W9-ANZ-507

THE BETHANY PARALLEL COMMENTARY
ON THE OLD TESTAMENT

THE BETHANY PARALLEL COMMENTARY
ON THE OLD TESTAMENT

FROM THE CONDENSED EDITIONS OF
MATTHEW HENRY • JAMIESON / FAUSSET / BROWN • ADAM CLARKE

THREE CLASSIC COMMENTARIES IN ONE VOLUME

Also includes supplementary commentary from
Alexander Maclaren ■ Charles H. Spurgeon ■ A.B. Simpson ■ Albert Barnes ■ F.B. Meyer ■ Martin Luther

BETHANY HOUSE PUBLISHERS
MINNEAPOLIS, MINNESOTA 55438

THE BETHANY PARALLEL COMMENTARY ON THE OLD TESTAMENT

ISBN 0-87123-617-6

Published by Bethany House Publishers
A Division of Bethany Fellowship, Inc.
6820 Auto Club Road, Minneapolis, MN 55438

Printed in the United States of America

PUBLISHER'S PREFACE

The idea for *The Bethany Parallel Commentary on the Old Testament* was generated and developed to provide a convenient method for comparing the comments and opinions of several Bible scholars without having to resort to many different volumes. Meeting the needs of pastors, Bible teachers and students for a manageable, convenient, practical and inspiring reference tool, here are three classic commentaries in one volume for easy comparison and helpful insight on specific texts.

The Bethany Parallel Commentary on the Old Testament gives background information, original word definitions, inspirational insights and interesting notations on every passage of the Old Testament from a wide spectrum of evangelical Christian thought.

When Matthew Henry's pastoral view, including practical application of the text to personal experience, is compared with Adam Clarke's and the Jamieson/Fausset/Brown's more technical and linguistic approach, the researcher will find this book to be an invaluable aid in discovering background information and interpreting particular scriptures. The three commentaries complement each other, giving the reader a more complete understanding and new insights on a certain passage or verse.

Nearly five hundred additional notes are included in appropriate sections throughout the book. Outstanding Bible scholars such as Charles Spurgeon, Alexander Maclaren, F. B. Meyer, A. B. Simpson, Albert Barnes, Martin Luther, Joseph Parker, Keil-Delitzsch, John Gill, John Lange, F. C. Cook, E. H. Plumptre, F. Gardiner, George Rawlinson, R. Payne Smith, Alfred Barry, and C. J. Ball give additional amplification to the scripture texts. These further notes are a very effective introduction to some of the great Bible scholars, and many of these also would make excellent quotations in sermons or Bible studies.

It is the publisher's hope that *The Bethany Parallel Commentary* will help pastors, Bible teachers, and laymen better to understand and apply the eternal truths of God's Word.

MATTHEW HENRY (1662-1714)

Born in a Welsh farmhouse at Iscoid, Flintshire, Matthew Henry was the son of an evangelical Church of England minister who had recently been ejected from the Anglican Church along with two thousand Presbyterian, Independent, and Baptist ministers. They had resisted universal adoption of the Elizabethan Prayer Book. A studious boy, Matthew Henry dated his conversion from 1672. In 1680 he was sent to the Academy (a Nonconformist school) at Islington, London, and went on to study law at Gray's Inn. His remarkable memory and eloquence showed the promise of a great future. In 1687 he received a private ordination, but in 1702 he obtained a document certifying the regularity of his Presbyterian ordination fifteen years earlier. His first pastorate was in Chester (1687-1712), followed by Hackney (1712-1714).

Greatly influenced by the Puritans, he made exposition of Scripture and its practical application to life the central concern of his ministry. In November of 1704 he began his commentary of the Bible and finished to the end of Acts before his death in 1714. The Epistles and Revelation were prepared by thirteen Nonconformist ministerial friends. His commentary set a style in detailed, often highly spiritualized exposition of Scripture which has shaped evangelical ministry ever since.

For two hundred and fifty years, this commentary has been the most widely used of all Bible commentaries. Charles Spurgeon is reported to have said that "every minister ought to read Matthew Henry entirely and carefully through once at least."

ADAM CLARKE (1762?-1832)

Born at Moybeg in County Londonderry, Ireland, no conclusive record of his birth is now available. His father was a man of English extraction who studied at the universities of Edinburgh and Glasgow (M.A.), and his mother was a devout Scottish Presbyterian. He received a local education through the influence of John Wesley at Kingswood School, Bristol. Becoming a Methodist in 1778, he was appointed a Methodist circuit rider by Wesley in 1782. Thirty-one towns and villages were covered regularly by horseback, and he often preached in the open air. From 1805 he lived chiefly in London and was three times president of the Methodist conference. Awarded an Aberdeen LL.D., his scholarship encompassed classics, patristics, oriental languages and literature, history, geology and natural science.

Actual work on his commentary began in May of 1798. The project was completed in March 1825. Clarke worked long hours before daybreak and after sunset during those years before the whole set, in eight large volumes, was published in 1826. For over one hundred and fifty years, its authoritative scholarship has been recognized by scholars from all evangelical backgrounds.

ROBERT JAMIESON (1802-1880)

He was born in Edinburgh, Scotland, and his father was a baker. Graduating from Edinburgh University, Jamieson was licensed as a Presbyterian preacher in 1827. He served a parish in Weststruther (1830-1837), in the presbytery of Laudes, and, for seven more years, the parish of Currie in the presbytery of Edinburgh. From 1844-1880 he served as minister of St. Paul's, Glasgow. In 1848 the University of Glasgow conferred on him the degree of Doctor of Divinity, and his church made him moderator of the General Assembly in 1872. In this commentary he wrote the section from Genesis through Esther.

ANDREW FAUSSET (1821-1910)

Born in County Fermanagh, Ireland, he was a brilliant Anglican scholar. Graduating from Trinity College, Dublin, in 1843, he went on to excel in Latin and Greek. He was ordained a priest in 1848 and from then to 1859 was the curate in Bishop Middleham, County Durham. From 1859-1910 he was of St. Cuthbert's, York.

He was a prolific writer, especially interested in prophecy. His works include *Scripture and the Prayer Book in Harmony* (1854); the editorship of the first ET of Bengel's *Gnomon of the New Testament* (1886); *The Englishman's Critical and Expository Bible Cyclopedia* (1878); and the JFB commentary. He wrote the sections from Job to Malachi and 1 Corinthians to Revelation, approximately half of the entire work.

DAVID BROWN (1803-1897)

He was born in Aberdeen, Scotland. Graduating from Aberdeen University, M.A., in 1821, he served as an assistant to Edward Irving from 1830-1832 and was influenced by Irving's prophetic teaching. In 1857 he was appointed professor of apologetics and the exegesis of the Gospels in the Free Church

College of Aberdeen, a professorship which he held for thirty years. In 1876 he was made principal of the college and remained in this office until his death. In 1885 he was appointed moderator of the General Assembly of the Free Church.

He was an industrious writer. His works include *Christ's Second Coming: Will It Be Premillenial?* (from a postmillennial standpoint); *The Handbook for Bible Classes* (a volume on Romans); *The Apocalypse: Its Structure and Preliminary Predictions.* Since his material for the JFB commentary includes only New Testament writings, his actual notes do not appear in this volume.

Combined as one effort, the JFB commentary came from differing positions and attitudes. Jamieson and Brown were Presbyterians, while Fausset was a clergyman in the Church of England. All three served as ministers of congregations in England and knew the needs of a minister's life. All were conservative in their theology.

TABLE OF CONTENTS

GENESIS 2
EXODUS 129
LEVITICUS 226
NUMBERS 274
DEUTERONOMY 333
JOSHUA 391
JUDGES 441
RUTH 494
1 SAMUEL 503
2 SAMUEL 572
1 KINGS 627
2 KINGS 682
1 CHRONICLES 737
2 CHRONICLES 771
EZRA 819
NEHEMIAH 834
ESTHER 856
JOB 869
PSALMS 965
PROVERBS 1198
ECCLESIASTES 1284
SONG OF SOLOMON 1313
ISAIAH 1337
JEREMIAH 1513
LAMENTATIONS 1652
EZEKIEL 1666
DANIEL 1765
HOSEA 1816
JOEL 1845
AMOS 1854
OBADIAH 1874
JONAH 1878
MICAH 1887
NAHUM 1904
HABAKKUK 1912
ZEPHANIAH 1922
HAGGAI 1930
ZECHARIAH 1937
MALACHI 1978

ACKNOWLEDGMENTS

GREAT VERSES THROUGH THE BIBLE by F. B. Meyer. Copyright © 1966, Marshall, Morgan and Scott, Ltd. Published by Zondervan Corporation. Used by permission.

BIBLE COMMENTARY by F. B. Meyer. Published by Tyndale House.

TODAY'S DICTIONARY OF THE BIBLE compiled by T. A. Bryant. Copyright © 1982, Bethany House Publishers. All rights reserved.

THE PEOPLE'S BIBLE by Joseph Parker, D.D. Published by Funk and Wagnalls Company.

COMMENTARY ON THE OLD TESTAMENT by C. F. Keil and F. Delitzsch. Published by Wm. B. Eerdmans Publishing Company.

COMMENTARY ON THE HOLY SCRIPTURES by John Peter Lange, D.D. Published by Zondervan Corporation.

CHRIST IN THE BIBLE by A. B. Simpson. Published by Christian Publications, Inc.

ELLICOTT'S COMMENTARY ON THE WHOLE BIBLE, edited by Charles John Ellicott. Published by Zondervan Corporation.

MACLAREN'S EXPOSITIONS OF HOLY SCRIPTURE by Alexander Maclaren. Copyright © 1905, Hodder & Stoughton. Published by Wm. B. Eerdmans Publishing Company.

THE TREASURY OF THE OLD TESTAMENT by Charles H. Spurgeon. Published by Zondervan Corporation.

THE TREASURY OF DAVID by Charles H. Spurgeon. Published by Zondervan Corporation.

LUTHER'S WORKS by Martin Luther. Copyright © 1964, Concordia Publishing House.

GILL'S COMMENTARY by John Gill. Published by Baker Book House.

BARNE'S NOTES by Albert Barnes. Published by Baker Book House.

THE BOOK OF GENESIS

I. Generation (1:1-2:25)
A. Of the material to man (1:1-2:3)
1. Origin (1:1)
2. Ruin (1:2a)
3. The revealed cosmogony (1:2b-2:3)
B. Of man, as to nature and office (2:4-25)
1. Created (2:4-7)
2. Crowned (2:8-15)
3. Conditioned (2:16, 17)
4. Completed (2:18-25)

II. Degeneration (3:1-11:32)
A. Of the individual (3:1-24)
1. The serpent and man (3:1-8)
2. Jehovah (3:9-24)
B. Of the family (4:1-5:32)
1. The first family (4:1-26)
2. The families (5:1-32)
C. Of society (6:1-10)
1. The mixture of the seeds (6:1-4)
2. The result of the mixture (6:5-10)
D. The divine interpolation (6:11-10:32)
1. The corruption of the earth (6:11-12)
2. The divine action (6:13-8:19)
3. The new departure (8:20-10:32)
E. Of the nations (11:1-32)
1. Confederacy (11:1-4)
2. Confusion (11:5-9)
3. Continuity (11:10-32)

III. Regeneration (12:1-50:26)
A. Of individuals (12:1-35:21)
1. Abraham—7 communications (12:1-25:10)
2. Isaac—2 communications (25:11-26:35)
3. Jacob—5 communications (27:1-35:21)
B. Of the family (35:22-38:30)
1. Preliminary (35:22-36:42)
2. Joseph at home and in exile (37:1-36)
3. Judah's corruption (38:1-30)
C. Of society (39:1-50:21)
1. Preparation in Egypt (39:1-45:28)
2. Segregation of Israel (46:1-50:21)
D. Of a nation (50:22-26)

We have now before us the holy Bible, or *book*, for so *bible* signifies. We call it *the book*, for it is incomparably the best book that ever was written, the book of books. We call it the holy book because it was written by holy men and given by inspiration of the Holy Ghost. The great things of God's law and gospel are here *written* for us that they might be transmitted to distant places and ages more pure and entire than possibly they could be by report and tradition. This is the "light that shines in a dark place" (2 Pet. 1:19), and a dark place indeed the world would be without the Bible.

We have before us that part of the Bible which we call the *Old Testament.* This is called a *testament*, or *covenant* because it was a settled declaration of the *will* of God concerning man in a federal way, and had its force from the designed death of the great testator, "the Lamb slain from the foundation of the world" (Rev. 8:8). It is called the *Old Testament* with relation to the *New*, which does not cancel and supersede it, but crowns and perfects it by the bringing in of that better hope which was typified and foretold in it.

We have before us that part of the Old Testament which we call the *Pentateuch*, or five books of Moses. In our Savior's distribution of the books of the Old Testament into the *law*, the *prophets*, and the *psalms*, these are the *law*.

We have before us the first and longest of those five books, which we call *Genesis*, written, some think, when Moses was in Midian, for the instruction and comfort of his suffering brethren in Egypt: I rather think he wrote it in the wilderness after he had been in the mount with God, where, probably, he received full and particular instructions for the writing of it. *Genesis* is a name borrowed from the Greek. It signifies the *original*, or *generation*: it is a history of originals—the creation of the world, the entrance of sin and death into it, the invention of arts, the rise of nations, and especially the planting of the church, and the state of it in its early days. It is also a history of the generations of Adam, Noah, Abraham, etc. The beginning of the New Testament is called *Genesis* too (Matt. 1:1), *Biblos genesos*, the book of the *genesis*, or *generation*, of Jesus Christ. Blessed be God for that book which shows us our remedy, as this opens our wound. Lord, open our eyes that we may see the wondrous things both of thy law and gospel!

MATTHEW HENRY

CHAPTER 1

Verses 1–2

The work of creation in its epitome and in its embryo.

I. In its epitome, *v.* 1, where we find the first article of our creed, that *God the Father Almighty is the Maker of heaven and earth.*

1. Observe, in this verse, four things:—

(1) The effect produced—the whole frame and furniture of the universe. The world is a great house, consisting of upper and lower stories, the structure stately and magnificent, uniform and convenient, and every room well and wisely furnished. The heavens are not only beautified to our eye with glorious lamps which garnish its outside, of whose creation we here read, but they are within replenished with glorious beings, out of our sight. In the visible world it is easy to observe, [1] Great variety, several sorts of beings vastly differing in their nature and constitution from each other. [2] Great beauty. The azure sky and verdant earth are charming to the eye of the curious spectator. How transcendent then must the beauty of the Creator be! [3] Great exactness and accuracy. To those that, with the help of microscopes, narrowly look into the works of nature, they appear far more fine than any of the works of art. [4] Great power. It is not a lump of dead and inactive matter, the earth itself has a magnetic power. [5] Great order, a mutual dependence of beings, an exact harmony of motions, and an admirable chain and connection of causes. [6] Great mystery. There are phenomena in nature which cannot be solved. But from what we see of heaven and earth we may infer the eternal power and Godhead of the great Creator. Our duty as Christians is always to keep heaven in our eye and the earth

JAMIESON, FAUSSET, BROWN

CHAPTER 1

Vss. 1, 2. THE CREATION OF HEAVEN AND EARTH.

TODAY'S DICTIONARY OF THE BIBLE:

Genesis. The five books of Moses were collectively called the *Pentateuch*, a word of Greek origin meaning "the fivefold book." The Jews called them the *Torah*—i.e., "the law." It is probable that the division of the Torah into five books proceeded from the Greek translators of the Old Testament. The names by which these several books are generally known are Greek.

The first book of the *Pentateuch* is called by the Jews *Berêshîth*—i.e., "in the beginning"—because this is the first word of the book. It is generally known among Christians by the name of *Genesis*—i.e., "creation" or "generation," being the name given to it in the LXX as designating its character, because it gives an account of the origin of all things. It contains, according to the usual computation, the history of about 2,369 years.

ADAM CLARKE

CHAPTER 1

1. Many attempts have been made to define the term GOD. As to the word itself, it is pure Anglo-Saxon, and among our ancestors signified, not only the Divine Being, now commonly designated by the word, but also "good," as in their apprehensions it appeared that "God" and "good" were correlative terms; and when they thought or spoke of Him, they were doubtless led from the word itself to consider Him as the Good Being, a Fountain of infinite benevolence and beneficence towards His creatures.

A general definition of this great First Cause, as far as human words dare attempt one, may be thus given: The eternal, independent, and self-existent Being; the Being whose purposes and actions spring from himself, without foreign motive or influence; He who is absolute in dominion; the most pure, the most simple, and most spiritual of all essences; infinitely benevolent, beneficent, true, and holy; the Cause of all being, the Upholder of all things; infinitely happy, because infinitely perfect; and eternally self-sufficient, needing nothing that He has made; illimitable in His immensity, inconceivable in His mode of existence, and indescribable in His essence; known fully only to himself, because an infinite mind can be fully apprehended only by itself. In a word, a Being who, from His infinite wisdom, cannot err or be deceived; and who, from His infinite goodness, can do nothing but what is eternally just, right, and kind.

The original word *Elohim*, God, is certainly the plural form of *El*, or *Eloah*, and has long been

MATTHEW HENRY

under our feet.

(2) The author and cause of this great work—GOD. The Hebrew word is *Elohim*, which bespeaks, [1] The power of God the Creator. *El* signifies *the strong God*; and what less than almighty strength could bring all things out of nothing? [2] The plurality of persons in the Godhead, Father, Son, and Holy Ghost. This plural name of God, in Hebrew, which speaks of him as many though he is one, confirming our faith in the doctrine of the Trinity, which, though but darkly intimated in the Old Testament, is clearly revealed in the New. We are often told that the world was made by him, and nothing made without him, John i. 3, 10; Eph. iii. 9; Col. i. 16; Heb. i. 2.

(3) The manner in which this work was effected: *God created it*, that is, made it out of nothing. There was not any pre-existent matter out of which the world was produced. No artificer can work, unless he has something to work on. But by the almighty power of God it is not only possible that something should be made of nothing (the God of nature is not subject to the laws of nature), but in the creation it is impossible it should be otherwise, for nothing is more injurious to the honour of the Eternal Mind than the supposition of eternal matter.

(4) When this work was produced: *In the beginning*, that is, in the beginning of time, when that clock was first set a-going: time began with the production of those beings that are measured by time. Before the beginning of time there was none but that Infinite Being that inhabits eternity. But to us it is enough to say, *In the beginning was the Word*, John i. 1.

2. Let us learn hence, (1) That atheism is folly, and atheists are the greatest fools in nature; for they see there is a world that could not make itself, and yet they will not own there is a God that made it. (2) That God is sovereign Lord of all by an incontestable right. (3) That with God all things are possible, and therefore happy are the people that have him for their God, and whose help and hope stand in his name, Ps. cxxi. 2; cxxiv. 8. (4) That the God we serve is worthy of all blessing and praise, Neh. ix. 5, 6. If all is of him, all must be to him.

II. The work of creation in its embryo, *v.* 2, where we have an account of the first matter and the first mover.

1. A chaos was the first matter. It is here called the earth; it is also called *the deep*, both for its vastness and because the waters which were afterwards separated from the earth were now mixed with it. The Creator could have made his work perfect at first, but by this gradual proceeding he would show what is, ordinarily, the method of his providence and grace. Observe the description of this chaos. (1) There was nothing in it desirable to be seen, for it was *without form and void. Tohu* and *Bohu*, *confusion* and *emptiness*; so these words are rendered, Isa. xxxiv. 11. To those who have their hearts in heaven this lower world, in comparison with that upper, still appears to be nothing but confusion and emptiness. (2) If there had been anything desirable to be seen, yet there was no light to see it by; for *darkness*, thick darkness, *was upon the face of the deep*. This chaos represents the state of an unregenerate graceless soul: *there* is disorder, confusion, and every evil work; it is empty of all good, for it is without God; it is dark till almighty grace effects a blessed change.

JAMIESON, FAUSSET, BROWN

God—the name of the Supreme Being, signifying in *Hebrew*, "Strong," "Mighty." It is expressive of omnipotent power; and by its use here in the *plural* form, is obscurely taught at the opening of the Bible, a doctrine clearly revealed in other parts of it, viz., that though God is one, there is a plurality of persons in the Godhead—Father, Son, and Spirit, who were engaged in the creative work (Prov. 8:27; John 1:3, 10; Eph. 3:9; Heb. 1:2; Job 26:13).

1. In the beginning—a period of remote and unknown antiquity, hid in the depths of eternal ages; and so the phrase is used in Proverbs 8:22, 23.

created—not formed from any pre-existing materials, but made out of nothing.

the heaven and the earth—the universe. This first verse is a general introduction to the inspired volume, declaring the great and important truth that all things had a beginning; that nothing throughout the wide extent of nature existed from eternity, originated by chance, or from the skill of any inferior agent; but that the whole universe was produced by the creative power of God (Acts 17:24; Rom. 11:36). After this preface, the narrative is confined to the earth.

2. the earth was without form and void—or in "confusion and emptiness," as the words are rendered in Isaiah 34:11. This globe, at some undescribed period, having been convulsed and broken up, was a dark and watery waste for ages perhaps, till out of this chaotic state, the present fabric of the world was made to arise.

ADAM CLARKE

supposed, by the most eminiently learned and pious men, to imply a plurality of Persons in the divine nature. As this plurality appears in so many parts of the sacred writings to be confined to three Persons, hence the doctrine of the Trinity, which has formed a part of the creed of all those who have been deemed sound in the faith, from the earliest ages of Christianity. The verb *bara*, "he created," being joined in the singular number with this plural noun, has been considered as pointing out the unity of the divine Persons in this work of creation. In the ever-blessed Trinity, from the infinite and indivisible unity of the Persons, there can be but one will, one purpose, and one infinite and uncontrollable energy.

In the beginning. Before the creative acts mentioned in this chapter all was *eternity*. Time signifies duration measured by the revolutions of the heavenly bodies; but prior to the creation of these bodies there could be no measurement of duration, and consequently no time; therefore *in the beginning* must necessarily mean the commencement of time which followed, or rather was produced by, God's creative acts, as an effect follows or is produced by a cause.

Created. Caused existence where previously to this moment there was no being. The rabbins, who are legitimate judges in a case of verbal criticism on their own language, are unanimous in asserting that the word *bara* expresses the commencement of the existence of a thing. The supposition that God formed all things out of a preexisting, eternal nature is certainly absurd, for if there had been an eternal nature besides an eternal God, there must have been two self-existing, independent, and eternal beings, which is a most palpable contradiction.

Eth hashshamayim. The word *eth*, which is generally considered as a particle, simply denoting that the word following is in the accusative or oblique case, is often understood by the rabbins in a much more extensive sense. "The particle *eth*," says Aben Ezra, "signifies the *substance* of the thing." On this ground these words should be translated, "God in the beginning created the substance of the heavens and the substance of the earth," i.e., the *prima materia*, or first elements, out of which the heavens and the earth were successively formed.

The heaven and the earth. As the word *shamayim* is plural, we may rest assured that it means more than the atmosphere, to which some have endeavored to restrict its meaning. Nor does it appear that the atmosphere is particularly intended here, as this is spoken of in v. 6 under the term "firmament." The word *heaven* must, therefore, comprehend the whole solar system, as it is very likely the whole of this was created in these six days. In the word *earth* everything relative to the globe is included, that is, all that belongs to the solid and fluid parts of our world with its surrounding atmosphere.

2. *The earth was without form, and void.* The original terms *tohu* and *bohu*, which we translate *without form, and void*, are of uncertain etymology; but in this place, and wherever else they are used, they convey the idea of confusion and disorder. God seems at first to have created the elementary principles of all things; and this formed the grand mass of matter, which in this state must be without arrangement, or any distinction of parts: a vast collection of indescribably confused materials, of nameless entities strangely mixed.

When this congeries of elementary principles was brought together, God was pleased to spend six days in asimilating, assorting, and arranging the materials, out of which He built up, not only the earth, but the whole of the solar system.

The Spirit of God. This has been variously and strangely understood. Some think a violent wind is meant, because *ruach* often signifies "wind," as well as "spirit," as *pneuma* does in Greek; and the term *God* is connected with it merely, as they think, to express the superlative degree. Others understand by it an elementary fire. Others, the sun, penetrating and drying up the earth with his rays. Others, the angels, who were supposed to have been employed as agents in creation. But it is sufficiently evident from the use of the word in other places that

MATTHEW HENRY

2. The Spirit of God was the first mover: He *moved upon the face of the waters.* The Spirit of God begins to work, and, if he work, who or what shall hinder? God is said to make the world by his Spirit, Ps. xxxiii. 6; Job xxvi. 13; and by the same mighty worker the new creation is effected. He moved upon the face of the deep. God is not only the author of all being, but the fountain of life and spring of motion. Dead matter would be for ever dead if he did not quicken it. And this makes it credible to us that God should raise the dead.

Verses 3–5

We have here a further account of the first day's work, in which observe, 1. That the first of all visible beings which God created was light, that by it we might see his works and his glory in them, and might work our works while it is day. Light is the great beauty and blessing of the universe. In the new creation, the first thing wrought in the soul is *light*: the blessed Spirit captivates the will and affections by enlightening the understanding. Those that by sin were darkness by grace become light in the world. 2. That the light was made by the word of God's power. He said, *Let there be light*; he willed and appointed it, and it was done immediately. The word of God is quick and powerful. Christ is the Word, the essential eternal Word, and by him the light was produced, for *in him was light, and he is the true light, the light of the world,* John i. 9; ix. 5. The divine light which shines in sanctified souls is wrought by the power of God, giving the knowledge of the glory of God in the face of Christ, as, at first, *God commanded the light to shine out of darkness,* 2 Cor. iv. 6. 3. That the light which God willed, when it was produced, he approved of: *God saw the light that it was good.* If the light is good, how good is he that is the fountain of light, from whom we receive it. 4. That God *divided the light from the darkness.* Yet he divided time between them, the day for light and the night for darkness, in a constant and regular succession to each other. Though the darkness was now scattered by the light, yet it takes its turn with the light, and has its place, because it has its use; for, as the light of the morning befriends the business of the day, so the shadows of the evening befriend the repose of the night, and draw the curtains about us, that we may sleep the better. 5. That God divided them from each other by distinguishing names: *He called the light day, and the darkness he called night.* He gave them names, as the Lord of both. Let us acknowledge God in the constant succession of day and night, and consecrate both to his honour, by working for him every day and resting in him every night. 6. That this was the first day's work, and a good day's work it was. *The evening and the morning were the first day.* This was not only the first day of the world, but the first day of the week. I observe it to the honour of that day, because the new world began on the first day of the week likewise, in the resurrection of Christ, as the light of the world, early in the morning. In him the dayspring from on high has visited the world.

Verses 6–8

We have here an account of the second day's work, the creation of the firmament, in which observe, 1. The command of God concerning it: *Let there be a firmament*, an *expansion*, so the Hebrew word signifies, like a sheet spread, or a curtain drawn out. This firmament is not a wall of partition, but a way of intercourse. See Job xxvi. 7; xxxvii. 18; Ps. civ. 3; Amos ix. 6. 2. The creation of it. Lest it should seem as if God had only commanded it to be done, and someone else had done it, he adds, *And God made the firmament.* What God requires of us he himself works in us, or it is not done. He that commands faith, holiness, and love, creates them by the power of his grace going along with his word. 3. The use and design of it—to *divide the waters from the waters,* that is, to distinguish between the waters that are wrapped up in the clouds and those that cover the sea. God has, in the firmament of his power, chambers, store-chambers, whence he *watereth the earth.* O what a great God is he who has thus provided for the comfort of all that serve him. 4. The naming of it: *He called the firmament heaven.* It is the visible heaven, the pavement of the holy city; above the firmament God is said to have his throne (Ezek. i. 26). We should be led by the contemplation of the heavens that are in our eye to consider *our Father who is in heaven.* The height of the heavens should remind us of God's supremacy and the infinite distance there is between us and him; the brightness of the heavens and their purity should remind us of his glory, and majesty, and perfect holiness; the vastness of the heavens, their encompassing of the earth, and the influence they have upon it, should remind us of his immensity and universal providence.

JAMIESON, FAUSSET, BROWN

the Spirit of God moved—lit., continued brooding over it, as a fowl does, when hatching eggs. The immediate agency of the Spirit, by working on the dead and discordant elements, combined, arranged, and ripened them into a state adapted for being the scene of a new creation. The account of this new creation properly begins at the end of this second verse; and the details of the process are described in the natural way an onlooker would have done, who beheld the changes that successively took place.

3-5. THE FIRST DAY. **3. God said**—This phrase, which occurs so repeatedly in the account means: willed, decreed, appointed; and the determining will of God was followed in every instance by an immediate result. Whether the sun was created at the same time with, or long before, the earth, the dense accumulation of fogs and vapors which enveloped the chaos had covered the globe with a settled gloom. But by the command of God, light was rendered visible; the thick murky clouds were dispersed, broken, or rarefied, and light diffused over the expanse of waters. The effect is described in the name "day," which in *Hebrew* signifies "warmth," "heat"; while the name "night" signifies a "rolling up," as night wraps all things in a shady mantle. **4. divided the light from darkness**—refers to the alternation or succession of the one to the other, produced by the daily revolution of the earth round its axis.

5. first day—a natural day, as the mention of its two parts clearly determines; and Moses reckons, according to Oriental usage, from sunset to sunset, saying not day and night as we do, but evening and morning.

6-8. SECOND DAY. **6. firmament**—an expanse—a beating out as a plate of metal: a name given to the atmosphere from its appearing to an observer to be the *vault* of heaven, supporting the weight of the *watery clouds.* By the creation of an atmosphere, the lighter parts of the waters which overspread the earth's surface were drawn up and suspended in the visible heavens, while the larger and heavier mass remained below. The air was thus "in the midst of the waters," i.e., separated them; and this being the apparent use of it, is the only one mentioned, although the atmosphere serves other uses, as a medium of life and light.

ADAM CLARKE

the Holy Spirit of God is intended; which our blessed Lord represents under the notion of "wind," John iii. 8; and which, as a "mighty rushing wind" on the Day of Pentecost, filled the house where the disciples were sitting, Acts ii. 2, which was immediately followed by their speaking with other tongues, because they were filled with the Holy Ghost, v. 4. These scriptures sufficiently ascertain the sense in which the word is used by Moses.

Moved. "Was brooding over"; for the word expresses that tremulous motion made by the hen while either hatching her eggs or fostering her young. It here probably signifies the communicating of a vital or prolific principle to the waters.

3. *And God said, Let there be light.* Nothing can be conceived more dignified than this form of expression. It argues at once uncontrollable authority, and omnific power; and in human language it is scarcely possible to conceive that God can speak more like himself.

Many have asked, "How could light be produced on the first day, and the sun, the fountain of it, not created till the fourth day?" I shall observe that the original word signifies not only *light* but "fire," see Isa. xxxi. 9; Ezek. v. 2. I therefore conclude that, as God has diffused the matter of caloric or latent heat through every part of nature, without which there could be neither vegetation nor animal life, it is caloric or latent heat which is principally intended by the original word.

4. *God divided the light from the darkness.* These words simply refer us by anticipation to the rotation of the earth round its own axis once in twenty-three hours, fifty-six minutes, and four seconds, which is the cause of the distinction between day and night, by bringing the different parts of the surface of the earth successively into and from under the solar rays; and it was probably at this moment that God gave this rotation to the earth, to produce this merciful provision of day and night.

6. *And God said, Let there be a firmament.* Our translators, by following the *firmamentum* of the Vulgate, have deprived this passage of all sense and meaning. The Hebrew word *rakia,* from *raka,* to "spread out as the curtains of a tent or pavilion," simply signifies an "expanse" or "space," and consequently that space or expansion separating the clouds which are in the higher regions of it, from the seas, etc., which are below it. This we call the "atmosphere"; but the word appears to have been used by Moses in a more extensive sense, and to include the whole of the planetary vortex, or the space which is occupied by the whole solar system.

MATTHEW HENRY

Verses 9–13

Hitherto the power of the Creator had been employed about the upper part of the visible world; the light of heaven was kindled, and the firmament of heaven fixed: but now he descends to this lower world, the earth, which was designed for the children of men, designed both for their habitation and for their maintenance; and here we have an account of the fitting of it for both, the building of their house and the spreading of their table.

I. How the earth was prepared to be a habitation for man, by the gathering of the waters together, and the making of the dry land to appear. 1. The waters which had covered the earth were ordered to retire, and to gather into one place. The waters thus collected he called *seas.* Waters and seas often, in scripture, signify troubles and afflictions, Ps. xlii. 7; lxix. 2, 14, 15. God's own people are not exempted from these in this world; but it is their comfort that they are only waters under the heaven (there are none in heaven), and that they are all in the place that God has appointed them and within the bounds that he has set for them. 2. The dry land was made to appear, and emerge out of the waters, and was called *earth,* and *given to the children of men.* The earth, it seems, was in being before; but it was of no use, because it was under water. Thus many of God's gifts are received in vain, because they are buried; make them to appear, and they become serviceable.

II. How the earth was furnished for the maintenance and support of man, *v.* 11, 12. Present provision was now made, by the immediate products of the upstart earth. It became fruitful, and brought forth grass for the cattle and herb for the service of man. Provision was likewise made for time to come, every one *having its seed in itself after its kind,* that, during the continuance of man upon the earth, food might be fetched out of the earth for his use and benefit. Observe here, 1. That not only the earth is the Lord's, but *the fulness thereof,* and he is the rightful owner and sovereign disposer, not only of it, but of all its furniture. The earth was *emptiness* (*v.* 2), but now, by a word's speaking, it has become full of God's riches. 2. That common providence is a continued creation, and in it *our Father worketh hitherto.* The earth still remains under the efficacy of this command, to bring forth grass, and herbs, and its annual products. They are standing instances of the unwearied power and unexhausted goodness of the world's great Maker and Master. 3. That though God, ordinarily, makes use of the agency of second causes, according to their nature, yet he neither needs them nor is tied to them. 4. That it is good to provide things necessary before we have occasions to use them: before the beasts and man were made, here were grass and herbs prepared for them. 5. That God must have the glory of all the benefit we receive from the products of the earth.

Verses 14–19

This is the history of the fourth day's work, the creating of the sun, moon, and stars, that garniture which is not only so much the beauty of the upper world, but so much the blessing of this lower. Of the creation of the lights of heaven we have an account,

I. In general, *v.* 14, 15, where we have, 1. The command given concerning them: *Let there be lights in the firmament of heaven.* God had said, *Let there be light* (*v.* 3), and there was light; but this was, as it were, a chaos of light, scattered and confused: now it was collected and modelled, and so rendered both more glorious and more serviceable. God is the God of order, and not of confusion; and, as he is light, so he is the Father and former of lights. 2. The use they were intended to be to this earth. (1) They must be for the distinction of times, of day and night, summer and winter, and thus, *under the sun,* there is *a season to every purpose,* Eccl. iii. 1. (2) They must be for the direction of actions. They are for signs of the change of weather, that the husbandman may order his affairs with discretion, foreseeing, by the face of the sky, when second causes have begun to work, whether it will be fair or foul, Matt. xvi. 2, 3. They do also *give light upon the earth,* that we may *walk* (John xi. 9), and *work* (John ix. 4), according as the duty of every day requires. The lights of heaven shine for us, for our pleasure and advantage. The lights of heaven are made to serve us, and they do it faithfully, and shine in their season, without fail: but we are set as lights in this world to serve God; and do we in like manner answer the end of our creation? We burn our Master's candles, but do not mind our Master's work.

JAMIESON, FAUSSET, BROWN

9-13. THIRD DAY. **9. let the waters under the heaven be gathered together into one place**—The world was to be rendered a terraqueous globe, and this was effected by a volcanic convulsion on its surface, the upheaving of some parts, the sinking of others, and the formation of vast hollows, into which the waters impetuously rushed, as is graphically described (Ps. 104:6-9) [HITCHCOCK]. Thus a large part of the earth was left "dry land," and thus were formed oceans, seas, lakes, and rivers which, though each having its own bed, or channel, are all connected with the sea (Job 38:10; Eccles. 1:7).

11. let the earth bring forth—The bare soil was clothed with verdure, and it is noticeable that the trees, plants, and grasses—the three great divisions of the vegetable kingdom here mentioned—were not called into existence in the same way as the light and the air; they were made to grow, and they grew as they do still out of the ground—not, however, by the slow process of vegetation, but through the divine power, without rain, dew, or any process of labor—sprouting up and flourishing in a single day.

14-19. FOURTH DAY. **14. let there be lights in the firmament**—The atmosphere being completely purified, the sun, moon, and stars were for the first time unveiled in all their glory in the cloudless sky; and they are described as "in the firmament" which to the eye they appear to be, though we know they are really at vast distances from it.

ADAM CLARKE

10. *And God called the dry land Earth; and the gathering together of the waters called he Seas.* These two constitute what is called the terraqueous globe, in which the earth and the water exist in a most judicious proportion to each other.

And God saw that it was good. This is the judgment which God pronounced on His own works. They were "beautiful" and "perfect" in their kind, for such is the import of the word *tob.* They were in weight and measure perfect and entire, lacking nothing. But the reader will think it strange that this approbation should be expressed once on the first, fourth, fifth, and sixth days, twice on the third, and not at all on the second! I suppose that the words, *And God saw that it was good,* have been either lost from the conclusion of the eighth verse, or that the clause in the tenth verse originally belonged to the eighth. It appears, from the Septuagint translation, that the words in question existed originally at the close of the eighth verse, in the copies which they used. If the account of the second day stood originally as it does now, no satisfactory reason can be given for the omission of this expression of the divine approbation of the work wrought by His wisdom and power on that day.

11. *Let the earth bring forth grass . . . herb . . . fruit tree.* In these general expressions all kinds of vegetable productions are included. *Fruit tree* is not to be understood here in the restricted sense in which the term is used among us; it signifies all trees, not only those which bear fruit, but also those which had the power of propagating themselves by seeds.

12. *Whose seed was in itself.* Which has the power of multiplying itself by seeds, slips, roots, etc., *ad infinitum;* which contains in itself all the rudiments of the future plant through its endless generations. The astonishing power with which God has endued the vegetable creation to multiply its different species may be instanced in the seed of the elm. This tree produces millions of seeds; and each of these seeds has the power of producing the same number. How astonishing is this produce!

14. *And God said, Let there be lights.* One principal office of these was to divide between day and night. When night is considered a state of comparative darkness, how can lights divide or distinguish it? The answer is easy: The sun is the monarch of the day, which is the state of light; the moon, of the night, the state of darkness.

And let them be for signs. Let them ever be considered as continual tokens of God's tender care for man, and as standing proofs of His continual miraculous interference; for so the word *oth* is often used. And is it not the almighty energy of God that upholds them in being? The sun and moon also serve as *signs* of the different changes which take place in the atmosphere, and which are so essential for all purposes of agriculture, commerce.

For days. Both the hours of the day and night, as well as the different lengths of the days and nights, are distinguished by the longer and shorter spaces of time the sun is above or below the horizon.

And years. That is, those grand divisions of time by which all succession in the vast lapse of duration is distinguished. This refers principally to a complete revolution of the earth round the sun.

MATTHEW HENRY

II. In particular, *v.* 16–18.

1. Observe, The lights of heaven are the sun, moon, and stars; and all these are the work of God's hands. (1) The sun is the greatest light of all. Let us learn from Ps. xix. 1–6 how to give unto God the glory due unto his name, as the Maker of the sun. (2) The moon is a less light, and yet is here reckoned one of the greater lights. Those are most valuable that are most serviceable; and those are the greater lights, not that have the best gifts, but that humbly and faithfully do the most good with them. (3) *He made the stars also,* for the scriptures were written, not to gratify our curiosity and make us astronomers, but to lead us to God, and make us saints. Now these lights are deputy-governors, rulers under him. Here the less light, the moon, is said to rule *the night*; but in Ps. cxxxvi. 9 the stars are mentioned as sharers in that government: *The moon and stars to rule by night.* The best and most honourable way of ruling is by giving light and doing good: those command respect that live a useful life, and so shine as lights.

2. Learn from all this, (1) The sin and folly of that ancient idolatry, the worshipping of the sun, moon, and stars. But the account here given of them plainly shows that they are both God's creatures and man's servants; and therefore it is both a great affront to God and a great reproach to ourselves to make deities of them and give them divine honours. (2) The duty and wisdom of daily worshipping that God who made all these things, and to offer the solemn sacrifice of prayer and praise every morning and evening.

Verses 20–23

We do not read of the creation of any living creature till the fifth day, of which these verses give us an account. It was on the fifth day that the fish and fowl were created, and both out of the waters. Observe, 1. The making of the fish and fowl, at first, *v.* 20, 21. God commanded them to be produced. He said, *Let the waters bring forth abundantly.* This command he himself executed: *God created great whales, &c.* Insects, which perhaps are as various and as numerous as any species of animals, and their structure as curious, were part of this day's work. Mr. Boyle (I remember) says he admires the Creator's wisdom and power as much in an ant as in an elephant. The curious formation of the bodies of animals, their different sizes, shapes, and natures, with the admirable powers of the sensitive life with which they are endued, when duly considered, serve, not only to silence and shame the objections of atheists and infidels, but to raise high thoughts and high praises of God in pious and devout souls, Ps. civ. 25, &c. 2. The blessing of them, in order to their continuance. Life is a wasting thing. Its strength is not the strength of stones. It is a candle that will burn out, if it be not first blown out; and therefore the wise Creator not only made the individuals, but provided for the propagation of the several kinds: *God blessed them, saying, Be fruitful, and multiply, v.* 22.

Verses 24–25

We have here the first part of the sixth day's work, and this day were made the beasts of the earth, the cattle, and the creeping things that pertain to the earth. Here, as before, 1. *The Lord gave the word*; he said, *Let the earth bring forth.* 2. He also did the work; he made them all after their kind, not only of divers shapes, but of divers natures, manners, food, and fashions—some living upon grass and herbs, others upon flesh—some bold, and others timorous—some for man's service, and not his sustenance, as the horse—others for his sustenance, and not his service, as the sheep—others for both, as the ox—and some for neither, as the wild beasts.

Verses 26–28

The second part of the sixth day's work, the creation of man.

I. That man was made last of all the creatures, that it might not be suspected that he had been, in any way, a helper to God in the creation of the world.

JAMIESON, FAUSSET, BROWN

16. two great lights—In consequence of the day being reckoned as commencing at sunset—the moon, which would be seen first in the horizon, would appear "a great light," compared with the little twinkling stars; while its pale benign radiance would be eclipsed by the dazzling splendor of the sun; when his resplendent orb rose in the morning and gradually attained its meridian blaze of glory, it would appear "the greater light" that ruled the day. Both these lights may be said to be "made" on the fourth day—not created, indeed, for it is a different word that is here used, but constituted, appointed to the important and necessary office of serving as luminaries to the world, and regulating by their motions and their influence the progress and divisions of time.

20-23. Fifth Day. The signs of animal life appeared in the waters and in the air. **20. moving creature**—all oviparous animals, both among the finny and the feathery tribes—remarkable for their rapid and prodigious increase.

fowl—means every flying thing: The word rendered "whales," includes also sharks, crocodiles, etc.; so that from the countless shoals of small fish to the great sea monsters, from the tiny insect to the king of birds, the waters and the air were suddenly made to swarm with creatures formed to live and sport in their respective elements.

24-31. Sixth Day. A farther advance was made by the creation of terrestrial animals, all the various species of which are included in three classes: (1) cattle, the herbivorous kind capable of labor or domestication. **24. beasts of the earth**—(2) wild animals, whose ravenous natures were then kept in check, and (3) all the various forms of **creeping things**—from the huge reptiles to the insignificant caterpillars.

26. The last stage in the progress of creation being now reached—**God said, Let us make man**—words which show the peculiar importance of the work to be done, the formation of a creature,

ADAM CLARKE

16. *And God made two great lights.* Moses speaks of the sun and moon here, not according to their bulk or solid contents, but according to the proportion of light they shed on the earth. The expression has been objected to by some who are as devoid of mental capacity as of candor. "The moon," say they, "is not a *great* body; on the contrary, it is the very smallest in our system." Well, and has Moses said the contrary? He has said it is a *great light;* had he said otherwise he had not spoken the truth. It is, in reference to the earth, next to the sun himself, the greatest light in the solar system; and so true is it that the moon is a great light that it affords more light to the earth than all the planets in the solar system, and all the innumerable stars in the vault of heaven, put together.

He made the stars also. Or rather, "He made the lesser light, with the stars, to rule the night."

20. *Let the waters bring forth abundantly.* There is a meaning in these words which is seldom noticed. Innumerable millions of animalcula are found in water. Eminent naturalists have discovered not less than 30,000 in a single drop! But the fecundity of fishes is another point intended in the text; no creatures are so prolific as these. A tench lays 1,000 eggs, a carp 20,000, and Leuwenhoek counted in a middling-sized cod 9,384,000! Thus, according to the purpose of God, *the waters bring forth abundantly.*

21. *And God created great whales.* Though this is generally understood by the different versions as signifying *whales,* yet the original must be understood rather as a general than a particular term, comprising all the great aquatic animals.

22. *Let fowl multiply in the earth.* It is truly astonishing with what care, wisdom, and minute skill God has formed the different genera and species of birds, whether intended to live chiefly on land or in water. The structure of a single feather affords a world of wonders; and as God made the fowls that they might fly in the firmament of heaven, v. 20, so He has adapted the form of their bodies, and the structure and disposition of their plumage, for that very purpose. The head and neck in flying are drawn principally within the breastbone, so that the whole underpart exhibits the appearance of a ship's hull. The wings are made use of as sails, or rather oars, and the tail as a helm or rudder. By means of these the creature is not only able to preserve the center of gravity, but also to go with vast speed through the air, either straight forward or downwards. In these also God has shown His skill and His power in the great and in the little—in the vast ostrich and in the beautiful hummingbird, which in plumage excels the splendor of the peacock, and in size is almost on a level with the bee.

24. *Let the earth bring forth the living creature.* A general term to express all creatures endued with animal life, in any of its infinitely varied graduations, from the half-reasoning elephant down to the polyp, which seems equally to share the vegetable and animal life. The word *chaitho,* in the latter part of the verse, seems to signify all wild animals, as lions, tigers, and especially such as are carnivorous, or live on flesh, in contradistinction from domestic animals, such as live on grass and other vegetables, and are capable of being tamed, and applied to domestic purposes. See on v. 29. These latter are probably meant by *behemah* in the text, which we translate *cattle,* such as horses, kine, sheep, dogs. *Creeping thing, remes,* all the different genera of serpents, worms, and such animals as have no feet. In *beasts* also God has shown His wondrous skill and power; in the vast elephant, or still more colossal mammoth or mastodon.

25. *And God made the beast of the earth after his kind.* Everything in both the animal and vegetable world was made so according to its kind, in both genus and species, as to produce its own kind through endless generations. Thus the several races of animals and plants have been kept distinct from the foundation of the world to the present day.

26. *And God said, Let us make man.* It is evident that God intends to impress the mind of man with a sense of something extraordinary in the formation of his body and soul, when He

MATTHEW HENRY

Yet it was both an honour and a favour to him that he was made last: an honour, for the method of the creation was to advance from that which was less perfect to that which was more so; and a favour, for it was not fit he should be lodged in the palace designed for him till it was completely fitted up and furnished for his reception. Man, as soon as he was made, had the whole visible creation before him, both to contemplate and to take the comfort of.

II. That man's creation was a more signal and immediate act of divine wisdom and power than that of the other creatures. Hitherto, it had been said, "Let there be light," and "Let there be a firmament," and "Let the earth, or waters, bring forth" such a thing; but now the word of command is turned into a word of consultation, "*Let us make man*, for whose sake the rest of the creatures were made: this is a work we must take into our own hands." In the former he speaks as one having authority, in this as one having affection; as if he had said, "Having at last settled the preliminaries, let us now apply ourselves to the business, *Let us make man*." Man was to be a creature different from all that had been hitherto made. Flesh and spirit, heaven and earth, must be put together in him, and he must be allied to both worlds. And therefore God himself not only undertakes to make him, but is pleased so to express himself as if he called a council to consider of the making of him: *Let us make man*. The three persons of the Trinity, Father, Son, and Holy Ghost, consult about it and concur in it. Let him rule man who said, *Let us make man*.

III. That man was made in God's image and after his likeness, two words to express the same thing and making each other the more expressive; *image* and *likeness* denote the likest image. Still between God and man there is an infinite distance. Christ only is the *express* image of God's person, as the Son of his Father, having the same nature. It is only some of God's honour that is put upon man, who is God's image only as the shadow in the glass, or the king's impress upon the coin. God's image upon man consists in these three things:—1. In his nature and constitution, not those of his body (for God has not a body), but those of his soul. This honour indeed God has put upon the body of man, that the Word was made flesh, the Son of God was clothed with a body like ours and will shortly clothe ours with a glory like that of his. But it is the soul, the great soul, of man, that does especially bear God's image. The soul of man, considered in its three noble faculties, understanding, will, and active power, is perhaps the brightest, clearest looking-glass in nature, wherein to see God. 2. In his place and authority: *Let us make man in our image, and let him have dominion.* As he has the government of the inferior creatures, he is, as it were, God's representative, or viceroy, upon earth. Yet his government of himself by the freedom of his will has in it more of God's image than his government of the creatures. 3. In his purity and rectitude. God's image upon man consists in knowledge, righteousness, and true holiness, Eph. iv. 24; Col. iii. 10. Thus holy, thus happy, were our first parents, in having the image of God upon them.

IV. That man was made male and female, and blessed with the blessing of fruitfulness and increase. God said, *Let us make man*, and immediately it follows, *So God created man*; he performed what he resolved. With us saying and doing are two things, but they are not so with God. It would seem that of the rest of the creatures God made many couples; but of man *did not he make one?* Whence Christ gathers an argument against divorce, Matt. xix. 4, 5. Our first father, Adam, was confined to one wife; and, if he had put her away, there was no other for him to marry, which plainly intimated that the bond of marriage was not to be dissolved at pleasure. God made but one male and one female, that all the nations of men might know themselves to be made of one blood, descendants from one common stock, and might thereby be induced to love one another. He gave them, 1. A large inheritance: *Replenish the earth;* it is this that is bestowed upon the children of men. They were made *to dwell upon the face of all the earth*, Acts xvii. 26. This is the place in which God has set man to be a probationer for a better state. 2. A numerous lasting family, to enjoy this inheritance.

V. That God gave to man, when he had made him, a dominion over the inferior creatures, *over the fish of the sea and over the fowl of the air*. Though man provides for neither, he has power over both. God designed hereby to put an honour upon man. God's providence continues so much of it to the safety and children of men as is necessary to the safety and support of their lives.

JAMIESON, FAUSSET, BROWN

who was to be God's representative, clothed with authority and rule as visible head and monarch of the world.

In our image, after our likeness—This was a peculiar distinction, the value attached to which appears in the words being twice mentioned. And in what did this image of God consist? Not in the erect form or features of man, not in his intellect, for the devil and his angels are, in this respect, far superior; not in his immortality, for he has not, like God, a past as well as a future eternity of being; but in the moral dispositions of his soul, commonly called *original righteousness* (Eccles. 7:29). As the new creation is only a restoration of this image, the history of the one throws light on the other; and we are informed that it is renewed after the image of God in knowledge, righteousness, and true holiness (Col. 3:10; Eph. 4:24).

28. Be fruitful, etc.—The human race in every country and age has been the offspring of the first pair. Amid all the varieties found among men, some black, some copper-colored, others white, the researches of modern science lead to a conclusion, fully accordant with the sacred history, that they are all of one species and of one family (Acts 17:26).

ADAM CLARKE

introduces the account of his creation thus: "Let *us* make man." The word *Adam*, which we translate *man*, is intended to designate the species of animal, as *chaitho* marks the wild beasts that live in general a solitary life; *behemah*, domestic or gregarious animals; and *remes*, all kinds of reptiles, from the largest snake to the microscopic eel. Though the same kind of organization may be found in man as appears in the lower animals, yet there is a variety and complication in the parts, a delicacy of structure, a nice arrangement, a judicious adaptation of the different members to their great offices and functions, a dignity of mien, and a perfection of the whole, which are sought for in vain in all other creatures.

In our image, after our likeness. What is said above refers only to the body of man; what is here said refers to his soul. This was made in the *image* and *likeness* of God. Now, as the Divine Being is infinite, He is neither limited by parts, nor definable by passions; therefore He can have no corporeal image after which He made the body of man. The image and likeness must necessarily be intellectual; his mind, his soul, must have been formed after the nature and perfections of his God. The human mind is still endowed with most extraordinary capacities; it was more so when issuing out of the hands of its Creator. God was now producing a spirit, and a spirit, too, formed after the perfections of His own nature. God is the Fountain whence this spirit issued; hence the stream must resemble the spring which produced it. God is holy, just, wise, good, and perfect; so must the soul be that sprang from Him: there could be in it nothing impure, unjust, ignorant, evil, low, base, mean, or vile. It was created after the image of God; and that image, St. Paul tells us, consisted in "righteousness," "true holiness," and "knowledge," Eph. iv. 24; Col. iii. 10. Hence man was wise in his mind, holy in his heart, and righteous in his actions.

Gregory Nyssen has very properly observed that the superiority of man to all other parts of creation is seen in this, that all other creatures are represented as the effect of God's *word*, but man is represented as the *work of God*, according to plan and consideration: "Let us make man in our image, after our likeness."

And let them have dominion. Hence we see that the dominion was not the image. God created man capable of governing the world, and when fitted for the office, He fixed him in it. We see God's tender care and parental solicitude for the comfort and well-being of this masterpiece of His workmanship, in creating the world previously to the creation of man. He prepared everything for his subsistence, convenience, and pleasure, before He brought him into being; so that, comparing little with great things, the house was built, furnished, and amply stored, by the time the destined tenant was ready to occupy it.

28. *And God blessed them.* Marked them as being under His especial protection, and gave them power to propagate and multiply their own kind on the earth. A large volume would be insufficient to contain what we know of the excellence and perfection of man, even in his present degraded, fallen state. Both his body and soul are adapted with astonishing wisdom to their residence and occupations; and also the place of their residence, as well as the surrounding objects, in their diversity, color, and mutual relations, to the mind and body of this lord of the creation. The contrivance, arrangement, action, and reaction of the different parts of the body show the admirable skill of the wondrous Creator; while the various powers and faculties of the mind, acting on and by the different organs of this body, proclaim the soul's divine origin, and demonstrate that he who was made in the image and likeness of God was a transcript of His own excellency, destined to know, love, and dwell with his Maker throughout eternity.

MATTHEW HENRY

Verses 29–30

The third part of the sixth day's work, a gracious provision of food for all flesh, Ps. cxxxvi. 25.

I. Food provided for man, *v.* 29. Herbs and fruits must be his meat. See here, 1. That which should make us humble. As we were made out of the earth, so we are maintained out of it. There is meat that endures to everlasting life; the Lord evermore give us this. 2. That which should make us thankful. The Lord is for the body; from him we receive all the supports and comforts of this life. He gives us all things richly to enjoy, not only for necessity, but plenty, dainties, and varieties, for ornament and delight. 3. That which should make us temperate and content with our lot. If God gives us food for our lives, let us not, with murmuring Israel, ask food for our lusts, Ps. lxxviii. 18; see Dan. i. 15.

II. Food provided for the beasts, *v.* 30. *Doth God take care for oxen?* Yes, certainly, he provides food convenient for them, and not for oxen only, but even the young lions and the young ravens are the care of his providence. He is a great housekeeper, a very rich and bountiful one, that satisfies the desire of every living thing. He that feeds his birds will not starve his babes.

Verse 31

The approbation and conclusion of the whole work of creation.

I. The review God took of his work: He *saw that every thing that he had made.* So he does still; all the works of his hands are under his eye. Omniscience cannot be separated from omnipotence. But this was the Eternal Mind's solemn reflection upon the copies of its own wisdom and the products of its own power. God has hereby set us an example of reviewing our works. When we have finished a day's work, and are entering upon the rest of the night, we should commune with our own hearts about what we have been doing that day.

II. The complacency God took in his work. He did not pronounce it good till he had seen it so, to teach us not to answer a matter before we hear it. 1. It was good. Good, for it is all agreeable to the mind of the Creator, just as he would have it to be. Good, for it answers the end of its creation, and is fit for the purpose for which it was designed. Good, for it is serviceable to man, whom God had appointed lord of the visible creation. Good, for it is all for God's glory. 2. It was very good. Of each day's work (except the second) it was said that it was good, but now, it is very good. For, (1) Now man was made, who was the chief of the ways of God, who was designed to be the visible image of the Creator's glory and the mouth of the creation in his praises. (2) Now all was made; every part was good, but all together very good. The glory and goodness, the beauty and harmony, of God's works, both of providence and grace, as this of creation, will best appear when they are perfected. Therefore judge nothing before the time.

III. The time when this work was concluded: *The evening and the morning were the sixth day*; so that in six days God made the world. We are not to think but that God could have made the world in an instant. He that said, *Let there be light, and there was light,* could have said, "Let there be a world," and there would have been a world, *in a moment, in the twinkling of an eye,* as at the resurrection, 1 Cor. xv. 52. But he did it in his own way and in his own time. So much would the sabbath conduce to the keeping up of religion in the world that God had an eye to it in the timing of his creation.

JAMIESON, FAUSSET, BROWN

What power in the word of God! "He spake and it was done. He commanded and all things stood fast." "Great and manifold are thy works, Lord God Almighty! in wisdom hast thou made them all." We admire that wisdom, not only in the regular progress of creation, but in its perfect adaptation to the end. God is represented as pausing at every stage to look at His work. No wonder He contemplated it with complacency. Every object was in its right place, every vegetable process going on in season, every animal in its structure and instincts suited to its mode of life and its use in the economy of the world. He saw everything that He had made answering the plan which His eternal wisdom had conceived; and, **31. Behold it was very good.**

ADAM CLARKE

31. *And, behold, it was very good.* "Superlatively, or only good"; as good as they could be. The plan wise, the work well executed, the different parts properly arranged; their nature, limits, mode of existence, manner of propagation, habits, mode of sustenance, properly and permanently established and secured; for everything was formed to the utmost perfection of its nature, so that nothing could be added or diminished.

And the evening and the morning were the sixth day. The word *ereb,* which we translate *evening,* comes from the root *arab,* to "mingle"; and properly signifies that state in which neither absolute darkness nor full light prevails. It has nearly the same grammatical signification as our "twilight." The Hebrews extended the meaning of this term to the whole duration of night, because it was ever a mingled state, the moon, the planets, or the stars, tempering the darkness with some rays of light.

The morning—boker; from *bakar,* he "looked out"; a beautiful figure which represents the morning as looking out at the east, and illuminating the whole of the upper hemisphere.

The evening and the morning were the sixth day. It is somewhat remarkable that through the whole of this chapter, whenever the division of days is made, the evening always precedes the morning. The reason of this may perhaps be that darkness was preexistent to light and, therefore, time is reckoned from the first act of God towards the creation of the world, which took place before light was called forth into existence. It is very likely, for this same reason, that the Jews began their day at six o'clock in the evening in imitation of Moses' division of time in this chapter.

F. B. MEYER:

Man—creation's crown. Creation reveals God's nature, as the picture the artist. His eternal power and Godhead are visible in his works (Rom. 1:20). And all things and beings were made through Jesus Christ (Col. 1:15, 16). The hands of the Son of God wove the blue curtains above us and filled them with luminaries. The seas are his; he made them and filled them with living creatures. The woodlands are the outcome of his mind, and he filled them with flowers and birds. He taught them to live without worry. He filled the tiny heart of the mother bird with love for her young. His are the cattle on a thousand hills. He molded the red earth into his own likeness and made man. We were made to have dominion (Ps. 8:6–8). Ask God to put all things, especially all the evil things of your heart, under your feet. The world is good, and if you are good you find it so. —*Bible Commentary*

MATTHEW HENRY

CHAPTER 2

Verses 1–3

I. The settlement of the kingdom of nature, in God's resting from the work of creation, *v.* 1, 2. Here observe, 1. The creatures made both in heaven and earth are disciplined, and under command. Every one knows and keeps his place. 2. The heavens and the earth are finished pieces, and so are all the creatures in them.

3. After the end of the first six days God ceased from all works of creation. He has so ended his work. In miracles, he has controlled nature, but never changed its settled course. 4. The eternal God did not rest, as one weary, but as one well-pleased.

JAMIESON, FAUSSET, BROWN

CHAPTER 2

Vs. 1. The Narrative of the Six Days' Creation Continued. The course of the narrative is improperly broken by the division of the chapter. **1. the heavens**—the firmament or atmosphere. **host**—a multitude, a numerous array, usually connected in Scripture with heaven only, but here with the earth also, meaning all that they contain. **were finished**—brought to completion. No permanent change has ever since been made in the course of the world, no new species of animals been formed, no law of nature repealed or added to. They could have been finished in a moment as well as in six days, but the work of creation was gradual for the instruction of man, as well, perhaps, as of higher creatures (Job 38:7).

2-7. The First Sabbath. **2. and he rested on the seventh day**—not to repose from exhaustion with labor (see Isa. 40:28), but ceased from working, an example equivalent to a command that we also

ADAM CLARKE

CHAPTER 2

1. *And all the host of them.* The word *host* signifies literally an army, composed of a number of companies of soldiers under their respective leaders; and seems here applied to the various celestial bodies in our system, placed by the divine wisdom under the influence of the sun.

2. *On the seventh day God ended.* It is the general voice of Scripture that God finished the whole of the creation in six days, and rested the seventh, giving us an example that we might labor six days and rest the seventh from all manual exercises. It is worthy of notice that the Septuagint, the Syriac, and the Samaritan read the sixth day instead of the seventh; and this should be considered the general reading, which appears from these versions to have been originally that of the Hebrew

MATTHEW HENRY

II. The commencement of the kingdom of grace, in the sanctification of the sabbath day, *v.* 3. Observe, 1. The solemn observance of one day in seven, as a day of holy rest and holy work, to God's honour, is the indispensable duty of all those to whom God has revealed his holy sabbaths. 2. Sabbaths are as ancient as the world; and I see no reason to doubt that the sabbath, being now instituted in innocency, was religiously observed by the people of God throughout the patriarchal age. 3. The sabbath of the Lord is truly honourable, and we have reason to honour it in obedience to him. 4. The sabbath day is a blessed day, for God blessed it, and that which he blesses is blessed indeed. God has promised, on that day, to meet us and bless us. 5. The sabbath day is a holy day, for God has sanctified it.

Verses 4–7

In these verses, I. Here is a name given to the Creator which we have not yet met with, and that is *Jehovah*—the LORD, in capital letters, which are constantly used in our English translation to intimate that in the original it is *Jehovah*. All along, in the first chapter, he was called *Elohim—a God of power*; but now *Jehovah Elohim—a God of power and perfection*, a finishing God. *Jehovah* is that great and incommunicable name of God which denotes his having his being of himself, and his giving being to all things.

II. Further notice taken of the production of plants and herbs, because they were made and appointed to be food for man, *v.* 5, 6. Here observe, 1. The earth did not bring forth its fruits of itself, but purely by the almighty power of God. Thus grace in the soul, that plant of renown, grows not of itself in nature's soil, but is the work of God's own hands. 2. Rain also is the gift of God; it came not till *the Lord God caused it to rain*. 3. Though God, ordinarily, works by means, yet he is not tied to them. 4. Some way or other God will take care to water the plants that are of his own planting. Though as yet there was no rain, God made a mist equivalent to a shower, and with it *watered the whole face of the ground*. Divine grace descends like a mist, or silent dew, and waters the church without noise, Deut. xxxii. 2.

III. A more particular account of the creation of man, *v.* 7. Man is a little world, consisting of heaven and earth, soul and body. Now here we have an account of the origin of both.

1. The mean origin, and yet the curious structure, of the body of man. (1) The matter was despicable. He was made *of the dust of the ground*, a very unlikely thing to make a man of; but the same infinite power that made the world of nothing made man, its masterpiece, of next to nothing. He was not made of gold-dust, powder of pearl, or diamond dust, but common dust, dust of the ground. Our fabric is earthly, and the fashioning of it like that of an earthen vessel, Job x. 9. What have we then to be proud of? (2) Yet the Maker was great, and the make fine. Of the other creatures it is said that they were *created* and *made*; but of man that he was *formed*, which denotes a gradual process in the work with great accuracy and exactness. ***The workmanship exceeded the materials.*** Let us present our bodies to God as living sacrifices (Rom. xii. 1).

2. The high origin and the admirable serviceableness of the soul of man. (1) It takes its rise from the breath of heaven. It was not made of the earth, as the body was; it came immediately from God. Let the soul which God has breathed into us breathe after him. Into his hands let us commit our spirits, for from his hands we had them. (2) The soul is the man. The body would be worthless, useless, loathsome carcase, if the soul did not animate it. Since the extraction of the soul is so noble, and its nature and faculties are so excellent, let us not be of those fools that despise their own souls, by preferring their bodies before them, Prov. xv. 32. He that made the soul is alone able to new-make it.

Verses 8–15

Man consisting of body and soul, a body made out of the earth and a rational immortal soul the breath of heaven, we have, in these verses, the provision that was made for the happiness of both; he that made him took care to make him happy, if he could but have kept himself so and known when he was well off.

I. A description of the garden of Eden, which was intended for the mansion and demesne of this great lord, the palace of this prince. The inspired penman, in this history, writing for the Jews first, and calculating his narratives for the infant state of the church, describes things by their outward sensible appearances, and leaves us, by further discoveries

JAMIESON, FAUSSET, BROWN

should cease from labor of every kind. **3. blessed and sanctified the seventh day**—a peculiar distinction put upon it above the other six days, and showing it was devoted to sacred purposes. The institution of the Sabbath is as old as creation, giving rise to that weekly division of time which prevailed in the earliest ages. It is a wise and beneficent law, affording that regular interval of rest which the physical nature of man and the animals employed in his service requires, and the neglect of which brings both to premature decay. Moreover, it secures an appointed season for religious worship, and if it was necessary in a state of primeval innocence, how much more so now, when mankind has a strong tendency to forget God and His claims?

4. These are the generations of the heavens and the earth—the history or account of their production. Whence did Moses obtain this account so different from the puerile and absurd fictions of the heathen? Not from any human source, for man was not in existence to witness it; not from the light of nature or reason, for though they proclaim the eternal power and Godhead by the things which are made, they cannot tell *how* they were made. None but the Creator Himself could give this information, and therefore it is through faith we understand that the worlds were framed by the word of God (Heb. 11:3).

rain, mist—See on ch. 1:12.

7. Here the sacred writer supplies a few more particulars about the first pair. **formed**—had FORMED MAN OUT OF THE DUST OF THE GROUND. Science has proved that the substance of his flesh, sinews, and bones, consists of the very same elements as the soil which forms the crust of the earth and the limestone that lies embedded in its bowels. But from that mean material what an admirable structure has been reared in the human body (Ps. 139:14).

breath of life—lit., of lives, not only animal but spiritual life. If the body is so admirable, how much more the soul with all its varied faculties. **breathed into his nostrils the breath of life**—not that the Creator literally performed this act, but respiration being the medium and sign of life, this phrase is used to show that man's life originated in a different way from his body—being implanted directly by God (Eccles. 12:7), and hence in the new creation of the soul Christ breathed on His disciples (John 20:22).

ADAM CLARKE

text.

3. *And God blessed the seventh day.* The original word *barach,* which is generally rendered "to bless," has a very extensive meaning. It is frequently used in Scripture in the sense of speaking good of or to a person; and hence literally and properly rendered by the Septuagint *eulogesen,* from *eu,* "good" or "well," and *lego,* "I speak." So God has spoken well of the Sabbath, and good to them who conscientiously observe it.

Because that in it he had rested. *Shabath,* "he rested"; hence "Sabbath," the name of the seventh day, signifying "a day of rest"—rest to the body from labor and toil, and rest to the soul from all worldly care and anxieties. He who labors with his mind by worldly schemes and plans on the Sabbath day is as culpable as he who labors with his hands in his accustomed calling. It is by the authority of God that the Sabbath is set apart for rest and religious purposes, as the six days of the week are appointed for labor. Without this consecrated day religion itself would fail, and the human mind, becoming sensualized, would soon forget its origin and end.

As God formed both the mind and the body of man on principles of activity, so He assigned him proper employment; and it is His decree that the mind shall improve by exercise, and the body find increase of vigor and health in honest labor. He who idles away his time in the six days is equally culpable in the sight of God as he who works on the seventh.

4. *In the day that the Lord God made.* The word *Yehovah* is for the first time mentioned here. What it signifies see on Exod. xxxiv. 5-6. Wherever this word occurs in the sacred writings we translate it LORD, which word is, through respect and reverence, always printed in capitals. Though our English term "Lord" does not give the particular meaning of the original word, yet it conveys a strong and noble sense. The word implies the "giver of bread," i.e., he who deals out all the necessaries of life. Our ancient English noblemen were accustomed to keep a continual open house, where all their vassals, and all strangers, had full liberty to enter and eat as much as they would; and hence those noblemen had the honorable name of "lords," i.e., "the dispensers of bread."

5. *Every plant of the field before it was in the earth.* It appears that God created everything, not only perfect as it respects its nature, but also in a state of maturity, so that every vegetable production appeared at once in full growth; and this was necessary that man, when he came into being, might find everything ready for his use.

6. *There went up a mist.* This passage appears to have greatly embarrassed many commentators. The plain meaning seems to be this, that the aqueous vapors, ascending from the earth, and becoming condensed in the colder regions of the atmosphere, fell back upon the earth in the form of dews, and by this means an equal portion of moisture was distributed to the roots of plants. As Moses had said, v. 5, that "the Lord had not caused it to rain upon the earth," He probably designed to teach us, in v. 6, how rain is produced, namely, by the condensation of the aqueous vapors, which are generally through the heat of the sun and other causes raised to a considerable height in the atmosphere, where, meeting with cold air, the watery particles which were before so small and light that they could float in the air, becoming condensed, i.e., many drops being driven into one, become too heavy to be any longer suspended, and then, through their own gravity, fall down in the form which we term rain.

7. *God formed man of the dust.* In the most distinct manner God shows us that man is a compound being, having a body and soul distinctly and separately created; the body out of the dust of the earth, the soul immediately breathed from God himself. Of the soul it is said, *God breathed into his nostrils the breath of life;* "the breath of lives," i.e., animal and intellectual. While this breath of God expanded the lungs and set them in play, His inspiration gave both spirit and understanding.

MATTHEW HENRY

of the divine light, to be led into the understanding of the mysteries couched under them. Therefore he does not so much insist upon the happiness of Adam's mind as upon that of his outward state.

1. The place appointed for Adam's residence was a garden; not an ivory house nor a palace overlaid with gold, but a garden, furnished and adorned by nature, not by art. The heaven was the roof of Adam's house, and never was any roof so curiously ceiled and painted. The earth was his floor, and never was any floor so richly inlaid. The shadow of the trees was his retirement; under them were his dining-rooms, his lodging-rooms, and never were any rooms so finely hung as these: Solomon's, in all their glory, were not arrayed like them. Nature is content with a little and that which is most natural, grace with less, but lust with nothing.

2. The contrivance and furniture of this garden were the immediate work of God's wisdom and power. The Lord God planted this garden. No delights can be agreeable nor satisfying to a soul but those that God himself has provided and appointed for it; no true paradise, but of God's planting.

3. The situation of this garden was extremely sweet. It was in *Eden*, which signifies *delight* and *pleasure*. The place is here particularly pointed out by such marks and bounds as were sufficient. Let it be our care to make sure of a place in the heavenly paradise, and then we need not perplex ourselves with a search after the place of the earthly paradise.

4. The trees with which this garden was planted. (1) It had all the best and choicest trees. God, as a tender Father, consulted not only Adam's profit, but his pleasure; for there is a pleasure consistent with innocency, nay, there is a true and transcendent pleasure in innocency. But, (2) It had two extraordinary trees peculiar to itself; on earth there were not their like. [1] There was *the tree of life in the midst of the garden*, which was chiefly intended to be a sign and seal to Adam, assuring him of the continuance of life and happiness, even to immortality and everlasting bliss, through the grace and favour of his Maker, upon condition of his perseverance in this state of innocency and obedience. Of this he might eat and live. Christ is now to us the tree of life (Rev. ii. 7; xxii. 2). [2] There was *the tree of the knowledge of good and evil*, so called, not because it had any virtue in it to beget or increase useful knowledge, but, *First*, Because there was an express positive revelation of the will of God concerning this tree, so that by it he might know moral good and evil. What is good? It is good not to eat of this tree. What is evil? It is evil to eat of this tree. The distinction between all other moral good and evil was written in the heart of man by nature; but this, which resulted from a positive law, was written upon this tree. *Secondly*, Because, in the event, it proved to give Adam an experimental knowledge of good by the loss of it and of evil by the sense of it. As the covenant of grace has in it, not only *Believe and be saved*, but also, *Believe not and be damned* (Mark xvi. 16), so the covenant of innocency had in it, not only "Do this and live," which was sealed and confirmed by the tree of life, but "Fail and die," which Adam was assured of by this other tree: "Touch it at your peril; " so that, in these two trees, God set before him *good and evil, the blessing and the curse*, Deut. xxx. 19. These two trees were as two sacraments.

5. The rivers with which this garden was watered, *v.* 10–14. These four rivers (or one river branched into four streams) contributed much both to the pleasantness and the fruitfulness of this garden. In the heavenly paradise there is a river infinitely surpassing these; for it is a river of the water of life, not coming out of Eden, as this, but proceeding out of the throne of God and of the Lamb (Rev. xxii. 1), a river that *makes glad the city of our God*, Ps. xlvi. 4. Havilah had gold, and spices, and precious stones; but Eden had that which was infinitely better, the tree of life, and communion with God. So we may say of the Africans and Indians: "They have the gold, but we have the gospel. The gold of their land is good, but the riches of ours are infinitely better."

II. The placing of man in this paradise of delight, *v.* 15, where observe,

1. How God put him in possession of it. (1) Man was made *out* of paradise; for, after God had formed him, he put him into the garden: he was made of common clay, not of paradise-dust. He could not plead a tenant-right to the garden, for he was not born upon the premises, nor had anything but what he received. (2) The same God that was the author of his being was the author of his bliss. He that made us is alone able to make us happy. (3) It adds much to the comfort of any condition if we have plainly

TODAY'S DICTIONARY OF THE BIBLE:

Eden—*delight.* The garden in which Adam and Eve lived (Gen. 2:8–17). No geographical question has been so much discussed as that bearing on its site. It has been placed in Armenia, in the region west of the Caspian Sea, in Media, near Damascus, in Palestine, in Southern Arabia, and in Babylonia. The site must undoubtedly be sought for somewhere along the course of the great rivers Tigris and the Euphrates of Western Asia, in "the land of Shinar" or Babylonia. The region from about lat. 33°30' to lat. 31°, which is a very rich and fertile tract, has been by the most competent authorities agreed on as the probable site of Eden. It is a region where streams abound, where they divide and reunite, where alone in the Mesopotamian tract can be found the phenomenon of a single river parting into four arms, each of which is or has been a river of consequence.

Among almost all nations there are traditions of the primitive innocence of our race in the garden of Eden. This was the "golden age" to which the Greeks looked back. Men then lived a "life free from care, and without labor and sorrow. Old age was unknown; the body never lost its vigor; existence was a perpetual feast without a taint of evil. The earth brought forth spontaneously all things that were good in profuse abundance."

JAMIESON, FAUSSET, BROWN

8-17. THE GARDEN OF EDEN. **8. Eden**—was probably a very extensive region in Mesopotamia, distinguished for its natural beauty and the richness and variety of its produce. Hence its name, signifying "pleasantness." God planted a garden eastward, an extensive park, a paradise, in which the man was put to be trained under the paternal care of his Maker to piety and usefulness.

tree of life—so called from its symbolic character as a sign and seal of immortal life. Its prominent position "in the midst of the garden," where it must have been an object of daily observation and interest, was admirably fitted to keep man habitually in mind of God and futurity.

9. tree of the knowledge of good and evil—so called because it was a *test* of obedience by which our first parents were to be tried, whether they would be good or bad, obey God or break His commands.

KEIL–DELITZSCH:

The tree of life was to impart the power of transformation into eternal life. The tree of knowledge was to lead man to the knowledge of good and evil; and, according to the divine intention, this was to be attained through his not eating of its fruit. This end was to be accomplished, not only by his discerning in the limit imposed by the prohibition the difference between that which accorded with the will of God and that which opposed it, but also by his coming eventually, through obedience to the prohibition, to recognize the fact that all that is opposed to the will of God is an evil to be avoided, and, through voluntary resistance to such evil, to the full development of the freedom of choice originally imparted to him into the actual freedom of a deliberate and self-conscious choice of good. By obedience to the divine will he would have attained to a godlike knowledge of good and evil, *i.e.* to one in accordance with his own likeness to God. He would have detected the evil in the approaching tempter; but instead of yielding to it, he would have resisted it, and thus have made good his own property acquired with consciousness and of his own free will, and in this way by proper self-determination would gradually have advanced to the possession of truest liberty.

—*Commentary on the Old Testament*

ADAM CLARKE

8. *A garden eastward in Eden.* Though the word *Eden* signifies "pleasure" or "delight," it is certainly the name of a place. See chap. iv. 16; 2 Kings xix. 12; Isa. xxxvii. 12; Ezek. xxvii. 23; Amos i. 5.

9. *Every tree that is pleasant to the sight.* If we take up these expressions literally, they may bear the following interpretation: the tree pleasant to the sight may mean every beautiful tree or plant which for shape, color, or fragrance, delights the senses, such as flowering shrubs.

And good for food. All fruit-bearing trees, whether of the pulpy fruits, as apples, or of the kernel or nut kind, such as dates and nuts.

The tree of life. It is likely that this *tree of life* which was placed *in the midst of the garden* was intended as an emblem of that life which man should ever live, provided he continued in obedience to his Maker. And probably the use of this tree was intended as the means of preserving the body of man in a state of continual vital energy, and an antidote against death. This seems strongly indicated from chap. iii. 22.

And the tree of knowledge of good and evil. Considering this also in a merely literal point of view, it may mean any tree or plant which possessed the property of increasing the knowledge of what was in nature. The prohibition was intended to exercise this faculty in man that should constantly teach him this moral lesson, that there were some things fit and others unfit to be done, and that in reference to this point the tree itself should be both a constant teacher and monitor. The eating of its fruit would not have increased this moral faculty, but the prohibition was intended to exercise the faculty he already possessed.

10. *A river went out of Eden.* The most probable account of its situation is that given by Hadrian Reland. He supposes it to have been in Armenia, near the sources of the great rivers Euphrates, Tigris, Phasis, and Araxes. He thinks *Pison* was the Phasis, a river of Colchis, emptying itself into the Black Sea. This country was famous for *gold*, whence the fable of the golden fleece, attempted to be carried away from that country by the heroes of Greece. The *Gihon* he thinks to be the Araxes, which runs into the Caspian Sea, both the words having the same signification, namely, a "rapid motion." The *Hiddekel* all agree to be the Tigris, and the other river, *Phrat*, or *Perath*, to be the Euphrates. All of these rivers rise in the same tract of mountainous country, though they do not arise from one head.

MATTHEW HENRY

seen God going before us and putting us into it. If we have not forced providence, but taken the hints of direction it has given us, we may hope to find a paradise. See Ps. xlvii. 4.

2. How God appointed him to dress the garden and to keep it. Paradise itself was not a place of exemption from work. Note here, (1) We were none of us sent into the world to be idle. He that made us these souls and bodies has given us something to work with; he that gave us being has given us business, to serve him and our generation, and to work out our salvation. (2) Secular employments will very well consist with a state of innocency and a life of communion with God. (3) The husbandman's calling is an ancient and honourable calling; it was needful even in paradise. It was a calling giving man an opportunity of admiring the Creator. While his hands were about his trees, his heart might be with his God. (4) There is a true pleasure in the business which God calls us to, and employs us in.

III. The command which God gave to man in innocency, and the covenant he then took him into. Hitherto we have seen God as man's powerful Creator and his bountiful Benefactor; now he appears as his Ruler and Lawgiver.

Verses 16–17

Observe here, I. God's authority over man, as a creature that had reason and freedom of will. The Lord God commanded the man, who stood now as the father and representative of all mankind, to receive law, as he had lately received a nature. The brute-creatures have their respective instincts; but man was made capable of performing reasonable service, and therefore received, not only the command of a Creator, but the command of a Prince and Master.

II. The particular act of this authority, in prescribing to him what he should do.

1. A confirmation of his present happiness to him, in that grant, *Of every tree in the garden thou mayest freely eat.* This was not only an allowance of liberty to him, but it was, withal, an assurance of life to him, immortal life, upon his obedience. Thus, upon condition of perfect personal and perpetual obedience, Adam was sure of paradise to himself and his heirs for ever.

2. A trial of his obedience, upon pain of the forfeiture of all his happiness: "Know, Adam, that thou art now upon thy good behaviour, thou art put into paradise upon trial; be observant, be obedient, and thou art made for ever; otherwise thou wilt be as miserable as now thou art happy." Here,

(1) Adam is threatened with death in case of disobedience. Observe, [1] Even Adam, in innocency, was awed with a threatening. [2] The penalty threatened is death. [3] This was threatened as the immediate consequence of sin.

(2) Adam is tried with a positive law, not to eat of the fruit *of the tree of knowledge.* [1] Because the reason of it is fetched purely from the will of the Law-maker. Adam had in his nature an aversion to that which was evil in itself, and therefore he is tried in a thing which was evil only because it was forbidden. [2] Because the restraint of it is laid upon the desires of the flesh and of the mind, which, in the corrupt nature of man, are the two great fountains of sin. This prohibition checked both his appetite towards sensitive delights and his ambition of curious knowledge, that his body might be ruled by his soul and his soul by his God.

Verses 18–20

I. An instance of the Creator's care of man and his fatherly concern for his comfort, *v.* 18. He lets him know, for his encouragement in his obedience, that he was a friend.

1. How God graciously pitied his solitude. He that made him knew both him and what was good for him, better than he did himself, and he said, "It is not good that he should continue thus alone." (1) It is not for his comfort; for man is a sociable creature. Perfect solitude would turn a paradise into a desert, and a palace into a dungeon. (2) It is not for the increase and continuance of his kind. God could have made a world of men at first, to replenish the earth. God saw fit to make up that number by a succession of generations, which, as God had formed man, must be from two, and those male and female; one will be ever one.

2. How God graciously resolved to provide society for him. The result of this reasoning concerning him was this kind resolution, *I will make a help-meet for him.* Note hence, (1) In our best state in this world we have need of one another's help. (2) It is God only who perfectly knows our wants, and is perfectly able to supply them all, Phil. iv. 19. In him alone

JAMIESON, FAUSSET, BROWN

15. put the man into the garden of Eden to dress it—not only to give him a pleasant employment, but to place him on his probation, and as the title of this garden, the garden of the Lord (ch. 13:10; Ezek. 28:13), indicates, it was in fact a temple in which he worshipped God, and was daily employed in offering the sacrifices of thanksgiving and praise.

JOSEPH PARKER:

What a chance man had in beginning life as a gardener! Beginning life in the open, sunny air without even a hothouse to try his temper! Surely he ought to have done something better than he did. The air was pure, the climate was bright, the soil was kindly: you had but to "tickle it with a spade and it laughed in flowers." And a river in the grounds! Woe to those who have their water far to fetch! But here in the garden is the stream, so broad that the moment it is liberated from the sacred place it divides itself into four evangelists, carrying everywhere the odors of Eden and the offer of kindly help. Surely, then, man was well housed to begin with. He did not begin life as a beggar. He farmed his own God-given land, without disease, or disability, or taxation to fret him; yet what did he make of the fruitful inheritance? Did the roots turn to poison in his mouth, and the flowers hang their heads in shame when his shadow fell on them? We shall see.—*The People's Bible*

17. thou shalt not eat of it . . . thou shalt surely die—no reason assigned for the prohibition, but death was to be the punishment of disobedience. A positive command like this was not only the simplest and easiest, but the only trial to which their fidelity could be exposed.

18-25. The Making of Woman, and Institution of Marriage. **18. it is not good for man to be alone**—In the midst of plenty and delights, he was conscious of feelings he could not gratify. To make him sensible of his wants,

ADAM CLARKE

15. *Put him into the garden . . . to dress it and to keep it.* Horticulture, or gardening, is the first kind of employment on record, and that in which man was engaged while in a state of perfection and innocence. Though the garden may be supposed to produce all things spontaneously, as the whole vegetable surface of the earth certainly did at the creation, yet dressing and tilling were afterwards necessary to maintain the different kinds of plants and vegetables in their perfection, and to repress luxuriance. Even in a state of innocence we cannot conceive it possible that man could have been happy if inactive. God gave him work to do, and his employment contributed to his happiness; for the structure of his body, as well as of his mind, plainly proves that he was never intended for a merely contemplative life.

17. *Of the tree of the knowledge . . . thou shalt not eat.* This is the first positive precept God gave to man; and it was given as a test of obedience, and a proof of his being in a dependent, probationary state. It was necessary that, while constituted lord of this lower world, he should know that he was only God's vicegerent, and must be accountable to Him for the use of his mental and corporeal powers, and for the use he made of the different creatures put under his care. The man from whose mind the strong impression of this dependence and responsibility is erased necessarily loses sight of his origin and end, and is capable of any species of wickedness. As God is sovereign, He has a right to give to His creatures what commands He thinks proper.

Thou shalt surely die. Literally, "a death thou shalt die"; or, "dying thou shalt die." Thou shalt not only die spiritually, by losing the life of God, but from that moment thou shalt become mortal, and shalt continue in a dying state till thou die. This we find literally accomplished; every moment of man's life may be considered as an act of dying, till soul and body are separated.

18. *It is not good that the man should be alone.* "Only himself."

I will make him an help meet for him; a help, a counterpart of himself, one formed from him, and a perfect resemblance of his person. If the word be rendered scrupulously literally, it signifies one "like," or "as himself," standing opposite to or before him. And this implies that the woman was to be a perfect resemblance of the man, possessing neither inferiority nor superiority, but being in all things like and equal to himself. As man was made a social creature, it was not proper that he should be alone; for to be alone, i.e., without a matrimonial companion, was not good.

MATTHEW HENRY

our help is, and from him are all our helpers. (3) A suitable wife is a help-meet, and is from the Lord. (4) Family-society, if it is agreeable, is a redress sufficient for the grievance of solitude. He that has a good God, a good heart, and a good wife, to converse with, and yet complains he wants conversation, would not have been easy and content in paradise.

II. An instance of the creatures' subjection to man, and his dominion over them (*v.* 19, 20). Thus God gave man livery and seisin of the fair estate he had granted him, and put him in possession of his dominion over the creatures. God brought them to him, that he might name them, and so might give, 1. A proof of his knowledge, as a creature endued with the faculties both of reason and speech. And, 2. A proof of his power. It is an act of authority to impose names. God gave names to the day and night, to the firmament, to the earth, and to the sea; and he *calleth the stars by their names*, to show that he is the supreme Lord of these. But he gave Adam leave to name the beasts and fowls, as their subordinate lord; for, having made him in his own image, he thus put some of his honour upon him.

III. An instance of the creatures' insufficiency to be a happiness for man: *But* (among them all) *for Adam there was not found a help-meet for him.* Observe here, 1. The dignity and excellency of the human nature. 2. The vanity of this world and the things of it; put them all together, and they will not make a help-meet for man. They will not suit the nature of his soul, nor supply its needs, nor satisfy its just desires, nor run parallel with its never-failing duration.

Verses 21–25

Here we have, I. The making of the woman, to be a help-meet for Adam. Observe, 1. That Adam was first formed, then Eve (1 Tim. ii. 13). If man is the head, she is the crown, a crown to her husband, the crown of the visible creation. The man was dust refined, but the woman was dust double-refined, one remove further from the earth. 2. That Adam slept while his wife was in making as one that had cast all his care on God, with a cheerful resignation of himself and all his affairs to his Maker's will and wisdom. Jehovah-jireh, let the Lord provide when and whom he pleases. 3. That *God caused a sleep to fall on Adam,* and made it a deep sleep. While he knows no sin, God will take care he shall feel no pain. 4. That the woman was *made of a rib out of the side of Adam*; not made out of his head to rule over him, nor out of his feet to be trampled upon by him, but out of his side to be equal with him, under his arm to be protected, and near his heart to be beloved.

II. The marriage of the woman to Adam. Marriage is honourable, but this surely was the most honourable marriage that ever was, in which God himself had all along an immediate hand. Marriages (they say) are made in heaven: we are sure this was, for the man, the woman, the match, were all God's own work; he, by his power, made them *both*, and now, by his ordinance, made them *one*. 1. God, as *her* Father, brought the woman to the man, as his second self, and a help-meet for him. That wife that is of God's making by special grace, and of God's bringing by special providence, is likely to prove a help-meet for a man. 2. From God, as *his* Father, Adam received her. God's gifts to us are to be received with a humble thankful acknowledgment of his wisdom in suiting them to us, and his favour in bestowing them on us. Further, in token of his acceptance of her, he gave her a name, not peculiar to her, but common to her sex: *She shall be called woman, Ishah,* a *she-man,* differing from man in sex only, not in nature.

III. The institution of the ordinance of marriage, and the settling of the law of it, *v.* 24. The sabbath and marriage were two ordinances instituted in innocency, the former for the preservation of the church, the latter for the preservation of the world of mankind. It appears (by Matt. xix. 4, 5) that it was God himself who said here, "A man must leave all his relations, to cleave to his wife." 1. See here how great the virtue of a divine ordinance is; the bonds of it are stronger even than those of nature. 2. See how necessary it is that children should take their parents' consent along with them in their marriage. 3. See what need there is both of prudence and prayer in the choice of this relation, which is so near and so lasting. 4. See how firm the bond of marriage is, not to be divided and weakened by having many wives (Mal. ii. 15) nor to be broken or cut off by divorce, for any cause but fornication, or voluntary desertion. 5. See how dear the affection

JAMIESON, FAUSSET, BROWN

19. God brought unto Adam—not all the animals in existence, but those chiefly in his immediate neighborhood to be subservient to his use. **whatsoever Adam called every living creature, that was the name thereof**—His powers of perception and intelligence were supernaturally enlarged to know the characters, habits, and uses of each species that was brought to him.

20. but for Adam there was not found an help meet for him—The design of this singular scene was to show him that none of the living creatures he saw were on an equal footing with himself, and that while each class came with its mate of the same nature, form, and habits, he alone had no companion. Besides, in giving names to them he was led to exercise his powers of speech and to prepare for social intercourse with his partner, a creature yet to be formed. **21. deep sleep**—probably an ecstasy or trance like that of the prophets, when they had visions and revelations of the Lord, for the whole scene was probably visible to the mental eye of Adam, and hence his rapturous exclamation. **took one of his ribs**—"She was not made out of his head to surpass him, nor from his feet to be trampled on, but from his side to be equal to him, and near his heart to be dear to him."

23. Woman—in *Hebrew*— "man-ess."

one flesh—The human pair differed from all other pairs, that by the peculiar formation of Eve, they were one. And this passage is appealed to by our Lord as the divine institution of marriage (Matt. 19:4, 5; Eph. 5:28). Thus Adam appears as a creature formed after the image of God—showing his *knowledge* by giving names to the animals, his *righteousness* by his approval of the marriage relation, and his *holiness* by his principles and feelings, and finding gratification in the service and enjoyment of God.

ADAM CLARKE

19. *Out of the ground.* Concerning the formation of the different kinds of animals, see the preceding chapter.

20. *And Adam gave names to all cattle.* Two things God appears to have had in view by causing man to name all the cattle: (1) To show him with what comprehensive powers of mind his Maker had endued him; and (2) To show him that no creature yet formed could make him a suitable companion. And that this twofold purpose was answered we shall shortly see; for,

(1) *Adam gave names;* but how? From an intimate knowledge of the nature and properties of each creature. Here we see the perfection of his knowledge; for it is well known that the names affixed to the different animals in Scripture always express some prominent feature and essential characteristic of the creatures to which they are applied.

(2) Adam was convinced that none of these creatures could be a suitable companion for him, and that, therefore, he must continue in the state that was not good, or be a farther debtor to the bounty of his Maker; for among all the animals which he had named *there was not found an help meet for him.* Hence we read,

21. *The Lord God caused a deep sleep to fall upon Adam.* This was neither swoon nor ecstasy, but what our translation very properly terms a deep sleep.

And he took one of his ribs. It is immaterial whether we render *tsela* a rib or a part of his side, for it may mean either: some part of man was to be used on the occasion, whether bone or flesh it matters not, though it is likely, from v. 23, that a part of both was taken; for Adam, knowing how the woman was formed, said, "This is *flesh* of my *flesh,* and *bone* of my *bones.*" As God formed her out of a part of the man himself, he saw she was of the same nature, the same identical flesh and blood, and of the same constitution in all respects, and consequently having equal powers, faculties, and rights. This at once ensured his affection, and excited his esteem.

23. *Adam said, This is now bone of my bones.* There is a very delicate and expressive meaning in the original which does not appear in our version. When the different genera of creatures were brought to Adam, that he might assign them their proper names, it is probable that they passed in pairs before him, and as they passed received their names. To this circumstance the words in this place seem to refer. Instead of *this now is* we should render more literally "this turn," this creature, which now passes or appears before me, is flesh of my flesh. The creatures that had passed already before him were not suitable to him, and therefore it was said, "For Adam there was not a help meet found," v. 20; but when the woman came, formed out of himself, he felt all that attraction which consanguinity could produce, and at the same time saw that she was in her person and in her mind every way suitable to be his companion.

She shall be called Woman. A literal version of the Hebrew would appear strange, and yet a literal version is the only proper one. *Ish* signifies "man," and the word used to express what we term woman is the same with a feminine termination, *ishshah,* and literally means "she-man."

24. *Therefore shall a man leave his father and his mother.* There shall be, by the order of God, a more intimate connection formed between the man and woman than can subsist even between parents and children.

And they shall be one flesh. These words may be understood in a twofold sense. (1) These two shall be one flesh, shall be considered as one body, having no separate or independent rights, privileges, cares, concerns, each being equally interested in all things that concern the marriage state. (2) These two shall be for the production of one flesh; from their union a posterity shall spring, as exactly resembling themselves as they do each other. Our Lord quotes these words, Matt. xix. 5, with some variation from this text: "They twain shall be one flesh." So in Mark x. 8. St. Paul quotes

MATTHEW HENRY

ought to be between husband and wife, such as there is to our own bodies, Eph. v. 28.

IV. An evidence of the purity and innocency of that state wherein our first parents were created, *v.* 25. They were both naked. They needed no clothes for defence against cold nor heat. Nay, they needed none for decency; they were naked, and had no reason to be ashamed. *They knew not what shame was,* so the Chaldee reads it. Those that had no sin in their conscience might well have no shame in their faces, though they had no clothes to their backs.

CHAPTER 3

Verses 1–5

I. The tempter, and that was the devil, in the shape and likeness of a serpent.

1. It is certain it was the devil that beguiled Eve. The devil and Satan is the old serpent (Rev. xii. 9), a malignant spirit, by creation an angel of light and an immediate attendant upon God's throne, but by sin become an apostate from his first state and a rebel against God's crown and dignity. He knew he could not destroy man but by debauching him. The game therefore which Satan had to play was to draw our first parents to sin, and so to separate between them and their God. The whole race of mankind had here, as it were, but one neck, and at that Satan struck.

2. It was the devil in the likeness of a serpent. (1) Many a dangerous temptation comes to us in gay fine colours that are but skin-deep, and seems to come from above; for Satan can seem an angel of light. And, (2) Because it is a subtle creature. Many instances are given of the subtlety of the serpent. Observe, There is not anything by which the devil serves himself and his own interest more than by unsanctified subtlety.

II. The person tempted was the woman, now alone, and at a distance from her husband, but near the forbidden tree. It was the devil's subtlety. 1. To assault the weaker vessel with his temptations. 2. It was his policy to enter into discourse with her when she was alone. There are many temptations to which solitude gives great advantage; but the communion of saints contributes much to their strength and safety. 3. He took advantage by finding her near the forbidden tree, and probably gazing upon the fruit of it, only to satisfy her curiosity. Those that would not eat the forbidden fruit must not come near the forbidden tree. 4. Satan tempted Eve, that by her he might tempt Adam.

III. The temptation itself, and the artificial management of it. That which the devil aimed at was to persuade Eve to eat forbidden fruit; and to do this, he took the same method that he does still. He questioned whether it was a sin or no, *v.* 1. He denied that there was any danger in it, *v.* 4. He suggested much advantage by it, *v.* 5. And these are his common topics.

1. He questioned whether it was a sin or no to eat of this tree, and whether really the fruit of it was forbidden.

(1) *He said to the woman, Yea, hath God said, You shall not eat?* The first word intimated something said before, perhaps some discourse Eve had with herself, which Satan took hold of, and grafted this question upon. Observe here, [1] He does not discover his design at first, but puts a question which seemed innocent: "I hear a piece of news, pray is it true? Has God forbidden you to eat of this tree?" [2] He quotes the command fallaciously as if it were a prohibition, not only of that tree, but of all. [3] He seems to speak it tauntingly, upbraiding the woman with her shyness of meddling with that tree. [4] It is the subtlety of Satan to blemish the reputation of the divine law as uncertain or unreasonable, and so to draw people to sin.

(2) In answer to this question the woman gives

JAMIESON, FAUSSET, BROWN

CHAPTER 3

Vss. 1-5. THE TEMPTATION. **1. the serpent**—The fall of man was effected by the seductions of a serpent. That it was a real serpent is evident from the plain and artless style of the history and from the many allusions made to it in the New Testament. But the material serpent was the instrument or tool of a higher agent, Satan or the devil, to whom the sacred writers apply from this incident the reproachful name of "the serpent"—"the old dragon." Though Moses makes no mention of this wicked spirit—giving only the history of the visible world—yet in the fuller discoveries of the Gospel, it is distinctly intimated that Satan was the author of the plot (John 8:44; II Cor. 11:3; I John 3:8; I Tim. 2:14; Rev. 20:2). **more subtile**—Serpents are proverbial for wisdom (Matt. 10:16). But these reptiles were at first, probably, far superior in beauty as well as in sagacity to what they are in their present state. **He said**—There being in the pure bosoms of the first pair no principle of evil to work upon, a solicitation to sin could come only from *without*, as in the analogous case of Jesus Christ (Matt. 4:3); and as the tempter could not assume the human form, there being only Adam and Eve in the world, the agency of an inferior creature had to be employed. The dragon-serpent [BOCHART] seemed the fittest for the vile purpose; and the devil was allowed by Him who permitted the trial, to bring articulate sounds from its mouth. **unto the woman**—the object of attack, from his knowledge of her frailty, of her having been but a short time in the world, her limited experience of the animal tribes, and, above all, her being alone, unfortified by the presence and counsels of her husband. Though sinless and holy, she was a free agent, liable to be tempted and seduced.

yea, hath God said—Is it true that He has restricted you in using the fruits of this delightful place? This is not like one so good and kind. Surely there is some mistake. He insinuated a doubt as to her sense of the divine will and appeared as "an angel of light" (II Cor. 11:14), offering to lead her to the true interpretation. It was evidently from her regarding him as specially sent on that errand, that, instead of being startled by the reptile's speaking, she received him as a heavenly messenger.

ADAM CLARKE

in the same way, 1 Cor. vi. 16, and in Eph. v. 31. The Vulgate Latin, the Septuagint, the Syriac, the Arabic, and the Samaritan, all read the word "two." That this is the genuine reading I have no doubt.

We have here the first institution of marriage, and we see in it several particulars worthy of our most serious regard. (1) God pronounces the state of celibacy to be not a good one. (2) God made the woman *for* the man, and thus He has shown us that every son of Adam should be united to a daughter of Eve to the end of the world. (3) God made the woman *out* of the man, to intimate that the closest union, and the most affectionate attachment, should subsist in the matrimonial connection, so that the man should ever consider and treat the woman as a part of himself.

25. *They were both naked.* The weather was perfectly temperate, and therefore they had no need of clothing, the air being of the same temperature with their bodies. And as sin had not yet entered into the world, and no part of the human body had been put to any improper use, therefore there was no shame, for shame can only arise from a consciousness of sinful or irregular conduct.

CHAPTER 3

1. *Now the serpent was more subtil.* We have here one of the most difficult as well as the most important narratives in the whole Book of God. The last chapter ended with a short but striking account of the perfection and felicity of the first human beings, and this opens with an account of their transgression, degradation, and ruin. That man is in a fallen state, the history of the world, with that of the life and miseries of every human being, establishes beyond successful contradiction.

A. B. SIMPSON:

Sin entered through unbelief. Eve's first error was to listen to the devil's question about God's word. "Hath God said?" is always the beginning of sin. Let us take heed lest there be in us "an evil heart of unbelief, in departing from the living God." We begin by doubting God's Word about sin, and then by doubting His Word about salvation. It was because sin entered through unbelief that salvation must come through faith.

Eve's unbelief was not the deliberate denial of God's word, but a shadow of suspicion about the kindness of His word. In the light of the devil's question it seemed a little hard, and her answer made it a little harder still. And then the tempter dared to deny it openly and challenge her to disobey it. "Ye shall not surely die." The doubt of divine retribution was one of the earliest forms of human sin, and it is the form which today rationalism is trying its best to inculcate into the Church of God. Again the serpent is whispering to the Church, "Ye shall not surely die." Let us believe all God's words, whether spoken in warning or in promise. God's promises are always easily trusted when we fully believe and receive His commands.

—*Christ in the Bible*

MATTHEW HENRY

him a plain and full account of the law they were under, *v.* 2, 3. Here observe, [1] It was her weakness to enter into discourse with the serpent. It is a dangerous thing to treat with a temptation, which ought at first to be rejected with disdain and abhorrence. The garrison that sounds a parley is not far from being surrendered. [2] It was her wisdom to take notice of the liberty God had granted them. "Yea," says she, "we may eat of the fruit of the trees, thanks to our Maker, we have plenty and variety enough allowed us." [3] It was an instance of her resolution that she adhered to the command, and faithfully repeated it, as of unquestionable certainty: "We must not eat, therefore we will not touch. It is forbidden in the highest degree, and the authority of the prohibition is sacred to us." [4] She seems a little to waver about the threatening, all she makes of that is, *Lest you die.*

2. He denies that there was any danger in it, insisting that, though it might be the transgressing of a precept, yet it would not be the incurring of a penalty: *You shall not surely die, v.* 4. Either, (1) "It is not certain that you shall die," so some. Satan teaches men first to doubt and then to deny; he makes them sceptics first, and so by degrees makes them atheists. Or, (2) "It is certain you shall not die," so others. He avers his contradiction with the same phrase of assurance that God had used in ratifying the threatening. He concealed his own misery, that he might draw them into the like: thus he still deceives sinners into their own ruin. Hope of impunity is a great support to all iniquity.

3. He promises them advantage by it, *v.* 5. He could not have persuaded them to run the hazard of ruining themselves if he had not suggested to them a great probability of bettering themselves.

(1) He insinuates to them the great improvements they would make by eating of this fruit. And he suits the temptation to the pure state they were now in, intellectual delights and satisfactions. These were the baits with which he covered his hook. [1] "*Your eyes shall be opened;* you shall have much more of the power and pleasure of contemplation than now you have; you shall see further into things than now you do." [2] "*You shall be as gods,* as *Elohim,* mighty gods; not only omniscient, but omnipotent too." [3] "You shall know *good and evil,* that is, every thing that is desirable to be known." To support this part of the temptation, he abuses the name given to this tree: he perverts the sense of it, as if this tree would give them a speculative notional knowledge of the natures, kinds, and originals, of good and evil. And [4] All this presently: "*In the day you eat thereof* you will find a sudden and immediate change for the better." Now in all these insinuations he aims to beget in them, *First,* Discontent with their present state. *Secondly,* Ambition of preferment, as if they were fit to be gods.

(2) He insinuates to them that God had no good design upon them, in forbidding them this fruit, as if he durst not let them eat of that tree because then they would know their own strength, and would be able to cope with him. Now, [1] This was a great affront to God, and the highest indignity that could be done him, a reproach to his power, as if he feared his creatures, and much more a reproach to his goodness, as if he hated the work of his own hands and would not have those whom he has made to be made happy. [2] It was a most dangerous snare to our first parents, as it tended to alienate their affections from God.

Verses 6–8

Satan, at length, gains his point, and the stronghold is taken by his wiles.

I. We have here the inducements that moved them to transgress. 1. She saw no harm in this tree, more than in any of the rest. It seemed as good for food as any of them, and why should this be forbidden them rather than any of the rest? We are often betrayed into snares by an inordinate desire to have our senses gratified. It was the more coveted because it was prohibited. In us (that is, in our flesh, in our corrupt nature) there dwells a strange spirit of contradiction. *Nitimur in vetitum—We desire what is prohibited.* 2. She imagined more virtue in this tree than in any of the rest, that it was a tree not only not to be dreaded, but *to be desired to make one wise.* See here how the desire of unnecessary knowledge, under the mistaken notion of wisdom, proves hurtful and destructive to many. Our first parents, who knew so much, did not know this—that they knew enough.

II. The steps of the transgression, not steps upward, but downward. 1. She *saw.* She should have turned away her eyes from beholding vanity; but she enters into temptation, by looking with pleasure on the

JAMIESON, FAUSSET, BROWN

2. the woman said, We may eat of the fruit of the trees of the garden—In her answer, Eve extolled the large extent of liberty they enjoyed in ranging at will amongst all the trees—one only excepted, with respect to which, she declared there was no doubt, either of the prohibition or the penalty. But there is reason to think that she had already received an injurious impression; for in using the words—"lest ye die," instead of "ye shall surely die"—she spoke as if the tree had been forbidden because of some poisonous quality of its fruit. The tempter, perceiving this, became bolder in his assertions.

4. Ye shall not surely die—He proceeded, not only to assure her of perfect impunity, but to promise great benefits from partaking of it.

5. your eyes shall be opened—His words meant more than met the ear. In one sense her eyes were opened; for she acquired a direful experience of "good and evil"—of the happiness of a holy, and the misery of a sinful, condition. But he studiously concealed this result from Eve, who, fired with a generous desire for knowledge, thought only of rising to the rank and privileges of her angelic visitants.

6-9. THE FALL. **6. And when the woman saw that the tree was good for food**—Her imagination and feelings were completely won; and the fall of Eve was soon followed by that of Adam. The history of every temptation, and of every sin, is the same; the outward object of attraction, the inward commotion of mind, the increase and triumph of passionate desire; ending in the degradation, slavery, and ruin of the soul (Jas 1:15; I John 2:16).

ADAM CLARKE

3. *Neither shall ye touch it.* Did not the woman add this to what God had before spoken?

4. *Ye shall not surely die.* Here the father of lies at once appears; and appears, too, in flatly contradicting the assertion of God. The tempter insinuates the impossibility of her dying, as if he had said, God has created thee immortal; thy death, therefore, is impossible; and God knows this, for as thou livest by the tree of life, so shalt thou get increase of wisdom by the tree of knowledge.

5. *Your eyes shall be opened.* Your understanding shall be greatly enlightened and improved; *and ye shall be as gods, kelohim,* "like God," so the word should be translated; for what idea could our first parents have of *gods* before idolatry could have had any being, because sin had not yet entered into the world? The Syriac has the word in the singular number, and is the only one of all the versions which has hit on the true meaning. As the original word is the same which is used to point out the Supreme Being, chap. i. 1, so it has here the same signification, and the object of the tempter appears to have been this: to persuade our first parents that they should, by eating of this fruit, become wise and powerful as God (for knowledge is power), and be able to exist forever, independently of Him.

6. *The tree was good for food.* (1) The fruit appeared to be wholesome and nutritive. *And that it was pleasant to the eyes.* (2) The beauty of the fruit tended to whet and increase appetite. *And a tree to be desired to make one wise,* which was (3) an additional motive to please the palate. From these three sources all natural and moral evil sprang: they are exactly what the apostle calls the "desire of the flesh," the tree was good for food; "the desire of the eye," it was pleasant to the sight; and "the pride of life," it was a tree to be desired to make one wise. God had undoubtedly created our first parents not only very wise and intelligent, but also with a great capacity and suitable propensity to increase in knowledge. We see at once how transgression came; it was natural for them to desire to be increasingly wise. God had implanted this desire in their minds; but He showed them that this desire should be gratified in a certain way; that prudence and judgment should always regulate it; that they should

MATTHEW HENRY

forbidden fruit. Observe, a great deal of sin comes in at the eyes. 2. She *took*. It was her own act and deed. The devil did not take it, and put it into her mouth, whether she would or no; but she herself took it. Satan may tempt, but he cannot force; may persuade us to cast ourselves down, but he cannot cast us down, Matt. iv. 6. 3. She *did eat*. Perhaps she did not intend, when she looked, to take, nor, when she took, to eat; but this was the result. Note, The way of sin is down-hill; a man cannot stop himself when he will. Suppress the first emotions of sin, and leave it off before it be meddled with. *Obsta principiis—Nip mischief in the bud*. 4. She *gave also to her husband with her*. She gave it to him, persuading him with the same arguments that the serpent had used with her, adding this to all the rest, that she herself had eaten of it, and found it so far from being deadly that it was extremely pleasant and grateful. As was the devil, so was Eve, no sooner a sinner than a tempter. 5. *He did eat*, overcome by his wife's importunity. In neglecting the tree of life of which he was allowed to eat, and eating of the tree of knowledge which was forbidden, he plainly showed a contempt of the favours God had bestowed on him, and a preference given to those God did not see fit for him. He would be both his own carver and his own master, would have what he pleased and do what he pleased: his sin was, in one word, *disobedience* (Rom. v. 19). The human nature being lodged entirely in our first parents, henceforward it could not but be transmitted from them under an attainder of guilt, a stain of dishonour, and an hereditary disease of sin and corruption. And can we say, then, that Adam's sin had but little harm in it?

III. The immediate consequences of the transgression.

1. Shame seized them unseen, *v*. 7.

(1) The strong convictions they fell under, in their own bosoms: *The eyes of them both were opened*. It is not meant of the eyes of the body, but the eyes of their consciences were opened, their hearts smote them for what they had done. Now, when it was too late, they saw the folly of eating forbidden fruit. They saw the happiness they had fallen from, and the misery they had fallen into. They saw a law in their members warring against the law of their minds. The text tells us that they saw *that they were naked*, that is, [1] That they were stripped, deprived of all the honours and joys of their paradise-state. They were disarmed; their defence had departed from them. [2] That they were shamed. They saw themselves laid open to the contempt and reproach of heaven, and earth, and their own consciences. Now see here, *First*, What a dishonour and disquietment sin is; it makes mischief wherever it is admitted. *Secondly*, What a deceiver Satan is. He told our first parents, when he tempted them, that their eyes should be opened; and so they were, but not as they understood it; they were opened to their shame and grief.

(2) The sorry shift they made to palliate these convictions, and to arm themselves against them: *They sewed*, or platted, *fig-leaves together*; and to cover, at least, part of their shame from one another, they *made themselves aprons*. See here what is commonly the folly of those that have sinned. [1] That they are more solicitous to save their credit before men than to obtain their pardon from God. [2] That the excuses men make, to cover and extenuate their sins, are vain and frivolous. Like the aprons of fig-leaves, they make the matter never the better, but the worse; the shame, thus hidden, becomes the more shameful.

2. Fear seized them immediately upon their eating the forbidden fruit, *v*. 8. Observe here, (1) What was the cause and occasion of their fear: They *heard the voice of the Lord God walking in the garden in the cool of the day*. It was the approach of the Judge that put them into a fright; and yet he came in such a manner as made it formidable only to guilty consciences. He came in the cool of the day, not in the night, when all fears are double fearful, nor in the heat of day, for he came not in the heat of his anger. They heard his voice, and probably it was a still small voice, like that in which he came to enquire after Elijah. (2) What was the effect and evidence of their fear: *They hid themselves from the presence of the Lord God*—a sad change ! God had become a terror to them, and then no marvel that they had become a terror to themselves. Their own consciences accused them, and set their sin before them in its proper colours. Their fig-leaves failed them, and would do them no service. Knowing themselves guilty, they durst not stand a trial, but absconded, and fled from justice. See here, [1] The falsehood of the tempter. He promised them they should be safe, but now they cannot so much as think themselves so; he promised them they should be knowing,

JAMIESON, FAUSSET, BROWN

ALEXANDER MACLAREN:

As long as the prohibition was undoubted and the fatal results certain, the fascinations of the forbidden thing were not felt. But as soon as these were tampered with, Eve saw "that the tree was good for food, and that it was a delight to the eyes." So it is still. Weaken the awe-inspiring sense of God's command, and of the ruin that follows the breach of it, and the heart of man is like a city without walls, into which any enemy can march unhindered. So long as God's "Thou shalt not, lest thou die," rings in the ears, the eyes see little beauty in the sirens that sing and beckon. But once that awful voice is deadened, they charm, and allure to dally with them.

In the undeveloped condition of primitive man temptation could assail him only through the senses and appetites, and its assault would be the more irresistible because reflection and experience were not yet his. But the act of yielding was, as sin ever is, a deliberate choice to please self and disobey God. The woman's more emotional, sensitive, compliant nature made here the first victim; and her greatest glory, her craving to share her good with him whom she loves and her power to sway his will and acts, made her his temptress. "As the husband is, the wife is," says Tennyson; but the converse is even truer: As the wife is, the man is.

The fatal consequences came with a rush. There is a gulf between being tempted and sinning, but the results of the sin are closely knit to it. They come automatically, as surely as a stream from a fountain. The promise of knowing good and evil was indeed kept, but instead of its making the sinners "like gods," it showed them that they were like beasts, and brought the first sense of shame. To know evil was, no doubt, a forward step intellectually; but to know it by experience, and as part of themselves, necessarily changed their ignorant innocence into bitter knowledge, and conscience awoke to rebuke them. The first thing that their opened eyes saw was themselves, and the immediate result of the sight was the first blush of shame. Before, they had walked in innocent unconsciousness, like angels or infants; now they had knowledge of good and evil, because their sin had made evil a part of themselves, and the knowledge was bitter.

—*Expositions of Holy Scripture*

they heard the voice of the Lord God walking in the garden—The divine Being appeared in the same manner as formerly—uttering the well-known tones of kindness, walking in some visible form—not running hastily, as one impelled by the influence of angry feelings. How beautifully expressive are these words of the familiar and condescending manner in which He had hitherto held intercourse with the first pair. **in the cool of the day**—lit., the breeze of the day—the evening. **hid themselves amongst the trees**—Shame, remorse, fear—a sense of guilt—feelings to which they had hitherto been strangers disordered their minds and led them to shun Him whose approach they used to welcome. How foolish to think of eluding His notice (Ps. 139:1-12).

ADAM CLARKE

carefully examine what God had opened to their view; and should not pry into what He chose to conceal. He alone who knows all things knows how much knowledge the soul needs to its perfection and increasing happiness, in what subjects this may be legitimately sought, and where the mind may make excursions and discoveries to its prejudice and ruin.

7. *The eyes of them both were opened*. They now had a sufficient discovery of their sin and folly in disobeying the command of God; they could discern between good and evil; and what was the consequence? Confusion and shame were engendered, because innocence was lost and guilt contracted.

8. *The voice of the Lord*. The *voice* is properly used here, for as God is an infinite Spirit, and cannot be confined to any form, so He can have no personal appearance. It is very likely that God used to converse with them in the garden, and that the usual time was the decline of the day, in the "evening breeze"; and probably this was the time that our first parents employed in the more solemn acts of their religious worship, at which God was ever present. The time for this solemn worship is again come, and God is in His place; but Adam and Eve have sinned, and therefore, instead of being found in the place of worship, are hidden among the trees!

MATTHEW HENRY

but they see themselves at a loss, and know not so much as where to hide themselves; he promised them they should be as gods, great, and bold, and daring, but they are as criminals discovered. [2] The folly of sinners, to think it either possible or desirable to hide themselves from God. [3] The fear that attends sin. All that amazing fear of God's appearances, the accusations of conscience, the approaches of trouble, the assaults of inferior creatures, and the arrests of death, which is common among men, is the effect of sin.

Verses 9–10

The arraignment of these deserters before the righteous Judge.

I. The startling question with which God pursued Adam and arrested him: *Where art thou?* Not, In what *place*? but, In what *condition*? "Is this all thou hast gotten by eating forbidden fruit? Note, 1. This enquiry after Adam may be looked upon as a gracious pursuit, in kindness to him, and in order to his recovery. Note, 2. If sinners will but consider where they are, they will not rest till they return to God.

II. The trembling answer which Adam gave to this question: *I heard thy voice in the garden, and I was afraid, v.* 10. He does not own his guilt, and yet in effect confesses it by owning his shame and fear.

Verses 11–13

The offenders found guilty by their own confession, and yet endeavouring to excuse and extenuate their fault.

I. How their confession was extorted from them. God put it to the man: *Who told thee that thou wast naked? v.* 11. "How camest thou to be sensible of thy nakedness as thy shame?" *Hast thou eaten of the forbidden tree?* Note, Though God knows all our sins, yet he will know them from us,'and requires from us an ingenuous confession of them; not that he may be informed, but that we may be humbled. The question put to the woman was, *What is this that thou hast done? v.* 13. Note, It concerns those who have eaten forbidden fruit themselves, and especially those who have enticed others to eat it likewise, seriously to consider what they have done. In eating forbidden fruit, we have offended a great and gracious God. In enticing others to eat of it, we do the devil's work, make ourselves guilty of other men's sins, and accessory to their ruin.

II. How their crime was extenuated by them in their confession. It was to no purpose to plead *not guilty*. Instead of aggravating the sin, and taking shame to themselves, they excuse the sin, and lay the shame and blame on others. 1. Adam lays all the blame upon his wife. Learn, hence, never to be brought to sin by that which will not bring us off in the judgment; let us therefore never act against our consciences, nor ever displease God, to please the best friend we have in the world. But this is not the worst of it. He not only lays the blame upon his wife, but expresses it so as tacitly to reflect on God himself. He insinuates that God was accessory to his sin: he gave him the woman, and she gave him the fruit. Note, There is a strange proneness in those that are tempted to say that they are tempted of God, as if our abusing God's gifts would excuse our violation of God's laws. 2. Eve lays all the blame upon the serpent: *The serpent beguiled me.* Sin is a brat that nobody is willing to own, a sign that it is a scandalous thing. Learn hence, (1) That Satan's temptations are all beguilings, his arguments are all fallacies, his allurements are all cheats. Sin deceives us, and, by deceiving, cheats us. It is by the *deceitfulness of sin* that the heart is hardened. See Rom. vii. 11; Heb. iii. 13. (2) Satan's subtlety will not justify us in sin: though he is the tempter, we are the sinners; and indeed it is our own lust that draws us aside and entices us, Jam. i. 14.

Verses 14–15

God immediately proceeds to pass sentence; and, in these verses, he begins (where the sin began) with the serpent, because he was already convicted of rebellion against God.

I. The sentence passed upon the tempter may be considered as lighting upon the serpent. The devil's instruments must share in the devil's punishments. Now, 1. The serpent is here laid under the curse of God: *Thou art cursed above all cattle.* Unsanctified subtlety often proves a great curse to a man; and the more crafty men are to do evil the more mischief they do. 2. He is here laid under man's reproach and enmity. (1) He is to be for ever looked upon as a vile and despicable creature. His crime was that he tempted Eve to eat that which she should not; his punishment was that he was necessitated to

JAMIESON, FAUSSET, BROWN

CHARLES H. SPURGEON:

And now hear the voice of God as he cries, "Adam, where art thou?" Oh! there were two truths in that short sentence. It showed that *Adam was lost,* or God would not have needed to ask him where he was. Until we have lost a thing, we need not inquire about it; but when God said, "Adam, where art thou?" it was the voice of a shepherd inquiring for his lost sheep; or better still, the cry of a loving parent asking for his child that has ran away from him, "Where art thou?" There are but three words, but they contain the dread doctrine of our lost estate. When *God* asks, "Where art thou?" man must be lost. When God himself inquires where man is, he must be lost in a more awful sense than you and I have as yet fully known. But then, there was also mercy upon man, or else he would have let him remain lost, and would not have said, "Where art thou?" Men do not inquire for what they do not value. There was a gospel sermon, I think, in those three divine words as they penetrated the dense parts of the thicket, and reached the tingling ears of the fugitives—"Where art thou?" Thy God is not willing to lose thee; He is come forth to seek thee, just as by and bye He means to come forth in the Person of His Son, not only to seek but to save that which now is lost.—*The Treasury of the Old Testament*

10-13. THE EXAMINATION. **10. afraid, because . . . naked**—apparently, a confession—the language of sorrow; but it was evasive—no signs of true humility and penitence—each tries to throw the blame on another.

12. The woman . . . gave me—He blames God [CALVIN]. As the woman had been given him for his companion and help, he had eaten of the tree from love to her; and perceiving she was ruined, was determined not to survive her [M'KNIGHT].

13. beguiled—cajoled by flattering lies. This sin of the first pair was heinous and aggravated—it was not simply eating an apple, but a love of self, dishonor to God, ingratitude to a benefactor, disobedience to the best of Masters—a preference of the creature to the Creator.

14-24. THE SENTENCE. **14. And the Lord God said unto the serpent**—The Judge pronounces a doom: first, on the material serpent, which is cursed above all creatures. From being a model of grace and elegance in form, it has become the type of all that is odious, disgusting, and low [LECLERC, ROSENMULLER]; or the curse has converted its natural condition into a punishment; it is now branded with infamy and avoided with horror; next, on the spiritual serpent, the seducer. Already fallen, he was to be still more degraded and his power wholly destroyed by the offspring of those he had deceived.

ADAM CLARKE

10. ***I was afraid, because I was naked.*** **See the immediate consequences of sin. (1) Shame, because of the ingratitude marked in the rebellion, and because that in aiming to be like God they were now sunk into a state of the greatest wretchedness. (2) Fear, because they saw they had been deceived by Satan, and were exposed to that death and punishment from which he had promised them an exemption. Shame and fear were the first fruits of sin, and fruits which it has invariably produced, from the first transgression to the present time.**

12-13. ***And the man said.*** **We have here some farther proofs of the fallen state of man, and that the consequences of that state extend to his remotest posterity. (1) On the question, "Hast thou eaten of the tree?" Adam is obliged to acknowledge his transgression; but he does this in such a way as to shift off the blame from himself, and lay it upon God and upon the woman! "This woman whom Thou didst give to be with me," to be my companion, (for so the word is repeatedly used,) "she gave me, and I did eat." I have no farther blame in this transgression; I did not pluck the fruit; she took it and gave it to me.**

(2) When the woman is questioned, she lays the blame upon God and the serpent, "The serpent beguiled me, and I did eat." Thou didst make him much wiser than Thou didst make me, and therefore my simplicity and ignorance were overcome by his superior wisdom and subtlety. I can have no fault here; the fault is his, and His who made him so wise and me so ignorant. Thus we find that, while the eyes of their body were opened to see their degraded state, the eyes of their understanding were closed, so that they could not see the sinfulness of sin; and at the same time their hearts were hardened through its deceitfulness.

14. ***And the Lord God said unto the serpent.*** **The tempter is not asked why he deceived the woman; he cannot roll the blame on any other; self-tempted, he fell, and it is natural for him, such is his enmity, to deceive and destroy all he can. His fault admits of no excuse, and therefore God begins to pronounce sentence on him first. And here we must consider a twofold sentence, one on Satan and the other on the agent he employed.**

MATTHEW HENRY | JAMIESON, FAUSSET, BROWN | ADAM CLARKE

MATTHEW HENRY

eat that which he would not: *Dust thou shalt eat.* (2) He is to be for ever looked upon as a venomous noxious creature, and a proper object of hatred and detestation. The serpent is hurtful to man, and often bruises his heel, because it can reach no higher; nay, notice is taken of his biting the horses' heels, *ch.* xlix. 17. But man is victorious over the serpent, and bruises his head, that is, gives him a mortal wound, aiming to destroy the whole generation of vipers. This sentence pronounced upon the serpent is much fortified by that promise of God to his people, *Thou shalt tread upon the lion and the adder* (Ps. xci. 13), and that of Christ to his disciples, *They shall take up serpents* (Mark xvi. 18). Observe here, The serpent and the woman had just now been very familiar and friendly in discourse about the forbidden fruit, and a wonderful agreement there was between them; but here they are irreconcilably set at variance. Note, Sinful friendships justly end in mortal feuds: those that unite in wickedness will not unite long.

II. This sentence may be considered as levelled at the devil, who only made use of the serpent as his vehicle in this appearance, but was himself the principal agent.

1. A perpetual reproach is here fastened upon that great enemy both to God and man. Under the cover of the serpent, he is here sentenced to be, (1) Degraded and accursed of God. *How art thou fallen, O Lucifer!* He that would be above God, and would head a rebellion against him, is justly exposed here to contempt, and God will humble those that will not humble themselves. (2) Detested and abhorred of all mankind. He is here condemned to a state of war and irreconcilable enmity. (3) Destroyed and ruined at last by *the great Redeemer*, signified by the breaking of his head. His subtle politics shall all be baffled, his usurped power shall be entirely crushed.

2. A perpetual quarrel is here commenced between the kingdom of God and the kingdom of the devil among men. It is the fruit of this enmity, (1) That there is a continual conflict between grace and corruption in the hearts of God's people. (2) That there is likewise a continual struggle between the wicked and the godly in this world.

3. A gracious promise is here made of Christ, as the deliverer of fallen man from the power of Satan. It was said in the hearing of our first parents, who, doubtless, saw a door of hope opened to them. Here was the dawning of the gospel day. No sooner was the wound given than the remedy was provided and revealed. Notice is here given them of three things concerning Christ:—(1) His incarnation, that he should be *the seed of the woman*, the seed of *that* woman; therefore his genealogy (Luke iii) goes so high as to show him to be the son of Adam, but God does the woman the honour to call him rather her seed, because she it was whom the devil had beguiled, and on whom Adam had laid the blame; herein God magnifies his grace, in that, though the woman was first in the transgression, yet she shall be saved *by* childbearing (as some read it), that is, by the promised seed who shall descend from her, 1 Tim. ii. 15. He was likewise to be the seed of a woman only, of a virgin. (2) His sufferings and death, pointed at in Satan's *bruising his heel*, that is, his human nature. Satan tempted Christ in the wilderness, to draw him into sin; and some think it was Satan that terrified Christ in his agony, to drive him to despair. It was the devil that put it into the heart of Judas to betray Christ, of Peter to deny him, of the chief priests to prosecute him, of the false witnesses to accuse him, and of Pilate to condemn him, aiming in all this, by destroying the Saviour, to ruin the salvation; but, on the contrary, it was by death that Christ *destroyed him that had the power of death*, Heb. ii. 14. Christ's heel was bruised when his feet were pierced and nailed to the cross, and Christ's sufferings are continued in the sufferings of the saints for his name. The devil tempts them, casts them into prison, persecutes and slays them, and so bruises the heel of Christ, who is afflicted in their afflictions. But, while the heel is bruised on earth, it is well that the head is safe in heaven. (3) His victory over Satan thereby. Satan had now trampled upon the woman, and insulted her; but the seed of the woman should be raised up in the fulness of time to *triumph over him*, Col. ii. 15. *He shall bruise his head* that is, he shall destroy all his politics and all his powers, and give a total overthrow to his kingdom and interest. Christ baffled Satan's temptations; by his death, he gave a fatal blow to the devil's kingdom, a wound to the head of this beast, that can never be healed.

Verse 16

We have here the sentence passed upon the woman for her sin.

I. She is here put into a state of sorrow, one particular of which only is specified, that in bringing

CHARLES H. SPURGEON:

This is the first gospel sermon that was ever delivered upon the surface of this earth. It was a memorable discourse indeed, with Jehovah himself for the preacher, and the whole human race and the prince of darkness for the audience. It must be worthy of our heartiest attention.

Is it not remarkable that this great gospel promise should have been delivered so soon after the transgression? As yet no sentence had been pronounced upon either of the two human offenders, but the promise was given under the form of a sentence pronounced upon the serpent. Not yet had the woman been condemned to painful travail, or the man to exhausting labor, or even the soil to the curse of thorn and thistle. Truly "mercy rejoiceth against judgment." Before the Lord had said "Dust thou art and unto dust thou shalt return," He was pleased to say that the seed of the woman should bruise the serpent's head. Let us rejoice, then, in the swift mercy of God, which in the early watches of the night of sin came with comfortable words unto us.

These words were not directly spoken to Adam and Eve, but they were directed distinctly to the serpent himself, and that by way of punishment to him for what he had done. It was a day of cruel triumph to him: such joy as his dark mind is capable of had filled him, for he had indulged his malice and gratified his spite. He had in the worst sense destroyed a part of God's works, he had introduced sin into the new world, he had stamped the human race with his own image and gained new forces to promote rebellion and to multiply transgression, and therefore he felt that sort of gladness which a fiend can know who bears a hell within him. But now God comes in, takes up the quarrel personally, and causes him to be disgraced on the very battlefield upon which he had gained a temporary success. He tells the dragon that He will undertake to deal with him; this quarrel shall not be between the serpent and man, but between God and the serpent. God says, in solemn words, "I will put enmity between thee and the woman, between thy seed and her seed," and He promises that there shall rise in fullness of time a Champion, who, though He suffer, shall smite in a vital part the power of evil, and bruise the serpent's head. This was the more, it seems to me, a comfortable message of mercy to Adam and Eve, because they would feel sure that the tempter would be punished; and as that punishment would involve blessing for them, the vengeance due to the serpent would be the guarantee of mercy to themselves. Perhaps, however, by thus obliquely giving the promise, the Lord meant to say, "Not for your sakes do I this, O fallen man and woman, nor for the sake of your descendants; but for My own name and honor's sake, that it be not profaned and blasphemed among the fallen spirits. I undertake to repair the mischief which has been caused by the tempter, that My name and My glory may not be diminished among the immortal spirits who look down upon the scene."—*The Treasury of the Old Testament*

JAMIESON, FAUSSET, BROWN

15. **thy seed**— not only evil spirits, but wicked men. **seed of the woman**—the Messiah, or His Church [CALVIN, HENGSTENBERG]. **I will put enmity between thee and the woman**—God can only be said to do so by leaving "the serpent and his seed to the influence of their own corruption; and by those measures which, pursued for the salvation of men, fill Satan and his angels with envy and rage."

thou shalt bruise his heel—The serpent wounds the heel that crushes him; and so Satan would be permitted to afflict the humanity of Christ and bring suffering and persecution on His people.

it shall bruise thy head—The serpent's poison is lodged in its head; and a bruise on that part is fatal. Thus, fatal shall be the stroke which Satan shall receive from Christ, though it is probable he did not at first understand the nature and extent of his doom.

ADAM CLARKE

15. ***I will put enmity between thee and the woman.*** This has been generally supposed to apply to a certain enmity subsisting between men and serpents; but this is rather a fancy than a reality.

There is a deeper meaning in the text than this, especially in these words, *it shall bruise thy head,* or rather, *He.* Who? The Seed of the woman; the Person is to come by the woman, and by her alone, without the concurrence of man. Therefore the address is not to Adam and Eve, but to Eve alone; and it was in consequence of this purpose of God that Jesus Christ was born of a virgin; this, and this alone, is what is implied in the promise of the Seed of the woman bruising the head of the serpent.

Jesus Christ died to put away sin by the sacrifice of himself, and to destroy him who had the power of death, that is, the devil. Thus He bruises his head—destroys his power and lordship over mankind, turning them from the power of Satan unto God; Acts xxvi. 18. And Satan bruises His heel—God so ordered it, that the salvation of man could only be brought about by the death of Christ; and even the spiritual seed of our blessed Lord have the heel often bruised, as they suffer persecution, temptation, which may be all that is intended by this part of the prophecy.

MATTHEW HENRY

forth children; but it includes grief and fear. Note, Sin brought sorrow into the world; had we known no guilt, we should have known no grief. The sorrows are here said to be multiplied; *greatly multiplied.* No marvel that our sorrows are multiplied when our sins are: both are innumerable evils. The sorrows of child-bearing are multiplied; and if the children prove wicked and foolish, they are, more than ever, the heaviness of her that bore them.

II. *Wives, be in subjection to your own husbands;* but the entrance of sin has made that duty a punishment, which otherwise it would not have been. If Eve had not eaten forbidden fruit herself, and tempted her husband to eat it, she would never have complained of her subjection; therefore it ought never to be complained of, though harsh; but sin must be complained of, that made it so. Those wives who not only despise and disobey their husbands, but domineer over them, do not consider that they not only violate a divine law, but thwart a divine sentence.

III. Observe here how mercy is mixed with wrath in this sentence. The woman shall have sorrow, but it shall be in bringing forth children, and the sorrow shall be *forgotten for joy that a child is born,* John xvi. 21. The sentence was not a curse, to bring her to ruin, but a chastisement, to bring her to repentance.

Verses 17–19

The sentence passed upon Adam, which is prefaced with a recital of his crime.

I. God put marks of his displeasure on Adam in three instances:—

1. His habitation is, by this sentence, cursed: *Cursed is the ground for thy sake*; and the effect of that curse is, *Thorns and thistles shall it bring forth unto thee.* What good fruits it produces must be extorted from it by the ingenuity and industry of man. But observe a mixture of mercy in this sentence. (1) Adam himself is not cursed, as the serpent was (*v.* 14). God had blessings in store for him. (2) He is yet above ground. The earth does not open and swallow him up, notwithstanding its degeneracy from its primitive beauty and fruitfulness.

2. His employments and enjoyments are all embittered to him.

(1) His business shall henceforth become a toil to him, and he shall go on with it *in the sweat of his face, v.* 19. His business, before he sinned, was a constant pleasure to him; the garden was then dressed without any uneasy labour. If Adam had not sinned, he had not sweated. Labour is our duty, which we must faithfully perform.

(2) His food shall henceforth become (in comparison with what it had been) unpleasant to him. *In sorrow* (*v.* 17) and *in the sweat of his face* (*v.* 19) he must eat of it. All, even the happiest in this world, have some allays to their joy: troops of diseases, disasters, and deaths, in various shapes, entered the world with sin, and still ravage it. Yet, in this part of the sentence, there is also a mixture of mercy. He shall sweat, but his toil shall make his rest the more welcome when he returns to his earth, as to his bed; he shall grieve, but he shall not starve; he shall have sorrow, but in that sorrow he shall eat bread, which shall strengthen his heart under his sorrows.

3. His life also is but short. Considering how full of trouble his days are, it is in favour to him that they are few; yet death being dreadful to nature (yea, even though life be unpleasant) *that* concludes the sentence. "Thou shalt *return to the ground out of which thou wast taken*; thy body, that part of thee which was taken out of the ground, shall return to it again; for *dust thou art.*" "Thy body shall be forsaken by thy soul, and become itself a lump of dust; and then it shall be lodged in the grave, the proper place for it, and mingle itself with the dust of the earth," *our dust*, Ps. civ. 29. *Earth to earth, dust to dust.* Observe here, (1) That man is a mean frail creature, *little* as dust, the small dust of the balance —*light* as dust, altogether lighter than vanity—*weak* as dust, and of no consistency. (2) That he is a mortal dying creature. A great man is but a great mass of dust, and must return to his earth. (3) That sin brought death into the world. If Adam had not sinned, he would not have died, Rom. v. 12.

II. We must not go off from this sentence upon our first parents till we have considered two things:— 1. How fitly the sad consequences of sin upon the soul of Adam and his sinful race were represented. Though that misery only is mentioned which affected the body, yet that was a pattern of spiritual miseries, the curse that entered into the soul. (1) The pains of a woman in travail represent the terrors and pangs of a guilty conscience, awakened to a sense of sin. (2) The state of subjection to which the woman was reduced represents that loss of spiritual liberty

JAMIESON, FAUSSET, BROWN

16. unto the woman he said, I will greatly multiply thy sorrow—She was doomed as a wife and mother to suffer pain of body and distress of mind. From being the help-meet of man and the partner of his affections, her condition would henceforth be that of humble subjection.

17-19. unto Adam he said—made to gain his livelihood by tilling the ground; but what before his fall he did with ease and pleasure, was not to be accomplished after it without painful and persevering exertion.

till thou return unto the ground—Man became mortal; although he did not die the moment he ate the forbidden fruit, his body underwent a change, and that would lead to dissolution; the union subsisting between his soul and God having already been dissolved, he had become liable to all the miseries of this life and to the pains of hell for ever. What a mournful chapter this is in the history of man! It gives the only true account of the origin of all the physical and moral evils that are in the world; upholds the moral character of God; shows that man, made upright, fell from not being able to resist a slight temptation; and becoming guilty and miserable, plunged all his posterity into the same abyss (Rom. 5:12). How astonishing the grace which at that moment gave promise of a Saviour and conferred on her who had the disgrace of introducing sin the future honor of introducing that Deliverer (I Tim. 2:15).

ADAM CLARKE

16. *Unto the woman he said.* She being second in the transgression is brought up the second to receive her condemnation, and to hear her punishment: *I will greatly multiply,* or "multiplying I will multiply"; i.e., I will multiply thy sorrows, and multiply those sorrows by other sorrows, and this during conception and pregnancy, and particularly so in parturition or childbearing. And this curse has fallen in a heavier degree on the woman than on any other female. It is added farther, *Thy desire shall be to thy husband*—thou shalt not be able to shun the great pain and peril for childbearing, for thy desire, thy appetite, shall be to thy husband; *and he shall rule over thee,* though at their creation both were formed with equal rights, and the woman had probably as much right to rule as the man; but subjection to the will of her husband is one part of her curse; and so very capricious is this will, often, that a sorer punishment no human being can well have, to be at all in a state of liberty, and under the protection of wise and equal laws.

17. *Unto Adam he said.* The man being the last in the transgression is brought up last to receive his sentence: *Because thou hast hearkened unto the voice of thy wife*—"Thou wast not deceived, she only gave and counselled thee to eat; this thou shouldst have resisted"; and that he did not is the reason of his condemnation. *Cursed is the ground for thy sake*—from henceforth its fertility shall be greatly impaired; *in sorrow shalt thou eat of it*—be in continual perplexity concerning the seedtime and the harvest, the cold and the heat, the wet and the dry.

18. *Thorns also and thistles.* Instead of producing nourishing grain and useful vegetables, noxious weeds shall be peculiarly prolific, injure the ground, choke the good seed, and mock the hopes of the husbandman; *and thou shalt eat the herb of the field*—thou shalt no longer have the privilege of this garden of delights, but must go to the common country, and feed on such herbs as thou canst find, till by labor and industry thou hast raised others more suitable to thee and more comfortable.

In the curse pronounced on the *ground* there is much more implied than generally appears. The amazing fertility of some of the most common thistles and thorns renders them the most proper instruments for the fulfillment of this sentence against man.

19. *In the sweat of thy face.* Though the whole body may be thrown into a profuse sweat, if hard labor be long continued, yet the *face* or "forehead" is the first part whence this sweat begins to issue; this is occasioned by the blood being strongly propelled to the brain, partly through stooping, but principally by the strong action of the muscles; in consequence of this the blood vessels about the head become turgid through the great flux of blood, the fibres are relaxed, the pores enlarged, and the sweat or serum poured out. Thus then the very commencement of every man's labor may put him in mind of his sin and its consequences.

Dust thou art, and unto dust shalt thou return. God had said that in the day they ate of the forbidden fruit, "dying they should die" —they should then become mortal, and continue under the influence of a great variety of unfriendly agencies in the atmosphere and in themselves, from heats, colds, drought, and damps in the one, and morbid increased and decreased action in the solids and fluids of the other, till the spirit, finding its earthly house no longer tenable, should return to God, who gave it; and the body, being decomposed, should be reduced to its primitive dust. It is evident from this that man would have been immortal had he never transgressed, and that this state of continual life and health depended on his obedience to his Maker.

MATTHEW HENRY

and freedom of will which is the effect of sin. (3) The curse of barrenness which was brought upon the earth, and its produce of briars and thorns, are a fit representation of the barrenness of a corrupt and sinful soul in that which is good and its fruitfulness in evil. (4) The toil and sweat bespeak the difficulty which, through the infirmity of the flesh, man labours under, in the service of God and the work of religion.

2. How admirably the satisfaction our Lord Jesus made by his death and sufferings answered to the sentence here passed upon our first parents. (1) Did travailing pains come in with sin? We read of the *travail of Christ's soul* (Isa. liii. 11). (2) Did subjection come in with sin? Christ was made under the law, Gal. iv. 4. (3) Did the curse come in with sin? Christ was made a curse for us, died a cursed death, Gal. iii. 13. (4) Did thorns come in with sin? He was crowned with thorns for us. (5) Did sweat come in with sin? He for us did sweat as it were great drops of blood. (6) Did sorrow come in with sin? He was a man of sorrows, his soul was, in his agony, exceedingly sorrowful. (7) Did death come in with sin? He became obedient unto death. Thus is the plaster as wide as the wound. Blessed be God for Jesus Christ!

Verse 20

God having named the man, and called him *Adam,* which signifies *red earth,* Adam named the woman, *Eve,* that is, *life.* Adam bears the name of the dying body, Eve that of the living soul. The reason of the name is here given: *Because she was* (that is, was to be) *the mother of all living.* He had before called her *Ishah—woman,* as a wife; here he calls her *Evah—life,* as a mother. Now, 1. If this was done by divine direction, it was an instance of God's favour, and was a seal of the covenant, and an assurance to them that he had not reversed that blessing wherewith he had blessed them: *Be fruitful and multiply.* It was likewise a confirmation of the promise now made, that the seed of the woman, of this woman, should break the serpent's head. 2. If Adam did it of himself, it was an instance of his faith in the word of God. (1) The blessing of a reprieve, that he should spare such sinners to be the parents of all living. (2) The blessing of a Redeemer, the promised seed, to whom Adam had an eye, in calling his wife *Eve—life.*

Verse 21

We have here a further instance of God's care concerning our first parents, notwithstanding their sin. Though he corrects his disobedient children, yet he does not disinherit them, but, like a tender father, provides the herb of the field for their food and *coats of skins* for their clothing. God is to be acknowledged with thankfulness, not only in giving us food, but in giving us clothes also, *ch.* xxviii. 20. The wool and the flax are his, as well as *the corn and the wine,* Hos. ii. 9. Adam and Eve made for themselves aprons of fig-leaves, a covering too narrow for them to *wrap themselves in,* Isa. xxviii. 20. Such are all the rags of our own righteousness. But God made them coats of skins, large, and strong, and durable, and fit for them; such is the righteousness of Christ. Therefore *put on the Lord Jesus Christ.*

Verses 22–24

Sentence being passed upon the offenders, we have here execution, in part, done upon them immediately.

I. How they were justly disgraced and shamed before God and the holy angels, by the ironical upbraiding of them with the issue of their enterprise: "*Behold, the man has become as one of us, to know good and evil!* A goodly god he makes! Does he not?" This was said to awaken and humble them, and to bring them to a sense of their sin and folly, and to repentance for it. God thus *fills their faces with shame, that they may seek his name,* Ps. lxxxiii. 16. He puts them to this confusion, in order to their conversion.

II. How they were justly discarded, and shut out of paradise.

1. The reason God gave why he shut man out of paradise; not only because he had put forth his hand, and taken of the tree of knowledge, which was his sin, but lest he should again put forth his hand, and take also of the tree of life and flatter himself with a conceit that thereby he should live for ever.

2. The method God took in expelling and excluding him from this garden of pleasure. He turned him out, and kept him out.

(1) He turned him out, from the garden to the common. This signified the exclusion of him, and all his guilty race, from that communion with God which was the bliss and glory of paradise. His acquaintance with God was lessened and lost, and

JAMIESON, FAUSSET, BROWN

KEIL–DELITZSCH:

As justice and mercy were combined in the divine sentence; justice in the fact that God cursed the tempter alone, and only punished the tempted with labor and mortality, mercy in the promise of eventual triumph over the serpent: so God also displayed his mercy to the fallen before carrying the sentence into effect. It was through the power of divine grace that Adam believed the promise with regard to the woman's seed, and manifested his faith in the name which he gave to his wife. *Eve,* signifying life or life-spring, is a substantive, and not a feminine adjective meaning "the living one," nor an abbreviated form of the life-receiving one. This name was given by Adam to his wife, "because," as the writer explains with the historical fulfillment before his mind, "she became the mother of all living," i.e., because the continuance and life of his race were guaranteed to the man through the woman.—*Commentary on the Old Testament*

20. Adam called his wife's name Eve—probably in reference to her being a mother of the promised Saviour, as well as of all mankind.

21. God made coats of skins—taught them to make these for themselves. This implies the institution of animal sacrifice, which was undoubtedly of divine appointment, and instruction in the only acceptable mode of worship for sinful creatures, through faith in a Redeemer (Heb. 9:22).

22. And God said, Behold, the man is become as one of us—not spoken in irony as is generally supposed, but in deep compassion. The words should be rendered, "Behold, what has become [by sin] of the man who was as one of us!" Formed, at first, in our image to know good and evil—how sad his condition now. **and now, lest he put forth his hand, and take of the tree of life**—This tree being a pledge of that immortal life with which obedience should be rewarded, man lost, on his fall, all claim to this tree; and therefore, that he might not eat of it or delude himself with the idea that eating of it would restore what he had forfeited, the Lord sent him forth from the garden.

ADAM CLARKE

20. *And Adam called his wife's name Eve; because she was the mother of all living.* A man who does not understand the original cannot possibly comprehend the reason of what is said here. What has the word *Eve* to do with being *the mother of all living?* Our translators often follow the Septuagint; it is a pity they had not done so here, as the Septuagint translation is literal and correct: "And Adam called his wife's name *Life,* because she was the mother of all the *living.*" This is a proper and faithful representation of the Hebrew text. It is probable that God designed by this name to teach our first parents these two important truths: (1) That though they had merited immediate death, yet they should be respited, and the accomplishment of the sentence be long delayed; they should be spared to propagate a numerous progeny on the earth. (2) That though much misery would be entailed on his posterity, and death should have a long and universal empire, yet One should in the fulness of time spring from the woman, who should destroy death, and bring life and immortality to light, 2 Tim. i. 10. Therefore Adam called his wife's name "Life," because she was to be the mother of all human beings, and because she was to be the mother of *Him* who was to give life to a world dead in trespasses, and dead in sins, Eph. ii. 1.

21. *God made coats of skins.* It is very likely that the *skins* out of which their clothing was made were taken off animals whose blood had been poured out as a sin offering to God; for as we find Cain and Abel offering sacrifices to God, we may fairly presume that God had given them instructions on this head; nor is it likely that the notion of a sacrifice could have ever occurred to the mind of man without an express revelation from God.

22. *Behold, the man is become as one of us.* On all hands this text is allowed to be difficult, and the difficulty is increased by our translation, which is opposed to the original Hebrew and the most authentic versions. The Hebrew signifies "was," not *is.* The Samaritan text, the Samaritan version, the Syriac, and the Septuagint have the same tense. These lead us to a very different sense, and indicate that there is an ellipsis of some words which must be supplied in order to make the sense complete. A very learned man has ventured the following paraphrase, which should not be lightly regarded: "And the Lord God said, The man who was like one of us in purity and wisdom, is now fallen and robbed of his excellence; he has added to the knowledge of the good, by his transgression, the knowledge of the evil; and now, lest he put forth his hand, and take also of the tree of life, and eat and live forever in this miserable state, I will remove him, and guard the place lest he should reenter. Therefore the Lord God sent him forth from the Garden of Eden." This seems to be the most natural sense of the place.

In chap. i. 26-27, we have seen man in the perfection of his nature, the dignity of his office, and the plenitude of his happiness. Here we find the same creature, but stripped of his glories and happiness, so that the word "man" no longer conveys the same ideas it did before. Man and intellectual excellence were before so intimately connected as to appear inseparable; man and misery are now equally so.

MATTHEW HENRY

JAMIESON, FAUSSET, BROWN

ADAM CLARKE

that correspondence which had been settled between man and his Maker was interrupted and broken off. But whither did he send him when he turned him out of Eden? He might justly have chased him out of the world (Job xviii. 18), but he only chased him out of the garden. But man was only sent to till the ground out of which he was taken. He was sent to a place of toil, not to a place of torment. He was sent to the ground, not to the grave—to the work-house, not to the dungeon, not to the prison-house—to hold the plough, not to drag the chain. His tilling the ground would be recompensed by his eating of its fruits; and his converse with the earth whence he was taken was improvable to good purposes, to keep him humble, and to remind him of his latter end. Observe, then, that though our first parents were excluded from the privileges of their state of innocency, yet they were not abandoned to despair, God's thoughts of love designing them for a second state of probation upon new terms.

(2) He kept him out, and forbade him all hopes of a re-entry; for he *placed at the east of the garden of Eden* a detachment of *cherubim,* God's hosts, armed with a dreadful and irresistible power, to keep the way that led to the tree of life, so that he could neither steal nor force an entry. Now this intimated to Adam, [1] That God was displeased with him. [2] That the angels were at war with him; no peace with the heavenly hosts, while he was in rebellion against their Lord and ours. [3] That the way to the tree of life was shut up, namely, that way which, at first, he was put into, the way of spotless innocency. It was henceforward in vain for him and his to expect righteousness, life, and happiness, by virtue of the first covenant, for it was irreparably broken. We are all undone if we be judged by that covenant. God revealed this to Adam, not to drive him to despair, but to oblige and quicken him to look for life and happiness in the promised seed, by whom the flaming sword is removed. God and his angels are reconciled to us, and a new and living way into the holiest is consecrated and laid open for us.

24. placed . . . cherubim—The passage should be rendered thus:—"And he dwelt between the cherubim at the East of the Garden of Eden and a fierce fire or Shekinah unfolding itself to preserve the way of the tree of life." This was the mode of worship now established to show God's anger at sin and teach the mediation of a promised Saviour as the way of life, as well as of access to God. They were the same figures as were afterwards in the tabernacle and temple; and now, as then, God said, "I will commune with thee from between the cherubim" (Exod. 25:22).

24. *So he drove out the man.* Three things are noted here: (1) God's displeasure against sinful man, evidenced by His expelling him from this place of blessedness; (2) Man's unfitness for the place, of which he had rendered himself unworthy by his ingratitude and transgression; and (3) His reluctance to leave this place of happiness. He was, as we may naturally conclude, unwilling to depart, and God *drove* him out.

He placed at the east. Or "before" *the garden of Eden,* before what may be conceived its gate or entrance; *Cherubims,* "The cherubim." Hebrew plurals in the masculine end in general in *im;* to add an *s* to this when we introduce such words into English is very improper; therefore the word should be written *cherubim,* not *cherubims.* But what were these? They are utterly unknown.

The word *kerub* never appears as a verb in the Hebrew Bible, and therefore is justly supposed to be a word compounded of *ke,* a particle of resemblance, "like to, like as," and *rab,* he was "great, powerful." On this ground, I suppose, the cherubim were emblematical representations of the eternal power and Godhead of the Almighty. These angelic beings were for a time employed in guarding the entrance to paradise, and keeping the way of or road to the tree of life. This, I say, for a time; for it is very probable that God soon removed the tree of life, and abolished the garden, so that its situation could never after be positively ascertained.

By a flaming sword which turned every way, or flame folding back upon itself, we may understand the formidable appearances which these cherubim assumed, in order to render the passage to the tree of life inaccessible.

CHAPTER 4

Verses 1–2

Adam and Eve had many sons and daughters, *ch.* v. 4. But Cain and Abel seem to have been the two eldest.

I. The names of their two sons. 1. *Cain* signifies *possession;* for Eve, when she bore him, said with joy, and thankfulness, and great expectation, *I have gotten a man from the* LORD. Observe, Children are God's gifts, and he must be acknowledged in the building up of our families. It doubles and sanctifies our comfort in them when we see them coming to us from the hand of God, who will not forsake the works and gifts of his own hand. 2. *Abel* signifies *vanity.* When she thought she had obtained the promised seed in Cain, she was so taken up with that possession that another son was as vanity to her.

II. The employments of Cain and Abel. 1. They both had a calling. God gave their father a calling, even in innocency, and he gave them one. Note, It is the will of God that we should every one of us have something to do in this world. Parents ought to bring up their children to business. "Give them a Bible and a calling (said good Mr. Dod), and God be with them." 2. Their employments were different, that they might trade and exchange with one another, as there was occasion. The members of the body politic have need one of another, and mutual love is helped by mutual commerce. 3. Their employments belonged to the husbandman's calling, their father's profession. 4. Abel, though the younger brother, yet entered first into his calling, and probably his example drew in Cain. 5. Abel chose that employment which most befriended contemplation and devotion, for to these a pastoral life has been looked upon as being peculiarly favourable.

Verses 3–5

Here we have, I. The devotions of Cain and Abel. *In the process of time* Cain and Abel brought to Adam, as the priest of the family, each of them *an offering to the Lord.* God would thus try Adam's faith in the promise and his obedience to the remedial law; he would thus settle a correspondence again between heaven and earth, and give *shadows of good things to come.* Observe here, 1. That the religious worship of God is no novel invention, but an ancient institution. It is that which was *from the beginning* (1 John i. 1); it is the *good old way,* Jer. vi. 16. 2. That it is a good thing for children

CHAPTER 4

Vss. 1-26. BIRTH OF CAIN AND ABEL. **1. Eve said, I have gotten a man from the Lord**—i.e., "by the help of the Lord"—an expression of pious gratitude—and she called him Cain, i.e., "a possession," as if valued above everything else; while the arrival of another son reminding her of the misery she had entailed on her offspring, led to the name Abel, i.e., either weakness, vanity (Ps. 39:5), or grief, lamentation. Cain and Abel were probably twins; and it is thought that, at this early period, children were born in pairs (ch. 5:4) [CALVIN].

Abel was a keeper of sheep—lit., "feeder of a flock," which, in Oriental countries, always includes goats as well as sheep. Abel, though the younger, is mentioned first, probably on account of the pre-eminence of his religious character.

3. in process of time—*Hebrew,* "at the end of days," probably on the Sabbath. **brought . . . an offering unto the Lord**—Both manifested, by the very act of offering, their faith in the being of God and in His claims to their reverence and worship; and had the kind of offering been left to themselves, what more natural than that the one should bring "of the fruits of the ground," and that the other should bring "of the firstlings of his flock and the fat thereof."

CHAPTER 4

1. *I have gotten a man from the Lord.* Cain signifies "acquisition"; hence Eve says *kanithi,* I have gotten or "acquired" a man, *eth Yehovah,* "the Lord." It is extremely difficult to ascertain the sense in which Eve used these words, which have been as variously translated as understood. Most expositors think that Eve imagined Cain to be the promised "seed" that should bruise the head of the serpent. This exposition really seems too refined for that period. It is very likely that she meant no more than to acknowledge that it was through God's peculiar blessing that she was enabled to conceive and bring forth a son, and that she had now a well-grounded hope that the race of man should be continued on the earth. Unless she had been under divine inspiration she could not have called her son (even supposing him to be the promised "seed") *Jehovah;* and that she was not under such an influence her mistake sufficiently proves, for Cain, so far from being the Messiah, was of the wicked one; 1 John iii. 12. We may therefore suppose that *eth Yehovah,* "the Lord," is an elliptical form of expression for *meeth Yehovah,* "from the Lord," or "through the divine blessing."

2. *And she again bare his brother Abel.* Literally, "She added to bear his brother." From the very face of this account it appears evident that Cain and Abel were twins. In most cases where a subject of this kind is introduced in the Holy Scriptures, and the successive births of children of the same parents are noted, the acts of conceiving and bringing forth are mentioned in reference to each child; here it is not said that she conceived and brought forth Abel, but simply "she added to bring forth Abel his brother"; that is, as I understand it, Cain was the firstborn; Abel, his twin brother, came next.

Abel was a keeper of sheep. Adam was originally a gardener, Abel a shepherd, and Cain an agriculturist or farmer. These were the three primitive employments, and I may add, the most rational, and consequently the best calculated to prevent strife and an immoderate love of the world.

3. *In process of time.* "At the end of days." Some think the anniversary of the creation to be here intended; it is more probable that it

MATTHEW HENRY

to be well taught when they are young, and trained up betimes in religious services, that when they come to be capable of acting for themselves they may, of their own accord, *bring an offering to God*. 3. That we should every one of us honour God with what we have, according as he has prospered us. 4. That hypocrites and evil doers may be found going as far as the best of God's people in the external services of religion. Cain brought an offering with Abel; nay, Cain's offering is mentioned first, as if he were the more forward of the two. The Pharisee and the publican went to the temple to pray, Luke xviii. 10.

II. The different success of their devotions. That which is to be aimed at in all acts of religion is God's acceptance: we speed well if we attain this, but in vain do we worship if we miss of it, 2 Cor. v. 9. God had *respect to Abel and to his offering*, and showed his acceptance of it, probably by fire from heaven; but to *Cain and his offering he had not respect*.

1. There was a difference in the characters of the persons offering. Cain was a wicked man and therefore his sacrifice was *a vain oblation*, Isa. i. 13. God had no respect to Cain himself, and therefore no respect to his offering. But Abel was a righteous man; he is called *righteous Abel* (Matt. xxiii. 35); his heart was upright and his life was pious. God had respect to him as a holy man, and therefore to his offering as a holy offering.

2. There was a difference in the offerings they brought. It is expressly said (Heb. xi. 4), Abel's was a *more excellent sacrifice* than Cain's: either, (1) In the nature of it, or, (2) In the qualities of the offering. Cain brought *of the fruit of the ground*, any thing that came next to hand, what he had not occasion for himself. But Abel was curious in the choice of his offering: not the lame, nor the lean, nor the refuse, but the *firstlings of the flock*—the best he had, *and the fat thereof*—the best of those best.

3. The great difference was this, that Abel offered in faith, and Cain did not. There was a difference in the principle upon which they went. Abel offered with an eye to God's will as his rule, and God's glory as his end, but Cain did what he did only for company's sake, or to save his credit, not in faith, and so it turned into sin to him. Abel was a penitent; Cain was unhumbled; his confidence was within himself.

III. Cain's displeasure at the difference God made between his sacrifice and Abel's. Cain was very wroth, which presently appeared in his very looks. This anger bespeaks, 1. His enmity to God. He should have been angry at himself for his own infidelity and hypocrisy, by which he had forfeited God's acceptance. Note, It is a certain sign of an unhumbled heart to quarrel with those rebukes which we have, by our own sin, brought upon ourselves. 2. His envy of his brother. He conceived a hatred of him as an enemy. Note, (1) It is common for those who have rendered themselves unworthy of God's favour to have indignation against those who are dignified by it. The Pharisees walked in this way of Cain, when they *neither entered into the kingdom of God themselves* nor *suffered those that were entering to go in*, Luke xi. 52. (2) Envy is a sin that commonly carries with it its own punishment, in the rottenness of the bones.

Verses 6–7

God is here reasoning with Cain, to convince him of the sin and folly of his anger and discontent, and to bring him into a good temper again, that further mischief might be prevented. Thus the father of the prodigal argued the case with the elder son (Luke xv. 28, &c.).

I. God puts Cain himself upon enquiring into the cause of his discontent: *Why is thy countenance fallen?* Observe, 1. That God takes notice of all our sinful passions and discontents. 2. "*Why am I wroth?* Is there a real cause, a just cause, a proportionable cause for it? Why am I so soon angry?"

II. To reduce Cain to his right mind again, it is here made evident to him,

1. That he had no reason to be angry at God.

(1) God sets before Cain life and a blessing: either, [1] "If thou hadst done well, as thy brother did, thou shouldst have been accepted, as he was." Or, [2] "If now thou do well, if thou repent of thy sin, reform thy heart and life, and bring thy sacrifice in a better manner, thou shalt yet be accepted, thy sin shall be pardoned, thy comfort and honour restored, and all shall be well." See how early the gospel was preached, and the benefit of it here offered even to one of the chief of sinners.

(2) He sets before him death and a curse: "If now thou wilt not do well, if thou persist in this wrath, and, instead of humbling thyself before God, harden thyself against him, *sin lies at the door*," that is, [1] Further sin. "Now that anger is in thy

JAMIESON, FAUSSET, BROWN

4. the Lord had respect unto Abel, not unto Cain, etc.—The words, "had respect to," signify in *Hebrew*—"to look at any thing with a keen earnest glance," which has been translated, "kindle into a fire," so that the divine approval of Abel's offering was shown in its being consumed by fire (see ch. 15:17; Judg. 13:20).

7. If thou doest well, shalt thou not be accepted?—A better rendering is, "Shalt thou not have the excellency?" which is the true sense of the words referring to the high privileges and authority belonging to the first-born in patriarchal times. **sin lieth at the door**—sin, i.e., a sin offering—a common meaning of the word in Scrip-

ALEXANDER MACLAREN:

Sin here appears as having power to bar men's way to God. Much ingenuity has been spent on the question why Abel's offering was accepted and Cain's rejected. But the narrative itself shows in the words of Jehovah, "If thou doest well, is there not acceptance?" that the reason lay in Cain's evil deeds. So, in 1 John 3:12, the act of murder is put down to the fact that "his works were evil, and his brother's righteous"; and Hebrews 11:4 differs from this view only in making the ground of righteousness prominent, when it ascribes the acceptableness of Abel's offering to faith. Both these passages are founded on the narrative, and we need not seek further for the reason of the different reception of the two offerings. Character, then, or, more truly, faith, which is the foundation of a righteous character, determines the acceptableness of worship. Cain's offering had no sense of dependence, no outgoing of love and trust, no adoration—though it may have had fear—and no moral element. So it had no sweet odor for God. Abel's was sprinkled with some drops of the incense of lowly trust, and came from a heart which fain would be pure; therefore it was a joy to God. So we are taught at the very beginning that as is the man, so is his sacrifice; that the prayer of the wicked is an abomination. Plenty of worship nowadays is Cain worship. Many reputable professing Christians bring just such sacrifices. The prayers of such never reach higher than the church ceiling. Of course, the lesson of the story is not that a man must be pure before his sacrifice is accepted. The faintest cry of trust is heard and a contrite heart, however sinful, is always welcome. But we are taught that our acts of worship must have our hearts in them, and that it is vain to pray and to love evil. Sin has the awful power of blocking our way to God.

—Expositions of Holy Scripture

ADAM CLARKE

means the Sabbath, on which Adam and his family undoubtedly offered oblations to God, as the divine worship was certainly instituted, and no doubt the Sabbath properly observed in that family. This worship was, in its original institution, very simple. It appears to have consisted of two parts: (1) Thanksgiving to God as the Author and Dispenser of all the bounties of nature, and oblations indicative of that gratitude. (2) Sacrifices to His justice and holiness, implying a conviction of their own sinfulness, confession of transgression, and faith in the promised Deliverer.

Cain brought of the fruit of the ground an offering [*minchah*] *unto the Lord.* The word *minchah* is explained, Lev. ii. 1, etc., to be an offering of fine flour, with oil and frankincense. It was in general a eucharistic or gratitude offering, and is simply what is implied in the *fruit of the ground* brought by Cain to the Lord, by which he testified his belief in Him as the Lord of the universe, and the Dispenser of secular blessings.

4. *Abel, he also brought of the firstlings of his flock.* It was by this alone that he acknowledged himself a sinner, and professed faith in the promised Messiah. To this circumstance the apostle seems evidently to allude, Heb. xi. 4: "By faith Abel offered a more or greater sacrifice." Thus his offerings were accepted, while those of Cain were rejected; for this, as the apostle says, was done by faith, and therefore he obtained witness that he was righteous, or a justified person, God testifying with his gifts, the thank offering and the sin offering, by accepting them, that faith in the promised Seed was the only way in which He could accept the services and offerings of mankind.

5. *Unto Cain.* As being unconscious of his sinfulness, and consequently unhumbled, *and to his offering*, as not being accompanied, as Abel's was, with faith and a sacrifice for sin, *he had not respect*—He could not, consistently with His holiness and justice, approve of the one or receive the other. Of the manner in which God testified His approbation we are not informed; it was probably, as in the case of Elijah, by sending down fire from heaven, and consuming the sacrifice.

Cain was very wroth. That displeasure which should have been turned against his own unhumbled heart was turned against his innocent brother, who, though not more highly privileged than he, made a much better use of the advantages which he shared in common with his ungodly and unnatural brother.

6. *Why art thou wroth?* This was designed as a gracious warning, and a preventive of the meditated crime.

7. *If thou doest well,* that which is right in the sight of God, *shalt thou not be accepted?* Does God reject any man who serves Him in simplicity and godly sincerity? *And if thou doest not well*, can wrath and indignation against thy righteous brother save thee from the displeasure under which thou art fallen? On the contrary, have recourse to thy Maker for mercy; "a sin offering lieth at thy door"; an animal proper to be offered as an atonement for sin is now "couching" at the door of thy fold.

MATTHEW HENRY

heart, murder is at the door." Or, [2] The punishment of sin. So near akin are sin and punishment that the same word in Hebrew signifies both. If sin be harboured in the house, the curse waits at the door, like a bailiff, ready to arrest the sinner whenever he looks out. "If thou doest not well, *sin* (that is, *the sin-offering*), lies at the door, and thou mayest take the benefit of it." The same word signifies *sin* and *a sacrifice for sin.* Christ, the great sin-offering, is said to *stand at the door,* Rev. iii. 20. All this considered, Cain had no reason to be angry at God, but at himself only.

2. That he had no reason to be angry at his brother: "*Unto thee shall be his desire,* he shall continue his respect to thee as an elder brother, and thou, as the first-born, shalt rule over him as much as ever." God's acceptance of Abel's offering did not transfer the birth-right to him. God did not so intend it; Abel did not so interpret it; why then should he be so much exasperated?

Verse 8

Abel's murder, which may be considered two ways:—

I. As Cain's sin; and a scarlet, crimson, sin it was, a sin of the first magnitude. See in it, 1. Adam's eating forbidden fruit seemed but a little sin, but it opened the door to the greatest. 2. A fruit of the enmity which is in the seed of the serpent against the seed of the woman. So early did he that was after the flesh *persecute him that was after the Spirit.* 3. See also what comes of *envy, hatred, malice, and all uncharitableness*; if they be indulged and cherished in the soul, they are in danger of involving men in the horrid guilt of murder itself. Many were the aggravations of Cain's sin. (1) It was his own brother that he murdered, his younger brother, whom he ought to have protected. (2) He was a good brother, one who had never done him any wrong. (3) God himself had told him what would come of it, yet he persisted in his barbarous design. (4) He covered it with a show of friendship and kindness. According to the Septuagint Cain said to Abel, *Let us go into the field.* The Chaldee paraphrase adds that Cain maintained that there was no judgment to come, no future state, and that when Abel spoke in defence of the truth Cain took that occasion to fall upon him. However, (5) That which the scripture tells us was the reason why he slew him was a sufficient aggravation of the murder; it was *because his own works were evil and his brother's righteous.* Nay, (6) In killing his brother, he directly struck at God himself; he hated Abel because God loved him.

II. As Abel's suffering. Death reigned ever since Adam sinned, but we read not of any taken captive by him till now; and now, 1. The first that dies is a saint, one that was accepted and beloved of God. The first that went to the grave went to heaven. Nay, 2. The first that dies is a martyr, and dies for his religion. Abel's death has not only no curse in it, but it has a crown in it.

Verses 9–12

The trial and condemnation of the first murderer.

I. The arraignment of Cain: *The Lord said unto Cain, Where is Abel thy brother?* He asks him, that he may draw from him a confession of his crime, for those who would be justified before God must accuse themselves, and the penitent will do so.

II. Cain's plea: he pleads *not guilty,* and adds rebellion to his sin. For, 1. He endeavours to cover a deliberate murder with a deliberate lie: *I know not.* Thus, in Cain, the devil was both a murderer and a liar from the beginning. Those are strangely blind that think it possible to conceal their sins from a God that sees all, and those are strangely hard that think it desirable to conceal them from a God who pardons those only that confess. 2. He impudently charges his Judge with folly and injustice, in putting this question to him: *Am I my brother's keeper?* He should have humbled himself, and have said, *Am I not my brother's murderer?* Some think he reflects on God and his providence, as if he had said, "Art not thou his keeper? If he be missing, on thee be the blame, and not on me, who never undertook to keep him." Note, Those who are unconcerned in the affairs of their brethren, and take no care, when they have opportunity, to prevent their hurt in their bodies, goods, or good name, especially in their souls, do, in effect, speak Cain's language. See Lev. xix. 17; Phil. ii. 4.

III. The conviction of Cain, *v.* 10. "The evidence against thee is clear and incontestable: *The voice of thy brother's blood cries.*" He speaks as if the blood itself were both witness and prosecutor, before God's own knowledge testified against him. Observe here, 1. Murder is a crying sin, none more so. The patient

JAMIESON, FAUSSET, BROWN

ture (as in Hos.4:8; II Cor. 5:21; Heb. 9:28). The purport of the divine rebuke to Cain was this, "Why art thou angry, as if unjustly treated? If thou doest well (i.e., wert innocent and sinless) a thank offering would have been accepted as a token of thy dependence as a creature. But as thou doest not well (i.e., art a sinner), a sin offering is necessary, by bringing which thou wouldest have met with acceptance and retained the honors of thy birthright." This language implies that previous instructions had been given as to the mode of worship; Abel offered through faith (Heb. 11:4). **unto thee shall be his desire**—The high distinction conferred by priority of birth is described (ch. 27:29); and it was Cain's conviction, that this honor had been withdrawn from him, by the rejection of his sacrifice, and conferred on his younger brother—hence the secret flame of jealousy, which kindled into a settled hatred and fell revenge.

8. And Cain talked with Abel his brother—Under the guise of brotherly familiarity, he concealed his premeditated purpose till a convenient time and place occurred for the murder (I John 3:12; 9:10).

9. I know not—a falsehood. One sin leads to another.

10. the voice of thy brother's blood crieth unto me—Cain, to lull suspicion, had probably been engaging in the solemnities of religion when he was challenged directly from the Shekinah itself.

ADAM CLARKE

The words *chattath* and *chattaah* frequently signify "sin"; but I have observed more than a hundred places in the Old Testament where they are used for "sin offering."

Unto thee shall be his desire. That is, Thou shalt ever have the right of primogeniture, and in all things shall thy brother be subject unto thee. These words are not spoken of sin, as many have understood them, but of Abel's submission to Cain as his superior, and the words are spoken to remove Cain's envy.

8. *Cain talked with Abel his brother.* "And Cain said"; not *talked,* for this construction the word cannot bear without great violence to analogy and grammatical accuracy. But why should it be thus translated? Because our translators could not find that anything was spoken on the occasion; and therefore they ventured to intimate that there was a conversation, indefinitely. In the most correct editions of the Hebrew Bible there is a small space left here in the text, and a circular mark which refers to a note in the margin, intimating that there is a hiatus or deficiency in the verse. Now this deficiency is supplied in the principal ancient versions, and in the Samaritan text. In this the supplied words are, "Let us walk out into the field." The Syriac has, "Let us go to the desert." The Vulgate, "Let us walk out." The Septuagint, "Let us go out into the field." The two Chaldee Targums have the same reading; so has the Coptic version. The words may therefore be safely considered as a part of the sacred text, and with them the whole passage reads clear and consistently: "And Cain said unto Abel his brother, Let us go out into the field: and it came to pass, when they were in the field, that Cain rose up."

10. *The voice of thy brother's blood.* It is probable that Cain, having killed his brother, dug a hole and buried him in the earth, hoping thereby to prevent the murder from being known; and that this is what is designed in

MATTHEW HENRY

sufferers cried for pardon (*Father, forgive them*), but their blood cries for vengeance. 2. The blood is said to cry from the ground, the earth, which is said *to open her mouth to receive his brother's blood from his hand, v.* 11. 3. In the original the word is plural, thy brother's *bloods*, not only his blood, but the blood of all those that might have descended from him. How well is it for us that the blood of Christ speaks better things than that of Abel! Heb. xii. 24. Abel's blood cried for vengeance, Christ's blood cries for pardon.

IV. The sentence passed upon Cain: *And now art thou cursed from the earth, v.* 11.

1. He is cursed. The curse for Adam's disobedience terminated on the ground: *Cursed is the ground for thy sake;* but that for Cain's rebellion fell immediately upon himself: *Thou art cursed.* We have all deserved this curse, and it is only in Christ that believers are saved from it and inherit the blessing, Gal. iii. 10, 13.

2. He is cursed from the earth. Cain found his punishment where he chose his portion and set his heart. Two things we expect from the earth, and by this curse both are denied to Cain and taken from him: *sustenance* and *settlement.* (1) Sustenance out of the earth is here withheld from him. It is a curse upon him in his enjoyments, and particularly in his calling: *When thou tillest the ground, it shall not henceforth yield unto thee its strength.* (2) Settlement on the earth is here denied him: *A fugitive and a vagabond shalt thou be in the earth.* By this he was condemned, [1] To perpetual disgrace and reproach among men. [2] To perpetual disquietude and horror in his own mind. His own guilty conscience should haunt him wherever he went, and make him *Magor-missabib,* a *terror round about.* What rest can those find, what settlement, that carry their own disturbance with them in their bosoms wherever they go? Those must needs be fugitives that are thus tossed.

This was the sentence passed upon Cain; and even in this there was mercy mixed, inasmuch as he was not immediately cut off, but had space given him to repent; for God is long-suffering to us-ward, not willing that any should perish.

Verses 13–15

A further account of the proceedings against Cain.

I. Here is Cain's complaint of the sentence passed upon him, as hard and severe. Some make him to speak the language of despair. There is forgiveness with the God of pardons for the greatest sins and sinners; but those forfeit it who despair of it. Just now Cain made nothing of his sin, but now he is in the other extreme: Satan drives his vassals from presumption to despair. He thinks himself rigorously dealt with when really he is favourably treated; and he cries out of wrong when he has more reason to wonder that he is out of hell. Now, to justify this complaint, Cain descants upon the sentence. 1. He sees himself excluded by it from the favour of his God. 2. He sees himself expelled from all the comforts of this life, and concludes that, being a fugitive, he is, in effect, *driven out this day from the face of the earth.* 3. He sees himself exposed by it to the hatred and ill-will of all mankind: *It shall come to pass that everyone that finds me shall slay me.* Wherever he wanders, he goes in peril of his life, at least he thinks so; and, like a man in debt, thinks everyone he meets a bailiff. There were none alive but his near relations; yet even of them he is justly afraid who had himself been so barbarous to his brother. He sees the whole creation armed against him.

II. Here is God's confirmation of the sentence; for when he judges he will overcome, *v.* 15. 1. How Cain is protected from wrath by this declaration, notified, we may suppose, to all that little world which was then in being: *Whosoever slayeth Cain, vengeance shall be taken on him seven-fold,* because thereby the sentence he was under (that he should be a fugitive and a vagabond) would be defeated. God having said in Cain's case, *Vengeance is mine, I will repay,* it would have been a daring usurpation for any man to take the sword out of God's hand. 2. *The Lord set a mark upon Cain,* to distinguish him from the rest of mankind and to notify that he was the man that murdered his brother.

Verses 16–18

A further account of Cain, and what became of him after he was rejected of God.

I. He tamely submitted to that part of his sentence by which he was hidden from God's face; for (*v.* 16) *he went out from the presence of the Lord,* that is, he willingly renounced God and religion, and was content to forego its privileges, so that he might not be

JAMIESON, FAUSSET, BROWN

11, 12. now art thou cursed from the earth—a curse superadded to the general one denounced on the ground for Adam's sin.

a fugitive—condemned to perpetual exile—a degraded outcast—the miserable victim of an accusing conscience.

13, 14. And Cain said . . . My punishment is greater than I can bear—What an overwhelming sense of misery; but no sign of penitence, nor cry for pardon.

every one that findeth me shall slay me—This shows that the population of the world was now considerably increased.

15. whosoever slayeth Cain—By a special act of divine forbearance, the *life* of Cain was to be spared in the then small state of the human race. **set a mark**—not any visible mark or brand on his forehead, but some *sign* or *token* of assurance that his life would be preserved. This sign is thought by the best writers to have been a wild ferocity of aspect that rendered him an object of universal horror and avoidance.

16. presence of the Lord—the appointed place of worship at Eden. Leaving it, he not only severed himself from his relatives but forsook the ordinances of religion, probably casting off all fear of God from his eyes so that the last end of this man is worse than the first (Matt. 12:45).

ADAM CLARKE

the words, "Thy brother's blood crieth unto me from the ground—which hath opened her mouth to receive it from thy hand." Some think that by *the voice of thy brother's blood* the cries of Abel's widow and children are to be understood, as it is very probable that he was father of a family; indeed his occupation and sacrifices seem to render this probable, and probability is all we can expect on such a subject. God represents these as calling aloud for the punishment of the murderer; and it is evident that Cain expected to fall by the hands of some person who had the right of the avenger of blood; for now that the murder is found out, he expects to suffer death for it. See. v. 14.

12. *A fugitive and a vagabond shalt thou be.* Thou shalt be expelled from the presence of God, and from thy family connections, and shalt have no fixed, secure residence in any place. The Septuagint renders this, "Thou shalt be groaning and trembling" upon the earth—the horror of thy crime shall ever haunt thee, and thou shalt never have any well-grounded hope that God will remit the punishment thou deservest.

13. *My punishment is greater than I can bear.* The margin reads, "Mine iniquity is greater than that it may be forgiven." The original words may be translated, "Is my crime too great to be forgiven?" words which we may presume he uttered on the verge of black despair. It is most probable that *avon* signifies rather the crime than the punishment; in this sense it is used, Lev. xxvi. 41, 43; 1 Sam. xxviii. 10; 2 Kings vii. 9; and *nasa* signifies to remit or forgive. The marginal reading is, therefore, to be preferred to that in the text.

14. *Behold, thou hast driven me out.* In verses 11-12, God states two parts of Cain's punishment: (1) The ground was cursed, so that it was not to yield any adequate recompense for his most careful tillage. (2) He was to be a fugitive and a vagabond, having no place in which he could dwell with comfort or security. To these Cain himself adds others. (1) His being hidden from the face of God; which appears to signify his being expelled from that particular place where God had manifested His presence, in or contiguous to paradise, whither our first parents resorted as to an oracle, and where they offered their daily adorations. So in verse 16, it is said, "Cain went out from the presence of the Lord," and was not permitted anymore to associate with the family in acts of religious worship. (2) The continual apprehension of being slain, as all the inhabitants of the earth were at that time of the same family, the parents themselves still alive, and each having a right to kill this murderer of his relative. Add to all this (3) the terrors of a guilty conscience; his awful apprehension of God's judgments, and of being everlastingly banished from the beatific vision. To this part of the punishment of Cain, St. Paul probably alludes, 2 Thess. i. 9: "Who shall be punished with everlasting destruction from the presence of the Lord, and from the glory of his power." The words are so similar that we can scarcely doubt of the allusion.

15. *The Lord set a mark upon Cain.* Dr. Shuckford observes that the Hebrew word *oth,* which we translate *a mark,* signifies "a sign" or "token." Thus, Gen. ix. 13, the bow was to be "for a sign" or "token" that the world should not be destroyed; therefore the words, *And the Lord set a mark upon Cain,* should be translated, "And the Lord appointed to Cain a token or sign," to convince him that no person should be permitted to slay him. To have *marked* him would have been the most likely way to have brought all the evils he dreaded upon him; therefore the Lord gave him some miraculous sign or token that he should not be slain, to the end that he should not despair, but, having time to repent, might return to a gracious God and find mercy.

MATTHEW HENRY

under its precepts. Cain went out now from the presence of the Lord, and we never find that he came into it again, to his comfort.

II. He endeavoured to confront that part of the sentence by which he was made a fugitive and a vagabond; for,

1. He chose his land. He went and *dwelt on the east of Eden*, somewhere distant from the place where Adam and his religious family resided. But his attempt to settle was in vain; for the land he dwelt in was to him *the land of Nod* (that is, of *shaking* or *trembling*), because of the continual restlessness and uneasiness of his own spirit. Note, Those that depart from God cannot find rest anywhere else. After Cain went out from the presence of the Lord, he never rested. "*Return therefore to thy rest, O my soul*, to thy rest in God; else thou art for ever restless."

2. He built a city for a habitation, *v.* 17. *He was building a city*, so some read it, ever building it, but, a curse being upon him and the work of his hands, he could not finish it. (1) Cain's defiance of the divine sentence. God said he should be a *fugitive and a vagabond*. Had he repented and humbled himself, this curse might have been turned into a blessing. (2) See what was Cain's choice, after he had forsaken God; he pitched upon a settlement in this world, as his rest for ever. (3) See what method Cain took to defend himself against the terrors with which he was perpetually haunted. He undertook this building, to divert his thoughts from the consideration of his own misery, and to drown the clamours of a guilty conscience with the noise of axes and hammers. Thus many baffle their convictions by thrusting themselves into a hurry of worldly business. (4) See how wicked people often get the start of God's people, and out-go them in outward prosperity. Cain and his cursed race dwell in a city, while Adam and his blessed family dwell in tents.

3. His family also was built up. Here is an account of his posterity, at least the heirs of his family, for seven generations.

Verses 19–22

Some particulars concerning Lamech, the seventh from Adam in the line of Cain.

Though he sinned, in marrying two wives, yet he was blessed with children by both, and those such as lived to be famous in their generation, not for their piety but for their ingenuity. They were not only themselves men of business, but men that were serviceable to the world, and eminent for the invention, or at least the improvement, of some useful arts. 1. Jabal was a famous shepherd. 2. Jubal was a famous musician, and particularly an organist, and the first that gave rules for the noble art or science of music. When Jabal had set them in a way to be rich, Jubal put them in a way to be merry. Jabal was their Pan and Jubal their Apollo. 3. Tubalcain was a famous smith, who greatly improved the art of working in brass and iron, for the service both of war and husbandry. He was their Vulcan. Even those who are destitute of the knowledge and grace of God may be endued with many excellent and useful accomplishments, which may make them famous and serviceable in their generation. Common gifts are given to bad men, while God chooses to himself the foolish things of the world.

Verses 23–24

By this speech of Lamech, which is here recorded, and probably was much talked of in those times, he further appears to have been a wicked man, as Cain's accursed race generally were. He owns himself a man of a fierce and cruel disposition, that would lay about him without mercy, and kill all that stood in his way. His wives, knowing what manner of spirit he was of, how apt both to give and to resent provocation, were afraid lest somebody or other would be the death of him. "Never fear," says he, "I defy any man to set upon me; whosoever does, let me alone to make my part good with him; I will slay him, be he a man or a young man."

Verses 25–26

This is the first mention of Adam in the story of this chapter. No question, the murder of Abel, and the impenitence and apostasy of Cain, were a very great grief to him and Eve, and the more because their own wickedness did now correct them and their backslidings did reprove them. But here we have that which was a relief to our first parents in their affliction.

I. God gave them to see the re-building of their family, which was sorely shaken and weakened by that sad event. For, 1. They saw their seed, *another seed instead of Abel, v.* 25. Observe God's kindness and tenderness towards his people, in his providential

JAMIESON, FAUSSET, BROWN

land of Nod—of flight or exile—thought by many to have been Arabia Petræa—which was cursed to sterility on his account.

17-22. builded a city—It has been in cities that the human race has ever made the greatest social progress; and several of Cain's descendants distinguished themselves by their inventive genius in the arts.

19. Lamech took unto him two wives—This is the first transgression of the law of marriage on record, and the practice of polygamy, like all other breaches of God's institutions, has been a fruitful source of corruption and misery.

23, 24. Lamech said unto his wives—This speech is in a poetical form, probably the fragment of an old poem, transmitted to the time of Moses. It seems to indicate that Lamech had slain a man in self-defense, and its drift is to assure his wives, by the preservation of Cain, that an *unintentional* homicide, as he was, could be in no danger.

ADAM CLARKE

16. *The land of Nod*. As *nod* signifies the same as *nad*, a "vagabond," some think this verse should be rendered, "And Cain went out from the presence of the Lord, from the east of Eden, and dwelt a vagabond on the earth"; thus the curse pronounced on him, verse 12, was accomplished.

17. *She . . . bare Enoch*. As *Chanoch* signifies "instructed, dedicated, or initiated," and especially in sacred things, it may be considered some proof of Cain's repentance, that he appears to have dedicated this son to God, who, in his father's stead, might minister in the sacerdotal office, from which Cain, by his crime, was forever excluded.

19. *Lamech took . . . two wives*. He was the first who dared to reverse the order of God by introducing polygamy; and from him it has been retained, practiced, and defended to the present day.

20. *Jabal . . . was the father*. The "inventor" or "teacher," for so the word is understood, 1 Sam. x. 12. He was the first who invented tent making, and the breeding and managing of cattle; or he was, in these respects, the most eminent in that time. Though Abel was a shepherd, it is not likely he was such on an extensive scale.

21. *Jubal . . . the father*. I.e., the "inventor" of musical instruments, such as the *kinnor*, which we translate *harp*, and the *ugab*, which we render *organ;* it is very likely that both words are generic, the former including under it all stringed instruments, and the latter, all wind instruments.

22. *Tubal-cain*. The first smith on record, who taught how to make warlike instruments and domestic utensils out of brass and iron. Agricultural instruments must have been in use long before, for Cain was a tiller of the ground, and so was Adam, and they could not have cultivated the ground without spades, hooks, etc. Some of these arts were useless to man while innocent and upright, but after his fall they became necessary. Thus is the saying verified: "God hath made man upright; but they have sought out many inventions." As the power to get wealth is from God, so also is the invention of useful arts.

23. *And Lamech said unto his wives*. The speech of Lamech to his wives is in hemistichs in the original, and consequently, as nothing of this kind occurs before this time, it is very probably the oldest piece of poetry in the world.

The following is, as nearly as possible, a literal translation:

"And Lamech said unto his wives,
Adah and Tsillah, hear ye my voice;
Wives of Lamech, hearken to my speech;
For I have slain a man for wounding me,
And a young man for having bruised me.
If Cain shall be avenged sevenfold,
Also Lamech seventy and seven."

It is supposed that Lamech had slain a man in his own defense, and that his wives being alarmed lest the kindred of the deceased should seek his life in return, to quiet their fears he makes this speech, in which he endeavors to prove that there was no room for fear on this account; for if the slayer of the wilful murderer, Cain, should suffer a sevenfold punishment, surely he who should kill Lamech for having slain a man in self-defense might expect a seventy-seven-fold punishment.

25. *God . . . hath appointed me another seed*

MATTHEW HENRY

dealings with them; when he takes away one comfort from them, he gives them another instead of it, which may prove a greater blessing to them than that was in which they thought their lives were bound up. Those who slay God's servants hope by this means to wear out the saints of the Most High; but they will be deceived. Christ shall still see his seed; God can out of stones raise up children for him, and make the blood of the martyrs the seed of the church. This son, by a prophetic spirit, they called *Seth* (that is, *set, settled,* or *placed*), because, in his seed, mankind should continue to the end of time, and from him the Messiah should descend. While Cain, the head of the apostasy, is made a wanderer, Seth, from whom the true church was to come, is one fixed. In Christ and his church is the only true settlement. 2. They saw their seed's seed, *v.* 26. *To Seth was born a son called Enos.*

II. God gave them to see the reviving of religion in their family: *Then began men to call upon the name of the Lord, v.* 26. It is small comfort to a good man to see his children's children, if he do not, withal, see peace upon Israel, and those that come of him walking in the truth. 1. The worshippers of God began to stir up themselves to do more in religion than they had done. Now men began to worship God, not only in their closets and families, but in public and solemn assemblies. 2. The worshippers of God began to distinguish themselves. The margin reads it, *Then began men to be called by the name of the Lord,* or to call themselves by it.

JAMIESON, FAUSSET, BROWN

26. men began to call upon the name of the Lord—rather, by the name of the Lord. God's people, a name probably applied to them in contempt by the world.

ADAM CLARKE

instead of Abel. Eve must have received on this occasion some divine communication, else how could she have known that this son was appointed in the place of Abel, to continue that holy line by which the Messiah was to come? From this we see that the line of the Messiah was determined from the beginning, and that it was not first fixed in the days of Abraham; for the promise was then only renewed, and that branch of his family designated by which the sacred line was to be continued. And it is worthy of remark that Seth's posterity alone continued after the Flood, when all the other families of the earth were destroyed, Noah being the tenth descendant from Adam through Seth.

26. *Then began men to call upon the name of the Lord.* The marginal reading is, "Then began men to call themselves *by the* name of the Lord"; which words are supposed to signify that in the time of Enos the true followers of God began to distinguish themselves, and to be distinguished by others, by the appellation of "sons of God"; those of the other branch of Adam's family, among whom the divine worship was not observed, being distinguished by the name "children of men."

MATTHEW HENRY

CHAPTER 5

Verses 1–5

The first words of the chapter are the title or argument of the whole chapter: it is *the book of the generations of Adam.* The genealogy begins with Adam himself.

I. His creation, *v.* 1, 2, where we have a brief rehearsal of what was before related concerning the creation of man. Observe here, 1. That *God created man.* Man is not his own maker, therefore he must not be his own master; but the Author of his being must be the director of his motions and the centre of them. 2. That there was a day in which God created man. He was not from eternity, but of yesterday. 3. That God made him in his own likeness, righteous and holy, and therefore, undoubtedly, happy. 4. That God created them male and female (*v.* 2), for their mutual comfort as well as for the preservation and increase of their kind.

II. The birth of his son *Seth, v.* 3. That which is most observable here concerning Seth is that Adam begat him *in his own likeness, after his image.* Adam was made in the image of God; but, when he was fallen and corrupt, he begat a son in his own image.

Verses 6–20

We have here all that the Holy Ghost thought fit to leave upon record concerning five of the patriarchs before the flood. Seth, Enos, Cainan, Mahalaleel, and Jared. There is nothing observable concerning any of these particularly, though we have reason to think they were men of eminence, both for prudence and piety, in their day.

I. Concerning each of them, except Enoch, it is said, *and he died.* It is implied in the numbering of the years of their life that their life, when those years were numbered and finished, came to an end; and yet it is still repeated, *and he died,* to show that death passed upon all men without exception. Such a one was a strong healthy man, but he died; such a one was a great and rich man, but he died; such a one was a wise politic man, but he died; such a one was a very good man, perhaps a very useful man, but he died, &c.

II. That which is especially observable is that they all lived very long. Long life to the pious patriarchs was a blessing and made them blessings.

Verses 21–24

The accounts here run on for several generations without anything remarkable, or any variation but of the names and numbers; but at length there comes in one that must not be passed over so, of whom special notice must be taken, and that is *Enoch,* the seventh from Adam: the rest, we may suppose, did virtuously, but he excelled them all, and was the brightest star of the patriarchal age. It is but little that is recorded concerning him; but this little is enough to make his name great, greater than the name of the other Enoch, who had a city called by his name. Here are two things concerning him:—

I. His gracious conversation in this world, which is twice spoken of: *Enoch walked with God after he*

JAMIESON, FAUSSET, BROWN

CHAPTER 5

VSS. 1-32. GENEALOGY OF THE PATRIARCHS. **1. book of the generations** (See ch. 11:4). **Adam**—used here either as the name of the first man, or of the human race generally. **5. all the days . . . Adam lived**—The most striking feature in this catalogue is the longevity of Adam and his immediate descendants. Ten are enumerated in direct succession whose lives far exceed the ordinary limits with which we are familiar—the shortest being 365, and the longest 930 years. It is useless to inquire whether and what secondary causes may have contributed to this protracted longevity—vigorous constitutions, the nature of their diet, the temperature and salubrity of the climate; or, finally—as this list comprises only the true worshippers of God—whether their great age might be owing to the better government of their passions and the quiet, even tenor of their lives. Since we cannot obtain satisfactory evidence on these points, it is wise to resolve the fact into the sovereign will of God. We can, however, trace some of the important uses to which, in the early economy of Providence, it was subservient. It was the chief means of reserving a knowledge of God, of the great truths of religion, as well as the influence of genuine piety. So that, as their knowledge was obtained by tradition, they would be in a condition to preserve it in the greatest purity.

ADAM CLARKE

CHAPTER 5

1. *The book of the generations. Sepher* in Hebrew, which we generally translate *book,* signifies a "register," an "account," any kind of writing, even a "letter," such as the bill of divorce. Here it means the account or register of the generations of Adam or his descendants to the five hundredth year of the life of Noah.

In the likeness of God made he him. This account is again introduced to keep man in remembrance of the heights of glory whence he had fallen; and to prove to him that the miseries and death consequent on his present state were produced by his transgression, and did not flow from his original state. For, as he was created in the image of God, he was created free from natural and moral evil. As the deaths of the patriarchs are now to be mentioned, it was necessary to introduce them by this observation, in order to justify the ways of God to man.

3. *And Adam lived an hundred and thirty years.* The Scripture chronology, especially in the ages of some of the antediluvian and postdiluvian patriarchs, has exceedingly puzzled chronologists, critics, and divines. The printed Hebrew text, the Samaritan, the Septuagint, and Josephus are all different, and have their respective vouchers and defenders.

And begat a son in his own likeness, after his image. Words nearly the same with those of chap. i. 26: "Let us make man in our image, after our likeness." What this *image* and *likeness* of God were, we have already seen, and we may rest assured that the same image and likeness are not meant here. The body of Adam was created provisionally immortal, i.e., while he continued obedient he could not die; but his obedience was voluntary, and his state a probationary one. The soul of Adam was created in the moral image of God, in knowledge, righteousness, and true holiness. He had now sinned, and consequently had lost his moral resemblance to his Maker; he had also become mortal through his breach of the law. His image and likeness were therefore widely different at this time from what they were before; and his begetting children in this image and likeness plainly implies that they were imperfect like himself, mortal like himself, sinful and corrupt like himself.

MATTHEW HENRY

begat Methuselah (*v.* 22), and again, *Enoch walked with God, v.* 24.

1. The nature of his religion and the scope and tenor of his conversation: he *walked with God,* which denotes, (1) True religion; what is godliness, but walking with God? The ungodly and profane are without God in the world, they walk contrary to him: but the godly walk with God, which presupposes reconciliation to God, for two cannot *walk together except they be agreed* (Amos iii. 3). To walk with God is to set God always before us, and to act as those that are always under his eye. It is to live a life of communion with God both in ordinances and providences. It is to make God's word our rule and his glory our end in all our actions. It is to comply with his will, to concur with his designs, and to be workers together with him. (2) Eminent religion. He was entirely dead to this world, and did not only walk after God, as all good men do, but he walked with God, as if he were in heaven already. (3) Activity in promoting religion among others. Executing the priest's office is called *walking before God,* 1 Sam. ii. 30, 35, and see Zech. iii. 7. Enoch, it should seem, was a priest of the most high God. Now the Holy Spirit instead of saying, Enoch *lived,* says, Enoch *walked with God*; for it is the life of a good man to walk with God. This was, [1] The business of Enoch's life. [2] It was the joy and support of his life.

II. His glorious removal to a better world. As he did not live like the rest, so he did not die like the rest (*v.* 24): *He was not, for God took him;* that is, as it is explained (Heb. xi. 5), *He was translated that he should not see death, and was not found, because God had translated him.*

Whenever a good man dies, God takes him, fetches him hence, and receives him to himself. The apostle adds concerning Enoch that, *before his translation, he had this testimony, that he pleased God.* Those whose conversation in the world is truly holy shall find their removal out of it truly happy.

Verses 25–27

Methuselah signifies, *he dies.* However, this is observable, that the longest liver that ever was carried death in his name, that he might be reminded of its coming surely, though it came slowly.

Verses 28–32

The first mention of Noah, of whom we shall read much in the following chapters.

I. His name, with the reason of it: *Noah* signifies *rest*; his parents gave him that name, with a prospect of his being a more than ordinary blessing to his generation.

II. His children, Shem, Ham, and Japheth. It should seem that Japheth was the eldest (*ch.* x. 21), but Shem is put first because on him the covenant was entailed, as appears by *ch.* ix. 26, where God is called the *Lord God of Shem.* To him, it is probable, the birth-right was given, and from him, it is certain, both Christ the head, and the church the body, were to descend. Therefore he is called *Shem,* which signifies a *name,* because in his posterity the name of God should always remain, till he should come out of his loins whose name is above every name; so that in putting Shem first Christ was, in effect, put first, who in all things must have the pre-eminence.

JAMIESON, FAUSSET, BROWN

24. And Enoch walked with God—a common phrase in Eastern countries denoting constant and familiar intercourse.

was not; for God took him—In Hebrews 11:5, we are informed that he was translated to heaven—a mighty miracle, designed to effect what ordinary means of instruction had failed to accomplish, gave a palpable proof to an age of almost universal unbelief that the doctrines which he had taught (Jude 14, 15) were true and that his devotedness to the cause of God and righteousness in the midst of opposition was highly pleasing to the mind of God. **21. Enoch . . . begat Methuselah**—This name signifies, "He dieth, and the sending forth," so that Enoch gave it as prophetical of the flood. It is computed that Methuselah died in the year of that catastrophe. **26. Lamech**—a different person from the one mentioned in preceding chapter. Like his namesake, however, he also spoke in numbers on occasion of the birth of Noah—i. e., "rest" or "comfort." "The allusion is, undoubtedly, to the penal consequences of the fall in earthly toils and sufferings, and to the hope of a Deliverer, excited by the promise made to Eve. That this expectation was founded on a divine communication we infer from the importance attached to it and the confidence of its expression" [PETER SMITH]. **32. Noah was five hundred years old: and . . . begat**—That he and the other patriarchs were advanced in life before children were born to them is a difficulty accounted for probably from the circumstance that Moses does not here record their first-born sons, but only the succession from Adam through Seth to Abraham.

ADAM CLARKE

22. *And Enoch walked with God . . . three hundred years. Enoch,* from *chanack,* which signifies to "instruct," to "initiate," to "dedicate." From his subsequent conduct we are authorized to believe he was early instructed in the things of God, initiated into the worship of his Maker, and dedicated to His service. By these means, under the influence of the Divine Spirit, which will ever attend pious parental instructions, his mind got that sacred bias which led him to act a part so distinguished through the course of a long life. He *walked with God;* "he set himself to walk"; he was fixedly purposed and determined to live to God.

27. *The days of Methuselah were nine hundred sixty and nine years.* This is the longest life mentioned in Scripture, and probably the longest ever lived; but we have not authority to say positively that it was the longest. Before the Flood, and before artificial refinements were much known and cultivated, the life of man was greatly protracted, and yet of him who lived within thirty-one years of a thousand it is said he *died;* and the longest life is but as a moment when it is past.

29. *This same shall comfort us.* This is an allusion, as some think, to the name of Noah, which they derive from *nacham,* "to comfort"; but it is much more likely that it comes from *nach* or *nuach,* "to rest, to settle." And what is more comfortable than rest after toil and labor? These words seem to have been spoken prophetically concerning Noah, who built the ark for the preservation of the human race, and who seems to have been a typical person; for when he offered his sacrifice after the drying up of the waters, it is said that God smelled a savor of rest and said He would not curse the ground anymore for man's sake, chap. viii. 21; and from that time the earth seems to have had upon an average the same degree of fertility; and the life of man, in a few generations after, was settled in the mean at threescore years and ten. See chap. ix. 3.

32. *Noah begat Shem, Ham, and Japheth.* From chap. x. 21; 1 Chron. i. 5, etc., we learn that Japheth was the eldest son of Noah, but Shem is mentioned first, because it was from him, in a direct line, that the Messiah came. Ham was certainly the youngest of Noah's sons, and from what we read, chap. ix. 22, the worst of them; and how he comes to be mentioned out of his natural order is not easy to be accounted for. When the Scriptures design to mark precedency, though the subject be a younger son or brother, he is always mentioned first; so Jacob is named before Esau, his elder brother, and Ephraim before Manasseh. See chap. xxviii. 5; xlviii. 20.

MATTHEW HENRY

CHAPTER 6

Verses 1–2

Now here we have an account of two things which occasioned the wickedness of the old world:—1. The increase of mankind: *Men began to multiply upon the face of the earth.* This was the effect of the blessing (*ch.* i. 28), and yet man's corruption so abused and perverted this blessing that it was turned into a curse. The more sinners the more sin. Infectious diseases are most destructive in populous cities; and sin is a spreading leprosy. 2. Mixed marriages (*v.* 2): *The sons of God* (that is, the professors of religion) *married the daughters of men,* that is, those that were profane, and strangers to God and godliness. The posterity of Seth did not keep by themselves, as they ought to have done. They intermingled themselves with the excommunicated race of Cain: *They took them wives of all that they chose.* But what was amiss in these marriages? (1) They chose only by the eye: *They saw that they were fair,* which was all they looked at. (2) They followed the choice which their own corrupt affections made. But, (3) That which proved of such bad consequence to them was that they *married strange wives, were unequally yoked with unbelievers,* 2 Cor. vi. 14. The bad will sooner debauch the good than the good reform the bad.

JAMIESON, FAUSSET, BROWN

CHAPTER 6

Vss. 1-22. WICKEDNESS OF THE WORLD. **2. the sons of God saw the daughters of men**—By the former is meant the family of Seth, who were professedly religious; by the latter, the descendants of apostate Cain. Mixed marriages between parties of opposite principles and practice were necessarily sources of extensive corruption. The women, irreligious themselves, would as wives and mothers exert an influence fatal to the existence of religion in their household, and consequently the people of that later age sank to the lowest depravity.

ADAM CLARKE

CHAPTER 6

1. *When men began to multiply.* It was not at this time that men began to multiply, but the inspired penman speaks now of a fact which had taken place long before. As there is a distinction made here between men and those called the "sons of God," it is generally supposed that the immediate posterity of Cain and that of Seth are intended. The first were mere men, such as fallen nature may produce, degenerate sons of a degenerate father, governed by the desire of the flesh, the desire of the eye, and the pride of life. The others were "sons of God," not angels, as some have dreamed, but such as were, according to our Lord's doctrine, born again, born from above, John iii. 3, 5-6, etc., and made children of God by the influence of the Holy Spirit, Gal. v. 6. The former were apostates from the true religion; the latter were those among whom it was preserved and cultivated.

MATTHEW HENRY

Verse 3

This comes in here as a token of God's displeasure.

I. God's resolution not always to strive with man by his Spirit. Note, 1. The blessed Spirit strives with sinners, by the convictions and admonitions of conscience, to turn them from sin to God. 2. If the Spirit be resisted, quenched, and striven against, though he strive long, he will not strive always, Hos. iv. 17.

II. The reason of this resolution: *For that he also is flesh*, that is, incurably corrupt, and carnal, and sensual. Note, 1. It is the corrupt nature, and the inclination of the soul towards the flesh, that oppose the Spirit's strivings and render them ineffectual. 2. None lose the Spirit's strivings but those that have first forfeited them.

III. A reprieve granted, notwithstanding: *Yet his days shall be one hundred and twenty years.* Note, The time of God's patience and forbearance towards provoking sinners is sometimes long, but always limited: reprieves are not pardons.

Verses 4–5

A further account of the corruption of the old world.

I. The temptation they were under to oppress and do violence. They were *giants*, and they were *men of renown*. 1. With their great bulk, as the sons of Anak, Num. xiii. 33. 2. With their great name, as the king of Assyria, Isa. xxxvii. 11. Note, Those that have so much power over others as to be able to oppress them have seldom so much power over themselves as not to oppress.

II. The charge exhibited and proved against them, *v.* 5. Now what did God take notice of? 1. He observed all the streams of sin that flowed along in men's lives, and the breadth and depth of those streams. The oppressors were *mighty men and men of renown*; and, *then, God saw that the wickedness of man was great*. Note, The wickedness of a people is great indeed when the most notorious sinners are men of renown among them. Wickedness is then great when great men are wicked. Note, All the sins of sinners are known to God the Judge. 2. He observed the fountain of sin that was in men's hearts. Anyone might see that *the wickedness of man was great*, for they declared their sin as Sodom; but God's eye went further: *He saw that every imagination of the thoughts of his heart was only evil continually.* (1) The thoughts of the heart were so. (2) The imagination of the thoughts of the heart was so, that is, their designs and devices were wicked. They did not do evil through mere carelessness, but they did evil deliberately and designedly, contriving how to do mischief.

Verses 6–7

Here is, I. God's resentment of man's wickedness. He did not see it as an unconcerned spectator, but as one injured and affronted by it; he saw it as a tender father sees the folly and stubbornness of a rebellious and disobedient child, which not only angers him, but grieves him. 1. This language does not imply any passion or uneasiness in God (nothing can create disturbance to the Eternal Mind), but it expresses his just and holy displeasure against sin and sinners. Does God thus hate sin? And shall we not hate it? Has our sin grieved him to the heart? And shall not we be grieved and pricked to the heart for it? 2. It does not imply any change of God's mind, but it expresses a change of his way. But, now that man had apostatized, he could not do otherwise than show himself displeased; so that the change was in man, not in God. God repented that he had made man; but we never find him repenting that he redeemed man.

II. God's resolution to destroy man for his wickedness, *v.* 7. We do but mock God in saying that we are sorry for our sin, and that it grieves us to the heart, if we continue to indulge it. The original word is very significant: *I will wipe off man from the earth* (so some), as dirt or filth is wiped off from a place which should be clean. Those forfeit their lives that do not answer the end of their living. God took up this resolution concerning man after his Spirit had been long striving with him in vain. None are ruined by the justice of God but those that hate to be reformed by the grace of God.

Verses 8–10

We have here Noah distinguished from the rest of the world, and a peculiar mark of honour put upon him. 1. When God was displeased with the rest of the world, he favoured Noah: there being one good man, he found him out, and smiled upon him. He was made a vessel of God's mercy. God made him greater and more truly honourable than all the giants that were in those days, who became

JAMIESON, FAUSSET, BROWN

3. flesh—utterly, hopelessly debased. **And the Lord said, My spirit shall not always strive**—Christ, as God, had by His Spirit inspiring Enoch, Noah, and perhaps other prophets (I Pet. 3:20); II Pet. 2:5; Jude 14), preached repentance to the antediluvians; but they were incorrigible. **yet his days shall be an hundred and twenty years**—It is probable that the corruption of the world, which had now reached its height, had been long and *gradually* increasing, and this idea receives support from the long respite granted.

4. giants—The term in *Hebrew* implies not so much the idea of great stature as of reckless ferocity, impious and daring characters, who spread devastation and carnage far and wide.

5, 6. God saw it . . . repented . . . grieved—God cannot change (Mal. 3:6; Jas. 1:17); but, by language *suited to our nature and experience*, He is described as about to alter His visible procedure towards mankind—from being merciful and long-suffering, He was about to show Himself a God of judgment; and, as that impious race had filled up the measure of their iniquities, He was about to introduce a terrible display of His justice (Eccles. 8:11).

8. But Noah found grace in the eyes of the Lord—favor. What an awful state of things when only one man or one family of piety and virtue was now existing among the professed sons of God!

ADAM CLARKE

3. *My spirit shall not always strive.* It is only by the influence of the Spirit of God that the carnal mind can be subdued and destroyed; but those who wilfully resist and grieve that Spirit must be ultimately left to the hardness and blindness of their own hearts, if they do not repent and turn to God. God delights in mercy, and therefore a gracious warning is given. Even at this time the earth was ripe for destruction; but God promised them 120 years' respite: if they repented in that interim, well; if not, they should be destroyed by a flood. See on v. 5.

4. *There were giants in the earth. Nephilim,* from *naphal,* "he fell." Those who had apostatized or fallen from the true religion. The Septuagint translates the original word by *gigantes,* which literally signifies "earth-born," and which we, following them, term *giants,* without having any reference to the meaning of the word, which we generally conceive to signify persons of enormous stature. But the word when properly understood makes a very just distinction between the sons of men and the sons of God; those were the nephilim, the fallen earth-born men, with the animal and devilish mind. These were the sons of God, who were born from above; children of the Kingdom, because children of God.

The same became mighty men . . . men of renown. Gibborim, which we render *mighty men,* signifies properly "conquerors, heroes," from *gabar,* "he prevailed, was victorious," and "men of the name"; the same as we render "men of renown," "twice named," as the word implies, having one name which they derived from their fathers, and another which they acquired by their daring exploits and enterprises.

It may be necessary to remark here that our translators have rendered seven different Hebrew words by the one term "giants," namely, *nephilim, gibborim, enachim, rephaim, emim,* and *zamzummim;* by which appellatives are probably meant in general persons of great knowledge, piety, courage, wickedness, etc., and not men of enormous stature, as is generally conjectured.

5. *The wickedness of man was great.* What an awful character does God give of the inhabitants of the antediluvian world! (1) They were "flesh" (v. 3), wholly sensual, the desires of the mind overwhelmed and lost in the desires of the flesh. (2) They were in a state of "wickedness." All was corrupt within, and all unrighteous without. (3) This wickedness was "great," *rabbah,* "was multiplied"; it was continually increasing and multiplying increase by increase, so that the whole earth was corrupt before God, and was filled with violence (v. 11). (4) "All the imaginations of their thoughts were evil"—the very first embryo of every idea, the figment of every thought, the very materials out of which perception, conception, and ideas were formed, were all *evil;* the fountain which produced them, with every thought, purpose, wish, desire, and motive, was incurably poisoned. (5) All these were evil without any mixture of good—the Spirit of God which strove with them was continually resisted, so that evil had its sovereign sway. (6) They were evil "continually"—there was no interval of good, no moment allowed for serious reflection, no holy purpose, no righteous act. What a finished picture of a fallen soul! (7) To complete the whole, God represents himself as "repenting" because he had made them, and as "grieved at the heart" because of their iniquities! (8) So incensed is the most holy and the most merciful God that He is determined to destroy the work of His hands: "And the Lord said, I will destroy man whom I have created," v. 7. Fools make a mock at sin, but none except fools.

MATTHEW HENRY

mighty men and men of renown. Those are highly favoured whom God favours. 2. Noah kept his integrity: *Noah was a just man, v.* 9. This character of Noah comes in here either, (1) As the reason of God's favour to him. God loves those that love him: or, (2) As the effect of God's favour to him. It was God's good-will to him that produced this good work in him. He was a very good man, but he was no better than the grace of God made him, 1 Cor. xv. 10. Now observe his character. [1] He *was a just man,* that is, justified before God by faith in the promised seed; for he was an *heir of the righteousness which is by faith,* Heb. xi. 7. God has sometimes chosen the foolish things of the world, but he never chose the knavish things of it. [2] He was *perfect,* not with a sinless perfection, but a perfection of sincerity; and it is well for us that by virtue of the covenant of grace, upon the score of Christ's righteousness, sincerity is accepted as our gospel perfection. [3] He *walked with God.* He lived a life of communion with God. God looks down with an eye of favour upon those who sincerely look up to him with an eye of faith. It is easy to be religious when religion is in fashion; but it is an evidence of strong faith and resolution to swim against a stream to heaven, and to appear for God when no one else appears for him.

Verses 11–12

The wickedness of that generation is here again spoken of. 1. All kinds of sin was found among them, for it is said (*v.* 11) that the earth was, (1) *Corrupt before God.* (2) *The earth was also filled with violence* and injustice towards men. Wickedness, as it is the shame of human nature, so it is the ruin of human society. Take away conscience and the fear of God, and men become beasts and devils to one another. Sin fills the earth with violence, and so turns the world into a wilderness, into a cock-pit. 2. The proof and evidence of it were undeniable; for *God looked upon the earth,* and was himself an eye-witness of the corruption that was in it. 3. That which most aggravated the matter was the universal spreading of the contagion: *All flesh had corrupted his way.* When wickedness has become general then universal ruin is not far off; while there is a remnant of praying people in a nation, to empty the measure as it fills, judgments may be kept off a great while.

Verses 13–21

It appears indeed that Noah *found grace in the eyes of the Lord.*

I. God here makes Noah the *man of his counsel,* communicating to him his purpose to destroy this wicked world by water, as, afterwards, he told Abraham his resolution concerning Sodom (*ch.* xviii. 17). *The secret of the Lord* was with *his servants the prophets* (Amos iii. 7), by a spirit of revelation, informing them particularly of his purposes; it is with all believers by a spirit of wisdom and faith, enabling them to understand.

1. God told Noah, in general, that he would destroy the world (*v.* 13). Noah, it is likely, in preaching to his neighbours, had warned them, and now God seconds his endeavours.

2. He told him, particularly, that he would destroy the world by a flood of waters: *And behold, I, even I, do bring a flood of waters upon the earth, v.* 17. The reasons, we may be sure, were wise and just, though to us unknown. God has many arrows in his quiver, and he may use which he please. He intimates the certainty of the judgment: *I, even I,* will do it.

II. God here makes Noah the *man of his covenant,* another Hebrew periphrasis of a friend (*v.* 18): *But with thee will I establish my covenant.* 1. The covenant of providence, that the course of nature shall be continued to the end of time, notwithstanding the interruption which the flood would give to it. This promise was immediately made to Noah and his sons, *ch.* ix. 8, &c. They were as trustees for all this part of the creation. 2. The covenant of grace, that God would be to him a God and that out of his seed God would take to himself a people.

III. God here makes Noah a monument of sparing mercy. Singular piety shall be recompensed with distinguishing salvations.

1. God directs Noah to *make an ark, v.* 14–16. This ark was like the hulk of a ship, fitted not to sail upon the waters (there was no occasion for that, when there should be no shore to sail to), but to float upon the waters, waiting for their fall. God chose to employ him in making that which was to be the means of his preservation, both for the trial of his faith and obedience and to teach us that none shall be saved by Christ but those only that *work out their salvation.* We cannot do it without God, and he will not without us. God gave him very particular

JAMIESON, FAUSSET, BROWN

9. Noah . . . just . . . and perfect—not absolutely; for since the fall of Adam no man has been free from sin except Jesus Christ. But as living by faith he was just (Gal. 3:2; Heb. 11:7) and perfect—i.e., sincere in his desire to do God's will.

11. the earth was filled with violence—In the absence of any well-regulated government it is easy to imagine what evils would arise. Men did what was right in their own eyes, and, having no fear of God, destruction and misery were in their ways.

13. And God said unto Noah—How startling must have been the announcement of the threatened destruction! There was no outward indication of it. The course of nature and experience seemed against the probability of its occurrence. The public opinion of mankind would ridicule it. The whole world would be ranged against him. Yet, persuaded the communication was from God, through faith (Heb. 11:7), he set about preparing the means for preserving himself and family from the impending calamity.

14. Make thee an ark—ark, a hollow chest (Exod.2:3).

ADAM CLARKE

8. *Noah found grace in the eyes of the Lord.* Why? Because he was (1) *A just man,* a man who "gave to all their due"; for this is the ideal meaning of the original word. (2) He was *perfect in his generations*—he was in all things a consistent character, never departing from the truth in principle or practice. (3) He *walked with God*—he was not only righteous in his conduct, but he was pious, and had continual communion with God. The same word is used here as before in the case of Enoch. See chap. v. 22.

13. *I will destroy them with the earth.* Not only the human race was to be destroyed, but all terrestrial animals, i.e., those which could not live in the waters.

14. *Make thee an ark. Tebath,* a word which is used only to express this vessel, and that in which Moses was preserved, Exod. ii. 3, 5. It signifies no more than our word "vessel" in its common acceptation—a hollow place capable of containing persons, goods, etc., without any particular reference to shape or form.

Gopher wood. Some think the cedar is meant; others, the cypress.

15. *Thou shalt make . . . the length of the ark . . . three hundred cubits, the breadth of it fifty cubits, and the height of it thirty cubits.*

MATTHEW HENRY

instructions concerning this building. (1) It must be made of *gopher-wood*. (2) He must make it three stories high within. (3) He must divide it into cabins, with partitions, places fitted for the several sorts of creatures, so as to lose no room. (4) Exact dimensions were given him. Those that work for God must take their measures from him and carefully observe them. (5) He must *pitch it within and without*—without, to shed off the rain, and to prevent the water from soaking in—within, to take away the bad smell of the beasts when kept close. (6) He must make a little window towards the top, to let in light. (7) He must make a door in the side of it, by which to go in and out.

2. God promises Noah that he and his shall be preserved alive in the ark (*v.* 18): *Thou shalt come into the ark.* Observe, (1) The care of good parents; they are solicitous not only for their own salvation, but for the salvation of their families, and especially their children. (2) The happiness of those children that have godly parents. Their parents' piety often procures them temporal salvation, as here; and it furthers them in the way to eternal salvation, if they improve the benefit of it.

JAMIESON, FAUSSET, BROWN

gopher wood—probably cypress, remarkable for its durability and abounding on the Armenian mountains. **rooms**—cabins or small cells. **pitch it within and without**—mineral pitch, asphalt, naphtha, or some bituminous substance, which, when smeared over and become hardened, would make it perfectly watertight. **15. And this is the fashion**—According to the description, the ark was not a ship, but an immense house in form and structure like the houses in the East, designed not to sail, but only to float. Assuming the cubit to be 21.888 inches, the ark would be 547 feet long, 91 feet 2 inches wide, and 47 feet 2 inches high. **16. A window**—probably a skylight, formed of some transparent substance unknown. **in a cubit shalt thou finish it above**—a direction to raise the roof in the middle, seemingly to form a gentle slope for letting the water run off. **17-22. And, behold, I, even I, do bring a flood**—The repetition of the announcement was to establish its certainty (ch. 41:32). Whatever opinion may be entertained as to the operation of natural laws and agencies in the deluge, it was brought on the world by God as a punishment for the enormous wickedness of its inhabitants. **18. But with thee will I establish my covenant**—a special promise of deliverance, called a covenant, to convince him of the confidence to be reposed in it. The substance and terms of this covenant are related between vss. 19 and 21.

ADAM CLARKE

Allowing the cubit, which is the length from the elbow to the tip of the middle finger, to be 18 inches, the ark must have been 450 feet in length, 75 in breadth, and 45 in height.

16. *A window shalt thou make.* What this was cannot be absolutely ascertained. The original word signifies "clear" or "bright." It is probably a word which should be taken in a collective sense, signifying apertures for air and light.

17. *I . . . do bring a flood. Mabbul,* a word used only to designate the general deluge, being never applied to signify any other kind of inundation; and does not the Holy Spirit intend to show by this that no other flood was ever like this, and that it should continue to be the sole one of the kind? There have been many partial inundations in various countries, but never more than one general deluge; and we have God's promise, chap. ix. 15, that there shall never be another.

18. *With thee will I establish my covenant.* The word *berith,* from *bar,* "to purify or cleanse," signifies properly a purification or purifier (see on chap. xv. 18), because in all covenants made between God and man, sin and sinfulness were ever supposed to be on man's side, and that God could not enter into any covenant or engagement with him without a purifier; hence, in all covenants, a sacrifice was offered for the removal of offenses, and the reconciliation of God to the sinner; and hence the word *berith* signifies not only a *covenant,* but also the sacrifice offered on the occasion, Exod. xxiv. 8; Ps. i. 5; and Jesus Christ, the great Atonement and Purifier, has the same word for His title, Isa. xlii. 6; xlix. 8; and Zech. ix. 11.

Almost all nations, in forming alliances, etc., made their covenants or contracts in the same way. A sacrifice was provided, its throat was cut, and its blood poured out before God; then the whole carcass was divided through the spinal marrow from the head to the rump; so as to make exactly two equal parts; these were placed opposite to each other, and the contracting parties passed between them, or entering at opposite ends met in the center, and there took the covenant oath. This is particularly referred to by Jeremiah, chap. xxxiv. 18-20: "I will give the men [into the hands of their enemies, v. 20] that have transgressed my covenant, which have not performed the words of the covenant which they had made before me, when they cut the calf in twain, and passed between the parts thereof." See also Deut. xxix. 12.

The covenant made with Noah signified, on God's part, that He should save Noah and his family from death by the ark. On Noah's part, that he should in faith and obedience make and enter into the ark—"Thou shalt come into the ark," so committing himself to God's preservation, Heb. xi. 7. And under this the covenant or testament of eternal salvation by Christ was also implied, the apostle testifying, 1 Pet. iii. 21, that the antitype, baptism, doth also now save us; for baptism is a seal of our salvation, Mark xvi. 16. To provide a Saviour, and the means of salvation, is God's part; to accept this is ours. Those who refuse the way and means of salvation must perish; those who accept of the great Covenant Sacrifice cannot perish, but shall have eternal life.

19. *To keep them alive.* God might have destroyed all the animal creation, and created others to occupy the new world, but He chose rather to preserve those already created.

21. *Of all food that is eaten.* That is, of the food proper for every species of animals.

22. *Thus did Noah.* He prepared the ark; and during 120 years preached righteousness to that sinful generation, 2 Pet. ii. 5. And this we are informed, 1 Pet. iii. 18-19, he did by the Spirit of Christ; for it was only through Him that the doctrine of repentance could ever be successfully preached. The people in Noah's time are represented as shut up in prison—arrested and condemned by God's justice, but graciously allowed the space of 120 years to repent in. This respite was an act of great mercy; and no doubt thousands who died in the interim availed themselves of it, and believed to the saving of their souls. But the great majority of the people did not, else the Flood had never come.

TODAY'S DICTIONARY OF THE BIBLE:

Covenant. In biblical use "covenant" differs from a contract in two ways. First, a covenant has no termination date, whereas a contract always does. Second, a covenant applies to the whole of a person, whereas a contract involves only a part, especially a skill, possessed by a person. For example, one may contract to have a house built, but in marriage, he makes a covenant with God and his spouse. In the Old Testament the Hebrew word *berîth* is always thus translated. *Berîth* is derived from a root which means, "to cut," and hence a covenant is a "cutting," with reference to the cutting or dividing of animals into two parts, and the contracting parties passing between them, in making a covenant (Gen. 15; Jer. 34:18, 19).

The corresponding word in the New Testament Greek is *diathéke*, which is, however, rendered "testament" generally in the KJV. It ought to be rendered, just as the word *berîth* of the Old Testament, "covenant."

The word is used with reference to God's revelation of himself in the way of promise or of favor to men. Thus God's promise to Noah after the Flood is called a covenant (Gen. 9; Jer. 33:20, "my covenant"). We have an account of God's covenant with Abraham (Gen. 17; comp. Lev. 26:42), of the covenant of the priesthood (Num. 25:12, 13; Deut. 33:9; Neh. 13:29), and of the covenant of Sinai (Ex. 34:27, 28; Lev. 26:15), which was afterward renewed at different times in the history of Israel (Deut. 29; Josh. 24; 2 Chron. 15; 23; 29; 34; Ezra 10; Neh. 9). In conformity with human custom, God's covenant is said to be confirmed with an oath (Deut. 4:31; Ps. 89:3), and to be accompanied by a sign (Gen. 9; 17). Hence the covenant is called God's "counsel," "oath," "promise" (Ps. 89:3, 4; 105:8–11; Heb. 6:13–20; Luke 1:68–75). God's covenant consists wholly in the bestowal of blessing (Isa. 59:21; Jer. 31:33, 34).

MATTHEW HENRY

IV. God here makes Noah a great blessing to the world, and herein makes him an eminent type of the Messiah. 1. God made him a preacher to the men of that generation. 2. God made him a saviour to the inferior creatures, to keep the several kinds of them from perishing and being lost in the deluge, *v.* 19–21. (1) He was to provide shelter for them, that they might not be drowned. (2) He was to provide sustenance for them, that they might not be starved, *v.* 21. Herein also he was a type of Christ, to whom it is owing that the world stands, by whom all things consist, and who preserves mankind from being totally cut off and ruined by sin. Noah saved those whom he was to rule, so does Christ, Heb. v. 9.

Verse 22

Noah's care and diligence in building the ark may be considered, 1. As an effect of his faith in the word of God. 2. As an act of obedience to the command of God. His neighbours would ridicule him for his credulity, and he would be the song of the drunkards; his building would be called *Noah's folly*. But these, and a thousand such objections, Noah by faith got over. He did all exactly according to the instructions given him, and, having begun to build, did not leave off till he had finished it; so did he, and so must we do. 3. We must prepare to meet the Lord in his judgments on earth, especially prepare to meet him at death and in the judgment of the great day, build upon Christ the Rock (Matt. vii. 24), go into Christ the Ark. 4. Every blow of his axes and hammers was a call to repentance, a call to them to prepare arks too.

JAMIESON, FAUSSET, BROWN

22. Thus did Noah—He began without delay to prepare the colossal fabric, and in every step of his progress faithfully followed the divine directions he had received.

MATTHEW HENRY

CHAPTER 7

Verses 1–4

I. A gracious invitation of Noah and his family into a place of safety, *v.* 1.

1. The call itself is very kind, like that of a tender father to his children, to come indoors, when he sees night or a storm coming. God does not bid him *go* into the ark, but *come* into it, implying that God would go with him, would lead him into it, accompany him in it, and in due time bring him safely out of it. It was this that made Noah's ark, which was a prison, to be to him not only a refuge, but a palace. This call to Noah was a type of the call which the gospel gives to poor sinners. Christ is an ark already prepared, in whom alone we can be safe when death and judgment come.

2. The reason for this invitation is a very honourable testimony to Noah's integrity. Observe, (1) Those are righteous indeed that are righteous before God, who searches the heart, and cannot be deceived in men's characters. (2) God takes notice of and is pleased with those that are righteous before him: *The Lord knows those that are his.* (3) God, that is a witness to, will shortly be a witness for, his people's integrity. (4) God is, in a special manner, pleased with those that are good in bad times and places. (5) Those that keep themselves pure in times of common iniquity God will keep safe in times of common calamity.

II. Here are necessary orders given concerning the brute-creatures that were to be preserved alive with Noah in the ark, *v.* 2, 3. They were not capable of receiving the warning, therefore man is charged with the care of them: being under his dominion, they must be under his protection.

III. Here is notice given of the now imminent approach of the flood. 1. "It shall be seven days *yet,* before I do it." God grants them a reprieve of seven days longer, but all in vain; these seven days were trifled away, after all the rest; they continued secure and sensual until the day that the flood came. 2. "It shall be *but* seven days." While Noah told them of the judgment at a distance, they were tempted to put off their repentance, because the vision was for a great while to come; but now he is ordered to tell them that it is at the door.

Verses 5–10

Here is Noah's ready obedience to the commands that God gave him. Observe, 1. He went into the ark, upon notice that the flood would come after seven days, though probably as yet there appeared no visible sign of its approach. He went into it by faith in this warning that it would come quickly, though he did not see that the second causes had yet begun to work. In every step he took, he walked by faith, and not by sense. 2. He took all his family along with him, his wife, his sons, and his sons' wives, that by them, not only his family, but the world of mankind, might be built up. 3. The brute creatures readily went in with him.

Verses 11–12

The date of this great event; this is carefully recorded, for the greater certainty of the story.

The years of the old world are reckoned, not by the reigns of the giants, but by the lives of the patriarchs; saints are of more account with God than princes. Noah was now a very old man, even as men's years went then. Note, 1. The longer we live in this world the more we see of the miseries and calamities of it. 2. Sometimes God exercises his old servants with extraordinary trials of obedient patience. The oldest of Christ's soldiers must not promise themselves a discharge from their warfare till death discharge them. Still they must gird on their harness, and not boast as though they had put it off.

II. The second causes that concurred to this deluge.

1. In the self-same day that Noah was fixed in the ark, the inundation began. See what was done on that day, that fatal day to the world of the ungodly. (1) *The fountains of the great deep were broken up.* The waters of the sea returned to cover the earth, as they had done at first, *ch.* i. 9. (2) *The windows of heaven were opened,* and *the waters which were above the firmament* were poured out upon the world. The rain, which ordinarily descends in drops, then came down in streams, or *spouts,* as they call them in the Indies, where clouds have been often known to *burst,* as they express it there, when the rain descends in a much more violent torrent than we have ever seen in the greatest shower.

2. Now learn from this, (1) That all the creatures are at God's disposal, and that he makes what use he pleases of them, whether *for correction, or for*

JAMIESON, FAUSSET, BROWN

CHAPTER 7

Vss. 1-24. ENTRANCE INTO THE ARK. **1. And the Lord said unto Noah, Come thou and all thy house into the ark**—The ark was finished; and Noah now, in the spirit of implicit faith, which had influenced his whole conduct, waited for directions from God.

2, 3. Of every clean beast . . . fowls—Pairs of every species of animals, except the tenants of the deep, were to be taken for the preservation of their respective kinds. This was the general rule of admission, only with regard to those animals which are styled "clean," three pairs were to be taken, whether of beasts or birds; and the reason was that their rapid multiplication was a matter of the highest importance, when the earth should be renovated, for their utility either as articles of food or as employed in the service of man. But what was the use of the seventh? It was manifestly reserved for sacrifice; and so that both during Noah's residence in the ark, and after his return to dry land, provision was made for celebrating the rites of worship according to the religion of fallen man. He did not, like many, leave religion behind. He provided for it during his protracted voyage. **4. For yet seven days**—A week for a world to repent! What a solemn pause! Did they laugh and ridicule his folly still? He whose eyes saw and whose heart felt the full amount of human iniquity and perverseness has told us of their reckless disregard (Luke 17:27). **9. There went in two and two**—Doubtless they were led by a divine impulse. The number would not be so large as at first sight one is apt to imagine. It has been calculated that there are not more than three hundred distinct species of beasts and birds, the immense varieties in regard to form, size, and color being traceable to the influence of climate and other circumstances.

ADAM CLARKE

CHAPTER 7

1. *Thee have I seen righteous.* See on chap. vi. 9.

2. *Of every clean beast.* So we find the distinction between clean and unclean animals existed long before the Mosaic law. This distinction seems to have been originally designed to mark those animals which were proper for sacrifice and food, from those that were not. See Leviticus xi.

4. *For yet seven days.* God spoke these words probably on the seventh or Sabbath day, and the days of the ensuing week were employed in entering the ark, in embarking the mighty troop, for whose reception ample provision had been already made.

***Forty days.* This period afterwards became sacred, and was considered a proper space for humiliation. Moses fasted forty days, Deut. ix. 9, 11; so did Elijah, 1 Kings xix. 8; so did our Lord, Matt. iv. 2.**

11. *In the six hundredth year.* This must have been in the beginning of the six hundredth year of his life; for he was a year in the ark, chap. viii. 13; and lived 350 years after the Flood, and died when he was nine hundred and fifty years old, chap. ix. 29.

MATTHEW HENRY

mercy. (2) That God often makes that which *should be for our welfare to become a trap*, Ps. lxix. 22. Nothing is more needful nor useful than water, both the springs of the earth and the showers of heaven; and yet now nothing was more hurtful, nothing more destructive: every creature is to us what God makes it. (3) That it is impossible to escape the righteous judgments of God when they come against sinners with commission.

Verses 13–16

Here is repeated what was related before of Noah's entrance into the ark, with his family and the creatures that were marked for preservation.

I. It is thus repeated for the honour of Noah, whose faith and obedience herein shone so brightly.

II. Notice is here taken of the beasts going in *each after his kind*, according to the phrase used in the history of the creation (*ch.* i. 21–25), and that this preservation was as a new creation: a life remarkably protected is, as it were, a new life.

III. It is added, *The Lord shut him in, v.* 16. As Noah continued his obedience to God, so God continued his care of Noah. God shut the door, 1. To secure him, and keep him safe in the ark. 2. To exclude all others. Hitherto the door of the ark stood open, and if any, even during the last seven days, had repented and believed, for aught I know they might have been welcomed into the ark; but now the door was shut.

IV. There is much of our gospel duty and privilege to be seen in Noah's preservation in the ark. Observe then, 1. It is our great duty, in obedience to the gospel call, by a lively faith in Christ, to come into that way of salvation which God has provided for poor sinners. When Noah came into the ark, he quitted his own house and lands; so must we quit our own righteousness and our worldly possessions, whenever they come into competition with Christ. Noah must, for a while, submit to the confinements and inconveniences of the ark, in order to his preservation for a new world; so those that come into Christ to be saved by him must deny themselves, both in sufferings and services. 2. Those that come into the ark themselves should bring as many as they can in with them, by good instructions, by persuasions, and by a good example. There is room enough in Christ for all comers. 3. Those that by faith come into Christ, the ark, shall by the power of God be shut in, and kept as in a stronghold *by the power of God*, 1 Pet. i. 5.

Verses 17–20

I. How long the flood was increasing—*forty days, v.* 17. The profane world, who believed not that it would come, probably when it came flattered themselves with hopes that it would soon abate; but it prevailed. The gradual approaches of God's judgments, which are designed to bring sinners to repentance, are often abused to the hardening of them in their presumption.

II. To what degree they increased: they rose so high that not only the low flat countries were deluged, but to make sure work, and that none might escape, the tops of the highest mountains were overflowed—*fifteen cubits*, that is, seven yards and a half. Thus the refuge of lies was swept away. There is no place on earth so high as to set men out of the reach of God's judgments, Jer. xlix. 16; Obad. 3, 4.

III. What became of Noah's ark when the waters thus increased: *It was lifted up above the earth* (*v.* 17), *and went upon the face of the waters, v.* 18. Observe, 1. The waters which broke down everything else bore up the ark. 2. The more the waters increased the higher the ark was lifted up towards heaven. Thus sanctified afflictions are spiritual promotions.

Verses 21–24

I. The general destruction of all flesh by the waters of the flood.

1. All the cattle, fowl, and creeping things, died, except the few that were in the ark. The destruction of the creatures was their deliverance from the bondage of corruption, which deliverance the whole creation now groans after, Rom. viii. 21, 22.

2. All the men, women, and children, that were in the world (except what were in the ark) died. Now, (1) We may easily imagine what terror and consternation seized on them when they saw themselves surrounded. (2) We may suppose that they tried all ways and means possible for their preservation, but all in vain. Those that are not found in Christ, the ark, are certainly undone.

Let us now pause awhile and consider this tremendous judgment ! Eliphaz appeals to this story as a standing warning to a careless world (Job xxii. 15, 16), *Hast thou marked the old way, which wicked*

JAMIESON, FAUSSET, BROWN

JOHN LANGE:

"As God had commanded him, and the Lord shut him in." Here most distinctly presents itself the contrasting relation of these two names. *Elohim* gives him the prescription in relation to the pairs of animals for the preservation of the animal world, but *Jehovah*, the covenant God, shuts him in; that is, makes sure the closing of the ark for the whole voyage, and for the salvation of his people. This inclusion was, at the same time, an exclusion of the race devoted to death.

—*Commentary on the Holy Scriptures*

16. and the Lord shut him in—lit., "covered him round about." The "shutting him in" intimated that he had become the special object of divine care and protection, and that to those without the season of grace was over (Matt. 25:10).

17. the waters increased, and bare up the ark—It seems to have been raised so gradually as to be scarcely perceptible to its occupants. **20. Fifteen cubits upward . . . and the mountains were covered**—twenty-two and a half feet above the summits of the highest hills. The language is not consistent with the theory of a partial deluge.

21. all flesh died . . . fowl . . . cattle, and . . . creeping thing—It has been a uniform principle in the divine procedure, when judgments were abroad on the earth, to include every thing connected with the sinful objects of His wrath (ch. 19:25; Exod. 9:6). Besides, now that the human race was reduced to one single family, it was necessary that the beasts should be proportionally diminished, otherwise by their numbers they would have acquired the ascendancy and overmastered the few that were to repeople the world. Thus goodness was mingled with severity; the Lord exercises judgment in wisdom and in wrath remembers mercy.

ADAM CLARKE

15. *And they went in.* It was physically impossible for Noah to have collected such a vast number of tame and ferocious animals, nor could they have been retained in their wards by mere natural means. How then were they brought from various distances to the ark and preserved there? Only by the power of God. He who first miraculously brought them to Adam that he might give them their names now brings them to Noah that he may preserve their lives. And now we may reasonably suppose that their natural enmity was so far removed or suspended that the lion might dwell with the lamb, and the wolf lie down with the kid, though each might still require his peculiar aliment. This can be no difficulty to the power of God, without the immediate interposition of which neither the deluge nor the concomitant circumstances could have taken place.

16. *The Lord shut him in.* This seems to imply that God took him under His especial protection, and as He shut him in, so He shut the others out. God had waited 120 years upon that generation; they did not repent; they filled up the measure of their iniquities, and then wrath came upon them to the uttermost.

22. *Of all that was in the dry land.* From this we may conclude that such animals only as *could not live in the water* were preserved in the ark.

MATTHEW HENRY

men have trodden, who were cut down out of time, and sent into eternity, *whose foundation was overflown with the flood?*

II. The special preservation of Noah and his family. Observe, 1. Noah lives. When all about him were monuments of justice, thousands falling on his right hand and ten thousands on his left, he was a monument of mercy. We have reason to think that, while the long-suffering of God waited, Noah not only preached to, but prayed for, that wicked world, and would have turned away the wrath; but his prayers return into his own bosom, and are answered only in his own escape, which is plainly referred to, Ezek. xiv. 14, *Noah, Daniel, and Job, shall but deliver their own souls.* 2. He but lives. Noah remains alive, and this is all; he is, in effect, buried alive—cooped up in a close place. But he comforts himself with this, that he is in the way of duty and in the way of deliverance.

JAMIESON, FAUSSET, BROWN

24. an hundred and fifty days—a period of five months. Though long before that every living creature must have been drowned, such a lengthened continuance of the flood was designed to manifest God's stern displeasure at sin and sinners. Think of Noah during such a crisis. We learn (Ezek. 14:14) that he was a man who lived and breathed habitually in an atmosphere of devotion; and having in the exercise of this high-toned faith made God his refuge, he did not fear "though the waters roared and were troubled; though the mountains shook with the swelling thereof."

ADAM CLARKE

24. *And the waters prevailed upon the earth an hundred and fifty days.* **The breaking up of the fountains of the great deep, and the raining 40 days and nights, had raised the waters 15 cubits above the highest mountains; after which 40 days it appears to have continued at this height for 150 days more.**

MATTHEW HENRY

CHAPTER 8

Verses 1–3

I. An act of God's grace: *God remembered Noah and every living thing.* This is an expression after the manner of men; for not any of his creatures (Luke xii. 6), much less any of his people, are forgotten of God, Isa. xlix. 15, 16. God's remembering Noah was the return of his mercy to mankind, of whom he would not make a full end. Noah himself, though one that had found grace in the eyes of the Lord, yet seemed to be forgotten in the ark, and perhaps began to think himself so; for we do not find that God had told him how long he should be confined and when he should be released. Very good men have sometimes been ready to conclude themselves forgotten of God, especially when their afflictions have been unusually grievous and long. Perhaps Noah, though a great believer, yet when he found the flood continuing so long after it might reasonably be presumed to have done its work, was tempted to fear lest he that shut him in would keep him in, and began to expostulate. *How long wilt thou forget me?* But at length God returned in mercy to him, and this is expressed by remembering him.

II. An act of God's power over wind and water, both of which are at his beck, though neither of them is under man's control.

1. He commanded the wind, and said to that, *Go,* and it went, in order to the carrying off of the flood: *God made a wind to pass over the earth.* See here, (1) What was God's remembrance of Noah: it was his relieving him. (2) What a sovereign dominion God has over the winds. Even stormy winds fulfil his word, Ps. cxlviii. 8. Now God sent a wind, a drying wind, such a wind as God sent to divide the Red Sea before Israel, Exod. xiv. 21.

2. He commanded the waters, and said to them, *Come,* and they came. (1) He took away the cause. Note, As God has a key to open, so he has a key to shut up again, and to stay the progress of judgments by stopping the causes of them: and the same hand that brings the desolation must bring the deliverance. He that wounds is alone able to heal. See Job xii. 14, 15. (2) Then the effect ceased; not all at once, but by degrees. God usually works deliverance for his people gradually, that the day of small things may not be despised, nor the day of great things despaired of, Zech. iv. 10. See Prov. iv. 18.

Verses 4–5

Here we have the effects and evidences of the ebbing of the waters. 1. The ark rested. This was some satisfaction to Noah, to feel the house he was in upon firm ground, and no longer movable. It rested upon a mountain, whither it was directed, not by Noah's prudence (he did not steer it), but by the wise and gracious providence of God, that it might rest the sooner. Note, God has times and places of rest for his people after their tossings; and many a time he provides for their seasonable and comfortable settlement without their own contrivance and quite beyond their own foresight. 2. The tops of the mountains were seen, like little islands, appearing above the water. We must suppose that they were seen by Noah and his sons; for there were none besides to see them. It is probable that they had looked through the window of the ark every day, like the longing mariners, after a tedious voyage, to see if they could discover land. They felt ground above forty days before they saw it, according to Dr. Lightfoot's computation, whence he infers that, if the waters decreased proportionably, the ark drew eleven cubits in water.

JAMIESON, FAUSSET, BROWN

CHAPTER 8

Vss. 1-14. Assuaging of the Waters. **1. God remembered Noah**—The divine purpose in this awful dispensation had been accomplished, and the world had undergone those changes necessary to fit it for becoming the residence of man under a new economy of Providence. **every living thing . . . in the ark**—a beautiful illustration of Matthew 10:29. **and God made a wind to pass over the earth**—Though the divine will could have dried up the liquid mass in an instant, the agency of a wind was employed (Ps. 104:4)—probably a hot wind, which, by rapid evaporation, would again absorb one portion of the waters into the atmosphere; and by which, the other would be gradually drained off by outlets beneath.

4. seventh month—of the year—not of the flood—which lasted only five months. **rested**—evidently indicating a calm and gentle motion. **upon the mountains of Ararat**—or Armenia, as the word is rendered (II Kings 19:37; Isa. 37:38). The mountain which tradition points to as the one on which the ark rested is now called Ara Dagh, the "finger mountain." Its summit consists of two peaks, the higher of which is 17,750 feet and the other 13,420 above the level of the sea. **5. And the waters decreased continually**—The decrease of the waters was for wise reasons exceedingly slow and gradual—the period of their return being nearly twice as long as that of their rise.

ADAM CLARKE

CHAPTER 8

1. *And God made a wind to pass over the earth.* **Such a wind as produced a strong and sudden evaporation.**

4. *The mountains of Ararat.* **That Ararat was a mountain of Armenia is almost universally agreed.**

MATTHEW HENRY

Verses 6–12

An account of the spies which Noah sent forth to bring him intelligence from abroad, a raven and a dove.

I. That though God had told Noah particularly when the flood would come, yet he did not give him a particular account by revelation at what times, and by what steps, it should *go away*, 1. Because the knowledge of the former was necessary to his preparing the ark, but the knowledge of the latter would serve only to gratify his curiosity, and the concealing of it from him would be the needful exercise of his faith and patience. And, 2. He could not foresee the flood, but by revelation; but he might, by ordinary means, discover the decrease of it.

II. That though Noah by faith expected his enlargement, and by patience waited for it, yet he was inquisitive concerning it, as one that thought it long to be thus confined. *He that believes does not make haste* to run before God, but he does make haste to go forth to meet him, Isa. xxviii. 16. Particularly, 1. Noah sent forth a raven through the window of the ark, which went forth, as the Hebrew phrase is, *going forth and returning*, that is, flying about, but returning to the ark for rest; probably not in it, but upon it. This gave Noah little satisfaction; therefore, 2. He sent forth a dove, which returned the first time with no good news, but probably wet and dirty; but, the second time, she brought an olive-leaf in her bill, which appeared to be first plucked off, a plain indication that now the trees, the fruit-trees, began to appear above water. Note here, (1) That Noah sent forth the dove the second time seven days after the first time, and the third time was after seven days too; and probably the first sending of her out was seven days after the sending forth of the raven. This intimates that it was done on the sabbath day, which, it should seem, Noah religiously observed in the ark. (2) The dove is an emblem of a gracious soul, which finding no rest for its foot, no solid peace or satisfaction in this world, returns to Christ as to its ark. The carnal heart, like the raven, takes up with the world, and feeds on the carrions it finds there. And as Noah put forth his hand, and took the dove, and pulled her in to him, into the ark, so Christ will graciously preserve, and help, and welcome, those that fly to him for rest. (3) The olive-branch, which was an emblem of peace, was brought, not by the raven, a bird of prey, nor by a gay and proud peacock, but by a mild, patient, humble, dove. It is a dove-like disposition that brings into the soul earnests of rest and joy. (4) Some make these things an allegory. The law was first sent forth like the raven, but brought no tidings; therefore, in the fulness of time, God sent forth his gospel, as the dove, in the likeness of which the Holy Spirit descended, and this presents us with an olive-branch and brings in a better hope.

Verses 13–14

1. The ground dry (*v.* 13), that is, all the water carried off it, of which, upon the first day of the first month (a joyful new-year's-day it was), Noah was himself an eyewitness. He *removed the covering of the ark* to give him a prospect of the earth about it; and a most comfortable prospect he had. For behold, behold and wonder, *the face of the ground was dry*. Note, (1) It is a great mercy to see ground about us. Noah was more sensible of it than we are; for mercies restored are much more affecting than mercies continued. (2) The divine power which now renewed the face of the earth can renew the face of an afflicted troubled soul and of a distressed persecuted church. 2. The ground dried (*v.* 14), so as to be a fit habitation for Noah. Note, God consults our benefit rather than our desires. We would go out of the ark before the ground is dried: and perhaps, if the door be shut, are ready to remove the covering. God's time of showing mercy is certainly the best time, when the mercy is ripe for us and we are ready for it.

Verses 15–19

I. Noah's dismission out of the ark, *v.* 15–17. Observe, 1. Noah did not stir till God bade him. Those only go under God's protection that follow God's direction and submit to his government. 2. Though God detained him long, yet at last he gave him his discharge. 3. God had said, *Come into the ark*, which intimated that God went in with him; now he says, not *Come forth*, but *Go forth*, which intimates that God, who went in with him, stayed with him all the while, till he sent him out safely.

II. Noah's departure when he had his dismission. When he found himself preserved there, not only for a new life, but for a new world, he saw no reason to complain of his long confinement. Now observe, 1.

JAMIESON, FAUSSET, BROWN

6. at the end of forty days—It is easy to imagine the ardent longing Noah and his family must have felt to enjoy again the sight of land as well as breathe the fresh air; and it was perfectly consistent with faith and patience to make inquiries whether the earth was yet ready.

7. And he sent forth a raven—The smell of carrion would allure it to remain if the earth were in a habitable state. But it kept hovering about the spot, and, being a solitary bird, probably perched on the covering. **8-11. Also he sent forth a dove**—a bird flying low and naturally disposed to return to the place of her abode. **10. again he sent forth a dove**—Her flight, judging by the time she was abroad, was pursued to a great distance, and the newly plucked olive leaf, she no doubt by supernatural impulse brought in her bill, afforded a welcome proof that the declivities of the hills were clear. **12. he . . . sent forth the dove: which returned not . . . any more**—In these results, we perceive a wisdom and prudence far superior to the inspiration of instinct—we discern the agency of God guiding all the movements of this bird for the instruction of Noah, and reviving the hopes of his household. **other seven days**—a strong presumptive proof that Noah observed the Sabbath during his residence in the ark.

13, 14. Noah removed the covering of the ark—probably only as much of it as would afford him a prospect of the earth around. Yet for about two months he never stirred from his appointed abode till he had received the express permission of God. We should watch the leading of Providence to direct us in every step of the journey of life.

15-22. DEPARTURE FROM THE ARK. **15, 16. And God spake . . . Go forth**—They went forth in the most orderly manner—the human occupants first—then each species "after their kinds," lit., according to their families, implying that there had been an increase in the ark.

ADAM CLARKE

7. *He sent forth a raven, which went forth to and fro.* It is generally supposed that the raven flew off, and was seen no more, but this meaning the Hebrew text will not bear: "and it went forth, going forth and returning." From which it is evident that she did return, but was not taken into the ark. She made frequent excursions, and continued on the wing as long as she could, having picked up such aliment as she found floating on the waters; and then, to rest herself, regained the ark, where she might perch, though she was not admitted. Indeed this must be allowed, as it is impossible she could have continued twenty-one days upon the wing, which she must have done had she not returned. But the text itself is sufficiently determinate.

8. *He sent forth a dove.* The dove was sent forth thrice; the first time she speedily returned, having, in all probability, gone but a little way from the ark, as she must naturally be terrified at the appearance of the waters. After seven days, being sent out a second time, she returned with an olive leaf plucked off, v. 11, an emblem of the restoration of peace between God and the earth; and from this circumstance the olive has been the emblem of peace among all civilized nations. At the end of the other seven days the dove, being sent out the third time, returned no more, from which Noah conjectured that the earth was now sufficiently drained and, therefore, removed the covering of the ark, which probably gave liberty to many of the fowls to fly off, which circumstance would afford him the greater facility in making arrangements for disembarking the beasts and reptiles, and heavy-bodied domestic fowls, which might yet remain.

14. *And in the second month, on the seven and twentieth day.* From this it appears that Noah was in the ark a complete solar year, or 365 days; for he entered the ark the seventeenth day of the second month, in the six hundredth year of his life, chap. vii. 11, 13, and continued in it till the twenty-seventh day of the second month, in the six hundredth and first year of his life, as we see above. The months of the ancient Hebrews were lunar; the first 6 consisted of 30 days each, the latter 6 of 29; the whole 12 months making 354 days: add to this 11 days (for though he entered the ark the preceding year on the seventeenth day of the second month, he did not come out till the twenty-seventh of the same month in the following year), which make exactly 365 days.

MATTHEW HENRY

Noah and his family came out alive. 2. Noah brought out all the creatures that went in with him, except the raven and the dove, which, probably, were ready to meet their mates at their coming out. Noah was able to give a very good account of his charge; for of all that were given to him he had lost none.

Verses 20–22

I. Noah's thankful acknowledgment of God's favour to him, in completing the mercy of his deliverance, *v.* 20. 1. He *built an altar*. God is pleased with free-will offerings, and praises that wait for him. Noah was now turned out into a cold and desolate world, where, one would have thought, his first care would have been to build a house for himself; but, behold, he begins with an altar for God: God, that is the first, must be first served; and he begins well that begins with God. 2. He offered a sacrifice upon his altar, *of every clean beast, and of every clean fowl*. Here observe, (1) He offered only those that were clean. (2) Though his stock of cattle was so small, and that rescued from ruin at so great an expense of care and pains, yet he did not grudge to give God his dues out of it. Serving God with our little is the way to make it more; and we must never think that wasted with which God is honoured. (3) See here the antiquity of religion: the first thing we find done in the new world was an act of worship, Jer. vi. 16. We are now to express our thankfulness, not by burnt-offerings, but by the sacrifices of praise and the sacrifices of righteousness, by pious devotions and a pious conversation.

II. God's gracious acceptance of Noah's thankfulness.

1. God was well pleased with the performance, *v.* 21. He *smelt a sweet savour*, or, as it is in the Hebrew, *a savour of rest*, from it. He was well pleased with Noah's pious zeal, and these hopeful beginnings of the new world. Having caused his anger to rest upon the world of sinners, he here caused his love to rest upon this little remnant of believers.

2. Hereupon, he took up a resolution never to drown the world again. Good security is here given, and that which may be relied upon.

(1) That this judgment should never be repeated. Noah might think, "To what purpose should the world be repaired, when, in all probability, for the wickedness of it, it will quickly be in like manner ruined again?" "No," says God, "it never shall." *Neither will I again smite any more every living thing*. "I will no more take this severe method; for," *First*, "He is rather to be pitied, for it is all the effect of sin dwelling in him; and it is but what might be expected from such a degenerate race: he is called a *transgressor from the womb*, and therefore it is not strange that he deals so very treacherously," Isa. xlviii. 8. Thus God *remembers that he is flesh*. *Secondly*, "He will be utterly ruined, for, if he be dealt with according to his deserts, one flood must succeed another till all be destroyed." See here, 1. That outward judgments, though they may terrify and restrain men, yet cannot of themselves sanctify and renew them; the grace of God must work with those judgments. 2. That God's reasons of mercy are all drawn from himself, not from any thing in us.

(2) That the course of nature should never be discontinued (*v.* 22): "*While the earth remaineth*, and man upon it, there shall be *summer and winter* (not all winter as had been this last year), *day and night*," not all night, as probably it was while the rain was descending. It is plainly intimated that this earth is not to remain always. As long as it does remain God's providence will carefully preserve the regular succession of times and seasons, and cause each to know its place. To this we owe it that the world stands, and the wheel of nature keeps its track. See here how changeable the times are and yet how unchangeable. *First*, The course of nature always changing—*day and night, summer and winter*, counter-changed. *Secondly*, Yet never changed. It is constant in this inconstancy. These seasons have never ceased, nor shall cease, while the sun continues such a steady measurer of time and the moon such a *faithful witness in heaven*. This is *God's covenant of the day and of the night*, the stability of which is mentioned for the confirming of our faith in the covenant of grace, which is no less inviolable, Jer. xxxiii. 20, 21.

JAMIESON, FAUSSET, BROWN

20. Noah builded an altar—lit., "a high place"—probably a mound of earth, on which a sacrifice was offered. There is something exceedingly beautiful and interesting to know that the first care of this devout patriarch was to return thanks for the signal instance of mercy and goodness which he and his family had experienced. **took of every clean beast, and . . . fowl**—For so unparalleled a deliverance, a special acknowledgment was due.

21. The Lord smelled a sweet savour—The sacrifice offered by a righteous man like Noah in faith was acceptable as the most fragrant incense.

Lord said in his heart—same as "I have sworn that the waters of Noah should no more go over the earth" (Isa. 54:9). **for**—i.e., "though the imagination is evil"; instead of inflicting another destructive flood, I shall spare them—to enjoy the blessings of grace, through a Saviour.

22. While the earth remaineth—The consummation, as intimated in II Peter 3:7, does not frustrate a promise which held good only during the continuance of that system. There will be no flood between this and that day, when the earth therein shall be burnt up [Chalmers].

ADAM CLARKE

20. *Noah builded an altar*. As we have already seen that Adam, Cain, and Abel offered sacrifices, there can be no doubt that they had altars on which they offered them; but this, builded by Noah, is certainly the first on record. The word which we render *altar* signifies properly a "place for sacrifice," as the root signifies simply to "slay." *Altar* comes from the Latin *altus*, high or elevated, because places for sacrifice were generally either raised very high or built on the tops of hills and mountains; hence they are called high places in the Scriptures; but such were chiefly used for idolatrous purposes.

Burnt offerings. See the meaning of every kind of offering and sacrifice largely explained on Leviticus vii.

21. *The Lord smelled a sweet savour*. That is, He was well pleased with this religious act, performed in obedience to His own appointment, and in faith of the promised Saviour. That this sacrifice prefigured that which was offered by our blessed Redeemer in behalf of the world is sufficiently evident from the words of Paul, Eph. v. 2: "Christ also hath loved us, and given himself for us an offering and a sacrifice to God for a sweetsmelling savour"; where the words of the apostle are the very words used by the Septuagint in this place.

I will not again curse the ground. "I will not add to curse the ground"—there shall not be another deluge to destroy the whole earth: *for the imagination of man's heart*, "although the imagination of man's heart should be evil," i.e., should they become afterwards as evil as they have been before, I will not destroy the earth by a flood. God has other means of destruction; and the next time He visits by a general judgment, fire is to be the agent, 2 Pet. iii. 7.

22. *While the earth remaineth, seedtime and harvest*. There is something very expressive in the original, "until all the days of the earth"; for God does not reckon its duration by centuries, and the words themselves afford a strong presumption that the earth shall not have an endless duration.

Seedtime and harvest. This is a very merciful promise to the inhabitants of the earth. There may be a variety in the seasons, but no season essentially necessary to vegetation shall utterly fail. The times which are of greatest consequence to the preservation of man are distinctly noted; there shall be both *seedtime* and *harvest*—a proper time to deposit the different grain in the earth, and a proper time to reap the produce of this seed.

MATTHEW HENRY

CHAPTER 9

Verses 1–7

In general, *God blessed Noah and his sons* (*v.* 1), that is, he assured them of his good-will to them and his gracious intentions concerning them. We read (*ch.* viii. 20) how *Noah blessed God*, by his altar and sacrifice.

Now here we have the *Magna Charta—the great charter* of this new kingdom of nature which was now to be erected, and incorporated, the former charter having been forfeited and seized.

I. The grants of this charter are kind and gracious to men.

1. A grant of lands of vast extent, and a promise of a great increase of men to occupy and enjoy them. The first blessing is here renewed: *Be fruitful, and multiply, and replenish the earth* (*v.* 1). Now, (1) God sets the whole earth before them, tells them it is all their own, *while it remains*, to them and their heirs. Though it is not a paradise, but a wilderness rather; yet it is better than we deserve. Blessed be God, it is not hell. (2) He gives them a blessing, so that in a little time all the habitable parts of the earth should be more or less inhabited. Though death should still reign, yet the earth should never again be dispeopled as now it was, but still replenished, Acts xvii. 24–6.

2. A grant of power over the inferior creatures, *v.* 2. Man in innocence ruled by love, fallen man rules by fear. Now this grant remains in force, and thus far we have still the benefit of it. Now here see, (1) That God is a good Master, and provides, not only that we may live, but that we may live comfortably, in his service; not for necessity only, but for delight. (2) That every *creature of God is good*, and nothing to be refused, 1 Tim. iv. 4.

II. The precepts and provisos of this charter are no less kind and gracious, and instances of God's good-will to man. The Jewish doctors speak so often of the seven precepts of Noah, or of the sons of Noah, which they say were to be observed by all nations, that it may not be amiss to set them down. The first against the worship of idols. The second against blasphemy, and requiring to bless the name of God. The third against murder. The fourth against incest and all uncleanness. The fifth against theft and rapine. The sixth requiring the administration of justice. The seventh against eating of flesh with the life.

1. Man must not prejudice his own life by eating that food which is unwholesome and prejudicial to his health (*v.* 4); they must not be greedy and hasty in taking their food; they must not be barbarous and cruel to the inferior creatures. During the continuance of the law of sacrifices, in which the blood made *atonement for the soul* (Lev. xvii. 11), signifying that the life of the sacrifice was accepted for the life of the sinner, blood must not be looked upon as a common thing, but must be *poured out before the Lord* (2 Sam. xxiii. 16). But, now that the great and true sacrifice has been offered, the obligation of the law ceases with the reason of it.

2. Man must not take away his own life: *Your blood of your lives will I require*, *v.* 5. Our lives are not so our own as that we may quit them at our own pleasure, but they are God's.

3. The beasts must not be suffered to hurt the life of man. This was confirmed by the law of Moses (Exod. xxi. 28), and I think it would not be unsafe to observe it still. Thus God showed his hatred of the sin of murder, that men might hate it the more, and not only punish, but prevent it.

4. Wilful murderers must be put to death. This is the sin which is here designed to be restrained by the terror of punishment. (1) God will punish murderers. One time or other, in this world or in the next, he will both discover concealed murders, which are hidden from man's eyes, and punish avowed and justified murders, which are too great for man's hand. (2) The magistrate must punish murderers (*v.* 6). There are those who are ministers of God for this purpose, to be a protection to the innocent, by being a terror to the malicious and evildoers, and they must not *bear the sword in vain*, Rom. xiii. 4. It is a sin *which the Lord would not pardon* in a prince (2 Kings xxiv. 3, 4), and which therefore a prince should not pardon in a subject. To this law there is a reason annexed: *For in the image of God made he man* at first. Man is a creature to his Creator, and therefore ought to be so to us. God put honour upon him, let not us then put contempt upon him. Such remains of God's image are still even upon fallen man as that he who unjustly kills a man defaces the image of God and does dishonour to him.

JAMIESON, FAUSSET, BROWN

CHAPTER 9

Vss. 1-7. COVENANT. **1. And God blessed Noah**—Here is republished the law of nature that was announced to Adam, consisting as it originally did of several parts.

Be fruitful, etc.—The first part relates to the transmission of life, the original blessing being reannounced in the very same words in which it had been promised at first.

2. And the fear of you and the dread of you—The second part re-establishes man's dominion over the inferior animals; it was now founded not as at first in love and kindness, but in terror; this dread of man prevails among all the stronger as well as the weaker members of the animal tribes and keeps away from his haunts all but those employed in his service. **3. Every moving thing that liveth shall be meat for you**—The third part concerns the means of sustaining life; man was for the first time, it would seem, allowed the use of animal food, but the grant was accompanied with one restriction.

4. But flesh . . . the blood . . . shall ye not eat—The sole intention of this prohibition was to prevent these excesses of cannibal ferocity in eating flesh of living animals, to which men in the earlier ages of the world were liable.

5. surely your blood of your lives will I require—The fourth part establishes a new power for *protecting* life—the institution of the civil magistrate (Rom. 13:4), armed with public and official authority to repress the commission of violence and crime. Such a power had not previously existed in patriarchal society.

6. Whoso sheddeth man's blood . . . for in the image of God made he man—It is true that image has been injured by the fall, but it is not lost. In this view, a high value is attached to the life of every man, even the poorest and humblest, and an awful criminality is involved in the destruction of it.

ADAM CLARKE

CHAPTER 9

1. *God blessed Noah.* Even the increase of families, which appears to depend on merely natural means, and sometimes fortuitous circumstance, is all of God. It is by His power and wisdom that the human being is formed, and it is by His providence alone that man is supported and preserved.

2. *The fear of you and the dread.* Prior to the Fall, man ruled the inferior animals by love and kindness, for then gentleness and docility were their principal characteristics. After the Fall untractableness, with savage ferocity, prevailed among almost all orders of the brute creation; enmity to man seems particularly to prevail; and had not God in His mercy impressed their minds with the *fear* and *terror* of man, so that some *submit* to his will while others *flee* from his residence, the human race would long ere this have been totally destroyed by the beasts of the field.

3. *Every moving thing . . . shall be meat.* There is no positive evidence that animal food was ever used before the Flood. Noah had the first grant of this kind, and it has been continued to all his posterity ever since.

4. *But flesh with the life thereof, which is the blood.* Though animal food was granted, yet the *blood* was most solemnly forbidden, because it was the life of the beast, and this life was to be offered to God as an atonement for sin. Hence the blood was ever held sacred, because it was the grand instrument of expiation, and because it was typical of that Blood by which we enter into the holiest.

5. *Surely your blood . . . will I require; at the hand of every beast.* This is very obscure, but if taken literally it seems to be an awful warning against cruelty to the brute creation.

6. *Whoso sheddeth man's blood, by man shall his blood.* Hence it appears that whoever kills a man, unless "unwittingly," as the Scripture expresses it, shall forfeit his own life.

MATTHEW HENRY	JAMIESON, FAUSSET, BROWN	ADAM CLARKE

Verses 8–11

Here is, I. The general establishment of God's covenant with this new world, and the extent of that covenant, *v.* 9, 10. Here observe, 1. That God is graciously pleased to deal with man in the way of a covenant, wherein God greatly encourages man's duty and obedience. 2. That all God's covenants with man are of his own making: *I, behold, I.* 3. That God's covenants are established more firmly than the pillars of heaven or the foundations of the earth, and cannot be disannulled. 4. That God's covenants are made with the covenanters and with their seed; the promise is to them and their children.

II. The particular intention of this covenant. It was designed to secure the world from another deluge: *There shall not any more be a flood.* It is owing to God's goodness and faithfulness, not to any reformation of the world, that it has not often been deluged, and that it is not deluged now. As the old world was ruined to be a monument of justice, so this world remains to this day, a monument of mercy, according to the oath of God, that the waters of Noah should no more return to cover the earth, Isa. liv. 9. If the sea should flow but for a few days, as it does twice every day for a few hours, what desolation would it make ! Let us give him the glory of his mercy in promising and of his truth in performing.

Verses 12–17

Articles of agreement among men are usually sealed. God therefore, being *willing more abundantly to show to the heirs of promise the immutability of his councils*, has confirmed his covenant by a seal (Heb. vi. 17). The seal of this covenant of nature was natural enough; it was the *rainbow*. Now, concerning this seal of the covenant, observe, 1. This seal is affixed with repeated assurances of the truth of that promise of which it was designed to be the ratification: *I do set my bow in the cloud* (*v.* 13); it *shall be seen in the cloud* (*v.* 14), that the eye may affect the heart and confirm the faith; and it shall be *the token of the covenant* (*v.* 12, 13), *and I will remember my covenant, that the waters shall no more become a flood*, *v.* 15. 2. The rainbow appears when the clouds are most disposed to wet, and returns after the rain; when we have most reason to fear the rain prevailing. Thus God obviates our fears. 3. The thicker the cloud the brighter the bow in the cloud. Thus, as threatening afflictions abound, encouraging consolations much more abound, 2 Cor. i. 5. 4. The rainbow appears when one part of the sky is clear, which intimates mercy remembered in the midst of wrath; and the clouds are hemmed as it were with the rainbow, that they may not overspread the heavens, for the bow is coloured rain or the edges of a cloud gilded. A bow bespeaks terror, but this bow has neither string nor arrow, and a bow alone will do little execution. It is a bow, but it is directed upwards, not towards the earth; for the seals of the covenant were intended to comfort, not to terrify.

Verses 18–23

Here is, I. Noah's family and employment. The business Noah applied himself to was that of *a husbandman*, Heb. *a man of the earth*, that is, a man dealing in the earth, that kept ground in his hand, and occupied it. Noah was by his calling led to trade in the fruits of the earth. He *began to be a husbandman*, that is, he returned to his old employment, from which he had been diverted by the building of the ark first, and probably afterwards by the building of a house on dry land for himself and family. For this good while he had been a carpenter, but now he began again to be a husbandman.

II. Noah's sin and shame: *He planted a vineyard*; and, when he had gathered his vintage, probably he appointed a day of mirth and feasting in his family, and had his sons and their children with him, to rejoice with him in the increase of his house as well as in the increase of his vineyard; and perhaps he appointed this feast with a design, at the close of it, to bless his sons. At this feast he *drank of the wine*. But he drank too liberally, for he was *drunk*. Observe, how he came now to be overtaken in this fault. It was his sin, and a great sin, so much the worse for its being so soon after a great deliverance; but God left him to himself, and has left this miscarriage of his upon record, to teach us, 1. That the fairest copy that ever mere man wrote since the fall had its blots and false strokes. 2. That sometimes those who, with watchfulness and resolution, have, by the grace of God, kept their integrity in the midst of temptation, have, through security, and carelessness, and neglect of the grace of God, been surprised into sin, when the hour of temptation has been over. 3. That we have need to be very careful, when we use God's good creatures plentifully, lest we use them

ALEXANDER MACLAREN:

The sign of the covenant is described at great length in verses 12–17. Note that verses 12, 13 state the general idea of a token or sign, that verses 14–16 deepen this by stating that the token to man is a reminder to God, and that verse 17 sums up the whole with emphatic repetition of the main points. The narrative does not imply, as has often been supposed, that the rainbow was visible for the first time after the deluge. To suppose that is to read more into the story than is there, or than common sense tolerates. If there were showers and sunshine, there must have been rainbows. But the fair vision strode across the sky with no articulate promise in its loveliness, though it must always have kindled wonder, and sometimes stirred deeper thoughts. Now, for the first time, it was made "a sign," the visible pledge of God's promise.

Mark the emphasis with which God's agency is declared and His ownership asserted. "I do set *my* bow." Neither Noah nor the writer knew anything about refraction or the prismatic spectrum. But perhaps they knew more about the rainbow than people do who know all about how it comes, except that God sets it in the cloud, and that it is His. Let us have the facts which science labels as such, by all means, and the more the better; but do not let us forget that there are other facts in nature which science has no means of attaining, but which are as solid and a great deal deeper than those which it supplies.

The natural adaptation of the rainbow for this office of a token is too plain to need dwelling on. It "fills the sky when storms prepare to part," and hence is a natural token that the downpour is being stayed. Somewhere there must be a bit of blue through which the sun can pierce; and the small gap, which is large enough to let it out, will grow till all the sky is one azure dome. It springs into sight in front of the cloud, without which it could not be, so it typifies the light which may glorify judgments, and is born of sorrows borne in the presence of God. It comes from the sunshine smiting the cloud; so it preaches the blending of love with divine judgment. It unites earth and heaven; so it proclaims that heavenly love is ready to transform earthly sorrows. It stretches across the land; so it speaks of an all-embracing care, which enfolds the earth and all its creatures.

—*Expositions of Holy Scripture*

8-29. RAINBOW. **13. I do set my bow in the cloud**—set, i.e., constitute or appoint. This common and familiar phenomenon being made the pledge of peace, its appearance when showers began to fall would be welcomed with the liveliest feelings of joy.

20. And Noah . . . planted a vineyard—Noah had been probably bred to the culture of the soil, and resumed that employment on leaving the ark. **21. And he drank of the wine, and was drunken**—perhaps at the festivities of the vintage season. This solitary stain on the character of so eminently pious a man must, it is believed, have been the result of age or inadvertency.

13. *I do set my bow in the cloud.* From the well-known cause of this phenomenon it cannot be rationally supposed that there was no rainbow in the heavens before the time mentioned in the text, for as the rainbow is the natural effect of the sun's rays falling on drops of water, and of their being refracted and reflected by them, it must have appeared at different times from the creation of the sun and the atmosphere. Nor does the text intimate that the bow was now created for a sign to Noah and his posterity; but that what was formerly created, or rather that which was the necessary effect in certain cases of the creation of the sun and atmosphere, should now be considered by them as an unfailing token of their continual preservation from the waters of a deluge; therefore the text speaks of what had already been done, and not of what was now done, "My bow I *have* given, or put in the cloud."

17. *This is the token.* The divine sign or portent: "The bow shall be in the cloud." For the reasons above specified it must be there, when the circumstances already mentioned occur; if therefore it cannot fail because of the reasons before assigned, no more shall My promise; and the bow shall be the proof of its perpetuity.

20. *Noah began to be an husbandman.* A man of the ground, a farmer; by his beginning to be a husbandman we are to understand his recommencing his agricultural operations, which undoubtedly he had carried on for six hundred years before, but this had been interrupted by the Flood. And the transaction here mentioned might have occurred many years posterior to the deluge, even after Canaan was born and grown up, for the date of it is not fixed in the text.

21. *He drank of the wine.* It is very probable that this was the first time the vine was cultivated; and it is as probable that the strength or intoxicating power of the expressed juice was never before known. Noah, therefore, might have drunk it at this time without the least blame, as he knew not till this trial the effects it would produce.

MATTHEW HENRY

to excess. Now the consequence of Noah's sin was shame. He was made naked to his shame, as Adam when he had eaten forbidden fruit. Observe here the great evil of the sin of drunkenness. (1) It discovers men. What infirmities they have, they betray when they are drunk, and what secrets they are entrusted with are then easily got out of them. Drunken porters keep open gates. (2) It disgraces men, and exposes them to contempt. Men say and do that when drunk which when they are sober they would blush at the thoughts of, Hab. ii. 15, 16.

III. Ham's impudence and impiety: He *saw the nakedness of his father, and told his two brethren, v.* 22. 1. He pleased himself with the sight. Perhaps Ham had sometimes been himself drunk. It is common for those who walk in false ways themselves to rejoice at the false steps which they sometimes see others make. But charity rejoices not in iniquity. 2. *He told his two brethren* in a scornful deriding manner, that his father might seem vile unto them. It is very wrong, (1) To make a jest of sin (Prov. xiv. 9). And, (2) To publish the faults of any, especially of parents, whom it is our duty to honour.

IV. The pious care of Shem and Japheth to cover their poor father's shame, *v.* 23. 1. There is a mantle of love to be thrown over the faults of all, 1 Pet. iv. 8. 2. Besides this, there is a robe of reverence to be thrown over the faults of parents.

Verses 24–27

I. Noah comes to himself. He *awoke from his wine.*

II. The spirit of prophecy comes upon him, and, like dying Jacob, he tells his sons what shall befall them, *ch.* xlix. 1.

1, He pronounces a curse on Canaan the son of Ham (*v.* 25), in whom Ham is himself cursed. The particular curse is, *A servant of servants* (that is, the meanest and most despicable servant) *shall he be,* even *to his brethren.* Note, (1) God often visits the iniquity of the fathers upon the children, when the children inherit the fathers' wicked dispositions, and imitate the fathers' wicked practices, and do nothing to cut off the entail of the curse. (2) Disgrace is justly put upon those that put disgrace upon others, especially that dishonour and grieve their own parents.

2. He entails a blessing upon Shem and Japheth. (1) He blesses Shem, or rather blesses God for him. Observe, [1] He calls the Lord *the God of Shem.* All blessings are included in this. Shem is sufficiently recompensed for his respect to his father by this, that the Lord himself puts this honour upon him, *to be his God.* [2] He gives to God the glory of that good work which Shem had done. When we see men's good works we should glorify, not them, but *our* Father, Matt. v. 16. It is an honour and a favour to be employed for God and used by him in doing good. [3] He foresees that God's gracious dealings with Shem and his family would be evidence to all the world that he was the God of Shem. [4] It is intimated that the church should be built up and continued in the posterity of Shem; for of him came the Jews, who were, for a great while, the only professing people God had in the world.

(2) He blesses Japheth, and, in him, *the isles of the Gentiles,* which were peopled by his seed: *God shall enlarge Japheth, and he shall dwell in the tents of Shem, v.* 27. Now, Some make this to belong wholly to Japheth, and to denote either, *First,* His outward prosperity, that his seed should be so numerous and so victorious that they should be masters of the tents of Shem, which was fulfilled when the people of the Jews, the most eminent of Shem's race, were tributaries to the Grecians first and afterwards to the Romans, both of Japheth's seed. Or, *Secondly,* It denotes the conversion of the Gentiles, and the bringing of them into the church; and then we should read it, *God shall persuade Japheth* (for so the word signifies), and then, being so persuaded, *he shall dwell in the tents of Shem,* that is, Jews and Gentiles shall be united together in the gospel fold. Note, It is God only that can bring those again into the church who have separated themselves from it. Souls are brought into the church, not by force, but by persuasion, Ps. cx. 3. They are persuaded by reason to be religious.

Verses 28–29

Here see, 1. How God prolonged the life of Noah; this long life was a further reward of his signal piety, and a great blessing to the world. 2. How God put a period to his life at last. Noah lived to see two worlds, but, being an heir of the righteousness which is by faith, when he died he went to see a better than either.

JAMIESON, FAUSSET, BROWN

24. This incident could scarcely have happened till twenty years after the flood; for Canaan, whose conduct was more offensive than that even of his father, was not born till after that event. It is probable that there is a long interval included between these verses and that this prophecy, like that of Jacob on his sons, was not uttered till near the close of Noah's life when the prophetic spirit came upon him; this presumption is strengthened by the mention of his death immediately after. **25. Cursed be Canaan**—This doom has been fulfilled in the destruction of the Canaanites—in the degradation of Egypt and the slavery of the Africans, the descendants of Ham.

26. Blessed be the Lord God of Shem—rather, "Blessed of Jehovah, my God, be Shem,"—an intimation that the descendants of Shem should be peculiary honored in the service of the true God—His Church being for ages established among them (the Jews), and of them, concerning the flesh, Christ came. They got possession of Canaan, the people of that land being made their "servants" either by conquest, or, like the Gibeonites, by submission.

27. God shall enlarge Japheth—pointing to a vast increase in posterity and possessions. Accordingly his descendants have been the most active and enterprising, spread over the best and largest portion of the world, all Europe and a considerable part of Asia. **he shall dwell in the tents of Shem**—a prophecy being fulfilled at the present day, as in India British Government is established and the Anglo-Saxons being in the ascendancy from Europe to India, from India over the American continent. What a wonderful prophecy in a few verses (Isa. 46:10; I Peter 1:25)!

ADAM CLARKE

22-24. *And Ham, the father of Canaan.* There is no occasion to enter into any detail here; the sacred text is circumstantial enough. Ham, and very probably his son Canaan, had treated their father on this occasion with contempt or reprehensible levity. Had Noah not been innocent, as my exposition supposes him, God would not have endued him with the spirit of prophecy on this occasion, and testified such marked disapprobation of their conduct.

The conduct of Shem and Japheth was such as became pious and affectionate children, who appear to have been in the habit of treating their father with decency, reverence, and obedient respect. On the one the spirit of prophecy (not the incensed father) pronounces a curse; on the others the same spirit (not parental tenderness) pronounces a blessing. The curse pronounced on Canaan neither fell immediately upon himself nor on his worthless father, but upon the Canaanites; and from the history we have of this people, in Leviticus xviii; xx; and Deut. ix. 4; xii. 31, we may ask, Could the curse of God fall more deservedly on any people than on these? Their profligacy was great, but it was not the effect of the curse; but, being foreseen by the Lord, the curse was the effect of their conduct.

29. *The days of Noah were nine hundred and fifty years.* The oldest patriarch on record, except Methuselah and Jared.

MATTHEW HENRY

CHAPTER 10

JAMIESON, FAUSSET, BROWN

CHAPTER 10

VSS. 1-32. GENEALOGIES. **1. sons of Noah**—The historian has not arranged this catalogue according to seniority of birth; for the account begins with the descendants of Japheth, and the line of Ham is given before that of Shem though he is expressly said to be the youngest or younger son of Noah; and Shem was the elder brother of Japheth (vs. 21), the true rendering of that passage. **generations**, etc.—the narrative of the settlement of nations existing in the time of Moses, perhaps only the principal ones; for though the list comprises the sons of Shem, Ham, and Japheth, *all their descendants* are not enumerated. Those descendants, with one or two exceptions, are described by names indicative of tribes and nations and ending in the Hebrew *im*, or the English "ite."

ADAM CLARKE

CHAPTER 10

1. *Now these are the generations.* It is extremely difficult to say what particular nations and people sprang from the three grand divisions of the family of Noah, because the names of many of those ancient people have become changed in the vast lapse of time from the deluge to the Christian era; yet some are so very distinctly marked that they can be easily ascertained, while a few still retain their original names.

Moses does not always give the name of the first settler in a country, but rather that of the people from whom the country afterwards derived its name. Thus *Mizraim* is the dual of *Mezer*, and could never be the name of an individual. The like may be said of *Kittim, Dodanim, Ludim, Anamim, Lehabim, Naphtuhim, Pathrusim, Casluhim, Philistim,* and *Caphtorim,* which are all plurals, and evidently not the names of individuals, but of families or tribes. See vv. 4, 6, 13-14. In the posterity of Canaan we find whole nations reckoned in the geneaology, instead of the individuals from whom they sprang; thus the *Jebusite, Amorite, Girgasite, Hivite, Arkite, Sinite, Arvadite, Zemarite,* and *Hamathite,* vv. 16-18, were evidently whole nations or tribes which inhabited the Promised Land, and were called *Canaanites* from *Canaan,* the son of Ham, who settled there.

Moses also, in this genealogy, seems to have introduced even the name of some places that were remarkable in the sacred history, instead of the original settlers. Such as *Hazarmaveth,* v. 26; and probably *Ophir* and *Havilah,* v. 29. But this is not infrequent in the sacred writings, as may be seen, I Chron. ii. 51, where *Salma* is called "the father of Bethlehem," which certainly never was the name of a man, but of a place sufficiently celebrated in the sacred history; and in chap. iv. 14, where Joab is called "the father of the valley of Charashim," which no person could ever suppose was intended to designate an individual, but the society of craftsmen or artificers who lived there.

2. *The sons of Japheth.* Japheth is supposed to be the same with the "Japetus" of the Greeks, from whom, in an extremely remote antiquity, that people were supposed to have derived their origin. *Gomer.* Supposed by some to have peopled Galatia; so Josephus, who says that the Galatians were anciently named Gomerites. *Magog.* Supposed by many to be the father of the Scythians and Tartars, or "Tatars," as the word should be written; and in great Tartary many names are still found which bear such a striking resemblance to the Gog and Magog of the Scriptures as to leave little doubt of their identity. *Javan.* It is almost universally agreed that from him sprang the Ionians, of Asia Minor. *Tubal.* Some think he was the father of the Iberians, and that a part at least of Spain was peopled by him and his descendants; and that *Meshech,* who is generally in Scripture joined with him, was the founder of the Cappadocians, from whom proceeded the Muscovites. *Tiras.* From this person, according to general consent, the Thracians derived their origin.

4. *Elishah.* As *Javan* peopled a considerable part of Greece, it is in that region that we must seek for the settlements of his descendants; *Elishah* probably was the first who settled at Elis, in Pelopennesus. *Tarshish.* He first inhabited Cilicia, whose capital anciently was the city of Tarsus, where the Apostle Paul was born. *Kittim.* We have already seen that this name was rather the name of a people than of an individual; some think by *Kittim* Cyprus is meant.

5. *Isles of the Gentiles.* Europe, of which this is allowed to be a general epithet. *Every one after his tongue.* This refers to the time posterior to the confusion of tongues and dispersion from Babel.

6. *Cush.* Who peopled the Arabic nome near the Red Sea in Lower Egypt. Some think the Ethiopians descended from him. *Mizraim.* This family certainly peopled Egypt; and both in the East and in the West, Egypt is called *Mizraim. Phut.* Who first peopled an Egyptian nome or district, bordering on Libya. *Canaan.* He who first peopled the land so called, known also by the name of the Promised Land.

JOSEPH PARKER:

A clear conception of the import of this marvellous chapter should enlarge and correct our notions insofar as they had been narrowed and perverted by our insular position. We should recognize in all the nations of the earth one common human nature. "God hath made of one blood all nations of men to dwell on the face of the earth." The reflection is both humbling and elevating. It is humbling to think that the cannibal is a relative of ours, that the slave is bone of our bone, and that the meanest scum of all the earth started from the same foundation as ourselves! On the other hand, it is elevating to think that all kings and mighty men, all soldiers renowned in song, all heroes canonized in history—the wise, the strong, the good—are our elder brothers and immortal friends. If we limit our life to families, clans, and sects, we shall miss the genius of human history and all its ennobling influences. Better join the common lot. Take it just as it is. Our ancestors have been robbers and oppressors, deliverers and saviors, mean and noble, cowardly and heroic; some hanged, some crowned, some beggars, some kings; take it so, for the earth is one, and humanity is one, and there is only one God over all blessed for evermore!

If we take this idea aright we shall get a clear notion of what are called home and foreign missions. What are foreign missions? Where are they? I do not find the word in the Bible. Where does home end; where does foreign begin? It is possible for a man to immure himself so completely as practically to forget that there is anybody beyond his own front gate; we soon grow narrow, we soon become mean; it is easy for us to return to the dust from whence we come. It is here that Christianity redeems us; not from sin only, but from all narrowness, meanness, and littleness of conception; it puts great thoughts into our hearts and bold words into our mouths, and leads us out from our village prisons to behold and to care for all nations of mankind. On this ground alone Christianity is the best educator in the world. It will not allow the soul to be mean. It forces the heart to be noble and hopeful. It says, "Go and teach all nations"; "Go ye into all the world"; "Look not every man on his own things, but every man also on the things of others." It is something for a nation to have a voice so divine ever stirring its will and mingling with its counsels. It is like a sea breeze blowing over a sickly land; like sunlight piercing the fogs of a long dark night. Truly we have here a standard by which we may judge ourselves. "If any man have not the Spirit of Christ, he is none of his." If we have narrow sympathies, mean ideas, paltry conceptions, we are not scholars in the school of Christ. Let us bring no reproach upon Christ by our exclusiveness. Let us beware of the bigotry of patriotism, as well as of the bigotry of religion. We are citizens of the world: we are more than the taxpayers of a parish.—*The People's Bible*

Verses 1–5

The posterity of Japheth were allotted to the isles of the Gentiles (*v.* 5), which were divided among them, and probably this island of ours among the rest; all places beyond the sea from Judæa are called *isles* (Jer. xxv. 22), and this directs us to understand that promise (Isa. xlii. 4), *the isles shall wait for his law*, of the conversion of the Gentiles to the faith of Christ.

5. the isles of the Gentiles—a phrase by which the Hebrews described all countries which were accessible by sea (Isa. 11:11; 20:6; Jer. 25:22). Such in relation to them were the countries of Europe, the peninsula of Lesser Asia, and the region lying on the east of the Euxine. Accordingly, it was in these quarters the early descendants of Japheth had their settlements. **6. sons of Ham**—emigrated southward, and their settlements were: Cush in Arabia, Canaan in the country known by his name, and Mizraim in Egypt, Upper and Lower. It is generally thought that his father accompanied him and personally superintended the formation of the settlement, whence Egypt was called "the land of Ham."

MATTHEW HENRY

Verses 6–14

That which is observable and improvable in these verses is the account here given of Nimrod, *v.* 8–10. He is here represented as a great man in his day: he was resolved to tower above his neighbours. The same spirit that actuated the giants before the flood now revived in him. There are some in whom ambition and affectation of dominion seem to be bred in the bone. Nothing on this side hell will humble and break the proud spirits of some men. Now,

I. Nimrod was a great hunter; with this he began, and for this became famous to a proverb. 1. Some think he did good with his hunting, served his country by ridding it of the wild beasts which infested it. 2. Others think that under pretence of hunting he gathered men under his command, in pursuit of another game he had to play, which was to make himself master of the country. Note, Great conquerors are but great hunters. Alexander and Cæsar would not make such a figure in scripture-history as they do in common history. Nimrod was a mighty hunter *against* the Lord, so the LXX; that is, (1) He set up idolatry. That he might set up a new government, he set up a new religion. *Babel was the mother of harlots.* Or, (2) He carried on his oppression and violence in defiance of God himself.

II. Nimrod was a great ruler: *The beginning of his kingdom was Babel, v.* 10. Some way or other, by arts or arms, he got into power, and so laid the foundations of a monarchy. If Nimrod and his neighbours began, other nations soon learned to incorporate under one head for their common safety and welfare, which, however it began, proved so great a blessing to the world that things were reckoned to go ill indeed when there *was no king in Israel.*

III. Nimrod was a great builder. Probably he was architect in the building of Babel, and there he began his kingdom; but, when his project to rule all the sons of Noah was baffled by the confusion of tongues, *out of that land he went forth into Assyria* (so the margin reads it, *v.* 11) *and built Nineveh,* &c.

Verses 15–20

Observe here, 1. The account of the posterity of Canaan, of the families and nations that descended from him, and of the land they possessed, very pleasantly situated. Canaan here has a better land than either Shem or Japheth, and yet they have a better lot, for they inherit the blessing.

Verses 21–32

Two things especially are observable in this account of the posterity of Shem:—

I. The description of Shem, *v.* 21. We have not only his name, *Shem,* which signifies *a name,* but two titles to distinguish him by:—

1. He was *the father of all the children of Eber.* Eber was his great grandson; but why should he be called the father of all *his* children, rather than of all Arphaxad's, or Salah's, &c.? Probably because Abraham and his seed, God's covenant-people, not only descended from Heber, but from him were called *Hebrews; ch.* xiv. 13, *Abram the Hebrew.* The holy tongue being commonly called from him the *Hebrew,* it is probable that he retained it in his family, in the confusion of Babel, as a special token of God's favour to him. Now, when the inspired penman would give Shem an honourable title, he calls him *the father of the Hebrews.* As Ham, though he had many sons, is disowned by being called *the father of Canaan,* so Shem, though he had many sons, is dignified with the title of *the father of Eber,* on whose seed the blessing was entailed. Goodness is true greatness.

2. He was *the brother of Japheth the elder.* The sacred historian had mentioned it as Shem's honour that he was the father of the Hebrews; but, lest Japheth's seed should therefore be looked upon as for ever shut out from the Church, he here reminds us that he *was the brother of Japheth,* not in birth only, but in blessing; for *Japheth was to dwell in the tents of Shem.*

JAMIESON, FAUSSET, BROWN

8. Nimrod—mentioned as eclipsing all his family in renown. He early distinguished himself by his daring and successful prowess in hunting wild beasts. By those useful services he earned a title to public gratitude; and, having established a permanent ascendancy over the people, he founded the first kingdom in the world.

10. the beginning of his kingdom—This kingdom, of course, though then considered great, would be comparatively limited in extent, and the towns but small forts.

11. Out of that land went forth Asshur—or, as the *Margin* has it, "He [Nimrod] at the head of his army went forth into Assyria," i.e., he pushed his conquests into that country. **and builded Nineveh**—opposite the town of Mosul, on the Tigris, and the other towns near it. This raid into Assyria was an invasion of the territories of Shem, and hence the name "Nimrod," signifying "rebel," is supposed to have been conferred on him from his daring revolt against the divine distribution.

21. Unto Shem—The historian introduces him with marked distinction as "the father of Eber," the ancestor of the Hebrews.

23. Aram—In the general division of the earth, the countries of Armenia, Mesopotamia, and Syria, fell to his descendants. **24. Arphaxad**—The settlement of his posterity was in the extensive valley of Shinar, on the Tigris, towards the southern extremity of Mesopotamia, including the country of Eden and the region on the east side of the river. **25. Peleg; for in his days was the earth divided**—After the flood (ch. 11:10-16) the descendants of Noah settled at pleasure and enjoyed the produce of the undivided soil. But according to divine instruction, made probably through Eber, who seems to have been distinguished for piety or a prophetic character, the earth was divided and his son's name, "Peleg," was given in memory of that event (see Deut. 32:8; Acts 17:26).

ADAM CLARKE

7. *Seba.* The founder of the Sabeans. There seem to be three different people of this name mentioned in this chapter, and a fourth in chap. xxv. 3.

8. *Nimrod.* Of this person little is known, as he is not mentioned except here and in 1 Chron. i. 10, which is evidently a copy of the text in Genesis. He is called "a mighty hunter before the Lord"; and from v. 10, we learn that he founded a "kingdom" which included the cities "Babel, and Erech, and Accad, and Calneh, in the land of Shinar." Though the words are not definite, it is very likely he was a very bad man. His name Nimrod comes from *marad,* "he rebelled"; and the Targum, on 1 Chron. i. 10, says: "Nimrod began to be a mighty man in sin, a murderer of innocent men, and a rebel before the Lord." The word which we render *hunter* signifies "prey"; and is applied in the Scriptures to the hunting of men by persecution, oppression, and tyranny. Hence it is likely that Nimrod, having acquired power, used it in tyranny and oppression; and by rapine and violence founded that domination which was the first distinguished by the name of a *kingdom* on the face of the earth.

10. *The beginning of his kingdom was Babel. Babel* signifies "confusion"; and it seems to have been a very proper name for the commencement of a kingdom that appears to have been founded in apostasy from God and to have been supported by tyranny, rapine, and oppression. *In the land of Shinar.* The same as mentioned in chap. xi. 2. It appears that, as Babylon was built on the river Euphrates, and the Tower of Babel was in the land of Shinar, consequently Shinar itself must have been in the southern part of Mesopotamia.

11. *Out of that land went forth Asshur.* The marginal reading is to be preferred here. "He—Nimrod—went out into Assyria and built Nineveh"; and hence Assyria is called the "land of Nimrod," Mic. v. 6. Thus did this mighty hunter extend his dominations in every possible way.

14. *Philistim.* The people called Philistines, the frequent oppressors of the Israelites, whose history may be seen at large in the Books of Samuel, Kings.

15. *Sidon.* Who probably built the city of this name, and was the father of the Sidonians. *Heth.* From whom came the Hittites, so remarkable among the Canaanitish nations.

16. *The Jebusite . . . Amorite, etc.* Are well-known as being the ancient inhabitants of Canaan, expelled by the children of Israel.

20. *These are the sons of Ham, after their families.* No doubt all these were well-known in the days of Moses, and for a long time after; but at this distance, when it is considered that the political state of the world has been undergoing almost incessant revolutions through all the intermediate portions of time, the impossibility of fixing their residences or marking their descendants must be evident, as both the names of the people and the places of their residences have been changed beyond the possibility of being recognized.

21. *Shem also, the father of all the children of Eber.* It is generally supposed that the Hebrews derived their name from Eber or Heber, son of Shem; but it appears much more likely that they had it from the circumstance of Abraham "passing over" (for so the word *abar* signifies) the river Euphrates to come into the land of Canaan.

22. *Elam.* From whom came the Elamites, near to the Medes, and whose chief city was Elymais. *Asshur.* Who gave his name to a vast province (afterwards a mighty empire) called Assyria. *Lud.* The founder of the Lydians, in Asia Minor; or of the Ludim, who dwelt at the confluence of the Euphrates and Tigris. *Aram.* The father of the Aramaeans, afterwards called Syrians.

23. *Uz.* Supposed to have been the founder of *Damascus.*

25. *Peleg.* From *palag,* "to divide," because *in his days,* which is supposed to be about one hundred years after the Flood, *the earth was divided* among the sons of Noah. Though some are of opinion that a physical division, and not a political one, is what is intended here, namely,

MATTHEW HENRY

JAMIESON, FAUSSET, BROWN

32. These are the families of the sons of Noah after their generations, in their nations, etc.—This division was made in the most orderly manner; and the inspired historian evidently intimates that the sons of Noah were ranged according to their nations, and every nation ranked by its families, so that every nation had its assigned territory, and in every nation the tribes, and in every tribe the families, were located by themselves.

ADAM CLARKE

a separation of continents and islands from the main land; the earthy parts having been united into one great continent previously to the days of Peleg. This opinion appears to me the most likely, for what is said, v. 5, is spoken by way of anticipation.

MATTHEW HENRY — CHAPTER 11

Verses 1–4

The close of the foregoing chapter tells us that *by* the sons of Noah, or *among* the sons of Noah, *the nations were divided in the earth after the flood,* that is, were distinguished into several tribes, and it was either appointed by Noah, or agreed upon among his sons, which way each several tribe or colony should steer its course. But the sons of men, it should seem, were loth to disperse into distant places; they thought the more the merrier and the safer, and therefore they contrived to keep together, thinking themselves wiser than either God or Noah. Now here we have,

I. The advantages which befriended their design of keeping together, 1. They were all of *one language, v.* 1. Now, while they all understood one another, they would be the more likely to love one another, and the more capable of helping one another, and the less inclinable to separate one from another. 2. They found a very convenient commodious place to settle in (*v.* 2), *a plain in the land of Shinar,* a spacious plain, able to *contain* them all, and a *fruitful* plain, able, according as their present numbers were, to support them all.

II. The method they took to bind themselves to one another, and to settle together in one body. Instead of coveting to enlarge their borders by a peaceful departure under the divine protection, they contrived to fortify them. Their unanimous resolution is, *Let us build ourselves a city and a tower.* Observe here,

1. How they excited and encouraged one another to set about this work. They said, *Go to, let us make brick* (*v.* 3), and again, (*v.* 4), *Go to, let us build ourselves a city;* by mutual excitements they made one another more daring and resolute.

2. What materials they used in their building. The country, being plain, yielded neither stone nor mortar, yet this did not discourage them from their undertaking, but they made brick to serve instead of stone, and slime or pitch instead of mortar. What shift those will make that are resolute in their purposes: were we but thus zealously affected in a good thing, we should not stop our work so often as we do, under pretence that we want conveniences for carrying it on.

3. For what ends they built. Three things, it seems, they aimed at in building this tower:—

(1) It seems designed for an affront to God himself; for they would build a tower *whose top might reach to heaven,* which bespeaks a defiance of God, or at least a rivalship with him.

(2) They hoped hereby to make themselves a name, and to give posterity to know that there had been such men as they in the world. They would leave this monument of their pride and ambition, and folly. We do not find in any history the name of so much as one of these Babel-builders.

(3) They did it to prevent their dispersion. It is probable that the hand of ambitious Nimrod was in all this. He aimed at universal monarchy, in order to which, under pretence of uniting for their common safety, he contrives to keep them in one body, that, having them all under his eye, he might not fail to have them under his power. It is God's prerogative to be universal monarch, Lord of all, and King of kings; the man that aims at it offers to step into the throne of God, who will not give his glory to another.

Verses 5–9

We have here the quashing of the project of the Babel-builders.

I. The cognizance God took of the design that was on foot. God is incontestibly just and fair in all his proceedings against sin and sinners, and condemns none unheard. They were the sons of *Adam,* so it is in the Hebrew; nay, of that Adam, that sinful disobedient Adam, whose children are by nature children of disobedience. Pious Eber is not found among this ungodly crew; for he and his are called the children of God.

II. The counsels and resolves of the Eternal God concerning this matter.

1. He suffered them to proceed a good way in

JAMIESON, FAUSSET, BROWN — CHAPTER 11

Vss. 1-32. Confusion of Tongues. **1. the whole earth was of one language**—The descendants of Noah, united by the strong bond of a common language, had not separated, and notwithstanding the divine command to replenish the earth, were unwilling to separate. The more pious and well-disposed would of course obey the divine will; but a numerous body, seemingly the aggressive horde mentioned (ch. 10:10), determined to please themselves by occupying the fairest region they came to.

2. land of Shinar—The fertile valley watered by the Euphrates and Tigris was chosen as the center of their union and the seat of their power.

3. brick—There being no stone in that quarter, brick is, and was, the only material used for building, as appears in the mass of ruins which at the Birs Nimroud may have been the very town formed by those ancient rebels. Some of these are sun-dried—others burnt in the kiln and of different colors. **slime**—bitumen, a mineral pitch, which, when hardened, forms a strong cement, commonly used in Assyria to this day, and forming the mortar found on the burnt-brick remains of antiquity.

4. a tower whose top may reach unto heaven—a common figurative expression for great height (Deut. 1:28; 9:1-6).

ADAM CLARKE — CHAPTER 11

1. *The whole earth was of one language. The whole earth*—all mankind—*was of one language,* in all likelihood the Hebrew; *and of one speech*—articulating the same words in the same way. It is generally supposed that, after the confusion mentioned in this chapter, the Hebrew language remained in the family of Heber. The proper names and their significations given in the Scripture seem incontestable evidences that the Hebrew language was the original language of the earth—the language in which God spake to man, and in which He gave the revelation of His will to Moses and the prophets.

2. *As they journeyed from the east.* Assyria, Mesopotamia, and the country on the borders and beyond the Euphrates are called the *east* in the sacred writings. Balaam said that the king of Moab had brought him "from the mountains of the east," Num. xxiii. 7. Now it appears, from chap. xxii. 5, that Balaam dwelt at Pethor, on the river Euphrates. And it is very probable that it was from this country that the wise men came to adore Christ; for it is said they came "from the east" to Jerusalem, Matt. ii. 1. Abraham is said to have come "from the east" to Canaan, Isa. xli. 2; but it is well-known that he came from Mesopotamia and Chaldea. Isa. xlvi. 11 represents Cyrus as coming "from the east" against Babylon.

Noah and his family, landing after the Flood on one of the mountains of Armenia, would doubtless descend and cultivate the valleys; as they increased, they appear to have passed along the banks of the Euphrates, till, at the time specified here, they came to the plains of Shinar, allowed to be the most fertile country in the east. That Babel was built in the land of Shinar we have the authority of the sacred text to prove; and that Babylon was built in the same country we have the testimony of Eusebius and Josephus.

3. *Let us make brick.* It appears they were obliged to make use of *brick,* as there was an utter scarcity of stones in that district; and on the same account they were obliged to use *slime for morter:* so it appears they had neither common stone nor limestone; hence they had *brick* for stone, and *asphaltus* or *bitumen* instead of mortar.

4. *Let us build us a city and a tower.* It is probable that their being "of one language, and of one speech" implies not only a sameness of language but also a unity of sentiment and design, as seems pretty clearly intimated in v. 6. Being therefore strictly united in all things, coming to the fertile plains of Shinar they proposed to settle themselves there, instead of spreading themselves over all the countries of the earth according to the design of God; and in reference to this purpose they encouraged one another to build a *city* and a *tower,* probably a temple, to prevent their separation, "lest," say they, "we be scattered abroad upon the face of the whole earth": but God, miraculously interposing, confounded or frustrated their rebellious design, which was inconsistent with His will; see Deut. xxxii. 8; Acts xvii. 26; and, partly by confounding their language, and disturbing their counsels, they could no longer keep in a united state.

MATTHEW HENRY

their enterprise before he put a stop to it, that they might have space to repent.

2. God had tried, by his commands and admonitions, to bring them off from this project, but in vain; therefore he must take another course to keep the world in some order and to tie the hands of those that will not be checked by law. Now observe here, The mercy of God, in moderating the penalty, and not making it proportionable to the offence; for *he deals not with us according to our sins.* He does not say, "*Let us go down* now in thunder and lightning, and consume those rebels in a moment." No; only, "*Let us go down*, and scatter them." They deserved death, but are only banished or transported; for the patience of God is very great towards a provoking world. Three things were done:—

1. Their language was confounded. Those unhappy controversies which are strifes of words, and arise from our misunderstanding one another's language, for aught I know are owing to this confusion of tongues.

2. Their building was stopped: *They left off to build the city.* This was the effect of the confusion of their tongues; for it not only incapacitated them for helping one another, but probably struck such a damp upon their spirits that they could not proceed, since they saw, in this, the hand of the Lord gone out against them. It is wisdom to leave off that which we see God fights against.

3. The builders were scattered abroad upon the face of the whole earth, *v.* 8, 9. They departed in companies, after their families, and after their tongues (*ch.* x. 5, 20, 31), to the several countries and places allotted to them. They left behind them a perpetual memorandum of their reproach, in the name given to the place. It was called *Babel, confusion.* Those that aim at a great name commonly come off with a *bad* name. The children of men were now finally scattered, and never did, nor ever will, come all together again, till the great day, when the Son of man shall sit upon the throne of his glory, and all nations shall be gathered before him, Matt. xxv. 31, 32.

Verses 10–26

We have here a genealogy, not an endless genealogy, for here it ends in Abram, the friend of God, and leads further to Christ, the promised seed, who was the son of Abram, and from Abram the genealogy of Christ is reckoned (Matt. i. 1, &c.). 1. Nothing is left upon record concerning those of this line but their names and ages, the Holy Ghost seeming to hasten through them to the story of Abram. How little do we know of those that have gone before us in this world, even those that lived in the same places where we live, as we likewise know little of those that are our contemporaries in distant places! we have enough to do to mind the work of our own day, and let God alone to *require that which is past*, Eccl. iii. 15. 2. There was an observable gradual decrease in the years of their lives. Shem reached to 600 years, which yet fell short of the age of the patriarchs before the flood; the next three came short of 500; the next three did not reach to 300; after them we read not of any that attained to 200, except Terah; and, not many ages after this, Moses reckoned seventy, or eighty, to be the utmost men ordinarily arrive at. 3. Eber, from whom the Hebrews were denominated, was the longest-lived of any that was born after the flood, which perhaps was the reward of his singular piety and strict adherence to the ways of God.

Verses 27–32

Here begins the story of Abram, whose name is famous, henceforward, in both Testaments.

I. His country: *Ur of the Chaldees.* This was the land of his nativity, an idolatrous country, where even the children of Eber themselves had degenerated. Note, Those who are, through grace, heirs of the land of promise, ought to remember what was the land of their nativity, what was their corrupt and sinful state by nature, the rock out of which they were hewn.

II. His relations, mentioned for his sake, and because of their interest in the following story. 1. His father was *Terah*, of whom it is said (Josh. xxiv. 2) that he served other gods, on the other side of the flood, so early did idolatry gain footing in the world, and so hard is it even for those that have some good principles to swim against the stream. We have, 2. Some account of his brethren. (1) *Nahor*, out of whose family both Isaac and Jacob had their wives. (2) *Haran*, the father of Lot, of whom it is here said (*v.* 28) *that he died before his father Terah.* Note, Children cannot be sure that they shall survive their parents; for death does not go by seniority, taking

JAMIESON, FAUSSET, BROWN

6. **now nothing will be restrained from them**—an apparent admission that the design was practicable, and would have been executed but for the divine interposition. **lest we be scattered**—To build a city and a town was no crime; but to do this to defeat the counsels of heaven by attempting to prevent emigration was foolish, wicked, and justly offensive to God.

7. **confound their language**—lit., "their lip"; it was a failure in utterance, occasioning a difference in dialect which was intelligible only to those of the same tribe. Thus easily by God their purpose was defeated, and they were compelled to the dispersion they had combined to prevent. It is only from the Scriptures we learn the true origin of the different nations and languages of the world. By one miracle of tongues men were dispersed and gradually fell from true religion. By another, national barriers were broken down—that all men might be brought back to the family of God.

TODAY'S DICTIONARY OF THE BIBLE:

Babel, Tower of, the name given to the tower which the primitive fathers of our race built in the land of Shinar after the Deluge (Gen. 11:1–9). Their object in building this tower was probably that it might be seen as a rallying point in the extensive plain of Shinar and so prevent their being scattered abroad. But God interposed and defeated their design by confounding their language. The name Babel, meaning Gate of God or Babylon, is a pun on "balal," meaning to confuse. In the Babylonian tablets there is an account of this event, and also of the creation and the deluge.

A temple of this type, known to its builders as a ziggurat, which is supposed to occupy its site, is described by the Greek historian Herodotus as a temple of great extent and magnificence, erected by the Babylonians for their god Bel. The treasures Nebuchadnezzar brought from Jerusalem were laid up in this temple (2 Chron. 36:7).

The *Birs Nimrûd,* at ancient Borsippa, about 7 miles southwest of Hillah, the modern town which occupies a part of the site of ancient Babylon, and 6 miles from the Euphrates, is an immense mass of broken and fire-blasted fragments, about 2,300 feet in circumference, rising suddenly to the height of 235 feet above the desert-plain. It is with probability regarded as the ruins of the tower of Babel. This is "one of the most imposing ruins in the country." Others think it to be the ruins of the Temple of Belus.

28. **Ur** (now Orfa)—i.e., light, or fire. Its name probably derived from its being devoted to the rites of fire worship. Terah and his family were equally infected with that idolatry as the rest of the inhabitants (Josh. 24:15).

ADAM CLARKE

7. *Go to.* A form of speech which, whatever it might have signified formerly, now means nothing. The Hebrew *habah* signifies "come, make preparation," as it were for a journey, the execution of a purpose, etc. Almost all the versions understand the word in this way; the Septuagint has *deute*, the Vulgate *venite*, both signifying *come*, or *come ye*. This makes a very good sense, "Come, let us go down."

9. *Therefore is the name of it called Babel. Babel*, from *bal*, to "mingle, confound, destroy"; hence *Babel*, from the mingling together and confounding of the projects and language of these descendants of Noah; and this confounding did not so much imply the producing new languages as giving them a different method of pronouncing the same words, and leading them to affix different ideas to them.

10. *These are the generations of Shem.* This may be called the "holy family," as from it sprang Abraham, Isaac, Jacob, the twelve patriarchs, David, Solomon, and all the great progenitors of the Messiah.

26. *And Terah lived seventy years, and begat Abram, Nahor, and Haran.* Haran was certainly the eldest son of Terah, and he appears to have been born when Terah was about seventy years of age, and his birth was followed in successive periods with those of *Nahor* his second, and *Abram* his youngest son. Many have been greatly puzzled with the account here, supposing because Abram is mentioned first, that therefore he was the eldest son of Terah; but he is only put first by way of dignity. An instance of this we have already seen, chap. v. 32, where Noah is represented as having Shem, Ham, and Japheth in this order of succession; whereas it is evident from other scriptures that Shem was the youngest son, who for dignity is named first, as Abram is here; and Japheth, the eldest, named last, as Haran is here. Terah died two hundred and five years old, v. 32; then Abram departed from Haran when seventy-five years old, chap. xii. 4; therefore Abram was born, not when his father, Terah, was seventy, but when he was one hundred and thirty.

MATTHEW HENRY

the eldest first. *The shadow of death is without any order*, Job x. 22. It is likewise said that he died *in Ur of the Chaldees*, before the happy removal of the family out of that idolatrous country. 3. His wife was *Sarai*, who, some think, was the same with Iscah, the daughter of Haran. Abram himself says of her that she was the daughter of his father, but not the daughter of his mother, *ch.* xx. 12. She was ten years younger than Abram.

III. His departure out of Ur of the Chaldees, with his father Terah, his nephew Lot, and the rest of his family, in obedience to the call of God, of which we shall read more, *ch.* xii. 1, &c. This chapter leaves them in Haran, or Charran, a place about midway between Ur and Canaan, where they dwelt till Terah's head was laid, probably because the old man was unable, through the infirmities of age, to proceed in his journey. Many reach to Charran, and yet fall short of Canaan; they are not far from the kingdom of God, and yet never come thither.

CHAPTER 12

Verses 1–3

We have here the call by which Abram was removed out of the land of his nativity, into the land of promise, and which was designed both to try his faith and obedience and also to separate him and set him apart for God, and for special services. We may be somewhat helped to the knowledge of the circumstances of the call by Stephen's speech, Acts vii. 2, where we are told, 1. That the God of glory appeared in such displays of his glory as left Abram no room to doubt the divine authority of this call. God spoke to him afterwards in divers manners; but this first time, when the correspondence was to be settled, he appeared to him as *the God of glory*, and spoke to him. 2. That this call was given him in Mesopotamia, before he dwelt in Charran. Some think that Haran was in Chaldea, and so was still a part of Abram's country, or that Abram, having stayed there five years, began to call it his country, and to take root there, till God let him know this was not the place he was intended for. Note, If God loves us, and has mercy in store for us, he will not suffer us to take up our rest anywhere short of Canaan, but will graciously repeat his calls, till the good work begun be performed, and our souls repose in God only. In the call itself we have a precept and a promise.

I. A trying precept: *Get thee out of thy country*, *v.* 1.

1. By this precept he was tried whether he loved his native soil and dearest friends, and whether he could willingly leave all, to go along with God. His country had become idolatrous, his kindred and his father's house were a constant temptation to him, and he could not continue with them without danger of being infected by them. This command which God gave to Abram is much the same with the gospel call by which all the spiritual seed of faithful Abram are brought into covenant with God. For, (1) Natural affection must give way to divine grace. (2) Sin, and all the occasions of it, must be forsaken, and particularly bad company; we must abandon all the idols of iniquity which have been set up in our hearts, willingly parting with that which is dearest to us, when we cannot keep it without hazard of our integrity. (3) The world, and all our enjoyments in it, must be looked upon with a holy indifference; we must no longer look upon it as our country, or home, but as our inn, and must accordingly sit loose to it, live above it, and get out of it in affection.

2. By this precept he was tried whether he could trust God further than he saw him; for he must leave his own country, to go to a *land that God would show him*. He does not say, "It is a land that I will give thee," but merely, "a land that I will show thee." He must follow God with an implicit faith, though he had no particular securities given him that he should be no loser by leaving his country, to follow God.

II. Here is an encouraging promise, nay, it is a complication of promises, many, and exceedingly great and precious. Note, All God's precepts are attended with promises to the obedient. If we obey the command, God will not fail to perform the promise. Here are six promises:—

1. *I will make of thee a great nation.* When God took him from his own people, he promised to make him the head of another; he cut him off from being the branch of a wild olive, to make him the root of a good olive. This promise was, (1) A great relief to Abram's burden; for he had now no child. Note, God knows how to suit his favours to the wants and necessities of his children. He that has a plaster for every sore will first provide one for that which

JAMIESON, FAUSSET, BROWN

31. **Sarai his daughter-in-law**—the same as Iscah, granddaughter of Terah, probably by a second wife, and by early usages considered marriageable to her uncle, Abraham.

and they came unto Haran—two days' journey south-southeast from Ur, on the direct road to the ford of the Euphrates at Rakka, the nearest and most convenient route to Palestine.

CHAPTER 12

Vss. 1-20. CALL TO ABRAM. **1. Now the Lord had said unto Abram**—It pleased God, who has often been found of them who sought Him not, to reveal Himself to Abraham perhaps by a miracle; and the conversion of Abraham is one of the most remarkable in Bible history.

Get thee out of thy country—His being brought to the knowledge and worship of the true God had probably been a considerable time before. This call included two promises: the first, showing the land of his future posterity; and the second, that in his posterity all the earth was to be blessed. Abraham obeyed, and it is frequently mentioned in the New Testament as a striking instance of his faith (Heb. 11:8).

ADAM CLARKE

29. *Milcah, the daughter of Haran.* Many suppose *Sarai* and *Iscah* are the same person under two different names; but this is improbable, as *Iscah* is expressly said to be the daughter of Haran, and *Sarai* was the daughter of Terah, and half sister of Abram.

CHAPTER 12

1. *Get thee out of thy country.* There is great dissension between commentators concerning the call of Abram; some supposing he had two distinct calls, others that he had but one. At the conclusion of the preceding chapter, v. 31, we find Terah and all his family leaving Ur of the Chaldees, in order to go to Canaan. This was, no doubt, in consequence of some divine admonition. While resting at Haran, on their road to Canaan, Terah died, chap. xi. 32; and then God repeats His call to Abram, and orders him to proceed to Canaan, chap. xii. 1.

Thy kindred. Nahor and the different branches of the family of Terah, Abram and Lot excepted. That Nahor went with Terah and Abram as far as Padan-aram, in Mesopotamia, and settled there, so that it was afterwards called Nahor's city, is sufficiently evident from the ensuing history, see chap. xxv. 20; xxiv. 10, 15; and that the same land was Haran, see chap. xxviii. 2, 10, and there were Abram's kindred and country here spoken of, chap. xxiv. 4.

Thy father's house. Terah being now dead, it is very probable that the family were determined to go no farther, but to settle at Charran; and as Abram might have felt inclined to stop with them in this place, hence the ground and necessity of the second call recorded here, and which is introduced in a very remarkable manner: "Go for thyself." If none of the family will accompany thee, yet go for thyself unto that land *that I will shew thee.* God does not tell him what land it is, that He may still cause him to walk by faith and not by sight. This seems to be particularly alluded to by Isaiah, chap. xli. 2: "Who raised up the righteous man [Abram] from the east, and called him to his foot"; that is, to follow implicitly the divine direction. The apostle assures us that in all this Abram had spiritual views; he looked for a better country, and considered the land of promise only as typical of the heavenly inheritance.

2. *I will make of thee a great nation.* i.e., The Jewish people; *and make thy name great,* alluding to the change of his name from Abram, Abraham, a high father, to Abraham, the father of a multitude.

MATTHEW HENRY

is most painful. (2) A great trial to Abram's faith; for his wife had been long barren.

2. *I will bless thee.* Leave thy father's house, and I will give thee a father's blessing.

3. *I will make thy name great.* By deserting his country, he lost his name there. Having no child, he feared he should have no name; but God will make him a great nation, and so make him a great name.

4. *Thou shalt be a blessing;* that is, (1) "Thy happiness shall be a sample of happiness, so that those who would bless their friends shall only pray that God would make them like Abram"; as Ruth iv. 11. (2) "Thy life shall be a blessing to the places where thou shalt sojourn."

5. *I will bless those that bless thee and curse him that curseth thee.* This made it a kind of a league, offensive and defensive, between God and Abram.

6. *In thee shall all the families of the earth be blessed.* This was the promise that crowned all the rest; for it points to the Messiah, in whom *all the promises are yea and amen.* Note, (1) Jesus Christ is the great blessing of the world, the greatest that ever the world was blessed with. He is a family blessing, by him salvation is brought to the house (Luke xix. 9).

Verses 4–5

I. Abram's removal out of his country, out of Ur first and afterwards out of Haran, in compliance with the call of God. He *went out, not knowing whither he went* (Heb. xi. 8), but knowing whom he followed.

II. His age when he removed: he was *seventy-five years old,* an age when he should rather have had rest and settlement; but, if God will have him to begin the world again now in his old age, he will submit. Here is an instance of an old convert.

III. The company and cargo that he took with him.

1. He took his wife, and his nephew Lot, with him. Note, It is very comfortable when husband and wife agree to go together in the way to heaven. Lot also, his kinsman, was influenced by Abram's good example, who was perhaps his guardian after the death of his father, and he was willing to go along with him too.

2. They took all their effects with them—*all their substance* and movable goods, *that they had gathered.* To have thrown away his substance, because God had promised to bless him, would have been to tempt God, not to trust him.

IV. Here is their happy arrival at their journey's end: *They went forth to go into the land of Canaan*; so they did before (*ch.* xi. 31), and then took up short, but now they held on their way, and, by the good hand of their God upon them, to the land of Canaan they came, where by a fresh revelation they were told that this was the land God promised to show them.

Verses 6–9

One would have expected that Abram having had such an extraordinary call to Canaan some great event should have followed upon his arrival there. Little notice is taken of him for God will have him to live by faith.

I. How little comfort he had in the land he came to; for, 1. He had it not to himself: He found the country peopled and possessed by Canaanites, who were likely to be but bad neighbours and worse landlords. 2. He had not a settlement in it. All good people must look upon themselves as strangers and sojourners in this world, and by faith sit loose to it as a strange country. We must be journeying, and going on still from strength to strength, as having not yet attained.

II. How much comfort he had in the God he followed.

1. God spoke to him good words and comfortable words: *Unto thy seed will I give this land.* Enemies may part us and our tents, us and our altars, but not us and our God. Mercies to the children are mercies to the parents. "I will give it, not to thee, but to thy seed"; it is a grant in reversion to his seed, which Abram understood also as a grant to himself, for he looked for a heavenly country, Heb. xi. 16.

2. Abram *built an altar unto the Lord who appeared to him, and called on the name of the Lord, v.* 7, 8. Thus he returned God's visit, and kept up his correspondence with heaven, as one that resolved it should not fail on his side. Wherever he had a tent God had an altar, and that an altar sanctified by prayer. The *souls he had gotten in Haran,* being discipled, must be further taught. The way of family worship is a good old way, is no novel invention, but the ancient usage of all the saints. Wherever we go, let us not fail to take our religion along with us.

JAMIESON, FAUSSET, BROWN

CHARLES H. SPURGEON:

"I will bless thee . . . and thou shalt be a blessing." This was to be the double result of Abraham's coming out from his own country and his father's house. Those Orientals clung with great tenacity to their native homes. We in these latter ages are not so restful; we think nothing of crossing the Atlantic, and many think little of going to the other side of the globe; but those Easterns trembled even to cross the Euphrates or the Tigris. They spoke of the land beyond those rivers as "across the flood," and a journey of two or three hundred miles seemed to them to be an event only second to death itself. Yet when the Lord said to Abraham, "Get thee out of thy country, and from thy kindred, and from thy father's house, unto a land that I will shew thee," he "departed, as the Lord had spoken unto him." His obedience was an act of heroic faith.

—*The Treasury of the Old Testament*

5. into the land of Canaan . . . they came—with his wife and an orphan nephew. Abram reached his destination in safety, and thus the first promise was made good.

6. the place of Sichem—or Shechem, a pastoral valley then unoccupied (cf. ch. 33:18). **plain of Moreh**—rather, the "terebinth tree" of Moreh, very common in Palestine, remarkable for its wide-spreading branches and its dark green foliage. It is probable that in Moreh there was a grove of these trees, whose inviting shade led Abram to choose it for an encampment. **7. Unto thy seed will I give this land**—God was dealing with Abram not in his private and personal capacity merely, but with a view to high and important interests in future ages. That land his posterity was for centuries to inhabit as a peculiar people; the seeds of divine knowledge were to be sown there for the benefit of all mankind; and considered in its geographical situation, it was chosen in divine wisdom as the fittest of all lands to serve as the cradle of a divine revelation designed for the whole world. **and there builded he an altar unto the Lord**—By this solemn act of devotion he made an open profession of his religion, established the worship of the true God, and declared his faith in the promise.

ADAM CLARKE

3. *In thee.* In thy posterity, in the Messiah, who shall spring from thee, shall all families of the earth be blessed.

4. *And Abram was seventy and five years old.* As Abram was now seventy-five years old, and his father, Terah, had just died, at the age of two hundred and five, consequently Terah must have been one hundred and thirty when Abram was born; and the seventieth year of his age mentioned in Gen. xi. 26 was the period at which Haran, not Abram, was born.

5. *The souls that they had gotten in Haran.* This may apply either to the persons who were employed in the service of Abram or to the persons he had been the instrument of converting to the knowledge of the true God; and in this latter sense the Chaldee paraphrasts understood the passage, translating it, "The souls of those whom they proselyted in Haran." *They went forth to go into the land of Canaan.* A good land, possessed by a bad people, who for their iniquities were to be expelled, see Lev. xviii. 25.

6. *The plain of Moreh. Elon* should be translated "oak," not *plain;* the Septuagint translates, "the lofty oak"; and it is likely the place was remarkable for a grove of those trees, or for one of a stupendous height and bulk. *The Canaanite was then in the land.* This is thought to be an interpolation, because it is supposed that these words must have been written after the Canaanites were expelled from the land by the Israelites under Joshua; but this by no means follows. All that Moses states is simply that at the time in which Abram passed through Sichem the land was inhabited by the descendants of Canaan.

7. *The Lord appeared.* In what way this appearance was made we know not; it was probably by the great Angel of the covenant, Jesus the Christ. The appearance, whatsoever it was, perfectly satisfied Abram, and proved itself to be supernatural and divine. It is worthy of remark that Abram is the first man to whom God is said to have shown himself or *appeared:* (1) In Ur of the Chaldees, Acts vii. 2; and (2) At the oak of Moreh, as in this verse. As Moreh signifies a "teacher," probably this was called the oak of Moreh because God manifested himself here and instructed Abram concerning the future possession of that land by his posterity, and the dispensation of the mercy of God to all the families of the earth through the promised Messiah.

8. *Beth-el.* The place which was afterwards called *Beth-el* by Jacob, for its first name was Luz. See chap. xxviii. 19. *Beith El* literally signifies "the house of God." *And pitched his tent . . . and . . . builded an altar unto the Lord.* Where Abram has a *tent,* there God must have an *altar,* as he well knows there is no safety but under the divine protection. The house in which the worship of God is not established cannot be considered as under the divine protection.

MATTHEW HENRY

Verses 10–13

Here is, I. A famine in the land of Canaan, *a grievous famine*, and a very sore trial it was; it tried what he would think. Nothing short of a strong faith could keep up good thoughts of God under such a providence. Now he was tried whether he could preserve an unshaken confidence that the God who brought him to Canaan would maintain him there, and whether he could rejoice in him as the God of his salvation when the fig-tree did not blossom, Hab. iii. 17, 18. It is possible for a man to be in the way of duty, and in the way to happiness, and yet meet with great troubles and disappointments.

II. Abram's removal into Egypt, upon occasion of this famine. See how wisely God provides that there should be plenty in one place when there was scarcity in another. We must not expect needless miracles. When he must, for a time, quit Canaan, he chooses to go to Egypt, which lay south-west, the contrary way, that he might not so much as seem to look back. See Heb. xi. 15, 16.

III. A great fault which Abram was guilty of, in denying his wife, and pretending that she was his sister. The scripture is impartial in relating the misdeeds of the most celebrated saints, which are recorded, not for our imitation, but for our admonition, that he *who thinks he stands may take heed lest he fall.* 2. That which was at the bottom of it was a jealous timorous fancy he had that some of the Egyptians would be so charmed with the beauty of Sarai that, if they should know he was her husband, they would find some way or other to take him off, that they might marry her. The grace Abram was most eminent for was faith; and yet he thus fell through unbelief and distrust of the divine Providence, even *after God had appeared to him twice.* Alas ! what will become of the willows, when the cedars are thus shaken ?

Verses 14–20

Here is, I. The danger Sarai was in of having her chastity violated by the king of Egypt. They recommended her to the king, and she was presently taken into Pharaoh's house, as Esther into the seraglio of Ahasuerus (Esth. ii. 8), in order to her being taken into his bed.

II. The deliverance of Sarai from this danger. For if God did not deliver us we should soon be ruined. He deals not with us according to our deserts.

1. God chastised Pharaoh, and so prevented the progress of his sin. Those are happy chastisements that hinder us in a sinful way, and effectually bring us to our duty.

2. Pharaoh reproved Abram, and then dismissed him with respect.

(1) The reproof was calm, but very just: *What is this that thou hast done?* Pharaoh reasons with him: *Why didst thou not tell me that she was thy wife?* intimating that, if he had known this, he would not have taken her into his house. We have often found more of virtue, honour, and conscience, in some people than we thought they possessed; and it ought to be a pleasure to us to be thus disappointed, as Abram was here, who found Pharaoh to be a better man than he expected. Charity teaches us to hope the best.

(2) The dismission was kind and very generous. He restored him his wife without offering any injury to her honour. *Pharaoh commanded his men concerning him.* He appointed them, when Abram was disposed to return home, after the famine, to conduct him safely out of the country, as his convoy.

Observe a resemblance between this deliverance of Abram out of Egypt and the deliverance of his seed thence: 430 years after Abram went into Egypt on occasion of a famine they went thither on occasion of a famine also; he was fetched out with great plagues on Pharaoh, so were they. For God's care of his people is the same *yesterday, to-day, and for ever.*

JAMIESON, FAUSSET, BROWN

10. there was a famine . . . and Abram went down into Egypt—did not go back to the place of his nativity, as regretting his pilgrimage and despising the promised land (Heb. 11:15), but withdrew for a while into a neighboring country. **11-13.** Sarai's complexion, coming from a mountainous country, would be fresh and fair compared with the faces of Egyptian women which were sallow. The counsel of Abram to her was true in words, but it was a deception, intended to give an impression that she was no more than his sister. His conduct was culpable and inconsistent with his character as a servant of God: it showed a reliance on worldly policy more than a trust in the promise; and he not only sinned himself, but tempted Sarai to sin also. **14. when Abram was come into Egypt**—It appears from the monuments of that country that at the time of Abram's visit a monarchy had existed for several centuries. The seat of government was in the Delta, the most northern part of the country, the very quarter in which Abram must have arrived. They were a race of shepherd kings, in close alliance with the people of Canaan.

15. the woman was taken into Pharaoh's house—Eastern kings have for ages claimed the privilege of taking to their harem an unmarried woman which they like. The father or brother may deplore the removal as a calamity, but the royal right is never resisted nor questioned. **16. he entreated Abram well for her sake**—The presents are just what one pastoral chief would give to another.

18-20. Here is a most humiliating rebuke, and Abram deserved it. Had not God interfered, he might have been tempted to stay in Egypt and forget the promise (Ps. 105:13, 15). Often still does God rebuke His people and remind them through enemies that this world is not their rest.

ADAM CLARKE

10. *There was a famine in the land.* Of Canaan. God made it desolate for the wickedness of those who dwelt in it.

11. *Thou art a fair woman to look upon.* Widely differing in her complexion from the swarthy Egyptians, and consequently more likely to be coveted by them. It appears that Abram supposed they would not scruple to take away the life of the husband in order to have the undisturbed possession of the wife.

13. *Say, I pray thee, thou art my sister.* Abram did not wish his wife to tell a falsehood, but he wished her to suppress a part of the truth. From chap. xx. 12, it is evident she was his stepsister, i.e., his sister by his father, but by a different mother.

15. *The woman was taken into Pharaoh's house. Pharaoh* appears to have been the common appellative of the shepherd kings of Egypt, who had conquered this land. The word is supposed to signify "king" in the ancient Egyptian language. When a woman was brought into the harem of the Eastern princes, she underwent for a considerable time certain purifications before she was brought into the king's presence. It was in this interim that God *plagued Pharaoh and his house with plagues,* so that Sarai was restored before she could have been taken to the bed of the Egyptian king.

16. *He had sheep, and oxen.* As some of these terms are liable to be confounded, and as they frequently occur, especially in the Pentateuch, it may be necessary to consider and fix their meaning in this place. *Sheep; tson,* from *tsaan,* to be "plentiful" or "abundant"; a proper term for the Eastern sheep, which almost constantly bring forth twins, Cant. iv. 2, and sometimes three and even four at a birth. Hence their great fruitfulness is often alluded to in the Scripture. See Ps. lxv. 13; cxliv. 13. But under this same term, which almost invariably means a "flock," both sheep and goats are included. *Oxen; bakar,* from the root, to "examine, look out," because of the full, broad, steady, unmoved look of most animals of the beef kind. *He asses; chamorim,* from *chamar,* to be "disturbed, muddy"; probably from the dull, stupid appearance of this animal, as if it were always affected with melancholy. *She asses; athonoth,* from *ethan,* "strength," probably the strong animal, as being superior in muscular force to every other animal of its size. Under this term both the male and female are sometimes understood. *Camels; gemallim,* from *gamal,* to "recompense, return, repay"; so called from its resentment of injuries, and revengeful temper, for which it is proverbial in the countries of which it is a native. From this enumeration of the riches of Abram we may conclude that this patriarch led a pastoral and itinerant life.

17. *The Lord plagued Pharaoh.* What these plagues were we know not. In the parallel case, chap. xx. 18, all the females in the family of Abimelech, who had taken Sarah in nearly the same way, were made barren; possibly this might have been the case here; yet much more seems to be signified by the expression *great plagues.* Whatever these plagues were, it is evident they were understood by Pharaoh as proofs of the disapprobation of God; and, consequently, even at this time in Egypt there was some knowledge of the primitive and true religion.

20. *Commanded his men concerning him.* Gave particular and strict orders to afford Abram and his family every accommodation for their journey; for having received a great increase of cattle and servants, it was necessary that he should have the favor of the king, and his permission to remove from Egypt with so large a property.

MATTHEW HENRY — CHAPTER 13

Verses 1–4

1. Abram's return out of Egypt, *v.* 1. He came himself and brought all his with him back again to Canaan.

II. His wealth: *He was very rich, v.* 2. He was very *heavy*, so the Hebrew word signifies; for *riches are a burden.* There is a burden of care in getting them, fear in keeping them, temptation in using them,

JAMIESON, FAUSSET, BROWN — CHAPTER 13

Vss. 1-18. Return from Egypt. **1. went up . . . south**—Palestine being a highland country, the entrance from Egypt by its southern boundary is a continual ascent. **2. very rich**—compared with the pastoral tribes to which Abraham belonged. An Arab sheik is considered rich who has a hundred or two hundred tents, from sixty to a hundred camels,

ADAM CLARKE — CHAPTER 13

1. *Abram went up out of Egypt . . . into the south.* Probably the south of Canaan.

2. *Abram was very rich.* The property of these patriarchal times did not consist in flocks only, but also in *silver* and *gold;* and in all these respects Abram was "exceeding rich."

MATTHEW HENRY

guilt in abusing them, sorrow in losing them, and a burden of account, at last, to be given up concerning them. God, in his providence, sometimes makes good men rich men, and teaches them how to abound, as well as how to suffer want. Though it is hard for a rich man to get to heaven, yet it is not impossible, Mark x. 23, 24. Outward prosperity, if well managed, furnishes an opportunity of doing so much the more good.

III. His removal to Beth-el, *v.* 3, 4. Thither he went, not only because there he had formerly had his tent, but because there he had formerly had his altar. Long afterwards God sent Jacob to this same place on that errand (*ch.* xxxv. 1). We have need to be reminded of our solemn vows; and perhaps the place where they were made may help to bring them afresh to mind, and it may therefore do us good to visit it.

IV. His devotion there. His altar was gone, so that he could not offer sacrifice; but *he called on the name of the Lord*, as he had done, *ch.* xii. 8. Abram did not leave his religion behind him in Egypt, as many do in their travels.

Verses 5–9

An unhappy falling out between Abram and Lot, who had hitherto been inseparable companions.

I. The occasion of their quarrel was their riches. Riches are often an occasion of strife and contention. Poverty and travail, wants and wanderings, could not separate between Abram and Lot; but riches did. Friends are soon lost; but God is a friend from whose love neither the height of prosperity nor the depth of adversity shall separate us.

II. The strife began between *the herdsmen of Abram's cattle and the herdsmen of Lot's cattle*, *v.* 7. They strove which should have the better pasture or the better water.

III. The aggravation of the quarrel was that *the Canaanite and the Perizzite dwelt then in the land*; this made the quarrel, 1. Very dangerous. 2. Very scandalous. The quarrels of professors are the reproach of profession, and give occasion, as much as anything, to the enemies of the Lord to blaspheme.

IV. The making up of this quarrel was very happy. It is best to preserve the peace, that it be not broken; but the next best is, if differences do happen, with all speed to accommodate them. The motion for staying this strife was made by Abram.

1. His petition for peace was very affectionate: *Let there be no strife, I pray thee.* Abram knew how to turn away wrath with a soft answer; he made the first overture of reconciliation. The people of God should always approve themselves a peaceable people; whatever others are for, they must be for peace.

2. His plea for peace was very cogent. (1) "Let there be no strife *between me and thee*. Let the Canaanites and Perizzites contend about trifles; but let not thee and me fall out, who know better things, and look for a better country." The remembrance of old friendships should quickly put an end to new quarrels which at any time happen. (2) Let it be remembered that *we are brethren*. We are rational creatures, and should be ruled by reason. We are men, and not brutes, men, and not children. We are brethren. Men of the same nature, of the same kindred and family, of the same religion, companions in obedience, companions in patience.

3. His proposal for peace was very fair. "Why should we quarrel for room, while there is room enough for us both?" He offers him a sufficient share of the land they were in. He gives him his choice, and offers to take up with his leavings: *If thou wilt take the left hand, I will go to the right.* There was all the reason in the world that Abram should choose first; yet he recedes from his right. It is a noble conquest to be willing to yield for the sake of peace; it is the conquest of ourselves, and our own pride and passion, Matt. v.

Verses 10–13

The choice that Lot made when he parted from Abram. Abram having offered him the choice, without compliment he accepted it, and made his election. Passion and selfishness make men rude.

I. How much he had an eye to the goodness of the land. He *beheld all the plain of Jordan*, the flat country in which Sodom stood, that it was admirably *well watered everywhere*. It would yield him a comfortable settlement, and in such a fruitful soil he should certainly thrive, and grow very rich: and this was all he looked at. But what came of it? Why, the next news we hear of him is that he is in the briars among them, he and his carried captive. At last, God fired the town over his head, and forced him to the mountain for safety who chose the plain

JAMIESON, FAUSSET, BROWN

a thousand sheep and goats respectively. And Abraham being very rich, must have far exceeded that amount of pastoral property. "Gold and silver" being rare among these peoples, his probably arose from the sale of his produce in Egypt.

3. went on his journeys—His progress would be by slow marches and frequent encampments as he had to regulate his movements by the prospect of water and pasturage. **unto the place . . . between Beth-el and Hai**—"a conspicuous hill—its topmost summit resting on the rocky slopes below, and distinguished by its olive groves—offering a natural base for the altar and a fitting shade for the tent of the patriarch" [STANLEY]. **4. there Abram called on the name of the Lord**—He felt a strong desire to reanimate his faith and piety on the scene of his former worship: it might be to express humility and penitence for his misconduct in Egypt or thankfulness for deliverance from perils—to embrace the first opportunity on returning to Canaan of leading his family to renew allegiance to God and offer the typical sacrifices which pointed to the blessings of the promise.

7. And there was a strife—Abraham's character appears here in a most amiable light. Having a strong sense of religion, he was afraid of doing anything that might tend to injure its character or bring discredit on its name, and he rightly judged that such unhappy effects would be produced if two persons whom nature and grace had so closely connected should come to a rupture. Waiving his right to dictate, he gave the freedom of choice to Lot. The conduct of Abraham was not only disinterested and peaceable, but generous and condescending in an extraordinary degree, exemplifying the Scripture precepts (Matt. 6:32; Rom. 12:10, 11; Phil. 2:4).

10. Lot lifted up his eyes—Travellers say that from the top of this hill, a little "to the east of Bethel," they can see the Jordan, the broad meadows on either bank, and the waving line of verdure which marks the course of the stream. **11. Then Lot chose him all the plain**—a choice excellent from a worldly point of view, but most inexpedient for his best interests. He seems, though a good man, to have been too much under the influence of a selfish and covetous spirit: and how many, alas! imperil the good of their souls for the prospect of worldly advantage.

ADAM CLARKE

F. B. MEYER:

Abram and Lot part. The patriarch, like a restored backslider, made his way back to the old spot on the highlands of Bethel, where his first tent and altar had stood. Throughout his wanderings hitherto there had been a depressing element of worldliness in his camp through the presence of Lot who, like many more, was swept along by his uncle's religion, but had little of his own. Feeling that separation was inevitable and that God would surely care for him, Abram offered Lot his choice (Ps. 16:5). The younger man chose according to the sight of his eyes. In his judgment he gained the world—but see 2 Pet. 2:7, 8. The world is full of Lots—shallow, impulsive, doomed to be revealed by their choice and end. "Let there be no strife!" Blessed are the peacemakers! Wherever the interests of peace can be conserved through the sacrifice of your own interests, be prepared to forfeit the advantage; but stand like a rock when God's truth is in balance.—*Bible Commentary*

6. *Their substance was great.* As their families increased, it was necessary their flocks should increase also, as from those flocks they derived their clothing, food, and drink. Many also were offered in sacrifice to God. *They could not dwell together.* (1) Because their flocks were great. (2) Because the Canaanites and the Perizzites had already occupied a considerable part of the land. (3) Because there appears to have been envy between the herdmen of Abram and Lot. To prevent disputes among them, that might have ultimately disturbed the peace of the two families, it was necessary that a separation should take place.

9. *Is not the whole land before thee?* As the patriarch or head of the family, Abram, by prescriptive right, might have chosen his own portion first, and appointed Lot his; but intent upon peace, and feeling pure and parental affection for his nephew, he permitted him to make his choice first.

11. *Then Lot chose him all the plain.* A little civility or good breeding is of great importance in the concerns of life. Lot either had none, or did not profit by it. He certainly should have left the choice to the patriarch and should have been guided by his counsel; but he took his own way, trusting to his own judgment, and guided only by the sight of his eyes. *He beheld all the plain of Jordan, that it was well watered;* so he chose the land without considering the character of the inhabitants or what advantages or disadvantages it might afford him in spiritual things. This choice, as we shall see in the sequel, had nearly proved the ruin of his body, soul, and family.

MATTHEW HENRY

for wealth and pleasure. Sensual choices are sinful choices, and seldom speed well. In all our choices this principle should overrule us, That that is best for us which is best for our souls.

II. *But the men of Sodom were wicked, v.* 13. Some sinners are the worse for living in a good land. So the Sodomites were. Filthy Sodomites dwell in a city, in a fruitful plain, while faithful Abram and his pious family dwell in tents upon the barren mountains. Now Lot's coming to dwell among the Sodomites may be considered a great mercy to them, and a likely means of bringing them to repentance; for now they had a prophet among them and a preacher of righteousness, and, if they had hearkened to him, they might have been reformed, and the ruin prevented.

Verses 14–18

An account of a gracious visit which God paid to Abram, to confirm the promise to him and his.

I. When it was that God renewed and ratified the promise: 1. After the quarrel was over. 2. After Abram's humble self-denying condescensions to Lot for the preserving of peace. 3. After he had lost the comfortable society of his kinsman, and his heart was saddened, then God came to him with these good words and comfortable words. Lot perhaps had the better land, yet Abram had the better *title.* Lot had the paradise, such as it was, but Abram had the promise.

II. The promises themselves with which God now comforted and enriched Abram. Two things he assures him of—a good land, and a numerous issue to enjoy it.

1. Here is the grant of a good land, a land famous above all lands, for it was to be the holy land, and Immanuel's land. Note, That which God has to show is infinitely better and more desirable than anything that the world has to offer to our view. He secures this land to him and his seed for ever (*v.* 15).

2. Here is the promise of a numerous issue to replenish this good land, so that it should never be lost for want of heirs (*v.* 16). The same God that provides the inheritance provides the heirs.

We are told what Abram did when God had thus confirmed the promise to him, *v.* 18. 1. He *removed his tent.* In compliance with God's will herein, *he removes his tent*, conforming himself to the condition of a pilgrim. 2. He *built there an altar*, in token of his thankfulness to God.

JAMIESON, FAUSSET, BROWN

14, 15. Lift up now thine eyes . . . all the land which thou seest—So extensive a survey of the country, *in all directions*, can be obtained from no other point in the neighborhood; and those plains and hills, then lying desolate before the eyes of the solitary patriarch, were to be peopled with a mighty nation "like the dust of the earth in number," as they were in Solomon's time (I Kings 4:20).

18. plain of Mamre . . . built . . . an altar—grove of Mamre—the renewal of the promise was acknowledged by Abram by a fresh tribute of devout gratitude.

ADAM CLARKE

13. *The men of Sodom were wicked. Raim,* from *ra*, "to break in pieces, destroy, and afflict"; meaning persons who broke the established order of things, destroyed and confounded the distinctions between right and wrong, and who afflicted and tormented both themselves and others. *And sinners, chattaim,* from *chata*, "to miss the mark, to step wrong, to miscarry"; so a sinner is one who is ever aiming at happiness and constantly missing his mark; because, being wicked—radically evil within, every affection and passion depraved and out of order, he seeks for happiness where it never can be found, in worldly honors and possessions, and in sensual gratifications, the end of which is disappointment, affliction, vexation, and ruin. The people of Sodom were "exceedingly sinful and wicked before," or against, the Lord—they were sinners of no common character; they excelled in unrighteousness, and soon filled up the measure of their iniquities.

14. *The Lord said unto Abram.* It is very likely that the Angel of the covenant appeared to Abram in open day, when he could take a distinct view of the length and the breadth of this good land. The revelation made in chap. xv. 5 was evidently made in the night; for then he was called to number the stars; here he is called on to number the dust of the earth. v. 16.

15. *To thee will I give it, and to thy seed for ever.* This land was given to Abram, that it might lineally and legally descend to his posterity; and though Abram himself cannot be said to have possessed it, Acts vii. 5, yet it was the gift of God to him in behalf of his seed; and this was always the design of God, not that Abram himself should possess it, but that his posterity should, till the manifestation of Christ in the flesh. And this is chiefly what is to be understood by the words *for ever,* to the end of the present dispensation and the commencement of the new.

18. *Abram removed his tent.* Continued to travel and pitch in different places, till at last he fixed his tent in the *plain*, or "by the oak," *of Mamre*, see chap. xii. 6, *which is in Hebron;* i.e., the district in which Mamre was situated was called Hebron. Mamre was an Amorite then living, with whom Abram made a league, chap. xiv. 13; and the oak probably went by his name, because he was the possessor of the ground. *Built there an altar unto the Lord.* On which he offered sacrifice, as the word *mizbach*, from *zabach*, "to slay," imports.

CHAPTER 14 (MATTHEW HENRY)

Verses 1–12

An account of the first war that ever we read of in scripture.

I. The parties engaged in it. The invaders were four kings, two of them no less than kings of Shinar and Elam (that is, Chaldea and Persia). The invaded were the kings of five cities that lay near together in the plain of Jordan, namely, Sodom, Gomorrah, Admah, Zeboiim, and Zoar.

II. The occasion of this war was the revolt of the five kings from under the government of Chedorlaomer. Twelve years they served him. Small joy they had of their fruitful land, while thus they were tributaries to a foreign power, and could not call what they had their own. In the thirteenth year, beginning to be weary of their subjection, they rebelled, denied their tribute, and attempted to shake off the yoke and retrieve their ancient liberties. In the fourteenth year, after some pause and preparation, Chedorlaomer, in conjunction with his allies, set himself to chastise and reduce the rebels.

CHAPTER 14 (JAMIESON, FAUSSET, BROWN)

Vss. 1-24. WAR. **1. And it came to pass**—This chapter presents Abram in the unexpected character of a warrior. The occasion was this: The king of Sodom and the kings of the adjoining cities, after having been tributaries for twelve years to the king of Elam, combined to throw off his yoke. To chastise their rebellion, as he deemed it, Chedorlaomer, with the aid of three allies, invaded the territories of the refractory princes, defeated them in a pitched battle where the nature of the ground favored his army (vs. 10), and hastened in triumph on his homeward march, with a large amount of captives and booty, though merely a stranger.

CHAPTER 14 (ADAM CLARKE)

1. *In the days of Amraphel.* Who this king was is not known; and yet, from the manner in which he is spoken of in the text, it would seem that he was a person well known, even when Moses wrote this account. *Tidal king of nations. Goyim,* different peoples or clans. Probably some adventurous person, whose subjects were composed of refugees from different countries.

2. *These made war with Bera.* It appears, from v. 4, that these five Canaanitish kings had been subdued by Chedorlaomer, and were obliged to pay him tribute; and that, having been enslaved by him twelve years, wishing to recover their liberty, they revolted in the thirteenth; in consequence of which Chedorlaomer, the following year, summoned to his assistance three of his vassals, invaded Canaan, fought with and discomfited the kings of the Pentapolis or five cities—Sodom, Gomorrah, Zeboiim, Zoar, and Admah, which were situated in the fruitful plain of Siddim, having previously overrun the whole land.

5. *Rephaims.* A people of Canaan: chap. xv. 20. *Emims.* A people great and many in the days of Moses, and tall as the Anakim. They dwelt among the Moabites, by whom they were reputed *giants;* Deut. ii. 10-11. *Shaveh Kiriathaim.* Rather, as the margin, the "plain of Kiriathaim," which was a city afterwards belonging to Sihon, king of Heshbon; Josh. xiii. 19.

6. *The Horites.* A people that dwelt in Mount Seir, till Esau and his sons drove them thence; Deut. ii. 22. *El-paran.* The "plain or oak of Paran," which was a city in the wilderness of Paran: chap. xxi. 21.

MATTHEW HENRY	JAMIESON, FAUSSET, BROWN	ADAM CLARKE

III. The progress and success of the war. The four kings laid the neighbouring countries waste and enriched themselves with the spoil of them (*v.* 5–7). 1. The forces of the king of Sodom and his allies were routed. 2. The cities were plundered, *v.* 11. 3. Lot was carried captive, *v.* 12. They took Lot among the rest, and his goods. Many an honest man fares the worse for his wicked neighbours. It is therefore our wisdom to separate ourselves and so deliver ourselves, Rev. xviii. 4. Note, When we go out of the way of our duty we put ourselves from under God's protection, and cannot expect that the choices which are made by our lusts should issue to our comfort.

Verses 13–16

We have here an account of the only military action we ever find Abram engaged in, and this he was prompted to, not by his avarice or ambition, but purely by a principle of charity; it was not to enrich himself, but to help his friend.

I. The tidings brought him of his kinsman's distress. 1. He is here called *Abram the Hebrew*, that is, the son and follower of Heber, in whose family the profession of the true religion was kept up in that degenerate age. 2. The tidings were brought by one that had escaped with his life for a prey.

II. The preparations he made for this expedition. This shows that Abram was, 1. A great man, who had so many servants depending upon him. 2. A good man, who not only served God himself, but instructed all about him in the service of God. 3. A wise man, for, though he was a man of peace, yet he disciplined his servants for war. Though our holy religion teaches us to be for peace, yet it does not forbid us to provide for war.

III. His allies and confederates in this expedition. He prevailed with his neighbours, *Aner, Eshcol, and Mamre*, to go along with him. Those who depend on God's help, yet, in times of distress, ought to make use of men's help, as Providence offers it; else they tempt God.

IV. His courage and conduct were very remarkable. 1. There was a great deal of bravery in the enterprise itself, considering the disadvantages he lay under. What could one family of husbandmen and shepherds do against the armies of four princes, who now came fresh from blood and victory? Religion tends to make men, not cowardly, but truly valiant. The true Christian is the true hero. 2. There was a great deal of policy in the management of it. Note, Honest policy is a good friend both to our safety and to our usefulness. The serpent's head (provided it be nothing akin to the old serpent) may well become a good Christian's body, especially if it have a dove's eye in it, Matt. x. 16.

V. His success was very considerable, *v.* 15, 16. He defeated his enemies, and rescued his friends; and we do not find that he sustained any loss.

1. He rescued his kinsman; twice here he is called his *brother Lot*. The remembrance of the relation that was between them, both by nature and grace, made him forget the little quarrel that had been between them. Note, (1) We ought to be ready, whenever it is in the power of our hands, to succour and relieve those that are in distress. (2) Though others have been wanting in their duty to us, yet we must not therefore deny our duty to them. Some have said that they can more easily forgive their enemies than their friends; but we shall see ourselves obliged to forgive both.

2. He rescued the rest of the captives, for Lot's sake, though they were strangers to him and such as he was under no obligation to at all. Note, As we have opportunity we must do good to all men.

Verses 17–20

This paragraph begins with the mention of the respect which the king of Sodom paid to Abram, but, before a particular account is given of this, the story of Melchizedek is briefly related.

I. Who he was. He was *king of Salem* and *priest of the most high God*; and other glorious things are said of him, Heb. vii. 1, &c. 1. Rabbinical writers conclude that Melchizedek was Shem the son of Noah. But why should his name be changed? And how came he to settle in Canaan? 2. Many Christian writers have thought that this was an appearance of the Son of God himself. He appeared to him as a righteous king, owning a righteous cause, and giving peace. It is difficult to imagine that any mere man should be said to *be without father, without mother, and without descent, having neither beginning of days nor end of life*, Heb. vii. 3. 3. The most commonly received opinion is that Melchizedek was a Canaanitish prince, that reigned in Salem, and kept up the true religion there; but, if so, why should his name

they took Lot . . . and his goods, and departed—How would the conscience of that young man now upbraid him for his selfish folly and ingratitude in withdrawing from his kind and pious relative! Whenever we go out of the path of duty, we put ourselves away from God's protection, and cannot expect that the choice we make will be for our lasting good. **13. there came one that had escaped**—Abram might have excused himself from taking any active concern in his "brother," i.e., nephew, who little deserved that he should incur trouble or danger on *his* account. But Abram, far from rendering evil for evil, resolved to take immediate measures for the rescue of Lot.

14. And when Abram heard that his brother was taken captive, he armed his trained servants—domestic slaves, such as are common in Eastern countries still and are considered and treated as members of the family. If Abram could spare three hundred and eighteen slaves and leave a sufficient number to take care of the flocks, what a large establishment he must have had. **15, 16. he divided himself . . . by night**—This war between the petty princes of ancient Canaan is exactly the same as the frays and skirmishes between Arab chiefs in the present day. When a defeated party resolves to pursue the enemy, they wait till they are fast asleep; then, as they have no idea of posting sentinels, they rush upon them from different directions, strike down the tent poles—if there is any fight at all, it is the fray of a tumultuous mob—a panic commonly ensues, and the whole contest is ended with little or no loss on either side.

18. Melchizedek—This victory conferred a public benefit on that part of the country; and Abram, on his return, was treated with high respect and consideration, particularly by the king of Sodom and Melchizedek, who seems to have been one of the few native princes, if not the only one, who knew and worshipped, "the most high God," whom Abram served. This king who was a type of the Saviour (Heb. 7:1), came to bless God for the victory which had been won, and in the name of God to bless Abram, by whose arms it had been achieved—a pious acknowledgment which we should imitate on succeeding in any lawful enterprise.

7. *En-mishpat.* The "well of judgment"; probably so called from the judgment pronounced by God on Moses and Aaron for their rebellion at that place; Num. xx. 1-10. *Amalekites.* So called afterwards, from Amalek, son of Esau; chap. xxxvi. 12. *Hazenon-tamar.* Called, in the Chaldee, Engaddi; a city in the land of Canaan, which fell to the lot of Judah; Josh. xv. 62. See also 2 Chron. xx. 2. It appears, from Cant. i. 13, to have been a very fruitful place.

8. *Bela (the same is Zoar).* That is, it was called Zoar after the destruction of Sodom, mentioned in chap. xix.

10. *Slimepits.* Places where *asphaltus* or *bitumen* sprang out of the ground; this substance abounded in that country. *Fell there.* It either signifies they were defeated on this spot, and many of them slain, or that multitudes of them had perished in the bitumen pits which abounded there; that the place was full of pits we learn from the Hebrew, which reads here *beeroth beeroth*, "pits, pits," i.e., multitudes of pits. A bad place to maintain a fight on or to be obliged to run through in order to escape.

12. *They took Lot.* The people, being exceedingly wicked, had provoked God to afflict them by means of those marauding kings; and Lot also suffered, being found in company with the workers of iniquity.

13. *Abram the Hebrew.* See on chap. x. 21. It is very likely that Abram had this appellation from his coming from beyond the river Euphrates to enter Canaan; for *haibri*, which we render *the Hebrew*, comes from *abar*, to "pass over," or come from beyond. *These were confederate with Abram.* It seems that a kind of convention was made between Abram and the three brothers, Mamre, Eshcol, and Aner, who were probably all chieftains in the vicinity of Abram's dwelling: all petty princes, similar to the nine kings before mentioned.

14. *He armed his trained servants.* These amounted to 318 in number: and how many were in the divisions of Mamre, Eshcol, and Aner, we know not; but they and their men certainly accompanied him in this expedition. See v. 24.

15. *And he divided himself against them.* It required both considerable courage and address in Abram to lead him to attack the victorious armies of these four kings with so small a number of troops, and on this occasion both his skill and his courage are exercised. His affection for Lot appears to have been his chief motive; he cheerfully risks his life for that nephew who had lately chosen the best part of the land and left his uncle to live as he might, on what he did not think worthy his own acceptance. But it is the property of a great and generous mind not only to forgive but to forget offenses, and at all times to repay evil with good.

16. *And he brought back . . . the women also.* This is brought in by the sacred historian with peculiar interest and tenderness. All who read the account must be in pain for the fate of wives and daughters fallen into the hands of a ferocious, licentious, and victorious soldiery. Other spoils the routed confederates might have left behind; and yet on their swift asses, camels, and dromedaries, have carried off the female captives. However, Abram had disposed his attack so judiciously, and so promptly executed his measures, that not only all the baggage, but all the females also, were recovered.

17. *The king of Sodom went out to meet him.* This could not have been Bera, mentioned in v. 2, for it seems pretty evident, from v. 10, that both he and Birsha, king of Gomorrah, were slain at the bitumen pits in the vale of Siddim; but another person in the meantime might have succeeded to the government.

18. *And Melchizedek king of Salem.* A thousand idle stories have been told about this man, and a thousand idle conjectures spent on the subject of his short history given here and in Hebrews vii. At present it is only necessary to state that he appears to have been as real a personage as Bera, Birsha, or Shinab, though we have no more of his genealogy than we have of theirs. *Brought forth bread and wine.* Certainly to refresh Abram and his men, exhausted with the late battle and fatigues of the journey; not in the way of *sacrifice;* this is an idle con-

MATTHEW HENRY

occur here only in all the story of Abram? The *Arabic Catena* gives this account of Melchizedek, That he was the son of Heraclim, the son of Peleg, the son of Eber, and that his mother's name was Salathiel, the daughter of Gomer, the son of Japheth, the son of Noah.

II. What he did. 1. He *brought forth bread and wine*, for the refreshment of Abram and his soldiers, and in congratulation of their victory. This he did as a king. 2. As priest of the most high God, he blessed Abram, which we may suppose a greater refreshment to Abram than his bread and wine were. Thus God, having raised up his Son Jesus, has sent him to bless us, as one having authority; and those whom he blesses are blessed indeed.

III. What he said, *v.* 19, 20. Two things were said by him:—1. He blessed Abram from God. Observe the titles he here gives to God, which are very glorious. (1) *The most high God.* (2) *Possessor of heaven and earth*, that is, rightful owner, and sovereign Lord, of all the creatures, because he made them. 2. He blessed God for Abram (*v.* 20): and *blessed be the most high God.*

IV. What was done to him: *Abram gave him tithes of all*, that is, of the spoils, Heb. vii. 4. This may be looked upon, 1. As a gratuity presented to Melchizedek, by way of return for his tokens of respect. 2. As an offering vowed and dedicated to the most high God, and therefore put into the hands of Melchizedek his priest. (1) When we have received some signal mercy from God, it is very fit that we should express our thankfulness by some special act of pious charity. (2) That the tenth of our increase is a very fit proportion to be set apart for the honour of God and the service of his sanctuary. (3) That Jesus Christ, our great Melchizedek, is to have homage done him, and to be humbly acknowledged by every one of us as our king and priest; and not only the tithe of all, but all we have, must be surrendered and given up to him.

Verses 21–24

We have here an account of what passed between Abram and the king of Sodom.

I. The king of Sodom's grateful offer to Abram (*v.* 21): *Give me the soul, and take thou the substance*; so the Hebrew reads it. Here he fairly begs the persons, but as freely bestows the goods on Abram.

II. Abram's generous refusal of this offer. He not only resigned the persons to him, but he restored all the goods too. He would not take *from a thread to a shoe-latchet.* What are all the ornaments and delights of sense to one that has God and heaven ever in his eye?

1. Abram ratifies this resolution with a solemn oath. The ceremony used in this oath: *I have lifted up my hand.* In religious swearing we appeal to God's knowledge of our truth and sincerity and imprecate his wrath if we swear falsely, and the *lifting up of the hand* is very significant and expressive of both.

2. He backs his refusal with a good reason: *Lest thou shouldest say, I have made Abram rich*, which would reflect reproach, (1) Upon the promise and covenant of God. And, (2) Upon the piety and charity of Abram. The people of God must, for their credit's sake, take heed of doing anything that looks mean or mercenary, or that savours of covetousness and self-seeking.

CHAPTER 15

Verse 1

The time when God made this treaty with Abram. 1. After that famous act of generous charity which Abram had done, in rescuing his friends and neighbours out of distress, and that, *not for price nor reward.* 2. After that victory which he had obtained over four kings.

II. The manner in which God conversed with Abram: which supposes Abram awake, and some visible appearance of the Shechinah, or some sensible token of the presence of the divine glory.

III. The gracious assurance God gave him of his favour to him.

1. He called him by name—*Abram.* God's good word does us good when it is spoken by his Spirit to us in particular. The word says, *Ho, every one* (Isa. lv. 1), the Spirit says, *Ho, such a one.*

2. He cautioned him against being disquieted and confounded: *Fear not, Abram.* Let the sinners

JAMIESON, FAUSSET, BROWN

TODAY'S DICTIONARY OF THE BIBLE:

Melchizedek—*king of righteousness*—the king of *Salem*. All we know of him is recorded in Gen. 14:18–20. He is subsequently mentioned only once in the Old Testament, in Ps. 110:4. The typical significance of his history is set forth in detail in Hebrews 7. The apostle there points out the superiority of his priesthood to that of Aaron in these several respects: (1) Even Abraham paid him tithes; (2) he blessed Abraham; (3) he is the type of a Priest who lives forever; (4) Levi, yet unborn, paid him tithes in the person of Abraham; (5) the permanence of his priesthood in Christ implied the abrogation of the Levitical system; (6) he was made priest not without an oath; and (7) his priesthood can neither be transmitted nor interrupted by death: "This man, because he continueth ever, hath an unchangeable priesthood."

His appearance in Scripture as the king of a city called *Salem* = peace and having a name meaning "king of righteousness" has made him the perfect object of speculation. A fragment of a document from cave eleven at Qumran gives evidence of the Jewish speculation about Melchizedek. It sees him as a divinely appointed judge in the court of heaven. Another Jewish tradition saw him as Shem, the son of Noah. Melchizedek was a Canaanite prince, a worshiper of the true God, and in his brief history and character an instructive type of our Lord, the great High Priest (Heb. 5:6, 7; 6:20).

he gave him tithes of all—Here is an evidence of Abram's piety, as well as of his valor; for it was to a priest or official mediator between God and him that Abram gave a tenth of the spoil—a token of his gratitude and in honor of a divine ordinance (Prov. 3:9). **21. the king of Sodom said . . . Give me the persons**—According to the war customs still existing among the Arab tribes, Abram might have retained the recovered goods—and his right was acknowledged by the king of Sodom. But with honest pride, and a generosity unknown in that part of the world, he replied with strong phraseology common to the East, "I have lifted up mine hand [i.e., I have sworn] unto the Lord that I will not take from a thread even to a sandal-thong—that I will not take any thing that is thine, lest thou shouldst say, I have made Abram rich."

CHAPTER 15

Vss. 1-21. Divine Encouragement. **1. After these things**—the conquest of the invading kings. **the word of the Lord**—a phrase used, when connected with a vision, to denote a prophetic message.

ADAM CLARKE

jecture. *He was the priest of the most high God.* He had preserved in his family and among his subjects the worship of the true God, and the primitive patriarchal institutions; by these the father of every family was both king and priest, so Melchizedek, being a worshipper of the true God, was priest among the people, as well as king over them.

Melchizedek is called here *king of Salem*, and the most judicious interpreters allow that by Salem, Jerusalem is meant. That it bore this name anciently is evident from Ps. lxxvi. 1-2: "In Judah is God known: his name is great in Israel. In Salem also is his tabernacle, and his dwelling place in Zion." From the use made of this part of the sacred history by David, Ps. cx. 4, and by St. Paul, Heb. vii. 1-10, we learn that there was something very mysterious, and at the same time typical, in the person, name, office, residence, and government of this Canaanitish prince. (1) In his *person* he was a representative and type of Christ; see the scriptures above referred to. (2) His name signifies "my righteous king," or "king of righteousness." (3) *Office;* he was a *priest of the most high God.* The word *cohen*, which signifies both "prince" and "priest," because the patriarchs sustained this double office, has both its root and proper signification in the Arabic; *kahana* signifies "to approach, draw near, have intimate access to"; and from hence to officiate as priest before God, and thus have intimate access to the divine presence. (4) His *residence;* he was king of *Salem. Shalam* signifies "to make whole, complete, or perfect"; and hence it means "peace." Christ is called "The Prince of Peace" because, by His incarnation, sacrifice, and mediation, He procures and establishes peace between God and man. His residence is peace and quietness and assurance forever in every believing, upright heart.

19. *And he blessed him.* This was a part of the priest's office, to bless in the name of the Lord forever. See the form of this blessing, Num. vi. 23-26; and for the meaning of the word "to bless," see Gen. ii. 3.

20. *And he gave him tithes.* A tenth part of all the spoils he had taken from the confederate kings. These Abram gave as a tribute to the most high God, who, being the "possessor of heaven and earth," dispenses all spiritual and temporal favors, and demands the gratitude, and submissive, loving obedience, of all His subjects. Almost all nations of the earth have agreed in giving a tenth part of their property to be employed in religious uses.

22. *I have lift up mine hand.* The primitive mode of appealing to God, and calling Him to witness a particular transaction.

23. *From a thread even to a shoelatchet.* This was certainly a proverbial mode of expression.

24. *Save only that which the young men have eaten.* His own servants had partaken of the victuals which the confederate kings had carried away; see v. 11. This was unavoidable, and this is all he claims; but as he had no right to prescribe the same liberal conduct to his assistants, Aner, Eshcol, and Mamre, he left them to claim the share that by right of conquest belonged to them of the recaptured booty.

CHAPTER 15

1. *The word of the Lord came unto Abram.* This is the first place where God is represented as revealing himself by His word. Some learned men suppose that the *debar Yehovah*, translated here *word of the Lord*, means the same with the *logos tou theou* of St. John, chap. i. 1. There have been various conjectures concerning the manner in which God revealed His will, not only to the patriarchs, but also to the prophets, evangelists, and apostles. It seems to have been done in different ways. (1) By a personal appearance of Him who was afterwards incarnated for the salvation of mankind. (2) By an audible voice, sometimes accompanied with emblematical appearances. (3) By visions which took place either in the night in ordinary sleep, or when the persons were cast into a temporary trance by daylight, or when about their ordinary business. (4) By the ministry of angels appearing

MATTHEW HENRY

in Sion be afraid, but fear not, Abram.

3. He assured him of safety and happiness, that he should for ever be, (1) As safe as God himself could keep him. Not only the God of Israel, but a God to Israel. (2) As happy as God himself could make him: I will be *thy exceedingly great reward*; not only thy rewarder, but thy reward. Abram had generously refused the rewards which the king of Sodom offered him.

Verses 2–6

The assurance given to Abram of a numerous offspring which should descend from him.

I. Abram's repeated complaint, *v.* 2, 3. This was that which gave occasion to this promise. The great affliction that sat heavy upon Abram was the want of a child. Though we must never complain of God, yet we have leave to complain to him, and it is some ease to a burdened spirit to open its case to a faithful and compassionate friend: such a friend God is. Now his complaint is four-fold:—1. That he had no child (*v.* 3). 2. That he was never likely to have any, intimated in that, *I go*, or "*I am going, childless*, going into years, going down the hill apace." 3. That his servants were for the present and were likely to be to him instead of sons. 4. That the want of a son was so great a trouble to him that it took away the comfort of all his enjoyments: "All is nothing to me, if I have not a son." But, If we suppose that Abram, herein, had an eye to the promised seed, the importunity of his desire was very commendable: all was nothing to him, if he had not an assurance of his relation to the Messiah, of which God had already encouraged him to maintain the expectation. "This, and the other, I have; but what will all this avail me, if I go Christless?"

II. God's gracious answer to this complaint. 1. God gave him an express promise of a son, *v.* 4. This that is born in thy house *shall not be thy heir*, as thou fearest, but one that shall *come forth out of thy own bowels shall be thy heir*. 2. To affect him the more with this promise, he took him out, and showed him the stars, and then tells him, *So shall thy seed be*, *v.* 5. (1) So numerous; the stars seem innumerable to a common eye: Abram feared he should have no child at all. (2) So illustrious, resembling the stars in splendour. Abram's seed, according to his flesh, were like the dust of the earth (*ch.* xiii. 16), but his spiritual seed are like the stars of heaven, not only numerous, but glorious, and very precious.

III. Abram's firm belief of the promise God now made him, and God's favourable acceptance of his faith, *v.* 6. See how the apostle magnifies this faith of Abram, and makes it a standing example, Rom. iv. 19–21. *God counted it to him for righteousness;* that is, upon the score of this he was accepted of God, and, as the rest of the patriarchs, by faith he *obtained witness that he was righteous*, Heb. xi. 4. This is urged in the New Testament to prove that we are justified by faith without the works of the law (Rom. iv. 3; Gal. iii. 6). All believers are justified as Abram was, and it was his faith that was *counted to him for righteousness.*

Verses 7–11

The assurance given to Abram of the land of Canaan for an inheritance.

I. God declares his purpose concerning it, *v.* 7. Those that are sure of an interest in the promised seed will see no reason to doubt of a title to the promised land. If Christ is ours, heaven is ours. When he believed the former promise (*v.* 6) then God explained and ratified this to him. Three things God here reminds Abram of, for his encouragement concerning the promise of this good land:—

1. What God is in himself: *I am the Lord Jehovah.* "I can give it to thee, whatever opposition may be made, though by the sons of Anak." God never promises more than he is able to perform, as men often do.

2. What he had done for Abram. He had brought him out of Ur of the Chaldees. The Jewish writers have a tradition that Abram was cast into a fiery furnace for refusing to worship idols, and was miraculously delivered. A foundation mercy, the beginning of mercy, peculiar mercy to Abram, and therefore a pledge and earnest of further mercy, Isa. lxvi. 9.

3. What he intended to do yet further for him: "*I brought thee* hither, on purpose *to give thee this land to inherit it*, not only to possess it, but to possess it as an inheritance, which is the sweetest and surest title." The great thing God designs in all his dealings with his people is to bring them safely to heaven.

II. Abram desires a sign: *Whereby shall I know that I shall inherit it ?*, *v.* 8. 1. For the strengthening and confirming of his own faith; he believed (*v.* 6), but

JAMIESON, FAUSSET, BROWN

Fear not, Abram—When the excitement of the enterprise was over, he had become a prey to despondency and terror at the probable revenge that might be meditated against him. To dispel his fear, he was favored with this gracious announcement. Having such a promise, how well did it become him (and all God's people who have the same promise) to dismiss fears, and cast all burdens on the Lord (Ps. 27:3).

2. Lord God, what wilt thou give?—To his mind the declaration, "I am thy exceeding great reward," had but one meaning, or was viewed but in one particular light, as bearing on the fulfilment of the promise, and he was still experiencing the sickness of hope deferred. **Eliezer of Damascus . . . one born in my house is mine heir**—According to the usage of nomadic tribes, his chief confidential servant would be heir to his possessions and honors. But this man could have become his son only by adoption; and how sadly would that have come short of the parental hopes he had been encouraged to entertain! His language betrayed a latent spirit of fretfulness or perhaps a temporary failure in the very virtue for which he is so renowned—and absolute submission to God's time, as well as way, of accomplishing His promise.

4. This shall not be thine heir—To the first part of his address no reply was given; but having renewed it in a spirit of more becoming submission, "whereby shall I know that I shall inherit it," he was delighted by a most explicit promise of Canaan, which was immediately confirmed by a remarkable ceremony.

JOHN LANGE:

"And he believed in the Lord." This cannot be either an element of a dream or the frame of mind prepared peculiarly for visions, for it is an act of faith on the part of Abram, which was counted to him for righteousness by Jehovah. Knobel remarks: "Abram did not laugh, incredulously, as in the Elohistic section (17:17)," as if a believer, in the long delay of the promise, could never fall into doubt (although there is no mention of any incredulity in the passage referred to). Keil asks: "How did Moses know that Abram believed? and that Jehovah counted it to him for righteousness?" He answers: "He proves his faith, because, according to the following directions, he brought the sacrifices, and because what Jehovah did with the animals was a real declaration on his part that he counted to Abram his faith for righteousness." We must distinguish, however, the inward events from these sacramental signs in which they are visibly manifested and sealed. The faith of Abram in the promise of a bodily heir was the central point in the development of his faith; with this faith he enjoyed the consciousness that Jehovah counted it to him for righteousness. Justification by faith, as an experience of the inner life, manifests itself in the peace of God; and Abram could have given testimony as to this to his children if nothing had occurred as to the sacrificial animals and their consumption by fire.

—*Commentary on the Holy Scriptures*

ADAM CLARKE

in human bodies, and performing certain miracles to accredit their mission. (5) By the powerful agency of the Spirit of God upon the mind, giving it a strong conception and supernatural persuasion of the truth of the things perceived by the understanding. We shall see all these exemplified in the course of the work. It was probably in the third sense that the revelation in the text was given; for it is said, God appeared to Abram in a vision.

I am thy shield. Can it be supposed that Abram understood these words as promising him temporal advantages at all corresponding to the magnificence of these promises? If he did he was disappointed through the whole course of his life, for he never enjoyed such a state of worldly prosperity as could justify the strong language in the text.

6. *And he believed in the Lord: and he counted it to him for righteousness.* This **I conceive to be one of the most important passages in the whole Old Testament. It properly contains and specifies that doctrine of justification by faith which engrosses so considerable a share of the Epistles of St. Paul, and at the foundation of which is the atonement made by the Son of God: *And he* (Abram) *believed* (put faith) in Jehovah, *and he counted it* (the faith he put in Jehovah) *to him for righteousness* (or justification), though there was no act in the case but that of the mind and heart, no work of any kind. Hence the doctrine of justification by faith, without any merit of works; for in this case there could be none—no works of Abram which could merit the salvation of the whole human race.**

8. *And he said, Lord God. Adonai Yehovah*, "my Lord Jehovah." *Adonai* is the word which the Jews in reading always substitute for Jehovah, as they count it impious to pronounce this name. *Adonai* signifies my "director, basis, supporter, prop, or stay"; and scarcely a more appropriate name can be given to that God who is the Framer and Director of every righteous word and action; the Basis or Foundation on which every rational hope rests; the Supporter of the souls and bodies of men, as well as of the universe in general; the Prop and Stay of the weak and fainting, and the Buttress that shores up the building, which otherwise must necessarily fall. This word often occurs in the Hebrew Bible, and is rendered in our translation *Lord*, the same term by which the word Jehovah is expressed; but to distinguish between the two, and to show the reader when the original is *Yehovah* and when *Adonai*, the first is always put in capitals, LORD, the latter in plain Roman characters, Lord. *Whereby shall I know?* By what sign shall I be assured that I shall inherit this land? It appears that he expected some sign, and that on such occasions one was ordinarily given.

MATTHEW HENRY

here he prays, *Lord, help me* against *my unbelief. Now* he believed, but he desired a sign to be treasured up against an hour of temptation. 2. For the ratifying of the promise to his posterity, that they also might be brought to believe it.

III. God directs Abram to make preparations for a sacrifice, intending by that to give him a sign, and Abram makes preparation accordingly (*v.* 9–11). Those that would receive the assurances of God's favour, and would have their faith confirmed, must attend instituted ordinances, and expect to meet with God in them. Abram took as God appointed him, though as yet he knew not how these things should become a sign to him. This was not the first instance of Abram's implicit obedience. He divided the beasts in the midst, according to the ceremony used in confirming covenants, Jer. xxxiv. 18, 19, where it is said, They cut *the calf in twain, and passed between the parts.* While God's appearing to own his sacrifice was deferred, Abram continued waiting, and his expectations were raised by the delay; when *the fowls came down upon the carcases* to prey upon them, *Abram drove them away* (*v.* 11). When vain thoughts, like these fowls, come down upon our sacrifices, we must drive them away, and *attend on God without distraction.*

Verses 12–16

A full and particular discovery made to Abram of God's purposes concerning his seed.

I. The time when God came to him with this discovery: *When the sun was going down,* or *declining,* about the time of the *evening oblation.* God often keeps his people long in expectation of the comforts he designs them, for the confirmation of their faith; but though the answers of prayer, and the performance of promises, come slowly, yet they come surely.

II. The preparatives for this discovery. 1. *A deep sleep fell upon Abram,* not a common sleep through weariness or carelessness, but a divine ecstasy. The doors of the body were locked up, that the soul might be private and retired, and might act the more freely. 2. With this sleep, *a horror of great darkness fell upon him.* This great darkness, which brought horror with it, was designed, (1) To strike an awe upon the spirit of Abram, and to possess him with an holy reverence. Holy fear prepares the soul for holy joy; the spirit of bondage makes way for the spirit of adoption. (2) To be a specimen of the methods of God's dealings with his seed. They must first be in the horror and darkness of Egyptian slavery, and then enter with joy into the good land.

III. The prediction itself. Several things are here foretold.

1. The suffering state of Abram's seed for a long time, *v.* 13. He must know that the promised seed should be a persecuted seed. Now we have here,

(1) The particulars of their sufferings. [1] They shall be strangers. Thus the heirs of heaven are first strangers on earth. [2] They shall be servants. The Canaanites serve under a curse, the Hebrews under a blessing. [3] They shall be sufferers. Those whom they serve shall afflict them; see Exod. i. 11.

(2) The continuance of their sufferings—*four hundred years.* This was a long time, but a limited time.

2. The judgment of the enemies of Abram's seed: *That nation whom they shall serve,* even the Egyptians, *will I judge, v.* 14. Though God may suffer persecutors and oppressors to trample upon his people a great while, yet he will certainly reckon with them at last; for his *day is coming,* Ps. xxxvii. 12, 13.

3. The deliverance of Abram's seed out of Egypt. That great event is here foretold: *afterwards shall they come out with great substance.* It is here promised, (1) That they should be enlarged. The destruction of oppressors is the redemption of the oppressed. (2) That they should be enriched. God took care they should have, not only a good land to go to, but a good stock to carry with them.

4. Their happy settlement in Canaan, *v.* 16. They shall not only come out of Egypt, but *they shall come hither again,* hither to the land of Canaan, wherein thou now art.

5. Abram's peaceful quiet death and burial, before these things should come to pass, *v.* 15. Note, Good men are sometimes greatly favoured by being *taken away from the evil to come,* Isa. lvii. 1. Let this satisfy Abram, that, for his part,

(1) He shall *go to his fathers in peace.* Note, [1] Even the friends and favourites of Heaven are not exempted from the stroke of death. [2] Good men die willingly; they are not fetched, they are not forced, but they go. [3] At death we go to our fathers, godly fathers that have gone before us to the state of the blessed, Heb. xii. 23. Outward peace, to the last, is promised to Abram, peace and truth in his days,

JAMIESON, FAUSSET, BROWN

9-12. Take me an heifer, etc.—On occasions of great importance, when two or more parties join in a compact, they either observe precisely the same rites as Abram did, or, where they do not, they invoke the lamp as their witness. According to these ideas, which have been from time immemorial engraven on the minds of Eastern people, the Lord Himself condescended to enter into covenant with Abram. The patriarch did not pass between the sacrifice and the reason was that in this transaction he was bound to nothing. He asked a sign, and God was pleased to give him a sign, by which, according to Eastern ideas, He bound Himself. In like manner God has entered into covenant with us; and in the glory of the only begotten Son, who passed through between God and us, all who believe have, like Abram, a sign or pledge in the gift of the Spirit, whereby they may know that they shall inherit the heavenly Canaan.

KEIL–DELITZSCH:

"And when the sun was just about to go down, and deep sleep (as in 2:21, a deep sleep produced by God) had fallen upon Abram, behold there fell upon him terror, great darkness." The vision here passes into a prophetic sleep produced by God. In this sleep there fell upon Abram dread and darkness. The reference of the time is intended to show "the supernatural character of the darkness and sleep, and the distinction between the vision and a dream" (O. v. Gerlach). It also possesses a symbolical meaning. The setting of the sun prefigured to Abram the departure of the sun of grace, which shone upon Israel, and the commencement of a dark and dreadful period of suffering for his posterity, the very anticipation of which involved Abram in darkness. For the words which he heard in the darkness were these (v. 13): "Know of a surety, that thy seed shall be a stranger in a land that is not theirs, and shall serve them [the lords of the strange land], and they [the foreigners] shall oppress them 400 years." That these words had reference to the sojourn of the children of Israel in Egypt is placed beyond all doubt by the fulfillment. The 400 years were, according to prophetic language, a round number for the 430 years that Israel spent in Egypt (Ex. 12:40).

—*Commentary on the Old Testament*

ADAM CLARKE

9. *Take me an heifer.* It is worthy of remark that every animal allowed or commanded to be sacrificed under the Mosaic law is to be found in this list. And is it not a proof that God was now giving to Abram an epitome of that law and its sacrifices which He intended more fully to reveal to Moses, the essence of which consisted in its sacrifices, which typified the Lamb of God that takes away the sin of the world?

10. *Divided them in the midst.* The ancient method of making covenants, as well as the original word, have been already alluded to and in a general way explained. See chap. vi. 18. The word "covenant" from *con,* "together," and *venio,* "I come," signifies an agreement, association, or meeting between two or more parties; for it is impossible that a covenant can be made between an individual and himself, whether God or man. Rabbi Solomon Jarchi says, "It was a custom with those who entered into covenant with each other to take a heifer and cut it in two, and then the contracting parties passed between the pieces." *But the birds divided he not.* According to the law, Lev. i. 17, fowls were not to be divided asunder but only cloven for the purpose of taking out the intestines.

11. *And when the fowls,* "birds of prey," *came down upon the carcases* to devour them. *Abram,* who stood by his sacrifice waiting for the manifestation of God, who had ordered him to prepare for the ratification of the covenant, *drove them away,* that they might neither pollute nor devour what had been thus consecrated to God.

12. *A deep sleep.* The same word which is used to express the sleep into which Adam was cast, previous to the formation of Eve; chap. ii. 21. *An horror of great darkness.* Which God designed to be expressive of the affliction and misery into which his posterity should be brought during the four hundred years of their bondage in Egypt, as the next verse particularly states.

14. *And also that nation.* How remarkably was this promise fulfilled, in the redemption of Israel from its bondage, in the plagues and destruction of the Egyptians, and in the immense wealth which the Israelites brought out of Egypt! Not a more circumstantial or literally fulfilled promise is to be found in the Sacred Writings.

15. *Thou shalt go to thy fathers in peace.* This verse strongly implies the immortality of the soul, and a state of separate existence.

MATTHEW HENRY

whatever should come afterwards (2 Kings xx. 19); peace with God, and everlasting peace, are sure to all the seed.

(2) He shall be *buried in a good old age*. He shall not only die in peace, but die in honour. Old age is a blessing, a great opportunity for usefulness.

Verses 17–21

The covenant ratified (*v.* 17); the sign which Abram desired was given.

1. The *smoking furnace* signified the affliction of his seed in Egypt.

2. The *burning lamp* denotes comfort in this affliction; and this God showed to Abram, at the same time that he showed him the *smoking furnace*. (1) Light denotes deliverance out of the furnace. (2) The lamp denotes direction in the smoke. God's word was their lamp: this word to Abram was so, it was a light shining in a dark place. (3) The burning lamp denotes the destruction of their enemies who kept them so long in the furnace.

3. The passing of these between the pieces was the confirming of the covenant God now made with him. It is probable that the furnace and lamp, which passed between the pieces, burnt and consumed them, and so completed the sacrifice, and testified God's acceptance of it, as of Gideon's (Judges vi. 21). 1. So it intimates, (1) That God's covenants with man are made by sacrifice (Ps. l. 5), by Christ, the great sacrifice: no agreement without atonement. (2) God's acceptance of our spiritual sacrifices is an earnest of further favours.

II. The covenant repeated and explained: *Unto thy seed have I given this land*, *v.* 18. Here is,

1. A rehearsal of the grant. God's promises are God's gifts, and are so to be accounted. The possession is as sure, in due time, as if it were now actually delivered to them. What God has promised is as sure as if it were already done; hence, it is said, *He that believes hath everlasting life* (John iii. 36), for he shall as surely go to heaven as if he were there already.

2. A recital of the particulars granted, such as is usual in the grants of lands. The land granted is here described in its utmost extent because it was to be a type of the heavenly inheritance, where there is room enough: in our father's house are many mansions.

JAMIESON, FAUSSET, BROWN

KEIL–DELITZSCH:

When the sun had gone down and thick darkness had come on, "behold a smoking furnace, and [with] a fiery torch, which passed between those pieces"—a description of what Abram saw in his deep prophetic sleep, corresponding to the mysterious character of the whole proceeding. A stove is a cylindrical fire-pot, such as is used in the dwelling houses of the East. The phenomenon, which passed through the pieces as they lay opposite to one another, resembled such a smoking stove, from which a fiery torch, i.e. a brilliant flame, was streaming forth. In this symbol Jehovah manifested himself to Abram, just as He afterwards did to the people of Israel in the pillar of cloud and fire. Passing through the pieces, He ratified the covenant which He made with Abram. His glory was enveloped in fire and smoke, the product of consuming fire—both symbols of the wrath of God (cf. Ps. 18:9), whose fiery zeal consumes whatever opposes it (Ex. 3:2). To establish and give reality to the covenant to be concluded with Abram, Jehovah would have to pass through the seed of Abram when oppressed by the Egyptians and threatened with destruction, and to execute judgment upon their oppressors (Ex. 7:4; 12:12). In this symbol, the passing of the Lord between the pieces meant something altogether different from the oath of the Lord by himself in 22:16, or by His life in Deut. 32:40, or by His soul in Amos 6:8 and Jer. 51:14. It set before Abram the condescension of the Lord to his seed, in the fearful glory of His majesty as the judge of their foes.

—*Commentary on the Old Testament*

ADAM CLARKE

16. *In the fourth generation.* In former times most people counted by generations, to each of which was assigned a term of years amounting to 20, 25, 30, 33, 100, 108, or 110; for the generation was of various lengths among various people, at different times. It is probable that the *fourth generation* here means the same as the "four hundred years" in v. 13.

17. *A smoking furnace, and a burning lamp.* Probably the *smoking furnace* might be designed as an emblem of the sore afflictions of the Israelites in Egypt; but the *burning lamp* was certainly the symbol of the divine presence, which, passing between the pieces, ratified the covenant with Abram, as the following verse immediately states.

18. *The Lord made a covenant. Carath berith* signifies to "cut a covenant," or rather the covenant sacrifice; for as no covenant was made without one, and the creature was cut in two that the contracting parties might pass between the pieces, hence cutting the covenant signified making the covenant. *From the river of Egypt.* Not the Nile, but the river called Sichor, which was on the border of Egypt, near to the isthmus of Suez; see Josh. xiii. 3; though some think that by this a branch of the Nile is meant. This promise was fully accomplished in the days of David and Solomon. See 2 Sam. viii. 3, etc., and 2 Chron. ix. 26.

19. *The Kenites.* Here are ten nations mentioned, though afterwards reckoned but seven; see Deut. vii. 1; Acts xiii. 19. Probably some of them which existed in Abram's time had been blended with others before the time of Moses, so that seven only out of the ten then remained; see part of these noticed in Genesis x.

MATTHEW HENRY

CHAPTER 16

Verses 1–3

We have here the marriage of Abram to Hagar, who was his secondary wife. It seems to have proceeded from an irregular desire to build up families for the speedier peopling of the world and the church. Certainly it must not be so now. Christ has reduced this matter to the first institution, and makes the marriage uinon to be between one man and one woman only.

I. The maker of this match was Sarai herself. It is the policy of Satan to tempt us by our nearest and dearest relations. It would have been much more for Sarai's interest if Abram had kept to the rule of God's law instead of being guided by her foolish projects.

II. The inducement to it was Sarai's barrenness. She used this as an argument with Abram to marry his maid; and he was prevailed upon by this argument to do it.

Abram's compliance with Sarai's proposal, we have reason to think, was from an earnest desire of the promised seed, on whom the covenant should be entailed. God had told him that his heir should be a son of his body, but had not yet told him that it should be a son by Sarai; therefore he thought, "Why not by Hagar, since Sarai herself proposed it?" Fleshly wisdom, as it anticipates God's time of mercy, so it puts us out of God's way. This would be happily prevented if we would ask counsel of God by the word and by prayer, before we attempt that which is important and suspicious.

Verses 4–6

The immediate bad consequences of Abram's unhappy marriage to Hagar. A great deal of mischief it made quickly. When we do not well both sin and trouble lie at the door. See it in this story.

I. Sarai is despised, and thereby provoked and put into a passion, *v.* 4. Hagar thinks herself a better woman than Sarai, more favoured by Heaven, and likely to be better beloved by Abram, and therefore she will not submit as she has done. 2. We justly suffer by those whom we have sinfully indulged, and it is a righteous thing with God to make those

JAMIESON, FAUSSET, BROWN

CHAPTER 16

Vss. 1-16. BESTOWMENT OF HAGAR. **1. Now Sarai . . . had a handmaid**—a female slave—one of those obtained in Egypt.

3. Sarai . . . gave her to . . . Abram to be his wife—Wife is here used to describe an inferior, though not degrading, relation, in countries where polygamy prevails. In the case of these female slaves, who are the personal property of his lady, being purchased before her marriage or given as a special present to her, no one can become the husband's secondary wife without her mistress' consent or permission. This usage seems to have prevailed in patriarchal times; and Hagar, Sarai's slave, of whom she had the entire right of disposing, was given by her mistress' spontaneous offer, to be the secondary wife of Abram, in the hope of obtaining the long-looked—for heir. It was a wrong step—indicating a want of simple reliance on God—and Sarai was the first to reap the bitter fruits of her device.

ADAM CLARKE

CHAPTER 16

1. *She had a handmaid, an Egyptian.* As Hagar was an Egyptian, St. Chrysostom's conjecture is very probable, that she was one of those female slaves which Pharaoh gave to Abram when he sojourned in Egypt; see chap. xii. 16. Her name, *Hagar,* signifies a "stranger" or "sojourner," and it is likely she got this name in the family of Abram, as the word is pure Hebrew.

2. *Go in unto my maid.* It must not be forgotten that female slaves constituted a part of the private patrimony or possessions of a wife, and that she had a right, according to the usages of those times, to dispose of them as she pleased, the husband having no authority in the case. *I may obtain children by her.* The slave, being the absolute property of the mistress, not only her person, but the fruits of her labor, with all her children, were her owner's property also. The children, therefore, which were born of the slave, were considered as the children of the mistress. It was on this ground that Sarai gave her slave to Abram; and we find, what must necessarily be the consequence in all cases of polygamy, that strifes and contentions took place.

MATTHEW HENRY

instruments of our trouble whom we have made instruments of our sin.

II. Abram is clamoured upon, and cannot be easy while Sarai is out of humour; she unjustly charges him with the injury (*v.* 5). She rashly appeals to God in the case: *The Lord judge between me and thee*; as if Abram had refused to right her. When passion is upon the throne, reason is out of doors, and is neither heard nor spoken. 2. Those are not always in the right who are most loud and forward in appealing to God. Rash and bold imprecations are commonly evidences of guilt and a bad cause.

III Hagar is afflicted, and driven from the house, *v.* 6. She herself had first given the provocation, by despising her mistress.

Verses 7–9

The first mention we have in scripture of an angel's appearance.

I. How the angel arrested her in her flight, *v.* 7. She was making towards her own country, towards Egypt. It were well if our afflictions would make us think of our home. But Hagar was now out of the way of her duty, and going further astray. 2. God suffers those that are out of the way to wander awhile, that when they see their folly, they may be the better disposed to return. Hagar was not stopped till she was in the wilderness. God brings us into a wilderness, and there meets us, Hos. ii. 14.

II. How he examined her, *v.* 8. Observe,

1. He called her *Hagar, Sarai's maid.* Though she was Abram's wife, yet he calls her *Sarai's maid,* to humble her. Note, Though civility teaches us to call others by their highest titles, yet humility and wisdom teach us to call ourselves by the lowest. Sarai's maid ought to be in Sarai's tent, and not wandering in the wilderness and sauntering by a fountain of water.

2. The questions the angel put to her were proper and very pertinent. (1) "*Whence comest thou?*" Consider that thou art running away from duty. (2) "*Whither wilt thou go?* Thou art running thyself into sin, in Egypt, and into danger, in the wilderness." Note, Those who are forsaking God and their duty would do well to remember not only *whence they have fallen,* but *whither they are falling.*

3. Her answer was honest, and a fair confession: *I flee from the face of my mistress.*

4. How he sent her back, with suitable and compassionate counsel: "*Return to thy mistress, and submit thyself under her hand, v.* 9.

Verses 10–14

We may suppose that the angel having given Hagar that good counsel (*v.* 9) to *return to her mistress* she immediately promised to do so, and was setting her face homeward; and then the angel went on to encourage her with an assurance of the mercy God had in store for her and her seed: for God will meet those with mercy that are returning to their duty. *I said, I will confess, and thou forgavest,* Ps. xxxii. 5.

I. A prediction concerning her posterity given her for her comfort in her present distress. Note, It is a great comfort to women with child to think that they are under the particular cognizance and care of the divine Providence. Now, 1. The angel assures her of a safe delivery, and that of a *son,* which Abram desired. She was saved in child-bearing, not only by providence, but by promise. 2. He names her child, which was an honour both to her and it: Call him *Ishmael, God will hear*; and the reason is, because the Lord has heard. Even where there is little cry of devotion, the God of pity sometimes graciously hears the cry of affliction. Tears speak as well as prayers. 3. He promises her a numerous offspring, *v.* 10. It is supposed that the Turks at this day descend from Ishmael; and they are a great people. He gives a character of the child she should bear. He *will be a wild man*; *a wild ass of a man* (so the word is), rude and bold, and fearing no man—untamed, untractable, living at large, and impatient of service and restraint. *His hand against every man*—this is his *sin; and every man's hand against him*—this is his *punishment.* Note, Those that have turbulent spirits have commonly troublesome lives. And yet, he should live in safety. Note, Many that are much exposed by their own imprudence are yet strangely preserved by the divine Providence, so much better is God to them than they deserve.

II. Hagar's pious reflection upon this gracious appearance of God to her, *v.* 13, 14. Observe in what she said,

1. Her awful adoration of God's omniscience and providence, with application of it to herself: *Thou God seest me*; this should be, with her, his name for ever. *God is* (as the ancients expressed it) *all eye.*

JAMIESON, FAUSSET, BROWN

5. And Sarai said . . . My wrong be upon thee—Bursts of temper, or blows, as the original may bear, took place till at length Hagar, perceiving the hopelessness of maintaining the unequal strife, resolved to escape from what had become to her in reality, as well as in name, a house of bondage.

7. And the angel of the Lord found her by a fountain—This well, pointed out by tradition, lay on the side of the caravan road, in the midst of Shur, a sandy desert on the west of Arabia Petræa, to the extent of 150 miles, between Palestine and Egypt. By taking that direction, she seems to have intended to return to her relatives in that country. Nothing but pride, passion, and sullen obstinacy, could have driven any solitary person to brave the dangers of such an inhospitable wild; and she would have died, had not the timely appearance and words of the angel recalled her to reflection and duty.

11. Ishmael—Like other Hebrew names, this had a signification, and it is made up of two words—"God hears." The reason is explained.

12. he will be a wild man—lit., "a wild ass man," expressing how the wildness of Ishmael and his descendants resembles that of the wild ass. **his hand will be against every man**—descriptive of the rude, turbulent, and plundering character of the Arabs. **dwell in the presence of all his brethren**—dwell, i.e., pitch tents; and the meaning is that they maintain their independence in spite of all attempts to extirpate or subdue them. **13. called the name**—common in ancient times to name places from circumstances; and the name given to this well was a grateful recognition of God's gracious appearance in the hour of her distress.

ADAM CLARKE

5. *My wrong be upon thee.* This appears to be intended as a reproof to Abram, containing an insinuation that it was his fault that she herself had not been a mother, and that now he carried himself more affectionately towards Hagar than he did to her, in consequence to which conduct the slave became petulant. To remove all suspicion of this kind, Abram delivers up Hagar into her hand, who was certainly under his protection while his concubine or secondary wife; but this right given to him by Sarai he restores, to prevent her jealousy and uneasiness.

6. *Sarai dealt hardly with her.* "She afflicted her"; the term implying stripes and hard usage, to bring down the body and humble the mind. If the slave was to blame in this business the mistress is not less liable to censure. She alone had brought her into those circumstances in which it was natural for her to value herself beyond her mistress.

7. *The angel of the Lord.* That Jesus Christ, in a body suited to the dignity of His nature, frquently appeared to the patriarchs, has been already intimated. That the person mentioned here was greater than any created being is sufficiently evident from the following particulars: (1) From his promising to perform what God alone could do, and foretelling what God alone could know: *"I will multiply thy seed exceedingly,"* v. 10; *"Thou art with child, and shalt bear a son,"* v. 11; *"He will be a wild man,"* v. 12. (2) Hagar considers the person who spoke to her as God, calls him Eli, and addresses him in the way of worship, which, had he been a created angel, he would have refused. See Rev. xix. 10; xxii. 9. (3) Moses, who relates the transaction, calls this angel expressly Jehovah; for, says he, she called *shem Yehovah,* the name of the Lord that spake to her. v. 13. (4) This person, who is here called *malach Yehovah,* the Angel of the Lord, is the same who is called "the redeeming Angel" or "the Angel the Redeemer," Gen. xlviii. 16; the Angel of God's presence, Isa. lxiii. 9; and the Angel of the Covenant, Mal. iii. 1. *In the way to Shur.* As this was the road from Hebron to Egypt, it is probable she was now returning to her own country.

8. *Hagar, Sarai's maid.* This mode of address is used to show her that she was known, and to remind her that she was the property of another.

10. *I will multiply thy seed exceedingly.* Who says this? The person who is called the Angel of the Lord; and he certainly speaks with all the authority which is proper to God.

11. *And shalt call his name Ishmael. Yishmael,* from *shama,* "he heard," and *El,* "God"; for, says the Angel, "the Lord hath heard thy affliction." Thus the name of the child must ever keep the mother in remembrance of God's merciful interposition in her behalf, and remind the child and the man that he was an object of God's gracious and providential goodness. Afflictions and distresses have a voice in the ears of God, even when prayer is restrained; but how much more powerfully do they speak when endured in meekness of spirit, with confidence in and supplication to the Lord!

12. *He will be a wild man. Pere adam.* As the root of this word does not appear in the Hebrew Bible, it is probably found in the Arabic *farra,* "to run away, to run wild." What is said of the wild ass, Job xxxix. 5-8, affords the very best description that can be given of the Ishmaelites (the Bedouins and wandering Arabs), the descendants of Ishmael.

13. *And she called the name of the Lord.* She "invoked the name of Jehovah who spake unto her," thus: *Thou God seest me!* She found that the eye of a merciful God had been upon her in all her wanderings and afflictions; and her words seem to intimate that she had been seeking the divine help and protection, for she says, *Have I also* (or *have I* not also) *looked after him that seeth me?*

MATTHEW HENRY

He that sees all sees me, as David (Ps. cxxxix. 1), *O Lord, thou hast searched me, and known me.* It is a proper word for a penitent:—"Thou seest the sincerity and seriousness of my return and repentance."

2. Her humble admiration of God's favour to her: "*Have I also here looked after him that seeth me?*" Probably she knew not who it was that talked with her till he was departing and then she looked after him, with a reflection like that of the two disciples, Luke xxiv. 31, 32. Not only in Abram's tent and at his altar, but *here* also, in this wilderness? Here, where I never expected it, where I was out of the way of my duty? *Lord, how is it?*" John xiv. 22.

III. The name which this gave to the place: *Beer-lahai-roi, The well of him that liveth and seeth me, v.* 14. This was the place where the God of glory manifested the special care he took of a poor woman in distress.

Verses 15–16

It is here taken for granted that Hagar did as the angel commanded her, returning to her mistress and then, in the fulness of time, she brought forth her son.

JAMIESON, FAUSSET, BROWN

TODAY'S DICTIONARY OF THE BIBLE:

Beerlahairoi—i.e., "the well of him that liveth and seeth me," or, as some render it, "the well of the vision of life"—the well where the Lord met with Hagar (Gen. 16:7–14). Isaac dwelt beside this well "Lahairoi" (24:62; 25:11). It has been identified with *'Ain Muweileh*, or *Moilahhi*, southwest of Beersheba, and about 12 miles west from Kadesh-barnea.

ADAM CLARKE

14. *Wherefore the well was called Beer-lahai-roi.* It appears, from v. 7, that Hagar had sat down by a fountain or well of water in the wilderness of Shur, at which the Angel of the Lord found her; and, to commemorate the wonderful discovery which God had made of himself, she called the name of the well *Beer-lahai-roi*, "A well to the Living One who seeth me." Two things seem implied here: (1) A dedication of the well to Him who had appeared to her; and (2) Faith in the promise; for He who is the Living One, existing in all generations, must have it ever in His power to accomplish promises which are to be fulfilled through the whole lapse of time.

15. *And Hagar bare Abram a son.* It appears, therefore, that Hagar returned at the command of the angel, believing the promise that God had made to her. *Called his son's name . . . Ishmael.* Finding by the account of Hagar that God had designed that he should be so called.

MATTHEW HENRY — CHAPTER 17

Verses 1–3

Here is, I. The time when God made Abram this gracious visit: full thirteen years after the birth of Ishmael. There are some special comforts which are not the daily bread, no, not of the best saints, but they are favoured with them now and then. On this side heaven they have convenient food, but not a continual feast. So long the promise of Isaac was deferred. Perhaps to correct Abram's over-hasty marrying of Hagar.

II. The way in which God made this covenant with him: *The Lord appeared to Abram*, in the *shechinah*, some visible display of God's immediate glorious presence with him.

III. The posture Abram put himself into upon this occasion: *He fell on his face while God talked with him, v.* 3. 1. As one overcome by the brightness of the divine glory. 2. As one ashamed of himself, and blushing to think of the honours done to one so unworthy.

IV. The general scope and summary of the covenant laid down as the foundation on which all the rest was built; it is no other than the covenant of grace still made with all believers in Jesus Christ, *v.* 1.

1. What we may expect God to be to us: *I am the Almighty God.* By this name he chose to make himself known to Abram rather than by his name *Jehovah*, Exod. vi. 3. He used it to Jacob, *ch.* xxxv. 11. They called him by this name, *ch.* xxviii. 3; xliii. 14; xlviii. 3. After Moses, *Jehovah* is more frequently used, and this, *El-shaddai*, very rarely; it bespeaks the almighty power of God, either, (1) As an avenger, or, (2) As a benefactor. He is a God that is enough; or, as our old English translation reads it here very significantly, *I am God all-sufficient.*

2. What God requires that we should be to him. The covenant is mutual: *Walk before me, and be thou perfect.* Observe, (1) That to be religious is to walk before God in our integrity. It is to be *inward with him*, in all the duties of religious worship, for in them particularly we walk before God (1 Sam. ii. 30). I know no religion but sincerity. (2) That upright walking with God is the condition of our interest in his all-sufficiency.

Verses 4–6

The covenant of grace is a covenant of God's own making; this he glories in (*as for me*), and so may we.

I. It is promised to Abram that he should be a *father of many nations*; that is, (1) That his seed after the flesh should be very numerous. 2. That all believers in every age should be looked upon as his spiritual seed, and that he should be called, not only *the friend of God*, but *the father of the faithful.*

II. In token of this his name was changed from *Abram, a high father*, to *Abraham, the father of a multitude.* This was, 1. To put an honour upon him. 2. To encourage and confirm his faith.

JAMIESON, FAUSSET, BROWN — CHAPTER 17

Vss. 1-27. Renewal of the Covenant. **1. Abram . . . ninety years old and nine**—thirteen years after the birth of Ishmael. During that interval he had enjoyed the comforts of communion with God but had been favored with no special revelation as formerly, probably on account of his hasty and blameable marriage with Hagar. **the Lord appeared**—some visible manifestation of the divine presence, probably the Shekinah or radiant glory of overpowering effulgence. **I am the Almighty God**—the name by which He made Himself known to the patriarchs (Exod. 6:3), designed to convey the sense of "all-sufficient" (Ps. 16:5, 6; 73:25). **walk . . . and be . . . perfect**—upright, sincere (Ps. 51:6) in heart, speech, and behavior.

3. Abram fell on his face—the attitude of profoundest reverence assumed by Eastern people. It consists in the prostrate body resting on the hands and knees, with the face bent till the forehead touches the ground. It is an expression of conscious humility and profound reverence. **4. my covenant is with thee**—Renewed mention is made of it as the foundation of the communication that follows. It is the covenant of grace made with all who believe in the Saviour. **5. but thy name shall be Abraham**—In Eastern countries a change of name is an advertisement of some new circumstance in the history, rank, or religion of the individual who bears it. The change is made variously, by the old name being entirely dropped for the new, or by conjoining the new with the old; or sometimes only a few letters are inserted, so that the altered form may express the difference in the owner's state or prospects. It is surprising how soon a new name is known and its import spread through the country. In dealing with Abraham and Sarai, God was pleased to adapt His procedure to the ideas and customs of the country and age. Instead of Abram, "a high father," he was to be called Abraham, "father of a multitude of nations" (Rev. 2:17).

ADAM CLARKE — CHAPTER 17

1. *The Lord appeared to Abram.* See on chap. xv. 1. *I am the Almighty God. El shaddai*, "God all-sufficient"; from *shadah*, to "shed," to "pour out." I am that God who pours out blessings, who gives them richly, abundantly, continually. *Walk before me.* "Set thyself to walk"—be firmly purposed, thoroughly determined to obey, *before me*; for My eye is ever on thee, therefore ever consider that God seeth thee. Who can imagine a stronger incitement to conscientious, persevering obedience? *Be thou perfect.* "And thou shalt be perfections," i.e., altogether perfect. Be just such as the holy God would have thee to be, as the almighty God can make thee, and live as the all-sufficient God shall support thee; for He alone who makes the soul holy can preserve it in holiness. Our blessed Lord appears to have had these words pointedly in view, Matt. v. 48: "Ye shall be perfect, as your Father who is in heaven is perfect." But what does this imply? Why, to be saved from all the power, the guilt, and the contamination of sin. This is only the negative part of salvation, but it has also a positive part; to be made perfect—to be perfect as our Father who is in heaven is perfect, to be filled with the fulness of God, to have Christ dwelling continually in the heart by faith, and to be rooted and grounded in love. This is the state in which man was created, for he was made in the image and likeness of God. This is the state from which man fell, for he broke the command of God. And this is the state into which every human soul must be raised, who would dwell with God in glory; for Christ was incarnated and died to put away sin by the sacrifice of himself. What a glorious privilege! And who can doubt the possibility of its attainment who believes in the omnipotent love of God, the infinite merit of the Blood of atonement, and the all-pervading and all-purifying energy of the Holy Ghost?

3. *And Abram fell on his face.* The Eastern method of prostration was thus: the person first went down on his knees, and then lowered his head to his knees, and touched the earth with his forehead. A very painful posture, but significative of great humiliation and reverence.

5. *Thy name shall be Abraham.* Abram literally signifies a "high or exalted father." Abraham differs from the preceding in only one letter; it has *he* before the last radical. Though this may appear very simple and easy, yet the true etymology and meaning of the word are very difficult to be assigned. The reason given for the change made in the patriarch's name is this: *For a father of many nations have I made thee*, "a father of a multitude of nations." This has led some to suppose that Abraham is a contraction for *ab-rab-hamon*, "the father of a great multitude."

The same difficulty occurs, v. 15, on the word *Sarai*, which signifies "my prince" or "princess," and *Sarah*, where the whole change is made by the substitution of a *he* for a *yod.* This latter might be translated "princess" in

MATTHEW HENRY | JAMIESON, FAUSSET, BROWN | ADAM CLARKE

KEIL–DELITZSCH:

As a pledge of this promise God changed his name "high father" into "father of the multitude." In this name God gave him a tangible pledge of the fulfillment of His covenant, inasmuch as a name which God gives cannot be a mere empty sound, but must be the expression of something real, or eventually acquire reality. On the part of Abraham, God required that he and his descendants in all generations should keep the covenant, and that as a sign he should circumcise himself and every male in his house. As a sign of the covenant, circumcision is called in verse 13, "the covenant in the flesh," so far as the nature of the covenant was manifested in the flesh. It was to be extended not only to the seed, the lineal descendants of Abraham, but to all the males in his house, even to every foreign slave not belonging to the seed of Abram, whether born in the house or acquired (i.e. bought) with money, and to the "son of eight days," i.e., the male child eight days old; with the threat that the uncircumcised should be exterminated from his people, because by neglecting circumcision he had broken the covenant with God.—*Commentary on the Old Testament*

Verses 7–14

Here is, I. The continuance of the covenant, intimated in three things:—1. It is established; not to be altered nor revoked. 2. It is entailed; it is a covenant, not with Abraham only but with his seed after him, not only his seed after the flesh, but his spiritual seed. 3. It is everlasting in the evangelical sense and meaning of it. The covenant of grace is everlasting.

II. The contents of the covenant: it is a covenant of promises. Here are two which indeed are all-sufficient:—1. That God would be their God, *v.* 7, 8. What God is himself, that he will be to his people: his wisdom theirs, to guide and counsel them; his power theirs, to protect and support them; his goodness theirs, to supply and comfort them. 2. That Canaan should be their everlasting possession, *v.* 8. It must be looked upon as a type of heaven's happiness, that everlasting rest which remains for the people of God, Heb. iv. 9. Canaan is here said to be the land wherein Abraham was a stranger; and the heavenly Canaan is a land to which we are strangers, for it does not yet appear what we shall be.

III. The token of the covenant, and that is circumcision, for the sake of which the covenant is itself called the *covenant of circumcision*, Acts vii. 8. It is called a sign and seal (Rom. iv. 11), for it was, 1. A confirmation to Abraham and his seed of those promises which were God's part of the covenant. (1) Circumcision was a bloody ordinance; for all things by the law were purged with blood, Heb. ix. 22. See Exod. xxiv. 8. But, the blood of Christ being shed, all bloody ordinances are now abolished; circumcision therefore gives way to baptism. (2) It was peculiar to the males, though the women were also included in the covenant, for the man is the head of the woman. (3) It was the flesh of the foreskin that was to be cut off, because it is by ordinary generation that sin is propagated. Christ having not yet offered himself for us, God would have man to enter into covenant by the offering of some part of his own body. It is a secret part of the body; for the true circumcision is that of the heart, 1 Cor. xii. 23, 24. (4) The ordinance was to be administered to children when they were eight days old. (5) The children of the strangers, of whom the master of the family was the true domestic owner, were to be circumcised (*v.* 12, 13), which looked favourably upon the Gentiles, who should in due time be brought into the family of Abraham, by faith. See Gal. iii. 14. (6) The contempt of circumcision was a contempt of the covenant; if the parents did not circumcise their children, it was at their peril, as in the case of Moses, Exod. iv. 24, 25.

Verses 15–22

I. The promise made to Abraham of a son by *Sarai*, for *she also shall be a mother of nations, and kings of people shall be of her*, *v.* 16. Note, 1. God reveals the purposes of his good-will to his people by degrees. God had told Abram long before that he should have a son, but never till now that he should have a son by *Sarai*. 2. The blessing of the Lord makes fruitful, and adds no sorrow with it, no such sorrow as was in Hagar's case. 3. Civil government and order are a great blessing to the church. It is promised, not only that *people*, but *kings of people*, should be of her; not a headless rout, but a well-modelled well-governed society.

II. The ratification of this promise was the change of *Sarai's* name into *Sarah* (*v.* 15). *Sarai* signifies *my princess*, as if her honour were confined to one family only. *Sarah* signifies *a princess*—namely, of *multitudes*.

III. Abraham's joyful, thankful, entertainment of this gracious promise, *v.* 17. Upon this occasion he expressed, 1. Great humility: He *fell on his face*.

6-8. I will give unto thee . . . the land—It had been previously promised to Abraham and his posterity (ch. 15:18). Here it is promised as an "everlasting possession," and was, therefore, a type of heaven, "the better country" (Heb. 11:16). **10. Every man child among you shall be circumcised**—This was the sign in the Old Testament Church as baptism is in the New, and hence the covenant is called "covenant of circumcision" (Acts 7:8; Rom. 4:11). The terms of the covenant were these: on the one hand Abraham and his seed were to observe the right of circumcision; and on the other, God promised, in the event of such observance, to give them Canaan for a perpetual possession, to be a God to him and his posterity, and that in him and his seed all nations should be blessed.

15, 16. As for Sarai . . . I will . . . give thee a son also of her—God's purposes are gradually made known. A son had been long ago promised to Abraham. Now, at length, for the first time he is informed that it was to be a child of Sarai.

17. Abraham fell upon his face, and laughed—It was not the sneer of unbelief, but a smile of delight at the improbability of the event (Rom. 4:20).

general; and while the former seems to point out her government in her own family alone, the latter appears to indicate her government over the nations of which her husband is termed the father or lord; and hence the promise states that *she shall be a mother of nations*, and that *kings of people shall be of her*. See vv. 15-16.

Now as the only change in each name is made by the insertion of a single letter, and that letter the same in both names, I cannot help concluding that some mystery was designed by its insertion; and therefore the opinion of Clarius and some others is not to be disregarded, which supposes that God shows He had conferred a peculiar dignity on both, by adding to their names one of the letters of His own; a name by which His eternal power and Godhead are peculiarly pointed out.

7. *An everlasting covenant. Berith olam.* See on chap. xiii. 15. Here the word *olam* is taken in its own proper meaning, as the words immediately following prove—*to be a God unto thee, and thy seed after thee;* for as the soul is to endure forever, so it shall eternally stand in need of the supporting power and energy of God; and as the reign of the gospel dispensation shall be as long as sun and moon endure, and its consequences eternal, so must the covenant be on which these are founded.

8. *Everlasting possession.* Here *olam* appears to be used in its accommodated meaning, and signifies the completion of the divine counsel in reference to a particular period or dispensation. And it is literally true that the Israelites possessed the land of Canaan till the Mosaic dispensation was terminated in the complete introduction of that of the gospel. But as the spiritual and temporal covenants are both blended together, and the former was pointed out and typified by the latter, hence the word even here may be taken in its own proper meaning, that of ever-during, or eternal; because the spiritual blessings pointed out by the temporal covenant shall have no end. And hence it is immediately added, *I will be their God,* not for a time, certainly, but for ever and ever.

11. *And it shall be a token.* For a sign of spiritual things; for the circumcision made in the flesh was designed to signify the purification of the heart from all unrighteousness, as God particularly showed in the law itself. See Deut. x. 16; see also Rom. ii. 25-29; Col. ii. 11. And it was a seal of that righteousness or justification that comes by faith, Rom. iv. 11. That some of the Jews had a just notion of its spiritual intention is plain from many passages in the Chaldee paraphrases and in the Jewish writers.

12. *He that is eight days old.* Because previously to this they were considered unclean, Lev. xii. 2-3, and circumcision was ever understood as a consecration of the person to God. Neither calf, lamb, nor kid, was offered to God till it was eight days old for the same reason, Lev. xxii. 27.

14. *The uncircumcised . . . shall be cut off from his people.* By being cut off some have imagined that a sudden temporal death was implied; but the simple meaning seems to be that such should have no right to nor share in the blessings of the covenant, which we have already seen were both of a temporal and spiritual kind; and if so, then eternal death was implied, for it was impossible for a person who had not received the spiritual purification to enter into eternal glory. The spirit of this law extends to all ages, dispensations, and people; he whose heart is not purified from sin cannot enter into the kingdom of God.

15. *Thou shalt not call her name Sarai, but Sarah.* See on v. 5.

16. *I will bless her.* Sarah certainly stands at the head of all the women of the Old Testament, on account of her extraordinary privileges. I am quite of Calmet's opinion that Sarah was a type of the blessed Virgin. St. Paul considers her a type of the New Testament and heavenly Jerusalem; and as all true believers are considered as the children of Abraham, so all faithful, holy women are considered the daughters of Sarah, Gal. iv. 22, 24, 26. See also 1 Pet. iii. 6.

17. *Then Abraham . . . laughed.* I am astonished to find learned and pious men considering

MATTHEW HENRY

2. Great joy: He *laughed*. It was a laughter of delight, not of distrust. There is the joy of faith as well as the joy of fruition. 3. Great admiration: *Shall a child be born to him that is a hundred years old?*

IV. Abraham's prayer for Ishmael: *O that Ishmael might live before thee! v.* 18. This he speaks, not as desiring that Ishmael might be preferred before the son he should have by Sarah; but, dreadful lest he should be abandoned and forsaken of God. Though we ought not to prescribe to God, yet he gives us leave, in prayer, to be humbly free with him, and particular in making known our requests, Phil. iv. 6. It is the duty of parents to pray for their children, for all their children, as Job, who offered burnt offerings according to the number of them all, Job i. 5. The great thing we should desire of God for our children is that they may live before him, that is, that they may be kept in covenant with him, and may have grace to walk before him in their uprightness.

V. God's answer to his prayer; and it is an answer of peace.

1. Common blessings are secured to Ishmael (*v.* 20): *As for Ishmael*, whom thou art in so much care about, *I have heard thee*; he shall find favour for thy sake; *I have blessed him.* His posterity shall be numerous: *I will multiply him exceedingly*, more than his neighbours. They shall be considerable: *Twelve princes shall he beget.*

2. Covenant blessings are reserved for Isaac, and appropriated to him, *v.* 19, 21. (1) God repeats to him the promise of a son by Sarah. (2) He names that child—calls him *Isaac, laughter*, because Abraham rejoiced in spirit when this son was promised him. God's mercies promised shall in due time be our *exceeding* joy. Christ will be laughter to those that look for him. (3) He entails the covenant upon that child.

Verses 23–27

We have here Abraham's obedience to the law of circumcision. He himself and all his family were circumcised, so receiving the token of the covenant and distinguishing themselves from other families, that had no part nor lot in the matter. 1. It was an implicit obedience. 2. It was a speedy obedience: *In the self-same day, v.* 23, 26. Sincere obedience is not dilatory, Ps. cxix. 60. 3. It was a universal obedience: He did not circumcise his family and excuse himself, but set them an example. Ishmael is blessed, and therefore circumcised.

JAMIESON, FAUSSET, BROWN

18. O that Ishmael might live before thee—natural solicitude of a parent. But God's thoughts are not as man's thoughts.

19, 20. The blessings of the covenant are reserved for Isaac, but common blessings were abundantly promised to Ishmael; and though the visible Church did not descend from his family, yet personally he might, and it is to be hoped *did*, enjoy its benefits.

ADAM CLARKE

this as a token of Abraham's weakness of faith or unbelief, when they have the most positive assurance from the Spirit of God himself that "Abraham was not weak but strong in the faith"; that "he staggered not at the promise through unbelief, but gave glory to God," Rom. iv. 19-20. It is true the same word is used, chap. xviii. 12, concerning Sarah, in whom it was certainly a sign of doubtfulness, though mixed with pleasure at the thought of the possibility of her becoming a mother; but we know how possible it is to express both faith and unbelief in the same way, and even pleasure and disdain have been expressed by a smile or laugh. By laughing Abraham undoubtedly expressed his joy at the prospect of the fulfilment of so glorious a promise; and from this very circumstance Isaac had his name. *Yitschak*, which we change into *Isaac*, signifies "laughter"; and it is the same word which is used in the verse before us.

18. *O that Ishmael might live before thee!* Abraham, finding that the covenant was to be established in another branch of his family, felt solicitous for his son Ishmael, whom he considered as necessarily excluded; on which God delivers that most remarkable prophecy which follows in the twentieth verse, and which contains an answer to the prayer and wish of Abraham: *And as for Ishmael, I have heard thee;* so that the object of Abraham's prayer was that his son Ishmael might be the head of a prosperous and potent people.

20. *Twelve princes shall he beget.* See the names of these twelve princes, chap. xxv. 12-16. From Ishmael proceeded the various tribes of the Arabs. They were anciently, and still continue to be, a very numerous and powerful people.

21. *My covenant will I establish with Isaac.* All temporal good things are promised to Ishmael and his posterity, but the establishment of the Lord's covenant is to be with Isaac. Hence it is fully evident that this covenant referred chiefly to spiritual things—to the Messiah, and the salvation which should be brought to both Jews and Gentiles by His incarnation, death, and glorification.

22. *God went up from Abraham.* Ascended evidently before him, so that he had the fullest proof that it was no human being, no earthly angel or messenger, that talked with him; and the promise of a son in the course of a single year, "at this set time in the next year," v. 21, which had every human probability against it, was to be the sure token of the truth of all that had hitherto taken place, and the proof that all that was farther promised should be fulfilled in its due time.

23. *And Abraham took Ishmael.* Had not Abraham, his son (who was of age to judge for himself), and all the family been fully convinced that this thing was of God, they could not have submitted to it. A rite so painful, so repugnant to every feeling of delicacy, and every way revolting to nature, could never have sprung up in the imagination of man. To this day the Jews practice it as a divine ordinance; and all the Arabians do the same.

MATTHEW HENRY — CHAPTER 18

Verses 1–8

This appearance of God to Abraham seems to have had in it freedom and familiarity, and therefore resembles that great visit when the Word would be made flesh, and appear as one of us.

I. How Abraham expected strangers, and how richly his expectations were answered (*v.* 1). God graciously visits those in whom he has first raised the expectation of him. Those that have been forward to entertain strangers have entertained angels, to their unspeakable honour and satisfaction. Where we see no cause to suspect ill, charity teaches us to hope well and to show kindness accordingly. It is better to feed five drones, or wasps, than to starve one bee.

II. How Abraham entertained those strangers, and how kindly his entertainment was accepted. Forgetting his age and gravity, he *ran to meet them* in the most obliging manner, and with all due courtesy. Religion does not destroy, but improve, good manners, and teaches us to honour all men.

JAMIESON, FAUSSET, BROWN — CHAPTER 18

Vss. 1-8. ENTERTAINMENT OF ANGELS. **1. the Lord appeared**—another manifestation of the divine presence, more familiar than any yet narrated; and more like that in the fulness of time, when the Word was made flesh. **plains of Mamre**—rather, terebinth or oak of Mamre—a tall-spreading tree or grove of trees. **sat in the tent door**—The tent itself being too close and sultry at noon, the shaded open front is usually resorted to for the air that may be stirring. **2. lift up his eyes . . . and, lo, three men**—Travellers in that quarter start at sunrise and continue till midday when they look out for some resting-place. **he ran to meet them**—When the visitor is an ordinary person, the host merely rises; but if of superior rank, the custom is to advance a little towards the stranger, and after a very low bow, turn and lead him to the tent, putting an arm round his waist, or tapping him on the shoulder as they go, to assure him of welcome. **3. My Lord, if now I have found favor**—The hospitalities offered are just of the kind that are necessary and most grateful, the refreshment of water, for feet exposed to dust and heat by the

ADAM CLARKE — CHAPTER 18

1. *And the Lord appeared.* See on chap. xv. 1. *Sat in the tent door.* For the purpose of enjoying the refreshing air *in the heat of the day,* when the sun had most power. A custom still frequent among the Asiatics.

2. *Three men stood by him.* Were "standing over against him"; for if they had been standing by him, as our translation says, he needed not to have "run from the tent door to meet them." To Abraham these appeared at first as *men;* but he "entertained angels unawares," see Heb. xiii. 2.

3. *And said, My Lord.* The word is *Adonai*, not *Yehovah*, for as yet Abraham did not know the quality of his guests. For an explanation of this word, see on chap. xv. 8.

4. *Let a little water . . . be fetched, and wash your feet.* In these verses we find a delightful picture of primitive hospitality. In those ancient times shoes such as ours were not in use; and the foot was protected only by sandals or soles,

MATTHEW HENRY

It becomes those whom God has blessed with plenty to be liberal and open-hearted. His entertainment, though it was very free, was yet plain and homely. His dining-room was an arbour under a tree. His feast was a joint or two of veal, and some cakes baked on the hearth. Here were no dainties, but good, plain, wholesome food, though Abraham was very rich and his guests were very honourable. He and his wife were busy, in accommodating their guests with the best they had. Sarah herself is cook and baker; Abraham runs to fetch the calf, brings out the milk and butter, and thinks it not below him to wait at table. Hearty friendship will stoop to anything but sin. Christ himself has taught us to wash one another's feet, in humble love.

Verses 9–15

These heavenly guests return his kindness. He receives angels, and has angels' rewards, a gracious message from heaven, Matt. x. 41.

I. Care is taken that Sarah should be within hearing. The women did not sit at meat with men, at least not with strangers, but confined themselves to their own apartments; therefore Sarah is here out of sight: but she must not be out of hearing. *Where is Sarah thy wife?* say the angels. *Behold, in the tent*, says Abraham. "Where should she be else? There she is in her place, as she uses to be." Those are most likely to receive comfort from God and his promises that are in their place and in the way of their duty, Luke ii. 8.

II. The promise is then renewed and ratified, that she should have a son (*v.* 10). Note, 1. The same blessings which others have from common providence believers have from the promise, which makes them very sweet and very sure. 2. The spiritual seed of Abraham owe their life, and joy, and hope, and all, to the promise. They are born by the word of God, 1 Pet. i. 23.

III. Sarah thinks this too good news to be true, and therefore cannot as yet find her heart to believe it: *Sarah laughed within herself, v.* 12—a laughter of doubting and mistrust. The great objection which Sarah could not get over was her age: "*I am waxed old*, and past child-bearing in the course of nature." Human improbability often sets up in contradiction to the divine promise. It is hard to cleave to the first Cause, when second causes frown.

IV. The angel reproves the indecent expressions of her distrust, *v.* 13, 14. God gave this reproof to Sarah by Abraham her husband. To him he said, *Why did Sarah laugh?* Our unbelief and distrust are a great offence to the God of heaven. He justly takes it ill to have the objections of sense set up in contradiction to his promise, as Luke i. 18. *Is any thing too hard for the Lord?*

V. Sarah foolishly endeavours to conceal her fault (*v.* 15): *She denied, saying, I did not laugh*; she told this lie, because *she was afraid*. There seems to be in Sarah a retraction of her distrust. Now she perceived, by laying circumstances together, that it was a divine promise which had been made concerning her, she renounced all doubting distrustful thoughts about it. There was withal a sinful attempt to cover a sin with a lie. It is a shame to do amiss, but a greater shame to deny it.

Verses 16–22

The messengers from heaven had now despatched one part of their business, which was an errand of grace to Abraham and Sarah, but now they have before them work of another nature. Sodom is to be destroyed.

I. The honour Abraham did to his guests: *He went with them to bring them on the way*, as one that was loth to part with such good company, and was desirous to pay his utmost respects to them.

II. The honour they did to him; for those that honour God he will honour. God communicated to Abraham his purpose to destroy Sodom.

1. But why must Abraham be of the cabinet-council? The Jews suggest that because God had granted the land of Canaan to Abraham and his seed therefore he would not destroy those cities which were a part of that land, without his knowledge and consent. But God here gives two other reasons:—

(1) Abraham must know, for he is a friend and a favourite. Those who by faith live a life of communion with God cannot but know more of his mind than other people. They have a better insight than others into what is present (Hos. xiv. 9; Ps. cvii. 43), and a better foresight of what is to come.

(2) Abraham must know, for he will teach his household. Those that expect family blessings must make conscience of family duty. If our children be the Lord's they must be nursed for him; if they

JAMIESON, FAUSSET, BROWN

sandals, being still the first observed among the pastoral people of Hebron.

5. for therefore are ye come—No questions were asked. But Abraham knew their object by the course they took—approaching directly in *front* of the chief sheik's tent, which is always distinguishable from the rest and thus showing their wish to be his guests. **6. Abraham hastened . . . unto Sarah . . . make cakes upon the hearth**—Bread is baked daily, no more than is required for family use, and always by the women, commonly the wife. It is a short process. Flour mixed with water is made into dough, and being rolled out into cakes, it is placed on the earthen floor, previously heated by a fire. The fire being removed, the cakes are laid on the ground, and being covered over with hot embers, are soon baked, and eaten the moment they are taken off. **7. Abraham ran unto the herd, and fetched a calf**—Animal food is never provided, except for visitors of a superior rank when a kid or lamb is killed. A calf is still a higher stretch of hospitality, and it would probably be cooked as is usually done when haste is required—either by roasting it whole or by cutting it up into small pieces and broiling them on skewers over the fire. It is always eaten along with boiled corn swimming in butter or melted fat, into which every morsel of meat, laid upon a piece of bread, is dipped, before being conveyed by the fingers to the mouth. **8. milk**—A bowl of camel's milk ends the repast. **he stood by them under the tree**—The host himself, even though he has a number of servants, deems it a necessary act of politeness to *stand* while his guests are at their food, and Abraham evidently did this before he was aware of the real character of his visitors.

9-15. Reproof of Sarah. An inquiry about his wife, so surprising in strangers, the subject of conversation, and the fulfilment of the fondly cherished promise within a specified time, showed Abraham that he had been entertaining more than ordinary travellers (Heb. 13:2). **10. Sarah heard it in the tent door, which was behind him**—The women's apartment is in the back of the tent, divided by a thin partition from the men's. **12. Therefore Sarah laughed within herself**—Long delay seems to have weakened faith. Sarah treated the announcement as incredible, and when taxed with the silent sneer, she added falsehood to distrust. It was an aggravated offense (Acts 5:4), and nothing but grace saved her (Rom. 9:18).

16-22. Disclosure of Sodom's Doom. **16. the men rose . . . Abraham went with them**—It is customary for a host to escort his guests a little way.

17. the Lord said, Shall I hide—The chief stranger, no other than the Lord, disclosed to Abraham the awful doom about to be inflicted on Sodom and the cities of the plain for their enormous wickedness.

ADAM CLARKE

which fastened round the foot with straps. It was, therefore, a great refreshment in so hot a country to get the feet washed at the end of a day's journey; and this is the first thing that Abraham proposes. *Rest yourselves under the tree.* We have already heard of the oak grove of Mamre, chap. xii. 6, and this was the second requisite for the refreshment of a weary traveller, namely, rest in the shade.

5. *I will fetch a morsel of bread.* This was the third requisite, and is introduced in its proper order, as eating immediately after exertion or fatigue is very unwholesome. *For therefore are ye come.* In those ancient days every traveller conceived he had a right to refreshment, when he needed it, at the first tent he met with on his journey. *So do, as thou hast said.* How exceedingly simple was all this! On neither side is there any compliment but such as a generous heart and sound sense dictate.

6. *Three measures of fine meal.* The *seah*, which is here translated "measure," contained, according to Bishop Cumberland, about two gallons and a half; and Mr. Ainsworth translates the word "peck." *Make cakes upon the hearth.* Or under the ashes. This mode is used in the East to the present day. When the hearth is strongly heated with the fire that has been kindled on it, they remove the coals, sweep off the ashes, lay on the bread, and then cover it with the hot cinders.

10. *I will certainly return.* Abraham was now ninety-nine years of age, and this promise was fulfilled when he was a hundred; so that the phrase *according to the time of life* must mean either a complete year, or nine months from the present time, the ordinary time of pregnancy. Taken in this latter sense, Abraham was now in the ninety-ninth year of his age, and Isaac was born when he was in his hundredth year.

11. *It ceased to be with Sarah after the manner of women.* And consequently, naturally speaking, conception could not take place; therefore, if she is to have a son it must be in a supernatural or miraculous way.

12. *Sarah laughed.* Partly through pleasure at the bare idea of the possibility of the thing, and partly from a conviction that it was extremely improbable. She appears to have been in the same spirit, and to have had the same feelings of those who, unexpectedly hearing of something of great consequence to themselves, smile and say, "The news is too good to be true"; see chap. xxi. 6. There is a case very similar to this mentioned in Ps. cxxvi. 1-2.

13. *And the Lord* [*Jehovah*] *said.* So it appears that One of those three persons was Jehovah, and as this name is never given to any created being, consequently the ever-blessed God is intended; and as He was never seen in any bodily shape, consequently the great Angel of the covenant, Jesus Christ, must be meant.

14. *Is any thing too hard for the Lord?* "Shall a word (or thing) be wonderful from the Lord?" i.e., Can anything be too great a miracle for Him to effect? It was to correct Sarah's unbelief, and to strengthen her faith, that God spoke these most important words; words which state that where human wisdom, prudence, and energy fail, and where nature herself ceases to be an agent, through lack of energy to act, or laws to direct and regulate energy, there also God has full sway, and by His own omnific power works all things after the counsel of His own will. Is there an effect to be produced? God can produce it as well without as with means.

16. *Abraham went with them to bring them on the way.* This was another piece of primitive hospitality—to direct strangers in the way. Public roads did not then exist, and guides were essentially necessary in countries where villages were seldom to be met with and where solitary dwellings did not exist.

17. *Shall I hide from Abraham?* That is, I will not hide. A common mode of speech in Scripture—a question asked when an affirmative is designed.

18. *Shall surely become a great and mighty nation.* The revelation that I make to him shall be preserved among his posterity; and the exact fulfilment of My promises, made so long before, shall lead them to believe in My name and

MATTHEW HENRY

wear his livery, they must be trained up in his work. Abraham made it his care and business to promote practical religion in his family. He did not fill their heads with matters of nice speculation, or doubtful disputation; but he taught them to keep *the way of the Lord, and to do judgment and justice*, that is, to be serious and devout in the worship of God and to be honest in their dealings with all men. Abraham was in care that his household after him should keep the way of the Lord, that religion might flourish in his family when he was in his grave.

2. God's friendly talk with Abraham. He tells him of the evidence there was against Sodom. Some sins, and the sins of some sinners, cry aloud to heaven for vengeance. Men are apt to suggest that his way is not equal; but let them know that his judgments are the result of an eternal counsel, and are never rash or sudden resolves. Perhaps the decree is here spoken of as not yet peremptory, that room and encouragement might be given to Abraham to make intercession for them. Thus God looked to see if there were any to intercede, Isa. lix. 16.

Verses 23–33

Communion with God is kept up by the word and by prayer. In the word God speaks to us; in prayer we speak to him. God had revealed to Abraham his purposes concerning Sodom; now from this Abraham takes occasion to speak to God on Sodom's behalf. Note, God's word then does us good when it furnishes us with matter for prayer and excites us to it.

I. The solemnity of Abraham's address to God on this occasion: *Abraham drew near, v.* 23. The expression intimates, 1. A holy concern: *He engaged his heart* to approach to God, Jer. xxx. 21. 2. A holy confidence: He drew near *with an assurance of faith.*

II. The general scope of this prayer. It is the first solemn prayer we have upon record in the Bible; and it is a prayer for the sparing of Sodom. Though sin is to be hated, sinners are to be pitied and prayed for. God delights not in their death, nor should we desire, but deprecate, the woeful day. 1. He begins with a prayer that the righteous among them might be spared, having an eye particularly to just Lot. 2. He improves this into a petition that all might be spared for the sake of the righteous that were among them, God himself countenancing this request.

III. The particular graces eminent in this prayer.

1. Here is great faith; and it is the prayer of faith that is the prevailing prayer. (1) Note, [1] The righteous are mingled with the wicked in this world. Among the best there are, commonly, some bad, and among the worst some good: even in Sodom, one Lot. [2] Though the righteous be among the wicked, yet the righteous God will not, certainly he will not, destroy the righteous with the wicked.

(2) That the righteous shall not *be as the wicked, v.* 25. Though they may suffer with them, yet they do not suffer like them.

2. Here is great humility.

(1) A deep sense of his own unworthiness (*v.* 27): *Behold now, I have taken upon me to speak unto the Lord, who am but dust and ashes*; and again, *v.* 31. He speaks as one amazed at his own boldness. Note, The access we have to the throne of grace, and the freedom of speech allowed us, are just matter of humble wonder, 2 Sam. vii. 18.

(2) An awful dread of God's displeasure. But he with whom we have to do is *God and not man;* and, however he may seem, is not really *angry with the prayers of the upright* (Ps. lxxx. 4), for they are *his delight* (Prov. xv. 8), and he is pleased when he is wrestled with.

3. Here is great charity. (1) A charitable opinion of Sodom's character: as bad as it was, he thought there were several good people in it. It becomes us to hope the best of the worst places. Of the two it is better to err in that extreme. (2) A charitable desire of Sodom's welfare: he used all his interest at the throne of grace for mercy for them.

4. Here are great boldness and believing confidence. Suppose there be fifty, *v.* 24. He advanced upon God's concessions, again and again.

IV. The success of the prayer. God's general goodwill appears in this, that he consented to spare the wicked for the sake of the righteous. See what great blessings good people are to any place. His particular favour to Abraham appeared in this, that he did not leave off granting till Abraham left off asking. Such is the power of prayer.

JAMIESON, FAUSSET, BROWN

21. I will go down . . . and see—language used after the manner of men. These cities were to be made examples to all future ages of God's severity; and therefore ample proof given that the judgment was neither rash nor excessive (Ezek. 18:23; Jer. 18:7).

23-33. ABRAHAM'S INTERCESSION. **23. Abraham drew near, and said,** etc.—The scene described is full of interest and instruction—showing in an unmistakable manner the efficacy of prayer and intercession. (See also Prov. 15:8; Jas. 5:16). Abraham reasoned justly as to the rectitude of the divine procedure (Rom. 3:5, 6), and many guilty cities and nations have been spared on account of God's people (Matt. 5:13; 24:22).

JOSEPH PARKER:

"Shall not the judge of all the earth do right?" There is a marked difference between the tone of Abraham and the tone of Noah. So far as we can learn from the record, Noah did not put any such inquiries as those before the Flood; though, perhaps, they were in some measure rendered needless by the distinct separation of himself on account of his righteousness. Still, the inquiries are intensely interesting as showing how divine judgments on a great scale strike a pious observer. Could such a thing be *right*? was Abraham's anxious question. A wonderful question, opening up a wonderful range of moral speculation! Remember from whom Abraham held moral nature, and you will see that this very question is itself a tribute to the righteousness of God. The question was an inspiration. And the course which God took in answering it shows that he has ever held it of the first consequence to secure the moral approbation of his creatures. In many things he has transcended their *reason*; in nearly all things he has baffled and even confounded and mocked their *speculations*; but in all instances he has been most careful not to excite controversy against himself in the human *conscience.—The People's Bible*

33. the Lord . . . left communing . . . and Abraham returned unto his place—Why did Abraham cease to carry his intercessions farther? Either because he fondly thought that he was now sure of the cities being preserved (Luke 13:9), or because the Lord restrained his mind from farther intercession (Jer. 7:16; 11:14). But there were not ten "righteous persons." There was only one, and he might without injustice have perished in the general overthrow (Eccles. 9:2). But a difference is sometimes made, and on this occasion the grace of God was manifested in a signal manner for the sake of Abraham. What a blessing to be connected with a saint of God!

ADAM CLARKE

trust in My goodness.

19. *And they shall keep the way of the Lord.* The true religion; God's way; that in which God walks himself, and in which, of course, His followers walk also.

22. *And the men turned their faces.* That is, the two angels who accompanied Jehovah were now sent towards Sodom; while the third, who is called the Lord or *Jehovah,* remained with Abraham for the purpose of teaching him the great usefulness and importance of faith and prayer.

23. *Wilt thou also destroy the righteous with the wicked?* A form of speech similar to that in verse 17, an invariable principle of justice, that the righteous shall not be punished for the crimes of the impious. And this Abraham lays down as the foundation of his supplications. Who can pray with any hope of success who cannot assign a reason to God and his conscience for the petitions he offers? The great sacrifice offered by Christ is an infinite reason why a penitent sinner should expect to find the mercy for which he pleads.

25. *Shall not the Judge of all the earth do right?* God alone is the Judge of all men. Abraham, in thus addressing himself to the person in the text, considers him either as the Supreme Being or His representative.

27. *Which am but dust and ashes. Aphar vaepher,* words very similar in sound, as they refer to matters which so much resemble each other. *Dust*—the lightest particles of earth. *Ashes*—the residuum of consumed substances. By these expressions he shows how deeply his soul was humbled in the presence of God. He who has high thoughts of himself must have low thoughts of the dignity of the divine nature, of the majesty of God, and the sinfulness of sin.

32. *Peradventure ten shall be found there.* Knowing that in the family of his nephew the true religion was professed and practiced, he could not suppose there could be less than ten righteous persons in the city; he did not think it necessary to urge his supplication farther; he therefore left off his entreaties, and the Lord departed from him. It is highly worthy of observation that while he continued to pray the presence of God was continued; and when Abraham ended, "the glory of the Lord was lifted up," as the Targum expresses it.

MATTHEW HENRY

CHAPTER 19

Verses 1–3

Observe here, 1. There was but one good man in Sodom, and these heavenly messengers soon found him out. 2. Lot sufficiently distinguished himself from the rest of his neighbours, at this time, which plainly set a mark upon him. He that did not act like the rest must not fare like the rest. (1) Lot sat in the gate of Sodom at even. (2) He was hospitable, and very free and generous in his invitations and entertainments. He courted these strangers to his house, and to the best accommodations he had, and gave them all the evidences that he could of his sincerity. When the angels accepted his invitation, he treated them nobly. Note, Good people should be (with prudence) generous people.

Verses 4–11

Now it appeared, beyond contradiction, that the cry of Sodom was no louder than there was cause for.

I. That they were all wicked, *v.* 4. Wickedness had become universal, and they were unanimous in any vile design.

II. That they had arrived at the highest pitch of wickedness; they were *sinners before the Lord exceedingly* (*ch.* xiii. 13); for, 1. It was the most unnatural and abominable wickedness that they were now set upon, a sin that still bears their name, and is called *Sodomy*. Those that have become impudent in sin generally prove impenitent in sin; and it will be their ruin. Those have hard hearts indeed that sin with a high hand, Jer. vi. 15. 3. When Lot interposed, with all the mildness imaginable, to check the rage and fury of their lust, they were most insolently rude and abusive to him. Being greatly disturbed at their vile attempt, he unadvisedly and unjustifiably offered to prostitute his two daughters to them, *v.* 8. It is true, of two evils we must choose the less; but of two sins we must choose neither, nor ever do evil that good may come of it. They threaten him, and lay violent hands upon him.

III. That nothing less than the power of an angel could save a good man out of their wicked hands. 1. They rescue Lot, *v.* 10. The saints, at death, are pulled like Lot into a house of perfect safety, and the door shut for ever against those that pursue them. 2. They chastise the insolence of the Sodomites: *They smote them with blindness*, *v.* 11. Yet these Sodomites, after they were struck blind, continued seeking the door, to break it down, till they were tired. No judgments will, of themselves, change the corrupt natures and purposes of wicked men. If their minds had not been blinded as well as their bodies, they would have said, as the magicians, *This is the finger of God*, and would have submitted.

Verses 12–14

We have here the preparation for Lot's deliverance.

I. Notice is given him of the approach of Sodom's ruin: *We will destroy this place*, *v.* 13.

II. He is directed to give notice to his friends and relations, that they, if they would, might be saved with him (*v.* 12). Note, Those who through grace are themselves delivered out of a sinful state should do what they can for the deliverance of others, especially their relations. 2. The offer of great favour. They ask what relations he had there, that, whether righteous or unrighteous, they might be saved with him. Note, Bad people often fare the better in this world for the sake of their good relations. It is good being akin to a godly man.

III. He applies himself accordingly to his sons-in-law, *v.* 14. Observe, 1. The fair warning that Lot gave them: *Up, get you out of this place*. 2. The slight they put upon this warning: *He seemed to them as one that mocked.* They thought, perhaps, that the assault which the Sodomites had just now made upon his house had disturbed his head. Those who lived a merry life, and made a jest of everything, made a jest of this warning, and so they perished in the overthrow.

Verses 15–23

Here is, I. The rescue of Lot out of Sodom, Ezek. xiv. 14. Early in the morning his own guests, in kindness to him, turned him out of doors, and his family with him, v. 15. His daughters that were married perished with their unbelieving husbands; but those that continued with him were preserved with him.

1. With what a gracious violence Lot was brought out of Sodom, *v.* 16. It seems he did not make so much haste as the case required. It might have been fatal to him if the angels had not *laid hold of his hand, and brought him forth*, and saved him with fear,

JAMIESON, FAUSSET, BROWN

CHAPTER 19

Vss. 1-38. LOT'S ENTERTAINMENT. **1. there came two angels**—most probably two of those that had been with Abraham, commissioned to execute the divine judgment against Sodom. **Lot sat in the gate of Sodom**—In Eastern cities it is the market, the seat of justice, of social intercourse and amusement, especially a favorite lounge in the evenings, the arched roof affording a pleasant shade. **2. turn in, I pray you . . . tarry all night**—offer of the same generous hospitalities as described in the preceding chapter, and which are still spontaneously practised in the small towns. **And they said, Nay; but we will abide in the street all night**—Where there are no inns and no acquaintance, it is not uncommon for travellers to sleep in the street wrapped up in their cloaks. **3. entered into his house**—On removing to the plain, Lot intended at first to live in his tent apart from the people. But he was gradually drawn in, dwelt in the city, and he and his family were connected with the citizens by marriage ties. **4. men of Sodom, compassed the house**—Appalling proofs are here given of their wickedness. It is evident that evil communications had corrupted good manners; otherwise Lot would never have acted as he did.

12, 13. Hast thou here any besides? . . . we will destroy this place—Apostolic authority has declared Lot was "a righteous man" (II Pet. 2:8), at bottom good, though he contented himself with lamenting the sins that he saw, instead of acting on his own convictions, and withdrawing himself and family from such a sink of corruption. But favor was shown him: and even his bad relatives had, for his sake, an offer of deliverance, which was ridiculed and spurned (II Pet. 3:4).

15-17. The kindly interest the angels took in the preservation of Lot is beautifully displayed. But he "lingered." Was it from sorrow at the prospect of losing all his property, the acquisition of many years? Or was it that his benevolent heart was paralyzed by thoughts of the awful crisis? This is the charitable way of accounting for a delay that would have been fatal but for the friendly urgency of the angel.

ADAM CLARKE

CHAPTER 19

1. *Two angels.* The two referred to in chap. xviii. 22. *Sat in the gate.* Probably, in order to prevent unwary travellers from being entrapped by his wicked townsmen, he waited at the gate of the city to bring the strangers he might meet with to his own house, as well as to transact his own business. Or, as the gate was the place of judgment, he might have been sitting there as magistrate to hear and determine disputes. *Bowed himself.* Not through religious reverence, for he did not know the quality of his guests; but through the customary form of civility.

2. *Nay; but we will abide in the street.* Instead of "nay" some MSS. have "to him"; "And they said unto him, For we lodge in the street," where, nevertheless, the negation is understood. Knowing the disposition of the inhabitants, and appearing in the mere character of travellers, they preferred the open street to any house; but as Lot pressed them vehemently, and they knew him to be a righteous man, not yet willing to make themselves known, they consented to take shelter under his hospitable roof. Our Lord, willing for the time being to conceal His person from the knowledge of the disciples going to Emmaus, made as though He would go farther, Luke xxiv. 13; but at last, like the angels here, yielded to the importunity of His disciples, and went into their lodgings.

5. *Where are the men which came in to thee?* This account justifies the character given of this depraved people in the preceding chapter, v. 20, and in chap. xiii. 13. As their crime was the deepest disgrace to human nature, so it is too bad to be described; in the sacred text it is sufficiently marked; and the iniquity which, from these most abominable wretches, has been called "Sodomy" is punished in our country with death.

8. *Behold now, I have two daughters.* Nothing but that sacred light in which the rights of hospitality were regarded among the Eastern nations could either justify or palliate this proposal of Lot. A man who had taken a stranger under his care and protection was bound to defend him even at the expense of his own life. In this light the rights of hospitality are still regarded in Asiatic countries; and on these high notions only, the influence of which an Asiatic mind alone can properly appreciate, Lot's conduct on this occasion can be at all excused: but even then, it was not only the language of anxious solicitude, but of unwarrantable haste.

9. *And he will needs be a judge.* So his sitting in the gate is perhaps a farther proof of his being there in a magisterial capacity, as some have supposed.

11. *And they smote the men . . . with blindness.* This has been understood two ways: (1) The angels, by the power which God had given them, deprived these wicked men of a proper and regular use of their sight; or (2) They caused such a deep darkness to take place that they could not find Lot's door. The author of the book of Wisdom was evidently of this latter opinion, for he says they were compassed about with horrible great darkness, chap. xix. 17. See a similar case of Elisha and the Syrians, 2 Kings vi. 18, etc.

12. *Hast thou here any besides? son in law.* Here there appears to be but one meant, as the word is in the singular number; but in v. 14 the word is plural, his sons-in-law. These were only two in number, as we do not hear that Lot had more than two daughters; and these daughters but only betrothed, as is evident from what Lot says, v. 8; for they had not known man, but were the spouses elect of those who are here called his sons-in-law. But though these might be reputed as a part of Lot's family, and entitled on this account to God's protection, yet it is sufficiently plain that they did not escape the perdition of these wicked men; and the reason is given, v. 14, they received the solemn warning as a ridiculous tale, the creature of Lot's invention, or the offspring of his fear. Therefore they made no provision for their escape, and doubtless perished, notwithstanding the sincerely offered grace, in the perdition that fell on this ungodly city.

16. *While he lingered.* Probably in affection-

MATTHEW HENRY

Jude 23. The salvation of the most righteous men must be attributed to God's mercy, not to their own merit. We are saved by grace.

2. With what a gracious vehemence he was urged to make the best of his way, when he was *brought forth, v.* 17. He must not hanker after Sodom: *Look not behind thee.* He must not loiter by the way: *Stay not in all the plain.* He must not take up short of the place of refuge appointed him: *Escape to the mountain.* Such as these are the commands given to those who through grace are delivered out of a sinful state. (1) Return not to sin and Satan, for that is looking back to Sodom. (2) Rest not in self and the world, for that is staying in the plain. And, (3) Reach towards Christ and heaven, for that is escaping to the mountain, short of which we must not take up.

II. The fixing of a place of refuge for him. The mountain was first appointed for him to flee to, but, 1. He begged for a city of refuge, one of the five that lay together, called *Bela, ch.* xiv. 2, 18–20. It was Lot's weakness to think a city of his own choosing safer than the mountain of God's appointing. Could not he that saved him from greater evils save him from the less? He insists much in his petition upon the smallness of the place: *It is a little one, is it not?* This gave a new name to the place; it was called *Zoar, a little one.* 2. God granted him his request, though there was much infirmity in it, *v.* 21, 22. See what favour God showed to a true saint, though weak. (1) Zoar was spared, to gratify him.

III. It is taken notice of that the sun had risen when Lot entered into Zoar; for when a good man comes into a place he brings light along with him, or should do.

Verses 24–25

Then, when Lot had got safely into Zoar, then this ruin came; for good men are taken away from the evil to come. *Then,* when the sun had risen bright and clear, promising a fair day, then this storm arose, to show that it was not from natural causes. It was a strange punishment, Job xxxi. 3. Never was the like before nor since. It was a judgment that laid all waste: *It overthrew the cities,* and destroyed all the inhabitants of them, the plain, and all that grew upon the ground, *v.* 25. It was an utter ruin, and irreparable. That fruitful valley remains to this day a great lake, or dead sea; it is called *the Salt Sea,* Num. xxxiv. 12. It is about thirty miles long and ten miles broad; it has no living creature in it; it is not moved by the wind; the smell of it is offensive; things do not easily sink in it. The Greeks call it *Asphaltites,* from a sort of pitch which it casts up. Jordan falls into it, and is lost there. It was a punishment that answered to their sin. Those that went after strange flesh were destroyed by strange fire, Jude 7. It is often referred to in the scripture, and made a pattern of the ruin of Israel (Deut. xxix. 23), of Babylon (Isa. xiii. 19), of Edom (Jer. xlix. 18), of Moab and Ammon (Zeph. ii. 9).

Verse 26

This also is written for our admonition. Our Saviour refers to it (Luke xvii. 32), *Remember Lot's wife.* As by the example of Sodom the wicked are warned to turn from their wickedness, so by the example of Lot's wife the righteous are warned not to turn from their righteousness. See Ezek. iii. 18, 20.

I. The sin of Lot's wife: *She looked back from behind him.* She disobeyed an express command. Probably she hankered after her house and goods in Sodom, and was loth to leave them. Christ intimates this to be her sin (Luke xvii. 31, 32); she too much regarded her *stuff.* Her looking back evinced an inclination to go back; and therefore our Saviour uses it as a warning against apostasy from our Christian profession. We have all renounced the world and the flesh, and have set our faces heavenward; we are in the plain, upon our probation; and it is at our peril if we return into the interests we profess to have abandoned.

II. The punishment of Lot's wife for this sin. Though she was a monument of distinguishing mercy in her deliverance out of Sodom, yet God did not connive at her disobedience. Since it is such a dangerous thing to look back, let us always press forward, Phil. iii. 13, 14.

Verses 27–29

I. Here is Abraham's pious regard to God in this event. *He got up early* to look towards Sodom; and, to intimate that his design herein was to see what became of his prayers. We must direct our prayer as a letter, and then look up for an answer, direct our prayer as an arrow, and then look up to see

JAMIESON, FAUSSET, BROWN

18, 19. Lot said . . . Oh! not so, my Lord . . . I cannot escape to the mountain—What a strange want of faith and fortitude, as if He who had interfered for his rescue would not have protected him in the mountain solitude. **21. See, I have accepted thee concerning this . . . also**—His request was granted him, the prayer of faith availed, and to convince him, from his own experience, that it would have been best and safest at once to follow implicitly the divine directions. **22. Haste . . . for I cannot do any thing till thou be come thither**—The ruin of Sodom was suspended till he was secure. What care God does take of His people (Rev. 7:3)! What a proof of the love which God bore to a good though weak man!

24. Then the Lord rained . . . brimstone and fire from . . . heaven—God, in accomplishing His purposes, acts immediately or mediately through the agency of means; and there are strong grounds for believing that it was in the latter way He effected the overthrow of the cities of the plain—that it was, in fact, by a volcanic eruption. The raining down of fire and brimstone from heaven is perfectly accordant with this idea since those very substances, being raised into the air by the force of the volcano, would fall in a fiery shower on the surrounding region. This view seems countenanced by Job. Whether it was miraculously produced, or the natural operation employed by God, it is not of much consequence to determine: it was a divine judgment, foretold and designed for the punishment of those who were sinners exceedingly.

26. Lot was accompanied by his wife and two daughters. But whether it was from irresistible curiosity or perturbation of feeling, or that she was about to return to save something, his wife lingered, and while thus disobeying the parting counsel, "to look not back, nor stay in all the plain," the torrent of liquid lava enveloped her so that she became the victim of her supine indolence or sinful rashness.

27. Abraham gat up early in the morning, etc.—Abraham was at this time in Mamre, near Hebron, and a traveller last year verified the truth of this passage. "From the height which overlooks Hebron, where the patriarch stood, the observer at the present day has an ex-

ADAM CLARKE

ate though useless entreaties to prevail on the remaining parts of his family to escape from the destruction that was now descending; *laid hold upon his hand*—pulled them away by mere force, *the Lord being merciful;* else they had been left to perish in their lingering.

17. *When they had brought them forth.* Every word here is emphatic, *Escape for thy life;* thou art in the most imminent danger of perishing; thy life and thy soul are both at stake. *Look not behind thee*—thou hast but barely time enough to escape from the judgment that is now descending; no lingering, or thou art lost! One look back may prove fatal to thee, and God commands thee to avoid it. *Neither stay thou in all the plain,* because God will destroy that as well as the city. *Escape to the mountain,* on which these judgments shall not light, and which God has appointed thee for a place of refuge, *lest thou be consumed.* It is not an ordinary judgment that is coming; a fire from heaven shall burn up the cities, the plain, and all that remain in the cities and in the plain.

19. *I cannot escape to the mountain.* He saw the destruction so near that he imagined he should not have time sufficient to reach the mountain before it arrived. He did not consider that God could give no command to His creatures that it would be impossible for them to fulfil; but the hurry and perturbation of his mind will at once account for and excuse this gross oversight.

20. *It is a little one.* Probably Lot wished to have it for an inheritance, and therefore pleaded its being a little one, that his request might be the more readily granted. Or he might suppose that, being a little city, it was less depraved than Sodom and Gomorrah, and therefore not so ripe for punishment; which was probably the case.

22. *I cannot do any thing till thou be come thither.* So these heavenly messengers had the strictest commission to take care of Lot and his family; and even the purposes of divine justice could not be accomplished on the rebellious till this righteous man and his family had escaped from the place. A proof of Abraham's assertion, "The Judge of all the earth will do right."

The name of the city was called Zoar. "Little," its former name being Bela.

24. *Brimstone and fire.* The word which we translate *brimstone* is of very uncertain derivation. It is evidently used metaphorically to point out the utmost degrees of punishment executed on the most flagitious criminals, in Deut. xxix. 23; Job xviii. 15; Ps. xi. 6; Isa. xxxiv. 9; Ezek. xxxviii. 22. And as hell, or an everlasting separation from God and the glory of His power, is the utmost punishment that can be inflicted on sinners, hence brimstone and fire are used in Scripture to signify the torments in that place of punishment. See Isa. xxx. 33; Rev. xiv. 10; xix. 20; xx. 10; xxi. 8. We may safely suppose that it was quite possible that a shower of nitrous particles might have been precipitated from the atmosphere, here, as in many other places, called heaven, which by the action of fire would be immediately ignited, and so consume the cities; and, as we have already seen that the plains about Sodom and Gomorrah abounded with asphaltus or bitumen pits (see chap. xiv. 10), that what is particularly meant here in reference to the plain is the setting fire to this vast store of inflammable matter by the agency of lightning.

26. *She became a pillar of salt.* The vast variety of opinions, both ancient and modern, on the crime of Lot's wife, her change, and the manner in which that change was effected, are in many cases as unsatisfactory as they are ridiculous. On this point the sacred Scripture says little. God had commanded Lot and his family not to look behind them; the wife of Lot disobeyed this command; she *looked back from behind him*—Lot, her husband, *and she became a pillar of salt.* This is all the information the inspired historian has thought proper to give us on this subject.

27. *Abraham gat up early in the morning.* Anxious to know what was the effect of the prayers which he had offered to God the preceding day; what must have been his astonishment when he found that all these cities, with

MATTHEW HENRY

whether it reach the mark, Ps. v. 3.

II. Here is God's favourable regard to Abraham, *v.* 29. As before, when Abraham prayed for Ishmael, God heard him for Isaac, so now, when he prayed for Sodom, he heard him for Lot. *He remembered Abraham, and,* for his sake, *sent Lot out of the overthrow.* Note, God will certainly give an answer of peace to the prayer of faith, in his own way and time; though, for a while, it seem to be forgotten, yet, sooner or later, it will appear to be remembered.

Verses 30–38

Here is, I. The great trouble and distress that Lot was brought into after his deliverance, *v.* 30. 1. He was frightened out of Zoar, durst not dwell there; probably because he found it as wicked as Sodom, and therefore concluded it could not long survive it. Note, Settlements and shelters of our own choosing, and in which we do not follow God, commonly prove uneasy to us. 2. He was forced to betake himself to the mountain, and to take up with a cave for his habitation there. Observe, (1) He was now glad to go to the mountain, the place which God had appointed for his shelter. (2) He that, awhile ago, could not find room enough for himself and his stock in the whole land, but must jostle with Abraham, and get as far from him as he could, is now confined to a hole in a hill, where he has scarcely room to turn himself, and there he is solitary and trembling.

II. The great sin that Lot and his daughters were guilty of, when they were in this desolate place. It is a sad story.

1. His daughters laid a very wicked plot to bring him to sin; and theirs was, doubtless, the greater guilt. (1) Some think that their pretence was plausible. Their father had no sons, they had no husbands, nor knew they where to have any of the holy seed, whilst if they had children by others, their father's name would not be preserved in them. But, (2) Whatever their pretence was, it is certain that their project was very wicked and vile, and an impudent affront to the very light and law of nature.

2. Lot himself, by his own folly and unwariness, was wretchedly overcome, and suffered himself so far to be imposed upon by his own children as, two nights together, to be drunk, and to commit incest, *v.* 33, &c. *Lord, what is man!* What are the best of men, when God leaves them to themselves ! (1) The peril of security. Lot, who kept himself sober and chaste in Sodom, was yet, in the mountain, where he was alone, and as he thought quite out of the way of temptation, shamefully overtaken. Let him therefore that thinks he stands, stands high and stands firm, *take heed lest he fall.* No mountain, on this side the holy hill above, can set us out of the reach of Satan's fiery darts. (2) The peril of drunkenness. It is not only a great sin itself, but it is the inlet of many sins; it may prove the inlet of the worst and most unnatural sins.

3. In the close we have an account of the birth of the two sons, or grandsons (call them which you will), of Lot, Moab and Ammon, the fathers of two nations, neighbours to Israel, and which we often read of in the Old Testament; both together are called *the children of Lot,* Ps. lxxxiii. 8.

Lastly, Observe, that, after this, we never read any more of Lot, but from the silence of the scripture concerning him henceforward we may learn that drunkenness, as it makes men forgetful, so it makes them forgotten.

JAMIESON, FAUSSET, BROWN

tensive view spread out before him towards the Dead Sea. A cloud of smoke rising from the plain would be visible to a person at Hebron now, and could have been, therefore, to Abraham as he looked toward Sodom on the morning of its destruction by God" [HACKETT]. It must have been an awful sight, and is frequently alluded to in Scripture (Deut. 29:23; Isa. 13:19; Jude 7). "The plain which is now covered by the Salt or Dead Sea shows in the great difference of level between the bottoms of the northern and southern ends of the lake—the latter being 13 feet and the former 1300—that the southern end was of recent formation, and submerged at the time of the fall of the cities" [LYNCH]. **29. when God destroyed the cities,** etc.—This is most welcome and instructive after so painful a narrative. It shows if God is a "consuming fire" to the wicked, He is the friend of the righteous. He "remembered" the intercessions of Abraham, and what confidence should not this give us that He will remember the intercessions of a greater than Abraham in our behalf.

ADAM CLARKE

the plain which resembled the garden of the Lord, chap. xiii. 10, burnt up, and the smoke ascending like the smoke of a furnace, and was thereby assured that even God himself could not discover ten righteous persons in four whole cities!

29. *God remembered Abraham.* Though he did not descend lower than ten righteous persons (see chap. xviii. 32), yet the Lord had respect to the spirit of his petitions, and spared all those who could be called righteous, and for Abraham's sake offered salvation to all the family of Lot, though neither his sons-in-law elect nor his own wife ultimately profited by it.

30. *Lot went up out of Zoar.* From seeing the universal desolation that had fallen upon the land, and that the fire was still continuing its depredations, *he feared to dwell in Zoar,* lest that also should be consumed, and then went to those very mountains to which God had ordered him at first to make his escape.

31. *Our father is old,* and consequently not likely to remarry, *and there is not a man in the earth*—none left, according to their opinion, in all the land of Canaan, of their own family and kindred.

32. *Come, let us make our father drink wine.* On their flight from Zoar it is probable they had brought with them certain provisions to serve them for the time being, and the wine here mentioned among the rest.

KEIL–DELITZSCH:

From Zoar Lot removed with his two daughters to the (Moabitish) mountains, for fear that Zoar might after all be destroyed, and dwelt in one of the caves in which the limestone rocks abound, and so became a dweller in a cave. While there, his daughters resolved to procure children through their father; and to that end on two successive evenings they made him intoxicated with wine, and then lay with him in the night, one after the other, that they might conceive seed. To this accursed crime they were impelled by the desire to preserve their family, because they thought there was no man on the earth to come in unto them, i.e. to marry them, "after the manner of all the earth." Not that they imagined the whole human race to have perished in the destruction of the valley of Siddim, but because they were afraid that no man would link himself with them, the only survivors of a country smitten by the curse of God. If it was not lust, therefore, which impelled them to this shameful deed, their conduct was worthy of Sodom, and shows quite as much as their previous betrothal to men of Sodom, that they were deeply imbued with the sinful character of that city. The words of verses 33 and 35, "And he knew not of her lying down and of her rising up," do not affirm that he was in an unconscious state, as the Rabbins are said by *Jerome* to have indicated. They merely mean that in his intoxicated state, though not entirely unconscious, yet he lay with his daughters without clearly knowing what he was doing.—*Commentary on the Old Testament*

CHAPTER 20 (Matthew Henry)

Verses 1–2

Here is, 1. Abraham's removal from Mamre. We are not told upon what occasion he removed. His sin in denying his wife had here a two-fold aggravation:—(1) He had been guilty of this same sin before, and had been reproved for it. Note, It is possible that a good man may, not only fall into sin, but relapse into the same sin, through the surprise and strength of temptation and the infirmity of the flesh. (2) Sarah, as it should seem, was now with child of the promised seed; he ought therefore to have taken particular care of her now, as Judg. xiii. 4.

CHAPTER 20 (Jamieson, Fausset, Brown)

Vss. 1-18. ABRAHAM'S DENIAL OF HIS WIFE. **1. Abraham journeyed from thence . . . and dwelled between Kadesh and Shur**—Leaving the encampment, he migrated to the southern border of Canaan. In the neighborhood of Gerar was a very rich and well-watered pasture land.

2. Abraham said of Sarah his wife, She is my sister—Fear of the people among whom he was, tempted him to equivocate. His conduct was highly culpable. It was deceit, deliberate and premeditated—there was no sudden pressure upon him—it was the second offense of the kind—it was a distrust of God every way surprising, and it was calculated to produce injurious effects on the heathen around. Its mischievous tendency was not long in being developed. **Abimelech** (father-king) **. . . sent and took Sarah**—to be one of his wives, in the exercise of a privilege claimed by Eastern sovereigns, already explained (ch. 12:19).

CHAPTER 20 (Adam Clarke)

1. *And Abraham journeyed.* It is very likely that this holy man was so deeply affected with the melancholy prospect of the ruined cities, and not knowing what was become of his nephew Lot and his family, that he could no longer bear to dwell within sight of the place. Having, therefore, struck his tents, and sojourned for a short time at Kadesh and Shur, he fixed his habitation in Gerar, which was a city of Arabia Petraea, under a king of the Philistines called Abimelech, "my father king," who appears to have been not only the father of his people, but also a righteous man.

2. *She is my sister.* See the parallel account, chap. xxii, and the notes there. Sarah was now about ninety years of age, and probably pregnant with Isaac. Her beauty, therefore, must have been considerably impaired since the time she was taken in a similar manner by Pharaoh, king of Egypt; but she was probably now chosen by Abimelech more on the account of forming an alliance with Abraham, who was very rich,

MATTHEW HENRY

Verses 3–7

It appears by this that God revealed himself by dreams even to those who were out of the pale of the church and covenant.

I. God gives him notice of his danger (*v.* 3), his danger of *sin*, telling him that the woman is a man's wife, so that if he take her he will wrong her husband; his danger of death for this sin: *Thou art a dead man.* If thou art a bad man, certainly thou art a dead man.

II. He pleads ignorance that Abraham and Sarah had agreed to impose upon him, and not to let him know that they were any more than brother and sister, *v.* 6. His heart condemns him not, 1 John iii. 21. If our consciences witness to our integrity, and if, however we may have been cheated into a snare, we have not knowingly and wittingly sinned against God, it will be our rejoicing in the day of evil.

III. God gives a very full answer to what he had said.

He allows his plea, and admits that what he did he did in the integrity of his heart: *Yea, I know it, v.* 6. Note, It is matter of comfort to those that are honest that God knows their honesty, and will acknowledge it, though perhaps men that are prejudiced against them either cannot be convinced of it or will not own that they are.

He charges him to make restitution: *Now therefore,* now that thou art better informed, *restore the man his wife, v.* 7. Note, Ignorance will excuse no longer than it continues. If we have entered upon a wrong course through ignorance this will not excuse our knowingly persisting in it. Lev. v. 3–5.

Verses 8–13

Abimelech, being thus warned of God in a dream, takes the warning, and, as one truly afraid of sin and its consequences, he rises early to obey the directions given him.

I. He has a caution for his servants, *v.* 8.

II. He has a chiding for Abraham.

1. The serious reproof which Abimelech gave to Abraham, *v.* 9, 10. His reasoning with Abraham upon this occasion was very strong, and yet very mild. Nothing could be said better; he does not reproach him, not insult over him, does not say, "Is this your profession? I see, though you will not swear, you will lie. If these be prophets, I will beg to be freed from the sight of them:" but he fairly represents the injury Abraham had done him, and calmly signifies his resentment of it. (1) He calls that sin which he now found he had been in danger of, a great sin. (2) He looks upon it that both himself and his kingdom would have been exposed to the wrath of God if he had been guilty of this sin, though ignorantly. Note, The sins of kings often prove the plagues of kingdoms: rulers should therefore, for their people's sake, dread sin. (3) He charges Abraham with doing that which was not justifiable, in disowning his marriage. (4) He takes it as a very great injury to himself and his family that Abraham had thus exposed them to sin: "*What have I offended thee?* If I had been thy worst enemy, thou couldst not have done me a worse turn, nor taken a more effectual course to be revenged on me." (5) He challenges him to assign a cause for his suspecting them as a dangerous people. What reason hadst thou to think that if we had known her to be thy wife thou wouldst have been exposed to any danger by it?" Note, A suspicion of our goodness is justly reckoned a greater affront than a slight upon our greatness.

2. The poor excuse that Abraham made for himself.

(1) He pleaded the bad opinion he had of the place, *v.* 11. "*Surely the fear of God is not in this place,* and then they will slay me." There are many places and persons that have more of the fear of God in them than we think they have: perhaps they are not called by our dividing name, they do not wear our badges, they do not tie themselves to that which we have an opinion of; and therefore we conclude they have not the fear of God in their hearts, which is very injurious both to Christ and Christians, and makes us obnoxious to God's judgment, Matt. vii. 1. Uncharitableness and censoriousness are sins that are the cause of many other sins. Men would not do ill if they did not first think ill.

(2) He excused it from the guilt of a downright lie by making it out that, in a sense, she was his sister, *v.* 12. But those to whom he said, *She is my sister,* understood that she was so his sister as not to be capable of being his wife; so that it was an equivocation, with an intent to deceive.

(3) He clears himself from the imputation of an affront designed against Abimelech by alleging that it had been his practice before, according to an agreement between him and his wife, when they first became sojourners (*v.* 13).

JAMIESON, FAUSSET, BROWN

3. But God came to Abimelech in a dream—In early times a dream was often made the medium of communicating important truths; and this method was adopted for the preservation of Sarah.

9. Then Abimelech called Abraham, and said . . . What hast thou done?—In what a humiliating plight does the patriarch now appear—he, a servant of the true God, rebuked by a heathen prince. Who would not rather be in the place of Abimelech than of the honored but sadly offending patriarch! What a dignified attitude is that of the king—calmly and justly reproving the sin of the patriarch, but respecting his person and heaping coals of fire on his head by the liberal presents made to him.

11. Abraham said . . . I thought, Surely the fear of God is not in this place—From the horrible vices of Sodom he seems to have taken up the impression that all other cities of Canaan were equally corrupt. There might have been few or none who feared God, but what a sad thing when men of the world show a higher sense of honor and a greater abhorrence of crimes than a true worshipper!

12. yet indeed she is my sister. (See on ch. 11:3). What a poor defense Abraham made. The statement absolved him from the charge of direct and absolute falsehood, but he had told a moral untruth because there was an intention to deceive (cf. ch. 12:11-13). "Honesty is always the best policy." Abraham's life would have been as well protected without the fraud as with it: and what shame to himself, what distrust to God, what dishonor to religion might have been prevented! "Let us speak truth every man to his neighbor."

ADAM CLARKE

than on account of any personal accomplishments.

3. *But God came to Abimelech.* Thus we find that persons who were not of the family of Abraham had the knowledge of the true God.

5. *In the integrity of my heart.* Had Abimelech any other than honorable views in taking Sarah, he could not have justified himself thus to his Maker; and that these views were of the most honorable kind God himself, to whom the appeal was made, asserts in the most direct manner, "Yea, I know that thou didst this in the integrity of thy heart."

7. *He is a prophet, and he shall pray for thee.* The word prophet, which we have from the Greek *prophetes,* and which is compounded of *pro,* "before," and *phemi,* "I speak," means, in its general acceptation, one who speaks of things before they happen, i.e., one who foretells future events. But that this was not the original notion of the word, its use in this place sufficiently proves. Abraham certainly was not a prophet in the present general acceptation of the term, and for the Hebrew *nabi* we must seek some other meaning. I have, in a discourse entitled "The Christian Prophet and His Work," proved that the proper ideal meaning of the original word is to "pray, entreat, make supplication," and this meaning of it I have justified at large both from its application in this place and from its pointed use in the case of Saul, mentioned in 1 Samuel x, and from the case of the priests of Baal, 1 Kings xviii, where prophesying most undoubtedly means making prayer and supplication. As those who were in habits of intimacy with God by prayer and faith were found the most proper persons to communicate His mind to man, both with respect to the present and the future, hence *nabi,* the "intercessor," became in process of time the public instructor or preacher, and also the predictor of future events, because to such faithful praying men God revealed the secret of His will.

8. *Abimelech rose early.* God came to Abimelech in a dream by night, and we find as the day broke he arose, assembled his servants, and communicated to them what he had received from God. They were all struck with astonishment, and discerned the hand of God in this business. Abraham is then called, and in a most respectful and pious manner the king expostulates with him for bringing him and his people under the divine displeasure, by withholding from him the information that Sarah was his wife, when by taking her he sought only an honorable alliance with his family.

11. *And Abraham said.* The best excuse he could make for his conduct, which in this instance is far from defensible.

12. *She is my sister.* I have not told a lie; I have suppressed only a part of the truth. In this place it may be proper to ask, What is a lie? It is any action done or word spoken, whether true or false in itself, which the doer or speaker wishes the observer or hearer to take in a contrary sense to that which he knows to be true. It is, in a word, any action done or speech delivered with the intention to deceive, though both may be absolutely true and right in themselves.

MATTHEW HENRY

Verses 14–18

Here is, I. The kindness which Abimelech showed to Abraham. See how unjust Abraham's jealousies were. 1. He gives him his royal licence to dwell where he pleased in his country. 2. He gives him his royal gifts. These he gave when he restored Sarah, by way of satisfacton for the wrong he had offered to do, in taking her to his house. The law appointed that when restitution was made something should be added to it. Lev. vi. 5.

II. The kindness of a prophet which Abraham showed to Abimelech: he *prayed for him, v.* 17, 18. God healed Miriam, when Moses, whom she had most affronted, prayed for her (Num. xii. 13), and was reconciled to Job's friends when Job, whom they had grieved, prayed for them (Job xlii. 8–10). Note, The prayers of good men may be a kindness to great men, and ought to be valued.

JAMIESON, FAUSSET, BROWN

TODAY'S DICTIONARY OF THE BIBLE:

Abimelech—*my father a king*, or *father of a king*—a common name of Philistine kings, as "Pharaoh" was of the Egyptian kings. The Philistine king of Gerar in the time of Abraham (Gen. 20:1–18). Through God's intervention, Sarah was delivered from his harem, and was restored to her husband Abraham. As a mark of respect, he gave to Abraham valuable gifts, and offered him a settlement in any part of his country, while at the same time he delicately and yet severely rebuked him for having deceived him in pretending that Sarah was only his sister. Among the gifts presented by the king were a thousand pieces of silver as a "covering of the eyes" for Sarah; i.e., either as an atoning gift and a testimony of her innocence in the sight of all, or rather for the purpose of procuring a veil for Sarah to conceal her beauty, and thus as a reproof to her for not having worn a veil which, as a married woman, she ought to have done. A few years after this, Abimelech visited Abraham, who had moved southward beyond his territory, and there entered into a league of peace and friendship with him. This league was the first of which we have any biblical record. It was confirmed by a mutual oath at Beersheba (Gen. 21:22–34).

ADAM CLARKE

16. *And unto Sarah he said.* But what did he say? Here there is scarcely any agreement among interpreters; the Hebrew is exceedingly obscure, and every interpreter takes it in his own sense. *A thousand pieces of silver.* Shekels are very probably meant here, and so the Targum understands it. *Behold, he is to thee a covering of the eyes.* "It"—the one thousand shekels (not *he*—Abraham)—is to thee for a covering—to procure thee a veil to conceal thy beauty (*unto all that are with thee, and with all other*) from all thy own kindred and acquaintance, and from all strangers, that none, seeing thou art another man's wife, may covet thee on account of thy comeliness.

Thus she was reproved. Paraphrased: "Behold, I have given thy brother (Abraham, gently alluding to the equivocation, vv. 2, 5) a thousand shekels of silver; behold, it is (that is, the silver is, or may be, or let it be) to thee a covering of the eyes (to procure a veil) with regard to all those who are with thee, and to all (or and in all) speak thou the truth." Correctly translated by the Septuagint "and in all things speak the truth"—not only tell a part of the truth, but tell the whole; say not merely, "He is my brother," but say also, "He is my husband too." Thus in all things speak the truth. I believe the above to be the *sense* of this difficult passage.

17. *So Abraham prayed.* This was the prime office of the *nabi;* see v. 7.

18. *For the Lord had fast closed up all the wombs.* Probably by means of some disease with which He had smitten them, hence it is said they were healed at Abraham's intercession; and this seems necessarily to imply that they had been afflicted by some disease that rendered it impossible for them to have children till it was removed.

MATTHEW HENRY — CHAPTER 21

Verses 1–8

Few under the Old Testament were brought into the world with such expectation as Isaac was, not for the sake of any great personal eminence at which he was to arrive, but because he was to be, in this very thing, a type of Christ, that seed which the holy God had so long promised and holy men so long expected.

I. The fulfilling of God's promise in the conception and birth of Isaac, *v.* 1, 2. 1. Isaac was born according to the promise. He was born *at the set time of which God had spoken, v.* 2. Note, God is always punctual to his time; though his promised mercies come not at the time we set, they will certainly come at the time he sets, and that is the best time. 2. It was not by the power of common providence, but by the power of a special promise, that Isaac was born. Note, True believers, by virtue of God's promises, are enabled to do that which is above the power of human nature, for *by them they partake of a divine nature,* 2 Pet. i. 4.

II. Abraham's obedience to God's precept concerning Isaac.

1. He named him, as God commanded him, *v.* 3. *Isaac, laughter.* There was good reason for the name, for, (1) When Abraham received the promise of him he laughed for joy, *ch.* xvii. 17. (2) When Sarah received the promise she laughed with distrust and diffidence. (3) Isaac was himself, afterwards, laughed at by Ishmael (*v.* 9), and perhaps his name bade him expect it. (4) The promise which he was the heir of, was to be the joy of all the saints in all ages.

III. The impressions which this mercy made upon Sarah.

1. It filled her with joy (*v.* 6): "*God has made me to laugh*; he has given me both cause to rejoice and a heart to rejoice." Thus the mother of our Lord, Luke i. 46, 47. Whatever is the matter of our joy, God must be acknowledged as the author of it, unless it be the *laughter of the fool.* It adds to the comfort of any mercy to have our friends rejoice with us in it: *All that hear will laugh with me*; for laughing is catching. See Luke i. 58.

2. It filled her with wonder, *v.* 7. "The thing was so highly improbable, so near to impossible, that if anyone but God had said it we could not have believed it." Note, God's favours to his covenant-people are such as surpass both their own and others' thoughts and expectations. Who would have said that God should send his Son to die for us, his Spirit to sanctify us, his angels to attend us? Who would have said that such great sins should be pardoned?

JAMIESON, FAUSSET, BROWN — CHAPTER 21

VSS. 1-13. BIRTH OF ISAAC. **1. the Lord visited Sarah**—The language of the historian seems designedly chosen to magnify the power of God as well as His faithfulness to His promise. It was God's grace that brought about that event, as well as the raising of spiritual children to Abraham, of which the birth of this son was typical [CALVIN].

3, 4. Abraham called the name of his son . . . Isaac . . . and circumcised—God was acknowledged in the name which, by divine command, was given for a memorial (cf. ch. 17:19), and also in the dedication of the child by administering the seal of the covenant (cf. ch. 17: 10-12).

ADAM CLARKE — CHAPTER 21

1. *The Lord visited Sarah.* That is, God fulfilled His promise to Sarah by giving her, at the advanced age of ninety, power to conceive and bring forth a son.

3. *Isaac.* See the reason and interpretation of this name in the note on chap. xvii. 7.

6. *God hath made me to laugh.* Sarah alludes here to the circumstance mentioned in chap. xviii. 12; and as she seems to use the word *to laugh* in this place, not in the sense of being incredulous, but to express such pleasure or happiness as almost suspends the reasoning faculty for a time, it justifies the observation on the above-named verse. See a similar case in Luke xxiv. 41, where the disciples were so overcome with the good news of our Lord's resurrection that it is said, "They believed not for joy."

MATTHEW HENRY

IV. A short account of Isaac's infancy: *The child grew, v.* 8. He grew so as not always to need milk, but was able to bear strong meat, and then he was weaned. See Heb. v. 13, 14. Abraham made a feast on the day that he was weaned because God's blessing upon the nursing of children, and the preservation of them through the perils of the infant age, are signal instances of the care and tenderness of the divine providence. See Ps. xxii. 9, 10; Hos. xi. 1.

Verses 9–13

The casting out of Ishmael is here considered of, and resolved on.

I. Ishmael himself gave the occasion by some affronts he gave to Isaac his little brother. Sarah herself was an eye-witness of the abuse. Ishmael is here called the *son of the Egyptian*, because, as some think, the 400 years' affliction of the seed of Abraham by the Egyptians began now, *ch.* xv. 13. Ishmael was fourteen years older than Isaac; and it argued a base disposition in Ishmael to be abusive to a child that was no way a match for him.

II. Sarah made the motion: *Cast out this bondwoman, v.* 10. This seems to be spoken in some heat, yet it is quoted (Gal. iv. 30) as if it had been spoken by a spirit of prophecy; and it is the sentence passed on all hypocrites and carnal people, though they have a place and a name in the visible church.

III. Abraham was averse to it: *The thing was very grievous in Abraham's sight, v.* 11. 1. It grieved him that Ishmael had given such a provocation. 2. It grieved him that Sarah insisted upon such a punishment. "Might it not suffice to correct him? would nothing less serve than to expel him?"

IV. God determined it, *v.* 12, 13. The covenant seed of Abraham must be a peculiar people, a people by themselves, from the very first, distinguished, not mingled with those that were out of covenant; for this reason Ishmael must be separated. The casting out of Ishmael should not be his ruin, *v.* 13. He shall be a *nation, because he is thy seed.* It is presumption to say that all those who are left out of the external dispensation of God's covenant, are therefore excluded from all his mercies. Though he was chased out of the church, he was not *chased out of the world. I will make him a nation.* Note, 1. Nations are of God's making: he founds them, he forms them, he fixes them. 2. Many are full of the blessings of God's providence that are strangers to the blessings of his covenant.

Verses 14–21

Here is, I. The casting out of the bondwoman and her son from the family of Abraham, *v.* 14. Abraham's obedience to the divine command in this matter was speedy—*early in the morning*. It was also submissive; it was contrary to his own inclination, to do it; yet as soon as he perceives that it is the mind of God he makes no objections, but silently does as he is bidden.

II. Their wandering in the wilderness, missing their way to the place Abraham designed them for a settlement.

1. They were reduced to great distress there. Their provisions were spent, and Ishmael was sick. Hagar is in tears, and sufficiently mortified. She despairs of relief, counts upon nothing but *the death of the child* (*v.* 15, 16).

JAMIESON, FAUSSET, BROWN

8. the child grew, and was weaned—children are suckled longer in the East than in the Occident—boys usually for two or three years. **Abraham made a great feast,** etc.—In Eastern countries this is always a season of domestic festivity, and the newly weaned child is formally brought, in presence of the assembled relatives and friends, to partake of some simple viands. Isaac, attired in the symbolic robe, the badge of birthright, was then admitted heir of the tribe [ROSENMULLER].

9. Sarah saw the son of Hagar . . . mocking—Ishmael was aware of the great change in his prospects, and under the impulse of irritated or resentful feelings, in which he was probably joined by his mother, treated the young heir with derision and probably some violence (Gal. 4:29).

10. Wherefore she said unto Abraham, Cast out this bondwoman—Nothing but the expulsion of both could now preserve harmony in the household. Abraham's perplexity was relieved by an announcement of the divine will, which in everything, however painful to flesh and blood, all who fear God and are walking in His ways will, like him, promptly obey. This story, as the apostle tells us, in "an allegory," and the "persecution" by the son of the *Egyptian* was the commencement of the four hundred years' affliction of Abraham's seed by the *Egyptians*.

12. in all that Sarah hath said—it is called the Scripture (Gal. 4:30). **13. also of the son of the bondwoman will I make a nation**—Thus Providence overruled a family brawl to give rise to two great and extraordinary peoples.

14-21. EXPULSION OF ISHMAEL. **14. Abraham rose up early,** etc.—early, that the wanderers might reach an asylum before noon. Bread includes all sorts of victuals—bottle, a leathern vessel, formed of the entire skin of a lamb or kid sewed up, with the legs for handles, usually carried over the shoulder. Ishmael was a lad of seventeen years, and it is quite customary for Arab chiefs to send out their sons at such an age to do for themselves: often with nothing but a few days' provisions in a bag. **wandered in the wilderness of Beer-sheba**—in the southern border of Palestine, but out of the common direction, a wide extending desert, where they lost their way.

15. the water was spent, etc.—Ishmael sank exhausted from fatigue and thirst—his mother laid his head under one of the bushes to smell the damp while she herself, unable to witness his distress, sat down at a little distance in hopeless sorrow.

ADAM CLARKE

8. *The child grew, and was weaned.* At what time children were weaned among the ancients is a disputed point. St. Jerome says there were two opinions on this subject. Some hold that children were always weaned at five years of age; others, that they were not weaned till they were twelve. From the speech of the mother to her son, 2 Mac. vii. 27, it seems likely that among the Jews they were weaned when three years old: "O my son, have pity upon me that bare thee nine months in my womb, and gave thee suck three years, and nourished thee and brought thee up." And this is farther strengthened by 2 Chron. xxxi. 16, where Hezekiah, in making provision for the Levites and priests, includes the children from three years old and upwards; which is a presumptive proof that previously to this age they were wholly dependent on the mother for their nourishment. The term among the Mohammedans is fixed by the Koran, chap. xxxi. 14, at two years of age.

9. *Mocking.* What was implied in this mocking is not known. St. Paul, Gal. iv. 29, calls it persecuting; but it is likely he meant no more than some species of ridicule used by Ishmael on the occasion, and probably with respect to the age of Sarah at Isaac's birth, and her previous barrenness.

10. *Cast out this bondwoman and her son.* Both Sarah and Abraham have been accused of cruelty in this transaction, because every word reads harsh to us. *Cast out; garash* signifies not only to "thrust out, drive away, and expel," but also to "divorce" (see Lev. xxi. 7); and it is in this latter sense the word should be understood here. The child of Abraham by Hagar might be considered as having a right at least to a part of the inheritance; and as it was sufficiently known to Sarah that God had designed that the succession should be established in the line of Isaac, she wished Abraham to divorce Hagar, or to perform some sort of legal act by which Ishmael might be excluded from all claim on the inheritance.

12. *In Isaac shall thy seed be called.* Here God shows the propriety of attending to the counsel of Sarah; and lest Abraham, in whose eyes the thing was grievous, should feel distressed on the occasion, God renews His promises to Ishmael and his posterity.

14. *Took bread, and a bottle.* By the word *bread* we are to understand the food or provisions which were necessary for her and Ishmael till they should come to the place of their destination; which, no doubt, Abraham particularly pointed out. The *bottle,* which was made of skin, ordinarily a goat's skin, contained water sufficient to last them till they should come to the next well; which, it is likely, Abraham particularly specified also. This well, it appears, Hagar missed, and therefore wandered about in the wilderness seeking more water, till all she had brought with her was expended. We may therefore safely presume that she and her son were sufficiently provided for their journey had they not missed their way. Travellers in those countries take only provisions sufficient to carry them to the next village or encampment, and water to supply them till they shall meet with the next well. What adds to the appearance of cruelty in this case is that our translation seems to represent Ishmael as being a young child; and that Hagar was obliged to carry him, the bread, and the bottle of water on her back or shoulder at the same time. But that Ishmael could not be carried on his mother's shoulder will be sufficiently evident when his age is considered; Ishmael was born when Abraham was eighty-six years of age, chap. xvi. 16; Isaac was born when he was one hundred years of age, chap. xxi. 5; hence Ishmael was fourteen years old at the birth of Isaac. Add to this the age of Isaac when he was weaned, which, from v. 8 of this chapter (see the note), was probably three, and we shall find that Ishmael was at the time of his leaving Abraham not less than seventeen years old.

15. *And she cast the child.* "And she sent the lad under one of the shrubs," namely, to screen him from the intensity of the heat. Here Ishmael appears to be utterly helpless, and this circumstance seems farther to confirm the opinion that he was now in a state of infancy; but the preceding observations do this supposition

MATTHEW HENRY

2. In this distress, God heard *the voice of the lad*, *v.* 17. An angel was sent to comfort Hagar, and it was not the first time that she had met with God's comforts in a wilderness (*ch.* xvi. 13). (1) The angel assures her *God has heard the voice of the lad where he is*, though he is in a wilderness (for, wherever we are, there is a way open heaven-ward); therefore *lift up the lad, and hold him in thy hand*, *v.* 18. (2) He repeats the promise concerning her son, that he should be *a great nation*, as a reason why she should bestir herself to help him. (3) He directs her to a present supply (*v.* 19): and then *she saw a well of water*. Note, Many that have reason enough to be comforted go mourning from day to day. There is a well of water by them in the covenant of grace, but they are not aware of it till the same God that opened their eyes to see their wound opens them to see their remedy, John xvi. 6, 7. Now the apostle tells us that those things concerning Hagar and Ishmael are ἀλληγορούμενα (Gal. iv. 24), they are to be allegorized; this then will serve to illustrate the folly, [1] Of those who, like the unbelieving Jews, seek for righteousness by the law and the carnal ordinances of it, and not by the promise made in Christ. [2] Of those who seek for satisfaction and happiness in the world and the things of it. Those that forsake the comforts of the covenant and communion with God wander endlessly in pursuit of satisfaction, and, at length, sit down short of it.

III. The settlement of Ishmael, at last, in the wilderness of Paran (*v.* 20, 21), a wild place, fittest for a wild man; and such a one he was, *ch.* xvi. 12. Observe, 1. He had some tokens of God's presence: *God was with the lad*. 2. By trade he was an archer. 3. He matched among his mother's relations; she took him a wife out of Egypt: as great an archer as he was, he did not think he could take his aim well, in the business of marriage, if he proceeded without his mother's advice and consent.

Verses 22–32

We have here an account of the treaty between Abimelech and Abraham. His friendship is valued, is courted, though a stranger, though a tenant at will to the Canaanites and Perizzites.

I. The league is proposed by Abimelech, and Phichol his prime-minister of state and general of his army.

1. The inducement to it was God's favour to Abraham (*v.* 22): "*God is with thee in all that thou doest*, and we cannot but take notice of it." It is good being in favour with those that are in favour with God. *We will go with you, for we have heard that God is with you*. We do well for ourselves if we have fellowship with those that have fellowship with God, 1 John i. 3.

2. The tenor of it was, in general, that there should be a firm and constant friendship between the two families. He would have his son, and his son's son, and his land likewise, to have the benefit of it.

II. It is consented to by Abraham, with a particular clause inserted about a well. In Abraham's part of this transaction observe,

1. He was ready to enter into this league with Abimelech, finding him to be a man of honour and conscience, and that had the fear of God before his eyes.

2. He prudently settled the matter concerning a well, about which Abimelech's servants had quarrelled with him. Wells of water, it seems, were choice goods in that country. Abraham mildly told Abimelech of it, *v.* 25; and no more can be expected from an honest man than that he be ready to do right as soon as he knows that he has done wrong.

3. He made a very handsome present to Abimelech, *v.* 27. The interchanging of kind offices is the improving of love: that which is mine is my friend's.

4. He ratified the covenant by an oath, and registered it by giving a new name to the place (*v.* 31), *Beer-sheba*, the *well of the oath*.

Verses 33–34

He sojourned many days, as many as would consist with his character, as Abraham the *Hebrew*, or *passenger*. 2. There he made, not only a constant practice, but an open profession, of his religion: *There he called on the name of the Lord, the everlasting God*, probably in the grove he planted, which was his oratory or house of prayer. Christ prayed in a garden, on a mountain.

JAMIESON, FAUSSET, BROWN

God opened her eyes—Had she forgotten the promise (ch. 16:11)? Whether she looked to God or not, He regarded her and directed her to a fountain close beside her, but probably hid amid brushwood, by the waters of which her almost expiring son was revived.

20, 21. God was with the lad, etc.—Paran (i.e., Arabia), where his posterity has ever dwelt (cf. ch. 16:12; also Isa. 48:19; I Pet. 1:25). **his mother took him a wife**—On a father's death, the mother looks out for a wife for her son, however young; and as Ishmael was now virtually deprived of his father, his mother set about forming a marriage connection for him, it would seem, among her relatives.

22-34. COVENANT. **22. Abimelech and Phichol**—Here a proof of the promise (ch. 12:2) being fulfilled, in a native prince wishing to form a solemn league with Abraham. The proposal was reasonable, and agreed to.

25-31. Abraham reproved Abimelech because of a well—Wells were of great importance to a pastoral chief and on the successful operation of sinking a new one, the owner was solemnly informed in person. If, however, they were allowed to get out of repair, the restorer acquired a right to them. In unoccupied lands the possession of wells gave a right of property in the land, and dread of this had caused the offense for which Abraham reproved Abimelech. Some describe four, others five, wells in Beer-sheba.

Abraham planted a grove—*Hebrew*, of tamarisks, in which sacrificial worship was offered, as in a roofless temple.

ADAM CLARKE

entirely away, and his present helplessness will be easily accounted for on this ground: (1) Young persons can bear much less fatigue than those who are arrived at mature age. (2) They require much more fluid from the greater quantum of heat in their bodies. (3) Their digestion is much more rapid, and hence they cannot bear hunger and thirst as well as the others. On these grounds Ishmael must be much more exhausted with fatigue than his mother.

19. *God opened her eyes*. These words appear to me to mean no more than that God directed her to a well, which probably was at no great distance from the place in which she then was; and therefore she is commanded, v. 18, to "support the lad," literally, to "make her hand strong in his behalf"—namely, that he might reach the well and quench his thirst.

20. *Became an archer*. And by his skill in this art, under the continual superintendence of the divine providence (for *God was with the lad*), he was undoubtedly enabled to procure a sufficient supply for his own wants and those of his parent.

21. *He dwelt in the wilderness of Paran*. This is generally allowed to have been a part of the desert belonging to Arabia Petraea, in the vicinity of Mount Sinai; and this seems to be its uniform meaning in the sacred writings.

22. *At that time*. This may either refer to the transactions recorded in the preceding chapter or to the time of Ishmael's marriage, but most probably to the former.

23. *Now therefore swear unto me*. The oath on such occasions probably meant no more than the mutual promise of both the parties, when they slew an animal, poured out the blood as a sacrifice to God, and then passed between the pieces. See this ceremony, chap. v. 18, and on chap. xv. *According to the kindness that I have done*. The simple claims of justice were alone set up among virtuous people in those ancient times.

25. *Abraham reproved Abimelech*. Wells were of great consequence in those hot countries, and especially where the flocks were numerous, because the water was scarce and digging to find it was accompanied with much expense of time and labor.

26. *I wot not who hath done this thing*. The servants of Abimelech had committed these depredations on Abraham without any authority from their master, who appears to have been a very amiable man.

27. *Took sheep and oxen*. Some think that these were the sacrifices which were offered on the occasion, and which Abraham furnished at his own cost, and in order to do Abimelech the greater honor gave them to him to offer before the Lord.

28. *Seven ewe lambs*. These were either given as a present or they were intended as the price of the well; and being accepted by Abimelech, they served as a witness that he had acknowledged Abraham's right to the well in question.

31. *He called that place Beer-sheba*. Literally, the "well of swearing" or "of the oath," because they both sware there—mutually confirmed the covenant.

33. *Abraham planted a grove*. The original word has been variously translated a "grove," a "plantation," an "orchard," a "cultivated field," and an "oak." As Abraham, agreeably, no doubt, to the institutes of the patriarchal religion, planted an oak in Beer-sheba, and called on the name of Jehovah, the everlasting God (compare Gen. xii. 8; xviii. 1), so we find that oaks were sacred among the idolaters also. "Ye shall be ashamed of the oaks ye have chosen," says Isaiah, chap. i. 29, to the idolatrous Israelites.

And called there on the name of the Lord. On this important passage Dr. Shuckford speaks thus: "Our English translation very erroneously renders this place, *he called upon the name of Jehovah;* but the expression never signifies 'to call upon the name'; *kara beshem* signifies 'to invoke in the name,' and seems to be used where the true worshippers of God offered their prayers in the name of the true Mediator." I believe this to be a just view of the subject, and therefore I admit it without scruple.

MATTHEW HENRY

In calling on the Lord, we must eye him as *the everlasting God. The everlasting God*, who was, before all worlds, and will be, when time and days shall be no more. See Isa. xl. 28.

JAMIESON, FAUSSET, BROWN

34. Abraham sojourned in the Philistines' land—a picture of pastoral and an emblem of Christian life.

ADAM CLARKE

The everlasting God. Yehovah el olam, "Jehovah, the strong God, the eternal one." This is the first place in Scripture in which *olam* occurs as an attribute of God, and here it is evidently designed to point out His eternal duration; that it can mean no limited time is self-evident, because nothing of this kind can be attributed to God.

MATTHEW HENRY — CHAPTER 22

Verses 1–2

Here is the trial of Abraham's faith. It was made to appear that he loved God better than his father; now that he loved him better than his son.

I. Now, perhaps, he was beginning to think the storms had all blown over; but, after all, this encounter comes, which is sharper than any yet.

II. The author of the trial: *God* tempted him, not to draw him to sin but to discover his graces, how strong they were, that they might be *found to praise, and honour, and glory*, 1 Pet. i. 7. Thus God tempted Job, that he might appear not only a good man, but a great man. *God did tempt Abraham;* he did *lift up Abraham*, so some read it; as a scholar that improves well is lifted up, when he is put into a higher form.

III. The trial itself. Probably he expected some renewed promise like those, *ch.* xv. 1, and xvii. 1. But, to his great amazement, that which God has to say to him is, in short, *Abraham, Go kill thy son.* Every word here is a sword in his bones: the trial is steeled with trying phrases.

1. The person to be offered. (1) "*Take thy son,* not thy bullocks and thy lambs." "No, *I will take no bullock* out of thy house" (Ps. l. 9). "I must have thy son." "Take *Isaac*, him, by name, *thy laughter*, that *son indeed*," *ch.* xvii. 19. That son *whom thou lovest*. In the Hebrew it is expressed more emphatically, and, I think, might very well be read thus: *Take now that son of thine, that only one of thine, whom thou lovest, that Isaac.*

2. The place: *In the land of Moriah*, three days' journey off; so that he might have time to consider it, that it might be a service the more reasonable and the more honourable.

3. The manner: *Offer him for a burnt-offering*. He must not only kill his son, but kill him as a sacrifice.

Verses 3–10

Abraham's obedience to this severe command. *Being tried, he offered up Isaac*, Heb. xi. 17.

I. The difficulties which he broke through in this act of obedience. 1. It seemed directly against an antecedent law of God, which forbids murder, under a severe penalty, *ch.* ix. 5, 6. 2. How would it consist with natural affection to his own son? 3. God gave him no reason for it. When Ishmael was to be cast out, a just cause was assigned, but here Isaac must die, and Abraham must kill him, and neither the one nor the other must know why or wherefore. If Isaac had been to die a martyr for the truth, or his life had been the ransom of some other life more precious, it would have been another matter. But the case is not so: he is a dutiful, obedient, hopeful son. "Lord, what profit is there in his blood?" 4. How would this consist with the promise? Was it not said that in *Isaac shall thy seed be called*? 5. How should he ever look Sarah in the face again? 6. What would the Egyptians say, and the Canaanites and the Perizzites who dwelt then in the land? It would be an eternal reproach to Abraham, and to his altars. "Welcome nature, if this be grace."

II. The several steps of obedience.

1. He rises early, *v.* 3, for the command was peremptory, and would not admit a debate. Note, those that do the will of God heartily will do it speedily.

2. He gets things ready for a sacrifice.

3. It is very probable that he said nothing about it to Sarah.

4. He carefully looked about him, to discover the place appointed for this sacrifice, when he said (*v.* 5), "We will go yonder, where you see the light, and worship."

5. He left his servants at some distance off (*v.* 5), lest they should interpose in his strange oblation. Thus, when Christ was entering upon his agony in the garden, he took only three of his disciples with him, and left the rest at the garden door.

6. He obliged Isaac to carry the wood while he himself carried the fatal knife and fire, *v.* 6.

7. Without any ruffle or disorder, he talks it over with Isaac, as if it had been but a common sacrifice, that he was going to offer, *v.* 7, 8.

(1) It was a very affecting question that Isaac asked him, as they were going together: *My father,*

JAMIESON, FAUSSET, BROWN — CHAPTER 22

Vss. 1-19. OFFERING ISAAC. **1. God did tempt Abraham**—not incite to sin (Jas. 1:13), but try, prove—give occasion for the development of his faith (I Pet. 1:7). **and he said, . . . Here I am**—ready at a moment's warning for God's service.

2. Take now thy son, etc.,—Every circumstance mentioned was calculated to give a deeper stab to the parental bosom. To lose his only son, and by an act of his own hand, too!—what a host of conflicting feelings must the order have raised! But he heard and obeyed without a murmur (Gal. 1:16; Luke 14:26).

3. Abraham rose . . . early, etc.—That there might be no appearance of delay or reluctance on his part, he made every preparation for the sacrifice before setting out—the materials, the knife, and the servants to convey them. From Beer-sheba to Moriah, a journey of two days, he had the painful secret pent up in his bosom. So distant a place must have been chosen for some important reason. It is generally thought that "the place of which God had told him" was one of the hills of Jerusalem, on which the Great Sacrifice was afterwards offered. **4. on the third day Abraham lifted up his eyes, etc.**—Leaving the servants at the foot, the father and son ascended the hill, the one bearing the knife, and the other the wood for consuming the sacrifice. But there was no victim; and to the question so naturally put by Isaac, Abraham contented himself by replying, "My son, God will provide himself a lamb for a burnt offering." It has been supposed that the design of this extraordinary transaction was to show him, by action instead of words, the way in which all the families of the earth should be blessed; and that in his answer to Isaac, he anticipated some substitution. It is more likely that his words were spoken evasively to his son in ignorance of the issue, yet in unbounded confidence that that son, though sacrificed, would, in some miraculous way, be restored (Heb. 11:19).

ADAM CLARKE — CHAPTER 22

1. *God did tempt Abraham.* The original here is very emphatic: "And the Elohim He tried this Abraham"; God brought him into such circumstances as exercised and discovered his faith, love, and obedience. Though the word *tempt* signifies no more than to "prove" or "try," yet as it is now generally used to imply a solicitation to evil, in which way God never tempts any man, it would be well to avoid it here.

2. *Take now thy son.* Bishop Warburton's observations on this passage are weighty and important. "The order in which the words are placed in the original gradually increases the sense, and raises the passions higher and higher: *Take now thy son* (rather, take I beseech thee), *thine only son whom thou lovest, even Isaac.* Abraham desired earnestly to be let into the mystery of *redemption;* and God, to instruct him in the infinite extent of the divine goodness to mankind, *who spared not his own Son, but delivered him up for us all,* let Abraham feel by experience what it was to lose a beloved son, the son born miraculously when Sarah was past childbearing, as Jesus was miraculously born of a virgin. The *duration,* too, of the action, v. 4, was the same as that between Christ's death and resurrection, both which are designed to be represented in it; and still farther not only the final archetypical sacrifice of the Son of God was figured in the command to offer Isaac, but the *intermediate typical* sacrifice in the Mosaic economy was represented by the *permitted* sacrifice of the ram offered up, v. 13, instead of Isaac." *Only son.* All that he had by Sarah, his legal wife. *The land of Moriah.* This is supposed to mean all the mountains of Jerusalem. Beer-sheba, where Abraham dwelt, is about forty-two miles distant from Jerusalem, and it is not to be wondered at that Abraham, Isaac, the two servants, and the ass laden with wood for the burnt offering did not reach this place till the third day; see v. 4.

5. *I and the lad will go . . . and come again.* How could Abraham consistently with truth say this, when he knew he was going to make his son a burnt offering? The apostle answers for him: "By faith Abraham, when he was tried, offered up Isaac . . . accounting that God was able to raise him up, even from the dead, from whence also he received him in a figure," Heb. xi. 17, 19. He knew that previously to the birth of Isaac both he and his wife were dead to all the purposes of procreation; that his birth was a kind of life from the dead; that the promise of God was most positive, "In Isaac shall thy seed be called", chap. xxi. 12; that this promise could not fail; that it was his duty to obey the command of his Maker; and that it was as easy for God to restore him to life after he had been a burnt offering as it was for Him to give him life in the beginning. Therefore he went fully purposed to offer his son, and yet confidently expecting to have him restored to life again.

MATTHEW HENRY

said Isaac; it was a melting word, which, one would think, would strike deeper into the breast of Abraham than his knife could into the breast of Isaac. Yet he keeps his temper, and keeps his countenance, to admiration; he calmly waits for his son's question, and this is it: *Behold the fire and the wood, but where is the lamb?* [1] A trying question to Abraham. How could he endure to think that Isaac was himself the lamb? So it is, but Abraham, as yet, dares not tell him so. [2] It is a teaching question to us all, that, when we are going to worship God, we should seriously consider. Where is the heart? Is that ready to be offered up to God, to ascend to him as a burnt-offering?

(2) It was a very prudent answer which Abraham gave him: *My son, God will provide himself a lamb.* This was the language, either, [1] Of his obedience. Or, [2] Of his faith. A sacrifice was provided instead of Isaac. Thus, *First*, Christ, the great sacrifice of atonement, was of God's providing. *Secondly*, All our sacrifices of acknowledgment are of God's providing too. It is he that prepares the heart, Ps. x. 17. The broken and contrite spirit is a sacrifice of God (Ps. li. 17), of his providing.

8. He goes on with a holy wilfulness, after many a weary step, and with a heavy heart he arrives at length at the fatal place, builds the altar, the saddest that ever he built, lays the wood in order for Isaac's funeral pile, and now tells him the amazing news: "Isaac, thou art the lamb which God has provided." Isaac, for aught that appears, is as willing as Abraham; we do not find that he attempted to make his escape or made any resistance. Yet it is necessary that a sacrifice be bound. But with what heart could tender Abraham tie those guiltless hands, which perhaps had often been lifted up to ask his blessing, and stretched out to embrace him, and were now the more straitly bound with the cords of love and duty! However, it must be done. Having bound him, he lays him upon the altar, and his hand upon the head of his sacrifice; and now, we may suppose, with floods of tears, he gives, and takes, the final farewell of a parting kiss. With a fixed heart, and an eye lifted up to heaven, he takes the knife, and stretches out his hand. Be astonished, O heavens! at this; and wonder, O earth! Here is an act of faith and obedience, which deserves to be a spectacle to God, angels, and men. Now this obedience of Abraham in offering up Isaac is a lively representation, (1) Of the love of God to us, in delivering up his only-begotten Son to suffer and die for us, as a sacrifice. It *pleased the Lord* himself to *bruise him*. See Isa. liii. 10; Zech. xiii. 7. (2) Of our duty to God, in return for that love. We must tread in the steps of this faith of Abraham. God, by his word, calls us to part with all for Christ.

Verses 11–14

Hitherto this story has been very melancholy, and seemed to hasten towards a most tragical period; but here the sky suddenly clears up, the sun breaks out, and a bright and pleasant scene opens. The same hand that had wounded and cast down here heals and lifts up.

I. Isaac is rescued, *v.* 11, 12. The command to offer him was intended only for trial, therefore the order is countermanded: *Lay not thy hand upon the lad.* The more imminent the danger is, the more wonderful and the more welcome is the deliverance.

II. Abraham is not only approved, but applauded. *Now know I that thou fearest God.* The best evidence of our fearing God is our being willing to serve and honour him with that which is dearest to us.

III. Another sacrifice is provided instead of Isaac, *v.* 13. God must be acknowledged with thankfulness for the deliverance of Isaac. Abraham's words must be made good: *God will provide himself a lamb.* Reference must be had to the promised Messiah, the blessed seed. (1) Christ was sacrificed in our stead, as this ram instead of Isaac, and his death was our discharge. (2) Though that blessed seed was lately promised, and now typified by Isaac, yet the offering of him up should be suspended: and in the mean time the sacrifice of beasts should be accepted, as this ram was, as a pledge of that expiation which should one day be made by that great sacrifice. And it is observable that the temple, the place of sacrifice, was afterwards built upon this Mount Moriah (2 Chron. iii. 1); and Mount Calvary, where Christ was crucified, was not far off.

IV. A new name is given to the place, and for the encouragement of all believers, cheerfully to trust in God: *Jehovah-jireh, The Lord will provide* (*v.* 14), probably alluding to what he had said (*v.* 8), *God will provide himself a lamb.*

JAMIESON, FAUSSET, BROWN

Abraham built an altar, etc.—Had not the patriarch been sustained by the full consciousness of acting in obedience to God's will, the effort would have been too great for human endurance; and had not Isaac, then upwards of twenty years of age displayed equal faith in submitting, this great trial could not have gone through.

11, 12. the angel . . . called, etc.—The sacrifice was virtually offered—the intention, the purpose to do it, was shown in all sincerity and fulness. The Omniscient witness likewise declared His acceptance in the highest terms of approval; and the apostle speaks of it as actually made (Heb. 11:17; Jas. 2:21).

13-19. Abraham lifted up his eyes . . . and behold . . . a ram, etc.—No method was more admirably calculated to give the patriarch a distinct idea of the purpose of grace than this scenic representation: and hence our Lord's allusion to it (John 8:56).

ADAM CLARKE

7. *Behold the fire and the wood: but where is the lamb?* Nothing can be conceived more tender, affectionate, and affecting then the question of the son and the reply of the father on this occasion. A paraphrase would spoil it; nothing can be added without injuring those expressions of affectionate submission on the one hand and dignified tenderness and simplicity on the other.

8. *My son, God will provide himself a lamb.* Here we find the same obedient, unshaken faith for which this pattern of practical piety was ever remarkable. But we must not suppose that this was the language merely of faith and obedience; the patriarch spoke prophetically, and referred to that Lamb of God which He had provided for himself, who in the fulness of time should take away the sin of the world, and of whom Isaac was a most expressive type.

9. *And bound Isaac his son.* If the patriarch had not been upheld by the conviction that he was doing the will of God, and had he not felt the most perfect confidence that his son should be restored even from the dead, what agony must his heart have felt at every step of the journey, and through all the circumstances of this extraordinary business? What must his affectionate heart have felt at the questions asked by his innocent and amiable son? What must he have suffered while building the altar, laying on the wood, binding his lovely son, placing him on the wood, taking the knife, and stretching out his hand to slay the child of his hopes? Every view we take of the subject interests the heart and exalts the character of this father of the faithful. But has the character of Isaac been duly considered? Is not the consideration of his excellence lost in the supposition that he was too young to enter particularly into a sense of his danger, and too feeble to have made any resistance, had he been unwilling to submit? Josephus supposes that Isaac was now twenty-five, some rabbins that he was thirty-six; but it is more probable that he was now about thirty-three. Allowing him to be only twenty-five, he might have easily resisted; for can it be supposed that an old man of at least one hundred and twenty-five years of age could have bound, without his consent, a young man in the very prime and vigor of life? In this case we cannot say that the superior strength of the father prevailed, but the piety, filial affection, and obedience of the son yielded. All this was most illustriously typical of Christ. In both cases the father himself offers up his only begotten son, and the father himself binds him on the wood or to the Cross; in neither case is the son forced to yield, but yields of his own accord; in neither case is the life taken away by the hand of violence; Isaac yields himself to the knife, Jesus lays down His life for the sheep.

11. *The angel of the Lord.* The very Person who was represented by this offering; the Lord Jesus, who calls himself Jehovah, v. 16, and on His own authority renews the promises of the covenant. He was ever the great Mediator between God and man.

12. *Lay not thine hand upon the lad.* As Isaac was to be the representative of Jesus Christ's real sacrifice, it was sufficient for this purpose that in his own will, and the will of his father, the purpose of the immolation was complete. Isaac was now fully offered both by his father and by himself. The father yields up the son, the son gives up his life; on both sides, as far as will and purpose could go, the sacrifice was complete.

14. *Jehovah-jireh.* Literally interpreted in the margin, "The Lord will see"; that is, God will take care that everything shall be done that is necessary for the comfort and support of them who trust in Him. Hence the words are usually translated, "The Lord will provide"; so our translators, v. 8. But all this seems to have been done under a divine impulse, and the words to have been spoken prophetically; hence Houbigant and some others render the words thus: "The Lord shall be seen"; and this translation the following clause seems to require, "As it is said to this day, on this mount the Lord shall be seen." From this it appears that the sacrifice offered by Abraham was understood to be a representative one, and a tradition was kept up that Jehovah should be seen in a sacrificial way

MATTHEW HENRY

Verses 15–19

Abraham's obedience was graciously accepted; but this was not all: here we have it recompensed. Observe, 1. God is pleased to make mention of Abraham's obedience as the consideration of the covenant; and he speaks of it with an encomium: *Because thou hast done this thing, and hast not withheld thy son, thine only son, v.* 16. 2. God now confirmed the promise with an oath. It was said and sealed before; but now it is sworn: *By myself have I sworn*; for he could swear by no greater, Heb. vi. 13. He did (to speak with reverence) even pawn his own life and being upon it (*As I live*), that by all those immutable things, in which it was impossible for God to lie, he and his might have strong consolation. 3. The particular promise here renewed is that of a numerous offspring: *Multiplying, I will multiply thee, v.* 17. What a figure does the seed of Abraham make in history ! How numerous, how illustrious, were his known descendants, who, to this day, triumph in this, that they have Abraham to their father ! 4. The promise, doubtless, points at the Messiah, and the grace of the gospel. This is the oath sworn to our father Abraham, which Zacharias refers to, Luke i. 73, &c. And so here is a promise, (1) Of the great blessing of the Spirit: *In blessing, I will bless thee*, namely, with that best of blessings, the gift of the Holy Ghost. (2) Of the increase of the church, that believers, his spiritual seed, should be numerous as the stars of heaven. (3) Of spiritual victories. Probably Zacharias refers to this part of the oath (Luke i. 74), *That we, being delivered out of the hand of our enemies, might serve him without fear*. But the crown of all is the last promise. (4) Of the incarnation of Christ: *In thy seed*, one particular person that shall descend from thee (for he speaks not of many, but of one, as the apostle observes, Gal. iii. 16), *shall all the nations of the earth be blessed*.

Verses 20–24

This is recorded here to show that though Abraham saw his own family highly dignified with peculiar privileges, yet he was glad to hear of the increase and prosperity of their families.

JAMIESON, FAUSSET, BROWN

KEIL–DELITZSCH:

After Abraham had offered the ram, the angel of the Lord called to him a second time from heaven, and with a solemn oath renewed the former promises as a reward for this proof of his obedience of faith (cf. 12:2, 3). To confirm their unchangeableness, Jehovah swore by himself (cf. Heb. 6:13), a thing which never occurs again in His intercourse with the patriarchs; so that subsequently not only do we find repeated references to this oath (Gen. 24:7; 26:3; 50:24; Ex. 8:5; 33:1, etc.), but, as Luther observes, all that is said in Psalms 89:36; 132:11; 150:4 respecting the oath given to David, is founded upon this. For in the promise upon which these psalms are based nothing is said about an oath (cf. 2 Sam. 7; 1 Chron. 17). The declaration on oath is still further confirmed by the addition of an "edict of Jehovah," which, frequently as it occurs in the prophets, is met with in the Pentateuch only in Num. 14:28 and (without Jehovah) in the oracles of Balaam (Num. 24:3, 15, 16). As the promise was intensified in form, so was it also in substance. To express the innumerable multiplication of the seed in the strongest possible way, a comparison with the sand of the seashore is added to the previous simile of the stars. And this seed is also promised the possession of the gate of its enemies, i.e. the conquest of the enemy and the capture of his cities (cf. 24:60).

—Commentary on the Old Testament

ADAM CLARKE

on this mount. And this renders the opinion on v. 1 more than probable, namely, that Abraham offered Isaac on that very mountain on which, in the fulness of time, Jesus suffered.

16. *By myself have I sworn.* So we find that the person who was called the "angel of the Lord" is here called "Jehovah"; see on v. 2.

17. *Shall possess the gate of his enemies.* By the gates may be meant all the strength, whether troops, counsels, or fortified cities of their enemies. So Matt. xvi. 18: "On this rock I will build my church, and the gates of hell shall not prevail against it"—the counsels, stratagems, and powers of darkness shall not be able to prevail against or overthrow the true Church of Christ.

18. *And in thy seed.* We have the authority of St. Paul, Gal. iii. 8, 16, 18, to restrain this to our blessed Lord, who was the Seed through whom alone all God's blessings of providence, mercy, grace, and glory should be conveyed to the nations of the earth.

20. *Behold, Milcah, she hath also borne children unto thy brother.* This short history seems introduced solely for the purpose of preparing the reader for the transactions related in chap. xxiv, and to show that the providence of God was preparing, in one of the branches of the family of Abraham, a suitable spouse for his son Isaac.

21. *Huz.* He is supposed to have peopled the land of *Uz* in Arabia Deserta, the country of Job. *Buz his brother.* From this person Elihu the Buzite, one of the friends of Job, is thought to have descended. *Kemuel the father of Aram.* "The father of the Syrians," according to the Septuagint.

23. *Bethuel begat Rebekah.* Who afterward became the wife of Isaac.

24. *His concubine.* We borrow this word from the Latin compound *concubina*, from *con*, "together," and *cubo*, "to lie," and apply it solely to a woman cohabiting with a man without being legally married. The concubine in Scripture is a kind of secondary wife, not unlawful in the patriarchal times, though the progeny of such could not inherit.

MATTHEW HENRY — CHAPTER 23

Verses 1–2

We have here, 1. Sarah's age, *v.* 1. 2. Her death, *v.* 2. She died in the land of Canaan, where she had been above sixty years a sojourner. 3. Abraham's mourning for her. Two words are used: he came both to *mourn* and to *weep*. Tears are a tribute due to our deceased friends. When the body is sown, it must be watered. But we must not sorrow as those that have no hope; for we have a good hope through grace both concerning them and concerning ourselves.

Verses 3–15

Here is, I. The humble request which Abraham made to his neighbours, the Hittites, for a burying-place among them, *v.* 3, 4. The convenient diversion which this affair gave, for the present, to Abraham's grief: *He stood up from before his dead.* There must

JAMIESON, FAUSSET, BROWN — CHAPTER 23

Vss. 1, 2. Age and Death of Sarah. **1. Sarah was an hundred and seven and twenty years old,** etc.—Sarah is the only woman in Scripture whose age, death, and burial are mentioned, probably to do honor to the venerable mother of the Hebrew people.

2. Abraham came to mourn for Sarah, etc.—He came from his own tent to take his station at the door of Sarah's. The "mourning" describes his conformity to the customary usage of sitting on the ground for a time; while the "weeping" indicates the natural outburst of his sorrow.

3-20. Purchase of a Burying-Place. **3. Abraham stood up,** etc.—Eastern people are always pro-

ADAM CLARKE — CHAPTER 23

1. *And Sarah was an hundred and seven and twenty years old.* It is worthy of remark that Sarah is the only woman in the sacred writings whose age, death, and burial are distinctly noted. And she has been deemed worthy of higher honor, for St. Paul, Gal. iv. 22-23, makes her a type of the Church of Christ; and her faith in the accomplishment of God's promise that she should have a son, when all natural probabilities were against it, is particularly celebrated in the Epistle to the Hebrews, chap. xi. 11. Sarah was about ninety-one years old when Isaac was born, and she lived thirty-six years after, and saw him grown up to man's estate. With Sarah the promise of the incarnation of Christ commenced, though a comparatively obscure prophecy of it had been delivered to Eve, chap. iii. 15; and with Mary it terminated, having had its exact completion. Thus God put more honor upon these two women than upon all the daughters of Eve besides.

2. *Sarah died in Kirjath-arba.* Literally "in the city of the four." It seems evidently to have had its name from a Canaanite, one of the Anakim, probably called Arba, who was the chief of the four brothers who dwelt there; the names of the others being Sheshai, Ahiman, and Talmai. See Judg. i. 10. *Abraham came to mourn for Sarah.* From verse 19 of the preceding chapter it appears that Abraham had settled at Beer-sheba; and here we find that Sarah died at Hebron, which was about twenty-four miles distant from Beer-sheba. For the convenience of feeding his numerous flocks, Abraham had probably several places of temporary residence, and particularly one at Beer-sheba, and another at Hebron; and it is likely that while he sojourned at Beer-sheba, Sarah died at Hebron; and his coming to mourn and weep for her signifies his coming from the former to the latter place on the news of her death.

3. *Abraham stood up from before his dead.* He had probably sat on the ground some days

MATTHEW HENRY

be a time of standing up from before their dead, and ceasing to mourn. Weeping must not hinder sowing. The death of our relations should effectually remind us that we are not at home in this world. When they are gone, say, "We are going."

II. The generous offer which the children of Heth made to him, *v.* 5, 6. They compliment him, 1. With a title of respect: *Thou art a prince of God among us.* 2. With a tender of the best of their burying-places. Note, Even the light of nature teaches us to be civil and respectful towards all, though they be strangers and sojourners.

III. The particular proposal which Abraham made to them, *v.* 7–9. He returns them his thanks. Though a great man, an old man, and now a mourner, yet he stands up, and bows himself humbly before them, *v.* 7. Note, Religion teaches good manners; and those abuse it that place it in rudeness and clownishness.

IV. The present which Ephron made to Abraham of his field: *The field give I thee, v.* 10, 11. Abraham thought he must be entreated to sell it; but, upon the first mention of it, without entreaty, Ephron freely gives it. Some men have more generosity than they are thought to have.

V. Abraham's modest and sincere refusal of Ephron's kind offer, *v.* 12, 13. Abundance of thanks he returns him for it (*v.* 12), but resolves to give him money for the field, even the full value of it. Abraham was rich in silver and gold (*ch.* xiii. 2) and was able to pay for the field, and therefore would not take advantage of Ephron's generosity. Note, Honesty, as well as honour, forbids us to sponge upon our neighbours.

VI. The price of the land fixed by Ephron but not insisted on: *The land is worth four hundred shekels of silver* (about fifty pounds of our money), *but what is that between me and thee? v.* 14, 15. He would rather oblige his friend than have so much money in his pocket. When we are tempted to be high in demanding our rights, or hard in denying a kindness, we should answer the temptation with this question: "What is that between me and my friend?"

Verses 16–20

We have here the conclusion of the treaty between Abraham and Ephron about the burying-place. The bargain was publicly made before all the neighbours, *in the presence and audience of the sons of Heth, v.* 16, 17. Abraham, thereupon, takes possession, and buries Sarah in the cave which was in the purchased field. It is worth noting, (1) That a burying-place was the first spot of ground Abraham possessed in Canaan. Note, When we are entering into the world it is good to think of our going out of it; for, as soon as we are born, we begin to die. (2) That it was the only piece of land he ever possessed, though the country was all his own in reversion. Abraham sought a better country, that is, a heavenly. Abraham is content to be still flitting, while he lives, but secures a place where, when he dies, his flesh may rest in hope.

JAMIESON, FAUSSET, BROWN

vided with family burying-places; but Abraham's life of faith—his pilgrim state—had prevented him acquiring even so small a possession (Acts 7:5). **spake unto the sons of Heth**—He bespoke their kind offices to aid him in obtaining possession of a cave that belonged to Ephron—a wealthy neighbor.

9. Machpelah—the "double" case. **10. Ephron dwelt**—lit., was "sitting" among the children of Heth in the gate of the city where all business was transacted. But, though a chief man among them, he was probably unknown to Abraham. **11-15. Ephron answered, Nay, my lord, etc.**—Here is a great show of generosity, but it was only a show; for while Abraham wanted only the cave, he joins "the field and the cave"; and though he offered them both as free gifts, he, of course, expected some costly presents in return, without which, he would not have been satisfied. The patriarch, knowing this, wished to make a purchase and asked the terms.

15. the land is worth four hundred shekels, etc.—as if Ephron had said, "Since you wish to know the value of the property, it is so and so; but that is a trifle, which you may pay or not as it suits you." They spoke in the common forms of Arab civility, and this indifference was mere affectation.

16. Abraham weighed . . . the silver—The money, amounting to £50 (about $1,000), was paid in presence of the assembled witnesses; and it was weighed. The practice of weighing money, which is often in lumps or rings, each stamped with their weight, is still common in many parts of the East; and every merchant at the gates or the bazar has his scales at his girdle. **19. Abraham buried Sarah**—Thus he got possession of Machpelah and deposited the remains of his lamented partner in a family vault which was the only spot of ground he owned.

ADAM CLARKE

in token of sorrow, as the custom then was (see Isa. xlvii. 1 and Gen. xxxvii. 35), and when this time was finished he arose and began to treat about a burying place.

4. *I am a stranger and a sojourner.* It appears from Heb. xi. 13-16; 1 Pet. ii. 11 that these words refer more to the state of his mind than of his body. He felt that he had no certain dwelling place, and was seeking by faith a city that had foundations. *Give me a possession of a buryingplace.* In different nations it was deemed ignominious to be buried in another's ground; probably this idea prevailed in early times in the East, and it may be in reference to a sentiment of this kind that Abraham refuses to accept the offer of the children of Heth to bury in any of their sepulchres, and earnestly requests them to sell him one, that he might bury his wife in a place that he could claim as his own.

6. *Thou art a mighty prince. Nesi Elohim,* "a prince of God"—a person whom we know to be divinely favored, and whom, in consequence, we deeply respect and reverence.

8. *Entreat for me to Ephron.* Abraham had already seen the cave and field, and finding to whom they belonged, and that they would answer his purpose, came to the gate of Hebron, where the elders of the people sat to administer justice, and where bargains and sales were made and witnessed, and having addressed himself to the elders, among whom was Ephron, though it appears he was not personally known to Abraham, he begged them to use their influence with the owner of the cave and field to sell it to him, that it might serve him and his family for a place of sepulture.

10. *And Ephron dwelt among the children of Heth.* "And Ephron was sitting among the children of Heth," but, as was before conjectured, was personally unknown to Abraham; he therefore answered for himself, making a free tender of the field to Abraham, in the presence of all the people, which amounted to a legal conveyance of the whole property to the patriarch.

13. *If thou wilt give it.* Instead of, *If thou wilt give it,* we should read, "But if thou wilt sell it, I will give thee money for the field"; silver, not coined money, for it is not probable that any such was then in use.

15. *The land is worth four hundred shekels of silver.* Though the words *is worth* are not in the text, yet they are necessarily expressed here to adapt the Hebrew to the idiom of our tongue. A shekel, according to the general opinion, was equal to 2 shillings and sixpence; but according to Dr. Prideaux, whose estimate I shall follow, 3 shillings English, 400 of which are equal to 60 pounds sterling; but it is evident that a certain weight is intended, and not a coin; for in verse 16 it is said, "And Abraham weighed . . . the silver," and hence it appears that this weight itself passed afterwards as a current coin.

16. *Current with the merchant.* "Passing to or with the traveller"—such as was commonly used by those who travelled about with merchandise of any sort.

17. *All the trees that were in the field.* It is possible that all these were specified in the agreement.

20. *And the field, etc., were made sure.* "Were established, caused to stand," the whole transaction having been regulated according to all the forms of law then in use.

CHAPTER 24

MATTHEW HENRY

Verses 1–9

Three things we may observe here concerning Abraham:—

I. The care he took of a good son, to get him married, well married. Now Abraham's pious care concerning his son was, (1) That he should not marry a daughter of Canaan, but one of his kindred. He saw that the Canaanites were degenerating into great wickedness. (2) That yet he should not leave the land of Canaan, to go himself among his kindred, not even for the purpose of choosing a wife, lest he should be tempted to settle there.

II. The charge he gave to a good servant, probably Eliezer of Damascus, one of whose conduct, fidelity, and affection to him and his family, he had had long experience. He trusted him with his great affair, and

CHAPTER 24

JAMIESON, FAUSSET, BROWN

Vss. 1-9. A MARRIAGE COMMISSION. **1. And Abraham was old . . . take a wife**—His anxiety to see his son married was natural to his position as a pastoral chief interested in preserving the honor of his tribe, and still more as a patriarch who had regard to the divine promise of a numerous posterity. **3. thou shalt not take a wife,** etc.—Among pastoral tribes the matrimonial arrangements are made by the parents, and a youth must marry, not among strangers, but in his own tribe—custom giving him a claim, which is seldom or never resisted, to the hand of his first cousin. But Abraham had a far higher motive—a fear lest, if his son married into a Canaanitish family, he might be gradually led away from the true God. **said unto his eldest servant**—Abraham being too old, and as the heir of the prom-

CHAPTER 24

ADAM CLARKE

1. *And Abraham was old.* He was now about one hundred and forty years of age, and consequently Isaac was forty, being born when his father was one hundred years old. See chap. xxi. 5; xxv. 20.

2. *Eldest servant.* As this eldest servant is stated to have been the ruler over all that he had, it is very likely that Eliezer is meant. See chap. xv. 2-3.

4. *My country.* Mesopotamia, called here Abraham's country because it was the place where the family of Haran, his brother, had settled; and where he himself had remained a considerable time with his father, Terah. In this family, as well as in that of Nahor, the true

MATTHEW HENRY

not Isaac himself, because he would not have Isaac go at all into that country, but marry there by proxy; and no proxy so fit as this *steward of his house*. 1. The servant must be bound by an oath to do his utmost to get a wife for Isaac from among his relations, *v.* 2–4. 2. He must be clear of this oath if, when he had done his utmost, he could not prevail.

III. The confidence he put in a good God, who, he doubts not, will give his servant success in this undertaking, *v.* 7. He remembers also the promise God had made and confirmed to him that he would give Canaan to his seed, and thence infers that God would own him in his endeavours to match his son, not among those devoted nations, but to one that was fit to be the mother of such a seed. God's promises, and our own experiences, are sufficient to encourage our dependence upon God, and our expectations from him, in all the affairs of this life.

Verses 10–28

Abraham's servant is not named, yet much is here recorded to his honour.

I. How faithful Abraham's servant approved himself to his master. Having received his charge, he with all expedition set out on his journey, with an equipage suitable to the object of his negotiation (*v.* 10).

II. How devoutly he acknowledged God in this affair, like one of that happy household which Abraham had *commanded to keep the way of the Lord*, &c., *ch.* xviii. 19. He arrived early in the evening (after many days' journeying) at the place of his destination, and reposed himself by a well of water, to consider how he might manage his business for the best. And,

1. He acknowledges God by a particular prayer (*v.* 12–14), wherein, (1) He petitions for prosperity and good success in this affair: *Send me good speed, this day.* Those that would have good speed must pray for it. (2) He pleads God's covenant with his master Abraham: *O God of my master Abraham, show kindness to him.* He desires that his master's wife might be a humble and industrious woman, bred up to care and labour, and willing to put her hand to any work that was to be done; and that she might be of a courteous disposition, and charitable to strangers. When he came to seek a wife for his master, he did not go to the playhouse or the park, and pray that he might meet one there, but to *the well of water*, expecting to find one there well employed.

2. God owns him by a particular providence. The answer to this prayer was, (1) Speedy—*before he had made an end of speaking* (*v.* 15). (2) Satisfactory: the first that came to draw water was, and did, in everything, according to his own heart. [1] She was so well qualified that in all respects she answered the characters he wished for in the woman that was to be his master's wife, handsome and healthful, humble and industrious, very courteous and obliging to a stranger, and having all the marks of a good disposition. When she came to the well (*v.* 16), she went down and *filled her pitcher, and came up* to go home with it. She did not stand to gaze upon the strange man and his camels, but minded her business, and would not have been diverted from it but by an opportunity of doing good. [2] Providence so ordered it that she did that which exactly answered to his sign, and was wonderfully the counterpart of his proposal: she not only gave him drink, but, which was more than could have been expected, she offered her services to give his camels drink, which was the very sign he proposed. Rebekah hereby, quite beyond her expectation at this time, was brought into the line of Christ and the covenant. There may be a great deal of obliging kindness in that which costs but little: our Saviour has promised a reward for a cup of cold water, Matt. x. 42. [3] Upon enquiry he found, to his great satisfaction, that she was a near relation to his master, and that the family she was of was considerable, and able to give him entertainment, *v.* 23–25.

3. He acknowledges God in a particular thanksgiving. He first paid his respects to Rebekah, in gratitude for her civility (*v.* 22). Having done this, he turns his wonder (*v.* 21) into worshipping. He had prayed for good speed (*v.* 12), and now that he had sped well he gives thanks. What we win by prayer we must wear with praise. He thinks himself very happy, that he was led to the *house of his master's brethren*, those of them that had come out of Ur of the Chaldees. They were not idolators, but worshippers of the true God, and inclinable to the religion of Abraham's family.

JAMIESON, FAUSSET, BROWN

ise not being at liberty to make even a temporary visit to his native land, was obliged to intrust this delicate mission to Eliezer, whom, although putting entire confidence in him, he on this occasion bound by a solemn oath. A pastoral chief in the present day would follow the same course if he could not go himself.

10-67. THE JOURNEY. **10. the servant took ten camels,** etc.—So great an equipage was to give the embassy an appearance worthy of the rank and wealth of Abraham; to carry provisions; to bear the marriage presents, which as usual would be distributed over several beasts; besides one or two spare camels in case of emergency. **went to Mesopotamia,** etc.—A stranger in those regions, who wishes to obtain information, stations himself at one of the wells in the neighborhood of a town, and he is sure to learn all the news of the place from the women who frequent them every morning and evening. Eliezer followed this course, and letting his camels rest, he waited till the evening time of water-drawing. **12. And he said, O Lord God of my master**—The servant appears worthy of the master he served. He resolves to follow the leading of Providence; and while he shows good sense in the tokens he fixes upon of ascertaining the temper and character of the future bride, he never doubts but that in such a case God will direct him. **15-21. before he had done speaking . . . behold, Rebekah came out**—As he anticipated, a young woman unveiled, as in pastoral regions, appeared with her pitcher on her shoulder. Her comely appearance, her affable manners, her obliging courtesy in going down the steps to fetch water not only to him but to pour in into the trough for his camels, afforded him the most agreeable surprise. She was the very person his imagination had pictured, and he proceeded to reward her civility.

22. the man took a golden earring, etc.—The ring was not for the ear, but the nose; and the armlets, such as young women in Syria and Arabia still appear daily at wells decked in. They are worn from the elbow to the wrist, commonly made of silver, copper, brass, or horn. **23-27. And said, Whose daughter art thou?**—After telling her name and family, the kind-hearted damsel hastened home to give notice of a stranger's arrival.

ADAM CLARKE

religion had been in some sort preserved, though afterwards considerably corrupted; see chap. xxxi. 19.

5. *Peradventure the woman will not be willing.* We may see by this and other passages of Scripture, Josh. ix. 18, what the sentiments of the ancients were relative to an oath. They believed they were bound precisely by what was spoken, and had no liberty to interpret the intentions of those to whom the oath was made.

7. *The Lord God.* He expresses the strongest confidence in God, that the great designs for which He had brought him from his own kindred to propagate the true religion in the earth would be accomplished; and that therefore, when earthly instruments failed, heavenly ones should be employed. *He shall send his angel*, probably meaning the Angel of the Covenant, of whom see chap. xv. 7.

9. *Put his hand under the thigh of Abraham.* When we put the circumstances mentioned in this and the third verse together, we shall find that they fully express the ancient method of binding by oath in such transactions as had a religious tendency. (1) The rite or ceremony used on the occasion: the person binding himself put his hand under the thigh of the person to whom he was to be bound; i.e., he put his hand on the part that bore the mark of circumcision, the sign of God's covenant. (2) The form of the oath itself: the person swore by Jehovah, the God of heaven and the God of the earth. Three essential attributes of God are here mentioned: (1) His self-existence and eternity in the name *Jehovah.* (2) His dominion of glory and blessedness in the kingdom of *Heaven.* (3) His providence and bounty in the *earth.* The meaning of the oath seems to be this: "As God is unchangeable in His nature and purposes, so shall I be in this engagement, under the penalty of forfeiting all expectation of temporal prosperity, the benefits of the mystical covenant, and future glory."

10. *Took ten camels.* It appears that Abraham had left the whole management of this business to the discretion of his servant, to take with him what retinue and what dowry he pleased; for it is added, *All the goods of his master were in his hand;* and in those times it was customary to give a dowry for a wife, and not to receive one with her.

11. *He made his camels to kneel down.* To rest themselves, or lie down.

15. *Behold, Rebekah came out.* How admirably had the providence of God adapted every circumstance to the necessity of the case, and so as in the most punctual manner to answer the prayer which His servant had offered up!

19. *I will draw water for thy camels also.* Had Rebekah done no more than Eliezer had prayed for, we might have supposed that she acted not as a free agent, but was impelled to it by the absolutely controlling power of God; but as she exceeds all that was requested, we see that it sprang from her native benevolence, and sets her conduct in the most amiable point of view.

21. *The man wondering at her.* And he was so lost in wonder and astonishment at her simplicity, innocence, and benevolence that he permitted this delicate female to draw water for ten camels, without ever attempting to afford her any kind of assistance! I know not which to admire most, the benevolence and condescension of Rebekah, or the cold and apparently stupid indifference of the servant of Abraham. Surely they are both of an uncommon cast.

22. *The man took a golden earring.* That this could not be an *earring* is very probable from its being in the singular number. The margin calls it a "jewel for the forehead"; but it most likely means a jewel for the nose, or nose ring, which is in universal use through all parts of Arabia and Persia, particularly among young women. They are generally worn in the left nostril. *Half a shekel.* For the weight of a shekel, see chap. xx. 16.

26. *Bowed down his head, and worshipped.* Two acts of adoration are mentioned here: (1) bowing the head; and (2) prostration upon the earth.

27. *The Lord led me.* By desire of his master he went out on this journey; and as he ac-

MATTHEW HENRY

Verses 29–53

We have here the making up of the marriage between Isaac and Rebekah.

I. The very kind reception given to Abraham's servant by Rebekah's relations. 1. The invitation was kind: *Come in, thou blessed of the Lord*, *v.* 31. Perhaps because they heard from Rebekah (*v.* 28) of the gracious words which proceeded out of his mouth. Note, Those that are blessed of God should be welcome to us. It is good owning those whom God owns. 2. The entertainment was kind, *v.* 32, 33. Particular care was taken of the camels; for a *good man regardeth the life of his beast*, Prov. xii. 10.

II. The full account which he gave them of his errand, and the court he made to them for their consent respecting Rebekah.

1. How intent he was upon his business; though he had come off a journey, and come to a good house, he would *not eat, till he had told his errand*, *v.* 33.

2. How ingenious he was in the management of it.

(1) He gives a short account of the state of his master's family, *v.* 34–36. Two things he suggests, to recommend his proposal:—[1] That his master Abraham, through the blessing of God, had a very good estate; and, [2] That he had settled it all upon Isaac, for whom he was now a suitor.

(2) He tells them the charge his master had given him, to fetch a wife for his son from among his kindred, with the reason of it, *v.* 37, 38. The highest degrees of divine affection must not divest us of natural affection.

(3) He relates to them the wonderful concurrence of providences, to countenance and further the proposal, plainly showing the finger of God in it.

(4) They freely and cheerfully close with the proposal upon a very good principle (*v.* 50): "*The thing proceedeth from the Lord*, Providence smiles upon it, and we have nothing to say against it."

(5) Abraham's servant makes a thankful acknowledgment of the good success he had met with, *He worshipped the Lord*, *v.* 52. God sent his angel before him, and so gave him success, *v.* 7, 40. But when he has the desired success, he worships God, not the angel.

JAMIESON, FAUSSET, BROWN

28. and told them of her mother's house these things—the female apartments. This family was in an advanced stage of pastoral life, dwelling in a settled place and a fixed habitation. **29-31. Rebekah had a brother ... Laban ran out**—From what we know of his character, there is reason to believe that the sight of the dazzling presents increased both his haste and his invitation.

32-49. the man came into the house, etc.—What a beautiful picture of piety, fidelity, and disinterestedness in a servant! He declined all attention to his own comforts till he had told his name and his errand.

50. Then Laban and Bethuel answered—The brothers conduct all the marriage negotiations, their father being probably dead, and without consulting their sister. Their language seems to indicate they were worshippers of the true God.

53. And the servant brought forth jewels of silver, and ... gold—These are the usual articles, with money, that form a woman's dowry among the pastoral tribes. Rebekah was betrothed and accompanied the servant to Canaan.

ADAM CLARKE

knowledged God in all his ways, the Lord directed all his steps.

28. *Her mother's house.* Some have conjectured from this that her father, Bethuel, was dead; and the person called Bethuel, verse 50, was a younger brother. This is possible, but the mother's house might be mentioned were even the father alive; for in Asiatic countries the women have apartments entirely separate from those of the men, in which their little children and grown-up daughters reside with them. This was probably the case here, though it is very likely that Bethuel was dead, as the whole business appears to be conducted by Rebekah's brothers.

31. *Thou blessed of the Lord.* Probably a usual mode of wishing prosperity, as he that is blessed of the Lord is worthy of all respect.

32. *Provender for the camels.* These were the first objects of his care; for a good man is merciful to his beast. *Water to wash his feet.* Thus it appears that he had servants with him; and as the fatigues of the journey must have fallen as heavily upon them as upon himself, so we find no distinction made, but water is provided to wash their feet also.

33. *I will not eat, until I have told.* Here is a servant who had his master's interest more at heart than his own. He refuses to take even necessary refreshment till he knows whether he is likely to accomplish the object of his journey. Did not our blessed Lord allude to the conduct of Abraham's servant, John iv. 34: "My meat is to do the will of him that sent me, and to finish his work"?

36. *Unto him hath he given all that he hath.* He has made Isaac his sole heir. These things appear to be spoken to show the relatives of Rebekah that his master's son was a proper match for her; for even in those primitive times there was regard to the suitableness of station and rank in life, as well as of education, in order to render a match comfortable.

42. *O Lord God of my master.* As Abraham was the friend of God, Eliezer makes use of this to give weight and consequence to his petitions.

43. *When the virgin. Haalmah*, from *alam*, to hide, cover, or conceal; a pure virgin, a woman not uncovered, and in this respect still concealed from man. The same as *bethulah*, v. 16, which, from the explanation there given, incontestably means a virgin in the proper sense of the word —a young woman, not that is covered or kept at home, but who was not uncovered in the delicate sense in which the Scripture uses this word.

45. *Before I had done speaking in mine heart.* So we find that the whole of this prayer, so circumstantially related in verses 12-14, and again in 42-44, was mental, and heard only by that God to whom it was directed. It would have been improper to use public prayer on the occasion, as his servants could have felt no particular interest in the accomplishment of his petitions because they were not concerned in them, having none of the responsibility of this mission.

49. *That I may turn to the right hand, or to the left.* That is, That I may go elsewhere and seek a proper match for the son of my master.

50. *Laban and Bethuel.* These seem both to be brothers, of whom Laban was the eldest and chief; for the opinion of Josephus appears to be very correct, namely, that Bethuel, the father, had been some time dead. See v. 28. *Bad or good.* We can neither speak for nor against; it seems to be entirely the work of God, and we cordially submit. Consult Rebekah; if she be willing, take her and go.

53. *Jewels of silver, and jewels of gold.* The word which we here translate *jewels* signifies properly "vessels" or "instruments"; and those presented by Eliezer might have been of various kinds. What he had given before, v. 22, was in token of respect; what he gave now appears to have been in the way of dowry. *Precious things.* This word is used to express exquisite fruits or delicacies, Deut. xxxiii. 13-16; precious plants or flowers, Cant. iv. 16; vii. 13. But it may mean gifts in general.

54. *And they did eat and drink.* When Eliezer had got a favorable answer, then he and his servants sat down to meat; this he had refused

F. B. MEYER:

Abraham's servant fulfills his mission. This worthy man was almost always talking about his master. Count the number of times in which he contrives to introduce those two words, "my master." He put the errand on which he had come before his necessary food and poured out his story in a stream of crystal utterance of the highest eloquence. This identification of his thought and speech with his master's interests is full of teaching for us all. He could talk of nothing else, was only anxious not to fail for Abraham's sake, and took the favorable reply as kindness shown to him whom he represented. We, too, are called to be ambassadors, as though God did beseech men by us. If we are in the way of God's will, be sure that the Lord will not only lead, but lead "in the right way," and will create for us a sympathetic reception wherever we go.—*Bible Commentary*

MATTHEW HENRY

Verses 54–61
Rebekah is here taking leave of her father's house. Rebekah's relations, from natural affection and according to the usual expression of kindness in that case, solicit her to stay some time among them, *v.* 55. They had consented to the marriage, and yet were loth to part with her. Rebekah herself determined the matter. Rebekah consented, not only to go, but to go immediately. Hereupon she is sent away with Abraham's servant; with suitable attendants; with hearty good wishes. Now that she was going to be a wife, they prayed that she might be a mother both of a numerous and of a victorious progeny.

Verses 62–67
Isaac and Rebekah are, at length, happily brought together.

I. Isaac was well employed when he met Rebekah: *He went out to meditate*, or pray, *in the field, at the even-tide, v.* 62, 63. He went to take the advantage of a silent evening and a solitary field for meditation and prayer, those divine exercises by which we converse with God and our own hearts. Note, 1. Holy souls love retirement. It will do us good to be often left alone, walking alone and sitting alone; and, if we have the art of improving solitude, we shall find we are never less alone than when alone. 2. Meditation and prayer ought to be both our business and our delight when we are alone. The exercises of devotion should be the refreshment and entertainment of the evening, to relieve us from the fatigue occasioned by the care and business of the day, and to prepare us for the repose and sleep of the night. Some think Isaac was now praying for good success in this affair that was depending, and now, when he sets himself, as it were, upon his watchtower, to see what God would answer him, as the prophet (Hab. ii. 1), *he sees the camels coming.*

II. Rebekah behaved herself very becomingly, when she met Isaac: understanding who he was, she *alighted off her camel* (*v.* 64), and *took a veil, and covered herself* (*v.* 65), in token of humility, modesty, and subjection.

III. They were brought together to their mutual comfort, *v.* 67. Observe here, 1. What an affectionate son he was to his mother: it was about three years since her death, and yet he was not, till now, comforted concerning it. 2. What an affectionate husband he was to his wife.

JAMIESON, FAUSSET, BROWN

KEIL–DELITZSCH:

Verses 61–67. When the caravan arrived in Canaan with Rebekah and her maidens, Isaac had just come from going to the well Lahai-Roi (16:14), as he was then living in the south country; and he went towards evening (at the turning, coming on, of the evening, Deut. 23:12) to the field "to meditate." It is impossible to determine whether Isaac had been to the well of Hagar which called to mind the omnipresence of God, and there, in accordance with his contemplative character, had laid the question of his marriage before the Lord (Delitzsch), or whether he had merely traveled thither to look after his flocks and herds (Knobel). But the object of his going *to the field to meditate* was undoubtedly to lay the question of his marriage before God in solitude. The caravan arrived at the time; and Rebekah, as soon as she saw the man in the field coming to meet them, sprang (signifying a hasty descent, 2 Kings 5:21) from the camel to receive him, according to Oriental custom, in the most respectful manner. She then inquired the name of the man; and as soon as she heard that it was Isaac, she enveloped herself in her veil, as became a bride when meeting the bridegroom.—*Commentary on the Old Testament*

64. she lighted off the camel—If Isaac was walking, it would have been most unmannerly for her to have continued seated; an inferior, if riding, always alights in presence of a person of rank, no exception being made for women. **65. she took a veil, and covered herself**—The veil is an essential part of female dress. In country places it is often thrown aside, but on the appearance of a stranger, it is drawn over the face, as to conceal all but the eyes. In a bride it was a token of her reverence and subjection to her husband. **67. And Isaac brought her into his mother's . . . tent**—thus establishing her at once in the rights and honors of a wife before he had seen her features. Disappointments often take place, but when Isaac saw his wife, "he loved her."

ADAM CLARKE

to do till he had told his message, v. 33.

55. *Let the damsel abide with us a few days, at the least ten.* The original is very abrupt and obscure, because we are not acquainted with the precise meaning of the form of speech which is here used; *days* or *ten* probably meaning a year or ten months, as the margin reads it, or a week or ten days. This latter is the most likely sense, as there would be no propriety after having given their consent that she should go in detaining her for a year or ten months. In matters of simple phraseology, or in those which concern peculiar customs, the Septuagint translation, especially in the Pentateuch, where it is most accurate and pure, may be considered a legitimate judge; this translation renders the words "about ten days."

58. *Wilt thou go with this man?* So it appears it was left ultimately to the choice of Rebekah whether she would accept the proposals now made to her, unless we suppose that the question meant, "Wilt thou go immediately, or stay with us a month longer?" *She said, I will go.* It fully appears to be the will of God that it should be so, and I consent. This at once determined the whole business.

59. *And her nurse.* Whose name, we learn from chap. xxxv. 8, was Deborah, and who, as a second mother, was deemed proper to accompany Rebekah. This was a measure dictated by good sense and prudence. Rebekah had other female attendants. See v. 61.

60. *Be thou the mother of thousands of millions.* "For thousands ten thousand," or "for myriads of thousands," a large family being ever considered, in ancient times, as a proof of the peculiar blessing and favor of God.

62. *And Isaac came.* Concerning this *well* see chap. xvi. 13, etc. As it appears from chap. xxv. 11 that Isaac dwelt at the well *Lahai-roi*, it has been conjectured that he had now come on a visit to his aged father at Beer-sheba, where he waited in expectation of his bride. *For he dwelt in the south country.* The southern part of the land of Canaan.

63. *Isaac went out to meditate.* "To bend down" the body, or the mind, or both. He was probably in deep thought, with his eyes fixed upon the ground.

65. *She took a veil.* This is the first time this word occurs, and it is of doubtful signification; but most agree to render it a veil or a cloak. The former is the most likely, as it was generally used by women in the East as a sign of chastity, modesty, and subjection.

67. *Sarah's tent.* Sarah being dead, her tent became now appropriated to the use of Rebekah. *And took Rebekah.* After what form this was done we are not told; or whether there was any form used on the occasion, more than solemnly receiving her as the person whom God had chosen to be his wife; for it appears from v. 66 that the servant told him all the especial providential circumstances which had marked his journey. The primitive form of marriage we have already seen, chap. ii. 23-24, which, it is likely, as far as form was attended to, was that which was commonly used in all the patriarchal times.

MATTHEW HENRY — CHAPTER 25

Verses 1–10
Abraham lived, after the marriage of Isaac, thirty-five years, and all that is recorded concerning him during that time lies here in a very few verses. We hear no more of God's extraordinary appearances to him or trials of him; for all the days, even of the best and greatest saints, are not eminent days, some slide on silently, and neither come nor go with observation; such were these last days of Abraham.

I. An account of his children by Keturah, another wife whom he married after the death of Sarah.

II. The disposition which Abraham made of his estate, *v.* 5, 6. After the birth of these sons, he set his house in order, with prudence and justice. 1. He made Isaac his heir, as he was bound to do, in justice to Sarah his first and principal wife, and to Rebekah who married Isaac upon the assurance of it, *ch.* xxiv.

JAMIESON, FAUSSET, BROWN — CHAPTER 25

Vss. 1-6. SONS OF ABRAHAM. **1. Abraham took a wife**—rather, "had taken"; for Keturah is called Abraham's concubine, or secondary wife (I Chronicles 1:32); and as, from her bearing six sons to him, it is improbable that he married after Sarah's death; and also as he sent them all out to seek their own independence, during his lifetime, it is clear that this marriage is related here out of its chronological order, merely to form a proper winding up of the patriarch's history.

5, 6. Abraham gave all that he had unto Isaac . . . unto the sons of the concubines . . . Abraham gave gifts—While the chief part of the inheritance went to Isaac, (the other sons, Ishmael included, migrated to "the East country," i.e., Arabia) but received each a portion of the

ADAM CLARKE — CHAPTER 25

2. *Medan, and Midian.* Probably those who peopled that part of Arabia Petraea contiguous to the land of Moab eastward of the Dead Sea. *Shuah.* Or *Shuach.* From this man the Sacceans, near to Batania, at the extremity of Arabia Deserta, towards Syria, are supposed to have sprung. Bildad the Shuhite, one of Job's friends, is supposed to have descended from this son of Abraham.

3. *Sheba.* From whom sprang the Sabeans, who robbed Job of his cattle. *Asshurim, and Letushim, and Leummim.* We know not who these were, but as each name is plural they must have been tribes or families, and not individuals.

5. *Gave all that he had unto Isaac.* His principal flocks, and especially his right to the land of Canaan, including a confirmation to him and his posterity of whatever was contained in the promises of God.

6. *Unto the sons of the concubines.* Namely,

MATTHEW HENRY

36. God having already made him the heir of the promise, Abraham therefore made him heir of his estate. 2. He gave portions to the rest of his children, both to Ishmael, though at first he was sent empty away, and to his sons by Keturah. It was justice to provide for them; parents that do not imitate him in this are worse than infidels. It was prudence to settle them in places distant from Isaac, that they might not pretend to divide the inheritance with him, nor be in any way a care or expense to him. Observe, He did this *while he yet lived*, lest it should not be done, or not so well done, afterwards.

III. The age and death of Abraham, *v.* 7, 8. He lived 175 years, just 100 years after he came to Canaan; so long he was a sojourner in a strange country. 1. He *gave up the ghost*. His life was not extorted from him, but he cheerfully resigned it; into the hands of the Father of spirits he committed his spirit.

2. He *died in a good old age, an old man*; so God had promised him. His death was his discharge from the burdens of his age. It was also the crown of the glory of his old age. 3. He was *full of years*, or full of *life*. He did not live till the world was weary of him, but till he was weary of the world; he had had enough of it, and desired no more. A good man, though he should not die old, dies full of days, satisfied with living here, and longing to live in a better place. 4. He *was gathered to his people*. His body was gathered to the congregation of the dead, and his soul to the congregation of the blessed. Death gathers us to our people. Those that are our people while we live, whether the people of God or the children of this world, are the people to whom death will gather us.

IV. His burial, *v.* 9, 10. 1. Who buried him: *His sons Isaac and Ishmael*. It was the last office of respect they had to pay to their good father. Some distance there had formerly been between Isaac and Ishmael; but it seems either that Abraham had himself brought them together while he lived, or at least that his death reconciled them. 2. Where they buried him: in his own burying-place, which he had purchased, and in which he had buried Sarah.

JAMIESON, FAUSSET, BROWN

patrimony, perhaps in cattle and other things; and this settlement of Abraham's must have given satisfaction, since it is still the rule followed among the pastoral tribes.

7-11. DEATH OF ABRAHAM. **7. these are the days of . . . Abraham**—His death is here related, though he lived till Jacob and Esau were fifteen years, just one hundred years after coming to Canaan; "the father of the faithful," "the friend of God," died; and even in his death, the promises were fulfilled (cf. ch. 15:15). We might have wished some memorials of his deathbed experience; but the Spirit of God has withheld them—nor was it necessary; for (see Matt. 7:16) from earth he passed into heaven (Luke 16:22). Though dead he yet liveth (Matt. 22:32).

ALEXANDER MACLAREN:

Here we have the calm picture of the old man going down into his grave and looking back over all those long days since he came away from his father's house and became a pilgrim and a stranger. How all the hot anxieties, desires, occupations of youth have quieted themselves down! How far away now seem the warlike days when he fought the invading kings! How far away the heaviness of heart when he journeyed to Mount Moriah with his boy and whetted the knife to slay his son! His love had all been buried in Sarah's grave. He has been a lonely man for many years; and yet he looks back, as God looked back over His creative week, and feels that all has been good. "It was all for the best; the great procession of my life has been ordered from the beginning to its end by the Hand that shapes beauty everywhere, and has made all things blessed and sweet. I have drunk a full draught; I have had enough; I bless the Giver of the feast, and push my chair back; and get up and go away." He died an old man, and satisfied with his life.—*Expositions of Holy Scripture*

9, 10. his sons . . . buried him—Death often puts an end to strife, reconciles those who have been alienated, and brings rival relations, as in this instance, to mingle tears over a father's grave.

ADAM CLARKE

Hagar and Keturah, Abraham gave gifts. Cattle for breed, seed to sow the land, and implements for husbandry may be what is here intended. *And sent them away . . . while he yet lived.* Lest after his death they should dispute a settlement in the Land of Promise with Isaac; therefore he very prudently sent them to procure settlements during his lifetime, that they might be under no temptation to dispute the settlement with Isaac in, Canaan. From this circumstance arose that law which has prevailed in almost all countries, of giving the estates to the eldest son by a lawful wife; for though concubines, or wives of the second rank, were perfectly legitimate in those ancient times, yet their children did not inherit, except in case of the failure of legal issue, and with the consent of the lawful wife; and it is very properly observed that it was in consequence of the consent of Leah and Rachel that the children of their slaves by Jacob had a common and equal lot with the rest. *Eastward, unto the east country.* Arabia Deserta, which was eastward of Beer-sheba, where Abraham lived.

7. *The days of the years.* There is a beauty in this expression which is not sufficiently regarded. Good men do not count their lives by *years,* but by *days,* living as if they were the creatures only of a day; having no more time that they can with any propriety call their own, and living that day in reference to eternity.

8. *Then Abraham gave up the ghost.* Highly as I value our translation for general accuracy, fidelity, and elegance, I must beg leave to dissent from this version. The original word signifies "to pant for breath, to expire, to cease from breathing, or to breathe one's last"; and here, and wherever the original word is used, the simple term "expired" would be the proper expression. In our translation this expression occurs in Gen. xxv. 8, 17; xxxv. 29; xliv. 33; Job iii. 11; x. 18; xi. 20; xiii. 19; xiv. 10; Lam. i. 19. Now as our English word *ghost,* from the Anglo-Saxon *gast,* an "inmate, inhabitant, guest" (a casual visitant), also "spirit," is now restricted among us to the latter meaning, always signifying the immortal spirit or soul of man, the guest of the body; and as giving up the spirit, ghost, or soul, is an act not proper to man, though commending it to God, in our last moments, is both an act of faith and piety; and as giving up the ghost, i.e., dismissing His spirit from His body, is attributed to Jesus Christ, to whom alone it is proper, I therefore object against its use in every other case.

An old man. Namely, one hundred and seventy-five, the youngest of all the patriarchs; *and full of years.* The word *years* is not in the text; but as our translators saw that some word was necessary to fill up the text, they added this in italics. It is probable that the true word is "days," as in Gen. xxxv. 29; and this reading is found in the Samaritan text, Septuagint, Vulgate, Syriac, Arabic, Persic, and Chaldee. On these authorities it might be safely admitted into the text.

It was the opinion of Aristotle that a man should depart from life as he should rise from a banquet. Thus Abraham died "full of days," and satisfied with life, but in a widely different spirit from that recommended by the above writers—he left life with a hope full of immortality, which they could never boast; for he saw the day of Christ, and was glad; and his hope was crowned, for here it is expressly said, "He was gathered to his fathers"; surely not to the bodies of his sleeping ancestors, who were buried in Chaldea and not in Canaan, nor with his fathers in any sense, for he was deposited in the cave where his wife alone slept; but he was gathered to the "spirits of just men made perfect, and to the Church of the firstborn, whose names are written in heaven," Heb. xii. 23.

9. *His sons Isaac and Ishmael buried him.* Though Ishmael and his mother had been expelled from Abraham's family on the account of Isaac, yet, as he was under the same obligation to a most loving, affectionate father as his brother, Isaac, if any personal feuds remained, they agreed to bury them on this occasion, that both might dutifully join in doing the last offices to a parent who was an honor to them and to human nature; and, considering the re-

MATTHEW HENRY

Verses 11–18

Immediately after the account of Abraham's death, Moses begins the story of Isaac (*v.* 11), and tells us where he dwelt and how remarkably God blessed him. But he presently digresses from the story of Isaac, to give a short account of Ishmael, forasmuch as he also was a son of Abraham, and God had made some promises concerning him. 1. Concerning his children. He had twelve sons, *twelve princes* they are called (*v.* 16), heads of families, which in process of time became nations, distinct tribes, numerous and very considerable. They peopled *Arabia*. The names of his twelve sons are recorded. Midian and Kedar we often read of in scripture. And some very good expositors have taken notice of the signification of those three names which are put together (*v.* 14), as containing good advice to us all, *Mishma, Dumah*, and *Massa*, that is, *hear, keep silence*, and *bear*; we have them together in the same order, Jam. i. 19, *Be swift to hear, slow to speak, slow to wrath.* The posterity of Ishmael had not only tents in the fields, wherein they grew rich in times of peace; but they had towns and castles (*v.* 16), wherein they fortified themselves in time of war.

2. Concerning himself. Here is an account of his age: He *lived* 137 *years* (*v.* 17), which is recorded to show the efficacy of Abraham's prayer for him (*ch.* xvii. 18), *O that Ishmael might live before thee!* Here is also an account of his death; he too *was gathered to his people*; but it is not said that he was *full of days*, though he lived to so great an age. He died with his friends about him, which is comfortable.

Verses 19–28

We have here an account of the birth of Jacob and Esau, the twin sons of Isaac and Rebekah: their entrance into the world was (which is not usual) one of the most considerable parts of their story. Isaac seems not to have been a man of action, nor much tried, but to have spent his days in quietness and silence. Now concerning Jacob and Esau we are here told,

I. That they were prayed for. Their parents, after they had been long childless, obtained them by prayer, *v.* 20, 21. *Isaac was forty years old when he was married.* He was sixty years old when his sons were born (*v.* 26), so that, after he was married, he had no child for twenty years. But, 1. He prayed. He prayed *for* his wife; some read it *with* his wife. Note, Husbands and wives should pray together. The Jews have a tradition that Isaac, at length, took his wife with him to Mount Moriah, where God had promised that he would multiply Abraham's seed (*ch.* xxii. 17), and there, in his prayer with her and for her, pleaded the promise made in that very place. 2. God heard his prayer, and was entreated of him.

II. That they were prophesied of before they were born, and great mysteries were wrapped up in the prophecies which went before of them, *v.* 22, 23. Now Rebekah being with child of these two sons, observe here,

1. How she was perplexed in her mind concerning her present case: *The children struggled together within her.* This struggle between Jacob and Esau in the womb represents the struggle that is maintained between the kingdom of God and the kingdom of Satan. A holy war is better than the peace of the devil's palace.

2. What course she took for her relief: *She went to enquire of the Lord.* It is a great relief to the mind to spread our case before the Lord, and ask counsel at his mouth. *Go into the sanctuary*, Ps. lxxiii. 17.

JAMIESON, FAUSSET, BROWN

12-18. DESCENDANTS OF ISHMAEL. Before passing to the line of the promised seed, the historian gives a brief notice of Ishmael, to show that the promises respecting that son of Abraham were fulfilled—first, in the greatness of his posterity (cf. ch. 17:20); and, secondly, in their independence.

TODAY'S DICTIONARY OF THE BIBLE:

Ishmael settled in the land of Paran, a region lying between Canaan and the mountains of Sinai; and "God was with him, and he became a great archer" (Gen. 21:9–21). The young man became a great desert chief, but little of his history is recorded. He was about ninety years of age when his father Abraham died, in connection with whose burial he once more for a moment reappears. On this occasion the two brothers met after being long separated. "Isaac with his hundreds of household slaves, Ishmael with his troops of wild retainers and half-savage allies, in all the state of a Bedouin prince, gathered before the cave of Machpelah, in the midst of the men of Heth, to pay the last duties to the 'father of the faithful,' would make a notable subject for an artist" (Gen. 25:9). Of the after events of his life little is known. He died at the age of one hundred and thirty-seven years, but where and when are unknown (25:17). He had twelve sons, who became the founders of so many Arab tribes or colonies—the Ishmaelites—who spread over the wide desert spaces of Northern Arabia from the Red Sea to the Euphrates (Gen. 37:25, 27, 28; 39:1), "their hand against every man, and every man's hand against them."

18. he died—rather, "it [their lot] fell in the presence of his brethren" (cf. ch. 16:12).

19-35. HISTORY OF ISAAC. **19. these are the generations**—account of the leading events in his life. **21. Isaac entreated the Lord for his wife**—Though tried in a similar way to his father, he did not follow the same crooked policy. Twenty years he continued unblessed with offspring, whose seed was to be "as the stars." But in answer to their mutual prayers (I Pet. 3:7), Rebekah was divinely informed that she was to be the mother of twins, who should be the progenitors of two independent nations; that the descendants of the younger should be the more powerful and subdue those of the other (Rom. 9:12; II Chron. 21:8).

ADAM CLARKE

jection of Ishmael from the inheritance, this transaction shows his character in an amiable point of view; for though he was "a wild man" (see chap. xvi. 12), yet this appellation appears to be more characteristic of his habits of life than of his disposition.

11. *God blessed his son Isaac.* The peculiar blessings and influences by which Abraham had been distinguished now rested upon Isaac; but how little do we hear in him of the work of faith, the patience of hope, and the labor of love!

12. *These are the generations of Ishmael.* The object of the inspired writer seems to be to show how the promises of God were fulfilled to both the branches of Abraham's family. Isaac has been already referred to; God blessed him according to the promise. He had also promised to multiply Ishmael, and an account of his generation is introduced to show how exactly the promise had also been fulfilled to him.

13. *Nebajoth*—from whom came the Nabatheans, whose capital was Petra.

14. *Mishma*, and *Dumah*, and *Massa*—These three names have passed into a proverb among the Hebrews, because of their signification. *Mishma* signified "hearing"; *Dumah*, "silence"; and *Massa*, "patience." Hence, "Hear much, say little, and bear much."

15. *Hadar*—This name should be read "Hadad" as in 1 Chron. i. 30. This reading is supported by more than three hundred manuscripts, versions, and printed editions. *Tema*—Supposed to be a place in Arabia Deserta, the same of which Job speaks, chap. vi. 19. *Jetur*—From whom came the Itureans, who occupied a small tract of country beyond Jordan, which was afterwards possessed by the half-tribe of Manasseh. *Naphish*—These are evidently the same people mentioned in 1 Chron. v. 19, who, with the Itureans and the people of Nadab, assisted the Hagarenes against the Israelites, but were overcome by the two tribes of Reuben and Gad, and the half-tribe of Manasseh. *Kedemah*—Probably the descendants of this person dwelt at *Kedemoth*, a place mentioned in Deut. ii. 26.

16. *These are their names*—by which their descendants were called. *Their towns*—places of encampment in the wilderness, such as have been used by the Arabs from the remotest times. *Their castles*, "their towers," probably mountaintops, fortified rocks, and fastnesses of various kinds in woods and hilly countries.

18. *They dwelt from Havilah unto Shur.* The descendants of Ishmael possessed all that country which extends from east to west, from *Havilah* on the Euphrates, near its junction with the Tigris, to the desert of *Shur* eastward of Egypt, and which extends along the isthmus of Suez. *He died in the presence of all his brethren.* The original will not well bear this translation. In v. 17 it is said, "He gave up the ghost and died; and was gathered unto his people." Then follows the account of the district occupied by the Ishmaelites, at the conclusion of which it is added, "It [the lot or district] fell [or was divided] to him in the presence of all his brethren"; and this was exactly agreeable to the promise of God, chap. xvi. 12, "He shall dwell in the presence of all his brethren"; and to show that this promise had been strictly fulfilled, it is here remarked that his lot or inheritance was assigned him by divine providence, contiguous to that of the other branches of the family. The same word, *naphal*, is used, Josh. xxiii. 4, for "to divide by lot."

19. *These are the generations of Isaac.* This is the history of Issac and his family.

21. *Isaac intreated the Lord for his wife.* Isaac and Rebekah had now lived nineteen years together without having a child; for he was forty years old when he married Rebekah, v. 20, and he was threescore years of age when Jacob and Esau were born, v. 26.

22. *The children struggled together.* They dashed against or bruised each other." There was a violent agitation, so that the mother was apprehensive both of her own and her children's safety; and, supposing this was an uncommon case, she went to inquire of the Lord, as the good women in the present day would go to consult a surgeon or physician. It appears she was in considerable perplexity, hence that im-

MATTHEW HENRY

3. The information given her, upon her enquiry, which expounded the mystery: *Two nations are in thy womb*, *v.* 23. She was now pregnant, not only with two children, but two nations, which should not only in their manners and dispositions greatly differ from each other, but in their interests clash and contend with each other; and the issue of the contest should be that the elder should serve the younger, which was fulfilled in the subjection of the Edomites, for many ages, to the house of David, till they revolted, 2 Chron. xxi. 8. In the struggle between grace and corruption in the soul, grace, the younger, shall certainly get the upper hand at last.

III. That when they were born there was a great difference between them.

1. There was a great difference in their bodies, *v.* 25. Esau, when he was born, was rough and hairy, as if he had been already a grown man, whence he had his name Esau, *made*, reared already. This was an indication of a very strong constitution, and gave cause to expect that he would be a very robust, daring, active man. But Jacob was smooth and tender as other children. It is God's usual way to choose the weak things of the world, and to pass by the mighty, 1 Cor. i. 26, 27.

2. There was a manifest contest in their births.

3. They were very unlike in the temper of their minds, and the way of living they chose, *v.* 27. (1) Esau was a man for this world. He was a man addicted to his sports, for he was a cunning hunter. He was a man of the field, like Nimrod and Ishmael. (2) Jacob was a man for the other world. He was not cut out for a statesman, nor did he affect to look great, but he was *a plain man, dwelling in tents*, an honest man that always meant well, and dealt fairly, that preferred the true delights of solitude and retirement to all the pretended pleasure of busy noisy sports: he dwelt in tents, [1] As a shepherd. He was attached to that safe and silent employment of keeping sheep, to which also he bred up his children, *ch.* xlvi. 34. Or, [2] As a student. He frequented the tents of Melchizedek, or Heber, as some understand it, to be taught by them divine things. And this was that son of Isaac on whom the covenant was entailed.

4. Their interest in the affections of their parents was likewise different. They had but these two children, and, it seems, one was the father's darling and the other the mother's, *v.* 28. (1) Isaac loved to have his son active. Esau knew how to please him, and showed a great respect for him, by treating him often with venison. (2) Rebekah was mindful of the oracle of God, which had given the preference to Jacob, and therefore she preferred him in her love.

Verses 29–34

We have here a bargain made between Jacob and Esau about the birthright, which was Esau's by providence but Jacob's by promise. It was a spiritual privilege, such a birthright as had then the blessing annexed to it, and the entail of the promise.

I. Jacob's pious desire of the birthright, which yet he sought to obtain by indirect courses. For this he is to be commended, that he coveted earnestly the best gifts; yet in this he cannot be justified, that he took advantage of his brother's necessity to make him a very hard bargain (*v.* 31): *Sell me this day thy birthright*. Note, Plain men that have their conversation in simplicity and godly sincerity, and without worldly wisdom, are often found wisest of all for their souls and eternity. Jacob's wisdom appeared in two things:—1. He chose the fittest time. 2. Having made the bargain, he made it sure, and got it confirmed by Esau's oath: *Swear to me this day*, *v.* 33.

II. Esau's profane contempt of the birthright, and the foolish sale he made of it. He is called *profane Esau* for it (Heb. xii. 16), because *for one morsel of meat he sold his birthright*, as dear a morsel as ever was eaten since the forbidden fruit; and he lived to regret it when it was too late. Note, There are those that are penny-wise and pound-foolish, cunning hunters that can out-wit others and draw them into their snares, and yet are themselves imposed upon by Satan's wiles and led captive by him at his will. Observe the instances of Esau's folly.

1. His appetite was very strong, *v.* 29, 30. Poor Jacob had got some bread and pottage (*v.* 34) for his dinner, when Esau came from hunting, hungry and weary. Give me (says he) some of *that red, that red*, as it is in the original. The gratifying of the sensual appetite is that which ruins thousands of precious souls: surely, if Esau was hungry and faint, he might have got a meal's meat cheaper than at the expense of his birthright.

2. His reasoning was very weak (*v.* 32): *Behold, I am at the point to die*; and, if he were, would nothing serve to keep him alive but this pottage? If the

JAMIESON, FAUSSET, BROWN

27. the boys grew—from the first, opposite to each other in character, manners, and habits.

28. The parents were divided in their affection; and while the grounds, at least of the father's partiality, were weak, the distinction made between the children led, as such conduct always does, to unhappy consequences.

29. Jacob sod pottage—made of lentils or small beans, which are common in Egypt and Syria. It is probable that it was made of Egyptian beans, which Jacob had procured as a dainty; for Esau was a stranger to it. It is very palatable; and to the weary hunter, faint with hunger, its odor must have been irresistibly tempting.

31. Jacob said, Sell me . . . thy birthright—i.e., the rights and privileges of the first-born, which were very important, the chief being that they were the family priests (Exod. 4:22) and had a double portion of the inheritance (Deut. 21:17).

32. Esau said . . . I am at the point to die—i.e., I am running daily risk of my life; and of what use will the birthright be to me: so he despised or cared little

ADAM CLARKE

perfect speech, "If so, why am I thus?" the simple meaning of which is probably this: If I must suffer such things, why did I ever wish to have a child?

23. *Two nations are in thy womb*. "We have," says Bishop Newton, "in the prophecies delivered respecting the sons of Isaac, ample proof that these prophecies were not meant so much of single persons as of whole nations descended from them; for what was predicted concerning Esau and Jacob was not verified in themselves, but in their posterity. The Edomites were the offspring of Esau, the Israelites were of Jacob; and who but the Author and Giver of life could foresee that two children in the womb would multiply into two nations? The Edomites and Israelites have been from the beginning two such different people in their manners, customs, and religion, as to be at perpetual variance among themselves. The children struggled together in the womb, which was an omen of their future disagreement." *The one people shall be stronger than the other people*. The same author continues to observe that "for some time the family of Esau was the more powerful of the two; but David and his captains made an entire conquest of the Edomites, slew several thousands of them, and compelled the rest to become tributaries.

24. *There were twins*. *Thomim*, from which comes "Thomas," properly interpreted by the word *Didymus*, which signifies a "twin."

25. *Red, all over like an hairy garment*. This simply means that he was covered all over with red hair or down; and that this must be intended here is sufficiently evident from another part of his history, where Rebekah, in order to make her favorite son, Jacob, pass for his brother, Esau, was obliged to take the skins of kids, and put them upon his hands and on the smooth part of his neck.

26. *His name was called Jacob*. *Yaacob*, from *akab*, to "defraud, deceive, to supplant," i.e., to overthrow a person by tripping up his heels. Hence this name was given to Jacob, because it was found he had laid hold on his brother's heel, which was emblematical of his supplanting Esau and defrauding him of his birthright.

27. *A man of the field*. One who supported himself and family by hunting and by agriculture. *Jacob was a plain man*. *Ish tam*, "a perfect or upright man"; *dwelling in tents*—subsisting by breeding and tending cattle, which was considered in those early times the most perfect employment; and in this sense the word *tam* should be here understood, as in its moral meaning it certainly could not be applied to Jacob till after his name was changed, after which time only his character stands fair and unblemished. See chap. xxxii. 26-30.

28. *Isaac loved Esau . . . but Rebekah loved Jacob*. This is an early proof of unwarrantable parental attachment to one child in preference to another. And in consequence of this the interests of the family were divided and the house set in opposition to itself. The fruits of this unreasonable and foolish attachment were afterwards seen in a long catalogue of both natural and moral evils among the descendants of both families.

29. *Sod pottage*. *Yazed nazid*, "he boiled a boiling"; and this we are informed, v. 34, was of "lentiles," a sort of pulse.

30. *I am faint*. He had been either hunting or laboring in the field, and was now returning for the purpose of getting some food, but had been so exhausted that his strength utterly failed before he had time to make the necessary preparations.

31. *Sell me this day thy birthright*. What the *bechorah* or birthright was has greatly divided both ancient and modern commentators. It is generally supposed that the following rights were attached to the primogeniture: (1) Authority and superiority over the rest of the family. (2) A double portion of the paternal inheritance. (3) The peculiar benediction of the father. (4) The priesthood, previous to its establishment in the family of Aaron.

34. *Pottage of lentiles*. See. v. 29. *Thus Esau despised his birthright*. On this account the apostle, Heb. xii. 16, calls Esau a "profane person," because he had by this act alienated

MATTHEW HENRY

famine were now in the land (*ch.* xxvi. 1), as Dr. Lightfoot conjectures, we cannot suppose Isaac so poor, or Rebekah so bad a housekeeper, but that he might have been supplied with food convenient, in other ways. Note, It is egregious folly to part with our interest in God, and Christ, and heaven, for the riches, honours, and pleasures, of this world, as bad a bargain as his that sold a birthright for a dish of broth.

3. Repentance was hidden from his eyes (*v.* 34): *He did eat and drink*, pleased his palate, and then carelessly rose up and went his way, without any show of regret. Thus Esau despised his birthright.

JAMIESON, FAUSSET, BROWN

about it, in comparison with gratifying his appetite—he threw away his religious privileges for a trifle; and thence he is styled "a profane person" (Heb. 12:16; also Job 31:7, 16; 6:13; Phil. 3:19). "There was never any meat, except the forbidden fruit, so dear bought, as this broth of Jacob" [BISHOP HALL].

ADAM CLARKE

from himself and family those spiritual offices connected with the rights of primogeniture. Jacob verified his right to the name of "supplanter," a name which in its first imposition appears to have had no other object in view than the circumstance of his catching his brother by the heel; but all his subsequent conduct proved that it was truly descriptive of the qualities of his mind, as his whole life, till the time his name was changed (and then he had a change of nature), was a tissue of cunning and deception, the principles of which had been very early instilled in him by a mother whose regard for truth and righteousness appears to have been very superficial. See on chap. xxvii.

MATTHEW HENRY — CHAPTER 26

Verses 1–5

I. God tried Isaac by his providence. Now there is *a famine in the land*, *v.* 1. What shall he think of the promise when the promised land will not find him bread ? Yes, Isaac will still cleave to the covenant. Note, The intrinsic worth of God's promises cannot be lessened in a believer's eye by any cross providences.

II. He directed him under this trial by his word. Isaac must go for supply. He set out for Egypt, whither his father went in the like strait, but he takes Gerar in his way. 1. God bade him stay where he was, and *not go down into Egypt*: *Sojourn in this land*, *v.* 2, 3. There was a famine in Jacob's days, and God bade him *go down into Egypt* (*ch.* xlvi. 3, 4), a famine in *Isaac's* days, and God made him *not to go down*, a famine in Abraham's days, and God left him to his liberty. This variety in the divine procedure some ground upon the different characters of these three patriarchs. Abraham was a man of very high attainments, and intimate communion with God; and to him all places and conditions were alike. Isaac was a very good man, but not cut out for hardship; therefore he is forbidden to go to Egypt. Jacob was inured to difficulties, strong and patient; and therefore he must go down into Egypt. Thus God proportions his people's trials to their strength. "*Abraham obeyed my voice;* do thou do so too, and the promise shall be sure to thee." Abraham's obedience is here celebrated, to his honour; for by it he obtained a good report both with God and men.

Verses 6–11

Isaac had now set up his staff in Gerar, the country in which he was born (*v.* 6), yet there he enters into temptation to deny his wife, and to give out that she was his sister.

I. How he sinned, *v.* 7. Because his wife was handsome, he fancied the Philistines would find some way or other to take him off, that some of them might marry her; and therefore she must pass for his sister.

II. How he was detected, and the cheat discovered, by the king himself. Abimelech (not the same that was in Abraham's days, *ch.* xx, for this was nearly 100 years after that, but this was the common name of the Philistine kings) saw Isaac more familiar with Rebekah than he knew he would be with his sister (*v.* 8): he saw him sporting with her, or *laughing*; it is the same word with that from which Isaac had his name. Nowhere may a man more allow himself to be innocently merry than with his own wife and children. Abimelech charged him with the fraud (*v.* 9), showed him what might have been the bad consequences of it (*v.* 10), and then, to convince him how groundless and unjust his jealousy of them was, took him and his family under his particular protection, forbidding any injury to be done to him or his wife upon pain of death, *v.* 11.

Verses 12–25

I. The tokens of God's good-will to Isaac. 1. His corn multiplied strangely, *v.* 12. He had no land of his own, but took land of the Philistines, and sowed it; and (be it observed for the encouragement of poor tenants, that occupy other people's lands, and are honest and industrious) God blessed him with a great increase. He reaped *a hundred fold* that *same year* when there was a famine in the land.

JAMIESON, FAUSSET, BROWN — CHAPTER 26

Vss. 1-35. SOJOURN IN GERAR. **1. And there was a famine in the land . . . And Isaac went unto . . . Gerar**—The pressure of famine in Canaan forced Isaac with his family and flocks to migrate into the land of the Philistines, where he was exposed to personal danger, as his father had been on account of his wife's beauty; but through the seasonable interposition of Providence, he was preserved (Ps. 105:14, 15).

12. Then Isaac sowed in that land—During his sojourn in that district he farmed a piece of land, which, by the blessing of God on his skill and industry, was very productive (Isa. 65:13; Ps. 37:19); and by his plentiful returns he increased so rapidly in wealth and influence that the Philistines, afraid or envious of his prosperity, obliged him to leave the place (Prov. 27:4; Eccles. 4:4). This may receive illustration from the fact that many Syrian shepherds at this day settle for a year or two in a place, rent some ground, in the produce of which they trade with the neighboring market, till the

F. B. MEYER:

"Because that Abraham obeyed my voice and kept my charge." It is awful to realize how our sins may repeat themselves in our children. Here is Isaac following in the precise steps of Abraham, who had acted in a similar manner towards Sarah when entering Egypt. In each case there was a sad lapse of faith; but it was even worse for Isaac, with Abraham's example to warn him. But a man may pass blessings on to his children, as well as the sad entail of evil habits.

He leaves the blessing of the divine covenant. God had entered into covenant with Abraham and was prepared to fulfil its provisions to his son. "I will be a God to thee, and to thy seed after thee." So a godly ancestor may be able to secure for all his seed a share in the divine grace and favor. The spirit that is put on him does not depart from his seed, or his seed's seed forever.

The blessing of his prayer. It is impossible to overestimate the effect of a good man's prayers; they are as streams or trees, which go on flowing and bearing fruit long after they were originated. The legacy of a good man's prayers is of priceless worth. He may have long since passed to his rest; but God remembers them, and answers them in blessings to the next generation. How often in this chapter we read that "God blessed Isaac."

The blessing of a noble name. We may all leave that, if we can transmit nothing else. To have had a father that knew God, walked with God, pleased God; who was on intimate terms with Him, and could speak to Him, as a man with his friend—illumined the ordinary nature and existence of Isaac with unearthly beauty. Let us live so that our children may be ranked as nobles because they bear our name.

—Great Verses Through the Bible

ADAM CLARKE — CHAPTER 26

1. *There was a famine.* When this happened we cannot tell; it appears to have been after the death of Abraham. Concerning the first famine, see chap. xii. 10. *Abimelech.* As we know not the time when the famine happened, so we cannot tell whether this was the same Abimelech, Phichol, etc., which are mentioned chap. xx. 1, etc., or the sons or other descendants of these persons.

2. *Go not down into Egypt.* As Abraham had taken refuge in that country, it is probable that Isaac was preparing to go thither also; and God, foreseeing that he would there meet with trials which might prove fatal to his peace or to his piety, warns him not to fulfil his intention.

3. *Sojourn in this land.* In Gerar, whither he had gone, v. 1, and where we find he settled, v. 6, though the land of Canaan in general might be here intended.

4. *I will make thy seed . . . as the stars of heaven.* A promise often repeated to Abraham, and which has been most amply fulfilled in both its literal and spiritual sense.

5. *Abraham obeyed my voice.* "My word." *My charge. Mishmarti, from shamar;* he kept, observed, the "ordinances" or "appointments" of God. These were always of two kinds: (1) such as tended to promote moral improvement, the increase of piety; and (2) such as were typical of the promised Seed, and the salvation which was to come by Him.

7. *He said, She is my sister.* It is very strange that in the same place, and in similar circumstances, Isaac should have denied his wife, precisely as his father had done before him! Isaac could not say of Rebekah, as Abraham had done of Sarah, "She is my sister." In the case of Abraham this was literally true; it was not so in the case of Isaac, for Rebekah was only his cousin.

8. *Isaac was sporting with Rebekah his wife.* Whatever may be the precise meaning of the word, it evidently implies that there were liberties taken and freedom used on the occasion which were not lawful but between man and wife.

10. *Thou shouldest have brought guiltiness upon us.* It is likely that Abimelech might have had some knowledge of God's intentions concerning the family of Abraham, and that it must be kept free from all impure and alien mixtures; and that consequently, had he or any of his people taken Rebekah, the divine judgment might have fallen upon the land. Abimelech was a good and holy man; and he appears to have considered adultery as a grievous and destructive crime.

11. *He that toucheth.* He who injures Isaac or defiles Rebekah shall certainly die for it. Death was the punishment for adultery among the Canaanites, Philistines, and Hebrews. See chap. xxxviii. 24.

12. *Isaac sowed in that land.* Being now perfectly free from the fear of evil, he betakes himself to agricultural and pastoral pursuits, in which he has the special blessing of God, so that his property becomes greatly increased. *An hundredfold.* Literally, "A hundredfold of barley;" and so the Septuagint. Perhaps such a crop of this grain was a rare occurrence in Gerar. The words, however, may be taken in a general way, as signifying a very great increase; so they are used by our Lord in the parable of the sower.

MATTHEW HENRY

2. His cattle also increased, *v.* 14. And then, 3. He had *great store of servants,* whom he employed and maintained.

II. The tokens of the Philistines' ill-will to him. They *envied him, v.* 14. That is a bad principle indeed which makes men *grieve at the good of others,* as if it must needs be ill with me because it is well with my neighbour. Because they had not flocks of their own to water at the wells, they would not leave them for the use of others; so absurd a thing is malice. The king of Gerar began to look upon him with a jealous eye. Isaac's house was like a court and therefore he must go further off. A wise and a good man will rather retire into obscurity, like Isaac here into a valley, than sit high to be the butt of envy and ill-will.

III. His constancy and continuance in his business still.

1. He kept up his husbandry, and continued industrious to find wells of water, and he set himself to make the best of the country he had come into, which it is every man's prudence to do.

(1) He opened the wells that his father had digged (*v.* 18). Note, In our searches after truth, that fountain of living water, it is good to make use of the discoveries of former ages, which have been clouded by the corruptions of later times. Enquire for the old way, the wells which our fathers digged, which the adversaries of truth have stopped up.

(2) His servants dug new wells, *v.* 19. Note, Though we must use the light of former ages, it does not therefore follow that we must rest in it, and make no advances. We must still be building upon their foundation.

(3) In digging his wells he met with much opposition, *v.* 20, 21. Those that open the fountains of truth must expect contradiction. The first two wells which they dug were called *Esek* and *Sitnah, contention* and *hatred.*

(4) At length he removed to a quiet settlement. He preferred quietness to victory. Note, Those that follow peace, sooner or later, shall find peace. This well they called *Rehoboth, enlargements,* room enough: in the two former wells we may see what the earth is, *straitness* and *strife.* This well shows us what heaven is; it is *enlargement* and *peace,* room enough there, for there are many mansions.

2. He continued firm to his religion, and kept up his communion with God. He came weary and uneasy to Beer-sheba. *Fear not,* says God to him, *I am with thee, and will bless thee.* Those may remove with comfort that are sure of God's presence with them wherever they go. *There he built an altar, and called upon the name of the Lord, v.* 25.

Verses 26–33

We have here the contests that had been between Isaac and the Philistines issuing in a happy peace and reconciliation.

I. Abimelech pays a friendly visit to Isaac, in token of the respect he had for him, *v.* 26.

II. Isaac prudently and cautiously questions his sincerity in this visit, *v.* 27.

III. Abimelech professes his sincerity, in this address to Isaac, and earnestly courts his friendship, *v.* 28, 29. Isaac complained they had *hated him, and sent him away.* No, said Abimelech, *we sent thee away in peace.* He acknowledges the tokens of God's favour to him, and makes this the ground of their desire, to be in league with him: *The Lord is with thee, and thou art the blessed of the Lord.*

JAMIESON, FAUSSET, BROWN

owners, through jealousy of their growing substance, refuse to renew their lease and compel them to remove elsewhere.

15. all the wells which his father's servants had digged . . . the Philistines had stopped, etc.—The same base stratagem for annoying those against whom they have taken an umbrage is practiced still by choking the wells with sand or stones, or defiling them with putrid carcases.

17. valley of Gerar—torrent-bed or wady, a vast undulating plain, unoccupied and affording good pasture. **18-22. Isaac digged again the wells of water**—The naming of wells by Abraham, and the hereditary right of his family to the property, the change of the names by the Philistines to obliterate the traces of their origin, the restoration of the names by Isaac, and the contests between the respective shepherds to the exclusive possession of the water, are circumstances that occur among the natives in those regions as frequently in the present day as in the time of Isaac.

26-33. Then Abimelech went to him—As there was a lapse of ninety years between the visit of Abraham and of Isaac, the Abimelech and Phichol spoken of must have been different persons' official titles. Here is another proof of the promise (ch. 12:2) being fulfilled, in an overture of peace being made to him by the king of Gerar. By whatever motive the proposal was dictated—whether fear of his growing power, or regret for the bad usage they had given him, the king and two of his courtiers paid a visit to the tent of Isaac (Prov. 16:7). His timid and passive temper had submitted to the annoyances of his rude neighbors; but now that they wish to renew the covenant, he evinces deep feeling at their conduct, and astonishment at their assurance, or artifice, in coming near him. Being, however, of a pacific disposition, he forgave their offense, accepted their proposals, and treated them to the banquet by which the ratification of a covenant was usually crowned.

ADAM CLARKE

13. *The man waxed great.* There is a strange and observable recurrence of the same term in the original: "And the man was great; and he went, going on, and was great, until that he was exceeding great." How simple is this language and yet how forcible!

14. *He had possession of flocks.* He who blessed him in the increase of his fields blessed him also in the increase of his flocks; and as he had extensive possessions, so he must have many hands to manage such concerns. Therefore it is added, *he had . . . great store of servants*—he had many domestics, some born in his house, and others purchased by his money.

15. *For all the wells . . . the Philistines had stopped them.* In such countries a good well was a great acquisition; and hence in predatory wars it was usual for either party to fill the wells with earth or sand, in order to distress the enemy. The filling up the wells in this case was a most unprincipled transaction, as they had pledged themselves to Abraham, by a solemn oath, not to injure each other in this or any other respect. See chap. xxi. 25-31.

16. *Go from us; for thou art much mightier than we.* This is the first instance on record of what was termed among the Greeks "ostracism"; i.e., the banishment of a person from the state, of whose power, influence, or riches, the people were jealous. The Philistines appear to have been jealous of Isaac's growing prosperity, and to have considered it, not as a due reward of his industry and holiness, but as their individual loss, as though his gain was at their expense; therefore they resolved to drive him out, and take his well-cultivated ground to themselves, and compelled Abimelech to dismiss him, who gave this reason for it, "Thou hast obtained much wealth among us," and my people are envious of thee.

18. *In the days of Abraham.* Instead of *bimey,* "in the days," Houbigant contends we should read *abdey,* "servants." Isaac digged again the wells which the servants of Abraham, his father, had digged. This reading is supported by the Samaritan, Septuagint, Syriac, and Vulgate; and it is probably the true one.

19. *A well of springing water.* "A well of living waters." This is the oriental phrase for a spring, and this is its meaning in both the Old and New Testaments: Lev. xiv. 5, 50; xv. 30; Num. xix. 17; Cant. iv. 15. See also John iv. 10-14; vii. 38; Rev. xxi. 6; xxii. 1. And by these scriptures we find that an unfailing spring was an emblem of the graces and influences of the Spirit of God.

21. *They digged another well.* Never did any man more implicitly follow the divine command, "Resist not evil," than Isaac; whenever he found that his work was likely to be a subject of strife and contention, he gave place, and rather chose to suffer wrong than to have his own peace of mind disturbed. Thus he overcame evil with good.

24. *The Lord appeared unto him.* He needed special encouragement when insulted and outraged by the Philistines.

25. *Builded an altar there.* That he might have a place for God's worship, as well as a place for himself and family to dwell in. *And called upon the name of the Lord.* And invoked in the name of Jehovah. See on chap. xii. 8; xiii. 15.

26. *Abimelech went to him.* When a man's ways please God, He makes even his enemies to be at peace with him; so Isaac experienced on this occasion. Whether this was the same Abimelech and Phichol mentioned in chap. xxi. 22 we cannot tell; it is possible both might have been now alive, provided we suppose them young in the days of Abraham; but it is more likely that *Abimelech* was a general name of the Gerarite kings, and that *Phichol* was a name of office.

27. *Seeing ye hate me.* He was justified in thinking thus, because if they did not injure him, they had connived at their servants doing it.

28. *Let there be now an oath betwixt us.* Let us make a covenant by which we shall be mutually bound and let it be ratified in the most solemn manner.

30. *He made them a feast.* Probably on the sacrifice that was offered on the occasion of

MATTHEW HENRY

IV. Isaac entertains him and his company, and enters into a league of friendship with him, *v.* 30, 31. Note, Religion teaches us to be neighbourly, and, as much as in us lies, to *live peaceably with all men.*

V. Providence smiled upon what Isaac did; for the same day that he made this covenant with Abimelech his servants brought him the tidings of a well of water they had found, *v.* 32, 33.

Verses 34–35

Here is, 1. Esau's foolish marriage—foolish, in marrying Canaanites, who were strangers to the blessing of Abraham, for which he is called *profane*; for hereby he intimated that he neither desired the blessing nor dreaded the curse of God. 2. The grief and trouble it created to his tender parents. It grieved them that he married the daughters of Hittites, who had no religion among them.

JAMIESON, FAUSSET, BROWN

34. Esau . . . took to wife—If the pious feelings of Abraham recoiled from the idea of Isaac forming a matrimonial connection with a Canaanitish woman, that devout patriarch himself would be equally opposed to such a union on the part of his children; and we may easily imagine how much his pious heart was wounded, and the family peace destroyed, when his favorite but wayward son brought no less than two idolatrous wives among them—an additional proof that Esau neither desired the blessing nor dreaded the curse of God. These wives never gained the affections of his parents, and this estrangement was overruled by God for keeping the chosen family aloof from the dangers of heathen influence.

ADAM CLARKE

making this covenant. This was a common custom.

31. *They rose up betimes.* Early rising was general among the primitive inhabitants of the world, and this was one cause which contributed greatly to their health and longevity.

33. *He called it Shebah.* This was probably the same well which was called Beer-sheba in the time of Abraham, which the Philistines had filled up, and which the servants of Isaac had reopened. *The name of the city is Beer-sheba.* This name was given to it a hundred years before this time; but as the well from which it had this name originally was closed up by the Philistines, probably the name of the place was abolished with the well; when therefore Isaac reopened the well, he restored the ancient name of the place.

34. *He took to wife . . . the daughter.* It is very likely that the wives taken by Esau were daughters of chiefs among the Hittites, and by this union he sought to increase and strengthen his secular power and influence.

35. *Which were a grief of mind.* Not the marriage, though that was improper, but the persons; they, by their perverse and evil ways, brought bitterness into the hearts of Isaac and Rebekah.

MATTHEW HENRY

Verses 1–5

Here is, I. Isaac's design to make his will, and to declare Esau his heir.

II. The directions he gave to Esau, pursuant to this design. He calls him to him, *v.* 1. For Esau, though he had greatly grieved his parents by his marriage, yet they had not expelled him, but made the best of it. Parents that are justly offended at their children yet must not be implacable towards them.

1. He tells him upon what considerations he resolved to do this now (*v.* 2).

2. He bids him to get things ready for the solemnity of executing his last will and testament, by which he designed to make him his heir, *v.* 3, 4. Esau must go a hunting, and bring some venison, which his father will eat of, and then bless him. Prayer is the work of the soul, and not of the lips only; as the soul must be employed in blessing God (Ps. ciii. 1), so it must be in blessing ourselves and others: the blessing will not come to the heart if it do not come from the heart.

Verses 6–17

Rebekah is here contriving to procure for Jacob the blessing which was designed for Esau.

I. The end was good. God had said it should be so, that the elder should *serve the younger*; and therefore Rebekah resolves it shall be so. But,

II. The means were bad, and no way justifiable. If it was not wrong to Esau to deprive him of the blessing (he himself having forfeited it by selling the birthright), yet it was a wrong to Isaac, taking advantage of his infirmity to impose upon him; it was a wrong to Jacob too, whom she taught to deceive. It would likewise expose him to endless scruples about the blessing, if he should obtain it thus fraudulently. If Rebekah had gone to Isaac, and put him in remembrance of that which God had said concerning their sons,—if she further had shown him how Esau had forfeited the blessing both by selling his birthright and by marrying strange wives, it is probable that Isaac would have been prevailed upon to confer the blessing upon Jacob.

JAMIESON, FAUSSET, BROWN

CHAPTER 27

Vss. 1-27. Infirmity of Isaac. **1. when Isaac was old, and his eyes were dim**—He was in his 137th year; and apprehending death to be near, he prepared to make his last will—an act of the gravest importance, especially as it included the conveyance through a prophetic spirit of the patriarchal blessing.

4. make . . . savory meat—perhaps to revive and strengthen him for the duty; or rather, "as eating and drinking" were used on all religious occasions, he could not convey the right, till he had eaten of the meat provided for the purpose by him who was to receive the blessing [Adam Clarke] (cf. ch. 18:7). **that my soul may bless thee**—It is difficult to imagine him ignorant of the divine purpose (cf. ch. 25:23). But natural affection, prevailing through age and infirmity prompted him to entail the honors and powers of the birthright on his elder son; and perhaps he was not aware of what Esau had done (ch. 25:34).

5-10. Rebekah spake unto Jacob—She prized the blessing as invaluable; she knew that God intended it for the younger son; and in her anxiety to secure its being conferred on the right object—on one who cared for religion—she acted in the sincerity of faith; but in crooked policy—with unenlightened zeal; on the false principle that the end would sanctify the means. **11. Jacob said, Esau my brother is an hairy man**—It is remarkable that his scruples were founded, not on the evil of the act, but on the risk and consequences of deception.

ADAM CLARKE

CHAPTER 27

1. *Isaac was old.* It is conjectured, on good grounds, that Isaac was now about one hundred and seventeen years of age, and Jacob about fifty-seven; though the commonly received opinion makes Isaac one hundred and thirty-seven, and Jacob seventy-seven. *And his eyes were dim.* This was probably the effect of that affliction, of what kind we know not, under which Isaac now labored; and from which, as well as from the affliction, he probably recovered, as it is certain he lived forty if not forty-three years after this time, for he lived till the return of Jacob from Padan-aram; chap. xxxv. 27-29.

2. *I know not the day of my death.* From his present weakness he had reason to suppose that his death could not be at any great distance, and therefore would leave no act undone which he believed it his duty to perform. He who lives not in reference to eternity lives not at all.

3. *Thy weapons.* The original word *keley* signifies "vessels" and "instruments" of any kind; and is probably used here for a hunting spear, javelin, sword, etc. *Quiver. Teli,* from *talah,* to "hang or suspend."

4. *Savoury meat. Matammim,* from *taam,* to "taste or relish." *That I may eat.* The blessing which Isaac was to confer on his son was a species of divine right, and must be communicated with appropriate ceremonies. As eating and drinking were used among the Asiatics on almost all religious occasions, and especially in making and confirming covenants, it is reasonable to suppose that something of this kind was essentially necessary on this occasion and that Isaac could not convey the right till he had eaten of the meat provided for the purpose by him who was to receive the blessing. As Isaac was now old and in a feeble and languishing condition, it was necessary that the flesh used on this occasion should be prepared so as to invite the appetite, that a sufficiency of it might be taken to revive and recruit his drooping strength, that he might be the better able to go through the whole of this ceremony.

5. *And Rebekah heard.* And was determined, if possible, to frustrate the design of Isaac, and procure the blessing for her favorite son. Some pretend that she received a divine inspiration to the purpose; but if she had she needed not to have recourse to deceit to help forward the accomplishment. Isaac, on being informed, would have had too much piety not to prefer the will of his Maker to his own partiality for his eldest son; but Rebekah had nothing of the kind to plead, and therefore had recourse to the most exceptionable means to accomplish her ends.

12. *I shall bring a curse upon me.* For even in those early times the spirit of that law was understood, Deut. xxvii. 18: "Cursed be he that maketh the blind to wander out of the way";

MATTHEW HENRY

Verses 18–29

Observe here, I. The art and assurance with which Jacob managed this intrigue. Who would have thought that his plain man could have played his part so well in a design of this nature? Note, Lying is soon learnt. I wonder how honest Jacob could so readily turn his tongue to say (*v.* 19), *I am Esau thy firstborn.* How could he say, *I have done as thou badest me*, when he had received no command from his father, but was doing as his mother bade him? How could he say, *Eat of my venison*, when he knew it came, not from the field, but from the fold? But especially I wonder how he could have the assurance to father it upon God, and to use his name in the cheat (*v.* 20): *The Lord thy God brought it to me.* Is this Jacob? Is this Israel, indeed, without guile? It is certainly written, not for our imitation, but for our admonition.

II. The success of this management. Jacob with some difficulty gained his point, and obtained the blessing.

1. Isaac was at first dissatisfied, and would have discovered the fraud if he could have trusted his own ears; for *the voice was Jacob's voice*, *v.* 22. His voice is Jacob's voice, but his hands are Esau's. He speaks the language of a saint, but does the works of a sinner; but the judgment will be, as here, by the hands.

2. At length he yielded to the power of the cheat, *because the hands were hairy* (*v.* 23), not considering how easy it was to counterfeit that circumstance; and now Jacob carries it on dexterously. That which in some small degree extenuates the crime of Rebekah and Jacob is that the fraud was intended, not so much to hasten the fulfilling, as to prevent the thwarting, of the oracle of God: the blessing was just going to be put upon the wrong head, and they thought it was time to bestir themselves. Now let us see how Isaac gave Jacob his blessing, *v.* 26–9. (1) He embraces him, in token of a particular affection to him. (2) He praised him. *He smelt the smell of his raiment, and said, See, the smell of my son is as the smell of a field which the Lord hath blessed.* (3) He rpayed for him, and therein prophesied concerning him. Three things Jacob is here blessed with:—[1] Plenty (*v.* 28). [2] Power (*v.* 29). [3] Prevalence with God, and a great interest in Heaven: "*Cursed be every one that curseth thee and blessed be he that blesseth thee.*"

Verses 30–40

Here is, I. The covenant-blessing denied to Esau. He that made so light of the birthright *would now have inherited the blessing.* Observe, 1. How carefully he sought it. When he understood that Jacob had obtained it surreptitiously, he *cried with a great and exceedingly bitter cry*, *v.* 34. Those that will not so much as ask and seek now, will knock shortly, and cry, *Lord, Lord.* Slighters of Christ will then be humble suitors to him. 2. How he was rejected. Isaac, when first made sensible of the imposition that had been practised on him, *trembled exceedingly*, *v.* 33. But he soon recovers himself, and ratifies the blessing he had given to Jacob: *I have blessed him, and he shall be blessed.* Having found himself more than ordinarily filled with the Holy Ghost when he gave the blessing to Jacob, he perceived that God did, as it were, say Amen to it. Now, (1) Jacob was hereby confirmed in his possession of the blessing. (2) Isaac hereby acquiesced in the will of God, though it contradicted his own expectation and affection. (3) Esau hereby was cut off from the expectation of that special blessing which he thought to have preserved to himself when he sold his birthright. The Jews, like Esau, hunted *after the law of righteousness* (*v.* 31), yet missed of the blessing of righteousness, *because they sought it by the works of the law* (*v.* 32); while the Gentiles, who, like Jacob, sought it by faith in the oracle of God, obtained it by force, with that violence which the kingdom of heaven suffers. See Matt. xi. 12. Those who undervalue their spiritual birthright, and can afford to sell it for a morsel of meat, forfeit spiritual blessings. Those that will part with their wisdom and grace, with their faith and a good conscience, for the honours, wealth, or pleasures, of this world, however they may pretend a zeal for the blessing, have already judged themselves unworthy of it.

II. Here is a common blessing bestowed upon Esau.

1. This he desired: *Bless me also*, *v.* 34. *Hast thou not reserved a blessing for me?*, *v.* 36. It is the folly of most men that they are willing to take up with any good (Ps. iv. 6), as Esau here, who desired but a second-rate blessing, a blessing separated from the birthright. As if he had said, "I will take up with any: though I have not the blessing of the church, yet let me have some blessing."

JAMIESON, FAUSSET, BROWN

13-17. and his mother said, Upon me be thy curse—His conscience being soothed by his mother, preparations were hastily made for carrying out the device; consisting, first, of a kid's flesh, which, made into a ragout, spiced with salt, onions, garlic, and lemon juice, might easily be passed off on a blind old man, with blunted senses, as game; second, of pieces of goat's skin bound on his hands and neck, its soft silken hair resembling that on the cheek of a young man; third, of the long white robe—the vestment of the first-born, which, transmitted from father to son and kept in a chest among fragrant herbs and perfumed flowers used much in the East to keep away moths, his mother provided for him. **18-27. he came unto his father**—The scheme planned by the mother was to be executed by the son in the father's bedchamber; and it is painful to think of the deliberate falsehoods, as well as daring profanity, he resorted to. The disguise, though wanting in one thing, which had nearly upset the whole plot, succeeded in misleading Isaac; and while giving his paternal embrace, the old man was roused into a state of high satisfaction and delight.

27. the smell of my son is as of a field—The aromatic odors of the Syrian fields and meadows, often impart a strong fragrance to the person and clothes, as has been noticed by many travellers.

28-46. THE BLESSING. **God give thee of the dew of heaven**—To an Oriental mind, this phraseology implied the highest flow of prosperity. The copious fall of dew is indispensable to the fruitfulness of lands, which would be otherwise arid and sterile through the violent heat; and it abounds most in hilly regions, such as Canaan, hence called the fat land (Neh. 9:25, 35). **plenty of corn and wine**—Palestine was famous for vineyards, and it produced varieties of corn, viz., wheat, barley, oats, and rye. **Let people serve thee**—fulfilled in the discomfiture of the hostile tribes that opposed the Israelites in the wilderness; and in the pre-eminence and power they attained after their national establishment in the promised land. This blessing was not realized to Jacob, but to his descendants; and the temporal blessings promised were but a shadow of those spiritual ones, which formed the grand distinction of Jacob's posterity. **30-35. Esau came in from his hunting**—Scarcely had the former scene been concluded, when the fraud was discovered. The emotions of Isaac, as well as Esau, may easily be imagined—the astonishment, alarm, and sorrow of the one—the disappointment and indignation of the other. But a moment's reflection convinced the aged patriarch that the transfer of the blessing was "of the Lord," and now irrevocable. The importunities of Esau, however, overpowered him; and as the prophetic afflatus was upon the patriarch, he added what was probably as pleasing to a man of Esau's character as the other would have been.

ADAM CLARKE

and Jacob seems to have possessed at this time a more tender conscience than his mother.

13. *Upon me be thy curse, my son.* What a dreadful responsibility did this woman take upon her at this time!

19. *I am Esau thy firstborn.* Here are many palpable falsehoods, and such as should neither be imitated nor excused.

23. *And he discerned him not, because his hands were hairy.* From this circumstance we may learn that Isaac's sense of feeling was much impaired by his present malady. When he could not discern the skin of a kid from the flesh of his son we see that he was, through his infirmity, in a fit state to be imposed on by the deceit of his wife and the cunning of his younger son.

27. *The smell of my son is as the smell of field.* The smell of these garments, the goodly raiment which had been laid up in the house, was probably occasioned by some aromatic herbs, which we may naturally suppose were laid up with the clothes—a custom which prevails in many countries to the present day.

29. *Let people serve thee.* It appears that Jacob was, on the whole, a man of more religion and believed the divine promises more than Esau. The posterity of Jacob likewise preserved the true religion and the worship of one God, while the Edomites were sunk in idolatry; and of the seed of Jacob was born at last the Saviour of the world. This was the peculiar privilege and advantage of Jacob, to be the happy instrument of conveying these blessings to all nations. This was his greatest superiority over Esau; and in this sense St. Paul understood and applied the prophecy: "The elder shall serve the younger," Rom. ix. 12.

33. *And Isaac trembled.* The marginal reading is very literal and proper, "And Isaac trembled with a great trembling greatly." And this shows the deep concern he felt for his own deception, and the iniquity of the means by which it had been brought about. Though Isaac must have heard of that which God had spoken to Rebekah, "The elder shall serve the younger," and could never have wished to reverse this divine purpose; yet he might certainly think that the spiritual blessing might be conveyed to Esau, and by him to all the nations of the earth, notwithstanding the superiority of secular dominion on the other side. *Yea, and he shall be blessed.* From what is said in this verse, collated with Heb. xii. 17, we see how binding the conveyance of the birthright was when communicated with the rites already mentioned. When Isaac found that he had been deceived by Jacob, he certainly would have reversed the blessing if he could; but as it had been conveyed in the sacramental way, this was impossible. "I have blessed him," says he, "yea, and he must, or will, be blessed." Hence it is said by the apostle, Esau "found no place of repentance"—no place for change of mind or purpose in his father—"though he sought it carefully with tears." The father could not reverse it because the grant had already been made and confirmed. But this had nothing to do with the final salvation of poor outwitted Esau, nor indeed with that of his unnatural brother.

35. *Hath taken away thy blessing.* This blessing, which was a different thing from the birthright, seems to consist of two parts: (1) The dominion, generally and finally, over the other part of the family; and (2) Being the progenitor of the Messiah.

36. *Is not he rightly named Jacob?* See on chap. xxv. 26. *He took away my birthright.* So he might say with considerable propriety; for though he sold it to Jacob, yet as Jacob had taken advantage of his perishing situation, he considered the act as a species of robbery.

MATTHEW HENRY

2. This he had; and let him make his best of it, *v.* 39, 40.

(1) It was promised him, [1] That he should have a competent livelihood—*the fatness of the earth, and the dew of heaven.* Note, Those that come short of the blessings of the covenant may yet have a very good share of outward blessings. [2] That by degrees he should recover his liberty. He shall serve, but he shall not starve; and, at length after much skirmishing, he shall break the yoke of bondage, and wear the marks of freedom. This was fulfilled (2 Kings viii. 20, 22) when the Edomites revolted.

(2) Yet it was far short of Jacob's blessing. For him God had reserved some better thing. In Jacob's blessing *the dew of heaven* is put first, as that which he most valued. In Esau's *the fatness of the earth* is put first, for it was this that he had the principal regard to. Jacob shall have dominion over his brethren: hence the Israelites often ruled over the Edomites. But the great difference is that there is nothing in Esau's blessing that points to Christ, nothing that brings him or his into the church and covenant of God, without which the fatness of the earth will stand him in little stead.

Verses 41–46

Here is, I. The malice Esau bore to Jacob upon account of the blessing which he had obtained, *v.* 41. Esau's hatred of Jacob was, 1. A causeless hatred. He hated him for no other reason but because his father blessed him and God loved him. 2. It was a cruel hatred. Nothing less would satisfy him than to slay his brother. 3. It was a politic hatred. He expected his father would soon die, and then titles must be tried and interests contested between the brothers, which would give him a fair opportunity for revenge.

II. The method Rebekah took to prevent the mischief.

1. She gave Jacob warning of his danger, and advised him to withdraw for a while, and shift for his own safety. Observe here, (1) What Rebekah feared—lest she *should be deprived of them both in one day* (*v.* 45). (2) What Rebekah hoped—that, if Jacob for a while kept out of sight, the affront which his brother resented so fiercely would by degrees go out of mind.

2. She impressed Isaac with an apprehension of the necessity of Jacob's going among her relations upon another account, which was to take a wife, *v.* 46.

JAMIESON, FAUSSET, BROWN

39, 40. **Behold thy dwelling shall be the fatness of the earth**—The first part is a promise of temporal prosperity, made in the same terms as Jacob's—the second refers to the roving life of hunting free-booters, which he and his descendants should lead. Though Esau was not personally subject to his brother, his posterity were tributary to the Israelites, till the reign of Joram when they revolted and established a kingdom of their own (II Kings 8:20; II Chron. 21:8-10).

41. **Esau hated Jacob**—It is scarcely to be wondered at that Esau resented the conduct of Jacob and vowed revenge. **The days of mourning for my father are at hand**—a common Oriental phrase for the death of a parent.

42-45. **these words of Esau were told Rebekah**—Poor woman! she now early begins to reap the bitter fruits of her fraudulent device; she is obliged to part with her son, for whom she planned it, never, probably, seeing him again; and he felt the retributive justice of heaven fall upon him heavily in his own future family.

45. **Why should I be deprived of you both**—This refers to the law of Goelism, by which the nearest of kin would be obliged to avenge the death of Jacob upon his brother.

46. **Rebekah said to Isaac**—Another pretext her cunning had to devise to obtain her husband's consent to Jacob's journey to Mesopotamia; and she succeeded by touching the aged patriarch in a tender point, afflicting to his pious heart—the proper marriage of their younger son.

ADAM CLARKE

40. *By thy sword shalt thou live.* This does not absolutely mean that the Edomites should have constant wars; but that they should be of a fierce and warlike disposition, gaining their sustenance by hunting, and by predatory excursions upon the possessions of others. *And when thou shalt have the dominion.* It is here foretold that there was to be a time when the elder was to have dominion and shake off the yoke of the younger. The word *tarid,* which we translate *have dominion,* is of rather doubtful meaning, as it may be deduced from three different roots: *yarad,* to "descend, to be brought down or brought low"; *radah,* to "obtain rule or have dominion"; and *rud,* to "complain"—meaning either that when reduced very low God would magnify His power in their behalf, and deliver them from the yoke of their brethren; or when they should be increased so as to venture to set up a king over them, or when they mourned for their transgressions, God would turn their captivity.

41. *The days of mourning for my father are at hand.* Such was the state of Isaac's health at that time, though he lived more than forty years afterwards, that his death was expected by all; and Esau thought that would be a favorable time for him to avenge himself on his brother, Jacob, as, according to the custom of the times, the sons were always present at the burial of the father. Ishmael came from his own country to assist Isaac to bury Abraham; and both Jacob and Esau assisted in burying their father, Isaac, but the enmity between them had happily subsided long before that time.

42. *Doth comfort himself, purposing to kill thee.* There is no doubt that Esau, in his hatred to his brother, felt himself pleased with the thought that he should soon have the opportunity of avenging his wrongs.

44. *Tarry with him a few days.* It was probably forty years before he returned, and it is likely Rebekah saw him no more; for it is the general opinion of the Jewish rabbins that she died before Jacob's return from Padan-aram, whether the period of his stay be considered twenty or forty years.

45. *Why should I be deprived also of you both?* If Esau should kill Jacob, then the nearest akin to Jacob, who was by the patriarchial law, Gen. ix. 6, the avenger of blood, would kill Esau; and both these deaths might possibly take place in the same day. This appears to be the meaning of Rebekah.

46. *I am weary of my life.* It is very likely that Rebekah kept many of the circumstances related above from the knowledge of Isaac; but as Jacob could not go to Padan-aram without his knowledge, she appears here quite in her own character, framing an excuse for his departure and concealing the true cause. Abraham had been solicitous to get a wife for his son Isaac from a branch of his own family; hence she was brought from Syria. She is now afraid, or pretends to be afraid, that her son Jacob will marry among the Hittites, as Esau had done; and therefore makes this to Isaac the ostensible reason why Jacob should immediately go to Padan-aram, that he might get a wife there. Isaac, not knowing the true cause of sending him away, readily falls in with Rebekah's proposal, and immediately calls Jacob, gives him suitable directions and his blessing, and sends him away. This view of the subject makes all consistent and natural; and we see at once the reason of the abrupt speech contained in this verse, which should be placed at the beginning of the following chapter.

MATTHEW HENRY — CHAPTER 28

Verses 1–5

Jacob had no sooner obtained the blessing than immediately he was forced to flee from his country. Now *Jacob fled into Syria,* Hos. xii. 12. He was blessed with plenty of corn and wine, and yet he went away poor, was blessed with government, and yet went out to service, a hard service. This was, 1. Perhaps to correct him for his dealing fraudulently with his father. The blessing shall be confirmed to him, and yet he shall smart for the indirect course he took to obtain it. However, 2. It was to teach us that

JAMIESON, FAUSSET, BROWN — CHAPTER 28

Vss. 1-19. JACOB'S DEPARTURE. **1. Isaac called Jacob and blessed him**—He entered fully into Rebekah's feelings, and the burden of his parting counsel to his son was to avoid a marriage alliance with any but the Mesopotamian branch of the family. At the same time he gave him a solemn blessing—pronounced before unwittingly, now designedly, and with a cordial spirit. It is more explicitly and fully given, and Jacob was thus acknowledged "the heir of the promise."

ADAM CLARKE — CHAPTER 28

1. *And Isaac called Jacob.* See the note on v. 46 of the preceding chapter. *And blessed him.* Now voluntarily and cheerfully confirmed to him the blessing, which he had before obtained through subtlety.

2. *Go to Padan-aram.* This mission, in its spirit and design, is nearly the same as that in chap. xxiv, which see. There have been several ingenious conjectures concerning the retinue which Jacob had, or might have had, for his journey; and by some he has been supposed

MATTHEW HENRY

those who inherit the blessing must expect persecution; those who have peace in Christ shall have tribulation in the world, John xvi. 33. Now Jacob is here dismissed by his father.

I. With a solemn charge: *He blessed him, and charged him*, v. 1, 2. Note, Those that have the blessing must keep the charge annexed to it, and not think to separate what God has joined. If Jacob be an heir of promise, he must *not take a wife of the daughters of Canaan*; those that profess religion should not marry those that are irreligious.

II. With a solemn blessing, v. 3, 4. He had before blessed him unwittingly; now he does it designedly, for the greater encouragement of Jacob in that melancholy condition to which he was now removing. This blessing is more express and full than the former; it is an entail of the blessing of Abraham. It is a gospel blessing, Gal. iii. 14. It is a blessing from God Almighty, by which name God appeared to the patriarchs, Exod. vi. 3.

1. The promise of heirs: *God make thee fruitful, and multiply thee*, v. 3. (1) And never was such a multitude of people so often gathered into one assembly as the tribes of Israel were in the wilderness, and afterwards. (2) Through his loins should descend from Abraham that person in whom all the families of the earth should be blessed, for all things in heaven and earth are united in Christ (Eph. i. 10).

2. The promise of an inheritance for those heirs: *That thou mayest inherit the land of thy sojournings*, v. 4. Canaan was hereby entailed upon the seed of Jacob, exclusive of the seed of Esau. He is here told that he should inherit the land wherein he sojourned. Those have the best enjoyment of present things that sit most loose to them. This was the better country, which Jacob, with the other patriarchs, had in his eye, when he confessed himself "a stranger and pilgrim upon the earth," Heb. xi. 13.

Away he went to Padan-aram, v. 5.

Verses 6–9

This passage concerning Esau comes in in the midst of Jacob's story, either, 1. To show the influence of a good example. Esau, though the greater man, now begins to think Jacob the better man, and disdains not to take him for his pattern in this particular instance of marrying with a daughter of Abraham. Or, 2. To show the folly of an afterwit. Esau did well, but he did it when it was too late. He *saw that the daughters of Canaan pleased not his father*, and he might have seen that long ago if he had consulted his father's judgment as much as he did his palate. And how did he now mend the matter? Why, truly, so as to make bad worse. He married a daughter of Ishmael, the son of the bond-woman, who was cast out. He did it only to please his father, not to please God. He rested in a partial reformation.

Verses 10–15

We have here Jacob upon his journey towards Syria, in a very desolate condition. The first night, he had made a long day's journey from Beersheba to Bethel, and there he had,

I. A hard lodging (v. 11), the *stones for his pillows*, and the heavens for his canopy and curtains.

II. In his hard lodging he had a pleasant dream. Any Israelite indeed would be willing to take up with Jacob's pillow, provided he might but have Jacob's dream. Then, and there, he *heard the words of God, and saw the visions of the Almighty*. It was the best night's sleep he ever had in his life.

1. The encouraging vision Jacob saw, v. 12. He saw a ladder which reached from earth to heaven, the angels ascending and descending upon it, and God himself at the head of it. Now this represents:—(1) The providence of God, by which there is a constant correspondence kept up between heaven and earth. Providence does its work gradually, and by steps. The wisdom of God is at the upper end of the ladder, directing all the motions of second causes to the glory of the first Cause. This vision gave very seasonable comfort to Jacob, letting him know that he had both a good guide and a good guard, in his going out and coming in. (2) The mediation of Christ. He is this ladder, the foot on earth in his human nature, the top in heaven in his divine nature: or the former in his humiliation, the latter in his exaltation. If God dwell with us, and we with him, it is by Christ. We have no way of getting to heaven, but by this ladder: if we climb up any other way we are thieves and robbers. To this vision our Saviour alludes when he speaks of the angels of God *ascending and descending upon the Son of man* (John i. 51).

JAMIESON, FAUSSET, BROWN

R. PAYNE SMITH:

"Isaac called Jacob." Though Rebekah's primary motive was her concern for Jacob's safety, yet we must not imagine that his marriage was a mere pretext. On the contrary, now that he was acknowledged as the firstborn, both he and she would have been abandoning his high position had they not arranged for the fulfillment of his duty in this respect. What is remarkable is the frankness of Isaac's conduct. There is no attempt to substitute Esau for Jacob, nor to lessen the privileges of the latter, but with hearty cheerfulness he blesses the younger son, and confirms him in the possession of the whole Abrahamic blessing.

—*Ellicott's Commentary on the Whole Bible*

6-9. when Esau saw that Isaac had blessed Jacob, etc.—Desirous to humor his parents and, if possible, get the last will revoked, he became wise when too late (see Matt. 25:10), and hoped by gratifying his parents in one thing to atone for all his former delinquencies. But he only made bad worse, and though he did not marry a "wife of the daughters of Canaan," he married into a family which God had rejected. It showed a partial reformation, but no repentance, for he gave no proofs of abating his vindictive purposes against his brother, nor cherishing that pious spirit that would have gratified his father—he was like Micah (see Judg. 17:13).

10. Jacob went out, etc.—His departure from his father's house was an ignominious flight; and for fear of being pursued or waylaid by his vindictive brother, he did not take the common road, but went by lonely and unfrequented paths, which increased the length and dangers of the journey. **11. he lighted upon a certain place**—By a forced march he had reached Bethel, about forty-eight miles from Beer-sheba, and had to spend the night in the open field.

he took of the stones, etc.—"The nature of the soil is an existing comment on the record of the stony territory where Jacob lay" [Clarke's Travels].

12. he dreamed . . . and behold a ladder—Some writers are of opinion that it was not a literal ladder that is meant, as it is impossible to conceive any imagery stranger and more unnatural than that of a ladder, whose base was on earth, while its top reached heaven, without having any thing on which to rest its upper extremity. They suppose that the little heap of stones, on which his head reclined for a pillow, being the miniature model of the object that appeared to his imagination, the latter was a gigantic mountain pile, whose sides, indented in the rock, gave it the appearance of a scaling ladder. There can be no doubt that this use of the original term was common among the early Hebrews; as Josephus, describing the town of Ptolemais (Acre), says it was bounded by a mountain, which, from its projecting sides, was called "the ladder," and the stairs that led down to the city are, in the original, termed a ladder (Neh. 3) thought they were only a flight of steps cut

ADAM CLARKE

to have been well attended. Of this nothing is mentioned here, and the reverse seems to be intimated elsewhere. It appears, from v. 11, that he lodged in the open air, with a stone for his pillow; and from chap. xxxii. 10, that he went on foot with his staff in his hand. He no doubt took provisions with him sufficient to carry him to the nearest encampment or village on the way, where he would naturally recruit his bread and water to carry him to the next stage, and so on. The oil that he poured on the pillar might be a little of that which he had brought for his own use.

3. *That thou mayest be a multitude of people.* There is something very remarkable in the original words: they signify literally "for an assembly, congregation, or church of peoples"; referring no doubt to the Jewish church in the wilderness, but more particularly to the Christian Church, composed of every kindred, and nation, and people, and tongue. This is one essential part of the blessing of Abraham.

4. *Give thee the blessing of Abraham.* May He confirm the inheritance with all its attendant blessings to thee, to the exclusion of Esau; as He did to me, to the exclusion of Ishmael. But, according to St. Paul, much more than this is certainly intended here. For it appears, from Gal. iii. 6-14, that the blessing of Abraham, which is to come upon the Gentiles through Jesus Christ, comprises the whole doctrine of justification by faith, and its attendant privileges, namely, redemption from the curse of the law, remission of sins, and the promise of the Holy Spirit, including the constitution and establishment of the Christian Church.

5. *Bethuel the Syrian.* Literally the "Aramean," so called, not because he was of the race of Aram, the son of Shem, but because he dwelt in that country which had been formerly possessed by the descendants of Aram.

9. *Then went Esau unto Ishmael.* Those who are apt to take everything by the wrong handle, and who think it was utterly impossible for Esau to do any right action, have classed his taking a daughter of Ishmael among his crimes, whereas there is nothing more plain than that he did this with a sincere desire to obey and please his parents. Having heard the pious advice which Isaac gave to Jacob, he therefore went and took a wife from the family of his grandfather Abraham, as Jacob was desired to do out of the family of his maternal uncle, Laban. *Mahalath,* whom he took to wife, stood in the same degree of relationship to Isaac, his father, as Rachel did to his mother, Rebekah. Esau married his father's niece; Jacob married his mother's niece. It was therefore most obviously to please his parents that Esau took this additional wife.

11. *A certain place, and tarried there.* From v. 19 we find this *certain place* was Luz, or some part of its vicinity. Jacob had probably intended to reach Luz; but the sun being set, and night coming on, he either could not reach the city or he might suspect the inhabitants, and rather prefer the open field. Or the gates might be shut by the time he reached it, which would prevent his admission. *He took of the stones.* He took one of the stones that were in that place; from v. 18 we find it was one stone only which he had for his pillow. Luz was about forty-eight miles distant from Beer-sheba, too great a journey for one day through what we may conceive very unready roads.

12. *He dreamed, and behold a ladder.* A multitude of fanciful things have been spoken of Jacob's vision of the ladder, and its signification. It might have several designs, as God chooses to accomplish the greatest number of ends by the fewest and simplest means possible. (1) It is very likely that its primary design was to point out the providence of God. (2) It might be intended also to point out the intercourse between heaven and earth, and the connection of both worlds by the means of angelic ministry. (3) It was probably a type of Christ, in whom both worlds meet, and in whom the divine and human nature are conjoined. The ladder was set up on the earth, and the top of it reached to heaven; for God was manifested in the flesh, and in Him dwelt all the fulness of the Godhead bodily. Nothing could be a more expressive emblem of the Incarnation and its effects;

MATTHEW HENRY

2. The encouraging words Jacob heard.

(1) The former promises made to his father were repeated and ratified to him, *v.* 13, 14. In general, God intimated to him that he would be the same to him that he had been to Abraham and Isaac. [1] The land of Canaan is settled upon him. [2] It is promised him that his posterity should multiply exceedingly as the dust of the earth. [3] It is added that the Messiah should come from his loins, in whom all the families of the earth should be blessed.

(2) Fresh promises were made him. [1] Jacob was apprehensive of danger from his brother Esau; but God promises to keep him. [2] He had now a long journey before him, had to travel alone, in an unknown road, to an unknown country; but, *behold, I am with thee*, says God. [3] He knew not, but God foresaw, what hardships he should meet with in his uncle's service, and therefore promises to preserve him in all places. [4] He was now going as an exile into a place far distant, but God promises him to bring him back again to this land. [5] He seemed to be forsaken of all his friends, but God here gives him this assurance, *I will not leave thee.* Note, Whom God loves he never leaves.

Verses 16–22

Behold his sleep was sweet to him. Here is much of Jacob's devotion on this occasion.

I. He expressed a great surprise at the tokens he had of God's special presence with him in that place: *Surely the Lord is in this place and I knew it not, v.* 16. Note, God can give undeniable demonstrations of his presence, satisfaction not communicable to others, but convincing to themselves. No place excludes divine visits (*ch.* xvi. 13, *here also*); wherever we are, in the city or in the desert, in the house or in the field, in the shop or in the street.

II. It struck an awe upon him (*v.* 17): *He was afraid.* He said, *How dreadful is this place!* What he saw there at this time was, as it were, *the house of God*, and *the gate of heaven.*

III. He took care to preserve the memorial of it two ways: 1. He set up the stone for a pillar (*v.* 18), because he had not time now to build an altar here, as Abraham did in the places where God appeared to him, *ch.* xii. 7. He therefore *poured oil on the top of this stone*, as an earnest of his building an altar when he should have conveniences for it, as afterwards he did, in gratitude to God for this vision, *ch.* xxxv. 7. 2. He gave a new name to the place, *v.* 19. It had been called *Luz, an almond-tree*; but he will have it henceforward called *Beth-el, the house of God.*

IV. He made a solemn vow upon this occasion, *v.* 20–22. When God ratifies his promises to us, it is proper for us to repeat our promises to him. Now in this vow observe, 1. Jacob's faith. God had said (*v.* 15), *I am with thee, and will keep thee.* Jacob takes hold of this, and infers, "I depend upon it." 2. Jacob's modesty and great moderation in his desires. He will cheerfully content himself with bread to eat, and raiment to put on. Nature is content with a little, and grace with less. 3. Jacob's piety, and his regard to God, which appear here, (1) In what he desired, that God would be with him and keep him. (2) In what he designed. His resolution is, [1] In general, to cleave to the Lord, as his God in covenant: *Then shall the Lord be my God.* [2] In particular, that he would perform some special acts of devotion, in token of his gratitude. *First*, "This pillar shall keep possession here till I come back in peace, and then an altar shall be erected here to the honour of God." *Secondly*, "The house of God shall not be unfurnished, nor his altar without a sacrifice: *Of all that thou shalt give me I will surely give the tenth unto thee*, to be spent either upon God's altars or upon his poor," both which are his receivers in the world.

JAMIESON, FAUSSET, BROWN

in the side of the rock. But whether the image presented to the mental eye of Jacob were a common ladder, or such a mountain pile as has been described, the design of this vision was to afford comfort, encouragement, and confidence to the lonely fugitive, both in his present circumstances and as to his future prospects. His thoughts during the day must have been painful—he would be his own self-accuser that he had brought exile and privation upon himself—and above all, that though he had obtained the forgiveness of his father, he had much reason to fear lest God might have forsaken him. Solitude affords time for reflection; and it was now that God began to bring Jacob under a course of religious instruction and training. To dispel his fears and allay the inward tumult of his mind, nothing was better fitted than the vision of the gigantic ladder, which reached from himself to heaven, and on which the angels were continually ascending and descending from God Himself on their benevolent errands (John 1:51). **13. The Lord stood above it, and said**—That Jacob might be at no loss to know the purport of the vision, he heard the divine voice; and the announcement of His name, together with a renewal of the covenant, and an assurance of personal protection, produced at once the most solemnizing and inspiring effect on his mind. **16. Jacob awaked out of his sleep**—His language and his conduct were alike that of a man whose mind was pervaded by sentiments of solemn awe, of fervent piety, and lively gratitude (Jer. 31:36).

18, 19. Jacob set up a stone, etc.—The mere setting up of the stone might have been as a future memorial to mark the spot; and this practice is still common in the East, in memory of a religious vow or engagement. But the pouring oil upon it was a consecration. Accordingly he gave it a new name, Beth-el, "the house of God" (Hos. 12:4); and it will not appear a thing forced or unnatural to call a stone a house, when one considers the common practice in warm countries of sitting in the open air by or on a stone, as are those of this place, "broad sheets of bare rock, some of them standing like the cromlechs of Druidical monuments" [STANLEY].

20-22. JACOB'S VOW. **20. Jacob vowed a vow**—His words are not to be considered as implying a doubt, far less as stating the condition or terms on which he would dedicate himself to God. Let "if" be changed into "since," and the language will appear a proper expression of Jacob's faith—an evidence of his having truly embraced the promise. How edifying often to meditate on Jacob at Beth-el.

ADAM CLARKE

Jesus Christ is the grand connecting Medium between heaven and earth, and between God and man. By Him, God comes down to man; through Him, man ascends to God. It appears that our Lord applies the vision in this way himself: First, in that remarkable speech to Nathanael, "Hereafter ye shall see heaven open, and the angels of God ascending and descending upon the Son of man," John i. 51. Secondly, in His speech to Thomas, John xiv. 6: "I am the way, the truth, and the life: no man cometh unto the Father, but by me."

13. *I am the Lord God of Abraham.* Here God confirms to him the blessing of Abraham, for which Isaac had prayed, vv. 3-4.

14. *Thy seed shall be as the dust.* The people that shall descend from thee shall be extremely numerous; *and in thee and in thy seed*—the Lord Jesus descending from thee, according to the flesh, *shall all the families of the earth*—not only all of thy race, but all the other families or tribes of mankind which have not proceeded from any branch of the Abrahamic family, *be blessed;* for Jesus Christ by the grace of God tasted death for every man, Heb. ii. 9.

16. *The Lord is in this place; and I knew it not.* That is, God has made this place His peculiar residence; it is a place in which He meets with and reveals himself to His followers.

18. *And Jacob . . . took the stone . . . and set it up for a pillar.* He placed the stone in an erect posture, that it might stand as a monument of the extraordinary vision which he had in this place; *and [he] poured oil upon . . . it,* thereby consecrating it to God, so that it might be considered an altar on which libations might be poured, and sacrifices offered unto God.

There is a foolish tradition that the stone set up by Jacob was afterwards brought to Jerusalem, from which, after a long lapse of time, it was brought to Spain, from Spain to Ireland, from Ireland to Scotland, and on it the kings of Scotland sat to be crowned. Edward I had it brought to Westminster; and there this stone, called Jacob's pillar, and Jacob's pillow, is now placed under the chair on which the king sits when crowned!

19. *He called the name of that place Beth-el.* That is, the "house of God"; for in consequence of his having anointed the stone, and thus consecrated it to God, he considered it as becoming henceforth His pecular residence. This word should be always pronounced as two distinct syllables, each strongly accented, Beth-el.

20. *Vowed a vow.* A vow is a solemn, holy promise, by which a man bound himself to do certain things in a particular way, time, etc., and for power to accomplish which he depended on God; hence all vows were made with prayer.

22. *This stone . . . shall be God's house.* That is, should I be preserved to return in safety, I shall worship God in this place. And this purpose he fulfilled, for there he built an altar, anointed it with oil, and poured a drink offering thereon.

MATTHEW HENRY — CHAPTER 29

Verses 1–8

1. We are here told how cheerfully he proceeded in his journey after the sweet communion he had with God at Beth-el: *Then Jacob lifted up his feet*; so the margin reads it, *v.* 1. 2. How happily he arrived at his journey's end. Providence brought him to the very field, where his uncle's flocks were to be watered, and there he met with Rachel, who was to be his wife. (1) The divine Providence is to be acknowledged in all the little circumstances which concur to make a journey, or other undertaking, comfortable and successful. If we meet seasonably with those that can direct us we must not say that it was by chance, but that it was by Providence, and that God therein favoured us.

JAMIESON, FAUSSET, BROWN — CHAPTER 29

Vss. 1-35. THE WELL OF HARAN. **1. Then Jacob went,** etc.—*Hebrew*, "lifted up his feet." He resumed his way next morning with a light heart and elastic step after the vision of the ladder; for tokens of the divine favor tend to quicken the discharge of duty (Neh. 8:10). **and came into the land,** etc.—Mesopotamia and the whole region beyond the Euphrates are by the sacred writers designated "the East" (Judg. 6:3; I Kings 4:32; Job 1:3). Between the first and the second clause of this verse is included a journey of four hundred miles.

ADAM CLARKE — CHAPTER 29

1. *Then Jacob went on his journey.* The original is very remarkable: "And Jacob lifted up his feet, and he travelled unto the land of the children of the east." There is a certain cheerfulness marked in the original which comports well with the state of mind into which he had been brought by the vision of the ladder and the promises of God. He now saw that, having God for his Protector, he had nothing to fear, and therefore he went on his way rejoicing. *People of the east.* The inhabitants of Mesopotamia and the whole country beyond the Euphrates are called "easterns" in the sacred writings.

MATTHEW HENRY

(2) What is here said of the constant care of the shepherds concerning their sheep (*v.* 2, 3, 7, 8) may serve to illustrate the tender concern which our Lord Jesus, the great Shepherd of the sheep, has for his flock, the church; for he is the good Shepherd, that knows his sheep, and is known of them, John x. 14. (3) When all the shepherds came together with their flocks, then, like loving neighbours, at watering-time, they watered their flocks together. (4) It becomes us to speak civilly and respectfully to strangers. The law of kindness in the tongue has a commanding power, Prov. xxxi. 26.

Verses 9–14

Here we see, 1. Rachel's humility and industry: *She kept her father's sheep* (*v.* 9). 2. Jacob's tenderness and affection. When he understood that this was his kinswoman he was wonderfully anxious to serve her (*v.* 10). 3. It is groundless conceit which some of the Jewish writers have, that Jacob, when he kissed Rachel, wept because he had been set upon in his journey by Eliphaz the eldest son of Esau, at the command of his father, and robbed of all his money and jewels, which his mother had given him when she sent him away. It was plain that it was his passion for Rachel, and the surprise of this happy meeting, that drew these tears from his eyes. 4. Laban, though none of the best-humoured men, bade him welcome, was satisfied in the account he gave of himself, and of the reason of his coming in such poor circumstances.

Verses 15–30

Here is, I. The fair contract made between Laban and Jacob, during the month that Jacob spent there as a guest, *v.* 14.

JAMIESON, FAUSSET, BROWN

2. And he looked, etc.—As he approached the place of his destination, he, according to custom, repaired to the well adjoining the town where he would obtain an easy introduction to his relatives.

3. thither were all the flocks gathered: and a stone, etc.—In Arabia, owing to the shifting sands and in other places, owing to the strong evaporation, the mouth of a well is generally covered, especially when it is private property. Over many is laid a broad, thick, flat stone, with a round hole cut in the middle, forming the mouth of the cistern. This hole is covered with a heavy stone which it would require two or three men to roll away. Such was the description of the well at Haran.

4. Jacob said, My brethren—Finding from the shepherds who were reposing there with flocks and who all belonged to Haran, that his relatives in Haran were well and that one of the family was shortly expected, he enquired why they were idling the best part of the day there instead of watering their flocks and sending them back to pasture.

8. They said, We cannot until all the flocks be gathered—In order to prevent the consequences of too frequent exposure in places where water is scarce, the well is not only covered, but it is customary to have all the flocks collected round it before the covering is removed in presence of the owner or one of his representatives; and it was for this reason that those who were reposing at the well of Haran with the three flocks were waiting the arrival of Rachel. **9-11. While he yet spake, Rachel came**—Among the pastoral tribes the young unmarried daughters of the greatest sheiks tend the flocks, going out at sunrise and continuing to watch their fleecy charges till sunset. Watering them, which is done twice a day, is a work of time and labor, and Jacob rendered no small service in volunteering his aid to the young shepherdess. The interview was affecting, the reception welcome, and Jacob forgot all his toils in the society of his Mesopotamian relatives. Can we doubt that he returned thanks to God for His goodness by the way?

12. Jacob told Rachel, etc.—According to the practice of the East, the term "brother" is extended to remote degrees of relationship, as uncle, cousin, or nephew. **14-20. he abode a month**—Among pastoral people a stranger is freely entertained for three days; on the fourth day he is expected to tell his name and errand; and if he prolongs his stay after that time, he must set his hand to work in some way, as may be agreed upon. A similar rule obtained in Laban's establishment, and the wages for which his nephew engaged to continue in his employment was the hand of Rachel.

ADAM CLARKE

2. *Three flocks of sheep.* Small cattle, such as sheep, goats, etc. The *three flocks,* if flocks and not shepherds be meant, which were lying now at the well, did not belong to Laban, but to three other chiefs; for Laban's flock was yet to come, under the care of Rachel, v. 6.

3. *All the flocks.* Instead of *hadarim, flocks,* the Samaritan reads *haroim,* "shepherds"; for which reading Houbigant strongly contends, as well in this verse as in v. 8. It is probable that the same reading was originally that of the second verse also. *And put the stone again upon the well's mouth.* It is very likely that the stone was a large one, which was necessary to prevent ill-minded individuals from either disturbing the water or filling up the well; hence a great stone was provided, which required the joint exertions of several shepherds to remove it; and hence those who arrived first waited till all the others were come up, that they might water their respective flocks in concert.

4. *My brethren, whence be ye?* The language of Laban and his family was Chaldee and not Hebrew; but from the names which Leah gave to her children we see that the two languages had many words in common, and therefore Jacob and the shepherds might understand each other with little difficulty. It is possible also that Jacob might have learned the Chaldee language from his mother, as this was his mother's tongue.

5. *Laban the son of Nahor. Son* is here put for grandson, for Laban was the son of Bethuel, the son of Nahor.

6. *Is he well? Hashalom lo?* Is there peace to him? Peace among the Hebrews signified all kinds of prosperity. Is he a prosperous man in his family and in his property? *And they said, He is well—shalom,* He prospers. *Rachel . . . cometh with the sheep. Rachel* (the *ch* sounded guttural) signifies a "sheep" or "ewe"; and she probably had her name from her fondness for these animals.

7. *It is yet high day.* The day is but about half run; *neither is it time that the cattle should be gathered together*—it is surely not time yet to put them into the folds; give them, therefore, water and take them again to pasture.

8. *We cannot, until all the flocks be gathered together.* It is a rule that the stone shall not be removed till all the shepherds and the flocks which have a right to this well be gathered together; then we may water the sheep.

9. *Rachel came with her father's sheep.* So we find that young women were not kept concealed in the house till the time they were married. Nor was it beneath the dignity of the daughters of the most opulent chiefs to carry water from the well, as in the case of Rebekah; or tend sheep, as in the case of Rachel. The chief property in those times consisted in flocks: and who so proper to take care of them as those who were interested in their safety and increase? Honest labor, far from being a discredit, is an honor to both high and low.

10. *Jacob went near, and rolled the stone.* Probably the flock of Laban was the last of those which had a right to the well; that flock being now come, Jacob assisted the shepherds to roll off the stone (for it is not likely he did it by himself) and so assisted his cousin, to whom he was as yet unknown, to water her flock.

11. *Jacob kissed Rachel.* A simple and pure method by which the primitive inhabitants of the earth testified their friendship to each other. *And lifted up his voice.* It may be, in thanksgiving to God for the favor He had shown him, in conducting him thus far in peace and safety. *And wept.* From a sense of the goodness of his Heavenly Father, and his own unworthiness of the success with which he had been favored. The same expressions of kindness and pure affection are repeated on the part of Laban, v. 13.

14. *My bone and my flesh.* One of my nearest relatives.

15. *Because thou art my brother.* Though thou art my nearest relative, yet I have no right to thy services without giving thee an adequate recompense. Jacob had passed a whole month in the family of Laban, in which he had undoubtedly rendered himself of considerable ser-

MATTHEW HENRY

Now Jacob had a fair opportunity to make known to Laban the affection he had for his daughter Rachel; and, having no worldly goods in his hand with which to endow her, he promises him seven years' service, upon condition that, at the end of the seven years, he would bestow her upon him for his wife.

II. Jacob's honest performance of his part of the bargain, *v.* 20. Jacob honestly served out his seven years. *They seemed to him but a few days, for the love he had to her*, as if it were more his desire to earn her than to have her.

III. The base cheat which Laban put upon him when he was out of his time: he put Leah into his arms instead of Rachel, *v.* 23. This was Laban's sin; he wronged both Jacob and Rachel. It is easy to observe here how Jacob was paid in his own coin. He had cheated his own father when he pretended to be Esau, and now his father-in-law cheated him.

IV. The excuse and atonement Laban made for the cheat. 1. The excuse was frivolous: *It must not be so done in our country*, *v.* 26. There was no such custom of his country as he pretends; only he banters Jacob with it, and laughs at his mistake. 2. His compounding the matter did but make bad worse: *We will give thee this also*, *v.* 27. Hereby he drew Jacob into the sin, and snare, and disquiet, of multiplying wives, which remains a blot in his escutcheon. Honest Jacob did not design it. He could not refuse Rachel, for he had espoused her; still less could he refuse Leah, for he had married her. The polygamy of the patriarchs was, in some measure excusable in them, because though there was a reason against it as ancient as Adam's marriage (Mal. ii. 15), yet there was no express command against it; it was in them a sin of ignorance. It will by no means justify the like practice now, when God's will is plainly made known, that one man and one woman only must be joined together, 1 Cor. vii. 2. Dr. Lightfoot makes Leah and Rachel to be figures of the two churches, the Jews under the law and the Gentiles under the gospel: the younger the more beautiful, and more in the thoughts of Christ when he came in the form of a servant; but the other, like Leah, first embraced.

Verses 31–35

We have here the birth of four of Jacob's sons, all by Leah. Observe, 1. That Leah, who was less beloved, was blessed with children, when Rachel was denied that blessing, *v.* 31.

JAMIESON, FAUSSET, BROWN

17. Leah tender-eyed—i.e., soft blue eyes—thought a blemish. **Rachel beautiful and well-favored**—i.e., comely and handsome in form. The latter was Jacob's choice. **18. I will serve thee seven years for Rachel thy daughter**—A proposal of marriage is made to the father without the daughter being consulted, and the match is effected by the suitor either bestowing costly presents on the family, or by giving cattle to the value the father sets upon his daughter, or else by giving personal services for a specified period. The last was the course necessity imposed on Jacob; and there for seven years he submitted to the drudgery of a hired shepherd, with the view of obtaining Rachel. The time went rapidly away; for even severe and difficult duties become light when love is the spring of action.

21. Jacob said, Give me my wife—At the expiry of the stipulated term the marriage festivities were held. But an infamous fraud was practised on Jacob, and on his showing a righteous indignation, the usage of the country was pleaded in excuse. No plea of kindred should ever be allowed to come in opposition to the claim of justice. But this is often overlooked by the selfish mind of man, and fashion or custom rules instead of the will of God. This was what Laban did, as he said, "It must not be so done in our country, to give the younger before the first-born." But, then, if that were the prevailing custom of society at Haran, he should have apprized his nephew of it at an early period in an honorable manner. This, however, is too much the way with the people of the East still. **The duty of marrying an elder daughter before a younger, the tricks which parents take to get off an elder daughter that is plain or deformed and in which they are favored by the long bridal veil that entirely conceals her features all the wedding day, and the prolongation for a week of the marriage festivities among the greater sheiks, are accordant with the habits of the people in Arabia and Armenia in the present day.**

28. gave him Rachel also—It is evident that the marriage of both sisters took place nearly about the same time, and that such a connection was then allowed, though afterwards prohibited (Lev. 18:18). **29. gave to Rachel his daughter Bilhah to be her maid**—A father in good circumstances still gives his daughter from his household a female slave, over whom the young wife, independently of her husband, has the absolute control. **31. Leah . . . hated**—i.e., not loved so much as she ought to have been. Her becoming a mother ensured her rising in the estimation both of her husband and of society.

ADAM CLARKE

vice. As Laban, who was of a very saving if not covetous disposition, saw that he was to be of great use to him in his secular concerns, he wished to secure his services, and therefore asked him what wages he wished to have.

17. *Leah was tender eyed.* "Soft, delicate, lovely." I believe the word means just the reverse of the signification generally given to it. The design of the inspired writer is to compare both the sisters together, that the balance may appear to be greatly in favor of Rachel. The chief recommendation of Leah was her soft and beautiful eyes; but Rachel was "beautiful in her shape, person, mien, and gait," and "beautiful in her countenance." The words plainly signify a fine shape and fine features, all that can be considered as essential to personal beauty. Therefore Jacob loved her and was willing to become a bond servant for seven years, that he might get her to wife; for in his destitute state he could produce no dowry, and it was the custom of those times for the father to receive a portion for his daughter, and not to give one with her.

21. *My days are fulfilled.* My seven years are now completed; let me have my wife, for whom I have given this service as a dowry.

22. *Laban . . . made a feast. Mishteh* signifies a feast of "drinking." As marriage was a very solemn contract, there is much reason to believe that sacrifices were offered on the occasion, and libations poured out; and we know that on festival occasions a cup of wine was offered to every guest; and as this was drunk with particular ceremonies, the feast might derive its name from this circumstance, which was the most prominent and observable on such occasions.

23. *In the evening . . . he took Leah his daughter.* As the bride was always veiled, and the bridechamber generally dark, or nearly so, and as Leah was brought to Jacob in the evening, the imposition here practiced might easily pass undetected by Jacob till the ensuing day discovered the fraud.

24. *And Laban gave . . . Zilpah his maid.* Slaves given in this way to a daughter on her marriage were the peculiar property of the daughter; and over them the husband had neither right nor power.

26. *It must not be so done in our country.* It was an early custom to give daughters in marriage according to their seniority; and it is worthy of remark that the Hindoos have this not merely as a custom, but as a positive law; and they deem it criminal to give a younger daughter in marriage while an elder daughter remains unmarried.

27. *Fulfil her week.* The marriage feast, it appears, lasted seven days; it would not, therefore, have been proper to break off the solemnities to which all the men of the place had been invited, v. 22, and probably Laban wished to keep his fraud from the public eye; therefore he informs Jacob that, if he will fulfil the marriage week for Leah, he will give him Rachel at the end of it, on condition of his serving seven other years. To this the necessity of the case caused Jacob to agree; and thus Laban had fourteen years' service instead of seven; for it is not likely that Jacob would have served even seven days for Leah, as his affection was wholly set on Rachel, the wife of his own choice. By this stratagem Laban gained a settlement for both his daughters. What a man soweth, that shall he reap. Jacob had practiced deceit, and is now deceived; and Laban, the instrument of it, was afterwards deceived himself.

28. *And Jacob did so . . . and he gave him Rachel.* It is perfectly plain that Jacob did not serve seven years more before he got Rachel to wife; but having spent a week with Leah, and in keeping the marriage feast, he then got Rachel, and served afterwards seven years for her.

31. *The Lord saw that Leah was hated.* From this and the preceding verse we get the genuine meaning of the word *sane*, "to hate," in certain disputed places in the Scriptures. The word simply signifies "a less degree of love"; so it is said, v. 30: Jacob "loved . . . Rachel more than Leah," i.e., he loved Leah less than Rachel; and this is called hating in v. 31: *When the Lord saw that Leah was hated*—that she had less affection

MATTHEW HENRY

2. The names she gave her children were expressive of her respectful regards both to God and to her husband. She called her first-born *Reuben* (*see a son*), with this pleasant thought, *Now will my husband love me*; and her third son *Levi* (*joined*), with this expectation, *Now will my husband be joined unto me*, *v.* 34. She thankfully acknowledges the kind providence of God in it: *The Lord hath looked upon my affliction*, *v.* 32. "*The Lord hath heard that I was hated, he has therefore given me this son.*" Her fourth she called *Judah* (*praise*), saying, *Now will I praise the Lord*, *v.* 35. And this was he of whom, as concerning the flesh, Christ came. He descended from him whose name was praise, for he is our praise. Is Christ formed in my heart? *Now will I praise the Lord.*

JAMIESON, FAUSSET, BROWN

32-35. son . . . called his name Reuben—Names were also significant; and those which Leah gave to her sons were expressive of her varying feelings of thankfulness or joy, or allusive to circumstances in the history of the family. There was piety and wisdom in attaching a signification to names, as it tended to keep the bearer in remembrance of his duty and the claims of God.

ADAM CLARKE

shown to her than was her due, as one of the legitimate wives of Jacob, *he opened her womb*—He blessed her with children. So "Jacob have I loved, but Esau have I hated," simply means, I have shown a greater degree of affection for Jacob and his posterity than I have done for Esau and his descendants, by giving the former a better earthly portion than I have given to the latter, and by choosing the family of Jacob to be the progenitors of the Messiah. But not one word of all this relates to the eternal state of either of the two nations.

32. *She called his name Reuben.* Literally, "behold a son"; *for Jehovah hath looked upon*, "beheld," *my affliction;* behold then the consequence, I have got a son!

33. *She called his name Simeon.* "Hearing"; i.e., God had blessed her with another son, because He had heard that she was hated—loved less than Rachel was.

34. *Therefore was his name called Levi.* "Joined"; because she supposed that, in consequence of all these children, Jacob would become joined to her in as strong affection, at least, as he was to Rachel. From Levi sprang the tribe of Levites, who, instead of the first-born, were joined unto the priests in the service of the sanctuary. See Num. xviii. 2, 4.

35. *She called his name Judah. Yehudah*, a "confessor"; one who acknowledges God, and acknowledges that all good comes from His hands, and gives Him the praise due to His grace and mercy. From this patriarch the Jews have their name, and could it be now rightly applied to them, it would intimate that they were a people that confess God, acknowledge His bounty, and praise Him for His grace. *Left bearing.* That is, for a time; for she had several children afterwards. Literally translated, "she stood still from bearing" certainly does not convey the same meaning as that in our translation; the one appearing to signify that she ceased entirely from having children; the other, that she only desisted for a time, which was probably occasioned by a temporary suspension of Jacob's company, who appears to have deserted the tent of Leah through the jealous management of Rachel.

F. B. MEYER:

Jacob marries Leah and Rachel. The chief lesson of this paragraph is its illustration of the awful nemesis which accompanies wrongdoing. No thoughtful person can watch the events of history or experience without realizing that we are already standing before the judgment seat of God, and that his sentences are in process of being executed. Jacob deceived his father, and was himself deceived. "With what measure ye mete, it shall be measured to you again."

What disappointments there are in life! We think that we are to be given Rachel, and lo! Leah is substituted. But in later days Jacob spoke of Reuben as his might, the beginning of his dignity and excellency. The names of Leah's sons suggest the blessings that accrue through heartbreak. For the Leahs of the world there are great compensations. God remembers and hears them. Broken-hearted and forsaken, they live again in the lives of those whom they have borne either naturally or spiritually.—*Bible Commentary*

MATTHEW HENRY

CHAPTER 30

Verses 1–13

We have here the bad consequences of that strange marriage which Jacob made with the two sisters. Here is,

I. An unhappy disagreement between him and Rachel (*v.* 1, 2), occasioned, not so much by her own barrenness as by her sister's fruitfulness.

1. Rachel frets. She *envied her sister*, *v.* 1. Envy is grieving at the good of another, than which no sin is more offensive to God, nor more injurious to our neighbour and ourselves.

2. Jacob chides, and most justly. He loved Rachel, and therefore reproved her for what she said amiss, *v.* 2. Note, Faithful reproofs are products and instances of true affection, Ps. cxli. 5; Prov. xxvii. 5, 6. He was angry, not at the person, but at the sin; he expressed himself so as to show his displeasure. It was a very grave and pious reply which Jacob gave to Rachel's peevish demand: *Am I in God's stead?* The Chaldee paraphrases it well, *Dost thou ask sons of me? Oughtest thou not to ask them from before the Lord?* The Arabic reads it, "*Am I above God?* Can I give thee that which God denies thee?"

II. An unhappy agreement between him and the two handmaids.

1. At the persuasion of Rachel, he took Bilhah her handmaid to wife, that, according to the usage of those times, his children by her might be adopted and owned as her mistress's children, *v.* 3, &c. She would rather have children by reputation than none at all, children that she might fancy to be her own, and call her own, though they were not so. She takes a pleasure in giving them names that carry in them nothing but marks of emulation with her sister, as if she had overcome her, (1) At law. She calls the first son of her handmaid *Dan* (*judgment*), saying, "*God hath judged me*" (*v.* 6), that is, "given sentence in my favour." (2) In battle. She calls the next *Naphtali* (*wrestlings*), saying, *I have wrestled with my sister, and have prevailed* (*v.* 8); as if all Jacob's sons must be born men of contention.

2. At the persuasion of Leah, he took Zilpah her handmaid to wife also, *v.* 9. Two sons Zilpah bore

JAMIESON, FAUSSET, BROWN

CHAPTER 30

Vss. 1-24. DOMESTIC JEALOUSIES. **1. Rachel envied her sister**—The maternal relation confers a high degree of honor in the East, and the want of that status is felt as a stigma and deplored as a grievous calamity. **Give me children or else I die**—either be reckoned as good as dead, or pine away from vexation. The intense anxiety of Hebrew women for children arose from the hope of giving birth to the promised seed. Rachel's conduct was sinful and contrasts unfavorably with that of Rebekah (cf. ch. 25:22) and of Hannah (I Sam. 1:11). **3-9. Bilhah, . . . Zilpah**—Following the example of Sarah with regard to Hagar, an example which is not seldom imitated still, she adopted the children of her maid. Leah took the same course. A bitter and intense rivalry existed between them, all the more from their close relationship as sisters; and although they occupied separate apartments, with their families, as is the uniform custom where a plurality of wives obtains, and the husband and father spends a day with each in regular succession, that did not allay their mutual jealousies. The evil lies in the system, which being a violation of God's original ordinance, cannot yield happiness.

ADAM CLARKE

CHAPTER 30

1. *Give me children, or else I die.* This is a most reprehensible speech, and argues not only envy and jealousy, but also a total want of dependence on God. She had the greatest share of her husband's affection, and yet was not satisfied unless she could engross all the privileges which her sister enjoyed! How true are those sayings, "Envy [is as] the rottenness of the bones," and, "Jealousy is cruel as the grave"!

2. *Am I in God's stead?* Am I greater than God, to give thee what He has refused?

3. *She shall bear upon my knees.* The handmaid was the sole property of the mistress, as has already been remarked in the case of Hagar; and therefore not only all her labor, but even the children borne by her, were the property of the mistress. These female slaves, therefore, bore children vicariously for their mistresses; and this appears to be the import. *That I may also have children by her.* "And I shall be built up by her." Hence *ben*, "a son," from *banah*, "to build"; because, as a house is formed of the stones that enter into its composition, so is a family by children.

6. *Called she his name Dan.* Because she found God had *judged* for her, and decided she should have a son by her handmaid; hence she called his name *Dan*, "judging."

8. *She called his name Naphtali.* "My wrestling," according to the common mode of interpretation.

11. *She called his name Gad.* This has been variously translated: a "troop," an "army," a "soldier." *A troop cometh. Ba gad*, the marginal reading, has it in two words, "a troop cometh"; whereas the textual reading has it only in one, *bagad*, "with a troop."

13. *And Leah said, Happy am I.* "In my happiness"; therefore *she called his name Asher*, that is, "blessedness" or "happiness."

MATTHEW HENRY

to Jacob, whom Leah looked upon herself as entitled to, in token of which she called one *Gad* (*v.* 11), promising herself a little *troop* of children. The other she called *Asher* (*happy*), thinking herself happy in him. There was much amiss in the contest and competition between these two sisters, yet God brought good out of this evil. Thus Jacob's family was replenished with twelve sons, heads of the thousands of Israel, from whom the celebrated twelve tribes descended and were named.

Verses 14–24

I. Reuben, a little lad, five or six years old, playing in the field, found *mandrakes, dudaim.* It is uncertain what they were, either fruits or flowers that were very pleasant to the smell. There are products of the earth in the exposed fields, as well as in the planted protected gardens, that are very valuable and useful. It is a laudable custom of the devout Jews, when they find pleasure, suppose in eating an apple, to lift up their hearts, and say, "Blessed be he that made this fruit pleasant!" Or, in smelling a flower, "Blessed be he that made this flower sweet." Some think these mandrakes were jessamine flowers. Whatever they were, Rachel could not see them in Leah's hands, where the child had placed them, but she must covet them. The learned bishop Patrick very well suggests here that the true reason of this contest between Jacob's wives for his company, and their giving him their maids to be his wives, was the earnest desire they had to fulfil the promise made to Abraham that his seed should be as the stars of heaven for multitude. And he thinks it would have been below the dignity of this sacred history to take such particular notice of these things if there had not been some such great consideration in them. Leah was now blessed with two sons; the first she called *Issachar* (*a hire*), reckoning herself well repaid for her mandrakes. The other she called *Zebulun* (*dwelling*), owning God's bounty to her: *God has endowed me with a good dowry, v.* 20. She reckons a family of children not a bill of charges, but a good dowry, Ps. cxiii. 9. Mention is made (*v.* 21) of the birth of a daughter, *Dinah,* because of the following story concerning her, *ch.* xxxiv.

II. Rachel fruitful at last (*v.* 22). Rachel called her son *Joseph,* which in Hebrew is akin to two words of a contrary signification, *Asaph* (*abstulit*), *He has taken away my reproach,* and *Jasaph* (*addidit*), *The Lord shall add to me another son.*

Verses 25–36

I. Jacob's thoughts of home. He faithfully served his time out with Laban, even his second apprenticeship. He retained his affection for the land of Canaan, not only because it was the land of his nativity, and his father and mother were there, whom he longed to see, but because it was the land of promise.

II. Laban's desire of his stay, *v.* 27. In love to himself, not to Jacob or to his wives or children, Laban endeavours to persuade him to continue his chief shepherd. Churlish selfish men know how to give good words when it is to serve their own ends. Laban found that his stock had wonderfully increased with Jacob's good management, and he owns it, with very good expressions of respect both to God and Jacob: *I have learned by experience that the Lord has blessed me for thy sake.*

III. The new bargain they came upon. Laban's craft and covetousness took advantage of Jacob's plainness, honesty, and goodnature. Jacob accordingly makes a proposal.

1. He shows what reason he had to insist upon so much, considering, (1) That Laban was bound in gratitude to do well for him. Yet here observe how he speaks, like himself, very modestly. Humble saints take more pleasure in doing good than in hearing of it again. (2) That he himself was bound in duty to take care of his own family.

2. He is willing to refer himself to the providence of God, which, he knew, extends itself to the smallest things, even the colour of the cattle; and he will be content to have for his wages the sheep and goats of such and such a colour, speckled, spotted, and brown, which should hereafter be brought forth, *v.* 32, 33. Laban was willing to consent to this bargain because he thought if the few he had that were now speckled and spotted were separated from the rest, which by agreement was to be done immediately, the body of the flock which Jacob was to tend, being of one colour, either all black or all white, would produce few or none of mixed colours, and so he should have Jacob's service for nothing, or next to nothing.

JAMIESON, FAUSSET, BROWN

20. Leah said, God hath endued me with a good dowry—The birth of a son is hailed with demonstrations of joy, and the possession of several sons confers upon the mother an honor and respectability proportioned to their number. The husband attaches a similar importance to the possession, and it forms a bond of union which renders it impossible for him ever to forsake or to be cold to a wife who has borne him sons. This explains the happy anticipations Leah founded on the possession of her six sons. **21. afterwards, she bare a daughter**—The inferior value set on a daughter is displayed in the bare announcement of the birth.

25-43. JACOB'S COVENANT WITH LABAN. **25. when Rachel had borne Joseph**—Shortly after the birth of this son, Jacob's term of servitude expired, and feeling anxious to establish an independence for his family, he probably, from knowing that Esau was out of the way, announced his intention of returning to Canaan (Heb. 13:14). In this resolution the faith of Jacob was remarkable, for as yet he had nothing to rely on but the promise of God (cf. ch. 28:15). **27. Laban said . . . I have learned**—His selfish uncle was averse to a separation, not from warmth of affection either for Jacob or his daughters, but from the damage his own interests would sustain. He had found, from long observation, that the blessing of heaven rested on Jacob, and that his stock had wonderfully increased under Jacob's management. This was a remarkable testimony that good men are blessings to the places where they reside. Men of the world are often blessed with temporal benefits on account of their pious relatives, though they have not always, like Laban, the wisdom to discern, or the grace to acknowledge it. **28. appoint me thy wages, and I will give it**—The Eastern shepherds receive for their hire not money, but a certain amount of the increase or produce of the flock; but Laban would at the time have done anything to secure the continued services of his nephew, and make a show of liberality, which Jacob well knew was constrained. **31. Jacob said, Thou shalt not give me any thing**—A new agreement was made, the substance of which was, that he was to receive remuneration in the usual way, but on certain conditions which Jacob specified. **32. I will pass through all thy flock to-day**—Eastern sheep being generally white, the goats black, and spotted or speckled ones comparatively few and rare, Jacob proposed to remove all existing ones of that description from the flock, and to be content with what might appear at the next lambing time. The proposal *seemed* so much in favor of Laban, that he at once agreed to it. But Jacob has been accused of taking advantage of his uncle, and though it is difficult to exculpate him from practising some degree of dissimulation, he was only availing himself of the results of his great skill and experience in the breeding of cattle. But it is evident from the next chapter (vss. 5-13) that there was something miraculous and that the means he had employed had been suggested by a divine intimation.

ADAM CLARKE

14. *Reuben . . . found mandrakes. Dudaim.* What these were is utterly unknown, and learned men have wasted much time and pains in endeavoring to guess out a probable meaning.

15. *Thou hast taken my husband.* It appears probable that Rachel had found means to engross the whole of Jacob's affection and company, and that she now agreed to let him visit the tent of Leah, on account of receiving some of the fruits or plants which Reuben had found.

16. *I have hired thee.* We may remark among the Jewish women an intense desire of having children; and it seems to have been produced, not from any peculiar affection for children, but through the hope of having a share in the blessing of Abraham, by bringing forth Him in whom all the nations of the earth were to be blessed.

18. *God hath given me my hire. Sechari. And she called his name Issachar.* This word is compounded of *yesh,* "is," and *sachar,* "wages," from *sachar,* to "content, satisfy, saturate"; hence a satisfaction or compensation for work done.

20. *Now will my husband dwell with me. Yizbeleni;* and *she called his name Zebulun,* "a dwelling or cohabitation," as she now expected that Jacob would dwell with her, as he had before dwelt with Rachel.

21. *And called her name Dinah.* "Judgment." As Rachel had called her son by Bilhah Dan, v. 6, so Leah calls her daughter Dinah, God having judged and determined for her, as well as for her sister in the preceding instance.

22. *And God hearkened to her.* After the severe reproof which Rachel had received from her husband, v. 2, it appears that she sought God by prayer, and that He heard her; so that her prayer and faith obtained what her impatience and unbelief had prevented.

24. *She called his name Joseph. Yoseph,* "adding," or "he who adds"; thereby prophetically declaring that God would add unto her another son, which was accomplished in the birth of Benjamin, chap. xxxv. 18.

25. *Jacob said unto Laban, Send me away.* Having now, as is generally conjectured, fulfilled the fourteen years which he had engaged to serve for Leah and Rachel.

27. *I have learned by experience. Nichashti,* from *nachash,* "to view attentively, to observe, to pry into." I have diligently considered the whole of thy conduct, and marked the increase of my property, and find that the Lord hath blessed me for thy sake.

30. *For it was little which thou hadst before I came.* Jacob takes advantage of the concession made by his father-in-law, and asserts that it was for his sake that the Lord had blessed him. *Since my coming,* "according to my footsteps"—every step I took in thy service, God prospered to the multiplication of thy flocks and property. *When shall I provide for mine own house?* Jacob had already laid his plan; and, from what is afterwards mentioned, we find him using all his skill and experience to provide for his family by a rapid increase of his flocks.

32. *I will pass through all thy flock.* All smaller cattle, such as sheep, goats. *All the speckled and spotted cattle. Seh,* which we translate *cattle,* signifies the young either of sheep or goats, what we call a lamb or a kid. *Speckled* signifies interspersed with variously colored spots. *Spotted.* Spotted with large spots, either of the same or different colors. I have never seen such sheep as are here described but in the islands of Zetland. There I have seen the most beautiful brown or fine chocolate color among the sheep; and several of the ringstreaked, spotted, speckled, and piebald among the same; and some of the latter description I have brought over, and can exhibit a specimen of Jacob's flock brought from the North Seas, feeding in Middlesex.

35. *The he goats that were ringstraked. The he goats* that had rings of black or other colored hair around their feet or legs.

It is extremely difficult to find out, from the thirty-second and thirty-fifth verses, in what the bargain of Jacob with his father-in-law properly consisted. The true meaning appears to be this: Jacob had agreed to take all the partly-colored for his wages. As he was now only beginning to act upon this agreement, consequently none of the cattle as yet belonged

MATTHEW HENRY

Verses 37–43

Now Jacob's contrivances were, 1. To set peeled sticks before the cattle where they were watered, that, looking much at those unusual party-coloured sticks, by the power of imagination they might bring forth young ones in like manner party-coloured, *v.* 37–39. Probably this custom was commonly used by the shepherds of Canaan, who coveted to have their cattle of this motley colour. When he began to have a stock of ring-straked and brown, he contrived to set them first, and to put the faces of the rest towards them, with the same design as in the former contrivance.

Thus *Jacob increased exceedingly* (*v.* 43), and grew very rich in a little time. Those who, while their beginning is small, are humble and honest, contented and industrious, are in a likely way to see their latter end greatly increasing. He that is faithful in a little shall be entrusted with more. He that is faithful in that which is another man's shall be entrusted with something of his own. Jacob, who had been a just servant, became a rich master.

JAMIESON, FAUSSET, BROWN

37. Jacob took rods, etc.—There are many varieties of the hazel, some of which are more erect than the common hazel, and it was probably one of these varieties Jacob employed. The styles are of a bright red color, when peeled; and along with them he took wands of other shrubs, which, when stripped of the bark, had white streaks. These, kept constantly before the eyes of the female at the time of gestation, his observation had taught him would have an influence, through the imagination, on the future offspring.

38. watering troughs—usually a long stone block hollowed out, from which several sheep could drink at once, but sometimes so small as to admit of only one drinking at a time.

ADAM CLARKE

to him; therefore Laban separated from the flock, v. 35, all such cattle as Jacob might afterwards claim in consequence of his bargain; therefore Jacob commenced his service to Laban with a flock that did not contain a single animal of the description of those to which he might be entitled; and the others were sent away under the care of Laban's sons, three days' journey from those of which Jacob had the care. The bargain, therefore, seemed to be wholly in favor of Laban; and to turn it to his own advantage, Jacob made use of the stratagems afterwards mentioned. This mode of interpretation removes all the apparent contradiction between the thirty-second and thirty-fifth verses, with which commentators in general have been grievously perplexed.

37. *Rods of green poplar. Libneh lach.* The *Libneh* is generally understood to mean the white poplar; and the word *lach,* which is here joined to it, does not so much imply greenness of color as being fresh, in opposition to witheredness. Had they not been fresh, just cut off, he could not have pilled the bark from them. *And of the hazel. Luz,* the nut or filbert tree, translated by others the almond tree; which of the two is here intended is not known. *And chestnut tree. Armon,* the plane tree, from *aram,* "he was naked." The plane tree is properly called by this name, because of the outer bark naturally peeling off, and leaving the tree bare in various places, having smooth places where it has fallen off. *Pilled white strakes in them.* Probably cutting the bark through in a spiral line, and taking it off in a certain breadth all round the rods, so that the rods would appear party-colored, the white of the wood showing itself where the bark was stripped off.

38. *And he set the rods which he had pilled before the flocks.* It has long been an opinion that whatever makes a strong impression on the mind of a female in the time of conception and gestation will have a corresponding influence on the mind or body of the fetus. This opinion is not yet rationally accounted for.

40. *Jacob did separate the lambs.* When Jacob undertook the care of Laban's flock, according to the agreement already mentioned, there were no partly-colored sheep or goats among them. Therefore the *ringstraked,* etc., mentioned in this verse, must have been born since the agreement was made; and Jacob makes use of them precisely as he used the pilled rods, that, having these before their eyes during conception, the impression might be made upon their imagination which would lead to the results already mentioned.

41. *Whensoever the stronger cattle did conceive.* The word which we translate *stronger* is understood by several of the ancient interpreters as signifying the "early, first-born, or early spring" cattle; and hence it is opposed to *feeble,* which Symmachus properly renders cattle of the "second birth." Now this more particularly refers to early and late lambs in the same year; as those that are born just at the termination of winter, and in the very commencement of spring, are every way more valuable than those which are born later in the same spring. Jacob therefore took good heed not to try his experiments with those late produced cattle, because he knew these would produce a degenerate breed, but with the early cattle, which were strong and vigorous, by which his breed must be improved.

43. *And the man increased exceedingly.* No wonder, when he used such means as the above. And had *maidservants, and menservants*—he was obliged to increase these as his cattle multiplied. *And camels and asses,* to transport his tents, baggage, and family from place to place, being obliged often to remove for the benefit of pasturage.

KEIL–DELITZSCH:

In the first place (vv. 37–39), he took fresh rods of storax, maple, and walnut trees, all of which have a dazzling white wood under their dark outside, and peeled white stripes upon them, "peeling the white naked in the rods." These partially peeled, and therefore mottled rods, he placed in the drinking troughs (lit. gutters, water-troughs), to which the flock came to drink, in front of the animals, in order that, if copulation took place at the drinking time, it might occur near the mottled sticks, and the young be speckled and spotted in consequence. This artifice was founded upon a fact frequently noticed, particularly in the case of sheep, that whatever fixes their attention in copulation is marked upon the young. Secondly (v. 40), Jacob separated the speckled animals thus obtained from those of a normal color, and caused the latter to feed so that the others would be constantly in sight, in order that he might in this way obtain a constant accession of mottled sheep. As soon as these had multiplied sufficiently, he formed separate flocks (viz. of the speckled additions), "and put them not unto Laban's cattle"; i.e., he kept them apart in order that a still larger number of speckled ones might be procured, through Laban's one-colored flock having this mottled group constantly in view.—*Commentary on the Old Testament*

CHAPTER 31

MATTHEW HENRY

Verses 1–16

Jacob is here taking up a resolution immediately to quit his uncle's service, to take what he had and go back to Canaan. This resolution he took.

I. Upon a just provocation; for Laban and his sons had become very ill-natured towards him.

1. Laban's sons showed their ill-will in what they said, *v.* 1.

JAMIESON, FAUSSET, BROWN

Vss. 1-21. Envy of Laban and Sons. **1. he heard the words of Laban's sons**—It must have been from rumor that Jacob got knowledge of the invidious reflections cast upon him by his cousins; for they were separated at the distance of three days' journey.

ADAM CLARKE

1. *And he heard the words of Laban's sons.* The multiplication of Jacob's cattle, and the decrease and degeneracy of those of Laban, were sufficient to arouse the jealousy of Laban's sons. This, with Laban's unfair treatment and the direction he received from God, determined him to return to his own country. *Hath he got-*

MATTHEW HENRY

2. Laban himself said little, but his countenance was not towards Jacob as it used to be; and Jacob could not but take notice of it, *v.* 2, 5. He was but a churl at the best, but now he was more churlish than formerly.

II. By divine direction and under the convoy of a promise: *The Lord said unto Jacob, Return, and I will be with thee, v.* 3. He came thither by orders from Heaven, and there he would stay till he was ordered back. It is our duty to set ourselves under God's guidance, both in our going out and in our coming in. Jacob was also encouraged by what is said in *v.* 13, *I am the God of Beth-el.* This was the place where the covenant was renewed with him. *Now arise* (*v.* 13) *and return,* (1) To thy devotions in Canaan, the solemnities of which had perhaps been much intermitted while he was with Laban. (2) To thy comforts in Canaan: *Return to the land of thy kindred.*

III. With the knowledge and consent of his wives. He sent for Rachel and Leah to him to the field (*v.* 4), that he might confer with them more privately. Husbands that love their wives will communicate their purposes and intentions to them. Where there is a mutual affection there will be a mutual confidence. He told them of the command God had given him, in a dream, to return to his own country (*v.* 13), that they might not suspect his resolution to arise from inconstancy, or any disaffection to their country or family, but might see it to proceed from a principle of obedience to his God.

His wives cheerfully consented to his resolution. They were willing to go along with their husband, and put themselves with him under the divine direction: *Whatsoever God hath said unto thee do.*

Verses 17–24

Here is, I. Jacob's flight from Laban. It was honestly done to take no more than his own with him, the *cattle of his getting, v.* 18. He took what Providence gave him, and was content with that. Yet Rachel was not so honest as her husband; she *stole her father's images* (*v.* 19) and carried them away with her. The Hebrew calls them *teraphim.* Some think they were only little representations of the ancestors of the family, in statues or pictures, which Rachel had a particular fondness for, and was desirous to have with her, now that she was going into another country. It should rather seem that they were images for a religious use, *penates, household-gods,* either worshipped or consulted as oracles; and we are willing to hope that she took them away out of a design hereby to convince her father of the folly of his regard to those as gods which could not secure themselves, Isa. xlvi. 1, 2.

II. Laban's pursuit of Jacob. Tidings were brought him, on the third day, that Jacob had fled; he immediately raises the whole clan. Seven days' journey he marched in pursuit of him, *v.* 23. But the truth is, bad men are more vehement in their anger than in their love. God interposed in the quarrel, rebuked Laban and sheltered Jacob, charging Laban not to *speak unto him either good or bad* (*v.* 24). The same Hebraism we have, *ch.* xxiv. 50. God comes to him, and with one word ties his hands, though he does not turn his heart. The safety of good men is very much owing to the hold God has of the consciences of bad men and the access he has to them.

JAMIESON, FAUSSET, BROWN

2. And Jacob beheld the countenance of Laban—lit., was not the same as yesterday, and the day before, a common Oriental form of speech. The insinuations against Jacob's fidelity by Laban's sons, and the sullen reserve, the churlish conduct, of Laban himself, had made Jacob's situation, in his uncle's establishment, most trying and painful. It is always one of the vexations attendant on worldly prosperity, that it excites the envy of others (Eccles. 4:4); and that, however careful a man is to maintain a good conscience, he cannot always reckon on maintaining a good name, in a censorious world. This, Jacob experienced; and it is probable that, like a good man, he had asked direction and relief in prayer. **3. the Lord said, . . . Return unto the land of thy fathers**—Notwithstanding the ill usage he had received, Jacob might not have deemed himself at liberty to quit his present sphere, under the impulse of passionate fretfulness and discontent. Having been conducted to Haran by God (ch. 28:15) and having got a promise that the same heavenly Guardian would bring him again into the land of Canaan, he might have thought he ought not to leave it, without being clearly persuaded as to the path of duty. So ought we to set the Lord before us, and to acknowledge Him in all our ways, our journeys, our settlements, and plans in life. **4. Jacob sent and called Rachel and Leah**—His wives and family were in their usual residence. Whether he wished them to be present at the festivities of sheep-shearing, as some think; or, because he could not leave his flock, he called them both to come to him, in order that, having resolved on immediate departure, he might communicate his intentions. Rachel and Leah only were called, for the other two wives, being secondary and still in a state of servitude, were not entitled to be taken into account. Jacob acted the part of a dutiful husband in telling them his plans; for husbands that love their wives should consult with them and trust in them (Prov. 31:11). **6. ye know that . . . I have served your father**—Having stated his strong grounds of dissatisfaction with their father's conduct and the ill requital he had got for all his faithful services, he informed them of the blessing of God that had made him rich notwithstanding Laban's design to ruin him; and finally, of the command from God he had received to return to his own country, that they might not accuse him of caprice, or disaffection to their family; but be convinced, that in resolving to depart, he acted from a principle of religious obedience. **14. Rachel and Leah answered**—Having heard his views, they expressed their entire approval; and from grievances of their own, they were fully as desirous of a separation as himself. They display not only conjugal affection, but piety in following the course described—"whatsoever God hath said unto thee, do." "Those that are really their husbands' helpmeets will never be their hindrances in doing that to which God calls them" [HENRY]. **17. Then Jacob rose up**—Little time is spent by pastoral people in removing. The striking down the tents and poles and stowing them among their other baggage; the putting their wives and children in *houdas* like cradles, on the backs of camels, or in panniers on asses; and the ranging of the various parts of the flock under the respective shepherds; all this is a short process. A plain that is covered in the morning with a long array of tents and with browsing flocks, may, in a few hours, appear so desolate that not a vestige of the encampment remains, except the holes in which the tent-poles had been fixed. **20. Jacob stole away**—The result showed the prudence and necessity of departing secretly; otherwise, Laban might have detained him by violence or artifice. **18. he carried the cattle of his getting**—i.e., his own and nothing more. He did not indemnify himself for his many losses by carrying off any thing of Laban's, but was content with what Providence had given him. Some may think that due notice should have been given; but when a man feels himself in danger—the law of self-preservation prescribes the duty of immediate flight, if it can be done consistently with conscience.

22-55. LABAN PURSUES JACOB—THEIR COVENANT AT GILEAD. **22. it was told Laban on the third day**—No sooner did the news reach Laban than he set out in pursuit, and he being not encumbered, advanced rapidly; whereas Jacob, with a young family and numerous flocks, had to march slowly, so that he overtook the fugitives after seven days' journey as they lay encamped on the brow of mount Gilead, an extensive range of hills forming the eastern boundary of Canaan. Being accompanied by a number of his people, he might have used violence had he not been divinely warned in a dream to give no interruption to his nephew's journey. How striking and sudden a change! For several days he

ADAM CLARKE

ten all this glory. All these riches, this wealth, or property. The original word signifies both to be "rich" and to be "heavy"; and perhaps for this simple reason, that riches ever bring with them heavy weight and burden of cares and anxieties.

3. *And the Lord said unto Jacob, Return . . . and I will be with thee.* I will take the same care of thee in thy return, as I took of thee on thy way to this place.

4. *Jacob sent and called Rachel and Leah.* He had probably been at some considerable distance with the flocks; and for the greater secrecy, he rather sends for them to the field, to consult them on this most momentous affair, than visit them in their tents, where probably some of the family of Laban might overhear their conversation, though Laban himself was at the time three days' journey off. It is possible that Jacob sheared his sheep at the same time; and that he sent for his wives and household furniture to erect tents on the spot, that they might partake of the festivities usual on such occasions. Thus they might all depart without being suspected.

7. *Changed my wages ten times.* There is a strange diversity among the ancient versions, and ancient and modern interpreters, on the meaning of these words. It is most natural to suppose that Jacob uses the word *ten times* for an indefinite number, which we might safely translate "frequently"; and that it means an indefinite number in other parts of the sacred writings is evident from Lev. xxvi. 26: "Ten women shall bake your bread in one oven." Eccles. vii. 19: "Wisdom strengtheneth the wise more than ten mighty men in the city." Num, xiv. 22: "Because all those men . . . have tempted me now these ten times." Job xix. 3: "These ten times have ye reproached me." Zech. viii. 23: "In those days . . . ten men shall take hold . . . of the skirt of him that is a Jew." Rev. ii. 10: "Ye shall have tribulation ten days."

12. *Grisled. Beruddim; barad* signifies "hail," and the meaning must be, they had white spots on them similar to hail. Our word *grisled* comes from the old French, *greslé,* "hail."

15. *Are we not counted of him strangers?* Rachel and Leah, who well knew the disposition of their father, gave him here his true character. He has treated us as *strangers*—as slaves whom he had a right to dispose of as he pleased; in consequence, *he hath sold us*—disposed of us on the mere principle of gaining by the sale. *And hath quite devoured also our money.* Has applied to his own use the profits of the sale, and has allowed us neither portion nor inheritance.

19. *Laban went to shear his sheep.* Laban had gone; and this was a favorable time not only to take his images, but to return to Canaan without being perceived. *Rachel had stolen the images. Teraphim.* In v. 30 they are termed *elohai,* "gods."

21. *Passed over the river.* The Euphrates. But how could he pass such a river with his flocks? There might have been fords well known to both Jacob and Laban, by which they might readily pass. *The mount Gilead.* What the ancient name of this mountain was we know not; but it is likely that it had not the name of *Gilead* till after the transaction mentioned in v. 47. The mountains of Gilead were eastward of the country possessed by the tribes of Reuben and Gad, and extended from Mount Hermon to the mountains of Moab.

24. *And God came to Laban.* God's caution to Laban was of high importance to Jacob—*Take heed that thou speak not to Jacob either good or bad;* or rather, as is the literal meaning of the Hebrew *ra,* "from good to evil," for had he neither spoken good nor evil to Jacob, they could have had no intercourse at all. The original is, therefore, peculiarly appropriate; for when people meet, the language at first is the language of friendship; the command therefore implies, "Do not begin with 'Peace be unto thee,' and then proceed to injurious language and acts of violence."

MATTHEW HENRY

Verses 25–35

We have here the reasoning, not to say the rallying, that took place between Laban and Jacob at their meeting, in that mountain which was afterwards called *Gilead*, *v.* 25.

I. The high charge which Laban exhibited against him. He accuses him,

1. As a renegade that had unjustly deserted his service. To represent Jacob as a criminal, he will have it thought that he intended kindness to his daughters (*v.* 27, 28). It is common for bad men, when they are disappointed in their malicious projects, to pretend that they designed nothing but what was kind and fair.

2. As a thief, *v.* 30. *Wherefore hast thou stolen my gods?* Foolish man! to call those his gods that could be stolen! Could he expect protection from those that could neither resist nor discover their invaders? Enemies may steal our goods, but not our God.

II. Jacob's apology for himself. 1. As to the charge of stealing away his own wives he clears himself by giving the true reason. He feared lest Laban would by force take away his daughters, and so oblige him, by the bond of his affection to his wives, to continue in his service. 2. As to the charge of stealing Laban's gods he pleads not guilty, *v.* 32. He not only did not take them himself (he was not so fond of them), but he did not know that they were taken.

III. The diligent search Laban made for his gods (*v.* 33–35). We do not find that he searched Jacob's flocks for stolen cattle; but he searched his furniture for stolen gods. Laban, after all his searches, missed of finding his gods, and was baffled in his enquiry with a sham; but our God will not only be found of those that seek him, but they shall find him their bountiful rewarder.

Verses 36–42

I. The power of provocation. Jacob's natural temper was mild and calm, yet Laban's unreasonable carriage towards him put him into a heat that transported him into some vehemence, *v.* 36, 37.

II. The comfort of a good conscience. Those that in any employment have dealt faithfully, if they cannot obtain the credit of it with men, yet shall have the comfort of it in their own bosoms.

III. The character of a good servant, and particularly of a faithful shepherd. 1. He was very careful, so that, through his oversight or neglect, the ewes did not cast their young. 2. He was very honest, and took none of that for his own eating which was not allowed him. 3. He was very laborious, *v.* 40. He stuck to his business, all weathers.

IV. The character of a hard master. Laban had been such an one to Jacob. Those are bad masters, 1. Who exact from their servants, that which is unjust, by obliging them to make good that which is not damaged by any default of theirs. This Laban did, *v.* 39. 2. Those also are bad masters who deny to their servants that which is just and equal. This Laban did, *v.* 41. It was unreasonable for him to make Jacob serve for his daughters, when he had in reversion so great an estate secure to him by the promise of God himself.

V. The care of providence for the protection of injured innocence, *v.* 42. God took cognizance of the wrong done to Jacob, and repaid him whom Laban would otherwise have sent empty away. Jacob speaks of God the God of Abraham, and the fear of Isaac; for Abraham was dead, and had gone to that world where perfect love casts out fear; but Isaac was yet alive, sanctifying the Lord in his heart, as his fear and his dread.

Verses 43–55

We have here the compromising of the matter between Laban and Jacob. Laban had nothing to say in reply to Jacob's remonstrance: he could neither justify himself nor condemn Jacob, but was convicted by his own conscience of the wrong he had done him.

I. He turns it off with a profession of kindness for Jacob's wives and children (*v.* 43): *These daughters are my daughters.* When he cannot excuse what he has done, he does, in effect, own what he should have done; he should have treated them as his own, but he had counted them as strangers, *v.* 15.

II. He proposes a covenant of friendship between them, to which Jacob readily agrees, without insisting upon Laban's submission, much less his restitution. Peace and love are such valuable jewels that we can scarcely buy them too dearly. Better sit down losers than go on in strife.

JAMIESON, FAUSSET, BROWN

had been full of rage, and was now in eager anticipation that his vengeance would be fully wreaked, when lo! his hands are tied by invisible power (Ps. 76:10). He did not dare to touch Jacob, but there was a war of words. **25-30. Laban said . . . What hast thou done?**—Not a word is said of the charge, (vs. 1). His reproaches were of a different kind. His first charge was for depriving him of the satisfaction of giving Jacob and his family the usual salutations at parting. In the East it is customary, when any are setting out to a great distance, for their relatives and friends to accompany them a considerable way with music and valedictory songs. Considering the past conduct of Laban, his complaint on this ground was hypocritical cant. But his second charge was a grave one—the carrying off his gods—*Hebrew*, teraphim, small images of human figures, used not as idols or objects of worship, but as talismans, for superstitious purposes.

31, 32. Jacob said, . . . With whomsoever thou findeth thy gods let him not live—Conscious of his own innocence and little suspecting the misdeed of his favorite wife, he boldly challenged a search and denounced the heaviest penalty on the culprit. A personal scrutiny was made by Laban, who examined every tent; and having entered Rachel's last, he would have infallibly discovered the stolen images had not Rachel made an appeal to him which prevented further search. **34. Rachel had taken the images, and put them in the camel's furniture, and sat upon them**—The common pack-saddle is often used as a seat or a cushion, against which a person squatted on the floor may lean.

36, 37. Jacob was wroth—Recrimination on his part was natural in the circumstances, and, as usual, when passion is high, the charges took a wide range. He rapidly enumerated his grievances for twenty years and in a tone of unrestrained severity described the niggard character and vexatious exactions of his uncle, together with the hardships of various kinds he had patiently endured. **38. The rams of thy flock have I not eaten**—Eastern people seldom kill the females for food except they are barren.

39. That which was torn of beasts I brought not unto thee—The shepherds are strictly responsible for losses in the flock, unless they can prove these were occasioned by wild beasts. **40. in the day the drought . . . and the frost by night**—The temperature changes often in twenty-four hours from the greatest extremes of heat and cold, most trying to the shepherd who has to keep watch by his flocks. Much allowance must be made for Jacob. Great and long-continued provocations ruffle the mildest and most disciplined tempers. It is difficult to "be angry and sin not." But these two relatives, after having given utterance to their pent-up feelings, came at length to a mutual understanding, or rather, God influenced Laban to make reconciliation with his injured nephew (Prov. 16:7). **44. Come thou, let us make a covenant**—The way in which this covenant was ratified was by a heap of stones being laid in a circular pile, to serve as seats, and in the center of this circle a large one was set up perpendicularly for an altar. It is probable that a sacrifice was first offered, and then that the feast of reconciliation was partaken of by both parties seated on the stones around it. To this day heaps of stones, which have been used as memorials, are found abundantly in the region where this transaction took place.

ADAM CLARKE

27. *I might have sent thee away with mirth.* "With rejoicing," making a feast or entertainment on the occasion; *and with songs*, odes either in the praise of God or to commemorate the splendid acts of their ancestors; *with tabret*, the "tympanum" used in the East to the present day, a thin, broad wooden hoop, with parchment extended over one end of it, to which are attached small pieces of brass, tin, etc., which make a jingling noise; it is held in the air with one hand, and beat on with the fingers of the other. It appears to have been precisely the same with that which is called the "tambourine," and which is frequently to be met with in our streets. *And with harp*, a sort of stringed instrument, a lute or harp. These four things seem to include all that was used in those primitive times as expressive of gladness and satisfaction on the most joyous occasions.

29. *It is in the power of my hand to do you hurt.* Literally, "My hand is unto God to do you evil," i.e., I have vowed to God that I will punish thee for thy flight, and the stealing of my teraphim; but the *God of your father* has prevented me from doing it.

32. *Let him not live.* It appears that anciently theft was punished by death; and we know that the patriarchs had the power of life and death in their hands. But previously to the law the punishment of death was scarcely ever inflicted but for murder. The rabbins consider that this was an imprecation used by Jacob, as if he had said, Let God take away the life of the person who has stolen them! And that this was answered shortly after in the death of Rachel, chap. xxxv.

35. *The custom of women is upon me.* This she knew must be a satisfactory reason to her father; for if the teraphim were used to any religious purpose, and they seem to have been used in this way, as Laban calls them his "gods," he therefore could not suspect that a woman in such a situation, whose touch was considered as defiling, would have sat upon articles that were either the objects of his adoration or used for any sacred purpose. The stratagem succeeded to her wish and Laban departed without suspicion.

36. *And Jacob was wroth, and chode with Laban.* The expostulation of Jacob with Laban and their consequent agreement are told in this place with great spirit and dignity. Jacob was conscious that, though he had made use of cunning to increase his flocks, yet Laban had been on the whole a great gainer by his services. He had served him at least twenty years, fourteen for Rachel and Leah, and six for the cattle. Laban's constitutional sin was covetousness, and it was an easily besetting sin; for it appears to have governed all his conduct, and to have rendered him regardless of the interests of his children, so long as he could secure his own. That he had frequently falsified his agreement with Jacob, though the particulars are not specified, we have already had reason to conjecture from v. 7, and with this Jacob charges his father-in-law, in the most positive manner, v. 41.

39. *That which was torn . . . of my hand didst thou require it.* This more particularly marks the covetous and rigorous disposition of Laban; for the law of God required that what had been torn by beasts the shepherd should not be obliged to make good, Exod. xxii. 10, 13. And it is very likely that this law was in force from the earliest times.

42. *The fear of Isaac.* It is strange that Jacob should say, the *God of Abraham* and the *fear of Isaac*, when both words are meant of the same Being. The reason perhaps was this: Abraham was long since dead, and God was his unalienable Portion forever. Isaac was yet alive in a state of probation, living in the fear of God, not exempt from the danger of falling; therefore God is said to be his *fear*—not only the Object of his religious worship in a general way, but that holy and just God before whom he was still working out his salvation with fear and trembling—fear lest he should fall, and trembling lest he should offend.

46. *Made an heap. Gal*, translated *heap*, signifies properly a round heap; and this heap was probably made for the double purpose of

MATTHEW HENRY

1. The substance of this covenant. Jacob left it wholly to Laban to settle it. (1) That Jacob should be a good husband to his wives. Jacob had never given him any cause to suspect that he would be any other than a kind husband; yet, as if he had, he was willing to come under this engagement. (2) That he should never be a bad neighbour to Laban, *v.* 52. It was agreed that Jacob should forgive and forget all the wrongs he had received.

2. The ceremony of this covenant. It was made and ratified with great solemnity, according to the usages of those times. (1) A pillar was erected (*v.* 45), and a heap of stones raised (*v.* 46), to perpetuate the memory of the thing. (2) A sacrifice was offered (*v.* 54), a sacrifice of peace-offerings. Our peace with God is that which puts true comfort into our peace with our friends. If parties contend, the reconciliation of both to him will facilitate their reconciliation one to another. (3) They did eat bread together (*v.* 46), jointly partaking of the feast upon the sacrifice, *v.* 54. Covenants of friendship were anciently ratified by the parties eating and drinking together. It was in the nature of a love-feast. (4) They solemnly appealed to God concerning their sincerity herein, [1] As a witness (*v.* 49): *The Lord watch between me and thee.* When we are out of one another's sight, let this be a restraint upon us, that wherever we are we are under God's eye. [2] As a Judge, *v.* 53. *The God of Abraham* (from whom Jacob descended), *and the God of Nahor* (from whom Laban descended), *the God of their father* (the common ancestor, from whom they both descended), *judge betwixt us.* God's relation to them is thus expressed to intimate that they worshipped one and the same God, upon which consideration there ought to be no enmity between them. (5) They gave a new name to the place, *v.* 47, 48. Laban called it in Syriac, and Jacob in Hebrew, *the heap of witness*; and (*v.* 49) it was called *Mizpah, a watch-tower.* These names are applicable to the seals of the gospel covenant, which are witnesses to us if we be faithful, but witnesses against us if we be false. The name Jacob gave this heap (*Galeed*) stuck by it, not the name Laban gave it. In all this rencounter, Laban was noisy and full of words, affecting to say much; Jacob was silent, and said little.

Lastly, After all this angry parley, they part friends, *v.* 55.

JAMIESON, FAUSSET, BROWN

This heap be witness—Objects of nature were frequently thus spoken of. But over and above, there was a solemn appeal to God; and it is observable that there was a marked difference in the religious sentiments of the two. Laban spake of the God of Abraham and Nahor, their common ancestors; but Jacob, knowing that idolatry had crept in among that branch of the family, swore by the "fear of his father Isaac." They who have one God should have one heart: they who are agreed in religion should endeavor to agree in everything else.

KEIL–DELITZSCH:

Verses 49, 50. After these words of Laban, which are introduced parenthetically and in which he enjoined upon Jacob fidelity to his daughters, the formation of the covenant of reconciliation and peace between them is first described, according to which neither of them was to pass the stone heap and memorial stone with a hostile intention towards the other. Of this the memorial was to serve as a witness, and the God of Abraham and the God of Nahor, the God of their father (Terah), would be umpire between them. To this covenant, in which Laban, according to his polytheistic views, placed the God of Abraham upon the same level with the God of Nahor and Terah, Jacob swore by "the fear of Isaac" (v. 42), the God who was worshiped by his father with sacred awe. He then offered sacrifices upon the mountain and invited his relations to eat, i.e. to partake of a sacrificial meal and seal the covenant by a feast of love.—*Commentary on the Old Testament*

ADAM CLARKE

an altar and a table, and Jacob's stone or pillar was set on it for the purpose of a memorial.

47. *Laban called it Jegar-sahadutha.* "The heap or round heap of witness"; *but Jacob called it Galeed,* which signifies the same thing. The first is pure Chaldee, the second pure Hebrew.

48-49. I think these two verses are badly divided, and should be read thus:

48. *And Laban said, This heap is a witness between me and thee this day.*

49. *Therefore was the name of it called Galeed and Mizpah; for he said, The Lord watch between me and thee, when we are absent one from another.*

Mizpah. Mitspah signifies a "watchtower"; and Laban supposes that in consequence of the consecration of the place, and the covenant now solemnly made and ratified, God would take possession of this heap, and stand on it as on a watchtower, to prevent either of them from trenching on the conditions of their covenant.

50. *No man is with us.* Though all were present at the sacrifice offered, yet it appears that in making the contract Jacob and Laban withdrew, and transacted the business in private, calling on God to witness it. Jacob had already four wives; but Laban feared that he might take others, whose children would naturally come in for a share of the inheritance to the prejudice of his daughters and grandchildren.

51. *And Laban said to Jacob . . . behold this pillar, which I have cast betwixt me and thee.* But this pillar, not *cast* but "set up," was certainly set up by Jacob; for in v. 45 we read, "And Jacob took a stone, and set it up for a pillar."

53. *The God of their father.* As Laban certainly speaks of the true God here, with what propriety can he say that this God was the God of Terah, the father of Abraham and Nahor? It is certain that Terah was an idolater; of this we have the most positive proof, Josh. xxiv. 2. Because the clause is not in the Septuagint, and is besides wanting in some MSS., Dr. Kennicott considers it an interpolation. But there is no need of having recourse to this expedient if we adopt the reading "your father," for "their father," which is supported by several of Kennicott's and De Rossi's MSS., and is precisely the same form made use of by Laban, v. 29, when addressing Jacob, and appears to me to be used here in the same way; for he there most manifestly uses the plural pronoun, when speaking only to Jacob himself. It is therefore to be considered as a form of speech peculiar to Laban; at least we have two instances of his use of it in this chapter. *Jacob sware by the fear of his father Isaac.* See on v. 42.

54. *Offered sacrifice upon the mount.* It is very likely that Laban joined in this solemn religious rite, and that, having offered the blood and fat to God, they feasted upon the sacrifice.

55. *Kissed his sons and his daughters.* That is, his grandchildren, Jacob's eleven sons with Dinah, their sister, and their mothers, Leah and Rachel. All these he calls his "children," v. 43. *And blessed them*—prayed heartily for their prosperity, though we find from v. 29 that he came having bound himself by a vow to God to do them some injury. Thus God turned his intended curse into a blessing.

MATTHEW HENRY

CHAPTER 32

Verses 1–2

1. Here is Jacob's convoy in his journey (*v.* 1): *The angels of God met him,* in a visible appearance, whether in a vision by day or in a dream by night, as when he saw them upon the ladder (*ch.* xxviii. 12), is uncertain. They had invisibly attended him all along, but now they appeared to him, because he had greater dangers before him than those he had hitherto encountered. God will have us, when we are in peace, to provide for trouble, and, when trouble comes, to live upon former observations and experiences; for *we walk by faith, not by sight.* God's people, at death, are returning to Canaan, to their Father's house; and then the angels of God will meet them. 2. The comfortable notice he took of this convoy, *v.* 2. *This is God's host.* To preserve the

JAMIESON, FAUSSET, BROWN

CHAPTER 32

Vss. 1, 2. VISION OF ANGELS. **1. angels of God met him**—It is not said whether this angelic manifestation was made in a vision by day, or a dream by night. There is an evident allusion, however, to the appearance upon the ladder (cf. ch. 28:12), and this occurring to Jacob on his return to Canaan, was an encouraging pledge of the continued presence and protection of God (Ps. 34:7; Heb. 1:14).

2. Mahanaim—two hosts or camps. The place was situated between mount Gilead and the Jabbok, near the banks of that brook.

ADAM CLARKE

CHAPTER 32

1. *The angels of God met him.* Our word *angel* comes from the Greek *aggelos,* which literally signifies a messenger; or, as translated in some of our old Bibles, a "tidings-bringer." The Hebrew word *malach,* from *laach,* "to send, minister to, employ," is nearly of the same import; and hence we may see the propriety of St. Augustine's remark: "It is a name, not of nature, but of office"; and hence it is applied indifferently to a human agent or messenger, 2 Sam. ii. 5; to a prophet, Hag. i. 13; to a priest, Mal. ii. 7; to celestial spirits, Ps. ciii. 19-20, 22; civ. 4.

2. *Mahanaim.* The "two hosts," if read by the points, the angels forming one, and Jacob

MATTHEW HENRY

remembrance of this favour, Jacob gave a name to the place from it, *Mahanaim, two hosts*, one on either side, or one in the front and the other in the rear, to protect him from Laban behind and Esau before, that they might be a complete guard. Thus he is *compassed* with God's favour. Perhaps in allusion to this the church is called *Mahanaim, two armies*, Cant. vi. 13. Here were Jacob's family, which made one army, representing the church militant and itinerant on earth; and the angels, another army, representing the church triumphant and at rest in heaven.

Verses 3–8

He takes occasion to remind himself of the enemies he had, particularly Esau. It is probable that Rebekah had sent him word of Esau's settlement in Seir, and of the continuance of his enmity to him. What shall poor Jacob do? He longs to see his father, and yet he dreads to see his brother.

I. He sends a very kind and humble message to Esau. Acts of civility may help to slay enmities. 1. He calls Esau his lord, himself his servant, to intimate that he did not insist upon the prerogatives of the birthright and blessing he had obtained for himself. 2. He gives him a short account of himself, that he was not a fugitive and a vagabond, and that he was not a beggar, nor did he come home, as the prodigal son, destitute of necessaries and likely to be a charge to his relations. And, 3. He courts his favour: *I have sent, that I might find grace in thy sight.*

II. He receives a very formidable account of Esau's warlike preparations against him (*v.* 6), *He comes to meet thee, and four hundred men with him.* 1. He remembers the old quarrel, and will now be avenged on him for the birthright and blessing, and, if possible, defeat Jacob's expectations from both. Angry men have good memories. 2. He envies Jacob what little estate he had, and, though he himself was now possessed of a much better, yet nothing will serve him but to feed his eyes upon Jacob's ruin, and fill his fields with Jacob's spoils. 3. He concludes it easy to destroy him, now that he was upon the road, a poor weary traveller, unfixed, and (as he thinks) unguarded. 4. He resolves to do it suddenly, and before Jacob had come to his father, lest he should interpose and mediate between them. Out he marches, spurred on with rage; four hundred men he had with him, armed, and now breathing nothing but threatenings and slaughter. The tenth part of these were enough to cut off poor Jacob, and his guiltless helpless family, root and branch. Jacob, though a man of great faith, yet was now greatly afraid. Note, A lively apprehension of danger may very well consist with a humble confidence in God's power and promise. Christ himself, in his agony, was sorely amazed.

III. He puts himself into the best posture of defence that his present circumstances will admit. It was absurd to think of making resistance, all his contrivance is to make an escape, *v.* 7, 8. He divided his company, not as Abraham (*ch.* xiv. 15), for fight, but for flight.

Verses 9–12

Our rule is to call upon God in the time of trouble; we have here an example to this rule, and the success encourages us to follow this example. In his distress he sought the Lord, and he heard him. Times of fear should be times of prayer; whatever frightens us should drive us to our knees, to our God. Now it is worth while to enquire what there was extraordinary in this prayer, that it should gain the petitioner all this honour.

I. The request itself is one, and very express: *Deliver me from the hand of my brother*, *v.* 11.

II. The pleas are many, and very powerful; never was cause better ordered, Job xxiii. 4. He offers up his request with great faith, fervency, and humility.

1. He addresses himself to God as the God of his fathers, *v.* 9. Such was the humble self-denying sense he had of his own unworthiness that he did not call God his own God, but a God in covenant with his ancestors. God's covenant with our fathers may be a comfort to us when we are in distress.

2. He produces his warrant: *Thou saidst unto me, Return unto thy country.* We may be going whither God calls us, and yet may think our way hedged up with thorns. If God be our guide, he will be our guard.

3. He humbly acknowledges his own unworthiness to receive any favour from God (*v.* 10): *I am not worthy*; it is an unusual plea. Christ never commended any of his petitioners so much as him who said, *Lord, I am not worthy* (Matt. viii. 8), and her who said, *Truth, Lord, yet the dogs eat of the crumbs which fall from their master's table*, Matt. xv. 27. Now observe, (1) How magnificently and honourably he speaks of the mercies of God to him. (2) How

JAMIESON, FAUSSET, BROWN

3-32. MISSION TO ESAU. **3. Jacob sent messengers before him to Esau**—i.e., had sent. It was a prudent precaution to ascertain the present temper of Esau, as the road, on approaching the eastern confines of Canaan, lay near the wild district where his brother was now established. **the land of Seir**—a highland country on the east and south of the Dead Sea, inhabited by the Horites, who were dispossessed by Esau or his posterity (Deut. 11:12). When and in what circumstances he had emigrated thither, whether the separation arose out of the undutiful conduct and idolatrous habits of his wives, which had made them unwelcome in the tent of his parents, or whether his roving disposition had sought a country from his love of adventure and the chase, he was living in a state of power and affluence, and this settlement on the outer borders of Canaan, though made of his own free-will, was overruled by Providence to pave the way for Jacob's return to the promised land. **4. Thus shall ye speak unto my lord Esau**—The purport of the message was that, after a residence of twenty years in Mesopotamia, he was now returning to his native land, that he did not need any thing, for he had abundance of pastoral wealth, but that he could not pass without notifying his arrival to his brother and paying the homage of his respectful obeisance. Acts of civility tend to disarm opposition and soften hatred (Eccles. 10:4). **Thy servant Jacob**—He had been made *lord* over his brethren (cf. ch. 27:29). But it is probable he thought this referred to a spiritual superiority; or if to temporal, that it was to be realized only to his posterity. At all events, leaving it to God to fulfil that purpose, he deemed it prudent to assume the most kind and respectful bearing. **6. The messengers returned to Jacob**—Their report left Jacob in painful uncertainty as to what was his brother's views and feelings. Esau's studied reserve gave him reason to dread the worst. Jacob was naturally timid; but his conscience told him that there was much ground for apprehension, and his distress was all the more aggravated that he had to provide for the safety of a large and helpless family.

9-12. **Jacob said, O God of my father Abraham**—In this great emergency, he had recourse to prayer. This is the first recorded example of prayer in the Bible. It is short, earnest, and bearing directly on the occasion. The appeal is made to God, as standing in a covenant relation to his family, just as we ought to put our hopes of acceptance with God in Christ. It pleads the special promise made to him of a safe return; and after a most humble and affecting confession of unworthiness, it breathes an earnest desire for deliverance from the impending danger. It was the prayer of a kind husband, an affectionate father, a firm believer in the promises.

ADAM CLARKE

and his company forming another; or simply "hosts" or "camps" in the plural. There was a city built afterwards here, and inhabited by the priests of God, Josh. xxi. 38. For what purpose the angels of God met Jacob does not appear from the text; probably it was intended to show him that he and his company were under the care of an especial providence, and consequently to confirm his trust and confidence in God.

3. *Jacob sent messengers. Malachim*, the same word which is before translated "angels." It is very likely that these messengers had been sent some time before he had this vision at Mahanaim, for they appear to have returned while Jacob encamped at the brook Jabbok, where he had the vision of angels; see vv. 6 and 23. *The land of Seir, the country of Edom.* This land which was, according to Dr. Wells, situated on the south of the Dead Sea, extending from thence to the Arabian Gulf, 1 Kings ix. 26, was formerly possessed by the Horites, Gen. xiv. 6; but Esau with his children drove them out, destroyed them, and dwelt in their stead, Deut. ii. 22; and thither Esau went from the face of his brother, Jacob, chap. xxxvi. 6-7. Thus we find he verified the prediction, "By thy sword shalt thou live," chap. xxvii. 40.

4. *Thus shall ye speak unto my lord Esau.* Jacob acknowledges the superiority of his brother; for the time was not yet come in which it could be said, "The elder shall serve the younger."

6. *Esau . . . cometh . . . and four hundred men with him.* Jacob, conscious that he had injured his brother, was now apprehensive that he was coming with hostile intentions, and that he had every evil to fear from his displeasure. Conscience is a terrible accuser. It does not appear that Esau in this meeting had any hostile intention, but was really coming with a part of his servants or tribe to do his brother honor. If he had had any contrary intention, God had removed it; and the angelic host which Jacob met with before might have inspired him with sufficient confidence in God's protection.

7. *He divided the people.* His prudence and cunning were now turned into a right channel, for he took the most effectual method to appease his brother, had he been irritated, and save at least a part of his family. This dividing and arranging of his flocks, family, and domestics, has something in it highly characteristic. To such a man as Jacob such expedients would naturally present themselves.

9. *O God of my father Abraham.* This prayer is remarkable for its simplicity and energy; and it is a model too for prayer, of which it contains the essential constituents: (1) Deep self-abasement. (2) Magnification of God's mercy. (3) Deprecation of the evil to which he was exposed. (4) Pleading the promises that God had made to him. And (5) Taking encouragement from what God had already wrought.

10. *I am not worthy of the least of all the mercies.* The marginal reading is more consistent with the original: "I am less than all the compassions, and than all the faithfulness, which thou hast showed unto thy servant." Probably St. Paul had his eye on this passage when he wrote, "Unto me, who am less than the least of all saints." A man who sees himself in the light of God will ever feel that he has no good

MATTHEW HENRY	JAMIESON, FAUSSET, BROWN	ADAM CLARKE

meanly and humbly he speaks of himself, disclaiming all thought of his own merit: "*I am not worthy of the least of all thy mercies*, much less am I worthy of so great a favour as this I am now suing for." *I am less than all thy mercies*; so the word is. Those are best prepared for the greatest mercies that see themselves unworthy of the least.

4. He thankfully owns God's goodness to him in his banishment, and how much it had outdone his expectations: "*With my staff I passed over this Jordan*, poor and desolate, like a forlorn and despised pilgrim"; "*and now I have become two bands*, now I am surrounded with a numerous and comfortable retinue of children and servants."

5. He urges the extremity of the peril he was in: *Lord, deliver me from Esau, for I fear him, v.* 11. The people of God have not been shy of telling God their fears. The fear that quickens prayer is itself pleadable.

6. He insists especially upon the promise God had made him (*v.* 9): *Thou saidst, I will deal well with thee*, and again, in the close (*v.* 12): *Thou saidst, I will surely do thee good.* The best we can say to God in prayer is what he has said to us.

Verses 13–23

Jacob, having piously made God his friend by a prayer, is here prudently endeavouring to make Esau his friend by a present. He had prayed to God to deliver him from the hand of Esau, nor did his prayer make him presume upon God's mercy, without the use of means. When we have prayed to God for any mercy, we must second our prayers with our endeavours. To pacify Esau,

I. Jacob sent him a very noble present of cattle, to the number of 580 in all, *v.* 13–15. It was a present that he thought would be acceptable to Esau, who had traded so much in hunting wild beasts that perhaps he was but ill furnished with tame cattle with which to stock his new conquests. Peace and love, though purchased dearly, will prove a good bargain to the purchaser. Jacob forgives and forgets.

II. He sent him a very humble message, which he ordered his servants to deliver in the best manner, *v.* 17, 18. They must call Esau their *lord*, and Jacob his *servant*; they must tell him the cattle they had was a small present which Jacob had sent him. They must especially take care to tell him that Jacob was coming after (*v.* 18–20), that he might not suspect he had fled through fear. If Jacob will seem not to be afraid of Esau, Esau, it may be hoped, will not be a terror to Jacob.

Verses 24–32

We have here the remarkable story of Jacob's wrestling with the angel and prevailing, which is referred to, Hos. xii. 4. Very early in the morning, a great while before day, Jacob had helped his wives and his children over the river, and he desired to be private, and was left alone, that he might again more fully spread his cares and fears before God in prayer. While Jacob was earnest in prayer, *stirring up himself to take hold on God*, an angel takes hold on him. Some think this was the *angel of his presence* (Isa. lxiii. 9), one of those that attend on the *shechinah*, or the divine Majesty. Others think it was Michael our prince, the eternal Word, the angel of the covenant. Observe,

I. How Jacob and this angel engaged, *v.* 24. Jacob was now full of care and fear about the interview he expected, next day, with his brother, and God himself seemed to oppose his entrance into the land of promise. We are told by the prophet (Hos. xii. 4) how *Jacob wrestled*: he *wept, and made supplication*; prayers and tears were his weapons.

II. What was the success of the engagement. 1. Jacob kept his ground; though the struggle continued long, the angel *prevailed not against him* (*v.* 25), that is, this discouragement did not shake his faith, nor silence his prayer. It was not in his own strength that he wrestled, nor by his own strength that he prevailed, but in and by strength derived from Heaven. Note, We cannot prevail with God but in his own strength. It is his Spirit that intercedes in us, and *helps our infirmities*, Rom. viii. 26. 2. The angel put out Jacob's thigh. Some think that Jacob felt little or no pain from this hurt; it is probable that he did not, for he did not so much as halt till the struggle was over (*v.* 31), and, if so, this was an evidence of a divine touch indeed, which wounded and healed at the same time. 3. The angel, by an admirable condescension, mildly requests Jacob to let him go (*v.* 26), as God said to Moses (Exod. xxxii. 10), *Let me alone.* Thus he would put an honour on Jacob's faith and prayer, and further try his constancy. 4. Jacob persists in his holy importunity:

13-23. took . . . a present for Esau his brother—Jacob combined active exertions with earnest prayer; and this teaches us that we must not depend upon the aid and interposition of God in such a way as to supersede the exercise of prudence and foresight. Superiors are always approached with presents, and the respect expressed is estimated by the quality and amount of the gift. The present of Jacob consisted of 550 head of cattle, of different kinds, such as would be most prized by Esau. It was a most magnificent present, skilfully arranged and proportioned. The milch camels alone were of immense value; for the she-camels form the principal part of Arab wealth; their milk is a chief article of diet; and in many other respects they are of the greatest use. **16. every drove by themselves**—There was great prudence in this arrangement; for the present would thus have a more imposing appearance; Esau's passion would have time to cool as he passed each successive company; and if the first was refused, the others would hasten back to convey a timely warning. **17. he commanded the foremost**—The messengers were strictly commanded to say the same words, that Esau might be more impressed and that the uniformity of the address might appear more clearly to have come from Jacob himself. **21. himself lodged**—not the whole night, but only a part of it. **22. ford Jabbok**—now the *Zerka*—a stream that rises among the mountains of Gilead, and running from east to west, enters the Jordan, about forty miles south of the Sea of Tiberias. At the ford it is ten yards wide. It is sometimes forded with difficulty: but in summer it is very shallow. **he rose up and took**—Unable to sleep, he waded the ford in the night-time by himself; and having ascertained its safety, he returned to the north bank and sent over his family and attendants, remaining behind, to seek anew, in silent prayer, the divine blessing on the means he had set in motion. **24, 25. There wrestled a man with him**—This mysterious person is called an angel (Hos. 12:5) and God (vss. 28, 30; Hos. 12:4); and the opinion that is most supported is that he was "the angel of the covenant," who, in a visible form, appeared to animate the mind and sympathize with the distress of his pious servant. It has been a subject of much discussion whether the incident described was an actual conflict or a visionary scene. Many think that as the narrative makes no mention in express terms either of sleep, or dream, or vision, it was a real transaction; while others, considering the bodily exhaustion of Jacob, his great mental anxiety, the kind of aid he supplicated, as well as the analogy of former manifestations with which he was favored—such as the ladder—have concluded that it was a vision [CALVIN, HESSENBERG, HENGSTENBERG]. The moral design of it was to revive the sinking spirit of the patriarch and to arm him with confidence in God, while anticipating the dreaded scenes of the morrow. To us it is highly instructive; showing that, to encourage us valiantly to meet the trials to which we are subjected, God allows us to ascribe to the efficacy of our faith and prayers, the victories which His grace alone enables us to make.

but what he has received, and that he deserves nothing of all that he has. *For with my staff.* i.e., "myself alone," without any attendants, as the Chaldee has properly rendered it.

11. *And the mother with the children.* He must have had an awful opinion of his brother when he used this expression, which implies the utmost cruelty, proceeding in the work of slaughter to total extermination.

12. *Make thy seed as the sand.* Having come to the promise by which the covenant was ratified both to Abraham and Isaac, he ceased, his faith having gained strong confirmation in a promise which he knew could not fail, and which he found was made over to him, as it had been to his father and grandfather.

13. *And took of that which came to his hand.* "Which came under his hand," i.e., what, in the course of God's providence, came under his power.

14. *Two hundred she goats.* This was a princely present, and such as was sufficient to have compensated Esau for any kind of temporal loss he might have sustained in being deprived of his birthright and blessing. The *thirty milch camels* were particularly valuable.

15. *Ten bulls.* The Syriac and Vulgate have "twenty"; but *ten* is a sufficient proportion to the *forty kine.* By all this we see that Jacob was led to make restitution for the injury he had done to his brother. Restitution for injuries done to man is essentially requisite if in our power. He who can and will not make restitution for the wrongs he has done can have no claim even on the mercy of God.

22. *Passed over the ford Jabbok.* This brook or rivulet rises in the mountains of Galaad, and falls into the Jordan at the south extremity of the lake of Gennesaret.

24. *And there wrestled a man with him.* This was doubtless the Lord Jesus Christ, who, among the patriarchs, assumed that human form which in the fulness of time He really took of a woman, and in which He dwelt thirty-three years among men.

25. *The hollow of Jacob's thigh was out of joint.* What this implies is difficult to find out; it is not likely that it was complete luxation of the thigh bone. It may mean no more than he received a stroke on the groin, not a "touch"; for the Hebrew word *naga* often signifies to "smite with violence," which stroke, even if comparatively slight, would effectually disable him for a time, and cause him to halt for many hours, if not for several days.

26. *Let me go, for the day breaketh.* Probably meaning that, as it was now morning, Jacob must rejoin his wives and children, and proceed on their journey.

MATTHEW HENRY

I will not let thee go, except thou bless me. The credit of a conquest will do him no good without the comfort of a blessing. In begging this blessing he owns his inferiority, though he seemed to have the upper hand in the struggle.

5. The angel puts a perpetual mark of honour upon him, by changing his name (*v.* 27, 28): "Thou art a brave combatant" (says the angel), "a man of heroic resolution; what is thy name?" "Jacob," says he, *a supplanter*; so *Jacob* signifies: "Well," says the angel, "thou shalt be called *Israel, a prince with God.*" Jacob is here knighted in the field, as it were, and has a title of honour which will remain, to his praise, to the end of time. Yet this was not all; having power with God, he shall have power with men too.

6. He dismisses him with a blessing, *v.* 29. Instead of telling him his name, he gave him his blessing, which was the thing he wrestled for. An interest in the angel's blessing is better than an acquaintance with his name. The tree of life is better than the tree of knowledge. 7. Jacob gives a new name to the place; he calls it *Peniel*, the *face of God* (*v.* 30). The name he gives to the place preserves and perpetuates, not the honour of his valour or victory, but only the honour of God's free grace. "In this place I saw God face to face, and my life was preserved"; not, "It was my praise that I came off a conqueror, but it was God's mercy that I escaped with my life."

8. The memorandum Jacob carried of this in his bones: *He halted on his thigh* (*v.* 31). The honour and comfort he obtained by this struggle were abundantly sufficient to countervail the damage, though he went limping to his grave. Notice is taken of the sun's rising upon him when he passed over *Penuel*; for it is sunrise with that soul that has communion with God. The inspired penman mentions a traditional custom which the seed of Jacob had, never to eat of that sinew, or muscle, in any beast, by which the hip-bone is fixed in its cup: thus they preserved the memorial of this story.

JAMIESON, FAUSSET, BROWN

26. I will not let thee go, except thou bless me—It is evident that Jacob was aware of the character of Him with whom he wrestled; and, believing that His power, though by far superior to human, was yet limited by His promise to do him good, he determined not to lose the golden opportunity of securing a blessing. And nothing gives God greater pleasure than to see the hearts of His people firmly adhering to Him. **28. Thy name shall be called no more Jacob, but Israel**—The old name was not to be abandoned; but, referring as it did to a dishonorable part of the patriarch's history, it was to be associated with another descriptive of his now sanctified and eminently devout character.

29. Jacob asked, Tell me . . thy name—The request was denied that he might not be too elated with his conquest nor suppose that he had obtained such advantage over the angel as to make him do what he pleased.

31. halted upon his thigh—As Paul had a thorn in the flesh given to humble him, lest he should be too elevated by the abundant revelations granted him, so Jacob's lameness was to keep him mindful of this mysterious scene, and that it was in gracious condescension the victory was yielded to him. In the greatest of these spiritual victories which, through faith, any of God's people obtain, there is always something to humble them. **32. the sinew which shrank**—the nerve that fastens the thigh-bone in its socket. The practice of the Jews in abstaining from eating this in the flesh of animals, is not founded on the law of Moses, but is merely a traditional usage. The sinew is carefully extracted; and where there are no persons skilled enough for that operation, they do not make use of the hind legs at all.

ADAM CLARKE

28. *Thy name shall be called no more Jacob, but Israel. Yisrael*, from *sar*, "a prince," or *sarah*, "he ruled as a prince," and *el*, "God"; or rather from *ish*, "a man," and *raah*, "he saw," *el*, "God"; and this corresponds with the name which Jacob imposed on the place, calling it *Peniel*, the "faces of God, or of Elohim," which faces being manifested to him caused him to say, v. 30, "I have seen the Elohim faces-to-faces (i.e., fully and completely without any medium), and my soul is redeemed."

We may learn from this that the redemption of the soul will be the blessed consequence of wrestling by prayer and supplication with God: "The kingdom of heaven suffereth violence, and the violent take it by force." From this time Jacob became a new man; but it was not till after a severe struggle that he got his name, his heart, and his character changed. After this he was no more Jacob, the supplanter, but Israel—the man who prevails with God, and sees Him face-to-face.

And hast prevailed. More literally, "Thou hast had power with God, and with man thou shalt also prevail." *In Elohim*, "with the strong God"; *im anashim*, "with weak, feeble man." There is a beautiful opposition here between the two words: Seeing thou hast been powerful with the Almighty, surely thou shalt prevail over perishing mortals; as thou hast prevailed with God, thou shalt also prevail with men.

29. *Tell me, I pray thee, thy name.* It is very likely that Jacob wished to know the name of this angel, that he might invoke him in his necessities: but this might have led him into idolatry, for the doctrine of the Incarnation could be but little understood at this time; hence He refuses to give himself any name, yet shows himself to be the true God, and so Jacob understood Him (see v. 28); but he wished to have heard from His own lips that name by which He desired to be invoked and worshipped. *Wherefore is it that thou dost ask after my name?* Canst thou be ignorant who I am? *And he blessed him there*—gave him the new heart and the new nature which God alone can give to fallen man, and by the change He wrought in him, sufficiently showed who He was.

31. *The sun rose upon him.* Did the Prophet Malachi refer to this, chap. iv. 2: "Unto you that fear my name shall the Sun of righteousness arise with healing in his wings"? Possibly with the rising of the sun, which may here be understood as emblematical of "the Sun of righteousness"—the Lord Jesus—the pain and weakness of his thigh passed away, and he felt in both soul and body that he was healed of his plagues.

32. *Therefore the children of Israel eat not of the sinew.* What this sinew was neither Jew nor Christian can tell; and it can add nothing either to science or to a true understanding of the text to multiply conjectures. I have already supposed that the part which the angel touched or "struck" was the groin; and if this be right, the *sinew*, nerve, or muscle that *shrank*, must be sought for in that place.

MATTHEW HENRY

CHAPTER 33

Verses 1–4

Here, I. Jacob discovered Esau's approach, *v.* 1. Some think that his lifting up his eyes denotes his cheerfulness and confidence, in opposition to a dejected countenance; having by prayer committed his case to God, he went on his way, *and his countenance was no more sad*, 1 Sam. i. 18.

II. He put his family into the best order he could to receive him. Observe what a different figure these two brothers made. Esau is attended with a guard of 400 men, and looks big; Jacob is followed by a cumbersome train of women and children that are his care, and he looks tender and solicitous for their safety; and yet Jacob had the birthright, and was to have the dominion, and was every way the better man. Jacob, at the head of his household, set a better example than Esau at the head of his regiment.

III. At their meeting, the expressions of kindness were interchanged in the best manner that could be between them.

1. Jacob bowed to Esau, *v.* 3. Though he feared Esau as an enemy, yet he did obeisance to him as an elder brother. Many preserve themselves by humbling themselves: the bullet flies over him that stoops.

JAMIESON, FAUSSET, BROWN

CHAPTER 33

Vss. 1-11. KINDNESS OF JACOB AND ESAU. **1. behold, Esau came, and with him four hundred men**—Jacob having crossed the ford and ranged his wives and children in order—the dearest last, that they might be the least exposed to danger—awaited the expected interview. His faith was strengthened and his fears gone (Ps. 27:3). Having had power to prevail with God, he was confident of the same power with man, according to the promise (cf. ch. 32:28).

3. he bowed himself . . . seven times—The manner of doing this is by looking towards a superior and bowing with the upper part of the body brought parallel to the ground, then advancing a

ADAM CLARKE

CHAPTER 33

1. *Behold, Esau came, and with him four hundred men.* It has been generally supposed that Esau came with an intention to destroy his brother, and for that purpose brought with him 400 armed men. But (1) There is no kind of evidence of this pretended hostility. (2) There is no proof that the 400 men that Esau brought with him were at all armed. (3) But there is every proof that he acted towards his brother, Jacob, with all openness and candor and with such a forgetfulness of past injuries as none but a great mind could have been capable of. Why then should the character of this man be perpetually vilified? Here is the secret. With some people, on the most ungrounded assumption, Esau is a reprobate and the type and figure of all reprobates, and therefore he must be everything that is bad.

2. *He put the handmaids and their children foremost.* There is something so artificial in this arrangement of Jacob's family that it must have had some peculiar design. Was Jacob still apprehensive of danger, and put those foremost

MATTHEW HENRY

2. Esau embraced Jacob (*v.* 4): *He ran to meet him*, not in passion, but in love; and, as one heartily reconciled to him. If there was not some wonderful change wrought upon the spirit of Esau at this time, I see not how wrestling Jacob could be said to obtain such power with men as to denominate him a *prince*. God has the hearts of all men in his hands, and can turn them when and how he pleases, by a secret, silent, but resistless power. He can, of a sudden, convert enemies into friends, as he did two Sauls, one by restraining grace (1 Sam. xxvi. 21, 25), the other by renewing grace, Acts ix. 21, 22.

They both wept. Jacob wept for joy, to be thus kindly received by his brother, and Esau perhaps wept for grief and shame.

Verses 5–15

We have here the discourse between the two brothers at their meeting. They converse,

I. About Jacob's retinue, *v.* 5–7. Eleven or twelve little ones, the eldest of them not fourteen years old, followed Jacob closely: *Who are these?* says Esau. Jacob returns a serious answer: They are *the children which God hath graciously given thy servant*. Jacob speaks of his children as God's gifts; they are a *heritage of the Lord*, Ps. cxxviii. 3; cxii. 9; cvii. 41.

II. About the present he had sent him.

1. Esau modestly refused it because he had enough, and did not need it, *v.* 9. It is a good thing for those that have much to know that they have enough, though they have not so much as some others have. Even Esau can say, *I have enough*.

2. Jacob affectionately urges him to accept it, and prevails, *v.* 10, 11. Jacob sent it, through fear (*ch.* xxxii. 20), but, the fear being over, he now importunes his acceptance of it for love, to show that he desires his brother's friendship, and did not merely dread his wrath. It is a very high compliment that he passes upon him: *I have seen thy face, as though I had seen the face of God*. The meaning is that Jacob saw God's favour to him in Esau's: it was a token for good to him that God had accepted his prayers. The competency he had of this world's goods: *God has dealt graciously with me*. "And *I have enough*; I have *all*," so the word is. Esau's enough was much, but Jacob's enough was all. He has all in prospect; he will have all shortly, when he comes to heaven: upon this principle Jacob urged Esau, and he took his present.

III. About the progress of their journey. 1. Esau offers himself to be his guide and companion, in token of sincere reconciliation, *v.* 12. Esau has become fond of Jacob's company, courts him to Mount Seir: let us never despair of any, nor distrust God in whose hand all hearts are. Yet Jacob saw cause modestly to refuse this offer (*v.* 13, 14), wherein he shows a tender concern for his own family and flocks, like a good shepherd and a good father. He must consider the children, and the flocks with young, and not lead the one, nor drive the other, too fast. This prudence and tenderness of Jacob ought to be imitated by those that have the care and charge of young people in the things of God. They must not be over-driven, at first, by heavy tasks in religious services, but led, as they can bear, having their work made as easy to them as possible. Christ, the good Shepherd, does so, Isa. xl. 11. 2. Esau offers some of his men to be his guard and convoy, *v.* 15. (1) Jacob is humble, and needs it not for state. (2) Jacob is under the divine protection, and needs it not for safety.

Verses 16–20

Here, 1. Having in a friendly manner parted with Esau, who had gone to his own country (*v.* 16), he comes to a place where, it should seem, he rested for some time. The place was afterwards known by the name of Succoth, a city in the tribe of Gad, on the other side Jordan (it signifies *booths*), that when his posterity afterwards dwelt in houses of stone, they might remember that *the Syrian ready to perish* was their father, who was glad of booths (Deut. xxvi. 5). 2. He comes to Shechem; we read it, to *Shalem, a city of Shechem*. After a perilous journey, in which he had met with many difficulties, he came safely, at last, into Canaan. Here, (1) He buys a field, *v.* 19. Though the land of Canaan was his by promise, yet, the time for taking possession not having yet come, he is content to pay for his own. (2) He builds an altar, *v.* 20. [1] In thankfulness to God. [2] That he might keep up the worship of God, in his family. Where we have a tent God must have an altar, where we have a house he must have a church in it. He dedicated this altar to the honour of *El-elohe-Israel—God, the God of Israel*. God had lately called him by the name of *Israel*, and now he calls God *the God of Israel*; though he is styled *a prince with God*, God shall still be a prince with him, his Lord and his God.

JAMIESON, FAUSSET, BROWN

few steps and bowing again, and repeating his obeisance till, at the seventh time, the suppliant stands in the immediate presence of his superior. The members of his family did the same. This was a token of profound respect, and, though very marked, it would appear natural; for Esau being the elder brother, was, according to the custom of the East, entitled to respectful treatment from his younger brother. His attendants would be struck by it, and according to Eastern habits, would magnify it in the hearing of their master. **4. Esau ran to meet him**—What a sudden and surprising change! Whether the sight of the princely present and the profound homage of Jacob had produced this effect, or it proceeded from the impulsive character of Esau, the cherished enmity of twenty years in a moment disappeared; the weapons of war were laid aside, and the warmest tokens of mutual affection reciprocated between the brothers. But doubtless, the efficient cause was the secret, subduing influence of grace (Prov. 21:1), which converted Esau from an enemy into a friend. **5. Who are those with thee?**—It might have been enough to say, They are my children; but Jacob was a pious man, and he could not give even a common answer but in the language of piety (Ps. 127:3; 113:9; 107:41).

11. He urged him and he took it—In the East the acceptance by a superior is a proof of friendship, and by an enemy, of reconciliation. It was on both accounts Jacob was so anxious that his brother should receive the cattle; and in Esau's acceptance he had the strongest proofs of a good feeling being established that Eastern notions admit of.

12-20. THE PARTING. **12. And he said, Let us take our journey**—Esau proposed to accompany Jacob and his family through the country, both as a mark of friendship and as an escort to guard them. But the proposal was prudently declined. Jacob did not need any worldly state or equipage. Notwithstanding the present cordiality, the brothers were so different in spirit, character, and habits—the one so much a man of the world, and the other a man of God, that there was great risk of something occurring to disturb the harmony. Jacob having alleged a very reasonable excuse for the tardiness of his movements, the brothers parted in peace. **14. until come unto my lord**—It seems to have been Jacob's intention, passing round the Dead Sea, to visit his brother in Seir, and thus, without crossing the Jordan, go to Beersheba to Isaac; but he changed his plan, and whether the intention was carried out then or at a future period has not been recorded.

17. Jacob journeyed to Succoth—i.e., "booths," that being the first station at which Jacob halted on his arrival in Canaan. His posterity, when dwelling in houses of stone, built a city there and called it Succoth, to commemorate the fact that their ancestor, "a Syrian ready to perish," was glad to dwell in booths. **18. Shalem**—i.e., "peace"; and the meaning may be that Jacob came into Canaan, arriving safe and sound at the city Shechem—a tribute to Him who had promised such a return (cf. ch. 28:15). But most writers take Shalem as a proper name—a city of Shechem, and the site is marked by one of the little villages about two miles to the northeast. A little further in the valley below Shechem "he bought a parcel of a field, where he spread his tent," thus being the first of the patriarchs who became a proprietor of land in Canaan. **19. an hundred pieces of money**—pieces, lit., "lambs"; probably a coin with the figure of a lamb on it. **20. and he erected . . . an altar**—A beautiful proof of his personal piety, a most suitable conclusion to his journey, and a lasting memorial of a distinguished favor in the name "God, the God of Israel." Wherever we pitch a tent, God shall have an altar.

ADAM CLARKE

whom he least esteemed, that if the foremost met with any evil, those who were behind might escape on their swift beasts? Or did he intend to keep his choicest treasure to the last, and exhibit his beautiful *Rachel* and favorite *Joseph* after Esau had seen all the rest, in order to make the deeper impression on his mind?

4. *Esau ran to meet him*. How sincere and genuine is this conduct of Esau, and at the same time how magnanimous! He had buried all his resentment, and forgotten all his injuries; and receives his brother with the strongest demonstrations, not only of forgiveness, but of fraternal affection. *And kissed him*. In the Masoretic Bibles each letter of this word is noted with a point over it to make it emphatic. And by this kind of notation the rabbins wished to draw the attention of the reader to the change that had taken place in Esau and the sincerity with which he received his brother, Jacob.

10. *Receive my present at my hand*. Jacob could not be certain that he had found favor with Esau unless the present had been received; for in accepting it Esau necessarily became his friend, according to the custom of those times and in that country. In the Eastern countries, if your present be received by your superior, you may rely on his friendship; if it be not received, you have everything to fear.

14. *Until I come unto my lord unto Seir*. It is very likely that Jacob was perfectly sincere in his expressed purpose of visiting Esau at Seir, but it is as likely that circumstances afterwards occurred that rendered it either improper or impracticable; and we find that Esau afterwards removed to Canaan, and he and Jacob dwelt there together for several years.

17. *Journeyed to Succoth*. So called from *succoth*, the "booths" or "tents" which Jacob erected there for the resting and convenience of his family, who in all probability continued there for some considerable time.

18. *And Jacob came to Shalem, a city of Shechem*. The word *shalem*, in the Samaritan *shalom*, should be translated here "in peace," or "in safety." After resting some time at Succoth, which was necessary for the safety of his flocks and the comfort of his family, he got safely to a city of Shechem, in health of body, without any loss of his cattle or servants, his wives and children being also in safety. Coverdale and Matthews translate this word as above, and with them agree the Chaldee and the Arabic; it is not likely to have been the name of a city, as it is nowhere else to be found.

20. *And he erected there an altar*. It appears that Jacob had a very correct notion of the providence and mercy of God; hence he says, v. 5: "The children which God hath graciously given thy servant"; and in v. 11 he attributes all his substance to the bounty of his Maker: "Take, I pray thee, my blessing . . . because God hath dealt graciously with me, and because I have enough." Hence he viewed God as the God of all grace, and to Him he erected an altar, dedicating it to "God, the God of Israel," referring to the change of his own name, and the mercies which he then received; and hence perhaps it would be best to translate the words, "The strong God [is] the God of Israel"; as by the power of His grace and goodness He had rescued, defended, blessed, and supported him from his youth up until now. The erecting altars with particular names appears in other places; so, Exod. xvii. 15, Moses calls his altar *Jehovah-nissi*, "the Lord is my banner."

(1) "When a man's ways please the Lord, he maketh even his enemies to be at peace with him." When Jacob had got reconciled to God, God reconciled his brother to him. The hearts of all men are in the hands of God, and He turns them howsoever He will.

(2) Since the time in which Jacob wrestled with the Angel of the covenant, we see in him much dependence on God, accompanied with a spirit of deep humility and gratitude. God's grace alone can change the heart of man, and it is by that grace only that we get a sense of our obligations; this lays us in the dust, and the more we receive the lower we shall lie.

MATTHEW HENRY

CHAPTER 34

Verses 1–5

Dinah, Jacob's only daughter, is reckoned now but fifteen or sixteen years of age when she here occasioned so much mischief. Observe, 1. Her vain curiosity. She went to *see*, yet that was not all, she went to be *seen* too; she went to see the daughters of the land, but, it may be, with some thoughts of the sons of the land too. I doubt she went to get an acquaintance with those Canaanites, and to learn their way. 2. The loss of her honour by this means (*v.* 2). Dinah went abroad to look about her; but, if she had looked about her as she ought, she would not have fallen into this snare. 3. The court Shechem made to her, after he had defiled her. 4. The tidings brought to poor Jacob, *v.* 5. The good man *held his peace*, as one astonished, that knows not what to say. He had left the management of his affairs very much (too much I doubt) to his sons, and he would do nothing without them. Note, Things never go well when the authority of a parent runs low in a family.

Verses 6–17

Jacob's sons, when they heard of the injury done to Dinah, showed a very great resentment of it, influenced perhaps rather by jealousy for the honour of their family than by a sense of virtue. Many are concerned at the shamefulness of sin that never lay to heart the sinfulness of it. It is here called *folly in Israel* (*v.* 7). Note, 1. Uncleanness is folly; for it sacrifices the favour of God, peace of conscience, and all the soul can pretend to that is sacred and honourable, to a base and brutish lust. 2. This folly is most shameful in *Israel*, in a family of Israel, where God is known and worshipped.

Hamor came to treat with Jacob himself, but he turns him over to his sons; and here we have a particular account of the treaty, in which the Canaanites were more honest than the Israelites.

I. Hamor and Shechem fairly propose this match, in order to a coalition in trade. Shechem is deeply in love with Dinah; he will have her upon any terms, *v.* 11, 12. His father not only consents, but solicits for him, and gravely insists upon the advantages that would follow from the union of the families, *v.* 9, 10.

II. Jacob's sons basely pretend to insist upon a coalition in religion, when really they designed nothing less. Jacob's sons meditate only revenge. The Shechemites must be circumcised; not to make them holy (they never intended that), but to make them sore, that they might become an easier prey to their sword. 1. The pretence was specious. 2. The intention was malicious, as appears by the sequel of the story; all they aimed at was to prepare them for the day of slaughter. Religion is never more injured, nor are God's sacraments more profaned, than when they are thus used for a cloak of maliciousness.

Verses 18–24

1. Hamor and Shechem gave consent themselves to be circumcised, *v.* 18, 19. To this perhaps they were moved by what they might have heard of the sacred and honourable intentions of this sign, in the family of Abraham, which, it is probable, they had some confused notions. Note, Many who know little of religion, yet know so much of it as makes them willing to join themselves with those that are religious. Jacob's sons were industrious thriving people, and promised themselves and their neighbours advantage by an alliance with them; it would improve ground and trade, and bring money into their country. Now, (1) It was bad enough to marry upon this principle. (2) It was worse to be circumcised upon this principle. There are many with whom gain is godliness, and who are more governed and influenced by their secular interest than by any principle of their religion.

Verses 25–31

Simeon and Levi, two of Jacob's sons, young men not much above twenty years old, cutting the throats of the Shechemites, and thereby breaking the heart of their good father.

I. The barbarous murder of the Shechemites.

1. Slaying the inhabitants of Shechem—*all the males*, Hamor and Shechem particularly, with whom they had been treating in a friendly manner but the other day, yet with a design upon their lives. Note, As nothing secures us better than true religion, so nothing exposes us more than religion only pretended to. But Simeon and Levi were most unrighteous. (1) It was true that Shechem had *wrought folly against Israel*, in defiling Dinah; but it ought to have been considered how far Dinah herself had been accessory to it. (2) It was true that Shechem had done ill;

JAMIESON, FAUSSET, BROWN

CHAPTER 34

Vss. 1-31. THE DISHONOR OF DINAH. **1-4.** Though freed from foreign troubles, Jacob met with a great domestic calamity in the fall of his only daughter. According to Josephus, she had been attending a festival; but it is highly probable that she had been often and freely mixing in the society of the place and that she, being a simple, inexperienced, and vain young woman, had been flattered by the attentions of the ruler's son. There must have been time and opportunities of acquaintance to produce the strong attachment that Shechem had for her. **5. Jacob held his peace**—Jacob, as a father and a good man, must have been deeply distressed. But he could do little. In the case of a family by different wives, it is not the father, but the full brothers, on whom the protection of the daughters devolves—they are the guardians of a sister's welfare and the avengers of her wrongs. It was for this reason that Simeon and Levi, the two brothers of Dinah by Leah, appear the chief actors in this episode; and though the two fathers would have probably brought about an amicable arrangement of the affair, the hasty arrival of these enraged brothers introduced a new element into the negotiations. **6. Hamor**—i.e., "ass"; and it is a striking proof of the very different ideas which, in the East, are associated with that animal, which there appears sprightly, well proportioned, and of great activity. This chief is called Emmor (Acts 7:16). **7. the men were grieved, and . . . very wroth**—Good men in such a case could not but grieve; but it would have been well if their anger had been less, or that they had known the precept "let not the sun go down upon your wrath." No injury can justify revenge (Deut. 32:35; Rom. 12:9); but Jacob's sons planned a scheme of revenge in the most deceitful manner. **8. Hamor communed with them**—The prince and his son seem at first sight to have acted honestly, and our feelings are enlisted on their side. They betray no jealousy of the powerful shepherds; on the contrary, they show every desire to establish friendly intercourse. But their conduct was unjustifiable in neither expressing regret nor restoring Dinah to her family; and this great error was the true cause of the negotiations ending in so unhappy a manner. **11. Shechem said unto her father . . . and brethren**—The consideration of the proposal for marriage belonged to Jacob, and he certainly showed great weakness in yielding so much to the fiery impetuosity of his sons. The sequel shows the unhappy consequences of that concession. **12. Ask me never so much dowry and gift**—The gift refers to the presents made at betrothal, both to the bride elect and her relations (cf. ch. 24:53), the dowry to a suitable settlement upon her. **13. The sons of Jacob answered**—The honor of their family consisted in having the sign of the covenant. Circumcision was the external rite by which persons were admitted members of the ancient Church. But that outward rite could not make the Shechemites true Israelites; and yet it does not appear that Jacob's sons required anything more. Nothing is said of their teaching the people to worship the true God, but only of their insisting on their being circumcised; and it is evident that they did not seek to convert Shechem, but only made a show of religion—a cloak to cover their diabolical design. Hypocrisy and deceit, in all cases vicious, are infinitely more so when accompanied with a show of religion; and here the sons of Jacob, under the pretense of conscientious scruples, conceal a scheme of treachery as cruel and diabolical as was, perhaps, ever perpetrated. **20. Hamor and Shechem . . . came unto the gate of their city**—That was the place where every public communication was made; and in the ready obsequious submission of the people to this measure we see an evidence either of the extraordinary affection for the governing family, or of the abject despotism of the East, where the will of a chief is an absolute command.

ADAM CLARKE

CHAPTER 34

1. *And Dinah . . . went out to see the daughters of the land.* It is supposed that Jacob had been now about seven or eight years in the land, and that Dinah, who was about seven years of age when Jacob came to Canaan, was now about fourteen or fifteen. Why or on what occasion she went out we know not, but the reason given by Josephus is very probable, namely, that it was on one of their festivals.

2. *Prince of the country.* I.e., Hamor was prince; Shechem was the son of the prince or chief.

3. *Spake kindly unto the damsel.* Literally, "he spake to the heart of the damsel"—endeavored to gain her affections, and to reconcile her to her disgrace. It appears sufficiently evident from this and the preceding verse that there had been no consent on the part of Dinah, that the whole was an act of violence, and that she was now detained by force in the house of Shechem. Here she was found when Simeon and Levi sacked the city, v. 26.

7. *He had wrought folly in Israel.* The land, afterwards generally called "Israel," was not as yet so named; and the sons of Jacob were called neither Israel, Israelites, nor Jews, till long after this. How then can it be said that Shechem had *wrought folly in Israel?* The words are capable of a more literal translation: "against Israel." Shechem wrought folly against *Israel*, the prince of God, in lying with the daughter of Jacob. Here both the names are given; *Jacob*, whose daughter was defiled, and *Israel*, the "prince of God," against whom the offense was committed.

12. *Ask me never so much dowry.* See the law relative to this, Exod. xxii. 16-17.

13. *Answered . . . deceitfully.* Which nothing could excuse; yet, to show that they had had much provocation, it is immediately subjoined, "they spoke thus because he had defiled Dinah their sister"; for so this parenthesis should be read.

14. *That were a reproach unto us.* Because the uncircumcised were not in the covenant of God; and to have given an heiress of the promise to one who had no kind of right to its spiritual blessings, from whom might spring children who would naturally walk in the way of their father, would have been absurd, reproachful, and wicked. Thus far they were perfectly right; but to make this holy principle a cloak for their deceitful and murderous purposes was the full sum of all wickedness.

17. *Then will we take our daughter, and we will be gone.* It is natural to suppose that the tribe of Hamor was very inconsiderable, else they would not have sought an alliance with the family of Jacob, and have come so readily into a painful, disgraceful measure, without having either the sanction of divine authority or reason; for it does not appear that the sons of Jacob urged either. And they are threatened here that, if they do not agree to be circumcised, Dinah shall be taken from them and restored to her family; and this is probably what the Shechemites saw they had not power at present to prevent.

23. *Shall not their cattle and their substance . . . be ours?* This was a bait held out for the poor, unsuspecting people of Hamor by their prince and his son, who were not much less deceived than the people themselves.

24. *Every male was circumcised.* These simple people must have had very great affection for their chief and his son, or have been under the influence of the most passive obedience, to have come so readily into this measure, and to have submitted to this rite. But the petty princes in Asiatic countries have ever been absolute and despotic, their subjects paying them the most prompt and blind obedience.

25. *On the third day, when they were sore.* When the inflammation was at the height, and a fever ensued which rendered the person utterly helpless, and his state critical, *Simeon and Levi*, the brothers of Dinah, *took each man his sword*, probably assisted by that portion of the servants which helped them to take care of the flock, *came upon the city boldly*, "securely"—without being suspected, and being in no danger of meeting with resistance—*and slew all the males.* Great as the provocation was, and it

MATTHEW HENRY

but he was endeavouring to atone for it, and was as honest and honourable, *ex post facto—after the deed*, as the case would admit. (3) It was true that Shechem had done ill; but what was that to all the Shechemites? Must the innocent fall with the guilty? (4) But that which above all aggravated the cruelty was the most perfidious treachery that was in it.

2. Seizing the prey of Shechem, and plundering the town. The Shechemites were willing to gratify the sons of Jacob by submitting to the penance of circumcision, upon this principle, *Shall not their cattle and their substance be ours?* (*v.* 23), and see what was the issue; instead of making themselves masters of the wealth of Jacob's family, Jacob's family become masters of their wealth.

II. Here is Jacob's resentment of this bloody deed of Simeon and Levi, *v.* 30. Two things he bitterly complains of:—1. The reproach they had brought upon him thereby: What will they say of us and our religion? 2. The ruin they had exposed him to. What could be expected, but that the Canaanites, who were numerous and formidable, would confederate against him, and he and his little family would become an easy prey to them? Note, When sin is in the house, there is reason to fear ruin at the door. One would think this should have made them to relent, but, instead of this, they justify themselves, and give him this insolent reply, *Should he deal with our sister as with a harlot?*

JAMIESON, FAUSSET, BROWN

30. Jacob said . . . Ye have troubled me—This atrocious outrage perpetrated on the defenseless citizens and their families made the cup of Jacob's affliction overflow. We may wonder that, in speaking of it to his sons, he did not represent it as a heinous sin, an atrocious violation of the laws of God and man, but dwelt solely on the present consequences. It was probably because that was the only view likely to rouse the cold-blooded apathy, the hardened consciences of those ruffian sons. Nothing but the restraining power of God saved him and his family from the united vengeance of the people (cf. ch. 35:5). All his sons had not been engaged in the massacre. Joseph was a boy, Benjamin not yet born, and the other eight not concerned in it. Simeon and Levi alone, with their retainers, had been the guilty actors in the bloody tragedy. But the Canaanites would not be discriminating in their vengeance; and if *all* the Shechemites were put to death for the offense of their chief's son, what wonder if the natives should extend their hatred to all the family of Jacob; and who probably equalled, in number, the inhabitants of that village.

ADAM CLARKE

certainly was very great, this was an act of unparalleled treachery and cruelty.

27. *The sons of Jacob.* The rest of Jacob's sons, the remaining brothers of Simeon and Levi, spoiled the city. Though the others could slay the defenseless males, it was not likely that they could have carried away all the booty, with the women, children, and cattle; it is therefore most natural to suppose that the rest of the sons of Jacob assisted at last in the business.

30. *Ye have troubled me.* Brought my mind into great distress, and endangered my personal safety; *to make me to stink*—to render me odious to the surrounding tribes, so that there is every reason to suspect that when this deed is come abroad they will join in a confederacy against me and extirpate my whole family. And had he not been under the peculiar protection of God, this in all human probability would have been the case; but he had prevailed with God, and he was also to prevail with men. That Jacob's resentment was not dissembled we have the fullest proof in his depriving these two sons of the birthright, which otherwise they had doubtless enjoyed. See chap. xlix. 5, 7.

31. *Should he deal with our sister as with an harlot?* On this outrage alone they vindicated their flagitious conduct. The word *harlot* first occurs here. The original is not *pilegesh*, which we render "concubine," but *zonah*, which ordinarily signifies "one who prostitutes herself to any person for hire."

MATTHEW HENRY

CHAPTER 35

Verses 1–5

I. God reminds Jacob of his vow at Beth-el, and sends him thither to perform it, *v.* 1. Jacob had said in the day of his distress, *If I come again in peace, this stone shall be God's house, ch.* xxviii. 22. Seven or eight years it was now since he came to Canaan; he had purchased ground there, and had built an altar in remembrance of God's last appearance to him when he called him *Israel* (*ch.* xxxiii. 19, 20); but still Beth-el is forgotten. Note, 1. As many as God loves he will remind of neglected duties, one way or other, by conscience or by providences. 2. When we have vowed a vow to God, it is best not to defer the payment of it (Eccles. v. 4), yet better late than never. In Beth-el, the house of God, we should desire to dwell, Ps. xxvii. 4. That should be our home, not our inn. God reminds him not expressly of his vow, but of the occasion of it: *When thou fleddest from the face of Esau.*

II. Jacob commands his household to prepare for this solemnity; not only for the journey and remove, but for the religious services that were to be performed, *v.* 2, 3. Observe the commands he gives his household, like Abraham, ch. xviii. 19. 1. They must *put away the strange gods.* Strange gods in Jacob's family! Strange things indeed! Could such a family, that was taught the good knowledge of the Lord, admit them? In those families where there is a face of religion, and an altar to God, yet many times there is much amiss, and more strange gods than one would suspect. 2. They must be clean, and *change their garments.* Simeon and Levi had their hands full of blood, it concerned them particularly to wash, and to put off their garments that were so stained. These were but ceremonies, signifying the purification and change of the heart. What are clean clothes, and new clothes, without a clean heart, and a new heart? 3. They must go with him to Bethel, *v.* 3.

JAMIESON, FAUSSET, BROWN

CHAPTER 35

Vss. 1-15. REMOVAL TO BETHEL. **1. God said unto Jacob, Arise,** etc.—This command was given seasonably in point of time and tenderly in respect of language. The disgraceful and perilous events that had recently taken place in the patriarch's family must have produced in him a strong desire to remove without delay from the vicinity of Shechem. Borne down by an overwhelming sense of the criminality of his two sons—of the offense they had given to God and the dishonor they had brought on the true faith; distracted, too, with anxiety about the probable consequences which their outrage might bring upon himself and family, should the Canaanite people combine to extirpate such a band of robbers and murderers; he must have felt this call as affording a great relief to his afflicted feelings. At the same time it conveyed a tender rebuke. **go up to Bethel**—Bethel was about thirty miles south of Shechem and was an ascent from a low to a highland country. There, he would not only be released from the painful associations of the latter place but be established on a spot that would revive the most delightful and sublime recollections. The pleasure of revisiting it, however, was not altogether unalloyed. **make there an altar unto God, that appeared**—It too frequently happens that early impressions are effaced through lapse of time, that promises made in seasons of distress, are forgotten; or, if remembered on the return of health and prosperity, there is not the same alacrity and sense of obligation felt to fulfil them. Jacob was lying under that charge. He had fallen into spiritual indolence. It was now eight or ten years since his return to Canaan. He had effected a comfortable settlement and had acknowledged the divine mercies, by which that return and settlement had been signally distinguished (cf. ch. 33:19). But for some unrecorded reason, his early vow at Bethel, in a great crisis of his life, remained unperformed. The Lord appeared now to remind him of his neglected duty, in terms, however, so mild, as awakened less the memory of his fault, than of the kindness of his heavenly Guardian; and how much Jacob felt the touching nature of the appeal to that memorable scene at Bethel, appears in the immediate preparations he made to *arise* and *go up* thither (Ps. 66:13). **2. Then Jacob said unto his household . . . Put away the strange gods that are among you**—*Hebrew*, "gods of the stranger," of foreign nations. Jacob had brought, in his service, a number of Mesopotamian retainers, who were addicted to superstitious practices; and there is some reason to fear that the same high testimony as to the religious superintendence of his household could not have been borne of him as was done of Abraham (ch. 18:19). He might have been too negligent hitherto in winking at these evils in his servants; or, perhaps, it was not till his arrival in Canaan, that he had learnt, for the first time, that one nearer and dearer to him was secretly infected with the same corruption (ch. 31:34). Be that as it

ADAM CLARKE

CHAPTER 35

1. *Arise, go up to Beth-el.* The transaction that had lately taken place rendered it unsafe for Jacob to dwell any longer at the city of Shechem; and it seems that while he was reflecting on the horrible act of Simeon and Levi, and not knowing what to do, God graciously appeared to him and commanded him to go up to Beth-el, build an altar there, and thus perform the vow he had made, chap. xxviii. 20, 22.

2. *Put away the strange gods.* "The gods of the foreigners." Jacob's servants were all Syrians, and no doubt were addicted more or less to idolatry and superstition. These gods might belong to them, or, as some have conjectured, they were the *teraphim* which Rachel stole. But it is more natural to suppose that these gods found now in Jacob's family were images of silver, gold, or curious workmanship, which were found among the spoils of the city of Shechem. Lest these should become incitements to idolatry, Jacob orders them to be put away. *Be clean, and change your garments.* Personal or outward purification, as emblematical of the sanctification of the soul, has been in use among all the true worshipers of God from the beginning of the world.

3. *Answered me in the day of my distress.* Not only when he fled from the face of his brother, but more particularly when he was in his greatest strait at the brook of Jabbok.

MATTHEW HENRY

III. His family surrendered all they had that was idolatrous or superstitious, *v.* 4. Jacob took care to bury their images, that they might not afterwards find them and return to them.

IV. He removes without molestation from Shechem to Bethel, *v.* 5. *The terror of God was upon the cities.* Note, The way of duty is the way of safety. While there was sin in Jacob's house, he was afraid of his neighbours; but now that the strange gods were put away, and they were all going together to Bethel, his neighbours were afraid of him.

Verses 6–15

Jacob and his retinue having safely arrived at Bethel, we are here told what passed there.

I. There he built an altar (*v.* 7), and offered sacrifice upon it. With these sacrifices he joined praises for former mercies. And he called the place (that is, *the altar*) *El-beth-el, the God of Bethel.* Note, The comfort which the saints have in holy ordinances is not so much from *Bethel, the house of God,* as from *El-beth-el, the God of the house.* The ordinances are but empty things if we do not meet with God in them.

II. There he buried Deborah, Rebekah's nurse, *v.* 8. Rebekah probably was dead, but her old nurse (of whom mention is made *ch.* xxiv. 59) survived her. Honour was done to this nurse, at her death, by Jacob's family, though she was not related to them, and though she was aged. Family afflictions may come even when family reformation and religion are on foot.

III. There God appeared to him (*v.* 9), to own his altar, to answer to the name by which he had called him, *The God of Bethel* (*v.* 7), and to comfort him under his affliction, *v.* 8. He renewed and ratified the covenant with him, by the name *El-Shaddai. I am God Almighty, God all-sufficient* (*v.* 11), able to make good the promise in due time. Two things are promised, 1. That he should be the father of a great nation. 2. That he should be the master of a good land (*v.* 12). He shall not have children without an estate, which is often the case of the poor, nor an estate without children, which is often the grief of the rich; but both. These two promises had a spiritual signification, for, without doubt, Christ is the promised seed, and heaven is the promised land. He then went up from him, or *from over him,* in some visible display of glory, which had hovered over him while he talked with him, *v.* 13.

IV. There Jacob erected a memorial of this, *v.* 14. He set up a pillar. In token of his intending it for a sacred memorial of his communion with God, he poured oil and the other ingredients of a drink-offering upon it. His vow was, *This stone shall be God's house,* that is, shall be set up for his honour, as houses to the praise of their builders.

JAMIESON, FAUSSET, BROWN

may, he resolved on an immediate and thorough reformation of his household; and in commanding them to put away the strange gods, he added, "be clean, and change your garments"; as if some defilement, from contact with idolatry, should still remain about them. In the law of Moses, many ceremonial purifications were ordained and observed by persons who had contracted certain defilements, and without the observance of which, they were reckoned unclean and unfit to join in the social worship of God. These bodily purifications were purely figurative; and as sacrifices were offered before the law, so also were external purifications, as appears from the words of Jacob; hence it would seem that types and symbols were used from the fall of man, representing and teaching the two great doctrines of revealed truth—viz., the atonement of Christ and the sanctification of our nature. **4. they gave unto Jacob all the strange gods . . . and earrings**—Strange gods—the seraphim (cf. ch. 31:30), as well, perhaps, as other idols acquired among the Shechemite spoil—earrings of various forms, sizes, and materials, which are universally worn in the East, and, then as now, connected with incantation and idolatry (cf. Hos. 2:13). The decided tone which Jacob now assumed was the probable cause of the alacrity with which those favorite objects of superstition were surrendered. **Jacob hid them under the oak**—or terebinth—a towering tree, which, like all others of the kind, was a striking object in the scenery of Palestine; and beneath which, at Shechem, the patriarch had pitched his tent. He hid the images and amulets, delivered to him by his Mesopotamian dependents, at the root of this tree. The oak being deemed a consecrated tree, to bury them at its root was to deposit them in a place where no bold hand would venture to disturb the ground; and hence it was called from this circumstance—"the plain of Meonenim"—i.e., the oak of enchantments" (Judg. 9:37); and from the great stone which Joshua set up—"the oak of the pillar" (Judg. 9:6). **5. the terror of God was upon the cities**—There was every reason to apprehend that a storm of indignation would burst from all quarters upon Jacob's family, and that the Canaanite tribes would have formed one united plan of revenge. But a supernatural panic seized them; and thus, for the sake of the "heir of the promise," the protecting shield of Providence was specially held over his family. **6. So Jacob came to Luz . . . that is, Bethel**—It is probable that this place was unoccupied ground when Jacob first went to it; and that after that period [CALVIN], the Canaanites built a town, to which they gave the name of Luz, from the profusion of almond trees that grew around. The name of Bethel, which would, of course, be confined to Jacob and his family, did not supersede the original one, till long after. It is now identified with the modern Beitin and lies on the western slope of the mountain on which Abraham built his altar (Gen. 12:8). **7. El-Beth-el**—i.e., "the God of Bethel." **8. Deborah, Rebekah's nurse, died**—This event seems to have taken place before the solemnities were commenced. Deborah, a "bee," supposing her to have been fifty years on coming to Canaan, had attained the great age of 180. When she was removed from Isaac's household to Jacob's, is unknown. But it probably was on his return from Mesopotamia; and she would have been of invaluable service to his young family. Old nurses, like her, were not only honored, but loved as mothers; and, accordingly, her death was the occasion of great lamentation. She was buried under *the* oak—hence called "the terebinth of tears" (cf. I Kings 13:14). God was pleased to make a new appearance to him after the solemn rites of devotion were over. By this manifestation of His presence, God testified His acceptance of Jacob's sacrifice and renewed the promise of the blessings guaranteed to Abraham and Isaac; and the patriarch observed the ceremony with which he had formerly consecrated the place, comprising a sacramental cup, along with the oil that he poured on the pillar, and reimposing the memorable name. The whole scene was in accordance with the character of the patriarchal dispensation, in which the great truths of religion were exhibited to the senses, and "the world's grey fathers" taught in a manner suited to the weakness of an infantine condition. **13. God went up from him**—The presence of God was indicated in some visible form and His acceptance of the sacrifice shown by the miraculous descent of fire from heaven, consuming it on the altar.

16-27. BIRTH OF BENJAMIN—DEATH OF RACHEL, etc. **16. they journeyed from Beth-el**—There can be no doubt that much enjoyment was experienced at Bethel, and that in the religious observances solemnized, as well as in the vivid recollections of the glorious vision seen there, the affections of

ADAM CLARKE

4. *And . . . earrings which were in their ears. Earrings* were worn as amulets and charms, first consecrated to some god, or formed under some constellation, on which magical characters and images were drawn.

5. *The terror of God.* A supernatural awe sent by the Almighty *was upon the cities that were round about,* so that they were not molested in their departure. This could be owing to nothing less than the especial providence of God.

7. *El-beth-el.* "The strong God, the house of the strong God."

8. *But Deborah Rebekah's nurse died.* She was sent with Rebekah when taken by Abraham's servant to be wife to Isaac, chap. xxiv. 59. How she came to be in Jacob's family, expositors are greatly puzzled to find out; but the text does not state that *she was in Jacob's family.* Her death is mentioned merely because Jacob and his family had now arrived at the place where she was buried, and the name of that place was called *Allon-bachuth,* "the oak of weeping," as it is likely her death had been greatly regretted, and a general and extraordinary mourning had taken place on the occasion. Of Rebekah's death we know nothing. After her counsel to her son, chap. xxvii. we hear no more of her history from the sacred writings, except of her burial in chap. xlix. 31. Her name is written in the dust. And is not this designed as a mark of the disapprobation of God? It seems strange that such an inconsiderable person as a nurse should be mentioned, when even the person she brought up is passed by unnoticed!

9. *God appeared unto Jacob again.* He appeared to him first at Shechem, when He commanded him to go to Beth-el; and now that he is arrived at the place, God appears to him the second time, and confirms to him the Abrahamic blessing. To Isaac and Jacob these frequent appearances of God were necessary, but they were not so to Abraham; for to him one word was sufficient—"Abraham believed God."

13. *And God went up from him.* This was not a vision, nor a strong mental impression, but a real manifestation of God. Jacob saw and heard Him speak, and before his eyes He *went up*—ascended to heaven. This was no doubt the future Saviour, the Angel of the covenant.

14. *A drink offering.* A "libation." These were afterwards very common in all countries. At first they consisted probably of water only, afterwards wine was used; see on Lev. vii. 1, etc. The *pillar* which Jacob set up was to commemorate the appearance of God to him; the *drink offering* and the *oil* were intended to express his gratitude and devotion to his Preserver. It was probably the same pillar which he had set up before, which had since been thrown down, and which he had consecrated afresh to God.

16. *There was but a little way to come to Ephrath. Ephrath,* called also Bethlehem, and Bethlehem Ephrata, was the birthplace of our blessed Redeemer. See its meaning, Matt. ii. 6.

MATTHEW HENRY

Verses 16–20

We have here the story of the death of Rachel, the beloved wife of Jacob. 1. She fell in travail by the way, not able to reach to Bethlehem, the next town, though they were near it. Her travail was to the life of the child, but to her own death. Her dying is here called *the departing of her soul.* Note, The death of the body is but the departure of the soul to the world of spirits. Her dying lips called her new-born son *Ben-oni, The son of my sorrow.* But Jacob, because he would not renew the sorrowful remembrance of the mother's death every time he called his son by his name, changed his name, and called him *Benjamin, The son of my right hand*; that is, "very dear to me, set on my right hand for a blessing, the support of my age, like the staff in my right hand." Jacob buried her near the place where she died. If the soul be at rest after death, it matters little where the body lies. Jacob set up a pillar upon her grave, so that it was known, long after, to be Rachel's sepulchre (1 Sam. x. 2), and Providence so ordered it that this place afterwards fell in the lot of Benjamin.

Verses 21–29

Here is, 1. Jacob's removal, *v.* 21. Immediately after the story of Rachel's death he is here called *Israel* (*v.* 21, 22), and not often so afterwards: the Jews say, "The historian does him this honour here because he bore that affliction with such admirable patience and submission to Providence." 2. The sin of Reuben. A piece of abominable wickedness it was that he was guilty of (*v.* 22). Though perhaps Bilhah was the greater criminal, and it is probable was abandoned by Jacob for it, yet Reuben's crime was so provoking that, for it, he lost his birthright and blessing, *ch.* xlix. 4. This was Reuben's sin, but it was Jacob's affliction. 3. A complete list of the sons of Jacob, now that Benjamin the youngest was born. This is the first time we have the names of these heads of the twelve tribes together.

4. The visit which Jacob made to his father Isaac at Hebron. Probably he did this now upon the death of Rebekah, by which Isaac was left solitary. 5. The age and death of Isaac are here recorded. Isaac, a mild quiet man, lived the longest of all the patriarchs. Particular notice is taken of the amicable agreement of Esau and Jacob, in solemnizing their father's funeral (*v.* 29), to show how wonderfully God had changed Esau's mind since he vowed his brother's murder immediately after his father's death, *ch.* xxvii. 41.

JAMIESON, FAUSSET, BROWN

the patriarch were powerfully animated and that he left the place a better and more devoted servant of God. When the solemnities were over, Jacob, with his family, pursued a route directly southward and they reached Ephrath, when they were plunged into mourning by the death of Rachel, who sank in childbirth, leaving a posthumous son. A very affecting death, considering how ardently the mind of Rachel had been set on offspring (cf. ch. 30:1). **18. She called his name Ben-oni**—The dying mother gave this name to her child, significant of her circumstances; but Jacob changed it into Benjamin. This is thought by some to have been originally Benjamin, "a son of days," i.e., of old age. But with its present ending it means "son of the right hand," i.e., particularly dear and precious. **19. Ephrath, which is Bethlehem**—The one the old, the other the later name, signifying "house of bread." **20. and Jacob set a pillar on her grave . . . unto this day**—The spot still marked out as the grave of Rachel exactly agrees with the Scriptural record, being about a mile from Bethlehem. Anciently it was surmounted by a pyramid of stones, but the present tomb is a Mohammedan erection. **22-26. Sons of Jacob . . . born to him in Padan-aram**—It is a common practice of the sacred historian to say of a company or body of men that which, though true of the majority, may not be applicable to every individual. (See Matt. 19:28; John 20:24; Heb. 11:13). Here is an example, for Benjamin was born in Canaan.

28, 29. DEATH OF ISAAC. **29. Isaac gave up the ghost**—The death of this venerable patriarch is here recorded by anticipation for it did not take place till fifteen years after Joseph's disappearance. Feeble and blind though he was, he lived to a very advanced age; and it is a pleasing evidence of the permanent reconciliation between Esau and Jacob that they met at Mamre to perform the funeral rites of their common father.

ADAM CLARKE

18. *As her soul was in departing.* "In the going away of her soul." *She called his name Ben-oni.* "The son of my sorrow," because of the hard labor she had in bringing him into the world; *but his father called him Benjamin,* "the son of my right hand," i.e., the son peculiarly dear to me.

20. *Jacob set a pillar upon her grave.* Was not this the origin of funeral monuments? In ancient times, and among rude nations, a heap of stones designated the burial place of the chief; many of these still remain in different countries. It is very likely from the circumstances of Jacob that a single stone constituted the *pillar* in this case.

21. *Tower of Edar.* Literally, "the tower of the flock," and so translated in Mic. iv. 8. By the "tower of the flock" we may understand a place built by the shepherds near to some well for the convenience of watering their flocks and keeping watch over them by night.

22. *And Israel heard it.* Not one word is added farther in the Hebrew text; but a break is left in the verse, opposite to which there is a Masoretic note, which simply states that there is a hiatus in the verse. This hiatus the Septuagint has thus supplied: "and it appeared evil in his sight." *Now the sons of Jacob were twelve.* Called afterwards the "twelve patriarchs," because they became heads or chiefs of numerous families or tribes, Acts vii. 8; and the people that descended from them are called the "twelve tribes," Acts xxvi. 7; Jas. i. 1. Twelve princes came from Ishmael, chap. xxv. 16, who were heads of families and tribes. And in reference to the twelve patriarchs, our Lord chose twelve apostles.

23. *The sons of Leah.* The children are arranged under their respective mothers, and not in order of their birth.

26. *Born to him in Padan-aram. I.e.,* all but Benjamin, who was born in Canaan, vv. 16-17. It is well known that Padan-aram is the same as Mesopotamia, and hence the Septuagint translate "Mesopotamia of Syria." The word signifies "between the two rivers." It is situated between the Euphrates and Tigris, having Assyria on the east, Arabia Deserta, with Babylonia, on the south, Syria on the west, and Armenia on the north.

27. *The city of Arbah, which is Hebron.* See chap. xxiii. 2. It has been conjectured that Jacob must have paid a visit to his father before this time, as previously to this he had been some years in Canaan; but now, as he was approaching to his end, Jacob is supposed to have gone to live with and comfort him in his declining days.

29. *Isaac gave up the ghost . . . and was gathered unto his people.* See on chap. xxv. 8. *Esau and Jacob buried him.* See chap. xxv. 9. Esau, as we have seen in chap. xxxiii, was thoroughly reconciled to his brother, Jacob, and now they both join in fraternal and filial affection to do the last kind office to their amiable father. It is generally allowed that the death of Isaac is mentioned here out of its chronological order, as several of the transactions mentioned in the succeeding chapters, especially xxxvii and xxxviii, must have happened during his life; but that the history of Joseph might not be disturbed, his death is anticipated in this place.

MATTHEW HENRY

CHAPTER 36

Verses 1–8

1. Concerning Esau himself, *v.* 1. He is called *Edom* (and again, *v.* 8), that name by which was perpetuated the remembrance of the foolish bargain he made, when he sold his birthright for *that red, that red pottage.* 2. Concerning his wives, and the children they bore him in the land of Canaan.

JAMIESON, FAUSSET, BROWN

CHAPTER 36

Vss. 1-43. POSTERITY OF ESAU. **1. these are the generations**—history of the leading men and events (cf. ch. 2:4). **Esau who is Edom**—A name applied to him in reference to the peculiar color of his skin at birth, rendered more significant by his inordinate craving for the *red* pottage and also by the fierce sanguinary character of his descendants (cf. Ezek. 25:12; Obad. 10). **2, 3. Esau took his wives of the daughters of Canaan**—There were three, mentioned under different names; for it is evident that Bashemath is the same as Mahalath (ch. 28:9), since they both stand in the relation of daughter to Ishmael and sister to Nebajoth; and hence it may be inferred that Adah is the same as Judith, Aholibamah as Bathsemath (ch. 26:34). It was not unusual for women, in that early age, to

ADAM CLARKE

CHAPTER 36

1. *These are the generations of Esau.* We have here the genealogy of Esau in his sons and grandsons, and also the genealogy of Seir the Horite. The genealogy of the sons of Esau, born in Canaan, is related in vv. 1-8; those of his grandchildren born in Seir, 9-19; those of Seir the Horite, 20-30. The generations of Esau are particularly marked, to show how exactly God fulfilled the promises He made to him, chaps. xxv and xxvii; and those of Seir the Horite are added, because his family became in some measure blended with that of Esau.

2. *His wives.* It appears that Esau's wives went by very different names. Aholibamah is named Judith, chap. xxvi. 34; Adah is called Bashemath in the same place; and she who is

MATTHEW HENRY

TODAY'S DICTIONARY OF THE BIBLE: Esau, at the age of forty years, to the great grief of his parents, married (Gen. 26:34, 35) two Canaanite maidens—Judith, the daughter of Beeri, and Bashemath, the daughter of Elon. When Jacob was sent away to Padan-aram, Esau tried to conciliate his parents (Gen. 28:8,9) by marrying his cousin Malalath, the daughter of Ishmael. This led him to cast in his lot with the Ishmaelite tribes; and driving the Horites out of Mount Seir, he settled in that region. After some thirty years' sojourn in Padan-aram, Jacob returned to Canaan and was reconciled to Esau, who came out to meet him (33:4). Twenty years after this, Isaac their father died, when the two brothers met, probably for the last time, beside his grave (35:29). Esau now permanently left Canaan, and established himself as a powerful and wealthy chief in the land of *Edom*.

Long after this, when the descendants of Jacob came out of Egypt, the Edomites remembered the old quarrel between the brothers, and with fierce hatred they warred against Israel.

3. Concerning his removal to Mount Seir, which was the country God had given him for a possession, when he reserved Canaan for the seed of Jacob. God owns it, long afterwards: *I gave to Esau Mount Seir* (Deut. ii. 5; Josh. xxiv. 4), which was the reason why the Edomites must not be disturbed in their possession. He wholly withdrew to Mount Seir, took with him what came to his share of his father's personal estate, and left Canaan to Jacob, not only because he had the promise of it, but because Esau perceived that if they should continue to thrive as they had begun there would not be room for both.

Verses 9–19

Observe here, 1. That only the names of Esau's sons and grandsons are recorded, only their names, not their history. Nor does the genealogy go any further than the third and fourth generation. It is only the pedigree of the Israelites, who were to be the heirs of Canaan, and of whom were to come the promised seed, and the holy seed, that is drawn out to any length, as far as there was occasion for it, even of all the tribes till Canaan was divided among them, and of the royal line till Christ came. 2. That these sons and grandsons of Esau are called *dukes*, or captains, that had soldiers under them; for Esau and his family lived *by the sword*, *ch.* xxvii. 40. Esau's sons were dukes when Jacob's sons were but plain shepherds, *ch.* xlvii. 3. This is not a reason why such titles should not be used among Christians; but it is a reason why men should not overvalue themselves, or others, for the sake of them. 3. Esau increases, and is enriched first. God's promise to Jacob began to work late, but the effect of it remained longer, and it had its complete accomplishment in the spiritual Israel.

Verses 20–30

In the midst of this genealogy of the Edomites here is inserted the genealogy of the Horites, those Canaanites, or Hittites (compare *ch.* xxvi. 34), that were the natives of Mount Seir. This comes in here, not only to give light to the story, but to be a standing reflection upon the Edomites for intermarrying with them. Esau having sold his birthright, and lost his blessing, and entered into alliance with the Hittites, his posterity and the sons of Seir are here reckoned together.

Verses 31–42

By degrees, it seems, the Edomites wormed out the Horites, obtained full possession of the country, and had a government of their own. 1. They were ruled by kings, and seem to have come to the throne by election, and not by lineal descent. These kings reigned in *Edom before there reigned any king over*

JAMIESON, FAUSSET, BROWN

have two names, as Sarai was also Iscah; and this is the more probable in the case of Esau's wives, who of course would have to take new names when they went from Canaan to settle in mount Seir.

6, 7. Esau . . . went into the country from the face of his brother Jacob—lit., "a country," without any certain prospect of a settlement. The design of this historical sketch of Esau and his family is to show how the promise (ch. 27:39, 40) was fulfilled. In temporal prosperity he far exceeds his brother; and it is remarkable that, in the overruling providence of God, the vast increase of his worldly substance was the occasion of his leaving Canaan and thus making way for the return of Jacob. **8. Thus dwelt Esau in mount Seir**—This was divinely assigned as his possession (Josh. 24:4; Deut. 2:5).

15-19. dukes—The Edomites, like the Israelites, were divided into tribes, which took their names from his sons. The head of each tribe was called by a term which in our version is rendered "duke"—not of the high rank and wealth of a British peer, but like the sheiks or emirs of the modern East, or the chieftains of highland clans. Fourteen are mentioned who flourished contemporaneously.

20-30. Sons of Seir, the Horite—native dukes, who were incorporated with those of the Edomite race.

24. This was that Anah that found the mules—The word "mules" is, in several ancient versions, rendered "water springs"; and this discovery of some remarkable fountain was sufficient, among a wandering or pastoral people, to entitle him to such a distinguishing notice.

31-39. kings of Edom—The royal power was not built on the ruins of the dukedoms, but existed at the same time.

ADAM CLARKE

here called Bashemath is called Mahalath, chap. xxviii. 9. These are variations which cannot be easily accounted for; and they are not of sufficient importance to engross much time. It is well known that the same persons in Scripture are often called by different names.

Anah the daughter of Zibeon. But this same Anah is said to be the son of Zibeon, v. 24, though in this and the fourteenth verse he is said to be the daughter of Zibeon. But the Samaritan, the Septuagint (and the Syriac, in v. 2), read "son" instead of "daughter," which Houbigant and Kennicott contend to be the true reading. Others say that "daughter" should be referred to Aholibamah, who was the daughter of Anah, and granddaughter of Zibeon. I should rather prefer the reading of the Samaritan, Septuagint, and Syriac, and read, both here and in v. 14, "Aholibamah, the daughter of Anah the son of Zibeon," and then the whole will agree with v. 24.

6. *Esau took his wives.* So it appears that Esau and Jacob dwelt together in Canaan, whither the former removed from Seir, probably soon after the return of Jacob. That they were on the most friendly footing this sufficiently proves; and Esau shows the same dignified conduct as on other occasions, in leaving Canaan to Jacob, and returning again to Mount Seir—certainly a much less fruitful region than that which he now in behalf of his brother voluntarily abandoned.

12. *Timna was concubine to Eliphaz.* As Timna was sister to Lotan the Horite, v. 22, we see how the family of Esau and the Horites got intermixed. This might give the sons of Esau a pretext to seize the land, and expel the ancient inhabitants, as we find they did, Deut. ii. 12. *Amalek.* The father of the Amalekites, afterwards bitter enemies to the Jews, and whom God commanded to be entirely exterminated, Deut. xxv. 17, 19.

15. *Dukes of the sons of Esau.* The word *duke* comes from the Latin *dux*, a "captain" or "leader." The Hebrew *alluph* has the same signification; and as it is also the term for a "thousand," which is a grand capital or leading number, probably the *dukes* had this name from being leaders of or captains over a company of one thousand men; just as those among the Greeks called *chiliarchs*, which signifies the same; and as the Romans called those *centurions* who were captains over one hundred men, from the Latin word *centum*, which signifies a hundred. The ducal government was that which prevailed first among the Idumeans, or descendants of Esau. Here fourteen dukes are reckoned to Esau: seven that came of his wife, Adah, four of Bashemath, and three of Aholibamah.

16. *Duke Korah.* This Dr. Kennicott pronounces to be an interpolation. Everything considered, I incline to the opinion that these words were not originally in the text.

20. *These are the sons of Seir the Horite.* These Horites were the original inhabitants of the country of Seir, called the land of the Horites, and afterwards the land of the Idumeans, when the descendants of Esau had driven them out. These people are first mentioned in chap. xiv. 6.

21. *These are the dukes of the Horites.* It appears pretty evident that the Horites and the descendants of Esau were mixed together in the same land, as before observed.

24. *This was that Anah that found the mules in the wilderness.* The word here translated *mules* has given rise to a great variety of conjectures and discordant opinions. St. Jerome, who renders it "warm springs," says there are as many opinions concerning it as there are commentators. My own opinion is that *mules* were not known before the time of Anah; and that he was probably the first who coupled the mare and ass together to produce this mongrel, or the first who met with creatures of this race in some very secluded part of the wilderness.

31. *Before there reigned any king over . . . Israel.* I suppose all the verses, from this to the thirty-ninth inclusive, have been transferred to this place from 1 Chron. i. 43-50, as it is not likely they could have been written by Moses; and it is quite possible they might have been, at a very early period, written in the margin of

MATTHEW HENRY

the children of Israel. Esau's blood becomes royal long before any of Jacob's did. We may suppose it was a great trial to the faith of God's Israel to hear of the pomp and power of the kings of Edom, while they were bond-slaves in Egypt; but those that look for great things from God must be content to wait for them; God's time is the best time. 2. They were afterwards governed by dukes, again here named, who, I suppose, ruled all at the same time in several places in the country. We read of the dukes of Edom (Exod. xv. 15), yet, long afterwards, of their kings again.

3. Mount Seir is called *the land of their possession, v.* 43. While the Israelites dwelt in the house of bondage, and their Canaan was only the land of promise, the Edomites dwelt in their own habitations, and Seir was in their possession. Note, The children of this world have their all in hand, and nothing in hope (Luke xvi. 25); while the children of God have their all in hope, and next to nothing in hand. But, all things considered, it is better to have Canaan in promise than Mount Seir in possession.

CHAPTER 37

Verses 1–4

The story of Jacob's family: *These are the generations of Jacob.* His is not a bare barren genealogy as that of Esau (*ch.* xxxvi. 1), but a memorable useful history. Here is, 1. Jacob a sojourner with his father Isaac, who was yet living, *v.* 1. 2. Joseph a shepherd, *feeding the flock with his brethren, v.* 2. Though he was his father's darling, yet he was not brought up in idleness or delicacy. Those that are trained up to do nothing are likely to be good for nothing.

3. Joseph, beloved by his father (*v.* 3), was the greatest comfort of his old age. Jacob proclaimed his affection to him by dressing him finer than the rest of his children: He *made him a coat of divers colours.*

4. Joseph hated by his brethren, (1) Because his father loved him; when parents make a difference, children soon take notice of it, and it often occasions feuds and quarrels in families. (2) Because he *brought to his father their evil report.* Jacob's sons did that, when they were from under his eye, which they durst not have done if they had been at home with him; but Joseph gave his father an account of their bad carriage.

Verses 5–11

Here, I. Joseph relates the prophetical dreams he had, *v.* 6, 7, 9, 10. His dreams were, 1. That his

JAMIESON, FAUSSET, BROWN

40-43. Recapitulation of the dukes according to their residences.

CHAPTER 37

Vss. 1-4. Parental Partiality. **1. Jacob dwelt in the land wherein his father was a stranger**—i.e., sojourner: father used collectively. The patriarch was at this time at Mamre, in the valley of Hebron (cf. ch. 35:27); and his dwelling there was continued in the same manner and prompted by the same motives as that of Abraham and Isaac (Heb. 11:13). **2. generations**—leading occurrences, in the domestic history of Jacob, as shown in the narrative about to be commenced. **Joseph . . . was feeding the flock**—lit., Joseph being seventeen years old was a shepherd over the flock—he a lad, with the sons of Bilhah and Zilpah. Oversight or superintendence is evidently implied. This post of chief shepherd in the party might be assigned him either from his being the son of a principal wife or from his own superior qualities of character; and if invested with this office, he acted not as a gossiping telltale, but as a "faithful steward" in reporting the scandalous conduct of his brethren. **3. son of his old age**—Benjamin being younger, was more the son of his old age and consequently on that ground might have been expected to be the favorite. Literally rendered, it is "son of old age to him"—*Hebrew* phrase, for "a wise son"—one who possessed observation and wisdom above his years—an old head on young shoulders. **made him a coat of many colors**—formed in those early days by sewing together patches of colored cloth, and considered a dress of distinction (Judg. 5:30; II Sam. 13:18). The passion for various colors still reigns among the Arabs and other people of the East, who are fond of dressing their children in this gaudy attire. But since the art of interweaving various patterns was introduced, "the coats of colors" are different now from what they seem to have been in patriarchal times, and bear a close resemblance to the varieties of tartan. **4. could not speak peaceably unto him**—did not say "peace be to thee," the usual expression of good wishes among friends and acquaintances. It is deemed a sacred duty to give all this form of salutation; and the withholding of it is an unmistakable sign of dislike or secret hostility. The habitual refusal of Joseph's brethren, therefore, to meet him with "the *salaam*," showed how ill-disposed they were towards him. It is very natural in parents to love the youngest, and feel partial to those who excel in talents or amiableness. But in a family constituted as Jacob's—many children by different mothers—he showed great and criminal indiscretion.

5-36. The Dreams of Joseph. **5. Joseph dreamed a dream**—Dreams in ancient times were

ADAM CLARKE

an authentic copy, to make out the regal succession in Edom, prior to the consecration of Saul; which words being afterwards found in the margin of a valuable copy, from which others were transcribed, were supposed by the copyist to be a part of the text; on this conviction he would not hesitate to transcribe them consecutively in his copy.

I know there is another way of accounting for those words on the ground of their being written originally by Moses; but to me it is not satisfactory. It is simply this: the word *king* should be considered as implying any kind of regular government, whether by chiefs, dukes, judges, and therefore when Moses says these are the *kings* which reigned in Edom, before there was any king in Israel, he may be only understood as saying that these kings reigned among the Edomites before the family of Jacob had acquired any considerable power, or before the time in which his twelve sons had become the fathers of numerous tribes.

Esau, after his dukes, had eight kings, who reigned successively over their people, while Israel was in affliction in Egypt.

40. *These are the names of the dukes that came of Esau.* These dukes did not govern the whole nation of the Idumeans, but they were chiefs in their respective *families,* in *their places* —the districts they governed, and to which they gave *their names.*

43. *He is Esau the father of the Edomites.* That is, the preceding list contains an account of the posterity of Esau, who was the father of Edom. Thus ends Esau's history; for after this there is no further account of his life, actions, or death, in the Pentateuch.

CHAPTER 37

1. *Wherein his father was a stranger.* Jacob dwelt in the land "of his father's sojournings," as the margin very properly reads it. The place was probably the vale of Hebron, see v. 14.

2. *These are the generations. Toledoth,* "the history of the lives and actions of Jacob and his sons"; for in this general sense the original must be taken, as in the whole of the ensuing history there is no particular account of any genealogical succession. Yet the words may be understood as referring to the tables or genealogical lists in the preceding chapter; and if so, the original must be understood in its common acceptation.

3. *A coat of many colours.* A coat made up of stripes of differently colored cloth. Similar to this was the *toga praetexta* of the Roman youth, which was white, striped or fringed with purple; this they wore till they were seventeen years of age, when they changed it for the *toga virilis,* or *toga pura,* which was all white. It is no wonder that his brethren should envy him when his father had thus made him such a distinguished object of his partial love.

4. *And could not speak peaceably unto him.* Does not this imply, in our use of the term, that they were continually quarrelling with him? But this is no meaning of the original: "they could not speak peace to him," i.e., they would not accost him in a friendly manner. They would not even wish him well. The Eastern method of salutation is, "Peace be to thee!" Now as "peace" among those nations comprehends all kinds of blessings spiritual and temporal, so they are careful not to say it to those whom they do not cordially wish well. It is not an unusual thing for an Arab or a Turk to hesitate to return the *salam,* if given by a Christian, or by one of whom he has not a favorable opinion; and this, in their own country, may be ever considered as a mark of hostility; not only as a proof that they do not wish you well, but that if they have an opportunity they will do you an injury. This was precisely the case with respect to Joseph's brethren; they would not give him the *salam,* and therefore felt themselves at liberty to take the first opportunity to injure him.

MATTHEW HENRY

brethren's sheaves all bowed to his, intimating upon what occasion they should be brought to do homage to him, namely, in seeking to him for corn; their empty sheaves should bow to his full one. 2. That the sun, and moon, and eleven stars, did obeisance to him, *v.* 9. Joseph was more of a prophet than a politician, else he would have kept this to himself, when he could not but know that his brethren did already hate him and that this would but the more exasperate them.

II. His brethren take it very ill, and are more and more enraged against him (*v.* 8): *Shalt thou indeed reign over us?* How scornfully they resented it: "*Shalt thou*, who art but one, *reign over us*, who are many? Thou, who art the youngest, over us who are older?"

III. His father gives him a gentle rebuke for it, yet observes the saying, *v.* 10, 11. Probably he checked him for it. He insinuated that it was but an idle dream. Jacob, like Mary (Luke ii. 51), kept these things in his heart, and no doubt remembered them long afterwards, when the event answered to the prediction.

Verses 12–22

Here is, I. The kind visit which Joseph, in obedience to his father's command, made to his brethren, who were feeding the flock at Shechem, many miles off. See in Joseph an instance, 1. Of dutifulness to his father. Though he was his father's darling, yet he was willing to be his father's servant. How readily does he wait his father's orders! 2. Of kindness to his brethren. Though he knew they hated him and envied him, yet he made no objections against his father's commands. Joseph was sent by his father to Shechem, to see whether his brethren were well there, and whether the country had not risen upon them and destroyed them, in revenge of their barbarous murder of the Shechemites some years before.

II. The bloody and malicious plot of his brethren against him, who rendered good for evil: it was not in a heat, or upon a sudden provocation, that they thought to slay him, but from malice prepense, and in cold blood. The more there is of a project and contrivance in a sin the worse it is; it is bad to do evil, but worse to devise it. How scornfully they reproached him for his dreams (*v.* 19): *This dreamer cometh*; and (*v.* 20), *We shall see what will become of his dreams.* This shows what it was that fretted and enraged them. They could not endure to think of doing homage to him. How they agreed to cover the murder with a lie: *We will say, Some evil beast hath devoured him.*

III. Reuben's project to deliver him, *v.* 21, 22. Reuben, of all the brothers, had most reason to be jealous of Joseph, for he was the first-born, yet he proves his best friend. Reuben made a proposal which they thought would effectually answer their intention of destroying Joseph, and yet which he designed should answer his intention of rescuing Joseph out of their hands and restoring him to his father. But God overruled all to serve his own purpose of making Joseph an instrument to save much people alive.

Verses 23–30

We have here the execution of their plot against Joseph. 1. They stripped him, each striving to seize the envied coat of many colours, *v.* 23. Thus, in imagination, they degraded him from the birthright, of which perhaps this was the badge. Thus our Lord Jesus was stripped of his seamless coat, and thus his suffering saints have first been industriously divested of their privileges and honours, and then made the off-scouring of all things. 2. They went about to starve him, throwing him into a dry pit, to perish there with hunger. Where envy reigns pity is banished, and humanity itself is forgotten, Prov. xxvii. 4. Is this he to whom his brethren must do homage? Note, God's providences often seem to contradict his purposes, even when they are serving them. 3. They slighted him when he was in distress, and were not grieved for the affliction of Joseph; they *sat down to eat bread*, *v.* 25. They felt no remorse of conscience for the sin; if they had, it would have spoiled their appetite for their meat, and the relish of it. They were now pleased to think how they were freed from the fear of their brother's dominion over them.

JAMIESON, FAUSSET, BROWN

much attended to, and hence the dream of Joseph, though but a mere boy, engaged the serious consideration of his family. But this dream was evidently symbolical. The meaning was easily discerned, and, from its being repeated under different emblems, the fulfilment was considered certain (cf. ch. 41:32), whence it was that "his brethren envied him, but his father observed the saying." **12. his brethren went to feed their father's flock in Shechem**—The vale of Shechem was, from the earliest mention of Canaan, blest with extraordinary abundance of water. Therefore did the sons of Jacob go from Hebron to this place, though it must have cost them near twenty hours' travelling—i.e., at the shepherd rate, a little more than fifty miles. But the herbage there was so rich and nutritious that they thought it well worth the pains of so long a journey, to the neglect of the grazing district of Hebron [VAN DE VELDE]. **13-17. Israel said, . . . Do not thy brethren feed the flock in Shechem?**—Anxious to learn how his sons were doing in their distant encampment, Jacob despatched Joseph; and the youth, accepting the mission with alacrity, left the vale of Hebron, sought them at Shechem, heard of them from a man in "the field," (the wide and richly cultivated plain of Esdraelon), and found that they had left that neighborhood for Dothan, probably being compelled by the detestation in which, from the horrid massacre, their name was held. **Joseph went after his brethren, and found them in Dothan**—*Hebrew, Dothaim*, or "two wells," recently discovered in the modern "Dothan," situated a few hours' distance from Shechem. **18. when they saw him afar off**—on the level grass-field, where they were watching their cattle. They could perceive him approaching in the distance from the side of Shechem, or rather, Samaria. **19. Behold, this dreamer cometh**—lit., "master of dreams"— a bitterly ironical sneer. Dreams being considered suggestions from above, to make false pretensions to having received one was detested as a species of blasphemy, and in this light Joseph was regarded by his brethren as an artful pretender. They already began to form a plot for his assassination, from which he was rescued only by the address of Reuben, who suggested that he should rather be cast into one of the wells, which are, and probably were, completely dried up in summer. **23. they stripped Joseph out of his coat . . . of many colors**—Imagine him advancing in all the unsuspecting openness of brotherly affection. How astonished and terrified must he have been at the cold reception, the ferocious aspect, the rough usage of his unnatural assailants! A vivid picture of his state of agony and despair was afterwards drawn by themselves (cf. ch. 42:21). **25. they sat down to eat bread**—What a view does this exhibit of those hardened profligates! Their common share in this conspiracy is not the only dismal feature in the story. The rapidity, the almost instantaneous manner in which the proposal was followed by their joint resolution, and the cool indifference, or rather the fiendish satisfaction, with which they sat down to regale themselves, is astonishing. It is impossible that mere envy at his dreams, his gaudy dress, or the doting partiality of their common father, could have goaded them on to such a pitch of frenzied resentment or confirmed them in such consummate wickedness. Their hatred to Joseph must have had a far deeper seat. It must have been produced by dislike to his piety and other excellencies, which made his character and conduct a constant censure upon theirs, and on account of which they found that they could never be at ease till they had rid themselves of his hated presence. This was the true solution of the mystery, just as it was in the case of Cain (I John 3:12). **they lifted up their eyes, . . . and, behold, a company of Ishmaelites**—They are called Midianites (vs. 28), and Medanites, *Hebrew* (vs. 36), being a travelling caravan composed of a mixed association of Arabians. Those tribes of Northern Arabia had already addicted themselves to commerce, and long did they enjoy a monopoly, the carrying trade being entirely in their hands. Their approach could easily be seen; for, as their road, after crossing the ford from the transjordanic district, led along the south side of the mountains of Gilboa, a party seated on the plain of Dothan could trace them and their string of camels in the distance as they proceeded through the broad and gently sloping valley that intervenes. Trading in the produce of Arabia and India, they were in the regular course of traffic on their way to Egypt: and the chief articles of commerce in which this clan dealt were "spicery" from

ADAM CLARKE

7. *We were binding sheaves in the field.* Though in these early times we read little of tillage, yet it is evident from this circumstance that it was practiced by Jacob and his sons.

14. *Go . . . see whether it be well with thy brethren.* Literally, "Go, I beseech thee, and see the peace of thy brethren, and the peace of the flock." Go and see whether they are all in prosperity. See on v. 4. As Jacob's sons were now gone to feed the flock on the parcel of ground they had bought from the Shechemites (see chap. xxxiii. 19), and where they had committed such a horrible slaughter, their father might feel more solicitous about their welfare, lest the neighboring tribes should rise against them and revenge the murder of the Shechemites. As Jacob appears to have been at this time in the vale of Hebron, it is supposed that Shechem was about sixty English miles distant from it, and that Dothan was about eight miles farther.

19. *Behold, this dreamer cometh.* This "master of dreams," this "master dreamer." A form of speech which conveys great contempt.

20. *Come now . . . and let us slay him.* What unprincipled savages these must have been to talk thus coolly about imbruing their hands in an innocent brother's blood!

21. *Reuben heard it.* Though Reuben appears to have been a transgressor of no ordinary magnitude, if we take chap. xxxv. 22 according to the letter, yet his bosom was not the habitation of cruelty. He determined, if possible, to save his brother from death and deliver him safely to his father, with whose fondness for him he was sufficiently acquainted.

23. *They stript Joseph out of his coat.* This probably was done that, if ever found, he might not be discerned to be a person of distinction, and consequently no inquiry made concerning him.

25. *They sat down to eat bread.* Every act is perfectly in character, and describes forcibly the brutish and diabolic nature of their ruthless souls.

A company of Ishmeelites. We may naturally suppose that this was a caravan, composed of different tribes that, for their greater safety, were travelling together, and of which Ishmaelites and Midianites made the chief.

MATTHEW HENRY

4. They sold him. A caravan of merchants very opportunely passed by, and Judah made the motion that they should sell Joseph to them, to be carried far enough off into Egypt, where, in all probability, he would be lost, and never heard of more. (1) Judah proposed it in compassion to Joseph (*v.* 26): "*What profit is it if we slay our brother?*

(2) They acquiesced in it, because they thought that if he were sold for a slave he would never be a lord. Reuben thought himself undone, because the child was sold: *I, whither shall I go? v.* 30. He being the eldest, his father would expect from him an account of Joseph; but, as it proved, they would all have been undone if he had not been sold.

Verses 31–36

I. Joseph would soon be missed, great enquiry would be made for him, and therefore his brethren have a further design, to make the world believe that Joseph was torn in pieces by a wild beast; and this they did, 1. To clear themselves, that they might not be suspected to have done him any mischief. Note, When the devil has taught men to commit one sin, he then teaches them to conceal it with another, theft and murder with lying and perjury; but he that covers his sin shall not prosper long. 2. To grieve their good father. It seems designed by them on purpose to be revenged upon him for his distinguishing love of Joseph. They sent him Joseph's coat of many colours with one colour more than it had had, a bloody colour, *v.* 32. They pretended they had found it in the fields, and Jacob himself must be scornfully asked, *Is this thy son's coat?* Now let those that know the heart of a parent suppose the agonies of poor Jacob. Sleeping or waking, he imagines he sees the wild beast setting upon Joseph. He fancies how the beast tore him limb from limb, and left no remains of him, but the coat of many colours. Now, (1) Endeavours were used to comfort him. His sons basely pretended to do it (*v.* 35); but miserable hypocritical comforters were they all. Had they really desired to comfort him, they might easily have done it, by telling him the truth, "Joseph is alive, he is indeed sold into Egypt, but it will be an easy thing to send thither and ransom him." But (2) It was all in vain: *Jacob refused to be comforted, v.* 35.

II. The Ishmaelites and Midianites having bought Joseph only to make their market of him, here we have him sold again to Potiphar, *v.* 36. How soon was the land of Egypt made a house of bondage to the seed of Jacob! Jacob little thought that ever his beloved Joseph would be thus bought and sold for a servant.

JAMIESON, FAUSSET, BROWN

India, i.e., a species of resinous gum, called *storax*, "balm of Gilead," the juice of the balsam tree, a native of Arabia-Felix, and "myrrh," an Arabic gum of a strong, fragrant smell. For these articles there must have been an enormous demand in Egypt as they were constantly used in the process of embalmment. **26-28. Judah said, . . . what profit is it if we slay our brother?**—The sight of these travelling merchants gave a sudden turn to the views of the conspirators; for having no wish to commit a greater degree of crime than was necessary for the accomplishment of their end, they readily approved of Judah's suggestion to dispose of their obnoxious brother as a slave. The proposal, of course, was founded on their knowledge that the Arabian merchants trafficked in slaves; and there is the clearest evidence furnished by the monuments of Egypt that the traders who were in the habit of bringing slaves from the countries through which they passed, found a ready market in the cities of the Nile. **they . . . lifted up Joseph out of the pit, and sold him**—Acting impulsively on Judah's advice, they had their poor victim ready by the time the merchants reached them; and money being no part of their object, they sold him for "twenty pieces of silver." The money was probably in rings or pieces (shekels), and silver is always mentioned in the records of that early age before gold, on account of its rarity. The whole sum, if in shekel weight, did not exceed $20.00. **they brought Joseph into Egypt**—There were two routes to Egypt—the one was overland by Hebron, where Jacob dwelt, and by taking which, the fate of his hapless son would likely have reached the paternal ears; the other was directly westward across the country from Dothan to the maritime coast, and in this, the safest and most expeditious way, the merchants carried Joseph to Egypt. Thus did an overruling Providence lead this murderous conclave of brothers, as well as the slave-merchants—both following their own free courses—to be parties in an act by which He was to work out, in a marvellous manner, the great purposes of His wisdom and goodness towards His ancient Church and people. **29, 30. Reuben returned unto the pit**—He seems to have designedly taken a circuitous route, with a view of secretly rescuing the poor lad from a lingering death by starvation. His intentions were excellent, and his feelings no doubt painfully lacerated when he discovered what had been done in his absence. But the thing was of God, who had designed that Joseph's deliverance should be accomplished by other means than his. **31-33. they took Joseph's coat**—The commission of one sin necessarily leads to another to conceal it; and the scheme of deception which the sons of Jacob planned and practised on their aged father was a necessary consequence of the atrocious crime they had perpetrated. What a wonder that their cruel sneer, "thy son's coat," and their forced efforts to comfort him, did not awaken suspicion! But extreme grief, like every other passion, is blind, and Jacob, great as his affliction was, did allow himself to indulge his sorrow more than became one who believed in the government of a supreme and all-wise Disposer. **34. Jacob rent his clothes, and put sackcloth upon his loins**—the common signs of Oriental mourning. A rent is made in the skirt more or less long according to the afflicted feelings of the mourner, and a coarse rough piece of black sackcloth or camel's hair cloth is wound round the waist. **35. and he said, For I will go down into the grave unto my son**—not the earth, for Joseph was supposed to be torn in pieces, but the unknown place—the place of departed souls, where Jacob expected at death to meet his beloved son.

ADAM CLARKE

28. *For twenty pieces of silver.* This, I think, is the first instance on record of selling a man for a slave. But the practice certainly did not commence now; it had doubtless been in use long before.

29. *Reuben returned unto the pit.* It appears he was absent when the caravan passed by, to whom the other brethren had sold Joseph.

32. *Sent the coat of many colours . . . to their father.* What deliberate cruelty to torture the feelings of their aged father, and thus harrow up his soul!

33-34. *Joseph is without doubt rent in pieces.* It is likely he inferred this from the lacerated state of the coat, which, in order the better to cover their wickedness, they had not only besmeared with the blood of the goat, but it is probable reduced to tatters. And what must a father's heart have felt in such a case! As this coat is rent, so is the body of my beloved son rent in pieces! *And Jacob rent his clothes.*

35. *All his sons and all his daughters.* He had only one daughter, Dinah; but his sons' wives may be here included. But what hypocrisy in his sons to attempt to comfort him concerning the death of a son who they knew was alive; and what cruelty to put their aged father to such torture, when, properly speaking, there was no ground for it!

36. *Potiphar, an officer of Pharaoh's.* The word *saris*, translated *officer*, signifies a "eunuch," and lest any person should imagine that, because this Potiphar had a wife, therefore it is absurd to suppose him to have been a eunuch, let such persons know that it is not uncommon in the East for eunuchs to have wives.

Captain of the guard. "Chief of the butchers"; a most appropriate name for the guards of an Eastern despot. If a person offend one of the despotic Eastern princes, the order to one of the life-guards is, "Go and bring me his head"; and this command is instantly obeyed, without judge, jury, or any form of law. Potiphar, we may therefore suppose, was captain of those guards whose business it was to take care of the royal person, and execute his sovereign will on all the objects of his displeasure.

MATTHEW HENRY — CHAPTER 38

Verses 1–11

Here is, 1. Judah's foolish friendship with a Canaanite-man. 2. His foolish marriage with a Canaanite-woman, a match made, not by his father, who, it should seem, was not consulted, but by his new friend Hirah, *v.* 2.

JAMIESON, FAUSSET, BROWN — CHAPTER 38

Vss. 1-30. Judah and Family. **1. at that time**—a formula frequently used by the sacred writers, not to describe any precise period, but an interval near about it. **2. Judah saw there a daughter of a certain Canaanite**—Like Esau, this son of Jacob, casting off the restraints of religion, married into a Canaanite family; and it is not surprising that the family which sprang from such an unsuitable connection should be infamous for bold and unblushing wickedness.

ADAM CLARKE — CHAPTER 38

1-2. *And it came to pass at that time.* The facts mentioned here could not have happened at the times mentioned in the preceding chapter, as those times are all unquestionably too recent, for the very earliest of the transactions here recorded must have occurred long before the selling of Joseph. *Adullamite.* An inhabitant of Adullam, a city of Canaan, afterwards given for a possession to the sons of Judah, Josh. xv. 1, 35. It appears as if this Adullamite had kept a kind of lodging house, for *Shuah* the Canaanite and his family lodged with him; and there Judah lodged also. As the woman was a Canaanitess, Judah had the example of his fathers to prove at least the impropriety of such a connection.

MATTHEW HENRY

3. Three sons he had by her, Er, Onan, and Shelah. Judah married too young, and very rashly; he also married his sons too young, when they had neither wit nor grace to govern themselves, and the consequences were very bad. (1) His first-born, *Er*, was notoriously wicked; he was so *in the sight of the Lord*, that is, in defiance of God and his law. (2) The next son, *Onan*, was, according to the ancient usage, married to the widow, to preserve the name of his deceased brother that died childless. The custom of marrying the brother's widow was afterwards made one of the laws of Moses, Deut. xxv. 5. Onan, though he consented to marry the widow, yet, to the great abuse of his own body, of the wife that he had married, and of the memory of his brother that was gone, refused to raise up seed unto his brother. (3) *Shelah*, the third son, was reserved for the widow (*v.* 11), yet with a design that he should not marry so young. However, Tamar acquiesced for the present, and waited the issue.

Verses 12–23

It is a very ill-favoured story that is here told concerning Judah. He was unjust to his daughter-in-law, either through negligence or design, in not giving her his surviving son, and this exposed her to temptation.

I. Tamar wickedly prostituted herself as a harlot to Judah, that, if the son might not, the father might raise up seed to the deceased. Bishop Patrick thinks it probable that she hoped Shelah, who was by right her husband, might have come along with his father, and that he might have been allured to her embraces. 1. She took an opportunity for it, when Judah had a time of mirth and feasting with his sheep-shearers. 2. She exposed herself as a harlot *in an open place*, *v.* 14. It should seem, it was the custom of harlots, in those times, to cover their faces, that, though they were not ashamed, yet they might seem to be so. The sin of uncleanness did not then go so barefaced as it does now.

II. Judah was taken in the snare, and though it was ignorantly that he was guilty of incest with his daughter-in-law (not knowing who she was), yet he was wilfully guilty of fornication: whoever she was, he knew she was not his wife, and therefore not to be touched. Observe, 1. Judah's sin began in the eye (*v.* 15): *He saw her.* We have need to make a covenant with our eyes, and to turn them from beholding vanity, lest the eye infect the heart. 2. It added to the scandal that the hire of a harlot (than which nothing is more infamous) was demanded, offered, and accepted—*a kid from the flock*, a goodly price at which her chastity and honour were valued! Nay, had the consideration been thousands of rams, and ten thousand rivers of oil, it had not been a valuable consideration. The favour of God, the purity of the soul, the peace of conscience, and the hope of heaven, are too precious to be exposed to sale at any such rates. 3. It turned to the reproach of Judah that he left his jewels in pawn for a kid.

III. He lost his jewels by the bargain; he sent the kid, according to his promise, to redeem his pawn, but the supposed harlot could not be found. Judah sits down content to lose his signet and his bracelets, and forbids any further enquiry, *lest we be shamed*, 23. He expresses no concern about the sin, to get that pardoned, only about the shame, to prevent that.

Verses 24–30

I. Judah's rigour against Tamar, when he heard she was an adulteress. She was, in the eye of the law, Shelah's wife, and therefore her being with child by another was looked upon as an injury and reproach to Judah's family: *Bring her forth therefore*, says Judah, the master of the family, and *let her be burnt*; not burnt to death, but burnt in the cheek or forehead, stigmatized for a harlot. Note, It is a common thing for men to be severe against those

JAMIESON, FAUSSET, BROWN

8. Judah said unto Onan . . . marry her, and raise up seed to thy brother—The first instance of a custom, which was afterwards incorporated among the laws of Moses, that when a husband died leaving a widow, his brother next of age was to marry her, and the issue, if any, was to be served heir to the deceased (cf. Deut. 25:5).

12. Judah . . . went up unto his sheep-shearers—This season, which occurs in Palestine towards the end of March, was spent in more than usual hilarity, and the wealthier masters invited their friends, as well as treated their servants, to sumptuous entertainments. Accordingly, it is said, Judah was accompanied by his friend Hirah. **Timnath**—in the mountains of Judah.

18. signet, etc.—Bracelets, including armlets, were worn by men as well as women among the Hebrews. But the *Hebrew* word here rendered "bracelets," is everywhere else translated "lace" or "ribbon"; so that as the signet alone was probably more than an equivalent for the kid, it is not easy to conjecture why the other things were given in addition, except by supposing the perforated seal was attached by a ribbon to the staff.

24. Bring her forth, and let her be burnt—In patriarchal times fathers seem to have possessed the power of life and death over the members of their families. The crime of adultery was anciently punished in many places by burning (Lev. 21:9; Judg. 15:6; Jer. 29:22). This chapter contains details, which probably would never have obtained a place in the inspired record, had it not been to exhibit the full links of the chain that connects the genealogy of

ADAM CLARKE

5. *And he was at Chezib, when she bare him.* This town is supposed to be the same with Achzib, which fell to the tribe of Judah, Josh. xv. 44.

7. *Er . . . was wicked in the sight of the Lord.* What this wickedness consisted in we are not told; but the phrase *sight of the Lord* being added proves that it was some very great evil. It is worthy of remark that the Hebrew word used to express Er's wickedness is his own name, the letters reversed. As if the inspired writer had said, "Er was altogether wicked, a completely abandoned character."

9. *Onan knew that the seed should not be his.* That is, that the child begotten of his brother's widow should be reckoned as the child of his deceased brother, and his name, though the real father of it, should not appear in the genealogical tables. We find from this history that long before the Mosaic law it was an established custom, probably founded on a divine precept, that if a man died childless his brother was to take his wife, and the children produced by this second marriage were considered as the children of the first husband, and in consequence inherited his possessions.

12. *In process of time.* This phrase, which is in general use in the Bible, needs explanation; the original is "and the days were multiplied." Though it implies an indefinite time, yet it generally embraces a pretty long period, and in this place may mean several years.

15. *Thought her to be an harlot.* See the original of this term, chap. xxxiv. 31. The Hebrew is *zonah* and signifies generally a person who prostitutes herself to the public for hire, or one who lives by the public. It appears that in very ancient times there were public persons of this description; and they generally veiled themselves, sat in public places by the highway side, and received certain hire.

17. *Wilt thou give me a pledge, till thou send it?* The word *erabon* signifies an "earnest" of something promised, a part of the price agreed for between a buyer and seller, by giving and receiving of which the bargain was ratified; or a deposit, which was to be restored when the thing promised should be given. St. Paul uses the same word in Greek letters, 2 Cor. i. 22; Eph. i. 14. From the use of the term in this history we may at once see what the apostle means by the Holy Spirit being the "earnest" of the promised inheritance; namely, a security given in hand for the fulfilment of all God's promises relative to grace and eternal life. We may learn from this that eternal life will be given in the great day to all who can produce this *erabon* or "pledge." He who has the earnest of the Spirit then in his heart shall not only be saved from death, but have that eternal life of which it is the pledge and the evidence. What the pledge given by Judah was, see on v. 25.

21. *Where is the harlot, that was openly by the way side?* Our translators often render different Hebrew words by the same term in English, and thus many important shades of meaning, which involve traits of character, are lost. In v. 15 Tamar is called a "harlot," *zonah*, which, as we have already seen, signifies a person who prostitutes herself for money. In this verse she is called a *harlot* in our version; but the original is *kedeshah*, a holy or "consecrated person," from *kadash*, "to make holy," or "to consecrate to religious purposes." And the word here must necessarily signify a person consecrated by prostitution to the worship of some impure goddess.

23. *Lest we be shamed.* Not of the act, for this he does not appear to have thought criminal; but lest he should fall under the raillery of his companions and neighbors for having been tricked out of his signet, bracelets, and staff, by a prostitute.

24. *Bring her forth, and let her be burnt.* As he had ordered Tamar to live as widow in her own father's house till his son Shelah should be marriageable, he considers her therefore as the wife of his son; and as Shelah was not yet given to her, and she is found with child, she is reputed by him as an adulteress, and burning, it seems, was anciently the punishment of this crime. Judah, being a patriarch or head of a family, had, according to the custom of those

MATTHEW HENRY

very sins in others in which yet they allow themselves; and so, in judging others, they condemn themselves, Rom. ii. 1; xiv. 22.

II. Judah's shame, when it was made to appear that he was the adulterer. She produced *the ring and the bracelets* in court, which justified the fathering of the child upon Judah, *v.* 25, 26. He owns that a perpetual mark of infamy should be fastened rather upon him, who had been so much accessory to it.

III. The building up of Judah's family in the birth of Pharez and Zarah, from whom descended the most considerable families of the illustrious tribe of Judah. The four eldest sons of Jacob fell under very foul guilt, Reuben and Judah under the guilt of incest, Simeon and Levi under that of murder; yet they were patriarchs, and from Levi descended the priests, from Judah the kings and Messiah. Thus they became examples of repentance, and monuments of pardoning mercy.

JAMIESON, FAUSSET, BROWN

the Saviour with Abraham; and in the disreputable character of the ancestry who figure in this passage, we have a remarkable proof that "He made himself of no reputation."

F. B. MEYER:

Judah. This was the destined heir of the birthright of which Reuben had shown himself unworthy; and yet this chapter is a dark story of his unbridled passion. Oh, my soul, remember that the possibilities of all these sins are latent in thee! Thou mightest have been as one of these men or women but for the grace of God.

There is nothing so absolutely priceless as the white flower of a pure and blameless life. The pure in heart are the children of the presence chamber—entrusted with secrets hidden from the wise and prudent—vessels by which God does not hesitate to quench the thirst of men, because the water of the crystal river will not be diluted or contaminated by contact with their natures. Above all other gifts, covet that of a cleansed heart. You may be very conscious of temptation and that naturally you are no better than others, and yet if you will constantly live in the Spirit and walk in the Spirit, you will be kept absolutely pure; and the sea of ink that is sweeping through the world will leave no stain on you.

The blood cleanseth: "The blood of Jesus Christ, his Son, cleanseth us from all sin" (1 John 1:7).

The Savior keepeth: "The Lord is faithful, who shall stablish you, and keep you from evil" (2 Thess. 3:3).

—*Great Verses Through the Bible*

ADAM CLARKE

times, the supreme magisterial authority over all the branches of his own family; therefore he only acts here in his juridicial capacity. How strange that in the very place where adultery was punished by the most violent death, prostitution for money and for religious purposes should be considered as no crime!

25. *The signet.* Properly a "seal," or instrument with which impressions were made to ascertain property. *Bracelets. Pethilim,* from *pathal,* "to twist, wreathe, twine," may signify a girdle or a collar by which precedency might be indicated. *Staff.* Either what we would call a common walking stick or the staff which was the ensign of his tribe.

26. ***She hath been more righteous than I.*** It is probable that Tamar was influenced by no other motive than that which was common to all the Israelitish women, the desire to have children who might be heirs of the promise made to Abraham. And as Judah had obliged her to continue in her widowhood under the promise of giving her his son Shelah when he should be of age, consequently his refusing or delaying to accomplish this promise was a breach of truth, and an injury done to Tamar.

28. ***The midwife . . . bound upon his hand a scarlet thread.*** The binding of the scarlet thread about the wrist of the child whose arm appeared first in the birth serves to show us how solicitously the privileges of the birthright were preserved. Had not this caution been taken by the midwife, Pharez would have had the right of primogeniture to the prejudice of his elder brother, Zarah. And yet Pharez is usually reckoned in the genealogical tables before Zarah; and from him, not Zarah, does the line of our Lord proceed. See Matt. i. 3. Probably the two brothers, as being twins, were conjoined in the privileges belonging to the birthright.

29. *How hast thou broken forth?* Thou shalt bear the name of the *breach* thou hast made, i.e., in coming first into the world. Therefore his name was called *Parets,* i.e., the person who made the breach.

30. *His name was called Zarah. Zarach,* "risen or sprung up," applied to the sun, rising and diffusing his light.

CHAPTER 39

Verses 1–6

I. Joseph was sold to an officer of Pharaoh, with whom he might get acquainted with public persons and public business, and so be fitted for the preferment for which he was designed. What God intends men for he will be sure, some way or other, to qualify them for.

II. Joseph blessed, wonderfully blessed, even in the house of his servitude.

1. God prospered him, *v.* 2, 3. Though, at first, we may suppose that his hand was put to the meanest services, even in those appeared his ingenuity and industry; a particular blessing of Heaven attended him, which, as he rose in his employment, became more and more discernible. Joseph's brethren had stripped him of his coat of many colours, but they could not strip him of his virtue and prudence. Joseph was separated from his brethren, but not from his God; banished from his father's house, but *the Lord was with him,* and this comforted him.

2. His master preferred him, and by degrees made him steward of his household, *v.* 4. It is the wisdom of those that are in any sort of authority to countenance and employ those with whom it appears that the presence of God is, Ps. ci. 6. Potiphar knew what he did when he put all into the hands of Joseph.

CHAPTER 39

Vss. 1-23. JOSEPH IN POTIPHAR'S HOUSE. **1. Potiphar**—This name, Potiphar, signifies one "devoted to the sun," the local deity of On or Heliopolis, a circumstance which fixes the place of his residence in the Delta, the district of Egypt bordering on Canaan. **officer**—lit., "prince of Pharaoh"—i.e., in the service of government. **captain of the guard**—The import of the original term has been variously interpreted, some considering it means "chief cook," others, "chief inspector of plantations"; but that which seems best founded is "chief of the executioners," "head of the police," the same as the captain of the watch, the *zabut* of modern Egypt [WILKINSON]. **bought him . . . of the Ishmaelites**—The age, appearance, and intelligence of the Hebrew slave would soon cause him to be picked up in the market. But the unseen, unfelt influence of the great Disposer drew the attention of Potiphar towards him, in order that in the house of one so closely connected with the court, he might receive that previous training which was necessary for the high office he was destined to fill, and in the school of adversity learn the lessons of practical wisdom that were to be of greatest utility and importance in his future career. Thus it is that when God has any important work to be done, He always prepares fitting agents to accomplish it. **2. he was in the house of his master**—Those slaves who had been war captives were generally sent to labor in the field and subjected to hard treatment under the "stick" of taskmasters. But those who were bought with money were employed in domestic purposes, were kindly treated, and enjoyed as much liberty as the same class does in modern Egypt. **3. his master saw that the Lord was with him**—Though changed in condition, Joseph was not changed in spirit; though stripped of the gaudy coat that had adorned his person, he had not lost the moral graces that distinguished his character; though separated from his father on earth, he still lived in communion with his Father in heaven; though in the house of an idolater, he continued a wor-

CHAPTER 39

CHARLES H. SPURGEON:

Scripture frequently sums up a man's life in a single sentence. Here is the biography of Joseph sketched by inspiration: "God was with him," so Stephen testified in his famous speech recorded in Acts 7:9. Here is the life story of Abraham: "Abraham believed God." Of Moses we read, "The man Moses was very meek." Take a New Testament life, such as that of John the Baptist, and you have it in a line: "John did no miracle: but all things that he spake concerning Jesus were true." The mere name of John—"that disciple whom Jesus loved"—would serve for an epitaph of him: it pictures both the man and his history. Holy Scripture excels in this kind of full length miniature painting. As Michaelangelo is said to have drawn a portrait with a single stroke of his crayon, so the Spirit of God sketches a man to the life in a single sentence: "The Lord was with Joseph."

—*The Treasury of the Old Testament*

4. *He made him overseer. Hiphkid,* from *pakad,* "to visit, take care of, superintend"; the same as *episcopos,* "overseer" or "bishop," among the Greeks. This is the term by which the Septuagint often express the meaning of the original.

MATTHEW HENRY

3. God favoured his master for his sake (*v.* 5): *He blessed the Egyptian's house,* though he was an Egyptian, a stranger to the true God, *for Joseph's sake.* Good men are the blessings of the places where they live.

Verses 7–12

I. A most shameful instance of impudence and immodesty in Joseph's mistress, the shame and scandal of her sex, perfectly lost to all virtue and honour.

1. Her sin began in the eye: She *cast her eyes upon Joseph* (*v.* 7), who *was a goodly person, and well-favoured, v.* 6. We have great need to make a covenant with our eyes (Job xxxi. 1), lest the eye infect the heart.

2. She was daring and shameless in the sin.

3. She was urgent and violent in the temptation. She *spoke to him day by day, v.* 10. Now this was, (1) Great wickedness in her, and (2) A great temptation to Joseph.

II. Here is a most illustrious instance of virtue and resolved chastity in Joseph, who, by the grace of God, was enabled to resist and overcome this temptation; and, all things considered, his escape was as great an instance of the divine power as the deliverance of the three children out of the fiery furnace.

1. The temptation he was assaulted with was very strong. The tempter was his mistress, a person of quality, whom it was his place to obey and his interest to oblige, whose favour would contribute more than anything to his preferment. On the other hand, it was at his utmost peril if he slighted her, and made her his enemy. Opportunity favoured the temptation. The tempter was in the house with him; his business led him to be, without any suspicion, where she was.

2. His resistance of the temptation was very brave, and the victory truly honourable.

(1) He would not wrong his master. He would not offend his God. This is the chief argument with which he strengthens his aversion to the sin. *How can I do this?* not only, How shall I? or, How dare I? but, *How can I? Id possumus, quod jure possumus—We can do that which we can do lawfully.* Three arguments Joseph urges upon himself. *First,* He considers who he was that was tempted. "*I;* others may perhaps take their liberty, but *I* cannot." *Secondly,* What the sin was to which he was tempted: *This great wickedness.* Others might look upon it as a small matter, a peccadillo, a trick of youth; but Joseph had another idea of it. Let sin appear sin (Rom. vii. 13), call it by its own name, and never go about to lessen it. *Thirdly,* Against whom he was tempted to sin—*against God,* against his nature and his dominion, against his love and his design. Those that love God do for this reason hate sin.

(2) By steadfastness of resolution. The grace of God enabled him to overcome the temptation by avoiding the tempter. He would not stay so much as to parley with the temptation, but flew out from it with the utmost abhorrence; he left his garment, as one escaping for his life. Note, It is better to lose a good coat than a good conscience.

Verses 13–18

Joseph's mistress, having tried in vain to make him a criminal, now endeavours to represent him as one; so to be revenged on him for his virtue. Chaste and holy love will continue, though slighted; but sinful love, like Amnon's to Tamar, is easily changed into sinful hatred. She accused him to his fellow servants (*v.* 13–15) and gave him a bad name among them. She accused him to his master, who had power in his hand to punish him. Observe, 1. What an improbable story she tells, but it was told to be revenged upon his virtue, a most malicious lie. And yet, 2. She manages it so as to incense her husband against him, reflecting upon him for bringing this Hebrew servant among them.

Verses 19–23

Here is, 1. Joseph wronged by his master. He believed the accusation, and there is no remedy, he is condemned to perpetual imprisonment, *v.* 19, 20. He should be shut up among the king's prisoners, the state-prisoners. Potiphar, it is likely, chose that prison because it was the worst. He was committed to the king's prison, that he might thence be preferred to the king's person. 2. Joseph was at a distance from all his friends, but *the Lord was with Joseph, and showed him mercy, v.* 21. No gates nor bars can shut out his gracious presence from his people; for he has promised that he will never leave them. Those that have a good conscience in a prison have a good God there. Joseph is not long a prisoner before he becomes a little ruler. God *gave him favour in the sight of the keeper of the prison.* Note, God

JAMIESON, FAUSSET, BROWN

shipper of the true God. **5. the Lord blessed the Egyptian's house for Joseph's sake,** etc.—It might be—it probably was—that a special, a miraculous blessing was poured out on a youth who so faithfully and zealously served God amid all the disadvantages of his place. But it may be useful to remark that such a blessing usually follows in the ordinary course of things; and the most worldly, unprincipled masters always admire and respect religion in a servant when they see that profession supported by conscientious principle and a consistent life. **made him overseer in his house**—We do not know in what capacity Joseph entered into the service of Potiphar; but the observant eye of his master soon discovered his superior qualities and made him his chief, his confidential servant (cf. Eph. 6:7; Col. 3:23). The advancement of domestic slaves is not uncommon, and it is considered a great disgrace not to raise one who has been a year or two in the family. But this extraordinary advancement of Joseph was the doing of the Lord, though on the part of Potiphar it was the consequence of observing the astonishing prosperity that attended him in all that he did. **7. his master's wife cast her eyes upon Joseph**—Egyptian women were not kept in the same secluded manner as females are in most Oriental countries now. They were treated in a manner more worthy of a civilized people—in fact, enjoyed much freedom both at home and abroad. Hence Potiphar's wife had constant opportunity of meeting Joseph. But the ancient women of Egypt were very loose in their morals. Intrigues and intemperance were vices very prevalent among the them, as the monuments too plainly attest [WILKINSON]. Potiphar's wife was probably not worse than many of the same rank, and her infamous advances made to Joseph arose from her superiority of station. **9. How then can I do this great wickedness, and sin against God?**—This remonstrance, when all inferior arguments had failed, embodied the true principle of moral purity—a principle always sufficient where it exists, and alone sufficient.

14. Then she called unto the men of her house—Disappointed and affronted, she vowed revenge and accused Joseph, first to the servants of the house, and on his return to her lord. **See, he hath brought in an Hebrew . . . to mock us**—an affected and blind aspersion of her husband for keeping in his house an Hebrew, the very abomination of Egyptians. **20. Joseph's master took him and put him into the prison**—the roundhouse, from the form of its construction, usually attached to the dwelling of such an officer as Potiphar. It was partly a subterranean dungeon (ch. 41:14), though the brick-built walls rose considerably above the surface of the ground, and were surmounted by a vaulted roof somewhat in the form of an inverted bowl. Into such a dungeon Potiphar, in the first ebullition of rage, threw Joseph and ordered him to be subjected further to as great harshness of treatment (Ps. 105:18) as he dared; for the power of masters over their slaves was very properly restrained by law, and the murder of a slave was a capital crime. **a place where the king's prisoners were bound**—Though prisons seem to have been an inseparable appendage of the palaces, this was not a common jail—it was the receptacle of state criminals; and, therefore, it may be presumed that more than ordinary strictness and vigilance were exercised over the prisoners. In general, however, the Egyptian, like other Oriental prisons, were used solely for the purposes of detention. Accused persons were cast into them until the charges against them could be investigated; and though the jailer was responsible for the appearance of those placed under his custody, yet, provided they were produced when called, he was never interrogated as to the way in which he had kept them. **21-23. The Lord . . . gave him favour in the sight of the keeper of the prison,** etc. It is highly probable, from the situation of this prison (ch. 40:3), that the keeper might have been previously acquainted with Joseph and have had access to know his innocence of the crime laid to his charge, as well as with all the high integrity of his character. That

ADAM CLARKE

6. *Joseph was a goodly person, and well favoured.* "Beautiful in his person," and "beautiful in his countenance." The same expressions are used relative to Rachel; see them explained in chap. xxix. 17. The beauty of Joseph is celebrated over all the East, and the Persian poets vie with each other in descriptions of his comeliness. Mohammed spends the twelfth chapter of the Koran entirely on Joseph, and represents him as a perfect beauty, and the most accomplished of mortals.

8. *My master wotteth not.* Knoweth not, from the old Anglo-Saxon *witan,* "to know"; hence "wit," intellect, understanding, wisdom, prudence.

9. *How then.* "And how?" Joseph gives two most powerful reasons for his noncompliance with the wishes of his mistress: (1) Gratitude to his master, to whom he owed all that he had. (2) His fear of God, in whose sight it would be a heinous offense, and who would not fail to punish him for it.

14. *He hath brought in an Hebrew unto us.* Potiphar's wife affects to throw great blame on her husband, whom we may reasonably suppose she did not greatly love. *He hath brought in*—he hath raised this person to all his dignity and eminence, to give him the greater opportunity to mock us. *Letsachek,* here translated "to mock," is the same word used in chap. xxvi. 8, relative to Isaac and Rebekah; and is certainly used by Potiphar's wife in v. 17 to signify some kind of familiar intercourse not allowable but between man and wife.

20. *Put him into the prison.* Literally the "round house"; in such a form the prison was probably built.

21. *The Lord was with Joseph.* It is but of little consequence where the lot of a servant of God may be cast; like Joseph he is ever employed for his Master, and God honors him and prospers his work.

MATTHEW HENRY

can raise up friends for his people even where they little expect to find them. The keeper saw that God was with him and that every thing prospered under his hand; and therefore entrusted him with the management of the affairs of the prison, *v.* 22, 23.

CHAPTER 40

Verses 1–4

We should not have had this story of Pharaoh's butler and baker recorded in scripture if it had not been serviceable to Joseph's preferment. Observe, 1. Two of the great officers of Pharaoh's court, having offended the king, are committed to prison. Many conjectures there are concerning the offence of these servants of Pharaoh; some make it no less than an attempt to take away his life, others no more than the casual lighting of a fly into his cup and a little sand into his bread.

2. The *captain of the guard* himself, who was Potiphar, charged Joseph with them (*v.* 4), which intimates that he began now to be reconciled to him, and perhaps to be convinced of his innocence, though he durst not release him for fear of disobliging his wife.

Verses 5–19

I. The special providence of God, which filled the heads of these two prisoners with unusual dreams, such as made extraordinary impressions upon them, and carried with them evidences of a divine origin, both in one night.

II. The impression which was made upon these prisoners by their dreams (*v.* 6): *They were sad.*

III. Joseph's great tenderness and compassion towards them. He enquired with concern, *Wherefore look you so sadly to-day? v.* 7. Joseph was their keeper, and was now a prisoner with them, and had been a dreamer too. Communion in sufferings helps to work compassion towards those that do suffer. It is some relief to those that are in trouble to be taken notice of.

IV. The dreams themselves, and the interpretation of them. *There is no interpreter* here in the prison, *v.* 8. Joseph hereupon directed them which way to look: *Do not interpretations belong to God?* Joseph suggests, "If interpretations belong to God, he is a free agent, and may communicate the power to whom he pleases, and therefore tell me your dreams." Now, 1. The chief butler's dream was a happy presage of his enlargement, and re-advancement, within three days; and so Joseph explained it to him, *v.* 12, 13. 2. The chief baker's dream portended his ignominious death, *v.* 18, 19. The happy interpretation of the other's dream encouraged him to relate his. It was not Joseph's fault that he brought him no better tidings. Ministers are but interpreters, they cannot make the thing otherwise than it is.

V. The improvement Joseph made of this opportunity to get a friend at court, *v.* 14, 15. He modestly bespoke the favour of the chief butler, whose preferment he foretold: *But think of me when it shall be well with thee.* What a modest representation he makes of his own case, *v.* 15. He does not reflect upon his brethren that sold him. Nor does he reflect on the wrong done him in this imprisonment by his mistress that was his prosecutrix, and his master that was his judge; but mildly avers his own innocence. When we are called to vindicate ourselves we should carefully avoid, as much as may be, speaking ill of others. Let us be content to prove ourselves innocent, and not be fond of upbraiding others with their guilt.

JAMIESON, FAUSSET, BROWN

may partly account for his showing so much kindness and confidence to his prisoner. But there was a higher influence at work; for "the Lord was with Joseph, and that which he did, the Lord made it to prosper."

CHAPTER 40

Vss. 1-8. TWO STATE PRISONERS. **1. the butler**—not only the cup-bearer, but overseer of the royal vineyards, as well as the cellars; having, probably, some hundreds of people under him. **baker**—or cook, had the superintendence of every thing relating to the providing and preparing of meats for the royal table. Both officers, especially the former, were, in ancient Egypt, always persons of great rank and importance; and from the confidential nature of their employment, as well as their access to the royal presence, they were generally the highest nobles or princes of the blood. **3. Pharaoh put them in ward,** etc.—Whatever was their crime, they were committed, until their case could be investigated, to the custody of the captain of the guard, i.e., Potiphar, in an outer part of whose house the royal prison was situated. **4. The captain of the guard charged Joseph with them**—not the keeper, though he was most favorably disposed; but Potiphar himself, who, it would seem, was by this time satisfied of the perfect innocence of the young Hebrew; though, probably, to prevent the exposure of his family, he deemed it prudent to detain him in confinement (see Ps. 37:5). **They continued a season in ward**—lit., "days," how long, is uncertain; but as they were called to account on the king's birthday, it has been supposed that their offense had been committed on the preceding anniversary [CALVIN]. **5-8. they dreamed a dream**—Joseph, influenced by the spirit of true religion, could feel for others (Eccles. 4:1; Rom. 12:15; Phil. 2:4). Observing them one day extremely depressed, he inquired the cause of their melancholy; and being informed it was owing to a dream they had respectively dreamed during the previous night, after piously directing them to God (Dan. 2:30; Isa. 26:10), he volunteered to aid them, through the divine help, in discovering the import of their vision. The influence of Providence must be seen in the remarkable fact of both officers dreaming such dreams in one night. He moves the spirits of men.

9-15. THE BUTLER'S DREAM. **9. In my dream, behold, a vine was before me**—The visionary scene described seems to represent the king as taking exercise and attended by his butler, who gave him a cooling draught. On all occasions, the kings of ancient Egypt were required to practice temperance in the use of wine [WILKINSON]; but in this scene, it is a prepared beverage he is drinking, probably the sherbet of the present day. Everything was done in the king's presence—the cup was washed, the juice of the grapes pressed into it; and it was then handed to him—not grasped; but lightly resting on the tips of the fingers. **12-15. Joseph said, . . . This is the interpretation**—Speaking as an inspired interpreter, he told the butler that within three days he would be restored to all the honors and privileges of his office; and while making that joyful announcement, he earnestly bespoke the officer's influence for his own liberation. Nothing has hitherto met us in the record indicative of Joseph's feelings; but this earnest appeal reveals a sadness and impatient longing for release, which not all his piety and faith in God could dispel.

16-23. THE BAKER'S DREAM. **16. I had three white baskets**—The circumstances mentioned exactly describe his duties, which, notwithstanding numerous assistants, he performed with his own hands. **white**—lit., "full of holes,"—i.e., wicker baskets. The meats were carried to table upon the head in three baskets, one piled upon the other; and in the uppermost, the bakemeats. And in crossing the open courts, from the kitchen to the dining rooms, the removal of the viands by a vulture, eagle, ibis, or other rapacious bird, was a frequent occurrence in the palaces of Egypt, as it is an everyday incident in the hot countries of the East still. The risk from these carnivorous birds was the greater in the cities of Egypt, where being held sacred, it was unlawful to destroy them; and they swarmed in such numbers as to be a great annoyance to the people. **18, 19. Joseph answered and said, This is the interpretation**—The purport was that in three days his execution should be ordered. The language of Joseph de-

ADAM CLARKE

CHAPTER 40

1. *The butler.* "Cupbearer." *Baker.* Rather "cook, confectioner," or the like. *Had offended.* They had probably been accused of attempting to take away the king's life, one by poisoning his drink, the other by poisoning his bread or confectionaries.

3. *Where Joseph was bound.* The place in which Joseph was now "confined"; this is what is implied in being *bound;* for, without doubt, he had his personal liberty. As the butler and the baker were state criminals they were put in the same prison with Joseph, which we learn from the preceding chapter, v. 20, was the king's prison.

4. *They continued a season.* Literally "days"; how long we cannot tell.

5. *Each man according to the interpretation.* Not like dreams in general, the disordered workings of the mind, the consequence of disease or repletion; these were dreams that had an interpretation, that is, that were prophetic.

6. *They were sad.* They concluded that their dreams portended something of great importance, but they could not tell what.

8. *There is no interpreter.* They either had access to none, or those to whom they applied could give them no consistent, satisfactory meaning. *Do not interpretations belong to God?* God alone, the Supreme Being, knows what is in futurity; and if He have sent a significant dream, He alone can give the solution.

11. *And I took the grapes, and pressed them into Pharaoh's cup.* From this we find that wine anciently was the mere expressed juice of the grape, without fermentation. The cupbearer took the bunch, pressed the juice into the cup, and instantly delivered it into the hands of his master.

12. *The three branches are three days.* That is, the three branches signify three days; a form of speech frequently used in the sacred writings, for the Hebrew has no proper word by which our terms "signifies, represents," etc., are expressed.

14. *Make mention of me unto Pharaoh.* One would have supposed that the very circumstance of his restoration, according to the prediction of Joseph, would have almost necessarily prevented him from forgetting so extraordinary a person. But what have mere courtiers to do with either gratitude or kindness?

15. *For indeed I was stolen.* "Stolen, I have been stolen"—most assuredly I was stolen; *and here also have I done nothing.* These were simple assertions, into the proof of which he was ready to enter if called on.

19. *Lift up thy head from off thee.* Thus we find that beheading, hanging, and gibbeting were modes of punishment among the ancient Egyptians; but the criminal was beheaded before he was hanged, and then either hanged on hooks or by the hands. See Lam. v. 12.

MATTHEW HENRY

Verses 20–23

The verifying of Joseph's interpretation of the dreams, on the very day prefixed. The chief butler and baker were both advanced, one to his office, the other to the gallows, and both at the three days' end.

Some observe the resemblance between Joseph and Christ in this story. Joseph's fellow-sufferers were like the two thieves that were crucified with Christ—the one saved, the other condemned. One of these, when Joseph said to him, *Remember me when it shall be well with thee*, forgot him; but one of those, when he said to Christ, *Remember me when thou comest into thy kingdom*, was not forgotten.

JAMIESON, FAUSSET, BROWN

scribes minutely one form of capital punishment that prevailed in Egypt; viz., that the criminal was decapitated and then his headless body gibbeted on a tree by the highway till it was gradually devoured by the ravenous birds. **20-22. it came to pass the third day, which was Pharaoh's birthday**—This was a holiday season, celebrated at court with great magnificence and honored by a free pardon to prisoners. Accordingly, the issue happened to the butler and baker, as Joseph had foretold. Doubtless, he felt it painful to communicate such dismal tidings to the baker; but he could not help announcing what God had revealed to him; and it was for the honor of the true God that he should speak plainly.

23. yet did not the chief butler remember Joseph—This was human nature. How prone are men to forget and neglect in prosperity, those who have been their companions in adversity (Amos 6:6)! But although reflecting no credit on the butler, it was wisely ordered in the providence of God that he should forget him. The divine purposes required that Joseph should obtain his deliverance in another way, and by other means.

ADAM CLARKE

20. *Pharaoh's birthday.* The distinguishing a birthday by a feast appears from this place to have been a very ancient custom. It probably had its origin from a correct notion of the immortality of the soul, as the commencement of life must appear of great consequence to that person who believed he was to live forever. St. Matthew, xiv. 6, mentions Herod's keeping his birthday; and examples of this kind are frequent to the present time in most nations. *Lifted up the head of the chief butler.* By lifting up the head, probably no more is meant than bringing them to trial, tantamount to what was done by Jezebel and the nobles of Israel to Naboth: "Set Naboth on high among the people: and set two men, sons of Belial . . . to bear witness against him," 1 Kings xxi. 9, etc. The issue of the trial was, the baker alone was found guilty and hanged; and the butler, being acquitted, was restored to his office.

23. *Yet did not the chief butler remember Joseph.* Had he mentioned the circumstance to Pharaoh, there is no doubt that Joseph's case would have been examined into, and he would in consequence have been restored to his liberty; but, owing to the ingratitude of the chief butler, he was left two years longer in prison.

MATTHEW HENRY

CHAPTER 41

Verses 1–8

Observe, 1. The delay of Joseph's enlargement. It was not till *the end of two full years* (*v.* 1). There is a time set for the deliverance of God's people; that time will come, though it seem to tarry; and, when it comes, it will appear to have been the best time. 2. The means of Joseph's enlargement, which were Pharaoh's dreams, here related. If we were to look upon them as ordinary dreams, we might observe from them the follies and absurdities of a roving working fancy, tame cows as beasts of prey (nay, more ravenous than any, eating up those of their own kind), and ears of corn as devouring one another. Foolish dreams related can make no better than foolish talk. But these dreams which Pharaoh dreamed carried their own evidence with them that they were sent of God; and therefore, when he awoke, his spirit was troubled, *v.* 8.

His magicians were puzzled, the rules of their art failed them. This was to make Joseph's performance by the Spirit of God the more admirable. Compare with this story, Dan. ii. 27; iv. 7; v. 8. Joseph's own dreams were the occasion of his troubles, and now Pharaoh's dreams were the occasion of his enlargement.

Verses 9–16

Here is, 1. The recommending of Joseph to Pharaoh for an interpreter. The chief butler did it more in compliment to Pharaoh, to oblige him, than in gratitude to Joseph, or in compassion for his case. The story he had to tell was, in short, That there was an obscure young man in the king's prison, who had very properly interpreted his dream, and the chief baker's (the event corresponding in each with the interpretation), and that he would recommend him to the king his master for an interpreter. Note, God's time for the enlargement of his people will appear at last to be the fittest time. If the chief butler had at first used his interest for Joseph's enlargement, and had obtained it, it is probable that upon his release he would have gone back to *the land of the Hebrews* again, which he spoke of so feelingly (*ch.* xl. 15), and then he would neither have been so blessed himself, nor such a blessing to his family, as afterwards he proved. But staying two years longer, and coming out now upon this occasion, at last, to interpret the king's dreams, way was made for his very great preferment. 2. The introducing of Joseph to Pharaoh. It is done with all possible expedition, and Joseph is brought in, perhaps almost as much surprised as Peter was, Acts xii. 9.

JAMIESON, FAUSSET, BROWN

CHAPTER 41

Vss. 1-24. PHARAOH'S DREAM. **1. at the end of two full years**—It is not certain whether these years are reckoned from the beginning of Joseph's imprisonment, or from the events described in the preceding chapter—most likely the latter. What a long time for Joseph to experience the sickness of hope deferred! But the time of his enlargement came when he had sufficiently learned the lessons of God designed for him; and the plans of Providence were matured. **Pharaoh dreamed**—Pharaoh, from an Egyptian word *Phre*, signifying the "sun," was the official title of the kings of that country. The prince, who occupied the throne of Egypt, was Aphophis, one of the Memphite kings, whose capital was On or Heliopolis, and who is universally acknowledged to have been a patriot king. Between the arrival of Abraham and the appearance of Joseph in that country, somewhat more than two centuries had elapsed. Kings sleep and dream, as well as their subjects. And this Pharaoh had two dreams in one night so singular and so similar, so distinct and so apparently significant, so coherent and vividly impressed on his memory, that his spirit was troubled. **8. he called for all the magicians of Egypt**—It is not possible to define the exact distinction between "magicians and wise men"; but they formed different branches of a numerous body, who laid claim to supernatural skill in occult arts and sciences, in revealing mysteries, explaining portents, and, above all, interpreting dreams. Long practice had rendered them expert in devising a plausible way of getting out of every difficulty and framing an answer suitable to the occasion. But the dreams of Pharaoh baffled their united skill. Unlike their Assyrian brethren (Dan. 2:4), they did not pretend to know the meaning of the symbols contained in them, and the providence of God had determined that they should all be nonplussed in the exercise of their boasted powers, in order that the inspired wisdom of Joseph might appear the more remarkable. **9-13. then spake the chief butler unto Pharaoh, saying, I do remember my faults**—This public acknowledgment of the merits of the young Hebrew would, tardy though it was, have reflected credit on the butler had it not been obviously made to ingratiate himself with his royal master. It is right to confess our faults against God, and against our fellow men when that confession is made in the spirit of godly sorrow and penitence. But this man was not much impressed with a sense of the fault he had committed against Joseph; he never thought of God, to whose goodness he was indebted for the prophetic announcement of his release, and in acknowledging his former fault against the king, he was practising the courtly art of pleasing his master. **14. Then Pharaoh sent and called Joseph**—Now that God's set time had come (Ps. 105:19), no human power nor policy could detain Joseph in prison. During his protracted confinement, he might have often been distressed with perplexing doubts; but the mystery of Providence was about to be cleared up, and all his sorrows forgotten in the course of honor and

ADAM CLARKE

CHAPTER 41

1. *Two full years.* "Two years of days," two complete solar revolutions, after the events mentioned in the preceding chapter. *The river.* The Nile, the cause of the fertility of Egypt.

2. *There came up out of the river seven well favoured kine.* This must certainly refer to the hippopotamus or river horse, as the circumstances of coming up out of the river and feeding in the field characterize that animal alone. The hippopotamus is the well-known inhabitant of the Nile and frequently by night comes out of the river to feed in the fields, or in the sedge by the riverside.

6. *Blasted with the east wind.* It has been very properly observed that all the mischief done to corn or fruit, by blasting, smutting, mildews, locusts is attributed to the *east wind.* See Exod. x. 13; xiv. 21; Ps. lxxviii. 26; Ezek. xvii. 10; Jonah iv. 8. In Egypt it is peculiarly destructive, because it comes through the parched deserts of Arabia, often destroying vast numbers of men and women. The action of this destructive wind is referred to by the Prophet Hosea, chap. xiii. 15: "Though he be fruitful among his brethren, an east wind shall come, the wind of the Lord shall come up from the wilderness, and his spring shall become dry, and his fountain shall be dried up: he shall spoil the treasure of all pleasant vessels."

8. *Called for all the magicians.* The word here used may probably mean no more than interpreters of abstruse and difficult subjects. They seem to have been such persons as Josephus (*Ant.*, lib. ii, c. 9, s. 2) calls "sacred scribes, or professors of sacred learning." *Wise men.* The persons who, according to Porphyry, "addicted themselves to the worship of God and the study of wisdom, passing their whole life in the contemplation of Divine things. Contemplation of the stars, self-purification, arithmetic, and geometry, and singing hymns in honour of their gods, was their continual employment."

9. *I do remember my faults.* It is not possible he could have forgotten the circumstance to which he here alludes; it was too intimately connected with all that was dear to him to permit him ever to forget it. But it was not convenient for him to remember this before; and probably he would not have remembered it now, had he not seen that giving this information in such a case was likely to serve his own interest.

14. *They brought him hastily out of the dungeon.* Pharaoh was in perplexity on account of his dreams; and when he heard of Joseph, he sent immediately to get him brought before him. *He shaved himself*—having let his beard grow all the time he was in prison, he now trimmed it, for it is not likely that either the Egyptians or Hebrews shaved themselves in our sense of the word. The change of raiment was, no doubt, furnished out of the king's wardrobe; as Joseph, in his present circumstances, could

MATTHEW HENRY

Pharaoh immediately, without enquiring who or whence he was, tells him his business, that he expected he should interpret his dream, *v.* 15. To which Joseph makes him a very modest decent reply (*v.* 16), in which, (1) He gives honour to God. "It is not in me, God must give it." (2) He shows respect to Pharaoh, and hearty good will to him and his government, in supposing that the interpretation would be an answer of peace.

Verses 17–32

I. Pharaoh relates his dream. He dreamt that he stood upon the bank of the river Nile, and saw the kine, both the fat ones and the lean ones, come out of the river.

II. Joseph interprets his dream, and tells him that it signified seven years of plenty now immediately to ensue, which should be succeeded by as many years of famine. Observe, 1. The two dreams signified the same thing, but the repetition was to denote the certainty, the nearness, and the importance of the event, *v.* 32. 2. Yet the two dreams had a distinct reference to the two things wherein we most experience plenty and scarcity, namely, grass and corn. The plenty and scarcity of grass for the cattle were signified by the fat kine and the lean ones; the plenty and scarcity of herb for the service of man by the full ears and the thin ones.

3. See what changes the comforts of this life are subject to. After great plenty may come great scarcity. 4. See the goodness of God in sending the seven years of plenty before those of famine, that provision might be made accordingly. With what wonderful wisdom has Providence, that great housekeeper, ordered the affairs of this numerous family from the beginning hitherto! Great variety of seasons there have been, and the produce of the earth is sometimes more and sometimes less; yet, take one time with another, what was miraculous concerning the manna is ordinarily verified in the common course of Providence, *He that gathers much has nothing over, and he that gathers little has no lack*, Exod. xvi. 18. 5. See the perishing nature of our worldly enjoyments. The great increase of the years of plenty was quite lost and swallowed up in the years of famine; and the overplus of it, which seemed very much, yet did but just serve to keep men alive, *v.* 29–31. Observe, God revealed this beforehand to Pharaoh, who, as king of Egypt, was to be the father of his country, and to make prudent provision for them.

Verses 33–45

I. The good advice that Joseph gave to Pharaoh, which was, 1. That in the years of plenty he should lay up for the years of famine, buy up corn when it was cheap, that he might both enrich himself and supply the country when it would be dear and scarce. 2. Because that which is everybody's work commonly proves nobody's work, he advises Pharaoh to appoint officers who should make it their business, and to select some one person to preside in the affair, *v.* 33.

II. The great honour that Pharaoh did to Joseph. 1. He gave him an honourable testimony: He is *a man in whom the Spirit of God is*; and this puts a great excellency upon any man; such men ought to be valued, *v.* 38. He is a nonsuch for prudence: *There is none so discreet and wise as thou art*, *v.* 39. Now he is abundantly recompensed for the disgrace that had been done him.

JAMIESON, FAUSSET, BROWN

public usefulness in which his services were to be employed. **shaved himself**—The Egyptians were the only Oriental nation that liked a smooth chin. All slaves and foreigners who were reduced to that condition, were obliged, on their arrival in that country, to conform to the cleanly habits of the natives, by shaving their beards and heads, the latter of which were covered with a close cap. Thus prepared, Joseph was conducted to the palace, where the king seemed to have been anxiously waiting his arrival. **15, 16. Pharaoh said, . . . I have dreamed a dream**—The king's brief statement of the service required brought out the genuine piety of Joseph; disclaiming all merit, he ascribed whatever gifts or sagacity he possessed to the divine source of all wisdom, and he declared his own inability to penetrate futurity; but, at the same time, he expressed his confident persuasion that God would reveal what was necessary to be known. **17. Pharaoh said, In my dream, behold, I stood upon the bank of the river**—The dreams were purely Egyptian, founded on the productions of that country and the experience of a native. The fertility of Egypt being wholly dependent on the Nile, the scene is laid on the banks of that river; and oxen being in the ancient hieroglyphics symbolical of the earth and of food, animals of that species were introduced in the first dream. **18. there came up out of the river seven kine**—Cows now, of the buffalo kind, are seen daily plunging into the Nile; when their huge form is gradually emerging, they seem as if rising "out of the river." **and they fed in a meadow**—Nile grass, the aquatic plants that grow on the marshy banks of that river, particularly the lotus kind, on which cattle were usually fattened. **19. behold, seven other kine . . . poor and ill-favoured**—The cow being the emblem of fruitfulness, the different years of plenty and of famine were aptly represented by the different condition of those kine—the plenty, by the cattle feeding on the richest fodder; and the dearth, by the lean and famishing kine, which the pangs of hunger drove to act contrary to their nature. **22. I saw in my dream, and, behold, seven ears**—that is, of Egyptian wheat, which, when "full and good," is remarkable in size—a single seed sprouting into seven, ten, or fourteen stalks—and each stalk bearing an ear. **23. blasted with the east wind**—destructive everywhere to grain, but particularly so in Egypt; where, sweeping over the sandy deserts of Arabia, it comes in the character of a hot, blighting wind, that quickly withers all vegetation (cf. Ezek. 19:12; Hos. 13:15). **24. the thin ears devoured the seven good ears**—*devoured* is a different word from that used in vs. 4 and conveys the idea of destroying, by absorbing to themselves all the nutritious virtue of the soil around them.

25-36. Joseph Interprets Pharaoh's Dreams. **25. Joseph said, . . . The dream . . . is one**—They both pointed to the same event—a remarkable dispensation of seven years of unexampled abundance, to be followed by a similar period of unparalleled dearth. The repetition of the dream in two different forms was designed to show the absolute certainty and speedy arrival of this public crisis; the interpretation was accompanied by several suggestions of practical wisdom for meeting so great an emergency as was impending. **33. Now therefore let Pharaoh look out a man**—The explanation given, when the key to the dreams was supplied, appears to have been satisfactory to the king and his courtiers; and we may suppose that much and anxious conversation arose, in the course of which Joseph might have been asked whether he had anything further to say. No doubt the providence of God provided the opportunity of his suggesting what was necessary. **34. and let him appoint officers over the land**—overseers, equivalent to the beys of modern Egypt. **take up the fifth part of the land**—i.e., of the land produce, to be purchased and stored by the government, instead of being sold to foreign corn merchants.

37-57. Joseph Made Ruler of Egypt. **38. Pharaoh said unto his servants**—The kings of ancient Egypt were assisted in the management of state affairs by the advice of the most distinguished members of the priestly order; and, accordingly, before admitting Joseph to the new and extraordinary office that was to be created, those ministers were consulted as to the expediency and propriety of the appointment. **a man in whom the Spirit of God is**—An acknowledgment of the being and power of the true God, though faint and feeble, continued to linger amongst the higher classes long after idolatry had come to prevail. **40. Thou**

ADAM CLARKE

not be supposed to have any changes of raiment.

16. *It is not in me.* "Without or independently of me"—I am not essential to thy comfort; God himself has thee under His care. And "he will send thee," or answer thee, "peace"; thou shalt have prosperity howsoever ominous thy dreams may appear. By this answer he not only conciliated the mind of the king, but led him to expect his help from that God from whom alone all comfort, protection, and prosperity must proceed.

18. *Seven kine, fatfleshed.* See on v. 2. And observe further that the seven fat and the seven lean kine coming out of the same river plainly show, at once, the cause of both the plenty and the dearth. It is well known that there is scarcely any rain in Egypt; and that the country depends for its fertility on the overflowing of the Nile; and that the fertility is in proportion to the duration and quantity of the overflow. We may therefore safely conclude that the seven years of plenty were owing to an extraordinary overflowing of the Nile; and that the seven years of dearth were occasioned by a very partial or total want of this essentially necessary inundation. Thus then the two sorts of cattle, signifying years of plenty and want, might be said to "come out of" the same river, as the inundation was either complete, partial, or wholly restrained.

21. *And when they had eaten them up.* Nothing can more powerfully mark the excess and severity of the famine than creatures eating each other, and yet without any effect, remaining as lean and as wretched as they were before.

25. *God hath shewed Pharaoh what he is about to do.* Joseph thus shows the Egyptian king that, though the ordinary cause of plenty or want is the river Nile, yet its inundations are under the direction of God; the dreams are sent by Him, not only to signify beforehand the plenty and want, but to show also that all these circumstances, however fortuitous they may appear to man, are under the direction of an overruling Providence.

31. *The plenty shall not be known in the land by reason of that famine following.* As Egypt depends for its fertility on the flowing of the Nile, and this flowing is not always equal, there must be a point to which it must rise to saturate the land sufficiently in order to produce grain sufficient for the support of its inhabitants. Pliny, *Hist. Nat.*, lib. v, c. 9, has given us a scale by which the plenty and the dearth may be ascertained. "The ordinary height of the inundations is sixteen cubits. When the waters are lower than this standard they do not overflow the whole ground; when above this standard, they are too long in running off. In the first place the ground is not saturated: by the second, the waters are detained so long on the ground that seed-time is lost. The province marks both. If it rise only twelve cubits, a famine is the consequence. Even at thirteen cubits hunger prevails; fourteen cubits produces general rejoicing; fifteen, perfect security; and sixteen, all the luxuries of life."

33. *A man discreet and wise.* As it is impossible that Joseph could have foreseen his own elevation, consequently he gave this advice without any reference to himself. The counsel, therefore, was either immediately inspired by God or was dictated by policy, prudence, and sound sense.

34. *Let him appoint officers.* "Visitors, overseers"; see chap. xxxix. 1.

37. *The thing was good.* Pharaoh and his courtiers saw that the counsel was prudent and should be carefully followed.

38. *In whom the Spirit of God is? Ruach Elohim*, the identical words used in chap. i. 2; and certainly to be understood here as in the preceding place. If the Egyptians were idolaters, they acknowledged Joseph's God.

40. *According unto thy word shall all my people be ruled.* Literally, "At thy mouth shall all my people kiss." In the Eastern countries it is customary to kiss anything that comes from a superior, and this is done by way of testifying respect and submission. In this sense the words in the text are to be understood: All the people shall pay the profoundest respect and obedience to all thy orders and commands. *Only in the*

MATTHEW HENRY	JAMIESON, FAUSSET, BROWN	ADAM CLARKE

MATTHEW HENRY

2. He put him into an honourable office; not only employed him to buy up corn, but made him prime-minister of state, comptroller of the household.

3. He put upon him all the marks of honour imaginable, to recommend him to the esteem and respect of the people as the king's favourite, and one whom he delighted to honour.

He gave him a new name, to show his authority over him, and yet such a name as bespoke the value he had for him. *Zaphnath-paaneah—A revealer of secrets.* He married him honourably to a prince's daughter. Where God had been liberal in giving wisdom and other merits, Pharaoh was not sparing in conferring honours.

Verses 46–57

Observe here, I. The building of Joseph's family in the birth of two sons, Manasseh and Ephraim, *v.* 50-52. In the names he gave them, he owned the divine Providence giving this happy turn to his affairs. He was made *fruitful in the land of his affliction.* It had been the land of his affliction, and in some sense it was still so, for it was not Canaan, the land of promise. His distance from his father was still his affliction. The afflictions of the saints promote their fruitfulness. *Ephraim* signifies *fruitfulness,* and *Manasseh forgetfulness,* for these two often go together; when Jeshurun waxed fat, he forgot God his Maker.

II. The accomplishment of Joseph's predictions. Pharaoh had great confidence in the truth of them. The seven plenteous years came (*v.* 47), and, at length, they were ended, *v.* 53. Years of plenty will end, therefore, Whatever thy hand finds to do, do it; and gather in gathering time. *The seven years of dearth began to come, v.* 54. This famine, it seems, was not only in Egypt, but in other lands, in *all lands,* that is, all the neighbouring countries. It is here said that *in the land of Egypt there was bread.*

JAMIESON, FAUSSET, BROWN

shalt be over my house—This sudden change in the condition of a man who had just been taken out of prison could take place nowhere, except in Egypt. In ancient as well as modern times, slaves have often risen to be its rulers. But the special providence of God had determined to make Joseph governor of Egypt; and the way was paved for it by the deep and universal conviction produced in the minds both of the king and his councillors, that a divine spirit animated his mind and had given him such extraordinary knowledge. **according unto thy word shall all my people be ruled**—lit., "kiss." This refers to the edict granting official power to Joseph, to be issued in the form of a firman, as in all Oriental countries; and all who should receive that order would kiss it, according to the usual Eastern mode of acknowledging obedience and respect for the sovereign [WILKINSON]. **41. Pharaoh said, . . . See, I have set thee over all the land**—These words were preliminary to investiture with the insignia of office, which were these: the signet ring, used for signing public documents, and its impression was more valid than the sign-manual of the king; the *khelaat* or dress of honor, a coat of finely wrought linen, or rather cotton, worn only by the highest personages; the gold necklace, a badge of rank, the plain or ornamental *form* of it indicating the degree of rank and dignity; the privilege of riding in a state carriage, the second chariot; and lastly— **43. they cried before him, Bow the knee**—*abrech,* an Egyptian term, not referring to prostration, but signifying, according to some, "father" (cf. ch. 45:8); according to others, "native prince"—i.e., proclaimed him naturalized, in order to remove all popular dislike to him as a foreigner.

44. These ceremonies of investiture were closed in usual form by the king in council solemnly ratifying the appointment. **I am Pharaoh, and without thee,** etc.—a proverbial mode of expression for great power. **45. Zaphnath-paaneah**—variously interpreted, "revealer of secrets"; "saviour of the land"; and from the hieroglyphics, "a wise man fleeing from pollution"—i.e., adultery. **gave him to wife Asenath, the daughter of**—His naturalization was completed by this alliance with a family of high distinction. On being founded by an Arab colony, Poti-pherah, like Jethro, priest of Midian, might be a worshipper of the true God; and thus Joseph, a pious man, will be freed from the charge of marrying an idolatress for worldly ends. **On**—called Aven (Ezek. 30:17) and also Beth-shemesh (Jer. 43:13). In looking at this profusion of honors heaped suddenly upon Joseph, it cannot be doubted that he would humbly yet thankfully acknowledge the hand of a special Providence in conducting him through all his checkered course to almost royal power; and we, who know more than Joseph did, cannot only see that his advancement was subservient to the most important purposes relative to the Church of God, but learn the great lesson that a Providence directs the minutest events of human life. **46. Joseph was thirty years old, when he stood before Pharaoh**—seventeen when brought into Egypt, probably three in prison, and thirteen in the service of Potiphar. **went out . . . all the land**—made an immediate survey to determine the site and size of the storehouses required for the different quarters of the country. **47. the earth brought forth by handfuls**—a singular expression, alluding not only to the luxuriance of the crop, but the practice of the reapers grasping the ears, which alone were cut. **48. he gathered up all the food of the seven years**—It gives a striking idea of the exuberant fertility of this land, that, from the superabundance of the seven plenteous years, corn enough was laid up for the subsistence, not only of its home population, but of the neighboring countries, during the seven years of dearth. **50-52. unto Joseph were born two sons**—These domestic events, which increased his temporal happiness, develop the piety of his character in the names conferred upon his children. **53-56. The seven years of plenteousness . . . ended**—Over and above the proportion purchased for the government during the years of plenty, the people could still have husbanded much for future use. But improvident as men commonly are in the time of prosperity, they found themselves in want, and would have starved by thousands had not Joseph anticipated and provided for the protracted calamity.

ADAM CLARKE

throne will I be greater than thou. This, in one word, is a perfect description of a prime minister. Thou shalt have the sole management, under me, of all state affairs.

42. *And Pharaoh took off his ring . . . and put it upon Joseph's hand.* In this ring was probably set the king's signet, by which the royal instruments were sealed; and thus Joseph was constituted what we would call lord chancellor, or lord keeper of the privy seal. *Vestures of fine linen.* Whether this means linen or cotton is not known. It seems to have been a term by which both were denominated; or it may be some other substance or cloth with which we are unacquainted. If the fine linen of Egypt was such as that which invests the bodies of the mummies, and these in general were persons of the first distinction, and consequently were enveloped in cloth of the finest quality, it was only fine comparatively speaking, Egypt being the only place at that time where such cloth was manufactured. I have often examined the cloth about the bodies of the most splendidly ornamented mummies, and found it sackcloth when compared with the fine Irish linens.

43. *He made him to ride in the second chariot.* That which usually followed the king's chariot in public ceremonies. *Bow the knee. Abrech,* which we translate *bow the knee,* and which we might as well translate anything else, is probably an Egyptian word, the signification of which is utterly unknown. If we could suppose it to be a Hebrew word, it might be considered as compounded of *ab,* "father," and *rach,* "tender"; for Joseph might be denominated a "father," because of his care over the people, and the provision he was making for their preservation; and tender because of his youth. Or it may be compounded of *ab,* "father," and *barech,* "blessing."

44. *I am Pharaoh.* The same as if he had said, "I am the king"; for "Pharaoh" was the common title of the sovereigns of Egypt.

45. *Zaphnath-paaneah.* The meaning of this title is as little known as that of *abrech* in the preceding verse. Some translate it, "The revealer of secrets"; others, "The treasury of glorious comfort." All the etymologies hitherto given of this word are, to say the least of them, doubtful. I believe it also to be an Egyptian epithet, designating the office to which he was now raised; and similar to our compound terms, prime minister, lord chancellor. *Asenath the daughter of Poti-pherah.* There is no likelihood that the Poti-pherah mentioned here is the same as the Potiphar who had purchased Joseph and on the false accusations of his wife cast him into prison. *Priest of On. On* is rendered Heliopolis (the city of the sun) by the Septuagint. *Joseph went out over all the land.* No doubt for the building of granaries, and appointing proper officers to receive the corn in every place.

46. *Joseph was thirty years old.* As he was seventeen years old when he was sold into Egypt, chap. xxxvii. 2, and was now thirty, he must have been thirteen years in slavery. *Stood before Pharaoh.* This phrase always means admission to the immediate presence of the sovereign, and having the honor of his most unlimited confidence.

47. *The earth brought forth by handfuls.* This probably refers principally to rice, as it grows in tufts, a great number of stalks proceeding from the same seed. In those years the Nile probably rose sixteen cubits; see on v. 31.

50. *Two sons.* Whom he called by names expressive of God's particular and bountiful providence towards him. Manasseh signifies "forgetfulness"; and Ephraim "fruitfulness"; and he called his sons by these names, because God had enabled him to forget all his toil, disgrace, and affliction, and had made him fruitful in the very land in which he had suffered the greatest misfortune and indignities.

54. *The seven years of dearth began to come.* Owing in Egypt to the Nile not rising more than twelve or thirteen cubits (see on v. 31); but there must have been other causes which affected other countries, not immediately dependent on the Nile, though remotely connected with Egypt and Canaan. *The dearth was in all lands.* All the countries dependent on the Nile.

MATTHEW HENRY

III. The performance of Joseph's trust. He was found faithful to it, as a steward ought to be. 1. He was diligent in laying up, while the plenty lasted, *v.* 48, 49. 2. He was prudent and careful in giving out, when the famine came, and kept the markets low by furnishing them at reasonable rates out of his stores. The people in distress cried to Pharaoh. He sent them to his treasurer, *Go to Joseph.* Joseph, no doubt, with wisdom and justice fixed the price of the corn he sold, so that the country might not be oppressed, nor advantage taken of their prevailing necessity. And let the price be determined by that golden rule of justice, to do as we would be done by.

CHAPTER 42

Verses 1–6

Though Jacob's sons were all married they were still incorporated in one society, under the conduct and presidency of their father Jacob.

I. The orders he gave them to go and buy corn in Egypt, *v.* 1, 2. Observe, 1. The famine was grievous in the land of Canaan. It is observable that all the three patriarchs, to whom Canaan was the land of promise, met with famine in that land, which was not only to try their faith, whether they could trust God though he should starve them, but to teach them to seek the better country, that is, the heavenly, Heb. xi. 14–16. 2. Still, when there was famine in Canaan, there was corn in Egypt. Thus Providence orders it, that one place should be a succour and supply to another; for we are all brethren. 3. *Jacob saw that there was corn in Egypt.* 4. He reproved his sons for delaying to provide corn for their families. *Why do you look one upon another?* 5. He quickened them to go to Egypt: *Get you down thither.*

II. Their obedience to these orders, *v.* 3. They *went down to buy corn*; they did not send their servants, but very prudently went themselves, to lay out their own money. Let none think themselves too great nor too good to take pains. Benjamin went not with them, for he was his father's darling. To Egypt they came, and, having a considerable cargo of corn to buy, they were brought before Joseph himself, *they bowed down themselves before him, v.* 6. Now their empty sheaves did obeisance to his full one.

Verses 7–20

We may well wonder that Joseph, during the twenty years that he had now been in Egypt, never made an excursion to Canaan, to visit his aged father, when he was in the borders of Egypt, that lay next to Canaan. It is a probable conjecture that his whole management of himself in this affair was by special direction from Heaven, that the purpose of God concerning Jacob and his family might be accomplished. When Joseph's brethren came, he knew them by many a satisfactory token, but they knew not him, little thinking to find him there, *v.* 8. Joseph had an eye to his dreams, in his carriage towards his brethren, and aimed at the bringing of his brethren to repentance for their former sins.

I. He showed himself very rigorous and harsh with them. He charged them with bad designs against the government (*v.* 9), treated them as dangerous persons, saying, *You are spies.* Now why was Joseph thus hard upon his brethren? We may be sure it was not from a spirit of revenge. It was to bring them to repentance. It was to get out of them an account of the state of their family, which he longed to know. Not seeing his brother Benjamin with them, perhaps he began to suspect that they had made away with him too, and therefore gives them occasion to speak of their father and brother.

II. They, hereupon, were very submissive. They spoke to him with all the respect imaginable: *Nay, my lord* (*v.* 10)—a great change since they said, *Behold, this dreamer comes.* They very modestly deny the charge: *We are no spies.* They tell him their business, that they came to buy food.

III. He clapped them all up in prison for three days, *v.* 17.

JAMIESON, FAUSSET, BROWN

57. The famine was sore in all lands—i.e., the lands contiguous to Egypt—Canaan, Syria, and Arabia.

CHAPTER 42

Vss. 1-38. JOURNEY INTO EGYPT. 1. Now when **Jacob saw that there was corn in Egypt**—learned from common rumor. It is evident from Jacob's language that his own and his sons' families had suffered greatly from the scarcity; and through the increasing severity of the scourge, those men, who had formerly shown both activity and spirit, were sinking into despondency. God would not interpose miraculously when natural means of preservation were within reach. **5. the famine was in the land of Canaan**—The tropical rains, which annually falling swell the Nile, are those of Palestine also; and their failure would produce the same disastrous effects in Canaan as in Egypt. Numerous caravans of its people, therefore, poured over the sandy desert of Suez, with their beasts of burden, for the purchase of corn; and among others, "the sons of Israel" were compelled to undertake a journey from which painful associations made them strongly averse. **6. Joseph was the governor**—in the zenith of his power and influence. **he it was that sold**—i.e., directed the sales; for it is impossible that he could give attendance in every place. It is probable, however, that he may have personally superintended the storehouses near the border of Canaan, both because that was the most exposed part of the country and because he must have anticipated the arrival of some messengers from his father's house. **Joseph's brethren came, and bowed down themselves before him**—His prophetic dreams were in the course of being fulfilled, and the atrocious barbarity of his brethren had been the means of bringing about the very issue they had planned to prevent (Isa. 60:14; Rev. 3:9, last clause). **7, 8. Joseph saw his brethren, and he knew them, . . . but they knew not him**—This is not strange. They were full-grown men—he was but a lad at parting. They were in their usual garb—he was in his official robes. They never dreamt of him as governor of Egypt, while he had been expecting them. They had but one face—he had ten persons to judge by. **made himself strange unto them, and spake roughly**—It would be an injustice to Joseph's character to suppose that this stern manner was prompted by any vindictive feelings—he never indulged any resentment against others who had injured him. But he spoke in the authoritative tone of the governor in order to elicit some much-longed-for information respecting the state of his father's family, as well as to bring his brethren, by their own humiliation and distress, to a sense of the evils they had done to him. **9-14. Ye are spies**—This is a suspicion entertained regarding strangers in all Eastern countries down to the present day. Joseph, however, who was well aware that his brethren were not spies, has been charged with cruel dissimulation, with a deliberate violation of what he knew to be the truth, in imputing to them such a character. But it must be remembered that he was sustaining the part of a ruler; and, in fact, acting on the very principle sanctioned by many of the sacred writers, and our Lord Himself, who spoke parables (fictitious stories) to promote a good end. **15. By the life of Pharaoh**—It is a very common practice in Western Asia to swear by the life of the king. Joseph spoke in the style of an Egyp-

ADAM CLARKE

And it appears that a general drought had taken place, at least through all Egypt and Canaan; for it is said, v. 57, "that the famine was sore in all lands"—Egypt and Canaan, and their respective dependencies.

55. *When all the land of Egypt was famished.* As Pharaoh, by the advice of Joseph, had exacted a fifth part of all the grain during the seven years of plenty, it is very likely that no more was left than what was merely necessary to supply the ordinary demand both in the way of home consumption and for the purpose of barter or sale to neighboring countries.

56. *Over all the face of the earth.* The original should be translated, "all the face of that land," namely, Egypt, as it is explained at the end of the verse.

57. *All countries came into Egypt . . . to buy.* As there had not been a sufficiency of rains to swell the Nile, to effect a proper inundation in Egypt, the same cause would produce drought, and consequently scarcity, in all the neighboring countries; and this may be all that is intended in the text.

CHAPTER 42

1. *Jacob saw that there was corn.* That is, Jacob heard from the report of others that there was plenty in Egypt. Before agriculture was properly known and practiced, famines were frequent; Canaan seems to have been peculiarly vexed by them. There was one in this land in the time of Abraham, chap. xii. 10; another in the days of Isaac, chap. xxvi. 1; and now a third in the time of Jacob.

6. *Joseph was the governor.* A "protector." *Bowed down themselves before him.* Thus fulfilling the prophetic dream, chap. xxxvii. 7-8, which they had taken every precaution to render null and void. But there is neither might nor counsel against the Lord.

9. *Ye are spies.* "Ye are footmen, trampers about, foot-pads, vagabonds," lying in wait for the property of others; persons who, under the pretense of wishing to buy corn, desire only to find out whether the land be so defenseless that the tribes to which ye belong (see v. 11) may attack it successfully, drive out the inhabitants, and settle in it themselves; or, having plundered it, retire to their deserts. Thus Joseph spake roughly to them merely to cover that warmth of affection which he felt towards them; and that being thus brought, apparently, into straits and dangerous circumstances, their consciences might be awakened to reflect on and abhor their own wickedness.

11. *We are all one man's sons.* We do not belong to different tribes, and it is not likely that one family would make a hostile attempt upon a whole kingdom. This seems to be the very ground that Joseph took, namely, that they were persons belonging to different tribes. Against this particularly they set up their defense, asserting that they all belonged to one family; and it is on the proof of this that Joseph puts them, v. 15, in obliging them to leave one as a hostage, and insisting on their bringing their remaining brother; so that he took exactly the same precautions to detect them as if he had had no acquaintance with them, and had every reason to be suspicious.

13. *One is not.* An elliptical sentence, "One is not alive."

15. *By the life of Pharaoh.* "Pharaoh liveth." As if he said, As surely as the king of Egypt lives, so surely shall ye not go hence unless your brother come hither. Here, therefore, is no oath; it is just what they themselves make it in their report to their father, chap. xliii. 3: "The man did solemnly protest unto us"; and our translators should not have put it in the form of an oath, especially as the original not only will bear another version, but is absolutely repugnant to this in our sense of the word.

MATTHEW HENRY

IV. He concluded with them, at last, that one of them should be left as a hostage, and the rest should go home and fetch Benjamin. It was a very encouraging word he said to them (*v.* 18): *I fear God;* as if he had said, "You may assure yourselves I will do you no wrong; I dare not, for I know that, high as I am, there is one higher than I." Note, With those that fear God we have reason to expect fair dealing. The fear of God will be a check upon those that are in power, to restrain them from abusing their power to oppression and tyranny. Those that have no one else to stand in awe of ought to stand in awe of their own consciences. See Neh. v. 15, *So did not I, because of the fear of God.*

Verses 21–28

I. The penitent reflection Joseph's brethren made upon the wrong they had formerly done to him, *v.* 21. They talked the matter over in the Hebrew tongue, not suspecting that Joseph, whom they took for a native of Egypt, understood them, much less that he was the person they spoke of.

They remembered with regret the barbarous cruelty wherewith they persecuted him. Now see here, 1. The office of conscience. As time will not wear out the guilt of sin, so it will not blot out the records of conscience. 2. The benefit of afflictions; they often prove the happy and effectual means of awakening conscience.

II. Joseph's tenderness towards them upon this occasion. This represents the tender mercies of our God towards repenting sinners. See Jer. xxxi. 20, *Since I spoke against him I do earnestly remember him still.* See Judg. x. 16.

III. The imprisonment of Simeon, *v.* 24. He chose him for the hostage probably because he remembered him to have been his most bitter enemy, or because he observed him now to be least humbled and concerned.

IV. The dismission of the rest of them. They came for corn, and corn they had; and not only so, but every man had his money restored in his sack's mouth.

1. It was really a merciful event; for I hope they had no wrong done to them when they had their money given them back, but a kindness; yet they were thus terrified by it. Guilty consciences are apt to take good providences in a bad sense. If they had been robbed of their money, they could not have been worse frightened than they were now when they found their money in their sacks.

2. They knew that the Egyptians abhorred a Hebrew (*ch.* xliii. 32), and therefore, since they could not expect to receive any kindness from them, they concluded that this was done with a design to pick a quarrel with them, because the lord of the land had charged them as spies. Their own consciences also were awake, and their sins set in order before them; and this put them into confusion. When men's spirits are sinking every thing helps to sink them.

Verses 29–38

1. The report which Jacob's sons made to their father of the great distress they had been in in Egypt; how they had been suspected, and threatened, and obliged to leave Simeon a prisoner there, till they should bring Benjamin with them thither. 2. The deep impression this made upon the good man. The very bundles of money which Joseph returned, in kindness to his father, frightened him (*v.* 35); for he concluded it was done with some mischievous design. (1) He has very melancholy apprehensions concerning the present state of his family. Jacob gives up Joseph for gone, and Simeon and Benjamin as being in danger; and he concludes, *All these things are against me.* It proved otherwise, that all these were for him, were working together for his good and the good of his family. Through our ignorance and mistake, and the weakness of our faith, we often apprehend that to be against us which is really for us. (2) He is at present resolved that Benjamin shall not go down. No, Jacob's present thoughts are, *My son shall not go down with you.* He plainly intimates a distrust of them, remembering that he never saw Joseph since he had been with them.

JAMIESON, FAUSSET, BROWN

tian and perhaps did not think there was any evil in it. But we are taught to regard all such expressions in the light of an oath (Matt. 5:34; Jas. 5:12). **17-24. put them . . . into ward three days**—Their confinement had been designed to bring them to salutary reflection. And this object was attained, for they looked upon the retributive justice of God as now pursuing them in that foreign land. The drift of their conversation is one of the most striking instances on record of the power of conscience.

24. took . . . Simeon, and bound him—He had probably been the chief instigator—the most violent actor in the outrage upon Joseph; and if so, his selection to be the imprisoned and fettered hostage for their return would, in the present course of their reflections, have a painful significance. **25-28. Joseph commanded to fill their sacks with corn, and to restore every man's money**—This private generosity was not an infringement of his duty—a defrauding of the revenue. He would have a discretionary power—he was daily enriching the king's exchequer—and he might have paid the sum from his own purse.

27. inn—a mere station for baiting beasts of burden. **he espied his money**—The discovery threw them into greater perplexity than ever. If they had been congratulating themselves on escaping from the ruthless governor, they perceived that now he would have a handle against them; and it is observable that they looked upon this as a judgment of heaven. Thus one leading design of Joseph was gained in their consciences being roused to a sense of guilt. **35. as they emptied their sacks, that behold, every man's . . . money was in his sack**—It appears that they had been silent about the money discovery at the resting-place, as their father might have blamed them for not instantly returning. However innocent they knew themselves to be, it was universally felt to be an unhappy circumstance, which might bring them into new and greater perils. **36. Me have ye bereaved**—This exclamation indicates a painfully excited state of feeling, and it shows how difficult it is for even a good man to yield implicit submission to the course of Providence. The language does not imply that his missing sons had got foul play from the hands of the rest, but he looks upon Simeon as lost, as well as Joseph, and he insinuates it was by some imprudent statements of theirs that he was exposed to the risk of losing Benjamin also. **37. Reuben spake, . . . Slay my two sons, if I bring him not to thee**—This was a thoughtless and unwarrantable condition—one that he never seriously expected his father would accept. It was designed only to give assurance of the greatest care being taken of Benjamin. But unforeseen circumstances might arise to render it impossible for all of them to preserve that young lad (Jas. 4:13), and Jacob was much pained by the prospect. Little did he know that God was dealing with him severely, but in kindness (Heb. 12:7, 8), and that all those things he thought against Him were working together for his good.

ADAM CLARKE

18. *I fear God.* He seems to say to his brethren, I am a worshipper of the true God, and ye have nothing to fear.

21. *We are verily guilty.* How finely are the office and influence of conscience exemplified in these words! It was about twenty-two years since they had sold their brother, and probably their consciences had been lulled asleep to the present hour. God combines and brings about those favorable circumstances which produce attention and reflection and give weight to the expostulations of conscience.

23. *For he spake unto them by an interpreter.* Either there was a very great difference between the two languages as then spoken, or Joseph, to prevent all suspicion, might affect to be ignorant of both. We have many evidences in this book that the Egyptians, Hebrews, Canaanites, and Syrians could understand each other in a general way, though there are also proofs that there was a considerable difference between their dialects.

25. *Commanded to fill their sacks.* "Their vessels"; probably large woolen bags, or baskets lined with leather. These vessels, of whatever sort, must have been different from those called *sak* in the twenty-seventh and following verses, which was probably only a small "sack" or "bag," in which each had reserved a sufficiency of corn for his ass during the journey; the larger vessels or bags serving to hold the wheat or rice they had brought, and their own packages. The reader will at once see that the English word "sack" is plainly derived from the Hebrew.

26. *They laded their asses.* Amounting, no doubt, to several scores, if not hundreds, else they could not have brought a sufficiency of corn for the support of so large a family as that of Jacob.

27. *One of them opened his sack.* From v. 35 we learn that each of the ten brethren on emptying his sack when he returned found his money in it; can we suppose that this was not discovered by them all before? It seems not; and the reason was probably this: the money was put in the mouth of the sack of one only, in the sacks of the others it was placed at or near to the bottom; hence only one discovered it on the road, the rest found it when they came to empty their sacks at their father's house. *In the inn.* Our word *inn* gives us a false idea here; there were no such places of entertainment at that time in the desert over which they had to pass, nor are there any to the present day. Travellers generally endeavor to reach a well, where they fill their leathern bottles with fresh water, and having clogged their camels, asses, etc., permit them to crop any little verdure there may be in the place, keeping watch over them by turns.

28. *Their heart failed them.* "Their heart went out." This refers to that spasmodic affection which is felt in the breast at any sudden alarm or fright. Among the common people in our own country we find an expression exactly similar, "My heart was ready to leap out at my mouth," used on similar occasions. *What is this that God hath done unto us?* Their guilty consciences, now thoroughly awakened, were in continual alarms; they felt that they deserved God's curse, and every occurrence served to confirm and increase their suspicions.

36. *All these things are against me.* Literally, "All these things are upon me." They lie upon me as heavy loads, hastening my death; they are more than I can bear.

37. *Slay my two sons, if I bring him not to thee.* What a strange proposal made by a son to his father, concerning his grandchildren! But they show the honesty and affection of Reuben's heart; he felt deeply for his father's distress, and was determined to risk and hazard everything in order to relieve and comfort him. There is scarcely a transaction in which Reuben is concerned that does not serve to set his character in an amiable point of view, except the single instance mentioned in chap. xxxv. 22.

38. *He is left alone.* That is, Benjamin is the only remaining son of Rachel; for he supposed Joseph, who was the other son, to be dead. *Shall ye bring down my gray hairs with sorrow.* Here he keeps up the idea of the

MATTHEW HENRY

CHAPTER 43

Verses 1–10

1. Jacob urges his sons to go and buy more corn in Egypt, *v.* 1, 2. The famine continued; and the corn they had bought was all spent. 2. Judah urges him to consent that Benjamin should go down with them. Judah's conscience had lately smitten him for what he had done a great while ago against Joseph (*ch.* xlii. 21); and, as an evidence of the truth of his repentance he would make some amends for the irreparable injury he had done him by doubling his care concerning Benjamin.

Verses 11–14

I. Jacob's persuasibleness. He would be ruled by reason. "*If it must be so now, take your brother.* If no corn can be had but upon those terms, we may as well expose him to the perils of the journey as suffer ourselves and families, and Benjamin amongst the rest, to perish for want of bread." Constancy is a virtue, but obstinacy is not.

II. Jacob's prudence and justice, which appeared in three things:—1. He sent back the money which they had found in the sacks' mouths, with this discreet construction of it, *Peradventure it was an oversight.* Though we get it by oversight, if we keep it when the oversight is discovered, it is kept by deceit. 2. He sent double money, as much again as they took the time before, upon supposition that the price of corn might have risen, or to show a generous spirit, that they might be the more likely to find generous treatment with *the man, the lord of the land.* 3. He sent a present of such things as the land afforded, and as were scarce in Egypt—*balm and honey*, &c. (*v.* 11), the commodities that Canaan exported, *ch.* xxxvii. 25. Honey and spice will never make up the want of bread-corn. The famine was sore in Canaan, and yet they had balm and myrrh, &c. We may live well enough upon plain food without dainties; but we cannot live upon dainties without plain food. Let us thank God that that which is most needful and useful is generally most cheap and common.

III. Jacob's piety appearing in his prayer: *God Almighty give you mercy before the man! v.* 14. Jacob had formerly turned an angry brother into a kind one with a present and a prayer; and here he betakes himself to the same tried method, and it sped well.

Verses 15–25

Jacob's sons, having got leave to take Benjamin with them, went down the second time into Egypt to buy corn. If we should ever know what a famine of the word means, let us not think it much to travel as far for spiritual food as they did for corporal food. Now here we have an account of what passed between them and Joseph's steward. *They were afraid, because they were brought into Joseph's house, v.* 18. Now they thought they should be reckoned with about the money in the sacks' mouths, and should be charged as cheats. They therefore laid the case before the steward, and, as a substantial proof of their honesty, before they were charged with taking back their money they produced it. The steward encouraged them (*v.* 23): *Peace be to you, fear not.* He directs them to look at the divine Providence in the return of their money: *Your God, and the God of your father, has given you treasure in your sacks.* Hereby he silences their further enquiry about it. "Ask not how it came thither; Providence brought it to you, and let that satisfy you." It appears by what he said that, by his good master's instructions, he was brought to the knowledge of the true God, the God of the Hebrews.

JAMIESON, FAUSSET, BROWN

CHAPTER 43

VSS. 1-14. PREPARATIONS FOR A SECOND JOURNEY TO EGYPT. **2. their father said, . . . Go again, buy us a little food**—It was no easy matter to bring Jacob to agree to the only conditions on which his sons could return to Egypt (ch. 42:15). The necessity of immediately procuring fresh supplies for the maintenance of themselves and their families overcame every other consideration and extorted his consent to Benjamin joining in a journey, which his sons entered on with mingled feelings of hope and anxiety—of hope, because having now complied with the governor's demand to bring down their youngest brother, they flattered themselves that the alleged ground of suspecting them would be removed; and of apprehension that some ill designs were meditated against them.

11. take of the best fruits . . . a present—It is an Oriental practice never to approach a man of power without a present, and Jacob might remember how he pacified his brother (Prov. 21:14)—balm, spices, and myrrh (ch. 37:25), honey, which some think was *dibs*, a syrup made from ripe dates [BOCHART]; but others, the honey of Hebron, which is still valued as far superior to that of Egypt; nuts, pistachio nuts, of which Syria grows the best in the world; almonds, which were most abundant in Palestine. **12. take double money**—the first sum to be returned, and another sum for a new supply. The restored money in the sacks' mouth was a perplexing circumstance. But it might have been done inadvertently by one of the servants—so Jacob persuaded himself—and happy it was for his own peace and the encouragement of the travellers that he took this view. Besides the duty of restoring it, honesty in their case was clearly the best—the safest policy. **14. God Almightly give you mercy before the man**—Jacob is here committing them all to the care of God and, resigned to what appears a heavy trial, prays that it may be overruled for good.

15-30. ARRIVAL IN EGYPT. **15. stood before Joseph**—We may easily imagine the delight with which, amid the crowd of other applicants, the eye of Joseph would fix on his brethren and Benjamin. But occupied with his public duties, he consigned them to the care of a confidential servant till he should have finished the business of the day. **16. ruler of his house**—In the houses of wealthy Egyptians one upper man-servant was intrusted with the management of the house (cf. ch. 39:5). **slay, and make ready**—*Hebrew*, "kill a killing"—implying preparations for a grand entertainment (cf. ch. 31:54; I Sam. 25:11; Prov. 9:2; Matt. 22:4). The animals have to be killed as well as prepared at home. The heat of the climate requires that the cook should take the joints directly from the hands of the flesher, and the Oriental taste is, from habit, fond of newly killed meat. A great profusion of viands, with an inexhaustible supply of vegetables, was provided for the repasts, to which strangers were invited, the pride of Egyptian people consisting rather in the quantity and variety than in the choice or delicacy of the dishes at their table. **dine . . . at noon**—The hour of dinner was at midday. **18. the men were afraid**—Their feelings of awe on entering the stately mansion, unaccustomed as they were to houses at all, their anxiety at the reasons of their being taken there, their solicitude about the restored money, their honest simplicity in communicating their distress to the steward and his assurances of having received their money in "full weight," the offering of their fruit-present, which would, as usual, be done with some parade, and the Oriental salutations that passed between their host and them—are all described in a graphic and animated manner.

ADAM CLARKE

oppressive burden mentioned in v. 36, to which every occurrence was adding an additional weight, so that he felt it impossible to support it any longer.

CHAPTER 43

8. *Send the lad with me.* As the original is not *yeled,* from which we have derived our word "lad," but *naar,* it would have been better had our translators rendered it by some other term, such as "the youth," or "the young man," and thus the distinction in the Hebrew would have been better kept up. Benjamin was at this time at least twenty-four years of age, some think thirty, and had a family of his own. See chap. xlvi. 21. *That we may live, and not die.* An argument drawn from self-preservation, what some have termed "the first law of nature." By your keeping Benjamin we are prevented from going to Egypt; if we go not to Egypt we shall get no corn; if we get no corn we shall all perish by famine; and Benjamin himself, who otherwise might live, must, with thee and the whole family, infallibly die.

9. *Let me bear the blame for ever.* "Then shall I sin against thee all my days," and consequently be liable to punishment for violating my faith.

11. *Carry down the man a present.* From the very earliest times presents were used as means of introduction to great men. This is particularly noticed by Solomon: "A man's gift maketh room for him, and bringeth him before great men," Prov. xviii. 16. But what was the present brought to Joseph on this occasion? After all the labor of commentators, we are obliged to be contented with probabilities and conjecture. According to our translation, the gifts were balm, honey, spices, myrrh, nuts, and almonds.

12. *Double money.* What was returned in their sacks, and what was farther necessary to buy another load.

14. This verse may be literally translated thus: "And God, the all-sufficient, shall give you tender mercies before the man, and send to you your other brother, and Benjamin; and I, as I shall be childless, so I shall be childless." That is, I will submit to this privation, till God shall restore my children. It appears that this verse is spoken prophetically; and that God at this time gave Jacob a supernatural evidence that his children should be restored.

16. *Slay, and make ready. Teboach tebach,* "slay a slaying," or make a great slaughter—let preparations be made for a great feast or entertainment. See a similar form of speech, Prov. ix. 2; 1 Sam. xxv. 11; and Gen. xxxi. 54.

18. *And the men were afraid.* A guilty conscience needs no accuser. Everything alarms them; they now feel that God is exacting retribution, and they know not what the degrees shall be, nor where it shall stop. *Fall upon us.* "Roll himself upon us." A metaphor taken from wrestlers; when a man has overthrown his antagonist, he rolls himself upon him, in order to keep him down. *And our asses.* Which they probably had in great number with them; and which, if captured, would have been a great loss to the family of Jacob, as such cattle must have constituted a principal part of its riches.

20. *O sir, we came indeed . . . to buy food.* There is a frankness now in the conduct of Joseph's brethren that did not exist before; they simply and honestly relate the whole circumstance of the money being found in their sacks on their return from their last journey. Afflictions from the hand of God, and under His direction, have a wonderful tendency to humble the soul. Did men know how gracious His designs are in sending such, no murmur would ever be heard against the dispensations of Divine Providence.

23. *And he said.* The address of the steward in this verse plainly proves that the knowledge of the true God was in Egypt. It is probable that the steward himself was a Hebrew, and that Joseph had given him intimation of the whole affair; and though he was not at liberty to reveal it, yet he gives them assurances that the whole business will issue happily. *I had*

MATTHEW HENRY

Verses 26-34

I. The great respect that Joseph's brethren paid to him. When they brought him the present, *they bowed themselves before him* (*v.* 26); and again, when they gave him an account of their father's health, *they made obeisance*, and called him, *Thy servant our father*, *v.* 28. Thus were Joseph's dreams fulfilled more and more.

II. The great kindness that Joseph showed to them, while they little thought it was a brotherly kindness. Here is,

1. His kind enquiry concerning Jacob: *Is he yet alive?*

2. The kind notice he took of Benjamin, his own brother. (1) He put up a prayer for him: *God be gracious unto thee, my son*, *v.* 29. (2) He shed some tears for him, *v.* 30. Tears of tenderness and affection are no disparagement at all, even to great and wise men.

3. When his weeping had subsided so that he could refrain himself, he sat down to dinner with them, treated them nobly, and yet contrived every thing to amuse them.

He ordered three tables to be spread, one for his brethren, another for the Egyptians that dined with him (for so different were their customs that they did not care to eat together), another for himself, who durst not own himself a Hebrew, and yet would not sit with the Egyptians.

He placed his brethren according to their seniority (*v.* 33).

He gave them a very plentiful entertainment, sent messes to them from his own table, *v.* 34. This was the more generous in him, and the more obliging to them, because of the present scarcity of provisions. Their cares and fears were now over, and they ate their bread with joy, concluding they were now upon good terms with the man, the lord of the land. Joseph gave them to understand that Benjamin was his favourite; for his mess was *five times as much as any of theirs*.

CHAPTER 44

Verses 1-17

Joseph heaps further kindnesses upon his brethren, fills their sacks, returns their money, and sends them away full of gladness; but he also exercises them with further trials. Joseph ordered his steward to put a fine silver cup which he had (and which, it is likely, was used at his table when they dined with him) into Benjamin's sack's mouth, that it might seem as if he had stolen it from the table, and put it there himself, after his corn was delivered to him.

I. How the pretended criminals were pursued and arrested, on suspicion of having stolen a silver cup. The steward charged them with ingratitude.

JAMIESON, FAUSSET, BROWN

31-34. THE DINNER. **31. Joseph said, Set on bread**—equivalent to having dinner served, bread being a term inclusive of all victuals. The table was a small stool, most probably the usual round form, "since persons might even then be seated according to their rank or seniority, and the modern Egyptian table is not without its post of honor and a fixed gradation of place" [WILKINSON]. Two or at most three persons were seated at one table. But the host being the highest in rank of the company had a table to himself; while it was so arranged that an Egyptian was not placed nor obliged to eat from the same dish as a Hebrew. **32. Egyptians might not eat bread with the Hebrews; for that is an abomination**—The prejudice probably arose from the detestation in which, from the oppressions of the shepherd-kings, the nation held all of that occupation. **34. took and sent messes . . . Benjamin's mess was five times**—In Egypt, as in other Oriental countries, there were, and are, two modes of paying attention to a guest whom the host wishes to honor—either by giving a choice piece from his own hand, or ordering it to be taken to the stranger. The degree of respect shown consists in the quantity, and while the ordinary rule of distinction is a double mess, it must have appeared a very distinguished mark of favor bestowed on Benjamin to have no less than five times any of his brethren. **they drank, and were merry with him**—*Hebrew*, "drank freely" (same as Solomon's Song, 5:1, John 2:10). In all these cases the idea of intemperance is excluded. The painful anxieties and cares of Joseph's brethren were dispelled, and they were at ease.

CHAPTER 44

VSS. 1-34. POLICY TO STAY HIS BRETHREN. **1. And Joseph commanded the steward**—The design of putting the cup into the sack of Benjamin was obviously to bring that young man into a situation of difficulty or danger, in order thereby to discover how far the brotherly feelings of the rest would be roused to sympathize with his distress and stimulate their exertions in procuring his deliverance. But for what purpose was the money restored? It was done, in the first instance, from kindly feelings to his father; but another and further design seems to have been the prevention of any injurious impressions as to the character of Benjamin. The discovery of the cup in *his* possession, if there had been nothing else to judge by, might have fastened a painful suspicion of guilt on the youngest brother; but the sight of the money in each man's sack would lead all to the same conclusion, that Benjamin was just as innocent as themselves, although the additional circumstance of the cup being found in his sack would bring him into greater trouble and danger. **2. put my cup, the silver cup, in the sack's mouth**—It was a large goblet, as the original denotes, highly valued by its owner, on account of its costly material or its elegant finish and which had probably graced his table at the sumptuous entertainment of the previous day. **3. As soon as the morning was light, the men were sent away**—They commenced their homeward journey at early dawn (see on ch. 18:2); and it may be readily supposed in high spirits, after so happy an issue from all their troubles and anxieties. **4. When they were gone out of the city . . . Joseph said unto his steward**—They were brought to a sudden halt by the stunning intelligence that an article of rare value was missing from the governor's house. It was a silver cup; so strong suspicions were entertained against them that a special messenger was

ADAM CLARKE

your money. "Your money comes to me." As I am the steward, the cash for the corn belongs to me. Ye have no reason to be apprehensive of any evil; the whole transaction is between myself and you; receive, therefore, the money as a present from the God of your father, no matter whose hands He makes use of to convey it. The conduct of the steward, as well as his words, had a great tendency to relieve their burdened minds.

24. *Brought the men into Joseph's house.* This is exactly the way in which a Hindoo receives a guest. As soon as he enters, one of the civilities is the presenting of water to wash his feet.

27. *And he asked them of their welfare.* This verse may be thus translated: "And he asked them concerning their prosperity; and he said, Is your father prosperous, the old man who ye told me was alive? And they said, Thy servant our father prospers; he is yet alive."

29. *He lifted up his eyes, and saw his brother Benjamin.* They were probably introduced to him successively; and as Benjamin was the youngest, he would of course be introduced last. *God be gracious unto thee, my son.* A usual salutation in the East from the aged and superiors to the younger and inferiors.

32. *They set on for him by himself.* From the text it appears evident that there were three tables, one for Joseph, one for the Egyptians, and one for the eleven brethren. *The Egyptians might not eat bread with the Hebrews.* There might have been some *political* reason for this, with which we are unacquainted; but independently of this, two may be assigned. (1) The Hebrews were shepherds; and Egypt had been almost ruined by hordes of lawless wandering banditti, under the name of *Hyksos*, or "king-shepherds." (2) The Hebrews sacrificed those animals which the Egyptians held sacred, and fed on their flesh.

33. *The firstborn according to his birthright.* This must greatly astonish these brethren, to find themselves treated with so much ceremony and at the same time with so much discernment of their respective ages.

34. *Benjamin's mess was five times so much as any of theirs.* The circumstance of Benjamin's having a mess five times as large as any of his brethren shows the peculiar honor which Joseph designed to confer upon him.

CHAPTER 44

2. *Put my cup . . . in the sack's mouth of the youngest.* The stratagem of the cup seems to have been designed to bring Joseph's brethren into the highest state of perplexity and distress, that their deliverance by the discovery that Joseph was their brother might have its highest effect.

MATTHEW HENRY

II. How they pleaded for themselves. They solemnly protested their innocence, and offered to submit to the severest punishment if they should be found guilty, *v.* 9, 10.

III. How the theft was fastened upon Benjamin. In his sack the cup was found. They dare not arraign Joseph's justice, nor so much as suggest that perhaps he that had put their money in their sacks' mouths had put the cup there; but they throw themselves upon Joseph's mercy.

IV. Here is their humble submission, *v.* 16. 1. They acknowledge the righteousness of God: *God hath found out the iniquity of thy servants,* perhaps referring to the injury they had formerly done to Joseph, for which they thought God was now reckoning with them. 2. They surrender themselves prisoners to Joseph: *We are my lord's servants.* Now Joseph's dreams were accomplished to the utmost.

V. Joseph, with an air of justice, gives sentence that Benjamin only should be kept in bondage, and the rest should be dismissed; for why should any suffer but the guilty? It is plain he intended hereby to try the affection of his brethren to Benjamin and to their father. If they had gone away contentedly, and left Benjamin in bonds, no doubt Joseph would soon have released and promoted him, and sent notice to Jacob, and would have left the rest of his brethren justly to suffer for their hard-heartedness; but they proved to be better affected to Benjamin than he feared. Those that had sold Joseph would not now abandon Benjamin. The worst may mend in time.

Verses 18–34

We have here a most ingenious and pathetic speech which Judah made to Joseph on Benjamin's behalf, to obtain his discharge. Perhaps Judah was a better friend to Benjamin than the rest were, or the rest chose him for their spokesman, because he had a greater command of language than any of them.

I. A great deal of unaffected art, and unstudied unforced rhetoric, there is in this speech. 1. He addresses himself to Joseph with a great deal of respect and deference. 2. He represented Benjamin as one well worthy of his compassionate consideration (*v.* 20); he was *a little one,* compared with the rest of them; the youngest, brought up tenderly with his father. It made the case the more pitiable that he alone was left of his mother, and his brother was dead, namely, *Joseph.* 3. He urged it very closely that Joseph had himself constrained them to bring Benjamin with them. Was he not brought to Egypt, in obedience, purely in obedience, to the command of Joseph? and would he not show him some mercy? 4. The great argument he insisted upon was the insupportable grief it would be to his aged father if Benjamin should be left behind in servitude: "*If he should leave his father, his father would die;* much more if now he be left behind, never more to return to him." This therefore Judah presses with a great deal of earnestness: "*His life is bound up in the lad's life*" (*v.* 30). 5. Judah, in honour to the justice of Joseph's sentence, and to show his sincerity in this plea, offers himself to become a bondsman instead of Benjamin, *v.* 33. Neither Jacob nor Benjamin needed an intercessor with Joseph; for he himself loved them.

II. Upon the whole matter let us take notice, 1. How prudently Judah suppressed all mention of the crime that was charged upon Benjamin. 2. What good reason dying Jacob had to say, *Judah, thou art he whom thy brethren shall praise* (*ch.* xlix. 8), for he excelled them all in boldness, wisdom, eloquence, and especially tenderness for their father and family. 3. Judah's faithful adherence to Benjamin, now in his distress, was recompensed long after by the constant adherence of the tribe of Benjamin to the tribe of Judah, when all the other ten tribes deserted it. 4. How fitly does the apostle, when he is discoursing of the mediation of Christ, observe, that *our Lord sprang out of Judah* (Heb. vii. 14); for, like his father Judah, he not only *made intercession for the transgressors,* but he became a surety for them.

JAMIESON, FAUSSET, BROWN

despatched to search them. **5. Is not this it in which my lord drinketh**—not only kept for the governor's personal use, but whereby he divines. Divination by cups, to ascertain the course of futurity, was one of the prevalent superstitions of ancient Egypt, as it is of Eastern countries still. It is not likely that Joseph, a pious believer in the true God, would have addicted himself to this superstitious practice. But he might have availed himself of that popular notion to carry out the successful execution of his stratagem for the last decisive trial of his brethren. **6, 7. he overtook them, and he spake . . . these words**—The steward's words must have come upon them like a thunderbolt, and one of their most predominant feelings must have been the humiliating and galling sense of being made so often objects of suspicion. Protesting their innocence, they invited a search. The challenge was accepted. Beginning with the eldest, every sack was examined, and the cup being found in Benjamin's, they all returned in an indescribable agony of mind to the house of the governor, throwing themselves at his feet, with the remarkable confession, "God hath found out the iniquity of thy servants." **16-34. Judah said, What shall we say?**—This address needs no comment—consisting at first of short, broken sentences, as if, under the overwhelming force of the speaker's emotions, his utterance were choked, it becomes more free and copious by the effort of speaking, as he proceeds. Every word finds its way to the heart; and it may well be imagined that Benjamin, who stood there speechless like a victim about to be laid on the altar, when he heard the magnanimous offer of Judah to submit to slavery for his ransom, would be bound by a lifelong gratitude to his generous brother, a tie that seems to have become hereditary in his tribe. Joseph's behavior must not be viewed from any single point, or in separate parts, but as a whole—a well-thought, deep-laid, closely, connected plan; and though some features of it do certainly exhibit an appearance of harshness, yet the pervading principle of his conduct was real, genuine, brotherly kindness. Read in this light, the narrative of the proceedings describes the continuous, though secret, pursuit of one end; and Joseph exhibits, in his management of the scheme, a very high order of intellect, a warm and susceptible heart, united to a judgment that exerted a complete control over his feelings—a happy invention in devising means towards the attainment of his ends and an inflexible adherence to the course, however painful, which prudence required.

ADAM CLARKE

5. *Whereby . . . he divineth?* Divination by cups has been from time immemorial prevalent among the Asiatics; and for want of knowing this, commentators have spent a profusion of learned labor upon these words, in order to reduce them to that kind of meaning which would at once be consistent with the scope and design of the history, and save Joseph from the impeachment of sorcery and divination. I take the word *nachash* here in its general acceptation of "to view attentively, to inquire." Now though it is not at all likely that Joseph practiced any kind of divination, yet probably, according to the superstition of those times, supernatural influence might be attributed to his cup; and as the whole transaction related here was merely intended to deceive his brethren for a short time, he might as well affect divination by his cup, as he affected to believe they had stolen it. The steward, therefore, uses the word *nachash* in its proper meaning: "Is not this it out of which my lord drinketh, and in which he inspecteth accurately?" And hence Joseph says, v. 15: *Wot ye not*—did ye not know, *that such a person as I* (having such a cup) *would accurately and attentively look into it?*

16. *What shall we say?* No words can more strongly mark confusion and perturbation of mind. They, no doubt, all thought that Benjamin had actually stolen the cup; and the probability of this guilt might be heightened by the circumstance of his having that very cup to drink out of at dinner; for as he had the most honorable mess, so it is likely he had the most honorable cup to drink out of at the entertainment.

18. *Thou art even as Pharaoh.* As wise, as powerful, and as much to be dreaded as he. In the Asiatic countries, the reigning monarch is always considered to be the pattern of all perfection; and the highest honor that can be conferred on any person is to resemble him to the monarch, as the monarch himself is likened, in the same complimentary way, to an angel of God. See 2 Sam. xiv. 17-18. Judah is the chief speaker here, because it was in consequence of his becoming surety for Benjamin that Jacob permitted him to accompany them to Egypt. See chap. xliii. 9.

No paraphrase can heighten the effect of Judah's address to Joseph. It is perhaps one of the most tender, affecting pieces of natural oratory ever spoken or penned; and we need not wonder to find that when Joseph heard it he could not refrain himself, but wept aloud. His soul must have been insensible beyond what is common to human nature had he not immediately yielded to a speech so delicately tender and so powerfully impressive. We cannot but deplore the unnatural and unscientific division of the narrative in our common Bibles, which obliges us to have recourse to another chapter in order to witness the effects which this speech produced on the heart of Joseph.

MATTHEW HENRY — CHAPTER 45

Verses 1–15

Judah and his brethren were waiting for an answer.

I. Joseph ordered all his attendants to withdraw, *v.* 1. The private conversations of friends are the most free. Thus Christ graciously manifests himself and his loving-kindness to his people, out of the sight and hearing of the world.

JAMIESON, FAUSSET, BROWN — CHAPTER 45

VSS. 1-28. JOSEPH MAKING HIMSELF KNOWN. **1. Then Joseph could not refrain himself**—The severity of the inflexible magistrate here gives way to the natural feelings of the man and the brother. However well he had disciplined his mind, he felt it impossible to resist the artless eloquence of Judah. He saw a satisfactory proof, in the return of *all* his brethren on such an occasion, that they were affectionately united to one another; he had heard enough to convince him that time, reflection,

ADAM CLARKE — CHAPTER 45

1. *Joseph could not refrain himself.* The word *hithappek* is very emphatic; it signifies to "force one's self, to do something against nature, to do violence to one's self." Joseph could no longer constrain himself to act a feigned part—all the brother and the son rose up in him at once, and overpowered all his resolutions; he felt for his father, he realized his disappointment and agony; and he felt for his brethren, "now at his feet submissive in distress"; and, that he might

MATTHEW HENRY

II. Tears were the preface or introduction to his discourse, *v.* 2. These were tears of tenderness and strong affection.

III. He very abruptly tells them who he was: *I am Joseph.* They knew him only by his Egyptian name, *Zaphnath-paaneah,* his Hebrew name being lost and forgotten in Egypt; but now he teaches them to call him by that. Thus when Christ would convince Paul he said, *I am Jesus;* and when he would comfort his disciples he said, *It is I, be not afraid.* Thus when Christ manifests himself to his people he encourages them to draw near to him with a true heart.

IV. He endeavours to assuage their grief for the injuries they had done him, by showing them that God had brought much good out of it (*v.* 5): *Be not grieved, nor angry with yourselves.* Sinners must grieve for their sins; but true penitents should be greatly affected when they see God thus bringing good out of evil. Now he tells them how long the famine was likely to last—*five years;* yet (*v.* 6) what a capacity he was in of being kind to his relations and friends. *God sent me before you, v.* 5, 7. 1. God's Israel is the particular care of God's providence. 2. Providence looks a great way forward, and has a long reach. The psalmist praises God for this (Ps. cv. 17): *He sent a man before them, even Joseph.* God sees his work from the beginning to the end, but we do not, Eccl. iii. 11. 3. God often works by contraries. Those that put Christ to death were many of them saved by his death. 4. God must have all the glory. *It was not you that sent me hither, but God, v.* 8. They must not be proud of it, because it was God's doing, and not theirs.

V. He promises to take care of his father and all the family during the rest of the years of famine. 1. His brethren must hasten to Canaan, and must inform Jacob that his son Joseph was *lord of all Egypt* (*v.* 9). If any thing would make him young again, this would. 2. He is very earnest that his father and all his family should come to him to Egypt: *Come down unto me, tarry not, v.* 9. He allots his dwelling in Goshen. He promises to provide for him: *I will nourish thee, v.* 11. Our Lord Jesus being, like Joseph, exalted to the highest honours and powers of the upper world, it is his will that all that are his should be with him where he is, John xvii. 24.

VI. Endearments were interchanged between him and his brethren. He began with the youngest, his own brother Benjamin, who was but about a year old when Joseph was separated from his brethren. After he had embraced Benjamin, he, in like manner, caressed them all (*v.* 15); and then *his brethren talked with him.*

JAMIESON, FAUSSET, BROWN

or grace had made a happy improvement on their characters; and he would probably have proceeded in a calm and leisurely manner to reveal himself as prudence might have dictated. But when he heard the heroic self-sacrifice of Judah and realized all the affection of that proposal—a proposal for which he was totally unprepared—he was completely unmanned; he felt himself forced to bring this painful trial to an end. **he cried, Cause every man to go out from me**—In ordering the departure of witnesses of this last scene, he acted as a warm-hearted and real friend to his brothers—his conduct was dictated by motives of the highest prudence—that of preventing their early iniquities from becoming known either to the members of his household, or among the people of Egypt. **2. he wept aloud**—No doubt, from the fulness of highly excited feelings; but to indulge in vehement and long-continued transports of sobbing is the usual way in which the Orientals express their grief. **3. I am Joseph**—The emotions that now rose in his breast as well as that of his brethren—and chased each other in rapid succession—were many and violent. He was agitated by sympathy and joy; they were astonished, confounded, terrified; and betrayed their terror, by shrinking as far as they could from his presence. So "troubled" were they, that he had to repeat his announcement of himself; and what kind, affectionate terms he did use. He spoke of their having sold him—not to wound their feelings, but to convince them of his identity; and then, to reassure their minds, he traced the agency of an overruling Providence, in his exile and present honor. Not that he wished them to roll the responsibility of their crime on God; no, his only object was to encourage their confidence and induce them to trust in the plans he had formed for the future comfort of their father and themselves. **6. and yet there are five years, in the which there shall neither be earing nor harvest**—"Ear" is an *old* English word, meaning "to plough" (cf. I Sam. 8:12; Isa. 30:24). This seems to confirm the view given (ch. 41:57) that the famine was caused by an extraordinary drought, which prevented the annual overflowing of the Nile; and of course made the land unfit to receive the seed of Egypt.

14, 15.

And he fell upon . . . Benjamin's neck—The sudden transition from a condemned criminal to a fondled brother, might have occasioned fainting or even death, had not his tumultuous feelings been re-

ADAM CLARKE

give free and full scope to his feelings, and the most ample play of the workings of his affectionate heart, he ordered all his attendants to go out, while he made himself known to his brethren.

2. *The Egyptians and the house of Pharaoh heard.* Pharaoh's servants, or any of the members of his household, such as those whom Joseph had desired to withdraw, and who might still be within hearing of his voice. The words may only mean that the report was brought to Pharaoh's house.

5. *Be not grieved, nor angry with yourselves.* This discovers a truly noble mind; he not only forgives and forgets, but he wishes even those who had wronged him to forget the injury they had done, that they might not suffer distress on the account; and with deep piety he attributes the whole to the providence of God; for, says he, *God did send me before you to preserve life.* On every word here a strong emphasis may be laid. It is not *you,* but *God;* it is not you that *sold* me, but God who *sent* me; Egypt and Canaan must both have perished had not a merciful provision been made; you were to come down hither, and God sent me before you; death must have been the consequence of this famine had not God sent me here to preserve life.

6. *There shall neither be earing nor harvest. Earing* has been supposed to mean collecting the ears of corn, which would confound it with harvest. The word, however, means ploughing or seedtime, and plainly means that there should be no seedtime, and consequently no *harvest;* and why? Because there should be a total want of rain in other countries, and the Nile should not rise above twelve cubits in Egypt; see on chap. xli. 31. But the expressions here must be qualified a little, as we find from chap. xlvii. 19 that the Egyptians came to Joseph to buy seed; and it is probable that even during this famine they sowed some of the ground, particularly on the borders of the river, from which a crop, though not an abundant one, might be produced. The passage, however, in the above chapter may refer to the last year of the famine, when they came to procure seed for the ensuing year.

8. *He hath made me a father to Pharaoh.* It has already been conjectured that father was a name of office in Egypt, and that "father of Pharaoh" might among them signify the same as prime minister or the king's minister does among us. In Judg. xvii. 10, Micah says to the young Levite, "Dwell with me, and be unto me a father and a priest."

10. *Thou shalt dwell in the land of Goshen.* Probably this district had been allotted to Joseph by the king of Egypt, else we can scarcely think he could have promised it so positively without first obtaining Pharaoh's consent. Goshen was the most easterly province of Lower Egypt, not far from the Arabian Gulf, lying next to Canaan, from whence it is supposed to have been about fourscore miles distant, though Hebron was distant from the Egyptian capital about three hundred miles. At Goshen, Jacob stayed till Joseph visited him, chap. xlvi. 28. It is also called the "land of Rameses," chap. xlvii. 11, from a city of that name, which was the metropolis of the country. Josephus, *Antiq.,* 1. ii, c. 4, makes Heliopolis, the city of Joseph's father-in-law, the place of the Israelites' residence. As *geshem* signifies "rain" in Hebrew, St. Jerome and some others have supposed that *Goshen* comes from the same root, and that the land in question was called thus because it had rain, which was not the case with Egypt in general; and as it was on the confines of the Arabian Gulf, it is very probable that it was watered from heaven, and it might be owing to this circumstance that it was peculiarly fertile, for it is stated to be the "best" of the land of Egypt. See chap. xlvii. 6, 11.

12. *That it is my mouth that speaketh unto you.* Undoubtedly Joseph laid considerable stress on his speaking with them in the Hebrew tongue, without the assistance of an interpreter, as in the case mentioned in chap. xlii. 23.

14. *He fell upon his brother Benjamin's neck.* Among the Asiatics kissing the beard, the neck, and the shoulders is in use to the present day; and probably falling on the neck signifies no more than kissing the neck or shoulders, with

MATTHEW HENRY

Verses 16-24

I. The kindness of Pharaoh to Joseph, and to his relations for his sake: he bade his brethren welcome (*v.* 16), though it was a time of scarcity, and they were likely to be a charge to him. He engaged Joseph to send for his father down to Egypt, and promised to furnish them with all conveniences both for his removal thither and his settlement there. If the good of all the land of Egypt would suffice him, he was welcome to it all, so that they need not *regard their stuff, v.* 20. What they had in Canaan he reckoned but stuff, in comparison with what he had for them in Egypt.

II. The kindness of Joseph to his father and brethren. Pharaoh was respectful to Joseph, in gratitude, because he had been an instrument of much good to him. Joseph likewise was respectful to his father and brethren. He gave them waggons and provisions for the way, both going and coming. To his brethren he gave two suits apiece of good clothes, to Benjamin five suits, and money besides in his pocket, *v.* 22. To his father he sent a very handsome present of the varieties of Egypt, *v.* 23. He dismissed them with a seasonable caution: *See that you fall not out by the way, v.* 24. Now Joseph, having forgiven them all, lays this obligation upon them, not to upbraid one another. This charge our Lord Jesus has given to us, *that we love one another.* For, 1. We are brethren, we have all one Father. 2. We are his brethren, and we shame our relation to him *who is our peace,* if we fall out. 3. We are guilty, *verily guilty,* and, instead of quarrelling with one another, have a great deal of reason to fall out with ourselves.

Verses 25-28

We have here the good news brought to Jacob. The relation of it, at first, sunk his spirits. To hear that *Joseph is alive* is too good news to be true; he faints, for he believes it not. Note, We faint, because we do not believe. Jacob had easily believed his son formerly when they told him, *Joseph is dead*; but he can hardly believe them now that they tell him, *Joseph is alive.* Weak and tender spirits are influenced more by fear than hope. But at length Jacob is convinced of the truth of the story, especially when he sees the waggons which were sent to carry him (for seeing is believing). He says nothing of Joseph's glory, of which they told him; it was enough to him that Joseph was alive.

JAMIESON, FAUSSET, BROWN

lieved by a torrent of tears. But Joseph's attentions were not confined to Benjamin. He affectionately embraced every one of his brothers in succession; and by those actions, his forgiveness was demonstrated more fully than it could be by words. **17-20. Pharaoh said unto Joseph, Say unto thy brethren**—As Joseph might have been prevented by delicacy, the king himself invited the patriarch and all his family to migrate into Egypt; and he made most liberal arrangements for their removal and their subsequent settlement. It displays the character of this Pharaoh to advantage, that he was so kind to the relatives of Joseph; but indeed the greatest liberality he could show could never recompense the services of so great a benefactor of his kingdom. **21. Joseph gave them wagons**—which must have been novelties in Palestine; for wheeled carriages were almost unknown there. **22. changes or raiment**—It was and is customary with great men, to bestow on their friends dresses of distinction, and in places where they are of the same description and quality, the value of these presents consists in their number. The great number given to Benjamin bespoke the warmth of his brother's attachment to him; and Joseph felt, from the amiable temper they now all displayed, he might, with perfect safety, indulge this fond partiality for his mother's son. **23. to his father he sent**—a supply of everything that could contribute to his support and comfort—the large and liberal scale on which that supply was given being intended, like the five messes of Benjamin, as a token of his filial love. **24. so he sent his brethren away**—In dismissing them on their homeward journey, he gave them this particular admonition: "See that ye fall not out by the way"—a caution that would be greatly needed; for not only during the journey would they be occupied in recalling the parts they had respectively acted in the events that led to Joseph's being sold into Egypt, but their wickedness would soon have to come to the knowledge of their venerable father.

ADAM CLARKE

the arms around.

20. *Regard not your stuff.* Literally, "Let not your eye spare your instruments" or vessels. *Keleychem,* a general term, in which may be included household furniture, agricultural utensils, or implements of any description. They were not to delay nor encumber themselves with articles which could be readily found in Egypt, and were not worth so long a carriage.

21. *Joseph gave them wagons. Agaloth,* from *agal,* which, though not used as a verb in the Hebrew Bible, evidently means to "turn round, roll round," and hence very properly applied to wheel carriages. It appears from this that such vehicles were very early in use, and that the road from Egypt to Canaan must have been very open and much frequented, else such carriages could not have passed by it.

22. *Changes of raiment.* It is a common custom with all the Asiatic sovereigns to give both garments and money to ambassadors and persons of distinction whom they particularly wish to honor. Hence they keep in their wardrobes several hundred changes of raiment, ready made up for presents of this kind. That such were given by way of reward and honor, see Judg. xiv. 12, 19; Rev. vi. 11.

23. *Meat for his father by the way. Mazon,* from *zan,* to "prepare, provide." Hence "prepared meat," some made-up dish. As the word is used, 2 Chron. xvi. 14, for aromatic preparations, it may be restrained in its meaning to something of that kind here.

24. *See that ye fall not out by the way.* This prudent caution was given by Joseph to prevent his brethren from accusing each other for having sold him; and to prevent them from envying Benjamin for the superior favor shown him by his brother. It is strange, but so it is, that children of the same parents are apt to envy each other, fall out, and contend; and therefore the exhortation in this verse must be always seasonable in a large family.

26. *Jacob's heart fainted.* Probably the good news so overpowered him as to cast him into a swoon. *He believed them not*—he thought it was too good news to be true.

27. *When he saw the wagons . . . the spirit of Jacob . . . revived.* The wagons were additional evidences of the truth of what he had heard from his sons; and the consequence was that he was restored to fresh vigor, he seemed as if he had gained new life, *vattechi,* "and he lived."

28. *It is enough; Joseph my son is yet alive.* It was not the state of dignity to which Joseph had arisen that particularly affected Jacob; it was the consideration that he was still alive. It was this that caused him to exclaim *rab;* "Much! Multiplied! My son is yet alive! I will go and see him before I die." None can realize this scene; the words, the circumstances, all refer to indescribable feelings.

This chapter, which contains the unravelling of the plot, and wonderfully illustrates the mysteries of these particular providences, is one of the most interesting in the whole account; the speech of Joseph to his brethren, vv. 1-13, is inferior only to that of Judah in the preceding chapter. He saw that his brethren were confounded at his presence, that they were struck with his present power, and that they keenly remembered and deeply deplored their own guilt. It was necessary to comfort them, lest their hearts should have been overwhelmed with overmuch sorrow. How delicate and finely wrought is the apology he makes for them! The whole heart of the affectionate brother is at once seen in it—art is confounded and swallowed up by nature—"Be not grieved, nor angry with yourselves . . . it was not *you* that sent me hither, but God." What he says also concerning his father shows the warmest feelings of a benevolent and filial heart. Indeed, the whole chapter is a masterpiece of composition, and it is the more impressive because it is evidently a simple relation of facts just as they occurred.

F. B. MEYER:

Joseph sends for his father. This is an Easter lesson. It must have seemed to Jacob and his children as though Joseph were indeed risen from the dead. Hardly more startling were the appearances of the risen Lord than the news carried back to Jacob that his long-lost and much-mourned son was the prime minister of Egypt. Joseph had not forgotten his father. His one desire was to bring him to share his glory. For this he sent the wagons to transport the whole family to his side. At first Jacob was incredulous. It seemed too good to be true. But when he saw the wagons that Joseph had sent, that touch of delicate thoughtfulness, in such striking contrast to the cheerless isolation and loneliness of the last few years, caused his aged spirit to revive. Let us talk of the glory of our risen and ascended Lord, and especially of his desire that where he is we may be also. Now let us thank him that he is not only willing to receive us, but provides the grace and help of the Spirit to transport us thither.—*Bible Commentary*

MATTHEW HENRY

CHAPTER 46

Verses 1–4

Jacob has here a very great concern before him.

I. How he acknowledged God in this way. He *came to Beersheba*, from Hebron, where he now dwelt; and there *he offered sacrifices to the God of his father Isaac, v.* 1. Abraham called on God there (*ch.* xxi. 33), so did Isaac (*ch.* xxvi. 25). In his devotion, 1. He had an eye to God as the God of his father Isaac, that is, a God in covenant with him. 2. He *offered sacrifices*, (1) By way of thanksgiving for the late blessed change of the face of his family, for the good news he had received concerning Joseph, and for the hopes he had of seeing him. (2) By way of petition for the presence of God with him in his intended journey. (3) By way of consultation. The heathen consulted their oracles by sacrifice. Jacob would not go till he had asked God's leave.

II. How God directed his paths: *In the visions of the night God spoke unto him, v.* 2. If we speak to him as we ought, he will not fail to speak to us. What has God to say to him?

1. He renews the covenant with him: *I am God, the God of thy father* (*v.* 3).

2. He encourages him to make this removal of his family: *Fear not to go down into Egypt*. We must always rejoice with trembling. Jacob had many careful thoughts about this journey, which God took notice of. (1) He was old. It was a long journey. (2) He feared lest his sons should be tainted with the idolatry of Egypt, and forget the God of their fathers, or enamoured with the pleasures of Egypt, and forget the land of promise.

3. He promises him comfort in the removal. (1) That he should multiply in Egypt. (2) That he should have God's presence with him: *I will go down with thee into Egypt*. (3) That neither he nor his should be lost in Egypt. Though Jacob died in Egypt, yet this promise was fulfilled, [1] In the bringing up of his body to be buried in Canaan. [2] In the bringing up of his seed to be settled in Canaan. Whatever low or darksome valley we are called into at any time, we may be confident, if God go down with us into it, that he will surely bring us up again. If he go with us down to death, he will surely bring us up again to glory. (4) That living and dying, his beloved Joseph should be a comfort to him: *Joseph shall put his hand upon thine eyes*.

Verses 5–27

Old Jacob is here flitting. Little did he think of ever leaving Canaan; he expected, no doubt, *to die in his nest*, and to leave his seed in actual possession of the promised land: but Providence orders it otherwise. It is good to be ready, not only for the grave, but for whatever may happen betwixt us and the grave. We have here a particular account of the names of Jacob's family, *his sons' sons*, most of whom are afterwards mentioned as heads of houses in the several tribes. When Jacob himself removed to a land of plenty, he would not leave any of his children behind him to starve in a barren land. It was now 215 years since God had promised Abraham to make him a great nation (*ch.* xii. 2); and yet that branch of his seed on which the promise was entailed had increased only to seventy. When God pleases, *a little one shall become a thousand*, Isa. lx. 22.

JAMIESON, FAUSSET, BROWN

CHAPTER 46

Vss. 1-4. SACRIFICE AT BEER-SHEBA. **1. Israel took his journey with all that he had**—that is, his household; for in compliance with Pharaoh's recommendation, he left his heavy furniture behind. In contemplating a step so important as that of leaving Canaan, which at his time of life he might never revisit, so pious a patriarch would ask the guidance and counsel of God. With all his anxiety to see Joseph, he would rather have died in Canaan without that highest of earthly gratifications than leave it without the consciousness of carrying the divine blessing along with him. **came to Beer-sheba**—That place, which was in his direct route to Egypt, had been a favorite encampment of Abraham (ch. 21:33) and Isaac (ch. 26:25), and was memorable for their experience of the divine goodness; and Jacob seems to have deferred his public devotions till he had reached a spot so consecrated by covenant to his own God and the God of his fathers. **2. God spake unto Israel**—Here is a virtual renewal of the covenant and an assurance of its blessings. Moreover, here is an answer on the chief subject of Jacob's prayer and a removal of any doubt as to the course he was meditating. At first the prospect of paying a personal visit to Joseph had been viewed with unmingled joy. But, on calmer consideration, many difficulties appeared to lie in the way. He may have remembered the prophecy to Abraham that his posterity was to be afflicted in Egypt and also that his father had been expressly told *not* to go; he may have feared the contamination of idolatry to his family and their forgetfulness of the land of promise. These doubts were removed by the answer of the oracle, and an assurance given him of great and increasing prosperity. **3. I will there make of thee a great nation**—How truly this promise was fulfilled, appears in the fact that the seventy souls who went down into Egypt increased, in the space of 215 years, to 180,000. **4. I will also surely bring thee up again**—As Jacob could not expect to live till the former promise was realized, he must have seen that the latter was to be accomplished only to his posterity. To himself it was literally verified in the removal of his remains to Canaan; but, in the large and liberal sense of the words, it was made good only on the establishment of Israel in the land of promise. **Joseph shall put his hand upon thine eyes**—shall perform the last office of filial piety; and this implied that he should henceforth enjoy, without interruption, the society of that favorite son.

5-27. IMMIGRATION TO EGYPT. **5. Jacob rose up from Beer-sheba**—to cross the border and settle in Egypt. However refreshed and invigorated in spirit by the religious services at Beer-sheba, he was now borne down by the infirmities of advanced age; and, therefore, his sons undertook all the trouble and toil of the arrangements, while the enfeebled old patriarch, with the wives and children, was conveyed by slow and leisurely stages in the Egyptian vehicles sent for their accommodation. **6. goods, which they had gotten in the land**—not furniture, but substance—precious things. **7. daughters**—As Dinah was his only daughter, this must mean daughters-in-law. **all his seed, brought he with him**—Though disabled by age from active superintendence, yet, as the venerable sheik of the tribe, he was looked upon as their common head and consulted in every step.

ADAM CLARKE

CHAPTER 46

1. *And came to Beer-sheba*. This place appears to be mentioned, not only because it was the way from Hebron, where Jacob resided, to Egypt, whither he was going, but because it was a consecrated place, a place where God had appeared to Abraham, chap. xxi. 33, and to Isaac, chap. xxvi. 23, and where Jacob is encouraged to expect a manifestation of the same goodness. He chooses, therefore, to begin his journey with a visit to God's house; and as he is going into a strange land, he feels it right to renew his covenant with God by sacrifice. There is an old proverb which applies strongly to this case: "Prayers and provender never hinder any man's journey." He who would travel safely must take God with him.

3. *Fear not to go down into Egypt*. It appears that there had been some doubts in the patriarch's mind relative to the propriety of this journey; he found, from the confession of his own sons, how little they were to be trusted. But every doubt is dispelled by this divine manifestation. (1) He may go down confidently; no evil shall befall him. (2) Even in Egypt the covenant shall be fulfilled: God will make of him there a great nation. (3) God himself will accompany him on his journey, be with him in the strange land, and even bring back his bones to rest with those of his fathers. (4) He shall see Joseph, and this same beloved son shall be with him in his last hours, and do the last kind office for him. "Joseph shall put his hand upon thine eyes." It is not likely that Jacob would have at all attempted to go down to Egypt had he not received these assurances from God; and it is very likely that he offered his sacrifice merely to obtain this information. It was now a time of famine in Egypt, and God had forbidden his father, Isaac, to go down to Egypt when there was a famine there, chap. xxvi. 1-3; besides, he may have had some general intimation of the prophecy delivered to his grandfather, Abraham, that his seed should be afflicted in Egypt, chap. xv. 13-14; and he also knew that Canaan, not Egypt, was to be the inheritance of his family, chap. xii. On all these accounts it was necessary to have the most explicit directions from God before he should take such a journey.

7. *All his seed brought he with him into Egypt*. When Jacob went down into Egypt he was in the one hundred and thirtieth year of his age, 215 years after the promise was made to Abraham, chap. xii. 1-4.

8. *These are the names of the children of Israel*. It may be necessary to observe here, *First*, that several of these names are expressed differently elsewhere; compare Num. xxvi. 12; 1 Chron. iv. 24. But it is no uncommon case for the same person to have different names, or the same name to be differently pronounced; see chap. xxv. 15. *Secondly*, that it is probable that some names in this list are brought in by prolepsis or anticipation, as the persons were born (probably) during the seventeen years which Jacob sojourned in Egypt, see v. 12. *Thirdly*, that the families of some are entered more at large than others because of their peculiar respectability, as in the case of Judah, Joseph, and Benjamin.

12. *The sons of Pharez were Hezron and Hamul*. It is not likely that Pharez was more than ten years of age when he came into Egypt, and if so he could not have had children; therefore it is necessary to consider Hezron and Hamul as being born during the seventeen years that Jacob sojourned in Egypt, see on v. 8; and it appears necessary, for several reasons, to take these seventeen years into the account, as it is very probable that what is called the going down into Egypt includes the seventeen years which Jacob spent there.

20. *Unto Joseph . . . were born Manasseh and Ephraim*. There is a remarkable addition here in the Septuagint, which must be noticed: "These were the sons of Manasseh whom his Syrian concubine bore unto him: Machir; and Machir begat Galaad. The sons of Ephraim, Manasseh's brother, were Sutalaam and Taam; and the sons of Sutalaam, Edem." These add five persons to the list, and make out the number given by Stephen, Acts vii. 14, which it seems he had taken from the text of the Sep-

MATTHEW HENRY

JOHN LANGE:

The numbering of the souls in Jacob's household evidently points to the important symbolic number 70. This appears in its significance throughout the history of the kingdom of God. It is reflected in the ethnological table, in the 70 elders of Moses, in the Jewish Sanhedrin, in the Alexandrian version of the LXX, in the 70 disciples of our Lord, in the Jewish reduction of the heathen world to 70 nations. Ten is the number of the completed human development, seven the number of perfection in God's work; seventy, therefore, is the development of perfection and holiness in God's people. But between the complete development and the germ there must be a correspondence; and this is the family of the patriarch, consisting of seventy souls.

—*Commentary on the Holy Scriptures*

Verses 28–34

I. The joyful meeting between Jacob and his son Joseph, in which observe,

1. Jacob's prudence in sending Judah before him to Joseph, to give him notice of his arrival in Goshen.

2. Joseph's filial respect to him. He went in his chariot to meet him, and, in the interview, showed, (1) How much he honoured him. (2) How much he loved him. Time did not wear out the sense of his obligations, but his tears which he shed abundantly upon his father's neck, for joy to see him, were real indications of the sincere and strong affection he had for him.

3. Jacob's great satisfaction in this meeting.

II. Joseph's prudent care concerning his brethren's settlement. Time was when they were contriving to get rid of him; now he is contriving to settle them to their satisfaction and advantage: this is rendering good for evil. Now, 1. He would have them to live *in the land of Goshen*, which lay nearest to Canaan, and which perhaps was more thinly peopled by the Egyptians, and well furnished with pastures for cattle. He desired they might live separately, that they might be in the less danger both of being infected by the vices of the Egyptians and of being insulted by the malice of the Egyptians. 2. He would have them to continue shepherds, and not to be ashamed to own that as their occupation before Pharaoh. It is better to be the credit of a mean post than the shame of a high one.

JAMIESON, FAUSSET, BROWN

8-27. all the souls of the house of Jacob, which came into Egypt, were threescore and ten—Strictly speaking, there were only sixty-six went to Egypt; but to these add Joseph and his two sons, and Jacob the head of the clan, and the whole number amounts to seventy. In the speech of Stephen (Acts 7:14) the number is stated to be seventy-five; but as that estimate includes five sons of Ephraim and Manasseh (I Chron. 7:14-20), born in Egypt, the two accounts coincide.

28-34. ARRIVAL TO EGYPT. **28. he sent Judah before him unto Joseph**—This precautionary measure was obviously proper for apprising the king of the entrance of so large a company within his territories; moreover, it was necessary in order to receive instruction from Joseph as to the *locale* of their future settlement.

29, 30. Joseph made ready his chariot—The difference between chariot and wagon was not only in the lighter and more elegant construction of the former, but in the one being drawn by horses and the other by oxen. Being a public man in Egypt, Joseph was required to appear everywhere in an equipage suitable to his dignity; and, therefore, it was not owing either to pride or ostentatious parade that he drove his carriage, while his father's family were accommodated only in rude and humble wagons. **presented himself unto him**—in an attitude of filial reverence (cf. Exod. 22:17). The interview was a most affecting one—the happiness of the delighted father was now at its height; and life having no higher charms, he could, in the very spirit of the aged Simeon, have departed in peace. **31-34. Joseph said, ... I will go up, and show Pharaoh**—It was a tribute of respect due to the king to inform him of their arrival. And the instructions which he gave them were worthy of his character alike as an affectionate brother and a religious man.

ADAM CLARKE

tuagint. The addition in the Septuagint is not found in either the Hebrew or the Samaritan at present; and some suppose that it was taken either from Num. xxvi. 29, 35 or 1 Chron. vii. 14-20, but in none of these places does the addition appear as it stands in the Septuagint, though some of the names are found interspersed. Various means have been proposed to find the seventy persons in the text, and to reconcile the Hebrew with the Septuagint and the New Testament.

Dr. Hales's method is, I think, satisfactory: "Moses states that all the souls that came with Jacob into Egypt, which issued from his loins (except his sons' wives), were sixty-six souls, Gen. xlvi. 26. . . . If to these sixty-six children, and grandchildren, and great-grandchildren, we add Jacob himself, Joseph and his two sons, the amount is seventy, the whole amount of Jacob's family which settled in Egypt.

"In this statement the wives of Jacob's sons, who formed part of the household, are omitted; but they amounted to nine, for of the twelve wives of the twelve sons of Jacob, Judah's wife was dead, chap. xxxviii. 12, and Simeon's also, as we may collect from his youngest son Shaul by a Canaanitess, v. 10, and Joseph's wife was already in Egypt. These nine wives, therefore, added to the sixty-six, give seventy-five souls, the whole amount of Jacob's household that went down with him to Egypt; critically corresponding with the statement in the New Testament, that 'Joseph sent for his father Jacob and all his kindred, amounting to seventy-five souls.'"

28. *He sent Judah before him unto Joseph.* Judah was certainly a man of sense, and also an eloquent man; and of him Joseph must have had a very favorable opinion from the speech he delivered before him, chap. xliv. 18, etc.; he was therefore chosen as the most proper person to go before and announce Jacob's arrival to his son Joseph.

29. *And Joseph made ready his chariot.* In chap. xli. 43 we have the first mention of a chariot, and if the translation be correct, it is a proof that the arts were not in a rude state in Egypt even at this early time. When we find wagons used to transport goods from place to place, we need not wonder that these suggested the idea of forming chariots for carrying persons, and especially those of high rank and authority.

30. *Now let me die, since I have seen thy face.* Perhaps old Simeon had this place in view when, seeing the salvation of Israel, he said, "Lord, now lettest thou thy servant depart in peace," Luke ii. 29.

34. *Thy servants' trade hath been about cattle.* As this land was both fruitful and pleasant, Joseph wished to fix his family in that part of Egypt; hence he advises them to tell Pharaoh that their trade had been in cattle from their youth: and because every shepherd is an abomination to the Egyptians, hence he concluded that there would be less difficulty to get them quiet settlement in Goshen, as they would then be separated from the Egyptians, and consequently have the free use of all their religious customs. This scheme succeeded, and the consequence was the preservation of both their religion and their lives. As it is well known that the Egyptians had cattle and flocks themselves, and that Pharaoh even requested that some of Joseph's brethren should be made rulers over his cattle, how could it be said, *Every shepherd is an abomination unto the Egyptians?* Three reasons may be assigned for this: (1) Shepherds and feeders of cattle were usually a sort of lawless, freebooting banditti. (2) They must have abhorred shepherds if Manetho's account of the Hyksos or king-shepherds can be credited. Hordes of marauders under this name, from Arabia, Syria, and Ethiopia, made a powerful irruption into Egypt, which they subdued and ruled with great tyranny for 259 years. (3) The last and probably the best reason why the Egyptians abhorred such shepherds as were the Israelites was that they sacrificed those very animals, the ox particularly, and the sheep, which the Egyptians held sacred.

MATTHEW HENRY

CHAPTER 47

Verses 1–12

I. The respect which Joseph, as a subject, showed to his prince. Though he had had particular orders from him to send for his father down to Egypt, yet he would not suffer him to settle till he had given notice of it to Pharaoh, *v.* 1.

II. The respect which Joseph, as a brother, showed to his brethren.

1. Though he was a great man, and they were comparatively mean and despicable, especially in Egypt, yet he owned them. Every branch of the tree is not a top branch; but, because it is a lower branch, is it therefore not of the tree? Our Lord Jesus, like Joseph here, is not *ashamed to call us brethren.*

2. They being strangers and no courtiers, he introduced some of them to Pharaoh. Being presented to Pharaoh, according to the instructions which Joseph had given them, they tell him, (1) What was their business—that they were shepherds, *v.* 3. Note, All that have a place in the world should have an employment in it according to their capacity. Magistrates should enquire into the occupation of their subjects, as those that have the care of the public welfare; for idle people are as drones in the hive, unprofitable burdens of the commonwealth. (2) What was their business in Egypt—to sojourn there for a time, while the famine so prevailed in Canaan.

3. He obtained for them a grant of a settlement in the land of Goshen, *v.* 5, 6. This was an instance of Pharaoh's gratitude to Joseph. He offered them preferment as shepherds over his cattle.

III. The respect Joseph, as a son, showed to his father.

1. He presented him to Pharaoh, *v.* 7. And here, (1) Pharaoh asks Jacob a common question: *How old art thou? v.* 8. A question usually put to old men, for it is natural to us to admire old age and to reverence it (Lev. xix. 32).

(2) Jacob gives Pharaoh an uncommon answer, *v.* 9. He speaks as becomes a patriarch, with an air of seriousness, for the instruction of Pharaoh. Observe here, [1] He calls his life *a pilgrimage,* looking upon himself as a stranger in this world, and a traveller towards another world: this earth his inn, not his home. [2] He reckons his life by *days.* [3] The character he gives of them is, *First,* That they were few. *Secondly,* That they were evil. Jacob's life, particularly, had been made up of evil days; and the pleasantest days of his life were yet before him. *Thirdly,* That they were short of the days of his fathers, not so many, not so pleasant, as their days.

(3) Jacob both addresses himself to Pharaoh and takes leave of him with a blessing (*v.* 7): *Jacob blessed Pharaoh,* and again, *v.* 10, he prayed for him, as one having the authority of a prophet and a patriarch.

Verses 13–26

Joseph now returns to the management of that great trust which Pharaoh had lodged in his hand. It would have been pleasing enough to him to have gone and lived with his father and brethren in Goshen; but his employment would not permit it. In Joseph's transactions with the Egyptians observe,

I. The great extremity that Egypt, and the parts adjacent, were reduced to by the famine. 1. See here what a dependence we have upon God's providence. If its usual favours are suspended but for a while, we die, we perish, we all perish. All our wealth would not keep us from starving if the rain of heaven were but withheld for two or three years. See how much we lie at God's mercy, and let us keep ourselves always in his love. 2. See how much we smart by our own improvidence. If all the Egyptians had done for themselves in the seven years of plenty as Joseph did for Pharaoh, they had not been now in these straits.

II. The price they had come up to, for their supply, in this exigency. 1. They parted with all their money which they had hoarded up, *v.* 14. Silver and gold would not feed them; they must have corn. 2. When the money failed, they parted with all their cattle, those for labour, as the horses and asses, and those for food, as the flocks and the herds, *v.* 17. Pharaoh saw in reality what he had before seen in vision, nothing but lean kine. 3. When they had sold their stocks off their land, it was easy to persuade themselves to sell their land too; for what good would that do them, when they had neither corn to sow it nor cattle to eat of it? They therefore sold that next, for a further supply of corn.

JAMIESON, FAUSSET, BROWN

CHAPTER 47

VSS. 1-31. PRESENTATION AT COURT. **1. Joseph . . . told Pharaoh, My father, and my brethren**—Joseph furnishes a beautiful example of a man who could bear equally well the extremes of prosperity and adversity. High as he was, he did not forget that he had a superior. Dearly as he loved his father and anxiously as he desired to provide for the whole family, he would not go into the arrangements he had planned for their stay in Goshen until he had obtained the sanction of his royal master. **2. he took some of his brethren**—probably the five eldest brothers: seniority being the least invidious principle of selection. **4. For to sojourn . . . are we come**—The royal conversation took the course which Joseph had anticipated (ch. 46:33), and they answered according to previous instructions—manifesting, however, in their determination to return to Canaan, a faith and piety which affords a hopeful symptom of their having become all, or most of them, religious men.

7. Joseph brought in Jacob his father—There is a pathetic and most affecting interest attending this interview with royalty; and when, with all the simplicity and dignified solemnity of a man of God, Jacob signalized his entrance by imploring the divine blessing on the royal head, it may easily be imagined what a striking impression the scene would produce (cf. Heb. 7:7). **8. Pharaoh said unto Jacob, How old art thou?**—The question was put from the deep and impressive interest which the appearance of the old patriarch had created in the minds of Pharaoh and his court. In the low-lying land of Egypt and from the artificial habits of its society, the age of man was far shorter among the inhabitants of that country than it had yet become in the pure bracing climate and among the simple mountaineers of Canaan. The Hebrews, at least, still attained a protracted longevity. **9. The days of the years of my pilgrimage,** etc.—Though 130 years, he reckons by days (cf. Ps. 90:12), which he calls *few,* as they appeared in retrospect, and *evil,* because his life had been one almost unbroken series of trouble. The answer is remarkable, considering the comparative darkness of the patriarchal age (cf. II Tim. 1:10). **11. Joseph placed his father and his brethren . . . in the best of the land**—best *pasture* land in lower Egypt. Goshen, "the land of verdure," lay along the Pelusiac or eastern branch of the Nile. It included a part of the district of Heliopolis, or "On," the capital, and on the east stretched out a considerable length into the desert. The ground included within these boundaries was a rich and fertile extent of natural meadow, and admirably adapted for the purposes of the Hebrew shepherds (cf. ch. 49:24; Ps. 34:10; 78:72). **13-15. there was no bread in all the land**—This probably refers to the second year of the famine (ch. 45:6) when any little stores of individuals or families were exhausted and when the people had become universally dependent on the government. At first they obtained supplies for payment. Before long money failed. **16. And Joseph said, Give your cattle**—"This was the wisest course that could be adopted for the preservation both of the people and the cattle, which, being bought by Joseph, was supported at the royal expense, and very likely returned to the people at the end of the famine, to enable them to resume their agricultural labors."

ADAM CLARKE

CHAPTER 47

2. *He took some of his brethren.* There is something very strange in the original; literally translated it signifies "from the end or extremity of his brethren he took five men." It is certain that in Judg. xviii. 2 the word may be understood as implying dignity, valor, excellence, and preeminence. But the word may be understood simply as signifying *some;* out of the whole of his brethren he took only five men.

6. *In the best of the land make thy father and brethren to dwell; in the land of Goshen let them dwell.* So it appears that the land of Goshen was the best of the land of Egypt. *Men of activity.* "Stout or robust men"—such as were capable of bearing fatigue, and of rendering their authority respectable. *Rulers over my cattle. Mikneh* signifies not only *cattle,* but "possessions" or "property" of any kind; though most usually cattle are intended, because in ancient times they constituted the principal part of a man's property. The word may be taken here in a more extensive sense, and the circumstances of the case seem obviously to require it. If every shepherd was an abomination to the Egyptians, however we may understand or qualify the expression, is it to be supposed that Pharaoh should desire that the brethren of his prime minister, of his chief favorite, should be employed in some of the very meanest offices in the land? We may therefore safely understand Pharaoh as expressing his will that the brethren of Joseph should be appointed as overseers or superintendents of his domestic concerns, while Joseph superintended those of the state.

7. *Jacob blessed Pharaoh.* Saluted him on his entrance with "Peace be unto thee," or some such expression of respect and goodwill.

9. *The days of the years of my pilgrimage.* Of my "sojourning" or "wandering." Jacob had always lived a migratory or wandering life, in different parts of Canaan, Mesopotamia, and Egypt, scarcely ever at rest; and in the places where he lived longest, always exposed to the fatigues of the field and the desert.

Have not attained unto the . . . life of my fathers. Jacob lived in the whole one hundred and forty-seven years; Isaac, his father, lived one hundred and eighty; and Abraham, his grandfather, one hundred and seventy-five.

14. *Gathered up all the money.* I.e., by selling corn out of the public stores to the people; and this he did till the money failed, v. 15, till all the money was exchanged for corn, and brought into Pharaoh's treasury. Besides the fifth part of the produce of the seven plentiful years, Joseph had bought additional corn with Pharaoh's money to lay up against the famine that was to prevail in the seven years of dearth; and it is very likely that this was sold out at the price for which it was bought, and the fifth part, which belonged to Pharaoh, sold out at the same price. And as money at that time could not be plentiful, the cash of the whole nation was thus exhausted, as far as that had circulated among the common people.

16. *Give your cattle.* This was the wisest measure that could be adopted, for the preservation both of the people and of the cattle also. As the people had not grain for their own sustenance, consequently they could have none for their cattle; hence the cattle were in the most imminent danger of starving; and the people also were in equal danger, as they must have divided a portion of that bought for themselves with the cattle, which for the sake of tillage they wished of course to preserve till the seven years of famine should end. The cattle being bought by Joseph were supported at the royal expense, and very likely returned to the people at the end of the famine; for how else could they cultivate their ground, transport their merchandise, etc.? For this part of Joseph's conduct he certainly deserves high praise and no censure.

18. *When that year was ended.* The sixth year of the famine, *they came unto him the second year,* which was the last or seventh year of the famine, in which it was necessary to sow the land that there might be a crop the succeeding year; for Joseph, on whose prediction

MATTHEW HENRY

4. When their land was sold, so that they had nothing to live on, they must of course sell themselves, that they might live purely upon their labour. Note, *Skin for skin, and all that a man hath,* even liberty and property (those darling twins), *will he give for his life;* for life is sweet.

III. The method which Joseph took to accommodate the matter between prince and people. 1. For their lands, he needed not to come to any bargain with them while the years of famine lasted; but when these were over he came to an agreement, which it seems both sides were pleased with, that the people should occupy and enjoy the lands, as he thought fit to assign them, and should have seed to sow them with out of the king's stores, for their own proper use and behoof, yielding and paying only a fifth part of the yearly profits as a chief rent to the crown. This became a standing law, *v.* 26. It is observable how faithful Joseph was to him that appointed him. He did not put the money into his own pocket, nor entail the lands upon his own family; but converted both entirely to Pharaoh's use. 2. For their persons, he removed them to cities, *v.* 21. He transplanted them. How hard soever this seems to have been upon them, they themselves were at this time sensible of it as a very great kindness, and were thankful they were not worse used: *Thou hast saved our lives, v.* 25.

IV. The reservation he made in favour of the priests. They were maintained on free cost, so that they needed not to sell their lands, *v.* 22.

Verses 27-31

1. The comfort Jacob lived in (*v.* 27, 28); while the Egyptians were impoverished in their own land, Jacob was replenished in a strange land. 2. The care Jacob died in. At last *the time drew nigh that Israel must die, v.* 29. Now Jacob's care was about his burial, (1) He would be buried in Canaan, because it was the land of promise, and because it was a type of heaven, that better country which he that said these things declared plainly that he was in expectation of, Heb. xi. 14. He aimed at a good land, which would be his rest and bliss on the other side death. (2) He would have Joseph sworn to bring him thither to be buried (*v.* 29, 31).

(3) When this was done *Israel bowed himself upon the bed's head,* yielding himself, as it were, to the stroke of death.

JAMIESON, FAUSSET, BROWN

21. as for the people, he removed them to the cities—obviously for the convenience of the country people, who were doing nothing, to the cities where the corn stores were situated.

22. Only the land of the priests, bought he not—These lands were inalienable, being endowments by which the temples were supported. The priests for themselves received an annual allowance of provision from the state, and it would evidently have been the height of cruelty to withhold that allowance when their lands were incapable of being tilled.

23-28. Joseph said, Behold, etc.—The lands being sold to the government (vss. 19, 20), seed would be distributed for the first crop after the famine; and the people would occupy them as tenants-at-will on the payment of a produce rent, almost the same rule as obtains in Egypt in the present day.

29-31. the time drew nigh that Israel must die—One only of his dying arrangements is recorded; but that one reveals his whole character. It was the disposal of his remains, which were to be carried to Canaan, not from a mere romantic attachment to his native soil, nor, like his modern descendants, from a superstitious feeling for the soil of the Holy Land but from faith in the promises. His address to Joseph—"if I have found grace in thy sight," i.e., as the vizier of Egypt, his exacting a solemn oath that his wishes would be fulfilled and the peculiar form of that oath, all pointed significantly to the promise and showed the intensity of his desire to enjoy its blessings (cf. Num. 10:29).

Israel bowed himself upon the bed's head—Oriental beds are mere mats, having no head, and the translation should be "the top of his staff," as the apostle renders it (Heb. 11:21).

ADAM CLARKE

they relied, had foretold that the famine should continue only seven years, and consequently they expected the eighth year to be a fruitful year provided the land was sowed, without which, though the inundation of the land by the Nile might amount to the sixteen requisite cubits, there could be no crop.

21. *And as for the people, he removed them to cities.* It is very likely that Joseph was influenced by no political motive in removing the people to the cities, but merely by a motive of humanity and prudence. As the corn was laid up in the cities, he found it more convenient to bring them to the place where they might be conveniently fed, each being within the reach of an easy distribution. Thus then the country which could afford no sustenance was abandoned for the time being, that the people might be fed in those places where the provision was deposited.

22. *The land of the priests bought he not.* From this verse it is natural to infer that whatever the religion of Egypt was, it was established by law and supported by the state. Hence when Joseph bought all the lands of the Egyptians for Pharaoh, he bought not the land of the priests, for that was a *portion assigned them of Pharaoh, and they did eat,* did live on, that *portion.* This is the earliest account we have of an established religion supported by the state.

23. *I have bought you this day and your land for Pharaoh.* It fully appears that the kingdom of Egypt was previously to the time of Joseph a very limited monarchy. The king had his estates; the priests had their lands; and the common people their patrimony independently of both. The land of Rameses, or Goshen, appears to have been the king's land, v. 11. The priests had their lands, which they did not sell to Joseph, vv. 22, 26; and that the people had lands independent of the crown is evident from the purchases Joseph made, vv. 19-20; and we may conclude from those purchases that Pharaoh had no power to levy taxes upon his subjects to increase his own revenue until he had bought the original right which each individual had in his possessions. And when Joseph bought this for the king he raised the crown an ample revenue, though he restored the lands, by obliging each to pay one-fifth of the product to the king, v. 24. And it is worthy of remark that the people of Egypt well understood the distinction between subjects and servants; for when they came to sell their land, they offered to sell themselves also, and said: "Buy us and our land . . . and we and our land will be servants unto Pharaoh," v. 19.

26. *And Joseph made it a law.* That the people should hold their land from the king and give him the fifth part of the produce as a yearly tax. Beyond this it appears the king had no further demands. The whole of this conduct of Joseph has been as strongly censured by some as applauded by others. It is natural for men to run into extremes in attacking or defending any position. Sober and judicious men will consider what Joseph did by divine appointment as a prophet of God, and what he did merely as a statesman from the circumstances of the case, the complexion of the times, and the character of the people over whom he presided.

30. *I will lie with my fathers.* As God had promised the land of Canaan to Abraham and his posterity, Jacob considered it as a consecrated place, under the particular superintendence and blessing of God: and as Sarah, Abraham, and Isaac were interred near Hebron, he in all probability wished to lie, not only in the same place, but in the same grace; and it is not likely that he would have been solicitous about this had he not considered that promised land as being a type of the rest that remains for the people of God, and a pledge of the inheritance among the saints in light.

31. *And Israel bowed himself upon the bed's head.* Jacob was now both old and feeble, and we may suppose him reclined on his couch when Joseph came; that he afterwards sat up erect (see chap. xlviii. 2) while conversing with his son, and receiving his oath and promise; and that when this was finished he *bowed himself upon the bed's head*—exhausted with the conversation, he again reclined himself on his bed

MATTHEW HENRY	JAMIESON, FAUSSET, BROWN	ADAM CLARKE

KEIL–DELITZSCH:

Verses 28–31. Jacob lived in Egypt for 17 years. He then sent for Joseph, as he felt that his death was approaching; and having requested him, as a mark of love and faithfulness, not to bury him in Egypt, but near his fathers in Canaan, he made him assure him on oath (by putting his hand under his hip) that his wishes should be fulfilled. When Joseph had taken this oath, "Israel bowed [in worship] upon the bed's head." He had talked with Joseph while sitting upon the bed; and when Joseph had promised to fulfill his wish, he turned towards the head of the bed, so as to lie with his face upon the bed, and thus worshipped God, thanking Him for granting his wish, which sprang from living faith in the promises of God; just as David also worshipped upon his bed (1 Kings 1:47, 48). But no fitting sense can be obtained from this rendering unless we think of the staff with which Jacob had gone through life, and assume that Jacob made use of the staff to enable him to sit upright in bed, and so prayed, bent upon or over it, though even then the expression remains a strange one.—*Commentary on the Old Testament*

as before. This seems to be the simple meaning which the text, unconnected with any religious system or prejudice, naturally proposes. But because *shachah* signifies not only to "bow" but to "worship," because acts of religious worship were performed by bowing or prostration, and because *mittah*, "a bed," by the change of the points, only becomes *matteh*, "a staff," in which sense the Septuagint took it, translating the original words thus: "And Israel worshipped upon the top of his staff," which the writer of the Epistle to the Hebrews, chap. xi. 21, quotes *literatim;* therefore some have supposed that Jacob bowed himself to the staff or scepter of Joseph, thus fulfilling the prophetic import of his son's dreams! The sense of the Hebrew text is given above. If the reader prefers the sense of the Septuagint and the Epistle to the Hebrews, the meaning is that Jacob, through feebleness, supported himself with a staff, and that, when he got the requisite assurance from Joseph that his dead body should be carried to Canaan, leaning on his staff he bowed his head in adoration to God, who had supported him all his lifelong, and hitherto fulfilled all His promises.

CHAPTER 48

Verses 1–7

I. Joseph goes to see his aged father, *v.* 1. Visiting the sick, to whom we lie under obligations, or may have opportunity of doing good, either for body or soul, is our duty. Joseph took his own sons with him, that they might receive their dying grandfather's blessing. Manasseh and Ephraim would never forget what passed at this time.

II. Jacob, upon notice of his son's visit, prepared himself as well as he could to entertain him, *v.* 2. Note, It is very good for sick and aged people to be as lively and cheerful as they can, that they may not faint in the day of adversity. *Strengthen thyself,* as Jacob here, and God will strengthen thee.

III. In recompense to Joseph for all his attentions to him, he adopted his two sons. In this charter of adoption there is, 1. A particular recital of God's promise to him, to which this had reference: "*God blessed me* (*v.* 3), and let that blessing be entailed upon them." 2. An express reception of Joseph's sons into his family: "Thy sons are mine (*v.* 5), not only my grandchildren, but as my own children." He explains this at *v.* 16, *Let my name be named upon them, and the name of my fathers.* Thus the aged dying patriarch teaches these young persons not to look upon Egypt as their home, nor to incorporate themselves with the Egyptians, but to take their lot with the people of God, as Moses afterwards in the like temptation, Heb. xi. 24–26. Those are worthy of double honour who, through God's grace, break through the temptations of worldly wealth and preferment, to embrace religion in disgrace and poverty. Mention is made of the death and burial of Rachel, Joseph's mother, and Jacob's best beloved wife (*v.* 7), referring to that story, *ch.* xxxv. 19. Those that were to us as our own souls are dead and buried; and shall we think it much to follow them in the same path?

Verses 8–22

Here is, I. The blessing with which Jacob blessed the two sons of Joseph, which is the more remarkable because the apostle makes such particular mention of it (Heb. xi. 21).

1. Jacob was blind with age, *v.* 10. Jacob, like his father before him, when he was old, was dim-sighted. Note, (1) Those that have the honour of age must therewith be content to take the burden of it. (2) The eye of faith may be very clear even when the eye of the body is very much clouded.

2. Jacob was very fond of Joseph's sons. With what satisfaction does Jacob say here (*v.* 11), *I had not thought to see thy face* (having many years given him up for lost), *and, lo, God has shown me also thy seed!*

CHAPTER 48

VSS. 1-22. JOSEPH'S VISIT TO HIS SICK FATHER. **1. one told Joseph, Behold, thy father is sick**—Joseph was hastily sent for, and on this occasion he took with him his two sons. **2. Israel strengthened himself, and sat upon the bed**—In the chamber where a good man lies, edifying and spiritual discourse may be expected. **3, 4. God Almighty appeared unto me at Luz**—The object of Jacob, in thus reverting to the memorable vision at Bethel—one of the great landmarks in his history—was to point out the splendid promises in reserve for his posterity—to engage Joseph's interest and preserve his continued connection with the people of God, rather than with the Egyptians. **Behold, I will make thee fruitful**—This is a repetition of the covenant (ch. 28:13-15, 35:12). Whether these words are to be viewed in a limited sense, as pointing to the many centuries during which the Jews were occupiers of the Holy Land, or whether the words bear a wider meaning and intimate that the scattered tribes of Israel are to be reinstated in the land of promise, as their "everlasting possession," are points that have not yet been satisfactorily determined. **5. thy two sons, Ephraim and Manasseh**—It was the intention of the aged patriarch to adopt Joseph's sons as his own, thus giving him a double portion. The reasons for this procedure are stated (I Chron. 5:1, 2). **are mine**—Though their connections might have attached them to Egypt and opened to them brilliant prospects in the land of their nativity, they willingly accepted the adoption (Heb. 11:25).

9. Bring them, I pray thee, unto me, and I will bless them—The apostle (Heb. 11:21) selected the blessing of Joseph's son as the chief, because the most comprehensive, instance of the patriarch's faith which his whole history furnishes.

13. Joseph took them both—The very act of pronouncing the blessing was remarkable, showing that Jacob's bosom was animated by the spirit of prophecy.

CHAPTER 48

1. *One told Joseph, Behold, thy father is sick.* He was ill before, and Joseph knew it; but it appears that a messenger had now been dispatched to inform Joseph that his father was apparently at the point of death.

2. *Israel strengthened himself, and sat upon the bed.* He had been confined to his bed before (see chap. xlvii. 31), and now, hearing that Joseph was come to see him, he made what efforts his little remaining strength would admit to sit up in bed to receive his son. This verse proves that a bed, not a staff, is intended in the preceding chapter, v. 31.

3. *God Almighty. El Shaddai,* "the all-sufficient God," the Outpourer and Dispenser of mercies (see chap. xvii. 1), *appeared unto me at Luz,* afterwards called Beth-el; see chap. xxviii. 13; xxxv. 6, 9.

5. *And now thy two sons, Ephraim and Manasseh . . . are mine.* I now adopt them into my own family, and they shall have their place among my twelve sons, and be treated in every respect as those, and have an equal interest in all the spiritual and temporal blessings of the covenant.

7. *Rachel died by me.* Rachel was the wife of Jacob's choice, and the object of his unvarying affection; he loved her in life—he loves her in death. "Many waters cannot quench love, neither can the floods drown it."

8. *Who are these?* At verse 10 it is said that Jacob's eyes were dim for age, that he "could not see"—could not discern any object unless it were near him; therefore, though he saw Ephraim and Manasseh, yet he could not distinguish them till they were brought nigh unto him.

11. *I had not thought to see thy face.* There is much delicacy and much tenderness in these expressions. He feels himself now amply recompensed for his long grief and trouble on account of the supposed death of Joseph, in seeing not only himself but his two sons, whom God, by an especial act of favor, is about to add to the number of his own. Thus we find that as Reuben and Simeon were heads of two distinct tribes in Israel, so were Ephraim and Manasseh; because Jacob, in a sort of sacramental way, had adopted them with equal privileges to those of his own sons.

12. *Joseph . . . bowed himself with his face to the earth.* Joseph, in thus reverencing his father, only followed the customs of the Egyptians among whom he lived, who, according to Herodotus, were particularly remarkable for the reverence they paid to old age. "For if a young person meet his senior, he instantly turns aside to make way for him; if an aged person enter an apartment, the youth always rise from their seats."

14. *Israel stretched out his right hand.* Laying hands on the head was always used among the Jews in giving blessings, designating men to any office, and in the consecration of solemn

MATTHEW HENRY

3. Before he entails his blessing, he recounts his experiences of God's goodness to him. (1) He had *fed him all his life long unto this day, v.* 15. Note, As long as we have lived in this world we have had continual experience of God's goodness to us, in providing for the support of our natural life. He that has fed us *all our life long* surely will not fail us at last. (2) He had by this angel *redeemed him from all evil, v.* 16.

4. When he confers the blessing and name of Abraham and Isaac upon them he recommends the pattern and example of Abraham and Isaac to them, *v.* 15. He calls God the *God before whom his fathers Abraham and Isaac walked,* that is, in whom they believed, whom they observed and obeyed.

5. In blessing them, he *crossed hands.* Joseph placed them so that Jacob's right hand should be put on the head of Manasseh the elder, *v.* 12, 13. But Jacob would put it on the head of Ephraim the younger, *v.* 14. But Jacob gave him to understand that he knew what he did, and that he did it not by mistake, nor in a humour, nor from a partial affection to one more than the other, but from a spirit of prophecy, and in compliance with the divine counsels. Manasseh should be great, but truly Ephraim should be greater. Joshua was of that tribe, so was Jeroboam. The tribe of Manasseh was divided, one half on one side Jordan, the other half on the other side, which made it the less powerful and considerable. In the foresight of this, *Jacob crossed hands.* Note, Grace observes not the order of nature, nor does God prefer those whom we think fittest to be preferred, but as it pleases him. It is observable how often God, by the distinguishing favours of his covenant, advanced the younger above the elder, Abel above Cain, Shem above Japheth, Abraham above Nahor and Haran, Isaac above Ishmael, Jacob above Esau; Judah and Joseph were preferred before Reuben, Moses before Aaron, David and Solomon before their elder brethren. See 1 Sam. xvi. 7.

JAMIESON, FAUSSET, BROWN

ADAM CLARKE

sacrifices. This is the first time we find it mentioned; but we often read of it afterwards. See Num. xxvii. 18, 23; Deut. xxxiv. 9; Matt. xix. 13, 15; Acts vi. 6; 1 Tim. iv. 14. Jacob laid his right hand on the head of the younger, which we are told he did *wittingly*—well knowing what he was about, *for* (or "although") *Manasseh was the firstborn,* knowing by the Spirit of prophecy that Ephraim's posterity would be more powerful than that of Manasseh. It is observable how God from the beginning has preferred the younger to the elder, as Abel before Cain, Shem before Japheth, Isaac before Ishmael, Jacob before Esau, Judah and Joseph before Reuben. Ephraim before Manasseh, Moses before Aaron, and David before his brethren.

15. *He blessed Joseph.* The father first, and then the sons afterwards. And this is an additional proof to what has been adduced under v. 12, of Jacob's superiority; for the less is always blessed of the greater. *The God which fed me all my life long.* Jacob is now standing on the verge of eternity, with his faith strong in God. He sees his life to be a series of mercies; and as he had been affectionately attentive, provident, and kind to his most helpless child, so has God been unto him; He has fed him all his lifelong; he plainly perceives that he owes every morsel of food which he has received to the mere mercy and kindness of God.

16. *The Angel which redeemed me from all evil. Hammalac haggoel.* "The Messenger, the Redeemer or Kinsman"; for so *goel* signifies; for this term, in the law of Moses, is applied to that person whose right it is, from his being nearest akin, to redeem or purchase back a forfeited inheritance. But of whom does Jacob speak? We have often seen, in the preceding chapters, an angel of God appearing to the patriarchs; and we have full proof that this was no created angel, but the Messenger of the Divine Council, the Lord Jesus Christ. Who then was the angel that *redeemed Jacob,* and whom he invoked to bless Ephraim and Manasseh? Is it not *Jesus?* He alone can be called *Goel,* the "redeeming Kinsman"; for He alone took part of our flesh and blood that the right of redemption might be His; and that the forfeited possession of the favor and image of God might be redeemed, brought back, and restored to all those who believe in His name. To have invoked any other angel or messenger in such a business would have been impiety.

Let my name be named on them. "Let them be ever accounted as a part of my own family; let them be true Israelites—persons who shall prevail with God as I have done; and *the name of . . . Abraham*—being partakers of his faith; and *the name of . . . Isaac*—let them be as remarkable for submissive obedience as he was. Let the virtues of Abraham, Isaac, and Jacob be accumulated in them, and invariably displayed by them!" These are the very words of adoption; and by the imposition of hands, the invocation of the Redeemer, and the solemn blessing pronounced, the adoption was completed. From this moment Ephraim and Manasseh had the same rights and privileges as Jacob's sons, which as the sons of Joseph they could never have possessed.

And let them grow into a multitude. "Let them increase like fishes into a multitude." This prophetic blessing was verified in a most remarkable manner; see Num. xxvi. 34, 37; Deut. xxxiii. 17; Josh. xvii. 17. At one time the tribe of Ephraim amounted to 40,500 effective men, and that of Manasseh to 52,700, amounting in the whole to 93,200.

18. *Joseph said . . . Not so, my father.* Joseph supposed that his father had made a mistake in laying his right hand on the head of the younger, because the right hand was considered as the most noble, and the instrument of conveying the highest dignities, and thus it has ever been considered among all nations, though the reason of it is not particularly obvious. Even in the heavens the right hand of God is the place of the most exalted dignity. It has been observed that Joseph spoke here as he was moved by natural affection, and that Jacob acted as he was influenced by the Holy Spirit.

20. *In thee shall Israel bless.* That is, In future generations the Israelites shall take their form of wishing prosperity to any nation or

CHARLES H. SPURGEON:

Joseph was one by himself. In Jacob's family he was like a swan in a duck's nest; he seemed to be of a different race from the rest, even from his childhood. He was the son of old age, the son of the elders, that is, a child who was old when he was young, in thoughtfulness and devotion. He reached an early ripeness, which did not end in early decay. In consequence of this, Joseph was one by himself in the peculiarity of his trials.

Through his brothers' hatred of him he was made to suffer greatly, and at last was sold into slavery, and underwent trials in Egypt of the severest kind. "The archers have sorely grieved him, and shot at him, and hated him." But, brethren, see the recompense; for he had blessings which were altogether his own. "His bow abode in strength, and the arms of his hands were made strong by the hands of the mighty God of Jacob." He was as distinguished by the favor of God as by the disfavor of his brethren. When Jacob was old and about to die, he gave Joseph a blessing all to himself, in addition to that which he received with his brothers. In the forty-ninth chapter we read, "Gather yourselves together, and hear, ye sons of Jacob: and hearken unto Israel your father"; and they did so, and received as a family such blessings as their father's prophetic eye foresaw; but before this, "by faith Jacob blessed the two sons of Joseph" at a private interview specially granted to them. Had not his tribulations abounded, his consolations would not have so abounded.

Do you seem yourself, my friend, to be marked out for peculiar sorrows? Do the arrows of affliction make your life their target, and are you chastened above all other men? Do not be regretful, for the arrows are winged by covenant love, which designs by their wounds to prepare you for a special work which will lead up to a special benediction from your Father who is in heaven. The day will come when you will be grateful for every smart you now endure; yes, grateful for that bitter pang of unkindness from your brethren, though now it tortures your heart. The abundance of the revelation of God is usually joined with a thorn in the flesh either before or after it. Notwithstanding your grief, there shall yet be born to you, as to Joseph, a Manasseh, for God shall make you to forget all your toil, and an Ephraim, for God shall make you fruitful in the land of your affliction. You shall be blessed above all others. "Even by the God of thy father, who shall help thee; and by the Almighty, who shall bless thee with blessings of heaven above, blessings of the deep that lieth under, blessings of the breasts, and of the womb; the blessings of thy father have prevailed above the blessings of my progenitors unto the utmost bound of the everlasting hills: they shall be on the head of Joseph, and on the crown of the head of him that was separate from his brethren." Surely it is good for a man that he bear the yoke in his youth: his shoulders shall be the better able to bear the government when God shall lay it upon them. Instructed by affliction, the man shall become a father to his people, and a comforter to the afflicted.—*The Treasury of the Old Testament*

MATTHEW HENRY

II. The particular tokens of his favour to Joseph. He left with him the promise of their return out of Egypt, as a sacred trust: *I die, but God shall be with you, and bring you again, v.* 21. These words of Jacob furnish us with comfort in reference to the death of our friends. He will bring us to the land of our fathers, the heavenly Canaan, whither our godly fathers have gone before us. If God be with us while we stay behind in this world, and will receive us shortly to be with those that have gone before to a better world, we ought not to sorrow as those that have no hope.

CHAPTER 49

Verses 1–4

I. The preface to the prophecy, in which, 1. The congregation is called together. It was a comfort to Jacob, now that he was dying, to see all his children about him. His calling upon them once and again to gather together intimated a precept to them to unite in love and all make one people. 2. A general idea is given of the intended discourse (*v.* 1): *That I may tell you that which shall befall you* (not your persons, but your posterity) *in the latter days.* 3. Attention is demanded (*v.* 2): "*Hearken to Israel your father*"; let Israel, that has prevailed with God, prevail with you."

II. The prophecy concerning Reuben. He begins with him (*v.* 3, 4), for he was the first-born; but by committing uncleanness with his father's wife he forfeited the prerogatives of the birthright. He shall

JAMIESON, FAUSSET, BROWN

21. Israel said unto Joseph, Behold, I die—The patriarch could speak of death with composure, but he wished to prepare Joseph and the rest of the family for the shock. **but God shall be with you**—Jacob, in all probability, was not authorized to speak of their bondage—he dwelt only on the certainty of their restoration to Canaan.

22. moreover, I have given to thee one portion above thy brethren—This was near Shechem (ch. 33:18; John 4:5; also Josh. 16:1; 20:7). And it is probable that the Amorites, having seized upon it during one of his frequent absences, the patriarch, with the united forces of his tribe, recovered it from them by his sword and his bow.

CHAPTER 49

VSS. 1-33. PATRIARCHAL BLESSING. **1. Jacob called unto his sons**—It is not to the sayings of the dying saint, so much as of the inspired prophet, that attention is called in this chapter. Under the immediate influence of the Holy Spirit he pronounced his prophetic benediction and described the condition of their respective descendants in the last days, or future times.

3-4. REUBEN forfeited by his crime the rights and honors of primogeniture. His posterity never made any figure; no judge, prophet, nor ruler, sprang from this tribe.

ADAM CLARKE

family from the circumstance of the good which it shall be known that God has done to Ephraim and Manasseh: "May God make thee as fruitful as Ephraim, and multiply thee as Manasseh!" So, to their daughters when married, the Jewish women are accustomed to say, "God make thee as Sarah and Rebekah!" The forms are still in use.

21. *Behold, I die.* With what composure is this most awful word expressed! Surely of Jacob it might be now said, "He turns his sight undaunted on the tomb"; for though it is not said that he was full of days, as were Abraham and Isaac, yet he is perfectly willing to bid adieu to earthly things, and lay his body in the grave. Could any person act as the patriarchs did in their last moments who had no hopes of eternal life, no belief in the immortality of the soul? Impossible! With such a conviction of the being of God, with such proofs of His tenderness and regard, with such experience of His providential and miraculous interference in their behalf, could they suppose that they were only creatures of a day, and that God had wasted so much care, attention, providence, grace, and goodness, on creatures who were to be ultimately like the beasts that perish? The supposition that they could have no correct notion of the immortality of the soul is as dishonorable to God as to themselves.

22. *Moreover I have given to thee one portion. Shechem achad,* one *shechem* or one "shoulder." We have already seen the transactions between Jacob and his family on one part, and Shechem and the sons of Hamor on the other. See chap. xxxiii. 18-19 and chap. xxxiv. As he uses the word *shechem* here, I think it likely that he alludes to the purchase of the field or parcel of ground mentioned in chap. xxxiii. 18-19. It has been supposed that this parcel of ground which Jacob bought from Shechem had been taken from him by the Amorites and that he afterwards had recovered it by his *sword* and by his *bow,* i.e., by force of arms. Shechem appears to have fallen to the lot of Joseph's sons (see Josh. xvii. 1 and xx. 7), and in our Lord's time there was a parcel of ground near to Sychar, or Shechem, which was still considered as that portion which Jacob gave to his son Joseph, John iv. 5; and on the whole it was probably the same that Jacob bought for a hundred pieces of money, chap. xxxiii. 18-19.

CHAPTER 49

1. *That which shall befall you in the last days.* It is evident from this, and indeed from the whole complexion of these important prophecies, that the twelve sons of Jacob had very little concern in them, personally considered, as they were to be fulfilled in the last days, i.e., in times remote from that period, and consequently to their posterity, and not to themselves, or to their immediate families. The whole of these prophetic declarations, from v. 2 to v. 27 inclusive, is delivered in strongly figurative language, and in the poetic form, which, in every translation, should be preserved as nearly as possible, rendering the version line for line with the original. This order I shall pursue in the succeeding notes, always proposing the verse first, in as literal a translation as possible, line for line with the Hebrew after the hemistich form, from which the sense will more readily appear; but to the Hebrew text and the common version the reader is ultimately referred.

Come together and hear, O sons of Jacob!
And hearken unto Israel your father.
Reuben, my firstborn art thou!
My might, and the prime of my strength,
Excelling in eminence, and excelling in power:
Pouring out like the waters:—thou shalt not excel,
For thou wentest up to the bed of thy father,—
Then thou didst defile: to my couch he went up!

3. Reuben as the *firstborn* had a right to a double portion of all that the father had; see Deut. xxi. 17.

The "eminence" or *dignity* mentioned here

MATTHEW HENRY

have all the privileges of a son, but not of a first-born. No judge, prophet, nor prince, is found of that tribe, nor any person of renown except Dathan and Abiram, who were noted for their impious rebellion against Moses. Reuben himself seems to have lost all that influence upon his brethren to which his birthright entitled him; for *when he spoke unto them they would not hear, ch.* xlii. 22. The character fastened upon Reuben, for which he is laid under this mark of infamy, is that he was *unstable as water*. 1. His virtue was unstable; he had not the government of himself and his own appetites. Men do not thrive because they do not fix. 2. His honour consequently was unstable; it departed from him, and became as water spilt upon the ground. Note, Those that throw away their virtue must not expect to save their reputation.

Verses 5–7

Observe, 1. The character of Simeon and Levi: they were brethren in disposition; but, unlike their father, they were passionate and revengeful, fierce and uncontrollable; their swords, which should have been only weapons of defence, were (as the margin reads it, *v.* 5) *weapons of violence*. It is not in the power of parents, no, not by education, to form the dispositions of their children; Jacob bred his sons to every thing that was mild and quiet, and yet they proved to be thus furious. 2. A proof of this is the murder of the Shechemites, which Jacob deeply resented at the time (*ch.* xxxiv. 30) and still continued to resent. Simeon and Levi would not be advised by their aged and experienced father; no, they would be governed by their own passion rather than by his prudence. 3. Jacob's protestation against this barbarous act of theirs: *O my soul, come not thou into their secret.* Hereby he professes not only his abhorrence of such practices in general, but his innocence particularly in that matter.

4. His abhorrence of those brutish lusts that led them to this wickedness: *Cursed be their anger.* He does not curse their persons, but their lusts. We ought carefully to distinguish between the sinner and the sin, so as not to love the sin for the sake of the person, nor to hate the person for the sake of the sin. 5. A token of displeasure which he foretells their posterity should lie under for this: *I will divide them.* The Levites were scattered throughout all the tribes, and Simeon's lot lay not together. This curse was afterwards turned into a blessing to the Levites; but the Simeonites, for Zimri's sin (Num. xxv. 14), had it bound on.

JAMIESON, FAUSSET, BROWN

KEIL–DELITZSCH:

Verses 3, 4. Reuben, "my first-born thou, my might and first-fruit of my strength; pre-eminence in dignity and pre-eminence in power." As the firstborn, the first sprout of the full virile power of Jacob, Reuben, according to natural right, was entitled to the first rank among his brethren, the leadership of the tribes and a double share of the inheritance (27:29; Deut. 21:17). But Reuben had forfeited this prerogative. "Effervescence like water—thou shalt have no preference; for thou didst ascend thy father's marriage bed: then hast thou desecrated; my couch has he ascended." Literally, "the boiling over of water," figuratively, the excitement of lust; hence the verb is used in Judg. 9:4, Zeph. 3:4 for frivolity and insolent pride. With this predicate, Jacob describes the moral character of Reuben. His crime was lying with Bilhah, his father's concubine (35:22). "Desecrated hast thou," what should have been sacred to thee (cf. Lev. 18:8). From this wickedness the injured father turns away with indignation, and passes to the third person as he repeats the words, "my couch he has ascended." By the withdrawal of the rank belonging to the firstborn, Reuben lost the leadership in Israel, so that his tribe attained no position of influence in the nation (cf. the blessing of Moses in Deut. 33:6). The leadership was transferred to Judah, the double portion to Joseph (1 Chron. 5:1, 2), by which, so far as the inheritance was concerned, the firstborn of the beloved Rachel took the place of the firstborn of the slighted Leah; not, however, according to the subjective will of the father, which is condemned in Deut. 21:15, but according to the leading of God, by which Joseph had been raised above his brethren but without the chieftainship being accorded to him.

—Commentary on the Old Testament

5-7. SIMEON AND LEVI were associate in wickedness, and the same prediction would be equally applicable to both their tribes. Levi had cities allotted to them (Josh. 21) in every tribe.

On account of their zeal against idolatry, they were honorably "divided in Jacob"; whereas the tribe of Simeon, which was guilty of the grossest idolatry and the vices inseparable from it, were ignominiously "scattered."

ADAM CLARKE

may refer to the priesthood; the "power," to the regal government or kingdom. In this sense it has been understood by all the ancient Targumists. The Targum of Onkelos paraphrases it thus: "Thou shouldst have received three portions, the birthright, the priesthood, and the kingdom"; and to this the Targums of Jonathan ben Uzziel and Jerusalem add: "But because thou hast sinned, the birthright is given to Joseph, the kingdom to Judah, and the priesthood to Levi." That the birthright was given to the sons of Joseph we have the fullest proof from 1 Chron. v. 1.

4. *"Pouring out* like *the waters."* This is an obscure sentence because unfinished. It evidently relates to the defilement of his father's couch; and the word *pachaz,* here translated "pouring out," and in our version "unstable," has a bad meaning in other places of the Scripture, being applied to dissolute, debauched, and licentious conduct. See Judg. ix. 4; Zeph. iii. 4; Jer. xxiii. 14, 32; xxix. 23. *Thou shalt not excel.*—This tribe never rose to any eminence in Israel; was not so numerous by one-third as either Judah, Joseph, or Dan, when Moses took the sum of them in the wilderness, Num. i. 21; and was among the first that were carried into captivity, 1 Chron. v. 26.

"Then thou didst defile." Another unfinished sentence, similar to the former, and upon the same subject, passing over a transaction covertly which delicacy forbade Jacob to enlarge upon. For the crime of Reuben, see chap. xxxv. 22.

Simeon and Levi, brethren:
They have accomplished their fraudulent purposes.
Into their secret council my soul did not come;
In their confederacy my honor was not united:
For in their anger they slew a man,
And in their pleasure they murdered a prince.
Cursed was their anger, for it was fierce!
And their excessive wrath, for it was inflexible!
I will divide them out in Jacob,
And I will disperse them in Israel.

5. *Simeon and Levi are brethren.* Not only springing from the same parents, but they have the same kind of disposition, headstrong, deceitful, vindictive, and cruel.

"They have accomplished." Our margin has it, "Their swords are weapons of violence," i.e., Their swords, which they should have used in defense of their persons or the honorable protection of their families, they have employed in the base and dastardly murder of an innocent people.

The Septuagint gives a different turn to this line from our translation, and confirms the translation given above: "They have accomplished the iniquity of their purpose"; with which the Samaritan Version agrees.

6. "Into their secret council." Jacob here exculpates himself from all participation in the guilt of Simeon and Levi in the murder of the Shechemites. He most solemnly declares that he knew nothing of the confederacy by which it was executed, nor of the secret council in which it was plotted. *For in their anger they slew a man. Ish,* a noble, an honorable man, namely, Shechem. "And in their pleasure." This marks the highest degree of wickedness and settled malice; they were delighted with their deed. As the original word *ratson* signifies, in general, "pleasure, benevolence, delight," it should neither be translated *selfwill* nor "wilfulness," as some have done, but simply as above; and the reasons appear sufficiently obvious. "They murdered a prince"—Hamor, the father of Shechem. Instead of *shor,* which we have translated *a wall,* and others an "ox," I read *sar,* "a prince," which makes a consistent sense.

7. "Cursed was their anger." The first motions of their violence were savage; "and their excessive (or overflowing) wrath, for it was inflexible"—neither the supplications of the males, nor the entreaties, tears, cries, and shrieks of the helpless females, could deter them from their murderous purpose; for this, v. 5, they are said to have accomplished.

"I will divide them out," *achallekem,* "I will make them into lots," giving a portion of them to one tribe, and a portion to another; but they shall never attain to any political consequence.

MATTHEW HENRY

Verses 8–12

Glorious things are here said of Judah. Judah's name signifies *praise*, in allusion to which he says, *Thou art he whom thy brethren shall praise*, *v.* 8. It is prophesied that, 1. The tribe of Judah should be victorious and successful in war. 2. It should be superior to the rest of the tribes; not only in itself more numerous and illustrious, but having a dominion over them: Judah was the *lawgiver*, Ps. lx. 7. That tribe led the van through the wilderness, and in the conquest of Canaan, Judges i. 2. 3. It should be a strong and courageous tribe, and so qualified for command and conquest: *Judah is a lion's whelp*, *v.* 9. The lion is the king of beasts; when he seizes his prey none can resist him. By this is foretold that the tribe of Judah should become very formidable, and should not only obtain great victories, but should peaceably and quietly enjoy what was obtained by those victories—that they should make war, not for the sake of war, but for the sake of peace. Judah is compared, not to a lion *rampant*, always tearing, always raging, always ranging; but to a lion *couchant*, enjoying the satisfaction of his power and success, without creating vexation to others: this is to be truly great. 4. It should be the royal tribe, and the tribe from which Messiah the Prince should come: *The sceptre shall not depart from Judah, till Shiloh come*, *v.* 10. Jacob here foresees and foretells, (1) That the sceptre should come into the tribe of Judah, which was fulfilled in David, on whose family the crown was entailed. (2) That Shiloh should be of this tribe—his seed, that promised seed, in whom the earth should be blessed: *that peaceable and prosperous one*, or *the Saviour*, so others translate it, he shall come of Judah. (3) That after the coming of the sceptre into the tribe of Judah it should continue in that tribe. Till the captivity, all along from David's time, the sceptre was in Judah, and subsequently the governors of Judea were of that tribe, or of the Levites that adhered to it (which was equivalent), till Judea became a province of the Roman Empire, just at the time of our Saviour's birth, and was at that time taxed as one of the provinces, Luke ii. 1. And at the time of his death the Jews expressly owned, *We have no king but Caesar*. Hence it is undeniably inferred against the Jews that our Lord Jesus is he that should come. 5. It should be a very fruitful tribe, especially that it should abound with milk for babes, and wine to make glad the heart of strong men (*v.* 11). Much of what is here said concerning Judah is to be applied to our Lord Jesus. In him there is plenty of all that which is nourishing and refreshing to the soul, and which maintains and cheers the divine life in it; in him we may have wine and milk, the riches of Judah's tribe, without money and without price, Isa. lv. 1.

Verses 13–21

Jacob's prophecy concerning six of his sons.

I. Concerning Zebulun (*v.* 13), that his posterity should have their lot upon the seacoast, and should be merchants, and mariners, and traders at sea. This was fulfilled when, two or three hundred years after, the land of Canaan was divided by lot, and the *border of Zebulun went up towards the sea*, Josh. xix. 11.

II. Concerning Issachar, *v.* 14, 15. That the men of that tribe should be strong and industrious, fit for labour and inclined to labour, particularly the toil of husbandry, like the ass, that patiently carried his burden, and, by using himself to it, makes it the easier. Issachar submitted to two burdens, tillage and tribute. It was a tribe that took pains, and, thriving thereby, was called upon for rents and taxes.

JAMIESON, FAUSSET, BROWN

8-12. JUDAH—A high pre-eminence is destined to this tribe (Num. 10:14; Judg. 1:2). Besides the honor of giving name to the Promised Land, David, and a greater than David—the Messiah—sprang from it. Chief among the tribes, "it grew up from a lion's whelp," i.e., a little power, till it became "an old lion"—i.e., calm and quiet, yet still formidable. **until Shiloh come**—Shiloh—this obscure word is variously interpreted to mean "the sent" (John 17:3), "the seed" (Isa. 11:1), the "peaceable or prosperous one" (Eph. 2:14)—i.e., the Messiah (Isa. 11:10; Rom. 15:12); and when He should come, "the tribe of Judah should no longer boast either an independent king or a judge of their own" [CALVIN]. The Jews have been for eighteen centuries without a ruler and without a judge since Shiloh came, and "to Him the gathering of the people has been."

13. ZEBULUN was to have its lot on the seacoast, close to Zidon, and to engage, like that state, in maritime pursuits and commerce.

14-15. ISSACHAR—a strong ass couching down between two burdens—i.e., it was to be active, patient, given to agricultural labors. It was established in lower Galilee— a "good land," settling down in the midst of the Canaanites, where, for the sake of quiet, they "bowed their shoulder to bear, and became a servant unto tribute."

ADAM CLARKE

This appears to have been literally fulfilled. Levi had no inheritance except forty-eight cities, scattered through different parts of the land of Canaan; and as to the tribe of Simeon, it is generally believed among the Jews that they became schoolmasters to the other tribes; and when they entered Canaan they had only a small portion, a few towns and villages in the worst part of Judah's lot, Josh. xix. 1, which afterwards finding too little, they formed different colonies in districts which they conquered from the Idumeans and Amalekites, 1 Chron. iv. 39, etc. Thus these two tribes were not only separated from each other, but even divided from themselves, according to this prediction of Jacob.

Judah! thou! Thy brethren shall praise thee.
Thy hand, in the neck of thine enemies:
The sons of thy father shall bow themselves
to thee.
A lion's whelp is Judah:
From the prey, my son, thou hast ascended.
He couched, lying down like a strong lion,
And like a lioness; who shall arouse him?
From Judah the sceptre shall not depart,
Nor a teacher from his offspring,
Until that Shiloh shall come,
And to him shall be assembled the peoples.
Binding his colt to the vine,
And to the choice vine the foals of his ass,
He washed his garments in wine,
His clothes in the blood of the grape.
With wine shall his eyes be red,
And his teeth shall be white with milk.

8. "Thy brethren shall praise thee." As the name Judah signifies "praise," Jacob takes occasion from its meaning to show that this tribe should be so eminent and glorious that the rest of the tribes should praise it; that is, they should acknowledge its superior dignity, as in its privileges it should be distinguished beyond all the others.

10. "From Judah the sceptre shall not depart." Judah shall continue a distinct tribe till the Messiah shall come; and it did so; and after His coming it was confounded with the others, so that all distinction has been ever since lost.

"Nor a teacher from his offspring." I am sufficiently aware that the literal meaning of the original is "from between his feet," and I am as fully satisfied that it should never be so translated; "from between the feet" and "out of the thigh" simply mean progeny, natural offspring, for reasons which surely need not be mentioned.

At the haven of the seas shall Zebulun dwell,
And he shall be a haven for ships.
And his border shall extend unto Sidon.
Issachar is a strong ass
Couching between two burdens.
And he saw the resting place that it was good,
And the land that it was pleasant;
And he inclined his shoulder to the load,
And he became a servant unto tribute.

13. Zebulun's lot or portion in the division of the Promised Land extended from the Mediterranean Sea on the west to the lake of Gennesareth on the east; see his division, Josh. xix. 10, etc. The Targum of Jonathan paraphrases the passage thus: "Zebulun shall be on the coasts of the sea, and he shall rule over the havens; he shall subdue the provinces of the sea with his ships, and his border shall extend unto Sidon."

14. *Issachar is a strong ass. Chamor garem* is properly a "strong-limbed ass"; *couching down between two burdens*—bearing patiently, as most understand it, the fatigues of agriculture, and submitting to exorbitant taxes rather than exert themselves to drive out the old inhabitants. The *two burdens* literally mean the two sacks or panniers, one on each side of the animal's body; and couching down between these refers to the well-known propensity of the ass, whenever wearied or overloaded, to lie down even with its burden on its back.

15. *He saw that rest.* The inland portion that was assigned to him between the other tribes. "He inclined his shoulder to the load"; the Chaldee paraphrase gives this a widely different turn to that given it by most commentators: "He saw his portion that it was good, and the

MATTHEW HENRY | JAMIESON, FAUSSET, BROWN | ADAM CLARKE

R. PAYNE SMITH:

Dan. In passing on to the sons of the handmaids it was necessary to assure them of an independent rank among their brethren. The four tribes descended from them did always hold an inferior position, but Jacob by his words to Dan prevented their ever becoming subject states. Playing, then, upon the name Dan (a *judge*), he says that he shall judge his people as a distinct and separate tribe, possessed of all those rights of self-government and tribal independence which this rank implied. It seems also that Dan's symbol was a serpent, and from this Jacob prophesies that though too weak a tribe to take the foremost place in war, yet that Dan should not be without military importance; and this was especially the case in the days of Samson. The word rendered *adder* is more exactly the *arrow-snake*, which lies in wait in the "path," a narrow track, and springs upon its prey as it passes. A horse bitten in this way would rear and throw its rider, who would then be in the power of his assailant.—*Ellicott's Commentary on the Whole Bible*

III. Concerning Dan, *v.* 16, 17. What is said concerning Dan has reference either, To that tribe in general, that though Dan was one of the sons of the concubines yet he should by art, and policy, and surprise, gain advantages against his enemies, like a serpent suddenly biting the heel of the traveller. Dan shall be incorporated by as good a charter as any of the other tribes. Some, like Dan, may excel in the subtlety of the serpent, as others, like Judah, in the courage of the lion; and both may do good service to the cause of God against the Canaanites.

Thus was Jacob going on with his discourse; but now he relieves himself with those words which come in as a parenthesis (*v.* 18), *I have waited for thy salvation, O Lord!*

IV. Concerning Gad, *v.* 19. He alludes to his name, which signifies a *troop*, foresees the character of that tribe, that it should be a warlike tribe, and so we find (1 Chron. xii. 8); the *Gadites were men of war fit for the battle.* He foresees that the situation of that tribe on the other side Jordan would expose it to the incursions of its neighbours, the Moabites and Ammonites; and he foretells that the troops of their enemies should, in many skirmishes, overcome them; yet he assures them that they should *overcome at the last*, which was fulfilled when, in Saul's time and David's, the Moabites and Ammonites were wholly subdued: see 1 Chron. v. 18, &c. Note, *Vincimur in praelio, sed non in bello—We are foiled in a battle, but not in a campaign.* Grace in the soul is often foiled in its conflicts, but the cause is God's and grace will in the issue come off conqueror, yea *more than conqueror*, Rom. viii. 37.

16-18. DAN—though the son of a secondary wife, was to be "as one of the tribes of Israel." Dan—"a judge."

a serpent, . . . an adder—A serpent, an adder, implies subtlety and stratagem; such was pre-eminently the character of Samson, the most illustrious of its judges.

19. GAD—This tribe should be often attacked and wasted by hostile powers on their borders (Judg. 10:8; Jer. 49:1). But they were generally victorious in the close of their wars.

land that it was fruitful; and he shall subdue the provinces of the people, and drive out their inhabitants, and those who are left shall be his servants, and his tributaries." Grotius understands it nearly in the same way. The pusillanimity which is generally attributed to this tribe certainly does not agree with the view in which they are exhibited in Scripture. In the song of Deborah this tribe is praised for the powerful assistance which it then afforded, Judg. v. 15. And in 1 Chron. vii. 1-5, they are expressly said to have been "valiant men of might in all their families, and in all their generations"; i.e., through every period of their history. It appears they were a laborious, hardy, valiant tribe, patient in labor, and invincible in war, bearing both these burdens with great constance whenever it was necessary. When Tola of this tribe judged Israel, the land had rest twenty-three years, Judg. x. 1.

Dan shall judge his people,
As one of the tribes of Israel.
Dan shall be a serpent on the way,
A cerastes upon the track,
Biting the heels of the horse,
And his rider shall fall backwards.

16. *Dan shall judge.* Dan, whose name signifies "judgment," was the eldest of Jacob's sons by Bilhah, Rachel's maid, and he is here promised an equal rule with those tribes that sprang from either Leah or Rachel, the legal wives of Jacob. Some Jewish and some Christian writers understand this prophecy of Samson, who sprang from this tribe, and judged, or as the word might be translated "avenged," the people of Israel twenty years. See Judg. xiii. 2; xv. 20.

17. *Dan shall be a serpent.* The original word is *nachash*, and this has a great variety of significations. It is probable that a serpent is here intended, but of what kind we know not. "A cerastes upon the track." The word *shephiphon*, which is nowhere else to be found in the Bible, is thus translated by the Vulgate. The cerastes has its name from two little horns upon its head, and is remarkable for the property here ascribed to the *shephiphon*. The word *orach*, which we translate *path*, signifies the track or rut made in the ground by the wheel of a cart, wagon, etc. And the description that Nicander gives of this serpent in his *Theriaca* perfectly agrees with what is here said of the *shephiphon*: "It lies under the sand, or in some cart rut by the way."

It is intimated that this tribe should gain the principal part of its conquests more by cunning and stratagem than by valor; and this is seen particularly in their conquest of Laish, Judges xviii, and even in some of the transactions of Samson, such as burning the corn of the Philistines, and at last pulling down their temple, and destroying 3,000 at one time; see Judg. xvi. 26-30.

For thy salvation have I waited, O Lord!

18. This is a remarkable ejaculation, and seems to stand perfectly unconnected with all that went before and all that follows; though it is probable that certain prophetic views which Jacob now had and which he does not explain gave rise to it; and by this he at once expressed both his faith and hope in God. As the tribe of Dan was the first that appears to have been seduced from the true worship of God (see Judg. xviii. 30), some have thought that Jacob refers particularly to this and sees the end of the general apostasy only in the redemption by Jesus Christ, considering the *nachash* above as the seducer and the Messiah the promised Seed.

Gad, an army shall attack him,
And he shall attack in return.

19. This is one of the most obscure prophecies in the whole chapter, and no two interpreters agree in the translation of the original words. The prophecy seems to refer generally to the frequent disturbances to which this tribe should be exposed, and their hostile, warlike disposition, that would always lead them to repel every aggression. It is likely that the prophecy had an especial fulfillment when this tribe, in conjunction with that of Reuben and the half-tribe of Manasseh, had a great victory over the Hagarites, taking captive 100,000 men, 2,000 asses, 50,000 camels, and 250,000 sheep; see 1 Chron. v. 18-22.

MATTHEW HENRY

V. Concerning Asher (*v.* 20), that it should be a very rich tribe, replenished not only with bread for necessity, but with fatness, with *dainties,* and these exported out of Asher to other tribes, perhaps to other lands.

VI. Concerning Naphtali (*v.* 21), a tribe that carries struggles in its name; it signifies *wrestling,* and the blessing entailed upon it signifies prevailing; it is *a hind let loose.* This tribe was, 1. As the loving hind, friendly and obliging. 2. As the loosened hind, zealous for their liberty. 3. As the swift hind (Ps. xviii. 33), quick in despatch of business. Note, Among God's Israel there is to be found a great variety of dispositions, contrary to each other, yet all contributing to the beauty and strength of the body, Judah like a lion, Issachar like an ass, Dan like a serpent, Naphtali like a hind.

JAMIESON, FAUSSET, BROWN

20. ASHER—"Blessed." Its allotment was the seacoast between Tyre and Carmel, a district fertile in the production of the finest corn and oil in all Palestine.

21. NAPHTALI—The best rendering we know is this, "Naphtali is a deer roaming at liberty; he shooteth forth goodly branches," or majestic antlers [TAYLOR's *Scripture Illustrations*], and the meaning of the prophecy seems to be that the tribe of Naphtali would be located in a territory so fertile and peaceable, that, feeding on the richest pasture, he would spread out, like a deer, branching antlers.

KEIL–DELITZSCH:

Verse 21. "Naphtali is a hind let loose, who giveth goodly words." The hind or gazelle is a simile of a warrior who is skillful and swift in his movements (2 Sam. 2:18; 1 Chron. 12:8, cf. Ps. 18:33; Hab. 3:19). A "hind" here is neither hunted not stretched out or grown slim; but let loose, running freely about (Job 39:5). The meaning and allusion are obscure, since nothing further is known of the history of the tribe of Naphtali, than that Naphtali obtained a great victory under Barak in association with Zebulun over the Canaanitish king Jabin, which the prophetess Deborah commemorated in her celebrated song (Judg. 4, 5).—*Commentary on the Old Testament*

MATTHEW HENRY

Verses 22–27

He closes with the blessings of his best beloved sons, Joseph and Benjamin; with these he will breathe his last.

I. The blessing of Joseph, which is very large and full. He is compared (*v.* 22) to *a fruitful bough,* or young tree; for God had made him fruitful in the land of his affliction; he owned it, *ch.* xli. 52. His two sons were as branches of a vine, or other spreading plants, *running over the wall.*

1. The providences of God concerning Joseph, *v.* 23, 24. Here observe (1) Joseph's straits and troubles, *v.* 23. Though he now lived at ease and in honour, Jacob reminds him of the difficulties he had formerly waded through. He had had many enemies, here called *archers,* being skilful to do mischief. His brethren, in his father's house, thought they had been the death of him. His mistress in the house of Potiphar impudently assaulted his chastity and shot arrows against which there is little fence but the hold God has in the consciences of the worst of men. Doubtless he had enemies in the court of Pharaoh, that envied his preferment, and sought to undermine him. (2) Joseph's strength and support under all these troubles (*v.* 24): *His bow abode in strength,* that is, his faith did not fail. The *arms of his hands were made strong,* that is, his other graces did their part, his wisdom, courage, and patience, which are better than weapons of war.

JAMIESON, FAUSSET, BROWN

22-26. JOSEPH—**a fruitful bough,** etc.—denotes the extraordinary increase of that tribe (cf. Num. 1:33-35; Josh. 17:17; Deut. 33:17). The patriarch describes him as attacked by envy, revenge, temptation, ingratitude; yet still, by the grace of God, he triumphed over all opposition, so that he became the sustainer of Israel; and then he proceeds to shower blessings of every kind upon the head of this favorite son. The history of the tribes of Ephraim and Manasseh shows how fully these blessings were realized.

ADAM CLARKE

From Asher his bread shall be fat,
And he shall produce royal dainties.

20. This refers to the great fertility of the lot that fell to Asher, and which appears to have corresponded with the name, which signifies **"happy" or "blessed." His great prosperity** is described by Moses in this figurative way: "Let Asher be blessed with children; let him be acceptable to his brethren, and let him dip his foot in oil," Deut. xxxiii. 24.

Naphtali is a spreading oak,
Producing beautiful branches.

21. This is Bochart's translation; and perhaps no man who understands the genius of the Hebrew language will attempt to dispute its propriety; it is as literal as it is correct. Our own translation scarcely gives any sense. The fruitfulness of this tribe in children may be here intended. But as great increase in this way was not an uncommon case in the descendants of Jacob, this may refer particularly to the fruitfulness of their soil, and the especial providential care and blessing of the Almighty; to which indeed Moses seems particularly to refer, Deut. xxxiii. 23: "O Naphtali, satisfied with favour, and full with the blessing of the Lord." So that he may be represented under the notion of a tree planted in a rich soil, growing to a prodigious size, extending its branches in all directions, becoming a shade for men and cattle and a harbor for the fowls of heaven.

The son of a fruitful [vine] is Joseph;
The son of a fruitful [vine] by the fountain:
The daughters [branches] shoot over the wall.
They sorely afflicted him and contended with him;
The chief archers had him in hatred.
But his bow remained in strength,
And the arms of his hands were made strong
By the hand of the Mighty One of Jacob:
By the name of the Shepherd, the Rock of Israel.
By the God of thy father, for He helped thee;
And God All-sufficient, He blessed thee.
The blessing of the heavens from above,
And the blessings lying in the deep beneath,
The blessings of the breasts and of the womb,
The blessings of thy father have prevailed
Over the blessings of the eternal mountains,
And the desirable things of the everlasting hills.
These shall be on the head of Joseph,
And on his crown who was separated from his brethren.

22. "The son of a fruitful vine." This appears to me to refer to Jacob himself, who was blessed with such a numerous posterity that in 215 years after this his own descendants amounted to upwards of 600,000 effective men; and the figures here are intended to point out the continual growth and increase of his posterity. Jacob was a fruitful tree planted by a fountain, which because it was good would yield good fruit; and because it was planted near a fountain, from being continually watered, would be perpetually fruitful. "The daughters," *banoth,* put here for "branches," shoot over or run upon the wall. Alluding probably to the case of the vine, which requires to be supported by a wall, trees, etc.

23. "The chief archers." "The masters of arrows"—Joseph's brethren, who either used such weapons, while feeding their flocks in the deserts, for the protection of themselves and cattle or for the purpose of hunting, and who probably excelled in archery. It may however refer to the bitter speeches and harsh words that they spoke to and of him, for "they hated him, and could not speak peaceably unto him," chap. xxxvii. 4. Thus they sorely afflicted him, and were incessantly scolding or finding fault.

24. "But his bow remained in strength." The more he was persecuted, either by his brethren or in Egypt, the more resplendent his uprightness and virtues shone. *And the arms*—his extended power and influence—*of his hands*—plans, designs, and particular operations of his prudence, judgment, and discretion—were all rendered successful by the "hand"—the powerful succor and protection, "of the Mighty One of Jacob"—that God who blessed and protected all the counsels and plans of Jacob, and protected and increased him also when he was in a strange

MATTHEW HENRY

ALEXANDER MACLAREN:

The Stone of Israel. Here, again, we have a name, that after ages have caught up and cherished, used for the first time. I suppose the Stone of Israel means much the same thing as the Rock. If so, that symbol, too, which is full of such large meanings, was coined by Jacob. It is, perhaps, not fanciful to suppose that it owes its origin to the scenery of Palestine. The wild cliffs of the eastern region where Peniel lay, or the savage fastnesses in the southern wilderness, a day's march from Hebron, where he lived so long, came back to his memory amid the flat, clay land of Egypt; and their towering height, their immovable firmness, their cool shade, their safe shelter, spoke to him of the unalterable might and impregnable defense which he had found in God. So there is in this name the same devout, reflective laying-hold upon experience which we have observed in the preceding.—*Expositions of Holy Scripture*

(3) The spring and fountain of this strength it was *by the hands of the mighty God.* All our strength for the resisting of temptations, and the bearing of afflictions, comes from God: his grace is sufficient, and his strength is perfected in our weakness. (4) The state of honour and usefulness to which he was subsequently advanced. Herein Joseph was a type, [1] Of Christ. [2] Of the church in general.

2. The promises of God to Joseph. Our experiences of God's power and goodness in strengthening us hitherto are our encouragements still to hope for help from him. We may build much upon our *Eben-ezers.* Observe the blessings conferred on Joseph. *Blessings of heaven above* (rain in its season, and fair weather in its season, and the benign influences of the heavenly bodies); *blessings of the deep that lieth under* this earth, which, compared with the upper world, is but a great deep, with subterraneous mines and springs. Eminent and transcendent blessings, which *prevail above the blessings of my progenitors, v.* 26. Durable and extensive blessings: *Unto the utmost bounds of the everlasting hills,* including all the productions of the most fruitful hills, and lasting as long as they last, Isa. liv. 10.

II. The blessing of Benjamin (*v.* 27): He *shall raven as a wolf*; it is plain by this that Jacob was guided in what he said by a spirit of prophecy, and not by natural affection; else he would have spoken with more tenderness of his beloved son Benjamin, concerning whom he only foresees and foretells this, that his posterity should be a warlike tribe, strong and daring, and that they should enrich themselves with the spoils of their enemies—that they should be active and busy in the world, and a tribe as much feared by their neighbours as any other. Blessed Paul was of this tribe (Rom. xi 1; Phil. iii. 5); and he did in the morning of his day, devour the prey as a persecutor, but, in the evening, divided the spoil as a preacher.

Verses 28–33

I. The summing up of the blessings of Jacob's sons, *v.* 28. Though Reuben, Simeon, and Levi were put under the marks of their father's displeasure, yet he is said to *bless them every one according to his blessing;* for none of them were rejected as Esau was.

II. The solemn charge Jacob gave them concerning his burial, which is a repetition of what he had before given to Joseph. See how he speaks of death: *I am to be gathered unto my people, v.* 29. Though it separates us from our children and our people in this world, it gathers us to our fathers and to our people in the other world.

III. The death of Jacob, *v.* 33: as one cheerfully

JAMIESON, FAUSSET, BROWN

27-33. BENJAMIN shall ravin like a wolf.—This tribe in its early history spent its energies in petty or inglorious warfare and especially in the violent and unjust contest (Judg. 19, 20), in which it engaged with the other tribes, when, notwithstanding two victories, it was almost exterminated. **28. all these are the twelve tribes of Israel**—or ancestors. Jacob's prophetic words obviously refer not so much to the sons as to the tribes of Israel.

29. he charged them—The charge had already been given and solemnly undertaken (ch. 47:31). But in mentioning his wishes now and rehearsing all the circumstances connected with the purchase of Machpelah, he wished to declare, with his latest breath, before all his family, that he died in the same faith as Abraham.

33. when Jacob had made an end of commanding his sons—It is probable that he was supernaturally

ADAM CLARKE

land, and often under the power of those who sought opportunities to oppress and defraud him.

"By the name of the Shepherd, the Rock of Israel." This appears to me to refer to the subject of the thirty-second chapter, where Jacob wrestled with God, had God's name revealed to him, and his own name changed from Jacob to Israel, in consequence of which he built an altar and dedicated it to God, who had appeared to him under the name of *Elohey-Israel,* the "strong God of Israel"; which circumstance led him to use the term "Rock," which, as an emblem of power, is frequently given to God in the sacred writings, and may here refer to the stone which Jacob set up. It is very probable that the word *shepherd* is intended to apply to our blessed Lord, who is the Shepherd of Israel, the Good Shepherd, John x. 11-17; and who, beyond all controversy, was the Person with whom Jacob wrestled.

25. *The God of thy father.* How frequently God is called the "God of Jacob" none needs to be told who reads the Bible. "God All-sufficient." Instead of *Eth Shaddai,* "The Almighty or All-sufficient," I read *El Shaddai,* "God All-sufficient," which is the reading of the Samaritan, Septuagint, Syriac, and Coptic. "The blessing of the heavens from above." A generally pure, clear, serene sky, frequently dropping down fertilizing showers and dews, so as to make a very fruitful soil and salubrious atmosphere. "Blessings lying in the deep beneath." Whatever riches could be gained from the sea or rivers, from mines and minerals in the bowels of the earth, and from abundant springs in different parts of his inheritance. Our translation of this line is excessively obscure: *Blessings of the deep that lieth under.* What is it that lies under the deep? By connecting "blessings" with "lying," all ambiguity is avoided, and the text speaks a plain and consistent sense. "The blessings of the breasts and of the womb." A numerous offspring, and an abundance of cattle. The progeny of Joseph by Ephraim and Manasseh amounted at the first census or enumeration (Numbers i) to 75,900 men, which exceeded the sum of any one tribe; Judah, the greatest of the others, amounting to no more than 74,600. Indeed, Ephraim and Manasseh had multiplied so greatly in the days of Joshua that a common lot was not sufficient for them. See their complaint, Josh. xvii. 14.

26. *The blessings of thy father.* **The blessings which thy father now prays for and pronounces are neither temporal nor transitory; they shall exceed in their duration the eternal mountains, and in their value and spiritual nature all the conveniences, comforts, and delicacies which the everlasting hills can produce. They shall last when the heavens and the earth are no more, and shall extend throughout eternity. They are the blessings which shall be communicated to the world by means of the Messiah.**

Benjamin is a ravenous wolf:
In the morning he shall devour the prey,
And in the evening he shall divide the spoil.

27. This tribe is very fitly compared to a ravenous *wolf,* because of the rude courage and ferocity which they have invariably displayed, particularly in their war with the other tribes, in which they killed more men than the whole of their own numbers amounted to.

28. *Every one according to his blessing.* That is, guided by the unerring Spirit of prophecy, Jacob now foretold to each of his sons the important events which should take place during their successive generations and the predominant characteristic of each tribe; and at the same time made some comparatively obscure references to the advent of the Messiah and the redemption of the world by Him.

29. *Bury me with my fathers.* From this it appears that the cave at Machpelah was a common burying place for Hebrews of distinction, and indeed the first public burying place mentioned in history. From v. 31 we find that Abraham, Sarah, Isaac, Rebekah, and Leah had already been deposited there, and among them Jacob wished to have his bones laid; and he left his dying charge with his children to bury him in this place, and this they conscientiously performed.

33. *He gathered up his feet into the bed.* It is very probable that while delivering these

MATTHEW HENRY

composing himself to rest, now that he was weary. *I will lay me down, and sleep.* He freely resigned his spirit into the hand of God, the Father of spirits: *He yielded up the ghost.* His separated soul went to the assembly of the souls of the faithful, which, after they are delivered from the burden of the flesh, are in joy and felicity: he was *gathered to his people.*

CHAPTER 50

Verses 1–6

Joseph is here paying his last respects to his deceased father. 1. With tears and kisses, and all the tender expressions of a filial affection, he takes leave of the deserted body, *v.* 1. The departed soul is out of the reach of our tears and kisses, but it is proper to show our respect to the poor body, of which we look for a glorious and joyful resurrection. 2. He ordered the body to be embalmed (*v.* 2), not only because he died in Egypt, and that was the manner of the Egyptians, but because he was to be carried to Canaan.

3. He observed the ceremony of solemn mourning for him, *v.* 3. Even the Egyptians, many of them out of the great respect they had for Joseph, put themselves into mourning for his father. 4. He asked and obtained leave of Pharaoh to go to Canaan, thither to attend the funeral of his father, *v.* 4–6. He promised to return: *I will come again.* When we return to our own houses from burying the bodies of our relations, we say, "We have left them behind"; but, if their souls have gone to our heavenly Father's house, we may say with more reason, "They have left us behind."

Verses 7–14

We have here an account of Jacob's funeral. He dies in honour, and is followed to the grave by all his children. 1. It was a stately funeral. He was attended to the grave, not only by his own family, but by the courtiers, and all the great men of the kingdom, who, in token of their gratitude to Joseph, showed this respect to his father for his sake, and did him honour at his death. Good old Jacob had conducted himself so well among them as to gain universal esteem. Note, Professors of religion should endeavour, by wisdom and love, to remove the prejudices which many may have conceived against them because they do not know them. 2. It was a sorrowful funeral (*v.* 10, 11). The solemn mourning for Jacob gave a name to the place, *Abel-Mizraim, the mourning of the Egyptians*, which served for a testimony against the next generation of the Egyptians, who oppressed the posterity of this Jacob to whom their ancestors showed such respect.

Verses 15–21

We have here the settling of a good correspondence between Joseph and his brethren, now that their father was dead. When Providence has removed the parents by death, the best methods ought to be taken for the preserving of acquaintance and love, that unity may continue even when that centre of unity is taken away.

I. Joseph's brethren humbly make their court to him for his favour. 1. While their father lived, they thought themselves safe under his shadow; but now that he was dead they feared the worst from Joseph. A guilty conscience exposes men to continual frights. Those that would be fearless must keep themselves guiltless.

JAMIESON, FAUSSET, BROWN

strengthened for this last momentous office of the patriarch, and that when the divine afflatus ceased, his exhausted powers giving way, he yielded up the ghost, and was gathered unto his people.

CHAPTER 50

Vss. 1-26. Mourning for Jacob. **1. Joseph fell upon his father's face,** etc.—On him, as the principal member of the family, devolved the duty of closing the eyes of his venerable parent (cf. ch. 46:4) and imprinting the farewell kiss. **2. Joseph commanded his servants the physicians to embalm his father,** etc.—In ancient Egypt the embalmers were a class by themselves. The process of embalmment consisted in infusing a great quantity of resinous substances into the cavities of the body, after the intestines had been removed, and then a regulated degree of heat was applied to dry up the humors, as well as decompose the tarry materials which had been previously introduced. Thirty days were alloted for the completion of this process; forty more were spent in anointing it with spices; the body, tanned from this operation, being then washed, was wrapped in numerous folds of linen cloth—the joinings of which were fastened with gum, and then it was deposited in a wooden chest made in the form of a human figure. **3. the Egyptians mourned,** etc.—It was made a period of public mourning, as on the death of a royal personage. **4. Joseph spake unto the house of Pharaoh,** etc.—Care was taken to let it be known that the family sepulchre was provided before leaving Canaan and that an oath bound his family to convey the remains thither. Besides, Joseph deemed it right to apply for a special leave of absence; and being unfit, as a mourner, to appear in the royal presence, he made the request through the medium of others. **7-9. Joseph went up to bury his father**—a journey of 300 miles. The funeral cavalcade, composed of the nobility and military, with their equipages, would exhibit an imposing appearance.

10. they came to the threshing-floor of Atad, etc.—"Atad" may be taken as a common noun, signifying "the plain of the thorn bushes." It was on the border between Egypt and Canaan; and as the last opportunity of indulging grief was always the most violent, the Egyptians made a prolonged halt at this spot, while the family of Jacob probably proceeded by themselves to the place of sepulture.

15-21. When Joseph's brethren saw that their father was dead, they said, Joseph will peradventure hate us, etc.—Joseph was deeply affected by this communication. He gave them the strongest assurances of his forgiveness and thereby gave both a beautiful trait of his own pious character, as well as appeared an eminent type of the Saviour.

ADAM CLARKE

prophetic blessings Jacob sat upon the side of his bed, leaning upon his staff; and having finished, he lifted up his feet into the bed, stretched himself upon it, and expired! *And was gathered unto his people.* The testimony that this place bears to the immortality of the soul, and to its existence separate from the body, should not be lightly regarded. In the same moment in which Jacob is said to have *gathered up his feet into the bed,* and to have expired, it is added, *and was gathered unto his people.*

CHAPTER 50

1. *Joseph fell upon his father's face.* Though this act appears to be suspended by the unnatural division of this verse from the preceding chapter, yet we may rest assured it was the immediate consequence of Jacob's death.

2. *The physicians.* The "healers," those whose business it was to heal or restore the body from sickness by the administration of proper medicines; and when death took place, to heal or preserve it from dissolution by embalming, and thus give it a sort of immortality or everlasting duration. In the art of embalming, the Egyptians excelled all nations in the world; with them it was a common practice. Instances of the perfection to which they carried this art may be seen in the numerous mummies which have been brought from Egypt.

3. *Forty days.* The body it appears required this number of days to complete the process of embalming; afterwards it lay thirty days more, making in the whole seventy days, during which the mourning was continued.

4. *Speak, I pray you, in the ears of Pharaoh.* But why did not Joseph apply himself? Because he was now in his mourning habits, and in such none must appear in the presence of the Eastern monarchs. See Esther iv. 2.

7. *The elders of his house.* Persons who, by reason of their age, had acquired much experience; and who on this account were deemed the best qualified to conduct the affairs of the king's household. The funeral procession of Jacob must have been truly grand. Joseph, his brethren and their descendants, the servants of Pharaoh, the elders of his house, and all the elders—all the principal men—of the land of Egypt, with chariots and horsemen, must have appeared a very great company indeed. He was a national blessing; and the nation mourns in his affliction, and unites to do him honor.

10. *The threshingfloor of Atad.* As *Atad* signifies a "bramble" or "thorn," it has been understood by the Arabic, not as a man's name, but as the name of a *place;* but all the other versions and the Targums consider it as the name of a man.

The mourning of the ancient Hebrews was usually of seven days' continuance, Num. xix. 19; 1 Sam. xxxi. 13; though on certain occasions it was extended to thirty days, Num. xx. 29; Deut. xxi. 13; xxiv. 8, but never longer. The seventy days' mourning mentioned above was that of the Egyptians, and was rendered necessary by the long process of embalming, which obliged them to keep the body out of the grave for seventy days, as we learn both from Herodotus and Diodorus. Seven days by the order of God a man was to mourn for his dead, because during that time he was considered as unclean: but when those were finished he was to purify himself, and consider the mourning as ended, Num. xix. 11, 19.

15. *Saw that their father was dead.* This at once argues both a sense of guilt in their own consciences and a want of confidence in their brother. They might have supposed that hitherto he had forborne to punish them merely on their father's account; but now that he was dead, and Joseph having them completely in his power they imagined that he would take vengeance on them for their former conduct towards him.

16. *Thy father did command.* Whether he did or not we cannot tell. Some think they had feigned this story, but that is not so likely. Jacob might have had suspicions too, and might have thought that the best way to prevent evil was to humble themselves before their brother and get a fresh assurance of his forgiveness.

MATTHEW HENRY

2. They humbled themselves before him, confessed their fault, and begged his pardon. *Forgive the trespass. We are thy servants.* 3. They pleaded their relation to Jacob and to Jacob's God. (1) To Jacob, urging that he directed them to make this submission. *Thy father did command.* (2) To Jacob's God. They plead (*v.* 17), *We* are the *servants of the God of thy father*; not only children of the same Jacob, but worshippers of the same Jehovah.

II. Joseph, with a great deal of compassion, confirms his reconciliation and affection to them; his compassion appears, *v.* 17. *He wept when they spoke to him.* These were tears of sorrow for their suspicion of him, and tears of tenderness upon their submission. In his reply, 1. He directs them to look up to God in their repentance (*v.* 19): *Am I in the place of God?* "Make your peace with God, and then you will find it an easy matter to make your peace with me." 2. He extenuates their fault, from the consideration of the great good which God wonderfully brought out of it, which, though it should not make them the less sorry for their sin, yet might make him the more willing to forgive it (*v.* 20). God often brings good out of evil, and promotes the designs of his providence even by the sins of men; not that he is the author of sin, far be it from us to think so; but his infinite wisdom so overrules events, that, in the issue, that ends in his praise which in its own nature had a direct tendency to his dishonour; as the putting of Christ to death, Acts ii. 23. 3. He assures them of the continuance of his kindness to them: *Fear not; I will nourish you, v.* 21.

Verses 22-26

I. The prolonging of Joseph's life in Egypt: he lived to be *a hundred and ten years old, v.* 22.

II. The building up of Joseph's family: he lived to see his great-grand-children by both his sons (*v.* 23), and probably he saw his two sons solemnly owned as heads of distinct tribes, equal to any of his brethren.

III. The last will and testament of Joseph published in the presence of his brethren, when he saw his death approaching. To those of them who yet survived, and to the sons of those who were gone, who stood up in their fathers' stead, he said this. 1. He comforted them with the assurance of their return to Canaan in due time: *I die, but God will surely visit you, v.* 24. He bids them be confident: *God will bring you out of this land,* and therefore, (1) They must not look upon it as their rest for ever; they must set their hearts upon the land of promise, and call that their home. (2) They must not fear sinking, and being ruined there. "*God will bring you* in triumph *out of this land* at last." 2. For a confession of his own faith, and a confirmation of theirs, he charges them to keep him unburied till they should be settled in the land of promise, *v.* 25. He makes them promise him with an oath that they would bury him in Canaan.

IV. The death of Joseph, and the reservation of his body for a burial in Canaan, *v.* 26. He was *put in a coffin in Egypt,* but not buried till his children had received their inheritance in Canaan, Josh. xxiv. 32.

JAMIESON, FAUSSET, BROWN

22, 23. Joseph dwelt in Egypt—He lived eighty years after his elevation to the chief power witnessing a great increase in the prosperity of the kingdom, and also of his own family and kindred—the infant Church of God.

24. Joseph said unto his brethren, I die—The national feelings of the Egyptians would have been opposed to his burial in Canaan; but he gave the strongest proof of the strength of his faith and full assurance of the promises, by "the commandment concerning his bones."

26. they embalmed him—His funeral would be conducted in the highest style of Egyptian magnificence and his mummied corpse carefully preserved till the Exodus.

ADAM CLARKE

17. *The servants of the God of thy father.* These words were wonderfully well chosen and spoken in the most forcible manner to Joseph's piety and filial affection. No wonder then that he *wept when they spake unto him.*

22. *Joseph dwelt in Egypt.* Continued in Egypt after his return from Canaan till his death; *he, and his father's house*—all the descendants of Israel, till the exodus or departure under the direction of Moses and Aaron, which was 144 years after.

23. *Were brought up upon Joseph's knees.* They were educated by him, or under his direction; his sons and their children continuing to acknowledge him as patriarch, or head of the family, as long as he lived.

24. *Joseph said . . . I die.* That is, I am dying; *and God will surely visit you*—He will yet again give you, in the time when it shall be essentially necessary, the most signal proof of His unbounded love towards the seed of Jacob. *And bring you out of this land.* Though ye have here everything that can render life comfortable, yet this is not the typical land, the land given by covenant, the land which represents the rest that remains for the people of God.

25. *Ye shall carry up my bones.* That I may finally rest with my ancestors in the land which God gave to Abraham, to Isaac, and to Jacob; and which is a pledge as it is a type of the kingdom of Heaven. Thus says the author of the Epistle to the Hebrews, chap. xi. 22: "By faith Joseph, when he died [when dying], made mention of the departing [of the Exodus] of the children of Israel; and gave commandment concerning his bones." From this it is evident that Joseph considered all these things as typical, and by this very commandment expressed his faith in the immortality of the soul and the general resurrection of the dead. This oath, by which Joseph then bound his brethren, their posterity considered as binding on themselves; and Moses took care, when he departed from Egypt, to carry up Joseph's body with him, Exod. xiii. 19; which was afterwards buried in Shechem, Josh. xxiv. 32, the very portion which Jacob had purchased from the Amorites, and which he gave to his son Joseph, Gen. lxviii. 22; Acts vii. 16.

26. *Joseph died, being an hundred and ten years old.* Literally, "the son of a hundred and ten years." *They embalmed him.* The same precautions were taken to preserve his body as to preserve that of his father, Jacob; and this was particularly necessary in his case, because his body was to be carried to Canaan 144 years after.

THE BOOK OF EXODUS

I. Bondage (1:1-5:23)
A. Israel in Egypt (1:1-22)
1. Growth of the nation (1:1-7)
2. Oppression (1:8-22)
B. Moses (2:1-4:31)
1. Birth and preservation (2:1-10)
2. Flight and residence in Midian (2:11-22)
3. His call (2:23-4:17)
4. His obedience (4:18-31)
C. Israel and Pharaoh (5:1-23)
1. Moses and Pharaoh (5:1-18)
2. Moses and Israel (5:19-21)
3. Moses and Jehovah (5:22-23)

II. Deliverance (6:1-18:27)
A. Jehovah and Moses—the charge (6:1-7:7)
1. Self-declaration of Jehovah (6:1-9)
2. The charge and fear (6:10-12)
(Parenthesis—6:13-27)
3. The charge and faith (6:28-7:7)
B. Jehovah and Pharaoh (7:8-11:10)
1. The approach (7:8-13)
2. First cycle—3 plagues (7:14-8:19)
3. Second cycle—3 plagues (8:20-9:12)
4. Third cycle—3 plagues (9:13-10:29)
5. Final (11:1-10)
C. Jehovah and Israel (12:1-18:27)
1. Deliverance (12:1-15:21)
2. Guidance (15:22-18:27)

III. Organization (19:1-40:38)
A. Preliminary and fundamental (19:1-20:26)
1. The purpose: grace (19:1-25)
2. The plan: law (20:1-26)
B. Laws (21:1-23:33)
1. Of the person (21:1-32)
2. Of property (21:33-22:15)
3. Of the state (22:16-23:19)
4. The angel promised (23:20-33)
C. The system of worship (24:1-40:38)
1. Instruction and equipment (24:1-31:18)
2. Interlude—the people's sin (32:1-34:35)
3. Construction and consecration (35:1-40:38)

Moses, having, in the first book of his history, preserved, and transmitted the records of the church, while it existed in private families, comes, in this second book, to give us an account of its growth into a great nation. The beginning of the former book shows us how God formed the world for himself; the beginning of this shows us how he formed Israel for himself, and both to show forth his praise (Isa. 43:21). There we have the creation of the world in history, here the redemption of the world in type. The Greek translators called this book "Exodus" (which signifies a *departure* or *going out*) because it begins with the story of the going out of the children of Israel from Egypt. The forming of Israel into a people was a new creation.

This book gives us the accomplishment of the promises made before to Abraham (ch. 1–19), and then, the establishment of the ordinances which were afterwards observed by Israel (ch. 20–40). Moses, in this book, begins, like Caesar, to write his own commentaries. But henceforward the penman is himself the hero, and gives us the history of those things of which he was himself an eye- and ear-witness and in which he bore a conspicuous part. There are more types of Christ in this book than perhaps in any other book of the Old Testament; for Moses wrote of him (John 5:46). The way of man's reconciliation to God and coming into covenant and communion with him by a Mediator is here variously represented; and it is of great use to us for the illustration of the New Testament, now that we have that to assist us in the explanation of the Old.

MATTHEW HENRY

CHAPTER 1

Verses 1–7

1. A recital of the names of the *twelve patriarchs*, as they are called, Acts vii. 8. 2. The account which was kept of the number of Jacob's family, when they went down into Egypt. Notice is here taken of this that their increase in Egypt might appear the more wonderful.

3. The death of Joseph, *v.* 6. *All that generation* by degrees wore off. Perhaps all Jacob's sons died much about the same time; for there was not more than seven years' difference in age between the eldest and the youngest of them, except Benjamin. 4. The strange increase of Israel in Egypt, *v.* 7. Here are four words used to express it: They *were fruitful*, and *increased abundantly*. They *multiplied* and *waxed exceedingly mighty*. This wonderful increase was the fulfilment of the promise long before made unto the fathers.

Verses 8–14

The land of Egypt here, at length, becomes to Israel a house of bondage, though hitherto it had been a happy shelter and settlement for them.

I. The obligations they lay under to Israel upon Joseph's account were forgotten: *There arose a new king*, after several successions in Joseph's time, *who knew not Joseph, v.* 8. If we work for men only, our works, at furthest, will die with us; if for God, they will follow us, Rev. xiv. 13.

JAMIESON, FAUSSET, BROWN

CHAPTER 1

Vss. 1-22. Increase of the Israelites. **1. Now these are the names**—(See on ch. 46:8-26).

children of Israel were fruitful—They were living in a land where, according to the testimony of an ancient author, mothers produced three and four sometimes at a birth; and a modern writer declares "the females in Egypt, as well among the human race as among animals, surpass all others in fruitfulness." To this natural circumstance must be added the fulfilment of the promise made to Abraham.

8. Now there arose up a new king—About sixty years after the death of Joseph a revolution took place—by which the old dynasty was overthrown, and upper and lower Egypt were united into one kingdom. Assuming that the king formerly reigned in Thebes, it is probable that he would know nothing about the Hebrews; and that, as foreigners and shepherds, the new government would, from the first, regard them with dislike and scorn.

ADAM CLARKE

CHAPTER 1

1. *These are the names.* Though this book is a continuation of the Book of Genesis, with which probably it was in former times conjoined, Moses thought it necessary to introduce it with an account of the names and number of the family of Jacob when they came to Egypt, to show that though they were then very few, yet in a short time, under the especial blessing of God, they had multiplied exceedingly; and thus the promise to Abraham had been literally fulfilled. See the notes on Genesis xlvi.

6. *Joseph died, and all his brethren.* That is, Joseph had now been some time dead, as also all his brethren, and all the Egyptians who had known Jacob and his twelve sons; and this is a sort of reason why the important services performed by Joseph were forgotten.

7. *The children of Israel were fruitful. Paru*, a general term, signifying that they were like healthy trees, bringing forth an abundance of fruit. *And increased.* "They increased like fishes," as the original word implies. *Abundantly. Yirbu*, "they multiplied"; this is a separate term, and should not have been used as an adverb by our translators. *And waxed exceeding mighty.* And they became strong beyond measure—"superlatively, superlatively"—so that *the land* (Goshen) *was filled with them.* This astonishing increase was, under the providence of God, chiefly owing to two causes: (1) The Hebrew women were exceedingly fruitful, suffered very little in parturition, and probably often brought forth twins. (2) There appear to have been no premature deaths among them. Thus in about two hundred and fifteen years they were multiplied to upwards of 600,000, independently of old men, women, and children.

8. *Which knew not Joseph.* The verb *yada*, which we translate "to know," often signifies to "acknowledge" or "approve." See Judg. ii. 10; Ps. i. 6; xxxi. 7; Hos. ii. 8; Amos iii. 2. We may therefore understand by the new king's not knowing Joseph his disapproving of that system of government which Joseph had established, as well as his haughtily refusing to acknowledge the obligations under which the whole land of

MATTHEW HENRY

II. Reasons of state were suggested for their dealing hardly with Israel, *v.* 9, 10. 1. They are represented as more and mightier than the Egyptians; certainly they were not so, but the king of Egypt, when he resolved to oppress them, would have them thought so, and looked on as a formidable body. 2. Hence it is inferred that if care were not taken to keep them under they would become dangerous to the government. Observe, The thing they feared was lest they should *get them up out of the land*, probably having heard them speak of the promise made to their fathers that they should settle in Canaan. 3. It is therefore proposed that a course be taken to prevent their increase: *Come on, let us deal wisely with them, lest they multiply.*

III. The method they took to suppress them, and check their growth, *v.* 11, 13, 14. 1. They took care to keep them poor, by charging them with heavy taxes. 2. By this means they took an effectual course to make them slaves. The Israelites, it should seem, were much more industrious laborious people than the Egyptians, and therefore Pharaoh took care to find them work, both in building and in husbandry, and this was exacted from them with the utmost rigour and severity. They had *taskmasters* set over them, directed *to afflict them with their burdens.* They made them *serve with rigour*, so that their lives became bitter to them, intending hereby, (1) To break their spirits. (2) To ruin their health and shorten their days, and so diminish their numbers. (3) To discourage them from marrying, since their children would be born to slavery. And it is to be feared that the oppression they were under brought over many of them to join with the Egyptians in their idolatrous worship. However, they were kept a distinct body, unmingled with the Egyptians, and by their other customs separated from them, which was *the Lord's doing, and marvellous.*

IV. The wonderful increase of the Israelites: *The more they afflicted them the more they multiplied*, sorely to the grief and vexation of the Egyptians. The blood of the martyrs was the seed of the church.

Verses 15–22

The Egyptians' indignation at Israel's increase, notwithstanding the many hardships they put upon them, drove them at length to the most barbarous and inhuman methods of suppressing them, by the murder of their children. Pharaoh and Herod sufficiently proved themselves agents for that *great red dragon, who stood to devour the man-child as soon as it was born*, Rev. xii. 3, 4. Pilate delivered Christ to be crucified, after he had confessed that he found no fault in him. It is well for us that, though man can kill the body, this is all he can do.

I. The midwives were commanded to murder them. Observe, 1. The orders given them, *v.* 15, 16. It added much to the barbarity of the intended executions that the *midwives* were appointed to be the executioners. Pharaoh's project was secretly to engage the midwives to stifle the men-children as soon as they were born, and then to lay it upon the difficulty of the birth, or some mischance common in that case, Job iii. 11. 2. Their pious disobedience to this impious command, *v.* 17. *They feared God*, regarded his law, and dreaded his wrath more than Pharaoh's, and therefore saved the men-children alive. 3. Their justifying themselves in this disobedience, when they were charged with it as a crime, *v.* 18. They gave a reason for it, that they came too late to do it, for generally the children were born before they came, *v.* 19. Some of the ancient Jews expound it thus, *Ere the midwife comes to them they pray to their Father in heaven, and he answereth them, and they do bring forth.* 4. The recompence God gave them for their tenderness towards his people: *He dealt well with them, v.* 20.

JAMIESON, FAUSSET, BROWN

9. he said . . . Behold, the . . . children of Israel are more and mightier than we—They had risen to great prosperity—as during the lifetime of Joseph and his royal patron, they had, probably, enjoyed a free grant of the land. Their increase and prosperity were viewed with jealousy by the new government; and as Goshen lay between Egypt and Canaan, on the border of which latter country were a number of warlike tribes, it was perfectly conformable to the suggestions of worldly policy that they should enslave and maltreat them, through apprehension of their joining in any invasion by those foreign rovers. The new king, who neither knew the name nor cared for the services of Joseph, was either *Amosis*, or one of his immediate successors [OSBURN]. **11. Therefore they did set over them taskmasters**—Having first obliged them, it is thought, to pay a ruinous rent and involved them in difficulties, that new government, in pursuance of its oppressive policy, degraded them to the condition of serfs—employing them exactly as the laboring people are in the present day (driven in companies or bands), in rearing the public works, with taskmasters, who anciently had sticks—now whips—to punish the indolent, or spur on the too languid. All public or royal buildings, in ancient Egypt, were built by captives; and on some of them was placed an inscription that no free citizen had been engaged in this servile employment. **they built for Pharaoh treasure cities**—These two store places were in the land of Goshen; and being situated near a border liable to invasion, they were fortified cities (cf. II Chron. 11-12). Pithom (*Greek, Patumos*), lay on the eastern Pelusiac branch of the Nile, about twelve Roman miles from Heliopolis; and Raamses, called by the LXX Heroöpolis, lay between the same branch of the Nile and the Bitter Lakes. These two fortified cities were situated, therefore, in the same valley; and the fortifications, which Pharaoh commanded to be built around both, had probably the same common object, of obstructing the entrance into Egypt, which this valley furnished the enemy from Asia [HENGSTENBERG]. **13, 14. The Egyptians . . . made their lives bitter with hard bondage, in mortar and in brick**—Ruins of great brick buildings are found in all parts of Egypt. The use of crude brick, baked in the sun, was universal in upper and lower Egypt, both for public and private buildings; *all* but the temples themselves were of crude brick. It is worthy of remark that more bricks bearing the name of Thothmes III, who is supposed to have been the king of Egypt at the time of the Exodus, have been discovered than of any other period [WILKINSON]. Parties of these brickmakers are seen depicted on the ancient monuments with "taskmasters," some standing, others in a sitting posture beside the laborers, with their uplifted sticks in their hands. **15. the king of Egypt spake to the Hebrew midwives**—Two only were spoken to—either they were the heads of a large corporation [LABORDE], or, by tampering with these two, the king designed to terrify the rest into secret compliance with his wishes [CALVIN]. **16. if it be a son, then ye shall kill him**—Opinions are divided, however, what was the method of destruction which the king did recommend. Some think that the "stools" were low seats on which these obstetric practitioners sat by the bedside of the Hebrew women; and that, as they might easily discover the sex, so, whenever a boy appeared, they were to strangle it, unknown to its parents; while others are of opinion that the "stools" were stone troughs, by the river side—into which, when the infants were washed, they were to be, as it were, accidentally dropped. **17. But the midwives feared God**—Their faith inspired them with such courage as to risk their lives, by disobeying the mandate of a cruel tyrant; but it was blended with weakness, which made them shrink from speaking the truth, the whole truth, and nothing but the truth.

20. God dealt well with the midwives—This represents God as rewarding them for telling a lie. This difficulty is wholly removed by a more correct translation. To make or build up

ADAM CLARKE

Egypt was laid to this eminent prime minister of one of his predecessors.

9. *He said unto his people.* He probably summoned a council of his nobles and elders to consider the subject; and the result was to persecute and destroy them, as is afterwards stated.

10. *They join also unto our enemies.* It has been conjectured that Pharaoh had probably his eye on the oppressions which Egypt had suffered under the shepherd-kings, who for a long series of years had, according to Manetho, governed the land with extreme cruelty. As the Israelites were of the same occupation (namely, shepherds), the jealous, cruel king found it easy to attribute to them the same motives, taking it for granted that they were only waiting for a favorable opportunity to join the enemies of Egypt, and so overrun the whole land.

11. *Set over them taskmasters.* "Chiefs or princes of burdens, works, or tribute"; Septuagint, "overseers of the works." The persons who appointed them their work, and exacted the performance of it. The work itself being oppressive, and the manner in which it was exacted still more so, there is some room to think that they not only worked them unmercifully, but also obliged them to pay an exorbitant tribute at the same time. *Treasure cities.* "Store cities—public granaries."

12. *But the more they afflicted them.* The margin has pretty nearly preserved the import of the original: "And as they afflicted them, so they multiplied and so they grew." That is, in proportion to their afflictions was their prosperity.

13. *To serve with rigour.* With cruelty, great oppression; being ferocious with them. This kind of cruelty to slaves, and ferociousness, unfeelingness, and hardheartedness, were particularly forbidden to the children of Israel. See Lev. xxv. 43, 46, where the same word is used: "Thou shalt not rule over him with rigour; but shalt fear thy God."

14. *They made their lives bitter.* So that they became weary of life, through the severity of their servitude. *With hard bondage.* "With grievous servitude." This was the general character of their life in Egypt; it was a life of the most painful servitude, oppressive enough in itself, but made much more so by the cruel manner of their treatment while performing their tasks. *In morter, and in brick. First,* in digging the clay, kneading, and preparing it, and *secondly,* forming it into bricks, drying them in the sun. *Service in the field.* Carrying these materials to the places where they were to be formed into buildings, and serving the builders while employed in those public works.

15. *Hebrew midwives. Shiphrah* and *Puah,* who are here mentioned, were probably certain chiefs, under whom all the rest acted and by whom they were instructed in the obstetric art.

17. *The midwives feared God.* Because they knew that God had forbidden murder of every kind; for though the law was not yet given, Exod. xx. 13, being Hebrews they must have known that God had from the beginning declared, "Whosoever sheddeth man's blood, by man shall his blood be shed," Gen. ix. 6. Therefore they saved the male children of all to whose assistance they were called.

19. *The Hebrew women are not as the Egyptian women.* This is a simple statement of what general experience shows to be a fact, namely, that women who during the whole of their pregnancy are accustomed to hard labor, especially in the open air, have comparatively little pain in parturition. With the strictest truth the midwives might say, *The Hebrew women are not as the Egyptian women.* The latter fare delicately, are not inured to labor, and are kept shut up at home; therefore they have hard, difficult, and dangerous labors. But the Hebrew women are *lively, chayoth,* are "strong, hale, and vigorous," and therefore *are delivered ere the midwives come in unto them.* In such cases we may naturally conclude that the midwives were very seldom even sent for.

20. *Therefore God dealt well with the midwives: and the people multiplied, and waxed very mighty.* This shows an especial providence and blessing of God; for though in all cases

MATTHEW HENRY

In particular, *he made them houses* (*v.* 21), built them up into families, blessed their children, and prospered them in all they did.

II. When this project did not take effect, Pharaoh gave public orders to all his people to drown all the male children of the Hebrews, *v.* 22.

CHAPTER 2

Verses 1–4

Moses was a Levite, both by father and mother. Jacob left Levi under marks of disgrace (Gen. xlix. 5); and yet, soon after, Moses appears a descendant from him, that he might typify Christ, who came in the likeness of sinful flesh and was made a curse for us. This tribe began to be distinguished from the rest by the birth of Moses, as afterwards it became remarkable in many other instances.

I. How he was hidden. The parents of Moses had Miriam and Aaron, both older than he, born to them before this edict came out. Probably the mother of Moses was full of anxiety in the expectation of his birth, now that this edict was in force. Yet this child proves the glory of his father's house. Just at the time when Pharaoh's cruelty rose to this height the deliverer was born. Note, When men are projecting the church's ruin God is preparing for its salvation. 1. His parents observed him to be a *goodly child*, more than ordinarily beautiful; he was *fair to God*, Acts vii. 20. 2. Therefore they were the more solicitous for his preservation, because they looked upon this as an indication of some kind purpose of God concerning him, and a happy omen of something great. *Three months* they hid him in some private apartment of their own house. Herein Moses was a type of Christ, who, in his infancy, was forced to abscond, and in Egypt too (Matt. ii. 13), and was wonderfully preserved, when many innocents were butchered. Duty is ours, events are God's. Faith in God will set us above the ensnaring fear of man.

II. How he was exposed. At three months' end they put him in an ark of bulrushes by the *river's brink* (*v.* 3), and set his little sister at some distance to watch what would become of him, and into whose hands he would fall, *v.* 4. God put it into their hearts to do this, to bring about his own purpose, that Moses might by this means be brought into the hands of Pharaoh's daughter. Moses seemed quite abandoned by his friends; his own mother durst not own him: but now the Lord took him up and protected him, Ps. xxvii. 10.

JAMIESON, FAUSSET, BROWN

a house in *Hebrew* idiom, means to have a numerous progeny. The passage then should be rendered thus: God protected the midwives, and the people waxed very mighty; and because the midwives feared, the Hebrews grew and prospered.

CHAPTER 2

Vss. 1-10. Birth and Preservation of Moses. **1. there went a man of the house of Levi,** etc.—Amram was the husband and Jochebed the wife (cf. ch. 6:2); Num. 26:59). The marriage took place, and two children, Miriam and Aaron, were born some years before the infanticidal edict.

the woman . . . bare a son, etc. Some extraordinary appearance of remarkable comeliness led his parents to augur his future greatness. Beauty was regarded by the ancients as a mark of the divine favor. **hid him three months**—The parents were a pious couple, and the measures they took were prompted not only by parental attachment, but by a strong faith in the blessing of God prospering their endeavors to save the infant.

3. she took for him an ark of bulrushes—papyrus, a thick, strong, and tough reed. **slime**—the mud of the Nile, which, when hardened, is very tenacious. **pitch**—mineral tar. Boats of this description are seen daily floating on the surface of the river, with no other caulking than Nile mud (cf. Isa. 18:2), and they are perfectly watertight, unless the coating is forced off by stormy weather. **flags**—a general term for sea- or river-weed. The chest was not, as is often represented, committed to the bosom of the water but laid on the bank, where it would naturally appear to have been drifted by the current and arrested by the reedy thicket. The spot is traditionally said to be the Isle of Rodah, near Old Cairo. **4. his sister**—Miriam would probably be a girl of ten or twelve years of age at the time.

ADAM CLARKE

where females are kept to hard labor they have comparatively easy and safe travail, yet in a state of slavery the increase is generally very small, as the children die for want of proper nursing, the women, through their labor, being obliged to neglect their offspring; so that in the slave countries the stock is obliged to be recruited by foreign imports.

21. *He made them houses.* That the *houses* in question were not made for the midwives, but for the Israelites in general, the Hebrew text seems pretty plainly to indicate, for the pronoun *lahem*, "to them," is the masculine gender; had the midwives been meant, the femine pronoun *lahen* would have been used.

22. *Ye shall cast into the river.* As the Nile, which is here intended, was a sacred river among the Egyptians, it is not unlikely that Pharaoh intended the young Hebrews as an offering to his god, having two objects in view: (1) To increase the fertility of the country by thus procuring, as he might suppose, a proper and sufficient annual inundation; and (2) To prevent an increase of population among the Israelites, and in process of time procure their entire extermination.

It is conjectured, with a great show of probability, that the edict mentioned in this verse was not made till after the birth of Aaron, and that it was revoked soon after the birth of Moses; as, if it had subsisted in its rigor during the eighty-six years which elapsed between this and the deliverance of the Israelites, it is not at all likely that their males would have amounted to six hundred thousand, and those all effective men.

CHAPTER 2

1. *There went a man.* Amram, son of Kohath, son of Levi, chap. vi. 16-20. *A daughter of Levi,* Jochebed, sister to Kohath, and consequently both the wife and aunt of her husband, Amram, chap. vi. 20; Num. xxvi. 59. Such marriages were at this time lawful, though they were afterwards forbidden, Lev. xviii. 12. But it is possible that *daughter of Levi* means no more than a descendant of that family, and that probably Amram and Jochebed were only cousins-german. As a new law was to be given and a new priesthood formed, God chose a religious family out of which the lawgiver and the high priest were both to spring.

2. *Bare a son.* This certainly was not her first child, for Aaron was fourscore and three years old when Moses was but fourscore, see chap. vii. 7: and there was a sister, probably Miriam, who was older than either; see below, v. 4, and see Num. xxvi. 59. Miriam and Aaron had no doubt both been born before the decree was passed for the destruction of the Hebrew male children, mentioned in the preceding chapter.

Goodly child. The text simply says "that he was good," which signifies that he was not only a perfect, well-formed child, but that he was very beautiful; hence the Septuagint translate the place, "Seeing him to be beautiful," which Stephen interprets, "He was comely to God," or "divinely beautiful." This very circumstance was wisely ordained by the kind providence of God to be one means of his preservation. Scarcely anything interests the heart more than the sight of a lovely babe in distress. His beauty would induce even his parents to double their exertions to save him, and was probably the sole motive which led the Egyptian princess to take such particular care of him, and to educate him as her own, which in all likelihood she would not have done had he been only an ordinary child.

3. *An ark of bulrushes.* A small boat or basket made of the Egyptian reed called papyrus, so famous in all antiquity. This plant grows on the banks of the Nile, and in marshy grounds; the stalk rises to the height of six or seven cubits above the water. This reed was of the greatest use to the inhabitants of Egypt, the pith contained in the stalk serving them for food, and the woody part to build vessels with, which vessels frequently appear on engraved stones and other monuments of Egyptian antiquity. *She laid it in the flags.* Not willing to trust it

MATTHEW HENRY

Verses 5–10

Here is, I. Moses saved from perishing. He lay in a bulrush-basket by the river's side. Had he been left to lie there, he must have perished in a little time with hunger, if he had not been sooner washed into the river or devoured by a crocodile. Had he fallen into any other hands than those he did fall into, either they would not, or durst not, have done otherwise than have thrown him straightway into the river; but Providence brings no less a person thither than Pharaoh's daughter, just at that juncture, guides her to the place where this poor forlorn infant lay, and inclines her heart to pity it, which she dares do when none else durst. Never did poor child cry so seasonably, so happily, as this did. God often raises up friends for his people even among their enemies. Pharaoh cruelly seeks Israel's destruction, but his own daughter charitably compassionates a Hebrew child, and not only so, but, beyond her intention, preserves Israel's deliverer.

II. Moses well provided with a good nurse, no less than his own dear mother, *v.* 7–9. Pharaoh's daughter thinks it convenient that he should have a Hebrew nurse, and the sister of Moses, with art and good management, introduces the mother into the place of a nurse, to the great advantage of the child; for mothers are the best nurses.

III. Moses preferred to be the son of Pharaoh's daughter (*v.* 10). The tradition of the Jews is that Pharaoh's daughter had no child of her own, and that she was the only child of her father, so that when he was adopted for her son he stood fair for the crown. Those whom God designs for great services he finds out ways to qualify and prepare beforehand. Moses, by having his education in a court, is the fitter to be a prince and *king in Jeshurun*; by having his education in a learned court (for such the Egyptian then was) is the fitter to be an historian; and by having his education in the court of Egypt is the fitter to be employed, in the name of God, as an ambassador to that court.

IV. Moses named. Pharaoh's daughter called him *Moses, Drawn out of the water*, so it signifies in the Egyptian language. The calling of the Jewish lawgiver by an Egyptian name is a happy omen to the Gentile world, and gives hopes of that day when it shall be said, *Blessed be Egypt my people*, Isa. xix. 25. And his tuition at court was an earnest of the performance of that promise, Isa. xlix. 23. *Kings shall be thy nursing fathers, and queens thy nursing mothers.*

Verses 11–15

Moses had now passed the first forty years of his life in the court of Pharaoh, preparing himself for business; and now it was time for him to enter upon action, and,

I. He boldly owns and espouses the cause of God's people: *When Moses was grown he went out unto his brethren, and looked on their burdens*, *v.* 11. The best exposition of these words we have from an inspired pen, Heb. xi. 24–26, where we are told that by this he expressed, 1. His holy contempt of the honours and pleasures of the Egyptian court; he *refused to be called the son of Pharaoh's daughter.* 2. His tender concern for his poor brethren in bondage, with whom (though he might easily have avoided it) he *chose to suffer affliction.*

II. He gives a specimen of the great things he was afterwards to do for God and his Israel in two little instances, related particularly by Stephen (Acts vii. 23, &c.).

1. Moses killed the Egyptian who smote the Hebrew (*v.* 11, 12); probably it was one of the Egyptian taskmasters, whom he found abusing his Hebrew slave. The Jews' tradition is that he did not slay him with any weapon, but, as Peter slew Ananias and Sapphira, with the word of his mouth.

JAMIESON, FAUSSET, BROWN

5. the daughter of Pharaoh came down to wash herself at the river—The occasion is thought to have been a religious solemnity which the royal family opened by bathing in the sacred stream. Peculiar sacredness was attached to those portions of the Nile which flowed near the temples. The water was there fenced off as a protection from the crocodiles; and doubtless the princess had an enclosure reserved for her own use, the road to which seems to have been well known to Jochebed. **walked along**—in procession or in file. **she sent her maid**—her immediate attendant. The term is different from that rendered "maidens." **6-9. when she had opened it, she saw the child**—The narrative is picturesque. No tale of romance ever described a plot more skilfully laid or more full of interest in the development. The expedient of the ark—the slime and pitch—the choice of the time and place—the appeal to the sensibilities of the female breast—the stationing of the sister as a watch of the proceedings—her timely suggestion of a nurse—and the engagement of the mother herself—all bespeak a more than ordinary measure of ingenuity as well as intense solicitude on the part of the parents. But the origin of the scheme was most probably owing to a divine suggestion, as its success was due to an overruling Providence, who not only preserved the child's life, but provided for his being trained in the nurture and admonition of the Lord. Hence it is said to have been done by faith (Heb. 11:23), either in the general promise of deliverance, or some special revelation made to Amram and Jochebed—and in this view, the pious couple gave a beautiful example of a firm reliance on the word of God, united with an active use of the most suitable means. **10. she brought him unto Pharaoh's daughter**—Though it must have been nearly as severe a trial for Jochebed to part with him the second time as the first, she was doubtless reconciled to it by her belief in his high destination as the future deliverer of Israel. His age when removed to the palace is not stated; but he was old enough to be well instructed in the principles of the true religion; and those early impressions, deepened by the power of divine grace, were never forgotten or effaced. **he became her son**—by adoption, and his high rank afforded him advantages in education, which in the Providence of God were made subservient to far different purposes from what his royal patroness intended. **she called his name Moses**—His parents might, as usual, at the time of his circumcision, have given him a name, which is traditionally said to have been Joachim. But the name chosen by the princess, whether of Egyptian or Hebrew origin, is the only one by which he has ever been known to the church; and it is a permanent memorial of the painful incidents of his birth and infancy.

11-25. HIS SYMPATHY WITH THE HEBREWS. **11. in those days, when Moses was grown**—not in age and stature only, but in power as well as in renown for accomplishments and military prowess (Acts 7:22). There is a gap here in the sacred history which, however, is supplied by the inspired commentary of Paul, who has fully detailed the reasons as well as extent of the change that took place in his worldly condition; and whether, as some say, his royal mother had proposed to make him co-regent and successor to the crown, or some other circumstances, led to a declaration of his mind, he determined to renounce the palace and identify himself with the suffering people of God (Heb. 11:24-29). The descent of some great sovereigns, like Diocletian and Charles V, from a throne into private life, is nothing to the sacrifice which Moses made through the power of faith. **he went out unto his brethren**—to make a full and systematic inspection of their condition in the various parts of the country where they were dispersed (Acts 7:23), and he adopted this proceeding in pursuance of the patriotic purpose that the faith, which is of the operation of God, was even then forming in his heart. **he spied an Egyptian smiting an Hebrew**—one of the taskmasters scourging a Hebrew slave without any just cause (Acts 7:24), and in so cruel a manner, that he seems to have died under the barbarous treatment—for the conditions of the sacred story imply such a fatal issue. The sight was new and strange to him, and though pre-eminent for meekness (Num. 12:3), he was fired with indignation. **12. he slew the Egyptian, and hid him in the sand**—This act of Moses may seem and indeed by some has been condemned as rash and unjustifiable—in plain terms, a deed of assassination. But we must not

ADAM CLARKE

in the stream for fear of a disaster, and probably choosing the place to which the Egyptian princess was accustomed to come for the purpose specified in the note on the following verse.

5. *To wash herself at the river.* Whether the daughter of Pharaoh went to bathe in the river through motives of pleasure, health, or religion, or whether she bathed at all, the text does not specify. It is merely stated by the sacred writer that she went down to the river to wash; for the word *herself* is not in the original.

6. *She had compassion on him.* The sight of a beautiful babe in distress could not fail to make the impression here mentioned; see on v. 2. It has already been conjectured that the cruel edict of the Egyptian king did not continue long in force; see chap. i. 22. And it will not appear unreasonable to suppose that the circumstance related here might have brought about its abolition. The daughter of Pharaoh, struck with the distressed state of the Hebrew children from what she had seen in the case of Moses, would probably implore her father to abolish this sanguinary edict.

7. *Shall I go and call . . . a nurse?* Had not the different circumstances marked here been placed under the superintendence of an especial providence, there is no human probability that they could have had such a happy issue. The parents had done everything to save their child that piety, affection, and prudence could dictate, and having done so, they left the event to God. "By faith," says the apostle, Heb. xi. 23, "Moses, when he was born, was hid three months of his parents, because they saw he was a proper child; and they were not afraid of the king's commandment." Because of the king's commandment they were obliged to make use of the most prudent caution to save the child's life; and their faith in God enabled them to risk their own safety, for they were not afraid of the king's commandment—they feared God, and they had no other fear.

10. *And he became her son.* From this time of his being brought home by his nurse his education commenced, and he "was learned in all the wisdom of the Egyptians," Acts vii. 22, who in the knowledge of nature probably exceeded all the nations then on the face of the earth. *And she called his name. Mosheh*, because "out of the waters have I drawn him." *Mashah* signifies "to draw out"; and *mosheh* is the person drawn out; the word is used in the same sense in Ps. xviii. 17 and 2 Sam. xxii. 17. What name he had from his parents we know not; but whatever it might be, it was ever after lost in the name given to him by the princess of Egypt.

11. *When Moses was grown.* Being full forty years of age, as Stephen says, Acts vii. 23, "it came into his heart to visit his brethren," i.e., he was excited to it by a divine inspiration; "and seeing one of them suffer wrong," by an Egyptian smiting him, probably one of the taskmasters, he "avenged him . . . and smote"—slew, "the Egyptian," supposing that God, who had given him commission, had given also his brethren to understand that they were to be delivered by his hand; see Acts vii. 23-25. Probably the Egyptian killed the Hebrew, and therefore on the Noahic precept Moses was justified in killing him; and he was authorized so to do by the commission which he had received from God, as all succeeding events amply prove.

MATTHEW HENRY

2. Moses was afterwards to be employed in governing Israel, and, as a specimen of this, we have him here trying to end a controversy between two Hebrews.

(1) The unhappy quarrel which Moses observed between two Hebrews, *v.* 13. When God raises up instruments of salvation for the church they will find enough to do, not only with oppressing Egyptians to restrain them, but with quarrelsome Israelites, to reconcile them.

(2) The way he took of dealing with them; he marked him that caused the division, that did the wrong, and mildly reasoned with him: *Wherefore smitest thou thy fellow?* Moses endeavoured to make them friends, a good office. The reproof Moses gave on this occasion may still be of use, *Wherefore smitest thou thy fellow?*

(3) The ill success of his attempt (*v.* 14): *He said, Who made thee a prince?* A man needs no great authority for the giving of a friendly reproof, it is an act of kindness; yet this man needs will interpret it an act of dominion, and represents his reprover as imperious and assuming. Thus when people dislike good discourse, or a seasonable admonition, they will call it *preaching*, as if a man could not speak a word for God and against sin but he took too much upon him. He upbraids him with what he had done in killing the Egyptian: *Intendest thou to kill me?* If the Hebrews had taken the hint, and come in to Moses as their head and captain, it is probable that they would have been delivered now; but, despising their deliverer, their deliverance was justly deferred, and their bondage prolonged forty years, as afterwards their despising Canaan kept them out of it forty years more. We must take heed of being prejudiced against the ways and people of God by the follies and peevishness of some particular persons that profess religion. Christ himself was set at nought by the builders, and is still rejected by those he would save.

(4) The flight of Moses to Midian, in consequence.. God ordered it for wise and holy ends. Things were not yet ripe for Israel's deliverance. Moses is to be further fitted for the service, and therefore is directed to withdraw for the present. God guided Moses to Midian because the Midianites were of the seed of Abraham. And through this country he was afterwards to lead Israel. Hither he came, and sat down by a well, tired and thoughtful, at a loss, and waiting to see which way Providence would direct him. It was a great change with him, since he was but the other day at ease in Pharaoh's court: thus God tried his faith.

Verses 16–22

Moses here gains a settlement in Midian, just as his father Jacob had gained one in Syria, Gen. xxix. 2, &c. Events that seem inconsiderable, and purely accidental, afterwards appear to have been designed by the wisdom of God for very good purposes. A casual transient occurrence has sometimes occasioned the greatest and happiest turns of a man's life.

I. Concerning the seven daughters of Reuel the priest or prince of Midian. 1. They were humble, and very industrious, they *drew water for their father's flock*, *v.* 16. Idleness can be no one's honour. 2. They were modest, and would not ask this strange Egyptian to come home with them till their father sent for him. Modesty is the ornament of woman.

II. Concerning Moses. He was taken for an Egyptian (*v.* 19). 1. How ready he was to help Reuel's daughters to water their flocks. Those that have had a liberal education yet should not be strangers to servile work, because they know not what necessity Providence may put them in of working for themselves, or what opportunity Providence may give them of being serviceable to others. He loved to be doing good. Wherever the Providence of God casts us we should desire and endeavour to be useful; and, when we cannot do the good we would, we must be ready to do the good we can. 2. How well he was paid for his serviceableness. When the young women acquainted their father, he sent to invite him to his house, and made much of him, *v.* 20. Moses soon recommended himself to the esteem and good affection of this prince of Midian, who took him into his house, and, in process of time, married one of his daughters to him (*v.* 21), by whom he had a son, whom he called *Gershom, a stranger there* (*v.* 22). Now this settlement of Moses in Midian was designed by Providence, (1) To shelter him for the present. (2) It was also designed to prepare him for the great services he was further designed for. His manner of life in Midian would be of use of him, [1] To inure him to hardship and poverty. [2] To inure him to contemplation and devotion. Egypt accomplished him as a scholar, a gentleman, a statesman, a soldier, but yet he lacked one thing, in which the court of Egypt could not befriend him. He must know what

JAMIESON, FAUSSET, BROWN

judge of his action in such a country and age by the standard of law and the notions of right which prevail in our Christian land; and, besides, not only is it not spoken of as a crime in Scripture or as distressing the perpetrator with remorse, but according to existing customs among nomadic tribes, he was bound to avenge the blood of a brother. The person he slew, however, being a government officer, he had rendered himself amenable to the laws of Egypt, and therefore he endeavored to screen himself from the consequences by concealment of the corpse. **13, 14. two men of the Hebrews strove together**—His benevolent mediation in this strife, though made in the kindest and mildest manner, was resented, and the taunt of the aggressor showing that Moses' conduct on the preceding day had become generally known, he determined to consult his safety by immediate flight (Heb. 11:27). These two incidents prove that neither were the Israelites yet ready to go out of Egypt, nor Moses prepared to be their leader (Jas. 1:20). It was by the staff and not the sword—by the meekness, and not the wrath of Moses that God was to accomplish that great work of deliverance. Both he and the people of Israel were for forty years more to be cast into the furnace of affliction, yet it was therein that He had chosen them (Isa. 48:10).

15. Moses fled from the face of Pharaoh—His flight took place in the second year of Thothmes I. **dwelt in the land of Midian**—situated on the eastern shore of the gulf of the Red Sea and occupied by the posterity of Midian the son of Cush. The territory extended northward to the top of the gulf and westward far across the desert of Sinai. And from their position near the sea, they early combined trading with pastoral pursuits (Gen. 37:28). The headquarters of Jethro are supposed to have been where Dahab-Madian now stands; and from Moses coming direct to that place, he may have travelled with a caravan of merchants. But another place is fixed by tradition in Wady Shuweib, or Jethro's valley, on the east of the mountain of Moses. **sat down by a well**—See on Genesis 29:3.

16-22. the priest of Midian—As the officers were usually conjoined, he was the ruler also of the people called Cushites or Ethiopians, and like many other chiefs of pastoral people in that early age, he still retained the faith and worship of the true God. **seven daughters**—were shepherdesses to whom Moses was favorably introduced by an act of courtesy and courage in protecting them from the rude shepherds of some neighboring tribe at a well. He afterwards formed a close and permanent alliance with this family by marrying one of the daughters, Zipporah, "a little bird," called a Cushite or Ethiopian (Num. 12:1), and whom he doubtless obtained in the manner of Jacob by service. He had by her two sons, whose names were, according to common practice, commemorative of incidents in the family history.

ADAM CLARKE

13. *Two men of the Hebrews strove together.* How strange that, in the very place where they were suffering a heavy persecution because they were Hebrews, the very persons themselves who suffered it should be found persecuting each other! It has been often seen that, in those times in which the ungodly oppressed the Church of Christ, its own members have been separated from each other by disputes concerning comparatively unessential points of doctrine and discipline, in consequence of which both they and the truth have become an easy prey to those whose desire was to waste the heritage of the Lord.

14. *And Moses feared.* He saw that the Israelites were not as yet prepared to leave their bondage; and that though God had called him to be their leader, yet His providence had not yet sufficiently opened the way; and had he stayed in Egypt he must have endangered his life. Prudence therefore dictated an escape for the present to the land of Midian.

15. *Pharaoh . . . sought to slay Moses. But Moses fled from the face of Pharaoh.* How can this be reconciled with Heb. xi. 27: "By faith he [Moses] forsook Egypt, not fearing the wrath of the king"? Very easily. The apostle speaks not of this forsaking of Egypt, but of his and the Israelites' final departure from it, and of the bold and courageous manner in which Moses treated Pharaoh and the Egyptians, disregarding his threatenings and the multitudes of them that pursued after the people whom, in the name and strength of God, he led in the face of their enemies out of Egypt. *Dwelt in the land of Midian.* A country generally supposed to have been in Arabia Petraea, on the eastern coast of the Red Sea, not far from Mount Sinai.

16. *The priest of Midian.* Or "prince," or both; for the original *cohen* has both meanings.

17. *The shepherds . . . drove them.* The verb being in the masculine gender seems to imply that the shepherds drove away the flocks of Reuel's daughters, and not the daughters themselves. The fact seems to be that, as the daughters of Reuel filled the troughs and brought their flocks to drink, the shepherds drove those away, and, profiting by the young women's labor, watered their own cattle. Moses resisted this insolence, and assisted them to water their flocks, in consequence of which they were enabled to return much sooner than they were wont to do, v. 18.

18. *Reuel their father.* In Num. x. 29 this person is called Raguel, but the Hebrew is the same in both places. The person in question appears to have several names. Here he is Reuel; in Num. x. 29, Raguel; in Exod. iii. 1, *Jethro;* in Judg. iv. 11, *Hobab;* and in Judg. i. 16 he is called *Keyni,* which in chap. iv we translate Kenite. Some suppose that Reuel was father to Hobab, who was also called Jethro. This is the most likely.

20. *That he may eat bread.* That he may be entertained, and receive refreshment to proceed on his journey. *Bread* among the Hebrews was used to signify all kinds of food commonly used for the support of man's life.

21. *Zipporah his daughter.* It appears that Moses obtained Zipporah something in the same way that Jacob obtained Rachel; namely, for the performnce of certain services, probably keeping of sheep; see chap. iii. 1.

22. *Called his name Gershom.* Literally, "a stranger"; the reason of which Moses immediately adds, "for I have been an alien in a strange land."

MATTHEW HENRY

it was to live a life of communion with God; and in this he would be greatly furthered by the solitude and retirement of a shepherd's life in Midian. By the former he was prepared to rule in Jeshurun, but by the latter he was prepared to converse with God in Mount Horeb, near which mount he had spent much of his time.

Verses 23–25

Here is, 1. The continuance of the Israelites' bondage in Egypt, *v.* 23. Probably the murdering of their infants did not continue. The Egyptians now were content with their increase, finding that Egypt was enriched by their labour; so that they might have them for slaves, they cared not how many they were. When one Pharaoh died, another rose up in his place that was governed by the same maxims, and was as cruel to Israel as his predecessors. 2. The preface to their deliverance at last. (1) *They cried, v.* 23. Now, at last, they began to think of God under their troubles, and to return to him from the idols they had served, Ezek. xx. 8. But before God unbound them he put it into their hearts to cry unto him, as it is explained, Num. xx. 16. (2) *God heard, v.* 24, 25. [1] *God heard their groaning.* He knows the burdens they groan under and the blessings they groan after. [2] *God remembered his covenant.* (3) *God looked upon the children of Israel.* Moses looked upon them and pitied them (*v.* 11); but now God looked upon them and helped them. (4) *God had a respect unto them,* a favourable respect to them as his own.

JAMIESON, FAUSSET, BROWN

23. the king of Egypt died: and the children of Israel sighed by reason of the bondage—The language seems to imply that the Israelites had experienced a partial relaxation, probably through the influence of Moses' royal patroness; but in the reign of her father's successor the persecution was renewed with increased severity.

ADAM CLARKE

23. *In process of time . . . the king of Egypt died.* According to Stephen (Acts vii. 30, compared with Exod. vii. 7), the death of the Egyptian king happened about forty years after the escape of Moses to Midian. The words which we translate, *And it came to pass in process of time,* signify, "And it was in many days from these."

24. *God remembered his covenant.* God's covenant is God's engagement; He had promised to Abraham, to Isaac, and to Jacob, to give their posterity a land flowing with milk and honey. They were now under the most oppressive bondage, and this was the most proper time for God to show them His mercy and power in fulfilling His promise. This is all that is meant by God's "remembering" His covenant, for it was now that He began to give it its effect.

25. *And God had respect unto them.* God "knew" them. i.e., He "approved" of them, and therefore it is said that their cry came up before God and He heard their groaning. The word *yada,* "to know," in the Hebrew Bible is frequently used in the sense of approving.

MATTHEW HENRY — CHAPTER 3

Verses 1–6

The years of the life of Moses are remarkably divided into three forties: the first forty he spent as a prince in Pharaoh's court, the second a shepherd in Midian, the third a king in Jeshurun. He had now finished his second forty, when he received his commission to bring Israel out of Egypt. Note, Sometimes it is long before God calls his servants out to that work which of old he designed them for, and has been graciously preparing them for.

I. How this appearance of God to him found him employed. He was keeping the flock (tending sheep) near Mount Horeb, *v.* 1. This was a poor employment for a man of his parts and education. It was the lot of Moses, who foresaw nothing to the contrary but that he should die, as he had lived a great while, a poor despicable shepherd. When we are alone, the Father is with us. Moses saw more of God in a desert than ever he had seen in Pharaoh's court.

II. What the appearance was. To his great surprise he saw a bush burning, when he perceived no fire either from earth or heaven to kindle it, and, which was more strange, it did not consume, *v.* 2. It was an extraordinary manifestation of the divine presence and glory. 1. He saw a flame of fire. When Israel's deliverance out of Egypt was promised to Abraham, he saw a burning lamp, which signified the light of joy which that deliverance should cause (Gen. xv. 17); but now it shines brighter, as a flame of fire. 2. This fire was not in a tall and stately cedar, but in a bush, *a thorny bush,* so the word signifies. 3. *The bush burned,* and yet *was not consumed.*

JAMIESON, FAUSSET, BROWN — CHAPTER 3

Vss. 1-22. Divine Appearance and Commission to Moses. **1. Now Moses kept the flock**—This employment he had entered on in furtherance of his matrimonial views (see on ch. 2:21), but it is probable he was continuing his service now on other terms like Jacob during the latter years of his stay with Laban (Gen. 30:28). **he led the flock to the back side of the desert**—i.e., on the west of the desert [Genesius], assuming Jethro's headquarters to have been at Dahab. The route by which Moses led his flock must have been west through the wide valley called by the Arabs, Wady-es-Zugherah [Robinson], which led into the interior of the wilderness. **Mountain of God**—so named either according to *Hebrew* idiom from its great height, as "great mountains," *Hebrew,* "mountains of God" (Ps. 36:6); "goodly cedars," *Hebrew,* "cedars of God" (Ps. 80:10); or some think from its being the old abode of "the glory"; or finally from its being the theater of transactions most memorable in the history of the true religion to Horeb—rather, Horeb-ward. Horeb, i.e., dry, desert, was the general name for the mountainous district in which Sinai is situated, and of which it is a part. (See on ch. 19). It was used to designate the region comprehending that immense range of lofty, desolate, and barren hills, at the base of which, however, there are not only many patches of verdure to be seen, but almost all the valleys, or *wadys,* as they are called, show a thin coating of vegetation, which, towards the south, becomes more luxuriant. The Arab shepherds seldom take their flocks to a greater distance than one day's journey from their camp. Moses must have gone at least two days' journey, and although he seems to have been only following his pastoral course, that region, from its numerous springs in the clefts of the rocks being the chief resort of the tribes during the summer heats, the Providence of God led him thither for an important purpose. **2, 3. the angel of the Lord appeared unto him in a flame of fire**—It is common in Scripture to represent the elements and operations of nature, as winds, fires, earthquakes, pestilence, everything enlisted in executing the divine will, as the "angels" or messengers of God. But in such cases God Himself is considered as really, though invisibly, present. Here the preternatural fire may be primarily meant by the expression "angel of the Lord"; but it is clear that under this symbol, the Divine Being was present, whose name is given (vss. 4, 6), and elsewhere called the angel of the covenant, Jehovah-Jesus. **out of the midst of a bush**—the wild acacia or thorn, with which that desert abounds, and which is generally dry and brittle, so much so, that at certain seasons, a spark might kindle a district far and wide into a blaze. A fire, therefore, being in the midst of such a desert bush was a "great sight." It is generally supposed to have been emblematic of the Israelites' condition in Egypt—oppressed by a grinding servitude and a bloody persecution, and yet, in

ADAM CLARKE — CHAPTER 3

1. *Jethro his father in law.* Concerning Jethro, see the note on chap. ii. 18. Learned men are not agreed on the signification of the word *chothen,* which we translate "father in law," and which in Gen. xix. 14 we translate "son in law." It seems to be a general term for a "relative by marriage," and the connection only in which it stands can determine its precise meaning. It is very possible that Reuel was now dead, it being forty years since Moses came to Midian; that Jethro was his son, and had succeeded him in his office of prince and priest of Midian; that Zipporah was the sister of Jethro; and that consequently the word *chothen* should be translated "brother-in-law" in this place: as we learn from Gen. xxxiv. 9; Deut. vii. 3; Josh. xxiii. 12, and other places, that it simply signifies to contract affinity by marriage. If this conjecture be right, we may well suppose that, Reuel being dead, Moses was continued by his brother-in-law, Jethro, in the same employment he had under his father.

Mountain of God. Sometimes named Horeb, at other times Sinai. The mountain itself had two peaks; one was called Horeb, the other Sinai. Horeb was probably the primitive name of the mountain, which was afterwards called the *mountain of God* because God appeared upon it to Moses; and Mount Sinai, from *seneh,* a "bush," because it was in a bush, in a flame of fire, that this appearance was made.

2. *The angel of the Lord.* Not a created angel certainly; for He is called Jehovah, v. 4, and has the most expressive attributes of the Godhead applied to Him, vv. 14, etc. Yet He is an *angel, malach,* a "Messenger," in whom was the name of God, chap. xxiii. 21; and in whom dwelt all the fulness of the Godhead bodily, Col. ii. 9; and who, in all these primitive times, was the Messenger of the covenant, Mal. iii. 1. And who was this but Jesus, the Leader, Redeemer, and Saviour of mankind? *A flame of fire out of the midst of a bush.* Fire was, not only among the Hebrews but also among many other ancient nations, a very significant emblem of the Deity. *And the bush was not consumed.* (1) An emblem of the state of Israel in its various distresses and persecutions: it was in the fire of adversity, but was not consumed. (2) An emblem also of the state of the Church of God in the wilderness, in persecutions often, in the midst of its enemies, in the region of the shadow of death—yet not consumed. (3) An emblem also of the state of every follower of Christ: cast down, but not forsaken; grievously tempted, but not destroyed; walking through the fire, but still unconsumed! Why are all these preserved in the midst of those things which have a natural tendency to destroy them? Because God is in the midst of them; it was this that preserved the

MATTHEW HENRY

III. The curiosity Moses had to enquire into this extraordinary sight: *I will turn aside and see, v.* 3.

IV. The invitation he had to draw near, yet with a caution not to come too near, nor rashly.

1. God gave him a gracious call, to which he returned a ready answer, *v.* 4. When he turned aside, God called to him. *Draw nigh to God, and he will draw nigh to you.* God called him by name, *Moses, Moses.* The word of the Lord always went along with the glory of the Lord, for every divine vision was designed for divine revelation, Job iv. 16, &c.; xxxiii. 14–16. Divine calls are effectual when we return an obedient answer to them, as Moses here, "*Here am I, what saith my Lord unto his servant?*"

2. God gave him a needful caution. He must draw near, but not too near. His conscience must be satisfied, but not his curiosity. He must express his reverence, and his readiness to obey: *Put off thy shoes from off thy feet,* as a servant. Putting off the shoe was then what putting off the hat is now, a token of respect and submission.

V. The solemn declaration God made of his name, by which he would be known to Moses: *I am the God of thy father, v.* 6. Abraham was dead, and yet God is the God of Abraham; therefore Abraham's soul lives, to which God stands in relation; and, to make his soul completely happy, his body must live again in due time. By these words it appears that God remembered his covenant, *ch.* ii. 24.

VI. The solemn impression this made upon Moses: He *hid his face,* as one both ashamed and afraid to look upon God. He was not afraid of a burning bush till he perceived that God was in it.

Verses 7–10

Now, after forty years of Israel's bondage and Moses's banishment, when we may suppose both he and they began to despair, at length the time has come, even the year of the redeemed.

Here is, I. The notice God takes of the afflictions of Israel (*v.* 7, 9): *Seeing I have seen,* not only, *I have surely seen,* but I have strictly observed and considered the matter. Three things God took cognizance of:—1. *Their sorrows, v.* 7. It is likely they were not permitted to make a remonstrance of their grievances to Pharaoh. But God observed their tears. 2. Their cry: *I have heard their cry* (*v.* 7), *it has come unto me, v.* 9. 3. The tyranny of their persecutors: *I have seen the oppression, v.* 9.

II. The promise God makes of their speedy deliverance and enlargement: *I have come down to deliver them, v.* 8. When God does something very extraordinary he is said to *come down* to do it, as Isa. lxiv. 1. This deliverance was typical of our redemption by Christ, in which the eternal Word did indeed come down from heaven to deliver us. He promises also their happy settlement in the land of Canaan, that they should exchange bondage for liberty, poverty for plenty, labour for rest.

III. The commission he gives to Moses in order hereunto, *v.* 10. He is not only sent as a prophet to Israel, but he is sent as an ambassador to Pharaoh, to treat with him; and he is sent as a prince to Israel, to conduct and command them. The same hand that now fetched a shepherd out of a desert, to be the planter of a Jewish church, afterwards fetched fishermen from their ships, to be the planters of the Christian church.

Verses 11–15

God, having spoken to Moses, allows him also a liberty of speech.

I. He objects his own insufficiency for the service he was called to (*v.* 11): *Who am I?* He thinks himself unworthy of the honour. He thinks he wants courage. He thinks he wants skill, and therefore cannot bring forth the children of Israel out of Egypt; they are unarmed, undisciplined, quite dispirited. 1. Moses was incomparably the fittest of any man living for this work, eminent for learning, wisdom, experience, valour, faith, holiness; and yet he says, *Who am I?* Note, The more fit any person is for service commonly the less opinion he has of himself: see Judges ix. 8, &c. 2. The difficulties of the work were indeed very great. Yet Moses is the man that does it at last; for God gives grace to the lowly.

II. God answers this objection, *v.* 12. 1. He promises him his presence: *Certainly I will be with thee,* and that is enough. 2. He assures him of success, and that the Israelites should serve God upon this mountain.

III. He begs instructions for the executing of his commission, and desires to know by what name God would at this time make himself known, *v.* 13.

1. He supposes the children of Israel would ask him, *What is his name?* This they would ask either, (1) To perplex Moses. Or (2) For their own informa-

JAMIESON, FAUSSET, BROWN

spite of the cruel policy that was bent on annihilating them, they continued as numerous and thriving as ever. The reason was "God was in the midst of them." The symbol may also represent the present state of the Jews, as well as of the Church generally in the world. **4. when the Lord saw that he turned aside to see**—The manifestations which God anciently made of Himself were always accompanied by clear, unmistakable signs that the communications were really from heaven. This certain evidence was given to Moses. He saw a fire, but no human agent to kindle it; he heard a voice, but no human lips from which it came; he saw no living Being, but One was in the bush, in the heat of the flames, who knew him and addressed him by name. Who could this be but the Divine Being? **5. put off thy shoes**—The direction was in conformity with a usage which was well known to Moses, for the Egyptian priests observed it in their temples, and it is observed in all Eastern countries where the people take off their shoes or sandals, as we do our hats. But the Eastern idea is not precisely the same as the Western. With us, the removal of the hat is an expression of reverence for the place we enter, or rather of Him who is worshiped there. With them the removal of the shoes is a confession of personal defilement and conscious unworthiness to stand in the presence of unspotted holiness.

6-8. I am the God . . . come down to deliver—The reverential awe of Moses must have been relieved by the divine Speaker (see on Matt. 22:32), announcing Himself in His covenant character, and by the welcome intelligence communicated. Moreover, the time, as well as all the circumstances of this miraculous appearance, were such as to give him an illustrious display of God's faithfulness to His promises. The period of Israel's journey and affliction in Egypt had been predicted (Gen. 15:13), and it was during the last year of the term which had still to run that the Lord appeared in the burning bush. **10-22. Come now therefore, and I will send thee**—Considering the patriotic views that had formerly animated the breast of Moses, we might have anticipated that no mission could have been more welcome to his heart than to be employed in the national emancipation of Israel. But he evinced great reluctance to it and stated a variety of objections, all of which were successfully met and removed—and the happy issue of his labors was minutely described.

ADAM CLARKE

bush from destruction; and it was this that preserved the Israelites; and it is this, and this alone, that preserves the Church, and holds the soul of every genuine believer in the spiritual life.

5. *Put off thy shoes.* It is likely that from this circumstance all the Eastern nations have agreed to perform all the acts of their religious worship barefooted. All the Mohammedans, Brahmins, and Parsees do so still. The Jews were remarked for this in the time of Juvenal; hence he speaks of their performing their sacred rites barefooted. It is probable that *nealim* in the text signifies "sandals," translated by the Chaldee *sandal* (see Gen. xiv. 23), which was the same as the Roman *solea,* a "sole" alone, strapped about the foot. As this sole must let in dust, gravel, and sand about the foot in travelling, hence the custom of frequently washing the feet in those countries where these sandals were worn. Pulling off the shoes was, therefore, an emblem of laying aside the pollutions contracted by walking in the way of sin.

6. *I am the God of thy father.* Though the word *abi,* "father," is here used in the singular, Stephen, quoting this place, Acts vii. 32, uses the plural, "The God of thy fathers"; and that this is the meaning the following words prove: *The God of Abraham, the God of Isaac, and the God of Jacob. And Moses hid his face.* For similar acts, see the passages referred to in the margin. *He was afraid to look*—he was overawed by God's presence, and dazzled with the splendor of the appearance.

7. *I have surely seen.* "Seeing, I have seen"—I have not only seen the afflictions of this people because I am omniscient, but I have considered their sorrows, and My eye affects My heart.

8. *And I am come down to deliver them.* This is the very purpose for which I am now come down upon this mountain, and for which I manifest myself to thee. *Large . . . land.* Canaan, when compared with the small tract of Goshen, in which they were now situated, and where, we learn from chap. i. 7, they were straitened for room, might be well called a large land. See a fine description of this land, Deut. viii. 7. *A land flowing with milk and honey.* Excellent for pasturage, because abounding in the most wholesome herbage and flowers; and from the latter an abundance of wild honey was collected by the bees.

11. *Who am I . . . that I should bring?* He was so satisfied that this was beyond his power, and all the means that he possessed, that he was astonished that even God himself should appoint him to this work! Such indeed was the bondage of the children of Israel, and the power of the people by whom they were enslaved, that had not their deliverance come through supernatural means, their escape had been utterly impossible.

12. *Certainly I will be with thee.* This great event shall not be left to thy wisdom and to thy power; My counsel shall direct thee, and My power shall bring all these mighty things to pass. *And this shall be a token.* Literally, "And this to thee for a sign," i.e., this miraculous manifestation of the burning bush shall be a proof that I have sent thee; or, "My being with thee," to encourage thy heart, strengthen thy hands, and enable thee to work miracles, shall be to thyself and to others the evidence of thy divine mission. *Ye shall serve God upon this mountain.* This was not the sign, but God shows him that in their return from Egypt they should take this mountain in their way, and should worship Him in this place. There may be a prophetic allusion here to the giving of the law on Mount Sinai. As Moses received his commands here, so likewise should the Israelites receive theirs in the same place.

13. *They shall say . . . What is his name?* Does not this suppose that the Israelites had an idolatrous notion even of the Supreme Being? They had probably drunk deep into the Egyptian superstitions, and had gods many and lords many; and Moses conjectured that, hearing of a supernatural deliverance, they would inquire who that God was by whom it was to be effected.

14. *I AM THAT I AM. Eheyeh asher Eheyeh.* These words have been variously understood. The Vulgate translates, "I am who am." The

MATTHEW HENRY

tion.

2. He desires instructions what answer to give them: "*What shall I say to them?* What name shall I vouch to them for the proof of my authority?"

IV. Two names God would now be known by:—

1. A name that denotes what he is in himself (*v.* 14): *I am that I am.* This explains his name *Jehovah*, and signifies, (1) That he is self-existent; he has his being of himself, and has no dependence upon any other. Being self-existent, he cannot but be self-sufficient, and therefore all-sufficient, and the inexhaustible fountain of being and bliss. (2) That he is eternal and unchangeable. (3) That we cannot by searching find him out. Let Israel know this, *I AM hath sent me unto you.*

2. A name that denotes what he is to his people. *The Lord God of your fathers hath sent me unto you* (*v.* 15): Thus God had made himself known to him (*v.* 6), and thus he must make him known to them, (1) That he might revive among them the religion of their fathers. (2) That he might raise their expectations of the speedy performance of the promises made unto their fathers. God will have this to be his name for ever, and it has been, is, and will be, his name, by which his worshippers know him, and distinguish him from all false gods; see 1 Kings xviii. 36.

Verses 16–22

Moses is here more particularly instructed in his work, and informed beforehand of his success. 1. He must deal with the elders of Israel, and raise their expectations of a speedy removal to Canaan, *v.* 16, 17.

His success with the elders of Israel would be good; so he is told (*v.* 18): *They shall hearken to thy voice*, and not thrust thee away as they did forty years ago. 2. He must deal with the king of Egypt (*v.* 18), he and the elders of Israel, and in this they must not begin with a demand, but with a humble petition. *We beseech thee, let us go.* Moreover, they must only beg leave of Pharaoh to go as far as Mount Sinai to worship God. If he would not give them leave to go and sacrifice at Sinai, justly did they go without leave to settle in Canaan. As to his success with Pharaoh, Moses is here told, (1) That petitions would not prevail with him: *I am sure he will not let you go*, *v.* 19.

(2) That plagues should compel him to it: *I will smite Egypt*, and then he will *let you go*, *v.* 20.

JAMIESON, FAUSSET, BROWN

JOSEPH PARKER:

Verses 13, 14. The wisdom of Moses is seen in the nature of the inquiry which he proposed. He was resolved not to go a warfare at his own charges. Every man should know upon *whose* business he is going in life. Who is sending me? is an inquiry which a man should put to himself before venturing upon any course that is doubtful, hazardous, or experimental. Moses wished to be able to identify the *personal* authority of his mission. It was not enough to have a message; he must also know the name of the Author. There are some doctrines which are independent of personality; there are others which depend upon personality for their authority and beneficence. Among the latter are all religious doctrines and appeals. The Giver is greater than the gift. The Speaker is greater than the speech. To know the Speaker is to have deep insight into the meaning of the words spoken.

The answer returned to Moses was the sublimest reply ever made to reverent inquiry. God announces himself as Personal, Independent, Self-existent. There is no word to qualify or limit his personality—it is, so to speak, pure *being*—it is infinite life—it is the fountain out of which all other lives start on their little course. Mark the comprehensiveness of the name. It relates not only to being, but to *character*, to self-completeness; it is the one life which can live without dependence and without society. The element of sublimity must be found in religion; the measure of sublimity is the measure of condescension. A man proceeding to his work under the influence of such a revelation as was granted to Moses must be superior to hardship and triumphant in the presence of difficulty. A man's inspiration should always be in excess of the duty which is imposed upon him. The inspired man descends upon his work and conducts his service with an overplus of power; but he whose inspiration falls below his duty toils fretfully and unsuccessfully, and eventually becomes the prey of the spirit of the hireling. It is here that the Christian worker actually triumphs in his labor, and rejoices even in persecution and tribulation: God the Holy Ghost is in him, and so the whole tone of his life is infinitely superior to the influences which seek to distract his attention and baffle his energy. In the absence of God the Holy Ghost, Christian service becomes a toil and ends in failure and mortification: but under the influence of the life-giving and light-giving Spirit of God, sorrow itself is turned into joy.

Notwithstanding this revelation, Moses was unable to overcome his infirmity; he still doubted, as well indeed he might, in the presence of such a vocation as had probably never been addressed to man. Let us listen to his excuses, and we shall see how unbecoming it would be on our part to sneer at a man upon whom the divine burden pressed so heavily. Moses himself was not disobedient unto the heavenly vision, nor did he doubt the authority with which he had been charged; but a difficulty presented itself from the other side.—*The People's Bible*

ADAM CLARKE

Septuagint, "I am he who exists." The Syriac, the Persic, and the Chaldee preserve the original words without any gloss. The Arabic paraphrases them, "The Eternal, who passes not away." As the original words literally signify, "I will be what I will be," some have supposed that God simply designed to inform Moses that what He had been to his fathers Abraham, Isaac, and Jacob, He would be to him and the Israelites; and that He would perform the promises He had made to his fathers, by giving their descendants the Promised Land. It is difficult to put a meaning on the words; they seem intended to point out the eternity and self-existence of God.

15. *This is my name for ever.* The name here referred to is that which immediately precedes, *Yehovah Elohim,* which we translate *the Lord God,* the name by which God had been known from the creation of the world (see Gen. ii. 4) and the name by which He is known among the same people to the present day. Even the heathen knew this name of the true God; and hence out of our *Yehovah* they formed their *Jove.* As to be self-existent and eternal must be attributes of God forever, does it not follow that the *leolam, for ever,* in the text signifies eternity?

16. *Elders of Israel.* Though it is not likely the Hebrews were permitted to have any regular government at this time, yet there can be no doubt of their having such a government in the time of Joseph, and for some considerable time after; the elders of each tribe forming a kind of court of magistrates, by which all actions were tried, and legal decisions made, in the Israelitish community. *I have surely visited you.* An exact fulfillment of the prediction of Joseph, Gen. 1 24, "God will surely visit you," and in the same words too.

18. *They shall hearken to thy voice.* This assurance was necessary to encourage him to an enterprise so dangerous and important. *Three days' journey into the wilderness.* Evidently intending Mount Sinai, which is reputed to be about three days' journey, the shortest way, from the land of Goshen. In ancient times, distances were computed by the time required to pass over them. Thus, instead of miles, furlongs. it was said, the distance from one place to another was so many days', so many hours' journey; and it continues the same in all countries where there are no regular roads or highways.

19. *I am sure that the king of Egypt will not let you go, no, not by a mighty hand.* When the facts detailed in this history have been considered in connection with the assertion as it stands in our Bibles, the most palpable contradiction has appeared. That the king of Egypt did let them go, and that by a mighty hand, the book itself amply declares. We should, therefore, seek for another meaning of the original word. *Velo,* which generally means "and not," has sometimes the meaning of "if not, unless, except"; and in Becke's Bible, 1549, it is thus translated: "I am sure that the kyng of Egypt wyl not let you go, except wyth a mighty hand." The meaning, therefore, is very plain: The king of Egypt, who now profits much by your servitude, will not let you go till he sees My hand stretched out, and he and his nation be smitten with ten plagues. Hence God immediately adds, v. 20: "I will stretch out my hand, and smite Egypt with all my wonders . . . and after that, he will let you go."

22. *Every woman shall borrow.* This is certainly not a correct translation: the original word *shaal* signifies simply to "ask, request, demand, require, inquire"; but it does not signify to *borrow* in the proper sense of that word, though in a very few places of Scripture it is thus used. In this and the parallel place, chap. xii. 35, the word signifies to "ask" or "demand," and not to *borrow,* which is a gross mistake into which scarcely any of the versions, ancient or modern, have fallen, except our own. The Septuagint has "she shall ask"; the Vulgate, "she shall demand." The European versions are generally correct on this point; and our common English version is almost the sole transgressor. God commanded the Israelites to "ask" or "demand" a certain recompense for their past services, and He inclined the hearts of the

MATTHEW HENRY

(3) That his people should furnish them at their departure with abundance of plate and jewels, to their great enriching: *I will give this people favour in the sight of the Egyptians, v.* 21, 22.

CHAPTER 4

Verses 1–9

I. Moses objects that in all probability the people would not *hearken to his voice* (*v.* 1), that is, they would not take his bare word, unless he showed them some sign. If there should be some gainsayers among them who would question his commission, how should he deal with them?

II. God empowers him to work miracles, directs him to three particularly, two of which were now immediately wrought for his own satisfaction.

1. The rod in his hand is made the subject of a miracle, a double miracle: it is but thrown out of his hand and it becomes a serpent; he resumes it and it becomes a rod again, *v.* 2–4. Here was an honour put upon Moses, that this change was wrought upon his throwing it down and taking it up, without any spell, or charm, or incantation: his being empowered thus to act under God, out of the common course of nature and providence, was a demonstration of his authority, under God, to settle a new dispensation of the kingdom of grace. There was a significance in the miracle itself. Pharaoh had turned the rod of government into the serpent of oppression, from which Moses had himself fled into Midian; but by the agency of Moses the scene was altered again.

2. His hand itself is next made the subject of a miracle. He puts it once into his bosom, and takes it out leprous; he puts it again into the same place, and takes it out well, *v.* 6, 7. This signified, (1) That Moses, by the power of God, should bring sore diseases upon Egypt, and that, at his prayer, they should be removed. (2) That whereas the Israelites in Egypt had become leprous, polluted by sin, by being taken into the bosom of Moses they should be cleansed and cured. (3) That Moses was not to work miracles by his own power.

3. He is directed, when he shall come to Egypt, to turn some of the water of the river into blood, *v.* 9.

Verses 10–17

Moses still continues backward to the service for which God had designed him; now we can no longer impute it to his humility and modesty, but must own that there was too much of cowardice, slothful-

JAMIESON, FAUSSET, BROWN

CHAPTER 4

Vss. 1-31. MIRACULOUS CHANGE OF THE ROD, etc. **1. But behold**—*Hebrew*, "If," "perhaps," "they will not believe me."—What evidence can I produce of my divine mission? There was still a want of full confidence, not in the character and divine power of his employer, but in His presence and power always accompanying him. He insinuated that his communication might be rejected and he himself treated as an impostor. **2. the Lord said, . . . What is that in thine hand?**—The question was put not to elicit information which God required, but to draw the particular attention of Moses. **A rod**—probably the shepherd's crook—among the Arabs, a long staff, with a curved head, varying from three to six feet in length.

6. Put now thine hand into thy bosom—the open part of his outer robe, worn about the girdle.

9. take of the water of the river—Nile. Those miracles, two of which were wrought then, and the third to be performed on his arrival in Goshen, were at first designed to encourage him as satisfactory proofs of his divine mission, and to be repeated for the special confirmation of his embassy before the Israelites. **10-13. I am not eloquent**—It is supposed that Moses labored under a natural defect of utterance or had a difficulty in the free and fluent expression of his ideas in the Egyptian language, which he had long disused. This new objection was also

ADAM CLARKE

Egyptians to give liberally; and this, far from a matter of oppression, wrong, or even charity, was no more than a very partial recompense for the long and painful services which we may say six hundred thousand Israelites had rendered to Egypt, during a considerable number of years.

Jewels of silver. The word *keley* we have already seen signifies "vessels, instruments, weapons," and may be very well translated by our English term "articles" or "goods." The Israelites got both gold and silver, and such raiment as was necessary for the journey which they were about to undertake.

Ye shall spoil the Egyptians. The verb *natsal* signifies, not only to "spoil, snatch away," but also to "get away, to escape, to deliver, to regain, or recover." Spoil signifies what is taken by violence; but this cannot be the meaning of the original word here, as the Israelites only asked, and the Egyptians without fear, terror, or constraint, freely gave. It is worthy of remark that the original word is used, 1 Sam. xxx. 22, to signify the recovery of property that had been taken away by violence. In this sense we should understand the word here. The Israelites recovered a part of their property—their wages, of which they had been most unjustly deprived by the Egyptians.

CHAPTER 4

1. *They will not believe me.* As if he had said, Unless I be enabled to work miracles, and give them proofs by extraordinary works as well as by words, they will not believe that Thou hast sent me.

2. *A rod. Matteh,* a "staff," probably his shepherd's crook; see Lev. xxvii. 32. As it was made the instrument of working many miracles, it was afterwards called the "rod of God"; see v. 20.

3. *A serpent.* Of what sort we know not, as the word *nachash* is a general name for serpents.

4. *He put forth his hand, and caught it.* Considering the light in which Moses had viewed this serpent, it required considerable faith to induce him thus implicitly to obey the command of God; but he obeyed, and the noxious serpent became instantly the miraculous rod in his hand! Implicit faith and obedience conquer all difficulties; and he who believes in God and obeys Him in all things has really nothing to fear.

5. *That they may believe.* This is an example of what is called an imperfect or unfinished speech, several of which occur in the sacred writings. It may be thus supplied: "Do this before them, that they may believe that the Lord hath appeared unto thee."

6. *His hand was leprous as snow.* That is, the leprosy spread itself over the whole body in thin white scales. The leprosy, at least among the Jews, was a most inveterate and contagious disorder and deemed by them incurable. Among the heathen it was considered as inflicted by their gods, and it was supposed that they alone could remove it. It is certain that a similar belief prevailed among the Israelites; hence, when the king of Syria sent his general, Naaman, to the king of Israel to cure him of his leprosy, he rent his clothes, saying, "Am I God, to kill and to make alive, that this man doth send unto me to recover a man of his leprosy?" 2 Kings v. 7. This appears, therefore, to be the reason why God chose this sign, as the instantaneous infliction and removal of this disease were demonstrations which all would allow of the sovereign power of God.

8. *If they will not believe . . . the voice of the first sign.* Probably intimating that some would be more difficult to be persuaded than others: some would yield to the evidence of the first miracle; others would hesitate till they had seen the second; and others would not believe till they had seen the water of the Nile turned into blood, when poured upon the dry land, v. 9.

10. *I am not eloquent. Lo ish debarim,* "I am not a man of words"; a periphrasis common in the Scriptures. So Job xi. 2, "a man of lips" signifies one that is talkative. But how could it be said that Moses was *not eloquent,* when

MATTHEW HENRY

ness, and unbelief in it.

I. How Moses endeavours to excuse himself.

1. He pleads that he was no good spokesman: *O my lord! I am not eloquent, v.* 10. God is pleased sometimes to make choice of those as his messengers who have fewest of the advantages of art or nature. Christ's disciples were no orators, till the Spirit made them such.

2. When this plea was overruled, and all his excuses were answered, he begged that God would send somebody else on this errand and leave him to keep sheep in Midian (*v.* 13).

II. How God condescends to answer all his excuses. Though *the anger of the Lord was kindled against him* (*v.* 14), yet he continued to reason with him, till he had overcome him.

1. To balance the weakness of Moses, he here reminds him of his own power, *v.* 11. *Who has made man's mouth? Have not I the Lord?* Moses knew that God made man, but he must be reminded now that God made man's mouth, and of His power in general over the other faculties. The perfections of our faculties are his work, he makes the *seeing*; he formed the eye (Ps. xciv. 9); he opens the understanding, the eye of the mind, Luke xxiv. 45.

2. To encourage him in this great undertaking, he repeats the promise of his presence, not only in general, *I will be with thee* (*ch.* iii. 12), but in particular, "*I will be with thy mouth*, so that the imperfection in thy speech shall be no prejudice to thy message." If others spoke more gracefully, none spoke more powerfully.

3. He joins Aaron in commission with him. He promises that Aaron shall meet him opportunely, and that he will be glad to see him, they having not seen one another (it is likely) for many years, *v.* 14. He directs him to make use of Aaron as his spokesman, *v.* 16, that their natural affection one to another might strengthen their union in the joint execution of their commission. Christ sent his disciples two and two, and some of the couples were brothers. The tongue of Aaron, with the head and heart of Moses, would make one completely fit for this embassy. God promises, *I will be with thy mouth, and with his mouth.* Even Aaron, that could speak well, yet could not speak to purpose unless God was with his mouth.

4. He bids him take the rod with him in his hand (*v.* 17). The rod he carried as a shepherd must be his staff of authority, and must be to him instead both of sword and sceptre.

Verses 18–23

I. Moses obtains leave of his father-in-law to return into Egypt, *v.* 18.

II. He receives from God further encouragements and directions in his work. And, 1. He assures Moses that the coasts were clear. Whatever new enemies he might make by his undertaking, his old enemies were *all dead, all that sought his life, v.* 19.

2. He orders him to do the miracles, not only before the elders of Israel, but before Pharaoh, *v.* 21. 3. That Pharaoh's obstinacy might be no surprise nor discouragement to him, God tells him before that he would *harden his heart.*

JAMIESON, FAUSSET, BROWN

overruled, but still Moses, who foresaw the manifold difficulties of the undertaking, was anxious to be freed from the responsibility.

14. the anger of the Lord was kindled against Moses—The Divine Being is not subject to ebullitions of passion; but His displeasure was manifested by transferring the honor of the priesthood, which would otherwise have been bestowed on Moses, to Aaron, who was from this time destined to be the head of the house of Levi (I Chron. 23:13). Marvellous had been His condescension and patience in dealing with Moses; and now every remaining scruple was removed by the unexpected and welcome intelligence that his brother Aaron was to be his colleague. God knew from the beginning what Moses would do, but He reserves this motive to the last as the strongest to rouse his languid heart, and Moses now fully and cordially complied with the call. If we are surprised at his backwardness amidst all the signs and promises that were given him, we must admire his candor and honesty in recording it.

18. Moses . . . returned to Jethro—Being in his service, it was right to obtain his consent, but Moses evinced piety, humility, and prudence, in not divulging the special object of his journey.

19. all the men are dead which sought thy life—The death of the Egyptian monarch took place in the four hundred and twenty-ninth year of the Hebrew sojourn in that land, and that event, according to the law of Egypt, took off his proscription of Moses, if it had been publicly issued. **20. Moses took his wife and sons, and set them upon an ass**—*Septuagint,* "asses." Those animals are not now used in the desert of Sinai except by the Arabs for short distances. **returned**—entered on his journey towards Egypt. **he took the rod of God**—so called from its being appropriated to His service, and because whatever miracles it might be employed in performing would be wrought not by its inherent properties, but by a divine power following on its use. (Cf. Acts 3:12).

ADAM CLARKE

Stephen asserts, Acts vii. 22, that he was "mighty in words" as well as in deeds? Though Moses was slow of speech, yet when acting as the messenger of God his word was with power, for at his command the plagues came and the plagues were stayed; thus was he mighty in words as well as in deeds: and this is probably the meaning of Stephen. By the expression *neither heretofore, nor since thou hast spoken unto thy servant,* he might possibly mean that the natural inaptitude to speak readily, which he had felt, he continued to feel, even since God has begun to discover himself; for though He had wrought several miracles for him, yet He had not healed this infirmity.

11. *Who hath made man's mouth?* Cannot He who formed the mouth, the whole organs of speech, and hath given the gift of speech also, cannot He give utterance? God can take away those gifts and restore them again. Do not provoke Him; He who created the eye, the ear, and the mouth, hath also made the blind, the deaf, and the dumb.

13. *Send . . . by the hand of him whom thou wilt send.* The Hebrew literally translated is, "Send now [or, I beseech Thee] by the hand thou wilt send"; which seems to intimate, Send a person more fit for the work than I am. So the Septuagint: "Elect another powerful person, whom thou wilt send."

14. *I know that he can speak well.* "I know that in speaking he will speak." That is, he is apt to talk, and has a ready utterance. *He cometh forth to meet thee.* He shall meet thee at My mount (v. 27), shall rejoice in thy mission, and most heartily cooperate with thee in all things. A necessary assurance to prevent Moses from suspecting that Aaron, who was his elder brother, would envy his superior call and office.

15. *I will be with thy mouth, and with his mouth.* Ye shall be both, in all things which I appoint you to do in this business, under the continual inspiration of the Most High.

16. *He shall be thy spokesman.* Literally, "He shall speak for thee [or in thy stead] to the people." *He shall be to thee instead of a mouth.* He shall convey every message to the people; *and thou shalt be to him instead of God*—thou shalt deliver to him what I communicate to thee.

18. *Let me go, I pray thee, and return unto my brethren.* Moses, having received his commission from God, and directions how to execute it, returned to his father-in-law, and asked permission to visit his family and brethren in Egypt, without giving him any intimation of the great errand on which he was going.

19. *In Midian.* This was a new revelation, and appears to have taken place after Moses returned to his father-in-law previous to his departure for Egypt.

20. *His wife and his sons.* Both Gershom and Eliezer, though the birth of the latter has not yet been mentioned in the Hebrew text. See the note on chap. ii. 22.

Set them upon an ass. The Septuagint reads the word in the plural "upon asses," as it certainly required more than one to carry Zipporah, Gershom, and Eliezer. *The rod of God.* The sign of sovereign power, by which he was to perform all his miracles; once the badge of his shepherd's office, and now that by which he is to feed, rule, and protect his people Israel.

21. *But I will harden his heart.* The case of Pharaoh has given rise to many fierce controversies, and to several strange and conflicting opinions. Would men but look at the whole account without the medium of their respective creeds, they would find little difficulty to apprehend the truth. If we take up the subject in a theological point of view, all sober Christians will allow the truth of this proposition of St. Augustine, when the subject in question is a person who has hardened his own heart by frequently resisting the grace and spirit of God: "God does not harden men by infusing malice into them, but by not imparting mercy to them." And this other will be as readily credited: "God does not work this hardness of heart in man; but he may be said to harden him whom he refuses to soften, to blind him whom he refuses to enlighten, and to repel him whom he

MATTHEW HENRY	JAMIESON, FAUSSET, BROWN	ADAM CLARKE

KEIL–DELITZSCH:

Verse 21. "In thy going [returning] to Egypt, behold, all the wonders which I have put into thy hand, thou doest them before Pharaoh." *Portentum* is any object (natural event, thing, or person) of significance which surpasses expectation or the ordinary course of nature, and excites wonder in consequence. It is frequently connected with "a sign" (Deut. 4:34; 6:22; 7:19, etc.), and embraces the idea of a "wonder sign." The expression, "all those wonders," does not refer merely to the three signs mentioned in chapter 4:2–9, but to all the miracles which were to be performed by Moses with the staff in the presence of Pharaoh, and which, though not named, were put into his hand potentially along with the staff. But all the miracles would not induce Pharaoh to let Israel go, for Jehovah would harden his heart. Literally, "I will make his heart *firm*," so that it will not move, his feelings and attitude towards Israel will not change. We find in 7:3, "I will make Pharaoh's heart *hard*, or unfeeling"; and in 10:1, "I have made his heart *heavy*," i.e., obtuse, or insensible to impressions or divine influences. These three words are expressive of the hardening of the heart.

The *hardening of Pharaoh* is ascribed to God, not only in the passages just quoted, but also in 9:12; 10:20, 27; 11:10; 14:8—that is to say, ten times in all; and that not merely as foreknown or foretold by Jehovah, but as caused and effected by Him. In the last five passages it is invariably stated that "Jehovah hardened Pharaoh's heart." But it is also stated just as often (ten times) that Pharaoh hardened his own heart, or made it heavy or firm; *e.g.* in 7:13, 22; 8:15; 9:35, "and Pharaoh's heart was [or became] hard"; 7:14, "Pharaoh's heart was heavy"; in 9:7, "the heart of Pharaoh was hardened"; in 9:34, "he sinned, yet more, and hardened his heart." According to this, the hardening of Pharaoh was quite as much his own act as the decree of God. But if, in order to determine the precise relation of the divine to the human causality, we look more carefully at the two classes of expressions, we shall find that not only in connection with the first sign, by which Moses and Aaron were to show their credentials as the messengers of Jehovah, sent with the demand that he would let the people of Israel go (7:13, 14), but after the first five penal miracles, the hardening is invariably represented as his own. After every one of these miracles, it is stated that Pharaoh's heart was firm, or dull, *i.e.* insensible to the voice of God, and unaffected by the miracles performed before his eyes, and the judgments of God suspended over him and his kingdom, and he did not listen to them (to Moses and Aaron with their demand), or let the people go (7:22; 8:8, 15, 28; 9:7). It is not till after the sixth plague that it is stated that Jehovah made the heart of Pharaoh firm (9:12). At the seventh the statement is repeated that "Pharaoh made his heart heavy" (9:34, 35); but the continued refusal on the part of Pharaoh after the eighth and ninth (10:20, 27) and his resolution to follow the Israelites and bring them back again are attributed to the hardening of his heart by Jehovah (14:8). This hardening of his own heart was manifested first of all in the fact that he paid no attention to the demand of Jehovah addressed to him through Moses, and would not let Israel go; and that not only at the commencement, so long as the Egyptian magicians imitated the signs performed by Moses and Aaron (though at the very first sign the rods of the magicians, when turned into serpents, were swallowed by Aaron's, 7:12, 13), but even when the magicians themselves acknowledged, "This is the finger of God" (8:19). It was also continued after the fourth and fifth plagues, when a distinction was made between the Egyptians and the Israelites, and the latter were exempted from the plagues—a fact of which the king took care to convince himself (9:7). And it was exhibited still further in his breaking his promise that he would let Israel go if Moses and Aaron would obtain from Jehovah the removal of the plague, and in the fact that even after he had been obliged to confess, "I have sinned, Jehovah is the righteous one, I and my people are unrighteous" (9:27), he sinned again as soon as breathing-time was given him, and would not let the people go (9:34, 35). Thus Pharaoh would not bend his self-will to the will of God, even after he had discerned the finger of God and the omnipotence of Jehovah in the plagues suspended over him and his nation; he would not withdraw his haughty refusal, not withstanding the fact that he was obliged to acknowledge that it was sin against Jehovah.

Looked at from this side, the hardening was a fruit of sin, a consequence of that self-will, high-mindedness, and pride which flow from sin, and a continuous and ever-increasing abuse of that freedom of the will which is innate in man, and which involves the possibility of obstinate resistance to the word and chastisement of God even until death. As the freedom of the will has its fixed limits in the unconditional dependence of the creature upon the Creator, so the sinner may resist the will of God as long as he lives. But such resistance plunges him into destruction, and is followed inevitably by death and damnation. God never allows any man to scoff at Him. Whoever will not suffer himself to be led, by the kindness and earnestness of the divine admonitions, to repentance and humble submission to the will of God must inevitably perish, and by his destruction subserve the glory of God and the manifestations of the holiness, righteousness, and omnipotence of Jehovah.

—Commentary on the Old Testament

refuses to call." It is but just and right that He should withhold those graces which He had repeatedly offered, and which the sinner had despised and rejected. Thus much for the general principle. The verb *chazak,* which we translate *harden,* literally signifies to "strengthen, confirm, make bold or courageous"; and is often used in the sacred writings to excite to duty, perseverance, etc., and is placed by the Jews at the end of most books in the Bible as an exhortation to the reader to take courage, and proceed with his reading and with the obedience it requires. It constitutes an essential part of the exhortation of God to Joshua, chap. i. 7: "Only be thou strong," *rak chazak.* And of Joshua's dying exhortation to the people, chap. xxiii. 6: "Be ye therefore very courageous," *vachazaktem,* "to keep and to do all that is written in the book of the law." Now it would be very strange in these places to translate the word "harden": "Only be thou hard"; "Be ye therefore very hard"; and yet if we use the word "hardy," it would suit the sense and context perfectly well: "Only be thou hardy"; "Be ye therefore very hardy." Now suppose we apply the word in this way to Pharaoh, the sense would be good, and the justice of God equally conspicuous. I will make his heart hardy, bold, daring, presumptuous; for the same principle acting against God's order is presumption which when acting according to it is undaunted courage. It is true that the verb *kashah* is used, chap. vii. 3, which signifies to render stiff, tough, or stubborn, but it amounts to nearly the same meaning with the above.

All those who have read the Scriptures with care and attention know well that God is frequently represented in them as doing what He only *permits* to be done. So because a man has grieved His Spirit and resisted His grace He withdraws that Spirit and grace from him, and thus he becomes bold and presumptuous in sin. Pharaoh made his own heart stubborn against God, chap. ix. 34; and God gave him up to judicial blindness, so that he rushed on stubbornly to his own destruction. From the whole of Pharaoh's conduct we learn that he was bold, haughty, and cruel; and God chose to *permit* these dispositions to have their full sway in his heart without check or restraint from divine influence. The consequence was what God intended: he did not immediately comply with the requisition to let the people go; and this was done that God might have the fuller opportunity of manifesting His power by multiplying signs and miracles, and thus impress the hearts both of the Egyptians and Israelites with a due sense of His omnipotence and justice. The whole procedure was graciously calculated to do endless good to both nations. The Israelites must be satisfied that they had the true God for their Protector, and thus their faith was strengthened. The Egyptians must see that their gods could do nothing against the God of Israel, and thus their dependence on them was necessarily shaken. These great ends could not have been answered had Pharaoh at once consented to let the people go. This consideration alone unravels the mystery, and explains everything. Let it be observed that there is nothing spoken here of the eternal state of the Egyptian king; nor does anything in the whole of the subsequent account authorize us to believe that God hardened his heart against the influences of His own grace, that He might occasion him so to sin that His justice might consign him to hell. This would be such an act of flagrant injustice as we could scarcely attribute to the worst of men. He who leads another into an offense that he may have a fairer pretense to punish him for it, or brings him into such circumstances that he cannot avoid committing a capital crime, and then hangs him for it, is surely the most execrable of mortals. What then should we make of the God of justice and mercy should we attribute to Him a decree, the date of which is lost in eternity, by which He has determined to cut off from the possibility of salvation millions of millions of unborn souls, and leave them under a necessity of sinning, by actually hardening their hearts against the influences of His own grace and Spirit, that He may, on the pretext of justice, consign them to endless perdition? Whatever may be pretended in behalf of such unqualified opinions, it must be evident to all who are not

MATTHEW HENRY

4. Words are put into his mouth with which to address Pharaoh, *v.* 22, 23. (1) He must deliver his message in the name of the great Jehovah: *Thus saith the Lord*; this is the first time *that* preface is used by any man which afterwards is used so frequently by all the prophets. (2) He must let Pharaoh know Israel's relation to God, and God's concern for Israel. (3) He must demand a discharge for them: "*Let my son go:* not only my servant whom thou hast no right to detain, but my son whose liberty and honour I am very jealous for." (4) He must threaten Pharaoh with the death of the first-born of Egypt, in case of a refusal: *I will slay thy son, even thy firstborn.*

III. Moses addresses himself to this expedition.

Verses 24–31

Moses is here going to Egypt, and we are told, I. How God met him in anger, *v.* 24-26. This is a very difficult passage.

1. The sin of Moses, which was neglecting to circumcise his son. This was probably the effect of his being unequally yoked with a Midianite, who was too indulgent of her child.

2. God's displeasure against him. Omissions are sins. God takes notice of, and is much displeased with, the sins of his own people. If they neglect their duty, let them expect to hear of it by their consciences, and perhaps to feel from it by cross providences.

3. The speedy performance of the duty for the neglect of which God had now a controversy with him. His son must be circumcised; Moses is unable to circumcise him; therefore, in this case of necessity, Zipporah does it.

4. The release of Moses thereupon: *So he let him go*; and all was well: only Zipporah cannot forget the fright she was in, and, upon this occasion (it is probable), he sent them back to his father-in-law.

II. How Aaron met him in love, *v.* 27, 28. God sent Aaron to meet him, and directed him where to find him, in the wilderness, that lay towards Midian. He met him *in the mount of God*, the place where God had met with him. They embraced one another as a pledge of their hearty concurrence in the work to which they were jointly called. Moses informed his brother of the commission he had received, *v.* 28.

III. How the elders of Israel met him in faith and obedience. When Moses and Aaron first opened their commission in Egypt they met with a better reception than they promised themselves, *v.* 29-31. *The people believed*, as God had foretold (*ch.* iii. 18). *They bowed their heads and worshipped.*

JAMIESON, FAUSSET, BROWN

24. inn—*Hebrew,* a halting-place for the night. **the Lord met him, and sought to kill him**—i.e., he was either overwhelmed with mental distress or overtaken by a sudden and dangerous malady. The narrative is obscure, but the meaning seems to be, that, led during his illness to a strict self-examination, he was deeply pained and grieved at the thought of having, to please his wife, postponed or neglected the circumcision of one of his sons, probably the younger. To dishonor that sign and seal of the covenant was criminal in any Hebrew, peculiarly so in one destined to be the leader and deliverer of the Hebrews; and he seems to have felt his sickness as a merited chastisement for his sinful omission. Concerned for her husband's safety, Zipporah overcomes her maternal feelings of aversion to the painful rite, performs herself, by means of one of the sharp flints with which that part of the desert abounds, an operation which her husband, on whom the duty devolved, was unable to do, and having brought the bloody evidence, exclaimed in the painful excitement of her feelings that from love to him she had risked the life of her child [CALVIN, BULLINGER, ROSENMULLER]. **26. So he let him go**—Moses recovered; but the remembrance of this critical period in his life would stimulate the Hebrew legislator to enforce a faithful attention to the rite of circumcision when it was established as a divine ordinance in Israel, and made their peculiar distinction as a people. **27. Aaron met him in the mount of God, and kissed him**—After a separation of forty years, their meeting would be mutually happy. Similar are the salutations of Arab friends when they meet in the desert still; conspicuous is the kiss on each side of the head. **29. Moses and Aaron went**—towards Egypt, Zipporah and her sons having been sent back. (Cf. ch. 18:2). **gathered . . . all the elders**—Aaron was spokesman, and Moses performed the appointed miracles—through which "the people," i.e., the elders, believed (I Kings 17:24; Josh. 3:2) and received the joyful tidings of the errand on which Moses had come with devout thanksgiving. Formerly they had slighted the message and rejected the messenger. Formerly Moses had gone in his own strength; now he goes leaning on God, and strong only through faith in Him who had sent him. Israel also had been taught a useful lesson, and it was good for both that they had been afflicted.

ADAM CLARKE

deeply prejudiced that neither the justice nor the sovereignty of God can be magnified by them.

22. *Israel is my son, even my firstborn.* That is, The Hebrew people are unutterably dear to Me.

23. *Let my son go, that he may serve me.* Which they could not do in Goshen, consistently with the policy and religious worship of the Egyptians; because the most essential part of the Israelites' worship consisted in sacrifice, and the animals which they offered to God were sacred among the Egyptians. Moses gives Pharaoh this reason in chap. viii. 26. *I will slay thy son, even thy firstborn.* Which, on Pharaoh's utter refusal to let the people go, was accordingly done; see chap. xii. 29.

24. *By the way in the inn.* See the note on Gen. xlii. 27. The meaning of the whole passage seems to be this: The son of Moses, Gershom or Eliezer, had not been circumcised, though it would seem that God had ordered the father to do it; but as he had neglected this, therefore Jehovah was about to have slain the child, because not in covenant with Him by circumcision, and thus He intended to have punished the disobedience of the father by the natural death of his son. Zipporah, getting acquainted with the nature of the case and the danger to which her firstborn was exposed, took a sharp stone and cut off the foreskin of her son. By this act the displeasure of the Lord was turned aside, and Zipporah considered herself as now allied to God because of this circumcision. The sharp stone mentioned in v. 25 was probably a knife made of flint, for such were anciently used, even where knives of metal might be had, for every kind of operation about the human body. Ancient authors are full of proofs of these facts. It is probable that Zipporah, being alarmed by this circumstance, and fearing worse evils, took the resolution to return to her father's house with her two sons. See chap. xviii. 1, etc.

27. *The Lord said to Aaron.* See v. 14. By some secret but powerful movement on Aaron's mind, or by some voice or angelic ministry, he was now directed to go and meet his brother, Moses; and so correctly was the information given to both that they arrived at the same time on the sacred mountain.

30. *Aaron spake all the words.* It is likely that Aaron was better acquainted with the Hebrew tongue than his brother, and on this account he became the spokesman. *Did the signs.* Turned the rod into a serpent, made the hand leprous, and changed the water into blood. See on vv. 8 and 9.

31. *The people believed.* They credited the account given of the divine appointment of Moses and Aaron to be their deliverers out of their bondage, the miracles wrought on the occasion confirming the testimony delivered by Aaron. *They bowed their heads and worshipped.* See a similar act mentioned, and in the same words, Gen. xxiv. 26. The bowing the head here may probably refer to the Eastern custom of bowing the head down to the knees, then kneeling down and touching the earth with the forehead.

CHAPTER 5

MATTHEW HENRY

Verses 1–2

Moses and Aaron are now to deal with Pharaoh.

I. Their demand is piously bold: *Thus saith the Lord God of Israel, Let my people go, v.* 1. Moses, in treating with the elders of Israel, is directed to call God *the God of their fathers*; but, in treating with Pharaoh, they call him *the God of Israel*, and it is the first time we find him called so in scripture: he is called *the God of Israel*, the *person* (Gen. xxxiii. 20); but here it is Israel, the *people*. They are just beginning to be formed into a people when God is called their God. In this great name they deliver their message: *Let my people go.*

II. Pharaoh's answer is impiously bold: *Who is the Lord, that I should obey his voice? v.* 2. He will not treat about it, nor so much as bear the mention of it. How scornfully he speaks of the God of Israel: "*Who is Jehovah?* I neither know him nor care for him, neither value him nor fear him." Ignorance and contempt of God are at the bottom of all the wickedness that is in the world. How

JAMIESON, FAUSSET, BROWN

VSS. 1-23. FIRST INTERVIEW WITH PHARAOH. **1. Moses and Aaron went in**—As representatives of the Hebrews, they were entitled to ask an audience of the king, and their thorough Egyptian training taught them how and when to seek it. **and told Pharaoh**—When introduced, they delivered a message in the name of the God of Israel. This is the first time He is mentioned by that national appellation in Scripture. It seems to have been used by divine direction (ch. 4:2) and designed to put honor on the Hebrews in their depressed condition (Heb. 11:16). **2. Pharaoh said, Who is the Lord**—rather "Jehovah." Lord was a common name applied to objects of worship; but Jehovah was a name he had never heard of; he estimated the character and power of this God by the abject and miserable condition of the worshippers and concluded that He held as low a rank among the gods as His people did in the nation. To demonstrate the supremacy of the true God over all the gods of Egypt, was the design of the plagues. I

ADAM CLARKE

1. *And afterward Moses and Aaron went.* This chapter is properly a continuation of the preceding, as the succeeding is a continuation of this; and to preserve the connection of the facts they should be read together.

How simply, and yet with what authority, does Moses deliver his message to the Egyptian king! "Thus saith JEHOVAH, God of Israel, Let My people go." It is well in this, as in almost every other case where "Jehovah" occurs, to **preserve the original word: our using the word Lord is not sufficiently expressive and often leaves the sense indistinct.**

2. *Who is the Lord?* Who is Jehovah, *that I should obey his voice?* What claims has He on me? I am under no obligation to Him. Pharaoh spoke here under the common persuasion that every place and people had a tutelary deity, and he supposed that this Jehovah might be the tutelary deity of the Israelites, to whom he, as

MATTHEW HENRY

proudly he speaks of himself: "*That I should obey his voice.* Shall I, that rule the Israel of God, obey the God of Israel?" Here is the core of the controversy: God must rule, but man will not be ruled.

Verses 3–9

Finding that Pharaoh had no veneration at all for God, Moses and Aaron next try whether he had any compassion for Israel.

I. Their request is very humble and modest, *v.* 3. They make no complaint of the rigour they were ruled with. What they ask is very reasonable, only for a short vacation, while they went three days' journey into the desert, "*We will sacrifice unto the Lord our God,* as other people do to theirs."

II. Pharaoh's denial of their request is very barbarous and unreasonable, *v.* 4–9.

1. That the people were idle, and that therefore they talked of going to sacrifice. The cities they built for Pharaoh were witnesses that they were not idle. The malice of Satan has often represented the service and worship of God as fit employment for those only that have nothing else to do.

2. His resolutions hereupon were most barbarous. (1) Moses and Aaron themselves must get to *their burdens* (*v.* 4); they must share in the common slavery of their nation. (2) The usual tale of bricks must be exacted, without the usual allowance of straw to mix with the clay, or to burn the bricks with.

Verses 10–14

Pharaoh's orders are here put in execution; straw is denied, and yet the work not diminished. 1. The Egyptian task-masters were very severe. These task-masters insisted upon the daily tasks, as when there was straw, *v.* 13. 2. The people hereby were dispersed throughout all the land of Egypt, to gather stubble, *v.* 12. 3. The Israelite-officers were used with particular harshness, *v.* 14. What a miserable thing slavery is, and what reason we have to be thankful to God that we are a free people, and not oppressed. Liberty and property are valuable jewels in the eyes of those whose services and possessions lie at the mercy of an arbitrary power. What strange steps God sometimes takes in delivering his people. The lowest ebbs go before the highest tides; and very cloudy mornings commonly introduce the fairest days, Deut. xxxii. 36.

Verses 15–23

It was a great strait that the head-workmen were in.

I. How justly they complained to Pharaoh: They *came and cried unto Pharaoh, v.* 15. *Thy servants are beaten* and yet *the fault is in thy own people,* the task-masters, who deny us what is necessary for carrying on our work. But what did they get by this complaint? It did but make bad worse. Pharaoh taunted them (*v.* 17); when they were almost killed with working, he told them they were idle. It is well for us that men are not to be our judges, but a God who knows what the principles are on which we act.

JAMIESON, FAUSSET, BROWN

know not the Lord, neither will I let Israel go—As his honor and interest were both involved he determined to crush this attempt, and in a tone of insolence, or perhaps profanity, rejected the request for the release of the Hebrew slaves. **3. The God of the Hebrews hath met with us**—Instead of being provoked into reproaches or threats, they mildly assured him that it was not a proposal originating among themselves, but a duty enjoined on them by their God. They had for a long series of years been debarred from the privilege of religious worship, and as there was reason to fear that a continued neglect of divine ordinances would draw down upon them the judgments of offended heaven, they begged permission to go three days' journey into the desert—a place of seclusion—where their sacrificial observances would neither suffer interruption nor give umbrage to the Egyptians. In saying this, they concealed their ultimate design of abandoning the kingdom, and by making this partial request at first, they probably wished to try the king's temper before they disclosed their intentions any farther. But they said only what God had put in their mouths (ch. 3:12, 18), and this "legalizes the specific act, while it gives no sanction to the general habit of dissimulation" [CHALMERS]. **4. Wherefore do ye, Moses and Aaron, let the people from their works?** etc.—Without taking any notice of what they had said, he treated them as ambitious demagogues, who were appealing to the superstitious feelings of the people, to stir up sedition and diffuse a spirit of discontent, which spreading through so vast a body of slaves, might endanger the peace of the country.

6. Pharaoh commanded—It was a natural consequence of the high displeasure created by this interview that he should put additional burdens on the oppressed Israelites. **taskmasters**—Egyptian overseers, appointed to exact labor of the Israelites. **officers**—Hebrews placed over their brethren, under the taskmasters, precisely analogous to the Arab officers set over the Arab Fellahs, the poor laborers in modern Egypt. **7. Ye shall no more give the people straw to make brick**—The making of bricks appears to have been a government monopoly as the ancient bricks are nearly all stamped with the name of a king, and they were formed, as they are still in Lower Egypt, of clay mixed with chopped straw and dried or hardened in the sun. The Israelites were employed in this drudgery; and though they still dwelt in Goshen and held property in flocks and herds, they were compelled in rotation to serve in the brick-quarries, pressed in alternating groups, just as the *fellaheen,* or peasants, are marched by press-gangs in the same country still. **let them go and gather straw for themselves**—The enraged despot did not issue orders to do an impracticable thing. The Egyptian reapers in the corn harvest were accustomed merely to cut off the ears and leave the stalk standing. **8. tale**—an appointed number of bricks. The materials of their labor were to be no longer supplied, and yet, as the same amount of produce was exacted daily, it is impossible to imagine more aggravated cruelty—a perfect specimen of Oriental despotism. **12. So the people were scattered**—It was an immense grievance to the laborers individually, but there would be no hindrance from the husbandmen whose fields they entered, as almost all the lands of Egypt were in the possession of the crown (Gen. 47:20). **13-19. taskmasters hasted them . . . officers . . . beaten**—As the nearest fields were bared and the people had to go farther for stubble, it was impossible for them to meet the demand by the usual tale of bricks. "The beating of the officers is just what might have been expected from an Eastern tyrant, especially in the valley of the Nile, as it appears from the monuments, that

ADAM CLARKE

an Egyptian, could be under no kind of obligation.

3. *Three days' journey.* The distance from Goshen to Sinai; see chap. iii. 18. *And sacrifice unto the Lord.* Great stress is laid on this circumstance. God required sacrifice; no religious acts which they performed could be acceptable to Him without this. He had now showed them that it was their indispensable duty thus to worship Him, and that if they did not they might expect Him to send the pestilence—some plague or death proceeding immediately from himself, or the *sword*—extermination by the hands of an enemy. The original word *deber,* from *dabar,* "to drive off, draw under," which we translate *pestilence* from the Latin *pestis,* "the plague," signifies any kind of disease by which an extraordinary mortality is occasioned, and which appears from the circumstances of the case to come immediately from God. The Israelites could not sacrifice in the land of Egypt, because the animals they were to offer to God were held sacred by the Egyptians; and they could not omit this duty, because it was essential to religion even before the giving of the law.

4. *Wherefore do ye, Moses and Aaron?* He hints that the Hebrews are in a state of revolt, and charges Moses and Aaron as being ringleaders of the sedition. This unprincipled charge has been, in nearly similar circumstances, often repeated since. Men who have labored to bring the mass of the common people from ignorance irreligion, and general profligacy of manners, to an acquaintance with themselves and God, and to a proper knowledge of their duty to Him and to each other, have often been branded as being disaffected to the state, and as movers of sedition among the people! *Let the people. Taphriu,* from *para,* to "loose or disengage," which we translate *to let,* from the Anglo-Saxon *lettan,* to "hinder." Ye hinder the people from working. "Get ye to your burdens." "Let religion alone, and mind your work." The language not only of tyranny, but of the basest irreligion also.

5. *The people of the land now are many.* The sanguinary edict had no doubt been repealed long before, or they could not have multiplied so greatly.

6. *The taskmasters of the people, and their officers.* The taskmasters were Egyptians (see on chap. i. 11), the officers were Hebrews; see v. 14. But it is probable that the taskmasters, chap. i. 11, who are called "princes of the burdens or taxes," were different from those termed *taskmasters* here, as the words are different; *nogesim* signifies "exactors" or "oppressors"—persons who exacted from them an unreasonable proportion of either labor or money. *Officers—shoterim;* those seem to have been an inferior sort of officers, who attended on superior officers or magistrates to execute their orders.

7. *Straw to make brick.* There have been many conjectures concerning the use of straw in making bricks. Some suppose it was used merely for burning them, but this is unfounded. The Eastern bricks are often made of clay and straw kneaded together, and then not burned, but thoroughly dried in the sun. This is expressly mentioned by Philo in his life of Moses, who says, describing the oppression of the Israelites in Egypt, that some were obliged to work in clay for the formation of bricks, and others to gather straw for the same purpose, "because straw is the bond by which the brick is held together."

8. *And the tale of the bricks. Tale* signifies the "number." *For they be idle; therefore they cry . . . Let us go and sacrifice.* Thus their desire to worship the true God in a proper manner was attributed to their unwillingness to work.

16. *The fault is in thine own people. Chatath,* the "sin," is in thy own people. *First,* Because they require impossibilities; and *Secondly,* Because they punish us for not doing what cannot be performed.

17. *Ye are idle: therefore ye say, Let us go and do sacrifice.* It is common for those who feel unconcerned about their own souls to attribute the religious earnestness of others, who

MATTHEW HENRY

II. How unjustly they complained of Moses and Aaron: *The Lord look upon you, and judge*, *v.* 21. This was not fair. Moses and Aaron had given sufficient evidence of their hearty good will to the liberties of Israel; and yet, because things succeed not immediately they are reproached as accessories to their slavery. Now what did Moses do in this strait? 1. He returned to the Lord (*v.* 22), to acquaint him with it. When we find ourselves, at any time, perplexed and embarrassed in the way of our duty, we ought to have recourse to God by faithful and fervent prayer. If we retreat, let us retreat to him, and no further. 2. Now he asks, (1) *Wherefore hast thou so evil entreated this people?* (2) *Why is it thou hast sent me?* Thus, [1] He complains of his ill success: "Pharaoh has done evil to this people, and not one step seems to be taken towards their deliverance." Or, [2] He enquires what was further to be done: *Why hast thou sent me?* that is, "What other method shall I take in pursuance of my commission?"

JAMIESON, FAUSSET, BROWN

ancient Egypt, like modern China, was principally governed by the stick" [TAYLOR]. "The mode of beating was by the offender being laid flat on the ground and generally held by the hands and feet while the chastisement was administered" [WILKINSON]. (Deut. 25:2). A picture representing the Hebrews on a brick-field, exactly as described in this chapter, was found in an Egyptian tomb at Thebes.

20, 21. they met Moses. . . . The Lord look upon you, and judge—Thus the deliverer of Israel found that this patriotic interference did, in the first instance, only aggravate the evil he wished to remove, and that instead of receiving the gratitude, he was loaded with the reproaches of his countrymen. But as the greatest darkness is immediately before the dawn, so the people of God are often plunged into the deepest affliction when on the eve of their deliverance; and so it was in this case.

ADAM CLARKE

feel the importance of eternal things, to idleness or a disregard of their secular concerns. Strange that they cannot see there is a medium! He who has commanded them to be "diligent in business" has also commanded them to be "fervent in spirit, serving the Lord."

19. *Did see that they were in evil case.* They saw that they could neither expect justice nor mercy; that their deliverance was very doubtful, and their case almost hopeless.

21. *The Lord look upon you, and judge.* These were hasty and unkind expressions; but the afflicted must be allowed the privilege of complaining. *Put a sword in their hand.* Given them a pretense which they had not before, to oppress us even unto death.

22. *And Moses returned unto the Lord.* This may imply, either that there was a particular place into which Moses ordinarily went to commune with Jehovah; or it may mean that kind of turning of heart and affection to God which every pious mind feels itself disposed to practice in any time or place. The old adage will apply here: "A praying heart never lacks a praying place." *Lord, wherefore hast thou so evil entreated this people?* It is certain that in this address Moses uses great plainness of speech. Whether the offspring of a testy impatience and undue familiarity, or of strong faith which gave him more than ordinary access to the throne of his gracious Sovereign, it would be difficult to say. The latter appears to be the most probable, as we do not find, from the succeeding chapter, that God was displeased with his freedom; we may therefore suppose that it was kept within due bounds and that the principles and motives were all pure and good. However, it should be noted that such freedom of speech with the Most High should never be used but on very special occasions and then only by His extraordinary messengers.

23. *He hath done evil to this people.* Their misery is increased instead of being diminished. *Neither hast thou delivered thy people at all.* The marginal reading is both literal and correct: "And delivering thou hast not delivered." Thou hast begun the work by giving us counsels and a commission, but Thou hast not brought the people from under their bondage.

MATTHEW HENRY

CHAPTER 6

Verses 1-9

Here, I. God silences Moses's complaints with the assurance of success in this negotiation, repeating the promise made him in *ch.* iii. 20, *After that, he will let you go. Then the Lord said unto Moses*, for the quieting of his mind, "*Now shalt thou see what I will do to Pharaoh*" (*v.* 1). See Ps. xii. 5, *Now will I arise.* Note, Man's extremity is God's opportunity of helping and saving. God takes the work into his own hands. *With a strong hand*, that is, being forced to it by a strong hand, *he shall let them go.*

II. He gives him further instructions, that both he and the people of Israel might be encouraged to hope for a glorious issue of this affair. Take comfort,

1. From God's name, Jehovah, *v.* 2, 3. God would now be known by his name *Jehovah*, that is, (1) A God performing what he had begun. (2) A God perfecting what he had begun. In the history of the creation, God is never called Jehovah till the heavens and the earth were finished, Gen. ii. 4. When the salvation of the saints is completed in eternal life, then he will be known by his name Jehovah (Rev. xxii. 13); in the meantime they shall find him, for their strength and support, *El-shaddai, a God all-sufficient*, a God that is enough.

JAMIESON, FAUSSET, BROWN

CHAPTER 6

Vss. 1-13. RENEWAL OF THE PROMISE. **1. Lord said unto Moses**—The Lord, who is long-suffering and indulgent to the errors and infirmities of His people, made allowance for the mortification of Moses as the result of this first interview and cheered him with the assurance of a speedy and successful termination to his embassy.

2. And God spake unto Moses—For his further encouragement, there was made to him an emphatic repetition of the promise (ch. 3:20). **3. I . . . God Almighty**—All enemies must fall, all difficulties must vanish before My omnipotent power, and the patriarchs had abundant proofs of this. **but by my name,** etc.—rather, interrogatively, by My name Jehovah was I not known to them? Am not I, the Almighty God, who pledged My honor for the fulfilment of the covenant, also the self-existent God who lives to accomplish it? Rest assured, therefore, that I shall bring it to pass. This passage has occasioned much discussion; and it has been thought by many to intimate that as the name Jehovah was not known to the patriarchs, at least in the full bearing or practical experience of it, the honor of the disclosure was reserved to Moses, who was the first sent with a message in the name of Jehovah, and enabled to attest it by a series of public miracles.

ADAM CLARKE

CHAPTER 6

1. *With a strong hand. Yad chazakah*, the same verb which we translate "to harden"; see on chap. iv. 21. The *strong hand* here means sovereign power, suddenly and forcibly applied. God purposed to manifest His sovereign power in the sight of Pharaoh and the Egyptians; in consequence of which Pharaoh would manifest his power and authority as sovereign of Egypt, in dismissing and thrusting out the people.

2. *I am the Lord.* It should be, "I am JEHOVAH," and without this the reason of what is said in the third verse is not sufficiently obvious.

3. *By the name of God Almighty. El-Shaddai*, "God All-sufficient"; God the Dispenser or Pourer-out of gifts.

But by my name JEHOVAH was I not known to them. This passage has been a sort of *crux criticorum*, and has been variously explained. It is certain that the name Jehovah was in use long before the days of Ab.aham, see Gen. ii. 4, where the words *Jehovah Elohim* occur, as they do frequently afterwards; and see Gen. xv. 2, where Abraham expressly addresses Him by the name *Adonai Jehovah;* and see the seventh verse, where God reveals himself to Abraham by this very name: "And he said unto him, I am Jehovah, that brought thee out of Ur of the Chaldees." How then can it be said that by His name Jehovah He was not known unto them?

I believe the simple meaning is this, that though from the beginning the name Jehovah was known as one of the names of the Supreme Being, yet what it really implied they did not know. *El-Shaddai*, "God All-sufficient," they knew well by the continual provision He made for them and the constant protection He afforded them; but the name Jehovah is particularly to be referred to the accomplishment of promises already made; to the giving them a being, and

MATTHEW HENRY

2. From his covenant: *I have established my covenant, v.* 4. We may venture our all upon this bottom.

3. From his compassions (*v.* 5): *I have heard the groaning of the children of Israel.*

4. From his present resolutions, *v.* 6–8. *I will bring you out. I will rid you. I will redeem you. I will bring you into the land of Canaan,* and *I will give it to you.*

5. From his gracious intentions in all these: (1) He intended their happiness: *I will take you to me for a people.* (2) He intended his own glory: *You shall know that I am the Lord.* But regardless of God's promises (*v.* 9): *They hearkened not unto Moses for anguish of spirit.* By indulging ourselves in discontent and fretfulness, we deprive ourselves of the comfort we might have both from God's word and from his providence, and must thank ourselves if we go comfortless.

Verses 10–13

I. God sends Moses the second time to Pharaoh (*v.* 11) upon the same errand as before, to command him, at his peril, that he *let the children of Israel go.*

II. Moses makes objections. He pleads, 1. The unlikelihood of Pharaoh's hearing: "*Behold the children of Israel have not hearkened unto me*; they give no heed, no credit, to what I have said; how then can I expect that Pharaoh should hear me?" If God's professing people hear not his messengers, how can it be thought that his professed enemy should? 2. He pleads the unreadiness and infirmity of his own speaking: *I am of uncircumcised lips.* To this objection God had given a sufficient answer for the sufficiency of grace can supply the defects of nature at any time.

III. God again joins Aaron in commission with Moses, and puts an end to the dispute by interposing his own authority, and giving them both a solemn charge. Moses himself has need to be charged, and so has Timothy, 1 Tim. vi. 13; 2 Tim. iv. 1.

Verses 14–30

I. We have here a genealogy, not an endless one, such as the apostle condemns (1 Tim. i. 4), for it ends in those two great patriots Moses and Aaron, and comes in here to show that they were Israelites, bone of their bone and flesh of their flesh whom they were sent to deliver. The heads of the houses of three of the tribes are here named, agreeing with the accounts we had, Gen. xlvi. Dr. Lightfoot thinks that Reuben, Simeon, and Levi, are thus dignified here by themselves because they were left under marks of infamy by their dying father, and therefore Moses would put this particular honour upon them, to magnify God's mercy in their repentance and remission. The two former seem rather to be mentioned only for the sake of a third, which was Levi, from whom Moses and Aaron descended, and all the priests of the Jewish church. Observe here, 1. That Kohath, from whom Moses and Aaron, and all the priests, derived their pedigree, was a younger son of Levi, *v.* 16. 2. That Aaron married Elisheba, daughter of Amminadab, one of the chief of the fathers of the tribe of Judah; for the tribes of Levi and Judah often intermarried, *v.* 23.

II. In the close of the chapter Moses returns to his narrative, from which he had broken off somewhat abruptly (*v.* 13), and repeats, 1. The charge God had given him to deliver his message to Pharaoh (*v.* 29): *Speak all that I say unto thee,* as a faithful ambassador. 2. His objection against it, *v.* 30. Note, Those that have at any time spoken unadvisedly with their lips ought often to reflect upon it with regret, as Moses seems to do here.

JAMIESON, FAUSSET, BROWN

9-11. Moses spake so unto the children of Israel—The increased severities inflicted on the Israelites seem to have so entirely crushed their spirits, as well as irritated them, that they refused to listen to any more communications (ch. 14:12). Even the faith of Moses himself was faltering; and he would have abandoned the enterprise in despair had he not received a positive command from God to revisit the people without delay, and at the same time renew their demand on the king in a more decisive and peremptory tone. **12. how then shall . . . who am of uncircumcised lips?**—A metaphorical expression among the Hebrews, who, taught to look on the circumcision of any part as denoting perfection, signified its deficiency or unsuitableness by uncircumcision. The words here express how painfully Moses felt his want of utterance or persuasive oratory. He seems to have fallen into the same deep despondency as his brethren, and to be shrinking with nervous timidity from a difficult, if not desperate, cause. If he had succeeded so ill with the people, whose dearest interests were all involved, what better hope could he entertain of his making more impression on the heart of a king elated with pride and strong in the possession of absolute power? How strikingly was the indulgent forbearance of God displayed towards His people amid all their backwardness to hail His announcement of approaching deliverance! No perverse complaints or careless indifference on their part retarded the development of His gracious purposes. On the contrary, here, as generally, the course of His providence is slow in the infliction of judgments, while it moves more quickly, as it were, when misery is to be relieved or benefits conferred.

14-30. THE GENEALOGY OF MOSES. **14. These be the heads of their fathers' houses**—chiefs or governors of their houses. The insertion of this genealogical table in this part of the narrative was intended to authenticate the descent of Moses and Aaron. Both of them were commissioned to act so important a part in the events transacted in the court of Egypt and afterwards elevated to so high offices in the government and Church of God, that it was of the utmost importance that their lineage should be accurately traced. Reuben and Simeon being the oldest of Jacob's sons, a passing notice is taken of them, and then the historian advances to the enumeration of the principal persons in the house of Levi. **20. Amram took him Jochebed his father's sister to wife**—The *Septuagint* and *Syriac* versions render it his cousin. **23. Elisheba**—i.e., Elizabethan. These minute particulars recorded of the family of Aaron, while he has passed over his own, indicate the real modesty of Moses. An ambitious man or an impostor would have acted in a different manner.

ADAM CLARKE

thus bringing them into existence, which could not have been done in the order of His providence sooner than here specified. This name, therefore, in its power and significancy was not known unto them; nor fully known unto their descendants till the deliverance from Egypt and the settlement in the Promised Land.

4. *I have also established my covenant.* I have now fully purposed to give present effect to all My engagements with your fathers in behalf of their posterity.

6. *Say unto the children of Israel, I am the Lord, and I will bring you out.* This confirms the explanation given of v. 3.

7. *I will take you to me for a people.* This was precisely the covenant that He had made with Abraham. See Gen. xvii. 7, and the notes there. *And ye shall know that I am the Lord your God.* By thus fulfilling My promises ye shall know what is implied in My name. See on v. 3.

8. *Which I did swear.* "I have lifted up my hand." The usual mode of making an appeal to God, and hence considered to be a form of swearing. It is thus that Isa. lxii. 8 is to be understood: "The Lord hath sworn by his right hand, and by the arm of his strength."

9. *But they hearkened not.* Their bondage was become so extremely oppressive that they had lost all hope of ever being redeemed from it. *Anguish of spirit. Kotzer ruach,* "shortness of spirit or breath." The words signify that their labor was so continual and their bondage so cruel and oppressive that they had scarcely time to breathe.

12. *Uncircumcised lips?* The word *aral,* which we translate *uncircumcised,* seems to signify anything exuberant or superfluous. The word must refer to some natural impediment in his speech; and probably means a want of distinct and ready utterance, either occasioned by some defect in the organs of speech or impaired knowledge of the Egyptian language after an absence of forty years.

14. *These be the heads.* The "chiefs" or "captains." The following genealogy was simply intended to show that Moses and Aaron came in a direct line from Abraham, and to ascertain the time of Israel's deliverance. The whole account from this verse to v. 26 is a sort of parenthesis, and does not belong to the narration; and what follows from v. 28 is a recapitulation of what was spoken in the preceding chapters.

20. *His father's sister. Dodatho.* The true meaning of this word is uncertain. Parkhurst observes that *dod* signifies "uncle" in 1 Sam. x. 14; Lev. x. 4, and frequently elsewhere. It signifies also an "uncle's son"; compare Jer. xxxii. 8 with v. 12, where the Vulgate renders *dodi* by "my paternal cousin"; and in Amos vi. 10, for *dodo,* the Targum has "his near relation." So the Vulgate, "his relative," and the Septuagint, "those of their household." The best critics suppose that Jochebed was the cousin-german of Amram, and not his aunt. *Bare him Aaron and Moses.* The Samaritan, Septuagint, Syriac, and one Hebrew MS. add, "And Miriam their sister."

21. *Korah.* Though he became a rebel against God and Moses (see Num. xvi. 1, etc.), yet Moses, in his great impartiality, inserts his name among those of his other progenitors.

22. *Uzziel.* He is called Aaron's uncle, Lev. x. 4.

23. *Elisheba.* The oath of the Lord. It is the same name as Elizabeth, so very common among Christians. She was of the royal tribe of Judah, and was sister to Nahshon, one of the princes; see Num. ii. 3. *Eleazar.* He succeeded to the high priesthood on the death of his father, Aaron, Num. xx. 25, etc.

25. *Phinehas.* Of the celebrated act of this person and the most honorable grant made to him and his posterity, see Num. xxv. 7-13.

26. *According to their armies.* Their "battalions"—regularly arranged troops.

28. *And it came to pass.* Here the seventh chapter should commence, as there is a complete ending of the sixth with v. 27, and the thirtieth verse of this chapter is intimately connected with the first verse of the succeeding.

MATTHEW HENRY

CHAPTER 7

Verses 1–7

Here, I. God encourages Moses to go to Pharaoh. 1. He clothes him with great power and authority (*v.* 1): *I have made thee a god to Pharaoh*; that is, my representative in this affair, as magistrates are called *gods*, because they are God's vicegerents. He was authorized to speak and act in God's name and stead. Moses was a god, but he was only a *made* god, not essentially one by nature; he was no god but by commission. He was a god, but he was a god only to Pharaoh; the living and true God is a God to all the world.

2. He again nominates him an assistant, his brother Aaron, a notable spokesman: "He shall be *thy prophet.* Thou shalt, as a god, inflict and remove the plagues, and Aaron, as a prophet, shall denounce them, and threaten Pharaoh with them." 3. He tells him that Pharaoh would not hearken to him, and yet the work should be done at last. The Egyptians, who would not know the Lord, should be made to know him.

II. Moses and Aaron apply themselves to their work without further objection: *They did as the Lord commanded them, v.* 6. Their obedience was celebrated by the Psalmist (Ps. cv. 28), *They rebelled not against his word*, namely, Moses and Aaron, whom he mentions, *v.* 26. Thus Jonah, though at first he was very averse, at length went to Nineveh.

Verses 8–13

The first time that Moses made his application to Pharaoh, he produced his instructions only; now he is directed to produce his credentials, and does accordingly. 1. Pharaoh will say, *Show a miracle*; not with any desire to be convinced, but with the hope that none will be wrought. 2. Orders are therefore given to turn the rod into a serpent, according to the instructions, *ch.* iv. 3.

Aaron cast his rod to the ground, and instantly it became a serpent, *v.* 10. This was proper, not only to affect Pharaoh with wonder, but to strike a terror upon him.

3. This miracle, though too plain to be denied, is enervated, and the conviction of it taken off, by the magicians' imitation of it, *v.* 11, 12. Moses had been originally instructed in the learning of the Egyptians, and was suspected to have improved himself in magical arts in his long

JAMIESON, FAUSSET, BROWN

CHAPTER 7

VSS. 1-25. SECOND INTERVIEW WITH PHARAOH. **1. the Lord said unto Moses**—He is here encouraged to wait again on the king—not, however, as formerly, in the attitude of a humble suppliant, but now armed with credentials as God's ambassador, and to make his demand in a tone and manner which no earthly monarch or court ever witnessed. **I have made thee a god**—made, i.e., set, appointed; "a god," i.e., he was to act in this business as God's representative, to act and speak in His name and to perform things beyond the ordinary course of nature. The Orientals familiarly say of a man who is eminently great or wise, "he is a god" among men. **Aaron thy brother shall be thy prophet**—i.e., interpreter or spokesman. The one was to be the vicegerent of God, and the other must be considered the speaker throughout all the ensuing scenes, even though his name is not expressly mentioned. **3. I will harden Pharaoh's heart**—This would be the *result.* But the divine message would be the *occasion,* not the *cause* of the king's impenitent obduracy. **4, 5. I may lay mine hand upon Egypt,** etc.—The succession of terrible judgments with which the country was about to be scourged would fully demonstrate the supremacy of Israel's God. **7. Moses was fourscore years**—This advanced age was a pledge that they had not been readily betrayed into a rash or hazardous enterprise, and that under its attendant infirmities they could not have carried through the work on which they were entering had they not been supported by a divine hand. **9. When Pharaoh shall speak unto you,** etc.—The king would naturally demand some evidence of their having been sent from God; and as he would expect the ministers of his own gods to do the same works, the contest, in the nature of the case, would be one of miracles. Notice has already been taken of the rod of Moses (ch. 4:2), but rods were carried also by all nobles and official persons in the court of Pharaoh. It was an Egyptian custom, and the rods were symbols of authority or rank. Hence God commanded His servants to use a rod.

10. Aaron cast down his rod before Pharaoh, etc.—It is to be presumed that Pharaoh had demanded a proof of their divine mission.

11. Then Pharaoh also called the wise men and the sorcerers, etc.—His object in calling them was to ascertain whether this doing of Aaron's was really a work of divine power or merely a feat of magical art. The magicians of Egypt in modern times have been long celebrated adepts in charming serpents, and particularly by pressing the nape of the neck, they throw them into a kind of catalepsy, which renders them stiff and immovable—thus seeming to change them into a rod. They conceal the serpent about their persons, and by acts of legerdemain produce it from their dress, stiff and straight as a rod. Just the same trick was played off by their ancient predecessors, the most renowned of whom, Jannes and Jambres (II Tim. 3:8), were called in on this occasion. They had time after the summons to make suitable preparations—and so it appears they succeeded by their "enchantments" in practising an illusion on the senses.

ADAM CLARKE

CHAPTER 7

1. *I have made thee a god.* At thy word every plague shall come, and at thy command each shall be removed. Thus Moses must have appeared as a god to Pharaoh. *Shall be thy prophet.* Shall receive the word from thy mouth, and communicate it to the Egyptian king, v. 2.

3. *I will harden Pharaoh's heart.* I will permit his stubbornness and obstinacy still to remain, that I may have the greater opportunity to multiply My wonders in the land, that the Egyptians may know that I only am Jehovah, the self-existent God.

5. *And bring out the children of Israel.* Pharaoh's obstinacy was either caused or permitted in mercy to the Egyptians, that he and his magicians being suffered to oppose Moses and Aaron to the uttermost of their power, the Israelites might be brought out of Egypt in so signal a manner, in spite of all the opposition of the Egyptians, their king, and their gods, that Jehovah might appear to be "All-mighty" and "All-sufficient."

7. *Moses was fourscore years old.* He was forty years old when he went to Midian, and he had tarried forty years in Midian (see chap. ii. 11 and Acts vii. 30); and from this verse it appears that Aaron was three years older than Moses. We have already seen that Miriam, their sister, was older than either, chap. ii. 4.

9. *Shew a miracle for you.* A miracle, *mopheth,* signifies an effect produced in nature which is opposed to its laws, or such as its powers are inadequate to produce. As Moses and Aaron professed to have a divine mission, and to come to Pharaoh on the most extraordinary occasion, making a most singular and unprecedented demand, it was natural to suppose, if Pharaoh should even give them an audience, that he would require them to give him some proof by an extraordinary sign that their pretensions to such a divine mission were well-founded and incontestable. For it appears to have ever been the sense of mankind that he who has a divine mission to effect some extraordinary purpose can give a supernatural proof that he has got this extraordinary commission. *Take thy rod.* This rod, whether a common staff, an ensign of office, or a shepherd's crook, was now consecrated for the purpose of working miracles; and is indifferently called the rod of God, the rod of Moses, and the rod of Aaron. God gave it the miraculous power, and Moses and Aaron used it.

10. *It became a serpent. Tannin.* What kind of serpent is here intended, learned men are not agreed. From the manner in which the original word is used in Ps. lxxiv. 13; Isa. xxvii. 1; li. 9; Job vii. 12, some very large creature, either aquatic or amphibious, is probably meant; some have thought that the crocodile, a well-known Egyptian animal, is here intended. In chap. iv. 3 it is said that this rod was changed into a "serpent," but the original word there is *nachash,* and here *tannin,* the same word which we translate "whale," Gen. i. 21.

11. *Pharaoh . . . called the wise men. Chacamim,* the men of learning. *Sorcerers, cashshephim,* those who "reveal" hidden things. *Magicians, chartummey,* "decipherers" of abstruse writings. *They also did in like manner with their enchantments.* The word *lahatim,* comes from *lahat,* "to burn, to set on fire"; and probably signifies such incantations as required lustral fires, sacrifices, fumigations, burning of incense, aromatic and odoriferous drugs, as the means of evoking departed spirits or assistant demons, by whose ministry, it is probable, the magicians in question wrought some of their deceptive miracles. There can be no doubt that real serpents were produced by the magicians. On this subject there are two opinions: *First,* That the serpents were such as they, either by juggling or sleight of hand, had brought to the place, and had secreted till the time of exhibition, as our common conjurers do in the public fairs, etc. *Secondly,* That the serpents were brought by the ministry of a familiar spirit, which, by the magic flames already referred to, they had evoked for the purpose. Both these opinions admit the serpents to be real and no illusion of the sight. The first opinion appears to me insufficient to account for the phenomena

MATTHEW HENRY

retirement; the magicians are therefore sent for, to vie with him. Their rods became serpents, some think, by the power of God, for the hardening of Pharaoh's heart; others think, by the power of evil angels. Note, God suffers the lying spirit to do strange things, that the faith of some may be tried and manifested (Deut. xiii. 3; 1 Cor. xi. 19). In this contest, Moses plainly gains the victory. The serpent which Aaron's rod was turned into swallowed up the others, which was sufficient to have convinced Pharaoh on which side the right lay. But Pharaoh was not wrought upon by this. The magicians having produced serpents, he had this to say, that the case between them and Moses was disputable.

Verses 14–25

Here is the first of the ten plagues, the turning of the water into blood, which was, 1. A dreadful plague, and very grievous. Fish was food (Num. xi. 5), but the changing of the waters was the death of the fish; it was a pestilence in that element (*v.* 21): *The fish died. He slew their fish*; and when another destruction of Egypt, long afterwards, is threatened, the disappointment of those that make sluices and ponds for fish is particularly noticed, Isa. xix. 10. It was a righteous plague, and justly inflicted upon the Egyptians. For, (1) Nilus, the river of Egypt, was their idol; they and their land derived so much benefit from it that they served and worshipped it more than the Creator. God punished them, and turned that into blood which they had turned into a god. Note, That creature which we idolize God justly removes from us, or embitters to us. He makes that a scourge to us which we make a competitor with him. Egypt had a great dependence upon their river (Zech. xiv. 18), so that in smiting the river they were warned of the destruction of all the productions of their country, till it came at last to their first-born; and this red river proved a direful omen of the ruin of Pharaoh and all his forces in the Red Sea. One of the first miracles Moses wrought was turning water into blood, but one of the first miracles our Lord Jesus wrought was turning water into wine; for the law was given by Moses, and it was a dispensation of death and terror; but grace and truth, which, like wine, make glad the heart, came by Jesus Christ.

I. Moses is directed to give Pharaoh warning of this plague. "Pharaoh's heart is hardened (*v.* 14), therefore go and try what this will do to soften it," *v.* 15. Moses is directed to meet him by the river's brink, whither God foresaw he would come in the morning to pay his morning devotions to the river. There Moses must be ready to give him a new summons to surrender, and, in case of a refusal, to tell him of the judgment that was coming upon that very river on the banks of which they were now standing. Notice is thus given him of it beforehand, that they might have no colour to say it was a chance, or to attribute it to any other cause, but that it might appear to be done by the power of the God of the Hebrews. That God warns before he wounds; for he is *long-suffering, not willing that any should perish, but that all should come to repentance.*

II. Aaron (who carried the mace) is directed to summon the plague by smiting the river with his rod, *v.* 19, 20. See here the almighty power of God. Every creature is that to us which he makes it to be, water or blood. See the mutability of all things under the sun, and what changes we may meet with in them. A river, at the best, is transient; but divine justice can quickly make it malignant. See what mischievous work sin makes. If the things that have been our comforts prove our crosses, we must thank ourselves: it is sin that turns our waters into blood.

III. Pharaoh endeavours to confront the miracle, because he resolves not to humble himself under the plague. He sends for the magicians, and, by God's permission, they ape the miracle with their enchantments (*v.* 22), and this serves Pharaoh for an excuse not to set his heart to this also (*v.* 23), and a pitiful excuse it was. Could they have turned the river of blood into water again, this would have been something to the purpose; then they would have proved their power, and Pharaoh would have been obliged to them as his benefactors.

IV. The Egyptians, in the meantime, are seeking for relief against the plague, digging round about the river for water to drink, *v.* 24. Probably they found some, with much ado, God remembering mercy in the midst of wrath; for he is full of compassion, and would not let the subjects smart too much for the obstinacy of their prince.

V. The plague continued seven days (*v.* 25), and, in all that time, Pharaoh's proud heart would not let him so much as desire Moses to intercede for the removal of it.

JAMIESON, FAUSSET, BROWN

12. but Aaron's rod swallowed up their rods. This was what they could not be prepared for, and the discomfiture appeared in the loss of their rods, which were probably real serpents.

14. Pharaoh's heart is hardened—Whatever might have been his first impressions, they were soon dispelled; and when he found his magicians making similar attempts, he concluded that Aaron's affair was a magical deception, the secret of which was not known to his wise men. **15. Get thee unto Pharaoh**—Now began those appalling miracles of judgment by which the God of Israel, through His ambassadors, proved His sole and unchallengeable supremacy over all the gods of Egypt, and which were the natural phenomena of Egypt, at an unusual season, and in a miraculous degree of intensity. The court of Egypt, whether held at Rameses, or Memphis, or Tanis in the field of Zoan (Ps. 78:12), was the scene of those extraordinary transactions, and Moses must have resided during that terrible period in the immediate neighborhood. **in the morning; lo, he goeth out unto the water, etc.**—for the purpose of ablutions or devotions perhaps; for the Nile was an object of superstitious reverence, the patron deity of the country. It might be that Moses had been denied admission into the palace; but be that as it may, the river was to be the subject of the first plague, and therefore he was ordered to repair to its banks with the miracle-working rod, now to be raised, not in demonstration, but in judgment, if the refractory spirit of the king should still refuse consent to Israel's departure for their sacred rites. **17-21. Aaron lifted up the rod and smote the waters,** etc.—Whether the water was changed into real blood, or only the appearance of it (and Omnipotence could effect the one as easily as the other), this was a severe calamity. How great must have been the disappointment and disgust throughout the land when the river became of a blood-red color, of which they had a national abhorrence; their favorite beverage became a nauseous draught, and the fish, which formed so large an article of food, were destroyed. The immense scale on which the plague was inflicted is seen by its extending to "the streams," or branches of the Nile—to the "rivers," the canals, the "ponds" and "pools," that which is left after an overflow, the reservoirs, and the many domestic vessels in which the Nile water was kept to filter. And accordingly the sufferings of the people from thirst must have been severe. Nothing could more humble the pride of Egypt than this dishonor brought on their national god. **22. The magicians . . . did so with their enchantments,** etc.—Little or no pure water could be procured, and therefore their imitation must have been on a small scale—the only drinkable water available being dug among the sands. It must have been on a sample or specimen of water dyed red with some coloring matter. But it was sufficient to serve as a pretext or command for the king to turn unmoved and go to his house.

ADAM CLARKE

of the case referred to.

12. *Aaron's rod swallowed up their rods.* As Egypt was remarkably addicted to magic, sorcery, etc., it was necessary that God should permit Pharaoh's wise men to act to the utmost of their skill in order to imitate the work of God, that His superiority might be clearly seen and His powerful working incontestably ascertained; and this was fully done when Aaron's rod swallowed up their rods.

13. *And he hardened Pharaoh's heart.* "And the heart of Pharaoh was hardened," the identical words which in v. 22 are thus translated, and which should have been rendered in the same way here, lest the hardening, which was evidently the effect of his own obstinate shutting of his eyes against the truth, should be attributed to God. See on chap. iv. 21.

14. *Pharaoh's heart is hardened. Cabed,* is become "heavy" or "stupid"; he receives no conviction, notwithstanding the clearness of the light which shines upon him.

15. *Lo, he goeth out unto the water.* Probably for the purpose of bathing, or of performing some religious ablution.

17. *Behold, I will smite.* Here commences the account of the ten plagues which were inflicted on the Egyptians by Moses and Aaron, by the command and through the power of God.

19. *That there may be blood . . . both in vessels of wood, and in vessels of stone.* Not only the Nile itself was to be thus changed into blood in all its branches, and the canals issuing from it, but all the water of lakes, ponds, and reservoirs was to undergo a similar change. And this was to extend even to the water already brought into their houses for culinary and other domestic purposes.

The First Plague— The Waters Turned into Blood

20. *All the waters . . . were turned to blood.* Not merely in appearance, but in reality; for these changed waters became corrupt so that even the fish that were in the river died; and the smell became highly offensive, so that the waters could not be drunk, v. 21.

22. *And the magicians . . . did so.* But if all the water in Egypt was turned into blood by Moses, where did the magicians get the water which they changed into blood? This question is answered in verse 24. The Egyptians digged round about the river for water to drink, and it seems that the water obtained by this means was not bloody like that in the river; on this water, therefore, the magicians might operate. Again, though a general commission was given to Moses, not only to turn the waters of the river (Nile) into blood, but also those of their streams, rivers, ponds, and pools, yet it seems pretty clear from verse 20 that he did not proceed thus far, at least in the first instance; for it is there stated that only the waters of the river were turned into blood. Afterwards the plague doubtless became general.

The plague of the bloody waters may be considered as a display of retributive justice against the Egyptians, for the murderous decree which enacted that all the male children of the Israelites should be drowned in that river, the waters of which, so necessary to their support and life, were now rendered not only insalubrious but deadly, by being turned into blood. As it is well known that the Nile was a chief object of Egyptian idolatry (see on v. 15) and that annually they sacrificed a girl, or as others say, both a boy and a girl, to this river, in gratitude for the benefits received from it, God might have designed this plague as a punishment for such cruelty; and the contempt poured upon this object of their adoration, by turning its waters into blood and rendering them fetid and corrupt, must have had a direct tendency to correct their idolatrous notions and lead them to acknowledge the power and authority of the true God.

25. *And seven days were fulfilled.* So we learn that this plague continued at least a whole week.

MATTHEW HENRY

CHAPTER 8

Verses 1–15

Pharaoh is here first threatened and then plagued with frogs, as afterwards, in this chapter, with lice and flies, little despicable inconsiderable animals, and yet by their vast numbers rendered sore plagues to the Egyptians. Some have thought that the power of God is shown as much in the making of an ant as in the making of an elephant; so is his providence in serving his own purposes by the least creatures as effectually as by the strongest, that he might humble Pharaoh's pride, and chastise his insolence. What a mortification must it needs be to this haughty monarch to see himself brought to his knees, and forced to submit by such despicable means! As to the plague of frogs we may observe,

I. How it was threatened. Moses is here directed to give notice to Pharaoh of another judgment coming upon him, in case he continue obstinate. Note, God does not punish men for sin unless they persist in it. The plague threatened, in case of refusal, was formidably extensive.

II. How it was inflicted. Pharaoh not being at all inclined to yield to the summons, Aaron is ordered to give the signal of battle. Shoals of frogs invade the land, and the Egyptians cannot check their progress. Compare this with that prophecy of an army of locusts and caterpillars, Joel ii. 2, &c.; and see Isa. xxxiv. 16, 17.

III. How the magicians were permitted to imitate it, *v.* 7. They also brought up frogs, but could not remove those that God sent. The magicians intended to deceive, but God intended by them to destroy those that would be deceived.

IV. How Pharaoh relented under this plague: it was the first time he did so, *v.* 8. He begs of Moses to intercede for the removal of the frogs, and promises fair that he will let the people go.

V. How Moses fixes the time with Pharaoh, and then prevails with God by prayer for the removal of the frogs. Pharaoh sets the time for *to-morrow, v.* 10. In answer to the prayer of Moses, the frogs that came up one day perished the next, or the next but one.

VI. What was the issue of this plague (*v.* 15): *When Pharaoh saw there was a respite,* without considering either what he had lately felt or what he had reason to fear, he hardened his heart. Note, 1. Till the heart is renewed by the grace of God, the impressions made by the force of affliction do not abide; the convictions wear off, and the promises that were extorted are forgotten. 2. God's patience is shamefully abused by impenitent sinners. He graciously allows them a truce, in order to the making of their peace. They take that opportunity to rally again the baffled forces of an obstinate infidelity. See Eccles. viii. 11; Ps. lxxviii. 34, &c.

JAMIESON, FAUSSET, BROWN

CHAPTER 8

Vss. 1-15. PLAGUE OF FROGS. **1. the Lord spake unto Moses, Go unto Pharaoh**—The duration of the first plague for a whole week must have satisfied all that it was produced not by any accidental causes, but by the agency of omnipotent power. As a judgment of God, however, it produced no good effect, and Moses was commanded to wait on the king and threaten him, in the event of his continued obstinacy, with the infliction of a new and different plague. As Pharaoh's answer is not given, it may be inferred to have been unfavorable, for the rod was again raised. **2. I will smite all thy borders with frogs**—Those animals, though the natural spawn of the river, and therefore objects familiar to the people, were on this occasion miraculously multiplied to an amazing extent, and it is probable that the ova of the frogs, which had been previously deposited in the mire and marshes, were miraculously brought to perfection at once. **3. bedchamber . . . bed**—mats strewed on the floor as well as more sumptuous divans of the rich. **ovens**—holes made in the ground and the sides of which are plastered with mortar. **kneading-troughs**—Those used in Egypt were bowls of wicker or rush work. What must have been the state of the people when they could find no means of escape from the cold, damp touch and unsightly presence of the frogs, as they alighted on every article and vessel of food!

5, 6. Stretch forth thine hand with thy rod over the streams, etc.—The miracle consisted in the reptiles leaving their marshes at the very time he commanded them. **7. the magicians did so with their enchantments**—required no great art to make the offensive reptiles appear on any small spot of ground. What they undertook to do already existed in abundance all around. They would better have shown their power by removing the frogs. **8. Pharaoh called, . . . Intreat the Lord, that he may take away the frogs from me**—The frog, which was now used as an instrument of affliction, whether from reverence or abhorrence, was an object of national superstition with the Egyptians, the god Ptha being represented with a frog's head. But the vast numbers, together with their stench, made them an intolerable nuisance so that the king was so far humbled as to promise that, if Moses would intercede for their removal, he would consent to the departure of Israel, and in compliance with this appeal, they were withdrawn at the very hour named by the monarch himself. But many, while suffering the consequences of their sins, make promises of amendment and obedience which they afterwards forget; and so Pharaoh, when he saw there was a respite, was again hardened.

ADAM CLARKE

CHAPTER 8

THE SECOND PLAGUE—FROGS

1. *Let my people go.* God, in great mercy to Pharaoh and the Egyptians, gives them notice of the evils He intends to bring upon them if they continue in their obstinacy. Having had therefore, such warning, the evil might have been prevented by a timely humiliation and return to God.

2. *If thou refuse.* Nothing can be plainer than that Pharaoh had it still in his power to dismiss the people, and that his refusal was the mere effect of his own wilful obstinacy.

3. *The river shall bring forth frogs abundantly.* The river Nile, which was an object of their adoration, was here one of the instruments of their punishment. The expression *bring forth . . . abundantly* not only shows the vast numbers of those animals which should now infest the land, but it seems also to imply that all the spawn or ova of those animals which were already in the river and marshes should be brought miraculously to a state of perfection. We may suppose that the animals were already in an embryo existence, but multitudes of them would not have come to a state of perfection had it not been for this miraculous interference. This supposition will appear the more natural when it is considered that the Nile was remarkable for breeding frogs.

Into thine ovens. In various parts of the East, instead of what we call *ovens* they dig a hole in the ground, in which they insert a kind of earthen pot, which having sufficiently heated, they stick their cakes to the inside, and when baked remove them and supply their places with others, and so on. To find such places full of frogs when they came to heat them, in order to make their bread, must be both disgusting and distressing in the extreme.

5. *Stretch forth thine hand . . . over the streams, over the rivers.* The streams and rivers here may refer to the grand divisions of the Nile in the Lower Egypt, which were at least seven, and to the canals by which these were connected, as there were no other streams but what proceeded from this great river.

9. *Glory over me. Hithpaer alai.* These words have greatly puzzled commentators in general; and it is not easy to assign their true meaning. The Septuagint render the words thus: "Appoint unto me when I shall pray." The Vulgate is exactly the same; and in this sense almost all the versions understood this place. This countenances the conjectural emendation of Le Clerc, who, by the change of a single letter, reading *hithbaer* for *hithpaer,* gives the same sense as that in the ancient versions. This appears to be the genuine import of the words, and the sense taken in this way is strong and good. Nothing could be a fuller proof that this plague was supernatural than the circumstance of Pharaoh's being permitted to assign himself the time of its being removed, and its removal at the intercession of Moses according to that appointment. And this is the very use made of it by Moses himself, v. 10, when he says, "Be it according to thy word: that thou mayest know that there is none like unto the Lord our God."

14. *They gathered them together upon heaps.* The killing of the frogs was a mitigation of the punishment; but the leaving them to rot in the land was a continual proof that such a plague had taken place, and that the displeasure of the Lord still continued.

The conjecture of Calmet is at least rational: he supposes that the plague of flies originated from the plague of frogs; that the former deposited their ova in the putrid masses and that from these the innumerable swarms afterwards mentioned were hatched. In vindication of this supposition it may be observed that God never works a miracle when the end can be accomplished by merely natural means; and in the operations of divine providence we always find that the greatest number of effects possible are accomplished by the fewest causes. As, therefore, the natural means for this fourth plague had been miraculously provided by the second, the Divine Being had a right to use the instruments which He had already prepared.

MATTHEW HENRY

Verses 16–19

Here is a short account of the plague of lice.

I. How this plague of lice was inflicted on the Egyptians, *v.* 16, 17. The frogs were produced out of the waters, but these lice out of *the dust of the earth.* The second woe was past, but behold the third woe came very quickly.

II. How the magicians were baffled by it, *v.* 18. They attempted to imitate it, but they could not.

This forced them to confess themselves overpowered: *This is the finger of God* (*v.* 19). Sooner or later God will extort, even from his enemies, an acknowledgment of his own sovereignty and overruling power. It is certain they must all (as we say) knock under at last, as Julian the apostate did, when his dying lips **confessed,** *Thou hast overcome me, O thou Galilean!* God will not only be too hard for all opposers, but will force them to own it.

III. How Pharaoh, notwithstanding this, was made more and more obstinate (*v.* 19). Note, Those that are not made better by God's word and providences are commonly made worse by them.

Verses 20–32

Here is the story of the plague of flies.

I. How it was threatened, like that of frogs, before it was inflicted. Moses is directed (*v.* 20) to rise early in the morning, to meet Pharaoh when he came forth to the water. Moses must *stand before Pharaoh,* proud as he was, and tell him that which was in the highest degree humbling, must challenge him (if he refused to release his captives) to engage with an army of flies, which would obey God's orders if Pharaoh would not.

II. How the Egyptians and the Hebrews were to be remarkably distinguished in this plague, *v.* 22, 23. Pharaoh must be made to know that *God is the Lord in the midst of the earth*; and by this it will be known beyond dispute. Observe how it is repeated: *I will put a division between my people and thy people, v.* 23. Note, The Lord knows those that are his, and will make it appear, perhaps in this world, certainly in the other, that he has set them apart for himself. A day will come when you shall *return and discern between the righteous and the wicked* (Mal. iii. 18), *the sheep and the goats* (Matt. xxv. 32; Ezek. xxxiv. 17), though now intermixed.

III. How it was inflicted, the day after it was threatened: *There came a grievous swarm of flies* (*v.* 24).

JAMIESON, FAUSSET, BROWN

16-19. Plague of Lice. **16. smite the dust of the land,** etc.—Aaron's rod, by the direction of Moses, who was commanded by God, was again raised, and the land was filled with gnats, mosquitoes—that is the proper meaning of the original term. In ordinary circumstances they embitter life in Eastern countries, and therefore the *terrible* nature of this infliction on Egypt may be imagined when no precautions could preserve from their painful sting. The very smallness and insignificance of these fierce insects made them a dreadful scourge.

The magicians never attempted any imitation, and what neither the blood of the river nor the nuisance of the frogs had done, the visitation of this tiny enemy constrained them to acknowledge "this is the finger of God," properly "gods," for they spoke as heathens.

20-32. Plague of Flies. **20. Rise up early . . . Pharaoh; lo, he cometh forth to the water,** etc.—Pharaoh still appearing obdurate, Moses was ordered to meet him while walking on the banks of the Nile and repeat his request for the liberation of Israel, threatening in case of continued refusal to cover every house from the palace to the cottage with swarms of flies—while, as a proof of the power that accomplished this judgment, the land of Goshen should be exempted from the calamity. The appeal was equally vain as before, and the predicted evil overtook the country in the form of what was not "flies," such as we are accustomed to, but divers sorts of flies (Ps. 78:45), the gad-fly, the cockroach, the Egyptian beetle, for all these are mentioned by different writers. They are very destructive, some of them inflicting severe bites on animals, others destroying clothes, books, plants, every thing. The worship of flies, particularly of the beetle, was a prominent part of the religion of the ancient Egyptians. The employment of these winged deities to chastise them must have been painful and humiliating to the Egyptians while it must at the same time have strengthened the faith of the Israelites in the God of their fathers as the only object of worship.

ADAM CLARKE

The Third Plague—Lice

16. *Smite the dust of the land, that it may become lice.* If the vermin commonly designated by this name be intended, it must have been a very dreadful and afflicting plague to the Egyptians, and especially to their priests, who were obliged to shave the hair off every part of their bodies, and to wear a single tunic, that no vermin of this kind might be permitted to harbor about them.

The circumstance of their being *in* man and *in* beast agrees so well with the nature of the "tick" that I am ready to conclude this is the insect meant. This animal buries both its sucker and head equally in man or beast; and can with very great difficulty be extracted before it is grown to its proper size, and filled with the blood and juices of the animal on which it preys. When fully grown, it has a glossy black, oval body. Not only horses, cows, and sheep are infested with it in certain countries, but even the common people, especially those who labor in the field, in woods. I know no insect to which the Hebrew term so properly applies. This is the fixed, established insect, which will permit itself to be pulled in pieces rather than let go its hold; and this is literally "in man and in beast," burying its trunk and head in the flesh of both.

18. *The magicians did so.* That is, They tried the utmost of their skill, either to produce these insects or to remove this plague. *But they could not;* no juggling could avail here, because insects must be produced which would stick to and infix themselves in man and beast, which no kind of trick could possibly imitate; and to remove them, as some would translate the passage, was to their power equally impossible. If the magicians even acted by spiritual agents, we find from this case that these agents had assigned limits, beyond which they could not go; for every agent in the universe is acting under the direction or control of the Almighty.

19. *This is the finger of God.* That is, The power and skill of God are here evident. Probably before this the magicians supposed Moses and Aaron to be conjurers, like themselves; but now they are convinced that no man could do these miracles which these holy men did, unless God were with him. God permits evil spirits to manifest themselves in a certain way that men may see that there is a spiritual world and be on their guard against seduction. He at the same time shows that all these agents are under His control, that men may have confidence in His goodness and power.

The Fourth Plague—Flies

21. *Swarms of flies upon thee.* It is not easy to ascertain the precise meaning of the original word *hearob;* as the word comes from *arab,* he "mingled," it may be supposed to express a multitude of various sorts of insects. And if the conjecture be admitted that the putrid frogs became the occasion of this plague (different insects laying their eggs in the bodies of those dead animals, which would soon be hatched, see on verse 14), then the supposition that a multitude of different kinds of insects is meant will seem the more probable. Though the plague of the locusts was miraculous, yet God both brought it and removed it by natural means; see chap. x. 13-19.

22. *I will sever in that day. Hiphleythi* has been translated by some good critics, "I will miraculously separate"; so the Vulgate: "I will do a marvellous thing." And the Septuagint, "I will render illustrious" the land of Goshen in that day; and this He did, by exempting that land and its inhabitants, the Israelites, from the plagues by which He afflicted the land of Egypt.

23. *And I will put a division. Peduth,* "a redemption," *between my people and thy people,* God hereby showing that He had redeemed them from those plagues to which He had abandoned the others.

24. *The land was corrupted.* Everything was spoiled, and many of the inhabitants destroyed, being probably stung to death by these venomous insects. This seems to be intimated by the Psalmist, "He sent divers sorts of flies among them, which devoured them," Ps. lxxviii. 45.

25. *Sacrifice to your God in the land.* That

MATTHEW HENRY

IV. How Pharaoh, upon this attack, entered into a treaty with Moses and Aaron about a surrender of his captives: but observe with what reluctance he yields.

1. He is content they should sacrifice to their God, provided they would do it in the land of Egypt, *v.* 25. But Moses will not accept his concession; he cannot do it, *v.* 26.

He insists: *We will go three days' journey into the wilderness, v.* 27. Those that would offer an acceptable sacrifice to God must retire from the distractions of the world. Israel cannot keep the feast of the Lord either among the brick-kilns or among the flesh-pots of Egypt. Though they were in the utmost degree of slavery to Pharaoh, yet, in the worship of God, they must observe his commands and not Pharaoh's.

2. When this proposal is rejected, he consents for them to go into the wilderness, provided they do not go *very far away*. We observe here a struggle between Pharaoh's convictions and his corruptions; his convictions said, "Let them go"; his corruptions said, "Yet not very far away": but he sided with his corruptions against his convictions, and this was his ruin. This proposal Moses so far accepted as that he promised the removal of this plague upon it, *v.* 29.

The issue of all was that God graciously removed the plague (*v.* 30, 31), but Pharaoh perfidiously returned to his hardness, and *would not let the people go, v.* 32. His pride would not let him part with such a flower of his crown as his dominion over Israel was, nor his covetousness with such a branch of his revenue as their labours were.

JAMIESON, FAUSSET, BROWN

25-32. Pharaoh called for Moses, . . . and said, Go ye, sacrifice to your God in the land, etc.—Between impatient anxiety to be freed from this scourge and a reluctance on the part of the Hebrew bondsmen, the king followed the course of expediency; he proposed to let them free to engage in their religious rites within any part of the kingdom. But true to his instructions, Moses would accede to no such arrangement; he stated a most valid reason to show the danger of it; and the king having yielded so far as to allow them a brief holiday *across the border,* annexed to this concession a request that Moses would entreat with Jehovah for the removal of the plague.

He promised to do so, and it was removed the following day. But no sooner was the pressure over than the spirit of Pharaoh, like a bent bow, sprang back to its wonted obduracy, and, regardless of his promise, he refused to let the people depart.

ADAM CLARKE

is, Ye shall not leave Egypt, but I shall cause your worship to be tolerated here.

26. *We shall sacrifice the abomination of the Egyptians.* That is, The animals which they hold sacred, and will not permit to be slain, are those which our customs require us to sacrifice to our God; and should we do this in Egypt the people would rise in a mass, and stone us to death. Perhaps few people were more superstitious than the Egyptians. Almost every production of nature was an object of their religious worship: the sun, moon, planets, stars, the river Nile, animals of all sorts, from the human being to the monkey, dog, cat, and ibis, and even the onions and leeks which grew in their gardens. Jupiter was adored by them under the form of a ram, Apollo under the form of a crow, Bacchus under that of a goat, and Juno under that of a heifer.

27. *And sacrifice to the Lord . . . as he shall command us.* It is very likely that neither Moses nor Aaron knew as yet in what manner God would be worshipped; and they expected to receive a direct revelation from Him relative to this subject when they should come into the wilderness.

28. *I will let you go . . . only ye shall not go very far away.* Pharaoh relented because the hand of God was heavy upon him; but he was not willing to give up his gain. The Israelites were very profitable to him; they were slaves of the state, and their hard labor was very productive: hence he professed a willingness, first to tolerate their religion in the land (v. 25); or to permit them to go into the wilderness, so that they went not far away and would soon return. How ready is foolish man, when the hand of God presses him sore, to compound with his Maker! He will consent to give up some sins, provided God will permit him to keep others. *Intreat for me.* Exactly similar to the case of Simon Magus, who, like Pharaoh, fearing the divine judgments, begged an interest in the prayers of Peter, Acts viii. 24.

31. *The Lord did according to the word of Moses.* How powerful is prayer! God permits His servant to prescribe even the manner and time in which He shall work. *He removed the swarms.* Probably by means of a strong wind which swept them into the sea.

32. *Pharaoh hardened his heart at this time also.* See v. 15. This hardening was the mere effect of his self-determining obstinacy. He preferred his gain to the will and command of Jehovah, and God made his obstinacy the means of showing forth His own power and providence in a supereminent degree.

MATTHEW HENRY — CHAPTER 9

Verses 1–7

Here is, I. Warning given or another plague, namely, the murrain of beasts. 1. *Let my people go, v.* 1. They are my people, therefore let them go.

2. He describes the plague that should come, if he refused, *v.* 2, 3. *The hand of the Lord is upon the cattle,* many of which should die by a sort of pestilence. *To-morrow* it shall be done. We know not what any day will bring forth, and therefore we cannot say what we will do to-morrow, but it is not so with God.

JAMIESON, FAUSSET, BROWN — CHAPTER 9

Vss. 1-7. MURRAIN OF BEASTS. **3. Behold, the hand of the Lord is upon thy cattle**—A fifth application was made to Pharaoh in behalf of the Israelites by Moses, who was instructed to tell him that, if he persisted in opposing their departure, a pestilence would be sent among all the flocks and herds of the Egyptians, while those of the Israelites would be spared. As he showed no intention of keeping his promise, he was still a mark for the arrows of the Almighty's quiver, and the threatened plague of which he was forewarned was executed. But it is observable that in this instance it was not inflicted through the instrumentality or waving of Aaron's rod, but directly by the hand of the Lord, and the fixing of the precise time tended still further to determine the true character of the calamity (Jer. 12:4).

ADAM CLARKE — CHAPTER 9

1. *The Lord God of the Hebrews.* It is very likely that the term Lord, *Yehovah,* is used here to point out particularly His eternal power and Godhead; and that the term God, *Elohey,* is intended to be understood in the sense of Supporter, Defender, Protector. Thus saith the self-existent, omnipotent, and eternal Being, the Supporter and Defender of the Hebrews, "Let My people go, that they may worship Me."

THE FIFTH PLAGUE—THE MURRAIN

3. *The hand of the Lord.* The power of God manifested in judgment. *Upon the horses. Susim.* This is the first place the horse is mentioned, a creature for which Egypt and Arabia were always famous. *Sus* is supposed to have the same meaning with *sas,* which signifies to be "active, brisk, or lively," all which are proper appellatives of the horse, especially in Arabia and Egypt. Because of their activity and swiftness they were sacrificed and dedicated to the sun, and perhaps it was principally on this account that God prohibited the use of them among the Israelites. *A very grievous murrain.* The murrain is a very contagious disease among cattle, the symptoms of which are a hanging down and swelling of the head, abundance of gum in the eyes, rattling in the throat, difficulty of breathing, palpitation of the heart, staggering, a hot breath, and a shining tongue; which symptoms prove that a general inflammation

MATTHEW HENRY

II. The plague itself inflicted. The cattle died, *v.* 6. The Egyptians afterwards, and (some think) now, worshipped their cattle; it was among them that the Israelites learned to make a god of a calf: in this therefore the plague here spoken of meets with them.

III. The distinction put between the cattle of the Egyptians and the Israelites' cattle, according to the word of God: Not *one of the cattle of the Israelites died, v.* 6, 7.

Verses 8–12

Concerning the plague of boils and blains.

I. When they were not wrought upon by the death of their cattle, God sent a plague that seized their own bodies, and touched them to the quick. If less judgments do not do their work, God will send greater.

II. The signal by which this plague was summoned. Sometimes God shows men their sin in their punishment; they had oppressed Israel in the furnaces, and now the ashes of the furnace are made as much a terror to them as ever their task-masters had been to the Israelites.

III. The plague itself was very grievous—these eruptions were inflammations, like Job's. This is afterwards called the *botch of Egypt* (Deut. xxviii. 27).

IV. The magicians themselves were struck with these boils, *v.* 11. Thus they were punished for helping to harden Pharaoh's heart. God will severely reckon with those that strengthen the hands of the wicked in their wickedness.

V. Pharaoh continued obstinate, for now *the Lord hardened* his heart, *v.* 12. Before, he had hardened his own heart, and resisted the grace of God; and now God justly gave him up to his own heart's lusts.

Verses 13–21

Here is, I. A general declaration of the wrath of God against Pharaoh for his obstinacy. Though God has hardened his heart (*v.* 12), yet Moses must repeat his applications to him. God would likewise show forth a pattern of long-suffering, and how he waits to be gracious to a *rebellious and gainsaying people*. Six times the demand had been made in vain, yet Moses must make it the seventh time: *Let my people go, v.* 13. A most dreadful message Moses is here ordered to deliver to him, whether he will hear or whether he will forbear. "I will send my plagues *upon thy heart*, not only temporal plagues upon thy body, but spiritual plagues upon thy soul." He must tell him that he is to remain in history a standing monument of the justice and power of God's wrath (*v.* 14): *"For this cause have I raised thee up* to the throne at this time, and made thee to stand the shock of the plagues hitherto, *to show in thee my power."* Every thing concurred to signalise this, that God's name (that is, his incontestable sovereignty, his irresistible power, and his inflexible justice) might be declared throughout all the earth, not only to all places, but through all ages while the earth remains. Pharaoh was a great king; God's people were poor shepherds at the best, and now poor slaves; and yet Pharaoh shall be ruined if he exalt himself against them, for it is considered as exalting himself against God.

JAMIESON, FAUSSET, BROWN

6. all the cattle of Egypt died—not absolutely every beast, for we find (vss. 19, 21) that there were still some left; but a great many died of each herd—the mortality was frequent and widespread. The adaptation of this judgment consisted in the Egyptians venerating the more useful animals, such as the ox, the cow, and the ram; in all parts of the country temples were reared and divine honors paid to these domesticated beasts, and thus while the pestilence caused a great loss in money, it also struck a heavy blow at their superstition.

7. Pharaoh sent . . . there was not one of the cattle of the Israelites dead—The despatch of confidential messengers indicates that he would not give credit to vague reports, and we may conclude that some impression had been made on his mind by that extraordinary exemption, but it was neither a good nor a permanent impression. His pride and obstinacy were in no degree subdued.

8-17. Plague of Boils. **8. Take to you handfuls of ashes**, etc.—The next plague assailed the persons of the Egyptians, and it appeared in the form of ulcerous eruptions upon the skin and flesh (Lev. 13:20; II Kings 20:7; Job 2:7). That this epidemic did not arise from natural causes was evident from its taking effect from the particular action of Moses done in the sight of Pharaoh. The attitude he assumed was similar to that of Eastern magicians, who, "when they pronounce an imprecation on an individual, a village, or a country, take the ashes of cows' dung (that is, from a common fire) and throw them in the air, saying to the objects of their displeasure, such a sickness or such a curse shall come upon you" [Roberts]. Moses took ashes from the furnace—*Hebrew*, brick-kiln.

The magicians, being sufferers in their own persons, could do nothing, though they had been called; and as the brick-kiln was one of the principal instruments of oppression to the Israelites, it was now converted into a means of chastisement to the Egyptians, who were made to read their sin in their punishment.

ADAM CLARKE

has taken place. The original word *deber* is variously translated. The Septuagint has "death"; the Vulgate has *pestis*, a "plague" or "pestilence." Our English word *murrain* comes either from the French *mourir*, "to die," or from the Greek *maraino*, to "grow lean, waste away." The term "mortality" would be the nearest in sense to the original, as no particular disorder is specified by the Hebrew word.

4. *The Lord shall sever.* See on chap. viii. 22.

5. *To morrow the Lord shall do this.* By thus foretelling the evil, he showed His prescience and power; and from this both the Egyptians and Hebrews must see that the mortality that ensued was no casualty, but the effect of a predetermined purpose in the divine justice.

6. *All the cattle of Egypt died.* That is, all the cattle that did die belonged to the Egyptians, but not one died that belonged to the Israelites, vv. 4 and 6. That the whole stock of cattle belonging to the Egyptians did not die we have the fullest proof, because there were cattle both to be killed and saved alive in the ensuing plague, vv. 19-25. By this judgment the Egyptians must see the vanity of the whole of their national worship, when they found the animals which they not only held sacred, but deified, slain without distinction among the common herd by a pestilence sent from the hand of Jehovah. One might naturally suppose that after this the animal worship of the Egyptians could nevermore maintain its ground.

7. *And Pharaoh sent.* Finding so many of his own cattle and those of his subjects slain, he sent to see whether the mortality had reached to the cattle of the Israelites, that he might know whether this were a judgment inflicted by their God, and probably designing to replace the lost cattle of the Egyptians with those of the Israelites.

The Sixth Plague—The Boils and the Blains

8. *Handfuls of ashes of the furnace.* As one part of the oppression of the Israelites consisted in their labor in the brickkilns, some have observed a congruity between the crime and the punishment. The furnaces, in the labor of which they oppressed the Hebrews, now yielded the instruments of their punishment; for every particle of those *ashes*, formed by unjust and oppressive labor, seemed to be a boil or a blain on the tyrannic king and his cruel and hard-hearted people.

9. *Shall be a boil. Shechin.* This word is generally expounded, "an inflammatory swelling, a burning boil"; one of the most poignant afflictions, not immediately mortal, that can well affect the surface of the human body. If a single boil on any part of the body throws the whole system into a fever, what anguish must a multitude of them on the body at the same time occasion! *Breaking forth with blains. Ababuoth,* supposed to come from *baah*, to "swell, bulge out"; any inflammatory swelling in any part of the body, but more especially in the more glandular parts, the neck, armpits, groin. The Septuagint translates it thus: "And it shall be an ulcer with burning pustules." It seems to have been a disorder of an uncommon kind, and hence it is called by way of distinction "the botch of Egypt," Deut. xxviii. 27, perhaps never known before in that or any other country.

11. *The boil was upon the magicians.* They could not produce a similar malady by throwing ashes in the air; and they could neither remove the plague from the people, nor from their own tormented flesh. Whether they perished in this plague we know not, but they are no more mentioned. If they were not destroyed by this awful judgment, they at least left the field and no longer contended with these messengers of God. The triumph of God's power was now complete, and both the Hebrews and the Egyptians must see that there was neither might, nor wisdom, nor counsel against the Lord.

15. *For now I will stretch out my hand.* In the Hebrew the verbs are in the past tense, and not in the future, as our translation improperly expresses them, by which means a contradiction appears in the text; for neither Pharaoh nor his people were smitten by a pestilence, nor was he by any kind of mortality *cut off from the earth.* It is true the firstborn were slain by a destroying angel, and Pharaoh

MATTHEW HENRY | JAMIESON, FAUSSET, BROWN | ADAM CLARKE

ADAM CLARKE

himself was drowned in the Red Sea; but these judgments do not appear to be referred to in this place. If the words be translated, as they ought, in the subjunctive mood, or in the past instead of the future, this seeming contradiction to facts, as well as all ambiguity, will be avoided: "For if now I had stretched out [*shalachti*, had set forth] My hand, and had smitten thee and thy people with the pestilence, thou shouldst have been cut off from the earth. 16. But truly on this very account, have I caused thee to subsist, that I might cause thee to see My power, and that My name might be declared throughout all the earth [or, *becol haarets*, in all this land]."

Thus God gave this impious king to know that it was in consequence of His especial providence that both he and his people had not been already destroyed by means of the past plagues; but God had preserved him for this very purpose, that He might have a further opportunity of manifesting that He, Jehovah, was the only true God for the full conviction of both the Hebrews and the Egyptians, that the former might follow and the latter fear before Him. Judicious critics of almost all creeds have agreed to translate the original as above, a translation which it not only can bear but requires, and which is in strict conformity to both the Septuagint and the Targum. Neither the Hebrew, "I have caused thee to stand"; nor the apostle's translation of it, Rom. ix. 17, "I have raised thee"; nor that of the Septuagint, "On this account art thou preserved," namely, in the past plagues, can countenance that most exceptionable meaning put on the words by certain commentators, namely, "That God ordained or appointed Pharaoh from all eternity, by certain means, to this end; that He made him to exist in time; that He raised him to the throne; promoted him to that high honor and dignity; that He preserved him, and did not cut him off as yet; that He strengthened and hardened his heart; irritated, provoked, and stirred him up against His people Israel, and suffered him to go all the lengths he did go in his obstinacy and rebellion; all which was done to show in him His power in destroying him in the Red Sea. The sum of which is, that this man was raised up by God in every sense for God to show His power in his destruction." So man speaks; thus God hath not spoken.

17. *As yet exaltest thou thyself against my people?* So it appears that at this time he might have submitted, and thus prevented his own destruction.

KEIL–DELITZSCH:

As the plagues had thus far entirely failed to bend the unyielding heart of Pharaoh under the will of the Almighty God, the terrors of that judgment, which would infallibly come upon him, were set before him in three more plagues, which were far more terrible than any that had preceded them. That these were to be preparatory to the last decisive blow is proved by the great solemnity with which they were announced to the hardened king (vv. 13–16). This time Jehovah was about to "send all his strokes at the heart of Pharaoh, and against his servants and his people" (v. 14). The strokes were to go the king's heart. "It announces that they will be plagues that will not only strike the head and arms, but penetrate the very heart, and inflict a mortal wound" (Calvin). From the plural "strokes," it is evident that his threat referred not only to the seventh plague (the hail), but to all the other plagues, through which Jehovah was about to make known to the king that "there was none like him in all the earth"; i.e., that not one of the gods whom the heathen worshipped was like Him, the only true God. For, in order to show this, Jehovah had not smitten Pharaoh and his people at once with pestilence and cut them off from the earth, but had set him up to make him see, i.e., discern or feel His power, and to glorify His name in all the earth (vv. 15, 16). In verse 15, "I have stretched out," is to be taken as the conditional clause: "If I had now stretched out My hand and smitten thee ... thou wouldest have been cut off." The reason why God had not destroyed Pharaoh at once was twofold: (1) that Pharaoh himself might experience ("to cause to see," i.e., to experience) the might of Jehovah, by which he was compelled more than once to give glory to Jehovah (v. 27; 10:16, 17; 12:31); and (2) that the name of Jehovah might be declared throughout the earth. As both the rebellion of the natural man against the word and will of God and the hostility of the world-power to the Lord and His people were concentrated in Pharaoh, so there were manifested in the judgments suspended over him the patience and grace of the living God, quite as much as His holiness, justice, and omnipotence, as a warning to impenitent sinners, and a support to the faith of the godly, in a manner that should be typical for all times and circumstances of the kingdom of God in conflict with the ungodly world. The report of this glorious manifestation of Jehovah spread at once among all the surrounding nations, and travelled not only to the Arabians, but to the Greeks and Romans also, and eventually with the Gospel of Christ to all the nations of the earth.—*Commentary on the Old Testament*

MATTHEW HENRY

II. A particular prediction of the plague of hail (*v.* 18), and a gracious advice to Pharaoh and his people to send for their servants and cattle out of the field, that they might be sheltered from the hail, *v.* 19. See here what care God took, not only to distinguish between Egyptians and Israelites, but between some Egyptians and others.

***Some believed the things that were spoken*, and they feared, and housed their servants and cattle (*v.* 20), like Noah (Heb. xi. 7), and it was their wisdom. Even among the servants of Pharaoh there were some that trembled at God's word.**

Verses 22–35

The threatened plague of hail is here summoned:

I. What desolations it made upon the earth. It killed both men and cattle, and battered down, not

JAMIESON, FAUSSET, BROWN

18-35. PLAGUE OF HAIL. **18. I will cause it to rain a very grievous hail,** etc.—The seventh plague which Pharaoh's hardened heart provoked was that of hail, a phenomenon which must have produced the greatest astonishment and consternation in Egypt as rain and hailstones, accompanied by thunder and lightning, were very rare occurrences. **such as hath not been in Egypt**—In the Delta, or lower Egypt, where the scene is laid, rain occasionally falls between January and March—hail is not unknown, and thunder sometimes heard. But a storm, not only exhibiting all these elements, but so terrific that hailstones of immense size fell, thunder pealed in awful volleys, and lightning swept the ground like fire, was an unexampled calamity. **20, 21. He that feared the word of the Lord . . . regarded not,** etc.—Due premonition, it appears, had been publicly given of the impending tempest—the cattle seem to have been sent out to graze, which is from January to April, when alone pasturage can be obtained, and accordingly the cattle were in the fields. This storm occurring at that season, not only struck universal terror into the minds of the people, but occasioned the destruction of all—people and cattle—which, in neglect of the warning, had been left in the fields, as well as of all vegetation. It was the more appalling because hailstones in Egypt are small and of little force; lightning also is scarcely ever known to produce fatal effects; and to enhance the wonder, not a trace of any storm was found in Goshen.

ADAM CLARKE

THE SEVENTH PLAGUE—THE HAIL

18. *To morrow about this time.* The time of this plague is marked thus circumstantially to show Pharaoh that Jehovah was Lord of heaven and earth, and that the water, the fire, the earth, and the air, which were all objects of Egyptian idolatry, were the creatures of His power, and subservient to His will; and that, far from being able to help them, they were now, in the hands of God, instruments of their destruction.

To rain a very grievous hail. "To rain hail" may appear to some superficial observers as an unphilosophical mode of expression, but nothing can be more correct. "Drops of rain falling through a cold region of the atmosphere are frozen and converted into hail"; and thus the *hail* is produced by *rain.* When it begins to fall it is rain; when it is falling it is converted into hail; thus it is literally true that it rains hail. The farther a hailstone falls the larger it generally is, because in its descent it meets with innumerable particles of water, which, becoming attached to it, are also frozen, and thus its bulk is continually increasing till it reaches the earth.

19. *Send . . . now, and gather thy cattle.* So in the midst of judgment, God remembered mercy. The miracle should be wrought that they might know He was the Lord; but all the lives both of men and beasts might have been saved had Pharaoh and his servants taken the warning so mercifully given them. While some regarded not the word of the Lord, others feared it, and their cattle and their servants were saved. See vv. 20-21.

23. *The Lord sent thunder. Koloth,* "voices"; but loud, repeated peals of thunder are meant. *And the fire ran along upon the ground.* "And

MATTHEW HENRY

only the herbs, but the trees, *v.* 25. The corn that was above ground was destroyed, and that only preserved which as yet had not come up, *v.* 31, 32. Notice is here taken (*v.* 26) of the land of Goshen's being preserved from receiving any damage by this plague.

II. What a consternation it put Pharaoh in. He humbled himself to Moses in the language of a penitent, *v.* 27, 28. He condemns himself and his land: "*I and my people are wicked,* and deserve what is brought upon us." He begs the prayers of Moses: "*Entreat the Lord* for me, that this direful plague may be removed." And, *lastly,* he promises to yield up his prisoners: *I will let you go.* Moses, hereupon, becomes an intercessor for him with God. Though he had all the reason in the world to think that he would immediately repent of his repentance, and told him so (*v.* 30), yet he promises to be his friend in the court of heaven. Note, Even those whom we have little hopes of, yet we should continue to pray for, and to admonish, 1 Sam. xii. 23. The place Moses chose for his intercession. Peace with God makes men thunderproof, for thunder is the voice of their Father.

The success of it. 1. He prevailed with God, *v.* 33. But, 2. He could not prevail with Pharaoh: *He sinned yet more, and hardened his heart, v.* 34, 35. Note, Little credit is to be given to confessions upon the rack.

JAMIESON, FAUSSET, BROWN

27-35. Pharaoh sent, and called for Moses and Aaron, and said unto them, I have sinned—This awful display of divine displeasure did seriously impress the mind of Pharaoh, and, under the weight of his convictions, he humbles himself to confess he has done wrong in opposing the divine will. At the same time he calls for Moses to intercede for cessation of the calamity. Moses accedes to his earnest wishes, and this most awful visitation ended. But his repentance proved a transient feeling, and his obduracy soon became as great as before.

31, 32. the flax and the barley was smitten, etc.—The peculiarities that are mentioned in these cereal products arise from the climate and physical constitution of Egypt. In that country flax and barley are almost ripe when wheat and rye (spelt) are green. And hence the flax must have been "bolled"—i.e., risen in stalk or podded in February, thus fixing the particular month when the event took place. Barley ripens about a month earlier than wheat. Flax and barley are generally ripe in March, wheat and rye (properly, spelt) in April.

KEIL–DELITZSCH:

The supernatural character of this plague was manifested not only in its being predicted by Moses, and in the exemption of the land of Goshen, but more especially in the terrible fury of the hailstorm, which made a stronger impression upon Pharaoh than all the previous plagues. For he sent for Moses and Aaron and confessed to them, "I have sinned this time: Jehovah is righteous; I and my people are the sinners" (v. 27). But the very limitation "this time" showed that his repentance did not go very deep, and that his confession was far more the effect of terror caused by the majesty of God, which was manifested in the fearful thunder and lightning, than a genuine acknowledgment of his guilt. This is apparent also from the words which follow: "Pray to Jehovah for me, and let it be enough of the being of the voices of God and of the hail"; *i.e.,* there has been enough thunder and hail, they may cease now.

Verse 29. Moses promised that his request should be granted that he might know "that the land belonged to Jehovah," *i.e.,* that Jehovah ruled as Lord over Egypt; at the same time he told him that the fear manifested by himself and his servants was no true fear of God. The true fear of God includes a voluntary subjection to the divine will. Observe the expression *Jehovah, Elohim:* Jehovah, who is Elohim, the Being to be honored as supreme, the true God.

—*Commentary on the Old Testament*

ADAM CLARKE

the fire walked upon the earth." It was not a sudden flash of lightning, but a devouring fire, walking through every part, destroying both animals and vegetables; and its progress was irresistible.

26. *Only in the land of Goshen . . . was there no hail.* What a signal proof of a most particular providence! Surely both the Hebrews and Egyptians profited by this display of the goodness and severity of God.

27. *The Lord is righteous, and I and my people are wicked.* The original is very emphatic: "The Lord is the righteous One [*hatstaddik*], and I and my people are the sinners [*hareshaim*]"; i.e., He is alone righteous, and we alone are transgressors. Who could have imagined that, after such an acknowledgment and confession, Pharaoh should have again hardened his heart?

28. *It is enough.* There is no need of any further plague; I submit to the authority of Jehovah and will rebel no more. *Mighty thunderings. Koloth Elohim,* "voices of God"—that is, superlatively loud thunder. So "mountains of God" (Ps. xxxvi. 6) means exceeding high mountains. So "a prince of God" (Gen. xxiii. 6) means a mighty prince. See a description of thunder, Ps. xxix. 3-8.

29. *I will spread abroad my hands.* That is, I will make supplication to God that He may remove this plague. This may not be an improper place to make some observations on the ancient manner of approaching the Divine Being in prayer. Kneeling down, stretching out the hands, and lifting them up to heaven were in frequent use among the Hebrews in their religious worship. Solomon kneeled down on his knees, and spread forth his hands to heaven, 2 Chron. vi. 13. So David, Ps. cxliii. 6: "I stretch forth my hands unto thee." So Ezra: "I fell upon my knees, and spread out my hands unto the Lord my God"; chap. ix. 5. See also Job xi. 13: "If thou prepare thine heart, and stretch out thine hands towards him." Most nations who pretended to any kind of worship made use of the same means in approaching the objects of their adoration, namely, kneeling down and stretching out their hands, which custom it is very likely they borrowed from the people of God. Kneeling was ever considered to be the proper posture of supplication, as it expresses humility, contrition, and subjection.

31. *The flax and the barley was smitten.* The word *pishtah, flax,* Mr. Parkhurst thinks, is derived from the root *pashat,* "to strip," because the substance which we term *flax* is properly the bark or rind of the vegetable, pilled or stripped off the stalks. From time immemorial Egypt was celebrated for the production and manufacture of flax: hence the linen and fine linen of Egypt, so often spoken of in ancient authors. *Barley. Seorah,* from *saar,* "to stand on end, to be rough, bristly"; hence *barley* because of the rough and prickly beard with which the ears are covered and defended. *The flax was bolled.* Meaning, I suppose, was grown up into a stalk: the original is *gibol,* "podded" or was "in the pod." The word well expresses that globous pod on the top of the stalk of flax which succeeds the flower and contains the seed, very properly expressed by the Septuagint, "but the flax was in seed or was seeding."

32. *But the wheat and the rie were not smitten. Wheat, chittah,* which Mr. Parkhurst thinks should be derived from the Chaldee and Samaritan *chati,* which signifies "tender, delicious, delicate," because of the superiority of its flavor to every other kind of grain. *Rie, cussemeth,* from *casam,* "to have long hair"; and hence, though the particular species is not known, the word must mean some bearded grain.

33. *Spread abroad his hands.* Probably with the rod of God in them. See what has been said on the spreading out of the hands in prayer, v. 29.

34. *He sinned yet more, and hardened his heart.* These were merely acts of his own.

35. *And the heart of Pharaoh was hardened.* In consequence of his sinning yet more, and hardening his own heart against both the judgments and mercies of God, we need not be

MATTHEW HENRY

JAMIESON, FAUSSET, BROWN

ADAM CLARKE

surprised that, after God had given him the means of softening and repentance, and he had in every instance resisted and abused them, he should at last have been left to the hardness and darkness of his own obstinate heart, so as to fill up the measure of his iniquity and rush headlong to his own destruction.

CHAPTER 10 (Matthew Henry)

Verses 1–11

I. Moses is instructed. These plagues are standing monuments of the greatness of God, the happiness of the church, and the sinfulness of sin, and standing monitors to the children of men in all ages not to *provoke the Lord to jealousy* nor to *strive with their Maker.*

II. Pharaoh is reproved (*v.* 3): *Thus saith the Lord God of the poor,* despised, persecuted Hebrews, *How long wilt thou refuse to humble thyself before me?* Those that will not humble themselves God will humble.

III. The plague of locusts is threatened, *v.* 4–6. The hail had broken down the fruits of the earth, but these locusts should come and devour them. Moses, when he had delivered his message, not expecting any better answer than he had formerly, *turned himself and went out from* Pharaoh, *v.* 6. Thus Christ appointed his disciples to depart from those who would not receive them, and to *shake off the dust of their feet for a testimony against them.*

IV. Pharaoh's attendants, his ministers of state, or privy-counsellors, interpose, to persuade him to come to some terms with Moses, *v.* 7. The Israelites had become a burdensome stone to the Egyptians, and now, at length, the princes of Egypt were willing to be rid of them, Zech. xii. 3.

V. A new treaty is, hereupon, set on foot between Pharaoh, and Moses, in which Pharaoh consents for the Israelites to go into the wilderness to do sacrifice; but the matter in dispute was who should go, *v.* 8. 1. Moses insists that they should take their whole families, and all their effects, along with them, *v.* 9.

2. Pharaoh will by no means grant this: he will allow the men to go, pretending that this was all they desired, though this matter was never yet mentioned in any of the former treaties; but, for the *little ones,* he resolves to keep them as hostages, to oblige them to return, *v.* 10, 11. 3. The treaty, hereupon, breaks off abruptly.

CHAPTER 10 (Jamieson, Fausset, Brown)

Vss. 1-20. PLAGUE OF LOCUSTS. **1. show these my signs,** etc.—Sinners even of the worst description are to be admonished even though there may be little hope of amendment, and hence those striking miracles that carried so clear and conclusive demonstration of the being and character of the true God were performed in lengthened series before Pharaoh to leave him without excuse when judgment should be finally executed. **2. And that thou mayest tell . . . of thy son, and of thy son's son,** etc.—There was a further and higher reason for the infliction of those awful judgments, viz., that the knowledge of them there, and the permanent record of them still, might furnish a salutary and impressive lesson to the Church down to the latest ages. Worldly historians might have described them as extraordinary occurrences that marked this era of Moses in ancient Egypt. But we are taught to trace them to their cause: the judgments of divine wrath on a grossly idolatrous king and nations.

4. to-morrow will I bring the locusts—Moses was commissioned to renew the request, so often made and denied, with an assurance that an unfavorable answer would be followed on the morrow by an invasion of locusts. This species of insect resembles a large, spotted, red and black, double-winged grasshopper, about three inches or less in length, with the two hind legs working like hinged springs of immense strength and elasticity. Perhaps no more terrible scourge was ever brought on a land than those voracious insects, which fly in such countless numbers as to darken the land which they infest; and on whatever place they alight, they convert it into a waste and barren desert, stripping the ground of its verdure, the trees of their leaves and bark, and producing in a few hours a degree of desolation which it requires the lapse of years to repair. **7-11. Pharaoh's servants said**—Many of his courtiers must have suffered serious losses from the late visitations, and the prospect of such a calamity as that which was threatened and the magnitude of which former experience enabled them to realize, led them to make a strong remonstrance with the king.

Finding himself not seconded by his counsellors in his continued resistance, he recalled Moses and Aaron, and having expressed his consent to their departure, inquired who were to go. The prompt and decisive reply, "all," neither man nor beast shall remain, raised a storm of indignant fury in the breast of the proud king. He would permit the grown-up men to go away; but no other terms would be listened to.

CHAPTER 10 (Adam Clarke)

1. *Hardened his heart.* God suffered his natural obstinacy to prevail, that He might have further opportunities of showing forth His eternal power and Godhead.

2. *That thou mayest tell in the ears of thy son.* That the miracles wrought at this time might be a record for the instruction of the latest posterity, that Jehovah alone, the God of the Hebrews, was the sole Maker, Governor, and Supporter of the heavens and the earth.

3. *How long wilt thou refuse to humble thyself?* Had it been impossible for Pharaoh, in all the preceding plagues, to have humbled himself and repented, can we suppose that God could have addressed him in such language as the preceding? We may rest assured that there was always a time in which he might have relented, and that it was because he hardened his heart at such times that God is said to harden him, i.e., to give him up to his own stubborn and obstinate heart.

THE EIGHTH PLAGUE—THE LOCUSTS

4. *To morrow will I bring the locusts.* The word *arbeh, a locust,* is probably from the root *rabah,* he "multiplied, became great, mighty"; because of the immense swarms of these animals by which different countries, especially the East, are infested. See this circumstance referred to, Judg. vi. 5; vii. 12; Ps. cv. 34; Jer. xlvi. 23; li. 14; Joel i. 6; Nah. iii. 15; where the most numerous armies are compared to the *arbeh* or "locust." The locust has a large, open mouth; and in its two jaws it has four incisive teeth, which traverse each other like scissors, being calculated, from their mechanism, to gripe or cut.

7. *How long shall this man be a snare unto us?* As there is no noun in the text, the pronoun *zeh* may refer either to the Israelites, to the plague by which they were then afflicted, or to Moses and Aaron, the instruments used by the Most High in their chastisement. *Let the men go, that they may serve the Lord their God.* Much of the energy of several passages is lost in translating *Yehovah* by the term "Lord." The Egyptians had their gods, and they supposed that the Hebrews had a god like unto their own; that this Jehovah required their services, and would continue to afflict Egypt till His people were permitted to worship Him in his own way. *Egypt is destroyed.* This last plague had nearly ruined the whole land.

8. *Who are they that shall go?* Though the Egyptians, about fourscore years before, wished to destroy the Hebrews, yet they found them now so profitable to the state that they were unwilling to part with them.

9. *We will go with our young and with our old.* As a feast was to be celebrated to the honor of Jehovah, all who were partakers of His bounty and providential kindness must go and perform their part in the solemnity. The men and the women must make the feast, the children must witness it, and the cattle must be taken along with them to furnish the sacrifices necessary on this occasion.

10. *Let the Lord be so with you.* This is an obscure sentence. Some suppose that Pharaoh meant it as a curse, as if he had said, "May your God be as surely with you, as I shall let you go!" For as he purposed not to permit them to go, so he wished them as much of the divine help as they should have of his permission.

Look . . . for evil is before you. "See ye that evil is before your faces"—if you attempt to go, ye shall meet with the punishment ye deserve. Probably Pharaoh intended to insinuate that they had some sinister designs, and that they wished to go in a body that they might the better accomplish their purpose; but if they had no such designs they would be contented for the

MATTHEW HENRY

Verses 12–20

I. The invasion of the land by the locusts—*God's great army*, Joel ii. 11. The locusts obey the summons, and fly upon the wings of the wind, the east wind, and *caterpillars without number*, as we are told, Ps. cv. 34, 35. A formidable army of horse and foot might more easily have been resisted than this host of insects.

II. The desolations they made in it (*v.* 15): They *covered the face of the earth*, and *ate up the fruit* of it. Herbs grow *for the service of man*; yet, when God pleases, those contemptible insects shall not only be fellow-consumers with him, but shall plunder him, and eat the bread out of his mouth.

III. Pharaoh's admission, hereupon, *v.* 16, 17. 1. Pharaoh confesses his fault: *I have sinned against the Lord your God, and against you.* He now sees his own folly in the slights and affronts he had put on God and his ambassadors, and *seems*, at least, to repent of it. 2. He begs pardon, not of God, as penitents ought, but of Moses. 3. He entreats Moses and Aaron to pray for him. Pharaoh desires their prayers *that this death* only might be taken away, not *this sin*: he deprecates the plague of locusts, not the plague of a hard heart, which yet was much the more dangerous.

IV. The removal of the judgment, upon the prayer of Moses, *v.* 18, 19. This was, 1. As great an instance of the power of God as the judgment itself. An east wind brought the locusts, and now a west wind carried them off. Note, Whatever point of the compass the wind is in, it is fulfilling God's word, and turns about by his counsel. 2. It was a proof of the authority of Moses, and a ratification of his commission. 3. It was also as strong an argument for their repentance as the judgment itself; for by this it appeared that God is ready to forgive, and swift to show mercy.

V. Pharaoh's return to his impious resolution again not to let the people go (*v.* 20).

Verses 21–29

Here is, I. The plague of darkness. Observe particularly concerning this plague, 1. That it was a total darkness. They *saw not one another.* Hell is *utter darkness.* The light of *a candle shall shine no more at all in thee*, Rev. xviii. 23. 2. That it was darkness which *might be felt* (*v.* 21). 3. No doubt it astonished and terrified them. The tradition of the Jews is that in this darkness they were terrified by the apparitions of evil spirits, or rather by dreadful sounds and murmurs which they made, or (which is no less frightful) by the horrors of their own consciences. 4. It continued three days, *six nights* (says bishop Hall) *in one.* Spiritual darkness is spiritual bondage; while Satan blinds men's eyes that they see not, he binds their hands and feet that they work not for God, nor move towards heaven. They *sit in darkness.* Never was mind so blinded as Pharaoh's, never was air so darkened as Egypt's. The Egyptians by their cruelty would have extinguished the lamp of Israel, and quenched their coal; justly therefore does God put out their lights.

II. Here is the impression made upon Pharaoh by this plague. 1. It awakened him so far that he renewed the treaty with Moses and Aaron, and now, at length, consented that they should take their little ones with them, only he would have their cattle left in pawn, *v.* 24.

JAMIESON, FAUSSET, BROWN

11. they were driven out from Pharaoh's presence—In the East, when a person of authority and rank feels annoyed by a petition which he is unwilling to grant, he makes a signal to his attendants, who rush forward and, seizing the obnoxious suppliant by the neck, drag him out of the chamber with violent haste. Of such a character was the impassioned scene in the court of Egypt when the king had wrought himself into such a fit of uncontrollable fury as to treat ignominiously the two venerable representatives of the Hebrew people. **13. the Lord brought an east wind**—The rod of Moses was again raised, and the locusts came. They are natives of the desert and are only brought by an east wind into Egypt, where they sometimes come in sun-obscuring clouds, destroying in a few days every green blade in the track they traverse. Man, with all his contrivances, can do nothing to protect himself from the overwhelming invasion. Egypt has often suffered from locusts. But the plague that followed the wave of the miraculous rod was altogether unexampled. Pharaoh, fearing irretrievable ruin to his country, sent in haste for Moses, and confessing his sin, implored the intercession of Moses, who entreated the Lord, and a "mighty strong west wind took away the locusts."

21-29. PLAGUE OF DARKNESS. **21. Stretch out thine hand toward heaven, that there may be darkness**—Whatever secondary means were employed in producing it, whether thick clammy fogs and vapors, according to some; a sandstorm, or the *chamsin*, according to others; it was such that it could be almost perceived by the organs of touch, and so protracted as to continue for three days, which the *chamsin* does [HENSTENBERG]. The appalling character of this calamity consisted in this, that the sun was an object of Egyptian idolatry; that the pure and serene sky of that country was never marred by the appearance of a cloud. And here, too, the Lord made a marked difference between Goshen and the rest of Egypt.

24-26. Pharaoh called unto Moses, and said, Go ye, serve the Lord—Terrified by the preternatural darkness, the stubborn king relents, and proposes another compromise—the flocks and herds to be left as hostages for their return. But the crisis is approaching, and Moses insists on every iota of his demand. The cattle would be needed for sacrifice—how many or how few could not be known till their arrival at the scene of religious observance. But the emancipation of Israel from Egyptian bondage was to be complete.

ADAM CLARKE

males to go, and leave their wives and children behind; for he well knew if the men went and left their families they would infallibly return, but that if he permitted them to take their families with them, they would undoubtedly make their escape; therefore he says, v. 11, "Go now ye that are men, and serve the Lord."

13. *The Lord brought an east wind.* As locusts abounded in those countries, and particularly in Ethiopia, and more especially at this time of the year, God had no need to create new swarms for this purpose; all that was requisite was to cause such a wind to blow as would bring those which already existed over the land of Egypt. The miracle in this business was the bringing the locusts at the appointed time and causing the proper wind to blow for that purpose; and then taking them away after a similar manner.

14. *Before them there were no such locusts.* They exceeded all that went before, or were since, in number and in the devastations they produced. Probably both these things are intended in the passage. See v. 15.

17. *Forgive, I pray thee, my sin only this once.* What a strange case! And what a series of softening and hardening, of sinning and repenting! Had he not now another opportunity of returning to God? But the love of gain, and the gratification of his own self-will and obstinacy, finally prevailed.

19. *A mighty strong west wind.* Literally the "wind of the sea"; the wind that blew from the Mediterranean Sea, which lay northwest of Egypt, which had the Red Sea on the east. Here again God works by natural means; He brought the locusts by the east wind, and took them away by the west or northwest wind, which carried them to the Red Sea, where they were drowned.

The Red sea. The "weedy sea"; so called, as some suppose, from the great quantity of seaweed which grows in it and about its shores. In the Septuagint it is called the "Red Sea," from which version we have borrowed the name. The *Red sea,* called also the Arabic Gulf, separates Arabia from Upper Ethiopia and part of Egypt.

THE NINTH PLAGUE—THICK DARKNESS

21. *Darkness which may be felt.* Probably this was occasioned by a superabundance of aqueous vapors floating in the atmosphere, which were so thick as to prevent the rays of the sun from penetrating through them; an extraordinarily thick mist supernaturally, i.e., miraculously, brought on. An awful emblem of the darkened state of the Egyptians and their king.

23. *They saw not one another.* So deep was the obscurity, and probably such was its nature, that no artificial light could be procured; as the thick, clammy vapors would prevent lamps from burning, or if they even could be ignited, the light through the palpable obscurity could diffuse itself to no distance from the burning body. The author of the Book of Wisdom, chap. xvii. 2-19, gives a fearful description of this plague. *All the children of Israel had light.* By thus distinguishing the Israelites, God showed the Egyptians that the darkness was produced by His power; that He sent it in judgment against them for their cruelty to His people; that because they trusted in Him they were exempted from these plagues; that in the displeasure of such a Being His enemies had everything to fear, and in His approbation His followers had everything to hope.

24. *Only let your flocks and your herds be stayed.* Pharaoh cannot get all he wishes; and as he sees it impossible to contend with Jehovah, he now consents to give up the Israelites, their wives, and their children, provided he may keep their *flocks* and their *herds.* The cruelty of this demand is not more evident than its avarice. Had six hundred thousand men, besides women and children, gone three days' journey into the wilderness without their cattle, they must have inevitably perished, being without milk for their little ones, and animal food for their own sustenance, in a place where little as a substitute could possibly be found. It is evident from this that Pharaoh intended the total destruction of the whole Israelitish host.

MATTHEW HENRY

Moses resolves not to abate in his terms: *Our cattle shall go with us, v.* 26. Moses gives a very good reason why they must take their cattle with them; they must go to do sacrifice, and therefore they must take wherewithal.

2. Yet it exasperated him so far that, when he might not make his own terms, he broke off the conference abruptly. Moses is dismissed in anger, forbidden the court upon pain of death. Moses takes him at his word (*v.* 29): *I will see thy face no more.* So that, after this interview, Moses came no more, till he was sent for.

JAMIESON, FAUSSET, BROWN

28. Pharaoh said . . . , Get thee from me—The calm firmness of Moses provoked the tyrant. Frantic with disappointment and rage, with offended and desperate malice, he ordered him from his presence and forbade him ever to return. **29. Moses said, Thou hast spoken well.**

ADAM CLARKE

26. *We know not with what we must serve the Lord.* The law was not yet given, the ordinances concerning the different kinds of sacrifices and offerings not known. What kind and what number of animals God should require to be sacrificed, even Moses himself could not as yet tell. He therefore very properly insists on taking the whole of their herds with them, and not leaving even *one hoof behind.*

27. *The Lord hardened Pharaoh's heart.* He had yet another miracle to work for the complete conviction of the Egyptians and triumph of His people; and till that was wrought He permitted the natural obstinacy of Pharaoh's haughty heart to have its full sway, after each resistance of the gracious influence which was intended to soften and bring him to repentance.

28. *See my face no more.* Hitherto Pharaoh had left the way open for negotiation; but now, in wrath against Jehovah, he dismisses His ambassador and threatens him with death if he should attempt anymore to come into his presence.

29. *I will see thy face again no more.* It is very likely that this was the last interview that Moses had with Pharaoh, for what is related, chap. xi. 4-8, might have been spoken on this very occasion, as it is very possible that God gave Moses to understand His purpose to slay the firstborn while before Pharaoh at this time; so, in all probability, the interview mentioned here was the last which Moses had with the Egyptian king. It is true that in v. 31 of chap. xii it is stated that Pharaoh "called for Moses and Aaron by night," and ordered them to leave Egypt, and to take all their substance with them, which seems to imply that there was another interview, but the words may imply no more than that Moses and Aaron received such a message from Pharaoh. If, however, this mode of interpreting these passages should not seem satisfactory to any, he may understand the words of Moses thus: *I will see thy face*—seek thy favor—*no more* in behalf of my people, which was literally true; for if Moses did appear anymore before Pharaoh, it was not as a supplicant, but merely as the ambassador of God, to denounce His judgments by giving him the final determination of Jehovah relative to the destruction of the firstborn.

MATTHEW HENRY

CHAPTER 11

Verses 1–3

Here is, I. The high favour Moses and Israel were in with God. Moses longed to see an end of this dreadful work, to see Egypt no more plagued and Israel no more oppressed. The Israelites were favourites of Heaven. This was the last day of their servitude; they were about to go away, and their masters, who had abused them in their work, would now have defrauded them of their wages, and have sent them away empty. Though the patient Israelites were content to lose their wages, yet God would not let them go without them.

II. The high favour Moses and Israel were in with the Egyptians, *v.* 3. 1. Even the people that had been hated and despised now came to be respected. 2. *The man Moses was very great.* How could it be otherwise when they saw what power he was clothed with, and what wonders were wrought by his hand? Thus the apostles, though otherwise despicable men, came to be magnified, Acts v. 13. Those that honour God he will honour. Though Pharaoh hated Moses, there were those of Pharaoh's servants that respected him. Thus in Caesar's household, even Nero's, there were some that had an esteem for blessed Paul, Phil. i. 13.

JAMIESON, FAUSSET, BROWN

CHAPTER 11

Vss. 1-10. DEATH OF THE FIRST-BORN THREATENED. **1. the Lord said**—rather HAD said unto Moses. It may be inferred, therefore, that he had been apprised that the crisis had now arrived, that the next plague would so effectually humble and alarm the mind of Pharaoh, that he would "thrust them out thence altogether"; and thus the word of Moses (ch. 10:29), must be regarded as a prediction.

2, 3. Speak now in the ears of the people—These verses, describing the communication which had been made in private to Moses, are inserted here as a parenthesis, and will be considered (ch. 12:35).

4. Thus saith the Lord, About midnight—Here is recorded the announcement of the last plague made in the most solemn manner to the king, on whose hardened heart all his painful experience had hitherto produced no softening, at least no permanently good effect. **will I go out into the midst of Egypt**—language used after the manner of men.

ADAM CLARKE

CHAPTER 11

1. *The Lord said unto Moses.* Calmet contends that this should be read in the pluperfect tense, "For the Lord had said to Moses," as the fourth, fifth, sixth, seventh, and eighth verses appear to have been spoken when Moses had the interview with Pharaoh mentioned in the preceding chapter; see the note there on verse 29. If, therefore, this chapter be connected with the preceding, as it should be, and the first three verses not only read in the past tense but also in a parenthesis, the sense will be much more distinct and clear than it now appears.

2. *Let every man borrow.* For a proper correction of the strange mistranslation of the word *shaal* in this verse, see the note on chap. iii. 22.

3. *The man Moses was very great.* The miracles which Pharaoh and his servants had already seen him work had doubtless impressed them with a high opinion of his wisdom and power. Had he not appeared in their sight as a very extraordinary person, whom it would have been very dangerous to molest, we may naturally conclude that some violence would long ere this have been offered to his person.

4. *About midnight will I go out.* Whether God did this by the ministry of a good or of an evil angel is a matter of little importance, though some commentators have greatly magnified it. Both kinds of angels are under His power and jurisdiction, and He may employ them as He pleases. Such a work of destruction as the slaying of the firstborn is supposed to be more proper for a bad than for a good angel. But the works of God's justice are not less holy and pure than the works of His mercy; and the highest archangel may, with the utmost propriety, be employed in either.

5. *The firstborn of Pharaoh.* From the heir

MATTHEW HENRY

Verses 4–10

Warning is here given to Pharaoh of the last and conquering plague which was now to be inflicted. This was the *death of all the first-born in Egypt* at once, which had been first threatened (*ch.* iv. 23, *I will slay thy son, thy first-born*), but is last executed. If the death of their cattle had humbled and reformed them, their children would have been spared. The extent of this plague is described, *v.* 5. The prince that was to succeed in the throne was not too high to be reached by it, nor were the slaves at the mill too low to be taken notice of.

When Moses had thus delivered his message, it is said, *He went out from Pharaoh in a great anger*, though he was the meekest of all the men of the earth. Probably he expected that the very threatening of the death of the first-born would have induced Pharaoh to comply. But it had not that effect; his proud heart would not yield, no, not to save all the first-born of his kingdom. Moses, hereupon, was provoked to a holy indignation, being grieved (as our Saviour afterwards) for the *hardness of his heart*, Mark iii. 5. Note, It is a great vexation to the spirits of good ministers to see people deaf to all the fair warnings given them, and running headlong upon ruin, notwithstanding all the kind methods taken to prevent it. Thus Ezekiel went in *the bitterness of his spirit* (Ezek. iii. 14), because God had told him that the house of Israel would not hearken to him, *v.* 7. To be angry at nothing but sin is the way not to sin in anger.

JAMIESON, FAUSSET, BROWN

5. all the first-born in the land . . . shall die—The time, the suddenness, the dreadful severity of this coming calamity, and the peculiar description of victims, among both men and beasts, on whom it was to fall, would all contribute to aggravate its character. **the maid-servant that is behind the mill**—The grinding of the meal for daily use in every household is commonly done by female slaves and is considered the lowest employment. Two portable millstones are used for the purpose, of which the uppermost is turned by a small wooden handle, and during the operation the maid sits behind the mill. **6. shall be a great cry throughout all the land**—In the case of a death, people in the East set up loud wailings, and imagination may conceive what "a great cry" would be raised when death would invade every family in the kingdom. **7. against any of the children of Israel shall not a dog move his tongue**—No town or village in Egypt or in the East generally is free from the nuisance of dogs, who prowl about the streets and make the most hideous noise at any passers-by at night. What an emphatic significance does the knowledge of this circumstance give to this fact in the sacred record, that on the awful night that was coming, when the air should be rent with the piercing shrieks of mourners, so great and universal would be the panic inspired by the hand of God, that not a dog would move his tongue against the children of Israel! **8. all these thy servants shall . . . bow down themselves unto me**—This would be the effect of the universal terror; the hearts of the proudest would be humbled and do reverential homage to God, in the person of His representative. **went out . . . in a great anger**—Holy and righteous indignation at the duplicity, repeated falsehood, and hardened impenitence of the king; and this strong emotion was stirred in the bosom of Moses, not at the ill reception given to himself, but the dishonor done to God (Matt. 19:8; Eph. 4:26).

ADAM CLARKE

to the Egyptian throne to the son of the most abject slave, or the principal person in each family. *The maidservant that is behind the mill.* The meanest slaves were employed in this work. In many parts of the East they still grind all their corn with a kind of portable millstones, the upper one of which is turned round by a sort of lever fixed in the rim.

6. *There shall be a great cry.* Of the dying and for the dead.

7. *Not a dog move his tongue.* This passage has been generally understood as a proverbial expression, intimating that the Israelites should not only be free from this death, but that they should depart without any kind of molestation. For though there must be much bustle and comparative confusion in the sudden removal of six hundred thousand persons with their wives, children, goods, cattle, yet this should produce so little alarm that even the dogs should not bark at them, which it would be natural to expect, as the principal stir was to be about midnight.

8. *And all these thy servants shall come.* A prediction of what actually took place. See chap. xii. 31-33.

9. *Pharaoh shall not hearken unto you.* Though *shall* and *will* are both reputed signs of the future tense, and by many indiscriminately used, yet they make a most essential difference in composition in a variety of cases. For instance, if we translate *lo yishma*, "Pharaoh shall not hearken," as in our text, the word *shall* strongly intimates that it was impossible for Pharaoh to hearken, and that God had placed him under that impossibility; but if we translate as we should do, "Pharaoh will not hearken," it alters the case most essentially, and agrees with the many passages in the preceding chapters, where he is said to have hardened his own heart; as this proves that he, without any impulsive necessity, obstinately refused to attend to what Moses said or threatened; and that God took the advantage of this obstinacy to work another miracle, and thus multiply His wonders in the land. "Pharaoh will not hearken unto you"; and because he would not, God hardened his heart—left him to his own obstinacy.

MATTHEW HENRY — CHAPTER 12

Verses 1–20

Moses and Aaron here *receive of the Lord* what they were afterwards to *deliver to the people* concerning the ordinance of the passover, to which is prefixed an order for a new style to be observed in their months (*v.* 1, 2): *This shall be to you the beginning of months.* They had hitherto begun their year from the middle of September, but henceforward they were to begin it from the middle of March, at least in all their ecclesiastical computations. Note, It is good to begin the day, and begin the year, and especially to begin our lives, with God. This new calculation began the year with the spring, which *reneweth the face of the earth*, and was used as a figure of the coming of Christ, Cant. ii. 11, 12. While Moses was bringing the ten plagues upon the Egyptians, he was directing the Israelites to prepare for their departure at an hour's warning. Their amazement and hurry, it is easy to suppose, were great; yet now they must apply themselves to the observance of a sacred rite, to the honour of God.

I. God appointed that on the night wherein they were to go out of Egypt they should, in each of their families, *kill a lamb*, or that two or three families, if they were small, should join for a lamb. The lamb was to be got ready four days before, and that afternoon they were to *kill it* (*v.* 6) as a religious ceremony, acknowledging God's goodness to them, not only in preserving them from, but in delivering them by, the plagues inflicted on the Egyptians.

JAMIESON, FAUSSET, BROWN — CHAPTER 12

Vss. 1-10. THE PASSOVER INSTITUTED. **1. the Lord spake unto Moses**—rather, *had* spoken unto Moses and Aaron; for it is evident that the communication here described must have been made to them on or before the tenth of the month. **2. this month shall be unto you the beginning of months**—the first not only in order but in estimation. It had formerly been the seventh according to the reckoning of the civil year, which began in September, and continued unchanged, but it was thenceforth to stand first in the national religious year which began in March, April.

3. Speak ye unto all the congregation of Israel—The recent events had prepared the Israelitish people for a crisis in their affairs, and they seem to have yielded implicit obedience at this time to Moses. It is observable that, amid all the hurry and bustle of such a departure, their serious attention was to be given to a solemn act of religion. **a lamb for an house**—a kid might be taken (vs. 5). The service was to be a domestic one, for the deliverance was to be from an evil threatened to every house in Egypt.

4. if the household be too little for the lamb, etc.—It appears from Josephus that ten persons were required to make up the proper paschal communion. **every man, according to his eating**—It is said that the quantity eaten of the paschal lamb, by each individual, was about the size of an olive.

ADAM CLARKE — CHAPTER 12

2. *This month shall be unto you the beginning of months.* It is supposed that God now changed the commencement of the Jewish year. The month to which this verse refers, the month *Abib*, answers to a part of our March and April; whereas it is supposed that previously to this the year began with *Tisri*, which answers to a part of our September; for in this month the Jews suppose God created the world, when the earth appeared at once with all its fruits in perfection. From this circumstance the Jews have formed a twofold commencement of the year, which has given rise to a twofold denomination of the year itself, to which they afterwards attended in all their reckonings: that which began with *Tisri* or September was called their civil year; that which began with *Abib* or March was called the sacred year.

3. *In the tenth day of this month.* In after times they began their preparation on the thirteenth day or day before the Passover, which was not celebrated till the fourteenth day, see v. 6; but on the present occasion, as this was their first Passover, they probably required more time in which to get ready, as a state of very great confusion must have prevailed at this time. *A lamb.* The original word *seh* signifies the young of sheep and of goats, and may be indifferently translated either "lamb" or "kid." See v. 5. *A lamb for an house.* The whole host of Israel was divided into twelve tribes, these tribes into families, the families into houses, and the houses into particular persons; Numbers i; Josh. vii. 14.

4. *If the household be too little.* That is, if there be not persons enough in one family to eat a whole lamb, then two families must join together. The rabbins allow that there should be at least ten persons to one paschal lamb, and not more than twenty. *Take it according to the number of the souls.* The persons who were to eat of it were to be first ascertained,

MATTHEW HENRY

1. The paschal lamb was typical. Christ is *our Passover*, 1 Cor. v. 7. (1) It was to be a *lamb*; and Christ is *the Lamb of God* (John i. 29), often in the Revelation called the *Lamb*, meek and innocent as a lamb, dumb before the shearers. (2) It was to be a *male of the first year* (*v.* 5), in its prime; Christ offered up himself in the midst of his days, not in infancy with the babes of Bethlehem. (3) It was to be *without blemish* (*v.* 5), denoting the purity of the Lord Jesus, a Lamb *without spot*, 1 Pet. i. 19. (4) It was to be set apart four days before (*v.* 3, 6), denoting the designation of the Lord Jesus to be a Saviour. It is very observable that as Christ was crucified at the passover, so he solemnly entered into Jerusalem four days before, the very day that the paschal lamb was set apart. (5) It was to be slain, and *roasted with fire* (*v.* 6–9), denoting the exquisite sufferings of the Lord Jesus, even unto death, the death of the cross. (6) It was to be killed by the whole congregation. Christ suffered in the *end of the world* (Heb. ix. 26), by the hand of the Jews, the whole multitude of them (Luke xxiii. 18), and for the good of all his spiritual Israel. (7) Not *a bone of it must be broken* (*v.* 46), which is expressly said to be fulfilled in Christ (John xix. 33, 36), denoting the unbroken strength of the Lord Jesus.

III. Before they ate the flesh of the lamb, they were to sprinkle the blood upon the door-posts, *v.* 7. By this their houses were to be distinguished from the houses of the Egyptians.

2. The sprinkling of the blood was typical. (1) It was not enough that the blood of the lamb was shed, but it must be sprinkled, denoting the application of the merits of Christ's death to our souls; we must *receive the atonement*, Rom. v. 11. (2) It was to be sprinkled with *a bunch of hyssop* (*v.* 22) *dipped in the basin*. Faith is the bunch of hyssop by which we apply the promises to ourselves. (3) It was to be sprinkled upon the *door-posts*, denoting the open profession we are to make of faith in Christ, and obedience to him. (4) It was to be sprinkled upon the *lintel* and the *side-posts*, but not upon the *threshold* (*v.* 7), which cautions us to take heed of trampling under foot the blood of the covenant, Heb. x. 29. (5) The blood, thus sprinkled, was a means of the preservation of the Israelites from the destroying angel, who had nothing to do where the blood was.

3. The solemn eating of the lamb was typical of our gospel-duty to Christ. (1) The paschal lamb was killed, not to be looked upon only, but to be fed upon; so we must by faith make Christ ours, as we do that which we eat, and we must receive spiritual strength and nourishment from him, as from our food: see John vi. 53–55. (2) It was to be all eaten; those that by faith feed upon Christ must feed upon a whole Christ; they must take Christ and his yoke, Christ and his cross, as well as Christ and his crown. (3) It was to be eaten immediately, not deferred till morning, *v.* 10. *To-day* Christ is offered, and is to be accepted while it is called to-day. (4) It was to be eaten *with bitter herbs* (*v.* 8), in remembrance of the bitterness of their bondage in Egypt. Christ will be sweet to us if sin be bitter. (5) It was to be eaten in a departing posture (*v.* 11); when we feed upon Christ by faith we must absolutely forsake the rule and dominion of sin, and we must forsake all for Christ, and reckon it no bad bargain, Heb. xiii. 13, 14.

II. The lamb so slain they were to eat, roasted, with unleavened bread and bitter herbs, because they were to eat it *in haste* (*v.* 11), and to leave none of it until the morning; for God would have them to depend upon him for their daily bread. He that led them would feed them.

JAMIESON, FAUSSET, BROWN

5. lamb . . . without blemish—The smallest deformity or defect made a lamb unfit for sacrifice—a type of Christ (Heb. 7:26; I Pet. 1:19). **a male of the first year**—Christ in the prime of life.

6. keep it up until the fourteenth day, etc.—Being selected from the rest of the flock, it was to be separated four days before sacrifice; and for the same length of time was Christ under examination and His spotless innocence declared before the world. **kill it in the evening**—i.e., the interval between the sun's beginning to decline, and sunset, corresponding to our three o'clock in the afternoon.

7. take of the blood, and strike it on the two side-posts, etc.—as a sign of safety to those within. The posts must be considered of tents, in which the Israelites generally lived, though some might be in houses. Though the Israelites were sinners as well as the Egyptians, God was pleased to accept the substitution of a lamb—the blood of which, being seen *sprinkled* on the doorposts, procured them mercy. It was to be on the sideposts and upper doorposts, where it might be *looked* to, not on the threshold, where it might be trodden under foot. This was an emblem of the blood of sprinkling (Heb. 12:24, 29). **8. roast with fire**—for the sake of expedition; and this difference was always observed between the cooking of the paschal lamb and the other offerings (II Chron. 35:13). **unleavened bread**—also for the sake of despatch (Deut. 16:3), but as a kind of corruption (Luke 12:1) there seems to have been a typical meaning under it (I Cor. 5:8). **bitter herbs**—lit., bitters—to remind the Israelites of their affliction in Egypt, and morally of the trials to which God's people are subject on account of sin. **9. Eat not of it raw**—i.e., with any blood remaining—a caveat against conformity to idolatrous practices. It was to be roasted whole, not a bone to be broken, and this pointed to Christ (John 19:36).

10. let nothing of it remain until the morning—which might be applied in a superstitious manner, or allowed to putrefy, which in a hot climate would speedily have ensued; and which was not becoming in what had been offered to God.

11-14. THE RITE OF THE PASSOVER. **11. thus shall ye eat it; with your loins girded, your shoes on your feet**—as prepared for a journey. The first was done by the skirts of the loose outer cloth being drawn up and fastened in the girdle, so as to leave the leg and knee free for motion. As to the other, the Orientals never wear shoes indoors, and the ancient Egyptians, as appears from the monuments, did not usually wear either shoes or sandals. These injunctions seem to have applied chiefly to the first celebration of the rite.

ADAM CLARKE

and then the lamb was to be slain and dressed for that number.

5. *Without blemish.* Having no natural imperfection, no disease, no deficiency or redundancy of parts. *From the sheep, or from the goats.* The *seh* means either; and either was equally proper if without blemish. The Hebrews however in general preferred the lamb to the kid.

6. *Ye shall keep it up until the fourteenth day.* The lamb or kid was to be taken from the flock on the tenth day, and kept up and fed by itself till the fourteenth day, when it was to be sacrificed. This was never commanded nor practiced afterwards. *The whole assembly . . . shall kill it.* Any person might kill it, the sacrificial act in this case not being confined to the priests. *In the evening.* "Between the two evenings." The Jews divided the day into morning and evening: till the sun passed the meridian all was morning or forenoon; after that, all was afternoon or evening. Their first evening began just after twelve o'clock, and continued till sunset; their second evening began at sunset and continued till night, i.e., during the whole time of twilight; between twelve o'clock, therefore, and the termination of twilight, the passover was to be offered.

7. *Take of the blood, and strike it on the two side posts.* This was to be done by dipping a bunch of hyssop into the blood, and thus sprinkling it upon the posts; see v. 22. That this sprinkling of the blood of the paschal lamb was an emblem of the sacrifice and atonement made by the death of Jesus Christ is most clearly intimated in the sacred writings, 1 Pet. i. 2; Heb. ix. 13-14; viii. 10.

8. *They shall eat the flesh . . . roast with fire.* As it was the ordinary custom of the Jews to boil their flesh, some think that the command given here was in opposition to the custom of the Egyptians, who ate raw flesh in honor of Osiris.

Unleavened bread. Matstsoth, from *matsah,* to "squeeze" or "compress," because the bread prepared without leaven or yeast was generally compressed. *Bitter herbs.* What kind of herbs or salad is intended by the word *merorim,* which literally signifies "bitters," is not well known.

9. *With the purtenance thereof.* All the intestines, for these were abused by the heathen to purposes of divination; and when roasted in the manner here directed they could not be thus used. The command also implies that the lamb was to be roasted whole; neither the head nor the legs were to be separated, nor the intestines removed. I suppose that these last simply included the heart, lungs, liver, kidneys, and not the intestinal canal.

10. *Ye shall let nothing of it remain until the morning.* Merely to prevent putrefaction; for it was not meet that a thing offered to God should be subjected to corruption, which in such hot countries it must speedily undergo. Thus the body of our blessed Lord "saw no corruption," Ps. xvi. 10; Acts ii. 27, because, like the paschal lamb, it was a sacrifice offered to God.

11. *And thus shall ye eat it; with your loins girded.* As in the Eastern countries they wear long, loose garments, whenever they travel they tuck up the foreparts of their garments in the girdle which they wear round their loins. *Your shoes on your feet.* This seems particularly mentioned because not customary. "The easterns throw off their shoes when they eat, because it would be troublesome," says Sir J. Chardin, "to keep their shoes upon their feet, they sitting cross-legged on the floor, and having no hinder quarters to their shoes, which are made like slippers; and as they do not use tables and chairs as we do in Europe, but have their floors covered with carpets, they throw off their shoes when they enter their apartments, lest they should soil those beautiful pieces of furniture." On the contrary the Israelites were to have their *shoes on,* because now about to commence their journey. *Your staff in your hand.* The same writer observes that the Eastern people universally make use of a *staff* when they travel on foot.

Ye shall eat it in haste. Because they were suddenly to take their departure: the destroying

MATTHEW HENRY

F. C. COOK:

"The Lord's passover." The great and most significant name for the whole ordinance. The word *passover* renders as nearly as possible the true meaning of the original, of which the primary sense is generally held to be "pass rapidly," like a bird with outstretched wings, but it undoubtedly includes the idea of sparing (v. 13). See. Isa. 31:5, which combines the two great ideas involved in the word.

12. "I will pass through." A word wholly distinct from that which means "pass over." The "passing through" was in judgment, the "passing over" in mercy.—*Barnes' Notes*

4. The feast of unleavened bread was typical of the Christian life, 1 Cor. v. 7, 8. Having received Christ Jesus the Lord, (1) We must keep a feast in holy joy, continually delighting ourselves in Christ Jesus. If true believers have not a continual feast, it is their own fault. (2) It must be a feast of unleavened bread, kept in charity, without the leaven of malice, and in sincerity, without the leaven of hypocrisy.

IV. This was to be annually observed as a feast of the Lord in their generations, to which the *feast of unleavened bread* was annexed, during which, for seven days, they were to eat no bread but what was unleavened, in remembrance of their being confined to such bread, of necessity, for many days after they came out of Egypt, *v.* 14–20.

JAMIESON, FAUSSET, BROWN

it is the Lord's passover—called by this name from the blood-marked dwellings of the Israelites being *passed* over figuratively be the destroying angel.

12. smite . . . gods of Egypt—perhaps used here for princes and grandees. But, according .o Jewish tradition, the idols of Egypt were all on that night broken in pieces (see Num. 33:4; Isa. 19:1).

14. for a memorial, etc.—The close analogy traceable in all points between the Jewish and Christian passovers is seen also in the circumstance that both festivals were instituted before the events they were to commemorate had transpired.

15-51. Unleavened Bread. **15. Seven days shall ye eat unleavened bread,** etc.—This was to commemorate another circumstance in the departure of the Israelites, who were urged to leave so hurriedly that their dough was unleavened (vs. 39), and they had to eat unleavened cakes (Deut. 16:3). The greatest care was always taken by the Jews to free their houses from leaven—the owner searching every corner of his dwelling with a lighted candle. A figurative allusion to this is made (I Cor. 5:7). The exclusion of leaven for seven days would not be attended with inconvenience in the East, where the usual leaven is dough kept till it becomes sour, and it is kept from one day to another for the purpose of preserving leaven in readiness. Thus even were there none in all the country, it could be got within twenty-four hours [Harmer]. **that soul shall be cut off**—excommunicated from the community and privileges of the chosen people.

16. there shall be an holy convocation—lit., *calling* of the people, which was done by sound of trumpets (Num. 10:2), a sacred assembly—for these days were to be regarded as Sabbaths—excepting only that meat might be cooked on them (ch. 16:23).

17. ye shall observe, etc.—The seven days of this feast were to commence the day after the passover. It was a distinct festival following that feast; but although this feast was instituted like the passover *before* the departure, the observance of it did not take place till *after*.

ADAM CLARKE

angel was at hand, their enemies were coming against them, and they had not a moment to lose.

It is the Lord's passover. That is, Jehovah is now about to "pass over" the land, and the houses only where the blood is sprinkled shall be safe from the stroke of death. The Hebrew word *pesach,* which we very properly translate *passover,* and which should always be pronounced as two words, has its name from the angel of God passing by or over the houses of the Israelites, on the posts and lintels of which the blood of the lamb was sprinkled, while he stopped at the houses of the Egyptians to slay their firstborn.

12. *Against all the gods of Egypt.* As different animals were sacred among the Egyptians, the slaying of the *firstborn* of all the beasts might be called executing judgment upon the gods of Egypt. As this however does not appear very clear and satisfactory, some have imagined that the word *elohey* should be translated "princes," which is the rendering in our margin; for as these princes, who were rulers of the kingdom under Pharaoh, were equally hostile to the Hebrews with Pharaoh himself, therefore these judgments fell equally heavy on them also.

13. *The blood shall be to you for a token.* It shall be the sign to the destroying angel that the house on which he sees this blood sprinkled is under the protection of God, and that no person in it is to be injured. See on v. 11.

14. *A memorial.* To keep up a remembrance of the severity and goodness, or justice and mercy, of God. *Ye shall keep it a feast*—it shall be annually observed, and shall be celebrated with solemn religious joy, *throughout your generations*—as long as ye continue to be a distinct people; an *ordinance*—a divine appointment, an institution of God himself, neither to be altered nor set aside by any human authority. *For ever. Chukkath olam,* an everlasting or endless statute, because representative of the Lamb of God, who taketh away the sin of the world; whose mediation, in consequence of His sacrifice, shall endure while time itself lasts; and to whose merits and efficacy the salvation of the soul shall be ascribable throughout eternity. This, therefore, is a statute and ordinance that can have no end, either in this world or in the world to come.

15. *Seven days shall ye eat unleavened bread.* This has been considered as a distinct ordinance, and not essentially connected with the Passover. The Passover was to be observed on the fourteenth day of the first month; the Feast of Unleavened Bread began on the fifteenth and lasted seven days, the first and last of which were holy convocations. *That soul shall be cut off.* There are thirty-six places in which this excision or cutting off is threatened against the Jews for neglect of some particular duty; and what is implied in the thing itself is not well known. Some think it means a violent death, some a premature death, and some an eternal death. It is very likely that it means no more than a separation from the rights and privileges of an Israelite; so that after this excision the person was considered as a mere stranger, who had neither lot nor part in Israel, nor any right to the blessings of the covenant. This is probably what St. Paul means, Rom. ix. 3.

16. *In the first day . . . and in the seventh day there shall be an holy convocation.* This is the first place where we meet with the account of an assembly collected for the mere purpose of religious worship. Such assemblies are called *holy convocations,* which is a very appropriate appellation for a religious assembly; they were called together by the express command of God, and were to be employed in a work of holiness.

17. *Selfsame day. Beetsem,* "in the body of this day," or "in the strength of this day"; probably they began their march about daybreak, called here the body or strength of the day, and in Deut. xvi. 1, by night—sometime before the sun rose.

19. *No leaven found in your houses.* To meet the letter of this precept in the fullest manner possible, the Jews, on the eve of this festival, institute the most rigorous search through every part of their houses, not only removing all

MATTHEW HENRY

Verses 21–28

I. Moses is here, as a faithful steward in God's house.

1. That this night, when the first-born were to be destroyed, no Israelite must *stir out of doors till morning*. They must not go out of the doors, lest they should straggle and be out of the way when they should be summoned to depart.

2. That hereafter they should carefully teach their children the meaning of this service, *v.* 26, 27.

(1) The question which the children would ask: "*What mean you by this service?* What is the meaning of all this care and exactness about eating this lamb, and this unleavened bread, more than about common food?" It concerns us all rightly to understand the meaning of those holy ordinances wherein we worship God, what is the nature and what the end of them.

(2) The answer which the parents were to return to this question (*v.* 27): *You shall say, It is the sacrifice of the Lord's passover*, that is, "By the killing and sacrificing of this lamb, we keep in remembrance the work of wonder and grace which God did for our fathers, when," [1] "To make way for our deliverance out of bondage" He slew the first-born of the Egyptians; and, [2] "Though there were *with us, even with us, sins against the Lord our God*, yet God graciously appointed and accepted the family-sacrifice of a lamb, as, of old, the ram instead of Isaac, and in every house where the lamb was slain the first-born were saved." The word *pesach* signifies a *leap*, or *transition*; it is a passing over; for the destroying angel passed over the houses of the Israelites, and did not destroy their first-born. It was designed to look forward as an earnest of the great sacrifice of the Lamb of God in the fulness of time, instead of us and our first-born. *Christ our passover was sacrificed for us*, his death was our life, and thus he was the *Lamb slain from the foundation of the world*, from the foundation of the Jewish church: Moses kept the passover by faith in Christ, for Christ was *the end of the law for righteousness*.

II. The people received these instructions with reverence and ready obedience. 1. They *bowed the head and worshipped* (*v.* 27). 2. They *went away and did* as they were commanded, *v.* 28. Here was none of that discontent and murmuring among them which we read of, *ch.* v. 20, 21. The plagues of Egypt had done them good, and raised their expectations of a glorious deliverance, which before they despaired of; and now they went forth to meet it in the way appointed.

Verses 29–36

Here we have, I. The Egyptians' sons, even their first-born, slain, *v.* 29, 30. If Pharaoh would have taken the warning which was given him of this plague, and would thereupon have released Israel, what a great many dear and valuable lives might have been preserved! But see what obstinate infidelity brings upon men. It reached from the throne to the dungeon. Prince and peasant stand upon the same level before God's judgments, for there is no respect of persons with him; see Job xxxiv. 19, 20. Let us learn hence, (1) To tremble before God, and to be *afraid of his judgments*, Ps. cxix. 120. (2) To be thankful to God for the daily preservation of ourselves and our families.

II. Now Pharaoh's pride is abased, and he yields to all that Moses had insisted on: *Serve the Lord as you have said* (*v.* 31), and *take your flocks as you have said*, *v.* 32. 1. They are commanded to depart: *Rise up and get you forth*, *v.* 31. Pharaoh had told Moses he should *see his face no more*; but now he sent for him. That he sent them out, not as men hated but as men feared, is plainly discovered by his humble request to them (*v.* 32): "*Bless me also*; let me have your prayers, that I may not be plagued for what is past, when you are gone."

JAMIESON, FAUSSET, BROWN

19. stranger—No foreigner could partake of the passover, unless circumcised; the "stranger" specified as admissible to the privilege must, therefore, be considered a Gentile *proselyte*.

21-25. Then Moses called for all the elders of Israel, etc.—Here are given special directions for the observance.

hyssop—a small red moss [HASSELQUIST]. The caper-plant [ROYLE]. It was used in the sprinkling, being well adapted for such purposes, as it grows in bushes—putting out plenty of suckers from a single root. And it is remarkable that it was ordained in the arrangements of an all-wise Providence that the Roman soldiers should undesignedly, on their part, make use of this symbolical plant to Christ when, as our Passover, He was sacrificed for us. **none . . . shall go out at the door of his house until the morning**—This regulation was peculiar to the first celebration, and intended, as some think, to prevent any suspicion attaching to them of being agents in the impending destruction of the Egyptians; there is an allusion to it (Isa. 26:20). **26. when your children shall say, . . . What mean ye by this service**—Independently of some observances which were not afterwards repeated, the usages practised at this yearly commemorative feast were so peculiar that the curiosity of the young would be stimulated, and thus parents had an excellent opportunity, which they were enjoined to embrace, for instructing each rising generation in the origin and leading facts of the national faith.

27, 28. the people bowed the head, and worshipped—All the preceding directions were communicated through the elders, and the Israelites, being deeply solemnized by the influence of past and prospective events, gave prompt and faithful obedience.

29. at midnight the Lord smote all the first-born in the land of Egypt—At the moment when the Israelites were observing the newly instituted feast in the singular manner described, the threatened calamity overtook the Egyptians. It is more easy to imagine than describe the confusion and terror of that people suddenly roused from sleep and enveloped in darkness—none could assist their neighbors when the groans of the dying and the wild shrieks of mourners were heard everywhere around. The hope of every family was destroyed at a stroke. This judgment, terrible though it was, evinced the equity of divine retribution. For eighty years the Egyptians had caused the male children of the Israelites to be cast into the river, and now all their own first-born fell under the stroke of the destroying angel. They were made, in the justice of God, to feel something of what they had made His people feel. Many a time have the hands of sinners made the snares in which they have themselves been entangled, and fallen into the pit which they have dug for the righteous. "Verily there is a God that judgeth in the earth." **30. there was not a house where there was not one dead**—Perhaps this statement is not to be taken absolutely. The Scriptures frequently use the words "all," "none," in a comparative sense—and so in this case. There would be many a house in which there would be no child, and many in which the first-born might be already dead. What is to be understood is, that almost every house in Egypt had a death in it. **31. called for Moses and Aaron**—a striking fulfilment of the words of Moses (ch. 11:8), and showing that they were spoken under divine suggestion.

ADAM CLARKE

leavened bread, but sweeping every part clean, that no crumb of bread shall be left that had any leaven in it. And so strict were they in the observance of the letter of this law that if even a mouse was seen to run across the floor with a crumb of bread in its mouth they considered the whole house as polluted, and began their purification afresh. Leaven was an emblem of sin, because it proceeded from corruption; and the putting away of this implied the turning to God with simplicity and uprightness of heart.

21. *Kill the passover.* That is, the lamb, which was called the paschal or passover lamb. The animal that was to be sacrificed on this occasion got the name of the institution itself. St. Paul copies the expression, 1 Cor. v. 7: "Christ our passover" (that is, our Paschal Lamb) "is sacrificed for us."

22. *A bunch of hyssop.* The original word *ezob* has been variously translated *musk, rosemary, mint, marjoram,* and *hyssop;* the latter seems to be the most proper. It was used in sprinkling the blood of the paschal lamb, in cleansing the leprosy, Lev. xiv. 4, 6, 51-52; in composing the water of purification, Num. xix. 6, and sprinkling it, v. 18. It was a type of the purifying virtue of the bitter sufferings of Christ. And it is plain, from Ps. li. 7, that the Psalmist understood its meaning.

26. *What mean ye by this service?* The establishment of this service annually was a very wise provision to keep up in remembrance this wonderful deliverance. From the remotest antiquity the institution of feasts, games, etc., has been used to keep up the memory of past grand events. Hence God instituted the Sabbath to keep up the remembrance of the creation, and the Passover to keep up the remembrance of the deliverance from Egypt. All the other feasts were instituted on similar reasons. The Jews never took their sons to the Tabernacle or Temple till they were twelve years of age, nor suffered them to eat of the flesh of any victim till they had themselves offered a sacrifice at the Temple, which they were not permitted to do before the twelfth year of their age. It was at this age that Joseph and Mary took our blessed Lord to the Temple, probably for the first time, to offer His sacrifice.

27. *It is the sacrifice of the Lord's passover.* We have already intimated that the paschal lamb was an illustrious type of Christ; and we shall find that everything in this account is typical or representative. The bondage and affliction of the people of Israel may be considered as emblems of the hard slavery and wretchedness consequent on a state of sinfulness.

29. *Smote all the firstborn.* If we take the term *firstborn* in its literal sense only, we shall be led to conclude that in a vast number of the houses of the Egyptians there could have been no death, as it is not at all likely that every firstborn child of every Egyptian family was still alive, and that all the firstborn of their cattle still remained. And yet it is said, v. 30, that there was "not a house where there was not one dead." The word, therefore, must not be taken in its literal sense only. From its use in a great variety of places in the Scriptures it is evident that it means the chief, most excellent, best beloved, most distinguished. In this sense our blessed Lord is called "the firstborn of every creature," Col. i. 15, and "the firstborn among many brethren," Rom. viii. 29; that is, He is more excellent than all creatures, and greater than all the children of men. And the people of Israel are often called by the same name, see Exod. iv. 22: "Israel is my son, my firstborn"; that is, the people in whom I particularly delight, and whom I will especially support and defend.

30. *There was a great cry.* No people in the universe were more remarkable for their mournings than the Egyptians, especially in matters of religion; they whipped, beat, tore themselves, and howled in all the excess of grief. When a relative died, the people left the house, ran into the streets, and howled in the most lamentable and frantic manner.

31. *Called for Moses and Aaron.* That is, he sent the message here mentioned to them; for it does not appear that he had any further interview with Moses and Aaron, after what is mentioned in chap. x. 28-29 and xi. 8. See the

MATTHEW HENRY

2. They are hired to depart by the Egyptians; they cried out (*v.* 33), *We be all dead men.*

When the Egyptians urged them to be gone, it was easy for them to say that the Egyptians had kept them poor, that they could not undertake such a journey with empty purses, but that, if they would give them wherewithal to bear their charges, they would be gone. The Israelites might receive and keep what they thus borrowed, or rather required, of the Egyptians, as justly as servants receive wages from their masters for work done, and sue for it if it be detained.

Verses 37–42

Here is the departure of the children of Israel out of Egypt. Pharaoh was now in a good mind; but they had reason to think he would not long continue so, and therefore it was no time to linger. We have here an account, 1. Of their number, about 600,000 men (*v.* 37), besides women and children, which, I think, we cannot suppose to make less than 1,200,000 more. What a vast increase was this, to arise from seventy souls in little more than 200 years' time! 2. Of their retinue (*v.* 38): *A mixed multitude went up with them,* hangers on to that great family, some perhaps willing to leave their country, because it was laid waste by the plagues, others went out of curiosity, to see the solemnities of Israel's sacrifice to their God, which had been so much talked of, and expecting to see some glorious appearances of their God to them in the wilderness. Probably the greatest part of this mixed multitude were but a rude unthinking mob, that followed the crowd they knew not why; we afterwards find that they proved a snare to them (Num. xi. 4), and it is probable that when, soon afterwards, they understood that the children of Israel were to continue forty years in the wilderness, they quitted them, and returned to Egypt. 3. Of their effects. They had with them *flocks and herds,* even *very much cattle.* 4. Of the provision made for the camp, which was very poor and slender. They brought some dough with them out of Egypt in their knapsacks, *v.* 34. They had prepared to bake, the next day, in order to their removal, understanding it was very near; but, being hastened away sooner than they thought of, by some hours, they took the dough as it was, unleavened; when they came to Succoth, their first stage, they baked unleavened cakes, and, though these were of course insipid, yet the liberty they were brought into made this the most joyful meal they had ever eaten in their lives. It was just 430 years from the promise made to Abraham (as the apostle explains it, Gal. iii. 17) at his first coming into Canaan. So long the promise of a settlement lay dormant and unfulfilled, but now, at length, it revived. The first passover-night was a night of the Lord *much to be observed*; but the last passover-night, in which Christ was betrayed (and in which the passover, with the rest of the ceremonial institutions, was superseded and abolished), was a night of the Lord *much more to be observed,* when a yoke heavier than that of Egypt was broken from off our necks, and a land better than that of Canaan set before us. That was a temporal deliverance to be celebrated *in their generation*; this is an eternal redemption to be celebrated in the praises of glorious saints, *world without end.*

JAMIESON, FAUSSET, BROWN

32. also take your flocks, etc.—All the terms the king had formerly insisted on were now departed from; his pride had been effectually humbled. Appalling judgments in such rapid succession showed plainly that the hand of God was against him. His own family bereavement had so crushed him to the earth that he not only showed impatience to rid his kingdom of such formidable neighbors, but even begged an interest in their prayers. **34. people took . . . kneading-troughs**—Having lived so long in Egypt, they must have been in the habit of using the utensils common in that country. The Egyptian kneading-trough was a bowl of wicker or rush-work, and it admitted of being hastily wrapped up with the dough in it and slung over the shoulder in their *hykes* or loose upper garments. **35. children of Israel borrowed of the Egyptians jewels of silver**—When the Orientals go to their sacred festivals, they always put on their *best jewels.* The Israelites themselves thought they were only going three days' journey to hold a feast unto the Lord, and in these circumstances it would be easy for them to *borrow* what was necessary for a sacred festival. But "borrow" conveys a wrong meaning. The word rendered *borrow* signifies properly to *ask, demand, require.* The Israelites had been kept in great poverty, having received little or no wages. They now insisted on full remuneration for all their labor, and it was paid in light and valuable articles adapted for convenient carriage. **36. the Lord gave the people favour in the sight of the Egyptians**—Such a dread of them was inspired into the universal minds of the Egyptians, that whatever they asked was readily given. **spoiled the Egyptians**—The accumulated earnings of many years being paid them at this moment, the Israelites were suddenly enriched, according to the promise made to Abraham (Gen. 15:14), and they left the country like a victorious army laden with spoil (Ps. 105:37; Ezek. 39:10). **37. The children of Israel journeyed from Rameses**—now generally identified with the ancient Heroöpolis, and fixed at the modern *Abu*-Keisheid. This position agrees with the statement that the scene of the miraculous judgments against Pharaoh was "in the field of Zoan." And it is probable that, in expectation of their departure, which the king on one pretext or another delayed, the Israelites had been assembled there as a general rendezvous. In journeying from Rameses to Palestine, there was a choice of two routes—the one along the shores of the Mediterranean to El-Arish, the other more circuitous round the head of the Red Sea and the desert of Sinai. The latter Moses was directed to take (ch. 13:17). **to Succoth**—i.e., booths, probably nothing more than a place of temporary encampment. The Hebrew word signifies a covering or shelter formed by the boughs of trees; and hence, in memory of this lodgment, the Israelites kept the feast of tabernacles yearly in this manner. **six hundred thousand . . . men**—It appears from Numbers 1 that the enumeration is of men above twenty years of age. Assuming, what is now ascertained by statistical tables, that the number of males above that age is as nearly as possible the half of the total number of males, the whole male population of Israel, on this computation, would amount to 1,200,000; and adding an equal number for women and children, the aggregate number of Israelites who left Egypt would be 2,400,000. **38. a mixed multitude went with them**—lit., a great rabble (see also Num. 11:4); Deut. 29:11); slaves, persons in the lowest grades of society, partly natives and partly foreigners, bound close to them as companions in misery, and gladly availing themselves of the opportunity to escape in the crowd. (Cf. Zech. 8:23). **40. the sojourning of the children of Israel . . . was four hundred and thirty years**—The *Septuagint* renders it thus: "The sojourning of the children and of their fathers, which they sojourned in the land of Canaan and in the land of Egypt." These additions are important, for the period of sojourn in Egypt did not exceed 215 years; but if we reckon from the time that Abraham entered Canaan and the promise was made in which the sojourn of his posterity in Egypt was announced, this makes up the time to 430 years. **41. even the selfsame day**—implying an exact and literal fulfilment of the predicted period.

ADAM CLARKE

notes there.

33. *The Egyptians were urgent upon the people.* They felt much, they feared more; and therefore wished to get immediately rid of a people on whose account they found they were smitten with so many and such dreadful plagues.

34. *The people took their dough before it was leavened.* There was no time now to make any regular preparation for their departure, such was the universal hurry and confusion. The Israelites could carry but little of their household utensils with them; but some, such as they kneaded their bread and kept their meal in, they were obliged to carry with them. The kneading troughs of the Arabs are comparatively small wooden bowls, which, after kneading their bread in, serve them as dishes out of which they eat their victuals. And as to these being bound up in their clothes, no more may be intended than their wrapping them up in their long, loose garments.

35. *They borrowed of the Egyptians.* See the note on chap. iii. 22, where the very exceptionable term *borrow* is largely explained.

37. *From Rameses to Succoth. Rameses* appears to have been another name for Goshen, though it is probable that there might have been a chief city or village in that land, where the children of Israel rendezvoused previously to their departure, called Rameses. As the term *Succoth* signifies "booths" or "tents," it is probable that this place was so named from its being the place of the first encampment of the Israelites. *Six hundred thousand.* That is, there was this number of effective men, twenty years old and upwards, who were able to go out to war.

40. *Now the sojourning of the children of Israel.* The statement in this verse is allowed on all hands to be extremely difficult and, therefore, the passage stands in especial need of illustration. The Samaritan Pentateuch, in all its manuscripts and printed copies, reads the place thus: "Now the sojourning of the children of Israel, and of their fathers, which they sojourned in the land of Canaan and in the land of Egypt, was 430 years." This same sum is given by St. Paul, Gal. iii. 17, who reckons from the promise made to Abraham, when God commanded him to go to Canaan, to the giving of the law, which soon followed the departure from Egypt; and this chronology of the apostle is concordant with the Samaritan Pentateuch, which, by preserving the two passages, "they and their fathers," and "in the land of Canaan," which are lost out of the present copies of the Hebrew text, has rescued this passage from all obscurity and contradiction. It may be necessary to observe that the Alexandrian copy of the Septuagint has the same reading as that in the Samaritan. That these three witnesses have the truth, the chronology itself proves; for from Abraham's entry into Canaan to the birth of Isaac was 25 years, Gen. xii. 4; xvii. 1-21; Isaac was 60 years old at the birth of Jacob, Gen. xxv. 26; and Jacob was 130 at his going down into Egypt, Gen. xlvii. 9; which three sums make 215 years. And then Jacob and his children having continued in Egypt 215 years more, the whole sum of 430 years is regularly completed.

42. *A night to be much observed.* A night to be held in everlasting remembrance, because of the peculiar display of the power and goodness of God, the observance of which annually was to be considered a religious precept while the Jewish nation should continue.

43. *This is the ordinance of the passover.* From the last verse of this chapter it appears pretty evident that this, to the fiftieth verse inclusive, constituted a part of the directions given to Moses relative to the proper observance of the first Passover, and should be read conjointly with the preceding account beginning at verse 21. It may be supposed that these latter parts contain such particular directions as God gave to Moses after He had given those general ones mentioned in the preceding verses, but they seem all to belong to this first Passover. *There shall no stranger eat thereof. Ben nechar,* the "son of a stranger or foreigner," i.e., one who was not of the genuine Hebrew stock, or one who had not received circumcision; for any

MATTHEW HENRY

Verses 43–51

Some further precepts are here given concerning the passover, as it should be observed in times to come.

I. *All the congregation of Israel must keep it, v.* 47. All that share in God's mercies should join in thankful praises for them. The New Testament passover, the Lord's supper, ought not to be neglected by any who are capable of celebrating it. 1. No stranger that was uncircumcised might be admitted to eat of it, *v.* 43, 45, 48. We must be born again by the word ere we can be nourished by it. Nor shall any partake of the benefit of Christ's sacrifice, or feast upon it, who are not first circumcised in heart, Col. ii. 11. 2. Any stranger that was circumcised might be welcome to eat of the passover, even *servants, v.* 44. If in sincerity and with that zeal which the thing requires and deserves, we give up ourselves to God, we shall, with ourselves, give up all we have to him, and do our utmost that all ours may be his too. Here is an early indication of favour to the poor Gentiles, that the stranger, if circumcised, stands upon the same level with the home-born Israelite. It was their dedication to God, not their descent from Abraham, that entitled them to their privileges.

II. *In one house shall it be eaten* (*v.* 46), that they might rejoice together, and edify one another in the eating of it.

The chapter concludes with a repetition of the whole matter, that the children of Israel did as they were bidden, and God did for them as he promised (*v.* 50, 51).

JAMIESON, FAUSSET, BROWN

KEIL–DELITZSCH:

Verses 43–50. *Regulations concerning the participants in the Passover.* These regulations, which were supplementary to the law of the Passover in verses 3–11, were not communicated before the exodus; because it was only by the fact that a crowd of foreigners attached themselves to the Israelites that Israel was brought into a connection with foreigners, which needed to be clearly defined, especially so far as the Passover was concerned, the festival of Israel's birth as the people of God. If the Passover was still to retain this signification, of course no foreigner could participate in it. This is the first regulation. But as it was by virtue of a divine call, and not through natural descent, that Israel had become the people of Jehovah, and as it was destined in that capacity to be a blessing to all nations, the attitude assumed towards foreigners was not to be an altogether repelling one. Hence the further directions in verse 44: purchased servants, who had been politically incorporated as Israel's property, were to be entirely incorporated by circumcision, so as even to take part in the Passover. But settlers, and servants working for wages, were not to eat of it, for they stood in a purely external relation, which might be any day dissolved. Literally, "to eat at anything," to take part in the eating (Lev. 22:11). The deeper ground for this was that in this meal Israel was to preserve and celebrate its unity and fellowship with Jehovah. This was the meaning of the regulations, which were repeated in verses 46 and 47 from verses 4, 9, and 10, where they had been already explained. If, therefore, a foreigner living among the Israelites wished to keep the Passover, he was first of all to be spiritually incorporated into the nation of Jehovah by circumcision (v. 48).

—Commentary on the Old Testament

49. One law shall be to him that is homeborn, and unto the stranger—This regulation displays the liberal spirit of the Hebrew institutions. Any foreigner might obtain admission to the privileges of the nation on complying with their sacred ordinances. In the Mosaic equally as in the Christian dispensation, privilege and duty were inseparably conjoined.

ADAM CLARKE

circumcised person might eat the Passover, as the total exclusion extends only to the uncircumcised, see v. 48.

45. *A foreigner. Toshab,* from *yashab,* to "sit down or dwell"; one who is a mere sojourner, for the purpose of traffic, merchandise, etc. *And an hired servant.* None of these shall eat of it, because not circumcised—not brought under the bond of the covenant; and not being under obligation to observe the Mosaic law, had no right to its privileges and blessings.

46. *In one house shall it be eaten.* In one family, if that be large enough; if not, a neighboring family might be invited, v. 4. *Thou shalt not carry forth ought of the flesh.* Every family must abide within doors because of the destroying angel, none being permitted to go out of his house till the next day, v. 22. *Neither shall ye break a bone thereof.* As it was to be eaten in haste (v. 11), there was no time either to separate the bones or to break them in order to extract the marrow; and lest they should be tempted to consume time in this way, therefore this ordinance was given. It is very likely that, when the whole lamb was brought to table, they cut off the flesh without even separating any of the large joints, leaving the skeleton, with whatever flesh they could not eat, to be consumed with fire, v. 10. This precept was also given to point out a most remarkable circumstance which fifteen hundred years after was to take place in the crucifixion of the Saviour of mankind, who was the true Paschal Lamb, that Lamb of God that takes away the sin of the world; who, though He was crucified as a common malefactor, and it was a universal custom to break the legs of such on the cross, yet so did the providence of God order it that a bone of Him was not broken. See the fulfillment of this wondrously expressive type, John xix. 33, 36.

48. *And when a stranger . . . will keep the passover.* Let all who sojourn among you, and who desire to partake of this sacred ordinance, not only be circumcised themselves, but all the males of their families likewise, that they may all have an equal right to the blessings of the covenant.

49. *One law shall be to him that is homeborn.* As this is the first place that the term *torah* or "law" occurs, a term of the greatest importance in divine revelation, and on the proper understanding of which much depends, I judge it best to give its genuine explanation once for all.

The word *torah* comes from the root *yarah,* which signifies to "aim at, teach, point out, direct, lead, guide, make straight or even"; and from these significations of the word (and in all these senses it is used in the Bible) we may see at once the nature, properties, and design of the law of God. It is a system of instruction in righteousness; it teaches the difference between moral good and evil; ascertains what is right and fit to be done, and what should be left undone, because improper to be performed.

The word *lex,* "law," among the Romans, has been derived from *lego,* "I read"; because when a law or statute was made, it was hung up in the most public places, that it might be seen, read, and known by all men, that those who were to obey the laws might not break them through ignorance, and thus incur the penalty. The Greeks call a law *nomos,* from *nemo,* to "divide, distribute, minister to, or serve," because the law divides to all their just rights, appoints or distributes to each his proper duty, and thus serves or ministers to the welfare of the individual and the support of society.

51. *By their armies. Tsibotham,* from *tsaba,* to "assemble, meet together," in an orderly or regulated manner, and hence to "war," to act together as troops in battle; whence *tsebaoth,* "troops, armies, hosts." It is from this that the Divine Being calls himself *Yehovah tsebaoth,* "the Lord of hosts or armies," because the Israelites were brought out of Egypt under His direction, marshalled and ordered by himself, guided by His wisdom, supported by His providence, and protected by His might. This is the true and simple reason why God is so frequently styled in Scripture the "Lord of hosts"; for *the Lord did bring the children of Israel out of the land of Egypt by their armies.*

MATTHEW HENRY

CHAPTER 13

Verses 1–10

Care is here taken to perpetuate the remembrance, I. Of the preservation of Israel's firstborn. God here lays claim in particular to the firstborn of the Israelites, by right of protection: *Sanctify to me all the firstborn.* God, who is the first and best, should have the first and best, and to him we should resign that which is most dear to us, and most valuable. The firstborn were the joy and hope of their families. Therefore *they shall be mine,* says God. It is the *church of the firstborn* that is sanctified to God, Heb. xii. 23. Christ is the *firstborn among many brethren* (Rom. viii. 29), and, by virtue of their union with him, all that are born again, and born from above, are accounted as firstborn. There is an *excellency of dignity and power* belonging to them; and, *if children, then heirs.*

II. The remembrance of their coming out of Egypt must also be perpetuated: "*Remember this day* (*v.* 3). Remember it by a good token, as the most remarkable day of your lives, the birthday of your nation, or the day of its coming of age, to be no longer under the rod." Thus the day of Christ's resurrection is to be remembered, for in it we were raised up with Christ out of death's *house of bondage.*

1. They must be sure to *keep the feast of unleavened bread, v.* 5–7. It was not enough that they remembered it, but they must celebrate the memorial of it in that way which God had appointed. Observe, How strict the prohibition of leaven is (*v.* 7); not only no leaven must be eaten, but none must be seen, no, not in all their quarters. Accordingly, the Jews' usage was, before the feast of the passover, to cast all the leavened bread out of their houses: they burnt it, or buried it, or broke it small and scattered it in the wind; they searched diligently with lighted candles in all the corners of their houses, lest any leaven should remain.

2. They must instruct their children in the meaning of it, and relate to them the story of their deliverance out of Egypt, *v.* 8. When they were celebrating the ordinance, they must explain it.

JAMIESON, FAUSSET, BROWN

CHAPTER 13

Vss. 1, 2. THE FIRST-BORN SANCTIFIED. **2. Sanctify unto me all the first-born**—To sanctify means to consecrate, to set apart from a common to a sacred use. The foundation of this duty rested on the fact that the Israelites, having had their first-born preserved by a distinguishing act of grace from the general destruction that overtook the families of the Egyptians, were bound in token of gratitude to consider them as the Lord's peculiar property (cf. Heb. 12:23).

3-10. MEMORIAL OF THE PASSOVER. **3. Moses said unto the people, Remember this day**—The day that gave them a national existence and introduced them into the privileges of independence and freedom, deserved to live in the memories of the Hebrews and their posterity; and, considering the signal interposition of God displayed in it, to be held not only in perpetual, but devout remembrance. **house of bondage**—lit., house of slaves—i.e., a servile and degrading condition. **for by strength of hand the Lord brought you out from this place**—The emancipation of Israel would never have been obtained except it had been wrung from the Egyptian tyrant by the appalling judgments of God, as had been at the outset of his mission announced to Moses (ch. 3:19). **There shall no leavened bread,** etc.—The words are elliptical, and the meaning of the clause may be paraphrased thus:—"For by strength of hand the Lord brought you out from this place, in such haste that there could or should be no leavened bread eaten." **4. month Abib**—lit., a green ear, and hence the month Abib is the month of green ears, corresponding to the middle of our March. It was the best season for undertaking a journey to the desert region of Sinai, especially with flocks and herds; for then the winter torrents had subsided, and the wadies were covered with an early and luxuriant verdure. **5-7. when the Lord shall bring thee**—The passover is here instituted as a permanent festival of the Israelites. It was, however, only a prospective observance; we read of only one celebration of the passover during the protracted sojourn in the wilderness; but on their settlement in the promised land, the season was hallowed as a sacred anniversary, in conformity with the directions here given. **8. thou shalt show thy son in that day, saying**—The establishment of this and the other sacred festivals presented the best opportunities of instructing the young in a knowledge of His gracious doings to their ancestors in Egypt. **9. it shall be for a sign unto thee upon thine hand,** etc.—There is no reason to believe that the Oriental tattooing—the custom of staining the hands with the powder of Hennah, as Eastern females now do—is here referred to. Nor is it probable that either this practice or the phylacteries of the Pharisees—parchment scrolls, which were worn on their wrists and foreheads—had so early an existence. The words are to be considered only as a figurative mode of expression. **that the Lord's law may be in thy mouth,** etc.—i.e., that it may be the subject of frequent conversation and familiar knowledge among the people.

ADAM CLARKE

CHAPTER 13

1. *The Lord spake unto Moses.* The commands in this chapter appear to have been given at Succoth, on the same day in which they left Egypt.

2. *Sanctify unto me all the firstborn.* To sanctify, *kadash,* signifies to "consecrate, separate, and set apart" a thing or person from all secular purposes to some religious use; and exactly answers to the import of the Greek *hagiazo,* from *a,* privative, and *ge,* "the earth," because everything offered or consecrated to God was separated from all earthly uses. Hence a holy person or saint is termed *hagios,* i.e., a person separated from the earth; one who lives a holy life, entirely devoted to the service of God. Thus the persons and animals sanctified to God were employed in the service of the Tabernacle and Temple; and the animals, such as were proper, were offered in sacrifice. *Whatsoever openeth the womb.* That is, the firstborn, if a male; for females were not offered, nor the first male, if a female had been born previously. Again, if a man had several wives, the firstborn of each, if a male, was to be offered to God. And all this was done to commemorate the preservation of the firstborn of the Israelites, when those of the Egyptians were destroyed.

5. *When the Lord shall bring thee into the land.* Hence it is pretty evident that the Israelites were not obliged to celebrate the Passover, or keep the Feast of Unleavened Bread, till they were brought into the Promised Land.

9. *And it shall be for a sign . . . upon thine hand.* This direction, repeated and enlarged in v. 16, gave rise to "phylacteries," and this is one of the passages which the Jews write upon them to the present day. The manner in which the Jews understood and kept these commands may appear in their practice. They wrote the following four portions of the law upon slips of parchment or vellum: "Sanctify unto me the firstborn," Exod. xiii, from verse 2 to 10 inclusive. "And it shall be, when the Lord shall bring thee into the land," Exod. xiii, from verse 11 to 16 inclusive. "Hear, O Israel: the Lord our God is one Lord," Deut. vi, from verse 4 to 9 inclusive. "And it shall come to pass, if ye shall hearken diligently," Deut. xi, from verse 13 to 21 inclusive. These four portions, making in all thirty verses, written as mentioned above, and covered with leather, they tied to the forehead and to the hand or arm.

These which were for the head (the frontlets) they wrote on four slips of parchment, and rolled up each by itself, and placed them in four compartments, joined together in one piece of skin or leather. Those which were designed for the hand were formed of one piece of parchment, the four portions being written upon it in four columns, and rolled up from one end to the other. These were all correct transcripts from the Mosaic text, without one redundant or deficient letter; otherwise they were not lawful to be worn. Those for the head were tied on so as to rest on the forehead. Those for the hand or arm were usually tied on the left arm, a little above the elbow, on the inside, that they might be near the heart, according to the command, Deut. vi. 6: "And these words which I command thee this day shall be in thine heart." These phylacteries formed no inconsiderable part of a Jew's religion; they wore them as a sign of their obligation to God, and as representing some future blessedness. Hence they did not wear them on feast days nor on the Sabbath, because these things were in themselves signs; but they wore them always when they read the law, or when they prayed, and hence they called them *tephillin,* "prayer ornaments, oratories, or incitements to prayer." In process of time the spirit of this law was lost in the letter, and when the word was not in their mouth, nor the law in their heart, they had their phylacteries on their heads and on their hands. And the Pharisees, who in our Lord's time affected extraordinary piety, made their phylacteries very broad, that they might have many sentences written upon them, or the ordinary portions in very large and observable letters.

It appears that the Jews wore these for three different purposes: (1) As signs or remembrancers. This was the original design, as the

MATTHEW HENRY

Verses 11–16

I. Further directions concerning the dedicating of their firstborn to God. 1. The firstlings of their cattle were to be dedicated to God, as part of their possessions. 2. The firstborn of their children were to be redeemed, and by no means sacrificed, as the Gentiles sacrificed their children to Moloch. The price of the redemption of the firstborn was fixed by the law (Num. xviii. 16) at *five shekels*.

II. Further directions concerning the catechising of their children, and all those of the rising generation, from time to time, in this matter. Note, 1. Children should be directed and encouraged to ask their parents questions concerning the things of God. 2. We should all be able to show cause for what we do in religion. As sacraments are sanctified by the word, so they must be explained and understood by it. God's service is reasonable, and it is then acceptable when we perform it intelligently, knowing what we do and why we do it. Mercies to our fathers are mercies to us; we reap the benefit of them. Much more reason have we to say that in the death and resurrection of Jesus Christ we were redeemed.

Verses 17–22

Here is, I. The choice God made of their way, *v.* 17, 18. He was their guide. Moses gave them direction, but as he received it from the Lord. There were two ways from Egypt to Canaan. One was a short cut from the north of Egypt to the south of Canaan, perhaps about four or five days' journey; the other was much further about, through the wilderness, and that was the way in which God chose to lead his people Israel, *v.* 18. 1. There were many reasons why God led them *through the way of the wilderness of the Red Sea.* The Egyptians were to be drowned in the Red Sea. The Israelites were to be humbled and proved in the wilderness, Deut. viii. 2. Matters must be settled between them and their God, laws must be given, ordinances instituted, covenants sealed, and the original contract ratified. God's way is the right way, though it seem *about*. If we think he leads not his people the nearest way, yet we may be sure he leads them the best way, and so it will appear when we come to our journey's end. 2. There was one reason why God did not lead them the nearest way, because they were not as yet fit for war, much less for war with the Philistines, *v.* 17. Their spirits were broken with slavery; it was not easy for them to turn their hands of a sudden from the trowel to the sword. The Philistines were formidable enemies, too fierce to be encountered by raw recruits. God is said to bring Israel out of Egypt as the eagle *brings up her young ones* (Deut. xxxii. 11), teaching them by degrees to fly. Orders being thus given which way they should go, we are told, (1) That they went up themselves, not as a confused rout, but in good order, rank and file: they *went up harnessed, v.* 18. (2) That they took the *bones of Joseph* along with them (*v.* 19). Joseph had particularly appointed that his bones should be carried up when God should visit them (Gen. l. 25, 26). They might think, "Joseph's bones must rest at last, and then we shall."

II. Here is the guidance they were blessed with in the way: *The Lord went before them,* the *shechinah* (or appearance of the divine Majesty, which was typical of Christ) or a previous manifestation of the eternal Word, which, in the fulness of time, was to be *made flesh,* and *dwell among us.* Christ was with the church in the wilderness, 1 Cor. x. 9. Note, Those whom God brings into a wilderness he will not leave nor lose there, but will take care to lead them through it. Those who made the glory of God their end, and the word of God their rule, the Spirit of God the guide of their affections, and the providence of God the guide of their affairs, may be confident that *the Lord goes before them,* as truly as he went before Israel in the wilderness, though not so sensibly; we must live by faith. 1. They all saw an appearance from heaven of a pillar, which in the bright day appeared cloudy, and in the dark night appeared fiery. God gave them this ocular demonstration of his presence, in compassion to the infirmity of their faith. 2. They had sensible effects of God's going before them in this pillar. For, (1) It led the way in that wilderness, in which there was no road, no track, of which they had no maps, through which they had no guides. When they marched, this pillar went before them, at the rate that they could follow. (2) It sheltered them by day from the heat. (3) It gave them light by night and at all times made the wilderness they were in less frightful.

JAMIESON, FAUSSET, BROWN

11-16. FIRSTLINGS OF BEASTS. **12. every firstling,** etc.—the injunction respecting the consecration of the first-born, as here repeated, with some additional circumstances. The firstlings of clean beasts, such as lambs, kids, and calves, if males, were to be devoted to God and employed in sacrifice. Those unclean beasts, as the ass's colt, being unfit for sacrifice, were to be redeemed (Num. 18:15).

17-21. JOURNEY FROM EGYPT. **17. God led them not through the way of the land of the Philistines, although that was near,** etc.—The shortest and most direct route from Egypt to Palestine was the usual caravan road that leads by Belbeis, El-Arish, to Ascalon and Gaza. The Philistines, who then possessed the latter, would have been sure to dispute their passage, for between them and the Israelites there was a hereditary feud (I Chron. 7:21, 22); and so early a commencement of hostilities would have discouraged or dismayed the unwarlike band which Moses led. Their faith was to be exercised and strengthened, and from the commencement of their travels we observe the same careful proportion of burdens and trials to their character and state, as the gracious Lord shows to His people still in that spiritual journey of which the former was typical. **18. God led the people about through the way of the wilderness of the Red Sea,** etc.—This wondrous expanse of water is a gulf of the Indian ocean. It was called in Hebrew "the weedy sea," from the forest of marine plants with which it abounds. But the name of the Red Sea is not so easily traced. Some think it was given from its contiguity to the countries of Edom (red); others derive it from its coral rocks; while a third class ascribe the origin of the name to an extremely red appearance of the water in some parts, caused by a numberless multitude of very small mollusca. This sea, at its northern extremity, separates into two smaller inlets—the eastern called anciently the Elanitic gulf, now the gulf of Akaba; and the western the Heroöpolite gulf, now the gulf of Suez, which, there can be no doubt, extended much more to the north anciently than it does now. It was toward the latter the Israelites marched. **went up harnessed**—i.e., girded, equipped for a long journey. (See Psalm 105:37). The margin renders it "five in a rank," meaning obviously five large divisions, under five presiding officers, according to the usages of all caravans; and a spectacle of such a mighty and motley multitude must have presented an imposing appearance, and its orderly progress could have been effected only by the superintending influence of God. **19. Moses took the bones of Joseph with him**—in fulfilment of the oath he exacted from his brethren (Gen. 50:25, 26). The remains of the other patriarchs—not noticed from their obscurity—were also carried out of Egypt (Acts 7:16); and there would be no difficulty as to the means of conveyance—a few camels bearing these precious relics would give a true picture of Oriental customs, such as is still to be seen in the immense pilgrimages to Mecca. **20. encamped in Etham**—This place is supposed by the most intelligent travellers to be the modern Ajrud, where is a watering-place, and which is the third stage of the pilgrim caravans to Mecca. "It is remarkable that either of the different routes eastward from Heliopolis, or southward from Heroöpolis, equally admit of Ajrud being Etham. It is twelve miles northwest from Suez, and is literally on the edge of the desert" [PICTORIAL BIBLE]. **21, 22. the Lord went before them**—by a visible token of His presence, the Shekinah, in a majestic cloud (Ps. 78:14; Neh. 9:12; I Cor. 10:1), called the angel of God (ch. 14:19; 23:20-23; Ps. 99:6, 7; Isa. 63:8, 9).

ADAM CLARKE

institution itself sufficiently proves. (2) To procure reverence and respect in the sight of the heathen. This reason is given in the *Gemara,* Berachoth, chap. i: "Whence is it proved that the phylacteries or tephillin are the strength of Israel? *Ans.* From what is written, Deut. xxviii. 10: 'All the people of the earth shall see that thou art called by the name of the Lord [Yehovah]; and they shall be afraid of thee.'" (3) They used them as amulets or charms, to drive away evil spirits. This appears from the Targum on Canticles viii. 3: "His left hand is under my head," etc. "The congregation of Israel hath said, I am elect above all people, because I bind my phylacteries on my left hand and on my head, and the scroll is fixed to the right side of my gate, the third part of which looks to my bed-chamber, that demons may not be permitted to injure me."

13. *Every firstling of an ass thou shalt redeem with a lamb.* Or a "kid," as in the margin. In Num. xviii. 15 it is said: "The firstborn of man shalt thou surely redeem; and the firstling of an unclean beast shalt thou redeem." Hence we may infer that *ass* is put here for any unclean beast, or for unclean beasts in general. The *lamb* was to be given to the Lord, that is, to His priest, Num. xviii. 8, 15. And then the owner of the ass might use it for his own service, which without this redemption he could not do; see Deut. xv. 19.

The firstborn of man . . . shalt thou redeem. This was done by giving to the priests five standard shekels, or shekels of the sanctuary, every shekel weighing twenty gerahs.

17. *God led them not through the way of the land of the Philistines.* Had the Israelites been obliged to commence their journey to the Promised Land by a military campaign, there is little room to doubt that they would have been discouraged, have rebelled against Moses and Aaron, and have returned back to Egypt. Their long slavery had so degraded their minds that they were incapable of any great or noble exertions; and it is only on the ground of this mental degradation, the infallible consequence of slavery, that we can account for their many dastardly acts, murmurings, and repinings after their escape from Egypt.

18. *Went up harnessed. Chamushim.* It is truly astonishing what a great variety of opinions are entertained relative to the meaning of this word. After having maturely considered all that I have met with on the subject, I think it probable that the word refers simply to that "orderly" or "well-arranged" manner in which the Israelites commenced their journey from Egypt. For to "arrange, array, or set in order" seems to be the ideal meaning of the word *chamash.*

19. *Moses took the bones of Joseph.* See the note on Gen. i. 25. It is supposed that the Israelites carried with them the bones or remains of all the twelve sons of Jacob, each tribe taking care of the bones of its own patriarch, while Moses took care of the bones of Joseph. Stephen expressly says, Acts vii. 15-16, that not only Jacob but the "fathers" were carried from Egypt into Sychem; and this was the only opportunity that seems to have presented itself for doing this; and certainly the reason that rendered it proper to remove the bones of Joseph to the Promised Land had equal weight in reference to those of the other patriarchs. See the notes on Gen. xlix. 29.

20. *Encamped in Etham.* As for the reasons assigned on v. 17, God would not lead the Israelites by the way of the Philistines' country, He directed them towards the wilderness of Shur, chap. xv. 22, upon the edge or extremity of which, next to Egypt, at the bottom of the Arabian Gulf, lay *Etham,* which is the second place of encampment mentioned.

21. *The Lord went before them.* That by the Lord here is meant the Lord Jesus, we have the authority of St. Paul to believe, 1 Cor. x. 9; it was He whose Spirit they tempted in the wilderness, for it was He who led them through the desert to the promised rest. *Pillar of a cloud.* This *pillar* or "column," which appeared as a *cloud* by day and a *fire* by night, was the symbol of the Divine Presence. This was the *Shechinah* or divine dwelling place, and was the continual proof of the presence and protection of *God.*

MATTHEW HENRY

III. These were constant standing miracles (*v.* 22): He *took not away the pillar of cloud.* It never left them, till it brought them to the borders of Canaan. It was a cloud which the wind could not scatter. There was something spiritual in this pillar of cloud and fire. Some make this cloud a type of Christ. The cloud of his human nature was a veil to the light and fire of his divine nature. Christ is our way, the light of our way and the guide of it.

CHAPTER 14

Verses 1-9

I. Instructions given to Moses concerning Israel's motions and encampments. That there might be no scruple nor dissatisfaction about it, Moses is told before, 1. Whither they must go, *v.* 1, 2. They had got to the edge of the wilderness (*ch.* xiii. 20), and a stage or two more would have brought them to Horeb, the place appointed for their serving God; but, instead of going forward, they are ordered to turn short off, on the right hand from Canaan, and to march towards the Red Sea.

2. Moses shall know, (1) That Pharaoh has a design to ruin Israel, *v.* 3. (2) That therefore God has a design to ruin Pharaoh, and he takes this way to effect it, *v.* 4.

II. Pharaoh's pursuit of Israel, in which, while he gratifies his own malice and revenge, he is furthering the accomplishment of God's counsels concerning him. *It was told him that the people fled, v.* 5. Now, hereupon,

1. He reflects upon it with regret that he had connived at their departure. He and his servants were now angry with themselves for it: *Why have we done thus?* (1) It vexed them that Israel had their liberty, that they had lost the profit of their labours, and the pleasure of chastising them. Note, The liberty of God's people is a heavy grievance to their enemies, Esther v. 12, 13; Acts v. 17, 23. (2) It aggravated the vexation that they themselves had consented to it. Thus God makes men's envy and rage against his people a torment to themselves, Ps. cxii. 10.

2. He resolves, if possible, either to reduce them or to be revenged on them; in order to this, he levies an army, musters all his force of chariots and horsemen, *v.* 17, 18, and thus he doubts not but he shall re-enslave them, *v.* 6, 7.

JAMIESON, FAUSSET, BROWN

CHAPTER 14

VSS. 1-41. GOD INSTRUCTS THE ISRAELITES AS TO THEIR JOURNEY. **2. Speak unto the children of Israel, that they turn and encamp**—The Israelites had now completed their three days' journey, and at Etham the decisive step would have to be taken whether they would celebrate their intended feast and return, or march onwards by the head of the Red Sea into the desert, with a view to a final departure. They were already on the borders of the desert, and a short march would have placed them beyond the reach of pursuit, as the chariots of Egypt could have made little progress over dry and yielding sand. But at Etham, instead of pursuing their journey eastward with the sea on their right, they were suddenly commanded to diverge to the south, keeping the gulf on their left; a route which not only detained them lingering on the confines of Egypt, but, in adopting it, they actually turned their backs on the land of which they had set out to obtain the possession. A movement so unexpected, and of which the ultimate design was carefully concealed, could not but excite the astonishment of all, even of Moses himself, although, from his implicit faith in the wisdom and power of his heavenly Guide, he obeyed. The object was to entice Pharaoh to pursue, in order that the moral effect, which the judgments on Egypt had produced in releasing God's people from bondage, might be still further extended over the nations by the awful events transacted at the Red Sea. **Pi-hahiroth**—the mouth of the defile, or pass—a description well suited to that of Bedea, which extended from the Nile and opens on the shore of the Red Sea. **Migdol**—a fortress or citadel. **Baal-zephon**—some marked site on the opposite or eastern coast. **3. the wilderness hath shut them in**—Pharaoh, who would eagerly watch their movements, was now satisfied that they were meditating flight, and he naturally thought from the error into which they appeared to have fallen by entering that defile, he could intercept them. He believed them now entirely in his power, the mountain chain being on one side, the sea on the other, so that, if he pursued them in the rear, escape seemed impossible. **5. the heart of Pharaoh and of his servants was turned against the people,** etc. —Alas, how soon the obduracy of this reprobate king reappears! He had been convinced, but not converted—overawed, but not sanctified by the appalling judgments of heaven. He bitterly repented of what he now thought a hasty concession. Pride and revenge, the honor of his kingdom, and the interests of his subjects, all prompted him to recall his permission to reclaim those runaway slaves and force them to their wonted labor. Strange that he should yet allow such considerations to obliterate or outweigh all his painful experience of the danger of oppressing that people. But those whom the Lord has doomed to destruction are first infatuated by sin. **6. he made ready his chariot**—His preparations for an immediate and hot pursuit are here described: a difference is made between "the chosen chariots and the chariots of Egypt." The first evidently composed the king's guard, amounting to six hundred, and they are called "chosen," lit., "third men"; three men being allotted to each chariot, the charioteer and two warriors. As to "the chariots of Egypt," the common cars contained only two persons, one for driving and the other for fighting"; sometimes only one person was in the chariot, the driver lashed the reins round his body and fought;

ADAM CLARKE

It was necessary that they should have a guide to direct them through the wilderness, even had they taken the most direct road; and how much more so when they took a circuitous route not usually travelled, and of which they knew nothing but just as the luminous pillar pointed out the way! Besides, it is very likely that even Moses himself did not know the route which God had determined on, nor the places of encampment, till the pillar that went before them became stationary, and thus pointed out, not only the road, but the different places of rest.

22. *He took not away the pillar of the cloud.* Neither Jews nor Gentiles are agreed how long the cloud continued with the Israelites. It is very probable that it first visited them at Succoth, if it did not accompany them from Rameses; and that it continued with them till they came to the river Jordan, to pass over opposite to Jericho, for after that it appears that the ark alone was their guide, as it always marched at their head. See Josh. iii. 10, etc.

CHAPTER 14

2. *Encamp before Pi-hahiroth. Pi hachiroth,* the "mouth, strait, or bay of Chiroth." Between *Migdol,* the "tower," probably a fortress that served to defend the bay. *Over against Baal-zephon,* the "lord or master of the watch," probably an idol temple, where a continual guard, watch, or light was kept up for the defense of one part of the haven or as a guide to ships.

3. *They are entangled in the land.* God himself brought them into straits from which no human power or art could extricate them. Consider their situation when once brought out of the open country, where alone they had room either to fight or fly. Now they had the Red Sea before them, Pharaoh and his host behind them, and on their right and left hand fortresses of the Egyptians to prevent their escape; nor had they one boat or transport prepared for their passage! If they be now saved, the arm of the Lord must be seen, and the vanity and nullity of the Egyptian idols be demonstrated. By bringing them into such a situation He took from them all hope of human help, and gave their adversaries every advantage against them, so that they themselves said, *They are entangled in the land, the wilderness hath shut them in.*

4. *I will harden Pharaoh's heart.* After relenting and giving them permission to depart, he now changes his mind and determines to prevent them; and without any further restraining grace, God permits him to rush on to his final ruin, for the cup of his iniquity was now full.

5. *And it was told the king . . . that the people fled.* Of their departure he could not be ignorant, because himself had given them liberty to depart; but the word *fled* here may be understood as implying that they had utterly left Egypt without any intention to return, which is probably what he did not expect, for he had only given them permsion to go three days' journey into the wilderness, in order to sacrifice to Jehovah; but from the circumstances of their departure, and the property they had received from the Egyptians, it was taken for granted that they had no design to return; and this was in all likelihood the consideration that weighed most with this avaricious king, and determined him to pursue, and either recover the spoil or bring them back, or both. Thus *the heart of Pharaoh and of his servants was turned against the people, and they said, Why have we . . . let Israel go from serving us?* Here was the grand incentive to pursuit; their service was profitable to the state, and they were determined not to give it up.

7. *Six hundred chosen chariots.* According to the most authentic accounts we have of warchariots, they were frequently drawn by two or by four horses, and carried three persons; one was charioteer, whose business it was to guide the horses, but he seldom fought; the second chiefly defended the charioteer; and the third alone was properly the combatant. It appears that in this case Pharaoh had collected all the cavalry of Egypt (see v. 17); and though these might not have been very numerous, yet,

MATTHEW HENRY

It is said (*v.* 8), The children of Israel went out with a great deal of courage. *But the Egyptians* (*v.* 9) *pursued after them.* Note, Those that in good earnest set their faces heaven-ward, and will live godly in Christ Jesus, must expect to be set upon by Satan's temptations and terrors. He will not tamely part with any out of his service, nor go out without raging, Mark ix. 26.

Verses 10–14

We have here, I. The fright that the children of Israel were in when they perceived that Pharaoh pursued them, *v.* 10. They knew very well the strength and rage of the enemy, and their own weakness. On the one hand was Pi-hahiroth, a range of craggy rocks impassable; on the other hand were Migdol and Baalzephon; before them was the sea; behind them were the Egyptians: so that there was no way open for them but upwards, and thence their deliverance came. 1. Some of them cried out unto the Lord; their fear set them praying, and that was a good effect of it. God brings us into straits that he may bring us to our knees. 2. Others of them cried out against Moses; their fear set them murmuring, *v.* 11, 12. How inexcusable was their distrust! They here express, (1) A sordid contempt of liberty, preferring servitude before it, only because it was attended with some difficulties. A generous spirit would have said, "Better live God's freemen in the open air of a wilderness than the Egyptians' bondmen in the smoke of the brick-kilns." (2) Base ingratitude to Moses, who had been the faithful instrument of their deliverance. They had as soon forgotten the miracles of mercy as the Egyptians had forgotten the miracles of wrath; and they, as well as the Egyptians, hardened their hearts, at last, to their own ruin; as Egypt after ten plagues, so Israel after ten provocations, of which this was the first (Num. xiv. 22), were sentenced to die in the wilderness.

II. The seasonable encouragement that Moses gave them in this distress, *v.* 12, 14. He answered not these fools according to their folly. Instead of chiding them, he comforts them, and with an admirable presence and composure of mind stills their murmuring, with the assurance of a speedy and complete deliverance: *Fear you not.* Note, It is our duty and interest, when we cannot get out of our troubles, yet to get above our fears, so that they may only serve to quicken our prayers and endeavours, but may not prevail to silence our faith and hope. He directs them to leave it to God, in a silent expectation of the event: "*Stand still,* and think not to save yourselves either by fighting or flying; wait God's orders. God is now about to work for you.

Verses 15–20

I. Direction given to Israel's leader.

1. What he must do himself. He must, for the present, leave off praying, and apply himself to his business (*v.* 15): *Wherefore cryest thou unto me?* But is God displeased with Moses for praying? No, he asks this question, *Wherefore cryest thou unto me?* (1) To satisfy his faith. "Wherefore shouldst thou press thy petition any further, when it is already granted? *I have accepted thy prayer.*" (2) To quicken his diligence. Moses had something else to do besides praying; he was to command the hosts of Israel, and it was now requisite that he should be at his post.

2. What he must order Israel to do. *Speak to them, that they go forward.* Moses had bidden them stand still, and expect orders from God; and now orders are given. They thought they must have been directed either to the right hand or to the left. "No," says God, "speak to them to go forward, directly to the sea-side"; as if there had lain a fleet of transport-ships ready for them to embark in.

3. What he might expect God to do. Let the children of Israel go as far as they can upon dry ground, and then God will divide the sea, and open a passage for them through it, *v.* 16–18.

II. A guard set upon Israel's camp where it now lay most exposed, which was *in the rear, v.* 19, 20. *The angel of God,* whose ministry was made use of in the pillar of cloud and fire, went from *before the camp of Israel,* where they did not now need a guide (there was no danger of missing their way through the sea, nor needed they any other word of command than to go forward), and it came behind them, where now they needed a guard and so was a wall of partition between them.

JAMIESON, FAUSSET, BROWN

infantry being totally unsuitable for a rapid pursuit, and the Egyptians having had no cavalry, the word "riders" is in the grammatical connection applied to war chariots employed, and these were of light construction, open behind, and hung on small wheels. **10. when Pharaoh drew nigh, the children of Israel lifted up their eyes**—The great consternation of the Israelites is somewhat astonishing, considering their vast superiority in numbers, but their deep dismay and absolute despair at the sight of this armed host receives a satisfactory explanation from the fact that the civilized state of Egyptian society required the absence of all arms, except when they were on service. If the Israelites were entirely unarmed at their departure, they could not think of making any resistance [WILKINSON & HENGSTENBERG]. **13, 14. Moses said, . . . Fear ye not, stand still, and see the salvation of the Lord**—Never, perhaps, was the fortitude of a man so severely tried as that of the Hebrew leader in this crisis, exposed as he was to various and inevitable dangers, the most formidable of which was the vengeance of a seditious and desperate multitude; but his meek, unruffled, magnanimous composure presents one of the sublimest examples of moral courage to be found in history. And whence did his courage arise? He saw the miraculous cloud still accompanying them, and his confidence arose solely from the hope of a divine interposition, although, perhaps, he might have looked for the expected deliverance in every quarter, rather than in the direction of the sea.

15-18. the Lord said unto Moses, Wherefore criest thou unto me? etc.—When in answer to his prayers, he received the divine command to go forward, he no longer doubted by what kind of miracle the salvation of his mighty charge was to be effected.

19. the angel of God, i.e., the pillar of cloud. The slow and silent movement of that majestic column through the air, and occupying a position behind them must have excited the astonishment of the Israelites (Isa. 58:8). It was an effectual barrier between them and their pursuers, not only protecting them, but concealing their movements. Thus, the same cloud produced light (a symbol of favor) to the people of God, and darkness (a symbol of wrath) to their enemies (cf. II Cor. 2:16).

21. Moses stretched out his hand, etc.—The waving of the rod was of great importance on this occasion to give public attestation in the presence of the assembled Israelites, both to the character of Moses and the divine mission with which he was charged.

ADAM CLARKE

humanly speaking, they might easily overcome the unarmed and encumbered Israelites, who could not be supposed to be able to make any resistance against cavalry and war-chariots.

10. *The children of Israel cried out unto the Lord.* Had their prayer been accompanied with faith, we should not have found them in the next verses murmuring against Moses, or rather against the Lord, through whose goodness they were now brought from under that bondage from which they had often cried for deliverance.

13. *Moses said . . . Fear ye not.* This exhortation was not given to excite them to resist, for of that there was no hope; they were unarmed, they had no courage, and their minds were deplorably degraded. *Stand still.* Ye shall not be even workers together with God; only be quiet, and do not render yourselves wretched by your fears and your confusion. *See the salvation of the Lord.* Behold the deliverance which God will work, independently of all human help and means. *Ye shall see them again no more.* Here was strong faith, but this was accompanied by the spirit of prophecy. God showed Moses what He would do; he believed, and therefore he spoke in the encouraging manner related above.

14. *The Lord shall fight for you.* Ye shall have no part in the honor of the day; God alone shall bring you off, and defeat your foes. *Ye shall hold your peace.* Your unbelieving fears and clamors shall be confounded, and ye shall see that by might none shall be able to prevail against the Lord, and that the feeblest shall take the prey when the power of Jehovah is exerted.

15. *Wherefore criest thou unto me?* We hear not one word of Moses' praying, and yet here the Lord asks him why he cries unto Him. From which we may learn that the heart of Moses was deeply engaged with God, though it is probable he did not articulate one word; but the language of sighs, tears, and desires is equally intelligible to God with that of words. This consideration should be a strong encouragement to every feeble, discouraged mind.

16. *Lift thou up thy rod.* Neither Moses nor his rod could be any effective instrument in a work which could be accomplished only by the omnipotence of God; but it was necessary that he should appear in it, in order that he might have credit in the sight of the Israelites, and that they might see that God had chosen him to be the instrument of their deliverance.

18. *Shall know that I am the Lord.* Pharaoh had just recovered from the consternation and confusion with which the late plagues had overwhelmed him, and now he is emboldened to pursue after Israel; and God is determined to make his overthrow so signal by such an exertion of omnipotence that He shall get himself honor by this miraculous act, and that the Egyptians shall know, i.e., "acknowledge," that He is Jehovah, the omnipotent, self-existing, eternal God.

19. *The angel of God.* It has been thought by some that the *angel,* i.e., "messenger," of the Lord and the pillar of cloud mean here the same thing. An angel might assume the appearance of a cloud; and even a material cloud thus particularly appointed might be called an angel or "messenger" of the Lord, for such is the literal import of the word *malach,* "an angel." It is however most probable that the Angel of the covenant, the Lord Jesus, appeared on this occasion in behalf of the people; for as this deliverance was to be an illustrious type of the deliverance of man from the power and guilt of sin by His incarnation and death, it might have been deemed necessary, in the judgment of divine wisdom, that He should appear Chief Agent in this most important and momentous crisis.

20. *It was a cloud and darkness to them.* That the Israelites might not be dismayed at the appearance of their enemies, and that these might not be able to discern the object of their pursuit, the pillar of cloud moved from the front to the rear of the Israelitish camp, so as perfectly to separate between them and the Egyptians. It appears also that this cloud had two sides, one dark and the other luminous: the luminous side gave light to the whole camp of Israel during the night of passage; and the dark side, turned towards the pursuing Egyptians,

MATTHEW HENRY

Verses 21-31

We have here the history of that work of wonder which is so often mentioned both in the Old and New Testament, the dividing of the Red Sea before the children of Israel. It was the terror of the Canaanites (Josh. ii. 9, 10), the praise and triumph of the Israelites, Ps. cxiv. 3; cvi. 9; cxxxvi. 13, 14. It was a type of baptism, 1 Cor. x. 1, 2. Israel's passage through it was typical of the conversion of souls (Isa. xi. 15).

I. An instance of God's almighty power in the kingdom of nature, in dividing the sea. It was a bay, or gulf, or arm of the sea, two or three leagues over, which was divided, *v.* 21. The natural sign was a strong east wind, signifying that it was done by the power of God, whom the winds and the seas obey.

II. An instance of his wonderful favour to his Israel. They went through the sea to the opposite shore. They *walked upon dry land in the midst of the sea, v.* 29. *The waters were a wall to them on their right hand and on their left.* Moses and Aaron, it is probable, ventured first into this untrodden path, and then all Israel after them; and this march through the paths of the great waters would make their march afterwards, through the wilderness, less formidable. Those who had followed God through the sea needed not to fear following him whithersoever he led them.

This was done, and recorded, in order to encourage God's people in all ages to trust in him in the greatest straits. We find the saints, long afterwards, making themselves sharers in the triumphs of this march (Ps. lxvi. 6).

III. An instance of his just and righteous wrath upon his and his people's enemies, the Egyptians. Observe here, 1. How they were infatuated. They were more advantageously provided with chariots and horses, while the Israelites were on foot. 2. How they were troubled and perplexed, *v.* 24, 25. But, *in the morning watch, the Lord looked upon the host of the Egyptians, and troubled them.* (1) They had hectored and boasted as if the day were their own; but now they were troubled and dismayed, struck with a panic-fear. (2) They had driven furiously; but now they drove heavily, and found themselves plunged and embarrassed at every step. As soon as ever the children of Israel had got safely to the shore, the waters returned to their place, and overwhelmed all the host of the Egyptians, *v.* 27, 28. Pharaoh and his servants, who had hardened one another in sin, now fell together, and not one escaped. An ancient tradition says that Pharaoh's magicians, Jannes and Jambres, perished with the rest. God reckoned with Pharaoh for all his proud and insolent conduct towards Moses his ambassador. Come and see the desolations he made, and write it, not in water, but with an iron pen in the rock for ever. This is Pharaoh and all his multitude, Ezek. xxxi. 18.

IV. Here is the notice which the Israelites took of this wonderful work which God wrought for them. Now they were ashamed of their distrusts and murmurings; they would never again quarrel with Moses, nor talk of returning to Egypt. They were now baptized unto Moses in the sea, 1 Cor. x. 2. Being brought thus triumphantly out of Egypt, they did not doubt that they should be in Canaan shortly, having such a God to trust to, and such a mediator between them and him. O that there had been such a heart in them as now there seemed to be! How well were it for us if we were always in as good a frame as we are in sometimes!

JAMIESON, FAUSSET, BROWN

the Lord caused . . . a strong east wind all that night—Suppose a mere ebb tide caused by the wind, raising the water to a great height on *one side,* still as there was not only "dry land," but, according to the tenor of the sacred narrative, a wall on the right hand and on the left, it would be impossible on the hypothesis of such a natural cause to rear the wall on the *other.* The idea of divine interposition, therefore, is imperative; and, assuming the passage to have been made at Mount Attakah, or at the mouth of Wady-Tawarik, an *east* wind would cut the sea in that line. The *Hebrew* word *kedem,* however, rendered in our translation, "east," means, in its primary signification, *previous;* so that this verse might, perhaps, be rendered, "the Lord caused the sea to go back by a strong *previous* wind all that night"; a rendering which would remove the difficulty of supposing the host of Israel marched over on the sand, in the teeth of a rushing column of wind, strong enough to heap up the waters as a wall on each side of a dry path, and give the intelligible narrative of divine interference. **22. the children of Israel went into the midst of the sea,** etc.—It is highly probable that Moses, along with Aaron, first planted his footsteps on the untrodden sand, encouraging the people to follow him without fear of the treacherous walls; and when we take into account the multitudes that followed him, the immense number who through infancy and old age were incapable of hastening their movements, together with all the appurtenances of the camp, the strong and steadfast character of the leaders' faith was strikingly manifested (Josh. 2:10; 4:23; Ps. 66:6; 74:13; 106:9; 136:13; Isa. 63:11-13; I Cor. 10:1; Heb. 11:29). **23. the Egyptians pursued, and went in after them to the midst of the sea** — From the darkness caused by the intercepting cloud, it is probable that they were not aware on what ground they were driving: they heard the sound of the fugitives before them, and they pushed on with the fury of the avengers of blood, without dreaming that they were on the bared bed of the sea. **24. Lord looked . . . through . . . the cloud, and troubled them**—We suppose the fact to have been that the side of the pillar of cloud towards the Egyptians was suddenly, and for a few moments, illuminated with a blaze of light, which, coming as it were in a refulgent flash upon the dense darkness which had preceded, so frightened the horses of the pursuers that they rushed confusedly together and became unmanageable. "Let us flee," was the cry that resounded through the broken and trembling ranks, but it was too late; all attempts at flight were vain [Bush]. **27. Moses stretched forth his hand over the sea,** etc.—What circumstances could more clearly demonstrate the miraculous character of this transaction than that at the waving of Moses' rod, the dividing waters left the channel dry, and on his making the same motion on the opposite side, they returned, commingling with instantaneous fury? Is such the character of any ebb tide? **28. there remained not so much as one of them** — It is surprising that, with such a declaration, some intelligent writers can maintain there is no evidence of the destruction of Pharaoh himself (Ps. 106:11). **30. Israel saw the Egyptians dead upon the sea-shore,** etc.—The tide threw them up and left multitudes of corpses on the beach; a result that brought greater infamy on the Egyptians, but that tended, on the other hand, to enhance the triumph of the Israelites, and doubtless enriched them with arms, which they had not before. The locality of this famous passage has not yet been, and probably never will be, satisfactorily fixed. Some place it in the immediate neighborhood of Suez; where, they say, the part of the sea is most likely to be affected by "a strong east wind"; where the road from the defile of Migdol (now Muktala) leads directly to this point; and where the sea, not above two miles broad, could be crossed in a short time. The vast majority, however, who have examined the spot, reject this opinion, and fix the passage, as does local tradition, about ten or twelve miles further down the shore at Wady-Tawarik. "The time of the miracle was the whole night, at the season of the year, too, when the night would be about its average length. The sea at that point extends from six and a half to eight miles in breadth. There was thus ample time for the passage of the Israelites from any part of the valley, especially considering their excitement and animation by the gracious and wonderful interposition of Providence in their behalf" [Wilson].

ADAM CLARKE

prevented them from receiving any benefit from that light. How easily can God make the same thing an instrument of destruction or salvation, as seems best to His godly wisdom!

21. *The Lord caused the sea to go back.* That part of the sea over which the Israelites passed was, according to Mr. Bruce and other travellers, about four leagues across and, therefore, might easily be crossed in one night. In the dividing of the sea two agents appear to be employed, though the effect produced can be attributed to neither. By stretching out the rod the waters were divided; by the blowing of the vehement, ardent, east wind the bed of the sea was dried.

22. *And the waters were a wall unto them on their right hand, and on their left.* This verse demonstrates that the passage was miraculous.

24. *The morning watch.* A *watch* was the fourth part of the time from sunsetting to sunrising. As the Israelites went out of Egypt at the vernal equinox, the morning watch, or, according to the Hebrew, the "watch of daybreak," would answer to our four o'clock in the morning. *The Lord looked unto.* This probably means that the cloud suddenly assumed a fiery appearance where it had been dark before; or they were appalled by violent thunders and lightning, which we are assured by the Psalmist did actually take place, together with great inundations of rain: "The clouds poured out water: the skies sent out a sound: thine arrows also went abroad. The voice of thy thunder was in the heaven: the lightnings lightened the world: the earth trembled and shook. Thy way is in the sea, and thy path in the great waters . . . Thou leddest thy people like a flock by the hand of Moses and Aaron," Ps. lxxvii. 17-20. Such tempests as these would necessarily terrify the Egyptian horses, and produce general confusion. By their dashing hither and thither the wheels must be destroyed, and the chariots broken; and foot and horse must be mingled together in one universal ruin; see v. 25. During the time that this state of horror and confusion was at its summit the Israelites had safely passed over; and then Moses, at the command of God (v. 26), having stretched out his rod over the waters, the "sea returned to his strength" (v. 27); i.e., the waters by their natural gravity resumed their level, and the whole Egyptian host were completely overwhelmed, v. 28. Thus the enemies of the Lord perished; and that people who decreed that the male children of the Hebrews should be drowned were themselves destroyed in the pit which they had destined for others. God's ways are all equal, and He renders to every man "according to his works."

30. *Israel saw the Egyptians dead upon the sea shore.* By the extraordinary agitation of the waters, no doubt multitudes of the dead Egyptians were cast on the shore, and by their spoils the Israelites were probably furnished with considerable riches, and especially clothing and arms; which latter were essentially necessary to them in their wars with the Amalekites and Amorites on their way to the Promised Land. If they did not get their arms in this way, we know not how they got them, as there is not the slightest reason to believe that they brought any with them out of Egypt.

31. *The people feared the Lord.* They were convinced by the interference of Jehovah that His power was unlimited, and that He could do whatsoever He pleased, both in the way of judgment and in the way of mercy. *And believed the Lord, and his servant Moses.* They now clearly discerned that God had fulfilled all His promises, and that not one thing had failed of all the good which He had spoken concerning Israel. And they *believed . . . his servant Moses*—they had now the fullest proof that he was divinely appointed to work all these miracles, and to bring them out of Egypt into the Promised Land.

MATTHEW HENRY

CHAPTER 15

Verses 1–21

Having read how that complete victory of Israel over the Egyptians was obtained, here we are told how it was celebrated. Moses, no doubt by divine inspiration, indited this song, and delivered it to the children of Israel, to be sung before they stirred from the place where they saw the Egyptians dead upon the shore. Observe, They expressed their joy in God, and thankfulness to him, by singing. It was a song of faith.

I. The song itself;

1. We may observe respecting this song, that it is, (1) An ancient song, the most ancient that we know of. (2) A most admirable composition, the style lofty and magnificent, the images lively and proper, and the whole very moving. (3) It is a holy song, consecrated to the honour of God, and intended to exalt his name and celebrate his praise, and his only.

2. What Moses chiefly aims at in this song.

(1) He gives glory to God, and triumphs in him; this is first in his intention (*v.* 1): *I will sing unto the Lord.* Israel rejoiced in God, [1] As their own God, and therefore their *strength, song,* and *salvation, v.* 2.

JAMIESON, FAUSSET, BROWN

CHAPTER 15

Vss. 1-27. Song of Moses. **1. Then sang Moses and the children of Israel**—The scene of this thanksgiving song is supposed to have been at the landing-place on the eastern shore of the Red Sea, at Ayoun Musa, the fountains of Moses. They are situated somewhat farther northward along the shore than the opposite point from which the Israelites set out. But the line of the people would be extended during the passage, and one extremity of it would reach as far north as these fountains, which would supply them with water on landing. The time when it was sung is supposed to have been the morning after the passage. This song is, by some hundred years, the oldest poem in the world. There is a sublimity and beauty in the language that is unexampled. But its unrivalled superiority arises not solely from the splendor of the diction. Its poetical excellencies have often drawn forth the admiration of the best judges, while the character of the event commemorated, and its being prompted by divine inspiration, contribute to give it an interest and sublimity peculiar to itself.

I will sing unto the Lord, for he hath triumphed gloriously—Considering the state of servitude in which they had been born and bred, and the rude features of character which their subsequent history often displays, it cannot be supposed that the children of Israel generally were qualified to commit to memory or to appreciate the beauties of this inimitable song. But they might perfectly understand its pervading strain of sentiment; and, with the view of suitably improving the occasion, it was thought necessary that all, old and young, should join their united voices in the rehearsal of its words. As every individual had cause, so every individual gave utterance to his feelings of gratitude.

ADAM CLARKE

CHAPTER 15

1. *Then sang Moses and the children of Israel this song.* Poetry has been cultivated in all ages and among all people, from the most refined to the most barbarous; and to it principally, under the kind providence of God, we are indebted for most of the original accounts we have of the ancient nations of the universe. Equally measured lines, with a harmonious collocation of expressive, sonorous, and sometimes highly metaphorical terms, the alternate lines either answering to each other in sense or ending with similar sounds, were easily committed to memory and easily retained. As these were often accompanied with a pleasing air or tune, histories formed thus became the amusement of youth, the softeners of the tedium of labor, and even the solace of age. In such a way the histories of most nations have been preserved. The interesting events celebrated, the rhythm or metre, and the accompanying tune rendered them easily transmissible to posterity; and by means of tradition they passed safely from father to son through the times of comparative darkness, till they arrived at those ages in which the pen and the press have given them a sort of deathless duration and permanent stability, by multiplying the copies. Though this is not the first specimen of poetry we have met with in the Pentateuch (see Lamech's speech to his wives, Gen. iv. 23-24; Noah's prophecy concerning his sons, chap. ix. 25-27; and Jacob's blessing to the twelve patriarchs, chap. xlix. 2-27), yet it is the first regular ode of any considerable length, having but one subject; and it is all written in hemistichs, or half-lines, the usual form in Hebrew poetry; and though this form frequently occurs, it is not attended to in our common printed Hebrew Bibles, except in this and three other places (Deuteronomy xxxii, Judges v, and 2 Samuel xxii).

I will sing unto the Lord. Moses begins the song, and in the first two hemistichs states the subject of it; and these first two lines became the grand chorus of the piece, as we may learn from v. 21. *Triumphed gloriously.* "He is exceedingly exalted," rendered by the Septuagint, "He is gloriously glorified"; and surely this was one of the most signal displays of the glorious majesty of God ever exhibited since the creation of the world. And when it is considered that the whole of this transaction shadowed out the redemption of the human race from the thraldom and power of sin and iniquity by the Lord Jesus, and the final triumph of the Church of God over all its enemies, we may also join in the song and celebrate Him who triumphed so gloriously, having conquered death and opened the kingdom of Heaven to all believers.

2. *The Lord is my strength and song.* How judiciously are the members of this sentence arranged! He who has God for his Strength will have Him for his Song; and he to whom Jehovah is become Salvation will exalt His name. It is worthy of observation that the word which we translate *Lord* here is not Jehovah in the original, but *Jah. Jah* is several times joined with the name *Jehovah,* so that we may be sure that it is not, as some have supposed, a mere abbreviation of that word. See Isa. xii. 2; xxvi. 4. Our blessed Lord solemnly claims to himself what is intended in this divine name *Jah,* John viii. 58: "Before Abraham was, I AM," not "I was," but "I am," plainly intimating His divine, eternal existence. Compare Isa. xliii. 13. And the Jews appear to have well understood Him, for "then took they up stones to cast at him" as a blasphemer. Compare Col. i. 16-17, where the Apostle Paul, after asserting that all things that are in heaven and that are in earth, visible and invisible, were created by and for Christ, adds, "And He is [not 'was'] before all things, and by Him all things have subsisted, and still subsist."

I will prepare him an habitation. It has been supposed that Moses, by this expression, intended the building of the Tabernacle; but it seems to come in very strangely in this place. Most of the ancient versions understood the original in a very different sense. The Vulgate has *et glorificabo eum;* the Septuagint, "I will glorify him"; with which the Syriac, Coptic, the Targum of Jonathan, and the Jerusalem Targum agree. From the Targum of Onkelos the pres-

ALEXANDER MACLAREN:

These words occur three times in the Bible: here, in Isa. 12:2, and in Ps. 118:14.

I. *The lessons from the various instances of their occurrence.* The first and second teach that the Mosaic deliverance is a picture-prophecy of the redemption in Christ. The third (Ps. 118:14), long after, and the utterance of some private person, teaches that each age and each soul has the same mighty hand working for it. "As we have heard, so have we seen."

II. *The lessons from the words themselves.*

A. True faith appropriates God's universal mercy as a personal possession. "*My* Lord and my God!" "He loved *me,* and gave himself for *me.*"

B. Each single act of mercy should reveal God more clearly as "My strength." The "and" in the second clause is substantially equivalent to "for." It assigns the reason for the assurance expressed in the first. Because of the experienced deliverance and God's manifestation of himself in it as the author of "salvation," my faith wins happy increase of confidence that He "is the strength of my heart." Blessed are they who bring that treasure out of all the sorrows of life!

C. The end of His deliverances is "praise." "He is my song." This is true for earth and for heaven. The "Song of Moses and the Lamb."—*Expositions of Holy Scripture*

MATTHEW HENRY

[2] *As their father's God.* This they take notice of, because, being conscious in themselves of their own unworthiness and provocations, they had reason to think that what God had now done for them was for their *father's sake*, Deut. iv. 37. [3] As a God of infinite power (*v.* 3). [4] As a God of matchless and incomparable perfection, *v.* 11. This is expressed, *First*, more generally: *Who is like unto thee, O Lord, among the gods!* Egypt was notorious for the multitude of its gods, but the *God of the Hebrews* was too hard for them and baffled them all, Deut. xxxii. 23–39. More particularly, [i] *He is glorious in holiness*; his holiness is his glory. God is *rich in mercy*—this is his treasure, *glorious in holiness*—this is his honour. [ii] *He is fearful in praises.* That which is the matter of our praise, though it is joyful to the servants of God, is dreadful and very terrible to his enemies, Ps. lxvi. 1–3. 3. He is *doing wonders*, wondrous to all, being above the power and out of the common course of nature. They were wonders of power and wonders of grace; in both God was to be humbly adored.

(2) He describes the deliverance they were now triumphing in, because the song was intended, not only to express and excite their thankfulness for the present, but to preserve and perpetuate the remembrance of this work of wonder to after-ages. Two things were to be taken notice of:—

[1] The destruction of the enemy; the waters were divided, *v.* 8. *The floods stood upright as a heap.* Pharaoh and all his hosts were buried in the waters. The proud waters went over the proud sinners. Their sin had made them hard like a stone, and now they justly sink like a stone.

[2] The protection and guidance of Israel (*v.* 13): *Thou in thy mercy hast led forth the people*, led them forth out of the bondage of Egypt, led them forth

JAMIESON, FAUSSET, BROWN

CHARLES H. SPURGEON:

The next is, "The Lord is my *song*," that is to say, the Lord is the giver of our songs; He breathes the music into the hearts of His people; He is the creator of their joy. The Lord is also the subject of their songs; they sing of Him and of all that He does on their behalf. Moreover, the Lord is the object of their song: they sing unto the Lord. Their praise is meant for Him alone. They do not make melody for human ears, but unto the Lord. "The Lord is my song." Then I ought always to sing; and if I sing my loudest, I can never reach the height of this great argument, nor come to the end of it. This song never changes. If I live by faith my song is always the same, for "the Lord is my song." Our song unto God is God himself. He alone can express our intensest joy. O God, Thou art my exceeding joy. Father, Son, and Holy Ghost, Thou art my hymn of everlasting delight.

"The Lord is my strength and song, and *he is become my salvation.*" The Father in His eternal purpose is my salvation; the Son in His complete redemption is my salvation—nay not in His redemption only, but in His life, His death, His resurrection, His intercession, His second coming, He has become my salvation. And the Holy Ghost indwelling in me, quickening me, instructing me, illuminating me, perfecting me, keeping me—He is become my salvation. Triune God, it is not alone that Thou dost save me, but Thou art my salvation. I look for nothing but what is in Thee, and if Thou givest thyself to me, Thou hast given me a perfect salvation, salvation from bondage, salvation from worldliness, salvation from death and hell, salvation into light, and liberty, and love, and joy, salvation that shall culminate in eternal glory. A full salvation is God to His people.

Next, "He is *my God.*" Perhaps this is the most joyous note of all. "He is become my salvation"—this is very sweet: "He is my God"—this is the sweetest of all. "He is my God." I choose Him to be my God, but I choose Him of necessity; I can do no other. Who else can be my God? In the Revised Version it is, "This is my God," and a very proper translation, too; as if Israel saw what God did at the Red Sea and then exclaimed, "This is my God!" This God of justice, this God of vengeance and power, is my God. Beloved, choose Jehovah to be your God: whom else can you choose? Let your hearts cling to Him.

But then comes the added word, "He is *my father's God,*" that is to say, the God of Abraham, of Isaac, and of Jacob—a God by covenant, the God who has given himself to us by His own purpose and promise, and therefore is our God, not by any right of merit on our behalf, but solely by the gift of His free, rich, covenant grace. Let us praise the triune God of free grace for He belongs to each of us.

—The Treasury of the Old Testament

ADAM CLARKE

ent translation seems to have been originally derived; he has translated the place, "And I will build him a sanctuary," which not one of the other versions, the Persian excepted, acknowledges. Our own old translations are generally different from the present: Coverdale, "This my God, I will magnify him"; Matthew's, Cranmer's, and the Bishops' Bible render it "glorify," and the sense of the place seems to require it. *My father's God.* I believe Houbigant to be right, who translates the original, *Elohey abi*, "My God is my Father." Every man may call the Divine Being his God; but only those who are His children by adoption through grace can call Him their Father. See Gal. iv. 6.

3. *The Lord is a man of war.* Perhaps it would be better to translate the words, "Jehovah is the Man or Hero of the battle." *The Lord is his name.* That is, *Jehovah.* He has now, as the name implies, given comple *existence* to all His promises. See the notes on Gen. ii. 4 and Exod. vi. 3.

4. *Pharaoh's chariots . . . his host . . . his chosen captains.* On such an expedition it is likely that the principal Egyptian nobility accompanied their king, and that the overthrow they met with here had reduced Egypt to the lowest extremity. Had the Israelites been intent on plunder or had Moses been influenced by a spirit of ambition, how easily might both have gratified themselves, as, had they returned, they might have soon overrun and subjugated the whole land!

6. *Thy right hand.* Thy omnipotence, manifested in a most extraordinary way.

7. *In the greatness of thine excellency.* To this wonderful deliverance the Prophet Isaiah refers, chap. lxiii. 11-14.

8. *The depths were congealed.* The strong east wind (chap. xiv. 21) employed to dry the bottom of the sea is here represented as the blast of God's nostrils that had *congealed* or "frozen" the waters, so that they stood in heaps like a wall on the right hand and on the left.

9. *The enemy said.* As this song was composed by divine inspiration, we may rest assured that these words were spoken by Pharaoh and his captains, and the passions they describe felt, in their utmost sway, in their hearts; but how soon was their boasting confounded? "Thou didst blow with thy wind, the sea covered them: they sank as lead in the mighty waters."

11. *Who is like unto thee, O Lord, among the gods?* We have already seen that all the Egyptian gods, or the objects of the Egyptians' idolatry, were confounded, and rendered completely despicable, by the ten plagues, which appear to have been directed principally against them. *Glorious in holiness.* Infinitely resplendent in this attribute, essential to the perfection of the divine nature. *Fearful in praises.* Such glorious holiness cannot be approached without the deepest reverence and fear, even by angels, who veil their faces before the majesty of God. *Doing wonders.* Every part of the work of God is wonderful; not only miracles, which imply an inversion or suspension of the laws of nature, but every part of nature itself. Who can conceive how a single blade of grass is formed; or how earth, air, and water become consolidated in the body of the oak? And who can comprehend how the different tribes of plants and animals are preserved, in all the distinctive characteristics of their respective natures? And who can conceive how the human being is formed, nourished, and its different parts developed? These are wonders which God alone works, and to himself only are they fully known.

12. *The earth swallowed them.* It is very likely there was also an earthquake on this occasion, and that chasms were made in the bottom of the sea, by which many of them were swallowed up, though multitudes were overwhelmed by the waters, whose dead bodies were afterward thrown ashore. The Psalmist strongly intimates that there was an earthquake on this occasion: "The voice of thy thunder was in the heaven: the lightnings lightened the world: the earth trembled and shook," Ps. lxxvii. 18.

13. *Thou hast guided them in thy strength unto thy holy habitation.* As this ode was dictated by the Spirit of God, it is most natural

MATTHEW HENRY

out of the perils of the Red Sea, *v.* 19.

(3) He sets himself to improve this wonderful appearance of God for them. God having preserved them, they resolve to spare no cost nor pains for the erecting of a tabernacle to his honour, and there they will exalt him. So confident is this Psalmist of the happy issue of the salvation which was so gloriously begun that he looks upon it as in effect finished already: "*Thou hast guided them to thy holy habitation*, *v.* 13. Two ways this great deliverance was encouraging:—*First*, It was such an instance of God's power as would terrify their enemies, and quite dishearten them, *v.* 14–16. It had this effect: the Edomites were afraid of them (Deut. ii. 4), so were the Moabites (Num. xxii. 3), and the Canaanites, Josh. ii. 9, 10; *v.* 1. *Secondly*, It was such a beginning of God's favour to them as gave them an earnest of the perfection of his kindness. *Thou shalt bring them in*, *v.* 17. If he thus *bring them out of Egypt*, notwithstanding their unworthiness, and the difficulties that lay in the way of their escape, doubtless he will bring them into Canaan. *Lastly*, The great ground of the encouragement which they draw from this work of wonder is, *The Lord shall reign for ever and ever*, *v.* 18. Note, It is the unspeakable comfort of all God's faithful subjects that he will reign eternally, and there shall be no end of his dominion.

II. The solemn singing of this song, *v.* 20, 21. Moses led the psalm, and gave it out for the men, and then Miriam for the women. Famous victories were wont to be applauded by the daughters of Israel (1 Sam. xviii. 6, 7); so was this.

JAMIESON, FAUSSET, BROWN

JOSEPH PARKER:

We, too, have a sea to cross. We are pursued; the enemy is not far behind any one of us. The Lord has promised to bring us to a city of rest, and, lie between us and our covenanted land what may, it shall be passed. That is the speech of faith. We, too, shall sing, "I heard the voice of many angels round about the throne and the beasts and the elders . . . saying with a loud voice, Worthy is the Lamb that was slain to receive power, and riches, and wisdom, and strength, and honor, and glory, and blessing. And every creature . . . saying, Blessing, and honor, and glory, and power, be unto him that sitteth upon the throne, and unto the Lamb for ever and ever." We, too, shall sing; the dumb shall break into praise, the cry will be, "O death, where is thy sting? O grave, where is thy victory?" "All the angels stood round about the throne, saying, Amen: Blessing, and glory, and wisdom, and thanksgiving, and honor, and power, and might, be unto our God for ever and ever. Amen."

It shall not always be grim silence with us. We shall learn the song of Moses and the Lamb. Then all argument will have ceased; controversy will have fought out its little wordy fight and have forgotten its bitterness and clamor, and all heaven shall be full of song. They shall sing who enter that city the song of Moses and of the Lamb. But we begin it upon earth. There is no magic in death; there is no evangelizing power in the grave, whither we haste. The song begins now, because it immediately follows the deliverances and benedictions of Providence. It may be a hoarse song, uttered very poorly, in the judgment of musical canons and according to pedantic and scholastic standards; but it shows that the soul is alive and would sing if it could; and God knows what our poor throats and lips would do were we equal to the passions of the soul, and therefore he accepts the broken hymn, the poorly-uttered psalm of adoration, as if it were uttered with thunder, and held in it all the majesty of heaven.—*The People's Bible*

20. Miriam the prophetess—so called from her receiving divine revelations (Num. 12:1; Mic. 6:4), but in this instance principally from her being eminently skilled in music, and in this sense the word "prophecy" is sometimes used in Scripture (I Chron. 25:1; I Cor. 11:5).

took a timbrel—or tabret—a musical instrument in the form of a hoop, edged round with rings or pieces of brass to make a jingling noise and covered over with tightened parchment like a drum. It was beat with the fingers, and corresponds to our tambourine. **all the women went out after her with timbrels and with dances**—We shall understand this by attending to the modern customs of the East, where the dance—a slow, grave, and solemn gesture, generally accompanied with singing and the sound of the timbrel, is still led by the principal female of the company, the rest imitating her movements and repeating the words of the song as they drop from her lips.

ADAM CLARKE

to understand this and the following verses, to the end of the eighteenth, as containing a prediction of what God would do for this people which He had so miraculously redeemed. On this mode of interpretation it would be better to read several of the verbs in the future tense.

15. *The dukes of Edom.* Idumea was governed at this time by those called *alluphim*, "heads, chiefs, or captains." See the note on Gen. xxxvi. 15.

16. *Till thy people pass over.* Not over the Red Sea, for that event had been already celebrated; but over the desert and Jordan, in order to be brought into the Promised Land.

17. *Thou shalt bring them in.* By Thy strength and mercy alone shall they get the promised inheritance. *And plant them.* Give them a fixed habitation in Canaan, after their unsettled, wandering life in the wilderness. *In the mountain.* Meaning Canaan, which was a very mountainous country, Deut. xi. 11; or probably Mount Zion, on which the Temple was built. Where the pure worship of God was established, there the people might expect both rest and safety.

18. *The Lord shall reign for ever and ever.* This is properly the grand chorus in which all the people joined. The words are expressive of God's everlasting dominion, not only in the world, but in the Church; not only under the law, but also under the gospel; not only in time, but through eternity. The original *leolam vaed* may be translated, "for ever and onward"; or, by our very expressive compound term, "for evermore," i.e., "for ever and more"—not only through time, but also through all duration. His dominion shall be ever the same, active and infinitely extending. With this verse the song seems to end, as with it the hemistichs, or poetic lines, terminate. The twentieth and beginning of the twenty-first are in plain prose, but the latter part of the twenty-first is in hemistichs, as it contains the response made by Miriam and the Israelitish women at different intervals during the song.

20. *And Miriam the prophetess.* We have already seen that Miriam was older than either Moses or Aaron; for when Moses was exposed on the Nile, she was a young girl capable of managing the stratagem used for the preservation of his life; and then Aaron was only three years and three months old, for he was fourscore and three years old when Moses was but fourscore (see chap. vii. 7); so that Aaron was older than Moses, and Miriam considerably older than either, not less probably than nine or ten years of age. The name *Miriam* is the same with the Greek *Mariam*, the Latin *Maria*, and the English *Mary*.

The prophetess. Hannebiah. For the meaning of the word prophet, *nabi*, see the note on Gen. xx. 7. It is very likely that Miriam was inspired by the Spirit of God to instruct the Hebrew women, as Moses and Aaron were to instruct the men; and when she and her brother Aaron sought to share in the government of the people with Moses, we find her laying claim to the prophetic influence, Num. xii. 2: "Hath the Lord indeed spoken only by Moses? hath he not spoken also by us?" And that she was constituted joint leader of the people with her two brothers, we have the express word of God by the Prophet Micah, chap. vi. 4: "For I brought thee up out of the land of Egypt . . . and I sent before thee Moses, Aaron, and Miriam." Hence it is very likely that she was the instructress of the women, and regulated the times, places, etc., of their devotional acts; for it appears that from the beginning to the present day the Jewish women all worshipped apart.

A timbrel. Toph, the same word which is translated "tabret," Gen. xxxi. 27. *And with dances. Mecholoth.* Many learned men suppose that this word means some instruments of wind music, because the word comes from the root *chalal*, the ideal meaning of which is to "perforate, penetrate, pierce, stab." Pipes or hollow tubes, such as flutes and the like, may be instruments. Both the Arabic and Persian understand it as meaning instruments of music of the pipe, drum, or sistrum kind; and this seems to comport better with the scope and design of the place than the term *dances*. Miriam is the first prophetess on record, and by this we find

MATTHEW HENRY

Verses 22–27

It should seem, it was with some difficulty that Moses prevailed with Israel to leave that triumphant shore on which they sang the foregoing song. Now here we are told,

I. That in the wilderness of Shur they had no water, *v.* 22.

II. That at Marah they had water, but it was bitter, so that though they had been three days without water they could not drink it. Now in this distress, 1. The people fretted and quarrelled with Moses, as if he had done ill by them. *What shall we drink?* is all their clamour, *v.* 24. 2. Moses prayed: *He cried unto the Lord*, *v.* 25. God is the guide of the church's guides; and to him, as the Chief Shepherd, the under-shepherds must upon all occasions apply. 3. God directed Moses to a tree, which he cast into the waters, in consequence of which, all of a sudden, they were made sweet. Some think this wood had a peculiar virtue in it for this purpose, because it is said, *God showed him the tree.* God is to be acknowledged, not only in the creating of things useful for man, but in discovering their usefulness. Some make this tree typical of the cross of Christ, which sweetens the bitter waters of affliction to all the faithful, and enables them to rejoice in tribulation. *There he made a statute and an ordinance*, and settled matters with them. *There he proved them*, that is, there he put them upon the trial, admitted them as probationers for his favour. In short, he tells them, *v.* 26, (1) What he expected from them, and that was, in one word, obedience. They must not think, now that they were delivered from their bondage in Egypt, that they were their own masters; they must look upon themselves as God's servants, because he had *loosed their bonds*, Ps. cxvi. 16; Luke i. 74, 75. (2) What they might then expect from him: *I will put none of these diseases upon thee*, that is, "I will not bring upon thee any of the plagues of Egypt." Let not the Israelites think God would connive at their sins and let them do as they would. No, God is no respecter of persons; a rebellious Israelite shall fare no better than a rebellious Egyptian; and so they found, to their cost, before they got to Canaan.

III. That at Elim they had good water, and enough of it, *v.* 27. Here were twelve wells for their supply, one for every tribe, that they might not strive for water, as their fathers had sometimes done; and, for their pleasure, there were seventy palm-trees.

JAMIESON, FAUSSET, BROWN

21. Miriam answered them—"them" in the *Hebrew* is masculine, so that Moses probably led the men and Miriam the women—the two bands responding alternately, and singing the first verse as a chorus. **22. wilderness of Shur** — comprehending all the western part of Arabia Petræa. The desert of Etham was a part of it, extending round the northern portion of the Red Sea, and a considerable distance along its eastern shore; whereas the "wilderness of Shur" (now Sudhr) was the designation of all the desert region of Arabia Petræa that lay next to Palestine. **23. when they came to Marah, they could not drink of the waters**—Following the general route of all travellers southward, between the sea and the tableland of the Tih (valley of wandering), Marah is almost universally believed to be what is now called Howarah, in Wady-Amarah, about thirty miles from the place where the Israelites landed on the eastern shore of the Red Sea—a distance quite sufficient for their march of three days. There is no other perennial spring in the intermediate space. The water still retains its ancient character, and has a bad name among the Arabs, who seldom allow their camels to partake of it. **25. the Lord showed him a tree, which when he had cast into the waters, the waters were made sweet**—Some travellers have pronounced this to be the Elvah of the Arabs—a shrub in form and flower resembling our hawthorn; others, the berries of the Ghurkhud—a bush found growing around all brackish fountains. But neither of these shrubs are known by the natives to possess such natural virtues. It is far more likely that God miraculously endowed some tree with the property of purifying the bitter water—a tree employed as the medium, but the sweetening was not dependent upon the nature or quality of the tree, but the power of God (cf. John 9:6). And hence the "statute and ordinance" that followed, which would have been singularly inopportune if no miracle had been wrought. **and there he proved them**—God now brought the Israelites into circumstances which would put their faith and obedience to the test (cf. Gen. 22:1).

27. they came to Elim, where were twelve wells of water—supposed to be what is now called Wady-Ghurandel, the most extensive watercourse in the western desert—an oasis, adorned with a great variety of trees, among which the palm is still conspicuous, and fertilized by a copious stream. It is estimated to be a mile in breadth, but stretching out far to the northeast. After the weary travel through the desert, this must have appeared a most delightful encampment from its shade and verdure, as well as from its abundant supply of sweet water for the thirsty multitude. The palm is called "the tree of the desert," as its presence is always a sign of water. The palms in this spot are greatly increased in number, but the wells are diminished.

ADAM CLARKE

that God poured out His Spirit not only upon men, but upon women also; and we learn also that Miriam was not only a prophetess, but a poetess also, and must have had considerable skill in music to have been able to conduct her part of these solemnities.

22. *The wilderness of Shur.* This was on the coast of the Red Sea on their road to Mount Sinai.

23. *Marah.* So called from the "bitter waters" found there.

24. *The people murmured.* They were in a state of great mental degradation, owing to their long and oppressive vassalage, and had no firmness of character. See the note on chap. xiii. 17.

25. *He cried unto the Lord.* Moses was not only their leader, but also their mediator. Of prayer and dependence on the Almighty, the great mass of Israelites appear to have had little knowledge at this time. Moses, therefore, had much to bear from their weakness, and the merciful Lord was long-suffering. *There he made for them.* Though it is probable that the Israelites are here intended, yet the word *lo* should not be translated *for them*, but "to him," for these statutes were given to Moses that he might deliver them to the people. *There he proved them. Nissahu,* "he proved him." By this murmuring of the people He proved Moses, to see, speaking after the manner of men, whether he would be faithful, and, in the midst of the trials to which he was likely to be exposed, whether he would continue to trust in the Lord and seek all his help from Him.

26. *If thou wilt diligently hearken.* What is contained in this verse appears to be what is intended by the *statute* and *ordinance* mentioned in the preceding: "If thou wilt diligently hearken to the voice of the Lord thy God, and wilt do that which is right in his sight, and wilt give ear to his commandments, and keep all his statutes, I will put none of these diseases upon thee." This statute and ordinance implied the three following particulars: (1) That they should acknowledge Jehovah for their God, and thus avoid all idolatry. (2) That they should receive His word and testimony as a divine revelation, binding on their hearts and lives, and thus be saved from profligacy of every kind, and from acknowledging the maxims or adopting the customs of the neighboring nations. (3) That they should continue to do so, and adorn their profession with a holy life. These things being attended to, then the promise of God was that they should have none of the diseases of the Egyptians put on them; that they should be kept in a state of health of body and peace of mind; and if at any time they should be afflicted, on application to God the evil should be removed, because He was their Healer or Physician—*I am the Lord that healeth thee.* That the Israelites had in general a very good state of health, their history warrants us to believe; and when they were afflicted, as in the case of the fiery serpents, on application to God they were all healed.

27. *They came to Elim.* This was in the desert of Sin. *Twelve wells of water.* One for each of the tribes of Israel, say the Targums of Jonathan and Jerusalem. *And threescore and ten palm trees.* One for each of the seventy elders (*ibid.*).

MATTHEW HENRY — CHAPTER 16

Verses 1–12

The host of Israel, it seems, took along with them out of Egypt a month's provisions, which, by the fifteenth day of the second month, was all spent.

I. Their discontent and murmuring upon that occasion, *v.* 2, 3. 1. They count upon being killed in the wilderness—nothing less, at the first appearance of disaster. It argues great distrust of God to talk of nothing but being speedily killed. 2. They invidiously charge Moses with a design to starve them when he brought them out of Egypt. 3. They so far

JAMIESON, FAUSSET, BROWN — CHAPTER 16

Vss. 1-36. Murmurs for Want of Bread. **1. they took their journey from Elim**—where they had remained several days. **came unto the wilderness of Sin**—It appears from Number 32, that several stations are omitted in this historical notice of the journey. This passage represents the Israelites as advanced into the great plain, which, beginning near El-Murkah, extends with a greater or less breadth to almost the extremity of the peninsula. In its broadest part northward of Tur it is called El-Kaa, which is probably the desert of Sin [Robinson]. **2. the whole congregation . . . murmured against Moses and Aaron**—Modern travellers through the desert of Sinai are accustomed to take as much as is sufficient for the sustenance of men and beasts during forty days. The Israelites having been rather more than a month on their journey, their store of corn or other provisions was altogether or

ADAM CLARKE — CHAPTER 16

1. *The wilderness of Sin.* This desert lies between Elim and Sinai. *The fifteenth day of the second month.* They had now left Egypt one month, during which it is probable they lived on the provisions they brought with them from Rameses, though it is possible they might have had a supply from the seacoast. Concerning Mount Sinai, see the note on chap. xix. 1.

2. *The whole congregation . . . murmured.* This is an additional proof of the degraded state of the minds of this people; see the note on chap. xiii. 17. And this very circumstance affords a convincing argument that a people so stupidly carnal could not have been induced to leave Egypt had they not been persuaded so to do by the most evident and striking miracles.

MATTHEW HENRY

undervalue their deliverance that they wish they had died in Egypt. They would rather die by the fleshpots of Egypt, where they found themselves with provision, than live under the guidance of the heavenly pillar in a wilderness and be provided for by the hand of God! We cannot suppose that they had any great plenty in Egypt, how largely soever they now talk of the flesh-pots; nor could they fear dying for want in the wilderness, while they had their flocks and herds with them. But discontent magnifies what is past, and vilifies what is present, without regard to truth or reason.

II. The care God graciously took for their supply.

1. How God makes known to Moses his kind intentions, that he might not be uneasy at their murmurings, nor be tempted to wish he had let them alone in Egypt. (1) He takes notice of the people's complaints. (2) He promises them a speedy, sufficient, and constant supply, *v.* 4. See what God designed in making this provision for them: *That I may prove them, whether they will walk in my law or no.* [1] Thus he tried whether they would trust him, and walk in the law of faith or no, whether they could rest satisfied with the bread of the day in its day, and depend upon God for fresh supplies tomorrow. [2] Thus he tried whether they would serve him, and be always faithful.

2. How Moses made known these intentions to Israel, as God ordered him. Here Aaron was his prophet, as he had been to Pharaoh. Moses directed Aaron what to *speak to the congregation of Israel* (*v.* 9). Note, God condescends to give even murmurers a fair hearing. (1) He convinces them of the evil of their murmurings. They thought they reflected only upon Moses and Aaron, but here they are told that God was struck at through their sides. Note, When we murmur against those who are instruments of any uneasiness to us, whether justly or unjustly, we should do well to consider how much we reflect upon God by it; men are but God's hand. (2) He assures them of the supply of their wants, that since they had harped upon the flesb-pots so much they should for once have flesh in abundance that evening, and bread the next morning, and so on every day thenceforward, *v.* 8, 12. Many there are of whom we say that they are better fed than taught; but the Israelites were thus fed, that they might be taught. [1] *By this you shall know that the Lord hath brought you out from the land of Egypt*, *v.* 6. That they were brought out of Egypt was plain enough; but so strangely sottish and short-sighted were they that they said it was Moses that brought them out, *v.* 3. [2] *By this you shall know that I am the Lord your God*, *v.* 12. When God plagued the Egyptians, it was to make them know that he was the Lord; when he provided for the Israelites, it was to make them know that he was their God.

3. How God himself manifested his glory, to still the murmurings of the people, and to put a reputation upon Moses and Aaron, *v.* 10. While Aaron was speaking, *the glory of the Lord appeared in the cloud.*

Verses 13–21

Now they begin to be provided for by the immediate hand of God.

I. He makes them a feast, at night, of delicate fowl. Quails, or pheasants, or some wild fowl, came up, and covered the camp, so tame that they might take up as many of them as they pleased.

II. Next morning he rained manna upon them, which was to be continued to them for their daily bread. 1. That which was provided for them was

JAMIESON, FAUSSET, BROWN

nearly exhausted; and there being no prospect of procuring any means of subsistence in the desert, except some wild olives and wild honey (Deut. 32: 13), loud complaints were made against the leaders. **3. Would to God we had died by the hand of the Lord in the land of Egypt**—How unreasonable and absurd the charge against Moses and Aaron! how ungrateful and impious against God! After all their experience of the divine wisdom, goodness, and power, we pause and wonder over the sacred narrative of their hardness and unbelief. But the expression of feeling is contagious in so vast a multitude, and there is a feeling of solitude and despondency in the desert which numbers cannot dispel; and besides, we must remember that they were men engrossed with the *present*—that the Comforter was not then given—and that they were destitute of all visible means of sustenance and cut off from every visible comfort, with only the promises of an *unseen* God to look to as the ground of their hope. And though we may lament they should tempt God in the wilderness and freely admit their sin in so doing, we can be at no loss for a reason why those who had all their lives been accustomed to walk by *sight* should, in circumstances of unparalleled difficulty and perplexity, find it hard to walk by *faith*. Do not even *we* find it difficult to walk by faith through the wilderness of this world, though in the light of a clearer revelation, and under a nobler leader than Moses? [FISK]. (See I Cor. 10:11, 12). **4. Then said the Lord unto Moses**—Though the outbreak was immediately against the human leaders, it was indirectly against God: yet mark His patience, and how graciously He promised to redress the grievance. **I will rain bread from heaven**—Israel, a type of the Church which is from above, and being under the conduct, government, and laws of heaven, received their food from heaven also (Ps. 78:24). **that I may prove them, whether they will walk in my law, or no**—The grand object of their being led into the wilderness was that they might receive a religious training directly under the eye of God; and the first lesson taught them was a constant dependence on God for their daily nourishment.

13. at even the quails came up, and covered the camp—This bird is of the gallinaceous kind, resembling the red partridge, but not larger than the turtledove. They are found in certain seasons in the places through which the Israelites passed, being migratory birds, and they were probably brought to the camp by "a wind from the Lord" as on another occasion (Num. 11:31).

13-31. and in the morning . . . a small round thing . . . manna—There is a gum of the same name distilled in this desert region from the

ADAM CLARKE

3. The *flesh pots.* As the Hebrews were in a state of slavery in Egypt, they were doubtless fed in various companies by their taskmasters in particular places, where large pots or boilers were fixed for the purpose of cooking their victuals.

4. *I will rain bread.* Therefore this substance was not a production of the desert; nor was the dew that was the instrument of producing it common there, else they must have had this bread for a month before.

6. *Ye shall know that the Lord hath brought you out.* After all the miracles they had seen, they appear still to suppose that their being brought out of Egypt was the work of Moses and Aaron; for though the miracles they had already seen were convincing for the time, yet as soon as they had passed by they relapsed into their former infidelity. God therefore saw it necessary to give them a daily miracle in the fall of the manna, that they might have the proof of His divine interposition constantly before their eyes. Thus they knew that *Jehovah* had brought them out, and that it was not the act of Moses and Aaron.

7. *Ye shall see the glory of the Lord.* Does it not appear that the *glory of the Lord* is here spoken of as something distinct from the Lord? for it is said, *He* (the glory) *heareth your murmurings against the Lord;* though *the Lord* may be here put for "himself," the antecedent instead of the relative. This passage may receive some light from Heb. 1. 3: "Who being the brightness of his glory, and the express image of his person." And as St. Paul's words are spoken of the Lord Jesus, is it not likely that the words of Moses refer to Him also? "No man hath seen God at any time"; hence we may infer that Christ was the visible Agent in all the extraordinary and miraculous interferences which took place both in the patriarchal times and under the law.

8. *In the evening flesh to eat.* Namely, the quails; *and in the morning bread to the full,* namely, the manna. *And what are we?* Only His servants, obeying His commands. *Your murmurings are not against us,* for we have not brought you up from Egypt; *but against the Lord,* who, by His own miraculous power and goodness, has brought you out of your slavery.

9. *Come near before the Lord.* This has been supposed to refer to some particular place where the Lord manifested His presence. The great Tabernacle was not yet built, but there appears to have been a small tabernacle, or tent, called the "tabernacle of the congregation," which, after the sin of the golden calf, was always placed without the camp; see chap. xxxiii. 7: "And Moses took the tabernacle, and pitched it without the camp, afar off from the camp, and called it the Tabernacle of the congregation. And it came to pass, that every one which sought the Lord went out unto the tabernacle of the congregation, which was without the camp." May we not conclude that Moses invited them to come near before the Lord, and so witness His glory, that they might be convinced it was God and not he that led them out of Egypt, and that they ought to submit to Him, and cease from their murmurings? It is said, chap. xix. 17, that Moses brought forth the people out of the camp "to meet with God." And in this instance there might have been a similar though less awful manifestation of the Divine Presence.

10. *As Aaron spake.* So he now became the spokesman or minister of Moses to the Hebrews, as he had been before unto Pharaoh; according to what is written, chap. vii. 1, etc.

13. *At even the quails came. Selav,* from *salah,* to be "quiet, easy, or secure"; and hence the quail, from their remarkably living at ease and plenty among the corn. "An amazing number of these birds," says Hasselquist, *Travels,* p. 209, "come to Egypt at this time (March), for in this month the wheat ripens. They conceal themselves among the corn, but the Egyptians know that they are thieves, and when they imagine the field to be full of them they spread a net over the corn and make a noise, by which the birds, being frightened, and endeavouring to rise, are caught in the net in great numbers, and make a most delicate and agreeable dish."

14. *Behold, upon the face of the wilderness there lay a small round thing.* It appears that this small, round thing fell with the dew, or

MATTHEW HENRY

manna, itself of such a consistency as to serve for nourishing strengthening food, without anything else. They called it *manna, manhu*, "What is this?"

2. They were to gather it every morning (*v.* 21), *the portion of a day in his day, v.* 4. To this daily raining and gathering of manna our Saviour seems to allude when he teaches us to pray, *Give us this day our daily bread.* We are hereby taught, (1) Prudence and diligence in providing food convenient for ourselves and our

JAMIESON, FAUSSET, BROWN

tamarisk, which is much prized by the natives, and preserved carefully by those who gather it. It is collected early in the morning, melts under the heat of the sun, and is congealed by the cold of night. In taste it is as sweet as honey, and has been supposed by distinguished travellers, from its whitish color, time, and place of its appearance, to be the manna on which the Israelites were fed: so that, according to the views of some, it was a production indigenous to the desert; according to others, there was a miracle, which consisted, however, only in the preternatural arrangements regarding its supply. But more recent and accurate examination has proved this gum of the tarfa-tree to be wanting in all the principal characteristics of the Scripture manna. It exudes only in small quantities, and not every year; it does not admit of being baked (Num. 11:8) or boiled (vs. 23). Though it may be exhaled by the heat and afterwards fall with the dew, it is a medicine, not food—it is well known to the natives of the desert, while the Israelites were strangers to theirs; and in taste as well as in the appearance of double quantity on Friday, none on Sabbath, and in not breeding worms, it is essentially different from the manna furnished to the Israelites.

ADAM CLARKE

rather the dew fell first, and this substance fell on it. The dew might have been intended to cool the ground, that the manna on its fall might not be dissolved; for we find, from v. 21, that the heat of the sun melted it. The ground therefore being sufficiently cooled by the dew, the manna lay unmelted long enough for the Israelites to collect a sufficient quantity for their daily use.

15. *They said one to another, It is manna: for they wist not what it was.* This is a most unfortunate translation, because it not only gives no sense, but it contradicts itself. The Hebrew *man hu* literally signifies, "What is this?" *for*, says the text, *they wist not what it was* and therefore they could not give it a name. Moses immediately answers the question, and says, *This is the bread which the Lord hath given you to eat.* From v. 31 we learn that this substance was afterwards called *man*, probably in commemoration of the question they had asked on its first appearance. Almost all our own ancient versions translate the words, "What is this?"

What this substance was we know not. It was nothing that was common to the wilderness. It is evident the Israelites never saw it before, for Moses says, Deut. viii. 3, 16: "He . . . fed thee with manna, which thou knewest not, neither did thy fathers know"; and it is very likely that nothing of the kind had ever been seen before; and by a pot of it being laid up in the ark, it is as likely that nothing of the kind ever appeared again, after the miraculous supply in the wilderness had ceased. It seems to have been created for the present occasion and, like Him whom it typified, to have been the only thing of the kind, the only bread from heaven, which God ever gave to preserve the life of man, as Christ is the True Bread that came down from heaven and was given for the life of the world. See John vi. 31-58.

16. *An omer for every man.* I shall here once for all give a short account of the measures of capacity among the Hebrews.

"Omer," from the root *amar*, to "press, squeeze, collect, and bind together." It is supposed that the *omer*, which contained about three quarts English, had its name from this circumstance; that it was the most contracted or the smallest measure of things dry known to the ancient Hebrews.

The "ephah," *eiphah*, from *aphah*, "to bake," because this was probably the quantity which was baked at one time. According to Bishop Cumberland the *ephah* contained seven gallons, two quarts, and about half a pint, wine measure; and as the *omer* was the tenth part of the ephah, v. 36, it must have contained about six pints English.

The "kab" is said to have contained about three pints and one-third English.

The "homer," *chomer*, mentioned in Lev. xxvii. 16, was quite a different measure from that above, and is a different word in the Hebrew. The *chomer* was the largest measure of capacity among the Hebrews, being equal to ten baths or ephahs, amounting to about seventy-five gallons, three pints, English. See Ezek. xlv. 11, 13-14. Goodwin supposes that this measure derived its name from *chamor*, an "ass," being the ordinary load of that animal.

The "bath" was the largest measure of capacity next to the homer, of which it was the tenth part. It was the same as the ephah, and consequently contained about seven gallons, two quarts, and half a pint, and is always used in Scripture as a measure of liquids.

The "seah" was a measure of capacity for things dry, equal to about two gallons and a half English. See 2 Kings vii. 1, 16, 18.

The "hin," according to Bishop Cumberland, was the one-sixth part of an ephah, and contained a little more than one gallon and two pints. See Exod. xxix. 40.

The "log" was the smallest measure of capacity for liquids among the Hebrews: it contained about three-quarters of a pint. See Lev. xiv. 10, 12.

Take ye . . . for them which are in his tents. Some might have been confined in their tents through sickness or infirmity, and charity required that those who were in health should gather a portion for them.

17. *Some more, some less.* According to their respective families, an *omer* for a man; and

TODAY'S DICTIONARY OF THE BIBLE:

Manna—Heb. *mân-hu*, "What is that?"—the name given by the Israelites to the food miraculously supplied to them during their wanderings in the wilderness (Ex. 16:15–35). The name is commonly taken as derived from man, an expression of surprise, "What is it?" but more probably it is derived from *mânan*, meaning "to allot," and hence denoting an "allotment" or a "gift." This "gift" from God is described as "a small round thing," like the "hoarfrost on the ground," and "like coriander seed," "of the color of bdellium," and in taste "like wafers made with honey." It was capable of being baked and boiled, ground in mills, or beaten in a mortar (Ex. 16:23; Num. 11:7). If any was kept over till the following morning, it became corrupt with worms; but as on the Sabbath none fell, on the preceding day a double portion was given, and that could be kept over to supply the wants of the Sabbath without becoming corrupt. Directions concerning the gathering of it are fully given (Ex. 16:16–18, 33; Deut. 8:3, 16). It fell for the first time after the eighth encampment in the desert of Sin, and was daily furnished, except on the Sabbath, for all the years of the wanderings, till they encamped at Gilgal, after crossing the Jordan, when it suddenly ceased, and where they "did eat of the old corn of the land; . . . neither had the children of Israel manna any more" (Josh. 5:11, 12). They now no longer needed the "bread of the wilderness."

This manna was evidently altogether a miraculous gift, wholly different from any natural product with which we are acquainted, and which bears this name. The manna of European commerce comes chiefly from Calabria and Cicily. It drops from the twigs of a species of ash during the months of June and July. At night it is fluid and resembles dew, but in the morning it begins to harden. The manna of the Sinaitic peninsula is an exudation from the "manna-tamarisk" tree (Tamarix mannifera), the eltarfah of the Arabs. This tree is found at the present day in certain well-watered valleys in the peninsula of Sinai. The manna with which the people of Israel were fed for forty years differs in many particulars from all these natural products.

Our Lord refers to the manna when he calls himself the "true bread from heaven" (John 6:31–35, 48–51). He is also the "hidden manna" (Rev. 2:17; comp. John 6:48, 51).

MATTHEW HENRY

household. What God graciously gives we must industriously gather. (2) Contentment and satisfaction with a sufficiency. They must gather, *every man according to his eating*; enough is as good as a feast, and more than enough is as bad as a surfeit. (3) Dependence upon Providence: *Let no man leave till morning* (*v.* 19), but let them learn to go to bed and sleep quietly, though they have not a bit of bread in their tent, nor in all their camp, trusting that God, with the following day, will bring them their daily bread." See here the folly of hoarding. The manna that was laid up by some putrefied, and bred worms, and became good for nothing. 3. Let us set ourselves to think, (1) Of that great power of God which fed Israel in the wilderness, and made miracles their daily bread. Never was there such a market of provisions as this, where so many hundred thousand men were daily furnished, without money and without price. Never was there such an open house kept as God kept in the wilderness for forty years together, nor such free and plentiful entertainment given. (2) Of that constant providence of God. The same wisdom, power, and goodness that now brought food daily out of the clouds, are employed in the constant course of nature, bringing food yearly out of the earth, and giving us all things richly to enjoy.

Verses 22–31

We have here the setting apart of one day in seven for holy work, and, in order to that, for holy rest, was a divine appointment ever since God created man upon the earth, and the most ancient of positive laws. The double provision which God made for the Israelites, and which they were to make for themselves, on the sixth day: God gave them *on the sixth day the bread of two days*, *v.* 29. Appointing them to rest on the seventh day, he took care that they should be no losers by it; and none ever will be losers by serving God. On that day they were to fetch in enough for two days, and to prepare it, *v.* 23. The law was very strict, that they must bake and seeth, the day before, and not on the sabbath day. This does not now make it unlawful for us to dress meat on the Lord's day, but directs us to contrive our family affairs so that they may hinder us as little as possible in the work of the sabbath. That which they kept for their food on the sabbath day did not putrefy, *v.* 24. Some, it seems, went out on the seventh day, expecting to find manna (*v.* 27); but they found none, for those that will find must seek in the appointed time. God, upon this occasion, said to Moses, *How long refuse you to keep my commandments? v.* 28. Why did he say this to Moses? He was not disobedient. No, but he was the ruler of a disobedient people, and God charges it upon him that he might the more warmly charge it upon them, and might take care that their disobedience should not be through any neglect or default of his.

Verses 32–36

God having provided manna to be his people's food in the wilderness, we are here told, 1. How the memory of it was preserved. An omer of this manna was laid up in *a golden pot*, as we are told (Heb. ix. 4), and kept *before the testimony*, or the ark, when it was afterwards made, *v.* 32–34. Note, Eaten bread must not be forgotten. God's miracles and mercies are to be had in everlasting remembrance, for our encouragement to trust in him at all times. 2. How the mercy of it was continued as long as they had occasion for it. The manna never ceased till they came to the borders of Canaan, where there was bread enough and to spare, *v.* 35. The manna is called *spiritual meat* (1 Cor. x. 3), because it was typical of spiritual blessings in heavenly things. Christ himself is the true manna, the bread of life, of which this was a figure, John vi. 49–51. The word of God is the manna by which our souls are nourished, Matt. iv. 4. The comforts of the Spirit are hidden manna, Rev. ii. 17. These come from heaven, as the manna did, and are the support and comfort of the divine life in the soul, while we are in the wilderness of this world. It is to be *gathered*; Christ in the word is to be applied to the soul, and the means of grace are to be used. We must every one of us gather for ourselves, and gather in the morning of our days, the morning of our opportunities, which if we let slip, it may be too late to gather. The manna they gathered must not be hoarded up, but eaten; those that have received Christ must by faith live upon him, and not receive his grace in vain. But those that did eat manna hungered again, died at last, and with many of them God was not well pleased; whereas those that feed on Christ by faith shall never hunger, and shall die no more, and with them God will be for ever well pleased. The Lord evermore give us this bread!

JAMIESON, FAUSSET, BROWN

KEIL–DELITZSCH:

Verses 22–31. Moreover, God bestowed His gift in such a manner that the Sabbath was sanctified by it, and the way was thereby opened for its sanctification by the law. On the sixth day of the week the quantity yielded was twice as much, viz., two omers for one (one person). When the princes of the congregation informed Moses of this, he said to them, "Let tomorrow be rest, a holy Sabbath to the Lord." They were to bake and boil as much as was needed for the day, and keep what was over for the morrow, for on the Sabbath they would find none in the field. They did this, and what was kept for the Sabbath neither stank nor bred worms. It is perfectly clear from this event that the Israelites were not acquainted with any sabbatical observance at that time, but that, while the way was practically opened, it was through the decalogue that it was raised into a legal institution.

Verse 27. On the seventh day some of the people went out to gather manna, notwithstanding Moses' command, but they found nothing. Whereupon God reproved their resistance to His commands and ordered them to remain quietly at home on the seventh day. Through the commandments which the Israelites were to keep in relation to the manna, this gift assumed the character of a temptation, or test of their obedience and faith.

—*Commentary on the Old Testament*

32-36. Fill an omer of it to be kept for your generations—The mere fact of such a multitude being fed for forty years in the wilderness, where no food of any kind is to be obtained, will show the utter impossibility of their subsisting on a natural production of the kind and quantity as this tarfa-gum; and, as if for the purpose of removing all such groundless speculations, Aaron was commanded to put a sample of it in a pot—a golden pot (Heb. 9:4)—to be laid before the Testimony—to be kept for future generations, that they might see the bread on which the Lord fed their fathers in the wilderness. But we have the bread of which that was merely typical (I Cor. 10:3; John 6:32).

ADAM CLARKE

according to the number of infirm persons, whose wants they undertook to supply.

18. *He that gathered much had nothing over.* Because his gathering was in proportion to the number of persons for whom he had to provide. And some having fewer, others more in family, and the gathering being in proportion to the persons who were to eat of it, therefore *he that gathered much had nothing over, and he that gathered little had no lack.* Probably every man gathered as much as he could; and then when brought home and measured by an omer, if he had a surplus, it went to supply the wants of some other family that had not been able to collect a sufficiency, the family being large, and the time in which the manna might be gathered, before the heat of the day, not being sufficient to collect enough for so numerous a household, several of whom might be so confined as not to be able to collect for themselves. Thus there was an equality, and in this light the words of St. Paul, 2 Cor. viii. 15, lead us to view the passage. Here the thirty-sixth verse should come in: "Now an omer is the tenth part of an ephah."

19. *Let no man leave of it till the morning.* For God would have them to take no thought for the morrow, and constantly to depend on Him for their daily bread. And is not that petition in our Lord's prayer founded on this very circumstance, "Give us day by day our daily bread"?

20. *It bred worms.* Their sinful curiosity and covetousness led them to make the trial; and they had a mass of loathsome putrefaction for their pains. How gracious is God! He is continually rendering disobedience and sin irksome to the transgressor; that finding his evil ways to be unprofitable, he may return to his Maker and trust in God alone.

22. *On the sixth day they gathered twice as much.* This they did that they might have a provision for the Sabbath, for on that day no manna fell, vv. 26-27. What a convincing miracle was this! No manna fell on the Sabbath! Had it been a natural production it would have fallen on the Sabbath as at other times; and had there not been a supernatural influence to keep it sweet and pure, it would have been corrupted on the Sabbath as well as on other days. By this series of miracles God showed His own power, presence, and goodness.

23. *To morrow is the rest of the holy sabbath.* There is nothing in either text or context that seems to intimate that the Sabbath was now first given to the Israelites, as some have supposed; on the contrary, it is here spoken of as being perfectly well known, from its having been generally observed. The commandment, it is true, may be considered as being now renewed; because they might have supposed that in their unsettled state in the wilderness they might have been exempted from the observance of it.

29. *Abide ye every man in his place.* Neither go out to seek manna nor for any other purpose; rest at home and devote your time to religious exercises.

34. *Laid it up before the Testimony.* The *Testimony* belonged properly to the Tabernacle, but that was not yet built. Some are of opinion that the Tabernacle, built under the direction of Moses, was only a renewal of one that had existed in the patriarchal times. The word signifies "reference to something beyond itself"; thus the Tabernacle, the manna, the tables of stone, Aaron's rod, all bore reference and testimony to that spiritual good which was yet to come, namely, Jesus Christ and His salvation.

MATTHEW HENRY

CHAPTER 17

Verses 1–7

I. The strait that the children of Israel were in for want of water.

II. Their discontent and distrust in this strait. It is said (*v.* 3), They *thirsted there for water*. This intimates that their passion sharpened their appetites and they were violent and impatient in their desire. See what was the language of this inordinate desire. 1. They challenged Moses to supply them (*v.* 2): *Give us water, that we may drink*, demanding it as a debt. 2. They quarrelled with him for bringing them out of Egypt, as if, instead of delivering them, he designed to murder them. To such a degree their malice against Moses rose that they were *almost ready to stone him*, *v.* 4. 3. They began to question whether God were with them or not: They *tempted the Lord, saying, "Is the Lord among us or not?" v.* 7. They question his essential presence—whether there was a God or not; his common providence—whether that God governed the world; and his special promise—whether he would be as good as his word to them. This is called their *tempting God*. They do, in effect, suppose that Moses was an impostor, that long series of miracles which had rescued them, served them, and fed them, a chain of cheats, and the promise of Canaan a banter upon them; it was all so, if *the Lord was not among them*.

III. The course that Moses took, 1. He reproved the murmurers (*v.* 2): *Why chide you with me?* Observe how mildly he answered them. He showed them whom their murmurings reflected upon, and that the reproaches they cast on him fell on God himself: *You tempt the Lord*; that is, "By distrusting his power, you try his patience, and so provoke his wrath." 2. He made his complaint to God (*v.* 4): *Moses cried unto the Lord*. When men unjustly censure us and quarrel with us, it will be a great relief to us to go to God, and by prayer lay the case before him and leave it with him: if men will not hear us, God will. Moses begs of God to direct him what he should do, for he was utterly at a loss.

IV. God's gracious appearance for their relief, *v.* 5, 6. He orders Moses to go on before the people. He must take his rod with him, not to summon some plague to chastise them, but to fetch water for their supply. O the wonderful patience and forbearance of God. If God had only shown Moses a fountain of water in the wilderness, as he did Hagar, that would have been a great favour; but that he might show his power as well as his pity, and make it a miracle of mercy, he gave them water out of a rock. He directed Moses whither to go, and appointed him to take some of the elders to be witnesses of what was done, that they might themselves be satisfied of the certainty of God's presence with them. He promised to meet him there in the cloud of glory, and ordered him to smite the rock; Moses obeyed, and immediately water came out of the rock in great abundance. It is called *a fountain of waters*, Ps. cxiv. 8. This fair water, that came out of the rock, is called *honey and oil* (Deut. xxxii. 13), because the people's thirst made it doubly pleasant; coming when they were in extreme want, it was like honey and oil to them. God can open fountains for our supply where we least expect them, *waters in the wilderness* (Isa. xliii. 20), because he makes a *way in the wilderness*, *v.* 19. Those who, in this wilderness, keep to God's way, may trust him to provide for them. The graces and comforts of the Spirit are compared to *rivers of living water*, John vii. 38, 39; iv. 14. These flow from Christ, who is the rock smitten by the law of Moses, for he was made under the law. Nothing will supply the needs, and satisfy the desires, of a soul, but water out of this rock, this fountain opened. The pleasures of sense are puddle-water; spiritual delights are rock water, so pure, so clear, so refreshing—rivers of pleasure.

V. A new name was, upon this occasion, given to the place, preserving the remembrance of the sin of their murmuring—*Massah, temptation*, because they tempted God; *Meribah, strife*, because they chid with Moses, *v.* 7.

Verses 8–16

Amalek was the first of the nations that Israel fought with, Num. xxiv. 20.

I. Amalek's attempt: They *came out, and fought with Israel*, *v.* 8. The Amalekites were the posterity of Esau, who hated Jacob because of the birthright and blessing, and this was an effort of the hereditary enmity. Consider this, 1. As Israel's affliction. 2. As Amalek's sin; so it is reckoned, Deut. xxv. 17, 18. They basely fell upon their rear, and smote those that were faint and feeble and could neither make resistance nor escape. In vain did they attack a camp guarded and victualled by miracles: verily they knew

JAMIESON, FAUSSET, BROWN

CHAPTER 17

Vss. 1-7. THE PEOPLE MURMUR FOR WATER. **1. the children of Israel journeyed from the wilderness of Sin**—In the succinct annals of this book, those places only are selected for particular notice by the inspired historian, which were scenes memorable for their happy or painful interest in the history of the Israelites. A more detailed itinerary is given in the later books of Moses, and we find that here two stations are omitted (Num. 33). **according to the commandment of the Lord,** etc.—not given in oracular response, nor a vision of the night, but indicated by the movement of the cloudy pillar. The same phraseology occurs elsewhere (Num. 9:18, 19). **pitched in Rephidim**—now believed, on good grounds, to be Wady Feiran, which is exactly a day's march from Mount Sinai, and at the entrance of the Horeb district. It is a long circuitous defile about forty feet in breadth, with perpendicular granite rocks on both sides. The wilderness of Sin through which they approached to this valley is very barren, has an extremely dry and thirsty aspect, little or no water, scarcely even a dwarfish shrub to be seen, and the only shelter to the panting pilgrims is under the shadow of the great overhanging cliffs. **2, 3. the people did chide with Moses, and said, Give us water that we may drink,** etc.—The want of water was a privation, the severity of which we cannot estimate, and it was a great trial to the Israelites, but their conduct on this new occasion was outrageous; it amounted even to "a tempting of the Lord." It was an opposition to His minister, a distrust of His care, an indifference to His kindness, an unbelief in His providence, a trying of His patience and fatherly forbearance. **4. Moses cried unto the Lord, saying, What shall I do unto this people?**—His language, instead of betraying any signs of resentment or vindictive imprecation on a people who had given him a cruel and unmerited treatment, was the expression of an anxious wish to know what was the best to be done in the circumstances (cf. Matt. 5:44; Rom. 12:21). **5. the Lord said unto Moses,** etc.—not to smite the rebels, but the rock; not to bring a stream of blood from the breast of the offenders, but a stream of water from the granite cliffs. The cloud rested on a particular rock, just as the star rested on the house where the infant Saviour was lodged. And from the rod-smitten rock there forthwith gushed a current of pure and refreshing water. It was perhaps the greatest miracle performed by Moses, and in many respects bore a resemblance to the greatest of Christ's: being done without ostentation and in the presence of a few chosen witnesses (I Cor. 10:4).

7. called the name of the place—Massah (temptation); Meribah (**chiding,** strife): the same word which is rendered "provocation" (Heb. 3:8).

8-16. ATTACK OF AMALEK. **8. Then came Amalek**—Some time probably elapsed before they were exposed to this new evil; and the presumption of there being such an interval affords the only ground on which we can satisfactorily account for the altered, the better, and former spirit that animated the people in this sudden contest. The miracles of the manna and the water from the rock had produced a deep impression and permanent conviction that God was indeed among them; and with feelings elevated by the conscious experience of the Divine Presence and aid, they remained calm, resolute, and

ADAM CLARKE

CHAPTER 17

1. *Pitched in Rephidim.* In Num. xxxiii. 12-14 it is said that when the Israelites came from Sin they encamped in Dophkah, and next in Alush, after which they came to Rephidim. Here, therefore, two stations are omitted, probably because nothing of moment took place at either.

2. *Why chide ye with me?* God is your Leader, complain to Him. *Wherefore do ye tempt the Lord?* As He is your Leader, all your murmurings against me He considers as directed against himself; why therefore do ye tempt Him? Has He not given you sufficient proofs that He can destroy His enemies and support His friends?

3. *And the people murmured.* The reader must not forget what has so often been noted relating to the degraded state of the minds of the Israelites. A strong argument however may be drawn from this in favor of their supernatural escape from Egypt. Had it been a scheme concerted by the heads of the people, provision would necessarily have been made for such exigencies as these. But as God chose to keep them constantly dependent upon himself for every necessity of life, and as they had Moses alone as their mediator to look to, they murmured against him when brought into straits and difficulties, regretted their having left Egypt, and expressed the strongest desire to return. This shows that they had left Egypt reluctantly; and as Moses and Aaron never appear to have any resources but those which came most evidently in a supernatural way, therefore the whole exodus or departure from Egypt proves itself to have been no human contrivance, but a measure concerted by God himself.

6. *I will stand before thee there upon the rock in Horeb. The rock.* It seems as if God had directed the attention of Moses to a particular rock, with which he was well acquainted; for every part of the mount and its vicinity must have been well known to Moses during the time he kept Jethro's flocks in those quarters.

7. *He called the name of the place Massah, and Meribah. Massah* signifies "temptation" or "trial"; and *Meribah*, "contention." From I Cor. x. 4, we learn that this rock was a type of Christ, and their drinking of it is represented as their being made partakers of the grace and mercy of God through Christ Jesus; and yet many who drank fell and perished in the wilderness in the very act of disobedience! Reader, be not high-minded, but fear!

8. *Then came Amalek, and fought with Israel.* The Amalekites seem to have attacked the Israelites in the same way and through the same motives that the wandering Arabs attack the caravans which annually pass through the same desert. It does not appear that the Israelites gave them any kind of provocation; they seem to have attacked them merely through the hopes of plunder. The Amalekites were the posterity of Amalek, one of the dukes of Eliphaz, the son of Esau, and consequently Israel's brother, Gen. xxxvi. 15-16. *Fought with Israel.* In the most treacherous and dastardly manner; for they came at the rear of the camp, smote the hindmost of the people, even all that were feeble behind, when they were faint and weary; see Deut. xxv. 18. The baggage, no doubt, was the object of their avarice; but finding the women, children, aged, and infirm persons behind with the baggage, they smote them and took away their spoils.

MATTHEW HENRY

not what they did.

II. Israel's defence against the aggressors.

1. The post assigned to Joshua, of whom this is the first mention: he is nominated commander-in-chief in this expedition, that he might be trained up to the services he was designed for after the death of Moses.

2. The post assumed by Moses: *I will stand on the top of the hill with the rod of God in my hand, v.* 9. Joshua fights, Moses prays, and held up *the rod of God in his hand.* This rod Moses held up to Israel, to animate them; the rod was held up as the banner to encourage the soldiers. Moses also held up this rod to God, by way of appeal to him. Moses was not only a standard-bearer, but an intercessor, pleading with God for success and victory. It is here the praying legion that proves the thundering legion. (1) How Moses was tired (*v.* 12): *His hands were heavy.* We do not find that Joshua's hands were heavy in fighting, but Moses's hands were heavy in praying. The more spiritual any service is the more apt we are to fail and flag in it. (2) What influence the rod of Moses had upon the battle (*v.* 11): *When Moses held up his hand* in prayer (so the Chaldee explains it) *Israel prevailed,* but, *when he let down his hand* from prayer, *Amalek prevailed.* (3) The care that was taken for the support of Moses. When he could not stand any longer he sat down upon a stone (*v.* 12); when he could not hold up his hands, he would have them held up. Moses, the man of God, is glad of the assistance of Aaron his brother, and Hur, who, some think, was his brother-in-law, the husband of Miriam. Moses's hands, thus stayed, were *steady till the going down of the sun.* No doubt it was a great encouragement to the people to see Joshua before them in the field of battle and Moses above them upon the top of the hill: Christ is both to us—our Joshua, the captain of our salvation who fights our battles, and our Moses, who, in the upper world, ever lives making intercession, that our faith fail not.

III. The defeat of Amalek. Victory had hovered awhile between the camps, but Israel carried the day, *v.* 13. Though Joshua fought with great disadvantages —his soldiers undisciplined, ill-armed, long inured to servitude, and apt to murmur; yet by them God wrought a great salvation.

IV. The trophies of this victory set up. 1. Moses took care that God should have the glory of it (*v.* 15); instead of setting up a triumphal arch to the honour of Joshua, he builds an altar to the honour of God, and that which is most carefully recorded is the inscription upon the altar, *Jehovah-nissi—The Lord is my banner,* which probably refers to the lifting up of the rod of God as a banner in this action. The presence and power of Jehovah were the banner under which they enlisted, by which they were animated and kept together, and therefore which they erected in the day of their triumph. 2. God took care that posterity should have the comfort and benefit of it: "*Write this for a memorial,* and then *rehearse it in the ears of Joshua,* let him be entrusted with this memorial, to transmit it to the generations to come." Moses must now begin to keep a diary or journal of occurrences; it is the first mention of writing that we find in scripture, and perhaps the command was not given till after the writing of the law upon the tables of stone: "Write it *in perpetuam rei memoriam—that the event may be had in perpetual remembrance*"; that which is written remains. (1) "Write what has been done. Let ages to come know that God fights for his people, and *he that touches them touches the apple of his eye.*" (2) Write what shall be done. [1] That in process of time Amalek shall be totally ruined and rooted out (*v.* 14). Israel will at last undoubtedly triumph in the fall of Amalek. This sentence was executed in part by Saul (1 Sam. xv.), and completely by David (*ch.* xxx.; 2 Sam. i. 1; viii. 12); after his time we never read so much as of the name of Amalek. [2] That in the meantime God would have a continual controversy with him (*v.* 16). This was written for direction to Israel never to make any league with the Amalekites.

JAMIESON, FAUSSET, BROWN

courageous under the attack of their unexpected foe. **fought with Israel**—The language implies that no occasion had been furnished for this attack; but, as descendants of Esau, the Amalekites entertained a deep-seated grudge against them, especially as the rapid prosperity and marvellous experience of Israel showed that the blessing contained in the birthright was taking effect. It seems to have been a mean, dastardly, insidious surprise on the rear (Num. 24: 20; Deut. 25:17), and an impious defiance of God. **9. Moses said unto Joshua**—or Jesus (Acts 7:45; Heb. 4:8). This is the earliest notice of a young warrior destined to act a prominent part in the history of Israel. He went with a number of picked men. There is not here a wide open plain on which the battle took place, as according to the rules of modern warfare. The Amalekites were a nomadic tribe, making an irregular attack on a multitude probably not better trained than themselves, and for such a conflict the low hills and open country around this wady would afford ample space [ROBINSON]. **10-12. Moses . . . went up . . . the hill . . . held up his hand**—with the wonder-working rod; he acted as the standard-bearer of Israel, and also their intercessor, praying for success and victory to crown their arms—the earnestness of his feelings being conspicuously evinced amid the feebleness of nature.

Joshua discomfited Amalek—Victory at length decided in favor of Israel, and the glory of the victory, by an act of national piety, was ascribed to God (cf. I John 5:4).

14-16. Write this for a memorial—If the bloody character of this statute seems to be at variance with the mild and merciful character of God, the reasons are to be sought in the deep and implacable vengeance they meditated against Israel (Ps. 83:4).

ADAM CLARKE

9. *Moses said unto Joshua.* This is the first place in which Joshua the son of Nun is mentioned; the illustrious part which he took in Jewish affairs, till the settlement of his countrymen in the Promised Land, is well known. He was captain-general of the Hebrews under Moses; and on this great man's death he became his successor in the government. Joshua was at first called Hoshea, Num. xiii. 16, and afterwards called Joshua by Moses. Both in the Septuagint and in the Greek Testament he is called Jesus. The name signifies "Saviour"; and he is allowed to have been a very expressive type of our blessed Lord. He fought with and conquered the enemies of his people, brought them into the Promised Land, and divided it to them by lot. *Top of the hill.* Probably some part of Horeb or Sinai, to which they were then near.

10. *Moses, Aaron, and Hur went up.* It is likely that the Hur mentioned here is the same with that Hur mentioned in 1 Chron. ii. 19, who appears from the chronology in that chapter to have been the son of Caleb, the son of Ezron, the son of Pharez, the son of Judah. The rabbins and Josephus say he was the brother-in-law of Moses, having married his sister, Miriam. He was a person in whom Moses put much confidence; for he left him conjoint governor of the people with Aaron, when he went to confer with God on the mount, chap. xxiv. 14. His grandson Bezaleel was the chief director in the work of the Tabernacle; see chap. xxxi. 2-5.

11. *When Moses held up his hand.* We cannot understand this transaction in any literal way; for the lifting up or letting down the hands of Moses could not, humanly speaking, influence the battle. It is likely that he held up the rod of God in his hand, v. 9, as an ensign to the people. We have already seen that in prayer the hands were generally lifted up and spread out (see the note on chap. ix. 29), and therefore it is likely that by this act prayer and supplication are intended.

13. *Joshua discomfited Amalek and his people. Amalek* might have been the name of the ruler of this people continued down from their ancestor (see on v. 8), as Pharaoh was the name of all succeeding kings in Egypt. If this were the case, then *Amalek and his people* mean the prince and the army that fought under him. But if *Amalek* stands here for the Amalekites, then *his people* must mean the confederates he had employed on this occasion.

14. *Write this for a memorial in a book.* This is the first mention of writing on record. *Rehearse it in the ears of Joshua.* Thus showing that Joshua was to succeed Moses, and that this charge should be given to every succeeding governor. *I will utterly put out the remembrance of Amalek.* This threatening was accomplished by Saul, 412 years after. Judgment is God's strange work; but it must take place when the sins which incensed it are neither repented of nor forsaken. This people, by their continued transgressions, proved themselves totally unworthy of a political existence; and therefore said God to Saul, "Go and utterly destroy the sinners the Amalekites," 1 Sam. xv. 18. So their continuance in sin was the cause of their final destruction.

15. *Jehovah-nissi.* "Jehovah is my Ensign or Banner." The hands and rod of Moses were held up as soldiers are wont to hold up their standards in the time of battle; and as these standards bear the arms of the country, the soldiers are said to fight under that banner, i.e., under the direction and in the defense of that government. Thus the Israelites fought under the direction of God, and in the defense of His truth; and therefore the name of Jehovah became the armorial bearing of the whole congregation. By His direction they fought, and in His name and strength they conquered, each one feeling himself, not his own, but the Lord's soldier.

16. *The Lord hath sworn that the Lord will have war with Amalek.* This is no translation of the words *ki yad al kes yah milcamah,* which have been variously rendered by different translators and critics, the most rational version of which is the following: "Because the hand of Amalek is against the throne of God, therefore will I have war with Amalek from generation to generation."

MATTHEW HENRY

CHAPTER 18

Verses 1–6

Jethro comes,

I. To congratulate the happiness of Israel, and particularly the honour of Moses his son-in-law; Jethro could not but hear what all the country rang of, the glorious appearances of God for his people Israel (*v.* 1); and he comes to enquire, and to rejoice with them, as one that had a true respect both for them and for their God. Though he, as a Midianite, was not to share with them in the promised land, yet he shared with them in the joy of their deliverance.

II. To bring Moses's wife and children to him. It seems he had sent them back home to his father-in-law. Jethro, we may suppose, was glad of his daughter's company, and fond of her children, yet he would not keep her from her husband, nor them from their father, *v.* 5, 6. Moses must have his family with him, that while he ruled the church of God he might set a good example of prudence in family-government, 1 Tim. iii. 5. Moses had now a great deal both of honour and care put upon him, and it was fit that his wife should be with him to share with him in both. Notice is taken of the significant names of his two sons. 1. The eldest was called *Gershom* (*v.* 3), *a stranger*. 2. The other he called *Eliezer* (*v.* 4), *My God a help*, as we translate it; it looks back to his deliverance from Pharaoh. I would rather translate it so as to look forward, which the original will bear, *The Lord is my help, and will deliver me* from the sword of Pharaoh.

JAMIESON, FAUSSET, BROWN

CHAPTER 18

VSS. 1-27. VISIT OF JETHRO. **1-5. Jethro . . . came . . . unto Moses,** etc.—It is thought by many eminent commentators that this episode is inserted out of its chronological order, for it is described as occurring when the Israelites were "encamped at the mount of God." And yet they did not reach it till the third month after their departure from Egypt (ch. 19:1, 2; cf. Deut. 1:6, 9-15).

ADAM CLARKE

CHAPTER 18

1. *When Jethro, the priest of Midian.* Concerning this person and his several names, see the notes on chap. ii. 15-16, 18; iii. 1; and iv. 20, 24. Jethro was probably the son of Reuel, the father-in-law of Moses, and consequently the brother-in-law of Moses; for the word *chothen,* which we translate *father in law,* in this chapter means simply a "relative by marriage."

2. *After he had sent her back.* Why Zipporah and her two sons returned to Midian is not certainly known. From the transaction recorded in chap. iv. 20, 24, it seems as if she had been alarmed at the danger to which the life of one of her sons had been exposed, and fearing worse evils, left her husband and returned to her father. It is however possible that Moses, foreseeing the troubles to which his wife and children were likely to be exposed had he taken them down to Egypt, sent them back till it should please God to deliver His people. Jethro, now finding that God had delivered them and totally discomfited the Egyptians, their enemies, thought it proper to bring Zipporah and her sons to Moses, while he was in the vicinity of Horeb.

3. *The name of the one was Gershom.* See the note on chap. ii. 22.

5. *Jethro . . . came with his sons.* There are several reasons to induce us to believe that the fact related here is out of its due chronological order, and that Jethro did not come to Moses till the beginning of the second year of the Exodus (see Num. x. 11), some time after the Tabernacle had been erected, and the Hebrew commonwealth established, both in things civil and ecclesiastical. This opinion is founded on the following reasons:

(1) On this verse, where it is said that Jethro came to Moses "while he encamped at the mount of God." Now it appears, from chap. xix. 1-2, that they were not yet come to Horeb, the mount of God, and that they did not arrive there till the third month after their departure from Egypt; and the transactions with which this account is connected certainly took place in the second month; see chap. xvi. 1.

(2) Moses, in Deut. i. 6, 9-10, 12-15, relates that when they were about to depart from Horeb, which was on the twentieth day of the second month of the second year from their leaving Egypt, he then complained that he was not able to bear the burden alone of the government of a people so numerous; and that it was at that time that he established judges and captains over thousands and hundreds and fifties and tens, which appears to be the very transaction recorded in this place; the measure itself being recommended by Jethro, and done in consequence of his advice.

(3) From Num. x. 11, 29, etc., we find that when the cloud was taken up, and the Israelites were about to depart from Horeb, Moses addressed Hobab, who is supposed to have been the same as Jethro, and who then was about to return to Midian, his own country, entreating him to stay with them as a guide while they travelled through the wilderness. It therefore seems necessary that the transaction recorded in this chapter should be inserted in Numbers x, between the tenth and eleventh verses.

(4) It has been remarked that shortly after they had departed from Sinai the dispute took place between Miriam, Aaron, and Moses, concerning the Ethiopian woman Zipporah, whom he had married (see Num. xii. 1, etc.); and this is supposed to have taken place shortly after she had been brought back by Jethro.

(5) In the discourse between Moses and Jethro, mentioned in this chapter, we find that Moses speaks of the statutes and laws of the Lord as things already revealed and acknowledged, which necessarily implies that these laws had already been given (v. 16), which we know did not take place till several months after the transactions mentioned in the preceding chapters.

(6) Jethro offers burnt offerings and sacrifices to God apparently in that way in which they were commanded in the law.

From all these reasons, but particularly from the first two and the last two, it seems most likely that this chapter stands out of its due

ALEXANDER MACLAREN:

In old times parents often used to give expression to their hopes or their emotions in the names of their children. Very clearly that was the case in Moses' naming of his two sons, who seem to have been the whole of his family. The significance of each name is appended to it in the text. The explanation of the first is, "For he said, I have been an alien in a strange land"; and that of the second, "For the God of my fathers, said he, was mine help, and delivered me from the sword of Pharaoh." These two names give us a glimpse of the feelings with which Moses began his exile, and of the better thoughts into which these gradually cleared. The first child's name expresses his father's discontent, and suggests the bitter contrast between Sinai and Egypt; the court and the sheepfold; the gloomy, verdureless, gaunt peaks of Sinai, blazing in the fierce sunshine, and the cool, luscious vegetation of Goshen, the land for cattle. The exile felt himself all out of joint with his surroundings, and so be called the little child that came to him "Gershom," which, according to one explanation, means "banishment," and, according to another means "a stranger here"; in the other case expressing the same sense of homelessness and want of harmony with his surroundings. But as the years went on, Moses began to acclimatize himself, and to become more reconciled to his position and to see things more as they really were. So, when the second child is born, all his murmuring has been hushed, and he looks beyond circumstances, and lays his hand upon God. "And the name of the second was Eliezer, for, he said, the God of my fathers was my help."

Now, there are the two main streams of thought that filled these forty years; and it was worthwhile to put Moses into the desert for all that time, and to break off the purposes and hopes of his life sharp and short, and to condemn him to comparative idleness, or work that was all unfitted to bring out his special powers, for that huge scantling out of his life, one-third of the whole of it, in order that there might be burnt into him, not either of these two thoughts separately, but the two of them in their blessed conjunction: "I am a stranger here"; "God is my help." And so these are the thoughts which, in like juxtaposition, ought to be ours; and in higher fashion with regard to the former of them than was experienced by Moses. —*Expositions of Holy Scripture*

MATTHEW HENRY | JAMIESON, FAUSSET, BROWN | ADAM CLARKE

KEIL–DELITZSCH:

Verses 1–12. The Amalekites had met Israel with hostility, as the prototype of the heathen who would strive against the people and kingdom of God. But Jethro, the Midianitish priest, appeared immediately after in the camp of Israel, not only as Moses' father-in-law, to bring back his wife and children, but also with a joyful acknowledgement of all that Jehovah had done to the Israelites in delivering them from Egypt, to offer burnt offerings to the God of Israel, and to celebrate a sacrificial meal with Moses, Aaron, and all the elders of Israel; so that in the person of Jethro the firstfruits of the heathen, who would hereafter seek the living God, entered into religious fellowship with the people of God. As both the Amalekites and Midianites were descended from Abraham, and stood in blood-relationship to Israel, the different attitudes which they assumed towards the Israelites foreshadowed and typified the twofold attitude which the heathen world would assume towards the kingdom of God.—*Commentary on the Old Testament*

MATTHEW HENRY

Verses 7–12

I. The kind greeting that took place between Moses and his father-in-law, *v.* 7. Those that stand high in the favour of God are not thereby discharged from the duty they owe to men. Moses went out to meet Jethro, did *homage to him, and kissed him.* Religion does not destroy good manners. *They asked each other of their welfare.*

II. The narrative that Moses gave his father-in-law of the great things God had done for Israel, *v.* 8.

III. The impressions this narrative made upon Jethro. 1. He congratulated God's Israel: *Jethro rejoiced, v.* 9. He not only rejoiced in the honour done to his son-in-law, but in *all the goodness done to Israel, v.* 9. Note, Public blessings are the joy of public spirits. While the Israelites were themselves murmuring, notwithstanding all God's goodness to them, here was a Midianite rejoicing. 2. He gave the glory to Israel's God (*v.* 10). 3. His faith was hereby confirmed, and he took this occasion to make a solemn profession of it: *Now know I that Jehovah is greater than all gods, v.* 11. Observe, (1) The matter of his faith: that the God of Israel is greater than all pretenders, all false and counterfeit deities. (2) The confirmation and improvement of his faith: *Now know I*; he knew it before, but now he knew it better; his faith grew up to a full assurance, upon this fresh evidence. (3) The ground and reason upon which he built it: *For wherein they dealt proudly, he was above them.* The magicians were baffled, the idols shaken, Pharaoh humbled, his powers broken, and, in spite of all their confederacies, God's Israel was rescued out of their hands.

IV. The expressions of their joy and thankfulness. They had communion with each other both in a feast and in a sacrifice, *v.* 12. Jethro was cheerfully admitted, though a Midianite, into fellowship with Moses and the elders of Israel, *forasmuch as he also was a son of Abraham,* though of a younger house. 1. They joined in a sacrifice of thanksgiving: *Jethro took burnt offerings for God,* and probably offered them himself, for he was a priest in Midian, and a worshipper of the true God. 2. They joined in a feast of rejoicing, a feast upon the sacrifice.

JAMIESON, FAUSSET, BROWN

6. thy wife, and her two sons—See on ch. 4:20. **7. Moses went out to meet his father-in-law,** etc.—Their salutations would be marked by all the warm and social greetings of Oriental friends (see on ch. 4:27)—the one going out to "meet" the other, the "obeisance," the "kiss" on each side of the head, the silent entrance into the tent for consultation; and their conversation ran in the strain that might have been expected of two pious men, rehearsing and listening to a narrative of the wonderful works and providence of God.

12. Jethro . . . took a burnt offering—This friendly interview was terminated by a solemn religious service—the *burnt offerings* were consumed on the altar, and the *sacrifices* were *peace* offerings, used in a feast of joy and gratitude at which Jethro, as priest of the true God, seems to have presided, and to which the chiefs of Israel were invited. This incident is in beautiful keeping with the character of the parties, and is well worthy of the imitation of Christian friends when they meet in the present day.

ADAM CLARKE

chronological order. As Moses had in the preceding chapter related the war with Amalek and the curse under which they were laid, he may be supposed to have introduced here the account concerning Jethro the Midianite, to show that he was free from that curse, although the Midianites and the Kenites, the family of Jethro, were as one people, dwelling with the Amalekites. See Judg. i. 16; I Chron. ii. 55; 1 Sam. xv. 6. For although the Kenites were some of those people whose lands God had promised to the descendants of Abraham (see Gen. xv. 18-19), yet, in consideration of Jethro, the relative of Moses, all of them who submitted to the Hebrews were suffered to live in their own country; the rest are supposed to have taken refuge among the Edomites and Amalekites.

6. *And he said unto Moses.* That is, by a messenger; in consequence of which Moses went out to meet him, as is stated in the next verse, for an interview had not yet taken place. This is supported by reading *hinneh,* "behold," for *ani,* "I," which is the reading of the Septuagint and Syriac, and several Samaritan MSS.; instead, therefore, of *I thy father,* we should read, "Behold thy father."

7. *And did obeisance.* "He bowed himself down" (see on Gen. xvii. 3 and Exod. iv. 31); this was the general token of respect. *And kissed him;* the token of friendship. *And they asked each other of their welfare;* literally, "and they inquired, each man of his neighbor, concerning peace" (or prosperity), the proof of affectionate intercourse. *And they came into the tent.* Some think that the Tabernacle is meant, which it is likely had been erected before this time; see the note on v. 5. Moses might have thought proper to take his relative first to the house of God, before he brought him to his own tent.

9. *And Jethro rejoiced for all the goodness.* Every part of Jethro's conduct proves him to have been a religious man and a true believer. His thanksgiving to Jehovah (v. 10) is a striking proof of it; he first blesses God for the preservation of Moses, and next for the deliverance of the people from their bondage.

11. *Now I know that the Lord is greater than all gods.* Some think that Jethro was now converted to the true God; but it is very probable that he enjoyed this blessing before he knew anything of Moses, for it is not likely that Moses would have entered into an alliance with this family had they been heathens. Jethro no doubt had the true patriarchal religion. *Wherein they dealt proudly.* Acting as tyrants over the people of God; enslaving them in the most unprincipled manner, and still purposing more tyrannical acts. *He was above them*—He showed himself to be infinitely superior to all their gods, by the miracles which He wrought. Various translations have been given of this clause; the above I believe to be the sense.

12. *Jethro . . . took a burnt offering. Olah.* Though it be true that in the patriarchal times we read of a "burnt offering" (see Gen. xxii. 2, etc.), yet we only read of one in the case of Isaac and, therefore, though this offering made by Jethro is not a decisive proof that the law relative to burnt offerings had already been given, yet, taken with other circumstances in this account, it is a presumptive evidence that the meeting between Moses and Jethro took place after the erection of the Tabernacle. See the note on v. 5.

Sacrifices for God. Zebachim, "slain beasts," as the word generally signifies. We have already seen that sacrifices were instituted by God himself as soon as sin entered into our world; and we see that they were continued and regularly practiced among all the people who had the knowledge of the only true God, from that time until they became a legal establishment. Jethro, who was a priest (chap. ii. 16), had a right to offer these sacrifices.

And Aaron came, and all the elders of Israel, to eat bread. The burnt offering was wholly consumed; every part was considered as the Lord's portion and, therefore, it was entirely burnt up. The other sacrifices mentioned here were such that, after the blood had been poured out before God, the officers and assistants might feed on the flesh. Thus, in ancient times, con-

MATTHEW HENRY

Verses 13–27

I. The great zeal and industry of Moses as a magistrate.

1. Having been employed to redeem Israel out of the house of bondage, herein he is a further type of Christ, that he is employed as a lawgiver and a judge among them. (1) He was to answer enquiries, and to explain the laws of God that were already given them, concerning the sabbath, the manna, &c., beside the laws of nature, relating both to piety and equity, *v.* 15. Moses made them *know the statutes of God and his laws, v.* 16. His business was, not to make laws, but to make known God's laws; his place was but that of a servant. (2) He was to decide controversies, judging between a man and his fellow, *v.* 16. And, if the people were as quarrelsome one with another as they were with God, no doubt he had a great many causes brought before him.

2. Such was the business Moses was called to, and it appears that he did it, (1) With great consideration. (2) With great condescension to the people, who stood *by him, v.* 14. (3) With great constancy and closeness of application.

II. The great prudence and consideration of Jethro as a friend.

1. He disliked the method that Moses took, and was so free with him as to tell him so, *v.* 14, 17, 18. He thought it was too much business for Moses to undertake alone. There may be overdoing even in well-doing.

2. He advised him to such a model of government as would better answer the intention, which was, (1) That he should reserve to himself all applications to God (*v.* 19): *Be thou for them to God-ward*; that was an honour in which it was not fit any other should share with him, Num. xii. 6–8.

Also whatever concerned the whole congregation in general must pass through his hand, *v.* 20. But, (2) That he should appoint judges in the several tribes and families, who should try causes between man and man, and determine them, which would be done with less noise, and more despatch, than in the general assembly wherein Moses himself presided. Yet, (3) An appeal might lie, if there were just cause for it, from these inferior courts to Moses himself. *Every great matter they shall bring unto thee, v.* 22.

3. He adds two qualifications to his counsel: (1) That great care should be taken in the choice of the persons who should be admitted into this trust (*v.* 21); they must *be able men,* &c. It was requisite that they should be men of the very best character, [1] For judgment and resolution—*able men.* Clear heads and stout hearts make good judges. [2] For piety and religion—*such as fear God.* Conscientious men, that dare not do a base thing, though they could do it ever so secretly and securely. [3] For integrity and honesty—*men of truth.* [4] For noble and generous contempt of worldly wealth—*hating covetousness.*

JAMIESON, FAUSSET, BROWN

13-26. on the morrow . . . Moses sat to judge the people, etc.—We are here presented with a specimen of his daily morning occupations; and among the multifarious duties his divine legation imposed, it must be considered only a small portion of his official employments. He appears in this attitude as a type of Christ in His legislative and judicial characters. **the people stood by Moses from the morning unto the evening,** etc.—Governors in the East seat themselves at the most public gate of their palace or the city, and there, amid a crowd of applicants, hear causes, receive petitions, redress grievances, and adjust the claims of contending parties.

17. Moses' father-in-law said unto him, The thing . . . is not good—not good either for Moses himself, for the maintenance of justice, or for the satisfaction and interests of the people. Jethro gave a prudent counsel as to the division of labor, and universal experience in the Church and State has attested the soundness and advantages of the principle.

JOSEPH PARKER:

The great leader of Israel, though leading a life of laborious self-sacrifice, was actually falling below the requirements of social justice. He seemed to be acting on the conviction that he only could manage, arrange, and otherwise successfully administer all the affairs of the people. It never occured to him that he was allowing the talent of others to lie idle. Talent requires to be evoked. It is true indeed that genius asserts itself, and clears for itself space and prominence equal to its measure of supremacy; on the other hand, it is equally true that much sound ability may become dormant, simply because the leaders of society do not call it into responsible exercise. The counsel which Moses received from Jethro inspired Israel with new life. From the moment that it was acted upon, talent rose to the occasion: energy was accounted of some value, and men who had probably been sulking in the background came to be recognized and honored as wise statesmen and cordial allies.

There is more talent in society than we suspect. It needs the sunshine of wise encouragement in order to develop it. There is a lesson in this suggestion for all who lead the lives of men. Specially, perhaps, there is a lesson to pastors of churches. It is a poor church in which there is not more talent than has yet been developed. When Saul saw any strong man and any valiant man, he took him to himself. This is the law of sure progress and massive consolidation in church life. Let us keep our eyes open for men of capacity and goodwill, and the more we watch the more shall our vigilance be rewarded. We should try men by imposing responsibilities upon them. There is range enough in church organization for the trial and strengthening of every gift. Better be a doorkeeper in the house of God than a sluggard, and infinitely better sweep the church floor than lounge upon the pew-top, and find fault with the sweeping of other people. Every man in the Church ought to be doing something.—*The People's Bible*

ADAM CLARKE

tracts were made and covenants sealed. It is very likely, therefore, that the sacrifices offered on this occasion were those on the flesh of which Aaron and the elders of Israel feasted with Jethro. *Before God.* Before the Tabernacle, where God dwelt; for it is supposed that the Tabernacle was now erected. See on v. 5; and see Deut. xii. 5-7 and 1 Chron. xxix. 21-22, where the same form of speech, "before the Lord," is used, and plainly refers to His manifested presence in the Tabernacle.

13. *To judge the people.* To hear and determine controversies between man and man, and to give them instruction in things appertaining to God. *From the morning unto the evening.* Moses was obliged to sit all day, and the people were continually coming and going.

15. *The people come unto me to enquire of God.* To know the mind and will of God on the subject of their inquiries. Moses was the mediator between God and the people; and as they believed that all justice and judgment must come from Him, therefore they came to Moses to know what God had spoken.

16. *I do make them know the statutes of God, and his laws.* These words are so very particular that they leave little room for doubt that the law had been given. Such words would scarcely have been used had not the *statutes* and *laws* been then in existence. And this is one of the proofs that the transaction mentioned here stands out of its due chronological order; see on v. 5.

18. *Thou wilt surely wear away. Nabol tibbol,* "in wearing away, thou wilt wear away" —by being thus continually employed, thou wilt soon become finally exhausted. *And this people that is with thee;* as if he had said, "Many of them are obliged to wait so long for the determination of their suit that their patience must be soon necessarily worn out, as there is no one to hear every cause but thyself."

19. *I will give thee counsel, and God shall be with thee.* Jethro seems to have been a man of great understanding and prudence. His advice to Moses was most appropriate and excellent; and it was probably given under the immediate inspiration of God, for after such sacrificial rites, and public acknowledgment of God, the prophetic spirit might be well expected to descend and rest upon him. God could have showed Moses the propriety and necessity of adopting such measures before, but He chose in this case to help man by man.

20. *Thou shalt teach them ordinances. Chukkim,* all such "precepts" as relate to the ceremonies of religion and political economy. *And laws, hattoroth,* the instructions relative to the whole system of morality. *And shalt shew them the way. Eth hadderech,* "that very way," that *only* way, which God himself has revealed, and in which they should walk in order to please Him and get their souls everlastingly saved. *And the work that they must do.* For it was not sufficient that they should know their duty both to God and man, but they must *do it too; yaasun,* they must do it "diligently, fervently, effectually"; for the paragogic *nun* deepens and extends the meaning of the verb.

21. *Able men.* Persons of wisdom, discernment, judgment, prudence, and fortitude; for who can be a ruler without these qualifications? *Such as fear God.* Who are truly religious, without which they will feel little concerned either for the bodies or souls of the people. *Men of truth.* Honest and true in their own hearts and lives; speaking the truth, and judging according to the truth. *Hating covetousness.* Doing all for God's sake, and love to man; laboring to promote the general good; never perverting judgment. *Rulers of thousands, etc.* "Millenaries, centurions, quinquagenaries, and decurions"; each of these, in all probability, dependent on that officer immediately above himself. So the decurion, or ruler over ten, if he found a matter too hard for him, brought it to the quinquagenary, or ruler of fifty; if, in the course of the exercise of his functions, he found a cause too complicated for him to decide on, he brought it to the centurion, or ruler over a hundred. In like manner the centurion brought his difficult case to the millenary, or ruler over a thousand; the case that was too hard for him to judge, he brought to Moses; and the case that was too hard

MATTHEW HENRY

(2) That he should attend God's direction in the case (*v.* 23): *If thou shalt do this thing, and God command thee so.*

Now Moses did not despise this advice but he *hearkened to the voice of his father-in-law, v.* 24.

III. Jethro's return to his own land, *v.* 27. It is supposed that the Kenites (mentioned 1 Sam. xv. 6) were the posterity of Jethro (compare Judges i. 16), and they are there taken under special protection, for the kindness their ancestor here showed to Israel.

CHAPTER 19

Verses 1–8

Here is, I. The date of that great charter by which Israel was incorporated. 1. The time when it bears date (*v.* 1)—*in the third month* after they came out of Egypt. 2. The place whence it bears date—from *Mount Sinai*, the highest in all that range of mountains. Thus God put contempt upon cities, and palaces, and magnificent structures, setting up his pavilion on the top of a high mountain, in a waste and barren desert, there to carry on this treaty. It is called *Sinai*, from the multitude of thorny bushes that overspread it.

II. The charter itself. Moses was called up to the mountain and was employed as the messenger of the covenant: *Thus shalt thou say to the house of Jacob, and tell the children of Israel, v.* 3. Now observe, 1. That the maker, and first mover, of the covenant, is God himself. In all our dealings with God, free grace anticipates us with the blessings of goodness, and all our comfort is owing, not to our knowing God, but rather to our being *known of him*, Gal. iv. 9. 2. That the matter of the covenant is kind and gracious, and such as gives them the greatest privileges and advantages imaginable. (1) He reminds them of what he had done for them, *v.* 4. *I bore you on eagles' wings*, a high expression of the wonderful tenderness God had shown for them. It is explained, Deut. xxxii. 11, 12. It denotes great speed. God not only came upon the wing for their deliverance, but he hastened them out, as it were, upon the wing. He did it with the strength as well as with the swiftness of an eagle. Egypt, that iron furnace, was the nest in which these young ones were hatched, where they were first formed as the embryo of a nation; when, by the increase of their numbers, they grew to some maturity, they were carried out of that nest. Other birds carry their young in their talons, but the eagle (they say) upon her wings, so that even those archers who shoot flying cannot hurt the young ones, unless they first shoot through the old one. *I brought you unto myself.* They were brought not only into a state of liberty and honour, but into covenant and communion with God. This, this was the glory of their deliverance, as it is of ours by Christ, that he died, *the just for the unjust, that he might bring us to God.* This God aims at in all the gracious methods of his providence and grace, to bring us back to himself, from whom we have revolted, and to bring us home to himself, in whom alone we can be happy. Some have well observed that the *Old Testament church* is said to be borne upon eagles' wings, but the *New Testament church* is said to be gathered by the Lord Jesus, *as a hen gathers her chickens under her wings* (Matt. xxiii. 37), denoting the grace and compassion of that dispensation, and the admirable condescension and humiliation of the redeemer. (2) He tells them plainly (*v.* 5), that they should *obey his voice in deed and keep his covenant.* Being thus saved by him, that which he insisted upon was that they should be ruled by him. (3) He assures them of the honour he would put upon them, and

JAMIESON, FAUSSET, BROWN

23. If thou shalt do this thing, etc.—Jethro's counsel was given merely in the form of a suggestion; it was not to be adopted without the express sanction and approval of a better and higher Counsellor; and although we are not informed of it, there can be no doubt that Moses, before appointing subordinate magistrates, would ask the mind of God, as it is the duty and privilege of every Christian in like manner to supplicate the divine direction in all his ways.

CHAPTER 19

Vss. 1-25. Arrival at Sinai. **1. In the third month**—according to Jewish usage, the *first* day of that month—"same day"—It is added, to mark the time more explicitly, i.e., forty-five days after Egypt—one day spent on the mount (vs. 3), one returning the people's answer (vss. 7, 8), three days of preparation, making the whole time fifty days from the first passover to the promulgation of the law. Hence the feast of pentecost, i.e., the fiftieth day, was the inauguration of the Old Testament church, and the divine wisdom is apparent in the selection of the same reason for the institution of the New Testament church (John 1:17; Acts 2:1). **2. were come to the desert of Sinai**—The desert has its provinces, or divisions, distinguished by a variety of names; and the "desert of Sinai" is that wild and desolate region which occupies the very center of the peninsula, comprising the lofty range to which the mount of God belongs. It is a wilderness of shaggy rocks of porphyry and red granite, and of valleys for the most part bare of verdure. **and there Israel camped before the mount**—Sinai, so called from Seneh, or acacia bush. It is now called Jebel Musa. Their way into the interior of the gigantic cluster was by Wady Feiran, which would lead the bulk of the hosts with their flocks and herds into the high valleys of Jebel Musa, with their abundant springs, especially into the great thoroughfare of the desert—the longest, widest, and most continuous of all the valleys, the Wady-es-Sheikh, while many would be scattered among the adjacent valleys; so that thus secluded from the world in a wild and sublime amphitheatre of rocks, they "camped before the mount." "In this valley—a long flat valley—about a quarter of a mile in breadth, winding northwards, Israel would find ample room for their encampment. Of all the wadys in that region, it seems the most suitable for a prolonged sojourn. The 'goodly tents' of Israel could spread themselves without limit" [Bonar]. **3-6. Moses went up unto God**—the Shekinah—within the cloud (ch. 33:20; John 1:18). **Thus shalt thou say to the house of Jacob,** etc.—The object for which Moses went up was to receive and convey to the people the message contained in these verses, and the purport of which was a general announcement of the terms on which God was to take the Israelites into a close and peculiar relation to Himself. In thus negotiating between God and His people, the highest post of duty which any mortal man was ever called to occupy, Moses was still but a servant. The only Mediator is Jesus Christ.

ADAM CLARKE

for Moses, he brought immediately to God. It is likely that each of these classes had a court composed of its own members, in which cases were heard and tried.

23. *If thou shalt do this thing, and God command thee.* Though the measure was obviously of the utmost importance, and plainly recommended itself by its expediency and necessity; yet Jethro very modestly leaves it to the wisdom of Moses to choose or reject it; and, knowing that in all things his relative was now acting under the immediate direction of God, intimates that no measure can be safely adopted without a positive injunction from God himself. As the counsel was doubtless inspired by the Divine Spirit, we find that it was sanctioned by the same, for Moses acted in every respect according to the advice he had received.

27. *And Moses let his father in law depart.* But if this be the same transaction with that mentioned in Num. x. 29, etc., we find that it was with great reluctance that Moses permitted so able a counsellor to leave him; for, having the highest opinion of his judgment, experience, and discretion, he pressed him to stay with them, that he might be instead of eyes to them in the desert. But Jethro chose rather to return to his own country, where probably his family were so settled and circumstanced that they could not be conveniently removed, and it was more his duty to stay with them, to assist them with his counsel and advice, than to travel with the Israelites.

CHAPTER 19

1. *In the third month.* This was called *Sivan*, and answers to our May. *The wilderness of Sinai.* Mount Sinai is called by the Arabs *Jibel Mousa* or the Mount of Moses, or, by way of eminence, *El Tor, The Mount.* It is one hill, with two peaks or summits; one is called Horeb, the other Sinai. Horeb was probably its most ancient name, and might designate the whole mountain; but as the Lord had appeared to Moses on this mountain in a "bush," *seneh*, chap. iii. 2, from this circumstance it might have received the name of *Sinai.*

3. *Moses went up unto God.* It is likely that the cloud which had conducted the Israelitish camp had now removed to the top of Sinai; and as this was the symbol of the divine presence, Moses went up to the place, there to meet the Lord. *The Lord called unto him.* This, according to Stephen, was the Angel of the Lord, Acts vii. 38. And from several scriptures we have seen that the Lord Jesus was the Person intended; see the notes on Gen. xvi. 7; xviii. 13; Exod. iii. 2.

4. *Brought you unto myself.* In this and the two following verses we see the design of God in selecting a people for himself. (1) They were to obey His voice, v. 5, to receive a revelation from Him, and to act according to that revelation. (2) They were to obey His voice *indeed, shamoa tishmen, in hearing they should hear;* they should consult His testimonies, hear them whenever read or proclaimed, and obey them as soon as heard, affectionately and steadily. (3) They must keep His covenant. (4) They should then be God's peculiar treasure, *segullah*, His own "patrimony," a people in whom He should have all right, and over whom He should have exclusive authority above all the people of the earth. (5) They should be a "kingdom of priests," v. 6. Their state should be a theocracy; and as God should be the sole Governor, so all His subjects should be priests, all worshippers, all sacrificers, every individual offering up the victim for himself. A beautiful representation of the gospel dispensation, to which the apostles Peter and John apply it, 1 Pet. ii. 5, 9; Rev. i. 6; v. 10; and xx. 6; under which dispensation every believing soul offers up for himself that Lamb of God which was slain for and which takes away the sin of the world and through which alone a man can have access to God.

MATTHEW HENRY

the kindness he would show them, in case they did thus keep his covenant (*v.* 5, 6): *Then you shall be a peculiar treasure to me.* [1] God here asserts his sovereignty over, and propriety in, the whole visible creation: *All the earth is mine.* [2] He appropriates Israel to himself, as a people dear unto him. *You shall be a peculiar treasure.* By giving them divine revelation, instituted ordinances, and promises inclusive of eternal life, by sending his prophets among them, and pouring out his Spirit upon them, he distinguished them from, and dignified them above, all people.

III. Israel's acceptance of this charter, and consent to the conditions of it. 1. Moses faithfully delivered God's message to them (*v.* 7): He *laid before their faces all those words.* His laying it to their faces denotes his laying it to their consciences. 2. They readily agreed to the covenant proposed. *All that the Lord hath spoken we will do.* 3. Moses, as a mediator, returned the words of the people to God, *v.* 8. Thus Christ, the Mediator between us and God, as a prophet reveals God's will to us, and then as a priest offers up to God our spiritual sacrifices. Thus he is that blessed *days-man who lays his hand upon us both.*

Verses 9–15

Here, I. God intimates to Moses his purpose of coming down upon Mount Sinai, in some visible appearance of his glory, in *a thick cloud* (*v.* 9). God would come down *in the sight of all the people* (*v.* 11); though they should see no manner of similitude, yet they should see so much as would convince them that God was among them of a truth. Thus the correspondence was to be first settled by a sensible appearance of the divine glory, which was afterwards to be carried on more silently by the ministry of Moses. In like manner, the Holy Ghost descended visibly upon Christ at his baptism, and all that were present heard God speak to him (Matt. iii. 17), that afterwards, without the repetition of such visible tokens, they might believe him. So likewise the Spirit descended in cloven tongues upon the apostles (Acts ii. 3), that they might be believed.

II. He orders Moses to make preparation for this great solemnity, giving him two days' time for it.

1. He must *sanctify the people* (*v.* 10). "*Sanctify them,*" that is, "Call them off from their worldly business, and call them to religious exercises, meditation and prayer, that they may receive the law from God's mouth with reverence and devotion. *Let them be ready,*" *v.* 11. Wandering thoughts must be gathered in, impure affections abandoned, disquieting passions suppressed, nay, and all cares about secular business, for the present, dismissed and laid by, that our hearts may be *engaged to approach unto God.* In token of their cleansing they must *wash their clothes* (*v.* 10), and they did so (*v.* 14); not that God regards our clothes; but while they were washing their clothes he would have them think of washing their souls by repentance. It becomes us to appear in clean clothes when we wait upon great men; so clean hearts are required in our attendance on the great God, who sees them as plainly as men see our clothes.

2. He must *set bounds about the mountain, v.* 12, 13. Probably he drew a line, or ditch, round at the foot of the hill, which none were to pass upon pain of death. This was to intimate, That humble awful reverence which ought to possess the minds of all those that worship God.

3. He must order the people to attend upon the summons that should be given (*v.* 13): "*When the trumpet soundeth long* then let them take their places at the foot of the mount, and so sit down at God's feet." No one man's voice could have reached so many, but the voice of God did.

Verses 16–25

Now, at length, comes that memorable day. Never was there such a sermon preached, before nor since, as this which was here preached to the church in the wilderness. For,

I. The preacher was God himself (*v.* 18): *The Lord descended in fire* and (*v.* 20), *The Lord came down upon Mount Sinai.* The *shechinah,* or glory of the Lord, appeared in the sight of all the people.

II. The pulpit (or throne rather) was mount Sinai, hung with a *thick cloud* (*v.* 16), covered with *smoke* (*v.* 18), and made to *quake* greatly.

III. The congregation was called together by the *sound of a trumpet, exceedingly loud* (*v.* 16), and *waxing louder and louder, v.* 19.

IV. Moses brought the hearers to the place of meeting, *v.* 17. He that had led them out of the bondage of Egypt now led them to receive the law from God's mouth. Moses, at the head of an assembly worshipping God, was as truly great as Moses

JAMIESON, FAUSSET, BROWN

ye shall be unto me a kingdom of priests—As the priestly order was set apart from the common mass, so the Israelites, compared with other people, were to sustain the same near relation to God; a community of spiritual sovereigns. **an holy nation**—set apart to preserve the knowledge and worship of God.

7, 8. Moses came and called for the elders of the people—The message was conveyed to the mighty multitude through their elders, who, doubtless, instructed them in the conditions required. Their unanimous acceptance was conveyed through the same channel to Moses, and by him reported to the Lord. Ah! how much self-confidence did their language betray! How little did they know what spirit they were of!

9-15. The Lord said unto Moses, Lo, I come . . . in a thick cloud, etc.—The deepest impressions are made on the mind through the medium of the senses; and so He who knew what was in man signalized His descent at the inauguration of the ancient church, by all the sensible tokens of august majesty that were fitted to produce the conviction that He is the great and terrible God. The whole multitude must have anticipated the event with feelings of intense solemnity and awe. The extraordinary preparations enjoined, the ablutions and rigid abstinence they were required to observe, the barriers erected all round the base of the mount, and the stern penalties annexed to the breach of any of the conditions, all tended to create an earnest and solemn expectation which increased as the appointed day drew near.

16. on the third day, in the morning, that there were thunders and lightning, etc.—The descent of God was signalized by every object imagination can conceive connected with the ideas of grandeur and of awe. But all was in keeping with the character of the law about to be proclaimed. As the mountain burned with fire, God was exhibited as a consuming fire to the transgressors of His law. The thunder and lightning, more awful amid the deep stillness of the region and reverberating with terrific peals among the mountains, would rouse the universal attention; a thick cloud was an apt emblem of the dark and shadowy dispensation (cf. Matt. 17:5). **the voice of a trumpet**—This gave the scene the character of a miraculous transaction, in which other elements than those of nature were at work, and some other than material trumpet was blown by other means than human breath. **17. Moses brought forth the people out of the camp to meet with God**—Wady-er-Raheh, where they stood, has a spacious sandy plain, immediately in front of Es-Suksafeh, considered by ROBINSON to be the mount from which the law was given. "We measured it, and estimate the whole plain at two geographical miles long, and ranging in breadth from one-third to two-thirds of a mile, or as equivalent to a surface

ADAM CLARKE

6. *And an holy nation.* They should be a *nation,* one people; firmly united among themselves, living under their own laws; and powerful, because united, and acting under the direction and blessing of God. They should be *an holy nation,* saved from their sins, righteous in their conduct, holy in their hearts.

7. *The elders of the people.* The head of each tribe, and the chief of each family, by whose ministry this gracious purpose of God was speedily communicated to the whole camp.

8. *And all the people answered.* The people, having such gracious advantages laid before them, most cheerfully consented to take God for their portion; as He had graciously promised to take them for His people. Thus a covenant was made, the parties being mutually bound to each other. *Moses returned the words.* When the people had on their part consented to the covenant, Moses appears to have gone immediately up to the mountain and related to God the success of his mission; for he was now on the mount, as appears from v. 14.

9. *A thick cloud.* This is interpreted by v. 18: "And mount Sinai was altogether on a smoke . . . and the smoke thereof ascended as the smoke of a furnace"; His usual appearance was in the cloudy pillar, which we may suppose was generally clear and luminous. *That the people may hear.* See the note on chap. xv. 9. The Jews consider this as the fullest evidence their fathers had of the divine mission of Moses; they themselves were permitted to see this awfully glorious sight, and to hear God himself speak out of the thick darkness.

10. *Sanctify them.* See the meaning of this term, chap. xiii. 2. *Let them wash their clothes.* And consequently bathe their bodies; for, according to the testimony of the Jews, these always went together. It was necessary that, as they were about to appear in the presence of God, everything should be clean and pure about them; that they might be admonished by this of the necessity of inward purity, of which the outward washing was the emblem.

12. *Thou shalt set bounds.* Whether this was a line marked out on the ground, beyond which they were not to go, or whether a fence was actually made to keep them off, we cannot tell. This verse strictly forbids the people from coming near and touching Mount Sinai, which was burning with fire. The words, therefore, in v. 15, *al tiggeshu el ishshah,* "come not at your wives," seem rather to mean, "come not near unto the fire." *Whosoever toucheth the mount shall be surely put to death.* The place was awfully sacred, because the dreadful majesty of God was displayed on it. And this taught them that "God is a consuming fire," and that "it is a fearful thing to fall into the hands of the living God."

13. *There shall not an hand touch it. Bo,* "him," not the mountain, but the man who had presumed to touch the mountain. He should be considered altogether as an unclean and accursed thing, not to be touched for fear of conveying defilement; but should be immediately stoned or pierced through with a dart, Heb. xii. 20.

16. *Thunders and lightnings, and a thick cloud . . . and the voice of the trumpet.* The thunders, lightnings, etc., announced the coming, as they proclaimed the majesty, of God. Of the thunders and lightnings, and the deep, dark, dismal, electric cloud, from which the thunders and lightnings proceeded, we can form a tolerable apprehension; but of the loud, long-sounding trumpet we can scarcely form a conjecture. Such were the appearances and the noise that all the people in the camp trembled, and Moses himself was constrained to say, "I exceedingly fear and quake," Heb. xii. 21.

17. *And Moses brought forth the people . . . to meet with God.* For though they might not tocuh the mount till they had permission, yet when the trumpet sounded long, it appears they might come up to *the nether part of the mount* (see v. 13 and Deut. iv. 11); and when the trumpet had ceased to sound, they might then go up unto the mountain, as to any other place. The whole scope and design of the chapter prove that no soul can possibly approach this holy and terrible Being but through a mediator; and this is the use made of this whole trans-

MATTHEW HENRY

at the head of an army in the field.

V. The introductions to the service were *thunders and lightnings, v.* 16. Thunder and lightning have natural causes, but the scripture directs us in a particular manner to take notice of the power of God, and his terror, in them.

VI. Moses is God's minister, who is spoken to, to command silence, and keep the congregatoin in order: *Moses spoke, v.* 19. God stilled his fear by his distinguishing favour to him, in calling him up to the top of the mount (*v.* 20), by which also he tried his faith and courage.

Neither the priests nor the people should offer to force the lines that were set, to *come up unto the Lord*, but Moses and Aaron only, the men whom God delighted to honour. Observe, what it was that God forbade them—breaking through to gaze; enough was provided to awaken their consciences, but they were not allowed to gratify their vain curiosity. They might see, but not gaze. It is at our peril if we break the bounds that God has set us, and intrude upon that which he has not allowed us.

JAMIESON, FAUSSET, BROWN

of one square mile. This space is nearly doubled by the recess on the west, and by the broad and level area of Wady-es-Sheikh on the east, which issues at right angles to the plain, and is equally in view of the front and summit of the mount. The examination convinced us that here was space enough to satisfy all the requisitions of the Scripture narrative, so far as it relates to the assembling of the congregation to receive the law. Here, too, one can see the fitness of the injunction to set bounds around the mount, that neither man nor beast might approach too near, for it rises like a perpendicular wall." But Jebel Musa, the old traditional Sinai, and the highest peak, has also a spacious valley, Wady-Seba'iyeh, capable of holding the people. It is not certain on which of these two they stood. **21. the Lord said unto Moses, Go down, charge the people**—No sooner had Moses proceeded a little up the mount, than he was suddenly ordered to return, in order to keep the people from breaking through to gaze—a course adopted to heighten the impressive solemnity of the secne. The strict injunctions renewed to all, whatever their condition, at a time and in circumstances when the whole multitude of Israel were standing at the base of the mount, was calculated in the highest degree to solemnize and awe every heart.

ADAM CLARKE

action by the author of the Epistle to the Hebrews, chap. xii. 18-24.

20. *The Lord came down.* This was undoubtedly done in a visible manner, that the people might witness the awful appearance. We may suppose that everything was arranged thus: The glory of the Lord occupied the top of the mountain, and near to this Moses was permitted to approach. Aaron and the seventy elders were permitted to advance some way up the mountain, while the people were permitted to come up only to its base. Moses, as the lawgiver, was to receive the statutes and judgments from God's mouth; Aaron and the elders were to receive them from Moses, and deliver them to the people; and the people were to act according to the direction received. Nothing can be imagined more glorious, terrible, majestic, and impressive than the whole of this transaction; but it was chiefly calculated to impress deep reverence, religious fear, and sacred awe; and he who attempts to worship God uninfluenced by these has a proper sense neither of the divine majesty nor of the sinfulness of sin. It seems in reverence to this that the apostle says, "Let us have grace, whereby we may serve God acceptably with reverence and godly fear: for our God is a consuming fire," Heb. xii. 28-29.

22. *Let the priests also . . . sanctify themselves.* That there were priests among the Hebrews before the consecration of Aaron and his sons cannot be doubted; though their functions might be in a considerable measure suspended while under persecution in Egypt, yet the persons existed whose right and duty it was to offer sacrifices to God. Moses requested liberty from Pharaoh to go into the wilderness to sacrifice; and had there not been among the people both sacrifices and priests, the request itself must have appeared absurd. Sacrifices from the beginning had constituted an essential part of the worship of God, and there certainly were priests whose business it was to offer them to God before the giving of the law; though this, for especial reasons, was restricted to Aaron and his sons after the law had been given.

23. *The people cannot come up.* Either because they had been so solemnly forbidden that they would not dare, with the penalty of instant death before their eyes, to transgress the divine command; or the bounds which were set about the mount were such as rendered their passing them physically impossible. *And sanctify it. Vekiddashto.* Here the word *kadash* is taken in its proper literal sense, signifying the "separating" of a thing, person, or place from all profane or common uses, and devoting it to sacred purposes.

24. *Let not the priests and the people break through.* God knew that they were heedless, criminally curious, and stupidly obstinate; and therefore His mercy saw it right to give them line upon line, that they might not transgress to their own destruction.

MATTHEW HENRY — CHAPTER 20

Verses 1-11

Here is, I. The preface of the law-writer, Moses: *God spoke all these words, v.* 1. The law of the ten commandments is, 1. A law of God's making. 2. It is a law of his own speaking. God has many ways of speaking to the children of men (Job xxxiii. 14); he never spoke, at any time, upon any occasion, as he spoke the ten commandments. This law God had given to man before (it was written in his heart by nature); but sin had so defaced that writing that it was necessary, in this manner, to revive the knowledge of it.

JAMIESON, FAUSSET, BROWN — CHAPTER 20

Vss. 1-26. THE TEN COMMANDMENTS. **1. God spake all these words**—The Divine Being Himself was the speaker (Deut. 5:12, 32, 33), in tones so loud as to be heard—so distinct as to be intelligible by the whole multitude standing in the valleys below, amid the most appalling phenomena of agitated nature. Had He been simply addressing rational and intelligent creatures, He would have spoken with the still small voice of persuasion and love. But He was speaking to those who were at the same time fallen and sinful creatures, and a corresponding change was required in the manner of God's procedure, in order to give a suitable impression of the character and sanctions of the law revealed from heaven (Rom. 11:5-9).

ADAM CLARKE — CHAPTER 20

1. *All these words.* Houbigant supposes, and with great plausibility of reason, that the clause *eth col haddebarim haelleh,* "all these words," belongs to the latter part of the concluding verse of chap. xix, which he thinks should be read thus: "And Moses went down unto the people, and spake unto them all these words"; i.e., delivered the solemn charge relative to their not attempting to come up to that part of the mountain on which God manifested himself in His glorious majesty. When Moses, therefore, had gone down and spoken *all these words,* and he and Aaron had reascended the mount, then the Divine Being, as supreme Legislator, is majestically introduced thus: *And God spake . . . saying.* This gives a dignity to the commencement of this chapter of which the clause above mentioned, if not referred to the speech of Moses, deprives it.

THE TEN COMMANDMENTS

The laws delivered on Mount Sinai have been variously named. In Deut. iv. 13, they are called *asereth haddebarim,* "the ten words." In the preceding chapter, v. 5, God calls them *eth berithi,* "my covenant," i.e., the agreement He

MATTHEW HENRY	JAMIESON, FAUSSET, BROWN	ADAM CLARKE

ALEXANDER MACLAREN:

An obscure tribe of Egyptian slaves plunges into the desert to hide from pursuit, and emerges, after forty years, with a code gathered into "ten words," so brief, so complete, so intertwining morality and religion, so free from local or national peculiarities, so close fitting to fundamental duties, that it is today, after more than three thousand years, authoritative in the most enlightened peoples. The voice that spoke from Sinai reverberates in all lands. The Old World had other lawgivers who professed to formulate their precepts by divine inspiration: they are all fallen silent. But this voice, like the trumpet on that day, waxes louder and louder as the years roll. Whose voice was it? The only answer explaining the supreme purity of the commandments, and their immortal freshness, is found in the first sentence of this paragraph, "God spake all these words."

We have first the revelation, which precedes and lays the foundation for the commandments: "I am the Lord thy God, which have brought thee out of the land of Egypt." God speaks to the nation as a whole, establishing a special relation between himself and them, which is founded on His redeeming act, and is reciprocal, requiring that they should be His people, as He is their God. The manifestation in act of His power and of His love precedes the claim for reverence and obedience. This is a universal truth. God gives before He asks us to give. He is not a hard taskmaster, "gathering where he has not strawn." Even in that system which is eminently "the law," the foundation is a divine act of deliverance, and only when He has won the people for himself by redeeming them from bondage does He call on them for obedience.—*Expositions of Holy Scripture*

II. The preface of the Law-maker: *I am the Lord thy God, v.* 2. Herein, 1. God asserts his own authority to enact this law in general. 2. He proposes himself as the sole object of that religious worship which is enjoined in the first four of the commandments. They are here bound to obedience by a threefold cord. (1) Because God *is the Lord.* He that gives being may give law; and therefore he is able to bear us out in our obedience, to reward it, and to punish our disobedience. (2) He was their God, a God in covenant with them, their God by their own consent. Though that covenant of peculiarity is now no more, yet there is another, by virtue of which all that are baptized are taken into relation to him as their God, and are therefore unjust, unfaithful, and very ungrateful, if they obey him not. (3) He had *brought them out of the land of Egypt.* By redeeming them, he acquired a further right to rule them; they owed their service to him to whom they owed their freedom. And thus Christ, having rescued us out of the bondage of sin, is entitled to the best service we can do him, Luke i. 74.

III. The law itself. The first four of the ten commandments, which concern our duty to God (commonly called *the first table*), we have in these verses. It was fit that those should be put first, because man had a Maker to love before he had a neighbour to love; and justice and charity are acceptable acts of obedience to God only when they flow from the principles of piety. It cannot be expected that he should be true to his brother who is false to his God.

1. The first commandment concerns the object of our worship, Jehovah, and him only (*v.* 3): *Thou shalt have no other gods before me.* The Egyptians, and other neighbouring nations, had many gods, the creatures of their own fancy, strange gods, *new gods.* The sin against this commandment which *we* are most in danger of is giving the glory and honour to any creature which are due to God only. Pride makes a god of self, coveteousness makes a god of money, sensuality makes a god of the belly, whatever is esteemed or loved, feared or served, delighted in or depended on, more than God, that (whatever it is) we do in effect make a god of. In the last words, *before me,* it is intimated, (1) That we cannot have any other God but he will certainly know it. (2) That it is a sin that dares him to his face, which he cannot, which he will not, overlook.

2. The second commandment concerns the ordinances of worship, or the way in which God will be worshipped.

(1) The prohibition: we are here forbidden to worship even the true God by images, *v.* 4, 5. The Jews (at least after the captivity) thought themselves forbidden by this commandment to make any image or picture whatsoever. Hence the very images which

2. I am the Lord thy God—This is a preface to the ten commandments—the latter clause being specially applicable to the case of the Israelites, while the former brings it home to all mankind; showing that the reasonableness of the law is founded in their eternal relation as creatures to their Creator, and their mutual relations to each other.

3. Thou shalt have no other gods before me—in My presence, beside, or except Me.

4, 5. Thou shalt not make . . . any graven image . . . thou shalt not bow down thyself to them—i.e., "make in order to bow." Under the auspices of Moses himself, figures of cherubim, brazen serpents, oxen, and many other things in the earth beneath, were made and never condemned. The mere making was no sin—it was the making with the intent to give idolatrous worship.

entered into with the people of Israel to take them for His peculiar people, if they took Him for their God and portion. "If ye will obey my voice indeed, and keep my covenant, then shall ye be a peculiar treasure unto me." And the word "covenant" here evidently refers to the laws given in this chapter, as is evident from Deut. iv. 13: "And he declared unto you his covenant, which he commanded you to perform, even ten commandments." Sometimes they have been termed *the law, hattorah,* by way of eminence, as containing the grand system of spiritual instruction, direction, guidance. See on the word "law," chap. xii. 49. And frequently "the Decalogue," which is a literal translation into Greek of the *asereth haddebarim,* or "ten words," of Moses.

Among divines they are generally divided into what they term the first and second tables: the first table containing the first, second, third, and fourth commandments and comprehending the whole system of theology, the true notions we should form of the divine nature, the reverence we owe and the religious service we should render to Him; the second containing the last six commandments, and comprehending a complete system of ethics, or moral duties, which man owes to his fellows. By this division the first table contains our duty to God; the second, our duty to our neighbor. This division, which is natural enough, refers us to the grand principle, love to God and love to man, through which both tables are observed. (1) Thou shalt love the Lord thy God with all thy heart, soul, mind, and strength. (2) Thou shalt love thy neighbor as thyself. On these two hang all the law and the prophets. See Matt. xxii. 37-40.

The First Commandment: Against mental or theoretic idolatry

2. *I am the Lord thy God. Yehovah eloheycha.* On the word Jehovah, which we here translate *Lord,* see the notes on Gen. ii. 4 and Exod. vi. 3. And on the word *Elohim,* here translated *God,* see on Gen. i. 1. It is worthy of remark that each individual is addressed here, and not the people collectively, though they are all necessarily included, that each might feel that he was bound for himself to hear and do all these words. Moses labored to impress this personal interest on the people's minds, when he said, Deut. v. 3-4: "The Lord made . . . this covenant . . . with us, even us, who are all of us here alive this day." *Brought thee out of the land of Egypt.* And by this very thing have proved myself to be superior to all gods, unlimited in power, and most gracious as well as fearful in operation. This is the preface or introduction, but should not be separated from the commandment. Therefore—

3. *Thou shalt have no other gods before me. Elohim acherim,* no "strange" gods—none that thou art not acquainted with, none who has not given thee such proofs of his power and godhead as I have done in delivering thee from the Egyptians, dividing the Red Sea, bringing water out of the rock, quails into the desert, manna from heaven to feed thee, and the pillar of cloud to direct, enlighten, and shield thee. By these miracles God had rendered himself familiar to them, they were intimately acquainted with the operation of His hands; and therefore with great propriety He says, Thou shalt have no strange gods *before me; al panai,* "before or in the place of" those manifestations which I have made of myself.

The Second Commandment: Against making and worshiping images

4. *Thou shalt not make unto thee any graven image.* As the word *pasal* signifies to "hew, carve, grave," *pesel* may here signify any kind of image, either of wood, stone, or metal, on which the axe, the chisel, or the graving tool has been employed. This commandment includes in its prohibitions every species of idolatry known to have been practiced among the Egyptians.

Or any likeness. To know the full spirit and extent of this commandment, this place must be collated with Deut. iv. 15, etc.: "Take ye therefore good heed unto yourselves . . . lest ye corrupt yourselves, and make you a graven image,

MATTHEW HENRY

the Roman armies had in their ensigns are called *an abomination* to them (Matt. xxiv. 15), especially when they were set up *in the holy place*. It is called the changing of the truth of God into a lie (Rom. i. 25), for an image is a teacher of lies; it insinuates to us that God has a body, whereas he is an infinite spirit, Hab. ii. 18. It also forbids us to make images of God in our fancies, as if he were a man as we are. Our religious worship must be governed by the power of faith, not by the power of imagination.

(2) The reasons to enforce this prohibition (*v.* 5, 6), which are, [1] God's jealousy in the matters of his worship: "*I the Lord* Jehovah, and *thy God, am a jealous God*, especially in things of this nature." [2] The punishment of idolaters. God looks upon them as haters of him. He will *visit it upon the children.* Nor is it an unrighteous thing with God (if the parents died in their iniquity, and the children tread in their steps, and keep up false worships, because they received them by tradition from their fathers), when the measure is full, and God comes by his judgments to reckon with them. Though he bear long with an idolatrous people, he will not bear always, but by the fourth generation, at furthest, he will begin to visit. [3] The favour God would show to his faithful worshippers: *Keeping mercy for thousands* of persons, thousands of generations *of those that love me, and keep my commandments.* As the first commandment requires the inward worship of love, desire, joy, hope, and admiration, so the second requires the outward worship of prayer and praise, and solemn attendance on God's word. Those that truly love God will make it their constant care to keep his commandments, particularly those that relate to his worship. Those that love God, and keep those commandments, shall receive grace to keep his other commandments. Gospel worship will have a good influence upon all manner of gospel obedience. This mercy shall extend to thousands, much further than the wrath threatened to those that hate him.

3. The third commandment concerns the manner of our worship.

(1) A strict prohibition: *Thou shalt not take the name of the Lord thy God in vain.* We take God's name in vain, [1] By hypocrisy, making a profession of God's name, but not living up to that profession. Those that name the name of Christ, but do not depart from iniquity, name it in vain. [2] By covenant-breaking; if we make promises to God, binding our souls with those bonds to that which is good, and yet perform not to the Lord our vows, we take his name in vain (Matt. v. 23). [3] By rash swearing, mentioning the name of God as a by-word, to no purpose at all, or to no good purpose. [4] By false swearing. One part of the religious regard the Jews were taught to pay to their God was to *swear by his name*, Deut. x. 20. But they affronted him, instead of doing him honour, if they called him to be witness to a lie.

JAMIESON, FAUSSET, BROWN

ALEXANDER MACLAREN:

The second commandment forbids all representations, whether of the one God or of false deities. The golden calf, which was a symbol of Jehovah, is condemned equally with the fair forms that haunted the Greek Olympus, or the half-bestial shapes of Egyptian mythology. The reasons for the prohibition may be considered as two—the impossibility of setting forth the glory of the Infinite Spirit in any form, and the certainty that the attempt will sink the worshiper deeper in the mire of sense. An image degrades God and damages men. By it religion reverses its nature, and becomes another clog to keep the soul among the things seen, and an ally of all fleshly inclinations. We know how idolatry seemed to cast a spell over the Israelites from Egypt to Babylon, and how their first relapse into it took place almost before the voice which "spake all these words" had ceased.

In its grosser form, we have no temptation to it. But there are other ways of breaking the commandment than setting up an image. All sensuous worship in which the treacherous aid of art is called in to elevate the soul, comes perilously near to contradicting its spirit, if not its letter. The attempt to make of the senses a ladder for the soul to climb to God by, is a great deal more likely to end in the soul's going down the ladder than up it. The history of public worship in the Christian Church teaches that the less it has to do with such slippery help the better. We need to remember that the God who is a Spirit is worshiped "in spirit," and that outward forms may easily choke, and outward aids hinder, that worship.

The especial difficulty of obedience to this commandment is marked by the reason or sanction annexed. That opens a wide field, on which it would be folly to venture here. There is a glimpse of God's character, and a statement of a law of His working. He is a "jealous" God. We need not be afraid of the word. It means nothing but what is congruous with the loftiest conception of a loving God. It means that He allows no rival in our hearts' affection, or in our submission for love's sake to Him. A half trust in God is no trust. How can worship be shared, or love be parted out, among a pantheon? Our poor hearts ask of one another and get from one another, wherever a man and a woman truly love, just what God asks—"All in all, or not at all." His jealousy is but infinite love seeking to be known as such, and asking for a whole heart.—*Expositions of Holy Scripture*

ADAM CLARKE

the similitude of any figure, the likeness of male or female." All who have even the slightest acquaintance with the ancient history of Egypt know that Osiris and his wife, Isis, were supreme divinities among that people. The likeness of any beast, *behemah*, such as the ox and the heifer: Among the Egyptians the ox was not only sacred but adored, because they supposed that in one of these animals Osiris took up his residence; hence they always had a living ox, which they supposed to be the habitation of this deity; and they imagined that on the death of one he entered into the body of another, and so on successively. This famous ox-god they called Apis. The likeness of any winged fowl: The ibis, or stork, or crane, and hawk, may be here intended, for all these were objects of Egyptian idolatry. The likeness of anything that creepeth: The crocodile, serpents, the scarabeus or beetle, were all objects of their adoration. The likeness of any fish: All fish were esteemed sacred animals among the Egyptians.

To countenance its image worship, the Roman Catholic church has left the whole of this second commandment out of the Decalogue, and thus lost one whole commandment out of the ten; but to keep up the number they have divided the tenth into two. This is totally contrary to the faith of God's elect and to the acknowledgment of that truth which is according to godliness. The verse is found in every MS. of the Hebrew Pentateuch that has ever been discovered. It is in all the ancient versions, Samaritan, Chaldee, Syriac, Septuagint, Vulgate, Coptic, and Arabic; also in the Persian, and in all modern versions.

This commandment prohibits every species of external idolatry, as the first does all idolatry that may be called internal or mental. All false worship may be considered of this kind, together with all image worship, and all other superstitious rites and ceremonies.

5. *Jealous God.* This shows in a most expressive manner the love of God to this people. He felt for them as the most affectionate husband could do for his spouse; and was *jealous* for their fidelity, because He willed their invariable happiness. *Visiting the iniquity of the fathers upon the children.* This necessarily implies—if the children walk in the steps of their fathers; for no man can be condemned by divine justice for a crime of which he was never guilty; see Ezekiel xviii. Idolatry is however particularly intended, and visiting sins of this kind refers principally to national judgments. By withdrawing the divine protection the idolatrous Israelites were delivered up into the hands of their enemies, from whom the gods in whom they had trusted could not deliver them. This God did to *the third and fourth generation*, i.e., "successively," as may be seen in every part of the Jewish history, and particularly in the Book of Judges. And this, at last, became the grand and the only effectual and lasting means in His hand of their final deliverance from idolatry; for it is well known that after the Babylonish captivity the Israelites were so completely saved from idolatry as nevermore to have disgraced themselves by it as they had formerly done. These national judgments, thus continued from generation to generation, appear to be what are designed by the words in the text, *Visiting the iniquity of the fathers upon the children.*

6. ***And shewing mercy unto thousands.*** Mark; even those who love God and keep His commandments merit nothing from Him, and therefore the salvation and blessedness which they enjoy come from the mercy of God: *shewing mercy*. What a disproportion between the works of justice and mercy! Justice works to the third or fourth, mercy to thousands of generations! *That love me, and keep my commandments.* It was this that caused Christ to comprise the fulfilment of the whole law in love to God and man; see the note on v. 1. And as love is the grand principle of obedience, and the only incentive to it, so there can be no obedience without it.

The Third Commandment:
Against false swearing, blasphemy, and irreverent use of the name of God

7. *Thou shalt not take the name of the Lord thy God in vain.* This precept not only forbids all false oaths, but all common swearing where

MATTHEW HENRY

(2) A severe penalty: *The Lord will not hold him guiltless*; magistrates, who punish other offences, may not think themselves concerned to take notice of this, because it does not immediately offer injury either to private property or the public peace. The sinner may perhaps hold himself guiltless. God will *not hold him guiltless*, and they will find it a fearful thing to fall into the hands of the living God.

4. The fourth commandment concerns the time of worship. God is to be served and honoured daily, but one day in seven is to be particularly dedicated to his honour and spent in his service.

(1) The command itself (*v.* 8): *Remember the sabbath day to keep it holy;* and (*v.* 10), *In it thou shalt do no manner of work.* We read of God's blessing and sanctifying a seventh day from the beginning (Gen. ii. 3), so that this was not the enacting of a new law, but the reviving of an old law. [1] They are told what is the day they must religiously observe—*a seventh, after six days' labour*; whether this was the seventh by computation from the first seventh, or from the day of their coming out of Egypt, or both, is not certain. [2] How it must be observed. *First,* As a day of rest; they were to do no manner of work on this day in their callings or worldly business. *Secondly,* As a holy day, set apart to the honour of the holy God, and to be spent in holy exercises. God, by blessing it, had made it holy; they, by solemnly blessing him, must keep it holy. [3] Who must observe it: *Thou, and thy son, and thy daughter*; the wife is not mentioned, because she is supposed to be one with the husband and present with him. God takes notice of what we do, particularly what we do on sabbath days, though we should be where we are strangers. [4] A particular memorandum put upon this duty: *Remember it.* It is intimated that the sabbath was instituted and observed before; but in their bondage in Egypt they had let fall the observance of it. Some think it denotes the preparation we are to make for the sabbath; we must think of it before it comes, that, when it does come, we may keep it holy.

(2) The reasons of this command. [1] We have time enough for ourselves on the other six days: *Six days must thou labour* and time enough to tire ourselves. On the seventh day let us serve God. On the seventh it will be a kindness to us to be obliged to rest. [2] This is God's day: it is the *sabbath of the Lord thy God,* not only instituted by him, but consecrated to him. [3] It is designed for a memorial of the creation of the world, and therefore to be observed to the glory of the Creator. By the sanctification of the sabbath, the Jews declared that they worshipped the God that made the world, and so distinguished themselves from all other nations, who worshipped gods which they themselves made. [4] God has given us an example of rest, after six days' work: he *rested the seventh day.* [5] He has himself *blessed the sabbath day and sanctified it.* He has put blessings into it, which he has encouraged us to expect from him in the religious observance of that day. It is *the day which the Lord hath made,* let us not do what we can to unmake it.

Verses 12–17

We have here the laws of the second table, as they are commonly called, the last six of the ten commandments, comprehending our duty to ourselves and to one another, and constituting a comment upon the second great commandment, *Thou shalt love thy neighbour as thyself.*

I. The fifth commandment concerns the duties we owe to our relations; those of children to their parents are alone specified: *Honour thy father and thy mother,* which includes, 1. A decent respect to their persons, an inward esteem of them outwardly expressed upon all occasions in our conduct. 2. Obedience to their lawful commands; so it is expounded (Eph. vi. 1–3): "*Children, obey your parents,*" from a principle of love. Though you have said, "We will not," yet afterwards repent and obey, Matt. xxi. 29. 3. Submission to their rebukes, instructions, and corrections; not only to the good and gentle, but also to the froward, out of conscience towards God. Endeavouring, in every thing, to be the comfort of their parents, and to make their old age easy to them, maintaining them if they stand in need of support, which our Saviour makes to be particularly intended in this commandment, Matt. xv. 4–6. The reason annexed to this commandment is a promise: *That thy days may be long in the land which the Lord thy God giveth thee.* He here, in the beginning of the second table, mentions his bringing them into Canaan. A long life in that good land is promised particularly to obedient children.

II. The sixth commandment concerns our own and our neighbour's life (*v.* 13): "*Thou shalt not kill;*

JAMIESON, FAUSSET, BROWN

8. Remember the sabbath day—implying it was already known, and recognized as a season of sacred rest. The first four commandments comprise our duties to God—the other six our duties to our fellow men; and as interpreted by Christ, they reach to the government of the heart as well as the lip (Matt. 5:17). "If a man do them he shall live in them." But, ah! what an *if* for frail and fallen man. Whoever rests his hope upon the law stands debtor to it all; and in this view every one would be without hope were not "the LORD OUR RIGHTEOUSNESS" (John 1:17).

GEORGE RAWLINSON:

"Honor thy father and thy mother." It is not a matter of much importance how we divide the commandments; nor is it historically certain how they were originally distributed between the two tables. But, practically, the view that the fifth commandment begins the second table, which lays down our duty towards our neighbors, is to be preferred for its convenience, though it trenches upon symmetrical arrangement. Of all our duties to our fellow men, the first and most fundamental is our duty towards our parents, which lies at the root of all our social relations, and is the first of which we naturally become conscious. Honor, reverence, and obedience are due to parents from the position in which they stand to their children: (1) As, in a certain sense, the authors of their being; (2) as their shelterers and nourishers; (3) as their protectors and educators, from whom they derive the foundation of their moral training and the first elements of their knowledge.

Even among savages the obligations of children towards their parents are felt and acknowledged to a greater or a lesser extent; and there has never been a civilized community of whose moral code they have not formed an important part. In Egypt the duty of filial piety was strictly inculcated from a very early date and a bad son forfeited the prospect of happiness in another life. Confucianism bases all morality upon the parental and filial relation, and requires the most complete subjection, even of the grown-up son, to his father and mother. Greek ethics taught that the relation of children to their parents was parallel to that of men to God, and Rome made the absolute authority of the father the basis of its entire state system. The divine legislation of Sinai is in full accord, here as elsewhere, with the voice of reason and conscience, affirming broadly the principles of parental authority and filial submission, but leaving the mode in which the principles should be carried out to the discretion of individuals or communities.

—*Ellicott's Commentary on the Whole Bible*

ADAM CLARKE

the name of God is used, or where He is appealed to as a Witness of the truth. It also necessarily forbids all light and irreverent mention of God, or any of His attributes, and this the original word *lashshav* particularly imports; and we may safely add to all these that every prayer, ejaculation, etc., that is not accompanied with deep reverence and the genuine spirit of piety is here condemned also. *The Lord will not hold him guiltless.* Whatever the person himself may think or hope, however he may plead in his own behalf, and say he intends no evil, if he in any of the above ways, or in any other way, takes the name of God in vain, God will not hold him guiltless—He will account him guilty and punish him for it.

THE FOURTH COMMANDMENT: AGAINST PROFANATION OF THE SABBATH, AND IDLENESS ON THE OTHER DAYS OF THE WEEK

8. *Remember the sabbath day, to keep it holy.* See what has been already said on this precept, Gen. ii. 2, and elsewhere. As this was the most ancient institution, God calls them to *remember* it: as if He had said, Do not forget that when I had finished My creation I instituted the Sabbath, and remember why I did so, and for what purposes. The word *shabbath* signifies "rest" or "cessation from labor"; and the sanctification of the seventh day is commanded, as having something representative in it; and so indeed it has, for it typifies the rest which remains for the people of God, and in this light it evidently appears to have been understood by the apostle, Hebrews iv. Because this commandment has not been particularly mentioned in the New Testament as a moral precept binding on all, therefore some have presumptuously inferred that there is no Sabbath under the Christian dispensation. The truth is, the Sabbath is considered as a type. All types are of full force till the thing signified by them takes place. But the thing signified by the Sabbath is that rest in glory which remains for the people of God; therefore the moral obligation of the Sabbath must continue till time be swallowed up in eternity.

9. *Six days shalt thou labour.* Therefore he who idles away time on any of the six days is as guilty before God as he who works on the Sabbath. No work should be done on the Sabbath that can be done on the preceding days, or can be deferred to the succeeding ones. Works of absolute necessity and mercy are alone excepted.

THE FIFTH COMMANDMENT: AGAINST DISRESPECT AND DISOBEDIENCE TO PARENTS

12. *Honour thy father and thy mother.* There is a degree of affectionate respect which is owing to parents that no person else can properly claim. For a considerable time parents stand as it were in the place of God to their children, and therefore rebellion against their lawful commands has been considered as rebellion against God. This precept therefore prohibits, not only all injurious acts, irreverent and unkind speeches to parents, but enjoins all necessary acts of kindness, filial respect, and obedience. We can scarcely suppose that a man honors his parents who, when they fall weak, blind, or sick, does not exert himself to the uttermost in their support. In such cases God as truly requires the children to provide for their parents as He required the parents to feed, nourish, support, instruct, and defend the children when they were in the lowest state of helpless infancy. *That thy days may be long.* This, as the apostle observes, Eph. vi. 2, is the first commandment to which God has annexed a promise; and therefore we may learn in some measure how important the duty is in the sight of God. In Deut. v. 16 it is said, "And that it may go well with thee"; we may therefore conclude that it will go ill with the disobedient.

THE SIXTH COMMANDMENT: AGAINST MURDER AND CRUELTY

13. *Thou shalt not kill.* This commandment, which is general, prohibits murder of every kind. (1) All actions by which the lives of our fellow creatures may be abridged. (2) All wars for extending empire, commerce, etc. (3) All sanguinary laws, by the operation of which the

MATTHEW HENRY

thou shalt not do any thing hurtful or injurious to the health, ease, and life, of thy own body, or any other person's unjustly." It does not forbid killing in lawful war, or in our own necessary defence, but it forbids all malice and hatred to the person of any (for *he that hateth his brother is a murderer*), and all personal revenge arising therefrom; also all rash anger upon sudden provocations, and hurt said or done, or aimed to be done, in passion: of this our Saviour expounds this commandment, Matt. v 22.

III. The seventh commandment concerns our own and our neighbour's chastity: *Thou shalt not commit adultery, v.* 14. This is put before the sixth by our Saviour (Mark x. 19): *Do not commit adultery, do not kill*; for our chastity should be as dear to us as our lives, and we should be as much afraid of that which defiles the body as of that which destroys it.

IV. The eighth commandment concerns our own and our neighbour's wealth, estate, and goods: *Thou shalt not steal, v.* 15. This command forbids us to rob ourselves of what we have by sinful spending, or of the use and comfort of it by sinful sparing, and to rob others by removing the ancient landmarks, invading our neighbour's rights, taking his goods from his person, or house, or field, forcibly or clandestinely, over-reaching in bargains, not restoring what is borrowed or found, withholding just debts, rents, or wages, and (which is worst of all) to rob the public in the coin or revenue, or that which is dedicated to the service of religion.

V. The ninth commandment concerns our own and our neighbour's good name: *Thou shalt not bear false witness, v.* 16. This forbids, 1. Speaking falsely in any matter, lying, equivocating, and any way devising and designing to deceive our neighbour. 2. Speaking unjustly against our neighbour, to the prejudice of his reputation. 3. Bearing false witness against him, laying to his charge things that he knows not, slandering, backbiting, tale-bearing, aggravating what is done amiss and making it worse than it is, and any way endeavouring to raise our own reputation upon the ruin of our neighbour's.

VI. The tenth commandment strikes at the root: *Thou shalt not covet, v.* 17. The foregoing commands implicitly forbid all desire of doing that which will be an injury to our neighbour; this forbids all inordinate desire of having that which will be a gratification to ourselves. St. Paul, when the grace of God caused the scales to fall from his eyes, perceived that this law, *Thou shalt not covet*, forbade all those irregular appetites and desires which are the beginnings of all the sin that is committed by us.

Verses 18–21

I. The extraordinary terror with which the law was given. It was designed to give a sensible discovery of the glorious majesty of God, to prepare the soul

JAMIESON, FAUSSET, BROWN

GEORGE RAWLINSON:

"Thou shalt not kill." From the peculiar duties owed by children to their parents, the divine legislator went on to lay down those general duties which men owe to their fellowmen. And of these the first is that of respecting their life. The security of life is the primary object of government; and it has been well said that men originally coalesced into states with a view to self-preservation. All written codes forbid murder; and in communities which are without written codes an unwritten law condemns it. When God "set a mark upon Cain" (Gen. 4:15), He marked thereby His abhorrence of the murderer. The "seven precepts of Noah" included one which distinctly forbade the taking of human life (Gen. 9:6). In all countries and among all peoples, a natural instinct or an unwritten tradition placed murder among the worst of crimes, and made its penalty death. The Mosaic legislation on the point was differenced from others principally by the care it took to distinguish between actual murder, manslaughter (21:13), death by misadventure (Num. 35:23), and justifiable homicide (22:2). Before, however, it made these distinctions, the great principle of the sanctity of human life required to be broadly laid down; and so the law was given in the widest possible terms—"Thou shalt not kill." Exceptions were reserved till later.

"Thou shalt not commit adultery." Next to the duty of respecting a man's life is placed that of respecting his domestic peace and honor. Adultery is an invasion of the household, a destruction of the bond which unites the family, a dissolution of that contract which is the main basis of social order. It was forbidden by all civilized communities, and in uncivilized ones frequently punished with death. The Mosaic enactments on the subject are peculiar chiefly in the absolute equality on which they place the man and the woman. Adulterers are as hateful as adulteresses, and are as surely to be put to death (Lev. 20:10; Deut. 22:22–24). The man who acts treacherously against "the wife of his covenant" is as great a sinner as the woman who breaks the marriage bond (Mal. 2:14–16). There is "no respect of persons" and no respect of sexes with God.

"Thou shalt not steal." Our third duty towards our neighbor is to respect his right to his property. The framers of Utopias, both ancient and modern, have imagined communities in which private property should not exist. But such a condition of things has never yet been realized in practice. In the laws of all known states private property has been recognized, and social order has been, in a great measure, based upon it. Here, again, law has but embodied natural instinct. The savage who hammers out a flint knife by repeated blows with a pebble, laboring long and undergoing pain in the process, feels that the implement which he has made is his own, and that his right to it is indisputable. If he is deprived of it by force or fraud, he is wronged.

—Ellicott's Commentary on the Whole Bible

18-21. all the people saw the thunderings and the lightnings—They were eye and ear witnesses of the awful emblems of the Deity's descent. But they perceived not the Deity

ADAM CLARKE

lives of men may be taken away for offenses of comparatively trifling demerit. (4) All bad dispositions which lead men to wish evil to, or meditate mischief against, one another; for, says the Scripture, He that hateth his brother in his heart is a murderer. (5) All want of charity to the helpless and distressed; for he who has it in his power to save the life of another by a timely application of succor, food, raiment, and does not do it, and the life of the person either fails or is abridged on this account, is in the sight of God a murderer. (6) All riot and excess, all drunkenness and gluttony, by which life may be destroyed or shortened; all these are point-blank sins against the sixth commandment.

The Seventh Commandment: Against adultery and uncleanness

14. *Thou shalt not commit adultery.* Adultery, as defined by our laws, is of two kinds: double, when between two married persons; single, when one of the parties is married, the other single. One principal part of the criminality of adultery consists in its injustice. (1) It robs a man of his right by taking from him the affection of his wife. (2) It does him a wrong by fathering on him and obliging him to maintain as his own a spurious offspring—a child which is not his. The act itself, and everything leading to the act, is prohibited by this commandment; for our Lord says, "He who looks on a woman to lust after her has already committed adultery with her in his heart." And not only adultery (the unlawful commerce between two married persons) is forbidden here, but also fornication and all kinds of mental and sensual uncleanness. All impure books, songs, paintings, etc., which tend to inflame and debauch the mind, are against this law.

The Eighth Commandment: Against stealing and dishonesty

15. *Thou shalt not steal.* All rapine and theft are forbidden by this precept; as well national and commercial wrongs as petty larceny, highway robberies, and private stealing; even the taking advantage of a seller's or buyer's ignorance, to give the one less and make the other pay more for a commodity than its worth, is a breach of this sacred law. All withholding of rights and doing of wrongs are against the spirit of it. But the word is principally applicable to clandestine stealing, though it may undoubtedly include all political injustice and private wrongs.

The Ninth Commandment: Against false testimony, perjury, etc.

16. *Thou shalt not bear false witness.* Not only false oaths, to deprive a man of his life or of his right, are here prohibited, but all whispering, talebearing, slander, and calumny; in a word, whatever is deposed as a truth, which is false in fact, and tends to injure another in his goods, person, or character, is against the spirit and letter of this law. Suppressing the truth when known, by which a person may be defrauded of his property or his good name, or lie under injuries or disabilities which a discovery of the truth would have prevented, is also a crime against this law. By the term *neighbour* any human being is intended, whether he rank among our enemies or friends.

The Tenth Commandment: Against covetousness

17. *Thou shalt not covet thy neighbour's house . . . wife. Covet* signifies to desire or long after in order to enjoy as a property the person or thing coveted. He breaks this command who by any means endeavors to deprive a man of his house or farm by taking them "over his head," as it is expressed in some countries; who lusts after his neighbor's wife, and endeavors to ingratiate himself into her affections and to lessen her husband in her esteem; and who endeavors to possess himself of the servants, cattle, etc., of another in any clandestine or unjustifiable manner.

18. *And all the people saw the thunderings.* They had witnessed all these awful things before (see chap. xix. 16) but here they seem to have been repeated; probably at the end of each

MATTHEW HENRY

for the comforts of the gospel. Thus was the law given by Moses in such a way as might humble men, that the *grace and truth which came by Jesus Christ* might be the more welcome.

II. The impression which this made upon the people: 1. *They removed, and stood afar off, v.* 18. 2. *They entreated that the word should not be so spoken to them any more* (Heb. xii. 19), but begged that God would speak to them by Moses, *v.* 19. Hereby also they teach us to acquiesce in that method which Infinite Wisdom takes, of speaking to us by men like ourselves.

III. The encouragement Moses gave them, by explaining the design of God in his terror (*v.* 20): *Fear not,* that is, "Think not that the thunder and fire are designed to consume you." They were intended, 1. To prove them, to try how they would like dealing with God immediately, without a mediator. 2. To keep them to their duty, and prevent their sinning against God. He encourages them, saying, *Fear not,* and yet tells them that God thus spoke to them, *that his fear might be before their face.* We must not fear with amazement, but we must always have in our minds a reverence of God's majesty, a dread of his displeasure, and an obedient regard to his sovereign authority over us: this fear will quicken us to our duty and make us circumspect in our walking.

IV. The progress of their communion with God by the mediation of Moses, *v.* 21. While the people continued to stand afar off, *Moses drew near unto the thick darkness;* he *was made to draw near.* Some of the rabbis suppose God sent an angel to take him by the hand, and lead him up.

Verses 22–26

Moses having gone into *the thick darkness, where God was,* God there spoke in his hearing only, privately and without terror, all that follows hence to the end of *ch.* xxiii., which is mostly an exposition of the ten commandments; and he was to transmit it by word of mouth first, and afterwards in writing, to the people. The laws in these verses related to God's worship.

I. They are here forbidden to make images for worship (*v.* 22, 23).

1. This repetition of the second commandment comes in here as pointing to that which might properly be inferred from God's speaking to them as he had done. He had given them sufficient demonstration of his presence among them; they needed not to make images of him, as if he were absent.

2. Though they pretended to worship them but as representations of God, yet really they made them rivals with God, which he would not endure.

II. They are here directed in making altars for worship.

1. To make their altars very plain, either of *earth* or of *unhewn stone, v.* 24, 25. That they might not be tempted to think of a graven image, they must not so much as hew into shape the stones that they made their altars of, but pile them up as they were, in the rough. Plainness should be accepted as the best ornament of the external services of religion, and gospel-worship should not be performed with external pomp and gaiety. The beauty of holiness needs no paint.

III. They are here assured of God's gracious acceptance of their devotions, wherever they were paid according to his will (*v.* 24). Under the gospel, when men are encouraged to pray everywhere, this promise revives in its full extent, that, wherever God's people meet in his name to worship him, he will be *in the midst of them.* There he will come unto them, and will bless them, and more than this we need not desire for the beautifying of our solemn assemblies.

JAMIESON, FAUSSET, BROWN

Himself. **19. let not God speak with us, lest we die,** etc.—The phenomena of thunder and lightning had been one of the plagues so fatal to Egypt, and as they heard God speaking to them now, they were apprehensive of instant death also. Even Moses himself, the mediator of the old covenant, did "exceedingly quake and fear" (Heb. 12:21). But doubtless God spake what gave *him* relief—restored him to a frame of mind fit for the ministrations committed to him; and hence immediately after he was enabled to relieve and comfort them with the relief and comfort which he himself had received from God (II Cor. 1:4).

22, 23. the Lord said unto Moses—It appears from Deuteronomy 4:14-16, that this injunction was a conclusion drawn from the scene on Sinai—that as no similitude of God was displayed then, they should not attempt to make any visible figure or form of Him.

24. An altar of earth thou shalt make unto me—a regulation applicable to special or temporary occasions.

25. thou shalt not build it of hewn stone, etc.—i. e., carved with figures and ornaments that might lead to superstition.

ADAM CLARKE

command, there was a peal of thunder, a blast of the trumpet, and a gleam of lightning, to impress their hearts the more deeply with a due sense of the divine majesty, of the holiness of the law which was now delivered, and of the fearful consequences of disobedience. This had the desired effect; the people were impressed with a deep religious fear and a terror of God's judgments; acknowledged themselves perfectly satisfied with the discoveries God had made of himself; and requested that Moses might be constituted the mediator between God and them, as they were not able to bear these tremendous discoveries of the divine majesty. "Speak thou with us, and we will hear; but let not God speak with us, lest we die," v. 19. This teaches us the absolute necessity of that great Mediator between God and man, Christ Jesus, as no man can come unto the Father but by Him.

20. *And Moses said . . . Fear not: for God is come to prove you, and that his fear may be before your faces.* The maxim contained in this verse is, "Fear not, that ye may fear"—do not fear with such a fear as brings consternation into the soul, and produces nothing but terror and confusion; but fear with that *fear* which reverence and filial affection inspire, *that ye sin not*—that, through the love and reverence ye feel to your Maker and Sovereign, ye may abstain from every appearance of evil, lest you should forfeit that love which is to you better than life.

22. *I have talked with you from heaven.* Though God manifested himself by the fire, the lightning, the earthquake, the thick darkness, yet the ten words or commandments were probably uttered from the higher regions of the air, which would be an additional proof to the people that there was no imposture in this case; for though strange appearances and voices might be counterfeited on earth—as was often, no doubt, done by the magicians of Egypt—yet it would be utterly impossible to represent a voice, in a long continued series of instruction, as proceeding from heaven itself, or the higher regions of the atmosphere. This, with the earthquake and repeated thunders (see on v. 18) would put the reality of this whole procedure beyond all doubt; and this enabled Moses, Deut. v. 26, to make such an appeal to the people on a fact incontrovertible and of infinite importance, that God had indeed talked with them face-to-face.

23. *Ye shall not make with me gods of silver.* The expressions here are very remarkable. Before it was said, "Thou shalt have no other gods before me," v. 3. Here they are commanded, "Ye shall not make gods of silver or gold with Me," as emblems or representatives of God, in order, as might be pretended, to keep these displays of His magnificence in memory; on the contrary, He would have only an *altar of earth*—of plain turf, on which they should offer those sacrifices by which they should commemorate their own guilt and the necessity of an atonement to reconcile themselves to God.

24. *Thy burnt offerings, and thy peace offerings.* The law concerning which was shortly to be given, though sacrifices of this kind were in use from the days of Abel. *In all places where I record my name.* Wherever I am worshipped, whether in the open wilderness, at the Tabernacle, in the Temple, the synagogues, or elsewhere, *I will come unto thee . . . and bless thee.* These words are precisely the same in signification with those of our Lord, Matt. xviii. 20: "For where two or three are gathered together in my name, there am I in the midst of them." And as it was JESUS who was the "angel" that spoke to them in the wilderness, Acts vii. 38; from the same mouth this promise in the law and that in the gospel proceeded.

25. *Thou shalt not build it of hewn stone.* Because they were now in a wandering state, and had as yet no fixed residence; and therefore no time should be wasted to rear costly altars, which could not be transported with them, and which they must soon leave. Besides, they must not lavish skill or expense on the construction of an altar; the altar of itself, whether costly or mean, was nothing in the worship; it was only the place on which the victim should be laid, and their mind must be attentively fixed on that God to whom the sacrifice was offered, and on the sacrifice itself, as that appointed by the Lord to make an atonement for their sins.

MATTHEW HENRY

2. To make their altars very low (*v.* 26), so that they might not go up by steps to them. That the higher the altar was, and the nearer heaven, the more acceptable the sacrifice was, was a foolish fancy of the heathen, who therefore chose high places; in opposition to this, and to show that it is the elevation of the heart, not of the sacrifice, that God looks at, they were here ordered to make their altars low.

CHAPTER 21

Verses 1–11

The first verse is the general title of the laws contained in this and the two following chapters, most of them relating to matters between man and man. These laws are called *judgments,* because they are framed in infinite wisdom and equity, and because their magistrates were to give judgment according to them. God delivered them privately to Moses, and he was to communicate them to the people. He begins with the laws concerning servants, commanding mercy and moderation towards them.

I. A law concerning men-servants, sold, either by themselves or their parents, through poverty, or by the judges, for their crimes; even those of the latter sort (if Hebrews) were to continue in slavery but seven years at the most.

At the seven years' end the servant should either go out free (*v.* 2, 3), or his servitude should thenceforward be his choice, *v.* 5, 6.

1. By this law God taught, (1) The Hebrew servants generosity, and a noble love of liberty, for they were the Lord's freemen. Thus Christians, being *bought with a price, and called unto liberty,* must not be the servants of men, nor of the lusts of men, 1 Cor. vii. 23. He likewise taught, (2) The Hebrew masters not to trample upon their poor servants.

2. This law will be further useful to us to illustrate the right God has to the children of believing parents, as such, and the place they have in his church.

II. Concerning maid-servants, whom their parents, through extreme poverty, had sold, when they were very young, to such as they hoped would marry them when they grew up; if they did not, yet they must not sell them to strangers, but rather study how to make them amends for the disappointment; if they did, they must maintain them handsomely, *v.* 7–11.

JAMIESON, FAUSSET, BROWN

26. by steps—a precaution taken for the sake of decency, in consequence of the loose, wide, flowing garments of the priests.

CHAPTER 21

Vss. 1-6. Laws for Menservants. **1. judgments**—rules for regulating the procedure of judges and magistrates in the decision of cases and the trial of criminals. The government of the Israelites being a theocracy, those public authorities were the servants of the Divine Sovereign, and subject to His direction. Most of these laws here noticed were primitive usages, founded on principles of natural equity, and incorporated, with modifications and improvements, in the Mosaic code.

2-6. If thou buy an Hebrew servant—Every Israelite was freeborn; but slavery was permitted under certain restrictions.

An Hebrew might be made a slave through poverty, debt, or crime; but at the end of six years he was entitled to freedom, and his wife, if she had voluntarily shared his state of bondage, also obtained release.

Should he, however, have married a female slave, she and the children, after the husband's liberation, remained the master's property; and if, through attachment to his family, the Hebrew chose to forfeit his privilege and abide as he was, a formal process was gone through in a public court, and a brand of servitude stamped on his ear (Ps. 40:6) for life, or at least till the Jubilee (Deut. 15:17).

7-36. Laws for Maidservants. **7. if a man sell his daughter**—Hebrew girls might be redeemed for a reasonable sum. But in the event of her parents or friends being unable to pay the redemption money, her owner was not at liberty to sell her elsewhere.

ADAM CLARKE

26. *Neither shalt thou go up by steps unto mine altar.* The word *altar* comes from *altus,* "high" or "elevated," though the Hebrew word *mizbach,* from *zabach,* to "slay, kill," signifies merely a place for sacrifice. But the heathen, who imitated the rites of the true God in their idolatrous worship, made their altars very high; whence they derived their name, *altaria,* "altars."

CHAPTER 21

1. *Now these are the judgments.* There is so much good sense, feeling, humanity, equity, and justice in the following laws that they cannot but be admired by every intelligent reader; and they are so very plain as to require very little comment. The laws in this chapter are termed political, those in the succeeding chapter judicial laws; and are supposed to have been delivered to Moses alone, in consequence of the request of the people, chap. xx. 19, that God should communicate His will to Moses, and that Moses should, as mediator, convey it to them.

2. *If thou buy an Hebrew servant.* Calmet enumerates six different ways in which a Hebrew might lose his liberty: (1) In extreme poverty he might sell his liberty, Lev. xxv. 39: "If thy brother . . . be waxen poor, and be sold unto thee." (2) A father might sell his children. "If a man sell his daughter to be a maidservant"; see v. 7. (3) Insolvent debtors became the slaves of their creditors. "My husband is dead . . . and the creditor is come to take unto him my two sons to be bondmen," 2 Kings iv. 1. (4) A thief, if he had not money to pay the fine laid on him by the law, was to be sold for his profit whom he had robbed. "If he have nothing, then he shall be sold for his theft," chap. xxii. 3-4. (5) A Hebrew was liable to be taken prisoner of war, and so sold for a slave. (6) A Hebrew slave who had been ransomed from a Gentile by a Hebrew might be sold by him who ransomed him, to one of his own nation.

Six years he shall serve. It was an excellent provision in these laws that no man could finally injure himself by any rash, foolish, or precipitate act. No man could make himself a servant or slave for more than seven years; and if he mortgaged the family inheritance, it must return to the family at the jubilee, which returned every fiftieth year. It is supposed that the term *six years* is to be understood as referring to the sabbatical years; for let a man come into servitude at whatever part of the interim between two sabbatical years, he could not be detained in bondage beyond a sabbatical year; so that if he fell into bondage the third year after a sabbatical year, he had but three years to serve; if the fifth, but one. See on chap. xxiii. 11, etc. Others suppose that this privilege belonged only to the year of jubilee, beyond which no man could be detained in bondage, though he had been sold only one year before.

3. *If he came in by himself.* If he and his wife came in together, they were to go out together; in all respects as he entered, so should he go out.

4. *The wife and her children shall be her master's.* It was a law among the Hebrews that, if a Hebrew had children by a Canaanitish woman, those children must be considered as Canaanitish only, and might be sold and bought, and serve forever. The law here refers to such a case only.

6. *Shall bring him unto the judges. El haelohim,* literally, "to God"; or, "to the judgment of God." *Bore his ear through with an aul.* This was a ceremony sufficiently significant, as it implied, (1) That he was closely attached to that house and family. (2) That he was bound to hear all his master's orders, and to obey them punctually. Boring of the ear was an ancient custom in the East.

7. *If a man sell his daughter.* This the Jews allowed no man to do but in extreme distress—when he had no goods, either movable or immovable, left, even to the clothes on his back; and he had this permission only while she was unmarriageable. It may appear at first view strange that such a law should have been given; but let it be remembered that this servitude could extend, at the utmost, only to six years; and that it was nearly the same as in some cases

MATTHEW HENRY

Verses 12–21

I. A law concerning murder. He had lately said, *Thou shalt not kill*; 1. For the punishing of wilful murder (*v.* 12): *Whoso sheddeth man's blood, by man shall his blood be shed.* 2. For the relief of such as killed by accident, when a man, without intent of hurt to any, happens to kill another. In this case God provided cities of refuge for the protection of those whose infelicity it was, but not their fault, to occasion the death of another, *v.* 13. With us, who know no avengers of blood but the magistrates, the law itself is a sufficient sanctuary.

II. Concerning rebellious children. It is here made a capital crime, to be punished with death, for children either, 1. To strike their parents (*v.* 15). Or, 2. To curse their parents (*v.* 17). The undutiful behaviour of children towards their parents is a very great provocation to God our common Father; and, if men do not punish it, he will.

III. Here is a law against man-stealing (*v.* 16): *He that steals a man* (that is, a person, man, woman, or child), with design to sell him to the Gentiles (for no Israelite would buy him), was adjudged to death by this statute.

IV. Care is here taken that satisfaction be made for hurt done to a person, though death do not ensue, *v.* 18, 19. He that did the hurt must be accountable for damages, and pay, not only for the cure, but for the loss of time.

V. Direction is given what should be done if a servant died by his master's correction. If he died under his hand, he should be punished for his cruelty, at the discretion of the judges, upon consideration of circumstances, *v.* 20.

Verses 22–36

I. The particular care which the law took of women with child, that no hurt should be done them which might occasion their miscarrying. On this occasion comes in that general law of retaliation which our Saviour refers to, Matt. v. 38, *An eye for an eye.* Now, 1. The execution of this law is not hereby put into the hands of private persons. The tradition of the elders seems to have put this corrupt gloss upon it, in opposition to which our Saviour commands us to forgive injuries, and not to meditate revenge, Matt. v. 39. 2. God often executes it in the course of his providence, making the punishment, in many cases, to answer to the sin, as Judges i. 7; Isa. xxxiii. 1; Hab. ii. 13; Matt. xxvi. 52. 3. Magistrates ought to have an eye to this rule in punishing offenders, and doing right to those that are injured. Consideration must be had of the nature, quality, and degree of the wrong done, that reparation may be made to the party injured, and others deterred from doing the like.

II. The care God took of servants. If their masters maimed them, though it was only striking out a tooth, that should be their discharge, *v.* 26, 27.

JAMIESON, FAUSSET, BROWN

Should she have been betrothed to him or his son, and either change their minds, a maintenance must be provided for her suitable to her condition as his intended wife, or her freedom instantly granted.

23-25. eye for eye—The law which authorized retaliation—a principle acted upon by all primitive people—was a civil one. It was given to regulate the procedure of the public magistrate in determining the amount of compensation in every case of injury, but did not encourage feelings of private revenge. The later Jews, however, mistook it for a moral precept, and were corrected by our Lord (Matt. 5:38-42).

F. C. COOK:

13, 14. There was no place of safety for the guilty murderer, not even the altar of Jehovah. Thus all superstitious notions connected with the right of sanctuary were excluded. Adonijah and Joab (1 Kings 1:50; 2:28) appear to have vainly trusted that the vulgar feeling would protect them if they took hold of the horns of the altar on which atonement with blood was made (Lev. 4:7). But for one who killed a man "at unawares," that is, without intending to do it, the Law afterwards appointed places of refuge (Num. 35:6–34; Deut. 4:41–43; 19:2–10; Josh. 20:2–9). It is very probable that there was some provision answering to the cities of refuge, that may have been based upon old usage, in the camp in the Wilderness.

15, 16, 17. The following offenses were to be punished with death:

Striking a parent (Deut. 27:16).

Cursing a parent.

Kidnapping, whether with a view to retain the person stolen, or to sell him.—*Barnes' Notes*

ADAM CLARKE

of apprenticeship among us, where the parents bind the child for seven years and have from the master so much per week during that period.

9. *Betrothed her unto his son, he shall deal with her.* He shall give her the same dowry he would give to one of his own daughters. From these laws we learn that if a man's son married his servant, by his father's consent, the father was obliged to treat her in every respect as a daughter; and if the son married another woman, as it appears he might do, v. 10, he was obliged to make no abatement in the privileges of the first wife, either in her food, raiment, or duty of marriage. The word *onathah* here is the same with the *homilian* of the Septuagint, which signifies the cohabitation of man and wife.

11. *These three.* (1) Her *food,* her "flesh," for she must not, like a common slave, be fed merely on vegetables. (2) Her *raiment*—her private wardrobe, with all occasional necessary additions. And, (3) The "marriage debt"—a due proportion of the husband's time and company.

13. *I will appoint thee a place whither he shall flee.* From the earliest times the nearest akin had a right to revenge the murder of his relation, and as this right was universally acknowledged, no law was ever made on the subject; but as this might be abused, and a person who had killed another accidentally, having had no previous malice against him, might be put to death by the avenger of blood, as the nearest kinsman was termed, therefore God provided the cities of refuge to which the accidental manslayer might flee till the affair was inquired into, and settled by the civil magistrate.

14. *Thou shalt take him from mine altar.* Before the cities of refuge were assigned, the altar of God was the common asylum.

15. *That smiteth his father, or his mother.* As such a case argued peculiar depravity, therefore no mercy was to be shown to the culprit.

16. *He that stealeth a man.* By this law every man-stealer, and every receiver of the stolen person, should lose his life.

19. *Shall pay for the loss of his time, and shall cause him to be thoroughly healed.* This was a wise and excellent institution, and most courts of justice still regulate their decisions on such cases by this Mosaic precept.

21. If the slave who had been beaten by his master died under his hand, the master was punished with death; see Gen. ix. 5-6. But if he survived the beating a day or two, the master was not punished, because it might be presumed that the man died through some other cause. And all penal laws should be construed as favorably as possible to the accused.

22. *And hurt a woman with child.* As a posterity among the Jews was among the peculiar promises of their covenant, and as every man had some reason to think that the Messiah should spring from his family, therefore any injury done to a woman with child, by which the fruit of her womb might be destroyed, was considered a very heavy offense; and as the crime was committed principally against the husband, the degree of punishment was left to his discretion. But if mischief followed, that is, if the child had been fully formed, and was killed by this means, or the woman lost her life in consequence, then the punishment was as in other cases of murder—the person was put to death, v. 23.

24. *Eye for eye.* This is the earliest account we have of the *lex talionis,* or law of like for like, which afterwards prevailed among the Greeks and Romans. Among the latter, it constituted a part of the "twelve tables," so famous in antiquity; but the punishment was afterwards changed to a pecuniary fine, to be levied at the discretion of the praetor. Nothing, however, of this kind was left to private revenge; the magistrate awarded the punishment when the fact was proved; otherwise the *lex talionis* would have utterly destroyed the peace of society and have sown the seeds of hatred, revenge, and all uncharitableness.

27. *If he smite out his . . . tooth.* It was a noble law that obliged unmerciful slaveholders to set the slave at liberty whose eye or tooth they had knocked out. If this did not teach them humanity, it taught them caution, as one rash blow might have deprived them of all right to

MATTHEW HENRY

III. *Does God take care for oxen?* Yes, it appears by the following laws in this chapter that he does, *for our sakes*, 1 Cor. ix. 9, 10. The Israelites are here directed what to do,

1. In case of hurt done by oxen, or any other brute-creature. (1) As an instance of God's care of the life of man. If an ox killed any man, woman, or child, the ox was to be *stoned* (*v.* 28). Thus God would keep up in the minds of his people a rooted abhorrence of the sin of murder and every thing that was barbarous. (2) To make men careful that none of their cattle might do hurt, but that, by all means possible, mischief might be prevented.

2. In case of hurt done to oxen, or other cattle. (1) If they fall into a pit, and perish there, he that opened the pit must make good the loss, *v.* 33, 34. Mischief done in malice is the great transgression; but mischief done through negligence is not without fault. (2) If cattle fight, and one kill another, the owners shall equally share in the loss, *v.* 35. In the wilderness where they lay closely encamped, and had their flocks and herds among them, such mischiefs as these last mentioned were likely enough to occur.

JAMIESON, FAUSSET, BROWN

28-36. If an ox gore a man or a woman, that they die—For the purpose of sanctifying human blood, and representing all injuries affecting life in a serious light, an animal that occasioned death was to be killed or suffer punishment proportioned to the degree of damage it had caused. Punishments are still inflicted on this principle in Persia and other countries of the East; and among a rude people greater effect is thus produced in inspiring caution, and making them keep noxious animals under restraint, than a penalty imposed on the owners. **30. If there be laid on him a sum of money**, etc.—Blood fines are common among the Arabs as they were once general throughout the East. This is the only case where a money compensation, instead of capital punishment, was expressly allowed in the Mosaic law.

ADAM CLARKE

the future services of the slave; and thus self-interest obliged them to be cautious and circumspect.

28. *If an ox gore a man.* It is more likely that a "bull" is here intended, as the word signifies both, see chap. xxii. 1; and the Septuagint translates the *shor* of the original by *tauros*, "a bull." *His flesh shall not be eaten.* This served to keep up a due detestation of murder, whether committed by man or beast; and at the same time punished the man as far as possible, by the total loss of the beast.

30. *If there be laid on him a sum of money . . . the ransom of his life.* So it appears that, though by the law he forfeited his life, yet this might be commuted for a pecuniary mulct, at which the life of the deceased might be valued by the magistrates.

32. *Thirty shekels.* Each worth about three shillings English; see Gen. xx. 16; xxiii. 15. So, counting the shekel at its utmost value, the life of a slave was valued at four pounds ten shillings. And at this price these same vile people valued the life of our blessed Lord; see Zech. xi. 12-13; Matt. xxvi. 15.

33. *And if a man shall open a pit, or . . . dig a pit.* That is, if a man shall open a well or cistern that had been before closed up, or dig a new one (for these two cases are plainly intimated), and if he did this in some public place where there was danger that men or cattle might fall into it; for a man might do as he pleased in his own grounds, as those were his private right. In the above case, if he had neglected to cover the pit, and his neighbor's ox or ass was killed by falling into it, he was to pay its value in money. The thirty-third and thirty-fourth verses seem to be out of their places. They probably should conclude the chapter, as where they are, they interrupt the statutes concerning the goring ox, which begin at verse 28.

CHAPTER 22

MATTHEW HENRY

Verses 1–6

Here are the laws,

I. Concerning theft, which are these:—1. If a man steal any cattle (in which the wealth of those times chiefly consisted), and they be found in his custody, he must restore double, *v.* 4. 2. If he had killed or sold the sheep or ox he had stolen, and thereby persisted in his crime, he must restore *five oxen for an ox, and four sheep for a sheep* (*v.* 1)

JAMIESON, FAUSSET, BROWN

VSS. 1-31. LAWS CONCERNING THEFT. **1. If a man shall steal an ox, or a sheep**—The law respects the theft of cattle which constituted the chief part of their property.

The penalty for the theft of a sheep which was slain or sold, was fourfold; for an ox fivefold, because of its greater utility in labor; but, should the stolen animal have been recovered alive, a *double* compensation was all that was required, because it was presumable he (the thief) was not a practised adept in dishonesty. A robber breaking into a house at *midnight* might, in self-defense, be slain with impunity; but if he was slain after *sunrise*, it would be considered murder, for it was not thought likely an assault would then be made upon the lives of the occupants.

ADAM CLARKE

1. *If a man shall steal.* This chapter consists chiefly of judicial laws, as the preceding chapter does of political; and in it the same good sense, and well-marked attention to the welfare of the community and the moral improvement of each individual, are equally evident.

In our translation of this verse, by rendering different Hebrew words by the same term in English, we have greatly obscured the sense. I shall produce the verse with the original words which I think improperly translated, because one English term is used for two Hebrew words, which in this place certainly do not mean the same thing. *If a man shall steal an ox* [*shor*], *or a sheep* [*seh*], *and kill it, or sell it; he shall restore five oxen* [*bakar*] *for an ox* [*shor*], *and four sheep* [*tson*] *for a sheep* [*seh*]. I think it must appear evident that the sacred writer did not intend that these words should be understood as above. A *shor* certainly is different from a *bakar*, and a *seh* from a *tson*. Where the difference in every case lies, wherever these words occur, it is difficult to say. The *shor* and the *bakar* are doubtless creatures of the beef kind, and are used in different parts of the sacred writings to signify the bull, the ox, the heifer, the steer, and the calf. The *seh* and the *tson* are used to signify the ram, the ewe, the lamb, the he-goat, the she-goat, and the kid. And the latter word *tson* seems frequently to signify the flock, composed of either of these lesser cattle, or both sorts conjoined.

As *shor* is used, Job xxi. 10, for a "bull," probably it may mean so here. "If a man steal a bull, he shall give five oxen for him," which we may presume was no more than his real value, as very few bulls could be kept in a country destitute of horses, where oxen were so necessary to till the ground. *Tson* is used for a flock either of sheep or goats, and *seh* for an individual of either species. For every *seh*, four, taken indifferently from the *tson* or flock, must be given; i.e., a sheep stolen might be recompensed with four out of the "flock," whether of sheep or goats.

2. *If a thief be found.* If a thief was found breaking into a house in the night season, he might be killed; but not if the sun had risen,

MATTHEW HENRY

. If he was not able to make restitution, he must be old for a slave, *v.* 3. 4. If a thief broke a house in the ight, and was killed in the doing of it, his blood was ipon his own head.

II. Concerning trespass, *v.* 5. He that wilfully ut his cattle into his neighbour's field must make estitution of the best of his own.

III. Concerning damage done by fire, *v.* 6. He that lesigned only the burning of thorns might become ccessory to the burning of corn, and should not be eld guiltless. Men must suffer for their carelessness, s well as for their malice.

Verses 7–15

I. Concerning trusts, *v.* 7–13. If a man deliver oods, and if a special confidence be reposed in the erson they are lodged with, in case these goods be tolen or lost, perish or be damaged, if it appear that t was not by any fault of the trustee, the owner must tand to the loss, otherwise he that has been false to is trust must be compelled to make satisfaction. This teaches us, 1. It is unjust and base, and that which ll the world cries shame on, to betray a trust. 2. That here is such a general failing of truth and justice upon arth as gives too much occasion to suspect men's onesty whenever it is their interest to be dishonest. The religion of an oath is very ancient, and a plain inlication of the universal belief of a God, and a providence, and a judgment to come.

II. Concerning loans, *v.* 14, 15. If a man (suppose) ent his team to his neighbour, if the owner was with t, or was to receive profit for the loan of it, whatever harm befell the cattle the owner must stand to the oss of: but if the owner was so kind to the borrower as to lend it to him gratis, then, if any harm happened, the borrower must make it good.

Verses 16–24

I. A law that he who debauched a young woman should be obliged to marry her, *v.* 16, 17. This law puts an honour upon marriage and shows likewise how improper a thing it is that children should marry without their parents' consent.

II. A law which makes witchcraft a capital crime, *v.* 18.

III. Unnatural abominations are here made capital; such beasts in the shape of men as are guilty of them are unfit to live (*v.* 19): *Whosoever lies with a beast shall die.*

IV. Idolatry is also made capital, *v.* 20.

V. A caution against oppression. Because those who were empowered to punish other crimes were themselves most in danger of this, God takes the punishing of it into his own hands.

1. Strangers must not be abused (*v.* 21), not wronged in judgment by the magistrates, not imposed upon in contracts, nor must any advantage be taken of their ignorance or necessity; no, nor must they be taunted, trampled upon, treated with contempt, or upbraided with being strangers. Note, (1) Humanity is one of the laws of religion. Those that are strangers to us are known to God, and he preserves them, Ps. cxlvi. 9. (2) Those that profess religion should study to oblige strangers, that they may thereby recommend religion.

2. Widows and fatherless must not be abused (*v.* 22): *You shall not afflict them,* that is, You shall comfort and assist them. Their condition must be considered, who have lost those that should deal for them, and protect them. It is a great comfort to those who are injured and oppressed by men that they have a God to go to who will do more than *give them the hearing.*

Verses 25–31

Here is, I. A law against extortion in lending. This law, in the strictness of it, seems to have been peculiar to the Jewish state; but, in the equity of it, it obliges us to show mercy to those of whom we might take advantage, and to be content to share, in loss as well as profit. It seems as lawful to receive interest for my money, which another takes pains with and improves, but runs the hazard of, in trade, as it is to receive rent for my land, which another takes pains with and improves, but runs the hazard of, in husbandry.

JAMIESON, FAUSSET, BROWN

In every case where a thief could not make restitution, he was sold as a slave for the usual term. **6. If fire break out, and catch in thorns**—This refers to the common practice in the East of setting fire to the dry grass before the fall of the autumnal rains, which prevents the ravages of vermin, and is considered a good preparation of the ground for the next crop. The very parched state of the herbage and the long droughts of summer, make the kindling of a fire an operation often dangerous, and always requiring caution from its liability to spread rapidly. **stacks**—or as it is rendered "shocks" (Judg. 15:5; Job 5: 26), means simply a bundle of loose sheaves.

GEORGE RAWLINSON:

The remainder of the chapter contains laws which it is impossible to bring under any general head or heads, and which can, therefore, only be regarded as miscellaneous. Moses may have recorded them in the order in which they were delivered to him; or have committed them to writing as they afterwards occurred to his memory.

16. "If a man entice a maid." The seduction of a maiden is regarded more seriously in primitive than in more advanced communities. The father looked to receive a handsome sum from the man to whom he consented to betroth his virgin daughter; and required compensation if his daughter's eligibility as a wife was diminished. If the seducer were a person to whom he felt it a degradation to marry his daughter, he might exact from him such a sum as would be likely to induce another to wed her; if he was one whom he could accept as a son-in-law, he might compel him to reestablish his daughter's status by marriage. It might be well if modern societies would imitate the Mosaic code on this point by some similar proviso.

"He shall surely endow her"—i.e., pay the customary sum to the father. See Deut. 22:29, where the sum is fixed at fifty shekels of silver.

17. "He shall pay money according to the dowry of virgins." It is not stated what the amount was to be in this case, but probably it was more than in the other.

18. "Thou shalt not suffer a witch to live." The word translated "witch" in this passage is the feminine singular of that rendered by "sorcerers" in chapter 7:11, and means "a mutterer of charms." The use of the feminine form can only be accounted for by supposing that, practically, witchcraft was at the time mainly professed by females. Whether "witches" had actual help from evil spirits, or only professed to work magical effects by their aid, the sin against God was the same. Jehovah was renounced, and a power other than His invoked and upheld. Witchcraft was as much rebellion against God as idolatry or blasphemy, and deserved the same punishment.

19. The sin here denounced was common among the Canaanitish nations (Lev. 18:24) and not unknown in Egypt (Herod 2:46). It was therefore necessary that God's abhorrence of it should be distinctly declared to Israel.

20. "He that sacrificeth." Sacrifice in this place represents worship generally, being its most essential act. Elsewhere the death penalty is affixed to any acknowledgment of false gods (Deut. 8:1–16).

"Shall be utterly destroyed." Heb., "Shall be devoted," i,e., devoted to destruction.

—*Ellicott's Commentary on the Whole Bible*

ADAM CLARKE

for then he might be known and taken, and the restitution made which is mentioned in the succeeding verse.

4. *He shall restore double.* In no case of theft was the life of the offender taken away; the utmost that the law says on this point is that if, when found breaking into a house, he should be smitten so as to die, no blood should be shed for him, v. 2. If he had stolen and sold the property, then he was to restore four- or five-fold, v. 1; but if the animal was found alive in his possession, he was to restore double.

7. *Deliver unto his neighbour.* This is called "pledging"; it is a deposit of goods by a debtor to his creditor, to be kept till the debt be discharged. Whatever goods were thus left in the hands of another person, that person, according to the Mosaic law, became responsible for them; if they were stolen, and the thief was found, he was to pay double; if he could not be found, the oath of the person who had them in keeping, made before the magistrates, that he knew nothing of them, was considered a full acquittance.

8. *Unto the judges.* See the note on chap. xxi. 6.

9. *Challengeth to be his.* It was necessary that such a matter should come before the judges, because the person in whose possession the goods were found might have had them by a fair and honest purchase; and, by sifting the business, the thief might be found out, and if found, be obliged to pay double to his neighbor.

11. *An oath of the Lord be between them.* So solemn and awful were all appeals to God considered in those ancient times that it was taken for granted that the man was innocent who could by an oath appeal to the omniscient God that he had not put his hand to his neighbor's goods.

13. *If it be torn in pieces . . . let him bring it for witness.* Rather, "Let him bring a testimony or evidence of the torn thing," such as the horns, hoofs, etc.

16. *If a man entice a maid.* This was an exceedingly wise and humane law, and must have operated powerfully against seduction and fornication; because the person who might feel inclined to take the advantage of a young woman knew that he must marry her, and give her a dowry, if her parents consented; and if they did not consent that their daughter should wed her seducer, in this case he was obliged to give her the full dowry which could have been demanded had she been still a virgin.

19. *Lieth with a beast.* If this most abominable crime had not been common, it never would have been mentioned in a sacred code of laws. It is very likely that it was an Egyptian practice.

20. *Utterly destroyed.* The word *cherem* denotes a thing utterly and finally separated from God and devoted to destruction, without the possibility of redemptio..

21. *Thou shalt neither vex a stranger, nor oppress him.* This was not only a very humane law, but it was also the offspring of a sound policy: "Do not vex a stranger; remember ye were strangers. Do not oppress a stranger; remember ye were oppressed. Therefore do unto all men as ye would they should do to you."

22. *Ye shall not afflict any widow, or fatherless child.* It is remarkable that offenses against this law are not left to the discretion of the judges to be punished; God reserves the punishment to himself, and by this He strongly shows His abhorrence of the crime.

25. *Neither shalt thou lay upon him usury. Neshech,* from *nashach,* to "bite, cut, or pierce with the teeth"; "biting usury." So the Latins call it *usura vorax,* "devouring usury."

It is evident that what is here said must be understood of accumulated usury, or what we call "compound interest" only; and accordingly *neshech* is mentioned with and distinguished from *tarbith* and *marbith,* "interest" or "simple interest," Lev. xxv. 36-37; Prov. xxviii. 8; Ezek. xviii. 8, 13, 17; and xxii. 12. Perhaps *usury* may be more properly defined "unlawful interest," receiving more for the loan of money than it is really worth and more than the law allows. It is a wise regulation in the laws of England that if a man be convicted of usury, taking unlawful

MATTHEW HENRY

They must not take a poor man's bed-clothes in pawn; but, if they did, must restore them by bed-time, *v.* 26, 27.

II. A law against the contempt of authority (*v.* 28): *Thou shalt not revile the gods,* that is, the *judges* and *magistrates,* for their executing these laws; they must do their duty, whoever suffer by it.

III. A law concerning the offering of their first-fruits to God, *v.* 29, 30. It was appointed before (*ch.* xiii.), and it is here repeated: *The firstborn of thy sons shalt thou give unto me;* and much more reason have we to give ourselves, and all we have, to God, who *spared not his own Son, but delivered him up for us all.* The first ripe of their corn they must not delay to offer. Let not young people delay to offer to God the first-fruits of their time and strength.

IV. A distinction put between the Jews and all other people: *You shall be holy men unto me;* and one mark of that honourable distinction is appointed in their diet, which was, that they should not *eat any flesh that was torn of beasts* (*v.* 31), not only because it was unwholesome, but because it was paltry to eat the leavings of the beasts of prey.

JAMIESON, FAUSSET, BROWN

26, 27. **If thou at all take thy neighbour's raiment to pledge,** etc.—From the nature of the case, this is the description of a poor man. No Orientals undress, but, merely throwing off their turbans and some of their heavy outer garments, they sleep in the clothes which they wear during the day. The bed of the poor is usually nothing else than a mat; and, in winter, they cover themselves with a cloak—a practice which forms the ground or reason of the humane and merciful law respecting the pawned coat.

28. **gods**—a word which is several times in this chapter rendered "judges" or magistrates. **the ruler of thy people**—and the chief magistrate who was also the high priest, at least in the time of Paul (Acts 23:1-5).

ADAM CLARKE

interest, the bond or security is rendered void and he forfeits treble the sum borrowed.

26. *If thou . . . take thy neighbour's raiment to pledge.* It seems strange that any pledge should be taken which must be so speedily restored; but it is very likely that the pledge was restored by night only; and that he who pledged it brought it back to his creditor next morning. The opinion of the rabbins is that whatever a man needed for the support of life he had the use of it when absolutely necessary, though it was pledged. Thus he had the use of his working tools by day, but he brought them to his creditor in the evening. His *hyke* was probably the *raiment* here referred to; it is a sort of coarse blanket, about six yards long, and five or six feet broad, which an Arab always carries with him, and on which he sleeps at night, it being his only substitute for a bed.

28. *Thou shalt not revile the gods.* Most commentators believe that the word *gods* here means "magistrates." The original is *Elohim,* and should be understood of the true God only: "Thou shalt not blaspheme or make light of God," the Fountain of justice and power, *nor curse the ruler of thy people,* who derives his authority from God.

29. *The first of thy ripe fruits.* This offering was a public acknowledgment of the bounty and goodness of God.

30. *Seven days it shall be with his dam.* For the mother's health it was necessary that the young one should suck so long; and prior to this time the process of nutrition in a young animal can scarcely be considered as completely formed.

31. *Neither shall ye eat . . . flesh . . . torn of beasts in the field.* The reason of the prohibition against eating the flesh of animals that had been torn appears to have been simply this: That the people might not eat the blood, which in this case must be coagulated in the flesh; and the blood, being the life of the beast, and emblematical of the blood of the covenant, was ever to be held sacred, and was prohibited from the days of Noah. See on Gen. ix. 4.

MATTHEW HENRY

CHAPTER 23

Verses 1-9

I. Cautions concerning judicial proceedings.

1. The witnesses are here cautioned that they neither occasion an innocent man to be indicted, by raising a false report of him, nor assist in the prosecution of an innocent man, by *putting their hand* in swearing as witnesses against him, *v.* 1. Bearing false witness has in it all the guilt of lying, perjury, malice, theft, murder. There is scarcely any one act of wickedness that a man can possibly be guilty of which has in it a greater complication of villainies than this has. Yet the former part of this caution is to be extended to common conversation; so that slandering and backbiting are a species of falsewitness-bearing. A man's reputation lies as much at the mercy of every company as his estate or life does at the mercy of a judge or jury; so that he who raises, or spreads, a false report against his neighbour, sins as much against the laws of truth, justice, and charity, as a false witness does.

2. The judges are here cautioned not to pervert judgment. (1) They might not be overruled, either by might or multitude, to go against their consciences in giving judgment, *v.* 2. The junior upon the bench voted first, that he might not be swayed nor overruled by the authority of the senior. We must enquire what we ought to do, not what the majority do; because we must be judged by our Master, not by our fellow-servants, and it is too great a compliment to be willing to go to hell for company. (2) They must not pervert judgment, no, not in favour of a poor man, *v.* 3. Let them not therefore fare the worse for being poor. They must dread the thoughts of assisting or abetting a bad cause (*v.* 7). Judges themselves are accountable to the great judge. They must not oppress a stranger, *v.* 9. Though aliens might not inherit lands among them, yet they must have justice done them, must peaceably enjoy their own, and be redressed if they were wronged, though they were strangers to the commonwealth of Israel.

II. Commands concerning neighbourly kindnesses. We must be ready to do all good offices, as there is occasion, for anybody, yea even for those that have done us ill offices, *v.* 4, 5. The command of loving our enemies, is not only a *new,* but an *old* command-

JAMIESON, FAUSSET, BROWN

CHAPTER 23

Vss. 1-33. LAWS CONCERNING SLANDER, ETC. 1. **put not thine hand**—join not hands.

2. **decline**—depart, deviate from the straight path of rectitude.

3. **countenance**—adorn, embellish—thou shalt not varnish the cause even of a poor man to give it a better coloring than it merits.

ADAM CLARKE

CHAPTER 23

1. *Thou shalt not raise a false report.* Acting contrary to this precept is a sin against the ninth commandment. And the inventor and receiver of false and slanderous reports are almost equally criminal. The word seems to refer to either, and our translators have very properly retained both senses, putting *raise* in the text, and "receive" in the margin. The original *lo tissa* has been translated, Thou shalt not "publish."

2. *Thou shalt not follow a multitude to do evil.* Be singular. But *rabbim,* which we translate *multitude,* sometimes signifies the "great, chiefs, or mighty ones"; and is so understood by some eminent critics in this place: "Thou shalt not follow the example of the great or rich, who may so far disgrace their own character as to live without God in the world, and trample under foot his laws." It is supposed that these directions refer principally to matters which come under the eye of the civil magistrate; as if He had said, "Do not join with great men in condemning an innocent or righteous person, against whom they have conceived a prejudice on the account of his religion."

3. *Neither shalt thou countenance a poor man in his cause.* The word *dal,* which we translate *poor man,* is probably put here in opposition to *rabbim,* the great, or noblemen, in the preceding verse. If so, the meaning is, Thou shalt neither be influenced by the great to make an unrighteous decision, nor by the poverty or distress of the poor to give thy voice against the dictates of justice and truth.

4. *If thou meet thine enemy's ox . . . going astray.* From the humane and heavenly maxim in this and the following verse, our blessed Lord has formed the following precept: "Love your enemies, bless them that curse you, do good to them that hate you, and pray for them which despitefully use you, and persecute you," Matt. v. 44.

6. *Thou shalt not wrest the judgment of thy poor.* Thou shalt neither countenance him in

MATTHEW HENRY

ment, Prov. xxv. 21, 22. Infer hence, 1. If we must do this kindness for an enemy, much more for a friend. 2. If it be wrong not to prevent our enemy's loss and damage, how much worse is it to occasion harm and loss to him, or anything he has. 3. If we must bring back our neighbours' cattle when they go astray, much more must we endeavour, by prudent admonitions and instructions, to bring back our neighbours themselves, when they go astray in any sinful path, see Jam. v. 19, 20. And, if we must endeavour to help up a fallen ass, much more should we endeavour to help up a sinking spirit, *saying to those that are of a fearful heart, Be strong.*

Verses 10–19

Here is, I. The institution of the sabbatical year, *v.* 10, 11. **Every seventh year the land was to rest;** they must not plough nor sow it at the beginning of the year, and then they could not expect any great harvest at the end of the year. Now this was designed, 1. To show what a plentiful land that was into which God was bringing them. 2. To remind them of their dependence upon God their great landlord, and their obligation to use the fruit of their land as he should direct. Afterwards we find that their disobedience to this command was a forfeiture of the promises, 2 Chron. xxxvi. 21. 3. To teach them a confidence in the divine Providence.

II. The repetition of the law of the fourth commandment concerning the weekly sabbath, *v.* 12. Some have endeavoured to take away the observance of the sabbath, by pretending that every day must be a sabbath day.

III. All manner of respect to the gods of the heathen is here strictly forbidden, *v.* 13. A general caution is prefixed to this, which has reference to all these precepts: *In all things that I have said unto you, be circumspect.*

IV. Their solemn religious attendance on God in the place which he should choose is here strictly required, *v.* 14–17. Thrice a year all their males must come together in a holy convocation. They must come together *before the Lord* (*v.* 17) to pay their homage to him. They must not *appear before God empty, v.* 15. Some free-will offering or other they must bring, and, as they were not allowed to come empty-handed, so we must not come to worship God empty-hearted; our souls must be filled with grace, with pious and devout affections, holy desires towards him, and dedications of ourselves to him. The passover, pentecost, and feast of tabernacles, in spring, summer, and autumn, were the three times appointed for their attendance.

V. Some particular directions are here given about the three feasts, though not so fully as afterwards. 1. As to the passover, it was not to be offered with leavened bread, nor was the fat of it to remain until the morning, lest it should become offensive, *v.* 18. 2. At the feast of pentecost, when they were to begin their harvest, they must bring *the first of their first-fruits* to God, by the pious presenting of which the whole harvest was sanctified, *v.* 19. 3. At the feast of *ingathering, as it is called* (*v.* 16), they must give God thanks for the harvest-mercies they had received, and must depend upon him for the next harvest, and must not think to receive benefit by that superstitious usage of some of the Gentiles, who, it is said, at the end of their harvest, *seethed a kid in its dam's milk*, and sprinkled that milk-potage, in a magical way, upon their gardens and fields, to make them more fruitful next year.

JAMIESON, FAUSSET, BROWN

10, 11. six years thou shalt sow thy land—intermitting the cultivation of the land every seventh year. But it appears that even then there was a spontaneous produce which the poor were permitted freely to gather for their use, and the beasts driven out fed on the remainder, the owners of fields not being allowed to reap or collect the fruits of the vineyard or oliveyard during the course of this sabbatical year. This was a regulation subservient to many excellent purposes; for, besides inculcating the general lesson of dependence on Providence, and of confidence in His faithfulness to His promise respecting the triple increase on the sixth year (Lev. 25:20, 21), it gave the Israelites a practical proof that they held their properties of the Lord as His tenants, and must conform to His rules on pain of forfeiting the lease of them. **12. Six days thou shalt do thy work, and on the seventh day thou shalt rest**—This law is repeated lest any might suppose there was a relaxation of its observance during the sabbatical year. **13. make no mention of the name of other gods,** etc.—i.e., in common conversation, for a familiar use of them would tend to lessen horror of idolatry.

14-18. Three times . . . keep a feast . . . in the year—This was the institution of the great religious festivals—"The feast of unleavened bread" or the passover—"the feast of harvest" or pentecost—"the feast of ingathering" or the feast of tabernacles, which was a memorial of the dwelling in booths in the wilderness, and which was observed "in the end of the year," or the seventh month (ch. 12:2).

All the males were enjoined to repair to the tabernacle and afterwards the temple, and the women frequently went. The institution of this national custom was of the greatest importance in many ways: by keeping up a national sense of religion and a public uniformity in worship, by creating a bond of unity, and also by promoting internal commerce among the people. Though the absence of all the males at these three festivals left the country defenseless, a special promise was given of divine protection, and no incursion of enemies was ever permitted to happen on those occasions.

19. Thou shalt not seethe a kid in his mother's milk—A prohibition against imitating the superstitious rites of the idolaters in Egypt, who, at the end of their harvest, seethed a kid in its mother's milk and sprinkled the broth as a magical charm on their gardens and fields, to render them more productive the following season.

ADAM CLARKE

his crimes, nor condemn him in his righteousness.

8. *Thou shalt take no gift.* A strong ordinance against selling justice, which has been the disgrace and ruin of every state where it has been practiced.

9. *Ye know the heart of a stranger.* Having been strangers yourselves, under severe, long continued, and cruel oppression, ye know the fears, cares, anxieties, and dismal forebodings which the heart of a stranger feels.

11. *The seventh year thou shalt let it rest.* As every seventh day was a Sabbath day, so every seventh year was to be a Sabbath year. That God intended to teach them the doctrine of providence by this ordinance, there can be no doubt; and this is marked very distinctly, Lev. xxv. 20-21: "And if ye shall say, What shall we eat the seventh year? behold, we shall not sow, nor gather in our increase: then I will command my blessing upon you in the sixth year, and it shall bring forth fruit for three years." That is, There shall be, not three crops in one year, but one crop equal in its abundance to three, because it must supply the wants of three years.

12. *Six days thou shalt do thy work.* Though they were thus bound to keep the sabbatical year, yet they must not neglect the seventh day's rest or weekly Sabbath; for that was of perpetual obligation, and was paramount to all others. That the sanctification of the Sabbath was of great consequence in the sight of God, we may learn from the various repetitions of this law; and we may observe that it has still for its object, not only the benefit of the soul, but the health and comfort of the body also. *The son of thy handmaid, and the stranger . . . be refreshed. Yinnaphesh,* may be "re-spirited" or "new-souled"; have a complete renewal of both bodily and spiritual strength.

14. *Three times thou shalt keep a feast unto me in the year.* The three feasts here referred to were Passover, Pentecost, Tabernacles. The Feast of the Passover was celebrated to keep in remembrance the wonderful deliverance of the Hebrews from Egypt. The Feast of Pentecost, called also the "feast of harvest" and the "feast of weeks," chap. xxxiv. 22, was celebrated fifty days after the Passover to commemorate the giving of the law on Mount Sinai. The Feast of Tabernacles, called also the "feast of the ingathering," was celebrated about the fifteenth of the month Tisri to commemorate the Israelites' dwelling in tents for forty years, during their stay in the wilderness. See on Leviticus xxiii.

17. *All thy males.* Old men, sick men, male idiots, and male children under thirteen years of age, excepted; for so the Jewish doctors understand this command.

18. *The blood of my sacrifice with leavened bread.* The sacrifice here mentioned is undoubtedly the Passover (see chap. xxxiv. 25); this is called by way of eminence *my sacrifice*, because God had instituted it for that especial purpose, the redemption of Israel from the Egyptian bondage, and because it typified the Lamb of God, who taketh away the sin of the world. We have already seen how strict the prohibition against leaven was during this festival, and what was signified by it. See on chap. xii.

19. *Thou shalt not seethe a kid in his mother's milk.* This passage has greatly perplexed commentators; but Dr. Cudworth is supposed to have given it its true meaning by quoting a MS. comment of a Karaite Jew, which he met with, on this passage. "It was a custom of the ancient heathens, when they had gathered in all their fruits, to take a kid and boil it in the milk of its dam; and then, in a magical way, to go about and besprinkle with it all their trees and fields, gardens and orchards; thinking by these means to make them fruitful, that they might bring forth more abundantly in the following year." After all the learned labor which critics have bestowed on this passage, the simple object of the precept seems to be this: "Thou shalt do nothing that may have any tendency to blunt thy moral feelings, or teach thee hardness of heart." Even human nature shudders at the thought of causing the mother to lend her milk

MATTHEW HENRY

Verses 20–33

Three gracious promises are here made to Israel, to engage them to their duty and encourage them in it.

I. It is here promised that they should be guided and kept in their way through the wilderness to the land of promise: *Behold, I send an angel before thee* (*v.* 20), *my angel* (*v.* 23), a created angel, say some, a minister of God's providence, employed in conducting and protecting the camp of Israel. Others suppose it to be the Son of God, the angel of the covenant; and we may as well suppose him God's messenger, and the church's Redeemer, before his incarnation, as *the Lamb slain from the foundation of the world.* It is promised that this blessed angel should *keep them in the way.* It is also promised that he should bring them into the place which God had not only designed but prepared for them: and thus Christ has prepared a place for his followers.

II. It is promised that they should have a comfortable settlement in the land of Canaan. Observe, 1. How reasonable the conditions of this promise are—only that they should serve their own God, who was indeed the only true God. 2. How rich the particulars of this promise are. (1) The comfort of their food. He shall *bless thy bread and thy water.* (2) The continuance of their health: "*I will take sickness away,* either prevent it or remove it." (3) The increase of their wealth. Their cattle should not be barren. (4) The prolonging of their lives to old age: "*The number of thy days I will fulfil,* and they shall not be cut off in the midst by untimely deaths." Thus hath godliness the *promise of the life that now is.*

III. It is promised that they should conquer and subdue their enemies, the present occupants of the land of Canaan, who must be driven out to make room for them. Hosts of hornets made way for the hosts of Israel; such mean creatures can God make use of for the chastising of his people's enemies, as in the plagues of Egypt. When God pleases, hornets can drive out Canaanites, as well as lions could, Josh. xxiv. 12.

The precept annexed to this promise is that they should not make any friendship, nor have any familiarity, with idolaters, *v.* 32, 33. Idolaters must not so much as sojourn in their land, unless they renounced their idolatry. Note, Those that would be kept from bad courses must keep from bad company.

JAMIESON, FAUSSET, BROWN

20-25. Behold, I send an Angel before thee, to keep thee in the way—The communication of these laws, made to Moses and by him rehearsed to the people, was concluded by the addition of many animating promises, intermingled with several solemn warnings that lapses into sin and idolatry would not be tolerated or passed with impunity.

my name is in him—This angel is frequently called Jehovah and Elohim, i.e., God.

28. I will send hornets before thee, etc. (Josh. 24: 12).—Some instrument of divine judgment, but variously interpreted, as hornets in a literal sense [BOCHART]. As a pestilential disease [ROSENMULLER]. As a terror of the Lord—an extraordinary dejection [JUNIUS]. **29, 30. I will not drive . . . out . . . in one year; lest the land become desolate**—Many reasons recommend a gradual extirpation of the former inhabitants of Canaan. But only one is here specified—the danger lest, in the unoccupied grounds, wild beasts should inconveniently multiply; a clear proof that the promised land was more than sufficient to contain the actual population of the Israelites.

ADAM CLARKE

to seethe the flesh of her young one!

20. *Behold, I send an Angel before thee.* Some have thought that this was Moses, others Joshua, because the word *malach* signifies an *angel* or "messenger"; but as it is said, v. 21, "My name is in him" (*bekirbo,* "intimately, essentially in him"), it is more likely that the great Angel of the Covenant, the Lord Jesus Christ, is meant, in whom dwelt "all the fulness of the Godhead bodily." Of Him, Joshua was a very expressive type, the names *Joshua* and *Jesus,* in Hebrew and Greek, being of exactly the same signification, from *yasha,* "he saved, delivered, preserved, or kept safe." Nor does it appear that the description given of the Angel in the text can belong to any other person.

21. *He will not pardon your transgressions.* He is not like a man, with whom ye may think that ye may trifle; were He either man or angel, in the common acceptation of the term, it need not be said, *He will not pardon your transgressions,* for neither man nor angel could do it. *My name is in him.* The Jehovah dwells in Him; in Him dwelt "all the fulness of the Godhead bodily"; and because of this He could either pardon or punish.

23. *Unto the Amorites.* There are only six of the seven nations mentioned here, but the Septuagint, Samaritan, Coptic, and one Hebrew MS., add Girgashite, thus making the seven nations.

24. *Break down their images.* "Pillars, anointed stones."

25. *Shall bless thy bread, and thy water.* That is, all thy provisions, no matter of what sort; the meanest fare shall be sufficiently nutritive when God's blessing is in it.

26. *There shall nothing cast their young, nor be barren.* Hence there must be a very great increase both of men and cattle. *The number of thy days I will fulfil.* Ye shall all live to a good old age, and none die before his time. This is the blessing of the righteous, for wicked men live not out half their days, Ps. lv. 23.

31. *I will set thy bounds from the Red sea,* on the southeast, *even unto the sea of the Philistines*—the Mediterranean, on the northwest; *and from the desert*—of Arabia, or the wilderness of Shur, on the west, *unto the river*—the Euphrates, on the northeast. Or in general terms, from the Euphrates on the east to the Mediterranean Sea on the west, from Mount Libanus on the north to the Red Sea on the south. This promise was not completely fulfilled till the days of David and Solomon. The general disobedience of the people before this time prevented a more speedy accomplishment; and their disobedience afterwards caused them to lose the possession.

32. *Thou shalt make no covenant with them.* They were incurable idolaters, and the cup of their iniquity was full. And had the Israelites contracted any alliance with them, either sacred or civil, they would have enticed them into their idolatries, to which the Jews were at all times most unhappily prone; and as God intended that they should be the preservers of the true religion till the coming of the Messiah, hence He strictly forbade them to tolerate idolatry.

33. *They shall not dwell in thy land.* They must be utterly expelled. The land was the Lord's, and He had given it to the progenitors of this people, to Abraham, Isaac, and Jacob.

MATTHEW HENRY — CHAPTER 24

Verses 1–8

Moses is directed to bring Aaron and his sons, and the seventy elders of Israel, that they might be witnesses of the glory of God, and that their testimony might confirm the people's faith. They must all be very reverent: *Worship you afar off, v.* 1.

In the following verses, we have the solemn covenant made between God and Israel, and the exchanging of the ratifications.

I. Moses told the people the words of the Lord, *v.* 3. He laid before them all the precepts, general and particular, in the foregoing chapters; and fairly put it to them whether they were willing to submit to these laws or no.

II. The people unanimously consented to the terms proposed, without reservation or exception: *All the*

JAMIESON, FAUSSET, BROWN — CHAPTER 24

Vss. 1-18. DELIVERY OF THE LAW AND COVENANT. **3. Moses came and told the people all the words of the Lord**—The rehearsal of the foregoing laws and

ADAM CLARKE — CHAPTER 24

1. *Come up unto the Lord.* Moses and Aaron were already on the mount, or at least some way up (chap. xix. 24), where they had heard the voice of the Lord distinctly speaking to them; and the people also saw and heard, but in a less distinct manner, probably like the hoarse grumbling sound of distant thunder; see chap. xx. 18.

2. *Moses alone shall come near.* The people stood at the foot of the mountain. Aaron and his two sons and the seventy elders went up, probably about halfway, and Moses alone went to the summit.

3. *Moses . . . told the people all the words of the Lord.* That is, the Ten Commandments,

MATTHEW HENRY

words which the Lord hath said will we do. This is the tenor of the covenant. That, if they would observe the foregoing precepts, God would perform the foregoing promises. "Obey, and be happy."

1. How it was engrossed in the book of the covenant: *Moses wrote the words of the Lord* (*v.* 4)

2. How it was sealed by the blood of the covenant, that Israel might receive strong consolations from the ratifying of God's promises to them, and might lie under strong obligations from the ratifying of their promises to God. The covenant must be made by sacrifice (Ps. l. 5), because, since man has sinned, and forfeited his Creator's favour, there can be no fellowship by covenant till there be first friendship and atonement by sacrifice.

(1) In preparation therefore [1] Moses builds an altar, to the honour of God, which was principally intended in all the altars that were built, and which was the first thing to be looked at in the covenant they were now to seal. [2] He erects twelve pillars, according to the number of the tribes. These were to represent the people, the other party to the covenant; and we may suppose that they were set up against the altar, and that Moses, as mediator, passed to and fro between them. Probably each tribe set up and knew its own pillar, and their elders stood by it.

[3] He appointed sacrifices to be offered upon the altar (*v.* 5), burnt-offerings and peace-offerings, which yet were designed to be expiatory.

(2) Preparation being thus made, the ratifications were very solemnly exchanged. [1] The blood of the sacrifice which the people offered was (part of it) sprinkled upon the altar (*v.* 6), which signifies the people's dedicating themselves, their lives, and beings, to God, and to his honour. [2] The blood of the sacrifice which God had owned and accepted was (the remainder of it) sprinkled either upon the people themselves (*v.* 8) or upon the pillars that represented them, which signified God's graciously conferring his favour upon them. Thus our Lord Jesus, the Mediator of the new covenant (of whom Moses was a type), having offered up himself a sacrifice upon the cross, that his blood might be indeed the blood of the covenant, sprinkles it upon the altar in his intercession (Heb. ix. 12), and sprinkles it upon his church by his word and ordinances and the influences and operations of the Spirit of promise, by whom we are sealed. He himself seemed to allude to this solemnity when, in the institution of the Lord's supper, he said, *This cup is the New Testament* (or covenant) *in my blood.* Compare with this, Heb. ix. 19, 20.

Verses 9–11

God here gives to their representatives some special tokens of his favour to them, and admits them nearer to him than they could have expected. Observe, 1. They saw the God of Israel (*v.* 10), that is, they had some glimpse of his glory, in light and fire, though they saw *no manner of similitude*, and his being *no man hath seen nor can see*, 1 Tim. vi. 16. They saw the place where the God of Israel stood (so the LXX.), something that came near a similitude, but was not; whatever they saw, it was certainly something of which no image or picture could be made, and yet enough to satisfy them that God was with them of a truth. Nothing is described but that which was under his feet; for our conceptions of God are all below him, and fall infinitely short of being adequate. At the bottom of the brightness, and as the footstool or pedestal of it, they saw a most rich and splendid pavement, as it had been of sapphires, azure or sky-coloured.

2. *Upon the nobles* (or elders) *of Israel, he laid not his hand, v.* 11. Though they were

JAMIESON, FAUSSET, BROWN

the ten commandments, together with the promises of special blessings in the event of their obedience, having drawn forth from the people a unanimous declaration of their consent, it was forthwith recorded as the conditions of the *national* covenant. The next day preparations were made for having it solemnly ratified, by building an altar and twelve pillars; the altar representing God, and the pillars the tribes of Israel—the two parties in this solemn compact—while Moses acted as typical mediator.

5. young men—priests (ch. 19:22), probably the oldest sons of particular families, who acted under the direction of Moses. **oxen**—Other animals, though not mentioned, were offered in sacrifice (Heb. 9:18-20). **6. Moses took half of the blood . . . sprinkled**—Preliminary to this was the public reading of the law and the renewed acceptance of the terms by the people; then the sprinkling of the blood was the sign of solemn ratification—half on each party in the transaction. **8. Moses took the blood, and sprinkled it on the people**—probably on the twelve pillars, as representing the people (also the book, Heb. 9:19), and the act was accompanied by a public proclamation of its import. It was setting their seal to the covenant (cf. I Cor. 11:25). It must have been a deeply impressive, as well as instructive scene, for it taught the Israelites that the covenant was made with them only through the sprinkling of blood—that the divine acceptance of themselves and services, was only by virtue of an atoning sacrifice, and that even the blessings of the *national* covenant were promised and secured to them only through grace. The ceremonial, however, had a further and higher significance, as is shown by the apostle (see as above). **9. Then went up Moses, and Aaron**—in obedience to a command given (vss. 1, 2; also ch. 19:24), previous to the religious engagement of the people, now described. **Nadab, and Abihu**—the two oldest sons of Aaron. **seventy of the elders**—a select number; what was the principle of selection is not said; but they were the chief representatives, the most conspicuous for official rank and station, as well as for their probity and weight of character in their respective tribes. **10. they saw the God of Israel**—That there was no visible form or representation of the divine nature, we have expressly intimated (Deut. 4:15). But a symbol or emblem of His glory was distinctly, and at a distance, displayed before those chosen witnesses. Many think, however, that in this private scene was discovered, amid the luminous blaze, the faint adumbrated form of the humanity of Christ (Ezek. 1:26; cf. Gal. 3:24). **sapphire**—one of the most valuable and lustrous of the precious gems—of a sky-blue or light azure color and frequently chosen to describe the throne of God (see Ezek. 1: 26; 10:1).

11. upon the nobles of the children of Israel he laid not his hand—The "nobles," i.e., the

ADAM CLARKE

and the various laws and ordinances mentioned from the beginning of the twentieth to the end of the twenty-third chapter.

4. *Moses wrote all the words of the Lord.* After the people had promised obedience (v. 3) and so entered into the bonds of the covenant, "it was necessary," says Calmet, "to draw up an act by which the memory of these transactions might be preserved, and confirm the covenant by authentic and solemn ceremonies." And this Moses does. (1) As legislator, he reduces to writing all the articles and conditions of the agreement, with the people's act of consent. (2) As their mediator and the deputy of the Lord, he accepts on his part the resolution of the people; and Jehovah on His part engages himself to Israel, to be their God, their King, and Protector, and to fulfil to them all the promises He had made to their fathers. (3) To make this the more solemn and affecting, and to ratify the covenant, which could not be done without sacrifice, shedding and sprinkling of blood, Moses builds an altar and erects twelve pillars, no doubt of unhewn stone, and probably set round about the altar. The altar itself represented the throne of God; the twelve stones, the twelve tribes of Israel. These were the two parties who were to contract, or enter into covenant, on this occasion.

5. *He sent young men.* Stout, able, reputable young men, chosen out of the different tribes, for the purpose of killing, flaying, and offering the oxen mentioned here. *Burnt offerings.* They generally consisted of sheep and goats, Lev. i. 10. These were wholly consumed by fire. *Peace offerings.* Bullocks or goats; see Heb. ix. 19. The blood of these was poured out before the Lord, and then the priests and people might feast on the flesh.

7. *The book of the covenant.* The writing containing the laws mentioned in the three preceding chapters. As this writing contained the agreement made between God and them, it was called *the book of the covenant;* but as no covenant was considered to be ratified and binding till a sacrifice had been offered on the occasion, hence the necessity of the sacrifices mentioned here. Half of the blood being sprinkled on the altar, and half of it sprinkled on the people, showed that both God and they were mutually bound by this covenant. God was bound to the people to support, defend, and save them; the people were bound to God to fear, love, and serve Him.

10. *They saw the God of Israel.* The seventy elders, who were representatives of the whole congregation, were chosen to witness the manifestation of God, that they might be satisfied of the truth of the revelation which He had made of himself and of His will; and on this occasion it was necessary that the people also should be favored with a sight of the glory of God; see chap. xx. 18. Thus the certainty of the revelation was established by many witnesses, and by those especially of the most competent kind. *A paved work of a sapphire stone.* Or "sapphire brickwork." I suppose that something of the mosaic pavement is here intended: floors inlaid with variously colored stones or small square tiles, disposed in a great variety of ornamental forms. *Sapphire* is a precious stone of a fine blue color, next in hardness to the diamond. The ruby is considered by most mineralogists of the same genus; so is also the topaz. Hence we cannot say that the sapphire is only of a blue color; it is blue, red, or yellow, as it **may be called sapphire, ruby, or topaz; and some of them are blue or green, according to the light in which they are held; and some white. The ancient oriental sapphire is supposed to have been the same with the *lapis lazuli.* Supposing that these different kinds of sapphires are here intended, how glorious must a pavement be, constituted of polished stones of this sort, perfectly transparent, with an effulgence of heavenly splendor poured out upon them! There is a similar description of the glory of the Lord in the Book of Revelation, chap. iv. 3: "And he that sat [upon the throne] was to look upon like a jasper and a sardine stone: and there was a rainbow round about the throne, in sight like unto an emerald."**

11. *Upon the nobles of . . . Israel he laid not his hand.* This laying on of the hand has been

MATTHEW HENRY

men, the dazzling splendour of his glory was so moderated that they were able to bear it.

3. *They saw God, and did eat and drink.* They had not only their lives preserved, but their vigour, courage, and comfort; it cast no damp upon their joy, but rather increased and elevated it.

Verses 12–18

The public ceremony of sealing the covenant being over, Moses is called up to receive further instructions.

I. He is called up into the mount, and there he remains six days at some distance. "Come up, and *I will give thee a law, that thou mayest teach them.*"

Having received these orders, 1. He appointed Aaron and Hur to be as lords-justices in his absence, to keep the peace and good order in the congregation, *v.* 14. 2. He took Joshua up with him into the mount, *v.* 13. Joshua was his minister, and it would be a satisfaction to him to have him with him as a companion, during the six days that he tarried in the mount, before God called to him. Joshua was to be his successor, and therefore thus he was honoured before the people, above the rest of the elders, that they might afterwards the more readily take him for their governor; and thus he was prepared for service, by being trained up in communion with God. 3. A cloud covered the mount six days, a visible token of God's special presence there. During these six days Moses stayed waiting upon the mountain for a call into the presence-chamber, *v.* 15, 16.

II. He is called up into a cloud on the seventh day, probably on the sabbath day, *v.* 16. Now, 1. The thick cloud opened in the sight of all Israel, and the glory of the Lord broke forth *like devouring fire, v.* 17.

2. The entrance of Moses into the cloud was very wonderful: *Moses went into the midst of the cloud, v.* 18, sure that he who called him would protect him. 3. His continuance in the cloud was no less wonderful; he was there *forty days and forty nights.* When Moses was called *into the midst of the cloud* he left Joshua without, who continued to eat and drink daily while he waited for Moses's return, but thenceforward Moses fasted.

JAMIESON, FAUSSET, BROWN

elders, after the sprinkling of the blood, were not inspired with terror in presence of the calm, benign, radiant symbol of the divine majesty; so different from the terrific exhibitions at the giving of the law. The report of so many competent witnesses would tend to confirm the people's faith in the divine mission of Moses. **eat and drink**—feasted on the peace offering—on the remnants of the late sacrifices and libations. This feast had a prophetic bearing, intimating God's dwelling with men.

12. I will give thee tables of stone—The ten commandments, which had already been spoken, were to be given in a permanent form. Inscribed on stone, for greater durability, by the hand of God Himself, they were thus authenticated and honored above the judicial or ceremonial parts of the law. **13. Moses went up into the mount of God**—He was called to receive the divine transcript. Joshua was taken a little higher, and it would be a great comfort for the leader to have his company during the six days he was in patient waiting for the call on the seventh or sabbath-day.

14. he said unto the elders, Tarry ye here for us—There is a circular valley or hollow a good way up on the brow of Jebel Musa, which was their halting-place, while he alone was privileged to ascend the highest peak. The people stood below, as in the "outer court," the elders in the "holy place," Moses, as a type of Christ, in "the holy of holies."

18. Moses went into the midst of the cloud—the visible token of God's presence. Divine grace animated and supported him to enter with holy boldness. **Moses was in the mount forty days and forty nights**—The six days spent in waiting are not included. During that protracted period he was miraculously supported (Deut. 9:9), on a peak scarcely thirty paces in compass.

ADAM CLARKE

variously explained. (1) He did not conceal himself from the nobles of Israel by covering them with His hand, as He did Moses, chap. xxxiii. 22. (2) He did not endue any of the nobles, i.e., the seventy elders, with the gift of prophecy; for so laying on of the hand has been understood. (3) He did not slay any of them; none of them received any injury; which is certainly one meaning of the phrase: see Neh. xiii. 21; Ps. lv. 20. *Also they saw God,* i.e., although they had this discovery of His majesty, yet they did eat and drink, i.e., were preserved alive and unhurt. Perhaps the eating and drinking here may refer to the peace offerings on which they feasted, and the libations that were then offered on the ratification of the covenant.

12. *Come up to me into the mount, and be there.* We may suppose Moses to have been, with Aaron, Nadab, Abihu, and the seventy elders, about midway up the mount.

13. *Moses rose up.* In verse 16 it is said that "the glory of the Lord abode upon mount Sinai, and the cloud covered it." The glory was probably above the cloud, and it was to the cloud that Moses and his servant Joshua ascended at this time, leaving Aaron and the elders below. After they had been in this region, namely, where the cloud encompassed the mountain, for six days, God appears to have called Moses up higher; compare the sixteenth and eighteenth verses. Moses then ascended to the glory, leaving Joshua in the cloud, with whom he had, no doubt, frequent conferences during the forty days he continued with God on the mount.

14. *Tarry ye here for us.* Probably Moses did not know that he was to continue so long on the mount, nor is it likely that the elders tarried the whole forty days where they were. They doubtless, after waiting some considerable time, returned to the camp; and their return is supposed to have been the grand cause why the Israelites made the golden calf, as they probably reported that Moses was lost. *Aaron and Hur are with you.* Not knowing how long he might be detained on the mount, and knowing that many cases might occur which would require the interference of the chief magistrate, Moses constituted them regents of the people during the time he should be absent.

16. *And the seventh day he called.* It is very likely that Moses went up into the mount on the first day of the week; and having with Joshua remained in the region of the cloud during six days, on the seventh, which was the Sabbath, God spake to him, and delivered successively to him, during forty days and forty nights, the different statutes and ordinances which are afterwards mentioned.

17. *The glory of the Lord was like devouring fire.* This appearance was well calculated to inspire the people with the deepest reverence and godly fear; and this is the use the apostle makes of it, Heb. xii. 28-29, where he evidently refers to this place. Seeing the glory of the Lord upon the mount like a devouring fire, Moses having tarried long, the Israelites probably supposed that he had been devoured or consumed by it, and therefore the more easily fell into idolatry. But how could they do this, with this tremendous sight of God's glory before their eyes?

18. *Forty days and forty nights.* During the whole of this time he neither ate bread nor drank water; see chap. xxxiv. 28; Deut. ix. 9. Both his body and soul were so sustained by the invigorating presence of God that he needed no earthly support, and this may be the simple reason why he took none. Elijah fasted forty days and forty nights, sustained by the same influence, 1 Kings xix. 8; as did likewise our blessed Lord, when He was about to commence the public ministry of His own gospel, Matt. iv. 2.

MATTHEW HENRY — CHAPTER 25

Verses 1–9

We may suppose that when Moses went into the midst of the cloud, and abode there so long, he saw and heard very glorious things relating to the upper world, but there were things which it was not lawful nor possible to utter.

In these verses God tells Moses his intention in

JAMIESON, FAUSSET, BROWN — CHAPTER 25

Vss. 1-40. CONCERNING AN OFFERING. **1. the Lord spake unto Moses,** etc.—The business that chiefly occupied Moses on the mount, whatever other disclosures were made to him there, was in receiving directions about the tabernacle, and they are here recorded as given to him. **2. bring me an offering: of every man that giveth it willingly,** etc.—

ADAM CLARKE — CHAPTER 25

2. *That they bring me an offering.* The offering here mentioned is the *terumah,* a kind of freewill offering, consisting of anything that was necessary for the occasion. It signifies properly anything that was "lifted up," the heave offering, because in presenting it to God it was lifted up to be laid on His altar; but see on chap. xxix. 26.

MATTHEW HENRY

general, that the children of Israel should build him a sanctuary, for he designed to *dwell among them* (v. 8). God had chosen the people of Israel. As their King, he had already given them laws for the government of themselves, and their dealings one with another, with some general rules for religious worship.

I. He orders a royal palace to be set up among them for himself, here called *a sanctuary*, or *holy place*, or *habitation*, of which it is said (Jer. xvii. 12), *A glorious high throne from the beginning is the place of our sanctuary.* This sanctuary is to be considered,

1. As ceremonial, consonant to the other institutions of that dispensation, which consisted in carnal ordinances (Heb. ix. 10); hence it is called a *worldly sanctuary*, Heb. ix. 1. (1) There he manifested his presence among them, a sign or token of his presence, that, while they had that in the midst of them, they might never again ask, *Is the Lord among us or not?* And, because in the wilderness they dwelt in tents, even this royal palace was ordered to be a tabernacle too, that it might move with them. (2) There he ordered his subjects to attend him with their homage and tribute. Thither they must bring their sacrifices, and there all Israel must meet, to pay their joint respects to the God of Israel.

2. As typical; the holy places made with hands were the *figures of the true*, Heb. ix. 24. The body of Christ, in and by which he made atonement, was the *greater and more perfect tabernacle*, Heb. ix. 11. The *Word was made flesh, and dwelt among us*, as in a tabernacle.

II. When Moses was to erect this palace, it was requisite that he should first be instructed where he must have the materials, and where he must have the model.

1. The people must furnish him with the materials, not by a tax imposed upon them, but by a voluntary contribution.

(1) *Speak unto the children of Israel that they bring me an offering.* Since we live upon him, we must live to him.

(2) This offering must be given willingly, and with the heart. We should ask, not only, "What must we do?" but, "What may we do for God?"

(3) The particulars are here mentioned which they must offer (*v.* 3–7), all of them things that there would be occasion for in the tabernacle. Some observe that here was gold, silver, and brass, provided, but no iron; that is the military metal, and this was to be a house of peace.

JAMIESON, FAUSSET, BROWN

Having declared allegiance to God as their sovereign, they were expected to contribute to His state, as other subjects to their kings; and the "offering" required of them was not to be imposed as a tax, but to come from their own loyal and liberal feelings. **3. this is the offering which ye shall take of them**—the articles of which the offerings should consist. **brass**—rather copper, brass being a composite metal.

4. goats' hair—or leather of goats' skin.

5. badgers' skins—The badger was an unclean animal, and is not a native of the East—rather some kind of fish, of the leather of which sandals are made in the East.

shittim wood—or *Shittah* (Isa. 41:19), the acacia, a shrub which grows plentifully in the deserts of Arabia, yielding a light, strong, and beautiful wood, in long planks.

7. ephod—a square cloak, hanging down from the shoulders, and worn by priests.

ADAM CLARKE

3. *This is the offering.* There were three kinds of metals: (1) *Gold, zahab,* which may properly signify "wrought gold"; what was bright and resplendent, as the word implies. (2) *Silver, keseph,* from *casaph,* to be "pale, wan, or white"; so called from its well-known color. (3) *Brass, nechosheth,* "copper"; unless we suppose that the factitious metal commonly called brass is intended; this is formed by a combination of the oxide or ore of zink with copper. Brass seems to have been very anciently in use, as we find it mentioned in Gen. iv. 22. Because brass was capable of so fine a polish as to become exceedingly bright and keep its luster a considerable time, hence it was used for all weapons of war and defensive armor among ancient nations; and copper seems to have been in no repute but for its use in making *brass*.

4. *Blue. Techeleth,* generally supposed to mean an "azure or sky color." *Purple. Argaman,* a very precious color, extracted from the *murex,* a species of shellfish, from which it is supposed the famous Tyrian purple came, so costly, and so much celebrated in antiquity. *Scarlet. Tolaath,* signifies a "worm," of which this coloring matter was made. *Fine linen. Shesh;* whether this means linen, cotton, or silk is not agreed on among interpreters. Because *shesh* signifies "six," the rabbins suppose that it always signifies the fine linen of Egypt, in which six folds constituted one thread. *Goats' hair. Izzim,* "goats," but used here elliptically for goats' hair. In different parts of Asia Minor, Syria, Cilicia, and Phyrgia, the goats have long, fine, and beautiful hair, in some cases almost as fine as silk, which they shear at proper times, and manufacture into garments.

5. *Rams' skins dyed red.* Literally, "the skins of red rams." It is a fact attested by many respectable travellers that in the Levant sheep are often to be met with that have red or violet-colored fleeces. And almost all ancient writers speak of the same thing. *Badgers' skins. Oroth techashim.* Few terms have afforded greater perplexity to critics and commentators than this. Bochart has exhausted the subject, and seems to have proved that no kind of animal is here intended, but a color. None of the ancient versions acknowledge an animal of any kind except the Chaldee, which seems to think the badger is intended, and from it we have borrowed our translation of the word. The Septuagint and Vulgate have skins dyed a violet color; the Syriac, azure; the Arabic, black; the Coptic, violet; the modern Persic, ram-skins. The color contended for by Bochart is a very deep blue. *Shittim wood.* By some supposed to be the finest species of the cedar; by others, the *acacia Nilotica,* a species of thorn, solid, light, and very beautiful. This acacia is known to have been plentiful in Egypt, and it abounds in Arabia Deserta, the very place in which Moses was when he built the Tabernacle; and hence it is reasonable to suppose that he built it of that wood, which was every way proper for his purpose.

6. *Oil for the light.* This they must have brought with them from Egypt, for they could not get any in the wilderness, where there were no olives; but it is likely that this and some other directions refer more to what was to be done when in their fixed and settled residence than while wandering in the wilderness. *Spices,* to make a confection *for sweet incense,* abounded in different parts of these countries.

7. *Onyx stones.* We have already met with the stone called *shoham,* Gen. ii. 12, and acknowledged the difficulty of ascertaining what is meant by it. Some think the onyx, some the sardine, and some the emerald, is meant. *Stones to be set in the ephod.* "Stones of filling up." Stones so cut as to be proper to be set in the gold work of the breastplate. *The ephod.* It is very difficult to tell what this was or in what form it was made. It was a garment of some kind peculiar to the priests, and ever considered essential to all the parts of divine worship for without it no person attempted to inquire of God. As the word itself comes from the root *aphad,* "he tied or bound close," Calmet supposes that it was a kind of girdle, which, brought from behind the neck and over the shoulders, and so hanging down before, was put cross upon the stomach, and then carried round the waist, and

MATTHEW HENRY

KEIL–DELITZSCH:

To give a definite external form to the covenant concluded with His people, and construct a visible bond of fellowship in which He might manifest himself to the people and they might draw near to Him as their God, Jehovah told Moses that the Israelites were to erect Him a sanctuary, that He might dwell in the midst of them (25:8). The construction and arrangement of this sanctuary were determined in all respects by God himself, who showed to Moses, when upon the mountain, a pattern of the dwelling and its furniture, and prescribed with great minuteness both the form and materials of all the different parts of the sanctuary and all the things required for the sacred service. If the sanctuary was to answer its purpose, the erection of it could not be left to the inventive faculty of any man whatever, but must proceed from Him, who was there to manifest himself to the nation, as the Holy One, in righteousness and grace. The people could only carry out what God appointed, and could only fulfill their covenant duty, by the readiness with which they supplied the materials required for the erection of the sanctuary and completed the work with their own hands.

—*Commentary on the Old Testament*

2. God himself would furnish him with the model: *According to all that I show thee, v.* 9.

Verses 10–22

The first thing which is here ordered to be made is the ark with its appurtenances, the furniture of the most holy place, and the special token of God's presence, for which the tabernacle was erected to be the receptacle.

I. The ark itself was a chest, or coffer, in which the two tables of the law were to be honourably deposited, and carefully kept. If the Jewish cubit was, as some learned men compute, three inches longer than our half-yard (twenty-one inches in all), this chest or cabinet was about fifty-two inches long, thirty-one broad, and thirty-one deep. It was overlaid within and without with thin plates of gold. It had a crown, or cornice, of gold, round it, with rings and staves to carry it with; and in it he must put the testimony, *v.* 10–16.

The tables of the law are called the *testimony* because God did in them testify his will. The gospel of Christ is also called a testimony or witness, Matt. xxiv. 14. It is observable, 1. That the tables of the law were carefully preserved in the ark for the purpose, to teach us to make much of the word of God, and to hide it in our hearts, in our innermost thoughts, as the ark was placed in the holy of holies. 2. That this ark was the chief token of God's presence, which teaches us that the first and great evidence and assurance of God's favour is the putting of his law in the heart. God dwells where that rules, Heb. viii. 10. 3. That provision was made for the carrying of this ark about with them in all their removals, which intimates to us that, wherever we go, we should take our religion along with us, always bearing about with us the love of the Lord Jesus, and his law.

II. The mercy-seat was the covering of the ark

JAMIESON, FAUSSET, BROWN

a sanctuary; that I may dwell among them—In one sense the tabernacle was to be a palace, the royal residence of the King of Israel, in which He was to dwell among His people, receive their petitions, and issue His responses. But it was also to be a place of worship, in which God was to record His name and to enshrine the mystic symbols of His presence.

According to all that I show thee, after the pattern of the tabernacle—The proposed erection could be, in the circumstances of the Israelites, not of a fixed and stable but of a temporary and movable description, capable of being carried about with them in their various sojournings. It was made after "the pattern" shown to Moses, by which is now generally understood, not that it was an unheard-of novelty, or an entirely original structure, for it is ascertained to have borne resemblance in form and arrangements to the style of an Egyptian temple, but that it was so altered, modified, and purified from all idolatrous associations, as to be appropriated to right objects, and suggestive of ideas connected with the true God and His worship. **10. an ark**—a coffer or chest, overlaid with gold, the dimensions of which, taking the cubit at eighteen inches, are computed to be three feet nine inches in length, two feet three inches in breadth. **11. a crown**—a rim or cornice. **12. rings**—staples for the poles, with which it was to be carried from place to place.

15. staves shall be in the rings of the ark—i.e., always remain in the rings, whether the ark be at rest or in motion.

16. the testimony—that is, the two tables of stone, containing the ten commandments, and called "the testimony," because by it God did testify His sovereign authority over Israel as His people, His selection of them as the guardians of His will and worship, and His displeasure in the event of their transgressing His laws; while on their part, by receiving and depositing this law in its appointed place, they testified their acknowledgment of God's right to rule over them, and their submission to the authority of His law. The superb and elaborate style of the ark that contained "the testimony" was emblematic of the great treasure it held; in other words, the incomparable value and excellence of the Word of God, while its being placed in this chest further showed the great care which God has ever taken for preserving it. **17. thou shalt make a mercy seat of pure gold**—to serve as a lid, covering

ADAM CLARKE

thus made a girdle to the tunic. Where the ephod crossed on the breast there was a square ornament called *choshen,* the *breastplate,* in which twelve precious stones were set, each bearing one of the names of the twelve sons of Jacob engraven on it. There were two sorts of ephods, one of plain linen for the priests, the other very much embroidered for the high priest. As there was nothing singular in this common sort, no particular description is given; but that of the high priest is described very much in detail, chap. xxviii. 6-8. It was distinguished from the common ephod by being composed of gold, blue, purple, scarlet, fine twisted linen, and cunning work, i.e., superbly ornamented and embroidered. This ephod was fastened on the shoulders with two precious stones, on which the names of the twelve tribes of Israel were engraved, six names on each stone.

8. *Let them make me a sanctuary. Mikdash,* a "holy place," such as God might dwell in; this was that part of the Tabernacle that was called the most holy place, into which the high priest entered only once a year, on the great Day of Atonement. *That I may dwell among them.* As the dwelling in this Tabernacle was the highest proof of God's grace and mercy towards the Israelites, so it typified Christ's dwelling by faith in the hearts of believers, and thus giving them the highest and surest proof of their reconciliation to God, and of His love and favor to them; see Eph. i. 22; iii. 17.

9. *After the pattern of the tabernacle.* It has been supposed that there had been a tabernacle before that erected by Moses, though it probably did not now exist; but the Tabernacle which Moses is ordered to make was to be formed exactly on the model of this ancient one, the pattern of which God showed him in the mount, v. 40. The word *mishcan* signifies literally the "dwelling" or "habitation"; and this was so called because it was the dwelling place of God.

10. *They shall make an ark. Aron* signifies an ark, chest, coffer, or coffin. It is used particularly to designate that chest or coffer in which the testimony or two tables of the covenant was laid up, on the top of which was the propitiatory or mercy seat (see on v. 17) and at the end of which were the cherubim of gold (vv. 18-20), between whom the visible sign of the presence of the supreme God appeared as seated upon His throne. The ark was the most excellent of all the holy things which belonged to the Mosaic economy, and for its sake the Tabernacle and the Temple were built, chap. xxvi. 33; xl. 18, 21. It was considered as conferring a sanctity wherever it was fixed, 2 Chron. viii. 11; 2 Sam. vi. 12.

15. *The staves . . . shall not be taken from it.* Because it should ever be considered as in readiness to be removed, God not having told them at what hour He should command them to strike their tents. If the staves were never to be taken out, how can it be said, as in Num. iv. 6, that when the camp should set forward, they should "put in the staves thereof," which intimates that when they encamped they took out the staves, which appears to be contrary to what is here said? To reconcile these two places, it has been supposed, with great show of probability, that besides the staves which passed through the rings of the ark, and by which it was carried, there were two other staves or poles in the form of a bier or hand-barrow, on which the ark was laid in order to be transported in their journeyings, when it and its own staves, still in their rings, had been wrapped up in the covering of what is called badgers' skins and blue cloth. The staves of the ark itself, which might be considered as its handles simply to lift it by, were never taken out of their rings; but the staves or poles which served as a bier were taken from under it when they encamped.

16. *The testimony.* The two tables of stone which were not yet given; these tables were called *eduth,* from "forward, onward, to bear witness to or of a person or thing." Not only the tables of stone, but all the contents of the ark, Aaron's rod, the pot of manna, the holy anointing oil, bore testimony to the Messiah in His prophetic, sacerdotal, and regal offices.

17. *A mercy seat. Capporeth,* from *caphar,* to "cover or overspread"; because by an act of

MATTHEW HENRY

or chest, made of solid gold, exactly to fit the dimensions of the ark, *v.* 17, 21.

JAMIESON, FAUSSET, BROWN

it exactly. It was "the propitiatory cover," as the term may be rendered, denoting that Christ, our great propitiation, has fully answered all the demands of the law, covers our transgressions, and comes between us and the curse of a violated law.

ADAM CLARKE

pardon sins are represented as being covered, so that they no longer appear in the eye of divine justice to displease and call for punishment; and the person of the offender is covered or protected from the stroke of the broken law. In the Greek version of the Septuagint the word *hilasterion* is used, which signifies a "propitiatory," and is the name used by the apostle, Heb. ix. 5. This mercy seat or propitiatory was made of pure gold; it was properly the lid or covering of that vessel so well known by the name of the "ark" and "ark of the covenant." On and before this, the high priest was to sprinkle the blood of the expiatory sacrifices on the great Day of Atonement: and it was in this place that God promised to meet the people (see v. 22), for there He dwelt, and there was the symbol of the Divine Presence. At each end of this propitiatory was a cherub, between whom this glory was manifested; hence in Scripture it is so often said that "he dwelleth between the cherubim," as the word "propitiatory" or "mercy seat," is applied to Christ, Rom. iii. 25, "whom God hath set forth to be a propitiation through faith in his blood . . . for the remission of sins that are past," hence we learn that Christ was the true Mercy Seat, the thing signified by the *capporeth*, to the ancient believers. And we learn further that it was by His blood that an atonement was to be made for the sins of the world. And as God showed himself between the cherubim over this propitiatory or mercy seat, so it is said, "God was in Christ, reconciling the world unto himself," 2 Cor. v. 19; etc. See on Leviticus vii.

TODAY'S DICTIONARY OF THE BIBLE:

Mercy Seat (Heb. *kappōreth*, a "covering"; LXX and N.T., *hilasterion*; Vulg., *propitiatorium*), the covering or lid of the ark of *covenant*. It was of acacia wood, overlaid with gold, or perhaps rather a plate of solid gold, 2½ cubits long and 1' broad (Ex. 25:17; 30:6; 31:7). It is compared to the throne of grace (Heb. 9:5; Eph. 2:6). The Holy of Holies is called the "place of the mercy seat" (1 Chron. 28:11; Lev. 16:2).

It has been conjectured that the censer (*thumiatērion*, meaning "anything having regard to or employed in the burning of incense") mentioned in Heb. 9:4 was the "mercy seat," at which the incense was burned by the high priest on the great day of atonement, and upon or toward which the blood of the goat was sprinkled (Lev. 16:11–16; comp. Ex. 25:22 and Num. 7:89).

III. The cherubim of gold were fixed to the mercy-seat, and of a piece with it, and spread their wings over it, *v.* 18. It is supposed that these cherubim were designed to represent the holy angels, who always attended the *shechinah*, or divine Majesty, not by any effigies of an angel, but some emblem of the angelical nature, probably some one of those four faces spoken of, Ezek. i. 10. Whatever the faces were, they looked one towards another, and both downward towards the ark, while their wings were stretched out so as to touch one another. The apostle calls them *cherubim of glory shadowing the mercy-seat*, Heb. ix. 5. God is said to dwell *between the cherubim*, on the mercy-seat (Ps. lxxx. 1), and thence he here promises, for the future, to meet with Moses, and to *commune with him*, *v.* 22. In allusion to this mercy-seat, we are said to come boldly to *the throne of grace* (Heb. iv. 16); for we *are not under the law*, which is covered, *but under grace*, which is displayed; its wings are stretched out, and we are invited to come under the shadow of them, Ruth ii. 12.

Verses 23–30

Here is, 1. A table ordered to be made of wood overlaid with gold, which was to stand, not in the holy of holies (nothing was in that but the ark with its appurtenances), but in the outer part of the tabernacle, called the *sanctuary*, or *holy place*, Heb. ix. 2, 23, &c. There must also be the usual furniture of the sideboard, dishes and spoons, &c., and all *of gold*, *v.* 29. 2. This table was to be always spread, and furnished with the show-bread (*v.* 30) or *bread of faces*, twelve loaves, one for each tribe, set in two rows, six in a row; see the law concerning them, Lev. xxiv. 6, &c. In the royal palace it was fit that there should be a royal table. Some make the twelve loaves to represent the twelve tribes. As the ark signified God's being present with them, so the twelve loaves signified their being presented to God. This bread was designed to be, (1) A thankful acknowledgment of God's goodness to them, in giving them their daily bread, manna in the wilderness, where he prepared a table for them, and, in Canaan, the corn of the land. Christ has taught us to pray every day for the bread of the day. (2) A token of their communion with God. This bread on God's table being made of the same corn with the bread on their own tables, God and Israel did, as it were, eat together, as a pledge of friendship and fellowship; he supped with them, and they with him. (3) A type of the spiritual provision which is made in the church, by the gospel of Christ, for all that are made priests to our God. *In our Father's house there is bread enough and to spare*, a loaf for every tribe.

Verses 31–40

I. The next thing ordered to be made for the furnishing of God's palace was a rich stately candlestick, all of pure gold. The particular directions here given concerning it show, 1. That it was a great

18. two cherubim—The real meaning of these figures, as well as the shape or form of them, is not known with certainty— probably similar to what was afterwards introduced into the temple, and described in Ezekiel 10. They stretched out their wings, and their faces were turned towards the mercy seat, probably in a bowing attitude. The prevailing opinion now is, that those splendid figures were symbolical not of angelic but of earthly and human beings—the members of the Church of God interested in the dispensation of grace, the redeemed in every age—and that these hieroglyphic forms symbolized the qualities of the true people of God—courage, patience, intelligence, and activity. **22. there I will meet with thee, and I will commune with thee from above the mercy seat**—The Shekinah, or symbol of the Divine Presence, rested on the mercy seat, and was indicated by a cloud, from the midst of which responses were audibly given when God was consulted on behalf of His people. Hence God is described as "dwelling" or "sitting" between the cherubim. **23. table of shittim wood**—of the same material and decorations as the ark, and like it, too, furnished with rings for the poles on which it was carried. The staves, however, were taken out of it when stationary, in order not to encumber the priests while engaged in their services at the table. It was half a cubit less than the ark in length and breadth, but of the same height. **24. crown**—the moulding or ornamental rim, which is thought to have been raised above the level of the table, to prevent anything from falling off. **29. dishes**—broad platters. **spoons**—cups or concave vessels, used for holding incense. **covers**—both for bread and incense. **bowls**—cups; for though no mention is made of wine, libations were undoubtedly made to God, according to JOSEPHUS and the rabbins, once a week, when the bread was changed. **to cover withal**—rather to pour out withal.

30. showbread lit., *presence bread*, so called because it was constantly exhibited before the Lord, or because the bread of His presence, like the angel of His presence, pointed symbolically to Christ. It consisted of twelve unleavened loaves, said traditionally to have been laid in piles of six each. This bread was designed to be a symbol of the full and never-failing provision which is made in the Church for the spiritual sustenance and refreshment of God's people.

31. candlestick—lit., a lamp-bearer. It was so constructed as to be capable of being taken to pieces for facility in removal. The shaft or stock rested on a pedestal. It had seven branches, shaped like reeds or canes—three on each side, with one in the center—and worked out into knobs, flowers, and bowls, placed alternately. The figure

18. *Thou shalt make two cherubims.* What these were we cannot distinctly say. It is probable that the term often means a figure of any kind, such as was ordinarily sculptured on stone, engraved on metal, carved on wood, or embroidered on cloth. It may be only necessary to add that "cherub" is the singular number; "cherubim," not *cherubims*, the plural.

22. *And there I will meet with thee.* That is, over the mercy seat, between the cherubim. In this place God chose to give the most especial manifestations of himself; here the divine glory was to be seen; and here Moses was to come in order to consult Jehovah relative to the management of the people.

23. *Thou shalt also make a table of shittim wood.* The same wood, the *acacia*, of which the ark staves were made.

29. *The dishes thereof. Kearothaiv,* probably the deep bowls in which they kneaded the mass out of which they made the shewbread. *And spoons thereof. Cappothaiv,* probably "censers," on which they put up the incense; as seems pretty evident from Num. vii. 14, 20, 26, 32, 38, 44, 50, 56, 62, 68, 74, 80, 86, where the same word is used, and the instrument, whatever it was, is always represented as being filled with incense. *Covers thereof. Kesothaiv,* supposed to be a large cup in which pure wine was kept on the table along with the shewbread for libations, which were poured out before the Lord every Sabbath, when the old bread was removed, and the new bread laid on the table. *Bowls thereof. Menakkiyothaiv,* from *nakah,* to "clear away, remove, empty"; supposed by Calmet to mean either the sieves by which the Levites cleansed the wheat they made into bread or the ovens in which the bread was baked.

30. *Shewbread. Lechem panim,* literally "bread of faces." The Hebrew text seems to intimate that they were called the "bread of faces" because, as the Lord says, they were set *lephanai,* "before My face." These loaves or cakes were twelve, representing, as is generally supposed, the twelve tribes of Israel. They were in two rows of six each. On the top of each row there was a golden dish with frankincense, which was burned before the Lord as a memorial at the end of the week, when the old loaves were removed and replaced by new ones, the priests taking the former for their domestic use.

31. *A candlestick of pure gold.* This *candlestick* or "chandelier" is generally described as having one shaft or stock, with six branches proceeding from it, adorned at equal distances with six flowers like lilies, with as many bowls and knops placed alternately. On each of the branches there was a lamp, and one on the top

MATTHEW HENRY

ornament; it had many branches drawn from the main shaft, which had not only their bowls (to put the oil and the kindled wick in) for necessity, but knops and flowers for ornament. 2. That it was very convenient, and admirably contrived both to scatter the light and to keep the tabernacle clean from smoke and snuffs. 3. That it was very significant. The tabernacle had no windows by which to let in the light of the day, all its light was candle-light. Yet God left not himself without witness, nor them without instruction; the commandment was a lamp, and the law a light, and the prophets were branches from that lamp, which gave light in their several ages to the Old Testament church. The church is still dark, as the tabernacle was, in comparison with what it will be in heaven; but the word of God is the candlestick, *a light shining in a dark place* (2 Pet. i. 19), and a dark place indeed the world would be without it. The Spirit of God, in his various gifts and graces, is compared to the *seven lamps* which *burn before the throne*, Rev. iv. 5. The churches are golden candlesticks, the lights of the world, *holding forth the word of life* as the candlestick does the light, Phil. ii. 15, 16. Ministers are to light the lamps, and snuff them (*v.* 37), by opening the scriptures.

II. There is in the midst of these instructions an express caution given to Moses, to take heed of varying from his model: *Make them after the pattern shown thee*, *v.* 40.

JAMIESON, FAUSSET, BROWN

represented on the arch of Titus gives the best idea of this candlestick. **33. knops**—old spelling for knobs—bosses. **37. they shall light the lamps . . . that they may give light**—The light was derived from pure olive oil, and probably kept continually burning (cf. ch. 30:7; Lev. 24:2). **38. tongs**—snuffers.

39. a talent of pure gold—in weight equivalent to 125 lbs. troy.

40. look that thou make them after their pattern—This caution, which is repeated with no small frequency in other parts of the narrative, is an evidence of the deep interest taken by the Divine King in the erection of His palace or sanctuary; and it is impossible to account for the circumstance of God's condescending to such minute details, except on the assumption that this tabernacle was to be of a typical character, and eminently subservient to the religious instruction and benefit of mankind, by shadowing forth in its leading features the grand truths of the Christian Church.

ADAM CLARKE

of the shaft which occupied the center; thus there were seven lamps in all, v. 37. These seven lamps were lighted every evening and extinguished every morning. We are not so certain of the precise form of any instrument or utensil of the Tabernacle or Temple as we are of this, the golden table, and the two silver trumpets.

Titus, after the overthrow of Jerusalem, A.D. 70, had the golden candlestick and the golden table of the shewbread, the silver trumpets, and the book of the law, taken out of the Temple and carried in triumph to Rome; and Vespasian lodged them in the temple which he had consecrated to the goddess of Peace. At the foot of Mount Palatine there are the ruins of an arch on which the triumph of Titus for his conquest of the Jews is represented, and on which the several monuments which were carried in the procession are sculptured, and particularly the golden candlestick, the table of the shewbread, and the two silver trumpets.

39. *Of a talent of pure gold shall he make it, with all these vessels*. That is, a talent of gold in weight was used in making the candlestick, and the different vessels and instruments which belonged to it. According to Bishop Cumberland, a talent was 3,000 shekels. A total of 7,013 pounds was expended on the candlestick and its furniture. It is no wonder that Titus should think it of sufficient consequence to be one of the articles, with the golden table and silver trumpets, that should be employed to grace his triumph.

40. *And look that thou make*. This verse should be understood as an order to Moses after the Tabernacle had been described to him; as if he had said: "When thou comest to make all the things that I have already described to thee, with the other matters of which I shall afterwards treat, see that thou make everything according to the pattern which thou didst see in the mount."

MATTHEW HENRY — CHAPTER 26

Verses 1–6

I. The house must be a *tabernacle* or *tent*. God manifested his presence among them thus in a tabernacle, 1. In compliance with their present condition in the wilderness, that they might have him with them wherever they went. 2. That it might represent the state of God's church in this world, it is a *tabernacle-state*, Ps. xv. 1. *We have here no continuing city*; being strangers in this world, and travellers towards a better, we shall never be fixed till we come to heaven.

II. The curtains of the tabernacle must correspond to a divine pattern. 1. They were to be very rich, the best of the kind, *fine twined linen*; and colours very pleasing, *blue*, and *purple*, and *scarlet*. 2. They were to be embroidered with cherubim (*v.* 1), to intimate that the angels of God pitch their tents round about the church, Ps. xxxiv. 7. 3. There were to be two hangings, five breadths in each, sewed together, and the two hangings coupled together with golden clasps, or tacks, so that it might be all one tabernacle, *v.* 6. Thus the churches of Christ and the saints, though they are many, are yet one, being *fitly joined together* in holy love, and by the *unity of the Spirit*, so growing into one *holy temple* in *the Lord*, Eph. ii. 21, 22; iv. 16.

Verses 7–14

Moses is here ordered to make a double covering for the tabernacle, that it might not rain in. 1. There was to be a covering of hair camlet curtains, which were somewhat larger every way than the inner curtains, because they were to enclose them, and probably were stretched out at some little distance from them, *v.* 7, &c. These were coupled together with brass clasps. 2. Over this there was to be another covering, and that a double one (*v.* 14), one of *rams' skins dyed red*, probably dressed with the wool on; another of *badgers' skins*, so we translate it, but it should rather seem to have been some strong sort of leather (but very fine), for we read of the best sort of shoes being made of it, Ezek. xvi. 10. Now observe here that the outside of the tabernacle was coarse and rough, the beauty of it was in the inner curtains. Those in whom God dwells must labour to be better than they seem to be. Let our adorning be that of the hidden man of the heart, which God values, 1 Pet. iii. 4.

JAMIESON, FAUSSET, BROWN — CHAPTER 26

Vss. 1-37. TEN CURTAINS. **1. cunning work**—i.e., of elegant texture, richly embroidered. The word "cunning," in old English, is synonymous with skilful. **2. length**—Each curtain was to be fifteen yards in length and a little exceeding two in breadth.

3. The five curtains shall be coupled together one to another, etc.—so as to form two grand divisions, each eleven yards wide.

6. taches—clasps; supposed in shape, as well as in use, to be the same as hooks and eyes.

7-13. curtains of goats' hair—These coarse curtains were to be one more in number than the others, and to extend a yard lower on each side, the use of them being to protect and conceal the richer curtains.

14. a covering . . . of rams' skins dyed red—i. e., of Turkey red leather.

ADAM CLARKE — CHAPTER 26

1. *Thou shalt make the tabernacle. Mischan*, from *shachan*, "to dwell," means simply a dwelling place or habitation of any kind, but here it means the dwelling place of Jehovah, who, as a king in his camp, had His dwelling or pavilion among His people, His table always spread, His lamps lighted, and the priests, His attendants, always in waiting. From the minute and accurate description here given, a good workman, had he the same materials, might make a perfect facsimile of the ancient Jewish Tabernacle. It was a movable building, and so constructed that it might be easily taken to pieces, for the greater convenience of carriage, as they were often obliged to transport it from place to place in their various journeyings.

Cunning work. Chosheb probably means a sort of diaper, in which the figures appear equally perfect on both sides; this was probably formed in the loom. Another kind of curious work is mentioned, v. 36, *rokem*, which we term "needlework"; this was probably similar to our embroidery or tapestry. The whole of this account shows that not only necessary but ornamental arts had been carried to a considerable pitch of perfection, among both the Israelites and the Egyptians. The inner curtains of the Tabernacle were ten in number, and each in length twenty-eight cubits, and four in breadth. The curtains were to be coupled together, five and five of a side, by fifty loops, v. 5, and as many golden clasps, v. 6, so that each might look like one curtain, and the whole make one entire covering, which was the *first*.

7. *Curtains of goats' hair*. See the note on chap. xxv. 4. This was the *second* covering.

14. *Rams' skins dyed red*. See on chap. xxv. 5. This was the *third* covering; and what is called the *badgers' skins* was the *fourth*. See the note on chap. xxv. 5. Why there should have been four coverings does not appear. They might have been designed partly for respect; and partly to keep off dust and dirt, and the extremely fine sand which in that desert rises as it were on every breeze; and partly to keep off the intense heat of the sun.

MATTHEW HENRY

Verses 15–30

Very particular directions are here given about the boards of the tabernacle, which were to bear up the curtains, as the stakes of a tent which had need to be strong, Isa. liv. 2. These boards had tenons which fell into the mortises that were made for them in silver bases. God took care to have every thing strong, as well as fine, in his tabernacle. The boards were coupled together with gold rings at top and bottom (*v.* 24), and kept firm with bars that ran through golden staples in every board (*v.* 26), and the boards and bars were all richly gilded, *v.* 29.

Verses 31–37

Two veils are here ordered to be made, 1. One for a partition between the holy place and the most holy, which not only forbade any to enter, but forbade them so much as to look into the holiest of all, *v.* 31, 33. Under that dispensation, divine grace was veiled, but now we behold it with open face, 2 Cor. iii. 18. The apostle tells us (Heb. ix. 8, 9) what was the meaning of this veil; it intimated that the ceremonial law *could not make the comers thereunto perfect,* nor would the observance of it bring men to heaven; the *way into the holiest of all was not made manifest while the first tabernacle was standing; life and immortality* lay concealed till they were *brought to light by the gospel,* which was therefore signified by the rending of this veil at the death of Christ, Matt. xxvii. 51. We have now *boldness to enter into the holiest,* in all acts of devotion, *by the blood of Jesus,* yet such as obliges us to a holy reverence and a humble sense of our distance. 2. Another veil was for the outer door of the tabernacle, *v.* 36, 37. Through this first veil the priests went in every day to minister in the holy place, but not the people, Heb. ix. 6. This veil, which was all the defence the tabernacle had against thieves and robbers, might easily be broken through, for it could be neither locked nor barred, and the abundance of wealth in the tabernacle, one would think, might be a temptation; but by leaving it thus exposed, (1) The priests and Levites would be so much the more obliged to keep a strict watch upon it, and, (2) God would show his care of his church on earth, though it is weak and defenceless, and continually exposed. A curtain shall be (if God please to make it so) as strong a defence to his house as gates of brass and bars of iron.

JAMIESON, FAUSSET, BROWN

15-30. thou shalt make boards . . . rear up the tabernacle according to the fashion . . . which was showed thee—The tabernacle, from its name as well as from its general appearance and arrangements, was a tent; but from the description given in these verses, the boards that formed its walls, the five (cross) bars that strengthened them, and the middle bar that "reached from end to end," and gave it solidity and compactness, it was evidently a more substantial fabric than a light and fragile tent, probably on account of the weight of its various coverings as well as for the protection of its precious furniture.

36. an hanging for the door of the tent—Curtains of rich and elaborate embroidery, made by the women, are suspended over the doors or entrances of the tents occupied by Eastern chiefs and princes. In a similar style of elegance was the hanging finished which was to cover the door of this tabernacle—the chosen habitation of the God and King of Israel. It appears from verses 12, 22, 23, that the ark and mercy seat were placed in the west end of the tabernacle, and consequently the door or entrance fronted the east, so that the Israelites in worshipping Jehovah, turned their faces towards the west, that they might be thus figuratively taught to turn from the worship of that luminary which was the great idol of the nations, and to adore the God who made it and them [HEWLETT].

ADAM CLARKE

15. *Thou shalt make boards.* These formed what might be called the walls of the Tabernacle, and were made of shittim wood, the *acacia Nilotica,* which Dr. Shaw says grows here in abundance.

29. *Thou shalt overlay the boards with gold.* It is not said how thick the gold was by which these boards were overlaid; it was no doubt done with gold plates, but these must have been very thin, else the boards must have been insupportably heavy.

31. *Thou shalt make a veil. Parocheth,* from *parach,* "to break or rend"; the inner veil of the Tabernacle or Temple (2 Chron. iii. 14), which broke, interrupted, or divided between the holy place and the most holy; "the holy Ghost this signifying, that the way into the holiest of all was not yet made manifest, while as the first tabernacle was yet standing." Compare Heb. ix. 8. Does not the Hebrew name *parocheth* intimate the typical correspondence of this veil to the body or flesh of Christ? For this veil was His flesh (Heb. x. 20), which, being rent, affords us "a new and living way" into the holiest of all, i.e., "into heaven itself." Compare Heb. x. 19-20; ix. 24. And accordingly when His blessed body was rent upon the Cross, this veil also "was rent in twain from the top to the bottom," Matt. xxvii. 51.

32. *Their hooks shall be of gold. Vaveyhem,* which we translate *their hooks,* is rendered "capitals" by the Septuagint, and *capita* by the Vulgate. On the whole it appears much more reasonable to translate the original by "capitals" than by *hooks.*

After this verse the Samaritan Pentateuch introduces the first ten verses of chap. xxx, and this appears to be their proper place. Those ten verses are not repeated in the thirtieth chapter in the Samaritan, the chapter beginning with the eleventh verse.

36. *A hanging for the door of the tent.* This may be called the "first veil," as it occupied the door or entrance to the Tabernacle; the veil that separated the holy place from the holy of holies is called the "second veil," Heb. ix. 3. These two veils and the inner covering of the Tabernacle were all of the same materials, and of the same workmanship. See chap. xxvii. 16.

MATTHEW HENRY — CHAPTER 27

Verses 1–8

As God intended in the tabernacle to manifest his presence among his people, so there they were to pay their devotions to him, not in the tabernacle itself (into that only the priests entered as God's domestic servants), but in the court before the tabernacle. There an altar was ordered to be set up, to which they must bring their sacrifices. Moses is here directed about, 1. The dimensions of it; it was square, *v.* 1. 2. The horns of it (*v.* 2), which were for ornament and for use; the sacrifices were *bound with cords to the horns of the altar,* and to them malefactors fled for refuge. 3. The materials; it was of wood overlaid with brass, *v.* 1, 2. 4. The appurtenances of it (*v.* 3), which were all of brass. 5. The grate, which was let into the hollow of the altar, about the middle of it, in which the fire was kept, and the sacrifice burnt. 6. The staves with which it must be carried, *v.* 6, 7. And, *lastly,* he is referred to the pattern shown him, *v.* 8.

Now this brazen altar was a type of Christ dying to make atonement for our sins. To the horns of this altar poor sinners fly for refuge when justice pursues them, and they are safe in virtue of the sacrifice there offered.

JAMIESON, FAUSSET, BROWN — CHAPTER 27

Vss. 1-21. ALTAR FOR BURNT OFFERING. **1. altar of shittim wood**—The dimensions of this altar which was placed at the entrance of the sanctuary were nearly three yards square, and a yard and a half in height. Under the wooden frame of this chest-like altar the inside was hollow, and each corner was to be terminated by "horns"—angular projections, perpendicular or oblique, in the form of horns. The animals to be sacrificed were bound to these (Ps. 118:27), and part of the blood was applied to them. **3. shovels**—fire shovels for scraping together any of the scattered ashes.

basons—for receiving the blood of the sacrifice to be sprinkled on the people. **fleshhooks**—curved, three-pronged forks (I Sam. 2: 13, 14).

fire-pans—A large sort of vessel, wherein the sacred fire which came down from heaven (Lev. 9:24) was kept burning, while they cleaned the altar and the grate from the coals and ashes, and while the altar was carried from one place to another in the wilderness [PATRICK, SPENCER, LE CLERC]. **4. a grate of network of brass**—sunk latticework to support the fire. **5. put it under the compass of the altar beneath**—i.e., the grating in which they were carried to a clean place (Lev. 4: 12). **4. four brazen rings**—by which the grating might be lifted and taken away as occasion required from the body of the altar. **6, 7. staves . . . rings**—Those rings were placed at the side through which the poles were inserted on occasions of removal.

ADAM CLARKE — CHAPTER 27

2. *Thou shalt make the horns of it.* The horns might have three uses: (1) For ornament. (2) To prevent carcasses from falling off. (3) To tie the victim to, previously to its being sacrificed. So David: "Bind the sacrifice with cords, even unto the horns of the altar," Ps. cxviii. 27.

3. *Thou shalt make his pans. Sirothaiv,* a sort of large brazen dishes, which stood under the altar to receive the ashes that fell through the grating. *His shovels. Yaaiv.* Some kind of fire shovels or scuttles, which were used to carry off the ashes that fell through the grating into the large pan. *His basons. Mizrekothaiv,* from *zarak,* to "sprinkle" or "disperse"; bowls or basins to receive the blood of the sacrifices, in order that it might be sprinkled on the people before the altar. *His fleshhooks. Mizlegothaiv.* That this word is rightly translated *fleshhooks* is fully evident from 1 Sam. ii. 13-14, where the same word is used in such a connection as demonstrates its meaning: "And the priest's custom with the people was, that, when any man offered sacrifice, the priest's servant came, while the flesh was in seething, with a fleshhook of three teeth [prongs] in his hand; and he struck it into the pan . . . all that the fleshhook brought up the priest took for himself." It was probably a kind of trident, or fork with three prongs, and these bent to a right angle at the middle, as the ideal meaning of the Hebrew seems to imply crookedness or curvature in general. *His firepans. Machtothaiv.* Bishop Patrick and others suppose that "this was a larger sort of vessel, wherein, probably, the sacred fire which came down from heaven (Lev. ix. 24) was kept burning, whilst they cleansed the altar and the grate from the coals and the ashes; and while the altar was carried from one place to another, as it often was in the wilderness."

8. *Hollow with boards.* It seems to have been

MATTHEW HENRY

Verses 9–19

Before the tabernacle there was to be a court or yard, enclosed with hangings of the finest linen that was used for tents. This court, according to the common computation of cubits, was fifty yards long, and twenty-five broad. Pillars were set up at convenient distances, in sockets of brass, the pillars filleted with silver, and silver tenter-hooks in them, on which the linen hangings were fastened: the hanging which served for the gate was finer than the rest, *v.* 16. Thanks be to God, now, under the gospel, the enclosure is taken down. God's will is that men *pray everywhere*; and there is room for all that in every place call on the name of Jesus Christ.

Verses 20–21

Here is an order given for the keeping of the lamps constantly burning in it; in every candlestick there should be a burning and shining light; candlesticks without candles are as *wells without water* or as *clouds without rain*. Now, 1. The people were to provide the oil.

2. The priests were to light the lamps, and to tend them; thus it is the work of ministers, by the preaching and expounding of the scriptures (which are as a lamp), to enlighten the church, God's tabernacle upon earth.

JAMIESON, FAUSSET, BROWN

9. the court of the tabernacle—The enclosure in which the edifice stood was a rectangular court, extending rather more than fifty yards in length and half that space in breadth, and the enclosing parapet was about three yards or half the height of the tabernacle. That parapet consisted of a connected series of curtains, made of fine twined linen yarn, woven into a kind of network, so that the people could see through; but that large curtain which overhung the entrance was of a different texture, being embroidered and dyed with variegated colors, and it was furnished with cords for pulling it up or drawing it aside when the priests had occasion to enter. The curtains of this enclosure were supported on sixty brazen pillars which stood on pedestals of the same metal, but their capitals and fillets were of silver, and the hooks on which they were suspended were of silver also. **19. pins**—were designed to hold down the curtains at the bottom, lest the wind should waft them aside.

20, 21. pure oil olive beaten—i.e., such as runs from the olives when bruised and without the application of fire.

for the light . . . Aaron and his sons—were to take charge of lighting it in all time coming. **shall order it from evening to morning**—The tabernacle having no windows, the lamps required to be lighted during the day. JOSEPHUS says that in his time only three were lighted; but his were degenerate times, and there is no Scripture authority for this limitation. But although the priests were obliged from necessity to light them by day, they might have let them go out at night had it not been for this express ordinance.

ADAM CLARKE

a kind of framework, and to have had nothing solid in the inside, and only covered with the grating at the top. This rendered it more light and portable.

9. *The court of the tabernacle*. The Tabernacle stood in an enclosure or court, open at the top. This court was made with pillars or posts, and hangings. It was *an hundred cubits* in length; the breadth we learn from verses 12 and 18; and *five cubits* high, v. 18. And as this was but half the height of the Tabernacle, chap. xxvi. 16, that sacred building might easily be seen by the people from without.

16. *And for the gate of the court*. It appears that the hangings of this gate were of the same materials and workmanship with that of the inner covering of the Tabernacle, and the outer and inner veil. See chap. xxvi. 36.

19. *All the vessels . . . shall be of brass*. It would have been improper to use instruments made of the more precious metals about this altar, as they must have been soon worn out by the severity of the service.

20. *Pure oil olive beaten*. That is, such oil as could easily be expressed from the olives after they had been bruised in a mortar. *To cause the lamp to burn always*. It was to be kept burning through the whole of the night, and some think all the day besides. This oil and continual flame were not only emblematical of the unction and influences of the Holy Ghost, but also of that pure spirit of devotion which ever animates the hearts and minds of the genuine worshippers of the true God.

21. *The tabernacle of the congregation*. The place where all the assembly of the people were to worship, where the God of that assembly was pleased to reside, and to which, as the habitation of their King and Protector, they were ever to turn their faces in all their adorations. *Before the testimony*. That is, the ark where the tables of the covenant were deposited. See chap. xxv. 16. *Aaron and his sons*. These and their descendants being the only legitimate priests, God having established the priesthood in this family. *Shall order it from evening to morning*. Josephus says the whole of the seven lamps burned all the night; in the morning four were extinguished, and three kept burning through the whole day. Others assert that the whole seven were kept lighted both day and night continually; but it appears sufficiently evident, from 1 Sam. iii. 3, that these lamps were extinguished in the morning: "And ere the lamp of God went out in the temple of the Lord, where the ark of God was, and Samuel was laid down to sleep." See also chap. xxx. 8: "And when Aaron lighteth the lamps at even."

MATTHEW HENRY

CHAPTER 28

Verses 1–5

I. The priests nominated: *Aaron and his sons*, *v.* 1. Moses, who had hitherto officiated, and is therefore reckoned among the *priests of the Lord* (Ps. xcix. 6), had enough to do as their prophet to consult the oracle for them, and as their prince to judge among them; but was well pleased to see his brother Aaron invested in this office. Aaron, who had humbly served as a prophet to his younger brother Moses, and did not decline the office (*ch.* vii. 1), is now advanced to be a priest, a high priest, to God. Because it was requisite that those who ministered at the altar should give themselves wholly to the service, and because that which is everybody's work will soon come to be nobody's work, God here chose from among them one to be a family of priests, the father and his four sons; and from Aaron's loins descended all the priests of the Jewish church, of whom we read so often, both in the Old Testament and in the New.

II. The priests' garments appointed, *for glory and beauty*, *v.* 2. The garments appointed were, 1. Four which both the high priest and the inferior priests wore, namely, the linen breeches, the linen coat, the linen girdle which fastened it to them, and the bonnet or turban; that which the high priest wore is called *a mitre*.

JAMIESON, FAUSSET, BROWN

CHAPTER 28

Vss. 1-43. APPOINTMENT TO THE PRIESTHOOD. **1. take thou unto thee Aaron thy brother, and his sons with him**—Moses had hitherto discharged the priestly functions (Ps. 99:6), and he evinced the piety as well as humility of his character, in readily complying with the command to invest his brother with the sacred office, though it involved the perpetual exclusion of his own family. The appointment was a special act of God's sovereignty, so that there could be no ground for popular umbrage by the selection of Aaron's family, with whom the office was inalienably established and continued in unbroken succession till the introduction of the Christian era. **2-5. holy garments**—No inherent holiness belonged either to the material or the workmanship. But they are called "holy" simply because they were not worn on ordinary occasions, but assumed in the discharge of the sacred functions (Ezek. 44:19). **for glory and for beauty**—It was a grand and sumptuous attire. In material, elaborate embroidery, and color, it had an imposing splendor. The tabernacle being adapted to the infantine aid of the church, it was right and necessary that the priests' garments should be of such superb and dazzling appearance, that the people might be inspired with a due respect for the ministers as well as the rites of religion. But they had also a further meaning; for being all made of linen, they were symbolical of the truth, purity, and other qualities in Christ that rendered Him such a high priest as became us.

ADAM CLARKE

CHAPTER 28

1. *Aaron . . . and his sons*. The priesthood was to be restrained to this family because the public worship was to be confined to one place; and previously to this the eldest in every family officiated as priest, there being no settled place of worship. It has been very properly observed that, if Moses had not acted by the divine appointment, he would not have passed by his own family, which continued in the condition of ordinary Levites, and established the priesthood, the only dignity in the nation, in the family of his brother, Aaron.

2. *For glory and for beauty*. Four articles of dress were prescribed for the priests in orinary, and four more for the high priest. Those for the priests in general were a coat, drawers, a girdle, and a bonnet. Besides these the high priest had a robe, an ephod, a breastplate, and a plate or diadem of gold on his forehead. The garments, says the sacred historian, were for honor and for beauty. They were emblematical of the office in which they ministered.

3. *Whom I have filled with the spirit of wisdom*. So we find that ingenuity in arts and sciences, even those of the ornamental kind, comes from God. It is not intimated here that these persons were filled with the spirit of wisdom for this purpose only; for the direction to Moses is to select those whom he found to be expert artists, and those who were such, God

MATTHEW HENRY

2. Four more, which were peculiar to the high priest, namely, the ephod, with the curious girdle of it, the breast-plate of judgment, the long robe with the bells and pomegranates at the bottom of it, and the golden plate on his forehead. Our adorning, now under the gospel, is not to be of gold, and pearl, and costly array, but the *garments of salvation, and the robe of righteousness*, Isa. lxi. 10; Ps. cxxxii. 9, 16.

Verses 6–14

Directions are here given concerning the ephod, which was the outmost garment of the high priest. *Linen* ephods were worn by the inferior priests, 1 Sam. xxii. 18. Samuel wore one when he was a child (1 Sam ii. 18), and David when he danced before the ark (2 Sam. vi. 14); but this which the high priest only wore was called a *golden ephod*, because there was a great deal of gold woven into it. It was a short coat without sleeves, buttoned closely to him, with a curious girdle of the same stuff (*v.* 6–8); the shoulder-pieces were buttoned together with two precious stones set in gold, one on each shoulder, on which were engraven the names of the *children of Israel, v.* 9–12.

Verses 15–30

The most considerable of the ornaments of the high priest was this breast-plate, a rich piece of cloth, curiously wrought with gold and purple, &c., two spans long and a span broad, so that, being doubled, it was a span square, *v.* 16. This was fastened to the ephod with wreathen chains of gold (*v.* 13, 14, 22, &c.) both at top and bottom, so that *the breast-plate might not be loosed from the ephod, v.* 28. The ephod was the garment of service; the breast-plate of judgment was an emblem of honour: these two must by no means be separated. In this breast-plate,

I. The tribes of Israel were recommended to God's favour in twelve precious stones, *v.* 17–21, 29. Aaron was to bear their names for a *memorial before the Lord continually*, being *ordained for men*, to represent them in things pertaining to God, herein typifying our great high priest, who always appears in the presence of God for us. 1. Though the people were forbidden to come near, yet by the high priest, who had their names on his breast-plate, they entered into the holiest; so believers, even while they are here on this earth, not only *enter into the holiest*, but by faith are made to *sit with Christ in heavenly places*, Eph. ii. 6. 2. The name of each tribe was engraven in a precious stone, to signify how precious, in God's sight, believers are and how honourable, Isa. xliii. 4. They shall be his in the day he *makes up his jewels*, Mal. iii. 1. 3. The high priest had the names of the tribes both on his shoulders and on his breast, intimating both the power and the love with which our Lord Jesus intercedes for those that are his. He not only bears them up in his arms with an almighty strength, but he bears them *upon his heart, as the expression here is* (*v.* 29), *carries them in his bosom* (Isa. xl. 11), with the most tender affection.

JAMIESON, FAUSSET, BROWN

6-14. ephod—It was a very gorgeous robe made of byssus, curiously embroidered, and dyed with variegated colors, and further enriched with golden tissue, the threads of gold being either originally interwoven or afterwards inserted by the embroiderer. It was short—reaching from the breast to a little below the loins—and though destitute of sleeves, retained its position by the support of straps thrown over each shoulder. These straps or braces, connecting the one with the back, the other with the front piece of which the tunic was composed, were united on the shoulder by two onyx stones, serving as buttons, and on which the names of the twelve tribes were engraved, and set in golden encasements. The symbolical design of this was, that the high priest, who bore the names along with him in all his ministrations before the Lord, might be kept in remembrance of his duty to plead their cause, and supplicate the accomplishment of the divine promises in their favor. The ephod was fastened by a girdle of the same costly materials, i.e., dyed, embroidered, and wrought with threads of gold. It was about a handbreadth wide and wound twice round the upper part of the waist; it fastened in front, the ends hanging down at great length (Rev. 1:13).

15-29. thou shalt make the breastplate of judgment with cunning work— a very splendid and richly embroidered piece of brocade, a span square, and doubled, to enable it the better to bear the weight of the precious stones in it. There were twelve different stones, containing each the name of a tribe, and arranged in four rows, three in each. The Israelites had acquired a knowledge of the lapidary's art in Egypt, and the amount of their skill in cutting, polishing, and setting precious stones, may be judged of by the diamond forming one of the engraved ornaments on this breastplate. A ring was attached to each corner, through which the golden chains were passed to fasten this brilliant piece of jewelry at the top and bottom tightly on the breast of the ephod.

ADAM CLARKE

shows by these words, had derived their knowledge from himself.

4. *Robe. Meil,* from *alah,* "to go up, go upon"; hence the *meil* may be considered as an upper coat. It is described by Josephus as a garment that reaches down to the feet, not made of two distinct pieces, but was one entire long garment, woven throughout. This was immediately under the ephod. *Broidered coat. Kethoneth,* what Parkhurst translates "a close, strait coat or garment"; according to Josephus, "a tunic circumscribing or closely encompassing the body, and having tight sleeves for the arms." This was immediately under the *meil* or robe, and answered the same purpose to the priests that our *shirts* do for us. *Mitre. Mitsnepheth.* As this word comes from the root *tsanaph,* "to roll or wrap round," it evidently means that covering of the head so universal in the Eastern countries which we call "turban." *A girdle. Abnet,* "a belt" or "girdle." This seems to have been the same kind of sash or girdle, so common in the Eastern countries, that confined the loose garments about the waist, and in which their long skirts were tucked up when they were employed in work or on a journey.

8. *The curious girdle of the ephod.* The word *chesheb,* rendered here *curious girdle,* signifies merely a kind of embroidered work (see the note on chap. xxvi. 1); and it is widely different from *abnet,* which is properly translated "girdle" in v. 4.

11. *Like the engravings of a signet.* So signets or seals were in use at this time, and engraving on precious stones was then an art, and this art, which was one of the most elegant and ornamental, was carried in ancient times to a very high pitch of perfection, particularly among the ancient Greeks; such a pitch of perfection as has never been rivalled and cannot now be even well imitated.

12. *Aaron shall bear their names before the Lord.* He was to consider that he was the representative of the children of Israel; and the stones on the ephod and the stones on the breastplate were for a memorial to put Aaron in remembrance that he was the priest and mediator of the twelve tribes.

13. *Ouches of gold. Mishbetsoth,* "straight places," sockets to insert the stones in, from *shabats,* "to close, inclose, straiten." "Socket" in this place would be a more proper translation, as *ouch* cannot be traced up to any legitimate authority.

15. *The breastplate of judgment. Choshen mishpat,* the same as the *choshen,* see chap. xxv. 7, but here called the *breastplate of judgment,* because the high priest wore it upon his breast when he went to ask counsel of the Lord, to give judgment in any particular case; as also when he sat as judge to teach the law, and to determine controversies. See Lev. x. 11; Deut. xvii. 8-9.

16. *Foursquare it shall be.* Here we have the exact dimensions of this breastplate, or more properly "breast piece." It was a *span* in length and breadth when *doubled,* and consequently two spans long one way before it was doubled. Between these doublings, it is supposed, the Urim and the Thummim were placed. See on v. 30.

17. *Four rows of stones.* With a name on each stone, making in all the twelve names of the twelve tribes. (1) A *sardius, odem,* from the root *adam,* he was "ruddy"; the ruby, a beautiful gem of a fine, deep *red* color. The *sardius* is defined to be a precious stone of a blood-red color, the best of which come from Babylon.

(2) A *topaz, pitdah,* a precious stone of a pale dead-green, with a mixture of yellow, sometimes of a fine yellow; and hence it was called "chrysolite" by the ancients, from its gold color. It is now considered by mineralogists as a variety of the sapphire.

(3) *Carbuncle, bareketh,* from *barak,* "to lighten, glitter, or glisten"; a very elegant gem of a deep red color, with an admixture of scarlet. From its bright, lively color it had the name *carbunculus,* which signifies a "little coal"; and among the Greeks *anthrax,* a "coal," because when held before the sun it appears like a piece of bright burning charcoal. It is found only in

MATTHEW HENRY	JAMIESON, FAUSSET, BROWN	ADAM CLARKE

the East Indies, and there but rarely.

(4) *Emerald, nophech;* it is one of the most beautiful of all the gems, and is of a bright green color, without any other mixture.

(5) *Sapphire, sappir.* See this described, chap. xxiv. 10.

(6) *Diamond, yahalom,* from *halam,* "to beat or smite upon." The diamond is supposed to have this name from its resistance to a blow, for the ancients have assured us that if it be struck with a hammer, upon an anvil, it will not break. This is a complete fable, as it is well known that the diamond can be easily broken. It is, however, the hardest, as it is the most valuable, of all the precious stones hitherto discovered.

(7) *Ligure, leshem,* the same as the jacinth or hyacinth; a precious stone of a dead red or cinnamon color, with a considerable mixture of yellow.

(8) *Agate, shebo.* This is a stone that assumes such a variety of hues and appearances that Mr. Parkhurst thinks it derives its name from the root *shab,* "to turn, to change." Agates have a white, reddish, yellowish, or greenish ground.

(9) *Amethyst, achlamah,* a gem generally of a purple color, composed of a strong blue and deep red.

(10) The *beryl, tarshish.* Mr. Parkhurst derives this name from *tar,* "to go round," and *shash,* "to be vivid or bright in color." If the beryl be intended, it is a pellucid gem of a bluish green color, found in the East Indies, and about the gold mines of Peru. But some of the most learned mineralogists and critics suppose the chrysolite to be meant. This is a gem of a yellowish green. Its name in Greek, *chrysolite,* literally signifies the "golden stone."

(11) The *onyx, shoham.* See the notes on Exod. xxv. 7. There are a great number of different sentiments on the meaning of the original; it has been translated beryl, emerald, prasius, sapphire, sardius, ruby, cornelian, onyx, and sardonyx. It is well known that the onyx is of a darkish horny color, resembling the hoof or nail, from which circumstance it has its name.

(12) *Jasper, yashepheh.* The similarity of the Hebrew name has determined most critics and mineralogists to adopt the *jasper* as intended by the original word. The jasper is usually defined a hard stone, of a beautiful bright green color, sometimes clouded with white, and spotted with red or yellow.

TODAY'S DICTIONARY OF THE BIBLE:

Thummim—meaning lost long before time of Christ—(LXX, "truth"; Vulg., "veritas")—Ex. 28:30; Deut. 33:8; Judg. 1:1; 20:18; 1 Sam. 14:3, 18; 23:9; 2 Sam. 21:1. What the "Urim and Thummim" were cannot be determined with any certainty. All we know for sure is that they were a certain divinely given means by which God imparted, through the high priest, direction and counsel to Israel when these were needed. The method by which this was done can be only a matter of mere conjecture. They were apparently material objects, quite distinct from the breastplate, but something added to it after all the stones had been set in it—something in addition to the breastplate and its jewels. They may have been, as some suppose, two small images, like the teraphim (comp. Judg. 17:5; 18:14, 17, 20; Hos. 3:4), which were kept in the bag of the breastplate, by which, in some unknown way, the high priest could give forth his divinely imparted decision when consulted. Probably lost at the destruction of the temple by Nebuchadnezzar, they were never seen after the return from captivity.

II. The urim and thummim, by which the will of God was made known in doubtful cases, were put in this breast-plate, which is therefore called the *breast-plate of judgment, v.* 30. *Urim* and *thummim* signify *light* and *integrity*: I think the words may be read thus, *And thou shalt give,* or *add,* or *deliver, to the breastplate of judgment, the illuminations and perfections, and they shall be upon the heart of Aaron*; that is, "He shall be endued with a power of knowing and making known the mind of God in all difficult doubtful cases, relating either to the civil or ecclesiastical state of the nation." Their government was a theocracy: God was their King, the high priest was, under God, their ruler, the urim and thummim were his cabinet-council; probably Moses wrote upon the breast-plate, or wove into it, these words, *urim* and *thummim,* to signify that the high priest, having on him this breast-plate, and asking counsel of God in any emergency relating to the public, should be directed to take those measures, and give that advice, which God would own. The answer was given either by a voice from heaven or rather by an impulse upon the mind of the high priest, which last is perhaps intimated in that expression, *He shall bear the judgment of the children of Israel upon his heart.* This oracle was of great use to Israel; Joshua consulted it (Num. xxvii. 21), and, it is likely, the judges after him. It was lost in the captivity, and never regained after. But it was a shadow of good things to come, and the substance is Christ. He is our oracle; by him God in these last days makes known himself and his mind to us, Heb. i. 2; John i. 18. Divine revelation centres in him, and comes to us through him.

Verses 31–39

1. Direction given concerning *the robe of the ephod, v.* 31–35. This was next under the ephod, and reached down to the knees, and was without sleeves. The hole on the top, through which the head was put, was carefully bound about, that it might not tear in the putting on. Round the skirts of the robe were hung golden bells, and the representations of pomegranates made of yarn of divers colours. The pomegranates added to the beauty of the robe, and the sound of the bells gave notice to the people in the outer court when he went into the holy place to burn incense, that they might then apply themselves to the devotions at the same time. Some make the bells of the holy robe to typify the sound of the gospel of Christ in the world, giving notice of his entrance within the veil for us. The adding of the pomegranates, which are a fragrant fruit, denotes the sweet savour of the gospel. 2. Concerning the golden plate fixed upon Aaron's forehead, on which must be engraven, *Holiness to the Lord* (*v.* 36, 37), Aaron must hereby be reminded that God is holy, and that his priests must be holy.

30. thou shalt put in the breastplate of judgment the Urim and Thummim—The words signify "lights" and "perfections"; and nothing more is meant than the precious stones of the breastplate already described (cf. ch. 39:8-21; Lev. 8:8). They received the name because the bearing of them qualified the high priest to consult the divine oracle on all public or national emergencies, by going into the holy place—standing close before the veil and putting his hand upon the Urim and Thummim, he conveyed a petition from the people and asked counsel of God, who, as the Sovereign of Israel, gave response from the midst of His glory. Little, however, is known about them. But it may be remarked that Egyptian judges wore on the breast of their official robes a representation of Justice, and the high priest in Israel long officiated also as a judge; so that some think the Urim and Thummim had a reference to his judicial functions. **31. the robe of the ephod all of blue**—It was the middle garment, under the ephod and above the coat. It had a hole through which the head was thrust, and was formed carefully of one piece, such as was the robe of Christ (John 19: 23). The high priest's was of a sky-blue color. The binding at the neck was strongly woven, and it terminated below in a fringe, made of blue, purple, and scarlet tassels, in the form of a pomegranate, interspersed with small bells of gold, which tinkled as the wearer was in motion. **34. a golden bell and a pomegranate**—The bells were hung between the pomegranates, which are said to have amounted to seventy-two, and the use of them seems to have been to announce to the people when the high priest entered the most holy place, that they might accompany him with their prayers, and also to remind himself to be attired in his official dress, to minister without which was death. **36-38. mitre**—crown-like cap for the head, not covering the entire head, but adhering closely to it, composed of fine linen. The Scripture has not described its form, but from JOSEPHUS we may gather that it was conical in shape, as he distinguishes the mitres of the common priests by saying that they were *not* conical—that it was encircled with swathes of blue embroidered, and that it was covered by one piece of fine linen to hide the seams. **plate**—lit., a petal

30. *Thou shalt put in the breastplate . . . the Urim and the Thummim.* What these were has, I believe, never yet been discovered. As the word *urim* signifies "lights," and the word *tummim,* "perfections," they were probably designed to point out the "light"—the abundant information, in spiritual things, afforded by the wonderful revelation which God made of himself by and under the law; and the "perfection," entire holiness and strict conformity to himself, which this dispensation required and which are introduced and accomplished by that dispensation of light and truth, the gospel.

31. *The robe of the ephod.* See on v. 4. From this description, and from what Josephus says, who must have been well acquainted with its form, we find that this *meil,* or robe, was one long, straight piece of blue cloth, with a hole or opening in the center for the head to pass through; which hole or opening was bound about, that it might not be rent in putting it on or taking it off, v. 32.

35. *His sound shall be heard.* The bells were doubtless intended to keep up the people's attention to the very solemn and important office which the priest was then performing, that they might all have their hearts engaged in the work; and at the same time to keep Aaron himself in remembrance that he ministered before Jehovah and should not come into His presence without due reverence.

36. *Thou shalt make a plate of pure gold.* The word *tsits,* which we render *plate,* means a "flower," or any appearance of this kind. The Septuagint translate it by "a leaf"; hence we might be led to infer that this plate resembled a wreath of flowers or leaves; it is called, chap. xxix. 6, *nezer,* a "crown."

HOLINESS TO THE LORD. This we may consider as the grand badge of the sacerdotal office. (1) The priest was to minister in holy

MATTHEW HENRY

Aaron must have this upon his forehead, that he may *bear the iniquity of the holy things* (*v.* 38), and that *they may be accepted before the Lord.* Herein he was a type of Christ, the great Mediator between God and man, through whom it is that we have to do with God. (1) Through him what is amiss in our services is pardoned. In many things we come short of our duty, so that we cannot but be conscious to ourselves of much iniquity cleaving even to our holy things. But Christ, our high priest, bears this iniquity, bears it for us so as to bear it from us, and through him it is forgiven to us and not laid to our charge. (2) Through him what is good is accepted; our persons, our performances, are pleasing to God upon the account of Christ's intercession, and not otherwise, 1 Pet. ii. 5. Having *such a high priest,* we come *boldly to the throne of grace,* Heb. iv. 14–16. 3. The rest of the garments are but named (*v.* 39). The embroidered coat of fine linen was the innermost of the priestly garments; it reached to the feet, and the sleeves to the wrists, and was bound to the body with a girdle or sash of needle-work. The mitre, or diadem, was of linen, such as kings anciently wore in the east, typifying the kingly office of Christ.

Verses 40–43

We have here, 1. Particular orders about the vestments of the inferior priests. They were to have coats, and girdles, and bonnets, of the same materials with those of the high priest; but there was a difference in shape between their bonnets and his mitre. Theirs, as his, were to be *for glory and beauty* (*v.* 40), yet all this glory was nothing compared with the glory of grace, this beauty nothing to the beauty of holiness, of which these holy garments were typical. 2. A general rule concerning the garments both of the high priest and of the inferior priests, that they were to be put upon them, at first, when they were consecrated, and then they were to wear them in all their ministrations, but not at other times (*v.* 43). To us these garments typify, (1) The righteousness of Christ; if we appear not before God in this, we shall *bear iniquity and die.* (2) *The armour of God* prescribed, Eph. vi. 13.

CHAPTER 29

Verses 1–37

I. The law concerning the consecration of Aaron and his sons to the priests' office.

1. The ceremonies wherewith it was to be done were very fully and particularly appointed, because nothing of this kind had been done before. Now,

(1) The work to be done was the consecrating of the persons whom God had chosen to be priests, by which they devoted and gave up themselves to the service of God and God declared his acceptance of them; and the people were made to know that they *glorified not themselves* to be made priests, but were *called of God,* Heb. v. 4, 5. Note, All that are to be employed for God are to be sanctified to him. The person must first be accepted, and then the performance.

(2) The person to do it was Moses, by God's appointment. By God's special appointment he now did the priest's work, and therefore that which was the priest's part of the sacrifice was here ordered to be his, *v.* 26.

(3) The place was at the *door of the tabernacle of meeting, v.* 4. They were consecrated at the door, for they were to be door-keepers.

(4) It was done with many ceremonies.

[1] They were to be washed (*v.* 4), signifying that those must be clean who *bear the vessels of the Lord,* Isa. lii. 11. Those that would *perfect holiness* must *cleanse themselves from all filthiness of flesh and spirit,* 2 Cor. vii. 1; Isa. i. 16–18.

[2] They were to be clothed with the holy garments (*v.* 5, 6, 8, 9), to signify that it was not sufficient for them to put away the pollutions of sin, but they must put on the graces of the Spirit, be *clothed with righteousness,* Ps. cxxxii. 9.

[3] The high priest was to be anointed with the *holy anointing oil* (*v.* 7), that the church might be filled and delighted with the sweet savour of his administrations and in token of the pouring out of the Spirit upon him, to qualify him for his work.

JAMIESON, FAUSSET, BROWN

of a flower, which seems to have been the figure of this golden plate, which was tied with a ribbon of blue on the front of the mitre, so that every one facing him could read the inscription.

39. coat of fine linen—a garment fastened at the neck, and reaching far down the person, with the sleeves terminating at the elbow. **girdle of needlework**—a piece of fine twined linen, richly embroidered, and variously dyed. It is said to have been very long, and being many times wound round the body, it was fastened in front and the ends hung down, which, being an impediment to a priest in active duty, were usually thrown across the shoulders. This was the outer garment of the common priests. **40. bonnets**—turbans. **42. linen breeches**—drawers, which encompassed the loins and reached half-way down the thighs. They are seen very frequently represented in Egyptian figures.

CHAPTER 29

Vss. 1-35. Consecrating the Priests and the Altar.—**1. hallow them, to minister unto me in the priest's office**—The act of inaugurating the priests was accompanied by ceremonial solemnities well calculated not only to lead the people to entertain exalted views of the office, but to impress those functionaries themselves with a profound sense of its magnitude and importance. In short, they were taught to know that the service was for them as well as for the people; and every time they engaged in a new performance of their duties, they were reminded of their personal interest in the worship, by being obliged to offer for themselves, before they were qualified to offer as the representatives of the people. **this is the thing that thou shalt do**—Steps are taken at the beginning of a society, which would not be repeated when the social machine was in full motion; and Moses, at the opening of the tabernacle, was employed to discharge functions which in later periods would have been regarded as sacrilege and punished with instant death. But he acted under the special directions of God. **4-10. Aaron and his sons thou shalt bring unto the door of the tabernacle**—as occupying the intermediate space between the court where the people stood, and the dwelling-place of Israel's king, and therefore the fittest spot for the priests being duly prepared for entrance, and the people witnessing the ceremony of inauguration. **wash them with water. And . . . take the garments**—The manner in which these parts of the ceremonial were performed is minutely described, and in discovering their symbolical import, which indeed, is sufficiently plain and obvious, we have inspired authority to guide us. It signified the necessity and importance of moral purity or holiness (Isa. 52:11; John 13:10; II Cor. 7:1; I Pet. 3:21). In like manner, the investiture with the holy garments signified their being clothed with righteousness (Rev. 19:8) and equipped as men active and well prepared for the service of God; the anointing the high priest with oil denoted that he was to be filled with the influences of the Spirit, for the edification and delight of the church (Lev. 10:7; Ps. 45:7; Isa. 61:1; I John 2:27), and as he was officially a type of Christ (Heb. 7:26; John 3:34; also Matt. 3:16; 11:29).

ADAM CLARKE

things. (2) He was the representative of a holy God. (3) He was to offer sacrifices to make an atonement for and to put away sin. (4) He was to teach the people the way of righteousness and true holiness. (5) As mediator, he was to obtain for them those divine influences by which they should be made holy, and be prepared to dwell with holy spirits in the Kingdom of glory. (6) In the sacerdotal office he was the type of that holy and just One who, in the fulness of time, was to come and put away sin by the sacrifice of himself.

38. *May bear the iniquity of the holy things.* "And Aaron shall bear [in a vicarious and typical manner] the sin of the holy or separated things"—offerings or sacrifices. Aaron was, as the high priest of the Jews, the type or representative of our blessed Redeemer; and as he offered the sacrifices prescribed by the law to make an atonement for sin, and was thereby represented as bearing their sins because he was bound to make an atonement for them, so Christ is represented as bearing their sins, i.e., the punishment due to the sins of the world, in His becoming a Sacrifice for the human race. See Isa. liii. 4, 12, where the same verb, *nasa,* is used; and see 1 Pet. ii. 24. By the inscription on the plate on his forehead Aaron was acknowledged as the holy minister of the holy God. *It shall be always upon his forehead.* The plate inscribed with "HOLINESS TO THE LORD" should be always on his forehead, to teach that the law required holiness; that this was its aim, design, and end. And the same is required by the gospel; for under this dispensation it is expressly said, Without holiness "no man shall see the Lord," Heb. xii. 14.

42. *Linen breeches.* This command had in view the necessity of purity and decency in every part of the divine worship, in opposition to the shocking indecency of the pagan worship in general, in which the priests often ministered naked, as in the sacrifices to Bacchus.

CHAPTER 29

1. *Take one young bullock.* This consecration did not take place till after the erection of the Tabernacle. See Lev. viii. 9-10.

2. *Unleavened bread.* Three kinds of bread as to its form are mentioned here, but all unleavened: (1) *matstsoth, unleavened bread,* no matter in what shape; (2) *challoth, cakes,* "pricked or perforated," as the root implies; (3) *rekikey,* an exceeding thin cake, from *rak,* "to be attenuated," properly enough translated *wafer.* The manner in which these were prepared is sufficiently plain from the text, and probably these were the principal forms in which flour was prepared for household use during their stay in the wilderness. These were all waved before the Lord, v. 24, as an acknowledgment that the bread that sustains the body, as well as the mercy which saves the soul, comes from God alone.

4. *Thou . . . shalt wash them.* This was done emblematically, to signify that they were to put away all filthiness of the flesh and spirit, and perfect holiness in the fear of God, 2 Cor. vii. 1.

5. *Thou shalt take the garments.* As most offices of spiritual and secular dignity had appropriate habits and insignia, hence, when a person was appointed to an office and habited for the purpose, he was said to be "invested" with that office, from *in,* used intensively, and *vestio,* "I clothe," because he was then clothed with the vestments peculiar to that office.

7. *Then shalt thou take the anointing oil.* It appears, from Isa. lxi. 1, that anointing with oil, in consecrating a person to any important office, whether civil or religious, was considered as an emblem of the communication of the gifts and graces of the Holy Spirit. This ceremony was used on three occasions, namely, the installation of prophets, priests, and kings, into their respective offices. In the Hebrew language *mashach* signifies to "anoint," and *mashiach,* the "anointed person." But as no man was ever dignified by holding the three offices, so no person ever had the title *mashiach,* the "anointed one," but Jesus the Christ. He alone is King of Kings and Lord of Lords: the King who governs

MATTHEW HENRY

[4] Sacrifices were to be offered for them. The covenant of priesthood, as all other covenants, must be *made by sacrifice*.

First, There must be a sin-offering, to make atonement for them, *v.* 10–14. It was used as other sin-offerings were; only, whereas the flesh of other sin-offerings was eaten by the priests (Lev. x. 18), in token of the priest's taking away the sin of the people, this was appointed to be all burnt without the camp (*v.* 14), to signify the imperfection of the legal dispensation.

Secondly, There must be a burnt-offering, a ram wholly burnt, to the honour of God, in token of the dedication of themselves wholly to God and to his service, as living sacrifices, kindled with the fire and ascending in the flame of holy love, *v.* 15–18.

Thirdly, There must be a peace-offering; it is called *the ram of consecration*, because there was more in this peculiar to the occasion than in the other two. In the burnt-offering God had the glory of their priesthood, in this they had the comfort of it; and, in token of a mutual covenant between God and them, [i] The blood of the sacrifice was divided between God and them (*v.* 20, 21); part of the blood was *sprinkled upon the altar round about*, and part put upon them, upon their bodies (*v.* 20), and upon their garments, *v.* 21. The blood of Christ, and the graces of the Spirit, which constitute and complete the beauty of holiness, recommend us to God; we read of robes *made white with the blood of the lamb*.

JAMIESON, FAUSSET, BROWN

Thou shalt cause a bullock to be brought before the tabernacle—This part of the ceremonial consisted of three sacrifices:

(1) The sacrifice of a bullock, as a sin offering; and in rendering it, the priest was directed to put his hand upon the head of his sacrifice, expressing by that act a consciousness of personal guilt, and a wish that it might be accepted as a vicarious satisfaction. (2) The sacrifice of a ram as a burnt offering—(vss. 15-18)—The ram was to be wholly burnt, in token of the priest's dedication of himself to God and His service. The sin offering was first to be presented, and *then* the burnt offering; for until guilt be removed, no acceptable service can be performed. (3) There was to be a peace offering, called the ram of consecration (vss. 19-22). And there was a marked peculiarity in the manner in which this other ram was to be disposed of. The former was for the glory of God—this was for the comfort of the priest himself; and as a sign of a mutual covenant being ratified, the blood of the sacrifice was divided—part sprinkled on the altar round about, and part upon the persons and garments of the priests. Nay, the blood was, by a singular act, directed to be put upon the extremities of the body, thereby signifying that the benefits of the atonement would be applied to the whole nature of man.

ADAM CLARKE

the universe, and rules in the hearts of His followers; the Prophet, to instruct men in the way wherein they should go; and the great High Priest, to make atonement for their sins. Hence He is called the Messias, a corruption of the word *hammashiach*, "the anointed one," in Hebrew; which gave birth to *ho Christos*, which has precisely the same signification in Greek. Of Him, Melchizedek, Abraham, Aaron, David, and others were illustrious types. But none of these had the title of the Messiah, or the Anointed of God.

10. *Shall put their hands upon the head of the bullock*. By this rite the animal was consecrated to God, and was then proper to be offered in sacrifice. Imposition of hands also signified that they offered the life of this animal as an atonement for their sins, and to redeem their lives from that death which, through their sinfulness, they had deserved. In the case of the sin offering and trespass offering, the person who brought the sacrifice placed his hands on the head of the animal between the horns, and confessed his sin over the sin offering, and his trespass over the trespass offering, saying, "I have sinned, I have done iniquity; I have trespassed, and have done thus and thus; and do return by repentance before Thee, and with *this* I make atonement." Then the animal was considered as vicariously bearing the sins of the person who brought it.

14. *It is a sin offering*. See the note on Lev. vii. 1, etc.

18. *It is a burnt offering*. See the note on Lev. vii. 1, etc.

19. *The other ram*. There were two rams brought on this occasion: one was for a burnt offering, and was to be entirely consumed; the other was the ram of consecration, v. 22, *eil milluim*, the "ram of filling up," because when a person was dedicated or consecrated to God his hands were filled with some particular offering proper for the occasion, which he presented to God. Hence the word "consecration" signifies the "filling up or filling the hands."

20. *Take of his blood*. The putting the blood of the sacrifice on the *tip* of the *right ear*, the *thumb* of the *right hand*, and the *great toe* of the *right foot* was doubtless intended to signify that they should dedicate all their faculties and powers to the service of God; their *ears* to the hearing and study of His law, their *hands* to diligence in the sacred ministry and to all acts of obedience, and their *feet* to walking in the way of God's precepts. And this sprinkling appears to have been used to teach them that they could neither hear, work, nor walk profitably, uprightly, and well pleasing in the sight of God without this application of the blood of the sacrifice.

22. *The fat and the rump*. The *rump* or "tail" of some of the Eastern sheep is the best part of the animal, and is counted a great delicacy. They are also very large, some of them weighing from twelve to forty pounds' weight.

23. *And one loaf of bread*. The bread of different kinds (see on v. 2) in this offering seems to have been intended as a *minchah*, or offering of grateful acknowledgment for providential blessings. The essence of worship consisted in acknowledging God, (1) As the Creator, Governor, and Preserver of all things, and the Dispenser of every good and perfect gift. (2) As the Judge of men, the Punisher of sin, and He who alone could pardon it. The *minchahs*, heave offerings, wave offerings, and thank offerings, referred to the *first* point. The burnt offerings, sin offerings, and sacrifices in general referred to the *second*.

24. *For a wave offering*. See the notes on Leviticus vii, where an ample account of all the offerings, sacrifices, etc., under the Mosaic dispensation, and the reference they bore to the great sacrifice offered by Christ, is given in detail.

25. *Thou shalt receive them of their hands*. Aaron and his sons are here considered merely as any common persons bringing an offering to God, and not having, as yet, any authority to present it themselves, but through the medium of a priest. Moses, therefore, was now to Aaron and his sons what they were afterwards to the children of Israel; and as the minister of

F. B. MEYER:

The consecration offerings. The second ram of the consecration ceremony yielded its blood to be placed on ear and hand and foot. We are thus taught that our senses, deeds, and goings are to be dedicated to God. Though the garments, which had just been put on, were perfectly new, they were besprinkled with blood and oil from head to foot. To our eyes that is a grievous disfigurement; but the Holy Spirit thus signified that even beauty is subordinate to the necessity for God's forgiveness and anointing. Whenever the priest beheld his dress he was reminded of his unworthiness, and of the abundant grace of God. Of course, the Lord Jesus needed no such preparation. He was holy, harmless, and separate from sinners.

Part of the flesh was waved heavenward and burned, as though God fed on it, while part was eaten by the priests. It was as though God and they feasted together in one holy sacrament, the symbol of their at-one-ment.—*Bible Commentary*

MATTHEW HENRY

[ii] The *flesh of the sacrifice*, with the meat-offering annexed to it, was likewise divided between God and them, that (to speak with reverence) God and they might feast together, in token of friendship and fellowship. Their eating of the things wherewith *the atonement was made* signified their *receiving the atonement*, as the expression is (Rom. v. 11), their thankful acceptance of the benefit of it, and their joyful communion with God thereupon, which was the true intent and meaning of a feast upon a sacrifice.

2. The time that was to be spent in this consecration: *Seven days shalt thou consecrate them, v.* 35. Though all the ceremonies were performed on the first day, yet, (1) They were not to look upon their consecration as completed till the seven days' end, which put a distance between this and their former state, and obliged them to enter upon their work with a pause, giving them time to consider the weight and seriousness of it. (2) Every day of the seven, in this first consecration, a bullock was to be offered for a sin-offering (*v.* 36), which was to intimate to them, [1] That though atonement was made, and they had the comfort of it, yet they must still keep up a penitent sense of sin and often repeat the confession of it. [2] That those sacrifices which were thus offered day by day to make atonement could not make the *comers thereunto perfect*, for then they would have ceased to be offered, as the apostle argues, Heb. x. 1, 2. They must therefore expect the *bringing in of a better hope*.

3. This consecration of the priests was a *shadow of good things to come.* (1) Our Lord Jesus is the great high-priest of our profession, clothed with the holy garments, even with glory and beauty, sanctified by his own blood, not that of bullocks and rams (Heb. ix. 12), *made perfect*, or consecrated, *through sufferings*, Heb. ii. 10. (2) All believers are spiritual priests, to offer spiritual sacrifices (1 Pet. ii. 5), washed in the blood of Christ. It is through Christ, the great sacrifice, that they are dedicated to this service.

II. The consecration of the altar, which seems to have been coincident with that of the priests, and the sin-offerings which were offered every day for seven days together had reference to the altar as well as the priests, *v.* 36, 37. The altar was also *sanctified*, not only set apart itself to a sacred use, but made so holy as to *sanctify the gifts* that were offered upon it, Matt. xxiii. 19. Christ is our altar; for our sakes he sanctified himself, that we and our performances might be sanctified and recommended to God, John xvii. 19.

Verses 38–46

I. The daily service appointed. A lamb was to be offered upon the altar every morning, and a lamb every evening, each with a meat-offering, both made by fire, as a *continual burnt-offering throughout their generations*, v. 38–41. Now, 1. This typified the con-

JAMIESON, FAUSSET, BROWN

Moreover, the flesh of this sacrifice was to be divided, as it were, between God and the priest—part of it to be put into his hand to be waved up and down, in token of its being offered to God, and then it was to be burnt upon the altar; the other part was to be eaten by the priests at the door of the tabernacle—that feast being a symbol of communion or fellowship with God. These ceremonies, performed in the order described, showed the qualifications necessary for the priests. (See Heb. 7:26, 27; 10:14).

35. seven days shalt thou consecrate them—The renewal of these ceremonies on the return of every day in the seven, with the intervention of a Sabbath, was a wise preparatory arrangement, in order to afford a sufficient interval for calm and devout reflection (Heb. 9:1; 10:1).

36, 37. CONSECRATION OF THE ALTAR. **36. thou shalt cleanse the altar**—The phrase, "when thou hast made an atonement for it," should be, *upon* it; and the purport of the direction is, that during all the time they were engaged as above from day to day in offering the appointed sacrifices, the greatest care was to be taken to keep the altar properly cleansed—to remove the ashes, and sprinkle it with the prescribed unction that, at the conclusion of the whole ceremonial, the altar itself should be consecrated as much as the ministers who were to officiate at it (Matt. 23:19). It was thenceforth associated with the services of religion.

38–46. INSTITUTION OF DAILY SERVICE. **38. two lambs of the first year day by day continually**—The sacred preliminaries being completed, Moses was instructed in the end or design to which these preparations were subservient, viz., the worship of God; and hence the institution of the morning and evening sacrifice. The institution was so imperative, that in no circumstances was this daily oblation to be dispensed with; and the due observance of it would secure the oft-promised grace and blessing of their heavenly King.

TODAY'S DICTIONARY OF THE BIBLE:

Wave Offerings, parts of peace offerings were so called, because they were waved by the priests (Ex. 29:24, 26, 27; Lev. 7:20–34; 8:27; 9:21; 10:14, 15, etc.), in token of a solemn special presentation of God. They then became the property of the priests. The firstfruits—a sheaf of barley—offered at the feast of Pentecost (Lev. 23:17–20), and wheatbread—the firstfruits of the second harvest—offered at the Passover (10:14), were wave offerings.

Heave Offering—Heb. *terúmah*—(Ex. 29:27) means simply an offering, a present, including all the offerings made by the Israelites as a present. This Hebrew word is frequently employed. Some of the rabbis attach to the word the meaning of elevation, and refer it to the *heave* offering, which consisted in presenting the offering by a motion up and down, distinguished from the *wave* offering, which consisted in a repeated movement in a horizontal direction—a "*wave offering* to the Lord as ruler of earth, a *heave offering* to the Lord as ruler of heaven." The right shoulder, which fell to the priests in presenting thank offerings, was called the *heave* shoulder (Lev. 7:34; Num. 6:20). The firstfruits offered in harvest time (Num. 15:20, 21) were heave offerings.

ADAM CLARKE

God he now consecrates them to the sacred office, and presents their offerings to Jehovah.

27. *The breast of the wave offering, and the shoulder of the heave offering.* As the *wave offering* was agitated to and fro, and the *heave offering* up and down, some have conceived that this twofold action represented the figure of the Cross, on which the great Peace Offering between God and man was offered in the personal sacrifice of our blessed Redeemer. The breast and the shoulder, thus waved and heaved, were by this consecration appointed to be the priests' portion forever. Moses, as priest, received on this occasion the breast and the shoulder, which became afterwards the portion of the priests; see v. 28, and Lev. vii. 34. It is worthy of remark that, although Moses himself had no consecration to the sacerdotal office, yet he acts here as high priest, consecrates a high priest, and receives the breast and the shoulder, which were the priests' portion! But Moses was an extraordinary messenger and derived his authority, without the medium of rites or ceremonies, immediately from God himself.

29. *The holy garments . . . shall be his sons' after him.* These garments were to descend from father to son, and no new garments were to be made.

30. *Seven days.* The priest in his consecration was to abide seven days and nights at the door of the Tabernacle, keeping the Lord's watch. See Lev. viii. 33, etc. The number *seven* is what is called among the Hebrews a number of "perfection"; and it is often used to denote the completion, accomplishment, fulness, or perfection of a thing, as this period contained the whole course of that time in which God created the world and appointed the day of rest. As this act of consecration lasted seven days, it signified a perfect consecration, and intimated to the priest that his whole body and soul, his time and talents, should be devoted to the service of God and His people.

33. *But a stranger shall not eat thereof.* That is, no person who was not of the family of Aaron—no Israelite, and not even a Levite.

34. *Burn the remainder with fire.* Common, voluntary, and peace offerings might be eaten even on the second day; see Lev. vii. 16; xix. 5-6. But this being a peculiar consecration, in order to qualify a person to offer sacrifices for sin, like that great sacrifice, the paschal lamb, that typified the atonement made by Christ, none of it was to be left till the morning lest putrefaction should commence, which would be utterly improper in a sacrifice that was to make expiation for sin and bring the soul into a state of holiness and perfection with God. See the note on Exod. xii. 10.

36. *Thou shalt cleanse the altar.* The altar was to be sanctified for seven days; and it is likely that on each day, previously to the consecration service, the altar was wiped clean, and the former day's ashes, etc., removed.

37. *Whatsoever toucheth the altar shall be holy.* To this our Lord refers in Matt. xxiii. 19, where He says the altar sanctifies the gift; and this may be understood as implying that whatever was laid on the altar became the Lord's property, and must be wholly devoted to sacred uses, for in no other sense could such things be sanctified by touching the altar.

39. *One lamb thou shalt offer in the morning.* These two lambs, one in the morning, and the other in the evening, were generally termed the morning and evening daily sacrifices, and were offered from the time of their settlement in the Promised Land to the destruction of Jerusalem by the Romans. The use of these sacrifices according to the Jews was this: "The morning sacrifice made atonement for the sins committed in the night, and the evening sacrifice expiated the sins committed during the day."

40. *A tenth deal of flour. Deal* signifies a "part." From Num. xxviii. 5 we learn that this *tenth deal* was the tenth part of an ephah, which constituted what is called an omer. See chap. xvi. 36. *The fourth part of an hin.* The *hin* contained one gallon and two pints. The *fourth* part of this was about one quart and a half of a pint. *Drink offering.* A libation poured out before the Lord. See its meaning, Lev. vii. 1, etc.

44. *I will sanctify . . . both Aaron and his sons.*

MATTHEW HENRY

tinual intercession which Christ ever lives to make, in virtue of his satisfaction, for the continual sanctification of his church: though he offered himself *once for all*, yet that one offering thus becomes a continual offering. 2. This teaches us to offer up to God the spiritual sacrifices of prayer and praise every day, morning and evening, in humble acknowledgment of our dependence upon him and our obligations to him. Prayer-time must be kept up as duly as meat-time.

II. Great and precious promises made of God's favour to Israel, and the tokens of his special presence with them. It is constancy in religion that brings in the comfort of it. If we do our part, God will do his, and will mark and fit that for himself which is in sincerity given up to him.

JAMIESON, FAUSSET, BROWN

F. B. MEYER:

The continual daily offerings. The consecration ceremony was repeated on seven succeeding days, and must have produced a profound impression. Thus line was upon line; and we may magnify God's patience in being willing through these repeated ordinances to educate the Hebrew people to the sublimest spirituality.

Notice the injunctions for daily services! No religious life can thrive without its regular hours and habits of devotion, such as these offerings suggest. Morning and evening prayers have been the custom in all ages. With the one we go forth to our labor till the evening, asking our Father to give guidance and protection. With the other, we entreat forgiveness and mercy (Ps. 55:17; Dan. 6:10). The chapter ends with many great and precious promises, which we who believe in Jesus may claim and enjoy.

—*Bible Commentary*

ADAM CLARKE

So we find the sanctification by Moses according to the divine institution was only symbolical; and that Aaron and his sons must be sanctified, i.e., made holy, by God himself before they could officiate in holy things. From this, as well as from many other things mentioned in the sacred writings, we may safely infer that no designation by man only is sufficient to qualify any person to fill the office of a minister of the sanctuary. The approbation and consecration of man have both their propriety and use, but must never be made substitutes for the unction and inspiration of the Almighty. Let holy men ordain, but let God sanctify; then we may expect that His Church shall be built up on its most holy faith.

45. *I will dwell among the children of Israel.* This is the great charter of the people of God, under both the Old and New Testaments; see chap. xxv. 8; Lev. xxvi. 11-12; 2 Cor. vi. 16; Rev. xxi. 3. God dwells among them: He is ever to be found in His Church to enlighten, quicken, comfort, and support it; to dispense the light of life by the preaching of His Word, and the influences of His Spirit for the conviction and conversion of sinners. And He dwells in those who believe; and this is the very tenor of the new covenant which God promised to make with the house of Israel; see Jer. xxxi. 31-34; Ezek. xxxvii. 24-28; Heb. viii. 7-12; and 2 Cor. vi. 16. And because God had promised to dwell in all His genuine followers, hence the frequent reference to this covenant and its privileges in the New Testament. And hence it is so frequently and strongly asserted that every believer is a habitation of God through the Spirit, Eph. ii. 22.

46. *And they shall know that I am the Lord their God.* That is, they shall "acknowledge" God, and their infinite obligations to Him. In a multitude of places in Scripture the word *know* should be thus understood. *That I may dwell among them.* For without this acknowledgment and consequent dependence on and gratitude and obedience to God, they could not expect Him to dwell among them.

CHAPTER 30

Verses 1–10

I. The orders given concerning the altar of incense are, 1. That it was to be made of wood, and covered with gold, with horns at the corners, a golden cornice round it, with rings and staves of gold, for the convenience of carrying it, *v.* 1–5. The measure of the altar of incense in Ezekiel's temple is double to what it is here (Ezek. xli. 22), and it is there called *an altar of wood*, and there is no mention of gold, to signify that the incense in gospel times should be spiritual, the worship plain, and the service of God enlarged.

2. That it was to be placed before the mercy-seat, which was within the veil, *v.* 6. For though he that ministered at the altar could not see the mercy-seat, the veil interposing, yet he must look towards it, and direct his incense that way, to teach us that though we cannot with our bodily eyes see the throne of grace, yet we must in prayer by faith set ourselves before it, direct our prayer, and look up.

3. That Aaron was to burn sweet incense upon this altar, every morning and every evening, intended, not only to take away the ill smell of the flesh that was burnt daily on the brazen altar, but to show the acceptableness of his people's services. As by the offerings on the brazen altar satisfaction was made for what had been done displeasing to God, so, by the offering on this, what

CHAPTER 30

Vss. 1-38. THE ALTAR OF INCENSE. **1. thou shalt make an altar to burn incense upon,** etc.—Its material was to be like that of the ark of the testimony, but its dimensions very small. **2. foursquare**—the meaning of which is not that it was to be entirely of a cubical form, but that upon its upper and under surface, it showed four equal sides. It was twice as high as it was broad, being twenty-one inches broad and three feet six inches high. It had "horns"; its top or flat surface was surmounted by an ornamental ledge or rim, called a crown, and it was furnished at the sides with rings for carriage. Its only accompanying piece of furniture was a golden censer or pan, in which the incense was set fire to upon the altar. Hence it was called the altar of incense, or the "golden altar," from the profuse degree in which it was gilded or overlaid with the precious metal. This splendor was adapted to the early age of the church, but in later times, when the worship was to be more spiritual, the altar of incense is prophetically described as not of gold but of wood, and double the size of that in the tabernacle, because the church should be vastly extended (Mal. 1:11). **6. thou shalt put it before the veil that is by the ark of the testimony**—which separated the holy from the most holy place. The altar was in the middle between the table of showbread and the candlestick next the holy of holies, at equal distances from the north and south walls; in other words, it occupied a spot on the outside of the great partition veil, but directly in front of the mercy seat, which was within that sacred enclosure; so that although the priest who ministered at this altar could not behold the mercy seat, he was to look towards it, and present his incense in that direction. This was a special arrangement, and it was designed to teach the important lesson that, though we cannot with the eye of sense, see the throne of grace, we must "direct our prayer to it and look up" (cf. II Cor. 3:14; Heb. 10:20; Rev. 4:1). **7. Aaron shall burn thereon sweet incense**—lit., incense of spices—Strong aromatic substances were burnt upon this altar to counteract by their odoriferous fragrance the offensive fumes of the sacrifices; or the incense was employed in an offering of tributary homage which the Orientals used to make as a mark of honor to kings; and as God was Theocratic Ruler of

CHAPTER 30

1. *Altar to burn incense.* The Samaritan omits the ten first verses of this chapter, because it inserts them after the thirty-second verse of chap. xxvi. See the note there. *Shittim wood.* The same of which the preceding articles were made, because it was abundant in those parts, and because it was very durable; hence everywhere the Septuagint translation, which was made in Egypt, renders the original by "incorruptible wood."

2. *Foursquare.* That is, on the upper or under surface, as it showed four equal sides; but it was twice as high as it was broad. It was called, not only the "altar of incense," but also the "golden altar," Num. iv. 11. For the *crown, horns, staves,* etc., see on the altar of burnt offering, chap. xxvi.

6. *Before the mercy seat that is over the testimony.* These words in the original are supposed to be a repetition, by mistake, of the preceding clause; the word *happarocheth,* the "veil," being corrupted by interchanging two letters into *haccapporeth,* the "mercy seat"; and this, as Dr. Kennicott observes, places the altar of incense before the mercy seat, and consequently in the holy of holies! Now this could not be, as the altar of incense was attended every day, and the holy of holies entered only once in the year. The five words which appear to be a repetition are wanting in twenty-six of Kennicott's and De Rossi's MMS., and in the Samaritan. The verse reads better without them and is more consistent with the rest of the account.

7. *When he dresseth the lamps.* Prepares the wicks and puts in fresh oil for the evening. *Shall burn incense upon it.* Where so many sacrifices were offered, it was essentially necessary to have some pleasing perfume to counteract the disagreeable smells that must have arisen

MATTHEW HENRY

hey did well was, as it were, recommended to the ivine acceptance; for our two great concerns with God are to be acquitted from guilt and accepted as ighteous in his sight.

II. This incense-altar typified, 1. The mediation of Christ. The brazen altar in the court was a type of Christ dying on earth; the golden altar in the anctuary was a type of Christ interceding in heaven. This altar was before the mercy-seat, for Christ always appears in the presence of God for us: he is our *advocate with the father* (1 John ii. 1), and his intercession is unto God of a sweet-smelling savour. This altar had a crown fixed to it; for Christ intercedes as a king. 2. The devotions of the saints. When the priest was burning incense the people were praying Luke i. 10), to signify that prayer is the true incense. The lamps were dressed or lighted at the same time hat the incense was burnt, to teach us that the eading of the scriptures (which are our light and amp) is a part of our daily work, and should ordinarily accompany our prayers and praises. When we peak to God we must hear what God says to us, and thus the communion is complete. And, if the heart and life be not holy, even *incense is an abomination* (Isa. i. 13), and he that offers it is *as if he blessed an idol*, Isa. lxvi. 3.

Verses 11–16

Moses is here ordered to levy money upon the people by way of poll, so much a head, for the service of the tabernacle. This he must do when he numbered the people. Some think that it refers only to the first numbering of them. Others think that it was afterwards repeated upon any emergency and always when the people were numbered. But many of the Jewish writers are of opinion that it was to be an annual tribute. This was that tribute-money which Christ paid, for fear of offending his adversaries (Matt. xvii. 27). Now, 1. The tribute to be paid was *half a shekel*. The rich were not to give more, nor the poor less (*v.* 15), to intimate that the souls of the rich and poor are alike precious, and that God is *no respecter of persons*, Acts x. 34. In other offerings men were to give according to their ability; but this, which was the *ransom of the soul*, must be alike for all. 2. This tribute was to be paid as a *ransom of the soul, that there might be no plague among them*. 3. This money that was raised was to be employed in the service of the tabernacle (*v.* 16); with it they bought sacrifices, flour, incense, wine, oil, fuel, salt, priests' garments. Note, Those that have the benefit of God's tabernacle among them must be willing to defray the expenses of it.

Verses 17–21

Orders are here given, 1. For the making of a laver, or font, of brass, a large vessel, that would contain a good quantity of water, which was to be set near the door of the tabernacle, *v.* 18. 2. For the using of this laver. Aaron and his sons must wash their hands and feet at this laver every time they went in to minister, every morning, at least, *v.* 19–21. This was designed, (1) To teach them purity in all their ministrations. He only shall *stand in God's holy place* that has *clean hands and a pure heart*, Ps. xxiv. 3, 4. And, (2) It was to teach us, who are daily to attend upon God, daily to renew our repentance for sin. *Cleanse your hands and purify your hearts*, and then *draw nigh to God*, Jam. iv. 8.

Verses 22–38

Directions are here given for the composition of the holy anointing oil and the incense that were to be used in the service of the tabernacle. 1. The holy anointing oil is here ordered to be made up; the ingredients, and their quantities, are prescribed, *v.* 23–25. It was to be compounded *secundum artem—after the art of the apothecary* (*v.* 25); the spices were to be infused in the oil, and then strained out, leaving an admirable sweet smell in the oil. With this oil God's tent and all the furniture of it were to be anointed; it was to be used also in the consecration of the priests, *v.* 26–30. Solomon was anointed with it (1 Kings i. 39), and some other of the kings; and all the high priests. Christ's name is said to be *as ointment poured forth* (Cant. i. 3), and the good name of Christians better than *precious ointment*, Eccles. vii. 1.

JAMIESON, FAUSSET, BROWN

Israel, *His* palace was not to be wanting in a usage of such significancy. Both these ends were served by this altar—that of fumigating the apartments of the sacred edifice, while the pure lambent flame, according to Oriental notions, was an honorary tribute to the majesty of Israel's King. But there was a far higher meaning in it still; for as the tabernacle was not only a palace for Israel's King, but a place of worship for Israel's God, this altar was immediately connected with a religious purpose. In the style of the sacred writers, incense was a symbol or emblem of prayer (Ps. 141:2; Rev. 5:8; 8:3). From the uniform combination of the two services, it is evident that the incense was an emblem of the prayers of sincere worshippers ascending to heaven in the cloud of perfume; and, accordingly, the priest who officiated at this altar typified the intercessory office of Christ (Luke 1:10; Heb. 7:25). **8. Aaron shall burn incense**—seemingly limiting the privilege of officiating at the altar of incense to the high priest alone, and there is no doubt that he and his successors exclusively attended this altar on the great religious festivals. But "Aaron" is frequently used for the whole priestly order, and in later times, any of the priests might have officiated at this altar in rotation (Luke 1:9). **every morning . . . at even**—In every period of the national history this daily worship was scrupulously observed. **9. Ye shall offer no strange incense**—i.e., of a different composition from that of which the ingredients are described so minutely. **11-16. When thou takest the sum of the children of Israel,** etc.—Moses did so twice, and doubtless observed the law here prescribed. The tax was not levied from women, minors, old men (Num. 1:42, 45), and the Levites (Num. 1:47), they being not numbered. Assuming the shekel of the sanctuary to be about half an ounce troy, though nothing certain is known about it, the sum payable by each individual was fifty cents. This was not a voluntary contribution, but a ransom for the soul or lives of the people. It was required from all classes alike, and a refusal to pay implied a wilful exclusion from the privileges of the sanctuary, as well as exposure to divine judgments. It was probably the same impost that was exacted from our Lord (Matt. 17:24-27), and it was usually devoted to repairs and other purposes connected with the services of the sanctuary. **18-21. Thou shalt . . . make a laver of brass**—Though not actually forming a component part of the furniture of the tabernacle, this vase was closely connected with it; and though from standing at the entrance it would be a familiar object, it possessed great interest and importance from the baptismal purposes to which it was applied. No data are given by which its form and size can be ascertained; but it was probably a miniature pattern of Solomon's—a circular basin. **his foot**—supposed not to be the pedestal on which it rested, but a trough or shallow receptacle below, into which the water, let out from a cock or spout, flowed; for the way in which all Eastern people wash their hands or feet is by pouring upon them the water which falls into a basin. This laver was provided for the priests alone. But in the Christian dispensation, all believers are priests, and hence the apostle exhorts them how to draw near to God (Josh. 13:10; Heb. 10:22). **22-33. Take thou also . . . principal spices,** etc.—Oil is frequently mentioned in Scripture as an emblem of sanctification, and anointing with it a means of designating objects as well as persons to the service of God. Here it is prescribed by divine authority, and the various ingredients in their several proportions described which were to compose the oil used in consecrating the furniture of the tabernacle. **myrrh**—a fragrant and medicinal gum from a little known tree in Arabia. **sweet cinnamon**—produced from a species of laurel or sweet bay, found chiefly in Ceylon, growing to a height of twenty feet: this spice is extracted from the inner bark, but it is not certain whether that mentioned by Moses is the same as that with which we are familiar. **sweet calamus**—or sweet cane, a product of Arabia and India, of a tawny color in appearance; it is like the common cane and strongly odoriferous. **cassia**—from the same species of tree as the cinnamon—some think the outer bark of that tree. All these together would amount to 120 lbs. troy weight. **hin**—a word of Egyptian origin, equal to ten pints. Being mixed with the olive oil—no doubt of the purest kind—this composition probably remained always in a liquid state, and the strictest prohibition issued against using it for any other purpose than anointing the tabernacle and its furniture. **34-38. the Lord said unto Moses, Take unto thee sweet spices**—These were: stacte, the finest myrrh; onycha, supposed to be an odoriferous shell; galbanum, a

ADAM CLARKE

from the slaughter of so many animals, the sprinkling of so much blood, and the burning of so much flesh. The perfume that was to be burnt on this altar is described in v. 34. No blood was ever sprinkled on this altar, except on the day of general expiation, which happened only once in the year, v. 10. But the perfume was necessary in every part of the Tabernacle and its environs.

9. *No strange incense.* None made in any other way. *Nor burnt sacrifice.* It should be an altar for incense, and for no other use.

10. *An atonement . . . once in a year.* On the tenth day of the seventh month. See Lev. xvi. 18, etc.

12. *Then shall they give every man a ransom for his soul.* This was a very important ordinance, and should be seriously considered.

13. *Half a shekel.* Each of the Israelites was ordered to give as a ransom for his soul (i.e., for his life) half a shekel, according to the shekel of the sanctuary. St. Peter seems to allude to this, and to intimate that this mode of atonement was ineffectual in itself, and only pointed out the great sacrifice which, in the fulness of time, should be made for the sin of the world. "Ye know," says he, "that ye were not redeemed with corruptible things, as silver and gold, from your vain conversation received by tradition from your fathers; but with the precious blood of Christ, as of a lamb without blemish and without spot: who verily was foreordained before the foundation of the world," 1 Pet. i. 18-20.

18. *A laver of brass. Kiyor* sometimes signifies a "caldron," 1 Sam. ii. 14; but it seems to signify any large, round vessel or basin used for washing the hands and feet. There were doubtless spigots in it to draw off the water, as it is not likely the feet were put into it in order to be washed. The *foot* of the laver must mean the pedestal on which it stood.

20. *They shall wash with water, that they die not.* This was certainly an emblematical washing; and as the hands and the feet are particularly mentioned, it must refer to the purity of their whole conduct. Their *hands* (all of their works), their *feet* (all their goings) must be *washed*—must be holiness unto the Lord. And this washing must be repeated every time they entered into the Tabernacle, or when they came near to the altar to minister. This washing was needful because the priests all ministered barefoot; but it was equally so because of the guilt they might have contracted, for the washing was emblematical of the putting away of sin, or what St. Paul calls the "washing [laver] of regeneration, and renewing of the Holy Ghost" (Titus iii. 5), as the influences of the Spirit must be repeated for the purification of the soul as frequently as any moral defilement has been contracted.

21. *And it shall be a statute for ever.* To continue in its literal meaning as long as the Jewish economy lasted, and in its spiritual meaning to the end of time. What an important lesson does this teach the ministers of the gospel of Christ! Each time they minister in public, whether in dispensing the Word or the sacraments, they should take heed that they have a fresh application of the grace and spirit of Christ to do away past transgressions or unfaithfulness and to enable them to minister with the greater effect, as being in the divine favor, and consequently entitled to expect all the necessary assistances of the divine unction to make their ministrations spirit and life to the people.

24. *Oil olive.* Olive oil is supposed to be the best preservative of odors. As the gifts and graces of the Holy Spirit are termed the anointing of the Holy Ghost, therefore this holy ointment appears to have been designed as emblematical of those gifts and graces. See Acts i. 5; x. 38; 2 Cor. i. 21; 1 John ii. 20, 27.

25. *After the art of the apothecary.* The original, *rokeach*, signifies a "compounder" or "confectioner"; any person who compounds *drugs, aromatics, etc.*

34. *Take unto thee sweet spices.* The holy perfume was compounded of the following ingredients: *Stacte. Nataph*, supposed to be the same with what was afterwards called the balm

MATTHEW HENRY

2. The incense which was burned upon the golden altar was prepared of sweet spices likewise, though not so rare and rich as those of which the anointing oil was compounded, *v.* 34, 35. 3. Concerning both these preparations the same law is here given (v. 32, 33, 37, 38), that the like should not be made for any common use.

CHAPTER 31

Verses 1–11

A great deal of fine work God had ordered to be done about the tabernacle; the materials the people were to provide, but who must put them into form? Moses himself was learned in all the learning of the Egyptians, but he knew not how to engrave or embroider. We may suppose that there were some very ingenious men among the Israelites; but, having lived all their days in bondage in Egypt, we cannot think they were any of them instructed in these curious arts. They knew how to make brick and work in clay, but to work in gold and in cutting diamonds was what they had never been brought up to. They had no goldsmiths or jewellers but what must be made out of masons and bricklayers? *Who was sufficient for these things?* But God takes care of this matter also.

I. He nominates the persons that were to be employed. 1. Bezaleel was to be the architect, or master workman, *v.* 2. He was of the tribe of Judah, a tribe that God delighted to honour; the grandson of Hur, probably that Hur who had helped to hold up Moses's hands (*ch.* xvii.). 2. Aholiab, of the tribe of Dan, is appointed next to Bezaleel, and partner with him, *v.* 6. Aholiab was of the tribe of Dan, which was one of the less honourable tribes, that the tribes of Judah and Levi might not be lifted up, as if they were to engross all the preferments. Hiram, who was the head workman in the building of Solomon's temple, was also of the tribe of Dan, 2 Chron. ii. 14. 3. There were others that were employed by and under these in the several operations about the tabernacle, *v.* 6.

II. He qualifies these persons for the service (*v.* 3): *I have filled him with the Spirit of God; and* (*v.* 6) *in the hearts of all that are wise-hearted I have put wisdom.* Note, 1. Skill in common arts and employments is the gift of God; from him are derived both the faculty and the improvement of the faculty. He teaches the husbandman discretion (Isa. xxviii. 26), and the tradesmen too; and he must have the praise of it. 2. God dispenses his gifts variously, one gift to one, another to another, and all for the good of the whole body, both of mankind and of the church. Moses was fittest of all to govern Israel, but Bezaleel was fitter than he to build the tabernacle. 3. Those whom God calls to any service he will either find, or make, fit for it. The work that was to be done here was to make the tabernacle and the utensils of it, which are here particularly reckoned up, *v.* 7, &c. And for this the persons employed were enabled to *work in gold, and silver, and brass.* When Christ sent his apostles to rear the gospel tabernacle, he poured out his Spirit upon them, to enable them to speak with tongues the wonderful works of God; not to work upon metal, but to work upon men; so much more excellent were the gifts, as the tabernacle to be pitched was a *greater and more perfect tabernacle*, as the apostle calls it, Heb. ix. 11.

Verses 12–18

I. A strict command for the sanctification of the sabbath day, *v.* 13-17. The law of the sabbath had been given them before any other law, by way of preparation (*ch.* xvi. 23); it had been inserted in the body of the moral law, in the fourth commandment; it had been annexed to the judicial law (*ch.* xxiii. 12); and here it is added to the first part of the ceremonial law, because the observance of the sabbath is indeed the hem and hedge of the whole law; where no conscience is made of that, farewell both godliness and honesty; for, in the moral law, it stands in the midst between the two tables. *Verily,* or *nevertheless, my*

JAMIESON, FAUSSET, BROWN

gumresin from an umbelliferous plant. **frankincense**—a dry, resinous, aromatic gum, of a yellow color, which comes from a tree in Arabia, and is obtained by incision of the bark. This incense was placed within the sanctuary, to be at hand when the priest required to burn on the altar. The art of compounding unguents and perfumes was well known in Egypt, where sweet-scented spices were extensively used not only in common life, but in the ritual of the temples. Most of the ingredients here mentioned have been found on minute examination of mummies and other Egyptian relics; and the Israelites, therefore, would have the best opportunities of acquiring in that country the skill in pounding and mixing them which they were called to exercise in the service of the tabernacle. But the recipe for the incense as well as for the oil in the tabernacle, though it receives illustration from the customs of Egypt, was peculiar, and being prescribed by divine authority, was to be applied to no common or inferior purpose.

CHAPTER 31

Vss. 1-18. BEZALEEL AND AHOLIAB. **2. See, I have called**—Though the instructions about the tabernacle were privately communicated to Moses, it was plainly impossible that he could superintend the work in person, amid the multiplicity of his other duties. A head director or builder was selected by God Himself; and the nomination by such high authority removed all ground of jealousy or discontent on the part of any who might have thought their merits overlooked (cf. Matt. 18:1). **by name Bezaleel**—signifying "in the shadow or protection of God"; and, as called to discharge a duty of great magnitude—to execute a confidential trust in the ancient Church of God, he has his family and lineage recorded with marked distinction. He belonged to the tribe of Judah, which, doubtless for wise and weighty reasons, God all along delighted to honor; and he was the grandson of Hur, a pious patriot (ch. 17:12), who was associated, by a special commission, with Aaron in the government of the people during the absence of Moses. Moreover, it may be noticed that a Jewish tradition affirms Hur to be the husband of Miriam; and if this tradition may be relied on, it affords an additional reason for the appointment of Bezaleel emanating from the direct authority of God. **3-5. I have filled him with the spirit of God**—It is probable that he was naturally endowed with a mechanical genius, and had acquired in Egypt great knowledge and skill in the useful, as well as liberal, arts so as to be a first-class artisan, competent to take charge of both the plain and ornamental work, which the building of the sacred edifice required. When God has any special work to be accomplished, He always raises up instruments capable of doing it; and it is likely that He had given to the son of Uri that strong natural aptitude and those opportunities of gaining mechanical skill, with an ultimate view to this responsible office. Notwithstanding that his grand duty was to conform with scrupulous fidelity to the pattern furnished, there was still plenty of room for inventive talent and tasteful exactness in the execution; and his natural and acquired gifts were enlarged and invigorated for the important work. **6. I have given with him Aholiab**—He belonged to the tribe of Dan, one of the least influential and honorable in Israel; and here, too, we can trace the evidence of wise and paternal design, in choosing the colleague or assistant of Bezaleel from an inferior tribe (cf. I Cor. 12:14-25; also Mark 6:7). **all that are wise-hearted I have put wisdom**—At that period, when one spirit pervaded all Israel, it was not the man full of heavenly genius who presided over the work; but all who contributed their skill, experience, and labor, in rendering the smallest assistance, showed their piety and devotedness to the divine service. In like manner, it was at the commencement of the Christian Church (Acts 6:5; 18:2).

ADAM CLARKE

of Jericho. *Stacte* is the gum which spontaneously flows from the tree which produces myrrh. *Onycha. Shecheleth,* allowed by the best critics to be the external crust of the shellfish *murex,* and is the basis of the principal perfumes made in the East Indies. *Galbanum, Chelbenah,* the African *ferula;* it rises with a ligneous stalk from eight to ten feet, and is garnished with leaves at each joint. When any part of the plant is broken, there issues out a little thin milk of a cream color. The gummy, resinous juice which proceeds from this plant is what is commonly called *galbanum,* from the *chelbenah* of the Hebrew. *Pure frankincense. Labonah Zaccah. Frankincense* is supposed to derive its name from *frank,* "free," because of its liberal or ready distribution of its odors. It is a dry, resinous substance in pieces or drops of a pale yellowish-white color, has a strong smell, and bitter, acrid taste.

CHAPTER 31

2. *I have called by name Bezaleel.* That is, I have particularly appointed this person to be the chief superintendent of the whole work. His name is significant, *betsal-el,* "in or under the shadow of God," meaning under the especial protection of the Most High.

3. *In wisdom. Chochmah,* from *chacham,* to be "wise, skilful, or prudent," denoting the compass of mind and strength of capacity necessary to form a wise man; hence our word "wisdom," the power of judging what is wise or best to be done. *Understanding. Tebunah,* from *ban,* to "separate, distinguish, discern"; capacity to comprehend the different parts of a work, how to connect, arrange, in order to make a complete whole. *Knowledge. Daath,* denoting particular "acquaintance" with a person or thing; practical, experimental knowledge.

4. *Cunning works. Machashaboth,* works of invention or genius, in the goldsmith and silversmith line.

5. *In cutting of stones.* Everything that concerned the lapidary's, jeweler's, and carver's art.

6. *In the hearts of all that are wise hearted I have put wisdom.* So every man that had a natural genius, as we term it, had an increase of wisdom by immediate inspiration from God, so that he knew how to execute the different works which divine wisdom designed for the Tabernacle and its furniture.

8. *The pure candlestick.* Called so either because of the pure gold of which it was made, or the brightness and splendor of its workmanship, or of the light which it imparted in the Tabernacle, as the purest, finest oil was always burnt in it.

9. *The altar of burnt offering.* See on chap. xxvii. 1. *The laver and his foot.* The pedestal on which it stood.

10. *Cloths of service.* Vestments for the ordinary work of their ministry; *the holy garments*—those which were peculiar to the high priest.

MATTHEW HENRY

sabbaths you shall keep. Though they must hasten the work, yet they must not make more haste than good speed; they must not break the law of the sabbath in their haste: even tabernacle-work must give way to the sabbath-rest.

1. The nature, meaning, and intention, of the sabbath, by the declaration of which God puts an honour upon it, and teaches us to value it. Divers things are here said of the sabbath. (1) *It is a sign between me and you* (*v.* 13), and again (*v.* 17). The institution of the sabbath was a sign that he had distinguished them from all other people. God, by sanctifying this day among them, let them know that he sanctified them, and set them apart for himself and his service. (2) *It is holy unto you* (*v.* 14), that is, "It is designed for your benefit as well as for God's honour"; *the sabbath was made for man.* (3) It is the *sabbath of rest, holy to the Lord, v.* 15. It is separated from common use, and designed for the honour and service of God. (4) It was to be observed *throughout their generations,* in every age, *for a perpetual covenant, v.* 16.

2. The law of the sabbath. They must keep it (*v.* 13, 14, 16), keep it as a treasure, as a trust.

3. The reason of the sabbath; for God's laws are not only backed with the highest authority, but supported with the best reason. God's own example is the great reason, *v.* 17.

4. The penalty to be inflicted for the breach of this law: "Every one that *defileth the sabbath,* by doing *any work therein* but works of piety and mercy, *shall be cut off from among his people* (*v.* 14); *he shall surely be put to death, v.* 15.

II. The delivering of the two tables of testimony to Moses. 1. The ten commandments which God had spoken upon Mount Sinai in the hearing of all the people were now written, *in perpetuam rei memoriam—for a perpetual memorial,* because that which is written remains. 2. They were written in *tables of stone.* The law was written in *tables of stone,* to denote the perpetual duration of it. 3. They were written *with the finger of God,* that is, by his will and power immediately. It is God only that can write his law in the heart; by his Spirit, which is the *finger of God,* he writes his will in the *fleshy tables of the heart,* 2 Cor. iii. 3. 4. They were written in two tables, being designed to direct us in our duty both towards God and towards man. 5. They are called *tables of testimony,* because this written law testified both the will of God concerning them and his good-will towards them, and would be a testimony against them if they were disobedient.

JAMIESON, FAUSSET, BROWN

12-17. Verily my sabbaths ye shall keep—The reason for the fresh inculcation of the fourth commandment at this particular period was, that the great ardor and eagerness, with which all classes betook themselves to the construction of the tabernacle, exposed them to the temptation of encroaching on the sanctity of the appointed day of rest. They might suppose that the erection of the tabernacle was a sacred work, and that it would be a high merit, an acceptable tribute, to prosecute the undertaking without the interruption of a day's repose; and therefore the caution here given, at the commencement of the undertaking, was a seasonable admonition.

18. tables of stone, written with the finger of God—containing the ten commandments (ch. 24:12), called "tables of testimony," because God testified His will in them.

ADAM CLARKE

13. *My sabbaths ye shall keep.* See the notes on Exod. xx. 8.

14. *Every one that defileth it.* By any kind of idolatrous or profane worship. *Shall surely be put to death.* The magistrates shall examine into the business, and if the accused be found guilty, he shall be stoned to death. *Shall be cut off.* Because that person who could so far contemn the Sabbath, which was a sign to them of the rest which remained for the people of God, was of course an infidel, and should be cut off from all the privileges and expectations of an Israelite.

16. *A perpetual covenant.* Because it is a sign of this future rest and blessedness, therefore the religious observance of it must be perpetually kept up.

17. *Rested, and was refreshed.* God, in condescension to human weakness, applies to himself here what belongs to man. If a man religiously rests on the Sabbath, both his body and soul shall be refreshed; he shall acquire new light and life.

18. *When he had made an end of communing.* When the forty days and forty nights were ended. *Two tables of testimony.* See on chap. xxxiv. 1. *Tables of stone.* That the record might be lasting, because it was a testimony that referred to future generations, and therefore the materials should be durable. *Written with the finger of God.* That these tables were written, not by the commandment but by the power of God himself, the following passages seem to prove: "And the Lord said unto Moses, Come up to me into the mount, and be there: and I will give thee tables of stone . . . which I have written; that thou mayest teach them," Exod. xxiv. 12. "And he gave unto Moses . . . upon mount Sinai, two tables of testimony, tables of stone, written with the finger of God," chap. xxxi. 18. "And Moses . . . went down from the mount, and the two tables of testimony were in his hand: the tables were written on both their sides . . . And the tables were the work of God, and the writing was the writing of God, graven upon the tables," chap. xxxii. 15-16. "These words [the Ten Commandments] the Lord spake . . . in the mount out of the midst of the fire, of the cloud, and of the thick darkness, with a great voice: and he added no more. And he wrote them in two tables of stone," Deut. v. 22.

MATTHEW HENRY

CHAPTER 32

Verses 1–6

While Moses was in the mount, receiving the law from God, the people had time to meditate upon what had been delivered, but there were those among them that were contriving how to break the laws they had already received. On the thirty-ninth day of the forty, the plot broke out of rebellion against the Lord.

I. A tumultuous address which the people made to Aaron, who was entrusted with the government in the absence of Moses: *Up, make us gods, which shall go before us, v.* 1.

1. See the ill effect of Moses's absence from them.

2. See the fury and violence of a multitude when they are influenced and corrupted by such as lie in wait to deceive.

(1) They were weary of waiting for the promised land. They are for hastening to the land *flowing with milk and honey,* and cannot stay to take their religion along with them. We must first wait for God's law before we catch at his promises.

(2) They were weary of waiting for the return of Moses. *As for this Moses, the man that brought us up out of Egypt, we wot not what has become of him. Observe,* [1] How slightly they speak of his person—*this Moses.* Thus ungrateful are they to Moses, who had shown such a tender concern for them, and thus do they walk contrary to God. If he tarried long, it was because God had a great deal to say to him, for their good; he resided upon the mount as their ambassador, and he would certainly return as soon as he had finished the business he went upon; and yet they make this the colour for their wicked proposal. Misinterpretations of our Redeemer's delays are the occasion of a great deal of wickedness. Our Lord Jesus has gone up into the mount of glory, where he is appearing in the presence of God for us, but out of our sight; the heavens must contain him, must conceal him, that we may live by faith. Weariness in waiting betrays us to a great many temptations. Israel here, if they could but have stayed one day longer, would have seen what had become of Moses.

JAMIESON, FAUSSET, BROWN

CHAPTER 32

Vss. 1-35. THE GOLDEN CALF. **1. when the people saw that Moses delayed**—They supposed that he had lost his way in the darkness or perished in the fire. **the people gathered themselves together unto Aaron**—rather "against" Aaron in a tumultuous manner, to compel him to do what they wished. The incidents related in this chapter disclose a state of popular sentiment and feeling among the Israelites that stands in singular contrast to the tone of profound and humble reverence they displayed at the giving of the law. Within a space of little more than thirty days, their impressions were dissipated. Although they were still encamped upon ground which they had every reason to regard as holy; although the cloud of glory that capped the summit of Sinai was still before their eyes, affording a visible demonstration of their being in close contact, or rather in the immediate presence, of God, they acted as if they had entirely forgotten the impressive scenes of which they had been so recently the witnesses.

ADAM CLARKE

CHAPTER 32

1. *When the people saw that Moses delayed.* How long this was before the expiration of the forty days, we cannot tell; but it certainly must have been some considerable time, as the ornaments must be collected, and the calf or ox, after having been founded, must require a considerable time to fashion it with the graving tool; and certainly not more than two or three persons could work on it at once. This work, therefore, must have required several days. *The people gathered themselves together.* They came in a tumultuous and seditious manner, insisting on having an object of religious worship made for them, as they intended under its direction to return to Egypt. See Acts vii. 39-40.

As for this Moses, the man that brought us up. This seems to be the language of great contempt, and by it we may see the truth of the character given them by Aaron, v. 22, "they are set on mischief." It is likely they might have supposed that Moses had perished in the fire, which they saw had invested the top of the mountain into which he went.

MATTHEW HENRY

(3) They were weary of waiting for a divine institution of religious worship among them. They were told that they must *serve God in this mountain*, but, because that was not appointed them so soon as they wished, they would set their own wits on work to devise signs of God's presence with them, and would glory in them, and have a worship of their own invention, probably such as they had seen among the Egyptians. To say, *Moses is lost, make us a god*, was the greatest absurdity imaginable. *Make us gods, which shall go before us! Gods!* How many would they have? Is not one sufficient? *Make us gods!* and what good would gods of their own making do them?

II. Here is the demand which Aaron makes of their jewels thereupon: *Bring me your golden ear-rings, v.* 2. We do not find that he said one word to discountenance their proposal, but seemed to approve the motion, and showed himself not unwilling to humour them in it. One would hope he designed, at first, only to make a jest of it, and, by setting up a ridiculous image among them, to expose the motion, and show them the folly of it. Some charitably suppose that when Aaron told them to break off their ear-rings, and bring them to him, he did it with design to crush the proposal, believing that though their coveteousness would have let them *lavish gold out of the bag* to make an idol of (Isa. xlvi. 6), yet their pride would not have suffered them to part with their golden ear-rings.

III. Here is the making of the golden calf, *v.* 3, 4. 1. The people brought in their ear-rings to Aaron, whose demand of them, instead of discouraging the motion, perhaps did rather gratify their superstition, and beget in them a fancy that the gold taken from their ears would be the most acceptable, and would make the most valuable god. 2. Aaron melted down their rings, and, having a mould prepared for the purpose, poured the melted gold into it, and then produced it in the shape of an ox or calf. Some think that Aaron chose this figure, for a sign or token of the divine presence, because he thought the head and horns of an ox a proper emblem of the divine power, and yet, being so plain and common a thing, he hoped the people would not be so sottish as to worship it. But it is probable that they had learnt of the Egyptians thus to represent the Deity, for it is said (Ezek. xx. 8), *They did not forsake the idols of Egypt*, and (*ch.* xxiii. 8), *Neither left she her whoredoms brought from Egypt. Thus they changed their glory into the similitude of an ox* (Ps. cvi. 20), and proclaimed their own folly, beyond that of other idolaters, who worshipped the host of heaven.

IV. Having made the calf in Horeb, they *worshipped the graven image*, Ps. cvi. 19. Aaron, seeing the people fond of their calf, was willing yet further to humour them, and he built an altar before it, and proclaimed a feast to the honour of it (*v.* 5), a feast of dedication. Yet he calls it *a feast to Jehovah*; for, brutish as they were, they did not imagine that this image was itself a god, but they made it for a representation of the true God, whom they intended to worship in and through this image. The people are forward enough to celebrate this feast (*v.* 6): *They rose up early on the morrow*, to show how well pleased they were with the solemnity, and, according to the ancient rites of worship, they offered sacrifice to this new-made diety, and then feasted upon the sacrifice; thus having, at the expense of their ear-rings, made their god, they endeavour, at the expense of their beasts, to make this god propitious. Now, 1. It was strange that any of the people, especially so great a number of them, should do such a thing. Had they not, but the other day, in this very place, heard the voice of the Lord God speaking to them out of the midst of the fire, *Thou shalt not make to thyself any graven image*? Nay, had they not themselves solemnly entered into covenant with God, and promised that all that which he had said unto them they *would do, and would be obedient*? *ch.* xxiv. 7. *They made a calf in Horeb*, the very place where the law was given. It was otherwise with those that received the gospel; they immediately *turned from idols*, 1 Thess. i. 9. 2. It was especially strange that Aaron should be so deeply implicated in this sin, that he should make the calf, and proclaim the feast! Is this Aaron, who had been with Moses in the mount (*ch.* xix. 24; xxiv. 9), and knew that there was no manner of similitude seen there, by which they might make an image? Is he aiding and abetting in this rebellion against the Lord? How was it possible that he should ever do so sinful a thing? Either he was strangely surprised into it, and did it when he was half asleep, or he was frightened into it by the outrages of the rabble. The Jews have a tradition that his colleague Hur opposing it the people fell upon him and stoned him (and therefore we never read of him after) and that this frightened Aaron into a compliance.

JAMIESON, FAUSSET, BROWN

said unto him, Up, make us gods; which shall go before us—The *Hebrew* word rendered "gods" is simply the name of God in its plural form. The image made was single, and therefore it would be imputing to the Israelites a greater sin than they were guilty of, to charge them with renouncing the worship of the true God for idols. The fact is, that they required, like children, to have something to strike their senses, and as the Shekinah, "the glory of God," of which they had hitherto enjoyed the sight, was now veiled, they wished for some visible material object as the symbol of the divine presence, which should go before them as the pillar of fire had done. **2. Aaron said, . . . Break off . . . earrings**—It was not an Egyptian custom for young men to wear earrings, and the circumstance, therefore, seems to point out "the mixed rabble," who were chiefly *foreign* slaves, as the ringleaders in this insurrection. In giving direction to break their earrings, Aaron probably calculated on gaining time; or, perhaps, on their covetousness and love of finery proving stronger than their idolatrous propensity. If such were his expectations, they were doomed to signal disappointment. Better to have calmly and earnestly remonstrated with them, or to have preferred duty to expediency, leaving the issue in the hands of Providence. **3. all the people brake off the golden earrings**—The Egyptian rings, as seen on the monuments, were round massy plates of metal; and as they were rings of this sort the Israelites wore, their size and number must, in the general collection, have produced a large store of the precious metal. **4. fashioned it with a graving tool, after he had made it a molten calf**—The words are transposed, and the rendering should be, "he framed with a graving tool the image to be made, and having poured the liquid gold into the mould, he made it a molten calf." It is not said whether it was of life size, whether it was of solid gold or merely a wooden frame covered with plates of gold. This idol seems to have been the god Apis, the chief deity of the Egyptians, worshipped at Memphis under the form of a live ox, three years old. It was distinguished by a triangular white spot on its forehead and other peculiar marks. Images of it in the form of a whole ox, or of a calf's head on the end of a pole, were very common; and it makes a great figure on the monuments where it is represented in the van of all processions, as borne aloft on men's shoulders. **they said, These be thy gods, O Israel, which brought thee up out of the land of Egypt**—It is inconceivable that they, who but a few weeks before had witnessed such amazing demonstrations of the true God, could have suddenly sunk to such a pitch of infatuation and brutish stupidity, as to imagine that human art or hands could make a god that should go before them. But it must be borne in mind, that though by election and in name they were the people of God, they were as yet, in feelings and associations, in habits and tastes, little, if at all different, from Egyptians. They meant the calf to be an image, a visible sign or symbol of Jehovah, so that their sin consisted not in a breach of the FIRST, but of the SECOND commandment. **5, 6. Aaron made proclamation, and said, To-morrow is a feast to the Lord**—a remarkable circumstance, strongly confirmatory of the view that they had not renounced the worship of Jehovah, but in accordance with Egyptian notions, had formed an image with which they had been familiar, to be the visible symbol of the divine presence. But there seems to have been much of the revelry that marked the feasts of the heathen.

ADAM CLARKE

2. *Golden earrings.* Both men and women wore these ornaments, and we may suppose that these were a part of the spoils which they brought out of Egypt.

3. *And all the people brake off the golden earrings.* The human being is naturally fond of dress, though this has been improperly attributed to the female sex alone, and those are most fond of it who have the shallowest capacities; but on this occasion the bent of the people to idolatry was greater than even their love of dress, so that they readily stripped themselves of their ornaments in order to get a molten god.

4. *Fashioned it with a graving tool.* There has been much controversy about the meaning of the word *cheret* in the text: some make it a mold; others a garment, cloth, or apron; some a purse or bag, and others a graver. It is likely that some mold was made on this occasion, that the gold when fused was cast into it, and that afterwards it was brought into form and symmetry by the action of the chisel and graver. *These be thy gods, O Israel.* Was it possible that Aaron could have imagined that he could make any god that could help them? Possibly he only intended to make them some symbolical representation of the divine power and energy. It must, however, be granted that Aaron does not appear to have even designed a worship that should supersede the worship of the Most High; hence we find him making proclamation, "To morrow is a feast to the Lord." It has been supposed that this calf was an exact resemblance of the famous Egyptian god Apis, who was worshipped under the form of an ox, which worship the Israelites no doubt saw often practiced in Egypt.

6. *The people sat down to eat and to drink.* The burnt offerings were wholly consumed; the peace offerings, when the blood had been poured out, became the food of the priests. They *rose up to play, letsachek*, a word of ominous import, which seems to imply here fornicating and adulterous intercourse; and in some countries the verb "to play" is still used precisely in this sense. In this sense the original is evidently used, Gen. xxxix. 14.

MATTHEW HENRY

Verses 7–14

Here, I. God acquaints Moses with what was doing in the camp while he was absent, *v.* 7, 8. God says to Moses concerning this sin, 1. That they had *corrupted themselves*. Sin is the corruption or depravation of the sinner, and it is a self-corruption. 2. That they had *turned aside out of the way*. Sin is a deviation from the way of our duty into a by-path. 3. That they had turned aside quickly after the law was given them and they had promised to obey it. 4. He tells him particularly what they had done: *They have made a calf, and worshipped it*. Those sins which are concealed from our governors are naked and open before God. We could not bear to see the thousandth part of that provocation which God sees every day and yet keeps silence. 5. He seems to disown them, in saying to Moses, They are *thy people whom thou broughtest up out of the land of Egypt*. Those that corrupt themselves not only shame themselves, but even make God himself ashamed of them and of his kindness to them. 6. He sends him down to them with all speed: *Go, get thee down*.

II. He expresses his displeasure against Israel for this sin, *v.* 9, 10. 1. He gives this people their true character: "*It is a stiff-necked people*." The righteous God sees, not only what we do, but what we are. 2. He declares what was their just desert—that his wrath should *wax hot against them*. Sin exposes us to the wrath of God; and that wrath, if it be not allayed by divine mercy, will burn us up as stubble. 3. He holds out inducements to Moses not to intercede for them: *Therefore, let me alone*. Thus he would put an honour upon prayer, intimating that nothing but the intercession of Moses could save them from ruin.

III. Moses earnestly intercedes with God on their behalf (*v.* 11–13): he besought the Lord his God. If God would not be called *the God of Israel*, yet he hoped he might address him as *his own God*. He wisely took the hint which God gave him when he said, *Let me alone*, which, though it seemed to forbid his interceding, did really encourage it, by showing what power the prayer of faith has with God. Observe, 1. His prayer (*v.* 12): *Turn from thy fierce wrath*; not as if he thought God was not justly angry, but he begs that he would not be so greatly angry as to consume them. 2. His pleas. He fills his mouth with arguments, not to move God, but to express his own faith and to excite his own fervency in prayer. He urges, (1) God's interest in them, the great things he had already done for them. God had said to Moses (*v.* 7), They are *thy people, whom thou broughtest up out of Egypt*; but Moses humbly turns them back upon God again: "They are *thy people*, thou art their Lord and owner; I am but their servant. *Thou broughtest them forth out of Egypt*. I was but the instrument in thy hand. "Thou *broughtest them out of Egypt*, though they were unworthy, and had there served the gods of the Egyptians, Josh. xxiv. 15. If thou didst that for them, notwithstanding their sins in Egypt, wilt thou undo it for their sins of the same nature in the wilderness?" (2) He pleads the concern of God's glory (*v.* 12): *Wherefore should the Egyptians say, For mischief did he bring them out?* He cannot bear to hear God reflected on, and therefore this he insists upon, *Lord, what will the Egyptians say?* If a people so strangely saved should be suddenly ruined, what would the world say of it, especially the Egyptians, who have such an implacable hatred both to Israel and to the God of Israel? They would say, "God was either weak, and could not, or fickle, and would not, complete the salvation he began." *What will the Egyptians say?* We ought always to be careful that the name of God and his doctrine be not blasphemed through us. (3) He pleads God's promise to the patriarchs that he would multiply their seed, and give them the land of Canaan. God's promises are to be our pleas in prayer.

IV. God graciously abated the rigour of the sentence, and *repented of the evil he thought to do* (*v.* 14). See here, 1. The power of prayer; God suffers himself to be prevailed with by the humble believing importunity of intercessors. 2. The compassion of God towards poor sinners, and how ready he is to forgive.

Verses 15–20

I. The favour of God to Moses, in trusting him with the two tables of the testimony, which, though of common stone, were far more valuable than all the precious stones that adorned the breastplate of Aaron.

II. The familiarity between Moses and Joshua. While Moses was in the cloud, as in the presence-chamber, Joshua continued as near as he might. When Moses came down he came with him, and not till then. Joshua, who was a military man, feared

JAMIESON, FAUSSET, BROWN

7-14. the Lord said unto Moses, Go, get thee down—Intelligence of the idolatrous scene enacted at the foot of the mount was communicated to Moses in language borrowed from human passions and feelings, and the judgment of a justly offended God was pronounced in terms of just indignation against the gross violation of the so recently promulgated laws. **make of thee a great nation**—Care must be taken not to suppose this language as betokening any change or vacillation in the divine purpose. The covenant made with the patriarchs had been ratified in the most solemn manner; it *could* not and never was intended that it *should* be broken. But the manner in which God spoke to Moses served two important purposes—it tended to develop the faith and intercessory patriotism of the Hebrew leader, and to excite the serious alarm of the people, that God would reject them and deprive them of the privileges they had fondly fancied were so secure.

15-18. Moses turned, and went down from the mount—The plain, Er-Raheh, is not visible from the top of Jebel Musa, nor can the mount be descended on the side towards that valley; hence Moses and his companion, who on duty had patiently waited his return in the hollow of the mountain's brow, heard the shouting some time before they actually saw the camp.

ADAM CLARKE

7. *Thy people . . . have corrupted themselves.* They had not only got into the spirit of idolatry, but they had become abominable in their conduct, so that God disowns them to be His: *Thy people* have broken the covenant, and are no longer entitled to My protection and love.

9. *A stiffnecked people.* Probably an allusion to the stiff-necked ox, the object of their worship.

10. *Now therefore let me alone.* Moses had already begun to plead with God in the behalf of this rebellious and ungrateful people; and so powerful was his intercession that even the Omnipotent represents himself as incapable of doing anything in the way of judgment unless His creature desists from praying for mercy!

14. *And the Lord repented of the evil.* This is spoken merely after the manner of men who, having formed a purpose, permit themselves to be diverted from it by strong and forcible reasons, and so change their minds relative to their former intentions.

F. C. COOK:

14. This states a fact which was not revealed to Moses till after his second intercession when he had come down from the mountain and witnessed the sin of the people (vv. 30–34). He was then assured that the Lord's love to His ancient people would prevail. God is said, in the language of Scripture, to "repent," when His forgiving love is seen by man to blot out the letter of His judgments against sin (2 Sam. 24:16; Joel 2:13; Jonah 3:10); or when the sin of man seems to human sight to have disappointed the purposes of grace (Gen. 6:6; 1 Sam. 15:35). The awakened conscience is said to "repent," when, having felt its sin, it feels also the divine forgiveness: it is at this crisis that God, according to the language of Scripture, repents towards the sinner. Thus the repentance of God made known in and through the One true Mediator reciprocates the repentance of the returning sinner, and reveals to him atonement.—*Barnes' Notes*

MATTHEW HENRY

there was *a noise of war in the camp*, and then he would be missed; but Moses, having received notice of it from God, better distinguished the sound, and was aware that it was *the voice of those that sing*.

III. The great and just displeasure of Moses against Israel, for their idolatry. He resented it as an offence to God, and the scandal of his people. Moses was the meekest man on the earth, and yet when he saw *the calf, and the dancing*, his *anger waxed hot*. Note, It is no breach of the law of meekness to show our displeasure at the wickedness of the wicked. It becomes us to be cool in our own cause, but warm in God's. 1. To convince them that they had forfeited and lost the favour of God, *he broke the tables*, *v.* 19, that the sight of it might the more affect them, and fill them with confusion, when they saw what blessings they had lost. 2. To convince them that they had betaken themselves to a God that could not help them, he *burnt the calf* (*v.* 20), melted it down, and then filed it to dust; and, that the powder to which it was reduced might be taken notice of throughout the camp, he strewed it upon that water of which they all drank. That it might appear that *an idol is nothing in the world* (1 Cor. viii. 4), he reduced this to atoms, that it might be as near nothing as could be.

Verses 21–29

Moses, having shown his just indignation against the sin of Israel by breaking the tables and burning the calf, now proceeds to reckon with the sinners and to call them to an account, herein acting as the representative of God. Now,

I. He begins with Aaron, as God began with Adam, because he was the principal person, though not first in the transgression, but drawn into it. Observe here,

1. The just reproof Moses gives him, *v.* 21. And having prevailed with God for him, to save him from ruin, he here expostulates with him, to bring him to repentance. He puts Aaron upon considering, (1) What he had done to this people: *Thou hast brought so great a sin upon them.* The people, as the first movers, might be said to bring the sin upon Aaron; but he being a magistrate, who should have suppressed it, and yet aiding and abetting it, might truly be said to bring it upon them, because he hardened their hearts and strengthened their hands in it. (2) What moved him to it: *What did this people unto thee?* Men can but tempt us to sin; they cannot force us. Men can but frighten us; if we do not comply, they cannot hurt us.

2. The frivolous excuse Aaron makes for himself. (1) He deprecates the anger of Moses only, whereas he should have deprecated God's anger in the first place: *Let not the anger of my lord wax hot*, *v.* 22. (2) He lays all the fault upon the people: *They are set on mischief, and they said, Make us gods.* It is natural to us to endeavour thus to transfer our guilt. Sin is a brat that nobody is willing to own. (3) It is well if he did not intend a reflection upon Moses, as accessory to the sin, by staying so long on the mount, in repeating, without need, that invidious surmise of the people, *As for this Moses, we know not what has become of him*, *v.* 23. (4) He extenuates and conceals his own share in the sin, and childishly insinuates that when he cast the gold into the fire it came out in this shape; but not a word of his graving and fashioning it, *v.* 24.

II. The people are next to be judged for this sin. The approach of Moses turned their dancing into trembling. Those that hectored Aaron into a compliance with them in their sin durst not look Moses in the face.

1. How they were exposed to shame by their sin: *The people were naked* (*v.* 25), not so much because they had some of them lost their ear-rings, but because they had lost their integrity. It was a shame to them, and a perpetual blot, that they *changed their glory into the similitude of an ox.* Thus were they *made naked*, stripped of their ornaments, and exposed to contempt.

2. The course that Moses took to roll away this reproach, not by concealing the sin, or putting any false colour upon it, but by punishing it, and so bearing a public testimony against it.

(1) By whom vengeance was taken—by the children of Levi (*v.* 26, 28); not by the immediate hand of God himself, as on Nadab and Abihu, but by the sword of man, to teach them that idolatry was an *iniquity to be punished by the judge*, being a *denial of the God that is above*, Job. xxxi. 28; Deut. xiii. 9. The innocent must be culled out to be the executioners of the guilty. Now here we are told, [1] How the Levites were called out to this service. *Moses clad himself with zeal* as with a robe, and summoned all those to appear forthwith that were on God's side, against the golden calf. *Who is on the Lord's side?* The interest of sin and

JAMIESON, FAUSSET, BROWN

19. Moses' anger waxed hot, and he cast the tables out of his hands—The arrival of the leader, like the appearance of a specter, arrested the revellers in the midst of their carnival, and his act of righteous indignation when he dashed on the ground the tables of the law, in token that as they had so soon departed from their covenant relation, so God could withdraw the peculiar privileges that He had promised them—that act, together with the rigorous measures that followed, forms one of the most striking scenes recorded in sacred history. **20. he took the calf which they had made, and burnt it in the fire,** etc.—It has been supposed that the gold was dissolved by *natron* or some chemical substance. But there is no mention of solubility here, or in Deuteronomy 9:21; it was "burned in the fire," to cast it into ingots of suitable size for the operations which follow—"grounded to powder"; the powder of malleable metals can be ground so fine as to resemble dust from the wings of a moth or butterfly; and these dust particles will float in water for hours, and in a running stream for days. These operations of grinding were intended to show contempt for such worthless gods, and the Israelites would be made to remember the humiliating lesson by the state of the water they had drunk for a time [NAPIER]. Others think that as the idolatrous festivals were usually ended with great use of sweet wine, the nauseous draught of the gold dust would be a severe punishment (ch. II Kings 23:6, 15; II Chron. 15:16; 34:7).

22. Aaron said, Let not the anger of my lord wax hot—Aaron cuts a poor figure, making a shuffling excuse and betraying more dread of the anger of Moses than of the Lord (cf. Deut. 9:20).

25. naked—either unarmed and defenseless, or ashamed from a sense of guilt. Some think they were literally naked, as the Egyptians performed some of their rites in that indecent manner.

26-28. Moses stood in the gate of the camp, and said—The camp is supposed to have been protected by a rampart after the attack of the Amalekites. **Who is on the Lord's side? let him**

ADAM CLARKE

16. *The tables were the work of God.* Because such a law could proceed from none but himself; God alone is the Fountain and Author of law, of what is right, just, holy, and good. *The writing was the writing of God.* For as He is the sole Author of law and justice, so He alone can write them on the heart of man. This is agreeable to the spirit of the new covenant which God had promised to make with men in the latter days: "I will make [a new covenant] with the house of Israel . . . I will put my laws into their mind, and write them in their hearts," Jer. xxxi. 33; Heb. viii. 10; 2 Cor. iii. 3.

17. *Joshua . . . said . . . There is a noise of war in the camp.* How natural was this thought to the mind of a military man! Hearing a confused noise, he supposed that the Israelitish camp had been attacked by some of the neighboring tribes.

18. *And he said.* That is, Moses returned this answer to the observations of Joshua.

19. *He cast the tables out of his hands, and brake them.* He might have done this through distress and anguish of spirit, on beholding their abominable idolatry and dissolute conduct; or he probably did it emblematically, intimating thereby that, as by this act of his the tables were broken in pieces, on which the law of God was written; so they, by their present conduct, had made a breach in the covenant, and broken the laws of their Maker.

20. *He took the calf . . . and burnt . . . and ground it to powder.* How truly contemptible must the object of their idolatry appear when they were obliged to drink their god, reduced to powder and strewed on the water!

21. *What did this people unto thee?* It seems, if Aaron had been firm, this evil might have been prevented.

22. *Thou knowest the people.* He excuses himself by the wicked and seditious spirit of the people, intimating that he was obliged to accede to their desires.

24. *I cast it into the fire, and there came out this calf.* What a silly and ridiculous subterfuge! He seems to insinuate that he only threw the metal into the fire, and that the calf came unexpectedly out by mere accident.

25. *Moses saw that the people were naked.* It is likely that the word *parua* implies that they were reduced to the most helpless and wretched state, being abandoned by God in the midst of their enemies. This is exactly similar to that expression, 2 Chron. xxviii. 19: "For the Lord brought Judah low because of Ahaz king of Israel; for he made Judah naked [*hiphria*], and transgressed sore against the Lord."

26. *Who is on the Lord's side?* That is, Who among you is free from this transgression? *And all the sons of Levi.* It seems they had no part in this idolatrous business.

MATTHEW HENRY

wickedness is the devil's interest, and all wicked people side with that interest; the interest of truth and holiness is God's interest, with which all godly people side; and it is a case that will not admit a neutrality. [2] How they were commissioned for this service (*v.* 27): *Slay every man his brother*, that is, "Slay all those that you know to have been active for the making and worshipping of the golden calf, though they were your own nearest relations, or dearest friends." Yet, it should seem, they were to slay those only whom they found *abroad in the streets* of the camp; for it might be hoped that those who had retired into their tents were ashamed of what they had done, and were upon their knees, repenting.

(2) On whom vengeance is taken: *There fell of the people that day about* 3,000 *men*, *v.* 28. Probably these were but few, in comparison with the many that were guilty; but these were the men that headed the rebellion, and were therefore picked out, to be made examples of, for terror to all others.

Verses 30–35

Moses, having executed justice upon the principal offenders, is here dealing both with the people and with God.

I. With the people, to bring them to repentance, *v.* 30.

1. When some were slain, lest the rest should imagine that, because they were exempt from the capital punishment, they were therefore looked upon as free from guilt, Moses here tells the survivors, *You have sinned a great sin*. To affect them with the greatness of their sin he intimates to them what a difficult thing it would be to make up the quarrel which God had with them for it. The malignity of sin appears in the price of pardons.

2. Yet it was some encouragement to the people (when they were told that they had *sinned a great sin*) to hear that Moses would *go up unto the Lord to make atonement* for them. Christ, the great Mediator, went upon greater certainty than this, for he had laid in the bosom of the Father, and perfectly knew all his counsels.

II. He intercedes with God for mercy. Observe, 1. How pathetic his address was. *Moses returned unto the Lord*, not to receive further instructions about the tabernacle. Moses in this address expresses, (1) His great detestation of the people's sin, *v.* 31. *Oh! this people have sinned a great sin*. God had first told him of it (*v.* 7), and now he tells God of it, by way of lamentation. He does not go about to excuse or extenuate the sin; but what he had said to them by way of conviction he says to God by way of confession: *They have sinned a great sin*; he came not to make apologies, but to make atonement. (2) His great desire of the people's welfare (*v.* 32): *Yet now* it is not too great a sin for infinite mercy to pardon, and therefore *if thou wilt forgive their sin*. It is an abrupt expression, *If thou wilt forgive*, is as much as, "O that thou wouldest forgive!" as Luke xix. 42, *If thou hadst known* is, *O that thou hadst known*. "But *if not, blot me, I pray thee, out of the book which thou hast written*"; that is, "If they must be cut off, let me be cut off with them, and cut short of Canaan; if all Israel must perish, I am content to perish with them; let not the land of promise be mine by survivorship." Thus he expresses his tender affection for the people, and is a type of the good Shepherd, that *lays down his life for the sheep* (John x. 11), who was to be *cut off from the land of the living for the transgression of my people*, Isa. liii. 8; Dan. ix. 26. He is also an example of public-spiritedness to all, especially to those in public stations.

2. Observe how prevalent his address was. God would not take him at his word; no, he will not blot any out of his book but those that by their wilful disobedience have forfeited the honour of being enrolled in it (*v.* 33). This was also an intimation of mercy to the people.

Further, in answer to the address of Moses, (1) God promises to go on with his intention of giving them the land of Canaan. Therefore he sends Moses back to them to lead them, though they were unworthy of him, and promises that his angel should go before them. (2) Yet he threatens to remember this sin against them when hereafter he should see cause to punish them for other sins.

JAMIESON, FAUSSET, BROWN

come unto me—The zeal and courage of Moses was astonishing, considering he opposed an intoxicated mob. The people were separated into two divisions, and those who were the boldest and most obstinate in vindicating their idolatry were put to death, while the rest, who withdrew in shame or sorrow, were spared.

29. Consecrate yourselves to-day to the Lord—or, ye have consecrated yourselves to-day. The Levites, notwithstanding the dejection of Aaron, distinguished themselves by their zeal for the honor of God and their conduct in doing the office of executioners on this occasion; and this was one reason that they were appointed to a high and honorable office in the service of the sanctuary. **30-33. Moses said unto the people, Ye have sinned a great sin**—Moses labored to show the people the heinous nature of their sin, and to bring them to repentance. But not content with that, he hastened more earnestly to intercede for them. **32. blot me . . . out of thy book**—an allusion to the registering of the living, and erasing the names of those who die. What warmth of affection did he evince for his brethren! How fully was he animated with the true spirit of a patriot, when he professed his *willingness* to die for them. But Christ actually died for His people (Rom. 5:8).

F. B. MEYER:

"Peradventure I shall make an Atonement for your sin" (Ex. 32:30).

The heart of Moses was full of that great, wonderful new word, *atonement*. For many days, God had been telling him about it, and speaking it over and over to his heart. He seemed, however, to feel that no ordinary sacrifices would avail: the blood of goats and bulls would surely be insufficient to put away the black transgression into which Israel had fallen. But there was rising in his heart a resolve, to which he gave expression when he returned to God: "Blot me, I pray thee, out of the book of which thou hast written." He did not realize that his blood would not avail, but that the blood of Christ, who should, in the fullness of time, offer himself without spot to God, alone could put away sin.

In every heart there is a deep conviction of the necessity of an atonement. This is the source of the temples, altars, and sacrifices which have marked the history of every nation under heaven. Man has felt as by a natural instinct that some reparation was necessary to the broken law.

The insufficiency of animal sacrifice. In the Levitical system there was a remembrance of sin made year by year; but the sin itself could not be purged by such rites. The fact that the worshipers so constantly came back to offer their sacrifices shows that they were not assured. The priests always stood: their attitude was an emblem of an unfinished work.

The sufficiency of Christ's atonement. He was willing to be cut off out of the land of the living for the transgression of his people; and because He died, there is no longer the "—" which in Moses' prayer speaks of uncertainty; but a blessed assurance that we are at one with God, with each other, and with all holy beings.

—Great Verses Through the Bible

ADAM CLARKE

28. *There fell . . . about three thousand men.* These were, no doubt, the chief transgressors; having broken the covenant by having other gods besides Jehovah, they lost the divine protection, and then the justice of God laid hold on and slew them. Moses, doubtless, had positive orders from God for this act of justice (see v. 27); for though, thorugh his intercession, the people were spared so as not to be exterminated as a nation, yet the principal transgressors, those who were "set on mischief," v. 22, were to be put to death.

29. *For Moses had said, Consecrate yourselves.* "Fill your hands" to the Lord. See the reason of this form of speech in the note on chap. xxiv. 19.

32. *Forgive their sin—; and if not, blot me . . . out of thy book.* "This people have sinned a great sin, and have made them gods of gold"; thus they had broken the covenant (see the first and second commandments), and by this had forfeited their right to Canaan. *Yet now*, he adds, *if thou wilt forgive their sin*, that they may yet attain the promised inheritance—; *and if not, blot me, I pray thee, out of thy book which thou hast written*—if Thou wilt blot out their names from this register, and never suffer them to enter Canaan, blot me out also; for I cannot bear the thought of enjoying that blessedness while my people and their posterity shall be forever excluded. And God, in kindness to Moses, spared him the mortification of going into Canaan without taking the people with him. They had forfeited their lives, and were sentenced to die in the wilderness; and Moses' prayer was answered in mercy to him, while the people suffered under the hand of justice. But the promise of God did not fail; for, although those who sinned were blotted out the book, yet their posterity enjoyed the inheritance.

This seems to be the simple and pure light in which this place should be viewed; and in this sense St. Paul is to be understood, Rom. ix. 3, where he says: "For I could wish that myself were accursed from Christ for my brethren, my kinsmen according to the flesh: who are Israelites; to whom pertaineth the adoption, and the glory, and the covenants." Moses could not survive the destruction of his people by the neighboring nations, nor their exclusion from the Promised Land; and St. Paul, seeing the Jews about to be cut off by the Roman sword for their rejection of the gospel, was willing to be deprived of every earthly blessing, and even to become a sacrifice for them, if this might contribute to the preservation and salvation of the Jewish state. Both those eminent men, engaged in the same work, influenced by a spirit of unparalleled patriotism, were willing to forfeit every blessing of a secular kind, even die for the welfare of the people. But certainly neither of them could wish to go to eternal perdition to save their countrymen from being cut off, the one by the sword of the Philistines, the other by that of the Romans. Even the supposition is monstrous.

33. *Whosoever hath sinned against me, him will I blot out.* As if the Divine Being had said: "All My conduct is regulated by infinite justice and righteousness: in no case shall the innocent ever suffer for the guilty. That no man may transgress through ignorance, I have given you My law, and thus published My covenant; the people themselves have acknowledged its justice and equity, and have voluntarily ratified it. He then that sins against Me (for sin is the transgression of the law, 1 John iii. 4, and the law must be published and known that it may be binding), him will I blot out of My book." And is it not remarkable that to these conditions of the covenant God strictly adhered, so that not one soul of these transgressors ever entered into the promised rest? Here was justice. And yet, though they deserved death, they were spared! Here was mercy. Thus, as far as justice would permit, mercy extended; and as far as mercy would permit, justice proceeded.

34. *Lead the people unto the place.* The word *place* is not in the text, and is with great propriety omitted. For Moses never led this people into that place; they all died in the wilderness except Joshua and Caleb. But Moses led them "towards" the place, and thus the particle *el* here should be understood, unless we suppose

MATTHEW HENRY

The Jews have a saying, grounded on this, that henceforward no judgment fell upon Israel but there was in it an ounce of the powder of the golden calf. Stephen says that when they *made a calf, and offered sacrifice to the idol, God turned, and gave them up to worship the host of heaven* (Acts vii. 41, 42); so that the strange addictedness of that people to the sin of idolatry was a just judgment upon them for making and worshipping the golden calf, and a judgment they were never quite freed from till the captivity of Babylon. See Rom. i. 23-25. Aaron was not plagued, but the people; for his was a sin of infirmity, theirs a presumptuous sin.

CHAPTER 33

Verses 1-6

Here is, I. The message which God sent by Moses to the children of Israel. 1. He applies to them a mortifying name, by giving them their just character —*a stiff-necked people, v.* 3, 5. God would have brought them under the yoke of his law, and into the bond of his covenant, but their necks were too stiff to bow to them. Note, God judges of men by the temper of their minds. We know what man does; God knows what he is: we know what proceeds from man; God knows what is in man, and nothing is more displeasing to him than stiff-neckedness. 2. He tells them what they deserved. Had he dealt with them according to their sins, he had taken them away with a swift destruction. 3. He bids them *depart and go up hence* to the land of Canaan, *v.* 1. 4. Though he promises to make good his covenant with Abraham, in giving them Canaan, yet he denies them the extraordinary tokens of his presence. "*I will send an angel before thee*, for thy protector, otherwise the evil angels would soon destroy thee; but *I will not go up in the midst of thee, lest I consume thee*" (*v.* 2, 3). Justice said, "Cut them off, and consume them." Mercy said, "*How shall I give thee up, Ephraim?*" Hos. xi. 8. Well, says God, *put off thy ornaments, that I may know what to do with thee*; that is, "Put thyself into the posture of a penitent, that mercy may rejoice against judgment," *v.* 5. Note, Calls to repentance are plain indications of mercy designed.

II. The people's melancholy reception of this message. 1. *They mourned* (*v.* 4), for their sin which had provoked God to withdraw from them, and mourned for this as the sorest punishment of their sin. Note, Of all the bitter fruits and consequences of sin, that which true penitents most lament, and dread most, is God's departure from them. 2. In token of great shame and humiliation, those that were undressed did *not put on their ornaments* (*v.* 4), and those that were dressed *stripped themselves of their ornaments, by the mount*; as some read it, *at a distance from the mount* (*v.* 6), standing afar off like the publican, Luke xviii. 13.

Verses 7-11

Here is, I. One mark of displeasure put upon them for their further humiliation: *Moses took the tabernacle*, the tent wherein he gave audience, heard causes, and enquired of God, the *guild-hall* (as it were) of their camp, and *pitched it without, afar off from the camp* (*v.* 7), to signify to them that they had rendered themselves unworthy of it, and that, unless peace was made, it would return to them no more.

II. Many encouragements given them, notwithstanding, to hope that God would yet be reconciled to them.

1. Though the tabernacle was removed, yet every one that was disposed to seek the Lord was welcome to follow it, *v.* 7. A place was appointed for them to go to *without the camp*, to solicit God's return to them. When God designs mercy, he stirs up prayer.

2. Moses undertook to mediate between God and Israel. He *went out to the tabernacle*, the place of treaty, probably pitched between them and the mount (*v.* 8), and he *entered into the tabernacle, v.* 9.

3. The people seemed to be in a very good mind and well disposed towards a reconciliation. (1) When Moses went out to go to the tabernacle, the people *looked after him* (*v.* 8), in token of their respect to him whom before they had slighted, and their entire dependence upon his mediation. (2) When they saw the cloudy pillar, that symbol of God's presence, they all *worshipped, every man at his tent door, v.* 10. Their worshipping in their tent doors declared plainly that they were not ashamed publicly to own their respect to God and Moses, as they had publicly worshipped the calf.

4. God was, in Moses, reconciling Israel to himself, and manifested himself very willing to be at peace. (1) God met Moses at the place of treaty, *v.* 9.

JAMIESON, FAUSSET, BROWN

35. the Lord plagued the people, because they made the calf—No immediate judgments were inflicted, but this early lapse into idolatry was always mentioned as an aggravation of their subsequent apostasies.

CHAPTER 33

Vss. 1-23. THE LORD REFUSES TO GO WITH THE PEOPLE. **1. the Lord said**—rather "had" said unto Moses. The conference detailed in this chapter must be considered as having occurred prior to the pathetic intercession of Moses, recorded at the close of the preceding chapter; and the historian, having mentioned the fact of his earnest and painful anxiety, under the overhelming pressure of which he poured forth that intercessory prayer for his apostate countrymen, now enters on a detailed account of the circumstances.

3. I will not go up . . . lest I consume thee—Here the Lord is represented as determined to do what He afterwards did not. (See on ch. 32:10). **4. when the people heard these evil tidings**— from Moses on his descent from the mount. **5. put off thy ornaments**—In seasons of mourning, it is customary with Eastern people to lay aside all gewgaws and divest themselves of their jewels, their gold, and every thing rich and splendid in their dress. This token of their sorrow the Lord required of His offending people. **that I may know what to do unto thee**—The language is accommodated to the feeble apprehensions of men. God judges the state of the heart by the tenor of the conduct. In the case of the Israelites, He cherished a design of mercy; and the moment He discerned the first symptoms of contrition, by their stripping off their ornaments, as penitents conscious of their error and sincerely sorrowful, this fact added its weight to the fervency of Moses' prayers, and gave them prevalence with God in behalf of the people.

7. Moses took the tabernacle, and pitched it without the camp—Not the tabernacle, of which a pattern had been given him, for it was not yet erected, but his own tent—conspicuous as that of the leader—in a part of which he heard cases and communed with God about the people's interests; hence called "the tabernacle of the congregation," and the withdrawal of which, in abhorrence from a polluted camp, was regarded as the first step in the total abandonment with which God had threatened them.

8. all the people rose up, and stood every man at his tent door—Its removal produced deep and universal consternation; and it is easy to conceive how anxiously all eyes would be directed towards it; how rapidly the happy intelligence would spread, when a phenomenon was witnessed from which an encouraging hope could be founded. **9-11. the cloudy pillar descended, and stood at the door of the tabernacle**—How would

ADAM CLARKE

that God designed to lead them "to" the borders of the land but not to take them into it. *I will visit their sin.* I will not destroy them, but they shall not enter into the Promised Land. They shall wander in the wilderness till the present generation become extinct.

35. *The Lord plagued the people.* Every time they transgressed afterwards, divine justice seems to have remembered this transgression against them. The Jews have a metaphorical saying, apparently founded on this text: "No affliction has ever happened to Israel in which there was not some particle of the dust of the golden calf."

CHAPTER 33

1. *Unto the land.* That is, towards it, or to the borders of it. See chap. xxxii. 34.

2. *I will send an angel.* In chap. xxiii. 20, God promises to send an angel to conduct them into the good land, in whom the name of God should be; that is, in whom God should dwell. Here He promises that an angel shall be their conductor; but as there is nothing particularly specified of him, it has been thought that an ordinary angel is intended, and not that Angel of the Covenant promised before. And this sentiment seems to be confirmed by the following verse.

3. *I will not go up in the midst of thee.* Consequently the angel here promised to be their guide was not that angel in whom Jehovah's name was; and so the people understood it; hence the mourning which is afterwards mentioned.

7. *Moses took the tabernacle. Eth haohel*, "the tent"; not *eth hammishcan*, "the tabernacle," the dwelling place of Jehovah, see chap. xxv. 11, for this was not as yet erected; but probably the tent of Moses, which was before in the midst of the camp, and to which the congregation came for judgment, and where, no doubt, God frequently met with His servant. This is now removed to a considerable distance from the camp, as God refuses to dwell any longer among this rebellious people. And as this was the place to which all the people came for justice and judgment, hence it was probably called the tabernacle, more properly the "tent," *of the congregation.*

9. *The cloudy pillar descended.* This very circumstance precluded the possibility of deception. The cloud descending at these times,

MATTHEW HENRY

if our hearts go forth towards God to meet him he will graciously come down to meet us. (2) God talked with Moses (*v.* 9), *spoke to him face to face, as a man speaks to his friend* (*v.* 11), which intimates that God revealed himself to Moses, not only with greater clearness and evidence of divine light than to any other of the prophets, but also with greater expressions of particular kindness and grace. *Moses turned again into the camp*, but, because he intended speedily to return to the tabernacle of the congregation, he left Joshua there, for it was not fit that the place should be empty, so long as the cloud of glory *stood at the door* (*v.* 9).

Verses 12–23

Moses, having returned to the door of the tabernacle, becomes a humble and importunate supplicant here for two very great favours.

I. He is very earnest with God for a grant of his presence with Israel in the rest of their march to Canaan, notwithstanding their provocations. Observe how admirably Moses orders this cause before God: how he pleads, and how he speeds.

1. How he pleads. (1) He insists upon the commission God had given him to *bring up this people*, *v.* 12. This he begins with: "Lord, it is thou thyself that employest me; and wilt thou not own me? (2) He improves the interest he himself had with God, and pleads God's gracious expressions of kindness to him: *Thou hast said, I know thee by name. Now, therefore*, says Moses, if it be indeed so, that *I have found grace in thy sight, show me thy way*, *v.* 13. By this therefore he takes hold on God: "Lord, if ever thou wilt do anything for me, do this for the people." Thus our Lord Jesus, in his intercession, presents himself to the Father, as one in whom he is always well pleased, and so obtains mercy for us with whom he is justly displeased; and we are *accepted in the beloved*. (3) He insinuates that the people also, though most unworthy, yet were in some relation to God: "*Consider that this nation is thy people*, a people that thou hast done great things for, redeemed to thyself, and taken into covenant with thyself; Lord, they are thy own, do not leave them." The offended father considers this, "My child is foolish and froward, but he is my child, and I cannot abandon him." (4) He expresses the great value he had for the presence of God. When God said, *My presence shall go with thee*, he caught at that word, as that which he could not live and move without: *If thy presence go not with me, carry us not up hence*," *v.* 15. (5) He concludes with an argument taken from God's glory (*v.* 16): "*Wherein shall it be known to the nations that I and thy people have found grace in thy sight*, so as to be *separated from all people upon earth?* How will it appear that we are indeed thus honoured? *Is it not in that thou goest with us?*"

2. Observe how he speeds. He obtained an assurance of God's favour, (1) To himself (*v.* 14): *I will give thee rest*. Moses never entered Canaan, and yet God made good his word that he would give him rest, Dan. xii. 13. (2) To the people for his sake. Gracious generous souls think it not enough to get to heaven themselves, but would have all their friends go thither too. God grants as long as he asks, *gives liberally*, and *does not upbraid* him. See the power of prayer, and be quickened hereby to ask, and seek, and knock, and to *continue instant in prayer*, to *pray always and not to faint*. See, in type, the prevalency of Christ's intercession, which he ever lives to make for all those that come to God by him, and the ground of that prevalency. It is purely his own merit, not any thing in those for whom he intercedes; it is because *thou hast found grace in my sight*. And now the matter is settled, God is perfectly reconciled to them, his presence in the pillar of cloud returns to them and shall continue with them; all is well again, and henceforth we hear no more of the golden calf.

II. Having gained this point, he next begs *a sight of God's glory*, and is heard in this matter also.

1. The humble request Moses makes: *I beseech thee, show me thy glory*, *v.* 18. Moses had wonderfully prevailed with God for one favour after another, and the success of his prayers emboldened him to go on still to seek God; the more he had the more he asked! "*Show me thy glory; make me to see it* (so the word is); "make it some way or other visible, and enable me to bear the sight of it." Not that he was so ignorant as to think God's essence could be seen with bodily eyes; but, having hitherto only heard a voice out of a pillar of cloud or fire, he desired to see some representation of the divine glory, such as God saw fit to gratify him with. Some think that Moses desired a sight of God's glory as a token of his reconciliation, and an earnest of that presence which he had promised them; but he knew not what he asked.

JAMIESON, FAUSSET, BROWN

the downcast hearts of the people revive—how would the tide of joy swell in every bosom, when the symbolic cloud was seen slowly and majestically to descend and stand at the entrance of the tabernacle! **as Moses entered**—It was when he appeared as their mediator, when he repaired from day to day to intercede for them, that welcome token of assurance was given that his advocacy prevailed, that Israel's sin was forgiven, and that God would again be gracious.

CHARLES H. SPURGEON:

"My presence shall go with thee, and I will give thee rest."

It is instructive to remember that a very short time before this promise was given, the Israelites had greatly grieved their God by setting up an image of gold, before which they prostrated themselves, saying, "These be thy gods, O Israel." They had seen the greatness and glory of God at the Red Sea, and during their journey in the wilderness up to that time, and yet they were so besotted that they bowed in worship before the image of an ox which eateth grass. We do not marvel that the living God was angry, but we are filled with astonishment that, after such wanton provocation, He should, nevertheless, turn away His wrath from them and say to them—for the promise was not to Moses only, but to them as a people—"My presence shall go with thee, and I will give thee rest." Will God then, go with sinners, with those who have provoked Him so grossly, with those who have sinned against light and knowledge in so shameful a manner? Will He put away the iniquity of great offenders and speak comfortably unto them? Yes, He will, for He is slow to wrath, and bears with our ill manners for many a day. Here is His own word: "For my name's sake will I defer mine anger, and for my praise will I refrain for thee, that I cut thee not off" (Isa. 48:9). Oh, my brethren and sisters, what a consolation it is to us, while laboring under a sense of sin, that the Lord is able to put away sin so that we shall not die; and He will come and walk with us and dwell in the midst of us, notwithstanding all our former wickednesses. You know what a righteous God He is, and how jealous He is, especially of those He loves; and yet, for all that, though He be a consuming fire, yet, so gracious is He that, passing by transgression, iniquity, and sin, He will return unto His people still, and yet again speak comfortably unto them.

—*The Treasury of the Old Testament*

18-23. I beseech thee, show me thy glory—This is one of the most mysterious scenes described in the Bible: he had, for his comfort and encouragement, a splendid and full display of the divine majesty, not in its unveiled effulgence, but as far as the weakness of humanity would admit. The face, hand, back parts, are to be understood figuratively.

ADAM CLARKE

and at none others, was a full proof that it was miraculous, and a pledge of the divine presence. It was beyond the power of human art to counterfeit such an appearance; and let it be observed that all the people saw this, v. 10.

11. *The Lord spake unto Moses face to face.* That there was no personal appearance here we may readily conceive; and that the communications made by God to Moses were not by visions, ecstasies, dreams, inward inspirations, or the mediation of angels, is sufficiently evident. We may therefore consider the passage as implying that familiarity and confidence with which the Divine Being treated His servant, and that He spake with him by articulate sounds in his own language, though no shape or similitude was then to be seen. *Joshua, the son of Nun, a young man.* There is a difficulty here. Joshua certainly was not a young man in the literal sense of the word; "but he was called so," says Mr. Ainsworth, "in respect of his service, not of his years; for he was now above fifty years old, as may be gathered from Josh. xxiv. 29." Perhaps the word *naar*, here translated *young man*, means a "single person, one unmarried."

12. *Moses said unto the Lord.* We may suppose that after Moses had quitted the tabernacle he went to the camp and gave the people some general information relative to the conversation he lately had with the Lord; after which he returned to the tabernacle or tent, and began to plead with God, as we find in this and the following verses. *Thou hast not let me know.* As God had said He would not go up with this people, Moses wished to know whom He would send with him, as He had only said in general terms that he would send an angel.

13. *Shew me now thy way.* Let me know the manner in which Thou wouldst have this people led up and governed, because this nation is *thy people* and should be governed and guided in Thy own way.

14. *My presence shall go with thee. Panai yelechu*, "My faces shall go." I shall give thee manifestations of My grace and goodness through the whole of thy journey. I shall vary My appearances for thee, as thy necessities shall require.

15. *If thy presence go not. Im ein paneycha holechim*, "if Thy faces do not go"—if we have not manifestations of Thy peculiar providence and grace, *carry us not up hence.* Without supernatural assistance, and a most particular providence, he knew that it would be impossible either to govern such a people or support them in the desert; and therefore he wishes to be well assured on this head, that he may lead them up with confidence and be able to give them the most explicit assurances of support and protection. But by what means should these manifestations take place? This question seems to be answered by the Prophet Isaiah, chap. lxiii. 9: "In all their affliction he was afflicted, and the angel of his presence [*panaiv*, of His faces] saved them." So we find that the goodness and mercy of God were to be manifested by the Angel of the Covenant, the Lord Jesus, the Messiah; and this is the interpretation which the Jews themselves give of this place.

16. *So shall we be separated.* By having this divine protection we shall be saved from idolatry and be preserved in Thy truth and in the true worshipping of Thee; and thus "shall we be separated . . . from all the people that are upon the face of the earth," as all the nations of the world, the Jews only excepted, were at this time *idolaters.*

17. *I will do this thing also.* "My presence shall go with thee," and I will keep thee separate from all the people of the earth. Both these promises have been remarkably fulfilled. God continued miraculously with them till He brought them into the Promised Land; and from the day in which He brought them out of Egypt to the present day He has kept them a distinct, unmixed people!

18. *Shew me thy glory.* Moses probably desired to see that which constitutes the peculiar glory or excellence of the divine nature as it stands in reference to man. By many this is thought to signify His eternal mercy in sending Christ Jesus into the world. Moses perceived that what God was now doing had the most

MATTHEW HENRY

2. The gracious reply God made to this request. (1) He denied that which was not fit to be granted, and which Moses could not bear: *Thou canst not see my face, v.* 20. A full discovery of the glory of God would quite overpower the faculties of any mortal man in this present state, and overwhelm him, even Moses himself. There is a knowledge and enjoyment of God which must be waited for in another world, when we shall *see him as he is,* 1 John iii. 2. In the meantime let us adore the height of what we do know of God, and the depth of what we do not. (2) He granted that which would be abundantly satisfying. [1] He should hear what would please him (*v.* 19): *I will make all my goodness pass before thee.* He had given him wonderful instances of his goodness in being reconciled to Israel; but that was only goodness in the stream; he would show him goodness in the spring—*all his goodness.* This was a sufficient answer to his request. "Show me thy glory," says Moses. "I will show thee my goodness," says God. Note, God's goodness is his glory; and he will have us to know him by the glory of his mercy more than by the glory of his majesty. It is never said "I will be angry at whom I will be angry," for his wrath is always just and holy; but *I will show mercy on whom I will show mercy,* for his grace is always free. He never damns by prerogative, but by prerogative he saves. [2] He should see what he could bear, and what would suffice him. *First,* Safe in a *cleft of the rock, v.* 21, 22. *That rock was Christ,* 1 Cor. x. 4. And it is only through Christ that we have *the knowledge of the glory of God.* None can see his glory to their comfort but those who stand upon this rock, and take shelter in it. *Secondly,* He should see more of God than any ever saw on earth, but not so much as those see who are in heaven. That sight of God Moses might not have, but such a sight as we have of a man who has gone past us, so that we only see his back, and have (as we say) a blush of him. When we see what God has done in his works, observe the goings of our God, our King, we see (as it were) his back-parts. If we faithfully improve the discoveries God gives us of himself while we are here, a brighter and more glorious scene will shortly be opened to us; for *to him that hath shall be given.*

JAMIESON, FAUSSET, BROWN

ALEXANDER MACLAREN:

Human language and thought are out of their depth here. We must be content to see a dim splendor shining through the cloudy words, to know that there was granted to one man a realization of God's presence, and a revelation of His character, so far transcending ordinary experiences as that it was fitly called sight, but yet as far beneath the glory of His being as the comparatively imperfect knowledge of a man's form, when seen only from behind, is beneath that derived from looking him in the face.

But whatever was the singular prerogative of the lawgiver, as he gazed from the cleft of the rock at the receding glory, we see more than he ever did; and the Christian child, who looks upon the "glory of God in the face of Jesus Christ," has a vision which outshines the flashing radiance that shone round Moses. It deepened his convictions, confirmed his faith, added to his assurance of his divine commission, but only added to his knowledge of God by the proclamation of the Name, and that Name is more fully proclaimed in our ears. Sinai, with all its thunders, is silent before Calvary. And he who has Jesus Christ to declare God's Name to him need not envy the lawgiver on the mountain, nor even the saints in heaven.

—*Expositions of Holy Scripture*

ADAM CLARKE

important and gracious designs which at present he could not distinctly discover; therefore he desires God to show him His glory. God graciously promises to indulge him in this request as far as possible by proclaiming His name and making all His goodness pass before him, v. 19. But at the same time He assures him that he could not see His face, the fulness of His perfections and the grandeur of His designs, and live, as no human being could bear, in the present state, this full discovery. But He adds, "Thou shalt see my back parts," *eth achorai,* probably meaning that appearance which He should assume in after times when it should be said, God is manifest in the flesh. This appearance did take place, for we find God putting him into a cleft of the rock, covering him with His hand, and passing by in such a way as to exhibit a human similitude.

19. *I will make all my goodness pass before thee.* Thou shalt not have a sight of My justice, for thou couldst not bear the infinite splendor of My purity; but I shall show myself to thee as the Fountain of inexhaustible compassion, the sovereign Dispenser of My own mercy.

20. *No man see me, and live.* The splendor would be insufferable to man; he only, whose mortality is swallowed up of life, can see God as He is. See I John iii. 2.

21. *Behold, there is a place by me.* There seems to be a reference here to a well-known place on the mount where God was accustomed to meet with Moses. This was a *rock;* and it appears there was a cleft or cave in it, in which Moses was to stand while the Divine Majesty was pleased to show him all that human nature was capable of bearing. But this appears to have referred more to the counsels of His mercy and goodness, relative to His purpose of redeeming the human race, than to any visible appearance of the Divine Majesty itself.

MATTHEW HENRY

CHAPTER 34

Verses 1–4

The treaty that was on foot between God and Israel being broken off abruptly, by their worshipping the golden calf, when peace was made all must be begun anew.

I. Moses must prepare for the renewing of the tables, *v.* 1. Thus, in the first writing of the law upon the heart of man in innocency, both the tables and the writing were the work of God; but when those were broken and defaced by sin, and the divine law was to be preserved in the scriptures, God therein made use of the ministry of man, and Moses first. But the prophets and apostles did only hew the tables, as it were; the writing was God's still, for *all scripture is given by inspiration of God.* Observe, When God was reconciled to them, he ordered the tables to be renewed, and wrote his law in them, which plainly intimates to us, 1. That even under the gospel of peace and reconciliation by Christ (of which the intercession of Moses was typical) the moral law should continue to bind believers. When our Saviour, in his sermon on the mount, expounded the moral law, and vindicated it from the corrupt glosses with which the scribes and Pharisees had broken it (Matt. v. 19), he did in effect renew the tables, and make them like the first, that is, reduce the law to its primitive sense and intention. 2. That the best evidence of the pardon of sin and peace with God is the writing of the law in the heart. 3. That, if we would have God to write the law in our hearts, we must prepare our hearts for the reception of it.

II. Moses must attend again on the top of mount Sinai, and present himself to God there, *v.* 2. Moses, accordingly, *rose up early* (*v.* 4), to go to the place appointed. It is good to be early at our devotions. The morning is perhaps as good a friend to the graces as it is to the muses.

Verses 5–9

No sooner had Moses got to the top of the mount than God gave him the meeting (*v.* 5): *The Lord descended,* by some sensible token of his presence, and manifestation of his glory. He descended *in the cloud.* His making a cloud his pavilion intimated that, though he made known much of himself, yet there was much more concealed.

I. How God proclaimed his name (*v.* 6, 7): he did it *in transitu—as he passed by him.* Fixed views of God are reserved for the future state; the best we

JAMIESON, FAUSSET, BROWN

CHAPTER 34

Vss. 1-35. THE TABLES ARE RENEWED. **1. the like unto the first**—God having been reconciled to repentant Israel, through the earnest intercession, the successful mediation of Moses, means were to be taken for the restoration of the broken covenant. Intimation was given, however, in a most intelligible and expressive manner, that the favor was to be restored with some memento of the rupture; for at the former time God Himself had provided the materials, as well as written upon them. Now, Moses was to prepare the stone tables, and God was only to retrace the characters originally inscribed for the use and guidance of the people. **2. present thyself . . . to me in the top of the mount**—Not absolutely the highest peak; for as the cloud of the Shekinah usually abode on the summit, and yet (vs. 5) it "descended," the plain inference is that Moses was to station himself at a point not far distant, but still below the loftiest pinnacle. **3. no man shall come up with thee . . . neither . . . flocks nor herds**—All these enactments were made in order that the law might be a second time renewed with the solemnity and sanctity that marked its first delivery. The whole transaction was ordered so as to impress the people with an awful sense of the holiness of God; and that it was a matter of no trifling moment to have subjected Him, so to speak, to the necessity of re-delivering the law of the ten commandments. **4. Moses . . . took in his hand the two tables of stone**—As he had no attendant to divide the labor of carrying them, it is evident that they must have been light, and of no great dimensions—probably flat slabs of shale or slate, such as abound in the mountainous region of Horeb. An additional proof of their comparatively small size appears in the circumstance of their being deposited in the ark of the most holy place (ch. 25:10). **5. the Lord descended in the cloud**—After graciously hovering over the tabernacle, it seems to have resumed its usual position on the summit of the mount. It was the shadow of God manifest to the outward senses; and, at the same time, of God manifest in the flesh. The emblem of a cloud seems to have been chosen to signify that, although He was pleased to make known much about himself, there was more veiled from mortal view. It was to check presumption and engender awe and give a humble sense of human attainments in divine knowledge, as now

ADAM CLARKE

CHAPTER 34

1. *Hew thee two tables of stone like unto the first.* In chap. xxxii. 16 we are told that the first two "tables were the work of God, and the writing was the writing of God"; but here Moses is commanded to provide tables of his own workmanship, and God promises to write on them the words which were on the first. That God wrote the first tables himself seems proved by different passages of Scripture at the end of chap. xxxii. But here, in v. 27, it seems as if Moses was commanded to "write . . . these words," and in v. 28 it is said, "And he wrote upon the tables"; but in Deut. x. 1-4 it is expressly said that God wrote the second tables as well as the first.

In order to reconcile these accounts let us suppose that the "ten words," or Ten Commandments, were written on both tables by the hand of God himself, and that what Moses wrote, v. 27, was a copy of these to be delivered to the people, while the tables themselves were laid up in the ark before the testimony, whither the people could not go to consult them, and therefore a copy was necessary for the use of the congregation; this copy, being taken off under the direction of God, was authenticated equally with the original, and the original itself was laid up as a record to which all succeeding copies might be continually referred, in order to prevent corruption.

6. *And the Lord passed by . . . and proclaimed, The Lord.* It would be much better to read this verse thus: "And the Lord passed by

MATTHEW HENRY

have in this world are transient. God now was performing what he had promised Moses, the day before, that his glory should pass by, *ch.* xxxiii. 22. He *proclaimed the name of the Lord*, by which he would make himself known. He had made himself known to Moses in the glory of his self-existence and self-sufficiency when he proclaimed that name, *I am that I am*; now he makes himself known in the glory of his grace, and goodness, and all-sufficiency to us. This is prefixed before the display of his mercy, to teach us to think and to speak even of God's grace and goodness with great seriousness and a holy awe. His greatness and goodness illustrate and set off each other. Many words are here heaped up, to acquaint us with, and convince us of, God's goodness. 1. He is *merciful.* This bespeaks his tender compassion, like that of a father to his children. 2. He is *gracious.* His mercy is grace, free grace; this teaches us to be not only pitiful, but courteous, 1 Pet. iii. 8. 3. He is *long-suffering*, that is, he is slow to anger, and delays the execution of his justice; he waits to be gracious, and lengthens out the offers of his mercy. 4. He is *abundant in goodness and truth.* It bespeaks promised goodness, goodness and truth put together, goodness engaged by promise, and his faithfulness pledged for the security of it. 5. He keepeth *mercy for thousands.* 6. He *forgiveth iniquity, transgression, and sin.* Pardoning mercy is specified, because it is this which opens the door to all other gifts of his divine grace.

II. How Moses received this declaration which God made of himself, and of his grace and mercy. It should seem as if Moses accepted this as a sufficient answer to his request that God would *show him his glory*. Now we are here told,

1. What impression it made upon him: *Moses made haste, and bowed his head, v.* 8.

2. What improvement he made of it. He immediately grounded a prayer upon it (*v.* 9); and a most earnest affectionate prayer it is, (1) For the presence of God with his people Israel in the wilderness: "*I pray thee, go among us*, for thy presence is all in all to our safety and success." (2) For pardon of sin: "*O pardon our iniquity and our sin*, else we cannot expect thee to go among us." And, (3) For the privileges of a peculiar people: "Take us for *thy inheritance*." These things God had already promised, and given Moses assurances of, and yet he prays for them, not as doubting the sincerity of God's grants, but as one solicitous for the ratification of them. Those who have some good hopes, through grace, that their sins are pardoned, must yet continue to pray for pardon, for the renewing of their pardon, and the clearing of it more and more to their souls. Thus Moses, like a man of a truly public spirit, intercedes even for the children that should be born. But it is a strange plea he urges: *For it is a stiff-necked people.* God had given this as a reason why he would not go along with them, *ch.* xxxiii. 3. "Yea," says Moses, "the rather go along with us; for the worse they are the more need they have of thy presence and grace to make them better."

Verses 10-17

Reconciliation being made, a covenant of friendship is here settled between God and Israel. The traitors are not only pardoned, but preferred and made favourites again. Well may the assurances of this be ushered in with a *behold*, a word commanding attention and admiration: *Behold, I make a covenant.*

1. God's part of this covenant, what he would do for them, *v.* 10, 11. (1) In general: *Before all thy people, I will do marvels.* Marvels indeed, for they were without precedent, *such as have not been done in all the earth.* They were the joy of Israel, and the confirmation of their faith: *Thy people shall see*, and own *the work of the Lord.* And they were the terror of their enemies: *It is a terrible thing that I will do.* Nay, even God's own people should see them with astonishment. 2. In particular: *I drive out before thee the Amorite.*

II. Their part of the covenant: *Observe that which I command thee*, We cannot expect the benefit of the promises unless we make conscience of the precepts.

Thou shalt worship no other gods (*v.* 14), not give divine honour to any creature, or any name whatsoever, the creature of fancy. Those cannot worship God aright who do not worship him alone. That they might not be tempted to worship other gods, they must not join in affinity or friendship with those that did (*v.* 12). *Make no covenant with the inhabitants of the land.* If God, in kindness to them, drove out the Canaanites, they ought, in duty to God, not to harbour them. They must particularly take heed of intermarrying with them, *v.* 15, 16. If they espoused their children, they would be in danger of espousing their gods. That they might not be tempted to make molten gods, they must utterly destroy those they

JAMIESON, FAUSSET, BROWN

man sees, but darkly. **6. the Lord passed by before him**—in this remarkable scene, God performed what He had promised to Moses the day before.

proclaimed, The Lord . . . merciful and gracious—At an earlier period He had announced Himself to Moses, in the glory of His self-existent and eternal majesty, as "I am"; now He makes Himself known in the glory of His grace and goodness—attributes that were to be illustriously displayed in the future history and experience of the church. Being about to republish His law—the sin of the Israelites being forgiven and the deed of pardon about to be signed and sealed by renewing the terms of the former covenant—it was the most fitting time to proclaim the extent of the divine mercy which was to be displayed, not in the case of Israel only, but of all who offend.

8-26. Moses bowed . . . and worshipped—In the East, people bow the head to royalty, and are silent when it passes by, while in the West, they take off their hats and shout. **9. he said, If now I have found grace in thy sight, O Lord, let my Lord, I pray thee, go among us**—On this proclamation, he, in the overflowing benevolence of his heart, founded an earnest petition for the Divine Presence being continued with the people; and God was pleased to give His favorable answer to his intercession by a renewal of His promise under the form of a covenant, repeating the leading points that formed the conditions of the former national compact.

F. B. MEYER:

The covenant of the law renewed (vv.1–17). Before we can behold the vision of Eternal Love, we must be willing to fulfill three conditions: (1) *Earliness:* "Be ready in the morning." (2) *Solitude:* "No man shall come up with thee." (3) *The open heart:* "And I will write . . ." God is always passing by and covering us with the shadow of his hand, and proclaiming his lovingkindness and tender mercy. He keeps mercy for thousands, and limits the consequence of sin to the third and fourth generation.

Whenever we get near to God, we should begin to think of and pray for others. As the last notes of the divine procession were dying away, Moses bowed his head and worshiped, saying, "Let the Lord go in the midst of us and forgive." It was as though he said, "If thou art a God like that, thou art the God that stiff-necked people need. Go with us, therefore, for thou canst bear with us." He went on to ask that they might be pardoned and that God would account them his heritage. His request was more than granted! God entered into covenant with them and promised to drive out their enemies on conditions which he proceeded to enumerate.

—*Bible Commentary*

ADAM CLARKE

before him, and proclaimed Jehovah," that is, showed Moses fully what was implied in this august name. Moses had requested God to show him His glory (see the preceding chapter, eighteenth verse) and God promised to proclaim or fully declare the name Jehovah (v. 19), by which proclamation or interpretation Moses should see how God "will be gracious to whom I will be gracious," and how He would be merciful to those to whom He would show mercy. Here, therefore, God fulfils that promise by proclaiming this name. It has long been a question what is the meaning of the word Jehovah. Some have maintained that it is utterly inexplicable. How strange is it that none of these learned men have discovered that God himself interprets this name in verses 6 and 7 of this chapter! "And the Lord passed by before him, and proclaimed, The Lord [Jehovah], The Lord God, merciful and gracious, longsuffering, and abundant in goodness and truth, keeping mercy for thousands, forgiving iniquity and transgression and sin, and that will by no means clear the guilty." These words contain the proper interpretation of the venerable and glorious name JEHOVAH.

7. *That will by no means clear the guilty.* This last clause is rather difficult; literally translated it signifies, "in clearing He will not clear." But the Samaritan, reading "to him," instead of the negative "not," renders the clause thus: "With whom the innocent shall be innocent"; i.e., an innocent or holy person shall never be treated as if he were a transgressor, by this just and holy God.

9. *O Lord, let my Lord, I pray thee, go among us.* The original is not *Jehovah,* but *Adonai* in both these places, and seems to refer particularly to the Angel of the Covenant, the Messiah.

10. *I will do marvels.* This seems to refer to what God did in putting them in possession of the land of Canaan, causing the walls of Jericho to fall down, making the sun and moon to stand still, etc. And thus God made His covenant with them; binding himself to put them in possession of the Promised Land, and binding them to observe the precepts laid down in the following verses, from the eleventh to the twenty-sixth inclusive.

13. *Ye shall destroy their . . . images.* See the subjects of this and all the following verses, to the twenty-eighth, treated at large in the notes on chap. xxiii.

MATTHEW HENRY

found and all that belong to them, the altars and groves (*v.* 13).

Verses 18–27

Several appointments relating to their solemn feasts. When they had made the calf, they proclaimed a feast in honour of it; now, that they might never do so again, they are here charged with the observance of the feasts which God had instituted. Note, Men need not be drawn from their religion by the temptation of mirth, for we serve a Master that has abundantly provided for the joy of his servants.

I. Once a week they must rest (*v.* 21), *even in earing time, and in harvest*, the most busy times of the year. Harvest-work will prosper the better for the religious observance of the sabbath day in harvest time.

II. Thrice a year they must feast (*v.* 23); they must then appear *before the Lord God, the God of Israel*. The country would be left exposed to the insults of their neighbours; and what would become of the poor women and children, and sick and aged, that were left at home? Trust God with them (*v.* 24): *Neither shall any man desire thy land*; not only they shall not invade it, but they shall not so much as think of invading it. The way of duty is the way of safety.

III. The three feasts are here mentioned, with their appendages. 1. The passover, and the feast of unleavened bread, in remembrance of their deliverance out of Egypt; and to this is annexed the law of the redemption of the first-born, *v.* 18–20. This feast was instituted, *ch.* xii. 13, and urged again, *ch.* xxiii. 15. 2. The feast of weeks, that is, that of pentecost, seven weeks after the passover; and to this is annexed the law of the first-fruits. 3. The feast of in-gathering at the year's end, which was the feast of tabernacles (*v.* 22): of these also he had spoken before, *ch.* xxiii. 16.

IV. These laws are here repeated to show that *not one jot or tittle of the law should pass away*. And in the close, 1. Moses is ordered to write these words (*v.* 27), that the people might be the better acquainted with them by a frequent perusal, and that they might be transmitted to the generations to come. We can never be thankful enough to God for the written word. 2. He is told that according to the tenor of these words God would make a covenant with Moses and Israel; not with Israel immediately, but with them in Moses as mediator.

Verses 28–35

I. The continuance of Moses in the mount, where he was miraculously sustained, *v.* 28. When we are weary of an hour or two spent in attendance upon God and adoration of him, we should think how many days and nights Moses spent with him. So long he continued without meat and drink (and probably without sleep too), for, 1. The power of God supported him, that he did not need it. 2. He had meat to eat which the world knew not of, for it was his meat and drink to hear the word of God and pray. When God would treat his favourite Moses, it was not with meat and drink, but with his light, law and love, with the knowledge of himself and his will. As Moses, so Elijah and Christ, fasted forty days and forty nights.

II. The coming down of Moses from the mount, greatly enriched and miraculously adorned.

1. He came down enriched with the best treasure; for he brought in his hands the two tables of the law.

2. He came down adorned with the best beauty; for the *skin of his face shone*, *v.* 29.

(1) This may be looked upon, [1] As a great honour done to Moses, that the people might never again question his mission. He carried his credentials in his very countenance, The Israelites could not look him in the face but they must there read his commission. Yet, after this, they murmured against him. [2] It was also a great favour to the people, and an encouragement to them, that God put this glory upon him, who was their intercessor, thereby giving them assurance that he was accepted, and they through him. [3] It was the effect of his sight of God. When we have been in the mount with God, we should let our *light shine before men*, that all we converse with may *take knowledge of us that we have been with Jesus*, Acts iv. 13.

(2) Concerning the shining of Moses's face observe here, [1] Moses was not aware of it himself: *He wist not that the skin of his face shone*, *v.* 29. Whatever beauty God puts upon us, we should still be filled with such a humble sense of our own unworthiness, and manifold infirmities, as will make us even overlook and forget that which makes our faces shine. [2] Aaron and the children of Israel saw it, and *were afraid*, *v.* 30. Probably they doubted whether it were

JAMIESON, FAUSSET, BROWN

GEORGE RAWLINSON:

21. The Law of the Sabbath meets us at every turn in Exodus. It was so fundamental to the entire polity that it naturally held a place in every section of the legislation. We have already found it (1) propounded at the giving of the manna (16:22–30); (2) reasserted in the fourth commandment (20:8–11); (3) introduced into the "Book of the Covenant" (23:12); and (4) appended to the directions given for the construction of the Tabernacle (31:13–17).

"In earing time and in harvest thou shalt rest." "Earing time" is ploughing time, "to ear" being an old English verb. There was a special temptation to trench on the Sabbatical rest at the times most critical in respect to agricultural operations.

—*Ellicott's Commentary on the Whole Bible*

27, 28. the Lord said unto Moses, Write thou these words—i. e., the ceremonial and judicial injunctions comprehended above (vss. 11-26); while the rewriting of the ten commandments on the newly prepared slabs was done by God Himself (cf. Deut. 10:1-4).

he was there with the Lord forty days and forty nights—as long as formerly, being sustained for the execution of his special duties by the miraculous power of God. A special cause is assigned for his protracted fast on this second occasion (Deut. 9:18).

29. Moses wist not that the skin of his face shone while he talked with him—It was an intimation of the exalted presence into which he had been admitted and of the glory he had witnessed (II Cor. 3:18); and in that view, it was a badge of his high office as the ambassador of God. No testimonial needed to be produced. He bore his credentials on his very face; and whether this extraordinary effulgence was a permanent or merely temporary distinction, it cannot be doubted that this reflected glory was given him as an honor before all the people.

30. they were afraid to come nigh him—Their fear arose from a sense of

ADAM CLARKE

21. *In earing time and in harvest thou shalt rest.* This commandment is worthy of especial note. Many break the Sabbath on the pretense of absolute necessity, because, if in harvest-time the weather happens to be what is called bad, and the Sabbath day be fair and fine, they judge it perfectly lawful to employ that day in endeavoring to save the fruits of the field, and think that the goodness of the day beyond the preceding is an indication from Providence that it should be thus employed. But is not the above command pointed directly against this?

24. *Neither shall any man desire thy land.* What a manifest proof was this of the power and particular providence of God! How easy would it have been for the surrounding nations to take possession of the whole Israelitish land with all their fenced cities when there were none left to protect them but women and children!

25. *The blood of my sacrifice.* That is, the paschal lamb. See on chap. xxiii. 18.

26. *Thou shalt not seethe a kid in his mother's milk.* See this amply considered in chap. xxiii. 19.

27. *Write thou these words.* Either a transcript of the whole law now delivered, or the words included from verse 11 to 26. God certainly wrote the "ten words" on both sets of tables. Moses either wrote a transcript of these and the accompanying precepts for the use of the people, or he wrote the precepts themselves in addition to the Ten Commandments, which were written by the finger of God. See on v. 1. Allowing this mode of interpretation, the accompanying precepts were, probably, what was written on the back side of the tables by Moses; the Ten Commandments, what were written on the front by the finger of Jehovah.

29. *The skin of his face shone. Karan*, "was horned": having been long in familiar intercourse with his Maker, his flesh, as well as his soul, was penetrated with the effulgence of the divine glory, and his looks expressed the light and life which dwelt within. Probably Moses appeared now as he did when in our Lord's transfiguration he was seen with Elijah on the mount, Matthew xvii. As the original word *karan* signifies to "shine out, to dart forth," as horns on the head of an animal, or rays of light reflected from a polished surface, we may suppose that the heavenly glory which filled the soul of this holy man darted out from his face in coruscations, in that manner in which light is generally represented. The Vulgate renders the passage, "And he did not know that his face was horned"; which version, misunderstood, has induced painters in general to represent Moses with two very large horns, one proceeding from each temple. But we might naturally ask, while they were indulging themselves in such fancies, why only two horns? for it is very likely that there were hundreds of these radiations, proceeding at once from the face of Moses.

30. *They were afraid to come nigh him.* A sight of his face alarmed them; their consciences were still guilty from their late transgression, and they had not yet received the atonement. The very appearance of superior sanctity often awes the guilty into respect.

33. *And till Moses had done speaking.* The meaning of the verse appears to be this: As often as Moses spoke in public to the people, he put the veil on his face, because they could not bear to look on the brightness of his countenance; but when he entered into the tabernacle to converse with the Lord, he removed this veil, v. 34. St. Paul, 2 Cor. iii. 7, etc., makes a very important use of the transactions recorded in this place. He represents the brightness of the face of Moses as emblematical of the glory or excellence of that dispensation; but he shows that, however glorious or excellent that was, it had no glory when compared with the superior excellence of the gospel. As Moses was glorious in the eyes of the Israelites, but that glory was absorbed and lost in the splendor of God when he entered into the tabernacle, or went to meet the Lord upon the mount, so the brightness and excellence of the Mosaic dispensation are eclipsed and absorbed in the transcendent brightness or excellence of the gospel of Christ. The apostle further considers the veil on the face of Moses as being emblematical of the meta-

MATTHEW HENRY

token of God's favour or of his displeasure; being conscious of guilt, they feared the worst. [3] Moses put a *veil upon his face*, when he perceived that it shone, *v.* 33, 35. This teaches us all a lesson of modesty and humility. [4] When Moses *went in before the Lord*, to speak with him in the tabernacle of meeting, he *put off the veil*, *v.* 34. Then there was no occasion for it, and, before God, every man does and must appear unveiled. This signified also, as it is explained (2 Cor. iii. 16), that when a soul turns to the Lord the veil shall be taken away, that with open face it may behold his glory.

JAMIESON, FAUSSET, BROWN

guilt— the beaming radiance of his countenance made him appear to their awe-struck consciences a flaming minister of heaven. **33. he put a veil upon his face**—That veil was with the greatest propriety removed when speaking with the Lord, for every one appears unveiled to the eye of Omniscience; but it was replaced on returning to the people—and this was emblematic of the dark and shadowy character of that dispensation (II Cor. 3:13, 14).

ADAM CLARKE

phorical nature of the different rites and ceremonies of the Mosaic dispensation, each "covering" some spiritual meaning or a spiritual subject; and that the Jews did not lift the veil to penetrate the spiritual sense, and did not look to "the end of the commandment," which was to be "abolished," but rested in the letter or literal meaning, which conferred neither light nor life. He considers the veil also as being emblematical of that state of intellectual darkness into which the Jewish people, by their rejection of the gospel, were plunged, and from which they have never yet been recovered. When a Jew, even at the present day, reads the law in the synagogue, he puts over his head an oblong woolen veil, with four tassels at the four corners, which is called the *taled*. This is a very remarkable circumstance, as it appears to be an emblem of the intellectual veil referred to by the apostle, which is still upon their hearts when Moses is read, and which prevents them from looking to the end of that which God designed should be abrogated, and which has been abolished by the introduction of the gospel. The veil is upon their hearts, and prevents the light of the glory of God from shining into them; "But we all," says the apostle, speaking of believers in Christ, "with open face," without any veil, "beholding as in a glass the glory of God, are changed into the same image from glory to glory, as by the Spirit of the Lord," 2 Cor. iii. 18.

MATTHEW HENRY — CHAPTER 35

Verses 1–19

The erecting and furnishing of the tabernacle being the work to which they were now immediately to apply themselves, here is particular mention of the orders given concerning it.

I. All the congregation is summoned to attend (*v.* 1).

II. Moses gave them in charge all that which God had commanded him. Both sides having reposed a trust in him, he was true to the trust; yet he was faithful as a servant only, but *Christ as a Son*, Heb. iii. 5, 6.

III. He begins with the law of the sabbath, *Six days shall work be done*, work for the tabernacle, *but on the seventh day* you must not strike a stroke. It is a sabbath of rest. It is a *sabbath of sabbaths* (so some read it), more honourable and excellent than any of the other feasts, and should survive them all. A *sabbath of sabbatism*, so others read it, being typical of that sabbatism or rest, both spiritual and eternal, which *remains for the people of God*, Heb. iv. 9. It is a sabbath and a little sabbath, so some of the Jews would have it read; not only observing the whole day as a sabbath, but an hour before the beginning of it, and an hour after the ending of it, *a little sabbath*, to show how glad they are of the approach of the sabbath and how loth to part with it.

IV. He orders preparation to be made for the setting up of the tabernacle. Two things were to be done:—

1. All that were able must contribute: *Take you from among you an offering*, *v.* 5. The rule is, *Whosoever is of a willing heart let him bring*. It was not to be a tax imposed upon them, but a benevolence or voluntary contribution, to intimate to us, (1) That God has not made our yoke heavy. (2) That God loves a cheerful giver, and is best pleased with the free-will offering. Those services are acceptable to him that come from the willing heart of a willing people, Ps. cx. 3.

2. All that were skilful must work: *Every wise-hearted among you shall come, and make*, *v.* 10. See how God dispenses his gifts variously; and, *as every man hath received the gift, so he must minister*, 1 Pet. iv. 10. Those that were rich must bring in materials to work on; those that were ingenious must serve the tabernacle with their ingenuity; as they needed one another, so the tabernacle needed them both, 1 Cor. xii. 7–21.

Verses 20–29

I. The offerings that were brought for the service of the tabernacle (*v.* 21, &c.). 1. It is intimated that they brought their offerings immediately. No season will be more convenient than the present season. 2. It is said that *their spirits made them willing* (*v.* 21), and *their hearts*, *v.* 29. 3. When it is said that as many as were willing-hearted brought their offerings (*v.* 22), it should seem as if there were some who were not, who loved their gold better than their God, and would

JAMIESON, FAUSSET, BROWN — CHAPTER 35

Vss. 1-35. CONTRIBUTIONS TO THE TABERNACLE. **1. Moses gathered all the congregation of the children of Israel,** etc.—On the occasion referred to in the opening of this chapter, the Israelites were specially reminded of the design to erect a magnificent tabernacle for the regular worship of God, as well as of the leading articles that were required to furnish that sacred edifice. (See on chs. 25, 27, 30, 31).

20, 21. all the congregation of Israel departed from the presence of Moses—No exciting harangues were made, nor had the people Bibles at home in which they could compare the requirements of their leader and see if these things were so. But they had no doubt as to his bearing to them the will of God, and they were impressed with so strong a sense of its being their duty, that they made a spontaneous offer of the best and most valuable treasures they possessed. **they came, every one whose heart stirred him up**—One powerful element doubtless of this extraordinary open-hearted liberality was the remembrance of their recent transgression, which made them "zealous of good works" (cf. II Cor. 7: 11). But along with this motive, there were others of a higher and nobler kind—a principle of love to God and devotedness to His service, an anxious desire to secure the benefit of His presence, and gratitude for the tokens of His divine favor: it was under the combined influence of these considerations that the people were so willing and ready to pour their contributions into that exchequer of the sanctuary. **every one whom his spirit made willing**—Human nature is always the same, and it is implied that while an extraordinary spirit of pious liberality reigned in the bosoms of the people at large, there were exceptions—some who were too fond of the world, who loved their possessions more than their God, and who could not part with these; no, not for the service of the tabernacle. **22. they came, both men and women,** etc.—lit., "the men over and above the women"; a phraseology which implies that the women acted a prominent part, presented their

ADAM CLARKE — CHAPTER 35

1. *And Moses gathered.* The principal subjects in this chapter have been already largely considered in the notes on chapters xxv, xvi, xxvii, xxviii, xxix, xxx, and xxxi, and to those the reader is particularly desired to refer, together with the parallel texts in the margin.

3. *Ye shall kindle no fire.* The Jews understand this precept as forbidding the kindling of fire only for the purpose of doing work or dressing victuals; but to give them light and heat they judge it lawful to light a fire on the Sabbath day, though themselves rarely kindle it—they get Christians to do this work for them.

5. *An offering. A terumah* or heave offering; see Lev. vii. 1, etc.

5 and 6. See on these metals and colors, chap. xxv. 3-4, etc.

7. *Rams' skins, etc.* See chap. xxv. 5.

8. *Oil for the light.* See chap. xxv. 6.

9. *Onyx stones.* See chap. xxv. 7.

11. *The tabernacle.* See chap. xxv. 8.

12. *The ark.* See chap. xxv. 10-17.

13. *The table.* See chap. xxv. 23-28.

14. *The candlestick.* See chap. xxv. 31-39.

15. *The incense altar.* The golden altar, see chap. xxx. 1-10.

16. *The altar of burnt offering.* The brazen altar, see chap. xxvii. 1-8.

17. *The hangings of the court.* See chap. xxvii. 9.

19. *The cloths of service.* Probably aprons, towels, and suchlike, used in the common service, and different from the vestments for Aaron and his sons. See these latter described, chap. xxviii. 1, etc.

21. *Every one whose heart stirred him up.* Literally, "whose heart was lifted up"—whose affections were set on the work, being cordially engaged in the service of God.

22. *As many as were willing hearted.* For no one was forced to lend his help in this sacred work; all was a freewill offering to the Lord. *Bracelets. Chach,* whatever "hooks to-

MATTHEW HENRY

not part with it, no, not for the service of the tabernacle. They are for the true religion, provided it be cheap and will cost them nothing. 4. The offerings were of divers kinds, according as they had. Those that had not precious stones to bring brought goats' hair, and rams' skins. Two mites from a pauper were more pleasing than so many talents from a Dives. God has an eye to the heart of the giver more than to the value of the gift. 5. Many of the things they offered were their ornaments, bracelets, and rings, and tablets or lockets (*v.* 22); and even the women parted with these. If we think those gospel rules concerning our clothing too strict (1 Tim. ii. 9, 10; 1 Pet. iii. 3, 4), I fear we should scarcely have done as these Israelites did. These rich things that they offered, we may suppose, were mostly the spoils of the Egyptians. Who would have thought that even the wealth of Egypt should have been so well employed? Let every man give *according as God hath prospered him,* 1 Cor. xvi. 2. Extraordinary successes should be acknowledged by extraordinary offerings. But then great care must be taken that Egypt's gods mingle not with Egypt's gold.

II. The work that was done for the service of the tabernacle (*v.* 25): *The women did spin with their hands.* Some spun fine work, of blue and purple; others coarse work, of goats' hair, and yet theirs also is said to be done in wisdom, *v.* 26. As it is not only rich gifts, so it is not only fine work that God accepts. Notice is here taken of the good women's work for God, as well as of Bezaleel's and Aholiab's. Mary's anointing of Christ's head shall be told for a memorial (Matt. xxvi. 13); and a record is kept of the women that laboured in the gospel tabernacle (Phil. iv. 3), and were helpers to Paul in Christ Jesus, Rom. xvi. 3. The poor may relieve the poor, and those that have nothing but their limbs and senses may be very charitable in the labour of love.

Verses 30–35

Here is the divine appointment of the master-workmen, that there might be no strife for the office. God is the God of order and not of confusion. 1. Those whom God called by name to this service he *filled with the Spirit of God,* to qualify them for it, *v.* 30, 31. Skill in secular employments is God's gift, and comes from above, Jam. i. 17. Thus when the apostles were appointed to be master-builders in setting up the gospel tabernacle they were *filled with the Spirit of God in wisdom and understanding.* 2. They were appointed, not only to devise, but to work (*v.* 32). 3. They were not only to devise and work themselves, but they were to teach others, *v.* 34. Not only had Bezaleel power to command, but he was to take pains to instruct. Those that rule should teach; and those to whom God has given knowledge should be willing to communicate it for the benefit of others, not coveting to monopolize it.

JAMIESON, FAUSSET, BROWN

offerings *first,* and then were followed by as many of their male companions as were similarly disposed. **brought bracelets,** etc.—There was in that early age no money in the form of coins or bullion. What money passed current with the merchant consisted of rings which were weighed, and principally of ornaments for personal decoration. Astonishment at the abundance of their ornaments is at an end when we learn that costly and elegant ornaments abounded in proportion as clothing was simple and scarce among the Egyptians, and some, entirely divested of clothing, yet wore rich necklaces [HENGSTENBERG]. Among people with Oriental sentiments and tastes, scarcely any stronger proof could have been given of the power of religion than their willingness not only to lay aside, but to devote those much-valued trinkets to the house of God; and thus all, like the Eastern sages, laid the best they had at the service of God.

30. See, the Lord hath called by name Bezaleel the son of Uri, etc.—Moses had made this communication before. But now that the collection had been made, the materials were contributed, and the operations of building about to be commenced, it was with the greatest propriety he reminded the people that the individuals entrusted with the application of their gold and silver had been nominated to the work by authority to which all would bow. **35. Them hath he filled with wisdom of heart**—A statement which not only testifies that skill in art and science is a direct gift from God, but that weaving was especially the business of men in Egypt (see ch. 38:22; 39:22, 27). And in perfect harmony with the testimony of the monuments is the account given by Moses to the artists who were divinely taught the arts necessary for the embellishment of the tabernacle. Others, whose limited means did not admit of these expensive contributions, offered their gratuitous services in fabricating such articles of tapestry as were needed; arts which the Israelitish females learned as bondwomen, in the houses of Egyptian princes.

ADAM CLARKE

gether"; ornaments for the wrists, arms, legs, or neck. *Earrings. Nezem,* see this explained, Gen. xxiv. 22. *Rings. Tabbaath,* from *taba,* to "penetrate, enter into"; probably rings for the fingers. *Tablets. Cumaz,* a word only used here and in Num. xxxi. 50, supposed to be a girdle to support the breasts.

25. *All the women that were wise hearted did spin.* They had before learned this art, they were wisehearted; and now they practice it, and God condescends to require and accept their services. In building this house of God, all were ambitious to do something by which they might testify their piety to God, and their love for His worship. The spinning practiced at this time was simple, and required little apparatus. It was the plain distaff or twirling pin, which might be easily made out of any wood they met with in the wilderness.

27. *The rulers brought onyx stones.* These being persons of consequence, might be naturally expected to furnish the more scarce and costly articles. See how all join in this service: The men worked and brought offerings; the women spun and brought their ornaments; the rulers united with them, and delivered up their jewels; and all the children of Israel "brought a willing offering unto the Lord," v. 29.

CHAPTER 36

MATTHEW HENRY

Verses 1–7

I. The workmen set in without delay. Then they wrought, *v.* 1. When God had qualified them for the work, then they applied themselves to it. They began when Moses called them, *v.* 2. Those are to be called to the building of the gospel tabernacle whom God has by his grace made in some measure fit for the work and free to engage in it. Ability and willingness (with resolution) are the two things to be regarded in the call of ministers. The materials which the people had contributed were delivered by Moses to the workmen, *v.* 3. Precious souls are the materials of the gospel tabernacle; they are *built up a spiritual house,* 1 Pet. ii. 5. To this end they are to offer themselves a free-will offering to the Lord, for his service (Rom. xv. 16), and they are then committed to the care of his ministers, as builders, to be framed and wrought upon by their edification and increase in holiness, till they all come, like the curtains of the tabernacle, *in the unity of the faith to be a holy temple,* Eph. ii. 21, 22; iv. 12, 13.

II. The contributions restrained. The people continued to bring *free offerings every morning, v.* 3.

JAMIESON, FAUSSET, BROWN

VSS. 1-38. OFFERINGS DELIVERED TO THE WORKMEN. **1. Then wrought Bezaleel and Aholiab, and every wise-hearted man,** etc.—Here is an illustrious example of zeal and activity in the work of the Lord. No unnecessary delay was allowed to take place; and from the moment the first pole was stuck in the ground till the final completion of the sacred edifice, he and his associates labored with all the energies both of mind and body engaged in the work. And what was the mainspring of their arduous and untiring diligence? They could be actuated by none of the ordinary motives that give impulse to human industry, by no desire for the acquisition of gain; no ambition for honor; no view of gratifying a mere love of power in directing the labors of a large body of men. They felt the stimulus—the strong irresistible impulse of higher and holier motives—obedience to the authority, zeal for the glory, and love to the service of God. **3. they brought yet unto him free offerings every morning,** etc.—Moses, in common with other Oriental magistrates, had his morning levees for receiving the people (see on ch. 18:13); and it was while he was performing his magisterial duties that the people brought unto him freewill offerings every morning. Some who had nothing but their manual labor to give would spend a great part of the night in hastening to complete their self-imposed task before the early dawn; others might find their hearts constrained by silent meditations on their beds to open their coffers and give a part of their hoarded treasure to the pious object. All whose hearts were touched by piety, penitence, or gratitude, repaired with eager haste into the presence of Moses, not as heretofore, to have their controversies

ADAM CLARKE

1. *Then wrought.* The first verse of this chapter should end the preceding chapter, and this should begin with the second verse; as it now stands, it does not make a very consistent sense. By reading the first word *veasah, then wrought,* in the future tense instead of the past, the proper connection will be preserved; for all grammarians know that the conjunction *vau* is often *conversive,* i.e., it turns the preterite tense of those verbs to which it is prefixed into the future, and the future into the preterite. This power it evidently has here; and joined with the last verse of the preceding chapter the connection will appear thus, chap. xxxv. 30, etc.: "The Lord hath called by name Bezeleel . . . and Aholiab . . . them hath he filled with wisdom of heart, to work all manner of work." Chap. xxxvi. 1: And Bezaleel and Aholiab shall work, "and every wise hearted man, in whom the Lord put wisdom."

MATTHEW HENRY

Now observe, 1. The honesty of the workmen. When they had cut out their work, and found how their stuff held out, they went in a body to Moses to tell him that there needed no more contributions, *v.* 4, 5. They were men of integrity, that scorned to do so mean a thing as to sponge upon the people, and enrich themselves with that which was offered to the Lord. Those are the greatest cheats that cheat the public. 2. The liberality of the people. A rare instance! Most need a spur to quicken their charity; few need a bridle to check it, yet these did.

Verses 8–13

The first work they set about was the framing of the house, not made of timber or stone, but of curtains curiously embroidered and coupled together. This served to typify the state of the church in this world, the palace of God's kingdom among men. It is mean and mutable, and in a militant state; shepherds dwelt in tents, and God is the Shepherd of Israel; soldiers dwelt in tents, and the Lord is a man of war, and his church marches through an enemy's country, and must fight its way. The kings of the earth enclose themselves in cedar (Jer. xxii. 15), but the ark of God was lodged in curtains only. Yet there is a beauty in holiness; the curtains were embroidered, so is the church adorned with the gifts and graces of the Spirit, that *raiment of needle-work*, Ps. xlv. 14.

Verses 14–34

1. The shelter and special protection that the church is under are signified by the curtains of hair-cloth, which were spread over the tabernacle, and the covering of rams' skins and badgers' skins over them, *v.* 14–19. God has provided for his people a *shadow from the heat, and a covert from storm and rain*, Isa. iv. 6. Those that dwell in God's house shall find, be the tempest ever so violent, or the dropping ever so continual, it does not rain in. 2. The strength and stability of the church, though it is but a tabernacle, are signified by the boards and bars with which the curtains were borne up, *v.* 20–34.

Verses 35–38

1. There was a veil made for a partition between the holy place and the most holy, *v.* 35, 36. This signified the darkness and distance of that dispensation, compared with the New Testament, which shows us the glory of God more clearly and invites us to draw near to it. 2. There was a veil made for the door of the tabernacle, *v,* 37, 38. At this door the people assembled, though forbidden to enter; for, while we are in this present state, we must get as near to God as we can.

JAMIESON, FAUSSET, BROWN

settled, but to lay on his tribunal their contributions to the sanctuary of God (II Cor. 9:7). **they** [the workmen] **received of Moses all the offering which the children of Israel had brought,** etc.—It appears that the building was begun after the first few contributions were made; it was progressively carried on, and no necessity occurred to suspend operations even for the shortest interval, from want of the requisite materials. **5. they spake unto Moses, saying, The people bring much more than enough,** etc. —By the calculations which the practised eyes of the workmen enabled them to make, they were unanimously of the opinion that the supply already far exceeded the demand and that no more contributions were required. Such a report reflects the highest honor on their character as men of the strictest honor and integrity, who, notwithstanding they had command of an untold amount of the most precious things and might, without any risk of human discovery, have appropriated much to their own use, were too high principled for such acts of peculation. Forthwith, a proclamation was issued to stop further contributions.

35. he made a veil of blue—the second or inner veil, which separated the holy from the most holy place, embroidered with cherubim and of great size and thickness. **37. made an hanging for the . . . door**—Curtains of elaborately wrought needlework are often suspended over the entrance to tents of the great nomad sheiks, and throughout Persia, at the entrance of summer tents, mosques, and palaces. They are preferred as cooler and more elegant than wooden doors. This chapter contains an instructive narrative: it is the first instance of donations made for the worship of God, given from the wages of the people's sufferings and toils. They were acceptable to God (Phil. 4:18), and if the Israelites showed such liberality, how much more should those whose privilege it is to live under the Christian dispensation (I Cor. 6:20; 16:2).

ADAM CLARKE

5. *The people bring much more than enough.* With what a liberal spirit do these people bring their freewill offerings unto the Lord! Moses is obliged to make a proclamation to prevent them from bringing any more, as there was at present more than enough! Had Moses been intent upon gain, and had he not been perfectly disinterested, he would have encouraged them to continue their contributions, as thereby he might have multiplied to himself gold, silver, and precious stones. But he was doing the Lord's work, under the inspiration of the Divine Spirit, and therefore he sought no secular gain. Everything necessary for the worship of God will be cheerfully provided by a people whose hearts are in that worship.

8. *Cherubims of cunning work.* See on chap. xxvi. 18. Probably the word means no more than figures of any kind wrought in the loom, or by the needle in embroidery, or by the chisel or graving tool in wood, stone, or metal; see on chap. xxv. 18. In some places the word seems to be restricted to express a particular figure then well-known; but in many other places it seems to imply any kind of figure commonly formed by sculpture on stone, by carving on wood, by engraving upon brass, and by weaving in the loom.

9. *The length of one curtain.* Concerning these curtains, see chap. xxvi. 1, etc.

20. *And he made boards.* See the notes on chap. xxvi. 15, etc.

31. *He made bars.* See on chap. xxvi. 26, etc.

35. *He made a veil.* See on chap. xxvi. 31, etc.

37. *Hanging for the . . . door.* See on chap. xxvi. 36.

38. *The five pillars of it with their hooks.* Their capitals. See the note on chap. xxvi. 32.

MATTHEW HENRY — CHAPTER 37

Verses 1–9

I. Moses had recorded so fully the instructions given him upon the mount for the making of all these things. Why then are so many chapters taken up with this narrative? We must consider, 1. That Moses wrote primarily for the people of Israel, to whom it would be of great use to read and hear often of these divine and sacred treasures with which they were entrusted. The great things of God's law and gospel we need to have inculcated upon us again and again. 2. Moses would thus show the great care which he and his workmen took to make every thing exactly according to the pattern shown him in the mount. Having before given us the original, he here gives us the copy, that we may compare them, and observe how exactly they agree.

II. In these verses we have an account of the making of the ark, with its glorious and most significant appurtenances, the mercy-seat and the cherubim. Consider these three together, and they represent the glory of a holy God, the sincerity of a holy heart, and the communion that is between them, in and by a Mediator.

Verses 10–24

Here is, 1. The making of the table on which the show-bread was to be continually placed. God is a good householder, that always keeps a plentiful table. Is the world his tabernacle? His providence in it spreads a table for all the creatures: he *provides food for all flesh.* Is the church his tabernacle? His grace in it spreads a table for all believers, furnished with the bread of life. But observe how much the dispensation of the gospel exceeds that of the law. Though here was a table furnished, it was only with *show-bread,* bread to be looked upon, not to be fed upon, while it was on this table, and afterwards only by the priests; but to the table which Christ has spread in the new covenant all real Christians are

JAMIESON, FAUSSET, BROWN — CHAPTER 37

Vss. 1-29. FURNITURE OF THE TABERNACLE. **1. Bezaleel made the ark**—The description here given of the things within the sacred edifice is almost word for word the same as that contained in chapter 25. It is not on that account to be regarded as a useless repetition of minute particulars; for by the enumeration of these details, it can be seen how exactly everything was fashioned according to the "pattern shown on the mount"; and the knowledge of this exact correspondence between the prescription and the execution was essential to the purposes of the fabric. **6-10. made the mercy seat of pure gold**—To construct a figure, whether the body of a beast or a man, with two extended wings, measuring from two to three feet from tip to tip, with the hammer, out of a solid piece of gold, was what few, if any, artisans of the present day could accomplish. **17-22. he made the candlestick of pure gold**—Practical readers will be apt to say, "Why do such works with the hammer, when they could have been cast so much easier—a process they were well acquainted with?" The only answer that can be given is, that it was done according to order. We have no doubt but there were reasons for so distinctive an order, something significant, which has not been revealed to us [NAPIER]. The whole of that sacred building was arranged with a view to inculcate through every part of its apparatus the great fundamental principles of revelation. Every object was symbolical of important truth—every piece of furniture was made the hieroglyphic of a doctrine or a duty—on the floor and along the sides of that movable edifice was exhibited, by emblematic signs addressed to the eye, the whole remedial scheme of the gospel. How far this spiritual instruction was received by every successive generation of the Israelites, it may not be easy to determine. But the tabernacle, like the law of which it was a part, was a schoolmaster to Christ. Just as the

ADAM CLARKE — CHAPTER 37

1. *And Bezaleel made the ark.* For a description of the ark, see chap. xxv. 10, etc.

6. *He made the mercy seat.* See this described in chap. xxv. 17.

10. *He made the table.* See chap. xxv. 23.

16. *He made the vessels.* See all these particularly described in the notes on chap. xxv. 29.

17. *He made the candlestick.* See this described in the note on chap. xxv. 31.

MATTHEW HENRY

invited guests; and to them it is said, *Eat, O friends, come eat of my bread.* What the law gave but a sight of at a distance, the gospel gives the enjoyment of, and a hearty welcome to. 2. The making of the candlestick, all beaten work of pure gold only, *v.* 17, 22. The Bible is a golden candlestick; it is of pure gold, Ps. xix. 10. From it light is diffused to every part of God's tabernacle.

Verses 25–29

Here is, 1. The making of the golden altar, on which incense was to be burnt daily, which signified both the prayers of saints and the intercession of Christ. The rings and staves, and all the appurtenances of this altar, were overlaid with gold, as all the vessels of the table and candlestick were of gold, for these were used in the holy place. 2. The preparing of the incense which was to be burnt upon this altar, and with it the holy anointing oil (*v.* 29).

JAMIESON, FAUSSET, BROWN

walls of schools are seen studded with pictorial figures, by which the children, in a manner level to their capacities and suited to arrest their volatile minds, are kept in constant and familiar remembrance of the lessons of piety and virtue, so the tabernacle was intended by its furniture and all its arrangements to serve as a "shadow of good things to come." In this view, the minute description given in this chapter respecting the ark and mercy seat, the table of showbread, the candlestick, the altar of incense, and the holy oil, were of the greatest utility and importance; and though there are a few things that are merely ornamental appendages, such as the knops and the flowers, yet, in introducing these into the tabernacle, God displayed the same wisdom and goodness as He has done by introducing real flowers into the kingdom of nature to engage and gratify the eye of man.

ADAM CLARKE

25. *He made the incense altar.* See this described in chap. xxx. 1.

29. *He made the holy anointing oil.* See this and the *perfume,* and the materials out of which they were made, described at large in the notes on chap. xxx. 23-25 and 34-38.

MATTHEW HENRY

CHAPTER 38

Verses 1–8

Bezaleel having finished the gold-work, which, though the richest, yet was ordered to lie most out of sight, in the tabernacle itself, here goes on to prepare the court, which lay open to the view of all. Two things the court was furnished with, and both made of brass:—

I. An altar of burnt-offering, *v.* 1–7. On this all their sacrifices were offered.

II. A laver, to hold water for the priests to wash in when they went in to minister, *v.* 8. This is here said to be made of the *looking-glasses* (or mirrors) of the women that assembled at the door of the tabernacle.

1. It should seem these women were eminent and exemplary for devotion. Anna was such a one long afterwards, who *departed not from the temple, but served God with fastings and prayers night and day,* Luke ii. 37.

2. These women parted with their mirrors for the use of the tabernacle. Rather than the workmen should want brass, or not have of the best, they would part with their mirrors, though they could not do well without them.

3. These mirrors were used for the making of the laver. Either they were artfully joined together, or else molten down and cast anew.

Verses 9–20

The walls of the court, or church yard, were like the rest curtains or hangings, made according to the appointment, *ch.* xxvii. 9, &c. This represented the state of the Old Testament church: it was a garden enclosed; the worshippers were then confined to a little compass. But the enclosure being of curtains only intimated that the confinement of the church in one particular nation was not to be perpetual. The dispensation itself was a tabernacle-dispensation, movable and mutable, and in due time to be taken down and folded up, when the place of the tent should be enlarged and its cords lengthened, to make room for the Gentile world, as is foretold, Isa. liv. 2, 3.

Verses 21–31

Here we have a breviat of the account which, by Moses's appointment, the Levites took and kept of the gold, silver, and brass, that was brought in for the tabernacle's use, and how it was employed. Ithamar the son of Aaron was appointed to draw up this account, and was thus by less services trained up and filled for greater, *v.* 21. Bezaleel and Aholiab must bring in the account (*v.* 22, 23), and Ithamar must audit it, and give it in to Moses. And it was thus:—1. All the gold was a free will offering. 2. The silver was levied by way of tax; every man was assessed half a shekel, a kind of poll-money.

JAMIESON, FAUSSET, BROWN

CHAPTER 38

Vss. 1-31. Furniture of the Tabernacle. **1. the altar of burnt offering**—The repetitions are continued, in which may be traced the exact conformity of the execution to the order. **8. laver of brass . . . of the looking glasses of the women**—The word *mirrors* should have been used, as those implements, usually round, inserted into a handle of wood, stone, or metal, were made of brass, silver, or bronze, highly polished [Wilkinson]. It was customary for the Egyptian women to carry mirrors with them to the temples; and whether by taking the looking glasses of the Hebrew women Moses designed to put it out of their power to follow a similar practice at the tabernacle, or whether the supply of brass from other sources in the camp was exhausted, it is interesting to learn how zealously and to a vast extent they surrendered those valued accompaniments of the female toilet. **of the women assembling . . . at the door**—not priestesses but women of pious character and influence, who frequented the courts of the sacred building (Luke 2: 37), and whose parting with their mirrors, like the cutting the hair of the Nazarites, was their renouncing the world for a season [Hengstenberg]. **9. the court**—It occupied a space of one hundred and fifty feet by seventy-five, and it was enclosed by curtains of fine linen about eight feet high, suspended on brazen or copper pillars. Those curtains were secured by rods fastened to the top, and kept extended by being fastened to pins stuck in the ground. **10. hooks**—The hooks of the pillars in the court were for hanging up the carcasses of the sacrificial beasts —those on the pillars at the entry of the tabernacle were for hanging the sacerdotal robes and other things used in the service. **11. sockets**—mortices or holes in which the end of the pillars stood. **17. chapiters**—or capitals of the pillars, were wooden posts which ran along their top, to which were attached the hooks for the hangings. **18. the height in the breadth**—or in the measure. The sense is that the hangings of the court gate, which was twenty cubits wide, were of the same height as the hangings all round the court [Wall]. **21. This is the sum of the tabernacle**—Having completed his description of the component parts of the tabernacle, the inspired historian digresses into a statement respecting the gold and silver employed in it, the computation being made according to an order of Moses—by the Levites, under the direction of Ithamar, Aaron's youngest son. **24. twenty and nine talents, and seven hundred and thirty shekels**— equivalent to approximately $450,000. **25. the silver of them that were numbered**—603,550 men at 50 cents each would contribute 301,775 dollars. It may seem difficult to imagine how the Israelites should be possessed of so much wealth in the desert; but it should be remembered that they were enriched first by the spoils of the Egyptians, and afterwards by those of the Amalekites. Besides, it is highly probable that during their sojourn they traded with the neighboring nations who bordered on the wilderness [Hewlett].

ADAM CLARKE

CHAPTER 38

1. *The altar of burnt offering.* See the notes on chap. xxvii. 1; and for its horns, pots, shovels, basins, etc., see the meaning of the Hebrew terms explained, chap. xxvii. 3-5.

8. *He made the laver.* See the notes on chap. xxx. 18, etc. *The lookingglasses.* The word *maroth,* from *raah,* "he saw," signifies reflectors or mirrors of any kind. Here metal, highly polished, must certainly be meant, as glass was not yet in use; and had it even been in use, we are sure that looking glasses could not make a brazen laver. The word, therefore, should be rendered "mirrors," not *lookingglasses,* which in the above verse is perfectly absurd, because from those *maroth* the brazen laver was made. *Of the women . . . which assembled at the door.* What the employment of these women was at the door of the Tabernacle is not easily known. Some think they assembled there for purposes of devotion. Others, that they kept watch there during the night; and this is the most probable opinion, for they appear to have been in the same employment as those who assembled at the door of the Tabernacle of the congregation in the days of Samuel, who were abused by the sons of the high priest Eli, 1 Sam. ii. 22. Among the ancients women were generally employed in the office of porters or doorkeepers.

9. *The court.* See on chap. xxvii. 9.

17. *The hooks . . . and their fillets.* The capitals, and the silver bands that went round them; see the note on chap. xxvi. 32.

21. *This is the sum of the tabernacle.* That is, the foregoing account contains a detail of all the articles which Bezaleel and Aholiab were commanded to make; and which were reckoned up by the Levites, over whom Ithamar, the son of Aaron, presided.

24. *All the gold that was occupied for the work,* etc. The total value of all the *gold, silver,* and *brass* of the Tabernacle will amount to 244,127£ 14s. 6d. And the total weight of all these three metals amounts to 29,124 pounds troy, which, reduced to avoirdupois weight, is nearly ten tons and a half. When all this is considered, besides the quantity of gold which was employed in the golden calf, and which was all destroyed, it is no wonder that the sacred text should say the Hebrews spoiled the Egyptians, particularly as in those early times the precious metals were probably not very plentiful in Egypt.

26. *A bekah for every man.* The Hebrew word *beka,* from *baka,* to "divide, separate into two," seems to signify, not a particular coin, but a shekel broken or cut in two; so, anciently, our farthing was a penny divided in the midst and then subdivided, so that each division contained the fourth part of the penny; hence its name *fourthing* or *fourthling,* since corrupted into "farthing."

MATTHEW HENRY

CHAPTER 39

'erses 1–31

In this account of the making of the priests' gar-
ıents, according to the instructions given (*ch.* xxviii),
'e may observe, 1. That the priests' garments are
alled here *clothes of service*, *v.* 1. It is said of those
ıat are arrayed in white robes that they *are before
he throne of God, and serve him day and night in his
emple*, Rev. vii. 13, 15. 2. That all the six para-
raphs here, which give a distinct account of the
ıaking of these holy garments, conclude with those
'ords, *as the Lord commanded Moses*, *v.* 5, 7, 21,
6, 29, 31. It is an intimation to all the Lord's
ıinisters to make the word of God their rule in all
ıeir ministrations, and to act in observance of and
bedience to the command of God. 3. That these
arments, in conformity to the rest of the furniture
f the tabernacle, were very rich and splendid; the
hurch in its infancy was thus taught, thus pleased,
'ith the rudiments of this world. 4. That they were
ll shadows of good things to come, but the sub-
tance is Christ, and the grace of the gospel; when
herefore the substance has come, it is a jest to be
ond of the shadow. (1) Christ is our great high-
riest; when he undertook the work of our re-
emption, he put on the clothes of service. (2) True
elievers are spiritual priests. The clean linen with
hich all their clothes of service must be made is
he righteousness of saints (Rev. xix. 8).

'erses 32–43

I. The builders of the tabernacle made very good
lespatch. It was not much more than five months
rom the beginning to the finishing of it.

II. They punctually observed their orders, and did
ıot in the least vary from them. They did it *according
o all that the Lord commanded Moses*, *v.* 32, 42.

III. They brought all their work to Moses, and
ubmitted it to his inspection and censure, *v.* 33.
Though they knew how to do the work better than
Moses, Moses had a better and more exact idea of
he model than they had, and therefore they could
ıot be well pleased with their own work, unless they
ıad his approbation.

**IV. Moses, upon search, found all done according
o the rule, *v.* 43. Behold they had done it according
o the pattern shown him, for the same Being that
howed him the pattern guided their hand in the work.**

V. Moses blessed them. 1. He commended them,
ınd signified his approbation of all they had done.
He did not find fault where there was none, as some
lo, who think they disparage their own judgment if
hey do not find something amiss in the best and
nost accomplished performance. In all this work
t is probable there might have been found here and
here a stitch amiss, and a stroke awry, but Moses was
oo candid to notice small faults where there were no
great ones. 2. He not only praised them, but prayed
or them.

JAMIESON, FAUSSET, BROWN

CHAPTER 39

Vss. 1-43. GARMENTS OF THE PRIESTS. **1. cloths of service**—official robes. The ephod of the high priest, the robe of the ephod, the girdle of needle-work, and the embroidered coat were all of fine linen; for on no material less delicate could such elaborate symbolical figures have been portrayed in embroidery, and all beautified with the same brilliant colors. (See on ch. 28). **3. cut the gold into wires to work it**—i.e., the metal was beaten with a hammer into thin plates—cut with scissors or some other instrument into long slips—then rounded into filaments or threads. "Cloth of golden tissue is not uncommon on the monuments, and specimens of it have been found rolled about mummies; but it is not easy to determine whether the gold thread was originally interwoven or subsequently inserted by the embroiderer" [TAYLOR].

30. a writing, like to the engravings of a signet—The seal-ring worn both by ancient and modern Egyptians on the little finger of the right hand, contained, inscribed on a cornelian or other precious stone, along with the owner's name, a religious sentiment or sacred symbol, intimating that he was the servant of God, or expressive of trust in Him. And it was to this practice the inscription on the high priest alludes (cf. Exod. 28:11). **34. the covering of rams' skin dyed red**—(See ch. 25:7). It was probably red morocco leather and "badgers' skins," rather "the skins of the *tahash*, supposed to be the dugong, or dolphin of the Red Sea, the skin of which is still used by the Arabs under the same appellation" [GOSS].

43. Moses did look upon all the work, and, behold, they had done it as the Lord had commanded—A formal inspection was made on the completion of the tabernacle, not only with a view to have the work transferred from the charge of the workmen, but to ascertain whether it corresponded with "the pattern." The result of a careful and minute survey showed that every plank, curtain, altar, and vase had been most accurately made of the form, and in the place designed by the Divine Architect—and Moses, in accepting it of their hands, thanked God for them, and begged Him to bless them.

ADAM CLARKE

CHAPTER 39

1. *Blue, and purple, and scarlet.* See this subject explained in the notes on chap. xxv. 4.

2. *Ephod.* See this described, chap. xxv. 7.

3. *They did beat the gold into thin plates.* For the purpose, as it is supposed, of cutting it into wires or threads; for to "twist" or "twine" is the common acceptation of the root *pathal.* I cannot suppose that the Israelites had not then the art of making gold thread, as they possessed several ornamental arts much more difficult.

6. *Onyx stones.* See chap. xxv. 7; xxviii. 17; etc.

8. *Breastplate.* See on chap. xxviii. 18.

10. *And they set in it four rows of stones.* See all these precious stones particularly explained in the notes on chap. xxviii. 17, etc.

23. *As the hole of an habergeon.* The *habergeon* was a small coat of mail, something in form of a half shirt, made of small iron rings curiously united together. It covered the neck and breast, was very light, and resisted the stroke of a sword. Sometimes it went over the whole head as well as over the breast. This kind of defensive armor was used among the Asiatics, particularly the ancient Persians, among whom it is still worn.

30. *The holy crown of pure gold.* On Asiatic monuments, particularly those that appear in the ruins of Persepolis and on many Egyptian monuments, the priests are represented as wearing crowns or tiaras, and sometimes their heads are crowned with laurel.

32. *Did according to all that the Lord commanded Moses.* This refers to the command given in chap. xxv. 40; and Moses has taken care to repeat everything in the most circumstantial detail, to show that he had conscientiously observed all the directions he had received.

37. *The pure candlestick.* See the note on chap. xxv. 31. *The lamps to be set in order.* To be trimmed and fresh oiled every day for the purpose of being lighted in the evening. See the note on chap. xxvii. 21.

43. *And Moses did look upon all the work.* As being the general superintendent of the whole, under whom Bezaleel and Aholiab were employed, as the other workmen were under them. *They had done it as the Lord had commanded.* Exactly according to the pattern which Moses received from the Lord, and which he laid before the workmen to work by. *And Moses blessed them.* Gave them that praise which was due to their skill, diligence, and fidelity. See this meaning of the original word in the note on Gen. ii. 3. It is very probable that Moses prayed to God in their behalf that they might be prospered in all their undertakings, saved from every evil, and be brought at last to the inheritance that fadeth not away. This blessing seems to have been given, not only to the workmen, but to all the people. The people contributed liberally, and the workmen wrought faithfully, and the blessing of God was pronounced upon all.

MATTHEW HENRY

CHAPTER 40

Verses 1–15

The materials and furniture of the tabernacle had been viewed severally and approved, and now they must be put together. 1. The time for doing this is fixed to *the first day of the first month* (*v.* 2). It is good to begin the year with some good work. Let him that is the first have the first; and let the things of his kingdom be first sought. In Hezekiah's time we find they began to sanctify the temple *on the first day of the first month*, 2 Chron. xxix. 17. Moses is particularly ordered to set up the tabernacle itself first, in which God would dwell and would be served (*v.* 2), then to put the ark in its place, and draw the veil before it (*v.* 3), then to fix the table, and the candlestick, and the altar of incense, without the veil (*v.* 4, 5), and to fix the hanging of the door before the door. Then in the court he must place the altar of burnt offering, and the laver (*v.* 6, 7); and, lastly, he must set up the curtains of the court, and a hanging for a court-gate. 2. He directs Moses, when he had set up the tabernacle and all the furniture of it, to consecrate it and them, by anointing them with the oil which was prepared for the purpose, *ch.* xxx. 25, &c. Everything was sanctified when it

JAMIESON, FAUSSET, BROWN

CHAPTER 40

Vss. 1-38. THE TABERNACLE REARED AND ANOINTED. **2. On the first day of the first month**—From a careful consideration of the incidents recorded to have happened after the exodus (ch. 12:2; 13:4; 19:1; 20:18; 34:28, etc.), it has been computed that the work of the tabernacle was commenced within six months after that emigration; and consequently, that other six months had been occupied in building it. So long a period spent in preparing the materials of a movable pavilion, it would be difficult to understand, were it not for what we are told of the vast dimensions of the tabernacle, as well as the immense variety of curious and elaborate workmanship which its different articles of furniture required. **the tabernacle**—the entire edifice. **the tent**—the covering that surmounted it (vs. 19). **15. anoint them, as thou didst anoint their fathers**—The sacred oil was used, but it does not appear that the ceremony was performed exactly in the same manner; for although the anointing oil was sprinkled over the garments both of Aaron and his sons (ch. 29:21; Lev. 8:30), it was not poured over the heads of the latter. This distinction was reserved for the high

ADAM CLARKE

CHAPTER 40

2. *The first day of the first month.* It is generally supposed that the Israelites began the work of the Tabernacle about the sixth month after they had left Egypt; and as the work was finished about the end of the first year of their exodus (for it was set up the first day of the second year), that therefore they had spent about six months in making it. Such a building, with such a profusion of curious and costly workmanship, was never put up in so short a time. But it was the work of the Lord, and the people did service as unto the Lord; for the people had a mind to work.

4. *Thou shalt bring in the table, and set in order the things.* That is, Thou shalt place the twelve loaves upon the table in the order before mentioned. See the note on chap. xxv. 30.

15. *For their anointing shall surely be an everlasting priesthood.* By this anointing a right was given to Aaron and his family to be high priests among the Jews forever; so that all who should be born of this family should have a right

MATTHEW HENRY

was put in its proper place. As everything is beautiful in its season, so is everything in its place. 3. He directs him to consecrate Aaron and his sons.

Verses 16–33

When the tabernacle and the furniture of it were prepared, they set it up in the midst of their camp, while they were in the wilderness.

Here we have an account of that new year's day's work. That which was to be veiled he veiled (*v.* 21), and that which was to be used he used immediately. What he did he did by special warrant and direction from God, rather as a prophet, or law-giver, than as a priest. He set the wheels a-going, and then left the work in the hands of the appointed ministry. (1) When he had placed the table, he set the show-bread in order upon it (*v.* 23). (2) As soon as he had fixed the candlestick, *he lighted the lamps before the Lord, v.* 25. (3) The golden altar being put in its place, immediately he *burnt sweet incense thereon* (*v.* 27). (4) The altar of burnt-offering was no sooner set up in the court of the tabernacle than he had a *burnt-offering, and a meat-offering, ready to offer upon it, v.* 29. (5) At the laver likewise, when he had fixed that, Moses himself washed his hands and feet.

Verses 34–38

As when, in the creation, God had finished this earth, which he designed for man's habitation, he made man, and put him in possession of it, so when Moses had finished the tabernacle, which was designed for God's dwelling-place among men, God came and took possession of it. Where God has a throne and an altar in the soul, there is a living temple. Accordingly, when God descended to take possession of his house, the *cloud covered it* on the outside, and *the glory of the Lord filled it* within.

I. *The cloud covered the tent.* This cloud was intended to be, 1. A token of God's presence constantly visible day and night (*v.* 38) to all Israel, even to those that lay in the remotest corners of the camp, that they might never again make a question of it, *Is the Lord among us, or is he not?* 2. A concealment of the tabernacle, and the glory of God in it. God did indeed dwell among them, but he dwelt in a cloud. 3. A protection of the tabernacle. They had sheltered it with one covering upon another, but, after all, the cloud that covered it was its best guard. Those that dwell in the house of the Lord are safe under the divine protection, Ps. xxvii. 4, 5. 4. A guide to the camp of Israel in their march through the wilderness, *v.* 36, 37. While the cloud continued on the tabernacle, they rested; when it removed, they removed and followed it, as being purely under divine direction.

II. *The glory of the Lord filled the tabernacle, v.* 34, 35. It was in light and fire, and (for aught we know) no otherwise, that the *shechinah* made itself visible; for *God is light.*

JAMIESON, FAUSSET, BROWN

priest (ch. 29:7; Lev. 8:12; Ps. 133:2). **16. Thus did Moses: according to all that the Lord commanded him**—On his part, the same scrupulous fidelity was shown in conforming to the "pattern" in the disposition of the furniture, as had been displayed by the workmen in the erection of the edifice. **33. So Moses finished the work**—Though it is not expressly recorded in this passage, yet, from what took place on all similar occasions, there is reason to believe that on the inauguration day the people were summoned from their tents—were all drawn up as a vast assemblage, yet in calm and orderly arrangement, around the newly erected tabernacle. **34. a cloud**—lit., "*The*" cloud,—the mystic cloud which was the well-known symbol of the Divine Presence. After remaining at a great distance from them on the summit of the mount, it appeared to be in motion; and if many among them had a secret misgiving about the issue, how the fainting heart would revive, the interest of the moment intensely increase, and the tide of joy swell in every bosom, when that symbolic cloud was seen slowly and majestically descending towards the plain below and covering the tabernacle. The entire and universal concealment of the tabernacle within the folds of an impervious cloud was not without a deep and instructive meaning; it was a protection to the sacred edifice from the burning heats of the Arabian climate; it was a token of the Divine Presence; and it was also an emblem of the Mosaic dispensation, which, though it was a revelation from heaven, yet left many things hid in obscurity; for it was a dark cloud compared with the bright cloud, which betokened the clearer and fuller discoveries of the divine character and glory in the gospel (Matt. 17:5). **the glory of the Lord filled the tabernacle**—i. e., light and fire, a created splendor, which was the peculiar symbol of God (I John 1:5). Whether this light was inherent in the cloud or not, it emanated from it on this occasion, and making its entry, not with the speed of a lightning flash as if it were merely an electric spark, but in majestic splendor, it passed through the outer porch into the interior of the most holy place (I Kings 8:10; John 1:14). Its miraculous character is shown by the fact, that, though "it filled the tabernacle," not a curtain or any article of furniture was so much as singed. **35. Moses was not able to enter into the tent of the congregation**—How does this circumstance show the incapacity of man, in his present state, to look upon the unveiled perfections of the Godhead! Moses could not endure the unclouded effulgence, nor the sublimest of the prophets (Isa. 6:5). But what neither Moses nor the most eminent of God's messengers to the ancient church through the weakness of nature could endure, we can all now do by an exercise of faith; looking unto Jesus, who reflected with chastened radiance the brightness of the Father's glory; and who, having as the Forerunner for us, entered within the veil, has invited us to come boldly to the mercy seat. While Moses was compelled, through the influence of overwhelming awe, to stand aloof and could not enter the tabernacle, Christ entered into the holy place not made with hands; nay, He is Himself the true tabernacle, filled with the glory of God, ever with the grace and truth which the Shekinah typified. What great reason we have to thank God for Jesus Christ, who, while He Himself was the brightness of the Father's glory, yet exhibited that glory in so mild and attractive a manner, as to allure us to draw near with confidence and love into the Divine Presence! **36. when the cloud was taken up from over the tabernacle**—In journeying through the sandy, trackless deserts of the East, the use of torches, exhibiting a cloud of smoke by day and of fire by night, has been resorted to from time immemorial. The armies of Darius and Alexander were conducted on their marches in this manner [FABER]. The Arab caravans in the present day observe the same custom; and materials for these torches are stored up among other necessary preparations for a journey. Live fuel, hoisted in chafing-dishes at the end of long poles, and being seen at a great distance, serves, by the smoke in the daytime and the light at night, as a better signal for march than the sound of a trumpet, which is not heard at the extremities of a large camp [LABORDE]. This usage, and the miracle related by Moses, mutually illustrate each other. The usage leads us to think that the miracle was necessary, and worthy of God to perform; and, on the other hand, the miracle of the cloudy pillar, affording double benefit of shade by day and light at night, implies not only that the usage was not unknown to the Hebrews, but supplied all the wants which they felt in common with other travellers through those dreary regions [FABER, HESS, GRANDPIERRE]. But

ADAM CLARKE

to the priesthood without the repetition of this unction, as they should enjoy this honor in their father's right, who had it by a particular grant from God. But it appears that the high priest, on his consecration, did receive the holy unction; see Lev. iv. 3; vi. 22; xxi. 10. And this continued till the destruction of the first Temple, and the Babylonish captivity; and according to Eusebius, Cyril of Jerusalem, and others, this custom continued among the Jews to the advent of our Lord, after which there is no evidence it was ever practiced. The Jewish high priest was a type of Him who is called the "high priest over the house of God," Heb. x. 21; and when He came, the functions of the other necessarily ceased.

19. *He spread abroad the tent over the tabernacle.* By the *tent,* in this and several other places, we are to understand the coverings made of rams' skins, goats' hair, etc., which were thrown over the building; for the Tabernacle had no other kind of roof.

20. *And put the testimony into the ark.* That is, the two tables on which the Ten Commandments had been written. See chap. xxv. 16. The ark, the golden table with the shewbread, the golden candlestick, and the golden altar of incense, were all in the Tabernacle, "within the veil" or curtains, which served as a door, vv. 22, 24, 26. And the altar of burnt offering was "by the door," v. 29. And the brazen laver, between the tent of the congregation and the brazen altar, v. 30; still farther outward, that it might be the first thing the priests met with when entering into the court to minister, as their hands and feet must be washed before they could perform any part of the holy service, vv. 31-32. When all these things were thus placed, then the *court* that surrounded the Tabernacle, which consisted of posts and hangings, was set up, v. 33.

34. *Then a cloud covered the tent.* Thus God gave His approbation of the work; and as this was visible, so it was a sign to all the people that Jehovah was among them. *And the glory of the Lord filled the tabernacle.* How this was manifested we cannot tell; it was probably by some light or brightness which was insufferable to the sight, for Moses himself could not enter in because of the cloud and the glory, v. 35. Precisely the same happened when Solomon had dedicated his Temple; for it is said that "the cloud filled the house of the Lord, so that the priests could not stand to minister because of the cloud: for the glory of the Lord had filled the house of the Lord," 1 Kings viii. 10-11. Previously to this the cloud of the divine glory had rested upon that tent which Moses had pitched without the camp, after the transgression in the matter of the molten calf; but now the cloud removed from that tabernacle and rested upon this one, which was made by the command and under the direction of God himself. And there is reason to believe that this Tabernacle was pitched in the center of the camp, all the twelve tribes pitching their different tents in a certain order around it.

36. *When the cloud was taken up.* The subject of these last three verses has been very largely explained in the notes on chap. xiii. 21, to which, as well as to the general remarks on that chapter, the reader is requested immediately to refer.

MATTHEW HENRY

JAMIESON, FAUSSET, BROWN

its peculiar appearance, unvarying character, and regular movements, distinguished it from all the common atmospheric phenomena. It was an invaluable boon to the Israelites, and being recognized by all classes among that people as the symbol of the Divine Presence, it guided their journeys and regulated their encampments (cf. Ps. 29 and 105). **38. the cloud of the Lord was upon the tabernacle,** etc.– While it had hitherto appeared sometimes in one place, sometimes in another, it was now found on the tabernacle only; so that from the moment that sanctuary was erected, and the glory of the Lord had filled the sacred edifice, the Israelites had to look to the place which God had chosen to put His name there, in order that they might enjoy the benefit of a heavenly Guide (Num. 9:15-23). In like manner, the church had divine revelation for its guide from the first—long before the WORD of God existed in a written form; but ever since the setting up of that sacred canon, it rests on that as its tabernacle and there only is it to be found. It accompanies us wherever we are or go, just as the cloud led the way of the Israelites. It is always accessible and can be carried in our pockets when we walk abroad; it may be engraven on the inner tablets of our memories and our hearts; and so true, faithful, and complete a guide is it, that there is not a scene of duty or of trial through which we may be called to pass in the world, but it furnishes a clear, a safe, and unerring direction (Col. 3:16).

ADAM CLARKE

38. *For the cloud of the Lord was upon the tabernacle by day.* This daily and nightly appearance was at once both a merciful providence and a demonstrative proof of the divinity of their religion: and these tokens continued with them *throughout all their journeys;* for, notwithstanding their frequently repeated disobedience and rebellion, God never withdrew these tokens of His presence from them, till they were brought into the Promised Land. When, therefore, the Tabernacle became fixed, because the Israelites had obtained their inheritance, this mark of the divine presence was no longer visible in the sight of all Israel, but appears to have been confined to the holy of holies, where it had its fixed residence upon the mercy seat between the cherubim; and in this place continued till the first Temple was destroyed, after which it was no more seen in Israel till God was manifested in the flesh.

THE BOOK OF LEVITICUS

I. Dedication: the offerings—provision for approach (1:1-7:38)
  A. The offerings: the worship (1:1-6:7)
    1. Burnt offering (1:1-17)
    2. Meal offering (2:1-16)
    3. Peace offering (3:1-17)
    4. Sin offering (4:1-35)
    5. Trespass offering (5:1-6:7)
  B. The laws of the offerings: the worshipper (6:8-7:38)

II. Meditation: the priests—appropriation for provision (8:1-10:20)
  A. Consecration of the priests (8:1-36)
    1. Preparation (8:1-9)
    2. Anointing (8:10-24)
    3. Sacrifice and new anointing (8:25-36)
  B. The priests at work (9:1-24)
    1. Offerings for themselves (9:1-14)
    2. Offerings for the people (9:15-24)
  C. Nadab and Abihu (10:1-20)
    1. Their sin (10:1-7)
    2. Consequent warnings (10:8-20)

III. Separation: the people—conditions of appropriation (11:1-22:33)
  A. A people God-governed (11:1-17:16)
    1. Of health (11:1-15:33)
    2. The Day of Atonement (16:1-34)
    3. General instructions concerning sacrifices (17:1-16)
  B. A people God-manifesting (18:1-22:33)
    1. Separation from evil practices (18:1-30)
    2. A call to holiness (19:1-37)
    3. Laws against unchastity and uncleanness (20:1-27)
    4. Responsibilities of the priests (21:1-22:33)

IV. Consecration: the feasts—benefits of approach (23:1-24:23)
  A. The feasts (23:1-44)
    1. The Sabbath (23:1-3)
    2. The Passover (23:4-5)
    3. Unleavened bread ((23:6-8)
    4. First fruits (23:9-14)
    5. Pentecost (23:15-22)
    6. Trumpets (23:23-25)
    7. Atonement (23:26-32)
    8. Tabernacles (23:33-44)
  B. Symbols of consecration (24:1-9)
    1. The oil (24:1-4)
    2. The shewbread (24:5-9)
  C. The blasphemer (24:10-23)

V. Ratification: the signs—symbols of relation (25:1-27:34)
  A. Obligatory (25:1-26:46)
    1. The land sabbath (25:1-7)
    2. Jubilee (25:8-55)
    3. Exhortations (26:1-46)
  B. Voluntary—vows (27:1-34)

There is nothing historical in all this book of Leviticus except the account which it gives us of the consecration of the priesthood (ch. 8, 9); of the punishment of Nadab and Abihu by the hand of God for offering strange fire (ch. 10); and of Shelomith's son by the hand of the magistrate for blasphemy (ch. 24). All the rest of the book is taken up with the laws, chiefly the ecclesiastical laws, which God gave to Israel by Moses, concerning their sacrifices and offerings, their meats, and drinks, and various form of washings, and the other peculiarities by which God set that people apart for himself and distinguished them from other nations: all which were shadows of good things to come which are realized and superseded by the gospel of Christ. We call the book Leviticus, from the Septuagint, because it contains the laws and ordinances of the *levitical priesthood* (as it is called, Heb. 7:11), and the ministrations of it.

MATTHEW HENRY

CHAPTER 1

Verses 1–2

Observe here, 1. It is taken for granted that people would be inclined to bring offerings to the Lord. Revealed religion supposes natural religion to be an ancient and early institution, since the fall had directed men to glorify God by sacrifice, which was an implicit acknowledgment of their having received all from God as creatures, and their having forfeited all to him as sinners. Provision is made that men should not indulge their own fancies, nor become vain about their sacrifices, lest, while they pretended to honour God, they should really dishonour him. Everything therefore is directed to be done so that the sacrifices might be most significant both of the great sacrifice of atonement which Christ was to offer in the fulness of time and of the spiritual sacrifices of acknowledgment which believers should offer daily. God gave those laws to Israel by Moses. By other prophets God sent messages to his people, but by Moses he gave them laws. As soon as ever the shechinah had taken possession of its new habitation, God talked with Moses from the mercy-seat, while he attended without the veil, or rather at the door, hearing a voice only. The tabernacle was set up to be a place of communion between God and Israel; there, where they performed their services to God, God revealed his will to them. The moral law was given with terror from a burning mountain in thunder and lightning; but the remedial law of sacrifice was given more gently from a mercy-seat, because that was typical of the grace of the gospel, which is the ministration of life and peace.

JAMIESON, FAUSSET, BROWN

CHAPTER 1

Vss. 1-17. Burnt Offerings of the Herd. **1. the Lord . . . spake . . . out of the tabernacle**—The laws that are contained in the previous record were delivered either to the people publicly from Sinai, or to Moses privately, on the summit of that mountain; but on the completion of the tabernacle, the remainder of the law was announced to the Hebrew leader by an audible voice from the divine glory, which surmounted the mercy seat.

2. Speak unto the children of Israel, and say unto them—If the subject of communication were of a temporal nature, the Levites were excluded; but if it were a spiritual matter, all the tribes were comprehended under this name (Deut. 27:12). **If any man of you bring an offering unto the Lord**—The directions given here relate solely to voluntary or freewill offerings—those rendered over and above such, as being of standing and universal obligation, could not be dispensed with or commuted for any other kind of offering (Exod. 29:38; ch. 23:37; Num. 28:3, 11-27, etc.). **bring your offering of the cattle,** etc.—i.e., those animals that were not only tame, innocent and gentle, but useful and adapted for food. This rule excluded horses, dogs, swine, camels, and asses, which were used in sacrifice by some heathen nations, beasts and birds of prey, as also hares and deers.

ADAM CLARKE

CHAPTER 1

1. *And the Lord called unto Moses.* From the manner in which this book commences, it appears plainly to be a continuation of the preceding; and indeed the whole is but one law, though divided into five portions, and why thus divided is not easy to be conjectured.

Previously to the erection of the Tabernacle, God had given no particular directions concerning the manner of offering the different kinds of sacrifices; but as soon as this divine structure was established and consecrated, Jehovah took it as His dwelling place; described the rites and ceremonies which He would have observed in His worship, that His people might know what was best pleasing in His sight; and that, when thus worshipping Him, they might have confidence that they pleased Him, everything being done according to His own directions. A consciousness of acting according to the revealed will of God gives strong confidence to an upright mind.

2. *Bring an offering.* The word *korban,* from *karab,* "to approach or draw near," signifies an *offering* or "gift" by which a person had access unto God; and this receives light from the universal custom that prevails in the East, no man being permitted to approach the presence of a superior without a present or gift; and the offering thus brought was called *korban,* which properly means the "introduction offering," or "offering of access." *Of the cattle. Habbehemah,* animals of the beef kind, such as the bull, heifer, bullock, and calf; and restrained to these alone by the term *herd, bakar,* which, from its general use in the Levitical writings, is known to refer to the ox, heifer, etc. And therefore other animals of the beef kind were excluded. *Of the flock. Tson,* "sheep" and "goats"; for we have already seen that this term implies both kinds; and we know, from its use, that no other animal of the smaller, clean, domestic quad-

MATTHEW HENRY

Verses 3–9

If a man were rich and could afford it, it is supposed that he would bring his burnt-sacrifice, with which he designed to honour God, out of his herd of larger cattle. 1. The beast to be offered must be a male, and without blemish, and the best he had in his pasture. 2. The owner must offer it voluntarily. What is done in religion, so as to please God, must be done by no other constraint than that of love. 3. It must be offered at the door of the tabernacle, where the brazen altar of burnt-offerings stood, which sanctified the gift. He must offer it at the door, as one unworthy to enter, and acknowledging that there is no admission for a sinner into covenant and communion with God, but by sacrifice.

4. The offerer must put his hand upon the head of his offering, *v.* 4, signifying thereby, (1) The transfer of all his right to, and interest in, the beast, to God. (2) An acknowledgment that he deserved to die, and would have been willing to die if God had required it. (3) A dependence upon the sacrifice, as an instituted type of the great sacrifice on which the iniquity of us all was to be laid. Though the burnt-offerings had not respect to any particular sin, as the sin-offering had, yet they were to make atonement for sin in general. 5. The sacrifice was to be killed by the priests or Levites, before the Lord, that is, in a devout religious manner. 6. The priests were to *sprinkle the blood upon the altar* (*v.* 5); for, the blood being the life, it was this that made atonement for the soul. 7. The beast was to be flayed and decently cut up, and divided into its several joints or pieces, and then all the pieces, with the head and the fat were to be burnt together upon the altar, *v.* 6–9. 8. This is said to be *an offering of a sweet savour*, or *savour of rest, unto the Lord*. The burning of flesh is unsavoury in itself; but this, as an act of obedience to a divine command, and a type of Christ, was well pleasing to God: he was reconciled to the offerer. Christ's offering of himself to God is said to be of *a sweet-smelling savour* (Eph. v. 2), and the spiritual sacrifices of Christians are said to be *acceptable to God, through Christ*, 1 Pet. ii. 5.

Verses 10–17

Here we have the laws concerning the burnt-offerings, which were of the flock or of the fowls. Those of the middle rank, that could not well afford to offer a bullock, would bring a sheep or a goat; and those that were not able to do that should be accepted of God if they brought a turtle-dove or a pigeon. It is observable that those creatures were chosen for sacrifice which were most mild and gentle, harmless and inoffensive, to typify the innocence and meekness that were in Christ, and to teach the innocence and meekness that should be in Christians. Directions are here given, 1. Concerning the burnt-offerings of the flock, *v.* 10. The method of managing these is much the same with that of the bullocks. 2. Concerning those of the fowls. They must be either turtle-doves or *pigeons*, and, if so, they must be *young* pigeons. The poor man's turtle-doves, or young pigeons, are here said to be *an offering of a sweet-smelling savour*, as much as that of an ox or bullock that hath horns or hoofs. Yet, after all, to *love God with all our heart, and to love our neighbour as ourselves, is better than all burnt-offerings and sacrifices*, Mark xii. 33.

JAMIESON, FAUSSET, BROWN

3. a burnt sacrifice—so called from its being wholly consumed on the altar; no part of it was eaten either by the priests or the offerer. It was designed to propitiate the anger of God incurred by original sin, or by particular transgressions; and its entire combustion indicated the self-dedication of the offerer—his whole nature—his body and soul—as necessary to form a sacrifice acceptable to God (Rom. 12:1; Phil. 1:20). This was the most ancient as well as the most conspicuous mode of sacrifice. **a male without blemish**—No animal was allowed to be offered that had any deformity or defect. Among the Egyptians, a minute inspection was made by the priest; and the bullock having been declared perfect, a certificate to that effect being fastened to its horns with wax, was sealed with his ring, and no other might be substituted. A similar process of examining the condition of the beasts brought as offerings, seems to have been adopted by the priests in Israel (John 6:27). **at the door of the tabernacle**—where stood the altar of burnt offering (Exod. 40:6). Every other place was forbidden, under the highest penalty (ch. 17:4). **4. shall put his hand upon the head**—This was a significant act which implied not only that the offerer devoted the animal to God, but that he confessed his consciousness of sin and prayed that his guilt and its punishment might be transferred to the victim. **and it shall be**—rather, "that it may be an acceptable atonement." **5. he shall kill the bullock**—The animal should be killed by the offerer, not by the priest, for it was not his duty in case of voluntary sacrifices; in later times, however, the office was generally performed by Levites. **before the Lord**—on the spot where the hands had been laid upon the animal's head, on the north side of the altar. **sprinkle the blood**—This was to be done by the priests. The blood being considered the life, the effusion of it was the essential part of the sacrifice; and the sprinkling of it—the application of the atonement—made the person and services of the offerer acceptable to God. The skin having been stripped off, and the carcass cut up, the various pieces were disposed on the altar in the manner best calculated to facilitate their being consumed by the fire. **8. the fat**—that about the kidneys especially, which is called "suet." **9. but his inwards and his legs shall he wash in water,** etc.—This part of the ceremony was symbolical of the *inward* purity, and the holy *walk*, that became acceptable worshippers. **a sweet savour unto the Lord**—is an expression of the offerer's piety, but especially as a sacrificial type of Christ. **10-13. if his offering be of the flocks**—Those who could not afford the expense of a bullock might offer a ram or a he-goat, and the same ceremonies were to be observed in the act of offering. **14-17. if the burnt sacrifice . . . be of fowls**—The gentle nature and cleanly habits of the dove led to its selection, while all other fowls were rejected, either for the fierceness of their disposition or the grossness of their taste; and in this case, there being from the smallness of the animal no blood for waste, the priest was directed to prepare it *at* the altar and sprinkle the blood. This was the offering appointed for the poor. The fowls were always offered in pairs, and the reason why Moses ordered two turtledoves or two young pigeons, was not merely to suit the convenience of the offerer, but according as the latter was in season; for pigeons are sometimes quite hard and unfit for eating, at which time turtledoves are very good in Egypt and Palestine. The turtledoves are not restricted to any age because they are always good when they appear in those countries, being birds of passage; but the age of the pigeons is particularly marked that they might not be offered to God at times when they are rejected by men [HARMER]. It is obvious, from the varying scale of these voluntary sacrifices, that the disposition of the offerer was the thing looked to – not the costliness of his offering.

ADAM CLARKE

rupeds is intended, as no other animal of this class, besides the sheep and goat, was ever offered in sacrifice to God. The animals mentioned in this chapter as proper for sacrifice are the very same which God commanded Abraham to offer; see Gen. xv. 9. And thus it is evident that God delivered to the patriarchs an epitome of that law which was afterwards given in detail to Moses, the essence of which consisted in its sacrifices; and those sacrifices were of clean animals.

3. *Burnt sacrifice.* The most important of all the sacrifices offered to God; called by the Septuagint *holokautoma,* because it was "wholly consumed," which was not the case in any other offering. *His own voluntary will. Lirtsono,* "to gain himself acceptance" before the Lord. In this way all the versions appear to have understood the original words, and the connection in which they stand obviously requires this meaning.

4. *He shall put his hand upon the head of the burnt offering.* By the imposition of hands the person bringing the victim acknowledged, (1) The sacrifice as his own. (2) That he offered it is an atonement for his sins. (3) That he was worthy of death because he had sinned, having forfeited his life by breaking the law. (4) That he entreated God to accept the life of the innocent animal in place of his own. (5) And all this, to be done profitably, must have respect to Him whose life, in the fulness of time, should be made a sacrifice for sin. (6) The blood was to be sprinkled round about upon the altar, v. 5, as by the sprinkling of blood the atonement was made; for the blood was the life of the beast, and it was always supposed that life went to redeem life.

6. *He shall flay.* Probably meaning the person who brought the sacrifice, who, according to some of the rabbins, killed, flayed, cut up, and washed the sacrifice, and then presented the parts and the blood to the priest, that he might burn the one, and sprinkle the other upon the altar. But it is certain that the priests also, and the Levites, flayed the victims, and the priest had the skin to himself; see chap. vii. 8, and 2 Chron. xxix. 34.

7. *Put fire.* The fire that came out of the Tabernacle from before the Lord, and which was kept perpetually burning; see chap. ix. 24. Nor was it lawful to use any other fire in the service of God. See the case of Nadab and Abihu, chap. x.

8. *The priests . . . shall lay the parts.* The sacrifice was divided according to its larger joints. The sacred fire was then applied, and the whole mass was consumed. This was the *holocaust,* or complete burnt offering.

9. *An offering . . . of a sweet savour.* A "fire offering, an odor of rest," or, as the Septuagint express it, "a sacrifice for a sweet-smelling savor"; which place St. Paul had evidently in view when he wrote Eph. v. 2: "Christ . . . hath loved us, and hath given himself for us an offering and a sacrifice to God for a sweet-smelling savour," where he uses the same terms as the Septuagint. Hence we find that the *holocaust,* or burnt offering, typified the sacrifice and death of Christ for the sins of the world.

16. *Pluck away his crop with his feathers.* In this sacrifice of fowls the head was violently wrung off, then the blood was poured out, then the feathers were plucked off, the breast was cut open, and the crop, stomach, and intestines taken out, and then the body was burnt. Though the bird was split up, yet it was not divided asunder.

MATTHEW HENRY — CHAPTER 2

Verses 1–10

The law of this chapter concerns those meat-offerings that were offered by themselves, whenever a man saw cause thus to express his devotion. The first offering we read of in scripture was of this kind (Gen. iv. 3): *Cain brought of the fruit of the ground an offering*.

I. This sort of offering was appointed, 1. In condescension to the poor, and their ability, that those who themselves lived only upon bread and cakes might offer an acceptable offering to God out of that which was their own coarse and homely fare. 2. As

JAMIESON, FAUSSET, BROWN — CHAPTER 2

Vss. 1-16. THE MEAT OFFERINGS. **1. when any will offer a meat offering**—or gift—distinguishing a bloodless from a bloody sacrifice. The word "meat," however, is improper, as its meaning as now used is different from that attached at the date of our English translation. It was then applied not to "flesh," but "food," generally, and here it is applied to the flour of wheat. The meat offerings were intended as a thankful acknowledgment for the bounty of Providence; and hence, although meat offerings accompanied some of the appointed

ADAM CLARKE — CHAPTER 2

1. *Meat offering. Minchah.* There are *five* kinds of the *minchah* mentioned in this chapter. (1) *Soleth,* simple flour or meal, v. 1. (2) Cakes and wafers, or whatever was baked in the oven, v. 4. (3) Cakes baked in the pan, v. 5. (4) Cakes baked on the frying pan, or probably, a gridiron, v. 7. (5) Green ears of corn parched, v. 14. All these were offered without honey or leaven, but accompanied with wine, oil, and frankincense. It is very likely that the *minchah,* in some or all of the above forms, was the earliest oblation

MATTHEW HENRY

a proper acknowledgment of the mercy of God to them in their food. This was like a quit-rent, by which they testified their dependence upon God, their thankfulness to him, and their expectations from him. Those that now, with a grateful charitable heart, deal out their bread to the hungry, offer unto God an acceptable meat-offering.

II. The laws of the meat-offerings were these:—1. The ingredients must always be fine flour and oil, two staple commodities of the land of Canaan, Deut. viii. 8. Oil was to them then in their food what butter is now to us. 2. If it was flour unbaked, besides the oil it must have frankincense put upon it, which was to be burnt with it (*v.* 1, 2), for the perfuming of the altar. 3. If it was prepared, this might be done in various ways; the offerer might bake it, or fry it, or mix the flour and oil upon a plate. The law was very exact even about those offerings that were least costly. 4. It was to be presented by the offerer to the priest, which is called *bringing it to the Lord* (*v.* 8). 5. Part of it was to be burnt upon the altar, for a memorial, that is, in token of their mindfulness of God's bounty to them, in giving them all things richly to enjoy. 6. The remainder of the meat-offering was to be given to the priests, *v.* 3, 10. Thus God provided that those who served at the altar should live upon the altar, and live comfortably.

Verses 11–16

I. Leaven and honey are forbidden to be put in any of their meat-offerings. 1. The leaven was forbidden in remembrance of the unleavened bread they ate when they came out of Egypt. 2. Honey was forbidden, though Canaan flowed with it. Some think the chief reason why these two things, leaven and honey, were forbidden, was because the Gentiles used them very much in their sacrifices, and God's people must not learn or use the way of the heathen. Some make this application of this double prohibition: leaven signifies grief and sadness of spirit (Ps. lxxiii. 21), *My heart was leavened*; honey signifies sensual pleasure and mirth.

II. Salt is required in all their offerings, *v.* 13. The altar was the table of the Lord; and therefore, salt being always set on our tables, God would have it always used at his. It is called *the salt of the covenant*, because, as men confirmed their covenants with each other by eating and drinking together, at all which collations salt was used, so God, by accepting his people's gifts and feasting them upon his sacrifices, supping with them and they with him (Rev. iii. 20), did confirm his covenant with them. Among the ancients salt was a symbol of friendship. The salt for the sacrifice was not brought by the offerers, but was provided at the public charge, as the wood was, Ezra vii. 20–22. And there was a chamber in the court of the temple called *the chamber of salt*, in which they laid it up. Christianity is the salt of the earth.

III. Directions are given about the first-fruits. 1. The oblation of their first-fruits at harvest, of which we read, Deut. xxvi. 2. These were offered to the Lord, not to be burnt upon the altar, but to be given to the priests as perquisites of their office, *v.* 12. 2. A meat-offering of their first-fruits. The former was required by the law; this was a free-will offering, *v.* 14–16. (1) Be sure to bring the first ripe and full ears, not such as were small and half-withered. (2) These green ears must be dried by the fire, that the corn, such as it was, might be beaten out of them. (3) Oil and frankincense must be put upon it. Thus wisdom and humility must soften and sweeten the spirits and services of young people. God takes a particular delight in the first ripe fruits of the Spirit and the expressions of early piety and devotion. (4) It must be used as other meat-offerings, *v.* 16, compare *v.* 9. He shall *offer all the frankincense; it is an offering made by fire*. Holy love to God is the fire by which all our offerings must be made; else they are not of a sweet savour to God. Frankincense denotes the mediation and intercession of Christ, by which all our services are perfumed and recommended to God's gracious acceptance.

JAMIESON, FAUSSET, BROWN

sacrifices, those here described being voluntary oblations, were offered alone. **pour oil upon it**—Oil was used as butter is with us—symbolically it meant the influences of the Spirit, of which oil was the emblem, as incense was of prayer. **2. shall burn the memorial**—rather "for a memorial,' i.e., a part of it. **3. the remnant of the meat offering shall be Aaron's and his sons'**—The circumstance of a portion of it being appropriated to the use of the priests distinguishes this from a burnt offering. They alone were to partake of it within the sacred precincts, as among "the most holy things." **4. if thou bring an oblation of a meat offering baken in the oven**—generally a circular hole excavated in the floor, from one to five feet deep, the sides of which are covered with hardened plaster, on which cakes are baked of the form and thickness of pancakes. (See on Genesis 18:6.) The shape of Eastern ovens varies considerably according to the nomadic or settled habits of the people. **5. baken in a pan**—a thin plate, generally of copper or iron, placed on a slow fire, similar to what the country people in Scotland called a "girdle" for baking oatmeal cakes. **6. part it in pieces, and pour oil thereon**—Pouring oil on bread is a common practice among Eastern people, who are fond of broken bread dipped in oil, butter, and milk. Oil only was used in the meat offerings, and probably for a symbolic reason. It is evident that these meat offerings were previously prepared by the offerer, and when brought, the priest was to take it from his hands and burn a portion on the altar. **11. ye shall burn no leaven, nor any honey, in any offering of the Lord**—Nothing sweet or sour was to be offered. In the warm climates of the East leavened bread soon spoils, and hence it was regarded as the emblem of hypocrisy or corruption. Some, however, think that the prohibition was that leaven and honey were used in the idolatrous rites of the heathen. **12. the oblation of the first-fruits**—voluntary offerings made by individuals out of their increase, and leaven and honey might be used with these (ch. 23:17; Num. 15:20). Though presented at the altar, they were not consumed, but assigned by God for the use of the priests. **13. every . . . meat offering shalt thou season with salt**—The same reasons which led to the prohibition of leaven, recommended the use of salt—if the one soon putrefies, the other possesses a strongly preservative property, and hence it became an emblem of incorruption and purity, as well as of a perpetual covenant—a perfect reconciliation and lasting friendship. No injunction in the whole law was more sacredly observed than this application of salt; for besides other uses of it that will be noticed elsewhere, it had a typical meaning referred to by our Lord concerning the effect of the Gospel on those who embrace it (Mark 9:49, 50); as when plentifully applied it preserves meat from spoiling, so will the Gospel keep men from being corrupted by sin. And as salt was indispensable to render sacrifices acceptable to God, so the Gospel, brought home to the hearts of men by the Holy Ghost, is indispensably requisite to their offering up of themselves as living sacrifices [BROWN]. **14. a meat offering of thy first-fruits**—From the mention of green ears, this seems to have been a voluntary offering before the harvest—the ears being prepared in the favorite way of Eastern people, by parching them at the fire, and then beating them out for use. It was designed to be an early tribute of pious thankfulness for the earth's increase, and it was offered according to the usual directions.

ADAM CLARKE

offered to the Supreme Being, and probably was in use before sin entered into the world, and consequently before bloody sacrifices had been ordained. The *minchah* of green ears of corn dried by the fire was properly the gratitude offering for a good seedtime, and the prospect of a plentiful harvest. This appears to have been the offering brought by Cain, Gen. iv. 3. The *flour*, whether of wheat, rice, barley, rye, or any other grain, was in all likelihood equally proper; for in Num. v. 15, we find the flour of barley, or barley meal, is called *minchah*. It is plain that in the institution of the *minchah* no animal was here included, though in other places it seems to include both kinds; but in general the *minchah* was not a bloody offering, nor used by way of atonement or expiation, but merely in a eucharistic way, expressing gratitude to God for the produce of the soil.

2. *His handful of the flour*. This was for a *memorial*, to put God in mind of His covenant with their fathers, and to recall to their minds His gracious conduct towards them and their ancestors. In this case a handful only was burnt, the rest was reserved for the priest's use; but all the frankincense was burnt, because from it the priest could derive no advantage.

4. *Baken in the oven. Tannur*, from *nar*, to "split, divide," says Mr. Parkhurst; and hence the *oven*, because of its burning, dissolving, and melting heat.

5. *Baken in a pan. Machabath*, supposed to be a flat iron plate, placed over the fire; such as is called a griddle in some countries.

7. *The fryingpan. Marchesheth*, supposed to be a shallow earthen vessel like a *fryingpan*, used not only to fry in, but for other purposes.

8. *Thou shalt bring the meat offering*. It is likely that the person himself who offered the sacrifice brought it to the priest, and then the priest presented it before the Lord.

11. *No meat offering . . . shall be made with leaven*. See the reason of this prohibition in the note on Exod. xii. 8. *Nor any honey*. Because it was apt to produce acidity, as some think, when wrought up with flour paste; or rather because it was apt to prove purgative. On this latter account the College of Physicians have totally left it out of all medicinal preparations.

13. *With all thine offerings thou shalt offer salt. Salt* was the opposite to leaven, for it preserved from putrefaction and corruption, and signified the purity and persevering fidelity that were necessary in the worship of God. Everything was seasoned with it, to signify the purity and perfection that should be extended through every part of the divine service and through the hearts and lives of God's worshippers. It was called the *salt of the covenant of thy God*, because as salt is incorruptible, so was the covenant made with Abram, Isaac, Jacob, and the patriarchs, relative to the redemption of the world by the incarnation and death of Jesus Christ.

14. *Green ears of corn dried by the fire*. Green or half-ripe ears of wheat parched with fire is a species of food in use among the poor people of Palestine and Egypt to the present day. As God is represented as keeping a table among His people (for the Tabernacle was His house, where He had the golden table, shewbread, etc.), so He represents himself as partaking with them of all the aliments that were in use, and even sitting down with the poor to a repast on parched corn!

MATTHEW HENRY — CHAPTER 3

Verses 1–5

The burnt-offerings were purely expressive of adoration, and therefore were wholly burnt. But the peace-offerings had regard to God as a benefactor to his creatures, and the giver of all good things to us; and therefore these were divided between the altar, the priest, and the owner. Peace signifies, 1. Reconciliation, concord, and communion. And so these were called *peace-offerings*, because in them God and his people did, as it were, feast together, in token of friendship. 2. It signifies prosperity and

JAMIESON, FAUSSET, BROWN — CHAPTER 3

VSS. 1-17. THE PEACE OFFERING OF THE HERD. **1. if his oblation be a sacrifice of peace offering,** etc.—"Peace" being used in Scripture to denote prosperity and happiness generally, a peace offering was a voluntary tribute of gratitude for health or other benefits. In this view it was eucharistic, being a token of thanksgiving for benefits already received, or it was sometimes votive, presented in prayer for benefits wished for in the future. **of the herd**—This kind of offering being of a festive character, either male or female, if without blemish,

ADAM CLARKE — CHAPTER 3

1. *Peace offering. Shelamim*, an offering to make peace between God and man.

MATTHEW HENRY

all happiness: *Peace be to you* was as much as, *All good* be to you; and so the peace-offerings were offered either, (1) By way of supplication or request for some good that was wanted and desired. Or, (2) By way of thanksgiving for some particular mercy received. It is called *a peace-offering of thanksgiving*, for so it was sometimes; as in other cases *a vow, ch.* vii. 15, 16. The sacrifice of praise shall please the Lord better than an ox.

Verses 6–17

Directions are here given concerning the peace-offering, if it was a sheep or a goat. Turtle-doves or young pigeons, which might be brought for whole burnt-offerings, were not allowed for peace-offerings, because they have not fat considerable enough to be burnt upon the altar. The laws concerning a lamb or goat offered for a peace offering are much the same with those concerning a bullock.

JAMIESON, FAUSSET, BROWN

might be used, as both of them were equally good for food, and, if the circumstances of the offerer allowed it, it might be a calf. **2. he shall lay his hand upon the head of his offering**—Having performed this significant act, he killed it before the door of the tabernacle, and the priests sprinkled the blood round about upon the altar. **3. he shall offer of the sacrifice of the peace offering**—The peace offering differed from the oblations formerly mentioned in this respect: while the burnt offering was wholly consumed on the altar, and the freewill offering was partly consumed and partly assigned to the priests; in this offering the fat alone was burnt; only a small part was allotted to the priests while the rest was granted to the offerer and his friends, thus forming a sacred feast of which the Lord, His priests, and people conjointly partook, and which was symbolical of the spiritual feast, the sacred communion which, through Christ, the great peace offering, believers enjoy. (See further on chs. 19, 22.) **the fat that covereth the inwards**—i.e., the web-work that presents itself first to the eye on opening the belly of a cow. **the fat . . . upon the inwards**—adhering to the intestines, but easily removable from them; or, according to some, that which was next the ventricle. **4-11. the two kidneys . . . of the flock . . . the whole rump**—There is, in Eastern countries, a species of sheep the tails of which are not less than four feet and a half in length. These tails are of a substance between fat and marrow. A sheep of this kind weighs sixty or seventy English pounds weight, of which the tail usually weights fifteen pounds and upwards. This species is by far the most numerous in Arabia, Syria, and Palestine, and, forming probably a large portion in the flocks of the Israelites, it seems to have been the kind that usually bled on the Jewish altars. The extraordinary size and deliciousness of their tails give additional importance to this law. To command by an express law the tail of a certain sheep to be offered in sacrifice to God, might well surprise us; but the wonder ceases, when we are told of those broad-tailed Eastern sheep, and of the extreme delicacy of that part which was so particularly specified in the statute [PAXTON]. **12. if his offering be a goat**—Whether this or any of the other two animals were chosen, the same general directions were to be followed in the ceremony of offering. **17. ye eat neither fat nor blood**—The details given above distinctly define the fat in animals which was not to be eaten, so that all the rest, whatever adhered to other parts, or was intermixed with them, might be used. The prohibition of blood rested on a different foundation, being intended to preserve their reverence for the Messiah, who was to shed His blood as an atoning sacrifice for the sins of the world [BROWN].

ADAM CLARKE

2. *Lay his hand upon the head of his offering.* See this rite explained on Exod. xxix. 10, and chap. i. 4. "As the *burnt offering* (chap. i)," says Mr. Ainsworth, "figured our reconciliation to God by the death of Christ, and the *meat offering* (chap. ii), our sanctification in him before God, so this *peace offering* signified both Christ's oblation of himself whereby he became our *peace* and salvation (Eph. ii. 14-16; Acts xiii. 47; Heb. v. 9; ix. 28), and our oblation of praise, thanksgiving, and prayer unto God."

5. *Aaron's sons shall burn it.* As the fat was deemed the most valuable part of the animal, it was offered in preference to all other parts.

9. *The whole rump, it shall he take off hard by the backbone.* The "tails" of the Eastern sheep (note on Exod. xxix. 22).

11. *It is the food of the offering.* We have already remarked that God is frequently represented as feasting with His people on the sacrifices they offered; and because these sacrifices were consumed by that fire which was kindled from heaven, therefore they were considered as the food of that fire, or rather of the Divine Being who was represented by it.

12. *A goat.* Implying the whole species, he-goat, she-goat, and kid, as we have already seen.

17. *That ye eat neither fat nor blood.* It is not likely that the *fat* should be forbidden in the same manner and in the same latitude as the *blood*. The blood was the life of the beast, and that was offered to make an atonement for their souls; consequently, this was never eaten in all their generations. But it was impossible to separate the fat from the flesh, which in many parts is so intimately intermixed with the muscular fibers. By the fat, therefore, mentioned here and in the preceding verse, we may understand any fat that exists in a separate or unmixed state.

MATTHEW HENRY — CHAPTER 4

Verses 1–12

Here begin the statutes of another session, another day. From the throne of glory between the cherubim God delivered these orders. Burnt-offerings, meat-offerings, and peace-offerings, it should seem, had been offered before the giving of the law upon Mount Sinai.

I. The general case we have supposed, *v.* 2. Here observe, 1. Concerning sin in general, that it is described to be against *any of the commandments of the Lord*; for *sin is the transgression of the law*, the divine law. It is said likewise, *if a soul sin*, for it is not sin if it be not some way or other the soul's act; hence it is called the *sin of the soul* (Mic. vi. 7), and it is the soul that is injured by it, Prov. viii. 36. 2. Concerning the sins for which those offerings were appointed. (1) They are supposed to be overt acts; for, had they been required to bring a sacrifice for every sinful thought or word, the task had been endless. Atonement was made for those in the gross, on the day of expiation, once a year; but these are said to be done against the commandments. (2) They are supposed to be sins of commission, things which ought not to be done. (3) They are supposed to be sins committed through ignorance. But if the offender were either ignorant of the law, as in divers instances we may suppose many were (so numerous and various were the prohibitions), or were surprised into the sin unawares, relief was provided by the remedial law of the sin-offering.

II. The law begins with the case of the anointed priest, that is, the high priest, provided he should sin through ignorance; for *the law made men priests who had infirmity*. Though his ignorance was of all others least excusable, yet he was allowed to bring his offering. Now the law concerning the sin-offering for the high priest is, 1. That he must bring a bullock

JAMIESON, FAUSSET, BROWN — CHAPTER 4

VSS. 1, 2. SIN OFFERING OF IGNORANCE. **2. If a soul shall sin through ignorance against any of the commandments of the Lord**—a soul—an individual. All sins may be considered, in a certain sense, as committed "through ignorance," error, or misapprehension of one's true interests. The sins, however, referred to in this law were unintentional violations of the ceremonial laws,— breaches made through haste, or inadvertency of some negative precepts, which, if done knowingly and wilfully, would have involved a capital punishment. **do against any of them**—To bring out the meaning, it is necessary to supply, "he shall bring a sin offering."

3-35. SIN OFFERING FOR THE PRIEST. **3. If the priest that is anointed do sin**—i.e., the high priest, in whom, considering his character as typical mediator, and his exalted office, the people had the deepest interest; and whose transgression of any part of the divine law, therefore, whether done unconsciously or heedlessly, was a very serious offense,

ADAM CLARKE — CHAPTER 4

2. *If a soul shall sin through ignorance.* That is, if any man shall do what God has forbidden, or leave undone what God has commanded, through ignorance of the law relative to these points; as soon as the transgression or omission comes to his knowledge he shall offer the sacrifice here prescribed, and shall not suppose that his *ignorance* is an excuse for his sin.

3. *If the priest that is anointed.* Meaning, most probably the high priest.

MATTHEW HENRY

without blemish for a sin-offering (*v.* 3), as valuable an offering as that for the whole congregation (*v.* 14). 2. The hand of the offerer must be laid upon the head of the offering (*v.* 4), with a solemn penitent confession of the sin he had committed, putting it upon the head of the sin-offering, *ch.* xvi. 21. 3. The bullock must be killed, and a great deal of solemnity there must be in disposing of the blood; for it was *the blood that made atonement*, and *without shedding of blood* there was *no remission*, *v.* 5–7. Some of the blood of the high-priest's sin-offering was to be *sprinkled seven times before the veil*, with an eye towards the mercy-seat, though it was veiled: some of it was to be put upon the horns of the golden altar, because at that altar the priest himself ministered; and thus was signified the putting away of that pollution which from his sins did cleave to his services. When this was done the remainder of the blood was poured at the foot of the brazen altar. By this rite, the sinner acknowledged that he deserved to have his blood thus poured out like water. It likewise signified the pouring out of the soul before God in true repentance, and typified our Saviour's *pouring out his soul unto death*. 4. The fat of the inwards was to be burnt upon the altar of burnt-offering, *v.* 8–10. By this the intention of the offering and of the atonement made by it was directed to the glory of God, who, having been dishonoured by the sin, was thus honoured by the sacrifice.

Verses 13–21

This is the law for expiating the guilt of a national sin, by a sin-offering. If the leaders of the people, through mistake concerning the law, caused them to err, when the mistake was discovered an offering must be brought, that wrath might not come upon the whole congregation. 1. It is possible that the church may err, and that her guides may mislead her. It is here supposed that the whole congregation may sin, and sin through ignorance. God will always have a church on earth; but he never said it should be infallible, or perfectly pure from corruption on this side heaven. 2. When a sacrifice was to be offered for the whole congregation, the elders were to lay their hands upon the head of it (three of them at least), as representatives of the people and agents for them. 3. The blood of this sin-offering, as of the former, was to be *sprinkled seven times before the Lord*, *v.* 17. It was not to be poured out there, but sprinkled only; for the cleansing virtue of the blood of Christ was then and is still sufficiently signified and represented by sprinkling, Isa. lii. 15. It was to be sprinkled seven times. Seven is a number of perfection, because when God had made the world in six days he rested the seventh; so this signified the perfect satisfaction Christ made, and the complete cleansing of the souls of the faithful by it; see Heb. x. 14. When the offering is completed, it is said, *atonement is made, and the sin shall be forgiven*, *v.* 20. The promise of remission is founded upon the atonement.

Verses 22–26

Observe here, 1. That God takes notice of and is displeased with the sins of rulers. 2. The sin of the ruler which he committed through ignorance is supposed afterwards to come to his knowledge (*v.* 23), which must be either by the check of his own conscience or by the reproof of his friends. 3. The sin-offering for a ruler was to be *a kid of the goats*, not a bullock, as for the priest and the whole congregation; nor was the blood of his sin-offering to be brought into the tabernacle, as of the other two, but it was all bestowed upon the brazen altar (*v.* 25); nor was the flesh of it to be burnt, as that of the other two, without the camp, which intimated that the sin of a ruler, though worse than that of a common person, yet was not so heinous, nor of such pernicious consequence, as the sin of the high priest, or of the whole congregation. 4. It is promised that the atonement shall be accepted and the sin forgiven (*v.* 26), that is, if he repent and reform.

Verses 27–35

I. Here is the law of the sin-offering for a common person, which differs from that for a ruler only in this, that a private person might bring either a kid or a lamb, a ruler only a kid; and that for a ruler must be a male, for the other a female. 1. The case supposed: *If any one of the common people sin through ignorance*, *v.* 27. If they sin through ignorance, they must bring a sin-offering. We have all need to pray with David to be cleansed from *secret faults*, the errors which we ourselves do not understand or are not aware of, Ps. xix. 12. 2. That the sins of ignorance committed by a single obscure person did require a sacrifice. 3. That a sin-offering was not only admitted, but accepted, even from one of the common people,

JAMIESON, FAUSSET, BROWN

both as regarded himself individually, and the influence of his example. He is the person principally meant, though the common order of the priesthood was included. **according to the sin of the people**—i.e., bring guilt on the people. He was to take a young bullock (the age and sex being expressly mentioned), and having killed it according to the form prescribed for the burnt offerings, he was to take it into the holy place and sprinkle the atoning blood seven times before the veil, and tip with the crimson fluid the horns of the golden altar of incense, on his way to the court of the priests,—a solemn ceremonial appointed only for very grave and heinous offenses, and which betokened that his sin, though done in ignorance, had vitiated all his services; nor could any official duty he engaged in be beneficial either to himself or the people, unless it were atoned for by blood. **11. the skin of the bullock, and all his flesh**—In ordinary circumstances, these were perquisites of the priests. But in the expiation necessary for a sin of the high priest, after the fat of the sacrifice was offered on the altar, the carcass was carried without the camp, in order that the total combustion of it in the place of ashes might the more strikingly indicate the enormity of the transgression, and the horror with which he regarded it (cf. Heb. 13:12, 13).

13. if the whole congregation of Israel sin through ignorance—In consequence of some culpable neglect or misapprehension of the law, the people might contract national guilt, and then national expiation was necessary. The same sacrifice was to be offered as in the former case, but with this difference in the ceremonial, that the elders or heads of the tribes, as representing the people and being the principal aggressors in misleading the congregation, laid their hands on the head of the victim. The priest then took the blood into the holy place, where, after dipping his finger in it seven times, he sprinkled the drops seven times before the veil.—This done, he returned to the court of the priests, and ascending the altar, put some portion upon its horns; then he poured it out at the foot of the altar. The fat was the only part of the animal which was offered on the altar; for the carcass, with its appurtenances and offals, was carried without the camp, into the place where the ashes were deposited, and there consumed with fire.

22-26. When a ruler hath sinned, and done somewhat through ignorance against any of the commandments—Whatever was the form of government, the king, judge, or subordinate, was the party concerned in this law. The trespass of such a civil functionary being less serious in its character and consequences than that either of the high priest or the congregation, a sin offering of inferior value was required—"a kid of the goats"; and neither was the blood carried into the sanctuary, but applied only to the altar of burnt offering; nor was the carcass taken without the camp; it was eaten by the priests-in-waiting.

27-34. if any one of the common people sin through ignorance—In this case the expiatory offering appointed was a female kid, or a ewe lamb without blemish; and the ceremonies were exactly the same as those observed in the case of the offending ruler. In these two latter instances, the blood of the sin offering was applied to the altar of burnt offering—the place where bloody sacrifices were appointed to be immolated. But the transgression of a high priest, or of the whole congregation, entailing a general taint on the ritual of the tabernacle, and vitiating its services, required a further expiation; and therefore, in these cases, the blood of the sin offering was

ADAM CLARKE

According to the sin of the people; for although he had greater advantages than the people could have, in being more conversant with the law of God, yet it was possible even for him to transgress through ignorance; and his transgression might have the very worst tendency, because the people might be thereby led into sin. Hence several critics understand this passage in this way, and translate it thus: "If the anointed priest shall lead the people to sin"; or, literally, "If the anointed priest shall sin to the sin of the people"; that is, so as to cause the people to transgress, the shepherd going astray, and the sheep following after him.

4. *Lay his hand upon the bullock's head.* See on chap. i. 4.

6. *Seven times.* See the note on Exod. xxix. 30. The blood of this sacrifice was applied in three different ways: (1) The priest put his finger in it, and sprinkled it seven times before the veil, v. 6. (2) He put some of it on the horns of the altar of incense. (3) He poured the remaining part at the bottom of the altar of burnt offerings, v. 7.

12. *Without the camp.* This was intended figuratively to express the sinfulness of this sin, and the availableness of the atonement. The sacrifice, as having the sin of the priest transferred from himself to it by his confession and imposition of hands, was become unclean and abominable, and was carried, as it were, out of the Lord's sight; from the Tabernacle and congregation it must be carried without the camp, and thus its own offensiveness was removed, and the sin of the person in whose behalf it was offered. The apostle (Heb. xiii. 11-13) applies this in the most pointed manner to Christ: "For the bodies of those beasts, whose blood is brought into the sanctuary by the high priest for sin, are burned without the camp. Wherefore Jesus also, that he might sanctify the people with his own blood, suffered without the gate. Let us go forth therefore unto him without the camp, bearing his reproach."

13. *If the whole congregation of Israel sin.* This probably refers to some oversight in acts of religious worship, or to some transgression of the letter of the law, which arose out of the peculiar circumstances in which they were then found, such as the case mentioned in 1 Sam. xiv. 32, etc., where the people, through their long and excessive fatigue in their combat with the Philistines, being faint, "flew on the spoil, and took sheep, and oxen, and calves, and slew them on the ground: and . . . did eat them with the blood"; and this was partly occasioned by the rash adjuration of Saul mentioned in v. 24: "Cursed be the man that eateth any food until evening." The sacrifices and rites in this case were the same as those prescribed in the preceding, only here the elders of the congregation, i. 3., three of the Sanhedrim, according to Maimonides, laid their hands on the head of the victim in the name of all the congregation.

22. *When a ruler hath sinned.* Under the term *nasi* it is probable that any person is meant who held any kind of political dignity among the people, though the rabbins generally understand it of the king. *A kid of the goats* was the sacrifice in this case, the rites nearly the same as in the preceding cases, only the fat was burnt as that of the peace offering. See v. 26, and chap. iii. 5.

27. *The common people. Am haarets,* "the people of the land," that is, any individual who was not a priest, king, or ruler among the people; any of the poor or ordinary sort. Any of these, having transgressed through ignorance, was obliged to bring a lamb or a kid, the ceremonies being nearly the same as in the preceding cases. The original may denote the very lowest of the people, the laboring or agricultural classes.

MATTHEW HENRY

and an atonement made by it, *v.* 31, 35. Here rich and poor, prince and peasant, meet together; they are both alike welcome to Christ upon the same terms. See Job xxxiv. 19.

II. From all these laws concerning the sin-offerings we may learn, 1. To hate sin, and to watch against it. 2. To value Christ, the great and true sin-offering, whose blood cleanses from all sin, which it was not possible that the *blood of bulls and of goats should take away.* And perhaps there was some allusion to this law concerning sacrifices for sins of ignorance in that prayer of Christ's, just when he was offering up himself a sacrifice, *Father, forgive them, for they know not what they do.*

CHAPTER 5

Verses 1–6

I. The offences here supposed are, 1. A man's concealing the truth when he was sworn as a witness to speak the truth, the whole truth, and nothing but the truth. Judges among the Jews had power to adjure not only the witnesses, as with us, but the person suspected, as appears by the high priest adjuring our Saviour, who thereupon answered, though before he stood silent, Matt. xxvi. 63, 64. Now (*v.* 1), *If a soul sin* (that is, a person, for the soul is the man), if he *hear the voice of swearing* (that is, if he be adjured to testify what he knows, if in such a case he refuses to give evidence, or gives it but in part, *he shall bear his iniquity.* Let all that are called out at any time to bear testimony think of this law, and be free and open in their evidence, and take heed of prevaricating. An oath of the Lord is a sacred thing, and not to be dallied with. 2. A man's touching anything that was ceremonially unclean, *v.* 2, 3. If a man, polluted by such touch, came into the sanctuary inconsiderately, or if he neglected to wash himself according to the law, then he was to look upon himself as under guilt, and must bring his offering. 3. Rash swearing. If a man bind himself by an oath that he will do or not do such a thing, and the performance of his oath afterwards proves either unlawful or impracticable, by which he is discharged from the obligation, yet he must bring an offering to atone for his folly in swearing so rashly.

II. Now in these cases, 1. The offender must confess his sin and bring his offering (*v.* 5, 6); and the offering was not accepted unless it was accompanied with a penitential confession and a humble prayer for pardon. 2. The priest must *make an atonement for him.*

Verses 7–13

Provision is here made for the poor of God's people, and the pacifying of their consciences under the sense of guilt. Those that were not able to bring a lamb might bring for a sin-offering a pair of *turtle doves* or *two young pigeons*; nay, if any were so extremely poor that they were not able to procure these, they might bring a pottle of fine flour, and this should be accepted. Thus the expense of the sin-offering was brought lower than that of any other offering, to teach us that no man's poverty shall ever be a bar in the way of his pardon. No man shall say that he had not wherewithal to bear the charges of a journey to heaven.

I. If the sinner brought two doves, one was to be offered for a sin-offering and the other for a burnt-offering, *v.* 7. Observe, 1. Before he offered the burnt-offering, which was for the honour and praise of God, he must offer the sin-offering, to make atonement. 2. After the sin-offering, which made atonement, came the burnt-offering, as an acknowledgment of the great mercy of God in appointing and accepting the atonement.

II. If he brought fine flour, a handful of it was to be offered, but without either oil or frankincense (*v.* 11), not only because this would make it too costly for the poor, but because it was a sin-offering, and therefore, to show the loathsomeness of the sin for which it was offered, it must not be made grateful either to the taste by oil or to the smell by frankincense.

Verses 14–19

Here we have the law concerning those that were properly and peculiarly *trespass-offerings*, which were offered to atone for trespass done against a neighbour. Now injuries done to another may be either in holy things or in common things; of the former we have the law in these verses; of the latter in the beginning of the next chapter. Now if a man did alienate or convert to his own use any thing that was dedicated to God, unwittingly, he was to bring this sacrifice; as suppose he had ignorantly made use of

JAMIESON, FAUSSET, BROWN

applied to the altar of incense. **35. it shall be forgiven him**—None of these sacrifices possessed any intrinsic value sufficient to free the conscience of the sinner from the pollution of guilt, or to obtain his pardon from God; but they gave a formal deliverance from a secular penalty (Heb. 9:13, 14); and they were figurative representations of the full and perfect sin offering which was to be made by Christ.

CHAPTER 5

VS. 1. TRESPASS OFFERINGS FOR CONCEALING KNOWLEDGE. **1. if a soul . . . hear the voice of swearing**—or, according to some, "the words of adjuration." A proclamation was issued calling any one who could give information, to come before the court and bear testimony to the guilt of a criminal; and the manner in which witnesses were interrogated in the Jewish courts of justice was not by swearing them directly, but adjuring them by reading the words of an oath: "the voice of swearing." The offense, then, for the expiation of which this law provides, was that of a person who neglected or avoided the opportunity of lodging the information which it was in his power to communicate.

2, 3. TOUCHING ANY THING UNCLEAN. **2. if a soul touch any unclean thing**—A person who, unknown to himself at the time, came in contact with any thing unclean, and either neglected the requisite ceremonies of purification or engaged in the services of religion while under the taint of ceremonial defilement, might be afterwards convinced that he had committed an offense.

4-19. FOR SWEARING. **4. if a soul swear**—a rash oath, without duly considering the nature and consequences of the oath, perhaps inconsiderately binding himself to do anything wrong, or neglecting to perform a vow to do something good. In all such cases a person might have transgressed one of the divine commandments unwittingly, and have been afterwards brought to a sense of his delinquency. **5. it shall be, when he shall be guilty . . . that he shall confess that he hath sinned in that thing**—make a voluntary acknowledgment of his sin from the impulse of his own conscience, and before it come to the knowledge of the world. A previous discovery might have subjected him to some degree of punishment from which his spontaneous confession released him, but still he was considered guilty of trespass, to expiate which he was obliged by the ceremonial law to go through certain observances. **6-14. he shall bring his trespass offering unto the Lord for his sins which he hath sinned**—A trespass offering differed from a sin offering in the following respects—that it was appointed for persons who had either done evil unwittingly, or were in doubt as to their own criminality; or felt themselves in such a special situation as required sacrifices of that kind [BROWN]. The trespass offering appointed in such cases was a female lamb or kid; if unable to make such an offering, he might bring a pair of turtledoves or two young pigeons—the one to be offered for a sin offering, the other for a burnt offering; or if even *that* was beyond his ability, the law would be satisfied with the tenth part of an ephah of fine flour without oil or frankincense.

15, 16. sin through ignorance, in the holy things of the Lord, etc.—This is a case of sacrilege committed ignorantly, either in not paying the full due of tithes, first-fruits, and similar tribute in eating of meats, which belonged to the priests alone—or he was required, along with the restitution in money, the amount of which was to be determined by the priest, to offer a ram for a trespass offering, as soon as he came to the knowledge of his involuntary fraud. **17-19. if a soul sin . . . though he wist it not, yet he is guilty**—This also refers to holy things, and it differs from the preceding in being one of the *doubtful* cases, i.e., where conscience suspects, though the understanding be in doubt whether criminality or sin has been

ADAM CLARKE

CHAPTER 5

1. *If a soul sin.* It is generally supposed that the case referred to here is that of a person who, being demanded by the civil magistrate to answer upon oath, refuses to tell what he knows concerning the subject; such a one *shall bear his iniquity*—shall be considered as guilty in the sight of God of the transgression which he has endeavored to conceal, and must expect to be punished by Him for hiding the iniquity to which he was privy, or suppressing the truth which, being discovered, would have led to the exculpation of the innocent, and the punishment of the guilty.

2. *Any unclean thing.* Either the dead body of a clean animal or the living or dead carcass of any unclean creature. All such persons were to wash their clothes and themselves in clean water, and were considered as unclean till the evening, chap. xi. 24-31. But if this had been neglected, they were obliged to bring a trespass offering. What this meant, see in the notes on chap. vii.

4. *To do evil, or to do good.* It is very likely that rash promises are here intended; for if a man vow to do an act that is evil, though it would be criminal to keep such an oath or vow, yet he is guilty because he made it, and therefore must offer the trespass offering. If he neglect to do the good he has vowed, he is guilty, and must in both cases confess his iniquity, and bring his trespass offering.

5. *He shall confess that he hath sinned.* Even restitution was not sufficient without this confession, because a man might make restitution without being much humbled; but the confession of sin has a direct tendency to humble the soul, and hence it is so frequently required in the Holy Scriptures, as without humiliation there can be no salvation.

7. *If he be not able to bring a lamb.* See the conclusion of chap. i.

10. *He shall offer the second for a burnt offering.* The pigeon for the burnt offering was wholly consumed, it was the Lord's property; that for the sin offering was the priest's property, and was to be eaten by him after its blood had been partly sprinkled on the side of the altar, and the rest poured out at the bottom of the altar. See also chap. vi. 26.

11. *Tenth part of an ephah.* About three quarts. The ephah contained a little more than seven gallons and a half.

15. *In the holy things of the Lord.* This law seems to relate particularly to sacrilege, and defrauds in spiritual matters; such as the neglect to consecrate or redeem the firstborn, the withholding of the firstfruits, tithes, and suchlike; and, according to the rabbins, making any secular gain of divine things, keeping back any part of the price of things dedicated to God, or witholding what man had vowed to pay. *With thy estimation.* The wrong done or the defraud committed should be estimated at the number of shekels it was worth, or for which it would sell. These the defrauder was to pay down, to which he was to add a fifth part more, and bring a ram without blemish for a sin offering

MATTHEW HENRY

the tithes, or first-fruits, or first-born of his cattle, or had eaten any of those parts of the sacrifices which were appropriated to the priests; this was a trespass. If it was done presumptuously, and in contempt of the law, the offender died without mercy, Heb. x. 28. But in case of negligence and ignorance this sacrifice was appointed. The trespasser must bring an offering to the Lord, which, in all those that were purely trespass-offerings, must be a *ram without blemish*. He must likewise make restitution to the priest, according to a just estimation of the thing which he had so alienated, adding a fifth part to it.

JAMIESON, FAUSSET, BROWN

committed. The Jewish rabbis give, as an example, the case of a person who, knowing that "the fat of the inwards" is not to be eaten, religiously abstained from the use of it; but should a dish happen to have been at table in which he had reason to suspect some portion of that meat was intermingled, and he had, inadvertently, partaken of that unlawful viand, he was bound to bring a ram as a trespass offering. These provisions were all designed to impress the conscience with the sense of responsibility to God and keep alive on the hearts of the people a salutary fear of doing any secret wrong.

ADAM CLARKE

besides. There is an obscurity in the text, but this seems to be its meaning.

16. *Shall make amends.* Make restitution for the wrong he had done according to what is laid down in the preceding verse.

19. *He hath certainly trespassed.* And because he hath sinned, therefore he must bring a sacrifice. On no other ground shall he be accepted by the Lord.

CHAPTER 6 (Matthew Henry)

Verses 1–7

The latter part of the law of the trespass-offering. I. The trespass supposed, *v.* 2, 3. Though all the instances relate to our neighbour, yet it is called a *trespass against the Lord.* He that speaks evil of his brother is said to speak evil of the law, and consequently of the Law-maker, Jam. iv. 11. The trespasses specified are, 1. Denying a trust: *If a man lie unto his neighbour in that which was delivered him to keep,* or, which is worse, which was lent him for his use. 2. Defrauding a partner: *If a man lie in fellowship,* claiming a sole interest in that wherein he has but a joint-interest. 3. Disowning a manifest wrong: *If a man* has the front to *lie in a thing taken away by violence,* which ordinarily cannot be hid. 4. Deceiving in commerce, or, as some think, by false accusation. 5. Detaining what is found, and denying it (*v.* 3).

II. The trespass-offering appointed. 1. *In the day of his trespass-offering* he must make satisfaction to his brother. Let him faithfully restore all that he has got by fraud or oppression, with a fifth part added. 2. He must *then come and offer his gift,* must *bring his trespass-offering to the Lord* whom he had offended; and the priest must make an atonement for him, *v.* 6, 7.

Verses 8–13

Moses was directed to give instructions to the priests; he must *command Aaron and his sons, v.* 9. In these verses we have the law of the burnt-offering, as far as it was the peculiar care of the priests. The daily sacrifice of a lamb, which was offered morning and evening for the whole congregation, is here chiefly referred to.

I. The priest must take care of the ashes of the burnt-offering, that they may be decently disposed of, *v.* 10, 11. He must clear the altar of them every morning, and put them on the east side of the altar, which was furthest from the sanctuary; this he must do in his linen garment, which he always wore when he did any service at the altar; and then he must put on other garments, and must *carry the ashes into a clean place without the camp.* The priest himself must not only kindle the fire, but clean the hearth, and carry out the ashes. God's servants must think nothing below them but sin.

CHAPTER 6 (Jamieson, Fausset, Brown)

VSS. 1-7. TRESPASS OFFERING FOR SINS DONE WITTINGLY. **2. If a soul sin, and commit a trespass against the Lord**—This law, the record of which should have been joined with the previous chapter, was given concerning things stolen, fraudulently gotten, or wrongfully kept. The offender was enjoined to make restitution of the articles to the rightful owner, along with a fifth part out of his own possessions. But it was not enough thus to repair the injury done to a neighbor and to society; he was required to bring a trespass offering, as a token of sorrow and penitence for having hurt the cause of religion and of God. That trespass offering was a ram without blemish, which was to be made on the altar of burnt offerings, and the flesh belonged to the priests. This penalty was equivalent to a mitigated fine; but being associated with a sacred duty, the form in which the fine was inflicted served the important purpose of rousing attention to the claims and reviving a sense of responsibility to God.

8-13. THE LAW OF THE BURNT OFFERING. **9. Command Aaron and his sons, saying, This . . . law of the burnt offering**—In this passage Moses received instructions to be delivered to the priests respecting their official duties, and first the burnt offering—*Hebrew,* "a sacrifice, which went up in smoke." The daily service consisted of two lambs, one offered in the morning at sunrise, the other in the evening, when the day began to decline. Both of them were consumed on the altar by means of a slow fire, before which the pieces of the sacrifice were so placed that they fed it all night. At all events, the observance of this daily sacrifice on the altar of burnt offering was a daily expression of national repentance and faith.

CHAPTER 6 (Adam Clarke)

2. *Lie unto his neighbour.* This must refer to a case in which a person delivered his property to his neighbor to be preserved for him, and took no witness to attest the delivery of the goods; such a person therefore might deny that he had ever received such goods, for he who had deposited them with him could bring no proof of the delivery. On the other hand, a man might accuse his neighbor of detaining property which had never been confided to him, or, after having been confided, had been restored again; hence the law here is very cautious on these points. And because in many cases it was impossible to come at the whole truth without a direct revelation from God, which should in no common case be expected, the penalties are very moderate; for in such cases, even when guilt was discovered, the man might not be so criminal as appearances might intimate. See the law concerning this laid down and explained on Exod. xxii. 7, etc.

3. *Have found that which was lost.* The Roman lawyers laid it down as a sound maxim of jurisprudence "that he who found any property and applied it to his own use should be considered as a thief whether he knew the owner or not; for in their view the crime was not lessened, supposing the finder was totally ignorant of the right owner."

5. *All that about which he hath sworn falsely.* That supposes the case of a man who, being convicted by his own conscience, comes forward and confesses his sin. *Restore it in the principal.* The property itself if still remaining, or the full value of it, to which a fifth part more was to be added.

8. *And the Lord spake unto Moses.* At this verse the Jews begin the twenty-fifth section of the law; and here, undoubtedly, the sixth chapter should commence, as the writer enters upon a new subject, and the preceding verses belong to the fifth chapter. The best edited Hebrew Bibles begin the sixth chapter at this verse.

9. *This is the law of the burnt offering.* This law properly refers to that burnt offering which was daily made in what was termed the morning and evening sacrifice; and as he had explained the nature of this burnt offering in general, with its necessary ceremonies, as far as the persons who brought them were concerned, he now takes up the same in relation to the priests who were to receive them from the hands of the offerer, and present them to the Lord on the altar of burnt offerings.

Because of the burning upon the altar all night. If the burnt offering were put all upon the fire at once, it could not be burning all night. We may therefore reasonably conclude that the priests sat up by turns the whole night, and fed the fire with portions of this offering till the whole was consumed, which they would take care to lengthen out till the time of the morning sacrifice. The same we may suppose was done with the morning sacrifice; it was also consumed by piecemeal through the whole day, till the time of offering the evening sacrifice. Thus there was a continual offering by fire unto the Lord; and hence in v. 13 it is said: "The fire shall ever be burning upon the altar; it shall never go out."

11. *And put on other garments.* The priests approached the altar in their holiest garments; when carrying the ashes from the altar, they put on other garments, the holy garments being only used in the holy place. *Clean place.* A place where no dead carcasses, dung, or filth of any kind was laid; for the ashes were holy, as being the remains of the offerings made by fire

MATTHEW HENRY

II. The priest must take care of the fire upon the altar. *The fire shall ever be burning upon the altar, it shall never go out*, *v.* 13. Though we be not always sacrificing, yet we must keep the fire of holy love always burning; and thus we must pray always.

Verses 14–23

The meat-offering was either that which was offered by the people or that by the priests at their consecration.

I. As to the common meat-offering,

1. Only a handful of it was to be burnt upon the altar; all the rest was allowed to the priests for their food.

2. The laws concerning the eating of it were, (1) That it must be *eaten unleavened*, *v.* 16. (2) It must be eaten in *the court of the tabernacle* (here called the *holy place*). (3) The males only must eat of it, *v.* 18. (4) The priests only that were clean might eat of it.

II. As to the consecration meat-offering, which was offered for the priests themselves, it was to be *wholly burnt, and none of it eaten*, *v.* 23. The Jewish writers say that the high priest was bound to offer it every day of his life, from the day in which he was anointed. Josephus says, "The high priest sacrificed twice every day at his own charges, and this was his sacrifice." The meat-offering of the priest was to be baked as if it were to be eaten, and yet it must be wholly burnt.

Verses 24–30

We have here so much of the law of the sin-offering as did peculiarly concern the priests that offered it. As, 1. That it must be killed *in the place where the burnt-offering was killed* (*v.* 25). 2. That the priest who offered it for the sinner was (with his sons, or other priests, *v.* 29) to eat the flesh of it, after the blood and fat had been offered to God, in the *court of the tabernacle*, *v.* 26. 3. The blood of the sin-offering was with great reverence to be washed out of the clothes on which it happened to light (*v.* 27). 4. The vessel in which the flesh of the sin-offering was boiled must be broken if it were an earthen one, and, if a brazen one, well washed, *v.* 28.

JAMIESON, FAUSSET, BROWN

The fire that consumed these sacrifices had been kindled from heaven at the consecration of the tabernacle, and to keep it from being extinguished and the sacrifices from being burned with common fire, strict injunctions are here given respecting not only the removal of the ashes, but the approaching near to the fireplace in garments that were not officially "holy."

14-18. THE LAW OF THE MEAT OFFERING. **14. this is the law of the meat offering**—Though this was a provision for the priests and their families, it was to be regarded as "most holy"; and the way in which it was prepared was: on any meat offerings being presented, the priest carried them to the altar, and taking a handful from each of them as an oblation, he salted and burnt it on the altar; the residue became the property of the priests, and was the food of those whose duty it was to attend on the service. They themselves as well as the vessels from which they ate were typically holy, and they were not at liberty to partake of the meat offering while they labored under any ceremonial defilement.

19-23. THE HIGH PRIEST'S MEAT OFFERING. **20. This is the offering of Aaron, and of his sons**—the daily meat offering of the high priest; for though his sons are mentioned along with him, it was probably only those of his descendants who succeeded him in that high office that are meant. It was to be offered, one half of it in the morning and the other half in the evening—being daily laid by the ministering priest on the altar of burnt offering, where, being dedicated to God, it was wholly consumed. This was designed to keep him and the other attendant priests in constant remembrance, that though they were typically expiating the sins of the people, their own persons and services could meet with acceptance only through faith, which required to be daily nourished and strengthened from above.

21-30. THE LAW OF THE SIN OFFERING. **25. This is the law of the sin offering**—It was slain, and the fat and inwards, after being washed and salted, were burnt upon the altar. But the rest of the carcass belonged to the officiating priest. He and his family might feast upon it—only, however, within the precincts of the tabernacle; and none else were allowed to partake of it but the members of a priestly family—and not even they, if under any ceremonial defilement. The flesh on all occasions was boiled or sodden, with the exception of the paschal lamb, which was roasted; and if an earthen vessel had been used, it being porous and likely to imbibe some of the liquid particles, it was to be broken; if a metallic pan had been used it was to be scoured and washed with the greatest care, not because the vessels had been defiled, but the reverse—because the flesh of the sin offering having been boiled in them, those vessels were now too sacred for ordinary use. The design of all these minute ceremonies was to impress the minds, both of priests and people, with a sense of the evil nature of sin and the care they should take to prevent the least taint of its impurities clinging to them.

ADAM CLARKE

unto the Lord.

13. *The fire shall ever be burning.* See on v. 9 and v. 20. In imitation of this perpetual fire, the ancient Persian Magi, and their descendants the Parsees, kept up a perpetual fire; the latter continue it to the present day.

15. *His handful, of the flour.* An omer of flour, which was the tenth part of an ephah, and equal to about three quarts of our measure, was the least quantity that could be offered even by the poorest sort, and this was generally accompanied with a log of oil, which was a little more than half a pint. This quantity both of flour and oil might be increased at pleasure, but no less could be offered.

20. *In the day when he is anointed.* Not only in that day, but from that day forward, for this was to them and their successors a statute forever. See v. 22.

23. *For every meat offering for the priest shall be wholly burnt.* Whatever the priest offered was wholly the Lord's and, therefore, must be entirely consumed. The sacrifices of the common people were offered to the Lord, but the priests partook of them; and thus they who ministered at the altar were fed by the altar. Had the priests been permitted to live on their own offerings as they did on those of the people, it would have been as if they had offered nothing, as they would have taken again to themselves what they appeared to give unto the Lord.

25. *In the place where the burnt offering is killed.* The place here referred to was the north side of the altar. See chap. i. 11.

26. *The priest . . . shall eat it.* From the expostulation of Moses with Aaron, chap. x. 17, we learn that the priest, by eating the sin offering of the people, was considered as bearing their sin, and typically removing it from them; and besides, this was a part of their maintenance, or what the Scripture calls their inheritance; see Ezek. xliv. 27-30. This was afterwards greatly abused; for improper persons endeavored to get into the priest's office merely that they might get a secular provision, which is a horrible profanity in the sight of God. See 1 Sam. ii. 36; Jer. xxiii. 1-2; Ezek. xxxiv. 2-4; and Hos. iv. 8.

28. *The earthen vessel . . . shall be broken.* Calmet states that this should be considered as implying the vessels brought by individuals to the court of the Temple or Tabernacle, and not of the vessels that belonged to the priests for the ordinary service. That the people dressed their sacrifices sometimes in the court of the Tabernacle, he gathers from 1 Sam. ii. 13-14, to which the reader is desired to refer.

In addition to what has been already said on the different subjects in this chapter, it may be necessary to notice a few more particulars. The perpetual meat offering, *minchah tamid*, v. 20, the perpetual fire, *esh tamid*, v. 13, and the perpetual burnt offering, *olath tamid*, Exod. xxix. 42, all cast much light on Heb. vii. 25, where it is said, Christ "is able also to save them to the uttermost [perpetually, to all intents and purposes] that come unto God by him, seeing he ever liveth [He is perpetually living] to make intercession for them"; in which words there is a manifest allusion to the perpetual *minchah*, the perpetual fire, and the perpetual burnt offering, mentioned here by Moses. As the *minchah* or gratitude offering should be perpetual, so our gratitude for the innumerable mercies of God should be perpetual. As the burnt offering must be perpetual, so should the sacrifice of our blessed Lord be considered as a perpetual offering, that all men, in all ages, should come unto God through Him who is ever living, in His sacrificial character, to make intercession for men. And as the fire on the altar must be perpetual, so should the influences of the Holy Spirit in every member of the Church, and the flame of pure devotion in the hearts of believers, be ever energetic and permanent.

TODAY'S DICTIONARY OF THE BIBLE:

Sin Offering (Heb. *hattāh*), the law of, is given in detail in Lev. 4—6:13; 9:7–11, 22–24; 12:6–8; 15:2, 14, 25–30; 14:19, 31; Num. 6:10–14. On the day of Atonement it was made with special solemnity (Lev. 16:5, 11, 15). The blood was then carried into the Holy of Holies and sprinkled on the mercy seat. Sin offerings were also presented at the five annual festivals (Num. 28, 29), and on the occasion of the consecration of the priests (Ex. 29:10–14, 36). As each individual—even the most private member of the congregation, as well as the congregation at large, and the high priest—was obliged, on being convicted by his conscience of any particular sin, to come with a sin offering, we see thus impressively disclosed the need in which every sinner stands of the salvation of Christ, and the necessity of making application to it as often as the guilt of sin renews itself upon his conscience. This resort of faith to the perfect sacrifice of Chirst is the one way that lies open for the sinner's attainment of pardon and restoration to peace. And then in the sacrifice itself there is the reality of that imcomparable worth and preciousness which were so significantly represented in the sin offering by the sacredness of its blood and the hallowed destination of its flesh. With reference to this the blood of Christ is called emphatically "the precious blood," and the blood that "cleanseth from all sin" (1 John 1:7).

MATTHEW HENRY

CHAPTER 7

Verses 1–10

Observe here, 1. Concerning the trespass-offering, that, being much of the same nature with the sin-offering, it was to be governed by the same rules, *v.* 6. When the blood and fat were offered to God to make atonement, the priests were to eat the flesh, as that of the sin-offering, in the holy place. The Jews have a tradition (as we have it from the learned bishop Patrick) concerning the sprinkling of the blood of the trespass-offering *round about upon the altar,* "That there was a scarlet line which went round about the altar exactly in the middle, and the blood of the burnt-offerings was sprinkled round about above the line, but that of the trespass-offerings and peace-offerings round about below the line." It seems the offerer was not himself to have any share of his trespass-offering, as he was to have of his peace-offering; but it was all divided between the altar and the priest. They offered peace-offerings in thankfulness for mercy, and then it was proper to feast; but they offered trespass-offerings in sorrow for sin, and then fasting was more proper, in token of holy mourning, and a resolution to abstain from sin. 2. Concerning the burnt-offering it is here appointed that the priest that offered it should have the skin (*v.* 8), which no doubt he might make money of. 3. Concerning the meat-offering, if it was dressed, it was fit to be eaten immediately; and therefore the priest that offered it was to have it, *v.* 9.

Verses 11–34

I. The nature and intention of the peace-offerings are here more distinctly opened. They were offered either, 1. In thankfulness for some special mercy received, such as recovery from sickness, preservation in a journey, deliverance at sea, redemption out of captivity. Or, 2. In performance of some vow which a man made when he was in distress (*v.* 16). Or, 3. In supplication for some special mercy, here called a *voluntary offering.* This accompanied a man's prayers, as the former did his praises.

II. The rites and ceremonies about the peace-offerings are enlarged upon.

1. If the peace-offering was offered for a thanksgiving, a meat-offering must be offered with it, cakes of several sorts, and wafers (*v.* 12), and (which was peculiar to the peace-offerings) leavened bread must be offered. Unleavened bread was less grateful to the taste, and therefore, though enjoined in the passover for a particular reason, yet in other festivals leavened bread, which was lighter and more pleasant, was appointed, that men might feast at God's table as well as at their own.

2. The flesh of the peace-offerings, both that which was the priest's share and that which was the offerer's, must be eaten quickly, and not kept long, either raw, or dressed, cold. Though they were not obliged to eat it in the holy place, as those offerings that are called most holy, but might take it to their own tents and feast upon it there, yet God would by this law make them to know a difference between that and other meat. (1) Because God would not have that holy flesh to be in danger of putrefying. (2) Because God would not have his people to be niggardly and sparing, and distrustful of providence. (3) The flesh of the peace-offerings was God's treat, and therefore God orders it to be used generously for the entertainment of their friends, and charitably for the relief of the poor.

3. But the flesh, and those that eat it, must be pure. (1) The flesh must *touch no unclean thing*; if it did, it must not be eaten, but burnt, *v.* 19. (2) It must not be eaten by any unclean person. When a person was upon any account ceremonially unclean it was at his peril if he presumed to eat of the flesh of the peace-offerings, *v.* 20, 21. If any dare to partake of the table of the Lord under the pollution of sin unrepented of, and so profane sacred things, they eat and drink *judgment to themselves,* as those did that ate of the peace-offerings in their uncleanness, 1 Cor. xi. 29.

4. The eating of blood and the fat of the inwards is here again prohibited; and the prohibition is annexed as before to the law of the peace-offerings, *ch.* iii. 17. To eat of the flesh of that which died of itself, or was torn of beasts, was unlawful; but to eat of the fat of such was doubly unlawful, *v.* 24. The prohibition of blood is more general (*v.* 26, 27), because the fat was offered to God only by way of acknowledgment, but the blood *made atonement for the soul,* and so typified Christ's sacrifice much more than the burning of the fat did; to this therefore a greater reverence must be paid, till these types had their accomplishment in the offering up of the body of Christ once for all.

JAMIESON, FAUSSET, BROWN

CHAPTER 7

Vss. 1-27. THE LAW OF THE TRESPASS OFFERING. **1. Likewise this is the law of the trespass offering**—This chapter is a continuation of the laws that were to regulate the duty of the priests respecting the trespass offerings. The same regulations obtained in this case as in the burnt offerings—part was to be consumed on the altar, while the other part was a perquisite of the priests—some fell exclusively to the officiating minister, and was the fee for his services; others were the common share of all the priestly order, who lived upon them as their provision, and whose meetings at a common table would tend to promote brotherly harmony and friendship.

8. the priest shall have to himself the skin of the burnt offering which he hath offered—All the flesh and the fat of the burnt offerings being consumed, nothing remained to the priest but the skin. It has been thought that this was a patriarchal usage, incorporated with the Mosaic law, and that the right of the sacrificer to the skin of the victim was transmitted from the example of Adam (see on Gen. 3:21). **11-14. this is the law of the sacrifice of peace offerings**—Besides the usual accompaniments of other sacrifices, leavened bread was offered with the peace offerings, as a thanksgiving, such bread being common at feasts.

15-17. the flesh of the sacrifice of his peace offerings . . . shall be eaten the same day that it is offered—The flesh of the sacrifices was eaten on the day of the offering or on the day following. But if any part of it remained till the third day, it was, instead of being made use of, to be burned with fire. In the East, butcher-meat is generally eaten the day it is killed, and it is rarely kept a second day, so that as a prohibition was issued against any of the flesh in the peace offerings being used on the third day, it has been thought, not without reason, that this injunction must have been given to prevent a superstitious notion arising that there was some virtue or holiness belonging to it. **18. if any of the flesh of the sacrifice . . . be eaten at all on the third day, it shall not be accepted, neither . . . imputed**—The sacrifice will not be acceptable to God nor profitable to him that offers it. **20. cut off from his people**—i.e., excluded from the privileges of an Israelite—lie under a sentence of excommunication. **21. abominable unclean thing**—Some copies of the Bible read, "any reptile." **22-27. Ye shall eat no manner of fat**—See on ch. 3:17.

ADAM CLARKE

CHAPTER 7

2. *In the place where they kill the burnt offering.* Namely, on the north side of the altar, chap. i. 11.

3. *The rump.* See the notes on chap. iii. 9, where the principal subjects in this chapter are explained, being nearly the same in both.

4. *The fat that is on them.* Chiefly the fat that was found in a detached state, not mixed with the muscles.

9. *Baken in the oven.* See the notes on chap. ii. 5, etc.

15. *He shall not leave any of it until the morning.* Because in such a hot country it was apt to putrefy, and as it was considered to be holy, it would have been very improper to expose that to putrefaction which had been consecrated to the Divine Being.

20. *Having his uncleanness upon him.* Having touched any unclean thing by which he became legally defiled, and had not washed his clothes, and bathed his flesh.

21. *The uncleanness of man.* Any ulcer, sore, or leprosy; or any sort of cutaneous disorder, either loathsome or infectious.

23. *Fat, of ox, or of sheep, or of goat.* Any other fat they might eat, but the fat of these was sacred, because they were the only animals which were offered in sacrifice, though many others ranked among the clean animals as well as these. But it is likely that this prohibition is to be understood of these animals when offered in sacrifice, and then only in reference to the inward fat, as mentioned on v. 4. Of the fat in any other circumstances it cannot be intended, as it was one of the especial blessings which God gave to the people. "Butter of kine, and milk of sheep, with fat of lambs, and rams of the breed of Bashan, and goats" were the provision that He gave to His followers. See Deut. xxxii. 12-14.

27. *Whatsoever soul . . . that eateth any manner of blood.* See the note on Gen. ix. 4. *Shall be cut off*—excommunicated from the people of God, and so deprived of any part in their inheritance, and in their blessings. See the note on Gen. xvii. 14.

29. *Shall bring his oblation.* Meaning those things which were given out of the peace offerings to the Lord and to the priest.

30. *Wave offering.* See on Exod. xxix. 27.

32. *The right shoulder.* See on Exod. xxix. 27.

36. *In the day that he anointed them.* See the note on Exod. xl. 15.

38. *In the wilderness of Sinai.* These laws were probably given to Moses while he was on the mount with God; the time was quite sufficient, as he was there with God not less than fourscore days in all; forty days at the giving, and forty days at the renewing of the law.

As in the course of this book the different kinds of sacrifices commanded to be offered are repeatedly occurring, I think it best, once for all, to give a general account of them, and a definition of the original terms, as well as of all others relative to this subject which are used in the Old Testament, and the reference in which they all stood to the great sacrifice offered by Christ.

(1) *Asham, trespass offering,* from *asham,* to be "guilty, or liable to punishment"; for in this sacrifice the guilt was considered as being transferred to the animal offered up to God, and the offerer redeemed from the penalty of his sin, v. 37. Christ is said to have made His soul an offering for sin, Isa. liii. 10.

(2) *Ishsheh, fire offering,* probably from *ashash,* to be "grieved, angered, inflamed"; either pointing out the distressing nature of sin, or its property of incensing divine justice against the offender, who, in consequence, deserving burning for his offense, made use of this sacrifice to be freed from the punishment due to his transgression. It occurs in Exod. xxix. 18, and in many places of this book.

(3) *Habhabim, iterated or repeated offerings,* from *yahab,* to "supply." The word occurs only in Hos. viii. 13, and probably means no more than the continual repetition of the accustomed offerings, or continuation of each part of the sacred service.

MATTHEW HENRY

5. The priest's share of the peace-offerings is here prescribed. Jesus Christ is our great peace-offering; for he made himself a sacrifice, not only to atone for sin, and so to save us from the curse, but to purchase a blessing for us, and all good. By our joyfully partaking of the benefits of redemption we *feast upon the sacrifice*, to signify which the Lord's supper was instituted.

Verses 35–38

Here is the conclusion of these laws concerning the sacrifices. They are to be considered, 1. As a grant to the priests, *v.* 35, 36. 2. As a statute for ever to the people, that they should bring these offerings according to the rules prescribed, and cheerfully give the priests their share out of them. God *commanded the children of Israel to offer their oblations*, *v.* 38. Note, The solemn acts of religious worship are commanded. The observance of the laws of Christ cannot be less necessary than the observance of the laws of Moses was.

JAMIESON, FAUSSET, BROWN

28-38. The Priests' Portion. **29. He that offereth the sacrifice of his peace offerings unto the Lord**—In order to show that the sacrifice was voluntary, the offerer was required to bring it with his own hands to the priest. The breast having been waved to and fro in a solemn manner as devoted to God, was given to the priests; it was assigned to the use of their order generally, but the right shoulder was the perquisite of the officiating priest. **35-38. This is the portion of the anointing of Aaron**—These verses contain a general summing up of the laws which regulate the privileges and duties of the priests. The word "anointing" is often used as synonymous with "office" or "dignity." So that the "portion of the anointing of Aaron" probably means the provision made for the maintenance of the high priest and the numerous body of functionaries which composed the sacerdotal order. **in the day when he presented them to minister unto the Lord**, etc.–i.e., from the day they approached the Lord in the duties of their ministry.

ADAM CLARKE

(4) *Zebach, a sacrifice*, a creature slain in sacrifice, from *zabach*, to "slay"; hence the altar on which such sacrifices were offered was termed *mizbeach*, the place of sacrifice. *Zebach* is a common name for sacrifices in general.

(5) *Chag*, a "festival," especially such as had a periodical return, from *chagag*, to "celebrate a festival, to dance round and round in circles." See Exod. v. 1; xii. 24.

(6) *Chattath* and *chattaah, sin offering*, from *chata*, to "miss the mark"; it also signifies sin in general, and is a very apt term to express its nature by. A sinner is continually aiming at and seeking happiness; but as he does not seek it in God, hence the Scripture represents him as missing his aim, or missing the mark. This is precisely the meaning of the Greek word *hamartia*, translated "sin" and "sin offering" in our version; and this is the term by which the Hebrew word is translated by both the Septuagint and the inspired writers of the New Testament. The sin offering was an acknowledgment of guilt. This word often occurs.

ADAM CLARKE: VERSE 38 CONTINUED

(7) *Copher*, the expiation or atonement, from *caphar*, to "cover," or annul a contract. Used often to signify the atonement or expiation made for the pardon or cancelling of iniquity.

(8) *Moed*, an appointed *annual festival*, from *yaad*, to "appoint or constitute," signifying such feasts as were instituted in commemoration of some great event or deliverance, such as the deliverance from Egypt. See Exod. xiii. 10, and thus differing from the *chag* mentioned above. See the note on Gen. i. 14.

(9) *Milluim*, consecrations or *consecration offerings*, from *mala*, to "fill"; those offerings made in consecrations, of which the priests partook, or, in the Hebrew phrase, had their "hands filled," or which had filled the hands of them that offered them. See the note on Exod. xxix. 19; and see 2 Chron. xiii. 9.

(10) *Minchah, meat offering*, from *nach*, to "rest, settle" after toil. It generally consisted of things without life, such as green ears of corn, full ears of corn, flour, oil, and frankincense (see on chap. ii. 1, etc.); and may be considered as having its name from that "rest" from labor and toil which a man had when the fruits of the autumn were brought in, or when, in consequence of obtaining any rest, ease, etc., a significant offering or sacrifice was made to God. If often occurs. See the note on Gen. iv. 3. The jealousy offering (Num. v. 15) was a simple *minchah*, consisting of barley meal only.

(11) *Mesech and mimsach*, a *mixture offering*, or mixed libation, called a *drink offering*, Isa. lv. 11, from *masach*, to "mingle"; it seems in general to mean old wine mixed with the lees, which made it extremely intoxicating. This offering does not appear to have had any place in the worship of the true God; but from Isa. lxv. 11 and Prov. xxiii. 30, it seems to have been used for idolatrous purposes.

(12) *Masseeth*, an oblation, things "carried" to the Temple to be presented to God, from *nasa*, to "bear or carry," to bear sin; typically, Exod. xxviii. 38; chap. x. 17; xvi. 21; really, Isa. liii. 4, 12. The sufferings and death of Christ were the true *masseeth* or vicarious bearing of the sins of mankind, as the passage in Isaiah above referred to sufficiently proves. See this alluded to by the Evangelist John, chap. i. 29.

(13) *Nedabah, freewill* or *voluntary offering;* from *nadab*, to be "free, liberal, princely." An offering not commanded, but given as a particular proof of extraordinary gratitude to God for especial mercies, or on account of some vow or engagement voluntarily taken, v. 16.

(14) *Nesech, libation*, or *drink offering*, from *nasach*, to "pour out." Water or wine poured out at the conclusion or confirmation of a treaty or covenant. To this kind of offering there is frequent allusion and reference in the New Testament, as it typified the blood of Christ poured out for the sin of the world; and to this our Lord himself alludes in the institution of the Holy Eucharist. The whole gospel economy is represented as a covenant or treaty between God and man, Jesus Christ being not only the Mediator, but the covenant Sacrifice, whose blood was poured out for the ratification and confirmation of this covenant or agreement between God and man.

(15) *Olah, burnt offering*, from *alah*, to "ascend," because this offering, as being wholly consumed, ascended as it were to God in smoke and vapor. It was a very expressive type of the sacrifice of Christ, as nothing less than His complete and full sacrifice could make atonement for the sin of the world. In most other offerings the priest, and often the offerer, had a share, but in the whole burnt offering *all* was given to God.

(16) *Ketoreth*, incense or perfume offering, from *katar*, to "burn," i.e., the frankincense, and other aromatics used as a perfume in different parts of the divine service. To this Paul compares the agreeableness of the sacrifice of Christ to God, Eph. v. 2: "Christ . . . hath given himself for us an offering . . . to God for a sweetsmelling savour." From Rev. v. 8 we learn that it was intended also to represent the prayers of the saints, which, offered up on the Altar, Christ Jesus, that sanctifies every gift, are highly pleasing in the sight of God.

(17) *Korban*, the *gift offering*, from *karab*, to "draw nigh or approach." See this explained on chap. i. 2. *Korban* was a general name for any kind of offering, because through these it was supposed a man had access to his Maker.

(18) *Shelamim, peace offering*, from *shalam*, to "complete, make whole"; for by these offerings that which was lacking was considered as being now made up, and that which was broken, viz., the covenant of God, by His creatures' transgression, was supposed to be made whole; so that after such an offering the sincere and conscientious mind had a right to consider that the breach was made up between God and it, and that it might lay confident hold on this covenant of peace. To this the apostle evidently alludes, Eph. ii. 14-19: "He is our peace [i.e., our *shalam* or Peace Offering], who hath made both one, and broken down the middle wall . . . having abolished in his flesh the enmity."

(19) *Todah, thank offering*, from *yadah*, to "confess"; offerings made to God with public confession of His power, goodness, mercy.

(20) *Tenuphah, wave offering*, from *naph*, to "stretch out"; an offering of the firstfruits stretched out before God, in acknowledgment of His providential goodness. This offering was moved from the right hand to the left.

(21) *Terumah, heave offering*, from *ram*, to "lift up," because the offering was lifted up towards heaven, as the wave offering, in token of the kindness of God in granting rain and fruitful seasons, and filling the heart with food and gladness. As the wave offering was moved from right to left, so the heave offering was moved up and down; and in both cases this was done several times. These offerings had a blessed tendency to keep alive in the breasts of the people a due sense of their dependence on the divine providence and bounty, and of their obligation to God for His continual and liberal supply of all their wants.

MATTHEW HENRY — CHAPTER 8

Verses 1–13

God had given Moses orders to consecrate Aaron and his sons to the priests' office, when he was with him the first time upon Mount Sinai, Exod. xxviii. and xxix.

I. The orders repeated. The tabernacle was newly set up, which, without the priests, would be as a candlestick without a candle; the law concerning sacrifices was newly given, but could not be observed without priests. Aaron and his sons were near relations to Moses, and therefore he would not consecrate them till he had further orders, lest he should seem too forward to bring honour into his family.

II. The congregation called together, *at the door*, that is, in the court *of the tabernacle*, *v.* 4. It was done thus publicly, 1. Because it was a solemn transaction between God and Israel, and therefore it was fit that both sides should appear, to own the appointment, at the door of the tabernacle of meeting.

JAMIESON, FAUSSET, BROWN — CHAPTER 8

Vss. 1-36. Moses Consecrates Aaron and His Sons. **2. Take Aaron and his sons**—The consecration of Aaron and his sons had been ordered long before (Exod. 29), but it is now described with all the details of the ceremonial, as it was gone through after the tabernacle was completed and the regulations for the various sacrifices enacted.

3-5. gather thou all the congregation together, etc.—It was manifestly expedient for the Israelitish people to be satisfied that Aaron's appointment to the high dignity of the priesthood was not a personal intrusion, nor a family arrangement between him and

ADAM CLARKE — CHAPTER 8

2. *Take Aaron and his sons.* The whole subject of this chapter has been anticipated in the notes on Exod. xxviii. 1, etc., and xxix. 1, etc., in which all the sacrifices, rites, and ceremonies have been explained in considerable detail. It is only necessary to observe that Aaron and his sons were not anointed until now. Before, the thing was commanded; now, first performed.

MATTHEW HENRY

2. The spectators of the solemnity could not but be possessed, by the sight of it, with a great veneration for the priests and their office. It was strange that any of those who were witnesses of what was here done should afterwards say, as some of them did, *You take too much upon you, you sons of Levi.*

III. The Commission read, *v.* 5. Moses, who was God's representative in this solemnity, produced his orders before the congregation: *This is the thing which the Lord commanded to be done.* The priesthood he delivered to them was that which he had received from the Lord.

IV. The ceremony performed according to the divine ritual. 1. Aaron and his sons were *washed with water* (*v.* 6), to signify that they ought now to purify themselves from all sinful dispositions and inclinations, and ever after to keep themselves pure. 2. They were clothed with the holy garments, Aaron with his (*v.* 7–9), which typified the dignity of Christ our great high priest, and his sons with theirs (*v.* 13), which typified the decency of Christians, who are spiritual priests. Christ wears the breast-plate of judgment and the holy crown; for the church's high priest is her prophet and king. All believers are clothed with the robe of righteousness, and girt with the girdle of truth, resolution, and close application; and their heads are *bound*, as the word here is, with the bonnet or diadem of beauty, the beauty of holiness. 3. The high priest was anointed. The tabernacle, and all its utensils, had some of the anointing oil put upon them with Moses's finger (*v.* 10), so had the altar (*v.* 11); but he poured it out more plentifully upon the head of Aaron (*v.* 12), so that it ran down to the *skirts of his garments*, because his unction was to typify the anointing of Christ with the Spirit, which was not given by measure to him.

Verses 14–30

Sacrifices of each kind must be offered for the priests, that they might with the more tenderness and concern offer the gifts and sacrifices of the people, with compassion on the ignorant, and on *those that were out of the way*, remembering that they themselves had had sacrifices offered for them, being *compassed with infirmity.* 1. A bullock, the largest sacrifice, was offered for a sin-offering (*v.* 14). Ministers, that are to declare the remission of sins to others, should give diligence to get it made sure to themselves in the first place that their own sins are pardoned. Those to whom is *committed the ministry of reconciliation* must first be reconciled to God themselves. 2. A ram was offered for a burnt-offering, *v.* 18–21. By this they gave to God the glory of this great honour which was now put upon them, and returned him praise for it, as Paul thanked Christ Jesus for *putting him into the ministry*, 1 Tim. i. 12. 3. Another ram, called the *ram of consecration*, was offered for a peace-offering, *v.* 22, &c. All the ceremonies about this offering, as those before, were appointed by the express command of God.

Verses 31–36

Moses, having done his part of the ceremony, now leaves Aaron and his sons to do theirs.

I. They must boil the flesh of their peace-offering, and eat it in the court of the tabernacle, and what remained they must burn with fire, *v.* 31, 32.

II. They must not stir out of the court of the tabernacle for seven days, *v.* 33. The priesthood being a good warfare, they must thus learn to endure hardness, and to disentangle themselves from the affairs of this life, 2 Tim. ii. 3, 4. The work lasted seven days; for it was a kind of creation: and this time was appointed in honour of the sabbath, which, probably, was the last day of the seven, for which they were to prepare during the six days. They attended to *keep the charge of the Lord*: we have every one of us a charge to keep, an eternal God to glorify, an immortal soul to provide for, needful duty to be done, our generation to serve; and it must be our daily care to keep this charge, for it is the charge of the Lord our Master. *Lastly*, We are told (*v.* 36) that *Aaron and his sons did all that was commanded.* But after all the ceremonies that were used in their consecration there was one point of ratification which was reserved to be the honour and establishment of Christ's priesthood, which was this, that they were *made priests without an oath*, but *Christ with an oath* (Heb. vii. 21), for neither such priests nor their priesthood could continue, but Christ's is a perpetual and unchangeable priesthood.

JAMIESON, FAUSSET, BROWN

Moses; and nothing, therefore, could be a more prudent or necessary measure, for impressing a profound conviction of the divine origin and authority of the priestly institution, than to summon a general assembly of the people, and in their presence perform the solemn ceremonies of inauguration, which had been prescribed by divine authority. **6. Moses . . . washed them with water**—At consecration they were subjected to entire ablution, though on ordinary occasions they were required, before entering on their duties, only to wash their hands and feet. This symbolical ablution was designed to teach them the necessity of inward purity, and the imperative obligation on those who bore the vessels and conducted the services of the sanctuary to be holy. **7-9. he put upon him the coat, and girded him with the girdle**—The splendor of the official vestments, together with the gorgeous tiara of the high priest, was intended, doubtless, in the first instance, to produce in the minds of the people a high respect for the ministers of religion; and in the next, from the predominant use of linen, to inculcate upon Aaron and his sons the duty of maintaining unspotted righteousness in their characters and lives.

10-12. took the anointing oil, etc.—which was designed to intimate that persons who acted as leaders in the solemn services of worship should have the unction of the Holy One both in His gifts and graces.

14-17. brought the bullock for the sin offering, etc.—a timely expression of their sense of unworthiness—a public and solemn confession of their personal sins and a transference of their guilt to the typical victim.

18-21. brought the ram, etc.—as a token of their entire dedication to the service of God.

22-30. brought the other ram, etc.—After the sin offering and burnt offering had been presented on their behalf, this was their peace offering, by which they declared the pleasure which they felt in entering upon the service of God and being brought into close communion with Him as the ministers of His sanctuary, together with their confident reliance on His grace to help them in all their sacred duties.

33. ye shall not go out of the door of the tabernacle of the congregation, etc.—After all these preliminaries, they had still to undergo a week's probation in the court of the tabernacle before they obtained permission to enter into the interior of the sacred building. During the whole of that period the same sacrificial rites were observed as on the first day, and they were expressly admonished that the smallest breach of any of the appointed observances would lead to the certain forfeiture of their lives.

ADAM CLARKE

8. *He put in the breastplate the Urim and the Thummim.* The Urim and Thummim are here supposed to be something different from the breastplate itself. See the note on Exod. xxviii. 30.

14. *The bullock for the sin offering.* This was offered each day during the seven days of consecration. See Exod. xxix. 36.

23. *Put it upon the tip of Aaron's right ear.* See this significant ceremony explained in the note on Exod. xxix. 20.

27. *And waved them for a wave offering.* See the nature of this and the *heave offering* in the note on Exod. xxix. 27.

30. *And Moses took . . . the blood . . . and sprinkled it upon Aaron.* Thus we find that the high priest himself must be sprinkled with the blood of the sacrifice.

33. *For seven days shall he consecrate you.* This number was the number of perfection among the Hebrews; and the seven days' consecration implied a perfect and full consecration to the sacerdotal office. See the note on Exod. xxix. 30.

36. *So Aaron and his sons did.* This chapter shows the exact fulfillment of the commands delivered to Moses, Exodus xxix; and consequently the complete preparation of Aaron and his sons to fill the awfully important office of priests and mediators between God and Israel, to offer sacrifices and make atonement for the sins of the people.

MATTHEW HENRY

CHAPTER 9

Verses 1–7

Orders are here given for another solemnity upon the eighth day. The priests had not so much as one day's respite from service, but were busily employed the very next day; for their consecration was the *filling of their hands.* Now, 1. Moses raises their expectation of a glorious appearance of God to them this day (*v.* 4): "*To day the Lord will appear to you* that are the priests." We are not now to expect such appearances; we Christians walk more by faith, and less by sight, than they did. But we may be sure that God draws nigh to those who draw nigh to him, and that the offerings of faith are really acceptable to him, though, the sacrifices being spiritual, the tokens of the acceptance are, as it is fit they should be, spiritual likewise. 2. He puts both priests and people upon preparing to receive this favour which God designed them. *Aaron and his sons,* and *the elders of Israel,* are all summoned to attend, *v.* 1. (1) Aaron is ordered to prepare his offerings: *A young calf for a sin-offering, v.* 2. The Jewish writers suggest that a *calf* was appointed for a sin-offering to remind him of his sin in making the golden calf. (2) Aaron must direct the people to get theirs ready. (3) Aaron must offer his own first, and then the people's, *v.* 7. [1] The high priest made atonement for himself, as one that was joined with sinners; but we have a high priest that was separated from sinners, and needed no atonement. When Messiah the prince was cut off as a sacrifice, it was not for himself; for he knew no sin. [2] He must *make an atonement for the people,* by offering their sacrifices. He must *make atonement as the Lord commanded.* See here the mercy of God, that he not only allows an atonement to be made, but commands it. No room therefore is left to doubt but that the atonement which is commanded will be accepted.

Verses 8–22

These being the first offerings that ever were offered by the levitical priesthood, according to the newly-enacted law of sacrifices, the manner of offering them is particularly related. 1. Aaron with his own hands *slew the offering* (*v.* 8), and did the work of the inferior priests. Therefore, as Moses before, so Aaron now offered some of each of the several sorts of sacrifices that were appointed. 2. He offered these *besides the burnt-sacrifice of the morning,* which was every day offered first, *v.* 17. When Aaron had done all that on his part was to be done about the sacrifices he *lifted up his hand towards the people, and blessed them, v.* 22. Aaron *lifted up his hands* in blessing them, to intimate whence he desired and expected the blessing to come, even from heaven, which is God's throne. Aaron could but crave a blessing, it is God's prerogative to command it. Aaron, when he had blessed, came down; Christ, when he blessed, went up.

Verses 23–24

We are not told what Moses and Aaron went into the tabernacle to do, *v.* 23. Some of the Jewish writers say, "They went in to pray for the appearance of the divine glory." But, when they came out, they both joined in blessing the people, who stood expecting the promised appearance of the divine glory; and it was now (when Moses and Aaron concurred in praying) that they had what they waited for. Note, God's manifestations of himself, of his glory and grace, are commonly given in answer to prayer. The glory of God appeared, not while the sacrifices were in offering, but when the priests prayed, which intimates that the prayers and praises of God's spiritual priests are more pleasing to God than all burnt-offerings and sacrifices.

I. *The glory of the Lord appeared unto all the people, v.* 23. What the appearance of it was we are not told; no doubt it was such as carried its own evidence along with it. Those that dwell in God's house with an eye of faith may *behold the beauty of the Lord.*

II. *There came a fire out from before the Lord, and consumed the sacrifice, v.* 24. Whether this fire came from heaven, or out of the most holy place, or from that visible appearance of the glory of God which all the people saw, it was a manifest token of God's acceptance of their service.

1. This fire did consume (or, as the word is, *eat up*) the present sacrifice. (1) It signified the turning away of God's wrath from them. Its fastening upon the sacrifice, and consuming that, signified God's acceptance of that as an atonement for the sinner. (2) It signified God's entering into covenant and communion with them.

2. This fire did, as it were, take possession of the altar. This also was a figure of good things to come.

JAMIESON, FAUSSET, BROWN

CHAPTER 9

Vss. 1-24. THE PRIESTS' ENTRY INTO OFFICE. **1, 2. Moses called . . . Take thee a young calf for a sin offering**—The directions in these sacred things were still given by Moses, the circumstances being extraordinary. But he was only the medium of communicating the divine will to the newly made priests. The first of their official acts was the sacrifice of another sin offering to atone for the defects of the inauguration services; and yet that sacrifice did not consist of a bullock—the sacrifice appointed for some particular transgression, but of a calf, perhaps not without a significant reference to Aaron's sin in the golden calf. Then followed a burnt offering, expressive of their voluntary and entire self-devotement to the divine service. The newly consecrated priests having done this on their own account, they were called to offer a sin offering and burnt offering for the people, ending the ceremonial by a peace offering, which was a sacred feast. This injunction "to make an atonement for himself and for the people" (*Septuagint,* "for thy family"), at the commencement of his sacred functions, furnishes a striking evidence of the divine origin of the Jewish system of worship. In all false or corrupt forms of religion, the studied policy has been to inspire the people with an idea of the sanctity of the priesthood as in point of purity and favor with the Divinity far above the level of other men. But among the Hebrews the priests were required to offer for the expiation of their own sins as well as the humblest of the people. This imperfection of Aaron's priesthood, however, does not extend to the gospel dispensation: for our great High Priest, who has entered for us into "the true tabernacle," "knew no sin" (Heb. 10:10, 11).

8. Aaron . . . went unto the altar, and slew the calf of the sin offering—Whether it had been enjoined the first time, or was unavoidable from the divisions of the priestly labor not being as yet completely arranged, Aaron, assisted by his sons, appears to have slain the victims with his own hands, as well as gone through all the prescribed ritual at the altar. **17-21. meat offering . . . wave offering**—It is observable that there is no notice taken of these in the offerings the priests made for themselves. They could not bear their own sins: and therefore, instead of eating any part of their own sin offering, as they were at liberty to do in the case of the people's offering, they had to carry the whole carcasses "*without* the camp and burn them with fire." **22. Aaron lifted up his hand . . . and blessed**—The pronouncing of a benediction on the people assembled in the court was a necessary part of the high priest's duty, and the formula in which it was to be given is described (Num. 6:23-27). **came down from offering**—The altar was elevated above the level of the floor, and the ascent was by a gentle slope (Exod. 20:26). **23. Moses and Aaron went into the tabernacle**—Moses, according to the divine instructions he had received, accompanied Aaron and his sons to initiate them into their sacred duties. Their previous occupations had detained them at the altar, and they now entered in company into the sacred edifice to bear the blood of the offerings within the sanctuary.

the glory of the Lord appeared unto all the people—perhaps in a resplendent effulgence above the tabernacle as a fresh token of the divine acceptance of that newly established seat of His worship.

there came a fire out from . . . the Lord—A flame emanating from that resplendent light that filled the holy place flashed upon the brazen altar and kindled the sacrifices. This miraculous fire—for the descent of which the people had probably been prepared, and which the priests were enjoined never to let go out (ch. 6:13)—was a sign, not only of the acceptance of the offerings and of the establishment of Aaron's authority, but of God's actual residence in that chosen dwelling-place.

ADAM CLARKE

CHAPTER 9

1. *On the eighth day.* This was the first day after their consecration, before which they were deemed unfit to minister in holy things, being considered as in a state of imperfection.

2. *Take thee a young calf.* As these sacrifices were for Aaron himself, they are furnished by himself and not by the people, for they were designed to make atonement for his own sin. See chap. iv. 3. And this is supposed by the Jews to have been intended to make an atonement for his sin in the matter of the golden calf. This is very probable, as no formal atonement for that transgression had yet been made.

3. *Take ye a kid.* In chap. iv. 14 a young bullock is commanded to be offered for the sin of the people; but here the offering is a *kid,* which was the sacrifice appointed for the sin of the ruler, chap. iv. 22-23, and hence some think that the reading of the Samaritan and the Septuagint is to be preferred. "Speak unto the elders of Israel," these being the only princes or rulers of Israel at that time; and for them it is possible this sacrifice was designed. It is however supposed that the sacrifice appointed in chap. iv. 14 was for a particular sin, but this for sin in general; and it is on this account that the sacrifices differ.

6. *And the glory of the Lord shall appear.* God shall give the most sensible signs of His presence among you; this He did in general by the cloud on the Tabernacle, but in this case the particular proof was the fire that came out from before the Lord, and consumed the burnt offering; see vv. 23-24.

7. *Make an atonement for thyself.* This showed the imperfection of the Levitical law; the high priest was obliged to make an expiation for his own sins before he could make one for the sins of the people. See the use made of this by the apostle, Heb. v. 3; vii. 27; ix. 7.

22. *And Aaron lifted up his hand toward the people, and blessed them.* On lifting up the hands in prayer, see Exod. ix. 29. The form of the blessing we have in Num. vi. 23, etc.: "The Lord bless thee, and keep thee: the Lord make his face shine upon thee, and be gracious unto thee: the Lord lift up his countenance upon thee, and give thee peace." *And came down from offering of the sin offering.* A sin offering, a burnt offering, a meat offering, and peace offerings, were made to God that His glory might appear to the whole congregation. This was the end of all sacrifice and religious service; not to confer any obligation on God, but to make an atonement for sin, and to engage Him to dwell among and influence His worshippers.

23. *Moses and Aaron went into the tabernacle.* It is supposed that Moses accompanied Aaron into the Tabernacle to show him how to offer the incense, prepare the lamps and the perfume, adjust the shewbread, etc. *And the glory of the Lord appeared.* To show that everything was done according to the divine mind, (1) The glory of Jehovah appeared unto all the people; (2) A fire came out from before the Lord, and consumed the burnt offering. This was the proof which God gave upon extraordinary occasions of His acceptance of the sacrifice.

24. *When all the people saw, they shouted, and fell on their faces.* (1) The miracle was done in such a way as gave the fullest conviction to the people of its reality. (2) They exulted in the thought that the God of almighty power and energy had taken up His abode among them. (3) They prostrated themselves in His presence, thereby intimating the deep sense they had of His goodness, of their unworthiness, and of the obligation they were under to live in subjection to His authority, and obedience to His will.

MATTHEW HENRY

The Spirit descended upon the apostles in *fire* (Acts ii. 3). And the descent of this holy fire into our souls to kindle in them pious and devout affections towards God, and such a holy zeal as burns up the flesh and the lusts of it, is a certain token of God's gracious acceptance of our persons and performances.

III. We are here told how the people were affected with this discovery of God's glory and grace; they received it, 1. With the highest joy: *They shouted*; so stirring up themselves and one another to a holy triumph. 2. With the lowest reverence: *They fell on their faces*, humbly adoring the majesty of that God who vouchsafed thus to manifest himself to them.

CHAPTER 10

Verses 1–2

Here is, I. The great sin that Nadab and Abihu were guilty of. But what was their sin? All the account here given of it is that they *offered strange fire before the Lord, which he commanded them not* (*v.* 1), and the same, Num. iii. 4. 1. Nadab and Abihu were so proud of the honour they were newly advanced to, and so ambitious of doing the highest and most honourable part of their work immediately, that though the service of this day was extraordinary, and done by particular direction from Moses, yet without receiving orders, they took their censers, and they would enter into the tabernacle and burn incense. And then their *offering strange fire* is the same with *offering strange incense*, which is expressly forbidden, Exod. xxx. 9. 2. Presuming thus to burn incense of their own without order, no marvel that they made a further blunder, and instead of taking of the fire from the altar, which was newly kindled from before the Lord and which henceforward must be used in offering both sacrifice and incense (Rev. viii. 5), they took common fire, probably from that with which the flesh of the peace-offerings was boiled, and this they made use of in burning incense; not being holy fire, it is called *strange fire*. 3. Incense was always to be burned by only one priest at a time, but here they would both go in together to do it. 4. They did it rashly, and with precipitation. They *snatched* their censers, without due reverence, when all the people *fell upon their faces*, before the *glory of the Lord*. 5. There is reason to suspect that they were drunk when they did it, because of the law which was given upon this occasion, *v.* 8. They had been feasting upon the peace-offerings, and the drink-offerings, and so their heads were light. 6. No doubt it was done presumptuously.

II. The dreadful punishment of this sin: *There went out fire from the Lord, and devoured them, v.* 2.

But why did the Lord deal thus severely with them? Were they not the sons of Aaron, the saint of the Lord, nephews to Moses, the great favourite of heaven? 1. The sin was greatly aggravated. It was a manifest contempt of Moses, and the divine law that was given by Moses. Hitherto it had been expressly observed concerning every thing that was done that they did it *as the Lord commanded Moses*, in opposition to which it is here said they did that *which the Lord commanded them not*, but they did it of their own heads. God was now teaching his people obedience, and to do every thing by rule, as becomes servants; for priests therefore to break rules and disobey was such a provocation as must by no means go unpunished. 2. Their punishment was a piece of necessary justice, now at the first settling of the ceremonial institutions. And no doubt this exemplary piece of justice at first prevented many irregularities afterwards. Thus Ananias and Sapphira were punished, when they presumed to lie to the Holy Ghost, that newly-descended fire.

Verses 3–7

We may well think that when Nadab and Abihu were struck with death, all about them were struck with horror. Moses was composed, though it touched him in a very tender part. He kept possession of his own soul.

I. He endeavours to pacify Aaron under this sad dispensation, *v.* 3.

1. What it was that Moses suggested to his poor brother upon this occasion: *This is it that the Lord spoke*. What was it that God spoke? It was this (the Lord by his grace speak it to all our hearts!) *I will be sanctified in those that come nigh me*, whoever they are, and *before all the people I will be glorified*. What was there in this to quiet Aaron? Two things:—(1) This must silence him, that his sons deserved their death; for they were thus cut off from their people because they did not sanctify and glorify God. (2) This must satisfy him, that the death of his sons redounded to the honour of God, and his impartial justice would for it be adored throughout all ages.

JAMIESON, FAUSSET, BROWN

The moment the solemn though welcome spectacle was seen, a simultaneous shout of joy and gratitude burst from the assembled congregation, and in the attitude of profoundest reverence they worshipped "a present Deity."

CHAPTER 10

Vss. 1-20. NADAB AND ABIHU BURNT. **1. the sons of Aaron,** etc.—If this incident occurred at the solemn period of the consecrating and dedicating the altar, these young men assumed an office which had been committed to Moses; or if it were some time after, it was an encroachment on duties which devolved on their father alone as the high priest. But the offense was of a far more aggravated nature than such a mere informality would imply. It consisted not only in their venturing unauthorized to perform the incense service—the highest and most solemn of the priestly offices—not only in their engaging together in a work which was the duty only of one, but in their presuming to intrude into the holy of holies, to which access was denied to all but the high priest alone. In this respect, "they offered strange fire before the Lord"; they were guilty of a presumptuous and unwarranted intrusion into a sacred office which did not belong to them. But their offense was more aggravated still; for instead of taking the fire which was put into their censers from the brazen altar, they seem to have been content with common fire and thus perpetrated an act which, considering the descent of the miraculous fire they had so recently witnessed and the solemn obligation under which they were laid to make use of that which was specially appropriated to the service of the altars, they betrayed a carelessness, an irreverence, a want of faith, most surprising and lamentable. A precedent of such evil tendency was dangerous, and it was imperatively necessary, therefore, as well for the priests themselves as for the sacred things, that a marked expression of the divine displeasure should be given for doing that which "God commanded them not." **2. there went out fire from the Lord, and devoured them**—rather, killed them; for it appears (vs. 5) that neither their bodies nor their robes were consumed. The expression, "from the Lord," indicates that this fire issued from the most holy place. In the destruction of these two young priests by the infliction of an awful judgment, the wisdom of God observed the same course, in repressing the first instance of contempt for sacred things, as he did at the commencement of the Christian dispensation (Acts 5: 1-11).

3. Moses said . . . This is it that the Lord spoke . . . I will be sanctified in them that come nigh me—"They that come nigh me," points, in this passage, directly to the priests; and they had received repeated and solemn warnings as to the cautious and reverent manner of their approach into the divine prescence (Exod. 19:22; 29:44; ch. 8:35).

ADAM CLARKE

This celestial fire was carefully preserved among the Israelites till the time of Solomon, when it was renewed, and continued among them till the Babylonish captivity. This divine fire was the emblem of the Holy Spirit. And as no sacrifice could be acceptable to God which was not "salted," i.e., as our Lord says, Mark ix. 49, so no soul can offer acceptable sacrifices to God but through the influences of the Divine Spirit. Hence the promise of the Spirit under the emblem of fire, Matt. iii. 11, and its actual descent in this similitude on the Day of Pentecost, Acts ii. 3-4.

CHAPTER 10

1. *And Nadab and Abihu . . . took either of them his censer*. In the preceding chapter we have seen how God intended that every part of His service should be conducted; and that every sacrifice might be acceptable to Him. He sent His own fire as the emblem of His presence, and the means of consuming the sacrifice. Here we find Aaron's sons neglecting the divine ordinance, and offering incense with strange, that is, common, fire—fire not of a celestial origin; and therefore the fire of God consumed them. So that very fire which, if properly applied, would have sanctified and consumed their gift, becomes now the very instrument of their destruction!

Which he commanded them not. Every part of the religion of God is divine. He alone knew what He designed by its rites and ceremonies, for that which they prefigured—the whole economy of redemption by Christ—was conceived in His own mind, and was out of the reach of human wisdom and conjecture. He therefore who altered any part of this representative system, who omitted or added anything, assumed a prerogative which belonged to God alone, and was certainly guilty of a very high offense against the wisdom, justice, and righteousness of his Maker. This appears to have been the sin of Nadab and Abihu, and this at once shows the reason why they were so severely punished. The most awful judgments are threatened against those who either add to, or take away from, the declarations of God. See Deut. iv. 2; Prov. xxx. 6; and Rev. xxii. 18-19.

MATTHEW HENRY

2. What good effects this had upon him: *Aaron held his peace*, that is, he patiently submitted to the holy will of God in this sad providence. When God corrects us or ours for sin, it is our duty to be silent under the correction, not to quarrel with God, arraign his justice, or charge him with folly, but to acquiesce in all that God does; not only bearing, but accepting, the punishment of iniquity. The most effectual arguments to quiet a gracious spirit under afflictions are those that are fetched from God's glory. Far be it from him that he should honour his sons more than God, or wish that God's name, or house, or law, should be exposed to reproach or contempt for the preserving of the reputation of his family.

II. Moses gives orders about the dead bodies. It was not fit that they should be left to lie where they fell. But Moses takes care of this matter, that though they died by the hand of justice in the act of sin, yet they should be decently buried, and they were so, *v.* 4, 5. They carried them out of the camp to be buried. It was a very awful affecting sight to the people. The names of Nadab and Abihu had become very great and honourable among them. Nadab and Abihu (who had been in the mount with God, Exod. xxiv. 1) were looked upon as the great favourites of heaven, and the hopes of their people; and now on a sudden, when the tidings of the event had scarcely reached their ears, to see them both carried out dead, with the visible marks of divine vengeance upon them, as sacrifices to the justice of God, they could not choose but cry out, *Who is able to stand before this holy Lord God?* 1 Sam. vi. 20.

III. He gives directions about the mourning.

1. That the priests must not mourn. But here it was forbidden both to Aaron and his sons, because, (1) They were now actually in waiting, doing a great work, which must by no means cease (Neh. vi. 3); and it was very much for the honour of God that their attendance on him should take place of their respects to their nearest relations, and that all services should give way to those of their ministry. (2) Their brethren were cut off for their transgression by the immediate hand of God, and therefore they must not mourn for them lest they should seem to countenance the sin, or impeach the justice of God in the punishment. It was very hard, no doubt, for Aaron and his sons to restrain themselves upon such an extraordinary occasion from inordinate grief, but reason and grace mastered the passion, and they bore the affliction with an obedient patience. Happy those who thus are themselves under God's government, and have their passions under their own government.

2. The people must mourn: *Let the whole house of Israel bewail the burning which the Lord has kindled.* The congregation must lament, not only the loss of their priests, but especially the displeasure of God which appeared in it.

Verses 8–11

Aaron having been very observant of what God said to him by Moses, now God does him the honour to speak to him immediately (*v.* 8): *The Lord spoke unto Aaron. Do not drink wine, nor strong drink, when you go into the tabernacle*, and this at his peril, *lest you die*, *v.* 9. Probably they had seen the ill effect of it in Nadab and Abihu, and therefore must take warning by them. Observe here, 1. The prohibition itself: *Do not drink wine nor strong drink.* At other times they were allowed (it was not expected that every priest should be a Nazarite), but during the time of their ministration they were forbidden it. This was one of the laws in Ezekiel's temple (Ezek. xliv. 21), and so it is required of gospel ministers that they be *not given to wine*, 1 Tim. iii. 3. 2. The penalty annexed to the prohibition: *Lest you die; lest you die* when you are in drink, *and so that day come upon you unawares*, Luke xxi. 34. Or, "Lest you do that which will make you liable to be cut off by the hand of God." 3. The reasons assigned for this prohibition. They must needs be sober, else they could not duly discharge their office; they will be in danger of *erring through wine*, Isa. xxviii. 7. They must be sure to keep sober, (1) That they might themselves be able to distinguish, in their ministrations, between that which was sacred and that which was common, and might never confound them, *v.* 10. (2) That they might be able to teach the people (*v.* 11), for that was a part of the priests' work (Deut. xxxiii. 10); and those that are addicted to drunkenness are very unfit to teach people God's statutes, both because those that live after the flesh can have no experimental acquaintance with the things of the Spirit, and because such teachers pull down with one hand what they build up with the other.

Verses 12–20

Moses is here directing Aaron to go on with his

JAMIESON, FAUSSET, BROWN

Aaron held his peace—The loss of two sons in so sudden and awful a manner was a calamity overwhelming to parental feelings. But the pious priest indulged in no vehement ebullition of complaint and gave vent to no murmur of discontent, but submitted in silent resignation to what he saw was "the righteous judgment of God."

4, 5. Moses called Mishael and Elzaphan—The removal of the two corpses for burial without the camp would spread the painful intelligence throughout all the congregation. The interment of the priestly vestments along with them, was a sign of their being polluted by the sin of their irreligious wearers; and the remembrance of so appalling a judgment could not fail to strike a salutary fear into the hearts both of priests and people. **6. Uncover not your heads**—They who were ordered to carry out the two bodies, being engaged in their sacred duties, were forbidden to remove their turbans, in conformity with the usual customs of mourning; and the prohibition, "neither rend your garments," was, in all probability, confined also to their official costume. For at other times the priests wore the ordinary dress of their countrymen and, in common with their families, might indulge their private feelings by the usual signs or expressions of grief.

8-11. Do not drink wine nor strong drink—This prohibition, and the accompanying admonitions, following immediately the occurrence of so fatal a catastrophe, has given rise to an opinion entertained by many, that the two disobedient priests were under the influence of intoxication when they committed the offense which was expiated only by their lives. But such an idea, though the presumption is in its favor, is nothing more than conjecture.

ADAM CLARKE

3. *And Aaron held his peace.* "And Aaron was dumb." How elegantly expressive is this of his parental affection, his deep sense of the presumption of his sons, and his own submission to the justice of God!

4. *Uzziel the uncle of Aaron.* He was brother to Amram, the father of Aaron; see Exod. vi. 18-22.

6. *Uncover not your heads.* They were to use no sign of grief or mourning: (1) Because those who were employed in the service of the sanctuary should avoid everything that might incapacitate them for that service; and (2) Because the crime of their brethren was so highly provoking to God, and so fully merited the punishment which *He* had inflicted, that their mourning might be considered as accusing the divine justice of undue severity.

7. *The anointing oil of the Lord is upon you.* They were consecrated to the divine service, and this required their constant attendance and most willing and cheerful service.

9. *Strong drink.* The word *shechar*, from *shachar*, to "inebriate," signifies any kind of fermented liquors. This is exactly the same prohibition that was given in the case of *John Baptist*, Luke i. 15: "Wine and sikera he shall not drink." Any inebriating liquor, says Jerome, is called *sicera*, whether made of corn, apples, honey, dates, or other fruit.

10. *That we may put difference between holy and unholy.* This is a strong reason why they should drink no inebriating liquor, that their understanding being clear, and their judgment correct, they might always be able to discern between the clean and the unclean, and ever pronounce righteous judgment.

MATTHEW HENRY

service after this interruption. Afflictions should rather quicken us to our duty than take us off from it. Observe (*v.* 12), He spoke unto Aaron and to his sons *that were left.* The notice taken of their survivorship intimates, 1. That Aaron should take comfort under the loss of two of his sons, from this consideration, that God had graciously spared him the other two. 2. That God's sparing them should be an engagement upon them to proceed in his service, and not to fly off from it. Here were four priests consecrated together, two were taken away, and two left; therefore the two that were left should endeavour to fill up the places of those that were gone, by double care and diligence in the services of the priesthood.

I. Moses repeats the directions he had formerly given them about eating their share of the sacrifices, *v.* 12–14, 15.

II. He enquires concerning one deviation from the appointment, which it seems had happened upon this occasion, which was this:—There was a goat to be sacrificed as a *sin-offering for the people, ch.* ix. 15. Now the law of the sin-offerings was that if the blood of them was brought into the holy place, as that of the sin-offerings for the priest was, then the flesh was to be burnt without the camp. Now the blood of this goat was not brought into the holy place, and yet, it seems, it was burnt without the camp. Moses charged the fault upon Eleazar and Ithamar (*v.* 16), but it is probable that what they did was by Aaron's direction, and therefore he apologized for it. He makes his affliction his excuse, *v.* 19. *Such things have befallen me,* such sad things, which could not but go near his heart, and make it very heavy. He was a high priest *taken from among men,* and could not put off natural affection when he put on the holy garments. He held his peace (*v.* 3), yet his sorrow was stirred. He makes this an excuse for his varying from the appointment about the sin-offering. He could not have eaten it but in his mourning, and with a sorrowful spirit; and would this have been accepted? The acquiescence of Moses in this excuse: *He was content, v.* 20. Perhaps he thought it justified what they had done. God had provided that what could not be eaten might be burnt.

JAMIESON, FAUSSET, BROWN

12-15. Moses spake unto Aaron, etc.—This was a timely and considerate rehearsal of the laws that regulated the conduct of the priests. Amid the distractions of their family bereavement, Aaron and his surviving sons might have forgotten or overlooked some of their duties. **16-20. Moses diligently sought the goat of the sin offering, and, behold, it was burnt**—In a sacrifice presented, as that had been, on behalf of the people, it was the duty of the priests, as typically representing them and bearing their sins, to have eaten the flesh after the blood had been sprinkled upon the altar. Instead of using it, however, for a sacred feast, they had burnt it without the camp; and Moses, who discovered this departure from the prescribed ritual, probably from a dread of some farther chastisements, challenged, not Aaron, whose heart was too much lacerated to bear a new cause of distress but his two surviving sons in the priesthood for the great irregularity. Their father, however, who heard the charge and by whose directions the error had been committed, hastened to give the explanation. The import of his apology is, that all the duty pertaining to the presentation of the offering had been duly and sacredly performed, except the festive part of the observance, which privately devolved upon the priest and his family; and that this had been omitted, either because his heart was too dejected to join in the celebration of a cheerful feast, or that he supposed, from the appalling judgments that had been inflicted, that all the services of that occasion were so vitiated that he did not complete them. Aaron was decidedly in the wrong. By the express command of God, the sin offering was to be eaten in the holy place; and no fanciful view of expediency or propriety ought to have led him to dispense at discretion with a positive statute. The law of God was clear and, where that is the case, it is sin to deviate a hair's breadth from the path of duty. But Moses sympathized with his deeply afflicted brother and, having pointed out the error, said no more.

ADAM CLARKE

14. *Wave breast and heave shoulder.* See chap. vii, and on Exod. xxix. 27.

16. *Moses diligently sought the goat.* The goat which was offered the same day for the sins of the priests and the people (see chap. ix. 15-16) and which, through the confusion that happened on account of the death of Nadab and Abihu, was burned instead of being eaten. See v. 18.

19. *And such things have befallen me.* The excuse which Aaron makes for not feasting on the sin offering according to the law is at once appropriate and dignified; as if he had said: "God certainly has commanded me to eat of the sin offering; but when such things as these have happened unto me, could it be good in the sight of the Lord? Does He not expect that I should feel as a father under such afflicting circumstances?" With this spirited answer Moses was satisfied.

20. *When Moses heard that, he was content.* The argument used by Aaron had in it both good sense and strong reason, and Moses, as a reasonable man, felt its force; and as God evidenced no kind of displeasure at this irregularity, which was, in a measure at least, justified by the present necessity, he thought proper to urge the matter no further.

MATTHEW HENRY — CHAPTER 11

Verses 1–8

Now that Aaron was consecrated a high priest over the house of God, God spoke to him with Moses, and appointed them both as joint-commissioners to deliver his will to the people. It was particularly required of the priests that they should put a difference between clean and unclean, and teach the people to do so. They might eat flesh, but not all kinds of flesh; some they must look upon as unclean and forbidden to them, others as clean and allowed them. But what reason can be given for this law? Most of the meats forbidden as unclean are such as were really unwholesome, and not fit to be eaten; and those of them that we think wholesome enough, and use accordingly, as the rabbit, the hare, and the swine, perhaps in those countries, and to their bodies, might be hurtful. The Lord is for the body, and it is not only folly, but sin against God to prejudice our health for the pleasing of our appetite. It should seem there had been, before this, some difference between the Hebrews and other nations in their food, kept up by tradition; for the Egyptians and they would not eat together, Gen. xliii. 32. The learned observe further, That most of the creatures which by this law were to be abominated as unclean were such as were had in high veneration among the heathen, not so much for food as for divination and sacrifice to their gods; and therefore those are here mentioned as unclean, and an abomination, which yet they would not be in any temptation to eat, that they might keep up a religious loathing of that for which the Gentiles had a superstitious value. The swine, with the later Gentiles, was sacred to Venus, the owl to Minerva, the eagle to Jupiter, the dog to Hecate, &c., and all these are here made unclean. As to the beasts, there is a general rule laid down, that those which both part the hoof and chew the cud were clean, and those only: these are particularly mentioned in the repetition of this law (Deut. xiv. 4, 5), where it appears that the Israelites had variety enough allowed them, and needed not to complain of the confinement they were under.

JAMIESON, FAUSSET, BROWN — CHAPTER 11

VSS. 1-47. BEASTS THAT MAY AND MAY NOT BE EATEN. **1. the Lord spake unto Moses and to Aaron**—These laws, being addressed to both the civil and ecclesiastical rulers in Israel, may serve to indicate the twofold view that is to be taken of them. Undoubtedly the first and strongest reason for instituting a distinction among meats was to discourage the Israelites from spreading into other countries, and from general intercourse with the world—to prevent them acquiring familiarity with the inhabitants of the countries bordering on Canaan, so as to fall into their idolatries or be contaminated with their vices: in short, to keep them a distinct and peculiar people. To this purpose, no difference of creed, no system of polity, no diversity of language or manner, was so subservient as a distinction of meats founded on religion; and hence the Jews, who were taught by education to abhor many articles of food freely partaken of by other people, never, even during periods of great degeneracy, could amalgamate with the nations among which they were dispersed. But although this was the principal foundation of these laws, dietetic reasons also had weight; for there is no doubt that the flesh of many of the animals here ranked as unclean, is everywhere, but especially in warm climates, less wholesome and adapted for food than those which were allowed to be eaten. These laws, therefore, being subservient to sanitary as well as religious ends, were addressed both to Moses and Aaron. **3-7. Whatsoever parteth the hoof, and is cloven-footed, and cheweth the cud**—Ruminating animals by the peculiar structure of their stomachs digest their food more fully than others. It is found that in the act of chewing the cud, a large portion of the poisonous properties of noxious plants eaten by them, passes off by the salivary glands. This power of secreting the poisonous effects of vegetables, is said to be particularly remarkable in cows and goats, whose mouths are often sore, and sometimes bleed, in consequence. Their flesh is therefore in a better state for food, as it contains more of the nutritious juices, is more easily digested in the human stomach, and is consequently more easily assimilated. Animals which do not chew the cud, convert their food less perfectly; their flesh is therefore unwholesome, from the gross animal juices with

ADAM CLARKE — CHAPTER 11

1. *And the Lord spake unto Moses.* Having delivered the law against drinking wine, Moses proceeds to deliver a series of ordinances, all well calculated to prevent the Israelites from mixing with the surrounding nations, and consequently from being contaminated by their idolatry. In chap. xi he treats of unclean meats. In chaps. xii, xiii, xiv, and xv he treats of unclean persons, garments, and dwellings. In chap. xvi he treats of the uncleanness of the priests and the people, and prescribes the proper expiations and sacrifices for both. In chap. xvii he continues the subject, and gives particular directions concerning the mode of offering. In chap. xviii he treats of unclean matrimonial connections. In chap. xix he repeats sundry laws relative to these subjects, and introduces some new ones. In chap. xx he mentions certain uncleannesses practiced among the idolatrous nations, and prohibits them on pain of death. In chap. xxi he treats of the mourning, marriages, and personal defects of the priests, which rendered them unclean. And in chap. xxii he speaks of unclean sacrifices, or such as should not be offered to the Lord. After this, to the close of the book, many important and excellent political and domestic regulations are enjoined, the whole forming an ecclesiastico-political system superior to anything the world ever saw.

3. *Whatsoever parteth the hoof, and is cloven-footed.* These two words mean the same thing—a divided hoof, such as that of the ox, where the hoof is divided into two toes, and each toe is cased with horn. *Cheweth the cud.* Ruminates; casts up the grass which had been taken into the stomach for the purpose of mastication.

MATTHEW HENRY

Those beasts that did not both *chew the cud and divide the hoof* were unclean, by which rule the flesh of swine, and of hares, and of rabbits, was prohibited to them, though commonly used among us.

Of all the creatures here forbidden as unclean, none has been more dreaded and detested by the pious Jews than swine's flesh. Many were put to death by Antiochus because they would not eat it. Some suggest that the prohibition of these beasts as unclean was intended to be a caution to the people against the bad qualities of these creatures. We must not be filthy nor wallow in the mire as swine, nor be timorous and faint-hearted as hares, nor dwell in the earth as rabbits; let not man that is in honour make himself like these beasts that perish.

Verses 9–19

Here is, 1. A general rule concerning fishes, which were clean and which not. All that had fins and scales they might eat, and only those odd sorts of water-animals that have not were forbidden, *v.* 9, 10. Concerning the prohibited fish it is said, *They shall be an abomination to you* (*v.* 10–12), that is, "You shall count them unclean, and not only not eat of them, but keep at a distance from them." Thus God's spiritual Israel, as they are dignified above others by the gospel-covenant of adoption and friendship, so they must be mortified more than others by the gospel-commands of self-denial and bearing the cross. 2. Concerning fowls here is no general rule given, but a particular enumeration of those fowls that they must abstain from as unclean, which implies an allowance of all others.

Of the fowls here forbidden, (1) Some are birds of prey, as the eagle, vulture, &c., and God would have his people to abhor every thing that is barbarous and cruel, and not to live by blood and rapine. Doves that are preyed upon were fit to be food for man and offerings to God; but kites and hawks that prey upon them must be looked upon as an abomination to God and man.

JAMIESON, FAUSSET, BROWN

which they abound, and is apt to produce scorbutic and scrofulous disorders. But the animals that may be eaten are those which "part the hoof as well as chew the cud," and this is another means of freeing the flesh of the animal from noxious substances. "In the case of animals with parted hoofs, when feeding in unfavorable situations a prodigious amount of fœtid matter is discharged, and passes off between the toes; while animals with undivided hoofs, feeding on the same ground, become severely affected in the legs, from the poisonous plants among the pasture" [WHITLAW'S *Code of Health*]. All experience attests this, and accordingly the use of ruminating animals (that is, those which both chew the cud and part the hoof) has always obtained in most countries though it was observed most carefully by the people who were favored with the promulgation of God's law. **4. the camel**–It does to a certain extent divide the hoof, for the foot consists of two large parts, but the division is not complete; the toes rest upon an elastic pad on which the animal goes; as a beast of burden its flesh is tough. An additional reason for its prohibition might be to keep the Israelites apart from the descendants of Ishmael. **5. the coney**–not the rabbit, for it is not found in Palestine or Arabia, but the hyrax, a little animal of the size and general shape of the rabbit, but differing from it in several essential features. It has no tail, singular, long hairs bristling like thorns among the fur on its back; its feet are bare, its nails flat and round, except those on each inner toe of the hind feet, which are sharp and project like an awl. It does not burrow in the ground but frequents the clefts of rocks. **6. the hare**–Two species of hare must have been pointed at: the Sinai hare–the hare of the desert, small and generally brown; the other, the hare of Palestine and Syria, about the size and appearance of that known in our own country. Neither the hare nor the coney are really ruminating. They only appear to be so from working the jaws on the grasses they live on. They are not cloven-footed; and besides, it is said that from the great quantity of down upon them, they are very much subject to vermin–that in order to expel these, they eat poisonous plants, and if used as food while in that state, they are most deleterious [WHITLAW]. **7. the swine**–It is a filthy, foul-feeding animal, and it lacks one of the natural provisions for purifying the system, "it cheweth not the cud"; in hot climates indulgence in swine's flesh is particularly liable to produce leprosy, scurvy, and various cutaneous eruptions. It was therefore strictly avoided by the Israelites. Its prohibition was further necessary to prevent their adopting many of the grossest idolatries practised by neighboring nations. **9. These shall ye eat . . . whatsoever hath fins and scales**–"The fins and scales are the means by which the excrescences of fish are carried off, the same as in animals by perspiration. I have never known an instance of disease produced by eating such fish; but those that have no fins and scales cause, in hot climates, the most malignant disorders when eaten; in many cases they prove a mortal poison" [WHITLAW]. **12. Whatsoever hath no fins nor scales,** etc.–Under this classification frogs, eels, shellfish of all descriptions, were included as unclean; "many of the latter (shellfish) enjoy a reputation they do not deserve, and have, when plentifully partaken of, produced effects which have led to a suspicion of their containing something of a poisonous nature." **13-19. these are they which ye shall have in** particularly ranked in the class unclean; all those **abomination among the fowls**–All birds of prey are which feed on flesh and carrion. No less than twenty species of birds, all probably then known, are mentioned under this category, and the inference follows that all which are not mentioned were allowed; that is, fowls which subsist on vegetable substances. From our imperfect knowledge of the natural history of Palestine, Arabia, and the contiguous countries at that time, it is not easy to determine exactly what some of the prohibited birds were; although they must have been all well known among the people to whom these laws were given. **the ossifrage**–*Hebrew*, "bone-breaker," rendered in the Septuagint *griffon*, supposed to be the *Gypætos barbatus*, the Lammer Geyer of the Swiss–a bird of the eagle or vulture species, inhabiting the highest mountain ranges in Western Asia as well as Europe. It pursues as its prey the chamois, ibex, or marmot, among rugged cliffs, till it drives them over a precipice–thus obtaining the name of "bone-breaker." **the ospray**–the black eagle, among the smallest, but swiftest and strongest of its kind. **the vulture**–The word so rendered in our version means more probably "the kite" or "glede" and describes

ADAM CLARKE

5. *The coney. Shaphan,* not the rabbit, but rather a creature nearly resembling it, which abounds in Judea, Palestine, and Arabia.

6. *The hare. Arnebeth,* as Bochart and others suppose, from *arah,* to "crop," and *nib,* the "produce of the ground," these animals being remarkable for destroying the fruits of the earth. That they are notorious for destroying the tender blade of the young corn is well known. It is very likely that different species of these animals are included under the general terms *shaphan,* and *arnebeth,* for some travellers have observed that there are four or five sorts of these animals, which are used for food in the present day in those countries.

7. *And the swine. Chazir,* one of the most gluttonous, libidinous, and filthy quadrupeds in the universe; and because of these qualities sacred to the Venus of the Greeks and Romans, and the Friga of our Saxon ancestors; and perhaps on these accounts forbidden, as well as on account of its flesh being strong and difficult to digest, affording a very gross kind of aliment, apt to produce disorders, especially in hot climates.

9. *Whatsoever hath fins and scales.* Because these, of all the fish tribe, are the most nourishing; the others which are without scales, or whose bodies are covered with a thick, glutinous matter, being in general very difficult of digestion.

13. *And these . . . among the fowls . . . the eagle. Nesher,* from *nashar,* to "lacerate, cut, or tear to pieces"; hence the *eagle,* a most rapacious bird of prey, from its tearing the flesh of the animals it feeds on; and for this purpose birds of prey have, in general, strong, crooked talons and a hooked beak. *The ossifrage.* Or bone-breaker, from *os,* a "bone," and *frango,* "I break," because it not only strips off the flesh, but breaks the bone in order to extract the marrow. In Hebrew it is called *peres,* from *paras,* to "break or divide in two," and probably signifies that species of the eagle anciently known by the name of *ossifraga,* and which we render "ossifrage." *Ospray. Ozniyah,* from *azan,* to be "strong, vigorous"; generally supposed to mean the black eagle, such as that described by Homer, *Iliad,* lib. xxi, v. 252. "Having the rapidity of the black eagle, that bird of prey, at once the swiftest and the strongest of the feathered race." Among the Greeks and Romans the eagle was held sacred, and is represented as carrying the thunderbolts of Jupiter.

14. *The vulture. Daah,* from the root "to fly," and therefore more probably the kite or glede, from its remarkable property of gliding or

MATTHEW HENRY

(2) Others of them are solitary birds, that abide in dark and desolate places, as the owl and the pelican (Ps. cii. 6), and the cormorant and raven (Isa. xxxiv. 11); for God's Israel should not be a melancholy people, nor affect sadness and constant solitude.

F. B. MEYER:

The distinction between clean and unclean. There were good and sufficient reasons for excluding certain animals from Israel's diet. Devout medical men insist that this is the finest sanitary code in existence, and that many of the diseases of modern life would disappear if it were universally adopted. God made these distinctions matters of religion that the well-being of his people might be doubly assured. These restrictions were also imposed to erect strong barriers between the Chosen People and the heathen. So long as they obeyed, it was clearly impossible to participate in the heathen festivals, where many of these animals were partaken of.

We are not now bound by these enactments. Our Lord made all meats clean (Mark 7:19). Peter was bidden to kill and eat all manner of creeping things, and his protest was overborne by the assurance that God had cleansed all (Acts 10:11–16). Religion consists not in outward rites, but in the inward temper (Heb. 9:9, 10). Note that touching was forbidden, because the least contact with evil hurts the soul.

—Bible Commentary

(3) Others of them feed upon that which is impure, as the stork on serpents, others of them on worms; and we must not only abstain from all impurity ourselves, but from communion with those that allow themselves in it. (4) Others of them were used by the Egyptians and other Gentiles in their divinations. Some birds were reckoned fortunate, others ominous; and their soothsayers had great regard to the flights of these birds, all which therefore must be an abomination to God's people, who must not learn the way of the heathen.

Verses 20–42

Here is the law, 1. Concerning flying insects, as flies, wasps, bees, &c.; these they might not eat (*v.* 20), nor indeed are they fit to be eaten;

JAMIESON, FAUSSET, BROWN

a varying but majestic flight, exactly that of the kite, which now darts forward with the rapidity of an arrow, now rests motionless on its expanded wings in the air. It feeds on small birds, insects, and fish. **the kite**—the vulture. In Egypt and perhaps in the adjoining countries also, the kite and vulture are often seen together flying in company, or busily pursuing their foul but important office of devouring the carrion and relics of putrefying flesh, which might otherwise pollute the atmosphere. **after his kind**—i.e., the prohibition against eating it extended to the whole species. **the raven**—including the crow, the pie. **the owl**—It is generally supposed the ostrich is denoted by the original word. **the nighthawk**—a very small bird, with which, from its nocturnal habits, many superstitious ideas were associated. **the cuckoo**—Evidently some other bird is meant by the original term, from its being ranged among rapacious birds. DR. SHAW thinks it is the safsaf; but that, being a graminivorous and gregarious bird, is equally objectionable. Others think that the sea mew, or some of the small seafowl, is intended. **the hawk**—The *Hebrew* word includes every variety of the falcon family—as the goshawk, the jerhawk, the sparrow hawk, etc. Several species of hawks are found in Western Asia and Egypt, where they find inexhaustible prey in the immense numbers of pigeons and turtledoves that abound in those quarters. The hawk was held pre-eminently sacred among the Egyptians; and this, besides its rapacious disposition and gross habits, might have been a strong reason for its prohibition as an article of food to the Israelites. **the little owl**—or horned owl, as some render it. The common barn owl, which is well known in the East. It is the only bird of its kind here referred to, although the word is thrice mentioned in our version. **cormorant**—supposed to be the gull. **the great owl**—according to some, the Ibis of the Egyptians. It was well known to the Israelites, and so rendered by the *Septuagint* (Deut. 14:16; Isa. 34:11): according to PARKHURST, the bittern, but not determined. **the swan**—found in great numbers in all the countries of the Levant. It frequents marshy places—the vicinity of rivers and lakes. It was held sacred by the Egyptians, and kept tame within the precincts of heathen temples. It was probably on this account chiefly that its use as food was prohibited. MICHAELIS considers it the goose. **the pelican**—remarkable for the bag or pouch under its lower jaw which serves not only as a net to catch, but also as a receptacle of food. It is solitary in its habits and, like other large aquatic birds, often flies to a great distance from its favorite haunts. **the gier eagle**—Being here associated with waterfowl, it has been questioned whether any species of eagle is referred to. Some think, as the original name *racham* denotes "*tenderness*," "*affection*," the halcyon or kingfisher is intended [CALMET]. Others think that it is the bird now called the *rachami*, a kind of Egyptian vulture, abundant in the streets of Cairo and popularly called Pharaoh's fowl. It is white in color, in size like a raven, and feeds on carrion; it is one of the foulest and filthiest birds in the world. **the stork**—a bird of benevolent temper and held in the highest estimation in all Eastern countries; it was declared unclean, probably, from its feeding on serpents and other venomous reptiles, as well as rearing its young on the same food.

the heron—The word so translated only occurs in the prohibited list of food and has been variously rendered—the crane, the plover, the woodcock, the parrot. In this great diversity of opinion nothing certain can be affirmed regarding it. Judging from the group with which it is classified, it must be an aquatic bird that is meant. It may as well be the heron as any other bird, the more especially as herons abound in Egypt and in the Hauran of Palestine.

the lapwing—or hoopoe—found in warm regions, a very pretty but filthy species of bird. It was considered unclean, probably from its feeding on insects, worms, and snails. **the bat**—the great or Ternat bat, known in the East, noted for its voracity and filthiness. **20. All fowls that creep,** etc.—By "fowls" here are to be understood all creatures with wings and "going upon all fours," not a restriction to animals which have exactly four feet, because many "creeping things" have more than that number. The prohibition is regarded generally as extending to insects, reptiles, and worms.

ADAM CLARKE

sailing with expanded wings through the air. The *daah* is a different bird from the *daiyah*, which signifies the vulture. *The kite. Aiyah*, thought by some to be the vulture. That it is a species of the hawk, most learned men allow.

15. *Every raven. Oreb*, a general term comprehending the raven, crow, rook, jackdaw, and magpie.

16. *The owl. Bath haiyaanah*, the "daughter of vociferation," the female ostrich, probably so called from the noise it makes. *The night hawk. Tachmas*, from *chamas*, to "force away, act violently and unjustly"; supposed by Bochart to signify the male ostrich, from its cruelty towards its young (see Job xxxix. 17-19); but others, with more reason, suppose it to be the bird described by Hasselquist, which he calls the Oriental owl. *The cuckow. Shachaph*, supposed rather to mean the sea mew; called *shachaph*, from *shachepheth*, a "wasting distemper," or "atrophy" (mentioned in chap. xxvi. 16; Deut. xxviii. 22), because its body is the leanest, in proportion to its bones and feathers, of most other birds, always appearing as if under the influence of a wasting distemper. *And the hawk. Nets*, from the root *natsah*, to "shoot forth or spring forward," because of the rapidity and length of its flight, the hawk being remarkable for both. As this is a bird of prey, it is forbidden, and all others of its kind.

17. *The little owl. Cos*, the bittern, night raven or night owl, according to most interpreters. *The cormorant. Shalach*, from the root which signifies to "cast down"; hence the Septuagint, the "cataract," or bird which falls precipitately down upon its prey. It probably signifies the diver, a sea fowl, which I have seen at sea dart down as swift as an arrow into the water and seize the fish which it had discovered while even flying, or rather soaring, at a very great height. *The great owl. Yanshuph*, according to the Septuagint and the Vulgate, signifies the ibis, a bird well known and held sacred in Egypt.

18. *The swan. Tinshemeth.* The Septuagint translate the word by *porphyrion*, "purple" or "scarlet" bird. Could we depend on this translation, we might suppose the flamingo or some such bird to be intended. *The pelican. Kaath.* As *kaah* signifies to "vomit up," the name is supposed to be descriptive of the pelican, who receives its food into the pouch under its lower jaw, and, by pressing it on its breast with its bill, throws it up for the nourishment of its young. *The gier eagle. Racham.* As the root of this word signifies "tenderness" and "affection," it is supposed to refer to some bird remarkable for its attachment to its young; hence some have thought that the pelican is to be understood.

19. *The stork. Chasidah*, from *chasad*, which signifies "to be abundant in kindness, or exuberant in acts of beneficence"; hence applied to the stork, because of its affection to its young, and its kindness in tending and feeding its parents when old, facts attested by the best informed and most judicious of the Greek and Latin natural historians. It is remarkable for destroying and eating serpents, and on this account might be reckoned by Moses among *unclean* birds. *The heron. Anaphah.* This word has been variously understood: some have rendered it the kite, others the woodcock, others the curlew, some the peacock, others the parrot, and others the crane. The root, *anaph*, signifies to "breathe short" through the nostrils, to "snuff," as in anger; hence "to be angry"; and it is supposed that the word is sufficiently descriptive of the heron, from its very irritable disposition. It will attack even a man in defense of its nest; and I have known a case where a man was in danger of losing his life by the stroke of a heron's bill, near the eye, who had climbed up into a high tree to take its nest. *The lapwing. Duchiphath*, the hoop, a crested bird, with beautiful plumage, but very unclean. *The bat. Atalleph*, so called, according to Parkhurst, from *at*, to "fly," and *alaph*, "darkness or obscurity," because it flies about in the dusk of the evening, and in the night.

20. *All fowls that creep.* Such as the bat, already mentioned, which has claws attached to its leathern wings, and which serve in place of feet to crawl by, the feet and legs not being distinct; but this may also include all the dif-

MATTHEW HENRY

but there were several sorts of locusts which in those countries were very good meat, and much used: John Baptist lived upon them in the desert, and they are here allowed them, *v.* 21, 22.

2. Concerning the creeping things on the earth; these were all forbidden (*v.* 29, 30), and again, *v.* 41, 42. Dust is the meat of the creeping things, and therefore they are not fit to be man's meat.

3. Concerning the dead carcases of all these unclean animals. (1) Every one that touched them was to be unclean until the evening, *v.* 24–28. It was a *ceremonial* uncleanness they contracted, which for the time forbade them to come into the tabernacle, or to eat of any of the holy things, or so much as to converse familiarly with their neighbours. But the uncleanness continued only till the evening. And we must learn, by daily renewing our repentance every night for the sins of the day, to cleanse ourselves from the pollution we contract by them, that we may not lie down in our uncleanness. (2) Even the vessels, or other things they fell upon, were thereby made unclean until the evening (*v.* 32), and if they were earthen vessels they must be broken, *v.* 33. We ought as industriously to preserve our precious souls from the pollutions of sin, and as speedily to cleanse them when they are polluted, as they were to preserve and cleanse their bodies and household goods from those ceremonial pollutions.

JAMIESON, FAUSSET, BROWN

21. Yet these may ye eat of every flying creeping thing that goeth upon all four, which have legs above their feet—Nothing short of a scientific description could convey more accurately the nature "of the locust after its kind." They were allowed as lawful food to the Israelites, and they are eaten by the Arabs, who fry them in olive oil.—When sprinkled with salt, dried, smoked, and fried, they are said to taste not unlike red herrings.

26. every beast . . . not cloven-footed—The prohibited animals under this description include not only the beasts which have a single hoof, as horses and asses, but those also which divided the foot into paws, as lions, tigers, etc.

29. the weasel—rather, the mole. **the mouse**—From its diminutive size it is placed among the reptiles instead of the quadrupeds. **the tortoise**—a lizard, resembling very nearly in shape, and in the hard pointed scales of the tail, the shaketail.

30. the ferret—the *Hebrew* word is thought by some to signify the newt or chameleon, by others the frog. **the chameleon**—called by the Arabs the warral, a green lizard.

the snail—a lizard which lives in the sand, and is called by the Arabs *chulca,* of an azure color. **the mole**—Another species of lizard is meant, probably the chameleon.

31-35. whosoever doth touch them, when . . . dead, shall be unclean until the even—These regulations must have often caused annoyance by suddenly requiring the exclusion of people from society, as well as the ordinances of religion. Nevertheless they were extremely useful and salutary, especially as enforcing attention to cleanliness. This is a matter of essential importance in the East, where venomous reptiles often creep into houses and are found lurking in boxes, vessels, or holes in the wall; and the carcass of one of them, or a dead mouse, mole, lizard, or other unclean animal, might be inadvertently touched by the hand, or fall on clothes, skin-bottles, or any article of common domestic use. By connecting, therefore, the touch of such creatures with ceremonial defile-

ADAM CLARKE

ferent kinds of insects, with the exceptions in the following verse. *Going upon all four.* May signify no more than walking regularly or progressively, foot after foot as quadrupeds do; for it cannot be applied to insects literally, as they have in general six feet, many of them more, some reputed to have a hundred, hence called "centipedes."

21. *Which have legs above their feet.* This appears to refer to the different kinds of locusts and grasshoppers, which have very remarkable hind legs, long, and with high joints, projecting above their backs, by which they are enabled to spring up from the ground, and leap high and far.

22. *The locust. Arbeh,* either from *arab,* to "lie in wait or in ambush," because often immense flights of them suddenly alight upon the fields, vineyards, etc., and destroy all the produce of the earth; or from *rabah,* he "multiplied," because of their prodigious swarms. *The bald locust. Solam,* compounded, says Mr. Parkhurst, from *sala,* to "cut, break," and *am,* "contiguity"; a kind of locust, probably so called from its rugged, craggy form. *The beetle. Chargol.* "The Hebrew name seems a derivative from *charag,* to shake, and *regel,* the foot; and so to denote the nimbleness of its motions. Thus in English we call an animal of the locust kind a grasshopper."—Parkhurst. This word occurs only in this place. The *beetle* never can be intended here, as that insect never was eaten by man, perhaps, in any country of the universe. *The grasshopper. Chagab.* Bochart supposes that this species of locust has its name from the Arabic verb *hajaba,* to "veil"; because when they fly, as they often do, in great swarms, they eclipse even the light of the sun.

27. *Whatsoever goeth upon his paws. Cappaiv,* his "palms" or "hands," probably referring to those animals whose feet resemble the hands and feet of the human being, such as apes, monkeys, and all creatures of that genus; together with bears, frogs, etc.

29. *The weasel. Choled,* from *chalad,* to "creep in." Bochart conjectures, with great propriety, that the mole, not the weasel, is intended by the Hebrew word; its property of digging into the earth, and creeping or burrowing under the surface, is well known. *The mouse. Achbar.* Probably the large field rat. *The tortoise. Tsab.* Most critics allow that the tortoise is not intended here, but rather the crocodile, the frog, or the toad. The frog is most probably the animal meant, and all other creatures of its kind.

30. *The ferret. Anakah,* from *anak,* to "groan, to cry out"; a species of lizard which derives its name from its piercing, doleful cry. *The chameleon. Coach. Cach,* to be "strong, firm, vigorous"; it is probably the same with the mongoose, a creature still well known in India, where it is often domesticated in order to keep the houses free from snakes, rats, mice. *The lizard. Letaah.* Bochart contends that this also is a species of lizard, which creeps close to the ground, and is poisonous. *The snail. Chomet,* another species of lizard, according to Bochart, which lives chiefly in the sand. *The mole. Tinshameth,* from *nasham,* to "breathe." Bochart seems to have proved that this is the chameleon, which has its Hebrew name from its wide, gaping mouth, very large lungs, and its deriving its nourishment from small animals which float in the air, so that it has been conjectured by some to feed on the air itself. A bird of the same name is mentioned v. 13, which Bochart supposes to be the night owl.

32. *Any vessel of wood.* Such as the wooden bowls still in use among the Arabs. *Or raiment, or skin*—any baskets covered with skins, another part of the furniture of an Arab tent; the goatskins, in which they churn their milk, also may be intended. *Or sack*—any haircloth used for the purpose of transporting goods from place to place.

33. *And every earthen vessel.* Such pitchers as are commonly used for drinking out of and for holding liquids. M. De la Roque observes that hair sacks, trunks, and baskets, covered with skin, are used among the travelling Arabs to carry their household utensils in, which are kettles or pots, great wooden bowls, hand mills,

MATTHEW HENRY

Verses 43-47

Here is, I. The exposition of this law, or a key to let us into the meaning of it. It was not intended merely for a bill of fare, or as the directions of a physician about their diet, but God would hereby teach them to sanctify themselves and to be holy, *v.* 44. These *rudiments of the world* were their tutors and governors (Gal. iv. 2, 3), to bring them to that which is the revival of our first state in Adam and the earnest of our best state with Christ, that is, *holiness*, without which no man shall see the Lord. This is indeed the great design of all the ordinances, that by them we may sanctify ourselves and learn to be holy. Even this law concerning their food, which seemed to stoop so very low, aimed thus high. *Without holiness no man shall see the Lord.* If it was such a provocation for a man to eat swine's flesh himself, much more it must be so to offer swine's blood at God's altar; see Prov. xv. 8.

II. The reasons of this law. 1. *I am the Lord your God, v.* 44. "Therefore you are bound to do thus, in pure obedience." 2. *I am holy, v.* 44, and again, *v.* 45. If God be holy, we must be so, else we cannot expect to be accepted of him. All these ceremonial restraints were designed to teach us that we must not *fashion ourselves according to our former lusts in our ignorance*, 1 Pet. 1. 14. 3. *I am the Lord that bringeth you out of the land of Egypt, v.* 45. He that had done more for them than for any other people might justly expect more from them.

III. The conclusion of this statute: *This is the law of the beasts, and of the fowl*, &c., *v.* 46, 47. This law was to them a statute for ever, that is, as long as that economy lasted; but under the gospel we find it expressly repealed by a voice from heaven to Peter (Acts x. 15), as it had before been virtually set aside by the death of Christ, with the other ordinances that *perished in the using*. And now we are sure that *meat commends us not to God* (1 Cor. viii. 8), and that *nothing is unclean of itself* (Rom. xiv. 14), nor does that defile a man which goes into his mouth, but that which comes out from the heart, Matt. xv. 11. Let us therefore, 1. Give thanks to God that we are not under this yoke, but that to us every creature of God is allowed as good. 2. *Stand fast in the liberty wherewith Christ has made us free.* 3. Be strictly and conscientiously temperate in the use of the good creatures God has allowed us. Nature is content with little, grace with less, but lust with nothing.

JAMIESON, FAUSSET, BROWN

ment, which required immediately to be removed, an effectual means was taken to prevent the bad effects of venom and all unclean or noxious matter.

47. make a difference between the unclean and the clean–i.e., between animals used and not used for food. It is probable that the laws contained in this chapter were not entirely new, but only gave the sanction of divine enactment to ancient usages. Some of the prohibited animals have, on physiological grounds, been everywhere rejected by the general sense or experience of mankind; while others may have been declared unclean from their unwholesomeness in warm countries of from some reasons, which are now imperfectly known, connected with contemporary idolatry.

ADAM CLARKE

and pitchers. It is very likely that these are nearly the same with those used by the Israelites in their journeyings in the wilderness.

35. *Ranges for pots.* To understand this, we must observe that the Arabs dig a hole in their tent, about a foot and a half deep; three-fourths of this they lay about with stones, and the fourth part is left open for the purpose of throwing in their fuel.

36. *A fountain or pit.* This must either refer to running water, the stream of which soon carries off all impurities, or to large reservoirs where the water soon purifies itself; the water in either which touched the unclean thing being considered as impure, the rest of the water being clean.

37. *Any sowing seed.* If any part of an impure carcass fall accidentally on seed about to be sown, it shall not on that account be deemed unclean; but if the water put to the seed to prepare it for being sown shall be touched by such impure carcass, the seed shall be considered as unclean, v. 38. Probably this may be the meaning of these passages.

42. *Whatsoever goeth upon the belly.* This is the middle verse of the Pentateuch. Whatsoever *hath more feet.* Than four; that is, all many-footed reptiles, as well as those which go upon the belly having no feet, such as serpents; besides the four-footed smaller animals mentioned above.

44. *Ye shall . . . sanctify yourselves.* You shall keep yourselves separate from all the people of the earth, that *ye shall be holy; for I am holy.* And this was the grand design of God in all these prohibitions and commands; for these external sanctifications were only the emblems of the internal purity which the holiness of God requires here, and without which none can dwell with Him in glory hereafter.

MATTHEW HENRY

CHAPTER 12

Verses 1-5

The law here pronounces women lying-in ceremonially unclean. The Jews say, "The law extended even to an abortion, if the child was so formed as that the sex was distinguishable." 1. There was some time of strict separation immediately after the birth. During these days she was separated from her husband and friends, and those that necessarily attended her were ceremonially unclean, which was one reason why the males were not circumcised till the eighth day, because they participated in the mother's pollution during the days of her separation. 2. There was also a longer time appointed for their purifying. During this time they were only separated from the sanctuary and forbidden to eat of the passover, or peace-offerings, or, if a priest's wife, to eat of any thing that was holy to the Lord. If sin had not entered, nothing but purity and honour had attended all the productions of that great blessing, *Be fruitful and multiply*. The exclusion of the woman for so many days from the sanctuary, and all participation of the holy things, signified that our original corruption would have excluded us for ever from the enjoyment of God and his favours if he had not graciously provided for our purifying.

Verses 6-8

A woman that had lain in, when the time set for her return to the sanctuary had come, must bring her offerings, *v.* 6. 1. A *burnt-offering*; a lamb if she was able; if poor, a pigeon. This she was to offer in thankfulness to God for his mercy to her, in bringing her safely through the pains of child-bearing and all the perils of child-bed, and in desire and hopes of God's further favour both to her and to the child. When a child is born there is joy and there is hope, and therefore it was proper to bring this offering. But, besides this, 2. She must offer a *sin-offering*, which must be the same for poor and rich, a turtle-dove or a young pigeon; for, whatever difference there may be between rich and poor in the sacrifices of acknowledgment, that of atonement is the same for both. This sin-offering was intended

JAMIESON, FAUSSET, BROWN

CHAPTER 12

VSS. 1-8. WOMAN'S UNCLEANNESS BY CHILDBIRTH. **2. If a woman,** etc.–The mother of a boy was ceremonially unclean for a week, at the end of which the child was circumcised (Gen. 17:12; Rom. 4:11-13); the mother of a girl for two weeks–a stigma on the sex (I Tim. 2:14, 15) for sin, which was removed by Christ; everyone who came near her during that time contracted a similar defilement. After these periods, visitors might approach her though she was still excluded from the public ordinances of religion.

6-8. the days of her purifying–Though the occasion was of a festive character, yet the sacrifices appointed were not a peace offering, but a burnt offering and sin offering, in order to impress the mind of the parent with recollections of the origin of sin, and that the child inherited a fallen and sinful nature. The offerings were to be presented the day after the period of her separation had ended–i.e., forty-first for a boy, eighty-first for a girl.

bring two turtles, etc.–(See on ch. 5:7). This was the offering made by Mary, the mother of Jesus, and it affords an incontestable proof of the poor and humble condition of the family (Luke 2:22-24).

ADAM CLARKE

CHAPTER 12

3. *And in the eighth day.* Before this time the child could scarcely be considered as having strength sufficient to bear the operation; after this time it was not necessary to delay it as the child was not considered to be in covenant with God, and consequently not under the especial protection of the divine providence and grace, till this rite had been performed. Circumcision was to every man a constant, evident sign of the covenant into which he had entered with God, and of the moral obligations under which he was thereby laid. It was also a means of purity, and was especially necessary among a people naturally incontinent, and in a climate not peculiarly favorable to chastity.

4. *The blood of her purifying.* The term *purifying* here does not imply that there is anything impure in the blood at this time; on the contrary, the blood is pure, perfectly so, as to its quality, but is excessive in quantity.

6. *When the days of her purifying.* It is not easy to account for the difference in the times of purification, after the birth of a male and female child. After the birth of a boy the mother was considered unclean for forty days; after the birth of a girl, fourscore days. There is probably no physical reason for this difference. *She shall bring . . . a burnt offering, and . . . a sin offering.* It is likely that all these ordinances were intended to show man's natural impurity and original defilement by sin, and the necessity of an atonement to cleanse the soul from unrighteousness.

8. *And if she be not able to bring a lamb, then she shall bring two turtles, or two young pigeons.* As the Virgin Mary brought only the latter, hence it is evident that she was not able, i.e., she was not rich enough to provide the former; for such a holy woman would not have brought the less offering had she been capable of bringing the greater. How astonishing is this! The

MATTHEW HENRY

either, (1) To complete her purification from that ceremonial uncleanness which, though it was not in itself sinful, yet was typical of moral pollution; or, (2) To make atonement for that which was really sin, either an inordinate desire of the blessing of children or discontent or impatience under the pains of child-bearing. According to this law, we find that the mother of our blessed Lord, though he was not conceived in sin as others, yet *accomplished the days of purification*, and then presented her son to the Lord, being a first-born, and brought her own offering, *a pair of turtle-doves*, Luke ii. 22-24. So poor were Christ's parents that they were not able to bring a lamb for a burnt-offering; and so early was Christ *made under the law, to redeem those that were under it.*

JAMIESON, FAUSSET, BROWN

ADAM CLARKE

only Heir to the throne of David was not able to bring a lamb to offer in sacrifice to God!

The priest shall make an atonement for her. Every act of man is sinful, but such as proceed from the influence of the grace and mercy of God. Her sorrow in conception, and her pain in bringing forth children, reminded the woman of her original offense—an offense which deserved death, an offense which she could not expiate, and for which a sacrifice must be offered; and in reference to better things the life of an animal must be offered as a ransom for her life. And being saved in childbed, though she deserved to die, she is required, as soon as the days of her separation were ended, to bring a sacrifice according to her ability to the priest, that he might offer it to God as an atonement for her. Thus, wherever God keeps up the remembrance of *sin*, He keeps up also the memorial of *sacrifice*, to show that the state of a sinner, howsoever deplorable, is not hopeless, for that He himself has found out a ransom.

MATTHEW HENRY

CHAPTER 13

Verses 1-17

I. Concerning the plague of leprosy we may observe in general, That it was rather an uncleanness than a disease; or, at least, so the law considered it, and therefore employed not the physicians but the priests about it. Christ is said to cleanse lepers, not to cure them. We do not read of any that died of the leprosy, but it rather buried them alive, by rendering them unfit for conversation with any but such as were infected like themselves. It is said to have begun first in Egypt, whence it spread into Syria. The Jews retained the idolatrous customs they had learnt in Egypt, and therefore God justly caused this with some others of the diseases of Egypt to follow them. Yet we read of Naaman the Syrian, who was a leper, 2 Kings v. 1. There were other breakings-out in the body which did very much resemble the leprosy, but were not it, which might make a man sore and loathsome and yet not ceremonially unclean. The judgment of it was referred to the priests. Lepers were looked upon as stigmatized by the justice of God, and therefore it was left to his servants the priests, who might be presumed to know his mark best, to pronounce who were lepers and who were not. It was a figure of the moral pollution of men's minds by sin, which is the leprosy of the soul, defiling to the conscience, and from which Christ alone can cleanse us; for herein the power of his grace infinitely transcends that of the legal priesthood, that the priest could only convict the leper (for by the law is the knowledge of sin), but Christ can cure the leper, he can take away sin. *Lord, if thou wilt, thou canst make me clean*, which was more than the priests could do, Matt. viii. 2. It is a work of great importance, but of great difficulty, to judge of our spiritual state: we have all cause to suspect ourselves, being conscious to ourselves of sores and spots, but whether clean or unclean is the question.

II. Several rules are here laid down by which the judgment of the priest must be governed. 1. If the sore was but *skin-deep*, it was to be hoped it was not the *leprosy*, *v.* 4. But, if it was *deeper than the skin*, the man must be pronounced unclean, *v.* 3. The infirmities that consist with grace do not sink deep into the soul, but *the mind* still *serves the law of God*, and the *inward man delights in it*, Rom. vii. 22, 25. But if the matter be really worse than it shows, and the inwards be infected, the case is dangerous.

JAMIESON, FAUSSET, BROWN

CHAPTER 13

VSS. 1-59. THE LAWS AND TOKENS IN DISCERNING LEPROSY. **2. When a man shall have in the skin,** etc.—The fact of the following rules for distinguishing the plague of leprosy being incorporated with the Hebrew code of laws, proves the existence of the odious disease among that people. But a short time, little more than a year (if so long a period had elapsed since the exodus) when symptoms of leprosy seem extensively to have appeared among them; and as they could not be very liable to such a cutaneous disorder amid their active journeyings and in the dry open air of Arabia, the seeds of the disorder must have been laid in Egypt, where it has always been endemic. There is every reason to believe that this was the case: that the leprosy was not a family complaint, hereditary among the Hebrews, but that they got it from intercourse with the Egyptians and from the unfavorable circumstances of their condition in the house of bondage. The great excitement and irritability of the skin in the hot and sandy regions of the East produce a far greater predisposition to leprosy of all kinds than in cooler temperatures; and cracks or blotches, inflammations or even contusions of the skin, very often lead to these in Arabia and Palestine, to some extent, but particularly in Egypt. Besides, the subjugated and distressed state of the Hebrews in the latter country, and the nature of their employment, must have rendered them very liable to this as well as to various other blemishes and misaffections of the skin; in the production of which there are no causes more active or powerful than a depressed state of body and mind, hard labor under a burning sun, the body constantly covered with the excoriating dust of brickfields, and an impoverished diet—to all of which the Israelites were exposed while under the Egyptian bondage. It appears that, in consequence of these hardships, there was, even after they had left Egypt, a general predisposition among the Hebrews to the contagious forms of leprosy—so that it often occurred as a consequence of various other affections of the skin. And hence all cutaneous blemishes or blains—especially such as had a tendency to terminate in leprosy—were watched with a jealous eye from the first [GOOD'S *Study of Medicine*]. A swelling, a pimple, or bright spot on the skin, created a strong ground of suspicion of a man's being attacked by the dreaded disease. **then he shall be brought unto Aaron the priest,** etc.—Like the Egyptian priests, the Levites united the character of physician with that of the sacred office; and on the appearance of any suspicious eruptions on the skin, the person having these was brought before the priest—not, however, to receive medical treatment, though it is not improbable that some purifying remedies might be prescribed, but to be examined with a view to those sanitary precautions which it belonged to legislation to adopt. **3-6. the priest shall look on the plague in the skin of the flesh,** etc.—The leprosy, as covering the person with a white, scaly scurf, has always been accounted an offensive blemish rather than a serious malady in the East, unless when it assumed its less common and malignant forms. When a Hebrew priest, after a careful inspection, discovered under the cutaneous blemish the distinctive signs of contagious leprosy, the person was immediately pronounced unclean, and is supposed to have been sent out of the camp to a lazaretto provided for that purpose. If the

ADAM CLARKE

CHAPTER 13

2. *The plague of leprosy.* This dreadful disorder has its name *leprosy* from the Greek *lepra*, from *lepis*, a "scale," because in this disease the body was often covered with thin, white scales, so as to give it the appearance of snow. Hence it is said of the hand of Moses, Exod. iv. 6, that it was "leprous as snow"; and of Miriam, Num. xii. 10, that she became "leprous, white as snow"; and of Gehazi, 2 Kings v. 27, that, being judicially struck with the disease of Naaman, he went out from Elisha's presence "a leper as white as snow." In Hebrew this disease is termed *tsaraath*, from *tsara*, to "smite or strike."

There were three signs by which the leprosy was known: (1) A bright spot; (2) A rising (enamelling) of the surface; (3) A scab; the enamelled place producing a variety of layers, or stratum super stratum, of these scales.

3. *The priest shall . . . pronounce him unclean. Vetimme otho*; literally, "shall pollute him," i.e., in the Hebrew idiom, shall "declare or pronounce him polluted"; and in v. 23 it is said, "the priest shall pronounce him clean," *vetiharo haccohen*, the "priest shall cleanse him," i.e., "declare him clean." In this phrase we have the proper meaning of Matt. xvi. 19: "Whatsoever thou shalt bind on earth shall be bound in heaven: and whatsoever thou shalt loose on earth shall be loosed in heaven." By which our Lord intimates that the disciples, from having

MATTHEW HENRY

2. If the sore *be at a stay*, and does not *spread*, it is no leprosy, *v*, 5, 6.

But if it *spread much abroad*, and continue to do so after several inspections, the case is bad, *v*. 7, 8. If men do not grow worse, but a stop be put to the course of their sins and their corruptions be checked, it is to be hoped they will grow better; but if sin gets ground, and they become worse every day, they are going downhill.

3. If there was *proud raw flesh* in the rising, the priest needed not to wait any longer, it was certainly a leprosy, *v*. 10, 11. Nor is there any surer indication of the badness of a man's spiritual state than the heart's rising in self-conceit, confidence in the flesh, and resistance of the reproofs of the word and strivings of the Spirit. 4. If the eruption, whatever it was, *covered all the skin* from head to foot, it was no leprosy (*v*. 12, 13); for it was an evidence that the vitals were sound and strong, and nature hereby helped itself, throwing out what was burdensome and pernicious. There is hope in the small-pox when they come out well: so if men freely confess their sins, and hide them not, there is no danger comparable to theirs that cover their sins. Some gather this from it, that there is more hope of the profane than of hypocrites. The publicans and harlots went into the kingdom of heaven before scribes and Pharisees. In one respect, the sudden breakings-out of passion, though bad enough, are not so dangerous as malice concealed. Others gather this, that, if we judge ourselves, we shall not be judged; if we see and own that there is *no health in us, no soundness in our flesh*, by reason of sin, we shall *find grace in the eyes of the Lord*. 5. The priest must take time in making his judgment, and not give it rashly.

Verses 18–37

The priest is here instructed what judgment to make if there was any appearance of a leprosy, either, 1. In an old ulcer or bile, that has been healed, *v*. 18, &c. When old sores, that seemed to be cured, break out again, it is to be feared there is a leprosy in them; such is the danger of those who, having escaped the pollutions of the world, are again *entangled therein and overcome*. Or, 2. In a burn by accident, for this seems to be meant, *v*. 24, &c. The burning of strife and contention often proves the occasion of the rising up and breaking out of that corruption which witnesses to men's faces that they are unclean.

Verses 38–46

I. Provisos that neither a *freckled skin* nor a *bald head* should be mistaken for a leprosy, *v*. 38–41. Every deformity must not forthwith be made a ceremonial defilement.

II. A particular brand set upon the leprosy if at any time it did appear in a *bald head*: *The plague is in his head, he is utterly unclean*, *v*. 44. If the leprosy of sin have seized the head, if the judgment be corrupted, and wicked principles which countenance and support wicked practices, be embraced, it is an *utter uncleanness*. Soundness in the faith keeps the leprosy from the head.

JAMIESON, FAUSSET, BROWN

symptoms appeared to be doubtful, he ordered the person to be kept in domestic confinement for seven days, when he was subjected to a second examination; and if during the previous week the eruption had subsided or appeared to be harmless, he was instantly discharged. But if the eruption continued unabated and still doubtful, he was put under surveillance another week; at the end of which the character of the disorder never failed to manifest itself, and he was either doomed to perpetual exclusion from society or allowed to go at large. A person who had thus been detained on suspicion, when at length set at liberty, was obliged to "wash his clothes," as having been tainted by ceremonial pollution; and the purification through which he was required to go was, in the spirit of the Mosaic dispensation, symbolical of that inward purity it was instituted to promote. **7, 8. But if the scab spread much abroad in the skin**—Those doubtful cases, when they assumed a malignant character, appeared in one of two forms, apparently according to the particular constitution of the skin or of the habit generally. The one was "somewhat dark"—i.e., the obscure or dusky leprosy, in which the natural color of the hair (which in Egypt and Palestine is black) is not changed, as is repeatedly said in the sacred code, nor is there any depression in the dusky spot, while the patches, instead of keeping stationary to their first size, are perpetually enlarging their boundary. The patient laboring under this form was pronounced unclean by the Hebrew priest or physician, and hereby sentenced to a separation from his family and friends—a decisive proof of its being contagious. **9-37. if the rising be white**—This BRIGHT WHITE leprosy is the most malignant and inveterate of all the varieties the disease exhibits, and it was marked by the following distinctive signs:—A glossy white and spreading scale, upon an elevated base, the elevation depressed in the middle, but without a change of color; the black hair on the patches participating in the whiteness, and the scaly patches themselves perpetually enlarging their boundary. Several of these characteristics, taken separately, belong to other blemishes of the skin as well; so that none of them was to be taken alone, and it was only when the whole of them concurred that the Jewish priest, in his capacity of physician, was to pronounce the disease a malignant leprosy. If it spread over the entire frame without producing any ulceration, it lost its contagious power by degrees; or, in other words, it ran through its course and exhausted itself. In that case, there being no longer any fear of further evil, either to the individual himself or to the community, the patient was declared clean by the priest, while the dry scales were yet upon him, and restored to society. If, on the contrary, the patches ulcerated and quick or fungous flesh sprang up in them, the purulent matter of which, if brought into contact with the skin of other persons, would be taken into the constitution by means of absorbent vessels, the priest was at once to pronounce it an inveterate leprosy. A temporary confinement was them declared to be totally unnecessary, and he was regarded as unclean for life [DR. GOOD]. Other skin affections, which had a tendency to terminate in leprosy, though they were not decided symptoms when alone, were: "a boil" (vss. 18-23); "a hot burning," i.e., a fiery inflammation or carbuncle (vss. 24-28); and "a dry scall" (vss. 29-37), when the leprosy was distinguished by being deeper than the skin and the hair became thin and yellow. **38, 39. If a man . . . or a woman have in the skin of their flesh bright spots**—This modification of the leprosy is distinguished by a dull white color, and it is entirely a cutaneous disorder, never injuring the constitution. It is described as not penetrating below the skin of the flesh and as not rendering necessary an exclusion from society. It is evident, then, that this common form of leprosy is not contagious; otherwise Moses would have prescribed as strict a quarantine in this as in the other cases. And hereby we see the great superiority of the Mosaic law (which so accurately distinguished the characteristics of the leprosy and preserved to society the services of those who were laboring under the uncontagious forms of the disease) over the customs and regulations of Eastern countries in the present day, where all lepers are indiscriminately proscribed and are avoided as unfit for free intercourse with their fellow men. **40, 41. bald . . . forehead bald**—The falling off of the hair, when the baldness commences in the back part of the head, is another symptom which creates a suspicion of leprosy. But it was not of itself a decisive sign unless taken in connection with other tokens, such as a "sore of a reddish white color." The Hebrews as well as

ADAM CLARKE

the "keys," i.e., the true knowledge of the doctrine, of the kingdom of Heaven, should, from particular evidences, be at all times able to distinguish between the clean and the unclean, the sincere and the hypocrite; and pronounce a judgment as infallible as the priest did in the case of the leprosy, from the tokens already specified.

13. *If the leprosy have covered all his flesh, he shall pronounce him clean.* Why is it that the partial leper was pronounced unclean, and the person totally covered with the disease clean? This was probably owing to a different species or stage of the disease; the partial disease was contagious, the total not contagious.

29. *A plague upon the head or the beard.* This refers to a disease in which, according to the Jews, the hair on either the head or the chin dropped out by the roots.

33. *The scall shall he not shave.* Lest the place should be irritated and inflamed, and assume in consequence other appearances besides those of a leprous infection, in which case the priest might not be able to form an accurate judgment.

MATTHEW HENRY

III. Directions what must be done with the convicted leper. When the priest, upon mature deliberation, had solemnly pronounced him unclean,

1. He must pronounce himself so, *v.* 45. He must put himself into the posture of a mourner and cry, *Unclean, unclean.* He must therefore, (1) Humble himself under the mighty hand of God, not insisting upon his cleanness when the priest had pronounced him unclean. He must signify this by *rending his clothes, uncovering* his head, and *covering his upper lip,* all tokens of shame and confusion of face, and very significant of that self-loathing and self-abasement which should fill the hearts of penitents, the language of which is self-judging. (2) He must give warning to others to take heed of coming near him. Wherever he went, he must cry to those he saw at a distance, "I am *unclean, unclean,* take heed of touching me." Not that the leprosy was catching, but by the touch of a leper ceremonial uncleanness was contracted. And this was all that the law could do. The law only shows us our disease; the gospel shows us our help in Christ.

2. He must then be shut out of the camp, and afterwards, when they came to Canaan, out of the city, town, or village, where he lived, and *dwell alone* (*v.* 46), associating with none but those that were lepers like himself.

Verses 47–59

This is the law concerning the plague of leprosy in a garment, whether linen or woollen. A leprosy in a garment, with discernible indications of it, is a thing which to us now is altogether unaccountable. The process was much the same with that concerning a leprous person. The garment suspected to be tainted was not to be burnt immediately, but it must be *shown to the priest.* If, upon search, it was found that there was a *leprous spot* it must be *burnt.* If the cause of the suspicion was gone, it must be *washed,* and then might be used, *v.* 58.

JAMIESON, FAUSSET, BROWN

other Orientals were accustomed to distinguish between the forehead baldness, which might be natural, and that baldness which might be the consequence of disease. **45. the leper in whom the plague is, his clothes shall be rent,** etc.—The person who was declared affected with the leprosy forthwith exhibited all the tokens of suffering from a heavy calamity. Rending garments and uncovering the head were common signs of mourning. As to "the putting a covering upon the upper lip," that means either wearing a moustache, as the Hebrews used to shave the upper lip [CALMET], or simply keeping a hand over it. All these external marks of grief were intended to proclaim, in addition to his own exclamation "Unclean!" that the person was a leper, whose company every one must shun. **46. he shall dwell alone; without the camp**—in a lazaretto by himself, or associated with other lepers (II Kings 7:3, 8). **47-59. The garment . . . that the . . . leprosy is in**—It is well known that infectious diseases, such as scarlet fever, measles, the plague, are latently imbibed and carried by the clothes. But the language of this passage clearly indicates a disease to which clothes themselves were subject, and which was followed by effects on them analogous to those which malignant leprosy produces on the human body—for similar regulations were made for the rigid inspection of suspected garments by a priest as for the examination of a leprous person. It has long been conjectured and recently ascertained by the use of a lens, that the leprous condition of swine is produced by myriads of minute insects engendered in their skin; and regarding all leprosy as of the same nature, it is thought that this affords a sufficient reason for the injunction in the Mosaic law to destroy the clothes in which the disease, after careful observation, seemed to manifest itself. Clothes are sometimes seen contaminated by this disease in the West Indies and the southern parts of America [WHITLAW'S *Code of Health*]; and it may be presumed that, as the Hebrews were living in the desert where they had not the convenience of frequent changes and washing, the clothes they wore and the skin mats on which they lay, would be apt to breed infectious vermin, which, being settled in the stuff, would imperceptibly gnaw it and leave stains similar to those described by Moses. It is well known that the wool of sheep dying of disease, if it had not been shorn from the animal while living, and also skins, if not thoroughly prepared by scouring, are liable to the effects described in this passage. The stains are described as of a greenish or reddish color, according, perhaps, to the color or nature of the ingredients used in preparing them; for acids convert blue vegetable colors into red and alkalies change then into green [BROWN]. It appears, then, that the leprosy, though sometimes inflicted as a miraculous judgment (Num. 12:10; II Kings 5:27) was a natural disease, which is known in Eastern countries still; while the rules prescribed by the Hebrew legislator for distinguishing the true character and varieties of the disease and which are far superior to the method of treatment now followed in those regions, show the divine wisdom by which he was guided. Doubtless the origin of the disease is owing to some latent causes in nature; and perhaps a more extended acquaintance with the archæology of Egypt and the natural history of the adjacent countries, may confirm the opinion that leprosy results from noxious insects or a putrid fermentation. But whatever the origin or cause of the disease, the laws enacted by divine authority regarding it, while they pointed in the first instance to sanitary ends, were at the same time intended, by stimulating to carefulness against ceremonial defilement, to foster a spirit of religious fear and inward purity.

ADAM CLARKE

45. *His clothes shall be rent.* The leprous person was required to be as one that mourned for the dead, or for some great and public calamity. He was to have his clothes rent in token of extreme sorrow; his head was to be made bare, the ordinary bonnet or turban being omitted; and he was to have a *covering upon his upper lip,* his jaws being tied up with a linen cloth, after the same manner in which the Jews bind up the dead. He was also to cry, *Unclean, unclean,* in order to prevent any person from coming near him, lest the contagion might be thus communicated and diffused through society.

47. *The garment also.* The whole account here seems to intimate that the garment was fretted by this contagion; and hence it is likely that it was occasioned by a species of small animals, which we know to be the cause of the itch; these, by breeding in the garments, must necessarily multiply their kind, and fret the garments, i.e., corrode a portion of the finer parts, after the manner of moths, for their nourishment. See v. 52.

52. *He shall therefore burn that garment.* There being scarcely any means of radically curing the infection. It is well known that the garments infected by the itch animal have been known to communicate the disease even six or seven years after the first infection. This has been also experienced by the sorters of rags at some paper mills.

54. *He shall shut it up seven days more.* To give time for the spreading of the contagion, if it did exist there; that there might be the most unequivocal marks and proofs that the garment was or was not infected.

58. *It shall be washed the second time.* According to the Jews the first washing was to put away the plague, the second to cleanse it.

MATTHEW HENRY

CHAPTER 14

Verses 1–9

I. It is supposed that the plague of the leprosy was not an incurable disease. Uzziah's indeed continued to the day of his death, but Miriam's lasted only seven days: we may suppose that it often wore off in process of time.

II. The judgment of the cure, as well as that of the disease, was referred to the priest. He must go out of the camp to the leper, to see whether his leprosy was healed, *v.* 3. It was in mercy to the poor lepers that the priests particularly had orders to attend them. When the leper was shut out, and could not go to the priests, it was well that the priests might come to him. *Is any sick? Let him send for the elders,* the ministers, Jam. v. 14. If we apply it

JAMIESON, FAUSSET, BROWN

CHAPTER 14

VSS. 1-57. THE RITES AND SACRIFICES IN CLEANSING OF THE LEPER. **2. law of the leper in the day of his cleansing**—Though quite convalescent, a leper was not allowed to return to society immediately and at his own will. The malignant character of his disease rendered the greatest precautions necessary to his re-admission among the people. One of the priests most skilled in the diagnostics of disease [GROTIUS], being deputed to attend such outcasts, the restored leper appeared before this official, and when after examination a certificate of health was given, the ceremonies here described were forthwith observed outside the camp. **4. two birds**—lit., sparrows. The *Septuagint,* however, renders the expression "little birds"; and it is evident

ADAM CLARKE

CHAPTER 14

3. *The priest shall go forth out of the camp.* As the leper was separated from the people, and obliged, because of his uncleanness, to dwell without the camp, and could not be admitted till the priest had declared that he was clean; hence it was necessary that the priest should go out and inspect him, and, if healed, offer for him the sacrifices required, in order to his readmission to the camp. As the priest alone had authority to declare a person clean or unclean, it was necessary that the healed person should show himself to the priest, that he might make a declaration that he was clean and fit for civil and religious society, without which, in no case, could he be admitted; hence, when Christ

MATTHEW HENRY

to the spiritual leprosy of sin, it intimates that when we withdraw from those who walk disorderly, that they may be ashamed, we must not count them as enemies, but admonish them as brethren, 2 Thess. iii. 15. And also that when God by his grace has brought those to repentance who were shut out of communion for scandal, they ought with tenderness, and joy, and sincere affection, to be received in again. Thus Paul orders concerning the excommunicated Corinthian that when he had given evidences of his repentance they should forgive him, and comfort him, and *confirm their love towards him*, 2 Cor. ii. 7, 8.

III. If it was found that the leprosy was healed, the priest must declare it with a particular solemnity. The leper or his friends were to get ready two birds caught for this purpose (any sort of wild birds that were clean), and cedar-wood, and scarlet, and hyssop. 1. A preparation was to be made of blood and water, with which the leper must be sprinkled. One of the birds was to be killed over an earthen cup of spring water, so that the blood of the bird might discolour the water. 2. The living bird, with a little scarlet wool, and a bunch of hyssop, must be fastened to a cedar stick, dipped in the water and blood, which must be so sprinkled upon him that was to be cleansed, *v.* 6, 7. The cedar-wood signified the restoring of the leper to his strength and soundness, for that is a sort of wood not apt to putrefy. The scarlet wool signified his recovering a florid colour again, for the leprosy made him white as snow. And the hyssop intimated the removing of the disagreeable scent which commonly attended the leprosy. The cedar the stateliest plant, and hyssop the meanest, are here used together in this service (see 1 Kings iv. 33). The leper must be sprinkled *seven times*, to signify a complete purification, in allusion to which David prays, *Wash me throughly*, Ps. li. 2. Naaman was directed to wash *seven times*, 2 Kings v. 10. 3. The living bird was then to be let loose in the open field, to signify that the leper, being cleansed, was now no longer under restraint and confinement, but might take his liberty to go where he pleased. But this being signified by the flight of a bird towards heaven was an intimation to him henceforward to seek the things that are above, and not to spend this new life to which God had restored him merely in the pursuit of earthly things. Those whose souls before *bowed down to the dust* (Ps. xliv. 25), in grief and fear, now fly in the open firmament of heaven, and soar upwards upon the wings of faith and hope, and holy love and joy. 4. The priest must, upon this, pronounce him clean. Those are clean indeed whom Christ pronounces so, and they need not regard what men say of them. But, though Christ was the *end of the law for righteousness*, yet being in the days of his flesh *made under the law*, which as yet stood unrepealed, he ordered those lepers whom he had cured miraculously to go and *show themselves to the priest*, and *offer for their cleansing according to the law*, Matt. viii. 4; Luke v. 14. 5. When the leper was pronounced clean, he must wash his body and his clothes, and shave *off all his hair* (*v.* 8), must still tarry seven days out of the camp, and on the seventh day must do it again, *v.* 9. The priest having pronounced him clean from the disease, he must make himself as clean as ever he could from all the remains of it, and from all other defilements.

Verses 10–20

Observe, I. To complete the purification of the leper, on the eighth day, after the former solemnity performed without the camp, he was to attend *at the door of the tabernacle*, and was there to be *presented to the Lord*, with his offering, *v.* 11. Observe here, 1. That the mercies of God oblige us to present ourselves to him, Rom. xii. 1. 2. When God has restored us to the liberty of ordinances again, after restraint by sickness, distance, or otherwise, we should take the first opportunity of testifying our respect to God, and our affection to his sanctuary.

II. Three lambs the cleansed leper was to bring, with a meat-offering, and a log of oil, which was about half a pint. Now, 1. Most of the ceremony peculiar to this case was about the trespass-offering, the lamb for which was offered first, *v.* 12. The Jews say that the leper stood without the gate of the tabernacle and the priest within, and thus the ceremony was performed through the gate, signifying that now he was admitted with other Israelites to attend in the courts of the Lord's house again, and was as welcome as ever; though perhaps the name might stick by him as long as he lived (as we read of one who probably was cleansed by our Lord Jesus, who yet afterwards is called *Simon the leper*, Matt. xxvi. 6). Cleansed lepers are as welcome to the blood and the oil as consecrated priests. 2. Besides

JAMIESON, FAUSSET, BROWN

that it is to be taken in this generic sense from their being specified as "clean"—a condition which would have been altogether superfluous to mention in reference to sparrows. In all the offerings prescribed in the law, Moses ordered only common and accessible birds; and hence we may presume that he points here to such birds as sparrows or pigeons, as in the desert it might have been very difficult to procure wild birds alive. **cedar wood, and scarlet, and hyssop**—The cedar here meant was certainly **not** the famous tree of Lebanon, and it is generally supposed to have been the juniper, as several varieties of that shrub are found growing abundantly in the clefts and crevices of the Sinaitic mountains. A stick of this shrub was bound to a bunch of hyssop by a scarlet ribbon, and the living bird was to be so attached to it, that when they dipped the branches in the water, the tail of the bird might also be moistened, but not the head nor the wings, that it might not be impeded in its flight when let loose. **5. the priest shall command that one of the birds be killed . . . over running water**—As the blood of a single bird would not have been sufficient to immerse the body of another bird, it was mingled with spring water to increase the quantity necessary for the appointed sprinklings, which were to be repeated *seven times,* denoting a complete purification. (See II Kings 5:10; Ps. 51:2; Matt. 8:4; Luke 5:14.) The living bird being then set free, in token of the leper's release from quarantine, the priest pronounced him clean; and this official declaration was made with all solemnity, in order that the mind of the leper might be duly impressed with a sense of the divine goodness, and that others might be satisfied they might safely hold intercourse with him. Several other purifications had to be gone through during a series of seven days, and the whole process had to be repeated on the seventh, ere he was allowed to re-enter the camp. The circumstance of a priest being employed seems to imply that instruction suitable to the newly recovered leper would be given, and that the symbolical ceremonies used in the process of cleansing leprosy would be explained. How far they were then understood we cannot tell. But we can trace some instructive analogies between the leprosy and the disease of sin, and between the rites observed in the process of cleansing leprosy and the provisions of the Gospel. The chief of these analogies is that as it was only when a leper exhibited a certain change of state that orders were given by the priest for a sacrifice, so a sinner must be in the exercise of faith and penitence ere the benefits of the gospel remedy can be enjoyed by him. The slain bird and the bird let loose are supposed to typify, the one the death, and the other the resurrection of Christ; while the sprinklings on him that had been leprous typified the requirements which led a believer to cleanse himself from all filthiness of the flesh and spirit, and to perfect his holiness in the fear of the Lord.

10-20. on the right day he shall take two he-lambs without blemish, and one ewe-lamb of the first year without blemish—The purification of the leper was not completed till at the end of seven days, after the ceremonial of the birds and during which, though permitted to come into the camp, he had to tarry abroad out of his tent, from which he came daily to appear at the door of the tabernacle with the offerings required. He was presented before the Lord by the priest that made him clean. And hence it has always been reckoned among pious people the first duty of a patient newly restored from a long and dangerous sickness to repair to the church to offer his thanksgiving, where his body and soul, in order to be an acceptable offering, must be presented by our great Priest, whose blood alone makes any clean. The offering was to consist of two lambs, the one was to be a sin offering and the an ephah of fine flour (two pints = $\frac{1}{10}$), and one log (half pint) of oil (ch. 2:1). One of the lambs was for a trespass offering, which was necessary from the inherent sin of his nature or from his defilement of the camp by his leprosy previous to his expulsion; and it is remarkable that the blood of the trespass offering was applied exactly in the same particular manner to the extremities of the restored leper, as that of the ram in the consecration of the priests. The parts sprinkled with this blood were

ADAM CLARKE

cleansed the lepers, Matt. viii. 2-4, He commanded them to go and show themselves to the priest.

4. *Two birds alive and clean.* Whether these birds were sparrows, or turtledoves, or pigeons, we know not; probably any kind of clean bird, or bird proper to be eaten, might be used on this occasion, though it is more likely that turtledoves or pigeons were employed, because these appear to have been the only birds offered in sacrifice. Of the cedarwood, hyssop, clean bird, and scarlet wool were made an instrument to *sprinkle* with. The cedarwood served for the handle; the hyssop and living bird were attached to it by means of the scarlet wool. The bird was so bound to this handle as that its tail should be downwards, in order to be dipped into the blood of the bird that had been killed. The whole of this made an instrument for the sprinkling of this blood, and when this business was done, the living bird was let loose, and permitted to go whithersoever it would.

5. *Over running water.* Literally, "living," that is, spring water. The meaning appears to be this: Some water was taken from a spring, and put into a clean earthen vessel, and they killed the bird over this water, that the blood might drop into it; and in this blood and water mixed they dipped the instrument before described, and sprinkled it seven times upon the person who was to be cleansed. The "living" or spring water was chosen because it was purer than what was taken from pits or wells, the latter being often in a putrid or corrupt state; for in a ceremony of purifying or cleansing, everything must be as pure and perfect as possible.

7. *Shall let the living bird loose.* The Jews teach that wild birds were employed on this occasion; no tame or domestic animal was used.

8. *And shave off all his hair.* That the water by which he was to be washed should reach every part of his body, that he might be cleansed from whatever defilement might remain on any part of the surface of his body.

10. *Two he lambs.* One for a trespass offering, v. 12, the other for a burnt offering, vv. 19-20. *One ewe lamb.* This was for a sin offering, v. 19. *Three tenth deals.* Three parts of an ephah, or three omers; see all these measures explained, Exod. xvi. 16. The *three tenth deals* of flour were for a *minchah,* meat or gratitude offering, v. 20. The sin offering was for his *impurity,* the trespass offering for his transgression, and the gratitude offering for his gracious cleansing. These constituted the offering which each was ordered to bring to the priest; see Matt. viii. 4.

12. *Wave offering.* See Exod. xxix. 27, and chap. vii., where the reader will find an ample account of all the various offerings and sacrifices used among the Jews.

MATTHEW HENRY

this there must be a sin-offering and a burnt-offering, a lamb for each, *v.* 19, 20. By each of these offerings, it is said, the priests shall *make an atonement for him.* (1) His moral guilt shall be removed. (2) His ceremonial pollution shall be removed, which had kept him from the participation of the holy things. And this is called *making an atonement for him,* because our restoration to the privileges of God's children, typified hereby, is owing purely to the great propitiation. The burnt-offering, besides the atonement that was made by it, was a thankful acknowledgment of God's mercy to him: and the more immediate the hand of God was both in the sickness and in the cure the more reason he had thus to give glory to him, and thus, as our Saviour speaks (Mark i. 44), to *offer for his cleansing* all *those things which Moses commanded for a testimony unto them.*

Verses 21–32

We have here the gracious provision which the law made for the cleansing of *poor lepers.* If they were not able to bring three lambs, and three tenth-deals of flour, they must bring one lamb, and one tenth-deal of flour, and, instead of the other two lambs, two turtle-doves or two young pigeons, *v.* 21, 22. Here see, 1. That the poverty of the person concerned would not excuse him if he brought no offerings at all. Let none think that because they are poor God requires no service from them, since he has considered them, and demands that which it is in the power of the poorest to give. "*My son, give me thy heart,* and with that the *calves of thy lips* shall be accepted instead of the *calves of the stall.*" 2. That God expected from those who were poor only according to their ability. If there be first a willing mind and an honest heart, two pigeons, when they are the utmost a man is able to get, are as acceptable to God as two lambs.

Verses 33–53

This is the law concerning the leprosy in a house. The leprosy in a house is as unaccountable as the leprosy in a garment. Now, 1. It is supposed that even in Canaan itself, the land of promise, their houses might be infected with a leprosy. 2. It is likewise taken for granted that the owner of the house will make the priest acquainted with it, as soon as he sees the least cause to suspect the leprosy in his house. Sin, where that reigns in a house, is a plague there, as it is in a heart. And masters of families should be aware and afraid of the first appearance of gross sin in their families, and put away the iniquity, whatever it is, far from their tabernacles, Job xxii. 23. 3. If the priest, upon search, found that the leprosy had got into the house, he must try to cure it, by taking out that part of the building that was infected, *v.* 40, 41. This was like cutting off a gangrened limb for the preservation of the rest of the body. 4. If yet it remained in the house, the whole house must be pulled down, and all the materials carried to the dunghill, *v.* 44, 45. 5. If the taking out the infected stones cured the house, and the leprosy did not spread any further, then the house must be cleansed; not only aired, that it might be healthful, but purified from the ceremonial pollution, that it might be fit to be the habitation of an Israelite. The ceremony of its cleansing was much the same with that of cleansing a leprous person, *v.* 49, &c. And the same care should we take to reform whatever is amiss in our families, that we and our houses may serve the Lord; see Gen. xxxv. 2.

Verses 54–57

This is the conclusion of this law concerning the leprosy. We may see in this law, 1. The gracious care God took of his people Israel. When Naaman the Syrian was cured of his leprosy he was not bidden to show himself to the priest, though he was cured in Jordan, as the Jews that were cured by our Saviour were. 2. The religious care we ought to take of ourselves, to keep our minds from the dominion of all sinful affections and dispositions, which are both their disease and their defilement, that we may be fit for the service of God.

JAMIESON, FAUSSET, BROWN

then anointed with oil—a ceremony which is supposed to have borne this spiritual import: that while the blood was a token of forgiveness, the oil was an emblem of healing—as the blood of Christ justifies, the influence of the Spirit sanctifies. Of the other two lambs the one was to be a sin offering and the other a burnt offering, which had also the character of a thank offering for God's mercy in his restoration. And this was considered to make atonement "for him"; i.e., it removed that ceremonial pollution which had excluded him from the enjoyment of religious ordinances, just as the atonement of Christ restores all who are cleansed through faith in His sacrifice to the privileges of the children of God. **21-32. if he be poor, and cannot get so much; then he shall take one lamb**—a kind and considerate provision for an extension of the privilege to lepers of the poorer class. The blood of their smaller offering was to be applied in the same process of purification and they were as publicly and completely cleansed as those who brought a costlier offering (Acts 10:34). **34-48. leprosy in a house**—This law was prospective, not to come into operation till the settlement of the Israelites in Canaan. The words, "I put the leprosy," has led many to think that this plague was a judicial infliction from heaven for the sins of the owner; while others do not regard it in this light, it being common in Scripture to represent God as doing that which He only permits in His providence to be done. Assuming it to have been a natural disease, a new difficulty arises as to whether we are to consider that the house had become infected by the contagion of leprous occupiers; or that the leprosy was in the house itself. It is evident that the latter was the true state of the case, from the furniture being removed out of it on the first suspicion of disease on the walls. Some have supposed that the name of leprosy was analogically applied to it by the Hebrews, as we speak of cancer in trees when they exhibit corrosive effects similar to what the disease so named produces on the human body; while others have pronounced it a mural efflorescence or species of mildew on the wall apt to be produced in very damp situations, and which was followed by effects so injurious to health as well as to the stability of a house, particularly in warm countries, as to demand the attention of a legislator. Moses enjoined the priests to follow the same course and during the same period of time for ascertaining the true character of this disease as in human leprosy. If found leprous, the infected parts were to be removed. If afterwards there appeared a risk of the contagion spreading, the house was to be destroyed altogether and the materials removed to a distance. The stones were probably rough, unhewn stones, built up without cement in the manner now frequently used in fences and plastered over, or else laid in mortar. The oldest examples of architecture are of this character. The very same thing has to be done still with houses infected with mural salt. The stones covered with the nitrous incrustation must be removed, and if the infected wall is suffered to remain, it must be plastered all over anew. **48-57. the priest shall pronounce the house clean, because the plague is healed**—The precautions here described show that there is great danger in warm countries from the house leprosy, which was likely to be increased by the smallness and rude architecture of the houses in the early ages of the Israelitish history. As a house could not contract any impurity in the sight of God, the "atonement" which the priest was to make for it must either have a reference to the sins of its occupants or to the ceremonial process appointed for its purification, the very same as that observed for a leprous person. This solemn declaration that it was "clean," as well as the offering made on the occasion, was admirably calculated to make known the fact, to remove apprehension from the public mind, as well as relieve the owner from the aching suspicion of dwelling in an infected house.

ADAM CLARKE

21. *And if he be poor . . . he shall take one lamb.* There could be no cleansing without a sacrifice. On this ground the apostle has properly observed that "all things are by the law purged with blood"; and that "without shedding of blood [there] is no remission." Even if the person be poor, he must provide one lamb; this could not be dispensed with. So every soul to whom the word of divine revelation comes must bring that Lamb of God, which takes away the sin of the world. There is no redemption but in His blood.

34. *When ye be come into the land . . . and I put the plague of leprosy.* It was probably from this text that the leprosy has been generally considered to be a disease inflicted immediately by God himself; but it is well known that in Scripture God is frequently represented as doing what, in the course of His providence, He only permits or suffers to be done.

53. *He shall let go the living bird.* This might as well be called the "scape-bird"; as the goat, in chap. xvi., is called the scapegoat. The rites are similar in both cases, and probably had nearly the same meaning.

MATTHEW HENRY

CHAPTER 15

Verses 1–18

We have here the law concerning the ceremonial uncleanness that was contracted by running issues in men, which was, usually, the effect of a dissolute life. A vile disease for vile deserts. Now whoever had this disease upon him, 1. He was himself unclean, *v.* 2. He must not dare to come near the sanctuary.

JAMIESON, FAUSSET, BROWN

CHAPTER 15

Vss. 1-18. UNCLEANNESS OF MEN. **2. When any man hath a running issue**—This chapter describes other forms of uncleanness, the nature of which is sufficiently intelligible in the text without any explanatory comment. Being the effects of licentiousness, they properly come within the notice of the legislator, and the very stringent rules here prescribed, both for the separation of the person diseased and for avoiding contamination from anything connected with him, were well calculated

ADAM CLARKE

CHAPTER 15

2. *When any man hath a running issue.* The cases of natural uncleanness, of both men and women, mentioned in this chapter, taken in a theological point of view, are not of such importance to us as to render a particular description necessary, the letter of the text being, in general, plain enough. The disease mentioned in the former part of this chapter appears to some to have been either the consequence of a very bad infection or of some criminal indul-

MATTHEW HENRY

2. He made every person and thing unclean that he touched, or that touched him, *v.* 4–12. This signified the contagion of sin, the danger we are in of being polluted by conversing with those that are polluted.

3. When he was cured of the disease, yet he could not be cleansed from the pollution without a sacrifice, for which he was to prepare by bathing in spring water, *v.* 13–15. This signified the great gospel duties of faith and repentance, and the great gospel privileges of the application of Christ's blood to our souls for our justification and his grace for our sanctification.

Verses 19–33

This is concerning the ceremonial uncleanness which women lay under from their issues. This made the woman unclean (*v.* 25) and every thing she touched unclean, *v.* 26, 27. And if she was cured, and found by seven days' trial that she was perfectly free from her issue of blood, she was to be cleansed by the offering of two turtle-doves or two young pigeons, to make an atonement for her, *v.* 28, 29.

By these laws they were taught that they were *purified unto God a peculiar people*, and were intended by the holy God for a kingdom of priests, a holy nation. They were also taught to preserve the honour of their purity, and to keep themselves from all sinful pollutions. In all these laws there seems to be a special regard had to the honour of the tabernacle, to which none must approach in their uncleanness, that they *defile not my tabernacle.* Thus they were taught never to draw near to God but with an awful humble sense of their distance and danger.

Let us bless God that we are not under the yoke of these carnal ordinances, that, as nothing can destroy us, so nothing can defile us, but sin. Those may now partake of the Lord's supper who durst not then eat of the peace-offerings. Let us all see how indispensably necessary real holiness is to our future happiness, and get our hearts purified by faith, that we may see God.

JAMIESON, FAUSSET, BROWN

not only to prevent contagion, but to discourage the excesses of licentious indulgence.

9. what saddle . . . he rideth upon that hath the issue shall be unclean—(See on Gen. 31:34). **12. the vessel of earth that he toucheth which hath the issue shall be broken**—It is thought that the pottery of the Israelites, like the earthenware jars in which the Egyptians kept their water, was unglazed and consequently porous, and that it was its porousness which, rendering it extremely liable to imbibe small particles of impure matter, was the reason why the vessel touched by an unclean person was ordered to be broken. **13, 14. then he shall number to himself seven days for his cleansing**—Like a leprous person he underwent a week's probation, to make sure he was completely healed. Then with the sacrifices prescribed, the priest made an atonement for him, i.e., offered the oblations necessary for the removal of his ceremonial defilement, as well as the typical pardon of his sins.

19-33. Uncleanness of Women. **19. if a woman have an issue**—Though this, like the leprosy, might be a natural affection, it was anciently considered contagious and entailed a ceremonial defilement which typified a moral impurity. This ceremonial defilement had to be removed by an appointed method of ceremonial expiation, and the neglect of it subjected any one to the guilt of defiling the tabernacle, and to death as the penalty of profane temerity. **31-33. Thus shall ye separate the children of Israel from their uncleanness**—The divine wisdom was manifested in inspiring the Israelites with a profound reverence for holy things; and nothing was more suited to this purpose than to debar from the tabernacle all who were polluted by any kind of uncleanness, ceremonial as well as natural, mental as well as physical. The better to mark out that people as His family, His servants and priests, dwelling in the camp as in a holy place, consecrated by His presence and His tabernacle, He required of them complete purity, and did not allow them to come before Him when defiled, even by involuntary or secret impurities, as a want of respect due to His majesty. And when we bear in mind that God was training a people to live in His presence in some measure as priests devoted to His service, we shall not consider these rules for the maintenance of personal purity either too stringent or too minute (I Thess. 4:4).

ADAM CLARKE

gence; for they find that it might be communicated in a variety of ways, which they imagine are here distinctly specified. On this ground the person was declared unclean, and all commerce and connection with him strictly forbidden. The Septuagint version renders *hazzab*, the man with the *issue*, by the man with a *gonorrhoea*, no less than nine times in this chapter; and that it means what in the present day is commonly understood by that disorder, taken not only in its mild but in its worst sense, they think there is little room to doubt. The disgraceful disorder referred to here is a foul blot which the justice of God in the course of providence has made in general the inseparable consequence of these criminal indulgences, and serves in some measure to correct and restrain the vice itself. In countries where public prostitution was permitted, where it was even a religious ceremony among those who were idolaters, this disease must necessarily have been frequent and prevalent. That the Israelites might have received it from the Egyptians, and that it must, through the Baal-peor and Ashteroth abominations which they learned and practiced, have prevailed among the Moabites, there can be little reason to doubt. Supposing this disease to be at all hinted at here, the laws and ordinances enjoined were at once wisely and graciously calculated to remove and prevent it. By contact, contagion of every kind is readily communicated; and to keep the whole from the diseased must be essential to the check and eradication of a contagious disorder. This was the wise and grand object of this enlightened Legislator in the ordinances which He lays down in this chapter.

11. *And whomsoever he toucheth.* Here we find that the saliva, sitting on the same seat, lying on the same bed, riding on the same saddle, or simple contact, was sufficient to render the person unclean, meaning, possibly, in certain cases, to communicate the disorder; and it is well known that in all these ways the contagion of this disorder may be communicated.

18. *They shall both bathe themselves.* What a wonderful tendency had these ordinances to prevent all excesses! The pains which such persons must take, the separations which they must observe, and the privations which, in consequence, they must be exposed to in the way of commerce, traffic, etc., would prevent them from making an unlawful use of lawful things.

24. In chap. xx. 18, persons guilty of this are condemned to death; here only to a seven days' separation; because, in the former case, Moses speaks of the act when both the man and the woman were acquainted with the situation; in the latter, he speaks of a case where the circumstance was not known till afterwards.

29. *Two turtles, or two young pigeons.* In all these cases moral pollution was ever considered as being less or more present, as even such infirmities sprang from the original defection of man. On these accounts sacrifices must be offered; and in the case of the woman, one of the birds above mentioned must be sacrificed as a sin offering, the other as a burnt offering, v. 30.

31. *Thus shall ye separate the children of Israel from their uncleanness.* By this separation the cause became less frequent, and the contagion, if it did exist, was prevented from spreading. So fever wards are constructed for the purpose of separating the infected from the sound; and thus contagion is lessened, and its diffusion prevented. *That they die not.* That life may be prolonged by these prudential cares; and that he who is morally and legally unclean may not presume to enter into the Tabernacle of God till purified, lest he provoke divine justice to consume him, while attempting to worship with a polluted mind and impure hands.

MATTHEW HENRY

CHAPTER 16

Verses 1–4

Here is, 1. The date of this law concerning the day of atonement: it was *after the death of the two sons of Aaron* (*v.* 1), which we read, *ch.* x. 1. 1. Lest Aaron should fear that any remaining guilt of that sin should cleave to his family, he is directed how to make atonement for his house. 2. The priests being warned by the death of Nadab and Abihu to approach to God with reverence and godly fear, directions are

JAMIESON, FAUSSET, BROWN

CHAPTER 16

Vss. 1-34. How the High Priest Must Enter into the Holy Place. **1. after the death of the two sons of Aaron, when they offered before the Lord, and died**—It is thought by some that this chapter has been transposed out of its right place in the sacred record, which was immediately after the narrative of the deaths of Nadab and Abihu. That appalling catastrophe must have filled Aaron with painful apprehensions lest the guilt of these two sons might

ADAM CLARKE

CHAPTER 16

1. *After the death of the two sons of Aaron.* It appears from this verse that the natural place of this chapter is immediately after the tenth, where probably it originally stood; but the transposition, if it did take place, must be very ancient, as all the versions acknowledge this chapter in the place in which it now stands.

MATTHEW HENRY

here given how the nearest approach might be made.

II. The design of this law. One intention of it was to preserve a veneration for the most holy place, within the veil, where the *Shechinah*, or divine glory, was pleased to dwell between the cherubim. Within the veil none must ever come but the high priest only, and he but on one day in the year. But see what a blessed change is made by the gospel of Christ; all good Christians have now *boldness to enter into the holiest*, through the veil, every day (Heb. x. 19, 20); and we *come boldly* (not as Aaron must, with fear and trembling) to the *throne of grace*, or mercy-seat, Heb. iv. 16. The objects of faith the more they are conversed with the more do they manifest of their greatness and goodness: now therefore we are welcome to come at all times into the *holy place not made with hands*. Then Aaron must not come near at all times, *lest he die*; we now must come near at all times that we may live: it is distance only that is our death.

III. The person to whom the work of this day was committed, and that was the high priest only: *Thus shall Aaron come into the holy place*, *v.* 3.

IV. The attire of the high priest in this service. He was not to be dressed up in his rich garments, he was not to put on the ephod, with the precious stones in it, but only the linen clothes which he wore in common with the inferior priests, *v.* 4. That meaner dress did best become him on this day of humiliation.

Verses 5–14

The Jewish writers say that for seven days before the day of expiation the high priest was to dwell in a chamber of the temple, that he might prepare himself. During those seven days he himself did the work of the inferior priests. 1. He was to begin the service of the day very early with the usual morning sacrifice, after he had first washed his whole body before he dressed himself, and his hands and feet again afterwords. He then burned the daily incense, dressed the lamps, and offered the extraordinary sacrifice appointed (Num. xxix. 8). 2. He must now put off his rich robes, bathe himself, put on the linen garments, and present unto the Lord his own bullock, which was to be a sin-offering for himself and his house, *v.* 6. 3. He must then cast lots upon the two goats, which were to make (both together) one sin-offering for the congregation. One of these goats must be slain, in token of a satisfaction to be made to God's justice for sin, the other must be sent away, in token of the remission or dismission of sin by the mercy of God. Both must be presented together to God (*v.* 7) before the lot was cast upon them, and afterwards the scape-goat by itself, *v.* 10. Some think that goats were chosen for the sin-offering because, by the disagreeableness of their smell, the offensiveness of sin is represented. 4. The next thing to be done was to kill the bullock for the sin-offering for himself and his house, *v.* 11. 5. He took a censer of burning coals and a dish full of the sweet incense and then went into the holy of holies, set the coals down upon the floor, and scattered the incense upon them, so that the room was immediately filled with smoke. The Jews say that he was to go in *side-ways*, that he might not look directly upon the ark where the divine glory was, then he must come out *backwards*, out of reverence to the divine majesty; and, after a short prayer, he was to show himself to the people. 6. He then fetched the blood of the bullock and took that in with him the second time into the holy of holies, which was now filled with the smoke of the incense, and sprinkled with his finger of that blood towards the mercy-seat, once over against the top of it and then seven times towards the lower part of it, *v.* 14.

Verses 15–19

When the priest had come out from sprinkling the blood of the bullock before the mercy-seat, 1. He must next kill the goat which was the sin-offering for the people (*v.* 15) and go the third time into the holy of holies, to sprinkle the blood of the goat, as he had done that of the bullock; and thus he was to *make atonement for the holy place* (*v.* 16). God, being reconciled to them, might continue with them. 2. He must then do the same for the outward part of the tabernacle that he had done for the inner room. The reason intimated is *because the tabernacle remained among them in the midst of their uncleanness*, *v.* 16. God would hereby show them how much their hearts needed to be purified. 3. He must then put some of the blood, both of the bullock and of the goat mixed together, upon the horns of the altar that is before the Lord, *v.* 18, 19.

JAMIESON, FAUSSET, BROWN

be entailed on his house, or that other members of his family might share the same fate by some irregularities or defects in the discharge of their sacred functions. And, therefore, this law was established, by the due observance of whose requirements the Aaronic order would be securely maintained and accepted in the priesthood. **2. Speak unto Aaron thy brother, that he come not at all times into the holy place within the veil,** etc.—Common priests went every day into the part of the sanctuary *without* the veil to burn incense on the golden altar. But none except the high priest was allowed to enter *within* the veil, and that only once a year with the greatest care and solemnity. This arrangement was evidently designed to inspire a reverence for the most holy place, and the precaution was necessary at a time when the presence of God was indicated by sensible symbols, the impression of which might have been diminished or lost by daily and familiar observation. **I will appear in the cloud**—i.e., the smoke of the incense which the high priest burnt on his yearly entrance into the most holy place: and this was the cloud which at that time covered the mercy seat. **3, 4. Thus shall Aaron come into the holy place**—As the duties of the great day of atonement led to the nearest and most solemn approach to God, the directions as to the proper course to be followed were minute and special. **with a young bullock . . . and a ram**—These victims he brought alive, but they were not offered in sacrifice till he had gone through the ceremonies described between this and the eleventh verse. He was not to attire himself on that occasion in the splendid robes that were proper to his sacred office, but in a plain dress of linen, like the common Levites, for, as he was then to make atonement for his own sins, as well as for those of the people, he was to appear in the humble character of a suppliant. That plain dress was more in harmony with a season of humiliation (as well as lighter and more convenient for the duties which on that occasion he had singly to perform) than the gorgeous robes of the pontificate. It showed that when all appeared as sinners, the highest and lowest were then on a level, and that there is no distinction of persons with God. **5-10. shall take of the congregation . . . two kids of the goats . . . and one ram**—The sacrifices were to be offered by the high priest respectively for himself and the other priests, as well as for the people. The bullock (vs. 3) and the goats were for sin offerings and the rams for burnt offerings. The goats, though used in different ways, constituted only one offering. They were both presented before the Lord, and the disposal of them determined by lot, which Jewish writers have thus described: The priest, placing one of the goats on his right hand and the other on his left, took his station by the altar, and cast into an urn two pieces of gold exactly similar, inscribed, the one with the words "for the Lord," and the other for "Azazel" (the scapegoat). After having well shaken them together, he put both his hands into the box and took up a lot in each: that in his right hand he put on the head of the goat which stood on his right, and that in his left he dropped on the other. In this manner the fate of each was decided. **11-14. Aaron shall bring the bullock of the sin offering which is for himself,** etc.—The first part of the service was designed to solemnize his own mind, as well as the minds of the people, by offering the sacrifices for their sins. The sin offerings being slain had the sins of the offerer judicially transferred to them by the imputation of his hands on their head (ch. 4); and thus the young bullock, which was to make atonement for himself and the other priests (called "his house," Ps. 135: 19), was killed by the hands of the high priest. While the blood of the victim was being received into a vessel, taking a censer of live coals in his right hand and a platter of sweet incense in his left, he, amid the solemn attention and the anxious prayers of the assembled multitude, crossed the porch and the holy place, opened the outer veil which led into the holy of holies and then the inner veil. Standing before the ark, he deposited the censer of coals on the floor, emptied the plate of incense into his hand, poured it on the burning coals; and the apartment was filled with fragrant smoke, intended, according to Jewish writers, to prevent any presumptuous gazer prying too curiously into the form of the mercy seat, which was the Lord's throne. The high priest having done this, perfumed the sanctuary, returned to the door, took the blood of the slain bullock, and, carrying it into the holy of holies, sprinkled it with his finger once upon the mercy seat "eastward,"—i.e., on the side next to himself; and seven times "before the mercy seat,"—i.e., on the front of the ark. Leaving the coals and

ADAM CLARKE

2. *That he come not at all times into the holy place.* By the holy place we are to understand here what is ordinarily called the "holy of holies," or "most holy place"; that place within the veil where the ark of the covenant, etc., were laid up; and where God manifested His presence between the cherubim. In ordinary cases the high priest could enter this place only once in the year, that is, on the day of annual atonement; but in extraordinary cases he might enter more frequently, viz., while in the wilderness, in decamping and encamping, he must enter to take down or adjust the things; and on solemn, pressing public occasions he was obliged to enter in order to consult the Lord. But he never entered without the deepest reverence and due preparation.

That it may appear that the grand subject of this chapter, the ordinance of the scapegoat, typified the death and resurrection of Christ, and the atonement thereby made, I beg leave to refer to Heb. ix. 7-12 and 24-26.

3. *With a young bullock for a sin offering.* The *bullock* was presented as a *sin offering* for himself, his family, the whole priesthood, and probably the Levites. The *ram* was for a *burnt offering,* to signify that he and his associates were wholly consecrated, and to be wholly employed in this work of the ministry. The ceremonies with which these two sacrifices were accompanied are detailed in the following verses.

4. *He shall put on the holy linen coat.* He was not to dress in his pontifical garments, but in the simple sacerdotal vestments, or those of the Levites, because it was a day of humiliation; and as he was to offer sacrifices for his own sins, it was necessary that he should appear in habits suited to the occasion. Hence he has neither the robe, the ephod, the breastplate, the mitre, etc.; these constituted his dress of dignity as the high priest of God, ministering for others and the representative of Christ. But now he appears before God as a sinner, offering an atonement for his transgressions, and his garments are those of humiliation.

7. *And he shall take the two goats.* It is allowed on all hands that this ceremony, taken in all its parts, pointed out the Lord Jesus dying for our sins and rising again for our justification; being put to death in the flesh, but quickened by the Spirit. *Two goats* are brought, one to be slain as a sacrifice for sin, the other to have the transgressions of the people confessed over his head, and then to be sent away into the wilderness. The animal by this act was represented as bearing away or carrying off the sins of the people. The two goats made only one sacrifice, yet only one of them was slain. One animal could not point out both the divine and human nature of Christ, nor show both His death and resurrection, for the goat that was killed could not be made alive. The divine and human natures in Christ were essential to the grand expiation; yet the human nature alone suffered, for the divine nature could not suffer; but its presence in the human nature, while agonizing unto death, stamped those agonies, and the consequent death, with infinite merit. The goat therefore that was slain prefigured His human nature and its death; the goat that escaped pointed out His resurrection. The one shows the atonement for sin, as the ground of justification; the other Christ's victory, and the total removal of sin in the sanctification of the soul.

8. *Aaron shall cast lots upon the two goats.* The Jews inform us that there were two *lots* made either of wood, stone, or any kind of metal. On one was written *lashshem,* "for the name," i.e., *Jehovah,* which the Jews will neither write nor pronounce; on the other was written *laazazel,* "for the scapegoat." Then they put the two lots into a vessel which was called *kalpey,* the goats standing with their faces towards the west. Then the priest came, and the goats stood before him, one on the right hand and the other on the left. The *kalpey* was then shaken, and the priest put in both his hands and brought out a lot in each. That which was in his right hand he laid on the goat that was on his right, and that in his left hand he laid on the goat that was on his left; and according to what was written on the lots, the scapegoat and the goat for sacrifice were ascertained. The determining

MATTHEW HENRY

Verses 20–28

The high priest having presented unto the Lord the expiatory sacrifices, by the sprinkling of their blood, 1. He is next to confess the sins of Israel, with both his hands upon the head of the scape-goat (*v.* 20, 21); and whenever hands were imposed upon the head of any sacrifice it was always done with confession. In the latter and more degenerate ages of the Jewish church they had a set form of confession prepared for the high priest. By this confession he must *put the sins of Israel upon the head of the goat*. 2. The goat was then to be sent away immediately by the hand of a fit person into a wilderness, a land not inhabited; and God allowed them to make this construction of it, that the sending away of the goat was the sending away of their sins, by a free and full remission: *He shall bear upon him all their iniquities*, *v.* 22. The later Jews had a custom to tie one shred of scarlet cloth to the horns of the goat and another to the gate of the temple, or to the top of the rock where the goat was lost, and they concluded that if it turned white, as they say it usually did, the sins of Israel were forgiven, as it is written, *Though your sins have been as scarlet, they shall be as wool*: and they add that for forty years before the destruction of Jerusalem by the Romans the scarlet cloth never changed colour at all, which is a fair confession that, having rejected the substance, the shadow stood them in no stead. 3. The high priest must then put off his linen garments in the tabernacle, and leave them there, the Jews say never to be worn again by himself or any other, for they made new ones every year; and he must bathe himself in water, put on his rich clothes, and then offer both his own and the people's burnt-offerings, *v.* 23, 24. When we have the comfort of our pardon God must have the glory of it. 4. The flesh of both those sin-offerings whose blood was taken within the veil was to be all burnt at a distance without the camp, to signify both our putting away sin by true repentance, and the spirit of burning, and God's putting it away by a full remission, so that it shall never rise up in judgment against us. 5. He that took the scape-goat into the wilderness, and those that burned the sin-offering, were to be looked upon as ceremonially unclean, and must not come into the camp till they had washed their clothes and bathed their flesh in water, which signified the defiling nature of sin. 6. When all this was done, the high priest went again into the most holy place to fetch his censer, and so returned to his own house with joy, because he had done his duty, and died not.

Verses 29–34

I. We have here some additional directions in reference to this great solemnity, particularly,

1. The day appointed for this solemnity. It must be observed yearly on *the tenth day of the seventh month*, *v.* 29.

2. The duty of the people on this day. (1) They must rest from all their labours: *It shall be a sabbath of rest*, *v.* 31. (2) They must afflict their souls. They must refrain from all bodily refreshments and delights, in token of inward humiliation and contrition of soul for their sins. They all fasted on this day from food (except the sick and children), and laid aside their ornaments.

3. The perpetuity of this institution: *It shall be a statute for ever*, *v.* 29, 34. It must not be intermitted any year, nor ever let fall till that constitution should be dissolved, and the type should be superseded by the antitype. The annual repetition of the sacrifices showed that there was in them only a faint and feeble effort towards making atonement; it could be done effectually only by the *offering up of the body of Christ once for all*, and that once was sufficient; that sacrifice needed not to be repeated.

II. Let us see what there was of gospel in all this.

1. Here are typified the two great gospel privileges of the remission of sin and access to God, both which we owe to the mediation of our Lord Jesus. Here then let us see,

(1) The expiation of guilt which Christ made for us. He is himself both the maker and the matter of the atonement; for he is, [1] The priest, the high priest, that *makes reconciliation for the sins of the people*, Heb. ii. 17. No man was to be with the high priest when he made atonement (*v.* 17); for our Lord Jesus was to *tread the wine-press alone*, and of the people there must be *none with him* (Isa. lxiii. 3); therefore, when he entered upon his sufferings, *all his disciples forsook him and fled*, for if any of them had been taken and put to death with him it would have looked as if they had assisted in making the atonement. But, whereas the atonement which the high priest made pertained only to the congregation of Israel, Christ is the propitiation, not for their sins only, that are Jews, but for the sins of the whole Gentile world. And in this also Christ infinitely ex-

JAMIESON, FAUSSET, BROWN

the incense burning, he went out a second time, to sacrifice at the altar of burnt offering the goat which had been assigned as a sin offering for the people; and carrying its blood into the holy of holies, he made similar sprinklings as he had done before with the blood of the bullock. While the high priest was thus engaged in the most holy place, none of the ordinary priests were allowed to remain within the precincts of the tabernacle. The sanctuary or holy place and the altar of burnt offering were in like manner sprinkled seven times with the blood of the bullock and the goat. The object of this solemn ceremonial was to impress the minds of the Israelites with the conviction that the whole tabernacle was stained by the sins of a guilty people, that by their sins they had forfeited the privileges of the divine presence and worship, and that an atonement had to be made as the condition of God's remaining with them. The sins and shortcomings of the past year having polluted the sacred edifice, the expiation required to be annually renewed. The exclusion of the priests indicated their unworthiness and the impurities of their service. The mingled blood of the two victims being sprinkled on the horns of the altar indicated that the priests and the people equally needed an atonement for their sins. But the sanctuary being thus ceremonially purified, and the people of Israel reconciled by the blood of the consecrated victim, the Lord continued to dwell in the midst of them, and to honor them with His gracious presence. **20-22. he shall bring the live goat**—Having already been presented before the Lord (vs. 10), it was now brought forward to the high priest, who, placing his hands upon its head, and "having confessed over it all the iniquities of the people of Israel, and all their transgressions in all their sins," transferred them by this act to the goat as their substitute. It was then delivered into the hands of a person, who was appointed to lead him away into a distant, solitary, and desert place, where in early times he was let go, to escape for his life; but in the time of Christ, he was carried to a high rock twelve miles from Jerusalem, and there, being thrust over the precipice, he was killed. Commentators have differed widely in their opinions about the character and purpose of this part of the ceremonial; some considering the word "Azazel," with the LXX and our translators, to mean, "the scapegoat"; others, "a lofty, precipitous rock" [BOCHART]; others, "a thing separated to God" [EWALD, THOLUCK]; while others think it designates Satan [GESENIUS, HENGSTENBERG]. This last view is grounded on the idea of both goats forming one and the same sacrifice of atonement, and it is supported by Zechariah 3, which presents a striking commentary on this passage. Whether there was in this peculiar ceremony any reference to an Egyptian superstition about Typhon, the spirit of evil, inhabiting the wilderness, and the design was to ridicule it by sending a cursed animal into his gloomy dominions, it is impossible to say. The subject is involved in much obscurity. But in any view there seems to be a typical reference to Christ who bore away our sins. **23-28. Aaron shall come into the tabernacle of the congregation, and shall put off the linen garments**—On the dismissal of the scapegoat, the high priest prepared for the important parts of the service which still remained; and for the performance of these he laid aside his plain linen clothes, and, having bathed himself in water, he assumed his pontifical dress. Thus gorgeously attired, he went to present the burnt offerings which were prescribed for himself and the people, consisting of the two rams which had been brought with the sin offerings, but reserved till now. The fat was ordered to be burnt upon the altar; the rest of the carcasses to be cut down and given to some priestly attendants to burn without the camp, in conformity with the general law for the sin offerings (ch. 4:8-12; 8:14-17). The persons employed in burning them, as well as the conductor of the scapegoat, were obliged to wash their clothes and bathe their flesh in water before they were allowed to return into the camp. **29-34. this shall be a statute for ever unto you, that in the seventh month, on the tenth day of the month, ye shall afflict your souls**—This day of annual expiation for all the sins, irreverences, and impurities of all classes in Israel during the previous year, was to be observed as a solemn fast, in which "they were to afflict their souls"; it was reckoned a sabbath—kept as a season of "holy convocation," or, assembling for religious purposes. All persons who performed any labor were subject to the penalty of death. It took place on the tenth day of the seventh month, corresponding to our third of October; and this chapter, together with chapter 23:27-32, as containing special

ADAM CLARKE

of this solemn business by *lot*, the disposal of which is with the Lord, Prov. xvi. 33, shows that God alone was to select and point out the person by whom this great atonement was to be made; hence He says: "Behold, I lay in Sion a . . . stone elect [that is, chosen by himself], precious"—of infinite value.

10. *To be the scapegoat. Azazel*, from *az*, a "goat," and *azal*, to "dismiss"; the dismissed or sent-away goat, to distinguish it from the goat that was to be offered in sacrifice. Most ancient nations had vicarious sacrifices, to which they transferred by certain rites and ceremonies the guilt of the community at large, in the same manner in which the scapegoat was used by the Jews.

21. *Aaron shall lay both his hands upon the head*. What this imposition of hands meant see in the notes on Exod. xxix. 10, and on chap. i. 4.

And confess over him all the iniquities . . . transgressions . . . sins. The three terms used here, *iniquities, avonoth*, from *avah*, to "pervert, distort, or turn aside"; *transgressions, peshaim*, from *pasha*, to "transgress, to rebel"; and *sins, chattaoth*, from *chata*, to "miss the mark," are supposed by the Jews to comprise everything that implies a breach of the divine law or an offense against God. Maimonides gives us the confession in the following words: "O Lord, thy people, the house of Israel, have sinned and done iniquity, and trespassed before thee. O Lord, make atonement now for the iniquities and transgressions and sins that thy people, the house of Israel, have sinned and transgressed against thee; as it is written in the law of Moses thy servant, saying: That in this day he shall make atonement for you, to cleanse you from all your sins before the Lord, and ye shall be clean."

When this confession was finished, the goat was sent by a proper hand to the wilderness, and there let loose; and nothing further was ever heard of it. Did not all this signify that Christ has so carried and borne away our sins that against them who receive Him as the only true atoning Sacrifice they should never more be brought to remembrance?

26. *He that let go the goat . . . shall wash*. Not only the person who led him away, but the priest who consecrated him, was reputed unclean, because the goat himself was unclean, being considered as bearing the sins of the whole congregation. On this account both the priest and the person who led him to the wilderness were obliged to wash their clothes and bathe themselves before they could come into the camp.

29. *The seventh month, on the tenth day of the month*. The commandment of fasting, and sanctifying this *tenth* day, is again repeated, chap. xxiii. 27-32; but in the last verse it is called the "ninth day . . . at even," because the Jewish day began with the evening. The sacrifices which the Day of Atonement should have more than other days are mentioned in Num. xxix. 7-11; and the jubilee which was celebrated every fiftieth year was solemnly proclaimed by sound of trumpet on this tenth day, chap. xxv. 8-9. This seventh month was Tisri, and answers to a part of our September and October.

MATTHEW HENRY

celled Aaron, that Aaron needed to offer sacrifice for his own sin first, of which he was to make confession upon the head of his sin-offering; but our Lord Jesus had no sin of his own to answer for. [2] As he is the high priest, so he is the sacrifice with which atonement is made; for he is all in all in our reconciliation to God. Thus he was prefigured by the two goats, which both made one offering: the slain goat was a type of Christ dying for our sins, the scape-goat a type of Christ rising again for our justification. *First,* The atonement is said to be completed by putting the sins of Israel upon the head of the goat. They deserved to have been abandoned and sent into a land of forgetfulness, but that punishment was here transferred to the goat that bore their sins, with reference to which God is said to have laid upon our Lord Jesus (the substance of all these shadows) *the iniquity of us all* (Isa. liii. 6), and he is said to have *borne our sins,* even the punishment of them, *in his own body upon the tree,* 1 Pet. ii. 24. *Secondly,* The consequence of this was that all the iniquities of Israel were *carried into a land of forgetfulness.* Thus Christ, the Lamb of God, *takes away the sin of the world,* by taking it upon himself, John i. 29. And, when God forgives sin, he is said to remember it no more (Heb. viii. 12), *to cast it behind his back* (Isa. xxxviii. 17), *into the depths of the sea* (Mic. vii. 19), and to separate it *as far as the east is from the west,* Ps. ciii. 12.

(2) The entrance into heaven which Christ made for us is here typified by the high priest's entrance into the most holy place. This the apostle has expounded (Heb. ix. 7, &c.), and he shows, [1] That heaven is the holiest of all, but not of that building, and that the way into it by faith, hope, and prayer, through a Mediator, was not then so clearly manifested as it is to us now by the gospel. [2] That Christ our high priest entered into heaven at his ascension once for all. [3] That he entered *by his own blood* (Heb. ix. 12), sprinkling his blood, as it were, before the mercy-seat, where it speaks better things than the blood of bulls and goats could do. Hence he is said to appear in the midst of the throne as *a lamb that had been slain,* Rev. v. 6. The intercession of Christ is there set forth before God as incense, as *this incense.* And as the high priest interceded for himself first, then for his household, and then for all Israel, so our Lord Jesus, in the xviith of St. John, recommended himself first to his Father, then his disciples who were his household, and then all that should believe on him through their word, as all Israel.

2. Here are likewise typified the two great gospel duties of faith and repentance, by which we are qualified for the atonement, and come to be entitled to the benefit of it. (1) By faith we must put our hands upon the head of the offering, relying on Christ as the Lord our Righteousness, pleading his satisfaction as that which was alone able to atone for our sins and procure us a pardon. *"Thou shalt answer, Lord, for me."* (2) By repentance we must afflict our souls; not only fasting for a time from the delights of the body, but inwardly sorrowing for our sins, and living a life of self-denial and mortification.

JAMIESON, FAUSSET, BROWN

allusion to the observances of the day, was publicly read. The rehearsal of these passages appointing the solemn ceremonial was very appropriate, and the details of the successive parts of it (above all the spectacle of the public departure of the scape-goat under the care of its leader) must have produced salutary impressions both of sin and of duty that would not be soon effaced.

ADAM CLARKE

CHARLES H. SPURGEON:

Before Adam transgressed he lived in communion with God; but after he had broken the covenant, and grieved God's Spirit, he could have no more familiar fellowship with God. Under the Mosaic dispensation, in which God was pleased in His grace to dwell among His people and walk with them in the wilderness, it was still under a reserve: there was a holy place wherein the symbol of God's presence was hidden away from mortal gaze. No man might come near to it except in one only way, and then only once in the year, "The Holy Ghost this signifying, that the way into the holiest of all was not yet made manifest, while as the first tabernacle was yet standing." This chapter shows that the way of access to God is by atonement, and by no other method. We cannot draw near unto the Most High except along the blood-sprinkled way of sacrifice. Our Lord Jesus said: "No man cometh unto the Father, but by me"; and this is true in many senses, and in this among them, that our way to God lies only through the sacrifice of His Son.

The reason for this is that sin lieth at the door. Brethren, a pure and holy God cannot endure sin: He cannot have fellowship with it, or with those who are rendered unclean by it, for it would be inconsistent with His nature so to do. On the other hand, sinful men cannot have fellowship with God: their evil nature could not endure the fire of His holiness. Who among us shall dwell with the devouring fire? Who among us shall dwell with everlasting burnings? What is that devouring fire, and what are those everlasting burnings, but the justice and holiness of God? The apostle saith, "Even our God is a consuming fire." A guilty soul would perish if it were possible for it to draw near to God apart from the Mediator and his atonement. The fire of God's nature must consume the stubble of our nature so long as there is sin in us or about us. Hence the difficulty of access, a difficulty which only a divine method can remove. God cannot commune with sinful men, for He is holy. Sinful men cannot commune with a holy God, because He must destroy them, even as he destroyed Nadab and Abihu when they intruded into His holy place. The terrible judgment is mentioned in the opening verses of the chapter before us as the reason why the ordinances herein contained were first of all made.

How, then, shall men come to God? Only in God's own way. He himself devised the way, and He has taught it to us by a parable in this chapter. It would be very wrong to prefer any one passage of Scripture beyond another, for all Scripture is given by inspiration; but if we might do so, we should set this chapter in a very eminent and prominent place for its fullness of instruction, and its clear yet deep doctrinal teaching. It treats upon a matter which is of the very highest importance to all of us. We are here taught the way by which the sin that blocks the door may be taken away, so that a seeking soul may be introduced into the presence of God and stand in His holy place and yet live. Here we learn how we may say, with the astonished prophet, "I have seen God, and my life is preserved." Oh, that we might today so learn the lesson that we may enter into the fullest fellowship with the Father, and with His Son Jesus Christ, in that safe way, that only way, which God has appointed for us! Oh, for the power and guidance of the Holy Spirit, that we may know and use "the new and living way"!—*The Treasury of the Old Testament*

CHAPTER 17

Verses 1-9

This statute obliged all the people of Israel to bring all their sacrifices to God's altar, to be offered there.

I. How it stood before. 1. It was allowed to all people to build altars, and offer sacrifices to God, where they pleased. 2. This liberty had been an occasion of idolatry. The Israelites themselves had learned in Egypt to sacrifice to demons. And some of them, it should seem, practised it even since the God of Israel had so gloriously appeared for them, and with them.

II. How this law settled it. It is hard to construe this as a temporary law, when it is expressly said to be a *statute for ever* (*v.* 7); and therefore it should seem rather to forbid only the killing of beasts for sacrifice anywhere but at God's altar. They must not offer sacrifice, as they had done, *in the open field* (*v.* 5), no, not to the true God, but it must be brought to the priest, to be offered on the altar of the Lord. If any should transgress this law, and offer sacrifice anywhere but at the tabernacle, 1. The guilt was great: *Blood shall be imputed to that man; he hath shed blood, v.* 4. Idolatrous sacrifices were looked upon, not only as adultery, but as murder: he that *offereth them is as if he slew a man,* Isa. lxvi. 3. 2. The punishment should be severe: *That man shall be cut off from among his people.*

III. How this law was observed. 1. While the Israelites kept their integrity they had a tender and

CHAPTER 17

Vss. 1-16. BLOOD OF BEASTS MUST BE OFFERED AT THE TABERNACLE DOOR. **3. What man . . . killeth an ox**—The Israelites, like other people living in the desert, would not make much use of animal food; and when they did kill a lamb or a kid for food, it would almost always be, as in Abraham's entertainment of the angels, an occasion of a feast, to be eaten in company. This was what was done with the peace offerings, and accordingly it is here enacted, that the same course shall be followed in slaughtering the animals as in the case of those offerings, viz., that they should be killed publicly, and after being devoted to God, partaken of by the offerers. This law, it is obvious, could only be observable in the wilderness while the people were encamped within an accessible distance from the tabernacle. The reason for it is to be found in the strong addictedness of the Israelites to idolatry at the time of their departure from Egypt; and as it would have been easy for any by killing an animal to sacrifice privately to a favorite object of worship, a strict prohibition was made against their slaughtering at home. (See on Deut. 12:13.) **5. To the end that the children of Israel may bring their sacrifices, which they offer in the open field**—"They" is supposed by some commentators to refer to the Egyptians, so that the verse will stand thus: "the children of Israel may bring their sacrifices which they (the Egyptians) offer in the open field." The law is

CHAPTER 17

4. ***And bringeth it not unto the door.*** As sacrifice was ever deemed essential to true religion, it was necessary that it should be performed in such a way as to secure the great purpose of its institution. God alone could show how this should be done so as to be pleasing in His sight, and therefore He has given the most plain and particular directions concerning it. The Israelites, from their long residence in Egypt, an idolatrous country, had doubtless adopted many of their usages; and many portions of the Pentateuch seem to have been written merely to correct and bring them back to the purity of the divine worship. *Blood shall be imputed unto that man.* Having poured out the blood improperly, he shall be considered as guilty of murder, because that blood, had it been properly and sacrificially employed, might have made atonement for the life of a man.

MATTHEW HENRY

very jealous regard to this law, as appears by their zeal against the altar which was erected by the two tribes and a half, which they would by no means have left standing if they had not been satisfied that it was never designed, nor should ever be used, for sacrifice or offering, Josh. xxii. 12, &c. 2. The breach of this law was for many ages the corruption of the Jewish church, witness that complaint which so often occurs in the history even of the good kings, *Howbeit the high places were not taken away*; and it was an inlet to the grossest idolatries.

IV. How the matter stands now, and what use we are to make of this law. 1. It is certain that the spiritual sacrifices we are now to offer are not confined to any one place. We have now no temple nor altar that sanctifies the gift, nor does the gospel unity lie in one place, but in one heart, and the *unity of the spirit*. 2. Christ is our altar, and the *true tabernacle* (Heb. viii. 2; xiii. 10); in Him God dwells among us, and it is in him that our sacrifices are acceptable to God, and in him only, 1 Pet. ii. 5.

Verses 10–16

We have here, A repetition and confirmation of the law against eating blood. We have met with this prohibition twice before in the levitical law (*ch.* iii. 17; vii. 26), besides the place it had in the precepts of Noah, Gen. ix. 4. But here, 1. The prohibition is repeated again and again, and reference had to the former laws to this purport (*v.* 12). A great stress is laid upon it, as a law which has more in it than at first view one would think. 2. It is made binding, not only on the *house of Israel*, but on *the strangers that sojourned among them* (*v.* 10). 3. The penalty annexed to this law is very severe (*v.* 10).

4. A reason is given for this law (*v.* 11): because *it is the blood that makes atonement for the soul*. The sinner deserved to die; therefore the sacrifice must die. Now, the blood being so—that ordinarily beasts were killed for man's use by the drawing out of all their blood—God appointed the sprinkling or pouring out of the blood of the sacrifice upon the altar to signify that the life of the sacrifice was given to God instead of the sinner's life, and as a ransom or counter-price for it; therefore *without shedding of blood there was no remission*, Heb. ix. 22. For this reason they must eat no blood, and, (1) It was then a very good reason; for God would by this means preserve the honour of that way of atonement which he had instituted. But, (2) This reason is now superseded, which intimates that the law itself was ceremonial, and is now no longer in force: the blood of Christ who has come is that alone which makes atonement for the soul, and of which the blood of the sacrifices was an imperfect type. The blood, provided it be so prepared as not to be unwholesome, is now allowed for the nourishment of our bodies, because it is no longer appointed to make an atonement for the soul.

JAMIESON, FAUSSET, BROWN

thought to have been directed against those whose Egyptian habits led them to imitate this idolatrous practice. **7. they shall no more offer their sacrifices unto devils**—lit., "goats." The prohibition evidently alludes to the worship of the hirei-footed kind, such as Pan, Faunus, and Saturn, whose recognized symbol was a goat. This was a form of idolatry enthusiastically practised by the Egyptians, particularly in the nome or province of Mendes. Pan was supposed especially to preside over mountainous and desert regions, and it was while they were in the wilderness that the Israelites seem to have been powerfully influenced by a feeling to propitiate this idol. Moreover, the ceremonies observed in this idolatrous worship were extremely licentious and obscene, and the gross impurity of the rites gives great point and significance to the expression of Moses, "they have gone a-whoring." **8, 9. Whatsoever man . . . offereth . . . And bringeth it not unto the door of the tabernacle**—Before the promulgation of the law, men worshipped wherever they pleased or pitched their tents. But after that event the rites of religion could be acceptably performed only at the appointed place of worship. This restriction with respect to place was necessary as a preventive of idolatry; for it prohibited the Israelites, when at a distance, from repairing to the altars of the heathen, which were commonly in groves or fields. **10. I will even set my face against that soul that eateth blood, and will cut him off from among his people**—The face of God is often used in Scripture to denote His anger (Ps. 34:16; Rev. 6:16; Ezek. 38:18). The manner in which God's face would be set against such an offender was, that if the crime were public and known, he was condemned to death; it it were secret, vengeance would overtake him. (See on Gen. 9:4.) But the practice against which the law is here pointed was an idolatrous rite. The Zabians, or worshippers of the heavenly host, were accustomed, in sacrificing animals, to pour out the blood and eat a part of the flesh at *the place* where the blood was poured out (and sometimes the blood itself) believing that by means of it, friendship, brotherhood, and familiarity were contracted between the worshippers and the deities. They, moreover, supposed that the blood was very beneficial in obtaining for them a vision of the demon during their sleep, and a revelation of future events. The prohibition against eating blood, viewed in the light of this historic commentary and unconnected with the peculiar terms in which it is expressed, seems to have been levelled against idolatrous practices, as is still farther evident from Ezek. 33:25, 26, I Cor. 10:20, 21. **11. the life of the flesh is in the blood; and I have given it to you upon the altar, to make an atonement for your souls**—God, as the sovereign author and proprietor of nature, reserved the blood to Himself and allowed men only one use of it—in the way of sacrifices. **13, 14. whatsoever man . . . hunteth**—It was customary with heathen sportsmen, when they killed any game or venison, to pour out the blood as a libation to the god of the chase. The Israelites, on the contrary, were enjoined, instead of leaving it exposed, to cover it with dust and, by this means, were effectually debarred from all the superstitious uses to which the heathen applied it. **15, 16. every soul that eateth that which died of itself** (Exod. 22:31; ch. 11:30; Acts 15:20), **be unclean until the even**—i.e., from the moment of his discovering his fault until the evening. This law, however, was binding only on an Israelite. (See Deut. 14:21.)

ADAM CLARKE

7. *They shall no more offer their sacrifices unto devils.* They shall not sacrifice *lasseirim*, to the "hairy ones," to goats. The famous heathen god, Pan, was represented as having the posteriors, horns, and ears of a goat. Herodotus says that all goats were worshipped in Egypt, but the he-goat particularly. *After whom they have gone a whoring.* Though this term is frequently used to express idolatry, yet we are not to suppose that it is not to be taken in a literal sense in many places in Scripture, even where it is used in connection with idolatrous acts of worship. It is well-known that Baal-peor and Ashtaroth were worshipped with unclean rites; and that public prostitution formed a grand part of the worship of many deities among the Egyptians, Moabites, Canaanites, Greeks, and Romans. The great god of the latter nations, Jupiter, was represented as the general corrupter of women.

11. *For the life of the flesh is in the blood.* This sentence, which contains a most important truth, had existed in the Mosaic writings for 3,600 [3,000] years before the attention of any philosopher was drawn to the subject. This is the more surprising, as the nations in which philosophy flourished were those which especially enjoyed the divine oracles in their respective languages. That the blood actually possesses a living principle, and that the life of the whole body is derived from it, is a doctrine of divine revelation, and a doctrine which the observations and experiments of the most accurate anatomists have served strongly to confirm. The proper circulation of this important fluid through the whole human system was first taught by Solomon in figurative language, Eccles. xii. 6; and discovered, as it is called, and demonstrated by Dr. Harvey in 1628, though some Italian philosophers had the same notion a little before. This accurate anatomist was the first who fully revived the Mosaic notion of the vitality of the blood; which notion was afterward adopted by the justly celebrated Dr. John Hunter, professor of anatomy in London, and fully established by him by a great variety of strong reasoning and accurate experiments.

15. *That which died of itself, or that which was torn.* Because, in both cases, the blood was retained in the body; hence the council at Jerusalem forbade "things strangled" as well as "blood," because in such beasts the blood was coagulated in the veins and arteries. See Acts xv. 28.

MATTHEW HENRY — CHAPTER 18

Verses 1–5

After divers ceremonial institutions, God here returns to the enforcement of moral precepts. The former are still of use to us as types, the latter still binding as laws. We have here, 1. The sacred authority by which these laws are enacted: *I am the Lord your God* (*v.* 2, 4, 30). 2. A strict caution to take heed of retaining the relics of the idolatries of Egypt, where they had dwelt, and of receiving the infection of the idolatries of Canaan, whither they were now going, *v.* 3. If we keep God's commandments in sincerity, though we come short of sinless perfection, we shall find that the way of duty is the way of comfort, and will be the way to happiness. It is the description of the *righteousness which is by the law, the man that doeth them shall live ἐν αὐτοῖς*—in *them* (Rom. x. 5), and is urged to prove that *the law is not of faith*, Gal. iii. 12. The alteration which the gospel has made is in the last word: still *the man that does them shall live*, but not live *in them*; for the law could not give

JAMIESON, FAUSSET, BROWN — CHAPTER 18

Vss. 1-30. UNLAWFUL MARRIAGES. **2-4. I am the Lord your God**—This renewed mention of the divine sovereignty over the Israelites was intended to bear particularly on some laws that were widely different from the social customs that obtained both in Egypt and Canaan; for the enormities, which the laws enumerated in this chapter were intended to put down, were freely practised or publicly sanctioned in both of those countries; and, indeed, the extermination of the ancient Canaanites is described as owing to the abominations with which they had polluted the land. **5. Ye shall therefore keep my statutes and my judgments; which if a man do, he shall live in them**—A special blessing was promised to the Israelites on condition of their obedience to the divine law; and this promise was remarkably verified at particular eras of their history, when pure and undefiled religion prevailed among them, in the public prosperity and domestic happiness enjoyed by them as a people. Obedience to the divine

ADAM CLARKE — CHAPTER 18

MATTHEW HENRY

life, because we could not perfectly keep it. He shall owe his life to the grace of Christ, and not to the merit of his own works; see Gal. iii. 21, 22.

Verses 6–18

These laws relate to the seventh commandment.

I. That which is forbidden as to the relations here specified is *approaching to them to uncover their nakedness, v.* 6.

1. It is chiefly intended to forbid the marrying of any of these relations. Marriage is a divine institution, intended for the comfort of human life, and the decent and honourable propagation of the human race, such as became the dignity of man's nature above that of the beasts. These prohibitions, besides their being enacted by an incontestable authority, are in themselves highly reasonable and equitable. (1) By marriage two were to become one flesh, therefore those that before were in a sense one flesh by nature could not, without the greatest absurdity, become one flesh by institution. (2) Marriage puts an equality between husband and wife. The inequality between master and servant, noble and ignoble, is founded in consent and custom, and there is no harm done if that be taken away by the equality of marriage; but the inequality between parents and children, uncles and nieces, aunts and nephews, either by blood or marriage, is founded in nature, and cannot without confusion be taken away by the equality of marriage. (3) No relations that are equals are forbidden, except brothers and sisters, by the whole blood or half blood, or by marriage. The making use of the ordinance of marriage for the patronising of incestuous mixtures is so far from justifying them, or extenuating their guilt, that it adds the guilt of profaning an ordinance of God, and prostituting that to the vilest of purposes which was instituted for the noblest ends. But,

2. Uncleanness, committed with any of these relations out of marriage, is likewise forbidden here.

II. The relations forbidden are most of them plainly described; and it is generally laid down as a rule that what relations of a man's own he is bound up from marrying the same relations of his wife he is likewise forbidden to marry, for they two are one. That law which forbids marrying a brother's wife (*v.* 16) had an exception peculiar to the Jewish state, that, if a man died without issue, his brother or next of kin should marry the widow, and raise up seed to the deceased (Deut. xxv. 5), for reasons which held good only in that commonwealth.

Verses 19–30

I. A law to preserve the honour of the marriage-bed, that it should not be unseasonably used (*v.* 19), nor invaded by an adulterer, *v.* 20.

II. A law against that which was the most unnatural idolatry, causing their children to *pass through the fire to Moloch, v.* 21. Moloch (as some think) was the idol in and by which they worshipped the sun, that great fire of the world; and therefore in the worship of it they made their own children either sacrifices to this idol, burning them to death before it, or devotees to it, causing them to pass between two fires, as some think, or to be thrown through one, to the honour of this pretended deity, imagining that the consecrating of but one of their children in this manner to Moloch would procure good fortune for all the rest of their children.

III. A law against unnatural lusts, sodomy and bestiality, sins not to be named nor thought of without the utmost abhorrence imaginable, *v.* 22, 23. Other sins level men with the beasts, but these sink them much lower.

JAMIESON, FAUSSET, BROWN

law always, indeed, ensures temporal advantages; and this, doubtless, was the primary meaning of the words, "which if a man do, he shall live in them." But that they had a higher reference to spiritual life is evident from the application made of them by our Lord (Luke 10:28) and the apostle (Rom. 10: 2). **6. None of you shall approach to any that is near of kin**—Very great laxity prevailed amongst the Egyptians in their sentiments and practice about the conjugal relation, as they not only openly sanctioned marriages between brothers and sisters, but even between parents and children. Such incestuous alliances Moses wisely prohibited, and his laws form the basis upon which the marriage regulations of this and other Christian nations are chiefly founded. This verse contains a general summary of all the particular prohibitions; and the forbidden intercourse is pointed out by the phrase, "to approach to." In the specified prohibitions that follow, all of which are included in this general summary, the prohibited familiarity is indicated by the phrases, to "uncover the nakedness," to "take," and to "lie with." The phrase in this sixth verse, therefore, has the same identical meaning with each of the other three, and the marriages in reference to which it is used are those of consanguinity or too close affinity, amounting to incestuous connections. **18. Neither shalt thou take a wife to her sister, to vex her.** The original is rendered in the margin, "neither shalt thou take one wife to another to vex her," and two different and opposite interpretations have been put upon this passage. The marginal construction involves an express prohibition of polygamy; and, indeed, there can be no doubt that the practice of having more wives than one is directly contrary to the divine will. It was prohibited by the original law of marriage, and no evidence of its lawfulness under the Levitical code can be discovered, although Moses—from "the hardness of their hearts"—tolerated it in the people of a rude and early age. The second interpretation forms the ground upon which the "vexed question" has been raised in our times respecting the lawfulness of marriage with a deceased wife's sister. Whatever arguments may be used to prove the unlawfulness or inexpediency of such a matrimonial relation, the passage under consideration cannot, on a sound basis of criticism, be enlisted in the service; for the crimes with which it is here associated warrant the conclusion that it points not to marriage with a deceased wife's sister, but with a sister in the wife's lifetime, a practice common among the ancient Egyptians, Chaldeans, and others. **21. thou shalt not let any of thy seed pass through the fire to Molech,** etc.—Molech, or Moloch, which signifies "king," was the idol of the Ammonites. His statue was of brass, and rested on a pedestal or throne of the same metal. His head, resembling that of a calf, was adorned with a crow, and his arms were extended in the attitude of embracing those who approached him. His devotees dedicated their children to him; and when this was to be done, they heated the statue to a high pitch of intensity by a fire within, and then the infants were either shaken over the flames, or passed through the ignited arms, by way of lustration to ensure the favor of the pretended deity. The fire-worshippers asserted that all children who did not undergo this purifying process would die in infancy; and the influence of this Zabian superstition was still so extensively prevalent in the days of Moses, that the divine lawgiver judged it necessary to prohibit it by an express statute. **neither shalt thou profane the name of thy God**—by giving it to false or pretended divinities; or, perhaps, from this precept standing in close connection with the worship of Molech, the meaning rather is, Do not, by devoting your children to him, give foreigners occasion to blaspheme the name of your God as a cruel and sanguinary deity, who demands the sacrifice of human victims, and who encourages cruelty in his votaries. **24. Defile not yourselves in any of these things**—In the preceding verses seventeen express cases of incest are enumerated; comprehending eleven of affinity, and six of consanguinity, together with some criminal enormities of an aggravated and unnatural character. In such prohibitions it was necessary for the instruction of a people low in the scale of moral perception, that the enumeration should be very specific as well as minute; and then, on completing it, the divine lawgiver announces his own views of these crimes, without any exception or modification, in the remarkable terms employed in this verse. **in all these the nations are defiled which I cast out before you,** etc.—Ancient history gives many appalling proofs that the enormous vices described in this chapter were very prevalent, nay, were regularly

ADAM CLARKE

6. *Any that is near of kin. Col shear besaro,* "any remnant of his flesh," i.e., to any particularly allied to his own family, the prohibited degrees in which are specified from the seventh to the seventeenth verse inclusive. Notwithstanding the prohibitions here, it must be evident that in the infancy of the world persons very near of kin must have been joined in matrimonial alliances, and that even brothers must have matched with their own sisters. This must have been the case in the family of Adam. In these first instances necessity required this; when this necessity no longer existed, the thing became inexpedient and improper for two reasons: (1) That the duties owing by nature to relatives might not be confounded with those of a social or political kind; for could a man be a brother and a husband, a son and a husband, at the same time, and fulfil the duties of both? (2) That by intermarrying with other families the bonds of social compact might be strengthened and extended, so that the love of our neighbor might at once be felt to be not only a maxim of sound policy, but also a very practicable and easy duty; and thus feuds, divisions, and wars be prevented.

16. *Thy brother's wife.* This was an illegal marriage, unless the brother died childless. In that case it was not only lawful for her to marry her brother-in-law, but he was obliged by the law, Deut. xxv. 5, to take her to wife.

18. *A wife to her sister.* You shall not marry two sisters at the same time, as Jacob did Rachel and Leah; but there is nothing in this law that rendered it illegal to marry a sister-in-law when her sister was dead; therefore the text says, Thou shalt not take her *in her life time, to vex her,* alluding probably to the case of the jealousies and vexations which subsisted between Leah and Rachel, and by which the family peace was so often disturbed. Some think that the text may be so understood as also to forbid polygamy.

21. *Pass through the fire to Molech.* The name of this idol is mentioned for the first time in this place. As the word *molech* or *melech* signifies "king" or "governor," it is very likely that this idol represented the sun; and more particularly as the fire appears to have been so much employed in his worship. There are several opinions concerning the meaning of passing through the fire to Molech. That some were actually burned alive to this idol several scriptures, according to the opinion of commentators, seem strongly to intimate; see, among others, Ps. cvi. 38; Jer. vii. 31; and Ezek. xxiii. 37-39. That others were only consecrated to his service by passing between two fires the rabbins strongly assert; and if Ahaz had but one son, Hezekiah (though it is probable he had others, see 2 Chron. xxviii. 3), he is said to have passed through the fire to Molech, 2 Kings xvi. 3, yet he succeeded his father in the kingdom, chap. xviii. 1; therefore this could only be a consecration, his idolatrous father intending thereby to initiate him early into the service of this demon.

22. *With mankind.* This abominable crime [was] frequent among the Greeks and Romans as well as the Canaanites.

23. *Any woman stand before a beast.* That this was often done in Egypt there can be no doubt; and we have the testimony of Herodotus that a fact of this kind actually took place while he was in Egypt.

MATTHEW HENRY

IV. Arguments against these and the like abominable wickednesses. 1. Sinners defile themselves with these abominations. All sin is defiling to the conscience, but these are sins that have a peculiar turpitude in them. 2. *The souls that commit them shall be cut off, v.* 29. Fleshly lusts war against the soul, and will certainly be the ruin of it if God's mercy and grace prevent not. For these and the like sins the Canaanites were to be destroyed.

V. The chapter concludes with a sovereign antidote against this infection: *Therefore you shall keep my ordinance that you commit not any one of these abominable customs, v.* 30. A close and constant adherence to God's ordinances is the most effectual preservative from the infection of gross sin. It is the grace of God only that will secure us, and that grace is to be expected only in the use of the means of grace.

JAMIESON, FAUSSET, BROWN

practised from religious motives in the temples of Egypt and the groves of Canaan; and it was these gigantic social disorders that occasioned the expulsion, of which the Israelites were, in the hands of a righteous and retributive Providence, the appointed instruments (Gen. 15:16). The strongly figurative language of "the land itself vomiting out her inhabitants," shows the hopeless depth of their moral corruption. **25 therefore I do visit the iniquity thereof upon it; and the land itself vomiteth out its inhabitants**—The Canaanites, as enormous and incorrigible sinners, were to be exterminated; and this extermination was manifestly a judicial punishment inflicted by a ruler whose laws had been grossly and perseveringly outraged. But before a law can be disobeyed, it must have been previously in existence; and hence a law, prohibiting all the horrid crimes enumerated above—a law obligatory upon the Canaanites as well as other nations—was already known and in force before the Levitical law of incest was promulgated. Some general law, then, prohibiting these crimes must have been published to mankind at a very early period of the world's history; and that law must either have been the moral law, originally written on the human heart, or a law on the institution of marriage revealed to Adam and known to the Canaanites and others by tradition or otherwise. **29. the souls that commit them shall be cut off**—This strong denunciatory language is applied to all the crimes specified in the chapter without distinction: to incest as truly as to bestiality, and to the eleven cases of affinity as fully as to the six of consanguinity. Death is the punishment sternly denounced against all of them. No language could be more explicit or universal; none could more strongly indicate intense loathing and abhorrence. **30. Therefore shall ye keep mine ordinance, that ye commit not any one of these abominable customs**—In giving the Israelites these particular institutions, God was only re-delivering the law imprinted on the natural heart of man; for there is every reason to believe that the incestuous alliances and unnatural crimes prohibited in this chapter were forbidden to all men by a law expressed or understood from the beginning of the world, or at least from the era of the flood, since God threatens to condemn and punish, in a manner so sternly severe, these atrocities in the practice of the Canaanites and their neighbors, who were not subject to the laws of the Hebrew nation.

ADAM CLARKE

25. *The land itself vomiteth out her inhabitants.* This is a personification. Here the *land* is represented as an intelligent being, with a deep and refined sense of moral good and evil. Information concerning the abominations of the people is brought to this personified land, with which it is so deeply affected that a nausea is produced, and it vomits out its abominable and accursed inhabitants.

30. *Shall ye keep mine ordinance.* The only way to be preserved from all false worship is seriously to consider and devoutly to observe the ordinances of the true religion. He who in the things of God goes no further than he can say, "Thus it is written, and thus it behooves me to do," is never likely to receive a false creed, nor perform a superstitious act of worship.

MATTHEW HENRY

CHAPTER 19

Verses 1–10

Moses is ordered to deliver the summary of the laws *to all the congregation of the children of Israel* (*v.* 2). Many of the precepts here given they had received before, but it was requisite that they should be repeated, that they might be remembered. In these verses it is required,

I. That Israel be a holy people, because the God of Israel is a holy God, *v.* 2. And this is now the law of Christ. *You shall be holy, for I am holy,* 1 Pet. i. 15, 16. Israel was sanctified by the types and shadows (*ch.* xx. 8), but we are *sanctified by the truth,* or substance of all those shadows, John xvii. 17; Tit. ii. 14.

II. That children be obedient to their parents: "*You shall fear every man his mother and his father,*" *v.* 3. 1. The fear here required includes inward reverence and esteem, outward expressions of respect, obedience to the lawful commands of parents, care and endeavour to please them and make them easy, and to avoid everything that may offend and grieve them, and incur their displeasure. The Jewish doctors ask, "What is this fear that is owing to a father?" And they answer, "It is not to stand in his way nor to sit in his place, not to contradict what he says nor to carp at it, not to call him by his name, either living or dead, but 'My Father,' or 'Sir'; it is to provide for him if he be poor, and the like." 2. Children, when they grow up to be men, must not think themselves discharged from this duty: every man, though he be a wise man, and a great man, yet must reverence his parents, because they are his parents. 3. The mother is put first, which is not usual, to show that the duty is equally owing to both. 4. It is added, *and keep my sabbaths.* If God provides by his law for the preserving of the honour of parents, parents must use their authority over their children for the preserving of the honour of God, particularly the honour of his sabbaths. The ruin of young people has often been observed to begin in the contempt of their parents and the profanation of the sabbath day. 5. The reason added to both these precepts is, "*I am the Lord your God;* the Lord of the sabbath

JAMIESON, FAUSSET, BROWN

CHAPTER 19

VSS. 1-37. A REPETITION OF SUNDRY LAWS. **2. Speak unto all the congregation of the children of Israel**—Many of the laws enumerated in this chapter had been previously announced. As they were, however, of a general application, not suited to particular classes, but to the nation at large, so Moses seems, according to divine instructions, to have rehearsed them, perhaps on different occasions and to successive divisions of the people, till "all the congregation of the children of Israel" were taught to know them. The will of God in the Old as well as the New Testament Church was not locked up in the repositories of an unknown tongue, but communicated plainly and openly to the people. **Ye shall be holy: for I . . . am holy**—Separated from the world, the people of God were required to be holy, for His character, His laws, and service were holy. (See I Pet. 1:15.) **3. Ye shall fear every man his mother and his father, and keep my sabbaths**—The duty of obedience to parents is placed in connection with the proper observance of the Sabbaths, both of them lying at the foundation of practical religion.

ADAM CLARKE

CHAPTER 19

3. *Ye shall fear every man his mother.* You shall have the profoundest reverence and respect for them. See the notes on Gen. xlviii. 12 and on Exod. xx. 8, 12.

MATTHEW HENRY

and the God of your parents."

III. That God only be worshipped, and not by images (*v.* 4): "*Turn you not to idols*, to *Elilim*, to vanities, things of no power, no value, gods that are no gods. You are the work of God's hands, be not so absurd as to worship gods *the work of your own hands*."

IV. That the sacrifices of their peace-offerings should always be offered, and eaten, according to the law, *v.* 5–8.

V. That they should leave the gleanings of their harvest and vintage for the poor, *v.* 9, 10. When they gathered in their corn, they must leave some standing in the corner of the field; the Jewish doctors say, "It should be a sixtieth part of the field"; and they must also leave the gleanings and the small clusters of their grapes, which at first were overlooked.

Verses 11–18

We are taught here.

I. To be honest and true in all our dealings, *v.* 11. Whatever we have in the world, we must see to it that it be honestly come by, for we cannot be truly rich, nor long rich, with that which is not.

II. To maintain a very reverent regard to the sacred name of God (*v.* 12).

III. Neither to take nor keep anyone's right from him, *v.* 13. We must not take that which is none of our own, either by fraud or robbery; nor detain that which belongs to another. Let the day-labourer have his wages as soon as he has done his day's work, if he desire it.

IV. To be particularly tender of the credit and safety of those that cannot help themselves, *v.* 14. 1. The credit of the deaf: *Thou shalt not curse the deaf*; that is, not only those that are naturally deaf, that cannot hear at all, but also those that are absent, and at present out of hearing. 2. The safety of the blind we must likewise be tender of, and not put a stumbling-block before them; for this is to add affliction to the afflicted. This prohibition implies a precept to help the blind, and remove stumbling-blocks out of their way. The Jewish writers, thinking it impossible that any should be so barbarous as to put a *stumbling-block in the way of the blind*, understood it figuratively, that it forbids giving bad counsel to those that are simple and easily imposed upon, by which they may be led to do something to their own prejudice.

V. Judges and all in authority are here commanded to give verdict and judgment without partiality (*v.* 15). *Thou shalt not respect the person of the poor*, Exod. xxiii. 3. Whatever may be given to a poor man as an alms, yet let nothing be awarded him as his right but what he is legally entitled to, nor let his poverty excuse him from any just punishment for a fault. The Jews say, "Judges were obliged by this law to be so impartial as not to let one of the contending parties sit while the other stood, nor permit one to say what he pleased and bid the other be short"; see James ii. 1–4.

VI. We are all forbidden to do anything injurious to our neighbour's good name (*v.* 16), either, 1. In common conversation: *Thou shalt not go up and down as a tale-bearer*. The word used for a tale-bearer signifies a *pedlar*, or *petty chapman*, the interlopers of trade; for tale-bearers pick up ill-natured stories at one house and utter them at another, and commonly barter slanders by way of exchange. See this sin condemned, Prov. xi. 13; xx. 19; Jer. ix. 4, 5; Ezek. xxii. 9. Or, 2. In witness-bearing: Neither *shalt thou stand* as a witness *against the blood of thy neighbour*, if his blood be innocent. The Jewish doctors put this further sense upon it: "He that can by his testimony clear one that is accused is obliged by this law to do it"; see Prov. xxiv. 11, 12.

VII. We are commanded to rebuke our neighbour in love (*v.* 17): 1. Rather rebuke him than hate him for an injury done to thyself. If we apprehend that our neighbour has any way wronged us, we must not conceive a secret grudge against him, and estrange ourselves from him. We must rather endeavour to convince our brother of the injury, reason the case fairly with him. This is the rule our Saviour gives in the case, Luke xvii. 3. 2. Therefore rebuke him for his sin against God, because thou lovest him. Note, Friendly reproof is a duty we owe to one another, and we ought both to give it and take it in love. *Let the righteous smite me, and it shall be a kindness*, Ps. cxli. 5.

VIII. We are here required to put off all malice, and to put on brotherly love, *v.* 18. 1. We must be ill-affected to none. 2. We must be well-affected to all: *Thou shalt love thy neighbour as thyself*. We must do to our neighbour as we would be done to ourselves (Matt. vii. 12), putting *our souls into his*

JAMIESON, FAUSSET, BROWN

5-8. if ye offer a sacrifice of peace offerings unto the Lord, ye shall offer it at your own will—Those which included thank offerings, or offerings made for vows, were always free-will offerings. Except the portions which, being waved and heaved, became the property of the priests (see ch. 3), the rest of the victim was eaten by the offerer and his friend, under the following regulations, however, that, if thank offerings, they were to be eaten on the day of their presentation; and if a freewill offering, although it might be eaten on the second day, yet if any remained of it till the third day, it was to be burnt, or deep criminality was incurred by the person who then ventured to partake of it. The reason of this strict prohibition seems to have been to prevent any mysterious virtue being superstitiously attached to meat offered on the altar. **9, 10. when ye reap the harvest of your land, thou shalt not wholly reap the corners of thy field**—The right of the poor in Israel to glean after reapers, as well as to the unreaped corners of the field, was secured by a positive statute; and this, in addition to other enactments connected with the ceremonial law, formed a beneficial provision for their support. At the same time, proprietors were not obliged to admit them into the field until the grain had been carried off the field; and they seem also to have been left at liberty to choose the poor whom they deemed the most deserving or needful (Ruth 2:2, 8). This was the earliest law for the benefit of the poor that we read of in the code of any people; and it combined in admirable union the obligation of a public duty with the exercise of private and voluntary benevolence at a time when the hearts of the rich would be strongly inclined to liberality. **11-16. Ye shall not steal**—A variety of social duties are inculcated in this passage, chiefly in reference to common and little-thought-of vices to which mankind are exceedingly prone; such as committing petty fraunds, or not scrupling to violate truth in transactions of business, ridiculing bodily infirmities, or circulating stories to the prejudice of others. In opposition to these bad habits, a spirit of humanity and brotherly kindness is strongly enforced.

17. thou shalt in any wise rebuke thy neighbour—Instead of cherishing latent feelings of malice or meditating purposes of revenge against a person who has committed an insult or injury against them, God's people were taught to remonstrate with the offender and endeavor, by calm and kindly reason, to bring him to a sense of his fault. **not suffer sin upon him**—lit., that ye may not participate in his sin.

18. thou shalt love thy neighbour as thyself--The word "neighbour" is used as synonymous with "fellow creature." The Israelites in a later age restricted its meaning as applicable only to their own countrymen. This narrow interpretation was refuted by our Lord in a beautiful parable (Luke 10:30).

ADAM CLARKE

4. *Turn ye not unto idols. Elilim*, literally "nothings"; and to this Paul seems to allude 1 Cor. viii. 4, where he says, "We know that an idol is nothing in the world."

5. *Peace offerings.* See the notes at the conclusion of chap. vii.

7. *If it be eaten . . . on the third day.* See the note on chap. vii. 15.

9. *When ye reap the harvest.* Liberty for the poor to glean both the cornfields and vineyards was a divine institution among the Jews; for the whole of the Mosaic dispensation, like the Christian, breathed love to God and benevolence to man. The poor in Judea were to live by gleanings from the cornfields and vineyards.

11. *Ye shall not steal.* See the notes on Exodus xx.

13. *The wages . . . shall not abide with thee all night.* For this plain reason, it is the support of the man's life and family, and they need to expend it as fast as it is earned.

14. *Thou shalt not curse the deaf.* Or "speak evil" of him, because he cannot hear, and so cannot vindicate his own character. *Nor put a stumbling block before the blind.* He who is capable of doing this must have a heart cased with cruelty. The spirit and design of these precepts are that no man shall in any case take advantage of the ignorance, simplicity, or inexperience of his neighbor, but in all things do to his neighbor as he would, on a change of circumstances, that his neighbor should do to him.

16. *Thou shalt not go up and down as a talebearer. Rachil* signifies a "trader," a "pedlar," and is here applied to the person who travels about dealing in scandal and calumny, getting the secrets of every person and family, and retailing them wherever he goes. A more despicable character exists not; such a person is a pest to society, and should be exiled from the habitations of men. *Neither shalt thou stand against the blood.* You shall not be as a false witness, because by such testimony the *blood*—the "life" of an innocent man—may be endangered.

17. *Thou shalt not hate thy brother.* You shall not only not do him any kind of evil, but you shall harbor no hatred in your heart towards him. On the contrary, thou shalt love him as thyself, v. 18. Many persons suppose, from misunderstanding our Lord's words, John xiii. 34, "A new commandment I give unto you, That ye love one another," that loving our neighbor as ourselves was first instituted under the gospel. This verse shows the opinion to be unfounded. But to love another as Christ has loved us, i.e., to lay down our lives for each other, is certainly a "new" commandment; we have it simply on the authority of Jesus Christ alone. *And not suffer sin upon him.* If you see him sin, or know him to be addicted to anything by which the safety of his soul is endangered, you shall mildly and affectionately reprove him, and by no means permit him to go on without counsel and advice in a way that is leading him to perdition. In a multitude of cases timely reproof has been the means of saving the soul. Speak to him privately if possible; if not, write to him in such a way that himself alone shall see it.

MATTHEW HENRY

soul's stead, Job xvi. 4, 5. Nay, we must in many cases deny ourselves for the good of our neighbour, as Paul, 1 Cor. ix. 19, &c. Herein the gospel goes beyond even that excellent precept of the law; for Christ, by laying down his life for us, has taught us even to *lay down our lives for the brethren*, in some cases (1 John iii. 16), and so to love our neighbour better than ourselves.

Verses 19–29

I. A law against mixtures, *v*. 19. God in the beginning made the cattle *after their kind* (Gen. i. 25), and we must acquiesce in the order of nature God hath established, believing that is best and sufficient, and not covet monsters. The sowing of mingled corn and the wearing of linsey-woolsey garments are forbidden, either as superstitious customs of the heathen or to intimate how careful they should be not to mingle themselves with the heathen nor to weave any of the usages of the Gentiles into God's ordinances. Ainsworth suggests that it was to lead Israel to the simplicity and sincerity of religion.

II. A law for punishing adultery committed with one that was a bondmaid that was espoused, *v*. 20–22. It was for the honour of marriage, though but begun by betrothing, that the crime should be punished; but it was for the honour of freedom that it should not be punished as the debauching of a free woman was, so great was the difference then made between bond and free (Gal. iv. 30); but the gospel of Christ knows no such distinction, Col. iii. 11.

III. A law concerning fruit trees, that for the first three years after they were planted, if they should happen to be so forward as to bear in that time, yet no use should be made of the fruit, *v*. 23–25. It was therefore the practice of the Jews to pluck off the fruit, as soon as they perceived it knit, from their young trees, as gardeners do sometimes, because their early bearing hinders their growing. If any did come to perfection, it was not to be used in the service either of God or man; but what they bore the fourth year was to be holy to the Lord, either given to the priests, or eaten before the Lord with joy, as their second tithe was, and thenceforward it was all their own. This law in the case of fruit trees seems to be parallel with that in the case of animals, that no creature should be accepted as an offering till it was past eight days old, nor till that day were children to be circumcised; see *ch*. xxii. 27. God would have the first-fruits of their trees, but, because for the first three years they were as inconsiderable as a lamb or a calf under eight days old, therefore God would not have them, for it is fit he should have every thing at its best; and yet he would not allow them to be used, because his first-fruits were not as yet offered: they must therefore be accounted as uncircumcised, that is, as an animal under eight days old, not fit for any use.

IV. A law against the superstitious usages of the heathen, *v*. 26–28. 1. Eating upon the blood, as the Gentiles did, who gathered the blood of their sacrifices into a vessel for their demons (as they fancied) to drink. The blood of God's sacrifices was to be sprinkled on the altar, and then poured at the foot of it, and conveyed away. 2. Enchantment and divination, and a superstitious observation of the times, some days and hours lucky and others unlucky. Curious arts of this kind, it is likely, had been of late invented by the Egyptian priests. It would be unpardonable in those *to whom were committed the oracles of God* to ask counsel of the devil, and yet worse in Christians to whom *the Son of God is manifested*, who has *destroyed the work of the devil*. For Christians to have their nativities cast, and their fortunes told them, to use spells and charms for the cure of diseases and the driving away of evil spirits, to be affected with the falling of the salt, a hare crossing the way, cross days, or the like, is an intolerable affront to the Lord Jesus, a support of paganism and idolatry, and a reproach both to themselves and to that worthy name by which they are called. 3. There was a superstition even in trimming themselves used by the heathen, which must not be imitated by the people of God: *You shall not round the corners of your heads*. Those that worshipped the hosts of heaven, in honour of them, cut their hair so that their heads might resemble the celestial globe; but, as the custom was foolish in itself, so, being done with respect to their false gods, it was idolatrous.

JAMIESON, FAUSSET, BROWN

19. Thou shalt not let thy cattle gender with a diverse kind—This prohibition was probably intended to discourage a practice which seemed to infringe upon the economy which God has established in the animal kingdom. **thou shalt not sow thy field with mingled seed**—This also was directed against an idolatrous practice, viz., that of the ancient Zabians, or fire-worshippers, who sowed different seeds, accompanying the act with magical rites and invocations; and commentators have generally thought the design of this and the preceding law was to put an end to the unnatural lusts and foolish superstitions which were prevalent among the heathen. But the reason of the prohibition was probably deeper: for those who have studied the diseases of land and vegetables tell us, that the practice of mingling seeds is injurious both to flowers and to grains. "If the various genera of the natural order Gramineæ, which includes the grains and the grasses, should be sown in the same field, and flower at the same time, so that the pollen of the two flowers mix, a spurious seed will be the consequence, called by the farmers *chess*. It is always inferior and unlike either of the two grains that produced it, in size, flavor, and nutritious principles. Independently of contributing to disease the soil, they never fail to produce the same in animals and men that feed on them" [WHITLAW]. **neither shall a garment mingled of linen and woollen come upon thee**—Although this precept, like the other two with which it is associated, was in all probability designed to root out some superstition, it seems to have had a farther meaning. The law, it is to be observed, did not prohibit the Israelites wearing many different kinds of cloths together, but only the two specified; and the observations and researches of modern science have proved that "wool, when combined with linen, increases its power of passing off the electricity from the body. In hot climates, it brings on malignant fevers and exhausts the strength; and when passing off from the body, it meets with the heated air, inflames and excoriates like a blister" [WHITLAW]. (See Ezek. 44:17, 18.) **23-25. ye shall count the fruit thereof as uncircumcised; three years . . . it shall not be eaten of**—"The wisdom of this law is very striking. Every gardener will teach us not to let fruit trees bear in their earliest years, but to pluck off the blossoms: and for this reason, that they will thus thrive the better, and bear more abundantly afterwards. The very expression, 'to regard them as uncircumcised,' suggests the propriety of pinching them off; I do not say *cutting* them off, because it is generally the hand, and not a knife, that is employed in this operation" [MICHAELIS]. **26. shall not eat any thing with the blood**—(See on ch. 17:10.) **neither . . . use enchantment, nor observe times**—The former refers to divination by serpents—one of the earliest forms of enchantment, and the other means the observation, lit., of *clouds*, as a study of the appearance and motion of clouds was a common way of foretelling good or bad fortune. Such absurd but deep-rooted superstitions often put a stop to the prosecution of serious and important transactions, but they were forbidden especially as implying a want of faith in the being, or of reliance on the providence of God. **27. Ye shall not round the corners of your heads**, etc.—It seems probable that this fashion had been learned by the Israelites in Egypt, for the ancient Egyptians had their dark locks cropped short or shaved with great nicety, so that what remained on the crown appeared in the form of a circle surrounding the head, while the beard was dressed into a square form. This kind of coiffure had a highly idolatrous meaning; and it was adopted, with some slight variations, by almost all idolaters in ancient times. (Jer. 9:25, 26; 25:23, where "in the utmost corners" means having the corners of their hair cut.) Frequently a lock or tuft of hair was left on the hinder part of the head, the rest being cut round in the form of a ring, as the Turks, Chinese, and Hindoos do at the present day. **neither shalt thou mar**, etc.—The Egyptians used to cut or shave off their whiskers, as may be seen in the coffins of mummies, and the representations of divinities on the monuments. But the Hebrews, in order to separate them from the neighboring nations, or perhaps to put a stop to some existing superstition, were forbidden to imitate this practice. It may appear surprising that Moses should condescend to such minutiæ as that of regulating the fashion of the hair and the beard—matters which do not usually occupy the attention of a legislator—and which appear widely remote from the province either of government or of a religion. A strong presumption, therefore, arises that he had in mind by these regulations to combat some superstitious

ADAM CLARKE

19. *Gender with a diverse kind*. These precepts taken literally seem to imply that they should not permit the horse and the she-ass, nor the he-ass and the cow, to couple together; nor sow different kinds of seeds in the same field or garden; nor have garments of silk and woolen, cotton and silk, linen and wool. And if all these were forbidden, there must have been some moral reason for the prohibitions, because domestic economy required several of these mixtures, especially those which relate to seeds and clothing. With respect to heterogeneous mixtures among *cattle*, there is something very unnatural in it, and it was probably forbidden to prevent excitements to such unnatural lusts as those condemned in the preceding chapter, vv. 22-23. As to *seed*, in many cases it would be very improper to sow different kinds in the same plot of ground. As to different kinds of *garments*, the prohibition here might be intended as much against pride and vanity as any thing else. But we really do not know what the original word *shaatnez*, which we translate *linen* and *woollen*, means. It is true that in Deut. xxii. 11, where it is again used, it seems to be explained by the words immediately following, "Thou shalt not wear a garment of divers sorts, as of linen and woollen together"; but this may as well refer to a garment made up of a sort of patchwork differently colored and arranged for pride and for show.

20. *A woman, that is a bondmaid*. Had she been free, the law required that she should be put to death (see Deut. xxii. 24); but as she was a slave, she is supposed to have less self-command, and therefore less guilt. But as it is taken for granted she did not make resistance, or did consent, she is to be scourged, and the man is to bring a ram for a trespass offering.

23. *Three years shall it be as uncircumcised*. I see no reason to seek for mystical meanings in this prohibition. The fruit of a young tree cannot be good; for not having arrived at a state of maturity, the juices cannot be sufficiently elaborated to produce fruit excellent in its kind. The Israelites are commanded not to eat of the fruit of a tree till the fifth year after its planting. In the first three years the fruit is unwholesome; in the fourth year the fruit is holy, it belongs to God, and should be consecrated to Him, v. 24; and in the fifth year and afterward the fruit may be employed for common use, v. 25.

26. *Neither shall ye use enchantment. Lo thenachashu*. Conjecture itself can do little towards a proper explanation of the terms used in this verse. *Nachash* in Gen. iii. 1 we translate "serpent." Possibly the superstition here prohibited may be what the Greeks called "divination by serpents." *Nor observe times. Velo teonenu*, you shall "not divine by clouds," which was also a superstition much in practice among the heathen, as well as divination by the flight of birds.

27. *Ye shall not round the corners of your heads*. This and the following verse evidently refer to customs which must have existed among the Egyptians when the Israelites sojourned in Egypt; and what they were it is now difficult, even with any probability, to conjecture. Herodotus observes that the Arabs shave or cut their hair round, in honor of Bacchus, who, they say, had his hair cut in this way. *The corners of thy beard*. Probably meaning the hair of the cheek that connects the hair of the head with the beard. This was no doubt cut in some peculiar manner, for the superstitious purposes mentioned above.

MATTHEW HENRY

4. The rites and ceremonies by which they expressed their sorrow at their funerals must not be imitated, *v.* 28. They must not make cuts or prints in their flesh for the dead; for the heathen did so to pacify the infernal deities. Christ by his sufferings has altered the property of death, and made it a true friend to every true Israelite; and now, as there needs nothing to make death propitious to us, so we sorrow not as those that have no hope. *Lastly,* The prostituting of their daughters to uncleanness, which is here forbidden (*v.* 29), seems to have been practised by the heathen in their idolatrous worships.

Verses 30–37

I. A law for the preserving of the honour of the time and place appropriated to the service of God, *v.* 30. 1. Sabbaths must be religiously observed. 2. The sanctuary must be reverenced. Though now there is no place holy by divine institution, as the tabernacle and temple then were, yet this law obliges us to respect the solemn assemblies of Christians for religious worship, as being held under a promise of Christ's special presence in them.

II. A caution against all communion with those that were in league with familiar spirits: "*Regard them not, seek not after them,* be not in fear of any evil from them nor in hopes of any good from them.

III. A charge to young people to show respect to the aged: *Thou shalt rise up before the hoary head, v.* 32. Those whom God has honoured with the common blessing of long life we ought to honour. Those who in age are wise and good are worthy of double honour; their credit and comfort must be carefully consulted, and their counsels asked and hearkened to, Job xxxii. 6, 7. Note, Religion teaches good manners, and obliges us to give honour to those to whom honour is due.

IV. A charge to the Israelites to be very tender of strangers, *v.* 33, 34. "*Thou shalt not vex a stranger,* but *love him as thyself,* and as one of thy own people." Strangers are God's particular care, as the widow and the fatherless are, because it is his honour to help the helpless, Ps. cxlvi. 9. It argues a generous disposition, and a pious regard to God, as a common Father, to be kind to strangers. But here is a reason added peculiar to the Jews: "*For you were strangers in the land of Egypt.* God then favoured you, therefore do you now favour the strangers."

V. Justice in weights and measures is here commanded. That there should be no cheat in them, *v.* 35. That they should be very exact, *v.* 36.

VI. The chapter concludes with a general command (*v.* 37): *You shall observe all my statutes, and do them.*

JAMIESON, FAUSSET, BROWN

practices of the Egyptians. **28. Ye shall not make any cuttings in your flesh for the dead**—The practice of making deep gashes on the face and arms and legs, in time of bereavement, was universal among the heathen, and it was deemed a becoming mark of respect for the dead, as well as a sort of propitiatory offering to the deities who presided over death and the grave. The Jews learned this custom in Egypt, and though weaned from it, relapsed in a later and degenerate age into this old superstition (Isa. 15:2; Jer. 16:6; 41:5). **nor print any marks upon you**—by *tattooing*—imprinting figures of flowers, leaves, stars, and other fanciful devices on various parts of their person—the impression was made sometimes by means of a hot iron, sometimes by ink or paint, as is done by the Arab females of the present day and the different castes of the Hindoos. It it probable that a strong propensity to adopt such marks in honor of some idol gave occasion to the prohibition in this verse; and they were wisely forbidden, for they were signs of apostasy; and, when once made, they were insuperable obstacles to a return. (See allusions to the practice, Isa. 44:5; Rev. 13:17; 14: 1.) **30. keep my sabbaths, and reverence my sanctuary**—This precept is frequently repeated along with the prohibition of idolatrous practices, and here it stands closely connected with the superstitions forbidden in the previous verses. **31. Regard not them that have familiar spirits**—The *Hebrew* word, rendered "familiar spirit," signifies the belly, and sometimes a leathern bottle, from its similarity to the belly. It was applied in the sense of this passage to ventriloquists, who pretended to have communication with the invisible world. The Hebrews were strictly forbidden to consult them as the vain but high pretensions of those impostors were derogatory to the honor of God and subversive of their covenant relations with Him as His people. **neither seek after wizards**—fortunetellers, who pretended, as the *Hebrew* word indicates, to prognosticate by palmistry (or an inspection of the lines of the hand) the future fate of those who applied to them. **33, 34. if a stranger sojourn with thee in your land, ye shall not vex him**—The Israelites were to hold out encouragement to strangers to settle among them, that they might be brought to the knowledge and worship of the true God; and with this in view, they were enjoined to treat them not as aliens, but as friends, on the ground that they themselves, who were strangers in Egypt, were at first kindly and hospitably received in that country.

37. I am the Lord—This solemn admonition, by which these various precepts are repeatedly sanctioned, is equivalent to "I, your Creator—your Deliverer from bondage, and your Sovereign, who have wisdom to establish laws, have power also to punish the violation of them." It was well fitted to impress the minds of the Israelites with a sense of their duty and God's claims to obedience.

ADAM CLARKE

28. *Any cuttings in your flesh for the dead.* That the ancients were very violent in their grief, tearing the hair and face, beating the breast, is well-known.

29. *Do not prostitute thy daughter.* This was a very frequent custom, and with examples of it writers of antiquity abound. The Cyprian women, according to Justin, gained that portion which their husbands received with them at marriage by previous public prostitution. And the Phoenicians, according to Augustine, made a gift to Venus of the gain acquired by the public prostitution of their daughters, previously to their marriage.

31. *Regard not them that have familiar spirits.* The Hebrew word *oboth* probably signifies a kind of ventriloquist, or such as the Pythoness mentioned Acts xvi. 16, 18; persons who, while under the influence of their demon became greatly "inflated," as the Hebrew word implies, and gave answers in a sort of frenzy. *Neither seek after wizards. Yiddeonim,* the "wise or knowing ones," from *yada,* to "know or understand"; called wizard in Scotland, "wise or cunning man" in England. Not only all real dealers with familiar spirits, or necromantic or magical superstitions, are here forbidden, but also all pretenders to the knowledge of futurity, fortunetellers, astrologers. To attempt to know what God has not thought proper to reveal is a sin against His wisdom, providence, and goodness.

33. *If a stranger sojourn.* This law to protect and comfort the stranger was at once humane and politic. None is so desolate as the stranger, and none needs the offices of benevolence and charity more; and we may add that he who is not affected by the desolate state of the stranger has neither benevolence nor charity. Moses also uses a powerful motive: *Ye were strangers in the land of Egypt.* The spirit of the precept here laid down may be well expressed in our Lord's words: "Do unto all men as ye would they should do unto you."

35. *Ye shall do no unrighteousness.* You shall not act contrary to the strictest justice in any case, and especially in the four following, which, properly understood, comprise all that can occur between a man and his fellow. (1) *Judgment* in all cases that come before the civil magistrate; he is to judge and decide according to the law. (2) *Meteyard, bammiddah,* in measures of length. (3) *Weight, bammishkal,* in anything that is weighed, the weights being all according to the standards kept for the purpose of trying the rest in the sanctuary, as appears from Exod. xxx. 13; 1 Chron. xxiii. 29. (4) *Measure, bammesurah,* from which we derive our term. This refers to all measures of capacity, such as the homer, ephah, seah, hin, omer, kab, and log. See all these explained, Exod. xvi. 16.

36. *Just balances*—"scales." *Weights, abanim*—"stones," as the weights appear to have been originally formed out of stones.

37. *Shall ye observe all my statutes. Chukkothi,* from *chak,* to "describe, mark, or trace out"; the righteousness which I have described, and the path of duty which I have traced out. *Judgments, mishpatai,* from *shaphat,* to "discern, determine, direct"; that which divine wisdom has discerned to be best for man, has determined shall promote his best interest, and has directed him conscientiously to use.

MATTHEW HENRY

CHAPTER 20

Verses 1–9

I. Three sins are in these verses threatened with death:—

1. Parents abusing their children, by sacrificing them to Molech, *v.* 2, 3. It was not enough to tell them they might spare their children, but they must be told, (1) That the criminal himself should be put to death as a murderer: *The people of the land shall stone him with stones* (*v.* 2), which was looked upon as the worst capital punishment among the Jews. (2) That all his aiders and abetters should be cut off likewise by the righteous hand of God. If his neighbours concealed him, and would not come in as witnesses against him,—if the magistrates connived at him, and would not pass sentence upon him, rather pitying his folly than hating his impiety,—God himself would reckon with them, *v.* 4, 5.

2. Children's abusing their parents, by cursing them, *v.* 9. If children should speak ill of their

JAMIESON, FAUSSET, BROWN

CHAPTER 20

VSS. 1-27. GIVING ONE'S SEED TO MOLECH. **2. Whosoever . . . giveth any of his seed unto Molech** [see on ch. 18:21], **the people of the land shall stone him with stones,** etc.—Criminals who were condemned to be stoned were led, with their hands bound, without the gates to a small eminence, where was a large stone placed at the bottom. When they had approached within ten cubits of the spot, they were exhorted to confess, that, by faith and repentance, their souls might be saved. When led forward to within four cubits, they were stripped almost naked, and received some stupefying draught, during which the witnesses prepared, by laying aside their outer garments, to carry into execution the capital sentence which the law bound them to do. The criminal, being placed on the edge of the precipice, was then pushed backwards, so that he fell down the perpendicular height on

ADAM CLARKE

CHAPTER 20

2. *That giveth any of his seed unto Molech.* To what has been said in the note on chap. xviii. 21 we may add, that the rabbins describe this idol, who was probably a representative or emblematical personification of the solar influence, as made of brass, in the form of a man, with the head of an ox; that a fire was kindled in the inside, and the child to be sacrificed to him was put in his arms, and roasted to death. The passing through the fire, so frequently spoken of, might mean no more than a simple rite of consecration to the service of this idol. See the note on chap. xviii. 21.

6. *Familiar spirits.* See the notes on chap. xix. 31; and Exod. xxii. 18.

9. *Curseth his father or his mother.* See the notes on Gen. xlviii. 12 and Exod. xx. 12. He

MATTHEW HENRY

parents, or wish ill to them, or carry it scornfully or spitefully towards them, it was an iniquity to be punished by the judges, who were employed as conservators both of God's honour and of the public peace, which were both attacked by this unnatural insolence.

3. Persons abusing themselves by consulting such as have *familiar spirits, v.* 6. By this, as much as any thing, a man diminishes, disparages, and deceives himself, and so abuses himself. What greater madness can there be than for a man to go to a liar for information, and to an enemy for advice? Those do so who turn after those that deal in the black art, and know the depths of Satan.

II. In the midst of these particular laws comes in that general charge, *v.* 7, 8, where we have,

1. The duties required; and they are two: (1) That in our principles, affections, and aims, we be holy: *Sanctify yourselves and be you holy.* (2) That in all our actions, and in the whole course of our conversation, we be obedient to the laws of God: *You shall keep my statutes.* Make the tree good, and the fruit will be good.

2. The reasons to enforce these duties. (1) "*I am the Lord your God*; therefore be holy, that you may resemble him whose people you are, and may be pleasing to him. Holiness becomes his house and household." (2) *I am the Lord who sanctifieth you.* God sanctifieth them by peculiar privileges, laws, and favours, which distinguished them from all other nations, and dignified them as a people set apart for God. He gave them his word and ordinances to be means of their sanctification, and his good Spirit to instruct them.

Verses 10–21

Sins against the seventh commandment are here ordered to be severely punished.

I. Lying with another man's wife was made a capital crime. The adulterer and the adulteress that had joined in the sin must fall alike under the sentence: they shall both be *put to death, v.* 10.

II. Incestuous connections, whether by marriage or not.

III. The unnatural lusts of sodomy and bestiality (sins not to be mentioned without horror) were to be punished with death.

Verses 22–27

The last verse is a particular law, which comes in after the general conclusion, as if omitted in its proper place: it is for the putting of those to death that dealt with familiar spirits, *v.* 27. Those that are in league with the devil have in effect made a covenant with death.

The rest of these verses repeat and inculcate what had been said before.

I. Their dignity. They had the *Lord for their God, v.* 24. They were his, his care, his choice, his treasure.

II. Their duty; this is inferred from their dignity. God had done more for them than for others, and therefore expected more from them than from others.

III. Their danger. They were going into an infected place (*v.* 24): *You shall inherit their land,* a land *flowing indeed with milk and honey,* which they would have the comfort of if they kept their integrity; but, withal, it was a land full of idols, idolatries, and superstitious usages, which they would be apt to fall in love with, having brought from Egypt with them a strange disposition to take that infection.

JAMIESON, FAUSSET, BROWN

the stone lying below: if not killed by the fall, the second witness dashed a large stone down upon his breast, and then the "people of the land," who were bystanders, rushed forward, and with stones completed the work of death (Matt. 21:44; Acts 7:58). **4. If the people of the land do any ways hide their eyes from the man,** etc.–i.e., connive at their countrymen practising the horrid rites of Molech. Awful was it that any Hebrew parents could so violate their national covenant, and no wonder that God denounced the severest penalties against them and their families.

7-19. Sanctify yourselves therefore, and be ye holy—The minute specification of the incestuous and unnatural crimes here enumerated shows their sad prevalence amongst the idolatrous nations around, and the extreme proneness of the Israelites to follow the customs of their neighbors. It is to be understood, that, whenever mention is made that the offender was "to be put to death" without describing the mode, stoning is meant. The only instance of another form of capital punishment occurs in verse 14, that of being burnt with fire; and yet it is probable that even here death was first inflicted by stoning, and the body of the criminal afterwards consumed by fire (Josh. 7:15).

20. they shall die childless—Either by the judgment of God they shall have no children, or their spurious offspring shall be denied by human authority the ordinary privileges of children in Israel.

24. I . . . have separated you from other people—Their selection from the rest of the nations was for the all-important end of preserving the knowledge and worship of the true God amid the universal apostasy; and as the distinction of meats was one great means of completing that separation, the law about making a difference between clean and unclean beasts is here repeated with emphatic solemnity.

ADAM CLARKE

who conscientiously keeps the fifth commandment can be in no danger of this judgment. The term *yekallel* signifies not only to "curse," but to speak of a person contemptuously and disrespectfully, to make light of; so that all speeches which have a tendency to lessen our parents in the eyes of others, or to render their judgment or piety suspected and contemptible, may be here included; though the act of cursing, or of treating the parent with injurious and opprobrious language, is that which is particularly intended.

10. *Committeth adultery.* The word *adultery* comes from the Latin *adulterium,* which is compounded of *ad,* "to or with," and *alter,* "another."

12. *They have wrought confusion.* See chap. xviii, and especially the note on v. 6.

14. *They shall be burnt with fire.* As there are worse crimes mentioned here (see vv. 11 and 17) where the delinquent is ordered simply to be put to death, or to be cut off, it is very likely that the crime mentioned in this verse was not punished by burning alive, but by some kind of branding, by which they were ever after rendered infamous. I need not add that the original, *baesh yishrephu,* may, without violence to its grammatical meaning, be understood as above, though in other places it is certainly used to signify a consuming by fire. But the case in question requires some explanation, It is this: A man marries a wife, and afterward takes his mother-in-law or wife's mother to wife also. Now for this offense the text says all three shall be *burned with fire,* and this is understood as signifying that they shall be burned alive. Now the first wife, we may safely presume, was completely innocent, and was legally married; for a man may take to wife the daughter if single, or the mother if a widow, and in neither of these cases can any blame attach to the man or the party he marries; the crime therefore lies in taking both. Either, therefore, they were all branded as infamous persons, and this certainly was severe enough in the case of the first wife; or the man and the woman taken last were burnt. But the text says, *both he and they;* therefore we should seek for another ininterpretation of *they shall be burnt with fire* than that which is commonly given. Branding with a hot iron would certainly accomplish every desirable end both for punishment and prevention of the crime; and because the Mosaic laws are so generally distinguished by humanity, it seems to be necessary to limit the meaning of the words as above.

22. *The land, whither I bring you to dwell therein, spue you not out.* See this explained in the note on chap. xviii. 25. From this we learn that the cup of the iniquities of the Canaanitish nations was full; and that, consistently with divine justice, they could be no longer spared.

24. *A land that floweth with milk and honey.* See this explained in Exod. iii. 8.

25. *Between clean beasts and unclean.* See the notes on chap. xi.

27. *A familiar spirit.* A spirit or demon, which, by magical rites, is supposed to be bound to appear at the call of his employer. See the notes on Gen. xli. 8; Exod. vii. 11, 22, 25; and chap. xix. 31.

MATTHEW HENRY — CHAPTER 21

Verses 1–9

It was before appointed that the priests should teach the people the statutes God had given concerning the *difference between clean and unclean, ch.* x. 10, 11. Now here it is provided that they should themselves observe what they were to teach the people. The priests were to draw nearer to God than any of the people, and to be more intimately conversant with sacred things, and therefore it was required of them that they should keep at a greater distance than others from every thing that was defiling.

I. They must take care not to disparage themselves in their mourning for the dead. "It made a man ceremonially unclean to come within six feet of a dead corpse"; nay, it is declared (Num. xix. 14) that all who come into the tent where the dead body lies shall be unclean seven days. 1. The priests should never put themselves under this incapacity of coming into the sanctuary, unless it were for one of their

JAMIESON, FAUSSET, BROWN — CHAPTER 21

Vss. 1-24. Of the Priests' Mourning. **1. There shall none be defiled for the dead among his people**—The obvious design of the regulations contained in this chapter was to keep inviolate the purity and dignity of the sacred office. Contact with a corpse, or even contiguity to the place where it lay, entailing ceremonial defilement (Num. 19: 14), all mourners were debarred from the tabernacle for a week; and as the exclusion of a priest during that period would have been attended with great inconvenience, the whole order were enjoined to abstain from all approaches to the dead, except at the funerals of relatives, to whom affection or necessity might call them to perform the last offices. Those exceptional cases, which are specified, were strictly confined to the members of their own family, within the nearest degrees of kindred.

ADAM CLARKE — CHAPTER 21

1. *There shall none be defiled for the dead.* No priest shall assist in laying out a dead body, or preparing it for interment. Any contact with the dead was supposed to be of a defiling nature, probably because putrefaction had then taken place; and animal putrefaction was ever held in detestation by all men.

MATTHEW HENRY

nearest relations, *v.* 1–3. 2. They must not be extravagant in the expressions of their mourning. Their mourning must not be either, (1) Superstitious, according to the manner of the heathen, who cut off their hair, and let out their blood, in honour of the imaginary deities which presided (as they thought) in the congregation of the dead, that they might engage them to be propitious to their departed friends. Nor, (2) Must it be passionate or immoderate. Note, God's ministers must be examples to others of patience under affliction, particularly that which touches in a very tender part, the death of their near relations.

II. They must take care not to degrade themselves in their marriage, *v.* 7. A priest must not marry a woman of ill fame, that either had been guilty or was suspected to have been guilty of uncleanness.

III. Their children must be afraid of doing any thing to disparage them (*v.* 9): *If the daughter of any priest play the whore*, her crime is great; she not only polluteth but *profaneth herself*: other women have not that honour to lose that she has, who, as one of a priest's family, has eaten of the holy things, and is supposed to have been better educated than others.

Verses 10–15

More was expected from a priest than from other people, but more from the high priest than from other priests, because upon his head the *anointing oil was poured*. It is called the *crown of the anointing oil of his God* (*v.* 12); for the anointing of the Spirit is, to all that have it, a *crown of glory*, and a *diadem of beauty*. The high priest being thus dignified,

I. He must not defile himself at all for the dead, no, not for his nearest relations, *his father or his mother*, much less his child or brother, *v.* 11. Our Lord Jesus, the great high priest of our profession, touched the dead body of Jairus's daughter, the bier of the widow's son, and the grave of Lazarus, to show that he came to alter the property of death, and to take off the terror of it, by breaking the power of it. Now that it cannot destroy it does not defile.

II. He might not marry a widow (as other priests might), much less one divorced, or a harlot, *v.* 13, 14. The reason of this was to put a difference between him and other priests in this matter.

III. He might not profane his seed among his people, *v.* 15. It may be a caution to him in disposing of his children; he must not profane his seed by marrying them unsuitably. Ministers' children are profaned if they be unequally yoked with unbelievers.

Verses 16–24

The priesthood being confined to one particular family, and entailed upon all the male issue of that family throughout their generations, it was very likely that some or other in after-ages that were born to the priesthood would have natural blemishes and deformities.

I. The law concerning priests that had blemishes was, 1. That they might *live upon the altar* (*v.* 22): *He shall eat* of the sacrifices with the other priests, even the *most holy things*, such as the show-bread and the sin-offerings, as well as the *holy things*, such as the tithes and first-fruits, and the priests' share of the peace-offerings. The blemishes were such as they could not help, and therefore, though they might not work, they must not starve. 2. Yet they must not *serve at the altar*, at either of the altars, nor be admitted to attend or assist the other priests in offering sacrifice of burning incense, *v.* 17, 21, 23. It was for the credit of the sanctuary that none should appear there who were any way disfigured, either by nature or accident.

II. Under the gospel, 1. Those that labour under any such blemishes as these have reason to thank God that they are not thereby excluded from offering spiritual sacrifices to God; nor, if otherwise qualified for it, from the office of the ministry. There is many a healthful beautiful soul lodged in a crazy deformed body. Yet, 2. We ought to infer hence how incapable those are to serve God acceptably whose minds are blemished and deformed by any reigning vice. Those are unworthy to be called Christians, and unfit to be employed as ministers, that are spiritually blind, and lame, and crooked, whose sins render them scandalous and deformed, so as that the offerings of the Lord are abhorred for their sakes.

JAMIESON, FAUSSET, BROWN

4. But he shall not defile himself—"for any other," as the sense may be fully expressed. "The priest, in discharging his sacred functions, might well be regarded as a chief man among his people, and by these defilements might be said to profane himself" [BISHOP PATRICK]. The word rendered "chief man" signifies also "a husband"; and the sense according to others is, "But he being a husband, shall not defile himself by the obsequies of a wife" (Ezek. 44:25). **5. They shall not make baldness upon their heads . . . nor . . . cuttings in their flesh**—The superstitious marks of sorrow, as well as the violent excesses in which the heathen indulged at the death of their friends, were forbidden by a general law to the Hebrew people (ch. 19:28). But the priests were to be laid under a special injunction, not only that they might exhibit examples of piety in the moderation of their grief, but also by the restraint of their passions, be the better qualified to administer the consolations of religion to others, and show, by their faith in a blessed resurrection, the reasons for sorrowing not as those who have no hope. **7-9. They shall not take a wife that is a whore, or profane**—Private individuals might form several connections, which were forbidden as inexpedient or improper in priests. The respectability of their office, and the honor of religion, required unblemished sanctity in their families as well as themselves, and departures from it in their case were visited with severer punishment than in that of others. **10-15. he that is the high priest among his brethren . . . shall not uncover his head, nor rend his clothes**—The indulgence in the excepted cases of family bereavement, mentioned above, which was granted to the common priests, was denied to him; for his absence from the sanctuary for the removal of any contracted defilement could not have been dispensed with, neither could he have acted as intercessor for the people, unless ceremonially clean. Moreover, the high dignity of his office demanded a corresponding superiority in personal holiness, and stringent rules were prescribed for the purpose of upholding the suitable dignity of his station and family. The same rules are extended to the families of Christian ministers (I Tim. 3:2; Titus 1:6).

16-24. Whosoever he be . . . that hath any blemish, let him not approach to offer the bread of his God—As visible things exert a strong influence on the minds of men, any physical infirmity or malformation of body in the ministers of religion, which disturbs the associations or excites ridicule, tends to detract from the weight and authority of the sacred office. Priests laboring under any personal defect were not allowed to officiate in the public service; they might be employed in some inferior duties about the sanctuary but could not perform any sacred office. In all these regulations for preserving the unsullied purity of the sacred character and office, there was a typical reference to the priesthood of Christ (Heb. 7:26).

ADAM CLARKE

4. *A chief man among his people.* The word *baal* signifies a "master, chief, husband" and is as variously translated here.

5. *They shall not make baldness.* See the note on chap. xix. 27. It is supposed that these things were particularly prohibited, because used superstitiously by the Egyptian priests, who, according to Herodotus, shaved the whole body every third day, that there might be no uncleanness about them when they ministered in their temple. This appears to have been a general custom among the heathen.

7. *That is a whore.* A prostitute, though even reclaimed. *Profane.* A heathen, or one who is not a cordial believer in the true God. *Put away from her husband.* Because this very circumstance might lead to suspicion that the priest and the divorced woman might have been improperly connected before.

9. *She shall be burnt with fire.* Probably not burned alive, but strangled first, and then burned afterward, though it is barely possible that some kind of branding may be intended.

10. *He that is the high priest.* This is the first place where this title is introduced; the title is very emphatic, *haccohen haggadol*, "that priest, the great one." For the meaning of *cohen*, see the note on Gen. xiv. 18. As the chief or high priest was a representative of our blessed Lord, therefore he was required to be especially holy; and he is represented as God's king among the people.

12. *The crown of the anointing oil . . . is upon him.* By his office the priest represented Christ in His sacrificial character; by his anointing, the prophetic influence; and by the crown, the regal dignity of our Lord.

13. *He shall take a wife in her virginity. Bethuleyha.* This is a full proof that *bethulah* is the proper Hebrew term for a "virgin," from the emphatic root *bathal*, to "separate"; because such a person was in her separate state, and had never been in any way united to man.

17. *Whosoever . . . hath any blemish, let him not approach to offer the bread of his God.* Never was a wiser, a more rational, and a more expedient law enacted relative to sacred matters. The man who ministers in holy things, who professes to be the interpreter of the will of God, should have nothing in his person nor in his manner which cannot contribute to render him respectable in the eyes of those to whom he ministers.

18. *A blind man.* That is, in one eye; for he that was utterly blind could not possibly be employed in such a service. *A flat nose,* like that of an ape; so the best versions. *Any thing superfluous,* such as six fingers, six toes.

19. *Brokenfooted, or brokenhanded.* Clubfooted, bandy-legged; or having the ankle, wrist, or fingers dislocated.

20. *Crookbackt.* Hunchbacked. *A dwarf, dak,* a person too "short" or too "thin," so as to be either particularly observable or ridiculous in his appearance. *A blemish in his eye.* A protuberance on the eye, observable spots or suffusions. *Stones broken.* Is ruptured; an infirmity which would render him incapable of fulfilling the duties of his office, which often might be very fatiguing.

MATTHEW HENRY

CHAPTER 22

Verses 1–9

Those that had a natural blemish, though they were forbidden to do the priests' work, were yet allowed to eat of the holy things: and the Jewish writers say that "to keep them from idleness they were employed in the wood-room, to pick out that which was worm-eaten, that it might not be used in the fire upon the altar; they might also be employed in the judgment of leprosy": but,

I. Those that were under any ceremonial uncleanness, which possibly they contracted by their own fault, might not so much as eat of the holy things while they continued in their pollution.

II. As to the design of this law we may observe, 1. This obliged the priests carefully to preserve their purity, and to dread every thing that would defile them. 2. This impressed the people with a reverence for the holy things.

Verses 10–16

The holy things were to be eaten by the priests and their families.

I. Here is a law that no stranger should eat of them, that is, no person whatsoever but the priests only, and those that pertained to them, *v.* 10.

JAMIESON, FAUSSET, BROWN

CHAPTER 22

VSS. 1-9. THE PRIESTS IN THEIR UNCLEANNESS. **2. Speak unto Aaron and to his sons, that they separate themselves from the holy thing**—"To separate" means, in the language of the Mosaic ritual, "to abstain"; and therefore the import of this injunction is that the priests should abstain from eating that part of the sacrifices which, though belonging to their order, was to be partaken of only by such of them as were free from legal impurities. **that they profane not my holy name in those things which they hallow unto me,** etc.—i.e., let them not, by their want of due reverence, give occasion to profane my holy name. A careless or irreverent use of things consecrated to God tends to dishonor the name and bring disrespect on the worship of God. **3. Whosoever he be . . . that goeth unto the holy things**—The multitude of minute restrictions to which the priests, from accidental defilement, were subjected, by keeping them constantly on their guard lest they should be unfit for the sacred service, tended to preserve in full exercise the feeling of awe and submission to the authority of God. The ideas of sin and duty were awakened in their breasts by every case to which either an interdict or an injunction was applied. But why enact an express statute for priests disqualified by the leprosy or polluting touch of a carcass, when a general law was already in force which excluded from society all persons in that condition? Because priests might be apt, from familiarity, to trifle with religion, and in committing irregularities or sins, to shelter themselves under the cloak of the sacred office. This law, therefore, was passed, specifying the chief forms of temporary defilement which excluded from the sanctuary, that priests might not deem themselves entitled to greater license than the rest of the people; and that so far from being in any degree exempted from the sanctions of the law, they were under greater obligations, by their priestly station, to observe it in its strict letter and its smallest enactments. **4-6. wash his flesh with water**—Any Israelite who had contracted a defilement of such a nature as debarred him from the enjoyment of his wonted privileges, and had been legally cleansed from the disqualifying impurity, was bound to indicate his state of recovery by the immersion of his whole person in water. Although all ceremonial impurity formed a ground of exclusion, there were degrees of impurity which entailed a longer or shorter period of excommunication, and for the removal of which different rites required to be observed according to the trivial or the malignant nature of the case. A person who came inadvertently into contact with an unclean animal was rendered unclean for a specified period; and then, at the expiry of that term, he washed, in token of his recovered purity. But a leper was unclean so long as he remained subject to that disease, and on his convalescence, he also washed, not to cleanse himself, for the water was ineffectual for that purpose, but to signify that he was clean. Not a single case is recorded of a leper being restored to communion by the use of water; it served only as an outward and visible sign that such a restoration was to be made. The Book of Leviticus abounds with examples which show that in all the ceremonial washings, as uncleanness meant loss of privileges, so baptism with water indicated a restoration to those privileges. There was no exemption; for as the unclean Israelite was exiled from the congregation, so the unclean priest was disqualified from executing his sacred functions in the sanctuary; and in the case of both, the same observance was required—a formal intimation of their being readmitted to forfeited privileges was intimated by the appointed rite of baptism. If any one neglected or refused to perform the washing, he disobeyed a positive precept, and he remained in his uncleanness; he forbore to avail himself of this privilege, and was therefore said to be "cut off" from the presence of the Lord. **8. dieth of itself**—The feelings of nature revolt against such food. It might have been left to the discretion of the Hebrews, who it may be supposed (like the people of all civilized nations) would have abstained from the use of it without any positive interdict. But an express precept was necessary to show them that whatever died naturally or from disease, was prohibited to them by the operation of that law which forbade them the use of any meat with its blood.

10-16. WHO OF THE PRIESTS' HOUSE MAY EAT OF THEM. **10. There shall no stranger eat the holy thing**—The portion of the sacrifices assigned for the support of the officiating priests was restricted to

ADAM CLARKE

CHAPTER 22

2. *Speak unto Aaron and to his sons, that they separate themselves.* The same subject is continued in this chapter as in the preceding, with this addition, that besides the perfection of the priests, it was indispensably necessary that the sacrifices also should be perfect. In the service of God, according to the law, neither an imperfect offering nor an imperfect offerer could be admitted. What need then of a mediator between a holy God and sinful men! And can we expect that any of our services, however sincere and well-intentioned, can be accepted, unless offered on that living Altar that sanctifies the gift?

4. *Is a leper, or hath a running issue.* See the case of the leper treated at large in the notes on chapters xiii and xiv; and for other uncleannesses, see the notes on chap. xv.

F. B. MEYER:

"He shall not eat of the holy things till he be clean" (Lev. 22:4).

The holy things referred to here are the offerings made by Israel to Jehovah, a part of which was presented to God in fire, and the rest partaken of by the priests and their families. None, however, might feed on them while ceremonially unclean. This suggests some useful precautions for ourselves if we would fully enjoy the privileges and blessings attending the worship of the holy God.

We must be clean before we can enjoy the private reading of the Word of God. We would wash our hands, soiled with the dust and grime of toil, before opening an exquisitely printed copy of the Scriptures; how much more should we seek cleansing at the hands of Christ before we feed on the holy things of Scripture!

We must be clean before entering the house of God. It is a holy habit for each intending worshiper to be quiet before leaving the house on the Lord's day; or to use carefully the moment of the bent head at the commencement of the public service, in order that the soul may be made clean from any contracted stain, and resolve henceforth to abstain from all evil.

We must be clean before partaking of the Lord's Supper. There we feed upon the bread of God; and as we wash our hands before we sit at the table of a friend, so should our hearts be cleansed ere we partake of the emblems of the body and blood of Christ. Holiness becomes God's house. Those that ascend the hill of the Lord must have clean hands and a pure heart. The reason why religious exercises do not profit you may lie in your failure to comply with this demand. "He shall not eat of the holy things until he be clean."

—Great Verses Through the Bible

MATTHEW HENRY

The priests are charged with this care, not to *profane the holy things* by permitting the strangers to eat of them (*v.* 15) or *suffer them to bear the iniquity of trespass* (*v.* 16). Note, We must not only be careful that we do not bear iniquity ourselves, but we must do what we can to prevent others bearing it.

II. Here is an explanation of the law, showing who were to be looked upon as belonging to the priest's family, and who not. 1. Sojourners and hired servants abode not in the house for ever; they were in the family, but not of it; and therefore they might not eat of the holy things (*v.* 10): but the servant that was born in the house or bought with money, being a heirloom to the family, though a servant, yet might eat of the holy things, *v.* 11. 2. As to the children of the family, concerning the sons there could be no dispute, they were themselves priests, but concerning the daughters there was a distinction. While they continued in their father's house they might eat of the holy things; but, if they married such as were not priests, they lost their right (*v.* 12). 3. Here is a demand of restitution to be made by him that had no right to the holy things, and yet should eat of them unwittingly, *v.* 14.

III. This law might be dispensed with in a case of necessity, as it was when David and his men ate of the show-bread, 1 Sam. xxi. 6. And our Saviour justifies them, and gives a reason for it, which furnishes us with a lasting rule in all such cases, that *God will have mercy and not sacrifice*, Matt. xii. 3, 4, 7. Rituals must give way to morals.

Verses 17–33

Here are four laws concerning sacrifices:—

I. Whatever was offered in sacrifice to God should be without blemish, otherwise it should not be accepted. Moreover a difference is made between what was brought as a free-will offering and what was brought as a vow, *v.* 23. According to this law great care was taken to search all the beasts that were brought to be sacrificed, that there might, to a certainty, be no blemish in them. The heathen priests were many of them not so strict in this matter, but would receive sacrifices for their gods that were ever so scandalous; but let strangers know that the God of Israel would not be so served. It is an instruction to us to offer to God the best we have in our spiritual sacrifices. If our devotions are ignorant, and cold, and trifling, and full of distractions, we offer *the blind, and the lame, and the sick, for sacrifice*.

II. That no beast should be offered in sacrifice before it was eight days old, *v.* 26, 27. It was provided before that the firstlings of their cattle, which were to be dedicated to God, should not be brought to him till after the eighth day, Exod. xxii. 30. Here it is provided that no creature should be offered in sacrifice till it was eight days old complete. Sooner than that it was not fit to be used at men's tables, and therefore not at God's altar.

III. That the dam and her young should not both be killed in one day, whether in sacrifice or for common use, *v.* 28. It looked ill-natured towards the species to kill two generations at once, as if one designed the ruin of the kind.

IV. That the flesh of their thank-offerings should be eaten on the same day that they were sacrificed, *v.* 29, 30. This is a repetition of what we had before, *ch.* vii. 15; xix. 6, 7. The chapter concludes with such a general charge as we have often met with, to *keep God's commandments*, and not to *profane his holy name*, *v.* 31, 32.

JAMIESON, FAUSSET, BROWN

the exclusive use of his own family. A temporary guest or a hired servant was not at liberty to eat of them; but an exception was made in favor of a bought or home-born slave, because such was a stated member of his household. On the same principle, his own daughter, who married a husband not a priest, could not eat of them. However, if a widow and childless, she was reinstated in the privileges of her father's house as before her marriage. But if she had become a mother, as her children had no right to the privileges of the priesthood, she was under a necessity of finding support for them elsewhere than under her father's roof. **13. there shall no stranger eat thereof**—The interdict recorded (vs. 10) is repeated to show its stringency. All the Hebrews, even the nearest neighbors of the priest, the members of his family excepted, were considered strangers in this respect, so that they had no right to eat of things offered at the altar. **14. if a man eat of the holy things unwittingly**—A common Israelite might unconsciously partake of what had been offered as tithes, first-fruits, etc., and on discovering his unintentional error, he was not only to restore as much as he had used, but be fined in a fifth part more for the priests to carry into the sanctuary. **15, 16. they shall not profane the holy things of the children of Israel**—There is some difficulty felt in determining to whom "they" refers. The subject of the preceding context being occupied about the priests, it is supposed by some that this relates to them also; and the meaning then is that the whole people would incur guilt through the fault of the priests, if they should defile the sacred offerings, which they would have done had they presented them while under any defilement [CALVIN]. According to others, "the children of Israel" is the nominative in the sentence; which thus signifies, the children of Israel shall not profane or defile their offerings, by touching them or reserving any part of them, lest they incur the guilt of eating what is divinely appointed to the priests alone [CALMET].

17-33. THE SACRIFICES MUST BE WITHOUT BLEMISH. **19. Ye shall offer at your own will**—rather, to your being accepted. **a male without blemish**—This law (ch. 1:3) is founded on a sense of natural propriety, which required the greatest care to be taken in the selection of animals for sacrifice. The reason for this extreme caution is found in the fact that sacrifices are either an expression of praise to God for His goodness, or else they are the designed means of conciliating or retaining His favor. No victim that was not perfect in its kind could be deemed a fitting instrument for such purposes if we assume that the significance of sacrifices is derived entirely from their relation to Jehovah. Sacrifices may be likened to gifts made to a king by his subjects, and hence the reasonableness of God's strong remonstrance with the worldly-minded Jews (Mal. 1:8). If the tabernacle, and subsequently the temple, were considered the palace of the great King, then the sacrifices would answer to presents as offered to a monarch on various occasions by his subjects; and in this light they would be the appropriate expressions of their feelings towards their sovereign. When a subject wished to do honor to his sovereign, to acknowledge allegiance, to appease his anger, to supplicate forgiveness, or to intercede for another, he brought a present; and all the ideas involved in sacrifices correspond to these sentiments—those of gratitude, of worship, of prayer, of confession and atonement [BIB. SAC]. **23. that mayest thou offer,** etc.—The passage should be rendered thus: if thou offer it either for a freewill offering, or for a vow, it shall not be accepted. This sacrifice being required to be "without blemish," symbolically implied that the people of God were to dedicate themselves wholly with sincere purposes of heart, and its being required to be "perfect to be accepted," led them typically to Him without whom no sacrifice could be offered acceptable to God. **27, 28. it shall be seven days under the dam**—Animals were not considered perfect nor good for food till the eighth day. As sacrifices are called the bread or food of God (vs. 25), to offer them immediately after birth, when they were unfit to be eaten, would have indicated a contempt of religion; and besides, this prohibition, as well as that contained in the following verse, inculcated a lesson of humanity or tenderness to the dam, as well as secured the sacrifices from all appearance of unfeeling cruelty.

ADAM CLARKE

14. *Then he shall put the fifth part thereof unto it.* The holy thing of which he has unknowingly eaten shall be fairly valued, and to this value he shall add one-fifth more, and give the whole to the priest.

20. *Whatsoever hath a blemish.* The same perfection is required in the sacrifice that was required in the priest; see on v. 2, and the notes on the preceding chapter.

23. *That hath any thing superfluous or lacking.* The term *sarua* signifies anything "extended" beyond the usual size, and the term *kalut* signifies anything unusually "contracted."

24. *Bruised, or crushed, or broken, or cut.* That is, no bullock or lamb that is injured in any of the above ways shall be offered unto the Lord.

25. *Their corruption is in them.* Viz., they are bruised, crushed, broken.

27. *When a bullock . . . is brought forth.* This is a most unfortunate as well as absurd translation. The creature called an ox is a bull castrated; surely then a *bullock* was never yet *brought forth!* The original word *shor* signifies a bull, a bullock, or indeed anything of the meat kind: here, even common sense required that it should be translated "calf"; and did I not hold myself sacredly bound to print the text of the common version with scrupulous exactness, I should translate the former clause of this verse thus, and so enter it into the text: "When a calf, or a lamb, or a kid is brought forth," instead of, *When a bullock, or a sheep, or a goat is brought forth,* the absurdity of which is glaring.

28. *Ye shall not kill it and her young . . . in one day.* This precept was certainly intended to inculcate mercy and tenderness of heart; and so the Jews understood it.

30. *Leave none of it until the morrow.* See the note on chap. vii. 18.

32. *Neither shall ye profane my holy name.* He profanes God's holy name who does not both implicitly believe and conscientiously obey all His words and all His precepts. *I will be hallowed among the children of Israel.* The words *children of Israel, beney Yishrael,* which so frequently occur, should be translated either "the descendants" or "posterity of Israel," or "the people of Israel." The word *children* has a tendency to beget a false notion, especially in the minds of young people, and lead them to think that children, in the proper sense of the word, i.e., "little ones," are meant.

33. *Brought you out of the land of Egypt.* By such a series of miraculous interferences, *to be your God*—to save you from all idolatry, false and superstitious worship, teach you the right way, lead and support you in it, and preserve you to My eternal kingdom and glory.

MATTHEW HENRY

CHAPTER 23

Verses 1-3

Here is, I. A general account of the holy times which God appointed (*v.* 2), and it is only his appointment that can make time holy; for he is the Lord of time, and as soon as ever he had set its wheels a-going it was he that sanctified and blessed one day above the rest, Gen. ii. 3. Man may by his appointment make a good day (Esth. ix. 19), but it is God's prerogative to make a holy day. Now, concerning the holy times here ordained, observe, 1. They are called *feasts*. The day of atonement, which was one of them, was a fast; yet, because most of them were appointed for joy and rejoicing, they are in the general called feasts. Some read it, *These are my assemblies*, but I would rather read it, These are *my solemnities*; and, reading it so here, the day of atonement was as great a solemnity as any of them. 2. They are the feasts of the Lord (*my feasts*). 3. They were proclaimed; for they were not to be observed by the priests only that attended the sanctuary, but by all the people. 4. They were to be sanctified and solemnized with holy convocations, that the services of these feasts might appear the more honourable and august, and the people the more unanimous in the performance of them.

II. A repetition of the law of the sabbath in the first place. Though the annual feasts were made more remarkable by the general attendance at the sanctuary, yet these must not eclipse the brightness of the sabbath, *v.* 3. Christ appointed the New Testament sabbath to be a holy convocation, by meeting his disciples once and again (and perhaps oftener) on the first day of the week. "Whether you have opportunity of sanctifying it in a holy convocation or not, yet let it be *the sabbath of the Lord in all your dwellings.* Put a difference between that day and other days in your families.

Verses 4-14

Here again the feasts are called the *feasts of the Lord*, because he appointed them. They were most of them times of joy and rejoicing. The weekly sabbath is so, and all their yearly solemnities, except the day of atonement. God would thus teach them that wisdom's ways are pleasantness, and engage them to his service by encouraging them to be cheerful in it and to sing at their work. Seven days were days of strict rest and holy convocations; the first day and the seventh of the feast of unleavened bread, the day of pentecost, the day of the feast of trumpets, the first day and the eighth of the feast of tabernacles, and the day of atonement: here were six for holy joy and one only for holy mourning.

I. A repetition of the law of the passover, which was to be observed on the fourteenth day of the first month, in remembrance of their deliverance out of Egypt and the distinguishing preservation of their first-born, mercies never to be forgotten.

II. An order for the offering of a sheaf of the first-fruits, upon the second day of the feast of unleavened bread; the first is called the *sabbath*, because it was observed as a sabbath (*v.* 11), and, on the morrow after, they had this solemnity. A sheaf or handful of new corn was brought to the priest, who was to heave it up, in token of his presenting it to the God of Heaven, and to wave it to and fro before the Lord, as the Lord of the whole earth, and this should be accepted for them as a thankful acknowledgment of God's mercy to them in clothing their fields with corn, and of their dependence upon God, and desire towards him, for the preserving of it to their use. And the offering of this sheaf of first-fruits in the name of the whole congregation did, as it were, sanctify to them their whole harvest. We find that when they came into Canaan the manna ceased upon the very day that the sheaf of first-fruits was offered; they had eaten of the old corn the day before (Josh. v. 11), and then on this day they offered the first-fruits, by which they became entitled to the new corn too (*v.* 12), so that there was no more occasion for manna. This sheaf of first-fruits was typical of our Lord Jesus, who has risen from the dead as the *first-fruits of those that slept*, 1 Cor. xv. 20. They were not to eat of their new corn till God's part was offered to him out of it (*v.* 14), for we must always begin with God, begin our lives with him, begin every day with him, begin every meal with him, begin every affair and business with him; *seek first the kingdom of God.*

Verses 15-22

Here is the institution of the feast of *pentecost*, or *weeks*, as it is called (Deut. xvi. 9), because it was observed fifty days, or seven weeks, after the passover. It is also called the *feast of harvest*, Exod. xxiii. 16. For as the presenting of the sheaf of first-fruits was an introduction to the harvest, and gave them liberty

JAMIESON, FAUSSET, BROWN

CHAPTER 23

VSS. 1-4. OF SUNDRY FEASTS. **2. Speak unto the children of Israel, . . . concerning the feasts of the Lord**— lit., "the times of assembling, or solemnities" (Isa. 33:20); and this is a preferable rendering, applicable to all sacred seasons mentioned in this chapter, even the day of atonement, which was observed as a fast. They were appointed by the direct authority of God and announced by a public proclamation, which is called "the joyful sound" (Ps. 89:15). Those "holy convocations" were evidences of divine wisdom, and eminently subservient to the maintenance and diffusion of religious knowledge and piety. **3. Six days shall work be done; but the seventh day is the sabbath of rest**—(See on Exod. 20:8, 9.) The Sabbath has the precedence given to it, and it was to be "a holy convocation," observed by families "in their dwellings"; where practicable, by the people repairing to the door of the tabernacle; at later periods, by meeting in the schools of the prophets, and in synagogues. **4. These are the feasts of the Lord, which ye shall proclaim in their seasons**—Their observance took place in the parts of the year corresponding to our March, May, and September. Divine wisdom was manifested in fixing them at those periods; in winter, when the days were short and the roads broken up, a long journey was impracticable; while in summer the harvest and vintage gave busy employment in the fields. Besides, another reason for the choice of those seasons probably was to counteract the influence of Egyptian associations and habits. And God appointed more sacred festivals for the Israelites in the month of September than the people of Egypt had in honor of their idols. These institutions, however, were for the most part prospective, the observance being not binding on the Israelites during their wanderings in the wilderness, while the regular celebration was not to commence till their settlement in Canaan.

5-8. THE PASSOVER. **the Lord's passover**—(See Exod. 12:2, 14, 18.) The institution of the passover was intended to be a perpetual memorial of the circumstances attending the redemption of the Israelites, while it had a typical reference to a greater redemption to be effected for God's spiritual people. On the first and last days of this feast, the people were forbidden to work; but while on the Sabbath they were not to do *any* work, on feast days they were permitted to dress meat—and hence the prohibition is restricted to "no servile work." At the same time, those two days were devoted to "holy convocation"—special seasons of social devotion. In addition to the ordinary sacrifices of every day, there were to be "offerings by fire" on the altar (see on Num. 28:19), while unleavened bread was to be eaten in families all the seven days (see I Cor. 5:8).

9-14. THE SHEAF OF FIRST FRUITS. **10. ye shall bring a sheaf of the first-fruits of your harvest unto the priest**—A sheaf, lit., an omer, of the first-fruits of the barley harvest. The barley being sooner ripe than the other grains, the reaping of it formed the commencement of the general harvest season. The offering described in this passage was made on the sixteenth of the first month, the day following the first Passover Sabbath, which was on the fifteenth (corresponding to the beginning of our April); but it was reaped after sunset on the previous evening by persons deputed to go with sickles and obtain samples from different fields. These, being laid together in a sheaf or loose bundle, were brought to the court of the temple, where the grain was winnowed, parched, and bruised in a mortar. Then, after some incense had been sprinkled on it, the priest waved it aloft before the Lord towards the four different points of the compass, took a part of it and threw it into the fire of the altar—all the rest being reserved to himself. It was a proper and beautiful act, expressive of dependence on the God of nature and providence—common among all people, but more especially becoming the Israelites, who owed their land itself as well as all it produced to the divine bounty. The offering of the wave-sheaf sanctified the whole harvest (Rom. 11:16). At the same time, this feast had a typical character, and pre-intimated the resurrection of Christ (I Cor. 15:20), who rose from the dead on the very day the first-fruits were offered.

15-22. FEAST OF PENTECOST. **15. ye shall count unto you from the morrow after the sabbath**—i.e., after the first day of the passover week, which was observed as a Sabbath. **16. number fifty days**—The forty-ninth day after the presentation of the first-fruits, or the fiftieth, including it, was the feast of Pentecost. (See also Exod. 23:16; Deut. 16:9.)

ADAM CLARKE

CHAPTER 23

2. ***These are my feasts.*** **The original word** ***moad*** **is properly applied to any solemn anniversary, by which great and important ecclesiastical, political, or providential facts were recorded; see Gen. i. 14. Anniversaries of this kind were observed in all nations; and some of them, in consequence of scrupulously regular observation, became chronological epochs of the greatest importance in history.**

3. ***The seventh day is the sabbath.*** **This, because the first and greatest solemnity, is first mentioned. He who kept not this, in the most religious manner, was not capable of keeping any of the others. The religious observance of the Sabbath stands at the very threshold of all religion. See Gen. ii. 3.**

5. ***The Lord's passover.*** **See this largely explained in the notes on Exod. xii. 21-27.**

11. ***He shall wave the sheaf.*** **He shall move it to and fro before the people, and thereby call their attention to the work of divine providence, and excite their gratitude to God for preserving to them the kindly fruits of the earth. See notes on Exod. xxix. 27 and chap. vii at end.**

14. ***Ye shall eat neither bread, nor parched corn, nor green ears.*** **It is right that God, the Dispenser of every blessing, should be acknowledged as such, and the firstfruits of the field, etc., dedicated to Him. Concerning the dedication of the firstfruits, see the note on Exod. xxii. 29. Parched ears of corn and green ears, fried, still constitute a part, and not a disagreeable one, of the food of the Arabs now resident in the Holy Land.**

15. ***Ye shall count unto you . . . seven sabbaths.*** **That is, from the sixteenth of the first month to the sixth of the third month. These seven weeks, called here** ***sabbaths,*** **were to be complete, i.e., the forty-nine days must be finished, and the next day, the fiftieth, is what, from the Septuagint, we call Pentecost.**

MATTHEW HENRY

to put in the sickle, so they solemnized the finishing of their corn-harvest at this feast. 1. Then they offered a handful of ears of barley, now they offered *two loaves of wheaten bread, v.* 17. This was leavened. At the passover they ate unleavened bread, but now at pentecost it was leavened, because it was an acknowledgment of God's goodness to them in their ordinary food, which was leavened. 2. With that sheaf of first-fruits they offered only one lamb for a burnt-offering, but with these loaves of first-fruits they offered seven lambs, two rams, and one bullock, all for a burnt-offering, so giving glory to God, as the Lord of their harvest. They offered likewise a kid for a sin-offering, and lastly, two lambs for a sacrifice of peace-offerings, to beg a blessing upon the corn they had gathered in. 3. That one day was to be kept with a holy convocation, *v.* 21. It was one of the days on which all Israel was to meet God and one another, at the place which the Lord should choose. Some suggest that whereas seven days were to make up the feast of unleavened bread there was only one day appointed for the feast of pentecost, because this was a busy time of the year with them, and God allowed them speedily to return to their work in the country. This annual feast was instituted in remembrance of the giving of the law upon Mount Sinai, the fiftieth day after they came out of Egypt. But the period and perfection of this feast was the pouring out of the Spirit upon the apostles on the day of this feast (Acts ii. 1), in which the law of faith was given, fifty days after Christ our passover was sacrificed for us.

To the institution of the feast of pentecost is annexed a repetition of that law by which they were required to leave the gleanings of their fields, and the corn that grew on the ends of the butts, for the poor, *v.* 22. It also taught them that the joy of harvest should express itself in charity to the poor.

Verses 23–32

I. The institution of the feast of trumpets, on the first day of the seventh month, *v.* 24, 25. That which is here made peculiar to this festival is that it was *a memorial of blowing of trumpets.* They blew the trumpet every new moon (Ps. lxxxi. 3), but in the new moon of the seventh month it was to be done with more than ordinary solemnity; for they began to blow at sun-rise and continued till sun-set. Now, 1. This is here said to be a *memorial,* perhaps of the sound of the trumpet upon Mount Sinai when the law was given, which must never be forgotten. 2. The Jewish writers suppose it to have a spiritual signification. Now at the beginning of the year they were called by this sound of trumpet to shake off their spiritual drowsiness, to search and try their ways, and to amend them: the day of atonement was the ninth day after this; and thus they were awakened to prepare for that day, by sincere and serious repentance. 3. It was typical of the preaching of the gospel, by which joyful sound souls were to be called in to serve God and keep a spiritual feast to him.

II. A repetition of the law of the day of atonement, that is, so much of it as concerned the people. 1. They must on this day rest from all manner of work. The reason is: *For it is a day of atonement.* He that would do the work of a day of atonement in its day, as it should be done, had need lay aside the thoughts of every thing else. 2. They must afflict their souls, and this upon pain of being cut off by the hand of God, *v.* 27, 29, 32. They must mortify the body, and deny the appetites of it. 3. The entire day must be observed: *From even to even you shall afflict your souls* (*v.* 32).

Verses 33–44

We have here, I. The institution of the feast of tabernacles, which was one of the three great feasts at which all the males were bound to attend, and celebrated with more expressions of joy than any of them.

1. As to the directions for regulating this feast, observe, (1) It was to be observed five days after the day of atonement. We may suppose, though they were not all bound to attend on the day of atonement, as on the three great festivals, yet that many of the devout Jews came up so many days before the feast of tabernacles as to enjoy the opportunity of attending on the day of atonement. The afflicting of their souls on the day of atonement prepared them for the joy of the feast of tabernacles. The more we are grieved and humbled for sin, the better qualified we are for the comforts of the Holy Ghost. (2) It was to continue eight days, the first and last of which were to be observed as sabbaths. (3) During the first seven days of this feast all the people were to leave their houses, and the women and children in them,

JAMIESON, FAUSSET, BROWN

17. Ye shall bring out of your habitations two wave loaves of two tenth deals, etc.–These loaves were made of "fine" or wheaten flour, the quantity contained in them being somewhat more than ten pounds in weight. As the wave-sheaf gave the signal for the commencement, the two loaves solemnized the termination of the harvest season. They were the first-fruits of that season, being offered unto the Lord by the priest in name of the whole nation. (See on Exod. 34:22.) The loaves used at the Passover were unleavened; those presented at Pentecost were leavened–a difference which is thus accounted for, that the one was a memorial of the bread hastily prepared at their departure, while the other was a tribute of gratitude to God for their daily food, which was leavened. **21. ye shall proclaim on the selfsame day, that it may be an holy convocation unto you: ye shall do no servile work therein**–Though it extended over a week, the first day only was held as a Sabbath, both for the national offering of first-fruits and a memorial of the giving of the law.

22. thou shalt not make clean riddance of the corners of thy fields when thou reapest, etc.–(See on ch. 19:9.) The repetition of this law here probably arose from the priests reminding the people, at the presentation of the first-fruits, to unite piety to God with charity to the poor.

23-25. FEAST OF TRUMPETS. **In the seventh month, the first day of the month, shall ye have a sabbath**–That was the first day of the ancient civil year. **a memorial of blowing of trumpets**–Jewish writers say that the trumpets were sounded thirty successive times, and the reason for the institution was for the double purpose of announcing the commencement of the new year, which was (vs. 25) to be religiously observed (see Num. 29:3), and of preparing the people for the approaching solemn feast.

27-32. there shall be a day of atonement . . . and ye shall affict your souls–an unusual festival, at which the sins of the whole year were expiated. (See ch. 16:29-34.) It is here only stated that the severest penalty was incurred by the violation of this day.

33-44. the feast of tabernacles, for seven days unto the Lord–This festival, which was instituted in grateful commemoration of the Israelites having securely dwelt in booths or tabernacles in the wilderness, was the third of the three great annual festivals, and, like the other two, it lasted a week. It began on the fifteenth day of the month, corresponding to the end of our September and beginning of October, which was observed as a Sabbath; and it could be celebrated only at the place of the sanctuary, offerings being made on the altar every day of its continuance. The Jews were commanded during the whole period of the festival to dwell in booths, which were erected on the flat roofs of houses, in the streets or fields; and the trees made use of are by some stated to be the citron, the palm, the myrtle, and the willow, while others maintain the people were allowed to take any trees they could obtain that were distinguished for verdure and fragrance. While the solid branches were reserved for the construction of the booths, the lighter

ADAM CLARKE

TODAY'S DICTIONARY OF THE BIBLE:

Pentecost—i.e., "fifieth"—found only in the New Testament (Acts 2:1; 20:16; 1 Cor. 16:8). The festival so named is first spoken of in Ex. 23:16 as "the feast of harvest," and again in Ex. 34:22 as "the feast of weeks." It is also called "the day of the firstfruits (Num. 28:26). From the sixteenth of the month of Nisan (the second day of the Passover), seven complete weeks—i.e., forty-nine days—were to be reckoned, and this feast was held on the fiftieth day. The manner in which it was to be kept is described in Lev. 23:15–19; Num. 28:27–29. Besides the sacrifices prescribed for the occasion, everyone was to bring to the Lord his "tribute of a free-will offering" (Deut. 16:9–11). The purpose of this feast was to commemorate the completion of the grain harvest. Its distinguishing feature was the offering of "two leavened loaves" made from the new corn of the completed harvest, which, with two lambs, were waved before the Lord as a thank offering.

The day of Pentecost is noted in the Christian Church as the day on which the Spirit descended upon the apostles, and on which, under Peter's preaching, so many thousands were converted in Jerusalem (Acts 2).

24. ***A memorial of blowing of trumpets.*** **This is generally called the Feast of Trumpets; and as it took place on the first day of the seventh month, Tisri, which answers to September, which month was the commencement of what was called the civil year, the feast probably had no other design than to celebrate the commencement of that year, if indeed such a distinction obtained among the ancient Jews.**

28. ***A day of atonement.*** **See the note on chap. xvi, 3, etc., where this subject is largely explained.**

34. ***The feast of tabernacles.*** **In this solemnity the people left their houses, and dwelt in booths or tents made of the branches of "goodly trees" and "thick trees" (of what kind the text does not specify), together with "palm trees" and "willows of the brook," v. 40. And in these they dwelt** ***seven days,*** **in commemoration of their forty years' sojourning and dwelling in tents in the wilderness while destitute of any fixed habitations.**

MATTHEW HENRY

and to dwell in booths made of the boughs of thick trees, particularly palm trees, *v.* 40, 42. (4) They were to *rejoice before the Lord God* during all the time of this feast, *v.* 40. The tradition of the Jews is that they were to express their joy by dancing, and singing hymns of praise to God, with musical instruments.

2. As to the design of this feast,

(1) It was to be kept in remembrance of their dwelling in tents in the wilderness.

(2) It was a feast of in-gathering, so it is called, Exod. xxiii. 16.

II. The summary and conclusion of these institutions.

1. God appointed these feasts (*v.* 37, 38), *besides the sabbaths and your free-will offerings.* God's institutions leave room for free-will offerings. The feasts of the Lord, declared unto us, are not so numerous, nor the observance of them so burdensome and costly, as theirs then were, but more spiritual and significant, and surer sweeter earnests of the everlasting feast, at the last in-gathering.

JAMIESON, FAUSSET, BROWN

branches were carried by men, who marched in triumphal procession, singing psalms and crying "Hosanna!" which signifies, "Save, we beseech thee!" (Ps. 118:15, 25, 26). It was a season of great rejoicing. But the ceremony of drawing water from the pool, which was done on the last day, seems to have been the introduction of a later period (John 7:37). That last day was the eighth, and, on account of the scene at Siloam, was called "the great day of the feast." The feast of ingathering, when the vintage was over, was celebrated also on that day, and, as the conclusion of one of the great festivals, it was kept as a sabbath.

ADAM CLARKE

40. *Boughs of goodly trees.* The Jews and many critics imagine the citron tree to be intended, and by *boughs of thick trees* the myrtle.

43. *That your generations may know.* By the institution of this feast God had two great objects in view: (1) To perpetuate the wonderful display of His providence and grace in bringing them out of Egypt, and in preserving them in the wilderness; (2) To excite and maintain in them a spirit of gratitude and obedience, by leading them to consider deeply the greatness of the favours which they had received for His most merciful hands.

CHAPTER 24 (Matthew Henry)

Verses 1–9

Care is here taken, and orders are given, for the decent furnishing of the candlestick and table in God's house.

I. The lamps must always be kept burning. 1. The people were to provide oil (*v.* 2), the best, *pure olive-oil, beaten,* probably it was double-strained. Ministers are as burning and shining lights in Christ's church, but it is the duty of people to provide comfortably for them, as Israel for the lamps. Scandalous maintenance makes a scandalous ministry. 2. The priests were to tend the lamps; they must snuff them, clean the candlestick, and supply them with oil, morning and evening, *v.* 3, 4. Thus it is the work of the ministers of the gospel to *hold forth that word of life,* not to set up new lights, but, by expounding and preaching the word, to make the light of it more clear and extensive.

II. The table must always be kept spread. This was appointed before, Exod. xxv. 30. 1. There was a loaf for every tribe, for *in our Father's house there is bread enough.* Even after the revolt of the ten tribes this number of loaves was continued (2 Chron. xiii. 11), for the sake of those few of each tribe that retained their affection to the temple and continued their attendance on it. 2. A handful of frankincense was put in a golden saucer. When the bread was removed, and given to the priests, this frankincense was burnt upon the golden altar for a memorial instead of the bread, as a humble acknowledgment, and all the loaves were consigned to the priests. 3. Every sabbath it was renewed. Christ's ministers should provide new bread for his house every sabbath day, the production of their fresh studies in the scripture, that *their proficiency may appear to all,* II Tim. iv. 1, 5.

Verses 10–23

Evil manners, we say, beget good laws. We have here an account of the evil manners of a certain nameless mongrel Israelite, and the good laws occasioned thereby.

I. The offender was the son of an Egyptian father and an Israelitish mother (*v.* 10); his mother was of the tribe of Dan, *v.* 11. This notice is taken of his parentage either, 1. To intimate what occasioned the quarrel he was engaged in. The Jews say, "He offered to set up his tent among the Danites in the right of his mother, but was justly opposed by some or other of that tribe, and informed that his father being an Egyptian he had no part nor lot in the matter, but must look upon himself as a stranger." Or, 2. To show the common ill effect of such mixed marriages.

II. The occasion of the offence was contention: He *strove with a man of Israel.*

III. The offence itself was blasphemy and cursing, *v.* 11. 1. He *blasphemed the name of the Lord.* It is probable that finding himself aggrieved by the divine appointment, which separated between the Israelites and strangers, he impudently reproached both the law and the Law-maker, and set him at defiance. 2. He cursed either God himself or the person with whom he strove.

IV. The caution with which he was proceeded against for this sin. Moses himself would not give judgment hastily, but committed the offender into custody, till he had consulted the oracle in this case. They waited to know what was *the mind of the Lord,* whether he was to be put to death by the hand of the magistrate or to be left to the judgment of God.

V. Sentence passed upon this offender by the righteous Judge of heaven and earth himself: *Let all the congregation stone him. v.* 14.

CHAPTER 24 (Jamieson, Fausset, Brown)

Vss. 1-23. OIL FOR THE LAMPS. **2. Command the children of Israel**—This is the repetition of a law previously given (Exod. 27:20, 21). **pure oil olive beaten**—or cold-drawn, which is always of great purity.

3, 4. Aaron shall order it from the evening unto the morning—The daily presence of the priests was necessary to superintend the cleaning and trimming. **upon the pure candlestick**—so called because of pure gold. This was symbolical of the light which ministers are to diffuse through the Church. **5-9. take fine flour, and bake twelve cakes**—for the showbread, as previously appointed (Exod. 25:30). Those cakes were baked by the Levites, the flour being furnished by the people (I Chron. 9:32; 23:29), oil, wine, and salt being the other ingredients (ch. 2:13). **two tenth deals**—i.e., of an ephah—thirteen and a half pounds weight each; and on each row or pile of cakes some frankincense was strewed, which, being burnt, led to the showbread being called "an offering made by fire." Every Sabbath a fresh supply was furnished; hot loaves were placed on the altar instead of the stale ones, which, having lain a week, were removed, and eaten only by the priests, except in cases of necessity (I Sam. 21:3-6; also Luke 6:3,4).

10. the son of an Israelitish woman, etc.—This passage narrates the enactment of a new law, with a detail of the circumstances which gave rise to it. The "mixed multitude" that accompanied the Israelites in their exodus from Egypt creates a presumption that marriage connections of the kind described were not infrequent. And it was most natural, in the relative circumstances of the two people, that the father should be an Egyptian and the mother an Israelite. **11. the Israelitish woman's son blasphemed the name of the Lord**—A youth of this half-blood, having quarrelled with an Israelite, vented his rage in some horrid form of impiety. It was a common practice among the Egyptians to curse their idols when disappointed in obtaining the object of their petitions. The Egyptian mind of this youth thought the greatest insult to his opponent was to blaspheme the object of his religious reverence. He spoke disrespectfully of One who sustained the double character of the King as well as the God of the Hebrew people; and as the offense was a new one, he was put in ward till the mind of the Lord was ascertained as to his disposal. **14. Bring forth him that hath cursed without the camp**—All executions took place without the camp; and this arrangement probably originated in the idea that, as the Israelites were to be "a holy people," all flagrant offenders should be thrust out of their society. **let all that heard him lay their hands upon his head,** etc.—The imposition of hands formed a public and solemn testimony against the crime, and at the same time made the punishment legal.

CHAPTER 24 (Adam Clarke)

5. *Bake twelve cakes.* See the whole account of the shewbread in the notes on Exod. xxv. 30; and relative to the table on which they stood, the golden candlestick and silver trumpets, carried in triumph to Rome, see the note on Exod. xxv. 31.

10. *The son of a Israelitish woman, whose father was an Egyptian.* What the cause of the strife between this mongrel person and the Israelitish man was is not even hinted at. The sacred text does not tell us what name he blasphemed; it is simply said *vaiyikkob eth hashshem,* "He pierced through, distinguished, explained, or expressed the name." As the Jews hold it impious to pronounce the name *Yehovah,* they always put either *Adonai, Lord,* or *hashshem,* "the name," in the place of it; but in this sense *hashshem* was never used prior to the days of rabbinical superstition, and therefore it cannot be put here for the word *Jehovah.* Blaspheming the name of the Lord is mentioned in v. 16, and there the proper Hebrew term is used *shem Yehovah,* and not the rabbinical *hashshem,* as in v. 11. The fifteenth verse seems to countenance the supposition that the god whose name was produced on this occasion was not the true God, for it is there said, "Whosoever curseth his god [*elohaiv*], shall bear his sin"—shall have the punishment due to him as an *idolater;* but "he that blasphemeth the name of the Lord [*shem Yehovah*], . . . shall surely be put to death . . . when he blasphemeth the name [*shem*]" he shall die, v. 16. The verb *nakab,* which we translate "blaspheme," signifies "to pierce, bore, make hollow"; also "to express or distinguish by name"; see Isa. lxii. 2; Num. i. 17; 1 Chron. xii. 31; xvi. 41; xxviii. 15. Hence all that we term blasphemy here may only signify the particularizing some false god, i.e., naming him by his name, or imploring his aid as a helper.

14. *Lay their hands upon his head.* It was by this ceremony that the people who heard him curse bore their public testimony in order to his being fully convicted, for without this his punishment would not have been lawful. By this ceremony also they in effect said to the man, "Thy blood be upon thy own head."

MATTHEW HENRY

VI. A standing law made upon this occasion for the stoning of blasphemers, *v.* 15, 16. Magistrates are the guardians of both tables, and ought to be as jealous for the honour of God against those that speak contemptuously of his being and government as for the public peace and safety against the disturbers of them.

VII. A repetition of some other laws annexed to this new law. 1. That murder should be punished with death (*v.* 17, and again *v.* 21). 2. That maimers should in like manner be punished by the law of retaliation, *v.* 19, 20. This law we had before, Exod. xxii. 4, 5. And it was more agreeable to that dispensation, in which were revealed the rigour of the law and what sin deserved, than to the dispensation we are under, in which are revealed the grace of the gospel and the remission of sins: and therefore our Saviour has set aside this law (Matt. v. 38, 39), not to restrain magistrates from executing public justice, but to restrain us all from returning personal injuries and to oblige us to forgive as we are and hope to be forgiven. 3. That hurt done wilfully to a neighbour's cattle should be punished by making good the damage, *v.* 18, 21. 4. That strangers, as well as native Israelites, should be both entitled to the benefit of this law, so as not to suffer wrong, and liable to the penalty of this law in case they did wrong.

JAMIESON, FAUSSET, BROWN

16. **as well the stranger, as he that is born in the land, when he blasphemeth the name of the Lord, shall be put to death**—Although strangers were not obliged to be circumcised, yet by joining the Israelitish camp, they became amenable to the law, especially that which related to blasphemy.

17-22. **he that killeth any man shall surely be put to death**—These verses contain a repetition of some other laws, relating to offenses of a social nature, the penalties for which were to be inflicted, not by the hand of private parties, but through the medium of the judges before whom the cause was brought.

23. **the children of Israel did as the Lord commanded**—The chapter closes with the execution of Shelomith's son—and stoning having afterwards become the established punishment in all cases of blasphemy, it illustrates the fate of Stephen, who suffered under a false imputation of that crime.

ADAM CLARKE

15. *Whosoever curseth his God. Yekallel Elohaiv,* he who "makes light" of Him, who does not treat Him and sacred things with due reverence, *shall bear his sin*—shall have the guilt of this transgression imputed to him, and may expect the punishment.

16. *Blasphemeth the name of the Lord. Venokeb shem Yehovah,* he who "pierces, transfixes," the name of Jehovah; see the note on the tenth verse. This being the name by which especially the Divine Essence was pointed out, it should be held peculiarly sacred. We have already seen that the Jews never pronounce this name, and so long has it been disused among them that the true pronunciation is now totally lost.

17. *He that killeth any man.* Blasphemy against God, i.e., speaking injuriously of His name, His attributes, His government, and His revelation, together with murder, is to be punished with death. He that blasphemes God is a curse in society, and he who takes away, wilfully and by malicious intent, the life of any man, should certainly be put to death. In this respect God has absolutely required that life shall go for life.

20. *Breach for breach.* This is a repetition of the *lex talionis,* which see explained Exod. xxi. 24.

22. *Ye shall have one manner of law, as well for the stranger, as for one of your own country.* Equal laws, where each individual receives the same protection and the same privileges, are the boast only of a sound political constitution. He who respects and obeys the laws has a right to protection and support, and his person and property are as sacred in the sight of justice as the person and property of the prince. He who does not obey the laws of his country forfeits all right and title to protection and privilege; his own actions condemn him, and justice takes him up on the evidence of his own transgressions.

23. *And stone him with stones.* We are not to suppose that the culprit was exposed to the unbridled fury of the thousands of Israel; this would be brutality, not justice, for the very worst of tempers and passions might be produced and fostered by such a procedure. The Jews themselves tell us that their manner of stoning was this: they brought the condemned person without the camp, because his crime had rendered him unclean, and whatever was unclean must be put without the camp. When they came within four cubits of the place of execution, they stripped the criminal, if a man, leaving him nothing but a cloth about the waist. The place on which he was to be executed was elevated, and the witnesses went up with him to it, and laid their hands upon him, for the purposes mentioned in v. 14. Then one of the witnesses struck him with a stone upon the loins; if he was not killed with that blow, then the witnesses took up a great stone, as much as two men could lift, and threw it upon his breast. This was the *coup de grace,* and finished the tragedy.

MATTHEW HENRY — CHAPTER 25

Verses 1-7

The law of Moses laid a great deal of stress upon the sabbath; that law not only revived the observance of the weekly sabbath, but, for the further advancement of the honour of them, added the institution of a sabbatical year: *In the seventh year shall be a sabbath of rest unto the land, v.* 4. This sabbatical year began in September, at the end of harvest, the seventh month of their ecclesiastical year: and the law was, 1. That at the seed-time, which immediately followed the end of their in-gathering, they should sow no corn in their land, and that they should not in the spring dress their vineyards, and consequently that they should not expect either harvest or vintage the next year. 2. That what their ground did produce of itself they should not claim any property or use in, otherwise than from hand to mouth, but leave it for the poor, servants, strangers, and cattle, *v.* 5-7. It must be a sabbath of rest to the land; they must neither do any work about it, nor expect any fruit from it; all annual labours must be intermitted in the seventh year, as much as daily labours on the seventh day. It was a kindness to their land to let it rest sometimes, and would keep it *in heart* (as our

JAMIESON, FAUSSET, BROWN — CHAPTER 25

VSS. 1-7. SABBATH OF THE SEVENTH YEAR. **2-4. When ye come into the land which I give unto you**—It has been questioned on what year, after the occupation of Canaan, the sabbatic year began to be observed. Some think it was the seventh year after their entrance. But others, considering that as the first six years were spent in the conquest and division of the land (Joshua 5:12), and that the sabbatical year was to be observed after six years of agriculture, maintain that the observance did not commence till the fourteenth year. **the land keep a sabbath unto the Lord**—This was a very peculiar arrangement. Not only all agricultural processes were to be intermitted every seventh year, but the cultivators had no right to the soil. It lay entirely fallow, and its spontaneous produce was the common property of the poor and the stranger, the cattle and game. This year of rest was to invigorate the productive powers of the land, as the weekly Sabbath was a refreshment to men and cattle. It commenced immediately after the feast of ingathering, and it was calculated to teach the people, in a remarkable manner, the reality of the presence and providential power of God.

ADAM CLARKE — CHAPTER 25

2. *The land keep a sabbath.* See this ordinance explained in the note on Exod. xxiii. 11. It may be asked here: If it required all the annual produce of the field to support the inhabitants, how could the people be nourished the seventh year, when no produce was received from the fields? To this it may be answered that God sent His blessing in an especial manner on the sixth year (see vv. 21-22) and it brought forth fruit for three years.

husbandmen express it) for posterity, whose satisfaction God would have them to consult, and not to use the ground as if it were designed only for one age. 3. This year of rest typified the spiritual rest which all believers enter into through Christ, our true Noah, who giveth us comfort and rest *concerning our work, and the toil of our hands, because of the ground which the Lord hath cursed*, Gen. v. 29.

Verses 8–22

The general institution of the jubilee, *v.* 8, &c.

1. When it was to be observed: after *seven sabbaths of years* (*v.* 8).

2. How it was to be proclaimed, with sound of trumpet in all parts of the country (*v.* 9), both to give notice to all persons of it, and to express their joy and triumph in it; and the word *jobel*, or *jubilee*, is supposed to signify some particular sound of the trumpet distinguishable from any other. The trumpet was sounded in the close of the day of atonement. When their peace was made with God, then liberty was proclaimed.

3. What was to be done in that year extraordinary; besides the common rest of the land, which was observed every sabbatical year (*v.* 11, 12), and the release of personal debts (Deut. xv. 2, 3), there was to be the legal restoration of every Israelite to all the property, and all the liberty, which had been alienated from him since the last jubilee.

(1) The property which every man had in his dividend of the land of Canaan could not be alienated any longer than till the year of jubilee. Now this was no wrong to the purchaser, because the year of jubilee was fixed, and every man knew when it would come, and made his bargain accordingly. They shall not have power to sell, but only to make leases for any term of years, not going beyond the next jubilee. By this means it was provided, That the distinction of tribes should be kept up; that none should grow exorbitantly rich, by laying *house to house, and field to field* (Isa. v. 8), but should rather apply themselves to the cultivating of what they had than the enlarging of their possessions.

(2) The liberty which every man was born to, if it were sold or forfeited, should likewise return at the year of jubilee: *You shall return every man to his family*, *v.* 10. Those that were sold into other families thereby became strangers to their own; but in this year of redemption they were to return.

II. A law upon this occasion against oppression in buying and selling of land; neither the buyer nor the seller must overreach, *v.* 14–17. It must be settled what the clear yearly value of the land was, and then how many years' purchase it was worth till the year of jubilee. It is easy to observe that the nearer the jubilee was the less must the value of the land be. *According to the fewness of the years thou shalt diminish the price.*

III. Assurance given them that they should be no losers, but great gainers, by observing these years of rest. It is promised, 1. That they should be safe: *You shall dwell in the land in safety*, *v.* 18, and again *v.* 19. The word signifies both outward safety and inward security and confidence of spirit. 2. That they should be rich: *You shall eat your fill.* 3. That they should not want food convenient that year in which they did neither sow nor reap: *I will command my blessing in the sixth year, and it shall bring forth fruit for three years*, *v.* 21. It was intended for an encouragement to all God's people, in all ages, to trust him in the way of duty, and to cast their care upon him.

Verses 23–38

Here is, I. A law concerning the real estates of the Israelites in the land of Canaan, and the transferring of them. No land should be sold for ever from the family to whose lot it fell in the division of the land. And the reason given is, *The land is mine, and you are strangers and sojourners with me*, *v.* 23. If a man was constrained through poverty to sell his land for the subsistence of his family, yet, if afterwards he was able, he might redeem it before the year of jubilee (*v.* 24, 26, 27), and the price must be settled according to the number of years since the sale and before the jubilee. If the person himself was not able to redeem it, his next kinsman might (*v.* 25): *The redeemer thereof, he that is near unto him, shall come and shall redeem*, so it might be read. The kinsman is called *Goel*, the redeemer (Num. v. 8; Ruth iii. 9), to whom belonged the right of redeeming the land. And this typified Christ, who assumed our nature, that he might be our *kinsman.* If the land was not redeemed before the year of jubilee, then it should return of course to him that had sold or mortgaged it: *In the jubilee it shall go out*, *v.* 28. This was a figure of the free grace of God towards us in Christ, by which we are restored to the favour

8-23. THE JUBILEE. **thou shalt number seven sabbaths of years**—This most extraordinary of all civil institutions, which received the name of "Jubilee" from a *Hebrew* word signifying a musical instrument, a horn or trumpet, began on the tenth day of the seventh month, or the great day of atonement, when, by order of the public authorities, the sound of trumpets proclaimed the beginning of the universal redemption. All prisoners and captives obtained their liberties, slaves were declared free, and debtors were absolved. The land, as on the sabbatic year, was neither sowed nor reaped, but allowed to enjoy with its inhabitants a sabbath of repose; and its natural produce was the common property of all. Moreover, every inheritance throughout the land of Judea was restored to its original owner. **ye shall hallow the fiftieth year**—Much difference of opinion exists as to whether the jubilee was observed on the forty-ninth, or, in round numbers, it is called the fiftieth. The prevailing opinion, both in ancient and modern times, has been in favor of the latter. **12. ye shall eat the increase thereof out of the field,** etc.—All that the ground yielded spontaneously during that period might be eaten for their necessary subsistence, but no persons were at liberty to hoard or form a private stock in reserve. **13. ye shall return every man unto his possession,** etc.—Inheritances, from whatever cause, and how frequently soever they had been alienated, came back into the hands of the original proprietors. This law of entail, by which the right heir could never be excluded, was a provision of great wisdom for preserving families and tribes perfectly distinct, and their genealogies faithfully recorded, in order that all might have evidence to establish their right to the ancestral property. Hence the tribe and family of Christ were readily discovered at his birth. **17. Ye shall not oppress one another, but thou shalt fear thy God**—This, which is the same as vs. 14, related to the sale or purchase of possessions and the duty of paying an honest and equitable regard, on both sides, to the limited period during which the bargain could stand. The object of the legislator was, as far as possible, to maintain the original order of families, and an equality of condition among the people. **21, 22. I will command my blessing upon you in the sixth year, and it shall bring forth fruit for three years,** etc.—A provision was made, by the special interposition of God, to supply the deficiency of food which would otherwise have resulted from the suspension of all labor during the sabbatic year. The sixth year was to yield a miraculous supply for three continuous years. And the remark is applicable to the year of Jubilee as well as the sabbatic year. (See allusions to this extraordinary provision in II Kings 19:29; Isa. 37:30.) None but a legislator who was conscious of acting under divine authority would have staked his character on so singular an enactment as that of the sabbatic year; and none but a people who had witnessed the fulfilment of the divine promise would have been induced to suspend their agricultural preparations on a recurrence of a periodical Jubilee.

23-28. The land shall not be sold for ever—or, "be quite cut off," as the margin better renders it. The land was God's, and, in prosecution of an important design, He gave it to the people of His choice, dividing it among their tribes and families—who, however, held it of Him merely as tenants at will and had no right or power of disposing of it to strangers. In necessitous circumstances, individuals might effect a temporary sale. But they possessed the right of redeeming it, at *any time,* on payment of an adequate compensation to the present holder; and by the enactments of the Jubilee they recovered it free—so that the land was rendered inalienable. (See an exception to this law, ch. 27: 20.)

8. *Thou shalt number seven sabbaths of years.* This seems to state that the jubilee was to be celebrated on the forty-ninth year; but in vv. 10 and 11 it is said, "Ye shall hallow the fiftieth year," and, "A jubile shall this fiftieth year be." Probably in this verse Moses either includes the preceding jubilee, and thus with the forty-ninth makes up the number fifty; or he speaks of proclaiming the jubilee on the forty-ninth, and celebrating it on the fiftieth year current.

11. *A jubile shall that fiftieth year be.* The literal meaning of the word *jubile, yobel* in Hebrew, has not been well ascertained. The most natural derivation is from *hobil,* to "cause to bring back," or "recall," because estates which had been alienated were then brought back to their primitive owners. This was a wise and excellent institution, but appears to have been little regarded by the Jews after the Babylonish captivity. Indeed, it is not mentioned under the second Temple, and the observance must have ceased among the Jews when they were brought under a foreign yoke.

The jubilee seems to have been typical, (1) Of the great time of release, the gospel dispensation, when all who believe in Christ Jesus are redeemed from the bondage of sin—repossess the favor and image of God, the only inheritance of the human soul, having all debts cancelled, and the right of inheritance restored. To this the prophet Isaiah seems to allude, chap. xxvi. 13, and particularly lxi. 1-3. (2) Of the general resurrection. It is worthy of remark that the jubilee was not proclaimed till the tenth day of the seventh month, on the very day when the great annual atonement was made for the sins of the people; and does not this prove that the great liberty or redemption from thraldom, published under the gospel, could not take place till the great atonement, the sacrifice of the Lord Jesus, had been offered up?

14. *Ye shall not oppress one another.* You shall not take advantage of each other's ignorance in either buying or selling; for he that buys an article at less than it is worth, or sells one for more than it is worth, taking advantage in both cases of the ignorance of the vender or buyer, is no better than a thief, as he actually robs his neighbor of as much property as he has bought the article at below or sold it above its current value.

15. *According to the number of years.* The purchases that were to be made of lands were to be regulated by the number of years unelapsed of the current jubilee. This was something like buying the unexpired term of a lease among us; the purchase is always regulated by the number of years between the time of purchase and the expiration of the term.

20. *What shall we eat the seventh year?* A very natural question, which could be laid at rest only by the sovereign promise in the next verse: "I will command my blessing upon you in the sixth year, and it shall bring forth fruit for three years."

23. *The land shall not be sold for ever . . . the land is mine.* As God in a miraculous manner gave them possession of this land, they were therefore to consider themselves merely as tenants to Him; and on this ground He, as the great Landholder or Lord of the soil, prescribes to them all the conditions on which they shall hold it.

25. *Any of his kin come to redeem it.* The land that was sold might be redeemed, in the interim between jubilee and jubilee, by the former owner or by one of his kinsmen or relatives. This kinsman is called in the text *goel* or "redeemer"; and was not this a lively emblem of the redemption of man by Christ Jesus? That *He* might have a right to redeem man, He took upon Him human nature, and thus became a Kinsman of the great family of the human race, and thereby possessed the right of redeeming that fallen nature of which He took part, and of buying back to man that inheritance which had been forfeited by transgression.

29. *Sell a dwelling house in a walled city.* A very proper difference is put between houses

MATTHEW HENRY

of God, and become entitled to paradise, from which our first parents were expelled for disobedience. A difference was made between houses in walled cities, and lands in the country, or houses in country villages. Houses in walled cities were more the fruits of their own industry than land in the country, which was the immediate gift of God's bounty; and therefore, if a man sold a house in a city, he might redeem it any time within a year after the sale, but otherwise it was confirmed to the purchaser for ever, and should not return, no, not at the year of the jubilee, *v.* 29, 30. This provision was made to encourage strangers and proselytes to come and settle among them. Though they could not purchase land in Canaan to them and their heirs, yet they might purchase houses in walled cities. A clause is added in favour of the Levites, by way of exception from these rules.

II. A law for the relief of the poor, and the tender usage of poor debtors, and these are of more general and perpetual obligation than the former.

1. The poor must be relieved, *v.* 35. Here is, (1) Our brother's poverty and distress supposed. All men are to be looked upon and treated as brethren, for *we have all one Father*, Mal. ii. 10. (2) Our duty enjoined: *Thou shalt relieve him.* By sympathy, pitying the poor; by service, doing for them; and by supply, giving to them according to their necessity and thy ability.

2. Poor debtors must not be oppressed: *If thy brother be waxen poor*, and have occasion to borrow money of thee for the necessary support of his family, *take thou no usury of him*, either for money or victuals, *v.* 36, 37.

Verses 39–55

We have here the laws concerning servitude, designed to preserve the honour of the Jewish nation as a free people, and rescued by a divine power out of the house of bondage, into the glorious liberty of God's sons, his first-born. Now the law is,

I. That a native Israelite should never be made a bondman for perpetuity. If he was sold for debt, or for a crime, by the house of judgment, he was to serve but six years, and to go out the seventh; this was appointed, Exod. xxi. 2. But if he sold himself through extreme poverty, having nothing at all left him to preserve his life, and if it was to one of his own nation that he sold himself, in such a case it is here provided, 1. That he should not *serve as a bond-servant* (*v.* 39), nor be *sold with the sale of a bondman* (*v.* 42). He shall serve thee as a *hired servant*, whom the master has the use of only. God had redeemed them out of Egypt, and therefore they must never be exposed to sale as bondmen. 2. That while he did serve he should not be ruled with rigour, as the Israelites were in Egypt, *v.* 43. Both his work and his usage must be such as were fitting for a son of Abraham. 3. That at the year of jubilee he should *go out free*, he *and his children*, and should *return to his own family*, *v.* 41. For ten days before the jubilee-trumpet sounded, the servants that were to be discharged by it did express their great joy by feasting, and wearing garlands on their heads.

II. That they might purchase bondmen of the heathen nations that were round about them for the year of jubilee should give no discharge to them, *v.* 44, 46.

III. That if an Israelite sold himself for a servant to a wealthy proselyte that sojourned among them care should be taken that he should have the same advantages as if he had sold himself to an Israelite, and in some respects greater. 1. That he should not serve as a bondman, but as a hired servant. Also he was to go free at the year of jubilee, *v.* 54. 2. That he should have this further advantage that he might be redeemed again before the year of jubilee, *v.* 48, 49.

JAMIESON, FAUSSET, BROWN

29-31. if a man sell a dwelling house in a walled city, then he may redeem it within a whole year after it is sold—All sales of houses were subject to the same condition. But there was a difference between the houses of villages (which, being connected with agriculture, were treated as parts of the land) and houses possessed by trading people or foreigners in walled towns, which could only be redeemed within the year after the sale; if not then redeemed, these did not revert to the former owner at the Jubilee. **32-34. Notwithstanding the cities of the Levites,** etc.—The Levites, having no possessions but their towns and their houses, the law conferred on them the same privileges that were granted to the lands of the other Israelites. A certain portion of the lands surrounding the Levitical cities was appropriated to them for the pasturage of their cattle and flocks (Num. 35:4, 5). This was a permanent endowment for the support of the ministry and could not be alienated for any time. The Levites, however, were at liberty to make exchanges among themselves; and a priest might sell his house, garden, and right of pasture to another priest, but not to an Israelite of another tribe (Jer. 41:7-9). **35-38. if thy brother be waxen poor, . . . relieve him**—This was a most benevolent provision for the poor and unfortunate, designed to aid them or alleviate the evils of their condition. Whether a native Israelite or a mere sojourner, his richer neighbor was required to give him food, lodging, and a supply of money without usury. Usury was severely condemned (Ps. 15:5; Ezek. 18:8, 17), but the prohibition cannot be considered as applicable to the modern practice of men in business, borrowing and lending at legal rates of interest. **39-46. if thy brother . . . be waxen poor, and be sold unto thee, thou shalt not compel him to serve as a bound-servant**—An Israelite might be compelled, through misfortune, not only to mortgage his inheritance, but himself. In the event of his being reduced to this distress, he was to be treated not as a slave, but a hired servant whose engagement was temporary, and who might, through the friendly aid of a relative, be redeemed at any time before the Jubilee. The ransom money was determined on a most equitable principle. Taking account of the number of years from the proposal to redeem and the Jubilee, of the current wages of labor for that time, and multiplying the remaining years by that sum, the amount was to be paid to the master for his redemption. But if no such friendly interposition was made for a Hebrew slave, he continued in servitude till the year of Jubilee, when, as a matter of course, he regained his liberty, as well as his inheritance. Viewed in the various aspects in which it is presented in this chapter, the Jubilee was an admirable institution, and subservient in an eminent degree to uphold the interests of religion, social order, and freedom among the Israelites.

ADAM CLARKE

in a city and houses in the country. If a man sold his house in the city, he might redeem it any time in the course of a year; but if it were not redeemed within that time, it could no more be redeemed, nor did it go out even in the jubilee. It was not so with a house in the country; such a house might be redeemed during any part of the interim; and if not redeemed, must go out at the jubilee. The reason in both cases is sufficiently evident. The house in the city might be built for purposes of trade or traffic merely; the house in the country was built on or attached to the inheritance which God had divided to the respective families, and it was therefore absolutely necessary that the same law should apply to the house as to the inheritance.

32. *The cities of the Levites.* The law in this and the following verses was also a very wise one. A Levite could not ultimately sell his house. If sold, he could redeem it at any time in the interim between the two jubilees; but if not redeemed, it must go out at the following jubilee. And why? They had no inheritance in Israel, only their cities, to dwell in: and because their houses in these cities were the whole that they could call their own, therefore these houses could not be ultimately alienated. All that they had to live on besides was from that most precarious source of support, the freewill offerings of the people, which depended on the prevalence of pure religion in the land.

36. *Take thou no usury of him.* Usury, at present, signifies unlawful interest for money. Properly, it means the reward or compensation given for the use of a thing, but is principally spoken of money. See the definition of the original term in the note on Exod. xxii. 25.

42. *For they are my servants.* As God redeemed every Israelite out of Egyptian bondage, they were therefore to consider themselves as His property, and that consequently they should not alienate themselves from Him. It was in being His servants, and devoted to His work, that both their religious and political service consisted. And although their political liberty might be lost, they knew that their spiritual liberty never could be forfeited except by an utter alienation from God. God therefore claims the same right to their persons which He does to their lands; see the note on v. 23.

50. *The price of his sale shall be.* This was a very equitable law, both for the sojourner to whom the man was sold and to the Israelite who had been thus sold. The Israelite might redeem himself, or one of his kindred might redeem him; but this must not be done to the prejudice of his master, the sojourner. They were therefore to reckon the years he must have served from that time till the jubilee; and then, taking the current wages of a servant per year at that time, multiply the remaining years by that sum, and the aggregate was the sum to be given to his master for his redemption. The Jews hold that the kindred of such a person were bound, if in their power, to redeem him, lest he should be swallowed up among the heathen; and we find, from Neh. v. 8, that this was done by the Jews on their return from the Babylonish captivity: "We after our ability have redeemed our brethren the Jews, which were sold unto the heathen."

55. *For unto me the children of Israel are servants.* The reason of this law we have already seen (see on v. 42) but we must look further to see the great end of it. The Israelites were a typical people; they represented those under the gospel dispensation who are children of God by faith in Christ Jesus. But these last have a peculiarity of blessing: they are not merely servants, but they are sons; though they also serve God, yet it is in the newness of the spirit, and not in the oldness of the letter. And to this difference of state the apostle seems evidently to allude, Gal. iv. 6, etc.: "And because ye are sons, God hath sent forth the Spirit of his Son into your hearts, crying, Abba, Father. Wherefore thou art no more a servant, but a son; and if a son, then an heir of God through Christ"—genuine believers in Christ not being heirs of an earthly inheritance, nor merely of a heavenly one, for they are heirs of God. God himself therefore is their Portion, without whom even heaven itself would not be a state of consummate blessedness to an immortal spirit.

MATTHEW HENRY

CHAPTER 26

Verses 1–13

Here is, I. The inculcating of those precepts of the law which were of the greatest consequence, and by which especially their obedience would be tried, *v.* 1, 2. They are the abstract of the second and fourth commandments. 1. "Be sure you never worship images, nor ever make any sorts of images or pictures for a religious use," *v.* 1. Next to God's being, unity, and universal influence, it is necessary that we know and believe that he is an infinite Spirit; and therefore to represent him by an image in the making of it, to confine him to an image in the consecrating of it, and to worship him by an image in bowing down to it, *changes his truth into a lie* and *his glory into shame*, as much as any thing. 2. "Be sure you keep up a great venèration for sabbaths and religious assemblies," *v.* 2. As nothing tends more to corrupt religion than the use of images in devotion, so nothing contributes more to the support of it than *keeping the sabbaths* and *reverencing the sanctuary*. These make up very much of the instrumental part of religion, by which the essentials of it are kept up.

II. Great encouragements given them to live in constant obedience to all God's commandments. Human governments enforce their laws with penalties to be inflicted for the breach of them; but God will be known as *the rewarder of those that seek and serve him*. 1. Plenty and abundance of the fruits of the earth. Before they had reaped their corn and threshed it, the vintage would be ready; and, before they had finished their vintage, it would be high time to begin their sowing. The plenty should be so great that they should *bring forth the old* to be given away to the poor *because of the new*, to make room for it in their barns. 2. Peace under the divine protection: "*You shall dwell in your land safely* (*v.* 5); both really safe, and safe in your own apprehensions; you shall lie down to rest in the power and promise of God, and not only none shall hurt you, but none shall so much as *make you afraid*," *v.* 6. See Ps. iv. 8. 3. Victory and success in their wars abroad, while they had peace and tranquillity at home, *v.* 7, 8. 4. The increase of their people: *I will make you fruitful and multiply you*, *v.* 9. 5. The favour of God, which is the fountain of all good: *I will have respect unto you*, *v.* 9. If the eye of our faith be unto God, the eye of his favour will be unto us. 6. Tokens of his presence in and by his ordinances: *I will set my tabernacle among you*, *v.* 11. 7. The grace of the covenant, as the fountain and foundation, the sweetness and security, of all these blessings: *I will establish my covenant with you*, *v.* 9. Let them perform their part of the covenant, and God would not fail to perform his. All covenant-blessings are summed up in the covenant-relation (*v.* 12): *I will be your God, and you shall be my people*; and they are all grounded upon their redemption: *I am your God*, because *I brought you forth out of the land of Egypt*, *v.* 13.

Verses 14–39

After God had set the blessing before them he here sets the curse before them, the death and evil which would make them miserable if they were disobedient.

I. How their sin is described, which would bring all this misery upon them. Not sins of ignorance and infirmity; God had provided sacrifices for those. Not the sins they repented of and forsook; but the sins that were presumptuously committed, and obstinately persisted in. Two things would certainly bring this ruin upon them:—

1. A contempt of God's commandments (*v.* 14). Their sin is supposed to begin in mere carelessness, and neglect, and omission. (1) *Despising God's statutes*, both the duties enjoined and the authority enjoining them, thinking meanly of the law and the Law-maker. (2) *Abhorring his judgments*, their very souls abhorring them. Those that turn from it will turn against it, and their hearts will rise at it. (3) *Breaking his covenant*. When men have come to such a pitch of impiety as to despise and abhor the commandment, the next step will be to disown God, and all relation to him. Those that reject the precept will come at least to renounce the covenant.

JAMIESON, FAUSSET, BROWN

CHAPTER 26

VSS. 1, 2. OF IDOLATRY. **1. Ye shall make you no idols**—Idolatry had been previously forbidden (Exod. 20:4, 5), but the law was repeated here with reference to some particular forms of it that were very prevalent among the neighboring nations. **a standing image**—i.e., upright pillar. **image of stone**—i.e., an obelisk, inscribed with hieroglyphical and superstitious characters; the former denoting the common and smaller pillars of the Syrians or Canaanites; the latter, pointing to the large and elaborate obelisks which the Egyptians worshipped as guardian divinities, or used as stones of adoration to stimulate religious worship. The Israelites were enjoined to beware of them. **2. Ye shall keep my sabbaths, and reverence my sanctuary**—Very frequently, in this Book of the Law, the Sabbath and the sanctuary are mentioned as antidotes to idolatry.

3-13. A BLESSING TO THE OBEDIENT. **3. If ye walk in my statutes**—In that covenant into which God graciously entered with the people of Israel, He promised to bestow upon them a variety of blessings, so long as they continued obedient to Him as their Almighty Ruler; and in their subsequent history that people found every promise amply fulfilled, in the enjoyment of plenty, peace, a populous country, and victory over all enemies. **4. I will give you rain in due season, and the land shall yield her increase**—Rain seldom fell in Judea except at two seasons—the former rain at the end of autumn, the seedtime; and the latter rain in spring, before the beginning of harvest (Jer. 5:24). **5. your threshing shall reach unto the vintage, and the vintage shall reach unto the sowing time,** etc.—The barley harvest in Judea was about the middle of April; the wheat harvest about six weeks after, or in the beginning of June. After the harvest came the vintage, and fruit gathering towards the latter end of July. Moses led the Hebrews to believe that, provided they were faithful to God, there would be no idle time between the harvest and vintage, so great would be the increase. (See Amos 9:13.) This promise would be very animating to a people who had come from a country where, for three months, they were pent up without being able to walk abroad because the fields were under water. **10. ye shall eat old store**—Their stock of old corn would be still unexhausted and large when the next harvest brought a new supply. **13. I have broken the bands of your yoke, and made you go upright**—a metaphorical expression to denote their emancipation from Egyptian slavery.

14-39. A CURSE TO THE DISOBEDIENT. **But if ye will not hearken unto me,** etc.—In proportion to the great and manifold privileges bestowed upon the Israelites would be the extent of their national criminality and the severity of their national punishments if they disobeyed.

ADAM CLARKE

CHAPTER 26

1. *Ye shall make you no idols*. See the note on Exod. xx. 4, and see the note on Gen. xxviii. 18-19, concerning consecrated stones. Not only idolatry in general is forbidden here, but also the superstitious use of innocent and lawful things. Probably the stones or pillars which were first set up, and anointed by holy men in commemoration of signal interposition of God in their behalf, were afterward abused to idolatrous and superstitious purposes, and therefore prohibited. This we know was the case with the brazen serpent, 2 Kings xviii. 4.

3. *If ye walk in my statutes*. For the meaning of this and similar words used in the law, see the note on v. 15.

5. *Your threshing shall reach unto the vintage*. According to Pliny, *Hist. Nat.*, 1. xviii., c. 18, the Egyptians reaped their barley six months, and their oats seven months, after seedtime; for they sowed all their grain about the end of summer, when the overflowings of the Nile had ceased. It was nearly the same in Judea: they sowed their corn and barley towards the end of autumn, and about the month of October; and they began their barley harvest after the Passover, about the middle of March; and in one month or six weeks after, about Pentecost, they began that of their wheat. After their wheat heavest their vintage commenced. Moses here leads the Hebrews to hope, if they continued faithful to God, that between their harvest and vintage, and between their vintage and seedtime, there should be no interval, so great should the abundance be. And these promises would appear to them the more impressive, as they had just now come out of a country where the inhabitants were obliged to remain for nearly three months shut up within their cities, because the Nile had then inundated the whole country.

11. *I will set my tabernacle among you*. This and the following verse contain the grand promise of the gospel dispensation, viz., the presence, manifestation, and indwelling of God in human nature, and His constant indwelling in the souls of His followers. So John i. 14: "The Word was made flesh, and dwelt [made His tabernacle] among us." And to this promise of the law Paul evidently refers, 2 Cor. vi. 16-18 and vii. 1.

15. *If ye shall despise my statutes . . . abhor my judgments*. As these words, and others of a similar import, which point out different properties of the revelation of God, are frequently occurring, I judge it best to take a general view of them, once for all, in this place, and show how they differ among themselves, and what property of the divine law each points out.

(1) *Statutes. Chukkoth,* from *chak,* "to mark out, define." This term seems to signify the things which God has defined, marked, and traced out, that men might have a perfect copy of pure conduct always before their eyes, to teach them how they might walk so as to please Him in all things, which they could not do without such instruction as God gives in His Word, and the help which He affords by His Spirit.

(2) *Judgments. Shephatim,* from *shaphat,* to "distinguish, regulate, and determine"; meaning those things which God has determined that men shall pursue, by which their whole conduct shall be regulated, making the proper distinction between virtue and vice, good and evil, right and wrong, justice and injustice; in a word, between what is proper to be done and what is proper to be left undone.

(3) *Commandments. Mitsvoth,* from *tsavah,* to "command, ordain, and appoint, as a legislator." This term is properly applied to those parts of the law which contain the obligation the people are under to act according to the statutes, judgments, etc., already established, and which prohibit them by penal sanctions from acting contrary to the laws.

(4) *Covenant. Berith,* from *bar,* to "clear, cleanse, or purify"; because the covenant, the whole system of revelation given to the Jews, was intended to separate them from all the people of the earth, and to make them holy. *Berith* also signifies the covenant sacrifice, which prefigured the atonement made by Christ

MATTHEW HENRY

2. A contempt of his corrections. Even their disobedience would not have been their destruction if they had not been obstinate and impenitent in it, notwithstanding the methods God took to reclaim them. Three ways this is expressed:—(1) "*If you will not for all this hearken to me,*" *v.* 18, 21, 27. (2) *If you walk contrary to me, v.* 21, 23, 27. All sinners walk contrary to God, to his truths, laws, and counsels; but those especially that are incorrigible under his judgments. (3) *If you will not be reformed by these things.* God's design in punishing is to reform, by giving men sensible convictions of the evil of sin, and obliging them to seek unto him for relief: this is the primary intention; but those that will not be reformed by the judgments of God must expect to be ruined by them.

II. How the misery is described which their sin would bring upon them, under two heads:—

1. God himself would be against them; and this is the root and cause of all their misery. Those that cast off God deserve that he should cast them off. Those that are obstinate and incorrigible, when they have weathered one storm must expect another more violent.

2. The whole creation would be at war with them.

(1) Temporal judgments threatened. [1] Diseases of body, which should be epidemical. [2] Famine and scarcity of bread. [3] Your choice men shall die in battle, and *those that hate you shall reign over you,* and justly, since you are not willing that the God that loved you should reign over you, 2 Chron. xii. 8. [4] Wild beasts, lions, bears, and wolves, which should increase upon them. [5] Captivity, or dispersion: *I will scatter you among the heathen* (*v.* 33), *in your enemies' land, v.* 34. Never were any people so incorporated and united among themselves as they were; but for their sin God would scatter them, so that they should be lost among the heathen, from whom God had graciously distinguished them, but with whom they had wickedly mingled themselves. [6] The utter ruin and desolation of their land, which should be so remarkable that their very enemies themselves, who had helped it forward, should in the review be astonished at it, *v.* 32. *First,* Their cities should be waste. *Secondly,* Their sanctuaries should be a desolation. *Thirdly,* The country itself should be desolate, not tilled or husbanded (*v.* 34, 35). [7] The destruction of their idols: *I will destroy your high places, v.* 30. Those that will not be parted from their sins by the commands of God shall be parted from them by his judgments; since they would not destroy their high places, God would.

(2) Spiritual judgments are here threatened. These should seize the mind; for he that made the mind can, when he pleases, make his sword approach to it. It is here threatened, [1] That they should find no acceptance with God: *I will not smell the savour of your sweet odours, v.* 31. [2] That they should have no courage in their wars, but should be quite disspirited and disheartened. [3] That they should have no hope of the forgiveness of their sins (*v.* 39).

JAMIESON, FAUSSET, BROWN

16. I will even appoint over you terror—the falling sickness [PATRICK]. **consumption, and the burning ague**—Some consider these as symptoms of the same disease—consumption followed by the shivering, burning, and sweating fits that are the usual concomitants of that malady. According to the Septuagint, ague is "the jaundice," which disorders the eyes and produces great depression of spirits. Others, however, consider the word as referring to a scorching wind; no certain explanation can be given. **18. if ye will not yet for all this hearken unto me, then I will punish you seven times more**—i.e., with far more severe and protracted calamities. **19. will make your heaven as iron, and your earth as brass**—No figures could have been employed to convey a better idea of severe and long-continued famine. **22. I will also send wild beasts among you**—This was one of the four judgments threatened (Ezek. 14:21; see also II Kings 2:4). **your highways shall be desolate**—Trade and commerce will be destroyed—freedom and safety will be gone—neither stranger nor native will be found on the roads (Isa. 33:8). This is an exact picture of the present state of the Holy Land, which has long lain in a state of desolation, brought on by the sins of the ancient Jews. **26. ten women shall bake your bread in one oven,** etc.—The bread used in families is usually baked by women, and at home. But sometimes also, in times of scarcity, it is baked in public ovens for want of fuel; and the scarcity predicted here would be so great, that one oven would be sufficient to bake as much as ten women used in ordinary occasions to provide for family use; and even this scanty portion of bread would be distributed by weight (Ezek. 4:16). **29. ye shall eat the flesh of your sons**—The revolting picture was actually exhibited at the siege of Samaria, at the siege of Jerusalem by Nebuchadnezzar (Lam. 4:10), and at the destruction of that city by the Romans. (See on Deut. 28.) **30. I will destroy your high places**—Consecrated enclosures on the tops of mountains, or on little hillocks, raised for practising the rites of idolatry. **cut down your images**—According to some, those images were made in the form of chariots (II Kings 23:11); according to others, they were of a conical form, like small pyramids. Reared in honor of the sun, they were usually placed on a very high situation, to enable the worshippers to have a better view of the rising sun. They were forbidden to the Israelites, and when set up, ordered to be destroyed. **cast your carcasses upon the carcasses of your idols,** etc.—Like the statues of idols, which, when broken, lie neglected and contemned, the Jews during the sieges and subsequent captivity often wanted the rites of sepulture. **31. I will make your cities waste**—This destruction of its numerous and flourishing cities, which was brought upon Judea through the sins of Israel, took place by the forced removal of the people during, and long after, the captivity. But it is realized to a far greater extent now. **bring your sanctuaries unto desolation, and I will not smell the savour of your sweet odours**—the tabernacle and temple, as is evident from the tenor of the subsequent clause, in which God announces that He will not accept or regard their sacrifices. **33. I will scatter you among the heathen,** etc.—as was done when the elite of the nation were removed into Assyria and placed in various parts of the kingdom. **34. Then shall the land enjoy her sabbaths, as long as it lieth desolate,** etc.—A long arrear of sabbatic years had accumulated through the avarice and apostasy of the Israelites, who had deprived their land of its appointed season of rest. The number of those sabbatic years seems to have been seventy, as determined by the duration of the captivity. This early prediction is very remarkable, considering that the usual policy of the Assyrian conquerors was to send colonies to cultivate and inhabit their newly acquired provinces.

ADAM CLARKE

for the sin of the world, by which He purifies believers unto himself, and makes them "a peculiar people, zealous of good works." Besides those four, we may add the following, from other places of Scripture.

(5) *Testimonies. Edoth,* from *ad,* "beyond, farther, besides"; because the whole ritual law referred to something farther on or beyond the Jewish dispensation, even to that Sacrifice which in the fulness of time was to be offered for the sins of men. Thus all the sacrifices of the Mosaic law referred to Christ, and bore *testimony* to Him who was to come.

(6) *Ordinances. Mishmaroth,* from *shamar,* to "guard, keep safe, watch over"; those parts of divine revelation which exhorted men to watch their ways, keep their hearts, and promised them, in consequence, the continual protection and blessing of God their Maker.

(7) *Precepts. Pikkudim,* from *pakad,* to "overlook, take care or notice of, to visit"; a very expressive character of the divine testimonies, the overseers of a man's conduct, those who stand by and look on to see whether he acts according to the commands of his Master.

(8) *Truth. Emeth,* from *am,* to "support, sustain, confirm"; because God is immutable, who has promised, threatened, commanded, and therefore all His promises, threatenings.

(9) *Righteousness. Tsedakah,* which, though not having a verb in the Hebrew Bible, seems to convey, from its use as a noun, the idea of giving just weight or good measure; see chap. xix. 36.

(10) *Word of Jehovah. Debar Yehovah,* from *dabar,* "to drive, lead, bring forward," hence to bring forward, or utter one's sentiments; so the word of God is what God has brought forth to man from His own mind and counsel.

(11) *Imrah,* "speech or word," variously modified from *amar,* to "branch out," because of the interesting details into which the word of God enters in order to instruct man and make him wise unto salvation.

(12) All these collectively are termed the *law torah,* or *torath Yehovah,* "the law of the Lord," from *yarah,* to "direct, set straight and true, as stones in a building, to teach and instruct," because this whole system of divine revelation is calculated to direct men to the attainment of present and eternal felicity.

16. *I will even appoint over you terror.* How dreadful is this curse! A whole train of evils are here personified and appointed to be the governors of a disobedient people. *Terror* is to be one of their keepers. *Consumption, shachepheth,* generally allowed to be some kind of atrophy by which the flesh was consumed and the whole body dried up by raging fever through lack of sustenance.

22. *I will also send wild beasts among you.* God fulfilled these threatenings at different times. He sent fiery serpents among them, Num. xxi. 6; lions, 2 Kings xvii. 25; bears, 2 Kings ii. 24, and threatened them with total desolation, so that their land should be overrun with *wild beasts,* etc., see Ezek. v. 17.

26. *Ten women shall bake your bread in one oven.* Though in general every family in the East bakes its own bread, yet there are some public bakehouses where the bread of several families is baked at a certain price. Moses here foretells that the desolation should be so great and the want so pressing that there should be many idle hands to be employed, many mouths to be fed, and very little for each.

29. *Ye shall eat the flesh of your sons.* This was literally fulfilled at the siege of Jerusalem. Josephus, *Wars of the Jews,* book vii, chap. ii, gives us a particular instance in dreadful detail of a woman named Mary, who, in the extremity of the famine during the siege, killed her sucking child, roasted, and had eaten part of it when discovered by the soldiers! See this threatened, Jer. xix. 9.

34. *Then shall the land enjoy her sabbaths.* This Houbigant observes to be a historical truth. "From Saul to the Babylonish captivity are numbered about four hundred and ninety years, during which period there were seventy Sabbaths of years; for 7, multiplied by 70, make 490. Now the Babylonish captivity lasted seventy years, and during that time the land of Israel *rested.* Therefore the land rested just as many

MATTHEW HENRY

Verses 40–46

Here the chapter concludes with gracious promises of the return of God's favour to them upon their repentance, that they might not (unless it were their own fault) *pine away in their iniquity*. As bad as things are, they may be mended. *Yet there is hope in Israel*.

I. How the repentance which would qualify them for this mercy is described, *v*. 40, 41. The instances of it are three:—1. Confession, by which they must give glory to God, and take shame to themselves. They must in their confession put sin under its worst character, as *walking contrary to God*. 2. Remorse and godly sorrow for sin: *If their uncircumcised heart be humbled*. An impenitent, unbelieving, unhumbled heart, is called an *uncircumcised* heart, the heart of a Gentile that is a stranger to God, rather than the heart of an Israelite in covenant with him. True circumcision is *of the heart* (Rom. ii. 29), without which the circumcision of the flesh avails nothing, Jer. ix. 26. A humble heart under humbling providences prepares for deliverance and true comfort. 3. Submission to the justice of God in all his dealings; if they then *accept of the punishment of their iniquity* (*v*. 41 and again *v*. 43), that is, if they justify God and condemn themselves, then they are penitents indeed.

II. How the mercy which they should obtain upon their repentance is described. 1. They should not be abandoned: *Though they have despised my judgments, yet, for all that, I will not cast them away*, *v*. 43, 44. He speaks as a tender Father that cannot find in his heart to disinherit a son that has been very provoking. 2. They should be remembered: *I will remember the land* with favour, which is grounded upon the promise before, *I will remember my covenant* (*v*. 42), which is repeated, *v*. 45. God is said *to remember the covenant* when he performs the promises of it, purely for his faithfulness' sake. The word covenant is thrice repeated, to intimate that God is ever mindful of it and would have us to be so. When those that have walked contrary to God in a way of sin return to him by sincere repentance, though he has walked contrary to them in a way of judgment he will return to them in a way of special mercy, pursuant to the covenant of redemption and grace. None are so ready to repent as God is to forgive upon repentance, through Christ, who is given for a covenant.

JAMIESON, FAUSSET, BROWN

38. the land of your enemies shall eat you up, etc.—On the removal of the ten tribes into captivity, they never returned, and all traces of them were lost. **40-45. If they shall confess their iniquity**, etc.—This passage holds out the gracious promise of divine forgiveness and favor on their repentance, and their happy restoration to their land, in memory of the covenant made with their fathers (Rom. 2).

46. These are the statutes and judgments and laws—It has been thought by some that the last chapter was originally placed after the twenty-fifth [ADAM CLARKE], while others consider that the next chapter was added as an appendix, in consequence of many people being influenced by the promises and threats of the preceding one, to resolve that they would dedicate themselves and their possessions to the service of God [CALMET].

ADAM CLARKE

years in the Babylonish captivity, as it should have rested Sabbaths if the Jews had observed the laws relative to the Sabbaths of the land."

38. *The land of your enemies shall eat you up*. Does this refer to the total loss of the ten tribes? These are so completely swallowed up in some enemies' land that nothing concerning their existence or place of residence remains but mere conjecture.

44. *Neither will I abhor them, to destroy them utterly*. Though God has literally fulfilled all His threatenings upon this people, in dispossessing them of their land, destroying their polity, overturning their city, demolishing their Temple, and scattering themselves over the face of the whole earth; yet He has, in His providence, strangely preserved them as a *distinct* people, and in very considerable numbers also.

46. *These are the statutes and judgments*. See on v. 15. This verse appears to be the proper concluding verse of the whole book; and I rather think that the twenty-seventh chapter originally followed the twenty-fifth. As the law was anciently written upon skins of parchment, sheep or goat skins, pasted or stitched together, and all rolled up in one roll, the matter being written in columns, one of those columns might have been very easily displaced, and thus whole chapters might have been readily interchanged. It is likely that this might have been the case in the present instance. Others endeavor to solve this difficulty by supposing that the twenty-seventh chapter was added after the book had been finished; and therefore there is apparently a double conclusion, one at the end of the twenty-sixth and the other at the end of the twenty-seventh chapter. However the above may have been, all the ancient versions agree in concluding both the chapters in nearly the same way; yet the twenty-sixth chapter must be allowed to be by far the most natural conclusion of the book.

MATTHEW HENRY

CHAPTER 27

Verses 1–13

This is part of the law concerning singular vows, extraordinary ones, which though God did not expressly insist on, yet, if they were consistent with and conformable to the general precepts, he would be well pleased with.

I. The case is here put of persons vowed to God by a singular vow, *v*. 2. If a man consecrated himself, or a child, to the service of the tabernacle, to be employed there in some inferior office, as sweeping the floor, carrying out ashes, running errands, or the like, *the person* so consecrated *shall be for the Lord*, that is, "God will graciously accept the good will." *Thou didst well that it was in thy heart*, 2 Chron. vi. 8.

JAMIESON, FAUSSET, BROWN

CHAPTER 27

VSS. 1-18. CONCERNING VOWS. **2-8. When a man shall make a singular vow**, etc.—Persons have, at all times and in all places, been accustomed to present votive offerings, either from gratitude for benefits received, or in the event of deliverance from apprehended evil. And Moses was empowered, by divine authority, to prescribe the conditions of this voluntary duty. **the persons shall be for the Lord**, etc.—better rendered thus:—"According to thy estimation, the persons shall be for the Lord." Persons might consecrate themselves or their children to the divine service, in some inferior or servile kind of work about the sanctuary (I Sam. 3:1). In the event of any change, the persons so devoted had the privilege in their power of redeeming themselves; and this chapter specifies the amount of the redemption money, which the priest had the discretionary power of reducing, as circumstances might seem to require.

Those of mature age, between twenty and sixty, being capable of the greatest service, were rated highest; young people, from five till twenty, less, because not so service-

ADAM CLARKE

CHAPTER 27

2. *When a man shall make a singular vow*. The verse is short and obscure, and may be translated thus: "A man who shall have separated a vow, according to thy estimation, of souls unto the Lord"; which may be paraphrased thus: He who shall have vowed or consecrated a soul, i.e., a living creature, whether man or beast, if he wish to redeem what he has thus vowed or consecrated, he shall ransom or redeem it according to the priest's estimation; for the priest shall judge of the properties, qualifications, and age of the person or beast, and the circumstances of the person who has vowed it, and shall regulate the value accordingly; and the money shall be put into his hands for the service of the sanctuary. A vow is a religious promise made unto the Lord, and for the most part with prayer, and paid with thanksgiving, Num. xxi. 2-3; Ps. lxvi. 13-14. Vows were either of abstinence, such as are spoken of in Numbers xxx, and the vow of the Nazarite, Numbers vi; or they were to give something to the Lord, as sacrifices, Lev. vii. 16, or the value of persons, beasts, houses, or lands, concerning which the law is here given. A man might vow or devote himself, his children (vv. 5-6), his domestics, his cattle, his goods. And in this chapter rules are laid down for the redemption of all these things. But if, after consecrating these things, he refused to redeem them, then they became the Lord's property forever. The persons continued all their lives devoted to the service of the sanctuary; the goods were sold for the profit of the Temple or the priests; the animals, if clean, were offered in sacrifice; if not proper for sacrifice, were sold, and the price devoted to sacred uses. This is a general view of the different laws relative to vows, mentioned in this chapter.

3. *From twenty years old even unto sixty . . . fifty shekels*. A man from twenty to sixty years of age, if consecrated to the Lord by a vow, might be redeemed for fifty shekels, which, at

MATTHEW HENRY

But forasmuch as he had no occasion to use their service about the tabernacle, a whole tribe being appropriated to the use of it, those that were thus vowed were to be redeemed, and the money paid for their redemption was employed for the repair of the sanctuary, or other uses of it, as appears by 2 Kings xii. 14, where it is called, in the margin, the *money of the souls of his estimation*. A book of rates is accordingly provided, by which the priests were to go in their estimation. The poor shall be valued according to their ability, *v.* 8. Something they must pay, that they might learn not to be rash in vowing to God. Yet not more than their ability, but that they might not ruin themselves and their families by their zeal.

II. The case is put of beasts vowed to God.

Verses 14–25

The law concerning real estates dedicated to the service of God by a singular vow.

I. Suppose a man, in his zeal for the honour of God, should *sanctify his house to God* (*v.* 14), the house must be valued by the priest, and the money got by the sale of it was to be converted to the use of the sanctuary, which by degrees came to be greatly enriched with *dedicated things*, 1 Kings xv. 15. If the owner be inclined to redeem it himself, he must not have it so cheap as another, but must add a fifth part to the price, for he should have considered before he had vowed it, *v.* 15.

II. Suppose a man should sanctify some part of his land to the Lord, giving it to pious uses, then a difference must be made between land that came to the donor by descent and that which came by purchase, and accordingly the case altered.

Verses 26–34

I. A caution given that no man should make such a jest of sanctifying things to the Lord as to sanctify any firstling to him, for that was his already by the law, *v.* 26.

II. Things or persons devoted are here distinguished from things or persons that were only sanctified. 1. Devoted things were most holy to the Lord, and could neither revert nor be alienated, *v.* 28. 2. Devoted persons were to be put to death, *v.* 29. Not that it was in the power of any parent or master thus to devote a child or a servant to death; but it must be meant of the public enemies of Israel.

III. A law concerning tithes, which were paid for the service of God before the law, as appears by Abraham's payment of them (Gen. xiv. 20), and Jacob's promise of them, Gen. xxviii. 22. It is here appointed, That they should pay tithe of all their increase, their corn, trees, and cattle, *v.* 30, 32. And we are taught in general to *honour the Lord with our substance* (Prov. iii. 9), and in particular to support and maintain his ministers, and to be *ready to communicate* to them, Gal. vi. 6; 1 Cor. ix. 11. And how this may be done in a fitter and more equal proportion than that of the tenth, which God himself appointed of old, I cannot see.

IV. The last verse seems to have reference to this whole book, of which it is the conclusion: *These are the commandments which the Lord commanded Moses, for the children of Israel.* Many of these commandments are moral, and of perpetual obligation; others of them, which were ceremonial and peculiar to the Jewish economy, have notwithstanding a spiritual significance, and are instructive to us who are furnished with a key to let us into the mysteries contained in them. Upon the whole matter, we may see cause to bless God that *we have not come to Mount Sinai*, Heb. xii. 18. 1. That we are not under the *dark shadows* of the law, but enjoy the clear light of the gospel, which shows us *Christ the end of the law for righteousness*, Rom. x. 4. The doctrine of our reconciliation to God by a Mediator is not clouded with the smoke of burning sacrifices, but cleared by the knowledge of *Christ and him crucified*. 2. That we are not under the *heavy yoke* of the law, and the carnal ordinances of it (as the apostle calls them, Heb. ix. 10), imposed till the time of reformation, a yoke which *neither they nor their fathers were able to bear* (Acts xv. 10), but under the sweet and easy institutions of the gospel, which pronounces those the *true worshippers that worship the Father in spirit and truth*, by Christ only, and in his name, who is our priest, temple, altar, sacrifice, purification, and all. *Having boldness to enter into the holiest by the blood of Jesus, let us draw near with a true heart, and in full assurance of faith*, worshipping God with so much the more cheerfulness and humble confidence, still saying, *Blessed be God for Jesus Christ!*

JAMIESON, FAUSSET, BROWN

able; infants, though devotable by their parents before birth (I Samuel 1:11), could not be offered nor redeemed till a month after birth; old people were valued below the young, but above children; and the poor—in no case freed from payment, in order to prevent the rash formation of vows—were rated according to their means.

9-13. if it be a beast, whereof men bring an offering unto the Lord—a clean beast. After it had been vowed, it could neither be employed in common purposes nor exchanged for an equivalent—it must be sacrificed—or if, through some discovered blemish, it was unsuitable for the altar, it might be sold, and the money applied for the sacred service. If an unclean beast—such as an ass or camel, for instance—had been vowed, it was to be appropriated to the use of the priest at the estimated value, or it might be redeemed by the person vowing on payment of that value, and the additional fine of a fifth more. **14-16. when a man shall sanctify his house to be holy unto the Lord,** etc.—In this case, the house having been valued by the priest and sold, the proceeds of the sale were to be dedicated to the sanctuary. But if the owner wished, on second thought, to redeem it, he might have it by adding a fifth part to the price. **16-24. if a man shall sanctify unto the Lord some part of a field of his possession,** etc.—In the case of acquired property in land, if not redeemed, it returned to the donor at the Jubilee; whereas the part of a hereditary estate, which had been vowed, did not revert to the owner, but remained attached in perpetuity to the sanctuary. The reason for this remarkable difference was to lay every man under an obligation to redeem the property, or stimulate his nearest kinsman to do it, in order to prevent a patrimonial inheritance going out from any family in Israel. **26, 27. Only the firstlings of the beasts**—These, in the case of clean beasts, being consecrated to God by a universal and standing law (Exod. 13:12; 34:19), could not be devoted; and in that of unclean beasts were subject to the rule mentioned (vss. 11, 12). **28, 29. no devoted thing, that a man shall devote unto the Lord of all that he hath, . . . shall be sold or redeemed**—This relates to vows of the most solemn kind—the devotee accompanying his vow with a solemn imprecation on himself not to fail in accomplishing his declared purpose. **shall surely be put to death**—This announcement imported not that the person was to be sacrificed or doomed to a violent death; but only that he should remain till death unalterably in the devoted condition. The preceding regulations were evidently designed to prevent rashness in vowing (Eccles. 5: 4) and to encourage serious and considerate reflection in all matters between God and the soul (Luke 21:4). **30-33. all the tithe of the land, whether of the seed of the land**—This law gave the sanction of divine authority to an ancient usage (Gen. 14:20; 28:22). The whole produce of the land was subjected to the tithe tribute—it was a yearly rent which the Israelites, as tenants, paid to God, the owner of the land, and a thank offering they rendered to Him for the bounties of His providence. (See Prov. 3: 9; I Cor. 9:11; Gal. 6:6.) **32. whatsoever passeth under the rod,** etc.—This alludes to the mode of taking the tithe of cattle, which were made to pass singly through a narrow gateway, where a person with a rod, dipped in ochre, stood, and counting them, marked the back of every tenth beast, whether male or female, sound or unsound. **34. These are the commandments,** etc.—The laws contained in this book, for the most part ceremonial, had an important spiritual bearing, the study of which is highly instructive (Rom. 10:4; Heb. 4:2; 12:18). They imposed a burdensome yoke (Acts 15:10), but yet in the infantine age of the Church formed the necessary discipline of "a schoolmaster to Christ."

ADAM CLARKE

3*s.* each, amounted to 7*l.* 10*s.* sterling.

4. *And if it be a female.* The woman, at the same age, vowed unto the Lord, might be redeemed for thirty shekels, 4*l.* 10*s.* sterling, a little more than one-half of the value of the man; for this obvious reason, that a woman, if employed, could not be of so much use in the service of the sanctuary as the man, and was therefore of much less value.

5. *From five years old.* The boy that was vowed might be redeemed for twenty shekels, 3*l.* sterling; the girl, for ten shekels, just one-half, 1*l.* 10*s.*

6. *A month old.* The male child, five shekels, 15*s.*; the female, three shekels, 9*s.* Being both in comparative infancy, they were nearly of an equal value. None were vowed under a month old; the firstborn, being always considered as the Lord's property, could not be vowed, see v. 26.

7. *Sixty years old.* The old man and the old woman, being nearly past labor, were nearly of an equal value; hence the one was estimated at fifteen shekels, 2*l.* 5*s.*, the other at ten shekels, 1*l.* 10*s.* This was about the same ratio as that of the children, v. 5, and for the same reason.

10. *He shall not alter it, nor change it, a good for a bad.* Whatever was consecrated to God by a vow, or purpose of heart, was considered from that moment as the Lord's property; to change which was impiety; to withhold it, sacrilege.

13. *Shall add a fifth part.* This was probably intended to prevent rash vows and covetous redemptions. The priest alone was to value the thing; and to whatever his valuation was, a fifth part must be added by him who wished to redeem the consecrated thing.

14. *Shall sanctify his house.* The yearly rent of which, when thus consecrated, went towards the repairs of the Tabernacle, which was the house of the Lord.

16. *Some part of a field.* Though the preceding words are not in the text, yet it is generally allowed they should be supplied here, as it was not lawful for a man to vow his whole estate, and thus make his family beggars, in order to enrich the Lord's sanctuary; this God would not permit.

21. *As a field devoted.* It is *cherem*, a thing so "devoted to God" as never more to be capable of being redeemed. See on v. 29.

25. *Shekel of the sanctuary.* A standard shekel, the standard being kept in the sanctuary by which to try and regulate all the weights in the land.

28. *No devoted thing . . . shall be sold or redeemed.* This is the *cherem*, which always meant an absolute, unredeemable grant to God.

29. *Which shall be devoted of men.* Every man who is devoted shall surely be put to death; or be the Lord's property, or be employed in His service, till death.

30. *All the tithe of the land.* This God claims as His own; and it is spoken of here as being a point perfectly settled, and concerning which there was neither doubt nor difficulty.

32. *Whatsoever passeth under the rod.* It seems to be in reference to this custom that the Prophet Ezekiel, speaking to Israel, says: "I will cause you to pass under the rod, and I will bring you into the bond of the covenant"—you shall be once more claimed as the Lord's property, and be in all things devoted to His service, being marked or ascertained, by especial providences and manifestations of His kindness, to be His peculiar people.

34. *These are the commandments.* This conclusion is very similar to that at the end of the preceding chapter. I have already supposed that this chapter should have followed the twenty-fifth and that the twenty-sixth originally terminated the book.

THE BOOK OF NUMBERS

I. On the margin of the land (1:1-10:36)
- *A. The order of the camp (1:1-4:49)*
  - 1. The census (1:1-54)
  - 2. The encampment (2:1-34)
  - 3. The Levites (3:1-4:49)
- *B. The purity of the camp (5:1-6:27)*
  - 1. Purification from pollution (5:1-31)
  - 2. Special dedication (6:1-27)
- *C. The worship of the camp (7:1-9:14)*
  - 1. Offerings of the princes (7:1-89)
  - 2. Order of worship (8:1-26)
  - 3. Passover and purification (9:1-14)
- *D. The movement of the camp (9:15-10:36)*
  - 1. Determined by the cloud (9:15-23)
  - 2. The method of summons and order of march (10:1-36)

II. Exclusion and wandering (11:1-25:18)
- *A. Discontent (11:1-12:16)*
  - 1. Against God—the people (11:1-3)
  - 2. Against circumstances—the mixed multitude (11:4-35)
  - 3. Against Moses—Miriam and Aaron (12:1-16)
- *B. Disaster (13:1-14:45)*
  - 1. Fear, sending of spies (13:1-33)
  - 2. Rebellion (14:1-35)
  - 3. Presumption (14:36-45)
- *C. Discipline (15:1-25:18)*
  - 1. Domestic (15:1-20:13)
    - a. The Sabbath-breaker (15:1-41)
    - b. Korah, Dathan, and Abiram (16:1-50)
    - c. Laws (17:1-19:22)
    - d. Death of Miriam (20:1)
    - e. Failure of Moses and Aaron (20:2-13)
  - 2. Foreign (20:14-25:18)
    - a. Edom (20:14-21)
    - b. Death of Aaron (20:22-29)
    - c. Victory over Canaanites (21:1-3)
    - d. Murmuring (21:4-9)
    - e. Sihon and Og (21:10-35)
    - f. Balaam (22:1-25:18)

III. On the margin of the land (26:1-36:13)
- *A. The census (26:1-65)*
- *B. The inheritance of women (27:1-11)*
- *C. The summons of Moses (27:12-23)*
- *D. Repetition of laws (28:1-30:16)*
- *E. War with Midian (31:1-54)*
- *F. Settlement of Reuben, Gad, and half-tribe of Manasseh (32:1-42)*
- *G. List of journeyings (33:1-49)*
- *H. Repetition of laws (33:50-36:13)*

The titles of the five books of Moses, which we use in our Bibles, are all borrowed from the Greek translation of the Seventy, the most ancient version of the Old Testament that we know of. But of the titles of the Five books, this is the only one we translate into English; in all the rest we retain the Greek word itself. This book was thus entitled because of the numbers of the children of Israel, so often mentioned in this book, and so well worthy to give a title to it because it was the remarkable accomplishment of God's promise to Abraham that his seed should be as the stars of heaven for multitude. It also relates to two numberings of them, one at Mount Sinai (ch.1), the other in the plains of Moab, thirty-nine years after (ch. 26). The book is almost equally divided between histories and laws, intermixed.

We have here:

I. The histories of the numbering and marshalling of the tribes (chs. 1–4), the dedication of the altar and Levites (chs. 7, 8), their march (chs. 9, 10), their murmuring and unbelief for which they were sentenced to wander forty years in the wilderness (chs. 11–14), the rebellion of Korah (chs. 16, 17), the history of the last year of the forty (chs. 20–26), the conquest of Midian and the settlement of the two tribes (chs. 31, 32), with an account of their journeys (ch. 33).

II. Various laws about the Nazarites, etc. (chs. 5, 6); and again about the priests' charge, etc. (chs. 18, 19), feasts (chs. 28, 29), and vows (ch. 30), and relating to their settlement in Canaan (chs. 27, 34–36).

MATTHEW HENRY

CHAPTER 1

Verses 1–16

I. We have here a commission issued out for the numbering of the people of Israel; and David, long after, paid dearly for doing it without a commission. Here is,

1. The date of this commission, *v.* 1. (1) The place: it is given at God's court *in the wilderness of Sinai,* from his royal palace, *the tabernacle of the congregation.* (2) The time: *In the second year* after they came up out of Egypt; we may call it the second year of that reign. The laws in Leviticus were given in the first month of that year; these orders were given in the beginning of the second month.

2. The directions given for the execution of it, *v.* 2, 3. (1) None were to be numbered but the males, and those only such as were fit for war. (2) Nor were any to be numbered who through age, or bodily infirmity, blindness, lameness, or chronical diseases, were unfit for war. (3) The account was to be taken *according to their families,* that it might not only be known how many they were, and what were their names, but of what tribe and family, or clan, nay, of what particular house every person was; or, reckoning it the muster of an army, to what regiment every man belonged, that he might know his place himself and the government might know where to find him. They were numbered a little before this, when their poll-money was paid for the service of the tabernacle, Exod. xxxviii. 25, 26. But it should seem they were not then registered *by the house of their fathers,* as now they were.

3. Commissioners are named for the doing of this work. Moses and Aaron were to preside (*v.* 3),

JAMIESON, FAUSSET, BROWN

CHAPTER 1

VSS. 1-54. MOSES NUMBERING THE MEN OF WAR. **1. on the first day of the second month,** etc.—Thirteen months had elapsed since the exodus. About one month had been occupied in the journey; and the rest of the period had been passed in encampment among the recesses of Sinai, where the transactions took place, and the laws, religious and civil, were promulgated, which are contained in the two preceding books. As the tabernacle was erected on the first day of the first month, and the order here mentioned was given on the first day of the second, some think the laws in Leviticus were all given in one month. The Israelites having been formed into a separate nation, undcr the special government of God as their King, it was necessary, before resuming their march towards the promised land, to put them into good order. And accordingly Moses was commissioned, along with Aaron, to take a census of the people. This census was incidentally noticed (Exod. 38:26), in reference to the poll tax for the works of the tabernacle; but it is here described in detail, in order to show the relative increase and military strength of the different tribes. The enumeration was confined to those capable of bearing arms, and it was to be made with a careful distinction of the tribe, family, and household to which every individual belonged. By this rule of summation many important advantages were secured: an exact genealogical register was formed, the relative strength of each tribe was ascertained, and the reason found for arranging the order of precedence in march as well as disposing the different tribes in camp around the tabernacle. The promise of God to Abraham was seen to be fulfilled in the extraordinary increase of his posterity, and provision made for tracing the regular descent of the Messiah. **3. Aaron shall number them by their armies**—or companies. In

ADAM CLARKE

CHAPTER 1

1. *The Lord spake unto Moses . . . on the first day of the second month.* As the Tabernacle was erected upon the first day of the first month, in the second year after their coming out of Egypt, Exod. xl. 17; and this muster of the people was made on the first day of the second month, in the same year; it is evident that the transactions related in the preceding book must all have taken place in the space of one month, and during the time the Israelites were encamped at Mount Sinai, before they had begun their journey to the Promised Land.

2. *Take ye the sum.* God, having established the commonwealth of Israel by just and equitable laws, ordained everything relative to the due performance of His own worship, erected His tabernacle, which was His throne, and the place of His residence among the people, and consecrated His priests who were to minister before Him; He now orders His subjects to be mustered.

3. *From twenty years old and upward.* In this census no women were reckoned, nor children,

MATTHEW HENRY

and one man of every tribe, that was renowned in his tribe, and was presumed to know it well, was to assist in it.

II. Why was this account ordered to be taken and kept? For several reasons. 1. To prove the accomplishment of the promise made to Abraham, that God would *multiply his seed exceedingly*, which promise was renewed to Jacob (Gen. xxviii. 14), that *his seed should be as the dust of the earth.* 2. It was to intimate the particular care which God himself would take of his Israel. God is called the *Shepherd of Israel*, Ps. lxxx. 1. Now the shepherds always kept count of their flocks, and delivered them by number to their under-shepherds, that they might know if any were missing; in like manner God numbers his flock. 3. It was to put a difference between the true-born Israelites and the mixed multitude that were among them; none were numbered but Israelites. 4. It was in order to their being marshalled into several districts, for the more easy administration of justice, and their more regular march through the wilderness.

Verses 17–43

We have here the speedy execution of the orders given for the numbering of the people. It was begun the same day that the orders were given, *The first day of the second month*; compare *v.* 18 with *v.* 1.

In the particulars here left upon record, we may observe, 1. That the numbers are registered in words at length (as I may say), and not in figures; to every one of the twelve tribes it is repeated, for the greater ceremony and solemnity of the account, that they were numbered *by their generations, after their families, by the house of their fathers, according to the number of the names.* Thus every man might know who were his relations or next of kin, on which some laws we have already met with did depend. 2. That they all end with hundreds, only Gad with fifty (*v.* 25), but none of the numbers descend to units or tens. 3. That Judah is the most numerous of them all, more than double to Benjamin and Manasseh, and almost 12,000 more than any other tribe, *v.* 27. It was Judah whom *his brethren must praise* because from him Messiah the Prince was to descend. Judah was to lead the van through the wilderness, and therefore was furnished accordingly with greater strength than any other tribe.

Verses 44–46

We have here the sum total at the foot of the account; they were in all 600,000 fighting men, and 3,550 over. Some think that when this was their number some months before (Exod. xxxviii. 26) the Levites were reckoned with them, but now that tribe was separated for the service of God, yet so many more had by this time attained to the age of twenty years as that still they were the same number, to show that whatever we part with for the honour and service of God it shall certainly be made up to us one way or other.

Verses 47–54

Care is here taken to distinguish from the rest of the tribes the tribe of Levi, which, in the matter of the golden calf, had distinguished itself, Exod xxxii. 26. Note, Singular services shall be recompensed with singular honours.

I. It was the honour of the Levites that they were made guardians of the spiritualities; to them was committed the care of the tabernacle and the treasures thereof, both in their camps and in their marches. 1. When they moved the Levites were to take down the tabernacle, to carry it and all that belonged to it, and then to set it up again in the place appointed, *v.* 50, 51. It was for the honour of the holy things that none should be permitted to see them, or touch them, but those only who were called of God to the service. 2. When they rested the Levites were to *encamp round about the tabernacle* (*v.* 50, 53), that they might be near their work, and resident upon their charge, always ready to attend, and that they might be a guard upon the tabernacle, to preserve it from being either plundered or profaned.

II. It was their further honour that as Israel, being a holy people, was not *reckoned among the nations*, so they, being a holy tribe, were not reckoned among other Israelites, but numbered afterwards by themselves, *v.* 49.

JAMIESON, FAUSSET, BROWN

their departure from Egypt they were divided into five grand companies (Exod. 13:18), but from the sojourn in the wilderness to the passage of the Jordan, they were formed into four great divisions. The latter is here referred to. **4-16. with you there shall be a man of every tribe,** etc.—The social condition of the Israelites in the wilderness bore a close resemblance to that of the nomad tribes of the East in the present day. The head of the tribe was a hereditary dignity, vested in the oldest son or some other to whom the right of primogeniture was transferred, and under whom were other inferior heads, also hereditary, among the different branches of the tribe. The Israelites being divided into twelve tribes, there were twelve chiefs appointed to assist in taking the census of the people. **5. these are the names of the men that shall stand with you,** etc.—Each is designated by adding the name of the ancestors of his tribe, the people of which were called "Beni-Reuben, Beni-Levi," sons of Reuben, sons of Levi, according to the custom of the Arabs still, as well as other nations which are divided into clans, as the Macs of Scotland, the Aps of Wales, and the O's and the Fitz's of Ireland [CHALMERS]. **16-18. These were the renowned**—lit., the called of the congregation, summoned by name; and they entered upon the survey the very day the order was given. **by their polls**—individually, one by one. **19. As the Lord commanded Moses,** etc.—The numbering of the people was not an act sinful in itself, as Moses did it by divine appointment; but David incurred guilt by doing it without the authority of God. (See on II Sam. 24:10.) **20-44. These are those that were numbered**—In this registration the tribe of Judah appears the most numerous; and accordingly, as the pre-eminence had been assigned to it by Jacob, it got the precedence in all the encampments of Israel. Of the two half tribes of Joseph, which is seen to be "a fruitful bough," that of Ephraim was the larger, as had been predicted. The relative increase of all, as in the two just mentioned, was owing to the special blessing of God, conformably to the prophetic declaration of the dying patriarch. But the divine blessing is usually conveyed through the influence of secondary causes; and there is reason to believe that the relative populousness of the tribes would, under God, depend upon the productiveness of the respective localities assigned to them.

46. all they that were numbered were six hundred thousand, etc.—What an astonishing increase from seventy-five persons who went down to Egypt about 215 years before, and who were subjected to the greatest privations and hardships! And yet this enumeration was restricted to men from 20 years and upwards. Including women, children, and old men, together with the Levites, the whole population of Israel, on the ordinary principles of computation, amounted to about 2,400,000.

47-54. But the Levites . . . were not numbered among them—They were obliged to keep a register of their own. They were consecrated to the priestly office, which in all countries has been exempted customarily, and in Israel by the express authority of God, from military service. The custody of the things devoted to the divine service was assigned to them so exclusively, that "no stranger"—i.e., no person, not even an Israelite of any other tribe, was allowed, under penalty of death, to approach these. Hence they encamped round the tabernacle in order that there should be no manifestation of the divine displeasure among the people. Thus the numbering of the people was subservient to the separation of the Levites from those Israelites who were fit for military service, and to the practical introduction of the law respecting the first-born, for whom the tribe of Levi became a substitute.

ADAM CLARKE

nor strangers, nor the Levites, nor old men, which, collectively, must have formed an immense multitude; the Levites alone amounted to 22,300. Trueborn Israelites only are reckoned; such as were able to carry arms, and were expert for war.

14. *Eliasaph, the son of Deuel.* This person is called Reuel, chap. ii. 14. As the *daleth* is very like the *resh*, it was easy to mistake the one for the other. The Septuagint and the Syriac have Reuel in this chapter; and in chap. ii. 14, the Vulgate, the Samaritan, and the Arabic have Deuel instead of Reuel, with which reading a vast number of MSS. concur; and this reading is supported by chap. x. 20. We may safely conclude therefore that *Deuel*, not *Reuel*, was the original reading.

16. *These were the renowned.* Literally, "the called," *of the congregation*—those who were summoned by name to attend.

33. *The tribe Ephraim . . . forty thousand and five hundred.* Ephraim, as he was blessed beyond his elder brother, Manasseh, Gen. xlviii. 20, so here he is increased by thousands more than Manasseh, and more than the whole tribe of Benjamin, and his blessing continued above his brother, Deut. xxxiii. 17. And thus the prophecy, Gen. xlviii. 19, was fulfilled: "His younger brother [Ephraim] shall be greater than he [Manasseh]."

46. *All they that were numbered were six hundred thousand and three thousand and five hundred and fifty.* What an astonishing increase from seventy souls that went down into Egypt, Gen. xlvi. 27, about two hundred fifteen years before, where latterly they had endured the greatest hardships!

In the second census, mentioned chap. xxvi. 34, Judah still has the preeminency; and Simeon, the third in number before, is become the least. Now we see also that the little tribe of Manasseh occupies the seventh place for number. Seven of the tribes had an increase; five, a decrease.

MATTHEW HENRY — CHAPTER 2

Verses 1–2

Here is the general appointment given both for their orderly encampment where they rested and their orderly march when they moved. 1. They all dwelt

JAMIESON, FAUSSET, BROWN — CHAPTER 2

VSS. 1-34. THE ORDER OF THE TRIBES IN THEIR TENTS. **2. Every man . . . shall pitch by his own standard, with the ensign of their father's house**—Standards were visible signs of a certain recognized

ADAM CLARKE — CHAPTER 2

MATTHEW HENRY

in tents, and when they marched carried all their tents along with them. 2. Those of a tribe were to pitch together, *every man by his own standard.* Those that are of kin to each other should, as much as they can, be acquainted with each other; and the bonds of nature should be improved for the strengthening of the bonds of Christian communion. 3. Every one must know his place and keep in it. 4. Every tribe had its standard, flag, or ensign, and it should seem every family had some particular ensign of their father's house. It is uncertain how these standards were distinguished: some conjecture that the standard of each tribe was of the same colour with the precious stone in which the name of that tribe was written in the high priest's ephod. Some of them say the four principal standards were, Judah a lion, Reuben a man, Joseph an ox, and Dan an eagle, making the appearances in Ezekiel's vision to allude to it. 5. They were to pitch about the tabernacle, which was to be in the midst of them, as the tent or pavilion of a general in the centre of an army. That they might be a guard and defence upon the tabernacle and the Levites on every side. 6. Yet they were to pitch afar off, in reverence to the sanctuary. It is supposed (from Josh. iii. 4) that the distance between the nearest part of the camp and the tabernacle was 2,000 cubits, that is, 1,000 yards, little more than half a measured mile with us.

Verses 3–34

We have here the particular distribution of the twelve tribes into four squadrons, three tribes in a squadron, one of which was to lead the other two. 1. God himself appointed them their place, to prevent strife and envy among them. If God in his providence advance others above us, and abase us, we ought to be as well satisfied in his doing it in that way as if he did it, as this was done here, by a voice out of the tabernacle. And as far as our place comes to be our choice our Saviour has given us a rule in Luke xiv. 8, *Sit not down in the highest room*; and another in Matt. xx. 27, *He that will be chief, let him be your servant.* Those that are most humble and most serviceable are really most honourable. 2. Every tribe had a captain, a prince, or commander-in-chief, whom God himself nominated, the same that had been appointed to number them, *ch.* i. 5. Most of them have *El, God,* at one end or other of their names. *Nethaneel, the gift of God; Eliab, my God a Father; Elizur, my God a rock; Shelumiel, God my peace; Eliasaph, God has added; Elishama, my God has heard; Gamaliel, God my reward; Pagiel, God has met me.* 3. Those tribes were placed together under the same standard that were nearest of kin to each other; Judah, Issachar, and Zebulun, were the three younger sons of Leah, and they were put together; and Issachar and Zebulun would not grudge to be under Judah, since they were his younger brethren. Reuben and Simeon would not have been content in their place. Therefore Reuben, Jacob's eldest son, is made chief of the next squadron; Simeon, no doubt, is willing to be under him, and Gad, the son of Zilpah, Leah's handmaid, is fitly added to them in Levi's room: Ephraim, Manasseh, and Benjamin, are all the posterity of Rachel. Dan, the eldest son of Bilhah, is made a leading tribe, though the son of a concubine, that more abundant honour might be bestowed on that which lacked; and it was said, *Dan should judge his people,* and to him were added the two younger sons of the handmaids. Thus unexceptionable was the order in which they were placed. 4. The tribe of Judah was in the first post of honour, encamped towards the rising sun, and in their marches led the van, not only because it was the most numerous tribe, but chiefly because from that tribe Christ was to come. Judah was the first of the twelve sons of Jacob that was blessed. He therefore being first in blessing, though not in birth, is put first, to teach children how to value the smiles of their godly parents and dread their frowns. 5. The tribe of Levi pitched closely about the tabernacle, within the rest of their tribes, *v.* 17. They must defend the sanctuary, and then the rest of the tribes must defend them. Civil powers should protect the religious interests of a nation, and be a defence upon that glory. 6. The camp of Dan, though posted in the left wing when they encamped, was ordered in their march to bring up the rear, *v.* 31. They were the most numerous, next to Judah, and therefore were ordered into a post which, next to the front, required the most strength.

JAMIESON, FAUSSET, BROWN

form for directing the movements of large bodies of people. As the Israelites were commanded to encamp "each by his own standard, with the ensign of their father's house," the direction has been considered as implying that they possessed three varieties: (1) the great tribal standards, which served as rallying points for the twelve large clans of the people; (2) the standards of the subdivided portions; and, (3) those of families or houses. The latter must have been absolutely necessary, as one ensign only for a tribe would not have been visible at the extremities of so large a body. We possess no authentic information as to their forms, material, colors, and devices. But it is probable that they might bear some resemblance to those of Egypt, only stripped of any idolatrous symbols. These were of an umbrella or a fanlike form, made of ostrich feathers, shawls, etc., lifted on the points of long poles, which were borne, either like the sacred central one, on a car, or on men's shoulders, while others might be like the beacon lights which are set on poles by Eastern pilgrims at night. Jewish writers say that the standards of the Hebrew tribes were symbols borrowed from the prophetic blessing of Jacob—Judah's being a lion, Benjamin's a wolf, etc.; and that the ensigns or banners were distinguished by their colors—the colors of each tribe being the same as that of the precious stone representing that tribe in the breastplate of the high priest. **far off about the tabernacle of the congregation shall they pitch**—i.e., over against, at a reverential distance. The place of every tribe is successively and specifically described because each had a certain part assigned both in the order of march and the disposition of the encampment. **3. on the east side toward the rising of the sun shall they of the standard of the camp of Judah pitch,** etc.—Judah, placed at the head of a camp composed of three tribes rallying under its standard, was said to have combined the united colors in the high priest's breastplate, but called by the name of Judah. They were appointed to occupy the east side and to take the lead in the march, which, for the most part, was in an easterly direction. **Nahshon** [or Naasson (Matt. 1:4)] **shall be captain**—It appears that the twelve men who were called to superintend the census were also appointed to be the captains of their respective tribes—a dignity which they owed probably to the circumstances, formerly noticed, of their holding the hereditary office of head or "prince." **5. those that pitch next unto him**—i.e., on the one side. **7. Then the tribe of Zebulun**—on the other side. While Judah's tribe was the most numerous, those of Issachar and Zebulun were also very numerous; so that the association of those three tribes formed a strong and imposing van. **10-31. On the south side the standard of the camp of Reuben**—The description given of the position of Reuben and his attendant tribes on the south, of Ephraim and his associates on the west, of Dan and his confederates on the north, with that of Judah on the east, suggests the idea of a square or quadrangle, which, allowing one square cubit to each soldier while remaining close in the ranks, has been computed to extend over an area of somewhat more than twelve square miles. But into our calculations of the occupied space must be taken not only the fighting men, whose numbers are here given, but also the families, tents, and baggage. The tabernacle or sacred tent of their Divine King, with the camp of the Levites around it (see on ch. 3:38), formed the center, as does the chief's in the encampment of all nomad people. In marching, this order was adhered to, with some necessary variations. Judah led the way, followed, it is most probable, by Issachar and Zebulun. Reuben, Simeon, and Gad formed the second great division. They were followed by the central company, composed of the Levites, bearing the tabernacle. Then the third and posterior squadron consisted of Ephraim, Manasseh, and Benjamin, while the hindmost place was assigned to Dan, Asher, and Naphtali. Thus Judah's, which was the most numerous, formed the van: and Dan's, which was the next in force, brought up the rear; while Reuben's and Ephraim's, with the tribes associated with them respectively, being the smallest and weakest, were placed in the center. (See on ch. 10:14.)

ADAM CLARKE

F. B. MEYER:

"The Children of Israel shall pitch every man by his own standard" (Num. 2:2–34).

Our God is a God of order; and it was needful for the order of the camp, whether at rest or on the march, that each man should know his place and keep to it. But though there were different standards and positions, there was one center, the ark, and one host of redeemed men.

Each believer has an appointed place in the great army of God. It is indicated by the voice of God and by the circumstances of our life; and it should be jealously retained. Repeatedly the Apostle bade his converts abide in the calling wherein they were called. Yours may be towards the bleak north of difficulty, or the warm south of privilege—in the home, the country parish, or the difficult foreign post. But, on the whole, you should stay where you are unless the Captain of our salvation moves you by some unmistakable indication of his will. The Apostle Paul ever lived in such dependence on the Holy Spirit for guidance, and for the unfolding of the divine purpose, that from some apparently trivial circumstance he would "gather" the movements of pillar of cloud by day and of fire by night. And interval there was none between his apprehension of the divine purpose and his endeavor to strike his tent and follow wherever it might lead (Acts 16:6, 7).

The main point with us all is to face the ark, to which the doors of all the tents looked, so that we may ever catch the first symptom of the movement of the cloud. On the whole, we do best to pitch and fight under our own standards. There is a closer bond of brotherhood possible between those who think alike. But while we are positive in what we affirm for ourselves, let us not deny that other standards represent necessary aspects of the common faith.

—*Great Verses Through the Bible*

MATTHEW HENRY

CHAPTER 3

II. A particular account is given of this family of Aaron; what we have met with before concerning them is here repeated. The two younger: Eleazar and Ithamar ministered *in the sight of Aaron*. They kept under their father's eye, and took instruction from him in all they did, because probably Nadab and Abihu got out of their father's sight when they offered strange fire.

III. A grant is made of the Levites to be assistants to the priests in their work: *Give the Levites to Aaron*, *v.* 9. Aaron was to have a greater propriety in, and power over, the tribe of Levi than any other of the princes had in and over their respective tribes. Here is, 1. The service for which the Levites were designed: they were to *minister to the priests* in their ministration to the Lord (*v.* 6), and to *keep Aaron's charge* (*v.* 7). The Levites killed the sacrifices, and then the priests needed only to sprinkle the blood and burn the fat: the Levites prepared the incense, the priests burnt it. They were to keep, not only Aaron's charge, but the *charge of the whole congregation.* 2. The consideration upon which the Levites were demanded; they were taken instead of the first-born.

I. The family of Aaron is confirmed in the priests' office, *v.* 10. They had been called to it before, and consecrated; here they are appointed to *wait on their priests' office*: the apostle uses this phrase (Rom. xii. 7), *Let us wait on our ministry*. The office of the ministry requires a constant attendance and great diligence; so frequent are the returns of its work, and yet so transient its favourable opportunities, that it must be waited on. *The stranger that cometh nigh shall be put to death*, which forbids the invading of the priests' office by any other person whatsoever; none must come nigh to minister but Aaron and his sons only, all others are strangers. It also lays a charge on the priests, as door-keepers in God's house, to take care that none should come near who were forbidden by the law.

Verses 14–39

The Levites being granted to Aaron to minister to him, they are here delivered to him by tale, that he might know what he had, and employ them accordingly.

I. By what rule they were numbered: *Every male from a month old and upward*, *v.* 15. The rest of the tribes were numbered only from twenty years old and upwards, and of them those only that were *able to go forth to war*; but into the number of the Levites they must take in both infants and infirm; being exempted from the war, it was not insisted upon that they should be of age and strength for the wars. Though it appears afterwards that little more than a third part of the Levites were fit to be employed in the service of the tabernacle (about 8,000 out of 22,000, *ch.* iv. 47, 48), yet God would have them all numbered as retainers to his family.

II. How they were distributed into three classes, according to the number of the sons of Levi, Gershon,

JAMIESON, FAUSSET, BROWN

CHAPTER 3

Vss. 1-51. THE LEVITES' SERVICE. **1. These . . . are the generations of Aaron and Moses,** etc.—This chapter contains an account of their families; and although that of Moses is not detailed like his brother's, his children are included under the general designation of the Amramites (vs. 27), a term which comprehends all the descendants of their common father Amram. The reason why the family of Moses was so undistinguished in this record is that they were in the private ranks of the Levites, the dignity of the priesthood being conferred exclusively on the posterity of Aaron; and hence, as the sacerdotal order is the subject of this chapter, Aaron, contrary to the usual style of the sacred history, is mentioned before Moses. **in the day that the Lord spake with Moses in mount Sinai**—This is added, because at the date of the following record the family of Aaron was unbroken. **2-4. these are the names of the sons of Aaron**—All the sons of Aaron, four in number, were consecrated to minister in the priest's office. The two oldest enjoyed but a brief term of office (Lev. 10:1, 2; ch. 26: 61); but Eleazar and Ithamar, the other two, were dutiful, and performed the sacred service during the lifetime of their father, as his assistants, and under his superintendence. **5-10. Bring the tribe of Levi near**—The *Heb.* word "bring near" is a sacrificial term, denoting the presentation of an offering to God; and the use of the word, therefore, in connection with the Levites, signifies that they were devoted as an offering to the sanctuary, no longer to be employed in any common offices. They were subordinate to the priests, who alone enjoyed the privilege of entering the holy place; but they were employed in discharging many of the humbler duties which belonged to the sanctuary, as well as in various offices of great utility and importance to the religion and morals of the people. **9. they are wholly given unto him out of the children of Israel,** etc.—The priests hold the place of God, and the Levites are the servants of God in the obedience they render to the priests. **11-13. I have taken the Levites,** etc.—The consecration of this tribe did not originate in the legislative wisdom of Moses, but in the special appointment of God, who chose them as substitutes for the first-born. By an appointment made in memory of the last solemn judgment on Egypt (from which the Israelitish households were miraculously exempt) all the first-born were consecrated to God (Exod. 13:12; 22:29), who thus, under peculiar circumstances, seemed to adopt the patriarchal usage of appointing the oldest to act as the priest of the family. But the privilege of redemption that was allowed the first-born opened the way for a change; and accordingly, on the full organization of the Mosaic economy, the administration of sacred things formerly committed to the first-born was transferred from them to the Levites, who received that honor partly as a tribute to Moses and Aaron, partly because this tribe had distinguished themselves by their zeal in the affair of the golden calf (Exod. 32:29), and also because, being the smallest of the tribes, they could ill find suitable employment and support in the work. (See on Deut. 33:9.) The designation of a special class for the sacred offices of religion was a wise arrangement; for, on their settlement in Canaan, the people would be so occupied that they might not be at leisure to wait on the service of the sanctuary, and sacred things might, from various causes, fall into neglect. But the appointment of an entire tribe to the divine service ensured the regular performance of the rites of religion. The subsequent portion of the chapter relates to the formal substitution of this tribe. **I am the Lord**—i.e., I decree it to be so; and being possessed of sovereign authority, I expect full obedience. **14-27. Number the children of Levi**—They were numbered as well as the other tribes; but the enumeration was made on a different principle—for while in the other tribes the number of males was calculated from twenty years and upward, in that of Levi they were counted from a month old and upward. The reason for the distinction is obvious. In the other tribes the survey was made for purposes of war, from which the Levites were totally exempt. But the Levites were appointed to a work on which they entered as soon as they were capable of instruction. They are mentioned under the names of Gershon, Kohath, and Merari, sons of Levi, and chiefs or ancestral heads of three subdivisions into which this tribe was distributed. Their duties were to assist in the conveyance of the tabernacle when the people were removing the various encampments, and to form its guard while stationary—the

ADAM CLARKE

CHAPTER 3

1. *The generations of Aaron and Moses.* Though Aaron and Moses are both mentioned here, yet the family of Aaron alone appears in the list; hence some have thought that the word *Moses* was not originally in the text. Others think that the words *veeleh toledoth*, "these are the generations," should be rendered "these are the acts," or transactions, or the history of the lives, as the same phrase may be understood in Gen. ii. 4; vi. 9. However this may be, it is evident that in this genealogy the family of Aaron are alone mentioned, probably because these belonged to the priesthood.

4. *Nadab and Abihu died.* See Lev. chap. x.

6. *Bring the tribe of Levi near.* The original word *hakreb* is properly a sacrificial word, and signifies the presenting of a sacrifice or offering to the Lord. As an offering, the tribe of Levi was given up entirely to the service of the sanctuary, to be no longer their own, but the Lord's property.

7. *The charge of the whole congregation.* They shall work for the whole congregation, and instead of the firstborn.

8. *All the instruments.* The Tabernacle itself and all its contents; see all described, vv. 25-26, 31, 36-37. The Levites were to perform the most common and laborious offices. It was their business to take down, put up, and carry the Tabernacle and its utensils; for it was the object of their peculiar care. In a word, they were the servants of the priests.

10. *Aaron and his sons . . . shall wait on their priest's office.* It was the business of the priests to offer the different sacrifices to God; to consecrate the shewbread, pour out the libations, burn the incense, sprinkle the blood of the victims, and bless the people. In a word, they were the servants of God alone.

12. *I have taken the Levites . . . instead of all the firstborn.* The Levites are taken for the service of the sanctuary in place of the firstborn. The firstborn were dedicated to God in commemoration of His slaying the firstborn of the Egyptians, and preserving those of the Israelites. Even the cattle of the Levites were taken in place of the firstborn of the cattle of the rest of the tribes. See v. 45.

Several reasons have been assigned why God should give this honor to the tribe of Levi in preference to all the others, but they do not seem to me to be conclusive. Their zeal in destroying those who had corrupted the worship of God in the business of the golden calf, Exod. xxxii. 28, has been thought a sufficient reason. A better reason is that this was the smallest tribe, and they were quite enough for the service. To have had a more numerous tribe at this time would have been very inconvenient.

15. *A month old and upward.* The males of all the other tribes were numbered from twenty years and upward; had the Levites been numbered in this way, they would not have been nearly equal in number to the firstborn of the twelve tribes. Add to this that, as there must have been firstborn of all ages in the other tribes, it was necessary that the Levites, who were to be their substitutes, should be also of all ages; and it appears to have been on this ground, at least partly, that the Levites were numbered from four weeks old and upward.

16. *Moses numbered them.* Though Moses and Aaron conjointly numbered the twelve tribes, yet Moses alone numbered the Levites; "for as the money with which the firstborn of Israel, who exceeded the number of Levites, were redeemed was to be paid to Aaron and his sons, v. 48, it was decent that he, whose advantage it was that the number of the firstborn of Israel should exceed, should not be authorized to take that number himself."

22. *Seven thousand* and *five hundred.* Perhaps originally *resh,* 200, instead of *caph,* 500; see the following note.

MATTHEW HENRY

Kohath and Merari, and these subdivided into several families, *v.* 17–20.

1. Concerning each of these three classes we have an account, (1) Of their number. (2) Of their post about the tabernacle on which they were to attend. The Gershonites pitched behind the tabernacle, westward, *v.* 23. The Kohathites on the right hand, southward, *v.* 29. The Merarites on the left hand, northward, *v.* 35. And, to complete the square, Moses and Aaron, with the priests, encamped in the front, eastward, *v.* 38. (3) Of their chief or head. As each class had its own place, so each had its own prince. (4) Of their charge, when the camp moved. The Gershonites were charged with the custody and carriage of all the curtains and hangings and coverings of the tabernacle and court (*v.* 25, 26), the Kohathites of all the furniture of the tabernacle—the ark, altar, table, &c. (*v.* 31, 32), the Merarites of the heavy carriage, boards, bars, pillars, &c., *v.* 36, 37.

2. Here we may observe, (1) That the Kohathites, though they were the second house, yet were preferred before the elder family of the Gershonites. Besides that Aaron and the priests were of that family, they were more numerous, and their post and charge more honourable, which probably was ordered to put an honour upon Moses, who was of that family. Yet, (2) The posterity of Moses were not at all dignified or privileged, but stood upon the level with other Levites.

III. The sum total of the numbers of this tribe. They are computed in all 22,000, *v.* 39. That which is especially observable here is that the tribe of Levi was by much the least of all the tribes.

Verses 40–51

Here is the exchange made of the Levites for the first-born. 1. The first-born were numbered from a month old, *v.* 42, 43. Bishop Patrick is decidedly of opinion that none were numbered but those only that were born since their coming out of Egypt, when the first-born were sanctified, Exod. xiii. 2. If there were 22,000 first-born males, we may suppose as many females, and all these brought forth in the first year after they came out of Egypt, we must hence infer that in the last year of their servitude, even when it was in the greatest extremity, there were abundance of marriages made among the Israelites; they were not discouraged by the present distress, but married in faith, expecting that God would shortly visit them with mercy, and that their children, though born in bondage, should live in liberty and honour. They were not only kept alive, but greatly increased, in a barren wilderness. 2. The number of the first-born, and that of the Levites, by a special providence, came pretty near to each other. 3. The small number of first-born which exceeded the number of the Levites (273 in all) were to be redeemed, at five shekels apiece, and the redemption money given to Aaron; for it would not do well to have them added to the Levites.

JAMIESON, FAUSSET, BROWN

Gershonites being stationed on the west, the Kohathites on the south, and the families of Merari on the north. The Kohathites had the principal place about the tabernacle, and charge of the most precious and sacred things—a distinction with which they were honored, probably, because the Aaronic family belonged to this division of the Levitical tribe. The Gershonites, being the oldest, had the next honorable post assigned them, while the burden of the drudgery was thrown on the division of Merari. **32. chief**—rather, chiefs of the Levites. Three persons are mentioned as chiefs of these respective divisions. And Eleazar presided over them; whence he is called "the second priest" (II Kings 25:18); and in the case of the high priest's absence from illness or other necessary occasions, he performed the duties (I Kings 4:4). **38. those that encamp,** etc.—That being the entrance side, it was the post of honor, and consequently reserved to Moses and the priestly family. But the sons of Moses had no station here. **39. twenty and two thousand**—The result of this census, though made on conditions most advantageous to Levi, proved it to be by far the smallest in Israel. The separate numbers stated in verses 22, 28, 34, when added together, amount to 22,300. The omission of the 300 is variously accounted for—by some, because they might be first-born who were already devoted to God and could not be counted as substitutes; and by others, because in Scripture style, the sum is reckoned in round numbers. The most probable conjecture is, that as *Heb.* letters are employed for figures, one letter was, in the course of transcription, taken for another of like form but smaller value. **40-51. Number all the first-born of the males of the children of Israel,** etc.—The principle on which the enumeration of the Levites had been made was now to be applied to the other tribes. The number of their male children, from a month old and upward, was to be reckoned, in order that a comparison might be instituted with that of the Levites, for the formal adoption of the latter as substitutes for the first-born. The Levites, amounting to 22,000, were given in exchange for an equal number of the first-born from the other tribes, leaving an excess of 273; and as there were no substitutes for these, they were redeemed at the rate of five shekels for each (ch. 18:15, 16). Every Israelite would naturally wish that his son might be redeemed by a Levite without the payment of this tax, and yet some would have to incur the expense, for there were not Levites enough to make an equal exchange. Jewish writers say the matter was determined by lot, in this manner: Moses put into an urn 22,000 pieces of parchment, on each of which he wrote "a son of Levi," and 273 more, containing the words, "five shekels." These being shaken, he ordered each of the first-born to put in his hand and take out a slip. If it contained the first inscription, the boy was redeemed by a Levite; if the latter, the parent had to pay. The ransom money, which, reckoning the shekel at half a dollar, would amount to $2.50 each, was appropriated to the use of the sanctuary. The excess of the general over the Levitical first-born is so small, that the only way of accounting for it is, by supposing those first-born only were counted as were males remaining in their parents' household, or that those first-born only were numbered which had been born since the departure from Egypt, when God claimed all the first-born as his special property. **41. the cattle of the Levites**—These, which they kept to graze on the glebes and meadows in the suburbs of their cities, to supply their families with dairy produce and animal food, were also taken as an equivalent for all the firstlings of the cattle which the Israelites at that time possessed. In consequence of this exchange the firstlings were not brought then, as afterwards, to the altar and the priests.

ADAM CLARKE

39. *Which Moses and Aaron numbered.* The word *veaharon*, "and Aaron," has a point over each of its letters, probably designed as a mark of spuriousness. The word is wanting in the Samaritan, Syriac, and Coptic; it is wanting also in eight of Dr. Kennicott's MSS., and in four of De Rossi's. Moses alone is commanded to take the number of the Levites; see vv. 5, 11, 40, 44, and 51.

All the males . . . were twenty and two thousand. This total does not agree with the particulars; for the Gershonites were 7,500, the Kohathites 8,600, the Merarites 6,200, total 22,300. Several methods of solving this difficulty have been proposed by learned men; Dr. Kennicott's is the most simple. Formerly the numbers in the Hebrew Bible were expressed by letters, and not by words at full length; and if two nearly similar letters were mistaken for each other, many errors in the numbers must be the consequence. Now it is probable that an error has crept into the number of the Gershonites, v. 22, where, instead of 7,500, we should read 7,200, as *caph*, 500, might have been easily mistaken for *resh*, 200, especially if the down stroke of the *caph* had been a little shorter than ordinary, which is often the case in MSS. The extra 300 being taken off, the total is just 22,000, as mentioned in the thirty-ninth verse.

43. *All the firstborn males . . . were twenty and two thousand two hundred and threescore and thirteen.* Thus we find there were 273 firstborn beyond the number of the Levites. These are ordered, v. 46, to be redeemed; and the redemption price is to be 5 shekels each, v. 47, about 15*s*. And this money, amounting to 1,365 shekels, equal to £204 15*s*. English, he took of the firstborn of Israel, v. 50.

MATTHEW HENRY — CHAPTER 4

Verses 1–20

We have here a second muster of the tribe of Levi. As that tribe was taken out of all Israel to be God's peculiar, so the middle-aged men of that tribe were taken from among the rest to be actually employed in the service of the tabernacle.

I. Who were to be taken into this number. All the males from thirty years old to fifty. The service of God requires the best of our strength, and the prime of our time, which cannot be better spent than to the honour of him who is the first and best. And a man may make a good soldier much sooner than a good minister.

1. They were not to be employed till they were

JAMIESON, FAUSSET, BROWN — CHAPTER 4

Vss. 1-49. Of the Levites' Service. **2, 3. sons of Kohath, from thirty years old and upward**—This age was specifically fixed (see on ch. 8:24) as the full maturity of bodily energy to perform the laborious duties assigned them in the wilderness, as well as of mental activity to assist in the management of the sacred services. And it was the period of life at which John the Baptist and Christ entered on their respective ministries. **even unto fifty**—The term perscribed for active duty was a period of twenty years, at the end of which they were exempted from the physical labors of the office, though still expected to attend in the tabernacle (ch. 8:26). **all that enter into the host**—so called from their

ADAM CLARKE — CHAPTER 4

3. *From thirty years old.* In chap. viii. 24, the Levites are ordered to enter on the service of the Tabernacle at the age of twenty-five years; and in 1 Chron. xxiii. 24, they were ordered to commence that work at twenty years of age. How can these different times be reconciled? (1) At the time of which Moses speaks here, the Levitical service was exceedingly severe, and consequently required men full-grown, strong, and stout, to perform it; the age therefore of thirty years was appointed as the period for commencing this service. (2) In chap. viii. 24, Moses seems to speak of the service in a general way; the severe, which was to be per-

MATTHEW HENRY

irty years old. They were entered as probationers twenty-five years old (*ch.* viii. 24), and in David's ne, when there was more work to be done, at enty (1 Chron. xxiii. 24, and so Ezra iii. 8); but ey must be five years learning and waiting, and so ting themselves for service; in David's time they ere ten years in preparation, from twenty to thirty. hn Baptist began his public ministry, and Christ s, at thirty years old. This gives us two good rules:—) That ministers must not be novices, 1 Tim. iii. 6. is a work that requires ripeness of judgment and eat steadiness. (2) That they must learn before ey teach, serve before they rule, and must *first be oved,* 1 Tim. iii. 10.

2. They were discharged at fifty years old from the ilsome part of the service, particularly that of rrying the tabernacle.

II. How their work is described. They are said to *ter into the host,* or warfare, *to do the work in the bernacle.* Those that enter into the ministry must ok upon themselves as entered into the *host,* and prove themselves *good soldiers,* 2 Tim. ii. 3. Now, to the sons of Kohath in particular, here is,

1. Their service appointed them, in the removes the tabernacle. Afterwards, when the tabernacle as fixed, they had other work assigned them; but is was the work of the day, which was to be done its day. Now the Kohathites were to carry all the ly things of the tabernacle. (1) Aaron, and his sons e priests, must pack up the things which the Kohaites were to carry, as here directed, *v.* 5, &c.

(2) All e holy things must be covered, the ark and table ith three coverings, all the rest with two. Even the hes of the altar, in which the holy fire was carelly preserved and raked up, must have a purple oth spread over them, *v.* 13. Even the brazen altar, ough in the court of the sanctuary it stood open the view of all, yet was covered in the carriage of This signified the darkness of that dispensation. hat which is now brought to light by the gospel, d revealed to babes, was then hidden from the ise and prudent. They saw only the coverings, not e holy things themselves (Heb. x. 1); but now hrist has *destroyed the face of the covering,* Isa. xv. 7. (3) When all the holy things were covered, en the Kohathites were to carry them on their oulders.

2. Eleazar, now the eldest son of Aaron, is appointed verseer of the Kohathites in this service (*v.* 16).

3. Great care must be taken to preserve the lives f these Levites, by preventing their irreverent pproach to the most holy things: *Cut you not off e Kohathites, v.* 18. (1) The Kohathites must not e the holy things till the priests had covered them, 20. And, (2) When the holy things were covered, ey might not touch them, at least not the ark, alled here *the holy thing,* upon pain of death, *v.* 15. hus were the Lord's ministers themselves then kept fear, and that was a dispensation of terror, as well s darkness; but now, through Christ, the case is ltered: we have *seen with our eyes,* and our *hands ave handled, the word of life* (1 John i. 1), and we are ncouraged to *come boldly to the throne of grace.*

erses 21–33

We have here the charge of the other two families f the Levites, which, though not so honourable as e first, yet was necessary, and was to be done egularly. 1. The Gershonites were charged with ll the drapery of the tabernacle, the curtains, and angings, and the coverings of badgers' skins, *v.* 2–26.

JAMIESON, FAUSSET, BROWN

ranks, and their special duty as guards of the tabernacle. The *Heb.* word, however, signifies also a station of office; and hence the passage may be rendered, "All that enter into the sacerdotal office" (vs. 23). **4-15. This shall be the service of the sons of Kohath,** etc.—They are mentioned first, from their close connection with Aaron; and the special department of duty assigned to them during the journeyings of Israel accorded with the charge they had received of the precious contents of the tabernacle. But these were to be previously covered by the common priests, who, as well as the high priest, were admitted on such necessary occasions into the holy place. This was an exception to the general rule, which prohibited the entrance of any but the high priest. But when the cloud removed from the tabernacle, the sanctuary might be entered by the common priests, as to them was reserved the exclusive privilege of packing the sacred utensils; and it was not till the holy things were thus ready for carriage, that the Kohathites were allowed to approach. **5. covering veil**—the inner veil, which separated the holy from the most holy place. (See on Exod. 36:3.) **6. covering of badgers' skins**—(See on Exod. 25:5.) The covering, however, referred to was not that of the tabernacle, but one made for the special purpose of protecting the ark. **put in the staves**—These golden staves were now taken out. (See on Exod. 25:15, compared with I Kings 8:8.) The *Hebrew* word rendered "put in," signifies also "dispose," and probably refers here to their insertion through the openings in the coverings made for receiving them, to preserve them from the touch of the carriers as well as from the influence of the weather. It is worthy of notice that the coverings did not consist of canvas or coarse tarpauling, but of a kind which united beauty with decency. **7. continual showbread**—Though the people were in the wilderness fed upon manna, the sacred loaves were constantly made of corn, which was probably raised in small quantities from the verdant patches of the desert. **10. a bar**—or bier, formed of two poles fastened by two crosspieces and borne by two men, after the fashion of a sedan chair. **12. instruments of ministry**—the official dress of the priests (Exod. 31:10). **13. shall take away the ashes from the altar,** etc.—The necessity of removing ashes from the altar plainly implies that sacrifices were offered in the wilderness (cf. Exod. 18:12; 24:4), though that rebellious race seems frequently to have neglected the duty (Amos 5:25). No mention is made of the sacred fire; but as, by divine command, it was to be kept constantly burning, it must have been transferred to some pan or brazier under the covering, and borne by the appointed carriers. **15. the sons of Kohath shall come to bear it, but they shall not touch any holy thing, lest they die**—The mode of transport was upon the shoulders of the Levites (see on ch. 7:9), although afterwards wheeled vehicles were employed (II Samuel 6:3; I Chron. 15:12). And it was allowed to touch the covering, but not the things covered, on the penalty of death, which was inflicted more than once (I Sam. 6:19; II Samuel 6:6, 7). This stern denunciation was designed to inspire a sentiment of deep and habitual reverence in the minds of those who were officially engaged about holy things. **16. to the office of Eleazar . . . pertaineth the oil for the light, and the sweet incense,** etc.—He was charged with the special duty of superintending the squadron who were employed in the carrying of the sacred furniture; besides, to his personal care were committed the materials requisite for the daily service, and which it was necessary he should have easily at his command (Exod. 29:38). **17-20. Cut ye not off the tribe of the families of the Kohathites from among the Levites,** etc.—a solemn admonition to Moses and Aaron to beware, lest, by any negligence on their part, disorder and improprieties should creep in, and to take the greatest care that all the parts of this important service be apportioned to the proper parties, lest the Kohathites should be disqualified for their high and honorable duties. The guilt of their death would be incurred by the superintending priest, if he failed to give proper directions or allowed any irreverent familiarity with sacred things. **24-28. This is the service of the families of the Gershonites,** etc.—They were appointed to carry "the curtains of the tabernacle"—i.e., the goats' hair covering of the tent—the ten curious curtains and embroidered hangings at the entrance, with their red morocco covering, etc. **28. their charge shall be under the hand of Ithamar the son of Aaron,** etc.—The Levites were generally subject to the official command of the priests in doing the ordinary work of the tabernacle. But during the journeyings Eleazar, who

ADAM CLARKE

formed by the full-grown Levites, and the less laborious work which younger men might assist in; hence the age of twenty-five is fixed. (3) In David's time and afterwards, in the fixed Tabernacle and Temple, the laboriousness of the service no longer existed, and hence twenty years was the age fixed on for all Levites to enter into the work of the sanctuary. *Until fifty years old.* This was allowing twenty years for public severe service, a very considerate and merciful ordinance.

20. *When the holy things are covered.* Literally, *keballa,* when they are "swallowed down"; which shows the promptitude with which everything belonging to the holy of holies was put out of sight, for these mysteries must ever be treated with the deepest reverence; and indeed without this they could not have been to them the representatives of heavenly realities.

KEIL–DELITZSCH:

Verse 4. The service of the Kohathites at the tabernacle is (relates to) "the most holy" (Ex. 30:10). This term includes, as is afterwards explained, the most holy things in the tabernacle, viz., the ark of the covenant, the table of shewbread, the candlestick, the altar of incense and altar of burnt offering, together with all the other things belonging to these. When the camp was broken up, the priest were to roll them up in wrappers, and hand them over in this state to the Kohathites, for them to carry (vv. 5–15). First of all (vv. 5, 6), Aaron and his sons were to take down the curtain between the holy place and the most holy (Ex. 26:31), and to cover the ark of testimony with it (Ex. 25:10). Over this they were to place a wrapper of sea-cow skin (*tachash,* Ex. 25:5), and over this again another covering of cloth made entirely of hyacinth-colored purple (as in Ex. 28:31). The sea-cow skin was to protect the inner curtain, which was covered over the ark, from storm and rain; the hyacinth purple, to distinguish the ark of the covenant as the throne of the glory of Jehovah. Lastly, they were to place the staves into the rings again, that is to say, the bearing poles, which were always left in their places on the ark (Ex. 25:15), but had necessarily to be taken out while it was being covered and wrapped up.

—*Commentary on the Old Testament*

MATTHEW HENRY

2. The Merarites were charged with the heavy carriage, the boards and bars, the pillars and sockets, the pins and cords, and these were delivered to them by name, *v.* 31, 32.

Verses 34-49

We have here a particular account of the numbers of the three families of the Levites respectively, that is, of the effective men, between thirty years old and fifty. The whole number of the able men of the tribe of Levi who entered into God's host to war his warfare was but 8,580, whereas the able men of the other tribes that entered into the host of Israel to war their warfare were many more. The least of the tribes had almost four times as many able men as the Levites, and some of them more than eight times as many; for those that are engaged in the service of this world, and war after the flesh, are many more than those that are devoted to the service of God, and *fight the good fight of faith.*

JAMIESON, FAUSSET, BROWN

was next in succession to his father, took the special charge of the Kohathites, while his brother Ithamar had the superintendence of the Gershonites and Merarites. **29-33. As for the sons of Merari**—They carried the coarser and heavier appurtenances, which, however, were so important and necessary, that an inventory was kept of them—not only on account of their number and variety, but of their comparative commonness and smallness, which might have led to their being lost or missing through carelessness, inadvertency, or neglect. It was a useful lesson, showing that God disregards nothing pertaining to His service, and that even in the least and most trivial matters, He requires the duty of faithful obedience. **34-49. Moses and Aaron and the chief of the congregation numbered the sons of the Kohathites,** etc.—This enumeration was made on a different principle from that which is recorded in the preceding chapter. That was confined to the males from a month old and upward, while this was extended to all capable of service in the three classes of the Levitical tribe. In considering their relative numbers, the wisdom of Divine Providence appears in arranging that, whereas in the Kohathites and Gershonites, whose burdens were few and easier, there were but about a third part of them which were fit for service; the Merarites, whose burdens were more and heavier, had above one-half of them fit for this work [POOLE]. The small population of this tribe, so inferior to that of the other tribes, is attempted to be explained (see on ch. 3: 39).

ADAM CLARKE

36. *Those that were numbered.* In chap. iii. 27, etc., we have an account of the whole number of the Levites, and here of those only who were able to serve the Lord in the sanctuary. Thus we find that the whole number of the Levites amounted to 22,300, of whom 8,580 were fit for service, and 13,720 unfit, being either too old or too young.

From this and the preceding chapter we see the very severe labor which the Levites were obliged to perform while the journeyings of the Israelites lasted. When we consider that there was almost ten tons and fourteen hundred pounds' weight of metal employed in the Tabernacle, besides the immense weight of the skins, hangings, cords, boards, and posts, we shall find it was no very easy matter to transport this movable Temple from place to place.

The Gershonites, who were 7,500 men in the service, had to carry the tent, coverings, veil, hangings of the court, etc., chap. iii. 25-26. The Kohathites, who were 8,600 men, had to carry the ark, table, candlestick, altars, and instruments of the sanctuary, chap. iii. 31. The Merarites, who were 6,200 men, had to carry the boards, bars, pillars, sockets, and all matters connected with these belonging to the Tabernacle, with the pillars of the court, their sockets, pins, and cords, chap. iii. 36-37.

MATTHEW HENRY

CHAPTER 5

Verses 1-10

I. A command for the purifying of the camp, by turning out from within its lines all those that were ceremonially unclean, by issues, leprosies, or the touch of dead bodies, until they were cleansed according to the law, *v.* 2, 3.

1. These orders are executed immediately, *v.* 4. The camp was now newly-modelled and put in order, and therefore, to complete the reformation of it, it is next to be cleansed. God's tabernacle was now fixed in the midst of their camp, and therefore they must be careful to keep it clean. The person, the place, *in the midst of which God dwells,* must not be defiled; for, if it be, he will be affronted, offended, and provoked to withdraw, 1 Cor. iii. 16, 17.

2. This expulsion of the unclean out of the camp was to signify, (1) What the governors of the church ought to do: they must *separate between the precious and the vile,* and purge out scandalous persons. It is for the glory of Christ and the edification of his church that those who are openly and incorrigibly profane and vicious should be put out and kept from Christian communion till they repent. (2) What God himself will do in the great day: he will *throughly purge his floor,* and *gather out of his kingdom all things that offend.* As here the unclean were shut out of the camp, so into the new Jerusalem *no unclean thing shall enter,* Rev. xxi. 27.

JAMIESON, FAUSSET, BROWN

CHAPTER 5

VSS. 1-4. THE UNCLEAN TO BE REMOVED OUT OF THE CAMP. **2. Command the children of Israel, that they put out of the camp every leper**—The exclusion of leprous persons from the camp in the wilderness, as from cities and villages afterwards, was a sanitary measure taken according to prescribed rules (Lev. 13, 14). This exclusion of lepers from society has been acted upon ever since; and it affords almost the only instance in which any kind of attention is paid in the East to the prevention of contagion. The usage still more or less prevails in the East among people who do not think the least precaution against the plague or cholera necessary; but judging from personal observation, we think that in Asia the leprosy has now much abated in frequency and virulence. It usually appears in a comparatively mild form in Egypt, Palestine, and other countries where the disorder is, or was, endemic. Small societies of excluded lepers live miserably in paltry huts. Many of them are beggars, going out into the roads to solicit alms, which they receive in a wooden bowl; charitable people also sometimes bring different articles of food, which they leave on the ground at a short distance from the hut of the lepers, for whom it is intended. They are generally obliged to wear a distinctive badge that people may know them at first sight and be warned to avoid them. Other means were adopted among the ancient Jews by putting their hand on their mouth and crying, "Unclean, unclean." But their general treatment, as to exclusion from society, was the same as now described. The association of the lepers, however, in this passage, with those who were subject only to ceremonial uncleanness, shows that one important design in the temporary exile of such persons was to remove all impurities that reflected dishonor on the character and residence of Israel's King. And this vigilant care to maintain external cleanliness in the people was typically designed to teach them the practice of moral purity, or cleansing themselves from all filthiness of the flesh and spirit. The regulations made for ensuring cleanliness in the camp suggest the adoption of similar means for maintaining purity in the church. And although, in large communities of Christians, it may be often difficult or delicate to do this, the suspension or, in flagrant cases of sin, the total excommunication of the offender from the privileges and communion of the church is an imperative duty, as necessary to the moral purity of the Christian as the exclusion of the leper from the camp was to physical health and ceremonial purity in the Jewish church.

5-10. RESTITUTION ENJOINED. **6. When a man or a woman shall commit any sin that men commit, to do a trespass against the Lord**—This is a wrong or injury done by one man to the property of another, and as it is called "a trespass against the Lord," it is implied, in the case supposed, that the offense has been aggravated by prevaricating—by a false oath, or a fraudulent lie in denying it, which is a "trespass" committed against God, who is the sole

ADAM CLARKE

CHAPTER 5

2. *Put out of the camp every leper.* According to the preceding plan, it is sufficiently evident that each camp had a space behind it, and on one side, whither the infected might be removed, and where probably convenient places were erected for the accommodation of the infected; for we cannot suppose that they were driven out into the naked wilderness. But the expulsion mentioned here was founded (1) On a purely physical reason, viz., the diseases were contagious, and therefore there was a necessity of putting those afflicted by them apart, that the infection might not be communicated. (2) There was also a spiritual reason; the camp was the habitation of God, and nothing impure should be permitted to remain where He dwelt.

4. *And the children of Israel . . . put them out.* This is the earliest account we have of such separations; and probably this ordinance gave the first idea of a hospital, where all those who are afflicted with contagious disorders are put into particular wards, under medical treatment.

7. *Shall confess their sin.* Without confession or acknowledgment of sin, there was no hope of mercy held out. *He shall recompense.* For without restitution, in every possible case, God will not forgive the iniquity of a man's sin. How can any person in a case of defraud, with his neighbor's property in his possession, expect to receive mercy from the hand of a just and holy God?

MATTHEW HENRY

II. A law concerning restitution, in case of wrong done to a neighbour. 1. He must *confess his sin,* confess it to God, confess it to his neighbour, and so take shame to himself. 2. He must bring a sacrifice, a *ram of atonement, v.* 8. Satisfaction must be made for the offence done to God, whose law is broken, as well as for the loss sustained by our neighbour; restitution in this case is not sufficient without faith and repentance. 3. Yet the sacrifices would not be accepted till full amends were made to the party wronged, not only the principal, but a fifth part added to it, *v.* 7. If the party wronged was dead, and he had no near kinsman who was entitled to the debt, it must be given to the priest, *v.* 8. Note, Some work of piety or charity is a piece of necessary justice to be done by those who are conscious to themselves that they have done wrong, but know not how otherwise to make restitution.

III. A general rule concerning hallowed things given upon this occasion, that, whatever was given to the priest, *his it shall be, v.* 9, 10.

Verses 11–31

We have here the law concerning the solemn trial of a wife whose husband was jealous of her.

I. What was the case supposed: That a man had some reason to suspect his wife to have committed adultery, *v.* 12–14. The sin of adultery is justly represented as an exceedingly sinful sin. It is committing a trespass against the husband, robbing him of his honour, alienating his right, introducing a spurious breed into his family to share with his children in his estate, and violating her covenant with him. Hence, 1. Let all wives be admonished not to give any the least occasion for the suspicion of their chastity. 2. Let all husbands be admonished not to entertain any causeless or unjust suspicions of their wives. If charity in general, much more conjugal affection, teaches to *think no evil,* 1 Cor. xiii. 5.

II. What was the course prescribed in this case, that, if the suspected wife was innocent, she might not continue under the reproach and uneasiness of her husband's jealousy, and, if guilty, her sin might find her out, and others might hear, and fear, and take warning. Her husband must *bring her to the priest,* with the witnesses that could prove the ground of his suspicion, and desire that she might be put upon her trial. If she confessed, saying, "I am defiled," she was not put to death, but was divorced and lost her dowry; if she said, "I am pure," then they proceeded. God will find out some way or other to clear the innocency of the innocent, and to bring forth their righteousness as the light. To *the pure all things are pure,* but *to the defiled nothing* is so, Tit. i. 15.

JAMIESON, FAUSSET, BROWN

judge of what is falsely sworn or spoken (Acts 5:3, 4). **and that person be guilty**—i.e., from the obvious tenor of the passage, conscience-smitten, or brought to a sense and conviction of his evil conduct. (See on Lev. 6:4.) In that case there must be: first, confession, a penitential acknowledgment of sin; secondly, restitution of the property, or the giving of an equivalent, with the additional fine of a fifth part, both as a compensation to the person defrauded, and as a penalty inflicted on the injurer, to deter others from the commission of similar trespasses. (See on Exod. 22:1.) The difference between the law recorded in that passage and this is that the one was enacted against flagrant and determined thieves, the other against those whose necessities might have urged them into fraud, and whose consciences were distressed by their sin. This law also supposes the injured party to be dead, in which case, the compensation due to his representatives was to be paid to the priest, who, as God's deputy, received the required satisfaction. **9, 10. every offering . . . shall be his**—Whatever was given in this way, or otherwise, as by freewill offerings, irrevocably belonged to the priest.

11-31. THE TRIAL OF JEALOUSY. **if any man's wife go aside**—This law was given both as a strong discouragement to conjugal infidelity on the part of a wife, and a sufficient protection of her from the consequences of a hasty and groundless suspicion on the part of the husband. His suspicions, however, were sufficient in the absence of witnesses (Lev. 20:10) to warrant the trial described; and the course of proceeding to be followed was for the jealous husband to bring his wife unto the priest with an offering of barley meal, because none were allowed to approach the sanctuary empty-handed (Exod. 23:15). On other occasions, there were mingled with the offering, oil which signified joy, and frankincense which denoted acceptance (Ps. 141:2). But on the occasion referred to, both these ingredients were to be excluded, partly because it was a solemn appeal to God in distressing circumstances, and partly because it was a sin offering on the part of the wife, who came before God in the character of a real or suspected offender. **17. the priest shall take holy water**—Water from the laver, which was to be mixed with dust—an emblem of vileness and misery (Gen. 3:14; Ps. 22:15). **in an earthen vessel**—This fragile ware was chosen because, after being used, it was broken in pieces (Lev. 6:28; 11:33). All the circumstances of this awful ceremony—her being placed with her face toward the ark—her uncovered head, a sign of her being deprived of the protection of her husband (I Cor. 11:7)—the bitter potion being put into her hands preparatory to an appeal to God—the solemn adjuration of the priest (vss. 19-22), all were calculated in no common degree to excite and appall the imagination of a person conscious of guilt. **21. The Lord make thee a curse, etc.**—a usual form of imprecation (Isa. 65:15; Jer. 29:22). **22. the woman shall say, Amen, Amen**—The Israelites were accustomed, instead of formally repeating the words of an oath merely to say, "Amen," a "so be it" to the imprecations it contained. The reduplication of the word was designed as an evidence of the woman's innocence, and a willingness that God would do to her according to her desert. **23, 24. write these curses in a book**—The imprecations, along with her name, were inscribed in some kind of record—on parchment, or more probably on a wooden tablet. **blot them out with the bitter water**—If she were innocent, they could be easily erased, and were perfectly harmless; but if guilty, she would experience the fatal effects of the water she had drunk. **29. This is the law of jealousies**—Adultery discovered and proved was punished with death. But strongly suspected cases would occur, and this law made provision for the conviction of the guilty person. It was, however, not a trial conducted according to the forms of judicial process, but an ordeal through which a suspected adulteress was made to go—the ceremony being of that terrifying nature, that, on the known principles of human nature, guilt or innocence could not fail to appear. From the earliest times, the jealousy of Eastern people has established ordeals for the detection and punishment of suspected unchastity in wives. The practice was deep-rooted as well as universal. And it has been thought, that the Israelites being strongly biassed in favor of such usages, this law of jealousies "was incorporated among the other institutions of the Mosaic economy, in order to free it from the idolatrous rites which the heathens had blended with it." Viewed in this light, its sanction by divine authority in a corrected and improved form exhibits a proof at once of the wisdom and condescension of God.

ADAM CLARKE

8. *If the man have no kinsman.* The Jews think that this law respects the stranger and the sojourner only, because every Israelite is in a state of affinity to all the rest; but there might be a stranger in the camp who has no relative in any of the tribes of Israel.

14. The spirit of jealousy. *Ruach kinah,* either a supernatural diabolic influence, exciting him to jealousy, or the passion or affection of jealousy, for so the words may be understood.

17. *Holy water.* Water out of the laver, called *holy* because consecrated to sacred uses. This is the most ancient case of the trial by ordeal. *In an earthen vessel.* Supposed by the Jews to be such as had never been previously used. *Dust that is in the floor.* Probably intended to point out the baseness of the crime of which she was accused.

18. *Uncover the woman's head.* To take off a woman's veil, and expose her to the sight of men, would be considered a very great degradation in the East. To this Paul appears to allude, 1 Cor. xi. 5-6, 10.

21. *The Lord make thee a curse and an oath.* Let thy name and punishment be remembered and mentioned as an example and terror to all others. Like that mentioned Jer. xxix. 22-23: "The Lord make thee like Zedekiah and like Ahab, whom the king of Babylon roasted in the fire; because they have committed villany in Israel, and have committed adultery with their neighbours' wives."

22. *Thy belly to swell, and thy thigh to rot.* What is meant by these expressions cannot be easily ascertained. *Lanpel yarech* signifies literally thy "thigh to fall." As the *thigh,* feet, etc., were used among the Hebrews delicately to express the parts which nature conceals (see Gen. xlvi. 26), the expression here is probably to be understood in this sense; and the falling down of the thigh here must mean something similar to the falling down of the womb, which might be a natural effect of the preternatural distension of the abdomen. *And the woman shall say, Amen, amen.* This is the first place where this word occurs in the common form of a concluding wish in prayer. The root *aman* signifies to be "steady, true, permanent." And in prayer it signifies, "Let it be so—make it steady—let it be ratified."

23. *The priest shall write these curses . . . and he shall blot them out.* It appears that the curses which were written down with a kind of ink prepared for the purpose, as some of the rabbins think, without any calx of iron or other material that could make a permanent dye, were washed off the parchment into the water which the woman was obliged to drink, so that she drank the very words of the execration. The ink used in the East is almost all of this kind—a wet sponge will completely efface the finest of their writings. The rabbins say that the trial by the waters of jealousy was omitted after the Babylonish captivity, because adulteries were so frequent among them that they were afraid of having the name of the Lord profaned by being so frequently appealed to! This is a most humiliating confession.

24. *The bitter water that causeth the curse.* Though the rabbins think that the priest put some bitter substance in the water, yet as nothing of the kind is intimated by Moses, we may consider the word as used here metaphorically for affliction, death, etc. These waters were afflicting and deadly to her who drank them, being guilty. In this sense afflictions are said to be bitter, Isa. xxxviii. 17; so also is death, 1 Sam. xv. 32; Eccles. vii. 26.

29. *This is the law of jealousies.* And this is the most singular law in the whole Pentateuch: a law that seems to have been copied by almost all the nations of the earth, whether civilized or barbarian, as we find that similar modes of trial for suspected offenses were used when complete evidence was wanting to convict; and where it was expected that the object of their worship would interfere for the sake of justice, in order that the guilty should be brought to punishment, and the innocent be cleared.

31. *This woman shall bear her iniquity.* That is, her belly shall swell, and her thigh shall rot; see on v. 22.

MATTHEW HENRY

CHAPTER 6

Verses 1–21

After the law for the discovery and shame of those that by sin had made themselves vile, there follows this for the direction and encouragement of those who by their eminent piety and devotion had made themselves honourable. There were those who went under the character of *Nazarites*, and were celebrated by that title as persons professing greater strictness and zeal in religion than other people. Joseph is called a Nazarite among his brethren (Gen. xlix. 26).

I. The general character of a Nazarite: it is a person *separated unto the Lord, v.* 2. Some were Nazarites for life, either by divine designation, as Samson (Judg. xiii. 5), and John Baptist (Luke i. 15), or by their parents' vow concerning them, as Samuel, 1 Sam. i. 11. Of these this law speaks not. Others were so for a certain time, and by their own voluntary engagement, and concerning them rules are given by this law. A woman might bind herself with the vow of a Nazarite, under the limitations we find, *ch.* xxx. 3. The Nazarites were, 1. Devoted to the Lord during the time of their Nazariteship, and, it is probable, spent much of their time in the study of the law, in acts of devotion, and instructing others. 2. They were separated from common persons and common things. 3. They separated themselves by vowing a vow. Every Israelite was bound by the divine law to love God with all his heart, but the Nazarites by their own act and deed bound themselves to some religious observances, as fruits and expressions of that love, which other Israelites were not bound to. Christ was called in reproach a Nazarene, so were his followers: but he was no Nazarite according to this law; he drank wine, and touched dead bodies, yet in him this type had its accomplishment, for in him all purity and perfection met; and every true Christian is a spiritual Nazarite, separated by vow unto the Lord.

II. The particular obligations that the Nazarites lay under.

1. They must have nothing to do with *the fruit of the vine, v.* 3, 4. They must drink no wine nor strong drink, nor eat grapes, no, not the kernel nor the husk: they might not so much as eat a raisin. Those who gave the Nazarites wine to drink did the tempter's work (Amos ii. 12), persuading them to that forbidden fruit. That it was reckoned a perfection and praise not to drink wine appears from the instance of the Rechabites, Jer. xxxv. 6. They were to *drink no* wine, (1) That they might be examples of temperance and mortification. Drinking *a little wine for the stomach's sake* is allowed, to help that, 1 Tim. v. 23. But drinking much wine for the *palate's sake,* to please that, does by no means become those who profess to walk not *after the flesh, but after the Spirit.* (2) That they might be qualified to employ themselves in the service of God. They must not drink, lest they should *forget the law* (Prov. xxxi. 5), lest they should *err through wine* Isa. xxviii. 7. Let all Christians oblige themselves to be very moderate in the use of wine and strong drink; for, if the love of these once gets the mastery of a man, he becomes a very easy prey to Satan.

2. They must not *cut their hair, v.* 5. They must neither poll their heads nor shave their beards; this was that mark of Samson's Nazariteship which we often read of in his story. Now, (1) This signified a noble neglect of the body and the ease and ornament of it, which became those who, being separated to God, ought to be wholly taken up with their souls, to secure their peace and beauty. (2) Some observe that long hair is spoken of as a badge of subjection (1 Cor. xi. 5, &c.); so that the long hair of the Nazarites denoted their subjection to God, and their putting themselves under his dominion.

3. They must not come near any dead body, *v.* 6, 7.

4. All *the days of their separation* they must be *holy to the Lord, v.* 8.

III. The provision that was made for the cleansing of a Nazarite, if he happened unavoidably to contract a ceremonial pollution by the touch of a dead body. He must be purified from the ceremonial pollution he had contracted, as others must, upon the seventh day, *v.* 9. Nay, more was required for the purifying of the Nazarite than of any other person that had touched a dead body; he must bring a sin-offering and a burnt-offering, and an atonement must be *made for him, v.* 10, 11. This teaches us that sins of infirmity, and the faults we are overtaken in by surprise, must be seriously repented of, and that an application must be made of the virtue of Christ's sacrifice to our souls for the forgiveness of them every day, 1 John ii. 1, 2.

IV. The law for the solemn discharge of a Nazarite from his vow, when he had completed the time he

JAMIESON, FAUSSET, BROWN

CHAPTER 6

Vss. 1-22. THE LAW OF THE NAZARITE IN HIS SEPARATION. **2-6. When either man or woman . . . shall vow a vow of a Nazarite**—i.e., "a separated one," from a Hebrew word, to separate. It was used to designate a class of persons who, under the impulse of extraordinary piety and with a view to higher degrees of religious improvement, voluntarily renounced the occupations and pleasures of the world to dedicate themselves unreservedly to the divine service. The vow might be taken by either sex, provided they had the disposal of themselves (ch. 30:4), and for a limited period—usually a month or a lifetime (Judg. 13:5; 16:17). We do not know, perhaps, the whole extent of abstinence they practised.

But they separated themselves from three things in particular— viz., from wine, and all the varieties of vinous produce; from the application of a razor to their head, allowing their hair to grow; and from pollution by a dead body. The reasons of the self-restrictions are obvious. The use of wine tended to inflame the passions, intoxicate the brain, and create a taste for luxurious indulgence. The cutting off the hair being a recognized sign of uncleanness (Lev. 14:8, 9), its unpolled luxuriance was a symbol of the purity he professed. Besides, its extraordinary length kept him in constant remembrance of his vow, as well as stimulated others to imitate his pious example. Moreover, contact with a dead body, disqualifying for the divine service, the Nazarite carefully avoided such a cause of unfitness, and, like the high priest, did not assist at the funeral rites of his nearest relatives, preferring his duty to God to the indulgence of his strongest natural affections.

8-11 if any man die suddenly by him, and he hath defiled the head of his consecration—Cases of sudden death might occur to make him contract pollution; and in such circumstances he was required, after shaving his head, to make the prescribed offerings necessary for the removal of ceremonial defilement (Lev. 15: 13; ch. 19:11). But by the terms of this law an accidental defilement vitiated the whole of his previous observances, and he was required to begin the period of his Nazaritism afresh. But even this full completion did not supersede the necessity of a sin offering at the close. Sin mingles with our best and holiest performances, and the blood of sprinkling is necessary to procure acceptance to us and our services.

ADAM CLARKE

CHAPTER 6

2. *When either man or woman shall separate* The word *nazir,* from *nazar,* to *separate,* signifies merely a separated person, i.e., one peculiarly devoted to the service of God by being separated from all service employments. From the Nazarites sprang the Rechabites, from the Rechabites the Essenes, from the Essenes the Anchorites or Hermits, and in imitation of those the different monastic orders.

3. *No vinegar of wine. Chomets* signifies fermented wine, and is probably used here to signify wine of a strong body, or any highly intoxicating liquor.

5. *There shall no razor come upon his head.* The vow of the Nazarite consisted in the following particulars: (1) He consecrated himself in a very especial and extraordinary manner to God. (2) This was to continue for a certain season, probably never less than a whole year, that he might have a full growth of hair to "burn in the fire which is under the sacrifice of the peace offerings," v. 18. (3) During the time of his separation, or *nazarate,* he drank no wine nor strong drink; nor used any vinegar formed from any inebriating liquor, nor ate the flesh or dried grapes, nor tasted even the kernels or husks of anything that had grown upon the vine. (4) He never shaved his head, but let his hair grow, as the proof of his being in this separated state, and under vows of peculiar austerity. (5) He never touched any dead body, nor did any of the last offices, even to his nearest kin; but was considered as the priests, who were wholly taken up with the service of God, and regarded nothing else. (6) All the days of his separation he was holy, v. 8. During the whole time he was to be incessantly employed in religious acts.

7. *The consecration of his God is upon his head.* Literally, "The separation of his God is upon his head"; meaning his hair, which was the proof and emblem of his separation.

10. *Two turtles, or two young pigeons.* The same kind of offering made by him who had an issue, Lev. xv. 14, etc.

MATTHEW HENRY

fixed to himself. The Jews say that the time of a Nazarite's vow could not be less than thirty days; and if a man said, "I will be a Nazarite but for two days," yet he was bound for thirty; but it should seem Paul's vow was for only seven days (Acts xxi. 27). When the time of the vowed separation was out, he was to be made free, 1. Publicly, *at the door of the tabernacle* (*v.* 13). 2. It was to be done with sacrifices, *v.* 14. He must bring one of each sort of the instituted offerings. (1) A burnt-offering. (2) A sin-offering. (3) A peace-offering, in thankfulness to God, who had enabled him to fulfil his vow. (4) To these were added the meat-offerings and drink-offerings. (5) Part of the peace-offering, with a cake and wafer, was to be waved for a wave-offering (*v.* 19, 20); and this was a gratuity to the priest, who had it for his pains, after it had been first presented to God. (6) Besides all this, he might bring his free-will offerings, *such as his hand shall get*, *v.* 21. And, to grace the solemnity, it was common upon this occasion to have their friends to be at *charges with them*, Acts xxi. 24. *Lastly*, One ceremony more was appointed, which was like the cancelling of the bond when the condition is performed, and that was the *cutting off of his hair*, which had been suffered to grow all the time of his being a Nazarite, and burning it in the fire over which the peace-offerings were boiling, *v.* 18. This intimated that his full performance of his vow was acceptable to God in Christ the great sacrifice, and not otherwise.

Verses 22–27

Here, I. The priests, among other good offices which they were to do, are appointed solemnly to bless the people in the *name of the Lord*, *v.* 23. Though the priest of himself could do no more than beg a blessing, yet being an intercessor by office, and doing that in his name who commands the blessing, the prayer carried with it a promise, and he pronounced it as one having authority with his hands lifted up and his face towards the people. Now, 1. This was a type of Christ's errand into the world, which was to *bless us* (Acts iii. 26), as the high priest of our profession. 2. It was a pattern to gospel ministers, the masters of assemblies, who are in like manner to dismiss their solemn assemblies with a blessing. The same that are God's mouth to his people, to teach and command them, are his mouth likewise to bless them.

II. A form of blessing is here prescribed them. Here observe, 1. That the blessing is commanded upon each particular person: *The Lord bless thee*. If we take the law to ourselves, we may take the blessing to ourselves, as if our names were inserted. 2. That the name *Jehovah* is three times repeated in it, and each with a different accent in the original. 3. That the favour of God is all in all in this blessing, for that is the fountain of all good. (1) *The Lord bless thee!* (2) *The Lord make his face shine upon thee*, alluding to the shining of the sun upon the earth, to enlighten and comfort it, and to renew the face of it. (3) *The Lord lift up his countenance upon thee.* This is to the same purport with the former, and it seems to allude to the smiles of a father upon his child, or of a man upon his friend whom he takes pleasure in. 4. That the fruits of this favour conveyed by this blessing are protection, pardon, and peace. (1) Protection from evil, *v.* 24. The Lord *keep thee.* (2) Pardon of sin, *v.* 25. The Lord be *gracious* or *merciful*, unto thee. (3) Peace (*v.* 26), including all that good which goes to make up a complete happiness.

III. God here promises to ratify and confirm the blessing: *They shall put my name upon the children of Israel*, *v.* 27.

CHAPTER 7

Verses 1–9

The offering of the princes to the service of the tabernacle.

I. When it was; not till it was *fully set up*, *v.* 1. When all things were done both about the tabernacle itself, and the camp of Israel which surrounded it.

JAMIESON, FAUSSET, BROWN

13-20. when the days of his separation are fulfilled, etc.—On the accomplishment of a limited vow of Nazaritism, Nazarites might cut their hair wherever they happened to be (Acts 18:18); but the hair was to be carefully kept and brought to the door of the sanctuary. Then after the presentation of sin offerings and burnt offerings, it was put under the vessel in which the peace offerings were boiled; and the priest, taking the shoulder (Lev. 7:32), when boiled, and a cake and wafer of the meat offering, put them on the hands of the Nazarites to wave before the Lord, as a token of thanksgiving, and thus released them from their vow.

23-27. THE FORM OF BLESSING THE PEOPLE. **Speak unto Aaron and unto his sons, saying, On this wise ye shall bless the congregation of Israel,** etc. —This passage records the solemn benediction which God appointed for dismissing the people at the close of the daily service. The repetition of the name "Lord" or "Jehovah" three times, expresses the great mystery of the Godhead—three persons, and yet one God. The expressions in the separate clauses correspond to the respective offices of the Father, to "bless and keep us"; of the Son, to be "gracious to us"; and of the Holy Ghost, to "give us peace." And because the benediction, though pronounced by the lips of a fellow man, derived its virtue, not from the priest but from God, the encouraging assurance was added, "I the Lord will bless them."

CHAPTER 7

Vss. 1-89. THE PRINCES' OFFERINGS. **1. the day that Moses had fully set up the tabernacle**— Those who take the word "day" as literally pointing to the exact date of the completion of the tabernacle, are under a necessity of considering the sacred narrative as disjointed, and this portion of the history from the seventh to the eleventh chapters as out of its place—the chronology requiring that it should have immediately followed the fortieth chapter of Exodus, which relates that the tabernacle was reared on the first day of the first month of the second year. But that the term "day" is used in a loose and indeterminate sense, as synonymous with *time*, is evident from the fact that not one day but several days were occupied with the transactions about to de described. So that this chapter stands in its proper place in the order of the history; after the tabernacle and its instruments (the altar and its

ADAM CLARKE

18. *Shall take the hair . . . and put it in the fire.* The hair was permitted to grow for this purpose; and as the Nazarite was a kind of sacrifice, offered to God through the whole term of his *nazarate* or separation, and no human flesh or blood could be offered on the altar of the Lord, he offered his hair at the conclusion of his separation, as a sacrifice—that hair which was the token of his complete subjection to the Lord and which was now considered as the Lord's property.

23. *On this wise ye shall bless the children of Israel.* The prayer which God makes for His followers and puts into their mouth we are sure must be right; and to it, when sincerely, faithfully, and fervently offered, we may confidently expect an answer. If He condescended to give us a form of blessings or a form of prayer, we may rest assured that He will accept what He himself has made. This consideration may produce great confidence in them who come with either prayer or praise to the throne of grace, both of which should be, as far as circumstances will admit, in the very words of Scripture; for we can readily attach a consequence to the words of God which we shall find difficult to attach to the best ordered words of men.

24. *The Lord bless thee.* There are three forms of blessing here, any or all of which the priests might use on any occasion. The following is a verbal translation:

May Jehovah bless thee and preserve thee!
May Jehovah cause His faces to shine upon thee, and be gracious unto thee!
May Jehovah lift up His faces upon thee, and may He put prosperity unto thee!

CHAPTER 7

1. *On the day that Moses had fully set up the tabernacle.* The transactions mentioned in this chapter took place on the second day of the second month of the second year after their departure from Egypt; and the proper place of this account is immediately after the tenth chapter of Leviticus.

MATTHEW HENRY

II. Who it was that offered: *The princes of Israel, heads of the house of their fathers*, v. 2.

III. What was offered: six waggons, with each of them a yoke of oxen to draw them, v. 3.

JAMIESON, FAUSSET, BROWN

vessels) had been anointed (Lev. 8:10), the Levites separated to the sacred service—the numbering of the people, and the disposal of the tribes about the tabernacle, in a certain order, which was observed by the princes in the presentation of their offerings. This would fix the period of the imposing ceremonial described in this chapter about a month after the completion of the tabernacle. **2, 3. the princes of Israel . . . brought their offering before the Lord**—The finishing of the sacred edifice would, it may well be imagined, be hailed as an auspicious occasion, diffusing great joy and thankfulness throughout the whole population of Israel. But the leading men, not content with participating in the general expression of satisfaction, distinguished themselves by a movement, which, while purely spontaneous, was at the same time so appropriate in the circumstances and so equal in character, as indicates it to have been the result of concerted and previous arrangement. It was an offer of the means of carriage, suitable to the migratory state of the nation in the wilderness, for transporting the tabernacle from place to place. In the pattern of that sacred tent exhibited on the mount, and to which its symbolic and typical character required a faithful adherence, no provision had been made for its removal in the frequent journeyings of the Israelites. That not being essential to the plan of the divine architect, it was left to be accomplished by voluntary liberality; and whether we look to the judicious character of the gifts, or to the public manner in which they were presented, we have unmistakable evidence of the pious and patriotic feelings from which they emanated and the extensive interest the occasion produced. The offerers were "the princes of Israel, heads of the house of their fathers," and the offering consisted of six covered wagons or little cars, and twelve oxen, two of the princes being partners in a wagon, and each furnishing an ox. **4, 5. The Lord spake unto Moses, saying, Take it of them, that they may be to do the service of the tabernacle of the congregation**—They exhibited a beautiful example to all who are great in dignity and in wealth, to be foremost in contributing to the support and in promoting the interests of religion. The strictness of the injunctions Moses had received to adhere with scrupulous fidelity to the divine model of the tabernacle probably led him to doubt whether he was at liberty to act in this matter without orders. God, however, relieved him by declaring His acceptance of the freewill offerings, as well as by giving instructions as to the mode of their distribution among the Levites. It is probable that in doing so, He merely sanctioned the object for which they were offered, and that the practical wisdom of the offerers had previously determined that they should be distributed "unto the Levites, to every man according to his service"; i.e., more or fewer were assigned to each of the Levitical divisions, as their department of duty seemed to require. This divine sanction it is of great importance to notice, as establishing the principle, that while in the great matters of divine worship and church government we are to adhere faithfully to the revealed rule of faith and duty, minor arrangements respecting them may be lawfully made, according to the means and convenience of God's people in different places. "There is a great deal left to human regulation—appendages of undoubted convenience, and which it were as absurd to resist on the ground that an express warrant cannot be produced for them, as to protest against the convening of the people to divine service, because there is no Scripture for the erection and ringing of a church bell" [CHALMERS]. **6-9. Moses took the wagons and the oxen**—The *Heb.* word seems to be fairly rendered by the word "wagons." Wheel carriages of some kind are certainly intended; and as they were covered, the best idea we can form of them is, that they bore some resemblance to our covered wagons. That wheel carriages were anciently used in Egypt, and in what is now Asiatic Turkey, is attested, not only by history, but by existing sculptures and paintings. Some of these the Israelites might have brought with them at their departure; and others, the skilful artisans, who did the mechanical work of the tabernacle, could easily have constructed, according to models with which they had been familiar. Each wagon was drawn by two oxen, and a greater number does not seem to have been employed on any of the different occasions mentioned in Scripture. Oxen seem to have been generally used for draught in ancient times among other nations as well as the Hebrews; and they continue still to be employed in dragging the few carts which are in use in some parts of Western Asia [KITTO]. **gave them unto the Levites**

ADAM CLARKE

KEIL–DELITZSCH:

This presentation took place at the time when Moses, after having completed the erection of the tabernacle, anointed and sanctified the dwelling and the altar, together with their furniture (Lev. 8:10, 11). Chronologically considered, this ought to have been noticed after Lev. 8:10. But in order to avoid interrupting the connection of the Sinaitic laws, it is introduced for the first time at this point, and placed at the head of the events which immediately preceded the departure of the people from Sinai, because these gifts consisted in part of materials that were indispensably necessary for the transport of the tabernacle during the march through the desert. Moreover, there was only an interval of at the most forty days between the anointing of the tabernacle, which commenced after the first day of the first month (cf. Ex. 40:16 and Lev. 8:10), and lasted eight days, and the departure from Sinai, on the twentieth day of the second month (10:11), and from this we have to deduct six days for the Passover, which took place before their departure (9:1); and it was within this period that the laws and ordinances from Lev. 11 to Num. 6 had to be published and the dedicatory offerings to be presented. Now, as the presentation itself was distributed, according to verse 11, over twelve or thirteen days, we may very well assume that it did not entirely precede the publication of the laws referred to, but was carried on in part contemporaneously with it. The presentation of the dedicatory gifts of one tribe-prince might possibly occupy only a few hours of the day appointed for the purpose; and the rest of the day, therefore, might very conveniently be made use of by Moses for publishing the laws. In this case the short space of a month and a few days would be amply sufficient for everything that took place.

—*Commentary on the Old Testament*

5. *According to his service*. That is, distribute them among the Levites as they may need them, giving most to those who have the heaviest burdens to bear.

MATTHEW HENRY

IV. How the offering was disposed of, and what use was made of it: the waggons and oxen were given to the Levites, to be used in carrying the tabernacle. 1. The Gershonites, that had the light carriage, the curtains and hangings, had but two waggons, and two yoke of oxen (*v.* 7). 2. The Merarites, that had the heavy carriage, and that which was most unwieldy, the boards, pillars, sockets, &c., had four waggons, and four yoke of oxen allotted them (*v.* 8). Observe here, How God wisely and graciously ordered the most strength to those that had the most work. Each had waggons *according to their service.*

3. The Kohathites, that had the most sacred carriage, had no waggons at all, because they were to carry their charges upon their shoulders (*v.* 9), with a particular care and veneration.

Verses 10–89

We have here an account of the great solemnity of dedicating the altars, both that of burnt-offerings and that of incense; they had been sanctified before, when they were anointed (Lev. viii. 10, 11), but now they were handselled, as it were, by the princes, with their free-will offerings. They began the use of them with rich presents, great expressions of joy and gladness, and extraordinary respect to those tokens of God's presence with them. Now observe here,

I. That the princes and great men were first and forwardest in the service of God. It is justly expected that those who have more than others should do more good than others with what they have, else they are unfaithful stewards, and will not make up their *account with joy.*

II. The offerings they brought were very rich and valuable.

1. They brought some things to remain for standing service, twelve large silver dishes, each about sixty ounces weight, as many large silver cups, or bowls, of about thirty-five ounces—the former to be used for the meat-offerings, the latter for the drink-offerings—the former for the flesh of the sacrifices, the latter for the blood. The golden spoons being filled with incense were intended, it is probable, for the service of the golden altar, for both the altars were anointed at the same time.

2. They brought some things to be used immediately, offerings of each sort. Hereby they signified their thankful acceptance of, and cheerful submission to, all those laws concerning the sacrifices which God had lately by Moses delivered to them. And, though it was a time of joy and rejoicing, yet it is observable that still in the midst of their sacrifices we find a *sin-offering.*

3. They brought their offerings each on a separate day, in the order that they had been lately put into, so that the solemnity lasted twelve days.

4. All their offerings were exactly the same, though it is probable that neither the princes nor the tribes were all alike rich; but thus it was intimated that all the tribes of Israel had an equal share in the altar, and an equal interest in the sacrifices that were offered upon it.

5. Nahshon, the prince of the tribe of Judah, offered first, because God had given that tribe the first post of honour in the camp; and the rest of the tribes acquiesced.

JAMIESON, FAUSSET, BROWN

—The principle of distribution was natural and judicious. The Merarites had twice the number of wagons and oxen appropriated to them that the Gershonites had, obviously because, while the latter had charge only of the coverings and hangings (the light but precious and richly-embroidered drapery) the former were appointed to transport all the heavy and bulky materials (the boards, bars, pillars, and sockets) in short, all the larger articles of furniture. Whoever thinks only of the enormous weight of metal, the gold, silver, brass, etc., that were on the bases, chapiters, and pillars, etc., will probably come to the conclusion that four wagons and eight oxen were not nearly sufficient for the conveyance of so vast a load. Besides, the Merarites were not very numerous, as they amounted only to 3200 men from thirty years and upward; and, therefore, there is reason to suppose that a much greater number of wagons would afterwards be found necessary, and be furnished, than were given on this occasion [CALMET]. Others, who consider the full number of wagons and oxen to be stated in the sacred record, suppose that the Merarites may have carried many of the smaller things in their hands—the sockets, for instance, which being each a talent weight, was one man's burden (II Kings 5:23). The Kohathites had neither wheeled vehicles nor beasts of burden assigned them, because, being charged with the transport of the furniture belonging to the holy place, the sacred worth and character of the vessels entrusted to them (see on ch. 4:15) demanded a more honorable mode of conveyance. These were carried by those Levites shoulder-high. Even in this minute arrangement every reflecting reader will perceive the evidence of divine wisdom and holiness; and a deviation from the prescribed rule of duty led, in one recorded instance, to a manifestation of holy displeasure, calculated to make a salutary and solemn impression (II Sam. 6:6-13). **10, 11. the princes offered for dedicating of the altar,** etc.—"Altar" is here used in the singular for the plural; for it is evident, from the kind of offerings, that the altars of burnt offering and incense are both referred to. This was not the first or proper dedication of those altars, which had been made by Moses and Aaron some time before. But it might be considered an additional *dedication*—those offerings being the first that were made for particular persons or tribes. **They shall offer . . ., each prince on his day,** etc.—Eastern princes were accustomed anciently, as they are in Persia still on a certain yearly festival, to sit upon their thrones in great state, when the princes and nobles, from all parts of their dominions, appear before them with tributary presents, which form a large proportion of their royal revenue. And in the offering of all gifts or presents to great personages, every article is presented singly and with ostentatious display. The tabernacle being the palace of their great King, as well as the sanctuary of their God, the princes of Israel may be viewed, on the occasion under notice, as presenting their tributary offerings, and in the same manner of successive detail, which accords with the immemorial usages of the East. A day was set apart for each, as much for the imposing solemnity and splendor of the ceremony, as for the prevention of disorder and hurry; and it is observable that, in the order of offering, regard was paid to priority not of birth, but of rank and dignity as they were ranked in the camp—beginning at the east, proceeding to the south, then to the west, and closing with the north, according to the course of the sun. **12-17. He that offered his offering the first day was Nahshon . . . of the tribe of Judah,** etc.—Judah having had the precedence assigned to it, the prince or head of that tribe was the first admitted to offer as its representative; and his offering, as well as that of the others, is thought, from its costliness, to have been furnished not from his own private means, but from the general contributions of each tribe. Some parts of the offering, as the animals for sacrifice, were for the ritual service of the day, the peace offerings being by much the most numerous, as the princes and some of the people joined with the priests afterwards in celebrating the occasion with festive rejoicing. Hence the feast of dedication became afterwards an anniversary festival. Other parts of the offering were intended for permanent use, as utensils necessary in the service of the sanctuary; such as an immense platter and bowl (Exod. 25:29). Being of silver, they were to be employed at the altar of burnt offering, or in the court, not in the holy place, all the furniture of which was of solid or plated gold; and there was a golden spoon, the contents of which show its destination to have been the altar of incense. The word rendered "spoon" means a

ADAM CLARKE

7. *Two wagons . . . unto the sons of Gershon.* The Gershonites carried only the curtains, coverings, and hangings, chap. iv. 25. And although this was a cumbersome carriage, and they needed the wagons, yet it was not a heavy one.

8. *Four wagons . . . unto the sons of Merari.* Because they had the boards, bars, pillars, and sockets of the Tabernacle to carry, chap. iv. 31-32, therefore they had as many more wagons as the Gershonites.

9. *Unto the sons of Kohath he gave none.* Because they had the charge of the ark, table, candlestick, altars, etc., chap. iv. 5-15, which were to be carried upon their shoulders; for those sacred things must not be drawn by beasts.

10. *And the princes offered.* Every prince or chief offered in the behalf, and doubtless at the expense, of his whole tribe.

13. *One silver charger. Kaarath,* a "dish," or deep bowl, in which they kneaded the paste. *One silver bowl. Mizrak,* a "bason," to receive the blood of the sacrifice in.

14. *One spoon. Caph,* a "censer," on which they put the incense.

MATTHEW HENRY

6. Though the offerings were all the same, yet the account of them is repeated at large for each tribe, in the same words. We find Christ taking particular notice of what was cast into the treasury, Mark xii. 41. Though what is offered be but little, yet if it be according to our ability it shall be recorded.

7. The sum total is added at the foot of the account (*v.* 84-88), to show how much God was pleased with the mention of his freewill-offerings, and what a great deal they amounted to in the whole, when every prince brought in his quota!

8. God signified his gracious acceptance of these presents that were brought him, by speaking familiarly to Moses, as a man speaks to his friend, from off the mercy-seat (*v.* 89, *ch.* xii. 8); and in speaking to him he did in effect speak to all Israel, showing them this token for good, Ps. ciii. 7.

JAMIESON, FAUSSET, BROWN

hollow cup, in the shape of a hand, with which the priests on ordinary occasions might lift a quantity from the incense-box to throw on the altar-fire, or into the censers; but on the ceremonial on the day of the annual atonement no instrument was allowed but the high priest's own hands (Lev. 16:12). **18. On the second day Nethaneel . . . prince of Issachar, did offer**—This tribe being stationed on the right side of Judah, offered next through its representative; then Zebulun, which was on the left side; and so on in orderly succession, every tribe making the same kind of offering and in the same amount, to show that, as each was under equal obligation, each rendered an equal tribute. Although each offering made was the same in quantity as well as quality, a separate notice is given of each, as a separate day was appointed for the presentation, that equal honor might be conferred on each, and none appear to be overlooked or slighted. And as the sacred books were frequently read in public, posterity, in each successive age, would feel a livelier interest in the national worship, from the permanent recognition of the offerings made by the ancestors of the respective tribes. But while this was done in one respect, as subjects offering tribute to their king, it was in another respect, a purely religious act. The vessels offered were for a sacrificial use—the animals brought were clean and fit for sacrifice, both symbolically denoting, that while God was to dwell among them as their Sovereign, they were a holy people, who by this offering dedicated themselves to God. **48. On the seventh day**—Surprise has been expressed by some that this work of presentation was continued on the Sabbath. But assuming that the seventh day referred to was a Sabbath (which is uncertain), the work was of a directly religious character, and perfectly in accordance with the design of the sacred day. **84-88. This was the dedication of the altar**—The inspired historian here sums up the separate items detailed in the preceding narrative, and the aggregate amount is as follows: 12 silver chargers, each weighing 130 shekels = 1560; 12 silver bowls, each 70 shekels = 840: total weight. A silver charger at 130 shekels, reduced to troy weight, made 75 oz., 9 dwts., 168.31 gr.; and a silver bowl at 70 shekels amounts to 40 oz., 12 dwts., 2121.31 gr. The total weight of the 12 chargers is therefore 905 oz., 16 dwts., 33.11 gr., and that of the 12 bowls 487 oz., 14 dwts., 204.31 gr.; making the total weight of silver vessels 1393 oz., 10 dwts., 237.31 gr. with an approximate value of $1200. The 12 golden spoons, allowing each to be 5 oz., 16 dwts., 3.31 gr., would have a value of about $1000. All this would make a grand total of about $2200. Besides these the offerings comprised 12 bullocks, 12 rams, 12 lambs, 24 goats, 60 rams, 60 he-goats, 60 lambs—amounting in all to 240. So large a collection of cattle offered for sacrifice on one occasion proves both the large flocks of the Israelites and the abundance of pastures which were then, and still are, found in the valleys that lie between the Sinaitic Mountains. All travellers attest the luxuriant verdure of those extensive wadies; and that they were equally or still more rich in pasture anciently, is confirmed by the numerous flocks of the Amalekites, as well as of Nabal, which were fed in the wilderness of Paran (I Sam. 15:9). **89. And when Moses was gone into the tabernacle of the congregation to speak with him**—As a king gives private andience to his minister, so special license was granted to Moses, who, though not a priest, was admitted into the sanctuary to receive instructions from his heavenly King as occasion demanded. **then he heard the voice of one speaking to him**—Though standing on the outer side of the veil, he could distinctly hear it, and the mention of this circumstance is important as the fulfilment, at the dedication of the tabernacle, of a special promise made by the Lord Christ Himself, the Angel of the Covenant, commanding its erection (Exod. 25:22). It was the reward of Moses' zeal and obedience; and, in like manner, to all who love Him and keep His commandments He will manifest Himself (John 14:21).

ADAM CLARKE

48. *On the seventh day.* Both Jewish and Christian writers have been surprised that this work of offering went forward on the seventh day, which they suppose to have been a Sabbath, as well as on the other days. But (1) There is no absolute proof that this seventh day of offering was a Sabbath. (2) Were it even so, could the people be better employed than in thus consecrating themselves and their services to the Lord?

72. *On the eleventh day.* The Hebrew form of expression, here and in the seventy-eighth verse, has something curious in it. *Beyom ashtey asar yom,* "In the day, the first and tenth day"; *beyom sheneym asar yom,* "In the day, two and tenth day." But this is the idiom of the language, and to an original Hebrew our almost anamalous words eleventh and twelfth, by which we translate the original, would appear as strange as his, literally translated, would appear to us. In reckoning after twelve, it is easy to find out the composition of the words thirteen, as three and ten, fourteen, four and ten, and so on; but eleven and twelve bear scarcely any analogy to ten and one, and ten and two, which nevertheless they intend.

84. *This was the dedication of the altar, in the day.* Meaning here the time in which it was dedicated; for as each tribe had a whole day for its representative or prince to present the offerings it had provided, consequently the dedication, in which each had his day, must have lasted twelve days. The words therefore, in this text, refer to the last day or twelfth, in which this dedication was completed.

88. *After that it was anointed.* By the anointing the altar was consecrated to God; by this dedication it was solemnly appointed to that service for which it had been erected.

89. *To speak with him.* To confer with God, and to receive farther discoveries of His will. *He heard the voice of one speaking unto him.* Though Moses saw no similitude, but only heard a voice, yet he had the fullest proof of the presence as well as of the being of the Almighty. In this way God chose to manifest himself during that dispensation. *The mercy seat.* See the note on Exod. xxv. 17. As God gave oracular answers from this place, and spoke to Moses as it were face-to-face, hence the place was called the "oracle," *debir,* or "speaking place," from *dabar,* "he spoke," 1 Kings vi. 23. And as this *mercy seat* represented our blessed Redeemer, so the apostle says that "God, who at sundry times and in divers manners spake in time past unto the fathers by the prophets, hath in these last days spoken unto us by his Son," Heb. i. 1-2. Hence the *incarnated* Christ is the true *debir* or "oracle," in and by whom God speaks unto man.

CHAPTER 8

MATTHEW HENRY

Verses 1-4

Directions were given long before this for the making of the golden candlestick (Exod. xxv. 31), and it was made according to the pattern shown to Moses in the mount, Exod. xxxvii. 17. But now it was that the lamps were first ordered to be lighted, when other things began to be used. Observe, 1. Who must light the lamps; Aaron himself, he *lighted the*

JAMIESON, FAUSSET, BROWN

Vss. 1-4. HOW THE LAMPS ARE TO BE LIGHTED. **1. the Lord spake unto Moses**—The order of this chapter suggests the idea that the following instructions were given to Moses while he was within the tabernacle of the congregation, after the princes had completed their offering. But from the tenor of the instructions, it is more likely that they were given immediately after the Levites had been given

MATTHEW HENRY

lamps, *v.* 3. As the people's representative to God, he thus did the office of a servant in God's house, lighting his Master's candle. The scripture is *a light shining in a dark place*, 2 Pet. i. 19. Now the work of ministers is to light these lamps, by expounding and applying the word of God. The priest lighted the middle lamp from the fire of the altar, and the rest of the lamps he lighted one from another, which (says Mr. Ainsworth) signifies that the fountain of all light and knowledge is in Christ, who has the *seven spirits of God* figured by the *seven lamps of fire* (Rev. iv. 5), but that in the expounding of scripture one passage must borrow light from another. He also supposes that, *seven* being a number of perfection, by the seven branches of the candlestick is shown the full perfection of the scripture, which are able to make us wise to salvation. 2. To what end the lamps were lighted. They were not lighted like tapers in an urn, to burn to themselves, but to give light to the other side of the tabernacle, for therefore candles are lighted, Matt. v. 15. Therefore we have light, that we may give light.

Verses 5–26

We read before of the separating of the Levites from among the children of Israel when they were numbered, and the numbering of them by themselves (*ch.* iii. 6, 15), that they might be employed in the service of the tabernacle. Now here we have directions given for their solemn ordination (*v.* 6), and the performance of it, *v.* 20. All Israel must know that they took not this honour to themselves, but were called of God to it; nor was it enough that they were distinguished from their neighbours, but they must be solemnly devoted to God. Note, All that are employed for God must be dedicated to him, according as the degree of the employment is. Christians must be baptized, ministers must be ordained; we must first give ourselves unto the Lord, and then our services. Observe, in what method this was done:

I. The Levites must be cleansed, and were so. The rites and ceremonies of their cleansing were to be performed, 1. By themselves. Those must be clean that bear the vessels of the Lord. 2. By Moses. He must *sprinkle the water of purifying upon them*, which was prepared by divine direction. It is our duty to cleanse ourselves, and God's promise that he will cleanse us.

II. The Levites, being thus prepared, must be brought before the Lord in a solemn assembly of all Israel, and the *children of Israel* must *put their hands upon them* (*v.* 10), so transferring their interest in them and in their service (to which, as a part, the whole body of the people was entitled) to God and to his sanctuary. This imposition of hands by the children of Israel upon the Levites did not make them ministers of the sanctuary, but only signified the people's parting with that tribe out of their militia, and civil incorporations, in order to their being made ministers by Aaron, who was to offer them before the Lord.

III. Sacrifices were to be offered for them, a sin-offering first (*v.* 12), and then a burnt-offering, to make an *atonement for the Levites*. See here, 1. That we are all utterly unworthy and unfit to be admitted into and employed in the service of God, till atonement be made for sin, and thereby our peace made with God. 2. That it is by sacrifice, by Christ the great sacrifice, that we are reconciled to God, and made fit to be offered to him. It is by him that Christians are sanctified to the work of their Christianity, and ministers to the work of their ministry.

IV. The Levites themselves were *offered before the Lord for an offering of the children of Israel*, *v.* 11. Aaron gave them up to God, as being first given up by themselves, and by the children of Israel.

V. God here declares his acceptance of them: *The Levites shall be mine*, *v.* 14. All whom God owns he employs; angels themselves have their services.

VI. They are then given as a gift to Aaron and his sons (*v.* 19), yet so as that the benefit accrued to the children of Israel. 1. The Levites must act under the priests as attendants on them. Aaron offers them to God (*v.* 11), and then God gives them back to Aaron, *v.* 19. Our hearts, our children, our estates, are never more ours, more truly, more comfortably ours, than when we have offered them up to God. 2. They must act for the people. God's ministers, while they keep within the sphere of their office and conscientiously discharge the duty of it, must be looked upon as some of the most useful servants of their country.

VII. The time of their ministration is fixed. 1. They were to enter upon the service at twenty-five years old, *v.* 24. A very good age for ministers to begin their public work at. 2. They were to have a writ of ease at fifty years old; then they were to return

JAMIESON, FAUSSET, BROWN

to the priests (see on chaps. 3, 4), and that the record of these instructions had been postponed till the narrative of other transactions in the camp had been made [PATRICK]. **2. Speak unto Aaron,** etc.—The candlestick, which was made of one solid, massive piece of pure gold, with six lamps supported on as many branches, a seventh in the center surmounting the shaft itself (Exod. 25:31; 37:17), and completed according to the pattern shown in the mount, was now to be lighted, when the other things in the sanctuary began to be applied to religious service. It was Aaron's personal duty, as the servant of God, to light His house, which, being without windows, required the aid of lights (II Pet. 1:19.) And the course he was ordered to follow was first to light the middle lamp from the altar-fire, and then the other lamps from each other—a course symbolical of all the light of heavenly truth being derived from Christ, and diffused by His ministers throughout the world (Rev. 4:5). **the seven lamps shall give light over against the candlestick**—The candlestick stood close to the boards of the sanctuary, on the south side, in full view of the table of showbread on the north (Exod. 26:35), having one set of its lamps turned towards the east, and another towards the west; so that all parts of the tabernacle were thus lighted up.

5-22. THE CONSECRATION OF THE LEVITES. **Take the Levites . . . and cleanse them**—This passage describes the consecration of the Levites. Although the tribe was to be devoted to the divine service, their hereditary descent alone was not a sufficient qualification for entering on the duties of the sacred office. They were to be set apart by a special ceremony, which, however, was much simpler than that appointed for the priests; neither washing nor anointing, nor investiture with official robes, was necessary. Their purification consisted, along with the offering of the requisite sacrifices (Lev. 1:4; 3:2; 4:4), in being sprinkled by water mixed with the ashes of a red heifer (ch. 19:9), and shaved all over, and their clothes washed—a combination of symbolical acts which was intended to remind them of the mortification of carnal and wordly desires, and the maintenance of that purity in heart and life which became the servants of God. **9. thou shalt gather the whole assembly of the children of Israel together,** etc.—As it was plainly impossible that the whole multitude of the Israelites could do this, a select portion of them must be meant. This party, who laid their hands upon the Levites, are supposed by some to have been the first-born, who by that act, transferred their peculiar privilege of acting as God's ministers to the Levitical tribe; and by others, to have been the princes, who thus blessed them. It appears, from this passage, that the imposition of hands was a ceremony used in consecrating persons to holy offices in the ancient, as, from the example of our Lord and His apostles, it has been perpetuated in the Christian Church. **11-13. Aaron shall offer the Levites**—*Heb.*, as a wave offering; and it has been thought probable that the high priest, in bringing the Levites one by one to the altar, directed them to make some simple movements of their persons, analogous to what was done at the presentation of the wave offerings before the Lord. Thus were they first devoted as an offering to God, and by Him surrendered to the priests to be employed in His service. The consecration ceremonial was repeated in the case of every Levite who was taken (as was done at a later period) to assist the priests in the tabernacle and temple. (See on II Chron. 29:34.) **14. the Levites shall be mine**—i.e., exempt from all military duty or secular work—free from all pecuniary imposition and wholly devoted to the custody and service of the sanctuary. **15. after that, shall the Levites go in to do the service of the tabernacle of the congregation**—into the court, to assist the priests; and at removal into the tabernacle—i.e., into the door of it—to receive the covered furniture. **19. to make an atonement for the children of Israel,** etc.—to aid the priests in that expiatory work; or, as the words may be rendered, "to make redemption for" the Levites being exchanged or substituted for the first-born for this important end, that there might be a sanctified body of men appointed to guard the sanctuary, and the people not allowed to approach or presumptuously meddle with holy things, which would expose them to the angry judgments of Heaven. **24. from twenty-five years old,** etc.—cf. ch. 4:3). They entered on their work in their 25th year, as pupils and probationers, under the superintendence and direction of their senior brethren; and at 30 they were admited to the full discharge of their official functions. **25. from the age of fifty they shall**

ADAM CLARKE

2. *The seven lamps shall give light.* The whole seven shall be lighted at one time, that seven may be ever burning.

4. *This work of the candlestick.* See many curious particulars relative to this candlestick in the notes on Exod. xxv. 31 and 39. The candlestick itself was an emblem of the Church of Christ; the oil, of the graces and gifts of the Spirit of God; and the light, of those gifts and graces in action among men. See Rev. i. 12-20. God builds His Church and sends forth His Spirit to dwell in it, to sanctify and cleanse it, that it may be shown unto the world as His own workmanship. The seven lights in the candlesticks point out "the seven Spirits of God," the Holy Ghost being thus termed, Rev. iii. 1, from the variety and abundance of His gifts and influences; seven being used among the Hebrews to denote anything full, complete, and perfect. A candlestick or lamp without oil is of no use; oil not burning is of no use. So a church or society of religious people without the influence of the Holy Ghost are dead while they have a name to live; and if they have a measure of this light, and do not let it shine by purity of living and holy zeal before men, their religion is neither useful to themselves nor to others.

7. *Sprinkle water of purifying. Mey chattath,* "water of sin," or "water of the sin offering." As this purifying water was made by the ashes of the red heifer, cedarwood, hyssop, and scarlet; and the blood of the heifer itself was sprinkled seven times before the Tabernacle, Num. xix. 3-6; she may be considered as a proper sacrifice for sin, and consequently the water thus prepared be termed the "water of the sin offering." As the ashes were kept ready at hand for purifying from all legal pollutions, the preparation might be considered as a concentration of the essential properties of the sin offering, and might be resorted to at all times with comparatively little expense or trouble and no loss of time. As there were so many things by which legal pollution might be contracted, it was necessary to have always at hand, in all their dwellings, a mode of purifying at once convenient and inexpensive. We see from Heb. ix. 13-14 that these ashes, mingled with water and sprinkled on the unclean, and which sanctified to the purification of the flesh, were intended to typify the blood of Christ, which purges the "conscience from dead works to serve the living God," v. 14. For as without this sprinkling with the water of the sin offering the Levites were not fit to serve God in the wilderness, so without this sprinkling of the blood of Christ no conscience can be purged "from dead works to serve the living God." See the notes on chap. xix. 1-10.

10. *Shall put their hands upon the Levites.* It has been argued from this that the congregation had a part in the appointment of their own ministers, and that this was done by the imposition of hands. However that may be, it appears that what was done on this occasion meant no more than that the people gave up this whole tribe to God in place of their firstborn; and that by this act they bound themselves to provide for them who, because of their sacred service, could follow no secular work.

17. *For all the firstborn . . . are mine.* See the manner of redeeming the firstborn, chap. xviii. 6.

21. *And Aaron made an atonement for them.* Though the Levites had been most solemnly consecrated to the Lord's service, and though all legal washings and purifications were duly performed on the occasion, yet they could not approach God till an atonement had been made for them. How strange is it, after all these significations, of the will and purpose of God relative to man, that any priest or any people will attempt to draw nigh to God without an atonement! As sure as God hath spoken it, there is no entrance into the holiest but through the blood of Jesus, Heb. x. 19-20.

24. *From twenty and five years old.* See the note on chap. iv. 47, where the two terms of twenty-five and thirty years are reconciled.

MATTHEW HENRY

from the warfare, as the phrase is (*v.* 25), not cashiered with disgrace, but preferred rather to the rest which their age required, to be loaded with the honours of their office, as hitherto they had been with the burdens of it. If God's grace provide that men shall have ability according to their work, man's prudence should take care that men have work only according to their ability. The aged are most fit for trusts, and to keep the charge; the younger are most fit for work, and to do the service.

CHAPTER 9

Verses 1–14

Here we have,

I. An order given for the solemnization of the passover, the day twelvemonth after they came out of Egypt, on the fourteenth day of the first month of the second year, some days before they were numbered, for that was done in the beginning of the second month. Observe, 1. God gave particular orders for the keeping of this passover. And, for aught that appears, after this they kept no passover till they came to Canaan, Josh. v. 10. This was an early indication of the abolishing of the ceremonial institutions at last. The ordinance of the Lord's supper (which came in the room of the passover) was not thus intermitted or set aside in the first days of the Christian church, though those were days of greater difficulty and distress than Israel knew in the wilderness; nay, in the times of persecution, the Lord's supper was celebrated more frequently than afterwards. The Israelites in the wilderness could not forget their deliverance out of Egypt. All the danger was when they came to Canaan. However, because the first passover was celebrated in a hurry it was the will of God that at the return of the year, when they were more composed, and better acquainted with the divine law, they should observe it again, that their children might more distinctly understand the solemnity and the better remember it hereafter. 2. Moses faithfully transmitted to the people the orders given him, *v.* 4. 3. The people observed the orders given them, *v.* 5. They kept the passover even in the wilderness. Thus is God's Israel provided for in a desert.

II. Instructions given concerning those that were ceremonially unclean when they were to eat the passover. The law of the passover required every Israelite to eat of it. They must therefore wash, and then *compass God's altar*. Now, *Certain men were defiled by the dead body of a man* (*v.* 6), and they lay under that defilement seven days (*ch.* xix. 11), and in that time might not eat of the holy things, Lev. vii. 20. This was not their iniquity, but their infelicity.

The directions which God gave in this case, and in other similar cases, explanatory of the law of the passover. This disagreeable accident produced good laws. Those that happened to be ceremonially unclean at the time when the passover should be eaten were allowed to eat it that day month, when they were clean; so were those that happened to be *in a journey afar off*, *v.* 10, 11.

Verses 15–23

We have here the history of the cloud; not a natural history: *who knows the balancings of the clouds?* but a divine history of a cloud that was appointed to be the visible sign and symbol of God's presence with Israel.

I. When the tabernacle was finished this cloud, which before had hung on high over their camp, settled upon the tabernacle, and covered it, to show that God manifests his presence with his people in and by his ordinances.

II. That which appeared as a cloud by day appeared as a fire by night. And thus we are taught to *set God always before us*, and to see him near us both

JAMIESON, FAUSSET, BROWN

cease waiting upon the service thereof, etc.—i.e., on the laborious and exhausting parts of their work. **26. But shall minister with their brethren**—in the performance of easier and higher duties, instructing and directing the young, or superintending important trusts. "They also serve who only wait" [MILTON].

CHAPTER 9

Vss. 1-5. THE PASSOVER ENJOINED. **2. Let the children of Israel also keep the passover at his appointed season,** etc.—The date of this command to keep the passover in the wilderness was given shortly after the erection and consecration of the tabernacle and preceded the numbering of the people by a month. (Cf. vs. 1 with ch. 1:1, 2.) But it is narrated after that transaction in order to introduce the notice of a particular case, for which a law was provided to meet the occasion. This was the first observance of the passover since the exodus; and without a positive injunction, the Israelites were under no obligation to keep it till their settlement in the land of Canaan (Exod. 12:25). The anniversary was kept on the exact day of the year on which they, twelve months before, had departed from Egypt; and it was marked by all the peculiar rites—the he-lamb and the unleavened bread. The materials would be easily procured—the lambs from their numerous flocks and the meal for the unleavened bread, by the aid of Jethro, from the land of Midian, which was adjoining their camp (Exod. 3:1). But their girded loins, their sandalled feet, and their staff in their hand, being mere circumstances attending a hurried departure and not essential to the rite, were not repeated. It is supposed to have been the only observance of the feast during their 40 years' wandering; and Jewish writers say that, as none could eat the passover except they were circumcised (Exod. 12:43, 44, 48), and circumsion was not practised in the wilderness, there could be no renewal of the paschal solemnity.

A SECOND PASSOVER ALLOWED. Vss. 6-14. **there were certain men who were defiled by the dead body of a man**—To discharge the last offices to the remains of deceased relatives was imperative; and yet attendance on a funeral entailed ceremonial defilement, which led to exclusion from all society and from the camp for seven days. Some persons who were in this situation at the arrival of the first paschal anniversary, being painfully perplexed about the course of duty because they were temporarily disqualified at the proper season, and having no opportunity of supplying their want were liable to a total privation of all their privileges, laid their case before Moses. Jewish writers assert that these men were the persons who had carried out the dead bodies of Nadab and Abihu. **8. Moses said unto them, Stand still, and I will hear what the Lord will command concerning you**—A solution of the difficulty was soon obtained, it being enacted, by divine authority, that to those who might be disqualified by the occurrence of a death in their family circle or unable by distance to keep the passover on the anniversary day, a special license was granted of observing it by themselves on the same day and hour of the following month, under a due attendance to all the solemn formalities. (See on II Chron. 30:2.) But the observance was imperative on all who did not labor under these impediments. **14. if a stranger shall sojourn among you, and will keep the passover**—Gentile converts, or proselytes, as they were afterwards called, were admitted, if circumcised, to the same privileges as native Israelites, and were liable to excommunication if they neglected the passover. But circumcision was an indispensable condition; and whoever did not submit to that rite, was prohibited, under the sternest penalties, from eating the passover.

15-23. A CLOUD GUIDES THE ISRAELITES. **the cloud covered the tabernacle**—The inspired historian here enters on an entirely new subject, which might properly have formed a separate chapter, beginning at this verse and ending at vs. 29 of the following chapter [CALMET]. The cloud was a visible token of God's special presence and guardian care of the Israelites (Exod. 14:20; Ps. 105:39). It was easily distinguishable from all other clouds by its peculiar form and its fixed position; for from the day of the completion of the tabernacle it rested by day as a dark, by night as a fiery, column on that part of the sanctuary which contained the ark of the testimony (Lev. 16:2). **17. when the cloud was taken up**—

ADAM CLARKE

26. *To keep the charge, and shall do no service.* They shall no longer be obliged to perform any laborious service, but act as general directors and counsellors. Therefore they were to be near the camp, sing praises to God, and see that no stranger or unclean person was permitted to enter. So the Jews and many other persons have understood this place.

CHAPTER 9

1. *The Lord spake unto Moses.* The first fourteen verses of this chapter certainly refer to transactions that took place at the time of those mentioned in the commencement of this book, before the numbering of the people, and several learned men are of opinion that these fourteen verses should be referred back to that place. We have already met with instances where transpositions have very probably taken place, and it is not difficult to account for them. As in very early times writing was generally on leaves of the Egyptian flag *papyrus*, facts and transactions thus entered were very liable to be deranged; so that when afterwards a series was made up into a book, many transactions might be inserted in wrong places, and thus the exact chronology of the facts be greatly disturbed. This one consideration will account for several transpositions, especially in the Pentateuch, where they occur more frequently than in any other part of the sacred writings.

3. *According to all the rites of it.* See all those rites and ceremonies largely explained in the notes on Exodus xii.

7. *We are defiled by the dead body of a man.* It is probable that the defilement mentioned here was occasioned by assisting at the burial of some person—a work of both necessity and mercy.

This circumstance however gave rise to the ordinance delivered in verses 10-14, so that on particular occasions the Passover might be twice celebrated: (1) At its regular time, the fourteenth of the first month; (2) An extra time, the fourteenth of the second month. But the man who had no legal hinderance, and did not celebrate it on one or other of these times, was to be cut off from the people of God; and the reason given for this cutting off is that he brought not the offering of God in His appointed season—therefore "that man shall bear his sin," v. 13.

15. *The cloud covered the tabernacle.* See the whole account of this supernatural cloud largely explained, Exod. xiii. 21 and xl. 34-38.

MATTHEW HENRY

night and day. Something of the nature of that divine revelation which the Old Testament church was governed by might also be signified by these visible signs of God's presence, the cloud denoting the darkness and the fire the terror of that dispensation, in comparison with the more clear and comfortable discoveries God has made of his glory in the face of Jesus Christ.

III. This pillar of cloud and fire directed and determined all the motions, marches, and encampments, of Israel in the wilderness. And the guidance of this cloud is spoken of as signifying the guidance of the blessed Spirit. We are not now to expect such sensible tokens of the divine presence and guidance as this was, but the promise is sure to all God's spiritual Israel that he will *guide them by his counsel* (Ps. lxxiii. 24), *even unto death* (Ps. xlviii. 14), that all the children of God shall be *led by the Spirit of God* (Rom. viii. 14). In our affections and actions we must follow the direction of his word and Spirit; all the motions of our souls must be guided by the divine will; at the commandment of the Lord our hearts should always move and rest.

JAMIESON, FAUSSET, BROWN

i.e., rose to a higher elevation, so as to be conspicuous at the remotest extremities of the camp. That was a signal for removal; and, accordingly, it is properly called (vs. 18) "the commandment of the Lord." It was a visible token of the presence of God; and from it, as a glorious throne, He gave the order. So that its motion regulated the commencement and termination of all the journeys of the Israelites. (See on Exod. 14:19.) **19. when the cloud tarried long upon the tabernacle, . . . then Israel kept the charge of the Lord and journeyed not**—A desert life has its attractions, and constant movements create a passionate love of change. Many incidents show that the Israelites had strongly imbibed this nomad habit and were desirous of hastening to Canaan. But still the phases of the cloud indicated the command of God: and whatsoever irksomeness they might have felt in remaining long stationary in camp, "when the cloud tarried upon the tabernacle many days, they kept the charge of the Lord, and journeyed not." Happy for them had they always exhibited this spirit of obedience! and happy for all if, through the wilderness of this world, we implicitly follow the leadings of God's Providence and the directions of God's Word!

ADAM CLARKE

21. *Whether . . . by day or by night.* As the heat of the day is very severe in that same desert, the night season is sometimes chosen for the performance of a journey, though it is very likely that in the case of the Israelites this was seldom resorted to.

23. *Kept the charge of the Lord.* When we consider the strong disposition which this people ever testified to follow their own will in all things, we may be well surprised to find them, in these journeyings, so implicitly following the directions of God. There could be no trick or imposture here. Moses, had he been the most cunning of men, never could have imitated the appearances referred to in this chapter. The cloud, and everything in its motion, was so evidently supernatural that the people had no doubt of its being the symbol of the divine presence.

CHAPTER 10

Verses 1-10

We have here directions concerning the public notices that were to be given to the people upon several occasions by sound of trumpet. The trumpets were to be sounded for the *calling of assemblies*, *v.* 2.

Thus they are told to blow the trumpet in Zion for the calling of a solemn assembly together, to sanctify a fast, Joel ii. 15. But, that the trumpet might not *give an uncertain sound*, they are directed, if only the princes and elders were to meet, to blow but one of the trumpets; but, if the body of the people were to be called together, both trumpets must be sounded. For the *journeying of the camps*, to give notice when each squadron must move. When the trumpets were blown for this purpose, they must *sound an alarm* (*v.* 5), a broken, quavering, interrupted sound, which was proper to excite and encourage the minds of people in their marches against their enemies; whereas a continued equal sound was more proper for the calling of the assembly together (*v.* 7): yet when the people were called together to deprecate God's judgments we find an alarm sounded, Joel ii. 1. At the first sounding, Judah's squadron marched, at the second Reuben's, at the third Ephraim's, at the fourth Dan's, *v.* 5, 6.

For the animating and encouraging of their armies, when they went out in battle (*v.* 9).

For the solemnizing of their sacred feasts, *v.* 10. One of their feasts was called *a memorial of the blowing of trumpets*, Lev. xxiii. 23, &c. Holy work should be done with holy joy.

CHAPTER 10

Vss. 1-36. The Use of the Silver Trumpets. **2. Make thee two trumpets of silver**—These trumpets were of a long form, in opposition to that of the Egyptian trumpets, with which the people were convened to the worship of Osiris and which were curved like rams' horns. Those which Moses made, as described by Josephus and represented on the arch of Titus, were straight, a cubit or more in length, the tubes of the thickness of a flute. Both extremities bore a close resemblance to those in use among us. They were of solid silver—so as, from the purity of the metal, to give a shrill, distinct sound; and there were two of them, probably because there were only two sons of Aaron; but at a later period the number was greatly increased (Josh. 6:8; II Chron. 5:12). And although the camp comprehended 2,500,000 of people, two trumpets would be quite sufficient, for sound is conveyed easily through the pure atmosphere and reverberated strongly among the valleys of the Sinaitic hills. **3. when they shall blow with them**—There seem to have been signals made by a difference in the loudness and variety in the notes, suited for different occasions, and which the Israelites learned to distinguish. A simple uniform sound by both trumpets summoned a general assembly of the people; the blast of a single trumpet convoked the princes to consult on public affairs; notes of some other kind were made to sound an alarm, whether for journeying or for war. One alarm was the recognized signal for the eastern division of the camp (the tribes of Judah, Issachar, and Zebulun) to march; two alarms gave the signal for the southern to move; and, though it is not in our present *Hebrew* text, the Septuagint has, that on three alarms being sounded, those on the west; while on four blasts, those on the north decamped. Thus the greatest order and discipline were established in the Israelitish camp—no military march could be better regulated. **8. Thet sons of Aaron the priests shall blow with the trumpets,** etc.—Neither the Levites nor any in the common ranks of the people could be employed in this office of signal-giving. In order to attract greater attention and more faithful observance, it was reserved to the priests alone, as the Lord's ministers; and as anciently in Persia and other Eastern countries the alarm trumpets were sounded from the tent of the sovereign, so were they blown from the tabernacle, the visible residence of Israel's King. **9. If ye go to war**—In the land of Canaan, either when attacked by foreign invaders or when they went to take possession according to the divine promise, "ye [i.e., the priests] shall blow an alarm." This advice was accordingly acted upon (ch. 31:6; II Chron. 13:12); and in the circumstances it was an act of devout confidence in God. A solemn and religious act on the eve of a battle has often animated the hearts of those who felt they were engaged in a good and just cause; and so the blowing of the trumpet, being an ordinance of God, produced that effect on the minds of the Israelites. But more is meant by the words—viz., that God would, as it were, be aroused by the trumpet to bless with His presence and aid. **10. Also in the days of your gladness, and in your solemn days**—Festive and thanksgiving occasions were to be ushered in with the trumpets, as all feasts

CHAPTER 10

2. *Make thee two trumpets of silver.* As the trumpets were to be blown by the priests only, the sons of Aaron, there were only 2, because there were only 2 such persons to use them at this time, Eleazar and Ithamar. In the time of Joshua there were 7 trumpets used by the priests, but these were made, according to our text, of rams' horns, Josh. vi. 4. In the time of Solomon, when the priests had greatly increased, there were 120 priests sounding with trumpets, 2 Chron. v. 12. Josephus intimates that one of these trumpets was always used to call the nobles together, the other to assemble the people; see v. 4. It is possible that these trumpets were made of different lengths and wideness, and consequently they would emit different tones. Thus the sound itself would at once show which was the summons for the congregation, and which for the princes only. These trumpets were allowed to be emblematical of the sound of the gospel, and in this reference they appear to be frequently used.

5. *When ye blow an alarm. Teruah*, probably meaning "short, broken, sharp" tones, terminating with long ones, blown with both the trumpets at once.

6. *When ye blow an alarm the second time.* A single alarm, as above stated, was a signal for the eastward division to march; two such alarms, the signal for the south division; and probably three for the west division, and four for the north. It is more likely that this was the case than that a single alarm served for each, with a small interval between them.

9. *If ye go to war.* These trumpets shall be sounded for the purpose of collecting the people together, to deliberate about the war, and to implore the protection of God against their enemies.

Ye shall be remembered before the Lord. When you decamp, encamp, make war, and hold religious festivals, according to His appointment, which appointment shall be signified to you by the priests, who at the command of God, for such purposes, shall blow the trumpets, then you may expect both the presence and blessing of Jehovah in all that you undertake.

10. *In the day of your gladness.* On every festival the people shall be collected by the same means.

MATTHEW HENRY

Verses 11–28

Here is, I. A general account of the removal of the camp of Israel from Mount Sinai, before which mountain it had lain now about a year, in which time and place a great deal of memorable business was done. Observe, 1. The signal given (*v.* 11): *The cloud was taken up.* 2. The march begun: *They took their journey according to the commandment of the Lord*, and just as the cloud led them, *v.* 13. Some think that mention is thus frequently made in this and the foregoing chapter of the *commandment of the Lord*, guiding and governing them in all their travels, to obviate the calumny and reproach which were afterwards thrown upon Israel, that they tarried so long in the wilderness, because they had lost themselves there, and could not find the way out. Note, Those that have given up themselves to the direction of God's word and Spirit steer a steady course, even when they seem to be bewildered. 3. The place they rested in, after three days' march: They went *out of the wilderness of Sinai*, and rested *in the wilderness of Paran*.

II. A particular draft of the order of their march, according to the late model. 1. Judah's squadron marched first, *v.* 14–16. The leading standard, now lodged with that tribe, was an earnest of the sceptre which in David's time should be committed to it, and looked further to the captain of our salvation, of whom it was likewise foretold that *unto him should the gathering of the people be*. 2. Then came those two families of the Levites which were entrusted to carry the tabernacle. 3. Reuben's squadron marched forward next, taking place after Judah, *according to the commandment of the Lord*, *v.* 18–20. 4. Then the Kohathites followed with their charge, the sacred furniture of the tabernacle, *in the midst of the camp*, the safest and most honourable place, *v.* 21. 5. Ephraim's squadron followed next after the ark (*v.* 22–24). 6. Dan's squadron followed last, *v.* 25–27. It is called the *rearward*, or *gathering host*, of all the camps, because it gathered up all that were left behind; not the women and children (these we may suppose were taken care of by the heads of their families in their respective tribes), but all the unclean, the mixed multitude, and all that were weak and feeble, and cast behind in their march.

Verses 29–36

Here is, I. An account of what passed between Moses and Hobab, now upon this advance which the camp of Israel made towards Canaan. Some think that Hobab was the same with Jethro, Moses's father-in-law, and that the story, Exod. xviii., should come in here; it seems more probably that Hobab was the son of Jethro, and that when the father, being aged, went to his own land (Exod. xviii. 27), he left his son Hobab with Moses. Now this Hobab stayed contentedly with Israel while they encamped at Mount Sinai, near his own country; but, now that they were removing, he was for going back to his own country and kindred, and his father's house. Here is, 1. The kind invitation Moses gives him to go forward with them to Canaan, *v.* 29. Note, Those that are bound for the heavenly Canaan should invite and encourage all their friends to go along with them. 2. Hobab's inclination, and present resolution, to go back to his own country, *v.* 30. He was indeed a son of Abraham's loins (for the Midianites descended from Abraham by Keturah), but not an heir of Abraham's faith (Heb. xi. 8), else he would not have given Moses this answer. 3. The great importunity Moses used with him to alter his resolution, *v.* 31, 32. He urges, That he might be serviceable to them: *We are to encamp in the wilderness* (a country well known to Hobab), *and thou mayest be to us instead of eyes.*

We do not find any reply that Hobab here made to Moses, and therefore we hope that his silence gave consent, and he did not leave them. And we find (Judg. i. 16; 1 Sam. xv. 6) that his family was no loser by it.

II. An account of the communion between God and Israel in this removal. They left *the mount of the Lord* (*v.* 33), that Mount Sinai where they had seen his glory and heard his voice. But when they left the *mount of the Lord* they took with them the *ark of the covenant of the Lord*, by which their stated communion with God was to be kept up. For,

1. By it God did *direct their paths.* The ark of the covenant went before them, some think in *place*, at least in this removal; others think only in *influence.* The ark (that is, the God of the ark) is said to *search out a resting place* for them.

2. By it they did *in all ways acknowledge God.* Moses, as the mouth of the congregation, lifted up a prayer, both at the removing and at the resting of the ark; and it is an example to us to begin and end

JAMIESON, FAUSSET, BROWN

afterwards were (Ps. 81:3; II Chron. 29:27) to intimate the joyous and delighted feelings with which they engaged in the service of God. **11. It came to pass on the twentieth day of the second month in the second year,** etc.—The Israelites had lain encamped in Wady-Er-Rahah and the neighboring valleys of the Sinaitic range for the space of 11 months and 29 days. (Cf. Exod. 19:1.) Besides the religious purposes of the highest importance to which their long sojourn at Sinai was subservient, the Israelites, after the hardships and oppression of the Egyptian servitude, required an interval of repose and refreshment. They were neither physically nor morally in a condition to enter the lists with the warlike people they had to encounter before obtaining possession of Canaan. But the wondrous transactions at Sinai—the arm of Jehovah so visibly displayed in their favor—the covenant entered into, and the special blessings guaranteed, beginning a course of moral and religious education which moulded the character of this people—made them acquainted with their high destiny and inspired them with those noble principles of divine truth and righteousness which alone make a great nation. **12. wilderness of Paran**—It stretched from the base of the Sinaitic group, or from Et-Tyh, over that extensive plateau to the southwestern borders of Palestine. **13-27. the children of Israel took their journey . . . by the hand of Moses**—It is probable that Moses, on the breaking up of the encampment, stationed himself on some eminence to see the ranks defile in order through the embouchure of the mountains. The marching order is described (ch. 2); but, as the vast horde is represented here in actual migration, let us notice the extraordinary care that was taken for ensuring the safe conveyance of the holy things. In the rear of Judah, which, with the tribes of Issachar and Zebulun, led the van, followed the Gershonites and Merarites with the heavy and coarser materials of the tabernacle. Next in order were set in motion the flank divisions of Reuben and Ephraim. Then came the Kohathites, who occupied the center of the moving mass, bearing the sacred utensils on their shoulder. They were so far behind the other portions of the Levitical body that these would have time at the new encampment to rear the framework of the tabernacle before the Kohathites arrived. Last of all, Dan, with the associated tribes, brought up the rear of the immense caravan. Each tribe was marshalled under its prince or chief and in all their movements rallied around its own standard. **29. Hobab, the son of Raguel the Midianite**—called also Reuel (the same as Jethro). Hobab, the son of this Midianite chief and brother-in-law to Moses, seems to have sojourned among the Israelites during the whole period of their encampment at Sinai and now on their removal proposed returning to his own abode. Moses urged him to remain, both for his own benefit from a religious point of view, and for the useful services his nomad habits could enable him to render.

31. Leave us not, I pray thee . . . and thou mayest be to us instead of eyes—The earnest importunity of Moses to secure the attendance of this man, when he enjoyed the benefit of the directing cloud, has surprised many. But it should be recollected that the guidance of the cloud, though it showed the general route to be taken through the trackless desert, would not be so special and minute as to point out the places where pasture, shade, and water were to be obtained and which were often hid in obscure spots by the shifting sands. Besides, several detachments were sent off from the main body; the services of Hobab, not as a single Arab, but as a prince of a powerful clan, would have been exceedingly useful. **32. if thou go with us . . . what goodness the Lord will show unto us, the same will we do unto thee**—A strong inducement is here held out; but it seems not to have changed the young man's purpose, for he departed and settled in his own district. (See on Judg. 1:16; I Sam. 15:6.) **33. they departed . . . three days' journey**—the first day's progress being very small, about 18 or 20 miles. **ark of the covenant went before them**—It was carried in the center, and hence some eminent commentators think the passage should be rendered, "the ark went in their presence," the cloud above upon it being conspicuous in their eyes. But it is probable that the cloudy pillar, which, while stationary, rested upon the ark, preceded them in the march—as, when in motion at one time (Exod. 14:19) it is expressly said to have shifted its place.

ADAM CLARKE

11. *The twentieth day of the second month.* The Israelites had lain encamped in the wilderness of Sinai about eleven months and twenty days; compare Exod. xix. 1 with this verse. They now received the order of God to decamp, and proceeded towards the Promised Land; and therefore the Samaritan introduces at this place the words which we find in Deut. i. 6-8: "The Lord our God spake unto us in Horeb, saying, Ye have dwelt long enough in this mount: turn you, and take your journey," etc.

12. *The cloud rested in the wilderness of Paran.* This was three days' journey from the wilderness of Sinai (see v. 33) and the people had three stations; the first at Kibroth-hattaavah, the second at Hazeroth, chap. xi. 35, and the third in the wilderness of Paran, see chap. xii. 16.

14. *The standard . . . of Judah.* The following is the order in which this vast company proceeded in their march:

Judah, Issachar, Zebulun, Gershonites and Merarites carrying the Tabernacle

Reuben, Simeon, Gad, and the Kohathites with the sanctuary

Ephraim, Manasseh, Benjamin, Dan, Asher, Naphtali

29. *Moses said unto Hobab.* For a circumstantial account of this person see the notes on Exod. ii. 15-16, 18; iii. 1; iv. 20, 24; and for the transaction recorded here, and which is probably out of its place, see Exod. xviii. 5, where the subject is discussed at large.

We are journeying. God has brought us out of thraldom, and we are thus far on our way through the wilderness, travelling towards the place of rest which He has appointed us, trusting in His promise, guided by His presence, and supported by His power. *Come thou with us, and we will do thee good.* Those who wish to enjoy the heavenly inheritance must walk in the way towards it, and associate with the people who are going in that way. True religion is ever benevolent. They who know most of the goodness of God are the most forward to invite others to partake of that goodness. *The Lord hath spoken good concerning Israel.* The name Israel is taken in a general sense to signify the followers of God, and to them all the promises in the Bible are made. God has spoken good of them, and He has spoken good to them; and not one word that He hath spoken shall fail.

30. *I will not go; but I will depart to mine own land, and to my kindred.* From the strong expostulations in verses 31 and 32, and from Judg. i. 16; iv. 11; and 1 Sam. xv. 6, it is likely that Hobab changed his mind; or that, if he did go back to Midian, he returned again to Israel, as the above scriptures show that his posterity dwelt among the Israelites in Canaan.

31. *Thou mayest be to us instead of eyes.* But what need had they of Hobab, when they had the pillar and fire continually to point out their way? Answer: The cloud directed their general journeys, but not their particular excursions. Parties took several journeys while the grand army lay still. (See chaps. xiii, xx, xxxi, xxxii, etc.) They therefore needed such a person as Hobab, who was well acquainted with the desert, to direct these particular excursions; to point them out watering places, and places where they might meet with fuel, etc.

33. *The ark . . . went before them.* We find from v. 21 that the ark was carried by the Kohathites in the center of the army; but as the army never moved till the cloud was taken up, it is said to go before them, i.e., to be the first to move, as without this motion the Israelites continued in their encampments.

MATTHEW HENRY

every day's journey, and every day's work, with prayer.

(1) Here is his prayer when the ark set forward: *Rise up, Lord, and let thy enemies be scattered, v.* 35. Note, [1] There are those in the world that are enemies to God, and haters of him: secret and open enemies; enemies of his truths, his laws, his ordinances, his people. [2] The scattering and defeating of God's enemies is a thing to be earnestly desired, and believingly expected, by all the Lord's people.

(2) His prayer when the ark rested, *v.* 36. [1] That God would cause his people to rest. So some read it, "*Return, O Lord, the many thousands of Israel,* return them to their rest again after this fatigue." [2] That God himself would take up his rest among them. So we read it: *Return to the thousands of Israel,* the *ten thousand thousand,* so the word is. The welfare and happiness of the Israel of God consist in the continual presence of God among them.

JAMIESON, FAUSSET, BROWN

35, 36. when the ark set forward that Moses said, Rise up, Lord, and let thine enemies be scattered—Moses, as the organ of the people, uttered an appropriate prayer both at the commencement and the end of each journey. Thus all the journeys were sanctified by devotion; and so should our prayer be, "If thy presence go not with us, carry us not hence."

ADAM CLARKE

35. *Rise up, Lord, and let thine enemies be scattered.* If God did not arise in this way and scatter His enemies, there could be no hope that Israel could get safely through the wilderness. God must go first, if Israel would wish to follow in safety.

36. *Return, O Lord, unto the many thousands of Israel.* These were the words spoken by Moses, at the moment the divisions halted in order to pitch their tents. In reference to this subject, and the history with which it is connected, Psalms 68 seems to have been composed, though applied by David to the bringing of the ark from Kirjath-jearim to Jerusalem. *Many thousands,* literally "the ten thousand thousands."

MATTHEW HENRY

CHAPTER 11

Verses 1–3

I. The people's sin. They *complained, v.* 1. The law discovered sin, but could not destroy it; checked it, but could not conquer it. They *complained.* When they were furnished with so much matter for thanksgiving, one may justly wonder where they found any matter for complaint.

II. God's just resentment of the affront given to him by this sin: *The Lord heard it,* and his *anger was kindled.*

III. The judgment wherewith God chastised them for this sin. We read of their murmurings several times, when they came first out of Egypt, Exod. xv., and xvi., and xvii. But we do not read of any plagues inflicted on them for their murmurings, as there were now; for now they had had great experience of God's care of them, and therefore now to distrust him was so much the more inexcusable.

IV. Their cry to Moses, who was their tried intercessor, *v.* 2. *When he slew them, then they sought him,* and made their application to Moses to stand their friend.

V. The prevalence of Moses's intercession for them: *When Moses prayed unto the Lord* God had respect to him and his offering, and *the fire was quenched.*

VI. A new name given hereupon to the place, to perpetuate the shame of a murmuring people. The place was called *Taberah,* a *burning* (*v.* 3), that others might hear, and fear, and take warning not to sin as they did.

Verses 4–15

These verses represent things sadly unhinged and out of order in Israel, both the people and the prince uneasy.

I. Here is the people fretting, and speaking against God himself.

1. Who were the criminals? (1) The *mixed multitude* began, they *fell a-lusting, v.* 4. The rabble that came with them out of Egypt, expecting only the land of promise, but not a state of probation in the way to it. These were the scabbed sheep that infected the flock, the leaven that leavened the whole lump. (2) Even *the children of Israel* took the infection, as we are informed, *v.* 4.

2. What was the crime? (1) They magnified the plenty and dainties they had had in Egypt (*v.* 5), as if God had done them a great deal of wrong in taking them thence. They *remember the cucumbers, and the melons, and the leeks, and the onions, and the garlick* (precious stuff indeed to be fond of!), but they do not remember the brick-kilns and the taskmasters, the voice of the oppressor and the smart of the whip.

(2) They were sick of the good provision God had made for them, *v.* 6. It was bread from heaven, angels' food. While they lived on manna, they seemed to be exempted from the curse which sin has brought on man, that in the *sweat of his face should he eat bread.* And yet they speak of the manna with such scorn, as if it were not good enough to be meat for swine: *Our soul is dried away.* (3) They could not be satisfied unless they had flesh to eat. (4) They distrusted the power and goodness of God as insufficient for their supply: *Who will give us flesh to eat?* taking it for granted that God could not. (5) They were eager and importunate in their desires; they *lusted a lust,* so the word is, lusted greatly and greedily, till they wept again for vexation.

JAMIESON, FAUSSET, BROWN

CHAPTER 11

Vss. 1-35. MANNA LOATHED. **1. When the people complained it displeased the Lord . . .**—Unaccustomed to the fatigues of travel and wandering into the depths of a desert, less mountainous but far more gloomy and desolate than that of Sinai, without any near prospect of the rich country that had been promised, they fell into a state of vehement discontent, which was vented at these irksome and fruitless journeyings. The displeasure of God was manifested against the ungrateful complainers by fire sent in an extraordinary manner. It is worthy of notice, however, that the discontent seems to have been confined to the extremities of the camp, where, in all likelihood, "the mixed multitude" had their station. At the intercession of Moses, the appalling judgment ceased, and the name given to the place, "Taberah" (a burning), remained ever after a monument of national sin and punishment. (See on vss. 34, 35.) **4. the mixed multitude that was among them fell a lusting**—These consisted of Egyptians. To dream of banquets and plenty of animal food in the desert becomes a disease of the imagination; and to this excitement of the appetite no people are more liable than the natives of Egypt. But the Israelites participated in the same feelings and expressed dissatisfaction with the manna on which they had hitherto been supported, in comparison with the vegetable luxuries with which they had been regaled in Egypt. **5. We remember the fish, which we did eat in Egypt freely**—(See on Exod. 7:21). The people of Egypt are accustomed to an almost exclusive diet of fish, either fresh or sun-dried, during the hot season in April and May—the very season when the Israelites were travelling in this desert. Lower Egypt, where were the brick-kilns in which they were employed, afforded great facilities for obtaining fish in the Mediterranean, the lakes, and the canals of the Nile. **cucumbers**—The Egyptian species is smooth, of a cylindrical form, and about a foot in length. It is highly esteemed by the natives and when in season is liberally partaken of, being greatly mellowed by the influence of the sun. **melons**—The watermelons are meant, which grow on the deep, loamy soil after the subsidence of the Nile; and as they afford a juicy and cooling fruit, all classes make use of them for food, drink, and medicine. **leeks**—by some said to be a species of grass cresses, which is much relished as a kind of seasoning. **onions**—the same as ours; but instead of being nauseous and affecting the eyes, they are sweet to the taste, good for the stomach, and form to a large extent the aliment of the laboring classes. **garlic**—is now nearly if not altogether extinct in Egypt although it seems to have grown anciently in great abundance. The herbs now mentioned form a diet very grateful in warm countries where vegetables and other fruits of the season are much used. We can scarcely wonder that both the Egyptian hangers-on and the general body of the Israelites, incited by their clamors, complained bitterly of the want of the refreshing viands in their toilsome wanderings. But after all their experience of the bounty and care of God, their vehement longing for the luxuries of Egypt was an impeachment of the divine arrangements; and if it was the sin that beset them in the desert, it became them more strenuously to repress a rebellious spirit, as dishonoring to God and unbecoming their relation to Him as a chosen people. **6-9. But now . . . there is nothing . . . beside this manna**—Daily familiarity had disgusted them with the sight and taste of the monotonous food; and, ungrateful for the heavenly gift, they longed for a change of fare. It may be

ADAM CLARKE

CHAPTER 11

1. *And when the people complained.* What the cause of this complaining was, we know not. The conjecture of Jerome is probable; they complained because of the length of the way. *It displeased the Lord.* For His extraordinary kindness was lost on such an ungrateful and rebellious people. *And his anger was kindled*—divine justice was necessarily incensed against such inexcusable conduct. *And the fire of the Lord burnt among them.* Either a supernatural fire was sent for this occasion, or the lightning was commissioned against them, or God smote them with one of those hot, suffocating winds which are very common in those countries. *And consumed . . . in the uttermost parts of the camp.* It pervaded the whole camp, from the center to the circumference, carrying death with it to all the murmurers; for we are not to suppose that it was confined to the uttermost parts of the camp, unless we could imagine that there were none culpable anywhere else. If this were the same with the case mentioned in v. 4, then, as it is possible that the mixed multitude occupied the outermost parts of the camp, consequently the burning might have been confined to them.

2. *The fire was quenched.* Was "sunk," or swallowed up, as in the margin. The plague, of whatever sort, ceased to act, and the people had respite.

4. *The mixt multitude. Hasaphsuph,* the "collected or gathered people." Such as came out of Egypt with the Israelites; and are mentioned Exod. xii. 38. This mongrel people, who had comparatively little of the knowledge of God, feeling the difficulties and fatigues of the journey, were the first to complain.

5. *We remember.* The choice aliments which those murmurers complained of having lost by their leaving Egypt were the following: fish, cucumbers, melons, leeks, onions, and garlic. This enumeration takes in almost all the commonly attainable delicacies in those countries.

MATTHEW HENRY

(6) Flesh is good food, and may lawfully be eaten; yet they are said to lust after evil things. What is lawful of itself becomes evil to us when it is what God does not allot to us and yet we eagerly desire it.

II. Moses himself, though so meek and good a man, is uneasy upon this occasion: *Moses also was displeased.* Now, 1. It must be confessed that the provocation was very great. These murmurings of theirs reflected great dishonour upon God, and Moses laid to heart the reproaches cast on him. 2. Yet Moses came short of his duty both to God and Israel in these expostulations. (1) He undervalues the honour God had put upon him. (2) He complains too much of a sensible grievance, and lays too near his heart a little noise and fatigue. (3) He magnifies his own performances, that *all the burden of the people lay upon him.* (4) He is not so sensible as he ought to be of the obligation he lay under, by virtue of the divine commission and command, to do the utmost he could for his people. (5) He takes too much to himself when he asks, *Whence should I have flesh to give them* (*v.* 13), as if he were the housekeeper, and not God. (6) He speaks distrustfully of the divine grace when he despairs of being *able to bear all this people, v.* 14. (7) It was worst of all passionately to wish for death, and desire to be killed out of hand. Is this Moses? Is this the meekest of all the men on the earth? The best have their infirmities, and fail sometimes in the exercise of that grace for which they are most eminent. *Lord, lead us not into temptation.*

Verses 16–23

God's gracious answer to both the foregoing complaints:

I. Provision is made for the redress of the grievances Moses complains of. If he find the weight of government lie too heavy upon him, though he was a little too passionate in his remonstrance, yet he shall be eased, not by being discarded from the government himself, but by having assistants appointed him.

1. Moses is directed to nominate the persons, *v.* 16. The number he is to choose is seventy men, according to the number of the souls that went down into Egypt.

2. God promises to qualify them.

II. Even the humour of the discontented people shall be gratified too, that every mouth may be stopped. They are ordered to *sanctify themselves* (*v.* 18), that is, to put themselves into a posture to receive such a proof of God's power as should be a token both of mercy and judgment.

1. God promises (shall I say?)—he threatens rather, that they shall have their fill of flesh, and, if they have not a better government of their appetites than now it appears they have, they shall be surfeited with it (*v.* 19, 20).

2. Moses objects the improbability of making good this word, *v.* 21, 22. It is an objection like that which the disciples made, Mark viii. 4, *Whence can a man satisfy these men?* He objects the number of the people, as if he that provided bread for them all could not, by the same unlimited power, provide flesh too. He reckons it must be the flesh either of beasts or fishes, little thinking that the flesh of birds, little birds, should serve the purpose.

3. God gives a short but sufficient answer to the objection in that question, *Has the Lord's hand waxed short? v.* 23. God here brings Moses to this first principle, sets him back in his lesson, to learn the ancient name of God, *The Lord God Almighty.*

Verses 24–30

The performance of God's word to Moses, that he should have help in the government of Israel.

I. Here is the case of the seventy privy-counsellors in general. Moses, though a little disturbed by the tumult of the people, yet was thoroughly composed by the communion he had with God, and soon came to himself again. 1. He did his part; he presented the seventy elders before the Lord, round the tabernacle (*v.* 24), that they might there stand ready to receive the grace of God, in the place where he manifested himself. 2. God was not wanting to do his part. *He gave of his Spirit to the seventy elders,* (*v.* 25).

II. Here is the particular case of two of them, *Eldad* and *Medad*, probably two brothers.

1. They were nominated by Moses to be assistants in the government, but they *went not out unto the tabernacle* as the rest did, *v.* 26.

2. The Spirit of God found them out in the camp, where they were hidden among the stuff, and there they prophesied, that is, they exercised their gift of praying, preaching, and praising God, in some private tent. There was a special providence in it that these

JAMIESON, FAUSSET, BROWN

noticed that the resemblance of the manna to coriander seed was not in the color, but in the size and figure; and from its comparison to bdellium, which is either a drop of white gum or a white pearl, we are enabled to form a better idea of it. Moreover, it is evident, from the process of baking into cakes, that it could not have been the natural manna of the Arabian desert, for that is too gummy or unctuous to admit of being ground into meal. In taste it is said (Exod. 16:31), to have been like "wafers made with honey," and here to have the taste of fresh oil. The discrepancy in these statements is only apparent; for in the latter the manna is described in its raw state; in the former, after it was ground and baked. The minute description given here of its nature and use was designed to show the great sinfulness of the people in being dissatisfied with such excellent food, furnished so plentifully and gratuitously. **10-15. Moses said unto the Lord, Wherefore hast thou afflicted thy servant,** etc.–It is impossible not to sympathize with his feelings although the tone and language of his remonstrances to God cannot be justified. He was in a most distressing situation–having a mighty multitude under his care, with no means of satisfying their clamorous demands. *Their* conduct shows how deeply they had been debased and demoralized by long oppression: while *his* reveals a state of mind agonized and almost overwhelmed by a sense of the undivided responsibilities of his office. **16, 17. the Lord said unto Moses, Gather unto me seventy men of the elders**–(Exod. 3:16; 5:6; 24:9; 18:21, 24; Lev. 4:15). An order of seventy was to be created, either by a selection from the existing staff of elders or by the appointment of new ones, empowered to assist him by their collective wisdom and experience in the onerous cares of government. The Jewish writers say that this was the origin of the Sanhedrim, or supreme appellate court of their nation. But there is every reason to believe that it was only a temporary expedient, adopted to meet a trying exigency. **17. I will come down**–i.e., not in a visible manner or by local descent, but by the tokens of the divine presence and operations. **and I will take of the spirit which is upon thee**–The spirit means the gifts and influences of the Spirit (ch. 27: 18; Joel 2:28; John 7:39; I Cor. 14:12), and by "taking the spirit of Moses, and putting it upon them," is not to be understood that the qualities of the great leader were to be in any degree impaired but that the elders would be endowed with a portion of the same gifts, especially of prophecy (vs. 25)–i.e., an extraordinary penetration in discovering hidden and settling difficult things. **18-20. say thou unto the people, Sanctify yourselves against to-morrow, and ye shall eat flesh**–i.e., "prepare yourselves," by repentance and submission, to receive to-morrow the flesh you clamor for. But it is evident that the tenor of the language implied a severe rebuke and that the blessing promised would prove a curse. **21-23. Moses said, The people, among whom I am, are six hundred thousand . . . . Shall the flocks and herds be slain for them, to suffice them?**–The great leader, struck with a promise so astonishing as that of suddenly furnishing, in the midst of the desert, more than two millions of people with flesh for a whole month, betrayed an incredulous spirit, surprising in one who had witnessed so many stupendous miracles. But it is probable that it was only a feeling of the moment–at all events, the incredulous doubt was uttered only to himself–and not, as afterwards, publicly and to the scandal of the people. (See on ch. 20:10.) It was, therefore, sharply reproved, but not punished. **24. Moses . . . gathered the seventy men of the elders of the people,** etc.–The tabernacle was chosen for the convocation, because, as it was there God manifested Himself, there His Spirit would be directly imparted–there the minds of the elders themselves would be inspired with reverential awe and their office invested with greater respect in the eyes of the people. **25. when the spirit rested upon them, they prophesied, and did not cease**–As those elders were constituted civil governors, their "prophesying" must be understood as meaning the performance of their civil and sacred duties by the help of those extraordinary endowments they had received; and by their not "ceasing" we understand, either that they continued to exercise their gifts uninterruptedly the first day (see I Sam. 19:24), or that these were permanent gifts, which qualified them in an eminent degree for discharging the duty of public magistrates. **26-29. But there remained two of the men in the camp**–They did not repair with the rest to the tabernacle, either from modesty in shrinking from the assumption of a public office, or being prevented by some ceremonial defilement.

ADAM CLARKE

7. *The manna was as coriander seed.* **Probably this short description is added to show the iniquity of the people in murmuring, while they had so adequate a provision. But the baseness of their minds appears in every part of their conduct.**

11-15. The complaint and remonstrance of Moses in these verses serve at once to show the deeply distressed state of his mind and the degradation of the minds of the people. We have already seen that the slavery they had so long endured had served to debase their minds, and to render them incapable of every high and dignified sentiment, and of every generous act.

22. *Shall the flocks and the herds be slain?* **There is certainly a considerable measure of weakness and unbelief manifested in the complaints and questions of Moses on this occasion; but his conduct appears at the same time so very simple, honest, and affectionate that we cannot but admire it, while we wonder that he had not stronger confidence in that God whose miracles he had so often witnessed in Egypt.**

23. *Is the Lord's hand waxed short?* **Have you forgotten the miracles which I have already performed? or think you that My power is decreased? The power that is unlimited can never be diminished.**

25. *When the spirit rested upon them, they prophesied.* **By prophesying here we are to understand their performing those civil and sacred functions for which they were qualified; exhorting the people to quiet and peaceable submission, to trust and confidence in the goodness and providence of God, would make no small part of the duties of their new office. The ideal meaning of the word** *naba* **is to "pray, entreat." The prophet is called** *nabi,* **because he prays, supplicates, in reference to God; exhorts, entreats, in reference to man.**

MATTHEW HENRY

wo should be absent, for thus it appeared that it was indeed a divine Spirit which the elders were actuated by, and that Moses gave them not that Spirit, but God himself.

3. Information of this was given to Moses (*v.* 27): *Eldad and Medad do prophesy in the camp.* Whoever the person was that brought the tidings, he seems to have looked upon it as an irregularity.

4. Joshua moved to have them silenced: *My lord Moses, forbid them, v.* 28. It is probable that Joshua himself was one of the seventy. He does not desire that they should be punished for what they had done, but only restrained for the future.

5. Moses rejected the motion, and reproved him that made it (*v.* 29): "*Enviest thou for my sake?*" Though Joshua was Moses's particular friend and confidant, though he said this out of a respect to Moses, whose honour he was very loth to see lessened by the call of those elders, yet Moses reproved him. We must not be forward to condemn and silence those that differ from us, as if they did not follow Christ because they do not follow *him with us,* Mark ix. 38. Shall we reject those whom Christ has owned, or restrain any from doing good because they are not in everything of our mind? Moses was of another spirit; so far from silencing these two, and quenching the Spirit in them, he wishes *all the Lord's people were prophets,* that is, that he would *put his Spirit upon them.*

6. The elders, now newly ordained, immediately entered upon their administration (*v.* 30); when their call was sufficiently attested by their prophesying, they went with Moses to the camp, and applied themselves to business.

Verses 31–35

God, having performed his promise to Moses by giving him assessors in the government. He here performs his promise to the people by giving them flesh. Observe, 1. How the people were gratified with flesh in abundance: *A wind* (a south-east wind, as appears, Ps. lxxviii. 26) *brought quails, v.* 31. It is uncertain what sort of animals they were; the psalmist calls them *feathered fowl, or fowl of wing.* The learned Bishop Patrick inclines to agree with some modern writers, who think they were *locusts,* a delicious sort of food well known in those parts, the rather because they were brought with a wind, lay in heaps, and were dried in the sun for use. Whatever they were, they answered the intention, they served for a month's feast for Israel, such an indulgent Father was God to his froward family. 2. How greedy they were of this flesh that God sent them. They *flew upon the spoil* with an insatiable appetite, not regarding what Moses had told them from God, that they would surfeit upon it, *v.* 32. 3. How dearly they paid for their feasts, when it came into the reckoning: *The Lord smote them with a very great plague* (*v.* 33), some bodily disease, which probably was the effect of their surfeit, and was the death of many of them.

The remembrance of this is preserved in the name given to the place, *v.* 34. Moses called it *Kibroth-hattaavah,* the *graves of lusters* or *of lust.*

JAMIESON, FAUSSET, BROWN

They, however, received the gifts of the Spirit as well as their brethren; and when Moses was urged to forbid their prophesying, his answer displayed a noble disinterestedness as well as zeal for the glory of God akin to that of our Lord (Mark 9:39). **31-35. There went forth a wind from the Lord, and brought quails from the sea,** etc.—These migratory birds (see on Exodus 16:13) were on their journey from Egypt, when "the wind from the Lord," an east wind (Ps. 78:26) forcing them to change their course, wafted them over the Red Sea to the camp of Israel. **let them fall a day's journey**—If the journey of an individual is meant, this space might be thirty miles; if the inspired historian referred to the whole host, ten miles would be as far as they could march in one day in the sandy desert under a vertical sun. Assuming it to be twenty miles this immense cloud of quails (Exod. 16:13) covered a space of forty miles in diameter. Others reduce it to sixteen. But it is doubtful whether the measurement be from the center or the extremities of the camp. It is evident, however, that the language describes the countless number of these quails. **as it were two cubits high**—Some have supposed that they fell on the ground above each other to that height—a supposition which would leave a vast quantity useless as food to the Israelites, who were forbidden to eat any animal that died of itself or from which the blood was not poured out. Others think that, being exhausted with a long flight, they could not fly more than three feet above the earth, and so were easily felled or caught. A more recent explanation applies the phrase, "two cubits high," not to the accumulation of the mass, but to the size of the individual birds. Flocks of large red-legged cranes, three feet high, measuring seven feet from tip to tip, have been frequently seen on the western shores of the Gulf of Akaba, or eastern arm of the Red Sea [STANLEY, SHUBERT]. **32. people stood up**—rose up in eager haste—some at one time, others at another—some, perhaps through avidity, both day and night. **ten homers**—ten asses' loads; or, "homers" may be used indefinitely (as in Exod. 8: 14; Judg. 15:16); and "ten" for many: so that the phrase "ten homers" is equivalent to great heaps. The collectors were probably one or two from each family; and, being distrustful of God's goodness, they gathered not for immediate consumption only, but for future use. In eastern and southern seas, innumerable quails are often seen, which, when weary, fall down, covering every spot on the deck and rigging of vessels; and in Egypt they come in such myriads that the people knock them down with sticks. **spread them all abroad for themselves**—salted and dried them for future use, by the simple process to which they had been accustomed in Egypt. **33. while the flesh was yet between their teeth, ere it was chewed**—lit., cut off—i.e., before the supply of quails, which lasted a month (vs. 20), was exhansted. The probability is, that their stomachs, having been long inured to manna (a light food), were not prepared for so sudden a change of regimen—a heavy, solid diet of animal food, of which they seem to have partaken to so intemperate a degree as to produce a general surfeit, and fatal consequences. On a former occasion their murmurings for flesh were raised (Exod. 16) because they were in want of food. Here they proceeded, not from necessity, but wanton, lustful desire; and their sin, in the righteous judgment of God, was made to carry its own punishment. **34. called the name of that place Kibrothhattaavah**—lit., the graves of lust, or those that lusted; so that the name of the place proves that the mortality was confined to those who had indulged inordinately. **35. Hazeroth**—The extreme southern station of this route was a watering-place in a spacious plain, now Ain Haderah.

ADAM CLARKE

27. *Eldad and Medad do prophesy.* These, it seems, made two of the seventy elders; they were written, though they went not out to the Tabernacle; they were enrolled as of the elders, but went not to meet God at the Tabernacle, probably at that time prevented by some legal hinderance, but they continued in the camp using their new function in exhorting the people.

28. *My lord Moses, forbid them.* Joshua was afraid that the authority and influence of his master Moses might be lessened by the part Eldad and Medad were taking in the government of the people, which might ultimately excite sedition or insurrection among them.

29. *Enviest thou for my sake?* Are you jealous of their influence only on my account? I am not alarmed; on the contrary, I would to God that all His people were endued with the same influence, and actuated by the same motives.

31. *A wind from the Lord.* An extraordinary one, not the effect of a natural cause. *And brought quails,* a bird which in great companies visits Egypt about the time of the year, March or April, at which the circumstance marked here took place. *Two cubits high upon the face of the earth.* We may consider the quails as flying within two cubits of the ground; so that the Israelites could easily take as many of them as they wished, while flying within the reach of their hands or their clubs. The common notion is that the quails were brought round about the camp, and fell there in such multitudes as to lie two feet thick upon the ground; but the Hebrew will not bear this version. The Vulgate has expressed the sense, "And they flew in the air, two cubits high above the ground."

32. *The people stood up.* While these immense flocks were flying at this short distance from the ground, fatigued with the strong wind and the distance they had come, they were easily taken by the people; and as various flocks continued to succeed each other for two days and a night, enough for a month's provision might be collected in that time. If the quails had fallen about the tents, there was no need to have stood up two days and a night in gathering them; but if they were on the wing, as the text seems to suppose, it was necessary for them to use dispatch, and avail themselves of the passing of these birds while it continued. *And they spread them all abroad.* Maillet observes that birds of all kinds come to Egypt for refuge from the cold of a northern winter; and that the people catch them, pluck, and bury them in the burning sand for a few minutes, and thus prepare them for use. This is probably what is meant by spreading them all abroad round the camp.

33. *The wrath of the Lord was kindled.* In what way, and with what effects, we cannot precisely determine. Some heavy judgment fell upon those murmurers and complainers, but of what kind the sacred writer says nothing.

34. *Kibroth-hattaavah.* "The graves of lust"; and thus their scandalous crime was perpetuated by the name of the place.

MATTHEW HENRY — CHAPTER 12

Verses 1–3

Here is, I. The unbecoming passion of Aaron and Miriam: they *spoke against Moses, v.* 1. It should seem that Miriam began the quarrel, and Aaron, not having been employed or consulted in the choice of the seventy elders, was for the present somewhat disgusted, and so was the sooner drawn in to take his sister's part. Two things they quarrelled with Moses about:—1. About his marriage: some think a late marriage with a Cushite or Arabian; others because of Zipporah, whom on this occasion they called, in scorn, an Ethiopian woman, and who, they insinuated, had too great an influence upon Moses in the choice of these seventy elders. 2. About his government; not the mismanagement of it, but the

JAMIESON, FAUSSET, BROWN — CHAPTER 12

VSS. 1-9. MIRIAM'S AND AARON'S SEDITION. **1. an Ethiopian woman**—*Heb.,* a Cushite woman—Arabia was usually called in Scripture the land of Cush, its inhabitants being descendants of that son of Ham (see on Exod. 2:15) and being accounted generally a vile and contemptible race (Amos 9:7). The occasion of this seditious outbreak on the part of Miriam and Aaron against Moses was the great change made in the government by the adoption of the seventy rulers. Their irritating disparagement of his wife (who, in all probability, was Zipporah, and not a second wife he had recently married) arose from jealousy of the relatives, through whose influence the innovation had been first made (Exod. 18), while they were overlooked or neglected.

ADAM CLARKE — CHAPTER 12

1. *Miriam and Aaron spake against Moses.* It appears that jealousy of the power and influence of Moses was the real cause of their complaint, though his having married an Ethiopian woman—*haishshah haccushith,* "that woman, the Cushite," probably meaning Zipporah, who was an Arab born in the land of Midian—was the ostensible cause.

MATTHEW HENRY

monopolizing of it (*v.* 2): "*Hath the Lord spoken only by Moses?*"

II. The wonderful patience of Moses under this provocation. He, *as a deaf man, heard not.* When God's honour was concerned, as in the case of the golden calf, no man more zealous than Moses; but, when his own honour was touched, no man more meek: as bold as a lion in the cause of God, but as mild as a lamb in his own cause. Sometimes the unkindness of our friends is a greater trial of our meekness than the malice of our enemies.

Verses 4–9

Moses did not resent the injury done him, nor complain of it to God, nor make any appeal to him; but God resented it. The more silent we are in our own cause the more is God engaged to plead it. The accused innocent needs to say little if he knows the judge himself will be his advocate.

I. The cause is called, and the parties are summoned forthwith to attend at the door of the tabernacle, *v.* 4, 5.

II. Aaron and Miriam were made to know that great as they were they must not pretend to be equal to Moses, nor set up as rivals with him, *v.* 6–8. 1. It was true that God put a great deal of honour upon the prophets. God *made himself known to them,* either by dreams when they were asleep, or by visions when they were awake, and by them made himself known to others. Now he does it not by dreams and visions, as of old, but by the *Spirit of wisdom and revelation.* 2. Yet the honour put upon Moses was far greater (*v.* 7): *My servant Moses is not so,* he excels them all. To recompense Moses for his meekly and patiently bearing the affronts which Miriam and Aaron gave him, God not only cleared him, but praised him. (1) Moses was a man of great integrity and tried fidelity. He is *faithful in all my house.* This is put first in his character, because grace excels gifts, love excels knowledge, and sincerity in the service of God puts a greater honour upon a man and recommends him to the divine favour more than learning, abstruse speculations, and an ability to *speak with tongues.* (2) Moses was therefore honoured with clearer discoveries of God's mind, and a more intimate communion with God, than any other prophet whatsoever.

Now let Miriam and Aaron consider who it was that they insulted: *Were you not afraid to speak against my servant Moses?*

III. God, having thus shown them their fault and folly, next shows them his displeasure (*v.* 9): *The anger of the Lord was kindled against them.* But indeed it was indication enough of his displeasure that he departed, and would not so much as hear their excuse. The removal of God's presence from us is the surest and saddest token of God's displeasure against us. Woe unto us if he depart; and he never departs till we by our sin and folly drive him from us.

Verses 10–16

Here is, I. God's judgment upon Miriam (*v.* 10): *The cloud departed from off* that part of *the tabernacle,* in token of God's displeasure, and presently Miriam became leprous. Her foul tongue (says Bishop Hall) is justly punished with a foul face. While Moses needs a veil to hide his glory, Miriam needs one to hide her shame. Miriam was struck with a leprosy, but not Aaron, because she was first in the transgression, and God would put a difference between those that mislead and those that are misled. Aaron as priest was to be the judge of the leprosy. He was struck through her side, and could not pronounce her leprous without blushing and trembling, knowing himself to be equally obnoxious.

II. Aaron's submission hereupon (*v.* 11, 12); he humbles himself to Moses, confesses his fault, and begs pardon. He that but just now joined with his sister in speaking against Moses is here forced for himself and his sister to make a penitent address to him. In his submission, 1. He confesses his own and his sister's sin, *v.* 11. 2. He begs Moses's pardon: *Lay not this sin upon us.* 3. He recommends the deplorable condition of his sister to Moses's compassionate consideration (*v.* 12): *Let her not be as one dead.*

III. The intercession made for Miriam (*v.* 13): He *cried unto the Lord* with a loud voice, because the cloud, the symbol of his presence, was removed and stood at some distance, and to express his fervency in this request, *Heal her now, O Lord, I beseech thee.* So Miriam here was healed by the prayer of Moses, whom she had abused.

IV. The accommodating of this matter so as that mercy and justice might meet together. 1. Mercy takes place so far as that Miriam shall be healed; Moses forgives her, and God will. See 2 Cor. ii. 10.

JAMIESON, FAUSSET, BROWN

Miriam is mentioned before Aaron as being the chief instigator and leader of the sedition. **2. Hath the Lord indeed spoken only by Moses? hath he not also spoken by us?**—The prophetical name and character was bestowed upon Aaron (Exod. 4:15, 16) and Miriam (Exod. 15:20); and, therefore, they considered the conduct of Moses, in exercising an exclusive authority in this matter, as an encroachment on their rights (Micah 6:4). **3. the man Moses was very meek**—(Exod. 14:13; 21:7; 32:12, 13; Deut. 9:18). This observation might have been made to account for Moses taking no notice of their angry reproaches and for God's interposing so speedily for the vindication of His servant's cause. The circumstance of Moses recording an eulogium on a distinguishing excellence of his own character is not without a parallel among the sacred writers, when forced to it by the insolence and contempt of opponents (II Cor. 11:5; 12:11, 12). But it is not improbable that, as this verse appears to be a parenthesis, it may have been inserted as a gloss by Ezra or some later prophet. Others, instead of "very meek," suggest "very afflicted," as the proper rendering. **4. the Lord spake suddenly unto Moses, and unto Aaron, and unto Miriam**—The divine interposition was made thus openly and immediately, in order to suppress the sedition and prevent its spreading among the people. **5. the Lord came down in the pillar of the cloud, and stood in the door of the tabernacle**—without gaining admission, as was the usual privilege of Aaron, though it was denied to all other men and women. This public exclusion was designed to be a token of the divine displeasure. **6. Hear now my words**—A difference of degree is here distinctly expressed in the gifts and authority even of divinely commissioned prophets. Moses, having been set over all God's house, (i.e., His church and people), was consequently invested with supremacy over Miriam and Aaron also and privileged beyond all others by direct and clear manifestations of the presence and will of God. **8. with him will I speak mouth to mouth**—immediately, not by an interpreter, nor by visionary symbols presented to his fancy. **apparently**—plainly and surely. **not in dark speeches**—parables or similitudes. **the similitude of the Lord shall he behold**—not the face or essence of God, who is invisible (Exod. 33:20; Col. 1:15; John 1:18); but some unmistakable evidence of His glorious presence (Exod. 33:2; 34:5). The latter clause should have been conjoined with the preceding one, thus: "not in dark speeches, and in a figure shall he behold the Lord." The slight change in the punctuation removes all appearance of contradiction to Deuteronomy 4:15.

10-16. HER LEPROSY. **10. the cloud departed from the tabernacle**—i.e., from the door to resume its permanent position over the mercy seat. **Miriam became leprous**—This malady in its most malignant form (Ex. 4:6; II Kings 5:27) as its color, combined with its sudden appearance, proved, was inflicted as a divine judgment; and she was made the victim, either because of her extreme violence or because the leprosy on Aaron would have interrupted or dishonored the holy service.

11-13. On the humble and penitential submission of Aaron, Moses interceded for both the offenders, especially for Miriam, who was restored; not, however, till she had been made, by ther exclusion, a public example.

ADAM CLARKE

2. *Hath the Lord indeed spoken only b Moses?* It is certain that both Aaron and Miriar had received a portion of the prophetic spiri (see Exod. iv. 15 and xv. 20), and therefore they thought they might have a share in the government; for though there was no kind of gair attached to this government and no honor bu such as came from God, yet the love of powe is natural to the human mind; and in many instances men will sacrifice even honor, pleasure, and profit to the lust of power.

3. *Now the man Moses was very meek.* Hov could Moses, who certainly was as humble anc modest as he was meek, write this encomiun upon himself? I think the word is not rightly understood; *anav,* which we translate *meek* comes from *anah,* to "act upon," to "humble depress, afflict," and is translated so in many places in the Old Testament; and in this sense it should be understood here: "Now this mar Moses was depressed or afflicted more thar any man [*haadamah*] of that land." And why was he so? Because of the great burden he had to bear in the care and government of thi people, and because of their ingratitude and rebellion both against God and himself; of thi depression and affliction, see the fullest proof ir the preceding chapter.

4. *And the Lord spake suddenly.* The sudden interference of God in this business shows a once the importance of the case and His displeasure.

6. *If there be a prophet.* We see here the different ways in which God usually made himself known to the prophets, viz., by *visions*—emblematic appearance, and by *dream,* in which the future was announced by *dark speeches, bechiaoth,* by enigmas or figurative representations, v. 8. But to Moses, God had communicated himself in a different way—He spoke to him face-to-face, *apparently,* showing him His glory, not in *dark* or enigmatical *speeches.* This could not be admitted in the case in which Moses was engaged, for he was to receive laws by divine inspiration, the precepts and expressions of which must all be within the reach of the meanest capacity. As Moses, therefore, was chosen of God to be the lawgiver, so was he chosen to see these laws duly enforced for the benefit of the people among whom he presided.

7. *Moses . . . is faithful. Neeman,* a "prefect" or "superintendent." So Samuel is termed 1 Sam. ii. 35; iii. 20; David is so called, 1 Sam. xviii. 27, *Neeman,* and son-in-law of the king Job xii. 20, speaks of the *Neemanim* as a name of dignity. It seems also to have been a title of respect given to ambassadors, Prov. xiii. 17; xxv. 13.

10. *Miriam became leprous.* It is likely Miriam was chief in this mutiny; and it is probable that it was on this ground she is mentioned first (see v. 1) and punished here, while Aaron is spared. Had he been smitten with the leprosy, his sacred character must have greatly suffered, and perhaps the priesthood itself have fallen into contempt.

MATTHEW HENRY

But, 2. Justice takes place so far as that Miriam shall be humbled (*v.* 14): *Let her be shut out from the camp seven days.*

V. The hindrance that this gave to the people's progress: *The people journeyed not till Miriam was brought in again, v.* 15. God did not remove the cloud, and therefore they did not remove their camp. This was intended, 1. As a rebuke to the people, who were conscious to themselves of having sinned after the similitude of Miriam's transgression, in speaking against Moses. 2. As a mark of respect to Miriam. If the camp had removed during the days of her suspension, her trouble and shame had been the greater. Those that are under censure and rebuke for sin ought to be treated with a great deal of tenderness, and not be over-loaded, no, not with the shame they have deserved, not *counted as enemies* (2 Thess. iii. 15), but *forgiven and comforted*, 2 Cor. ii. 7. Sinners must be cast out with grief and penitents taken in with joy.

JAMIESON, FAUSSET, BROWN

14. her father had but spit in her face, should she not be ashamed seven days?—The Jews, in common with all people in the East, seem to have had an intense abhorrence of spitting, and for a parent to express his displeasure by doing so on the person of one of his children, or even on the ground in his presence, separated that child as unclean from society for seven days. **15. the people journeyed not till Miriam was brought in again**—Either not to crush her by a sentence of overwhelming severity or not to expose her, being a prophetess, to popular contempt. **16 pitched in the wilderness of Paran**—The station of encampments seems to have been Rithma (ch. 33:19).

ADAM CLARKE

14. *If her father had but spit in her face.* This appears to have been done only in cases of great provocation on the part of the child, and strong irritation on the side of the parent. Spitting in the face was a sign of the deepest contempt. See Job xxx. 10; Isa. 1. 6; Mark xiv. 65. In a case where a parent was obliged by the disobedient conduct of his child to treat him in this way, it appears he was banished from the father's presence for seven days. If then this was an allowed and judged case in matters of high provocation on the part of a child, should not the punishment be equally severe where the creature has rebelled against the Creator? Therefore Miriam was shut out of the camp for seven days, and thus debarred from coming into the presence of God, her Father, who is represented as dwelling among the people.

MATTHEW HENRY — CHAPTER 13

Verses 1–20

Here we have, I. Orders given to send spies to search out the land of Canaan. It is here said, God directed Moses to send them (*v.* 1, 2), but it appears (Deut. i. 22) that the motion came originally from the people; they came to Moses, and said, *We will send men before us.* They would not take God's word that it was a good land. How absurd was it for them to send to spy out a land which God himself had spied out for them. But thus we ruin ourselves by giving more credit to the reports and representations of sense than to divine revelation; we walk by sight, not by faith. The people making this motion to Moses, he consulted God in the case, who bade him gratify the people in this matter, and send spies before them: "Let them walk in their own counsels."

II. The persons nominated that were to be employed in this service (*v.* 4, &c.), one of each tribe, that it might appear to be the act of the people in general. This was designed for the best, but it proved to have this ill effect that the quality of the persons occasioned the evil report they brought up to be the more credited and the people to be the more influenced by it. Some think that they are all named for the sake of two good ones that were among them, Caleb and Joshua. Notice is taken of the change of Joshua's name upon this occasion, *v.* 16. The name by which he was generally called and known in his own tribe was *Oshea*, but Moses called him *Joshua*, and now he ordered others to call him so. *Oshea* signifies a prayer for salvation, *Save thou*; *Joshua* signifies a promise of salvation, *He will save*, in answer to that prayer: so near is the relation between prayers and promises. Prayers prevail for promises, and promises direct and encourage prayers. *Jesus* is the same name with *Joshua*, and it is the name of our Lord Christ, of whom Joshua was a type as successor to Moses, Israel's captain, and conqueror of Canaan. Joshua was the saviour of God's people from the powers of Canaan, but Christ is their Saviour from the powers of hell.

III. The instructions given to those spies. They were sent into the land of Canaan to take account of its present state, *v.* 17. Two heads of enquiry were given them: 1. Concerning the land itself: *See* whether it be *good or bad*, and (*v.* 20) *whether it be fat or lean.* Moses himself was well satisfied that Canaan was a very good land, but he sent these spies to bring an account of it for the satisfaction of the people. 2. Concerning the inhabitants—their number, few or many,—their size and stature, whether strong able-bodied men or weak.

IV. Moses dismisses the spies with this charge, *Be of good courage*, intimating that they should bring an encouraging account to the people and make the best of everything.

Verses 21–25

We have here a short account of the survey which the spies made of the promised land. 1. They went quite through it, from Zin in the south, to Rehob, near Hamath, in the north, *v.* 21. See *ch.* xxxiv. 3, 8. They divided themselves into several companies, and so passed unsuspected, as wayfaring men. 2. They took particular notice of Hebron (*v.* 22), probably because near there was the field of Machpelah, where the patriarchs were buried (Gen. xxiii. 19). To this sepulchre they made a particular visit, and found the adjoining city in the possession of the sons of Anak. Where the bodies of their ancestors kept possession for them the giants kept possession against them. 3. They brought a bunch of grapes with them, and some other of the fruits of the land, as a proof

JAMIESON, FAUSSET, BROWN — CHAPTER 13

Vss. 1-35. THE NAMES OF THE MEN WHO WERE SENT TO SEARCH THE LAND. **1, 2. The Lord spake unto Moses, Send thou men, that they may search the land, of Canaan**—Cf. Deuteronomy 1:22, whence it appears, that while the proposal of delegating confidential men from each tribe to explore the land of Canaan emanated from the people who petitioned for it, the measure received the special sanction of God, who granted their request at once as a trial, and a punishment of their distrust. **3. those men were heads of the children of Israel**—Not the princes who are named (ch. 10), but chiefs, leading men though not of the first rank. **16. Oshea**—i.e., a desire of salvation. Jehoshua, by prefixing the name of God, means "divinely appointed," "head of salvation," "Saviour," the same as Jesus. **17. Get you up this way . . . , and go up into the mountain**—Mount Seir (Deut. 1:2), which lay directly from Sinai across the wilderness of Paran, in a northeasterly direction into the southern parts of the promised land. **20. Now the time was the time of the first grapes**—This was in August, when the first clusters are gathered. The second are gathered in September, and the third in October. The spies' absence for a period of forty days determines the grapes they brought from Eshcol to have been of the second period. **21-24. So they . . . searched the land**—They advanced from south to north, reconnoitering the whole land. **the wilderness of Zin**—a long level plain, or deep valley of sand, the monotony of which is relieved by a few tamarisk and rethem trees. Under the names of El Ghor and El Araba, it forms the continuation of the Jordan valley, extending from the Dead Sea to the Gulf of Akaba. **Rehob—or,** Beth-rehob, was a city and district situated, according to some, eastward of Sidon; and, according to others, it is the same as El Hule, an extensive and fertile champaign country, at the foot of Anti-libanus, a few leagues below Paneas. **as men come unto Hamath**—or, "the entering in of Hamath" (II Kings 14:25), now the valley of Balbeck, a mountain pass or opening in the northern frontier, which formed the extreme limit in that direction of the inheritance of Israel. From the mention of these places, the route of the scouts appears to have been along the course of the Jordan in their advance; and their return was by the western border through the territories of the Sidonians and Philistines. **22. unto Hebron**—situated in the heart of the mountains of Judah, in the southern extremity of Palestine. The town or "cities of Hebron," as it is expressed in the *Heb.*, consists of a number of sheikdoms distinct from each other, standing at the foot of one of those hills that form a bowl round and enclose it. "The children of Anak," mentioned in this verse, seem to have been also chiefs of townships; and this coincidence of polity, existing in ages so distant from each other, is remarkable [VERE MONRO]. Hebron (Kirjath-Arba, Gen. 23:2) was one of the oldest cities in the world. **Zoan**—(the Tanis of the Greeks). It was situated on one of the eastern branches of the Nile, near the lake Menzala, and was the early royal residence of the Pharaohs. It boasted a higher antiquity than any other city in Egypt. Its name, which signifies flat and level, is descriptive of its situation in the low grounds of the Delta. **23. they came unto the brook of Eshcol**—i.e., "the torrent of the cluster." Its location was a little to the southwest of Hebron. The valley and its sloping hills are still covered with vineyards, the character of whose fruit corresponds to its ancient celebrity. **and cut down from thence a branch with**

ADAM CLARKE — CHAPTER 13

2. *Send thou men, that they may search.* It appears from Deut. i. 19-24 that this was done in consequence of the request of the people. *Every one a ruler.* Not any of the princes of the people (see chap. i.), for these names are different from those; but these now sent were men of consideration and importance in their respective tribes.

18. *See the land, what it is.* What sort of country it is; how situated; its natural advantages or disadvantages. *And the people . . . whether they be strong or weak.* Healthy, robust, hardy men; or little, weak, and pusillanimous.

20. *The land . . . whether it be fat or lean.* Whether the soil be rich or poor; which might be known by its being well wooded, and by the fruits it produced; and therefore they were desired to examine it as to the trees, and to bring some of the fruits with them.

21. *From the wilderness of Zin.* The place called *Tsin*, here, is different from that called *Sin*, Exod. xvi. 1; the latter was nigh to Egypt, but the former was near Kadesh-barnea, not far from the borders of the Promised Land.

22. *Hebron was built seven years before Zoan in Egypt.* The Zoan of the Scriptures is allowed to be the Tanis of the heathen historians, which was the capital of Lower Egypt. Some think it was to humble the pride of the Egyptians, who boasted the highest antiquity, that this note concerning the higher antiquity of Hebron was introduced by Moses. Some have supposed that it is more likely to have been originally a marginal note, which in process of time crept into the text; but all the versions and all the MSS. that have as yet been collated acknowledge it.

23. *They bare it between two upon a staff.* It would be very easy to produce a great number of witnesses to prove that grapes in the Promised Land, and indeed in various other hot countries, grow to a prodigious size. From the most authentic accounts the Egyptian grape is very small, and this being the only one with

MATTHEW HENRY

of the extraordinary goodness of the country. The place whence they took it was called the *valley of the cluster*, that famous cluster which was to Israel both the earnest and the specimen of all the fruits of Canaan.

Verses 26–33

At length the messengers return, but they agree not in their report.

I. The major part discourage the people from going forward to Canaan.

1. Observe their report. (1) They could not deny but that the land of Canaan was a very fruitful land: the bunch of grapes they brought with them was an ocular demonstration of it, *v.* 27. And yet afterwards they contradict themselves, when they say (*v.* 32), *It is a land that eateth up the inhabitants thereof*; some think that there was a great plague in the country at the time they surveyed it. They invidiously imputed it to the unwholesomeness of the air, and thence took occasion to disparage the country. But (2) They represented the conquest of it as altogether impracticable, and that it was to no purpose to attempt it. Nothing served their ill purpose more than a description of the giants, on whom they lay a great stress. They gave it in as their judgment, *We are not able to go up against them* (*v.* 31), and therefore must think of taking some other course.

2. Now, even if they had been to judge only by human probabilities, they could not have been excused from the imputation of cowardice. Were not the hosts of Israel very numerous? Effective men, well marshalled and modelled, closely embodied, and entirely united in interest and affection. Moses, their commander-in-chief, was wise and brave; and if the people had put on resolution, and behaved themselves valiantly, what could have stood before them?

3. But, though they deserved to be posted for cowards, this was not the worst, the scripture brands them for unbelievers. (1) They had tokens of God's presence with them. The Canaanites were stronger than Israel; suppose they were, but were they stronger than the God of Israel? Their cities are walled against us, but can they be walled against heaven? Besides this, (2) They had had very great experience of the length and strength of God's arm, lifted up and made bare on their behalf. Were not the Egyptians as much stronger than they as the Canaanites were? And yet, without a sword drawn by Israel or a stroke struck, the chariots and horsemen of Egypt were quite routed and ruined; the Amalekites were discomfited. (3) They had particular promises made them of victory and success in their wars against the Canaanites. God had given Abraham all possible assurances that he would put his seed into possession of that land, Gen. xv. 18; xvii. 8. He had expressly promised them by Moses that he would *drive out the Canaanites* from *before them* (Exod. xxxiii. 2), and that he would do it *by little and little*, Exod. xxiii. 30. And after all this, for them to say, *We are not able to go up against them*, was in effect to say, "God himself is not able to make his words good."

II. Caleb encouraged them to go forward, though he was seconded by Joshua only (*v.* 30): *Caleb stilled the people. Caleb* signifies *all heart*, and he answered his name, was hearty himself, and would have made the people so if they would have hearkened to him. 1. He speaks very confidently of success: *We are well able to overcome them*, as strong as they are. 2. He animates the people to go on, and, his lot lying in the van, he speaks as one resolved to lead them on with bravery: "*Let us go up at once. Let us go up and possess it.*"

JAMIESON, FAUSSET, BROWN

one cluster of grapes—The grapes reared in this locality are still as magnificent as formerly—they are said by one to be equal in size to prunes, and compared by another to a man's thumb. One cluster sometimes weights 10 or 12 pounds. The mode of carrying the cluster cut down by the spies, though not necessary from its weight, was evidently adopted to preserve it entire as a specimen of the productions of the promised land; and the impression made by the sight of it would be all the greater because the Israelites were familiar only with the scanty vines and small grapes of Egypt. **26. they came . . . to Kadesh**—an important encampment of the Israelites. But its exact situation is not definitely known, nor is it determined whether it is the same or a different place from Kadesh-barnea. It is supposed to be identical with Ain-el-Weibeh, a famous spring on the eastern side of the desert [ROBINSON], or also with Petra [STANLEY].

27, 28. they told him, and said, We came unto the land whither thou sentest us, and surely it floweth with milk and honey—The report was given publicly in the audience of the people, and it was artfully arranged to begin their narrative with commendations of the natural fertility of the country in order that their subsequent slanders might the more readily receive credit. **29. The Amalekites dwell in the land of the south**—Their territory lay between the Dead and the Red Seas, skirting the borders of Canaan. **Hittites . . . dwell in the mountains**—Their settlements were in the southern and mountainous part of Palestine (Gen. 23:7). **the Canaanites dwell by the sea**—The remnant of the original inhabitants, who had been dispossessed by the Philistines, were divided into two nomadic hordes—one settled eastward near the Jordan; the other westward, by the Mediterranean. **32. a land that eateth up the inhabitants**—i.e., an unhealthy climate and country. Jewish writers say that in the course of their travels they saw a great many funerals, vast numbers of the Canaanites being cut off at that time, in the providence of God, by a plague or the hornet (Joshua 24:12). **men of a great stature**—This was evidently a false and exaggerated report, representing, from timidity or malicious artifice, what was true of a few as descriptive of the people generally. **33. there we saw the giants, the sons of Anak**—The name is derived from the son of Arba—a great man among the Arabians (Josh. 15:14), who probably obtained his appellation from wearing a splendid collar or chain round his neck, as the word imports. The epithet "giant" evidently refers here to stature. (See on Gen. 6:4.) And it is probable the Anakims were a distinguished family, or perhaps a select body of warriors, chosen for their extraordinary size. **we were in our own sight as grasshoppers**—a strong Orientalism, by which the treacherous spies gave an exaggerated report of the physical strength of the people of Canaan.

ADAM CLARKE

which the Israelites were acquainted, the great size of the grapes of Hebron would appear still more extraordinary. I myself once cut down a bunch of grapes nearly twenty pounds in weight. From what is mentioned v. 20, "Now the time was the time of the firstripe grapes," it is very probable that the spies received their orders about the beginning of August, and returned about the middle of September, as in those countries grapes, pomegranates, and figs are ripe about this time.

27. *We came unto the land.* It is astonishing that men so dastardly as these should have had courage enough to risk their persons in searching the land. But probably though destitute of valor they had a sufficiency of cunning, and this carried them through. The report they brought was exceedingly discouraging, and naturally tended to produce the effect mentioned in the next chapter. The conduct of Joshua and Caleb was alone magnanimous, and worthy of the cause in which they were embarked.

32. *Men of a great stature. Anshey middoth,* "men of measures"—two men's height; i.e., exceedingly tall men.

33. *There we saw the giants. Nephilim.* It is evident that they had seen a robust, sturdy, warlike race of men, and of great stature; for the asserted fact is not denied by Joshua or Caleb.

MATTHEW HENRY

CHAPTER 14

Verses 1–4

What mischief the evil spies made by their unfair representation.

I. How the people fretted themselves: *They lifted up their voices and cried* (*v.* 1); giving credit to the report of the spies rather than to the word of God. Those that cried when nothing hurt them deserved to have something given them to cry for.

II. How they flew in the face of their governors—*murmured against Moses and Aaron*, and in them reproached the Lord, *v.* 2, 3. The congregation of elders began the discontent (*v.* 1). 1. They look back with a causeless discontent. They wish that they had died in Egypt. Never were so many months spent so pleasantly as these which they had spent since they came out of Egypt. How base were the spirits of these degenerate Israelites, who desired rather to die in the wilderness. 2. They look for-

JAMIESON, FAUSSET, BROWN

CHAPTER 14

VSS. 1-45. 1. THE PEOPLE MURMUR AT THE SPIES' REPORT. **all the congregation lifted up their voice and cried**—Not literally all, for there were some exceptions.

2-4. Would God that we had died in Egypt—Such insolence to their generous leaders, and such base ingratitude to God, show the deep degradation of the Israelites, and the absolute necessity of the decree that debarred that generation from entering the promised land. They were punished by their wishes being granted to die in

ADAM CLARKE

CHAPTER 14

1. *Cried; and . . . wept that night.* In almost every case this people gave deplorable evidence of the degraded state of their minds. With scarcely any mental firmness, and with almost no religion, they could bear no reverses, and were ever at their wit's end. They were headstrong, presumptuous, pusillanimous, indecisive, and fickle. And because they were such, therefore the power and wisdom of God appeared the more conspicuously in the whole of their history.

MATTHEW HENRY

ward with a groundless despair, taking it for granted (*v.* 3) that if they went on they must fall by the sword. And here is a most wicked blasphemous reflection upon God himself, as if he had brought them hither on purpose that their wives and children, those poor innocents, should be a prey.

III. How they came at last to this desperate resolve, that, instead of going forward to Canaan, they would go back again to Egypt. *Were it not better for us to return to Egypt? Let us make a captain and return to Egypt.* 1. It was the greatest folly in the world to wish themselves in Egypt, or to think that if they were there it would be better with them than it was. 2. It was a most senseless, ridiculous thing to talk of returning thither through the wilderness. We are uneasy at that which is, complain of our place and lot, and we would shift; but is there any place or condition in this world that has not something in it to make us uneasy if we are disposed to be so? The way to better our condition is to get our spirits into a better frame; and instead of asking, "Were it not better to go to Egypt?" ask, "Were it not better to be content, and make the best of that which is?"

Verses 5–10

The friends of Israel here interpose to save them if possible from ruining themselves, but in vain.

I. The best endeavours were used to still the tumult.

1. The clamour and noise of the people were so great that Moses and Aaron could not be heard; and, therefore, to gain audience in the sight of all the assembly, they fell on their faces, thus expressing, (1) Their humble prayers to God to still the tumult of the people. (2) The great trouble and concern of their own spirits. They fall down as men astonished and even thunderstruck, amazed to see a people throw away their own mercies. What they said to the people Moses relates in the repetition of this story. Deut. i. 29, 30, *Be not afraid; the Lord your God shall fight for you.*

2. Caleb and Joshua did their part: they rent their clothes in a holy indignation at the sin of the people, and a holy dread of the wrath of God, which they saw ready to break out against them. No reasoning could be more pertinent and pathetic than theirs was (*v.* 7–9), and they spoke as with authority.

(1) They assured them of the goodness of the land they had surveyed, and that it was really worth venturing for.

(2) They made nothing of the difficulties that seemed to lie in the way of their gaining the possession of it: *Fear not the people of the land*, *v.* 9. Whatever formidable ideas have been given you of them, the lion is not so fierce as he is painted. *They are bread for us*, that is, "they are set before us rather to be fed upon than to be fought with." Though the Canaanites dwell in walled cities, they are naked: *Their defence has departed from them.* The other spies took notice of their strength, but these of their wickedness, and thence inferred that God had forsaken them, and therefore *their defence had departed.*

(3) They showed them plainly that all the danger they were in was from their own discontents, and that they would succeed against all their enemies if they did not make God their enemy.

II. It was all to no purpose; they were deaf to this fair reasoning; nay, they were exasperated by it, and grew more outrageous: *All the congregation bade stone them with stones*, *v.* 10. Caleb and Joshua knew they appeared for God and his glory, and therefore doubted not but God would appear for them and their safety. And they were not disappointed, for immediately *the glory of the Lord appeared*, to the terror and confusion of those that were for stoning the servants of God.

Verses 11–19

When the glory of the Lord *appeared in the tabernacle* we may suppose that Moses took it for a call to him immediately to come and attend there. Now here we are told what God said to him there.

1. He showed him the great evil of the people's sin, *v.* 11. Two things God justly complains of to Moses:—(1) Their sin. They *provoke me*, or (as the word signifies) they *reject, reproach, despise* me, for *they will not believe me.* It was their unbelief that made this a day of provocation in the wilderness, Heb. iii. 8. (2) Their continuance in it: *How long will they do so?* The more God has done for us the greater is the provocation if we distrust him.

2. He showed him the sentence which justice passed upon them for it, *v.* 12. What remains now but that I should make a full end of them? They wish to die; and let them die, and neither root nor branch be left of them.

II. The humble intercession Moses made for

JAMIESON, FAUSSET, BROWN

that wilderness. A leader to reconduct them to Egypt is spoken of (Neh. 9:17) as actually nominated. The sinfulness and insane folly of their conduct are almost incredible. Their conduct, however, is paralleled by too many among us, who shrink from the smallest difficulties and rather remain slaves to sin than resolutely try to surmount the obstacles that lie in their way to the Canaan above.

5. Moses and Aaron fell on their faces—as humble and earnest suppliants—either to the people, entreating them to desist from so perverse a design;—or rather, to God, as the usual and only refuge from the violence of that tumultuous and stiff-necked rabble—and a hopeful means of softening and impressing their hearts. **6. Joshua . . . and Caleb, which were of them that searched the land, rent their clothes**—The two honest spies testified their grief and horror, in the strongest manner, at the mutiny against Moses and the blasphemy against God; while at the same time they endeavored, by a truthful statement, to persuade the people of the ease with which they might obtain possession of so desirable a country, provided they did not, by their rebellion and ingratitude, provoke God to abandon them. **8. a land flowing with milk and honey**—a general expression, descriptive of a rich and fertile country. The two articles specified were among the principal products of the Holy Land.

9. their defence is departed—*Heb.*, their shadow. The Sultan of Turkey and the Shah of Persia are called "the shadow of God," "the refuge of the world." So that the meaning of the phrase, "their defence is departed" from them, is, that the favor of God was now lost to those whose iniquities were full (Gen. 15:16), and transferred to the Israelites.

10. the glory of the Lord appeared—It was seasonably manifested on this great emergency to rescue His ambassadors from their perilous situation.

11. the Lord said, . . . I will smite them with the pestilence—not a final decree, but a threatening, suspended, as appeared from the issue, on the intercession of Moses and the repentance of Israel.

ADAM CLARKE

4. *Let us make a captain.* Here was a formal renunciation of the authority of Moses, and flat rebellion against God. And it seems from Neh. ix. 17 that they had actually appointed another leader, under whose direction they were about to return to Egypt. How astonishing is this! Their lives were made bitter because of the rigor with which they were made to serve in the land of Egypt; and yet they were willing, yes, eager, to get back into the same circumstances again! Great evils, when once some time past, affect the mind less than present ills, though much inferior. They had partly forgotten their Egyptian bondage, and now smart under a little discouragement, having totally lost sight of their high calling, and of the power and goodness of God.

9. *Their defence. Tsillam,* "their shadow," a metaphor highly expressive of protection and support in the sultry Eastern countries. The protection of God is so called; see Ps. xci. 1; cxxi. 5; see also Isa. li. 16; xlix. 2; xxx. 2.

10. *The glory of the Lord appeared.* This timely appearance of the divine glory prevented these faithful servants of God from being stoned to death by this base and treacherous multitude.

MATTHEW HENRY

them.

1. The prayer of his petition is, in one word, *Pardon. I beseech thee, the iniquity of this people* (*v.* 19), that is, "Do not bring upon them the ruin they deserve." This was Christ's prayer for those that crucified him, *Father, forgive them.*

2. The pleas are many, and strongly urged.

(1) He insists most upon the plea that is taken from the glory of God, *v.* 13-16. "If this people that have made so great a noise be all consumed, if their mighty pretensions come to nothing, and their light go out in a snuff, it will be told with pleasure in Gath, and published in the streets of Askelon; and what construction will the heathen put upon it? It will be impossible to make them understand it as an act of God's justice, but they will impute it to the failing of God's power.

(2) He pleads God's proclamation of his name at Horeb (*v.* 17, 18); *Let the power of the Lord be great.* To enforce this petition, he refers to the word which God had spoken: *The Lord is long-suffering and of great mercy.* God's goodness had there been spoken of as his glory; God gloried in it, Exod. xxxiv. 6, 7. Now here he prays that upon this occasion he would glorify it. He does not ask that they may not be corrected, but that they may not be disinherited.

(3) He pleads past experience: *As thou hast forgiven this people from Egypt, v.* 19. Moses looks upon it as a good plea, *Lord, forgive, as thou hast forgiven.* It will be no more a reproach to thy justice, nor any less the praise of thy mercy, to forgive now, than it has been formerly.

Verses 20–35

God's answer to the prayer of Moses, which sings both of mercy and judgment.

I. The extremity of the sentence is receded from (*v.* 20). See what countenance and encouragement God gives to our intercessions for others, that we may be public-spirited in prayer. Here is a whole nation rescued from ruin by the effectual fervent prayer of one righteous man.

II. The glorifying of God's name is, in the general, resolved upon, *v.* 21. Moses in his prayer had shown a great concern for the glory of God. All the world shall see how God hates sin even in his own people, and will reckon for it, and yet how gracious and merciful he is, and how slow to anger. Thus when our Saviour prayed, *Father, glorify thy name,* he was immediately answered, *I have glorified it, and will glorify it yet again,* John xii. 28.

III. The sin of this people which provoked God to proceed against them is here aggravated, *v.* 22, 27. 1. They tempted God—tempted his power. They tempted his justice, whether he would resent their provocations and punish them or no. 2. They murmured against him. This is much insisted on, *v.* 27. 3. They did this after they had seen God's miracles in Egypt and in the wilderness, *v.* 2. 4. They had repeated the provocations ten times, that is, very often.

IV. The sentence passed upon them for this sin. 1. That they should not see the promised land (*v.* 23), nor *come into it, v.* 30. The promise of God should be fulfilled to their posterity, but not to them. 2. That they should immediately *turn back into the wilderness, v.* 25. Their next remove should be a retreat. 3. That all those who had now grown up to men's estate should die in the wilderness, not all at once, but by degrees. They wished that they might die in the wilderness, and God said *Amen* to their passionate wish. 4. That in pursuance of this sentence they should wander to and fro in the wilderness, like travellers that have lost themselves, for forty years. (1) That hereby they might be brought to repentance, and find mercy with God in the other world, whatever became of them in this. (2) That they might sensibly feel what a dangerous thing it is for God's covenant-people to break with him. For God never leaves any till they first leave him. (3) That a new generation might in this time be raised up, which could not be done all of a sudden. And the children, being brought up under the tokens of God's displeasure against their fathers, might take warning not to tread in the steps of their fathers' disobedience.

V. The mercy that was mixed with this severe sentence.

1. Mercy to Caleb and Joshua, that though they should wander with the rest in the wilderness, yet they, and they only of all that were now above twenty years old, should survive the years of banishment, and live to enter Canaan. Caleb only is spoken of (*v.* 24), and a particular mark of honour put upon him, both, (1) In the character given of him: he had *another spirit,* different from the rest of the spies, an *after-spirit,* which furnished him with second thoughts, and he *followed the Lord fully,* kept close to his

JAMIESON, FAUSSET, BROWN

17. let the power of my Lord be great—be magnified.

21. all the earth shall be filled with the glory of the Lord—This promise, in its full acceptation, remains to be verified by the eventual and universal prevalence of Christianity in the world. But the terms were used restrictively in respect to the occasion, to the report which would spread over all the land of the "terrible things in righteousness" which God would do in the infliction of the doom described, to which that rebellious race was now consigned. **ten times**—very frequently.

25. (Now the Amalekites and the Canaanites dwelt in the valley)—i.e., on the other side of the Idumean mountain, at whose base they were then encamped. Those nomad tribes had at that time occupied it with a determination to oppose the further progress of the Hebrew people. Hence God gave the command that they seek a safe and timely retreat into the desert, to escape the pursuit of those resolute enemies, to whom, with their wives and children, they would fall a helpless prey because they had forfeited the presence and protection of God. The 25th verse forms an important part of the narrative and should be freed from the parenthetical form which our English translators have given it.

24. my servant Caleb—Joshua was also excepted, but he is not named because he was no longer in the ranks of the people, being a constant attendant on Moses. **because he had another spirit, and hath followed me fully**—Under the influence of God's Spirit, Caleb was a man of bold, generous, heroic courage, above worldly anxieties and fears.

ADAM CLARKE

14. *That thy cloud standeth over them.* This cloud, the symbol of the divine glory, and proof of the divine presence, appears to have assumed three different forms for three important purposes. (1) It appeared by day in the form of a pillar of sufficient height to be seen by all the camp, and thus went before them to point out their way in the desert, Exod. xl. 38. (2) It appeared by night as a pillar of fire to give them light while travelling by night, which they probably sometimes did (see chap. ix. 21); or to illuminate their tents in their encampment; Exod. xiii. 21-22. (3) It stood at certain times above the whole congregation, overshadowing them from the scorching rays of the sun; and probably at other times condensed the vapors and precipitated rain or dew for the refreshment of the people. "He spread a cloud for a covering; and fire to give light in the night," Ps. cv. 39. It was probably from this circumstance that the shadow of the Lord was used to signify the divine protection.

19. *Pardon, I beseech thee, the iniquity of this people.* From v. 13 to v. 19 inclusive we have the words of Moses' intercession. They need no explanation; they are full of simplicity and energy. His arguments with God (for he did reason and argue with his Maker) are pointed, cogent, and respectful; and while they show a heart full of humanity, they evidence the deepest concern for the glory of God.

20. *I have pardoned.* That is, They shall not be cut off as they deserve, because you have interceded for their lives.

21. *All the earth shall be filled. Kol haarets,* "all this land," i.e., the land of Canaan, which was fulfilled to the letter only when the preaching of Christ and His apostles was heard through all the cities and villages of Judea. It does not appear that the whole of the terraqueous globe is meant by this expression in any of the places where it occurs connected with this promise of the diffusion of the divine light. See Ps. lxxii. 19; Isa. xl. 5; Hab. ii. 14.

24. *But my servant Caleb.* Caleb had *another spirit*—not only a bold, generous, courageous, noble, and heroic spirit; but the Spirit and influence of the God of heaven thus raised him above human inquietudes and earthly fears. Therefore he *followed* God, *fully; vaimalle acharai,* literally, "he filled after Me." God showed him the way he was to take, and the line of conduct he was to pursue, and he filled up this line, and in all things followed the will of his Maker. He therefore shall see the Promised Land, and his seed shall possess it.

MATTHEW HENRY

duty, and went through with it, though deserted and threatened; and, (2) In the recompence promised to him: *Him will I bring in due time into the land whereinto he went.* When Caleb is again mentioned (*v.* 30) Joshua stands with him, compassed with the same favours and crowned with the same honours, having stood with him in the same services.

2. Mercy to the children even of these rebels. They should have a seed preserved, and Canaan secured to that seed: *Your little ones,* now under twenty years old, *which you,* in your unbelief, *said should be a prey, them will I bring in, v.* 31.

Verses 36–45

Here is, I. The sudden death of the ten evil spies. While the sentence was passing upon the people, before it was published, they *died of the plague before the Lord, v.* 36, 37. 1. They sinned themselves, in bringing up a slander upon the land of promise. Note, Those greatly provoke God who misrepresent religion, cast reproach upon it, and raise prejudices in men's minds against it, or give occasion to those to do so who seek occasion. 2. They *made Israel to sin.* They designedly *made all the congregation murmur* against God.

II. The special preservation of Caleb and Joshua: *They lived still, v.* 38.

III. The publication of the sentence to all the people, *v.* 36. He told them all what the decree was which had gone forth concerning them, and which could not be reversed, that they must all die in the wilderness, and Canaan must be reserved for the next generation.

IV. The foolish fruitless attempts of some of the Israelites to enter Canaan, notwithstanding the sentence.

1. They were now eager to go forward towards Canaan, *v.* 40. They were up early, mustered all their force, got together in a body, and begged of Moses to lead them on against the enemy. But, though God was glorified by this recantation of theirs, they were not benefited by it, because it came too late.

2. Moses utterly disallows their motion, and forbids the expedition they were meditating: *Go not up, v.* 41–43. He gives them warning of the danger: "*The Canaanites are before you* to attack you, and *the Lord is not among you* to protect you and fight for you, and therefore look to yourselves *that you be not smitten before your enemies.*" Those that are out of the way of their duty are from under God's protection, and go at their peril.

3. They venture notwithstanding. Never was people so perverse and so desperately resolved in every thing to walk contrary to God. God bade them go, and they would not; he forbade them, and they would.

4. The expedition speeds accordingly, *v.* 45. The enemy had posted themselves upon the top of the hill, to make good that pass against the invaders, and, being informed by their scouts of their approach, sallied out upon them, and defeated them, and it is probable that many of the Israelites were killed.

JAMIESON, FAUSSET, BROWN

30. save Caleb . . . and Joshua—These are specially mentioned, as honorable exceptions to the rest of the scouts, and also as the future leaders of the people. But it appears that some of the old generation did not join in the mutinous murmuring, including in that number the whole order of the priests (Josh. 14:1). **34. ye shall known my breach of promise**—i.e., in consequence of your violation of the covenant betwixt you and Me, by breaking the terms of it, it shall be null and void on My part, as I shall withhold the blessings I promised in that covenant to confer on you on condition of your obedience. **36-38. those men that did bring up the evil report upon the land, died by the plague before the Lord**—Ten of the spies were struck dead on the spot—either by the pestilence, or some other judgment. This great and appalling mortality clearly betokened the hand of the Lord.

40-45. they rose up early in the morning, and gat them into the top of the mountain—Notwithstanding the tidings that Moses communicated and which diffused a general feeling of melancholy and grief throughout the camp, the impression was of very brief continuance. They rushed from one extreme of rashness and perversity to another, and the obstinacy of their rebellious spirit was evinced by their active preparations to ascend the hill, notwithstanding the divine warning they had received not to undertake that enterprise. **for we have sinned**—i.e., realizing our sin, we now repent of it, and are eager to do as Caleb and Joshua exhorted us—or, as some render it, *though* we have sinned, we trust God will yet give us the land of promise. The entreaties of their prudent and pious leader, who represented to them that their enemies, scaling the other side of the valley, would post themselves on the top of the hill before them, were disregarded. How strangely perverse the conduct of the Israelites, who, shortly before, were afraid that, though their Almighty King was with them, they could not get possession of the land; and yet now they act still more foolishly in supposing that, though God were not with them, they could expel the inhabitants by their unaided offorts. The consequences were such as might have been anticipated. The Amalekites and Canaanites, who had been lying in ambuscade expecting their movement, rushed down upon them from the heights and became the instruments of punishing their guilty rebellion. **even unto Hormah**—The name was afterwards given to that place in memory of the immense slaughter of the Israelites on this occasion.

ADAM CLARKE

34. *After the number of the days.* The spies were forty days in searching the land, and the people who rebelled on their evil report are condemned to wander forty years in the wilderness! Now let them make them a captain and go back to Egypt if they can. God had so hedged them about with His power and providence that they could neither go back to Egypt nor get forward to the Promised Land! *And ye shall know my breach of promise.* This is certainly a most harsh expression; and most learned men agree that the words *eth tenuathi* should be translated "my vengeance," which is the rendering of the Septuagint, Vulgate, Coptic, and Anglo-Saxon, and which is followed by almost all our ancient English translations. The meaning however appears to be this: As God had promised to bring them into the good land, provided they kept His statutes, ordinances, etc., and they had now broken their engagements, He was no longer held by His covenant; and therefore, by excluding them from the Promised Land, He showed them at once His annulling of the covenant which they had broken and His vengeance because they had broken it.

37. *Those men that did bring up the evil report . . . died.* Thus ten of the twelve that searched out the land were struck dead, by the justice of God, on the spot! Caleb, of the tribe of Judah, and Joshua, of the tribe of Ephraim, alone escaped, because they had followed God fully.

40. *We . . . will go up unto the place.* They found themselves on the very borders of the land, and they heard God say they should not enter it, but should be consumed by a forty years' wandering in the wilderness; notwithstanding, they are determined to render vain this purpose of God, probably supposing that the temporary sorrow they felt for their late rebellion would be accepted as a sufficient atonement for their crimes. They accordingly went up, and were cut down by their enemies; and why? God went not with them.

MATTHEW HENRY — CHAPTER 15

Verses 1–21

I. Full instructions given concerning the meat-offerings and drink-offerings, which were appendages to all the sacrifices of animals. The beginning of this law is very encouraging: *When you come into the land of your habitation which I give unto you,* then you shall do so and so, *v.* 2. This was a plain intimation, not only that God was reconciled to them, but that he would secure the promised land to their seed. Now the intent of this law is to direct what proportion the meat-offering and drink-offering should bear to the several sacrifices to which they were annexed.

II. Natives and strangers are here set upon a level, in this as in other matters (*v.* 13–16): "*One law shall be for you and for the stranger* that is proselyted to the Jewish religion." Now, 1. This was an invitation to the Gentiles to become proselytes, and to embrace the faith and worship of the true God. In civil things there was a difference between strangers and true-born Israelites, but not in the things of God. 2. This was an obligation upon the Jews to be kind to strangers, and not to oppress them, because they saw them owned and accepted of God. Communion in religion should slay all enmities. It was a happy presage of the calling of the Gentiles, and of their admission into the church. If the law made so little difference between Jew and Gentile, much less would the gospel make, which broke down the partition-wall, and reconciled both to God in one sacrifice, without the observance of the legal ceremonies.

III. A law for the offering of the first of their dough

JAMIESON, FAUSSET, BROWN — CHAPTER 15

Vss. 1-41. THE LAW OF SUNDRY OFFERINGS. **1, 2. The Lord spake unto Moses, saying, Speak unto the children of Israel**—Some infer from vs. 23 that the date of this communication must be fixed towards the close of the wanderings in the wilderness; and, also, that all the sacrifices prescribed in the law were to be offered only after the settlement in Canaan. **3. make an offering by fire unto the Lord, a burnt offering**—It is evident that a peace offering is referred to because this term is frequently used in such a sense (Exod. 18:12; Lev. 17:5). **4. tenth deal**—i.e., an omer, the tenth part of an ephah (Exod. 16:36). **fourth part of an hin of oil**—This element shows it to have been different from such meat offerings as were made by themselves, and not merely accompaniments of other sacrifices. **6-12. two tenth deals**—The quantity of flour was increased because the sacrifice was of superior value to the former. The accessory sacrifices were always increased in proportion to the greater worth and magnitude of its principal. **13-16. a stranger**—one who had become a proselyte. There were scarcely any of the national privileges of the Israelites, in which the Gentile stranger might not, on conforming to certain conditions, fully participate.

ADAM CLARKE — CHAPTER 15

2. *When ye be come into the land.* Some learned men are of opinion that several offerings prescribed by the law were not intended to be made in the wilderness, but in the Promised Land, the former not affording those conveniences which were necessary to the complete observance of the divine worship in this and several other respects.

3. *And will make an offering.* For the different kinds of offerings, sacrifices, etc., see Lev. i. 2 and vii.

5. *The fourth part of an hin.* The quantity of meal and flour was augmented in proportion to the size of the sacrifice with which it was offered. With a lamb or a kid were offered one-tenth deal of flour (the tenth part of an ephah, see on Exod. xxix. 40), the fourth part of a hin of oil, and *the fourth part of an hin of wine.* With a ram, two tenth deals of flour, a third part of a hin of oil, a third part of a hin of wine. With a bullock, three tenth deals of flour, half a hin of oil, and half a hin of wine. See vv. 4-11.

14. *If a stranger sojourn.* See the notes on Lev. xix. 33; xxii. 9. When the case of the Jewish people is fairly considered, and their situation with respect to the surrounding idolatrous nations, we shall see the absolute necessity of having but one form of worship in the land. That alone was genuine which was pre-

MATTHEW HENRY

unto the Lord. This, as the former, goes upon the comfortable supposition of their having *come into the promised land*, *v.* 18. They must not only offer him the first-fruits and tenths of the corn in their fields, but when they had it in their houses, in their kneading troughs, when it was almost ready to be set upon their tables, God must have a further tribute, part of their dough must be heaved or offered up to God (*v.* 20, 21), and the priest must have it for the use of his family. Thus they must own their dependence upon God for their daily bread. Christ has taught us to pray not, *Give us this year our yearly harvest*, but *Give us this day our daily bread.*

Verses 22–29

We have here the laws concerning sacrifices for sins of ignorance; the Jews understand it of idolatry, or false worship, through the error of their teachers. If they had failed in the offerings they must bring an offering of atonement, though the omission had been through forgetfulness or mistake. 1. The case is put of a national sin, committed through ignorance, and become customary through a vulgar error (*v.* 24). Now, if there should appear to have been a general neglect of that appointment, then a sacrifice must be offered for the whole congregation. It is likewise supposed to be the case of a particular person. Thus atonement shall be made *for the soul that sins, when he sins through ignorance*, *v.* 28. Sins committed ignorantly shall be forgiven, through Christ the great sacrifice, who, when he offered up himself once for all upon the cross, seemed to explain the intention of his offering in that prayer, *Father, forgive them, for they know not what they do.* And Paul seems to allude to this law concerning sins of ignorance (1 Tim. i. 13), *I obtained mercy, because I did it ignorantly and in unbelief.* And it looked favourably upon the Gentiles that this law of atoning for sins of ignorance is expressly made to extend to those who were strangers to the commonwealth of Israel (*v.* 29), but supposed to be *proselytes of righteousness.* Thus the blessing of Abraham comes upon the Gentiles.

Verses 30–36

Here is, I. The general doom passed upon presumptuous sinners. Those are to be reckoned presumptuous sinners that sin *with a high hand*, as the original phrase is (*v.* 30), that is, that fight against God, and dare him to do his worst, see Job xv. 25. It imputes folly to Infinite Wisdom, and iniquity to the righteous Judge of heaven and earth; such is the malignity of wilful sin. The sentence passed on such is dreadful. There remains no sacrifice for those sins; the law provided none.

II. A particular instance of presumption in the sin of sabbath-breaking. The offence was the gathering of sticks on the sabbath day (*v.* 32), which, it is probable, were designed to make a fire of, whereas they were commanded to bake and seethe what they had occasion for the day before, Exod. xvi. 23. It appears by the context to have been done presumptuously, and in affront both of the law and to the Law-maker. It seems, even common Israelites, though there was much amiss among them, yet would not contentedly see the sabbath profaned. The law had already made the profanation of the sabbath a capital crime (Exod. xxxi. 14, *ch.* xxxv. 2); but they were in doubt, either concerning the offence (whether this that he had done should be deemed a profanation or no) or concerning the punishment, what death he should die. Sentence was passed; the prisoner was adjudged a sabbath-breaker, according to the intent of that law, and as such he must be put to death; and to show how great the crime was, and how displeasing to God, and that others might hear and fear and not do in like manner presumptuously, that death is appointed him which was looked upon as most terrible: He must be *stoned with stones*, *v.* 35. Note, God is jealous for the honour of his sabbaths, and will not hold those guiltless, whatever men do, that profane them. Execution was done pursuant to the sentence. *v.* 36. He was *stoned* to death *by the congregation.* As many as could were employed in the execution, that those, at least, might be afraid of breaking the sabbath, who had thrown a stone at this sabbath-breaker. This intimates that the open profanation of the sabbath is a sin which ought to be punished and restrained by the civil magistrate, who, as far as overt acts go, is keeper of both tables. See Neh. xiii. 17. One would think there could be no great harm in gathering a few sticks, on what day soever it was, but God intended the exemplary punishment of him that did so for a standing warning to us all, to make conscience of keeping holy the sabbath.

JAMIESON, FAUSSET, BROWN

19. when ye eat of the bread of the land, ye shall offer up an heave offering—The offering prescribed was to precede the act of eating. **unto the Lord**—i.e., the priests of the Lord (Ezek. 44:30). **20. heave offering of the threshing-floor**—meaning the corn on the threshing-floor—i.e., after harvest. **so shall ye heave it**—to the priests accompanying the ceremony with the same rites.

22. if ye have erred and not observed all these commandments, etc.—respecting the performance of divine worship, and the rites and ceremonies that constitute the holy service. The law relates only to any omission and consequently is quite different from *that* laid down in Leviticus 4:13, which implies a transgression or positive neglect of some observances required. *This* law relates to private parties or individual tribes; *that* to the whole congregation of Israel. **24-26. if aught be committed by ignorance**—The Mosaic ritual was complicated, and the ceremonies to be gone through in the various instances of purification which are specified, would expose a worshipper, through ignorance, to the risk of omitting or neglecting some of them. This law includes the stranger in the number of those for whom the sacrifice was offered for the sin of general ignorance. **27-29. if any soul sin through ignorance**—not only in common with the general body of the people, but his personal sins were to be expiated in the same manner.

30. the soul that doeth aught presumptuously—*Heb. with an high or uplifted hand*—i.e., knowingly, wilfully, obstinately. In this sense the phraseology occurs (Exod. 14:8; Lev. 26:21; Ps. 19:13). **the same reproacheth the Lord**—sets Him at open defiance and dishonors His majesty. **31. his iniquity shall be upon him**—The punishment of his sins shall fall on himself individually; no guilt shall be incurred by the nation, unless there be a criminal carelessness in overlooking the offense. **32-34. a man that gathered sticks upon the sabbath day**—This incident is evidently narrated as an instance of presumptuous sin. The mere gathering of sticks was not a sinful act and might be necessary for fuel to warm him or to make ready his food. But its being done on the Sabbath altered the entire character of the action. The law of the Sabbath being a plain and positive commandment, this transgression of it was a known and wilful sin, and it was marked by several aggravations. For the deed was done with unblushing boldness in broad daylight, in open defiance of the divine authority—in flagrant inconsistency with His religious connection with Israel, as the covenant people of God; and it was an application to improper purposes of time, which God had consecrated to Himself and the solemn duties of religion. The offender was brought before the rulers, who, on hearing the painful report, were at a loss to determine what ought to be done. That they should have felt any embarrassment in such a case may seem surprising, in the face of the sabbath law (Exod. 31:14). Their difficulty probably arose from this being the first public offense of the kind which had occurred; and the appeal might be made to remove all ground of complaint—to produce a more striking effect, so that the fate of this criminal might be a beacon to warn all Israelites in the future. **35, 36. The Lord said, The man shall surely be put to death**—The Lord was King, as well as God of Israel, and the offense being a violation of the law of the realm, the Sovereign Judge gave orders that this man should be put to death; and, moreover, He required the whole congregation unite in executing the fatal sentence.

ADAM CLARKE

scribed by the Almighty, and no others could be tolerated, because they were idolatrous. All strangers, all that came to sojourn in the land, were required to conform to it; and it was right that those who did conform to it should have equal rights and privileges with the Hebrews themselves, which we find was the case.

20. *Ye shall offer . . . the first of your dough.* Concerning the offerings of firstfruits, see the notes on Exod. xxii. 29.

24. *If ought be committed by ignorance.* See the notes on Lev. iv. 2 and v. 17. The case here probably refers to the whole congregation; the cases above, to the sin of an individual.

25. *The priest shall make an atonement.* Even sins committed through ignorance required an atonement; and God in His mercy has provided one for them.

30. *But the soul that doeth ought presumptuously.* Bold, daring acts of transgression against the fullest evidence, and in despite of the divine authority, admitted of no atonement; the person was to be cut off—to be excluded from God's people, and from all their privileges and blessings.

32. *They found a man that gathered sticks upon the sabbath.* This was in all likelihood a case of that kind supposed above: the man despised the word of the Lord, and therefore broke His commandment; see v. 31. On this ground he was punished with the utmost rigor of the law.

36. *Stoned him.* See the note on Lev. xxiv. 23.

MATTHEW HENRY

Verses 37–41

Provision had been just now made by the law for the pardon of sins of ignorance and infirmity; now here is an expedient provided for the preventing of such sins. They are ordered to make fringes upon the borders of their garments, which were to be memorandums to them of their duty. The sign appointed is a fringe of silk, and a blue riband bound on the top of it to keep it tight, *v.* 38. Our Saviour, being made under the law, wore these fringes; hence we read of the hem or border of his garment, Matt. ix. 20. These borders the Pharisees enlarged, that they might be thought more holy and devout than other people. Many look upon their ornaments to feed their pride, but they must look upon these ornaments to awaken their consciences to a sense of their duty.

After the repetition of some ceremonial appointments, the chapter closes with that great and fundamental law of religion, *Be holy unto your God.*

JAMIESON, FAUSSET, BROWN

38. bid them that they make fringes in the border of their garments—These were narrow strips, in a wing-like form, wrapped over the shoulders and on various parts of the attire. "Fringe," however, is the English rendering of two distinct Hebrew words—the one meaning a narrow lappet or edging, called the "hem" or "border" (Matt. 23:5; Luke 8:44), which, in order to make it more attractive to the eye and consequently more serviceable to the purpose described, was covered with a riband of blue or rather purple color; the other term signifies strings with tassels at the end, fastened to the corners of the garment. Both of these are seen on the Egyptian and Assyrian frocks; and as the Jewish people were commanded by express and repeated ordinances to have them, the fashion was rendered subservient, in their case, to awaken high and religious associations—to keep them in habitual remembrance of the divine commandments. **41. I am the Lord your God**—The import of this solemn conclusion is, that though He was displeased with them for their frequent rebellions, for which they would be doomed to forty years' wanderings, He would not abandon them but continue His divine protection and care of them till they were brought into the land of promise.

ADAM CLARKE

38. *Bid them . . . make them fringes.* **We learn from v. 39 that these fringes were emblematical of the various commands of God.**

MATTHEW HENRY

CHAPTER 16

Verses 1–11

Here is, I. An account of the rebels, who and what they were, men of distinction and quality, that made a figure. Korah was the ring-leader: he formed and headed the faction. With him joined Dathan and Abiram, chief men of the tribe of Reuben, the eldest son of Jacob. Probably Korah was disgusted both at the preferment of Aaron to the priesthood and the constituting of Elizaphan to the head of the Kohathites (*ch.* iii. 30); and perhaps the Reubenites were angry that the tribe of Judah had the first post of honour in the camp. And, these being themselves *men of renown,* they seduced into the conspiracy *two hundred and fifty princes of the assembly* (*v.* 2).

II. The rebels' remonstrance, *v.* 3. That which they quarrel with is the settlement of the priesthood upon Aaron and his family. 1. They proudly boast of the holiness of the congregation, and the presence of God in it. Small reason they had to boast of the people's purity, or of God's favour, as the people had been so frequently and so lately polluted with sin. 2. They unjustly charge Moses and Aaron with taking the honour they had to themselves, whereas it was evident, beyond contradiction, that they were called of God to it, Heb. v. 4. See here, (1) What spirit levellers are of, and those that despise dominions, and resist the powers that God has set over them; they are proud, envious, ambitious, turbulent, wicked, and unreasonable men. (2) What usage even the best and most useful men may expect.

III. Moses's conduct when this remonstrance was published against him.

1. He *fell on his face* (*v.* 4), as before, *ch.* xiv. 5. He applied to God, by prayer, for direction what to say and to do upon this sad occasion.

2. He agrees to refer the case to God, and leave it to him to decide it, as one well assured of the goodness of his title, and yet well content to resign, if God thought fit, to gratify this discontented people with another nomination.

3. He argues the case fairly with them, to still the mutiny with fair reasoning, if possible, before the appeal came to God's tribunal, for then he knew it would end in the confusion of his complainants.

(1) He calls them *the sons of Levi, v.* 7, and again *v.* 8. Levites, and yet rebels.

(2) He retorts their charge upon themselves. They had unjustly charged Moses and Aaron with taking too much upon them, though they had done no more than what God put upon them; nay, says Moses, *You take too much upon you, you sons of Levi.*

(3) He shows them the privilege they had as Levites, which was sufficient for them, they needed not to aspire to the honour of the priesthood, *v.* 9, 10.

(4) He convicts them of the sin of undervaluing those privileges: *Seemeth it a small thing unto you?*

(5) He interprets their mutiny to be a rebellion against God (*v.* 11); while they pretended to assert the holiness and liberty of the Israel of God, they really took up arms against the God of Israel: *You are gathered together against the Lord.*

Verses 12–22

Here is, I. The insolence of Dathan and Abiram, and their treasonable remonstrance. Moses had heard what Korah had to say, and had answered it;

JAMIESON, FAUSSET, BROWN

CHAPTER 16

VSS. 1-30. THE REBELLION OF KORAH. **1, 2. Now Korah, the son of Izhar**—Izhar, brother of Amram (Exod. 6:18), was the second son of Kohath, and for some reason unrecorded he had been supplanted by a descendant of the fourth son of Kohath, who was appointed prince or chief of the Kohathites (Ch. 3:30). Discontent with the preferment over him of a younger relative was probably the originating cause of this seditious movement on the part of Korah. **Dathan, and Abiram, . . . and On**—These were confederate leaders in the rebellion, but On seems to have afterwards withdrawn from the conspiracy. **took men**—The latter mentioned individuals, being all sons of Reuben, the eldest of Jacob's family, had been stimulated to this insurrection on the pretext that Moses had, by an arbitrary arrangement, taken away the right of primogeniture, which had vested the hereditary dignity of the priesthood in the first-born of every family, with a view of transferring the hereditary exercise of the sacred functions to a particular branch of his own house; and that this gross instance of partiality to his own relations, to the permanent detriment of others, was a sufficient ground for refusing allegiance to his government. In addition to this grievance, another cause of jealousy and dissatisfaction that rankled in the breasts of the Reubenites was the advancement of Judah to the leadership among the tribes. These malcontents had been incited by the artful representations of Korah (Jude 11), with whom the position of their camp on the south side afforded them facilities of frequent intercourse. In addition to his feeling of personal wrongs, Korah participated in their desire (if he did not originate the attempt) to recover their lost rights of primogeniture. When the conspiracy was ripe, they openly and boldly declared its object, and at the head of 250 princes, charged Moses with an ambitious and unwarrantable usurpation of authority, especially in the appropriation of the priesthood, for they disputed the claim of Aaron also to pre-eminence. **3. they gathered themselves together against Moses and against Aaron**—The assemblage seems to have been composed of the whole band of conspirators; and they grounded their complaint on the fact that the whole people, being separated to the divine service (Exod. 19:6), were equally qualified to present offerings on the altar, and that God, being graciously present among them by the tabernacle and the cloud, evinced His readiness to receive sacrifices from the hand of any others as well as from theirs. **4. when Moses heard it he fell upon his face**—This attitude of prostration indicated not only his humble and earnest desire that God would interpose to free him from the false and odious imputation, but also his strong sense of the daring sin involved in this proceeding. Whatever feelings may be entertained respecting Aaron, who had formerly headed a sedition himself, it is impossible not to sympathize with Moses in this difficult emergency. But he was a devout man, and the prudential course he adopted was probably the dictate of that heavenly wisdom with which, in answer to his prayers, he was endowed. **5-11. he spake unto Korah and unto all his company**—They were first addressed, not only because they were a party headed by his own cousin

ADAM CLARKE

CHAPTER 16

1. *Now Korah . . . took men.* **Had not these been the most brutish of men, could they have possibly so soon forgotten the signal displeasure of God manifested against them so lately for their rebellion? The word *men* is not in the original; and the verb *vaiyikkach,* "and he took," is not in the plural but the singular; hence it cannot be applied to the act of all these chiefs. In every part of the Scripture where this rebellion is referred to it is attributed to Korah (see chap. xxvi. 3 and Jude, v. 11). Therefore the verb here belongs to him, and the whole verse should be translated thus: "Now Korah, son of Yitsar, son of Kohath, son of Levi, he took even Dathan and Abiram, the sons of Eliab, and On, son of Peleth, son of Reuben; and they rose up . . ."**

3. *Ye take too much upon you.* **The original is simply *rab lachem,* "too much for you." The spirit of this saying appears to me to be the following: "Holy offices are not equally distributed: you arrogate to yourselves the most important ones, as if your superior holiness entitled you alone to them; whereas all the congregation are holy, and have an equal right with you to be employed in the most holy services." Moses retorts this saying, v. 7: "Ye take too much upon you," *rab lachem;* You have too much already, "ye sons of Levi"; i.e., by your present spirit and disposition you prove yourselves to be wholly unworthy of any spiritual employment.**

MATTHEW HENRY

now he summons Dathan and Abiram to bring in their complaints (*v.* 12); but they would not obey his summons. They send their articles of impeachment against Moses; and the charge runs very high. 1. They charge him with having done them a great deal of wrong in bringing them out of Egypt, invidiously calling that *a land flowing with milk and honey*, *v.* 13. 2. They charge him with a design upon their lives, that he intended to *kill them in the wilderness*. 3. They charge him with a design upon their liberties, that he meant to enslave them, by *making himself a prince over them*. A prince over them! Was he not a tender father to them? nay, their devoted servant for the Lord's sake? 4. They charge him with cheating them, raising their expectations of a good land, and then defeating them (*v.* 14): *Thou hast not brought us*, as thou promisedst us, *into a land that floweth with milk and honey*; and pray whose fault was that? He had brought them to the borders of it, and was just ready, under God, to put them in possession of it; but they thrust it away from them, and shut the door against themselves; so that it was purely their own fault that they were not now in Canaan, and yet Moses must bear the blame.

II. Moses's just resentment of their insolence, *v.* 15. In this discomposure,

1. He appeals to God concerning his own integrity; God was his witness, (1) That he never got any thing by them: *I have not taken one ass from them*, not only not by way of bribery and extortion, but not by way of recompence or gratuity for all the good offices he had done them. He got more in his estate when he kept Jethro's flock than when he came to be king in Jeshurun. (2) That they never lost any thing by him: *Neither have I hurt any one of them.*

2. He begs of God to plead his cause, and clear him, by showing his displeasure at the incense which Korah and his company were to offer, with whom Dathan and Abiram were in confederacy. Lord, says he, *Respect not thou their offering*.

III. Issue joined between Moses and his accusers. 1. Moses challenges them to appear with Aaron next morning, at the time of offering up the morning incense, and refer the matter to God's judgment, *v.* 16, 17. 2. Korah accepts the challenge, and makes his appearance with Moses and Aaron *at the door of the tabernacle*, to make good his pretensions, *v.* 18, 19. They *took every man his censer*. Perhaps these were some of the censers which these heads of families had made use of at their family-altars.

IV. The judgment set, and the Judge taking the tribunal, and threatening to give sentence against the whole congregation. 1. The *glory of the Lord appeared*, *v.* 19. The same glory that appeared to install Aaron in his office at first (Lev. ix. 23) now appeared to confirm him in it, and to confound those that oppose him. 2. God threatened to *consume them all in a moment*, and, in order to that, bade Moses and Aaron stand from among them, *v.* 21.

V. The humble intercession of Moses and Aaron for the congregation, *v.* 22. 1. Their posture was importuning: they *fell on their faces*, prostrating themselves before God, as supplicants in good earnest, that they might prevail for sparing mercy. Though the people had treacherously deserted them, and struck in with those that were in arms against them, yet they approved themselves faithful to the trusts reposed in them, as shepherds of Israel, who were to stand in the breach when they saw the flock in danger. Note, If others fail in their duty to us, this does not discharge us from our duty to them, nor take off the obligations we lie under to seek their welfare. 2. Their prayer was a pleading prayer, and it proved a prevailing one. Observe in the prayer, (1) The title they give to God: *The God of the spirits of all flesh*. See what man is; he is a spirit in flesh, a soul embodied, a creature wonderfully compounded of heaven and earth. See what God is; he is the God of the spirits of all mankind. (2) The argument they insist on; it is much the same with that which Abraham urged in his intercession for Sodom (Gen. xviii. 23): *Wilt thou destroy the righteous with the wicked?* Such is the plea here: *Shall one man sin and wilt thou be wroth with all the congregation?*

Verses 23–34

We have here the determining of the controversy with Dathan and Abiram, who rebelled against Moses, as in the next paragraph the determining of the controversy with Korah and his company, who would be rivals with Aaron. It should seem that Dathan and Abiram had set up a spacious tabernacle in the midst of the tents of their families, where they kept court, met in council, and hung out their flag of defiance against Moses; it is here called *the tabernacle of Korah, Dathan and Abiram*, *v.* 24, 27.

I. Public warning is given to the congregation to

JAMIESON, FAUSSET, BROWN

and Moses might hope to have more influence in that quarter, but because they were stationed near the tabernacle; and especially because an expostulation was the more weighty coming from him who was a Levite himself, and who was excluded along with his family from the priesthood. But to bring the matter to an issue, he proposed a test which would afford a decisive evidence of the divine appointment. **Even to-morrow**—lit., "in the morning," the usual time of meeting in the East for the settlement of public affairs. **the Lord will show who are his, . . . even him whom he hath chosen will he cause to come near unto him**—i.e., will bear attestation to his ministry by some visible or miraculous token of His approval. **6. Take your censers, Korah, and all his company,** etc.—i.e., since you aspire to the priesthood, then go, perform the highest function of the office—that of offering incense; and if you are accepted—well. How magnanimous the conduct of Moses, who was now as willing that God's people should be priests, as formerly that they should be prophets (Ch. 11:29). But he warned them that they were making a perilous experiment. **12-14. Moses sent to call Dathan and Abiram**—in a separate interview, the ground of their mutiny being different; for while Korah murmured against the exclusive appropriation of the priesthood to Aaron and his family, they were opposed to the supremacy of Moses in civil power. They refused to obey the summons; and their refusal was grounded on the plausible pretext that their stay in the desert was prolonged for some secret and selfish purposes of the leader, who was conducting them like blind men wherever it suited him. **15. Moses was very wroth**—Though the meekest of all men, he could not restrain his indignation at these unjust and groundless charges; and the higly excited state of his feeling was evinced by the utterance of a brief exclamation in the mixed form of a prayer and an impassioned assertion of his integrity. (Cf. I Sam. 12:3.) **and said unto the Lord, Respect not thou their offering**—He calls it *their* offering, because, though it was to be offered by Korah and his Levitical associates, it was the united appeal of all the mutineers for deciding the contested claims of Moses and Aaron. **16-18. Moses said unto Korah, Be thou and all thy company before the Lord**—i.e., at "the door of the tabernacle" (vs. 18), that the assembled people might witness the experiment and be properly impressed by the issue. **two hundred and fifty censers**—probably the small platters, common in Egyptian families, where incense was offered to household deities and which had been among the precious things borrowed at their departure. **20. 21 the Lord spake unto Moses and Aaron, saying, Separate yourselves from among this congregation**—Curiosity to witness the exciting spectacle attracted a vast concourse of the people, and it would seem that the popular mind had been incited to evil by the clamors of the mutineers against Moses and Aaron. There was something in their behavior very offensive to God; for after His glory had appeared—as at the installation of Aaron (Lev. 9:23), so now for his confirmation in the sacred office—He bade Moses and Aaron withdraw from the assembly "that He might consume them in a moment." **22. they fell upon their faces, and said, O God, the God of the spirits of all flesh**—The benevolent importunity of their prayer was the more remarkable that the intercession was made for their enemies.

ADAM CLARKE

TODAY'S DICTIONARY OF THE BIBLE:

Korah. A Levite, the son of Izhar, the brother of Amram, the father of Moses and Aaron (Ex. 6:21). The institution of the Aaronic priesthood and the Levitical service at Sinai was a great religious revolution. The old priesthood of the heads of families passed away. This gave rise to murmurings and discontent—while the Israelites were encamped at Kadesh for the first time—which came to be a head in a rebellion against Moses and Aaron, headed by Korah, Dathan, and Abiram. Two hundred and fifty princes, "men of renown"—i.e., well-known men from among the other tribes—joined this conspiracy. The whole company demanded of Moses and Aaron that the old state of things should be restored, alleging that "they took too much upon them" (Num. 16:1–3). On the morning after the outbreak, Korah and his associates presented themselves at the door of the tabernacle, and "took every man his censer, and put fire in them, and laid incense thereon." But immediately "fire from the Lord" burst forth and destroyed them all (Num. 16:35). Dathan and Abiram "came out and stood in the door of their tents, and their wives, and their sons, and their little children," and it came to pass "that the ground clave asunder that was under them; and the earth opened her mouth and swallowed them up." A plague thereafter began among the people who sympathized in the rebellion, and was only halted by Aaron's appearing between the living and the dead, and making "an atonement for the people" (16:46).

The descendants of the sons of Korah who did not participate in the rebellion afterward rose to eminence in the Levitical service.

15. *Respect not thou their offering.* There was no danger of this; they wished to set up a priesthood and a sacrificial system of their own and God never has blessed, and never can bless any scheme of salvation which is not of His own appointment.

MATTHEW HENRY

withdraw immediately from the tents of the rebels. . God bids Moses speak to this purport, *v.* 24. This was in answer to Moses's prayer. He had begged that God would not *destroy the whole congregation.* God never promised to save by miracles those that would not save themselves by means. Moses that had prayed for them must preach this to them, and warn them to *flee from this wrath to come.* 2. Moses accordingly repairs to the head-quarters of the rebels, leaving Aaron at the door of the tabernacle, *v.* 25. Dathan and Abiram had contumaciously refused to come up to him (*v.* 12), yet he humbly condescends to go down to them, to try if he could yet convince and reclaim them. 3. Proclamation is made that all manner of persons, as they tendered their own safety, should forthwith *depart from the tents of these wicked men* (*v.* 26).

II. The congregation takes the warning, but the rebels themselves continue obstinate, *v.* 27. 1. God, in mercy, inclined the people to forsake the rebels. . God, in justice, left the rebels to the obstinacy and hardness of their own hearts. They impudently *stood in the doors of their tents,* as if they would outface God himself, and dare him to his worst.

III. Sentence is solemnly pronounced upon them by Moses in the name of the Lord, and the decision of the controversy is put upon the execution of that sentence by the almighty power of God.

IV. Execution is immediately done. It appeared that God and his servant Moses understood one another very well; for, as soon as ever Moses had spoken the word, God did the work, the earth *clave asunder* (*v.* 31), *opened her mouth, and swallowed them all up,* them and theirs (*v.* 32), and then *closed upon them, v.* 33. This judgment was, 1. Unparalleled. . It was very terrible to the sinners themselves to go down alive into their own graves. 3. It was severe upon their poor children, though we cannot particularly tell how bad they might be to deserve it or how good God might be otherwise to them to compensate it, yet of this we are sure in general, that infinite Justice did them no wrong.

V. All Israel is alarmed at the judgment: *They fled at the cry of them, v.* 34. Note, Others' ruins should be our warnings.

Verses 35–40

We must now look back to the door of the tabernacle, where we left the pretenders to the priesthood, with their censers in their hands ready to offer incense; and here we find,

I. Vengeance taken on them, *v.* 35. This punishment was no less strange or dreadful, and in it it appeared, 1. That *our God is a consuming fire.* . That it is at our peril if we meddle with that which does not belong to us. God is jealous of the honour of his own institutions, and will not have them invaded. Had they been content with their office as Levites, which was sacred and honourable, and better than they deserved, they might have lived and died with joy and reputation.

II. Care is taken to perpetuate the remembrance of this vengeance. Orders are given about their censers, . That they be secured, because they are hallowed. Eleazar is charged with this, *v.* 37. Now Eleazar is ordered to scatter the fire, with the incense that was kindled with it, in some unclean place without the camp, to signify God's abhorrence of their offering as a polluted thing: *The sacrifice of the wicked is an abomination to the Lord.* But he is to gather up the censers out of the mingled burning, God's fire and theirs, because *they are hallowed.* 2. That they be used in the service of the sanctuary. They must be beaten into *broad plates for a covering of the brazen altar, v.* 38–40. These pretenders thought to have ruined the altar, by laying the priesthood in common again; but, to show that Aaron's office was so far from being shaken by their impotent malice that it was rather confirmed by it, their censers, which offered to rival his, were used both for the adorning and for the preserving of the altar at which he ministered. These censers were preserved *in terrorem,* that others might hear and fear, and do no more presumptuously.

Verses 41–50

Here is, I. A new rebellion raised the very next day against Moses and Aaron. *On the morrow* (*v.* 41) the body of the people mutinied. 1. Though they were so lately terrified by the sight of the punishment of the rebels. The same sins were re-acted and all these warnings slighted. 2. Though they were so lately saved from sharing in the same punishment. Their charge runs very high: *You have killed the people of the Lord.* Could anything have been said more unjustly and maliciously? It was plain enough that Moses and Aaron had no hand in their death (they did what they could to save them), so that in

JAMIESON, FAUSSET, BROWN

24-26. Speak unto the congregation, . . . Get you up from about the tabernacle—Moses was attended in the execution of this mission by the elders. The united and urgent entreaties of so many dignified personages produced the desired effect of convincing the people of their crime, and of withdrawing them from the company of men who were doomed to destruction, lest, being partakers of their sins, they should perish along with them.

27. the tabernacle of Korah, Dathan, and Abiram—Korah being a Kohathite, his tent could not have been in the Reubenite camp, and it does not appear that he himself was on the spot where Dathan and Abiram stood with their families. Their attitude of defiance indicated their daring and impenitent character, equally regardless of God and man. **28-34. Moses said, Hereby ye shall know that the Lord hath sent me to do all these works**—The awful catastrophe of the earthquake which, as predicted by Moses, swallowed up those impious rebels in a living tomb, gave the divine attestation to the mission of Moses and struck the spectators with solemn awe.

35. there came out a fire from the Lord—i.e., from the cloud—This seems to describe the destruction of Korah and those Levites who with him aspired to the functions of the priesthood. (See on ch. 26:11, 58; I Chron. 6:22, 37.)

37-39. Speak unto Eleazar—He was selected lest the high priest might contract defilement from going among the dead carcasses. **the brazen censers . . . made broad plates to be a memorial**—The altar of burnt offerings, being made of wood and covered with brass, this additional covering of broad plates not only rendered it doubly secure against the fire, but served as a warning-beacon to deter all from future invasions of the priesthood.

41. the children of Israel murmured against Moses and against Aaron, saying, Ye have killed the people of the Lord—What a strange exhibition of popular prejudice and passion—to blame the leaders for saving the rebels! Yet Moses and Aaron interceded for the people—the high priest perilling his own life in doing good to that perverse race.

ADAM CLARKE

30. *If the Lord make a new thing. Veim beriah yibra Yehovah,* "And if Jehovah should create a creation," i.e., do such a thing as was never done before. *And they go down quick into the pit. Sheolah,* a proof, among many others, that *sheol* signifies here a "chasm" or "pit" of the earth, and not the place called hell; for it would be absurd to suppose that their houses had gone to hell; and it would be wicked to imagine that their little innocent children had gone thither, though God was pleased to destroy their lives with those of their iniquitous fathers.

33. *They, and all that appertained to them.* Korah, Dathan, and Abiram, and all that appertained to their respective families, went down into the pit caused by this supernatural earthquake; while the fire from the Lord consumed the 250 men that bare censers. Thus there were two distinct punishments, the pit and the fire, for the two divisions of these rebels.

37. *The censers . . . are hallowed. Kadeshu,* are "consecrated," i.e., to the service of God, though in this instance improperly employed.

41. *On the morrow all the congregation . . . murmured.* It is very likely that the people persuaded themselves that Moses and Aaron had used some cunning in this business, and that the earthquake and fire were artificial; else, had they discerned the hand of God in this punishment, could they have dared the anger of the Lord in the very face of justice?

MATTHEW HENRY	JAMIESON, FAUSSET, BROWN	ADAM CLARKE

charging them with murder they did in effect charge God himself with it. The terrors of his judgments as they were here executed on the disobedient, shows how necessary the grace of God is to the effectual change of men's hearts and lives. Love will do what fear could not.

II. God's speedy appearance against the rebels. When they had *gathered against Moses and Aaron*, perhaps with a design to depose or murder them, they *looked towards the tabernacle*, as if their misgiving consciences expected some frowns thence, and, *behold, the glory of the Lord appeared* (*v.* 42), for the protection of his servants, and the confusion of his and their accusers and adversaries.

III. The intercession which Moses and Aaron made for them. 1. They both *fell on their faces*, humbly to intercede with God for mercy. This they had done several times before, upon similar occasions; and, though the people had basely requited them for it, yet, God having graciously accepted them, they still have recourse to the same method. This is praying always. 2. Moses, perceiving that the *plague had begun in the congregation* of the rebels, sent Aaron by an act of his priestly office to make atonement for them, *v.* 46. And Aaron readily went and burned incense between the living and the dead. By this it appeared, (1) That Aaron was a very good man, and a man that had a true love for the children of his people, though they hated and envied him. (2) That Aaron was a very bold man—bold to venture into the midst of an enraged rabble, bold to venture into the midst of the infection. To save their lives he put his own into his hand, not counting it dear to him, so that he might but fulfil his ministry. (3) That Aaron was a man of God, and *ordained for men, in things pertaining to God.* His call to the priesthood was hereby abundantly confirmed and set above all contradiction. (4) That Aaron was a type of Christ, who came into the world to make an atonement for sin.

IV. The result and issue of the whole matter. God showed them what he could do by his power, and what he might do in justice, but then showed them what he would do in his love and pity: he would, notwithstanding all this, preserve them a people to himself in and by a mediator.

CHARLES H. SPURGEON:

Aaron deserves to be very highly praised for his patriotic affection for a people who were the most rebellious and stiffnecked that ever grieved the heart of a good man. You must remember that in this case *he* was the aggrieved party. The clamor was made against Moses and against Aaron, yet it was Moses and Aaron who interceded and saved the people. They were the offended ones, yet were they the saving ones. Aaron had a special part in the matter, for no doubt the conflict of Korah especially was rather against the priesthood, which belonged exclusively to Aaron, than against the prophetical dispensation which God had granted to Moses. Aaron must have felt when he saw Korah there and two hundred and fifty men, all of them with their censers, that the plot was against *him*; that they wished to strip from him his mitre, to take from him his embroidered vest, and the glittering stones that shone upon his breast; that they wished to reduce him to the position of a common Levite, and take to themselves his office and his dignity. Yet, forgetting himself, he does not say, "Let them die; I will wait awhile till they have been sufficiently smitten." But the old man with generous love hastened into the midst of the people, though he was himself the aggrieved person. Is not this the very picture of our sweet Lord Jesus?—*The Treasury of the Old Testament*

48. he stood between the living and the dead—The plague seems to have begun in the extremities of the camp. Aaron, in this remarkable act, was a type of Christ.

46. *The plague is begun.* God now punishe them by a secret blast, so as to put the matte beyond all dispute; His hand, and His alone, wa seen, not only in the plague, but in the manne in which the mortality was arrested. It wa necessary that this should be done in this wa that the whole congregation might see that thos men who had perished were not the people o the Lord; and that God, not Moses and Aaro had destroyed them.

48. *He stood between the dead and the living and the plague.* What the plague was we kno not, but it seems to have begun at one part o the camp and to have proceeded regularly on ward; and Aaron went to the quarter where was then prevailing, and stood with his atone ment where it was now making its ravage *And the plague was stayed;* but not befor **14,700 had fallen victims to it, v. 49.**

CHAPTER 17

Verses 1–7

Here we have, I. Orders given for the bringing in of a rod for every tribe that God by a miracle might make it known on whom he had conferred the honour of the priesthood. 1. It seems then the priesthood was a preferment worth seeking and striving for, even by the princes of the tribes. 2. It seems there were those who would not acquiesce in the divine appointment, but would make an interest in opposition to it. God will rule, but Israel will not be ruled; and this is the quarrel. 3. It is an instance of the grace of God that, having wrought divers miracles to punish sin, he would work one more on purpose to prevent it. The directions are, (1) That twelve rods or staves should be brought in. It is probable that they were all made of the almond-tree. It should seem they were but twelve in all, with Aaron's, for, when Levi comes into the account, Ephraim and Manasseh make but one, under the name of Joseph. (2) That the name of each prince should be written upon his rod. (3) That they should be laid up in the tabernacle, for one night, before the testimony, that is, before the ark, which, with its mercy-seat, was a symbol, token, or testimony, of God's presence with them. (4) They were to expect that the rod of the tribe, or prince, whom God chose to the priesthood, should bud and blossom, *v.* 5.

II. The preparing of the rods accordingly. The princes brought them in, and *Moses laid them up before the Lord.*

Verses 8–13

Here is, I. The final determination of the controversy concerning the priesthood by a miracle, *v.* 8, 9. The rods or staves were brought out from the most holy place where they were laid up, and publicly produced before the people; and, while all the rest of the rods remained as they were, Aaron's rod only, of a dry stick, became a living branch, budded, and blossomed, and yielded almonds. This was miraculous, and took away all suspicion of a fraud, as if in the night Moses had taken away Aaron's rod, and put a living branch of an almond tree in the room, of it; for no ordinary branch would have buds, blossoms, and fruits upon it, all at once. Now,

1. This was a plain indication to the people that

CHAPTER 17

Vss. 1-13. AARON'S ROD FLOURISHES. **2. Speak unto the children of Israel**—The controversy with Moses and Aaron about the priesthood was of such a nature and magnitude as required a decisive and authoritative settlement. For the removal of all doubts and the silencing of all murmuring in the future regarding the holder of the office, a miracle was wrought of a remarkable character and permanent duration; and in the manner of performing it, all the people were made to have a direct and special interest. **take of every one . . . princes . . . twelve rods**—As the princes, being the oldest sons of the chief family, and heads of their tribes, might have advanced the best claims to the priesthood, if that sacred dignity was to be shared among all the tribes, they were therefore selected, and being twelve in number—that of Joseph being counted only one—Moses was ordered to see that the name of each was inscribed—a practice borrowed from the Egyptians—upon his rod or wand of office. The name of Aaron rather than of Levi was used, as the latter name would have opened a door of controversy among the Levites; and as there was to be one rod only for the head of each tribe, the express appointment of a rod for Aaron determined him to be the head of that tribe, as well as that branch or family of the tribe to which the priestly dignity should belong. These rods were to be laid in the tabernacle close to the ark (cf. vs. 10 and Heb. 9:4), where a divine token was promised that would for all time terminate the dispute. **6. the rod of Aaron was among their rods**—either one of the twelve, or, as many suppose, a thirteenth in the midst (Heb. 9:4). The rods were of dry sticks or wands, probably old, as transmitted from one head of the family to a succeeding. **8. Moses went into the tabernacle**—being privileged to do so on this occasion by the special command of God; and he there beheld the remarkable spectacle of Aaron's rod—which, according to Josephus, was a stick of an almond tree, bearing fruit in three different stages at once—buds, blossoms, and fruit.

CHAPTER 17

2. *And take of every one of them a rod Matteh,* the "staff" or "scepter," which the prince or chief of each tribe bore, and which was the sign of office or royalty among almos all the people of the earth.

5. *The man's rod, whom I shall choose, shal blossom.* It was necessary that something furthe should be done to quiet the minds of the people and forever to settle the dispute in what trib the priesthood should be fixed. God therefor took the method described in the text, and i had the desired effect; the Aaronical priesthoo was never after disputed.

8. *The rod of Aaron . . . was budded.* Tha is, on the same rod or staff were found buds blossoms, and ripe fruit. This fact was so un questionably miraculous as to decide the busi ness forever; and probably this was intended t show that in the priesthood, represented by tha of Aaron, the beginning, middle, and end o every good work must be found. The buds o good desires, the blossoms of holy resolution and promising professions, and the ripe fruit o faith, love, and obedience, all spring from th priesthood of the Lord Jesus.

MATTHEW HENRY

Aaron was chosen to the priesthood. Bishop Hall here observes that fruitfulness is the best evidence of a divine call, and that the plants of God's setting, and the boughs cut off from them, will flourish. See Ps. xcii. 12–14. The trees of the Lord, though they seem dry trees, are full of sap.

2. It was a very proper sign to represent the priesthood itself, which was hereby confirmed to Aaron. (1) That it should be fruitful and serviceable to the church of God. (2) That there should be a succession of priests. Here were not only almonds for the present, but buds and blossoms promising more hereafter. (3) That yet this priesthood should not be perpetual, but in process of time, like the branches and blossoms of a tree, should fail and wither.

3. It was a type and figure of Christ and his priesthood. He was to *grow up before God*, as this before the ark, *like a tender plant, and a root out of a dry ground*, Isa. liii. 2.

II. The record of this determination, by the preserving of the rod before the testimony, *in perpetuam rei memoriam—that it might be had in perpetual remembrance*, *v.* 10, 11. 1. The design of God in all his providences is to take away sin, and to prevent it. 2. What God does for the taking away of sin is done in real kindness to us, *that we die not*. All the bitter potions he gives, and all the sharp methods he uses with us, are for the cure of a disease which otherwise would certainly be fatal.

III. The outcry of the people hereupon (*v.* 12, 13): *Behold, we die, we perish, we all perish. Shall we be consumed with dying?* This may be considered as the language either, 1. Of a repining people quarrelling with the judgments of God, which, by their own pride and obstinacy, they had brought upon themselves. They seem to speak despairingly, as if God was a hard Master, that sought advantage against them. Or, 2. Of a repenting people. We submit to the divine will in this appointment; we will not contend any more, lest we all perish.

CHAPTER 18

Verses 1–7

The coherence of this chapter with that foregoing is very observable.

I. The people, in the close of that chapter, had complained of the difficulty and peril that there were in drawing near to God. Now, in answer to this complaint, God here gives them to understand by Aaron that the priests should come near for them as their representatives.

II. A great deal of honour God had now lately put upon Aaron. Now God comes to him to remind him of the burden that was laid upon him, and the duty required from him as a priest. He would see reason to receive the honours of his office with reverence and holy trembling, when he considered how great was the charge committed to him.

1. God tells him of the danger that attended his dignity, *v.* 1. (1) That both the priests and Levites (*thou, and thy sons, and thy father's house*) should *bear the iniquity of the sanctuary*; that is, if the sanctuary were profaned by the intrusion of strangers, or persons in their uncleanness, the blame should lie upon the Levites and priests, who ought to have kept them off. (2) That the priests should themselves *bear the iniquity of the priesthood*; that is, if they either neglected any part of their work or permitted any other persons to invade their office, and take their work out of their hands, they should bear the blame of it.

2. He tells him of the duty that attended his dignity. (1) That he and his sons must *minister before the tabernacle of witness* (*v.* 2); that is (as bishop Patrick explains it), *before the most holy place*, in which the ark was, on the outside of the veil of that tabernacle, but within the door of the tabernacle of the congregation. They were to attend the golden altar, the table, and candlestick, which no Levite might approach to. *You shall serve*, *v.* 7. Not, "You shall rule". Ministers must remember that they are ministers, that is, servants, of whom it is required that they be humble, diligent, and faithful. (2) That the Levites must assist him and his sons, and minister to them in all the *service of the tabernacle* (*v.* 2–4), though they must by no means come nigh the vessels of the sanctuary. (3) That both priests and Levites must carefully watch against the profanation of sacred things. The Levites must *keep the charge of the tabernacle*. And the priests must *keep the charge of the sanctuary* (*v.* 5), must instruct the people, and admonish them concerning the due distance they were to keep.

JAMIESON, FAUSSET, BROWN

TODAY'S DICTIONARY OF THE BIBLE:

Rod—is sometimes used interchangeably for "staff." In the Hebrew there are three words translated rod: *maqqel*, Gen. 30:37 f.; *matteh*, Ex. 4:2; 7:15 f.; *choter*, Isa. 11:1. It can refer to a shepherd's staff or rod, usually fashioned from a tree limb and sometimes tipped with metal for use as a weapon to protect the flock from wolves and other predators. This is the rod spoken of in Ps. 23:4 as a guiding instrument. Moses had such a rod which miraculously turned into a serpent (Ex. 4:1–5; 7:9–12, 17 f.). Each of the twelve tribes of Israel had its own rod with it name symbolically indicated (Num. 17:2, 5–11). God used a "rod" to correct and chastise his people (Job 9:34; Ps. 2:9; Isa. 10:5, 24; Ezek. 20:37). The rod was used by fathers for punishing disobedient children (Prov. 13:24; 22:15), or it could also be used as a public instrument of punishment (2 Cor. 11:25). The rod could also be a measuring instrument to determine distance (Ezek. 40:3).

10. Bring Aaron's rod again before the testimony, to be kept for a token against the rebels—For if, after all admonitions and judgments, seconded by miracles, the people should still rebel, they would certainly pay the penalty by death.

12, 13. Behold we die, we perish—an exclamation of fear, both from the remembrance of former judgments, and the apprehension of future relapses into murmuring. **cometh any thing near**—i.e., nearer than he ought to do; an error into which many may fall. Will the stern justice of God overtake every slight offense? We shall all be destroyed. Some, however, regard this exclamation as the symptom or a new discontent, rather than the indication of a reverential and submissive spirit. Let us fear and sin not.

CHAPTER 18

VSS. 1-7. THE CHARGE OF THE PRIESTS AND LEVITES. **1. the Lord said unto Aaron, Thou and thy sons and thy father's house with thee shall bear the iniquity of the sanctuary**—Security is here given to the people from the fears expressed (ch. 17:12), by the responsibility of attending to all sacred things being devolved upon the priesthood, together with the penalties incurred through neglect; and thus the solemn responsibilities annexed to their high dignity, of having to answer not only for their own sins, but also for the sins of the people, were calculated in a great measure to remove all feeling of envy at the elevation of Aaron's family, when the honor was weighed in the balance with its burdens and dangers.

2-7. thy brethren also of the tribe of Levi—The departments of the sacred office, to be filled respectively by the priests and Levites, are here assigned to each. To the priests was committed the charge of the sanctuary and the altar, while the Levites were to take care of everything else about the tabernacle. The Levites were to attend the priests as servants—bestowed on them as "gifts" to aid in the service of the tabernacle—while the high and dignified office of the priesthood was a "service of gift." "A stranger," i.e., one, neither a priest nor a Levite, who should intrude into any departments of the sacred office, should incur the penalty of death.

ADAM CLARKE

12. *Behold, we die, we perish, we all perish. Gavaenu* signifies not so much to *die* simply, as to feel an extreme difficulty of breathing, which, producing suffocation, ends at last in death. See the folly and extravagance of this sinful people. At first every person might come near to God, for all, they thought, were sufficiently holy, and every way qualified to minister in holy things. Now no one, in their apprehension, can come near to the Tabernacle without being consumed, v. 13. In both cases they were wrong; some there were who might approach, others there were who might not. God had put the difference. His decision should have been final with them.

CHAPTER 18

1. *Thou and thy sons . . . shall bear the iniquity of the sanctuary.* That is, They must be answerable for its legal pollutions, and must make the necessary atonements and expiations. By this they must feel that, though they had a high and important office confirmed to them by a miraculous interference, yet it was a place of the highest responsibility; and that they must not be high-minded, but fear.

2. *Thy brethren also of the tribe of Levi . . . may be joined unto thee.* There is a fine paronomasia, or play upon words, in the original. *Levi* comes from the root *lavah*, to "join to, couple, associate"; hence Moses says, The *Levites, yillavu*, shall be *joined*, or associated, with the priests; they shall conjointly perform the whole of the sacred office, but the priests shall be principal, the Levites only their associates or assistants.

MATTHEW HENRY

Verses 8–19

The priest's service is called a *warfare*; and who goes a-warring at his own charges? As they were well employed, so they were well provided for. Those that *served at the altar lived upon the altar*, So those that preach the gospel should *live upon the gospel*, and live comfortably, 1 Cor. ix. 13, 14. Scandalous maintenance makes scandalous ministers. Now observe, 1. That much of the provision that was made for them arose out of the sacrifices which they themselves were employed to offer. 2. Their maintenance was such as left them altogether *disentangled from the affairs of this life*. Thus provision is made that a gospel ministry should continue till Christ comes, by an ordinance for ever. *Lo, I am with you* (that is their maintenance and support) *always, even to the end of the world*.

Verses 20–32

A further account of the provision that was made both for the Levites and for the priests, out of the country.

I. They must have *no inheritance in the land*; only cities to dwell in were afterwards allowed them, but no ground to occupy. God dispenses his favours variously. The Levites have the honour of attending the tabernacle, which is denied the Israelites; but then the Israelites have the honour of inheritances in Canaan, which is denied the Levites.

II. But they must both have tithes of the land. Besides the first-fruits which were appropriated to the priests, the tithe also was appropriated. 1. The Levites had the tithes of the people's increase (*v.* 21). The Levites were the smallest tribe of the twelve, and yet, besides all other advantages, they had a tenth part of the yearly profits, without the trouble and expense of ploughing and sowing. 2. The priests had the tenths of the Levites' tithes settled upon them. The order for this Moses is directed to give to the Levites, whom God would have to pay it with cheerfulness, rather than the priests to demand it with authority. (1) The Levites were to give God his dues out of their tithes, as well as the Israelites out of their increase. Those that are employed to assist the devotions of others must be sure to pay their own, as a heave-offering to the Lord. Prayers and praises lifted up to God, or rather the heart lifted up in them, are now our heave-offerings. (2) This was to be given to *Aaron the priest* (*v.* 28), and to his successors the high priests, to be divided and disposed of in such proportions as they should think fit among the inferior priests.

JAMIESON, FAUSSET, BROWN

8-20. THE PRIESTS' PORTION. **8-13. the Lord spake unto Aaron, I also have given thee the charge of my heave offerings**—A recapitulation is made in this passage of certain perquisites specially appropriated to the maintenance of the priests. They were parts of the votive and freewill offerings, including both meat and bread, wine and oil, and the first-fruits, which formed a large and valuable item. **14. Every thing devoted in Israel shall be thine**—provided it was adapted for food or consumable by use; for the gold and silver vessels that were dedicated as the spoils of victory were not given to the priests, but for the use and adornment of the sacred edifice. **19. it is a covenant of salt**—i.e., a perpetual ordinance. This figurative form of expression was evidently founded on the conservative property of salt, which keeps meat from corruption; and hence it became an emblem of inviolability and permanence. It is a common phrase among Oriental people, who consider the eating of salt a pledge of fidelity, binding them in a covenant of friendship. Hence the partaking of the altar meats, which were appropriated to the priests on condition of their services and of which salt formed a necessary accompaniment, was naturally called a covenant of salt (Lev. 2:13).

21-32. THE LEVITES' PORTION. **21, 22. I have given to the children of Levi all the tenth in Israel for an inheritance, for their service which they serve**—Neither the priests nor the Levites were to possess any allotments of land but to depend entirely upon Him who liberally provided for them out of His own portion; and this law was subservient to many important purposes—such as that, being exempted from the cares and labors of worldly business, they might be exclusively devoted to His service; that a bond of mutual love and attachment might be formed between the people and the Levites, who, as performing religious services for the people, derived their subsistence from them; and further, that being the more easily dispersed among the different tribes, they might be more useful in instructing and directing the people. **23. But the Levites shall do the service of the congregation: they shall bear their iniquity**—They were to be responsible for the right discharge of those duties that were assigned to them, and consequently to bear the penalty that was due to negligence or carelessness in the guardianship of the holy things. **26. the Levites . . . offer . . . a tenth of the tithe**—Out of their own they were to pay tithes to the priests equally as the people gave to them. The best of their tithes was to be assigned to the priests, and afterwards they enjoyed the same liberty to make use of the remainder that other Israelites had of the produce of their threshing-floors and winepresses. **32. ye shall bear no sin by reason of it,** etc.—Neglect in having the best entailed sin in the use of such unhallowed food, and the holy things would be polluted by the reservation to themselves of what should be offered to God and the priests.

ADAM CLARKE

15. *The firstborn of man . . . and the firstling of unclean beasts*. Thus vain man is ranked with the beasts that perish; and with the worst kinds of them too, those deemed unclean.

16. *Shalt thou redeem . . . for the money of five shekels*. Redemption of the firstborn is one of the rites which is still practiced among the Jews.

19. *It is a covenant of salt*. That is, an incorruptible, everlasting covenant. As *salt* was added to different kinds of viands, not only to give them a relish, but to preserve them from putrefaction and decay, it became the emblem of incorruptibility and permanence. Hence, *a covenant of salt* signified an everlasting covenant.

20. *I am thy part and thine inheritance*. The principal part of what was offered to God was the portion of the priests; therefore they had no inheritance of land in Israel—independently of that they had a very ample provision for their support.

21. *Behold, I have given the children of Levi all the tenth*. (1) The Levites had the tenth of all the productions of the land. (2) They had 48 cities, each forming a square of 4,000 cubits. (3) They had 2,000 cubits of ground round each city. (4) They had the firstfruits and certain parts of all the animals killed in the land.

28. *Thus ye also shall offer an heave offering*. As the Levites had the tithe of the whole land, they themselves were obliged to give the tithe of this tithe to the priests, so that this considerably lessened their revenue. And this tithe or tenth they were obliged to select from the best part of the substance they had received, vv. 29, etc. A portion of all must be given to God, as an evidence of His goodness, and their dependence on Him. See the end of chap. xx.

MATTHEW HENRY — CHAPTER 19

Verses 1–10

We have here the divine appointment concerning the solemn burning of a red heifer to ashes, and the preserving of the ashes, that of them might be made, not a beautifying, but a purifying, water, for that was the utmost the law reached to; it offered not to adorn as the gospel does, but to cleanse only.

I. There was a great deal of care employed in the choice of the heifer that was to be burnt, much more than in the choice of any other offering, *v.* 2. It must not only be without blemish, typifying the spotless purity and sinless perfection of the Lord Jesus, but it must be a red heifer, because of the rarity of the colour, that it might be the more remarkable. And it must be one on which never came yoke, which was not insisted on in other sacrifices, but thus was typified the voluntary offer of the Lord Jesus, when he said, *Lo, I come*. He was bound and held with no other cords than those of his own love.

II. There was to be a great deal of ceremony in the burning of it. The care of doing it was committed to Eleazar. By him that was next to Aaron in dignity. Now,

1. The heifer was to be slain without the camp, as an impure thing, which bespeaks the insufficiency of the methods prescribed by the ceremonial law to take away sin.

2. Eleazar was to *sprinkle the blood directly before the door of the tabernacle*, and looking steadfastly towards it, *v.* 4. This made it in some sort an expiation; for the sprinkling of the blood before the Lord was the chief solemnity in all the sacrifices of atonement.

JAMIESON, FAUSSET, BROWN — CHAPTER 19

VSS. 1-22. THE WATER OF SEPARATION. **2. This is the ordinance of the law**—an institution of a peculiar nature ordained by law for the purification of sin, and provided at the public expense because it was for the good of the whole community. **Speak unto the children of Israel, that they bring thee a red heifer without spot,** etc.—This is the only case in which the color of the victim is specified. It has been supposed the ordinance was designed in opposition to the superstitious notions of the Egyptians. That people never offered a vow but they sacrificed a red bull, the greatest care being taken by their priests in examining whether it possessed the requisite characteristics, and it was an annual offering to Typhon, their evil being. By the choice, both of the sex and the color, provision was made for eradicating from the minds of the Israelites a favorite Egyptian superstition regarding two objects of their animal worship. **3. ye shall give her unto Eleazar, that he may bring her forth without the camp**—He was the second or deputy high priest, and he was selected for this duty because the execution of it entailed temporary defilement, from which the acting high priest was to be preserved with the greatest care. It was led "forth without the camp," in accordance with the law regarding victims laden with the sins of the people, and thus typical of Christ (Heb. 13:12; also Lev. 24:14). The priest was to sprinkle the blood "seven times" before—lit., *towards or near* the tabernacle, a description which seems to imply either that he carried a portion of the blood in a basin to the door of the tabernacle (Lev. 4:17), or that in the act of sprinkling he turned

ADAM CLARKE — CHAPTER 19

2. *Speak unto the children of Israel, that they bring thee*. The ordinance of the *red heifer* was a sacrifice of general application. All the people were to have an interest in it, and therefore the people at large were to provide the sacrifice. This Jewish rite certainly had a reference to things done under the gospel, as the author of the Epistle to the Hebrews has remarked: "For if," says he, "the blood of bulls and of goats," alluding probably to the sin offerings and the scapegoat, "and the ashes of an heifer sprinkling the unclean, sanctifieth to the purifying of the flesh: how much more shall the blood of Christ, who through the eternal Spirit offered himself without spot to God, purge your conscience from dead works to serve the living God?" Heb. ix. 13-14.

MATTHEW HENRY

3. The heifer was to be *wholly burnt*, *v.* 5. The priest was to cast into the fire, while it was burning, cedarwood, hyssop, and scarlet, which were used in the cleansing of lepers (Lev. xiv. 6, 7), that the ashes of these might be mingled with the ashes of the heifer, because they were designed for purification.

4. The ashes of the heifer (separated as well as they could from the ashes of the wood wherewith it was burnt) were to be carefully gathered up by the hand of a clean person, and laid up for the use of the congregation, as there was occasion (*v.* 9).

5. All those that were employed in this service were made ceremonially unclean by it; even Eleazar himself, though he did but sprinkle the blood, *v.* 7. All the sacrifices which were offered for sin were therefore looked upon as impure, because the sins of men were laid upon them, as all our sins were upon Christ, who therefore is said to be *made sin for us*, 2 Cor. v. 21.

Verses 11–22

Directions are here given concerning the use and application of the ashes which were prepared for purification.

I. In what cases there needed a purification with these ashes. No other is mentioned here than the ceremonial uncleanness that was contracted by the touch of a dead body, or of the bone or grave of a dead man, or being in the tent or house where a dead body lay, *v.* 11, 14–16. The law could not conquer death, nor abolish it and alter the property of it, as the gospel does by bringing life and immortality to light, and so introducing a better hope. Since our Redeemer was dead and buried, death is no more destroying to the Israel of God, and therefore dead bodies are no more defiling; but while the church was under the law, the pollution contracted by dead bodies could not but form in their minds melancholy and uncomfortable notions concerning death, while believers now through Christ can triumph over it. *O grave! where is thy victory?* Where is thy pollution?

II. How the ashes were to be used and applied in these cases. 1. A small quantity of the ashes must be put into a cup of spring water, and mixed with the water, which thereby was made, as it is here called, a *water of separation*, because it was to be sprinkled on those who were separated or removed from the sanctuary by their uncleanness. As the ashes of the heifer signified the merit of Christ, so the running water signified the power and grace of the blessed Spirit, who is compared to rivers of living water; and it is by his operation that the righteousness of Christ is applied to us for our cleansing. 2. This water must be applied by a bunch of hyssop dipped in it, with which the person or thing to be cleansed must be sprinkled (*v.* 18), in allusion to which David prays, *Purge me with hyssop*. Faith is the bunch of hyssop wherewith the conscience is sprinkled and the heart purified. The blood of Christ is said to be the *blood of sprinkling* (Heb. xii. 24), and with it we are said to be *sprinkled from an evil conscience* (Heb. x. 22), that is, we are freed from the uneasiness that arises from a sense of our guilt. And it is foretold that Christ, by his baptism, shall *sprinkle many nations*, Isa. lii. 15.

JAMIESON, FAUSSET, BROWN

his face towards the sacred edifice, being disqualified through the defiling influence of this operation from approaching close to it. By this attitude he indicated that he was presenting an expiatory sacrifice, for the acceptance of which he hoped, in the grace of God, by looking to the mercy seat. Every part of it was consumed by fire except the blood used in sprinkling, and the ingredients mixed with the ashes were the same as those employed in the sprinkling of lepers (Lev. 14:4-7). It was a water of separation—i.e., of "sanctification" for the people of Israel. **7. the priest shall be unclean until the even**—The ceremonies prescribed show the imperfection of the Levitical priesthood, while they typify the condition of Christ when expiating our sins (II Cor. 5:21). **11-22. He that toucheth the dead body of any man shall be unclean**—This law is noticed here to show the uses to which the water of separation was applied. The case of a death is one; and as in every family which sustained a bereavement the members of the household became defiled, so in an immense population, where instances of mortality and other cases of uncleanness would be daily occurring, the water of separation must have been in constant requisition. To afford the necessary supply of the cleansing mixture, the Jewish writers say that a red heifer was sacrificed every year, and that the ashes, mingled with the sprinkling ingredients, were distributed through all the cities and towns of Israel. **12. He shall purify himself . . . the third day**—The necessity of applying the water on the third day is inexplicable on any natural or moral ground; and, therefore, the regulation has been generally supposed to have had a typical reference to the resurrection, on that day, of Christ, by whom His people are sanctified; while the process of ceremonial purification being extended over seven days, was intended to show that sanctification is progressive and incomplete till the arrival of the eternal Sabbath. Every one knowingly and presumptuously neglecting to have himself sprinkled with this water was guilty of an offense which was punished by excommunication. **14. when a man dieth in a tent**, etc.—The instances adduced appear very minute and trivial; but important ends, both of a religious and of a sanitary nature, were promoted by carrying the idea of pollution from contact with dead bodies to so great an extent. While it would effectually prevent that Egyptianized race of Israelites imitating the superstitious custom of the Egyptians, who kept in their houses the mummied remains of their ancestors, it ensured a speedy interment to all, thus not only keeping burial-places at a distance, but removing from the habitations of the living the corpses of persons who died from infectious disorders, and from the open field the unburied remains of strangers and foreigners who fell in battle. **21. he that sprinkleth . . . ; and he that toucheth the water of separation shall be unclean until even**—The opposite effects ascribed to the water of separation—of cleansing one person and defiling another—are very singular, and not capable of very satisfactory explanation. One important lesson, however, was thus taught, that its purifying efficacy was not inherent in itself, but arose from the divine appointment, as in other ordinances of religion, which are effectual means of salvation, not from any virtue in them, or in him that administers them, but solely through the grace of God communicated thereby.

ADAM CLARKE

9. *For a water of separation.* That is, the ashes were to be kept, in order to be mixed with water, v. 17, and sprinkled on those who had contracted any legal defilement.

11. *He that toucheth the dead body of any man shall be unclean seven days.* How low does this lay man! He who touched a dead beast was unclean for only one day, Lev. xi. 24, 27, 39; but he who touches a dead man is unclean for seven days. This was certainly designed to mark the peculiar impurity of man, and to show his sinfulness—seven times worse than the vilest animal!

12. *He shall purify himself with it. Yithchatta bo*, literally, "He shall sin himself with it." This Hebrew form of speech is common enough among us in other matters. Thus to fleece, to bark, and to skin do not signify to add a fleece, another bark, or a skin, but to take one away; therefore to "sin himself," in the Hebrew idiom, is not to add sin, but to take it away, to purify. The verb *chata* signifies to "miss the mark, to sin, to purify from sin, and to make a sin offering."

MATTHEW HENRY

CHAPTER 20

Verses 1–13

After thirty-eight years' tedious marches, or rather tedious rests, in the wilderness, backward towards the Red Sea, the armies of Israel now at length set their faces towards Canaan again, and had come not far off from the place where they were when, by the righteous sentence of divine Justice, they were made to begin their wanderings. Hitherto they had been led about as in a maze of labyrinth. They were now brought into the right way again; they abode in Kadesh (*v.* 1).

I. Here dies Miriam, the sister of Moses and Aaron, and as it should seem older than either of them. She must have been so if she was that sister that was set to watch Moses when he was put into the ark of bulrushes, Exod. ii. 4. *Miriam died there*, *v.* 1. She was a prophetess, and had been an instrument of much good to Israel, Mic. vi. 4. When Moses and Aaron with their rod went before them, to work wonders for them, Miriam with her timbrel went before them in praising God for these wondrous works (Exod. xv. 20), and therein did them real service; yet she had once been a murmurer (*ch.* xii. 1),

JAMIESON, FAUSSET, BROWN

CHAPTER 20

Vss. 1-29. The Death of Miriam. **1. Then came the children of Israel . . . into the desert of Zin in the first month**—i.e., of the fortieth year (cf. vss. 22, 23, with ch. 33:38). In this history only the principal and most important incidents are recorded, those confined chiefly to the first or second and the last years of the journeyings in the wilderness, thence called Et-Tih. Between the last verse of the preceding and the first verse of this chapter there is a long and undescribed interval of thirty-seven years. **the people abode in Kadesh**—supposed to be what is now known as Ain El-Weibeh, three springs surrounded by palms. (See on ch. 13:26.) It was their second arrival after an interval of thirty-eight years (Deut. 11:16). The old generation had nearly all died, and the new one encamped in it with the view of entering the promised land, not, however, as formerly on the south, but by crossing the Edomite region on the east. **Miriam died there**—four months before Aaron.

ADAM CLARKE

CHAPTER 20

1. *Then came the children of Israel.* This was the first month of the fortieth year after their departure from Egypt. See chap. xxxiii. 38, compared with v. 28 of this chapter, and Deut. i. 3. The transactions of thirty-seven years Moses passes by, because he writes not as a historian but as a legislator; and gives us particularly an account of the laws, ordinances, and other occurrences of the first and last years of their peregrinations. The year now spoken of was the last of their journeyings; for from the going out of the spies, chap. xiii, unto this time, was about thirty-eight years, Deut. i. 22-23; ii. 14.

And Miriam died there. Miriam was certainly older than Moses. When he was an infant, exposed on the river Nile, she was entrusted by her parents to watch the conduct of Pharaoh's daughter, and to manage a most delicate business, that required much address and prudence. See Exodus ii. It is supposed that she was at the time of her death one hundred and thirty years of age, having been at least ten years old

MATTHEW HENRY

and must not enter Canaan.

II. Here there is another Meribah.

1. *There was no water for the congregation,* v. 2. It is probable that for some time they had been in a country where they were supplied in an ordinary way, and when common providence supplied them it was fit that the miracle should cease. But in this place it fell out that there was no water, or not sufficient for the congregation.

2. Hereupon they murmured, mutinied (*v.* 2), *gathered themselves together,* and took up arms *against Moses and Aaron.* (1) They wished they had died as malefactors by the hands of divine justice, rather than thus seem for a while neglected by the divine mercy. (2) They were angry that they were brought out of Egypt, and led through this wilderness. The present want was of water only, yet, now that they are disposed to find fault, it shall be looked upon as an insufferable hardship put upon them that they have not vines and figs.

3. Moses and Aaron made them no reply, but retired to the door of the tabernacle to know God's mind in this case, *v.* 6.

4. God appeared, to determine the matter; not on his tribunal of justice, to sentence the rebels according to their deserts. But he appeared, (1) On his throne of glory, to silence their unjust murmuring (*v.* 6). Note, A believing sight of the glory of the Lord would be an effectual check to our lusts and passions, and would keep our mouths as with a bridle. (2) On his throne of grace, to satisfy their just desires. It was requisite that they should have water. Moses must a second time in God's name command water out of a rock for them, to show that God is as able as ever to supply his people with good things. (3) He bids him speak to the rock, which would do as it was bidden, to shame the people who had been so often spoken to, and would not hear nor obey. (4) He promises that the rock should give forth water (*v.* 8), and it did so (*v.* 11).

5. Moses and Aaron acted improperly in the management of this matter, so much so that God in displeasure told them immediately that they should not have the honour of bringing Israel into Canaan, *v.* 10–12.

(1) It is uncertain what it was in this management that was so provoking to God. The fault was complicated. *First,* God bade them *speak to the rock,* and they spoke *to the people,* and *smote the rock,* which at this time they were not ordered to do, but they thought speaking would not do. *Secondly,* They assumed too much of the glory of this work of wonder to themselves: *Must we fetch water?* as if it were done by some power or worthiness of theirs. *Thirdly,* Unbelief was the great transgression (*v.* 12): *You believed me not.* Dr. Lightfoot's notion of their unbelief is that they doubted whether now at last, when the forty years had expired, they should enter Canaan, and whether they must not for the murmurings of the people be condemned to another period of toil, because a new rock was now opened for their supply, which they took for an indication of their longer stay. *Fourthly,* They said and did all in heat and passion. *Fifthly,* That which aggravated all the rest, and made it the more provoking, was that it was public, *before the eyes of the children of Israel,* to whom they should have been examples of faith, and hope, and meekness.

(2) From the whole we may learn, [1] That the best of men have their failings. [2] That God judges not as man judges concerning sins.

Lastly, The place is hereupon called *Meribah, v.* 13. It is called *Meribah-Kadesh* (Deut. xxxii. 51), to distinguish it from the other Meribah. It is the *water of strife;* to perpetuate the remembrance of the people's sin, and Moses's, and yet of God's mercy, who supplied them with water, and owned and honoured Moses notwithstanding.

Verses 14–21

We have here the application made by Israel to the Edomites. The nearest way to Canaan from the place where Israel now lay encamped was through the country of Edom.

I. Moses sends ambassadors to treat with the king of Edom for leave to pass through his country. 1. They are to claim kindred with the Edomites. Both nations descended from Abraham and Isaac, their common ancestors. 2. They are to give a short account of the history and present state of Israel. And in this there was a double plea: (1) Israel had been abused by the Egyptians, and therefore ought to be pitied and succoured by their relations. (2) Israel had been wonderfully saved by the Lord, and therefore ought to be countenanced and favoured (*v.* 16). 3. They are humbly to beg a passport through their country. 4. They are to give security for the good

JAMIESON, FAUSSET, BROWN

2-13. there was no water for the congregation—There was at Kadesh a fountain, En-Mishpat (Gen. 14:7), and at the first encampment of the Israelites there was no want of water. It was then either partially dried up by the heat of the season, or had been exhausted by the demands of so vast a multitude.

6. Moses and Aaron went from the presence of the assembly—Here is a fresh ebullition of the untamed and discontented spirit of the people. The leaders fled to the precincts of the sanctuary, both as an asylum from the increasing fury of the highly excited rabble, and as their usual refuge in seasons of perplexity and danger, to implore the direction and aid of God.

8. Take the rod—which had been deposited in the tabernacle (ch. 17:10), the wonder-working rod by which so many miracles had been performed, sometimes called "the rod of God" (Exod. 4:20), sometimes Moses' (vs. 11) or Aaron's rod (Exod. 7:12). **10.** [Moses] **said unto them, Hear now, ye rebels, must we fetch you water out of this rock?**—The conduct of the great leader on this occasion was hasty and passionate (Ps. 106:33). He had been directed to *speak* to the rock, but he *smote it twice* in his impetuosity, thus endangering the blossoms of the rod, and, instead of speaking to the *rock,* he spoke to the *people* in a fury. **11. the congregation drank, and their beasts**—Physically the water afforded the same kind of needful refreshment to both. But from a religious point of view, this, which was only a common element to the cattle, was a sacrament to the people (I Cor. 10:3, 4)—It possessed a relative sanctity imparted to it by its divine origin and use. **12. The Lord spake unto Moses and Aaron, Because ye believed me not,** etc.—The act of Moses in smiting twice betrayed a doubt, not of the power, but of the will of God to gratify such a rebellious people, and his exclamation seems to have emanated from a spirit of incredulity akin to Sarai's (Gen. 18:13). These circumstances indicate the influence of unbelief, and there might have been others unrecorded which led to so severe a chastisement.

13. This is the water of Meribah—The word Kadesh is added to it to distinguish it from another Meribah (Exod. 17:7). **14-16. Moses sent messengers . . . to the king of Edom**—The encampment at Kadesh was on the confines of the Edomite territory, through which the Israelites would have had an easy passage across the Arabah by Wady-el-Ghuweir, so that they could have continued their course around Moab, and approached Palestine from the east [ROBERTS]. The Edomites, being the descendants of Esau and tracing their line of descent from Abraham as their common stock, were recognized by the Israelites as brethren, and a very brotherly message was sent to them. **17. we will go by the king's highway**—probably Wady-el-Ghuweir [ROBERTS], through which ran one of the great lines of road, constructed for commercial caravans, as well as for the progress of armies. The engineering necessary for carrying them over marshes or mountains, and the care requisite for protecting them from the shifting sands, led to their being under the special care of the state. Hence the expression, "the king's highway," which is of great antiquity.

ADAM CLARKE

at her brother's birth.

2. *And there was no water for the congregation.* The same occurrence took place to the children of Israel at Kadesh as did formerly to their fathers at Rephidim, see Exod. xvii. 1; and as the fathers murmured, so also did the children

12. *Because ye believed me not.* What was the offense for which Moses was excluded from the Promised Land? It appears to have consisted in some or all of the following particulars: (1) God had commanded him (v. 8) to take the rod in his hand, and go and speak to the rock, and it should give forth water. It seems Moses did not think speaking would be sufficient; therefore he smote the rock without any command so to do. (2) He did this twice, which certainly in this case indicated a great perturbation of spirit and want of attention to the presence of God. (3) He permitted his spirit to be carried away by a sense of the people's disobedience, and thus, being provoked, he was led to speak unadvisedly with his lips: "Hear now, ye rebels," v. 10. (4) He did not acknowledge God in the miracle which was about to be wrought, but took the honor to himself and Aaron: "Must we fetch you water out of this rock?" Thus it plainly appears that they did not properly believe in God, and did not honor Him in the sight of the people; for in their presence they seem to express a doubt whether the thing could possibly be done. As Aaron appears to have been consenting in the above particulars, therefore he is also excluded from the Promised Land.

14. *Thus saith thy brother Israel.* The Edomites were the descendants of Edom or Esau, the brother of Jacob or Israel, from whom the Israelites were descended.

17. *We will go by the king's high way.* This is the first time this phrase occurs; it appears to have been a public road made by the king's authority at the expense of the state.

MATTHEW HENRY

behaviour of the Israelites in this march.

II. The ambassadors returned with a refusal, *v.* 18. Edom, that is, the king of Edom, threatened, if they attempted to enter his country, it should be at their peril. This was owing, 1. To their jealousy of the Israelites. 2. It was owing to the old enmity which Esau bore to Israel. If they had no reason to fear damage by them, yet they were not willing to show so much kindness to them. Esau hated Jacob because of the blessing.

Verses 22–29

The chapter began with the funeral of Miriam, and it ends with the funeral of her brother Aaron.

I. God bids Aaron die, *v.* 24. 1. There is something of displeasure in these orders. Aaron must not enter Canaan, because he had failed in his duty at the waters of strife. The mention of this, no doubt, went to the heart of Moses, who knew himself, perhaps, at that time, to be the guiltier of the two. 2. There is much of mercy in them. Aaron, though he dies for his transgression, is not put to death as a malefactor, by a plague, or fire from heaven, but dies with ease and in honour. He is not *cut off from his people*, as the expression usually is concerning those that die by the hand of divine justice, but he is *gathered to his people*, as one that died in the arms of divine grace. 3. There is much of type and significancy in them. Aaron must not enter Canaan, to show that the Levitical priesthood could make nothing perfect: that must be done by the bringing in of a better hope.

II. Aaron submits, and dies in the method and manner appointed, and, for aught that appears, with as much cheerfulness as if he had been going to bed.

1. He puts on his holy garments to take his leave of them, and goes up with his brother and son to the top of Mount Hor, and probably some of the elders of Israel with him, *v.* 27. His going up the hill to die signified that the death of saints (and Aaron is called *the saint of the Lord*) is their ascension; they rather go up than go down to death.

2. Moses, whose hands had first clothed Aaron with his priestly garments, now strips him of them; for, in reverence to the priesthood, it was not fit that he should die in them.

3. Moses immediately puts the priestly garments upon Eleazar his son, clothes him with his father's robe, and *strengthens him with his girdle*, Isa. xxii. 21. Now, (1) This was a great comfort to Moses, a happy earnest and indication to the church of the care God would take that as one generation of ministers and Christians (spiritual priests) passes away another generation should come up instead of it. (2) It was a great satisfaction to Aaron to see his son, who was dear to him, thus preferred, and his office, which was dearer, thus preserved and secured. (3) It was a great kindness to the people.

CHAPTER 21

Verses 1–3

1. The descent which Arad the Canaanite made upon the camp of Israel, hearing that they came *by way of the spies*; for, though the spies which Moses had sent thirty-eight years before then passed and repassed unobserved, yet their coming, and their errand, it is likely, were afterwards known to the Canaanites, gave them an alarm, and induced them to keep an eye upon Israel. 2. His success at first in this attempt. His advance-guards picked up some straggling Israelites, and took them prisoners, *v.* 1. 3. Israel's humble address to God upon this occasion, *v.* 2. It was a temptation to them to murmur as their fathers did, and to despair of getting possession of Canaan; but God, who thus tried them by his providence, enabled them by his grace to quit themselves well in the trial, and to trust in him for relief. 4. The victory which the Israelites obtained over the Canaanites, *v.* 3. A strong party was sent out, probably under the command of Joshua, which not only drove back these Canaanites, but followed them to their cities and utterly destroyed them, and so returned to the camp. *Vincimur in praelio, sed non in bello—We lose a battle, but we finally triumph.* What is said of the tribe of Gad is true of all God's Israel, a troop may overcome them, but they shall overcome at the last.

Verses 4–9

I. The fatigue of Israel by a long march round the land of Edom, because they could not obtain passage through it the nearest way: *The soul of the people was much discouraged because of the way*, *v.* 4.

II. Their unbelief and murmuring upon this

JAMIESON, FAUSSET, BROWN

19. if I and my cattle drink of thy water, then I will pay for it—From the scarcity of water in the warm climates of the East, the practice of levying a tax for the use of the wells is universal; and the jealousy of the natives, in guarding the collected treasures of rain, is often so great that water cannot be procured for money. **21. Edom refused to give Israel passage through his border, etc.**—A churlish refusal obliged them to take another route. (See on chapter 21:4; Deut. 2:4; Judg. 11:18; see also I Sam. 14:47; II Sam. 8:14, which describe the retribution that was taken.) **22. the children of Israel . . . came unto mount Hor**—now Gebel Haroun, the most striking and lofty elevation in the Seir range, called emphatically "the mount" (vs. 28). It is conspicuous by its double top. **24-28. Aaron shall be gathered unto his people**—In accordance with his recent doom, he, attired in the high priest's costume, was commanded to ascend that mountain and die. But although the time of his death was hastened by the divine displeasure as a punishment for his sins, the *manner* of his death was arranged in tenderness of love, and to do him honor at the close of his earthly service. His ascent of the mount was to afford him a last look of the camp and a distant prospect of the promised land. The simple narrative of the solemn and impressive scene implies, though it does not describe, the pious resignation, settled faith, and inward peace of the aged pontiff.

26. strip Aaron of his garments—i.e., his pontifical robes, in token of his resignation. (See Isa. 22:20-25.) **put them on his son**—as the inauguration into his high office. Having been formerly anointed with the sacred oil, that ceremony was not repeated, or, as some think, it was done on his return to the camp. **28. Aaron died there in the top of the mount**—(See on Deut. 10:6). A tomb has been erected upon or close by the spot where he was buried. **29. When all the congregation saw that Aaron was dead**—Moses and Eleazar were the sole witnesses of his departure. According to the established law, the new high priest could not have been present at the funeral of his father without contracting ceremonial defilement (Lev. 21:11). But that law was dispensed with in the extraordinary circumstances. The people learned the event not only from the recital of the two witnesses, but from their visible signs of grief and change; and this event betokened the imperfection of the Levitical priesthood (Heb. 7:12). **they mourned for Aaron thirty days**—the usual period of public and solemn mourning. (See on Deut. 34:8.)

CHAPTER 21

Vss. 1-35. Israel Attacked by the Canaanites. **1. King Arad the Canaanite**—rather, the Canaanite king of Arad—an ancient town on the southernmost borders of Palestine, not far from Kadesh. A hill called Tell Arad marks the spot. **heard tell that Israel came by the way of the spies**—in the way or manner of spies, stealthily, or from spies sent by himself to ascertain the designs and motions of the Israelites. The Septuagint and others consider the *Heb.* word "spies" a proper name, and render it: "Came by the way of Atharim towards Arad" [Kennicott]. **he fought against Israel, and took some of them prisoners**—This discomfiture was permitted to teach them to expect the conquest of Canaan not from their own wisdom and valor, but solely from the favor and help of God (Deut. 9:4; Ps. 44:3, 4). **2, 3. Israel vowed a vow unto the Lord**—Made to feel their own weakness, they implored the aid of Heaven, and, in anticipation of it, *devoted* the cities of this king to future destruction. The nature and consequence of such anathemas are described (Lev. 27; Deut. 13). This vow of extermination against Arad gave name to the place Hormah (slaughter and destruction) though it was not accomplished till after the passage of the Jordan. Others think Hormah the name of a town mentioned (Josh. 12:14). **4. they journeyed from mount Hor**—On being refused the passage requested, they returned through the Arabah, "the way of the Red Sea," to Elath, at the head of the eastern gulf of the Red Sea, and thence passed up through the mountains to the eastern desert, so as to make the circuit of the land of Edom (ch. 33:41, 42). **the soul of the people was much discouraged because of the way**—Disappoint-

ADAM CLARKE

21. *Thus Edom refused to give Israel passage through his border.* Though every king has a right to refuse passage through his territories to any strangers, yet in a case like this, and in a time also in which emigrations were frequent and universally allowed, it was both cruelty and oppression in Edom to refuse a passage to a comparatively unarmed and inoffensive multitude, who were all their own near kinsmen. It appears however that it was only the Edomites of Kadesh that were thus unfriendly and cruel; for from Deut. ii. 29 we learn that the Edomites who dwelt in Mount Seir treated them in a hospitable manner. This cruelty in the Edomites of Kadesh is strongly reprehended, and threatened by the Prophet Obadiah, vv. 10, etc.

26. *Strip Aaron of his garments.* This was, in effect, depriving him of his office; and putting the clothes on his son Eleazar implied a transfer of that office to him. A transfer of office, from this circumstance of putting the clothes of the late possessor on the person intended to succeed him, was called "investing" or "investment" (clothing), as removing a person from an office was termed divesting or unclothing.

CHAPTER 21

1. *The way of the spies. Atharim.* Some think that this signifies the way that the spies took when they went to search the land. But this is impossible, as Dr. Kennicott justly remarks, because Israel had now marched from Meribath-kadesh to Mount Hor, beyond Eziongaber, and were turning round Edom to the southeast; and therefore the word is to be understood here as the name of a place.

3. *The Lord hearkened to the voice of Israel.* The whole of this verse appears to me to have been added after the days of Joshua. It is certain the Canaanites were not utterly destroyed at the time here spoken of, for this did not take place till after the death of Moses. If, instead of *utterly destroyed them, vaiyacharem*, we translate, "They devoted them to utter destruction," it will make a good sense, and not repugnant to the Hebrew; though some think it more probable that the verse was added afterwards by Joshua or Ezra, in testimony of the fulfillment of God's promise; for Arad, who is mentioned as being destroyed here, is mentioned among those destroyed by Joshua long after (see Josh. xii. 14). But this is quite consistent with their being "devoted to destruction," as this might be fulfilled any time after.

MATTHEW HENRY

occasion, *v.* 5. They have *bread enough and to spare;* and yet they complain *there is no bread,* because, though they eat angels' food, yet they are weary of it; manna itself is loathed, and called *light bread,* fit for children, not for men and soldiers. What will those be pleased with whom manna will not please? Let not the contempt which some cast upon the word of God cause us to value it the less: it is the bread of life, substantial bread, and will nourish those who by faith feed upon it to eternal life, whoever calls it light bread.

III. The righteous judgment which God brought upon them for their murmurings, *v.* 6. He sent *fiery serpents among them,* which bit or stung many of them to death. The wilderness through which they had passed was all along infested with those fiery serpents, as appears, Deut. viii. 15. But hitherto God had wonderfully preserved his people from receiving hurt by them, till now that they murmured. These serpents are called *fiery,* from their colour, or from their rage, or from the effects of their bitings. They in their pride had lifted themselves up against God and Moses, and now God humbled and mortified them, by making these despicable animals a plague to them.

IV. Their repentance and supplication to God under this judgment, *v.* 7. They confess their fault: *We have sinned.* It is to be feared that they would not have owned the sin if they had not felt the smart. They beg the prayers of Moses for them. Afflictions often change men's sentiments concerning God's people, and teach them to value those prayers which, at a former period, they had scorned. Moses, to show that he had heartily forgiven them, blesses those who had cursed him, and *prays for those who had despitefully used him.* Herein he was a type of Christ, who interceded for his persecutors, and a pattern to us to go and do likewise, and thus to show that we *love our enemies.*

V. The wonderful provision which God made for their relief. God ordered Moses to make the representation of a fiery serpent, which he did, in brass, and set it up on a very long pole, so that it might be seen from all parts of the camp, and every one that was stung with a fiery serpent was healed by looking up to this serpent of brass. The people prayed that God would *take away the serpents from them* (*v.* 7), but God saw fit not to do this: for he gives effectual relief in the best way, though not in our way. The Jews themselves say that it was not the sight of the brazen serpent that cured them, but, in looking up to it, they looked up to God as the Lord that healed them. But there was much of gospel in this appointment. Our Saviour has told us so (John iii. 14, 15), that *as Moses lifted up the serpent in the wilderness so the Son of man must be lifted up,* that *whosoever believeth in him should not perish.* Observe then a resemblance,

1. Between their disease and ours. The devil is the old serpent, a fiery serpent, hence he appears (Rev. xii. 3) as a *great red dragon.* Sin is the biting of this fiery serpent; it is painful to the startled conscience, and poisonous to the seared conscience. Satan's temptations are called his *fiery darts,* Eph. vi. 16.

2. Between their remedy and ours. (1) It was God himself that devised and prescribed this antidote against the fiery serpents; so our salvation by Christ was the contrivance of Infinite Wisdom; God himself has found the ransom. (2) It was a very unlikely method of cure; so our salvation by the death of Christ is *to the Jews a stumbling-block and to the Greeks foolishness.* (3) That which cured was shaped in the likeness of that which wounded. So Christ, though perfectly free from sin himself, yet was *made in the likeness of sinful flesh* (Rom. viii. 3), so like that it was taken for granted that this man was a sinner, John ix. 24. (4) The brazen serpent was lifted up; so was Christ. He was lifted up upon the cross (John xii. 33, 34), for he was made a spectacle to the world. He was lifted up by the preaching of the gospel. The word here used for a *pole* signifies a *banner,* or *ensign,* for Christ crucified *stands for an ensign of the people,* Isa. xi. 10. Some make the lifting up of the serpent to be a figure of Christ's triumphing over Satan, the old serpent, whose head he bruised, when in his cross he made an open show of the principalities and powers which he had spoiled and destroyed, Col. ii. 15.

3. Between the application of their remedy and ours. They looked and lived, and we, if we believe, shall not perish; it is by faith that we look unto Jesus, Heb. xii. 2. *Look unto me, and be you saved,* Isa. xlv. 22. Whoever looked up to this healing sign, though from the outmost part of the camp, though with a weak and weeping eye, was certainly healed; so whosoever believes in Christ, though as

JAMIESON, FAUSSET, BROWN

ment on finding themselves so near the confines of the promised land without entering it; vexation at the refusal of a passage through Edom and the absence of any divine interposition in their favor; and above all, the necessity of a retrograde journey by a long and circuitous route through the worst parts of a sandy desert and the dread of being plunged into new and unknown difficulties—all this produced a deep depression of spirits. But it was followed, as usually, by a gross outburst of murmuring at the scarcity of water, and of expressions of disgust at the manna. **5. our soul loatheth this light bread**—i.e., bread without substance or nutritious quality. The refutation of this calumny appears in the fact, that on the strength of this food they performed for forty years so many and toilsome journeys. But they had been indulging a hope of the better and more varied fare enjoyed by a settled people; and disappointment, always the more bitter as the hope of enjoyment seems near, drove them to speak against God and against Moses (I Cor. 10:9). **6. The Lord sent fiery serpents among the people**—That part of the desert where the Israelites now were—near the head of the gulf of Akaba—is greatly infested with venomous reptiles, of various kinds, particularly lizards, which raise themselves in the air and swing themselves from branches; and scorpions, which, being in the habit of lying in long grass, are particularly dangerous to the barelegged, sandalled people of the East. The only known remedy consists in sucking the wound, or, in the case of cattle, in the application of ammonia. The exact species of serpents that caused so great mortality among the Israelites cannot be ascertained. They are said to have been "fiery," an epithet applied to them either from their bright, vivid color, or the violent inflammation their bite occasioned. **7-9. the people came to Moses, and said, We have sinned**—The severity of the scourge and the appalling extent of mortality brought them to a sense of sin, and through the intercessions of Moses, which they implored, they were miraculously healed.

He was directed to make the figure of a serpent in brass, to be elevated on a pole or standard, that it might be seen at the extremities of the camp and that every bitten Israelite who looked to it might be healed. This peculiar method of cure was designed, in the first instance, to show that it was the efficacy of God's power and grace, not the effect of nature or art, and also that it might be a type of the power of faith in Christ to heal all who look to Him because of their sins (John 3:14, 15; see also on II Kings 18: 4).

ADAM CLARKE

5. *This light bread. Hakkelokel,* a word of excessive scorn; as if they had said, This innutritive, unsubstantial, cheat-stomach stuff.

6. *Fiery serpents. Hannechashim hasseraphim. Seraphim* is one of the orders of angelic beings, Isa. vi. 2, 6; but as it comes from the root *saraph,* which signifies to "burn," it has been translated *fiery* in the text.

8. *Make thee a fiery serpent.* Literally, make thee a seraph. *And set it upon a pole. Al nes,* upon a standard or ensign.

9. *And Moses made a serpent of brass. Nechash nechosheth.* Hence we find that the word for brass or copper comes from the same root with *nachash,* which here signifies a serpent, probably on account of the color; as most serpents, especially those of the bright spotted kind, have a very glistening appearance, and those who have brown or yellow spots appear something like burnished brass. But the true meaning of the root cannot be easily ascertained. On the subject of the cure of the serpent-bitten Israelites, by looking at the brazen serpent, there is a good comment in the book of Wisdom, chap. xvi. 4-12, in which are these remarkable words: "They were admonished, having a sign of salvation (i.e., the brazen serpent), to put them in remembrance of the commandments of thy law. For he that turned himself towards it was not saved by the thing that he saw, but by thee, that art the Saviour of all." To the circumstance of looking at the brazen serpent in order to be healed, our Lord refers, John iii. 14-15: "As Moses lifted up the serpent in the wilderness, even so must the Son of man be lifted up: that whosoever believeth in him should not perish, but have eternal life."

MATTHEW HENRY

yet but weak in faith, shall not perish.

Verses 10–20

We have here an account of the several stages and removals of the children of Israel, till they came into the plains of Moab, out of which they at length passed over Jordan into Canaan, as we read in the beginning of Joshua. Natural motions are quicker the nearer they are to their centre. The Israelites were now drawing near to the promised rest, and now they *set forward*, as the expression is, *v.* 10. It were well if we would do thus in our way to heaven, and the nearer we come to heaven be so much the more active and abundant in the work of the Lord. Two things especially are observable:

1. The wonderful success which God blessed his people with, near the brooks of Arnon, *v.* 13–15. They had now compassed the land of Edom. It is well that there are more ways than one to Canaan. The enemies of God's people may retard their passage, but cannot prevent their entrance into the promised rest. Care is taken to let us know that the Israelites in their march religiously observed the orders which God gave them to use no hostility against the Moabites (Deut. ii. 9), because they were the posterity of righteous Lot.

2. The wonderful supply which God blessed his people with at *Beer* (*v.* 16), which signifies the *well* or *fountain*. Hitherto we have found, when they were supplied with water, they asked it in unjust discontent, and God gave it in just displeasure; but here we find, (1) That God gave it in love (*v.* 16): *Gather the people together*, to be witnesses of the wonder, and joint-sharers in the favour, *and I will give them water*. Before they prayed, God granted. (2) That they received it with joy and thankfulness, which made the mercy doubly sweet to them, *v.* 17. Then they sang this song, to the glory of God and the encouragement of one another, *Spring up, O well!* Thus they pray that it may spring up, for promised mercies must be fetched in by prayer. As the brazen serpent was a figure of Christ, who is lifted up for our cure, so is this well a figure of the Spirit, who is poured forth for our comfort, and from whom flow to us *rivers of living waters*, John vii. 38. (3) That whereas before the remembrance of the miracle was perpetuated in the names given to the places, which signified the people's strife and murmuring, now it was perpetuated in a song of praise. *The princes digged the well*—the seventy elders; with their staves they made holes in the soft sandy ground, and God caused the water miraculously to spring up in the holes which they made. God promised to give them water, but they must open the ground to receive it, and give it vent. God's favours must be expected in the use of such means as lie within our power, but still the excellency of the power is of God.

Verses 21–35

An account of the victories obtained by Israel over Sihon and Og.

I. Israel sent a peaceable message to Sihon king of the Amorites (*v.* 21), but received an unpeaceable return. Sihon's army was routed, and not only so, but all his country came into the possession of Israel, *v.* 24, 25. This seizure is justified, 1. Against the Amorites themselves, for they were the aggressors, and provoked the Israelites to battle. 2. Against the Moabites, who had formerly been the lords-proprietors of this country. (1) The justification itself is that though it was true this country had belonged to the Moabites, yet the Amorites had taken it from them some time before, and were now in full and quiet possession of it, *v.* 26. This country being designed in due time for Israel, it is beforehand put into the hand of the Amorites, who little think that they have it but as trustees till Israel come of age, and then must surrender it. We understand not the vast reaches of Providence, but known unto God are all his works, as appears in this instance. (2) For proof of the allegation, he refers to the authentic records of the country, for so their proverbs or songs were, one of which he quotes some passages out of (*v.* 27–30), which sufficiently proves what is vouched for, namely, [1] That such and such places that are here named, though they had been in the possession of the Moabites, had by right of war become the dominion of Sihon king of the Amorites. [2] That the Moabites were utterly disabled and even Chemosh their god had given them up, as unable to rescue them out of the hands of Sihon, *v.* 29.

II. Og king of Bashan, instead of being warned by the fate of his neighbours to make peace with Israel, is instigated by it to make war with them, which proves in like manner to be his destruction. Og was also an Amorite, and more likely to prevail, because of his own gigantic strength and stature.

JAMIESON, FAUSSET, BROWN

10. the children of Israel set forward—along the eastern frontier of the Edomites, encamping in various stations. **12. pitched in the valley**—lit., the woody brook-valley of Zared (Deut. 2:13; Isa. 15:7; Amos 6:14). This torrent rises among the mountains to the east of Moab, and flowing west, empties itself into the Dead Sea. Ije-Abarim is supposed to have been its ford [CALMET].

13. pitched on the other side of Arnon—now El-Mojib, a deep, broad, and rapid stream, dividing the dominions of the Moabites and Amorites. **14. book of the wars of the Lord**—A fragment or passage is here quoted from a poem or history of the wars of the Israelites, principally with a view to decide the position of Arnon. **15. Ar**—the capital of Moab.

16. from thence they went to Beer—i.e., a well. The name was probably given to it afterwards, as it is not mentioned (ch. 33).

17, 18. Then Israel sang—This beautiful little song was in accordance with the wants and feelings of travelling caravans in the East, where water is an occasion both of prayer and thanksgiving. From the princes using their official rods only, and not spades, it seems probable that this well was concealed by the brushwood or the sand, as is the case with many wells in Idumea still. The discovery of it was seasonable, and owing to the special interposition of God.

21-23, Israel sent messengers unto Sihon—The rejection of their respectful and pacific message was resented—Sihon was discomfited in battle—and Israel obtained by right of conquest the whole of the Amorite dominions. **24. from Arnon unto the Jabbok**—now the Zurka. These rivers formed the southern and northern boundaries of his usurped territory. **for the border of . . . Ammon was strong**—a reason stated for Sihon not being able to push his invasion further. **25. Israel dwelt in all the cities**—after exterminating the inhabitants who had been previously doomed (Deut. 2:34). **26. Heshbon**—(Song of Sol. 7:4)—situated sixteen English miles north of the Arnon, and from its ruins it appears to have been a large city.

27-30. Wherefore they that speak in proverbs—Here is given an extract from an Amorite song exultingly anticipating an extension of their conquests to Arnon. The quotation from the poem of the Amorite bard ends at verse 28. The two following verses appear to be the strains in which the Israelites expose the impotence of the usurpers. **29. people of Chemosh**—the name of the Moabite idol (I Kings 11:7-33; II Kings 23:13; Jer. 48:46). **he**—i.e., their god, hath surrendered his worshippers to the victorious arms of Sihon. **33. they turned and went up by the way of Bashan**—a name given to that district from the richness of the soil—now Batanea or El-Bottein—a hilly region east of the Jordan lying between the mountains of Hermon on the north and those of Gilead on the south. **Og**—a giant, an

ADAM CLARKE

12. *They . . . pitched in the valley of Zared. Nachal zared.* This should be translated "the brook Zared," as it is in Deut. ii. 13-14. This stream has its origin in the mountains eastward of Moab, and runs from east to west, and discharges itself into the Dead Sea.

13. *Arnon.* Another river which takes its rise in the mountains of Moab, and, after having separated the ancient territories of the Moabites and Ammonites, falls into the Dead Sea, near the mouth of Jordan.

14. *The book of the wars of the Lord.* There are endless conjectures about this book, among both ancients and moderns. Dr. Lightfoot's opinion is the most simple, and to me bears the greatest appearance of being the true one. "This book seems to have been some book of remembrances and directions, written by Moses for Joshua's private instruction for the management of the wars after him. See Exod. xvii. 14-16. It may be that this was the same book which is called the *book of Jasher*, i.e., the *book of the upright*, or a directory for Joshua, from Moses, what to do and what to expect in his wars; and in this book it seems as if Moses directed the setting up of *archery*, see 2 Sam. i. 18, and warrants Joshua to command the sun, and expect its obedience, Josh. x. 13."

What he did in the Red sea, and in the brooks of Arnon. This clause is impenetrably obscure. All the versions, all the translators, all the commentators have been puzzled with it. Scarcely any two agree. The original is *eth vaheb besuphah*, which our translators render, *What he did in the Red sea*, following here the Chaldee Targum. As I judge the whole clause to have been a common proverb in those days, and *Vaheb* to be a proper name, I therefore propose the following translation, which I believe to be the best: "From Vaheb unto Suph, and unto the streams of Arnon." If we allow it to have been a proverbial expression, used to point out extensive distance, then it was similar to that well-known phrase, "From Dan even unto Beer-sheba."

17. *Spring up, O well.* This is one of the most ancient war songs in the world, but is not easily understood, which is commonly the case with all very ancient compositions, especially the poetic.

18. *The princes digged the well . . . with their staves.* This is not easily understood. Who can suppose that the princes dug this well with their *staves*? And is there any other idea conveyed by our translation? The word *chapharu*, which is translated *they digged*, should be rendered "they searched out," which is a frequent meaning of the root; and *bemishanotham*, which we render *with their staves*, should be translated "on their borders or confines," from the root *shaan*, to "lie along."

26. *For Heshbon was the city of Sihon.* It appears therefore that the territory now taken from Sihon by the Israelites was taken from a former king of Moab, in commemoration of which an *epikedion* or war song was made, several verses of which, in their ancient poetic form, are here quoted by Moses.

27. *They that speak in proverbs. Hammoshelim*, from *mashal*, to "rule, to exercise authority"; hence a weighty proverbial saying, because admitted as an axiom for the government of life.

The ode from verses 27 to 30 is composed of three parts. The first takes in verses 27 and 28; the second, verse 29; and the third, verse 30. The first records with bitter irony the late insults of Sihon and his subjects over the conquered Moabites. The second expresses the compassion of the Israelites over the desolations of Moab, with a bitter sarcasm against their god Chemosh, who had abandoned his votaries in their distress, or was not able to rescue them out of the hands of their enemies. The third sets forth the revenge taken by Israel upon the

MATTHEW HENRY

Here observe, 1. That the Amorite begins the war (*v.* 33). His country was very rich and pleasant. Bashan was famous for the best timber (witness the oaks of Bashan), and the best breed of cattle, witness the bulls and kine of Bashan, and the lambs and rams of that country, which are celebrated, Deut. xxxii. 14. 2. That God interests himself in the cause, bids Israel not to fear this threatening force. Giants are but worms before God's power. 3. That Israel not only routs the enemies' army, but gains the enemies' country, which afterwards was part of the inheritance of the two tribes and a half that were first seated on the other side Jordan.

CHAPTER 22

Verses 1–14

The children of Israel have at length finished their wanderings in the wilderness out of which they went up (*ch.* xxi. 18), and are now encamped in the plains of Moab near Jordan, where they continued till they passed through Jordan under Joshua, after the death of Moses.

I. The fright which the Moabites were in upon the approach of Israel, *v.* 2–4. Notwithstanding the old friendship between Abraham and Lot, the Moabites resolved to ruin Israel if they could, and therefore they will take it for granted, without any ground for the suspicion, that Israel resolves to ruin them. These fears they communicated to their neighbours, the elders of Midian, that some measures might be concerted between them for their common safety. They had reason to court Israel's friendship, and to come in to their assistance; but having forsaken the religion of their father Lot, and being sunk into idolatry, they hated the people of the God of Abraham.

II. The project which the king of Moab formed to get the people of Israel cursed, that is, to set God against them. He trusted more to his arts than to his arms, and had a notion that if he could get but some prophet or other, with his powerful charms, to imprecate evil upon them, and to pronounce a blessing upon himself and his forces, then, though otherwise too weak, he should be able to deal with them. This notion arose, 1. Out of the remains of some religion; for it owns a dependence upon some visible sovereign powers that rule in the affairs of the children of men. 2. Out of the ruins of the true religion; for if the Midianites and Moabites had not wretchedly degenerated from the faith and worship of their pious ancestors, Abraham and Lot, they could not have imagined it possible to do any mischief with their curses to a people who alone adhered to the service of the true God, from whose service they had themselves revolted.

III. The court which he made to Balaam the son of Beor, a famous conjurer to engage him to curse Israel. This Balaam lived a great way off, in that country whence Abraham came, and where Laban lived. And to gain him, 1. He makes him his friend. 2. In effect he makes him his god, by the great power he attributes to his word.

IV. The restraint God lays upon Balaam, forbidding him to curse Israel. He lodges the messengers, and takes a night's time to consider what he shall do, and to receive instructions from God, *v.* 8. In the night God comes to him, probably in a dream, and enquires what business those strangers had with him. He knows it, but he will know it from him. Balaam gives him an account of their errand (*v.* 9–11), and God thereupon charges him not to go with them, nor attempt to curse that blessed people, *v.* 12. Balaam is charged not only not to go to Balak, but not to offer to curse this people, which he might have attempted at a distance; and the reason is given: *They are blessed.*

V. The return of the messengers without Balaam. 1. Balaam is not faithful in returning God's answer to the messengers, *v.* 13. He only tells them, *The Lord refuseth to give me leave to go with you.* He did not tell them, as he ought to have done, that Israel was a blessed people, and must by no means be cursed.

Verses 15–21

A second embassy sent to Balaam, to fetch him over to curse Israel.

I. The temptation Balak laid before Balaam. Now he tempted him with honours, laid a bait not only for his covetousness, but for his pride and ambition. See how artfully Balak managed the temptation. 1. The messengers he sent were *more,* and *more honourable, v.* 15. 2. The request was very urgent. This powerful prince becomes a suitor to him: "*Let nothing, I pray thee, hinder thee* (*v.* 16), no, not God, nor conscience, nor any fear either of sin or

JAMIESON, FAUSSET, BROWN

Amoritish prince, who, having opposed the progress of the Israelites, was defeated. **34. The Lord said unto Moses, Fear him not**—a necessary encouragement, for his gigantic stature (Deut. 3:11) was calculated to inspire terror. He and all his were put to the sword.

CHAPTER 22

VSS. 1-20. BALAK'S FIRST MESSAGE FOR BALAAM REFUSED. **1. Israel . . . pitched in the plains of Moab**—so called from having formerly belonged to that people, though wrested from them by Sihon. It was a dry, sunken, desert region on the east of the Jordan valley, opposite Jericho. **2. Balak**—i.e., empty. Terrified (Deut. 2:25; Exod. 15:15) at the approach of so vast a multitude and not daring to encounter them in the field, he resolved to secure their destruction by other means. **4. elders of Midian**—called kings (ch. 31:8) and princes (Josh. 13:21). The Midianites, a distinct people on the southern frontier of Moab, united with them as confederates against Israel, their common enemy. **5. He sent messengers therefore unto Balaam**—i.e., "lord" or "devourer" of people, a famous soothsayer (Josh. 13:22). **son of Beor,** or, in the Chaldee form, *Bosor*—i.e., "destruction." **Pethor**—a city of Mesopotamia, situated on the Euphrates. **6. Come . . . , curse me this people**—Among the heathen an opinion prevailed that prayers for evil or curses would be heard by the unseen powers as well as prayers for good, when offered by a prophet or priest and accompanied by the use of certain rites. Many examples are found in the histories of the Greeks and Romans of whole armies being devoted to destruction, and they occur among the natives of India and other heathen countries still. In the Burmese war, magicians were employed to curse the British troops. **7. the elders of Moab and . . . of Midian departed with the rewards of divination**—like the fee of a fortuneteller, and being a royal present, it would be something handsome.

8-14. Lodge here this night, and I will bring you word again, as the Lord shall speak unto me, etc.—God usually revealed His will in visions and dreams; and Balaam's birth and residence in Mesopotamia, where the remains of patriarchal religion still lingered, account for his knowledge of the true God. His real character has long been a subject of discussion. Some, judging from his language, have thought him a saint; others, looking to his conduct, have described him as an irreligious charlatan; and a third class consider him a novice in the faith, who had a fear of God, but who had not acquired power over his passions [HENGSTENBERG]. **13. the Lord refuseth to give me leave to go with you**—This answer has an *appearance* of being good, but it studiously concealed the reason of the divine prohibition, and it intimated his own willingness and desire to go—if permitted. Balak despatched a second mission, which held out flattering prospects, both to his avarice and his ambition (Gen. 31:30).

ADAM CLARKE

whole country of Sihon, from Heshbon to Dibon, and from Nophah even to Medeba. See Isa. xv. 1-2.

CHAPTER 22

1. *And pitched in the plains of Moab.* They had taken no part of the country that at present appertained to the Moabites; they had taken only that part which had formerly belonged to this people, but had been taken from them by Sihon, king of the Amorites. *On this side Jordan.* On the east side. By Jericho, that is, over against it.

5. *To Pethor, which is by the river of the land of the children of his people.* "Twelve Hebrew MSS. confirm the Samaritan text here in reading, instead of *ammo,* 'his people,' *Ammon,* with the Syriac and Vulgate versions." It should therefore stand thus: "by the river of the land of the children of Ammon"; and thus it agrees with Deut. xxiii. 4.

6. *Come now therefore, I pray thee, curse me this people.* Balaam, once a prophet of the true God, appears to have been one of the *Moshelim* who had added to his poetic gift that of sorcery or divination. It was supposed that prophets and sorcerers had a power to curse persons and places so as to confound all their designs, frustrate their counsels, enervate their strength, and fill them with fear, terror, and dismay. See Gen. ix. 25; Ps. cix. 6, 20; Josh. vi. 26; Jer. xvii. 5-6.

7. *The rewards of divination.* Whoever went to consult a prophet took with him a present, as it was on such gratuitous offerings the prophets lived; but here more than a mere present is intended, perhaps everything necessary to provide materials for the incantation. The drugs, etc., used on such occasions were often very expensive. It appears that Balaam was very covetous, and that he "loved the wages of unrighteousness," and probably lived by them; see 2 Pet. ii. 15.

8. *I will bring you word again, as the Lord shall speak.* So it appears he knew the true God and had been in the habit of consulting Him, and receiving oracles from His mouth.

12. *Thou shalt not go with them; thou shalt not curse the people.* That is, You shalt not go with them to curse the people. With them he might go, as we find he afterwards did by God's own command, but not to curse the people; this was wholly forbidden. Probably the command, *Thou shalt not go,* refers here to that time, viz., the first invitation; and in this sense it was most punctually obeyed by Balaam; see v. 13.

MATTHEW HENRY

shame." 3. The proffers were high: "*I will promote thee to very great honour* among the princes of Moab."

II. Balaam's seeming resistance of, but real yielding to, this temptation. We may here discern in Balaam a struggle between his convictions and his corruptions. 1. His convictions charged him to adhere to the command of God, and he spoke their language, *v.* 18. Nor could any man have said better: "*If Balak would give me his house full of silver and gold*, and that is more than he can give or I can ask, *I cannot go beyond the word of the Lord my God*." 2. His corruptions at the same time strongly inclined him to go contrary to the command. He seemed to refuse the temptation, *v.* 18. But even then he expressed no abhorrence of it, as Christ did when he had the kingdoms of the world offered him (*Get thee hence, Satan*), and as Peter did when Simon Magus offered him money: *Thy money perish with thee.* But it appears (*v.* 19) that he had a strong inclination to accept the proffer; for he would further attend, to know what God would say to him, hoping that he might alter his mind and give him leave to go. This was a vile reflection upon God Almighty, as if he could change his mind. Note, It is a very great affront to God, and a certain evidence of the dominion of corruption in the heart, to beg leave to sin.

III. The permission God gave him to go, *v.* 20. God came to him, probably by an angel, and told him he might, if he pleased, go with Balak's messengers. *So he gave him up to his own heart's lust.* Note, As God sometimes denies the prayers of his people in love, so sometimes he grants the desires of the wicked in wrath.

Verses 22–35

An account of the opposition God gave to Balaam in his journey towards Moab.

I. Here is God's displeasure against Balaam for undertaking this journey: God's *anger was kindled because he went*, *v.* 22. Note, 1. The sin of sinners is not to be thought the less provoking to God because he permits it. 2. Nothing is more displeasing to God than malicious designs against his people; he that touches them touches the apple of his eye.

II. The way God took to let Balaam know his displeasure against him: *An angel stood in the way for an adversary.*

1. Balaam had notice given him of God's displeasure, by the ass, and this *did not startle him.* The *ass saw the angel*, *v.* 23. How vainly did Balaam boast that he was a man whose *eyes were open*, and that he *saw the visions of the Almighty* (*ch.* xxiv. 3, 4), when the ass he rode on saw more than he did, his eyes being blinded with covetousness and ambition. Let none be puffed up with a conceit of visions and revelations, when even an ass saw an angel; to save both herself and her senseless rider, (1) She *turned aside out of the way*, *v.* 23. Balaam should have taken the hint of this, and considered whether he was not out of the way of his duty; but, instead of this, he *beat her into the way again.* Thus those who by wilful sin are running headlong into perdition are angry at those that would prevent their ruin. (2) She had not gone much further before she saw the angel again, and then, to avoid him, *ran up to a wall*, and *crushed her rider's foot*, *v.* 24, 25. The crushing of Balaam's foot, though it was the saving of his life, provoked him so much that he smote his ass the second time. (3) Upon the next encounter with the angel, the ass fell down under Balaam, *v.* 26, 27. Balaam the third time smote his ass, though she had now done him the best piece of service that ever she did him, saving him from the sword of the angel, and by her falling down teaching him to do likewise. (4) When all this would not work upon him, God opened the mouth of the ass, and she spoke to him once and again; and yet neither did this move him. Here Mr. Ainsworth observes that the devil, when he tempted our first parents to sin, employed a subtle serpent, but that God, when he would convince Balaam, employed a silly ass, a creature dull and sottish to a proverb. [1] The ass complained of Balaam's cruelty (*v.* 28): *What have I done unto thee, that thou hast smitten me?* Note, The righteous God will not see the meanest and weakest abused; but either they shall be enabled to speak in their own defence or he will some way or other speak for them. His brutish head-strong passion so blinded him that he could not observe or consider the strangeness of the thing. Nothing besots men worse than unbridled anger. [2] The ass reasoned with him, *v.* 30. God enabled not only a dumb creature to speak, but a dull creature to speak to the purpose.

2. Balaam at length had notice of God's displeasure by the angel, and this did startle him. When God opened his eyes *he saw the angel* (*v.* 31), and then he himself *fell flat upon his face.* God has many ways of breaking and bringing down the hard and unhumbled

JAMIESON, FAUSSET, BROWN

19. tarry ye also here this night, that I may know what the Lord will say unto me more—The divine will, as formerly declared, not being according to his desires, he hoped by a second request to bend it, as he had already bent his own conscience, to his ruling passions of pride and covetousness. The permission granted to Balaam is in accordance with the ordinary procedure of Providence. God often gives up men to follow the impulse of their own lusts; but there is no approval in thus leaving them to act at the prompting of their own wicked hearts (Josh. 13:27).

21-41. THE JOURNEY. **21. Balaam . . . saddled his ass**—probably one of the white sprightly animals which persons of rank were accustomed to ride. The saddle, as usually in the East, would be nothing more than a pad or his outer cloak.

22. God's anger was kindled because he went—The displeasure arose partly from his neglecting the condition on which leave was granted him—viz., to wait till the princes of Moab "came to call him," and because, through desire for "the wages of unrighteousness," he entertained the secret purpose of acting in opposition to the solemn charge of God.

24. the angel of the Lord stood in a path of the vineyards—The roads which lead through fields and vineyards are so narrow that in most parts a man could not pass a beast without care and caution. A stone or mud fence flanks each side of these roads, to prevent the soil being washed off by the rains.

28. the Lord opened the mouth of the ass—to utter, like a parrot, articulate sounds, without understanding them. That this was a visionary scene is a notion which seems inadmissible, because of the improbability of a vision being described as an actual occurrence in the middle of a plain history. Besides, the opening of the ass's mouth must have been an external act, and that, with the manifest tenor of Peter's language, strongly favors the literal view. The absence of any surprise at such a phenomenon on the part of Balaam may be accounted for by his mind being wholly engrossed with the prospect of gain, which produced "the madness of the prophet." "It was a miracle, wrought to humble his proud heart, which had to be first subjected in the school of an ass before he was brought to attend to the voice of God speaking by the angel" [CALVIN].

ADAM CLARKE

18. *I cannot go beyond the word of the Lord my God.* Balaam knew God too well to suppose he could reverse any of His purposes; and he respected Him too much to attempt to do anything without His permission. Though he was covetous, yet he dared not, even when strongly tempted by both riches and honors, to go contrary to the command of his God.

19. *What the Lord will say unto me more.* He did not know but God might make a further discovery of His will to him, and therefore he might very innocently seek further information.

20. *If the man come . . . go with them.* This is a confirmation of what was observed on the twelfth verse, though we find his going was marked with the divine displeasure because he wished, for the sake of the honors and rewards, to fulfil as far as possible the will of the king of Moab. Mr. Shuckford observes that the pronoun *hu* is sometimes used to denote a person's doing a thing out of his own head, without regard to the directions of another. Thus in the case of Balaam, when God had allowed him to go with the messengers of Balak, if they came in the morning to call him; because he was more hasty than he ought to have been, and went to them instead of staying till they should come to him, it was said of him, not *ki halach*, "He went," but *ki holech hu*, i.e., "He went of his own head"—without being called; and in this, Mr. Shuckford supposes, his iniquity chiefly lay.

23. *And the ass saw the angel.* When God granted visions, those alone who were particularly interested saw them while others in the same company saw nothing; see Dan. x. 7; Acts ix. 7.

26. *And the angel . . . stood in a narrow place.* In this carriage of the angel, says Mr. Ainsworth, the Lord shows us the proceedings of His judgments against sinners. First, He mildly shakes His rod at them but lets them go untouched. Secondly, He comes nearer and touches them with an easy correction as it were wringing their foot against the wall. Thirdly when all this is ineffectual, He brings them into such straits that they can neither turn to the right hand nor to the left, but must fall before His judgments if they do not fully turn to Him.

28. *The Lord opened the mouth of the ass.* And where is the wonder of all this? If the ass had opened her own mouth, and reproved the rash prophet, we might well be astonished; but when God opens the mouth, an ass can speak as well as a man. It is worthy of remark here that Balaam testifies no surprise at this miracle, because he saw it was the Lord's doing.

MATTHEW HENRY

heart. (1) The angel reproved him for his outrageousness (*v.* 32, 33): *Wherefore hast thou smitten thy ass?* (2) Balaam then seemed to relent (*v.* 34): "*I have sinned,* sinned in undertaking this journey, sinned in pushing on so violently"; but he excused it with this, that he saw not the angel; yet, now that he did see him, he was willing to go back again. Here is no sign that his heart is turned, but, if his hands are tied, he cannot help it. Thus many leave their sins only because their sins have left them. There seems to be a reformation of the life, but what will this avail if there be no renovation of the heart? (3) The angel however continued his permission: "*Go with the men, v.* 35. Go, if thou hast a mind to be made a fool of, and to be shamed before Balak, and all the princes of Moab. *Go, only the word that I shall speak unto thee, that thou shalt speak,* whether thou wilt or no," for this seems not to be a precept but a prediction of the event, that he should not only not be able to curse Israel, but should be forced to bless them.

Verses 36–41

We have here the meeting between Balak and Balaam, confederate enemies to God's Israel; but here they seem to differ in their expectations of the success. 1. Balak speaks of it with confidence, not doubting but to gain his point now that Balaam had come. 2. Balaam speaks doubtfully of the issue, and bids Balak not depend too much upon him (*v.* 38): "*Have I now any power at all to say any thing?* Gladly would I curse Israel; but I must not, I cannot, God will not suffer me." 3. They address themselves with all speed to the business. Balaam is nobly entertained over night, a sacrifice of thanksgiving is offered to the gods of Moab, for the safe arrival of this welcome guest, and he is treated with a feast upon the sacrifice, *v.* 40. And the next morning, that no time might be lost, Balak takes Balaam in his chariot to the high places of his kingdom. And now Balaam is really as solicitous to please Balak as ever he had pretended to be to please God.

JAMIESON, FAUSSET, BROWN

34, 35. I have sinned . . . if it displease thee, I will get me back again—Notwithstanding this confession, he evinced no spirit of penitence, as he speaks of desisting only from the outward act. The words "go with the men" was a mere withdrawal of farther restraint, but the terms in which leave was given are more absolute and peremptory than those in verse 20.

36, 37. when Balak heard that Balaam was come, he went out to meet him—Politeness requires that the higher the rank of the expected guest, greater distance is to be gone to welcome his arrival.

38. the word that God putteth in my mouth, that shall I speak—This appears a pious answer. It was an acknowledgment that he was restrained by a superior power. **39. Kirjath-huzoth**—a city of streets. **40. Balak offered oxen and sheep**—made preparations for a grand entertainment to Balaam and the princes of Midian. **41. high places of Baal**—eminences consecrated to the worship of Baal-peor (ch. 25:3) or Chemosh.

ADAM CLARKE

33. *Surely now also I had slain thee.* How often are the meanest animals, and the most trivial occurrences, instruments of the preservation of our lives and of the salvation of our souls! The messenger of justice would have killed Balaam had not the mercy of God prevented the ass from proceeding.

34. *If it displease thee, I will get me back again.* Here is a proof that, though he "loved the wages of unrighteousness," yet he still feared God; and he is now willing to drop the enterprise if God be displeased with his proceeding.

38. *The word that God putteth in my mouth that shall I speak.* Here was a noble resolution and he was certainly faithful to it. Though he wished to please the king, and get wealth and honor, yet he would not displease God to realize even these bright prospects. Many who slander this poor prophet have not half his piety.

40. *And Balak offered oxen.* This was to gain the favor of his gods, and perhaps to propitiate Jehovah, that the end for which he had sent for Balaam might be accomplished.

41. *That . . . he might see the utmost part of the people.* As he thought Balaam must have them all in his eye when he pronounced his curse, lest it might not extend to those who were not in sight. On this account he took him up into the high places of Baal.

MATTHEW HENRY — CHAPTER 23

Verses 1–12

I. Great preparation made for the cursing of Israel. That which was aimed at was to engage the God of Israel to forsake them, and either to be on Moab's side or to stand neutral, as if he would *eat the flesh of bulls or drink the blood of goats.* Ridiculous nonsense, to think that these would please God, and gain his favour, when there could be in them no exercise either of faith or obedience! Yet, it should seem, they offered these sacrifices to the God of heaven, the supreme *Numen—Divinity,* and not to any of their local deities.

II. The turning of the curse into a blessing, by the overruling power of God, in love to Israel, which is the account Moses gives of it, Deut. xxiii. 5.

1. God puts the blessing into the mouth of Balaam. While the sacrifices were burning, Balaam retired: he *went solitary,* into some dark grove on the top of the high place, *v.* 3, marg. Thus much he knew, that solitude gives a good opportunity for communion with God. But Balaam retired with a peradventure only, having some thoughts that God might meet him; but being conscious to himself of guilt, and knowing that God had lately met him in anger, he had reason to speak doubtfully: *Peradventure the Lord will come to meet me, v.* 3. But, whatever he intended, God designed to serve his own glory by him, and therefore *met Balaam, v.* 4. God would constrain him to utter such a confession, to the honour of God and Israel, as should render those for ever inexcusable who should appear in arms against them. When Balaam was aware that God met him, he boasted of his performances: *I have prepared seven altars, and offered upon every altar a bullock and a ram.* However, though the sacrifice was an abomination, God took the occasion of Balaam's expectation to *put a word into his mouth* (*v.* 5).

2. Balaam pronounces the blessing in the ears of Balak. He pronounces Israel safe and happy, and so blesses them.

(1) He pronounces them safe, and out of the reach of his envenomed darts. [1] He owns that the design was to curse them, that Balak sent for him out of his own country, and that he came, with that intent, *v.* 7. [2] He owns the design defeated, and his own inability to accomplish it. He could not so much as give them an ill word or an ill wish: *How shall I curse those whom God has not cursed? v.* 8. Not that therefore he would not do it, but therefore he could not do it. This is a fair confession, *First,* Of the weakness and impotency of his own magic skill. *Secondly,*

JAMIESON, FAUSSET, BROWN — CHAPTER 23

Vss. 1-30. BALAK'S SACRIFICES. **1. Balaam said unto Balak, Build me here seven altars**—Balak, being a heathen, would naturally suppose these altars were erected in honor of Baal, the patron deity of his country. It is evident, from verse 4 that they were prepared for the worship of the true God; although in choosing the high places of Baal as their site and rearing a number of altars (II Kings 18:22; Isa. 17:8; Jer. 11:13; Hos. 8:11; 10:1), instead of one only, as God had appointed, Balaam blended his own superstitions with the divine worship. The heathen, both in ancient and modern times, attached a mysterious virtue to the number *seven;* and Balaam, in ordering the preparation of so many altars, designed to mystify and delude the king. **3. Stand by thy burnt offering**—as one in expectation of an important favor.

peradventure the Lord will come to meet me: and whatsoever he showeth me—i.e., makes known to me by word or sign. **he went to an high place**—apart by himself, where he might practise rites and ceremonies, with a view to obtain a response of the oracle. **4–6. God met Balaam**—not in compliance with his incantations, but to frustrate his wicked designs and compel him, contrary to his desires and interests, to pronounce the following benediction.

7. took up his parable—i.e., spoke under the influence of inspiration, and in the highly poetical, figurative, and oracular style of a prophet. **brought me from Aram**—This word, joined with "the mountains of the East," denotes the upper portion of Mesopotamia, lying on the east of Moab. The East enjoyed an infamous notoriety for magicians and soothsayers (Isa. 2:6). **8. How shall I curse, whom God hath not cursed?**—A divine blessing has been pronounced over the posterity of Jacob; and therefore, whatever prodigies can be achieved by my charms, al magical skill, all human power, is utterly impotent to counteract the decree of God.

ADAM CLARKE — CHAPTER 23

1. *Build me here seven altars.* The *oxen* and the *rams* were such as the Mosaic law had ordered to be offered to God in sacrifice; the building of seven altars was not commanded As *seven* was a number of perfection, Balaam chose it on this occasion because he intended to offer a grand sacrifice, and to offer a bullock and a ram upon each of the altars, the whole to be made a burnt offering at the same time. And as he intended to offer seven bullocks and seven rams at the same time, it could not be conveniently done on one altar; therefore he ordered seven to be built.

3. *Stand by thy burnt offering.* We have already seen that blessing and cursing in this way were considered as religious rites, and therefore must always be preceded by sacrifice. See this exemplified in the case of Isaac, before he blessed Jacob and Esau, Genesis xxvii, and the notes there. The venison that was brought to Isaac, of which he did eat, was properly the preparatory sacrifice.

7. *And he took up his parable. Meshalo,* see on chap. xxi. 27. All these oracular speeches of Balaam are in hemistich meter in the original. They are highly dignified, and may be considered as immediate poetic productions of the Spirit of God; for it is expressly said, v. 5, that God put the word in Balaam's mouth, and that "the spirit of God came upon him," chap. xxiv. 2.

8. *How shall I curse, whom God hath not cursed?* It was granted on all hands that no incantations nor imprecations could avail unless God concurred and ratified them. From God's communication to Balaam he saw that God was determined to bless and defend Israel, and therefore all endeavors to injure them must be in vain.

MATTHEW HENRY

It is a confession of the sovereignty and dominion of the divine power. He owns that he could do no more than God would suffer him to do. *Thirdly*, It is a confession of the inviolable security of the people of God.

(2) He pronounces them happy in three things:—

[1] Happy in their peculiarity, and distinction from the rest of the nations: *From the top of the rock I see him, v.* 9. And it seems to have been a great surprise to him that whereas, it is probable, they were represented to him as a rude and disorderly rabble, that infested the countries round about in rambling parties, he saw them a regular incorporated camp, in which appeared all the marks of discipline and good order. Note, It is the duty and honour of those that are dedicated to God to be separated from the world. Those who make conscience of peculiar duties may take the comfort of peculiar privileges.

[2] Happy in their numbers, not so few and despicable as they were represented to him, but an innumerable company, which made them both honourable and formidable (*v.* 10): *Who can count the dust of Jacob?* The number of the people was the thing that Balak was vexed at (*ch.* xxii. 3). He takes notice of the number, *First*, Of the *dust of Jacob*; that is, the people of Jacob, concerning whom it was foretold that they should be as the dust for number, Gen. xxviii. 14. *Secondly*, Of the *fourth part of Israel*, alluding to the form of their camp, which was cast into four squadrons, under four standards.

[3] Happy in their end: *Let me die the death of the righteous* Israelites, that are in covenant with God, and let my *last end, or future state, be like theirs, or my recompence*, namely, in the other world. Here, *First*, It is taken for granted that death is the end of all men; the righteous themselves must die: and it is good for us to think of this with application, as Balaam himself does here, speaking of his own death. *Secondly*, He goes upon the supposition of the soul's immortality, and a different state on the other side death, to which this is a noble testimony, and an evidence of its being anciently known and believed. *Thirdly*, He pronounces the righteous truly blessed, not only while they live, but when they die. *Fourthly*, He shows his opinion of religion to be better than his resolution; there are many who desire to die the death of the righteous, but do not endeavour to live the life of the righteous. Gladly would they have their end like theirs, but not their way. They would be saints in heaven, but not saints on earth. Now,

III. We are told, 1. How Balak fretted at it, *v.* 11. He pretended to honour the Lord with his sacrifices, and to wait for the answer God would send him; and yet, when it did not prove according to his mind, he forgot God. 2. How Balaam was forced to acquiesce in it. He submits because he cannot help it.

Verses 13–30

Here is, I. Preparation made the second time, as before, for the cursing of Israel. 1. The place is changed, *v.* 13. 2. The sacrifices are repeated, new altars are built, a bullock and a ram offered on every altar, and Balak attends his sacrifice as closely as ever, *v.* 14, 15. 3. Balaam renews his attendance on God, and God meets him the second time, and puts another word into his mouth, not to reverse the former, but to ratify it, *v.* 16, 17.

II. A second conversion of the curse into a blessing by the overruling power of God; and this blessing is both larger and stronger than the former, and quite cuts off all hopes of altering it. Balak having been so forward to ask what the Lord had spoken (*v.* 17), Balaam now addresses himself particularly to him (*v.* 18): *Rise up, Balak, and hear*.

1. Two things Balaam in this discourse informs Balak of:—

(1) That he had no reason to hope that he should ruin Israel.

[1] It would be to no purpose to attempt to ruin them.

First, Because God is unchangeable. He never changes his mind, and therefore never recalls his promise.

Secondly, Because Israel are at present unblamable. There was no idolatry among them, which is in a particular manner called iniquity and perverseness. Balaam knew that nothing would separate between them and God but sin.

Thirdly, Because the power of both was irresistible. They had the presence of God with them. They had the joy of that presence, and were always made to triumph in it.

[2] From all this he infers that it was to no purpose for him to think of doing them a mischief by all the arts he could use, *v.* 23. The curses of hell can never take place against the blessings of heaven.

(2) Balaam shows him that he had more reason to fear being ruined by them, for they were likely to

JAMIESON, FAUSSET, BROWN

9. from the top—lit., "a bare place" on the rocks, to which Balak had taken him, for it was deemed necessary to see the people who were to be devoted to destruction. But that commanding prospect could contribute nothing to the accomplishment of the king's object, for the destiny of Israel was to be a distinct, peculiar people, separated from the rest of the nations in government, religion, customs, and divine protection (Deut. 33:28). So that although I might be able to gratify your wishes against other people, I can do nothing against them (Exod. 19:5; Lev. 20:24). **10. Who can count the dust of Jacob?**—an Oriental hyperbole for a very populous nation, as Jacob's posterity was promised to be (Gen. 13:16; 28:14).

the number of the fourth part of Israel—i.e., the camp consisted of four divisions; every one of these parts was formidable in numbers. **Let me die the death of the righteous**—*Heb.*, of Jeshurun; or, the Israelites. The meaning is: they are a people happy, above all others, not only in life, but at death, from their knowledge of the true God, and their hope through His grace. Balaam is a representative of a large class in the world, who express a wish for the blessedness which Christ has promised to His people but are averse to imitate the mind that was in Him.

13-15. Come, . . . with me unto another place, from whence thou mayest see them—Surprised and disappointed at this unexpected eulogy on Israel, Balak hoped that, if seen from a different point of observation, the prophet would give utterance to different feelings; and so, having made the same solemn preparations, Balaam retired, as before, to wait the divine afflatus. **14. he brought him into the field of Zophim . . . top of Pisgah**—a flat surface on the summit of the mountain range, which was cultivated land. Others render it "the field of sentinels," an eminence where some of Balak's guards were posted to give signals [CALMET]. **18. Rise up**—As Balak was already standing (vs. 17), this expression is equivalent to "now attend to me." The counsels and promises of God respecting Israel are unchangeable; and no attempt to prevail on Him to reverse them will succeed, as they may with a man.

21. He hath not beheld iniquity in Jacob—Many sins were observed and punished in this people. But no such universal and hopeless apostasy had as yet appeared, to induce God to abandon or destroy them. **the Lord his God is with him**—has a favor for them. **and the shout of a king is among them**—such joyful acclamations as of a people rejoicing in the presence of a victorious prince. **22. he hath as it were the strength of an unicorn**—Israel is not as they were at the Exodus, a horde of poor, feeble, spiritless people, but powerful and invincible as a *reem*—i.e., a rhinoceros (Job 39:9; Ps. 22:21; 92:10). **23. Surely there is no enchantment against Jacob**—No art can ever prevail against a people who are under the shield of Omnipotence, and for whom miracles have been and yet shall be performed, which will be a theme of admiration in succeeding ages.

ADAM CLARKE

9. *From the top of the rocks I see him.* That is, from the high places of Baal where he went, chap. xxii. 41, that he might the more advantageously see the *whole* camp of Israel. *The people shall dwell alone.* They shall ever be preserved as a distinct nation. This prophecy has been literally fulfilled through a period of 3,300 years to the present day. This is truly astonishing.

10. *Let me die the death of the righteous.* Probably Balaam had some presentiment that he should be taken off by a premature death, and therefore he lodges this petition against it. The death of the righteous in those times implied being gathered to one's fathers in a good old age, having seen his children and children's children; and to this, probably, the latter part of this petition applies: *And let my last end be like his!* ("And let my posterity be like his!")

13. *Thou shalt see but the utmost part of them.* Balak thought that the sight of such an immense camp had intimidated Balaam, and this he might gather from what he said in the tenth verse: "Who can count the dust of Jacob?" He thought therefore that he might get Balaam to curse them in detached parties, till the whole camp should be devoted to destruction by successive execrations.

17. *What hath the Lord spoken?* Balak himself now understood that Balaam was wholly under the influence of Jehovah, and would say nothing but what God commanded him; but not knowing Jehovah as Balaam did, he hoped that he might be induced to change his mind, and curse a people whom he had hitherto determined to bless.

19. *God is not a man, that he should lie.* This seems to be spoken to correct the foregoing supposition of Balak that God could change his mind.

21. *He hath not beheld iniquity in Jacob, neither hath he seen perverseness in Israel.* This is a difficult passage; for if we take the words as spoken of the people Israel, as their *iniquity* and their *perverseness* were almost unparalleled, such words cannot be spoken of them with strict truth. If we consider them as spoken of the patiarch Jacob and Israel, or of Jacob after he became Israel, they are most strictly true, as after that time a more unblemished and noble character (Abraham excepted) is not to be found in the page of history, whether sacred or profane; and for his sake, and for the sake of his father, Isaac, and his grandfather, Abraham, God is ever represented as favoring, blessing, and sparing a rebellious and undeserving people. In this way, I think, this difficult text may be safely understood.

There is another way in which the words may be interpreted, which will give a good sense. *Aven* not only signifies *iniquity*, but most frequently "trouble, labor, distress, and affliction"; and these indeed are its ideal meanings, and *iniquity* is only an accommodated or metaphorical one, because of the pain, distress, etc., produced by sin. *Amal*, translated here *perverseness*, occurs often in Scripture, but is never translated "perverseness" except in this place. It signifies simply "labor," especially that which is of an afflictive or oppressive kind. The words may therefore be considered as implying that God will not suffer the people either to be exterminated by the sword or to be brought under a yoke of slavery. Either of these methods of interpretation gives a good sense, but our common version gives none.

22. *The strength of an unicorn. Reem* and *reim.* It is generally allowed that there is no such beast in nature as the *unicorn;* i.e., a creature of the horse kind, with one long, rich, curled horn in the forehead. The creature painted from fancy is represented as one of the supporters of the royal arms of Great Britain. It is difficult to say what kind of beast is intended by the original word. But I believe the rhinoceros is that intended by the sacred writers.

23. *There is no enchantment.* Because God has determined to save them, therefore no enchantment can prevail against them. *According to this time.* I think this clause should be read thus: "As at this time it shall be told to Jacob and to Israel what God worketh"; i.e., this people shall always have prophetic information of what God is about to work. And indeed they are the

MATTHEW HENRY | JAMIESON, FAUSSET, BROWN | ADAM CLARKE

make bloody work among his neighbours; and, if he and his country escaped, it was not because he was too great for them to meddle with, but because he fell not within their commission, *v.* 24.

2. Now what was the issue of this disappointment? (1) Balak and Balaam were both of them sick of the cause. Balak is now willing to have his conjurer silenced. If thou canst not curse them, I beseech thee not to bless them. Balaam is still willing to own himself overruled, and appeals to what he had said in the beginning of this enterprise (*ch.* xxii. 38): *All that the Lord speaketh, that I must do, v.* 26.

(2) Yet they resolve to make another attempt. The place to which Balak now took Balaam was the top of Peor, the most eminent high place in all his country, where, it is probable, Baal was worshipped, and it was thence called *Baal-peor.*

26. All that the Lord speaketh, that I must do—a remarkable confession that he was divinely constrained to give utterances different from what it was his purpose and inclination to do. **28. Balak brought Balaam unto the top of Peor**—or, Beth-peor (Deut. 3:29), **the eminence on which a temple of Baal stood. that looketh toward Jeshimon**—the desert tract in the south of Palestine, on both sides of the Dead Sea.

only people under heaven who ever had this privilege. When God himself designed to punish them because of their sins, He always forewarned them by the prophets, and also took care to apprise them of all the plots of their enemies against them.

24. *Behold, the people shall rise up as a great lion. Labi,* the "great, mighty, or old lion," the king of the forest, who is feared and respected by all the other beasts of the field; so shall Israel be the subduer and possessor of the whole land of Canaan. And *as a young lion, ari* from *arah,* "to tear off," the predatory lion, or the lion in the act of seizing and tearing his prey; the nations against whom the Israelites are now going shall be no more able to defend themselves against their attacks than the feeblest beasts of the forest are against the attacks of the strong lion.

28. *Unto the top of Peor.* Probably the place where the famous Baal-peor had his chief temple. He appears to have been the Priapus of the Moabites, and to have been worshipped with the same obscene and abominable rites.

CHAPTER 24

Verses 1-9

The blessing itself which Balaam here pronounces upon Israel is much the same with the two we had in the foregoing chapter; but the introduction to it is different.

I. The method of proceeding here varies. Balaam laid aside the enchantments which he had hitherto depended on, used no spells, or charms, or magic arts, finding they did him no service; it was to no purpose to deal with the devil for a curse, when it was plain that God was determined immovably to bless, *v.* 1. He did not now retire into a solitary place as before, but set his face directly towards the wilderness where Israel lay encamped. Now *the Spirit of God came upon him,* that is, the Spirit of prophecy. He used a different preface now from what he had used before (*v.* 3, 4), yet savouring very much (as some think) of pride and vain-glory, taking all the praise of this prophecy to himself, and magnifying himself as one of the cabinet-council of heaven. When he attempted to curse Israel, he owns, he was in a mistake, but now he began to see his error, and yet still he remained blinded by covetousness and ambition, those foolish and hurtful lusts. Many have their eyes open that have not their hearts open, are enlightened, but not sanctified.

II. Yet the blessing is for substance the same with those before. Several things he admires in Israel:—

1. Their beauty (*v.* 5): *How goodly are thy tents, O Jacob!* Though they dwelt not in stately palaces, but in coarse and homely tents, and these, no doubt, sadly weather-beaten, yet Balaam sees a beauty in those tents, because of their admirable order, according to their tribes, *v.* 2. Nothing recommends religion more to the good opinion of those that look upon it at a distance than the unity and harmony of its professors, Ps. cxxxiii. 1.

2. Their fruitfulness and increase. This may be intended by those similitudes (*v.* 6) of the valleys, gardens, and trees, as well as by those expressions (*v.* 7), *He shall pour the water out of his buckets*; that is, God shall water them with his blessing like rain from heaven, and then his *seed shall be in many waters.*

CHAPTER 24

VSS. 1-25. BALAAM FORETELLS ISRAEL'S HAPPINESS. **1. to seek for**—i.e., to use enchantments. His experience on the two former occasions had taught him that these superstitious accompaniments of his worship were useless, and therefore he now simply looked towards the camp of Israel, either with a secret design to curse them, or to await the divine afflatus.

2. he saw Israel abiding in his tents according to their tribes—i.e., in the orderly distribution of the camp (ch. 2). **the spirit of God came upon him**—Before the regular ministry of the prophets was instituted, God made use of various persons as the instruments through whom He revealed His will, and Balaam was one of these (Deut. 23:5). **3. the man whose eyes are open**—i.e., a seer (I Sam. 9:9), a prophet, to whom the visioned future was disclosed—sometimes when falling into a sleep (Gen. 15:12-15), frequently into "a trance."

5-7. How goodly are thy tents, . . . O Israel!—a fine burst of admiration, expressed in highly poetical strains. All travellers describe the beauty which the circular area of Bedouin tents impart to the desert. How impressive, then, must have been the view, as seen from the heights of Abarim, of the immense camp of Israel extended over the subjacent plains. **6. As the valleys**—*Heb.*, brooks, the watercourses of the mountains. **lign aloes**—an aromatic shrub on the banks of his native Euphrates, the conical form of which suggested an apt resemblance to a tent. The redundant imagery of these verses depicts the humble origin, rapid progress, and prosperity of Israel.

CHAPTER 24

1. *He went not, as at other times, to seek for enchantments.* We have already had occasion to observe that the proper meaning of the word *nachash* is not easily ascertained. Here the plural *nechashim* is rendered *enchantments,* but it probably means no more than the knowledge of future events. When Balaam saw that it pleased God to bless Israel, he therefore thought it unnecessary to apply for any further propetic declarations of God's will as he had done before, for he could safely infer every good to this people from the evident disposition of God towards them.

2. *The spirit of God came upon him.* This divine afflatus he had not expected on the present occasion, but God had not yet declared the whole of His will.

3. *He took up his parable.* His prophetic declaration couched in highly poetic terms, and in regular meter, as the preceding were. *The man whose eyes are open.* I believe the original *shethum* should be translated "shut," not *open;* for in the next verse, where the opening of his eyes is mentioned, a widely different word is used, *galah,* which signifies to "open" or "reveal." At first the eyes of Balaam were shut, and so closely too that he could not *see* the angel who withstood him, till God opened his eyes; nor could he see the gracious intentions of God towards Israel, till the eyes of his understanding were opened by the powers of the Divine Spirit.

4. *Falling into a trance.* There is no indication in the Hebrew that he fell into a *trance;* these words are added by our translators, but they are not in the original. *Nophel* is the only word used, and simply signifies "falling, or falling down," perhaps in this instance by way of religious prostration.

6. *Lign aloes which the Lord hath planted.* Or, "as the tents which the Lord hath pitched"; for it is the same word, *ohalim,* which is used in the fifth verse. But from other parts of Scripture we find that the word also signifies a species of tree called by some the sandal tree, and by others the lignum or wood aloes. This tree is described as being eight or ten feet high, with very large leaves growing at the top; and it is supposed that a forest of those at some distance must bear some resemblance to a numerous encampment. As the word comes from the root *ahal,* which signifies to "spread or branch out," and therefore is applied to tents, because of their being extended or spread out on the ground, so when it is applied to trees it must necessarily mean such as were remarkable for their widely extended branches; but what the particular species is cannot be satisfactorily ascertained. By the Lord's planting are probably meant such trees as grow independently of the cultivation of man.

7. *He shall pour the water out of his buckets.* Here is a very plain allusion to their method of raising water in different parts of the East. By the well a tall pole is erected, which serves as a fulcrum to a very long lever, to the smaller

MATTHEW HENRY

3. Their honour and advancement. As the multitude of the people is the honour of the prince, so the magnificence of the prince is the honour of the people; Balaam therefore foretells that their *king shall be higher than Agag*. Agag, it is probable, was the most potent monarch in those parts.

4. Their power and victory, *v.* 8. (1) He looks back upon what they had done, or rather what had been done for them: *God brought them forth out of Egypt*; this he had spoken of before, *ch.* xxiii. 22. (2) He looks down upon their present strength. (3) He looks forward to their future conquests.

5. Their courage and security: *He lay down as a lion, as a great lion, v.* 9. Lions do not retire into places of shelter to sleep, but lie down anywhere, knowing that none dares meddle with them.

6. Their interest, and influence upon their neighbours. Their friends, and those in alliance with them, were happy.

Verses 10–14

We have here the conclusion of this vain attempt to curse Israel, and the total abandonment of it. 1. Balak made the worst of it. He broke out into a rage against Balaam (*v.* 10). He forbade him his presence, expelled him his country, upbraided him with the preferments he had designed to bestow upon him, but now would not (*v.* 11). 2. Balaam made the best of it. (1) He endeavours to excuse the disappointment. Balak could not say that he had cheated him, since he had given him fair notice of the check he found himself under. (2) He endeavours to atone for it, *v.* 14. He will gratify his curiosity with some predictions concerning the nations about him. He will satisfy him with an assurance that, whatever this formidable people should do to his people, it should not be till the latter days. He will put him into a method of doing Israel a mischief without the ceremonies of enchantment and execration. Since he could not have leave from God to curse them, he puts him in a way of getting help from the devil to tempt them.

Verses 15–25

The office of prophets was both to bless and to prophesy in the name of the Lord.

I. He personates a true prophet admirably well, God permitting and directing him to do so, because, whatever he was, the prophecy itself was a true prophecy. *He saw the vision of the Almighty*, but not so as to be *changed into the same image*. He calls God the *Most High*, and the *Almighty*. Yet he had no true fear of him, love to him, or faith in him, so far may a man go towards heaven, and yet come short.

II. Here is his prophecy concerning him that should be the crown and glory of his people Israel, who is, 1. David, the type under whom the forces of Israel should *do valiantly, v.* 18. This was fulfilled when David smote Moab, 2 Sam. viii. 2. And at the same time the Edomites likewise were brought into obedience to Israel, *v.* 14. But, 2. Our Lord Jesus, the promised Messiah, is chiefly pointed at in the antitype, and of him it is an illustrious prophecy; it was the will of God that notice should thus be given of his coming, a great while before, not only to the people of the Jews, but to other nations, because his gospel and kingdom were to extend themselves so far beyond the borders of the land of Israel. It is here foretold, (1) That his coming should not be yet for a great while: "*I shall see him, but not now*; I do see him in vision, but at a very great distance, through the interposing space of 1,500 years at least. (2) That he shall come out of Jacob, and Israel, as a star and a sceptre, the former denoting his glory and lustre, as the *bright and morning star*, the latter his power and authority; it is *he that shall have dominion*. (3) That his kingdom shall be universal, and victorious over all opposition, which was typified by David's victories over Moab and Edom. Christ shall be king, not only of Jacob and Israel, but of all the world.

III. Here is his prophecy concerning the Amalekites and Kenites, part of whose country, it is probable, he had now in view. 1. The Amalekites were now the *chief of the nations* (*v.* 20). Here Balaam confirms that doom of Amalek which Moses had read (Exod. xvii. 14, 16).

JAMIESON, FAUSSET, BROWN

7. his king shall be higher than Agag—The Amalekites were then the most powerful of all the desert tribes, and Agag a title common to their kings.

10-14. Balak's anger was kindled against Balaam, and he smote his hands together—The "smiting of the hands together" is, among Oriental people, an indication of the most violent rage (see Ezek. 21:17; 22:13) and ignominious dismissal.

15. he took up his parable—or prophecy, uttered in a poetical style.

17. I shall see him—rather, "I do see" or "I have seen him"—a prophetic sight, like that of Abraham (John 8:56). **him**—i.e., Israel. **there shall come a Star out of Jacob, and a Sceptre shall rise out of Israel**—This imagery, in the hieroglyphic language of the East, denotes some eminent ruler—primarily David; but secondarily and pre-eminently, the Messiah (see on Gen. 49:10). **corners**—border, often used for a whole country (Exod. 8:2; Ps. 74:17). **children of Sheth**—some prince of Moab; or, according to some, "the children of the East." **18. Edom shall be a possession**—This prophecy was accomplished by David (II Sam. 8:14). **Seir**—seen in the south, and poetically used for Edom. The double conquest of Moab and Edom is alluded to (Ps. 60:8; 108:9). **19. Out of Jacob shall come he that shall have dominion** David, and particularly Christ. **that remaineth of the city**—those who flee from the field to fortified places (Ps. 60:9). **20. Amalek . . . his latter end shall be that he perish for ever**—Their territory was seen at the remote extremity of the desert. (See on Exod. 17:14; also I Sam. 15.)

ADAM CLARKE

end of which a bucket is appended. On the opposite end, which is much larger, are many notches cut in the wood, which serve as steps for a man, whose business it is to climb into the well. When the bucket is filled, he raises it by walking back on the opposite arm, till his weight brings the bucket above the well's mouth. A person standing by the well empties the bucket into a trench, which communicates with the ground intended to be watered. *His seed shall be in many waters.* Another simple allusion to the sowing of rice. The ground must not only be well-watered, but flooded, in order to serve for the proper growth of this grain. The rice that was sown in *many waters* must be the most fruitful. By an elegant and chaste metaphor all this is applied to the procreation of a numerous posterity.

His king shall be higher than Agag. This name is supposed to have been as common to all the Amalekitish kings as Pharaoh was to those in Egypt. But several critics, with the Septuagint, suppose that a small change has taken place here in the original word, and that instead of *meagag*, "than Agag," we should read *miggog*, "than Gog." As Gog in Scripture seems to mean the enemies of God's people, then the promise here may imply that the true worshippers of the Most High shall ultimately have dominion over all their enemies.

8. *God brought him forth out of Egypt.* They were neither expelled thence nor came voluntarily away. God alone, with a high hand and uplifted arm, brought them forth. Concerning the *unicorn*, see on chap. xxiii. 22.

9. *He couched, he lay down as a lion.* See the original terms explained, chap. xxiii. 24.

These oracles, delivered by Balaam, are evident prophecies of the victories which the Israelites should gain over their enemies, and of their firm possession of the Promised Land. They may also refer to the great victories to be obtained by the Lord Jesus Christ, that Lion of the tribe of Judah, over sin, death, and Satan, the grand enemies of the human race; and to that most numerous posterity of spiritual children which should be begotten by the preaching of the gospel.

11. *Lo, the Lord hath kept thee back from honor.* A bitter and impious sarcasm. "Hadst thou cursed this people, I would have promoted thee to great honor; but thou hast chosen to follow the directions of Jehovah rather than mine, and what will He do for thee?"

15. *The man whose eyes are open.* See on v. 3. It seems strange that our version should have fallen into such a mistake as to render *shethum* "open," which it does not signify, when the very sound of the word expresses the sense. The Vulgate has very properly preserved the true meaning, by rendering the clause "he whose eyes are shut." The Targum first paraphrased the passage falsely, and most of the versions followed it.

17. *I shall see him, but not now.* Or, "I shall see him, but he is not now." *I shall behold him, but not nigh*—I shall have a full view of him, but the time is yet distant. That is, The person of whom I am now prophesying does not at present exist among these Israelites, nor shall he appear in this generation. *There shall come a Star out of Jacob, and a Sceptre shall rise out of Israel*—a person eminent for wisdom, and formidable for strength and power, shall arise as king among this people. *He shall smite the corners of Moab*—he shall bring the Moabites perfectly under subjection (see 2 Sam. viii. 2), *and destroy all the children of Sheth.*

19. *Out of Jacob shall come.* This is supposed to refer to Christ, because of what is said in Gen. xlix. 10.

20. *Amalek was the first of the nations.* The most ancient and most powerful of all the nations or states then within the view of Balaam; *but his latter end shall be that he perish for ever*, or "his posterity [*acharitho*] shall be destroyed, or shall utterly fail." This oracle began to be fulfilled by Saul, 1 Sam. xv. 7-8, who overthrew the Amalekites and took their king, Agag, prisoner. Afterwards they were nearly destroyed by David, 1 Sam. xxvii. 8, and they were finally exterminated by the sons of Simeon in the days of Hezekiah, 1 Chron. iv. 41-43; since that time they have ceased to exist as a people,

MATTHEW HENRY

2. The Kenites were now the securest of the nations; their situation was such as that nature was their engineer, and had strongly fortified them: "*Thou puttest thy nest* (like the eagle) *in a rock*, *v.* 21. Thou thinkest thyself safe, and yet the *Kenites shall be wasted* (*v.* 22) and gradually brought to decay, till they be carried away captive by the Assyrians," which was done at the captivity of the ten tribes. Even a nest in a rock will be no perpetual security.

IV. Here is a prophecy that looks as far forward as the Greeks and Romans, for theirs is supposed to be meant by the *coast of Chittim*, *v.* 24.

1. The introduction to this parable; this article of his prophecy is very observable (*v.* 23): *Alas! who shall live when God doeth this?* Either, (1) These events are so distant, and so far off to come, that it is hard to say *who shall live till they come*. Or, (2) They will be so dismal, and make such desolations, that scarcely any will escape or be left alive.

2. The prophecy itself is observable. Both Greece and Italy lie much upon the sea, and therefore their armies were sent forth mostly in ships. Now he seems here to foretell, (1) That the forces of the Grecians should humble and bring down the Assyrians, who were united with the Persians, which was fulfilled when the eastern country was overrun by Alexander. (2) That theirs and the Roman forces should afflict the Hebrews, or Jews, who were called *the children of Eber*; this was fulfilled in part when the Grecian empire was oppressive to the Jewish nation, but chiefly when the Roman empire ruined it. But, (3) That Chittim, that is, the Roman empire, in which the Grecian was at length swallowed up, should itself perish when the stone cut out of the mountain without hands shall consume all these kingdoms, and particularly the *feet of iron and clay*, Dan. ii. 34. Thus (says Dr. Lightfoot) Balaam, instead of cursing the church, curses Amalek the first, and Rome the last enemy of the church.

JAMIESON, FAUSSET, BROWN

21. **Kenites . . . nest in a rock**—Though securely established among the clefts in the high rocks of Engedi towards the west, they should be gradually reduced by a succession of enemies till the Assyrian invader carried them into captivity (Judg. 1:16; 4:11; 16:17; also II Kings 15:29; 17:6).

23. **who shall live when God doeth this!**—Few shall escape the desolation that shall send a Nebuchadnezzar to scourge all those regions.

24. **Chittim**—the countries lying on the Mediterranean, particularly Greece and Italy (Dan. 11:29, 30). The Assyrians were themselves to be overthrown—first, by the Greeks under Alexander the Great and his successors; secondly, by the Romans. **Eber**—the posterity of the Hebrews (Gen. 10:24). **he also shall perish**—i.e., the conqueror of Asher and Eber, namely, the Greek and Roman empires.

25. **Balaam rose up, and went . . . to his place**—Mesopotamia, to which, however, he did not return. (See on ch. 31:8.)

ADAM CLARKE

and now no vestige of them remains on the face of the earth.

21. *He looked on the Kenites.* Commentators are not well agreed who the Kenites were. Dr. Dodd's opinion is, I think, nearest to the truth. Jethro, the father-in-law of Moses, is called a priest or prince of Midian, Exod. iii. 1, and in Judg. i. 16 he is called a Kenite; we may infer, therefore, says he, that the Kenites and the Midianites were the same, or at least that the Kenites and the Midianites were confederate tribes. Some of these, we learn from Judges i, followed the Israelites; others abode still among the Midianites and Amalekites.

22. *Until Asshur shall carry thee away captive.* The Assyrians and Babylonians who carried away captive the ten tribes, 2 Kings xvii. 6, and the Jews into Babylon, 2 Kings xxv, probably carried away the Kenites also. Indeed this seems pretty evident, as we find some Kenites mentioned among the Jews after their return from the Babylonish captivity, 1 Chron. ii. 55.

24. *Ships shall come from the coast of Chittim.* Some think by Chittim the Romans, others the Macedonians under Alexander the Great, are meant. *And shall afflict Eber.* Probably not the Hebrews, as some think, but the people on the other side the Euphrates, from *abar*, "to pass over, go beyond"; all which people were discomfited and their empire destroyed by Alexander the Great.

25. *And Balaam . . . returned to his place.* Intended to have gone to Mesopotamia, his native country (see Deut. xxiii. 4), but seems to have settled among the Midianites, where he was slain by the Israelites; see chap. xxxi. 8.

MATTHEW HENRY — CHAPTER 25

Verses 1–5

I. The sin of Israel, to which they were enticed by the daughters of Moab and Midian; they were guilty both of corporal and spiritual whoredoms, for *Israel joined himself unto Baal-peor*, *v.* 3. Not all, nor the most, but very many, were taken in this snare. Now concerning this observe, That whoredom and idolatry went together. They first defiled and debauched their consciences, by committing lewdness with the women, and then were easily drawn, in complaisance to them, and in contempt of the God of Israel, to bow down to their idols. And they were more likely to do so if, as it is commonly supposed, and seems probable by the joining of them together, the uncleanness committed was a part of the worship and service performed to Baal-peor. It was a great aggravation of the sin that *Israel abode in Shittim*, where they had the land of Canaan in view, and were just ready to enter and take possession of it.

II. God's just displeasure against them for this sin. Israel's whoredoms did that which all Balaam's enchantments could not do. 1. A plague immediately broke out. Epidemical diseases are the just punishments of epidemical sins; one infection follows the other. 2. The ringleaders are ordered to be put to death by the hand of public justice, which will be the only way to stay the plague (*v.* 4). The judges must first order them to be *slain with the sword* (*v.* 5), and their dead bodies must be hanged up, that the stupid Israelites might be possessed with a sense of the evil of the sin.

Verses 6–15

Here is a remarkable contest between wickedness and righteousness, and righteousness carries the day, as no doubt it will at last.

I. Never was vice more daring than it was in Zimri, *a prince of a chief house* in the tribe of Simeon. He publicly appeared leading a Midianitish harlot in the sight of Moses, and all the good people of Israel. It was an affront to the justice of the nation, and bade defiance to that. It was an affront to the religion of the nation, and put a contempt upon that.

II. Never was virtue more daring than it was in Phinehas. Being aware of the insolence of Zimri, in a holy indignation at the offenders he rises up from his prayers, takes his sword or half-pike, follows those impudent sinners into their tent, and stabs them both, *v.* 7, 8. It is not at all difficult to justify Phinehas in what he did; for, being now heir-apparent to the high-priesthood, no doubt he was one of those judges of Israel whom Moses had ordered, by the divine appointment, to slay all those whom they knew to

JAMIESON, FAUSSET, BROWN — CHAPTER 25

Vss. 1-18. The Israelites' Whoredom and Idolatry with Moab. **1. Israel abode in Shittim**—a verdant meadow, so called from a grove of acacia trees which lined the eastern side of the Jordan. (See ch. 33:49.) **3. Israel joined himself unto Baal-peor**—Baal was a general name for "lord," and Peor for a "mount" in Moab. The real name of the idol was Chemosh, and his rites of worship were celebrated by the grossest obscenity. In participating in this festival, then, the Israelites committed the double offense of idolatry and licentiousness.

4. The Lord said unto Moses, Take all the heads of the people, and hang them up—Israelite criminals, who were capitally punished, were first stoned or slain, and *then* gibbeted. The persons ordered here for execution were the principal delinquents in the Baal-peor outrage—the subordinate officers, rulers of tens or hundreds. **before the Lord**—for vindicating the honor of the true God. **against the sun**—i.e., as a mark of public ignominy; but they were to be removed towards sunset (Deut. 21:23). **5. judges of Israel**—the seventy elders, who were commanded not only to superintend the execution within their respective jurisdictions, but to inflict the punishment with their own hands. (See on I Sam. 15:33.) **6, 7. behold, one of the children of Israel . . . brought . . . a Midianitish woman**—This flagitious act most probably occurred about the time when the order was given and before its execution. **who were weeping before the door of the tabernacle**—Some of the rulers and well-disposed persons were deploring the dreadful wickedness of the people and supplicating the mercy of God to avert impending judgments. **8. the plague**—some sudden and widespread mortality. **9. those that died in the plague were twenty and four thousand**—Only 23,000 perished (I Cor. 10:8) from pestilence. Moses includes those who died by the execution of the judges.

ADAM CLARKE — CHAPTER 25

3. *Israel joined himself unto Baal-peor.* The same as the Priapus of the Romans, and worshipped with the same obscene rites as we have frequently had occasion to remark. The joining to Baal-peor, mentioned here, was probably what Paul had in view when he said, 2 Cor. vi. 14: "Be ye not unequally yoked together with unbelievers." And this joining, though done even in a matrimonial way, was nevertheless fornication (see Rev. ii. 14), as no marriage between an Israelite and a Midianite could be legitimate, according to the law of God.

4. *Take all the heads of the people.* Meaning the chiefs of those who had transgressed; as if he had said, "Assemble the chiefs and judges, institute an inquiry concerning the transgressors, and hang them who shall be found guilty before the Lord, as a matter required by his justice." *Against the sun*—in the most public manner, and in daylight.

5. *Slay ye every one his men.* In the different departments where you preside over thousands, hundreds, fifties, and tens, slay all the culprits that shall be found.

6. *One of the children of Israel.* Zimri, the son of Salu, a prince of a chief family in the tribe of Simeon, v. 14, *brought . . . a Midianitish woman,* Cozbi, daughter of Zur, head over a people of one of the chief families in Midian, v. 15. The condition of these two persons plainly proves it to have been a matrimonial alliance; the one was a prince, the other a princess. Therefore I must conclude that fornication or whoredom, in the common sense of the word, was not practiced on this occasion. Josephus positively says that Zimri had married Cozbi, *Antiq.*, l. iv, chap. 6; and if he had not said so, still the thing is nearly self-evident.

The children of Israel, who were weeping. This aggravated the crime, because the people were then in a state of great humiliation because of the late impure and illegal transactions.

8. *Thrust both of them through.* Inspired undoubtedly by the Spirit of the God of justice to do this act, which can never be a precedent on any common occasion.

9. *Those that died . . . were twenty and four thousand.* Paul, 1 Cor. x. 8, reckons only twenty-three thousand; though some MSS. and versions, particularly the latter Syriac and the Armenian, have twenty-four thousand, with

MATTHEW HENRY

have joined themselves to Baal-peor. God testified his acceptance of the pious zeal of Phinehas. He put an honour upon Phinehas. Though he did no more than it was his duty to do as a judge, yet because he did it with extraordinary zeal against sin, and did it when the other judges, out of respect to Zimri's character as a prince, were afraid, God showed himself particularly well pleased with him, and it *was counted to him for righteousness*, Ps. cvi. 31. Phinehas, upon this occasion, though a young man, is pronounced his country's patriot and best friend, *v.* 11. The priesthood is entailed by covenant upon his family. It was designed for him before, but now it was confirmed to him.

Verses 16–18

God had punished the Israelites for their sin with a plague; as a Father he corrected his own children with a rod. The mischief which the Midianites did to Israel by enticing them to whoredom must be remembered and punished with as much severity as that which the Amalekites did in fighting with them when they came out of Egypt, Exod. xvii. 14.

JAMIESON, FAUSSET, BROWN

10-13. Phinehas . . . hath turned my wrath away—This assurance was a signal mark of honor that the stain of blood, instead of defiling, confirmed him in office and that his posterity should continue as long as the national existence of Israel.

14. Zimri, . . . a prince . . . among the Simeonites—The slaughter of a man of such high rank is mentioned as a proof of the undaunted zeal of Phinehas, for there might be numerous avengers of his blood. **17. Vex the Midianites, and smite them**—They seem to have been the most guilty parties. (Cf. ch. 22:4; 31:8.) **18. they vex you with their wiles**—Instead of open war, they plot insidious ways of accomplishing your ruin by idolatry and corruption. **their sister**—their countrywoman.

ADAM CLARKE

the Hebrew text. Allowing the 24,000 to be the genuine reading, and none of the Hebrew MSS. exhibit any various reading here, the two places may be reconciled thus: 1,000 men were slain in consequence of the examination instituted, v. 4, and 23,000 in consequence of the orders given, v. 5, making 24,000 in the whole. Paul probably refers only to the latter number.

12-13. *My covenant of peace . . . of an everlasting priesthood.* As the word *peace* implied all kinds of blessings, both spiritual and temporal, it may mean no more here than the promise of God to grant him and his family the utmost prosperity in reference to both worlds. The *everlasting priesthood* refers properly to the priesthood of Christ, which was shadowed out by the priesthood under the law, no matter in what family it was continued. Therefore the *kehunnath olam,* or "eternal priesthood," does not merely refer to any sacerdotal ministrations which should be continued in the family of Phinehas during the Mosaic dispensation, but to that priesthood of Christ typified by that of Aaron and his successors.

17. *Vex the Midianites.* See this order fulfilled, chap. xxxi. 1-20. Twelve thousand Israelites attacked the Midianites, destroyed all their cities, slew their five kings, every male, and every grown-up woman, and took all their spoils.

MATTHEW HENRY — CHAPTER 26

Verses 1–4

Moses did not number the people but when God commanded him. David in his time did it without a command, and paid dearly for it. God now appointed him to take the sum of them. Eleazar was joined in commission with him, as Aaron had been before, by which God confirmed his succession. They were now to go by the same rule that they had gone by in the former numbering, counting those only that were able to go forth to war, for this was the service now before them.

Verses 5–51

This is the register of the tribes as they were now enrolled, in the same order that they were numbered in *ch.* i.

I. The account that is here kept of the families of each tribe, which must not be understood of such as we call families, those that live in a house together, but such as were the descendants of the several sons of the patriarchs. The families of the twelve tribes are thus numbered:—Of Dan but one, for Dan had but one son, and yet that tribe was the most numerous of all except Judah, *v.* 42, 43. Zebulun was divided into three families, Ephraim into four, Issachar into four, Naphtali into four, and Reuben into four; Judah, Simeon, and Asher had five families apiece, Gad and Benjamin seven apiece, and Manasseh eight. Benjamin brought ten sons into Egypt (Gen. xlvi. 21), but three of them, it seems, either died childless or their families were extinct, for here we find seven only of those names preserved.

II. The numbers of each tribe. In this account we may observe, 1. That all the three tribes that were encamped under the standard of Judah, who was the ancestor of Christ, had increased. 2. That none of the tribes had increased so much as that of Manasseh, which in the former account was the smallest of all the tribes, only 32,200, while here it is one of the most considerable. 3. That none of the tribes decreased so much as Simeon did; from 59,300, it sunk to 22,000, little more than a third part of what it was. Some conjecture that most of those 24,000 who were cut off by the plague for the iniquity of Peor were of that tribe; for Zimri, who was a ringleader in that iniquity, was a prince of that tribe.

III. In the account of the tribe of Reuben mention is made of the rebellion of Dathan and Abiram, who were of that tribe, in confederacy with Korah a Levite, *v.* 9–11.

Verses 52–56

If any ask why such a particular account is kept of the tribes, and families, and numbers, of the people of Israel, here is an answer for them; as they were multiplied, so they were portioned, not by common providence, but by promise; and, for the support of the honour of divine revelation, God will have the fulfilling of the promise taken notice of both in their increase and in their inheritance.

JAMIESON, FAUSSET, BROWN — CHAPTER 26

Vss. 1-51. ISRAEL NUMBERED. **1. after the plague**—That terrible visitation had swept away the remnant of the old generation, to whom God sware in His wrath that they should not enter Canaan (Ps. 95:11). **2. Take the sum of all the congregation**—The design of this new census, after a lapse of thirty-eight years, was primarily to establish the vast multiplication of the posterity of Abraham in spite of the severe judgments inflicted upon them; secondarily, it was to preserve the distinction of families and to make arrangements, preparatory to an entrance into the promised land, for the distribution of the country according to the relative population of the tribes. **7. These are the families of the Reubenites**—the principal households, which were subdivided into numerous smaller families. Reuben had suffered great diminution by Korah's conspiracy and other outbreaks. **10. the earth opened her mouth and swallowed them up together with Korah**—rather, the things of Korah. (See on ch. 16:32-35; cf. Ps. 106:17.) **11. Notwithstanding the children of Korah died not**—Either they were not parties to their father's crime, or they withdrew from it by timely repentance. His descendants became famous in the time of David, and are often mentioned in the Psalms, also in I Chronicles 6:22, 38. **12. The sons of Simeon**—It is supposed that this tribe had been pre-eminent in the guilt of Baal-peor and had consequently been greatly reduced in numbers.

Thus God's justice and holiness, as well as His truth and faithfulness, were strikingly displayed: His justice and holiness in the sweeping judgments that reduced the ranks of some tribes; and His truth and faithfulness in the extraordinary increase of others so that the posterity of Israel continued a numerous people. **53. the land shall be divided according to the number of names**—The portion of each tribe was to be greater or less, according to its populousness. **54. To many thou shalt give the more**—i.e., to the more numerous tribes a larger allotment shall be granted. **according to those that were numbered**—the number of persons twenty years old at the time of the census being made, without taking into account either the increase of those who might have attained that age, when the land should be actually distributed, or the diminution from that amount, occasioned during the war of invasion. **55. the land shall be divided by lot**—The appeal to the lot did not place the matter beyond the control of God; for it is at His disposal (Prov. 16:33), and He has fixed to all the bounds of their habitation. The manner in which the lot was taken has not been recorded. But it is evident that the lot was cast for determining the section of the country in which each tribe should be located—not the quantity of their possessions. In other words, when the lot had decided that a particular tribe was to be settled in the north or the south, the east or the west, the extent of territory was allocated according to the rule (vs. 54). **58. families of the Levites**—The census of this tribe was taken

ADAM CLARKE — CHAPTER 26

2. *Take the sum of all the congregation.* After thirty-eight years God commands a second census of the Israelites to be made, to preserve the distinction in families and to regulate the tribes previously to their entry into the Promised Land, and to ascertain the proportion of land which should be allowed to each tribe. For though the whole was divided by lot, yet the portions were so disposed that a numerous tribe did not draw where the lots assigned small inheritances. See verses 53-56, and also the note on chap. i. 1.

10. *Together with Korah.* The Samaritan text does not intimate that Korah was *swallowed . . . up,* but that he was burned, as appears, in fact, to have been the case. "And the earth swallowed them up, what time that company died; and the fire devoured Korah with the two hundred and fifty men, who became a sign."

11. *The children of Korah died not.* It is difficult to reconcile this place with chap. xvi. 27, 31-33, where it seems to be intimated that not only the men, but the wives, and the sons, and the little ones of Korah, Dathan, and Abiram, were swallowed up by the earthquake; see especially v. 27, collated with v. 33, of chap. xvi. But the text here expressly says, *The children of Korah died not;* and on a close inspection of v. 27 of the above-mentioned chapter, we shall find that the sons and the little ones of Dathan and Abiram alone are mentioned. "So they gat up from the tabernacle of Korah, Dathan, and Abiram, on every side: and Dathan and Abiram came out . . . and their wives, and their sons, and their little ones." Here is no mention of the children of Korah; they therefore escaped, while it appears those of Dathan and Abiram perished with their fathers.

51. *These were the numbered of the children of Israel, six hundred thousand and a thousand seven hundred and thirty.* Let it be observed, (1) That among these there was not a man of the former census, save Joshua and Caleb, see vv. 64-65. (2) That though there was an increase in seven tribes of not less than 74,800 men, yet so great was the decrease in the other five tribes that the balance against the present census is 1,820.

55. *The land shall be divided by lot.* The word *goral,* translated *lot,* is supposed by some to signify the stone or pebble formerly used for the purpose of what we term casting lots. A *lot* in the promised land was evidently typical of a place in eternal glory. "That they may receive forgiveness of sins, and an inheritance [a *lot*] among them which are sanctified," Acts xxvi. 18. Who "hath made us meet to be par-

MATTHEW HENRY

Verses 57–62

Levi was God's tribe, a tribe that was to have no inheritance with the rest in the land of Canaan, and therefore was not numbered with the rest, but by itself; so it had been numbered in the beginning of this book at Mount Sinai, and therefore came not under the sentence passed upon all that were then numbered, that none of them should enter Canaan but Caleb and Joshua; for of the Levites that were not numbered with them, nor were to go forth to war, Eleazar and Ithamar, and perhaps others who were above twenty years old then (as appears, *ch.* iv. 16, 28), entered Canaan; and yet this tribe, now at its second numbering, had increased but 1,000, and was still one of the smallest tribes.

Verses 63–65

That which is observable in this conclusion of the account is the execution of the sentence passed upon the murmurers (*ch.* xiv. 29), that not one of those who *were numbered from twenty years old and upwards* should enter Canaan, except Caleb and Joshua. In the muster now made it appeared that there was not one man numbered now that was numbered then except Caleb and Joshua, *v.* 64, 65. Herein appeared, 1. The righteousness of God, and his faithfulness to his threatenings, when once the *decree has gone forth.* 2. The goodness of God to this people, notwithstanding their provocations. And, though the number fell a little short of what it was at Mount Sinai, yet those now numbered had this advantage, that they were all middle-aged men, between twenty and sixty, in the prime of their time for service; and during the thirty-eight years of their wandering and wasting in the wilderness they had an opportunity of acquainting themselves with the laws and ordinances of God.

JAMIESON, FAUSSET, BROWN

separately, and on a different principle from the rest. (See Exod. 6:16-19). **62. twenty and three thousand**—so that there was an increase of a thousand (ch. 3:39). **males from a month old and upward**—(See on ch. 3:15.) **64. among these there was not a man . . . numbered . . . in the wilderness of Sinai**—The statement in this verse must not be considered absolute. For, besides Caleb and Joshua, there were alive at this time Eleazar and Ithamar, and in all probability a considerable number of Levites, who had no participation in the popular defections in the wilderness. The tribe of Levi, having neither sent a spy into Canaan, nor being included in the enumeration at Sinai, must be regarded as not coming within the range of the fatal sentence; and therefore it would exhibit a spectacle not to be witnessed in the other tribes of many in their ranks above sixty years of age.

Tribes	Chap. 1	Chap. 26	Increase	Decrease
Reuben	46,500	43,730	—	2,770
Simeon	59,300	22,200	—	37,100
Gad	45,650	40,500	—	5,150
Judah	74,600	76,500	1,900	—
Issachar	54,400	64,300	9,900	—
Zebulun	57,400	60,500	3,100	—
Ephraim	40,500	32,500	—	8,000
Manasseh	32,200	52,700	20,500	—
Benjamin	35,400	45,600	10,200	—
Dan	62,700	64,400	1,700	—
Asher	41,500	53,400	11,900	—
Naphtali	53,400	45,400	—	8,000
	603,550	601,730	59,200	61,020
Total decrease				1,820

ADAM CLARKE

takers of the inheritance [of the *lot*] of the saints in light," Col. i. 12. "Which is the earnest **of our inheritance"** (of our *allotted portion*)," Eph. i. 14. "What [is] the riches of the glory of his inheritance" (*allotted portion*), Eph. i. 18.

MATTHEW HENRY

CHAPTER 27

Verses 1–11

Mention is made of the case of these daughters of Zelophehad in the chapter before, *v.* 33. It was a singular case, and the like did not at this time occur in all Israel, that the head of a family had no sons, but daughters only. Their case is again debated (*ch.* xxxvi.) upon another article of it; and, according to the judgments given in their case, we find them put in possession, Josh., xvii. 3, 4. One would suppose that their personal character was such as added weight to their case.

Here is, I. Their case stated by themselves, and their petition upon it presented to the highest court of judicature. We find not that they had any advocate to speak for them, but they managed their own cause ingeniously enough, which they could do the better because it was plain and honest, and spoke for itself.

1. What it is they petition for: That they might have a possession in the land of *Canaan, among the brethren of their father, v.* 4. God had said to Moses (*ch.* xxvi. 53) that the land of Canaan was to be divided among those that were now numbered; these daughters knew that they were not numbered, and therefore by this rule must expect no inheritance. If they had had a brother, they would not have applied to Moses for an order to inherit with him. But, having no brother, they beg for a possession. There is a debt which children owe to the memory of their parents, required by the fifth commandment: *Honour thy father and mother.*

2. What their plea is: That their father did not die under any attainder which might be thought to have corrupted his blood and forfeited his estate, but he *died in his own sin* (*v.* 3), chargeable only with the common iniquities of mankind, for which to his own Master he was to stand or fall, but laid not himself open to any judicial process before Moses and the princes.

II. Their case determined by the divine oracle. 1. The petition is granted (*v.* 7). 2. The point is settled for all future occasions. These daughters of Zelophehad consulted, not only their own comfort and the credit of their family, but the honour and happiness of their sex likewise; for on this particular occasion a general law was made that, in case a man had no son, his estate should go to his daughters (*v.* 8); not to the eldest as the eldest son, but to them all in co-partnership, share and share alike. "If a man have no issue at all his estate shall go to his brethren; if no brethren, then to his father's brethren; and, if there be no such, then to his next kinsman."

Verses 12–14

1. God tells Moses of his fault, his speaking unadvisedly with his lips at the waters of strife, where

JAMIESON, FAUSSET, BROWN

CHAPTER 27

Vss. 1-11. The Daughters of Zelophehad Ask for an Inheritance. **4. Give unto us a possession among the brethren of our father**—Those young women perceived that the males only in families had been registered in the census. Because there were none in their household, their family was omitted. So they made known their grievance to Moses, and the authorities conjoined with him in administering justice. The case was important; and as the peculiarity of daughters being the sole members of a family would be no infrequent or uncommon occurrence, the law of inheritance, under divine authority, was extended not only to meet all similar cases, but other cases also—such as when there were no children left by the proprietor, and no brothers to succeed him. A distribution of the promised land was about to be made; and it is interesting to know the legal provision made in these comparatively rare cases for preserving a patrimony from being alienated to another tribe. (See on ch. 36:6, 7.) **3. Our father died in the wilderness, and he was not . . . in the company of . . . Korah**—This declaration might be necessary because his death might have occurred about the time of that rebellion; and especially because, as the children of these conspirators were involved along with their fathers in the awful punishment, their plea appeared the more proper and forcible that their father did not die for any cause that doomed his family to lose their lives or their inheritance. **died in his own sin**—i.e., by the common law of mortality to which men, through sin, are subject.

ADAM CLARKE

CHAPTER 27

1. *The daughters of Zelophehad.* The singular case of these women caused an additional law to be made to the civil code of Israel, which satisfactorily ascertained and amply secured the right of succession in cases of inheritance. The law, which is as reasonable as it is just, stands thus: (1) On the demise of the father the estate goes to the sons; (2) If there be no son, the daughters succeed; (3) If there be no daughter, the brothers of the deceased inherit; (4) If there be no brethren or paternal uncles, the estate goes to the brothers of his father; (5) If there be no granduncles or brothers of the father of the deceased, then the nearest akin succeeds to the inheritance.

TODAY'S DICTIONARY OF THE BIBLE:

Zelophehad—*protection from fear*—of the tribe of Manasseh, and of the family of Gilead; died in the wilderness. Having left no sons, his daughters, concerned lest their father's name should be "done away from among his family," made an appeal to Moses, who, by divine direction, appointed it as "a statue of judgment" in Israel that daughters should inherit their father's portion when no sons were left (Num. 27:1–11). But that the possession of Zelophehad might not pass away in the year of jubilee from the tribe to which he belonged, it was ordained by Moses that his daughters should not marry anyone out of their father's tribe; and this afterward became a general law (Num. 36).

MATTHEW HENRY

he did not express, so carefully as he ought to have done, a regard to the honour both of God and Israel, *v.* 14. 2. He tells Moses of his death. Notice is given him of it in such a manner as might best serve to sweeten and mollify the sentence, and reconcile him to it. (1) Moses must die, but he shall first have the satisfaction of seeing the land of promise, *v.* 12. (2) Moses must die, but death does not *cut him off,* it only gathers him to his people, brings him to rest with the holy patriarchs that had gone before him. (3) Moses must die, but only as Aaron died before him, *v.* 13. And Moses had seen how easily and cheerfully Aaron had put off the priesthood first and then the body; let not Moses therefore be afraid of dying; it was but to be *gathered to his people,* as Aaron was gathered.

Verses 15–23

Here, I. Moses prays for a successor. Envious spirits do not love their successors, but Moses was not one of these. We should concern ourselves, both in our prayers and in our endeavours, for the rising generation, that religion may flourish. In this prayer Moses expressed, 1. A tender concern for the people of Israel: *That the congregation of the Lord be not as sheep which have no shepherd.* 2. A believing dependence upon God, as the *God of the spirits of all flesh.* Moses prays to God, not to send an angel but to *set a man over the congregation,* that is, to nominate and appoint one whom he would qualify and own as ruler of his people Israel.

II. God, in answer to his prayer, appoints him a successor, even Joshua, who had long since signalized himself by his courage in fighting Amalek, his humility in ministering to Moses, and his faith and sincerity in witnessing against the report of the evil spies.

1. God directs Moses how to secure the succession to Joshua. (1) He must ordain him: *Lay thy hand upon him, v.* 18. This was done in token of Moses's transferring the government to him, as the laying of hands on the sacrifice put the offering in the place and stead of the offerer; also in token of God's conferring the blessing of the Spirit upon him, which Moses obtained by prayer. It is said (Deut. xxxiv. 9), *Joshua was full of the spirit of wisdom, for Moses had laid his hands on him.* This rite of imposing hands we find used in the New Testament in the setting apart of gospel ministers, denoting a solemn designation of them to the office and an earnest desire that God would qualify them for it and own them in it. It is the offering of them to Christ and his church for living sacrifices. (2) He must present him to Eleazar and the people, set him before them, that they might know him to be designed of God for this great trust and consent to that designation. (3) He must *give him a charge, v.* 19. (4) He must *put some of his honour upon him, v.* 20. (5) He must appoint Eleazar the high priest, with his breastplate of judgment, to be his privy-council (*v.* 21). This was a direction to Joshua. Though he was full of the Spirit, and had all this honour put upon him, yet he must do nothing without asking counsel of God, not leaning to his own understanding. Thus the government of Israel was now purely divine, for both the designation and direction of their princes were entirely so.

2. Moses does according to these directions, *v.* 22, 23. He cheerfully ordained Joshua, (1) Though it was a present lessening to himself, and amounted almost to a resignation of the government. (2) Though it might appear a perpetual slur upon his family, first to ordain Eleazar high priest, and then Joshua, one of another tribe, chief ruler, while his own children had no preferment at all, but were left in the rank of common Levites, this was such an instance of self-denial and submission to the will of God as was more his glory than the highest advancement of his family could have been.

CHAPTER 28

Verses 1–8

Here is, I. A general order given concerning the offerings of the Lord, which were to be brought in their season, *v.* 2. God saw fit now to repeat the law of sacrifices, 1. Because this was a new generation of men, that were most of them unborn when the former laws were given. 2. Because they were now entering upon war, and might be tempted to think that while they were engaged in that they should be excused from offering sacrifices. *Inter arma silent leges—law is little regarded amidst the clash of arms.* They were peculiarly concerned to keep their peace with God when they were at war with their enemies. 3. Because possession was now to be given them of the land of promise, that land flowing with milk and

JAMIESON, FAUSSET, BROWN

12-17. Moses, Being Told of His Approaching Death, Asks for a Successor. **12. The Lord said unto Moses, Get thee up into this mount Abarim, and see the land**—Although the Israelites were now on the confines of the promised land, Moses was not privileged to cross the Jordan, but died on one of the Moabitic range of mountains, to which the general name of Abarim was given (ch. 33:47). The privation of this great honor was owing to the unhappy conduct he had manifested in the striking of the rock at Meribah; and while the pious leader submitted with meek acquiescence to the divine decree, he evinced the spirit of genuine patriotism in his fervent prayers for the appointment of a worthy and competent successor.

16. God of the spirits of all flesh, set a man over the congregation—The request was most suitably made to God in this character, as the Author of all the intellectual gifts and moral graces with which men are endowed, and who can raise up qualified persons for the most arduous duties and the most difficult situations.

18-23. Joshua Appointed to Succeed Him. **18. Take Joshua . . . a man in whom is the spirit, and lay thine hand upon him**—A strong testimony is here borne to the personality of the divine Spirit—the imposition of hands was an ancient ceremony. (See on Gen. 48:14; Lev. 1:4; I Tim. 4:14.)

20. Thou shalt put some of thine honour upon him—In the whole history of Israel there arose no prophet or ruler in all respects like unto Moses till the Messiah appeared, whose glory eclipsed all. But Joshua was honored and qualified in an eminent degree, through the special service of the high priest, who asked counsel for him after the judgment of Urim before the Lord.

CHAPTER 28

Vss. 1-31. Offerings to Be Observed. **2. Command the children of Israel, and say unto them**—The repetition of several laws formerly enacted, which is made in this chapter, was seasonable and necessary, not only on account of their importance and the frequent neglect of them, but because a new generation had sprung up since their first institution and because the Israelites were about to be settled in the land where those ordinances were to be observed. **My offering, and my bread**—used generally for the appointed offerings, and the import of the prescription is to enforce regularity and care in their observance.

ADAM CLARKE

12. *Get thee up into this mount Abarim.* The mountain which Moses was commanded to ascend was certainly Mount Nebo, see Deut. xxxii. 49, etc., which was the same as Pisgah, see Deut. xxxiv. 1. The mountains of Abarim, according to Dr. Shaw, are a long ridge of frightful, rocky, precipitous hills, which are continued all along the eastern coast of the Dead Sea, as far as the eye can reach. As in Hebrew *abar* signifies to "pass over," *Abarim* here probably signifies "passages"; and the ridge in this place had its name in all likelihood from the passage of the Israelites, as it was opposite to these that they passed the Jordan into the Promised Land.

17. *That the congregation of the Lord be not as sheep which have no shepherd.* This is a beautiful expression, and shows us in what light Moses viewed himself among his people. He was their shepherd; he sought no higher place; he fed and guided the flock of God under the direction of the Divine Spirit, and was faithful in all his Master's house. To this saying of Moses our Lord alludes, Matt. ix. 36.

18. *In whom is the spirit.* This must certainly mean the Spirit of God; and because he was endued with this Spirit, therefore he was capable of leading the people.

20. *And thou shalt put. Mechodecha,* of "thine honor or authority" upon him. You shall show to the whole congregation that you have associated him with yourself in the government of the people.

21. *Eleazar the priest . . . shall ask counsel for him.* Here was a remarkable difference between him and Moses. God talked with Moses face-to-face, but to Joshua only through the medium of the high priest.

23. *He laid his hands upon him.* As a proof of his being appointed to and qualified for the work. So at the word of Joshua they were to go out, and at his word to come in, v. 21. And thus he was a type of our blessed Lord as to his mediatorial office and divine appointment as man to the work of our salvation.

CHAPTER 28

2. *Command the children of Israel.* It is not easy to account for the reason of the introduction of these precepts here, which had been so circumstantially delivered before in different parts of the Books of Exodus and Leviticus. It is possible that the daily, weekly, monthly, and yearly services had been considerably interrupted for several years, owing to the unsettled state of the people in the wilderness, and that it was necessary to repeat these laws for two reasons: (1) Because they were now about to enter into the Promised Land, where these services must be established and constant. (2) Because the former generations being all dead,

MATTHEW HENRY

honey, where they would have plenty of all good things. "Now" (says God), "when you are feasting yourselves, forget not to offer the bread of your God."

II. The particular law of the daily sacrifice, a lamb in the morning and a lamb in the evening, which, for the constancy of it duly as the day came, is called a *continual burnt-offering* (*v.* 3), which intimates that when we are bidden to *pray always, and to pray without ceasing*, it is intended that at least every morning and every evening we offer up our solemn prayers and praises to God.

Verses 9–15

The new moons and the sabbaths are often spoken of together, as great solemnities in the Jewish church. Now we have here the sacrifices appointed, 1. For the sabbaths. Every sabbath day the offering must be doubled. 2. For the new moons. Some suggest that, as the sabbath was kept with an eye to the creation of the world, so the new moons were sanctified with an eye to the divine providence, which *appoints the moon for seasons*, guiding the revolutions of time by its changes.

Verses 16–31

The appointment of the passover sacrifices; not that which was the chief, the paschal lamb (sufficient instructions had formerly been given concerning that), but those which were to be offered upon the seven days of unleavened bread, which followed it, *v.* 17–25. The first and last of those seven days were to be sanctified as sabbaths, by a holy rest and a holy convocation, and on each of the seven days they were to be liberal in their sacrifices, in token of their great and constant thankfulness for their deliverance out of Egypt. The sacrifices are likewise appointed which were to be offered at the feast of pentecost, here called the *day of the first-fruits, v.* 26. In the feast of unleavened bread they offered a *sheaf of their first-fruits* of barley (which with them was first ripe) to the priest (Lev. xxiii. 10), as an introduction to the harvest; but now, about seven weeks after, they were to bring a *new meat-offering to the Lord*, at the end of harvest. It was at this feast that *the Spirit was poured out* (Acts ii. 1, &c.), and thousands were converted by the preaching of the apostles, and were presented to Christ, to be *a kind of first-fruits of his creatures.*

CHAPTER 29

Verses 1–11

There were more sacred solemnities in the seventh month than in any other month of the year, not only because it had been the first month till the deliverance of Israel out of Egypt, but because still it continued the first month in the civil reckonings of the jubilees and years of release, and also because it was the time of vacation between harvest and seedtime, when they had most leisure to attend the sanctuary. 1. We have here the appointment of the sacrifices that were to be offered on the first day of the month, the day of *blowing the trumpets*, which was a preparative for the two great solemnities of holy mourning on the day of atonement and of holy joy in the feast of tabernacles. On the *day of atonement* itself, besides all the services of that day, which we had the institution of, Lev. xvi., here are burnt-offerings ordered to be offered, *v.* 8–10.

Verses 12–40

Soon after the day of atonement, that day in which men were to afflict their souls, followed the feast of the tabernacles, in which they were to rejoice before the Lord; for, those that *sow in tears* shall soon *reap in joy*. To the former laws about this feast, which we had, Lev. xxiii. 34, &c., here are added directions about the *offerings made by fire*, which they were to offer unto the Lord during the *seven days of that feast*, Lev. xxiii. 36. Observe here, 1. Their days of rejoicing were to be days of sacrifices. 2. All the days of their dwelling in booths they must offer sacrifices.

JAMIESON, FAUSSET, BROWN

9, 10. This is the burnt offering of every sabbath—There is no previous mention of a Sabbath burnt offering, which was additional to the daily sacrifices. **11-15. In the beginnings of your months ye shall offer up a burnt offering unto the Lord**—These were held as sacred festivals; and though not possessing the character of solemn feasts, they were distinguished by the blowing of trumpets over the sacrifices (ch. 10:10), by the suspension of all labor except the domestic occupations of women (Amos 8:5), by the celebration of public worship (II Kings 4:23), and by social or family feasts (I Sam. 20:5). These observations are not prescribed in the law though they obtained in the practice of a later time. The beginning of the month was known, not by astronomical calculations, but, according to Jewish writers, by the testimony of messengers appointed to watch the first visible appearance of the new moon; and then the fact was announced through the whole country by signal-fires kindled on the mountain tops. The new-moon festivals having been common among the heathen, it is probable that an important design of their institution in Israel was to give the minds of that people a better direction; and assuming this to have been one of the objects contemplated, it will account for one of the kids being offered unto the Lord (vs. 15), not unto the moon, as the Egyptians and Syrians did. The Sabbath and the new moon are frequently mentioned together. **16-25. in the fourteenth day of the first month is the passover**—The law for that great annual festival is given (Lev. 23:5), but some details are here introduced, as certain specified offerings are prescribed to be made on each of the seven days of unleavened bread. **26, 27. in the day of the first fruits . . . offer the burnt offering**—A new sacrifice is here ordered for the celebration of this festival, in addition to the other offering, which was to accompany the first fruits (Lev. 23:18).

CHAPTER 29

Vss. 1-40. THE OFFERING AT THE FEAST OF TRUMPETS. **1. in the seventh month**—of the ecclesiastical year, but the first month of the civil year, corresponding to our September. It was, in fact, the New Year's Day, which had been celebrated among the Hebrews and other contemporary nations with great festivity and joy and ushered in by a flourish of trumpets. This ordinance was designed to give a religious character to the occasion by associating it with some solemn observances. (Cf. Exod. 12:2; Lev. 23:24.) **it is a day of blowing the trumpets unto you**—This made it a solemn preparation for the sacred feasts—a greater number of which were held during this month than at any other season of the year. Although the institution of this feast was described before, there is more particularity here as to what the burnt offering should consist of; and, in addition to it, a sin offering is prescribed. The special offerings, appointed for certain days, were not to interfere with the offerings usually requisite on these days, for in verse 6 it is said that the daily offerings, as well as those for the first day of the month, were to take place in their ordinary course. **7-11. ye shall have on the tenth day of this seventh month an holy convocation**—This was the great day of atonement. Its institution, together with the observance to which that day was devoted, was described (Lev. 16:29, 30). But additional offerings seem to be noticed, viz., the large animal sacrifice for a general expiation, which was a sweet savor unto the Lord, and the sin offering to atone for the sins that mingled with that day's services. The prescriptions in this passage appear supplementary to the former statement in Leviticus. **12-34. on the fifteenth day**—was to be held the feast of booths or tabernacles. (See on Lev. 23:34, 35.) The feast was to last seven days, the first and last of which were to be kept as Sabbaths, and a particular offering was prescribed for each day, the details of which are given with a minuteness suited to the infant state of the church. Two things are deserving of notice: First, that this feast was distinguished by a greater amount and variety of sacrifices than any other—partly because, occurring at the end of the year, it might be

ADAM CLARKE

multitudes of the present might be ignorant of these ordinances.

In their due season. Moses divides these offerings into (1) *Daily.* The morning and evening sacrifices: a lamb each time, vv. 3-4.

(2) *Weekly.* The Sabbath offerings, two lambs of a year old, vv. 9, etc. (3) *Monthly.* At the beginning of each month two young bullocks, one ram, and seven lambs of a year old, and a kid for a sin offering, vv. 11, etc. (4) *Annually.* (*a*) The Passover to last seven days; the offerings, two young bullocks, one ram, seven lambs of a year old, and a he-goat for a sin offering, vv. 16, etc. (*b*) The day of firstfruits. The sacrifices, the same as on the beginning of the month, vv. 26, etc. With these sacrifices were offered libations, or drink offerings, of strong wine, vv. 7, 14, and *minchahs*, or meat offerings, composed of fine flour mingled with oil, vv. 8, 12, etc. For an ample account of all these offerings, see the notes on Leviticus vii and Exodus xii.

7. *Strong wine. Sikera:* see the note on chap. x. 9, where this is largely explained.

26. *Day of the firstfruits.* Called also the Feast of Weeks, and the Feast of Pentecost. See it explained, Exod. xxiii. 14 and Lev. xxiii. 15.

31. *Without blemish.* This is to be understood as applying, not only to the animals, but also to the flour, wine, and oil; everything must be perfect in its kind.

CHAPTER 29

1. *And in the seventh month.* This was the beginning of their civil year, and was a time of great festivity, and was ushered in by the blowing of trumpets. It answers to a part of our September.

7. *On the tenth day.* See the notes on Lev. xvi. 29; xxiii. 24.

12. *On the fifteenth day of the seventh month.* On this day there was to be a solemn assembly, and for seven days sacrifices were to be offered; on the first day 13 young bullocks, 2 rams, and 14 lambs. On each succeeding day one bullock less, till on the seventh day there were only 7, making in all 70. What an expensive service! How should we magnify God for being delivered from it! Yet these were all the taxes they had to pay. At the public charge there were annually offered to God, independently of trespass offer-

MATTHEW HENRY

3. The sacrifices for each of the seven days, though differing in nothing but the number of the bullocks, are severally and particularly appointed. 4. The number of the bullocks (which were the most costly part of the sacrifice) decreased every day. The multitude of their sacrifices should end in one great sacrifice, infinitely more worthy than all of them. It was on the last day of the feast, after all these sacrifices had been offered, that our Lord Jesus stood and cried to those who still thirsted after righteousness (being sensible of the insufficiency of these sacrifices to justify them) *to come unto him and drink*, John vii. 37. 5. The meat-offerings and drink-offerings attended all the sacrifices. 6. Every day there must be a sin-offering presented, as we observed in the other feasts. 7. Even when all these sacrifices were offered, yet the continual burnt-offering must not be omitted either morning or evening, but each day this must be offered first in the morning and last in the evening. No extraordinary services should jostle out our stated devotions.

8. Though all these sacrifices were required to be presented by the body of the congregation, at the common charge, yet, besides these, particular persons were to glorify God with their vows and their free-will offerings, *v.* 39.

JAMIESON, FAUSSET, BROWN

intended to supply any past deficiencies—partly because, being immediately after the ingathering of the fruits, it ought to be a liberal acknowledgment —and partly, perhaps, because God consulted the weakness of mankind, who naturally grow weary both of the charge and labor of such services when they are long continued, and made them every day less toilsome and expensive [PATRICK]. Secondly, it will be remarked that the sacrifices varied in a progressive ratio of decrease every day. **after the manner**—according to the ritual order appointed by divine authority—that for meat offerings (vss. 3-10), and drink offerings. (See on ch. 28:7, 14.) **35-40. On the eighth day ye shall have a solemn assembly**—The feast of tabernacles was brought to a close on the eighth day, which was the great day (Lev. 23: 39). Besides the common routine sacrifices, there were special offerings appointed for that day though these were fewer than on any of the preceding days; and there were also, as was natural on that occasion when vast multitudes were convened for a solemn religious purpose, many spontaneous gifts and services, so that there was full scope for the exercise of a devout spirit in the people, both for their obedience to the statutory offerings, and by the presentation of those which were made by free will or in consequence of vows. **39. These things ye shall do unto the Lord in your set feasts**—From the statements made in this and the preceding chapter, it appears that the yearly offerings made to the altar at the public expense, without taking into account a vast number of voluntary vow and trespass offerings, were calculated at the following amount: —goats, 15; kids, 21; rams, 72; bullocks, 132; lambs, 1,101; sum total of animals sacrificed at public cost, 1,241. This, of course, is exclusive of the prodigious addition of lambs slain at the passover, which in later times, according to Josephus, amounted in a single year to the immense number of 255,600.

ADAM CLARKE

ings and voluntary vows, 15 goats, 21 kids, 72 rams, 132 bullocks, and 1,101 lambs! But how little is all this when compared with the lambs slain every year at the Passover, which amounted in one year to the immense number of 255,600 slain in the Temple itself, which was the answer that Cestius, the Roman general, received when he asked the priests how many persons had come to Jerusalem at their annual festivals; the priests, numbering the people by the lambs that had been slain, said, "twenty-five myriads, five thousand and six hundred." For an account of the Feast of Tabernacles, see on Lev. xxiii. 34.

35. *On the eighth day ye shall have a solemn assembly.* This among the Jews was esteemed the chief or high day of the feast, though fewer sacrifices were offered on it than on the others. The people seem to have finished the solemnity with a greater measure of spiritual devotion, and it was on this day of the feast that our blessed Lord called the Jews from the letter to the spirit of the law, proposing himself as the sole Fountain whence they could derive the streams of salvation, John vii. 37. On the subject of this chapter see the notes on Leviticus xii; xvi; and xxiii.

MATTHEW HENRY

CHAPTER 30

Verses 1–2

This law was delivered to the heads of the tribes that they might instruct those who were under their charge.

1. The case supposed is that a person vows a vow unto the Lord, making God a party to the promise. The matter of the vow is supposed to be something lawful: no man can be by his own promise bound to do that which he is already by the divine precept prohibited from doing. He that vows is here said to *bind his soul with a bond.* It is a vow to God, who is a Spirit, and to him the soul, with all its powers, must be bound. A promise to a man is a bond upon the estate, but a promise to God is a bond upon the soul. 2. The command given is that these vows be conscientiously performed.

Verses 3–16

It is here taken for granted that all such persons as are *sui juris—at their own disposal*, and are likewise of sound understanding and memory, are bound to perform whatever they vow that is lawful and possible; but, if the person vowing be under the dominion and at the disposal of another, the case is different. Two cases much alike are here put and determined:—

I. The case of a daughter in her father's house. The rule is general, If a man vow, he must pay. But for a daughter it is express: her vow is nugatory or in suspense till her father knows it, and (it is

JAMIESON, FAUSSET, BROWN

CHAPTER 30

Vss. 1-16. VOWS ARE NOT TO BE BROKEN. **1. This is the thing which the Lord hath commanded** —The subject of this chapter relates to vowing, which seems to have been an ancient usage, allowed by the law to remain, and by which some people declared their intention of offering some gift on the altar or abstaining from particular articles of meat or drink, of observing a private fast, or doing something to the honor or in the service of God, over and above what was authoritatively required. In verse 39 of the preceding chapter, mention was made of "vows and freewill offerings," and it is probable, from the explanatory nature of the rules laid down in this chapter, that these were given for the removal of doubts and difficulties which conscientious persons had felt about their obligation to perform their vows in certain circumstances that had arisen. **2. If a man vow a vow unto the Lord** —A mere secret purpose of the mind was not enough to constitute a vow; it had to be actually expressed in words; and though a purely voluntary act, yet when once the vow was made, the performance of it, like that of every other promise, became an indispensable duty—all the more because, referring to a sacred thing, it could not be neglected without the guilt of prevarication and unfaithfulness to God. **he shall not break his word**—lit., profane his word—render it vain and contemptible (Ps. 55:20; 89:34). But as it would frequently happen that parties would vow to do things which were neither good in themselves nor in their power to perform, the law ordained that their natural superiors should have the right of judging as to the propriety of those vows, with discretionary power to sanction or interdict their fulfilment. Parents were to determine in the case of their children, and husbands in that of their wives—being, however, allowed only a day for deliberation after the matter became known to them; and their judgment, if unfavorable, released the devotee from all obligation. **3. If a woman also vow a vow unto the Lord, and bind herself by a bond, being in her father's house in her youth**—Girls only are specified; but minors of the other sex, who resided under the parental roof, were included, according to Jewish writers, who also consider the name "father" as comprehending all guardians of youth. We are also told that the age at which young people were deemed capable of vowing was 13 for boys and 12 for girls. The judgment of a father or guardian on the vow of any under his charge might be given either by an expressed approval or by silence, which was to be construed as approval. But in the case

ADAM CLARKE

CHAPTER 30

2. *If a man vow a vow.* A vow is a religious promise made to God. Vows were of several kinds: (1) Of abstinence or humiliation, see v. 13; (2) Of the Nazarite, see chap. vi; (3) Of giving certain things or sacrifices to the Lord, Lev. vii. 16; (4) Of alms given to the poor, see Deut. xxiii. 21. The law in this chapter must have been very useful, as it both prevented and annulled rash vows, and provided a proper sanction for the support and performance of those that were rationally and piously made. Besides, this law must have acted as a great preventive of lying and hypocrisy. If a vow was properly made, a man or woman was bound, under penalty of the displeasure of God, to fulfil it.

3. *In her youth.* That is, say the rabbins, under twelve years of age; and under thirteen in case of a young man. Young persons of this age were considered to be under the authority of their parents, and had consequently no power to vow away the property of another. A married woman was in the same circumstances, because she was under the authority of her husband. If however the parents or the husband heard of the vow, and objected to it in the same day in which they heard of it (v. 5), the vow was annulled; or if, having heard of it, they held their peace, this was considered a ratification of the vow.

MATTHEW HENRY

supposed) knows it from her; for, when it comes to his knowledge, it is in his power either to ratify or nullify it. But in favour of the vow, 1. Even his silence shall suffice to ratify it: If he *hold his peace*, her *vows shall stand*, *v.* 4. *Qui tacet, consentire videtur—Silence gives consent.* But, 2. His protestation against it shall perfectly disannul it, because it is possible that such vow may be prejudicial to the affairs of the family. She showed her good-will in making the vow, and, if her intentions therein were sincere, she shall be accepted, and to obey her father shall be accounted better than sacrifice.

II. The case of a wife is much the same. As for a woman that is a widow or divorced, she has neither father nor husband to control her, so that, whatever vows she binds her soul with, they shall *stand against her* (*v.* 9), it is at her peril if she run back.

JAMIESON, FAUSSET, BROWN

of a husband who, after silence from day to day, should ultimately disapprove or hinder his wife's vow, the sin of non-performance was to be imputed to him and not to her. **9. every vow of a widow**—In the case of a married woman, who, in the event of a separation from her husband, or of his death, returned, as was not uncommon, to her father's house, a doubt might have been entertained whether she was not, as before, subject to paternal jurisdiction and obliged to act with the paternal consent. The law ordained that the vow was binding if it had been made in her husband's lifetime, and he, on being made aware of it, had not interposed his veto; as, for instance, she might have vowed, when not a widow, that she would assign a portion of her income to pious and charitable uses, of which she might repent when actually a widow; but by this statute she was required to fulfil the obligation, provided her circumstances enabled her to redeem the pledge. The rules laid down must have been exceedingly useful for the prevention or cancelling of rash vows, as well as for giving a proper sanction to such as were legitimate in their nature, and made in a devout, reflecting spirit.

ADAM CLARKE

12. *Concerning the bond of her soul.* Her life is at stake if she fulfil not the obligation under which she has laid herself.

16. *These are the statutes.* It is very probable that this law, like that concerning the succession of daughters (chap. xxvii), rose from the exigency of some particular case that had just then occurred.

CHAPTER 31

Verses 1–6

Here, I. The Lord of hosts gives orders to Moses to make war upon the Midianites. The Midianites were the posterity of Abraham by Keturah, Gen. xxv. 2. Some of them settled south of Canaan, among whom Jethro lived, and they retained the worship of the true God; but these were settled east of Canaan, and had fallen into idolatry, neighbours to, and in confederacy with, the Moabites. They made themselves obnoxious by sending their bad women among them to draw them to whoredom and idolatry. This was the provocation, this was the quarrel. For this (says God) *avenge Israel of the Midianites*, *v.* 2. 1. God would have the Midianites chastised. Israel's quarrel with Amalek, that fought against them, was not avenged till long after: but their quarrel with Midian, that debauched them, was speedily avenged, for they were looked upon as much the more dangerous and malicious enemies. 2. God would have it done by Moses, in his life time, that he who had so deeply resented that injury might have the satisfaction of seeing it avenged.

II. Moses gives orders to the people to prepare for this expedition, *v.* 3.

III. A detachment is drawn out accordingly for this service, 1,000 *out of every tribe*, 12,000 in all, a small number in comparison with what they could have sent. But God would teach them that it is all one to him *to save by many or by few*, 1 Sam. xiv. 6.

IV. Phinehas the son of Eleazar is sent along with them. The war being a holy war, Phinehas was their common head. He therefore took with him the holy instruments or vessels, probably the breastplate of judgment, by which God might be consulted in any emergency.

Verses 7–12

Here is, 1. The descent which this little army of Israelites made upon the country of Midian. It is very probable that they first published their manifesto, showing the reasons of the war, and requiring them to give up the ringleaders of the mischief to justice; for such afterwards was the *law* (Deut. xx. 10), and such the *practice*, Judg. xx. 12, 13. 2. The execution (the military execution) they did in this descent. (1) They *slew all the males* (*v.* 7), that is, all they met with as far as they went; they put them all to the sword, and gave no quarter. (2) They *slew the kings of Midian*, the same that are called *elders of Midian* (*ch.* xxii. 4), and *dukes of Sihon*, Josh. xiii. 21. Five of these princes are here named, one of whom is *Zur*, probably the same Zur whose daughter Cozbi was, *ch.* xxv. 15.

(3) They slew Balaam. Whatever was the occasion of his being there, God's overruling providence brought him thither, and there his just vengeance found him.

CHAPTER 31

VSS. 1-54. THE MIDIANITES SPOILED AND BALAAM SLAIN. **1, 2. the Lord spake unto Moses, Avenge the children of Israel of the Midianites**—a semi-nomad people, descended from Abraham and Keturah, occupying a tract of country east and southeast of Moab, which lay on the eastern coast of the Dead Sea. They seem to have been the principal instigators of the infamous scheme of seduction, planned to entrap the Israelites into the double crime of idolatry and licentiousness, by which, it was hoped, the Lord would withdraw from that people the benefit of His protection and favor. Moreover, the Midianites had rendered themselves particularly obnoxious by entering into a hostile league with the Amorites (Josh. 13:21). The Moabites were at this time spared in consideration of Lot (Deut. 2:9) and because the measure of their iniquities was not yet full. God spoke of avenging "the children of Israel"; Moses spoke of avenging the Lord, as dishonor had been done to God and an injury inflicted on His people. The interests were identical. God and His people have the same cause, the same friends, and the same assailants. This, in fact, was a religious war, undertaken by the express command of God against idolaters, who had seduced the Israelites to practise their abominations. **3. Arm some of yourselves**—This order was issued but a short time before the death of Moses. The announcement to him of that approaching event seems to have accelerated, rather than retarded, his warlike preparations. **5. there were delivered**—i.e., drafted, chosen, an equal amount from each tribe, to prevent the outbreak of mutual jealousy or strife. Considering the numerical force of the enemy, this was a small quota to furnish. But the design was to exercise their faith and animate them to the approaching invasion of Canaan. **6. Moses sent . . . Eleazar the priest, to the war**—Although it is not expressly mentioned, it is highly probable that Joshua was the general who conducted this war. The presence of the priest, who was always with the army (Deut. 20:2), was necessary to preside over the Levites, who accompanied the expedition, and to inflame the courage of the combatants by his sacred services and counsels. **holy instruments**—As neither the ark nor the Urim and Thummim were carried to the battlefield till a later period in the history of Israel, the "holy instruments" must mean the "trumpets" (ch. 10:9). And this view is agreeable to the text, by simply changing "and" into "even," as the *Hebrew* particle is frequently rendered. **7. they slew all the males**—This was in accordance with a divine order in all such cases (Deut. 20:13). But the destruction appears to have been only partial—limited to those who were in the neighborhood of the Hebrew camp and who had been accomplices in the villainous plot of Baal-peor, while a large portion of the Midianites were absent on their pastoral wanderings or had saved themselves by flight. (Cf. Judg. 6:1.) **8. the kings of Midian**—so called, because each was possessed of absolute power within his own city or district—called also dukes or princes of Sihon (Josh. 13:21), having been probably subject to that Amorite ruler, as it is not uncommon in the East to find a number of governors or pachas tributary to one great king. **Zur**—father of Cozbi (ch. 25:15). **Balaam also . . . they slew with the sword**—This unprincipled man, on his dismissal from Balak, set out for his home in

CHAPTER 31

2. *Gathered unto thy people.* Where? Not in the grave surely. Moses was gathered with none of them; his burial place no man ever knew. "But being gathered unto one's people means dying." It does imply dying, but it does not mean this only. The truth is, God considers all those who are "dead" to men in a state of conscious existence in another world. Therefore He calls himself the "God of Abraham, and the God of Isaac, and the God of Jacob. [Now] God is not the God of the dead, but of the living," because all live to Him, whether dead to men or not. Moses therefore was to be gathered to his people—to enter into that republic of Israel which, having died in the faith, fear, and love of God, were now living in a state of conscious blessedness beyond the confines of the grave.

3. *Avenge the Lord of Midian.* It was God's quarrel, not their own, that they were now to take up. These people were idolaters; idolatry is an offense against God. The civil power has no authority to meddle with what belongs to Him, without especial directions, certified in the most unequivocal way. Private revenge, extension of territory, love of plunder were to have no place in this business; the Lord is to be avenged, and through Him the children of Israel (v. 2), because their souls as well as their bodies had been well-nigh ruined by their idolatry.

6. *A thousand of every tribe.* Twelve thousand men in the whole. *And Phinehas the son of Eleazar;* some think he was made general in this expedition, but this is not likely. The ark and its contents must proceed to this battle, because the battle was the Lord's and He dwelt between the cherubim over the ark; and Phinehas, who had before got a grant in the eternal priesthood, was chosen to accompany the ark in place of his father, Eleazar, who was probably now too far advanced in years to undergo the fatigue. Who then was general? Joshua, without doubt, though not here mentioned, because the battle being the Lord's, He alone is to have the supreme direction, and all the glory. Besides, it was an extraordinary war, and not conducted on the common principle, for we do not find that peace was offered to the Midianites, and that they refused it; see Deut. xx. 10, etc. In such a case only hostilities could lawfully commence; but they were sinners against God; the cup of their iniquity was full, and God thought proper to destroy them.

8. *Balaam . . . they slew with the sword.* This man had probably committed what John calls the "sin unto death"—a sin which God

MATTHEW HENRY

(4) They took all the *women and children captives, v.* 9. (5) They *burnt their cities and goodly castles* (*v.* 10). (6) They plundered the country, and carried off all the cattle and valuable goods, and so returned to the camp of Israel laden with a very rich booty, *v.* 9, 11, 12.

Verses 13–24

The triumphant return to the army of Israel from the war with Midian, and here,

I. They were met with great respect, *v.* 13.

II. They were severely reproved for saving the women alive. The execution having reference to that crime, their drawing them in to the worship of Peor, it was easy to conclude that the women, who were the principal criminals, must not be spared. "It is dangerous to let them live; they will be still tempting the Israelites to uncleanness, and so your captives will be your conquerors and a second time your destroyers."

III. They were obliged to purify themselves, according to the ceremony of the law, and to abide without the camp seven days, till their purification was accomplished. Thus God would preserve in their minds a dread and detestation of murder.

IV. They must likewise purify the spoil they had taken, the captives (*v.* 19) and all the goods, *v.* 21–23. What would bear the fire must pass through the fire, and what would not must be washed with water.

Verses 25–47

The distribution of the spoil which was taken in this expedition against Midian.

I. The prey is ordered to be divided into two parts, one for the 12,000 men that undertook the war, and the other for the congregation. The prey that was divided seems to have been only the captives and the cattle; as for the plate, and jewels, and other goods, every man kept what he took, as is intimated, *v.* 50–53. That only was distributed which would be of use for the stocking of that good land into which they were going.

II. God was to have a tribute out of it, as an acknowledgment of his sovereignty over them in general, and that he was their king to whom *tribute was due.*

Verses 48–54

Here is a great example of piety and devotion in the officers of the army. They came to Moses as their general and commander-in-chief, and very humbly and respectfully addressed themselves to him, calling themselves his *servants.* 1. The pious notice they take

JAMIESON, FAUSSET, BROWN

Mesopotamia (ch. 24:25). But, either diverging from his way to tamper with the Midianites, he remained among them without proceeding further, to incite them against Israel and to watch the effects of his wicked counsel; or, learning in his own country that the Israelites had fallen into the snare which he had laid and which he doubted not would lead to their ruin, he had, under the impulse of insatiable greed, returned to demand his reward from the Midianites. He was an object of merited vengeance. In the immense slaughter of the Midianitish people—in the capture of their women, children, and property and in the destruction of all their places of refuge—the severity of a righteous God fell heavily on that base and corrupt race. But, more than all others, Balaam deserved and got the just reward of his deeds. His conduct had been atrociously sinful, considering the knowledge he possessed, and the revelations he had received, of the will of God. For any one in his circumstances to attempt defeating the prophecies he had himself been the organ of uttering, and plotting to deprive the chosen people of the divine favor and protection, was an act of desperate wickedness, which no language can adequately characterize. **13. Moses, and Eleazar the priest, . . . went forth to meet them without the camp**—partly as a token of respect and congratulation on their victory, partly to see how they had executed the Lord's commands, and partly to prevent the defilement of the camp by the entrance of warriors stained with blood. **14-18. Moses was wroth with the officers of the host**—The displeasure of the great leader, though it appears the ebullition of a fierce and sanguinary temper, arose in reality from a pious and enlightened regard to the best interests of Israel. No order had been given for the slaughter of the women, and in ancient war they were commonly reserved for slaves. By their antecedent conduct, however, the Midianitish women had forfeited all claims to mild or merciful treatment; and the sacred character, the avowed object of the war (vss. 2, 3), made their slaughter necessary without any special order. But why "kill every male among the little ones"? It was designed to be a war of extermination, such as God Himself had ordered against the people of Canaan, whom the Midianites equalled in the enormity of their wickedness. **19-24. abide without the camp seven days; whosoever hath killed any person . . . purify both yourselves and your captives**—Though the Israelites had taken the field in obedience to the command of God, they had become defiled by contact with the dead. A process of purification was to be undergone, as the law required (Lev. 15:13; ch. 19:9-12), and this purifying ceremony was extended to dress, houses, tents, to everything on which a dead body had lain, which had been touched by the blood-stained hands of the Israelitish warriors, or which had been the property of idolaters. This became a standing ordinance in all time coming (Lev. 6:28; 11:33; 15:12). **25-39. Take the sum of the prey that was taken**—i.e., of the captives and cattle, which, having been first lumped together according ot ancient usage (Exod. 15:9; Judg. 5:30), were divided into two equal parts: the one to the people at large, who had sustained a common injury from the Midianites and who were all liable to serve: and the other portion to the combatants, who, having encountered the labors and perils of war, justly received the largest share. From both parts, however, a certain deduction was taken for the sanctuary, as a thank offering to God for preservation and for victory. The soldiers had greatly the advantage in the distribution; for a five-hundredth part only of their half went to the priest, while a fiftieth part of the congregation's half was given to the Levites. **32. the booty, being the rest of the prey which the men of war had caught**—Some of the captives having been killed (vs. 17) and part of the cattle taken for the support of the army, the total amount of the booty remaining was in the following proportions: —Sheep, 675,000—half to soldiers, 337,500; deducted to God, 675; half to congregation, 337,500; deducted to the Levites, 6,750. Beeves, 72,000—half to soldiers, 36,000; deducted to God, 72; half to congregation, 36,000; deducted to the Levites, 720. Asses, 61,000—half to soldiers, 30,500; deducted to God, 61; half to congregation, 30,500; deducted to the Levites, 610. Persons, 32,000—half to soldiers, 16,000, deducted to God, 32; half to congregation, 16,000; deducted to the Levites, 320. **48–54. officers . . . said . . . there lacketh not one man of us**—A victory so signal, and the glory of which was untarnished by the loss of a single Israelitish soldier, was an astonishing miracle. So clearly betokening the direct interposition of

ADAM CLARKE

punishes with temporal death, while at the same time He extends mercy to the soul.

17. *Kill every male among the little ones.* For this action I account simply on the principle that God, who is the Author and Supporter of life, has a right to dispose of it when and how He thinks proper; and the Judge of all the earth can do nothing but what is right. Of the women killed on this occasion it may be safely said their lives were forfeited by their personal transgressions; and yet even in this case there can be little doubt that God showed mercy to their souls. The little ones were safely lodged; they were taken to heaven and saved from the evil to come.

23. *The water of separation.* The water in which the ashes of the red heifer were mingled; see on chap. viii. 7; xix. 2, etc. Garments, whether of cloth or skins, were to be washed. Gold, silver, brass, iron, tin, and lead, to pass through the fire, probably to be melted down.

28. *And levy a tribute unto the Lord . . . one soul of five hundred.* The person to be employed in the Lord's service, under the Levites—the cattle either for sacrifice or for the use of the Levites, v. 30.

32. *The booty.* It appears from the enumeration here that the Israelites, in this war against the Midianites, took 32,000 female prisoners, 61,000 asses, 72,000 beeves, 675,000 sheep and small cattle; besides the immense number of males who fell in battle, and the women and children who were slain by the divine command, v. 17. And it does not appear that in this expedition a single man of Israel fell! This was naturally to be expected, because the battle was the Lord's, v. 49.

MATTHEW HENRY

of God's wonderful goodness to them in this late expedition, in preserving not only their own lives, but the lives of all the men of war that they had under their charge; so that, upon the review of their muster-roll, it appeared there was not one missing, *v.* 49. They looked upon it as a mercy to themselves that none of those under their charge miscarried. Instead of coming to Moses to demand a recompence for the good service they had done in *avenging the Lord of Midian*, or to set up trophies of their victory for the immortalizing of their own names, they bring an oblation to *make atonement for their souls*.

JAMIESON, FAUSSET, BROWN

Heaven, it might well awaken the liveliest feelings of grateful acknowledgment to God (Ps. 44:2, 3). The oblation they brought for the Lord "was partly an atonement" or reparation for their error (vss. 14-16), for it could not possess any expiatory virtue, and partly a tribute of gratitude for the stupendous service rendered them. It consisted of the "spoil," which, being the acquisition of individual valor, was not divided like the "prey," or livestock, each soldier retaining it in lieu of pay; it was offered by the "captains" alone, whose pious feelings were evinced by the dedication of the spoil which fell to their share. There were jewels to the amount of 16,750 shekels, or about $305,000.

ADAM CLARKE

50. *We have . . . brought an oblation for the Lord.* So it appears there was a great deal of booty taken which did not come into the general account; and of this the soldiers, of their own will, made a very extensive offering to God because He had preserved them from falling in battle. *To make an atonement for our souls.* That is, to make an acknowledgment to God for the preservation of their lives.

MATTHEW HENRY

CHAPTER 32

Verses 1–15

Israel's tents were now pitched in the plains of Moab. While they were at a pause, the disposal of the conquests they had already made was here settled, not by any particular order or appointment of God, but at the special instance and request of two of the tribes, to which Moses consented.

I. Here is a motion made by the Reubenites and Gadites, that the land which they had lately possessed themselves of, and which in the right of conquest belonged to Israel in common, might be assigned to them in particular for their inheritance. Two things common in the world induced these tribes to make this choice and this motion upon it, the *lust of the eye* and the *pride of life*, 1 John ii. 16. 1. The *lust of the eye*. This land which they coveted was not only beautiful for situation, and pleasant to the eye, but it was good for food, food for cattle; and they had a great multitude of cattle, above the rest of the tribes. Now they, having these large stocks, coveted land proportionable. 2. Perhaps there was something of the *pride of life* in it. Reuben was the first-born of Israel, but he had lost his birthright. He here catches at the first lot, though it was out of Canaan, and far off from the tabernacle. The tribe of Gad descended from the first-born of Zilpah, and were like pretenders with the Reubenites; and Manasseh too was a first-born, but knew he must be eclipsed by Ephraim his younger brother, and therefore he also coveted to get precedency.

II. Moses's dislike of this motion, and the severe rebuke he gives to it, as a faithful prince and prophet.

1. It must be confessed that, *prima facie—at first sight*, the thing looked ill, especially the closing words of their petition: *Bring us not over Jordan, v.* 5. It seemed to proceed from a bad principle, a contempt of the land of promise. There seemed also to be covetousness in it; for that which they insisted on was that it was convenient for their cattle. It argued likewise a neglect of their brethren, as if they cared not what became of Israel, while they themselves were well provided for.

2. Moses is therefore very warm upon them. (1) He shows them what he apprehended to be evil in this motion, that it would discourage the heart of their brethren, *v.* 6, 7. (2) He reminds them of the fatal consequences of the unbelief and faint-heartedness of their fathers, when they were just ready to enter Canaan, as they themselves now were. He recites the story very particularly (*v.* 8–13). (3) He gives them fair warning of the mischief that would be likely to follow upon this separation which they were about to make from the camp of Israel; they would be in danger of bringing wrath upon the whole congregation, and hurrying them all back again into the wilderness (*v.* 14, 15).

Verses 16–27

We have here the accommodating of the matter between Moses and the two tribes, about their settlement on this side Jordan. After some consultation, they return with this proposal, that their men of war should go and assist their brethren in the conquest of Canaan, and they would leave their families and flocks behind them in this land: and thus they might have their request, and no harm would be done.

I. Their proposal is very fair and generous, and such as, instead of disheartening, would rather encourage their brethren. 1. That their *men of war*, who were fit for service, would go *ready armed before the children of Israel* into the land of Canaan. 2. That they would leave behind them their families and cattle (which would otherwise be but the incumbrance of their camp), and so they would be the more serviceable to their brethren, *v.* 16. 3. That they would not return to their possessions till the conquest of Canaan was completed, *v.* 18. 4. That yet they would not expect any share of the land that was yet to be conquered (*v.* 19).

JAMIESON, FAUSSET, BROWN

CHAPTER 32

Vss. 1-42. The Reubenites and Gadites Ask for an Inheritance. **1. the land of Jazer, and the land of Gilead**—A complete conquest had been made of the country east of the Jordan, comprising "the land of Jazer," which formed the southern district between the Arnon and Jabbok and "the land of Gilead," the middle region between the Jabbok and Jarmouk, or Hieromax, including Bashan, which lay on the north of that river. The whole of this region is now called the Belka. It has always been famous for its rich and extensive pastures, and it is still the favorite resort of the Bedouin shepherds, who frequently contend for securing to their immense flocks the benefit of its luxuriant vegetation. In the camp of ancient Israel, Reuben and Gad were pre-eminently pastoral; and as these two tribes, being placed under the same standard, had frequent opportunities of conversing and arranging about their common concerns, they united in preferring a request that the transjordanic region, so well suited to the habits of a pastoral people, might be assigned to them. **6-19. Moses said unto the children of Gad and to the children of Reuben, Shall your brethren go to war, and shall ye sit here**—Their language was ambiguous; and Moses, suspicious that this proposal was an act of unbelief, a scheme of self-policy and indolence to escape the perils of warfare and live in ease and safety, addressed to them a reproachful and passionate remonstrance. Whether thev had really meditated such a withdrawal from all share in the war of invasion, or the effect of their leader's expostulation was to drive them from their original purpose, they now, in answer to his impressive appeal, declared it to be their sincere intention to co-operate with their brethren; but, if so, they ought to have been more explicit at first. **16. they came near**—The narrative gives a picturesque description of this scene. The suppliants had shrunk back, dreading from the undisguised emotions of their leader that their request would be refused. But, perceiving, from the tenor of his discourse, that his objection was grounded only on the supposition that they would not cross the Jordan to assist their brethren, they became emboldened to approach him with assurances of their goodwill. **We will build sheepfolds here for our cattle, and cities for our little ones**—i.e., rebuild, repair. It would have been impossible within two months to found new cities, or even to reconstruct those which had been razed to the ground. Those cities of the Amorites were not absolutely demolished, and they probably consisted only of mud-built, or dry-stone walls. **17. and our little ones shall dwell in the fenced cities, because of the inhabitants of the land**—There was good policy in leaving a sufficient force to protect the conquered region lest the enemy should attempt reprisals; and as only 40,000 of the Reubenites and the Gadites, and a half of Manasseh, passed over the Jordan (Josh. 4:13), there were left for the security of the new possessions 70,580 men, besides women and children under 20 years (cf. ch. 26:17). **We ourselves will go ready armed**—i.e., all of us in a collective body, or as many as may be deemed necessary, while the rest of our number shall remain at home to provide for the sustenance and secure the protection of our families and flocks. (See on Josh. 4:12, 13.) **20-33. Moses said unto them, If ye will do this thing**—with sincerity and zeal. **go before the Lord to war**—The phrase was used in allusion to the order of march in which the tribes of Reuben and Gad immediately preceded the ark (Num. 10:18-21), or to the passage over the Jordan, in which the ark stood in mid-channel, while all the tribes marched by in succession (Josh. 3:4), of course including those of Reuben and Gad, so that, literally, they *passed over before the Lord* and before the rest of Israel (Josh. 4:13). Perhaps, however, the phrase is used merely in a general

ADAM CLARKE

CHAPTER 32

3. *Ataroth, and Dibon.* The places mentioned here belonged to Sihon, king of the Amorites, and Og, king of Bashan, which, being conquered by the Israelites, constituted ever after a part of their territories, v. 33.

5. *Let this land be given unto thy servants.* Because it was good for pasturage, and they had many flocks, v. 1.

12. *Caleb the son of Jephunneh the Kenezite.* It was Jephunneh that was the Kenezite, and not Caleb. Kenaz was probably the father of Jephunneh.

16. *We will build . . . cities for our little ones.* It was impossible for these, numerous as they might be, to build cities and fortify them for the defense of their families in their absence.

17. *Because of the inhabitants of the land.* These were the Ammonites, Moabites, Idumeans, and the remains of the Midianites and Amorites. But could the women and children even keep the defensed cities when placed in them? This certainly cannot be supposed possible. Many of the man of war must, of course, stay behind. In the last census, chap. xxvi., the tribe of Reuben consisted of 43,730 men; the tribe of Gad, 40,500; the tribe of Manasseh, 52,700, the half of which is 26,350. Add this to the sum of the other two tribes, and the amount is 110,580. Now from Joshua iv. 13 we learn that of the tribes of Reuben and Gad, and the half of the tribe of Manasseh, only 40,000 armed men passed over Jordan to assist their brethren in the reduction of the land; consequently the number of 70,580 men were left behind for the defense of the women, the children, and the flocks. This was more than sufficient to defend them against a people already panic-stuck by their late discomfitures and reverses.

MATTHEW HENRY

II. Moses thereupon grants their request, upon consideration that they would adhere to their proposals. 1. He insists much upon it that they should never lay down their arms till their brethren laid down theirs. They promised to go armed *before the children of Israel, v.* 17. "Nay," says Moses, "you shall go armed *before the Lord, v.* 20, 21. It is God's cause more than your brethren's. 2. Upon this condition he grants them this land for their possession. But, 3. He warns them of the danger of breaking their word: "If you fail, you *sin against the Lord* (*v.* 23), and not against your brethren only, and *be sure your sin will find you out.*" Note, Sin will, without doubt, find out the sinner sooner or later. It concerns us therefore to find our sins out, that we may repent of them and forsake them, lest our sins find us out to our ruin and confusion.

III. They unanimously agree to the provisos and conditions of the grant, and do, as it were, give bond for performance, by a solemn promise: *Thy servants will do as my lord commandeth, v.* 25.

Verses 28–42

1. Moses settles this matter with Eleazar, and with Joshua who was to be his successor, knowing that he himself must not live to see it perfected, *v.* 28–30. He gives them an estate upon condition, leaving it to Joshua, if they fulfilled the condition, to declare the estate absolute. Hereupon they repeat their promise to adhere to their brethren, *v.* 31, 32. 2. Moses settles them in the land they desired. Here is the first mention of the half tribe of Manasseh coming in with them for a share.

Concerning the settlement of these tribes observe, (1) They built the cities, that is, repaired them.

(2) They changed the names of them (*v.* 38). Nebo and Baal were names of their gods, which they were forbidden to make mention of (Exod. xxiii. 13), and which, by changing the names of these cities, they endeavoured to bury in oblivion.

JAMIESON, FAUSSET, BROWN

sense to denote their marching on an expedition, the purpose of which was blessed with the presence, and destined to promote the glory, of God. The displeasure which Moses had felt on the first mention of their proposal had disappeared on the strength of their solemn assurances. But a lurking suspicion of their motives seems still to have been lingering in his mind—he continued to speak to them in an admonitory strain; and he concluded by warning them that in case of their failing to redeem their pledge, the judgments of an offended God would assuredly fall upon them. This emphatic caution against such an eventuality throws a strong doubt on the honesty of their first intentions; and yet, whether through the opposing attitude or the strong invectives of Moses they had been brought to a better state of mind, their final reply showed that now all was right. **28-32. concerning them Moses commanded**—The arrangement itself, as well as the express terms on which he assented to it, was announced by the leader to the public authorities. The pastoral country the two tribes had desired was to be granted them on condition that they would lend their aid to their brethren in the approaching invasion of Canaan. If they refused or failed to perform their promise, those possessions should be forfeited, and they themselves compelled to go across the Jordan and fight for a settlement like the rest of their brethren. **33. half the tribe of Manasseh**—It is nowhere explained in the record how they were incorporated with the two tribes, or what broke this great tribe into two parts, of which one was left to follow the fortunes of its brethren in the settled life of the western hills, while the other was allowed to wander as a nomadic tribe over the pasture lands of Gilead and Bashan. They are not mentioned as accompanying Reuben and Gad in their application to Moses; neither were they included in his first directions (vs. 25); but as they also were a people addicted to pastoral pursuits and possessed as immense flocks as the other two, Moses invited the half of them to remain, in consequence, probably, of finding that this region was more than sufficient for the pastoral wants of the others, and he may have given them the preference, as some have conjectured, for their valorous conduct in the contests with the Amorites (cf. vs. 39, with Josh. 17:1). **34-36. the children of Gad built**—(see on vs. 16)—Dibon, identified with Dheban, now in ruins, an hour's distance from the Arnon (Mojeb). **Ataroth** (crowns)—There are several towns so called in Scripture, but this one in the tribe of Gad has not been identified. Aroer, now Arair, standing on a precipice on the north bank of the Arnon. **35. Atroth, Shophan, and Jaazer . . .:**—Jaazer, near a famed fountain, Ain Hazier, the waters of which flow into Wady Schaib, about 15 miles from Hesbon. Beth-nimrah, now Nimrin; Heshbon, now Hesban; Elealeh (the high), **now Elaal; Kirjathaim (the double city)**; Nebo, now Neba, near the mountain of that name; Baal-meon, now Myoun, in ruins, where was a temple of Baal (Josh. 13:17; Jer. 48:23); Shibmah, or Shebam (vs. 2), near Heshbon, famous for vines (Isa. 16:9, 10; Jer. 48:32). **38. (their names being changed)**—either because it was the general custom of conquerors to do so; or, rather, because from the prohibition to *mention the names of other gods* (Exod. 23:13), as Nebo and Baal were, it was expedient on the first settlement of the Israelites to obliterate all remembrance of those idols. (See on Josh. 13:17-20.) **39. Gilead**—now Jelud. **41. Havoth-jair**—i.e., tent-villages. Jair, who captured them, was a descendant of Manasseh on his mother's side (I Chron. 1:21, 22). **42. Nobah**—also a distinguished person connected with the eastern branch of this tribe.

ADAM CLARKE

F. B. MEYER:

Warning against forsaking their brethren. These two and a half tribes never entered the national life as did those on the other side of Jordan. They were far from the center of religious life, first at Shiloh and then at Jerusalem. On them first the tide of invasion broke, sweeping them and their cattle into captivity.

In Deborah's great song Reuben is rebuked for sitting "among the sheepfolds to hear the pipings for the flocks," instead of coming to the help of the Lord against the mighty. The Brahmins say that the holy man dies to every other sin earlier and easier than to the love of money. Their cattle kept these tribes on the wrong side of the river of separation! Let us beware of the cares of this world if we are poor, and of the deceitfulness of riches if we are rich. Better lose all than the soul (Matt. 16:26).

—Bible Commentary

34. *The children of Gad built . . . Aroer.* This was situated on the river Arnon, Deut. ii. 36; 2 Kings x. 33. It was formerly inhabited by the *Emim,* a warlike and perhaps gigantic people. They were expelled by the Moabites; the Moabites, by the Amorites; and the Amorites, by the Israelites. The Gadites then possessed it till the captivity of their tribe, with that of Reuben and the half of the tribe of Manasseh, by the Assyrians, 2 Kings xv. 29, after which the Moabites appear to have repossessed it, as they seem to have occupied it in the days of Jeremiah, chap. xlviii. 15-20.

38. *And Nebo . . . (their names being changed).* That is, Those who conquered the cities called them after their own names. Thus the city Kenath, being conquered by Nobah, was called after his name, v. 42.

41. *Havoth-jair.* That is, the "villages" or "habitations of Jair"; and thus they should have been translated. As these two tribes and a half were the first, says Ainsworth, who had their inheritance assigned to them in the Promised Land, so they were the first of all Israel that were carried captive out of their own land, because of their sins. "For they transgressed against the God of their fathers, and went a whoring after other gods. And God delivered them into the hands of Pul and Tiglath-Pilneser, kings of Assyria, and they brought them to Halah, Habor, Hara, and Gozan, unto this day." See 1 Chron. v. 25-26.

MATTHEW HENRY — CHAPTER 33

Verses 1–49

This is a review and brief rehearsal of the travels of the children of Israel through the wilderness.

JAMIESON, FAUSSET, BROWN — CHAPTER 33

Vss. 1-15. TWO AND FORTY JOURNEYS OF THE ISRAELITES—FROM EGYPT TO SINAI. **1. These are the journeys of the children of Israel**—This chapter may be said to form the winding-up of the history of the travels of the Israelites through the wilderness; for the three following chapters relate to matters connected with the occupation and division of the promised land. As several apparent discrepancies will be discovered on comparing the records here given of the journeyings from Sinai with the detailed accounts of the events narrated in the Book of Exodus and the occasional notices of places that are found in that of Deuteronomy, it is probable that this itinerary comprises a list of only the *most important* stations in their journeys—those where they formed prolonged encampments,

ADAM CLARKE — CHAPTER 33

MATTHEW HENRY

I. Now the account was kept: *Moses wrote their goings out*, *v.* 2. It may be of good use to private Christians, but especially to those in public stations, to preserve in writing an account of the providences of God concerning them, the constant series of mercies they have experienced, especially those turns and changes which have made some days of their lives more remarkable. Our memories are deceitful and need this help, that we may *remember all the way which the Lord our God has led us in this wilderness*, Deut. viii. 2.

II. What the account itself was. It began with their departure out of Egypt, continued with their march through the wilderness, and ended in the plains of Moab, where they now lay encamped.

1. Some things are observed here concerning their departure out of Egypt, which they are reminded of upon all occasions, as a work of wonder never to be forgotten. They *went forth with their armies* (*v.* 1), rank and file, as an army with banners. They did not steal away clandestinely (Isa. lii. 12), but in defiance of their enemies, to whom God had made them such a burdensome stone that they neither could, nor would, nor durst, oppose them.

2. Concerning their travels towards Canaan. Observe, (1) They were continually upon the remove. Such is our state in this world; we have here no continuing city. (2) Most of their way lay through a wilderness, uninhabited, untracked, unfurnished even with the necessaries of human life, which magnifies the wisdom and power of God, by whose wonderful conduct and bounty the thousands of Israel not only subsisted for forty years in that desolate place, but came out at least as numerous and vigorous as they went in. At first they pitched *in the edge of the wilderness* (*v.* 6), but afterwards in the heart of it; by less difficulties God prepares his people for greater. (3) They were led to and fro, forward and backward, as in a maze or labyrinth, and yet were all the while under the direction of the pillar of cloud and fire. The way which God takes in bringing his people to himself is always the best way, though it does not always seem to us the nearest way.

JAMIESON, FAUSSET, BROWN

and whence they dispersed their flocks and herds to pasture on the adjacent plains till the surrounding herbage was exhausted. The catalogue extends from their departure out of Egypt to their arrival on the plains of Moab. **went forth . . . with their armies**—i.e., a vast multitude marshalled in separate companies, but regular order. **2. Moses wrote their goings out according to their journeys by the commandment of the Lord**—The wisdom of this divine order is seen in the importance of the end to which it was subservient—viz., partly to establish the truth of the history, partly to preserve a memorial of God's marvellous interpositions on behalf of Israel, and partly to confirm their faith in the prospect of the difficult enterprise on which they were entering, the invasion of Canaan. **3. Rameses**—generally identified with Heroöpolis, now the modern Abu-Keisheid (see on Exod. 12:37), which was probably the capital of Goshen, and, by direction of Moses, the place of general rendezvous previous to their departure. **4. upon their gods**—used either according to Scripture phraseology to denote their rulers (the first-born of the king and his princes) or the idolatrous objects of Egyptian worship. **5. pitched in Succoth**—i.e., booths—a place of no note except as a temporary halting-place, at Birketel-Hadji, the Pilgrim's Pool [Calmet]. **6. Etham**—edge, or border of all that part of Arabia Petræa which lay contiguous to Egypt and was known by the general name of Shur. **7. Pi-hahiroth, Baal-zephon, and Migdol**—(See on Exod. 14:1-4). **8.** Marah—thought to be Ain Howarah, both from its position and the time (three days) it would take them with their children and flocks to march from the water of Ayun Musa to that spot. **9. Elim**—supposed to be Wady Ghurundel. (See on Exod. 15:27.) **10. encamped by the Red Sea**—The road from Wady Ghurundel leads into the interior, in consequence of a high continuous ridge which excludes all view of the sea. At the mouth of Wady-et-Tayibeh, after about three days' march, it opens again on a plain along the margin of the Red Sea. The minute accuracy of the Scripture narrative, in corresponding so exactly with the geographical features of this region, is remarkably shown in describing the Israelites as proceeding by the only practicable route that could be taken. This plain, where they encamped, was the Desert of Sin (see on Exod. 16:1). **12-14. Dophkah . . . Alush . . . Rephidim**—These three stations, in the great valleys of El Sheikh and Feiran, would be equivalent to four days' journey for such a host. Rephidim (Exod. 17:6) was in Horeb, the burnt region—a generic name for a hot, mountainous country. **15. wilderness of Sinai**—the Wady Er-Raheh.

16-56. From Sinai to Kadesh and Plains of Moab. **16-37. Kibroth-Hattaavah** (the graves of lust, see on ch. 11:4-34)—The route, on breaking up the encampment at Sinai, led down Wady Sheikh; then crossing Jebel-et-Tih, which intersected the peninsula, they descended into Wady Zalaka, pitching successively at two brief, though memorable, stations (Deut. 9:22); then they encamped at Hazeroth (unwalled villages), supposed to be at Ain-Hadera (ch. 11:35). Kadesh or Kadesh-barnea, is supposed to be the great valley of the Ghor, and the city Kadesh to have been situated on the border of this valley [Burckhardt, Robinson]. But as there are no less than *eighteen stations* inserted between Hazeroth and Kadesh, and only eleven days were spent in performing that journey (Deut. 1:2), it is evident that the intermediate stations here recorded belong to another and totally different visit to Kadesh. The first was when they left Sinai in the second month (ch. 1:11; ch. 13:20), and were in Kadesh in August (Deut. 1:45), and "abode many days" in it. Then, murmuring at the report of the spies, they were commanded to return into the desert "by the way of the Red Sea." The arrival at Kadesh, mentioned in this catalogue, corresponds to the *second* sojourn at that place, being the *first* month, or April (ch. 20:1). Between the two visits there intervened a period of thirty-eight years, during which they wandered hither and thither through all the region of El-Tih (wanderings), often returning to the same spots as the pastoral necessities of their flocks required; and there is the strongest reason for believing that the stations named between Hazeroth (vs. 8) and Kadesh (vs. 36) belong to the long interval of wandering. No certainty has yet been attained in ascertaining the locale of many of these stations. There must have been more than are recorded; for it is probable that those only are noted where they remained some time, where the tabernacle was pitched, and where Moses and the elders encamped, the people being scattered for pasture in various directions. From Ezion-geber,

ADAM CLARKE

2. *And Moses wrote their goings out according to their journeys.* We may consider the whole Book of Numbers as a diary, and indeed the first book of travels ever published.

3. *From Rameses.* This appears to have been the metropolis of the land of Goshen, and the place of rendezvous whence the whole Israelitish nation set out on their journey to the Promised Land; and is supposed to be the same as Cairo.

[There follows in verses 5-49 an outline of the journey in which the forty-two stations or stopping places are listed.]

F. B. MEYER:

"They journeyed from Marah, and came unto Elim: and in Elim . . ." (Num. 33:9).

In his enumeration of the halting places of Israel, Moses mentions Marah and Elim. In the case of the former, he does not dwell on the murmuring of the people over the bitter stream; but in the case of Elim, he loves to dilate on the twelve springs of water, and the three-score and ten palm trees, under which they pitched. Years of weary travel had not obliterated the memory of the refreshment afforded by those seventy palms.

We should remember the blessings of the past. God has so made us that we soon forget pain; but memory is willing to keep the fresco-pictures of sunny scenes unobliterated upon the walls of her galleries. Thus we may encourage our faith and comfort our hearts by musing on the hand of the Lord which has been upon us for good. You have had many hard tracks of desert sand to traverse; but never forget those three-score and ten palm trees. Let their gracious shade and fruit still refresh you. And remember that God will restore them whenever needed. If not, you can always find your palm trees and wells in Himself.

God does not remember the sins of the past. There is no word of their murmurings, either at Marah or Rephidim. It is thus that God deals with us. "I, even I, am he that blotteth out thy transgressions for mine own sake, and will not remember thy sins." When God forgives, He forgets. He erases the record from His book, and deals with us as though no sin had been committed. When we get to heaven and study the way-book, we shall find all the deeds of love and self-denial carefully recorded, though we have forgotten them; and all the sins blotted out, though we remember them.

—*Great Verses Through the Bible*

MATTHEW HENRY

Verses 50–56

While the children of Israel were in the wilderness their total separation from all other people kept them out of the way of temptation to idolatry. But now that they were to pass over Jordan they were entering again into that temptation, and therefore, 1. They are here strictly charged utterly to destroy all the remnants of idolatry. 2. They were assured that, if they did so, God would by degrees put them in full possession of the land of promise, *v.* 53, 54. 3. They were threatened that, if they spared either the idols or the idolaters, they should be beaten with their own rod and their sin would certainly be their punishment. If we do not drive sin out, sin will drive us out; if we be not the death of our lusts, our lusts will be the death of our souls.

JAMIESON, FAUSSET, BROWN

for instance, which stood at the head of the gulf of Akaba, to Kadesh, could not be much less than the whole length of the great valley of the Ghor, a distance of not less than 100 miles, whatever might be the exact situation of Kadesh; and, of course, there must have been several intervening stations, though none are mentioned. The incidents and stages of the rest of the journey to the plains of Moab are sufficiently explicit from the preceding chapters. **Rithmah**—the place of the broom, a station possibly in some wady extending westward of the Ghor (ch. 10:40). **Rimmon-parez,** or Rimmon—a city of Judah and Simeon (Josh. 15:32); Libnah, so called from its white poplars (Joshua 10:29), or, as some think, a white hill between Kadesh and Gaza (Josh. 10:29); Rissah (Elarish); mount Shapher (Cassius); Moseroth, adjacent to mount Hor, in Wady Mousa. Ezion-geber, near Akaba, a seaport on the western shore of the Elanitic gulf; Wilderness of Zin, on the east side of the peninsula of Sinai; Punon, in the rocky ravines of mount Hor and famous for the mines and quarries in its vicinity as well as for its fruit trees, now Tafyle, on the border of Edom; Abarim, a ridge of rugged hills northwest of the Arnon—the part called Nebo was one of its highest peaks—opposite Jericho. (See on Deut. 10:6.) **50-53. ye shall drive out all the inhabitants of the land from before you**—not, however, by expulsion, but extermination (Deut. 7:1). **destroy all their pictures**—obelisks for idolatrous worship (see on Lev. 26:1). **and destroy all their molten images**—by metonymy for all their groves and altars, and materials of worship on the tops of hills. **54. ye shall divide the land by lot**—The particular locality of each tribe was to be determined in this manner while a line was to be used in measuring the proportion (Josh. 18:10; Ps. 16:5, 6). **55. But if ye will not drive out the inhabitants of the land from before you**—No associations were to be formed with the inhabitants; otherwise, "if ye let remain, they will be pricks in your eyes, and thorns in your sides"—i.e., they would prove troublesome and dangerous neighbors, enticing to idolatry, and consequently depriving you of the divine favor and blessing. The neglect of the counsel against union with the idolatrous inhabitants became fatal to them. This earnest admonition given to the Israelites in their peculiar circumstances conveys a salutary lesson to us to allow no lurking habits of sin to remain in us. That spiritual enemy must be eradicated from our nature; otherwise it will be ruinous to our present peace and future salvation.

ADAM CLARKE

52. *Ye shall . . . destroy all their pictures. Maskiyotham,* from *sachah,* "to be like, or resemble," either pictures, carved work, or embroidery, as far as these things were employed to exhibit the abominations of idolatry. *Molten images, tsalmey massechotham,* metallic talismanical figures, made under certain constellations, and supposed in consequence to be possessed of some extraordinary influences and virtues.

55. *Shall be pricks in your eyes.* Under these metaphors the continual mischief that should be done to them, in both soul and body, by these idolaters is set forth in a very expressive manner. What can be more vexatious than a continual goading of each side, so that the attempt to avoid the one throws the body more forcibly on the other? And what can be more distressing than a continual pricking in the eye?

MATTHEW HENRY — CHAPTER 34

Verses 1–15

We have here a particular draft of the line by which the land of Canaan was meted, and bounded, on all sides. There was a much larger possession promised them, which in due time they would have possessed if they had been obedient, reaching even to the river Euphrates, Deut. xi. 24. And even so far the dominion of Israel did extend in David's time and Solomon's, 2 Chron. ix. 26. But this which is here described is Canaan only, which was the lot of the nine tribes and a half, for the other two and a half were already settled, *v.* 14, 15. Now concerning the limits of Canaan observe,

I. That it was limited within certain bounds: 1. That they might know whom they were to dispossess, and how far the commission which was given them extended (*ch.* xxxiii. 53), that they should *drive out the inhabitants.* 2. That they might know what to expect the possession of themselves.

II. That it lay comparatively in a very little compass: as it is here bounded, it is reckoned to be but about 160 miles in length and about fifty in breadth; perhaps it did not contain more than half as much ground as England, and yet this is the country which was promised to the father of the faithful and was the possession of the seed of Israel. This was that little spot of ground in which alone, for many ages, *God was known, and his name was great,* Ps. lxxvi. 1. See here then, 1. How small a part of the world God has for himself. 2. How small a share of the world God often gives to his own people.

III. It is observable what the bounds and limits of it were. 1. Canaan was itself a *pleasant land* (so it is called Dan. viii. 9), and yet it bordered upon wilderness and seas, and was surrounded with divers melancholy prospects. 2. Many of its borders were its defences and natural fortifications. 3. The border reached to the *river of Egypt* (*v.* 5), that the sight of that country which they could look into out of their own might remind them of their bondage there, and

JAMIESON, FAUSSET, BROWN — CHAPTER 34

Vss. 1-29. THE BORDERS OF THE LAND OF CANAAN. **2. this is the . . . land of Canaan**—The details given in this chapter mark the general boundary of the inheritance of Israel west of the Jordan. The Israelites never actually possessed all the territory comprised within these boundaries, even when it was most extended by the conquests of David and Solomon. **3-5. your south quarter**—The line which bounded it on the south is the most difficult to trace. According to the best biblical geographers, the leading points here defined are as follows: The southwest angle of the southern boundary should be where the wilderness of Zin touches the border of Edom, so that the southern boundary should extend eastward from the extremity of the Dead Sea, wind around the precipitous ridge of Akrabbim (scorpions), thought to be the high and difficult Pass of Safeh, which crosses the stream that flows from the south into the Jordan—i.e., the great valley of the Arabah, reaching from the Dead to the Red Sea. **river of Egypt**—the ancient brook Sihor, the Rhinocolura of the Greeks, a little to the south of El-Arish, where this wady gently descends towards the Mediterranean (Josh. 13:3). **6. the western border**—There is no uncertainty about this boundary, as it is universally allowed to be the Mediterranean, which is called "the great sea" in comparison with the small inland seas or lakes known to the Hebrews. **7-9. north border**—The principal difficulty in understanding the description here arises from what our translators have called mount Hor. The Hebrew words, however, *Hor-ha-Hor,* properly signify "the mountain of the mountain"—"the high double mountain," which, from the situation, can mean nothing else than the mountain Amana (Song of Sol. 4:8), a member of the great Lebanon range (Josh. 13:5). **entrance of Hamath**—The northern plain between those mountain ranges, now the valley of Balbeck (see on ch. 13:21-24). **Zedad**—identified as the

ADAM CLARKE — CHAPTER 34

2. *The land of Canaan with the coasts thereof.* All description here is useless. The situation and boundaries of the land of Canaan can be known only by actual survey, or by consulting a good map.

3. *The salt sea.* The Dead Sea, or Lake Asphaltites.

5. *The river of Egypt.* The eastern branch of the river Nile; or, according to others, a river which is south of the land of the Philistines.

6. *Ye shall even have the great sea for a border.* The Mediterranean Sea, called here the Great Sea, to distinguish it from the Dead Sea, the Sea of Tiberias, etc., which were only a sort of lakes. In Hebrew there is properly but one term, *yam,* which is applied to all collections of water apparently stagnant, and which is generally translated "sea."

11. *The sea of Chinnereth.* The same as the sea of Galilee, Sea of Tiberias, and Sea of Gennesareth.

12. *The border shall go down to Jordan.* This river is famous in both the Old and New Testaments. It takes its rise at the foot of Mount Libanus, passes through the Sea of Chinnereth or Tiberias, and empties itself into the Lake Asphaltites or Dead Sea, from which it has no outlet. In and by it God wrought many miracles. God cut off the waters of this river as He did those of the Red Sea, so that they stood on a heap on each side, and the people passed over on dry ground. Both Elijah and Elisha separated its waters in a miraculous way, 2 Kings ii. 8-14. Naaman, the Syrian general, by washing in it at the command of the prophet, was miraculously cured of his leprosy, 2 Kings v. 10-14. In this

MATTHEW HENRY

their wonderful deliverance thence. 4. Their border is here made to begin at the *Salt Sea* (*v.* 3), and there it ends, *v.* 12. That pleasant fruitful vale in which these cities stood became a lake, which was never stirred by any wind, bore no vessels, was replenished with no fish, no living creature of any sort being found in it, therefore called the *Dead Sea.* 5. Their western border was the *Great Sea* (*v.* 6), which is now called the *Mediterranean.*

Verses 16–29

God here appoints commissioners for the dividing of the land to them. The conquest of it is taken for granted, though as yet there was never a stroke struck towards it. 1. The principal commissioners, who were of the *quorum,* were Eleazar and Joshua (*v.* 17). 2. Besides these, that there might be no suspicion of partiality, a prince of each tribe was appointed to inspect this matter, and to see that the tribe he served for was in no respect injured.

JAMIESON, FAUSSET, BROWN

present Sudud (Ezek. 17:15). **Ziphron**—(sweet odor); **Hazar-enan**—(village of fountains); but the places are unknown. "An imaginary line from mount Cassius, on the coast along the northern base of Lebanon to the entering into the Bekaa (Valley of Lebanon) at the Kamosa Hermel," must be regarded as the frontier that is meant [VAN DE VELDE]. **10-12. east border**—This is very clearly defined. Shephan and Riblah, which were in the valley of Lebanon, are mentioned as the boundary line, which commenced a little higher than the sources of the Jordan. Ain is supposed to be the source of that river; and thence the eastern boundary extended along the Jordan, the sea of Chinnereth (Lake of Tiberias), the Jordan; and again terminated at the Dead Sea. The line being drawn on the east of the river and the seas included those waters within the territory of the western tribes. **13-15. The two tribes and the half tribe have received their inheritance on this side Jordan**—The conquered territories of Sihon and Og, lying between the Arnon and mount Hermon, were allotted to them—that of Reuben in the most southerly part, Gad north of it, and the half Manasseh in the northernmost portion.

16-29. names of the men . . . who shall divide the land—This appointment by the Lord before the Jordan tended not only to animate the Israelites' faith in the certainty of the conquest, but to prevent all subsequent dispute and discontent, which might have been dangerous in presence of the natives. The nominees were ten princes for the nine and a half tribes, one of them being selected from the western section of Manasseh, and all subordinate to the great military and ecclesiastical chiefs, Joshua and Eleazar. The names are mentioned in the exact order in which the tribes obtained possession of the land, and according to *brotherly* connection.

ADAM CLARKE

river John baptized great multitudes of Jews; and in it was Christ himself baptized, and the Spirit of God descended upon Him, and the voice from heaven proclaimed Him the great and only Teacher and Saviour of men, Matt. iii. 16-17; Mark i. 5-11.

13. *This is the land which ye shall inherit by lot.* Much of what is said concerning this land is peculiarly emphatic. It is a land that contains a multitude of advantages in its climate, its soil, situation, etc. It is bounded on the south by a ridge of mountains, which separate it from Arabia, and screen it from the burning and often pestiferous winds which blow over the desert from that quarter. On the west it is bounded by the Mediterranean Sea; on the north, by Mount Libanus, which defends it from the cold northern blasts; and on the east by the river Jordan, and its fertile, well-watered plains. It is described by God himself as "a good land, a land of brooks of water, of fountains and depths that spring out of valleys and hills; a land of wheat, and barley, and vines, and fig trees, and pomegranates; a land of olive oil and honey"; a land wherein there was no scarcity of bread, and where both iron and copper mines abounded, Deut. viii. 7-9; a land finely diversified with hills and valleys, and well watered by the rain of heaven, in this respect widely different from Egypt; a land which God cared for, on which His eyes were continually placed from the beginning to the end of the year; watched over by a most merciful Providence; in a word, a land which flowed with milk and honey, and was the most pleasant of all lands, Deut. xi. 11-12; Ezek. xx. 6.

19, etc. *And the names of the men are these.* It is worthy of remark that Moses does not follow any order hitherto used of placing the tribes, neither that in chap. i, nor that in chap. vii, nor that in chap. xxvi, nor any other; but places them here exactly in that order in which they possessed the land: Judah, Simeon, Benjamin, Dan, Manasseh, Ephraim, Zebulun, Issachar, Asher, Naphtali. Judah is first, having the first lot; and he dwelt in the south part of the land, Josh. xv. 1, etc.; and next to him Simeon, because his inheritance was "within the inheritance of the children of Judah," Josh. xix. 1. Benjamin was third; he had his inheritance by Judah, "between the children of Judah and the children of Joseph," Josh. xviii. 11. Dan was the fourth; his lot fell westward of that of Benjamin, in the country of the Philistines, as may be seen in Josh. xix. 40-41, etc. Fifth, Manasseh; and sixth, by him, his brother, Ephraim, whose inheritances were behind that of Benjamin, Josh. xvi. 7. Next to these dwelt, seventh, Zebulun; and eighth, Issachar; concerning whose lots see Josh. xix. 10-17. Ninth, Asher; and tenth, Naphtali; see Josh. xix. 24, 32, etc. And as in encamping about the Tabernacle they were arranged according to their fraternal relationship, so they were in the division and inheriting of the Promised Land. Judah and Simeon, both sons of Leah, dwelt abreast of each other. Benjamin, son of Rachel, and Dan, son of Rachel's maid, dwelt next abreast. Manasseh and Ephraim, both sons of Joseph, son of Rachel, had the next place abreast. Zebulun and Issachar, who dwelt next together, were both sons of Leah; and the last pair were Asher, of Leah's maid, and Naphtali, of Rachel's maid. Thus God, in nominating princes that should divide the land, signified beforehand the manner of their possession, and that they should be so situated as to dwell together as brethren in unity, for the mutual help and comfort of each other.

MATTHEW HENRY — CHAPTER 35

Verses 1–8

The laws about the tithes and offerings had provided very plentifully for the maintenance of the Levites; but it was not to be thought, nor indeed was it for the public good, that when they came to Canaan they should all live about the tabernacle, as they had done in the wilderness, and therefore care must be taken to provide habitations for them, in which they might live comfortably and usefully. It is this which is here taken care of.

I. Cities were allotted them, with their suburbs, *v.* 2. They were not to have any ground for tillage.

JAMIESON, FAUSSET, BROWN — CHAPTER 35

VSS. 1-5. EIGHT AND FORTY CITIES GIVEN TO THE LEVITES. **2. give unto the Levites of the inheritance of their possession cities to dwell in**—As the Levites were to have no territorial domain allocated to them like the other tribes on the conquest of Canaan, they were to be distributed throughout the land in certain cities appropriated to their use; and these cities were to be surrounded by extensive suburbs. There is an apparent discrepancy between verses 4 and 5, with regard to the extent of these suburbs; but the statements in the two verses refer to totally different things—the one

ADAM CLARKE — CHAPTER 35

MATTHEW HENRY

1. Cities were allotted them, that they might live near together, and converse with one another about the law, and that in doubtful cases they might consult one another. 2. These cities had suburbs annexed to them for their cattle (*v.* 3), a thousand cubits from the wall was allowed them for out-houses to keep their cattle in, and then two thousand more for fields to graze their cattle in, *v.* 4, 5.

II. These cities were to be assigned them out of the possessions of each tribe, *v.* 8. 1. That each tribe might thus make a grateful acknowledgment to God. 2. That each tribe might have the benefit of the Levites dwelling among them, to *teach them the good knowledge of the Lord.*

III. The number allotted them was forty-eight in all, four out of each of the twelve tribes, one with another.

Verses 9–34

We have here the orders given concerning the cities of refuge. In this part of the constitution there is a great deal both of good law and pure gospel.

I. Here is a great deal of good law, in the case of murder and manslaughter.

1. That wilful murder should be punished with death, and in that case no sanctuary should be allowed, no ransom taken, nor any commutation of the punishment accepted. Where wrong has been done restitution must be made; and, since the murderer cannot restore the life he has wrongfully taken away, his own must be exacted from him in lieu of it, not (as some have fancied) to satisfy the manes or ghost of the person slain, but to satisfy the law and the justice of a nation, and to be a warning to all others not to do likewise. Not only the prosecution, but the execution, of the murderer, is committed to the next of kin, who, as he was to be the redeemer of his kinsman's estate if it were mortgaged, so he was to be the *avenger of his blood if he were murdered* (*v.* 19): *The avenger of blood himself shall slay the murderer.*

2. But if the homicide was not voluntary, nor done designedly, if it was *without enmity, or lying in wait* (*v.* 22), not *seeing* the person or not *seeking his harm* (*v.* 23), which our law calls chance-medley, or homicide *per infortunium—through misfortune*, in this case there were cities of refuge appointed for the man-slayer to flee to. By our law this incurs a forfeiture of goods, but a pardon is granted of course upon the special matter found. Concerning the cities of refuge the law was, (1) That, if a man killed another, in these cities he was safe, and under the protection of the law, till he had his trial *before the congregation*, that is, before the judges in open court. (2) If, upon trial, it were found to be wilful murder, the city of refuge should no longer be a protection to him; it was already determined: *Thou shalt take him from my altar, that he may die*, Exod. xxi. 14. (3) But if it were found to be by error or accident, and that the stroke was given without any design upon the life of the person slain or any other, then the man-slayer should continue safe in *the city of refuge*, and the avenger of blood might not meddle with him, *v.* 25. There he was to remain in banishment from his own house and patrimony *till the death of the high priest.* Now, [1] By the preservation of the life of the man-slayer God would teach us that men ought not to suffer for that which is rather their unhappiness than their crime. [2] By the banishment of the man-slayer from his own city, and his confinement to the city of refuge, God would teach us to conceive a dread and horror of the guilt of blood, and to be very careful of life. [3] By the limiting of the time of the offender's banishment to the death of the high priest, an honour was put upon that sacred office. The cities of refuge being all of them Levites' cities, and the high priest being the head of that tribe, those that were confined to them might properly be looked upon as his prisoners, and so his death must be their discharge.

JAMIESON, FAUSSET, BROWN

to the extent of the suburbs from the walls of the city, the other to the space of 2000 cubits from their extremity. In point of fact, there was an extent of ground, amounting to 3000 cubits, measured from the wall of the city. One thousand were most probably occupied with outhouses for the accommodation of shepherds and other servants, with gardens, vineyards, or oliveyards. And these which were portioned out to different families (I Chron. 6:60) might be sold by one Levite to another, but not to any individual of another tribe (Jer. 32:7). The other two thousand cubits remained a common for the pasturing of cattle (Lev. 25:34) and, considering their number, that space would be fully required.

6-8. CITIES OF REFUGE. **there shall be six cities for refuge, which ye shall appoint for the manslayer**—The establishment of those privileged sanctuaries among the cities of the Levites is probably traceable to the idea, that they would be the most suitable and impartial judges—that their presence and counsels might calm or restrain the stormy passions of the blood avenger—and that, from their being invested with the sacred character, they might be types of Christ, in whom sinners find a refuge from the destroyer (see Deut. 4:43; Josh. 20:8). **the cities which ye shall give shall be of the possession of the children of Israel**—The burden of furnishing those places for the residence and support of the Levitical order was to fall in equitable proportions upon the different tribes (see ch. 33:54; Josh. 20:7).

9-34. THE BLOOD AVENGER. **that the slayer may flee thither, which killeth any person at unawares**—The practice of Goelism, i.e., of the nearest relation of an individual who was killed being bound to demand satisfaction from the author of his death, existed from a very remote antiquity (Gen. 4:14; 27:45). It seems to have been an established usage in the age of Moses; and although in a rude and imperfect state of society, it is a natural and intelligible principle of criminal jurisprudence, it is liable to many great abuses; the chief of the evils inseparable from it is that the kinsman, who is bound in duty and honor to execute justice, will often be precipitate—little disposed, in the heat of passion or under the impulse of revenge, to examine into the circumstances of the case, to discriminate between the premeditated purpose of the assassin and the misfortune of the unintentional homicide. Moreover, it had a tendency, not only to foster a vindictive spirit, but in case of the Goel being unsuccessful in finding his victim, to transmit animosities and feuds against his descendants from one generation to another. This is exemplified among the Arabs in the present day. Should an Arab of one tribe happen to kill one of another tribe, there is "blood" between the tribes, and the stain can only be wiped out by the death of some individual of the tribe with which the offense originated. Sometimes the penalty is commuted by the payment of a stipulated number of sheep or camels. But such an equivalent, though offered, is as often refused, and blood has to be repaid only by blood. This practice of Goelism obtained among the Hebrews to such an extent that it was not perhaps expedient to abolish it; and Moses, while sanctioning its continuance, was directed, by divine authority, to make some special regulations, which tended both to prevent the unhappy consequences of sudden and personal vengeance, and, at the same time, to afford an accused person time and means of proving his innocence. This was the humane and equitable end contemplated in the institution of cities of refuge. There were to be six of these legalized asyla, three on the east of Jordan, both because the territory there was equal in length, though not in breadth, to Canaan, and because it might be more convenient for some to take refuge across the border. They were appointed for the benefit, not of the native Israelites only, but of all resident strangers. **16-21. If he smite him with an instrument of iron so that he die,** etc.—Various cases are here enumerated in which the Goel or avenger was at liberty to take the life of the murderer; and every one of them proves a premeditated purpose. **22-28. But if he thrust him suddenly without enmity, or have cast upon him any thing without laying of wait,** etc.—Under the excitement of a sudden provocation, or violent passion, an injury might be inflicted issuing in death; and for a person who had thus undesignedly committed slaughter, the Levitical cities offered the **benefit** of full protection. Once having reached the nearest, for one or other of them was within a day's journey of all parts of the land, he was secure. But he had to "abide in it." His confinement

ADAM CLARKE

4. *And the suburbs of the cities . . . shall reach from the wall of the city and outward a thousand cubits round about.*

5. *And ye shall measure from without the city . . . two thousand cubits.* Commentators have been much puzzled with the accounts in these two verses. In v. 4 the measure is said to be 1,000 cubits from the wall; in v. 5 the measure is said to be 2,000 from without the city. It is likely these two measures mean the same thing; at least so it was understood by the Septuagint and Coptic, who have 2,000 cubits in the fourth as well as in the fifth verse; but this reading of the Septuagint and Coptic is not acknowledged by any other of the ancient versions, nor by any of the MSS. collated by Kennicott and De Rossi. We must seek therefore for some other method of reconciling this apparently contradictory account. Sundry modes have been proposed by commentators, which appear to me, in general, to require fully as much explanation as the text itself. Maimonides is the only one intelligible on the subject. "The suburbs," says he, "of the cities are expressed in the law to be 3,000 cubits on every side from the wall of the city and outwards. The first thousand cubits are the suburbs, and the 2,000, which they measured without the suburbs, were for fields and vineyards."

11. *Ye shall appoint . . . cities of refuge.* The cities of refuge among the Israelites were widely different from the *asyla* among the Greeks and Romans, as also from the privileged altars among the Roman Catholics. Those among the Hebrews were for the protection of such only as had slain a person involuntarily. The temples and altars among the latter often served for the protection of the most profligate characters. Cities of refuge among the Hebrews were necessary because the old patriarchal law still remained in force, viz., that the nearest akin had a right to avenge the death of his relation by slaying the murderer; for the original law enacted that "whoso sheddeth man's blood, by man shall his blood be shed," Gen. ix. 6, and none was judged so proper to execute this law as the man who was nearest akin to the deceased.

12. *Until he stand before the congregation in judgment.* So one of these cities was not a perpetual asylum; it was only a *pro tempore* refuge, till the case could be fairly examined by the magistrates in the presence of the people, or the elders—their representatives; and this was done in the city or place where he had done the murder, Josh. xx. 4, 6. If he was found worthy of death, they delivered him to the avenger that he might be slain, Deut. xix. 12; if not, they sent him back to the city of refuge, where he remained till the death of the high priest, v. 25. Before the cities of refuge were appointed, the altar appears to have been a sanctuary for those who had killed a person unwittingly.

19. *The revenger of blood. Goel haddam,* the "redeemer of blood," the next in blood to him who was slain.

MATTHEW HENRY

II. Here is a great deal of good gospel couched under the type and figure of the cities of refuge; and to them the apostle seems to allude when he speaks of our *fleeing for refuge to the hope set before us* (Heb. vi. 18), and being *found in Christ*, Phil. iii. 9. 1. There were several cities of refuge, and they were so appointed in several parts of the country that the man-slayer, wherever he dwelt in the land of Israel, might in half a day reach one or other of them; so, though there is but one Christ appointed for our refuge, yet, wherever we are, he is a refuge at hand, a very present help, for *the word is nigh us* and Christ in the word. 2. The man-slayer was safe in any of these cities; so in Christ believers that flee to him, and rest in him, are protected from the wrath of God and the curse of the law. *There is no condemnation to those that are in Christ Jesus*, Rom. viii. 1. 3. They were all Levites' cities; it was a kindness to the poor prisoner that the Levites would comfort and encourage him, and bid him welcome; so it is the work of gospel ministers to bid poor sinners welcome to Christ, and to assist and counsel those that through grace are in him. 4. Even strangers and sojourners, though they were not native Israelites, might take the benefit of these cities of refuge, *v.* 15. So in Christ Jesus no difference is made between Greek and Jew. 5. Even the suburbs or borders of the city were a sufficient security to the offender, *v.* 26, 27. So there is virtue even in the hem of Christ's garment for the healing and saving of poor sinners.

JAMIESON, FAUSSET, BROWN

within its walls was a wise and salutary rule, designed to show the sanctity of human blood in God's sight, as well as to protect the manslayer himself, whose presence and intercourse in society might have provoked the passions of the deceased's relatives. But the period of his release from this confinement was not until the death of the high priest. That was a season of public affliction, when private sorrows were sunk or overlooked under a sense of the national calamity, and when the death of so eminent a servant of God naturally led all to serious consideration about their own mortality. The moment, however, that the refugee broke through the restraints of his confinement and ventured beyond the precincts of the asylum, he forfeited the privilege, and, if he was discovered by his pursuer, he might be slain with impunity. **29-34. these things shall be for a statute of judgment unto you throughout your generations**—The law of the blood avenger, as thus established by divine authority, was a vast improvement on the ancient practice of Goelism. By the appointment of cities of refuge, the manslayer was saved, in the meantime, from the blind and impetuous fury of vindictive relatives; but he might be tried by the local court, and, if proved guilty on sufficient evidence, condemned and punished as a murderer, without the possibility of deliverance by any pecuniary satisfaction. The enactment of Moses, which was an adaptation to the character and usages of the Hebrew people, secured the double advantage of promoting the ends both of humanity and of justice.

ADAM CLARKE

30. *But one witness shall not testify against any.* This was a just and necessary provision. One may be mistaken, or so violently prejudiced as to impose even on his own judgment, or so wicked as to endeavor through malice to compass the life of his neighbor, but it is not likely that two or more should be of this kind; and even were they, their separate examination would lead to a discovery of the truth, and to their conviction.

31. *Ye shall take no satisfaction for the life of a murderer.* No atonement could be made for him, nor any commutation, so as to save him from death.

32. *Until the death of the priest.* Probably intended to typify that no sinner can be delivered from his banishment from God, or recover his forfeited inheritance, till Jessus Christ, the great High Priest, had died for his offenses and risen again for his justification.

33. *For blood it defileth the land.* The very land was considered as guilty till the blood of the murderer was shed in it.

MATTHEW HENRY

CHAPTER 36

Verses 1-4

We have here the humble address which the heads of the tribe of Manasseh made to Moses and the princes, on occasion of the order lately made concerning the daughters of Zelophehad. 1. They fairly recite the former order made in this case, and do not move to have that set aside, but are very willing to acquiesce in it (*v.* 2). 2. They represent the inconvenience which might, possibly, follow hereupon, if the daughters of Zelophehad should see cause to marry into any other tribes, *v.* 3. Two things they aimed at in their representation:—(1) It would break in upon the divine appointment if such a considerable part of the lot of Manasseh should, by their marriage, be transferred to any other tribe. (2) To prevent contests and quarrels among posterity. If those of other tribes should come among them perhaps it might occasion some contests.

Verses 5-13

Here is, I. The matter settled by express order from God between the daughters of Zelophehad and the rest of the tribe of Manasseh. The petition is assented to, and care taken to prevent the inconvenience feared: *The tribe of the sons of Joseph hath said well, v.* 5. 1. They are not determined to any particular persons; there was choice enough in the family of their father: *Let them marry to whom they think best.* As children must preserve the authority of their parents, and not marry against their minds, so parents must consult the affections of their children in disposing of them, and not compel them to marry such as they cannot love. Forced marriages are not likely to prove blessings. 2. Yet they are confined to their own relations, that their inheritance may not go to another family.

II. The law, in this particular case, was made perpetual.

III. The submission of the daughters of Zelophehad to this appointment.

IV. The conclusion of this whole book, referring to the latter part of it. Whatever new condition God is by his providence bringing us into, we must beg of him to teach us the duty of it, and to enable us to do it, that we may do the work of the day in its day, of the place in its place.

JAMIESON, FAUSSET, BROWN

CHAPTER 36

Vss. 1-13. THE INCONVENIENCE OF THE INHERITANCE. **1. the chief fathers of the families of the children of Gilead**—Being the tribal governors in Manasseh, they consulted Moses on a case that affected the public honor and interests of their tribe. It related once more to the daughters of Zelophehad. Formerly they had applied, at their own instance, to be recognized, for want of male heirs in their family, as entitled to inherit their father's property; now the application was made on behalf of the tribe to which they belonged—that steps might be taken to prevent the alienation of their patrimony by their alliance with husbands of another tribe. The unrestricted marriages of daughters in such circumstances threatened seriously to affect the tenure of land in Israel, as their inheritance would go to their children, who, by the father's side, would belong to another tribe, and thus lead, through a complication of interests and the confusion of families, to an evil for which even the Jubilee could not afford a remedy. (See on Lev. 25:13.) **5-12. Moses commanded the children of Israel according to the word of the Lord**—The plea appeared just and reasonable; and, accordingly an enactment was made by which the daughters of Zelophehad, while left to the free choice of their husbands, were restricted to marry not only within their own tribe, but *within the family* of their father's tribe—i.e., one of their cousins. This restriction, however, was imposed only on those who were heiresses. The law was not applicable to daughters in different circumstances (I Chron. 23:22)—for they might marry into another tribe; but if they did so, they were liable to forfeit their patrimonial inheritance, which, on the death of their father or brothers, went to the nearest of the family kinsmen. Here was an instance of progressive legislation (see also Exod. ch. 18:27) in Israel, the enactments made being suggested by circumstances. But it is deserving ot special notice that those additions to, or modifications of, the law were confined to civil affairs; while the slightest change was inadmissible in the laws relating to worship or the maintenance of religion. **13. These are the commandments and the judgments, which the Lord commanded by the hand of Moses unto the children of Israel in the plains of Moab**—The Israelitish encampment was on an extensive plateau north of the Arnon, which, though wrested from the Moabites by Sihon and Og, still retained the name of its original possessors. The particular site, as indicated by the words "Jordan near Jericho," is now called El-Koura—a large plain lying not far from Nebo, between the Arnon and a small tributary stream, the Wael [BURCKHARDT]. It was a desert plain on the eastern bank, and marked only by groves of the wild, thorny acacia tree.

ADAM CLARKE

CHAPTER 36

2. *To give the inheritance of Zelophehad . . . unto his daughters.* See this case spoken of at large on chap. xxvii. Either the first eleven verses of chap. xxvii should come in before this chapter or this chapter should come in immediately after those eleven verses; they certainly both make parts of the same subject. Here Moses determines that heiresses should marry in their own tribe, that no part of the ancient inheritance might be alienated from the original family.

6. *Let them marry to whom they think best.* Here was latitude sufficient, and yet a salutary and reasonable restraint, which prevented a vexatious mixture of property and possession.

8. *Every daughter, that possesseth an inheritance.* This law affected none but heiresses; all others were at liberty to marry into any of the other tribes. The priests and Levites, who could have no inheritance, were exempt from the operation of this law. Jehoiada had the king of Judah's daughter to wife, 2 Chron. xxii. 11. And another priest had for wife one of the daughters of Barzillai the Gileadite, Ezra ii. 61.

THE BOOK OF DEUTERONOMY

I. Retrospect (1:1-4:43)
- *A. Introduction—the place (1:1-5)*
- *B. The discourse (1:6-4:40)*
  - 1. Review of the forty years (1:6-3:29)
  - 2. Exhortation to obedience (4:1-40)
    - a. Retrospective (4:1-24)
    - b. Prospective (4:25-31)
    - c. Introspective (4:32-40)
- *C. Sequel—cities of refuge (4:41-43)*

II. Resume of laws (4:44-27:10)
- *A. Introduction—character and place (4:44-49)*
- *B. The discourse (5:1-26:19)*
  - 1. "Testimonies" (5:1-11:31)
    - a. The Decalogue (5:1-6:25)
    - b. Obedience (7:1-11:31)
  - 2. "Statutes" (11:32-16:17)
    - a. Worship (11:32-14:2)
    - b. Some effects of worship on conduct (14:3-16:17)
  - 3. "Judgments" (16:18-26:19)
    - a. Principles of law (16:18-20)
    - b. Administration of law (16:21-26:19)
- *B. Sequel—provision for the land (27:1-10)*

III. Warnings (27:11-28:68)
- *A. Introduction—the curses (27:11-26)*
- *B. The discourse (28:1-68)*
  - 1. The blessing of obedience (28:1-14)
  - 2. The cursing of disobedience (28:15-68)

IV. The Covenant (29:1-31:13)
- *A. Introduction (29:1-2a)*
- *B. The discourse (29:2b-30:20)*
  - 1. The appeal of the past (29:2b-9)
  - 2. The terms of the covenant (29:10-29)
  - 3. The appeal of the future (30:1-20)
- *C. Sequel (31:1-13)*

V. The song (31:14-32:47)
- *A. Introduction (31:14-30)*
- *B. The song (32:1-43)*
  - 1. Introduction (32:1-3a)
  - 2. A contrast (32:3b-5)
  - 3. An appeal (32:6a)
  - 4. A contrast (32:6b-18)
  - 5. Judgment (32:19-28)
  - 6. Lament (32:29-30)
  - 7. Final deliverance (32:31-43)
- *C. Sequel (32:44-47)*

VI. The blessing (32:48-33:29)
- *A. Introduction (32:48-52)*
- *B. The blessing (33:1-29)*

VII. Historical conclusion (34:1-12)

This book is a repetition of much of the history and the laws contained in the three preceding books. There is no new history in it except that of the death of Moses in the last chapter. But the former laws are repeated and commented upon, explained and enlarged, and some particular precepts added to them, with abundant reasonings for the enforcing of them. The Greek interpreters call it Deuteronomy, which signifies the *second law*, or a *second edition of the law*, not with amendments, for there needed none, but with additions, for the further direction of the people in various cases not mentioned before.

It was much for the honor of the divine law that it should be thus repeated. There might be a particular reason for the repeating of it now; the men of that generation to which the law was first given were all dead, and a new generation had sprung up to whom God would have it repeated by Moses himself, that, if possible, it might make a lasting impression upon them. Now that they were going to take possession of the land of Canaan, Moses must read the articles of agreement to them that they might know upon what terms and conditions they were to hold and enjoy that land. It would be of great use to the people to have those parts of the law thus gathered up and put together which did more immediately concern them and their practice; for the laws which concerned the priests and Levites and the execution of their offices are not repeated. The great and needful truths of the gospel should be often pressed upon people by the ministers of Christ. "To write the same things [says Paul, Phil. 3:1] to me indeed is not grievous, but for you it is safe." What God has spoken once we have need to hear twice, to hear many times, and it is well if, after all, it be duly perceived and regarded. The gospel is a kind of Deuteronomy, a second law, a remedial law, a spiritual law, a law of faith.

This book of Deuteronomy begins with a brief rehearsal of the most remarkable events that had befallen the Israelites since they came from Mount Sinai. In the fourth chapter we have a most pathetic exhortation to obedience. In the twelfth chapter, and so on to the twenty-seventh, are repeated many particular laws, which are enforced (chs. 27, 28) with promises and threatenings, blessings and curses, formed into a covenant (chs. 29, 30). Care is taken to perpetuate the remembrance of these things among them (ch. 31), particularly by a song (ch. 32), and so Moses concludes with a blessing (ch. 33). All this was delivered by Moses to Israel in the last month of his life. When our Savior would answer the devil's temptations with, "It is written," he fetched all his quotations out of this book (Matt. 4:4, 7, 10).

MATTHEW HENRY

CHAPTER 1

Verses 1–8

We have here, I. The date of this sermon which Moses preached to the people of Israel. 1. The place where they were now encamped was *in the plain, in the land of Moab* (*v.* 1, 5), where they were just ready to enter Canaan, and engage in a war with the Canaanites. Yet he discourses not to them concerning military affairs, but concerning their duty to God.

JAMIESON, FAUSSET, BROWN

CHAPTER 1

Vss. 1-46. MOSES' SPEECH AT THE END OF THE FORTIETH YEAR. **1. These be the words which Moses spake unto all Israel**—The mental condition of the people generally in that infantine age of the Church, and the greater number of them being of young or tender years, rendered it expedient to repeat the laws and counsels which God had given. Accordingly, to furnish a recapitulation of the leading branches of their faith and duty was among the last public services which Moses rendered to Israel. The scene of their delivery was on the plains of Moab where the encampment was pitched "on this side Jordan," or, as the Hebrew word may be rendered "on the bank of the Jordan." **in the wilderness, in the plain**—the Arabah, a desert plain, or steppe, extended the whole way from the Red Sea north to the Sea of Tiberias. While the high tablelands of Moab were "cultivated fields," the Jordan valley, at the foot of the mountains where Israel was encamped, was a part of the great desert plain, little more inviting than the desert of Arabia. The locale is indicated by the names of the most prominent places around it. Some of these places are unknown to us. The Hebrew word, *Suph*, red (for "sea," which our translators have inserted, is not in the original, and Moses was now farther from the Red Sea than ever), probably meant a place noted for its reeds (Num. 21:14). **Tophel**—identified as Tafyle or Tafeilah, lying between Bozrah and Kerak. Hazeroth is a different place from

ADAM CLARKE

CHAPTER 1

1. *These be the words which Moses spake.* The first five verses of this chapter contain the introduction to the rest of the book; they do not appear to be the work of Moses, but were added probably by either Joshua or Ezra.

On this side Jordan. Beeber, "at the passage" of Jordan, i.e., near or opposite to the place where the Israelites passed over after the death of Moses. Though *eber* is used to signify both on "this side" and on "the other side," and the connection in which it stands can only determine the meaning, yet here it signifies neither, but simply the place or ford where the Israelites passed over Jordan. *In the plain.* That is, of Moab; *over against the Red sea*—not the Red Sea, for they were now farther from it than they had been: the word *sea* is not in the text, and the word *suph,* which we render *red,* does not signify the Red Sea, unless joined with *yam,* "sea"; here it must necessarily signify a place in or adjoining to the plains of Moab. *Paran.* This could not have been the Paran which was contiguous to the Red Sea, and not far from Mount Horeb; for the place here mentioned lay on the very borders of the Promised Land, at a vast distance from the former. *Dizahab.* The word should be separated, as it is in the Hebrew, *Di Zahab.* As *Zahab* signifies "gold," the Septuagint have translated it "the

MATTHEW HENRY

The time was near the end of the fortieth year since they came out of Egypt. Now that a new and more pleasant scene was to be introduced, as a token for good, Moses repeats the law to them.

II. The discourse itself. In general, Moses spoke unto them *all that the Lord had given him in commandment* (*v.* 3). He begins his narrative with their removal from Mount Sinai (*v.* 6), and relates here, 1. The orders which God gave them to decamp, and proceed in their march (*v.* 6, 7): *You have dwelt long enough in this mount.* Thither God brought them to humble them, and by the terrors of the law to prepare them for the land of promise. Though God brings his people into spiritual trouble and affliction of mind, he knows when they have dwelt long enough in it, and will certainly find a time, to advance them from the terrors of the spirit of bondage to the comforts of the spirit of adoption. See Rom. viii. 15. 2. The prospect which he gave them of a happy and early settlement in Canaan. When God commands us to go forward in our Christian course he sets the heavenly Canaan before us for our encouragement.

Verses 9–18

Moses here reminds them of the happy constitution of their government, which was such as might make them all safe and easy if it was not their own fault. In this part of his narrative he insinuates to them,

I. That he greatly rejoiced in the increase of their numbers. He owns the accomplishment of God's promise to Abraham (*v.* 10): *You are as the stars of heaven for multitude* (*v.* 11): *God make you a thousand times more.* We are not straitened in the power and goodness of God, why should we be straitened in our own faith and hope, which ought to be as large as the promise? larger they need not be. They might become a thousand times more than they were now when they were now ten thousand times more than they were when they went down into Egypt.

II. That he was not ambitious of monopolizing the honour of the government, and ruling them himself alone, as an absolute monarch, *v.* 9.

III. That he was not desirous to prefer his own creatures, or such as should have a dependence upon him; for he leaves it to the people to choose their own judges, to whom he would grant commissions. He directs them to *take wise men and understanding,* whose personal merit would recommend them.

IV. That he was in this matter very willing to please the people. And they agreed to the proposal. The government they quarrelled with was what they themselves had consented to.

V. That he aimed to edify them as well as to gratify them; for,

1. He appointed men of good characters (*v.* 15), *wise men and men known,* men that would be faithful to their trust and to the public interest.

2. He gave them a good charge, *v.* 16, 17. (1) He charges them to be diligent and patient. Hear both sides, hear them fully, hear them carefully; for nature has provided us with two ears. The ear of the learner is necessary to the tongue of the learned, Isa. l. 4. (2) To be just and impartial. No faces must be known in judgment, but unbribed unbiassed equity must always pass sentence. (3) To be resolute and courageous. You are God's vicegerents, you act for him, and therefore must act like him; you are his representatives, but, if you judge unrighteously, you misrepresent him.

3. He allowed them to bring all difficult cases to him, and he would always be ready to hear and determine, and to make both the judges and the people easy.

Verses 19–46

Moses here makes a large rehearsal of the fatal turn which was given to their affairs by their own sins. It was a memorable story; we read it Num. xiii. and xiv., but divers circumstances are found here which are not related there.

I. He reminds them of their march from Horeb to Kadesh-barnea (*v.* 19), through *that great and terrible wilderness.* This he takes notice of to make them sensible of the great goodness of God to them, in guiding them through so great a wilderness. The remembrance of our dangers should make us thankful for our deliverances.

II. He shows them how fair they stood for Canaan at that time, *v.* 20, 21. He lets them see how near they were to a happy settlement when they put a bar in their own door.

JAMIESON, FAUSSET, BROWN

that at which the Israelites encamped after leaving "the desert of Sinai." **2. There are eleven days' journey from Horeb**—Distances are computed in the East still by the hours or days occupied by the journey. A day's journey on foot is about twenty miles—on camels, at the rate of three miles an hour, thirty miles—and by caravans, about twenty-five miles. But the Israelites, with children and flocks, would move at a slow rate. The length of the Ghor from Ezion-geber to Kadesh is 100 miles. The days here mentioned were not necessarily successive days [ROBINSON], for the journey can be made in a much shorter period. But this mention of the *time* was made to show that the great number of years spent in travelling from Horeb to the plain of Moab was not owing to the length of the way, but to a very different cause; viz., banishment for their apostasy and frequent rebellions. **mount Seir**—the mountainous country of Edom. **3-8. in the fortieth year . . . Moses spake unto the children of Israel,** etc.—This impressive discourse, in which Moses reviewed all that God had done for His people, was delivered about a month before his death, and after peace and tranquillity had been restored by the complete conquest of Sihon and Og. **Ashtaroth**—the royal residence of Og, so called from Astarte (the moon), the tutelary goddess of the Syrians. Og was slain at Edrei—now Edhra, the ruins of which are fourteen miles in circumference [BURCKHARDT]; its general breadth is about two leagues. **5. On this side Jordan, in the land of Moab, began Moses to declare this law**—declare, i.e., explain this law. He follows the same method here that he elsewhere observes; viz., that of first enumerating the marvellous doings of God in behalf of His people, and reminding them what an unworthy requital they had made for all His kindness—then he rehearses the law and its various precepts. **6. The Lord our God spake unto us in Horeb, saying, Ye have dwelt long enough in this mount**—Horeb was the general name of a mountainous district—lit., "the parched or burnt region," whereas Sinai was the name appropriated to a particular peak. About a year had been spent among the recesses of that wild solitude, in laying the foundation, under the immediate direction of God, of a new and peculiar community, as to its social, political, and, above all, religious character; and when this purpose had been accomplished, they were ordered to break up their encampment in Horeb. The command given them was to march straight to Canaan, and possess it. **8. I have set the land before you**—lit., before your faces—it is accessible—there is no impediment to your occupation. **The order of the journey as indicated by the places mentioned would have led to a course of invasion, the opposite of what was eventually followed; viz., from the seacoast eastward—instead of from the Jordan westward (see on Num. 20:1). 7. the mount of the Amorites**—the hilly tract lying next to Kadesh-barnea in the south of Canaan. **to the land of the Canaanites, and unto Lebanon**—i.e., Phœnicia, the country of Sidon, and the coast of the Mediterranean—from the Philistines to Lebanon. The name Canaanite is often used synonymously with that of Phœnician. **9-18. I spake unto you at that time, saying, I am not able to bear you myself alone**—a little before their arrival in Horeb. Moses addresses that new generation as the representatives of their fathers, in whose sight and hearing all the transactions he recounts took place. A reference is here made to the suggestion of Jethro (Exod. 18: 18). In noticing his practical adoption of a plan by which the administration of justice was committed to a select number of subordinate officers, Moses, by a beautiful allusion to the patriarchal blessing, ascribed the necessity of that memorable change in the government to the vast increase of the population. **ye are this day as the stars . . . for multitude**—This was neither an Oriental hyperbole nor a mere empty boast. Abraham was told (Gen. 15:5, 6) to look to the stars, and though they *appear* innumerable, yet those seen by the naked eye amount, in reality, to no more than 3010 in both hemispheres. The Israelites already far exceeded that number, being at the last census above 600,000. It was a seasonable memento, calculated to animate their faith in the accomplishment of other parts of the divine promise. **19-21. we went through all that great and terrible wilderness**—of Paran, which included the desert and mountainous space lying between the wilderness of Shur westward, or towards Egypt and mount Seir, or the land of Edom eastwards; between the land of Canaan northwards, and the Red Sea southwards; and thus it appears to have comprehended really the wilderness of Sin and Sinai [FISK]. It is called by the Arabs El Tih, "the

ADAM CLARKE

gold mines"; and the Vulgate, "where there is much gold." It is more likely to be the name of a place.

2. *There are eleven days' journey.* The Israelites were eleven days in going from Horeb to Kadesh-barnea, where they were near the verge of the Promised Land; after which they were thirty-eight years wandering up and down in the vicinity of this place, not being permitted, because of their rebellions, to enter into the promised rest, though they were the whole of that time within a few miles of the land of Canaan!

3. *The fortieth year.* This was a melancholy year to the Hebrews in different respects; in the first month of this year Miriam died, Numbers xx.; on the first day of the fifth month Aaron died, Num. xxxiii. 38; and about the conclusion of it, Moses himself died.

5. *Began Moses to declare this law. Began, hoil,* "willingly undertook"; *to declare, beer,* "to make bare, clear," "fully to explain," *this law.*

6. *Ye have dwelt long enough.* They came to Sinai in the third month after their departure from Egypt, Exod. xix. 1-2, and left it the twentieth of the second month of the second year; so it appears they had continued there nearly a whole year.

7. *Go to the mount of the Amorites.* On the south of the land of Canaan, towards the Dead Sea. *The river Euphrates.* Thus Moses fixes the bounds of the land, to which on all quarters the territories of the Israelites might be extended should the land of Canaan, properly so called, be found insufficient for them. Their south border might extend to the mount of the Amorites, their west to the borders of the Mediterranean Sea, their north to Lebanon, and their east border to the river Euphrates; and to this extent Solomon reigned; see 1 Kings iv. 21. So that in his time, at least, the promise to Abraham was literally fulfilled.

10. *Ye are this day as the stars of heaven for multitude.* This was the promise God made to Abraham, Gen. xv. 5-6; and Moses considers it now as amply fulfilled. But was it really so? Many suppose the expression to be hyperbolical; and others, no friends to revelation, think it a vain, empty boast, because the stars amount to innumerable millions. Let us consider this subject. How many in number are the stars which appear to the naked eye? For it is by what appears to the naked eye we are to be governed in this business, for God brought Abraham forth abroad, i.e., out of doors, and bade him look towards heaven, not with a telescope, but with his naked eyes, Gen. xv. 5. Now I shall beg the objector to come forth abroad, and look up in the brightest and most favorable night, and count the stars; and I shall pledge myself to find a male Israelite in the very last census taken of this people, Numbers xxvi., for every star he finds in the whole upper hemisphere of heaven. The truth is, only about 3,010 stars can be seen by the naked eye in both the northern and southern hemispheres; and the Israelites, independently of women and children, were at the above time more than 600,000.

13. *Take you wise men. Chachamim,* such as had gained knowledge by great labor and study. *Understanding, nebonim,* persons of discernment, judicious men. *Known, yeduim,* persons practiced in the operations of nature, capable of performing important works.

15. *Captains over thousands.* What a well-regulated economy was that of the Israelites! See its order and arrangement: (1) God, the King and Supreme Judge; (2) Moses, God's prime minister; (3) The priests, consulting Him by *Urim* and *Thummim;* (4) The chiefs or princes of the twelve tribes; (5) Chiliarchs, or captains over thousands; (6) Centurions, or captains over hundreds; (7) Tribunes, or captains over fifty men; (8) Decurions, or captains over ten men; and (9) Officers, persons who might be employed by the different chiefs in executing particular commands. All these held their authority from God, and yet were subject and accountable to each other.

17. *Ye shall not respect persons.* Hebrew,

MATTHEW HENRY

III. He lays the blame of sending the spies upon them, which did not appear in Numbers; there it is said (*ch.* xiii. 1, 2) that the Lord directed the sending of them, but here we find that the people first desired it, and God, in permitting it, gave them up to their counsels: *You said, We will send men before us, v.* 22. Moses had given them God's word (*v.* 20, 21), but they could not find in their hearts to rely upon that: human policy goes further with them than divine wisdom, and they will needs light a candle to the sun.

IV. He repeats the report which the spies brought of the goodness of the land which they were sent to survey, *v.* 24, 25. Yet they represented the difficulties of conquering it as insuperable (*v.* 28).

V. He tells them what pains he took with them to encourage them, when their brethren had said so much to discourage them (*v.* 29). He assured them that God was present with them. And for proof of his power over their enemies he refers them to what they had seen done in Egypt. And for proof of God's goodwill to them he refers them to what *they had seen in the wilderness* (*v.* 31, 33), through which they had been guided with as much care and tenderness as were ever shown to any child borne in the arms of a nursing father. And was there any room left to distrust this God?

VI. He charges them with the sin which they were guilty of upon this occasion. 1. Disobedience, and rebellion against God's law. 2. Invidious reflections upon God's goodness. 3. An unbelieving heart at the bottom of all this: *You did not believe the Lord your God, v.* 32.

VII. He repeats the sentence passed upon them. 1. They were all condemned to die in the wilderness, and none of them must be suffered to enter Canaan except Caleb and Joshua, *v.* 34–38. It was not the breach of any of the commands of the law that shut them out of Canaan, no, not the golden calf, but their disbelief of that promise which was typical of gospel grace, to signify that no sin will ruin us but unbelief, which is a sin against the remedy. 2. Moses himself afterwards fell under God's displeasure for a hasty word which they provoked him to speak: *The Lord was angry with me for your sakes, v.* 37. 3. Yet here is mercy mixed with wrath. (1) That, though Moses might not bring them into Canaan, Joshua should (*v.* 38): (2) That, though this generation should not enter into Canaan, the next should, *v.* 39.

VIII. He reminds them of their foolish and fruitless attempt to get this sentence reversed when it was too late. 1. They tried it by their reformation in this particular; whereas they had refused to go up against the Canaanites, now they would go up. But this, which looked like a reformation, proved but a further rebellion. They were chased and destroyed. 2. They tried by their prayers and tears to get the sentence reversed: *They returned and wept before the Lord, v.* 45. These were tears of repentance and humiliation *before* God. But their weeping was all to no purpose. *The Lord would not hearken to your voice,* because you would not hearken to his.

JAMIESON, FAUSSET, BROWN

wandering." It is a dreary waste of rock and of calcareous soil covered with black sharp flints; all travellers, from a feeling of its complete isolation from the world, describe it as a great and terrible wilderness. **22-33. ye came . . . and said, We will send men before us, and they shall search us out the land**—The proposal to despatch spies emanated from the people through unbelief; but Moses, believing them sincere, gave his cordial assent to this measure, and God on being consulted permitted them to follow the suggestion (see on Num. 13:1, 2). The issue proved disastrous to them, only through their own sin and folly. **28. the cities are great, and walled up to heaven**—an Oriental metaphor, meaning very high. The Arab marauders roam about on horseback, and hence the walls of St. Catherine's monastery on Sinai are so lofty that travellers are drawn up by a pulley in a basket. **Anakims**—(see on Num. 13:33). The honest and uncompromising language of Moses, in reminding the Israelites of their perverse conduct and outrageous rebellion at the report of the treacherous and faint-hearted scouts, affords a strong evidence of the truth of this history as well as of the divine authority of his mission. There was great reason for his dwelling on this dark passage in their history, as it was their unbelief that excluded them from the privilege of entering the promised land (Heb. 3: 19); and that unbelief was a marvellous exhibition of human perversity, considering the miracles which God had wrought in their favor, especially in the daily manifestations they had of His presence among them as their leader and protector. **34-36. the Lord heard the voice of your words, and was wroth**—In consequence of this aggravated offense (unbelief followed by open rebellion), the Israelites were doomed, in the righteous judgment of God, to a life of wandering in that dreary wilderness till the whole adult generation had disappeared by death. The only exceptions mentioned are Caleb and Joshua, who was to be Moses' successor. **37. Also the Lord was angry with me for your sakes**—This statement *seems* to indicate that it was on this occasion Moses was condemned to share the fate of the people. But we know that it was several years afterwards that Moses betrayed an unhappy spirit of distrust at the waters of strife (Ps. 106:32, 33). This verse must be considered therefore as a parenthesis. **39. your children . . . who in that day had no knowledge between good and evil**—All ancient versions read "to-day" instead of "that day"; and the sense is—"your children who now know," or "who know not *as yet* good or evil." As the children had not been partakers of the sinful outbreak, they were spared to obtain the privilege which their unbelieving parents had forfeited. God's ways are not as man's ways. **40-45. turn you, and take your journey into the wilderness by the . . . Red Sea**—This command they disregarded, and, determined to force an onward passage in spite of the earnest remonstrances of Moses, they attempted to cross the heights then occupied by the combined forces of the Amorites and Amalekites (cf. Num. 14:43), but were repulsed with great loss. People often experience distress even while in the way of duty. But how different their condition who suffer in situations where God is with them from the feelings of those who are conscious that they are in a position directly opposed to the divine will! The Israelites were grieved when they found themselves involved in difficulties and perils; but their sorrow arose not from a sense of the guilt so much as the sad effects of their perverse conduct; and "though they wept," they were not true penitents. So the Lord would not hearken to their voice, nor give ear unto them. **46. So ye abode at Kadesh many days**—That place had been the site of their encampment during the absence of the spies, which lasted forty days, and it is supposed from this verse that they prolonged their stay there after their defeat for a similar period.

ADAM CLARKE

"faces." Let not the bold, daring countenance of the rich or mighty induce you to give an unrighteous decision; and let not the abject look of the poor man induce you either to favor him in an unrighteous cause or to give judgment against him at the demand of the oppressor. Be uncorrupt and incorruptible, for *the judgment is God's.* You minister in the place of God; act like Him.

22. *We will send men before us.* See on Numbers xiii.

28. *Cities . . . walled up to heaven.* That is, with very high walls which could not be easily scaled.

34. *The Lord . . . was wroth.* That is, His justice was incensed, and He evidenced His displeasure against you; and He could not have been a just God if He had not done so.

36. *Caleb . . . wholly followed the Lord.* See on Num. xiv. 24.

37. *The Lord was angry with me.* See on Num. xx. 10, etc., where a particular account is given of the sin of Moses.

44. *The Amorites . . . chased you.* See the note on Num. xiv. 40; *as bees do*—by irresistible numbers.

46. *According unto the days that ye abode there.* They had been a long time at this place; see Num. xiii. 27; xx. 1, 14, 21. And some think that the words mean, "Ye abode as long at Kadesh, when you came to it the second time, as ye did at the first." Or, according to others, "While ye were in that part of the desert, ye encamped at Kadesh."

MATTHEW HENRY — CHAPTER 2

Verses 1–7

I. A short account of the long stay of Israel in the wilderness: *We compassed Mount Seir many days, v.* 1. Nearly *thirty-eight* years they wandered in the deserts of Seir; probably in some of their rests they stayed several years.

JAMIESON, FAUSSET, BROWN — CHAPTER 2

Vss. 1-37. The Story Is Continued. **1. Then we turned, and took our journey into the wilderness by the way of the Red Sea.** After their unsuccessful attack upon the Canaanites, the Israelites broke up their encampment at Kadesh, and journeying southward over the west desert of Tih as well as through the great valley of the Ghor and Arabah, they extended their removals as far as the gulf of Akaba. **we compassed mount Seir many days**—In these few words Moses comprised the whole of that wandering nomadic life through which they passed during 38 years, shifting from place to place, and reg-

ADAM CLARKE — CHAPTER 2

MATTHEW HENRY

II. Orders given them to turn towards Canaan.

III. A charge given them not to annoy the Edomites. 1. They must not offer any hostility to them as enemies: *Meddle not with them, v.* 4, 5.

2. They must trade with them as neighbours, buy meat and water of them, and pay for what they bought, *v.* 6. Religion must never be made a cloak for injustice.

Verses 8–23

It is observable here that Moses, speaking of the Edomites (*v.* 8), calls them *our brethren, the children of Esau.* Though they had been unkind to Israel, in refusing them a peaceable passage through their country, yet he calls them brethren. Now in these verses we have,

I. The account which Moses gives of the origin of the Moabites, Edomites, and Ammonites. Here he tells us how they came to those countries in which Israel found them; they were not the *aborigines*, or first planters. But, 1. The Moabites dwelt in a country which had belonged to a numerous race of giants, called *Emim* (that is, *terrible ones*), as tall as the Anakim, and perhaps more fierce, *v.* 10, 11. 2. The Edomites in like manner dispossessed the Horim from Mount Seir, and took their country (*v.* 12 and again *v.* 22), of which we read, Gen. xxxvi. 20. 3. The Ammonites likewise got possession of a country that had formerly been inhabited by giants, called *Zamzummim, crafty men*, or *wicked men* (*v.* 20, 21), probably the same that are called *Zuzim*, Gen. xiv. 5. He illustrates these remarks by an instance older than any of these; the Caphtorim (who were akin to the Philistines, Gen. x. 14) drove the Avim out of their country, and took possession of it, *v.* 23. The learned bishop Patrick supposes these Avites, being expelled hence, to have settled in Assyria, and to be the same people we read of under that name, 2 Kings xvii. 31.

II. The advances which Israel made towards Canaan. They *passed by the way of the wilderness of Moab* (*v.* 8), and then went over the brook or vale of Zered (*v.* 13), and there Moses takes notice of the fulfilling of the word which God had spoken concerning them, that none of those that were numbered at Mount Sinai should see the land that God had promised, Num. xiv. 23.

JAMIESON, FAUSSET, BROWN

ulating their stations by the prospect of pasturage and water. Within the interval they went northward a second time to Kadesh, but being refused a passage through Edom and opposed by the Canaanites and Amalekites, they again had no alternative but to traverse once more the great Arabah southwards to the Red Sea, where turning to the left and crossing the long, lofty mountain chain to the eastward of Ezion-geber (Num. 21:4, 5), they issued into the great and elevated plains, which are still traversed by the Syrian pilgrims in their way to Mecca. They appear to have followed northward nearly the same route, which is now taken by the Syrian hadji, along the western skirts of this great desert, near the mountains of Edom [ROBINSON]. It was on entering these plains they received the command, "Ye have compassed this mountain (this hilly tract, now Jebel Shera) long enough, turn ye northward." **4. the children of Esau which dwell in Seir . . . shall be afraid of you**—The same people who had haughtily repelled the approach of the Israelites from the western frontier were alarmed now that they had come round upon the weak side of their country. **5. Meddle not with them**—i.e., "which dwell in Seir" (vs. 4)—for there was another branch of Esau's posterity, viz., the Amalekites, who were to be fought against and destroyed (Gen. 36:12; Exod. 17: 14; Deut. 25:17). But the people of Edom were not to be injured, either in their persons or property. And although the approach of so vast a nomadic horde as the Israelites naturally created apprehension, they were to take no advantage of the prevailing terror to compel the Edomites to accept whatever terms they imposed. They were merely to pass "through" or along their border, and to buy meat and water of them for money (vs. 6). The people, kinder than their king, did sell them bread, meat, fruits, and water in their passage along their border (vs. 29), in the same manner as the Syrian caravan of Mecca is now supplied by the people of the same mountains, who meet the pilgrims as at a fair or market on the hadji route [ROBINSON]. Although the Israelites still enjoyed a daily supply of the manna, there was no prohibition against their eating other food when opportunity afforded. Only they were not to cherish an inordinate desire for it. Water is a scarce commodity and is often paid for by travellers in those parts. It was the more incumbent on the Israelites to do so, as, by the blessing of God, they possessed plenty of means to purchase, and the long-continued experience of the extraordinary goodness of God to them, should inspire such confidence in Him as would suppress the smallest thought of resorting to fraud or violence in supplying their wants. **8-18. we passed . . . through the way of the plain**—the Arabah or great valley, from Elath (trees), (the Ailah of the Greeks and Romans). The site of it is marked by extensive mounds of rubbish. Ezion-geber, now Akaba, both were within the territory of Edom; and after making a circuit of its southeastern boundary, the Israelites reached the border of Moab on the southeast of the Salt Sea. They had been forbidden by divine command to molest the Moabites in any way; and this special honor was conferred on that people not on their own account, for they were very wicked, but in virtue of their descent from Lot. (See on ch. 23:3.) Their territory comprised the fine country on the south, and partly on the north of the Arnon. They had won it by their arms from the original inhabitants, the Emims, a race, terrible, as their name imports, for physical power and stature (Gen. 14:5), in like manner as the Edomites had obtained their settlement by the overthrow of the original occupiers of Seir, the Horims (Gen. 14: 6), who were troglodytes, or dwellers in caves. Moses alluded to these circumstances to encourage his countrymen to believe that God would much more enable them to expel the wicked and accursed Canaanites. At that time, however, the Moabites, having lost the greater part of their possessions through the usurpations of Sihon, were reduced to the small but fertile region between the Zered and the Arnon. **13. Now rise up, and get you over the brook Zered**—The southern border of Moab, *Zered* (woody), now Wady Ahsy, separates the modern district of Kerak from Jebal, and, indeed, forms a natural division of the country between the north and south. Ar, called in later times Rabbah, was the capital of Moab and situated 25 miles south of the Arnon on the banks of a small but shady stream, the Beni-Hamed. It is here mentioned as representative of the country dependent on it, a rich and well-cultivated country, as appears from the numerous ruins of cities, as well as from the traces of tillage still visible on the fields. **16. all the men of war were consumed and dead from among the**

ADAM CLARKE

3. *Turn you northward.* From Mount Seir, in order to get to Canaan. This was not the way they went before, viz., by Kadesh-barnea, but they were to proceed between Edom on the one hand, and Moab and Ammon on the other, so as to enter into Canaan through the land of the Amorites.

5. *Meddle not with them.* That is, the Edomites. See on Num. xx. 14-21.

7. *The Lord . . . hath blessed thee.* God had given them much property, and therefore they had no need of plunder; they had gold and silver to buy the provender they needed, and therefore God would not permit them to take anything by violence.

10. *The Emims dwelt therein.* They are generally esteemed as giants; probably they were a hardy, fierce, and terrible people, who lived, like the wandering Arabs, on the plunder of others.

11. *Which also were accounted giants.* This is not a fortunate version. The word is not *giants*, but *Rephaim*, the name of a people. It appears that the *Emim*, the *Anakim*, and the *Rephaim* were probably the same people, called by different names in the different countries where they dwelt; for they appear originally to have been a kind of wandering freebooters, who lived by plunder. It must be granted, however, that there were several men of this race of extraordinary stature. And hence all gigantic men have been called *Rephaim*.

12. *The Horims also dwelt in Seir.* The whole of this verse was probably added by Joshua or Ezra.

MATTHEW HENRY

III. The caution given them not to meddle with the Moabites or Ammonites, whom they must not disseize, nor so much as disturb in their possessions: *Distress them not, nor contend with them*, v. 9. But why must not the Moabites and Ammonites be meddled with? 1. Because they were the *children of Lot* (v. 9, 19), righteous Lot who kept his integrity in Sodom. 2. Because the land they were possessed of was what God had given them, and he did not design it for Israel.

Verses 24–37

God having tried the self-denial of his people in forbidding them to meddle with the Moabites and Ammonites, and they having quietly passed by those rich countries, and, though superior in number, not made any attack upon them, here he recompenses them for their obedience by giving them possession of the country of Sihon king of the Amorites.

I. God gives them commission to seize upon the country of Sihon king of Heshbon, v. 24, 25. This was then God's way of disposing of kingdoms, but such particular grants are not now either to be expected or pretended.

II. Moses sends to Sihon a message of peace, and only begs a passage through his land, with a promise to give his country no disturbance, but the advantage of trading for ready money with so great a body, v. 26–29.

III. Sihon began the war (v. 32).

IV. Israel was victorious. 1. They put all the Amorites to the sword, men, women, and children (v. 33, 34). They died, not as Israel's enemies, but as sacrifices to divine justice, in the offering of which sacrifices Israel was employed, as a kingdom of priests. 2. They took possession of all they had; their cities (v. 34), their goods (v. 35), and their land, v. 36.

JAMIESON, FAUSSET, BROWN

people—The outbreak at Kadesh on the false report of the spies had been the occasion of the fatal decree by which God doomed the whole grown-up population to die in the wilderness; but that outbreak only filled up the measure of their iniquities. For that generation, though not universally abandoned to heathenish and idolatrous practices, yet had all along displayed a fearful amount of ungodliness in the desert, which this history only hints at obscurely, but which is expressly asserted elsewhere (Ezek. 20:25, 26; Amos 5:25, 27; Acts 7:42, 43). **19-37. when thou comest nigh over against the children of Ammon, distress them not, nor meddle with them**—The Ammonites, being kindred to the Moabites, were, from regard to the memory of their common ancestor, to remain undisturbed by the Israelites. The territory of this people had been directly north from that of Moab. It extended as far as the Jabbok, having been taken by them from a number of small Canaanitish tribes, viz., the Zamzummins, a bullying, presumptuous band of giants, as their name indicates; and the Avims, the aborigines of the district extending from Hazerim or Hazeroth (El Hudhera) even unto Azzah (Gaza), but of which they had been dispossessed by the Caphtorim (Philistines), who came out of Caphtor (Lower Egypt) and settled in the western coast of Palestine. The limits of the Ammonites were now compressed; but they still possessed the mountainous region beyond the Jabbok (Josh. 11:2). What a strange insight does this parenthesis of four verses give into the early history of Palestine! How many successive wars of conquest had swept over its early state—what changes of dynasty among the Canaanitish tribes had taken place long prior to the transactions recorded in this history! **24. Rise ye up . . . and pass over the river Arnon**—At its mouth, this stream is 82 feet wide and 4 deep. It flows in a channel banked by perpendicular cliffs of sandstone. At the date of the Israelitish migration to the east of the Jordan, the whole of the fine country lying between the Arnon and the Jabbok including the mountainous tract of Gilead, had been seized by the Amorites, who, being one of the nations doomed to destruction (see ch. 7:2; 20:16), were utterly exterminated. Their country fell by right of conquest into the hands of the Israelites. Moses, however, considering this doom as referring solely to the Amorite possessions west of Jordan, sent a pacific message to Sihon, requesting permission to go through his territories, which lay on the east of that river. It is always customary to send messengers before to prepare the way; but the rejection of Moses' request by Sihon and his opposition to the advance of the Israelites (Num. 21:23; Judg. 11:26) drew down on himself and his Amorite subjects the predicted doom on the first pitched battlefield with the Canaanites. It secured to Israel not only the possession of a fine and pastoral country, but, what was of more importance to them, a free access to the Jordan on the east.

ADAM CLARKE

20. *That also was accounted a land of giants.* That was accounted the land or territory of the *Rephaim. Zamzummims.* Supposed to be the same as the *Zuzim*, Gen. xiv. 5. From the tenth to the twelfth, and from the twentieth to the twenty-third verse inclusive, we have certain historical remarks introduced which do not seem to have been made by Moses, but rather by Joshua or Ezra. By the introduction of these verses the thread of the narrative suffers considerable interruption. That they could not have made a part of the speech of Moses originally needs little proof.

29. *As the children of Esau which dwell in Seir.* See the note on Num. xx. 21.

30. *The Lord . . . hardened his spirit.* See the notes on Exod. iv. 21; ix. 15; etc.

36. *From Aroer . . . by the brink of the river of Arnon.* See on Num. xxi. 13, etc.

37. *Only unto the land of the children of Ammon thou camest not.* God gave them their commission; and those only were to be cut off, the cup of whose iniquity was full. Though the Moabites and Ammonites were thus spared, they requited good with evil, for they fought against the Israelites, and cast them out of their possessions, Judg. xi. 4-5; 2 Chron. xx. 1; etc., and committed the most shocking cruelties; see Amos i. 13. Hence God enacted a law that none of these people should enter into the congregation of the Lord even to their tenth generation; see chap. xxiii. 3-6.

MATTHEW HENRY — CHAPTER 3

Verses 1–11

Another brave country delivered into the hand of Israel, that of Bashan.

I. How they got the mastery of Og, a very formidable prince, 1. He was very strong, for he was of the remnant of the giants (v. 11). When God pleads his people's cause he can deal with giants as with grasshoppers. No man's might can secure him against the Almighty. The army of Og was very powerful, for he had the command of sixty fortified cities, besides unwalled towns, v. 5. 2. He was very bold and daring. He trusted to his own strength, and so was hardened to his destruction. God bade Moses not fear him, v. 2. If Moses himself was so strong in faith as not to need the caution, yet it is probable that the people needed it, and for them these fresh assurances are designed: "*I will deliver him into thy hand.*"

JAMIESON, FAUSSET, BROWN — CHAPTER 3

VSS. 1-20. CONQUEST OF OG, KING OF BASHAN. **1. we turned, and went up the way to Bashan**—Bashan (fruitful or flat), now El-Bottein, lay situated to the north of Gilead and extended as far as Hermon. It was a rugged mountainous country, valuable however for its rich and luxuriant pastures. **Og the king of Bashan came out against us**—Without provocation, he rushed to attack the Israelites, either disliking the presence of such dangerous neighbors, or burning to avenge the overthrow of his friends and allies. **2. The Lord said unto me, Fear him not; for I will deliver him, and all his people, and his land, into thy hand**—His gigantic appearance and the formidable array of forces he will bring to the field, need not discourage you; for, belonging to a doomed race, he is destined to share the fate of Sihon. **3-8. Argob** was the capital of a district in Bashan of the same name, which, together with other 59 cities in the same province, were conspicuous for their lofty and fortified walls. It was a war of extermination. Houses and cities were razed to the ground; all classes of people were put to the sword; and nothing was saved but the cattle, of which an immense amount fell as spoil into the hands of the conquerors. Thus, the two Amorite kings and the entire population of their dominions were extirpated. The whole country east of the Jordan—first upland downs from the torrent of the Arnon on the south to that of the Jabbok on the north; next the high mountain tract of Gilead and Bashan from

ADAM CLARKE — CHAPTER 3

4. *All the region of Argob. Col chebel Argob*, all the "cable" or "cord of Argob." This expression, which is used in various other parts of Scripture (see, in the original, Amos vii. 17; Mic. ii. 5; Deut. xxii. 9; Ps. xv. 6), shows that anciently land was measured by lines or cords of a certain length.

MATTHEW HENRY

II. How they got possession of Bashan, a very desirable country. They took all the cities (*v.* 4), and all the spoil of them, *v.* 7. They made them all their own, *v.* 10. So that now they had in their hands all that fruitful country which lay east of Jordan, from *the river Arnon unto Hermon, v.* 8.

Verses 12–20

Having shown how this country which they were now in was conquered, in these verses he shows how it was settled upon the Reubenites, Gadites, and half tribe of Manasseh, which we had the story of before, Num. xxxii. 1. Moses specifies the particular parts of the country that were allotted to each tribe, especially the distribution of the lot to the half tribe of Manasseh, the subdividing of which tribe is observable. 2. He repeats the condition of the grant which they had already agreed to, *v.* 18–20. That they should send a strong detachment over Jordan to lead the van in the conquest of Canaan, who should not return to their families till they had seen their brethren in as full possession of their respective allotments as they themselves were now in of theirs. A good man cannot rejoice much in the comforts of his family unless withal he sees *peace upon Israel*, Ps. cxxviii. 6.

Verses 21–29

Here is, I. The encouragement which Moses gave to Joshua, who was to succeed him in the government, *v.* 21, 22. He commanded him not to fear. Two things he would have him consider for his encouragement:—1. What God had done. Joshua had seen what a total defeat God had given by the forces of Israel to these two kings. He must not only infer thence that thus the Lord can do with them all, for his arm is not shortened, but thus he will do, for his purpose is not changed; he that has begun will finish. 2. What God had promised. The *Lord your God he shall fight for you*; and that cause cannot but be victorious which the Lord of hosts fights for.

II. The prayer which Moses made for himself, and the answer which God gave to that prayer.

1. His prayer was that, if it were God's will, he might go before Israel over Jordan into Canaan. *Let me go over and see the good land there*. Not, "Let me go over and be a prince and a ruler there"; he seeks not his own honour, is content to resign the government to Joshua; but, "Let me go to be a spectator of thy kindness to Israel, to see what I believe concerning the goodness of the land of promise."

2. God's answer to this prayer had in it a mixture of mercy and judgment, that he might sing unto God of both.

(1) There was judgment in the denial of his request, and that in something of anger too: *The Lord was wroth with me for your sakes, v.* 26. But how was he wroth with Moses *for the sake of Israel?* Either, [1] For that sin which they provoked him to; see Ps. cvi. 32, 33. Or, [2] The removal of Moses at that time, when he could so ill be spared, was a rebuke to all Israel, and a punishment of their sin. Though Moses, being one of the wrestling seed of Jacob, did not seek in vain, yet he had not the thing itself which he sought for. God may accept our prayers, and yet not grant us the very thing we pray for.

(2) Here is mercy mixed with this wrath in several things:—[1] God quieted the spirit of Moses, *Let it suffice thee*. With this word, no doubt, a divine power went to reconcile Moses to the will of God, and to bring him to acquiesce in it. If God does not by his providence give us what we desire, yet, if by his grace he makes us content without it, it comes to the same. [2] He put an honour upon his prayer in directing him not to insist upon this request: *Speak no more to me of this matter*. [3] He promised him a sight of Canaan *from the top of Pisgah, v.* 27. Though

JAMIESON, FAUSSET, BROWN

the deep ravine of Jabbok—became the possession of the Israelites. **9. Hermon**—now Jebel-Es-Sheick—the majestic hill on which the long and elevated range of Anti-Lebanon terminates. Its summit and the ridges on its sides are almost constantly covered with snow. It is not so much one high mountain as a whole cluster of mountain peaks, the highest in Palestine. According to the survey taken by the English Government Engineers in 1840, they were about 9376 feet above the sea. Being a mountain chain, it is no wonder that it should have received different names at different points from the different tribes which lay along the base—all of them designating extraordinary height: Hermon, the lofty peak, "Sirion," or in an abbreviated form "Sion" (ch. 4:48), the upraised "Shenir," the glittering breastplate of ice. **11. only Og king of Bashan remained of the remnant of giants**—lit., of Rephaim. He was not the last giant, but the only living remnant in the transjordanic country (Josh. 15:14), of a certain gigantic race, supposed to be the most ancient inhabitants of Palestine. **behold, his bedstead was a bedstead of iron**—Although beds in the East are with the common people nothing more than a simple mattress, bedsteads are not unknown. They are in use among the great, who prefer them of iron or other metals, not only for strength and durability, but for the prevention of the troublesome insects which in warm climates commonly infest wood. Taking the cubit at half a yard, the bedstead of Og would measure 13½ feet, so that as beds are usually a little larger than the persons who occupy them, the stature of the Amorite king may be estimated at about 11 or 12 feet; or he might have caused his bed to be made much larger than was necessary, as Alexander the Great did for each of his foot soldiers, to impress the Indians with an idea of the extraordinary strength and stature of his men [LECLERC]. But how did Og's bedstead come to be in Rabbath, of the children of Ammon? In answer to this question, it has been said, that Og had, on the eve of engagement, conveyed it to Rabbath for safety. Or it may be that Moses, after capturing it, may have sold it to the Ammonites, who had kept it as an antiquarian curiosity till their capital was sacked in the time of David. This is a most unlikely supposition, and besides renders it necessary to consider the latter clause of this verse as an interpolation inserted long after the time of Moses. To avoid this, some eminent critics take the Hebrew word rendered "bedstead" to mean "coffin." They think that the king of Bashan having been wounded in battle, fled to Rabbath, where he died and was buried; hence the dimensions of his "coffin" are given [DATHE, ROS]. **12. this land, which we possessed at that time, from Aroer . . . gave I unto the Reubenites and to the Gadites**—The whole territory occupied by Sihon was parcelled out among the pastoral tribes of Reuben and Gad. It extended from the north bank of the Arnon to the south half of mount Gilead—a small mountain ridge, now called Djelaad, about six or seven miles south of the Jabbok, and eight miles in length. The northern portion of Gilead and the rich pasture lands of Bashan—a large province, consisting, with the exception of a few bleak and rocky spots, of strong and fertile soil—was assigned to the half tribe of Manasseh. **14. Jair the son of Manasseh took all the country of Argob**—The original inhabitants of the province north of Bashan, comprising sixty cities (vs. 4), not having been extirpated along with Og, this people were afterwards brought into subjection by the energy of Jair. This chief, of the tribe of Manasseh, in accordance with the pastoral habits of his people, called these newly acquired towns by a name which signifies "Jair's Bedouin Villages of Tents." **unto this day**—This remark must evidently have been introduced by Ezra, or some of the pious men who arranged and collected the books of Moses. **15. I gave Gilead unto Machir**—It was only the half of Gilead (vss. 12, 13) which was given to the descendants of Machir, who was now dead. **16. from Gilead**—i.e., not the mountainous region, but the town Ramoth-gilead, **even unto the river Arnon half the valley**—The word "valley" signifies a wady, either filled with water or dry, as the Arnon is in summer, and thus the proper rendering of the passage will be—"even to the half middle of the river Arnon" (cf. Josh. 12:2). This prudent arrangement of the boundaries was evidently made to prevent all disputes between the adjacent tribes about the exclusive right to the water. **25. I pray thee, let me go over, and see the good land that is beyond Jordan, that goodly mountain, and Lebanon**—The natural and very earnest wish of Moses to be allowed to cross the Jordan was founded on the idea that the divine threatening

ADAM CLARKE

9. *Hermon the Sidonians call . . . Shenir.* I suppose this verse to have been a marginal remark, which afterwards got incorporated with the text, or an addition by Joshua or Ezra.

11. *Og king of Bashan remained.* Og was the last king of the Amorites; his kingdom appears to have taken its name from the hill of Bashan; the country has been since called Batanaea. *Remnant of giants.* Of the *Rephaim.* See on chap. ii. 10-11. *His bedstead was . . . of iron.* Iron was probably used partly for its strength and durability, and partly to prevent noxious vermin from harboring in it. *Is it not in Rabbath, of the children of Ammon?* The bedstead was probably taken in some battle between the Ammonites and Amorites, in which the former had gained the victory. The bedstead was carried a trophy and placed in Rabbath, which appears, from 2 Sam. xii. 26, to have been the royal city of the children of Ammon. *Nine cubits was the length . . . four cubits the breadth.* Allowing the bedstead to have been one cubit longer than Og, which is certainly sufficient, and allowing the cubit to be about *eighteen* inches long, for this is perhaps the average of the cubit of a man, then Og was twelve feet high.

14. *Bashan-havoth-jair.* Bashan of the cities of Jair; see Num. xxxii. 41.

17. *From Chinnereth.* See on Num. xxxiv. 11.

24-25. The prayer of Moses recorded in these two verses, and his own reflections on it, v. 26, are very affecting. He had suffered much in both body and mind in bringing the people to the borders of the Promised Land; and it was natural enough for him to wish to see them established in it, and to enjoy a portion of that inheritance himself, which he knew was a type of the heavenly country. But notwithstanding his very earnest prayer, and God's especial favor towards him, he was not permitted to go over Jordan! He had grieved the Spirit of God, and He passed a sentence against him of exclusion from the Promised Land. Yet He permitted him to see it, and gave him the fullest assurances that the people whom he had brought out of Egypt should possess it. Thus God may choose to deprive those of earthly possessions to whom He is nevertheless determined to give a heavenly inheritance.

26. *Let it suffice thee. Rab lach,* "there is an abundance to thee"—you have had honor enough already, and may well dispense with going over Jordan. He surely has no reason to complain who is taken from earthly felicity to heavenly glory. In this act God showed to Moses both His goodness and severity.

28. *But charge Joshua.* Give him authority in the sight of the people; let them see that he has the same commission which I gave to you. *Encourage him,* for he will meet with many difficulties in the work to which he is called. *And strengthen him*—show him My unfailing promises, and exhort him to put his trust in Me

MATTHEW HENRY

he should not have the possession of it, he should have the prospect of it; not to tantalize him, but such a sight of it as would yield him true satisfaction, and would enable him to form a very clear and pleasing idea of that promised land. [4] He provided him a successor, one who should support the honour of Moses and carry on and complete that glorious work which the heart of Moses was so much upon, the bringing of Israel to Canaan, and settling them there (*v.* 28).

JAMIESON, FAUSSET, BROWN

might be conditional and revertible. "That goodly mountain" is supposed by Jewish writers to have pointed to the hill on which the temple was to be built (chapter 12:5; Exod. 15:2). But biblical scholars now, generally, render the words—"that goodly mountain, even Lebanon," and consider it to be mentioned as typifying the beauty of Palestine, of which hills and mountains were so prominent a feature. **26. speak no more unto me of this matter** —i.e., My decree is unalterable.

ADAM CLARKE

alone; *for he shall go over before this people, and shall cause them to inherit the land*—of this let him rest perfectly assured.

29. *Beth-peor.* This was a city in the kingdom of Sihon, king of the Amorites; and as *beth* signifies a "house," the place probably had its name from a temple of the god Peor, who was worshipped there. Peor was nearly the same among the Moabites that Priapus was among the Romans—the obscene god of an obscene people.

CHAPTER 4

Verses 1–40

This most lively and excellent discourse is often repeated.

I. In general, it is the use and application of the foregoing history. This use we should make of the review of God's providences concerning us, we should by them be quickened and engaged to duty and obedience.

II. The scope and drift of his discourse is to persuade them to keep close to God and to his service, and not to forsake him for any other god.

1. See here how he charges and commands them, and shows them *what the Lord requires of them.*

(1) He demands their diligent attention to the word of God: *Hearken, O Israel.* He means, not only that they must now give him the hearing, but that whenever the book of the law was read to them, or read by them, they should be attentive to it.

(2) He charges them to preserve the divine law pure and entire among them, *v.* 2. Keep it pure, and do not add to it; keep it entire, and do not diminish from it.

(3) He charges them to keep God's *commandments* (*v.* 2), to *do them* (*v.* 5, 14), to *keep and do them* (*v.* 6), to *perform the covenant*, *v.* 13. Hearing must be in order to doing, knowledge in order to practice.

(2) He urges their relation to this God, his authority over them and their obligations to him. He is the *Lord God of your fathers* (*v.* 1), so that you are his by inheritance: your fathers were his, and you were born in his house. "He is the *Lord your God* (*v.* 2), so that you are his by your own consent. He is the *Lord my God* (*v.* 5), so that I treat with you as his agent and ambassador."

(7) He urges God's righteous appearance against them sometimes for their sins. He specifies particularly the matter of Peor, *v.* 3, 4. This had happened very lately: their eyes had seen but the other day the sudden destruction of those that joined themselves to Baal-peor and the preservation of those that clave to the Lord, from which they might easily infer the danger of apostasy from God and the benefit of adherence to him.

(3) He urges the wisdom of being religious: *For this is your wisdom in the sight of the nations*, *v.* 6. Great things may justly be looked for from those who are guided by divine revelation, and unto whom are committed the oracles of God.

(4) He urges the singular advantages which they enjoyed by virtue of the happy establishment they were under, *v.* 7, 8. Our communion with God (which is the highest honour and happiness we are capable of in this world) is kept up by the word and prayer; in both these Israel were happy above any people under heaven. The law of God is far more excellent than the law of nations. No law so consonant to natural equity and the unprejudiced dictates of right reason, so consistent with itself in all the parts of it, and so conducive to the welfare and interest of mankind, as the scripture-law is, Ps. cxix. 128. Those that magnify the law shall be magnified by it.

(4) He charges them to be very strict and careful in their observance of the law (*v.* 9): *Only take heed to thyself, and keep thy soul diligently*; and (*v.* 15), *Take you therefore good heed unto yourselves*; and again (*v.* 23), *Take heed to yourselves.*

(6) He charges them to teach their children to observe the laws of God: *Teach them to thy sons, and thy sons' sons* (*v.* 9), *that they may teach their children*, *v.* 10.

(5) He urges God's glorious appearances to them at Mount Sinai, when he gave them this law. This he insists much upon. Take heed *lest thou forget the day that thou stoodest before the Lord thy God in Horeb*, *v.* 10. By what we see of God sufficient ground is given us to believe him to be a Being of infinite power and perfection, but no occasion given us to suspect him to have a body such as we have. What they heard at Mount Sinai (*v.* 12): "*The Lord spoke unto you* with an intelligible voice, in your own language, and you heard it." God manifests himself to all the world in the works of creation, without

CHAPTER 4

Vss. 1-13. An Exhortation to Obedience. **1. hearken, O Israel, unto the statutes and unto the judgments which I teach you**—By statutes were meant all ordinances respecting religion and the rites of divine worship; and by judgments, all enactments relative to civil matters. The two embraced the whole law of God. **2. Ye shall not add unto the word which I command you**—by the introduction of any heathen superstition or forms of worship different from those which I have appointed (ch. 12:32; Num. 15:39; Matt. 15:9). **neither shall ye diminish aught from it**—by the neglect or omission of any of the observances, however trivial or irksome, which I have prescribed. The character and provisions of the ancient dispensation were adapted with divine wisdom to the instruction of that infant state of the church. But it was only a temporary economy; and although God here authorizes Moses to command that all its institutions should be honored with unfailing observance, this did not prevent Him from commissioning other prophets to alter or abrogate them when the end of that dispensation was attained. **3, 4. Your eyes have seen what the Lord did because of Baal-peor . . . the Lord thy God hath destroyed them from among you**—It appears that the pestilence and the sword of justice overtook only the guilty in that affair (Num. 25) while the rest of the people were spared. The allusion to that recent and appalling judgment was seasonably made as a powerful dissuasive against idolatry, and the fact mentioned was calculated to make a deep impression on people who knew and felt the truth of it. **5, 6. this is your wisdom and your understanding in the sight of the nations, which shall hear all these statutes**—Moses predicted that the faithful observance of the laws given them would raise their national character for intelligence and wisdom. In point of fact it did do so; for although the heathen world generally ridiculed the Hebrews for what they considered a foolish and absurd exclusiveness, some of the most eminent philosophers expressed the highest admiration of the fundamental principle in the Jewish religion—the unity of God; and their legislators borrowed some laws from the constitution of the Hebrews. **7-9. what nation is there so great**—Here he represents their privileges and their duty in such significant and comprehensive terms, as were peculiarly calculated to arrest their attention and engage their interest. The former, their national advantages, are described (vss. 7, 8), and they were twofold: 1. God's readiness to hear and aid them at all times; and 2. the excellence of that religion in which they were instructed, set forth in the "statutes and judgments so righteous" which the law of Moses contained. Their duty corresponding to these pre-eminent advantages as a people, was also twofold: 1. their own faithful obedience to that law; and 2. their obligation to imbue the minds of the young and rising generation with similar sentiments of reverence and respect for it. **10. the day thou stoodest before the Lord . . . in Horeb**—The delivery of the law from Sinai was an era never to be forgotten in the history of Israel. Some of those whom Moses was addressing had been present, though very young; while the rest were federally represented by their parents, who in their name and for their interest entered into the national covenant. **12. ye heard the voice of the words, but saw no similitude**—Although articulate sounds were heard emanating from the mount, no form or representation of the Divine Being who spoke was seen to indicate His nature or properties according to the notions of the heathen.

14-40. A Particular Dissuasive against Idolatry. **15. Take . . . good heed . . . for ye saw no manner of similitude**—The extreme proneness of the Israelites to idolatry, from their position in the midst of surrounding nations already abandoned to its seductions, accounts for their attention being repeatedly drawn to the fact that God did not appear on Sinai in any visible form; and an earnest caution, founded on that remarkable circumstance,

CHAPTER 4

1. *Harken . . . unto the statutes.* Everything that concerned the rites and ceremonies of religion; *judgments*—all that concerned matters of civil right and wrong.

2. *Ye shall not add.* Any book, chapter, verse, or word which I have not spoken; nor give any comment that has any tendency to corrupt, weaken, or destroy any part of this revelation. *Neither shall ye diminish.* You shall not only not take away any larger portion of this word, but you shall not take one jot or tittle from the law; it is that word of God that abideth forever.

6. *Keep . . . and do them; for this is your wisdom.* There was no mode of worship at this time on the face of the earth that was not wicked, obscene, puerile, foolish, or ridiculous, except that established by God himself among the Israelites. And every part of this, taken in its connection and reference, may be truly called a wise and reasonable service. *The nations . . . and say, Surely this great nation is a wise and understanding people.* Almost all the nations in the earth showed that they had formed this opinion of the Jews, by borrowing from them the principal part of their civil code.

9. *Only take heed to thyself.* Be circumspect and watchful. *Keep thy soul diligently.* Be mindful of your eternal interests. Whatever becomes of the body, take care of the soul. *Lest thou forget.* God does His work that they may be had in everlasting remembrance; and he that forgets them forgets his own mercies. *Lest they depart from thy heart.* It is not sufficient to lay up divine things in the memory; they must be laid up in the *heart.* "Thy word have I hid in mine heart," says David, "that I might not sin against thee." The life of God in the soul of man can alone preserve the soul to life everlasting; and this grace must be retained all the days of our life. *But teach them thy sons.* If a man know the worth of his own soul, he will feel the importance of the salvation of the souls of his family. Those who neglect family religion neglect personal religion; if more attention were paid to the former, even among those called religious people, we should soon have a better state of civil society. On family religion God lays much stress; and no head of a family can neglect it without endangering the final salvation of his own soul.

15. *Ye saw no manner of similitude.* Howsoever God chose to appear or manifest himself, he took care never to assume any describable form. He would have no image worship, because He is a Spirit, and they who worship Him "must worship him in spirit and in truth."

MATTHEW HENRY

speech or language, and yet their voice is heard (Ps. xix. 1-3); but to Israel he made himself known by speech and language, condescending to the weakness of the church's infant state.

(5) He charges them particularly to take heed of the sin of idolatry. Two sorts of idolatry he cautions them against:—[1] The worship of images, however by them they might intend to worship the true God, as they had done in the golden calf, so changing the *truth of God into a lie* and his *glory into shame.* The second commandment is expressly directed against this, and is here enlarged upon, *v.* 15-18. To represent an infinite Spirit by an image, and the great Creator by the image of a creature, is the greatest affront we can put upon God and the greatest cheat we can put upon ourselves. As an argument against their making images of God, he urges it very much upon them that when God made himself known to them at Horeb he did it by a voice of words which sounded in their ears, to teach them that *faith comes by hearing*, and God in the word is nigh us; but no image was presented to their eye, for to see God as he is is reserved for our happiness in the other world, and to see him as he is not will do us hurt and no good in this world. You saw *no similitude* (*v.* 12), *no manner of similitude*, *v.* 15. [2] The worship of the sun, moon, and stars, is another sort of idolatry which they are here cautioned against, *v.* 19. This was the most ancient species of idolatry and the most plausible. And the plausibleness of it made it the more dangerous. *When thou seest the sun, moon, and stars*, thou wilt so admire their height and brightness, their regular motion and powerful influence, that thou wilt be strongly tempted to give that glory to them which is due to him that made them. It seems there was need of a great deal of resolution to arm them against this temptation, so weak was their faith in an invisible God and an invisible world. These pretended deities, the *sun, moon, and stars*, were only blessings which the Lord their God had imparted to all nations. It is absurd to worship them, for they are man's servants, were made and ordained to give light on earth.

(6) He urges God's gracious appearances for them, in bringing them out of Egypt, from the iron furnace, where they laboured in the fire, forming them into a people, and then taking them to be his own people, a *people of inheritance* (*v.* 20); this he mentions again, *v.* 34, 37, 38. They were designed for a happy settlement in Canaan, *v.* 38.

(7) He charges them never to forget their duty: *Take heed lest you forget the covenant of the Lord your God*, *v.* 23.

2. Let us see now what are the motives or arguments with which he backs these exhortations.

(1) He urges the greatness, glory, and goodness, of God. Did we consider what a God he is with whom we have to do, we should surely make conscience of our duty to him and not dare to sin against him. He reminds them here that the Lord Jehovah is the *one only living and true God.* All the deities of the heathen were counterfeits and usurpers; nor did any of them so much as pretend to be universal monarchs in heaven and earth, but only local deities. The Israelites, who worshipped no other than the supreme *Numen—Divinity*, were for ever inexcusable if they either changed their God or neglected him. Take heed of offending him, for he must have your entire affection and adoration, and will by no means endure a rival. Even in the New Testament we find the same argument urged upon us as a reason why we should serve *God with reverence* (Heb. xii. 28, 29), because though he is our God, and a rejoicing light to those that serve him faithfully, yet he is a consuming fire to those that trifle with him. Yet he is *a merciful God*, *v.* 31. It comes in here as an encouragement to repentance, but might serve as an inducement to obedience, and a consideration proper to prevent their apostasy.

(8) He urges the certain advantage of obedience.

(9) He urges the fatal consequences of their apostasy from God, that it would undoubtedly be the ruin of their nation. This he enlarges upon, *v.* 25-31. Here observe, *First*, That whatever place we are in we may *thence seek the Lord our God*, though ever so remote from our own land or from his holy temple. There is no part of this earth that has a gulf fixed between it and heaven. *Secondly*, Those, and those only, shall find God to their comfort, who seek him with all their heart. *Thirdly*, Afflictions are sent to engage and quicken us to see God, and, by the grace of God working with them, many are thus reduced to their right mind.

Now let all these arguments be laid together, and then say whether religion has not reason on its side. None cast off the government of their God but those that have first abandoned the understanding of a man.

JAMIESON, FAUSSET, BROWN

is given to beware, not only of making representations of false gods, but also any fancied representation of the true God. **16-19. Lest ye corrupt yourselves, and make you a graven image**—The things are here specified of which God prohibited any image or representation to be made for the purposes of worship; and, from the variety of details entered into, an idea may be formed of the extensive prevalence of idolatry in that age. In whatever way idolatry originated, whether from an intention to worship the true God through those things which seemed to afford the strongest evidences of His power, or whether a divine principle was supposed to reside in the things themselves, there was scarcely an element or object of nature but was deified. This was particularly the case with the Canaanites and Egyptians, against whose superstitious practices the caution, no doubt, was chiefly directed. The former worshipped Baal and Astarte, the latter Osiris and Isis, under the figure of a male and a female. It was in Egypt that animal worship most prevailed, for the natives of that country deified among beasts the ox, the heifer, the sheep, and the goat, the dog, the cat, and the ape; among birds, the ibis, the hawk, and the crane; among reptiles, the crocodile, the frog, and the beetle; among fishes, all the fish of the Nile; some of these, as Osiris and Isis, were worshipped over all Egypt, the others only in particular provinces. In addition they embraced the Zabian superstition, the adoration of the Egyptians, in common with that of many other people, extending to the whole starry host. The very circumstantial details here given of the Canaanitish and Egyptian idolatry were owing to the past and prospective familiarity of the Israelites with it in all these forms. **20. But the Lord hath taken you, and brought you forth out of the iron furnace**—i.e., furnace for smelting iron. A furnace of this kind is round, sometimes 30 feet deep, and requiring the highest intensity of heat. Such is the tremendous image chosen to represent the bondage and affliction of the Israelites [ROSENMULLER]. **to be unto him a people of inheritance**—His peculiar possession from age to age; and therefore for you to abandon His worship for that of idols, especially the gross and debasing system of idolatry that prevails among the Egyptians, would be the greatest folly—the blackest ingratitude. **26. I call heaven and earth to witness against you**—This solemn form of adjuration has been common in special circumstances among all people. It is used here figuratively, or as in other parts of Scripture where inanimate objects are called up as witnesses (ch. 32:1; Isa. 1:2). **28. there ye shall serve gods, the work of men's hands**—The compulsory measures of their tyrannical conquerors would force them into idolatry, so that their choice would become their punishment. **30. in the latter days, if thou turn to the Lord thy God**—either towards the destined close of their captivities, when they evinced a returning spirit of repentance and faith, or in the age of Messiah, which is commonly called "the latter days," and when the scattered tribes of Israel shall be converted to the Gospel of Christ. The occurrence of this auspicious event will be the most illustrious proof of the truth of the promise made in verse 31.

ADAM CLARKE

16. *The likeness of male or female.* Such as Baal-peor and the Roman Priapus, Ashtaroth or Astarte, and the Greek and Roman Venus, after whom most nations of the world literally went a whoring.

17. *The likeness of any beast.* Such as the Egyptian god Apis, who was worshipped under the form of a white bull; the ibis and hawk, among the fowls, had also divine honors paid to them; serpents and the crocodile, among reptiles.

19. *When thou seest the sun and the moon, and the stars.* The worship of the heavenly bodies was the oldest species of idolatry. Those who had not the knowledge of the true God were led to consider the sun, moon, planets, and stars as not only self-existing, but the authors of all the blessings possessed by mankind.

21. *The Lord was angry with me.* And if with me, so as to debar me from entering into the Promised Land, can you think to escape if guilty of greater provocations?

24. *Thy God is a consuming fire.* They had seen Him on the mount as an unconsuming fire, while appearing to Moses, and giving the law; and they had seen Him as a consuming fire in the case of Korah, Dathan, Abiram, and their company. They had, therefore, every good to expect from His approbation, and every evil to dread from His displeasure.

26. *I call heaven and earth to witness against you.* A most solemn method of adjuration, in use among all nations in the world.

27. *The Lord shall scatter you among the nations.* This was amply verified in their different captivities and dispersions.

28. *There ye shall serve gods . . . wood and stone.* This was also true of the Israelites, not only in their captivities, but also in their own land.

29. *But if from thence thou shalt seek the Lord.* God is long-suffering, and of tender mercy; and waits, ever ready, to receive a backsliding soul when it returns to Him.

30. *When thou art in tribulation . . . in the latter days.* Are not these the times spoken of? And is there not still hope for Israel?

33. *Did ever people hear the voice of God?* It seems to have been a general belief that if God appeared to men it was for the purpose of destroying them; and indeed most of the extraordinary manifestations of God were in the way of judgment. But here it was different; God did appear in a sovereign and extraordinary manner, but it was for the deliverance and support of the people. They heard His voice speaking with them in a distinct, articulate manner. They saw the fire, the symbol of His presence, the appearances of which demonstrated it to be supernatural. Notwithstanding God appeared so terrible, yet no person was destroyed, for He came, not to destroy, but to save.

34. *From the midst of another nation.* This was a most extraordinary thing, that a whole people, consisting of upwards of 600,000 effective men, besides women and children, should, without striking a blow, be brought out of the midst of a very powerful nation, to the political welfare of which their services were so essential: that they should be brought out in so open and public a manner; that the sea itself should be supernaturally divided to afford this mighty host a passage; and that, in a desert utterly unfriendly to human life, they should be sustained for forty years. These were such instances of the almighty power and goodness of God as never could be forgotten.

In this verse Moses enumerates seven different means used by the Almighty in effecting Israel's deliverance. (1) *Temptations, massoth,* from *nasah,* "to try or prove"; the miracles which God wrought to try the faith and prove the obedience of the children of Israel. (2) *Signs, othoth,* from *athah,* "to come near"; such signs as God gave them of His continual presence and especial providence, particularly the pillar of cloud and pillar of fire, keeping near to them night and day, and always directing their journeys. (3) *Wonders, mophethim,* from *yaphath,* "to persuade." It probably means "typical" representations; in this signification the word is used, Zech. iii. 8. Joshua, the high priest, and his companions were *anshey mopheth,* "typical men," raised up by God as types of Christ, and

MATTHEW HENRY

JAMIESON, FAUSSET, BROWN

ADAM CLARKE

proofs that God would bring His Servant, the Branch. (4) *War, milchamah,* "hostile engagements"; such as those with the Amalekites, the Amorites, and the Bashanites, in which the hand of God was seen rather than the hand of man. (5) *A mighty hand, yad chazakah;* one that is strong to deal its blows, irresistible in its operations, and grasps its enemies hard, so that they cannot escape, and protects its friends so powerfully that they cannot be injured. (6) *A stretched out arm, zeroa netuyah;* a series of almighty operations, following each other in quick, astonishing succession. Let it be noted that in the Scriptures: The *finger* of God denote any manifestation of the divine power where effects are produced beyond the power of art or nature. The *hand* of God signifies the same power, but put forth in a more signal manner. The *arm* of God, the divine omnipotence manifested in the most stupendous miracles. The *arm* of God *stretched out,* this same omnipotence exerted in a continuation of stupendous miracles, in the way of both judgment and mercy. In this latter sense it appears to be taken in the text: the judgments were poured out on the Egyptians; the mercies wrought in favor of the Israelites. (7) *Great terrors, moraim gedolim;* such terror, dismay, and consternation as were produced by the ten plagues, to which probably the inspired penman here alludes; or, as the Septuagint has it, "with great or portentous sights"; such as that when God looked out of the cloud upon the Egyptians, and their chariot wheels were taken off, Exod. xiv. 24-25 More awful displays of God's judgments, power, and might, were never witnessed by man.

41. *Then Moses severed three cities.* See the law relative to the cities of refuge explained, Num. xxxv. 9, etc.

43. *Bezer in the wilderness.* As the cities of refuge are generally understood to be types of the salvation provided by Christ for sinners, so their names have been thought to express some attribute of the Redeemer of mankind.

I suppose the last nine verses of this chapter to have been added by either Joshua or Ezra.

JOSEPH PARKER:

"Know therefore this day, and consider it in thine heart, that the Lord he is God in heaven above, and upon the earth beneath: there is none else" (v. 39).

I can imagine a man of average education and intelligence asking me some such question as this: "How is it that God does not show himself more clearly to us than he does, and so put an end to all uncertainty concerning himself?" I answer: Are we capable of understanding what is and what is not the proper degree and method of divine manifestation? Have we so proved our own wisdom as to be justified even to ourselves in saying that we are competent to judge how far God has manifested himself, and how much further he ought to have done so? Every day, as a matter of mere fact, we convict ourselves of making mistakes in the commonest affairs of life. Each day is marked by its own special sin. We are always going too far or not far enough. If we are just to ourselves, we shall apply the scourge of self-reproach to our hearts and understanding every day. Are we, then, with all these mistakes, like so many wrecks lying about us; are we, after all, the men to say how God should manifest himself, and when he should do so? Is it decent that we should take upon ourselves this high task of dictation? Is it becoming in men, who cannot certainly tell what will happen in one single hour, that they should write a program for God and appoint the way of the Almighty?—*The People's Bible*

Verses 41–49

Here is, 1. The nomination of the cities of refuge on that side Jordan where Israel now lay encamped. Three cities were appointed for that purpose, one in the lot of Reuben, another in that of Gad, and another in that of the half tribe of Manasseh, *v.* 41–43. 2. The introduction to another sermon that Moses preached to Israel, which we have in the following chapters. Probably it was preached the next sabbath day after, when the congregation attended to receive instruction. He had in general exhorted them to obedience in the former chapter; here he comes to repeat the law which they were to observe, for he demands a universal but not an implicit obedience. How can we do our duty if we do not know it? Here therefore he sets the law before them as the rule they were to work by.

41-43. Then Moses severed three cities on this side Jordan—(See on Josh. 20:7, 8). **44-49. this is the law which Moses set before the children of Israel**—This is a preface to the rehearsal of the law, which, with the addition of various explanatory circumstances, the following chapters contain. **46. Beth-peor**—i.e., house or temple of Peor. It is probable that a temple of this Moabite idol stood in full view of the Hebrew camp, while Moses was urging the exclusive claims of God to their worship, and this allusion would be very significant if it were the temple where so many of the Israelites had grievously offended. **49. The springs of Pisgah**—more frequently Ashdoth-pisgah (ch. 3:17; Josh. 12:3; 13:20), the roots or foot of the mountains east of the Jordan.

CHAPTER 5

Verses 1–5

Here, 1. Moses summons the assembly. He *called all Israel.* 2. He demands attention.

3. He refers them to the covenant made with them in Horeb, as that which they must govern themselves by. See the wonderful condescension of divine grace in turning the command into a covenant. Observe, (1) The parties to this covenant. "The covenant was made with us, or our immediate parents that represented us, before Mount Sinai, and transacted for us."

(2) The publication of this covenant. God himself did, as it were, read the articles to them (*v.* 4): He *talked with you face to face; word to word,* so the Chaldee.

(3) The mediator of the covenant: *Moses stood between God and them,* at the foot of the mount (*v.* 5). Herein Moses was a type of Christ, who *stands between God and man, to show us the word of the Lord,* a blessed days-man, that has laid his hand upon us both, so that we may both hear from God and speak to him without trembling.

CHAPTER 5

VSS. 1-29. A COMMEMORATION OF THE COVENANT IN HOREB. **1. Hear, O Israel, the statutes and judgments**—Whether this rehearsal of the law was made in a solemn assembly, or as some think at a general meeting of the elders as representatives of the people, is of little moment; it was addressed either directly or indirectly to the Hebrew people as principles of their peculiar constitution as a nation; and hence, as has been well observed, "the Jewish law has no obligation upon Christians, unless so much of it as given or commanded by Jesus Christ; for whatever in this law is conformable to the laws of nature, obliges us, not as given by Moses, but by virtue of an antecedent law common to all rational beings" [BISHOP WILSON]. **3. The Lord made not this covenant with our fathers, but with us**—The meaning is, "not with our fathers" only, "but with us" also, assuming it to be "a covenant" of grace. It may mean "not with our fathers" at all, if the reference is to the peculiar establishment of the covenant of Sinai; a law was not given to them as to us, nor was the covenant ratified in the same public manner and by the same solemn sanctions. Or, finally, the meaning may be "not with our fathers" who died in the wilderness, in consequence of their rebellion, and to whom God did not give the rewards promised only to the faithful; but "with us," who alone, strictly speaking, shall enjoy the benefits of this covenant by entering on the possession of the promised land. **4. The Lord talked with you face to face in the mount**—not in a visible and corporeal form, of which there was no trace (ch. 4:12, 15), but freely, familiarly, and in such a manner that no doubt could be entertained of His presence. **5. I stood between the Lord and you at that time**—as the messenger and interpreter of thy heavenly King, bringing near two objects formerly removed from each other at a vast distance, viz., God and the people (Gal. 10:19). In this character Moses was a type of Christ, who is the only mediator between God and men (I Tim. 11:5), the Mediator of a better covenant (Heb. 8:6; 9:15; 12:24). **to show you the word of the Lord**—not the ten commandments—for they were proclaimed directly by the Divine Speaker Himself, but the statutes and judgments which are repeated in

CHAPTER 5

1. *And Moses called all Israel, and said . . . Hear.* (1) God speaks to the people. (2) The people are called to *hear* what God speaks. (3) To *learn* what they heard, that they may be thoroughly instructed in the will of God. (4) To *keep* God's testimonies ever in mind, and to treasure them up in a believing and upright heart. (5) That they might *do them*—obey the whole will of God, taking His word for the invariable rule of their conduct. Should not all these points be kept in view by every Christian assembly?

3. *The Lord made not this covenant with our fathers* (only), *but with us* (also).

MATTHEW HENRY

Verses 6-22

Here is the repetition of the ten commandments, in which observe, 1. Though they had been spoken before, and written, yet they are again rehearsed. 2. There is some variation here from that record (Exod. xx.). 3. The most considerable variation is in the fourth commandment. In Exod. xx. the reason annexed is taken from the creation of the world; here it is taken from their deliverance out of Egypt, because that was typical of our redemption by Jesus Christ, in remembrance of which the Christian sabbath was to be observed: *Remember that thou wast a servant, and God brought thee out, v.* 15. And therefore, (1) "It is fit that thy servants should be favoured by the sabbath-rest; for thou knowest the heart of a servant, and how welcome one day's ease will be after six days' labour." (2) "It is fit that thy God should be honoured by the sabbath-work, and the religious services of the day, in consideration of the great things he has done for thee." In the resurrection of Christ we were brought into the glorious liberty of the children of God, *with a mighty hand and an outstretched arm*: therefore, by the gospel-edition of the law, we are directed to observe the first day of the week, in remembrance of that glorious work of power and grace. 4. It is added in the fifth commandment, *That it may go well with thee*, which addition the apostle quotes, and puts first (Eph. vi. 3), *that it may be well with thee, and that thou mayest live long*. 5. The last five commandments are connected or coupled together, which they are not in Exodus: *Neither shalt thou commit adultery, neither shalt thou steal,* &c., which intimates that God's commands are all of a piece. 6. That these commandments were given with a great deal of awful solemnity, *v.* 22.

Verses 23-33

I. Moses reminds them of the agreement of both the parties that were now treating, in the mediation of Moses.

1. Here is the consternation that the people were put into by that extreme terror with which the law was given. They owned that they could not bear it any more: "*This great fire will consume us*; this dreadful voice will be fatal to us; we shall certainly die if we hear it any more," *v.* 25.

2. Their earnest request that God would henceforward speak to them by Moses, with a promise that they would hear what he said as from God himself, and do it, *v.* 27.

3. God's approbation of their request. He appoints Moses to be his messenger to them, to receive the law from his mouth and to communicate it to them, *v.* 31. God should henceforward speak to us by men like ourselves, by Moses and the prophets, by the apostles and the evangelists, and, if we believe not these, neither should we be persuaded though God should speak to us as he did to Israel at Mount Sinai.

II. Hence he infers a charge to them to observe and do all that God had commanded them, *v.* 32, 33.

JAMIESON, FAUSSET, BROWN

the subsequent portion of this book. **6-20. I am the Lord thy God**—The word "Lord" is expressive of authority or dominion; and God, who by natural claim as well as by covenant relation was entitled to exercise supremacy over His people Israel, had a sovereign right to establish laws for their government. The commandments which follow are, with a few slight verbal alterations, the same as formerly recorded (Exod. 20), and in some of them there is a distinct reference to that promulgation. **12. Keep the sabbath day to sanctify it, as the Lord thy God hath commanded thee**—i.e., keep it in mind as a sacred institution of former enactment and perpetual obligation. **14. that thy manservant and thy maidservant may rest as well as thou**—This is a different reason for the observance of the Sabbath from what is assigned in Exodus 20, where that day is stated to be an appointed memorial of the creation. But the addition of another motive for the observance does not imply any necessary contrariety to the other; and it has been thought probable that, the commemorative design of the institution being well known, the other reason was specially mentioned on this repetition of the law, to secure the privilege of sabbatic rest to servants, of which, in some Hebrew families, they had been deprived. In this view, the allusion to the period of Egyptian bondage (vs. 15), when they themselves were not permitted to observe the Sabbath either as a day of rest or of public devotion, was peculiarly seasonable and significant, well fitted to come home to their business and bosoms. **16. that it may go well with thee**—This clause is not in Exodus, but admitted into Ephesians 6:3. **21. Neither shalt thou desire thy neighbour's wife, . . . house, his field**—An alteration is here made in the words (see Exod. 20), but it is so slight ("wife" being put in the first clause and house in the second) that it would not have been worth while noticing it, except that the interchange proves, contrary to the opinion of some eminent critics, that these two objects are included in one and the same commandment. **22. he added no more**—(Exod 20:1). The pre-eminence of these ten commandments was shown in God's announcing them directly: other laws and institutions were communicated to the people through the instrumentality of Moses. **23-28. And . . . ye came near unto me**—(See on Exod. 20:19). **29. Oh, that there were such an heart in them, that they would fear me**—God can bestow such a heart, and has promised to give it, wherever it is asked (Jer. 32:40). But the wish which is here expressed on the part of God for the piety and steadfast obedience of the Israelites did not relate to them as individuals, so much as a nation, whose religious character and progress would have a mighty influence on the world at large.

ADAM CLARKE

6. *I am the Lord thy God.* See these commandments explained in the notes on Exodus xx.

15. *And remember that thou wast a servant.* In this and the latter clause of the preceding verse Moses adds another reason why one day in seven should be sanctified, viz., that the servants might rest, and this is urged upon them on the consideration of their having been servants in the land of Egypt. We see therefore that God had three grand ends in view by appointing a Sabbath: (1) To commemorate the creation. (2) To give a due proportion of rest to man and beast. When in Egypt they had no rest; their cruel taskmasters caused them to labor without intermission; now God had given rest, and as He had showed them mercy, He teaches them to show mercy to their servants: *Remember that thou wast a servant.* (3) To afford peculiar spiritual advantages to the soul, that it might be kept in remembrance of the rest which remains at the right hand of God.

Therefore the Lord thy God commanded thee to keep the sabbath day. Here is a variation in the manner of expression, *sabbath day* for "seventh," owing, it is supposed, to a change of the day at the Exodus from Sunday to Saturday, effected upon the gathering of the manna, Exod. xvi. 23. The Sabbath now became a twofold memorial of the deliverance, as well as of the creation; and this accounts for the new reason assigned for its observance: "Therefore the Lord thy God commanded thee to keep the sabbath day."

21. *His field.* This clause is not in the tenth commandment as it stands in Exod. xx. 17.

29. *O that there were such an heart in them*—or rather, *mi yitten vehayah lebabam zeh,* "Who will give such a heart to them"—*that they may fear,* etc.! They refuse to receive such a heart from Me; who then can supply it?

32. *Ye shall observe to do.* He who marks not the word of God is never likely to fulfil the will of God. *Ye shall not turn aside to the right hand or to the left.* The way of truth and righteousness is a right line; a man must walk straight forward who wishes to go to glory; no crooked or devious path ever led to God or happiness.

33. *Ye shall walk in all the ways.* God never gave a commandment to man which He did not design that he should obey. He who selects from the divine testimonies such precepts as he feels but little inclination to transgress, and lives in the breach of others, sins against the grand legislative authority of God, and shall be treated as a rebel. *That ye may live. Ticheyun,* that ye "may enjoy life" (for the paragogic *nun,* at the end of the word, deepens the sense), *that it may be well with you, vetob lachem,* "and good shall be to you"—God will prosper you in all things essential to the welfare of your bodies, and the salvation of your souls. *That ye may prolong your days in the land.* That you may arrive at a good old age, and grow more and more meet for the inheritance among the saints in light.

MATTHEW HENRY

CHAPTER 6

Verses 1-3

Observe here, 1. That Moses taught the people all that, and that only, which God commanded him to teach them, *v.* 1. Thus Christ's ministers are to teach his churches *all that he has commanded,* and neither more nor less, Matt. xxviii. 20. 2. That the end of their being taught was that they might do as they were taught (*v.* 1), might *keep God's statutes* (*v.* 2), and *observe to do them, v.* 3. 3. That Moses carefully endeavoured to fix them for God and godliness, now that they were entering upon the land of Canaan.

JAMIESON, FAUSSET, BROWN

CHAPTER 6

VSS. 1-25. MOSES EXHORTS ISRAEL TO HEAR GOD AND TO KEEP HIS COMMANDMENTS. **1. Now these are the commandments, the statutes, and the judgments which the Lord your God commanded to teach you, that ye might do them . . . whither ye go to possess it**—The grand design of all the institutions prescribed to Israel was to form a religious people, whose national character should be distinguished by that fear of the Lord their God which would ensure their divine observance of His worship and their steadfast obedience to His will.

ADAM CLARKE

CHAPTER 6

1. *Now these are the commandments.* See the difference between commandments, statutes, judgments, etc., pointed out in Lev. xxvi. 15. *Do them.* That is, live in the continual practice of them; for by this they were to be distinguished from all the nations of the world, and all these were to be in force till the Son of God should come. *Whither ye go, oberim,* whither "ye pass over," referring to the river Jordan, across which they must pass to get into Canaan.

2. *That thou mightest fear the Lord.* Respect His sovereign authority as a Lawgiver, and ever feel thyself bound to obey Him. No man can walk either conscientiously or safely who has not the fear of God continually before his eyes. *Thou, and thy son, and thy son's son.* Through all thy successive generations. Whoever fears God will endeavor to bring up his children in the way of righteousness.

3. *Hear therefore, O Israel, and observe to do it.* Literally, "Ye shall hear, O Israel, and thou shalt keep to do them."

4. *Hear, O Israel. Shema Yisrael, Yehovah Eloheinu, Yehovah achad.* These words may

MATTHEW HENRY

Verses 4–16

Here is, I. A brief summary of religion, containing the first principles of faith and obedience, *v.* 4, 5. These two verses the Jews reckon one of the choicest portions of scripture: they write it in their phylacteries, and think themselves not only obliged to say it at least twice every day, but very happy in being so obliged, having this saying among them, *Blessed are we, who every morning and evening say, Hear, O Israel, the Lord our God is one Lord.*

1. What we are here taught to believe concerning God: That *Jehovah our God is one Jehovah.* (1) That the God whom we serve is Jehovah, a Being infinitely and eternally perfect, self-existent, and self-sufficient. (2) That he is the one only living and true God; he only is God, and he is but one. The firm belief of this self-evident truth would effectually arm them against all idolatry, which was introduced by that fundamental error, that there are gods many. Happy they that have this one Lord for their God; for they have but one master to please, but one benefactor to seek to. It is better to have one fountain than a thousand cisterns, one all-sufficient God than a thousand insufficient ones.

2. What we are here taught concerning the duty which God requires of man. It is all summed up in this as its principle, *Thou shalt love the Lord thy God with all thy heart.* Did ever any prince make a law that his subjects should love him? Yet such is the condescension of the divine grace that this is made the first and great commandment of God's law, that we love him, and that we perform all other parts of our duty to him from a principle of love. With an intelligent love; for so it is explained, Mark xii. 33. To love him with all the heart, and with all the understanding, we must know him, and therefore love him as those that see good cause to love him.

II. Means are here prescribed for the maintaining and keeping up of religion in our hearts and houses, that it might not wither and go to decay. And they are these:—1. Meditation: *These words which I command thee shall be in thy heart, v.* 6. 2. The religious education of children (*v.* 7): "*Thou shalt teach them diligently to thy children*; and by communicating thy knowledge thou wilt increase it." Take all occasions to discourse with those about thee of divine things; not of unrevealed mysteries, or matters of doubtful disputation, but of the plain truths and laws of God, and the things that belong to our peace. The more conversant we are with them the more we shall admire them and be affected with them, and may thereby be instrumental to communicate divine light and heat. God appointed them, at least for the present, to write some select sentences of the law, that were most weighty and comprehensive, upon their walls, or in scrolls of parchment to be worn about their wrists; and some think that hence the phylacteries so much used among the Jews took rise. Christ blames the Pharisees, not for wearing them, but for affecting to have them broader than other people's, Matt. xxiii. 5. It was prudently and piously provided by the first reformers of the English church that then, when Bibles were scarce, some select portions of scripture should be written on the walls and pillars of the churches, which the people might make familiar to them.

III. A caution is here given not to forget God in a day of prosperity and plenty, *v.* 10–12. He raises their expectations of the goodness of their God, taking it for granted that he would bring them into the good land that he had promised (*v.* 10), that they should no longer dwell in tents as shepherds and poor travellers, but should settle in great and goodly cities, should no longer wander in a barren wilderness, but should enjoy houses well furnished and gardens well planted (*v.* 11), *Cities which thou buildest not, houses which thou filledst not,* &c.

JAMIESON, FAUSSET, BROWN

The basis of their religion was an acknowledgment of the unity of God with the understanding and the love of God in the heart (vss. 4, 5). Compared with the religious creed of all their contemporaries, how sound in principle, how elevated in character, how unlimited in the extent of its moral influence on the heart and habits of the people! Indeed, it is precisely the same basis on which rests the purer and more spiritual form of it which Christianity exhibits (Matt. 22:37; Mark 12:30; Luke 10:27).

Moreover, to help in keeping a sense of religion in their minds, it was commanded that its great principles should be carried about with them wherever they went, as well as meet their eyes every time they entered their homes. A further provision was made for the earnest inculcation of them on the minds of the young by a system of parental training, which was designed to associate religion with all the most familiar and oft-recurring scenes of domestic life. It is probable that Moses used the phraseology in the seventh verse merely in a figurative way, to signify assiduous, earnest, and frequent instruction; and perhaps he meant the metaphorical language in the eighth verse to be taken in the same sense also. But as the Israelites interpreted it literally, many writers suppose that a reference was made to a superstitious custom borrowed from the Egyptians, who wore jewels and ornamental trinkets on the forehead and arm, inscribed with certain words and sentences, as amulets to protect them from danger. These, it has been conjectured, Moses intended to supersede by substituting sentences of the law; and so the Hebrews understood him, for they have always considered the wearing of the *Tephilim* or frontlets a permanent obligation. The form was as follows: Four pieces of parchment, inscribed, the first with Exodus 13:2-10; the second with Exodus 13:11-16; the third with Deuteronomy 6:1-8; and the fourth with Deuteronomy 11:18-21, were enclosed in a square case or box of tough skin, on the side of which was placed the Hebrew letter (*shin*), and bound round the forehead with a thong or ribbon. When designed for the arms, those four texts were written on one slip of parchment, which, as well as the ink, was carefully prepared for the purpose. With regard to the other usage supposed to be alluded to, the ancient Egyptians had the lintels and imposts of their doors and gates inscribed with sentences indicative of a favorable omen [WILKINSON]; and this is still the case, for in Egypt and other Mohammedan countries, the front doors of houses—in Cairo, for instance—are painted red, white, and green, bearing conspicuously inscribed upon them such sentences from the Koran, as "God is the Creator," "God is one, and Mohammed is his prophet." Moses designed to turn this ancient and favorite custom to a better account and ordered that, instead of the former superstitious inscriptions, there should be written the words of God, persuading and enjoining the people to hold the laws in perpetual remembrance.

ADAM CLARKE

be variously rendered into English; but almost all possible verbal varieties in the translation amount to the same sense: "Israel, hear! Jehovah, our God, is one Jehovah"; or, "Jehovah is our God, Jehovah is one"; or, "Jehovah is our God, Jehovah alone"; or, "Jehovah is our God, Jehovah who is one"; or, "Jehovah, who is our God, is the one Being." On this verse the Jews lay great stress; it is one of the four passages which they write on their phylacteries, and they write the last letter in the first and last words very large, for the purpose of exciting attention to the weighty truth it contains.

5. *Thou shalt love the Lord.* Here we see the truth of that word of the apostle, 1 Tim. i. 5: "Now the end of the commandment is . . . [love] out of a pure heart." See the whole of the doctrine contained in this verse explained on Matt. xxii. 36-40.

6. *Shall be in thine heart.* For where else can love be? If it be not in the heart, it exists not. And if *these words* be not *in thine heart*—if they are not esteemed, prized, and received as a high and most glorious privilege—what hope is there that this love shall ever reign there?

7. *Thou shalt teach them diligently. Shinnantam,* from *shanan,* "to repeat, iterate, or do a thing again and again"; hence to whet or sharpen any instrument, which is done by reiterated friction or grinding. We see here the spirit of this divine injunction. God's testimonies must be taught to our children, and the utmost diligence must be used to make them understand them. This is a most difficult task; and it requires much patience, much prudence, much judgment, and much piety in the parents, to enable them to do this good, this most important work, in the best and most effectual manner. *And shalt talk of them when thou sittest in thine house.* You shall have religion at home, as well as in the Temple and Tabernacle. *And when thou walkest by the way.* You shall be religious abroad as well as at home, and not be ashamed to own God wherever you are. *When thou liest down, and when thou risest up.* You shall begin and end the day with God, and thus religion will be the great business of your life.

8. *Thou shalt bind them for a sign upon thine hand.* Is not this an allusion to an ancient and general custom observed in almost every part of the world? When a person wishes to remember a thing of importance, and is afraid to trust to the common operations of memory, he ties a knot on some part of his clothes, or a cord on his hand or finger, that his memory may be whetted to recollection, and his eye affect his heart. God, who knows how slow of heart we are to understand, graciously orders us to make use of every help, and through the means of things sensible, to rise to things spiritual. *And they shall be as frontlets. Totaphoth* seems to have the same meaning as "phylacteries" has in the New Testament; and for the meaning and description of these appendages to a Jew's dress and to his religion, see the notes on Exod. xiii. 9 and on Matt. xxiii. 5.

9. *Write them upon the posts of thy house, and on thy gates.* The Jews, forgetting the spirit and design of this precept, used these things as superstitious people do amulets and charms, and supposed, if they had these passages of Scripture written upon slips of pure parchment, wrapped round their foreheads, tied to their arm, or nailed to their doorposts, that they should then be delivered from every evil!

12. *Beware lest thou forget the Lord.* In earthly prosperity men are apt to forget heavenly things. While the animal senses have everything they can wish, it is difficult for the soul to urge its way to heaven; the animal man is happy, and the desires of the soul are absorbed in those of the flesh. God knows this well; and therefore, in His love to man, makes comparative poverty and frequent affliction his general lot. Should not every soul therefore magnify God for this lot in life? "Before I was afflicted," says David, "I went astray"; and had it not been for poverty and affliction, as instruments in the hands of God's grace, multitudes of souls now happy in heaven would have been

MATTHEW HENRY

IV. Some special precepts and prohibitions are here given, 1. They must upon all occasions give honour to God (*v.* 13). Swear by his name in all treaties and covenants with the neighbouring nations, and do not compliment them so far as to swear by their gods.

They must take heed of dishonouring God by *tempting him* (*v.* 16): "You shall not in any exigence distrust the power, presence, and providence of God."

Verses 17–25

I. Moses charges them to keep God's commandments themselves: *You shall diligently keep God's commandments*, *v.* 17–19.

II. He charges them to instruct their children in the commands of God, not only that they might in their tender years intelligently and affectionately join in religious services, but that afterwards they might in their day keep up religion, and convey it to those that should come after them. Now,

1. Here is a proper question which it is supposed the children would ask (*v.* 20): "*What mean the testimonies and the statutes?* What is the meaning of the feasts we observe, the sacrifices we offer, and the many peculiar customs we keep up?" Observe, (1) All divine institutions have a certain meaning, and there is something great designed in them. (2) It concerns us to know and understand the meaning of them, that we may perform a reasonable service, and may not *offer the blind for sacrifice*.

2. Here is a full answer put into the parents' mouths to be given to this good question. Did the children ask the meaning of God's laws? Let them be told that they were to be observed, (1) In a grateful remembrance of God's former favours to them, especially their deliverance out of Egypt, *v.* 21–23. (2) As the prescribed condition of his further favours (*v.* 24): *The Lord commanded us all these statutes for our good.* Could we perfectly fulfil but that one command of loving God with all our heart, soul,

JAMIESON, FAUSSET, BROWN

MARTIN LUTHER:

13. "And you shall swear by his name." Here two things are to be noted. First, in Matt. 5:34, Christ simply forbids swearing; but here swearing is commanded. But we have also said elsewhere that the use of an oath is twofold. One use is to swear without cause for our own sake in our frivolity; this Christ totally forbids. The other is to swear for the glory of God and the safety of the neighbor, from faith and love, for confirming the truth; this Moses commands. Thus he does not command you to swear but urges that if you must swear, you do not swear except by the name of God.

But how does this relate to the preceding? He had said: "Him alone you shall serve." Under this service he did not distinguish those religious and ceremonial works of worship of God from other, secular ones; but he draws them all together into one, whether they are done to God or to men, that all of them may be exhibited to God alone from the heart. So we should understand "the name of God" here too. He does not want only that name "God" to be taken into the mouth when one must swear. Thus Paul says (1 Cor. 15:31): "By your glory I die daily"; and Christ says (John 16:23): "Verily, verily I say unto you"; and Paul (Rom 9:1): "My conscience is my witness." Therefore you swear by the name of God if you relate that by which you swear to God and grasp it in the name of God; otherwise you would not swear if you knew it displeased Him. Similarly, you serve God alone when you serve men in the name of God; otherwise you would not serve. By such swearing you safeguard your service to God alone and are not drawn toward a godless work or oath. Thus Christ also says in Matt. 23:16–22 that he who swears by the temple and altar and heaven swears by God; and in Matt. 5:35, 36 He forbids to swear by Jerusalem, by one's head, by heaven, or by anything else, because in all these one swears by God. But to swear by God frivolously and emptily is to take the name of God in vain.

When, therefore, He desires oaths to be made by the name of God and by no other, the reason is not only this, that for the truth (which is God) the confirmation of no one should be introduced except that of God himself, but also this, that man should remain in the service of God alone, learn to relate everything to Him, and to do, possess, use, and endure all in His name. Otherwise, if they employ another name, they would be diverted and become used to swearing as if it had nothing to do with God; and finally through bad usage they would begin to distinguish between the deeds by which God is served and those by which He is not served, when He wants to be served in all and wants all things to be done in fear, because He is present to see and judge.—*Luther's Works*

20-25. when thy son asketh thee in time to come, saying—The directions given for the instruction of their children form only an extension of the preceding counsels.

ADAM CLARKE

wretched in hell. It is not too much to speak thus far, because we ever see that the rich and the affluent are generally negligent of God and the interests of their souls. It must however be granted that extreme poverty is as injurious to religion as excessive affluence. Hence the wisdom as well as piety of Agur's prayer, Prov xxx. 7-9: "Give me neither poverty nor riches . . . lest I be full, and deny thee . . . or lest I be poor, and steal."

13. *Thou shalt fear the Lord thy God.* You shall respect and reverence Him as your Lawgiver and Judge; as your Creator, Preserver and the sole Object of your religious adoration. *And serve him.* Our blessed Lord, in Matt. iv. 10; Luke iv. 8, quotes these words thus: "And him *only* shalt thou serve." It appears, therefore that *lebaddo* was anciently in the Hebrew text, as it was and is in the Septuagint, from which our Lord quoted it. The Coptic preserves the same reading; so do also the Vulgate (*illi soli*) and the Anglo-Saxon. Dr. Kennicott argues that without the word "only" the text would not have been conclusive for the purpose for which our Lord advanced it; for as we learn from Scripture that some men worshipped false gods in conjunction with the true, the quotation here would not have been full to the point without this exclusive word. It may be proper to observe that the omitted word *lebaddo*, retained in the above versions, does not exist in the Hebrew printed text, nor in any MS. hitherto discovered. *Shalt swear by his name. Tishshabea*, from *shaba*, "he was full, satisfied, or gave that which was full or satisfactory." Hence an oath and swearing, because appealing to God, and taking Him for Witness in any case of promise, etc., gave full and sufficient security for the performance; and if done in evidence, or to the truth of any particular fact, it gave full security for the truth of that evidence. An oath, therefore, is an appeal to God, who knows all things of the truth of the matter in question; and when a religious man takes such an oath, he gives full and reasonable satisfaction that the thing is so, as stated.

14. *Ye shall not go after other gods.* The object of religious worship among every people, whether that object be true or false, is ever considered as the pattern or exemplar to his worshippers. Christians are termed the "followers" of God; they take God for their Pattern, and "walk"—act—as He does. Hence we see the meaning of the terms in this verse: *Ye shall not go after*—you shall not take false gods for your patterns. The Canaanites, Greeks, Romans, etc., were a most impure people, because the objects of their worship were impure, and they went after them, i.e., were like their gods. This serves to show us that such as our Redeemer is, such should we be; and indeed this is the uniform language of God to man: "Be ye holy, for I am holy," see Lev. xxi. 8; "Be ye therefore perfect, even as your Father which is in heaven is perfect," Matt. v. 48.

15. *A jealous God.* Jehovah has betrothed you to himself as a bride is to her husband. Do not be unfaithful, else that love wherewith He has now distinguished you shall assume the form of jealousy, and so divorce and consume you.

16. *Ye shall not tempt the Lord.* You shall not provoke Him by entertaining doubts of His mercy, goodness, providence, and truth. *As ye tempted him in Massah.* How did they tempt Him in Massah? They said, "Is the Lord among us, or not?" Exod. xvii. 1-7. After such proofs as they had of His presence and His kindness, this was exceedingly provoking. Doubting God's kindness where there are so many evidences of it is highly insulting to God Almighty.

17. *Ye shall diligently keep.* On this and the following verse see the note on v. 3.

20. *And when thy son asketh thee.* "Here," as Mr. Ainsworth justly remarks, "followeth a brief *catechism*, containing the grounds of religion." *What mean the testimonies?* The Hebrew language has no word to express to "mean" or "signify," and therefore uses simply the substantive verb "what is?" i.e., "what mean or signify?" The seven thin ears are, i.e., "signify," seven years of famine. This form of speech frequently occurs.

MATTHEW HENRY

and might, and could we say, "We have never done otherwise," this would be so our righteousness as to entitle us to the benefits of the covenant of innocency; had we continued in every thing that is written in the book of the law to do it, the law would have justified us. But this we cannot pretend to, therefore our sincere obedience shall be accepted through a Mediator.

CHAPTER 7

Verses 1–11

I. A very strict caution against all friendship and fellowship with idols and idolaters.

1. These devoted nations are here named and numbered (*v.* 1). They are specified that Israel might know the bounds and limits of their commission. The confining of this commission to the nations here mentioned plainly intimates that after-ages were not to draw this into a precedent; this will not serve to justify those barbarous laws which give no quarter. If God cast them out, Israel must not take them in, no, not as tenants, nor tributaries, nor servants. The iniquity of the Amorites was now full, and the longer it had been in the filling the sorer was the vengeance when it came at last. The people of these abominations must not be mingled with the holy seed, lest they corrupt them. Thus we must deal with our lusts that war against our souls; God has delivered them into our hands by that promise, *Sin shall not have dominion over you*, unless it be your own faults; let not us then make covenants with them, nor show them any mercy, but mortify and crucify them, and utterly destroy them.

2. They must make no marriages with those of them that escaped the sword, *v.* 3, 4. There is more ground of fear in mixed marriages that the good will be perverted than of hope that the bad will be converted. One of the Chaldee paraphrases adds here, as a reason of this command (*v.* 3), *For he that marries with idolaters does in effect marry with their idols.*

3. They must destroy all the relics of their idolatry, *v.* 5. Their altars and pillars, their groves and graven images, all must be destroyed, both in a holy indignation against idolatry and to prevent infection.

II. Here are very good reasons to enforce this caution.

1. The choice which God had made of this people for his own, *v.* 6.

JAMIESON, FAUSSET, BROWN

CHAPTER 7

VSS. 1-26. ALL COMMUNION WITH THE NATIONS FORBIDDEN. **1. the Hittites**—This people were descended from Heth, the second son of Canaan (Gen. 10:15), and occupied the mountainous region about Hebron, in the south of Palestine. **the Girgashites**—supposed by some to be the same as the Gergesenes (Matt. 8:28), who lay to the east of Lake Gennesareth; but they are placed on the west of Jordan (Josh 24:11), and others take them for a branch of the large family of the Hivites, as they are omitted in nine out of ten places where the tribes of Canaan are enumerated; in the tenth they are mentioned, while the Hivites are not. **the Amorites**—descended from the fourth son of Canaan. They occupied, besides their conquest on the Moabite territory, extensive settlements west of the Dead Sea, in the mountains. **the Canaanites**—located in Phoenicia, particularly about Tyre and Sidon, and being sprung from the oldest branch of the family of Canaan, bore his name. **the Perizzites**—i.e., *villagers,* a tribe who were dispersed throughout the country and lived in unwalled towns. **the Hivites**—who dwelt about Ebal and Gerizim, extending towards Hermon. They are supposed to be the same as the Avims. **the Jebusites**—resided about Jerusalem and the adjacent country. **seven nations greater and mightier than thou**—Ten were formerly mentioned (Gen. 15:19-21). But in the lapse of near five hundred years, it cannot be susprising that some of them had been extinguished in the many intestine feuds that prevailed among those warlike tribes. It is more than probable that some, stationed on the east of Jordan, had fallen under the victorious arms of the Israelites. **2-6. thou shalt smite them, and utterly destroy them; thou shalt make no covenant with them**—This relentless doom of extermination which God denounced against those tribes of Canaan cannot be reconciled with the attributes of the divine character, except on the assumption that their gross idolatry and enormous wickedness left no reasonable hope of their repentance and amendment. If they were to be swept away like the antediluvians or the people of Sodom and Gomorrah, as incorrigible sinners who had filled up the measure of their iniquities, it mattered not to them in what way the judgment was inflicted; and God, as the Sovereign Disposer, had a right to employ any instruments that pleased Him for executing His judgments. Some think that they were to be exterminated as unprincipled usurpers of a country which God had assigned to the posterity of Eber and which had been occupied ages before by wandering shepherds of that race, till, on the migration of Jacob's family into Egypt through the pressure of famine, the Canaanites overspread the whole land, though they had no legitimate claim to it, and endeavored to retain possession of it by force. In this view their expulsion was just and proper. The strict prohibition against contracting any alliances with such infamous idolaters was a prudential rule, founded on the experience that "evil communications corrupt good manners," and its importance or necessity was attested by the unhappy examples of Solomon and others in the subsequent history of Israel. **5. thus shall ye deal with them; ye shall destroy their altars, . . .**—The removal of the temples, altars, and everything that had been enlisted in the service, or might tend to perpetuate the remembrance, of Canaanite idolatry, was likewise highly expedient for preserving the Israelites from all risk of contamination. It was imitated by the Scottish Reformers, and although many ardent lovers of architecture and the fine arts have anathematized their proceedings as vandalism, yet there was profound wisdom in the favorite maxim of Knox—"pull down the nests, and the rooks will disappear." **6-10. For thou art an holy people unto the Lord thy God**—i.e., set apart to the service of God, or chosen to execute the important purposes of His providence. Their selection to this high destiny was neither on account of their numerical amount (for, till after the death of Joseph, they were but a handful of people); nor be-

ADAM CLARKE

25. *It shall be our righteousness.* The evidence that we are under the influence of the fear and love of God. Moses does not say that this righteousness could be wrought without the influence of God's mercy, nor does he say that they should purchase heaven by it; but God required them to be conformed to His will in all things, that they might be holy in heart, and righteous in every part of their moral conduct.

CHAPTER 7

1. *Seven nations greater and mightier than thou.* In several places of the Hebrew text, each of these seven nations is not enumerated, some one or other being left out, which the Septuagint in general supplies.

2. *Thou shalt smite them.* These idolatrous nations were to be utterly destroyed, and all the others also which were contigious to the boundaries of the promised land, provided they did not renounce their idolatry and receive the true faith. For if they did not, then no covenant was to be made with them on any secular or political consideration whatever; no mercy was to be shown to them, because the cup of their iniquity also was now full; and they must either embrace, heartily embrace, the true religion, or be cut off.

3. *Neither shalt thou make marriages.* The heart being naturally inclined to evil, there is more likelihood that the idolatrous wife should draw aside the believing husband than that the believing husband should be able to bring over his idolatrous wife to the true faith.

6. *Thou art an holy people.* And therefore should have no connection with the workers of iniquity.

MATTHEW HENRY

2. The freeness of that grace which made this choice. God fetched the reason of it purely from himself, *v.* 8. All that God loves he loves freely, Hos. xiv. 4.

3. The tenor of the covenant into which they were taken; it was in short this, That as they were to God so God would be to them.

Verses 12–26

I. The caution against idolatry is repeated, and against communion with idolaters. Here is also a repetition of the charge to destroy the images, *v.* 25, 26. The idols which the heathen had worshipped were an abomination to God, and therefore must be so to them: all that truly love God hate what he hates.

II. The promise of God's favour to them if they would be obedient is enlarged upon. All possible assurance is here given them. Let us be constant in our duty, and we cannot question the constancy of God's mercy. If they would keep themselves pure from the idolatries of Egypt, God would keep them clear from the *diseases of Egypt, v.* 15. It seems to refer not only to those plagues of Egypt by the force of which they were delivered, but to some other epidemical country disease (as we call it), which they remembered the prevalence of among the Egyptians, and by which God had chastised them for their national sins. Let them not be disheartened by the slow progress of their arms, nor think that the Canaanites would never be subdued if they were not expelled the first year; no, they must be *put out by little and little,* and not *all at once, v.* 22. Note, We must not think that, because the deliverance of the church and the destruction of its enemies are not effected immediately, therefore they will never be effected. God will do his own work in his own method and time, and we may be sure that they are always the best. Thus corruption is driven out of the hearts of believers *by little and little.* The work of sanctification is carried on gradually; but that judgment will at length be brought forth into a complete victory.

CHAPTER 8

Verses 1–9

The charge here given them is the same as before, to keep and do all God's commandments. He directs them,

I. To look back upon the wilderness through which God had now brought them. Now that they had come of age, and were entering upon their inheritance, they must be reminded of the discipline they had been under during their minority and the method God had taken to train them up for himself. The wilderness was the school in which they had been for forty years boarded and taught, under tutors and governors; and this was a time to bring it all to remembrance. Here let us set up our Ebenezer.

1. They must remember the straits they were sometimes brought into, (1) For the mortifying of their pride. (2) For the manifesting of their perverseness. God thereby proved them whether they would trust his promises, the word which he commanded to a thousand generations, and, in dependence on his promises, obey his precepts.

2. They must remember the supplies which were always granted them. Though God has appointed bread for the strengthening of man's heart, and that is ordinarily made the staff of life, yet God can, when he pleases, command support and nourishment without it, and make something else, very unlikely, to answer the intention as well. We might live upon air if it were sanctified for that use by *the word of God.* Our Saviour quotes this scripture in answer to that temptation of Satan, *Command that these stones be made bread.* "What need of that?" says Christ; "my heavenly Father can keep me alive without bread," Matt. iv. 3, 4. It may be applied spiritually; the *word of God,* as it is the revelation of God's will and grace duly received and entertained by faith, is the food of the soul. The life which is supported by that is the life of the man, and not only that life which is supported by bread. The manna typified Christ, *the bread of life.* He is *the Word of God*; by him we live.

3. They must also remember the rebukes they had been under, *v.* 5. During these years of their education they had been kept under a strict discipline, and not without need. They were chastened that they might not be condemned, chastened with the rod of men. Not as a man wounds and slays his enemies whose destruction he aims at, but as a man

JAMIESON, FAUSSET, BROWN

cause of their extraordinary merits (for they had often pursued a most perverse and unworthy conduct); but it was in consequence of the covenant or promise made with their pious forefathers; and the motives that led to that special act were such as tended not only to vindicate God's wisdom, but to illustrate His glory in diffusing the best and most precious blessings to all mankind. **11-26. Thou shalt therefore keep the commandments, and the statutes, and the judgments, which I command thee this day**—In the covenant into which God entered with Israel, He promised to bestow upon them a variety of blessings so long as they continued obedient to Him as their heavenly King. He pledged His veracity that His infinite perfections would be exerted for this purpose, as well as for delivering them from every evil to which, as a people, they would be exposed. That people accordingly were truly happy as a nation, and found every promise which the faithful God made to them amply fulfilled, so long as they adhered to that obedience which was required of them. See a beautiful illustration of this in Psalm 144:12-15. **15. the evil diseases of Egypt**—(See Exod. 15:26). Besides those with which Pharaoh and his subjects were visited, Egypt has always been dreadfully scourged with diseases. The testimony of Moses is confirmed by the reports of many modern writers, who tell us that, notwithstanding its equal temperature and sereneness, that country has some indigenous maladies which are very malignant, such as ophthalmia, dysentery, smallpox, and the plague. **20. God will send the hornet among them**—(See on Josh. 24:11-13). **22. lest the beasts of the field increase upon thee**—(See on Exod. 23:28-30). The omnipotence of their Almighty Ruler could have given them possession of the promised land at once. But, the unburied corpses of the enemy and the portions of the country that might have been left desolate for a while, would have drawn an influx of dangerous beasts. This evil would be prevented by a progressive conquest and by the use of ordinary means, which God would bless.

CHAPTER 8

Vss. 1-20. AN EXHORTATION TO OBEDIENCE. **1. All the commandments which I command thee this day shall ye observe to do, that ye may live**—In all the wise arrangements of our Creator duty has been made inseparably connected with happiness; and the earnest enforcement of the divine law which Moses was making to the Israelites was in order to secure their being a happy (because a moral and religious) people: a course of prosperity is often called life (Gen. 17:18; Prov. 3:2). **live, and multiply**—This reference to the future increase of their population proves that they were too few to occupy the land fully at first. **2. thou shalt remember all the way which the Lord thy God led thee these forty years in the wilderness**—The recapitulation of all their checkered experience during that long period was designed to awaken lively impressions of the goodness of God. First, Moses showed them the object of their protracted wanderings and varied hardships. These were trials of their obedience as well as chastisements for sin. Indeed, the discovery of their infidelity, inconstancy, and their rebellions and perverseness which this varied discipline brought to light, was of eminently practical use to the Israelites themselves, as it has been to the church in all subsequent ages. Next, he enlarged on the goodness of God to them, while reduced to the last extremities of despair, in the miraculous provision which, without anxiety or labor, was made for their daily support (see on Exod. 16:12). Possessing no nutritious properties inherent in it, this contributed to their sustenance, as indeed all food does (Matt. 4:4) solely through the ordinance and blessing of God. This remark is applicable to the means of spiritual as well as natural life. **4. Thy raiment waxed not old upon thee, neither did thy foot swell, these forty years**—What a striking miracle was this! No doubt the Israelites might have brought from Egypt more clothes than they wore at their outset; they might also have obtained supplies of various articles of food and raiment in barter with the neighboring tribes for the fleeces and skins of their sheep and goats; and in furnishing them with such opportunities the care of Providence appeared. But the strong and pointed terms which Moses here uses (see also ch. 29:5) indicate a special or miraculous interposition of their loving Guardian in preserving

ADAM CLARKE

8. *But because the Lord loved you.* It was no good in them that induced God to choose them at this time to be His peculiar people; He had His reasons, but these sprang from His infinite goodness. He intended to make a full discovery of His goodness to the world, and this must have a commencement in some particular place, and among some people. He chose that time, and He chose the Jewish people, but not because of their goodness or holiness.

12. *The Lord . . . shall keep unto thee the covenant.* So we find their continuance in the state of favor was to depend on their faithfulness to the grace of God. If they should rebel, though God had chosen them through His love, yet He would cast them off in His justice. The elect, we see, may become unfaithful, and so become reprobates. So it happened to 24,000 of them, whose carcasses fell in the wilderness because they had sinned; yet these were of the elect that came out of Egypt. Let him that standeth take heed lest he fall.

22. *Put out those nations . . . by little and little.* The Israelites were not as yet sufficiently numerous to fill the whole land occupied by the seven nations mentioned in v. 1. And as wild and ferocious animals might be expected to multiply where either there are no inhabitants or the place is but thinly peopled, therefore God tells them that, though at present by force of arms they might be able to expel them, it would be impolitic so to do, lest the beasts of the field should multiply upon them.

25. *Thou shalt not desire the silver or gold that is on them.* Some of the ancient idols were plated over with gold, and God saw that the value of the metal and the excellence of the workmanship might be an inducement for the Israelites to preserve them; and this might lead, remotely at least, to idolatry. As the idols were accursed, all those who had them, or anything appertaining to them, were accursed also, v. 26.

CHAPTER 8

2. *Thou shalt remember all the way.* The various dealings of God with you; the dangers and difficulties to which you were exposed, and from which God delivered you; together with the various miracles which He wrought for you, and His long-suffering towards you.

3. *He . . . suffered thee to hunger, and fed thee.* God never permits any tribulation to befall His followers which He does not design to turn to their advantage. When He permits us to hunger, it is that His mercy may be the more observable in providing us with the necessaries of life. Privations, in the way of providence, are the forerunners of mercy and goodness abundant.

4. *Thy raiment waxed not old.* The plain meaning of this much-tortured text appears to me to be this: "God so amply provided for them all the necessaries of life that they never were obliged to wear tattered garments, nor were their feet injured for lack of shoes or sandals." If they had carvers, engravers, silversmiths, and jewellers among them, as plainly appears from the account we have of the Tabernacle and its utensils, is it to be wondered at if they also had habit and sandal makers, as we are certain they had weavers, embroiderers, and suchlike? And the traffic which we may suppose they carried

MATTHEW HENRY

chastens his son whose happiness and welfare he designs: so did their God chasten them; he chastened and taught them, Ps. xciv. 12.

II. He directs them to look forward to Canaan, into which God was now bringing them. Look which way we will, both our reviews and our prospects will furnish us with arguments for obedience.

Verses 10–20

Moses, having mentioned the great plenty they would find in the land of Canaan, finds it necessary to caution them against the abuse of that plenty, which was a sin they would be the more prone to now that they came into that vineyard of the Lord, immediately out of a barren desert.

I. He directs them to the duty of a prosperous condition, *v.* 10. Whatever they had the comfort of, God must have the glory of. As our Saviour has taught us to bless before we eat (Matt. xiv. 19, 20), so we are here taught to bless after meat. That is our *Hosanna—God bless*; this is our *Hallelujah—Blessed be God. In every thing we must give thanks.* From this law the religious Jews took up a laudable usage of blessing God, not only at their solemn meals, but upon other occasions; if they drank a cup of wine they lifted up their hands and said, *Blessed be he that created the fruit of the vine to make glad the heart.* If they did but smell at a flower, they said, *Blessed be he that made this flower sweet.*

II. He arms them against the temptations of a prosperous condition. 1. "Then take heed of pride." When the estate rises, the mind is apt to rise with it, in self-conceit, self-conplacency, and self-confidence. 2. "Then take heed of forgetting God." When men grow rich they are tempted to think religion a needless thing. They are happy without it, think it a thing below them and too hard upon them. Their dignity forbids them to stoop, and their liberty forbids them to serve.

JAMIESON, FAUSSET, BROWN

them amid the wear and tear of their nomadic life in the desert. Thirdly, Moses expatiated on the goodness of the promised land. **7. For the Lord thy God bringeth thee into a good land**—All accounts, ancient and modern, concur in bearing testimony to the natural beauty and fertility of Palestine, and its great capabilities if properly cultivated. **a land of brooks of water, of fountains and depths that spring out of valleys and hills**—These characteristic features are mentioned first, as they would be most striking; and all travellers describe how delightful and cheerful it is, after passing through the barren and thirsty desert, to be among running brooks and swelling hills and verdant valleys. It is observable that water is mentioned as the chief source of its ancient fertility. **8. A land of wheat, and barley**—These cereal fruits were specially promised to the Israelites in the event of their faithful allegiance to the covenant of God (Ps. 81:16; 147:14). The wheat and barley were so abundant as to yield sixty and often an hundredfold (Gen. 26:12; Matt. 13:8). **vines, and fig trees, and pomegranates**—The limestone rocks and abrupt valleys were entirely covered, as traces of them still show, with plantations of figs, vines, and olive trees. Though in a southern latitude, its mountainous formations tempered the excessive heat, and hence, figs, pomegranates, etc., were produced in Palestine equally with wheat and barley, the produce of northern regions. **honey**—The word honey is used often in a loose, indeterminate sense, very frequently to signify a syrup of dates or of grapes, which under the name of *dibs* is much used by all classes, wherever vineyards are found, as a condiment to their food. It resembles thin molasses, but is more pleasant to the taste [ROBINSON]. This is esteemed a great delicacy in the East, and it was produced abundantly in Palestine. **9. a land whose stones are iron**—The abundance of this metal in Palestine, especially among the mountains of Lebanon, those of Kesraoun, and elsewhere, is attested not only by Josephus, but by Volney, Buckingham, and other travellers. **brass**—not the alloy brass, but the ore of copper. Although the mines may now be exhausted or neglected, they yielded plenty of those metals anciently (I Chron. 22:3; 29:2-7; Isa. 60:17). **11-20. Beware that thou forget not the Lord**—After mentioning those instances of the divine goodness, Moses founded on them an argument for their future obedience. **15. Who led thee through that great and terrible wilderness, wherein were fiery serpents, and scorpions**—Large and venomous reptiles are found in great numbers there still, particularly in autumn. Travelers must use great caution in arranging their tents and beds at night; even during the day the legs not only of men, but of the animals they ride, are liable to be bitten. **who brought thee forth water out of the flinty rock**—(See on chap. 9:21).

ADAM CLARKE

on with the Moabites, or with travelling hordes of Arabians, doubtless supplied them with the materials; though, as they had abundance of sheep and meat cattle, they must have had much of the materials within themselves. It is generally supposed that God, by a miracle, preserved their clothes from wearing out; but if this sense be admitted, it will require, not one miracle, but a chain of the most successive and astonishing miracles ever wrought, to account for the thing.

9. *A land whose stones are iron.* Not only meaning that there were iron mines throughout the land, but that the loose stones were strongly impregnated with iron, ores of this metal. *Out of whose hills thou mayest dig brass.* As there is no such thing in nature as a *brass* mine, the word *nechosheth* should be translated "copper"; of which, by the addition of the *lapis calaminaris,* brass is made. See on Exod. xxv. 3.

15. *Who led thee through that . . . terrible wilderness.* See the account of their journeying in the notes on Exod. xvi. 1, etc.; Numbers xxi, etc. *Fiery serpents.* Serpents whose bite occasioned a most violent inflammation, accompanied with an unquenchable thirst, and which terminated in death. See on Num. xxi. 6.

16. *Who fed thee . . . with manna.* See this miracle described in Exod. xvi. 13, etc.

18. *God . . . giveth thee power to get wealth.* Who among the rich and wealthy believes this saying? Who gives wisdom, understanding, skill, bodily strength, and health? Is it not God? And without these, how can wealth be acquired?

MATTHEW HENRY — CHAPTER 9

Verses 1–6

The call to attention (*v.* 1), *Hear, O Israel,* intimates that this was a new discourse.

I. Moses represents to the people the formidable strength of the enemies which they were now to encounter, *v.* 1. This representation is much the same with that which the evil spies had made (Num. xiii. 28, 33), but made with a very different intention: that was designed to drive them from God and to discourage their hope in him; this to drive them to God and to engage their hope in him.

II. He assures them of victory, by the presence of God with them, notwithstanding the strength of the enemy, *v.* 3.

III. He cautions them not to entertain the least thought of their own righteousness, as if that had procured them this favour at God's hand. Note, Our gaining possession of the heavenly Canaan, as it must be attributed to God's power and not to our own might, so it must be ascribed to God's grace and not to our own merit.

IV. He intimates to them the true reasons why God would take this good land out of the hands of the Canaanites, and settle it upon Israel.

JAMIESON, FAUSSET, BROWN — CHAPTER 9

VSS. 1-25. MOSES DISSUADES THEM FROM THE OPINION OF THEIR OWN RIGHTEOUSNESS. **1. this day**—means *this time.* The Israelites had reached the confines of the promised land, but were obliged, to their great mortification, to return. But now they certainly were to enter it. No obstacle could prevent their possession; neither the fortified defenses of the towns, for the resistance of the gigantic inhabitants of whom they had received from the spies so formidable a description. **cities great and fenced up to heaven**—Oriental cities generally cover a much greater space than those in Europe; for the houses often stand apart with gardens and fields intervening. They are almost all surrounded with walls built of burnt or sun-dried bricks, about forty feet in height. All classes in the East, but especially the nomad tribes, in their ignorance of engineering and artillery, would have abandoned in despair the idea of an assault on a walled town, which today would be demolished in a few hours. **4. Speak not thou in thine heart, . . . saying, For my righteousness the Lord hath brought me in to possess this land**—Moses takes special care to guard his countrymen against the vanity of supposing that their own merits had procured them the distinguished privilege. The Canaanites were a hopelessly corrupt race, and deserved extermination; but history relates many remarkable instances in which God punished corrupt and guilty nations by the instrumentality of other people as bad as themselves. It was not for the sake of the Israelites, but for His own sake, for the promise made to their pious ancestors, and in furtherance of high and comprehensive purposes of good to the world, that God

ADAM CLARKE — CHAPTER 9

1. *Thou art to pass over Jordan this day. Haiyom,* "this time"; they had come thirty-eight years before this nearly to the verge of the Promised Land, but were not permitted at that day or time to pass over, because of their rebellions; but "this time" they shall certainly pass over. This was spoken about the eleventh month of the fortieth year of their journeying, and it was on the first month of the following year they passed over; and during this interim Moses died.

5. *For the wickedness of these nations.* So then it was not by any sovereign act of God that these people were cast out, but for their wickedness; they had transgressed the law of their Creator; they had resisted His Spirit, and could no longer be tolerated. The Israelites were to possess their land, not because they deserved it, but first, because they were less wicked than the others; and secondly, because God thus

MATTHEW HENRY

Verses 7–29

That they might have no pretence to think that God brought them to Canaan *for their righteousness*, Moses here shows them what a miracle of mercy it was that they had not long ere this been destroyed in the wilderness: "*Remember, and forget not, how thou provokedst the Lord thy God* (v. 7); so far from purchasing his favour, thou hast many a time laid thyself open to his displeasure." They had been a provoking people ever since they came out of Egypt, *v.* 7. Though the Mosaic history records little more than the occurrences of the first and last year of the forty, yet it seems by this general account that the rest of the years were not much better, but one continued provocation.

Now let them lay all this together, and it will appear that whatever favour God should hereafter show them, in subduing their enemies and putting them in possession of the land of Canaan, it was not for their righteousness. It is good for us often to remember against ourselves, with sorrow and shame, our former sins, and to review the records conscience keeps of them, that we may see how much we are indebted to free grace, and may humbly own that we never merited at God's hand any thing but wrath and the curse.

JAMIESON, FAUSSET, BROWN

was about to give them a grant of Canaan. **7. Remember, and forget not, how thou provokedst the Lord**—To dislodge from their minds any presumptuous idea of their own righteousness, Moses rehearses their acts of disobedience and rebellion committed so frequently, and in circumstances of the most awful and impressive solemnity, that they had forfeited all claims to the favor of God. The candor and boldness with which he gave, and the patient submission with which the people bore, his recital of charges so discreditable to their national character, has often been appealed to as among the many evidences of the truth of this history. **8. Also in Horeb**—rather, even in Horeb, where it might have been expected they would have acted otherwise. **12-29. Arise, get thee down quickly from hence: for the people . . . have corrupted themselves**—With a view to humble them effectually, Moses proceeds to particularize some of the most atrocious instances of their infidelity. He begins with the impiety of the golden calf—an impiety which, while their miraculous emancipation from Egypt, the most stupendous displays of the Divine Majesty that were exhibited on the adjoining mount, and the recent ratification of the covenant by which they engaged to act as the people of God, were fresh in memory, indicated a degree of inconstancy or debasement almost incredible. **17. I took the two tables, . . . and broke them before your eyes**—not in the heat of intemperate passion, but in righteous indignation, from zeal to vindicate the unsullied honor of God, and by the suggestion of His Spirit to intimate that the covenant had been broken, and the people excluded from the divine favor. **18. I fell down before the Lord**—The sudden and painful reaction which this scene of pagan revelry produced on the mind of the pious and patriotic leader can be more easily imagined than described. Great and public sins call for seasons of extraordinary humiliation, and in his deep affliction for the awful apostasy, he seems to have held a miraculous fast as long as before. **20. The Lord was very angry with Aaron to have destroyed him**—By allowing himself to be overborne by the tide of popular clamor, Aaron became a partaker in the guilt of idolatry and would have suffered the penalty of his sinful compliance, had not the earnest intercession of Moses on his behalf prevailed. **21. I cast the dust thereof into the brook that descended out of the mount**—i.e., the smitten rock (El Leja) which was probably contiguous to, or a part of, Sinai. It is too seldom borne in mind that though the Israelites were supplied with water from this rock when they were stationed at Rephidim (Wady Feiran), there is nothing in the Scripture narrative which should lead us to suppose that the rock was in the immediate neighborhood of that place (see on Exod. 17:5, 6). The water on this smitten rock was probably the brook that descended from the mount. The water may have flowed at the distance of many miles from the rock, as the winter torrents do now through the wadies of Arabia Petræa (Ps. 78:15, 16). And the rock may have been smitten at such a height, and at a spot bearing such a relation to the Sinaitic valleys, as to furnish in this way supplies of water to the Israelites during the journey from Horeb by the way of mount Seir and Kadesh-barnea (ch. 1:1, 2). On this supposition new light is, perhaps, cast on the figurative language of the apostle, when he speaks of "the rock following" the Israelites (I Cor. 10:4) [WILSON'S LAND OF THE BIBLE]. **25. Thus I fell down before the Lord forty days and forty nights, as I fell down at the first**—After the enumeration of various acts of rebellion, he had mentioned the outbreak at Kadesh-barnea, which, on a superficial reading of this verse, would seem to have led Moses to a third and protracted season of humiliation. But on a comparison of this passage with Numbers 14:5, the subject and language of this prayer show that only the second act of intercession (vs. 18) is now described in fuller detail.

ADAM CLARKE

chose to begin the great work of His salvation among men. Thus then the Canaanites were cut off, and the Israelites were grafted in; and the Israelites, because of their wickedness, were afterwards cut off, and the Gentiles grafted in. Let the latter not be high-minded, but fear. "If God spared not the natural branches, take heed lest he also spare not thee."

10. *Tables of stone.* See the notes on Exod. xxxi. 18 and xxxii. 15-16.

12. *Thy people . . . have corrupted themselves.* Debased themselves by making and worshipping an Egyptian idol. See on Exodus xxxii.

21. *I took your sin, the calf which ye had made.* See this fully explained, Exod. xxxii. 20.

22. *At Kibroth-hattaavah.* See the note on Num. xi. 18.

27. *Remember thy servants, Abraham, Isaac, and Jacob.* As if he had said: "These are their descendants, and the covenant was made with those patriarchs in behalf of these."

MATTHEW HENRY — CHAPTER 10

Verses 1–11

There were four things in and by which God showed himself reconciled to Israel and made them truly great and happy.

I. He gave them his law, gave it to them in writing, as a standing pledge of his favour. Note, God's putting his law in our hearts, and writing it in our inward parts, furnish the surest evidence of our reconciliation to God and the best earnest of our happiness in him. God will send his law and gospel to those whose hearts are prepared as arks to receive them.

JAMIESON, FAUSSET, BROWN — CHAPTER 10

VSS. 1-22. GOD'S MERCY IN RESTORING THE TWO TABLES. **1. At that time the Lord said unto me, Hew thee two tables of stone like unto the first**—It was when God had been pacified through the intercessions of Moses with the people who had so greatly offended Him by the worship of the golden calf. The obedient leader executed the orders he had received as to the preparation both of the hewn stones, and the ark or chest in which those sacred archives were to be laid. **3. I made an ark of shittim wood**—It appears, however, from Exodus

ADAM CLARKE — CHAPTER 10

1. *Hew thee two tables of stone.* See the notes on Exod. xxxiv. 1.

3. *Shittim wood.* See the note on Exod. xxv. 5, and succeeding verses.

MATTHEW HENRY

Christ is the ark in which now our salvation is kept safely, that it may not be lost as it was in the first Adam, when he had it in his own hand. These two tables, thus engraven, were faithfully laid up in the ark. *And there they be*, said Moses, pointing it is probable towards the sanctuary, *v.* 5. That good thing which was committed to him, he transmitted to them, and left it pure and entire in their hands; now let them look to it at their peril. Thus we may say to the rising generation, "God has entrusted us with Bibles, sabbaths, sacraments, &c., as tokens of his presence and favour, and there they be; we lodge them with you," 2 Tim. i. 13, 14.

II. He led them forward towards Canaan, though they in their hearts turned back towards Egypt, and he might justly have chosen their delusions, *v.* 6, 7.

III. He appointed a standing ministry among them, to deal for them in holy things. Note, A settled ministry is a great blessing to a people, and a special token of God's favour. Under the law, a succession in the ministry was kept up, by an entail of the office on a certain tribe and family. But now, under the gospel, when the effusion of the Spirit is more plentiful and powerful, the succession is kept up by the Spirit's operation on men's hearts, qualifying men for, and inclining men to, that work, some in every age.

IV. He accepted Moses as an advocate or intercessor for them, and therefore constituted him their prince and leader (*v.* 10, 11): *The Lord hearkened to me and said, Arise, go before the people.* It was a mercy to them that they had such a friend, so faithful both to him that appointed him and to those for whom he was appointed.

Verses 12–22

A most pathetic exhortation to obedience.

I. We are here most plainly directed in our duty to God, to our neighbour, and to ourselves.

1. We are here taught our duty to God. We must *fear the Lord our God*, *v.* 12, and again *v.* 20. Fear him as a great God, and Lord, and love him as a good God and Father and benefactor. We must *serve him* (*v.* 20), *serve him with all our heart and soul* (*v.* 12), and what we do for him we must do cheerfully and with a good will. We must *keep his commandments and his statutes*, *v.* 13.

2. We are here taught our duty to our neighbour (*v.* 19): *Love the stranger*; and, if the stranger, much more our brethren, as ourselves. Two arguments are here urged to enforce this duty:—(1) God's common providence, which extends itself to all nations of men, they being all *made of one blood*. *God loveth the stranger* (*v.* 18), that is, he gives to all life, and breath, and all things, even to those that are Gentiles, and *strangers to the commonwealth of Israel* and to Israel's God. (2) The afflicted condition which the Israelites themselves had been in, when they were strangers in Egypt. Those that have themselves been in distress, and have found mercy with God, should sympathize most feelingly with those that are in the like distress and be ready to show kindness to them. The people of the Jews conceived a rooted antipathy to the Gentiles, and this brought a final ruin upon themselves.

3. We are here taught our duty to ourselves (*v.* 16): *Circumcise the foreskin of your hearts*, that is, "Cast away from you all corrupt affections and inclinations, which hinder you from fearing and loving God. The circumcision of the heart makes it ready to yield to God, and draw in his yoke.

II. We are here most pathetically persuaded to our duty. Let but reason rule us, and religion will.

1. Consider the greatness and glory of God, and therefore fear him, and from that principle serve and obey him.

2. Consider the goodness and grace of God, and therefore love him, and from that principle serve and obey him. His goodness is his glory as much as his greatness.

JAMIESON, FAUSSET, BROWN

37:1, that the ark was not framed till his return from the mount, or most probably, he gave instructions to Bezaleel, the artist employed on the work, before he ascended the mount,—that, on his descent, it might be finished, and ready to receive the precious deposit. **4, 5. he wrote on the tables, according to the first writing**—i.e., not Moses, who under the divine direction acted as amanuensis, but God Himself who made this inscription a second time with His own hand, to testify the importance He attached to the ten commandments. Different from other stone monuments of antiquity, which were made to stand upright and in the open air, those on which the divine law was engraven were portable, and designed to be kept as a treasure. Josephus says that each of the tables contained five precepts. But the tradition generally received, both among Jewish and Christian writers is, that one table contained four precepts, the other six. **I . . . put the tables in the ark which I had made; there they be, as the Lord commanded me**—Here is another minute, but important circumstance, the public mention of which at the time attests the veracity of the sacred historian. **6-9. the children of Israel took their journey from Beeroth of the children of Jaakan to Mosera**—So sudden a change from a spoken discourse to a historical narrative has greatly puzzled the most eminent biblical scholars, some of whom reject the parenthesis as a manifest interpolation. But it is found in the most ancient Hebrew MSS., and, believing that all contained in this book was given by inspiration and is entitled to profound respect, we must receive it as it stands, although acknowledging our inability to explain the insertion of these encampment details in this place. There is another difficulty in the narrative itself. The stations which the Israelites are said successively to have occupied are enumerated here in a different order from Numbers 33:31. That the names of the stations in both passages are the same there can be no doubt; but, in Numbers, they are probably mentioned in reference to the *first* visit of the Hebrews during the long wandering southwards, before their return to Kadesh the second time; while here they have a reference to the *second* passage of the Israelites, when they again marched south, in order to compass the land of Edom. It is easy to conceive that Mosera (Hor) and the wells of Jaakan might lie in such a direction that a nomadic horde might, in different years, at one time take the former *first* in their way, and at another time the latter [ROBINSON]. **10-22.** Moses here resumes his address, and having made a passing allusion to the principal events in their history, concludes by exhorting them to fear the Lord and serve Him faithfully.

16. Circumcise therefore the foreskin of your heart—Here he teaches them the true and spiritual meaning of that rite, as was afterwards more strongly urged by Paul (Rom. 2:25, 29), and should be applied by us to our baptism, which is "not the putting away of the filth of the flesh, but the answer of a good conscience toward God."

ADAM CLARKE

4. *Ten commandments.* See the note on Exod. xx. 1, etc.

12. *Now, Israel, what doth the Lord . . . require of thee?* An answer is immediately given. God requires: (1) That ye *fear* Him as Jehovah your God; Him who made, preserves, and governs you. (2) That ye *walk in all his ways*—that, having received His precepts, ye obey the whole; walking in God's ways, not your own, nor in the ways of the people of the land. (3) That ye *love him*—have confidence in Him as your Father and Friend, have recourse to Him in all your necessities, and love Him in return for His love. (4) That you *serve* Him—give Him that worship which He requires, performing it with all your *heart*—the whole of your affections, and with all your *soul*—your will, understanding, and judgment. In a word, putting forth your whole strength and energy of body and soul in the sacred work.

14. *Behold, the heaven and the heaven of heavens.* All these words in the original are in the plural number: *hen hashshamayim, ushemey hashshamayim;* "behold, the heavens and the heavens of heavens." But what do they mean? To say that the first means the atmosphere, the second the planetary system, and the third the region of the blessed, is saying but very little in the way of explanation. The words were probably intended to point out the immensity of God's creation, in which we may readily conceive one system of heavenly bodies, and others beyond them, and others still in endless progression through the whole vortex of space, every star in the vast abyss of nature being a sun, with its peculiar and numerous attendant worlds! Thus there may be systems of systems in endless gradation up to the throne of God!

16. *Circumcise . . . the foreskin of your heart.* A plain proof from God himself that this precept pointed out spiritual things, and that it was not the cutting away a part of the flesh that was the object of the divine commandment, but the purification of the soul, without which all forms and ceremonies are of no avail. Loving God with all the heart, soul, mind, and strength, the heart being circumcised to enable them to do it, was, from the beginning, the end, design, and fulfillment of the whole law.

17. *God of gods, and Lord of lords.* That is, He is the Source whence all being and power proceed; every agent is finite but himself; and He can counteract, suspend, or destroy all the actions of all creatures whensoever He pleases. If He determine to save, none can destroy; if He purpose to destroy, none can save. How absolutely necessary to have such a God for our Friend! *A great God . . . mighty. Hael haggibbor*, "the mighty God"; this is the very title that is given to our blessed Lord and Saviour, Isa. ix. 6.

21. *He is thy praise.* It is an eternal honor to any soul to be in the friendship of God. Why are people ashamed of being thought religious? Because they know nothing of religion. He who knows his Maker may glory in his God, for without Him what has any soul but disgrace, pain, shame, and perdition?

22. *With threescore and ten persons.* And now, from so small a beginning, they were multiplied to more than 600,000 souls; and this indeed in the space of forty years, for the 603,000 which came out of Egypt were at this time all dead but Moses, Joshua, and Caleb. How easily can God increase and multiply, and how easily diminish and bring low! In all things, because of His unlimited power, He can do whatsoever He will; and He will do whatsoever is right.

MATTHEW HENRY — CHAPTER 11

Verses 1–7

Thou shalt *keep his charge*, that is, the oracles of his word and ordinances of his worship, with which they were entrusted and for which they were accountable. It is a phrase often used concerning the office of the priests and Levites, for all Israel was a kingdom of priests, a holy nation. Observe the connection of these two: *Thou shalt love the Lord*, and *keep his charge*, since love will work in obedience, and that only is acceptable obedience which flows

JAMIESON, FAUSSET, BROWN — CHAPTER 11

VSS. 1-32. AN EXHORTATION TO OBEDIENCE. **1. Therefore thou shalt love the Lord thy God, and keep his charge**—The reason for the frequent repetition of the same or similar counsels is to be traced to the infantine character and state of the church, which required line upon line and precept upon precept. Besides, the Israelites were a headstrong and perverse people, impatient of control, prone to rebellion, and, from their long stay in Egypt, so violently addicted to idolatry, that they ran im-

ADAM CLARKE — CHAPTER 11

1. *Thou shalt love the Lord.* Because without this there could be no obedience to the divine testimonies, and no happiness in the soul; for the heart that is destitute of the love of God is empty of all good, and consequently miserable.

MATTHEW HENRY

from a principle of love. 1 John v. 3.

Verses 8–17

Still Moses urges the same subject, as loth to conclude till he had gained his point. *"If thou wilt enter into life*, if thou wilt enter into Canaan, a type of that life, and find it a good land indeed to thee, *keep the commandments: Keep all the commandments which I command you this day*; love God, and serve him with all your heart."

He does not go about to teach them the art of war, how to draw the bow, and use the sword, and keep ranks, that they might be strong, and go in and possess the land; no, but let them keep God's commandments, and their religion, while they are true to it, will be their strength and secure their success. Sin tends to the shortening of the days of particular persons and to the shortening of the days of a people's prosperity; but obedience will be a lengthening out of their tranquillity. Note, The better God has provided, by our outward condition, for our ease and convenience, the more we should abound in his service: the less we have to do for our bodies the more we should do for God and our souls. To awaken them to take heed, Moses here tells them plainly that if they should *turn aside to other gods*, 1. They would provoke the wrath of God against them. 2. Good things would be turned away from them; the heaven would withhold its rain, and then of course the earth would not yield its fruit.

Verses 18–25

I. Moses repeats the directions he had given for the guidance and assistance of the people in their obedience. Let us all be directed by the three rules here given:—1. Let our hearts be filled with the word of God: *Lay up these words in your heart and in your soul.* 2. Let our eyes be fixed upon the word of God. Bind these words for a sign *upon your hand*, which is always in view (Isa. xlix. 16), *and as frontlets between your eyes.* 3. Let our tongues be employed about the word of God. Let it be the subject of our familiar discourse, wherever we are; especially with our children.

II. He repeats the assurances he had before given them, in God's name, of prosperity and success if they were obedient. Nothing contributes more to the making of a nation considerable abroad, valuable to its friends and formidable to its enemies, than religion reigning in it; for who can be against those that have God for them? And he is certainly for those that are sincerely for him, Prov. xiv. 24.

JAMIESON, FAUSSET, BROWN

minent risk of being seduced by the religion of the country to which they were going, which, in its characteristic features, bore a strong resemblance to that of the country they had left. **2-9. I speak not to your children which have not known . . . But your eyes have seen all the great acts of the Lord which he did**—Moses is here giving a brief summary of the marvels and miracles of awful judgment which God had wrought in effecting their release from the tyranny of Pharaoh, as well as those which had taken place in the wilderness. He knew that he might dwell upon these, for he was addressing many who had been witnesses of those appalling incidents. For it will be remembered that the divine threatening that they should die in the wilderness, and its execution, extended only to males from 20 years and upward, who were able to go forth to war. No males under 20 years of age, no females, and none of the tribe of Levi, were objects of the denunciation (see Num. 14:28-30; 16:49). There might, therefore, have been many thousands of the Israelites at that time of whom Moses could say, "Your eyes have seen all the great acts which He did"; and with regard to those the historic review of Moses was well calculated to stir up their minds to the duty and advantages of obedience. **10-12. For the land, whither thou goest in to possess it, is not as the land of Egypt, from whence ye came out**—The physical features of Palestine present a striking contrast to those of the land of bondage. A widely extending plain forms the cultivated portion of Egypt, and on the greater part of this low and level country rain never falls. This natural want is supplied by the annual overflow of the Nile, and by artificial means from the same source when the river has receded within its customary channel. Close by the bank the process of irrigation is very simple. The cultivator opens a small sluice on the edge of the square bed in which seed has been sown, making drill after drill; and when a sufficient quantity of water has poured in, he shuts it up with his foot. Where the bank is high, the water is drawn up by hydraulic engines, of which there are three kinds used, of different power, according to the subsidence of the stream. The water is distributed in small channels or earthen conduits, simple in construction, worked by the foot, and formed with a mattock by the gardener who directs their course, and which are banked up or opened, as occasion may require, by pressing in the soil with the foot. Thus was the land watered in which the Israelites had dwelt so long. Such vigilance and laborious industry would not be needed in the promised land. Instead of being visited with moisture only at one brief season and left during the rest of the year under a withering blight, every season it would enjoy the benign influences of a genial climate. The hills would attract the frequent clouds, and in the refreshing showers the blessing of God would especially rest upon the land. **A land which the Lord thy God careth for**—i.e., watering it, as it were, with His own hands, without human aid or mechanical means. **14. the first rain and the latter rain**—The early rain commenced in autumn, i.e., chiefly during the months of September and October, while the latter rain fell in the spring of the year, i.e., during the months of March and April. It is true that occasional showers fell all the winter; but, at the autumnal and vernal seasons, they were more frequent, copious, and important; for the early rain was necessary, after a hot and protracted summer, to prepare the soil for receiving the seed; and the latter rain, which shortly preceded the harvest, was of the greatest use in invigorating the languishing powers of vegetation (Jer. 5:24; Joel 11:23; Amos 4:7; Jas. 5:7). **15-17. I will send grass in thy fields for thy cattle**—Undoubtedly the special blessing of the former and the latter rain was one principal cause of the extraordinary fertility of Canaan in ancient times. That blessing was promised to the Israelites as a temporal reward for their fidelity to the national covenant. It was threatened to be withdrawn on their disobedience or apostasy; and most signally is the execution of that threatening seen in the present sterility of Palestine. Mr. Lowthian, an English farmer, who was struck during his journey from Joppa to Jerusalem by not seeing a blade of grass, where even in the poorest localities of Britain some wild vegetation is found, directed his attention particularly to the subject, and pursued the inquiry during a month's residence in Jerusalem, where he learned that a miserably small quantity of milk is daily sold to the inhabitants at a dear rate, and that chiefly asses' milk. "Most clearly," says he, "did I perceive that the barrenness of large portions of the country was owing to the cessation of the early and latter rain, and that the

ADAM CLARKE

6. *What he did unto Dathan.* See the notes on Numbers xvi.

8. *Therefore shall ye keep all the commandments.* Because God can execute such terrible judgments, and because He has given such proofs of His power and justice; and because in similar provocations, He may be expected to act in a similar way; therefore keep His charge, that He may keep you unto everlasting life.

10. *Wateredst it with thy foot.* Rain scarcely ever falls in Egypt, and God supplies the lack of it by the inundations of the Nile. In order to water the grounds where the inundations do not extend, water is collected in ponds, and directed in streamlets to different parts of the field where irrigation is necessary. It is no unusual thing in the East to see a man, with a small mattock, making a little trench for the water to run by, and as he opens the passage, the water following, he uses his *foot* to raise up the mold against the side of this little channel, to prevent the water from being shed unnecessarily before it reaches the place of its destination. Thus he may be said to water the ground with his foot. But after all, the expression *wateredst it with thy foot* may mean no more than doing it by labor; for, as in the land of Egypt there is scarcely any rain, the watering of gardens, etc., must have been all artificial. But in Judea it was different, as there they had their proper seasons of rain. The compound word *beregel*, "with, under, or by the foot," is used to signify anything under the power, authority, etc., of a person; and this very meaning it has in the sixth verse, "all the substance that was in their possession" is, literally, all the substance that was "under their feet," *beragleyhem*, that is, in their power, possession, or what they had acquired by their labor.

14. *The rain . . . in his due season, the first rain and the latter rain.* By the *first* or "former" *rain* we are to understand that which fell in Judea about November, when they sowed their seed, and this served to moisten and prepare the ground for the vegetation of the seed. The *latter rain* fell about April, when the corn was well grown up, and served to fill the ears, and render them plump and perfect. Rain rarely fell in Judea at any other seasons than these. If the former rain were withheld, or not sent in due season, there could be no vegetation; if the latter rain were withheld, or not sent in its due season, there could be no full corn in the ear, and consequently no harvest. Of what consequence then was it that they should have their rain in *due season!* God, by promising this provided they were obedient, and threatening to withhold it should they be disobedient, shows that it is not a general providence that directs these things, but that the very rain of heaven falls by particular direction, and the showers are often regulated by an especial providence.

18. *Therefore shall ye lay up these my words.* See chap. vi. 4-8, and see on Exod. xiii. 9.

24. *From the river*—Euphrates, which was on the east—*unto the uttermost sea*—the Mediterranean, which lay westward of the Promised Land. This promise, notwithstanding the many provocations of the Israelites, was fulfilled in the time of Solomon, for "he reigned over all the kings from the river [Euphrates] even unto the land of the Philistines, and to the border of Egypt," 2 Chron. ix. 26.

26. *Behold, I set before you . . . a blessing and a curse.* If God had not put it in the power of this people either to obey or disobey; if they had not had a free will, over which they had complete authority, to use it either in the way of willing or nilling; could God, with any propriety, have given such precepts as these, sanctioned with such promises and threatenings? If they were not free *agents*, they could not be punished for disobedience, nor could they, in any sense of the word, have been rewardable for obedience.

29. *Thou shalt put the blessing upon mount Gerizim, and the curse upon mount Ebal.* The etymology of these names may be supposed to cast some light on this institution. *Gerizim*, from *garaz*, "to cut, cut off, cut down"; hence *gerizim*, the "cutters down, fellers, and reapers or harvestmen," this mountain being supposed to have its name from its great fertility, or the abundance of the crops it yielded. Of *ebal* or

MATTHEW HENRY

Verses 26–32

Moses concludes his general exhortation to obedience.

I. He sums up all his arguments for obedience in two words, *the blessing and the curse* (*v.* 26), taking hold of hope and fear, those two handles of the soul, by which it is caught, held, and managed.

II. He appoints a public and solemn proclamation to be made of the blessing and curse which he had set before them, upon the two mountains of Gerizim and Ebal, *v.* 29, 30. We have more particular directions for this solemnity in *ch.* xxvii. 11, &c., and an account of the performance of it, Josh. viii. 33, &c. It was to be done, and was done, immediately upon their coming into Canaan, that when they first took possession of that land they might know upon what terms they stood.

JAMIESON, FAUSSET, BROWN

absence of grass and flowers made it no longer the land (vs. 9) flowing with milk and honey." **18-25. lay up these my words in your heart and in your soul, and bind them**—(See on ch. 6:8). **Every place whereon the soles of your feet shall tread shall be yours**—not as if the Jews should be lords of the world, but of very place within the promised land. It should be granted to them and possessed by them, on conditions of obedience:—**from the wilderness**—the Arabah on the south; **Lebanon**—the northern limit; **Euphrates**—their boundary on the east. Their grant of dominion extended so far, and the right was fulfilled to Solomon. **even unto the uttermost sea**—the Mediterranean. **26-32. Behold, I set before you this day a blessing and a curse**—(See on ch. 27:11).

ADAM CLARKE

eybal the root is not found in Hebrew; but in Arabic *abala* signifies "rough, rugged, curled"; and *abalo,* from the same root, signifies "white stones," and a mountain in which such stones are found; *alabalo,* "the mount of white stones." And as it is supposed that the mountain had this name because of its barrenness, on this metaphorical interpretation the sense of the passage would appear to be the following: God will so superintend the land, and have it continually under the eye of His watchful providence, that no change can happen in it but according to His divine counsel, so that its fertility shall ever be the consequence of the faithful obedience of its inhabitants, and a proof of the blessing of God upon it; on the contrary, its barrenness shall be a proof that the people have departed from their God, and that His curse has in consequence fallen upon the land. See the manner of placing these blessings and curses, chap. xxvii. 12, etc. That Gerizim is very fruitful, and that Ebal is very barren, is the united testimony of all who have travelled in those parts.

MATTHEW HENRY — CHAPTER 12

Verses 1–4

From those great original truths, That there is a God, and that there is but one God, arise those great fundamental laws, That that God is to be worshipped, and he only, and that therefore we are to have no other God before him: this is the first commandment, and the second is a guard upon it, or a hedge about it. To prevent a revolt to false gods, we are forbidden to worship the true God in such a way and manner as the false gods were worshipped in, and are commanded to observe the instituted ordinances of worship that we may adhere to the proper object of worship. For this reason Moses is very large in his exposition of the second commandment. What is contained in this and the four following chapters mostly refers to that.

I. They are here charged to abolish and extirpate all those things that the Canaanites had served their idol-gods with, *v.* 2, 3. The places that had been used, and were now to be levelled, were enclosures for their worship on *mountains and hills* (as if the height of the ground would give advantage to the ascent of their devotions), and under green trees, either because pleasant or because awful. He begins the statutes that relate to divine worship with this, because there must first be an abhorrence of that which is evil before there can be a steady adherence to that which is good, Rom. xii. 9. The kingdom of God must be set up, both in persons and places, upon the ruins of the devil's kingdom; for they cannot stand together, nor can there be any communion between Christ and Belial.

II. They are charged not to transfer the rites and usages of idolaters into the worship of God; no, not under colour of beautifying and improving it (*v.* 4).

Verses 5–32

There is not any one particular precept (as I remember) in all the law of Moses, so largely pressed and inculcated as this, by which they are all tied to bring their sacrifices to that one altar which was set up in the court of the tabernacle, and there to perform all the rituals of their religion; for, as to moral services, then, no doubt, as now, men might pray everywhere, as they did in their synagogues. The command to do this, and the prohibition of the contrary, are here repeated. 1. Because of the strange proneness there was in the hearts of the people to idolatry and superstition. 2. Because of the great use which the observance of this appointment would be to preserve among them unity and brotherly love, that, meeting all in one place, they might continue both of one way and of one heart. 3. Because of the significance of this appointment. They must keep to one place, in token of their belief of those two great truths, which we find together (1 Tim. ii. 5), That *there is one God,* and *one Mediator between God and man.*

Let us now reduce this long charge to its proper heads.

I. It is here promised that when they were settled in Canaan, when they had *rest from their enemies, and dwelt in safety,* God would choose a certain place, which he would appoint to be the centre of their unity, to which they should bring all their offerings, *v.* 10, 11. He does not appoint the place now, as he had appointed Mounts Gerizim and Ebal, for the pronouncing of the blessings and curses (*ch.*

JAMIESON, FAUSSET, BROWN — CHAPTER 12

VSS. 1-15. MONUMENTS OF IDOLATRY TO BE DESTROYED. **1. These are the statutes and judgments which ye shall observe**—Having in the preceding chapter inculcated upon the Israelites the general obligation to fear and love God, Moses here enters into a detail of some special duties they were to practise on their obtaining possession of the promised land. **2. Ye shall utterly destroy all the places, wherein the nations which ye shall possess served their gods**—This divine command was founded on the tendencies of human nature; for to remove out of sight everything that had been associated with idolatry, that it might never be spoken of and no vestige of it remain, was the only effectual way to keep the Israelites from temptations to it. It is observable that Moses does not make any mention of temples, for such buildings were not in existence at that early period. The "places" chosen as the scene of heathen worship were situated either on the summit of a lofty mountain, or on some artificial mound, or in a grove, planted with particular trees, such as oaks, poplars, and elms (Isa. 57:5-7; Hos. 4:13). The reason for the selection of such sites was both to secure retirement and to direct the attention upward to heaven; and the "place" was nothing else than a consecrated enclosure, or at most, a canopy or screen from the weather. **3. ye shall overthrow their altars**—piles of turf or small stones. **and break their pillars**—Before the art of sculpture was known, the statues of idols were only rude blocks of colored stones. **5. unto the place which the Lord thy God shall choose . . . to put his name there . . . thou shalt come**—They were forbidden to worship either in the impure superstitious manner of the heathen, or in any of the places frequented by them. A particular place for the general rendezvous of all the tribes would be chosen by God Himself; and the choice of one common place for the solemn rites of religion was an act of divine wisdom, for the security of the true religion. It was admirably calculated to prevent the corruption which would otherwise have crept in from their frequenting groves and high hills—to preserve uniformity of worship and keep alive their faith in Him to whom all their sacrifices pointed. The place was successively Mizpeh, Shiloh, and especially Jerusalem. But in all the references made to it by Moses, the name is never mentioned. This studied silence was maintained partly lest the Canaanites within whose territories it lay might have concentrated their forces to frustrate all hopes of obtaining it; partly lest the desire of possessing a place of such importance might have become a cause of strife or rivalry amongst the Hebrew tribes, as about the appointment to the priesthood (Num. 16). **7. there ye shall eat before the Lord**—of the things mentioned (vs. 6); but of course, none of the parts assigned to the priests before the Lord—in the place where the sanctuary should be established, and in those parts of the Holy City which the people were at liberty to frequent and inhabit. **12. ye shall rejoice before the Lord your God, ye, your sons, and your daughters . . .**—Hence it appears that, although males only were commanded to appear before God at the annual solemn feasts (Exod. 23:17), the women were allowed to accompany them (I Sam. 1:3-23). **15. Notwithstanding thou mayest kill and eat flesh in all thy gates**—Every animal designed for

ADAM CLARKE — CHAPTER 12

3. *Ye shall overthrow their altars,* where unholy sacrifices have been offered; *and break their pillars,* probably meaning statues and representations of their gods cut out of stone; and burn their groves, such as those about the temple of Ashtaroth, the Canaanitish Venus, whose impure rites were practiced in different parts of the enclosures or groves round her temples; *and ye shall hew down the graven images,* probably implying all images carved out of wood; *and destroy the names of them,* which, no doubt were at first graven on the stones, and carved on the trees, and then applied to the surrounding districts. In various instances the names of whole mountains, valleys, and districts were borrowed from the gods worshipped there.

14. *The place which the Lord shall choose.* To prevent idolatry and bring about a perfect uniformity in the divine worship, which at that time was essentially necessary. Because every rite and ceremony had a determinate meaning, and pointed out the good things which were to come, therefore one place must be established where those rites and ceremonies should be carefully and punctually observed. Had it not been so, every man would have formed his worship according to his own mind, and the whole beauty and importance of the grand representative system would have been destroyed, and the Messiah and the glories of His kingdom could not have been seen through the medium of the Jewish ritual.

15. *Thou mayest kill and eat flesh in all thy gates.* With the proviso that the blood be poured

MATTHEW HENRY

xi. 29), but reserves the doing of it till hereafter, that hereby they might be made to expect further directions from heaven, and a divine conduct, after Moses should be removed. The ark was the token of God's presence, and where that was put there God put his name, and that was his habitation. The place which God first chose for the ark to reside in was Shiloh; and, after that place had sinned away its honours, we find the ark at Kirjath-jearim and other places; but at length, in David's time, it was fixed at Jerusalem, and God said concerning Solomon's temple, more expressly than ever he had said concerning any other place, *This I have chosen for a house of sacrifice*, 2 Chron. vii. 12. Compare 2 Chron. vi. 5. Now, under the gospel, we have no temple that sanctifies the gold, no altar that sanctifies the gift, but Christ only; and, as to the places of worship, the prophets foretold that *in every place* the spiritual *incense should be offered*, Mal. i. 11. And our Saviour has declared that those are accepted as true worshippers who worship God in sincerity and truth, without regard either to this mountain or Jerusalem, John iv. 23.

II. They are commanded to bring all their burnt-offerings and sacrifices to this place that God would choose (*v.* 6 and again *v.* 11).

III. They are commanded to feast upon their hallowed things before the Lord, with holy joy. If we glorify God, we edify ourselves, and cultivate our own minds, through the grace of God, by the increase of our knowledge and faith, the enlivening of devout affections, and the confirming of gracious habits and resolutions: thus is the soul nourished. Now while they were before the Lord they must rejoice, *v.* 12. It is the will of God that we should serve him with gladness; none displeased him more than those that *covered his altar with tears*, Mal. ii. 13. See what a good Master we serve, who has made it our duty to sing at our work.

It should seem that while they were in the wilderness they did not eat the flesh of any of those kinds of beasts that were used in sacrifice, but what was killed at the door of the tabernacle, and part of it presented to God as a peace-offering, Lev. xvii. 3, 4. But when they came to Canaan, where they must live at a great distance from the tabernacle, they might kill what they pleased for their own use of their flocks and herds, without bringing part to the altar. They must not eat blood (*v.* 16, and again, *v.* 23). When they could not bring the blood to the altar, to pour it out there before the Lord, as belonging to him, they must pour it out upon the earth, as not belonging to them, because it was the life, and therefore, as an acknowledgment, belonged to him who gives life, and, as an atonement, belonged to him to whom life is forfeited. Bishop Patrick thinks one reason why they were forbidden thus strictly the eating of blood was to prevent the superstitions of the old idolators about the blood of their sacrifices, which they thought their demons delighted in, and by eating of which they imagined that they had communion with them.

Never was there a better governor than Moses, and one would think never a better opportunity of keeping up good order and discipline than now among the people of Israel, when they lay so closely encamped under the eye of their governor; and yet it seems there was much amiss and many irregularities had crept in among them. But (says Moses) when you come to Canaan, you *shall not do as we do here*. Note, When the people of God are in an unsettled condition, that may be tolerated and dispensed with which would by no means be allowed at another time. Moses was now about to lay down his life and government, and it was a comfort to him to foresee that Israel would be better in the next reign than they had been in his.

JAMIESON, FAUSSET, BROWN

food, whether ox, goat, or lamb, was during the abode in the wilderness ordered to be slain as a peace offering at the door of the tabernacle; its blood to be sprinkled, and its fat burnt upon the altar by the priest. The encampment, being then round about the altar, made this practice, appointed to prevent idolatry, easy and practicable. But on the settlement in the promised land, the obligation to slay at the tabernacle was dispensed with. The people were left at liberty to prepare their meat in their cities or homes. **according to the blessing of the Lord thy God which he hath given thee**—The style of living should be accommodated to one's condition and means—profuse and riotous indulgence can never secure the divine blessing. **the unclean and the clean may eat thereof**—The unclean here are those who were under some slight defilement, which, without excluding them from society, yet debarred them from eating any of the sacred meats (Lev. 7:20). They were at liberty freely to partake of common articles of food. **of the roebuck**—the gazelle. **and as of the hart**—The Syrian deer (*Cervus barbatus*) is a species between our red and fallow deer, distinguished by the want of a bis-antler, or second branch on the horns, reckoning from below, and for a spotted livery which is effaced only in the third or fourth year.

16-25. BLOOD PROHIBITED. **ye shall not eat the blood; ye shall pour it upon the earth as water**—The prohibition against eating or drinking blood as an unnatural custom accompanied the announcement of the divine grant of animal flesh for food (Gen. 9:4), and the prohibition was repeatedly renewed by Moses with reference to the great objects of the law (Lev. 17:2), the prevention of idolatry, and the consecration of the sacrificial blood to God. In regard, however, to the blood of animals slain for food, it might be shed without ceremony and poured on the ground as a common thing like water—only for the sake of decency, as well as for preventing all risk of idolatry, it was to be covered over with earth (Lev. 17:13), in opposition to the practice of heathen sportsmen, who left it exposed as an offering to the god of the chase. **22-28. Even as the roebuck and the hart is eaten, so shalt thou eat them . . .**—Game when procured in the wilderness had not been required to be brought to the door of the tabernacle. The people were now to be as free in the killing of domestic cattle as of wild animals. The permission to hunt and use venison for food was doubtless a great boon to the Israelites, not only in the wilderness, but on their settlement in Canaan, as the mountainous ranges of Lebanon, Carmel, and Gilead, on which deer abounded in vast numbers, would thus furnish them with a plentiful and luxuriant repast.

26-32. HOLY THINGS TO BE EATEN IN THE HOLY PLACE. **Only thy holy things which thou hast**—The tithes mentioned (vs. 17) are not to be considered ordinary tithes, which belonged to the Levites, and of which private Israelites had a right to eat; but they are other extraordinary tithes or gifts, which the people carried to the sanctuary to be presented as peace offerings, and on which, after being offered and the allotted portion given to the priest, they feasted with their families and friends (Lev. 27:30). **29-32. Take heed to thyself that thou be not snared by following them . . . saying, How did these nations serve their gods?**—The Israelites, influenced by superstitious fear, too often endeavored to propitiate the deities of Canaan. Their Egyptian education had early impressed that bugbear notion of a set of local deities, who expected their dues of all who came to inhabit the country which they honored with their protection, and severely resented the neglect of payment in all newcomers [WARBURTON]. Taking into consideration the prevalence of this idea among them, we see that against an Egyptian influence was directed the full force of the wholesome caution with which this chapter closes.

ADAM CLARKE

out on the ground. (1) The blood should not be eaten.

(2) It should be poured out by way of sacrifice. *The roebuck, and . . . the hart.* It is very likely that by *tsebi* the antelope is meant; and by *aiyal*, the *hart* or deer.

19. *Forsake not the Levite.* These had no inheritance, and were to live by the sanctuary; if therefore the offerings were withheld by which the Levites were supported, they of course must perish. Those who have devoted themselves to the service of God in ministering to the salvation of the souls of men certainly should be furnished at least with all the necessaries of life.

23. *For the blood is the life.* And the life being offered as an atonement, consequently the blood should not be eaten. See the notes on Lev. xvii. 11.

31. *Their sons and their daughters they have burnt in the fire.* Almost all the nations in the world agreed in offering human victims to their gods on extraordinary occasions, by which it is evident that none of those nations had any right notion of the divine nature. How necessary, then, was the volume of revelation, to teach men what that religion is with which God can be well pleased!

CHAPTER 13

Verses 1–5

Here is, I. A very strange supposition, *v.* 1, 2. 1. It is strange that there should arise any among themselves, especially any pretending to vision and prophecy, who should instigate them to *go and serve other gods*. Could an Israelite ever be guilty of such impiety? We see it in our own day and therefore may think it the less strange; multitudes that profess both learning and religion yet exciting both themselves and others, not only to worship God by images, but to give divine honour to saints and angels. So here, 2. It is to fortify them against the danger of

CHAPTER 13

VSS. 1-5. ENTICERS TO IDOLATRY TO BE PUT TO DEATH. **1. If there arise among you a prophet**—The special counsels which follow arose out of the general precept contained in the last verse of the preceding chapter; and the purport of them is, that every attempt to seduce others from the course of duty which that divine standard of faith and worship prescribes must not only be strenuously resisted, but the seducer punished by the law of the land. This is exemplified in three cases of enticement to idolatry. **a prophet**—i.e., some notable person laying claim to the character and authority of the pro-

CHAPTER 13

1. *If there arise among you a prophet.* Any pretending to have a divine influence, so as to be able perfectly to direct others in the way of salvation; *or a dreamer of dreams*—one who pretends that some deity has spoken to him in the night season; *and giveth thee a sign, oth*, what appears to be a miraculous proof of his mission; *or a wonder, mopheth*, some type or representation of what he wishes to bring you over to, as some have pretended to have received a consecrated image from heaven. But here the word seems to mean some portentous

MATTHEW HENRY

impostures and lying wonders (2 Thess. ii. 9).

II. A very necessary charge given,

1. Not to yield to the temptation: "*Thou shalt not hearken to the words of that prophet, v.* 3. Not only thou shalt not do the thing he tempts thee to, but thou shalt not so much as patiently hear the temptation, but reject it with the utmost disdain and detestation. Keep close to your duty, and you keep out of harm's way. God never leaves us till we leave him.

2. Not to spare the tempter, *v.* 5. The infection must be kept from spreading by cutting off the gangrened limb, and putting away the mischief-makers. Such dangerous diseases as these must be taken in time.

Verses 6–11

Further provision is made by this branch of the statute against receiving the infection of idolatry from those that are near and dear to us. Satan tempted Adam by Eve and Christ by Peter.

Verses 12–18

Here the case is put of a city revolting from its allegiance to the God of Israel, *and serving other gods.*

I. The crime is supposed to be committed, 1. By one of the cities of Israel, that lay within the jurisdiction of their courts. The city that is here supposed to have become idolatrous is one that formerly worshipped the true God, but had now withdrawn to other gods, which intimates how great the crime is. 2. It is supposed to be committed by the generality of the inhabitants of the city. 3. They are supposed to be drawn to idolatry by *certain men, the children of Belial.* Belial is put for *the devil* (2 Cor. vi. 15), and the children of Belial are his children.

II. The cause is ordered to be tried with a great deal of care (*v.* 14): *Thou shalt enquire and make search.*

III. If the crime were proved, and the criminals were incorrigible, the city was to be wholly destroyed. If there were a few righteous men in it, no doubt they would remove themselves and their families out of such a dangerous place. The faithful worshippers of the true God must take all occasions to show their just indignation against idolatry, much more against atheism, infidelity, and irreligion. They might think it impolitic, and against the interest of their nation, to ruin a whole city for a crime relating purely to religion, and that they should be more sparing of the blood of Israelites: "Fear not that" (says Moses), "God will multiply you the more; the body of your nation will lose nothing by the letting out of this corrupt blood." Though idolaters may escape punishment from men (nor is this law in the letter of it binding now, under the gospel), yet the Lord our God will not suffer them to escape his righteous judgments.

JAMIESON, FAUSSET, BROWN

phetic office (Num. 12:6; I Sam. 10:6), performing feats of dexterity or power in support of his pretensions, or even predicting events which occurred as he foretold; as, for instance, an eclipse which a knowledge of natural science might enable him to anticipate (or, as Caiaphas, John 18:14). Should the aim of such a one be to seduce the people from the worship of the true God, he is an impostor and must be put to death. No prodigy, however wonderful, no human authority, however great, should be allowed to shake their belief in the divine character and truth of a religion so solemnly taught and so awfully attested (cf. Gal. 1:8). The modern Jews appeal to this passage as justifying their rejection of Jesus Christ. But He possessed all the characteristics of a true prophet, and He was so far from alienating the people from God and His worship that the grand object of His ministry was to lead to a purer, more spiritual and perfect observance of the law.

6-18. WITHOUT REGARD TO NEARNESS OF RELATION. **6. If thy brother . . . entice thee secretly**—This term being applied very loosely in all Eastern countries (Gen. 20:13), other expressions are added to intimate that no degree of kindred, however intimate, should be allowed to screen an enticer to idolatry, to conceal his crime, or protect his person. Piety and duty must overcome affection or compassion, and an accusation must be lodged before a magistrate. **9. thou shalt surely kill him**—not hastily, or in a private manner, but after trial and conviction; and his relative, as informer, was to cast the first stone (see on ch. 17:7; Acts 7:58). It is manifest that what was done in secret could not be legally proved by a single informer; and hence Jewish writers say that spies were set in some private part of the house, to hear the conversation and watch the conduct of a person suspected of idolatrous tendencies. **12-18. Certain men, the children of Belial**—lawless, designing demagogues (Judg. 19:22; I Sam. 1:16; 25:25), who abused their influence to withdraw the inhabitants of the city to idol worship. **14. Then shalt thou inquire**—i.e., the magistrate, to whom it officially belonged to make the necessary investigation. In the event of the report proving true, the most summary proceedings were to be commenced against the apostate inhabitants. The law in this chapter has been represented as stern and sanguinary, but it was in accordance with the national constitution of Israel. God being their King, idolatry was treason, and a city turned to idols put itself into a state, and incurred the punishment, of rebellion. **16. it shall be an heap for ever; it shall not be built again**—Its ruins shall be a permanent monument of the divine justice, and a beacon for the warning and terror of posterity. **17. there shall cleave naught of the cursed thing to thine hand**—No spoil shall be taken from a city thus solemnly devoted to destruction. Every living creature must be put to the sword—everything belonging to it reduced to ashes—that nothing but its infamy may remain.

ADAM CLARKE

sign, such as an eclipse, which he who knew when it would take place might predict to the people who knew nothing of the matter, and thereby accredit his pretensions.

3. *The Lord your God proveth you.* God permits such imposters to arise to try the faith of His followers, and to put their religious experience to the test; for he who experimentally knows God cannot be drawn away after idols. He who has no experimental knowledge of God may believe anything. Experience of the truths contained in the Word of God can alone preserve any man from false religion. They who have not this are a prey to the pretended prophet, and to the dreamer of dreams.

6. *If thy brother . . . or thy son.* The teacher of idolatry was to be put to death; and so strict was this order that a man must neither spare nor conceal his *brother, son, daughter, wife,* or *friend,* because this was the highest offense that could be committed against God, and the most destructive to society; hence the severest laws were enacted against it.

13. *Children of Belial.* From *bal,* "not," and *yaal,* "profit"; Septuagint, "lawless men"; persons good for nothing to themselves or others, and capable of nothing but mischief.

15. *Thou shalt surely smite the inhabitants.* If one city were permitted to practice idolatry, the evil would soon spread; therefore the contagion must be destroyed in its birth.

17. *And there shall cleave nought of the cursed thing.* As God did not permit them to take the spoils of these idolatrous cities, they could be under no temptation to make war upon them. It could be done only through a merely religious motive, in obedience to the command of God, as they could have no profit by the subversion of such places. How few religious wars would there ever have been in the world had they been regulated by this principle: "Thou shalt neither extend thy territory, nor take any spoils"!

MATTHEW HENRY — CHAPTER 14

Verses 1–21

Moses here tells the people of Israel,

I. How God had dignified them, as a peculiar people, with three distinguishing privileges. 1. Here is election: *The Lord hath chosen thee, v.* 2. He did not choose them because they were by their own dedication and subjection a peculiar people to him above other nations, but he chose them that they might be so by his grace. 2. Here is adoption (*v.* 1): "*You are the children of the Lord your God,* formed by him into a people, owned by him as his people, nay, his family, *a people near unto him,* nearer than any other." 3. Here is sanctification (*v.* 2): "*Thou art a holy people,* separated and set apart for God, devoted to his service, designed for his praise, governed by a holy law, graced by a holy tabernacle, and the holy ordinances relating to it."

II. How they ought to distinguish themselves by a sober singularity from all the nations that were about them. *Be you the children of the Lord your God*: so the Seventy read it, as a command, that is, "Carry yourselves as becomes the children of God, and do nothing to disgrace the honour and forfeit the privileges of the relation." In two things particularly they must distinguish themselves:—

1. In their mourning: *You shall not cut yourselves, v.* 1. This forbids (as some think), not only their cutting themselves at their funerals, either to express their grief or with their own blood to appease the infernal deities, but their wounding and mangling

JAMIESON, FAUSSET, BROWN — CHAPTER 14

VSS. 1, 2. GOD'S PEOPLE MUST NOT DISFIGURE THEMSELVES IN MOURNING. **1. ye shall not cut yourselves . . . for the dead**—It was a common practice of idolaters, both on ceremonious occasions of their worship (I Kings 18:28), and at funerals (cf. Jer. 16:6; 41:5), to make ghastly incisions on their faces and other parts of their persons with their finger nails or sharp instruments. The making a large bare space between the eyebrows was another heathen custom in honor of the dead (see on Lev. 19:27, 28; 21:5). Such indecorous and degrading usages, being extravagant and unnatural expressions of hopeless sorrow (I Thess. 4:13), were to be carefully avoided by the Israelites, as derogatory to the character, and inconsistent with the position, of those who were the people of God.

3-21. WHAT MAY BE EATEN, AND WHAT NOT. **Thou shalt not eat any abominable thing**—i.e., anything forbidden as unclean (see on Lev. 11). OF BEASTS.

ADAM CLARKE — CHAPTER 14

1. *Ye are the children of the Lord.* The very highest character that can be conferred on any created beings; *ye shall not cut yourselves,* i.e., their hair, for it was a custom among idolatrous nations to consecrate their hair to their deities, though they sometimes also made incisions in their flesh.

4. *These are the beasts which ye shall eat.* On Leviticus xi I have entered into considerable detail relative to the clean and unclean animals there mentioned. For the general subject, the reader is referred to the notes on that chapter; but as there are particulars mentioned here which Moses does not introduce in Leviticus, it will be necessary to consider them in this place. *The ox. Shor.* This term includes all clean animals of the beef kind; not only the *ox* properly so called, but also the bull, the cow, heifer, and calf. *The sheep. Seh*: including the ram, the wether, the ewe, and the lamb. *The goat. Az*: including the he-goat, she-goat, and kid. The words in the text, *seh chesabim,* signify the lamb or young of sheep; and *seh izzim,* the young or kid of goats: but this is a Hebrew idiom which signifies every creature of the genus. The flesh of these animals is universally allowed to be the most wholesome and nutritive. They live on the very best vegetables; and having several stomachs, their food is well concocted, and the chyle formed from it the most

MATTHEW HENRY

themselves in the worship of their gods, as Baal's prophets did (1 Kings xviii. 28). They are forbidden to disturb and afflict their own minds with inordinate grief for the loss of near and dear relations. We that have a God to hope in, and a heaven to hope for, must bear up ourselves with that hope under every burden of this kind.

2. They must be singular in their meat. Observe, (1) Many sorts of flesh which were wholesome enough, and which other people did commonly eat, they must religiously abstain from as unclean. [1] Concerning beasts, here is a more particular enumeration of those which they were allowed to eat than was in Leviticus.

[2] Concerning fish there is only one general rule given, that whatsoever had not fins and scales (as shell-fish and eels, besides leeches and other animals in the water that are not proper food) was *unclean and forbidden, v.* 9, 10. [3] No general rule is given concerning fowl, but those are particularly mentioned that were to be unclean to them, and there are few or none of them which are here forbidden that are now commonly eaten. [4] They are further forbidden, *First,* To eat the flesh of any creature that died of itself, because the blood was not separated from it, and, besides the ceremonial uncleanness which it lay under (from Lev. xi. 39), it is not wholesome food. *Secondly,* To *seethe a kid in its mother's milk,* either to gratify their own luxury, supposing it a dainty bit, or in conformity to some superstitious custom of the heathen.

(2) Now as to all these precepts concerning their food, [1] It is plain in the law itself that they belonged only to the Jews, and were not moral, nor of perpetual use, because not of universal obligation; for what they might not eat themselves they might give to a stranger, or they might sell it to an alien, a mere Gentile, that came into their country for trade, *v.* 21. [2] It is plain in the gospel that they are now antiquated and repealed. For *every creature of God is good, and nothing now to be refused,* or *called common and unclean,* 1 Tim. iv. 4.

Verses 22–29

We have here a part of the statute concerning tithes. The productions of the ground were twice tithed, so that, putting both together, a fifth part was devoted to God out of their increase, and only four parts of five were for their own common use. The first tithe was for the maintenance of their Levites. But it is the second tithe that is here spoken of, which was to be taken out of the remainder when the Levites had had theirs.

I. They are here charged to separate it, and set it apart for God: *Thou shalt truly tithe all the increase of thy seed, v.* 22.

II. They are here directed how to dispose of it when they had separated it. This second tithe may be disposed of,

1. In works of piety, for the first two years after the year of release.

2. Every third year this tithe must be disposed of at home in works of charity (*v.* 28, 29): *Lay it up within thy own gates,* and let it be given to the poor. "Thither let them come, and eat and be satisfied."

JAMIESON, FAUSSET, BROWN

4-8. The hart–(see on ch. 12:15). **fallow deer**–The Hebrew word (*Jachmur*) so rendered, does not represent the fallow deer, which is unknown in Western Asia, but an antelope (*Oryx leucoryx*), called by the Arabs, jazmar. It is of a white color, black at the extremities, and a bright red on the thighs. It was used at Solomon's table.

wild goat–The word *akko* is different from that commonly used for a wild goat (I Sam. 24:2; Ps. 104:18; Prov. 5:19), and it is supposed to be a goat-deer, having the body of a stag, but the head, horns, and beard of a goat. An animal of this sort is found in the East, and called *Lerwee* [SHAW'S TRAVELS].

pygarg–a species of antelope (*Oryx addax*) with white buttocks, wreathed horns two feet in length, and standing about three feet seven inches high at the shoulders. It is common in the tracks which the Israelites had frequented [SHAW]. **wild ox**–supposed to be the *Nubian Oryx,* which differs from the *Oryx leucoryx* (formerly mentioned) by its black color; and it is, moreover, of larger stature and more slender frame, with longer and more curved horns. It is called *Bekkar-El-Wash* by the Arabs. **chamois**–rendered by the Sept. Cameleopard; but, by others who rightly judge it must have been an animal more familiar to the Hebrews, it is thought to be the Kebsch (*Ovis tragelaphus*), rather larger than a common sheep, covered not with wool, but with reddish hair–a Syrian sheep-goat.

OF BIRDS.

11-20. Of all clean birds ye shall eat–(see on Lev. 11:21). **13. glede**–thought to be the same as that rendered "*Kulture*" (Lev. 11:14). **the cuckow**–more probably the sea-gull. **the swan**–rather the goose (MICHAELIS). **gier eagle**–The Hebrew word *Rachemah* is manifestly identical with *Rachamah,* the name which the Arabs give to the common vulture of Western Asia and Egypt. (*Neophron percnopterus.*) **cormorant**–rather the *plungeon;* a seafowl. **the lapwing**–the upupa or hoop: a beautiful bird, but of the most unclean habits. **21. Ye shall not eat of any thing that dieth of itself**–(see on Leviticus 17:15; 22:8). **thou shalt give it unto the stranger that is in thy gates**–not a proselyte, for he, as well as an Israelite, was subject to this law; but a heathen traveller or sojourner. **Thou shalt not seethe a kid in his mother's milk**–This is the third place in which the prohibition is repeated. It was pointed against an annual pagan ceremony (see on Exod. 23:19; 34:26). **22-27. Thou shalt truly tithe all the increase of thy seed**–The dedication of a tenth part of the year's produce in everything was then a religious duty. It was to be brought as an offering to the sanctuary; and, where distance prevented its being taken in kind, it was by this statute convertible into money.

28-29. At the end of three years . . . the Levite . . . shall come, etc.–The Levites having no inheritance like the other tribes, the Israelites were not to forget them, but honestly to tithe their increase. Besides the tenth of all the land produce, they had forty-eight cities, with the surrounding grounds, "the best of the land," and a certain proportion of the sacrifices as their allotted perquisites. They had, therefore, if not an affluent, yet a comfortable and independent, fund for their support.

ADAM CLARKE

pure because the best elaborated, as it is well refined before it enters into the blood. On ruminating or chewing the cud, see the note on Lev. xi. 3.

5. *The hart. Aiyal,* the deer, according to Dr. Shaw. *The roebuck. Tsebi,* generally supposed to be the antelope. It has round, twisted, spiral horns, hairy tufts on the knees, browses on tender shoots, lives in hilly countries, is fond of climbing rocks, and is remarkable for its beautiful black eyes. The flesh is good and well-flavored. *The fallow deer. Yachmur,* from *chamar,* to be "troubled, disturbed, disordered"; this is supposed to mean, not the *fallow deer,* but the "buffalo." According to 1 Kings iv. 23, this was one of the animals which was daily served up at the table of Solomon. Though the flesh of the buffalo is not considered very delicious, yet in the countries where it abounds it is eaten as frequently by all classes of persons as the ox is in England. The *yachmur* is not mentioned in the parallel place, Leviticus xi. *The wild goat. Akko.* It is not easy to tell what creature is intended by the *akko.* Dr. Shaw supposed it to be a kind of very timorous goat, bearing a resemblance to both the goat and the stag, whence the propriety of the name given it by the Septuagint and Vulgate, the "goat-stag"; probably the rock goat. The word is found nowhere else in the Hebrew Bible.

The pygarg. Dishon. As this word is nowhere else used, we cannot tell what animal is meant by it. The word *pygarg* literally signifies "white buttocks," and is applied to a kind of eagle with a white tail; but here it evidently means a quadruped. It was probably some kind of goat, common and well-known in Judea. *The wild ox. Teo.* This is supposed to be the *oryx* of the Greeks, which is a species of large "stag." *The chamois. Zemer.* This was probably a species of goat or deer, but of what kind we know not; that it cannot mean the *chamois* is evident from this circumstance, "that the chamois inhabits only the regions of snow and ice, and cannot bear the heat." The Septuagint and Vulgate translate it the *Camelopard,* but this creature is only found in the torrid zone and probably was never seen in Judea; consequently could never be prescribed as a clean animal, to be used as ordinary food. Once more I must be permitted to say that to ascertain the natural history of the Bible is a hopeless case. Of a few of its animals and vegetables we are comparatively certain, but of the great majority we know almost nothing.

13. *The vulture after his kind.* The word *daiyah* in this verse is not only different from that in Leviticus, but means also a different animal, properly enough translated *vulture.* See the note on Lev. xi. 14.

21. *Thou shalt not seethe a kid in his mother's milk.* Mr. Calmet thinks that this precept refers to the paschal lamb only, which was not to be offered to God till it was weaned from its mother; but see the note on Exod. xxiii. 19.

22. *Thou shalt truly tithe.* Meaning the second tithe, which themselves were to eat, v. 23, for there was a first tithe that was given to the Levites, out of which they paid a tenth part to the priests, Num. xviii. 24-28; Neh. x. 37-38. Then of that which remained, the owners separated a second tithe, which they ate before the Lord the first and second year; and in the third year it was given to the Levites and to the poor, Deut. xiv. 28-29. In the fourth and fifth years it was eaten again by the owners, and in the sixth year it was given to the poor. The seventh year was a Sabbath to the land, and then all things were common, Exod. xxiii. 10-11.

26. *Or for strong drink.* What the *sikera* or strong drink of the Hebrews was, see in the note on Lev. x. 9.

29. *And the Levite* (*because he hath no part nor inheritance*). And hence much of his support depended on the mere freewill offerings of the people. God chose to make His ministers thus dependent on the people, that they might be induced (among other motives) to labor for their spiritual profiting, that the people, thus blessed under their ministry, might feel it their duty and privilege to support and render them comfortable.

MATTHEW HENRY

CHAPTER 15

Verses 1–11

Here is, I. A law for the relief of poor debtors. Every seventh year was a year of release, in which the ground rested from being tilled and servants were discharged from their services; and, among other acts of grace, this was one, that those who had borrowed money, and had not been able to pay it before, should this year be released from it; and though, if they were able, they were afterwards bound in conscience to repay it, yet thenceforth the creditor should never recover it by law. Many good expositors think it only forbids the exacting of the debt in the year of release, because, no harvest being gathered in that year, it could not be expected that men should pay their debts then, but that afterwards it might be sued for and recovered: so that the release did not extinguish the debt, but only stayed the process for a time. But others think it was a release of the debt for ever, and this seems more probable. The law is not that the creditor shall not receive the debt if the debtor, or his friends for him, can pay it; but he shall not exact it by a legal process. The reasons of this law are, 1. To put an honour upon the sabbatical year: *Because it is called the Lord's release*, *v.* 2. 2. It was to prevent the falling of any Israelite into extreme poverty: so the margin reads (*v.* 4), *To the end there shall be no poor among you.* 3. God's security is here given by a divine promise that, whatever they lost by their poor debtors, it should be made up to them in the blessing of God upon all they had and did, *v.* 4–6.

II. Here is a law in favour of poor borrowers, that they might not suffer damage by the former law. 1. It is taken for granted that there would be poor among them, who would have occasion to borrow (*v.* 7), and that there would never cease to be some such objects of charity (*v.* 11). 2. In such a case we are here commanded to lend or give, according to our ability and the necessity of the case: *Thou shalt not harden thy heart, nor shut thy hand*, *v.* 7. Thou shalt *open thy hand wide unto him*, to *lend him sufficient*, *v.* 8. Sometimes there is as much charity in prudent lending as in giving, as it obliges the borrower to industry and honesty and may put him into a way of helping himself. When we have an occasion of charitable lending, if we cannot trust the borrower, we must trust God, and lend, hoping for nothing again in this world, but expecting it will be recompensed in the resurrection of the just, Luke vi. 35; xiv. 14.

III. Here is a command to give cheerfully whatever we give in charity: *Thy heart shall not be grieved when thou givest*, *v.* 10.

Verses 12–18

Here is, I. A repetition of the law that had been given concerning Hebrew servants who had sold themselves for servants, or were sold by their parents through extreme poverty, or were sold by the court of judgment for some crime committed. The law was, 1. That they should serve but six years, and in the seventh should go out free, *v.* 12. Compare Exod. xxi. 2. And, if the year of jubilee happened before they served out their time, that would be their discharge. 2. That if, when their six years' service had expired, they had no mind to go out free, but would rather continue in service, they must lay themselves under an obligation to serve for ever, that is, for life, by having *their ears bored to the door-posts*, *v.* 16, 17.

II. Here is an addition to this law, requiring them to put some small stock into their servants' hands to set up with for themselves, when they sent them out of their service, *v.* 13, 14.

Verses 19–23

Here is, 1. A repetition of the law concerning the firstlings of their cattle. 2. An addition to that law, for the further explication of it, directing them what to do with the firstlings, (1) That were females: "Thou shalt *do no work with the* female *firstlings of the cow*, nor shear those of the sheep" (*v.* 19). (2) But what must they do with that which was blemished, ill-blemished? *v.* 21. Were it male or female, it must not be brought near the sanctuary, nor used either for sacrifice or for holy feasting, for it would not be fit to honour God with. What a mercy is it that we are not under this yoke! We are not dieted as they were; we make no difference between a first calf, or lamb, and the rest that follow. Let us therefore realize the gospel meaning of this law, devoting ourselves and the first of our time and strength to God, as a kind of first-fruits of his creatures.

JAMIESON, FAUSSET, BROWN

CHAPTER 15

Vss. 1-11. The Seventh Year a Year of Release for the Poor. **1. At the end of every seven years**—during the last of the seven, i.e., the sabbatical year (Exod. 21:2; 23:11; Lev. 25:4; Jer. 34:14). **2. Every creditor that lendeth ought unto his neighbour shall release it**—not by an absolute discharge of the debt, but by passing over that year without exacting payment. The relief was temporary and peculiar to that year during which there was a total suspension of agricultural labor. **he shall not exact it . . . of his brother**—i.e., an Israelite, so called in opposition to a stranger or foreigner. **because it is called the Lord's release**—The reason for acquitting a debtor at that particular period proceeded from obedience to the command, and a regard for the honor, of God; an acknowledgment of holding their property of Him, and gratitude for His kindness. **3. Of a foreigner thou mayest exact it again**—Admission to all the religious privileges of the Israelites was freely granted to heathen proselytes, though this spiritual incorporation did not always imply an equal participation of civil rights and privileges (Lev. 25:44; Jer. 34:14; cf. I Chron. 22:2; II Chron. 2:17). **4. Save when there shall be no poor man among you**—Apparently a qualifying clause added to limit the application of the foregoing statement; so that "the brother" to be released pointed to a poor borrower, whereas it is implied that if he were rich, the restoration of the loan might be demanded even during that year. But the words may properly be rendered (as on marg.) to the *end, in order that there may be no poor among you*—i.e., that none be reduced to inconvenient straits and poverty by unseasonable exaction of debts at a time when there was no labor and no produce, and that all may enjoy comfort and prosperity, which will be the case through the special blessing of God on the land, provided they are obedient. **7-11. If there be among you a poor man . . . thou shalt not harden thine heart**—Lest the foregoing law should prevent the Israelites lending to the poor, Moses here admonishes them against so mean and selfish a spirit and exhorts them to give in a liberal spirit of charity and kindness, which will secure the divine blessing (Rom. 12:8; II Cor. 9:7). **11. For the poor shall never cease out of the land**—Although every Israelite on the conquest of Canaan became the owner of property, yet in the providence of God who foresaw the event, it was permitted, partly as a punishment of disobedience and partly for the exercise of benevolent and charitable feelings, that "the poor should never cease out of the land."

12-19. Hebrew Servants' Freedom. **12. if thy brother, an Hebrew man, or an Hebrew woman, be sold unto thee**—The last extremity of an insolvent debtor, when his house or land was not sufficient to cancel his debt, was to be sold as a slave with his family (Lev. 25:39; II Kings 4:1; Neh. 5:1-13; Job 24:9; Matt. 18:25). The term of servitude could not last beyond six years. They obtained their freedom either after six years from the time of their sale or before the end of the seventh year. At the year of jubilee, such slaves were emancipated even if their six years of service were not completed. **13-15. thou shalt not let him go away empty**—A seasonable and wise provision for enabling a poor unfortunate to regain his original status in society, and the motive urged for his kindness and humanity to the Hebrew slave was the remembrance that the whole nation was once a degraded and persecuted band of helots in Egypt. Thus, kindness towards their slaves, unparalleled elsewhere in those days, was inculcated by the Mosaic law; and in all their conduct towards persons in that reduced condition, leniency and gentleness were enforced by an appeal which no Israelite could resist. **16, 17. if he say unto thee, I will not go away from thee**—If they declined to avail themselves of the privilege of release and chose to remain with their master, then by a peculiar form of ceremony they became a party to the transaction, voluntarily sold themselves to their employer, and continued in his service till death. **18. he hath been worth a double hired servant to thee**—i.e., he is entitled to double wages because his service was more advantageous to you, being both without wages and for a length of time, whereas hired servants were engaged yearly (Lev. 25:53), or at most for three years (Isa. 16:14). **19. All the firstling males of thy herd and of thy flock thou shalt sanctify unto the Lord thy God**—(See on Exod. 22: 30). **thou shalt do not work with the firstling of thy bullock**—i.e., the second firstlings (see on ch. 12:17, 18; 14:23).

ADAM CLARKE

CHAPTER 15

1. *At the end of every seven years thou shalt make a release.* For an explanation of many things in this chapter, see the notes on Exodus xxi and xxiii and Leviticus xxv.

4. *There shall be no poor.* That is, comparatively; see v. 11.

8. *Thou shalt open thine hand wide.* Your benevolence shall be in proportion to his distress and poverty, and your ability. You shall have no other rule to regulate your charity by.

9. *Beware that there be not a thought in thy wicked heart. Lebabecha beliyaal*, "thy belial heart," that is, thy good-for-nothing or unprofitable heart; see on chap. xiv. 13. *And thine eye be evil.* An evil eye signifies a covetous disposition. See the same form of expression used by our Lord in the same sense, Matt. vi. 23. "If thine eye be evil"—if you are a covetous person. "Evil eye" is by our Lord opposed to "single eye," i.e., a person of a liberal, benevolent mind. Covetousness darkens the soul; liberality and benevolence enlighten it. *And he cry unto the Lord against thee.* What a consolation to the poor and the oppressed, that they have a sure Friend in God, who will hear their cry and redress their grievances!

11. *For the poor shall never cease out of the land.* To this passage our Lord appears to allude in Mark xiv. 7: "For ye have the poor with you always." God leaves these in mercy among men to exercise the feelings of compassion, tenderness, mercy. And without occasions afforded to exercise these, man would soon become a Stoic or a brute.

13. *Thou shalt not let him go away empty.* Because during the time he served you he made no property for himself, having been always honest towards you; and now when he leaves you, he has nothing to begin the world with.

14. *Thou shalt furnish him . . . out of thy flock.* You shall give him some cattle to breed with; *out of thy floor*—some corn for seed and for bread; *and out of thy winepress*—an adequate provision of wine for present necessity.

17. *Thou shalt take an aul.* See the note on Exod. xxi. 6.

20. *Thou shalt eat it . . . in the place which the Lord shall choose.* Thus God in His mercy made their duty and interest go hand in hand. And in every case God acts thus with His creatures.

21. *If there be any blemish.* See the notes on Lev. xxii. 20. God will have both a perfect priest and a perfect offering.

MATTHEW HENRY

CHAPTER 16

Verses 1–17
Much of the communion between God and his people Israel was kept up, and a face of religion preserved in the nation, by the three yearly feasts, the institution of which, and the laws concerning them, we have several times met with already; and here they are repeated.

I. The law of the passover, so great a solemnity that it made the whole month, in the midst of which it was placed, considerable: *Observe the month Abib*, *v.* 1. Though one week only of this month was to be kept as a festival, yet their preparations before must be so solemn, and their reflections upon it and improvements of it afterwards so serious, as to amount to an observance of the whole month. The laws concerning it are, 1. That they must be sure to sacrifice the passover in the place that God should choose (*v.* 2), and in no other place, *v.* 5–7.

2. That they must eat unleavened bread for seven days, and no leavened bread must be seen in all their coasts, *v,* 3, 4, 8. The gospel meaning of this feast of unleavened bread the apostle gives us, 1 Cor. v. 7. *Christ our passover being sacrificed for us*, and we having participated in the blessed fruits of that sacrifice to our comfort, *let us keep the feast* in a holy conversation, free from *the leaven of malice* towards our brethren and hypocrisy towards God, and *with the unleavened bread of sincerity* and love.

II. Seven weeks after the passover the feast of pentecost was to be observed. They must *bring an offering unto God*, *v.* 10. It is here called a *tribute of a freewill-offering.* The law did not determine the *quantum*, but it was left to every man's generosity to bring what he chose, and whatever he brought he must give cheerfully, it is therefore called a *free-will offering.*

III. They must keep the feast of tabernacles, *v.* 13–15. When we rejoice in God ourselves we should do what we can to assist others also to rejoice in him, by comforting the mourners and supplying the necessitous, that even *the stranger, the fatherless, and the widow may rejoice with us.* See Job xxix. 13. Those that make God their joy may *rejoice in hope*, for he is faithful that has promised.

JAMIESON, FAUSSET, BROWN

CHAPTER 16

Vss. 1-22. The Feast of the Passover. **1. Observe the month of Abib**—or first-fruits. It comprehended the latter part of our March and the beginning of April. Green ears of the barley, which were then full, were offered as first fruits, on the second day of the passover. **for in the month of Abib the Lord thy God brought thee out of Egypt by night**—This statement is apparently at variance with the prohibition (Exod. 12:22) as well as with the recorded fact that their departure took place in the *morning* (Exod. 13:3; Num. 33:3). But it is susceptible of easy reconciliation. Pharaoh's permission, the first step of emancipation, was extorted during the night, the preparations for departure commenced, the rendezvous at Rameses made, and the march entered on in the morning. **2. Thou shalt therefore sacrifice the passover**—not the paschal lamb, which was strictly and properly the passover. The whole solemnity is here meant, as is evident from the mention of the additional victims that required to be offered on the subsequent days of the feast (Num. 28:18, 19; II Chron. 35:8, 9), and from the allusion to the continued use of unleavened bread for seven days, whereas the passover itself was to be eaten at once. The words before us are equivalent to "thou shalt observe the feast of the passover." **3. seven days shalt thou eat unleavened bread**—a sour, unpleasant, unwholesome kind of bread, designed to be a memorial of their Egyptian misery and of the haste with which they departed, not allowing time for their morning dough to ferment. **5, 6. Thou mayest not sacrifice the passover within any of thy gates**—The passover was to be observed nowhere but in the court of the tabernacle or temple, as it was not a religious feast or sacramental occasion merely, but an actual sacrifice (Exod. 12:27; 23:18; 34:25). The blood had to be sprinkled on the altar and in the place where the true Passover was afterwards to be sacrificed for us at even, at the going down of the sun—lit., between the evenings. **at the season**—i.e., the month and day, though not perhaps the precise hour. The immense number of victims that had to be immolated on the eve of the passover—i.e., within a space of four hours—has appeared to some writers a great difficulty. But the large number of officiating priests, their dexterity and skill in the preparation of the sacrifices, the wide range of the court, the extraordinary dimensions of the altar of burnt offering and orderly method of conducting the solemn ceremonial, rendered it easy to do that in a few hours, which would otherwise have required as many days. **7. thou shalt roast and eat it**—(See on Exod. 12:8; cf. II Chron. 35:13). **thou shalt turn in the morning, and go unto thy tents**—The sense of this passage, on the first glance of the words, seems to point to the morning after the first day—the passover eve. Perhaps, however, the divinely appointed duration of this feast, the solemn character and important object, the journey of the people from the distant parts of the land to be present, and the recorded examples of their continuing all the time (II Chron. 30:21), (though these may be considered extraordinary, and therefore exceptional occasions), may warrant the conclusion that the leave given to the people to return home was to be on the morning after the completion of the seven days. **9-12. Seven weeks shalt thou number**—The feast of weeks, or a Week of Weeks: The feast of pentecost (see on Exod. 34:22; Lev. 23:10; Acts 2:1). As on the second day of the passover a sheaf of new barley, reaped on purpose, was offered, so on the second day of pentecost a sheaf of new wheat was presented as first fruits (Exod. 23:16; Num. 28:26), a freewill, spontaneous tribute of gratitude to God for His temporal bounties. This feast was instituted in memory of the giving of the law, that spiritual food by which man's soul is nourished (Deut. 8:3). **13-17. Thou shalt observe the feast of tabernacles seven days**—(See on Exod. 23:16; Lev. 23:34; Num. 29:12). Various conjectures have been formed to account for the appointment of this feast at the conclusion of the whole harvest. Some imagine that it was designed to remind the Israelites of the time when they had no cornfields to reap but were daily supplied with manna; others think that it suited the convenience of the people better than any other period of the year for dwelling in booths; others that it was the time of Moses' second descent from the mount; while a fourth class are of opinion that this feast was fixed to the time of the year when the Word was made flesh and *dwelt*—lit., *tabernacled*—among us (Josh. 1:14), Christ being actually born at that season. **15. in all the works of thine hands . . . repoice**—i.e., praising God with a warm

ADAM CLARKE

CHAPTER 16

1. *Keep the passover.* A feast so called because the angel that destroyed the firstborn of the Egyptians, seeing the blood of the appointed sacrifice sprinkled on the lintels and doorposts of the Israelites' houses, "passed over them," and did not destroy any of their firstborn. See the notes on Exod. xii. 2, etc.

3. *Bread of affliction.* Because, being baked without leaven, it was unsavory, and put them in mind of their afflictive bondage in Egypt.

11. *Thou shalt rejoice.* The offerings of the Israelites were to be eaten with festivity, communicated to their friends with liberality, and bestowed on the poor with great generosity, that they might partake with them in these repasts with joy before the Lord. To answer these views it was necessary to eat the flesh while it was fresh, as in that climate putrefaction soon took place; therefore they were commanded to let nothing remain until the morning, v. 4.

MATTHEW HENRY

IV. The laws concerning the three solemn feasts are summed up (*v.* 16, 17). The general commands concerning them are, 1. That all the males must then make their personal appearance before God. 2. That none must appear before God empty, but every man must bring some offering or other.

Verses 18–22

Here is, I. Care taken for the due administration of justice among them, that controversies might be determined, matters in variance adjusted, the injured redressed, and the injurious punished. While they were encamped in the wilderness, they had *judges and officers* according to their numbers, rulers of thousands and hundreds, Exod. xviii. 25. When they came to Canaan, they must have them according to their towns and cities, in all their gates; for the courts of judgment sat in the gates.

II. Care taken for the preventing of all conformity to the idolatrous customs of the heathen, *v.* 21, 22. They must not plant a grove, nor so much as a tree, near God's altar, lest they should make it look like the altars of the false gods. Nothing tends more to corrupt and debauch the minds of men, than representing and worshipping by an image that God who is an infinite and eternal Spirit.

JAMIESON, FAUSSET, BROWN

and elevated heart. According to Jewish tradition, no marriages were allowed to be celebrated during these great festivals, that no personal or private rejoicings might be mingled with the demonstrations of public and national gladness. **16. Three times in a year shall all thy males appear before the Lord thy God**—No *command* was laid on women to undertake the journeys, partly from regard to the natural weakness of their sex, and partly to their domestic cares. **18-20. Judges and officers shalt thou make**—These last meant heralds or bailiffs, employed in executing the sentence of their superiors. **in all thy gates**—The gate was the place of public resort among the Israelites and other Eastern people, where business was transacted and cases decided. The Ottoman Porte derived its name from the administration of justice at its gates. **21. Thou shalt not plant thee a grove**—A grove has in Scripture a variety of significations—a group of overshadowing trees, or a grove adorned with altars dedicated to a particular deity, or a wooden image in a grove (Judg. 6:25; II Kings 23:4-6). They might be placed near the earthen and temporary altars erected in the wilderness, but they could not exist either at the tabernacle or temples. They were places, which, with their usual accompaniments, presented strong allurements to idolatry; and therefore the Israelites were prohibited from planting them. **22. Neither shalt thou set up any image**—erroneously rendered so for "pillar"; pillars of various kinds, and materials of wood or stone were erected in the neighborhood of altars. Sometimes they were conical or oblong, at other times they served as pedestals for the statues of idols. A superstitious reverence was attached to them, and hence they were forbidden.

ADAM CLARKE

16. *Three times in a year.* See Exod. xxiii. 14, where all the Jewish feasts are explained. See also Lev. xxiii. 34.

18. *Judges and officers shalt thou make. Judges, shophetim,* among the Hebrews, were probably the same as our magistrates or "justices of the peace." *Officers, shoterim,* seem to have been the same as our sergeants, whose office it was to go into the houses, shops, etc., and examine weights, measures, and the civil conduct of the people. When they found anything amiss, they brought the person offending before the magistrate, and he was punished by the officer on the spot.

21. *Thou shalt not plant thee a grove.* We have already seen that groves were planted about idol temples for the purpose of the obscene worship performed in them. On this account God would have no groves or thickets about His altar, that there might be no room for suspicion that anything contrary to the strictest purity was transacted there. Every part of the divine worship was publicly performed, for the purpose of general edification.

MATTHEW HENRY — CHAPTER 17

Verses 1–7

Here is, I. A law for preserving the honour of God's worship, by providing that no creature that had any blemish should be offered in sacrifice to him, *v.* 1. The Old Testament sacrifices in a special manner were types of Christ, who is a *Lamb without blemish or spot* (1 Pet. i. 19). In the latter times of the Jewish church, when by the captivity in Babylon they were cured of idolatry, yet they were charged with profaneness in the breach of this law, with *offering the blind, and the lame, and the sick for sacrifice,* Mal. i. 8.

II. A law for the punishing of those that worshipped false gods. That which was the most ancient and plausible idolatry is specified, worshipping the sun, moon, and stars; and, if that was so detestable a thing, much more was it so to worship stocks and stones, or the representations of mean and contemptible animals. How heinous and dangerous soever the crime is, yet they must not punish any for it, unless there were good proof against them, by two witnesses at least. So great a punishment as death, so great a death as stoning, must be inflicted on the idolater, whether man or woman, for the infirmity of the weaker sex would be no excuse, *v.* 5. The hands of the witnesses, in this as in other cases, must be first upon him, that is, they must cast the first stone at him, thereby avowing their testimony, and solemnly imprecating the guilt of his blood upon themselves if their evidence were false. This custom might be of use to deter men from false-witness bearing.

Verses 8–13

Courts of judgment were ordered to be erected in every city (*ch.* xvi. 18), and they were empowered to hear and determine causes according to law, both those which we call pleas of the crown and those between party and party; and we may suppose that ordinarily they ended the matters that were brought before them, and their sentence was definitive; but, 1. It is here taken for granted that sometimes a case might come into their court too difficult for those inferior judges to determine. These difficult cases, which hitherto had been brought to Moses, according to Jethro's advice, were, after his death, to be brought to the supreme power, wherever it was lodged, whether in a judge (when there was such an extraordinary person raised up and qualified for that great service, as Othniel, Deborah, Gideon, &c.) or in the high-priest (when he was by the eminency of his gifts called of God to preside in public affairs, as Eli), or, if no single person were marked by heaven for this honour, then in the priests and Levites.

Verses 14–20

After the laws which concerned subjects fitly followed the laws which concern kings; for those that

JAMIESON, FAUSSET, BROWN — CHAPTER 17

VS. 1. THINGS SACRIFICED MUST BE SOUND. **1. Thou shalt not sacrifice . . . any bullock or sheep wherein is blemish**—Under the name of bullock were comprehended bulls, cows, and calves; under that of sheep, rams, lambs, kids, he and she-goats. An ox, from mutilation, was inadmissible. The qualifications required in animals destined for sacrifice are described (Exod. 12:5; Lev. 1:3).

2-7. IDOLATERS MUST BE SLAIN. **2-7. If there be found among you . . . man or woman, that hath wrought wickedness**—The grand object contemplated in choosing Israel was to preserve the knowledge and worship of the one true God; and hence idolatry of any kind, whether of the heavenly bodies or in some grosser form, is called "a transgression of His covenant." No rank or sex could palliate this crime. Every reported case, even a flying rumor of the perpetration of so heinous an offense, was to be judicially examined; and if proved by the testimony of competent witnesses, the offender was to be taken without the gates and stoned to death, the witnesses casting the first stone at him. The object of this special arrangement was partly to deter the witnesses from making a rash accusation by the prominent part they had to act as executioners, and partly to give a public assurance that the crime had met its due punishment.

8-13. THE PRIESTS AND JUDGES TO DETERMINE CONTROVERSIES. **8-13. If there arise a matter too hard for thee in judgment**—In all civil or criminal cases, where there was any doubt or difficulty in giving a decision, the local magistrates were to submit them by reference to the tribunal of the Sanhedrim—the supreme council, which was composed partly of civil and partly of ecclesiastical persons. "The priests and Levites," should rather be "the priests—the Levites"; i.e., the Levitical priests, including the high priest, who were members of the legislative assembly; and who, as forming one body, are called "the judge." Their sittings were held in the neighborhood of the sanctuary because in great emergencies the high priest had to consult God by Urim (Num. 27:21). From their judgment there was no appeal; and if a person were so perverse and refractory as to refuse obedience to their sentences, his conduct, as inconsistent with the maintenance of order and good government, was then to be regarded and punished as a capital crime.

14-20. THE ELECTION AND DUTY OF A KING. **14. When thou . . . shalt say, I will set a king over me**—In the following passage Moses *prophetically* announces a revolution which should occur at a later period in the national history of Israel. No sanction or recommendation was indicated; on the contrary, when the popular clamor had effected that constitutional change on the theocracy by the

ADAM CLARKE — CHAPTER 17

1. *Wherein is blemish.* God must not have that offered to Him which you would not use yourself. This not only refers to the perfect sacrifice offered by Christ Jesus, but to that sincerity and uprightness of heart which God requires in all those who approach Him in the way of worship.

4. *If it be told thee*—in a private way by any confidential person. *And thou hast heard of it*—so that it appears to be notorious, very likely to be true, and publicly scandalous. *And enquired diligently*—sought to find out the truth of the report by the most careful examination of persons reporting, circumstances of the case, etc. *And, behold, it be true*—the report is not founded on vague rumor, hearsay, or malice. *And the thing certain*—substantiated by the fullest evidence. *Then shalt thou bring forth that man,* v. 5. As the charge of idolatry was the most solemn and awful that could be brought against an Israelite, because it affected his life, therefore God required that the charge should be substantiated by the most unequivocal facts, and the most competent witnesses. Hence all the precautions mentioned in the fourth verse must be carefully used, in order to arrive at so affecting and so awful a truth.

6. *Two witnesses.* One might be deceived, or be prejudiced or malicious; therefore God required two substantial witnesses for the support of the charge.

8. *If there arise a matter too hard for thee.* These directions are given to the common magistrates, who might not be able to judge of or apply the law in all cases that might be brought before them. The priests and Levites, who were lawyers by birth and continual practice, were reasonably considered as the best qualified to decide on difficult points.

12. *The man that will do presumptuously!* The man who refused to abide by this final determination forfeited his life, as being then in a state of rebellion against the highest authority, and consequently the public could have no pledge for his conduct.

MATTHEW HENRY

rule others must themselves remember that they are under command. Here are laws given,

I. To the electors of the empire, what rules they must go by in making their choice, *v.* 14, 15. 1. It is here supposed that the people would, in process of time, be desirous of a king, whose royal pomp and power would be thought to make their nation look great among their neighbours. 2. They are directed in their choice. If they will have a king over them, as God foresaw they would (though it does not appear that ever the motion was made till almost 400 years after), then they must, (1) Ask counsel at God's mouth, and make him king whom God shall choose. Accordingly, when the people desired a king, they applied to Samuel a prophet of the Lord; and afterwards David, Solomon, Jeroboam, Jehu, and others, were chosen by the prophets. (2) They must not choose a foreigner under pretence of strengthening their alliances, lest a strange king should introduce strange customs or usages.

II. Laws are here given to the prince that should be elected for the due administration of the government.

1. He must carefully avoid every thing that would divert him from God and religion. Riches, honours, and pleasures are the three great hindrances of godliness (*the lusts of the flesh, the lusts of the eye, and the pride of life*), especially to those in high stations: against these therefore the king is here warned.

2. He must carefully apply himself to the law of God, and make that his rule. This must be to him better than all riches, honours, and pleasures, than many horses or many wives, better than thousands of gold and silver.

(1) He must write himself a copy of the law out of the original, which was in the custody of the priests that attended the sanctuary, *v.* 18. Note, It is of great use for each of us to write down what we observe as most affecting and edifying to us, out of the scriptures and good books, and out of the sermons we hear. A prudent pen may go far towards making up the deficiencies of the memory, and the furnishing of the treasures of the good householder with things new and old.

(2) His writing and reading were all nothing if he did not reduce to practice what he wrote and read, *v.* 19, 20. Let him know, what dominion his religion must have over him, and what influence it must have upon him. *First,* It must possess him with a very reverent and awful regard to the divine majesty and authority. *Secondly,* It must engage him to a constant observance of the law of God, and a conscientious obedience to it, as the effect of that fear. *Thirdly,* It must keep him humble. How much soever he is advanced, let him keep his spirit low, and let the *fear of his God prevent the contempt of his brethren.*

JAMIESON, FAUSSET, BROWN

appointment of a king, the divine disapproval was expressed in the most unequivocal terms (I Sam. 8:7). Permission at length was granted, God reserving to Himself the nomination of the family and the person who should be elevated to the regal dignity (I Sam. 9:15; 10:24; 16:12; I Chron. 28:4). In short, Moses foreseeing that his ignorant and fickle countrymen, insensible to their advantages as a peculiar people, would soon wish to change their constitution and be like other nations, provides to a certain extent for such an emergency and lays down the principles on which a king in Israel must act. He was to possess certain indispensable requisites. He was to be an Israelite, of the same race and religion, to preserve the purity of the established worship, as well as be a type of Christ, a spiritual king, one of their brethren. **15. thou mayest not set a stranger over thee, which is not thy brother**—i.e., by their free and voluntary choice. But God, in the retributions of His providence, did allow foreign princes to usurp the dominion (Jer. 38:17; Matt. 22:17). **16. he shall not multiply horses to himself**—The use of these animals was not absolutely prohibited, nor is there any reason to conclude that they might not be employed as part of the state equipage. But the multiplication of horses would inevitably lead to many evils, to increased intercourse with foreign nations, especially with Egypt, to the importation of an animal to which the character of the country was not suited, to the establishment of an Oriental military despotism, to proud and pompous parade in peace, to a dependence upon Egypt in time of war, and a consequent withdrawal of trust and confidence in God. (II Sam. 8:4; I Kings 10:26; II Chron. 1:16; 9:28; Isa. 31:3.) **17. Neither shall he multiply wives to himself, that his heart turn not away**—There were the strongest reasons for recording an express prohibition on this point, founded on the practice of neighboring countries in which polygamy prevailed, and whose kings had numerous harems; besides, the monarch of Israel was to be absolutely independent of the people and had nothing but the divine law to restrain his passions. The mischievous effects resulting from the breach of this condition were exemplified in the history of Solomon and other princes, who, by trampling on the restrictive law, corrupted themselves as well as the nation. **neither shall he greatly multiply . . . silver and gold**—i.e., the kings were forbidden to accumulate money for private purposes. **18-20. he shall write him a copy of this law in a book**—The original scroll of the ancient Scriptures was deposited in the sanctuary under the strict custody of the priests (see on ch. 31:26; II Kings 22:8). Each monarch, on his accession, was to be furnished with a true and faithful copy, which he was to keep constantly beside him, and daily peruse it, that his character and sentiments being cast into its sanctifying mould, he might discharge his royal functions in the spirit of faith and piety, of humility and a love or righteousness.

that he may prolong his days in his kingdom, he, and his children—From this it appears that the crown in Israel was to be hereditary, unless forfeited by personal crime.

ADAM CLARKE

15. *One from among thy brethren shalt thou set king over thee.* It was on the ground of His command that the Jews proposed that insidious question to our Lord, "Is it lawful to give tribute unto Caesar, or not?" Matt. xxii. 17; for they were then under the authority of a foreign power. Had Christ said, "Yes," then they would have condemned Him by this law; had He said, "No," then they would have accused Him to Caesar.

16. *He shall not multiply horses.* As horses appear to have been generally furnished by Egypt, God prohibits these: (1) Lest there should be such commerce with Egypt as might lead to idolatry; (2) Lest the people might depend on a well-appointed cavalry as a means of security, and so cease from trusting in the strength and protection of God; and (3) That they might not be tempted to extend their dominion by means of cavalry, and so get scattered among the surrounding idolatrous nations, and thus cease, in process of time, to be that distinct and separate people which God intended they should be, and without which the prophecies relative to the Messiah could not be known to have their due and full accomplishment.

17. *Neither shall he multiply wives.* For this would necessarily lead to foreign alliances, and be the means of introducing the manners and customs of other nations, and their idolatry also. Solomon sinned against this precept, and brought ruin on himself and on the land by it; see 1 Kings xi. 4.

18. *He shall write him a copy of this law. Mishneh hattorah hazzoth,* and "iteration or duplicate of this law"; translated by the Septuagint, "this deuteronomy." From this version both the Vulgate Latin and all the modern versions have taken the name of this book; and from the original word the Jews call it *Mishneh.* See the preface to this book.

Out of that which is before the priests the Levites. It is likely this means that the copy which the king was to write out was to be taken from the autograph kept in the Tabernacle before the Lord, from which, as a standard, every copy was taken, and with which doubtless every copy was compared; and it is probable that the priests and Levites had the revising of every copy that was taken off, in order to prevent errors from creeping into the sacred text.

19. *And it shall be with him.* It was the surest way to bring the king to an acquaintance with the divine law to oblige him to write out a fair copy of it with his own hand, in which he was to read daily. This was essentially necessary, as these laws of God were all permanent, and no Israelitish king could make any new law, the kings of this people being ever considered as only the vicegerents of Jehovah.

20. *He, and his children, in the midst of Israel.* From this verse it has been inferred that the crown of Israel was designed to be hereditary, and this is very probable; for long experience has proved to almost all the nations of the world that hereditary succession in the regal government is, on the whole, the safest, and best calculated to secure the public tranquillity.

CHAPTER 18 (Matthew Henry)

Verses 1-8

Magistracy and ministry are two divine institutions of admirable use for the support and advancement of the *kingdom of God among men.* Laws concerning the former we had in the close of the foregoing chapter, directions are in this given concerning the latter. Land marks are here set between the estates of the priests and those of the people.

I. Care is taken that the priests entangle not themselves with the affairs of this life, nor enrich themselves with the wealth of this world; they have better things to mind.

II. Care is likewise taken that they want not any of the comforts and conveniences of this life. Though God, who is a Spirit, is their inheritance, it does not therefore follow that they must live upon the air. The people must provide for them. They must have their *due from the people, v.* 3. Their maintenance must not depend upon the generosity of the people, but they must be by law entitled to it.

CHAPTER 18 (Jamieson, Fausset, Brown)

Vss. 1-8. THE LORD IS THE PRIESTS' AND THE LEVITES' INHERITANCE. **1. The priests the Levites . . . shall eat the offerings**—As the tribe of Levi had no inheritance allotted them like the other tribes but were wholly consecrated to the priestly office, their maintenance was to arise from tithes, first fruits, and certain portions of the oblations presented on the altar, which God having by express appointment reserved to Himself made over, after being offered, to His ministers. **3 this shall be the priests' due from the people**—All who offered sacrifices of thanksgiving or peace offerings (Lev. 7: 31-33) were ordered to give the breast and shoulder as perquisites to the priests. Here "the two cheeks" or head and "the maw" or stomach, deemed anciently a great dainty, are specified. But whether this is a new injunction, or a repetition of the old with the supplement of more details, it is not easy to determine.

CHAPTER 18 (Adam Clarke)

2. *The Lord is their inheritance.* He is the portion of their souls; and as to their bodies, they shall live by the offerings of the Lord made by fire, i.e., the meat offering, the sin offering, and the trespass offering; and whatever was the Lord's right, in these or other offerings, He gave to the priests.

3. *Offer a sacrifice. Zobechey hazzebach.* The word *zebach* is used to signify, not only an animal sacrificed to the Lord, but also one killed for common use. See Gen. xliii. 15; Prov. xvii. 1; Ezek. xxv. 6. And in this latter sense it probably should be understood here; and, consequently, the command in this verse relates to what the people were to allow the priests and Levites from the animals slain for common use. The parts to be given to the priests were: (1) The *shoulder;* (2) The *two cheeks,* which may include the whole head; (3) The *maw*—the whole of those intestines which are commonly used for food.

MATTHEW HENRY

Verses 9–14

One would not think there had been so much need as it seems there was to arm the people of Israel against the infection of the idolatrous customs of the Canaanites. After many cautions, they are here charged not to do after the abominations of those nations, *v.* 9.

I. Some particulars are specified; as, 1. The consecrating of their children to Moloch, an idol that represented the sun, by making them to *pass through the fire*, and sometimes consuming them as sacrifices in the fire, *v.* 10. See the law against this before, Lev. xviii. 21. 2. Using arts of divination, to get the unnecessary knowledge of things to come, *enchantments, witchcrafts, charms*, &c.

II. Some reasons are given against their conformity to the customs of the Gentiles. 1. Because it would make them abominable to God. 2. Because these abominable practices had been the ruin of the Canaanites, of which ruin they were not only the witnesses but the instruments. 3. Because they were *better taught*, *v.* 13, 14. It is an argument like that of the apostle against Christians walking as the Gentiles walked (Eph. iv. 17, 18, 20): *You have not so learned Christ.*

Verses 15–22

I. The promise of the great prophet, with a command to receive him, and hearken to him.

1. Some think it is the promise of a succession of prophets, that should for many ages be kept up in Israel. Besides the priests and Levites, their ordinary ministers, whose office it was to teach Jacob God's law, they should have prophets, extraordinary ministers, to reprove them for their faults, remind them of their duty, and foretell things to come, judgments for warning and deliverances for their comfort.

2. Whether a succession of prophets be included in this promise or not, we are sure that it is primarily intended as a promise of Christ, and it is the clearest promise of him that is in all the law of Moses. It is expressly applied to our Lord Jesus as the Messiah promised (Acts iii. 22; vii. 37), and the people had an eye to this promise when they said concerning him, *This is of a truth that prophet that should come into the world* (John vi. 14); and it was his Spirit that spoke in all the other prophets, 1 Pet. i. 11. It is also a charge and command given to all people to hear and believe, hear and obey, this great prophet here promised: *Unto him you shall hearken* (*v.* 15); and whoever will not hearken to him shall be surely and severely reckoned with for his contempt (*v.* 19): *I will require it of him.*

II. Here is a caution against false prophets. Whatever is directly repugnant to sense, to the light and law of nature, and to the plain meaning of the written word, we may be sure is not that which the Lord has spoken; nor that which gives countenance and encouragement to sin, or has a manifest tendency to the destruction of piety or charity.

JAMIESON, FAUSSET, BROWN

6-8. if a Levite . . . come with all the desire of his mind—It appears that the Levites served in rotation from the earliest times; but, from their great numbers, it was only at infrequent intervals they could be called into actual service. Should any Levite, however, under the influence of eminent piety, resolve to devote himself wholly and continually to the sacred duties of the sanctuary, he was allowed to realize his ardent wishes; and as he was admitted to a share of the work, so also to a share of the remuneration. Though he might have private property, that was to form no ground for withholding or even diminishing his claim to maintenance like the other ministering priests. The reason or principle of the enactment is obvious (I Cor. 9:13). At the same time, while every facility was afforded for the admission of such a zealous and self-denying officer, this admission was to be in an orderly manner: he was to minister "as all his brethren"—i.e., a Gershonite with Gershonites; a Merarite with Merarites; so that there might be no derangement of the established courses.

9-14. THE ABOMINATIONS OF THE NATIONS ARE TO BE AVOIDED. **9-14. thou shalt not learn to do after the abominations of those nations**—(See on Lev. 18:21; 19:26-31; 20:6). In spite of this express command, the people of Canaan, especially the Philistines, were a constant snare and stumbling block to the Israelites, on account of their divinations and superstitious practices.

15-19. CHRIST THE PROPHET IS TO BE HEARD. **15-19. The Lord thy God will raise up unto thee a prophet**—The insertion of this promise, in connection with the preceding prohibition, might warrant the application (which some make of it) to that order of true prophets whom God commissioned in unbroken succession to instruct, to direct, and warn His people; and in this view the purport of it is, "There is no need to consult with diviners and soothsayers, as I shall afford you the benefit of divinely appointed prophets, for judging of whose credentials a sure criterion is given" (vss. 20-22). But the prophet here promised was pre-eminently the Messiah, for He alone was "like unto Moses (see on ch. 34:10) in His mediatorial character; in the peculiar excellence of His ministry; in the number, variety, and magnitude of His miracles; in His close and familiar communion with God; and in His being the author of a new dispensation of religion." This prediction was fulfilled 1500 years afterwards and was expressly applied to Jesus Christ by Peter (Acts 3:22, 23), and by Stephen (Acts 7:37). **19. whosoever will not hearken unto my words which he shall speak in my name, I will require it of him**—The direful consequences of unbelief in Christ, and disregard of His mission, the Jewish people have been experiencing during 1800 years.

ADAM CLARKE

4. *The firstfruit also of thy corn, of thy wine, and of thine oil.* All these firstfruits and firstlings were the Lord's portion, and these He gave to the priests.

8. *The sale of his patrimony.* So we find that, though the Levites might have no part of the land by lot, yet they were permitted to make purchases of houses, goods, and cattle, yea, of fields also. See the case of Abiathar, 1 Kings ii. 26, and of Jeremiah, Jer. xxxii. 7-8.

10. *To pass through the fire.* Probably in the way of consecration to Molech, or some other deity. *Divination. Kosem kesamim,* one who endeavors to find out futurity by auguries, using lots, etc. *Observer of times. Meonen,* one who pretends to foretell future events by present occurrences, and who predicts great political or physical changes from the aspects of the planets, eclipses, motion of the clouds, etc. *Enchanter. Menachesh,* from *nichesh,* to "view attentively"; one who inspected the entrails of beasts, observed the flight of birds, etc., and drew auguries thence. Some think divination by serpents is meant, which was common among the heathen. *A witch. Mechashsheph,* probably those who by means of drugs, herbs, perfumes, etc., pretended to bring certain celestial influences to their aid. See the note on Lev. xix. 26.

11. *A charmer. Chober chaber,* one who uses spells; a peculiar conjunction, as the term implies, of words, or things, tying knots, etc., for the purposes of divination. This was a custom among the heathen. *A consulter with familiar spirits. Shoel ob,* a Pythoness, one who inquires by the means of one spirit to get oracular answers from another of a superior order. See on Lev. xix. 31. *A wizard. Yiddeoni,* "a wise one," a knowing one. *Wizard* was formerly considered as the masculine of "witch," both practicing divination by similar means. See on Exod. xxii. 18 and Lev. xix. 31. *Or a necromancer. Doresh el hammethim,* one who seeks from or inquires of the dead, such as the witch at Endor, who professed to evoke the dead, in order to get them to disclose the secrets of the spiritual world.

15. *The Lord thy God will raise up unto thee a Prophet.* Instead of diviners, observers of times, etc., God here promises to give them an infallible Guide, who should tell them all things that make for their peace, so that His declarations should completely answer the end of all the knowledge that was pretended to be gained by the persons already specified. *Like unto me.* Viz., a Prophet, a Legislator, a King, a Mediator, and the Head or Chief of the people of God. This was the very Person of whom Moses was the type, and who should accomplish all the great purposes of the Divine Being. Such a Prophet as had never before appeared, and who should have no equal till the consummation of the world. This Prophet is the Lord Jesus, who was in the bosom of the Father, and who came to declare Him to mankind. Every word spoken by Him is a living, infallible oracle from God himself; and must be received and obeyed as such, on pain of the eternal displeasure of the Almighty. See v. 19, and Acts iii. 22-23.

22. *If the thing follow not.* It is worthy of remark that the prophets in general predicted those things which were shortly to come to pass, that the people might have the fullest proof of their divine mission, and of the existence of God's providence in the administration of the affairs of men.

MATTHEW HENRY

CHAPTER 19

Verses 1–13

It was one of the precepts given to the sons of Noah that *whoso sheddeth man's blood by man shall his blood be shed*, that is, by the avenger of blood, Gen. ix. 6. Now here we have the law settled between blood and blood, between the blood of the murdered and the blood of the murderer, and effectual provision made.

I. That the cities of refuge should be a protection to him that slew another casually, so that he should not die for that as a crime which was not his voluntary act, but only his unhappiness.

1. The appointing of three cities in Canaan for this purpose. The country was to be divided into three districts, and a city of refuge in the centre of

JAMIESON, FAUSSET, BROWN

CHAPTER 19

VSS. 1-13. OF THE CITIES OF REFUGE. **2. Thou shalt separate three cities in the midst of thy land**—Goelism, or the duty of the nearest kinsmen to avenge the death of a slaughtered relative, being the customary law of that age (as it still is among the Arabs and other people of the East), Moses incorporated it in an improved form with his legislative code. For the protection of the unintentional homicide, he provided certain cities of refuge—three had been destined for this purpose on the east of Jordan (ch. 4:41; Num. 35:11); three were to be invested with the same privilege on the west of that river when Canaan should be conquered. **in the midst of the land**—in such a position that they would be conspicuous and accessible, and equi-

ADAM CLARKE

CHAPTER 19

2. *Thou shalt separate three cities.* See on Num. xxxv. 10, etc.

MATTHEW HENRY

each, so that every corner of the land might have one within reach.

2. The use to be made of these cities, *v.* 4–6. (1) It is supposed that it might so happen that a man might be the death of his neighbour without any design upon him either from a sudden passion or malice prepense, but purely by accident, as by the flying off of an axe-head, which is the instance here given, with which every case of this kind was to be compared, and by it adjudged. (2) It is supposed that the relations of the person slain would be forward to avenge the blood. Though the law did not allow the avenging of any other affront or injury with death, yet the avenger of blood, the blood of a relation, shall have great allowances made for the heat of his heart upon such a provocation as that, and his killing the man-slayer, though he was so by accident only, should not be accounted murder if he did it before he got to the city of refuge. (3) It is provided that, if an avenger of blood should be so unreasonable as to demand satisfaction for blood shed by accident only, then the city of refuge should protect the slayer.

3. The appointing of three cities more for this use in case God should hereafter enlarge their territories and the dominion of their religion, that all those places which came under the government of the law of Moses in other instances might enjoy the benefit of that law in this instance, *v.* 8–10.

II. It is provided that the cities of refuge should be no sanctuary or shelter to a wilful murderer, but even thence he should be fetched, and delivered to the avenger of blood, *v.* 11–13. Before the Reformation, there were some churches and religious houses (as they called them) that were made sanctuaries for the protection of all sorts of criminals that fled to them, wilful murderers not excepted, so that (as Stamford says, in his *Pleas of the Crown, lib.* II, *c.* xxxviii.) the government follows not Moses but Romulus, and it was not till about the latter end of Henry VIII's time that this privilege of sanctuary for wilful murder was taken away.

Verses 14–21

Here is a statute for the preventing of frauds and perjuries; for the divine law takes care of men's rights and properties, and has made a hedge about them.

I. A law against frauds, *v.* 14. 1. Here is an implicit direction given to the first planters of Canaan to fix land marks, according to the distribution of the land to the several tribes and families by lot. 2. An express law to posterity not to remove those land-marks. It forbids, (1) The invading of any man's right, and taking to ourselves that which is not our own, by any fraudulent arts or practices, as by forging, concealing, destroying, or altering deeds and writings (which are our land marks, to which appeals are made), or by shifting hedges, meer-stones, and boundaries. (2) It forbids the sowing of discord among neighbours, and doing any thing to occasion strife and law-suits.

II. A law against perjuries, which enacts two things:—1. That a single witness should never be admitted to give evidence in a criminal cause, so as that sentence should be passed upon his testimony, *v.* 15. 2. That a false witness should incur the same punishment which was to have been inflicted upon the person he accused, *v.* 16–21.

JAMIESON, FAUSSET, BROWN

distant from the extremities of the land and from each other. **3. Thou shalt prepare thee a way**—The roads leading to them were to be kept in good condition and the brooks or rivers to be spanned by good bridges; the width of the roads was to be 32 cubits; and at all the crossroads signposts were to be erected with the words, *Mekeleth, Mekeleth,* "refuge, refuge," painted on them. **divide the coasts of thy land . . . into three parts**—the whole extent of the country from the south to the north. The three cities on each side of Jordan were opposite to each other, "as two rows of vines in a vineyard" (see on Josh. 20:7, 8). **6. Lest the avenger of blood pursue the slayer, while his heart is hot**—This verse is a continuation of the third (for vss. 4, 5, which are explanatory, are in a parenthetical form), and the meaning is that if the kinsman of a person inadvertently killed should, under the impulse of sudden excitement and without inquiring into the circumstances, inflict summary vengeance on the homicide, however guiltless, the law tolerated such an act; it was to pass with impunity. But to prevent such precipitate measures, the cities of refuge were established for the reception of the homicide, that "innocent blood might not be shed in thy land" (vs. 10). In the case of premeditated murder (vss. 11, 12), they afforded no immunity; but, if it were only manslaughter, the moment the fugitive was within the gates, he found himself in a safe asylum (Num. 35:26-28; Josh. 20:6). **8, 9. And if the Lord thy God enlarge thy coast**—Three additional sanctuaries were to be established in the event of their territory extending over the country from Hermon and Gilead to the Euphrates. (See on Gen. 15:18; Exod. 23:31.) But it was obscurely hinted that this last provision would never be carried into effect, as the Israelites would not fulfil the conditions, viz., "that of keeping the commandments, to love the Lord, and walk ever in his ways." In point of fact, although that region was brought into subjection by David and Solomon, we do not find that cities of refuge were established; because those sovereigns only made the ancient inhabitants tributary, instead of sending a colony of Israelites to possess it. The privilege of sanctuary cities, however, was given only for Israelites; and besides, that conquered territory did not remain long under the power of the Hebrew kings.

14. THE LANDMARK IS NOT TO BE REMOVED. **14. Thou shalt not remove thy neighbour's landmark, which they of old have set in thine inheritance**—The state of Palestine in regard to enclosures is very much the same now as it has always been. Though gardens and vineyards are surrounded by dry stone walls or hedges of prickly-pear, the boundaries of arable fields are marked by nothing but by a little trench, a small cairn, or a single erect stone, placed at certain intervals. It is manifest that a dishonest person could easily fill the gutter with earth, or remove these stones a few feet without much risk of detection and so enlarge his own field by a stealthy encroachment on his neighbor's. This law, then, was made to prevent such trespasses.

15. TWO WITNESSES REQUIRED. **15. One witness shall not arise against a man for any iniquity**—The following rules to regulate the admission of testimony in public courts are founded on the principles of natural justice. A single witness shall not be admitted to the condemnation of an accused person.

16-21. PUNISHMENT OF A FALSE WITNESS. But if convicted of perjury, it will be sufficient for his own condemnation, and his punishment shall be exactly the same as would have overtaken the object of his malignant prosecution. (See on Exod. 21:24; Lev. 24:20.)

ADAM CLARKE

3. *Thou shalt prepare thee a way.* The Jews inform us that the roads to the cities of refuge were made very broad, thirty-two cubits; and even, so that there should be no impediments in the way; and were constantly kept in good repair.

9. *Shalt thou add three cities more.* This was afterwards found necessary, and accordingly six cities were appointed, three on either side Jordan. See Josh. xxi. 1, etc. In imitation of these cities of refuge the heathens had their *asyla,* and the Catholics their privileged altars.

11. *If any man hate his neighbour.* See on Exod. xxi. 13.

14. *Thou shalt not remove thy neighbour's landmark.* Before the extensive use of fences, landed property was marked out by stones or posts, set up so as to ascertain the divisions of family estates. It was easy to remove one of these landmarks, and set it in a different place; and thus the dishonest man enlarged his own estate by contracting that of his neighbor. The *termini* or landmarks among the Romans were held very sacred, and were at last deified.

15. *One witness shall not rise up, etc.* See Num. xxxv. 30.

19. *Then shall ye do unto him as he had thought to have done unto his brother.* Nothing can be more equitable or proper than this, that if a man endeavor to do any injury to or take away the life of another, on detection he shall be caused to undergo the same evil which he intended for his innocent neighbor.

21. *Life . . . for life, eye for eye.* The operation of such a law as this must have been very salutary; if a man prized his own members, he would naturally avoid injuring those of others.

MATTHEW HENRY — CHAPTER 20

Verses 1–9

Israel was at this time to be considered rather as a camp than as a kingdom, entering upon an enemy's country, and not yet settled in a country of their own; and, besides the war they were now entering upon in order to their settlement, even after their settlement they could neither protect nor enlarge their coast without hearing the alarms of war. It was therefore needful that they should have directions given them in their military affairs.

I. Those that were disposed to fight must be encouraged and animated against their fears. 1. The presence of God with them: "*The Lord thy God is with thee*, and therefore thou art not in danger, nor needest thou be afraid." See Isa. xli. 10. 2. The experience they and their fathers had had of God's

JAMIESON, FAUSSET, BROWN — CHAPTER 20

VSS. 1-20. THE PRIESTS' EXHORTATION TO ENCOURAGE THE PEOPLE TO BATTLE. **1. When thou goest out to battle against thine enemies**—In the approaching invasion of Canaan, or in any just and defensive war, the Israelites had reason to expect the presence and favor of God. **2. when ye are come nigh unto the battle, the priest shall approach and speak unto the people**—Jewish writers say that there was a war priest appointed by a special ceremonial to attend the army. It was natural that the solemn objects and motives of religion should have been applied to animate patriotism, and so give additional impulse to valor; other people have done this. But in the case of Israel, the regular attendance of a priest on the battlefield was in accordance with their theocratic government, in which

ADAM CLARKE — CHAPTER 20

1. *When thou goest out to battle.* This refers chiefly to the battles they were to have with the Canaanites, in order to get possession of the Promised Land; for it cannot be considered to apply to any wars which they might have with the surrounding nations for political reasons, as the divine assistance could not be expected in wars which were not undertaken by the divine command.

2. *The priest shall approach and speak unto the people.* The priest on these occasions was the representative of that God whose servant he was, and whose worship he conducted. It is remarkable that almost all ancient nations took their priests with them to battle, as they did not

MATTHEW HENRY

power and goodness in *bringing them out of the land of Egypt*, in defiance of Pharaoh and all his hosts. *Let not your hearts be tender* (so the word is), to receive all the impressions of fear, but let a believing confidence in the power and promise of God harden them. *Fear not, and do not make haste* (so the word is), for he that believeth doth not make more haste than good speed. "Do not make haste either rashly to anticipate your advantages or basely to fly off upon every disadvantage." The giving of this encouragement by a priest, one of the Lord's ministers, intimates, (1) That it is very fit that armies should have chaplains, not only to pray for them, but to preach to them, both to reprove that which would hinder their success and to raise their hopes of it. (2) That it is the work of Christ's ministers to encourage his good soldiers in their spiritual conflicts with the world and the flesh, and to assure them of a conquest, yea, more than a conquest, through Christ that loved us.

II. Those that were indisposed to fight must be discharged. 1. The Jewish writers agree that this liberty to return was allowed only in those wars which they made voluntarily (as bishop Patrick expresses it), not those which were made by the divine command against Amalek and the Canaanites, in which every man was bound to fight.

2. If a man's indisposition to fight arose from the weakness and timidity of his own spirit, he had leave to return from the war, *v.* 8. It was partly in kindness to them that they had their discharge (for, though shamed, they were eased); but much more in kindness to the rest of the army, who were hereby freed from the incumbrance of such as were useless and unserviceable, while the danger of infection from their cowardice and flight was prevented.

III. It is here ordered that, when all the cowards were dismissed, then captains should be nominated (*v.* 9), for it was in a special manner necessary that the leaders and commanders should be men of courage.

Verses 10–20

They are here directed what method to take in dealing with the cities (these only are mentioned, *v.* 10, but doubtless the armies in the field, and the nations they had occasion to deal with, are likewise intended) upon which they made war. They must not make a descent upon any of their neighbours till they had first given them fair notice, by a public manifesto, or remonstrance, stating the ground of their quarrel with them.

I. Even to the proclamation of war must be subjoined a tender of peace, if they would accept of it upon reasonable terms. They must first proclaim peace to them. Let this show, 1. God's grace in dealing with sinners: though he might most justly and easily destroy them, yet, having no pleasure in their ruin, he proclaims peace, and beseeches them to be reconciled. 2. Let it show us our duty in dealing with our brethren: if any quarrel happen, let us not only be ready to hearken to the proposals of peace, but forward to make such proposals. We should never make use of the law till we have first tried to accommodate matters in variance amicably, and without expense and vexation. *We* must be for peace, whoever are for war.

II. If the offers of peace were not accepted, then they must proceed to push on the war.

III. The nations of Canaan are excepted from the merciful provisions made by this law. Remnants might be left of the cities that were very far off (*v.* 15), because by them they were not in so much danger of being infected with idolatry, but of the cities which were given to Israel for an inheritance no remnants must be left of their inhabitants (*v.* 16), because, since it could not be expected that they should be cured of their idolatry, if they were left with that plague-sore upon them they would be in danger of infecting God's Israel, who were too apt to take the infection.

IV. Care is here taken that in the besieging of cities there should not be any destruction made of fruit trees, *v.* 19, 20. The intent of many of the divine precepts is to restrain us from destroying that which is our life and food. Armies and their commanders are not allowed to make what desolation they please in the countries that are the seat of war. No fruit tree is to be destroyed unless it be barren, and cumber the ground. "Nay," they maintain, "whoso wilfully breaks vessels, tears clothes, stops wells, pulls down buildings, or destroys meat, transgresses this law: *Thou shalt not destroy*."

JAMIESON, FAUSSET, BROWN

everything was done directly by God through His delegated ministers. It was the province of this priest to sound the trumpets (Num. 10:9; 31:6), and he had others under him who repeated at the head of each battalion the exhortations which he addressed to the warriors in general. The speech (vss. 3, 4) is marked by a brevity and expressiveness admirably suited to the occasion, viz., when the men were drawn up in line. **4. your God is he that goeth with you, to fight for you against your enemies, to save you**—According to Jewish writers, the ark was always taken into the field of combat. But there is no evidence of this in the sacred history; and it must have been a sufficient ground of encouragement to be assured that God was on their side. **5. the officers shall speak unto the people**—lit., *Shoterim*, who are called "scribes" or "overseers" (Exod. 5:6). They might be keepers of the muster-roll, or perhaps rather military heralds, whose duty it was to announce the orders of the generals (II Chron. 26:11). This proclamation (vss. 5, 8) must have been made previous to the priest's address, as great disorder and inconvenience must have been occasioned if the serried ranks were broken by the departure of those to whom the privilege was granted. Four grounds of exemption are expressly mentioned: (1) The dedication of a new house, which, as in all Oriental countries still, was an important event, and celebrated by festive and religious ceremonies (Neh. 12:27); exemption for a year. (2) The planting of a vineyard. The fruit of the first three years being declared unfit for use, and the first fruits producible on the fourth, the exemption in this case lasted at least four years. (3) The betrothal of a wife, which was always a considerable time before marriage. It was deemed a great hardship to leave a house unfinished, a new property half cultivated, and a recently contracted marriage; and the exemptions allowed in these cases were founded on the principle that a man's heart being deeply engrossed by something at a distance, he would not be very enthusiastic in the public service. (4) The ground of exemption was cowardice. From the composition of the Israelitish army, which was an irregular militia, all above twenty years being liable to serve, many totally unfit for war must have been called to the field; and it was therefore a prudential arrangement to rid the army of such unwarlike elements—persons who could render no efficient service, and the contagion of whose craven spirit might lead to panic and defeat. **9. they shall make captains of the armies to lead the people**—When the exempted parties have withdrawn, the combatants shall be ranged in order of battle. **10-20. When thou comest nigh unto a city to fight against it, then proclaim peace unto it**—An important principle is here introduced into the war law of Israel regarding the people they fought against and the cities they besieged. With "the cities of those people which God doth give thee" in Canaan, it was to be a war of utter extermination (vss. 17, 18). But when on a just occasion, they went against other nations, they were first to make a proclamation of peace, which if allowed by a surrender, the people would become dependent, and in the relation of tributaries the conquered nations would receive the highest blessings from alliance with the chosen people; they would be brought to the knowledge of Israel's God and of Israel's worship, as well as a participation of Israel's privileges. But if the besieged city refused to capitulate and be taken, a universal massacre was to be made of the males while the women and children were to be preserved and kindly treated (vss. 13, 14). By this means a provision was made for a friendly and useful connection being established between the captors and the captives; and Israel, even through her conquests, would prove a blessing to the nations. **19. thou shalt not destroy the trees thereof by forcing an axe against them**—In a protracted siege, wood would be required for various purposes, both for military works and for fuel. But fruit-bearing trees were to be carefully spared; and, indeed, in warm countries like India, where the people live much more on fruit than we do, the destruction of a fruit tree is considered a sort of sacrilege. **20. thou shalt build bulwarks against the city that maketh war with thee**—It is evident that some sort of military engines were intended; and accordingly we know, that in Egypt, where the Israelites learned their military tactics, the method of conducting a siege was by throwing up banks, and making advances with movable towers, or with the testudo [WILKINSON].

ADAM CLARKE

expect success without having the object of their adoration with them, and they supposed they secured his presence by having that of his representative.

5. *That hath built a new house, and hath not dedicated it?* From the title of Psalms xxx—"A Psalm and Song at the Dedication of the House of David," it is evident that it was a custom in Israel to dedicate a new house to God with prayer, praise, and thanksgiving; and this was done in order to secure the divine presence and blessing, for no pious or sensible man could imagine he could dwell safely in a house that was not under the immediate protection of God.

7. *Betrothed a wife, and hath not taken her?* It was customary among the Jews to contract matrimony, espouse, or betroth, and for some considerable time to leave the parties in the houses of their respective parents; when the bridegroom had made proper preparations, then the bride was brought home to his house, and thus the marriage was consummated. The provisions in this verse refer to a case of this kind; for it was deemed an excessive hardship for a person to be obliged to go to battle, where there was a probability of his being slain, who had left a new house unfinished, a newly purchased heritage half-tilled, or a wife with whom he had just contracted marriage.

8. *What man is there that is fearful and fainthearted?* The original *rach* signifies "tender" or "softhearted." And a soft heart the man must have who, in such a contest, after such a permission, could turn his back upon his enemies and his brethren. However, such were the troops commanded by Gideon in his war against the Midianites; for after he gave this permission, out of 32,000 men only 10,000 remained to fight! Judges vii. 3. There could be no deception in a business of this kind; for the departure of the 22,000 was the fullest proof of their dastardliness which they could possibly give.

10. *Proclaim peace unto it.* The text, taken in connection with the context (see vv. 15-18), appears to state that this proclamation or offer of peace to a city is to be understood only of those cities which were situated beyond the limits of the seven anathematized nations, because these latter are commanded to be totally destroyed. Nothing can be clearer than this from the bare letter of the text.

19. (*For the tree of the field is man's life*) *to employ them in the siege.* The original is exceedingly obscure, and has been variously translated. The following are the chief versions: "For, O man, the trees of the field are for thee to employ them in the siege"; or, "For it is man, and the tree of the field, that must go before thee for a bulwark"; or, "For it is a tree, and not men, to increase the number of those who come against thee to the siege"; or, lastly, "The tree of the field (is as) a man, to go before thy face for a bulwark." The sense is sufficiently clear, though the strict grammatical meaning of the words cannot be easily ascertained: it was a merciful provision to spare all fruit-bearing trees, because they yielded the fruit which supported man's life; and it was sound policy also, for even the conquerors must perish if the means of life were cut off.

MATTHEW HENRY

CHAPTER 21

Verses 1–9

Care had been taken by some preceding laws for the vigorous and effectual prosecution of a wilful murderer (*ch.* xix. 11, &c.), the putting of whom to death was the putting away of the guilt of blood from the land; but if this could not be done, the murderer not being discovered, they must not think that the land was in no danger of contracting any pollution because it was not through any neglect of theirs that the murderer was unpunished; no, a great solemnity is here provided for the putting away of the guilt, as an expression of their dread and detestation of that sin.

I. The case supposed is that *one is found slain, and it is not known who slew him, v.* 1.

II. Directions are given concerning what is to be done in this case. The priests were to pray to God for the country and nation, that God would be merciful to them, and not bring upon them the judgments which the connivance at the sin of murder would deserve.

Verses 10–14

By this law a soldier is allowed to marry his captive if he pleased. For the hardness of their hearts Moses gave them this permission, lest, if they had not had liberty given them to marry such, they should have taken liberty to defile themselves with them, and by such wickedness the camp would have been troubled. The man is supposed to have a wife already, and to take this wife for a secondary wife, as the Jews called them. This indulgence of men's inordinate desires, in which their hearts walked after their eyes, is by no means agreeable to the law of Christ, which therefore in this respect, among others, far exceeds in glory the law of Moses.

Verses 15–17

This law restrains men from disinheriting their eldest sons out of mere caprice, and without just provocation.

I. The case here put (*v.* 15) is very instructive. 1. It shows the great mischief of having more wives than one, which the law of Moses did not restrain. 2. It shows how Providence commonly sides with the weakest. For the first-born son is here supposed to be *hers that was hated*; it was so in Jacob's family: because *the Lord saw that Leah was hated*, Gen. xxix. 31.

II. The law in this case is still binding on parents; they must give their children their right without partiality. In the case supposed, the eldest son, though the son of the less-beloved wife, must have his birthright privilege, which was a double portion of the father's estate, because he was the beginning of his strength. No son should be abandoned by his father till he manifestly appear to be abandoned of God, which is hard to say of any while there is life.

Verses 18–23

Here is, I. A law for the punishing of a rebellious son. Having in the former law provided that parents should not deprive their children of their right, it was fit that it should next be provided that children withdraw not the honour and duty which are owing to their parents.

1. How the criminal is here described. He is a *stubborn and rebellious son, v.* 18. No child was to fare the worse for the weakness of his capacity, the slowness or dullness of his understanding, but for his wilfulness and obstinacy. He is particularly supposed (*v.* 20) to be a *glutton or a drunkard.* This intimates either, (1) That these were sins which his parents did in a particular manner warn him against. Or, (2 That his being a *glutton and a drunkard* was the cause of his insolence and obstinacy towards his parents. When men take to drink they forget the law, they forget all law (Prov. xxxi. 5), even that fundamental law of honouring parents.

2. How this criminal is to be proceeded against. His own father and mother are to be his prosecutors, *v.* 19, 20.

JAMIESON, FAUSSET, BROWN

CHAPTER 21

VSS. 1-9. EXPIATION OF UNCERTAIN MURDER. **1. If one be found slain . . . lying in the field, and it be not known who hath slain him**—The ceremonies here ordained to be observed on the discovery of a slaughtered corpse show the ideas of sanctity which the Mosaic law sought to associate with human blood, the horror which murder inspired, as well as the fears that were felt lest God should avenge it on the country at large, and the pollution which the land was supposed to contract from the effusion of innocent, unexpiated blood. According to Jewish writers, the Sanhedrim, taking charge of such a case, sent a deputation to examine the neighborhood. They reported to the nearest town to the spot where the body was found. An order was then issued by their supreme authority to the elders or magistrates of that town, to provide the heifer at the civic expense and go through the appointed ceremonial. The engagement of the public authorities in the work of expiation, the purchase of the victim heifer, the conducting it to a "rough valley" which might be at a considerable distance, and which, as the original implies, was a wady, a perennial stream, in the waters of which the polluting blood would be wiped away from the land, and a desert withal, incapable of cultivation; the washing of the hands, which was an ancient act symbolical of innocence—the whole of the ceremonial was calculated to make a deep impression on the Jewish, as well as on the Oriental, mind generally; to stimulate the activity of the magistrates in the discharge of their official duties; to lead to the discovery of the criminal, and the repression of crime.

10-23. THE TREATMENT OF A CAPTIVE TAKEN TO WIFE. **10-14. When thou goest to war . . and seest among the captives a beautiful woman . . . that thou wouldest have her to be thy wife**—According to the war customs of all ancient nations, a female captive became the slave of the victor, who had the sole and unchallengeable control of right to her person. Moses improved this existing usage by special regulations on the subject. He enacted that, in the event that her master was captivated by her beauty and contemplated a marriage with her, a month should be allowed to elapse, during which her perturbed feelings might be calmed, her mind reconciled to her altered condition, and she might bewail the loss of her parents, now to her the same as dead. A month was the usual period of mourning with the Jews, and the circumstances mentioned here were the signs of grief—the shaving of the head, the allowing the nails to grow uncut, the putting off her gorgeous dress in which ladies, on the eve of being captured, arrayed themselves to be the more attractive to their captors. The delay was full of humanity and kindness to the female slave, as well as a prudential measure to try the strength of her master's affections. If his love should afterwards cool and he become indifferent to her person, he was not to lord it over her, neither to sell her in the slave-market, nor retain her in a subordinate condition in his house; but she was to be free to go where her inclinations led her. **15-17. If a man have two wives, one beloved, and another hated**—In the original and all other translations, the words are rendered "have had," referring to events that have already taken place; and that the "had" has, by some mistake, been omitted in our version, seems highly probable from the other verbs being in the past tense—"hers that was hated," not "hers that is hated"; evidently intimating that she (the first wife) was dead at the time referred to. Moses, therefore, does not here legislate upon the case of a man who has two wives at the same time, but on that of a man who has married twice in succession, the second wife after the decease of the first; and there was an obvious necessity for legislation in these circumstances; for the first wife, who was hated, was dead, and the second wife, the favorite, was alive; and with the feelings of a stepmother, she would urge her husband to make her own son the heir. This case has no bearing upon polygamy, which there is no evidence that the Mosaic code legalized. **18-21. If a man have a stubborn and rebellious son**—A severe law was enacted in this case. But the consent of both parents was required as a prevention of any abuse of it; for it was reasonable to suppose that they would not both agree to a criminal information against their son except from absolute necessity, arising from his inveterate and hopeless wickedness; and, in that view, the law was wise and salutary, as such a person would be a pest and nuisance to society. The punishment was that to which blasphemers

ADAM CLARKE

CHAPTER 21

4. *Shall bring down the heifer unto a rough valley. Nachal eythan* might be translated a "rapid stream," probably passing through a piece of uncultivated ground where the elders of the city were to strike off the head of the heifer, and to wash their hands over her in token of their innocence. The spot of ground on which this sacrifice was made must be uncultivated, because it was considered to be a sacrifice to make atonement for the murder, and consequently would pollute the land. This regulation was calculated to keep murder in abhorrence, and to make the magistrates alert in their office, that delinquents might be discovered and punished, and thus public expense saved.

6. *Shall wash their hands over the heifer.* Washing the hands, in reference to such a subject as this, was a rite anciently used to signify that the persons thus washing were innocent of the crime in question. It was probably from the Jews that Pilate learned this symbolical method of expressing his innocence.

11. *And seest . . . a beautiful woman.* No forcible possession was allowed even in this case, when the woman was taken in war, and was, by the general consent of ancient nations adjudged as a part of the spoils. The person to whose lot or share such a woman as is here described fell might, if he chose, have her for a wife on certain conditions; but he was not permitted to use her under any inferior character.

12. *She shall shave her head.* This was in token of her renouncing her religion, and becoming a proselyte to that of the Jews. This is still a custom in the East; when a Christian turns Mohammedan his head is shaven, and he is carried through the city crying, *La alahila allah we Mohammed resooli Allah,* "There is no God but God, and Mohammed is the prophet of God." *Pare her nails.* "She shall make her nails." Now whether this signifies paring or letting them grow is greatly doubted among learned men. Possibly it means neither, but coloring the nails, staining them red with the hennah, which is much practiced in India to the present day, and which was undoubtedly practiced among the ancient Egyptians, as is evident from the nails of mummies which are found thus stained.

15. *One beloved, and another hated.* That is one loved less than the other. This is the true notion of the word *hate* in Scripture. So "Jacob hated Leah," that is, he loved her less than he did Rachel; and "Jacob have I loved, but Esau have I hated"—that is, I have shown a more particular affection to the posterity of Jacob than I have to the posterity of Esau. See the note on Gen. xxix. 31. From this verse we see that polygamy did exist under the Mosaic laws, and that it was put under certain regulations. But it was not enjoined; Moses merely suffered it, because of the hardness of their hearts, as our Lord justly remarks in Matt. xix. 8.

MATTHEW HENRY

II. A law for the burying of the bodies of malefactors that were hanged, *v.* 22. Of such as were stoned to death, it was usual, by order of the judges, to hang up the dead bodies upon a post for some time, as a spectacle to the world, to express the ignominy of the crime. Now it is here provided that, whatever time of the day they were thus hanged up, at sun set they should be taken down and buried. Now, 1. God would thus preserve the honour of human bodies and tenderness towards the worst of criminals. 2. Yet it is plain there was something ceremonial in it; by the law of Moses the touch of a dead body was defiling, and therefore dead bodies must not be left hanging up in the country, because, by the same rule, this would defile the land. 3. *He that is hanged is accursed of God,* that is, it is the highest degree of disgrace and reproach that can be done to a man, and proclaims him under the curse of God as much as any external punishment can. Those that see him thus hang between heaven and earth will conclude him abandoned of both and unworthy of either; and therefore let him not hang all night, for that would carry it too far.

JAMIESON, FAUSSET, BROWN

were doomed; for parents are considered God's representatives and invested with a portion of his authority over their children. **22, 23. if a man have committed a sin . . . and thou hang him on a tree**—Hanging was not a Hebrew form of execution—gibbeting is meant—but the body was not to be left to rot or be a prey to ravenous birds: it was to be buried "that day," either because the stench in a hot climate would corrupt the air, or the spectacle of an exposed corpse bring ceremonial defilement on the land.

ADAM CLARKE

23. *His body shall not remain all night upon the tree.* Its exposure for the space of one day was judged sufficient. The law which required this answered all the ends of public justice, exposed the shame and infamy of the conduct, but did not put to torture the feelings of humanity by requiring a perpetual exhibition of a human being, a slow prey to the most loathsome process of putrefaction. *For he that is hanged is accursed of God.* That is, he has forfeited his life to the law; for it is written, "Cursed is every one that continueth not in all things which are written in the book of the law to do them"; and on his body, in the execution of the sentence of the law, the curse was considered as alighting; hence the necessity of removing the accursed thing out of sight.

MATTHEW HENRY — CHAPTER 22

Verses 1–4

The kindness that was commanded to be shown in reference to an enemy (Exod. xxiii. 4, &c.) is here required to be much more done for a neighbour, though he were not an Israelite. 1. That strayed cattle should be brought back, either to the owner or to the pasture out of which they had gone astray, *v.* 1, 2. If such care must be taken of a neighbour's ox or ass going astray, much more of himself going astray from God and his duty; we should do our utmost to convert him (Jam. v. 19), and restore him, considering ourselves, Gal. vi. 1. 2. That lost goods should be brought to the owner, *v.* 3. The Jews say, "He that found the lost goods was to give public notice of them three or four times."

Verses 5–12

Here are several laws in these verses which seem to stoop very low, and to take cognizance of things mean and minute.

I. The distinction of sexes by the apparel is to be kept up, for the preservation of our own and our neighbour's chastity, *v.* 5. 1. Some think it refers to the idolatrous custom of the Gentiles: in the worship of Venus, women appeared in armour, and men in women's clothes. 2. It forbids the confounding of the dispositions and affairs of the sexes. 3. Probably this confounding of garments had been used to gain opportunity of committing uncleanness, and is therefore forbidden.

II. In taking a bird's nest, the dam must be let go, *v.* 6, 7. But *doth God take care* for birds? 1 Cor. ix. 9. Yes, certainly; and perhaps to this law our Saviour alludes. Luke xii. 6, *Are not five sparrows sold for two farthings, and not one of them is forgotten before God?* This law, 1. Forbids us to be cruel to the brute creatures, or to take a pleasure in destroying them. 2. It teaches us compassion to those of our own kind, and to abhor the thought of everything that looks barbarous, and cruel, and ill-natured, especially towards those of the weaker and tender sex, who always ought to be treated with the utmost respect, in consideration of the sorrows wherein they bring forth children.

III. In building a house, care must be taken to make it safe, that none might receive mischief by falling from it, *v.* 8. The roofs of their houses were flat for people to walk on. They must compass them with battlements, which (the Jews say) must be three feet and a half high. See here, 1. How precious men's lives are to God, who protects them, not only by his providence, but by his law. 2. How precious, therefore, they ought to be to us, and what care we should take to fence, or remove, every thing by which life may be endangered, to cover draw-wells, keep bridges in repair, and the like.

JAMIESON, FAUSSET, BROWN — CHAPTER 22

Vss. 1-4. Of Humanity toward Brethren. **1. Thou shalt not see thy brother's ox or his sheep go astray, and hide thyself from them . . .**—"Brother" is a term of extensive application, comprehending persons of every description; not a relative, neighbor, or fellow countryman only, but any human being, known or unknown, a foreigner, and even an enemy (Exod. 23:4). The duty inculcated is an act of common justice and charity, which, while it was taught by the law of nature, was more clearly and forcibly enjoined in the law delivered by God to His people. Indifference or dissimulation in the circumstances supposed would not only be cruelty to the dumb animals, but a violation of the common rights of humanity; and therefore the dictates of natural feeling, and still more the authority of the divine law, enjoined that the lost or missing property of another should be taken care of by the finder, till a proper opportunity occurred of restoring it to the owner.

5-12. The Sex to Be Distinguished by Apparel. **5. The woman shall not wear that which pertaineth unto a man, neither shall a man put on a woman's garment**—Though disguises were assumed at certain times in heathen temples, it is probable that a reference was made to unbecoming levities practised in common life. They were properly forbidden; for the adoption of the habiliments of the one sex by the other is an outrage on decency, obliterates the distinctions of nature by fostering softness and effeminacy in the man, impudence and boldness in the woman as well as levity and hypocrisy in both; and, in short, it opens the door to an influx of so many evils that all who wear the dress of another sex are pronounced "an abomination unto the Lord." **6, 7. If a bird's nest chance to be before thee**—This is a beautiful instance of the humanizing spirit of the Mosaic law, in checking a tendency to wanton destructiveness and encouraging a spirit of kind and compassionate tenderness to the tiniest creatures. But there was wisdom as well as humanity in the precept; for, as birds are well known to serve important uses in the economy of nature, the extirpation of a species, whether of edible or ravenous birds, must in any country be productive of serious evils. But Palestine, in particular, was situated in a climate which produced poisonous snakes and scorpions; and the deserts and mountains would have been overrun with them as well as immense swarms of flies, locusts, mice, and vermin of various kinds if the birds which fed upon them were extirpated [Michaelis]. Accordingly, the counsel given in this passage was wise as well as humane, to leave the hen undisturbed for the propagation of the species, while the taking of the brood occasionally was permitted as a check to too rapid an increase. **8. thou shalt make a battlement for thy roof, that thou bring not blood upon thine house, if any man fall from thence**—The tops of houses in ancient Judea, as in the East still, were flat, being composed of branches or twigs laid across large beams, and covered with a cement of clay or strong plaster. They were surrounded by a parapet breast high. In summer the roof is a favorite resort for coolness, and accidents would frequently happen from persons incautiously approaching the edge and falling into the street or court; hence it was a wise and prudent precaution in the Jewish legislator to provide that a stone balustrade or timber railing round

ADAM CLARKE — CHAPTER 22

1. *Thou shalt not see thy brother's ox or his sheep go astray.* The same humane, merciful, and wise regulations which we met with before, Exod. xxiii. 4-5, well calculated to keep in remembrance the second grand branch of the law of God, "Thou shalt love thy neighbour as thyself." A humane man cannot bear to see even an ass fall under his burden, and not endeavor to relieve him; and a man who loves his neighbor as himself cannot see his property in danger without endeavoring to preserve it. These comparatively small matters were tests and proofs of matters great in themselves, and in their consequences.

3. *Thou mayest not hide thyself.* You shall not keep out of the way of affording help, nor pretend you did not see occasion to render your neighbor any service. The priest and the Levite, when they saw the wounded man, passed by on the other side of the way, Luke x. 31-32. This was a notorious breach of the merciful law mentioned above.

5. *The woman shall not wear that which pertaineth unto a man. Keli geber,* "the instruments or arms of a man." As the word *geber* is here used, which properly signifies a "strong man" or "man of war," it is very probable that armor is here intended; especially as we know that in the worship of Venus, to which that of Astarte or Ashtaroth among the Canaanites bore a striking resemblance, the women were accustomed to appear in armor before her. It certainly cannot mean a simple change in dress, whereby the men might pass for women, and vice versa. This would have been impossible in those countries where the dress of the sexes had but little to distinguish it, and where every man wore a long beard.

7. *Thou shalt . . . let the dam go, and take the young to thee; that it may be well with thee.* This passage may be understood literally. If they destroyed both young and old, must not the breed soon fail, and would it not in the end be ill with them; and by thus cutting off the means of their continual support, must not their days be shortened on the land? But we may look for a humane precept in this law. The young never knew the sweets of liberty; the dam did. They might be taken and used for any lawful purpose, but the dam must not be brought into a state of captivity.

8. *A battlement for thy roof.* Houses in the East are in general built with flat roofs, and on them men walk to enjoy the fresh air, converse together, sleep, etc.; it was therefore necessary to have a sort of battlement or balustrade to prevent persons from falling off. If a man neglected to make a sufficient defense against such accidents, and the death of another was occasioned by it, the owner of the house must be considered in the light of a murderer.

9. *Divers seeds.* See the note on Lev. xix. 19.

10. *Thou shalt not plow with an ox and an ass.* It is generally supposed that mixtures of different sorts in seed, breed, etc., were employed for superstitious purposes, and therefore prohibited in this law. It is more likely, however, that there was a physical reason for this;

MATTHEW HENRY

IV. Odd mixtures are here forbidden, *v.* 9, 10. Much of this we met with before, Lev. xix. 19. There appears not any thing at all of moral evil in these things, and therefore we now make no conscience of sowing wheat and rye together, ploughing with horses and oxen together, and of wearing linsey-woolsey garments; but hereby is forbidden either, 1. A conformity to some idolatrous customs of the heathen. Or, 2. That which is contrary to the plainness and purity of an Israelite. They must not gratify their own vanity and curiosity by putting those things together which the Creator in infinite wisdom had made asunder.

V. The law concerning fringes upon their garments, and memorandums of the commandments, which we had before (Num. xv. 38, 39), is here repeated, *v.* 12. By these they were distinguished from other people, so that it might be said, upon the first sight, There goes an Israelite.

Verses 13–30

These laws relate to the seventh commandment, laying a restraint by laying a penalty upon those fleshly lusts which war against the soul.

I. If a man, lusting after another woman, to get rid of his wife slander her and falsely accuse her, upon the disproof of his slander he must be punished, *v.* 13–19. The nearer any are in relation to us the greater sin it is to belie them and blemish their reputation.

II. If the woman that was married as a virgin was not found to be one she was to be stoned to death at her father's door, *v.* 20, 21. Now, 1. This gave a powerful caution to young women to flee fornication, since, however concealed before, so as not to mar their marriage, it would very likely be discovered afterwards, to their perpetual infamy and utter ruin. 2. It is intimated to parents that they must by all means possible preserve their children's chastity, by giving them good advice and admonition, setting them good examples, keeping them from bad company, praying for them, and laying them under needful restraints.

III. If any man, single or married, lay with a married woman, they were both to be put to death, *v.* 22. This law we had before, Lev. xx. 10.

IV. If a damsel were betrothed and not married, she was from under the eye of her intended husband, and therefore she and her chastity were taken under the special protection of the law.

JAMIESON, FAUSSET, BROWN

the roof should form an essential part of every new house. **9. Thou shalt not sow thy vineyard with divers seeds**—(See on Lev. 19:19). **10. Thou shalt not plough with an ox and an ass together**—Whether this association, like the mixture of seeds, had been dictated by superstitious motives and the prohibition was symbolical, designed to teach a moral lesson (II Cor. 6:14), may or may not have been the case. But the prohibition prevented a great inhumanity still occasionally practised by the poorer sort in Oriental countries. An ox and ass, being of different species and of very different characters, cannot associate comfortably, nor unite cheerfully in drawing a plough or a wagon. The ass being much smaller and his step shorter, there would be an unequal and irregular draft. Besides, the ass, from feeding on coarse and poisonous weeds, has a fetid breath, which its yoke-fellow seeks to avoid, not only as poisonous and offensive, but producing leanness, or, if long continued, death; and hence, it has been observed always to hold away its head from the ass and to pull only with one shoulder. **11. thou shalt not wear a garment of divers sorts**—The essence of the crime (Zeph. 1:8) consisted, not in wearing a woollen and a linen robe, but in the two stuffs being woven together, according to a favorite superstition of ancient idolaters (see on Lev. 19:19). **12. thou shalt make thee fringes upon the four quarters**—or, according to some eminent biblical interpreters, *tassels on the coverlet of the bed*. The precept is not the same as Num. 15:38. **13-30. If a man take a wife,** etc.—The regulations that follow might be imperatively needful in the *then* situation of the Israelites; and yet, it is not necessary that *we* should curiously and impertinently inquire into them. So far was it from being unworthy of God to leave such things upon record, that the enactments must heighten our admiration of His wisdom and goodness in the management of a people so perverse and so given to irregular passions. Nor is it a better argument that the Scriptures were not written by inspiration of God to object that this passage, and others of a like nature, tend to corrupt the imagination and will be abused by evil-disposed readers, than it is to say that the sun was not created by God, because its light *may* be abused by wicked men as an assistant in committing crimes which they have meditated [HORNE].

ADAM CLARKE

two beasts of a different species cannot associate comfortably together, and on this ground never pull pleasantly either in cart or plough; and every farmer knows that it is of considerable consequence to the comfort of the cattle to put those together that have an affection for each other. This may be very frequently remarked in certain cattle, which, on this account, are termed true yokefellows. After all, it is very probable that the general design was to prevent improper alliances in civil and religious life. And to this Paul seems evidently to refer, 2 Cor. vi. 14: "Be ye not unequally yoked together with unbelievers," which is simply to be understood as prohibiting all intercourse between Christians and idolaters in social, matrimonial, and religious life. And to teach the Jews the propriety of this, a variety of precepts relative to improper and heterogeneous mixtures were interspersed through their law, so that in civil and domestic life they might have them ever before their eyes.

12. *Fringes.* See on Num. xv. 38.

15. *Tokens of the damsel's virginity.* This was a perfectly possible case in all places where girls were married at ten, twelve, and fourteen years of age, which is frequent in the East. I have known several instances of persons having had two or three children at separate births before they were fourteen years of age. Such tokens, therefore, as the text speaks of must be infallibly exhibited by females so very young on the consummation of their marriage.

17. *They shall spread the cloth.* A usage of this kind argues a roughness of manners which would ill comport with the refinement of European ideas on so delicate a subject. Attempts have been made to show that the law here is to be understood metaphorically; but they so perfectly fail to establish anything like probability that it would be wasting my own and my reader's time to detail them. A custom similar to that above is observed among the Mohammedans to the present day.

22. *Shall both of them die.* Thus we find that in the most ancient of all laws adultery was punished with death in both the parties.

25. *And the man force her.* A rape also, by these ancient institutions, was punished with death, because a woman's honor was considered equally as precious as her life; therefore the same punishment was inflicted on the ravisher as upon the murderer.

30. *A man shall not take his father's wife.* This is to be understood as referring to the case of a stepmother. A man in his old age may have married a young wife, and on his dying, his son by a former wife may desire to espouse her; this the law prohibits. It was probably on pretense of having broken this law that Solomon put his brother Adonijah to death, because he had desired to have his father's concubine to wife, 1 Kings ii. 13-25.

MATTHEW HENRY

CHAPTER 23

Verses 1–8

Interpreters are not agreed what is here meant by *entering into the congregation of the Lord*, which is here forbidden to eunuchs and to bastards, Ammonites and Moabites, for ever, but to Edomites and Egyptians only till the third generation. 1. Some think they are hereby excluded from communicating with the people of God in their religious services. 2. Others think they are hereby excluded from bearing office in the congregation. 3. Others think they are excluded only from marrying with Israelites. With the daughters of these nations (though out of the nations of Canaan), it should seem, the men of Israel might marry, if they were completely proselyted to the Jewish religion; but with the men of these nations the daughters of Israel might not marry, nor could the men be naturalized, otherwise than as here provided.

Verses 9–14

Israel was now encamped, and this vast army was just entering upon action, which was likely to keep them together for a long time, and therefore it was fit to give them particular directions for the good ordering of their camp. And the charge is in one word to be *clean*. They must take care to keep their camp pure from moral, ceremonial, and natural

JAMIESON, FAUSSET, BROWN

CHAPTER 23

VSS. 1-25. WHO MAY AND WHO MAY NOT ENTER INTO THE CONGREGATION. **1. He that is wounded . . . , shall not enter into the congregation of the Lord**—"To enter into the congregation of the Lord" means either admission to public honors and offices in the Church and State of Israel, or, in the case of foreigners, incorporation with that nation by marriage. The rule was that strangers and foreigners, for fear of friendship or marriage connections with them leading the people into idolatry, were not admissible till their conversion to the Jewish faith. But this passage describes certain limitations of the general rule. The following parties were excluded from the full rights and privileges of citizenship: (1) Eunuchs—It was a very ancient practice for parents in the East by various arts to mutilate their children, with a view to training them for service in the houses of the great. (2) Bastards—such an indelible stigma in both these instances was designed as a discouragement to practices that were disgraceful, but too common from intercourse with foreigners. (3) Ammonites and Moabites—without provocation they had combined to engage a soothsayer to curse the Israelites; and had further endeavored, by ensnaring them into the guilt and licentious abominations of idolatry, to seduce them from their allegiance to God. **3. even**

ADAM CLARKE

CHAPTER 23

1. *Shall not enter into the congregation.* If by entering the congregation be meant the bearing a civil office among the people, such as magistrate, judge, etc., then the reason of the law is very plain; no man with any such personal defect as might render him contemptible in the sight of others should bear rule among the people, lest the contempt felt for his personal defects might be transferred to his important office, and thus his authority be disregarded. The general meaning of these words is simply that the persons here designated should not be so incorporated with the Jews as to partake of their civil privileges.

2. *A bastard shall not enter. Mamzer,* which is here rendered *bastard,* should be understood as implying the offspring of an illegitimate or incestuous mixture.

MATTHEW HENRY

pollution.

I. From moral pollution (*v.* 9): *When the host goes forth against thy enemy* then look upon thyself as in a special manner engaged to *keep thyself from every evil thing.* 1. The soldiers themselves must take heed of sin, for sin takes off the edge of valour; guilt makes men cowards. Soldiers must keep themselves from the idols, or accursed things, they found in the camps they plundered. 2. Even those that tarried at home must at that time especially keep from every wicked thing. Times of war should be times of reformation, else how can we expect God should hear and answer our prayers for success? Ps. lxvi. 18. See 1 Sam. vii. 3.

II. From ceremonial pollution. By this trouble and reproach, which even involuntary pollutions exposed men to, they were taught to keep up a very great dread of all fleshly lusts.

III. From natural pollution; the camp of the Lord must have nothing offensive in it, *v.* 12–14. If there must be this care taken to preserve the body clean and sweet, much more should we be solicitous to keep the mind so. This is the reason here given: *For the Lord thy God walketh* by his ark, the special token of his presence, *in the midst of thy camp*; with respect to that external symbol this external purity is required, which teaches us to preserve inward purity of soul, in consideration of the eye of God, which is always upon us.

Verses 15–25

Orders are here given about five several things which have no relation one to another:—

I. The land of Israel is here made a sanctuary, or city of refuge, for servants that were wronged and abused by their masters, and fled thither for shelter from the neighbouring countries, *v.* 15, 16. 1. It is an honourable thing to shelter and protect the weak, provided they be not wicked. The angel bid Hagar return to her mistress, and Paul sent Onesimus back to his master Philemon, because they had neither of them any cause to go away, nor was either of them exposed to any danger in returning. 2. If it appeared that the servant was abused, they must not only protect him, but, supposing him willing to embrace their religion, they must give him all the encouragement that might be to settle among them.

II. The land of Israel must be no shelter for the unclean; no whore, no Sodomite, must be suffered to live among them (*v.* 17, 18), neither a whore nor a whoremonger. No houses of uncleanness must be kept either by men or women.

III. The matter of usury is here settled, *v.* 19, 20. 1. They must not lend upon usury to an Israelite. It was seldom or never that they had occasion to borrow any great sums, only what was necessary for the subsistence of their families when the fruits of their ground had met with any disaster, or the like. Where the borrower gets, or hopes to get, it is just that the lender should share in the gain; but to him that borrows for his necessary food pity must be shown, and we must lend, hoping for nothing again, if we have wherewithal to do it, Luke vi. 35. 2. They might lend upon usury to a stranger, who was supposed to live by trade, and (as we say) by turning the penny, and therefore got by what he borrowed, and came among them in hopes to do so. By this it appears that usury is not in itself oppressive; for they must not oppress a stranger, and yet might exact usury from him.

IV. The performance of the vows wherewith we have bound our souls is here required. 1. We are here left at our liberty whether we will make vows or no. God had already signified his readiness to accept a free-will offering thus vowed, though it were but a little fine flour (Lev. ii. 4, &c.). But lest the priests, who had the largest share of those vows and voluntary offerings, should sponge upon the people, by pressing it upon them as their duty to make such vows, beyond their ability and inclination, they are here expressly told that it should not be reckoned a sin in them if they did not make any such vows. 2. We are here laid under the highest obligations, when we have made a vow, to perform it, and to perform it speedily.

V. Allowance is here given, when they passed through a cornfield or vineyard, to pluck and eat of the corn or grapes that grew by the road side. Now, 1. This law intimated to them what great plenty of corn and wine they should have in Canaan. 2. It provided for the support of poor travellers, to relieve the fatigue of their journey. 3. It teaches us not to insist upon property in a small matter, of which it is easy to say, *What is that between me and thee?* 4. It used them to hospitality.

JAMIESON, FAUSSET, BROWN

to the their tenth generation shall they not enter—Many eminent writers think that this law of exclusion was applicable only to males; at all events that a definite is used for an indefinite number (Neh. 13:1; Ruth 4:10; II Kings 10:2). Many of the Israelites being established on the east side of Jordan in the immediate neighborhood of those people, God raised this partition wall between them to prevent the consequences of evil communications. More favor was to be shown to Edomites and Egyptians—to the former from their near relationship to Israel; and to the latter, from their early hospitalities to the family of Jacob, as well as the many acts of kindness rendered them by private Egyptians at the Exodus (Exod. 12:36). The grandchildren of Edomite or Egyptian proselytes were declared admissible to the full rights of citizenship as native Israelites; and by this remarkable provision, God taught His people a practical lesson of generosity and gratitude for special deeds of kindness, to the forgetfulness of all the persecution and ill services sustained from those two nations. **9-14. When the host goeth forth against thine enemies, keep thee from every wicked thing**—from the excesses incident to camp life, as well as from habits of personal neglect and impurity.

15, 16. Thou shalt not deliver unto his master the servant which has escaped from his master unto thee—evidently a servant of the Canaanites or some of the neighboring people, who was driven by tyrannical oppression, or induced, with a view of embracing the true religion, to take refuge in Israel.

19, 20. Thou shalt not lend upon usury to thy brother . . . Unto a stranger thou mayest lend upon usury—The Israelites lived in a simple state of society, and hence they were encouraged to lend to each other in a friendly way without any hope of gain. But the case was different with foreigners, who, engaged in trade and commerce, borrowed to enlarge their capital, and might reasonably be expected to pay interest on their loans.

21, 22. When thou shalt vow a vow—(See on Num. 30:2).

24, 25. When thou comest into thy neighbour's vineyard, then thou mayest eat grapes thy fill at thine own pleasure—Vineyards, like cornfields mentioned in the next verse, were often unenclosed. In vine-growing countries grapes are amazingly cheap; and we need not wonder, therefore, that all within reach of a person's arm, was free; the quantity plucked was a loss never felt by the proprietor, and it was a kindly privilege afforded to the poor and wayfaring man.

ADAM CLARKE

3. *An Ammonite or Moabite.* These nations were subjected for their impiety and wickedness (see vv. 4 and 5) to peculiar disgrace, and on this account were not permitted to hold any office among the Israelites. But this did not disqualify them from being proselytes; Ruth, who was a Moabitess, was married to Boaz, and she became one of the progenitors of our Lord. *Even to their tenth generation.* That is, "for ever," as the next clause explains; see Neh. xiii. 1.

12-14. These directions may appear trifling to some, but they were essentially necessary to this people in their present circumstances. Decency and cleanliness promote health, and prevent many diseases.

15. *Thou shalt not deliver . . . the servant which is escaped . . . unto thee.* That is, a servant who left an idolatrous master that he might join himself to God and to His people. In any other case, it would have been injustice to harbor the runaway.

17. *There shall be no whore.* See on Gen. xxxviii. 15-21.

18. *The hire of a whore, or the price of a dog.* Many public prostitutes dedicated to their gods a part of their impure earnings; and some of these prostitutes were publicly kept in the temple of Venus Melytta, whose gains were applied to the support of her abominable worship.

19. *Usury.* See on Lev. xxv. 36.

21. *When thou shalt vow.* See on Num. xxx. 1, etc.

24. *Thou shalt not put any in thy vessel.* You shall carry none away with you. The old English proverb, "Eat thy fill but pocket none," seems to have been founded on this law.

25. *Thou mayest pluck the ears with thine hand.* It was on the permission granted by this law that the disciples plucked the ears of corn, as related Matt. xii. 1. This was both a considerate and humane law, and is no dishonor to the Jewish code.

MATTHEW HENRY

CHAPTER 24

Verses 1–4

This is that permission which the Pharisees erroneously referred to as a precept, Matt. xix. 7, *Moses commanded to give a writing of divorcement.* It was not so; our Saviour told them that he only suffered it lest, if they had not had liberty to divorce their wives, they should have ruled them with rigour, and, it may be, have been the death of them. It is probable that divorces were in use before (they are taken for granted, Lev. xxi. 14), and Moses thought it needful here to give some rules concerning them. 1. That a man might not divorce his wife unless he *found some uncleanness in her, v.* 1. It was not sufficient to say that he did not like her, or that he liked another better, but he must show cause for his dislike. 2. That it must be done, not by word of mouth, for that might be spoken hastily, but by writing, and that put in due form, and solemnly declared, before witnesses, to be his own act and deed, which was a work of time, and left room for consideration, that it might not be done rashly. 3. That the husband must give it into the hand of his wife, and send her away, which some think obliged him to endow her. 4. That being divorced it was lawful for her to marry another husband, *v.* 2. The divorce had dissolved the bond of marriage as effectually as death could dissolve it; so that she was free to marry again as if her first husband had been naturally dead. 5. That if her second husband died, or divorced her, then still she might marry a third, but her first husband should never take her again (*v.* 3, 4). The Jewish writers say that this was to prevent a most vile and wicked practice which the Egyptians had of changing wives.

Verses 5–13

Here is, I. Provision made for the preservation and confirmation of love between new-married people, *v.* 5. This fitly follows upon the laws concerning divorce, which would be prevented if their affection to each other were well settled at first. If the husband were much abroad from his wife the first year, his love to her would be in danger of cooling, and of being drawn aside to others whom he would meet with abroad; therefore his service to his country in war, embassies, or other public business that would call him from home, shall be dispensed with, *that he may cheer up the wife that he has taken.* 1. It is of great consequence that love be kept up between husband and wife. 2. One of the duties of that relation is to cheer up one another under the cares and crosses that happen, as helpers of each other's joy; for a cheerful heart does good like a medicine.

II. A law against man-stealing, *v.* 7. It was not death by the law of Moses to steal cattle or goods; but to steal a child, or a weak and simple man, or one that a man had in his power, and to make merchandize of him, this was a capital crime. It was taking away a man's liberty, the liberty of a freeborn Israelite, which was next in value to his life.

III. A memorandum concerning the leprosy, *v.* 8, 9. The laws concerning it must be carefully observed. The laws concerning it we had, Lev. xiii. 14.

IV. Some necessary orders given about pledges for the security of money lent. 1. They must not take the millstone for a pledge (*v.* 6), for with that they ground the corn that was to be bread for their families, and so it forbids the taking of any thing for a pledge by the want of which a man was in danger of being undone. Consonant to this is the ancient common law of England, which provides that no man be distrained of the utensils or instruments of his trade or profession, as the axe of a carpenter, or the books of a scholar. That creditor who cares not though his debtor and his family starve so he may but get his money, goes contrary, not only to the law of Christ, but even to the law of Moses too. 2. They must not go into the borrower's house to fetch the pledge. It is provided that he shall take not what he pleases, but what the borrower can best spare. A poor man's bed-clothes should never be taken for a pledge, *v.* 12, 13. This we had before, Exod. xxii. 26, 27. If they were taken in the morning, they must be brought back again at night, which is in effect to say that they must not be taken at all.

Verses 14–22

I. Masters are commanded to be just to their poor servants, v. 14, 15. 1. They must not oppress them. "For *thou wast a bondman* in the land where thou wast a stranger (*v.* 18), and thou knowest what a grievous thing it is to be oppressed by a taskmaster, and therefore, *thou shalt not oppress a servant.*" 2. They must be faithful and punctual in paying them their wages. He that works by day-

JAMIESON, FAUSSET, BROWN

CHAPTER 24

Vss. 1-22. Of Divorces. **1. When a man hath taken a wife, and married her, and it come to pass that she find no favour in his eyes**—It appears that the practice of divorces was at this early period very prevalent amongst the Israelites, who had in all probability become familiar with it in Egypt [Lane]. The usage, being too deep-rooted to be soon or easily abolished, was tolerated by Moses (Matt. 19:8). But it was accompanied under the law with two conditions, which were calculated greatly to prevent the evils incident to the permitted system; viz.: (1) The act of divorcement was to be certified on a written document, the preparation of which, with legal formality, would afford time for reflection and repentance; and (2) In the event of the divorced wife being married to another husband, she could not, on the termination of that second marriage, be restored to her first husband, however desirous he might be to receive her.

5. When a man hath taken a new wife, he shall not go out to war—This law of exemption was founded on good policy and was favorable to matrimony, as it afforded a full opportunity for the affections of the newly married pair being more firmly rooted, and it diminished or removed occasions for the divorces just mentioned. **6. No man shall take the nether or the upper millstone to pledge**—The "upper" stone being concave, covers the "nether" like a lid; and it has a small aperture, through which the corn is poured, as well as a handle by which it is turned. The propriety of the law was founded on the custom of grinding corn every morning for daily consumption. If either of the stones, therefore, which composed the handmill was wanting, a person would be deprived of his necessary provision. **7. If a man be found stealing any of his brethren**—(See on Exod. 21:16).

8, 9. Take heed in the plague of leprosy—(See on Lev. 13:14. **10-13. When thou dost lend thy brother anything, thou shalt not go into his house to fetch his pledge**—The course recommended was, in kind and considerate regard, to spare the borrower's feelings.

In the case of a poor man who had pledged his cloak, it was to be restored before night, as the poor in Eastern countries have commonly no other covering for wrapping themselves in when they go to sleep than the garment they have worn during the day. **14, 15. Thou shalt not oppress a hired servant that is poor and needy**—Hired servants in the East are paid at the close of the day; and for a master to defraud the laborer of his hire, or to withhold it wrongfully for a night, might have subjected a poor man with his family to suffering and was therefore an injustice to be avoided (Lev. 19:13). **16-18 The fathers shall not be put to death for the children**—The rule was addressed for the guidance of magistrates, and it established the equitable principle that none should be responsible for the crimes

ADAM CLARKE

CHAPTER 24

1. *Some uncleanness.* Any cause of dislike, for this great latitude of meaning the fact itself authorizes us to adopt, for it is certain that a Jew might put away his wife for any cause that seemed good to himself; and so hard were their hearts that Moses suffered this; and we find they continued this practice even to the time of our Lord, who strongly reprehended them on the account, and showed that such license was wholly inconsistent with the original design of marriage; see Matt. v. 31, etc.; xix. 3, etc., and the notes there.

3. *And write her a bill of divorcement.* These bills, though varying in expression, are the same in substance among the Jews in all places.

4. *She is defiled.* Does not this refer to her having been divorced, and married in consequence to another? Though God, for the hardness of their hearts, suffered them to put away their wives, yet He considered all after-marriages in that case to be pollution and defilement; and it is on this ground that our Lord argues in the places referred to above that whoever marries the woman that is put away is an adulterer. Now this could not have been the case if God had allowed the divorce to be a legal and proper separation of the man from his wife; but in the sight of God nothing can be a legal cause of separation but adultery on either side. In such a case, according to the law of God, a man may put away his wife, and a wife may put away her husband; see Mark x. 12.

5. *When a man hath taken a new wife.* Other people made a similar provision for such circumstances. Alexander ordered those of his soldiers who had married that year to spend the winter with their wives, while the army was in winter quarters.

6. *The nether or the upper millstone.* Small hand-mills which can be worked by a single person were formerly in use among the Jews, and are still used in many parts of the East. As therefore the day's meal was generally ground for each day, they keeping no stock beforehand, hence they were forbidden to take either of the stones to pledge, because in such a case the family must be without bread. On this account the text terms the millstone the *man's life.*

8-9. *The plague of leprosy.* See on Leviticus xiii and xiv.

12. *And if the man be poor.* Did not this law preclude pledging entirely, especially in case of the abjectly poor? For who would take a pledge in the morning which he knew, if not redeemed, he must restore at night? However, he might resume his claim in the morning, and have the pledge daily returned, and thus keep up his property in it till the debt was discharged; see the note on Exod. xii. 26. The Jews in several cases did act contrary to this rule, and we find them cuttingly reproved for it by the Prophet Amos, chap. ii. 8.

15. *He is poor, and setteth his heart upon it.* How exceedingly natural is this! The poor servant who seldom sees money, yet finds from his master's affluence that it procures all the conveniences and comforts of life, longs for the time when he shall receive his wages. Should his pay be delayed after the time is expired, he may naturally be expected to cry unto God against him who withholds it. See most of these subjects treated at large on Exod. xxii. 21-27.

16. *The fathers shall not be put to death for the children.* This law is explained and illustrated in sufficient detail, Ezekiel xviii.

18. *Thou shalt remember that thou wast a bondman.* Most people who have affluence rose from comparative penury; such therefore should remember what their feelings, their fears, and anxieties were when *they* were poor and abject. A want of attention to this most wholesome precept is the reason why pride and arrogance are the general characteristics of those who have risen in the world from poverty to affluence;

MATTHEW HENRY

wages is supposed to live from hand to mouth, and cannot have to-morrow's bread for his family till he is paid for this day's labour.

II. Magistrates and judges are commanded to be just in their administrations.

III. The rich are commanded to be kind and charitable to the poor. Many ways they are ordered to be so by the law of Moses. The particular instance of charity here prescribed is that they should not be greedy in gathering in their corn, and grapes, and olives, so as to be afraid of leaving any behind them, but be willing to overlook some, and let the poor have the gleanings, *v.* 19–22.

JAMIESON, FAUSSET, BROWN

of others. **19-22. When thou cuttest down thine harvest in thy field**—The grain, pulled up by the roots or cut down with a sickle, was laid in loose sheaves; the fruit of the olive was obtained by striking the branches with long poles; and the grape clusters, severed by a hook, were gathered in the hands of the vintager. Here is a beneficent provision for the poor. Every forgotten sheaf in the harvest field was to lie; the olive tree was not to be beaten a second time; nor were grapes to be gathered, in order that, in collecting what remained, the hearts of the stranger, the fatherless, and the widow might be gladdened by the bounty of Providence.

ADAM CLARKE

and it is the conduct of those men which gave rise to the rugged proverb, "Set a beggar on horseback, and he will ride to the devil."

19. *When thou cuttest down thine harvest* This is an addition to the law, Lev. xix. 9; xxiii. 22. The corners of the field, the gleanings, and the forgotten sheaf were all the property of the poor. This the Hebrews extended to any part of the fruit or produce of a field which had been forgotten in the time of general ingathering, as appears from the concluding verses of this chapter.

MATTHEW HENRY — CHAPTER 25

Verses 1–4

I. A direction to the judges in scourging malefactors, *v.* 1–3. A great many precepts we have met with which have not any particular penalty annexed to them, the violation of most of which, according to the constant practice of the Jews, was punished by scourging. The directions here given for the scourging of criminals are, 1. That it be done solemnly; not tumultuously through the streets, but in open court before the judges' face, and with so much deliberation as that the stripes might be numbered. The Jews say that while execution was in doing the chief justice of the court read with a loud voice Deut. xxviii. 58, 59, and xxix. 9, and concluded with those words (Ps. lxxviii. 38), *But he, being full of compassion, forgave their iniquity.* Thus it was made a sort of religious act, and so much the more likely to reform the offender himself and to be a warning to others. 2. That it be done in proportion to the crime. 3. That how great soever the crime were the number of stripes should never exceed *forty, v.* 3. Forty *save one* was the common usage, as appears, 2 Cor. xi. 24. They abated one for fear of having miscounted or because they would never go to the utmost rigour, or because the execution was usually done with a whip of three lashes, so that thirteen stripes (each one being counted for three) made up thirty-nine, but one more by that reckoning would have been forty-two.

II. A charge to husbandmen not to hinder their cattle from eating when they were working, if meat were within their reach, *v.* 4.

Verses 5–12

Here is, I. The law settled concerning the marrying of a brother's widow. It appears from the story of Judah's family that this had been an ancient usage (Gen. xxxviii. 8). The case put is a case that often happens, of a man's dying without issue, while his brethren were yet so young as to be unmarried. Now in this case, 1. The widow was not to marry again into any other family, unless all the relations of her husband did refuse her, that the estate she was endowed with might not be alienated. 2. The husband's brother, or next of kin, must marry her, partly out of respect to her, who, having forgotten her own people and her father's house, should have all possible kindness shown her by the family into which she was married; and partly out of respect to the deceased husband, that though he was dead and gone he might not be forgotten, nor lost out of the genealogies of his tribe; for the first-born child, which the brother or next kinsman should have by the widow, should be denominated from him that was dead, and entered in the genealogy as his child, *v.* 5, 6. But, 3. If the brother, or next of kin, declined to do this good office to the memory of him that was gone, what must be done in that case? Why, (1) He shall not be compelled to do it, *v.* 7. (2) Yet he shall be publicly disgraced for not doing it.

II. A law for the punishing of an immodest woman, *v.* 11, 12.

Verses 13–19

Here is, I. A law against deceitful weights and measures: they must not only not use them, but they must not have them, for, if they had them, they would be strongly tempted to use them. They must not have a great weight and measure to buy by and a small one to sell by, for that was to cheat both ways. But *thou shalt have a perfect and just weight, v.* 15.

II. A law for the rooting out of Amalek.

1. The mischief Amalek did to Israel must be here remembered, *v.* 17, 18. They had no occasion at all to quarrel with Israel nor did they give them any

JAMIESON, FAUSSET, BROWN — CHAPTER 25

Vss. 1-19. Stripes Must Not Exceed Forty. **2. if the wicked man be worthy to be beaten**—In judicial sentences, which awarded punishment short of capital, scourging, like the Egyptian bastinado, was the most common form in which they were executed. The Mosaic law, however, introduced two important restrictions; viz.: (1) The punishment should be inflicted in presence of the judge instead of being inflicted in private by some heartless official; and (2) The maximum amount of it should be limited to forty stripes, instead of being awarded according to the arbitrary will or passion of the magistrate. The Egyptian, like Turkish and Chinese rulers, often applied the stick till they caused death or lameness for life. Of what the scourge consisted at first we are not informed; but in later times, when the Jews were exceedingly scrupulous in adhering to the letter of the law and, for fear of miscalculation, were desirous of keeping within the prescribed limit, it was formed of three cords, terminating in leathern thongs, and thirteen strokes of this counted as thirty-nine stripes (II Cor. 11:24). **4. Thou shalt not muzzle the ox when he treadeth out the corn**—In Judea, as in modern Syria and Egypt, the larger grains were beaten out by the feet of oxen, which, yoked together, day after day trod round the wide open spaces which form the threshing-floors. The animals were allowed freely to pick up a mouthful, when they chose to do so: a wise as well as humane regulation, introduced by the law of Moses (cf. I Cor. 9:9; I Tim. 5:17, 18).

5-10. the wife of the dead shall not marry without unto a stranger; her husband's brother . . . shall take her to him to wife—This usage existed before the age of Moses (Gen. 38:8). But the Mosaic law rendered the custom obligatory (Matt. 22:25) on younger brothers, or the nearest kinsman, to marry the widow (Ruth 4:4), by associating the natural desire of perpetuating a brother's name with the preservation of property in the Hebrew families and tribes. If the younger brother declined to comply with the law, the widow brought her claim before the authorities of the place at a public assembly (the gate of the city); and he having declared his refusal, she was ordered to loose the thong of his shoe—a sign of degradation—following up that act by spitting on the ground—the strongest expression of ignominy and contempt among Eastern people. The shoe was kept by the magistrate as an evidence of the transaction, and the parties separated.

13-16. Thou shalt not have . . . divers weights—Weights were anciently made of stone and are frequently used still by Eastern shopkeepers and traders, who take them out of the bag and put them in the balance. The man who is not cheated by the trader and his bag of divers weights must be blessed with more acuteness than most of his fellows [Roberts]. (Cf. Prov. 16:11; 20:10.)

ADAM CLARKE — CHAPTER 25

1. *They shall justify the righteous.* This is a very important passage, and is a key to several others. The word *tsadak* is used here precisely in the same sense in which Paul sometimes uses the corresponding word, not to "justify" or "make just," but to "acquit, declare innocent, to remit punishment, or give reasons why such a one should not be punished"; so here the magistrates, *hitsdiku,* "shall acquit" *the righteous*—declare him innocent, because he is found to be righteous and not wicked. So the Septuagint: "they shall make righteous the righteous"—declare him free from blame, not liable to punishment, acquitted; using the same word with Paul when he speaks of a sinner's justification, i.e., his acquittance from blame and punishment, because of the death of Christ in his stead.

3. *Forty stripes he may give him, and not exceed.* According to God's institution a criminal may receive forty stripes; not one more! But is the institution from above or not that for any offense sentences a man to receive 300, yes, 1,000 stripes? *Thy brother should seem vile,* or be contemptible. By this God teaches us to hate and despise the sin, not the sinner, who is by this chastisement to be amended; as the power which the Lord hath given is "to edification, and not to destruction," 2 Cor. xiii. 10.

4. *Thou shalt not muzzle the ox.* While the oxen were at work, some muzzled their mouths to hinder them from eating the corn, which Moses here forbids, instructing the people by this symbolical precept to be kind to their servants and laborers, but especially to those who ministered to them in holy things; so Paul applies it in 1 Cor. ix. 9, etc.; 1 Tim. v. 18.

9. *And loose his shoe.* It is difficult to find the reason of these ceremonies of degradation. Perhaps the *shoe* was the emblem of power; and by stripping it off, deprivation of that power and authority was represented. Spitting in the face was a mark of the utmost ignominy; but the Jews, who are legitimate judges in this case, say that the spitting was not in his face, but before his face on the ground. And this is the way in which the Asiatics express their detestation of a person to the present day, intelligent travellers assure us. It has been remarked that the prefix *beth* is seldom applied to *peney;* but when it is it signifies as well "before" as *in* the face. See Josh. xxi. 44; xxiii. 9; Esther ix. 2; and Ezek. xliii. 12, which texts are supposed to be proofs in point. The act of spitting, whether *in* or *before* the face, marked the strong contempt the woman felt for the man who had slighted her. And it appears that the man was ever after disgraced in Israel; for so much is certainly implied in the saying, v. 10: "And his name shall be called in Israel, The house of him that hath his shoe loosed."

13. *Divers weights. Eben vaaben,* "a stone and a stone," because the weights were anciently made of stone, and some had two sets of stones, a light and a heavy. With the latter they bought their wares; by the former they sold them. In our own country this was once **a** common case; smooth, round, or oval stones were generally chosen by the simple country people for selling their wares, especially such as were sold in pounds and half pounds. And hence the term a "stone weight," which is still in use, though lead or iron be the matter that is used as a counterpoise; but the name itself shows us that a stone of a certain weight was the material formerly used as a weight. See the notes on Lev. xix. 35-36.

14. *Divers measures.* Literally, "an ephah and an ephah"; one large, to buy your neighbor's

MATTHEW HENRY

notice, by a manifesto or declaration of war; but took them at an advantage, when they had just come out of the house of bondage, and, for aught that appeared to them, were only going to *sacrifice to God in the wilderness.*

2. This mischief must in due time be revenged, *v.* 19. It was nearly 400 years after this that Saul was ordered to put this sentence in execution (1 Sam. xv.), and was rejected of God because he did not do it effectually.

CHAPTER 26

Verses 1–11

Here is, I. A good work ordered to be done, and that is the presenting of a basket of their first-fruits to God every year, *v.* 1, 2. When a man went into the field or vineyard at the time when the fruits were ripening, he was to mark that which he observed most forward, and to lay it by for first-fruits, wheat, barley, grapes, figs, pomegranates, olives, and dates, some of each sort must be put in the same basket, with leaves between them, and presented to God in the place which he should choose. Now from this law we may learn, 1. To acknowledge God as the giver of all those good things which are the support and comfort of our natural life. 2. To deny ourselves. What is first ripe we are most fond of; those that are nice and curious expect to be served with each fruit at its first coming in. 3. To give to God the first and best we have. Those that consecrate the days of their youth, and the prime of their time, to the service and honour of God, bring him their first-fruits.

II. Good words put into their mouths to be said in the doing of this good work. Two things they must own for this purpose:—1. The meanness of their common ancestor: *A Syrian ready to perish was my father, v.* 5. Jacob is here called an *Aramite,* or *Syrian,* because he lived twenty years in Padan-Aram. 2. The miserable condition of their nation in its infancy. They sojourned in Egypt as strangers, they served there as slaves (*v.* 6).

Verses 12–15

Concerning the disposal of their tithe the third year we had the law before, *ch.* xiv. 28, 29. The second tithe, which in the other two years was to be spent in extraordinaries at the feasts, was to be spent the third year at home, in entertaining the poor.

I. They must make a solemn protestation to this purport, *v.* 13, 14. 1. That no hallowed things were hoarded up: "*I have brought them away out of my house,* nothing now remains there but my own part." 2. That the poor, and particularly poor ministers, poor strangers, and poor widows, had had their part according to the commandment. 3. That none of this tithe had been misapplied to any common use, much less to any ill use. The Jews say that this protestation of their integrity was to be made with a low voice, because it looked like a self-condemnation, but that the foregoing confession of God's goodness was to be made with a loud voice to his glory. He that durst not make this protestation must bring his *trespass-offering,* Lev. v. 15.

II. To this solemn protestation they must add a ***solemn prayer* (*v.* 15), not particularly for themselves,** but for *God's people Israel*; for in the common peace and prosperity every particular person prospers and has peace.

Verses 16–19

Two things Moses here urges to enforce all these precepts:—1. That they were the commands of God, *v.* 16. They were not the dictates of his own wisdom, nor were they enacted by any authority of his own, but infinite wisdom framed them, and the power of the King of kings made them binding to them: *The Lord thy God commands thee.* 2. That their covenant with God obliged them to keep these commands.

JAMIESON, FAUSSET, BROWN

17-19. Remember what Amalek did—This cold-blooded and dastardly atrocity is not narrated in the previous history (Exod. 17:14). It was an unprovoked outrage on the laws of nature and humanity, as well as a daring defiance of that God who had so signally shown His favor towards Israel.

CHAPTER 26

Vss. 1-15. The Confession of Him That Offers the Basket of First fruits. **2. Thou shalt take of the first of all the fruit of the earth**—The Israelites in Canaan, being God's tenants at will, were required to give Him tribute in the form of first fruits and tithes. No Israelite was at liberty to use any productions of his field until he had presented the required offerings. The tribute began to be exigible after the settlement in the promised land, and it was yearly repeated at one of the great feasts (Lev. 2:14; 23:10; 23:15; Num. 28: 26; ch. 16:9). Every master of a family carried it on his shoulders in a little basket of osier, peeled willow, or palm leaves, and brought it to the sanctuary. **5. thou shalt say . . . , A Syrian ready to perish was my father**—rather, a wandering Syrian. The ancestors of the Hebrews were nomad shepherds, either Syrians by birth as Abraham, or by long residence as Jacob. When they were established as a nation in the possession of the promised land, they were indebted to God's unmerited goodness for their distinguished privileges, and in token of gratitude they brought this basket of first fruits.

11. thou shalt rejoice—feasting with friends and the Levites, who were invited on such occasions to share in the cheerful festivities that followed oblations (ch. 12:7; 16:10-15).

12-15. When thou hast made an end of tithing all the tithes of thine increase the third year—Among the Hebrews there were two tithings. The first was appropriated to the Levites (Numbers 18:21). The second, being the tenth of what remained, was brought to Jerusalem in kind; or it was converted into money, and the owner, on arriving in the capital, purchased sheep, bread, and oil (ch. 14:22, 23). This was done for two consecutive years. But this second tithing was eaten at home, and the third year distributed among the poor of the place (ch. 14:28, 29). **13. thou shalt say before the Lord thy God, I have brought away the hallowed things out of mine house**—This was a solemn declaration that nothing which should be devoted to the divine service had been secretly reserved for personal use. **14. I have not eaten thereof in my mourning**—in a season of sorrow, which brought defilement on sacred things; under a pretense of poverty, and grudging to give any away to the poor. **neither . . . for any unclean use**—i.e., any common purpose, different from what God had appointed and which would have been a desecration of it. **nor given aught thereof for the dead**—on any funeral service, or, to an *idol,* which is a dead thing.

ADAM CLARKE

wares, another small, to sell your own by. See the notes on Exod. xvi. 16 and Lev. xix. 35.

18. *Smote the hindmost of thee.* See the note on Exod. xvii. 8. It is supposed that this command had its final accomplishment in the death of Haman and his ten sons, Esther iii, vii, ix, as from this time the memory and name of Amalek were blotted out from under heaven, for through every period of their history it might be truly said, They "feared not God."

CHAPTER 26

2. *Thou shalt take of the first of all the fruit.* This was intended to keep them in continual remembrance of the kindness of God, in preserving them through so many difficulties and literally fulfilling the promises He had made to them. God being the Author of all their blessings, the firstfruits of the land were consecrated to Him, as the Author of every good and perfect gift.

5. *A Syrian ready to perish was my father.* This passage has been variously understood, both by the ancient versions and by modern commentators. The Vulgate renders it thus: "A Syrian persecuted my father." The Septuagint thus: "My father abandoned Syria." The Targum thus: "Laban the Syrian endeavoured to destroy my father." The Syriac: "My father was led out of Syria into Egypt." The Arabic: "Surely, Laban the Syrian had almost destroyed my father." The Targum of Jonathan ben Uzziel: "Our father Jacob went at first into Syria of Mesopotamia, and Laban sought to destroy him." It is pretty evident from the text that by a *Syrian* we are to understand Jacob, so called from his long residence in Syria with his father-in-law, Laban. And his being ready to perish may signify the hard usage and severe labor he had in Laban's service, by which, as his health was much impaired, so his life might have often been in imminent danger.

8. *With a mighty hand.* See on Deut. iv. 34.

11. *Thou shalt rejoice.* God intends that His followers shall be happy; that they shall eat their bread with gladness and singleness of heart, praising Him. Those who eat their meat grudgingly, under the pretense of their unworthiness, profane God's bounties and shall have no thanks for their voluntary humility. *Thou, and the Levite, and the stranger.* They were to take care to share God's bounties among all those who were dependent on them. The *Levite* has no inheritance; let him rejoice with you. The *stranger* has no home; let him feel you to be his friend and his father.

12. *The third year, which is the year of tithing.* This is supposed to mean the third year after the seventh or sabbatical year, in which the tenths were to be given to the poor. See the law, chap. xiv. 28. But from the letter in both these places it would appear that the tithe was for the Levites, and that this tithe was drawn only once in three years.

14. *I have not . . . given ought thereof for the dead.* That is, I have not consecrated any of it to an idol, which was generally a dead man whom superstition and ignorance had deified. From 1 Cor. x. 27-28 we learn that it was customary to offer that flesh to idols which was afterwards sold publicly in the shambles; probably the blood was poured out before the idol in imitation of the sacrifices offered to the true God. Perhaps the text here alludes to a similar custom.

17. *Thou hast avouched the Lord.* The people *avouch,* publicly declare, that they have taken Jehovah to be their God.

18. *And the Lord hath avouched.* Publicly declared, by the blessings He pours down upon them, that He has taken them to be His peculiar people. Thus the covenant is made and ratified between God and His followers.

19. *Make thee high above all nations.* It is written, "Righteousness exalteth a nation, but sin is a reproach to any people," Prov. xiv. 34. While Israel regarded God's word and kept His testimonies, they were the greatest and most respectable of all nations; but when they forsook God and His law, they became the most contemptible.

MATTHEW HENRY

CHAPTER 27

Verses 1–10

Here is, I. A general charge to the people to keep God's commandments. This is pressed upon them, with all authority. *Moses with the elders of Israel*, the rulers of each tribe (*v.* 1), and again, *Moses and the priests the Levites* (*v.* 9), commanded their people to *keep God's law*.

II. A particular direction to them with great solemnity to register *the words of this law*, as soon as they came into Canaan. There was a solemn ratification of the covenant between God and Israel at Mount Sinai, when an altar was erected, with twelve pillars, and the book of the covenant was produced, Exod. xxiv. 4. That which is here appointed is a somewhat similar solemnity.

1. They must set up a monument on which they must *write the words of this law*.

2. They must also set up an altar. By the words of the law which were written upon the plaster, God *spoke to them*; by the altar, and the sacrifices offered upon it, they spoke to God; and thus was communion kept up between them and God.

Verses 11–26

There were, it seems, in Canaan, that part of it which afterwards fell to the lot of Ephraim (Joshua's tribe), two mountains that lay near together, with a valley between, one called *Gerizim* and the other *Ebal*. On the sides of these two mountains, which faced one another, all the tribes were to be drawn up, six on one side and six on the other. Then when silence was proclaimed, and attention commanded, one of the priests pronounced with a loud voice one of the curses here following, and all the people that stood on the side and foot of Mount Ebal said *Amen*; then the contrary blessing was pronounced, "Blessed is he that doth not so or so," and then those that stood on the side, and at the foot, of Mount Gerizim, said *Amen*.

I. Something is to be observed, in general, concerning this solemnity, which was to be done but once, but would be talked of to posterity. 1. God appointed which tribes should stand upon Mount Gerizim and which on Mount Ebal (*v.* 12, 13). The six tribes that were appointed for blessing were all the children of the free women, for to such the promise belongs, Gal. iv. 31. Levi is here put among the rest, to teach ministers to apply to themselves the blessing and curse which they preach to others, and by faith to set their own *Amen* to it. 2. Of those tribes that were to say *Amen* to the blessings it is said, *They stood to bless the people*, but of the other, *They stood to curse*, not mentioning the people, as loth to suppose that any of this people whom God had taken for his own should lay themselves under the curse. 3. The Levites or priests, such of them as were appointed for that purpose, were to pronounce the curses as well as the blessings. 4. The curses are here expressed, but not the blessings. In Christ's sermon upon the mount, which was the true Mount Gerizim, we have blessings only, Matt. v. 3, &c. 5. To each of the curses the people were to say *Amen*. The Jews have a saying to encourage people to say *Amen* to the public prayers, *Whosoever answereth* Amen, *after him that blesseth, he is as he that blesseth*. But how could they say *Amen* to the curses? When they said *Amen*, they did in effect say, not only, *It is certain it shall be so*, but, *It is just it should be so*.

II. Let us now observe what are the particular sins against which the curses are here denounced.

1. Sins against the second commandment. This flaming sword is set to keep that commandment first, *v.* 15. Those are here cursed, not only that worship images, but that make them or keep them, if they be such (or like such) as idolators used in the service of their gods.

2. Against the fifth commandment, *v.* 16. The contempt of parents is a sin so heinous that it is put next to the contempt of God himself.

3. Against the eighth commandment. The curse of God is here fastened, (1) Upon an unjust neighbour that *removes the land marks*, *v.* 17. See *ch.* xix. 14. (2) Upon an unjust counsellor. (3) Upon an unjust judge, that *perverteth the judgment of the stranger, fatherless, and widow*, whom he should protect and vindicate, *v.* 19.

4. Against the seventh commandment. Incest is a cursed sin, with a *sister, a father's wife, or a mother-in-law*, *v.* 20, 22, 23.

5. Against the sixth commandment. Two of the worst kinds of murder are here specified:—(1) Murder unseen, when a man does not set upon his neighbour as a fair adversary, giving him an opportunity to defend himself, but *smites him secretly* (*v.* 24), as by poison or otherwise, when he sees not who hurts

JAMIESON, FAUSSET, BROWN

CHAPTER 27

VSS. 2-10. THE PEOPLE ARE TO WRITE THE LAW UPON STONES. **2. it shall be on the day when ye shall pass over Jordan**—"Day" is often put for "time"; and it was not till some days after the passage that the following instructions were acted upon. **thou shalt set thee up great stones, and plaister them with plaister**—These stones were to be taken in their natural state, unhewn, and unpolished—the occasion on which they were used not admitting of long or elaborate preparation; and they were to be daubed over with paint or whitewash, to render them more conspicuous. Stones and even rocks are seen in Egypt and the peninsula of Sinai, containing inscriptions made 3000 years ago, in paint or plaister. By some similar method those stones may have been inscribed, and it is most probable that Moses learned the art from the Egyptians. **3. thou shalt write upon them all the words of this law**—It might be, as some think, the Decalogue; but a greater probability is that it was "the blessings and curses," which comprised in fact an epitome of the law (Josh. 8:34). **5-10. there shalt thou build an altar . . . of whole stones**—The stones were to be in their natural state, as if a chisel would communicate pollution to them. The stony pile was to be so large as to contain all the conditions of the covenant, so elevated as to be visible to the whole congregation of Israel; and the religious ceremonial performed on the occasion was to consist: first, of the elementary worship needed for sinful men; and secondly, of the peace offerings, or lively, social feasts, that were suited to the happy people whose God was the Lord. There were thus, the law which condemned, and the typical expiation—the two great principles of revealed religion.

11-13. THE TRIBES DIVIDED ON GERIZIM AND EBAL. **11-13. These shall stand upon mount Gerizim to bless the people . . . these shall stand upon mount Ebal to curse**—Those long, rocky ridges lay in the province of Samaria, and the peaks referred to were near Shechem (Nablous), rising in steep precipices to the height of about 800 feet and separated by a green, well-watered valley of about 500 yards wide. The people of Israel were here divided into two parts. On mount Gerizim (now Jebel-et-Tur) were stationed the descendants of Rachel and Leah, the two principal wives of Jacob, and to them was assigned the most pleasant and honorable office of pronouncing the benedictions; while on the twin hill of Ebal (now Imad-el-Deen) were placed the posterity of the two secondary wives, Zilpah and Bilhah, with those of Reuben, who had lost the primogeniture, and Zebulun, Leah's youngest son; to them was committed the necessary but painful duty of pronouncing the maledictions (see on Judg. 9:7). The ceremony might have taken place on the lower spurs of the mountains, where they approach more closely to each other; and the course observed was as follows: Amid the silent expectations of the solemn assembly, the priests standing round the ark in the valley below, said aloud, looking to Gerizim, "Blessed is the man that maketh not any graven image," when the people ranged on that hill responded in full simultaneous shouts of "Amen"; then turning round to Ebal, they cried, "Cursed is the man that maketh any graven image"; to which those that covered the ridge answered, "Amen." The same course at every pause was followed with all the blessings and curses (see on Josh. 8:33, 34). These curses attendant on disobedience to the divine will, which had been revealed as a law from heaven, be it observed, are given in the form of a *declaration*, not a *wish*, as the words should be rendered, "Cursed is he," and not, "Cursed be he."

ADAM CLARKE

CHAPTER 27

2. *Thou shalt set thee up great stones.* How many is not specified, possibly twelve, and possibly only a sufficient number to make a surface large enough to write the blessings and the curses on. *Plaister them with plaister.* Perhaps the original should be translated, "Thou shalt cement them with cement," because this was intended to be a durable monument. In similar cases it was customary to set up a single stone, or a heap, rudely put together, where no cement or mortar appears to have been used; and because this was common, it was necessary to give particular directions when the usual method was not to be followed.

3. *All the words of this law.* After all that has been said by ingenious critics concerning the *law* ordered to be written on these stones, some supposing the whole Mosaic law to be intended, others, only the Decalogue, I am fully of opinion that the (*torah*) law or ordinance in question simply means the blessings and curses mentioned in this and in the following chapter; and indeed these contained a very good epitome of the whole law in all its promises and threatenings, in reference to the whole of its grand moral design.

4. *Set up these stones . . . in mount Ebal.* So the present Hebrew text, but the Samaritan has "Mount Gerizim." On all hands it is allowed that Gerizim abounds with springs, gardens, and orchards, and that it is covered with a beautiful verdure, while Ebal is as naked and as barren as a rock. On this very account the former was highly proper for the ceremony of blessing, and the latter for the ceremony of cursing.

12. *These shall stand upon mount Gerizim to bless the people.* Instead of *upon* we may translate "by," as the particle *al* is sometimes used; for we do not find that the tribes did stand on either mount, for in Josh. viii. 88, when this direction was reduced to practice, we find the people did not stand on the mountains, but "over against" them on the plain.

15. *Cursed be the man.* Other laws, previously made, had prohibited all these things; and penal sanctions were necessarily understood; but here God more openly declares that he who breaks them is cursed—falls under the wrath and indignation of his Maker and Judge.

16. *Setteth light by his father or his mother.* See the note on Exod. xx. 12.

17. *Removeth his neighbour's landmark.* See before on Deut. xix. 14 and on Exod. xx. 17. And for all the rest of these curses, see the notes on Exodus xx.

18. *The blind to wander out of the way.* A sin against the sixth commandment. See on Exod. xx. 13.

MATTHEW HENRY

him. See Ps. x. 8, 9. (2) Murder under colour of law. Cursed therefore is he that will be hired, or bribed, to accuse, or to convict, or to condemn, and so *to slay, an innocent person, v.* 25. See Ps. xv. 5.

6. The solemnity concludes with a general curse upon him *that confirmeth not all the words of this law to do them, v.* 26. By our obedience to the law we set our seal to it, and so confirm it, as by our disobedience we do what lies in us to disannul it, Ps. cxix. 126.

CHAPTER 28

Verses 1–14

The blessings are here put before the curses, to intimate, 1. That God is slow to anger, but swift to show mercy: he has said it, and sworn, that he would much rather we would obey and live than sin and die. 2. That obedience pleases best which comes from a principle of delight in God's goodness.

The particulars of this blessing.

I. It is promised that the providence of God should prosper them in all their outward concerns. These blessings are said to *overtake them, v.* 2. Thus in the great day the blessing will overtake the righteous that say, *Lord, when saw we thee hungry and fed thee?* Matt. xxv. 37.

1. Several things are enumerated in which God by his providence would bless them:—(1) They should be safe and easy; a blessing should rest upon their persons wherever they were, *in the city or in the field, v.* 3. Their persons should be protected, and the affair they went about should succeed well. (2) Their families should be built up in a numerous issue. (3) They should be rich, and have an abundance of all the good things of this life. A blessing is promised, *First,* On all they had without doors, corn and cattle in the field (*v.* 4, 11), their cows and sheep particularly. *Secondly,* On all they had within doors, the basket and the store (*v.* 5), the store-houses or barns, *v.* 8. We depend upon God and his blessing, not only for our yearly corn out of the field, but for our daily bread out of our basket and store, and therefore are taught to pray for it every day. (4) They should have success in all their employments, God would own their industry, and *bless the work of their hand* (*v.* 12). (5) They should have honour among their neighbours (*v.* 1). Two things should help to make them great among the nations:—*First,* Their wealth (*v.* 12): "*Thou shalt lend to many nations* upon interest" (which they were allowed to take from the neighbouring nations), "but thou shalt not have occasion to borrow." *Secondly,* Their power (*v.* 13): "*The Lord shall make thee the head,* to give law to all about thee, to exact tribute, and to arbitrate all controversies." Religion among them, and the blessing of God upon them, would make them formidable to all their neighbours, terrible as an army with banners. (6) They should be victorious over their enemies, and prosper in all their wars.

2. From the whole we learn (though it were well if men would believe it) that religion and piety are the best friends to outward prosperity. Though temporal blessings do not take up so much room in the promises of the New Testament as they do in those of the Old, yet it is enough that our Lord Jesus has given us his word (and surely we may take his word) that if we *seek first the kingdom of God, and the righteousness thereof, all other things* shall be added to us, as far as Infinite Wisdom sees good; and who can desire them further? Matt. vi. 33.

II. It is likewise promised that the grace of God should *establish them a holy people, v.* 9. This establishment of their religion would be the establishment of their reputation (*v.* 10).

Verses 15–44

Having viewed the bright side of the cloud, which is towards the obedient, we have now presented to us the dark side, which is towards the disobedient. If we do not keep God's commandments, we not only come short of the blessing promised, but we lay ourselves under the curse, which is as comprehensive of all misery as the blessing is of all happiness.

I. The equity of this curse. It is not a curse causeless, nor for some light cause; God seeks not occasion against us, nor is he apt to quarrel with us. That which is here mentioned as bringing the curse is, 1. Despising God, refusing to *hearken to his voice* (*v.* 15), which bespeaks the highest contempt imaginable. 2. Disobeying him, *not doing his commandments.* 3. Deserting him. God never casts us off till we first cast him off.

II. The extent and efficacy of this curse.

1. In general, it is declared, "*All these curses shall*

JAMIESON, FAUSSET, BROWN

CHAPTER 28

Vss. 1-68. THE BLESSINGS FOR OBEDIENCE. **1. if thou shalt hearken diligently unto the voice of the Lord thy God**—In this chapter the blessings and curses are enumerated at length, and in various minute details, so that on the first entrance of the Israelites into the land of promise, their whole destiny was laid before them, as it was to result from their obedience or the contrary. **2. all these blessings shall come on thee**—Their national obedience was to be rewarded by extraordinary and universal prosperity.

7. flee before thee seven ways—i.e., in various directions, as always happens in a rout.

10. called by the name of the Lord—They are really and actually His people (ch. 14:1; 26:18). **11. the Lord shall make thee plenteous in goods**—Beside the natural capabilities of Canaan, its extraordinary fruitfulness was traceable to the special blessing of Heaven. **12. The Lord shall open unto thee his good treasure**—The seasonable supply of the early and latter rain was one of the principal means by which their land was so uncommonly fruitful. **thou shalt lend unto many nations, and thou shalt not borrow**—i.e., thou shalt be in such affluent circumstances, as to be capable, out of thy superfluous wealth, to give aid to thy poorer neighbors. **13, 14. the head, and not the tail**—an Oriental form of expression, indicating the possession of independent power and great dignity and acknowledged excellence (Isa. 9:14; 19:15). **15-20. But . . . if thou wilt not hearken unto the voice of the Lord**—Curses that were to follow them in the event of disobedience are now enumerated, and they are almost exact counterparts of the blessings which were described in the preceding context as the reward of a faithful adherence to the covenant. **21. pestilence**—some fatal epidemic. There is no reason, however, to think that the plague, which is the great modern scourge of the East, is referred to.

22. a consumption—a wasting disorder; but the modern tuberculosis is almost unknown in Asia.

ADAM CLARKE

26. *That confirmeth not all the words of this law.* The word *col, all,* is not found in any printed copy of the Hebrew text; but the Samaritan preserves it, and so do six MSS. in the collections of Kennicott and De Rossi, besides several copies of the Chaldee Targum. The Septuagint also, and Paul in his quotations of this place, Gal. iii. 10. Jerome says that the Jews suppressed the word, that it might not appear that they were bound to fulfill all the precepts in the law of Moses.

CHAPTER 28

2. *All these blessings shall come on thee.* God shall pour out His blessing from heaven upon thee. *And overtake thee.* Upright men are represented as going to the kingdom of God, and God's blessings as following and overtaking them in their heavenly journey.

3. *In the city*—in all civil employments. *In the field*—in all agricultural pursuits.

4. *Fruit of thy body*—all your children. *Increase of thy kine,* etc.—every animal employed in domestic and agricultural purposes shall be under the especial protection of divine providence.

5. *Thy basket.* Your olive gathering and vintage, as the *basket* was employed to collect those fruits. *Store. Mishereth,* kneading trough, or "remainder"; all that is laid up for future use, as well as what is prepared for present consumption. Some think that by *basket* all their property abroad may be meant, and by *store* all that they have at home, i.e., all that is in the fields, and all that is in the houses.

6. *When thou comest in,* from your employment, you shall find that no evil has happened to the family or dwelling in your absence. *When thou goest out.* Your way shall be made prosperous before you, and you shall have the divine blessing in all your labors. 7. *The Lord shall cause thine enemies.* This is a promise of security from foreign invasion, or total discomfiture of the invaders should they enter the land. *They shall come out against thee one way*—in the firmest and most united manner. *And flee . . . seven ways*—shall be utterly broken, confounded, and finally routed.

8. *The Lord shall command the blessing upon thee.* Everything that you have shall come by divine appointment; you shall have nothing casually, but everything, both spiritual and temporal, shall come by the immediate *command* of God.

9. *The Lord shall establish thee an holy people unto himself.* This is the sum of all blessings, to be made *holy,* and be preserved in holiness. *If thou shalt keep.* Here is the solemn condition; if they did not keep God's testimonies, taking them for the regulators of their lives, and according to their direction walking in His ways, under the influence and aids of His grace, then the curses, and not the blessings, must be their portion. See vv. 15, etc.

12. *The Lord shall open unto thee his good treasure.* The clouds, so that a sufficiency of showers should descend at all requisite times, and the vegetative principle in the earth should unfold and exert itself, so that their crops should be abundant.

14. *Thou shalt not go aside . . . to the right hand, or to the left.* The way of obedience is a straight way; it goes right forward; he who declines either to right or left from this path goes astray and misses heaven.

20. *Cursing*—this shall be your state; *vexation*—grief, trouble, and anguish of heart; *rebuke*—continual judgments, and marks of God's displeasure.

21. *The pestilence cleave unto thee.* "The Lord shall cement the pestilence or plague to thee." Septuagint, "The Lord will glue the death unto thee." How dreadful a plague it must be that ravages without intermission, any person may conceive who has ever heard the name.

22. *Consumption. Shachepheth,* atrophy through lack of food; from *shacaph,* "to be in want." *Fever. Kaddachath,* from *kadach,* "to be kindled, burn, sparkle"; a burning, inflammatory fever. *Inflammation. Dalleketh,* from *dalak,* "to

MATTHEW HENRY

come upon thee from above, *and shall overtake thee*; **though thou endeavour to escape them."** There is no running from God but by running to him, no fleeing from his justice but by fleeing to his mercy. See Ps. xxi. 7, 8. To those whose *mind and conscience are defiled* everything else is so, Tit. i. 15. This curse is just the reverse of the blessing in the former part of the chapter.

2. Many particular judgments are here enumerated, which would be the fruits of the curse. Note, God's judgments can reach the minds of men, to fill them with darkness and horror, as well as their bodies and estates; and those are the sorest of all judgments which make men a terror to themselves, and their own destroyers.

F. B. MEYER:

The fearful results of disobedience. If we compare this chapter with Exodus 23:20–23 and Leviticus 26, we shall see how Moses resumes and amplifies the promises and threatenings already set forth in the earlier editions of the Law. The blessings are declared in fourteen verses, while the curses require four times as much space. This is due to God's eagerness that men should be warned from courses that injure, and shut up to those that lead to blessedness. Note the language, which rises to the sublimest level, especially in the latter part. The forecasts of the dispersion and the degradation of the Hebrew people are specially remarkable.

It is not only that God goes out of his way to reward the obedient and to punish the ungodly, but these rewards and punishments are part of the nature of things, just as fire stings and burns when we transgress its laws, but blesses when we obey. If we are at one with God, through Jesus Christ, we are at one with the universe. But if not, "the stars in their courses" fight against us (Judg. 5:20).—*Bible Commentary*

JAMIESON, FAUSSET, BROWN

fever . . . inflammation . . . extreme burning—Fever is rendered "burning ague" (Lev. 26:16), and the others mentioned along with it evidently point to those febrile affections which are of malignant character and great frequency in the East.

the sword—rather "dryness,"—the effect on the human body of such violent disorders. **blasting, and with mildew**—two atmospheric influences fatal to grain.

23. heaven . . . brass . . . earth . . . iron—strong Oriental figures used to describe the effects of long-continued drought. This want of regular and seasonable rain is allowed by the most intelligent observers to be one great cause of the present sterility of Palestine.

24. the rain of thy land powder and dust—an allusion probably to the dreadful effects of tornadoes in the East, which, raising the sands in immense twisted pillars, drive them along with the fury of a tempest. These shifting sands are most destructive to cultivated lands; and in consequence of their encroachments, many once fertile regions of the East are now barren deserts. **27. the botch of Egypt**—a troublesome eruption, marked by red pimples, to which, at the rising of the Nile, the Egyptians are subject. **emerods**—fistulæ or piles. **scab**—scurvy.

itch—the disease commonly known by that name; but it is far more malignant in the East than is ever witnessed in our part of the world.

28. madness, and blindness, and astonishment of heart—They would be bewildered and paralyzed with terror at the extent of their calamities.

29-33. thou shalt grope at noonday—a general description of the painful uncertainty in which they would live. During the middle ages the Jews were driven from society into hiding-places which they were afraid to leave, not knowing from what quarter they might be assailed and their children dragged into captivity, from which no friend could rescue, and no money ransom them.

ADAM CLARKE

pursue eagerly, to burn after"; probably a rapidly consuming cancer. *Extreme burning. Charchur,* "burning upon burning," scald upon scald; from *char,* to be "heated, enraged." This probably refers not only to excruciating inflammations on the body but also to the irritation and agony of a mind utterly abandoned by God, and lost to hope. What an accumulation of misery! how formidable! and especially in a land where great heat was prevalent and dreadful. *Sword.* War in general, enemies without, and civil broils within. This was remarkably the case in the last siege of Jerusalem. *Blasting.* Probably either the blighting east wind that ruined vegetation or those awful pestilential winds which suffocate both man and beast wherever they come. These often prevail in different parts of the East. *Mildew. Yerakon,* an exudation of the vegetative juice from different parts of the stalk, by which the maturity and perfection of the plant are utterly prevented. It comes from *yarak,* "to throw out moisture."

Of these seven plagues, the five former were to fall on their bodies, the two latter upon their substance. What a fearful thing it is to fall into the hands of the living God!

23. *Thy heaven . . . shall be brass, and the earth . . . iron.* The atmosphere should not be replenished with aqueous vapors, in consequence of which they should have neither the early nor the latter rain; hence the *earth*—the ground—must be wholly intractable, and through its hardness, incapable of cultivation. God shows them by this that He is Lord of nature; and that drought and sterility are not casualties, but proceed from the immediate appointment of the Lord.

24. *The rain of thy land powder and dust.* As their heavens—atmosphere, clouds, etc.—were to be as brass—yielding no rain—so the surface of the earth must be reduced to powder; and this, being frequently taken up by the strong winds, would fall down in showers instead of rain.

27. *The Lord will smite thee with the botch. Shechin,* a violent, inflammatory swelling. *Emerods. Ophalim,* from *aphal,* "to be elevated, raised up"; swellings, protuberances; probably the bleeding piles. *Scab. Garab* does not occur as a verb in the Hebrew Bible, but *gharb,* in Arabic, signifies a distemper in the corner of the eye, and may amount to the Egyptian ophthalmia, which is so epidemic and distressing in that country; some suppose the scurvy to be intended. *Itch. Cheres,* a burning itch, probably what is commonly called "St. Anthony's fire." *Whereof thou canst not be healed.* For as they were inflicted by God's justice, they could not, of course, be cured by human art.

28. *The Lord shall smite thee with madness. Shiggaon,* "distraction," so that you shall not know what to do. *And blindness. Ivvaron,* blindness, both physical and mental; the *garab* (v. 27) destroying their eyes, and the judgments of God confounding their understandings. *Astonishment. Timmahon,* stupidity and amazement. By the just judgments of God they were so completely confounded as not to discern the means by which they might prevent or remove their calamities, and to adopt those which led directly to their ruin.

29. *Thou shalt be only oppressed.* Perhaps no people under the sun have been more oppressed and spoiled than the rebellious Jews. And still they *grope at noonday, as the blind gropeth in darkness*—they do not yet discover, notwithstanding the effulgence of the light by which they are encompassed, that the rejection of their own Messiah is the cause of all their calamities.

30. *Thou shalt betroth a wife.* Can any heart imagine anything more grievous than the evils threatened in this and the following verses? To be on the brink of all social and domestic happiness, and then to be suddenly deprived of all, and see an enemy possess and enjoy everything that was dear to them, must excite them to the utmost pitch of distraction and madness.

32. *Thy sons and thy daughters shall be given unto another people.* In several countries, particularly in Spain and Portugal, the children of the Jews have been taken from them by order of government, and educated in the popish faith. There have been some instances of Jewish children being taken from their parents even in

MATTHEW HENRY

Verses 45–68

One would have thought that enough had been said to possess them with a dread of that *wrath of God* which is *revealed from heaven against the ungodliness and unrighteousness of men.* But to show how deep the treasures of that wrath are, and that still there is more and worse behind, Moses, when one would have thought that he had concluded this dismal subject, begins again, and adds to this roll of curses many similar words; as Jeremiah did to his, Jer. xxxvi. 32. Here, in this latter part, he foretells their last destruction by the Romans and their dispersion thereupon. And the present deplorable state of the Jewish nation, and of all that have incorporated themselves with them, by embracing their religion, does so fully and exactly answer to the prediction in these verses that it serves for an incontestable proof of the truth of prophecy, and consequently of the divine authority of the scripture. And, this last destruction being here represented as more dreadful than the former, it shows that their sin, in rejecting Christ and his gospel, was more heinous. Under this last destruction now for above 1600 years they continue incurably averse to the Lord Jesus.

I. It is amazing to think that a people so long the favourites of Heaven should be so perfectly abandoned and cast off, that a people so closely incorporated should be so universally dispersed, and yet that a people so scattered in all nations should preserve themselves distinct and not mix with any, but like Cain be fugitives and vagabonds, and yet marked to be known.

II. The destruction threatened is described. Moses is here upon the same melancholy subject that our Saviour is discoursing of to his disciples in his farewell sermon (Matt. xxiv.), namely, The destruction of Jerusalem and the Jewish nation.

1. Five things are here foretold as steps to their ruin:—

(1) That they should be invaded by a foreign enemy (*v.* 49, 50): A *nation from far,* namely, the Romans, *as swift as the eagle* hastening to the prey. Our Saviour makes use of this similitude, in foretelling this destruction, that *where the carcase is there will the eagles be gathered together,* Matt. xxiv. 28. And bishop Patrick observes that the ensign of the Roman armies was an eagle.

(2) That the country should be laid waste, and all the fruits of it eaten up by this army of foreigners, which is the natural consequence of an invasion, especially when it is made, as that by the Romans was, for the chastisement of rebels.

(3) That their cities should be besieged, and that such would be the obstinacy of the besieged, and such the vigour of the besiegers, that they would be reduced to the last extremity, and at length fall into the hands of the enemy, *v.* 52.

(4) That multitudes of them should perish, so that they should become *few in number, v.* 62.

(5) That the remnant should be scattered throughout the nations. This completes their woe: *The Lord shall scatter thee among all people, v.* **64.**

2. Upon the whole matter, (1) The accomplishment of these predictions upon the Jewish nation shows that Moses spoke by the Spirit of God. (2) Let us all hence learn to stand in awe and not to sin. I have heard of a wicked man, who, upon reading the threatenings of this chapter, was so enraged that he tore the leaf out of the Bible, as Jehoiakim cut Jeremiah's roll; but to what purpose is it to deface a copy, while the original remains upon record in the divine counsels, by which it is unalterably determined that *the wages of sin is death,* whether men will hear or whether they will forbear?

JAMIESON, FAUSSET, BROWN

35. the Lord shall smite thee in the knees, and in the legs—This is an exact description of elephantiasis, a horrible disease, something like leprosy, which attacks particularly the lower extremities. **35. The Lord shall smite thee in the knees, and in** shows how widespread would be the national calamity; and at the same time how hopeless, when he who should have been their defender shared the captive fate of his subjects. **there shalt thou serve other gods, wood and stone**—The Hebrew exiles, with some honorable exceptions, were seduced or compelled into idolatry in the Assyrian and Babylonish captivities (Jer. 44:17-19). Thus, the sin to which they had too often betrayed a perverse fondness, a deep-rooted propensity, became their punishment and their misery. **37. thou shalt become an astonishment, a proverb, and a byword among all nations whither the Lord shall . . .**—The annals of almost every nation, for eighteen hundred years, afford abundant proofs that this has been, as it still is, the case—the very name of Jew being a universally recognized term for extreme degradation and wretchedness. **49. The Lord shall bring a nation against thee from far**—the invasion of the Romans—"they came from far." The soldiers of the invading army were taken from France, Spain, and Britain—then considered "the end of the earth." Julius Severus, the commander, afterwards Vespasian and Hadrian, left Britain for the scene of contest. Moreover, the ensign on the standards of the Roman army was "an eagle"; and the dialects spoken by the soldiers of the different nations that composed that army were altogether unintelligible to the Jews. **50. A nation of fierce countenance**—a just description of the Romans, who were not only bold and unyielding, but ruthless and implacable. **51. he shall eat the fruit of thy cattle,** etc.—According to the Jewish historian, every district of the country through which they passed was strewn with the wrecks of their devastation. **52. he shall besiege thee . . . until thy high and fenced walls come down**—All the fortified places to which the people betook themselves for safety were burnt or demolished, and the walls of Jerusalem itself razed to the ground. **53-57. thou shalt eat the fruit of thine own body**—(See on II Kings 6:29; Lam. 4:10). Such were the dreadful extremities to which the inhabitants during the siege were reduced that many women sustained a wretched existence by eating the flesh of their own children. Parental affection was extinguished, and the nearest relatives were jealously avoided, lest they should discover and demand a share of the revolting viands. **62. ye shall be left few in number**—There has been, ever since the destruction of Jerusalem, only an inconsiderable remnant of Jews existing in that land—aliens in the land of their fathers; and of all classes of the inhabitants they are the most degraded and miserable beings, dependent for their support on contributions from other lands. **63. ye shall be plucked from off the land**—Hadrian issued a proclamation, forbidding any Jews to reside in Judea, or even to approach its confines. **64. the Lord shall scatter thee among all people**—There is, perhaps, not a country in the world where Jews are not to be found. Who that looks on this condition of the Hebrews is not filled with awe, when he considers the fulfilment of this prophecy? **68. The Lord shall bring thee into Egypt again with ships**—The accomplishment of this prediction took place under Titus, when, according to Josephus, multitudes of Jews were transported in ships to the land of the Nile, and sold as slaves. "Here, then, are instances of prophecies delivered above three thousand years ago; and yet, as we see, being fulfilled in the world at this very time; and what stronger proofs can we desire of the divine legation of Moses? How these instances may affect others I know not; but for myself, I must acknowledge, they not only convince but amaze and astonish me beyond expression; they are truly, as Moses foretold (vss. 45, 46) they would be, 'a sign and a wonder for ever' " [BISHOP NEWTON].

ADAM CLARKE

Protestant countries.

35. *With a sore botch. Shechin,* an inflammatory swelling, a burning boil. See v. 27.

36-45. Can anything be conceived more dreadful than the calamities threatened in these verses?

48. *Therefore shalt thou serve thine enemies.* Because they would not serve God, therefore they became slaves to men.

49. *A nation . . . from far.* Probably the Romans. *As the eagle flieth.* The very animal on all the Roman standards. The Roman eagle is proverbial. *Whose tongue thou shalt not understand.* The Latin language, than which none was more foreign to the structure and idiom of the Hebrew.

52. *He*—Nebuchadnezzar first (2 Kings xxv. 1-2, etc.), and Titus next; *shall besiege thee*—beset you round on every side, and cast a trench around you, viz., lines of circumvallation, as our Lord predicted (see Matt. xxiv. 1, etc., and Luke xxi. 5, etc.); *in all thy gates throughout all thy land*—all your fenced cities, which points out that their subjugation should be complete, as both Jerusalem and all their fortified places should be taken. This was done literally by Nebuchadnezzar and the Romans.

56. *The tender and delicate woman.* This was literally fulfilled when Jerusalem was besieged by the Romans; a woman named Mary, of a noble family, driven to distraction by famine, boiled and ate her own child! See a similar case 2 Kings vi. 29; and see on Lev. xxvi. 29.

64. *The Lord shall scatter thee among all people.* How literally has this been fulfilled! The people of the Jews are scattered over every nation under heaven.

65. *No ease . . . a trembling heart, and failing of eyes.* The trembling of heart may refer to their state of continual insecurity, being, under every kind of government, proscribed, and, even under the most mild, uncertain of toleration and protection; and the failing of eyes, to their vain and ever-disappointed expectation of the Messiah.

68. *And the Lord shall bring thee into Egypt again.* That is, into another state of slavery and bondage similar to that of Egypt, out of which they had been lately brought. *And there ye shall be sold,* that is, be exposed to sale, or "expose yourself to sale," as the word *hithmaccartem* may be rendered. They were vagrants, and wished to become slaves that they might be provided with the necessaries of life. *And no man shall buy you;* even the Romans thought it a reproach to have a Jew for a slave, they had become so despicable to all mankind. When Jerusalem was taken by Titus, many of the captives which were above seventeen years of age were sent into the works in Egypt. See Josephus, *antiq.,* b. xii., c. 1, 2, *War* b. vi., c. 9, s. 2.

MATTHEW HENRY — CHAPTER 29

Verses 1–9

Now that Moses had largely repeated the commands which the people were to observe as their part of the covenant, and the promises and threatenings which God would make good (according as they behaved themselves) as his part of the covenant, the whole is here summed up in a federal transaction. The covenant formerly made is here renewed, and Moses, who was before, is still, the mediator of it (*v.* 1): *The Lord commanded Moses to make it.* It

JAMIESON, FAUSSET, BROWN — CHAPTER 29

VSS. 1-29. AN EXHORTATION TO OBEDIENCE. **1. These are the words of the covenant**—The discourse of Moses is continued, and the subject of that discourse was Israel's covenant with God, the privileges it conferred, and the obligations it imposed. **beside the covenant which he made with them in Horeb**—It was substantially the same; but it was renewed now, in different circumstances. They had violated its conditions. Moses rehearses these,

ADAM CLARKE — CHAPTER 29

1. *These are the words of the covenant.* This verse seems properly to belong to the preceding chapter, as a widely different subject is taken up at v. 2 of this; and it is distinguished as the sixty-ninth verse in some of the most correct copies of the Hebrew Bible. *Commanded Moses to make. Lichroth,* "to cut," alluding to the covenant sacrifice which was offered on the occasion and divided, as is explained, Gen. xv.

MATTHEW HENRY

s probable that some now living, though not of age to be mustered, were of age to consent for themselves to the covenant made at Horeb, and yet it is here renewed. But the far greater part were a new generation, and therefore the covenant must be made afresh with them, for it is fit that the covenant should be renewed to the children of the covenant.

I. It is usual for indentures to begin with a recital; this does so, with a rehearsal of the great things God had done for them, 1. As an encouragement to them to believe that God would indeed be to them a God, for he would not have done so much for them if he had not designed more, to which all he had hitherto done was but a preface. 2. As an engagement upon them to be to him an obedient people, in consideration of what he had done for them.

II. For the proof of what he here advances he appeals to their own eyes (*v.* 2): *You have seen all that the Lord did.* Their own senses were incontestable evidence of the matter of fact: *Keep therefore the words of this covenant, v.* 9.

III. These things he specifies, to show the power and goodness of God in his appearances for them. 1. Their deliverance out of Egypt, *v.* 2, 3. 2. Their conduct through the wilderness for forty years, *v.* 5, 6. There they were led, and clad, and fed, by miracles. By these miracles they were made to know that the Lord was God, and by these mercies that he was their God. 3. The victory they had lately obtained over Sihon and Og, and that good land which they had taken possession of, *v.* 7, 8.

IV. By way of inference from these memoirs, Moses laments their stupidity: *Yet the Lord has not given you a heart to perceive, v.* 4. Note, 1 The hearing ear, the seeing eye, and the understanding heart, are the gift of God. 2 God gives not only food and raiment, but wealth and large possessions, to many to whom he does not give grace. Many enjoy the gifts who have not hearts to perceive the giver, nor the true intention and use of the gifts. 3 God's readiness to do us good in other things is a plain evidence that if we have not grace, that best of gifts, it is our own fault and not his.

Verses 10–29

It appears by the length of the sentences here, and by the copiousness and pungency of the expressions, that Moses, now that he was drawing near to the close of his discourse, was very zealous, and very desirous to impress what he said upon the minds of this unthinking people. To bind them the faster to God and duty, he here concludes a bargain (as it were) between them and God, an everlasting covenant. He requires not their explicit consent, but lays the matter plainly before them, and then leaves it between God and their own consciences.

I. The parties to this covenant. 1. It is the Lord their God they are to covenant with, *v.* 12. 2. They are all to be taken into covenant with him. They were all summoned to attend (*v.* 2). (1) Even their great men, the captains of their tribes, their elders and officers, must not think it any disparagement to put their necks under the yoke of this covenant, and to draw in it. (2) Not the men only, but their wives and children, must come into this covenant, *v.* 11. (3) Not the men of Israel only, but the stranger that was in their camp, provided he was so far proselyted to their religion as to renounce all false gods. This was an early indication of favour to the Gentiles, and of the kindness God had in store for them. (4) Not the freemen only, but the hewers of wood and drawers of water, the meanest drudge they had among them. (5) Not only those that were now present before God in this solemn assembly, but those also that were not here with them were taken into covenant (*v.* 15). That is, [1] Those that tarried at home were included; though detained either by sickness or necessary business. [2] The generations to come are included. And so, taking this covenant as a typical dispensation of the covenant of grace, it is a noble testimony to the Mediator of that covenant, who is *the same yesterday, to-day, and for ever.*

II. The summary of this covenant. All the precepts and all the promises of the covenant are included in the covenant-relation between God and them, *v.* 13.

III. The principal design of the renewing of this covenant at this time was to fortify them against temptations to idolatry. Idolaters were like drunkards, violently set upon their idols themselves and industrious to draw others in with them. Revellings commonly accompanied their idolatries (1 Pet. iv. 3), so that this speaks a woe to drunkards. Drunkenness is a sin that hardens the heart, and debauches the conscience, as much as any other, a sin to which men are strangely tempted themselves even when they have lately felt the mischiefs of it, and to which they are strangely fond of drawing others.

JAMIESON, FAUSSET, BROWN

that they might have a better knowledge of its conditions and be more disposed to comply with them.

2. Moses called unto all Israel, . . . Ye have seen all that the Lord did . . .—This appeal to the experience of the people, though made generally, was applicable only to that portion of them who had been very young at the period of the Exodus, and who remembered the marvellous transactions that preceded and followed that era. Yet, alas! those wonderful events made no good impression upon them (vs. 4). They were strangers to that grace of wisdom which is liberally given to all who ask it; and their insensibility was all the more inexcusable that so many miracles had been performed which might have led to a certain conviction of the presence and the power of God with them. The preservation of their clothes and shoes, the supply of daily food and fresh water—these continued without interruption or diminution during so many years' sojourn in the desert. They were miracles which unmistakably proclaimed the immediate hand of God and were performed for the express purpose of training them to a practical knowledge of, and habitual confidence in, Him. Their experience of this extraordinary goodness and care, together with their remembrance of the brilliant successes by which, with little exertion or loss on their part, God enabled them to acquire the valuable territory on which they stood, is mentioned again to enforce a faithful adherence to the covenant, as the direct and sure means of obtaining its promised blessings. **10-29. Ye stand this day, all of you, before the Lord**—The whole congregation of Israel, of all ages and conditions, all—young as well as old; menials as well as masters; native Israelites as well as naturalized strangers—all were assembled before the tabernacle to renew the *Sinaitic* covenant. None of them were allowed to consider themselves as exempt from the terms of that national compact, lest any lapsing into idolatry might prove a root of bitterness, spreading its noxious seed and corrupt influence all around (cf. Heb. 12:15). It was of the greatest consequence thus to reach the heart and conscience of everyone, for some might delude themselves with the vain idea that by taking the oath (vs. 12) by which they engaged themselves in covenant with God, they would surely secure its blessings. Then, even though they would not rigidly adhere to His worship and commands, but would follow the devices and inclinations of their own hearts, yet they would think that He would wink at such liberties and not punish them. It was of the greatest consequence to impress all with the strong and abiding conviction, that while the covenant of grace had special blessings belonging to it, it at the same time had curses in reserve for transgressors, the infliction of which would be as certain, as lasting and severe. This was the advantage contemplated in the law being rehearsed a second time. The picture of a once rich and flourishing region, blasted and doomed in consequence of the sins of its inhabitants, is very striking, and calculated to awaken awe in every reflecting mind. Such is, and long has been, the desolate state of Palestine; and, in looking at its ruined cities, its blasted coast, its naked mountains, its sterile and parched soil—all the sad and unmistakable evidences of a land lying under a curse—numbers of travellers from Europe, America, and the Indies ("strangers from a far country," vs. 22) in the present day see that the Lord has executed His threatening. Who can resist the conclusion that it has been inflicted "because the inhabitants had forsaken the covenant of the Lord God of their fathers, . . . and the anger of the Lord was kindled against this land, to bring upon it all the curses that are written in this book"?

ADAM CLARKE

18. *Beside the covenant which he made . . . in Horeb.* What is mentioned here is an additional institution to the ten words given on Horeb; and the curses denounced here are different from those denounced against the transgressors of the Decalogue.

4. *The Lord hath not given you an heart.* Some critics read this verse interrogatively: "And hath not God given you a heart?" because they suppose that God could not reprehend them for the nonperformance of a duty, when He had neither given them a mind to perceive the obligation of it nor strength to perform it had that obligation been known. Though this is strictly just, yet there is no need for the interrogation, as the words only imply that they had not such a heart, not because God had not given them all the means of knowledge, and helps of His grace and Spirit, which were necessary; but they had not made a faithful use of their advantages, and therefore they had not that wise, loving, and obedient heart which they otherwise might have had. Hence God himself is represented as grieved because they were unchanged and disobedient: "O that there were such an heart in them, that they would fear me, and keep all my commandments always, that it might be well with them, and with their children for ever!" See chap. v. 29.

5. *Your clothes are not waxen old.* See on chap. viii. 4.

6. *Ye have not eaten bread.* That is, you have not been supported in an ordinary providential way; I have been continually working miracles for you, *that ye might know that I am the Lord.* Thus we find that God had furnished them with all the means of this knowledge, and that the means were ineffectual, not because they were not properly calculated to answer God's gracious purpose, but because the people were not workers with God; consequently they received the grace of God in vain. See 2 Cor. vi. 1.

10. *Ye stand . . . all of you before the Lord.* They were about to enter into a covenant with God; and as a covenant implies two parties contracting, God is represented as being present, and they and all their families, old and young, come before Him.

12. *That thou shouldest enter. Leaber,* "to pass through," that is, between the separated parts of the covenant sacrifice. See Gen. xv. 18.

15. *Him that standeth here.* The present generation. *Him that is not here*—all future generations of this people.

18. *A root that beareth gall and wormwood.* That is, as the apostle expresses it, Heb. iii. 12, "an evil heart of unbelief, in departing from the living God," for to this place he evidently refers.

19. *To add drunkenness to thirst.* A proverbial expression denoting the utmost indulgence in all sensual gratifications.

26. *Gods . . . whom he had not given unto them.* This is an unhappy translation. *Chalak* signifies a "portion, lot, inheritance," and God is frequently represented in Scripture as the Portion or Inheritance of His people. Here, therefore, I think the original should be rendered, "And there was no portion to them," that is, the gods they served could neither supply their wants nor save their souls.

MATTHEW HENRY

Idolatry would be the ruin of their nation; it would bring plagues upon the land that connived at this root of bitterness and received the infection; as far as the sin spread, the judgment should spread likewise. We are forbidden curiously to enquire into the secret counsels of God. A full answer is given to that question, *Wherefore has the Lord done thus to this land?* sufficient to justify God and admonish us. But if any ask further why God would be at such a vast expense of miracles to form such a people, whose apostasy and ruin he plainly foresaw, why he did not by his almighty grace prevent it, or what he intends yet to do with them, let such know that these are questions which cannot be answered. See Acts i. 7; John xxi. 22; Col. ii. 18. We are directed and encouraged diligently to enquire into that which God has made known: things *revealed belong to us and to our children.* Note, 1. Though God has kept much of his counsel secret, yet there is enough revealed to satisfy and save us. He has *kept back nothing that is profitable for us.* 2. We ought to acquaint ourselves, and our children too, with the things of God that are revealed. We are not only allowed to search into them, but are concerned to do so. They are things which we and ours are closely interested in. They are the rules we are to live by, the grants we are to live upon; and therefore we are to learn them diligently ourselves, and to teach them diligently to our children. 3. All our knowledge must be in order to practise, for this is the end of all divine revelation, not to furnish us with curious subjects of speculation and discourse, with which to entertain ourselves and our friends, *but that we may do all the words of this law,* and be blessed in our deed.

CHAPTER 30

Verses 1–10

These verses may be considered either as a conditional promise or as an absolute prediction.

I. They are chiefly to be considered as a conditional promise, and so they belong to all persons and all people, and not to Israel only; and the design of them is to assure us that the greatest sinners, if they repent and be converted, shall have their sins pardoned, and be restored to God's favour. This is the purport of the covenant of grace, it leaves room for repentance in case of misdemeanour, and promises pardon upon repentance. Now observe here,

1. How the repentance is described which is the condition of these promises. (1) It begins in *serious consideration, v.* 1. "Thou shalt call to mind that which thou hadst forgotten or not regarded." Note, Consideration is the first step towards conversion. Isa. xlvi. 8, *Bring to mind, O you transgressors.* The prodigal son came to himself first, and then to his father. That which they should call to mind is the blessing and the curse. If sinners would but seriously consider the happiness they have lost by sin and the misery they have brought themselves into, and that by repentance they may escape that misery and recover that happiness, they would not delay to *return to the Lord their God.* The prodigal *called to mind the blessing and the curse* when he considered his present poverty and the plenty of bread *in his father's house,* Luke xv. 17. (2) It consists in sincere conversion. The effect of the consideration cannot but be godly sorrow and shame, Ezek. vi. 9; vii. 16. But that which is the life and soul of repentance, and without which the most passionate expressions are but a jest, is *returning to the Lord our God, v.* 2. If thou turn (*v.* 10) *with all thy heart and with all thy soul.* (3) It is evidenced by a constant obedience to the holy will of God. [1] This obedience must be with an eye to God: Thou shalt *obey his voice* (*v.* 8), and hearken to it, *v.* 10. [2] It must be sincere, and cheerful, and entire: *With all thy heart, and with all thy soul, v.* 2. [3] It must be from a principle of love, and that love must be *with all thy heart and with all thy soul, v.* 6.

2. What the favour is which is promised upon this repentance. Though they are brought to God by their trouble and distress, in the nations whither they were driven (*v.* 1), yet God will graciously accept of them notwithstanding; for on this errand afflictions are sent, to bring us to repentance. *Undique ad cœlos tantundem est viæ—From every place there is the same way to heaven.* It is here promised, (1) That God would have compassion upon them, as proper objects of his pity, *v.* 3. (2) That he would *turn their captivity, and gather them from the nations whither they were scattered* (*v.* 3), though ever so remote, *v.* 4. (3) That he would *bring them into their land again, v.* 5. Note, Penitent sinners are not only delivered out of their misery, but restored to true happiness in the favour of God.

JAMIESON, FAUSSET, BROWN

29. The secret things belong unto the Lord—This verse has no apparent connection with the thread of discourse. It is thought to have been said in answer to the looks of astonishment or the words of inquiry as to whether they would be ever so wicked as to deserve such punishments. The recorded history of God's providential dealings towards Israel presents a wonderful combination of "goodness and severity." There is much of it involved in mystery too profound for our limited capacities to fathom; but, from the comprehensive wisdom displayed in those parts which have been made known to us, we are prepared to enter into the full spirit of the apostle's exclamation, "How unsearchable are his judgments" (Rom. 11:33).

CHAPTER 30

VSS. 1-10. GREAT MERCIES PROMISED UNTO THE PENITENT. **1-3. when all these things are come upon thee, . . . and** [thou] **shalt return . . . then the Lord thy God will turn thy captivity**—The hopes of the Hebrew people are ardently directed to this promise, and they confidently expect that God, commiserating their forlorn and fallen condition, will yet rescue them from all the evils of their long dispersion. They do not consider the promise as fulfilled by their restoration from the captivity in Babylon, for Israel was not then scattered in the manner here described—"among all the nations," unto the utmost parts of heaven" (vs. 4). When God recalled them from that bondage, all the Israelites were not brought back. They were not multiplied above their fathers (vs. 5), nor were their hearts and those of their children circumcised to love the Lord (vs. 6). It is not, therefore, of the Babylonish captivity that Moses was speaking in this passage; it must be of the dispersed state to which they have been doomed for 1800 years. This prediction may have been partially accomplished on the return of the Israelites from Babylon; for, according to the structure and design of Scripture prophecy, it may have pointed to several similar eras in their national history; and this view is sanctioned by the prayer of Nehemiah (Neh. 1: 8, 9). But undoubtedly it will receive its full and complete accomplishment in the conversion of the Jews to the Gospel of Christ. At the restoration from the Babylonish captivity, that people were changed in many respects for the better. They were completely weaned from idolatry; and this outward reformation was a prelude to the higher attainments they are destined to reach in the age of Messiah, "when the Lord God will circumcise their hearts and the hearts of their seed to love the Lord." The course pointed out seems clearly to be this: that the hearts of the Hebrew people shall be circumcised (Col. 2:2); in other words. by the combined influences of the Word and spirit of God, their hearts will be touched and purified from all their superstition and unbelief. They will be converted to the faith of Jesus Christ as their Messiah—a spiritual deliverer, and the effect of their conversion will be that they will return and obey the voice (the Gospel, the evangelical law) of the Lord. The words may be interpreted either wholly in a spiritual sense (John 11:51, 52), or, as many think, in a literal sense also (Rom. 11). They will be recalled from all places of the dispersion to their own land and enjoy the highest prosperity. The mercies and favors of a bountiful Providence will not then be abused as formerly (ch. 31:20; 32:15). They will be received in a better spirit and employed to nobler purposes. They will be happy, "for the Lord will again repoice over them for good, as He rejoiced over their fathers."

ADAM CLARKE

29. *The secret things belong unto the Lord.* This verse has been variously translated. The simple general meaning seems to be this: "What God has thought proper to reveal He has revealed; what He has revealed is essential to the well-being of man, and this revelation is intended not for the present time merely, nor for one people, but for all succeeding generations. The things which He has not revealed concern not man but God alone, and are therefore not to be inquired after." Thus, then, the things that are hidden belong unto the Lord, those that are revealed belong unto us and our children.

CHAPTER 30

3. *Gather thee from all the nations.* This must refer to a more extensive captivity than that which they suffered in Babylon.

5. *Will bring thee into the land.* As this promise refers to a return from a captivity in which they had been scattered among all nations, consequently it is not the Babylonish captivity which is intended; and the repossession of their land must be different from that which was consequent on their return from Chaldea.

6. *God will circumcise thine heart.* This promise remains yet to be fulfilled. Their heart, as a people, has never yet been circumcised; nor have the various promises in this chapter ever yet been fulfilled. There remaineth, therefore, a rest for this people of God. Now, as the law, properly speaking, made no provision for the circumcision of the heart, which implies the remission of sins, and purification of the soul from all unrighteousness; and as circumcision itself was only a sign of spiritual good, consequently the promise here refers to the days of the Messiah, and to this all the prophets and all the apostles give witness: for "circumcision is that of the heart, in the spirit, and not in the letter," Rom. ii. 29; and the genuine followers of God "are circumcised with the circumcision made without hands . . . by the circumcision of Christ," Col. ii. 11-12. Hence we see these promises cannot be fulfilled to the Jews but in their embracing the gospel of Christ.

MATTHEW HENRY

II. This may also be considered as a prediction of the repentance and restoration of the Jews: *When all these things shall have come upon thee* (*v.* 1), the blessing first, and after that the curse, then the mercy in reserve shall take place. Though their hearts were wretchedly hardened, yet the grace of God could soften and change them; and then, though their case was deplorably miserable, the providence of God would redress all their grievances. Now, 1. It is certain that this was fulfilled in their return from their captivity in Babylon. It was a wonderful instance of their repentance and reformation that Ephraim, who had been joined to idols, renounced them, and said, *What have I to do any more with idols?* That captivity effectually cured them of idolatry; and then God planted them again in their own land and did them good. But, 2. Some think that it is yet further to be accomplished in the conversion of the Jews who are now dispersed, their repentance for the sin of their fathers in crucifying Christ, their return to God through him, and their accession to the Christian church.

Verses 11–14

Moses here urges them to obedience from the consideration of the plainness and easiness of the command.

I. This is true of the law of Moses. They could never plead in excuse of their disobedience that God had enjoined them that which was either unintelligible or impracticable, impossible to be known or to be done (*v.* 11): *It is not hidden from thee.* That is, 1. "It is not too high for thee; thou needest not send messengers to heaven (*v.* 12), to enquire what thou must do to please God; nor needest thou go *beyond sea* (*v.* 13), as the philosophers did, that travelled through many and distant regions in pursuit of learning." 2. "It is not too *hard* nor *heavy* for thee": so the Septuagint reads it, *v.* 11. "There is that in thee which *consents to the law that it is good*, Rom. vii. 16. Thou hast therefore no reason to complain of any insuperable difficulty in the observance of it."

II. This is true of the gospel of Christ, to which the apostle applies it, and makes it the language of the *righteousness which is of faith*, Rom. x. 6–8. This is God's commandment now under the gospel that we *believe in the name of his Son Jesus Christ*, 1 John iii. 23. But the word is nigh us, and Christ in that word; so that if we believe with the heart that the promises of the incarnation and resurrection of the Messiah are fulfilled in our Lord Jesus, and receive him accordingly, and confess him with our mouth, we have then Christ with us, and we shall be saved. He is near, very near, that justifies us. The law was plain and easy, but the gospel much more so.

Verses 15–20

Moses here concludes with a very bright light, and a very strong fire, that, if possible, what he had been preaching of might find entrance into the understanding and affections of this unthinking people.

I. He states the case very fairly. 1. Every man covets to obtain life and good, and to escape death and evil, desires happiness and dreads misery. "Well," says he, "I have shown you the way to obtain all the happiness you can desire and to avoid all misery. Be obedient, and all shall be well, and nothing amiss." 2. Every man is moved and governed in his actions by hope and fear, hope of good and fear of evil, real or apparent. "Now," says Moses, "I have tried both ways; if you will be either drawn to obedience by the certain prospect of advantage by it, or driven to obedience by the no less certain prospect of ruin in case you be disobedient—if you will be wrought upon either way, you will be kept close to God and your duty; but, if you will not, you are utterly inexcusable."

II. Having thus stated the case, he fairly puts them to their choice, with a direction to them to choose well.

III. In the last verse, He shows them, in short, what their duty is, *to love God*, and to love him as *the Lord*, a Being most amiable, and as *their God*, a God in covenant with them. *He is thy life, and the length of thy days.*

JAMIESON, FAUSSET, BROWN

11-14. THE COMMANDMENT IS MANIFEST. **11-14. For this commandment . . . is not hidden . . . , neither is it far off**—That law of loving and obeying God, which was the subject of Moses' discourse, was well known to the Israelites. They could not plead ignorance of its existence and requirements. It was not concealed as an impenetrable mystery in heaven, for it had been revealed; nor was it carefully withheld from the people as a dangerous discovery; for the youngest and humblest of them were instructed in those truths, which were subjects of earnest study and research among the wisest and greatest of other nations. They were not under a necessity of undertaking long journeys or distant voyages, as many ancient sages did in quest of knowledge. They enjoyed the peculiar privilege of a familiar acquaintance with it. It was with them a subject of common conversation, engraven on their memories, and frequently explained and inculcated on their hearts. The apostle Paul (Rom. 10:6-8) has applied this passage to the Gospel, for the law of Christ is substantially the same as that of Moses, only exhibited more clearly in its spiritual nature and extensive application; and, accompanied with the advantages of Gospel grace, it is practicable and easy.

15-20. DEATH AND LIFE ARE SET BEFORE THE ISRAELITES. **15-20. See, I have set before thee this day, life and good, and death and evil**—the alternative of a good and happy, or a disobedient and miserable life. Love of God and compliance with His will are the only ways of securing the blessings and avoiding the evils described. The choice was left to them, and in urging upon them the inducements to a wise choice, Moses warmed as he proceeded into a tone of solemn and impressive earnestness similar to that of Paul to the elders of Ephesus (Acts 20:26, 27).

ADAM CLARKE

1. *When all these things are come upon thee, the blessing and the curse.* So fully did God foresee the bad use these people would make of their free agency in resisting the Holy Ghost that He speaks of their sin and punishment as certain; yet at the same time shows how they might turn to himself and live, even while He was pouring out His indignation upon them because of their transgressions.

11. *This commandment . . . is not hidden.* Not too "wonderful" or difficult for thee to comprehend or perform, as the word *niphleth* implies. *Neither is it far off*—the word or doctrine of salvation shall be proclaimed in your own land; for He is to be born in Bethlehem of Judah, who is to feed and save Israel; and the Prophet who is to teach them is to be raised up from among their brethren.

12. *It is not in heaven.* Shall not be communicated in that way in which the prophets received the living oracles; but the Word shall be made flesh, and dwell among you.

13. *Neither is it beyond the sea.* You shall not be obliged to travel for it to distant nations, because "salvation is of the Jews."

14. *But the word is very nigh unto thee.* The doctrine of salvation preached by the apostles; *in thy mouth*—the promises of redemption made by the prophets forming a part of every Jew's creed; *in thy heart*—the power to believe with the heart unto righteousness, that the tongue may make confession unto salvation. In this way, it is evident, Paul understood these passages; see Rom. x. 6, etc.

15. *Life and good.* Present and future blessings. *Death and evil.* Present and future miseries: termed, v. 19, "Life and death, blessing and cursing." Were there no such thing as *free will* in man, who could reconcile these sayings with either sincerity or common sense? God has made the human will free, and there is no power or influence either in heaven, earth, or hell, except the power of God, that can deprive it of its free volitions; of its power to will and nill, to choose and refuse, to act or not act or force it to sin against God. Hence man is accountable for his actions, because they are his; were he necessitated by fate, or sovereign constraint, they could not be his.

20. *That thou mayest love the Lord.* Without love there can be no obedience. *Obey his voice.* Without obedience love is fruitless and dead. *And . . . cleave unto him.* Without close attachment and perseverance, temporary love, however sincere and fervent—temporary obedience, however disinterested, energetic, and pure while it lasts—will be ultimately ineffectual. He alone who "endureth to the end shall be saved."

MATTHEW HENRY — CHAPTER 31

Verses 1–8

Loth to part (we say) *bids oft farewell.* Moses does so to the children of Israel; not because he was loth to go to God, but because he was loth to leave them, fearing that when he had left them they would leave God. Here he calls them together to give them a word

JAMIESON, FAUSSET, BROWN — CHAPTER 31

VSS. 1-8. MOSES ENCOURAGES THE PEOPLE AND JOSHUA. **1. Moses went and spake**—It is probable that this rehearsal of the law extended over several successive days; and it might be the last and most important day on which the return of Moses to the

ADAM CLARKE — CHAPTER 31

MATTHEW HENRY

of encouragement. It was a discouragement to them that Moses was to be removed at a time when he could so ill be spared: though Joshua would continue to fight for them in the valley, they would want Moses to intercede for them on the hill, as he did, Exod. xvii. 10. 1. He is 120 *years old*, and it is time for him to think of resigning his honour and returning to his rest. 2. He is under a divine sentence: *Thou shalt not go over Jordan.*

I. He encourages the people; and never could any general animate his soldiers upon such good grounds as those on which Moses here encourages Israel. 1. He assures them of the constant presence of God with them (*v.* 3): *The Lord thy God* that has led thee and kept thee hitherto *will go over before thee.* This is applied by the apostle to all God's spiritual Israel, for the encouragement of their faith and hope; unto us is this gospel preached, as well as unto them. *He will never fail thee, nor forsake thee*, Heb. xiii. 5. 2. He commends Joshua to them for a leader, one whose conduct, and courage, and sincere affection to their interest, they had had long experience of; and one whom God had ordained and appointed to be their leader, and therefore, no doubt, would own and bless, and make a blessing to them. See Num. xxvii. 18. 3. He ensures their success. Two things might encourage their hopes of this:—(1) The victories they had already obtained over Sihon and Og (*v.* 4), from which they might infer both the power of God, that he could do what he had done, and the purpose of God, that he would finish what he had begun to do. (2) The command God had given them to destroy the Canaanites (*ch.* vii. 2; xii. 2), and from which they might infer that no doubt he would put it into the power of their hands to do it.

II. He encourages Joshua, *v.* 7, 8. Observe, 1. Joshua was an experienced general, and a man of approved gallantry and very well pleased to be admonished by Moses to be strong and of good courage. 2. He gives him this charge *in the sight of all Israel*, that they might be the more observant of him whom they saw thus solemnly inaugurated. 3. He gives him the same assurances of the divine presence, and consequently of a glorious success, that he had given the people.

Verses 9-13

The law was given by Moses; so it is said, John i. 17. He was not only entrusted to deliver it to that generation, but to transmit it to the generations to come; and here it appears that he was faithful to that trust.

I. *Moses wrote this law, v.* 9. 1. That those who had heard it might often review it themselves, and call it to mind. 2. That it might be the more safely handed down to posterity. Note, The church has received abundance of advantage from the writing, as well as from the preaching, of divine things; faith comes not only by hearing, but by reading. The same care that was taken of the law, thanks be to God, is taken of the gospel too; soon after it was preached it was written, that it might reach to those on whom the ends of the world shall come.

II. Having written it, he committed it to the care and custody of the priests and elders. He delivered one authentic copy to the priests, to be laid up by the ark (*v.* 26), there to remain as a standard by which all other copies must be tried.

III. He appointed the public reading of this law in a general assembly of all Israel every seventh year. The pious Jews (it is very probable) read the law daily in their families, and *Moses of old time was read in the synagogue every sabbath day*, Acts. xv. 21. But once in seven years, that the law might be the more magnified and made honourable, it must be read in a general assembly. Now here he gives direction,

1. When this solemn reading of the law must be, that the time might add to the solemnity; it must be done, (1) In the year of release. In that year the land rested, so that they could the better spare time to attend this service. Servants who were then discharged, and poor debtors who were then acquitted from their debts, must know that, having the benefit of the law, it was justly expected they should yield obedience to it, and therefore give up themselves to be God's servants, because he had loosed their bonds. The year of release was typical of gospel grace, which therefore is called the *acceptable year of the Lord*; for our remission and liberty by Christ engage us to keep his commandments, Luke i. 74, 75. (2) At the feast of tabernacles in that year. In that feast they were particularly required to *rejoice before God*, Lev. xxiii. 40.

2. To whom it must be read: To *all Israel* (*v.* 11), *men, women, and children, and the strangers, v.* 12. The women and children were not obliged to go up to the other feasts, but to this only in which the law

JAMIESON, FAUSSET, BROWN

place of assembly is specially noticed. In drawing his discourse towards a conclusion, he adverted to his advanced age; and although neither his physical nor intellectual powers had suffered any decay (ch. 34:7), yet he knew, by a special revelation, that the time had arrived when he was about to be withdrawn from the superintendence and government of Israel.

2-8. also the Lord hath said—should be "*for* the Lord hath said" thou shalt not go over this Jordan. While taking a solemn leave of the people, he exhorted them not to be intimidated by the menacing opposition of enemies; to take encouragement from the continued presence of their covenanted God; and to rest assured that the same divine power, which had enabled them to discomfit their first assailants on the east of Jordan, would aid them not less effectually in the adventurous enterprise which they were about to undertake, and by which they would obtain possession of "the land which He had sworn unto their fathers to give them."

9-13. HE DELIVERS THE LAW TO THE PRIESTS, TO READ IT EVERY SEVENTH YEAR TO THE PEOPLE. **9-13. Moses wrote this law, and delivered it unto the priests**—The law thus committed to writing was either the whole book of Deuteronomy, or the important part of it contained between the twenty-seventh and thirtieth chapters. It was usual in cases of public or private contract for two copies of the engagement to be made—one to be deposited in the national archives or some secure place for reference, should occasion require. The other was to remain in the hands of the contracting parties (Jer. 32:12-14). The same course was followed on this renewal of the covenant between God and Israel. Two written copies of the law were prepared, the one of which was delivered to the public representatives of Israel; viz., the priests and the elders. **the priests, . . . who bare the ark of the covenant**—In all ordinary journeys, it was the common duty of the Levites to carry the ark and its furniture (Num. 4: 15); but, on solemn or extraordinary occasions, that office was discharged by the priests (Josh. 3:3-8; 6:6; I Chron. 15:11, 12). **all the elders of Israel**—They were assistants to the priests and overseers to take care of the preservation, rehearsal, and observance of the law. **10, 11. At the end of every seven years, . . . thou shalt read this law**—At the return of the sabbatic year and during the feast of tabernacles, the law was to be publicly read. This order of Moses was a future and prospective arrangement; for the observance of the sabbatic year did not commence till the conquest and peaceful occupation of Canaan.

The ordinance served several important purposes. For, while the people had opportunities of being instructed in the law every Sabbath and daily in their own homes, this

ADAM CLARKE

2. *I am an hundred and twenty years old.* The life of Moses, the great prophet of God and lawgiver of the Jews, was exactly the same in length as the time Noah employed in preaching righteousness to the antediluvian world. These 120 years were divided into three remarkable periods: 40 years he lived in Egypt, in Pharaoh's court, acquiring all the learning and wisdom of the Egyptians (see Acts vii. 20, 23); 40 years he sojourned in the land of Midian in a state of preparation for his great and important mission (Acts vii. 29-30); and 40 years he guided, led, and governed the Israelites under the express direction and authority of God.

3. *Joshua, he shall go over before thee.* See on Num. xxvii. 17, etc.

6. *Be strong. Chizku,* the same word that is used Exod. iv. 21; ix. 15, for hardening Pharaoh's heart. The Septuagint, in this and the following verse, have, "Play the man, and be strong"; and from this Paul seems to have borrowed his ideas, 1 Cor. xvi. 13: "Stand firm in the faith; play the man"—act like heroes; be vigorous.

8. *The Lord . . . doth go before thee.* To prepare your way, and to direct you. *He will be with thee.* Accompany you in all your journeys, and assist you in all your enterprises. *He will not fail thee.* Your expectation, however strong and extensive, shall never be disappointed; you cannot expect too much from Him. *Neither forsake thee.* He knows that without Him you can do nothing, and therefore He will continue with you, and in such a manner too that the excellence of the power shall appear to be of Him, and not of man.

9. *Moses wrote this law.* Not the whole Pentateuch, but either the discourses and precepts mentioned in the preceding chapters or the Book of Deuteronomy, which is most likely.

10-11. *At the end of every seven years . . . thou shalt read this law.* Every seventh year was a year of release, chap. xv. 1, at which time the people's minds, being under a peculiar degree of solemnity, were better disposed to hear and profit by the words of God. I suppose on this ground also that the whole Book of Deuteronomy is meant, as it alone contains an epitome of the whole Pentateuch. And in this way some of the chief Jewish rabbins understand this place.

It is strange that this commandment, relative to a public reading of the law every seven years, should have been rarely attended to. It does not appear that from the time mentioned in Josh. viii. 30, at which time this public reading first took place, till the reign of Jehoshaphat, 2 Chron. xvii. 7, there was any public seventh-year reading—a period of 530 years. The next

MATTHEW HENRY

was read.

3. By whom it must be read: *Thou shalt read it* (*v.* 11), "Thou, O Israel," by a proper person appointed for that purpose; or, "Thou, O Joshua," their chief ruler; accordingly we find that he did read the law himself, Josh. viii. 34, 35. So did Josiah, 2 Chron. xxxiv. 30, and Ezra, Neh. viii. 3.

4. For what end it must be thus solemnly read. That the present generation might hereby keep up their acquaintance with the law of God, *v.* 12. They must hear, that they may learn, and *fear God, and observe to do their duty*. See here what we are to aim at in hearing the word; we must hear, that we may learn and grow in knowledge; and every time we read the scriptures we shall find that there is still more and more to be learned out of them.

Verses 14–21

Here, I. Moses and Joshua are summoned to attend the divine majesty at the door of the tabernacle, *v.* 14. Moses is told again that he must shortly die. He must also bring Joshua with him to be presented to God for a successor, and to receive his commission and charge.

II. God graciously gives them the meeting: *He appeared in the tabernacle* (as the shechinah used to appear) *in a pillar of a cloud, v.* 15.

III. He tells Moses that, after his death, the covenant which he had taken so much pains to make between Israel and their God would certainly be broken. 1. That Israel would *forsake God, v.* 16. Worshipping the gods of the Canaanites would undoubtedly be counted a violation of the covenant. Thus still those are revolters from Christ, who either make a god of their money by allowing covetousness to reign, or a god of their belly by allowing sensuality to reign. Those that *turn to other gods* (*v.* 18) forsake their own mercies. 2. That then God would forsake Israel; and justly does he cast those off who had so unjustly cast him off (*v.* 17). Those that have sinned away their God will find that thereby they pull all mischiefs upon their own heads.

IV. He directs Moses to deliver them a song, in the composing of which he should be divinely inspired, and which should remain a standing testimony for God as faithful to them in giving them warning. The wisdom of man has devised many ways of conveying the knowledge of good and evil, by laws, histories, prophecies, proverbs, and, among the rest, by songs; each has its advantages. And the wisdom of God has in the scripture made use of them all, that ignorant and careless men might be left inexcusable. 1. This song, if rightly improved, might be a means to prevent their apostasy. 2. If this song did not prevent their apostasy, yet it might help to bring them to repentance. When their troubles come upon them, this *song shall not be forgotten*, but may serve as a glass to show them their own faces, that they may humble themselves, and return to him from whom they have revolted. Note, Those for whom God has mercy in store he may leave to fall, yet he will provide means for their recovery. Medicines are prepared beforehand for their cure.

Verses 22–30

Here, I. The charge is given to Joshua, which God had said (*v.* 14) he would give him. Joshua had now heard from God so much of the wickedness of the people whom he was to have the conduct of as could not but be a discouragement to him: "Nay," says God, "how bad soever they are, thou shalt go through thy undertaking, for *I will be with thee*. Therefore *be of good courage*."

II. The solemn delivery of the book of the law to the Levites, to be deposited in the side of the ark, is here again related (*v.* 24–26). Only they are here directed where to treasure up this precious original, not in the ark (there only the two tables were preserved), but in another box *by the side of the ark*. It is probable that this was the very book that was found in the house of the Lord (having been somehow or other misplaced) in the days of Josiah (2 Chron. xxxiv. 14).

III. The song which follows in the next chapter is here delivered to Moses, and by him to the people. 1. He declares what little joy he had had of them while he was with them, *v.* 27. Their rebellions against himself he makes no mention of: these he had long since forgiven and forgotten; but they must be made to hear of their rebellions against God, that they may be ever repented of and never repeated. 2. What little hopes he had of them now that he was leaving them. *I know that after my death you will utterly corrupt yourselves.*

JAMIESON, FAUSSET, BROWN

public periodical rehearsal at meetings in the courts of the sanctuary, where women and children of twelve years were present (as they usually were at the great festivals), was calculated to produce good and pious impressions of divine truth amid the sacred associations of the time and place. Besides, it formed a public guarantee for the preservation, integrity, and faithful transmission of the Sacred Book to successive ages.

14-15. the Lord said unto Moses, . . . call Joshua, and present yourselves in the tabernacle of the congregation—Joshua had been publicly designated to the office of commander by Moses; and God was pleased to confirm his appointment by the visible symbols of His presence and approval. As none but the priests were privileged to enter the sanctuary, it is probable that this significant manifestation of the cloudy pillar was made while the leaders stood at the door of the tabernacle. **16-22. the Lord said unto Moses, . . . this people will rise up**—In this remarkable interview, Moses was distinctly apprised of the infidelity of Israel, their corruptions of the true religion through intercourse with the idolatrous inhabitants of Canaan (Amos 5:26), and their chastisements in consequence of those national defections. **17. Then my anger shall be kindled, . . . and I will hide my face from them**—an announcement of the withdrawal of the divine favor and protection of which the Shekinah was the symbol and pledge. It never appeared in the second temple; and its non-appearance was a prelude of "all the evils that came upon them, because their God was not among them." **19. Now therefore write ye this song**—National songs take deep hold of the memories and have a powerful influence in stirring the deepest feelings of a people. In accordance with this principle in human nature, a song was ordered to be composed by Moses, doubtless under divine inspiration, which was to be learnt by the Israelites themselves and to be taught to their children in every age, embodying the substance of the preceding addresses, and of a strain well suited to inspire the popular mind with a strong sense of God's favor to their nation.

26. Take this book of the law, and put it in the side of the ark—The second copy of the law (see on vs. 9) was deposited for greater security and reverence in a little chest *beside* the ark of the covenant, for there was nothing contained within it but the tables of stone (I Kings 8:9). Others think it was put *within* the ark, it being certain, from the testimony of Paul (Heb. 9:4), that there were once other things inside the ark, and that this was the copy found in the time of Josiah (II Kings 22:8).

ADAM CLARKE

seventh-year reading was not till the eighteenth year of the reign of Josiah, 2 Chron. xxxiv. 30, a space of 282 years. Nor do we find any other publicly mentioned from this time till the return from the Babylonish captivity, Neh. viii. 2. Nor is there any other on record from that time to the destruction of Jerusalem.

16. *Behold, thou shalt sleep with thy fathers. Shocheb,* thou "shalt lie down"; it signifies to rest, take rest in sleep, and, metaphorically, "to die."

18. *I will surely hide my face.* Withdraw My approbation and My protection. This is a general meaning of the word in Scripture.

19. *Write ye this song.* The song which follows in the next chapter. Things which were of great importance and of common concern were, among the ancients, put into verse, as this was found the best method of keeping them in remembrance, especially in those times when writing was little practiced.

21. *This song shall testify against them.* Because in it their general defection is predicted, but in such a way as to show them how to avoid the evil; and if they did not avoid the evil, and the threatened punishment should come upon them, then the song should testify against them, by showing that they had been sufficiently warned, and might have lived to God, and so escaped those disasters.

26. *Take this book of the law.* The standard copy to which all transcripts must ultimately refer; another copy was put into the hands of the priests. See the note on v. 9.

27. *While I am yet alive . . . ye have been rebellious.* Such was the disposition of this people to act contrary to moral goodness that Moses felt himself justified in inferring what would take place from what had already happened.

MATTHEW HENRY

CHAPTER 32

Verses 1–6

Here is, I. A commanding preface or introduction to this song of Moses, *v.* 1, 2. He begins, 1. With a solemn appeal to heaven and earth concerning the truth and importance of what he was about to say, and the justice of the divine proceedings against a rebellious and backsliding people. Heaven and earth will be witnesses against sinners, witnesses of the warning given them and of their refusal to take the warning (see Job xx. 27). 2. He begins with a solemn application of what he was about to say to the people (*v.* 2): *My doctrine shall drop as the rain.* "It shall be a beating sweeping rain to the rebellious"; so one of the Chaldee paraphrasts expounds the first clause. Rain is sometimes sent for judgment, and the word of God, while to some it is so refreshing —a *savour of life unto life,* is to others terrifying. It shall be as a sweet and comfortable dew to those who are rightly prepared to receive it. Observe, (1) The subject of this song is doctrine; he had given them a song of praise and thanksgiving (Exod. xv.), but this is a song of instruction, for in psalms, and hymns, and spiritual songs, we are not only to give glory to God, but to *teach and admonish one another,* Col. iii. 16. Hence many of David's psalms are entitled *Maschil—to give instruction.* (2) This doctrine is fitly compared to rain and showers which come from above, to make the earth fruitful. (3) He promises that his doctrine shall drop and distil as the dew, and the small rain, which descend silently and without noise. The word preached is likely to profit when it comes gently, and sweetly insinuates itself into the hearts and affections of the hearers. (4) He bespeaks their acceptance and entertainment of it.

II. An awful declaration of the greatness and righteousness of God, *v.* 3, 4.

1. He begins with this, and lays it down as his first principle. To justify God in his dealings with them; we must abide by it, that God is righteous, even when his *judgments are a great deep,* Jer. xii. 1; Ps. xxxvi. 6.

2. Moses here sets himself to *publish the name of the Lord* (*v.* 3), that Israel might never be such fools as to exchange him for a false god. It will be of great use to us for the preventing of sin, and the preserving of us in the way of our duty, always to keep up high and honourable thoughts of God, and to take all occasions to express them: *Ascribe greatness to our God.* Now, when Moses would set forth the greatness of God, he does it, not by explaining his eternity and immensity, or describing the brightness of his glory in the upper world, but by showing the faithfulness of his word, the perfection of his works, and the wisdom and equity of all the administrations of his government; for in these his glory shines most clearly to us, and these are the things revealed concerning him, which *belong to us and our children, v.* 4. (1) *He is the rock.* God is the rock, for he is in himself immutable, immovable, and he is to all that seek him and fly to him an impenetrable shelter, and to all that trust in him an everlasting foundation. (2) *His work is perfect.* His work of creation was so, *all very good;* his works of providence are so, or will be so in due time, and when the mystery of God shall be finished the perfection of his works will appear to all the world. Nothing that God does can be mended, Eccl. iii. 14. God was now perfecting what he had promised and begun for his people Israel. (3) *All his ways are judgment.* The ends of his ways are all righteous, and he is wise in the choice of the means in order to those ends. *Judgment* signifies both *prudence* and *justice.* (4) He is *a God of truth,* whose word we may take and rely upon, for he cannot lie who is faithful to all his promises, nor shall his threatenings fall to the ground. (5) He is *without iniquity,* one who never cheated any that trusted in him, never wronged any that appealed to his justice, nor ever was hard upon any that cast themselves upon his mercy. (6) *Just and right is he.* As he will not wrong any by punishing them more than they deserve, so he will not fail to recompense all those that serve him or suffer for him.

III. A high charge exhibited against the Israel of God, whose character was in all respects the reverse of that of the *God of Israel, v.* 5. 1. *They have corrupted themselves.* 2. *Their spot is not the spot of his children.* Even God's children have their spots, while they are in this imperfect state; for if we say we have no sin, no spot, we deceive ourselves. But the sin of Israel was none of those; it was not an infirmity which they strove against, watched and prayed against, but an evil which their hearts were fully set in them to do. For, 3. They were a *perverse and crooked generation,* that were actuated by a spirit of contra-

JAMIESON, FAUSSET, BROWN

CHAPTER 32

VSS. 1-43. MOSES' SONG, WHICH SETS FORTH THE PERFECTIONS OF GOD. **1. Give ear, O ye heavens; . . . hear, O earth**—The magnificence of the exordium, the grandeur of the theme, the frequent and sudden transitions, the elevated strain of the sentiments and language, entitle this song to be ranked amongst the noblest specimens of poetry to be found in the Scriptures.

2, 3. My doctrine shall drop . . .—The language may justly be taken as uttered in the form of a wish or prayer, and the comparison of wholesome instruction to the pure, gentle, and insinuating influence of rain or dew, is frequently made by the sacred writers (Isa. 5:6; 55: 10, 11).

4. He is the Rock—a word expressive of power and stability. The application of it in this passage is to declare that God had been true to His covenant with their fathers and them. Nothing that He had promised had failed; so that if their national experience had been painfully checkered by severe and protracted trials, notwithstanding the brightest promises, that result was traceable to their own undutiful and perverse conduct; not to any vacillation or unfaithfulness on the part of God (Jas. 1:17), whose procedure was marked by justice and judgment, whether they had been exalted to prosperity or plunged into the depths of affliction. **5. They have corrupted themselves**—i.e., the Israelites by their frequent lapses and their inveterate attachment to idolatry. **their spot is not the spot of his children**—This is an allusion to the marks which idolaters inscribe on their foreheads or their arms with paint or other substances, in various colors and forms—straight, oval, or circular, according to the favorite idol of their worship.

ADAM CLARKE

CHAPTER 32

1. On the inimitable excellence of this ode much has been written by commentators, critics, and poets; and it is allowed by the best judges to contain a specimen of almost every species of excellence in composition. It is so thoroughly poetic that even the dull Jews themselves found they could not write it in the prose form; and hence it is distinguished as poetry in every Hebrew Bible by being written in its own hemistichs or short half-lines, which is the general form of the Hebrew poetry; and were it translated in the same way it would be more easily understood. The song itself has suffered by both transcribers and translators, the former having mistaken some letters in different places, and made wrong combinations of them in others. *Give ear, O ye heavens.* Let angels and men hear, and let this testimony of God be registered in both heaven and earth. Heaven and earth are appealed to as *permanent* witnesses.

2. *My doctrine. Likchi,* from *lakach,* to "take, carry away"; to "attract or gain over the heart" by eloquence or persuasive speech. *Shall drop as the rain.* It shall come drop by drop as the shower, beginning slowly and distinctly, but increasing more and more till the plenitude of righteousness is poured down, and the whole canon of divine revelation completed. *My speech shall distil as the dew. Imrathi;* My familiar, friendly, and affectionate speeches shall descend gently and softly, on the ear and the heart, as the dew, moistening and refreshing all around. In hot regions *dew* is often a substitute for rain; without it there could be no fertility, especially in those places where rain seldom falls. And in such places only can the metaphor here used be felt in its perfection. *As the small rain. Seirim,* from *saar,* to be "rough" or "tempestuous"; sweeping showers, accompanied with a strong gale of wind. *And as the showers. Rebibim,* from *rabah,* "to multiply, to increase greatly"; shower after shower, or rather a continual rain, whose drops are multiplied beyond calculation, upon the earth; alluding perhaps to the rainy seasons in the East, or to those early and latter rains so essentially necessary for the vegetation and perfection of the grain.

No doubt these various expressions point out that great variety in the word or revelation of God whereby it is suited to every place, occasion, person, and state; being profitable for doctrine, reproof, and edification in righteousness. Hence the apostle says that God "at sundry times and in divers manners spake in time past unto the fathers by the prophets," and "in these last times [has] spoken unto us by his Son, Heb. i. 1-2. By every prophet, evangelist, and apostle, God speaks a particular language; all is His *doctrine,* His great system of instruction, for the information and salvation of the souls of men. But some portions are like the "sweeping showers," in which the tempest of God's wrath appears against sinners. Others are like the "incessant showers of gentle rain," preparing the soil for the germination of the grain, and causing it to take root. And others still are like the "dew," mildly and gently insinuating convictions, persuasions, reproofs, and consolations.

4. *He is the Rock.* The word *tsur* is rendered "Creator" by some eminent critics. Rab. Moses ben Maimon observes that the word *tsur,* which is ordinarily translated "rock," signifies "origin, fountain, first cause," and in this way it should be translated here: "He is the First Principle; His work is perfect."

5. *Their spot is not the spot of his children.* This verse is variously translated and variously understood. "They are corrupted, not his, children of pollution."—Kennicott. "They are corrupt, they are not his children, they are blotted." —Houbigant. This is according to the Samaritan. The interpretation commonly given to these words is as unfounded as it is exceptionable: "God's children have their spots, i.e., their sins, but sin in them is not like sin in others; in others sin is exceedingly sinful, but God does not see the sins of His children as He sees the sins of His enemies." Unfortunately for this bad doctrine, there is no foundation for it in the sacred text, which, though very obscure, may be thus translated: "He [Israel] hath corrupted

MATTHEW HENRY

diction, and therefore would do what was forbidden because it was forbidden.

IV. A pathetic expostulation with this provoking people for their ingratitude (*v.* 6): *Do you thus requite the Lord?* 1. He reminds them of the obligations God had laid upon them to serve him, and to cleave to him. He had been a Father to them. And are not our obligations, as baptized Christians, equally great and strong to our Creator that made us, our Redeemer that bought us, and our Sanctifier that has established us? 2. Hence he infers the evil of deserting him and rebelling against him. For, (1) It was base ingratitude. (2) It was prodigious madness.

Verses 7–14

Moses, having in general represented God to them as their great benefactor, in these verses gives particular instances of God's kindness to them and concern for them. 1. Some instances were ancient, and for proof of them he appeals to the records (*v.* 7): *Remember the days of old.* Note, The authentic histories of ancient times are of singular use, and especially the history of the church in its infancy, both the Old Testament and the New Testament church. 2. Others were more modern, and for proof of them he appeals to their fathers and elders that were now alive and with them.

Three things are here enlarged upon as instances of God's kindness to his people Israel.

I. The early designation of the land of Canaan for their inheritance; for herein it was a type and figure of our heavenly inheritance, that it was of old ordained and prepared in the divine counsels, *v.* 8. Observe,

1. When the earth was divided among the sons of men, God had Israel in his thoughts.

2. The reason given for the particular care God took for this people, so long before they were either born or thought of (as I may say), in our world, does yet more magnify the kindness, and make it obliging beyond expression (*v.* 9): *For the Lord's portion is his people.*

II. The forming of them into a people, that they might be fit to enter upon this inheritance, like an heir of age, at the time appointed of the Father. And herein also Canaan was a figure of the heavenly inheritance; for, as it was from eternity proposed and designed for all God's spiritual Israel, so they are, in time (and it is a work of time), fitted and made meet for it, Col. i. 12. A great deal was done to model this people, to cast them into some shape, and to fit them for the great things designed for them in the land of promise.

1. *He found him in a desert land*, *v.* 10. This refers, no doubt, to the wilderness through which God brought them to Canaan, and in which he took so much pains with them; it is called *the church in the wilderness*, Acts vii. 38. There it was born, and nursed, and educated. (1) Their condition was forlorn. Egypt was to them a desert land, and a waste howling wilderness, for they were bond-slaves in it. (2) Their disposition was very unpromising. So ignorant were the generality of them in divine things, so stupid and unapt to receive the impressions of them, so peevish and humoursome, that they might well be said to be found in a desert land.

2. *He led him about and instructed him.* When God had them in the wilderness he did not bring them directly to Canaan, but made them go a great way about, and so he instructed them. Learners must have time to learn. By this means he tried their faith, and patience, and dependence upon God, and inured them to the hardships of the wilderness, and so instructed them. Every stage had something in it that was instructive. We may well imagine how unfit that people would have been for Canaan had they not first gone through the discipline of the wilderness.

3. *He kept him as the apple of his eye*, with all the care and tenderness that could be, from the malignant influences of an open sky and air, and all the perils of an inhospitable desert. The pillar of cloud and fire was both a guide and a guard to them.

4. He did that for them which the eagle does for her nest of young, *v.* 11, 12. The similitude was touched upon, Exod. xix. 4, *I bore you on eagles' wings*; here it is enlarged upon. The eagle is observed to have a strong affection for her young, by protecting them and making provision for them, by educating them and teaching them to fly. For this purpose she stirs them out of the nest where they lie dozing, flutters over them, to show them how they must use their wings, and then accustoms them to fly upon her wings till they have learnt to fly upon their own. This, by the way, is an example to parents to train up their children to business, and not to indulge them in idleness and the love of ease. God did thus

JAMIESON, FAUSSET, BROWN

6. is not he thy father that hath bought thee—or emancipated thee from Egyptian bondage. **and made thee**—advanced the nation to unprecedented and peculiar privileges. **8, 9. When the Most High divided to the nations their inheritance**—In the division of the earth, which Noah is believed to have made by divine direction (Gen. 10:5; ch. 2:5-9; Acts 17:26, 27), Palestine was reserved by the wisdom and goodness of Heaven for the possession of His peculiar people and the display of the most stupendous wonders. The theater was small, but admirably suited for the convenient observation of the human race—at the junction of the two great continents of Asia and Africa, and almost within sight of Europe. From this spot as from a common center the report of God's wonderful works, the glad tidings of salvation through the obedience and sufferings of His own eternal Son, might be rapidly and easily wafted to every part of the globe. **he set the bounds of the people according to the number of the children of Israel**—Another rendering, which has received the sanction of eminent scholars, has been proposed as follows: "When the Most High divided to the nations their inheritance, when He separated the sons of Adam and set the bounds of every people, the children of Israel were few in numbers, when the Lord chose that people and made Jacob His inheritance" (cf. ch. 30:5; Gen. 34:30; Ps. 105:9-12).

10. found him in a desert land—took him into a covenant relation at Sinai, or rather "sustained," "provided for him" in a desert land. **a waste howling wilderness**—a common Oriental expression for a desert infested by wild beasts.

11. As an eagle . . . fluttereth over her young—This beautiful and expressive metaphor is founded on the extraordinary care and attachment which the female eagle cherishes for her young. When her newly fledged progeny are sufficiently advanced to soar in their native element, she, in their first attempts at flying, supports them on the tip of her wing, encouraging, directing, and aiding their feeble efforts to longer and sublimer flights. So did God take the most tender and powerful care of His chosen people; He carried them out of Egypt and led them through all the horrors of the wilderness to the promised inheritance.

13, 14. He made him ride on the high places . . .—All these expressions seem to have peculiar reference to their home in the transjordanic territory, that being the extent

ADAM CLARKE

himself. They [the Israelites] are not His children: they are spotted." Coverdale renders the whole passage thus: "The froward and overthwart generation have marred themselves to himward, and are not his children because of their deformity." This is the sense of the verse. Let it be observed that the word *spot*, which is repeated in our translation, occurs but once in the original, and the marginal reading is greatly to be preferred: "He hath corrupted to himself, that they are not his children, that is their blot."

8. *When the most High divided to the nations.* Verses 8 and 9, says Dr. Kennicott, give us express authority for believing that the earth was very early divided in consequence of a divine command, and probably by *lot* (see Acts xvii. 26); and as Africa is called the land of Ham (Ps. lxxviii. 51; cv. 23, 27; cvi. 22), probably that country fell to him and to his descendants, at the same time that Europe fell to Japheth, and Asia to Shem, with a particular reserve of Palestine to be the Lord's portion, for some one peculiar people. *He set the bounds of the people according to the number of the children of Israel.* The Septuagint is very curious, "He established the bounds of the nations according to the number of the angels of God." The meaning of the passage seems to be that, when God divided the earth among mankind, He reserved twelve lots, according to the number of the sons of Jacob, which He was now about to give to their descendants, according to His promise.

9. *The Lord's portion is his people.* What an astonishing saying! As holy souls take God for their portion, so God takes them for His portion. He represents himself as happy in His followers; and they are infinitely happy in, and satisfied with, God as their portion. This is what is implied in being a saint. He who is seeking for an earthly portion has little commerce with the Most High.

10. *He*—the Lord, *found him*—Jacob, in his descendants, *in a desert land*—the wilderness. *He led him about* forty years in this wilderness, Deut. viii. 2, or *yesobebenhu;* "he compassed him about," i.e., God defended them on all hands, and in all places. *He instructed him*—taught them that astonishing law through which we have now almost passed, giving them statutes and judgments which, for depth of wisdom, and correct political adaptation to times, places, and circumstances, are so wondrously constructed as essentially to secure the comfort, peace, and happiness of the individual, and the prosperity and permanency of the moral system. *He kept him as the apple of his eye.* Nothing can exceed the force and delicacy of this expression. As deeply concerned and as carefully attentive as man can be for the safety of his eyesight, so was God for the protection and welfare of this people. How amazing this condescension!

11. *As an eagle stirreth up her nest,* flutters over her brood to excite them to fly; or, as some think, disturbs her nest to oblige the young ones to leave it; so God by His plagues in Egypt obliged the Israelites, otherwise very reluctant, to leave a place which He appeared by His judgments to have devoted to destruction. *Fluttereth over her young. Yeracheph,* broodeth over them, communicating to them a portion of her own vital warmth. So did God, by the influences of His Spirit, enlighten, encourage, and strengthen their minds. It is the same word which is used in Gen. i. 2. *Spreadeth abroad her wings.* In order, not only to teach them how to fly, but to bear them when weary. For to this fact there seems an allusion, it having been generally believed that the eagle, through extraordinary affection for her young, takes them upon her back when they are weary of flying. The same figure is used in Exod. xix. 4.

12. *So the Lord alone did lead him.* By His power, and by His only, were they brought out of Egypt, and supported in the wilderness. *And there was no strange god.* They had help from no other quarter. The Egyptian idols were not able to save their own votaries; but God not only saved His people, but destroyed the Egyptians.

13. *He made him ride. Yarkibehu,* "he will cause him to ride." All the verbs here are in the future tense, because this is a prophecy of the prosperity they should possess in the Prom-

MATTHEW HENRY

by Israel; when they were in love with their slavery, and loth to leave it, God, by Moses, stirred them up to aspire after liberty. He carried them out of Egypt, led them into the wilderness, and now at length had led them through it.

III. The settling of them in a good land. This was done in part already, in the happy planting of the two tribes and a half, an earnest of what would speedily and certainly be done for the rest of the tribes, with great plenty of all good things. *Honey out of the rock, and oil out of the flinty rock.* Ainsworth makes the plenty of good things in Canaan to be a figure of the fruitfulness of Christ's kingdom, and the heavenly comforts of his word and Spirit: for the children of his kingdom he has butter and milk, the sincere milk of the word; and strong meat for strong men, with the wine that makes glad the heart.

Verses 15–18

We have here a description of the apostasy of Israel from God, which would shortly come to pass, and to which already they had a disposition. Here are two great instances of their wickedness.

I. Security and sensuality, pride and insolence, and the other common abuses of plenty and prosperity, *v.* 15. They *kicked*; they grew proud and insolent, and *lifted up the heel* even against God himself. They *kicked against the goad*, as an *untamed heifer*, or a *bullock unaccustomed to the yoke*, and in their rage persecuted the prophets, and flew in the face of providence itself.

II. Idolatry was the great instance of their apostasy, and which the former led them to, as it made them sick of their religion, self-willed, and fond of changes. Observe,

1. What sort of gods they chose and offered sacrifice to, when they forsook the God that made them, *v.* 16, 17. Those very services which they should have done to the true God they did, (1) To *strange gods,*

JAMIESON, FAUSSET, BROWN

of Palestine that they had seen at the time when Moses is represented as uttering these words. "The high places" and "the fields" are specially applicable to the tablelands of Gilead as are the allusions to the herds and flocks, the honey of the wild bees which hive in the crevices of the rocks, the oil from the olive as it grew singly or in small clumps on the tops of hills where scarcely anything else would grow, the finest wheat (Ps. 81:16; 147:14), and the prolific vintage.

15. But Jeshurun waxed fat, and kicked—This is a poetical name for Israel. The metaphor here used is derived from a pampered animal, which, instead of being tame and gentle, becomes mischievous and vicious, in consequence of good living and kind treatment. So did the Israelites conduct themselves by their various acts of rebellion, murmuring, and idolatrous apostasy.

17. They sacrificed unto devils—(See on Lev. 17:7).

ALEXANDER MACLAREN:

I. God is a Rock to them that trust Him.

We note the singular frequency of that designation in this song, in which it occurs six times. It is also found often in the Psalms. If Moses were the singer, we might see in this often-repeated metaphor a trace of influence of the scenery of the Sinaitic peninsula, which would be doubly striking to eyes accustomed to the alluvial plains of Egypt. What are the aspects of the divine nature set forth by this name?

A. Firm foundation: the solid eternity of the rock on which we can build.

Petra: faithfulness to promises, unchanging.

B. Refuge: "refuge from the storm"; "my rock and my fortress and my high tower."

C. Refreshment: rock from which water gushed out.

D. Repose: "shadow of a great rock"; "shadow from the heat."

Trace the image through Scripture, from this song till Christ's parable of the man who "built his house on a rock."—*Expositions of Holy Scripture*

ADAM CLARKE

ised Land. The Israelites were to *ride*—exult, *on the high places*, the mountains and hills of their land, in which they are promised the highest degrees of prosperity, as even the rocky part of the country should be rendered fertile by the peculiar benediction of God. *Suck honey out of the rock, and oil out of the flinty rock.* This promise states that even the most barren places in the country should yield an abundance of aromatic flowers, from which the bees should collect *honey* in abundance; and even the tops of the rocks afford sufficient support for olive trees, from the fruit of which they should extract oil in abundance; and all this should be occasioned by the peculiar blessing of God upon the land.

14. *Fat of kidneys of wheat.* Almost every person knows that the kidney is enveloped in a coat of the purest fat in the body of the animal, for which several anatomical reasons might be given. As the kidney itself is to the abundantly surrounding fat, so is the germ of the grain to the lobes. The expression here may be considered as a very strong and peculiarly happy figure to point out the finest wheat, containing the healthiest and most vigorous germ, growing in a very large and nutritive grain; and consequently the whole figure points out to us a species of wheat, equally excellent for both seed and bread. *Pure blood of the grape.* Red wine, or the pure juice of whatever color, expressed from the grapes, without any adulteration or mixture with water; *blood* here is synonymous with juice. This intimates that their vines should be of the best kind, and their wine in abundance, and of the most delicious flavor.

15. *Jeshurun.* The "upright." This appellative is here put for Israel, and as it comes from *yashar*, "he was right, straight," may be intended to show that the people who once not only promised fair, but were really upright, walking in the paths of righteousness, should, in the time signified by the prophet, not only revolt from God, but actually fight against Him; like a full-fed horse, who not only will not bear the harness, but breaks away from his master, and endeavors to kick him as he struggles to get loose. All this is spoken prophetically, and is intended as a warning, that the evil might not take place. For were the transgression unavoidable, it must be the effect of some necessitating cause, which would destroy the turpitude of the action, as it referred to Israel; for if evil were absolutely unavoidable, no blame could attach to the unfortunate agent, who could only consider himself the miserable instrument of a dire necessity. See a case in point, 1 Sam. xxiii. 11-12, where the prediction appears in the most absolute form, and yet the evil was prevented by the person receiving the prediction as a warning.

The Rock of his salvation. He ceased to depend on the fountain whence his salvation issued; and thinking highly of himself, he lightly esteemed his God; and having ceased to depend on Him, his fall became inevitable. The figure is admirably well supported through the whole verse. We see, first, a miserable, lean steed, taken under the care and into the keeping of a master who provides him with an abundance of provender. We see, secondly, this horse waxing fat under this keeping. We see him, thirdly, breaking away from his master, leaving his rich pasturage, and running to the wilderness, unwilling to bear the yoke or harness, or to make any returns for his master's care and attention. We see, fourthly, whence this conduct proceeds —from a want of consciousness that his strength depends upon his master's care and keeping; and a lack of consideration that leanness and wretchedness must be the consequence of his leaving his master's service, and running off from his master's pasturage. How easy to apply all these points to the case of the Israelites! and how illustrative of their former and latter state! And how powerfully do they apply to the case of many called Christians who, having increased in riches, forget that God from whose hand alone those mercies flowed!

17. *They sacrificed unto devils.* The original word *shedim* has been variously understood. The Syriac, Chaldee, Targums of Jerusalem and Jonathan, and the Samaritans retain the original word: the Vulgate, Septuagint, Arabic, Persic,

MATTHEW HENRY

that could not pretend to have done them any kindness. (2) To *new gods, that came newly up*. A new god! can there be a more monstrous absurdity? (3) They were such as were no gods at all, their names the invention of men's fancies, and their images the work of men's hands. Nay, (4) They were devils. So far from being *gods*, they really were *destroyers* (so the word signifies), such as aimed to do mischief.

2. What a great affront this was to Jehovah their God. (1) It was justly interpreted a forgetting of him (*v.* 18): *Of the Rock that begat thee thou art unmindful*. (2) It was justly resented as an inexcusable offence.

Verses 19–25

The method of this song follows the method of the predictions in the foregoing chapter.

I. He had delighted in them, but now he would reject them. Note, The nearer any are to God in profession the more noisome are they to him if they are defiled in a sinful way, Ps. cvi. 39, 40.

II. He had given them the tokens of his presence with them and his favour to them; but now he would withdraw and *hide his face from them, v.* 20. His *hiding his face* signifies his great displeasure, but here it denotes also the slowness of God's proceedings against them in a way of judgment. 1. They were froward. 2. They were faithless, and a people that could not be trusted.

III. He had done every thing to make them easy, but now the punishment here answers the sin, *v.* 21. 1. They had provoked God with despicable deities which were not gods at all. 2. God would therefore plague them with despicable enemies. The more base the people were that tyrannised over them the more barbarous they would be (none so insolent as a beggar on horseback).

IV. He had planted them in a good land, and replenished them with all good things; but now he would strip them of all their comforts, and bring them to ruin. The particular judgments here threatened are, 1. Famine. 2. Pestilence. 3. The insults of the inferior creatures: *the teeth of beasts and the poison of serpents, v.* 24. 4. War and the fatal consequences of it, *v.* 25.

Verses 26–38

After many terrible threatenings of deserved wrath and vengeance, we have here surprising intimations of mercy, undeserved mercy, which rejoices against judgment, and by which it appears that God has *no pleasure in the death of sinners*, but would rather they should *turn and live*.

I. In jealousy for his own honour, he will not *make a full end* of them, *v.* 26–28. Mercy prevails for the sparing of a remnant and the saving of that unworthy people from utter ruin: *I feared the wrath of the enemy*. It is an expression after the manner of men; it is certain that God fears no man's wrath, but he acted in this matter as if he had feared it. He needed not Moses to plead it with him, but reminded himself of it: *What will the Egyptians say?* How much soever we deserve to be disgraced, God will never *disgrace the throne of his glory*.

II. In concern for their welfare, he earnestly desires their conversion. God delights not to see sinners ruin themselves, but desires they will help themselves; and, if they will, he is ready to help them. It will contribute much to the return of sinners to God, seriously to consider the latter end, or the future state. It is here meant particularly of that which God by Moses had foretold concerning this people in the latter days: but it may be applied more generally.

JAMIESON, FAUSSET, BROWN

21. those which are not a people—i.e., not favored with such great and peculiar privileges as the Israelites (or, rather poor, despised heathens). The language points to the future calling of the Gentiles.

23. I will spend mine arrows upon them—War, famine, pestilence (Ps. 77:17) are called in Scripture the arrows of the Almighty.

29. Oh, . . . that they would consider their latter end—The terrible judgments, which, in the event of their continued and incorrigible disobedience, would impart so awful a character to the close of their national history.

ADAM CLARKE

Coptic, and Anglo-Saxon have devils or demons. The Septuagint has, "They sacrificed to demons"; the Vulgate copies the Septuagint. *New gods that came newly up. Mikkarob bau*, "which came up from their neighbours"; viz., the Moabites and Amorites, whose gods they received and worshipped on their way through the wilderness, and often afterwards.

18. *Of the Rock that begat thee. Tsur*, the "first cause," the Fountain of your being. See the note on v. 4.

19. *When the Lord saw it*. More literally, "And the Lord saw it, and through indignation He reprobated His sons and His daughters." That is, When the Lord shall see such conduct, He shall be justly incensed, and so reject and deliver up to captivity His sons and daughters.

20. *Children in whom is no faith. Lo emon bam*, "There is no steadfastness in them"; they can never be depended on. They are fickle, because they are faithless.

21. *They have moved me to jealousy*. This verse contains a very pointed promise of the calling of the Gentiles, in consequence of the rejection of the Jews, threatened in v. 19; and to this great event it is applied by Paul, Rom. x. 19.

22. *The lowest hell. Sheol tachtith*, the very deepest destruction; a total extermination, so that *the earth*, their land, and its *increase*, and all their property, should be seized; and the *foundations of the mountains*, their strongest fortresses, should be razed to the ground. All this was fulfilled in a most remarkable manner in the last destruction of Jerusalem by the Romans, so that of the fortifications of that city not one stone was left on another. See the notes on Matthew xxiv.

23. *I will spend mine arrows upon them*. The judgments of God in general are termed the "arrows of God," Job vi. 4; Ps. xxxviii. 2-3; xci. 5; see also Ezek. v. 16; Jer. i. 14; 2 Sam. xxii. 14-15. In this and the following verses, to the twenty-eighth inclusive, God threatens this people with every species of calamity that could possibly fall upon man. How strange it is that, having this law continually in their hands, they should not discern those threatened judgments, and cleave to the Lord that they might be averted!

24. *They shall be burnt with hunger*. Their land shall be cursed, and famine shall prevail. This is one of the arrows. *Burning heat*. No showers to cool the atmosphere; or rather boils, blains, and pestilential fevers; this was a second. *Bitter destruction*. The plague; this was a third. *Teeth of beasts . . . with the poison of serpents*. The beasts of the field should multiply upon and destroy them—this was a fourth; and poisonous serpents, infesting all their steps, and whose mortal bite should produce the utmost anguish, were to be a fifth arrow. Added to all these, the *sword* of their enemies—*terror* among themselves, v. 25, and captivity were to complete their ruin, and thus the arrows of God were to be spent upon them.

27. *Were it not that I feared the wrath of the enemy*. Houbigant and others contend that *wrath* here refers not to the *enemy*, but to God, and that the passage should be thus translated: "Indignation for the adversary deters me, lest their enemies should be alienated, and say, The strength of our hands, and not of the Lord's, hath done this." Had not God punished them in such a way as proved that His hand and not the hand of man had done it, the heathens would have boasted of their prowess, and Jehovah would have been blasphemed, as not being able to protect His worshippers or to punish their infidelities. Titus, when he took Jerusalem, was so struck with the strength of the place that he acknowledged that, if God had not delivered it into his hands, the Roman armies never could have taken it.

29. *That they would consider their latter end! Archaritham*, properly, "their latter times"—the glorious days of the Messiah, who, according to the flesh, should spring up among them. Should they carefully consider this subject, and receive the promised Saviour, they would consequently act as persons under infinite obligations to God; His strength would be their shield, and then—

30. *How should one chase a thousand?* If

MATTHEW HENRY

III. He calls to mind the great things he had done for them formerly, as a reason why he should not quite cast them off. This seems to be the meaning of (*v.* 30, 31), "How should one Israelite have been too hard for a thousand Canaanites, as they have been many a time, but that God, who is greater than all gods, fought for them!" And so it corresponds with, Isa. lxiii. 10, 11. When he was *turned to be their enemy*, as here, *and fought against them* for their sins, *then he remembered the days of old*, saying, *Where is he that brought them out of the sea?* God would soon have subdued their enemies (Ps. lxxxi. 14), but that the wickedness of Israel delivered them into their hands.

IV. He resolves upon the destruction of those at last that had been their persecutors and oppressors. God will in due time bring down the church's enemies.

1. In displeasure against their wickedness, which he takes notice of, and keeps an account of, *v.* 34, 35. Some understand it of the sin of Israel, especially their persecuting the prophets, which was laid up in store against them from the *blood of righteous Abel*, Matt. xxiii. 35. However, it teaches us that the wickedness of the wicked is all laid up in store with God.

2. He will do it in compassion to his own people, who, though they had greatly provoked him, yet stood in relation to him, and their misery appealed to his mercy (*v.* 36). This plainly points at the deliverances God wrought for Israel by the judges out of the hands of those to whom he had sold them for their sins (see Judges ii. 11–18), and how *his soul was grieved for the misery of Israel* (Judges x. 16), and this when they were reduced to the last extremity. God helped them when they could not help themselves.

3. He will do it in contempt and to the reproach of the idol-gods, *v.* 37, 38. *Where are their gods?* Two ways it may be understood:—(1) That God would do that for his people which the idols they had served could not do for them. Or, (2) That God would do that against his enemies which the idols they had served could not save them from. Sennacherib and Nebuchadnezzar boldly challenged the God of Israel to deliver his worshippers (Isa. xxxvii. 10; Dan. iii. 15), and he did deliver them, to the confusion of their enemies. But the God of Israel challenged Bel and Nebo to deliver their worshippers, to rise up and help them, and to be their protection (Isa. xlvii. 12, 13); but they were so far from helping them that they themselves, that is, their images, which was all that was of them, *went into captivity*, Isa. xlvi. 1, 2.

Verses 39–43

This conclusion of the song speaks three things:—

I. Glory to God, *v.* 39. The great God here demands the glory, 1. Of a self-existence: *I, even I, am he.* Thus Moses concludes with the name of God by which he was first made to know him (Exod. iii. 14), "*I am that I am.* I am he that I have been, that I will be, that I have promised to be, that I have threatened to be; all shall find me true to my word." The Targum of Uzzielides paraphrases it thus: *When the Word of the Lord shall reveal himself to redeem his people, he shall say to all people, See that I now am what I am, and have been, and I am what I will be,* which we know very well how to apply to him who said to John, *I am he who is, and was, and is to come,* Rev. i. 8. These words, *I, even, I, am he,* we meet with often in those chapters of Isaiah where God is encouraging his people to hope for their deliverance out of Babylon, Isa. xli. 4; xliii. 11, 13, 25; xlvi. 4. 2. Of a sole supremacy. "There *is no god with me.* None to help with me, none to cope with me." See Isa. xliii. 10, 11. 3. Of an absolute sovereignty, a universal agency: *I kill, and I make alive.* 4. Of an irresistible power.

II. Terror to his enemies, *v.* 40–42. Terror indeed to those that hate him, as all those do that serve other gods, that persist in wilful disobedience to the divine law, and that malign and persecute his faithful servants. In order to alarm such in time to repent. 1. The divine sentence is ratified with an oath (*v.* 40): He *lifts up his hand to heaven*, the habitation of his holiness; this was an ancient and very significant sign used in swearing, Gen. xiv. 22. The sin of sinners shall be their ruin if they go on in it. 2. Preparation is made for the execution: The *glittering sword is whet.* See Ps. vii. 12. 3. The execution itself will be very terrible.

III. Comfort to his own people (*v.* 43): *Rejoice, O you nations, with his people.* He concludes the song with words of joy; for in God's Israel there is a remnant whose end will be peace. God's people will rejoice at last, will rejoice everlastingly. Three things are here mentioned as matter of joy:—1. The enlarging of the church's bounds. The apostle applies the first words of this verse to the conversion of the

JAMIESON, FAUSSET, BROWN

32. vine of Sodom . . . grapes of gall—This fruit, which the Arabs call "Lot's Sea Orange," is of a bright yellow color and grows in clusters of three or four. When mellow, it is tempting in appearance, but on being struck, explodes like a puff-ball, consisting of skin and fiber only.

JOSEPH PARKER:

"For their vine is of the vine of Sodom, and of the fields of Gomorrah: their grapes are grapes of gall, their clusters are bitter, their wine is the poison of dragons, and the cruel venom of asps" (vv. 32, 33).

This is perversion; this is the embittering of God's sweetness; this is what is meant by the light that is in a man becoming darkness. Israel has spoiled the vine, Israel has turned wine of heaven into poison, Israel has made productive fields barren as the ashes of Gomorrah. This always lies within our power. We can dwarf the Church, we can prostitute the altar, we can make the sweetest things the bitterest. This corrupting, pestilential power seems to belong to the man who was made in the image and likeness of God. We can so treat the Church as to hate it; we can so worship ourselves, our vanity, our ability, our love of so-called progress, that we can only go back to the altar to spit upon it, and to the ministers of God to call them liars. This possibility is quite within the compass of our faculty; the heart can perform this astounding and iniquitous miracle. Israel performed it in the wilderness, and men are performing it with awful repetition today.

—*The People's Bible*

ADAM CLARKE

therefore they had not forgotten their Rock, God, their Author and Defense, it could not possibly have come to pass that a thousand of them should flee before *one* of their enemies.

31. *For their rock.* The gods and pretended protectors of the Romans. *Is not as our Rock.* Have neither power nor influence like our God. *Our enemies themselves being judges.* For they often acknowledged the irresistible power of that God who fought for Israel. See Exod. xiv. 25; Num. xxiii. 8-12, 19-21; 1 Sam. iv. 8.

32. *For their vine is of the vine of Sodom.* The Jews are as wicked and rebellious as the Sodomites; for by the *vine* the inhabitants of the land are signified; see Isa. v. 2, 7. *Their grapes.* Their actions, are *gall* and wormwood—producing nothing but mischief and misery to themselves and others. *Their clusters are bitter.* Their united exertions, as well as their individual acts, are sin, and only sin, continually. That by *vine* is meant the people, and by *grapes* their moral conduct, is evident from Isa. v. 1-7. It is very likely that the grapes produced about the Lake Asphaltitis, where Sodom and Gomorrah formerly stood, were not only of an acrid, disagreeable taste, but of a deleterious quality; and to this, it is probable, Moses here alludes.

33. *Their wine.* Their system of doctrines and teaching, *is the poison of dragons,* fatal and destructive to all them who follow it.

34. *Sealed up among my treasures?* Deeds or engagements by which persons were bound at a specified time to fulfil certain conditions were *sealed* and *laid up* in places of safety; so here God's justice is pledged to avenge the quarrel of His broken covenant on the disobedient Jews, but the time and manner were sealed in His treasures, and known only to himself. Hence it is said,

35. *Their foot shall slide in due time.* But Calmet thinks that this verse is spoken against the Canaanites, the enemies of the Jewish people.

36. *The Lord shall judge his people.* He has an absolute right over them as their Creator, and authority to punish them for their rebellions as their Sovereign; yet He will *repent himself*—He will change His manner of conduct towards them, *when he seeth that their power is gone*—when they are entirely subjugated by their adversaries, so that their political power is entirely destroyed; *and there is none shut up, or left*—not one strong place untaken, and not one family left, all being carried into captivity, or scattered into strange lands. Or, He will do justice to His people, and avenge them of their adversaries; see v. 35.

37. *He shall say.* He shall begin to expostulate with them, to awaken them to a due sense of their ingratitude and rebellion. This may refer to the preaching of the gospel to them in the latter days.

39. *See now that I . . . am he.* Be convinced that God alone can save, and God alone can destroy, and that your idols can neither hurt nor help you. *I kill, and I make alive.* My mercy is as great as my justice, for I am as ready to save the penitent as I was to punish the rebellious.

40. *For I lift up my hand to heaven.* See concerning oaths and appeals to God in the note on chap. vi. 13.

42. *From the beginning of revenges.* The word *paroth,* rendered *revenges,* a sense in which it never appears to be taken, has rendered this place very perplexed and obscure. Probably *merosh paroth* may be properly translated, "from the naked head"—The enemy shall have nothing to shield him from My vengeance; the crown of dignity shall fall off, and even the helmet be no protection against the sword and arrows of the Lord.

43. *Rejoice, O ye nations.* You Gentiles, for the casting off of the Jews shall be the means of your ingathering with *his people,* for they shall not be utterly cast off. (See Rom. xv. 9, for in this way the apostle applied it.) But how shall the Gentiles be called, and the Jews have their iniquity purged? *He will be merciful unto his land, and to his people; vechipper,* "He shall cause an atonement" to be made for His land and people; i.e., Jesus Christ, the long-promised Messiah, shall be crucified for Jews

MATTHEW HENRY

Gentiles. Rom. xv. 10, *Rejoice you Gentiles with his people.* 2. The avenging of the church's controversies upon her adversaries. 3. The mercy God has in store for his church, and for all that belong to it: He will be *merciful to his land, and to his people,* that is, to all everywhere that fear and serve him.

Verses 44–52

Here is, I. The solemn delivery of this song to the children of Israel, *v.* 44, 45. Moses spoke it to as many as could hear him, while Joshua, in another assembly at the same time, delivered it to as many as his voice would reach. Though they changed their commander, there was no change in the divine command; Joshua, as well as Moses, would be a witness against them if ever they forsook God.

II. An earnest charge to them to mind these and all the rest of the good words that Moses had said to them.

1. The duties he charges upon them are, (1) Carefully to attend to these themselves: "Set your hearts both to the laws, and to the promises and threatenings, the blessings and curses, and now at last to this song." (2) Faithfully to transmit these things to those that should come after them. Those that are good themselves cannot but desire that their children may be so likewise.

2. The arguments he uses to persuade them to make religion their business and to persevere in it are, (1) The vast importance of the things themselves which he had charged upon them (*v.* 47): "*It is not a vain thing, because it is your life.* It is not an indifferent thing, but of absolute necessity. (2) The vast advantage it would be of to them: *Through this thing you shall prolong your days* in Canaan, which is a typical promise of that eternal life which Christ has assured us those shall enter into that keep the commandments of God, Matt. xix. 17.

III. Orders given to Moses concerning his death. Now that this renowned witness for God had finished his testimony, he must go up to Mount Nebo and die. Orders were given to Moses that self-same day, *v.* 48. Now that he had done his work, why should he desire to live a day longer? He had indeed formerly prayed that he might go over Jordan, but now he is entirely satisfied, and, as God had bidden him, *saith no more of that matter.* 1. God here reminds him of the sin he had been guilty of, for which he was excluded Canaan (*v.* 51). 2. He reminds him of the death of his brother Aaron (*v.* 50), to make his own the more familiar and the less formidable. 3. He sends him up to a high hill, thence to take a view of the land of Canaan and then die, *v.* 49, 50. The remembrance of his sin might make death terrible, but the sight God gave him of Canaan took off the terror of it, as it was a token of God's being reconciled to him, and a plain indication to him that though his sin shut him out of the earthly Canaan, yet it should not deprive him of that better country which in this world can only be seen, and that with an eye of faith.

JAMIESON, FAUSSET, BROWN

44-47. Moses . . . spake all the words of this song in the ears . . .—It has been beautifully styled "the Song of the Dying Swan" [LOWTH]. It was designed to be a national anthem, which it should be the duty and care of magistrates to make well known by frequent repetition, to animate the people to right sentiments towards a steadfast adherence to His service.

48-51. Get thee up . . . and die . . . Because ye trespassed . . . at Meribah—(See on Num. 20:12).

thou shalt see the land, but thou shalt not go thither—(Num. 27:12). Notwithstanding so severe a disappointment, not a murmur of complaint escapes his lips. He is not only resigned but acquiescing; and in the near prospect of his death, he pours forth the feelings of his devout heart in sublime strains and eloquent blessings.

ADAM CLARKE

and Gentiles, and the way to the holiest be made plain by His blood. The people have long been making atonements for themselves, but to none effect, for their atonements were but signs. and not the thing signified, for the body is Christ; now the Lord himself makes an atonement. for the Lamb of God alone taketh away the sin of the world. This is a very proper and encouraging conclusion to the awfully important matter of this poem. Israel shall be long scattered, peeled, and punished, but they shall have mercy in the latter times; they also shall rejoice with the Gentiles, in the common salvation purchased by the blood of the Saviour of all mankind.

44. *And Moses came.* Probably from the Tabernacle, where God had given him this prophetic ode, and he rehearsed it in the ears of the people.

46. *Set your hearts unto all the words.* Another proof that all these awful denunciations of divine wrath, though delivered in an absolute form, were only declaratory of what God would do if they rebelled against Him.

47. *Through this thing ye shall prolong your days.* Instead of being cut off, as God here threatens, you shall be preserved and rendered prosperous in the land which, when they passed over Jordan, they should possess.

49. *Get thee up into this mountain Abarim.* The mount of the "passages," i.e., of the Israelites when they entered into the Promised Land. See the notes on Num. xxvii. 12.

50. *And die in the mount . . . as Aaron.* Some have supposed that Moses was translated; but if so, then Aaron was translated, for what is said of the death of the one is said of the death of the other.

51. *Ye trespassed against me . . . at the waters of Meribah.* See the note on Num. xx. 8.

52. *Thou shalt see the land before thee.* See Num. xxvii. 12, etc. How glorious to depart out of this life with God in his heart and heaven in his eye! his work, his great, unparalleled usefulness, ending only with his life. The serious reader will surely join in the following pious ejaculation of Charles Wesley, one of the best Christian poets:

O that without a lingering groan
I may the welcome word receive;
My body with my charge lay down,
And cease at once to work and live!

MATTHEW HENRY — CHAPTER 33

Verses 1–5

The first verse is the title of the chapter: it is a blessing. In the foregoing chapter he had thundered out the terrors of the Lord against Israel for their sin. Now that he might not seem to part in anger, he here subjoins a blessing. Thus Christ's last work on earth was to bless his disciples (Luke xxiv. 50), like Moses here, in token of parting as friends. Moses blessed them, 1. As a prophet—a *man of God.* 2. As a parent to Israel; for so good princes are to their subjects. Jacob upon his death-bed blessed his sons (Gen. xlix. 1), in conformity to whose example Moses here blesses the tribes that were descended from them. He desired their happiness, though he must die and not share in it.

He begins his blessing with a lofty description of the glorious appearances of God to them in giving them the law, and the great advantage they had by it.

I. There was a visible and illustrious discovery of the divine majesty, enough to convince and for ever silence atheists and infidels, to awaken and affect those that were most stupid and careless, and to put to shame all secret inclinations to other gods, *v.* 2. His retinue was glorious; he came with his holy myriads, as Enoch had long since foretold he should come in the last day to judge the world, Jude 14. Hence the law is said to *be given by the disposition of angels,* Acts vii. 53; Heb. ii. 2.

II. He gave them his law, which is, 1. Called *a fiery law,* because it was given them *out of the midst of the fire* (Deut. iv. 33), and because it works like

JAMIESON, FAUSSET, BROWN — CHAPTER 33

Vss. 1-28. THE MAJESTY OF GOD. **1. Moses the man of God**—This was a common designation of a prophet (I Sam. 2:27; 9:6), and it is here applied to Moses, when, like Jacob, he was about to deliver ministerially before his death, a prophetic benediction to Israel.

2-4. The Lord came—Under a beautiful metaphor, borrowed from the dawn and progressive splendor of the sun, the Majesty of God is sublimely described as a divine light which appeared in Sinai and scattered its beams on all the adjoining region in directing Israel's march to Canaan. In these descriptions of a *theophania,* God is represented as coming from the south, and the allusion is in general to the thunderings and lightnings of Sinai; but other mountains in the same direction are mentioned with it. The location of Seir was on the east of the Ghor; mount Paran was either the chain on the west of the Ghor, or rather the mountains on the southern border of the desert towards the peninsula [ROBINSON]. (Cf. Judg. 5:4, 5; Ps. 68:7, 8; Hab. 3:3.) **ten thousands of saints**—rendered by some, "with the ten thousand of

ADAM CLARKE — CHAPTER 33

1. *And this is the blessing, wherewith Moses . . . blessed.* The general nature of this solemn introduction, says Kennicott, is to show the foundation which Moses had for blessing his brethren, viz., because God had frequently manifested His glory in their behalf; and the several parts of this introduction are disposed in the following order: (1) The manifestation of the divine glory on Sinai, as it was prior in time and more magnificent in splendor, is mentioned first. (2) That God manifested His glory at Seir is evident from Judg. v. 4: "Lord. when thou wentest out of Seir, when thou marchedst out of the fields of Edom. the earth trembled. and the heavens dropped." (3) The next place is Paran, where the "glory of the Lord appeared . . . before all the children of Israel," Num. xiv. 10.

2. Instead of *he came with ten thousands of saints,* by which our translators have rendered *meribeboth kodesh,* Kennicott reads Meribah-Kadesh, the name of a place; for we find that, towards the end of forty years, the Israelites came to Kadesh, Num. xx. 1, which was also called Meribah, on account of their contentious opposition to the determinations of God in their favor, v. 13; and there the glory of the Lord again appeared, as we are informed in v. 6. These four places, *Sinai, Seir, Paran,* and *Meribah-Kadesh,* mentioned by Moses in the text, are the identical places where God manifested

MATTHEW HENRY

fire; if it be received, it is melting, warming, purifying, and burns up the dross of corruption; if it be rejected, it hardens, sears, torments, and destroys. The Spirit descended in cloven tongues as of fire; for the gospel also is a fiery law. 2. It is said to *go from his right hand*, to denote the power and energy of the law and the divine strength that goes along with it, that it may not return void. It came as a gift to them, and a precious gift it was, a righthand blessing. 3. It was an instance of the special kindness he had for them: *Yea, he loved the people* (*v.* 3), and therefore, though it was a fiery law, yet it is said to *go for them* (*v.* 2), that, is, in favour to them. Note, The law of God written in the heart is a certain evidence of the love of God shed abroad there: we must reckon God's law one of the gifts of his grace. *All his saints are in his hand.* They were in his hand to be covered and protected, used and disposed of, as the seven stars were in the hand of Christ, Rev. i. 16.

III. He disposed them to receive the law which he gave them: *They sat down at thy feet*, as scholars at the feet of their master, in token of reverence, in attendance and humble submission to what is taught; so Israel sat at the foot of Mount Sinai, and promised to hear and do whatever God should say. Every one then stood ready to receive God's words, and did so again when the law was publicly read to them, as Josh. viii. 34.

1. They are taught to speak with great respect of the law, and to call it *the inheritance of the congregation of Jacob*.

2. They are taught to speak with great respect of Moses; and they were the more obliged to keep up his name because he had not provided for the keeping of it up in his family; his posterity were never called the *sons of Moses*, as the priests were the *sons of Aaron*.

Verses 6–7

Here is, I. The blessing of Reuben. Though Reuben had lost the honour of his birthright, yet Moses begins with him; for we should not insult over those that are disgraced, nor desire to perpetuate marks of infamy upon any, *v.* 6. Moses desires and foretells, 1. The preserving of this tribe. Though a frontier tribe on the other side Jordan, yet, "*Let it live*, and not be either ruined by its neighbours or lost among them." And perhaps he refers to those chosen men of that tribe who, having had their lot assigned them already, left their families in it, and were now ready to *go over armed before their brethren*, Num. xxxii. 27. 2. The increase of this tribe: *Let not his men be few*; or, *Let his men be a number. Let Reuben live and not die, though his men be few*; so bishop Patrick thinks it may be rendered. All the Chaldee paraphrasts refer this to the other world: *Let Reuben live in life eternal, and not die the second death*, so Onkelos. *Let Reuben live in this world, and not die that death which the wicked die in the world to come*, so Jonathan and the Jerusalem Targum.

II. The blessing of Judah, which is put before Levi because our *Lord sprang out of Judah*. The blessing (*v.* 7) may refer either, 1. To the whole tribe in general. Moses prays for, and prophesies, the great prosperity of that tribe. It is taken for granted that the tribe of Judah would be both a praying tribe and an active tribe. Or, 2. It may refer in particular to David, as a type of Christ, that God *would hear his prayers*, as that he would give him victory over his enemies, and success in his great undertakings. And that prayer that God would *bring him to his people* seems to refer to Jacob's prophecy concerning Shiloh, That *to him should the gathering of the people be*, Gen. xlix. 10. The tribe of Simeon is omitted in the blessing, because Jacob had left it under a brand, and it had never done any thing, as Levi had done, to retrieve its honour. It was lessened in the wilderness more than any other of the tribes; and Zimri, who was so notoriously guilty in the matter of Peor was of that tribe. Or, because the lot of Simeon was an appendage to that of Judah, that tribe is included in the blessing of Judah.

Verses 8–11

In blessing the tribe of Levi, Moses expresses himself more at large, not so much because it was his own tribe (for he takes no notice of his relation to it) as because it was God's tribe. The blessing of Levi has reference,

I. To the high priest, here called God's *holy one* (*v.* 8), because his office was holy, in token of which, *Holiness to the Lord* was written upon his forehead. 1. He seems to acknowledge that God might justly have displaced Aaron and his seed, for his sin at Meribah, Num. xx. 12. So many understand it. It seems rather probable to me that, on the contrary,

JAMIESON, FAUSSET, BROWN

Kadesh," or perhaps better still, "from Meribah" [EWALD]. **a fiery law**—so called both because of the thunder and lightning which accompanied its promulgation (Exod. 19:16-18; ch. 4:11), and the fierce, unrelenting curse denounced against the violation of its precepts (II Cor. 3:7-9). Notwithstanding those awe-inspiring symbols of Majesty that were displayed on Sinai, the law was really given in kindness and love (vs. 3), as a means of promoting both the temporal and eternal welfare of the people. And it was "the inheritance of the congregation of Jacob," not only from the hereditary obligation under which that people were laid to observe it, but from its being the grand distinction, the peculiar privilege of the nation.

6. Let Reuben live, and not die—Although deprived of the honor and privileges of primogeniture, he was still to hold rank as one of the tribes of Israel. He was more numerous than several other tribes (Num. 1:21; 2:11). Yet gradually he sank into a mere nomadic tribe, which had enough to do merely "to live and not die." Many eminent biblical scholars, resting on the most ancient and approved manuscripts of the Septuagint, consider the latter clause as referring to Simeon; "and Simean, let his men be few," a reading of the text which is in harmony with other statements of Scripture respecting this tribe (Num. 25: 6-14; 1:23; 26:14; Josh. 19:1).

7. this is the blessing of Judah—Its general purport points to the great power and independence of Judah, as well as its taking the lead in all military expeditions.

ADAM CLARKE

His glory in a fiery appearance, the more illustriously to proclaim His special providence over and care of Israel.

3. *Yea, he loved the people.* This is the inference which Moses makes from those glorious appearances, that God truly loved the people; and that all His saints, *kedoshaiv*, the people whom He had "consecrated" to himself, were under His especial benediction; and that in order to make them a holy nation, God had displayed His glory on Mount Sinai, where they had fallen prostrate at His feet with the humblest adoration, sincerely promising the most affectionate obedience; and that God had there commanded them a *law* which was to be the possession and inheritance of the children of Jacob, v. 4. And to crown the whole, He had not only blessed them as their Lawgiver, but had also vouchsafed to be their King, v. 5.

6. *Let Reuben live, and not die.* Though his life and his blessings have been forfeited by his transgression with his father's concubine, Gen. xlix. 3-4, and in his rebellion with Korah, Num. xvi. 1, etc., let him not become extinct as a tribe in Israel. "It is very usual," says Mr. Ainsworth, "in the Scripture, to set down things of importance and earnestness, by affirmation of the one part, and denial of the other; Isa. xxxviii. 1: 'Thou shalt die, and not live'; Num. iv. 19: 'That they may live, and not die'; Ps. cxviii. 17: 'I shall not die, but live'; Gen. xliii. 8: 'That we may live, and not die.' "

And let not his men be few. It is possible that this clause belongs to Simeon. In the Alexandrian copy of the Septuagint the clause stands thus: "Let Simeon be very numerous," but none of the other versions insert the word. As the negative particle is not in the Hebrew, but is supplied in our translation, and the word Simeon is found in one of the most ancient and most authentic copies of the Septuagint version; and as Simeon is nowhere else mentioned here, if not implied in this place, probably the clause anciently stood: "Let Reuben live, and not die; but let the men of Simeon be few." That this tribe was small when compared with the rest, and with what it once was, is evident enough from the first census, taken after they came out of Egypt, and that in the plains of Moab nearly forty years after. In the first, Simeon was 59,300; in the last, 22,200, a decrease of 37,100 men!

7. *And this is the blessing of Judah.* Though the word *blessing* is not in the text, yet it may be implied from v. 1; but probably the words, "he spake," are those which should be supplied: "And this he spake of Judah, Lord, hear the voice of Judah." *Let his hands be sufficient for him*—let him have a sufficiency of warriors always to support the tribe, and vindicate its rights; and let his enemies never be able to prevail against him! Three things are expressed here: (1) That the tribe of Judah, conscious of its weakness, shall depend on the Most High, and make prayer and supplication to Him; (2) That God will hear such prayer; and, (3) That his hands shall be increased, and that he shall prevail over his enemies. This blessing has a striking affinity with that which this tribe received from Jacob, Gen. xlix. 9; and both may refer to our blessed Lord, who sprang from this tribe, as is noticed on the above passage, who has conquered our deadly foes by His death, and whose praying posterity ever prevail through His might.

8. *Of Levi he said.* Concerning the *Urim* and *Thummim* see Exod. xxviii. 30. *Thy holy one.* Aaron primarily, who was anointed the high priest of God, and whose office was the most holy that man could be invested with. Therefore Aaron was called God's *holy one*, and the more especially so as he was the type of the most holy and blessed Jesus, from whom the *Urim*—all light and wisdom, and *Thummim*—all excellence, completion, and perfection, are derived. *Whom thou didst prove.* God contended with Aaron as well as with Moses at the waters of Meribah, and excluded him from the Promised Land because he did not sanctify the Lord before the people. From the words of Paul, 1 Cor. x. 8-12, it is evident that these words, at least in a secondary sense, belong to Christ. He is the Holy One who was tempted by them at Massah, who suffered their manners in the wilderness,

MATTHEW HENRY

he pleads with God the zeal and faithfulness of Aaron, and his boldness in stemming the tide of the people's murmurings at the other Meribah (Exod. xvii. 7). All the Chaldee paraphrasts agree that it was a trial in which he was *found perfect and faithful*. 2. He prays that the office of the high priest might ever remain: *Let thy thummim and thy urim be with him.* It was given him for some eminent piece of service, as appears, Mal. ii. 5. "Lord, let it never be taken from him." Notwithstanding this blessing, the urim and thummim were lost in the captivity, and never restored under the second temple. *Thummim* signifies *integrity*, and *Urim illumination*: Let these be with thy holy one, that is, "Lord, let the high priest ever be both an upright man and an understanding man." A good prayer to be put up for the ministers of the gospel, that they may have clear heads and honest hearts; light and sincerity make a complete minister.

II. To the inferior priests and Levites, *v.* 9–11. 1. He commends the zeal of this tribe for God when they sided with Moses (and so with God) against the worshippers of the golden calf (Exod. xxxii. 26, &c.). And those who not only keep themselves pure from the common iniquities of the times and places in which they live, but, as they are capable, bear testimony against them, and *stand up for God against the evil-doers*, shall have special marks of honour put upon them. Perhaps Moses may have an eye to the sons of Korah, who refused to join with their father in his gainsaying, Num. xxvi. 11. Also to Phinehas, who *executed judgment*, and *stayed the plague*.

2. He confirms the commission granted to this tribe to minister in holy things, which was the recompense of their zeal and fidelity, *v.* 10. (1) They were to deal for God with the people: "*They shall teach Jacob thy judgments and Israel thy laws*, both as preachers in thy religious assemblies, reading and expounding the law (Neh. viii. 7, 8), and as judges, determining doubtful and difficult cases that were brought before them," 2 Chron. xvii. 8, 9. (2) They were to deal for the people with God, in burning incense to the praise and glory of God, and offering sacrifices to make atonement for sin and to obtain the divine favour. This was the work of the priests, but the Levites attended and assisted in it.

3. He prays for them, *v.* 11. (1) That God would prosper them in their estates. *Bless, Lord, his substance. Bless, Lord, his virtue*; so some read it. "Lord, increase thy graces in them, and make them more and more fit for their work." (2) That he would accept them in their services: "*Accept the work of his hands*, both for himself and for the people for whom he ministers." (3) That he would take his part against all his enemies.

Verses 12–17

Here is, I. The blessing of Benjamin, *v.* 12. Benjamin is put next to Levi, because the temple, where the priests' work lay, was just upon the edge of the lot of this tribe; and it is put before Joseph because of the dignity of Jerusalem (part of which was in this tribe) above Samaria, which was in the tribe of Ephraim, and because Benjamin adhered to the house of David, and to the temple of the Lord, when the rest of the tribes deserted both with Jeroboam. 1. Benjamin is here called the *beloved of the lord*, as the father of this tribe was Jacob's beloved son, the *son of his right hand*. Saul the first king, and Paul the great apostle, were both of this tribe. 2. He is here assured of the divine protection: he shall *dwell safely*. 3. It is here intimated that the temple in which God would dwell should be built in the borders of this tribe. Jerusalem the holy city was in the lot of this tribe (Josh. xviii. 28); and though Zion, the city of David, is supposed to belong to Judah, yet Mount Moriah, on which the temple was built, was in Benjamin's lot. God is *therefore* said to dwell *between his shoulders*, because the temple stood on that mount, as the head of a man upon his shoulders.

II. The blessing of Joseph, including both Manasseh and Ephraim. In Jacob's blessing (Gen. xlix.) that of Joseph is the largest, and so it is here; and thence Moses here borrows the title he gives to Joseph (*v.* 16), that he was *separated from his brethren*. His brethren separated him from them by making him a slave, but God distinguished him from them by making him a prince.

1. Great plenty, *v.* 13–16. In general: *Blessed of the Lord be his land.* Those were very fruitful countries that fell into the lot of Ephraim and Manasseh, yet Moses prays they might be watered with the blessing of God.

(1) He enumerates many particulars which he prays may contribute to the wealth and abundance of those two tribes. He prays, [1] For seasonable rains and dews, *the precious things of heaven*; and so precious

JAMIESON, FAUSSET, BROWN

8-10. of Levi he said—The burden of this blessing is the appointment of the Levites to the dignified and sacred office of the priesthood (Lev. 10:11; ch. 22:8; 17:8-11), a reward for their zeal in supporting the cause of God, and their unsparing severity in chastising even their nearest and dearest relatives who had participated in the idolatry of the molten calf (Exod. 32:25-28; cf. Mal. 2:4-6).

12. of Benjamin he said—A distinguishing favor was conferred on this tribe in having its portion assigned near the temple of God.

between his shoulders—i.e., on his sides or borders. Mount Zion, on which stood the city of Jerusalem, belonged to Judah; but Mount Moriah, the site of the sacred edifice, lay in the confines of Benjamin.

13-17. of Joseph he said—The territory of this tribe, diversified by hill and dale, wood and water, would be rich in all the productions—olives, grapes, figs, etc., which are reared in a mountainous region, as well as in the grain and herbs that grow in the level fields. "The firstling of the bullock and the horns of the unicorn" (rhinceros), indicate glory and strength, and it is supposed that under these emblems were shadowed

ADAM CLARKE

who slew 23,000 of the most incorrigible transgressors, and who brought them into the Promised Land by His deputy, Joshua, whose name and that of Jesus have the same signification.

9. *Who said unto his father.* There are several difficulties in this and the following verses. Some think they are spoken of the tribe of Levi; others, of all the tribes; others, of the Messiah; but several of the interpretations founded on these suppositions are too recondite, and should not be resorted to till a plain literal sense is made out. I suppose the whole to be primarily spoken of Aaron and the tribe of Levi. Let us examine the words in this way, *Who said unto his father.* The law had strictly enjoined that if the father, mother, brother, or child of the high priest should die, he must not mourn for them, but act as if they were not his kindred; see Lev. xxi. 11-12. Neither must Aaron mourn for his sons Nadab and Abihu, though not only their death, but the circumstances of it, were the most afflicting that could possibly affect a parent's heart. Besides, the high priest was forbidden, on pain of death, to go out from the door of the Tabernacle, Lev. x. 2-7, for God would have them more to regard their function and duty in His service than any natural affection whatever. And herein Christ was figured, who, when He was told that His mother and brethren stood without, and wished to speak with Him, said: "Who is my mother? and who are my brethren? . . . whosoever shall do the will of my Father which is in heaven, the same is my brother, and sister, and mother," Matt. xii. 46-50. It is likely also that Moses may refer here to the fact of the Levites, according to the command of Moses, killing every man his brother, friend, neighbor, and even son, who had sinned in worshipping the golden calf, Exod. xxxii. 26; and in this way the Chaldee paraphrast understands the words.

10. *They shall teach Jacob.* This was the office of the Levites, to teach, by their significant service and typical ceremonies, the way of righteousness and truth to the children of Israel. And of their faithfulness in this respect God bears testimony by the prophet, "My covenant was with him of life and peace," Mal. ii. 5; and, "The law of truth was in his mouth, and iniquity was not found in his lips: he walked with me in peace and equity, and did turn many away from iniquity," v. 6. These words are a sufficient comment on the words of the text.

11. *Bless, Lord, his substance.* The blessing of God to the tribe of Levi was peculiarly necessary, because they had no inheritance among the children of Israel, and lived more immediately than others upon the providence of God. Yet, as they lived by the offerings of the people and the tithes, the increase of their substance necessarily implied the increase of the people at large: the more fruitful the land was, the more abundant would the tithes of the Levites be: and thus in the increased fertility of the land the substance of Levi would be blessed.

12. *Of Benjamin . . . The beloved of the Lord.* Alluding to his being particularly beloved of his father, Jacob, Gen. xlix. 27. *Shall dwell in safety by him.* That is, by the Lord, whose Temple, which is considered as His dwelling place, was in the tribe of Benjamin, for a part of Jerusalem belonged to this tribe. *Shall cover him all the day.* Be his continual Protector; *and he shall dwell between his shoulders*—within his coasts, or in his chief city, viz., Jerusalem, where the temple of God was built, on his mountains Zion and Moriah, here poetically termed his shoulders.

13. *Blessed . . . be his land.* The whole of this passage certainly relates to the peculiar fertility of the soil in the portion that fell to this tribe, which, the Jews say, yielded a greater abundance of all good things than any other part of the Promised Land. *The precious things of heaven.* The peculiar mildness and salubrity of its atmosphere. *For the dew.* A plentiful supply of which was a great blessing in the dry soil of a hot climate. *The deep that coucheth beneath.* Probably referring to the plentiful supply of water which should be found in digging wells; hence the Septuagint has "fountains of the deeps." Some suppose there has been a slight change made in the word *mittal, for the dew*, which was probably at first *meal*, "from above," and then the passage would read thus:

MATTHEW HENRY

they are, though but pure water, that without them the fruits of the earth would all fail and be cut off. [2] For plentiful springs, which help to make the earth fruitful, called here *the deep that coucheth beneath.* [3] For the benign influences of the heavenly bodies (*v.* 14), *for the precious fruits* put forth by the quickening heart of the sun, and the cooling moisture of the moon. [4] For the fruitfulness even of their hills and mountains, which in other countries used to be barren (*v.* 15). [5] For the productions of the lower grounds (*v.* 16): *For the precious things of the earth.* Though the earth itself seems a useless worthless lump of matter, yet there are precious things produced out of it, for the support and comfort of human life. Some make these precious things here prayed for to be figures of *spiritual blessings in heavenly things by Christ*, the gifts, graces, and comforts of the Spirit.

(2) He crowns all with the goodwill, or favourable acceptance, of him that *dwelt in the bush* (*v.* 16), that is, of God, that God who appeared to Moses in the bush that burned and was not consumed (Exod. iii. 2), to give him his commission for the bringing of Israel out of Egypt. Though God's glory appeared there but for a while, yet it is said to dwell there: *the goodwill of the shechinah in the bush*; so it might be read, for *shechinah* signifies *that which dwelleth.* Many a time God had appeared to Moses, but now that he is just dying he seems to have the most pleasing remembrance of that which was the first time, when his acquaintance with the visions of the Almighty first began: that was a time of love never to be forgotten. So that, when he prays for the goodwill of him that *dwelt in the bush*, he has an eye to the covenant then and there renewed, on which all our hopes of God's favour must be bottomed.

2. Great power Joseph is here blessed with, *v.* 17. Here are three instances of his power foretold:—(1) His authority among his brethren: *His glory is like the firstling of his bullock*, or young bull, which is a stately creature, and therefore was formerly used as an emblem of royal majesty. (2) His force against his enemies and victory over them: *His horns are like the horn of a unicorn*, that is, "The forces he shall bring into the field shall be very strong and formidable, and *with them he shall push the people.*" (3) The numbers of his people, in which Ephraim, though the younger house, exceeded, Jacob having, in the foresight of the same thing, crossed hands, Gen. xlviii. 18. *They are the ten thousands of Ephraim, and the thousands of Manasseh.*

Verses 18–21

Here we have, I. The blessings of Zebulun and Issachar put together, for they were both the sons of Jacob by Leah, and by their lot in Canaan they were neighbours; it is foretold,

1. That they should both have a comfortable settlement and employment, *v.* 18. Zebulun must rejoice, for he shall have cause to rejoice; and Moses prays that he may have cause in his going out, either to war or to sea, for Zebulun was a *haven of ships*, Gen. xlix. 13. And Issachar must rejoice in his tents, that is, in his business at home, his husbandry, to which the men of that tribe generally confined themselves. Observe here, (1) That the providence of God, as it variously appoints the bounds of men's habitation, some in the city and some in the country, some in the seaports and some in the inland towns, so it wisely disposes men's inclinations to different employments. The genius of some men leads them to a book, of others to the sea, of others to the sword; some are inclined to rural affairs, others to trade, and some have a turn for mechanics; and it is well it is so. *If the whole body were an eye, where were the hearing?* 1 Cor. xii. 17. It was for the common good of Israel that the men of Zebulun were merchants and that the men of Issachar were husbandmen. (2) That whatever our place and business are it is our wisdom and duty to accommodate ourselves to them, and it is a great happiness to be well pleased with them.

2. That they should both be serviceable in their places to the honour of God and the interests of religion in the nation (*v.* 19). It has been often observed that though those that with Zebulun dwell in the haven of ships, which are places of concourse, have commonly more of the *light* of religion, those that with Issachar dwell in tents in the country have more of the *life* and *heat* of it. (1) It is here foretold that both these tribes should grow rich. Zebulun that goes abroad shall *suck of the abundance of the seas*, which are full breasts to the merchants, while Issachar, that tarries at home, shall enrich himself with *treasures hid in the sands*, either the fruits of the earth or the underground treasures of metals and minerals, or (because the word for sand here signifies properly the

JAMIESON, FAUSSET, BROWN

forth the triumphs of Joshua and the new kingdom of Jeroboam, both of whom were of Ephraim (cf. Gen. 58:20).

18, 19. Rejoice, Zebulun, in thy going out–on commercial enterprises and voyages by sea.

and, Issachar in thy tents–preferring to reside in their maritime towns.

shall suck of the abundance of the seas, and of treasures hid in the sand–**Both tribes should traffic with the Phœnicians in gold and silver, pearl and coral, especially in *murex*, the shellfish that yielded the famous Tyrian dye, and in glass, which was manufactured from the sand of the river Belus, in their immediate neighborhood.**

ALEXANDER MACLAREN:

"The goodwill of Him that dwelt in the bush" (v.16).

I think this is the only reference in the Old Testament to that great vision which underlay Moses' call and Israel's deliverance. It occurs in what is called "the blessing wherewith Moses, the man of God, blessed the children of Israel before his death," although modern opinion tends to decide that this hymn is indeed much more recent than the days of Moses. There seems a peculiar appropriateness in this reference being put into the mouth of the ancient Lawgiver, for to him even Sinai, with all its glories, cannot have been so impressive and so formative of his character as was the vision granted to him when solitary in the wilderness. It is to be noticed that the characteristic by which God is designated here never occurs elsewhere than in this one place. It is intended to intensify the conception of the greatness, and preciousness, and all-sufficiency of that "goodwill." If it is that "of him that dwelt in the bush," it is sure to be all that a man can need. I need not remind you that the words occur in the blessing pronounced on Joseph—that is, the two tribes which represented Joseph—in which all the greatest material gifts that could be desired by a pastoral people are first called down upon them, and then the ground of all these is laid in "the goodwill of him that dwelt in the bush." "The blessing—let it come on the head of Joseph."—*Expositions of Holy Scripture*

ADAM CLARKE

"For the precious things of heaven from above, and for the deep that coucheth beneath." This reading is confirmed by several of Kennicott's and De Rossi's MSS. The Syriac and Chaldee have both readings: "The dew of heaven from above."

14. *The precious fruits brought forth by the sun.* All excellent and important productions of the earth, which come to perfection once in the year. So *the precious things put forth by the moon* may imply those vegetables which require but about a month to bring them to perfection, or vegetables of which several crops may be had in the course of a year.

15. *The chief things of the ancient mountains. Umerosh harerey kedem,* "and from the head or top of the ancient or eastern mountains," the precious things or productions being still understood. And this probably refers to the large trees growing on the mountaintops, and the springs of water issuing from them. The mountains of Gilead may be here intended, as they fell to the half-tribe of Manasseh. And *the precious things of the lasting hills* may signify the metals and minerals which might be digged out of them.

16. *The good will of him that dwelt in the bush.* The favour of Him who appeared in the burning bush on Mount Sinai, who there, in His *good will*, mere love and compassion, took Israel to be His people; and who has preserved and will preserve, in tribulation and distress, all those who trust in Him, so that they shall as surely escape unhurt as the bush, though enveloped with fire, was unburnt. *The top of the head.* The same words are used by Jacob in blessing this tribe, Gen. xlix. 26. The meaning appears to be that God should distinguish this tribe in a particular way, as Joseph himself was separated, *nazir*, a Nazarite, a consecrated prince to God, from among and in preference to all his brethren. See the notes on Gen. xlix. 25, etc.

17. *His glory is like the firstling of his bullock.* This similitude is very obscure. A bullock was the most excellent of animals among the Jews, not only because of its acceptableness in sacrifice to God, but because of its great usefulness in agriculture. There is something peculiarly noble and dignified in the appearance of the ox, and his greatest ornaments are his fine horns; these the inspired penman has particularly in view, as the following clause proves; and it is well known that in scriptural language *horns* are the emblem of strength, glory, and sovereignty; Ps. lxxv. 5, 10; lxxxix. 17, 24; cxii. 9; Dan. viii. 3, etc.; Luke i. 69; Rev. xvii. 3, etc. *His horns are like the horns of unicorns. Reem,* which we interpret *unicorn*, signifies, according to Bochart, the "mountain goat"; and according to others, the "rhinoceros," a very large quadruped with one great horn on his nose, from which circumstance his name is derived. See the notes on Num. xxiii. 22; xxiv. 8. *Reem* is in the singular number, and because the horns of a unicorn, a one-horned animal, would have appeared absurd, our translators, with an unfaithfulness not common to them, put the word in the plural number. *To the ends of the earth.* Of the land of Canaan, for Joshua with his armies conquered all this land, and drove the ancient inhabitants out before him. *They are the ten thousands of Ephraim.* That is, The *horns* signify the ten thousands of Ephraim, and the thousands of Manasseh. Jacob prophesied, Gen. xlviii. 19, that the younger should be greater than the elder; so here *tens of thousands* are given to Ephraim, and only *thousands* to Manasseh. See the census, Num. i. 33-35.

18. *Rejoice, Zebulun, in thy going out.* That is, You shall be very prosperous in your coasting voyages; for this tribe's situation was favorable for traffic, having many seaports. *And, Issachar, in thy tents.* That is, as Zebulon should be prosperous in his shipping and traffic, so should Issachar be in his *tents*—his agriculture and pasturage.

19. *They shall call the people unto the mountain.* By their traffic with the "Gentiles" (for so I think *ammim* should be understood here) they shall be the instruments in God's hands of converting many to the true faith; so that instead of sacrificing to idols, they should offer *sacrifices of righteousness. They shall suck of*

MATTHEW HENRY

sand of the sea) the rich things thrown up by the sea, for the lot of Issachar reached to the sea-side. (2) It is foretold, that these tribes, being thus enriched, should *consecrate their gain unto the Lord, and their substance unto the Lord of the whole earth,* Mic. iv. 13.

II. The blessing of the tribe of Gad comes next, *v.* 20, 21. This was one of the tribes that was already seated on that side Jordan where Moses now was.

1. He foretells what this tribe would be, *v.* 20. (1) That it would be enlarged, as at present it had a spacious allotment. We find how this tribe was enlarged by their success in a war which it seems they carried on very religiously against the Hagarites, 1 Chron. v. 19, 20, 22. (2) That it would be a valiant and victorious tribe, would, if let alone, dwell secure and fearless as a lion; but, if provoked, would, like a lion, *tear the arm with the crown of the head;* that is, would pull in pieces all that stood in his way, both the arm (that is, the strength) and the crown of the head (that is, the policy and authority) of his enemies.

2. He commends this tribe for what they had done and were now doing, *v.* 21.

Verses 22–25

Here is, I. The blessing of Dan, *v.* 22. Jacob in his blessing had compared him to a serpent for subtlety; Moses compares him to a lion for courage and resolution: and what could stand before those that had the head of a serpent and the heart of a lion? He is compared to the lions that leaped from Bashan, a mountain noted for fierce lions, whence they came down to leap upon their prey in the plains. A party of them, upon information brought them of the security of Laish, which lay in the furthest part of the land of Canaan from them, surprised it, and soon made themselves masters of it. See Judges xviii. 27. And, the mountains of Bashan lying not far from that city, probably thence they made their descent upon it; and therefore are here said to *leap from Bashan.*

II. The blessing of Naphtali, *v.* 23. He looks upon this tribe with wonder, and applauds it: "O Naphtali, thou art happy, thou shalt be so, mayest thou be ever so!" Jacob had described this tribe to be, generally, courteous obliging people, giving goodly words, as the loving hind, Gen. xlix. 21. Now what should they get by being so? Moses here tells them they should have an interest in the affections of their neighbours, and be satisfied with favour. "The portion of the tribe of Naphtali" (the Jews say) "was so fruitful, and the productions so forward, though it lay north, that those of that tribe were generally the first that brought their first-fruits to the temple; and so they had first the blessing from the priest, which was the blessing of the Lord." Capernaum, in which Christ chiefly resided, lay in this tribe. Be thou *in possession of the sea and the south;* so it may be read, that is, of that sea which shall lie south of thy lot, that was the sea of Galilee, which we so often read of in the gospels, directly north of which the lot of this tribe lay, and which was of great advantage to this tribe, witness the wealth of Capernaum and Bethsaida.

JAMIESON, FAUSSET, BROWN

20, 21. **of Gad he said**—Its possessions were larger than they would have been had they lain west of Jordan; and this tribe had the honor of being settled by Moses himself in the first portion of land conquered. In the forest region, south of the Jabbok, "he dwelt as a lion" (cf. Gen. 30:11; 49:19).

Notwithstanding, they faithfully kept their engagement to join the "heads of the people" in the invasion of Canaan.

22. **Dan is a lion's whelp**—His proper settlement in the south of Canaan being too small, he by a sudden and successful irruption, established a colony in the northern extremity of the land. This might well be described as the leap of a young lion from the hills of Bashan.

23. **of Naphtali he said**—The pleasant and fertile territory of this tribe lay to "the west," on the borders of lakes Merom and Chinnereth, and to "the south" of the northern Danites.

ADAM CLARKE

the abundance of the seas. That is, grow wealthy by merchandise. *And of treasures hid in the sand.* Jonathan ben Uzziel has probably hit upon the true meaning of this difficult passage: "From the sand," says he, "are produced looking-glasses and glass in general; the *treasures*—the method of finding and working this, was revealed to these tribes." Several ancient writers inform us that there were havens in the coasts of the Zebulunites in which the vitreous sand, or sand proper for making glass, was found. See Strabo, lib. xvi.; see also Pliny, *Hist. Nat.* 1. xxxvi., c. 26; Tacitus, *Hist.* 1. v., c. 7. The words of Tacitus are remarkable: "The river Belus falls into the Jewish sea, about whose mouth those sands, mixed with nitre, are collected, out of which glass is formed," or which is melted into glass. Some think that the celebrated shellfish called *murex,* out of which the precious purple dye was extracted, is here intended by the *treasures hid in the sand;* this also Jonathan introduces in this verse.

20. *Blessed be he that enlargeth Gad.* As deliverance out of distress is termed "enlarging" (see Ps. iv. 1), this may refer to God's deliverance of the tribe of Gad out of that distress mentioned Gen. xlix. 19, and to the enlargement obtained through means of Jephthah, Judg. xi. 33, and probably also the victories obtained by Gad and Reuben over the Hagarites, 1 Chron. v. 18-20. *He dwelleth as a lion.* Probably the epithet of *lion* or lionlike was applied to this tribe from their fierce and warlike disposition. And on this supposition, 1 Chron. xii. 8, will appear to be a sufficient comment: "And of the Gadites there [were] . . . men of might, and men of war for the battle, that could handle shield and buckler, whose faces were like the faces of lions, and were as swift as the roes upon the mountains." Tearing the *arm* or "shoulder" *with the crown of the head* seems simply to mean that no force should be able to prevail over them, or stand against them; as the arm or shoulder signifies dominion, and the crown of the head, sovereign princes.

21. *He provided the first part.* That is, he chose for himself a very excellent portion, viz., the land of Sihon and Og, in which this tribe had requested to be settled by the lawgiver, viz., Moses, from whom they requested this portion, Num. xxxii. 1-5. *He came with the heads of the people.* Notwithstanding this portion fell unto them on the east side of Jordan, yet they proceeded with the *heads of the people,* the chiefs of the other tribes. To execute *the justice of the Lord.* To extirpate the old inhabitants of the country, according to the decree and purpose of the Lord. See on Num. xxxii.

22. *Dan is a lion's whelp: he shall leap from Bashan.* The Jewish interpreters observe that Bashan was a place much frequented by lions, who issued thence into all parts to look for prey. By this probably Moses intended to point out the strength and prowess of this tribe, that it should extend its territories, and live a sort of predatory life. It appears from Josh. xix. 47 that the portion originally assigned to this tribe was not sufficient for them; hence we find them going out to war against Leshem and taking it, adding it to their territories, and calling it by the name of the tribe. Jacob, in his prophetic blessing of this tribe, represents it under the notion of a "serpent in the path," Gen. xlix. 17. The character there, and that given here, constitute the complete warrior—stratagem and courage.

23. *O Naphtali, satisfied with favour.* Though this may refer to the very great fertility of the country that fell to this tribe, yet certainly something more is intended. Scarcely any of the tribes was more particularly favored by the wondrous mercy and kindness of god than this and the tribe of Zebulun. The light of the glorious gospel of Christ shone brightly here, Matt. iv. 13, 15-16. Christ's chief residence was at Capernaum in this tribe, Matt. ix. 1; Mark ii. 1, and this city, through Christ's constant residence, and the mighty miracles He wrought in it, is represented as being "exalted unto heaven," Matt. xi. 23. And it is generally allowed that the apostles were principally of the tribe of Naphtali, who were to *possess . . . the west and the south*—to dispense the gospel through all the other tribes. The word *yam,* which we here

MATTHEW HENRY

III. The blessing of Asher, *v.* 24, 25. Four things he prays for and prophecies concerning this tribe, which carries blessedness in its name; for Leah called the father of it *Asher*, saying *Happy am I*, Gen. xxx. 13. 1. The increase of their numbers. 2. Their interest in their neighbours: *Let him be acceptable to his brethren.* 3. The richness of their land. (1) Above ground: *Let him dip his foot in oil*, that is, "Let him have such plenty of it in his lot that he may not only anoint his head with it, but, if he please, wash his feet in it." (2) Under ground: *Thy shoes shall be iron and brass*, that is, "Thou shalt have great plenty of these metals (mines of them) in thy own ground. The Chaldee paraphrasts understand this figuratively: "Thou shalt be strong and bright, as iron and brass." 4. The continuance of their strength and vigour: *As thy days, so shall thy strength be.* Many paraphrase it thus, "The strength of thy old age shall be like that of thy youth; thou shalt not feel a decay, nor be the worse for the wearing, but shalt renew thy youth; as if not thy shoes only, but thy bones, were iron and brass." Have they work appointed them? They shall have strength to do it. Have they burdens appointed them? They shall have strength to bear them; and never be *tempted above that they are able.*

Verses 26–29

Moses, the man of God, with his last breath magnifies both the God of Israel and the Israel of God.

I. No God like the God of Israel. None of the gods of the nations were capable of doing that for their worshippers which Jehovah did for his: *There is none like unto the God of Jeshurun, v.* 26. 1. His sovereign power and authority: *He rides upon the heavens.* When he has any thing to do for his people he *rides upon the heavens* to do it; for he does it swiftly and strongly: no enemy can either anticipate or obstruct the progress of him that rides on the heavens. 2. His boundless eternity; he is the eternal God, and his arms are *everlasting, v.* 27. The gods of the heathen were but lately invented, and would shortly perish; but the God of Jeshurun is eternal: he was before all worlds, and will be when time and days shall be no more. See Hab. i. 12.

II. No people like the Israel of God. Having pronounced each tribe happy, in the close he pronounces all together very happy, so happy in all respects that there was no nation under the sun comparable to them (*v.* 29). If Israel honour God as a non-such God, he will favour them so as to make them a non-such people. What is here said of the church of Israel is certainly to be applied to *the church of the first-born*, that are written in heaven. The Christian church is the Israel of God, as the apostle calls it (Gal. vi. 16).

1. Never were people so well seated and sheltered (*v.* 27): *The eternal God is thy refuge.* Or, as the word signifies, "thy *habitation*, or *mansion-house*, in which thou art safe, and easy, and at rest, as a man in his own house." Every Israelite indeed is at home in God; the soul returns to him, and reposes in him as its resting-place (Ps. cxvi. 7), its hiding-place, Ps. xxxii. 7.

2. Never were people so well supported and borne up: *Underneath are the everlasting arms*; that is, the almighty power of God. The everlasting covenant, and the everlasting consolations that flow from it, are indeed everlasting arms, with which believers have been wonderfully sustained, and kept cheerful in the worst of times; divine grace is sufficient for them, 2 Cor. xii. 9.

3. Never were people so well commanded and led on to battle: "*He shall thrust out the enemy from before thee* by his almighty power, which will make room for thee. Thus believers are more than conquerors over their spiritual enemies, through Christ that loved them. The captain of our salvation *thrust out the enemy from before us* when he overcame the world and spoiled principalities and powers on the cross.

4. Never were people so well secured and protected (*v.* 28): *Israel shall then dwell in safety alone.* Those that dwell in God, and make his name their strong tower, *dwell in safety*; the *place of their defence is the munitions of rocks*, Isa. xxxiii. 16. They shall dwell in safety alone. (1) Though alone. Though they contract no alliances with their neighbours. (2) Because alone. They shall dwell in safety as long as they continue pure, and unmixed with the heathen.

5. Never were people so well provided for: *The fountain of Jacob* (that is, the present generation of that people, which is as the fountain to all the streams that shall hereafter descend and be derived from it) shall now presently be fixed upon a good land. *The eye of Jacob* (so it might be read, for the same word

JAMIESON, FAUSSET, BROWN

24, 25. of Asher he said—The condition of this tribe is described as combining all the elements of earthly felicity. **dip his foot in oil**—These words allude either to the process of extracting the oil by foot presses, or to his district as particularly fertile and adapted to the culture of the olive.

shoes of iron and brass—These shoes suited his rocky coast from Carmel to Sidon. Country people as well as ancient warriors had their lower extremities protected by metallic greaves (I Sam. 17:6; Eph. 6:15) and iron-soled shoes.

ALEXANDER MACLAREN:

We have first that thought that God gives us an equipment of strength proportioned to our work—shoes fit for our road. God does not turn people out to scramble over rough mountains with thin-soled boots on; that is the plain English of the words. When an Alpine climber is preparing to go away into Switzerland for rock work, the first thing he does is to get a pair of strong shoes, with plenty of iron nails in the soles of them. So Asher had to be shod for his rough roads, and so each of us may be sure that if God sends us on stony paths, He will provide us with strong shoes and will not send us out on any journey for which He does not equip us well.

There are no difficulties to be found in any path of duty for which he that is called to tread it is not prepared by Him that sent him. Whatsoever may be the road, our equipment is calculated for it and is given to us from Him that has appointed it.

—Expositions of Holy Scripture

26-29. There is none like unto the God of Jeshurun—The chapter concludes with a congratulatory address to Israel on their peculiar happiness and privilege in having Jehovah for their God and protector.

who rideth upon the heaven in thy help—an evident allusion to the pillar of cloud and fire, which was both the guide and shelter of Israel.

28. the fountain of Jacob—The posterity of Israel shall dwell in a blessed and favored land.

ADAM CLARKE

translate *west*, literally signifies the "sea," and probably refers to the Sea of Gennesareth, which was in this tribe.

24. *Let Asher be blessed with children.* Let him have a numerous posterity, continually increasing. *Let him be acceptable to his brethren.* May he be in perfect union and harmony with the other tribes. *Let him dip his foot in oil.* Let him have a fertile soil, and an abundance of all the conveniences and comforts of life.

25. *Thy shoes shall be iron and brass.* Some suppose this may refer to the iron and copper mines in their territory; but it is more likely that it relates to their warlike disposition, as we know that greaves, boots, shoes, etc., of iron, brass, and tin, were used by ancient warriors. Goliath had greaves of brass on his legs, 1 Sam. xvii. 6; and "the brazen-booted Greeks" is one of the epithets given by Homer to his heroes.

And as thy days, so shall thy strength be. If we take this clause as it appears here, we have at once an easy sense; and the saying, I have no doubt, has comforted the souls of multitudes. The meaning is obvious: "Whatever thy trials or difficulties may be, I shall always give thee grace to support thee under and bring thee through them." The original is only two words, the latter of which has been translated in a great variety of ways, *ucheyameycha dobecha.* Of the first term there can be no doubt; it literally means, *and as thy days;* the second word, *dobe*, occurs nowhere else in the Hebrew Bible. The Septuagint have rendered it by *strength*, and most of the versions have followed them; but others have rendered it "affliction, old age, fame, weakness," etc. It would be almost endless to follow interpreters through their conjectures concerning its meaning. It is allowed among learned men that where a word occurs not as a verb in the Hebrew Bible its root may be legitimately sought in the Arabic. He who controverts this position knows little of the ground on which he stands. In this language the root is found; *daba* signifies "he rested, was quiet." This gives a very good sense, and a very appropriate one; for as the borders of this tribe lay on the vicinity of the Phoenicians, it was naturally to be expected that they should be constantly exposed to pillage; but God, to give them confidence in His protection, says, "According to thy days [all circumstances and vicissitudes], so shall thy rest be"—While faithful to your God, no evil shall touch you; your days shall increase, and your quiet be lengthened out. This is an unfailing promise of God: "I will keep him in perfect peace, whose mind is stayed upon Me, because he trusteth in Me"; therefore "trust ye in the Lord for ever: for in the Lord Jehovah is everlasting strength," Isa. xxvi. 4.

26. *There is none like unto the God of Jeshurun.* We have already seen the literal meaning of Jeshurun, chap. xxxii. 15; but besides its literal meaning, it seems to be used as an expression of particular affection. Hence the Septuagint seem to have apprehended the full force of the word by translating it "the beloved one," the object of God's especial delight. *Rideth upon the heaven.* Unites heaven and earth in your defense and support, and comes with irresistible velocity to succor and defend you, and to discomfit your adversaries.

27. *The eternal God. Elohey kedem*, the "former God," He who was of old. Not like the gods which were lately come up. He who ever was and ever will be; and He who was, is, and will be unchangeably holy, wise, just, and merciful. *Everlasting arms.* As the arm is the emblem of power, and of power in a state of exertion, the words here state that an unlimited and unconquerable power shall be eternally exerted in the defense of God's Church, and in the behalf of all those who trust in Him. *Thrust out the enemy.* He will expel all the ancient inhabitants, and put you in possession of their land.

28. *Israel then shall dwell . . . alone.* This people shall not be incorporated with any other people under heaven. A prophecy which continues to be fulfilled to the very letter. Every attempt to unite them with any other people has proved absolutely ineffectual. *The fountain of Jacob.* His "offspring" shall possess a most

MATTHEW HENRY

signifies a fountain and an eye) *is upon the land of corn and wine*, just before their faces, on the other side the river.

6. Never were people so well helped. If they were in any strait, God himself rode upon the heavens for *their help*, *v.* 26. And they were *a people saved by the Lord*, *v.* 29.

7. Never were people so well armed. God himself was the shield of their help by whom they were armed defensively, and he was the *sword of their excellency*, by whom they were armed offensively, and made formidable.

8. Never were people so well assured of victory over their enemies: *They shall be found liars unto thee*; that is, "shall be forced to submit to thee sorely against their will, so that it will be but a counterfeit submission. *If thy enemies be found liars to thee* (so some read it), *thou shalt tread upon their high places*.

CHAPTER 34

Verses 1–4

I. Moses climbing upwards towards heaven, as high as the top of Pisgah, there to die; for that was the place appointed, *ch.* xxxii. 49, 50. Israel lay encamped upon the flat grounds in the plains of Moab, and thence he went up, according to order, to the mountain of Nebo, to the highest point or ridge of that mountain, which was called *Pisgah*, *v.* 1. Pisgah is an appellative name for all such eminences. It should seem Moses went up alone to the top of Pisgah, *alone without help*. When he had made an end of blessing Israel, we may suppose, he solemnly took leave of Joshua, and Eleazar, and the rest of his friends, who probably brought him to the foot of the hill; but then he gave them such a charge as Abraham gave to his servants at the foot of another hill: *Tarry you here while I go yonder and die*. 1. To show that he was willing to die. When he knew the place of his death, he was so far from avoiding it that he cheerfully mounted a steep hill to come at it. 2. To show that he looked upon death as his ascension. The soul of a man, of a good man, when it leaves the body, *goes upwards* (Eccles. iii. 21). When God's servants are sent for out of the world, the summons runs thus, *Go up and die*.

II. Moses looking downward again towards this earth, to see the earthly Canaan into which he must never enter, but therein by faith looking forwards to the heavenly Canaan into which he should now immediately enter. 1. If he went up alone to the top of Pisgah, yet he *was not alone, for the Father was with him*, John xvi. 32. 2. Note, All the pleasant prospects we have of the better country we are beholden to the grace of God for; it is he that gives the *spirit of wisdom* as well as the *spirit of revelation*, the eye as well as the object. 3. He saw it at a distance. Such a sight believers now have, through grace, of the bliss and glory of their future state. The word and ordinances are to them what Mount Pisgah was to Moses. 4. He saw it, but must never enjoy it. Glorious things are spoken of the kingdom of Christ in the latter days, its advancement, enlargement, and flourishing state; we foresee it, but we are not likely to live to see it. Those that shall come after us, we hope, will enter that promised land, which is a comfort to us. 5. Canaan was *Immanuel's land* (Isa. viii. 8), so that in viewing it he had a view of the blessings we enjoy by Christ.

Verses 5–8

Here is, I. The death of Moses (*v.* 5): *Moses the servant of the Lord died*. It bore hard upon Moses himself, when he had gone through all the fatigues of the wilderness, to be prevented from enjoying the pleasures of Canaan. But *the man Moses was very meek*; God will have it so, and he cheerfully submits. 1. He is here called *the servant of the Lord*, not only as a good man (all the saints are God's servants), but as a useful man, eminently useful, who had served God's counsels in bringing Israel out of Egypt, and leading them through the wilderness. 2. Yet he dies. Neither his piety nor his usefulness would exempt him from the stroke of death. God's servants must die that they may rest from their labours, receive their recompense, and make room for others. When God's servants are removed, and must serve him no longer on earth, they go to serve him better, to serve him *day and night in his temple*. He dies *according to the word of the Lord*. *At the mouth of the Lord*; so the word is. The Jews say, "with a kiss from the mouth of God." Note, The servants of the Lord, when they have done all their other work, must die at last, in obedience to their Master, and be freely

JAMIESON, FAUSSET, BROWN

CHAPTER 34

Vss. 1-12. Moses from Mount Nebo Views the Land. **1. Moses went up from the plains of Moab**—This chapter appears from internal evidence to have been written subsequently to the death of Moses, and it probably formed, at one time, an introduction to the Book of Joshua. **unto the mountain of Nebo, to the top of Pisgah**—lit., the head or summit of *the Pisgah*,—i.e., the height (cf. Num. 23: 14; ch. 3:17-27; 4:49). The general name given to the whole mountain range east of Jordan, was Abarim (cf. ch. 32:49), and the peak to which Moses ascended was dedicated to the heathen Nebo, as Balaam's standing-place had been consecrated to Peor. Some modern travellers have fixed on Jebel-Attarus, a high mountain south of the Jabbok (Zurka), as the Nebo of this passage [Burckhardt, Seetzen, etc.]. But it is situated too far north for a height which, being described as "over against Jericho," must be looked for above the last stage of the Jordan. **the Lord showed him all the land of Gilead**—That pastoral region was discernible at the northern extremity of the mountain-line on which he stood, till it ended, far beyond his sight in Dan. Westward, there were on the horizon, the distant hills of "all Naphtali." Coming nearer, was "the land of Ephraim and Manasseh." Immediately opposite was "all the land of Judah," a title at first restricted to the portion of this tribe, beyond which were "the utmost sea" (the Mediterranean) and the Desert of the "South." These were the four great marks of the future inheritance of his people, on which the narrative fixes our attention. Immediately below him was "the circle" of the plain of Jericho, with its oasis of palm trees; and far away on his left, the last inhabited spot before the great desert "Zoar." The foreground of the picture alone was clearly discernible. There was no miraculous power of vision imparted to Moses. That he should see all that is described is what any man could do, if he attained sufficient elevation. The atmosphere of the climate is so subtle and free from vapor that the sight is carried to a distance of which the beholder, who judges from the more dense air of Europe, can form no idea [Vere Monro]. But between him and that "good land," the deep valley of the Jordan intervened; "he was not to go over thither."

5. So Moses . . . died—After having governed the Israelites forty years.

ADAM CLARKE

fertile land; such was Palestine.

29. *Happy art thou*. Oh, the happiness of Israel! it is ineffable, inconceivable, because they are a *people saved by the Lord*—have such a salvation as it becomes the infinite perfections of God to bestow; He is their *help*, their never-failing Strength, and the *shield* of that help—He defends their defense, saves them and preserves them in the state of salvation. *Sword of thy excellency*. Or "whose sword"—His all-conquering Word, "is thine excellency," in its promises, threatenings, precepts. Paul, in his exhortation to the Christians at Ephesus, uses the same metaphor, "Take unto you . . . the sword of the Spirit, which is the word of God." *Thine enemies shall be found liars*. Who said you should never be able to gain the possession of this good land; for you *shall tread on*, subdue, their *high places*—even their best fortified cities.

CHAPTER 34

1. *And Moses went up*. This chapter could not have been written by Moses. A man certainly cannot give an account of his own death and burial. We may therefore consider Moses' words as ending with the conclusion of the preceding chapter, as what follows could not possibly have been written by himself. To suppose that he anticipated these circumstances, or that they were shown to him by an especial revelation, is departing far from propriety and necessity, and involving the subject in absurdity; for God gives no prophetic intimations but such as are absolutely necessary to be made. But there is no necessity here, for the Spirit which inspired the writer of the following book would naturally communicate the matter that concludes this. I believe, therefore, that Deuteronomy xxxiv should constitute the first chapter of the Book of Joshua.

On this subject the following note from an intelligent Jew cannot be unacceptable to the reader: "Most commentators are of opinion that Ezra was the author of the last chapter of Deuteronomy; some think it was Joshua, and others the seventy elders, immediately after the death of Moses; adding, that the book of Deuteronomy originally ended with the prophetic blessing upon the twelve tribes: 'Happy art thou, O Israel: who is like unto thee, O people saved by the Lord!' and that what now makes the last chapter of Deuteronomy was formerly the first of Joshua, but was removed from thence and joined to the former by way of supplement."

5. *So Moses . . . died . . . according to the word of the Lord*. *Al pi Yehovah*, "at the mouth of Jehovah," i.e., by the especial command and authority of the Lord; but it is possible that what is here said refers only to the sentence of his exclusion from the Promised Land, when he offended at the waters of Meribah.

MATTHEW HENRY

willing to go home whenever he sends for them, Acts xxi. 13.

II. His burial, *v.* 6. God takes care of the dead bodies of his servants; as their death is precious, so is their dust, but the covenant with it shall be remembered. He was buried in a valley *over against Beth-peor.* If the soul be at rest with God, the matter is not great where the body rests. The particular place was not known, lest the children of Israel, who were so very prone to idolatry, should have enshrined and worshipped the dead body of Moses, that great founder and benefactor of their nation.

III. His age, *v.* 7. His life was prolonged, 1. To old age. He was 120 years old, which, though far short of the years of the patriarchs, yet much exceeded the years of most of his contemporaries. The years of the life of Moses were three forties. The first forty he lived a courtier, at ease and in honour in Pharaoh's court; the second forty he lived a poor desolate shepherd in Midian; the third forty he lived a king in Jeshurun, in honour and power, but encumbered with a great deal of care and toil. 2. To a good old age: *His eye was not dim* (as Isaac's, Gen. xxvii. 1, and Jacob's, Gen. xlviii. 10), *nor was his natural force abated.*

IV. The solemn mourning that there was for him, *v.* 8. Observe, 1. Who the mourners were: *The children of Israel.* 2. How long they mourned: *Thirty days.* Yet the *ending of the days of weeping and mourning* for Moses is an intimation that, how great soever our losses have been, we must not abandon ourselves to perpetual grief; we must suffer the wound at least to heal up in time. If we hope to go to heaven rejoicing, why should we resolve to go to the grave mourning?

Verses 9–12

A very honourable encomium passed both on Moses and Joshua; each has his praise, and should have. Let God be glorified in both.

I. Joshua is praised as a man admirably qualified for the work to which he was called, *v.* 9. Moses brought Israel to the borders of Canaan and then died and left them, to signify that *the law made nothing perfect,* Heb. vii. 19. It brings men into a wilderness of conviction, but not into the Canaan of rest and settled peace. It is an honour reserved for Joshua (our Lord Jesus, of whom Joshua was a type) to do that for us which *the law could not do, in that it was weak through the flesh,* Rom. viii. 3. Through him we enter into rest, the spiritual rest of conscience and eternal rest in heaven. Two things concurred to clear Joshua's call to this great undertaking:—1. God fitted him for it: *He was full of the spirit of wisdom.* Conduct is as requisite in a general as courage. 2. Moses, by the divine appointment, had ordained him to it: *He had laid his hands upon him,* so substituting him to be his successor, and praying to God to qualify him for the service to which he had called him.

II. Moses is praised (*v.* 10–12), and with good reason.

1. He was indeed a very great man, especially upon two accounts:—(1) His intimacy with the God of nature: *God knew him face to face,* and so he knew God. See Num. xii. 8. (2) His interest and power in the kingdom of nature. The miracles of judgment he wrought in Egypt before Pharaoh, and his miracles of mercy he wrought in the wilderness before Israel, served to demonstrate that he was a particular favourite of Heaven, and had an extraordinary commission to act as he did on this earth. Never was there any man whom Israel had more reason to love, or whom the enemies of Israel had more reason to fear.

2. He was greater than any other of the prophets of the Old Testament. Though they were men of great interest in heaven and great influence upon earth, yet they were none of them to be compared with this great man; none of them either so evidenced or executed a commission from heaven as Moses did. This encomium of Moses seems to have been written long after his death, yet then there had not arisen any prophet *like unto Moses.* By Moses God gave the law, and moulded and formed the Jewish church; by the other prophets he only sent particular reproofs, directions, and predictions. The last of the prophets concludes with a charge *to remember the law of Moses,* Mal. iv. 4. Christ himself often appealed to the writings of Moses, and vouched him for a witness, as one that *saw his day* at a distance *and spoke of him.* Moses was faithful as a servant, but Christ as a Son. The history of Moses leaves him buried in the plains of Moab, and concludes with the period of his government; but the history of our Saviour leaves him sitting *at the right hand of the Majesty on high,* and we are assured that *of the increase of his government and peace there shall be no end.*

JAMIESON, FAUSSET, BROWN

he buried him—or, "he was buried in a valley," i.e., a ravine or gorge of the Pisgah. Some think that he entered a cave and there died, being, according to an ancient tradition of Jews and Christians, buried by angels (Jude 9; Num. 21:20). **6. no man knoweth of his sepulchre unto this day**—This concealment seems to have been owing to a special and wise arrangement of Providence, to prevent its being ranked among "holy places," and made the resort of superstitious pilgrims or idolatrous veneration, in after ages.

8. wept for Moses . . . thirty days—Seven days was the usual period of mourning, but for persons in high rank or official eminence, it was extended to thirty (Gen. 50:3-10; 20:29).

9. Joshua . . . was full of the spirit of wisdom—He was appointed to a peculiar and extraordinary office. He was not the successor of Moses, for he was not a prophet or civil ruler, but the general or leader, called to head the people in the war of invasion and the subsequent allocation of the tribes.

10-12. there arose not a prophet since—In whatever light we view this extraordinary man, the eulogy pronounced in these inspired words will appear just. No Hebrew prophet or ruler equalled him in character or official dignity, or in knowledge of God's will and opportunities of announcing it.

ADAM CLARKE

6. *He buried him.* It is probable that the reason why Moses was buried thus privately was lest the Israelites, prone to idolatry, should pay him divine honors; and God would not have the body of His faithful servant abused in this way.

7. *His eye was not dim.* Even at the advanced age of a hundred and twenty; *nor his natural force abated*—he was a young man even in old age, notwithstanding the unparalleled hardships he had gone through.

9. *Laid his hands upon him.* See on Num. xxvii. 18-23.

10. *There arose not a prophet.* Among all the succeeding prophets none was found so eminent in all respects nor so highly privileged as Moses; with him God spoke *face to face*—admitted him to the closest familiarity and greatest friendship with himself. Now all this continued true till the advent of Jesus Christ, of whom Moses said, "A prophet shall the Lord your God raise up unto you of your brethren, like unto me"; but how great was this Person when compared with Moses! Moses desired to see God's glory; this sight he could not bear; he saw his "back parts," probably meaning God's design relative to the latter days. But Jesus, the almighty Saviour, in whom dwells all the fulness of the Godhead bodily, who lay in the bosom of the Father, He hath "declared" God to man.

Now to the ever blessed and glorious Trinity, Father, Word, and Spirit, the infinite and eternal One, from whom alone wisdom, truth, and goodness can proceed, be glory and dominion for ever and ever. Amen.

THE BOOK OF JOSHUA

I. The conquest of the land (1:1-12:24)
- *A. Mobilization (1:1-2:24)*
  - 1. The call to arms (1:1-18)
    - a. God's call to Joshua (1:1-9)
    - b. Joshua's call to the people (1:10-18)
  - 2. The mission of the spies (2:1-24)
- *B. Advance (3:1-5:15)*
  - 1. Crossing the Jordan (3:1-4:24)
    - a. The crossing (3:1-17)
    - b. The final movements (4:1-24)
  - 2. Ceremonies of consecration (5:1-15)
- *C. War (6:1-11:23)*
  - 1. Jericho (6:1-27)
  - 2. Ai (7:1-8:35)
    - a. Defeat "but" (7:1-26)
    - b. Victory (8:1-35)
  - 3. Beth-horon (9:1-10:43)
    - a. The deceit of the Gibeonites (9:1-27)
    - b. The defeat of five kings (10:1-27)
    - c. The following conquests (10:28-43)
  - 4. The northern kings (11:1-23)
- *D. Extent of the conquest (12:1-24)*

II. The settlement of the people (13:1-21:45)
- *A. Settlement according to the Mosaic promise (13:1-14:15)*
  - 1. The two-and-a-half tribes (13:1-33)
  - 2. The possession of Caleb (14:1-15)
- *B. Settlement of nine-and-a-half tribes (15:1-19:51)*
  - 1. Judah (15:1-63)
  - 2. Ephraim (16:1-10)
  - 3. Manasseh (17:1-18)
  - 4. Benjamin (18:1-28)
  - 5. The rest (19:1-51)
- *C. Settlement of cities of refuge and Levites (20:1-21:45)*
  - 1. Cities of refuge (20:1-9)
  - 2. The Levites (21:1-45)

III. Joshua's farewell (22:1-24:33)
- *A. The two-and-a-half tribes (22:1-34)*
- *B. Farewell addresses (23:1-24:15)*
  - 1. First address (23:1-16)
  - 2. Second address (24:1-15)
- *C. Final things (24:16-33)*

In this book and those that follow it to the end of the book of Esther, we have before us the history of the Jewish nation. They were part of the oracles of God, which were committed to the Jews, and were so received and referred to by our Savior and the apostles.

In the five books of Moses we had a very full account of the rise, advance, and constitution of the Old Testament church; the family out of which it was raised; the promise, that great charter by which it was incorporated; the miracles by which it was built up; and the laws and ordinances by which it was to be governed. A nation that had statutes and judgments so righteous, one would think, should have been very holy and very happy.

We have before us the "book of Joshua," so called, perhaps, not because it was written by him, for that is uncertain. Dr. Lightfoot thinks that Phinehas wrote it. Bishop Patrick is clear that Joshua wrote it himself. However that be, it is written concerning him, and, if any other wrote it, it was collected out of his journals or memoirs. It contains the history of Israel under the command and government of Joshua, how he presided as general of their armies in their entrance into Canaan (chs. 1–5), in their conquest of Canaan (chs. 6–12), in the distribution of the land of Canaan among the tribes of Israel (chs. 13–21), and in the settlement and establishment of religion among them (chs. 22–24).

We may see in it much of God and his providence—his power, his justice, his faithfulness, and his kindness to his people Israel, notwithstanding their provocations. And we see much of Christ and his grace. Though Joshua is not expressly mentioned in the New Testament as a type of Christ, yet all agree that he was a very eminent one. He bore our Savior's name, as did also another type of him, Joshua the high priest (Zech. 6:11, 12). The LXX, giving the name of Joshua a Greek termination, calls him all along "Jesus," and so he is called in Acts 7:45 and Hebrews 4:8. It signifies, "He shall save."

MATTHEW HENRY

CHAPTER 1

Verses 1–9

Honour is here put upon Joshua, and great power lodged in his hand, by him that is the fountain of honour and power, and by whom kings reign. God speaks to him (*v.* 1), probably as he spoke to Moses (Lev. i. 1) *out of the tabernacle of the congregation,* for his greater encouragement, God here speaks to him immediately, some think in a dream or vision (as Job xxxiii. 15). Concerning Joshua's call observe here,

I. The time when it was given him: *After the death of Moses.* As soon as ever Moses was dead, Joshua took upon him the administration, by virtue of his solemn ordination in Moses's life-time. God did not speak to him to go forward towards Canaan till after the thirty days of mourning for Moses were ended; God would give time to the people not only to lament their loss of him, but to repent of their miscarriages towards him.

II. The place Joshua had been in before he was thus preferred. He was Moses's minister, that is, an assistant in business. The LXX translate it ὑπουργος, a workman under his direction. Observe, 1. He had been long bred to business. 2. He was trained up in subjection and under command. Those are fittest to rule that have learnt to obey. 3. He that was to succeed Moses was intimately acquainted with him, that he might take the same measures, walk in the same spirit, having to carry on the same work. 4. He was herein a type of Christ, who might therefore be called Moses's minister, because he was made under the law and fulfilled all the righteousness of it.

III. The call itself that God gave him,

1. The consideration upon which he was called to the government: *Moses my servant is dead, v.* 2. Moses, when he has done his work as a servant, dies and goes to *rest from his labours, and enters into the joy of his Lord.*

2. The call itself. *Now therefore arise.* (1) "Though Moses is dead, the work must go on; therefore arise, and go about it." When God has work to do, he will either find or make instruments fit to carry it

JAMIESON, FAUSSET, BROWN

CHAPTER 1

VSS. 1-18. THE LORD APPOINTS JOSHUA TO SUCCEED MOSES. **1. Now after the death of Moses**—Joshua, having been already appointed and designated leader of Israel (Num. 27:18-23), in all probability assumed the reins of government *immediately* "after the death of Moses." **the servant of the Lord**—This was the official title of Moses as invested with a special mission to make known the will of God; and it conferred great honor and authority. **the Lord spake unto Joshua**—probably during the period of public mourning, and either by a direct revelation to the mind of Joshua, or by means of Urim and Thummim (Num. 27:21). This first communication gave a pledge that the divine instructions which, according to the provisions of the theocracy, had been imparted to Moses, would be continued to the new leader, though God might not perhaps speak to him "mouth to mouth" (Num. 12:8). **Joshua**—The original name, Oshea, (Num. 13:8), which had been, according to Eastern usage, changed like those of Abram and Sarai (Gen. 17:5-15) into Jehoshua or Joshua (i.e., "God's salvation") was significant of the services he was to render, and typified those of a greater Saviour (Heb. 4:8). **Moses' minister**—i.e., his official attendant, who, from being constantly employed in important services and early initiated into the principles of the government, would be well trained for undertaking the leadership of Israel.

ADAM CLARKE

CHAPTER 1

1. *Now after the death of Moses. Vayehi,* "and it was or happened" after the death of Moses. Even the first words in this book show it to be a continuation of the preceding, and intimately connected with the narrative in the last chapter in Deuteronomy, of which I suppose Joshua to have been the author, and that chapter to have originally made the commencement of this book. The time referred to here must have been at the conclusion of the thirty days in which they mourned for Moses.

2. *Moses my servant.* The word *servant,* as applied both to Moses and Joshua, is to be understood in a very peculiar sense. It signifies God's prime minister, the person by whom He issued His orders, and by whom He accomplished all his purposes and designs. No person ever bore this title in the like sense but the Redeemer of mankind, of whom Moses and Joshua were types.

MATTHEW HENRY

on. Moses the *servant* is dead, but God the *Master* is not: he lives for ever. (2) "Because Moses is dead, therefore the work devolves upon thee as his successor." Joshua must arise to finish what Moses began. Thus the latter generations enter into the labours of the former. And thus Christ, our Joshua, does that for us which could never be done by the law of Moses, —*justifies* (Acts xiii. 39), and *sanctifies*, Romans viii. 3. The life of Moses made way for Joshua, and prepared the people for what was to be done by him. Thus the law is a schoolmaster to bring us to Christ.

3. The particular service he was now called out to: "*Arise, go over this Jordan*, this river which you have in view, and on the banks of which you lie encamped." This was a trial to the faith of Joshua. He had no pontoons or bridge of boats by which to convey them over, and yet he must believe that God, who had ordered them over, would open a way for them. Going over Jordan was going into Canaan.

4. The grant of the land of Canaan to the children of Israel is here repeated (*v.* 2–4): *I do give it them.* To the patriarchs it was promised, *I will give it*; but, now that the fourth generation had expired, the time had come for the performance of the promise (*v.* 3), *I have given it*; though it be yet unconquered, it is as sure to you as if it were in your hands." Observe, (1) The persons to whom the conveyance is made: *To them, even to the children of Israel* (*v.* 2), because they are the seed of Jacob, who was called *Israel* at the time when this promise was made to him, Gen. xxxv. 10, 12. (2) The land itself that is conveyed: From the river Euphrates eastward, to the Mediterranean Sea westward, *v.* 4. Had they been obedient, God would have given them this and much more. Out of all these countries, and many others, there were in process of time proselytes to the Jewish religion, as appears, Acts ii. 5, &c. (3) The condition is here implied upon which this grant is made, in those words, *as I said unto Moses*, that is, "upon the terms that Moses told you of many a time, *if you will keep my statutes*, you shall go in and possess that good land. Take it under those provisos and limitations, and not otherwise." (4) "*Every place that the sole of your foot shall tread upon* (within the following bounds) shall be your own. Do but set your foot upon it and you have it."

5. The promises God here makes to Joshua for his encouragement. (1) That he should be sure of the presence of God (*v.* 5): "*As I was with Moses*, in bringing Israel out of Egypt and leading them through the wilderness, so I will be with thee to enable thee to settle them in Canaan." What Moses did was done by virtue of the presence of God with him, and, though Joshua had not always the same presence of mind that Moses had, yet, if he had always the same presence of God, he would do well enough. Note, It is a great comfort to the rising generation of ministers and Christians that the same grace which was sufficient for those that went before them shall not be wanting to them if they be not wanting to themselves in the improvement of it. It is repeated here again (*v.* 9). Note, Those that go where God sends them shall have him with them wherever they go. (2) That the presence of God should never be withdrawn from him: *I will not fail thee, nor forsake thee, v.* 5. Moses had assured him of this (Deut. xxxi. 8), that, though he must now leave him, God never would: of this we may be sure, that *the Lord is with us while we are with him*. This promise here made to Joshua is applied to all believers. (3) That he should have victory over all the enemies of Israel (*v.* 5): *There shall not any man* that comes against **thee** *be able to stand before thee*. Note, There is no standing before those that have God on their side. *If he be for us, who can be against us*? (4) That he should himself have the dividing of this land among the people of Israel, *v.* 6. He should be of good courage, because of the bad character of the people whom he must cause to inherit that land. He knew well what a froward discontented people they were, and how unmanageable they had been in his predecessor's time.

6. The charge or command he gives to Joshua, which is,

(1) That he conform himself in every thing to the law of God, and make this his rule, *v.* 7, 8. God does, as it were, put the book of the law into Joshua's hand; And he is charged, [1] To *meditate therein day and night*. If ever any man's business might have excused him from meditation, and other acts of devotion, one would think Joshua's might at this time. It was a great trust that was lodged in his hands; the care of it was enough to fill him, if he had had ten souls, and yet he must find time and thoughts for meditation. [2] Not to let it depart out of his mouth; that is, all his orders to the people, must be consonant to the law of God; upon all occasions he must *speak*

JAMIESON, FAUSSET, BROWN

2-9. now therefore arise, go over this Jordan—Joshua's mission was that of a military leader. This passage records his call to begin the work, and the address contains a literal repetition of the promise made to Moses (Deut. 11: 24, 25; 31:6-8, 23).

3, 4. Every place that the sole of your foot shall tread upon, that have I given you—meaning, of course, not universal dominion, but only the territory comprised within the boundaries here specified (see on Deut. 19:8, 9). **all the land of the Hittites**—These occupied the southern extremities and were the dominant tribe of Canaan. Their superior power and the extent of their dominions are attested by the mention of them under the name of Khita, on the Assyrian inscriptions, and still more frequently on the Egyptian inscriptions of the 18th and 19th Dynasties. What life and encouragement must have been imparted to Joshua by the assurance that his people, who had been overwhelmed with fear of that gigantic race, were to possess "all the land of the Hittites"!

5-9. There shall not any man be able to stand before thee—Canaan was theirs by a divine grant; and the renewed confirmation of that grant to Joshua when about to lead the people into it, intimated not only a certain but an easy conquest. It is remarkable, however, that his courage and hope of victory were made to depend (see on Deut. 17:19) on his firm and inflexible adherence to the law of God, not only that regarding the extirpation of the Canaanites, but the whole divine code.

ADAM CLARKE

3. *The sole of your foot shall tread upon.* That is, the whole land occupied by the seven Canaanitish nations, and as far as the Euphrates on the east; for this was certainly the utmost of the grant now made to them; and all that was included in what is termed the Promised Land, the boundaries of which have already been defined. See Deut. xxxiv. 1-4, and see v. 4 below. It has been supposed that the words *Every place that the sole of your foot shall tread upon* were intended to express the ease with which they were to conquer the whole land, an instance of which occurs in the taking of Jericho. It was only their unfaithfulness to God that rendered the conquest in any case difficult.

4. *From the wilderness and this Lebanon.* The utmost of their limits should be from the desert of Arabia Petraea on the south to Lebanon on the north, and from the Euphrates on the east to the Mediterranean Sea on the west. The Israelites did not possess the full extent of this grant till the days of David. See 2 Sam. viii. 3, etc., and 2 Chron. ix. 26.

Land of the Hittites. These are generally reputed to have been the most hardy and warlike of all the Canaanitish nations; and as they occupied the mountainous countries on the south of the land of Canaan, it is natural to suppose that they would be the most difficult to subdue, and on this account, it is supposed, God particularly specifies these. But it is probable that under this one term all the other nations are included, as it is certain they are in other places under the term *Amorites.*

Great sea—the Mediterranean, called *great* in respect of the lakes in the land of Judea, such as the Sea of Galilee and the Dead Sea, which were comparatively small lakes; but the Hebrews gave the name of *sea, yam,* to every large collection of waters.

5. *Be able to stand before thee.* Because God shall be with you, therefore you shall be irresistible. This promise was most punctually and literally fulfilled.

8. *This book of the law shall not depart out of thy mouth.* Though there was a copy of the law laid up in the sanctuary, yet this was not

MATTHEW HENRY

according to this rule, Isa. viii. 20. There was no occasion to make new laws; but *that good thing which was committed to him*, he must carefully and faithfully keep, 2 Tim. i. 14. [3] He must *observe to do according to all this law*. Joshua was a man of great power and authority, yet he must himself be under command and do as he is bidden. No man's dignity or dominion, how great soever, sets him above the law of God. *First*, He must do what was written. *Secondly*, He must do according to what was written, exactly observing the law as his copy. *Thirdly*, He must do according to all that was written, without exception or reserve. *Fourthly*, He must observe the checks of conscience, the hints of providence, and all the advantages of opportunity. *Fifthly*, He must *not turn from it*, either in his own practice or in any act of government, for virtue is in the mean. *Sixthly*, He must be *strong and courageous*. And, *lastly*, he assures him that then he shall *do wisely* (as it is in the margin) and *make his way prosperous*, *v.* 7, 8.

(2) That he encourage himself herein with the promise and presence of God, and make these his stay (*v.* 6, 7, 9). Joshua had long since signalized his valour, in the war with Amalek, and in his dissent from the report of the evil spies. Joshua was humble not distrustful of God, but diffident of himself, and of his sufficiency for the work, and therefore God repeats this so often, "*Be strong and of a good courage; Have not I commanded thee?* [1] "I have commanded the work to be done, and therefore it shall be done." It will help very much to animate and embolden us if we keep our eye upon the divine warrant, and hear God saying, "*Have not I commanded thee?* I will therefore help thee, succeed thee, accept thee, reward thee."

Verses 10–13

Joshua, being settled in the government, immediately applies himself to further the work of God among the people over whom God had set him.

I. He issues out orders to the people to provide for a march. The officers of the people that commanded under Joshua in their respective tribes and families attended him for orders, which they were to transmit to the people. What could Joshua have done without officers ? We are required to be subject, not only to *the king as supreme, but to governors as to those that are sent by him*, 1 Pet. ii. 13, 14. By these officers, 1. Joshua gives public notice that they were *to pass over Jordan within three days*. Observe with what assurance Joshua says to the people, because God had said it to him, *You shall pass over Jordan, and shall possess* the land. We greatly honour the truth of God when we stagger not at the promise of God. 2. He gives them directions to prepare victuals, not to prepare transport vessels. He that bore them out of Egypt would in like manner bear them into Canaan, Exod. xix. 4. But those that were desirous to have other victuals besides the manna, which had not yet ceased, must prepare it, and have it ready against the time appointed. Perhaps, though the manna did not quite cease till they came into Canaan (*ch.* v. 12), yet since they had come *into a land inhabited* (Exod. xvi. 35), where they might be furnished in part with other provisions, it did not fall so plentifully. See Exod. xix. 10, 11.

II. He reminds the two tribes and a half of the obligations they were under to go over Jordan with their brethren, though they left their possessions and families on this side. It was an act of self-denial, and against the grain; therefore it was needful to produce the argeement which Moses had made with them (*v.* 13): *Remember the word which Moses commanded you*. Though Moses was dead, his commands and their promises were still in full force. He reminds them. 1, Of the advantages they had received in being first settled: "*The Lord your God hath given you rest*. He has given your minds rest; you are not as the rest of the tribes waiting the issue of the war first and then of the lot. He has also given your families rest, giving you this land, this good land." Note, When God by his providence has given us rest we ought to consider what service we may do to our brethren who are unsettled. When God had given David rest (2 Sam. vii. 1), see how restless he was till he had *found out a habitation* for the ark, Ps. cxxxii. 4, 5. 2. He reminds them of their agreement to help their brethren in the wars of Canaan till God had in like manner given them rest, *v.* 14, 15. This was, (1) Reasonable in itself. (2) It was enjoined them by Moses, the servant of the Lord; (3) It was the only expedient they had to save themselves from the guilt of a great sin in settling on that side Jordan, a sin which would one time or other find them out, Num. xxxii. 23. (4) It was the condition of the grant Moses had made them, of *the land*

JAMIESON, FAUSSET, BROWN

CHARLES H. SPURGEON:

Joshua was very highly favored in the matter of promises. The promises given him by God were broadly comprehensive and exceedingly encouraging. But Joshua was not therefore to say within himself, "These covenant engagements will surely be fulfilled, and I may therefore sit still and do nothing." On the contrary, because God had decreed that the land should be conquered, Joshua was to be diligent to lead the people onward to battle. He was not to use the promise as a couch upon which his indolence might luxuriate, but as a girdle wherewith to gird up his loins for future activity.

As a spur to energy, let us always regard the gracious promises of our God. We should sin against Him most ungratefully and detestably were we to say within ourselves, "God will not desert His people; therefore let us venture into sin"; and we are almost equally wicked if we whisper in our own minds, "God will assuredly fulfill His own decrees, and give the souls of His redeemed as a reward to His Son Jesus; therefore let us do nothing, and refrain altogether from zealous Christian service." This is not proper language for true children. This is the talk of the indolently ignorant, or of mere pretenders, who do but mock God while they pretend to reverence His decrees. By the oath, by the promise, by the covenant, and by the blood which seals it, we are exhorted continually to be at work for Christ, since we are saved in order that we may serve Him, in the power of the Holy Spirit, with heart, and soul, and strength.

—The Treasury of the Old Testament

10-18. Then Joshua commanded the officers of the people—These were the Shoterim (see on Exod. 5:6; Deut. 20:5). **11. command the people, saying, Prepare you victuals**—not manna, which, though it still fell, would not keep; but corn, sheep, and articles of food procurable in the conquered countries. **for within three days ye shall pass over this Jordan**—i.e., the third day according to *Hebrew* idiom)—the time allotted for getting ready before the encampment in Abel-Shittim broke up and they removed to the desert bank of the river where no victuals were available.

At the same time Joshua himself convened the two and a half tribes which had settled east of Jordan, to remind them of their promise (Num. 32:1-42) to assist their brethren in the conquest of western Canaan. Their readiness to redeem their pledge and the terms in which they answered the appeal of Joshua displayed to great advantage their patriotic and pious feelings at so interesting a crisis.

14. ye shall pass . . . armed—i.e., officered or marshalled under five leaders in the old and approved caravan order (see on Exod. 13:18). **all the mighty men of valour**—The words are not to be interpreted strictly as meaning the whole, but only the flower or choice of the fighting men (see on ch. 4:12, 13).

ADAM CLARKE

sufficient. Joshua must have a copy for himself, and he was to consult it incessantly, that his way might be made prosperous. If he kept God's word, God would keep him in body and soul; if he should observe to do according to that word, then God would cause all his way to be prosperous.

7. *Only be thou strong, and very courageous*. "Be strong therefore, and play the man to the uttermost." Though God had promised him that no man should be able to stand before him, yet it was on condition that he should use all his military skill, and avail himself to the uttermost of all the means, natural and providential, which God should place within his reach. God will not help them who refuse to help themselves.

10. *Commanded the officers. Shoterim*. These were different from the *shophetim*, who were judges among the people, and whose business it was to determine in all civil cases. The *shoterim* have been supposed to be subordinate officers, whose business it was to see the decisions of the *shophetim* carried into effect.

11. *Prepare you victuals. Tsedah*, such prey or provisions as they had taken from the conquered countries, such as corn, oxen, sheep, etc.; for the word signifies "prey," or what is taken by hunting. This was necessary, as they were about to undergo considerable fatigue in marching, and in making preparations for the passage of the Jordan; for although the manna had not ceased to fall, yet such other provisions as are mentioned above were necessary on this occasion. *For within three days he shall pass*. The text is supposed to mean, "Prepare victuals for three days' march," for "on the third day after your decampment from Shittim ye shall pass over this Jordan."

13. *Remember the word*. He puts the Reubenites, etc., in remembrance of the agreement they had made with Moses (see Num. xxxii. 20) when he granted them their portion on the east side of Jordan.

14. *Your wives, your little ones*. And with these it appears, from Num. xxxii. 17, were left behind 70,580 effective men to guard them and their property, only 40,000 having passed over Jordan to assist the nine tribes and a half to conquer the land. See chap. iv. 13, *Armed, chamushim*, "by fives"; in several lines, five in

MATTHEW HENRY

of their possession, as it is here called (*v.* 15). (5) They themselves had covenanted and agreed thereunto (Num. xxxii. 25): *Thy servants will do as my Lord commandeth.*

Verses 16–18

This answer was given by the *officers of all the people* (*v.* 10), as their representatives.

I. They promise him obedience (*v.* 16), as subjects to their prince, as soldiers to their general. Thus the people of Israel here engage themselves to Joshua: "*All that thou commandest us we will readily do*, without murmuring or disputing." We must thus swear allegiance to our Lord Jesus, as the captain of our salvation, and bind ourselves to do what he commands us by his word, and to go where he sends us by his providence. The people had no reason to boast of their obedience to Moses; he had found them a stiff-necked people, Deut. ix. 13. But they meant that they would be as observant of Joshua as they should have been of Moses. Note, We must not so magnify those that are gone as to be wanting in the honour and duty we owe to those that succeed them. Obedience for conscience's sake will continue, though Providence change the hands by which it rules and acts.

II. They pray for the presence of God with him (*v.* 17): "*Only the Lord thy God be with thee*, to bless and prosper thee, and give thee success, *as he was with Moses*." The best thing we can ask of God for our magistrates is that they may have the presence of God with them. Those that we have reason to think have favour from God should have honour and respect from us. Some understand it as a limitation of their obedience: "We will obey only as far as we perceive the Lord is with thee, but no further. While thou keepest close to God we will keep close to thee; hitherto shall our obedience come, but no further."

III. They pass an act to make it death for any Israelite to disobey Joshua's orders, or *rebel against his commandments*, *v.* 18. There was a special reason for the making of this law now that they were entering upon the wars of Canaan; for in times of war the severity of military discipline is more necessary than at other times.

IV. It very much heartens those that lead in a good work to see those that follow with a good will. Joshua, though of approved valour, did not take it as an affront, but as a great kindness, for the people to bid him be strong and of a good courage.

JAMIESON, FAUSSET, BROWN

JOSEPH PARKER:

A charge was delivered to the people, interpreting the divine will, and promising great blessedness, possession, and rest. The people having heard the appeal answered Joshua saying, "All that thou commandest us we will do, and whithersoever thou sendest us, we will go." We see men occasionally at their best, and then the revelation of human nature is not without enchantment and great comfortableness. Men like to speak in crowds, to multiply their voices by a thousand and ten thousand; and then they imagine that they are revealing the strength and enjoying the confidence of what is termed unanimity. It is a beautiful thing to see forty thousand men all intent upon one purpose, and to hear them uttering one cry, and to know that their utterance is expressive of an obedient spirit. This is the answer which ought to have been given, and which ought now to be given to every divine appeal. We should answer love by love; we should answer music by music; when heaven descends to earth with some unusual blessing, earth should become almost heaven in its grateful appreciation and response. We see this sometimes in the sanctuary. A sublime revelation of divine care, providence, grace is made, and hearts are melted into one, and the final hymn becomes a pledge, a solemn vow, a great musical consecration of the heart. It is beautiful now and again to see what ought to be—occasionally to see the ideal, now and again to hear a common sentiment uttered by an inspired heart—surely such are sights and sounds which might do us good evermore!

—The People's Bible

ADAM CLARKE

front, probably the usual method of marching; but it seems to signify "arrayed, equipped, accoutred, well-armed," and ready for battle. See the note on Exod. xiii. 18.

16. *All that thou commandest us we will do.* Here they acknowledge the divine mission of Joshua, as they had done that of Moses, and consequently promise to follow his directions in all things.

17. *Only the Lord thy God be with thee.* Provided God be with thee, as He was with Moses, we will implicitly obey thee. The words however may mean no more than an earnest prayer for Joshua's prosperity: May God be with thee, as He was with Moses!

18. *He shall be put to death.* This was martial law; he who disobeyed the command of his general should be put to death. To this the people agreed, and it was essentially necessary in order that proper discipline should be kept up in this great army. By insubordination their fathers had suffered much in the wilderness; they rejected the authority of Moses, mutinied, and made themselves a leader to conduct them back to Egypt (see Num. xiv. 4). And Joshua himself, for attempting to encourage them against their fears, was near being stoned to death. It was necessary, therefore, that they should give him the most positive assurance that they would not act as their fathers had done.

MATTHEW HENRY — CHAPTER 2

Verses 1–7

In these verses we have,

I. The prudence of Joshua, in sending spies to observe this important pass, which was likely to be disputed at the entrance of Israel into Canaan (*v.* 1). *Go view the land, even Jericho.* Moses had sent spies (Num. xiii.); Joshua himself was one of them. Joshua now sent spies, not, as the former were sent, to survey the whole land, but Jericho only. Joshua was particularly careful to take the first step well and not to stumble at the threshold. Observe, 1. Great men must see with other people's eyes, which makes it very necessary that they be cautious in the choice of those they employ. 2. Faith in God's promise ought not to supersede but encourage our diligence in the use of proper means. We do not trust God, but tempt him, if our expectations slacken our endeavours. 3. See how ready these men were to go upon this hazardous enterprise. In obedience to Joshua their general, in zeal for the service of the camp, and in dependence upon the power of God.

II. The providence of God directing the spies to the house of Rahab. How they got over Jordan, we are not told; but into Jericho they came, which was about seven or eight miles from the river, and there seeking for a convenient inn were directed to the house of Rahab, here called a *harlot*, a woman that had formerly been of ill fame, the reproach of which stuck to her name, though of late she had repented and reformed. Rahab the harlot is so called in the New Testament, where both her faith and her good works are praised, to teach us, 1. That the greatness of sin is no bar to pardoning mercy if it be truly repented of in time. We read of publicans and harlots entering into the kingdom of the Messiah, and being welcomed to all the privileges of that kingdom, Matt. xxi. 31. 2. That there are many who before their conversion were very wicked and vile, and yet afterwards come to great eminence in faith and holiness. 3. Even those that through grace have repented of the sins of their youth must expect to bear the reproach of them. God's Israel, for aught that appears, had but one well-wisher in all Jericho,

JAMIESON, FAUSSET, BROWN — CHAPTER 2

VSS. 1-7. RAHAB RECEIVES AND CONCEALS THE TWO SPIES. **1. Joshua . . . sent . . . two men to spy secretly**—Faith is manifested by an active, persevering use of means (Jas. 2:22); and accordingly Joshua, while confident in the accomplishment of the divine promise (ch. 1:3), adopted every precaution which a skilful general could think of to render his first attempt in the invasion of Canaan successful. Two spies were despatched to reconnoitre the country, particularly in the neighborhood of Jericho; for in the prospect of investing that place, it was desirable to obtain full information as to its site, its approaches, the character, and resources of its inhabitants. This mission required the strictest privacy, and it seems to have been studiously concealed from the knowledge of the Israelites themselves, lest any unfavorable or exaggerated report, publicly circulated, might have dispirited the people, as that of the spies did in the days of Moses. **Jericho**—Some derive this name from a word signifying *"new moon,"* in reference to the crescent-like plain in which it stood, formed by an amphitheater of hills; others from a word signifying *"its scent,"* on account of the fragrance of the balsam and palm trees in which it was embosomed. Its site was long supposed to be represented by the small mud-walled hamlet Er-Riha; but recent researches have fixed on a spot about half an hour's journey westward, where large ruins exist about six or eight miles distant from the Jordan. It was for that age a strongly fortified town, the key of the eastern pass through the deep ravine, now called Wady-Kelt, into the interior of Palestine. **they . . . came into an harlot's house**—Many expositors, desirous of removing the stigma of this name from an ancestress of the Saviour (Matt. 1:5), have called her a hostess or tavern-keeper. But Scriptural usage (Lev. 21:7-14; Deut. 23:18; Judg. 11:1; I Kings 3:16), the authority of the Septuagint, followed by the apostles (Heb. 11:31; Jas. 2:25), and the immemorial style of Eastern khans, which are never kept by women, establish the propriety of the term employed in our

ADAM CLARKE — CHAPTER 2

1. *Joshua . . . sent . . . two men to spy secretly.* It is very likely that these spies had been sent out soon after the death of Moses, and therefore our marginal reading, "had sent," is to be preferred. *Secretly*—It is very probable also that these were confidential persons, and that the transaction was between them and him alone. As they were to pass over the Jordan opposite to Jericho, it was necessary that they should have possession of this city, that in case of any reverses they might have no enemies in their rear.

An harlot's house. Harlots and innkeepers seem to have been called by the same name, as no doubt many who followed this mode of life, from their exposed situation, were not the most correct in their morals. I am fully satisfied that the term *zonah* in the text, which we translate *harlot*, should be rendered "tavern or innkeeper," or "hostess." The spies who were sent out on this occasion were undoubtedly the most confidential persons that Joshua had in his host;

MATTHEW HENRY

and that was Rahab a harlot. God has often served his own purposes and his church's interests by men of indifferent morals. Had these scouts gone to any other house than this they would certainly have been betrayed. But God knew where they had a friend, though they did not, and directed them thither. Those that faithfully acknowledge God in their ways he will *guide with his eye*. See Jer. xxxvi. 19, 26.

III. The piety of Rahab in receiving and protecting these Israelites. Rahab showed her guests more than common civility; it was *by faith* that she received those with peace against whom her king and country had denounced war, Heb. xi. 31. 1. She bade them welcome to her house; they lodged there, though she knew both whence they came and what their business was. 2. She hid them upon the roof of the house, which was flat, and covered them with stalks of flax (*v.* 6). By these stalks of flax, which she herself had lain in order upon the roof to dry in the sun, in order to the beating of it and making it ready for the wheel, it appears she had one of the good characters of the virtuous woman, Prov. xxxi. 13. 3. When she was examined concerning them, she denied they were in her house. Nor marvel that the king of Jericho sent to enquire after them (*v.* 2, 3). Rahab not only disowned that she knew them, but, that no further search might be made for them in the city, told the pursuers they had gone away again, and in all probability might be overtaken, *v.* 4, 5. Now, (1) We are sure this was a good work: it is canonized by the apostle (James ii. 25), where she is said to be *justified by works*, and this is specified, that *she received the messengers, and sent them out another way*, and she did it by faith, above the fear of man, even of the wrath of the king. She believed, upon the report she had heard of the wonders wrought for Israel, that their God was the only true God, and that therefore their declared design upon Canaan would undoubtedly take effect. Note, Those that by faith take the Lord for their God take his people for their people, and cast in their lot among them. Those that have God for their refuge must shelter his people when there is occasion. *Let my outcasts dwell with thee*, Isa. xvi. 3, 4. And we must be glad of an opportunity of testifying the sincerity and zeal of our love to God by hazardous services to his church and kingdom among men. But, (2) There is that in it which it is not easy to justify, [1] It is plain that she betrayed her country by harbouring the enemies of it. That which justifies her in this is that *she knew the Lord had given Israel this land* (*v.* 9), knew it by the incontestable miracles God had wrought for them, which confirmed that grant; and her obligations to God were higher than her obligations to any other. If she knew *God had given them* this land, it would have been a sin to join with those that hindered them from possessing it. [2] It is plain that she deceived the officers that examined her with an untruth. What shall we say to this? If she had either told the truth or been silent, she would have betrayed the spies, and it does not appear that she had any other way of concealing them than by this ironical direction to the officers to pursue them another way. This case was altogether extraordinary, and therefore cannot be drawn into a precedent. Yet divines generally conceive that it was a sin, which however admitted of this extenuation, that being a Canaanite she was not better taught the evil of lying. However it was in this case, we are sure it is our duty to speak every man the truth to his neighbour, to dread and detest lying, and never to *do evil, that good may come of it*, Rom. iii. 8. But God accepts what is sincerely and honestly intended, though there be a mixture of frailty and folly in it, and is not extreme to mark what we do amiss.

Verses 8–21

The matter is here settled between Rahab and the spies respecting the service she was now to do for them, and the favour they were afterwards to show to her.

I. Having got clear of the officers, she comes up to them to the *roof of the house* where they lay hid. 1. She lets them know that the report of the great things God had done for them had come to Jericho (*v.* 10), to the amazement of everybody. 2. She tells them what impressions the tidings of these things had made upon the Canaanites: Your *terror has fallen upon us* (*v.* 9); *our hearts did melt*, *v.* 11. If she kept a public house, this would give her an opportunity of understanding the sense of various companies and of travellers from other parts of the country. It would put courage into the most cowardly Israelite to hear how their enemies were dispirited, and it was easy to conclude that those who now fainted before them would infallibly fall before them, it

JAMIESON, FAUSSET, BROWN

version. Her house was probably recommended to the spies by the convenience of its situation, without any knowledge of the character of the inmates. But a divine influence directed them in the choice of that lodging-place.

2, 3. it was told the king—by the sentinels who at such a time of threatened invasion would be posted on the eastern frontier and whose duty required them to make a strict report to headquarters of the arrival of all strangers. **4-6. the woman took the two men, and hid them**—lit., "him," i.e., each of them in separate places, of course previous to the appearance of the royal messengers and in anticipation of a speedy search after her guests. According to Eastern manners, which pay an almost superstitious respect to a woman's apartment, the royal messengers did not demand admittance to search but asked her to bring the foreigners out. **6. she had brought them up to the roof of the house, and hid them with the stalks of flax**—Flax, with other vegetable productions, is at a certain season spread out on the flat roofs of Eastern houses to be dried in the sun; and, after lying awhile, it is piled up in numerous little stacks, which, from the luxuriant growth of the flax, rise to a height of three or four feet. Behind some of these stacks Rahab concealed the spies. **5. the time of shutting the gates**—The gates of all Oriental cities are closed at sunset, after which there is no possibility either of admission or egress. **the men went out**—This was a palpable deception. But, as lying is a common vice among heathen people, Rahab was probably unconscious of its moral guilt, especially as she resorted to it as a means for screening her guests; and she might deem herself bound to do it by the laws of Eastern hospitality, which make it a point of honor to preserve the greatest enemy, if he has once eaten one's salt. Judged by the divine law, her answer was a sinful expedient; but her infirmity being united with faith, she was graciously pardoned and her service accepted (Jas. 2:25). **7. the men pursued after them the way to Jordan unto the fords**—That river is crossed at several well-known fords. The first and second immediately below the sea of Galilee; the third and fourth immediately above and below the pilgrims' bathing-place, opposite Jericho. **as soon as they which pursued after them were gone, they shut the gate**—This precaution was to ensure the capture of the spies, should they have been lurking in the city.

8-21. The Covenant between Her and Them. **8-13. she came up unto them upon the roof and said**—Rahab's dialogue is full of interest, as showing the universal panic and consternation of the Canaanites on the one hand (ch. 24:11; Deut. 2:25), and her strong convictions on the other, founded on a knowledge of the divine promise, and the stupendous miracles that had opened the way of the Israelites to the confines of the promised land. She was convinced of the supremacy of Jehovah, and her earnest stipulations for the preservation of her relatives amid the perils of the approaching invasion, attest the sincerity and strength of her faith.

ADAM CLARKE

they went on an errand of the most weighty importance, and which involved the greatest consequences. The risk they ran of losing their lives in this enterprise was extreme. Is it therefore likely that persons who could not escape apprehension and death, without the miraculous interference of God, should in despite of that law go into a place where they might expect, not the blessing, but the curse, of God? Is it not therefore more likely that they went rather to an inn to lodge than to a brothel? But what completes in my judgment the evidence on this point is that this very Rahab, whom we call a harlot, was actually married to Salmon, a Jewish prince, see Matt. i. 5. And is it probable that a prince of Judah would have taken to wife such a person as our text represents Rahab to be?

3. *The king of Jericho sent unto Rahab.* This appears to be a proof of the preceding opinion. Had she been a prostitute or a person of ill fame he could at once have sent officers to seize the persons lodged with her as vagabonds; but if she kept a house of entertainment, the persons under her roof were sacred, according to the universal custom of the Asiatics, and could not be molested on any trifling grounds.

4. *And hid them.* Probably she secreted them for the time being in some private corner, till she had the opportunity of concealing them on the housetop in the manner mentioned v. 6

5. *When it was dark.* So it appears that it was after night that the king of Jericho sent to Rahab, ordering her to produce the persons who lodged with her. The season itself was friendly to the whole plot; had these transactions taken place in daylight, it is scarcely possible that the spies could have escaped. But this is no excuse for the woman's prevarication; for God could have saved His messengers independently of her falsity. God never says to any, Do evil that good may come of it.

6. *Hid them with the stalks of flax.* As this was about the season, viz., the end of March or the beginning of April, in which the flax is ripe in that country, consequently Rahab's flax might have been recently pulled, and was now drying on the roof of her house. *Upon the roof.* We have already seen that all the houses in the east were made flat-roofed; for which a law is given Deut. xxii. 8. On these flat roofs the Asiatics to this day walk, converse, and oftentimes even sleep and pass the night.

9. *I know that the Lord hath given you the land.* It is likely she had this only from conjecture, having heard of their successes against the Amorites, their prodigious numbers, and seeing the state of terror and dismay to which the inhabitants of her own land were reduced.

MATTHEW HENRY

would be an earnest of the accomplishment of all the other promises God had made to them. Let not God's Israel be afraid of their most powerful enemies. 3. She hereupon makes profession of her faith in God and his promise. (1) She believes God's power and dominion over all the world (*v.* 11): "Jehovah your God, whom you worship and call upon, is so far above all gods that he is the only true God; for *he is God in heaven above and in earth beneath,* and is served by all the hosts of both." (2) She believes his promise to his people Israel (*v.* 9): *I know that the Lord hath given you the land.* The most powerful means of conviction will not of themselves attain the end without divine grace, and by that grace Rahab the harlot, who had only heard of the wonders God had wrought, speaks with more assurance of the truth of the promise made to the fathers than all the elders of Israel had done who were eye-witnesses of those wonders, many of whom perished through unbelief of this promise.

II. She engaged them to take her and her relations under their protection, *v.* 12, 13. Now, 1. It was an evidence of the sincerity and strength of her faith. Those who truly believe the divine revelation concerning the ruin of sinners, and the grant of the heavenly land to God's Israel, will give diligence to flee from the wrath to come, and to lay hold on eternal life, by joining themselves to God and to his people. 2. The provision she made for the safety of her relations, as well as for her own, is a laudable instance of natural affection, and an intimation to us to do all we can for the salvation of the souls of those that are dear to us. 3. Her request that they would swear unto her by Jehovah is an instance of her acquaintance with the only true God, and her faith in him. 4. Her petition is very just and reasonable, that since she had protected them, they should protect her. Note, Those that show mercy may expect to find mercy. Rahab was afterwards advanced to be a princess in Israel, the wife of Salmon, and one of the ancestors of Christ, Matt. i. 5.

III. They solemnly engaged for her preservation in the common destruction (*v.* 14): "*Our life for yours.*" She had pawned her life for theirs, and now they in requital pawn their lives for hers, and (as public persons) with them they pawn the public faith and the credit of their nation. The law of gratitude is one of the laws of nature. Now observe here, 1. The promises they made her. In general, "*We will deal kindly and truly with thee, v.* 14. We will not only be kind in promising now, but kind in outdoing thy demands and expectations." 2. The provisos and limitations of their promises. Though they were in haste, yet we find them very cautious in settling this agreement, not to bind themselves to more than was fit for them to perform. Note, Covenants must be made with care. Those that will be conscientious in keeping their promises will be cautious in making them. Their promise is here accompanied with three provisos. They will protect Rahab, and all her relations always, provided, (1) That she tie the scarlet cord with which she was now about to let them down in the window of her house, *v.* 18. That no soldier might offer any violence to the house that was thus distinguished. This was like the blood sprinkled upon the door-post, which secured the first-born from the destroying angel. The same cord that she made use of for the preservation of these Israelites was to be made use of for her preservation. What we serve and honour God with we may expect he will bless and make comfortable to us. (2) That she should have all those whose safety she had desired in the house with her and keep them there, and that, at the time of taking the town, none of them should dare to stir out of doors, *v.* 18, 19. It was a *reasonable* proviso that, since they were saved purely for Rahab's sake, her house should have the honour of being their castle. It was likewise a *significant* proviso, intimating to us that those who are added to the church that they may be saved must keep close to the society of the faithful. (3) That she should keep counsel (*v.* 14, 20): *If thou utter this our business,* that is, "If thou betray us when we are gone, we will be clear of thy oath." Those are unworthy of *the secret of the Lord* that know not how to keep it to themselves when there is occasion.

IV. She then took effectual care to secure her new friends, and *sent them out another way,* James ii. 25 (*v.* 15), the situation of her house befriending them herein: thus Paul made his escape out of Damascus, 2 Cor. xi. 33. She also directed them which way to go for their own safety, *v.* 16. She directs them to leave the high road, and abscond in the mountains till the pursuers returned. Those that are in the way of God may expect that Providence will protect them, but this will not excuse them from taking all prudent methods for their own safety. Providence

JAMIESON, FAUSSET, BROWN

F. B. MEYER:

A heathen woman's act of faith. To "view the land" was a hazardous undertaking. The physiognomy of the Hebrews would certainly betray them, and it did. The sacred writer does not commend Rahab's mode of life, nor her lies. Her morality was faulty enough, but beneath it, slowly smoldering, was a spark of pure love and faith, and this would consume the rubbish and burn clear (Heb. 11:31).

The stalks of flax were probably laid out on the roof to dry. She believed, on the ground of the wonders wrought in Egypt, that Jehovah was the true God, and that his word was sure. Her faith proved itself in her works—in her efforts to save others, and in the confidence with which she rested behind her scarlet cord. That she was sneered at and persecuted is quite likely, but she persisted and became an ancestress of Christ (Matt. 1:5). How faith greatens the soul (James 2:25)!—*Bible Commentary*

14. the men answered, Our life for yours, if ye utter not this our business—This was a solemn pledge—a virtual oath, though the name of God is not mentioned; and the words "if ye utter not this our business," were added, not as a condition of their fidelity, but as necessary for her safety, which might be endangered if the private agreement was divulged.

16-21. she said—rather "she had said," for what follows must have been part of the previous conversation. **Get you to the mountain**—A range of white limestone hills extends on the north, called Quarantania (now Jebel-karantu), rising to a height of from 1200 to 1500 feet, and the sides of which are perforated with caves. Some one peak adjoining was familiarly known to the inhabitants as "the mountain." The prudence and propriety of the advice to flee in that direction rather than to the ford, were made apparent by the sequel. **21. she bound the scarlet line in the window**—probably soon after the departure of the spies. It was not formed, as some suppose, into network, as a lattice, but simply to hang down the wall. Its red color made it conspicuous, and it was thus a sign and pledge of safety to Rahab's house, as the bloody mark on the lintels of the houses of the Israelites in Egypt to that people.

15. her house was upon the town wall—In many Oriental cities houses are built on the walls with overhanging windows; in others the town wall forms the back wall of the house, so that the window opens into the country. Rahab's was probably of this latter description, and the cord or rope sufficiently strong to bear the weight of a man.

ADAM CLARKE

11. *He is God in heaven above, and in earth beneath.* This confession of the true God is amazingly full, and argues considerable light and information, as if she had said, "I know your God to be omnipotent and omnipresent"; and in consequence of this faith she hid the spies, and risked her own life in doing it. But how had she this clear knowledge of the divine nature? Possibly she received this instruction from the spies, with whom she appears to have had a good deal of conversation; or she had it from a supernatural influence of God upon her own soul.

12. *Swear unto me by the Lord.* This is a further proof that this woman had received considerable instruction in the Jewish faith; she acknowledged the true God by His essential character Jehovah, and knew that an oath in His name was the deepest and most solemn obligation under which a Jew could possibly come. Does not this also refer to the command of God, "Thou shalt fear the Lord, and shalt swear by his name"? See the note on Deut. vi. 13.

13. *Deliver our lives from death.* She had learned, either from the spies or otherwise, that all the inhabitants of the land were doomed to destruction, and therefore she obliges them to enter into a covenant with her for the preservation of herself and her household.

14. *Our life for yours.* "May our life be destroyed if we suffer yours to be injured!"

15. *Then she let them down by a cord.* The natural place of this verse is after the first clause of v. 21; for it is certain that she did not let them down in the basket till all those circumstances marked from vv. 16-20 inclusive had taken place. *She dwelt upon the wall.* That is, either the wall of the city made a part of her house or her house was built close to the wall, so that the top or battlements of it were above the wall, with a window that looked out to the country. As the city gates were now shut, there was no way for the spies to escape but through this window; and in order for them to do this she let them down through the window in a basket suspended by a cord, till they reached the ground on the outside of the wall.

16. *Hide yourselves there three days.* They were to travel by night, and hide themselves in the daytime; otherwise they might have been discovered by the pursuers who were in search of them.

18. *This line of scarlet thread.* Probably this may mean "this piece of scarlet cloth," or "this cloth [made] of scarlet thread." When the Israelites took the city, this piece of red cloth seems to have been hung out of the window by way of flag; and this was the sign on which she and the spies had agreed.

20. *If thou utter this our business.* It was prudent to make her life depend on her secrecy; had it been otherwise she might have been tempted to give information, not only concerning the spies, but concerning the designs of the Israelites.

MATTHEW HENRY

must be trusted, but not tempted.

Verses 22-24

We have here the safe return of the spies Joshua had sent, and the great encouragement they brought with them to Israel to proceed in their descent upon Canaan. They might have told them what they had observed of the height and strength of the walls of Jericho, but they were of another spirit, and, depending themselves upon the divine promise, they animated Joshua likewise. 1. Their return in safety was itself an encouragement to Joshua, and a token for good. That they had come back in peace, was such an instance of God's great care concerning them for Israel's sake as might assure the people of the divine guidance and care. He that so wonderfully protected their scouts would preserve their men of war. 2. The report they brought was much more encouraging (*v.* 24): "*All the inhabitants of the country*, though resolved to stand it out, yet *do faint because of us*, they have neither wisdom to yield nor courage to fight," whence they conclude, "*Truly the Lord has delivered into our hands all the land.*" Sinners' frights are sometimes sure presages of their fall. If we resist our spiritual enemies they will flee before us.

CHAPTER 3

Verses 1-6

Rahab, in mentioning to the spies the *drying up of the Red Sea* (*ch.* ii. 10), intimates that those on that side the water expected that Jordan, that great defence of their country, would in like manner give way to them. God often *did things for them which they looked not for*, Isa. lxiv. 3. Now here we are told,

I. That they *came to Jordan and lodged there*, *v.* 1. Though they were not yet told how they should pass the river, they went forward in faith, having been told (*ch.* i. 11) that they should pass it. Let us proceed as far as we can, and depend on divine sufficiency. In this march Joshua led them, and particular notice is taken of his early rising (*ch.* vi. 12; vii. 16; viii. 10), which intimates how little he loved his ease. Those that would bring great things to pass must rise early.

II. That the people were directed to follow the ark. 1. They might depend upon the ark to lead them; that is, upon God himself, of whose presence the ark was an instituted sign and token. It is called here the *ark of the covenant of the Lord their God.* What greater encouragement could they have than this, that the Lord was their God, a God in covenant with them? Here was the *ark of the covenant.* Formerly the ark was carried in the midst of the camp, but now it went before them to *search out a resting-place* for them (Num. x. 33), and, as it were, to give them livery and seisin of the promised land, and put them in possession of it. In the ark the tables of the law were, and over it the mercy-seat; for the divine law and grace reigning in the heart are the surest pledges of God's presence and favour.

2. They might depend upon the priests and Levites, appointed to carry the ark before them. The work of ministers is to hold forth the word of life, and to take care of the administration of those ordinances which are the tokens of God's presence and the instruments of his power and grace.

3. The people must follow the ark: *Remove from your place and go after it*, (1) Wherever God's ordinances are, there we must be; if they flit, we must remove and go after them. (2) Thus must we walk after the rule of the word and the direction of the Spirit in everything, so shall *peace be upon us*, as it now was upon the Israel of God. They must follow the priests as far as they carried the ark, but no further; so we must follow our ministers only as they follow Christ.

4. In following the ark, they must *keep their distance*, *v.* 4. They must none of them come within a thousand yards of the ark. (1) They must thus express reverent regard lest its familiarity with them should breed contempt. This charge was agreeable to that dispensation of darkness, bondage, and terror: but we now through Christ have access with boldness. (2) The ark was able to protect itself, and needed not to be guarded by the men of war, but was itself a guard to them. (3) Thus it was the better seen by those that were to be led by it: *That you may know the way by which you must go.* They would all have the satisfaction of seeing it, and would be animated by the sight. *For you have not passed this way heretofore.* It was an untrodden path, especially through Jordan. Our way through the *valley of the shadow of death* is a way we have not gone before. But, if we have the assurance of God's presence, we need

JAMIESON, FAUSSET, BROWN

CHAPTER 3

VSS. 1-6. JOSHUA COMES TO JORDAN. **1. Joshua rose early in the morning**—On the day following that on which the spies had returned with their encouraging report, the camp was broken up in "Shittim" (the acacia groves), and removed to the eastern bank of the Jordan. The duration of their stay is indicated (vs. 2), being, according to *Hebrew* reckoning, only one entire day, including the evening of arrival and the morning of the passage; and such a time would be absolutely necessary for so motley an assemblage of men, women, and children, with all their gear and cattle to make ready for going into an enemy's country.

2-4. the officers went through the host; And they commanded the people—The instructions given at this time and in this place were different from those described (ch. 1:11). **When ye see the ark . . . , and the priests of the Levites bearing it . . .**—The usual position of the ark, when at rest, was in the center of the camp; and, during a march, in the middle of the procession. On this occasion it was to occupy the van, and be borne, not by the Kohathite Levites, but the priests, as on all solemn and extraordinary occasions (cf. Num. 4:15; ch. 6:6; I Kings 8:3-6). **then ye shall . . . go after it. Yet there shall be a space between you and it**—These instructions refer exclusively to the advance into the river. The distance which the people were to keep in the rear of the ark was nearly a mile. Had they crowded too near the ark, the view would have been intercepted, and this intervening space, therefore, was ordered, that the chest containing the sacred symbols might be distinctly visible to all parts of the camp, and be recognized as their guide in the untrodden way.

ADAM CLARKE

23. *So the two men returned.* Having concealed themselves in the mountains that night, all the next day, and the night ensuing, on the third day they returned to Joshua.

24. *Truly the Lord hath delivered into our hands all the land.* How different was this report from that brought by the spies on a former occasion! They found that all the inhabitants of the land were panic-struck. The people had heard of the great exploits of the Israelites on the other side of Jordan; and as they had destroyed the potent kings of the Amorites, they took it for granted that nothing could stand before them. This information was necessary to Joshua to guide him in forming the plan of his campaign.

CHAPTER 3

1. *Joshua rose early.* From Shittim, where they had lately been encamped, to Jordan, was about sixty stadia, according to Josephus; that is, about eight English miles.

2. *After three days.* These three days are probably to be thus understood: As soon as Joshua took the command of the army, he sent the spies to ascertain the state of Jericho; as we have seen chap. i. 12. They returned at the end of three days, or rather on the third day, and made their report. It was at this time, immediately on the return of the spies, that he made the proclamation mentioned here; in consequence of which the people immediately struck their tents, and marched forward to Jordan.

4. *About two thousand cubits.* This distance they were to keep, (1) for the greater respect, because the presence of the ark was the symbol and pledge of the divine presence; (2) that the ark, which was to be their pilot over these waters, might be the more conspicuous, which it could not have been had the people crowded upon it.

MATTHEW HENRY

not fear.

III. They were commanded to sanctify themselves, for *to-morrow the Lord will do wonders among you*, *v.* 5. Joshua could tell beforehand what God would do, and when. See what preparation we must make to receive the discoveries of God's glory and the communications of his grace: we must sanctify ourselves; we must separate ourselves from all other cares, devote ourselves to God's honour, and *cleanse ourselves from all filthiness of flesh and spirit*.

IV. The priests were ordered to take up the ark and carry it *before the people*, *v.* 6. It was the Levites' work ordinarily to carry the ark, Num. iv. 15. And now we may suppose that prayer of Moses used, when the ark set forward (Num. x. 35), *Rise up, Lord, and let thy enemies be scattered.* Magistrates are here instructed to stir up ministers to their work. Ministers must likewise learn to go before in the way of God. They must expect to be most struck at, but they *know whom they have trusted*.

Verses 7–13

God honours Joshua and Joshua honours God. Thus those that honour God he will honour.

I. *v.* 7, 8. 1. It was a great honour God did him that he spoke to him, as he had done to Moses from off the mercy-seat. 2. That he designed to *magnify him in the sight of all Israel*. He had told him before that he would be with him (*ch.* i. 5), but now all Israel shall see it. Those are truly great with whom God is and whom he employs and owns in his service. Pious magistrates are to be highly honoured and esteemed as public blessings, and the more we see of God with them the more we should honour them. By the dividing of Jordan, they shall be convinced that God is in like manner with Joshua in bringing them into Canaan. It was at the banks of Jordan that God began to magnify Joshua, and at the same place he began to magnify our Lord Jesus as Mediator; for John was baptizing at Bethabara, *the house of passage*, and there it was that when our Saviour was baptized it was proclaimed, *This is my beloved Son.* 3. That by him he gave orders to the priests themselves, to stand still at the brink of Jordan while the waters part, *at the presence of the Lord*, Ps. cxiv. 5, 7. God could have divided the river without the priests, but they could not without him.

II. Joshua speaks to the people, and therein honours God.

1. He had commanded them to sanctify themselves, and therefore calls them to *hear the word of God*, for that is the ordinary means of sanctification, John xvii. 17.

2. He now tells them, at length, by what way they should pass over Jordan, by the stopping of its streams (*v.* 13): *The waters of Jordan shall be cut off.* The dividing of the Red Sea is here repeated, to show that God has the same power to finish the salvation of his people that he had to begin it, and that *the word of the Lord* was as truly with Joshua as it was with Moses. The God whom they worshipped was the same God that made the world and it was the same power that was engaged and employed for them.

3. The people having been directed before to follow the ark are here told that it should *pass before them into Jordan*, *v.* 11. Observe, (1) The ark of the covenant must be their guide. Divine grace under the Mosaic dispensation was wrapt up as in a cloud and covered with a veil, while by Christ, our Joshua, it is revealed in the ark of the covenant unveiled. (2) It is called *the ark of the covenant of the Lord of all the earth.* "It is your honour and happiness to have him in covenant with you: if he be yours, all the creatures are at your service, and when he pleases shall be employed for you." (3) They are told that the ark should *pass before them into Jordan.* They might safely venture, even into Jordan itself, if the ark of the covenant led them. Isa. xliii. 2, *When thou passest through the waters I will be with thee, and through the rivers they shall not overflow thee.*

4. From what God was now about to do for them he infers an assurance of what he would yet further do. The dividing of Jordan was intended to be to them, (1) A sure token of God's presence with them. (2) A sure pledge of the conquest of Canaan. If the living God is among you, *expelling he will expel* (so the Hebrew phrase is) *from before you the Canaanites.* The forcing of the lines was a certain presage of the ruin of all their hosts. This assurance which Joshua here gives them was so well grounded that it would enable one Israelite to chase a thousand Canaanites. Note, God's glorious appearances for his church and people ought to be improved by us for the encouragement of our faith and hope for the

JAMIESON, FAUSSET, BROWN

5. Joshua said unto the people—rather "had said," for as he speaks of "to-morrow," the address must have been made previous to the day of crossing, and the sanctification was in all probability the same as Moses had commanded before the giving of the law, consisting of an outward cleansing (Exod. 19: 10-15) preparatory to that serious and devout state of mind with which so great a manifestation should be witnessed. **6. Joshua spake unto the priests**—This order to the priests would be given privately, and involving as it did an important change in the established order of march, it must be considered as announced in the name and by the authority of God. Moreover, as soon as the priests stepped into the waters of Jordan, they were to stand still. The ark was to accomplish what had been done by the rod of Moses.

7, 8. THE LORD ENCOURAGES JOSHUA. **7, 8. the Lord said to Joshua, This day will I . . . magnify thee in the sight of all Israel**—Joshua had already received distinguished honors (Exod. 24:13; Deut. 31:7). But a higher token of the divine favor was now to be publicly bestowed on him, and evidence given in the same unmistakable manner that his mission and authority were from God as was that of Moses (Exod. 14:31).

9-13. JOSHUA ENCOURAGES THE PEOPLE. **9-13. Come hither, and hear the words of the Lord**—It seems that the Israelites had no intimation how they were to cross the river till shortly before the event. The premonitory address of Joshua, taken in connection with the miraculous result exactly as he had described it, would tend to increase and confirm their faith in the God of their fathers as not a dull, senseless, inanimate thing like the idols of the nations, but a Being of life, power, and activity to defend them and work for them.

ADAM CLARKE

5. *Sanctify yourselves.* What was implied in this command we are not informed; but it is likely that it was the same as that given by Moses, Exod. xix. 10-14. They were to wash themselves and their garments, and abstain from everything that might indispose their minds from a profitable attention to the miracle about to be wrought in their behalf.

6. *Spake unto the priests, saying, Take up the ark.* It is remarkable that the priests, not the Levites, whose ordinary business it was, were employed to carry the ark on this occasion.

7. *This day will I begin to magnify thee.* By making him the instrument in this miraculous passage, He did him honor and gave him high credit in the sight of the people; hence his authority was established, and obedience to him as their leader fully secured. What must have confirmed this authority was his circumstantially foretelling how the waters should be cut off as soon as the feet of the priests had touched them, v. 13. This demonstrated that the secret of the Lord was with him.

8. *Ye shall stand still in Jordan.* The priests proceeded first with the ark, and entered into the bed of the river, the course of which was immediately arrested, the waters collecting above the place where the priests stood, while the stream fell off towards the Dead Sea, so that the whole channel below where the priests were standing became dry. The whole camp, therefore, passed over below where the priests were standing, keeping at the distance of two thousand cubits from the ark; this they would readily do, as the whole bed of the river was dry for many miles below the place where the priests entered.

10. *Hereby ye shall know that the living God is among you.* The Israelites were apt to be discouraged, and to faint at even the appearance of danger; it was necessary, therefore, that they should have the fullest assurance of the presence and assistance of God in the important enterprise on which they were now entering. They were to combat idolaters, who had nothing to trust in and help them but gods of wood, stone, and metal; whereas they were to have the living God in the midst of them—He who is the Author of life and of being—who can give, or take it away, at His pleasure; and who by this miracle proved that He had undertaken to guide and defend them; and Joshua makes this manifestation of God the proof that He will drive out the Hittites, Hivites, etc., before them.

MATTHEW HENRY

future. *As for God, his work is perfect.* If Jordan's flood cannot keep them out, Canaan's force cannot turn them out again.

5. He directs them to get twelve men ready, one of each tribe, who must be within call, to receive orders.

Verses 14–17

Here we have a short and plain account of the dividing of the river Jordan.

I. This river was now broader and deeper than usually it was at other times of the year, *v.* 15. The melting of the snow on the mountains of Lebanon, near which this river had its rise, was the occasion that at the time of harvest, barley-harvest, which was the spring of the year, Jordan overflowed all his banks. This great flood magnified the power of God and his kindness to Israel. Let the banks of Jordan be filled to the brink, it is as easy to Omnipotence to divide them, and dry them up, as if they were ever so narrow, ever so shallow.

II. As soon as ever the feet of the priests dipped in the brim of the water the stream stopped immediately, *v.* 15, 16. The waters above swelled, stood on a heap, and ran back, and yet did not spread. The waters on the other side this invisible dam ran down and left the bottom of the river dry. When they passed through the Red Sea, the waters were a wall on either hand, here only on the right-hand. What cannot God do? What will he not do for the perfecting of his people's salvation? When we have finished our pilgrimage through this wilderness, death will be like this Jordan between us and the heavenly Canaan, but the ark of the covenant has prepared us a way through it; it is the last enemy that shall be destroyed.

III. *The people passed over right against Jericho*, which was, 1. An instance of their boldness, and a noble defiance of their enemies. 2. It was an encouragement to them to venture through Jordan, for Jericho was a goodly city and the country about it extremely pleasant. 3. It would increase the confusion and terror of their enemies.

IV. The priests *stood still in the midst of Jordan while all the people passed over, v.* 17. There the ark was appointed to be, to show that the same power that parted the waters kept them parted as long as there was occasion. There the priests were appointed to stand still. 1. To try their faith. As they made a bold step when they set the first foot into Jordan, so now they made a bold stand when they tarried longest in Jordan; but they knew they carried their own protection with them. 2. It was to encourage the faith of the people, that they might go triumphantly into Canaan, and *fear no evil*, no, not in this *valley of the shadow of death*, being assured of God's presence, which interposed between them and the proud waters, which otherwise had gone over their souls.

JAMIESON, FAUSSET, BROWN

14-17. THE WATERS OF JORDAN ARE DIVIDED. **14. And it came to pass, when the people removed from their tents . . .**—To understand the scene described we must imagine the band of priests with the ark on their shoulders, standing on the depressed edge of the river, while the mass of the people were at a mile's distance. Suddenly the whole bed of the river was dried up; a spectacle the more extraordinary in that it took place in the time of harvest, corresponding to our April or May—when "the Jordan overfloweth all its banks." The original words may be more properly rendered "fills all its banks." Its channel, snow-fed from Lebanon, was at its greatest height—brimful; a translation which gives the only true description of the state of Jordan in harvest as observed by modern travellers. The river about Jericho is, in ordinary appearance, about 50 or 60 yards in breadth. But as seen in harvest, it is twice as broad; and in ancient times, when the hills on the right and left were much more drenched with rain and snow than since the forests have disappeared, the river must, from a greater accession of water, have been broader still than at harvest-time in the present day. **16. the waters which came down from above**—i.e., the Sea of Galilee "stood and rose up in a heap," a firm, compact barrier (Exod. 15:8; Ps. 18:13), "very far," high up the stream; "from the city Adam, that is beside Zaretan," near mount Sartabeh, in the northern part of the Ghor (I Kings 7:46); i.e., a distance of thirty miles from the Israelitish encampment; and "those that came down towards the sea of the desert"—the Dead Sea—failed and were cut off (Ps. 114:2, 3). The river was thus dried up as far as the eye could reach. This was a stupendous miracle; Jordan takes its name, "the Descender," from the force of its current, which, after passing the Sea of Galilee, becomes greatly increased as it plunges through twenty-seven "horrible rapids and cascades," besides a great many lesser through a fall of 1000 feet, averaging from four to five miles an hour [LYNCH]. When swollen "in time of harvest," it flows with a vastly accelerated current. **16. the people passed over right against Jericho**—The exact spot is unknown; but it cannot be that fixed by Greek tradition—the pilgrims' bathing-place—both because it is too much to the north, and the eastern banks are there sheer precipices 10 or 15 feet high. **17. the priests . . . and all the Israelites passed over on dry ground**—the river about Jericho has a firm pebbly bottom, on which the host might pass, without inconvenience when the water was cleared off.

ADAM CLARKE

15. *And the feet of the priests . . . were dipped in the brim of the water.* Thus we find that everything occurred exactly in the way in which Joshua had foretold it. This must have greatly increased his credit among the people. *For Jordan overfloweth all his banks.* It has often been remarked that there was no need of a miracle in crossing Jordan, as it is but an inconsiderable stream, easily fordable, being but about twenty yards in breadth. But the circumstance marked here by the sacred historian proves that there was a time in the year, viz., in the harvest, that this river overflowed its banks; and this is confirmed by another place in Scripture, 1 Chron. xii. 15. As the miracle reported here took place about the beginning of April, a time in which rivers in general are less than in winter, it may be asked how there could be such an increase of waters at this time. The simple fact is that the Jordan, as we have already seen, has its origin at the foot of Mount Lebanon, which mountain is always covered with snow during the winter months; in those months therefore the river is low. But when the summer's sun has melted these snows, there is consequently a prodigious increase of waters, so that the old channel is not capable of containing them.

16. *Rose up upon an heap.* That is, they continued to accumulate, filling up the whole of the channel toward the source, and the adjacent ground over which they were now spread, to a much greater depth, the power of God giving a contrary direction to the current. We need not suppose them to be gathered up "like a mountain," as the Vulgate expresses it, but that they continued to flow back in the course of the channel; and ere they could have reached the lake of Gennesareth, where they might have been easily accumulated, the whole Israelitish army would have all got safely to the opposite side. *Very far from the city Adam . . . beside Zaretan.* Where these places were it is difficult to say. The city *Adam* is wholly unknown.

17. *The priests . . . stood firm on dry ground.* They stood in the mid channel and shifted not their position till the camp, consisting of nearly six hundred thousand effective men, besides women, children, etc., had passed over.

MATTHEW HENRY — CHAPTER 4

Verses 1–9

How busy Joshua and all the men of war were while they were passing over Jordan, marching into an enemy's country. They had their wives, and children, cattle, and tents, bag and baggage, to convey by this strange and untrodden path, yet care must be taken to perpetuate the memorial of this wondrous work of God. Note, How much soever we have to do of business we must not omit what we have to do for the glory of God, for that is our best business. Now,

I. God gave orders for the preparing of this memorial. Had Joshua done it without divine direction, it might have looked like a design to perpetuate his own name. Note, God's works of wonder ought to be kept in everlasting remembrance. Some of the Israelites perhaps felt no concern to have it remembered; while others, it may be, had such deep impressions made upon them by it, that they thought there needed no memorial of it to be erected. But God, knowing how apt they had been soon to forget his works, ordered an expedient for the keeping of this in remembrance to all generations. 1. Joshua, as chief captain, must give direction about it (*v.* 1): *When all the people had clean passed over Jordan* God spoke unto Joshua to provide materials for this monument. 2. One man out of each tribe must be employed to prepare materials that each tribe might have the story told them by one of themselves, and each tribe might contribute something to the glory of God thereby (*v.* 2, 4): *Out of every tribe a man.* 3. The stones that must be set up for this memorial are ordered to be taken out of the midst

JAMIESON, FAUSSET, BROWN — CHAPTER 4

Vss. 1-8. TWELVE STONES TAKEN FOR A MEMORIAL OUT OF JORDAN. **1, 2. the Lord spake unio Joshua, Take you twelve men**—each representing a tribe. They had been previously chosen for this service (ch. 3:12), and the repetition of the command is made here solely to introduce the account of its execution. Though Joshua had been divinely instructed to erect a commemorative pile, the representatives were not apprised of the work they were to do till the time of the passage. **4, 5. Joshua called the twelve men**—They had probably, from a feeling of reverence, kept back, and were standing on the eastern bank. They were now ordered to advance. Picking up each a stone, probably as large as he could carry, from around the spot "where the priests stood," they pass over before the ark and deposit the stones in the place of next encampment (vss. 19, 20), viz., Gilgal.

ADAM CLARKE — CHAPTER 4

2. *Take you twelve men.* From chap. iii. 12, it appears that the twelve men had been before appointed, one taken out of each of the twelve tribes; and now they are employed for that purpose for which they had been before selected.

3. *Where ye shall lodge this night.* This was in the place that was afterwards called Gilgal. See v. 19.

4. *Twelve men, whom he had prepared.* This must refer to their appointment, chap. iii. 12.

MATTHEW HENRY

of the channel and as near as might be from the very place where the priests stood *with the ark*, *v.* 3, 5. Let posterity know by this that Jordan was driven back, for these very stones were then fetched out of it. 4. The use of these stones is here appointed for a sign (*v.* 6), a memorial, *v.* 7. They would give occasion to the children to ask their parents in time to come, *How came these stones hither?*

II. According to these orders the thing was done. 1. Twelve stones were taken up out of the midst of Jordan. By these stones which they were ordered to take up God did, as it were, give them livery and seisin of this good land; it is all their own, let them enter and take possession; therefore what these twelve did the children of Israel are said to do (*v.* 8), because they were the representatives of their respective tribes. When the Lord Jesus, our Joshua, having overcome the sharpness of death and dried up that Jordan, had opened the kingdom of heaven to all believers, he appointed his twelve apostles by the memorial of the gospel to transmit the knowledge of this to remote places and future ages. 2. Other twelve stones were set up *in the midst of Jordan* (*v.* 9), to notify the very place where the ark stood.

Verses 10–19

Joshua pursued the orders God gave him, and did nothing without divine direction, finishing all that *the Lord had commanded* him (*v.* 10).

I. *The people hasted and passed over*, *v.* 10. 1. Some hasted because they were not able to trust God. 2. Others because they were not willing to tempt God to continue the miracle longer than needs must. 3. Others because they were eager to be in Canaan. 4. Those that considered least, yet hasted because others did. He that believeth doth not make haste to *anticipate* God's counsels, but he makes haste to *attend* them, Isa. xxviii. 16.

II. The two tribes and a half led the van, *v.* 12, 13. They were all chosen men, and fit for service, ready armed. And the two tribes had no reason to complain: the post of danger is the post of honour.

III. When all the people had got clear to the other side, the priests with the ark came up out of Jordan. Joshua did not order them out of Jordan till God directed him to do so, *v.* 15–17. How low a condition soever God may at any time bring his priests or people to, let them patiently wait, till by his providence he shall call them up out of it, and let them not be weary of waiting, while they have the tokens of God's presence with them, in the depth of their adversity.

IV. As soon as ever the priests and the ark had come up out of Jordan, the waters of the river, which had stood on a heap, gradually flowed down according to their nature and usual course, *v.* 18. When Israel's turn was served, and the token of God's presence was removed, immediately the water went forward again.

V. Notice is taken of the honour put upon Joshua by all this (*v.* 14): *On that day the Lord magnified Joshua*, both by the fellowship he admitted him to with himself, and by the authority he confirmed him in over both priests and people. The best and surest way to command the respect of inferiors is not by blustering and threatening, but by holiness and love, and a constant regard to their welfare, and to God's will and honour. Those that are sanctified are truly magnified, and are worthy of double honour.

VI. An account is kept of the time of this great event (*v.* 19): it was *on the tenth day of the first month*, just forty years since they came out of Egypt, wanting five days. God had said in his wrath that they should wander forty years in the wilderness, and at last he brought them into Canaan five days before the forty years were ended, to show how little pleasure God takes in punishing, how swift he is to show mercy. God ordered it so that they should enter Canaan four days before the annual solemnity of the passover, and on the very day when the preparation for it was to begin (Exod. xii. 3), because he would have them then to be reminded of their deliverance out of Egypt.

Verses 20–24

The twelve stones which were *laid down in Gilgal* (*v.* 8) are here set up either one upon another, or one by another in rows; for after they were fixed they are not called *a heap of stones*, but *these stones*.

I. Posterity would enquire into the meaning of them: *Your children shall ask their fathers, What mean these stones?* Note, Those that will be wise when they are old must be inquisitive when they are young. Our Lord Jesus, though he had in himself the fulness of knowledge, has by his example taught children and young people to hear and ask questions, Luke ii. 46.

II. The parents are here directed what answer to

JAMIESON, FAUSSET, BROWN

6, 7. That this may be a sign among you—The erection of cairns, or huge piles of stones, as monuments of remarkable incidents has been common among all people, especially in the early and crude periods of their history. They are the established means of perpetuating the memory of important transactions, especially among the nomadic people of the East. Although there be no inscription engraved on them, the history and object of such simple monuments are traditionally preserved from age to age. Similar was the purpose contemplated by the conveyance of the twelve stones to Gilgal: it was that they might be a standing record to posterity of the miraculous passage of the Jordan. **8. the children of Israel did so as Joshua commanded**—i.e., it was done by their twelve representatives.

9. TWELVE STONES SET UP IN THE MIDST OF JORDAN. **9. Joshua set up twelve stones . . . in the place where the feet of the priests . . . stood**—In addition to the memorial just described, there was another memento of the miraculous event, a duplicate of the former, set up in the river itself, on the very spot where the ark had rested. This heap of stones might have been a large and compactly built one and visible in the ordinary state of the river. As nothing is said where these stones were obtained, some have imagined that they might have been gathered in the adjoining fields and deposited by the people as they passed the appointed spot. **they are there unto this day**—at least twenty years after the event, if we reckon by the date of this history (ch. 24:26), and much later, if the words in the latter clause were inserted by Samuel or Ezra.

10-13. THE PEOPLE PASS OVER. **10. the priests which bare the ark stood in the midst of Jordan**—This position was well calculated to animate the people, who probably crossed *below* the ark, as well as to facilitate Joshua's execution of the minutest instructions respecting the passage (Num. 27:21-23). The unfaltering confidence of the priests contrasts strikingly with the conduct of the people, who "hasted and passed over." Their faith, like that of many of God's people, was, through the weakness of nature, blended with fears. But perhaps their "haste" may be viewed in a more favorable light, as indicating the alacrity of their obedience, or it might have been enjoined in order that the the whole multitude might pass in one day. **11. the ark of the Lord passed over, and the priests, in the presence of the people**—The ark is mentioned as the efficient cause; it had been the first to move—it was the last to leave; and its movements arrested the deep attention of the people, who probably stood on the opposite bank, wrapt in admiration and awe of this closing scene. It was a great miracle, greater even than the passage of the Red Sea in this respect: that, admitting the fact, there is no possibility of rationalistic insinuations as to the influence of natural causes in producing it, as have been made in the former case. **12, 13. the children of Reuben . . . passed over armed before the children of Israel**—There is no precedency to the other tribes indicated here; for there is no reason to suppose that the usual order of march was departed from; but these are honorably mentioned to show that, in pursuance of their promise (ch. 1:16-18), they had sent a complement of fighting men to accompany their brethern in the war of invasion. **to the plains of Jericho**—That part of the Arabah or Ghor, on the west, is about seven miles broad from the Jordan to the mountain entrance at Wady-Kelt. Though now desert, this valley was in ancient times richly covered with wood. An immense palm forest, seven miles long, surrounded Jericho.

14-24. GOD MAGNIFIES JOSHUA. **14-17. On that day the Lord magnified Joshua in the sight of all Israel**—It appeared clear from the chief part he acted, that he was the divinely appointed leader; for even the priests did not enter the river or quit their position, except at his command; and thenceforward his authority was as firmly established as that of his predecessor. **18. it came to pass, when the priests that bare the ark . . . were come out of the midst of Jordan . . . that the waters of Jordan returned unto their place**—Their crossing, which was the final act, completed the evidence of the miracle; for then, and not till then, the suspended laws of nature were restored, the waters returned to their place, and the river flowed with as full a current as before. **19. the people came out of Jordan on the tenth day of the first month**—i.e., the month Nisan, four days before the passover, and the very day when the paschal lamb required to be set apart, the providence of God having arranged that the entrance into the promised land should be at the feast. **and encamped in Gilgal**—The name is here given by

ADAM CLARKE

6. *This may be a sign.* Stand as a continual memorial of this miraculous passage, and consequently a proof of their lasting obligation to God.

9. *And Joshua set up twelve stones in the midst of Jordan.* It seems from this chapter that there were two sets of stones erected as a memorial of this great event: twelve at Gilgal, v. 20; and twelve in the bed of Jordan, v. 9. The twelve stones in the bed of Jordan might have been so placed on a base of strong stonework so high as always to be visible, and serve to mark the very spot where the priests stood with the ark. The twelve stones set up at Gilgal would stand as a monument of the place of the first encampment after this miraculous passage.

10. *And the people hasted and passed over.* How very natural is this circumstance! The people seeing the waters divided, and Jordan running back, might be apprehensive that it would soon resume its wonted course; and this would naturally lead them to hasten to get over, with as much speed as possible. The circumstance itself thus marked is a proof that the relater was an eyewitness of this miraculous passage.

14. *The Lord magnified Joshua.* See the note on chap. iii. 7.

18. *The waters of Jordan returned unto their place.* It is particularly remarked by the sacred historian that as soon as the soles of the priests' feet touched the water the stream of the Jordan was cut off, chap. iii. 15, and the course of the river continued to be inverted all the time they continued in its channel; and that as soon as the soles of their feet had touched the dry land, on their return from the bed of the river, the waters immediately resumed their natural course.

19. *On the tenth day of the first month.* As the Israelites left Egypt on the fifteenth day of the first month (see Exodus xiv) and they entered into Canaan the tenth of the first month, it is evident that forty years, wanting five days, had elapsed from the time of their exodus from Egypt to their entrance into the promised inheritance. *Encamped in Gilgal.* That is, in the place that was afterwards called Gilgal, see chap. v. 9; for here the name is given it by anticipation. In Hebrew, *gal* signifies to "roll"; and the doubling of the root, *galgal* or *gilgal*, signifies "rolling round and round," or "rolling off or away," because, in circumcising the children that had been born in the wilderness, Joshua rolled away, rolled off completely, the reproach of the people. Gilgal was about ten furlongs from Jericho, and fifty from Jordan—Jericho being on the west, and Jordan on the east, Gilgal being between both.

MATTHEW HENRY

give to this enquiry (*v.* 22): "*You shall let your children know* that which you have yourselves learned from the written word and from your fathers." Note, It is the duty of parents to acquaint their children betimes with the word and works of God.

1. They must let their children know that Jordan was driven back before Israel, who *went through it upon dry land*, and that this was the very place where they passed over. Note, God's mercies to our ancestors were mercies to us; and we should revive the remembrance of the great things God did for our fathers *in the days of old*.

2. They must take that occasion to tell their children of the drying up of the Red Sea forty years before: *As the Lord your God did to the Red Sea.* Note, (i) By making the comparison, it appears that God is the same yesterday, to-day, and for ever. (ii) Later mercies should bring to remembrance former mercies, and revive our thankfulness for them.

(1) The power of God was hereby magnified. The deliverances of God's people are instructions to all people, and fair warnings not to contend with Omnipotence. (2) The remembrance of this wonderful work should effectually restrain them from the worship of other gods, and constrain them to abide and abound in the service of their own God.

JAMIESON, FAUSSET, BROWN

anticipation (see on ch. 5:9). It was a tract of land, according to Josephus, fifty stadia ($6\frac{1}{4}$ miles) from Jordan, and ten stadia ($1\frac{1}{4}$ miles) from Jericho, at the eastern outskirts of the palm forest, now supposed to be the spot occupied by the village Riha. **20-24. those twelve stones which they took out of Jordan, did Joshua pitch in Gilgal**—Probably to render them more conspicuous, they might be raised on a foundation of earth or turf. The pile was designed to serve a double purpose—that of impressing the heathen with a sense of the omnipotence of God, while at the same time it would teach an important lesson in religion to the young and rising Israelites in after ages.

ADAM CLARKE

20. *Those twelve stones.* It is very likely that a base of masonwork was erected of some considerable height, and then the twelve stones placed on the top of it, and that this was the case both in Jordan and Gilgal. For twelve such stones as a man could carry a considerable way on his shoulder, see v. 5, could scarcely have made any observable altar, or pillar of memorial; but erected on a high base of masonwork they would be very conspicuous, and thus properly answer the end for which God ordered them to be set up.

22. *Then ye shall let your children know.* The necessity of an early religious education is inculcated through the whole oracles of God. The parents who neglect it have an awful account to give to the Judge of quick and dead.

24. *That all the people of the earth might know.* It is very likely that *col ammey haarets* means simply, "all the people of this land"—all the Canaanitish nations.

MATTHEW HENRY — CHAPTER 5

Verses 1–9

A vast show, no doubt, the numerous camp of Israel made in the plains of Jericho, where now they had pitched their tents. The *church in the wilderness has now come up from the wilderness.* How terrible she was in the eyes of her enemies we are here told, *v.* 1. How fair and clear she was made in the eyes of her friends, by the rolling away of the reproach of Egypt, we are told in the following verses.

I. Here are impressions the tidings made upon the kings of this land: *Their heart melted* like wax before the fire, *neither was there spirit in them any more.* The kings have till now kept up their spirits pretty well, being in possession, their country populous, and their cities fortified, they should be able to make their part good against the invaders; but when they heard not only that they had come over Jordan, but that they had come over by a miracle, the God of nature manifestly fighting for them, *their hearts failed them* too, and they were now at their wits' end. And, 1. They had reason enough to be afraid; Israel itself was a formidable body, and much more so when God was its head, a God of almighty power. 2. God impressed these fears upon them, and dispirited them, as he had promised (Exod. xxiii. 27).

II. *At that time* (*v.* 2), when the country about them was in that great consternation, God ordered Joshua to circumcise the children of Israel.

1. The occasion there was for this general circumcision. All that came out of Egypt were circumcised, *v.* 5. But when the edict was made for the destruction of their male infants, the administration of this ordinance was interrupted; many of them were uncircumcised, of whom there was a general circumcision. It is with reference to that general circumcision that this is called a *second*, *v.* 2. Under the government of Moses himself, to have all their children that were born for thirty-eight years together left uncircumcised is unaccountable. Now, (1) Some think circumcision was omitted because it was needless: it was appointed to be a mark of distinction between the Israelites and other nations, and therefore in the wilderness there was no occasion for it. (2) Others think that they did not look upon the precept of circumcision as obligatory till they came to settle in Canaan. (3) Others think that God favourably dispensed with the observance of this ordinance in consideration of the unsettledness of their state. (4) To me it seems to have been a continued token of God's displeasure against them for their unbelief and murmuring. And this was such a significant indication of God's wrath as the breaking of the tables of the covenant was when Israel had broken the covenant by making the golden calf. Whatever the reason was, it seems that this great ordinance was omitted in Israel for almost forty years together, which is a plain indication that it was not of absolute necessity, nor was to be of perpetual obligation.

2. The orders given to Joshua for this general circumcision (*v.* 2). Why was this ordered to be done now? (1) Because now the promise of which circumcision was instituted to be the seal was performed. The seed of Israel was brought safely into the land of Canaan. (2) Because now the threatening was fully executed by the expiring of the forty years,

JAMIESON, FAUSSET, BROWN — CHAPTER 5

Vs. 1. The Canaanites Afraid. **1. the kings of the Amorites, which were on the side of Jordan westward, and all the kings of the Canaanites which were by the sea**—Under the former designation were included the people who inhabited the mountainous region, and under the latter those who were on the seacoast of Palestine. **heard that the Lord had dried up the waters of Jordan . . . that their heart melted**—They had probably reckoned on the swollen river interposing for a time a sure barrier of defense. But seeing it had been completely dried up, they were completely paralyzed by so incontestable a proof that God was on the side of the invaders. In fact, the conquest had already begun in the total prostration of spirit among the native chiefs. "Their heart melted," but unhappily not into faith and penitent submission.

2-12. Circumcision Is Renewed. **2. At that time**—on the encampment being made after the passage. **the Lord said unto Joshua, Make thee sharp knives**—Stone knives, collect and make them ready. Flints have been used in the early times of all people; and although the use of iron was known to the Hebrews in the days of Joshua, probably the want of a sufficient number of metallic implements dictated the employment of flints on this occasion (cf. Exod. 4:25). **circumcise again the children of Israel the second time**—lit., return and circumcise. The command did not require him to repeat the operation on those who had undergone it, but to resume the observance of the rite, which had been long discontinued. The language, however, evidently points to a general circumcising on some previous occasion, which, though unrecorded, must have been made before the celebration of the passover at Sinai (cf. Exod. 12:48; Num. 9:5), as a mixed multitude accompanied the camp. "The second time" of general circumcising was at the entrance into Canaan. **3. at the hill**—probably one of the argillaceous hills that form the highest terrace of the Jordan, on a rising ground at the palm forest.

4-7. this is the cause why Joshua did circumcise—The omission to circumcise the children born in the wilderness might have been owing to the incessant movements of the people; but it is most generally thought that the true cause was a temporary suspension of the covenant with the unbelieving race who, being rejected of the Lord, were doomed to

ADAM CLARKE — CHAPTER 5

1. *The Amorites, which were on the side of Jordan westward.* It has already been remarked that the term *Amorites* is applied sometimes to signify all the nations or tribes of Canaan. It appears from this verse that there were people thus denominated that dwelt on both sides of the Jordan. Those on the east side had already been destroyed in the war which the Israelites had with Sihon and Og; with those on the west side Joshua had not yet waged war. It is possible however that the *Amorites*, of whom we read in this verse, were the remains of those who dwelt on the east side of the Jordan, and who had taken refuge here on the defeat of Og and Sihon.

2. *Make thee sharp knives.* "Knives of rock, stone, or flint." *Circumcise again the children of Israel the second time.* This certainly does not mean that they should repeat circumcision on those who had already received it. This would have been as absurd as impracticable. But the command implies that they were to renew the observance of a rite which had been neglected in their travels in the desert.

4. *This is the cause why Joshua did circumcise.* The text here explains itself. Before the Israelites left Egypt all the males were circumcised; and some learned men think that all those who were born during their encampment at Sinai were circumcised also, because there they celebrated the Passover; but after that time, during the whole of their stay in the

MATTHEW HENRY

therefore now the seal of the covenant is revived again. [1] God would hereby show that the camp of Israel was not governed by the ordinary rules and measures of war, but by immediate direction from God. [2] God would hereby animate his people Israel against the difficulties they were now to encounter, by confirming his covenant with them, which gave them unquestionable assurance of victory and success, and the full possession of the land of promise. [3] God would hereby teach them, and us with them, in all great undertakings to *begin with God*, to make sure of his favour, by offering ourselves to him *a living sacrifice* (for that was signified by the blood of circumcision). [4] The reviving of circumcision, after it had been so long disused, was designed to revive the observance of other institutions. [5] This *second* circumcision, as it is here called, was typical of the spiritual circumcision with which the Israel of God, when they enter into the gospel rest, are circumcised; it points to *Jesus as the true circumciser*, the author of *another circumcision* than that *of the flesh*, commanded by the law, even the *circumcision of the heart* (Rom. ii. 29), called the *circumcision of Christ*, Col. ii. 11.

3. The people's obedience to these orders. Joshua *circumcised the children of Israel* (*v.* 3), and here they gave an instance of their dutifulness by submitting to this painful institution.

4. (1) Their circumcision rolled away the reproach of Egypt. They were tainted with the idolatry of Egypt, and that was their reproach; but now that they were circumcised it was to be hoped they would be so entirely devoted to God that the reproach would be rolled away. (2) Their coming safely to Canaan rolled away the reproach of Egypt, for it silenced that spiteful suggestion of the Egyptians, that *for mischief they were brought out, the wilderness had shut them in*, Exod. xiv. 3.

Verses 10–12

We may well imagine that the people of Canaan were astonished. Joshua opens the campaign with one act of devotion after another. That is likely to end well which begins with God.

I. A solemn passover kept, at the time appointed by the law, *the fourteenth day of the first month*, and in the same place where they were circumcised, *v.* 10. While they were wandering in the wilderness they were denied the benefit and comfort of this ordinance, but now God comforted them again, and therefore that joyful ordinance is revived. The solemn passover followed immediately after the solemn circumcision; thus, when those that received the word were baptized, immediately we find them *breaking bread*, Acts ii. 41, 42. They kept this passover in the plains of Jericho, as it were in defiance of the Canaanites. He now *prepared a table before them in the presence of their enemies*, Ps. xxiii. 5.

II. Provision made for their camp of the *corn of the land*, and the *ceasing of the manna* thereupon, *v.* 11, 12. Manna was a wonderful mercy to them when they needed it. But it was the mark of a wilderness state; more acceptable to them to eat of the *corn of the land*, and this they are now furnished with.

1. The country people, having retired for safety into Jericho, had left their barns and fields, and all that was in them. And the supply came very seasonably, for, (1) After the passover they were to keep *the feast of unleavened bread*, which they could not do according to the appointment when they had nothing but manna to live upon; now they found old corn enough in the barns of the Canaanites to supply them plentifully for that occasion. (2) On the morrow after the passover-sabbath they were to *wave the sheaf of first-fruits before the Lord*, Lev. xxiii. 10, 11. And this they were particularly ordered to do when they *came into the land which God would give them*: and they were furnished for this with the *fruit of the land that year* (*v.* 12), which was then growing and beginning to be ripe.

2. Notice is taken of the ceasing of the manna as soon as ever they had eaten the *old corn of the land*, (1) It came just when they needed it, so it continued as long as they had occasion for it and no longer. (2) To teach us not to expect extraordinary supplies when supplies may be had in an ordinary way. Now that they needed it not God withdrew it. He is a wise Father, who knows the necessities of his children, and accommodates his gifts to *them*, not to their humours. The word and ordinances of God are spiritual manna, with which God nourishes his people in this wilderness, but when we come to the heavenly Canaan this manna will cease, for we shall no longer have need of it.

Verses 13–15

We have hitherto found God often speaking to Joshua, but we read not till now of any appearance of God's glory to him; now that his difficulties

JAMIESON, FAUSSET, BROWN

perish in the wilderness, and whose children had to bear the iniquity of their fathers (Num. 14:33), though, as the latter were to be brought into the promised land, the covenant would be renewed with them. **8. when they had done circumcising all the people**—As the number of those born in the wilderness and uncircumcised must have been immense, a difficulty is apt to be felt how the rite could have been performed on such a multitude in so short a time. But it has been calculated that the proportion between those already circumcised (under twenty when the doom was pronounced) and those to be circumcised, was one to four, and consequently the whole ceremony could easily have been performed in a day. Circumcision being the sign and seal of the covenant, its performance was virtually an investment in the promised land, and its being delayed till their actual entrance into the country was a wise and gracious act on the part of God, who postponed this trying duty till the hearts of the people, animated by the recent astonishing miracle, were prepared to obey the divine will. **they abode in their places . . . till they were whole**—It is calculated that, of those who did not need to be circumcised, more than 50,000 were left to defend the camp if an attack had been then made upon it. **9. the Lord said unto Joshua, This day have I rolled away the reproach of Egypt**—The taunts industriously cast by that people upon Israel as *nationally* rejected by God by the cessation of circumcision and the renewal of that rite was a practical announcement of the restoration of the covenant [KEIL]. *Gigal*—No trace either of the name or site is now to be found; but it was about two miles from Jericho [JOSEPHUS], and well suited for an encampment by the advantages of shade and water. It was the first place pronounced "holy" in the Holy Land (vs. 15).

10. kept the passover on the fourteenth day of the month at even—The time fixed by the law (see Exod. 12:18; Lev. 23:5; Num. 28:16). Thus the national existence was commenced by a solemn act of religious dedication.

11, 12. they did eat of the old corn of the land—found in storehouses of the inhabitants who had fled into Jericho. **parched corn**—new grain (see on Lev. 23:10), probably lying in the fields. This abundance of food led to the discontinuance of the manna; and the fact of its then ceasing, viewed in connection with its seasonable appearance in the barren wilderness, is a striking proof of its miraculous origin.

ADAM CLARKE

wilderness, there were none circumcised till they entered into the Promised Land. Owing to their unsettled state, God appears to have dispensed, for the time being, with this rite. But as they were about to celebrate another Passover, it was necessary that all the males should be circumcised; for without this they could not be considered within the covenant, and could not keep the Passover, which was the seal of that covenant.

8. *They abode . . . in the camp, till they were whole*. This required several days; see the notes on Genesis xxxiv.

9. *The reproach of Egypt*. Their being uncircumcised made them like the uncircumcised Egyptians, and the Hebrews ever considered all those who were uncircumcised as being in a state of the grossest impurity. Being now circumcised, the reproach of uncircumcision was rolled away. *The place is called Gilgal*. "A rolling away" or "rolling off." See the note on chap. iv. 19, where the word is largely explained.

11. *They did eat of the old corn of the land*. The Hebrew word *abur*, which we translate "old corn," occurs only in this place in such a sense, if that sense be legitimate. The noun, though of doubtful signification, is evidently derived from *abar*, "to pass over, to go beyond"; and here it may be translated simply "the produce," that which passes from the land into the hands of the cultivator; or according to Cocceius, what passes from person to person in the way of traffic; hence bought corn, what they purchased from the inhabitants of the land. *On the morrow after the passover*. That is, on the fifteenth day, for then the Feast of Unleavened Bread began. But they could eat neither bread, nor parched corn, nor green ears, till the firstfruits of the harvest had been waved at the Tabernacle (see Lev. xxiii. 9, etc.); and therefore in this case we may suppose that the Israelites had offered a sheaf of the barley harvest, the only grain that was then ripe, before they ate of the unleavened cakes and parched corn.

12. *And the manna ceased . . . after they had eaten of the old corn*. This miraculous supply continued with them as long as they needed it. While they were in the wilderness they required such a provision; nor could such a multitude, in such a place, be supported without a miracle. Now as they entered into the Promised Land, and there was an ample provision made in the ordinary way of Providence, there was no longer any need of a miraculous supply; therefore the manna ceased which they had enjoyed for forty years.

MATTHEW HENRY

increased his encouragements were increased in proportion.

I. The time when he was favoured with this vision. It was immediately after he had performed the great solemnities of circumcision and the passover. Note, We may then expect the discoveries of the divine grace when we are found in the way of our duty.

II. The place where he had this vision. It was *by Jericho*. There, it should seem, he was all alone, fearless of danger, because sure of the divine protection. There he was (some think) meditating and praying. Or perhaps to take a view of the city, and contrive how to attack it; when God came and directed him. Note, God will *help those that help themselves. Vigilantibus non dormientibus succurrit lex—The law succours those who watch, not those who sleep.* Joshua was in his post as a general, when God came and made himself known as Generalissimo.

III. The appearance itself. Joshua, as is usual with those that are full of thought and care, was looking downwards, his eyes fixed on the ground, when of a sudden he was surprised with the appearance of a man who stood before him at some little distance, which obliged him to lift up his eyes. Now, 1. We have reason to think that this man was the Son of God, the eternal Word, who, before he assumed the human nature for a perpetuity, frequently appeared in a human shape. 2. He here appeared as a soldier, with *his sword drawn in his hand.* To Abraham in his tent he appeared as a traveller; to Joshua in the field as a man of war. Christ will be to his people what their faith expects and desires. He came to encourage him to carry it on with vigour; for Christ's sword drawn in his hand denotes how ready he is for the defence and salvation of his people, who through him shall do valiantly.

IV. The bold question with which Joshua accosted him. This shows, 1. His great courage and resolution. He was not ruffled by the suddenness of the appearance. 2. His great concern for the people and their cause. It should seem, he suspected him for an enemy. Thus apt are we to look upon that as against us which is most for us. The cause between the Israelites and the Canaanites, between Christ and Beelzebub, will not admit of a neutrality. *He that is not with us is against us.*

V. The account he gave of himself, *v.* 14. "Nay, not for your adversaries, you may be sure, but *as captain of the host of the Lord have I now come*, not only for you as a friend, but over you as commander in chief." He, as captain of both, conducts the host of Israel and commands the host of angels to their assistance. Perhaps in allusion to this Christ is called the *captain of our salvation* (Heb. ii. 10), *and a leader and commander to the people*, Isa lv. 4.

VI. He perceived that he was a divine person, and not a man. 1. Joshua paid homage to him: He *fell on his face to the earth and did worship.* Joshua was himself general of the forces of Israel, and yet cheerfully submitted to him as his commander. 2. He begged to receive commands and directions from him: *What saith my Lord unto his servant?* His former question was not more bold and soldier-like than this was pious and saint-like; nor was it any disparagement to the greatness of Joshua's spirit: even crowned heads cannot bow too low before the throne of the Lord Jesus, who is *King of kings*, Ps. ii. 10, 11; lxxii. 10, 11; Rev. xix. 16. Observe, (1) The relation he owns between himself and Christ, that Christ was his Lord and himself his servant and under his command, Christ his Captain and himself a soldier under him, to do as he is bidden, Matt. viii. 9. (2) The enquiry he makes pursuant to this relation: *What saith my Lord?* which implies an earnest desire to know the will of Christ, and a cheerful readiness and resolution to do it. This temper of mind shows him fit for the post he was in; for those know best how to command that know how to obey.

VII. The further expressions of reverence which this divine captain required from Joshua (*v.* 15): *Loose thy shoe from off thy foot*, in token of reverence and respect (which with us are signified by uncovering the head). We are accustomed to say of a person for whom we have a great affection that we love the very ground he treads upon. Outward expressions of inward reverence well become us, and are required of us. Bishop Patrick well observes here that the very same orders that God gave to Moses at the bush (Exod. iii. 5), he here gives to Joshua; as he had been with Moses so he would be with him, *ch.* i. 5.

JAMIESON, FAUSSET, BROWN

13-15. AN ANGEL APPEARS TO JOSHUA. **13. when Joshua was by Jericho**—in the immediate vicinity of that city, probably engaged in surveying the fortifications, and in meditating the best plan of a siege.

there stood a man over against him with his sword drawn—It is evident from the strain of the context that this was not a mere vision, but an actual appearance; the suddenness of which surprised, but did not daunt, the intrepid leader.

14. the host of the Lord—either the Israelitish people (Exod. 7:4; 12:41; Isa. 55:4), or the angels (Ps. 148:2), or both included, and the Captain of it was the angel of the covenant, whose visible manifestations were varied according to the occasion. His attitude of equipment betokened his approval of, and interest in, the war of invasion. **Joshua fell on his face . . . , and did worship**—The adoption by Joshua of this absolute form of prostration demonstrates the sentiments of profound reverence with which the language and majestic bearing of the stranger inspired him.

The real character of this personage was disclosed by His accepting the homage of worship (cf. Acts 10:25, 26; Rev. 19:10), and still further in the command, "Loose thy shoe from off thy foot" (Exod. 3:5).

ADAM CLARKE

13. *When Joshua was by Jericho.* The sixth chapter should have commenced here, as this is an entirely new relation; or these two chapters should have made but one, as the present division has most unnaturally divided the communication which Joshua had from the angel of the Lord, and which is continued to v. 5 of chap. vi. It is very likely that Joshua had gone out privately to reconnoiter the city of Jericho when he had this vision; and while he was contemplating the strength of the place, and probably reflecting on the extreme difficulty of reducing it, God, to encourage him, granted him this vision, and instructed him in the means by which the city should be taken.

There stood a man over against him. It has been a very general opinion, both among the ancients and moderns, that the person mentioned here was no other than the Lord Jesus in that form which, in the fulness of time, He was actually to assume for the redemption of man. *And Joshua went unto him.* The whole history of Joshua shows him to have been a man of the most undaunted mind and intrepid courage—a genuine hero. An ordinary person, seeing this man armed, with a drawn sword in his hand, would have endeavored to regain the camp, and sought safety in flight; but Joshua, undismayed, though probably slightly armed, walked up to this terrible person and immediately questioned him, *Art thou for us, or for our adversaries?* probably at first supposing that he might be the Canaanitish general, coming to reconnoitre the Israelitish camp, as himself was come out to examine the city of Jericho.

14. *But as captain of the host of the Lord am I now come.* By this saying Joshua was both encouraged and instructed. As if he had said, "Fear not; Jehovah hath sent from heaven to save thee and thy people from the reproach of them that would swallow thee up. Israel is the Lord's host; and the Lord of hosts is Israel's Captain. Thou thyself shalt only be captain under me, and I am now about to instruct thee relative to thy conduct in this war." *And Joshua . . . did worship.* Nor was he reprehended for offering divine worship to this person, which he would not have received had he been a created angel. See Rev. xxii. 8-9.

15. *Loose thy shoe from off thy foot.* These were the same words which the angel, on Mount Sinai spoke to Moses (see Exod. iii. 5-8); and from this it seems likely that it was the same person that appeared in both places: in the first, to encourage Moses to deliver the oppressed Israelites, and bring them to the Promised Land; in the second, to encourage Joshua in his arduous labor in expelling the ancient inhabitants, and establishing the people in the inheritance promised to their fathers.

There is scarcely a more unfortunate division of chapters in the whole Bible than that here. Through this very circumstance many persons have been puzzled to know what was intended by this extraordinary appearance, because they supposed that the whole business ends with the chapter, whereas it is continued in the succeeding one, the first verse of which is a mere parenthesis, simply relating the state of Jericho at the time that Joshua was favored by this encouraging vision.

MATTHEW HENRY

CHAPTER 6

Verses 1–5

We have here a contest between God and the men of Jericho.

I. Jericho resolves Israel shall *not* be its master, *v.* 1. None went out as deserters or to treat of peace, nor were any admitted in to offer peace.

II. God resolves Israel *shall* be its master, and that quickly. 1. The captain of the Lord's host gives directions how the city should be besieged. No trenches are to be opened, nor any military preparations made; but the ark of God must be carried by the priests round the city once a day for six days together, and seven times the seventh day, attended by the men of war in silence, the priests all the while blowing with trumpets of rams' horns, *v.* 3, 4. This was all they were to do. 2. He assures them that on the seventh day before night they should, without fail, be masters of the town. Upon a signal given, they must all shout, and immediately the wall should fall down, *v.* 5. God appointed this way, (1) To magnify his own power, that he might be *exalted in his own strength* (Ps. xxi. 13), not in the strength of instruments. (2) To put an honour upon his ark, the instituted token of his presence, and to give a reason for the laws by which the people were obliged to look upon it with the most profound veneration and respect. (3) It was likewise to put honour upon the priests, who were appointed upon this occasion to carry the ark and sound the trumpets. (4) It was to try the faith, obedience, and patience, of the people, to try whether they would observe a precept which to human policy seemed foolish to obey and believe a promise which in human probability seemed impossible to be performed. Thus by faith, not by force, the walls of Jericho fell down. (5) It was to encourage the hope of Israel with reference to the remaining difficulties that were before them. The strongest and highest walls cannot hold out against Omnipotence.

Verses 6–16

We have here an account of the cavalcade which Israel made about Jericho, the orders Joshua gave concerning it, as he had received them from the Lord and their punctual observance of these orders.

I. Wherever the ark went the people attended it, *v.* 9. The armed men went before it to clear the way, pioneers to the ark of God. It is an honour to the greatest men to do any good office to the ark and to serve the interests of religion in their country. The *rereward,* either another body of armed men, or Dan's squadron, which marched last through the wilderness, or, as some think, the multitude of the people who were not armed, followed the ark.

II. Seven priests went immediately before the ark, having trumpets in their hands, with which they were continually sounding, *v.* 4, 5, 9, 13. 1. They proclaimed war with the Canaanites, and so struck a terror upon them. Thus God's ministers, by the solemn declarations of his wrath against all ungodliness and unrighteousness of men, must blow the trumpet in Zion, that the sinners in Zion may be afraid. 2. They proclaimed God's gracious presence with Israel, and so put life and courage into them.

III. The trumpets they used were not silver trumpets, but trumpets of rams' horns, bored hollow for the purpose. These trumpets were of the basest matter, dullest sound, and least show, that the excellency of the power might be of God. Thus by the foolishness of preaching, fitly compared to the sounding of these rams' horns, the devil's kingdom is thrown down; and the *weapons of our warfare,* though they are not carnal, are yet *mighty through God to the pulling down of strong-holds,* 2 Cor. x. 4, 5.

IV. All the people were commanded to be silent, not to speak a word, nor make any noise (*v.* 10), that they might the more carefully attend to the sound of the sacred trumpets, which they were now to look upon as the voice of God among them; and it does not become us to speak when God is speaking.

V. They were to do this once a day for six days together and seven times the seventh day, and they did so, *v.* 14, 15. As promised deliverances must be expected in God's way, so they must be expected in his time.

VI. One of these days must needs be a sabbath day, and the Jews say that it was the last, but this is not certain; however, if he that appointed them to rest on the other sabbath days appointed them to walk on this, that was sufficient to justify them in it; he never intended to bind himself by his own laws, but that when he pleased he might dispense with them. And, besides, the law of the sabbath forbids our own work,

JAMIESON, FAUSSET, BROWN

CHAPTER 6

Vss. 1-7. Jericho Shut Up. **1. Now Jericho was straitly shut up**—This verse is a parenthesis introduced to prepare the way for the directions given by the Captain of the Lord's host. **See, I have given into thine hand Jericho**—The language intimates that a purpose already formed was about to be carried into immediate execution; and that, although the king and inhabitants of Jericho were fierce and experienced warriors, who would make a stout and determined resistance, the Lord promised a certain and easy victory over them. **3-5. ye shall compass the city, all ye men of war.... Thus shalt thou do six days . . .**—Directions are here given as to the mode of procedure. *Heb.,* "horns of jubilee"; i.e., the bent or crooked trumpets with which the jubilee was proclaimed. It is probable that the horns of this animal were used at first; and that afterwards, when metallic trumpets were introduced, the primitive name, as well as form of them, was traditionally continued. The design of this whole proceeding was obviously to impress the Canaanites with a sense of the divine omnipotence, to teach the Israelites a memorable lesson of faith and confidence in God's promises, and to inspire sentiments of respect and reverence for the ark as the symbol of His presence. The length of time during which those circuits were made tended the more intensely to arrest the attention, and to deepen the impressions, both of the Israelites and the enemy. The number seven was among the Israelites the symbolic seal of the covenant between God and their nation [Keil, Hengstenberg].

6, 7. Joshua . . . called the priests—The pious leader, whatever military preparations he had made, surrendered all his own views, at once and unreservedly, to the declared will of God.

8-19. The City Compassed Six Days. **8-11. the seven priests bearing the seven trumpets . . . passed on before the Lord**—before the ark, called "the ark of the covenant," for it contained the tables on which the covenant was inscribed. The procession was made in deep and solemn silence, conforming to the instructions given to the people by their leader at the outset, that they were to refrain from all acclamation and noise of any kind until he should give them a signal. It must have been a strange sight; no mound was raised, no sword drawn, no engine planted, no pioneers undermining—here were armed men, but no stroke given; they must walk and not fight. Doubtless the people of Jericho made themselves merry with the spectacle [Bishop Hall]. **12-14. Joshua rose early in the morning, and the priests took up the ark of the Lord**—The second day's procession seems to have taken place in the morning. In all other respects, down even to the smallest details, the arrangements of the first day continued to be the rule followed on the other six.

15. on the seventh day they rose early about the dawning of the day, and compassed the city . . . seven times—on account of the seven circuits they had to make that day. It is evident, however, that the militia only of the Israelites had been called to the march—for it is inconceivable that two millions of people could have gone so frequently round the city in a day.

ADAM CLARKE

CHAPTER 6

1. *Now Jericho was straitly shut up.* The king of Jericho, finding that the spies had escaped, though the city was always kept shut by night, took the most proper precaution to prevent everything of the kind in future by keeping the city shut both day and night, having no doubt laid in a sufficiency of provisions to stand a siege, being determined to defend himself to the uttermost.

2. *And the Lord said unto Joshua.* This is the same person who in the preceding chapter is called the captain or prince of the Lord's host, the discourse being here continued that was begun at the conclusion of the preceding chapter, from which the first verses of this are unnaturally divided. *I have given into thine hand Jericho.* From v. 11 of chap. xxiv. it seems as if there had been persons of all the seven Canaanitish nations then in Jericho, who might have come together at this time to help the king of Jericho against the invading Israelites.

3. *Ye shall compass the city.* In what order the people marched round the city does not exactly appear from the text. Some think they observed the same order as in their ordinary marches in the desert; others think that the soldiers marched first, then the priests who blew the trumpets, then those who carried the ark, and lastly the people.

4. *Seven trumpets of rams' horns.* The Hebrew word *yobelim* does not signify *rams' horns;* nor do any of the ancient versions, the Chaldee excepted, give it this meaning. The instruments used on this occasion were evidently of the same kind with those used on the jubilee, and were probably made of horn or of silver; and the text in this place may be translated, "And seven priests shall bear before the ark the seven jubilee trumpets." *Seven times.* The time was thus lengthened out that the besiegers and the besieged might be the more deeply impressed with that supernatural power by which *alone* the walls fell.

5. *The wall of the city shall fall down flat.* Several commentators, both Jews and Christians, have supposed that the ground under the foundation of the walls opened, and the wall sunk into the chasm, so that there remained nothing but plain ground for the Israelites to walk over. Of this the text says nothing; literally, "The wall of the city shall fall down under itself," which appears to mean no more than, "The wall shall fall down from its very foundations." And this probably was the case in every part, though large breaches in different places might be amply sufficient to admit the armed men first, after whom the whole host might enter, in order to destroy the city.

9. *The rereward came after the ark.* The word *measseph,* from *asaph,* to "collect" or "gather up," may signify either the *rearward,* as our translation understands it, or the people who carried the baggage of the army; for on the seventh day this was necessary, as much fighting might be naturally expected in the assault, and they would need a supply of arms, darts, etc., as well as conveniences for those who might happen to be wounded. Or the persons here intended might be such as carried the sacred articles belonging to the ark, or merely such people as might follow in the procession, without observing any particular order. The Jews think the division of Dan is meant, which always brought up the rear. See Numbers x.

14. *So they did six days.* It is not likely that the whole Israelitish host went each day round the city. This would have been utterly impossible; the fighting men alone amounted to nearly six hundred thousand, independently of the people, who must have amounted at least to two or three millions. We may therefore safely assert that only a select number, such as was deemed necessary for the occasion, were employed.

15. *The seventh day . . . they rose early.* Because on this day they had to encompass the city seven times; a proof that the city could not have been very extensive, else this going round it seven times, and having time sufficient left to sack and destroy it, would have been

MATTHEW HENRY

which is servile and secular, but this which they did was a religious act. It is certainly no breach of the sabbath rest to do the sabbath work.

VII. They continued to do this during the time appointed, and seven times the seventh day, though they saw not any effect of it. We may suppose the oddness of the thing did at first amuse the besieged. Probably they bantered the besiegers, as those mentioned in Neh. vi. 2, "*What do these feeble Jews?*"

VIII. At last they were to give a shout, and did so, and immediately the walls fell, *v.* 16. This was a triumphant shout; a shout of prayer, an echo to the sound of the trumpets which proclaimed the promise that God would remember them. And at the end of time, when our Lord shall descend from heaven with a shout, and the sound of a trumpet, Satan's kingdom shall be completely ruined, and not till then, when all opposing rule, principality, and power, shall be effectually and eternally put down.

Verses 17–27

The people had religiously observed the orders given them concerning the besieging of Jericho, and now at length Joshua had told them (*v.* 16), '*The Lord hath given you the city*, enter and take possession."

I. The rules they were to observe in taking possession. 1. The city shall be a *cherem*, a devoted thing, it and all therein, to the Lord. No life in it might be ransomed upon any terms. Only, when this severity is ordered, Rahab and her family are excepted: *She shall live and all that are with her*. She had distinguished herself from her neighbours by the kindness she showed to Israel. 2. All the treasure of it, the money and plate and valuable goods, must be consecrated to the service of the tabernacle. God had promised them a land *flowing with milk and honey*, not a land abounding with silver and gold. He would have them to reckon themselves enriched in the enriching of the tabernacle. 3. A particular caution is given them to take heed of meddling with the forbidding spoil; "*In any wise keep yourselves from the accursed thing*; check yourselves, and frighten yourselves from having anything to do with it." He speaks as if he foresaw the sin of Achan, which we have an account of in the next chapter.

II. The entrance that was opened to them into the city by the sudden fall of the walls. That which the inhabitants trusted to for defence proved their destruction. The sudden fall of the wall, no doubt, put the inhabitants into such a consternation that they had no strength nor spirit to make any resistance, but they became an easy prey to the sword of Israel. Thus shall Satan's kingdom fall, nor shall any prosper that harden themselves against God.

III. The execution of the orders given concerning this devoted city. 1. All that breathed were put to the sword. If they had not had a divine warrant under the seal of miracles for this execution, it could not have been justified, nor can it justify the like now, when we are sure no such warrant can be produced. The spirit of the gospel is very different, for Christ came not to destroy men's lives but to save them, Luke ix. 56. Christ's victories were of another nature. 2. The city was *burnt with fire, and all that was in it*, v. 24. 3. All the silver and gold, and all those vessels which were capable of being purified by fire, were brought into the treasury of the house of the Lord.

IV. The preservation of Rahab the harlot, or innkeeper, who *perished not with those that believed not*, Heb. xi. 31. The public faith was engaged for her safety by the two spies. The same persons that she had secured were employed to secure her, *v.* 22, 23. All her kindred were saved with her. Now being preserved alive, 1. She was left for some time without the camp to be purified from the Gentile superstition, which she was to renounce, and to be prepared for her admission as a proselyte. 2. She was in due time incorporated with the church of Israel, and she and her posterity dwelt in Israel, and her family was remarkable long after. We find her the wife of Salmon, prince of Judah, mother of Boaz, and named among the ancestors of our Saviour, Matt. i. 5.

V. Jericho is condemned to a perpetual desolation, and a curse pronounced upon the man that at any time hereafter should offer to rebuild it (*v.* 26). The situation of the city was very pleasant, and probably its nearness to Jordan was an advantage to it, which would tempt men to build upon the same spot; but they are here told it is at their peril if they do it. Men build for their posterity, but he that builds Jericho shall have no posterity to enjoy what he builds. This curse did come upon that man who long after rebuilded Jericho (1 Kings xvi. 34), but we are not to think it made the place ever the worse when it was built, or brought any hurt to those that inhabited it.

JAMIESON, FAUSSET, BROWN

16. it came to pass at the seventh time, . . . Joshua said unto the people, Shout; for the Lord hath given you the city—This delay brought out their faith and obedience in so remarkable a manner, that it is celebrated by the apostle (Heb. 11:30). **17-19. the city shall be accursed**—(See on Lev. 27:28, 29). **The *cherem*, or** anathema, was a devotion to utter destruction (Deut. 7:2; 20:17; I Sam. 15:3). When such a ban was pronounced against a hostile city, the men and animals were killed—no booty was allowed to be taken. The idols and all the precious ornaments on them were to be burned (Deut. 7:25; cf. I Chron. 14:12). Everything was either to be destroyed or consecrated to the sanctuary. Joshua pronounced this ban on Jericho, a great and wealthy city, evidently by divine direction. The severity of the doom, accordant with the requirements of a law which was holy, just, and good, was justified, not only by the fact of its inhabitants being part of a race who had filled up their iniquities, but by their resisting the light of the recent astonishing miracle at the Jordan. Besides, as Jericho seems to have been defended by reinforcements from all the country (ch. 24:11), its destruction would paralyze all the rest of the devoted people, and thus tend to facilitate the conquest of the land; showing, as so astounding a military miracle did, that it was done, not by man, but by the power and through the anger, of God. **18. and ye, in any wise keep yourselves from the accursed thing**—Generally they were at liberty to take the spoil of other cities that were captured (Deut. 2:35; 3:7; ch. 8:27). But this, as the first fruits of Canaan, was made an exception; nothing was to be spared but Rahab and those in her house. A violation of these stringent orders would not only render the guilty persons obnoxious to the curse, but entail distress and adversity upon all Israel, by provoking the divine displeasure. These were the instructions given, or repeated (Deut. 13:17; 7:26), previous to the last act of the siege.

20, 21. THE WALLS FALL DOWN. **20. So the people shouted when the priests blew with the trumpets**—Towards the close of the seventh circuit, the signal was given by Joshua, and on the Israelites' raising their loud war cry, the walls fell down, doubtless burying multitudes of the inhabitants in the ruins, while the besiegers, rushing in, consigned everything animate and inanimate to indiscriminate destruction (Deut. 20:16, 17.) Jewish writers mention it as an immemorial tradition that the city fell on the Sabbath. It should be remembered that the Canaanites were incorrigible idolaters, addicted to the most horrible vices, and that the righteous judgment of God might sweep them away by the sword, as well as by famine or pestilence. There was mercy mingled with judgment in employing the sword as the instrument of punishing the guilty Canaanites, for while it was directed against one place, time was afforded for others to repent.

22-25. RAHAB IS SAVED. **22, 23. Joshua had said . . . Go into the harlot's house, and bring out thence the woman, and all that she hath**—It is evident that the town walls were not demolished universally, at least all at once, for Rahab's house was allowed to stand until her relatives were rescued according to promise. **they brought out all her kindred, and left them without the camp of Israel**—a temporary exclusion, in order that they might be cleansed from the defilement of their native idolatries and gradually trained for admission into the society of God's people. **24. burned the city . . . and all . . . therein**—except the silver, gold, and other metals, which, as they would not burn, were added to the treasury of the sanctuary. **25. she** [Rahab] **dwelleth in Israel unto this day**—a proof that this book was written not long after the events related.

26, 27. THE REBUILDER OF JERICHO CURSED. **26. Joshua adjured them at that time**—i.e., imposed upon his countrymen a solemn oath, binding on themselves as well as their posterity, that they would never rebuild that city. Its destruction was designed by God to be a permanent memorial of His abhorrence of idolatry and its attendant vices. **Cursed be the man . . . that riseth up and buildeth this city Jericho**—i.e., makes the daring attempt to build. **he shall lay the foundation thereof in his first-born, and in his youngest son shall he set up the gates of it**—shall become childless—the first beginning being marked by the death of his oldest

ADAM CLARKE

impossible.

17. *The city shall be accursed.* That is, it shall be devoted to destruction; you shall take no spoils, and put all that resist to the sword. Though this may be the meaning of the word *cherem* in some places (see the note on Lev. xxvii. 29), yet here it seems to imply the total destruction of all the inhabitants, (see v. 21); but it is likely that peace was offered to this city, and that the extermination of the inhabitants was in consequence of the rejection of this offer.

20. *The people shouted with a great shout, that the wall fell down.* There has been much learned labor spent to prove that the shouting of the people might be the natural cause that the wall fell down! The whole relation evidently supposes it to have been a supernatural interference.

21. *They utterly destroyed . . . both man and woman.* As this act was ordered by God himself, who is the Maker and Judge of all men, it must be right; for the Judge of all the earth cannot do wrong. Nothing that breathed was permitted to live; hence the oxen, sheep, and asses were destroyed, as well as the inhabitants.

23. *Brought out Rahab, and her father.* Rahab having been faithful to her vow of secrecy, the Israelites were bound by the oath of the spies, who acted as their representatives in this business, to preserve her and her family alive. *And left them without the camp.* They were considered as persons unclean, and consequently left without the camp (see Lev. xiii. 46; Num. xii. 14). When they had abjured heathenism, were purified, and the males had received circumcision, they were doubtless admitted into the camp and became incorporated with Israel.

24. *Only the silver, and the gold . . . they put into the treasury.* The people were to have no share of the spoils, because they had no hand in the conquest. God alone overthrew the city; and only into His treasury the spoils were brought.

25. *And she dwelleth in Israel even unto this day.* This is one proof that the book was written in the time to which it is commonly referred; and certainly might have been done by the hand of Joshua himself, though doubtless many marginal notes may have since crept into the text, which, to superficial observers, give it the appearance of having been written after the days of Joshua. See the Preface to this book.

26. *And Joshua adjured them at that time.* It appears that he had received intimations from God that this idolatrous city should continue a monument of the divine displeasure; and having convened the princes and elders of the people, he bound them by an oath that they should never rebuild it; and then, in their presence, pronounced a curse upon the person who should attempt it. The ruins of this city continuing would be a permanent proof, not only of God's displeasure against idolatry, but of the miracle which He had wrought in behalf of the Israelites.

He shall lay the foundation thereof. This is a strange execration, but it may rather be considered in the light of a prediction. It seems to intimate that he who should attempt to rebuild this city should lose all his children in the interim from laying the foundation to the completion of the walls; which the author of 1 Kings xvi. 34 says was accomplished in Hiel

MATTHEW HENRY

We find Jericho afterwards graced with the presence, not only of those two great prophets Elijah and Elisha, but of our blessed Saviour himself, Luke xviii. 35; xix. 1; Matt. xx. 29.

CHAPTER 7

Verses 1-5

The story of this chapter begins with a *but. The Lord was with Joshua, and his fame was noised through all that country*, so the foregoing chapter ends. *But the children of Israel committed a trespass*, and so set God against them. If we lose our God, we lose our friends, who cannot help us unless God be for us.

I. Achan sinning, *v.* 1. The sin is here said to be *taking of the accursed thing*, in disobedience to the command and in defiance of the threatening, *ch.* vi. 18. In the sacking of Jericho compassion was put off and yielded to the law, but covetousness was indulged. The love of the world is that root of bitterness which of all others is most hardly rooted up. Yet the history of Achan is a plain intimation that he of all the thousands of Israel was the only delinquent in this matter. And yet, though it was a single person that sinned, the children of Israel are said *to commit the trespass*, because one of their body did it, and he was not as yet separated from them, nor disowned by them. They did it, that is, by what Achan did guilt was brought upon the whole society of which he was a member. This should be a warning to us to take heed of sin ourselves, lest by it many be defiled or disquieted (Heb. xii. 15). Many a careful tradesman has been broken by a careless partner. And it concerns us to watch over one another for the preventing of sin.

II. The camp of Israel suffering for the same: *The anger of the Lord was kindled against Israel*; he saw the offence, though they did not, and takes a course to make them see it. 1. Joshua sends a detachment to seize upon the next city that was in their way, and that was Ai. Only 3000 men were sent, advice being brought him by his spies that the place was inconsiderable, and needed no greater force for the reduction of it, *v.* 2, 3. *They are but few* (say the spies), but, as few as they were, they were too many for them. It will awaken our care and diligence in our Christian warfare to consider that *we wrestle with principalities and powers.* 2. The party he sent, in their first attack upon the town, were repulsed with some loss (*v.* 4, 5). It served, (1) To humble God's Israel. (2) To harden the Canaanites, and to make them the more secure. (3) To be an evidence of God's displeasure against Israel, and a call to them to *purge out the old leaven.* And this was principally intended in their defeat. 3. The retreat of this party in disorder put the whole camp of Israel into a fright: *The hearts of the people melted*, not so much for the loss as for the disappointment. To every thinking man among them it appeared an indication of God's displeasure.

Verses 6-9

An account of the deep concern Joshua was in upon this sad occasion.

I. How he grieved: He *rent his clothes* (*v.* 6), in token of great sorrow for this public disaster, and especially a dread of God's displeasure, which was certainly the cause of it. One of the bravest soldiers that ever was owned that his *flesh trembled for fear of God*, Ps. cxix. 120. As one *humbling himself under the mighty hand of God, he fell to the earth upon his face.* The elders of Israel, being interested in the cause and influenced by his example, prostrated themselves with him, and, in token of deep humiliation, *put dust upon their heads*, not only as mourners, but as penitents. His eye is upon God as displeased, and that troubles him.

II. How he prayed, or pleaded rather, humbly expostulating the case with God, not sullen, as David when *the Lord had made a breach upon Uzzah*, but much affected; his spirit seemed to be somewhat ruffled and discomposed, yet not so as to be put out of frame for prayer; but, by giving vent to his trouble in a humble address to God, he keeps his temper and it ends well. 1. Now he wishes they had all taken up with the lot of the two tribes on the other side Jordan, *v.* 7. Those words, *wherefore hast thou brought us over Jordan to destroy us?* are too like what the murmurers often said (Exod. xiv. 11, 12; xvi. 3; xvii. 3; Num. xiv. 2, 3); but he that searches the heart knew they came from another spirit, and therefore was not extreme to mark what he said amiss. 2. He speaks as one quite at a loss concerning the meaning of this event (*v.* 8). Is the Lord's arm shortened? Note, The methods of Providence are

JAMIESON, FAUSSET, BROWN

son, and his only surviving child dying at the time of its completion. This curse was accomplished 550 years after its denunciation (See on I Kings 16: 34.)

CHAPTER 7

VS. 1. ACHAN'S TRESPASS. **1. the children of Israel committed a trespass in the accursed thing**—There was one transgressor against the *cherem*, or ban, on Jericho, and his transgression brought the guilt and disgrace of sin upon the whole nation. **Achan**—called afterwards Achar (trouble) (I Chron. 2:7). **Zabdi**—or Zimri (I Chron. 2:6). **Zerah**—or Zarah, son of Judah and Tamar (Gen. 38:30.) His genealogy is given probably to show that from a parentage so infamous the descendants would not be carefully trained in the fear of God.

2-26. THE ISRAELITES SMITTEN AT AI. **2. Joshua sent men from Jericho to Ai**—After the sacking of Jericho, the next step was to penetrate into the hills above. Accordingly, spies went up the mountain pass to view the country. The precise site of Ai, or Hai, is indicated with sufficient clearness (Gen. 12:8; 13:3) and has been recently discovered in an isolated tell, called by the natives Tell-el-hajar, "the mount of stones," at two miles', or thirty-five minutes' distance, east-southeast from Bethel [VAN DE VELDE]. **Beth-aven**—("house of vanity")—a name afterwards given derisively (Hos. 4:15; 5:8; 10:5), on account of its idolatries, to Bethel, "house of God," but here referred to another place, about six miles east of Bethel and three north of Ai. **3. Let not all the people go up, . . . for they are but few**—As the population of Ai amounted to 12,000 (ch. 8:25), it was a considerable town; though in the hasty and distant reconnoitre made by the spies, it probably appeared small in comparison to Jericho; and this may have been the reason for their proposing so small a detachment to capture it. **4, 5. they fled before the men of Ai**—An unexpected resistance, and the loss of thirty-six of their number diffused a panic, which ended in an ignominious rout. **chased them from before the gate even unto Shebarim**—i.e., unto the "breakings" or "fissures" at the opening of the passes. **and smote them in the going down**—i.e., the declivity or slope of the deep, rugged, adjoining wady. **wherefore the hearts of the people melted, and became as water**—It is evident that the troops engaged were a tumultuary, undisciplined band, no better skilled in military affairs than the Bedouin Arabs, who become disheartened and flee on the loss of ten or fifteen men. But the consternation of the Israelites arose from another cause—the evident displeasure of God, who withheld that aid on which they had confidently reckoned.

6-9. Joshua rent his clothes, and fell to the earth . . . before the ark . . . , he and the elders—It is evident, from those tokens of humiliation and sorrow, that a solemn fast was observed on this occasion. The language of Joshua's prayer is thought by many to savor of human infirmity and to be wanting in that reverence and submission he owed to God. But, although apparently breathing a spirit of bold remonstrance and complaint, it was in reality the effusion of a deeply humbled and afflicted mind, expressing his belief that God could not, after having so miraculously brought His people over Jordan into the promised land, intend to destroy them, to expose them to the insults of their triumphant enemies, and bring reproach upon His own name for inconstancy or unkindness to His people, or inability to resist their enemies. Unable to understand the cause of the present calamity, he owned the hand of God.

ADAM CLARKE

the Beth-elite, who rebuilt Jericho under the reign of Ahab, and "laid the foundation thereof in Abiram his firstborn, and set up the gates thereof in his youngest son Segub."

CHAPTER 7

1. *The children of Israel committed a trespass* It is certain that one only was guilty, and yet the trespass is imputed here to the whole congregation; and the whole congregation soon suffered shame and disgrace on the account, as their armies were defeated, thirty-six persons slain, and general terror spread through the whole camp. Being one body, God attributed the crime of the individual to the whole till the trespass was discovered, and by a public act of justice inflicted on the culprit the congregation had purged itself of the iniquity. *The accursed thing.* A portion of the spoils of the city of Jericho, the whole of which God had commanded to be destroyed. *For Achan, the son of Carmi.* Judah had two sons by Tamar: Pharez and Zarah. Zarah was father of Zabdi, and Zabdi of Carmi, the father of Achan.

2. *Sent men from Jericho to Ai.* This is the place called Hai, Gen. xii. 8. It was in the east of Bethel, north of Jericho, from which it was distant about ten or twelve miles. From verses 4 and 5 it appears to have been situated upon a hill, and belonged to the Amorites, as we learn from v. 7. It is very likely that it was a strong place, as it chose to risk a siege, notwithstanding the extraordinary destruction of Jericho, which it had lately witnessed.

4. *About three thousand men.* The spies sent to reconnoitre the place (v. 3) reported that the town was meanly garrisoned, and that two or three thousand men would be sufficient to take it. These were accordingly sent up, and were repulsed by the Amorites.

5. *They chased them from before the gate even unto Shebarim.* They seem to have presumed that the men of Ai would have immediately opened their gates to them, and therefore they marched up with confidence; but the enemy appearing, they were put to flight, their ranks utterly broken, and thirty-six of them killed. *Shebarim* signifies "breaches" or "broken places," and may here apply to the ranks of the Israelites, which were broken by the men of Ai; for the people were totally routed, though there were but few slain. *The hearts of the people melted.* They were utterly discouraged, and by this gave an ample proof that without the supernatural assistance of God they could never have conquered the land.

6. *Joshua rent his clothes.* It was not in consequence of this slight discomfiture, simply considered in itself, that Joshua laid this business so much to heart; but (1) because the people melted, and became as water, and there was little hope that they would make any stand against the enemy; and (2) because this defeat evidently showed that God had turned His hand against them. *Put dust upon their heads.* Rending the clothes, beating the breast, tearing the hair, putting dust upon the head, and falling down prostrate were the usual marks of deep affliction and distress. Most nations have expressed their sorrow in a similar way.

7. *Alas, O Lord God.* Particles of exclamations and distress, or what are called interjections, are nearly the same in all languages; and the reason is because they are the simple voice of nature. The Hebrew word which we translate *alas* is *ahah.* The complaint of Joshua in this and the following verses seems principally to have arisen from his deep concern for the glory of God, and the affecting interest he took in behalf of the people. He felt for the thousands of Israel, whom he considered as abandoned to destruction; and he felt for the glory of God, for he knew should Israel be destroyed God's name would be blasphemed among the heathen. His expostulations with his Maker,

MATTHEW HENRY

often intricate and perplexing, and such as the wisest and best of men know not what to say to; but *they shall know hereafter*, John xiii. 7. 3. He pleads the danger Israel was now in of being ruined. Thus even good men, when things go against them a little, are too apt to fear the worst. But this comes in here as a plea: "Lord, let not Israel's name, which has been so dear to thee and so great in the world, be cut off." 4. He pleads the reproach that would be cast on God, and that if Israel were ruined his glory would suffer by it. He feared it would reflect on God, his wisdom and power, his goodness and faithfulness; what would the Egyptians say? Note, Nothing is more grievous to a gracious soul than dishonour done to God's name. We cannot urge a better plea than this, Lord, *What wilt thou do for thy great name?* Let God in all be glorified, and then welcome his whole will.

Verses 10–15

God's answer to Joshua's address. And let those that find themselves under the tokens of God's displeasure never complain *of* him, but complain *to* him, and they shall receive an answer of peace. The answer came immediately.

I. God encourages Joshua against his present despondencies: "*Get thee up*, suffer not thy spirits to droop and sink thus; *wherefore liest thou thus upon thy face?*" Now God told him it was enough, he would not have him continue any longer in that melancholy posture, for God delights not in the grief of penitents when they afflict their souls further than as it qualifies them for pardon and peace. Joshua continued his mourning *till eventide* (*v.* 6). It is time for him to lay aside his mourning weeds, and put on his judge's robes, and *clothe himself with zeal as a cloak*. Weeping must not hinder sowing, nor one duty of religion jostle out another.

II. He informs him of the true and only cause of this disaster (*v.* 11): *Israel hath sinned*. The sinner is not named, though the sin is described, but it is spoken of as the act of Israel in general. Observe how the sin is here made to appear exceedingly sinful. 1. *They have transgressed my covenant*, an express precept with a penalty annexed to it. It was agreed that God should have all the spoil of Jericho, and they should have the spoil of the rest of the cities of Canaan; but, in robbing God of his part, they *transgressed this covenant*. 2. *They have even taken of the devoted thing*. 3. They *have also stolen*; they did it clandestinely, as if they could conceal it from the divine omniscience. 4. They have *dissembled* also. Achan joined with the rest in a general protestation of innocency, and kept his countenance, like the adulterous woman that *eats and wipes her mouth, and says, I have done no wickedness*. Nay, 5. They have put the accursed thing *among their own goods*, as if they had as good a title to that as to anything they have. God could at this time have told him who the person was that had done this thing, but he does not, (1) To exercise the zeal of Joshua and Israel, in searching out the criminal. (2) To give the sinner himself space to repent and make confession. But Achan never discovering himself till the lot discovered him evidenced the hardness of his heart, and therefore he found no mercy.

III. He awakens him to enquire further into it, by telling him, 1. That this was the only ground for the controversy so that when this accursed thing was put away he needed not fear. 2. That if this accursed thing were not destroyed they could not expect the return of God's gracious presence. By personal repentance and reformation, we destroy the accursed thing in our own hearts, and, unless we do this, we must never expect the favour of the blessed God.

IV. He directs him in what method to make this enquiry and prosecution. 1. He must *sanctify the people*, now over-night, that is, as it is explained, he must command them to *sanctify themselves*, *v.* 13. And what can either magistrates or ministers do more towards sanctification? They must put themselves into a suitable frame to appear before God and submit to the divine scrutiny. 2. He must bring them all under the scrutiny of the lot (*v.* 14); the tribe which the guilty person was of should first be discovered by lot, then the family, then the household, and last of all the person. The conviction came upon him thus gradually that he might have some space given him to come in and surrender himself; for God is *not willing that any should perish, but that all should come to repentance*. 3. When the criminal was found out he must be put to death *without mercy* (Heb. x. 28). It was *sacrilege*; this was the crime to be thus severely punished, for warning to all people in all ages to take heed how they rob God.

Verses 16–26

I. The discovery of Achan by the lot. In the

JAMIESON, FAUSSET, BROWN

10-15. **the Lord said unto Joshua, Get thee up**—The answer of the divine oracle was to this effect: the crisis is owing not to unfaithfulness in Me, but sin in the people.

The conditions of the covenant have been violated by the reservation of spoil from the doomed city; wickedness, emphatically called folly, has been committed in Israel (Ps. 14:1), and dissimulation, with other aggravations of the crime, continues to be practised. The people are liable to destruction equally with the accursed nations of Canaan (Deut. 7:26). Means must, without delay, be taken to discover and punish the perpetrator of this trespass that Israel may be released from the ban, and things be restored to their former state of prosperity.

ALEXANDER MACLAREN:

We learn the power of one man to infect a whole community and to inflict disaster on it. One sick sheep taints a flock. The effects of the individual's sin are not confined to the doer. We have got a fine new modern word to express this solemn law, and we talk now of "solidarity," which sounds very learned and "advanced." But it means just what we see in this story: Achan was the sinner, all Israel suffered. We are knit together by a mystical but real bond, so that "no man," be he good or bad, "liveth unto himself," and no man's sin terminates in himself. We see the working of that unity in families, communities, churches, nations. Men are not merely aggregated together like a pile of cannon balls, but are knit together like the myriad lives in a coral rock. Put a drop of poison anywhere, and it runs by a thousand branching veins through the mass, and tints and taints it all. No man can tell how far the blight of his secret sins may reach, nor how wide the blessing of his modest goodness may extend. We should seek to cultivate the sense of being members of a great whole, and to ponder our individual responsibility for the moral and religious health of the church, the city, the nation. We are not without danger from an exaggerated individualism, and we need to realize more constantly and strongly that we are but threads in a great network, endowed with mysterious vitality and power of transmitting electric impulses, both good and evil.

—*Expositions of Holy Scripture*

ADAM CLARKE

which have been too hastily blamed by some as savoring of too great freedom and impatience, are founded on God's own words, Deut. xxxii. 26-27, and on the practice of Moses himself, who had used similar expressions on a similar occasion; see Exod. v. 22-23; Num. xiv. 13-18.

10. *Wherefore liest thou thus upon thy face?* It is plain there was nothing in Joshua's prayer or complaint that was offensive to God, for here there is no reprehension.

11. *Israel hath sinned.* It is impossible that God should turn against His people, if they had not turned away from Him. *They have taken of the accursed thing,* notwithstanding My severe prohibition. They *have also stolen,* supposing, if not seen by their brethren, I should either not see or not regard it. They have *dissembled*—pretended to have kept strictly the command I gave them; *and they have put it even among their own stuff*—considered it now as a part of their own property.

12. *Because they were accursed.* From this verse it appears that the nature of the execration or anathema was such that those who took of the thing doomed to destruction fell immediately under the same condemnation.

13. *Up, sanctify the people.* Joshua, all the time that God spake, lay prostrate before the ark; he is now commanded to get up, and sanctify the people, i.e., cause them to wash themselves, and get into a proper disposition to hear the judgment of the Lord relative to the late transactions.

14. *Ye shall be brought according to your tribes.* It has been a subject of serious inquiry in what manner and by what means the culpable tribe, family, household, and individual were discovered. It is probable that the whole was determined by the lot; and that God chose this method to detect the guilty *tribe,* next the *family,* thirdly the *household,* and lastly the individual. This was nearly the plan pursued in the election of Saul by Samuel, 1 Sam. x. 19-20. The same mode was used to find out who it was that transgressed the king's command, when it was found that Jonathan had eaten a little honey, 1 Sam. xiv. 40-43.

MATTHEW HENRY

scrutiny observe, 1. That the guilty tribe was that of Judah, which was, and was to be, of all the tribes, the most honourable and illustrious. The Jews' tradition is that when the tribe of Judah was taken the valiant men of that tribe drew their swords, and professed they would not sheathe them again till they saw the criminal punished and themselves cleared who knew their own innocency. 2. That the guilty person was at length fastened upon, and the language of the lot was, *Thou art the man, v.* 18. It was strange that Achan, being conscious to himself of guilt, when he saw the lot come nearer and nearer to him, had not either the wit to make an escape or the grace to make a confession. See here, (1) The folly of those that promise themselves secrecy in sin: the righteous God has many ways of bringing to light the hidden works of darkness. (2) How much it is our concern, when God is contending with us, to find out what the particular sin is, and pray earnestly with holy Job, *Lord, show me wherefore thou contendest with me.*

II. His arraignment and examination, *v.* 19. Joshua sits judge, and urges him to make a penitent confession, that his soul might be saved by it in the other world. Observe, 1. How he accosts him with the greatest tenderness. He might justly have called him "thief", and "rebel", "Raca", and "thou fool", but he calls him "son"; he might have adjured him to confess, as the high priest did our blessed Saviour, or threatened him with the torture to extort a confession, but for love's sake he rather beseeches him: *I pray thee make confession.* This is an example to all not to insult over those that are in misery, though they have brought themselves into it by their own wickedness. It is likewise an example to magistrates never to be transported into any indecencies of behaviour or language towards those that have given the greatest provocations. *The wrath of man worketh not the righteousness of God.* 2. What he wishes him to do, to confess the fact. Joshua was to him in God's stead, so that in confessing to him he confessed to God. Note, In confessing sin, as we take shame to ourselves, so we give glory to God as a righteous God, owning him justly displeased with us, and as a good God, who will not improve our confessions as evidences against us, but is faithful and just to forgive when we are brought to own that he would be faithful and just if he should punish. By sin we have injured God in his honour. Christ by his death has made satisfaction for the injury; but it is required that we by repentance show our good will to his honour, and, as far as in us lies, give glory to him.

III. His confession, which now at last, when he saw it was to no purpose to conceal his crime, was free and ingenuous enough, *v.* 20, 21. Here is, 1. A penitent acknowledgment of the fault. 2. A particular narrative of the fact: *Thus and thus have I done.* Note, It becomes penitents, in the confession of their sins to God, to be very particular; not only, "I have sinned," but, "In this and that instance I have sinned." He confesses, (1) To the things taken. In plundering a house in Jericho he found a goodly Babylonish garment; the word signifies a robe, such as princes wore when they appeared in state. "A thousand pities" (thinks Achan) "that it should be burnt; it will serve me many a year for my best garment." Under these pretences he makes bold with this first, but, his hand being thus in, he proceeds to take a bag of money, *two hundred shekels,* that is, one hundred ounces of silver, and a *wedge of gold* which weighed *fifty shekels,* that is, twenty-five ounces. He could not plead that, in taking these, he saved them *from the fire,* but those that make a slight excuse to serve in daring to commit one sin will venture upon the next without such an excuse; for the way of sin is downhill. See what a poor prize it was for which Achan ran this desperate hazard. See Matt. xvi. 26. (2) He confesses the manner of taking them. [1] The sin began in the eye. He saw these fine things, as Eve saw the forbidden fruit, and was strangely charmed with the sight. See what comes of suffering the heart to walk after the eyes, and what need we have to make this covenant with our eyes, that if they wander they shall be sure to weep for it. *Look not thou upon the wine that is red,* upon the woman that is fair. [2] It proceeded out of the heart. He owns, *I coveted them.* Thus lust conceived and brought forth this sin. Those that would be kept from sinful actions must mortify and check in themselves sinful desires. It was not the looking, but the lusting that ruined him. [3] When he had committed it he was very industrious to conceal it. See the *deceitfulness of sin*; that which is pleasing in the commission is bitter in the reflection; at the last it bites like a serpent.

IV. His conviction. God had convicted him by the lot; he had convicted himself by his own confession. Joshua has him further convicted by the searching of his tent, in which the goods were found

JAMIESON, FAUSSET, BROWN

16-18. So Joshua rose up early, and brought Israel by their tribes—i.e., before the tabernacle. The lot being appealed to (Prov. 16:33), he proceeded in the inquiry from heads of tribes to heads of families, and from heads of households in succession to one family, and to particular persons in that family, until the criminal was found to be Achan, who, on Joshua's admonition, confessed the fact of having secreted for his own use, in the floor of his tent, spoil both in garments and money. How dreadful must have been his feelings when he saw the slow but certain process of discovery! (Num. 32:23).

19. Joshua said unto Achan, My son, give . . . glory to God—a form of adjuration to tell the truth.

21. a goodly Babylonish garment—lit., a mantle of Shinar. The plain of Shinar was in early times celebrated for its gorgeous robes, which were of brilliant and various colors, generally arranged in figured patterns, probably resembling those of modern Turkish carpets, and the colors were either interwoven in the loom or embroidered with the needle. **two hundred shekels of silver**—about $200.00 according to the old Mosaic shekel, or the half of that sum, reckoning by the common shekel. **a wedge of gold**—lit., an ingot or bar in the shape of a tongue worth about $500.00.

22, 23. Joshua sent messengers, and they ran unto the tent—from impatient eagerness not only to test the truth of the story, but to clear Israel from the imputation of guilt. Having discovered the stolen articles, they laid them out before the Lord, "as a token of their belonging to Him" on account of the ban.

ADAM CLARKE

19. *My son, give . . . glory to the Lord God.* The person being now detected, Joshua wishes him to acknowledge the omniscience of God, and confess his crime. And doubtless this was designed, not only for the edification of the people, and a vindication of the righteous judgment of God, but in reference to his own salvation; for as his life was now become forfeited to the law, there was the utmost necessity of humiliation before God, that his soul might be saved. *Give . . . glory to God* signifies the same as, Make a thorough confession as in the presence of God, and disguise no part of the truth. In this way and in these very words the Jews adjured the man who had been born blind that he would truly tell who had healed him, John ix. 24.

20. *I have sinned against the Lord God.* This seems a very honest and hearty confession, and there is hope that this poor culprit escaped perdition.

21. *A goodly Babylonish garment. Addereth shinar,* a "splendid or costly robe of Shinar"; but as Babylon or Babel was built in the plain of Shinar, the word has in general been translated Babylon in this place. It is very probable that this was the robe of the king of Jericho, for the same word is used, Jon. iii. 6, to express the royal robe of the king of Nineveh, which he laid aside in order to humble himself before God. *A wedge of gold.* A tongue of gold, *leshon zahab* what we commonly call an "ingot of gold," a corruption of the word *lingot,* signifying a "little tongue." This verse gives us a notable instance of the progress of sin. It (1) enters by the eye; (2) sinks into the heart; (3) actuates the hand, and (4) leads to secrecy and dissimulation.

MATTHEW HENRY

which he confessed to.

V. His condemnation. Joshua passes sentence upon him (*v.* 25): *Why hast thou troubled us?* Note, Sin is a very troublesome thing, not only to the sinner himself, but to all about him. Now (says Joshua) *God shall trouble thee.* See why Achan was so severely dealt with, not only because he had robbed God, but because he had troubled Israel; over his head he had (as it were) this accusation written, "Achan, *the troubler of Israel,*" as Ahab, 1 Kings xviii. 18. Some of the Jewish doctors, from that word which determines the troubling of him to *this day*, infer that therefore he should not be troubled in the world to come; the flesh was destroyed that the spirit might be saved, and, if so, the dispensation was really less severe than it seemed.

VI. His execution.

1. The place of execution. The execution was at a distance, that the camp which was disturbed by Achan's sin might not be defiled by his death.

2. The persons employed in his execution. It was the act of all Israel, *v.* 24, 25.

3. The partakers with him in the punishment; for *he perished not alone in his iniquity, ch.* xxii. 20. (1) The stolen goods were destroyed with him. (2) All his other goods were destroyed likewise, not only his tent, and the furniture of that, but his *oxen, asses, and sheep.* Those lose their own that grasp at more than their own. (3) His sons and daughters were put to death with him. Some indeed think that they were *brought out* (*v.* 24) only to be the spectators of their father's punishment. Perhaps his sons and daughters were aiders and abettors in the villainy, had helped to carry off the accursed thing. It is very probable that they assisted in the concealment.

4. The punishment itself that was inflicted on him. He was stoned (some think as a sabbath breaker, supposing that the sacrilege was committed on the sabbath day), and then his dead body was burnt.

5. The pacifying of God's wrath hereby (*v.* 26): *The Lord turned from the fierceness of his anger.* Take away the cause, and the effect will cease.

VII. The record of his conviction and execution. Care was taken to preserve the remembrance of it, for warning and instruction to posterity. 1. A heap of stones was raised on the place where Achan was executed, every one perhaps of the congregation throwing a stone to the heap, in token of his detestation of the crime. 2. A new name was given to the place; it was called the *Valley of Achor,* or *trouble.* The *Valley of Achor* is said to be given for a *door of hope*, because when we put away the accursed thing then there begins to be hope in Israel, Hos. ii. 15; Ezra x. 2.

JAMIESON, FAUSSET, BROWN

24-26. Joshua, and all Israel with him, took Achan—He with his children and all his property, cattle as well as movables, were brought into one of the long broad ravines that open into the Ghor, and after being stoned to death (Num. 15:30-35), his corpse, with all belonging to him, was consumed to ashes by fire. "All Israel" was present, not only as spectators, but active agents, as many as possible, in inflicting the punishment—thus testifying their abhorrence of the sacrilege, and their intense solicitude to regain the divine favor. As the divine law expressly forbade the children to be put to death for their father's sins (Deut. 24:16), the conveyance of Achan's "sons and daughters" to the place of execution might be only as spectators, that they might take warning by the parental fate; or, if they shared his punishment (ch. 22:20), they had probably been accomplices in his crime, and, indeed, he could scarcely have dug a hole within his tent without his family being aware of it.

they raised over him a great heap of stones—It is customary to raise cairns over the graves of criminals or infamous persons in the East still. **the name of that place was called, The valley of Achor** [trouble], **unto this day**—So painful an episode would give notoriety to the spot, and it is more than once noted by the sacred writers of a later age (Isa. 65:10; Hos. 2:15).

ADAM CLARKE

24. *Joshua . . . took Achan . . . and all that he had.* He and his cattle and substance were brought to the valley to be consumed; his sons and his daughters, probably, to witness the judgments of God inflicted on their disobedient parent. See v. 25.

25. *Why hast thou troubled us?* Here is a reference to the meaning of Achan's or Achar's name, *meh achar-tanu;* and as *achar* is used here, and not *achan,* and the valley is called the "valley of Achor," and not the "valley of Achan," hence some have supposed that Achar was his proper name, as it is read in 1 Chron. ii. 7.

And all Israel stoned him with stones, and burned them with fire, after they had stoned them with stones. With great deference to the judgment of others, I ask, Can it be fairly proved from the text that the sons and daughters of Achan were stoned to death and burned as well as their father? The text certainly leaves it doubtful, but seems rather to intimate that Achan alone was stoned, and that his substance was burned with fire. The reading of the present Hebrew text is, "They stoned him with stones, and burned them with fire, after they had stoned them with stones." The singular number being used in the first clause of the verse, and the plural in the last, leaves the matter doubtful. The Vulgate is very clear: "All Israel stoned him: and all that he had was consumed with fire." The Septuagint add this and the first clause of the next verse together: "And all Israel stoned him with stones, and raised over him a great heap of stones." The Syriac says simply, "They stoned him with stones, and burned what pertained to him with fire."

CHAPTER 8

(MATTHEW HENRY)

Verses 1–2

It should seem, Joshua was now at a stand and could not think, without fear and trembling, of pushing forward, lest there should be in the camp another Achan; then God spoke to him, either by vision, as before (*ch.* v), as a man of war with his sword drawn, or by the breastplate of judgment. Note, When we have faithfully put away sin, that accursed thing, we may expect to hear from God to our comfort; and God's directing us how to go on in our Christian work and warfare is a good evidence of his being reconciled to us.

I. The encouragement God gives to Joshua to proceed: *Fear not, neither be thou dismayed, v.* 1. Corruptions within the church weaken the hands, and damp the spirits, of her guides and helpers, more than oppositions from without; treacherous Israelites are to be dreaded more than malicious Canaanites. But God bids Joshua not be dismayed; the same power that keeps Israel from being ruined by their enemies shall keep them from ruining themselves. To animate him, 1. He assures him of success against Ai, tells him it is all his own; but he must take it as God's gift. 2. He allows the people to take the spoil to themselves. Here the spoil was not consecrated to God as that of Jericho.

II. The direction he gives him in attacking Ai. It must not be such a work of time as the taking of Jericho was. Nor was it, as that, to be taken by miracle, but now their own conduct and courage must be exercised; having seen God work for them, they must now bestir themselves. God directs him, 1. To take all the people. 2. To lay an ambush behind the city.

Verses 3–22

We have here an account of the taking of Ai by stratagem. Nothing was dissembled, nothing counterfeited, but a retreat. The enemy ought to have been

CHAPTER 8

(JAMIESON, FAUSSET, BROWN)

Vss. 1-28. God Encourages Joshua. **1. The Lord said unto Joshua, Fear not**—By the execution of justice on Achan, the divine wrath was averted, the Israelites were reassured, defeat was succeeded by victory; and thus the case of Ai affords a striking example of God's disciplinary government, in which chastisements for sin are often made to pave the way for the bestowment of those temporal benefits, which, on account of sin, have been withdrawn, or withheld for a time. Joshua, who had been greatly dispirited, was encouraged by a special communication promising him (see ch. 1:6; Deut. 31:6-8) success in the next attempt, which, however, was to be conducted on different principles. **take all the people of war with thee, and arise, go up to Ai**—The number of fighting men amounted to 600,000, and the whole force was ordered on this occasion, partly because the spies, in their self-confidence, had said that a few were sufficient to attack the place (ch. 7:3), partly to dispel any misgivings which the memory of the late disaster might have created, and partly that the circumstance of the first spoil obtained in Canaan being shared among all, might operate both as a reward for obedience in refraining from the booty of Jericho, and as an incentive to future exertions (Deut. 6:10). The rest of the people, including the women and children, remained in the camp at Gilgal. Being in the plains of Jericho, it was an ascent to Ai, which was on a hill. **I have given into thy hand the king of Ai, and his people, and his city, and his land . . . lay thee an ambush for the city**—God assured him of its capture, but allowed him to follow his own tactics in obtaining the possession. **3. So Joshua . . . chose out thirty thousand mighty men of valour**—Joshua despatched 30,000 men under cover of night, to station themselves at the place appointed for the ambuscade. Out of this number a detachment of

CHAPTER 8

(ADAM CLARKE)

1. *Fear not.* The iniquity being now purged away, because of which God had turned His hand against Israel, there was now no cause to dread any other disaster, and therefore Joshua is ordered to take courage.

Take all the people of war with thee. From the letter of this verse it appears that all that were capable of carrying arms were to march out of the camp on this occasion: 30,000 chosen men formed an ambuscade in one place; 5,000 Joshua placed in another, who had all gained their positions in the night season; with the rest of the army he appeared the next morning before Ai, which the men of that city would naturally suppose were the whole of the Israelitish forces, and consequently be the more emboldened to come out and attack them. But some think that 30,000 men were the whole that were employed on this occasion; 5,000 of whom were placed as an ambuscade on the west side of the city between Bethel and Ai, v. 12, and with the rest Joshua appeared before the city in the morning. The king of Ai seeing but about 25,000 coming against him, and being determined to defend his city and crown to the last extremity, though he had but 12,000 persons in the whole city, v. 25, scarcely one-half of wnom we can suppose to be effective men, he was determined to risk a battle; and accordingly issued out, and was defeated by the stratagem mentioned in the preceding part of this chapter.

Several eminent commentators are of opinion that the whole Israelitish force was employed on this occasion, because of what is said in the first verse; but this is not at all likely. (1) It appears that but 30,000 were chosen out of the whole camp for this expedition, the rest being

MATTHEW HENRY	JAMIESON, FAUSSET, BROWN	ADAM CLARKE

upon their guard, and to have kept within the defence of their own walls. Common prudence, had they been governed by it, would have directed them not to venture on the pursuit of an army which they saw was so far superior to them in numbers, and leave their city unguarded; but *si populus vult decipi, decipiatur—if the people will be deceived, let them.*

I. There is some difficulty in adjusting the numbers that were employed to effect it. Mention is made (*v.* 3) of 30,000 that were *chosen and sent away by night,* to whom the charge was given to surprise the city as soon as ever they perceived it was evacuated, *v.* 4, 7, 8. And yet afterwards (*v.* 12) it is said, Joshua *took* 5000 *men and set them to lie in ambush* behind the city, and that *ambush entered the city,* and *set it on fire, v.* 19. Now, 1. Some think there were two parties sent out to lie in ambush, and that Joshua made his open attack upon the city with all the thousands of Israel. But, 2. Others think that all the people were taken only to encamp before the city, and that out of them Joshua chose out 30,000 men to be employed in the action, out of which he sent out 5000 to lie in ambush, which were as many as could be supposed to march *incognito—without being discovered.*

II. Yet the principal parts of the story are plain enough, that a detachment being secretly marched behind the city, on the other side to that on which the main body of the army lay, Joshua, and the forces with him, faced the city; the garrison made a vigorous sally out upon them, whereupon they withdrew, gave ground, and retreated in some seeming disorder towards the wilderness, which being perceived by the men of Ai, they drew out all the force they had to pursue them. This gave a fair opportunity for those that lay in ambush to make themselves masters of the city, whereof when they had given notice by a smoke to Joshua, he, with all his force, returned upon the pursuers, who now, when it was too late, were aware of the snare they were drawn into, and, their retreat being intercepted, they were every man of them cut off.

1. What a brave commander Joshua was. Though an army of Israelites had been repulsed before Ai, yet he resolves to lead them on in person the second time, *v.* 5. He *went that night into the midst of the valley,* to make the necessary dispositions for an attack. It is the pious conjecture of the learned bishop Patrick that he went into the valley alone, to pray to God. When he had stretched out his spear towards the city (*v.* 18, a spear almost as fatal and formidable to the enemies of Israel as the rod of Moses was) he never drew back his hand till the work was done. Those that have stretched out their hands against their spiritual enemies must never draw them back. Joshua conquered by yielding, as if he had himself been conquered; so our Lord Jesus, when he bowed his head and gave up the ghost, seemed as if death had triumphed over him, and as if he and all his interests had been routed and ruined; but in his resurrection he rallied again and gave the powers of darkness a total defeat; he broke the serpent's head, by suffering him to bruise his heel. A glorious stratagem!

2. What an obedient people Israel was. What *Joshua commanded them to do, according to the commandment of the Lord* (*v.* 8), they did it without murmuring or disputing.

3. What an infatuated enemy the king of Ai was! He did not by his scouts discover those that lay in ambush behind the city, *v.* 14. From the killing of thirty-six men out of 3000, when Israel made the former attack upon his city, he inferred the total routing of so great an army as now he had to deal with (*v.* 6): *They flee before us as at the first.* See how the prosperity of fools destroys them and hardens them to their ruin.

4. What a complete victory Israel obtained over them by the favour and blessing of God. Each did his part.

Verses 23–29

We have here an account of the improvement which the Israelites made of their victory over Ai. 1. They put all to the sword. Here it is said (*v.* 26) that *Joshua drew not his hand back wherewith he stretched out the spear* (*v.* 18). Some think the spear he stretched out was not to slay the enemies, but to animate and encourage his own soldiers. He kept the inferior post of a standard-bearer, and did not quit it till the work was done. By the spear stretched out, he directed the people to expect their help from God, and to him to give the praise. 2. They plundered the city and took all the spoil to themselves, *v.* 27. 3. They laid the city in ashes, and left it to remain so, *v.* 28. Israel must yet dwell in tents, and therefore this city, as well as Jericho, must be burnt. 4. The king of Ai

5000 was sent forward to conceal themselves in the immediate precincts of the town, in order to seize the first opportunty of throwing themselves into it. **4. behind the city**—is rendered (vs. 9) "on the west of Ai." **9. between Beth-el and Ai**—Beth-el, though lying quite near in the direction of west by north, cannot be seen from Tell-el-hajar; two rocky heights rise between both places, in the wady El-Murogede, just as the laying of an ambush to the west of Ai would require [Van de Velde, Robinson]. **10. Joshua . . . numbered the people**—i.e., the detachment of liers-in-wait; he did this, to be furnished with clear evidence afterwards, that the work had been done without any loss of men, whereby the people's confidence in God would be strengthened and encouragement given them to prosecute the war of invasion with vigor. **he and the elders of Israel**—the chief magistrates and rulers, whose presence and official authority were necessary to ensure that the cattle and spoil of the city might be equally divided between the combatants and the rest of the people (Num. 31:27)—a military rule in Israel, that would have been very liable to be infringed, if an excited soldiery, eager for booty, had been left to their own will. **11-14. there was a valley** [lit., "*the* valley"] **between them and Ai. Joshua went that night into the midst of the valley**—The deep and steep-sided glen to the north of Tell-el-hajar, into which one looks down from the tell, fully agrees with this account [Van de Velde]. Joshua himself took up his position on the north side of "the ravine"—the deep chasm of the wady El-Murogede; "*that* night"—means, while it was dark, probably after midnight, or very early in the morning (John 20:1). The king of Ai, in the early dawn, rouses his slumbering subjects and makes a hasty sally with all his people who were capable of bearing arms, once more to surprise and annihilate them. **at a time appointed**—either an hour concocted between the king and people of Ai and those of Beth-el, who were confederates in this enterprise, or perhaps they had fixed on the same time of day, as they had fought successfully against Israel on the former occasion, deeming it a lucky hour (Judg. 20:38). **but he wist not that there were liers in ambush against him behind the city**—It is evident that this king and his subjects were little experienced in war; otherwise they would have sent out scouts to reconnoitre the neighborhood; at all events, they would not have left their town wholly unprotected and open. Perhaps an ambuscade may have been a war stratagem hitherto unknown in that country, and among that people. **15-17. Joshua and all Israel made as if they were beaten before them**—the pretended flight in the direction of the wilderness—i.e., southeast, into the Ghor, the desert valley of the Jordan, decoyed all the inhabitants of Ai out of the city, while the people of Beth-el hastened to participate in the expected victory. It is supposed by some, from "the city," and not "cities," being spoken of, that the effective force of Beth-el had been concentrated in Ai, as the two places were closely contiguous, and Ai the larger of the two. (See on ch. 12:16.) It may be remarked, however, that the words, "or Beth-el," are not in the Sept., and are rejected by some eminent scholars, as an interpolation not found in the most ancient MSS. **18-25. Joshua stretched out the spear that he had in his hand toward the city**—The uplifted spear had probably a flag, or streamer on it, to render it the more conspicuous from the height where he stood. At the sight of this understood signal the ambush nearest the city, informed by their scouts, made a sudden rush and took possession of the city, telegraphing to their brethren by raising a smoke from the walls. Upon seeing this, the main body, who had been feigning a flight, turned round at the head of the pass upon their pursuers, while the 25,000 issuing from their ambuscade, fell back upon their rear. The Ai-ites surprised, looked back, and found their situation now desperate. **23. the king of Ai they took alive, and brought him to Joshua**—to be reserved for a more ignominious death, as a greater criminal in God's sight than his subjects. In the mingled attack from before and behind, all the men were massacred. **24. all the Israelites returned unto Ai, and smote it with the edge of the sword**—the women, children, and old persons left behind, amounting, in all, to 12,000 people. **Joshua drew not his hand back**—Perhaps, from the long continuance of the posture, it might have been a means appointed by God, to animate the people, and kept up in the same devout spirit as Moses had shown, in lifting up his hands, until the work of slaughter had been completed—the ban executed. (See on Exod. 17:11, 12.) **28. Joshua burnt Ai, and made it an heap for ever**—"For ever" often signifies

drawn up in readiness should their cooperation be necessary. See vv. 3 and 10. (2) That all the people were mustered in order to make this selection, v. 1. (3) That these 30.000 were sent off by night, v. 3, Joshua himself continuing in the camp a part of that night, v. 9, with the design of putting himself at the head of the army next morning. (4) That of the 30,000 men 5,000 were directed to lie in ambush between Bethel and Ai, on the west side of the city, v. 12, the 25,000 having taken a position on the north side of the city, v. 11.

8. *Ye shall set the city on fire.* Probably this means no more than that they should kindle a fire in the city, the smoke of which should be an indication that they had taken it. For as the spoils of the city were to be divided among the people, had they at this time set fire to the city itself, all the property must have been consumed, for the 5,000 men did not wait to save anything, as they immediately issued out to attack the men of Ai in the rear.

10. *Numbered the people.* "He visited the people"—inspected their ranks to see whether everything was in perfect readiness, that in case they should be needed they might be led on to the attack. There is no doubt that Joshua had left the rest of the army so disposed and ready, part of it having probably advanced towards Ai, that he might easily receive reinforcements in case of any disaster to the 30,000 which had advanced against the city; and this consideration will serve to remove a part of the difficulty which arises from vv. 1, 3, and 10, collated with other parts of this chapter. Had he brought all his troops in sight, the people of Ai would not have attempted to risk a battle, and would consequently have kept within their walls, from which it was the object of Joshua to decoy them.

17. *There was not a man left in Ai or Beth-el.* It is very likely that the principal strength of Bethel had been previously brought into Ai, as the strongest place to make a stand in, Bethel being but about three miles distant from Ai, and probably not greatly fortified. Therefore Ai contained on this occasion all the men of Bethel—all the warriors of that city, as well as its own troops and inhabitants. Others think that the Bethelites, seeing the Israelites flee, sallied out of their city as against a common enemy; but that, finding the men of Ai discomfited and the city taken, they returned to Bethel, which Joshua did not think proper to attack at this time. From Judg. i. 24 we find that Bethel was then a walled city, in the hands of the Canaanites, and was taken by the house of Joseph.

18. *Stretch out the spear.* It is very probable that Joshua had a flag or ensign at the end of his spear, which might be easily seen at a considerable distance; and that the unfurling or waving of this was the sign agreed on between him and the ambush.

19. *Set the city on fire.* See on v. 8.

20. *They had no power to flee this way or that way.* They were in utter consternation. They saw that the city was taken; they found themselves in the midst of their foes; that their wives, children, and property, had fallen a prey to their enemies, in consequence of which they were so utterly panic-struck as to be incapable of making any resistance.

24. *Returned unto Ai, and smote it with the edge of the sword.* This must refer to the women, children, and old persons, left behind; for it is likely that all the effective men had sallied out when they imagined the Israelites had fled.

26. *Joshua drew not his hand back.* He was not only the general, but the standard-bearer or ensign of his own army, and continued in this employment during the whole of the battle. Some commentators understand this and v. 18 figuratively, as if they implied that Joshua continued in prayer to God for the success of his troops; nor did he cease till the armies of Ai were annihilated and the city taken and destroyed. The Hebrew word *kidon,* which we render *spear,* is rendered by the Vulgate "buckler"; and it must be owned that it seems to have this signification in several passages of Scripture (see 1 Sam. xvii. 6, 45; Job xxxix. 23). But it is clear enough also that it means a spear, or some kind of offensive armor, in other places (see Job xli. 29; Jer. vi. 23). I cannot therefore think that it has any metaphorical meaning,

MATTHEW HENRY

was taken prisoner and hanged, and his dead body thrown at the gate of his own city, *under a heap of stones*, *v.* 23, 29. It is likely he had been notoriously wicked and vile, and a blasphemer of the God of Israel, perhaps upon occasion of the repulse he had given to the forces of Israel in their first onset.

Verses 30–35

This religious solemnity of which we have here an account comes in somewhat surprisingly in the midst of the history of the wars of Canaan. Here a scene opens of quite another nature; the camp of Israel is drawn out into the field, not to engage the enemy, but to offer sacrifice, to hear the law read, and to say *Amen* to the blessings and the curses. It is a remarkable instance, 1. Of the zeal of Israel for the service of God and for his honour. The business of the war shall stand still, while they make a long march to the place appointed, and there attend this solemnity. The way to prosper is to begin with God, Matt. vi. 33. 2. It is an instance of the care of God concerning his faithful servants and worshippers. Though they were in an enemy's country, as yet unconquered, yet in the service of God they were safe. It was a federal transaction: the covenant was now renewed between God and Israel upon their taking possession of the land of promise, that they might be encouraged in the conquest of it, and might know upon what terms they held it, and come under fresh obligations to obedience. In token of the covenant,

I. They built an altar, and offered sacrifice to God (*v.* 30, 31), in token of their dedication of themselves to God, as living sacrifices to his honour, in and by a Mediator, who is the altar that sanctifies this gift. This altar was erected on Mount *Ebal*. The curses pronounced on Mount Ebal would immediately have been executed if atonement had not been made by sacrifice. By the sacrifices offered on this altar they did likewise give God the glory of the victories they had already obtained, as Exod. xvii. 15. The altar they built was of rough unhewn stone, according to the law (Exod. xx. 25), for that which is most plain and natural, and least artful and affected, in the worship of God, he is best pleased with.

II. They received the law from God; and this those must do that would find favour with him, and expect to have their offerings accepted. Now here,

1. The law of the ten commandments was written upon stones in the presence of all Israel, as an abridgement of the whole, *v.* 32. But the stones were plastered, and it was written upon the plaster, Deut. xxvii. 4, 8. It was written, that all might see what it was that they consented to.

2. The blessings and the curses, the sanctions of the law, were publicly read, and the people (we may suppose), according to Moses's appointment, said *Amen* to them, *v.* 33, 34.

(1) The auditory was very large. [1] The greatest prince was not excused. [2] The poorest stranger was not excluded. This was an encouragement to proselytes, and a happy presage of the kindnesses intended for the poor Gentiles in the latter days.

(2) The tribes were posted, as Moses directed, six towards Gerizim and six towards Ebal. And the ark in the midst of the valley was between them, for it was the *ark of the covenant*; and in it were shut up the close rolls of that law which was copied out and shown openly upon the stones. The covenant was commanded, and the command covenanted. The priests that attended the ark, or some of the Levites that attended them, after the people had all taken their places, and silence was proclaimed, pronounced distinctly the blessings and the curses, as Moses had drawn them up, to which the tribes said *Amen*; and yet it is here only said that they should *bless the people*, for the blessing was that which was first and chiefly intended, and which God designed in giving the law. If they fell under the curse, that was their own fault.

3. The law itself also containing the precepts and prohibitions was read (*v.* 35), it should seem by Joshua himself.

JAMIESON, FAUSSET, BROWN

"a long time" (Gen. 6:3). One of the remarkable things with regard to the tell we have identified with Ai is its name—the tell of the heap of stones—a name which to this day remains [Van de Velde].

29. The King Hanged. **29. The king of Ai he hanged on a tree**—i.e., gibbeted. In ancient, and particularly Oriental wars, the chiefs, when taken prisoners, were usually executed. The Israelites were obliged, by the divine law, to put them to death. The execution of the king of Ai would tend to facilitate the conquest of the land, by striking terror into the other chiefs, and making it appear a judicial process, in which they were inflicting the vengeance of God upon His enemies. **take his carcass down . . . and raise thereon a great heap of stones**—It was taken down at sunset, according to the divine command (Deut. 21:23), and cast into a pit dug "at the entering of the gate," because that was the most public place. An immense cairn was raised over his grave—an ancient usage, still existing in the East, whereby is marked the sepulchre of persons whose memory is infamous.

30, 31. Joshua Builds an Altar. **30, 31. Then Joshua built an altar unto the Lord God of Israel in mount Ebal**—(See on Deut. 27:1, 2). This spot was little short of twenty miles from Ai. The march through a hostile country and the unmolested performance of the religious ceremonial observed at this mountain, would be greatly facilitated, through the blessing of God, by the disastrous fall of Ai. The solemn duty was to be attended to at the first convenient opportunity after the entrance into Canaan (Deut. 27:2); and with this in view Joshua seems to have conducted the people through the mountainous region that intervened though no details of the journey have been recorded. Ebal was on the north, opposite to Gerizim, which was on the south side of the town Sichem (Nablous). **an altar of whole stones**—according to the instructions given to Moses (Exod. 20:25; Deut. 27:5). **over which no man hath lifted up any iron**—i.e., iron tool. The reason for this was that every altar of the true God ought properly to have been built of earth (Exod. 20:24); and if it was constructed of stone, rough, unhewn stones were to be employed that it might retain both the appearance and nature of earth, since every bloody sacrifice was connected with sin and death, by which man, the creature of earth, is brought to earth again [Keil]. **they offered thereon burnt offerings unto the Lord, and sacrificed peace offerings**—This had been done when the covenant was established (Exod. 24:5); and by the observance of these rites (Deut. 27:6), the covenant was solemnly renewed—the people were reconciled to God by the burnt offering, and this feast accompanying the peace or thank offering, a happy communion with God was enjoyed by all the families in Israel. **32. he wrote there upon the stones a copy of the law**—(see on Deut. 27: 2-8); i.e., the blessings and curses of the law. Some think that the stones which contained this inscription were the stones of the altar: but this verse seems rather to indicate that a number of stone pillars were erected alongside of the altar, and on which, after they were plastered, this duplicate of the law was inscribed. **33. all Israel, and their elders, and officers, and their judges, stood on this side the ark and on that side**—One half of Israel was arranged on Gerizim, and the other half on Ebal—along the sides and base of each. **before the priests the Levites**—in full view of them. **34. afterward he read all the words of the law**—caused the priests or Levites to read it (Deut. 27:14). Persons are often said in Scripture to do that which they only command to be done. **35. There was not a word of all that Moses commanded, which Joshua read not**—It appears that a much larger portion of the law was read on this occasion than the brief summary inscribed on the stones; and this must have been the essence of the law as contained in Deuteronomy (Deut. 4:44; 6:9; 27:8). It was not written on the stones, but on the plaster. The immediate design of this rehearsal was attained by the performance of the act itself. It only related to posterity, in so far as the record of the event would be handed down in the Book of Joshua, or the documents which form the groundwork of it [Hengstenberg]. Thus faithfully did Joshua execute the instructions given by Moses. How awfully solemn must have been the assemblage and the occasion! The eye and the ear of the people being both addressed, it was calculated to leave an indelible impression; and with spirits elevated by their brilliant victories in the land of promise, memory would often revert to the striking scene on mounts Ebal and Gerizim, and in the vale of Sychar.

ADAM CLARKE

such as that attributed to the holding up of Moses' hands, Exod. xvii. 10-12.

27. *Only the cattle and the spoil*. In the case of Jericho these were all consigned to destruction, and therefore it was criminal to take anything pertaining to the city, as we have already seen; but in the case before us the cattle and spoils were expressly given to the conquerors by the order of God.

28. *Unto this day*. This last clause was probably added by a later hand.

29. *The king of Ai he hanged on a tree*. He had gone out at the head of his men, and had been taken prisoner, v. 23; and the battle being over, he was ordered to be hanged, probably after having been strangled, or in some way deprived of life, as in the case mentioned chap. x. 26, for in those times it was not customary to hang people alive. *As soon as the sun was down*. It was not lawful to let the bodies remain all night upon the tree. See the note on Deut. xxi. 23. *Raise thereon a great heap of stones*. This was a common custom through all antiquity in every country, as we have already seen in the case of Achan, chap. vii. 20.

30. *Then Joshua built an altar*. This was done in obedience to the express command of God, Deut. xxvii. 4-8.

32. *A copy of the law of Moses. Mishneh torath*, the "repetition of the law"; that is, a copy of the blessings and curses, as commanded by Moses; not a copy of the Decalogue, as some imagine, nor of the Book of Deuteronomy, as others think; much less of the whole Pentateuch; but merely of that part which contained the blessings and curses, and which was to be read on this solemn occasion.

35. *With the women, and the little ones*. It was necessary that all should know that they were under the same obligations to obey; even the *women* are brought forward, not only because of their personal responsibility, but because to them was principally intrusted the education of the children. The *children* also witness this solemn transaction, that a salutary fear of offending God might be early, diligently, and deeply impressed upon their hearts.

MATTHEW HENRY

CHAPTER 9

Verses 1–2

Hitherto the Canaanites had acted defensively; the Israelites were the aggressors upon Jericho and Ai. But here the kings of Canaan are in consultation to attack Israel, and concert matters for a vigorous effort of their united forces to check the progress of their victorious arms. When they *heard thereof* (*v.* 1), not only of the conquest of Jericho and Ai, but of the convention of the states of Mount Ebal—when they heard that Joshua, as if he thought himself already completely master of the country, had had all his people together, and had read the laws to them by which they must be governed, and taken their promises to submit to those laws—then they perceived the Israelites were in good earnest, and thought it was high time for them to bestir themselves. Though they were many kings of different nations, Hittites, Amorites, Perizzites, &c., doubtless of different interests, and that had often been at variance one with another, yet they determined, *nemine contradicente—unanimously*, to unite against Israel.

Verses 3–14

I. The Gibeonites desire to make peace with Israel, being alarmed by the tidings they heard of the destruction of Jericho, *v.* 3. Other people heard those tidings, and were irritated thereby to make war upon Israel; but the Gibeonites heard them and were induced to make peace with them. The same sun softens wax and hardens clay. These four united cities (mentioned *v.* 17) seem to have been governed by elders, or senators (*v.* 11), who consulted the common safety more than their own personal dignity. The inhabitants of Gibeon did well for themselves.

II. The method they took to compass it. They knew that all the inhabitants of the land of Canaan were to be cut off, and therefore there was no way of saving their lives from the sword of Israel unless they could, by disguising themselves, make Joshua believe that they came from some very far country, which the Israelites were not commanded to make war upon nor forbidden to *make peace with*, but were particularly appointed to *offer peace to*, Deut. xx. 10, 15. This therefore is the only game they have to play, and observe,

1. They play it very artfully and successfully. Never was any such thing more craftily managed.

(1) They come under the character of ambassadors from a foreign state, which they thought would please the princes of Israel, and make them proud of the honour of being courted by distant countries.

(2) They pretended to have undergone the fatigues of a very long journey, and produced what passed for an ocular demonstration of it. Now they here pretended that their provision, when they brought it from home, was fresh and new, but now it appeared to be old and dry. Their shoes and clothes were worse than those of the Israelites in forty years, and their bread was mouldy, *v.* 4, 5, and again, *v.* 12, 13.

(3) When they were suspected, and more strictly examined as to whence they came, they industriously declined telling the name of their country, till the agreement was settled. [1] The men of Israel suspected a fraud (*v.* 7): "*Peradventure you dwell among us*, and then we may not, we must not, make any league with you." [2] Joshua put the questions to them, *Who are you? and whence come you?* [3] They would not tell whence they came; but still repeat the same thing: *We have come from a very far country*, *v.* 9.

(4) They profess a respect for the God of Israel, the more to ingratiate themselves with Joshua, and we charitably believe they were sincere in this profession: *We have come because of the name of the Lord thy God* (*v.* 9).

(5) They fetch their inducements from what had been done some time before in Moses's reign, the plagues of Egypt and the destruction of Sihon and Og (*v.* 9, 10), but prudently say nothing of the destruction of Jericho and Ai because they will have it supposed that they came from home long before those conquests were made.

(6) They make a general submission—*We are your servants*; and humbly sue for a general agreement—*Make a league with us*, *v.* 11. But,

2. There is a mixture of good and evil in their conduct. (1) Their falsehood cannot be justified, nor ought it to be drawn into a precedent. It is observable that when they had once said, *We have come from a far country* (*v.* 6), they found themselves necessitated to say it again (*v.* 9), and to say what was utterly false concerning their bread, their bottles, and their clothes (*v.* 12, 13), for one lie is an inlet to another, and that to a third, and so on. But, (2) Their faith and prudence are to be greatly commended. Our Lord commended even the unjust steward, because

JAMIESON, FAUSSET, BROWN

CHAPTER 9

Vss. 1-29. THE KINGS COMBINE AGAINST ISRAEL. **1. all the kings which were on this side**—i.e., the western side of Jordan—**in the hills, and in the valleys, and in all the coasts of the great sea**—This threefold distinction marks out very clearly a large portion of Canaan. The first designates the hill country, which belonged afterwards to the tribes of Judah and Ephraim: the second, all the low country from Carmel to Gaza; and the third, the shores of the Mediterranean, from the Isthmus of Tyre to the plain of Joppa. (As for the tribes mentioned, see on ch. 3:10.) **heard** (*thereof*)—that is, of the sacking of Jericho and Ai, as well as the rapid advance of the Israelites into the interior of the country. **2. they gathered themselves together, to fight with Joshua and with Israel, with one accord**—Although divided by separate interests and often at war with each other, a sense of common danger prompted them to suspend their mutual animosities, that by their united forces they might prevent the land from falling into the hands of foreign masters.

3-15. THE GIBEONITES OBTAIN A LEAGUE BY CRAFT. **3-15. when the inhabitants of Gibeon heard**—This town, as its name imports, was situated on a rocky eminence, about six miles northwest from Jerusalem, where the modern village of El-Jib now stands. It was the capital of the Hivites, and a large important city (ch. 10:2). It seems to have formed, in union with a few other towns in the neighborhood, a free independent state (vs. 17) and to have enjoyed a republican government (vs. 11).

They did work wilily—They acted with dexterous policy, seeking the means of self-preservation, not by force, which they were convinced would be unavailing, but by artful diplomacy. **took old sacks upon their asses**—Travellers in the East transport their luggage on beasts of burden; the poorer sort stow all their necessaries, food, clothes, utensils together, in a woollen or hair-cloth sack, laid across the shoulders of the beast they ride upon. **wine bottles, old, and rent, and bound up**—Goat-skins, which are better adapted for carrying liquor of any kind fresh and good, than either earthenware, which is porous, or metallic vessels, which are soon heated by the sun. These skin bottles are liable to be rent when old and much used; and there are various ways of mending them—by inserting a new piece of leather, or by gathering together the edges of the rent and sewing them in the form of a purse, or by putting a round flat splinter of wood into the hole. **5. old shoes and clouted**—Those who have but one ass or mule for themselves and baggage frequently dismount and walk—a circumstance which may account for the worn shoes of the pretended travellers. **bread . . . dry and mouldy**—This must have been that commonly used by travellers—a sort of biscuit made in the form of large rings, about an inch thick, and four or five inches in diameter. Not being so well baked as our biscuits, it becomes hard and mouldy from the moisture left in the dough. It is usually soaked in water previous to being used. **6-14. they went to Joshua unto the camp at Gilgal**—Arrived at the Israelitish headquarters, the strangers obtained an interview with Joshua and the elders, to whom they opened their business. **7. the men of Israel said unto the Hivites, Peradventure ye dwell among us**—The answer of the Israelites implied that they had no discretion, that their orders were imperative, and that if the strangers belonged to any of the native tribes, the idea of an alliance with them was unlawful since God had forbidden it (Exod. 23:32; 34:12; Deut. 7:2). **9. From a very far country thy servants are come, because of the name of the Lord thy God**—They pretended to be actuated by religious motives in seeking to be allied with His people. But their studied address is worthy of notice in appealing to instances of God's miraculous doings at a distance, while they pass by those done in Canaan, as if the report of these had not yet reached their ears.

ADAM CLARKE

CHAPTER 9

1. *And it came to pass, when all the kings . . . heard thereof.* From this account it appears that the capture and destruction of Jericho and Ai had been heard of to the remotest parts of the land, that a general fear of the Israelitish arms prevailed, and that the different dynasties or petty governments into which the land was divided, felt all their interests at stake and determined to make the defense of their country a common cause.

3. *The inhabitants of Gibeon heard.* These alone did not join the confederation. Gibeon is supposed to have been the capital of the Hivites. In the division of the land it fell to the lot of Benjamin, chap. xviii. 25, and was afterwards given to the priests, chap. xxi. 17.

4. *Old sacks . . . and wine bottles, old.* They pretended to have come from a very distant country, and that their sacks and the goatskins that served them for carrying their wine and water were worn out by the length of the journey.

5. *Old shoes and clouted.* Their sandals they pretended had been worn out by long and difficult travelling, and they had been obliged to have them frequently patched during the way; their garments also were worn thin; and what remained of their bread was moldy—spotted with age, or, as our old version has it, "bored"—pierced with many holes by the vermin which had bred in it, through the length of the time it had been in their sacks; and this is the most literal meaning of the original *nikkudim*, which means "spotted or pierced with many holes."

7. *Peradventure ye dwell among us.* It is strange they should have had such a suspicion, as the Gibeonites had acted so artfully; and it is as strange that, having such a suspicion, they acted with so little caution.

8. *We are thy servants.* This appears to have been the only answer they gave to the question of the Israelitish elders, and this they gave to Joshua, not to them, as they saw that Joshua was commander in chief of the host. *Who are ye? and from whence come ye?* To these questions, from such an authority, they felt themselves obliged to give an explicit answer; and they do it very artfully by a mixture of truth, falsehood, and hypocrisy.

9. *Because of the name of the Lord thy God.* They pretend that they had undertaken this journey on a religious account, and seem to intimate that they had the highest respect for Jehovah, the object of the Israelites' worship; this was hypocrisy. *We have heard the fame of him.* This was true: the wonders which God did in Egypt, and the discomfiture of Sihon and Og, had reached the whole land of Canaan; and it was on this account that the inhabitants of it were panic-struck. The Gibeonites, knowing that they could not stand where such mighty forces had fallen, wished to make the Israelites their friends. This part of their relation was strictly true.

11. *Wherefore our elders.* All this, and what follows to the end of verse 13, was false, contrived merely for the purpose of deceiving the Israelites, and this they did to save their own lives, as they expected all the inhabitants of Canaan to be put to the sword.

MATTHEW HENRY

he had done wisely and well for himself, Luke xvi. 8. In submitting to Israel, they submitted to the God of Israel, which implied a renunciation of the god they had served. They did not stay till Israel had besieged their cities; then it would have been too late to capitulate; but when they were at some distance they desired conditions of peace. The way to avoid a judgment is to meet it by repentance. Let us imitate these Gibeonites, and make our peace with God in the rags of humiliation, godly sorrow, and mortification, so our iniquity shall not be our ruin. Let us be servants to Jesus, our blessed Joshua, and make a league with him and the Israel of God, and we shall live.

Verses 15–21

Here is, I. The treaty soon concluded with the Gibeonites, *v.* 15. The thing was not done with much formality, but in short, 1. They agreed to let them live, and more the Gibeonites did not ask. 2. This agreement was made not by Joshua only, but by the princes of the congregation in conjunction with him. 3. It was ratified by an oath; they swore unto them, not by any of the gods of Canaan, but by the God of Israel only, *v.* 19. 4. Nothing appears to have been culpable in all this but that it was done rashly. Making use of their senses only, but not their reason, *they received the men* (as the margin reads it) *because of their victuals,* upon the view and taste of their bread. But *they asked not counsel at the mouth of the Lord.* Joshua himself was not altogether without blame herein. Note, We make more haste than good speed in any business when we stay not to take God along with us, and by the word and prayer to consult him.

II. The fraud soon discovered, by which this league was procured. *A lying tongue is but for a moment,* and truth will be the daughter of time. Within three days they found, to their great surprise, that the cities which these ambassadors had treated for were very near them, but one night's footmarch from the camp at Gilgal, *ch.* x. 9.

III. The disgust of the congregation at this. They did indeed submit to the restraints which this league laid upon them, and smote not the cities of the Gibeonites, neither slew the persons nor seized the prey; but it vexed them to have their hands thus tied, and they *murmured against the princes* (*v.* 18).

IV. The prudent endeavour of the princes to pacify the discontented congregation doubtless disposed the people to acquiesce.

1. They resolved to spare the lives of the Gibeonites, for so they had expressly sworn to do (*v.* 15), to let them live. (1) The oath was lawful. (2) The oath being lawful, both the princes and the people for whom they transacted were bound by it, bound in conscience, bound in honour to the God of Israel, by whom they had sworn, and whose name would have been blasphemed by the Canaanites if they had violated this oath. The princes would keep their word, [1] Though they lost by it. A citizen of Zion *swears to his own hurt and changes not,* Ps. xv. 4. [2] Though the people were uneasy at it, and their discontent might have ended in a mutiny, yet the princes would not violate their engagement to the Gibeonites; we must never be overawed, either by majesty or multitude, to do a sinful thing, and go against our consciences. [3] Though they were drawn into this league by a wile, and might have had a very plausible pretence to declare it null and void, yet they adhered to it. Let this convince us all how religiously we ought to perform our promises, and make good our bargains; and what conscience we ought to make of our words when they are once given. If a covenant obtained by so many lies and deceits might not be broken, shall we think to evade the obligation of those that have been made with all possible honesty and fairness?

2. Though they spared their lives, yet they seized their liberties, and sentenced them to be *hewers of wood and drawers of water to the congregation, v.* 21. By this proposal the discontented congregation was pacified.

Verses 22–27

The matter is here settled between Joshua and the Gibeonites.

I. Joshua reproves them for their fraud, *v.* 22. And they excuse it as well as they can, *v.* 24. 1. Joshua gives the reproof very mildly: *Wherefore have you beguiled us?* 2. They make the best excuse for themselves, that the thing would bear, *v.* 24. They considered that God's sovereignty is incontestable, his justice inflexible, his power irresistible, and therefore resolved to try what his mercy was, and found it was not in vain to cast themselves upon it. They do not go about to justify their lie, but in effect beg pardon

JAMIESON, FAUSSET, BROWN

14, 15. the men took of their victuals, and asked not counsel at the mouth of the Lord—The mouldy appearance of their bread was, after examination, accepted as guaranteeing the truth of the story. In this precipitate conclusion the Israelites were guilty of excessive credulity and culpable negligence, in not asking by the high priest's Urim and Thummim the mind of God, before entering into the alliance. It is not clear, however, that had they applied for divine direction they would have been forbidden to spare and connect themselves with any of the Canaanite tribes who renounced idolatry and embraced and worshipped the true God. At least, no fault was found with them for making a covenant with the Gibeonites; while, on the other hand, the violation of it was severely punished (II Sam. 21:1; and ch. 11:19, 20). **16, 17. at the end of three days . . . they heard that they were their neighbours, and dwelt among them**—This information was obtained in their further progress through the country; for as vs. 17 should be rendered, "when the children of Israel journeyed, they came to their cities." Gibeon was about eighteen or twenty miles from Gilgal; *Chephirah* (ch. 18:26; Ezra 2:25; Neh. 7:29); Beeroth (II Samuel 4:2), now *El Berich,* about twenty minutes' distance from El Jib (Gibeon); Kirjath-jearim, "the city of forests," now Kuryet-el-Enab [ROBINSON]. **18-27. the children of Israel smote them not**—The moral character of the Gibeonites' stratagem was bad. The princes of the congregation did not vindicate either the expediency or the lawfulness of the connection they had formed; but they felt the solemn obligations of their oath; and, although the popular clamor was loud against them, caused either by disappointment at losing the spoils of Gibeon, or by displeasure at the apparent breach of the divine commandment, they determined to adhere to their pledge, "because they had sworn by the Lord God of Israel."

ADAM CLARKE

14. *The men took of their victuals.* This was done in all probability in the way of friendship; for, from time immemorial to the present day, eating together, in the Asiatic countries, is considered a token of unalterable friendship; and those who eat even salt together feel themselves bound thereby in a perpetual covenant. But the marginal reading of this clause should not be hastily rejected. *And asked not counsel at the mouth of the Lord.* They made the covenant with the Gibeonites without consulting God by Urim and Thummim, which was highly reprehensible in them, as it was a state transaction in which the interests and honor of God, their King, were intimately concerned.

15. *Joshua made peace with them.* Joshua agreed to receive them into a friendly connection with the Israelites, and to respect their lives and properties; and the elders of Israel bound themselves to the observance of it, and confirmed it with an oath. As the same words are used here as in verse 6, we may suppose that the covenant was made in the ordinary way, a sacrifice being offered on the occasion, and its blood poured out before the Lord.

16. *At the end of three days.* Gibeon is reputed to be only about eight leagues distant from Gilgal, and on this account the fraud might be easily discovered in the time mentioned above.

17. *The children of Israel . . . came unto their cities.* Probably when the fraud was discovered, Joshua sent out a detachment to examine their country, and to see what use could be made of it in the prosecution of their war with the Canaanites. Some of the cities mentioned here were afterwards in great repute among the Israelites; and God chose to make one of them, Kirjath-jearim, the residence of the ark of the covenant for twenty years, in the reigns of Saul and David. There is no evidence that the preservation of the Gibeonites was displeasing to Jehovah.

18. *All the congregation murmured.* Merely because they were deprived of the spoils of the Gibeonites. They were now under the full influence of a predatory spirit; God saw their proneness to this and therefore, at particular times, totally interdicted the spoils of conquered cities, as in the case of Jericho.

19. *We have sworn unto them.* Although the Israelites were deceived in this business, and the covenant was made on a certain supposition which was afterwards proved to have had no foundation in truth, and consequently the whole engagement on the part of the deceived was hereby vitiated and rendered null and void, yet because the elders had eaten with them, offered a covenant sacrifice, and sworn by Jehovah, they did not consider themselves at liberty to break the terms of the agreement, as far as the lives of the Gibeonites were concerned. That their conduct in this respect was highly pleasing to God is evident from this, that Joshua is nowhere reprehended for making this covenant and sparing the Gibeonites; and that Saul, who four hundred years after this thought himself and the Israelites loosed from this obligation, and in consequence oppressed and destroyed the Gibeonites, was punished for the breach of this treaty, being considered as the violator of a most solemn oath and covenant engagement (see 2 Sam. xxi. 2-9 and Ezek. xvii. 18-19). All these circumstances laid together prove that the command to destroy the Canaanites was not so absolute as is generally supposed, and should be understood as rather referring to the destruction of the political existence of the Canaanitish nations than to the destruction of their lives.

21. *Hewers of wood and drawers of water.* Perhaps this is a sort of proverbial expression, signifying the lowest state of servitude, though it may also be understood literally.

MATTHEW HENRY

for it, pleading it was purely to save their lives that they did it.

II. Joshua condemns them to servitude, as a punishment of their fraud (*v.* 23), and they submit to the sentence (*v.* 25), and for aught that appears both sides are pleased.

1. Joshua pronounces them perpetual bondmen. Observe how the judgment is given against them. (1) Their servitude is made a curse to them. (2) Yet this curse is turned into a blessing; they must be servants, but it shall be for *the house of my God.* The princes would have them slaves *unto all the congregation* (*v.* 21), but Joshua mitigates the sentence, both in honour to God and in favour to the Gibeonites. Even servile work becomes honourable when it is done for the house of our God and the offices thereof. [1] They were hereby excluded from the liberties and privileges of true-born Israelites. [2] They were hereby employed in such services as required their personal attendance upon *the altar of God in the place which he should choose* (*v.* 27), which would bring them to the knowledge of the law of God. [3] This would be a great advantage to the priests and Levites to have so many, and those mighty men, constant attendants upon them, and engaged by office to do all the drudgery of the tabernacle. A great deal of wood must be hewed for fuel for God's house. And a great deal of water must be drawn for the divers washings which the law prescribed. [4] They were herein servants to the congregation too; for whatever promotes and helps forward the worship of God is real service to the commonwealth. Gibeonites were afterwards called *Nethinim,* men given to the Levites, as the Levites were to the priests (Num. iii. 9), to minister to them in the service of God. [5] This may be looked upon as typifying the admission of the Gentiles into the gospel church.

2. They submit to this condition, *v.* 25. *Do as it seemeth right unto thee.* Accordingly the matter was determined. And thus Israel's bondmen became the Lord's freemen, for his service in the meanest office is liberty, and his work is its own wages. Let us, in like manner, submit to our Lord Jesus, and refer our lives to him. If he appoint us to bear his cross, and draw in his yoke, and serve at his altar, this shall be afterwards neither shame nor grief to us.

JAMIESON, FAUSSET, BROWN

The Israelitish princes acted conscientiously; they felt themselves bound by their solemn promise; but to prevent the disastrous consequences of their imprudent haste, they resolved to degrade the Gibeonites to a servile condition as a means of preventing their people from being ensnared into idolatry, and thus acted up, as they thought, to the true spirit and end of the law.

27. hewers of wood and drawers of water—The menials who performed the lowest offices and drudgery in the sanctuary; whence they were called Nethinims (I Chron. 9:2; Ezra 2:43; 8: 20); i.e., given, appropriated. Their chastisement thus brought them into the possession of great religious privileges (Ps. 84:10).

ADAM CLARKE

23. *Now therefore ye are cursed.* Does not this refer to what was pronounced by Noah, Gen. ix. 25, against Ham and his posterity? Did not the curse of Ham imply slavery, and nothing else? "Cursed be Canaan; a servant of servants shall he be"; and does it not sufficiently appear that nothing else than perpetual slavery is implied in the curse of the Gibeonites? *Hewers of wood and drawers of water.* The disgrace of this state lay not in the laboriousness of it, but in its being the common employment of the females, if the ancient customs among the same people were such as prevail now.

24. *We were sore afraid of our lives.* Self-preservation, which is the most powerful law of nature, dictated to them those measures which they adopted; and they plead this as the motive of their conduct.

25. *We are in thine hand.* Entirely in thy power. *As it seemeth good and right unto thee . . . do.* Whatever justice and mercy dictate to thee to do to us, that perform. They expect justice, because they deceived the Israelites; but they expect mercy also, because they were driven to use this expedient for fear of losing their lives.

26. *And so did he unto them.* That is, he acted according to justice and mercy. He delivered them out of the hands of the people, so that they slew them not—here was mercy; and he made them hewers of wood and drawers of water for the congregation, and to the altar of God—here was justice. Thus Joshua did nothing but what was good and right, not only in his own eyes, but also in the eyes of the Lord.

MATTHEW HENRY — CHAPTER 10

Verses 1–6

Joshua and the hosts of Israel were made masters of Jericho by a miracle, of Ai by stratagem, and of Gibeon by surrender, and that was all. Those among them that were impatient of delays, it is probable, complained of Joshua's slowness, and asked why they did not immediately penetrate into the heart of the country, before the enemy could rally their forces. Thus Joshua's prudence, perhaps, was censured as slothfulness, cowardice, and want of spirit. But, 1. Canaan was not to be conquered in a day. God had said that *by little and little* he would drive out the Canaanites, Exod. xxiii. 30. 2. Joshua waited for the Canaanites to be the aggressors.

After Israel had waited awhile for an occasion to make war upon the Canaanites, a fair one offers itself. 1. Five kings combine against the Gibeonites. Adonizedec king of Jerusalem was the first mover and ringleader of this confederacy. It seems he was a bad man, and an implacable enemy to the posterity of that Abraham to whom his predecessor, Melchizedek, was such a faithful friend. *Come,* says he, *and help me, that we may smite Gibeon.* This he resolves to do, either, (1) In policy, that he might retake the city, because it was a strong city, and of great consequence to his country in whose hands it was; or, (2) In passion, that he might chastise the citizens for making peace with Joshua, pretending that they had perfidiously betrayed their country. 2. The Gibeonites send notice to Joshua of the distress and danger they are in, *v.* 6. They think Joshua obliged to help them, (1) In conscience, because they were his servants. (2) In honour, because the ground of their enemies' quarrel with them was the respect they had shown to Israel. When our spiritual enemies set themselves in array against us, and threaten to swallow us up, let us, by faith and prayer, apply to Christ, our Joshua, for strength and succour, as Paul did, and we shall receive the same answer of peace, *My grace is sufficient for thee,* 2 Cor. xii. 8, 9.

Verses 7–14

Here, I. Joshua resolves to assist the Gibeonites, and God encourages him in this resolve. 1. He ascended from Gigal (*v.* 7), determined to relieve Gibeon. He knew that when they embraced the faith and worship of the God of Israel they came to trust under

JAMIESON, FAUSSET, BROWN — CHAPTER 10

Vss. 1-5. Five Kings War against Gibeon. **1. Adoni-zedek**—"lord of righteousness,"—nearly synonymous with Melchizedek, "king of righteousness." These names were common titles of the Jebusite kings. **Jerusalem**—The original name, "Salem" (Gen. 14:18; Ps. 76:2), was superseded by that here given, which signifies "a peaceful possession," or "a vision of peace," in allusion, as some think, to the strikingly symbolic scene (Gen. 22:14) represented on the mount whereon that city was afterwards built. **inhabitants of Gibeon had made peace with Israel, and were among them**—i.e., the Israelites—had made an alliance with that people, and acknowledging their supremacy, were living on terms of friendly intercourse with them. **2. they feared greatly**—The dread inspired by the rapid conquests of the Israelites had been immensely increased by the fact of a state so populous and so strong as Gibeon having found it expedient to submit to the power and the terms of the invaders. **as one of the royal cities**—Although itself a republic (ch. 9:3), it was large and well fortified, like those places in which the chiefs of the country usually established their residence. **3. Wherefore Adoni-zedek . . . sent, . . . saying, Come up unto me, and help me**—A combined attack was meditated on Gibeon, with a view not only to punish its people for their desertion of the native cause, but by its overthrow to interpose a barrier to the farther inroads of the Israelites. This confederacy among the mountaineers of Southern Palestine was formed and headed by the king of Jerusalem, because his territory was most exposed to danger, Gibeon being only six miles distant, and because he evidently possessed some degree of pre-eminence over his royal neighbors. **5. the five kings of the Amorites**—The settlement of this powerful and warlike tribe lay within the confines of Moab; but having also acquired extensive possessions on the southwest of the Jordan, their name, as the ruling power, seems to have been given to the region generally (II Sam. 21:2), although Hebron was inhabited by Hittites or Hivites (ch. 11:19), and Jerusalem by Jebusites (ch. 15:63).

6-9. Joshua Rescues It. **6-8. the men of Gibeon sent unto Joshua**—Their appeal was urgent and their claim to protection irresistible, on the ground, not only of kindness and sympathy, but of justice.

ADAM CLARKE — CHAPTER 10

1. *Adoni-zedec.* This name signifies the "Lord of justice or righteousness"; and it has been conjectured that the Canaanitish kings assume this name in imitation of that of the ancient patriarchal king of this city, Melchizedek, whose name signifies "king of righteousness," or "my righteous king." *Jerusalem. Yerushalam.* This word has been variously explained; if it be compounded of *shalam,* "peace, perfection," and *raah,* "he saw," it may signify "the vision of peace"—or "he shall see peace or perfection."

2. *As one of the royal cities.* Not a regal city, but great, well-inhabited and well-fortified, as those cities which served for the royal residence generally were.

3. *Hoham king of Hebron.* This city was situated in the mountains, southward of Jerusalem, from which it was about thirty miles distant. It fell to the tribe of Judah. *Piram king of Jarmuth.* There were two cities of this name; one belonged to the tribe of Issachar, see chap. xxi. 29; that mentioned here fell to the tribe of Judah, see chap. xv. 35; it is supposed to have been about eighteen miles distant from Jerusalem. *Japhia king of Lachish.* This city is celebrated in Scripture. In that city Amaziah was slain by conspirators, 2 Kings xiv. 19. It was besieged by Sennacherib, 2 Kings xviii. 14, 17; and without effect by the king of Assyria, as we learn from Isa. xxxvii. 8; it was also besieged by the army of Nebuchadnezzar, see Jer. xxxiv. 7. It also fell to the lot of Judah, chap. xv. 39.

5. *The five kings of the Amorites.* This is a general name for the inhabitants of Canaan, otherwise called Canaanites; and it is very likely that they had this appellation because the Amorites were the most powerful tribe or nation in that country.

MATTHEW HENRY

the shadow of his wings (Ruth ii. 12), and therefore, as his servants, he was bound to protect them. 2. God animated him for his undertaking, (*v.* 8): *Fear not*, that is, (1) "Doubt not of the goodness of thy cause and the clearness of thy call." (2) "Dread not the power of the enemy; *I have delivered them into thy hand.*"

II. Joshua applies himself to execute this resolve, and God assists him in the execution. Here we have,

1. The great industry of Joshua, and the power of God working with it for the defeat of the enemy. In this action, Joshua showed his goodwill in the haste he made for the relief of Gibeon (*v.* 9). Now that things were ripe for execution no man more expeditious than Joshua, who before had seemed slow. He marched all night, resolving not to give sleep to his eyes, nor slumber to his eye-lids, till he had accomplished this enterprise. Let the *good soldiers of Jesus Christ* learn hence to *endure hardness, in following the Lamb whithersoever he goes*, and not think themselves undone if their religion lose them now and then a night's sleep; it will be enough to rest when we come to heaven. But why needed Joshua to put himself and his men so much to the stretch? Had not God promised him that without fail he would *deliver the enemies into his hand*? It is true he had; but God's promises are intended, not to slacken and supersede, but to quicken and encourage our endeavours. *The Lord discomfited them before Israel.* Israel did what they could, and yet God did all.

2. The great faith of Joshua, and the power of God crowning it with the miraculous arrest of the sun, that the day of Israel's victories might be prolonged, and so the enemy totally defeated. The hailstones had their rise no higher than the clouds, but, to show that Israel's help came from above the clouds, the sun itself, who by his constant motion serves the whole earth, by halting when there was occasion served the Israelites, and did them a kindness. *The sun and moon stood still in their habitation, at the light of thy arrows* which gave the signal, Hab. iii. 11.

(1) Now, *First*, It looked great for Joshua to say, *Sun, stand thou still.* His ancestor Joseph had indeed dreamed that the sun and moon did homage to him; but who would have thought that, after it had been fulfilled in the figure, it should be again fulfilled in the letter to one of his posterity? He bids the sun stand still upon Gibeon, the place of action and the seat of war, intimating that what he designed in this request was the advantage of Israel against their enemies; it is probable that the sun was now declining, and here he mentions the valley of Ajalon, which was near to Gibeon, because there he was at that time. *Secondly*, It was bold indeed to say so before Israel, and argues a very strong assurance of faith.

(2) The wonderful answer to this prayer. No sooner said than done (*v.* 13): *The sun stood still, and the moon staid.* The same God that rules in heaven above rules at the same time on this earth, and, when he pleases, even *the heavens shall hear the earth*, as here. Concerning this great miracle it is here said, [1] *That it continued a whole day*, that is, the sun continued as long again above the horizon as otherwise it would have done. [2] That hereby the people had full time to avenge themselves of their enemies, and to give them a total defeat. Note, Sometimes God completes a great salvation in a little time, and makes but one day's work of it. This is said to be written *in the book of Jasher*, a collection of state-poems, in which the poem made upon this occasion was preserved among the rest. Those words, *Sun, stand thou still upon Gibeon, and thou moon in the valley of Ajalon*, sounding metrical, are supposed to be taken from the narrative of this event as it was found in the book of Jasher. The sun, the eye of the world, must be fixed for some hours upon Gibeon and the valley of Ajalon, as if to contemplate the great works of God there for Israel, and so to engage the children of men to look that way, and to *enquire of this wonder done in the land*, 2 Chron. xxxii. 31. He would hereby convince and confound those idolaters that worshipped the sun and moon and gave divine honours to them, by demonstrating that they were subject to the command of the God of Israel. This miracle signified that in the latter days, when the light of the world was tending towards a night of darkness, the *Sun of righteousness*, even our Joshua, should arise (Mal. iv. 2), give check to the approaching night, and be the true light.

Verses 15–27

The five kings were all routed. And now Joshua thought, his work being done, he might go with his army into quarters, but he soon finds he has more work cut out for him. The victory must be pursued, that the spoils might be divided.

I. The forces that had dispersed themselves must be followed. He directs his men to pursue the com-

JAMIESON, FAUSSET, BROWN

In attacking the Canaanites, Joshua had received from God a general assurance of success (ch. 1:5). But the intelligence of so formidable a combination among the native princes seems to have depressed his mind with the anxious and dispiriting idea that it was a chastisement for the hasty and inconsiderate alliance entered into with the Gibeonites. It was evidently to be a struggle of life and death, not only to Gibeon, but to the Israelites. And in this view the divine communication that was made to him was seasonable and animating. He seems to have asked the counsel of God and received an answer, before setting out on the expedition. **9. Joshua therefore came upon them suddenly**—This is explained in the following clause, where he is described as having accomplished, by a forced march of picked men, in one night, a distance of twenty-six miles, which, according to the slow pace of Eastern armies and caravans, had formerly been a three days' journey (ch. 9:17).

10, 11. GOD FIGHTS AGAINST THEM WITH HAILSTONES. **10, 11. the Lord discomfited them**—*Heb.*, terrified, confounded the Amorite allies, probably by a fearful storm of lightning and thunder. So the word is usually employed (I Sam. 7:10; Ps. 18:13; 144:6). **and slew them with a great slaughter at Gibeon**—This refers to the attack of the Israelites upon the besiegers. It is evident that there had been much hard fighting around the heights of Gibeon, for the day was far spent before the enemy took to flight. **chased them along the way that goeth up to Beth-horon**—i.e., the House of Caves, of which there are still traces existing. There were two contiguous villages of that name, upper and nether. Upper Beth-horon was nearest Gibeon—about ten miles distant, and approached by a gradual ascent through a long and precipitous ravine. This was the first stage of the flight. The fugitives had crossed the high ridge of Upper Beth-horon, and were in full flight down the descent to Beth-horon the Nether. The road between the two places is so rocky and rugged that there is a path made by means of steps cut in the rock [ROBINSON]. Down this pass Joshua continued his victorious rout. Here it was that the Lord interposed, assisting His people by means of a storm, which, having been probably gathering all day, burst with such irresistible fury, that "they were more which died with hailstones than they whom the children of Israel slew with the sword." The Oriental hailstorm is a terrific agent; the hailstones are masses of ice, large as walnuts, and sometimes as two fists; their prodigious size, and the violence with which they fall, make them always very injurious to property, and often fatal to life. The miraculous feature of *this* tempest, which fell on the Amorite army, was the entire preservation of the Israelites from its destructive ravages.

12-15. THE SUN AND MOON STAND STILL AT THE WORD OF JOSHUA. **12-15. Then spake Joshua to the Lord . . . and . . . he said in the sight of all Israel, Sun, stand thou still . . . and thou, Moon**—The inspired author here breaks off the thread of his history of this miraculous victory to introduce a quotation from an ancient poem, in which the mighty acts of that day were commemorated. The passage, which is parenthetical, contains a *poetical* description of the victory which was miraculously gained by the help of God, and forms an extract from "the book of Jasher," i.e., "the upright"—an anthology, or collection of national songs, in honor of renowned and eminently pious heroes. The language of a poem is not to be literally interpreted; and therefore, when the sun and moon are personified, addressed as intelligent beings, and represented as standing still, the explanation is that the light of the sun and moon was supernaturally prolonged by the same laws of refraction and reflection that ordinarily cause the sun to appear above the horizon, when it is in reality below it [KEIL, BUSH]. Gibeon (a hill) was now at the back of the Israelites, and the height would soon have intercepted the rays of the setting sun. The valley of Ajalon (stags) was before them, and so near that it was sometimes called "the valley of Gibeon" (Isa. 28:21). It would seem, from vs. 14, that the command of Joshua was in reality a prayer to God for the performance of this miracle; and that, although the prayers of eminently good men like Moses often prevailed with God, never was there on any other occasion so astonishing a display of divine power made in behalf of His people, as in answer to the prayer of Joshua. Verse 15 is the end of the quotation from Jasher; and it is necessary to notice this, as the fact described in it is recorded in due course, and the same words, by the sacred historian (vs. 43).

ADAM CLARKE

9. *Joshua . . . came unto them suddenly.* This he did by a forced march during the night, for he *went up from Gilgal all night;* from Gilgal to Gibeon was about eighteen or twenty miles; and, having fallen so unexpectedly on these confederate kings, they were immediately thrown into confusion.

10. *Slew them with a great slaughter at Gibeon.* Multitudes of them fell in the onset; after which they fled, and the Israelites pursued them by the way of *Beth-horon.* There were two cities of this name, the upper and lower, both in the tribe of Ephraim, and built by Sherah, the daughter of Ephraim, 1 Chron. vii. 24. *To Azekah, and unto Makkedah.* These two cities were in the tribe of Judah, chap. xv. 35-41.

11. *The Lord cast down great stones from heaven upon them.* Some have contended that stones, in the common acceptation of the word, are intended here; and that the term *hailstones* is used only to point out the celerity of their fall, and their quantity. But it is more likely that hailstones, in the proper sense of the word, are meant as well as expressed in the text. That God on other occasions has made use of hailstones to destroy both men and cattle we have ample proof in the plague of hail that fell on the Egyptians. See the note on Exod. ix. 18.

12. *Then spake Joshua to the Lord.* Though Joshua saw that the enemies of his people were put to flight, yet he well knew that all which escaped would rally again, and that he should be obliged to meet them once more in the field of battle if permitted now to escape. Finding that the day was drawing towards a close, he feared that he should not have time sufficient to complete the destruction of the confederate armies. In this moment, being suddenly inspired with divine confidence, he requested the Lord to perform the most stupendous miracle that had ever been wrought, which was no less than to arrest the sun in his course, and prolong the day till the destruction of his enemies had been completed!

Sun, stand thou still upon Gibeon; and thou, Moon, in the valley of Ajalon. The terms in this command are worthy of particular note. Joshua does not say to the sun, "Stand still," as if he had conceived him to be running his race round the earth; but, "Be silent," or "inactive"; that is, as I understand it, "Restrain thy influence"—no longer act upon the earth, to cause it to revolve round its axis, a mode of speech which is certainly consistent with the strictest astronomical knowledge. And the writer of the account, whether Joshua himself or the author of the book of Jasher, in relating the consequence of this command is equally accurate, using a word widely different when he speaks of the effect the retention of the solar influence had on the moon. In the first case the sun was "silent" or "inactive," *dom;* in the latter, the moon "stood still," *amad.* The standing still of the moon, or its continuance above the horizon, would be the natural effect of the cessation of the solar influence, which obliged the earth to discontinue her diurnal rotation, which of course would arrest the moon; and thus both it and the sun were kept above the horizon, probably for the space of a whole day. As to the address to the moon, it is not conceived in the same terms as that to the sun, and for the most obvious philosophical reasons; all that is said is simply, ". . . and the moon on the vale of Ajalon," which may be thus understood: "Let the sun restrain his influence or be inactive, as he appears now upon Gibeon, that the moon may continue as she appears now over the vale of Ajalon." It is worthy of remark that every word in this poetic address is apparently selected with the greatest caution and precision.

13. *Book of Jasher.* The book of the upright. See the note on Num. xxi. 14. Probably this was a book which, in reference to Joshua and his transactions, was similar to the commentaries of Caesar on his wars with the Gauls.

14. *And there was no day like that.* There was no period of time in which the sun was kept so long above the horizon as on that occasion.

15. *And Joshua returned . . . unto the camp to Gilgal.* That the Israelitish army did not return to the camp at Gilgal till after the hanging of the five kings and the destruction of their

MATTHEW HENRY

mon soldiers, as much as might be, to prevent their escaping to the garrisons. The result of this vigorous pursuit was, 1. That a very great slaughter was made of the enemies of God and Israel. And, 2. The field was cleared of them, so that none remained but such as got into fenced cities. 3. *None moved his tongue against any of the children of Israel, v.* 21. This expression intimates, (1) Their perfect safety and tranquillity. They were not threatened by any danger at all after their victory, no, not so much as the barking of a dog. (2) Their honour and reputation; no man had any reproach to cast upon them, nor an ill word to give them.

II. The kings that had hidden themselves must now be called to an account, as rebels against the Israel of God.

1. How they were secured. The cave which they fled to, and trusted in for a refuge, became their prison, in which they were clapped up, till Joshua sat in judgment on them, *v.* 18.

2. How they were triumphed over. Joshua ordered them to be brought forth out of the cave, set before him as at the bar, and their names called over, *v.* 22, 23. And when they either were bound and cast upon the ground, unable to help themselves, or threw themselves upon the ground, humbly to beg for their lives, he called for the general officers and great men, and commanded them to trample upon these kings, and set their feet upon their necks. The thing does indeed look barbarous, thus to insult over men in misery, who had suddenly fallen from the highest pitch of honour into this disgrace. Certainly it ought not to be drawn into a precedent, for the case was extraordinary. (1) God would hereby, by this public act of justice done upon these ringleaders of the Canaanites in sin, possess his people with the greater dread and detestation of those sins of *the nations that God cast out from before them*, which they would be tempted to imitate. (2) He would hereby have the promise by Moses made good (Deut. xxxiii. 29), *Thou shalt tread upon their high places.* (3) He would hereby encourage the faith and hope of his people Israel in reference to the wars that were yet before them. Therefore Joshua said (*v.* 25): *Fear not, nor be dismayed.* [1] "Fear not these things, nor any of theirs." [2] "Fear not any other kings, who may at any time be in confederacy against you, for you see these brought down, whom you thought formidable." (4) He would hereby give a type and figure of Christ's victories over the powers of darkness, and believers' victories through him. All the enemies of the Redeemer shall be *made his footstool*, Ps. cx. 1. Sooner or later we shall see all things put under him (Heb. ii. 8), and *principalities and powers* made a show of, Col. ii. 15.

3. How they were put to death. Joshua smote them with the sword, and then hanged up their bodies till evening, when they were taken down, and thrown *into the cave in which they had hidden themselves*, *v.* 26, 27. If these five kings had humbled themselves in time, and had begged peace instead of waging war, they might have saved their lives.

Verses 28–43

I. Here is a particular account of the several cities which he immediately made himself master of. 1. The cities of three of the kings whom he had conquered in the field he went and took possession of, Lachish (*v.* 31, 32), Eglon (*v.* 34, 35), and Hebron, *v.* 36, 37. The other two, Jerusalem and Jarmuth, were not taken at this time. 2. Three other cities, and royal cities too, he took: Makkedah (*v.* 28), Libnah (*v.* 29, 30) and Debir, *v.* 38, 39. 3. One king that brought in his forces for the relief of Lachish, Horam king of Gezer, was cut off with all his forces, *v.* 33.

JAMIESON, FAUSSET, BROWN

16-27. THE FIVE KINGS HANGED. **16-27. these five kings . . . hid themselves in a cave** [*Heb.*, the cave] **at Makkedah**—The pursuit was continued, without interruption, to Makkedah at the foot of the western mountains, where Joshua seems to have halted with the main body of his troops while a detachment was sent forward to scour the country in pursuit of the remaining stragglers, a few of whom succeeded in reaching the neighboring cities. The last act, probably the next day, was the disposal of the prisoners, among whom the five kings were consigned to the infamous doom of being slain (Deut. 20:16, 17); and then their corpses were suspended on five trees till the evening. **24. put your feet upon the necks of these kings**—not as a barbarous insult, but a symbolical action, expressive of a complete victory (Deut. 33:29; Ps. 110:5; Mal. 4:3).

28-42. SEVEN MORE KINGS CONQUERED. **28-42. that day Joshua took Makkedah**—In this and the following verses is described the rapid succession of victory and extermination which swept the whole of southern Palestine into the hands of Israel.

F. B. MEYER:

Joshua's victories over Israel's foes. The cave of Makkedah was a perpetual reminder of this wonderful victory which God gave his people. The details as to the placing of the princes' feet on the necks of their foes are related with this precision to indicate the completeness of the conquest. So at the end of this age (1 Cor. 15:25). We may therefore appropriate Joshua's words about the enemies of the Church and ourselves.

Joshua's career was one of unbroken success, because the Lord went before him, delivering kings and armies, cities and peoples into his hands. It was a war of utter extermination; but God's justice had waited long (Gen. 15:16), and this was the only way of stamping out the infection. The lesson for us is that no quarter can be given in the inner war. *All* our thoughts must be brought into capitivity (2 Cor. 10:5).
—*Bible Commentary*

ADAM CLARKE

cities is sufficiently evident from the subsequent parts of this chapter. When all this business was done, and not before, they returned unto the camp to Gilgal; see v. 43. This verse is omitted by the Septuagint and by the Anglo-Saxon, and it does not appear to have existed in the ancient hexaplar versions; it stands in its proper place in v. 43, and is not only useless where it is, but appears to be an encumbrance to the narrative.

16. *Hid themselves in a cave.* It is very likely that this cave was a fortified place among some rocks, for there were many such places in different parts of Palestine.

21. *None moved his tongue.* The whole transaction of this important day had been carried on so evidently under the direction of God that there was not the least murmuring, nor cause for it, among them, for their enemies were all discomfited. There is an expression similar to this in Exod. xi. 7.

24. *Put your feet upon the necks of these kings.* This act was done symbolically, as a token, not only of the present complete victory, but of their approaching triumph over all their adversaries, which is the interpretation given of it by Joshua in the succeeding verse.

28. *That day Joshua took Makkedah.* It is very possible that Makkedah was taken on the evening of the same day in which the miraculous solstice took place; but as to the other cities mentioned in this chapter, they certainly were subdued some days after, as it is not possible that an army, exhausted as this must have been with a whole night's march and two days' hard fighting, could have proceeded farther than Makkedah that night; the other cities were successively taken in the following days.

29. *Fought against Libnah.* This city was near Makkedah, see chap. xv. 42, and fell to the tribe of Judah, vv. 20, 42, and was given to the priests, chap. xxi. 13. Sennacherib besieged it, after he had been obliged to raise the siege of Lachish (see 2 Kings xix. 8; Isa. xxxvii. 8).

32. *Lachish.* It appears that this was anciently a very strong place; notwithstanding the people were panic-struck, and the Israelites flushed with success, yet Joshua could not reduce it till the second day, and the king of Assyria afterwards was obliged to raise the siege.

33. *Horam king of Gezer.* It is likely that Horam was in a state of alliance with the king of Lachish, and therefore came to his assistance as soon as it appeared that he was likely to be attacked. Joshua probably sent a detachment against him before he was able to form a junction with the forces of Lachish, and utterly destroyed him and his army.

36-38. *Hebron . . . and the king thereof.* See the note on v. 3. From v. 23 we learn that the king of Hebron was one of those five whom Joshua slew and hanged on five trees at Makkedah. How then can it be said that he slew the king of Hebron when he took the city, which was some days after the transactions at Makkedah? Either this slaying of the king of Hebron must refer to what had already been done, or the Hebronites, finding that their king fell in battle, had set up another in his place.

It appears that the city of *Hebron* had fallen back into the hands of the Canaanites, for it was again taken from them by the tribe of Judah, Judg. i. 10. *Debir* had also fallen into their hands, for it was reconquered by Othniel, the son-in-law of Caleb, Judg. i. 11-13. The manner in which Calmet accounts for this is very natural; Joshua, in his rapid conquests, contented himself with taking, demolishing, and burning those cities; but did not garrison any of them, for fear of weakening his army. In several instances no doubt the scattered Canaanites returned, repeopled, and put those cities in a state of defense. Hence the Israelites were obliged to conquer them a second time.

39. *Destroyed all the souls.* They brought every person under an anathema; they either slew them or reduced them to a state of slavery. Is it reasonable to say those were slain who were found in arms, of the others they made slaves?

40. *All the country of the hills.* See the note on Deut. i. 7. Destroyed all that breathed. Every person found in arms who continued to resist; these were all destroyed. Those who submitted were spared; but many no doubt made their escape, and afterwards reoccupied

MATTHEW HENRY

II. The country which was hereby reduced and brought into Israel's hands (*v.* 40–42) lay south of Jerusalem, and afterwards fell, for the most part, to the lot of the tribe of Judah. Observe in his narrative,

1. The great speed Joshua made in taking these cities.

2. The great severity Joshua used towards those he conquered. He gave no quarter to man, woman, nor child, put to the sword *all the souls* (*v.* 28, 30, 32, 35, &c.), *utterly destroyed all that breathed* (*v.* 40), and *left none remaining*. God would hereby, (1) Manifest his hatred of the idolatries and other abominations which the Canaanites had been guilty of. (2) He would hereby magnify his love to his people Israel.

3. The great success of this expedition. The Lord *fought for Israel*, *v.* 42. They could not have gotten the victory if God had not undertaken the battle.

JAMIESON, FAUSSET, BROWN

"All these kings and their land did Joshua take *at one time,* because the Lord God of Israel fought for Israel. And Joshua returned, and all Israel with him, unto the camp to Gilgal."

ADAM CLARKE

certain parts of the land. See vv. 36-37.

41. *And all the country of Goshen.* It appears plain that there was a city named *Goshen* in the tribe of Judah (see chap. xv. 51); and this probably gave name to the adjacent country, which may be that referred to above.

42. *Did Joshua take at one time.* That is, he defeated all those kings, and took all their cities, in one campaign; this appears to be the rational construction of the Hebrew. But these conquests were so rapid and stupendous that they cannot be attributed either to the generalship of Joshua or to the valor of the Israelites; and hence the author himself, disclaiming the merit of them, modestly and piously adds, *because the Lord God of Israel fought for Israel.*

MATTHEW HENRY — CHAPTER 11

Verses 1–9

We are here entering upon the story of another campaign that Joshua made. In respect of miracles it was inferior to it in glory. The wonders God then wrought for them were to animate and encourage them to act vigorously themselves. Thus the war carried on by the preaching of the gospel against Satan's kingdom was at first forwarded by miracles; but, the war being by them sufficiently proved to be of God, the managers of it are now left to the ordinary assistance of divine grace in the use of the sword of the Spirit, and must not expect hailstones nor the standing still of the sun.

I. The Canaanites taking the field against Israel. They were the aggressors. Note, Sinners bring ruin upon their own heads, so that *God will be justified when he speaks*, and they alone shall bear the blame for ever. Now, 1. Several nations joined in this confederacy, some *in the mountains* and some *in the plains*, *v.* 2. They here unite against Israel as against a common enemy. Thus are *the children of this world* more unanimous, and therein *wiser, than the children of light*. The oneness of the church's enemies should shame the church's friends out of their discords and divisions and engage them to be one. 2. The head of this confederacy was *Jabin king of Hazor* (*v.* 1). When they had all drawn up their forces together, they were a very great army; they had horses and chariots very many, which we do not find the southern kings had.

II. The encouragement God gave to Joshua to give them the meeting, even upon the ground of their own choosing (*v.* 6): *Be not afraid because of them.* Joshua was remarkable for his courage—it was his master grace, and yet it seems he had need to be

JAMIESON, FAUSSET, BROWN — CHAPTER 11

VSS. 1-9. DIVERS KINGS OVERCOME AT THE WATERS OF MEROM. **1-9. And it came to pass, when Jabin king of Hazor had heard those things**—The scene of the sacred narrative is here shifted to the north of Canaan, where a still more extensive confederacy was formed among the ruling powers to oppose the further progress of the Israelites. Jabin ("the Intelligent"), which seems to have been a hereditary title (Judg. 4:2), took the lead, from Hazor being the capital of the northern region (vs. 10). It was situated on the borders of lake Merom. The other cities mentioned must have been in the vicinity though their exact position is unknown.

2. **the kings that were on the north of the mountains**—the Anti-libanus district. **the plains south of Chinneroth**—the northern part of the Arabah, or valley of the Jordan. **the valley**—the low and level country, including the plain of Sharon. **borders of Dor on the west**—the highlands of Dor, reaching to the town of Dor on the Mediterranean coast, below mount Carmel.

3. **the Canaanites on the east and on the west**—a particular branch of the Canaanitish population who occupied the western bank of the Jordan as far northward as the Sea of Galilee, and also the coasts of the Mediterranean Sea. **under Hermon**—now Jebel-es-sheikh. It was the northern boundary of Canaan on the east of the Jordan. **land of Mizpeh**—now Cœlo-Syria.

4, 5. **they went out, . . . as the sand upon the seashore in multitude**—The chiefs of these several tribes were summoned by Jabin, being all probably tributary to the kingdom of Hazor. Their combined forces, according to Josephus, amounted to 300,000 infantry, 10,000 cavalry, and 20,000 war chariots. **with horses and chariots very many**—The war chariots were probably like those of Egypt, made of wood, but nailed and tipped with iron. These appear for the first time in the Canaanite war, to aid this last determined struggle against the invalers; and "it was the use of these which seems to have fixed the place of rendezvous by the lake Merom (now Huleh), along whose level shores they could have full play for their force." A host so formidable in numbers, as well as in military equipments, was sure to alarm and dispirit the Israelites. Joshua, therefore, was favored with a renewal of the divine promise of victory (vs. 6), and thus encouraged, he, in the full confidence of faith, set out to face the enemy. **6. to-morrow, about this time, will I deliver them up all slain before Israel**—As it was impossible to have marched from Gilgal to Merom in one day, we must suppose Joshua already moving northward and within a day's distance of the Canaanite camp,

ADAM CLARKE — CHAPTER 11

1. *Jabin king of Hazor.* It is probable that *Jabin* was the common name of all the kings of Hazor. That king, by whom the Israelites were kept in a state of slavery for twenty years, and who was defeated by Deborah and Barak, was called by this name; see Judg. iv. 2-3, 23. The name signifies "wise" or "intelligent." The city of Hazor was situated above the Lake Semechon, in upper Galilee, according to Josephus, *Antiq.* lib. v., c. 6. It was given to the tribe of Naphtali, Josh. xix. 36, who it appears did not possess it long; for though it was burned by Joshua, v. 11, it is likely that the Canaanites rebuilt it, and restored the ancient government, as we find a powerful king there about one hundred and thirty years after the death of Joshua, Judg. iv. 1. It is the same that was taken by Tiglath-pileser, together with Kadesh, to which it is contiguous; see 2 Kings xv. 29. *Jobab king of Madon.* This royal city is nowhere else mentioned in Scripture except in chap. xii. 19. *King of Shimron.* This city is supposed to be the same with Symira, joined to Maron or Marath, by Pliny. It cannot be Samaria, as that had its name long after by Omri, king of Israel. See 1 Kings xvi. 24.

2. *On the north of the mountains.* Or "the mountain," probably Hermon, or some mountain not far from the Lake of Gennesareth. *And of the plains.* That is, the valleys of the above mountains, which had the Sea of Chinneroth or Gennesareth on the south. *Chinneroth.* This city is supposed by Jerome and several others since his time to be the same as was afterwards called Tiberias. From this city or village the Sea of Chinneroth or Gennesareth probably had its name.

3. *The Canaanite on the east.* Those who dwelt on the borders of Jordan, south of the Sea of Tiberias. *The Hivite under Hermon.* Mount Hermon was to the east of Libanus and the fountains of Jordan; it is the same with Syrion and Baal-hermon in Scripture. *The land of Mizpeh.* There were several cities of this name: one in the tribe of Judah (chap. xv. 38); a second in the tribe of Benjamin (chap. xviii. 26); a third beyond Jordan, in the tribe of Gad; and a fourth beyond Jordan, in the tribe of Manasseh, which is that mentioned in the text.

4. *Much people, even as the sand.* This form of speech, by some called a hyperbole, conveys simply the idea of a vast or unusual number—a number of which no regular estimate could be easily formed. That *chariots* were frequently used in war all the records of antiquity prove; but it is generally supposed that among the Canaanites they were armed with iron scythes fastened to their poles and to the naves of their wheels. Terrible things are spoken of these, and the havoc made by them when furiously driven among the ranks of infantry. Of what sort the cavalry was, we know not; but from the account here given we may see what great advantages these allies possessed over the Israelites, whose armies consisted of infantry only.

5. *The waters of Merom.* Where these waters were, interpreters are not agreed. Whether they were the waters of the Lake Semechon, or the waters of Megiddo, mentioned Judg. v. 19, cannot be easily determined. The latter is the more probable opinion.

6. *Be not afraid . . . of them.* To meet such a formidable host so well-equipped, in their own country, furnished with all that was necessary

MATTHEW HENRY

again and again cautioned not to be afraid. For his encouragement, 1. God assures him of success, and fixes the hour: *To-morrow about this time.* 2. He appoints him to *hough their horses, hamstring* them, *lame* them, and *burn their chariots*, not only that Israel might not use them hereafter, but they might not fear them now. Let Israel look upon their chariots but as rotten wood designed for the fire, and their horses of war as disabled things, scarcely good enough for the cart.

III. Joshua's march against these confederate forces, *v.* 7. He *came upon them suddenly*, and surprised them in their quarters.

IV. His success, *v.* 8. He obtained the honour and advantage of a complete victory; he smote them and chased them, in the several ways they took in their flight.

V. His obedience to the orders given him, in destroying the horses and chariots (*v.* 9), which was an instance, of his care to keep up in the people the like confidence in God, by taking that from them which they would be tempted to trust too much to. This was *cutting off a right hand.*

Verses 10–14

We have here the same improvement made of this victory as was made of that in the foregoing chapter. 1. The destruction of Hazor is particularly recorded, because in it, and by the king thereof, this daring design against Israel was laid, *v.* 10, 11. 2. The rest of the cities of that part of the country are spoken of only in general, that Joshua got them all into his hands, but did not burn them as he did Hazor, for Israel was to dwell in *great and goodly cities which they builded not* (Deut. vi. 10) and in these among the rest.

Verses 15–23

We have here the conclusion of this whole matter. I. A short account is here given of what was done in four things:—1. The obstinacy of the Canaanites in their opposition to the Israelites. It is intimated that other cities might have made as good terms for themselves, without ragged clothes and clouted shoes, if they would have humbled themselves, but they never so much as *desired conditions of peace.* To punish them for all their other follies, God left them to this, to make those their enemies whom they might have made their friends.

2. The constancy of the Israelites in prosecuting this war (*v.* 18): *Joshua made war a long time*; some reckon it five years, others seven, that were spent in subduing this land. 3. The conquest of the Anakim at last, *v.* 21, 22. Either this was done as they met with them where they were dispersed, as some think, or rather it should seem the Anakim had retired to their fastnesses, and so were hunted out and cut off at last, after all the rest of Israel's enemies. The mountains of Judah and Israel were the habitations of those mountains of men; but not their height, nor the strength of their caves, nor the difficulty of the passes to them, could secure, no, not these mighty men, from the sword of Joshua. The cutting off of the sons of Anak is particularly mentioned because these had been such a terror to the spies forty years before, and their bulk and strength had been thought an insuperable difficulty in the way of the reducing of Canaan, Num. xiii. 28, 33. Giants are dwarfs to Omnipotence; yet this struggle with the Anakim was reserved for the latter end of the war, when the Israelites had become more expert in the arts of war, and had had more experience of the power and goodness of God. Note, God sometimes reserves the sharpest trials of his people by affliction and temptation for the latter end of their days. Death, that tremendous son of Anak, is the last enemy that is to be encountered; but it is *to be destroyed*, 1 Cor. xv. 26. 4. The end and issue of this long war. The Canaanites were rooted out: *Joshua took all that land, v.* 16, 17. And we may suppose the people dispersed themselves and their families into the countries they had conquered, at least those that lay nearest to the head-quarters at Gilgal.

JAMIESON, FAUSSET, BROWN

when the Lord gave him this assurance of success. With characteristic energy he made a sudden advance, probably during the night, and fell upon them like a thunderbolt, when scattered along the rising grounds (Sept.), before they had time to rally on the plain. In the sudden panic "the Lord delivered them into the hand of Israel, who smote them, and chased them." The rout was complete; some went westward, over the mountains, above the gorge of the Leontes, to Sidon and Misrephoth-maim (glass-smelting houses), in the neighborhood, and others eastward to the plain of Mizpeh. **8. they left none remaining**—of those whom they overtook. All those who fell into their hands alive were slain. **9. Joshua did unto them as the Lord** [vs. 6] **bade him**—Houghing the horses is done by cutting the sinews and arteries of their hinder legs, so that they not only become hopelessly lame, but bleed to death. The reasons for this special command were that the Lord designed to lead the Israelites to trust in Him, not in military resources (Ps. 20:7); to show that in the land of promise there was no use of horses; and, finally, to discourage their travelling as they were to be an agricultural, not a trading, people. **11. he burnt Hazor with fire**—calmly and deliberately, doubtless, according to divine direction. **13. as for the cities that stood still in their strength**—lit., "on their heaps." It was a Phœnician custom to build cities on heights, natural or artificial [HENGSTENBERG].

16. So Joshua took all that land—Here follows a general view of the conquest. The division of the country there into five parts; viz., the hills, the land of Goshen, i.e., a pastoral land near Gibeon (ch. 10:41); the valley, the plains and the mountains of Israel.

17. from the mount Halak [*Heb.*, "the smooth mountain"], **that goeth up to Seir**—an irregular line of white naked hills, about eighty feet high, and seven or eight geographical miles in length that cross the whole Ghor, eight miles south of the Dead Sea, probably "the ascent of Akrabbim" [ROBINSON]. **unto Baal-gad in the valley of Lebanon**—the city or temple of the god of destiny, in Baalbec.

ADAM CLARKE

to supply a numerous army, required more than ordinary encouragement in Joshua's circumstances. This communication from God was highly necessary, in order to prevent the people from desponding on the eve of a conflict in which their all was at stake.

7. *By the waters of Merom suddenly.* Joshua, being apprised of this grand confederation, lost no time, but marched to meet them; and before they could have supposed him at hand, fell suddenly upon them, and put them to the rout.

9. *He houghed their horses.* The Hebrew word *akar*, which we render to "hough" or "hamstring," signifies to "wound, cut, or lop off." It is very likely that it means here an act by which they were not only rendered useless, but destroyed.

13. *The cities that stood still in their strength.* The word *tillam*, which we translate *their strength*, and the margin, "their heap," has been understood two ways: (1) As signifying those cities which had made peace with the Israelites, when conditions of peace were offered according to the command of the law; and consequently were not destroyed, such as the cities of the Hivites; see v. 19; (2) The cities which were situated upon hills and mountains, which, when taken, might be retained with little difficulty. In this sense the place is understood by the Vulgate, as pointing out the cities "which were situated on hills and eminences."

14. *All the spoil of these cities . . . Israel took.* With the exception of those things which had been employed for idolatrous purposes; see Deut. vii. 25.

16. *The mountain of Israel, and the valley of the same.* This place has given considerable trouble to commentators; and it is not easy to assign such a meaning to the place as may appear in all respects satisfactory. (1) If we consider this verse and the twenty-first to have been added after the times in which the kingdoms of Israel and Judah were divided, the difficulty is at once removed. (2) The difficulty will be removed if we consider that *mountain* and *valley* are put here for "mountains" and "valleys," and that these include all mountains and valleys which were not in the lot that fell to the tribe of Judah. Or, (3) If by *mountain of Israel* we understand Bethel, where God appeared to Jacob, afterwards called Israel, and promised him the land of Canaan, a part of the difficulty will be removed. But the first opinion seems best founded; for there is incontestable evidence that several notes have been added to this book since the days of Joshua. See the Preface.

17. *From the mount Halak.* All the mountainous country that extends from the south of the land of Canaan towards *Seir* unto *Baal-gad*, which lies at the foot of Mount Libanus or Hermon, called by some the mountains of "Separation," which serve as a limit between the land of Canaan and that of Seir; see chap. xii. 7. *The valley of Lebanon.* The whole extent of the plain which is on the south, and probably north, of Mount Libanus.

18. *Joshua made war a long time.* The whole of these conquests were not effected in one campaign; they probably required six or seven years. Calmet allows the term of seven years for the conquest of the whole land. "Caleb was forty years old when sent from Kadesh-barnea to spy out the land. At the conclusion of the war he was eighty-five years old, as himself says, chap. xiv. 10. From this sum of eighty-five subtract forty, his age when he went from Kadesh-barnea, and the thirty-eight years which he spent in the wilderness after his return, and there will remain the sum of seven years, which was the time spent in the conquest of the land."

20. *It was of the Lord to harden their hearts.* They had sinned against all the light they had received, and God left them justly to the hardness, obstinacy, and pride of their own hearts; for as they chose to retain their idolatry, God was determined that they should be cut off. For as no city made peace with the Israelites but Gibeon and some others of the Hivites, v. 19, it became therefore necessary to destroy them; for their refusal to make peace was the proof that they willfully persisted in their idolatry.

MATTHEW HENRY

II. That which was now done is here compared with that which had been said to Moses. It is here observed in the close, 1. That all the precepts God had given to Moses relating to the conquest of Canaan were obeyed on the people's part, at least while Joshua lived. Joshua was himself a great commander, and yet nothing was more his praise than his obedience. Joshua, in his zeal for the Lord of hosts, spared neither the idols nor the idolaters. Saul's disobedience, or rather his partial obedience, to the command of God, for the utter destruction of the Amalekites, cost him his kingdom. 2. That all the promises God had given to Moses relating to his conquest were accomplished *on his part*, *v.* 23. God had promised to drive out the nations before them (Exod. xxxiii. 2; xxxiv. 11), and to *bring them down*, Deut. ix. 3. And now it was done.

CHAPTER 12

Verses 1–6

Joshua, or whoever else is the historian, before he comes to sum up the new conquests Israel had made, in these verses recites their former conquests in Moses's time, under whom they became masters of the great and potent kingdoms of Sihon and Og. Joshua's services and achievements are confessedly great, but let not those under Moses be overlooked and forgotten. Here is, 1. A description of this conquered country (*v.* 1): *From the river Arnon* in the south, to *Mount Hermon* in the north.

In particular, here is a description of the kingdom of Sihon (*v.* 2, 3), and that of Og, *v.* 4, 5. Moses had described this country very particularly (Deut. ii. 36; iii. 4, &c.), and this description here agrees with his. King Og is said to dwell at Ashtaroth and Edrei (*v.* 4), probably because they were both his royal cities; he had palaces in both. But Israel took both from him, and made one grave to serve him that could not be content with one palace. 2. The distribution of this country. Moses assigned it to the two tribes and a half, at their request, and divided it among them (*v.* 6), of which we had the story at large, Num. xxxii. The dividing of it when it was conquered by Moses is here mentioned as an example to Joshua what he must do now that he had conquered the country on this side Jordan. Moses, in his time, gave to one part of Israel a very rich and fruitful country, but it was on the outside of Jordan; but Joshua gave to all Israel the holy land, the mountain of God's sanctuary, within Jordan.

Verses 7–24

We have here a breviate of Joshua's conquests.

I. The limits of the country he conquered. It lay between Jordan on the east and the Mediterranean Sea on the west, and extended from Baal-gad near Lebanon in the north to Halak, which lay upon the country of Edom in the south, *v.* 7. The boundaries are more largely described, Num. xxxiv. 2, &c. God had been as good as his word, and had given them possession of all he had promised them by Moses.

II. The various kinds of land that were found in this country, which contributed both to its pleasantness and to its fruitfulness, *v.* 8. There were mountains, not craggy, and rocky, and barren, but fruitful hills, such as put forth *precious things* (Deut. xxxiii. 15). And valleys, not mossy and boggy, but *covered with corn*, Ps. lxv. 13. There were plains, and springs to

JAMIESON, FAUSSET, BROWN

23. Joshua took the whole land—The battle of the lake of Merom was to the north what the battle of Beth-horon was to the south; more briefly told and less complete in its consequences; but still the decisive conflict by which the whole northern region of Canaan fell into the hands of Israel [STANLEY].

CHAPTER 12

VSS. 1-6. THE TWO KINGS WHOSE COUNTRIES MOSES TOOK AND DISPOSED OF. **1. Now these are the kings of the land which the children of Israel smote, and possessed their land on the other side Jordan**—This chapter contains a recapitulation of the conquests made in the promised land, with the additional mention of some places not formerly noted in the sacred history. The river Arnon on the south and mount Hermon on the north were the respective boundaries of the land acquired by the Israelites beyond Jordan (see on Num. 21:21; Deut. 2:36; 3:6-16).

7-24. THE ONE AND THIRTY KINGS ON THE WEST SIDE OF JORDAN, WHICH JOSHUA SMOTE. **7. Baal-gad . . . even unto . . . Halak**—(see on ch. 11:17). A list of thirty-one chief towns is here given; and, as the whole land contained a superficial extent of only fifteen miles in length by fifty in breadth, it is evident that these capital cities belonged to petty and insignificant kingdoms. With a few exceptions, they were not the scenes of any important events recorded in the sacred history, and therefore do not require a particular notice.

ADAM CLARKE

21. *Cut off the Anakims . . . from Hebron . . . from Debir.* This is evidently a recapitulation of the military operations detailed in chap. x. 36-41. *Destroyed . . . their cities.* That is, those of the Anakims; for from v. 13 we learn that Joshua preserved certain other cities.

22. *In Gaza, in Gath, and in Ashdod.* The whole race of the Anakims was extirpated in this war, except those who had taken refuge in the above cities, which belonged to the Philistines, and in which some of the descendants of Anak were found even in the days of David.

23. *So Joshua took the whole land.* All the country described here and in the preceding chapter. *And Joshua gave it for an inheritance unto Israel.* He claimed no peculiar jurisdiction over it; his own family had no peculiar share of it, and himself only the ruined city of Timnath-serah, in the tribe of Ephraim, which he was obliged to rebuild. See chap. xix. 49-50. *And the land rested from war.* The whole territory being now conquered, which God designed the Israelites should possess at this time.

CHAPTER 12

1. *From the river Arnon unto Mount Hermon.* Arnon was the boundary of all the southern coast of the land occupied by the Israelites beyond Jordan, and the mountains of Hermon were the boundaries on the north. Arnon takes its rise in the mountains of Gilead, and having run a long way from north to south falls into the Dead Sea, near the same place into which Jordan discharges itself. *And all the plain on the east.* All the land from the plains of Moab to Mount Hermon.

2. *From Aroer.* Aroer was situated on the western side of the river Arnon, in the middle of the valley through which this river takes its course. The kingdom of Sihon extended from the river Arnon and the city of Aroer on the south to the river Jabbok on the north. *And from half Gilead.* The mountains of Gilead extended from north to south from Mount Hermon towards the source of the river Arnon, which was about the midst of the extent of the kingdom of Sihon; thus Sihon is said to have possessed the half of Gilead, that is, the half of the mountains and of the country which bore the name of Gilead on the east of his territories. *River Jabbok.* This river has its source in the mountains of Gilead, and running from east to west, falls into Jordan. It bounds the territories of Sihon on the north and those of the Ammonites on the south.

3. *The sea of Chinneroth.* Or Gennesareth, the same as the Lake or Sea of Tiberias. *The salt sea on the east.* Some think that the Dead Sea is here intended. *Beth-jeshimoth.* A city near the Dead Sea in the plains of Moab. *Ashdoth-pisgah.* Supposed to be a city at the foot of Mount Pisgah.

4. *Coast of Og king of Bashan.* Concerning this person see the notes on Deut. iii. 11 and on Num. xxi. 35, etc. *The remnant of the giants.* Or Rephaim. See the notes on Gen. vi. 4; xiv. 5; and Deut. ii. 7, 11.

5. *The border of the Geshurites.* The country of Bashan, in the days of Moses and Joshua, extended from the river Jabbok on the south to the frontiers of the Geshurites and Maachathites on the north, to the foot of the mountains of Hermon.

7. *From Baal-gad.* A repetition of what is mentioned chap. xi. 17.

9. *The king of Jericho.* On this and the following verses see the notes on chap. x. 1-3.

14. *The king of Hormah.* Supposed to be the place where the Israelites were defeated by the Canaanites, see Num. xiv. 45; and which probably was called Hormah, or "destruction," from this circumstance.

15. *Adullam.* A city belonging to the tribe of Judah, chap. xv. 35. In a cave at this place David often secreted himself during his persecution by Saul, 1 Sam. xxii. 1.

18. *Aphek.* There were several cities of this name: one in the tribe of Asher, chap. xix. 30; another in the tribe of Judah, 1 Sam. iv. 1 and xxix. 1; and a third in Syria, 1 Kings xx. 26 and 2 Kings xiii. 17. Which of the two former

MATTHEW HENRY

water them; and even in that rich land there were wildernesses too, or forests.

III. The several nations that had been in possession of this country—Hittites, Amorites, Canaanites, &c., all of them descended from Canaan, the accursed son of Ham, Gen. x. 15–18. Seven nations they are called (Deut. vii. 1), and so many are there reckoned up, but here six only are mentioned, the Girgashites being either lost or left out, though we find them, Gen. x. 16 and xv. 21. Either they were incorporated with some other of these nations, or, as the tradition of the Jews is, upon the approach of Israel under Joshua they all withdrew and went into Africa.

IV. A list of the kings that were conquered and subdued by the sword of Israel, the kings of Jericho and Ai, the king of Jerusalem and the princes of the south that were in confederacy with him, and then those of the northern association. This shows what a very fruitful country Canaan then was, which could support so many kingdoms.

JAMIESON, FAUSSET, BROWN

JOSEPH PARKER:

The twelfth chapter deals with the slaughter of many kings. Their names are given, or the names of their cities. Men were not slain and forgotten. This was not a heedless fight, wherein the soldiers on the victorious side struck in the dark and knew not what men they slew or what progress they made. The whole matter is detailed, put down—simply, clearly, and definitely. Moses seems to figure but poorly in the record of slaughter. He killed but two kings; and Joshua killed thirty-one kings. But who are the kings that Joshua killed compared with the kings Moses slew? The two which Moses slew have famous names; they were great and mighty men. The thirty-one slain by Joshua did not add up to the two slain by Moses. Thus work is estimated by quality. We do not reckon by number in the sanctuary, but by quality and by relation, by just standards, and the weighing is done in scales of gold. The poor woman who gave all she had gave more than all the rich: for they gave out of the margin, out of the abundant and all but unreckonable profit, the surplus of their earnings or savings; but she plucked out her whole heart and cast it into God's treasury.

—The People's Bible

ADAM CLARKE

is here intended cannot be ascertained.

21. *Taanach.* A city in the half-tribe of Manasseh, to the west of Jordan, not far from the frontiers or Zebulun, chap. xvii. 11. This city was assigned to the Levites, chap. xxi. 25.

22. *Kedesh.* There was a city of this name in the tribe of Naphtali, chap. xix. 37. It was given to the Levites, and was one of the cities of refuge, chap. xx. 7.

23. *The king of Dor.* The city of this name fell to the lot of the children of Manasseh, chap. xvii. 11. Bochart observes that it was one of the oldest royal cities in Phoenicia. The Canaanites held it, Judg. i. 27. *The king of the nations of Gilgal.* This is supposed to mean the higher Galilee, surnamed "Galilee of the Gentiles" or "nations," as the Hebrew word *goyim* means. On this ground it should be read "king of Galilee of the nations." Others suppose it is the same country with that of which Tidal was king; see Gen. xiv. 1. The place is very uncertain, and commentators have rendered it more so by their conjectures.

24. *King of Tirzah.* This city appears to have been for a long time the capital of the kingdom of Israel, and the residence of its kings. See 1 Kings xiv. 17; xv. 21, 33. Its situation cannot be exactly ascertained; but it is supposed to have been situated on a mountain about three leagues south of Samaria. *All the kings thirty and one.* So many kings in so small a territory shows that their kingdoms must have been very small indeed. The kings of Bethel and Ai had but about twelve thousand subjects in the whole; but in ancient times all kings had very small territories.

MATTHEW HENRY — CHAPTER 13

Verses 1–6

I. God puts Joshua in mind of his old age, *v.* 1. 1. It is said that Joshua was *old and stricken in years*, and he and Caleb were at this time the only old men among the thousands of Israel, none except them of all those who were numbered at Mount Sinai being now alive. Joshua had not the same strength and vigour in his old age that Moses had; all that come to old age do not find it alike good. 2. God takes notice of it to him: *God said to him, Thou art old.* (1) As a reason why he should now lay by the thoughts of pursuing the war. As he had entered into the labours of Moses, so let others enter into his, and bring forth the top-stone, the doing of which was reserved for David long after. (2) As a reason why he should speedily apply himself to the dividing of that which he had conquered. That work must be done, and done quickly; he being *old and stricken in years*, and not likely to continue long, let him make this his concluding piece of service to God and Israel.

II. He gives him a particular account of the land that yet remained unconquered, which was intended for Israel, and which, in due time, they should be masters of if they did not put a bar in their own door.

Divers places are here mentioned, some in the south, as the country of the Philistines, governed by five lords, and the land that lay towards Egypt (*v.* 2, 3), some westward, as that which lay towards the Sidonians (*v.* 4), some eastward, as all Lebanon (*v.* 5), some towards the north, as that in the entering in of Hamath, *v.* 5.

JAMIESON, FAUSSET, BROWN — CHAPTER 13

Vss. 1-33. Bounds of the Land Not Yet Conquered. **1. Now Joshua was old and stricken in years**—He was probably above a hundred years old; for the conquest and survey of the land occupied about seven years, the partition one; and he died at the age of 110 years (ch. 24:29). The distribution, as well as the conquest of the land, was included in the mission of Joshua; and his advanced age supplied a special reason for entering on the immediate discharge of that duty; viz., of allocating Canaan among the tribes of Israel—not only the parts already won, but those also which were still to be conquered.

2-6. This is the land that yet remaineth—i.e., to be acquired. This section forms a parenthesis, in which the historian briefly notices the districts yet unsubdued; viz., first, the whole country of the Philistines—a narrow tract stretching about sixty miles along the Mediterranean coast, and that of the Geshurites to the south of it (I Sam. 27:8). Both included that portion of the country "from Sihor, which is before Egypt," a small brook near El-Arish, which on the east was the southern boundary of Canaan, to Ekron, the most northerly of the five chief lordships or principalities of the Philistines.

also the Avites: From [on] **the south**—The two clauses are thus connected in the Septuagint and many other versions. On being driven out (Deut. 2:23), they established themselves in the south of Philistia. The second division of the unconquered country comprised **all the land of the Canaanites, and Mearah** [the cave] **that is beside the Sidonians**—a mountainous region of Upper Galilee, remarkable for its caves and fastnesses, eastward **unto Aphek** (now Afka), in Lebanon, **to the borders of the Amorites**—a portion of the north-eastern territory that had belonged to Og.

ADAM CLARKE — CHAPTER 13

1. *Joshua was old.* He is generally reputed to have been at this time about a hundred years of age. He had spent about seven years in the conquest of the land, and is supposed to have employed about one year in dividing it; and he died about ten years after, aged one hundred and ten years. It is very likely that he intended to subdue the whole land before he made the division of it among the tribes, but God did not think proper to have this done. So unfaithful were the Israelites that He appears to have purposed that some of the ancient inhabitants should still remain to keep them in check, and that the respective tribes should have some labor to drive out from their allotted borders the remains of the Canaanitish nations. *There remaineth yet very much land to be possessed.* That is, very much when compared with that on the other side Jordan, which was all that could as yet be said to be in the hands of the Israelites.

2. *The borders of the Philistines, and all Geshuri.* The borders of the Philistines may mean the land which they possessed on the seacoast, southwest of the land of Canaan.

3. *From Sihor, which is before Egypt.* Supposed by some to be the Pelusiac branch of the Nile, near to the Arabian Desert. *Ekron northward.* Ekron was one of the five lordships of the Philistines, and the most northern of all the districts they possessed. Baal-zebub, its idol, is famous in Scripture; see 2 Kings i. 2, etc. The five lordships of the Philistines were Gaza, Ashdod, Askelon, Gath, and Ekron. There is no proof that the Israelites ever possessed Ekron.

Counted to the Canaanite. It is generally allowed that the original possessors of this country were the descendants of Canaan, the youngest son of Ham. The Philistines sprang from Mizraim, the second son of Ham, and, having dispossessed the Avim from the places they held in this land, dwelt in their stead. See Gen. x. 13-14. *Five lords of the Philistines.* These dynasties are famous in the Scriptures for their successful wars against the Israelites, of whom they were almost the perpetual scourge. *Also the Avites.* These must not be confounded with the Hivites. The Avites seem to have been a very inconsiderable tribe, who dwelt in some of the outskirts of Palestine. They had been originally deprived of their country by the Caphtorim; and though they lived as a distinct people, they had never afterwards ar-

MATTHEW HENRY

III. He promises that he would make the Israelites masters of all those countries that were yet unsubdued, though Joshua was old. God will do his own work in his own time (*v.* 6): *I will drive them out.* This promise that he would drive them out from before the children of Israel plainly supposes it as the condition of the promise that the children of Israel must themselves attempt their extirpation, else they could not be said to be driven out before them; if afterwards Israel, through sloth, or cowardice, sit still and let them alone, they must blame themselves, and not God, if they be not driven out. We must work out our salvation, and then God will work in us and work with us.

Verses 7–33

I. Orders given to Joshua to assign to each tribe its portion of this land, including that which was yet unsubdued.

1. The land must be divided among the several tribes, and they must not always live in common, as now they did.

2. That it must be divided for an inheritance, though they got it by conquest. (1) The promise of it came to them as an inheritance from their fathers; the land of promise pertained to the children of promise. (2) The possession of it was to be transmitted by them, as an inheritance to their children.

3. That Joshua must not divide it by his own will. Though he was a very wise, just, and good man, it must not be left to him to give what he pleased to each tribe; but he must do it by lot, which referred the matter wholly to God, and to his determination. Joshua must have the honour of dividing the land, (1) Because he had undergone the fatigue of conquering it. (2) That he might be herein a type of Christ, who has not only conquered for us the gates of hell, but has opened to us the gates of heaven, and, having purchased the eternal inheritance for all believers, will in due time put them all in possession of it.

II. An account is here given of the distribution of the land on the other side Jordan among the Reubenites, and Gadites, and half the tribe of Manasseh.

1. How this account is introduced. It comes in, (1) As the reason why this land within Jordan must be divided only to the nine tribes and a half, because the other two and a half were already provided for. (2) As a pattern to Joshua in the work he had now to do. (3) As an inducement to Joshua to hasten the dividing of this land, that the nine tribes and a half might not be kept any longer than was necessary out of their possession, since their brethren of the two tribes and a half were so well settled in theirs.

2. The particulars of this account.

(1) Here is a general description of the country that was given to the two tribes and a half, *which Moses gave them, even as Moses gave them, v.* 8. The repetition implies a ratification of the grant by Joshua. Here we have, [1] The fixing of the boundaries of this country, by which they were divided from the neighbouring nations, *v.* 9, &c. Israel must know their own and keep to it. [2] An exception of one part of this country from Israel's possession, though it was in their grant, namely, the Geshurites and the Maachathites, *v.* 13.

(2) A very particular account of the inheritances of these two tribes and a half. This is very fully and exactly set down in order that posterity might, in reading this history, be the more affected with the goodness of God to their ancestors, and also that the limits of every tribe being punctually set down in this authentic record disputes might be prevented.

[1] We have here the lot of the tribe of Reuben, Jacob's first-born, who, though he had lost the dignity and power which pertained to the birthright, yet, it seems, had the advantage of being first served. The separation of this tribe from the rest, by the river Jordan, was that which Deborah lamented; and the preference they gave to their private interests was what she censured, Judges v. 15, 16. In this tribe lay Heshbon and Sibmah, famed for their fruitful fields and vineyards. This tribe, with that of Gad, was sorely shaken by Hazael king of Syria (2 Kings x. 33), and afterwards dislodged and carried into captivity, twenty years before the general captivity of the ten tribes by the king of Assyria, 1 Chron. v. 26.

[2] The lot of the tribe of Gad, *v.* 24–28. This lay north of Reuben's lot; the country of Gilead lay in this tribe, so famous for its balm and the cities of Jabesh-Gilead and Ramoth-Gilead which we often read of in scripture. Succoth and Penuel, which we read of in the story of Gideon, were in this tribe. Sharon, famous for roses, was in this tribe. And within the limits of this tribe lived those Gadarenes that loved their swine better than their Saviour, fitter to be called *Girgashites* than *Israelites.*

JAMIESON, FAUSSET, BROWN

The third district that remained unsubdued was: **5. all the land of the Giblites**—Their capital was Gebal or Bylbos (*Gr.*), on the Mediterranean, forty miles north of Sidon. **all Lebanon, toward the sunrising**—i.e., Anti-libanus; the eastern ridge, which has its proper termination in Hermon. **entering into Hamath**—the valley of Baalbec. **6, 7. All the inhabitants of the hill country from Lebanon unto Misrephoth-main** (see on ch. 11:8)—i.e., "all the Sidonians and Phœnicians." **them will I drive out**—The fulfilment of this promise was conditional. In the event of the Israelites proving unfaithful or disobedient, they would not subdue the districts now specified; and, in point of fact, the Israelites never possessed them though the inhabitants were subjected to the power of David and Solomon. **only divide thou it by lot unto the Israelites for an inheritance**—The parenthetic section being closed, the historian here resumes the main subject of this chapter—the order of God to Joshua to make an immediate allotment of the land. The method of distribution by lot was, in all respects, the best that could have been adopted, as it prevented all ground of discontent, as well as charges of arbitrary or partial conduct on the part of the leaders; and its announcement in the life of Moses (Num. 33:54), as the system according to which the allocations to each tribe should be made, was intended to lead the people to the acknowledgment of God as the proprietor of the land and as having the entire right to its disposal. Moreover, a solemn appeal to the lot showed it to be the dictate not of human, but divine, wisdom. It was used, however, only in determining the part of the country where a tribe was to be settled—the extent of the settlement was to be decided on a different principle (Num. 26:54). The overruling control of God is conclusively proved because each tribe received the possession predicted by Jacob (Gen. 49) and by Moses (Deut. 33).

8. With whom—*Heb.,* him. The antecedent is evidently to Manasseh, not, however, the half tribe just mentioned, but the other half; for the historian, led, as it were, by the sound of the word, breaks off to describe the possessions beyond Jordan already assigned to Reuben, Gad, and the half of Manasseh (see on Num. 32; Deut. 3:8-17). It may be proper to remark that it was wise to put these boundaries on record. In case of any misunderstanding or dispute arising about the exact limits of each district or property, an appeal could always be made to this authoritative document, and a full knowledge as well as grateful sense obtained of what they had received from God (Ps. 16:5, 6).

ADAM CLARKE

rived to any authority.

5. *The land of the Giblites.* This people dwelt beyond the precincts of the land of Canaan, on the east of Tyre and Sidon. See Ezek. xxvii. 9; Ps. lxxxiii. 7; their capital was named Gebal.

6. *Them will I drive out.* That is, if the Israelites continued to be obedient; but they did not, and therefore they never fully possessed the whole of that land which, on this condition alone, God had promised them. The Sidonians were never expelled by the Israelites, and were only brought into a state of comparative subjection in the days of David and Solomon.

7. *The nine tribes, and the half tribe of Manasseh.* The other half-tribe of Manasseh, and the two tribes of Reuben and Gad, received their inheritance on the other side of Jordan, in the land formerly belonging to Og, king of Bashan, and Sihon, king of the Amorites.

9. *From Aroer.* See on chap. xii. 2.

11. *Border of the Geshurites.* See on chap. xii. 5.

17. *Bamoth-baal.* The high places of Baal, probably so called from altars erected on hills for the impure worship of this Canaanitish Priapus.

18. *Jahaza.* A city near Medeba and Dibon. It was given to the Levites, 1 Chron. vi. 78. *Kedemoth.* Mentioned in Deut. ii. 26; supposed to have been situated beyond the river Arnon. *Mephaath.* Situated on the frontiers of Moab, on the eastern part of the desert. It was given to the Levites, chap. xxi. 37.

19. *Sibmah.* A place remarkable for its vines. See Isa. xvi. 8-9; Jer. xlviii. 32. *Zareth-shahar, in the mount of the valley.* This probably means a town situated on or near to a hill in some flat country.

20. *Beth-peor.* The "house" or temple of Peor, situated at the foot of the mountain of the same name. See Num. xxv. 3.

21. *The princes of Midian.* See the history of this war, Num. xxxi. 1, etc.; and from that place this and the following verse seem to be borrowed, for the introduction of the death of Baalam here seems quite irrelevant.

23. *The cities and the villages.* By *villages* it is likely that movable villages or tents are meant, such as are in use among the Bedouin Arabs, places where they were accustomed to feed and pen their cattle.

25. *Half the land of the children of Ammon.* This probably was land which had been taken from the Ammonites by Sihon, king of the Amorites, and which the Israelites possessed by right of conquest. For although the Israelites were forbidden to take the land of the Ammonites, Deut. ii. 37, yet this part, as having been united to the territories of Sihon, they might possess when they defeated that king and subdued his kingdom.

26. *Ramath-mizpeh.* The same as Ramoth-gilead. It was one of the cities of refuge, chap. xx. 8; Deut. iv. 47. *Mahanaim.* Or the "two camps." Situated on the northern side of the brook Jabbok, celebrated for the vision of the two camps of angels which Jacob had there; see Gen. xxxii. 2.

27. *Succoth.* A place between Jabbok and Jordan where Jacob pitched his "tents," from which circumstance it obtained its name; see Genesis xxxiii. 17.

MATTHEW HENRY

[3] The lot of the half-tribe of Manasseh, *v.* 29–31. Bashan, the kingdom of Og, was in this allotment, famous for the best timber, witness the oaks of Bashan—and the best breed of cattle, witness the bulls and rams of Bashan. This tribe lay north of Gad, reached to Mount Hermon, and had in it part of Gilead. Mizpeh was in this half-tribe, and Jephthah was one of its ornaments; so was Elijah, for in this tribe was Thisbe, whence he is called the Tishbite; and Jair was another. In the edge of the tribe stood Chorazin, honoured with Christ's wondrous works, but ruined by his righteous woe for not improving them.

[4] To the tribe of Levi *Moses gave no inheritance* (*v.* 14, 33), for so God had appointed, Num. xviii. 20. Their habitations must be scattered in all the tribes, and their maintenance brought out of all the tribes, Deut. x. 9; xviii. 2.

JAMIESON, FAUSSET, BROWN

ADAM CLARKE

29. *The half tribe of Manasseh.* When the tribes of Reuben and Gad requested to have their settlement on the east side of Jordan, it does not appear that any part of the tribe of Manasseh requested to be settled in the same place. But as this tribe was numerous, and had much cattle, Moses thought proper to appoint one half of it to remain on the east of Jordan, and the other to go over and settle on the west side of that river.

30. *The towns of Jair.* These were sixty cities; they are mentioned afterwards, and in 1 Chron. ii. 21, etc. They are the same with the Havoth-jair mentioned Num. xxxii. 41. Jair was son of Segub, grandson of Esron or Hezron, and great-grandson of Machir on his grandmother's side, who married Hezron of the tribe of Judah. See his genealogy, 1 Chron. ii. 21-24.

32. *Which Moses did distribute.* Moses had settled everything relative to these tribes before his death, having appointed them to possess the territories of Og, king of Bashan, and Sihon, king of the Amorites.

MATTHEW HENRY

CHAPTER 14

Verses 1–5

The historian now comes to tell us what they did with the countries in the land of Canaan. They were not conquered to be left desert. Canaan would have been subdued in vain if it had not been inhabited. Yet every man might not go and settle where he pleased. God had given Moses directions how this distribution should be made. See Num. xxvi. 53, &c.

I. The managers of this great affair were Joshua the chief magistrate, Eleazar the chief priest, and ten princes, one of each of the tribes, that were now to have their inheritance, whom God himself had nominated (Num. xxxiv. 17, &c.).

II. The tribes among whom this dividend was to be made were nine and a half. Not the tribe of Levi; this was to be otherwise provided for. Joseph made two tribes, Manasseh and Ephraim, pursuant to Jacob's adoption of Joseph's two sons, and so the number of the tribes was kept up to twelve, though Levi was taken out, which is intimated here (*v.* 4).

III. The rule by which they went was the lot, *v.* 2. *The disposal* of that is *of the Lord*, Prov. xvi. 33. It was here used in an affair of weight, and which could not otherwise be accommodated to universal satisfaction, and it was used in a solemn religious manner as an appeal to God, by consent of parties.

Verses 6–15

Before the lot was cast into the lap for the determining of the portions of the respective tribes, the particular portion of Caleb was assigned to him. He was now, except Joshua, not only the oldest man in all Israel, but was twenty years older than any of them, for all that were above twenty years old when he was forty were dead in the wilderness; it was fit therefore that this phoenix of his age should have some particular marks of honour put upon him in the dividing of the land.

I. Caleb here presents his petition, or rather makes his demand, to have Hebron given him for a possession (*this mountain* he calls it, *v.* 12), and not to have that put into the lot with the other parts of the country. To justify his demand, he shows that God had long since, by Moses, promised him *that very mountain.*

1. To enforce his petition, (1) He brings the children of Judah, that is, the heads and great men of that tribe, along with him, to present it. (2) He appeals to Joshua himself concerning the truth of the allegations upon which he grounded his petition: *Thou knowest the thing*, *v.* 6.

2. In his petition he sets forth,

(1) The testimony of his conscience concerning the spying out of the land. [1] That he made his report as it was in his heart, as we find he did, Num. xiii. 30; xiv. 7–9. He did not do it merely to please Moses, or to keep the people quiet, much less from a spirit of contradiction to his fellows, but from a full conviction of the truth of what he said and a firm belief of the divine promise. [2] That herein he *wholly followed the Lord his God*, and therefore it was not vain-glory in him to speak of it, any more than it is for those who have *God's Spirit witnessing with their spirits* that they are the children of God humbly and thankfully to tell others for their encouragement what God has done for their souls. [3] That he did this when all his brethren and companions in that service, except Joshua, did otherwise.

(2) The experience he had had of God's goodness

JAMIESON, FAUSSET, BROWN

CHAPTER 14

VSS. 1-5. THE NINE TRIBES AND A HALF TO HAVE THEIR INHERITANCE BY LOT. **1. these are the countries which the children of Israel inherited in the land of Canaan**—This chapter forms the introduction to an account of the allocation of the land west of Jordan, or Canaan proper, to the nine tribes and a half. It was also made by lot in presence of a select number of superintendents, appointed according to divine directions given to Moses (see on Num. 34:16-29). In everything pertaining to civil government, and even the division of the land, Joshua was the acknowledged chief. But in a matter to be determined by lot, a solemn appeal was made to God, and hence Eleazar, as high priest, is named before Joshua. **4. The children of Joseph were two tribes, Manasseh and Ephraim**—As two and a half tribes were settled on the east Jordan, and the Levites had no inheritance assigned them in land, there would have been only eight and a half tribes to provide for. But Ephraim and Manasseh, the two sons of Joseph, had been constituted two tribes (Gen. 48:5), and although Levi was excluded, the original number of the tribes of Israel was still preserved. **5. the children of Israel . . . divided the land**—i.e., they made the preliminary arrangements for the work. A considerable time was requisite for the survey and measurement.

6-15. CALEB BY PRIVILEGE REQUESTS AND OBTAINS HEBRON. **6-11. Then the children of Judah came to Joshua in Gilgal; and Caleb . . . said**—This incident is recorded here because it occurred while the preparations were being made for casting the lots, which, it appears, were begun in Gilgal. The claim of Caleb to the mountains of Hebron as his personal and family possessions was founded on a solemn promise of Moses, forty-five years before (Num. 14:24; Deut. 1:36), to give him that land on account of his fidelity. Being one of the nominees appointed to preside over the division of the country, he might have been charged with using his powers as a commissioner to his own advantage, had he urged his request in private; and therefore he took some of his brethren along with him as witness of the justice and propriety of his conduct.

ADAM CLARKE

CHAPTER 14

1. *Eleazar the priest.* Eleazar, as being the minister of God in sacred things, is mentioned first. Joshua, as having the supreme command in all things civil, is mentioned next. And the heads or princes of the twelve tribes, who in all things acted under Joshua, are mentioned last. These *heads* or "princes" were twelve, Joshua and Eleazar included; and the reader may find their names in Num. xxxiv. 19-28. It is worthy of remark that no prince was taken from the tribes of Reuben and Gad, because these had already received their inheritance on the other side of Jordan, and therefore could not be interested in this division.

2. *By lot was their inheritance.* Concerning the meaning and use of the lot, see the note on Num. xxxvi. 55.

4. *The children of Joseph were two tribes.* This was ascertained by the prophetic declaration of their grandfather Jacob, Gen. xlviii. 5-6; and as Levi was taken out of the tribes for the service of the sanctuary, one of these sons of Joseph came in his place, and Joseph was treated as the firstborn of Jacob, in the place of Reuben, who forfeited his right of primogeniture.

5. *They divided the land.* This work was begun some time before at Gilgal, and was finished some time after at Shiloh. It must have required a very considerable time to make all the geographical arrangements that were necessary for this purpose.

6. *Caleb the son of Jephunneh the Kenezite.* In the note on the parallel place, Num. xxxii. 12, it is said Kenaz was probably the father of Jephunneh, and that Jephunneh, not Caleb, was the Kenezite; but still, allowing this to be perfectly correct, Caleb might also be called the Kenezite, as it appears to have been a family name, for Othniel, his nephew and son-in-law, is called the son of Kenaz, chap. xv. 17; Judg. i. 13; and 1 Chron. iv. 13; and a grandson of Caleb is also called the son of Kenaz, 1 Chron. iv. 15. In 1 Chron. ii. 18, Caleb is called the son of Hezron, but this is only to be understood of his having Hezron for one of his ancestors; and *son* here may be considered the same as descendant.

Thou knowest the thing that the Lord said. In the place to which Caleb seems to refer, viz., Num. xiv. 24, there is not a word concerning a promise of Hebron to him and his posterity, nor in the place (Deut. i. 36) where Moses repeats what had been done at Kadesh-barnea; but it may be included in what is there spoken. God promised, because he had another spirit within him, and had followed God fully, therefore he should enter into the land whereinto he came, and his seed should possess it. Probably this relates to Hebron, and was so understood by all parties at that time. This seems tolerably evident from the pointed reference made by Caleb to this transaction.

7. *As it was in mine heart.* Neither fear nor favor influenced him on the occasion; he told

MATTHEW HENRY

to him ever since to this day. [1] That he was kept alive in the wilderness, not only notwithstanding the common perils and fatigues of that tedious march, but though all that generation of Israelites, except himself and Joshua, were one way or other cut off by death. With what a grateful sense of God's goodness to him does he speak it! (*v.* 10). *Now behold* (behold and wonder) *the Lord hath kept me alive these forty and five years,* thirty-eight years in the wilderness, through the plagues of the desert, and seven years in Canaan through the perils of war! Note, The longer we live the more sensible we should be of God's goodness to us in keeping us alive, his care in prolonging our frail lives, his patience in prolonging our forfeited lives. [2] That he was fit for business, now that he was in Canaan. Though eighty-five years old, yet as hearty and lively as when he was forty (*v.* 11): *As my strength was then, so is it now.* This was the fruit of the promise, and out-did what was said; for God not only gives what he promises, but he gives more: life by promise shall be life, and health, and strength, and all that which will make the promised life a blessing and comfort.

(3) The promise Moses had made him in God's name that he should have *this mountain, v.* 9. This was the place from which, more than any other, the spies took their report, for here they met with the sons of Anak (Num. xiii. 22), the sight of whom made such an impression upon them, *v.* 33. We may suppose that Caleb, observing what stress they laid upon the difficulty of conquering Hebron, a city garrisoned by the giants, bravely desired to have that city which they called *invincible* assigned to himself for his own portion: "I will undertake to deal with that, and, if I cannot get it for my inheritance, I will be without." He chose this place only because it was the most difficult to be conquered. And, to show that his soul did not decay any more than his body, now forty-five years after he adheres to his choice and is still of the same mind.

(4) The hopes he had of being master of it, though the sons of Anak were in possession of it (*v.* 12): ***If the Lord will be with me, then I shall be able to drive them out.*** The city of Hebron Joshua had already reduced (*ch.* x. 37), but the mountain which belonged to it, and which was inhabited by the sons of Anak, was yet unconquered. Here, [1] He seems to speak doubtfully of God's being with him from a humble sense of his own unworthiness. [2] But he expresses without the least doubt his assurance that if God were with him he should be able to dispossess the sons of Anak. Herein Caleb answered his name, which signifies *all heart.*

II. Joshua grants his petition (*v.* 13): *Joshua blessed him,* commended his bravery, applauded his request, and gave him what he asked. Hebron was settled on Caleb and his heirs (*v.* 14), *because he wholly followed the Lord God of Israel.* Hebron had been the city of Arba, a great man among the Anakim (*v.* 15); we find it called *Kirjatharba* (Gen. xxiii. 2), as the place where Sarah died. Hereabouts Abraham, Isaac, and Jacob lived most of their time in Canaan, and near to it was the cave of Machpelah, where they were buried, which perhaps had led Caleb hither when he went to spy out the land, and had made him covet this rather than any other part for his inheritance. It was one of the cities belonging to the priests (Josh. xxi. 13), and a *city of refuge,* Josh. xx. 7. When Caleb had it, he contented himself with the country about it, and cheerfully gave the city to the priests, the Lord's ministers. It was a royal city, and, in the beginning of David's reign, the metropolis of the kingdom of Judah; thither the people resorted to him, and there he reigned seven years.

JAMIESON, FAUSSET, BROWN

12. give me this mountain, whereof the Lord spake in that day—this highland region. **for thou heardest in that day how the Anakims were there**—The report of the spies, who tried to kindle the flame of sedition and discontent, related chiefly to the people and condition of this mountain district, and hence it was promised as the reward of Caleb's truth, piety, and faithfulness.

13, 14. Joshua blessed him, and gave unto Caleb Hebron for an inheritance—Joshua, who was fully cognizant of all the circumstances, not only admitted the claim, but in a public and earnest manner prayed for the divine blessing to succor the efforts of Caleb in driving out the idolatrous occupiers. **15. Kirjath-arba**—i.e., the city of Arba, a warrior among the native race remarkable for strength and stature. **the land had rest from war**—Most of the kings having been slain and the natives dispirited, there was no general or systematic attempt to resist the progress and settlement of the Israelites.

ADAM CLARKE

what he believed to be the truth, the whole truth, and nothing but the truth.

9. *The land whereon thy feet have trodden.* This probably refers to Hebron, which was no doubt mentioned on this occasion.

11. *Even so is my strength now.* I do not ask this place because I wish to sit down now, and take my ease; on the contrary, I know I must fight to drive out the Anakim, and I am as able and willing to do it as I was forty-five years ago, when Moses sent me to spy out the land.

12. *I shall be able to drive them out.* He cannot mean Hebron merely, for that had been taken before by Joshua; but in the request of Caleb doubtless all the circumjacent country was comprised, in many parts of which the Anakim were still in considerable force.

13. *Joshua blessed him.* As the word bless often signifies to "speak good or well of or to" any person, here it may mean the praise bestowed on Caleb's intrepidity and faithfulness by Joshua, as well as a prayer to God that he might have prosperity in all things; and especially that the Lord might be with him, as himself had expressed in the preceding verse.

14. *Hebron therefore became the inheritance of Caleb.* Joshua admitted his claim, recognized his right, and made a full conveyance of Hebron and its dependencies to Caleb and his posterity; and this being done in the sight of all the elders of Israel, the right was publicly acknowledged, and consequently this portion was excepted from **the general determination by lot, God having long before made the cession of this place to** him and to his descendants.

15. *And the name of Hebron before was Kirjath-arba.* That is, "the city of Arba," or rather, "the city of the four," for thus *kiryath arba* may be literally translated. It is very likely that this city had its name from four Anakim, gigantic or powerful men, probably brothers, who built or conquered it. This conjecture receives considerable strength from chap. xv. 14, where it is said that Caleb drove from Hebron the three sons of Anak, Sheshai, Ahiman, and Talmai. Now it is quite possible that Hebron had its former name, Kirjath-arba, "the city of the four," from these three sons and their father, who, being men of uncommon stature or abilities, had rendered themselves famous by acts proportioned to their strength and influence in the country. It appears however from chap. xv. 13 that Arba was a proper name, as there he is called the father of Anak.

The land had rest from war. There were no more general wars; the inhabitants of Canaan collectively could make no longer any head, and when their confederacy was broken by the conquests of Joshua, he thought proper to divide the land and let each tribe expel the ancient inhabitants that might still remain in its own territories.

MATTHEW HENRY — CHAPTER 15

Verses 1–12

Judah and Joseph were the two sons of Jacob on whom Reuben's forfeited birthright devolved. Judah had the dominion entailed on him, and Joseph the double portion, and therefore these two tribes were first seated, Judah in the southern part of the land of Canaan and Joseph in the northern part.

In these verses, we have the borders of the lot of Judah, which, as the rest, is said to be *by their families,* that is, with an eye to the number of their families. And it intimates that Joshua and Eleazar, and the rest of the commissioners, when they had by lot given each tribe its portion, did afterwards subdivide those larger portions, and assign to each family its inheritance, and then to each household.

JAMIESON, FAUSSET, BROWN — CHAPTER 15

Vss. 1-12. Borders of the Lot of Judah. **1. This then was the lot of the tribe of the children of Judah**—In what manner the lot was drawn on this occasion the sacred historian does not say; but it is probable that the method adopted was similar to that described in ch. 18. Though the general survey of the country had not been completed, some rough draft or delineation of the first conquered part must have been made, and satisfactory evidence obtained that it was large enough to furnish three cantons, before all the tribes cast lots for them; and they fell to Judah, Ephraim, and the half-tribe of Manasseh. The lot of Judah came first, in token of the pre-eminence of that tribe over all the others; and its destined superiority thus received the visible sanction of God. The territory, assigned to it as a possession, was large and extensive, being

ADAM CLARKE — CHAPTER 15

1. *By their families.* It is supposed that the family divisions were not determined by lot. These were left to the prudence and judgment of Joshua, Eleazar, and the ten princes, who appointed to each family a district in proportion to its number, etc., the general division being that alone which was determined by the lot. *To the border of Edom.* The tribe of Judah occupied the most southerly part of the land of Canaan. Its limits extended from the extremity of the Dead Sea southward, along Idumea, possibly by the desert of Sin, and proceeding from east to west to the Mediterranean Sea.

2. *From the bay that looketh southward.* These were the southern limits of the tribe of Judah, which commenced at the extremity of the Dead Sea and terminated at Sihor or the river

MATTHEW HENRY

1. The eastern border was all, and only, the Salt Sea, *v.* 5. 2. The southern border was that of the land of Canaan in general, as will appear by comparing *v.* 1–4 with Num. xxxiv. 3–5. So that this powerful and warlike tribe of Judah guarded the frontiers of the whole land, on that side which lay towards their old sworn enemies the Edomites. 3. The northern border divided it from the lot of Benjamin. In this, mention is made of *the stone of Bohan* a Reubenite (*v.* 6), who died in the camp at Gilgal, and was buried not far off under this stone. The valley of Achor likewise lies upon this border (*v.* 7), to remind the men of Judah of the trouble which Achan, one of their tribe, gave to the congregation of Israel. This northern line touched closely upon Jerusalem (*v.* 8), so closely as to include in the lot of this tribe Mount Zion and Mount Moriah, though the greater part of the city lay in the lot of Benjamin.

JAMIESON, FAUSSET, BROWN

bounded on the south by the wilderness of Zin, and the southern extremity of the Salt Sea (Num. 34: 3-5); on the east, by that sea, extending to the point where it receives the waters of the Jordan; on the north, by a line drawn nearly parallel to Jerusalem, across the country, from the northern extremity of the Salt Sea to the southern limits of the Philistine territory, and to the Mediterranean; and on the west this sea was its boundary, as far as Sihor (Wady El-Arish). **2. the bay**—*Heb.*, "tongue." It pushes its waters out in this form to a great distance [ROBINSON]. **3. Maaleh-akrabbim**—*Heb.*, "the ascent of scorpions"; a pass in the "bald mountain" (see on ch. 11:17), probably much infested by these venomous reptiles. **5. the end**—i.e., the mouth of the Jordan.

6. Beth-hogla—now Ain Hadjla, a fine spring of clear and sweet water, at the northern extremity of the Dead Sea, about two miles from the Jordan [ROBINSON]. **Beth-arabah**—the house or place of solitude, in the desert of Judah (vs. 61). **stone of Bohan the son of Reuben**—the sepulchral monument of a Reubenite leader, who had been distinguished for his bravery, and had fallen in the Canaanite war. **7. Achor**—(see on ch. 7:26). **Adummim**—a rising ground in the wilderness of Jericho, on the south of the little brook that flowed near Jericho (ch. 16:1). **En-shemesh**—the fountain of the sun; "either the present well of the apostle, below Bethany, on the road to Jericho, or the fountain near to St. Saba" [ROBINSON]. **En-rogel**—the fuller's fountain, on the southeast of Jerusalem, below the spot where the valleys of Jehoshaphat and Hinnom unite.

ADAM CLARKE

of Egypt and Mediterranean Sea.

3. *Maaleh-acrabbim.* The ascent of the Mount of Scorpions, probably so called from the multitude of those animals found in that place. *Kadesh-barnea.* This place was on the edge of the Wilderness of Paran, and about twenty-four miles from Hebron. Here Miriam, the sister of Moses and Aaron, died; and here Moses and Aaron rebelled against the Lord.

4. *Toward Azmon.* This was the last city they possessed toward Egypt.

5. *The east border was the salt sea.* The Salt Sea is the same as the Dead Sea. And here it is intimated that the eastern border of the tribe of Judah extended along the Dead Sea, from its lowest extremity to the *end of Jordan,* i.e., to **the place where Jordan falls into this sea.**

6. *Beth-hogla.* A place between Jericho and the Dead Sea, belonging to the tribe of Benjamin, chap. xviii. 21, though here serving as a frontier to the tribe of Judah.

7. *The valley of Achor.* The *valley of Achor* had its name from the punishment of Achan. See the account, chap. vii. 24, etc. *En-shemesh.* The "fountain of the sun"; it was eastward of Jerusalem, on the confines of Judah and Benjamin.

8. *The valley of the son of Hinnom.* It was situated on the east of Jerusalem, and is often mentioned in Scripture. The image of the idol Molech appears to have been set up there; and there the idolatrous Israelites caused their sons and daughters to pass through the fire in honor of that demon, 2 Kings xxiii. 10. It was also called Tophet; see Jer. vii. 32. When King Josiah removed the image of this idol from this valley, it appears to have been held in such universal execration that it became the general receptacle of all the filth and impurities which were carried out of Jerusalem; and it is supposed that continual fires were there kept up, to consume those impurities and prevent infection. From the Hebrew words *gei ben Hinnom,* "the valley of the son of Hinnom," and by contraction, *gei Hinnom,* the "valley of Hinnom," came the *Gehenna* of the New Testament, called also the *Gehenna of fire,* which is the emblem of hell, or the place of the damned. See Matt. v. 22, 29-30; x. 28; xviii. 9.

The same is Jerusalem. This city was formerly called Jebus; a part of it was in the tribe of Benjamin. Zion, called its citadel, was in the tribe of Judah. *The valley of the giants.* Of the *Rephaim.* See the notes on Gen. vi. 4; xiv. 5; Deut. ii. 7, 11.

9. *Baalah, which is Kirjath-jearim.* This place was rendered famous in Scripture, in consequence of its being the residence of the ark for twenty years after it was sent back by the Philistines; see 1 Sam. v; vi; and vii. 1-2.

10. *Beth-shemesh.* The "house or temple of the sun." It is evident that the sun was an object of adoration among the Canaanites; and hence fountains, hills, etc., were dedicated to him. Beth-shemesh is remarkable for the slaughter of its inhabitants, in consequence of their prying curiously into the ark of the Lord, when sent back by the Philistines. See 1 Samuel vii.

12. *The great sea.* The Mediterranean.

15. *Kirjath-sepher.* The "city of the book." Why so named is uncertain.

16. *Will I give Achsah my daughter.* In ancient times fathers assumed an absolute right over their children, especially in disposing of them in marriage; and it was customary for a king or great man to promise his daughter in marriage to him who should take a city, kill an enemy, etc. So Saul promised his daughter in marriage to him who should kill Goliath, 1 Sam. xvii. 25; and Caleb offers his on this occasion to him who should take Kirjath-sepher.

18. *As she came.* As she was now departing from the house of her father to go to that of her husband. *She moved him.* Othniel, *to ask of her father a field,* one on which she had set her heart, as contiguous to the patrimony already granted. *She lighted off her ass.* She "hastily, suddenly" alighted, as if she had forgotten something, or was about to return to her father's house. Which being perceived by her

TODAY'S DICTIONARY OF THE BIBLE:

Hinnom, a deep, narrow ravine separating Mount Zion from the so-called "Hill of Evil Counsel." It took its name from "some ancient hero, the son of Hinnom." It is first mentioned in Josh. 15:8. It had been the place where the idolatrous Jews burned their children alive to Moloch and Baal. A particular part of the valley was called Tophet, or the "firestove," where the children were burned. After the Exile, to show their abhorrence of the locality, the Jews made this valley the receptacle of the offal of the city, for the destruction of which a fire was, as is supposed, kept constantly burning there.

The Jews associated with this valley these two ideas—(1.) that of the sufferings of the victims that had there been sacrificed; and (2.) that of filth and corruption. Thus to the popular mind, it became a symbol of the abode of the wicked hereafter. It came to signify hell as the place of the wicked. "It might be shown by infinite examples that the Jews expressed hell, or the place of the damned, by this word. The word *Gehenna,* the Greek contraction of Hinnom, was never used in the time of Christ in any other sense than to denote the place of future punishment." About this fact there can be no question. In this sense the word is used eleven times in our Lord's discourses (Matt. 5:22; 23:33; Luke 12:5, etc.).

MATTHEW HENRY

4. The west border went near to the great sea at first (*v.* 12), but afterwards the lot of the tribe of Dan took off a good part of Judah's lot on that side. Judah's inheritance had its boundaries determined.

Verses 13–19

The historian seems pleased with every occasion to make mention of Caleb because he had honoured God.

I. The grant Joshua made him of the mountain of Hebron for his inheritance is here repeated (*v.* 13).

II. Caleb having obtained this grant, we are told,

1. How he signalized his own valour in the conquest of Hebron (*v.* 14): *He drove thence the three sons of Anak,* he and those that he engaged to assist him in this service.

2. How he encouraged the valour of those about him in the conquest of Debir, *v.* 15, &c. It seems, though Joshua had once made himself master of Debir (*ch.* x. 39), yet the Canaanites had regained the possession in the absence of the army, so that the work had to be done a second time; and when Caleb had completed the reduction of Hebron, which was for himself and his own family, to show his zeal for the public good, as much as for his own private interest, he pushes on his conquest to Debir.

The proffer that Caleb made of his daughter, and

JAMIESON, FAUSSET, BROWN

13-15. CALEB'S PORTION AND CONQUEST. **13. unto Caleb he gave a part among the children of Judah**—(See on ch. 14:6-15). **14. drove thence the three sons of Anak**—rather three chiefs of the Anakim race. This exploit is recorded to the honor of Caleb, as the success of it was the reward of his trust in God. **15. Debir**—oracle. Its former name, Kirjath-sepher, signifies "city of the book," being probably a place where public registers were kept.

16-20. OTHNIEL, FOR HIS VALOR, HAS ACHSAH TO WIFE. **16-20. He that smiteth Kirjath-sepher**—This offer was made as an incentive to youthful bravery (see on I Sam. 17:25); and the prize was won by Othniel, Caleb's *younger* brother (Judg. 1: 13; 3:9). This was the occasion of drawing out the latent energies of him who was destined to be the first judge in Israel. **18. as she came unto him**—i.e., when about to remove from her father's to her husband's house. She suddenly alighted from her travelling equipage—a mark of respect to her father, and a sign of making some request. She had urged

MATTHEW HENRY

a good portion with her, to any one that would undertake to reduce that city. Caleb's family was not only honourable and wealthy, but religious. The place was bravely taken by Othniel, a nephew of Caleb, whom probably Caleb had thoughts of when he made the proffer, *v.* 17. Othniel married his cousin-german Achsah, Caleb's daughter. The historian gives us an account of Achsah's portion. Some land she obtained by Caleb's free grant. He *gave her a south land, v.* 19. Land indeed, but *a south land,* dry, and apt to be parched. She obtained more upon her request. When her father brought her home to the house of her husband, she *lighted off her ass,* in token of respect and reverence to her father. She was sure that, since she married not only with her father's consent, but in obedience to his command, he would not deny her his blessing. She asks only for the *water,* without which the ground she had would be of little use either for tillage or pasture, but she means the field in which the springs of water were. Achsah gained her point; her father gave her what she asked, and perhaps more, for *he gave her the upper springs and the nether springs,* two fields so called from the springs that were in them, as we commonly distinguish between the higher field and the lower field.

From this story we learn it is no breach of the tenth commandment moderately to desire those comforts and conveniences of this life which we see attainable in a fair and regular way. Husbands and wives should mutually advise, and jointly agree, about that which is for the common good of their family. Parents must never think that lost which is bestowed upon their children for their real advantage.

Verses 20–63

We have here a list of the several cities that fell within the lot of the tribe of Judah.

I. The cities are here named, and numbered in several classes. Here are, 1. Some that are said to be the uttermost cities *towards the coast of Edom, v.* 21–32. Here are thirty-eight named, and yet said to be *twenty-nine* (*v.* 32), because nine of these were afterwards transferred to the lot of Simeon. 2. Others that are said to be *in the valley* (*v.* 33) are counted to be fourteen, yet fifteen are named; but it is probable that Gederah and Gederathaim were two parts of one and the same city. 3. Then sixteen are named without any head of distinction, *v.* 37–41, and nine more, *v.* 42–44. 4. Then the three Philistine-cities, Ekron, Ashdod, and Gaza, *v.* 45–47. 5. Cities *in the mountains.*

JAMIESON, FAUSSET, BROWN

Othniel to broach the matter, but he not wishing to do what appeared like evincing a grasping disposition, she resolved herself to speak out. Taking advantage of the parting scene when a parent's heart was likely to be tender, she begged (as her marriage portion consisted of a field which, having a southern exposure, was comparatively an arid and barren waste) he would add the adjoining one, which abounded in excellent springs. The request being reasonable, it was granted; and the story conveys this important lesson in religion, that if earthly parents are ready to bestow on their children that which is good, much more will our heavenly Father give every necessary blessing to them who ask Him.

21-63. CITIES OF JUDAH. **21-63. the uttermost cities of the tribe of the children of Judah**—There is given a list of cities within the tribal territory of Judah, arranged in four divisions, corresponding to the districts of which it consisted—the cities in the southern part (21-32), those in the lowlands (33-47), those in the highlands (48-60), and those in the desert (61, 62). One gets the best idea of the relative situation of these cities by looking at the map.

F. B. MEYER:

"He gave her the upper springs, and the nether springs" (Josh. 15:19). Caleb had conquered his giants, and so he was able to give his daughter an inheritance of land and springs of water. It was when Jesus had overcome the sharpness of death that He opened the Kingdom of Heaven to all believers; it was as He trampled under his victorious feet the principalities and powers of darkness that He gave to his Church the upper and the nether springs.

There are two departments in our life, which are closely related and yet one. We occupy the one in our contact with men and our work in the world; the other, in our holy moments of meditation and prayer. Christ's sheep go out to their manifold activities, and come in to feed on the green pastures beside waters of rest. In each of these we stand in daily need of the springs that are fed from the River which proceeds from the throne of God, and which is an emblem of the Holy Ghost.

On the Lord's Day, in the House of God, or in private prayer, we climb the hills and stand on the margin of the upper springs that rise there; in the solemn hush we hear the murmur of their waters. On Monday we descend into the valley amid the clang of the battle and the cries of human need; but, thank God! plentiful springs are there also. Upper springs from the Mount of Transfiguration; nether springs for the Valley of Humiliation. Upper springs for the days of health and abounding activity; nether springs for days of depression, and pain, and death. Upper springs in praise, adoration, and rapture; nether springs for taking the yoke, bearing the burden, and drinking of his cup. Let us partake freely of the refreshing water which flows from the River of God.

—*Great Verses Through the Bible*

ADAM CLARKE

father, he said, *What wouldest thou?* What is the matter? What do you want?

19. *Give me a blessing.* Do me an act of kindness. Grant me a particular request. *Thou hast given me a south land.* Which was probably dry, or very ill-watered. *Give me also springs of water.* Let me have some fields in which there are brooks or wells already digged. *The upper springs, and the nether springs.* He gave her even more than she requested; he gave her a district among the mountains and another in the plains well-situated and well-watered.

24. *Ziph.* There were two cities of this name in the tribe of Judah: that mentioned here, and another in v. 55. One of these two is noted for the refuge of David when persecuted by Saul, and the attempts made by its inhabitants to deliver him into the hands of his persecutor. See 1 Sam. xxiii. 14-24.

28. *Beer-sheba.* A city famous in the Book of Genesis as the residence of the patriarchs Abraham and Jacob, chap. xxii. 19; xxviii. 10; xlvi. 1, (see the note on Gen. xxi. 31). It lay on the way between Canaan and Egypt, about forty miles from Jerusalem.

30. *Hormah.* A place rendered famous by the defeat of the Hebrews by the Canaanites. See Num. xiv. 45; Deut. i. 44.

31. *Ziklag.* The Philistines seem to have kept possession of this city till the time of David, who received it from Achish, king of Gath, 1 Sam. xxvii. 6; after which time it remained in the possession of the kings of Judah.

32. *All the cities are twenty and nine, with their villages.* But on a careful examination we shall find thirty-eight; but it is supposed that nine of these are excepted, viz., Beer-sheba, Moladah, Hazar-shual, Baalah, Azem, Hormah, Ziklag, Ain, and Rimmon, which were afterwards given to the tribe of Simeon. This may appear satisfactory, but perhaps the truth will be found to be this: Several cities in the Promised Land are expressed by compound terms; not knowing the places, different translations combine what should be separated, and in many cases separate what should be combined. On this ground we have thirty-eight cities as the sum here, instead of twenty-nine.

33. *Eshtaol, and Zoreah.* Here Samson was buried, it being the burial place of his fathers; see Judg. xvi. 31. These places, though first given to Judah, afterwards fell to the lot of Dan, chap. xix. 41.

35. *Jarmuth.* See the note on chap. x. 3. *Adullam.* See the note on chap. xii. 15. *Socoh.* It was near this place that David fought with and slew Goliath, the champion of the Philistines, 1 Sam. xvii. 1.

36. *Gederah.* See the note on chap. xii. 13. *Fourteen cities.* Well-reckoned, we shall find fifteen cities here; but probably Gederah and Gederothaim (v. 36) are the same. See the note on v. 32.

39. *Lachish . . . and Eglon.* See on chap. x. 3.

41. *Beth-dagon.* The "house" or temple of Dagon. This is a well-known idol of the Philistines, and probably the place mentioned here was in some part of their territories; but the situation at present is unknown.

42. *Libnah.* See the note on chap. x. 29. *Ether.* From chap. xix. 7 we learn that this city was afterwards given to the tribe of Simeon.

44. *Keilah.* This town was near Hebron, and is said to have been the burying place of the prophet Habakkuk. David obliged the Philistines to raise the siege of it (see 1 Sam. xxiii. 1-13); but finding that its inhabitants had purposed to deliver him into the hands of Saul, who was coming in pursuit of him, he made his escape. *Mareshah.* Called also Maresheth and Marasthi; it was the birthplace of the prophet Micah. Near this place was the famous battle between Asa, king of Judah, and Zera, king of Cush or Ethiopia, who was at the head of "a thousand thousand [men], and three hundred chariots." Asa defeated this immense host and took much spoil, 2 Chron. xiv. 9-15.

46. *Ekron.* One of the five Philistine lordships (see the note on chap. xiii. 3).

MATTHEW HENRY

II. Now here, 1. We do not find Bethlehem, which was afterwards the city of David, and was ennobled by the birth of our Lord Jesus in it. But that city was but *little among the thousands of Judah* (Mic. v. 2), except that it was thus dignified. Christ came to give honour to the places he was related to, not to receive honour from them.

2. Jerusalem is said to continue in the hands of the Jebusites (*v.* 63), *for the children of Judah could not drive them out*, through their sluggishness, stupidity, and unbelief. 3. Among the cities of Judah (in all 114) we meet with Libnah, which in Joram's days revolted, and probably set up for a free independent state (2 Kings viii. 22), and Lachish, where king Amaziah was slain (2 Kings xiv. 19); it led the dance in idolatry (Mic. i. 13); it was the *beginning of sin to the daughter of Zion*. Many of the cities of this tribe occur in the history of David's troubles. Adullam, Ziph, Keilah, Maon, Engedi, Ziklag, here reckoned in this tribe, were places near which David had most of his haunts.

JAMIESON, FAUSSET, BROWN

TODAY'S DICTIONARY OF THE BIBLE:

Jerusalem, called also Salem, Ariel, Jebus, the "city of God," the "holy city"; by the modern Arabs *el-Khuds*, meaning "the holy"; once "the city of Judah" (2 Chron. 25:28). This name is in the original in the dual form, and means "possession of peace," or "foundation of peace." The dual form probably refers to the two mountains on which the city was built—viz., Zion and Moriah; or, as some suppose, to the two parts of the city, the "upper" and the "lower city." Jerusalem is a "mountain city enthroned on a mountain fastness" (comp. Ps. 68:15, 16; 87:1; 76:1, 2; 122:3; 125:2). It stands on the edge of one of the highest tablelands in Palestine, and is surrounded on the southeast, the south, and the west by deep and precipitous ravines.

Jerusalem is first mentioned in Scripture under the name Salem (Gen. 14:18; comp. Ps. 76:2). When it is first alluded to under the name Jerusalem, Adoni-zedek was its king (Josh. 10:1). It is afterward named among the cities of Benjamin (Judg. 19:10; 1 Chron. 11:4); but in the time of David it was divided between Benjamin and Judah. After the death of Joshua the city was taken and set on fire by the men of Judah (Judg. 1:1–8); but the Jebusites were not wholly driven out of it. The city is not mentioned again till we are told that David brought the head of Goliath there (1 Sam. 17:54). David afterward led his forces against the Jebusites still residing within its walls, and drove them out, establishing his own dwelling on Zion, which he called "the city of David" (2 Sam. 5:5–9; 1 Chron. 11:4–8). Here he built an altar to the Lord on the threshing floor of Araunah the Jebusite (2 Sam. 24:15–25), and brought up the ark of the covenant and placed it in the new tabernacle. Jerusalem now became the capital of the kingdom.

ADAM CLARKE

Ashdod. Called also Azotus, Acts viii. 40. *The great sea.* The Mediterranean.

51. *Giloh.* The country of the traitor Ahithophel, 2 Sam. xv. 12.

53. *Beth-tappuah.* The "house of the apple" or citron tree. Probably a place where these grew in great abundance and perfection.

55. *Maon.* In a desert to which this town gave name David took refuge for a considerable time from the persecution of Saul; and in this place Nabal the Carmelite had great possessions. See 1 Sam. xxiii. 24-25; xxv. 2. *Carmel.* Not the celebrated mount of that name, but a village, the residence of Nabal. See 1 Sam. xxv. 2. It was near Maon, mentioned above, and was about ten miles eastward of Hebron. It is the place where Saul erected a trophy to himself after the defeat of the Amalekites; see 1 Sam. xv. 12.

57. *Timnah.* A frontier town of the Philistines. It was in this place that Samson got his wife; see Judges xiv and xv.

62. *The city of Salt.* Or of Melach. This city was somewhere in the vicinity of the Lake Asphaltites, the waters of which are the saltiest perhaps in the world. The whole country abounds with salt; see the note on Gen. xix. 25. *En-gedi.* The "well of the kid." It was situated between Jericho and the Lake of Sodom or Dead Sea.

63. *The Jebusites dwell . . . at Jerusalem unto this day.* The whole history of Jerusalem, previously to the time of David, is encumbered with many difficulties. Sometimes it is attributed to Judah, sometimes to Benjamin; and it is probable that, being on the frontiers of both those tribes, each possessed a part of it. If the Jebusites were ever driven out before the time of David, it is certain they recovered it again, or at least a part of it—what is called the citadel or stronghold of Zion (see 2 Sam. v. 7), which he took from them, after which the city fell wholly into the hands of the Israelites. This verse is an additional proof that the Book of Joshua was not written after the times of the Jewish kings, as some have endeavored to prove; for when this verse was written, the Jebusites dwelt with the children of Judah, which they did not after the days of David. Therefore the book was written before there were any kings in Judea.

MATTHEW HENRY — CHAPTER 16

Verses 1–4

Though Joseph was one of the younger sons of Jacob, yet he was his eldest by his most just and best beloved wife Rachel, was himself *his best beloved son*. His posterity were very much favoured by the lot. Their portion lay in the very heart of the land of Canaan. It extended from Jordan in the east (*v.* 1) to the sea, the Mediterranean Sea, in the west, and the fruitfulness of the soil answered the blessings both of Jacob and Moses, Gen. xlix. 25, 26, and Deut. xxxiii. 13, &c. The portions allotted to Ephraim and Manasseh are not so particularly described as those of the other tribes; we have only the limits and boundaries of them, not the particular cities in them.

Verses 5–10

Here, 1. The border of the lot of Ephraim is set down, by which it was divided on the south from Benjamin and Dan, who lay between it and Judah, and on the north from Manasseh; for east and west it reached from Jordan to the great sea. 2. Some separate cities are spoken of, that lay not within these borders, at least not if the line was drawn direct, but lay within the lot of Manasseh (*v.* 9), which might better be read, *and there were separate cities for the children of Ephraim among the inheritance of the children of Manasseh.* 3. A brand is put upon the Ephraimites, that they did not drive out the Canaanites from Gezer (*v.* 10), putting them under tribute. It shows that they spared them out of covetousness, that they might be profited by their labours, and by dealing with them for their tribute they were in danger of being infected with their idolatry; yet some think that, when they brought them under tribute, they obliged them to renounce their idols. Samaria, built by Omri after the burning of the royal palace of Tirzah, was in this tribe, and was long the royal city of the kingdom of the ten tribes; not far from it were Shechem, and the mountains Ebal and Gerizim,

JAMIESON, FAUSSET, BROWN — CHAPTER 16

Vss. 1-4. THE GENERAL BORDERS OF THE SONS OF JOSEPH. **1. the lot of the children of Joseph fell**—*Heb.*, went forth, referring either to the lot as drawn out of the urn, or to the tract of land thereby assigned. The first four verses describe the territory allotted to the family of Joseph in the rich domains of central Palestine. It was drawn in one lot, that the brethren might be contiguously situated; but it was afterwards divided. The southern boundary only is described here; that on the north being irregular and less defined (ch. 17:10, 11), is not mentioned. **water of Jericho** (II Kings 2:19)—at the joint of its junction with the Jordan. **mount Beth-el**—the ridge south of Beth-el. Having described the position of Joseph's family generally the historian proceeds to define the territory; first, that of Ephraim.

5-9. THE BORDERS OF THE INHERITANCE OF EPHRAIM. **5-9. the border of their inheritance . . . was Ataroth-addar**—Ataroth-addar (now Atara), four miles south of Jetta [ROBINSON], is fixed on as a center, through which a line is drawn from Upper Beth-horon to Michmethah, showing the western limit of their actual possessions. The tract beyond that to the sea was still unconquered. **6, 7. Michmethah on the north side**—The northern boundary is traced from this point eastward to the Jordan. **8. from Tappuah westward unto the river Kanah**—It is retraced from east to west, to describe the prospective and intended boundary, which was to reach to the sea. Kanah (reedy) flows into the Mediterranean. **9. separate cities for the children of Ephraim were among the inheritance of Manasseh**—(ch. 17:9), because it was found that the tract allotted to Ephraim was too small in proportion to its population and power. **10. they drave not out the Canaanites . . . but the Canaanites dwell among the Ephraimites unto this day, and serve under tribute**—This is the first mention of the fatal policy of the Israelites, in neglecting the divine command

ADAM CLARKE — CHAPTER 16

1. *The children of Joseph.* Ephraim and Manasseh, and their descendants. The limits of the tribe of Ephraim extended along the borders of Benjamin and Dan, from Jordan on the east to the Mediterranean on the west.

2. *From Beth-el to Luz.* From Gen. xxviii. 19 it appears that the place which Jacob called Bethel was formerly called Luz (see the note there), but here they seem to be two distinct places. It is very likely that the place where Jacob had the vision was not in Luz, but in some place within a small distance of that city or village (see the note on Gen. xxviii. 12) and that sometimes the whole place was called Bethel, at other times Luz, and sometimes, as in the case above, the two places were distinguished. *Archi to Ataroth.* Archi was the country of Hushai, the friend of David, 2 Sam. xv. 32, who is called Hushai the Archite. Ataroth, called Ataroth-addar, "Ataroth the illustrious," v. 5, and simply Ataroth, v. 7, is supposed to have been about fifteen miles from Jerusalem.

3. *Beth-horon the nether.* This city was about twelve miles from Jerusalem, on the side of Nicopolis, formerly Emmaus.

8. *Tappuah.* This was a city in the tribe of Manasseh, and gave name to a certain district called the "land of Tappuah." *The sea.* The Mediterranean, as before.

9. *And the separate cities.* That is, the cities that were separated from the tribe of Manasseh to be given to Ephraim; see chap. xvii. 9.

10. *The Canaanites that dwelt in Gezer.* It appears that the Canaanites were not expelled from this city till the days of Solomon, when it was taken by the king of Egypt, his father-in-law, who made it a present to his daughter,

MATTHEW HENRY

and Sychar, near which was Jacob's well, where Christ talked with the woman of Samaria. We read much of Mount Ephraim in the story of the Judges, and of a city called *Ephraim,* it is probable in this tribe, to which Christ retired, John xi. 54. The whole kingdom of the ten tribes is often, in the prophets, especially in Hosea, called *Ephraim.*

CHAPTER 17

Verses 1–6

Manasseh was itself but one half of the tribe of Joseph, and yet was divided and subdivided. 1. It was divided into two parts, one already settled on the other side Jordan, consisting of those who were the posterity of Machir, *v.* 1. This Machir was born to Manasseh in Egypt; there he had signalized himself as a man of war, probably in the contests between the Ephraimites and the men of Gath, 1 Chron. vii. 21. 2. That part on this side Jordan was subdivided into ten families, *v.* 5. Here is, (1) The claim which the daughters of Zelophehad made, grounded upon the command God gave to Moses concerning them, *v.* 4. They had themselves, when they were young, pleaded their own cause before Moses, and obtained the grant of an inheritance with their brethren, and now they would not lose the benefit of that grant for want of speaking to Joshua. (2) The assignment of their portions according to their claim. Joshua knew very well what God had ordered in their case, and did not object that they having not served in the wars of Canaan there was no reason why they should share in the possessions of Canaan, but readily *gave them an inheritance among the brethren of their father.*

Verses 7–13

We have here a short account of the lot of this half tribe. It reached from Jordan on the east to the great sea on the west; on the south it lay all along contiguous to Ephraim, but on the north it abutted upon Asher and Issachar. Some things are particularly observed concerning this lot:—1. That there was great communication between this tribe and that of Ephraim. The city of Tappuah belonged to Ephraim, but the country adjoining to Manasseh (*v.* 8); there were likewise many cities of Ephraim that lay within the border of Manasseh (*v.* 9), of which before, *ch.* xvi. 9. 2. That Manasseh likewise had cities with their appurtenances in the tribes of Issachar and Asher (*v.* 11), God so ordering it, that though every tribe had its peculiar inheritance, which might not be alienated from it, yet they should thus intermix one with another, as became those who, though of different tribes, were all one Israel. 3. That they suffered the Canaanites to live among them, contrary to the command of God, serving their own ends by conniving at them, for they made them tributaries, *v.* 12, 13. The most remarkable person of this half tribe in after-time was Gideon, whose great actions were done within this lot.

Verses 14–18

I. The children of Joseph quarrel with their lot. Joshua makes them know that in the discharge of his office, as a public person, he had no more regard to his own tribe than to any other. Two things they suggest, 1. That they were very numerous, through the blessing of God upon them (*v.* 14): *I am a great people, for the Lord has blessed me;* and we have reason to hope that he that hath sent mouths will send meat. 2. That a good part of that country which had now fallen to their lot was in the hands of the Canaanites, and that they were formidable enemies, who brought into the field of battle *chariots of iron* (*v.* 16), that is, chariots with long scythes fastened to the sides of them, or the axle-tree, which made great destruction of all that came in their way, mowing them down like corn.

II. Joshua endeavours to reconcile them to their lot. He owns they were a *great people,* and being two tribes ought to have more than *one lot only* (*v.* 17), but tells them that what had fallen to their share would be a sufficient lot for them both, if they would but work and fight. "If thou hast many mouths to be filled, thou hast twice as many hands to be employed; earn, and then eat." 1. He bids them work for more (*v.* 15): "*Get thee up to the wood-country,* which is within thy own border, and let all hands be set to work to cut down the trees, rid the rough lands, and make them, with art and industry, good arable ground." Note, Many wish for larger possessions who do not cultivate and make the best of what they have. 2. He bids them fight for more (*v.* 17, 18), when they pleaded that they could not

JAMIESON, FAUSSET, BROWN

(Deut. 20:16) to exterminate the idolaters.

CHAPTER 17

Vss. 1-6. LOT OF MANASSEH. **1. There was also a lot for the tribe of Manasseh**—Ephraim was mentioned, as the more numerous and powerful branch of the family of Joseph (Gen. 48:19, 20); but Manasseh still retained the right of primogeniture and had a separate inheritance assigned. **Machir**—his descendants. **the father of Gilead**—Though he had a son of that name (Num. 26:29; 27:1), yet, as is evident from the use of the *Heb.* article, reference is made, not to the person, but the province of Gilead. "Father" here means lord or possessor of Gilead. This view is confirmed by the fact that it was not Machir, but his descendants, who subdued Gilead and Bashan (Num. 32:41; Deut. 3:13-15). These Machirites had their portion on the east side of Jordan. The western portion of land, allotted to the tribe of Manasseh, was divided into ten portions because the male descendants who had sons consisted of five families, to which, consequently, five shares were given; and the sixth family, viz., the posterity of Hepher, being all women, the five daughters of Zelophehad were, on application to the valuators, endowed each with an inheritance in land (see on Num. 27:1).

7-11. THIS COAST. **7-11. the coast of Manasseh was from Asher to Michmethah**—The southern boundary is here traced from the east. Asher (now Yasir), the starting-point, was a town fifteen Roman miles east of Shechem, and anciently a place of importance. **9. the coast descended unto the river Kanah, southward of the river**—The line which separated the possessions of the two brothers from each other ran to the south of the stream. Thus the river was in the territory of Manasseh; but the cities which were upon the river, though all were within the limits of Manasseh's possessions, were assigned partly to Ephraim, and partly to Manasseh; those on the south side being given to the former; those upon the north to the latter [KEIL]. It appears (vs. 10) that Manasseh was still further interlaced with other neighboring tribes. **11. Beth-shean and her towns**—*Gr.,* Scythopolis (now Beisan), in the valley of the Jordan, towards the east end of the plain of Jezreel. "Beth-shean" means "house of rest," so called from its being the halting-place for caravans travelling between Syria or Midian, and Egypt, and the great station for the commerce between these countries for many centuries. **Ibleam and her towns**—in the neighborhood of Megiddo (II Kings 9:27). **the inhabitants of Dor and her towns**—(now Tantoura), anciently a strong fortress; a wall of wild precipitous rock defended the shore fortifications against attack from the land side. **En-dor and her towns**—situated on a rocky eminence, four Roman miles south of Tabor. **Taanach and . . . Megiddo**—These were near to each other, and they are generally mentioned in Scripture together. They were both royal and strongly fortified places (see on Judg. 1:27). **three countries**—districts or provinces. It is computed that Manasseh possessed in Asher and Issachar portions of ground to the extent of more than 200 square miles.

12, 13. CANAANITES NOT DRIVEN OUT. **12, 13. Manasseh could not drive out the inhabitants of those cities**—probably due to indolence, a love of ease. Perhaps a mistaken humanity, arising from a disregard or forgetfulness of the divine command, and a decreasing principle of faith and zeal in the service of God, were the causes of their failure.

14-18. THE CHILDREN OF JOSEPH ASK FOR ANOTHER LOT. **14-18. the children of Joseph spake unto Joshua**—The two tribes join in laying a complaint before the leader, as to the narrow boundaries of their allotment and its insufficiency to be the residence of tribes so vastly increased. But Joshua's answer was full of wisdom as well as patriotism. Knowing their character, he treated them accordingly, and sarcastically turned all their arguments against themselves. Thus he rebuked their unbelief and cowardice. **mount Ephraim**—called so here by anticipation. The Gilboa range between Beth-shean and the plain of Jezreel is meant, anciently covered with an extensive forest. **chariots of iron**—unusually strengthened with that metal,

ADAM CLARKE

Solomon's queen (see 1 Kings ix. 16). The Ephraimites, however, had so far succeeded in subjecting these people as to oblige them to pay tribute, though they could not, or at least did not, totally expel them.

CHAPTER 17

1. *There was also a lot for the tribe of Manasseh.* It was necessary to mark this because Jacob, in his blessing (Gen. xlviii. 19-20), did in a certain sense set Ephraim before Manasseh, though the latter was the firstborn; but the place here shows that this preference did not affect the rights of primogeniture. *For Machir . . . because he was a man of war.* It is not likely that Machir himself was now alive; if he were, he must have been nearly two hundred years old. It is therefore probable that what is spoken here is spoken of his children, who now possessed the lot that was originally designed for their father, who it appears had signalized himself as a man of skill and valor in some of the former wars, though the circumstances are not marked. His descendants, being of a warlike, intrepid spirit, were well-qualified to defend a frontier country, which would be naturally exposed to invasion.

2. *The rest of the children of Manasseh.* That is, his grandchildren; for it is contended that Manasseh had no other son than Machir; and these were very probably the children of Gilead, the son of Machir.

3. *Zelophehad . . . had no sons, but daughters.* See this case considered at large in the notes on Num. xxvii. 1-7, and xxxvi. 1, etc.

5. *There fell ten portions to Manasseh.* The Hebrew word *chabley,* which we translate *portions,* signifies literally "cords" or "cables," and intimates that by means of a cord, cable, or what we call a chain, the land was divided. As there were six sons and five daughters, among whom this division was to be made, there should be eleven portions; but Zelophehad, son of Hepher, having left five daughters in his place, neither he nor Hepher is reckoned. The lot of Manasseh therefore was divided into ten parts: five for the five sons of Gilead, who were Abiezer, Helek, Asriel, Shechem, and Shemida; and five for the five daughters of Zelophehad, viz., Mahlah, Noah, Hoglah, Milcah, and Tirzah.

9. *Unto the river Kanah.* Literally, the "river or valley of the reeds." The tribe of Manasseh appears to have been bounded on the north by this torrent or valley, and on the south by the Mediterranean Sea.

11. *Beth-shean.* Called afterwards Scythopolis; the city of the Scythians or Cuthites, those who were sent into the different Samaritan cities by the kings of Assyria. *Dor.* On the Mediterranean Sea, about eight miles from Caesarea, on the road to Tyre. *En-dor.* The "well or fountain of Dor," the place where Saul went to consult the witch; 1 Sam. xxviii. 7, etc.

12. *Could not drive out.* They had neither grace nor courage to go against their enemies, and chose rather to share their territories with those whom the justice of God had proscribed than exert themselves to expel them. But some commentators give a different turn to this expression, and translate the passage thus: "But the children of Manasseh could not (resolve) to destroy those cities, but the Canaanites consented to dwell in the land."

15. *If thou be a great people.* Joshua takes them at their own word; they said, v. 14, that they were a great people; then said he, "If thou be a great people [or seeing thou art a great people, go to the wood country, and clear away for thyself." Joshua would not reverse the decision of the lot; but as there was much woodland country, he gave them permission to clear away as much of it as they found necessary to extend themselves as far as they pleased.

16. *The hill is not enough for us.* The mountain of Gilboa being that which had fallen to them by lot. *Chariots of iron.* We cannot possess the plain country, because that is occupied by the Canaanites; and we cannot con-

MATTHEW HENRY

come at the woodlands he spoke of because in the valley between them and it there were Canaanites whom they durst not enter the lists with.

CHAPTER 18

Verse 1

In the midst of the story of the dividing of the land comes in this account of the setting up of the tabernacle, which had hitherto continued in its old place in the centre of their camp; but now that three of the four squadrons that used to surround it in the wilderness were broken and diminished, it was time to think of removing the tabernacle itself into a city. Many a time the priests and Levites had taken it down, carried it, and set it up again in the wilderness, according to the directions given them (Num. iv. 5, &c.); but now they must do it for good and all.

I. The place to which the tabernacle was removed, and in which it was set up. It was *Shiloh*, a city in the lot of Ephraim, but lying close upon the lot of Benjamin. This place was pitched upon, 1. Because it was in the heart of the country. It had been in the midst of their camp in the wilderness, and therefore must now be in the midst of their nation. 2. The setting up of the tabernacle in Shiloh gave them a hint that in that Shiloh which Jacob spoke of all the ordinances of this worldly sanctuary should have their accomplishment in a greater and more perfect tabernacle, Heb. ix. 1, 11.

II. The solemn manner of doing it: *The whole congregation assembled together* to attend the solemnity, to do honour to the ark of God, as the token of his presence. It was a good presage of a comfortable settlement to themselves in Canaan, when their first care was to see the ark well settled as soon as they had a safe place ready to settle it in. Here the ark continued about 300 years, till the sins of Eli's house forfeited the ark, lost it and ruined Shiloh, and its ruins were long after made use of as warnings to Jerusalem. *Go, see what I did to Shiloh*, Jer. vii. 12; Ps. lxxviii. 60.

Verses 2–10

I. Joshua reproves those tribes which were yet unsettled that they did not bestir themselves to gain a settlement in the land which God had given them. Joshua reasons (*v.* 3): *How long are you slack?* 1. They were too well pleased with their present condition. The spoil of the cities they had taken served them to live plentifully upon for the present, and they banished the thoughts of time to come. 2. They were slothful and dilatory. Note, Many are diverted from real duties, and debarred from real comforts, by seeming difficulties. God by his grace has given us a title to a good land, the heavenly Canaan, but we are *slack to take possession*; we enter not into that rest, as we might by faith, and hope, and holy joy; we live not in heaven, as we might by setting our affections on things above and having our conversation there.

II. He puts them in a way to settle themselves.

1. The land that remained must be surveyed, an account taken of the cities, and the territories belonging to them, *v.* 4. These must be divided into seven equal parts. The Levites were to have no temporal estate. Gad and Reuben, with half of the tribe of Manasseh, were already fixed, and needed not to have any further care taken of them. Now, (1) The surveyors were three men out of each of the seven tribes that were to be provided for (*v.* 4). (2) The survey was accordingly made, and brought in to Joshua, *v.* 8, 9. [1] The faith and courage of the persons employed: abundance of Canaanites remained in the land, and all raging against Israel, *as a bear robbed of her whelps*. [2] The good providence of God in protecting them from the many deaths they were exposed to, and bringing them all safely again to the host at Shiloh.

2. When it was surveyed, and reduced to seven lots, then Joshua would, by appeal to God, and direction from him, determine which of these lots should belong to each tribe (*v.* 6). *That I may cast lots for you here* at the tabernacle (because it was a sacred transaction) *before the Lord our God.*

Verses 11–28

We have here the lot of the tribe of Benjamin, which Providence cast next to Joseph on the one hand, because Benjamin was own and only brother to Joseph, and was little Benjamin (Ps. lxviii. 27), that needed the protection of great Joseph. And it was next to Judah on the other hand, that this tribe might hereafter unite with Judah in an adherence to the

JAMIESON, FAUSSET, BROWN

and perhaps armed with projecting scythes.

CHAPTER 18

Vs. 1. The Tabernacle Set Up at Shiloh. **1. the whole congregation . . . assembled together at Shiloh**—The main body of the Israelites had been diminished by the separation of the three tribes, Judah, Ephraim, and Manasseh into their respective allotments; and the country having been in a great measure subdued, the camp was removed to Shiloh—now Seilun. It was twenty or twenty-five miles north of Jerusalem, twelve north of Bethel, and ten south of Shechem, and embosomed in a rugged and romantic glen. This sequestered spot in the heart of the country might have been recommended by the dictates of convenience. There the allotment of the territory could be most conveniently made, north, south, east, and west, to the different tribes. But "the tabernacle of the congregation was also set up there," and its removal therefore must have been made or sanctioned by divine intimation (Deut. 12:11). It remained in Shiloh for more than 300 years (I Sam. 4:1-11).

2-9. The Remainder of the Land Described. **2. there remained . . . seven tribes which had not yet received their inheritance**—The selection of Shiloh for the seat of worship, together with the consequent removal of the camp thither, had necessarily interrupted the casting of lots, which was commenced by fixing localities for the tribes of Judah and Joseph. Various causes led to a long delay in resuming it. The satisfaction of the people with their change to so pleasant and fertile a district, their preference of a nomad life, a love of ease, and reluctance to renew the war, seem to have made them indifferent to the possession of a settled inheritance. But Joshua was too much alive to the duty laid on him by the Lord to let matters continue in that state; and accordingly, since a general conquest of the land had been made, he resolved to proceed immediately with the lot, believing that when each tribe should receive its inheritance, a new motive would arise to lead them to exert themselves in securing the full possession. **3. How long are ye slack to go to possess the land which the Lord God of your fathers hath given you**—This reproof conveys an impression that the seven tribes were dilatory to a criminal extent. **4-9. Give out from among you three men for each tribe**—Though the lot determined the part of the country where each tribe was to be located, it could not determine the extent of territory which might be required; and the dissatisfaction of the children of Joseph with the alleged smallness of their possession gave reason to fear that complaints might arise from other quarters, unless precautions were taken to make a proper distribution of the land. For this purpose a commission was given to twenty-one persons—three chosen from each of the seven tribes which had not yet received their inheritance, to make an accurate survey of the country. "The men went and passed through the land, and described it by cities into seven parts in a book" (vs. 9); dividing the land according to its value, and the worth of the cities which it contained, into seven equal portions. This was no light task to undertake. It required learning and intelligence which they or their instructors had, in all probability, brought with them out of Egypt. Accordingly, Josephus says that the survey was performed by men expert in geometry. And, in fact, the circumstantial account which is given of the boundaries of each tribe and its situation, well proves it to have been the work of no mean or incompetent hands.

10. Divided by Lot. **10. Joshua cast lots for them in Shiloh before the Lord**—before the tabernacle, where the divine presence was manifested, and which associated with the lot the idea of divine sanction. **11. the lot of . . . Benjamin came up**—It has been supposed that there were two urns or vessels, from which the lots were drawn: one containing the names of the tribes, the other containing those of the seven portions; and that the two were drawn out simultaneously. **the coast of their lot came forth between the children of Judah and the children of Joseph**—Thus the prophecy of Moses respecting the inheritance of Benjamin was remarkably accomplished. (See on Deut. 33:12.)

ADAM CLARKE

quer them, because they have *chariots of iron*, that is, very strong chariots, and armed with scythes, as is generally supposed.

CHAPTER 18

1. *Israel assembled together at Shiloh.* This appears to have been a considerable town about fifteen miles from Jerusalem, in the tribe of Ephraim, and nearly in the center of the whole land. To this place both the camp of Israel and the ark of the Lord were removed from Gilgal, after a residence there of 7 years. Here the Tabernacle remained 120 years, as is generally supposed, being the most conveniently situated for access to the different tribes, and for safety, the Israelites having possession of the land on all sides; for it is here added, *The land was subdued before them*—the Canaanites were so completely subdued that there was no longer any general resistance to the Israelitish arms.

3. *How long are ye slack to go to possess the land?* We find an unaccountable backwardness in this people to enter on the inheritance which God had given them! They had so long been supported by miracle, without any exertions of their own, that they found it difficult to shake themselves from their inactivity.

4. *Three men for each tribe.* Probably meaning only three from each of the seven tribes who had not yet received their inheritance. It is likely that these twenty-one men were accompanied by a military guard, for without this they might have been easily cut off by straggling parties of the Canaanites. *They shall . . . describe it.* It is likely they were persons well-acquainted with geography, without which it would have been impossible for them to divide the land in the way necessary on this occasion.

5. *Judah shall abide . . . on the south, and the house of Joseph . . . on the north.* Joshua does not mean that the tribe of Judah occupied the south and the tribe of Ephraim and Manasseh the north of the Promised Land; this was not the fact. But being now at Shiloh, a considerable way in the territory of Ephraim, and not far from that of Judah, he speaks of them in relation to the place in which he then was.

7. *The priesthood of the Lord is their inheritance.* We have already seen that the priests and Levites had the sacrifices, oblations, tithes, firstfruits, redemption money of the firstborn, etc., for their inheritance; they had no landed possessions in Israel; the Lord was their Portion.

9. *And described it . . . in a book.* This, as far as I can recollect, is the first act of surveying on record. These men and their work differed widely from those who had searched the land in the time of Moses; they went only to discover the nature of the country and the state of its inhabitants, but these went to take an actual geographical survey of it, in order to divide it among the tribes which had not yet received their portions. We may suppose that the country was exactly described *in a book*, that is, a map, pointing out the face of the country, accompanied with descriptions of each part.

11. *And the lot . . . of Benjamin came up.* There were probably two urns, one of which contained the names of the seven tribes, and the other that of the seven portions. They therefore took out one name out of the first urn, and one portion out of the second, and thus the portion was adjudged to that tribe.

12. *The wilderness of Beth-aven.* This was the same as Bethel, but this name was not given to it till Jeroboam had fixed one of his golden calves there. It first name signifies the "house of God"; its second, "the house of iniquity."

16. *To the side of Jebusi.* The mountain of Zion, that was near Jerusalem; for Jebusi, or Jebus, was the ancient name of this city.

17. *En-shemesh.* The fountain of the sun; a proof of the idolatrous nature of the ancient inhabitants of this land. *Geliloth.* As the word signifies "borders" or "limits," it is probably not the proper name of a place: "And went forth towards the borders which are over against the ascent to Adummim."

MATTHEW HENRY

throne of David and the temple at Jerusalem. Here we have, 1. The exact borders and limits of this tribe. The western border is said to *compass the corner of the sea southward* (*v.* 14). Bishop Patrick thinks the meaning is that it ran along in a parallel line to the great sea, though at a distance. 2. The particular cities in this tribe, not all, but the most considerable. Twenty-six are here named. Jericho is put first, though dismantled, and forbidden to be rebuilt as a city with gates and walls. Gilgal, where Israel first encamped when Saul was made king (1 Sam. xi. 15), was in this tribe. It was afterwards a very profane place. Hos. ix. 15, *All their wickedness is in Gilgal.* Beth-el was in this tribe, a famous place.

JAMIESON, FAUSSET, BROWN

ADAM CLARKE

19. *The north bay of the salt sea. Leshon* signifies the "tongue."

21. *Now the cities.* Some of these cities have been mentioned before, and described; of others we know nothing but the name.

24. *And Gaba.* Supposed to be the same as Gibeah of Saul, a place famous for having given birth to the first king of Israel; and infamous for the shocking act towards the Levite's wife, mentioned in Judges xix, which was the cause of a war in which the tribe of Benjamin was nearly exterminated, Judges xx.

25. *Gibeon.* See before, chap. x. This place is famous for the confederacy of the five kings against Israel, and their miraculous defeat. *Ramah,* a place about six or eight miles north of Jerusalem. *Beeroth,* i.e., "wells"; one of the four cities which belonged to the Gibeonites, who made peace with the Israelites by stratagem.

26. *And Mizpeh.* This place is celebrated in the sacred writings. Here the people were accustomed to assemble often in the presence of the Lord, as in the deliberation concerning the punishment to be inflicted on the men of Gibeah, for the abuse of the Levite's wife, Judg. xx. 1-3. Samuel assembled the people here to exhort them to renounce their idolatry, 1 Sam. vii. 5-6. In this same place Saul was chosen to be king, 1 Sam. x. 17. It was deemed a sacred place among the Israelites; for we find, from 1 Mac. iii. 46, that the Jews assembled here to seek God, when their enemies were in possession of the Temple.

28. *And Zelah.* This was the burying place of Saul, Jonathan, and the family of Kish. See 2 Sam. xxi. 14. *Jebusi, which is Jerusalem.* We often meet with this name, and it is evident that it was the ancient name of Jerusalem, which was also called Salem, and was probably the place in which Melchizedek reigned in the days of Abraham. That this was a name of Jerusalem is evident from Ps. lxxvi. 1-2: "In Judah is God known: his name is great in Israel. In Salem also is his tabernacle, and his dwelling place in Zion." This must refer to Jerusalem, where the Temple was situated. Whether Jebus or Jebusi had its name from the Jebusites, or the Jebusites from it, cannot be ascertained.

JOHN LANGE:

Gibeath. This is the Gibeah of Saul (1 Sam. 10:26; 11:4; 15:34); as was already shown above on verse 24, to be sought on the hill Tuleil el-Ful. Here occurred before Saul's time the outrage reported in Judges 19 which resulted in the destruction of the city, and the extirpation of the Benjamites except six hundred (Judg. 20). After Saul's death its inhabitants hung seven of his descendants on the mountain of Gibeah (2 Sam. 21:6–9), but Mephibosheth was spared. Furrer accomplished the way from Jerusalem to Tel el-Ful, on foot, in one hour and twenty-five minutes. He found the summit completely strewn with ruins. There the traveller was rewarded with a wide and glorious prospect scarcely inferior to that of Mizpeh. "The land of Benjamin with its many famous old cities lay spread out around me. Over the heights of Hizmeh, Anathoth, and Isawijeh, the eye swept downward to the Jordan valley, which here appeared more beautiful than on the mount of Olives. In the southeast the dark blue of the Dead Sea enlivened wonderfully the stiff yellow mountain rocks of its neighborhood. On the far distant horizon the mountain chains of Moab were traced in soft and hazy lines. Northward lay Ramah and the hill of Geba. Further west and around toward the south followed Gibeon, 'the glorious height,' Mizpeh, the queen among the mountains of Benjamin, and then in the south, the most beautiful of all, the Holy City." Excellently descriptive!—*Commentary on the Holy Scriptures*

CHAPTER 19

Verses 1–9

Simeon's lot was drawn after Judah's, Joseph's, and Benjamin's, because Jacob had put that tribe under disgrace. Not one person of note, neither judge nor prophet, was of this tribe, that we know of. I. The situation of their lot was within that of Judah (*v.* 1) and was taken from it, *v.* 9. 1. The men of Judah did not oppose the taking away of the cities again, which by the first distribution fell within their border, when they were convinced that they had more than their proportion. 2. That which was thus taken off from Judah to be put into a new lot Providence directed to the tribe of Simeon. The cities of Simeon were scattered in Judah. This brought them into a confederacy with the tribe of Judah (Judg. i. 3), and afterwards was a happy occasion of the adherence of many of this tribe to the house of David, at the time of the revolt of the ten tribes to Jeroboam.

II. The cities within their lot are here named. Beersheba, or Sheba, for these names seem to refer to the same place, is put first. Ziklag, which we read of in David's story, is one of them.

Verses 10–16

This is the lot of Zebulun, who, though born of Leah after Issachar, yet was blessed by Jacob and Moses before him. 1. The lot of this tribe was washed by the great sea on the west, and by the sea of Tiberias on the east, answering Jacob's prophecy (Gen. xlix. 13), *Zebulun shall be a haven of ships,* trading ships on the great sea and fishing ships on the sea of Galilee. 2. Though there were some places in this tribe which were made famous in the Old Testament, especially *Mount Carmel,* yet it was made much more illustrious in the New Testament; for within the lot of this tribe was Nazareth, where our blessed Saviour spent so much of his time on earth, and that coast of the sea of Galilee on which Christ preached so many sermons and wrought so many miracles.

Verses 17–23

The lot of Issachar ran from Jordan in the east to

CHAPTER 19

Vss. 1-9. THE LOT OF SIMEON. **1. the second lot came forth to Simeon**—The next lot that was drawn at Shiloh, gave the tribe of Simeon his inheritance within the territory, which had been assigned to that of Judah. The knowledge of Canaan possessed by the Israelites, when the division of the land commenced, was but very general, being derived from the rapid sweep they had made over it during the course of conquest; and it was on the ground of that rough survey alone that the distribution proceeded, by which Judah received an inheritance. Time showed that this territory was too large (vs. 9), either for their numbers, however great, to occupy and their arms to defend, or too large in proportion to the allotments of the other tribes. Justice therefore required (what kind and brotherly feeling readily dictated) a modification of their possession; and a part of it was appropriated to Simeon. By thus establishing it within the original domain of another tribe, the prophecy of Jacob in regard to Simeon was fulfilled (Gen. 49:7); for from its boundaries being not traced, there is reason to conclude that its people were divided and dispersed among those of Judah; and though one group of its cities named (2-6), gives the idea of a compact district, as it is usually represented by mapmakers, the other group (7, 8) were situated, two in the south, and two elsewhere, with tracts of the country around them.

10-16. OF ZEBULUN. **10-14. the third lot came up for the children of Zebulun**—The boundaries of the possession assigned to them extended from the Lake of Chinnereth (Sea of Galilee) on the east, to the Mediterranean on the west. Although they do not seem at first to have touched on the western shore—a part of Manasseh running north into Asher (ch. 17:10)—they afterwards did, according to the prediction of Moses (Deut. 33:19). The extent from north to south cannot be very exactly traced; the sites of many of the places through which the boundary line is drawn being unknown. Some of the cities were of note.

17-23. OF ISSACHAR. **17-20. the fourth lot**

CHAPTER 19

1. *The second lot came forth to Simeon.* In this appointment the providence of God may be especially remarked. For the iniquitous conduct of Simeon and Levi, in the massacre of the innocent Shechemites, Genesis xxxiv, Jacob, in the spirit of prophecy, foretold that they should be "divided in Jacob," and "scattered in Israel," Gen. xlix. 7. And this is most literally fulfilled in the manner in which God disposed of both these tribes afterwards. Levi was scattered through all Palestine, not having received any inheritance, only cities to dwell in, in different parts of the land; and Simeon was dispersed in Judah, with what could scarcely be said to be their own or a peculiar lot. See the note on Gen. xlix. 7.

2. *Beer-sheba.* The "well of the oath." See the note on Gen. xxi. 31.

3. *Hazar-shual.* For this and several of the following places, see the notes on chap. xv.

5. *Beth-marcaboth.* The "house or city of chariots."

6. *Beth-lebaoth.* The "house or city of lionesses."

8. *Baalath-beer.* The "well of the mistresses." Probably so called from some superstitious or impure worship set up there.

13. *Gittah-hepher.* The same as Gath-hepher, the birthplace of the prophet Jonah.

15. *Shimron.* See on chap. xii. *Beth-lehem.* The "house of bread"; a different place from that in which our Lord was born.

17. *The fourth lot came out to Issachar.* It is remarkable that, though Issachar was the eldest brother, yet the lot of Zebulun was drawn before his lot; and this is the order in which Jacob himself mentions them, Gen. xlix. 13-14.

18. *Shunem.* This city was rendered famous by being the occasional abode of the prophet Elisha, and the place where he restored the son

MATTHEW HENRY

the great sea in the west, Manasseh on the south, and Zebulun on the north. Places in this tribe were, 1. Jezreel, in which was Ahab's palace, and near it Naboth's vineyard. 2. Shunem, where lived the good Shunamite that entertained Elisha. 3. The river Kishon, on the banks of which, in this tribe, Sisera was beaten by Deborah and Barak. 4. The mountains of Gilboa, on which Saul and Jonathan were slain, which were not far from Endor, where Saul consulted the witch. 5. The valley of Megiddo, where Josiah was slain near Hadad-rimmon, 2 Kings xxiii. 29; Zech. xii. 11.

Verses 24–31

The lot of Asher lay upon the coast of the great sea. We read not of any famous person of this tribe but Anna the prophetess, who was a constant resident in the temple at the time of our Saviour's birth, Luke ii. 36. But close adjoining to this tribe were the celebrated seaport towns of Tyre and Sidon.

Verses 32–39

Naphtali lay furthest north of all the tribes, bordering on Mount Libanus. The city of Leshem, or Laish, lay on the utmost edge of it to the north, and therefore when the Danites had made themselves masters of it, and called it *Dan*, the length of Canaan from north to south was reckoned from Dan to Beersheba. It was in the lot of this tribe, near the waters of Merom, that Joshua fought and routed Jabin, *ch.* xi. 1, &c. In this tribe stood Capernaum and Bethsaida, on the north end of the sea of Tiberias, in which Christ did so many mighty works.

Verses 40–48

Dan, though commander of one of the four squadrons of the camp of Israel, in the wilderness, that which brought up the rear, yet was last provided for in Canaan, and his lot fell in the southern part of Canaan, between Judah on the east and the land of the Philistines on the west, Ephraim on the north and Simeon on the south. Providence ordered this numerous and powerful tribe into a post of danger, as best able to deal with those vexatious neighbours the Philistines, and so it was found in Samson. Japho, or Joppa was in this lot.

JAMIESON, FAUSSET, BROWN

came out to Issachar—Instead of describing the boundaries of this tribe, the inspired historian gives a list of its principal cities. These cities are all in the eastern part of the plain of Esdraelon.

24-31. OF ASHER. **24-31. the fifth lot came out for the tribe of the children of Asher**—The western boundary is traced from north to south through the cities mentioned; the site of them, however, is unknown. **to Carmel . . . and Shihor-libnath**—i.e., the black or muddy river; probably the Nahr Belka, below Dor (Tantoura); for that town belonged to Asher (ch. 17:10). Thence the boundary line turned eastward to Beth-dagon, a town at the junction of Zebulun and Naphtali, and ran northwards as far as Cabul, with other towns, among which is mentioned (vs. 28) "great Zidon," so called on account of its being even then the flourishing metropolis of the Phœnicians. Though included in the inheritance of Asher, this town was never possessed by them (Judg. 1:31).

29. and then the coast turneth to Ramah—now El-Hamra, which stood where the Leontes (Litany) ends its southern course and flows westward. **and to the strong city Tyre**—The original city appears to have stood on the mainland, and was well fortified. From Tyre the boundary ran to Hosah, an inland town; and then, passing the unconquered district of Achzib (Judg. 1:31), terminated at the seacoast.

32-39. OF NAPHTALI. **32-39. the sixth lot came out to the children of Naphtali**—Although the cities mentioned have not been discovered, it is evident, from Zaanannim, which is by Kedesh, i.e., on the northwest of Lake Merom (Judg. 4:11), that the boundary described (vs. 34) ran from the southwest towards the northeast, up to the sources of the Jordan. **Aznoth-tabor**—on the east of Tabor towards the Jordan, for the border ran thence to Hukkok, touching upon that of Zebulun; and as the territory of Zebulun did not extend as far as the Jordan, Aznoth-tabor and Hukkok must have been border towns on the line which separated Naphtali from Issachar. **to Judah upon Jordan toward the sunrising**—The sixty cities, Havoth-jair, which were on the eastern side of the Jordan, opposite Naphtali, were reckoned as belonging to Judah, because Jair, their possessor, was a descendant of Judah (I Chron. 2:4-22) [KEIL].

40-48. OF DAN. **40-46. the seventh lot came out for the tribe . . . of Dan**—It lay on the west of Benjamin and consisted of portions surrendered by Judah and Ephraim. Its boundaries are not stated, as they were easily distinguishable from the relative position of Dan to the three adjoining tribes.

47. the children of Dan went up to fight against Leshem—The Danites, finding their inheritance too small, decided to enlarge its boundaries by the sword; and, having conquered Leshem (Laish), they planted a colony there, calling the new settlement by the name of Dan (see on Judg. 18).

ADAM CLARKE

of a pious woman to life, 2 Kings iv. 8. It was the place where the Philistines were encamped on that ruinous day in which the Israelites were totally routed at Gilboa, and Saul and his sons killed, 1 Sam. xxviii. 4; xxxi. 1, etc.

22. *Beth-shemesh.* "The house or temple of the sun"; there were several cities or towns of this name in Palestine, an ample proof that the worship of this celestial luminary had generally prevailed in that idolatrous country.

26. *Carmel.* "The vineyard of God"; a place greatly celebrated in Scripture, and especially for the miracles of Elijah; see 1 Kings xviii. The mountain of Carmel was so very fruitful as to pass into a proverb. There was another Carmel in the tribe of Judah (see chap. xv. 55), but this, in the tribe of Asher, was situated about one hundred and twenty furlongs south from Prolemais, on the edge of the Mediterranean Sea.

27. *Cabul on the left hand.* That is, to the north of Cabul, for so the *left hand,* when referring to place, is understood among the Hebrews.

28. *Unto great Zidon.* The city of Sidon and the Sidonians are celebrated from the remotest antiquity. They are frequently mentioned by Homer.

29. *The strong city Tyre.* I suspect this to be an improper translation. Perhaps the words of the original should be retained: "And the coast turneth to Ramah and to the city." Our translators have here left the Hebrew, and followed the Septuagint and Vulgate, a fault of which they are sometimes guilty. The word *Tsor,* which we translate or change into *Tyre,* signifies a "rock" or "strong place"; and as there were many rocks in the land of Judea that with a little art were formed into strong places of defense, hence several places might have the name of Tyre. *Achzib.* Called now Zib; it is about nine miles' distance from Ptolemais, towards Tyre.

30. *Twenty and two cities.* There are nearly thirty cities in the above enumeration instead of twenty-two, but probably several are mentioned that were but frontier towns, and that did not belong to this tribe, their border only passing by such cities; and on this account, though they are named, yet they do not enter into the enumeration in this place. Perhaps some of the villages are named as well as the cities.

34. *And to Judah upon Jordan.* It is certain that the tribe of Naphtali did not border on the east upon Judah, for there were several tribes betwixt them. Some think that, as these two tribes were bounded by Jordan on the east, they might be considered as in some sort conjoined, because of the easy passage to each other by means of the river; but this might be said of several other tribes as well as of these. There is considerable difficulty in the text as it now stands. But if, with the Septuagint, we omit *Judah,* the difficulty vanishes, and the passage is plain; but this omission is supported by no MS. hitherto discovered.

38. *Nineteen cities.* But if these cities be separately enumerated they amount to twenty-three; this is probably occasioned by reckoning frontier cities belonging to other tribes, which are mentioned here only as the boundaries of the tribe. See on v. 30.

41. *Ir-shemesh.* "The city of sun"; another proof of the idolatry of the Canaanites. Some think this was the same as Beth-shemesh.

42. *Shaalabbin.* "The foxes." Of this city the Amorites kept constant possession. See Judg. i. 35. *Ajalon.* There was a place of this name about two miles from Nicopolis or Emmaus, on the road to Jerusalem.

43. *Thimnathah.* Probably the same as Timnah. See on chap. xv. 57. *Ekron.* A well-known city of the Philistines, and the metropolis of one of their five dynasties.

45. *Jehud, and Bene-berak.* Or Jehud of the children of Berak.

46. *Japho.* The place since called Joppa, lying on the Mediterranean, and the chief seaport, in the possession of the twelve tribes.

47. *Went out too little for them.* This is certainly the meaning of the passage, but our translators have been obliged to add the words

MATTHEW HENRY

Verses 49–51

Here is an account of the particular inheritance assigned to Joshua. 1. He was last served, though the eldest and greatest man of all Israel. In all he did he sought the good of his country, and not any private interest of his own. He was content to be unfixed till he saw them all settled. 2. He had his lot *according to the word of the Lord*. It is probable that, when God by Moses told Caleb what inheritance he should have (*ch.* xiv. 9), he gave the like promise to Joshua. 3. He chose it in Mount Ephraim, which belonged to his own tribe. 4. The *children of Israel* are said to *give it to him* (*v.* 49), which bespeaks his humility, that he would not take it to himself without the people's consent and approbation. 5. It was a city that must be built before it was fit to be dwelt in.

JAMIESON, FAUSSET, BROWN

49-51. The Children of Israel Give an Inheritance to Joshua. **50. According to the word of the Lord, they gave him the city which he asked**—It was most proper that the great leader should receive an inheritance suited to his dignity, and as a reward for his public services. But the gift was not left to the spontaneous feelings of a grateful people. It was conferred "according to the word of the Lord"—probably an unrecorded promise, similar to what had been made to Caleb (ch. 14:9). **Timnath-serah**—or Heres, on Mount Gaash (Judg. 2:9). Joshua founded it, and was afterwards buried there (ch. 24:30).

51. These are the inheritances—This verse is the formal close of the section which narrates the history of the land distribution; and to stamp it with due importance, the names of the commissioners are repeated, as well as the spot where so memorable a transaction took place.

ADAM CLARKE

too little to make this sense apparent. *And called Leshem, Dan.* This city was situated near the origin of Jordan, at the utmost northern extremity of the Promised Land, as Beersheba was at that of the south; and as after its capture by the Danites it was called Dan, hence arose the expression "from Dan even to Beer-sheba," which always signified the whole extent of the Promised Land.

50. *Timnath-serah.* Called Timnath-heres in Judg. ii. 9, where we find that the mountain on which it was built was called Gaash. It is generally allowed to have been a barren spot in a barren country.

51. *At the door of the tabernacle.* All the inheritances were determined by lot, and this was cast *before the Lord*—everything was done in his immediate presence, as under his eye; hence there was no murmuring, each having received his inheritance as from the hand of God himself, though some of them thought they must have additional territory because of the great increase of their families.

MATTHEW HENRY — CHAPTER 20

Verses 1–6

Many things were by the law of Moses ordered to be done when they came to Canaan and this among the rest, the appointing of sanctuaries for the protecting of those that were guilty of casual murder. It was for the interest of the land that the blood of an innocent person, whose hand only was guilty but not his heart, should not be shed, no, not by the avenger of blood: of this law, which was so much for their advantage, God here reminds them. 1. Orders are given for the appointing of these cities (*v.* 2), Deut. xix. 3. Yet it is probable that it was not done till after the Levites had their portion assigned them, because the cities of refuge were all to be Levites' cities. As soon as ever God had given them cities of rest, he bade them appoint cities of refuge, to which none of them knew but they might be glad to escape. And it intimates what God's spiritual Israel have and shall have, in Christ and heaven, not only rest to repose themselves in, but refuge to secure themselves in. 2. Instructions are given for the using of these cities. The laws in this matter we had before, Num. xxxv. 10, &c., where they were opened at large. It is provided that if upon trial it appeared that the murder was done purely by accident, and not by design, either upon an old grudge or a sudden passion, then the slayer should be sheltered from the avenger of blood in any one of these cities, *v.* 4–6. By this law he was entitled to a dwelling in that city, but was confined to it, as a prisoner at large.

Verses 7–9

We have here the nomination of the cities of refuge in the land of Canaan. 1. They are said to *sanctify* these cities, that is the original word for *appointed*, *v.* 7. Not that any ceremony was used to signify the consecration of them, only they did by a public act of court solemnly declare them cities of refuge, and as such sacred to the honour of God, as the protector of exposed innocency. 2. These cities (as those also on the other side Jordan) stood in the three several parts of the country, so conveniently that a man might (they say) in half a day reach some one of them from any corner of the country. 3. They were all Levites' cities, which put an honour upon God's tribe, making them judges in those cases wherein divine Providence was so nearly concerned, and protectors to oppressed innocency. If he must be confined, it shall be to a Levite-city, where he may, if he will, improve his time. 4. These cities were upon hills to be seen afar off, for though therefore his way at last was uphill, yet this would comfort him, that he would be in his place of safety quickly. 5. Some observe a significancy in the names of these cities with application to Christ our refuge. *Kedesh* signifies *holy*, and our refuge is the holy Jesus. *Shechem, a shoulder*, and the government is upon his shoulder. *Hebron, fellowship*, and believers are called into the fellowship of Christ Jesus our Lord. *Bezer, a fortification*, for he is a stronghold to all those that trust in him. *Ramoth, high* or *exalted*, for him hath God exalted with his own right hand. *Golan, joy* or *exultation*, for in him all the saints are justified, and shall glory. *Lastly*, Besides all these, the horns of the altar, wherever it was, were a refuge to those who took hold of them, if the crime were such as that sanctuary allowed. This is implied in that law (Exod. xxi. 14), that a wilful murderer shall be taken from God's altar to be put to death.

JAMIESON, FAUSSET, BROWN — CHAPTER 20

Vss. 1-6. The Lord Commands the Cities of Refuge. **1. The Lord spake unto Joshua, . . . Appoint out for you cities of refuge**—(See Num. 35:9-28; Deut. 19:1-13). The command here recorded was given on their going to occupy their allotted settlements. The sanctuaries were not temples or altars, as in other countries, but inhabited cities; and the design was not to screen criminals, but only to afford the homicide protection from the vengeance of the deceased's relatives until it should have been ascertained whether the death had resulted from accident and momentary passion, or from premeditated malice. The institution of the cities of refuge, together with the rules prescribed for the guidance of those who sought an asylum within their walls, was an important provision, tending to secure the ends of justice as well as of mercy. **4. he that doth flee unto one of those cities shall stand at the entering of the gate of the city**—It was the place of public resort, and on arriving there he related his tale of distress to the elders, who were bound to give him shelter and the means of support, until the local authorities (vs. 6), having carefully investigated the case, should have pronounced the decision. If found guilty, the manslayer was surrendered to the blood-avenger; if extenuating circumstances appeared, he was to remain in the city of refuge, where he would be safe from the vindictive feelings of his pursuers; but he forfeited the privilege of immunity the moment he ventured beyond the walls. **6. until the death of the high priest**—His death secured the complete deliverance of the manslayer from his sin, only because he had been anointed with the holy oil (Num. 35:25), the symbol of the Holy Ghost; and thus the death of the earthly high priest became a type of that of the heavenly one (Heb. 9:14, 15).

7-9. The Israelites Appoint by Name the Cities of Refuge. **7-9. they appointed . . . cities**—There were six: three on the west, and three on the east, of Jordan. In the first instance, they were a provision of the criminal law of the Hebrews, necessary in the circumstances of that people (see on Num. 35:9-15; Deut. 19). At the same time they were designed also typically to point out the sinner's way to Christ (Heb. 6:18).

ADAM CLARKE — CHAPTER 20

2. *Cities of refuge.* An institution of this kind was essentially necessary wherever the patriarchal law relative to the right of redemption and the avenging of blood was in force. We have already seen that the nearest of kin to a deceased person had not only the right of redeeming an inheritance that had been forfeited or alienated, but had also authority to slay on the spot the person who had slain his relative. Now, as a man might casually kill another against whom he had no ill will, and with whom he had no quarrel, and might have his life taken away by him who was called the avenger of blood, though he had not forfeited his life to the law; therefore these privileged cities were appointed, where the person might have protection till the cause had been fully heard by the magistrates, who certainly had authority to deliver him up to the avenger if they found, on examination, that he was not entitled to this protection. On this subject see the notes on Num. xxxv. 11 to the end.

7. *They appointed Kedesh in Galilee.* The cities of refuge were distributed through the land at proper distances from each other, that they might be convenient to every part of the land; and it is said they were situated on eminences, that they might be easily seen at a distance, the roads leading to them being broad, even, and always kept in good repair. In the concluding note on Numbers xxxv it has been stated that these cities were a type of our blessed Lord, and that the apostle refers to them as such, Heb. vi. 17-18. Hence their names have been considered as descriptive of some character or office of Christ. I shall give each and its signification, and leave the application to others.

(1) *Kedesh*, from *kadash*, to "separate" or "set apart," because it implies the consecration of a person or thing to the worship or service of God alone; hence to "make or be holy," and hence *Kedesh*, "holiness," the full consecration of a person to God. (2) *Shechem*, from *shacham*, "to be ready, forward, and diligent"; hence Shechem, the "shoulder," because of its readiness to bear burdens, prop up, sustain, and from this ideal meaning it has the metaphorical one of government. (3) *Hebron*, from *chabar*, "to associate, join, conjoin, unite as friends"; and hence *chebron*, "fellowship, friendly association." (4) *Bezer*, from *batsar*, "to restrain, enclose, shut up, or encompass with a wall"; and hence the goods or treasure thus secured, and hence a fortified place, a fortress. (5) *Ramoth*, from *raam*, "to be raised, made high or exalted," and hence *Ramoth*, high places, eminences. (6) *Golan*, from *galah*, "to remove, transmigrate, or pass away"; hence Golan, a transmigration or passage.

Kedesh and *Hebron* were at the two extremities of the Promised Land; one was in Galilee, the other in the tribe of Judah, both in mountainous countries; and *Shechem* was in the tribe of Ephraim, nearly in the middle, between both. *Bezer* was on the east side of Jordan, in the plain, opposite to Jericho. *Ramoth* was about the midst of the country

MATTHEW HENRY

JAMIESON, FAUSSET, BROWN

ADAM CLARKE

occupied by the two tribes and a half, about the middle of the mountains of Gilead. *Golan* was the capital of a district called Gaulonitis, in the land of Bashan, towards the southern extremity of the lot of Manasseh.

9. *For all the children of Israel, and for the stranger.* As these typified the great provision which God was making for the salvation of both Jews and Gentiles, hence the stranger as well as the Israelite had the same right to the benefits of these cities of refuge. *Until he stood before the congregation.* The judges and elders of the people, in trying civil and criminal causes, always sat; the persons who came for judgment, or who were tried, always stood; hence the expressions so frequent in Scripture, "standing before the Lord, the judges, the elders."

MATTHEW HENRY — CHAPTER 21

Verses 1–8

Here is, I. The Levites' petition presented to this general convention of the states, now sitting at Shiloh, *v.* 1, 2. Observe, 1. They had not their lot assigned them till they made their claim. They build their claim upon a very good foundation, not their own merits nor services, but the divine precept: "*The Lord commanded by the hand of Moses to give us cities,* commanded you to grant them, which implied a command to us to ask them." Note, The maintenance of ministers is not an arbitrary thing, left purely to the good-will of the people, who may let them starve if they please; no, as the God of Israel commanded that the Levites should be well provided for, so has the Lord Jesus, the King of the Christian church, ordained that *those who preach the gospel should live of the gospel* (1 Cor. ix. 14). 2. They did not make their claim till all the rest of the tribes were provided for, and then they did it immediately. They were willing to be served last, and they fared never the worse for it. Let not God's ministers complain if at any time they find themselves postponed in men's thoughts and cares, but let them make sure of the favour of God and the honour that comes from him, and then they may well enough afford to bear the slights and neglects of men.

II. The Levites' petition granted immediately, without any dispute. 1. The children of Israel are said to give the cities for the Levites. God had appointed how many they should be in all, forty-eight. God had appointed, Num. xxxv. 8, *Every one shall give of his cities to the Levites.* It appears by the following catalogue that the cities they gave to the Levites were generally some of the best and most considerable in each tribe. 2. They gave them *at the commandment of the Lord.* 3. When the forty-eight cities were pitched upon, they were divided into four lots, as they lay next together, and then by lot were determined to the four several families of the tribe of Levi. (1) The family of Aaron, who were the only priests, had for their share the thirteen cities that were given by the tribes of Judah, Simeon, and Benjamin, *v.* 4. (2) The Kohathite-Levites (among whom were the posterity of Moses, though never distinguished from them) had the cities that lay in the lot of Dan, which lay next to Judah, and in that of Ephraim, and the half-tribe of Manasseh, which lay next to Benjamin. So those who descended from Aaron's father joined nearest to Aaron's sons. (3) Gershon was the eldest son of Levi, and therefore, though the younger house of the Kohathites was preferred before his, yet his children had the precedency of the other family of Merari, *v.* 6. (4) The Merarites, the youngest house, had their lot last, and it lay furthest off, *v.* 7.

Verses 9–42

Several things may be observed in this account, besides what was observed in the law concerning it, Num. xxxv.

I. That the Levites were dispersed into all the tribes, and not suffered to live all together in any one part of the country. Christ left his twelve disciples together in a body, but left orders that they should in due time disperse themselves, that they might *preach the gospel to every creature.*

II. That every tribe of Israel was adorned and enriched with its share of Levites' cities in proportion to its compass, even those that lay most remote. 1. To show kindness to, as God appointed them, Deut. xii. 19; xiv. 29. 2. To receive advice and instruction from; when they could not go up to the tabernacle, to consult those who attended there, they might go to a Levites' city, and be taught the good knowledge of the Lord. Thus God set up a

JAMIESON, FAUSSET, BROWN — CHAPTER 21

Vss. 1-8. EIGHT AND FORTY CITIES GIVEN BY LOT OUT OF THE OTHER TRIBES UNTO THE LEVITES. **1. Then came near the heads of the fathers of the Levites**—The most venerable and distinguished members of the three Levitical families, on behalf of their tribe, applied for the special provision that had been promised them to be now awarded (see on Num. 35:1-5). Their inheritance lay within the territory of every tribe. It was assigned in the same place and manner, and by the same commissioners as the other allotments.

While the people, knowing the important duties they were to perform, are described (vs. 3) as readily conceding this "peculiar" to them, it had most probably been specified and reserved for their use while the distribution of the land was in progress.

4-8. the lot came out for the families of the Kohathites—The Levites were divided into Kohathites, Gershonites, and Merarites. Among the former the family of Aaron were exclusively appointed to the priesthood, and all the rest were ranked in the common order of Levites. The first lot was drawn by the Kohathites; and the first of theirs again by the priests, to whom thirteen cities were granted , and ten to the rest of the Kohathites (vs. 5); thirteen to the Gershonites (vs. 6), and twelve to the Merarites (vs. 7).

9-42. THE CITIES OF THE PRIESTS. **9-40. they gave . . . these cities which are here mentioned by name**—It was overruled by the unerring providence of the Divine Lawgiver that the cities of the priests lay within the territories of Judah and Benjamin. This was a provision, the admirable wisdom and propriety of which were fully manifested on the schism that took place in the reign of Rehoboam.

ADAM CLARKE — CHAPTER 21

1. *The heads of the fathers of the Levites.* The Levites were composed of three grand families, the Gershonites, Koathites, and Merarites, independently of the family of Aaron, who might be said to form a fourth. To none of these had God assigned any portion in the division of the land. But in this general division it must have been evidently intended that the different tribes were to furnish them with habitations; and this was according to a positive command of God, Num. xxxv. 2, etc. Finding now that each tribe had its inheritance appointed to it, the heads of the Levites came before Eleazar, Joshua, and the chiefs of the tribes who had been employed in dividing the land, and requested that cities and suburbs should be granted them according to the divine command.

3. *And the children of Israel gave unto the Levites.* They cheerfully obeyed the divine command, and cities for habitations were appointed to them out of the different tribes by lot, that it might as fully appear that God designed them their habitations as He designed the others their inheritances.

4. *Out of the tribe of Judah . . . Simeon, and . . . Benjamin, thirteen cities.* These tribes furnished more habitations to the Levites in proportion than any of the other tribes, because they possessed a more extensive inheritance; and Moses had commanded, Num. xxxv. 8, "From them that have many ye shall give many; but from them that have few ye shall give few: every one shall give of his cities unto the Levites according to his inheritance." It is worthy of remark that the principal part of this tribe, whose business was to minister at the sanctuary, which sanctuary was afterwards to be established in Jerusalem, had their appointment nearest to that city, so that they were always within reach of the sacred work which God had appointed them.

5. *And the rest of the children of Kohath.* That is, the remaining part of that family that were not priests, for those who were priests had their lot in the preceding tribes. Those, therefore, of the family of Kohath who were simply Levites, and not of the priests or Aaron's family (see v. 10), had their habitations in Ephraim, Dan, and the half-tribe of Manasseh.

12. *The fields of the city . . . gave they to Caleb.* This was an exclusive privilege to him and his family, with which the grant to the Levites did not interfere.

18. *Anathoth.* Celebrated as the birthplace of Jeremiah, about three miles northward of Jerusalem, according to Jerome.

MATTHEW HENRY

candle in every room of his house, to give light to all his family.

III. That there were thirteen cities, and those some of the best, appointed for the priests, the sons of Aaron, *v.* 19. Aaron left but two sons, Eleazar and Ithamar, yet his family was now so much increased, and it was foreseen that it would in process of time grow so numerous, as to replenish all these cities. We read in both Testaments of such numbers of priests that we may suppose none of all the families of Israel that came out of Egypt increased afterwards so much as that of Aaron did; and the promise afterwards to the house of Aaron is, *God shall increase you more and more, you and your children*, Ps. cxv. 12, 14.

IV. That some of the Levites' cities were afterwards famous upon other accounts. Hebron was the city in which David began his reign, and in Mahanaim, another Levites' city (*v.* 38), he lay, and had his headquarters when he fled from Absalom. The first Israelite that ever wore the title of king (namely, Abimelech, the son of Gideon) reigned in Shechem, another Levites' city, *v.* 21.

Verses 43–45

We have here the foregoing history summed up.

I. God had promised to give the seed of Abraham the land of Canaan for a possession, and now at last he performed this promise (*v.* 43): *They possessed it, and dwelt therein.*

II. God had promised to give them rest in that land, and now they had rest round about, rest from their travel through the wilderness, rest from their wars in Canaan. They now dwelt, not only in habitations of their own, but those quiet and peaceable ones. This rest continued till they by their own sin and folly put thorns into their own beds and their own eyes.

III. God had promised to give them victory and success in their wars, and this promise likewise was fulfilled: *There stood not a man before them*, *v.* 44. Israel's experience of God's fidelity is here upon record, and is an acquittance under their hands to the honour of God, the vindication of his promise which had been so often distrusted, and the encouragement of all believers to the end of the world: *There failed not any good thing*, no, nor *aught* of any good thing (so full is it expressed), *which the Lord had spoken unto the house of Israel*, but in due time *all came to pass*, *v.* 45.

JAMIESON, FAUSSET, BROWN

41. All the cities of the Levites within the possession of the children of Israel were forty and eight cities with their suburbs—This may appear too great a proportion compared with those of the other tribes. But it must be borne in mind that the list given here contains the names of every Levitical city (see on I Chron. 6:39-66); whereas only those cities of the other tribes are mentioned which lay on the frontier or along the boundary line. Besides, the Levites were not the exclusive inhabitants of those forty-eight cities; for there must have been also a considerable number of people kept there to cultivate the glebe lands and tend the cattle. Still further, the Levitical cities had nothing but "their suburbs—a limited circuit of ground—round about them"; whereas the other cities in Israel possessed a group of independent villages (see chaps. 17-19).

43-45. GOD GAVE THEM REST. **43-45. the Lord gave unto Israel all the land which he sware to give unto their fathers**—This is a general winding up of the history from chapter 13, which narrates the occupation of the land by the Israelites. All the promises made, whether to the people or to Joshua (ch. 1:5), had been, or were in the course of being fulfilled; and the recorded experience of the Israelites (vs. 45), is a ground of hope and confidence to the people of God in every age, that all other promises made to the Church will, in due time, be accomplished.

ADAM CLARKE

19. *Thirteen cities with their suburbs.* At the time mentioned here certainly thirteen cities were too large a proportion for the *priests*, as they and their families amounted to a very small number; but this ample provision was made in reference to their great increase in after times, when they formed twenty-four courses, as in the days of David.

27. *Golan in Bashan.* On this and the other cities of refuge mentioned here, see the note on chap. xx. 7.

35. *Dimnah with her suburbs.* It is well known to every Hebrew scholar that the two following verses are wholly omitted by the Masora, and are left out in some of the most correct and authentic Hebrew Bibles.

43. *And the Lord gave . . . all the land which he sware.* All was now divided by lot unto them, and their enemies were so completely discomfited that there was not a single army of the Canaanites remaining to make head against them; and those which were left in the land served under tribute, and the tribute that they paid was the amplest proof of their complete subjugation.

MATTHEW HENRY — CHAPTER 22

Verses 1–9

The war being ended, and ended gloriously, Joshua, as a prudent general, disbands his army, who never designed to make war their trade, and sends them home, to enjoy what they had conquered, and to beat their swords into plough-shares and their spears into pruning-hooks; and particularly the forces of these separate tribes, who had received their inheritance on the other side Jordan. Joshua publicly and solemnly in Shiloh gives them their discharge. It was not done till after Shiloh was made the headquarters (*v.* 2), and the land was begun to be divided before they removed from Gilgal, *ch.* xiv. 6.

It is probable that this army of Reubenites and Gadites, which had led the van in all the wars of Canaan, had sometimes made a step over Jordan, for it was not far, to visit their families, but still these two tribes and a half had their quota of troops ready, 40,000 in all, which, whenever there was occasion, presented themselves at their respective posts, and now attended in a body to receive their discharge. So must we stay on earth till our warfare be accomplished, wait for a due discharge, and not anticipate the time of our removal.

I. Joshua dismisses them to the *land of their possession*, *v.* 4. Those that were first in the assignment of their lot were last in the enjoyment of it.

II. He dismisses them with their pay; for who goes a warfare at his own charge? *Return with much riches unto your tents*, *v.* 8. "Go," says Joshua, "go home to your tents," that is, "your houses," which he calls *tents*, because they had been so much used to tents in the wilderness. "Go home *with much riches*, not only cattle, the spoil of the country, but silver and gold, the plunder of the cities, and let your brethren whom you go to, who abode by the stuff, have some share of the spoil: *Divide the spoil with your brethren*."

III. He dismisses them with a very honourable character. 1. For the readiness of their obedience to their commanders, *v.* 2. 2. For the constancy of their affection and adherence to their brethren: *You*

JAMIESON, FAUSSET, BROWN — CHAPTER 22

VSS. 1-9. JOSHUA DISMISSES THE TWO TRIBES AND A HALF, WITH A BLESSING. **1. Then Joshua called the Reubenites, and the Gadites, and the half tribe of Manasseh**—The general war of invasion being ended and the enemy being in so dispirited and isolated a condition that each tribe, by its own resources or with the aid of its neighboring tribe, was able to repress any renewed hostilities, the auxiliary Israelites from the eastern side of the Jordan were now discharged from service. Joshua dismissed them with high commendations for their fidelity and earnest admonitions to cultivate perpetual piety in life. The redundancy of the language is remarkable. It shows how important, in the judgment of the venerable leader, a steadfast observance of the divine law was to personal happiness, as well as national prosperity.

4-7. get you unto your tents—i.e., home; for their families had been left in fortified towns (Num. 32:17).

8. he spake unto them, saying, Return with much riches—in cattle, clothes, and precious metals. **divide the spoil of your enemies with your brethren**—See on Numbers 31:25-39.

ADAM CLARKE — CHAPTER 22

1. *Then Joshua called the Reubenites.* We have already seen that 40,000 men of the tribes of Reuben and Gad and the half-tribe of Manasseh had passed over Jordan armed, with their brethren, according to their stipulation with Moses. The war being now concluded, Joshua assembles these warriors, and with commendations for their services and fidelity he dismisses them, having first given them the most pious and suitable advices. They had now been about seven years absent from their respective families; and though there was only the river Jordan between the camp at Gilgal and their own inheritance, yet it does not appear that they had during that time ever revisited their own home, which they might have done anytime in the year, the harvest excepted, as at all other times that river was easily fordable.

8. *Return with much riches.* It appears they had their full proportion of the spoils that were taken from the Canaanites, and that these spoils consisted in cattle, silver, gold, brass, iron, and raiment. *Divide the spoil . . . with your brethren.* It was right that those who stayed at home to defend the families of those who had been in the wars, and to cultivate the ground, should have a proper proportion of the spoils taken from the enemy; for had they not acted as they did, the others could not have safely left their families.

MATTHEW HENRY

have not left them these many days. 3. For the faithfulness of their obedience to the divine law. They had not only done their duty to Joshua and Israel, but, which was best of all, they had made conscience of their duty to God: *You have kept the charge*, or, as the word is, *You have kept the keeping*, that is, "You have carefully and circumspectly kept the *commandment of the Lord your God*, not only in this particular instance of continuing in the service of Israel to the end of the war, but, in general, you have kept up religion in your part of the camp, a rare and excellent thing among soldiers, and where it is worthy to be praised."

IV. He dismisses them with good counsel, not to cultivate their ground, fortify their cities, and, now that their hands were inured to war and victory, to invade their neighbours, and so enlarge their own territories, but to keep up serious godliness among them in the power of it.

V. He dismisses them with a blessing (*v.* 6), particularly the half tribe of Manasseh, to which Joshua, as an Ephraimite, was somewhat nearer akin than to the other two, and who perhaps were the more loth to depart because they left one half of their own tribe behind them, and therefore, bidding often farewell, and lingering behind, had a second dismission and blessing, *v.* 7. Joshua not only prayed for them as a friend, but blessed them as a father in the name of the Lord, recommending them, their families, and affairs, to the grace of God.

Verses 10–20

I. The pious care of the separated tribes to keep their hold of Canaan's religion. In order to this, they built a great altar on the borders of Jordan, to be a witness for them that they were Israelites, and as such *partakers of the altar of* the Lord, 1 Cor. x. 18. When they came to Jordan (*v.* 10) their relation to the church of God, together with their interest in the communion of saints, is that which they are solicitous to preserve, and therefore without delay, immediately they erected this altar, which served as a bridge to keep up their fellowship with the other tribes in the things of God. This altar was very innocently and honestly designed, but it would have been well if, since it had in it an appearance of evil, and might be an occasion of offence to their brethren, they had consulted the oracle of God about it before they did it, or at least acquainted their brethren with their purpose, and given them the same explication of their altar before, to prevent their jealousy, which they did afterwards, to remove it.

II. The holy jealousy of the other tribes for the honour of God and his altar at Shiloh. Notice was immediately brought to the princes of Israel of the setting up of this altar, *v.* 11. And they were soon apprehensive that the setting up of another altar was an affront to the choice which God had lately made of a place to put his name in, and had a direct tendency to the worship of some other God. Now,

1. Their suspicion was very excusable, for it must be confessed the thing, *prima facie—at first sight*, looked ill, and seemed to imply a design to set up and maintain a competitor with the altar at Shiloh.

2. Their zeal, upon this suspicion, was very commendable, *v.* 12. They all gathered together, and Shiloh was the place of their rendezvous, because it was in defence of the divine charter lately granted to that place that they now appeared; their resolution was as became a kingdom of priests, who, being devoted to God and his service, did not *acknowledge their brethren* nor *know their own children*, Deut. xxxiii. 9. They would immediately *go up to war against them* if it appeared they had revolted from God, and were in rebellion against him.

3. Their prudence in the prosecution of this zealous resolution is no less commendable. They resolve here not to send forth their armies, to wage war, till they had first sent their ambassadors to enquire into the merits of the cause, and these men of the first rank, one out of each tribe, and Phinehas at the head of them to be their spokesman, *v.* 13, 14.

4. The ambassadors' management of this matter bespeaks much both of zeal and prudence.

(1) The charge they draw up against their brethren is indeed very high, and admits no other excuse than that it was in their zeal for the honour of God, and was now intended to justify the resentments of the congregation at Shiloh and to awaken the supposed delinquents to clear themselves.

(2) The aggravation of the crime charged upon their brethren is somewhat far-fetched: Is *the iniquity of Peor too little for us? v.* 17. The building of this altar seemed but a small matter, but it might lead to an iniquity as bad as that of Peor, and therefore must be crushed in its first rise.

(3) The reason they give for their concerning them-

JAMIESON, FAUSSET, BROWN

3. Ye have not left your brethren these many days unto this day—for the space of seven years.

10. THEY BUILD THE ALTAR OF TESTIMONY ON THEIR JOURNEY. **10. when they came unto the borders of Jordan, that are in the land of Canaan, the children of Reuben . . . built there an altar**—This altar was probably an immense pile of stones and earth. The generality of our translators supposes that it was reared on the banks of the Jordan, within the limits of Canaan proper. But a little closer examination seems to make the conclusion irresistible that its position was on the eastern side of the river, for these two reasons; first, because it is said (vs. 11) to have been built "over against," or in the sight of the land of Canaan—not within it; and secondly, because the declared motive of the transjordanic Israelites in erecting it was to prevent their brethren in Canaan ever saying, "in time to come, What have ye to do with the Lord God of Israel? For the Lord hath made Jordan a border between us and you . . . ." Such a taunt would be obviously prevented or confuted by the two tribes and a half having on the eastern side of Jordan, within their own land, a facsimile of the altar at Shiloh, as a witness that they acknowledged the same God and practised the same rites of worship as the brethren in Canaan.

11-29. CONTENTION THEREUPON. **11-29. and the children of Israel heard say**—Fame speedily spread intelligence of what the transjordanic tribes had done. The act being suspected of some idolatrous design, the tribes rose in a mass, and repairing to the tabernacle at Shiloh, resolved to declare war against the two tribes and a half as apostates from God. On calmer and more mature consideration, however, they determined, in the first instance, to send a deputation consisting of the son of the high priest, and ten eminent persons from each tribe, to make inquiry into this rumored rebellion against God (Deut. 13:13-15).

The quality of the deputies evinced the deep solicitude that was felt on the occasion to maintain the purity of the divine worship throughout Israel. In the presumptive belief that the two tribes and a half had really built an altar, the deputies expressed astonishment at their so soon falling into such a heinous crime as that of violating the unity of divine worship (Exod. 20:24; 17:8, 9; Deut. 12:5-13).

ADAM CLARKE

5. *But take diligent heed.* Let us examine the force of this excellent advice; they must ever consider that their prosperity and continued possession of the land depended on their fidelity and obedience to God; to this they must take diligent heed. *Do the commandment.* They must pay the strictest regard to every moral precept. *And the law.* They must observe all the rites and ceremonies of their holy religion. *Love the Lord your God.* Without an affectionate filial attachment to their Maker, duty would be irksome, grievous, and impossible. *Walk in all his ways.* They must not only believe and love, but obey: Walk not in your own ways, but walk in those which God has pointed out. *Keep his commandments.* They must love Him with all their heart, soul, mind, and strength, and their neighbor as themselves. *Cleave unto him.* They must be cemented to Him in a union that should never be dissolved. *Serve him.* They must consider Him as their Master, having an absolute right to appoint them when, where, how, and in what measure they should do His work. *With all your heart.* Having all their affections and passions sanctified and united to Him. *And with all your soul.* Giving up their whole life to Him, and employing their understanding, judgment, and will in the contemplation and adoration of His perfections, that their love and obedience might increase in proportion to the cultivation and improvement of their understanding.

7. *Then he blessed them.* Spoke respectfully of their fidelity and exertions, wished them every spiritual and temporal good, prayed to God to protect and save them, and probably gave some gifts to those leaders among them that had most distinguished themselves in this seven years' war. In all the above senses the word *bless* is frequently taken in Scripture.

17. *Is the iniquity of Peor too little?* See this history, Num. xxv. 3, etc. Phinehas takes it for granted that this altar was built in opposition to the altar of God erected by Moses, and that they intended to have a separate service, priesthood, etc., which would be rebellion against God, and bring down His curse on them and their posterity.

MATTHEW HENRY

selves so warmly in this matter is very sufficient. They were obliged to it, in their own necessary defence, by the law of self-preservation: "For, if you revolt from God to-day, who knows but to-morrow his judgments may break in upon the *whole congregation* (*v.* 18), as in the case of Achan? *v.* 20. He sinned, and we all smarted for it.

(4) The offer they make is very fair and kind (*v.* 19), that if they thought the land of their possession unclean, for want of an altar, and therefore could not be easy without one, rather than they should set up another in competition with that at Shiloh they should be welcome to come back to the land *where the Lord's tabernacle was,* and settle there, and they would very willingly straiten themselves to make room for them.

Verses 21–29

Their reply to the warm remonstrance of the ten tribes is very fair and ingenuous. They do not retort their charge, nor reproach them for their rash and hasty censures, but give them a soft answer which turns away wrath. They demur not to their jurisdiction, nor plead that they were not accountable to them for what they had done, nor bid them mind their own business, but, by a free and open declaration of their sincere intention in what they did, free themselves from the imputation they were under, and set themselves right in the opinion of their brethren.

I. They solemnly protest against any design to use this altar for sacrifice or offering, and therefore were far from setting it up in competition with the altar at Shiloh, or from entertaining the least thought of deserting that. They had indeed set up that which had the shape and fashion of an altar, but they had not dedicated it to a religious use. To gain credit to this protestation here is,

1. A solemn appeal to God concerning it, with which they begin their defence, intending thereby to give glory to God first, and then to give satisfaction to their brethren, *v.* 22. (1) A profound awe and reverence of God are expressed in the form of their appeal: *The Lord God of gods, the Lord God of gods, he knows.* This brief confession of their faith would help to obviate and remove their brethren's suspicion of them, as if they intended to desert the God of Israel, and worship other gods. (2) It is a great confidence of their own integrity which they express in the matter of their appeal. Nothing but a clear conscience would have thus imprecated divine justice to avenge the rebellion if there had been any.

2. A sober apology presented to their brethren: *Israel, he shall know.*

3. A serious abjuration or renunciation of the design which they were suspected to be guilty of. With this they conclude their defence (*v.* 29): "*God forbid that we should rebel against the Lord.* We have as great a value and veneration for the altar of the Lord at Shiloh as any of the tribes of Israel have, and are as firmly resolved to adhere to it and constantly to attend it; we have the same concern that you have for the purity of God's worship and the unity of his church; far be it, far be it from us, to think of turning away from following God."

II. They fully explain their true intent and meaning in building this altar. In their vindication, they make it out that the building of this altar was so far from being a step towards a separation from their brethren, and from the altar of the Lord at Shiloh, that, on the contrary, it was really designed for a pledge and preservative of their communion with their brethren and with the altar of God, and a token of their resolution to *do the service of the Lord before him* (*v.* 27), and to continue to do so.

1. They gave an account of the fears they had lest, in process of time, their posterity, being seated at such a distance from the tabernacle, should be looked upon and treated as strangers to the commonwealth of Israel (*v.* 24). Those that are cut off from public ordinances are likely to lose all religion, and will by degrees cease from fearing the Lord. Though the form and profession of godliness are kept up by many without the life and power of it, yet the life and power of it will not long be kept up without the form and profession. You take away grace if you take away the means of grace.

2. The project they had to prevent this, *v.* 26–28. "Therefore, to secure an interest in the altar of God to those who shall come after us, and to prove their title to it, *we said, Let us build an altar, to be a witness between us and you,*" that, having this copy of the altar in their custody, it might be produced as an evidence of their right to the privileges of the original.

Verses 30–34

We have here the good issue of this controversy, which, if there had not been on both sides a dis-

JAMIESON, FAUSSET, BROWN

They reminded their eastern brethren of the disastrous consequences that were entailed on the nation at large by the apostasy at Peor and by the sin of Achan, and finally exhorted them, if they felt the want of the tabernacle and altar and repented of their rash choice in preferring worldly advantages to religious privileges, to remove to the western side of the Jordan, where all the tribes would form a united and obedient community of worshippers.

21. Then the children of Reuben . . . answered—repudiating, in the strongest terms, the alleged crime, and deponing that so far from entertaining the intention imputed to them, their only object was to perpetuate the memory of their alliance with Israel, and their adherence to the worship of Israel's God.

KEIL–DELITZSCH:

Verses 21–29. In utter amazement at the suspicion expressed by the delegates of the congregation, the two tribes and a half affirm with a solemn oath that it never entered into their minds to build an altar as a place of sacrifice, to fall away from Jehovah. The combination of the three names of God—El, the strong one; Elohim, the Supreme Being to be feared; and Jehovah, the truly existing One, the covenant God (v. 22)—serves to strengthen the invocation of God, as in Ps. 1:1; and this is strengthened still further by the repetition of these three names. God knows, and let Israel also know, what they intended and what they have done. "Verily [it was] not in rebellion, nor in apostasy from Jehovah," that this was done, or that we built the altar. "Mayest thou not help us today" if we did it in rebellion against God. An appeal addressed immediately to God in the heat of the statement, and introduced in the midst of the asseveration, which was meant to remove all doubt as to the truth of their declaration.

—*Commentary on the Old Testament*

ADAM CLARKE

19. *If the land of your possessions be unclean.* The generous mind of Phinehas led him to form this excuse for them. If you suppose that this land is impure, as not having been originally included in the covenant, and you think that you cannot expect the blessing of God unless you have an altar, sacrifices, etc., then *pass ye over unto the land of the possession of the Lord, wherein the Lord's tabernacle dwelleth,* the only legitimate place where sacrifices and offerings can be made. We will divide this land with you, and rather straiten ourselves than that you should conceive yourselves to be under any necessity of erecting a new altar *beside the altar of the Lord our God.*

20. *Did not Achan the son of Zerah?* Your sin will not be merely against yourselves; your transgressions will bring down the wrath of God upon all the people. This was the case in the transgression of Achan; he alone sinned, and yet God on that account turned His face against the whole congregation, so that they fell before their enemies.

21. *Then the children of Reuben . . . answered.* Though conscious of their own innocency they permitted Phinehas to finish his discourse, though composed of little else than accusations.

22. *The Lord God of gods.* The original words are exceedingly emphatic, and cannot be easily translated. *El Elohim Yehovah* are the three principal names by which the supreme God was known among the Hebrews, and may be thus translated, "the strong God, Elohim, Jehovah." And the Reubenites, by using these in their very solemn appeal, expressed at once their strong, unshaken faith in the God of Israel; and by this they fully showed the deputation from the ten tribes that their religious creed had not been changed; and in the succeeding part of their defense they show that their practice corresponded with their creed. The repetition of these solemn names by the Reubenites shows their deep concern for the honor of God, and their anxiety to wipe off the reproach which they consider cast on them by the supposition that they had been capable of defection from the pure worship of God, or of disaffection to their brethren.

Save us not this day. This was putting the affair to the most solemn issue; and nothing but the utmost consciousness of their own integrity could have induced them to make such an appeal, and call for such a decision. "Let God, the Judge, cause us to perish this day if **in principle or practice we have knowingly departed from Him."**

24. *For fear of this thing.* The motive that actuated us was directly the reverse of that of which we have been suspected.

26. *An altar, not for burnt offering, nor for sacrifice.* **Because this would have been in flat opposition to the law, Lev. xvii. 8-9; Deut. xii. 4-6, 10-11, 13-14, which most positively forbade any sacrifice or offering to be made in any other place than that one which the Lord should choose. Therefore the altar built by the Reubenites, etc., was for no religious purpose, but merely to serve as a testimony that they were one people with those on the west of Jordan, having the same religious and civil constitution, and bound by the same interests to keep that constitution inviolate.**

MATTHEW HENRY

position to peace, as there was on both sides a zeal for God, might have been of ill consequence; for quarrels about religion, for want of wisdom and love, often prove the most fierce and most difficult to be accommodated.

I. The ambassadors were exceedingly pleased when the separate tribes had given in a protestation of the innocency of their intentions in building this altar. 1. The ambassadors did not call in question their sincerity in that protestation. 2. They did not upbraid them with the rashness and unadvisedness of this action. 3. Much less did they go about to fish for evidence to make out their charge, because they had once exhibited it, but were glad to have their mistake rectified, and were not at all ashamed to own it. Proud and peevish spirits, when they have passed an unjust censure upon their brethren, though ever so much convincing evidence be brought of the injustice of it, will stand to it, and can by no means be persuaded to retract it.

II. The congregation was abundantly satisfied when their ambassadors reported to them their brethren's apology for what they had done.

III. The separate tribes were gratified, and, since they had a mind to preserve among them this pattern of the altar of God, though there was not likely to be that occasion for it which they fancied, yet Joshua and the princes let them have their humour, and did not give orders for the demolishing of it. Only care was taken that they having explained the meaning of their altar, that it was intended for no more than a testimony of their communion with the altar at Shiloh, this explanation should be recorded, by giving a name to it signifying so much (*v.* 34); they called it *Ed, a witness* to that, and no more, a witness of the relation they stood in to God and Israel.

JAMIESON, FAUSSET, BROWN

30-34. THE DEPUTIES SATISFIED. **33, 34. the thing pleased the children of Israel**—The explanation not only gave perfect satisfaction to the deputies, but elicited from them expressions of unbounded joy and thankfulness. "This day we perceive that the Lord is among us," i.e., by His gracious presence and preventing goodness, which has kept you from falling into the suspected sin and rescued the nation from the calamity of a fratricidal war or providential judgments. This episode reflects honor upon all parties and shows that piety and zeal for the honor and worship of God animated the people that entered Canaan to an extent far beyond what was exemplified in many other periods of the history of Israel.

ADAM CLARKE

33. *And did not intend to go up against them in battle.* That is, they now relinquished the intention of going against them in battle, as this explanation proved there was no cause for the measure.

34. *Called the altar Ed.* The word *Ed,* which signifies "witness" or "testimony," is not found in the common editions of the Hebrew Bible, and is supplied in italics by our translators, at least in our modern copies; for in the first edition of this translation it stands in the text without any note of this kind.

MATTHEW HENRY

CHAPTER 23

Verses 1–10

As to the date of this edict of Joshua,

I. No mention at all is made of the place where this general assembly was held; some think it was at Timnath-serah, Joshua's own city, where he lived, and whence, being old, he could not well remove. It is more probable this meeting was at Shiloh, where the tabernacle of meeting was.

II. There is only a general mention of the time when this was done. It was *long after the Lord had given them rest,* but it is not said how long, *v.* 1. It was, 1. So long as that Israel had time to feel the comforts of their rest and possessions in Canaan, and to enjoy the advantages of that good land. 2. So long as that Joshua had time to observe which way their danger lay of being corrupted, namely, by their intimacy with the Canaanites that remained, against which he is therefore careful to arm them.

III. The persons to whom Joshua made this speech: *To all Israel, even their elders, &c.* So it might be read, *v.* 2.

IV. Joshua's circumstances when he gave them this charge: He *was old and stricken in age* (*v.* 1), probably it was in the last year of his life, and he lived to be 110 years old, *ch.* xxiv. 29. *I am old and stricken in age.* He uses it, 1. As an argument with himself to give them this charge, because being old he could expect to be but a little while with them, to advise and instruct them. 2. As an argument with them to give heed to what he said. He was old and experienced, and he had grown old in their service, and had spent himself for their good, and therefore was to be the more regarded by them.

V. The discourse itself.

1. He puts them in mind of the great things God had done for them, now in his days. For the proof of this he appeals to their own eyes (*v.* 3): "*You have seen all that the Lord your God has done*; not what I have done, or what you have done but what God himself has done by me and for you." (1) Many great and mighty nations (as the rate of nations then went) were driven out from as fine a country as any was at that time upon the face of the earth, to make room for Israel. (2) They were not only driven out, they were subdued before them, which made the possessing of their land so much the more glorious. (3) They had not only conquered the Canaanites, but were put in full possession of their land (*v.* 4).

2. He assures them of God's readiness to carry on and complete this glorious work in due time. He tells them what little need they had to be in care about the numbers of their forces (*v.* 10): *One man of you shall chase a thousand,* as Jonathan did, 1 Sam. xiv. 13. "The Lord your God, *he it is that fighteth for you*; and how many do you reckon him for?"

JAMIESON, FAUSSET, BROWN

CHAPTER 23

VSS. 1, 2. JOSHUA'S EXHORTATION BEFORE HIS DEATH. **1. a long time after the Lord had given rest unto Israel from all their enemies**—about fourteen years after the conquest of Canaan, and seven after the distribution of that country among the tribes.

2. Joshua called for all Israel—The clause which follows seems to restrict this general expression as applicable only to the officers and representatives of the people. The place of assembly was most probably Shiloh. The occasion of convening it was the extreme age and approaching death of the venerable leader; and the purport of this solemn address was to animate the chosen people and their posterity to a faithful and unswerving continuance in the faith and worship of the God of Israel.

3. BY FORMER BENEFITS. **ye have seen all that the Lord your God hath done unto all these nations because of you**—The modesty and humility of Joshua are remarkably displayed at the commencement of this address. Dismissing all thoughts of his personal services, he ascribed the subjugation and occupation of Canaan entirely to the favoring presence and aid of God; and in doing so, he spoke not more piously than truly. This had been promised (Deut. 1:30; 3:22); and the reality of the divine aid was seen in the rapid overthrow of the Canaanites, which had already led to the division of the whole land among the tribes.

ADAM CLARKE

CHAPTER 23

1. *A long time after that the Lord had given rest.* This is supposed to have been in the last or one hundred and tenth year of the life of Joshua, about thirteen or fourteen years after the conquest of Canaan, and seven after the division of the land among the tribes.

2. *Joshua called for all Israel.* There are four degrees of civil distinction mentioned here: (1) *zekenim,* the *elders* or senate, the princes of the tribes; (2) *rashim,* the chiefs or *heads* of families; (3) *shophetim,* the *judges* who interpreted and decided according to the law; (4) *shoterim,* the *officers,* sergeants, etc., who executed the decisions of the judges. Whether this assembly was held at Timnath-serah, where Joshua lived, or at Shiloh, where the ark was, or at Shechem, as in chap. xxiv. 1, we cannot tell.

3. *For the Lord your God is he that hath fought for you.* There is much of both piety and modesty in this address. It was natural for the Israelites to look on their veteran, worn-out general, who had led them on from conquest to conquest, with profound respect; and to be ready to say, "Had we not had such a commander, we had never got possession of this good land." Joshua corrects this opinion, and shows them that all their enemies had been defeated because the Lord their God had fought for them; that the battle was the Lord's, and not his; and that God alone should have the glory.

4. *I have divided . . . these nations that remain.* The whole of the Promised Land had been portioned out, as well as those parts which had not yet been conquered as those from which the ancient inhabitants had been expelled. The Canaanitish armies had long ago been broken in pieces, so that they could make no head against the Israelites, but in many districts the old inhabitants remained, more through the supineness of the Israelites than through their own bravery.

10. *One man of you shall chase a thousand.* Do not remain inactive on the supposition that you must be much more numerous before you can drive out your enemies, for it is the Lord that shall drive out nations great and strong; and under His direction and influence *one . . . of you shall chase a thousand.*

MATTHEW HENRY

3. He hereupon most earnestly charges them to adhere to their duty, to go on and persevere in the good ways of the Lord wherein they had so well set out. He exhorts them,

(1) To be very courageous (*v.* 6): "God fighteth for you against your enemies, do you therefore *behave yourselves valiantly* for him."

(2) To be very cautious. [1] They must not acquaint themselves with idolaters, nor come among them to visit them or be present at any of their feasts or entertainments, for they could not contract any intimacy nor keep up any conversation with them, without danger of infection. [2] They must not show the least respect to any idol, nor *make mention of the name of their gods*, but endeavour to bury the remembrance of them in perpetual oblivion, that the worship of them may never be revived. [3] They must not countenance others in showing respect to them. They must not only not swear by them themselves, but they must not cause others to swear by them, which supposes that they must not make any covenants with idolaters, because they, in the confirming of their covenants, would swear by their idols; never let Israelites admit such an oath.

(3) To be very constant (*v.* 8): *Cleave unto the Lord your God*, that is, "delight in him, depend upon him, devote yourselves to his glory, and continue to do so to the end."

Verses 11–16

Here, I. Joshua directs them what to do, that they might persevere in religion, *v.* 11. Would we cleave to the Lord, and not forsake him, 1. We must always stand upon our guard, for many a precious soul is lost and ruined through carelessness: "Take heed therefore, *take good heed to yourselves*, to your *souls* (so the word is). 2. What we do in religion we must do from a principle of love, not by constraint or from a slavish fear of God, but of choice and with delight. "*Love the Lord your God*, and you will not leave him."

II. He urges God's fidelity to them as an argument why they should be faithful to him (*v.* 14): "*I am going the way of all the earth*, I am old and dying. Now that I am near my end it is proper to look back upon the years that are past; you know that *not one thing hath failed of all the good things which the Lord spoke concerning you*" (and he spoke a great many); see *ch.* xxi. 45.

III. He gives them fair warning what would be the fatal consequences of apostasy (*v.* 12, 13, 15, 16): "If you go back, know for a certainty it will be your ruin."

1. How he describes the apostasy which he warns them against. The first step would be (*v.* 12) growing intimate with idolaters. The next step would be intermarrying with them. And the consequence of that would be (*v.* 16) *serving other gods* (which were pretended to be the ancient deities of the country) and bowing down to them.

2. How he describes the destruction which he warns them of. He tells them, (1) That these remainders of the Canaanites would be snares and traps to them, both to draw them to sin and also to draw them into foolish bargains, unprofitable projects, and all manner of inconveniences. (2) That the anger of the Lord would be kindled against them. Their making leagues with the Canaanites would not only give those idolaters the opportunity of doing them a mischief, and be the fostering of snakes in their bosoms, but it would likewise provoke God to become their enemy, and would kindle the fire of his displeasure against them. (3) That all the threatenings of the word would be fulfilled, as the promise had been, for the God of eternal truth is faithful to both (*v.* 15): "*As all good things have come upon you* according to the promise, so long as you have kept close to God, so all evil things will come upon you according to the threatening, if you forsake him."

JAMIESON, FAUSSET, BROWN

5-11. BY PROMISES. **5-11. the Lord your God, he shall expel them from before you, as the Lord your God has promised you,** etc.—The actual possessions which God had given were a pledge of the complete fulfilment of His promise in giving them the parts of the country still unconquered. But the accomplishment of the divine promise depended on their inviolable fidelity to God's law—on their keeping resolutely aloof from all familiar intercourse and intimate connections with the Canaanites, or in any way partaking of their idolatrous sins. In the event of their continuing in steadfast adherence to the cause of God, as happily distinguished the nation at that time, His blessing would secure them a course of brilliant and easy victories (Lev. 26:7; Deut. 28:7; 32:30).

11. Take good heed, therefore, that ye love the Lord your God—The sum of his exhortation is comprised in the love of God, which is the end or fulfilment of the law (Deut. 6:5; 11:13; Matt. 22:37).

12. BY THREATENINGS IN CASE OF DISOBEDIENCE. **12. Else if ye do in any wise go back, and cleave unto the remnant of these nations**—By "going back" is meant transgression of the divine law; and as marriage connections with the idolatrous Canaanites would present many and strong temptations to transgress it, these were strictly prohibited (Exod. 34:12-16; Deut. 7:3). With his eye, as it were, upon those prohibitions, Joshua threatens them with the certain withdrawal of the divine aid in the further expulsion of the Canaanites (a threat founded on Exod. 23:33; Numb. 33:55; Deut. 7:16).

ADAM CLARKE

5. *And drive them . . . out . . . and ye shall possess.* The same Hebrew word *yarash* is used here to signify to "expel from an inheritance," and to "succeed" those thus expelled. "Ye shall disinherit them from your sight, and ye shall inherit their land."

6. *Be ye therefore very courageous to keep and to do.* It requires no small courage to keep a sound creed in the midst of scoffers, and not less to maintain a godly practice among the profane and profligate. *That is written in the book.* By the Word of God alone His followers are bound. Nothing is to be received as an article of faith which God has not spoken.

7. *Come not among these nations.* Have no civil or social contracts with them (see v. 12), as these will infallibly lead to spiritual affinities, in consequence of which you will make honorable *mention of the name of their gods . . . swear by them* as the judges of your motives and actions, *serve them* in their abominable rites, and *bow yourselves* unto them as your creators and preservers, thus giving the whole worship of God to idols—and all this will follow from simply coming among them.

11. *Take good heed . . . unto yourselves, that ye love the Lord.* "Take heed to your souls," literally; but *nephesh* and *nefs,* both in Hebrew and Arabic, signify the whole self, as well as soul and life. Both soul and body must be joined in this work, for it is written, "Thou shalt love the Lord thy God with all thy heart . . . soul . . . mind, and . . . strength."

12. *Else if ye do . . . go back.* The soldier who draws back when going to meet the enemy forfeits his life. These were the Lord's soldiers, and if they drew back they drew back unto perdition, their lives being forfeited by their infidelity.

13. *They shall be snares. Lephach,* a net set by the artful fowler to catch heedless birds. *And traps. Mokesh,* any snare, toil, or trap placed on the ground to catch the unwary traveller or wild beast by the foot. *Scourges in your sides, and thorns in your eyes.* Nothing can be conceived more vexatious and distressing than a continual goad in the side or thorn in the eye.

14. *The way of all the earth.* I am about to die; I am going into the grave. Not one thing *hath failed.* God had so remarkably and literally fulfilled His promises that not one of His enemies could state that even the smallest of them had not had its most literal accomplishment; this all Israel could testify.

15. *So shall the Lord bring upon you all evil things.* His faithfulness in fulfilling His promises is a proof that He will as faithfully accomplish His threatenings, for the veracity of God is equally pledged for both.

MATTHEW HENRY

CHAPTER 24

Verses 1–14

Joshua thought he had taken his last farewell of Israel in the solemn charge he gave them in the foregoing chapter, when he said, *I go the way of all the earth*; but God graciously continuing his life longer than expected, he was desirous to improve it for the good of Israel. He summons them together again, that he might try what more he could do to engage them for God.

I. The place appointed for their meeting is *Shechem*, not only because that lay nearer to Joshua than Shiloh, and therefore more convenient now that he was infirm and unfit for travelling, but because it was the place where Abraham, the first trustee of God's

JAMIESON, FAUSSET, BROWN

CHAPTER 24

Vs. 1. JOSHUA ASSEMBLING THE TRIBES. **1. Joshua gathered all the tribes of Israel to Shechem**—Another and final opportunity of dissuading the people against idolatry is here described as taken by the aged leader, whose solicitude on this account arose from his knowledge of the extreme readiness of the people to conform to the manners of the surrounding nations. This address was made to the representatives of the people convened at Shechem, and which had already been the scene of a solemn renewal of the covenant (ch. 8:30, 35). The transaction now to be entered upon being in principle and object the same, it was desirable to

ADAM CLARKE

CHAPTER 24

1. *Joshua gathered all the tribes.* This must have been a different assembly from that mentioned in the preceding chapter, though probably held not long after the former.

MATTHEW HENRY

covenant with this people, settled at his coming to Canaan, and where God appeared to him (Gen. xii. 6, 7), and near which stood Mounts Gerizim and Ebal, where the people had renewed their covenant with God at their first coming into Canaan, Josh. viii. 30.

II. They presented themselves not only before Joshua, but before God, in this assembly. Joshua ordered the ark of God to be brought by the priests to Shechem, which, they say, was about ten miles from Shiloh, and to be set down in the place of their meeting, which is therefore called (*v.* 26) *the sanctuary of the Lord*, the presence of the ark making it so at that time. We have not now any such sensible tokens of the divine presence, but are to believe that *where two or three are gathered together* in Christ's name he is as really in the midst of them as God was where the ark was, and they are indeed presenting themselves before him.

III. Joshua spoke to them in God's name, and as from him, in the language of a prophet (*v.* 2): "*Thus saith the Lord.*" Note, The word of God is to be received by us as his, whoever is the messenger that brings it, whose greatness cannot add to it, nor his meanness diminish from it.

1. The doctrinal part is a history of the great things God had done for his people, and for their fathers before them. (1) He brought Abraham out of Ur of the Chaldees, *v.* 2, 3. Abraham, who afterwards was the friend of God and the great favourite of heaven, was bred up in idolatry, and lived long in it, till God by his grace snatched him as a brand out of that burning. Hence Abraham's justification is made by the apostle an instance of God's *justifying the ungodly*, Rom. iv. 5. (2) He brought him to Canaan, and built up his family, led him through the land to Shechem, where they now were, multiplied his seed by Ishmael, who begat twelve princes, but at last gave him Isaac the promised son, and in him multiplied his seed. When Isaac had two sons, Jacob and Esau, God provided an inheritance for Esau elsewhere in Mount Seir, that the land of Canaan might be reserved entire for the seed of Jacob, and the posterity of Esau might not pretend to a share in it. (3) He delivered the seed of Jacob out of Egypt with a high hand (*v.* 5, 6), and rescued them out of the hands of Pharaoh and his host at the Red Sea, *v.* 6, 7. The same waters were the Israelites' guard and the Egyptians' grave, and this in answer to prayer; for, though we find in the story that they in that distress murmured against God (Exod. xiv. 11, 12), notice is here taken of their *crying to God*; he graciously accepted those that prayed to him, and overlooked the folly of those that quarrelled with him. (4) He protected them in the wilderness, where they are here said, not to *wander*, but to *dwell for a long season*, *v.* 7. (5) He gave them the land of the Amorites, on the other side Jordan (*v.* 8), and there defeated the plot of Balak and Balaam against them, so that Balaam could not curse them as he desired, and therefore Balak durst not fight them as he designed, and as, because he designed it, he is here said to have done it. (6) He brought them safely and triumphantly into Canaan, delivered the Canaanites into their hand (*v.* 11), *sent hornets before them*, when they were actually engaged in battle with the enemy, which with their stings tormented them and with their noise terrified them, so that they became a very easy prey to Israel. *Lastly*, They were now in the peaceable possession of a good land, and lived comfortably upon the fruit of other people's labours, *v.* 13.

2. The application of this history of God's mercies to them is by way of exhortation to fear and serve God, in gratitude for his favour, and that it might be continued to them, *v.* 14. It should seem by this charge, which is repeated (*v.* 23), that there were some among them that privately kept in their closets the images or pictures of these dunghill-deities, which came to their hands from their ancestors, as heirlooms of their families, though, it may be, they did not worship them; these Joshua earnestly urges them to throw away: "Deface them, destroy them, lest you be tempted to serve them."

Verses 15–28

Never was any treaty carried on with better management, nor brought to a better issue, than this of Joshua with the people, to engage them to serve God.

I. Would it be any obligation upon them if they made the service of God their choice?—he here puts them to their choice, because it would have a great influence upon their perseverance in religion if they embraced it with the reason of men and with the resolution of men. These two things he here brings them to.

1. He brings them to embrace their religion ration-

JAMIESON, FAUSSET, BROWN

give it all the solemn impresiveness which might be derived from the memory of the former ceremonial, as well as from other sacred associations of the place (Gen. 12:6, 7; 33:18-20; 35:2-4). **they presented themselves before God**—It is generally assumed that the ark of the covenant had been transferred on this occasion to Shechem; as on extraordinary emergencies it was for a time removed (Judg. 20:1-18; I Sam. 4:3; II Sam. 15:24). But the statement, not necessarily implying this, may be viewed as expressing only the religious character of the ceremony [HENGSTENBERG].

2-13. RELATES GOD'S BENEFITS. **2. Joshua said unto all the people**—His address briefly recapitulated the principal proofs of the divine goodness to Israel from the call of Abraham to their happy establishment in the land of promise; it showed them that they were indebted for their national existence as well as their peculiar privileges, not to any merits of their own, but to the free grace of God. **Your fathers dwelt on the other side of the flood**—The Euphrates, viz., at Ur. **Terah, the father of Abraham, and the father of Nahor**—(see on Gen. 11:27). Though Terah had three sons, Nahor only is mentioned with Abraham, as the Israelites were descended from him on the mother's side through Rebekah and her nieces, Leah and Rachel. **served other gods**—conjoining, like Laban, the traditional knowledge of the true God with the domestic use of material images (Gen. 31:19, 34). **3. I took your father Abraham from the other side of the flood, and led him throughout all the land of Canaan**—It was an irresistible impulse of divine grace which led the patriarch to leave his country and relatives, to migrate to Canaan, and live a "stranger and pilgrim" in that land. **4. I gave unto Esau mount Seir**—(see on Gen. 36:8, 9.) In order that he might be no obstacle to Jacob and his posterity being the exclusive heirs of Canaan.

12. I sent the hornet before you—a particular species of wasp which swarms in warm countries and sometimes assumes the scourging character of a plague; or, as many think, it is a figurative expression for uncontrollable terror (Exod. 23:27, 28).

14-28. Now therefore fear the Lord, and serve him in sincerity and in truth—After having enumerated so many grounds for national gratitude, Joshua calls on them to declare, in a public and solemn manner, whether they will be faithful and obedient to the God of Israel.

ADAM CLARKE

To Shechem. As it is immediately added that *they presented themselves before God,* this must mean the Tabernacle; but at this time the Tabernacle was not at Shechem but at Shiloh. The Septuagint appear to have been struck with this difficulty, and therefore read "Shiloh," both here and in v. 25.

2. *On the other side of the flood.* The river Euphrates. *They served other gods.* Probably Abraham as well as Terah, his father, was an idolater, till he received the call of God to leave that land. See on Gen. xi. 31; xii. 1.

9. *Then Balak . . . arose and warred against Israel.* This circumstance is not related in Numbers xxii, nor does it appear in that history that the Moabites attacked the Israelites; and probably the warring here mentioned means no more than his attempts to destroy them by the curses of Balaam and the wiles of the Midianitish women.

11. *The men of Jericho fought against you.* See the notes on chap. iii and chap. vi. 1, etc. The people of Jericho are said to have fought against the Israelites because they opposed them by shutting their gates.

14. *Fear the Lord.* Reverence Him as the sole Object of your religious worship. *Serve him.* Perform His will by obeying His commands. *In sincerity.* Having your whole heart engaged in His worship. *And in truth.* According to the directions He has given you in His infallible word. *Put away the gods.* From this exhortation of Joshua we learn of what sort the gods were, to the worship of whom these Israelites were still attached: (1) those which their fathers worshipped on the other side of the flood: i.e., the gods of the Chaldeans, fire, light, the sun; (2) those of the Egyptians, Apis, Anubis, the ape, serpents, vegetables; (3) those of the Canaanites, Moabites, Baal-peor or Priapus, Astarte or Venus.

MATTHEW HENRY

ally and intelligently, for it is a reasonable service. Accordingly,

(1) Joshua fairly puts the matter to their choice, *v.* 15. Here, [1] He proposes the candidates that stand for the election. The Lord, Jehovah, on one side, and on the other side either the gods of their ancestors, or the *gods of their neighbours*, the Amorites, in *whose land they dwelt*, which would insinuate themselves into the affections of those that were complaisant and fond of good fellowship. [2] He supposes there were those to whom, upon some account or other, it would *seem evil to serve the Lord*. There are prejudices and objections which some people raise against religion. It seems evil to them, hard and unreasonable, to be obliged to deny themselves, mortify the flesh, take up their cross, &c. [3] He refers it to themselves: "*Choose you whom you will serve*, choose this day, now that the matter is laid thus plainly before you, speedily bring it to a head, and do not stand hesitating." Elijah, long after this, referred the decision of the controversy between Jehovah and Baal to the consciences of those with whom he was treating, 1 Kings xviii. 21. Joshua's putting the matter here to this issue plainly intimates two things:—*First*. That it is the will of God we should every one of us make religion our serious and deliberate choice. *Secondly*, That religion has so much self-evident reason and righteousness on its side that it may safely be referred to every man that allows himself a free thought either to choose or refuse it; for the merits of the cause are so plain that no considerate man can do otherwise but choose it. [4] He directs their choice in this matter by an open declaration of his own resolutions: "*But as for me and my house*, whatever you do, *we will serve the Lord*, and I hope you will all be of the same mind."

(2) The matter being thus put to their choice, they immediately determine it by a free, rational, and intelligent declaration, for the God of Israel, against all competitors whatsoever, *v.* 16–18. *We will also serve the Lord* (*v.* 18). They give very substantial reasons for their choice, to show that they did not make it purely in compliance to Joshua, but from a full conviction of the reasonableness and equity of it.

2. He brings them to embrace their religion resolutely, and to express a full purpose of heart to cleave to the Lord. Now that he has them in a good mind he follows his blow, and drives the nail to the head, that it might, if possible, be a nail in a sure place. Fast bind, fast find.

(1) In order to this he sets before them the difficulties of religion, and that in it which might be thought discouraging (*v.* 19, 20): *You cannot serve the Lord, for he is a holy God. He will not forgive*, And, *if you forsake him, he will do you hurt.* Certainly Joshua does not intend hereby to deter them from the service of God as impracticable and dangerous. But, [1] He perhaps intends to represent here the suggestions of seducers, who tempted Israel from their God, with insinuations that he was a hard master, his work impossible to be done, and he not to be pleased. It is probable that this was then commonly objected against the Jewish religion. Or, [2] He thus expresses his godly jealousy over them, and his fear concerning them, that, notwithstanding the profession they now made of zeal for God and his service, they would afterwards draw back. Or, [3] He resolves to let them know the worst of it. "*You cannot serve the Lord*, except you put away all other gods." Thus, though our Master has assured us that *his yoke is easy*, yet lest we should grow remiss and careless, he has also told us that the gate is strait, and the way narrow, that leads to life, that we may therefore strive to enter, and not seek only. Or, [4] Joshua thus urges on them the seeming discouragements which lay in their way, that he might sharpen their resolutions.

(2) Notwithstanding this statement of the difficulties of religion, they declare a firm and fixed resolution to continue and persevere therein (*v.* 21): "*Nay, but we will serve the Lord*."

II. The service of God being thus made their deliberate choice, Joshua binds them to it by a solemn covenant, *v.* 25. Moses had twice publicly ratified this covenant between God and Israel, at Mount Sinai (Exod. xxiv.) and in the plains of Moab, Deut. xxix. 1. Joshua had likewise done it once (*ch.* viii. 31, &c.) and now the second time. Now to give it the formalities of a covenant, 1. He calls witnesses, no other than themselves (*v.* 22): *You are witnesses that you have chosen the Lord*. 2. He put it in writing, and inserted it, as we find it here, in the sacred canon: He *wrote it in the book of the law* (*v.* 26). He *set up a great stone under an oak*, as a monument of this covenant, and perhaps wrote an inscription upon it (by which stones are made to speak) signifying the intention of it.

JAMIESON, FAUSSET, BROWN

He avowed this to be his own unalterable resolution, and urged them, if they were sincere in making a similar avowal, "to put away the strange gods that were among them"—a requirement which seems to imply that some were suspected of a strong hankering for, or concealed practice of, the idolatry, whether in the form of Zabaism, the fire-worship of their Chaldean ancestors, or the grosser superstitions of the Canaanites.

CHARLES H. SPURGEON:

Joshua knew that the people who surrounded him, while ostensibly serving Jehovah, were many of them secretly worshiping the ancient idols of their Mesopotamian fathers, those teraphim which were once hidden in Rachel's tent, and were never quite purged from Jacob's family. Some of them also harbored the Eygptian emblems, and some had even fallen into the worship of the gods of the people whom they had displaced, and were setting up the images of Baalim in their habitations. The people were nominally worshippers of Jehovah, but in very deed many of them had turned aside unto strange gods. Never in their best days had the children of Israel been quite divorced from idols, for, as Stephen said of them, even in the wilderness they took up the tabernacle of Moloch, and the star of their god Remphan, figures which they made to worship. Now, being a thorough-going, decided, downright man, Joshua could not endure double-mindedness, and therefore he pushed the people to decision, urging them to serve the Lord with sincerity, and, if they did so, to put away altogether all their graven images. He demanded from them a determination for one thing or the other, and cried, "If it seem evil unto you to serve Jehovah, choose you this day whom ye will serve; whether the gods which your fathers served that were on the other side of the flood, or gods of the Amorites among whom ye dwell." He shut them up to a present choice, between the true God and the idols, and gave them no rest in their half-heartedness. Anticipating the cry of Elias, upon Carmel, he demanded in effect, "How long halt ye between two opinions? If God be God, serve Him, but if Baal be God, serve him." Decision he demanded, and rightly so. Can either earth or heaven be quiet while such a matter is in suspense?

—The Treasury of the Old Teatament

26. Joshua wrote these words in the book of the law of God—registered the engagements of that solemn covenant in the book of sacred history. **took a great stone**—according to the usage of ancient times to erect stone pillars as monuments of public transactions. **set it up there under an oak**—or terebinth, in all likelihood, the same as that at the root of which Jacob buried the idols and charms found in his family. **that was by the sanctuary of the Lord**—either the spot where the ark had stood, or else the place around, so called from that religious meeting, as Jacob named Beth-el the house of God.

ADAM CLARKE

15. *Choose you this day whom ye will serve.* Joshua well knew that all service that was not free and voluntary could be only deceit and hypocrisy. He therefore calls upon the people to make their choice, for God himself would not force them—they must serve Him with all their hearts if they served Him at all.

16. *God forbid that we should forsake the Lord.* That they were now sincere cannot be reasonably doubted, for they served the Lord all the days of Joshua, and the elders that outlived him, v. 31; but afterwards they turned aside, and did serve other gods.

19. *Ye cannot serve the Lord: for he is an holy God.* If we are to take this literally, we cannot blame the Israelites for their defection from the worship of the true God; for if it was impossible for them to serve God, they could not but come short of His kingdom. But surely this was not the case. Instead of *lo thuchelu*, "ye cannot serve," some eminent critics read *lo thechallu*, "ye shall not cease to serve." This is a very ingenious emendation, but there is not one MS. in all the collections of Kennicott and De Rossi to support it. If the common reading be preferred, the meaning of the place must be, "Ye cannot serve the Lord, for He is holy and jealous, *unless* ye put away the gods which your fathers served beyond the flood. For He is a jealous God, and will not give to nor divide His glory with any other. He is a holy God, and will not have His people defiled with the impure worship of the Gentiles."

21. *And the people said . . . Nay; but we will serve.* So they understood the words of Joshua to imply no moral impossibility on their side; and had they earnestly sought the gracious assistance of God, they would have continued steady in His covenant.

22. *Ye are witnesses against yourselves.* You have been sufficiently apprised of the difficulties in your way—of God's holiness—your own weakness and inconstancy—the need you have of divine help, and the awful consequences of apostasy; and now you deliberately make your choice. Remember, then, that you are witnesses against yourselves.

23. *Now therefore put away.* As you have promised to reform, begin instantly the work of reformation. A man's promise to serve God soon loses its moral hold of his conscience if he do not instantaneously begin to put it in practice. The grace that enables him to promise is that by the strength of which he is to begin the performance.

25. *Joshua made a covenant.* Literally, "Joshua cut the covenant," alluding to the sacrifice offered on the occasion. *And set them a statute and an ordinance.* He made a solemn and public act of the whole, which was signed and witnessed by himself and the people, in the presence of Jehovah; and having done so, he wrote the words of the covenant in the book of the law of God, probably in some part of the skin constituting the great roll, on which the laws of God were written, and of which there were some blank columns to spare. Having done this, he took a great stone and set it up under an oak—that this might be ed or "witness" that, at such a time and place, this covenant was made, the terms of which might be found written in the book of the law, which was laid up beside the ark. See Deut. xxxi. 26.

27. *This stone . . . hath heard all the words.* That is, the stone itself, from its permanency, shall be in all succeeding ages as competent and as substantial a witness as one who had been present at the transaction, and heard all the words which on both sides were spoken on the occasion.

28. *So Joshua.* After this verse the Septuagint insert v. 31.

MATTHEW HENRY	JAMIESON, FAUSSET, BROWN	ADAM CLARKE

MATTHEW HENRY

Verses 29–33

We have here, 1. The burial of Joseph, *v.* 32. He died about 200 years before in Egypt, but *gave commandment concerning his bones,* that they should not rest in their grave until Israel had rest in the land of promise; now therefore the children of Israel, who had brought this coffin full of bones with them out of Egypt, carried it along with them in all their marches through the wilderness and kept it in their camp till Canaan was perfectly reduced. Now at last they deposited his bones in that piece of ground which his father gave him near Shechem, Gen. xlviii. 22. Probably the sermon in this chapter served both for Joseph's funeral sermon and his own farewell sermon. 2. The death and burial of Joshua, *v.* 29, 30. He is here called the *servant of the Lord,* the same title that was given to Moses (*ch.* i. 1) when mention was made of his death. Joshua's burying-place is here said to be *on the north side of the hill Gaash,* or *the quaking hill*; the Jews say it was so called because it trembled at the burial of Joshua, to upbraid the people of Israel with their stupidity in that they did not lament the death of that great and good man as they ought to have done. 3. The death and burial of Eleazar the chief priest, who, it is probable, died about the same time that Joshua did, as Aaron in the same year with Moses, *v.* 33. He was buried in a hill that pertained to Phinehas his son. 4. A general idea given us of the state of Israel at this time, *v.* 31. While Joshua lived, religion was kept up among them under his care and influence; but soon after he and his contemporaries died it went to decay. How well is it for the gospel church that Christ, our Joshua, is still with it, by his Spirit, and will be always, even *unto the end of the world*!

JAMIESON, FAUSSET, BROWN

14-33. HIS AGE AND DEATH. **29, 30. Joshua . . . died**—Lightfoot computes that he lived seventeen, others twenty-seven years, after the entrance into Canaan. He was buried, according to the Jewish practice, within the limits of his own inheritance. The eminent public services he had long rendered to Israel and the great amount of domestic comfort and national prosperity he had been instrumental in diffusing among the several tribes, were deeply felt—were universally acknowledged; and a testimonial in the form of a statue or obelisk would have been immediately raised to his honor, in all parts of the land, had such been the fashion of the times. The brief but noble epitaph by the historian is, Joshua, "the servant of the Lord."

31. Israel served the Lord all the days of Joshua—The high and commanding character of this eminent leader had given so decided a tone to the sentiments and manners of his contemporaries and the memory of his fervent piety and many virtues continued so vividly impressed on the memories of the people, that the sacred historian has recorded it to his immortal honor. "Israel served the Lord all the days of Joshua, and all the days of the elders that overlived Joshua." **32. the bones of Joseph**—They had carried these venerable relics with them in all their migrations through the desert, and deferred the burial, according to the dying charge of Joseph himself, till they arrived in the promised land. The sarcophagus, in which his mummied body had been put, was brought thither by the Israelites, and probably buried when the tribe of Ephraim had obtained their settlement, or at the solemn convocation described in this chapter. **in a parcel of ground which Jacob bought . . . for an hundred pieces of silver**—*Kestitah,* translated, "piece of silver," is supposed to mean a lamb, the weights being in the form of lambs or kids, which were, in all probability, the earliest standard of value among pastoral people. The tomb that now covers the spot is a Mohammedan *Welce,* but there is no reason to doubt that the precious deposit of Joseph's remains may be concealed there at the present time. **33. Eleazar the son of Aaron died, and they buried him . . . in mount Ephraim**—The sepulchre is at the modern village Awertah, which, according to Jewish travellers, contains the graves also of Ithamar, the brother of Phinehas, the son of Eleazar [VAN DE VELDE].

ADAM CLARKE

29. *Joshua the son of Nun . . . died.* This event probably took place shortly after this public assembly; for he was old and stricken in years when he held the assembly mentioned in chap. xxiii. 2; and as his work was now all done, and his soul ripened for a state of blessedness, God took him to himself, being one hundred and ten years of age, exactly the same age as that of the patriarch Joseph. See Gen. i. 26.

30. *And they buried him . . . in Timnath-serah.* This was his own inheritance, as we have seen chap. xix. 50. It is very strange that there is no account of any public mourning for the death of this eminent general; probably, as he was buried in his own inheritance, he had forbidden all funeral pomp, and it is likely was privately interred.

31. *And Israel served the Lord.* Though there was private idolatry among them, for they had strange gods, yet there was no public idolatry all the days of Joshua and of the elders that overlived Joshua, most of whom must have been advanced in years at the death of this great man.

32. *And the bones of Joseph.* See the note on Gen. i. 25 and on Exod. xiii. 19. This burying of the bones of Joseph probably took place when the conquest of the land was completed, and each tribe had received its inheritance; for it is not likely that this was deferred till after the death of Joshua.

33. *And Eleazar . . . died.* Probably about the same time as Joshua, or soon after, though some think he outlived him six years. Thus, nearly all the persons who had witnessed the miracles of God in the wilderness were gathered to their fathers; and their descendants left in possession of the great inheritance, with the law of God in their hands, and the bright example of their illustrious ancestors before their eyes. *A hill that pertained to Phinehas his son.* This grant was probably made to Phinehas as a token of the respect of the whole nation, for his zeal, courage, and usefulness; for the priests had properly no inheritance.

The last six verses in this chapter were, doubtless, not written by Joshua; for no man can give an account of his own death and burial. Eleazar, Phinehas, or Samuel might have added them, to bring down the narration so as to connect it with their own times and thus preserve the thread of the history unbroken.

THE BOOK OF JUDGES

I. After Joshua (1:1-3:6)
- *A. Israel and the Canaanites (1:1-36)*
  - 1. Judah (1:1-21)
  - 2. Joseph (1:22-29)
  - 3. The rest (1:30-36)
- *B. Israel's failure (2:1-3:6)*
  - 1. Jehovah's messenger (2:1-5)
  - 2. The people under Joshua (2:6-10)
  - 3. Synopsis of history (2:11-23)
  - 4. The enemies (3:1-6)

II. The judges (3:7-16:31)
- *A. First declension (3:7-11)*
  - 1. Sin: idolatry (3:7)
  - 2. Punishment: 8 years' oppression (3:8)
  - 3. Deliverance: Othniel (3:9-11)
- *B. Second declension (3:12-31)*
  - 1. Sin (3:12a)
  - 2. Punishment: Eglon 18 years (3:12b-14)
  - 3. Deliverance: Ehud (Shamgar) (3:15-31)
- *C. Third declension (4:1-5:31)*
  - 1. Sin (4:1)
  - 2. Punishment: Jabin 20 years (4:2-3)
  - 3. Deliverance: Deborah, Barak (4:4-5:31)
- *D. Fourth declension (6:1-8:32)*
  - 1. Sin (6:1a)
  - 2. Punishment: Midian 7 years (6:1b-6)
  - 3. Deliverance: Gideon (6:7-8:32)
- *E. Fifth declension (8:33-10:5)*
  - 1. Sin: Baal worship (8:33-35)
  - 2. Punishment: Abimelech (9:1-57)
  - 3. Deliverance: Tola, Jair (10:1-5)
- *F. Sixth declension (10:6-12:15)*
  - 1. Sin: idolatry multiplied (10:6)
  - 2. Punishment: Philistines, Ammon 18 years (10:7-18)
  - 3. Deliverance: Jephthah (11:1-12:15)
- *G. Seventh declension (13:1-16:31)*
  - 1. Sin (13:1a)
  - 2. Punishment: Philistines 40 years (13:1b)
  - 3. Deliverance: Samson (13:2-16:31)

Appendix (17:1-21:25)
- *A. Micah (17-18:31)*
  - 1. Micah's idolatry (17:1-13)
  - 2. Its punishment by Dan (18:1-31)
- *B. The Levite (19:1-21:25)*
  - 1. The outrage (19:1-30)
  - 2. War between Israel and Benjamin (20:1-48)
  - 3. Preservation of Benjamin (21:1-25)

This is called in the Hebrew *Shepher Shoptim*, the *Book of Judges*, which the Syriac and Arabic versions enlarge upon and call it, *The Book of the Judges of the Children of Israel*. The LXX entitles it only *Judges*. It is the history of the commonwealth of Israel, during the government of the judges from Othniel to Eli. It contains the history (according to Dr. Lightfoot's computation) of 299 years.

Now as to the state of the commonwealth of Israel during this period:

I. They do not appear here either so great or so good as one might have expected the character of such a peculiar people would be, that were governed by such laws and enriched by such promises. We find them wretchedly corrupted and wretchedly oppressed by the neighbors about them.

II. We may hope that though the historian in this book enlarges most upon their provocations and grievances, yet there was a face of religion upon the land; and, however there were those among them that were drawn aside to idolatry, yet the tabernacle service, according to the law of Moses, was kept up and there were many that attended it.

III. It should seem that in these times each tribe had very much its own government and acted separately, without one common head or council, which occasioned many differences among themselves and kept them from being or doing anything considerable.

IV. The government of the judges was not constant but occasional—when it is said that after Ehud's victory the land rested eighty years and after Barak's forty, it is not certain that they lived, much less that they governed, so long; but they and the rest were raised up and animated by the Spirit of God to do particular service to the public when there was occasion, to "avenge Israel of their enemies" and to purge Israel of their idolatries, which are the two things principally meant by their judging Israel. Yet Deborah, as a prophetess, was attended for judgment by all Israel before there was occasion for her agency in war (4:4).

V. During the government of the judges God was in a more especial manner Israel's king; so Samuel tells them when they were resolved to throw off this form of government (1 Sam. 12:12). Four of the judges of Israel are canonized (Heb. 11:32): Gideon, Barak, Samson, and Jephtha. The learned bishop Patrick thinks the prophet Samuel was the penman of this Book.

MATTHEW HENRY

CHAPTER 1

Verses 1–8

I. The children of Israel consult the oracle of God for direction which of all the tribes should first attempt to clear their country of the Canaanites. The question they ask is, *Who shall go up first? v.* 1. By this time, we may suppose, they were so multiplied that the places they were in possession of began to be too strait for them. Whether each tribe was ambitious of being first, and so strove for the honour of it, or whether each was afraid of being first, and so strove to decline it, does not appear.

II. God appointed that Judah should go up first, and promised him success (*v.* 2): ***"I have delivered the land into his hand*, to be possessed, and therefore will** deliver the enemy that keeps him out of possession, into his hand, to be destroyed." And why must Judah be first in this undertaking? 1. Judah was the most numerous and powerful tribe. 2. Judah was first in dignity, and therefore must be first in duty. Judah was the tribe out of which our Lord was to spring: so that in Judah, Christ, the Lion of the tribe of Judah, went before them. Christ engaged the powers of darkness first, and foiled them, which animates us for our conflicts; and it is in him that we are *more than conquerors.*

III. Judah hereupon prepares to go up, but courts his brother and neighbour the tribe of Simeon to join forces with him, *v.* 3. The strongest should not despise but desire the assistance even of those that are weaker. Judah was the most considerable of all the tribes, and Simeon the least considerable, and yet

JAMIESON, FAUSSET, BROWN

CHAPTER 1

Vss. 1-3. The Acts of Judah and Simeon. **1. Now after the death of Joshua**—probably not a long period, for the Canaanites seem to have taken advantage of that event to attempt recovering their lost position, and the Israelites were obliged to renew the war. **the children of Israel asked the Lord**—The divine counsel on this, as on other occasions, was sought by **Urim and Thummim, by applying to the high priest,** who, according to Josephus, was Phinehas. **saying, Who shall go up for us against the Canaanites first**—The elders, who exercised the government **in** their respective tribes, judged rightly, that in entering upon an important expedition, they should have a leader nominated by divine appointment; and in consulting the oracle, they adopted a prudent course, whether the object of their inquiry related to the choice of an individual commander, or to the honor of precedency among the tribes. **2. the Lord said, Judah shall go up**—The predicted pre-eminence (Gen. 49:8) was thus conferred upon Judah by divine direction, and its appointment to take the lead in the ensuing hostilities was of great importance, as the measure of success by which its arms were crowned, would animate the other tribes to make similar attempts against the Canaanites within their respective territories. **I have delivered the land into his hand**—not the whole country, but the district assigned for his inheritance. **3. Judah said unto Simeon, Come up with me . . . , that we may fight against the Canaanites**—Being conterminous tribes (Josh. 19:1,

ADAM CLARKE

CHAPTER 1

1. *Now after the death of Joshua.* How long after the death of Joshua this happened we cannot tell; it is probable that it was not long. The enemies of the Israelites, finding their champion dead, would naturally avail themselves of their unsettled state and make incursions on the country.

Who shall go up? Joshua had left no successor, and everything relative to the movements of this people must be determined either by caprice or an especial direction of the Lord.

2. *The Lord said, Judah shall go up.* They had inquired of the Lord by Phinehas, the high priest; and he had communicated to them the divine counsel.

3. *Come up with me into my lot.* It appears that the portions of Judah and Simeon had not been cleared of the Canaanites, or that these were the parts which were now particularly invaded.

MATTHEW HENRY

Judah begs Simeon's friendship, and prays an aid from him; the head cannot say to the foot, *I have no need of thee*, for we are *members one of another*.

IV. The confederate forces of Judah and Simeon take the field: *Judah went up* (*v.* 4), and Simeon with him, *v.* 3. Caleb, it is probable, was commander-in-chief of this expedition. It should seem by what follows (*v.* 10, 11), that he was not yet in possession of his own allotment. It was happy for them that they had such a general as, according to his name, was all heart.

V. God gave them great success. Whether they invaded the enemy, or the enemy first gave them the alarm, *the Lord delivered them into their hand*, *v.* 4. Now, 1. We are told how the army of the Canaanites was routed in the field, in or near Bezek, the place where they drew up, which afterwards Saul made the place of a general rendezvous (1 Sam. xi. 8); they slew 10,000 men, which blow, if followed, could not but be a very great weakening to those that were already brought so very low. 2. How their king was taken and mortified. His name was Adoni-bezek, which signifies, *lord of Bezek*. He was taken prisoner after the battle, and we are here told how they used him; they cut off his thumbs, to disfit him for fighting, and his great toes, that he might not be able to run away, *v.* 6. It had been barbarous thus to triumph over a man in misery, and that lay at their mercy, but that he was a devoted Canaanite, and one that had in like manner abused others. Here observe, (1) What a great man this Adoni-bezek had been, yet now himself a prisoner and reduced to the extremity of meanness and disgrace. (2) What desolations he had made among his neighbours: he had wholly subdued seventy kings. "Judah," says Dr. Lightfoot, "in conquering Adoni-bezek, did, in effect, conquer seventy kings." (3) How justly he was treated as he had treated others. (4) How honestly he owned the righteousness of God herein: *As I have done, so God has requited me*.

VI. Particular notice is taken of the conquest of Jerusalem, *v.* 8.

Verses 9–20

A further account of that glorious and successful campaign which Judah and Simeon made. 1. The lot of Judah was pretty well cleared of the Canaanites, yet not thoroughly. Those that *dwelt in the mountain* (the mountains that were round about Jerusalem) were driven out (*v.* 9, 19), but those in the valley kept their ground against them, having *chariots of iron*, such as we read of, Josh. xvii. 16. They had iron chariots, and therefore it was thought not safe to attack them: but had not Israel God on their side, *whose chariots are thousands of angels* (Ps. lxviii. 17). Yet they suffered their fears to prevail against their faith, they could not trust God under any disadvantages, but meanly withdrew their forces, when with one bold stroke they might have completed their victories. 2. Caleb was put in possession of Hebron, which, though given him by Joshua ten or twelve years before, yet being employed in public service, for the settling of the tribes, which he preferred before his own private interests, it seems he did not till now make himself master of; so well content was that good man to serve others, while he left himself to be served last. Yet now the men of Judah all came in to his assistance for the reducing of Hebron (*v.* 10), slew the sons of Anak, and put him in possession of it, *v.* 20. They gave Hebron unto Caleb. And now Caleb, that he might return the kindness of his countrymen, is impatient to see Debir reduced and put into the hands of the men of Judah, to expedite which he proffers his daughter to the person that will undertake to command in the siege of that important place, *v.* 11, 12. Othniel bravely undertakes it, and wins the town and the lady (*v.* 13).

4. The Kenites gained a settlement in the tribe of Judah, choosing it there rather than in any other tribe, because it was the strongest, and there they hoped to be safe and quiet, *v.* 16. These were the posterity of Jethro. They had at first seated themselves in the *city of palm-trees*, that is, Jericho, a city which never was to be rebuilt, and therefore the fitter for those who *dwelt in tents*, and did not mind building. But afterwards they removed into the wilderness of Judah. This respect Israel showed them, to let them fix where they pleased, being a quiet people, who, wherever they were, were content with a little. Those that molested none were molested by none. *Blessed are the meek, for thus they shall inherit the earth.*

JAMIESON, FAUSSET, BROWN

2), they had a common interest, and were naturally associated in this enterprise.

4-21. Adoni-bezek Justly Requited. **Bezek**—This place lay within the domain of Judah, about twelve miles south of Jerusalem. **5. found Adoni-bezek**—i.e., lord of Bezek—he was "found," i.e., surprised and routed in a pitched battle, whence he fled; but being taken prisoner, he was treated with a severity unusual among the Israelites, for they "cut off his thumbs and great toes." Barbarities of various kinds were commonly practised on prisoners of war in ancient times, and the object of this particular mutilation of the hands and feet was to disable them for military service ever after. The infliction of such a horrid cruelty on this Canaanite chief would have been a foul stain on the character of the Israelites if there were not reason for believing it was done by them as an act of retributive justice, and as such it was regarded by Adoni-bezek himself, whose conscience read his atrocious crimes in their punishment. **7. Threescore and ten kings**—So great a number will not appear strange, when it is considered that anciently every ruler of a city or large town was called a king. It is not improbable that in that southern region of Canaan, there might, in earlier times, have been even more till a turbulent chief like Adoni-bezek devoured them in his insatiable ambition.

8. Now the children of Judah had fought against Jerusalem, and had taken it—The capture of this important city, which ranks among the early incidents in the war of invasion (Josh. 15:63), is here noticed to account for its being in the possession of the Judahites; and they brought Adoni-bezek thither, in order, probably, that his fate being rendered so public, might inspire terror far and wide. Similar inroads were made into the other unconquered parts of Judah's inheritance.

The story of Caleb's acquisition of Hebron is here repeated (Josh. 15:16-19). **16. the children of the Kenite, Moses' father-in-law, went up out of the city of palm trees with the children of Judah**—called "the Kenite," as probably descended from the people of that name (Num. 24:21, 22). If he might not himself, his posterity did accept the invitation of Moses (Num. 10:32) to accompany the Israelites to Canaan. Their first encampment was in the "city of palm trees"—not Jericho, of course, which was utterly destroyed, but the surrounding district, perhaps En-gedi, in early times called Hazezon-tamar (Gen. 14:7), from the palm-grove which sheltered it. Thence they removed for some unknown cause, and associating themselves with Judah, joined in an expedition against Arad, in the southern part of Canaan (Num. 21:1). On the conquest of that district, some of this pastoral people pitched their tents there, while others migrated to the north (ch. 4:17).

ADAM CLARKE

5. *And they found Adoni-bezek*. The word *matsa*, "he found," is used to express a hostile encounter between two parties; to "attack, surprise." This is probably its meaning here. *Adoni-bezek* is literally the "lord of Bezek." It is very probable that the different Canaanitish tribes were governed by a sort of chieftains.

6. *Cut off his thumbs*. That he might never be able to draw his bow or handle his sword; and *great toes*, that he might never be able to pursue or escape from an adversary.

7. *Threescore and ten kings*. Chieftains, heads of tribes, or military officers. For the word *king* cannot be taken here in its proper and usual sense. *Having their thumbs and their great toes cut off*. That this was an ancient mode of treating enemies we learn from Aelian, who tells us that "the Athenians, at the instigation of Cleon, son of Cleaenetus, made a decree that all the inhabitants of the island of Aegina should have the thumb cut off from the right hand, so that they might ever after be disabled from holding a spear, yet might handle an oar."

Gathered their meat under my table. I think this was a proverbial mode of expression, to signify reduction to the meanest servitude. *So God hath requited me*. The king of Bezek seems to have had the knowledge of the true God, and a proper notion of a divine providence. He now feels himself reduced to that state to which he had cruelly reduced others. Those acts in him were acts of tyrannous cruelty; the act towards him was an act of retributive justice. *And there he died*. He continued at Jerusalem in a servile and degraded condition till the day of his death. How long he lived after his disgrace we know not.

8. *Had fought against Jerusalem*. We read this verse in a parenthesis, because we suppose that it refers to the taking of this city by Joshua; for as he had conquered its armies and slew its king, Josh. x. 26, it is probable that he took the city. Yet we find that the Jebusites still dwelt in it, Josh. xv. 63; and that the men of Judah could not drive them out, which probably refers to the stronghold or fortress on Mount Zion, which the Jebusites held till the days of David, who took it, and totally destroyed the Jebusites. See 2 Sam. v. 6-9, and 1 Chron. xi. 4-8. It is possible that the Jebusites, who had been discomfited by Joshua, had again become sufficiently strong to possess themselves of Jerusalem; and that they were now defeated, and the city itself set on fire, but that they still were able to keep possession of their strong fort on Mount Zion, which appears to have been the citadel of Jerusalem.

9. *The Canaanites, that dwelt in the mountain*. The territories of the tribe of Judah lay in the most southern part of the Promised Land, which was very mountainous, though towards the west it had many fine plains. In some of these the Canaanites had dwelt, and the expedition marked here was for the purpose of finally expelling them. But probably this is a recapitulation of what is related Josh. x. 36; xi. 21; xv. 13.

12-15. *And Caleb*. See this whole account, which is placed here by way of recapitulation, in Josh. xv. 13-19.

16. *The children of the Kenite, Moses' father in law*. For an account of Jethro, the father-in-law of Moses, see Exod. xviii. 1-27; Num. x. 29, etc. *The city of palm trees*. This seems to have been some place near Jericho, which city is expressly called "the city of palm trees," Deut. xxxiv. 3; and though destroyed by Joshua, it might have some suburbs remaining where these harmless people had taken up their residence.

The Kenites, the descendants of Jethro, the father-in-law of Moses, were always attached to the Israelites. They received there a lot with the tribe of Judah, and remained in the city of palm trees during the life of Joshua; but after his death, not contented with their portion, or molested by the original inhabitants, they united with the tribe of Judah, and went with them to attack Arad. After the conquest of that country, the Kenites established themselves there, and remained in it till the days of Saul, mingled with the Amalekites. When this king received a commandment from God to destroy the Amalekites, he sent a message to the Kenites to

MATTHEW HENRY

3. Simeon got ground of the Canaanites in his border, *v.* 17, 18. In the eastern part of Simeon's lot, they destroyed the Canaanites in Zephath, and called it *Hormah—destruction.* In the western part they took Gaza, Askelon, and Ekron, cities of the Philistines; they gained present possession of the cities, but, not destroying the inhabitants, the Philistines in process of time recovered the cities, and proved inveterate enemies to the Israel of God, and no better could come of doing their work by the halves.

Verses 21–36

We are here told upon what terms the rest of the tribes stood with the Canaanites that remained.

I. Benjamin neglected to drive the Jebusites out of that part of the city of Jerusalem which fell to their lot, *v.* 21. Judah had set them a good example, and gained them great advantages by what they did (*v.* 9), but they did not follow the blow for want of resolution.

II. 1. The house of Joseph bestirred themselves a little to get possession of Beth-el, *v.* 22. That city is mentioned in the tribe of Benjamin, Josh. xviii. 22. Yet it is spoken of there (*v.* 13), as a city in the borders of that tribe, and, it should seem, the line went through it, so that one half of it only belonged to Benjamin, the other half to Ephraim. In this account of the expedition of the Ephraimites against Beth-el observe,

(1) Their interest in the divine favour: *The Lord was with them*, and would have been with the other tribes if they would have exerted their strength.

(2) The prudent measures they took to gain the city. They sent spies to observe what part of the city was weakest, *v.* 23. These spies got very good information from a man who showed them a private way into the town. It seems, he would not join himself to the people of Israel, and therefore he removed after a colony of the Hittites, which had gone into Arabia and settled there upon Joshua's invasion of the country; with them this man chose to dwell, and built a city, and in the name of it preserved the ancient name of his native city, *Luz, an almond-tree*, preferring this before its new name, which carried religion in it, *Bethel—the house of God.*

(3) Their success. The spies brought or sent notice of the intelligence they had gained to the army, which improved their advantages, surprised the city, and put them all to the sword, *v.* 25.

2. Besides this achievement, it seems, the children of Joseph did nothing remarkable.

JAMIESON, FAUSSET, BROWN

17-29. And Judah went with Simeon his brother—The course of the narrative is here resumed from verse 9, and an account given of Judah returning the services of Simeon (vs. 3), by aiding in the prosecution of the war within the neighboring tribes. **slew the Canaanites that inhabited Zephath**—or Zephathah (II Chron. 14:10), a valley lying in the southern portion of Canaan. **Hormah**—destroyed in fulfilment of an early vow of the Israelites (see on Num. 21:1-3). The confederate tribes, pursuing their incursions in that quarter, came successively to Gaza, Askelon, and Ekron, which they took. But the Philistines seem soon to have regained possession of these cities.

19. the Lord was with Judah; ... but they could not drive out the inhabitants of the valley—The war was of the Lord, whose omnipotent aid would have ensured their success in every encounter, whether on the mountains or the plains, with foot soldiers or cavalry. It was distrust, the want of a simple and firm reliance on the promise of God, that made them afraid of the iron chariots (see on Josh. 11:4-9).

21. the children of Benjamin did not drive out the Jebusites that inhabited Jerusalem—Judah had expelled the people from their part of Jerusalem (vs. 8). The border of the two tribes ran through the city—Israelites and natives must have been closely intermingled.

22-26. SOME CANAANITES LEFT. **22, 23. the house of Joseph**—the tribe of Ephraim, as distinguished from Manasseh (vs. 27).

24. the spies ... said, ... Show us, ... the entrance into the city—i.e., the avenues to the city, and the weakest part of the walls. **we will show thee mercy**—The Israelites might employ these means of getting possession of a place which was divinely appropriated to them: they might promise life and rewards to this man, though he and all the Canaanites were doomed to destruction (Josh. 2:12-14); but we may assume the promise was suspended on his embracing the true religion, or quitting the country, as he did. If they had seen him to be firmly opposed to either of these alternatives, they would not have constrained him by promises any more than by threats to betray his countrymen. But if they found him disposed to be

ADAM CLARKE

depart from among them, as God would not destroy them with the Amalekites. From them came Hemath, who was the father of the house of Rechab, 1 Chron. ii. 55, and the Rechabites, of whom we have a remarkable account Jer. xxxv. 1, etc.

17. *The city was called Hormah.* This appears to be the same transaction mentioned in Num. xxi. 1, etc.

18. *Judah took Gaza . . . and Askelon . . . and Ekron.* There is a most remarkable variation here in the Septuagint: "But Judah did not possess Gaza, nor the coast thereof; neither Askelon, nor the coasts thereof; neither Ekron, nor the coasts thereof; neither Azotus, nor its adjacent places: and the Lord was with Judah." This is the reading of the Vatican and other copies of the Septuagint; but the Alexandrian MS. and the text of the Complutensian and Antwerp Polyglots agree more nearly with the Hebrew text. St. Augustine and Procopius read the same as the Vatican MS.; and Josephus expressly says that the Israelites took only Askelon and Azotus, but did not take Gaza nor Ekron. And the whole history shows that these cities were not in the possession of the Israelites, but of the Philistines; and if the Israelites did take them at this time, as the Hebrew text states, they certainly lost them in a very short time after.

19. *And the Lord was with Judah; and he drave out the inhabitants of the mountain; but could not drive out the inhabitants of the valley, because they had chariots of iron.* Strange! were the iron chariots too strong for Omnipotence? The whole of this verse is improperly rendered. The first clause, *The Lord was with Judah,* should terminate the eighteenth verse, and this gives the reason for the success of this tribe. Here then is a complete period; the remaining part of the verse refers either to a different time or to the rebellion of Judah against the Lord, which caused Him to withdraw His support. This is the turn given to the verse by Jonathan ben Uzziel, the Chaldee paraphrast: "And the word of Jehovah was in the support of the house of Judah, and they extirpated the inhabitants of the mountains; but afterwards, when they sinned, they were not able to extirpate the inhabitants of the plain country, because they had chariots of iron."

20. *They gave Hebron unto Caleb.* See this whole transaction explained Josh. xiv. 12, etc.

21. *The Jebusites dwell with the children of Benjamin.* Jerusalem was situated partly in the tribe of Judah and partly in the tribe of Benjamin the northern part belonging to the latter tribe, the sourthern to the former. The Jebusites had their strongest position in the part that belonged to Benjamin, and from this place they were not wholly expelled till the days of David. See the notes on v. 8. What is said here of Benjamin is said of Judah, Josh. xv. 63. There must be an interchange of the names in one or other of these places. *Unto this day.* As the Jebusites dwelt in Jerusalem till the days of David, by whom they were driven out, and the author of the Book of Judges states them to have been in possession of Jerusalem when he wrote, therefore this book was written before the reign of David.

22. *The house of Joseph, they also went up against Beth-el.* That is, the tribe of Ephraim and the half-tribe of Manasseh. who dwelt beyond Jordan. Bethel was not taken by Joshua, though he took Ai, which was nigh to it.

23. *Beth-el . . . the name of the city before was Luz.* Concerning this city and its names, see the notes on Gen. xxviii. 19.

24. *Shew us . . . the entrance into the city.* Taken in whatever light we choose, the conduct of this man was execrable. He was a traitor to his country, and he was accessory to the destruction of the lives and property of his fellow citizens, which he most sinfully betrayed, in order to save his own. According to the rules and laws of war, the children of Judah might avail themselves of such men and their information, but this does not lessen, on the side of this traitor, the turpitude of the action.

26. *The land of the Hittites.* Probably some place beyond the land of Canaan, in Arabia, whither this people emigrated when expelled

MATTHEW HENRY

III. Zebulun, perhaps inclining to the sea-trade, for it was foretold that it should be a haven for ships, neglected to reduce Kitron and Nahalol (*v.* 30), and only made the inhabitants of those places tributaries to them.

IV. Asher quitted itself worse than any of the tribes (*v.* 31, 32), not only in leaving more towns than any of them in the hands of the Canaanites, but in submitting to the Canaanites instead of making them tributaries.

V. Naphtali also permitted the Canaanites to live among them (*v.* 33), only by degrees they got them so far under as to exact contributions from them.

VI. Dan was so far from extending his conquests where his lot lay that, wanting spirit to make head against the Amorites, he was forced by them to retire into the mountains and inhabit the cities there, but durst not venture into the valley, where, it is probable, the chariots of iron were, *v.* 34. In Jacob's blessing Judah is compared to a lion, Dan to a serpent; now observe how Judah with his lion-like courage prospered and prevailed, but Dan with all his serpentine subtlety could get no ground; craft and artful management do not always effect the wonders they pretend to.

Upon the whole matter it appears that the people of Israel were generally very careless both of their duty and interest in this thing; they did not what they might have done to expel the Canaanites and make room for themselves. The same thing that kept their fathers forty years out of Canaan kept them now out of the full possession of it, and that was unbelief. Distrust of the power and promise of God lost them their advantages, and ran them into a thousand mischiefs.

CHAPTER 2

Verses 1–5

It was the privilege of Israel that they had particular messages sent them from heaven, as there was occasion, for reproof, for correction, and for instruction. Besides the written word which they had before them to read, they often *heard a word behind them, saying, This is the way,* Isa. xxx. 21. Here begins that way of God's dealing with them. In these verses we have a very awakening sermon that was preached to them when they began to cool in their religion.

I. The preacher was an *angel of the Lord* (*v.* 1). Such extraordinary messengers we sometimes find in this book employed in the raising up of the judges that delivered Israel, as Gideon and Samson; and now, to show how various are the good offices they do for God's Israel, here is one sent to preach to them, to prevent their falling into sin and trouble.

II. The persons to whom this sermon was preached were *all the children of Israel, v.* 4. A great congregation for a great preacher! The place is called *Bochim* (*v.* 1), because it gained that name upon this occasion. All Israel needed the reproof and warning here given.

III. The sermon itself is short, but very close. God here tells them plainly, 1. What he had done for them, *v.* 1. He had brought them out of Egypt, a land of slavery and toil, into Canaan, a land of rest, liberty, and plenty. 2. What he had promised them: *I said, I will never break my covenant with you.* 3. What were his just and reasonable expectations from them (*v.* 2): that being taken into covenant with God they should make no league with the Canaanites, who were both his enemies and theirs,—that having set up his altar they should throw down their altars, lest they should be a temptation to them to serve their gods. 4. How they had in this very thing, which he had most insisted on, disobeyed him: "But you have not in so small a matter obeyed my voice." 5. How they must expect to smart by and by for this their folly, *v.* 3. Those deceive themselves who expect advantage by friendship with those that are enemies to God.

IV. The good success of this sermon is very remarkable: The people *lifted up their voice and wept, v.* 4. But this was not enough; they wept, but we do not find that they reformed, that they went home and destroyed all the remains of idolatry and idolaters among them. Many are melted under the word that harden again before they are cast into a new mould. However, this general weeping, 1. Gave a new name to the place (*v.* 5): they called it *Bochim, Weepers.* 2. It gave occasion for a solemn sacrifice: They *sacrificed there unto the Lord,* having (as is supposed) met at Shiloh, where God's altar was.

Verses 6–23

The angel had foretold that the Canaanites and

JAMIESON, FAUSSET, BROWN

serviceable, and to aid the invaders in executing the will of God, they might promise to spare him. **26. Luz**—(See on Gen. 12:8, 28:19). **27-36.** The same course of subjugation was carried on in the other tribes to a partial extent, and with varying success. Many of the natives, no doubt, during the progress of this exterminating war, saved themselves by flight and became, it is thought, the first colonists in Greece, Italy, and other countries. But a large portion made a stout resistance and retained possession of their old abodes in Canaan. In other cases, when the natives were vanquished, avarice led the Israelites to spare the idolaters, contrary to the express command of God; and their disobedience to His orders in this matter involved them in many troubles which this book describes.

CHAPTER 2

VSS. 1-10. AN ANGEL SENT TO REBUKE THE PEOPLE AT BOCHIM. **1, 2, an angel . . . came from Gilgal to Bochim**—We are inclined to think, from the authoritative tone of his language, that he was the Angel of the Covenant (Exod. 23:20; Josh. 5: 14); the same who appearerd in human form and announced himself captain of the Lord's host. His coming from Gilgal had a peculiar significance, for there the Israelites made a solemn dedication of themselves to God on their entrance into the promised land; and the memory of that religious engagement, which the angel's arrival from Gilgal awakened, gave emphatic force to his rebuke of their apostasy.

Bochim, "the weepers," was a name bestowed evidently in allusion to this incident or the place, which was at or near Shiloh.

I said, I will never break my covenant with you . . . but ye have not obeyed my voice—The burden of the angel's remonstrance was that God would inviolably keep His promise; but they, by their flagrant and repeated breaches of their covenant with Him, had forfeited all claim to the stipulated benefits. Having disobeyed the will of God by voluntarily courting the society of idolaters and placing themselves in the way of temptation, He left them to suffer the punishment of their misdeeds.

4, 5. when the Lord spake these words . . . the people lifted up their voice, and wept—The angel's expostulation made a deep and painful impression. But the reformation was but temporary, and the gratifying promise of a revival which this scene of emotion held out, was, ere long, blasted by speedy and deeper relapses into the guilt of defection and idolatry.

ADAM CLARKE

by Joshua. The man himself appears to have been a Hittite, and to perpetuate the name of his city he called the new one which he now founded Luz, this being the ancient name of Bethel.

27. *Beth-shean.* Called by the Septuagint Scythopolis, or "the city of the Scythians." On these towns see the notes, Josh. xvii. 12-13.

29. *Neither did Ephraim.* See the notes on the parallel passages, Josh. xvi. 5-10.

30. *Neither did Zebulun drive out.* See on Josh. xix. 10-15.

31. *Neither did Asher.* See on Josh. xix. 24-31.

Accho. Supposed to be the city of Ptolemais, near to Mount Carmel.

33. *Neither did Naphtali.* See the notes on Josh. xix. 32-39.

35. *The Amorites would dwell in mount Heres.* They perhaps agreed to dwell in the mountainous country, being unable to maintain themselves on the plain, and yet were so powerful that the Danites could not totally expel them; they were, however, laid under tribute, and thus the house of Joseph had the sovereignty.

36. *Akrabbim.* Of "scorpions"; probably so called from the number of those animals in that place. *From the rock, and upward.* The Vulgate understand by *sela,* "a rock," the city Petra, which was the capital of Arabia Petraea.

CHAPTER 2

1. *An angel of the Lord.* In the preceding chapter we have a summary of several things which took place shortly after the death of Joshua, especially during the time in which the elders lived (that is, the men who were contemporary with Joshua, but survived him) and while the people continued faithful to the Lord. In this chapter, and some parts of the following, we have an account of the same people abandoned by their God and reduced to the heaviest calamities because they had broken their covenant with their Maker. This chapter, and the first eight verses of the next, may be considered as an epitome of the whole book, in which we see on one hand the crimes of the Israelites, and on the other the punishments inflicted on them by the Lord; their repentance, and return to their allegiance; and the long-suffering and mercy of God, shown in pardoning their backslidings and delivering them out of the hands of their enemies.

The *angel of the Lord,* mentioned here, is variously interpreted. Some think it was Phinehas, the high priest, which is possible; others, that it was a prophet, sent to the place where they were now assembled, with an extraordinary commission from God, to reprove them for their sins, and to show them the reason why God had not rooted out their enemies from the land; this is the opinion of the Chaldee paraphrast, consequently of the ancient Jews. Others think that an angel, properly such, is intended; and several are of opinion that it was the Angel of the Covenant, the Captain of the Lord's host, which had appeared unto Joshua, chap. v. 14, and no less than the Lord Jesus Christ himself. I think it more probable that some extraordinary human messenger is meant, as such messengers, and indeed prophets, apostles, etc., are frequently termed *angels,* that is, "messengers" of the Lord. The person here mentioned appears to have been a resident at Gilgal, and to have come to Bochim on this express errand.

I will never break my covenant. Nor did God ever break it. A covenant is never broken but by him who violates any of the conditions, the covenant is then broken, and by that party alone; and the conditions on the other side are null and void.

3. *I will not drive them out from before you.* Their transgressions, and breach of the covenant, were the reasons why they were not put in entire possession of the Promised Land. See note at the end of this chapter.

5. *They called the name of that place Bochim.* The word *bochim* signifies "weepings" or "lamentations"; and is translated by the Septuagint

MATTHEW HENRY

their idols would be a snare to Israel; now the historian undertakes to show that they were so, and, that this may appear the more clear, he looks back a little, and takes notice, 1. Of their happy settlement in the land of Canaan. Joshua, having distributed this land among them, dismissed them to the quiet and comfortable possession of it (*v.* 6). 2. Of their continuance in the faith and fear of God's holy name as long as Joshua lived, *v.* 7. 3. Of the death and burial of Joshua, which gave a fatal stroke to the interests of religion among the people, *v.* 8, 9. 4. Of the rising of a new generation, *v.* 10. They were so entirely devoted to the world, so intent upon the business of it or so indulgent of the flesh in ease and luxury, that they never minded the true God and his holy religion, and so were easily drawn aside to false gods and their abominable superstitions.

A general idea of the series of things in Israel during the time of the judges,

I. The people of Israel forsook the God of Israel. In general, *they did evil*, nothing could be more evil, that is, more provoking to God, nor more prejudicial to themselves, and it was *in the sight of the Lord*. In particular, 1. They *forsook the Lord* (*v.* 12, and again *v.* 13); this was one of the two great evils they were guilty of, Jer. ii. 13. They had been joined to the Lord in covenant, but now they forsook him, as a wife *treacherously departs from her husband*. 2. When they forsook the only true God they did not turn atheists, nor were they such fools as to say, *There is no God*; but they followed other gods: so much remained of pure nature as to own a God, yet so much appeared of corrupt nature as to multiply gods, and take up with any, and to follow the fashion, not the rule, in religious worship. *Baalim* signifies *lords*, and *Ashtaroth blessed ones*, both plural, for when they forsook Jehovah, who is one, they had gods many and lords many.

II. The God of Israel was hereby provoked to anger, and delivered them up into the hand of their enemies, *v.* 14. 15. 1. The scale of victory turned against them. God would rather give the success to those that had never known nor owned him than to those that had done both, but had now deserted him. 2. The balance of power then turned against them of course.

III. The God of infinite mercy took pity on them in their distresses, though they had brought themselves into them by their own sin and folly, and wrought deliverance for them. Here observe, 1. The inducement of their deliverance. It came purely from God's pity and tender compassion; the reason was fetched from within himself. It is not so much the burden of sin as the burden of affliction that they are said to groan under. It is true they deserved to perish for ever under his curse, yet, this being the day of his patience and our probation, he does not stir up all his wrath. 2. The instruments of their deliverance. God raised up judges from among themselves, as there was occasion, men to whom God gave extraordinary qualifications to reform and deliver Israel, and whose great attempts he crowned with wonderful success: *The Lord was with the judges* when he raised them up, and so they became saviours. Observe, (1) In the days of the greatest degeneracy and distress of the church there shall be some whom God will make fit to redress its grievances and set things to rights. (2) God endues men with wisdom and courage, gives them hearts to act and venture. All that are in any way the blessings of their country must be looked upon as the gifts of God.

IV. The degenerate Israelites were not effectually and thoroughly reformed, no, not by their judges, *v.* 17–19. They had been espoused to God, but broke the marriage-covenant, and went a-whoring after these gods. Idolatry is spiritual adultery. *They corrupted themselves more than their fathers*, strove to outdo them in multiplying strange gods and inventing profane and impious rites of worship, as it were in contradiction to their reformers.

V. God's just resolution hereupon was still to continue the rod over them. After Joshua's death, little was done for a long time against the Canaanites: Israel indulged them, and grew familiar with them, and therefore God would not drive them out any more, *v.* 21. God chose their delusions, Isa. lxvi. 4. Thus men cherish and indulge their own corrupt appetites and passions, and therefore God justly leaves them to themselves under the power of their sins, which will be their ruin. *So shall their doom be; they themselves have decided it.*

JAMIESON, FAUSSET, BROWN

6-10. And when Joshua had let the people go—This passage is a repetition of Joshua 24:29-31. It was inserted here to give the reader the reasons which called forth so strong and severe a rebuke from the angel of the Lord. During the lifetime of the first occupiers, who retained a vivid recollection of all the miracles and judgments which they had witnessed in Egypt and the desert, the national character stood high for faith and piety. But, in course of time, a new race arose who were strangers to all the hallowed and solemnizing experience of their fathers, and too readily yielded to the corrupting influences of the idolatry that surrounded them.

11-19. Wickedness of the New Generation after Joshua. **11-19. the children of Israel did evil in the sight of the Lord**—This chapter, together with the first eight verses of the next, contains a brief but comprehensive summary of the principles developed in the following history. An attentive consideration of them, therefore, is of the greatest importance to a right understanding of the strange and varying phases of Israelitish history, from the death of Joshua till the establishment of the monarchy.

served Baalim—The plural is used to include all the gods of the country. **13. Ashtaroth**—Also a plural word, denoting all the female divinities, whose rites were celebrated by the most gross and revolting impurities. **14. the anger of the Lord was hot against Israel, and he delivered them into the hands of the spoilers that spoiled them**—Adversities in close and rapid succession befell them.

But all these calamities were designed only as chastisements—a course of correctional discipline by which God brought His people to see and repent of their errors; for as they returned to faith and allegiance, He "raised up judges" (vs. 16), **which delivered them out of the hand of those that spoiled them**—The judges who governed Israel were strictly God's vicegerents in the government of the people, He being the supreme ruler. Those who were thus elevated retained the dignity as long as they lived; but there was no regular, unbroken succession of judges. Individuals, prompted by the inward, irresistible impulse of God's Spirit when they witnessed the depressed state of their country, were roused to achieve its deliverance. It was usually accompanied by a special call, and the people seeing them endowed with extraordinary courage or strength, accepted them as delegates of Heaven, and submitted to their sway. Frequently they were appointed only for a particular district, and their authority extended no farther than over the people whose interests they were commissioned to protect. They were without pomp, equipage, or emoluments attached to the office. They had no power to make laws; for these were given by God; nor to explain them, for that was the province of the priests—but they were officially upholders of the law, defenders of religion, avengers of all crimes, particularly of idolatry and its attendant vices.

ADAM CLARKE

"bewailings"; and it is supposed that the place derived its name from these lamentations of the people. Some think the place itself, where the people were now assembled, was Shiloh, now named *Bochim* because of the above circumstance. It should be observed that the angel speaks here in the person of God, by whom he was sent, as the prophets frequently do.

11. *Served Baalim.* The word *baalim* signifies "lords." Their false gods they considered supernatural rulers or governors, each having his peculiar district and office; but when they wished to express a particular *baal,* they generally added some particular epithet, a Baal-zephon, Baal-peor, Baal-zebub, Baal-shamayim. The two former were adored by the Moabites; Baal-zebub, by the Ekronites. Baal-berith was honored at Shechem; and Baal-shamayim, the "lord or ruler of the heavens," was adored among the Phoenicians, Syrians, Chaldeans.

12. *Which brought them out of the land of Egypt.* This was one of the highest aggravations of their offense; they forsook the God who brought them out of Egypt, a place in which they endured the most grievous oppression, and were subjected to the most degrading servitude, from which they never could have rescued themselves; and they were delivered by such a signal display of the power, justice, and mercy of God as should never have been forgotten, because the most stupendous that had ever been exhibited.

14. *The hands of spoilers.* Probably marauding parties of the Canaanites, making frequent incursions in their lands, carrying away cattle, spoiling their crops.

15. *The hand of the Lord was against them.* The "power" which before protected them when obedient was now turned against them because of their disobedience. They not only had not God with them, but they had God against them.

16. *The Lord raised up judges.* That is, leaders, generals, and governors, raised up by an especial appointment of the Lord, to deliver them from, and avenge them on, their adversaries.

17. *Went a whoring after other gods.* Idolatry, or the worship of strange gods, is frequently termed adultery, fornication, and whoredom in the sacred writings. As many of their idolatrous practices were accompanied with impure rites, the term was not only metaphorically but literally proper.

18. *The Lord was with the judge.* God himself was King, and the judge was His representative. *It repented the Lord.* He changed His purpose towards them; He purposed to destroy them because of their sin; they repented and turned to Him, and He changed this purpose.

19. *When the judge was dead.* It appears that in general the office of the judge was for life. *Their stubborn way.* Their "hard or difficult way." Most sinners go through great tribulation in order to get to eternal perdition; they would have had less pain in their way to heaven.

20. *The anger of the Lord was hot.* They were as fuel by their transgressions; and the displeasure of the Lord was as a fire about to kindle and consume that fuel.

22. *That through them I may prove Israel.* There appeared to be no other way to induce this people to acknowledge the true God but by permitting them to fall into straits from which they could not be delivered but by His especial providence.

23. *Without driving them out hastily.* Had God expelled all the ancient inhabitants at once, we plainly see from the subsequent conduct of the people that they would soon have abandoned His worship, and in their prosperity forgotten their Deliverer. At first He drove out as many as were necessary in order to afford the people, as they were then, a sufficiency of room to settle in; as the tribes increased in population, they were to extend themselves to the uttermost of their assigned borders, and expel all the remaining inhabitants.

MATTHEW HENRY

CHAPTER 3

Verses 1–7

We are here told what remained of the old inhabitants of Canaan. 1. There were some of them that kept together in united bodies, unbroken (*v.* 3): *The five lords of the Philistines*, namely, Ashdod, Gaza, Askelon, Gath, and Ekron, 1 Sam. vi. 17. There was a particular nation called *Canaanites*, that kept their ground with the Sidonians, upon the coast of the great sea. And in the north the Hivites held much of Mount Lebanon. But, besides these, 2. There were everywhere in all parts of the country some scatterings of the nations (*v.* 5), Hittites, Amorites, &c.

Now concerning these remnants of the natives observe,

I. How wisely God permitted them to remain. It is mentioned in the close of the foregoing chapter as an act of God's justice, that he let them remain for Israel's correction. But here another construction is put upon it, and it appears to have been an act of God's *wisdom*, that he let them remain for Israel's real advantage, that those who *had not known the wars of Canaan* might *learn war*, *v.* 1, 2. Because their country lay very much in the midst of enemies it was therefore necessary they should be well disciplined, that they might defend their coasts when invaded, and might hereafter enlarge their coast as God had promised them.

II. How wickedly Israel mingled themselves with those that did remain. 1. They joined in marriage with the Canaanites (*v.* 6), though they could not advance either their honour or their estate by marrying with them. 2. Thus they were brought to join in worship with them; they served their *gods* (*v.* 6), *Baalim and the groves* (*v.* 7), that is, the images that were worshipped in groves of thick trees, which were a sort of natural temple. In such unequal matches there is more reason to fear that the bad will corrupt the good than to hope that the good will reform the bad, as there is in laying two pears together, the one rotten and the other sound. When they inclined to worship other gods they *forgot the Lord their God.*

Verses 8–11

We now come to the records of the government of the particular judges, the first of which was Othniel, in whom the story of this book is knit to that of Joshua. In this short narrative of Othniel's government we have,

I. The distress that Israel was brought into for their sin, *v.* 8. God being justly displeased with them laid them open to the nations, set them to sale as goods he would part with, and the first that laid hands on them was Chushan-rishathaim, king of that Syria which lay between the two great rivers of Tigris and Euphrates, thence called *Mesopotamia*, which signifies *in the midst of rivers.* Aiming to enlarge his dominions, he invaded the two tribes first on the other side Jordan that lay next him, and afterwards, perhaps by degrees, penetrated into the heart of the country, and as far as he went put them under contribution, exacting it with rigour, and perhaps quartering soldiers upon them.

II. Their return to God in this distress: *When he slew them, then they sought him* whom before they had slighted. The *children of Israel*, even the generality of them, *cried unto the Lord*, *v.* 9. Those who in the day of their mirth had cried to Baalim and Ashtaroth now that they are in trouble cry to the Lord.

III. God's return in mercy to them for their deliverance. 1. The deliverer was Othniel, who married Caleb's daughter, one of the old stock that had *seen the works of the Lord.* He was now, we may suppose, far advanced in years, when God raised him up to this honour. 2. Whence he had his commission, not of man, nor by man; but *the Spirit of the Lord came upon him* (*v.* 10), the spirit of wisdom and courage to qualify him for the service, and a spirit of power to excite him to it. 3. What method he took. He first judged Israel, reproved them, and reformed them, and then went out to war. This was the right method. Let sin at home be conquered, and then enemies abroad will be the more easily dealt with. Thus let Christ be our Judge and Law-giver, and then *he will save us*, and on no other terms, Isa. xxxiii. 22. 4. What good success he had. He prevailed to break the yoke of the oppression, for it is said, *The Lord delivered Chushan-rishathaim into his hand.* 5. The happy consequence of Othniel's good services. The land had rest, forty years; and the benefit would have been perpetual if they had kept close to God and their duty.

Verses 12–30

Ehud is the next of the judges whose achievements

JAMIESON, FAUSSET, BROWN

CHAPTER 3

Vss. 1-4. NATIONS LEFT TO PROVE ISRAEL. **1. these are the nations which the Lord left, to prove Israel**—This was the special design of these nations being left, and it evinces the direct influence of the theocracy under which the Israelites were placed. These nations were left for a double purpose: in the first instance, to be instrumental, by their inroads, in promoting the moral and spiritual discipline of the Israelites; and also to subserve the design of making them acquainted with war, in order that the young, more especially, who were total strangers to it, might learn the use of weapons and the art of wielding them.

5-7. BY COMMUNION WITH THESE THE ISRAELITES COMMIT IDOLATRY. **5-7. the children of Israel dwelt among the Canaanites**—The two peoples by degrees came to be on habits of intercourse. Reciprocal alliances were formed by marriage till the Israelites, relaxing the austerity of their principles, showed a growing conformity to the manners and worship of their idolatrous neighbors.

8-11. OTHNIEL DELIVERS ISRAEL. **8-11. sold them**—i.e., delivered them into the hand of Chushan-rishathaim, or Chushan, "the wicked." This name had been probably given him from his cruel and impious character. **served Chushan-rishathaim eight years**—by the payment of a stipulated tribute yearly, the raising of which must have caused a great amount of labor and privation.

9. when the children of Israel cried unto the Lord—In their distress they had recourse to earnest prayer, accompanied by humble and penitent confession of their errors.

Othniel—(See on Josh. 15:17; ch. 1: 13). His military experience qualified him for the work, while the gallant exploits he was known to have performed, gained him the full confidence of his countrymen in his ability as a leader. **10. The Spirit of the Lord came upon him, and he judged Israel, and went out to war**—Impelled by a supernatural influence, he undertook the difficult task of government at this national crisis—addressing himself to promote a general reformation of manners, the abolition of idolatry, and the revival of pure religion. After these preliminary measures, he collected a body of choice warriors to expel the foreign oppressors. **the Lord delivered Chushan-rishathaim king of Mesopotamia into his hand; and his hand prevailed against Chushan-rishathaim**—No details are given of this war, which, considering the resources of so potent a monarch, must have been a determined struggle But the Israelitish arms were crowned through the blessing of God with victory, and Canaan regained its freedom and independence. **11. Othniel . . . died**—How powerful the influence of one good man is, in church or state, is best found in his loss [BISHOP HALL].

ADAM CLARKE

CHAPTER 3

1. *Now these are the nations.* The nations left to prove the Israelites were the five lordships or satrapies of the Philistines, viz., Gath, Askelon, Ashdod, Ekron, and Gaza; the Sidonians, the Hivites of Lebanon, Baal-hermon, etc.; with the remains of the Canaanites, viz., the Hittites, Amorites, Perizzites, and Jebusites.

2. *That . . . Israel might know, to teach them war.* This was another reason why the Canaanites were left in the land, that the Israelites might not forget military discipline, but habituate themselves to the use of arms, that they might always be able to defend themselves against their foes. Had they been faithful to God, they would have had no need of learning the art of war; but now arms became a sort of necessary substitute for that spiritual strength which had departed from them.

4. *To know whether they would hearken.* This would be the consequence of the Canaanites being left among them: if they should be faithful to God, their enemies would not be able to enslave them; should they be rebellious, the Lord would abandon them to their foes.

6. *And they took their daughters.* They formed matrimonial alliances with those proscribed nations, served their idols, and thus became *one* with them in politics and religion.

7. *Served Baalim and the groves.* No *groves* were ever worshipped, but the deities who were supposed to be resident in them; and in many cases temples and altars were built in groves, and the superstition of consecrating groves and woods to the honor of the deities was a practice very usual with the ancients. But it is very probable that the word *asheroth,* which we translate *groves,* is a corruption of the word *ashtaroth,* the moon or Venus. *Ashtaroth* is read in this place by the Chaldee Targum, the Syriac, the Arabic, and the Vulgate.

8. *Chushan-rishathaim. Kushan,* the "wicked" or "impious"; and so the word is rendered by the Chaldee Targum, the Syriac, and the Arabic, wherever it occurs in this chapter. *King of Mesopotamia.* King of *Aram naharayim,* "Syria of the two rivers," translated *Mesopotamia* by the Septuagint and Vulgate. It was the district situated between the Tigris and Euphrates. *Served Chushan . . . eight years.* He overran their country, and forced them to pay a very heavy tribute.

9. *Raised up . . . Othniel the son of Kenaz.* This noble Hebrew was of the tribe of Judah, and nephew and son-in-law to Caleb, whose praise stands without abatement in the sacred records. Othniel had already signalized his valor in taking Kirjath-sepher, which appears to have been a very hazardous exploit. By his natural valor, experience in war, and the peculiar influence of the Divine Spirit, he was well qualified to inspire his countrymen with courage, and to lead them successfully against their oppressors.

10. *His hand prevailed.* We are not told of what nature this war was, but it was most decisive; and the consequence was an undisturbed peace of forty years, during the whole life of Othniel. By *the spirit of the Lord* coming upon him the Chaldee understands the spirit of prophecy; others understand the spirit of fortitude and extraordinary courage, as opposed to the spirit of fear or faintness of heart; but as Othniel was judge, and had many offices to fulfil besides that of a general, he had need of the Spirit of God, in the proper sense of the word, to enable him to guide and govern this most refractory and fickle people; and his receiving it for these purposes shows that the political state of the Jews was still a theocracy.

MATTHEW HENRY

are related in this history, and here is an account of his actions.

I. When Israel sins again God raises up a new oppressor, *v.* 12–14. Perhaps they thought they might make the more bold with their old sins because they saw themselves in no danger from their old oppressor; the powers of that kingdom were weakened and brought low. But God *strengthened Eglon king of Moab against them.* This oppressor lay nearer to them than the former, and therefore would be the more mischievous to them. The king of Moab took to his assistance the Ammonites and Amalekites (*v.* 13), and this strengthened him; and we are here told how they prevailed. 1. They beat them in the field: They *went and smote Israel* (*v.* 13), not only those tribes that lay next them on the other side Jordan, but those also within Jordan, for they made themselves masters of *the city of palm-trees*, near the place where Jericho had stood, for that was so called (Deut. xxxiv. 3). 2. They made them to serve (*v.* 14), that is, exacted tribute from them, either the fruits of the earth in kind or money in lieu of them.

II. When Israel prays again God raises up a new deliverer (*v.* 15), named *Ehud.*

1. That he was a Benjamite. The city of palm-trees lay within the lot of this tribe, by which it is probable that they suffered most, and therefore stirred first to shake off the yoke. The weakest of all the tribes, yet out of it God raised up this deliverer.

2. That he was left-handed, as it seems many of that tribe were, *ch.* xx. 16. Benjamin signifies *the son of the right hand*, and yet multitudes of them were left-handed; for men's natures do not always answer their names. God chose this left-handed man to be the man of his right hand, whom he would *make strong for himself*, Ps. lxxx. 17. It was *God's right hand* that gained Israel the victory (Ps. xliv. 3), not the right hand of the instruments he employed.

3. We are here told what Ehud did for the deliverance of Israel out of the hands of the Moabites.

(1) He put to death Eglon the king of Moab; I say, *put him to death*, not murdered or assassinated him, but as a judge, or minister of divine justice, executed the judgments of God upon him.

[1] He had a fair occasion of access to him. Being an ingenious active man, and fit to stand before kings, his people chose him to carry a present in the name of all Israel, over and above their tribute, to their great lord the king of Moab, that they might find favour in his eyes, *v.* 15. Ehud went on his errand to Eglon, offered his present with the usual ceremony and expressions of dutiful respect, the better to colour what he intended and to prevent suspicion.

[2] It should seem, from the first, he designed to be the death of him. That he compassed and imagined the death of this tyrant appears by the preparation he made of a weapon for the purpose, a short dagger, which might easily be concealed under his clothes (*v.* 16). This he wore on his right thigh, that it might be the more ready to his left hand, and might be the less suspected.

[3] He contrived how to be alone with him, which he might the more easily be now that he had not only made himself known to him, but ingratiated himself by the present. He begged a private audience, and obtained it in a withdrawing-room, here called a *summer parlour*. He told the king he had a secret errand to him, who thereupon ordered all his attendants to withdraw, *v.* 19.

[4] When he had him alone he soon dispatched him. Ehud demands his attention to *a message from God* (*v.* 20), and that message was a dagger. The message was delivered, not to his ear, but immediately, and literally, to his heart, into which the fatal knife was thrust, and was left there, *v.* 21, 22. Eglon signifies a *calf*, and he fell like a fatted calf, by the knife, an acceptable sacrifice to divine justice. No such commissions are now given, and to pretend to them is to blaspheme God, and make him patronize the worst of villainies.

[5] Providence wonderfully favoured his escape, when he had done the execution. The tyrant fell silently, without any shriek or out-cry, which might have been overheard by his servants at a distance. The heroic executioner of this vengeance shut the doors after him, took the key with him, and passed through the guards with an air of innocence, and boldness, and unconcernedness. The servants that attended in the antechamber, coming to the door of the inner parlour, when Ehud had gone, to know their master's pleasure, and finding it locked and all quiet, concluded he had lain down to sleep. Thus by their care not to disturb his sleep they lost the opportunity of revenging his death. The servants at length opened the door, and found their master had *slept indeed his long sleep*, *v.* 25. Ehud by this

JAMIESON, FAUSSET, BROWN

12-30. EHUD SLAYS EGLON. **12-14. the children of Israel did evil again in the sight of the Lord**—The Israelites, deprived of the moral and political influences of Othniel, were not long in following their native bias to idolatry. **the Lord strengthened Eglon king of Moab**—The reigning monarch's ambition was to recover that extensive portion of his ancient territory possessed by the Israelites. In conjunction with his neighbors, the Ammonites and the Amalekites, sworn enemies of Israel, he first subjected the eastern tribes; then crossing the Jordan, he made a sudden incursion on western Canaan, and in virtue of his conquests, erected fortifications in the territory adjoining Jericho [JOSEPHUS], to secure the frontier, and fixed his residence there. This oppressor was permitted, in the providence of God, to triumph for eighteen years.

15. Ehud son of Gera—descended from Gera, one of Benjamin's sons (Gen. 46:21). **left-handed**—This peculiarity distinguished many in the Benjamite tribe (ch. 20:16). But the original word is rendered in some versions "both-handed," a view countenanced by I Chron. 12:2.

by him the children of Israel sent a present unto Eglon the king of Moab—the yearly tribute, which, according to Eastern fashion, would be borne with ostentatious ceremony and offered (vs. 18) by several messengers.

16. Ehud made him a dagger . . . and he did gird it . . . upon his right thigh—The sword was usually worn on the left side; so that Ehud's was the more likely to escape detection.

19. quarries—rather graven images (Deut. 7:25; Jer. 8:19; 51:52); statues of Moabite idols, the sight of which kindled the patriotic zeal of Ehud to avenge this public insult to Israel on its author. **I have a secret errand unto thee, O king; who said, Keep silence**—"Privacy"—a signal for all to withdraw. **20. a summer parlour**—*Heb.*, chamber of cooling—one of those retired edifices which Oriental grandees usually have in their gardens, and in which they repose during the heat of the day. **21. Ehud put forth his left hand**—The whole circumstance of this daring act—the death of Eglon without a shriek, or noise—the locking of the doors—the carrying off the key—the calm, unhurried deportment of Ehud—show the strength of his confidence that he was doing God service.

ADAM CLARKE

12. *The children of Israel did evil.* They forgot the Lord and became idolaters, and God made those very people, whom they had imitated in their idolatrous worship, the means of their chastisement. *The Lord strengthened Eglon the king of Moab.* The success he had against the Israelites was by the especial appointment and energy of God. *Eglon* is supposed to have been the immediate successor of Balak. Some great men have borne names which, when reduced to their grammatical meaning, appear very ridiculous; the word *Eglon* signifies a "little calf"!

13. *The city of palm trees.* This the Targum renders "the city of Jericho"; but Jericho had been destroyed by Joshua, and certainly was not rebuilt till the reign of Ahab, long after this, 1 Kings xvi. 34. However, as Jericho is expressly called "the city of palm trees," Deut. xxxiv. 3, the city in question must have been in the vicinity or plain of Jericho, and the king of Moab had seized it as a frontier town contiguous to his own estates.

15. *Ehud the son of Gera . . . a man left-handed.* "A man lame in his right hand," and therefore obliged to use his left. The Septuagint render it "an ambidexter," a man who could use both hands alike. It is well known that to be an ambidexter was in high repute among the ancients. In chap. xx. 16 of this book we have an account of 700 men of Benjamin, each of whom was "lame of his right hand," and yet slinging stones to a hair's breadth without missing; these are generally thought to be ambidexters. *Sent a present unto Eglon.* This is generally understood to be the tribute money which the king of Moab had imposed on the Israelites.

17. *Eglon was a very fat man.* The *ish bari* of the text is translated by the Septuagint "a very beautiful or polite man," and in the Syriac, "a very rude man." It probably means what we call lusty or corpulent.

18. *Made an end to offer the present.* Presents, tribute, etc., in the Eastern countries were offered with very great ceremony; and to make the more parade several persons, ordinarily slaves, sumptuously dressed, and in considerable number, were employed to carry what would not be a burden even to one. This appears to have been the case in the present instance.

19. *He . . . turned . . . from the quarries. Pesilim.* Some of the versions understand this word as meaning idols or graven images, or some spot where the Moabites had a place of idolatrous worship. As *pasal* signifies to "cut, hew, or engrave," it may be applied to the images thus cut, or the place or quarry whence they were digged; but it is most likely that idols are meant.

20. *I have a message from God unto thee. Debar elohim li aleycha,* "a word of the gods to me, unto thee." It is very likely that the word *elohim* is used here to signify idols, or the *pesilim* mentioned above, v. 19. Ehud, having gone so far as this place of idolatry, might feign he had there been worshipping, and that the *pesilim* had inspired him with a message for the king; and this was the reason why the king commanded silence, why every man went out, and why he rose from his seat or throne, that he might receive it with the greater respect. This, being an idolater, he would not have done to any message coming from the God of Israel.

22. *The haft also went in after the blade.* As the instrument was very short, and Eglon very corpulent, this might readily take place.

24. *He covereth his feet.* He has lain down on his sofa in order to sleep; when this was done they dropped their slippers, lifted up their feet, and covered them with their long, loose garments.

MATTHEW HENRY

means made his escape to Sierath, *a thick wood*, *v.* 26.

(2) Ehud, having slain the king of Moab, gave a total rout to the forces of the Moabites that were among them, and so effectually shook off the yoke of their oppression. [1] He raised an army immediately in Mount Ephraim, at some distance from the headquarters of the Moabites, and headed them himself, *v.* 27. The trumpet he blew was indeed a jubilee-trumpet, proclaiming liberty, and a joyful sound it was to the oppressed Israelites, who for a long time had heard no other trumpets than those of their enemies. [2] Like a pious man, and as one that did all this in faith, he took encouragement himself, and gave encouragement to his soldiers, from the power of God engaged for them (*v.* 28): "*Follow me, for the Lord hath delivered your enemies into your hands.*" [3] Like a politic general, he first secured the fords of Jordan, set strong guards upon all those passes, to cut off the communications. He then fell upon them, and put them all to the sword: *There escaped not a man* of them. The consequence of this victory was that the power of the Moabites was wholly broken in the land of Israel. The country was cleared of these oppressors, and *the land had rest eighty years*, *v.* 30.

Verse 31

The other side of the country which lay south-west was in that time infested by the Philistines, against whom Shamgar made head. 1. It seems Israel needed deliverance, for *he delivered Israel*; how great the distress was, Deborah afterwards related in her song (*ch.* v. 6), that *in the days of Shamgar the highways were unoccupied*, &c. 2. God raised him up to deliver them, as it should seem, while Ehud was yet living. So inconsiderable were the enemies for number that it seems the killing of 600 of them amounted to a deliverance of Israel, and so many he slew with an ox-goad, or, as some read it, *a plough share*. He that has the residue of the Spirit could, when he pleased, make ploughmen judges and generals, and fishermen apostles. It is no matter how weak the weapon is if God direct and strengthen the arm. An ox-goad, when God pleases, shall do more than Goliath's sword.

JAMIESON, FAUSSET, BROWN

27. he blew a trumpet in the mount of Ephraim—summoned to arms the people of that mountainous region, which, adjoining the territory of Benjamin, had probably suffered most from the grievous oppression of the Moabites.

28. they went down after him, and took the fords—(See on Josh. 2:7). With the view of preventing all escape to the Moabite coast, and by the slaughter of 10,000 men, Ehud rescued his country from a state of ignominious vassalage.

31. after him was Shamgar—No notice is given of the tribe or family of this judge; and from the Philistines being the enemy that roused him into public service, the suffering seems to have been local—confined to some of the western tribes. **slew . . . six hundred men with an oxgoad**—This instrument is eight feet long and about six inches in circumference. It is armed at the lesser end with a sharp prong for driving the cattle, and on the other with a small iron paddle for removing the clay which encumbers the plough in working. Such an instrument, wielded by a strong arm, would do no mean execution. We may suppose, however, for the notice is very fragmentary, that Shamgar was only the leader of a band of peasants, who by means of such implements of labor as they could lay hold of at the moment, achieved the heroic exploit recorded.

ADAM CLARKE

26. *Passed beyond the quarries.* Beyond the *pesilim*, which appear to have been the Moabitish borders, where they had set up those hewn stones as landmarks, or sacred boundary stones.

28. *Took the fords of Jordan.* It is very likely that the Moabites, who were on the western side of Jordan, hearing of the death of Eglon, were panic-struck, and endeavored to escape over Jordan at the fords near Jericho, when Ehud blew his trumpet in the mountains of Ephraim, and thus to get into the land of the Moabites, which lay on the east of Jordan; but Ehud and his men, seizing the only pass by which they could make their escape, slew 10,000 of them in their attempt to cross at those fords. What is called here *the fords* was doubtless the place where the Israelites had passed over Jordan when they (under Joshua) took possession of the Promised Land.

29. *All lusty, and all men of valour.* Picked, chosen troops, which Eglon kept among the Israelites to reduce and overawe them.

31. *And after him was Shamgar the son of Anath.* Dr. Hales supposes that "Shamgar's administration in the West, included Ehud's administration of eighty years in the East; and that, as this administration might have been of some continuance, so this Philistine servitude, which is not noticed elsewhere, might have been of some duration; as may be incidentally collected from Deborah's thanksgiving, chap. v. 6."

MATTHEW HENRY

CHAPTER 4

Verses 1–3

I. Israel backsliding from God: They again *did evil in his sight*. See in this, 1. The strange strength of corruption, which hurries men into sin notwithstanding the most frequent experience of its fatal consequences. 2. The common ill effects of a long peace. The land had rest eighty years, which should have confirmed them in their religion; but, on the contrary, it made them secure and wanton. 3. The great loss which a people sustains by the death of good governors. *They did evil, because Ehud was dead.*

II. Israel oppressed by their enemies. When they forsook God, he forsook them; and then they became an easy prey to every spoiler. Jabin reigned in Hazor, as another of the same name, and perhaps his ancestor, had done before him, whom Joshua routed and slew, and burnt his city, Josh. xi. 1, 10. But it seems, in process of time, the city was rebuilt. Jabin, and his general Sisera, did mightily oppress Israel. That which aggravated the oppression was, that these Canaanites had formerly been conquered and subdued by Israel, were of old sentenced to be their servants (Gen. ix. 25), and might now have been under their feet if their own slothfulness, cowardice, and unbelief, had not suffered them thus to get ahead.

III. Israel returning to their God: They *cried unto the Lord*, when distress drove them to him, and they saw no other way of relief.

Verses 4–9

The year of the redeemed at length came, when Israel was to be delivered out of the hands of Jabin.

I. The preparation of the people for their deliverance, by the prophetic conduct and government of Deborah, *v.* 4, 5. Her name signifies a *bee*; and she answered her name by her industry, sagacity, and great usefulness to the public, her sweetness to her friends and sharpness to her enemies. She is said to be *the wife of Lapidoth*; but, the termination not being commonly found in the name of a man, some make this the name of a place: she was *a woman of Lapidoth*. Others take it appellatively, Lapidoth signifies *lamps*. The Rabbis say she had employed herself in making wicks for the lamps of the tabernacle. Or she was a woman of *illuminations*, or of *splendours*, one that was extraordinarily knowing and

JAMIESON, FAUSSET, BROWN

CHAPTER 4

Vss. 1-17. DEBORAH AND BARAK DELIVER ISRAEL FROM JABIN AND SISERA. **1. The children of Israel again did evil in the sight of the Lord, when Ehud was dead**—The removal of the zealous judge Ehud again left his infatuated countrymen without the restraint of religion.

2. Jabin, king of Canaan—Jabin, a royal title (Josh. 11:1). The second Jabin built a new capital on the ruins of the old (Josh. 11: 10, 11). The northern Canaanites had recovered from the effect of their disastrous overthrow in the time of Joshua, and now triumphed in their turn over Israel. This was the severest oppression to which Israel had been subjected. But it fell heaviest on the tribes in the north, and it was not till after a grinding servitude of twenty years that they were awakened to view it as the punishment of their sins and to seek deliverance from God.

Deborah, a prophetess—A woman of extraordinary knowledge, wisdom, and piety, instructed in divine knowledge by the Spirit and accustomed to interpret His will; who acquired an extensive influence, and was held in universal respect, insomuch that she became the animating spirit of the government and discharged all the special duties of a judge, except that of military leader. **wife of Lapidoth**—rendered by some "a woman of splendors."

ADAM CLARKE

CHAPTER 4

1. *When Ehud was dead.* Why not "when Shamgar was dead"? Does this not intimate that Shamgar was not reckoned in the number of the judges?

2. *Jabin king of Canaan.* Probably a descendant of the Jabin mentioned Josh. xi. 1, etc., who had gathered together the wrecks of the army of that Jabin defeated by Joshua.

3. *Nine hundred chariots of iron.* Chariots armed with iron scythes, as is generally supposed; they could not have been made all of iron, but they might have been shod with iron, or had iron scythes projecting from the axle on each side, by which infantry might be easily cut down or thrown into confusion.

4. *Deborah, a prophetess.* One on whom the Spirit of God descended, and who was the instrument of conveying to the Israelites the knowledge of the divine will, in things sacred and civil. *She judged Israel.* This is, I believe, the first instance of female government on record. Deborah seems to have been supreme in both civil and religious affairs; and *Lapidoth*, her husband, appears to have had no hand in the government. But the original may as well be translated "a woman of Lapidoth" as *the wife of Lapidoth*.

MATTHEW HENRY

wise. Concerning her we are here told, 1. That she was intimately acquainted with God; she was *a prophetess*. 2. That she was entirely devoted to the service of Israel. She judged Israel at the time that Jabin oppressed them. She judged, not as a princess, by any civil authority conferred upon her, but as a prophetess, and as God's mouth to them. It is said she *dwelt*, or, as some read it, she *sat* under a palm-tree, called ever after from her *the palm-tree of Deborah*. Either she had her house under that tree or she had her judgment-seat in the open air, under the shadow of that tree, which was an emblem of the justice she sat there to administer, which will thrive and grow against opposition, as palms under pressures.

II. The project laid for their deliverance. She was not herself fit to command an army in person, being a woman; but she nominated one that was fit, Barak of Naphtali. He could do nothing without her head, nor she without his hands; but both together made a complete deliverer, and effected a complete deliverance.

1. By God's direction, she orders Barak to raise an army, and engage Jabin's forces, that were under Sisera's command, *v.* 6, 7. Barak, it may be, had been meditating some great attempt against the common enemy. But two things discouraged him: (1) He wanted a commission to levy forces; this therefore Deborah here gives him under the broad seal of heaven, which, as a prophetess, she had a warrant to affix to it: "*Hath not the Lord God of Israel commanded it? Go and draw towards Mount Tabor.*" [1] She directs him what number of men to raise—10,000. [2] Whence he should raise them—only out of his own tribe, and that of Zebulun next adjoining. And, [3] She orders him where to make his rendezvous—at Mount Tabor, in his own neighbourhood.

(2) When he had an army raised, he knew not how he should have an opportunity of engaging the enemy. "Well," says Deborah, "*I will draw unto thee Sisera and his army.*" She gave him an express promise of success: *I will* (that is, God will, in whose name I speak) *deliver them into thy hand.*

2. At Barak's request, she promises to go along with him to the field of battle. (1) Barak insisted much upon the necessity of her presence, which would be to him better than a council of war (*v.* 8): "*If thou wilt go with me* to direct and advise me, and in every difficult case to let me know God's mind, *then I will go* with all my heart, and not fear the chariots of iron; otherwise not." Nothing would be a greater satisfaction to him than to have the prophetess with him to animate the soldiers and to be consulted as an oracle upon all occasions. (2) Deborah promised to go with him, *v.* 9. No toil nor peril shall discourage her from doing the utmost that becomes her for the service of her country. Deborah was the weaker vessel, yet had the stronger faith. But though she agrees to go with Barak, if he insists upon it, she gives him a hint proper enough to move a soldier not to insist upon it: "*The journey thou undertakest shall not be for thy honour*; not so much for thy honour as if thou hadst gone by thyself; for *the Lord shall sell Sisera into the hands of a woman*"; that is, [1] The world would ascribe the victory to the hand of Deborah. [2] God would complete the victory by the hand of Jael, which would be some eclipse to his glory. But Barak values the good success of his enterprise more than his honour; and therefore will by no means drop his request.

Verses 10–16

I. Barak beats up for volunteers, and soon has his quota of men ready, *v.* 10. Though the tribes of Zebulun and Naphtali were chiefly depended on, yet it appears by Deborah's song that some had come in to him from other tribes (Manasseh and Issachar), and more were expected that came not, from Reuben, Dan, and Asher, *ch.* v. 14–17. The 11th verse, concerning the removal of Heber, one of the families of the Kenites, out of the wilderness of Judah, in the south, comes in for the sake of what was to follow concerning the exploit of Jael, a wife of that family.

II. Sisera takes the field with a very numerous and powerful army (*v.* 12, 13). Sisera's confidence was chiefly in his chariots; therefore particular notice is taken of them, 900 *chariots of iron*, which, with the scythes fastened to their axle-trees, when they were driven into an army of footmen, did terrible execution.

III. Deborah gives orders to engage the enemy, *v.* 14. Josephus says that when Barak saw Sisera's army drawn up, and attempting to surround the mountain on the top of which he and his forces lay encamped, his heart quite failed him, but Deborah animated him to make a descent upon Sisera, "*The Lord hath delivered Sisera into thy hand.*" It was well for Barak that he had Deborah with him; for

JAMIESON, FAUSSET, BROWN

5. she dwelt under the palm tree—or, collectively, palm grove. It is common still in the East to administer justice in the open air, or under the canopy of an umbrageous tree.

6. she sent and called Barak—by virtue of her official authority as judge. **Kedesh-naphtali**—situated on an eminence, little north of the Sea of Galilee, and so called to distinguish it from another Kedesh in Issachar.

Hath not the Lord of Israel commanded—a Hebrew form of making an emphatic communication. **Go and draw toward Mount Tabor**—an isolated mountain of Galilee, northeast corner of the plain of Esdraelon. It was a convenient place of rendezvous, and the enlistment is not to be considered as limited to 10,000, though a smaller force would have been inadequate.

8. Barak said unto her, If thou wilt go with me, then I will go—His somewhat singular request to be accompanied by Deborah was not altogether the result of weakness. The Orientals always take what is dearest to the battlefield along with them; they think it makes them fight better. The policy of Barak, then, to have the presence of the prophetess is perfectly intelligible as it would no less stimulate the valor of the troops, than sanction, in the eyes of Israel, the uprising against an oppressor so powerful as Jabin.

9. the Lord shall sell Sisera into the hand of a woman—This was a prediction which Barak could not understand at the time; but the strain of it conveyed a rebuke of his unmanly fears.

11. Now Heber the Kenite . . . pitched his tent—It is not uncommon, even in the present day, for pastoral tribes to feed their flocks on the extensive commons that lie in the heart of inhabited countries in the East (see on ch. 1:16). **plain of Zaanaim**—This is a mistranslation for "the oaks of the wanderers." The site of the encampment was under a grove of oaks, or terebinths, **in the upland valley of Kedesh. 13. the river of Kishon**—The plain on its bank was chosen as the battlefield by Sisera himself, who was unconsciously drawn thither for the ruin of his army. **14. Barak went down from mount Tabor**—It is a striking proof of the full confidence Barak and his troops reposed in Deborah's assurance of victory, that they relinquished their advantageous position on the hill and rushed into the plain in face of the iron chariots they so much dreaded.

ADAM CLARKE

6. *She sent and called Barak.* She appointed him to be general of the armies on this occasion, which shows that she possessed the supreme power in the state.

9. *The Lord shall sell Sisera into the hand of a woman.* Does not this mean, If I go with thee, the conquest shall be attributed to me, and thou wilt have no honor? Or is it a prediction of the exploit of Jael? In both these senses the words have been understood. It seems, however, more likely that Jael is intended.

The Septuagint made a remarkable addition to the speech of Barak: "If thou wilt go with me I will go; but if thou wilt not go with me, I will not go; because I know not the day in which the Lord will send his angel to give me success." By which he appears to mean that, although he was certain of a divine call to this work, yet, as he knew not the time in which it would be proper for him to make the attack, he wished that Deborah, on whom the Divine Spirit constantly rested, would accompany him to let him know when to strike that blow, which he knew would be decisive.

10. *Ten thousand men at his feet.* Ten thousand footmen. He had no chariots; his army was all composed of infantry.

11. *Hohab the father in law of Moses.* For a circumstantial account of this person, and the meaning of the original word *chothen*, which is translated "son in law" in Gen. xix. 14, see the notes on Exod. ii. 15-16, 18; iii. 1; iv. 20, 24; and xviii. 5.

14. *Up; for this is the day.* This is exactly the purpose for which the Septuagint states, v. 8, that Barak wished Deborah to accompany him. *Went down from mount Tabor.* He had probably encamped his men on and near the summit of this mount.

MATTHEW HENRY

she made up what was defective, 1. In his conduct, by telling him, *This is the day*. 2. In his courage, by assuring him of God's presence.

IV. God himself routs the enemy's army, *v*. 15. It was not so much the bold and surprising alarm which Barak gave their camp that dispirited and dispersed them, but God's terror seized their spirits. *The stars*, it seems, fought against them, *ch*. v. 20. Josephus says that a violent storm of hail which beat in their faces drove them back; so that they became a very easy prey to the army of Israel, and Deborah's words were made good: "*The Lord has delivered them into thy hand*."

V. Barak pursues the scattered forces, even to their general's headquarters at Harosheth (*v*. 16), and spares none whom God had delivered into his hand to be destroyed: *There was not a man left*.

Verses 17–24

We have seen the army of the Canaanites totally routed.

I. The fall of their general, Sisera, captain of the host. Let us trace the steps of this mighty man's fall.

1. He quitted his chariot, and took to his feet, *v*. 15, 17. How miserable doth Sisera look now he is dismounted! He who but lately trusted to his arms with so much assurance must now trust to his heels only with so little.

2. He fled for shelter to the tents of the Kenites, having no stronghold, nor any place of his own in reach to retire to. And that which encouraged him to go thither was that at this time there was peace between his master and the house of Heber. Sisera thought he might therefore be safe among them.

3. Jael invited him in, and bade him very welcome. Probably she stood at the tent door, to enquire what news from the army, and what was the success of the battle which was fought not far off. (1) She invited him in. Perhaps she stood waiting for an opportunity to show kindness to any distressed Israelite, if there should be occasion for it. (2) She made very much of him, and seemed mighty careful to have him easy, as her invited guest. We must suppose she kept her tent as quiet as she could, and free from noise, that he might sleep the sooner and the faster. And now was Sisera least safe when he was most secure.

4. When he lay fast asleep she drove a long nail through his temples, so fastened his head to the ground, and killed him, *v*. 21. It was a divine warrant that justified her in the doing of it; and therefore, since no such extraordinary commissions can now be pretended, it ought not in any case to be imitated. The laws of friendship and hospitality must be religiously observed, and we must abhor the thought of betraying any whom we have invited and encouraged to put a confidence in us. And, as to this act of Jael (like that of Ehud in the chapter before), we have reason to think she was conscious of such a divine impulse upon her spirit to do it as did abundantly satisfy herself that it was well done. He that thought to destroy Israel with his many iron chariots is himself destroyed with one iron nail.

II. The glory and joy of Israel hereupon. 1. Barak their leader finds his enemy dead, (*v*. 22), and no doubt, he was very well pleased to find his work done so well to his hand, and so much to the glory of God and the confusion of his enemies. 2. Israel is completely delivered out of the hands of Jabin king of Canaan, *v*. 23, 24. They not only shook off his yoke by this day's victory, but they afterwards prosecuted the war against him, till they had destroyed him.

JAMIESON, FAUSSET, BROWN

15. the Lord discomfited Sisera—*Heb*., threw his army into confusion; men, horses, and chariots being intermingled in wild confusion. The disorder was produced by a supernatural panic (see on ch. 5:20). **so that Sisera lighted down off his chariot, and fled away on his feet**—His chariot being probably distinguished by its superior size and elegance, would betray the rank of its rider, and he saw therefore that his only chance of escape was on foot. **16. But Barak pursued . . . unto Harosheth**—Broken and routed, the main body of Sisera's army fled northward; others were forced into the Kishon and drowned (see on ch. 5:21).

17, 18. Sisera fled . . . to the tent of Jael—According to the usages of nomadic people, the duty of receiving the stranger in the sheik's absence devolves on his wife, and the moment the stranger is admitted into his tent, his claim to be defended or concealed from his pursuers is established. **19. she . . . gave him drink, and covered him**—Sisera reckoned on this as a pledge of his safety, especially in the tent of a friendly sheik. This pledge was the strongest that could be sought or obtained, after he had partaken of refreshments, and been introduced in the inner or women's apartment. **20. he said unto her, . . . when any man doth come and inquire of thee and say, Is there any man here? thou shalt say, No**—The privacy of the harem, even in a tent, cannot be intruded on without express permission.

21. Then Jael took a nail of the tent—most probably one of the pins with which the tent ropes are fastened to the ground. Escape was almost impossible for Sisera. But the taking of his life by the hand of Jael was murder. It was a direct violation of all the notions of honor and friendship that are usually held sacred among pastoral people, and for which it is impossible to conceive a woman in Jael's circumstances to have had any motive, except that of gaining favor with the victors. Though predicted by Deborah, it was the result of divine foreknowledge only—not the divine appointment or sanction; and though it is praised in the song, the eulogy must be considered as pronounced not on the moral character of the woman and her deed, but on the public benefits which, in the overruling providence of God, would flow from it.

ADAM CLARKE

15. *The Lord discomfited Sisera*. "The Lord confounded, threw them all into confusion, drove them pell-mell"—caused chariots to break and overthrow chariots, and threw universal disorder into all their ranks. In this case Barak and his men had little to do but kill and pursue, and Sisera, in order to escape, was obliged to abandon his chariot. There is no doubt all this was done by supernatural agency; God sent His angel and confounded them.

18. *Jael went out to meet Sisera*. He preferred the woman's tent because of secrecy; for, according to the etiquette of the Eastern countries, no person ever intrudes into the apartments of the women.

19. *She opened a bottle of milk*. She gave more than he requested, and her friendship increased his confidence and security.

20. *Stand in the door of the tent*. As no man would intrude into the women's apartment without permission, her simply saying, "There is no man in my tent," would preclude all search.

21. *A nail of the tent*. One of the spikes by which they fasten to the ground the cords which are attached to the cloth or covering. *He was fast asleep and weary*. As he lay on one side, and was overwhelmed with sleep through the heat and fatigues of the day, the piercing of his temples must have in a moment put him past resistence.

24. *The hand of the children of Israel prospered*. "It went, going"—they followed up this victory, and the consequence was, they utterly destroyed Jabin and his kingdom.

MATTHEW HENRY — CHAPTER 5

Verses 1–5

I. God is praised by a song, which is, 1. A very natural expression of rejoicing. *Is any merry? Let him sing*; and holy joy is the very soul and root of praise and thanksgiving. 2. A very proper expedient for perpetuating the remembrance of great events. Neighbours would learn this song one of another and children of their parents; and *one generation* would thus *praise God's works to another*, and *declare his mighty acts*, Ps. cxlv. 4, &c.

II. Deborah herself penned this song, as appears by *v*. 7. 1. She used her gifts as a prophetess in composing the song, and the strain throughout is very fine and lofty, the images are lively, the expressions elegant, and an admirable mixture there is in it of sweetness and majesty. 2. We may suppose she used her power as a princess, in obliging the conquering army of Israel to learn and sing this song. She had been the first wheel in the action, and now is so in the thanksgiving.

JAMIESON, FAUSSET, BROWN — CHAPTER 5

VSS. 1-31. DEBORAH AND BARAK'S SONG OF THANKSGIVING. **1. Then sang Deborah and Barak . . . on that day**—This noble triumphal ode was evidently the composition of Deborah herself.

ADAM CLARKE — CHAPTER 5

1. *Then sang Deborah and Barak*. There are many difficulties in this very sublime song, and learned men have toiled much to remove them. That there are several gross mistakes in our version will be instantly acknowledged by all who can critically examine the original.

MATTHEW HENRY

1. She begins with a general Hallelujah: *Praise* (or *bless*, for that is the word) *you the Lord*, *v.* 2. The design of the song is to give glory to God; this therefore is put first, to explain and direct all that follows, like the first petition of the Lord's prayer, *Hallowed be thy name*.

2. She calls to the great ones of the world, that sit at the upper end of its table, to attend to her song, and take notice of the subject of it: *Hear, O you kings! give ear, O you princes!* (1) She would have them know that horses and chariots are vain things for safety. (2) She would have them to join with her in praising the God of Israel, and no longer to praise their counterfeit deities. (3) She would have them take warning by Sisera's fate, and not dare to offer any injury to the people of God.

3. She looks back upon God's former appearances, and compares this with them. What God is doing should bring to our mind what he has done; for he is the same yesterday, to-day, and for ever (*v.* 4): *Lord, when thou wentest out of Sair*. This may be understood either, (1) Of the appearances of God's power and justice against the enemies of Israel to subdue and conquer them. God had led his people Israel from the country of Edom; he brought down under their feet Sihon and Og, striking them and their armies with such terror and amazement that they seemed apprehensive heaven and earth were coming together. Or it notes the glorious displays of the divine majesty, and the surprising effects of the divine power, enough to make the earth tremble, the heavens drop like snow before the sun, and the mountains to melt. Or, (2) It is meant of the appearances of God's glory and majesty to Israel, when he gave them his law at Mount Sinai. It was then literally true, *the earth trembled, and the heavens dropped*, &c. The Chaldee paraphrase applies it to the giving of the law, but has a strange descant on those words, *the mountains melted. Tabor, Hermon, and Carmel, contended among themselves: one said, Let the divine majesty dwell upon me; the other said, Let it dwell upon me; but God made it to dwell upon Mount Sinai, the meanest and least of all the mountains.* I suppose it means the least valuable, because barren and rocky.

Verses 6–11

I. Deborah describes the distressed state of Israel under the tyranny of Jabin. *From the days of Shamgar*, who did something towards the deliverance of Israel from the Philistines, to the days of Jael, the present day, in which Jael has so signalized herself, the country has been in a manner desolate. 1. No trade. All commerce ceased, and the highways were unoccupied; no caravans of merchants, as formerly. 2. No travelling. 3. No tillage. The fields must needs be laid waste and unoccupied when the inhabitants of the villages were obliged to take shelter for themselves and their families in walled and fenced cities. 4. No administration of justice. There was war in the gates where their courts were kept, *v.* 8. 5. No peace to him that went out nor to him that came in. The gates through which they passed and repassed were infested by the enemy; nay, the places of drawing water were alarmed by the archers—a mighty achievement to terrify the drawers of water. 6. Neither arms nor spirit to help themselves with, not a *shield nor spear seen among forty thousand*, *v.* 8.

II. She shows in one word what it was that brought all this misery upon them: *They chose new gods*, *v.* 8. It was their idolatry that provoked God to give them up thus into the hands of their enemies.

III. She takes notice of God's great goodness to Israel in raising up such as should redress these grievances. Herself first (*v.* 7): *Till that I Deborah arose*, to restrain and punish those who disturbed the public peace. Thus she became a mother in Israel, a nursing mother, such was the affection she bore to her people. Under her there were other governors of Israel (*v.* 9). Of these governors she says, *My heart is towards them*.

IV. She calls upon those who had a particular share in the advantages of this great salvation, to offer up particular thanks to God for it, *v.* 10, 11. 1. *You that ride on white asses*, that is, the nobility and gentry. Let such as are by this salvation restored, not only to their liberty as other Israelites, but to their dignity, speak God's praises. 2. Let those that *sit in judgment* be sensible of it, and thankful that the sword of justice is not struck out of their hand by the sword of war. 3. Let those that *walk by the way*, and meet with none there to make them afraid, speak of the goodness of God in ridding the roads of those banditti that had so long infested them. 4. Let those that have not their wells taken from them, or stopped up, nor are in danger of being caught by the enemy when they go forth to draw, *rehearse the acts of the Lord*, not Deborah's acts, nor Barak's, but the Lord's,

JAMIESON, FAUSSET, BROWN

2-3. The meaning is obscurely seen in our version; it has been better rendered thus, "Praise ye Jehovah; for the free are freed in Israel—the people have willingly offered themselves" [ROBINSON].

4, 5. Allusion is here made, in general terms, to God's interposition on behalf of His people. **Seir . . . the field of Edom**—represent the mountain range and plain extending along the south from the Dead Sea to the Elanitic Gulf. **thou wentest out**—indicates the storm to have proceeded from the south or southeast.

6-8. The song proceeds in these verses to describe the sad condition of the country, the oppression of the people, and the origin of all the national distress in the people's apostasy from God. Idolatry was the cause of foreign invasion and internal inability to resist it.

9. expresses gratitude to the respective leaders of the tribes which participated in the contest; but, above all, to God, who inspired both the patriotic disposition and the strength. **Speak**—i.e., join in this song of praise. **white asses**—Those which are purely white are highly prized, and being costly, are possessed only by the wealthy and great. "Ye that sit in judgment," has been rendered, "ye that repose on tapestries."

11-14. The wells which are at a little distance from towns in the East, are, in unsettled times, places of danger. But in peace they are scenes of pleasant and joyous resort.

ADAM CLARKE

4. *When thou wentest out of Seir.* Here is an illusion to the giving of the law, and the manifestation of God's power and glory at that time; and as this was the most signal display of His majesty and mercy in behalf of their forefathers, Deborah very properly begins her song with a commemoration of this transaction.

6. *The highways are unoccupied.* The land was full of anarchy and confusion, being everywhere infested with banditti. No public road was safe.

7. *The villages ceased.* The people were obliged to live together in fortified places; or in great numbers, to protect each other against the incursions of bands of spoilers.

8. *They chose new gods.* This was the cause of all their calamites; they forsook Jehovah, and served other gods; and *then was war in their gates*—they were hemmed up in every place, and besieged in all their fortified cities. And they were defenseless, they had no means of resisting their adversaries; for even *among forty thousand* men, there was neither spear nor shield to be seen.

10. *Ye that ride on white asses.* Perhaps *athonoth tsechoroth* should be rendered "sleek or well-fed asses." *Ye that sit in judgment. Yoshebey al middin;* some have rendered this, "ye who dwell in Middin." This was a place in the tribe of Judah, and is mentioned in Josh. xv. 61. *And walk by the way.* Persons who go from place to place for the purposes of traffic.

11. *In the places of drawing water.* As wells were very scarce in every part of the East, and travellers in such hot countries must have water, robbers and banditti generally took their sta-

MATTHEW HENRY

taking notice of his hand making peace in their borders. Observe in these acts of his, (1) Justice executed on his daring enemies. (2) Kindness shown to his trembling people, *the inhabitants of the villages*, who lay most open to the enemy. It is the glory of God to protect those that are most exposed, and to help the weakest.

Verses 12–23

I. Deborah stirs up herself and Barak to celebrate this victory in the most solemn manner. 1. Deborah, as a prophetess, must do it by a song, to compose and sing which she excites herself: *Awake, awake*, and again, *awake, awake*. 2. Barak, as a general, must do it by a triumph: *Lead thy captivity captive*. Though the army of Sisera was cut off in the field, and no quarter given, yet we may suppose in the prosecution of the victory, when the war was carried into the enemy's country, many not found in arms were seized and made prisoners of war.

II. She gives good reason for this praise and triumph, *v.* 13. 1. The Israelites had become few and inconsiderable, and yet to them God gave dominion over nobles. As long as any of God's Israel remain (and a remnant God will have in the worst of times) there is hope, be it ever so small a remnant, for God can make him that remains, though it should be but one single person, triumph over the most proud and potent. 2. Deborah was herself of the weaker sex, and the sex that from the fall had been sentenced to subjection, and yet the Lord authorized her to rule over the mighty men of Israel, who willingly submitted to her direction, and enabled her to triumph over the mighty men of Canaan.

III. She makes particular remarks on the several parties concerned in this great action, taking notice who fought against them, who fought for them, and who stood neutral.

1. Who fought against them. Jabin and Sisera had been mentioned in the history, but here it appears, (1) That Amalek was in league with Jabin. Ephraim is here said to act against Amalek (*v.* 14), probably intercepting and cutting off some forces of the Amalekites that were upon their march to join Sisera. (2) That others of the kings of Canaan, who had somewhat recovered themselves since their defeat by Joshua, joined with Jabin, and strengthened his army with their forces. These kings *came and fought*, *v.* 19. It is said of these kings that *they took no gain of money*, they were not mercenary troops hired into the service of Jabin.

2. Who fought for them. The several tribes that assisted in this great exploit are here spoken of with honour.

(1) Ephraim and Benjamin, those tribes among whom Deborah herself lived, bestirred themselves, and did bravely. Herein Benjamin had set them a good example among his people. "Ephraim moved *after thee, Benjamin*"; though Benjamin was the junior tribe, and much inferior, especially at this time, to Ephraim, both in number and wealth, yet when they led Ephraim followed.

(2) The ice being broken by Ephraim and Benjamin, Machir (the half-tribe of Manasseh beyond Jordan) and Zebulun sent in men that were very serviceable to this great design.

(3) Issachar did good service too; though he *saw that rest was good*, and therefore *bowed his shoulder to bear*, which is the character of that tribe (Gen. xlix. 15), yet they disdained to bear the yoke of Jabin's tribute, and now preferred the generous toils of war to a servile rest.

(4) Zebulun and Naphtali were the most bold and active of all the tribes, not only out of a particular affection to Barak their countryman, but because, they lying nearest to Jabin, the yoke of oppression lay heavier on their necks than on those of any other tribe.

(5) The stars from heaven appeared, or acted at least, on Israel's side (*v.* 20): *The stars in their courses*, according to the order and direction of him who is the great Lord of their hosts, *fought against Sisera*, by their malignant influences, or by causing the storms of hail and thunder which contributed so much to the rout of Sisera's army.

(6) The river of Kishon fought against their enemies. It swept away multitudes of those that hoped to make their escape through it, *v.* 21. Ordinarily, it was but a shallow river, and yet now, probably by the great rain that fell, it was so swollen, and the stream so deep and strong, that those who attempted to pass it were drowned.

(7) Deborah's own soul fought against them; she speaks of it with a holy exultation (*v.* 21): *O, my soul, thou hast trodden down strength.*

3. In this great engagement she observes who stood *neutral*, and did not side with Israel as might have been expected. No mention is made of Judah

JAMIESON, FAUSSET, BROWN

The poetess anticipates that this song may be sung, and the righteous acts of the Lord rehearsed at these now tranquil "places of drawing water." Deborah now rouses herself to describe, in terms suitable to the occasion, the preparation and the contest, and calls in a flight of poetic enthusiasm on Barak to parade his prisoners in triumphal procession.

19-22. describes the scene of battle and the issue. It would seem (vs. 19) that Jabin was reinforced by the troops of other Canaanite princes. The battlefield was near Taanach (now Ta'annuk), on a tell or mound in the level plain of Megiddo (now Leijun), on its southwestern extremity, by the left bank of the Kishon. **they took no gain of money**—They obtained no plunder.

Then follows a eulogistic enumeration of the tribes which raised the commanded levy, or volunteered their services—the soldiers of Ephraim who dwelt near the mount of the Amalekites, the small quota of Benjamin; "the governors," valiant leaders "out of Machir," the western Manasseh; and out of Zebulun.

the stars in their courses fought—A fearful tempest burst upon them and threw them into disorder.

the river of Kishon swept them away—The enemy was defeated near "the waters of Megiddo"—the sources and side streams of the Kishon: they that fled had to cross the deep and marshy bed of the torrent, but the Lord had sent a heavy rain—the waters suddenly rose—the warriors fell into the quicksands, and sinking deep into them, were drowned or washed into the sea [VAN DE VELDE]. **22. Then were the horse hoofs broken by the means of the prancings**—Anciently, as in many parts of the East still, horses were not shod. The breaking of the hoofs denotes the hot haste and heavy irregular tramp of the routed foe.

ADAM CLARKE

tions near tanks, pools, and springs, in order that they might suddenly fall upon those who came to drink; and when the country was badly governed, annoyances of this kind were very frequent. The victory gained now by the Israelites put the whole country under their own government, and the land was cleansed from such marauders. *Go down to the gates.* They may go down to the gates to receive judgment and justice as usual. It is well known that the gate was the place of judgment in the East.

12. *Lead thy captivity captive.* Make those captives who have formerly captivated us.

13. *Made him that remaineth.* This appears to be spoken of Barak, who is represented as being only a remnant of the people.

19. *The kings came and fought.* It is conjectured that Jabin and his confederates had invaded Manasseh, as both Taanach and Megiddo were in that tribe, and that they were discomfited by the tribes of Zebulun and Naphtali at Taanach and Megiddo, while Barak defeated Sisera at Mount Tabor. *They took no gain of money.* They expected much booty in the total rout of the Israelites; but they were defeated, and got no prey; or, if applied to the Israelites. They fought for liberty, not for plunder.

14. *Out of Ephraim . . . a root of them.* Deborah probably means that out of Ephraim and Benjamin came eminent warriors. Joshua, who was of the tribe of *Ephraim,* routed the Amalekites a short time after the Israelites came out of Egypt, Exod. xvii. 10. Ehud, who was of the tribe of *Benjamin,* slew Eglon, and defeated the Moabites, the friends and allies of the Ammonites and Amalekites. *Machir,* in the land of Gilead, produced eminent warriors; and *Zebulun* produced eminent statesmen, and men of literature. Probably Deborah speaks here of the past wars, and not of anything that was done on this occasion; for we know that no person from Gilead were present in the war between Jabin and Israel. See v. 17: "Gilead abode beyond Jordan."

15. *The princes of Issachar.* They were at hand and came willingly forth, at the call of Deborah, to this important war. *Barak . . . was sent on foot.* Should be translated "with his footmen or infantry." Thus the Alexandrian Septuagint understood it, rendering the clause thus: "Barak also sent forth his footmen into the valley." Luther has perfectly hit the meaning, "Barak with his footmen."

18. *Zebulun and Naphtali . . . jeoparded their lives.* The original is very emphatic, "They desolated their lives to death"—they were determined to conquer or die, and therefore plunged into the thickest of the battle.

20. *They fought from heaven.* The angels of God came to the assistance of Israel, and "the stars in their orbits fought against Sisera"; probably some thunderstorm, or great inundation from the river Kishon, took place at that time, which in poetic language was attributed to the stars.

21. *The river of Kishon swept them away.* This gives plausibility to the above conjecture, that there was a storm at this time which produced an inundation in the river Kishon, which the routed Canaanites attempting to ford were swept away.

22. *Then were the horsehoofs broken.* In very ancient times horses were not shod, nor are they to the present day in several parts of the East. Sisera had iron chariots when his hosts were routed; the horses that drew these, being strongly urged on by those who drove them, had their hoofs broken by the roughness of the roads; in consequence of which they became lame, and could not carry off their riders. This is marked as one cause of their disaster.

MATTHEW HENRY

nor Simeon among the tribes concerned, because they, lying so very remote from the scene of action, had not an opportunity to appear.

(1) Reuben basely declined the service, *v.* 15, 16. Two things hindered them from engaging:—[1] Their divisions. Not only for their division from Canaan by the river Jordan, which needed not to have hindered them had they been hearty in the cause, but it means either that they were divided among themselves, could not agree who should go or who should lead, or that they were divided in their opinion of this war from the rest of the tribes, and thought the attempt either not justifiable or not practicable. [2] Their business in the world: *Reuben abode among the sheepfolds,* a warmer and safer place than the camp, pretending they could not conveniently leave the sheep they tended.

(2) Dan and Asher did the same, *v.* 17. These two lay on the seacoast, and [1] Dan pretended he could not leave his ships but they would be exposed, and therefore *I pray thee have me excused.* [2] Asher pretended he must stay at home to repair the breaches which the sea had in some places made upon his land, and to fortify his works against the encroachments of it, or he abode in his creeks, or small havens, where his trading vessels lay to attend them.

(3) But above all Meroz is condemned, and a curse pronounced upon the inhabitants of it, *Because they came not to the help of the Lord, v.* 23. Probably this was some city that lay near the scene of action, and therefore the inhabitants had a fair opportunity of showing their obedience to God and their concern for Israel, and of doing good service to the common cause; but they basely declined it, for fear of Jabin's iron chariots, being willing to sleep in a whole skin. God looks upon those as against him that are not with him. This city of Meroz seems to have been at this time a considerable place, since something great was expected from it.

Verses 24–31

Deborah here concludes this triumphant song,

I. With the praises of Jael, her sister-heroine, whose valiant act had completed and crowned the victory. Her poetry is finest and most florid here in the latter end of the song. How honourably does she speak of Jael (*v.* 24), who preferred her peace with the God of Israel before her peace with the king of Canaan. *Blessed shall she be above women in the tent.* Those whose lot is cast in the tent, in a very low and narrow sphere of activity, if they serve God in that according to their capacity, shall in no wise lose their reward.

II. She concludes all with a prayer to God, 1. For the destruction of all his foes: "*So,* so shamefully, so miserably, *let all thy enemies perish, O Lord.*" 2. For the exaltation and comfort of all his friends. "But let those that love him, and heartily wish well to his kingdom among men, *be as the sun when he goeth forth in his strength.*"

The victory here celebrated with this song was of such happy consequence to Israel that for the best part of one age they enjoyed the peace which it opened the way to: *The land had rest forty years.*

JAMIESON, FAUSSET, BROWN

15. Then comes a reproachful notice of the tribes which did not obey the summons to take the field against the common enemy of Israel. By the "divisions," i.e., the watercourses which descend from the eastern hills unto the Jordan and Dead Sea. **For the divisions of Reuben there were great thoughts of heart**—They felt the patriotic impulse and determined, at first, to join the ranks of their western brethren, but resiled from the purpose, preferring their peaceful shepherd songs to the trumpet sound of war.

17. Gilead abode beyond Jordan—i.e., Both Gad and the eastern half to Manasseh chose to dwelt at ease in their Havoth-jair, or villages of tents, while Dan and Asher, both maritime tribes, continued with their ships and in their "breaches" (havens). The mention of these craven tribes is concluded (vs. 18) with a fresh burst of commendation on Zebulun and Naphtali.

23. Curse ye Meroz—a village on the confines of Issachar and Naphtali, which lay in the course of the fugitives, but the inhabitants declined to aid in their destruction.

24-27. is a most graphic picture of the treatment of Sisera in the tent of Jael. **butter**—curdled milk; a favorite beverage in the East.

28-30. In these verses a sudden transition is made to the mother of the Canaanite general, and a striking picture is drawn of a mind agitated between hope and fear—impatient of delay, yet anticipating the news of victory and the rewards of rich booty. **the lattice**—a lattice window—common to the houses in warm countries for the circulation of air. **her wise ladies**—maids of honor. **to every man a damsel or two**—Young maidens formed always a valued part of Oriental conquerors' war-spoils. But Sisera's mother wished other booty for him; namely, the gold-threaded, richly embroidered, and scarlet-colored cloaks which were held in such high esteem. The ode concludes with a wish in keeping with the pious and patriotic character of the prophetess.

ADAM CLARKE

For the divisions of Reuben. Either the Reubenites were divided among themselves into factions, which prevented their cooperation with their brethren, or they were divided in their judgment concerning the measures now to be pursued, which prevented them from joining with the other tribes till the business was entirely settled. The *thoughts of heart* and *searchings of heart* might refer to the doubts and uneasiness felt by the other tribes when they found the Reubenites did not join them; for they might have conjectured that they were either unconcerned about their liberty or were meditating a coalition with the Canaanites.

17. *Gilead abode beyond Jordan.* That is, the Gadites, who had their lot in those parts, and could not well come to the aid of their brethren at a short summons. But the words of Deborah imply a criminal neglect on the part of the Danites; they were intent upon their traffic, and trusted in their ships. Joppa was one of their seaports. *Asher continued on the sea shore.* The lot of Asher extended along the Mediterranean Sea; and being contiguous to Zebulun and Naphtali, they might have easily succored their brethren; but they had the pretense that their posts were unguarded, and they abode in their *breaches,* in order to defend them.

23. *Curse ye Meroz.* Where Meroz was is not known. *Curse ye bitterly.* "Curse with cursing"—use the most awful execrations. *Said the angel of the Lord.* That is, Barak, who was Jehovah's *angel* or "messenger" in this war; the person sent by God to deliver His people. *To the help of the Lord.* That is, to the help of the people of the Lord. *Against the mighty. Baggibborim,* "with the heroes"; that is, Barak and his men, together with Zebulun and Naphtali. These were the mighty men, or heroes, with whom the inhabitants of Meroz would not join.

24. *Blessed above women shall Jael . . . be.* She shall be highly celebrated as a most heroic woman; all the Israelitish women shall glory in her. I do not understand these words as expressive of the divine approbation towards Jael. The word *bless,* in both Hebrew and Greek, often signifies "to praise, to speak well of, to celebrate." This is most probably its sense here.

25. *She brought forth butter.* As the word *chemah,* here translated *butter,* signifies "disturbed, agitated," it is probable that buttermilk is intended.

26. *She smote off his head.* The original does not warrant this translation, nor is it supported by fact. "She smote his head," and transfixed him through the temples. It was his head that received the death wound, and the place where this wound was inflicted was the temples. The manner in which Jael dispatched Sisera seems to have been this: (1) Observing him to be in a profound sleep, she took a *workmen's hammer* and with one blow on the head deprived him of all sense. (2) She then took a tent nail and drove it through his temples, and thus pinned him to the earth, which she could not have done had she not previously stunned him with the blow on the head.

27. *At her feet he bowed. Bein ragleyha,* "between her feet." After having stunned him she probably sat down, for the greater convenience of driving the nail through his temples. *He bowed . . . he fell.* He probably made some struggles after he received the blow on the head, but could not recover his feet.

28. *Cried through the lattice.* This is very natural; in the women's apartments in the East the windows are latticed, to prevent them from sending or receiving letters, etc. The latticing is the effect of the jealousy which universally prevails in those countries. *Why is his chariot so long in coming?* Literally, Why is his chariot ashamed to come?

CHAPTER 6 (MATTHEW HENRY)

Verses 1–6

I. Israel's sin renewed: *They did evil in the sight of the Lord, v.* 1.

II. Israel's troubles repeated. This would follow of course; let all that sin expect to suffer; let all that return to folly expect to return to misery. Now as to this trouble, 1. It arose from a very despicable enemy. God delivered them into the hand of Midian

CHAPTER 6 (JAMIESON, FAUSSET, BROWN)

Vss. 1-6. The Israelites, for Their Sins, Oppressed by Midian. **1. the Lord delivered them into the hand of Midian**—Untaught by their former experiences, the Israelites again apostatized, and new sins were followed by fresh judgments. Midian had sustained a severe blow in the time of Moses (Num. 31:1-18); and the memory of that

CHAPTER 6 (ADAM CLARKE)

1. *Delivered them into the hand of Midian.* The Midianites were among the most ancient and inveterate of the enemies of Israel. They joined with the Moabites to seduce them to idolatry, and were nearly extirpated by them, Numbers xxxi. The Midianites dwelt on the

MATTHEW HENRY

(*v.* 1), that joined to Moab (Num. xxii. 4), a people that all men despised as uncultivated and unintelligent; a people that Israel had formerly subdued, and in a manner destroyed (see Num. xxxi. 7), and yet by this time so magnified, that they were capable of being made a very severe scourge to Israel. 2. It arose to a very formidable height (*v.* 2): *The hand of Midian prevailed*, purely by their multitude. God had promised to increase Israel as the sand on the sea shore; but their sin stopped their growth and diminished them, and then their enemies, though otherwise every way inferior to them, overpowered them with numbers. Here we have, (1) The Israelites imprisoned, or rather imprisoning themselves, in dens and caves, *v.* 2. This was owing purely to their own timorousness and faint-heartedness, that they would rather fly than fight; it was the effect of a guilty conscience. (2) The Israelites impoverished, greatly impoverished, *v.* 6. The Midianites made frequent incursions into the land of Canaan. This fruitful land was a great temptation to them. They came up against them (*v.* 3), pitched their camps among them (*v.* 4), and penetrated through the heart of the country as far as Gaza on the western side, *v.* 4. They let the Israelites alone to sow their ground, but towards harvest they came and seized all, and ate up and destroyed it, both grass and corn, and when they went away took with them the sheep and oxen. Now here we may see, [1] The justice of God in the punishment of their sin. [2] The consequence of God's departure from a people; when he goes all good goes and all mischiefs break in.

III. Israel's sense of God's hand revived at last. Seven years, year after year, did the Midianites make these inroads upon them, each we may suppose worse than the other (*v.* 1), until at last, all other succours failing, *Israel cried unto the Lord* (*v.* 6).

Verses 7–10

I. The cognizance God took of the cries of Israel, when at length they were directed towards him. Thus would he show how ready he is to forgive, how swift he is to show mercy, and how inclinable to hear prayer.

II. The method God took of working deliverance for them.

1. Before he sent an angel to raise them up a saviour he sent a prophet to reprove them for sin, and to bring them to repentance, *v.* 8. His errand was to convince them of sin, that, in their crying to the Lord, they might confess that with sorrow and shame, and not spend their breath in only complaining of their trouble. Note, (1) We have reason to hope God is designing mercy for us if we find he is by his grace preparing us for it. (2) The sending of prophets to a people, and the furnishing of a land with faithful ministers, is a token for good, and an evidence that God has mercy in store for them.

2. We have here the heads of the message which this prophet delivered to Israel, in the name of the Lord.

(1) He sets before them the great things God had done for them (*v.* 8, 9). [1] He brought them out of Egypt, where otherwise they would have continued in perpetual poverty and slavery. [2] He *delivered them out of the hands of all that oppressed them*; this is mentioned to intimate that the reason why they were not now delivered out of the hands of the oppressing Midianites was not for want of any power or goodwill in God. [3] He put them in quiet possession of this good land; this not only aggravated their sin, and affixed the brand of base ingratitude to it, but it justified God, and cleared him from blame upon account of the trouble they were now in.

(2) He shows the easiness and equity of God's demands and expectations from them (*v.* 10): "*I am the Lord your God*, to whom you lie under the highest obligations, *fear not the gods of the Amorites*."

(3) He charges them with rebellion against God, who had laid this injunction upon them: *But you have not obeyed my voice*.

Verses 11–24

It is not said what effect the prophet's sermon had upon the people, but we may hope it had a good effect, and that some of them at least repented and reformed upon it; for here, immediately after, we have the dawning of the day of their deliverance, by the effectual calling of Gideon to take upon him the command of their forces against the Midianites.

I. The person to be commissioned for this service was Gideon, the son of Joash, *v.* 14. The father kept up in his own family the worship of Baal (*v.* 25), which we may suppose this son, as far as was in his power, witnessed against. He was of the half tribe of Manasseh that lay in Canaan, of the family of Abiezer; the eldest house of that tribe, Josh. xvii. 2.

JAMIESON, FAUSSET, BROWN

disaster, no doubt, inflamed their resentment against the Israelites. They were wandering herdsmen, called "children of the East," from their occupying the territory east of the Red Sea, contiguous to Moab. The destructive ravages they are described as at this time committing in the land of Israel are similar to those of the Bedouin Arabs, who harass the peaceful cultivators of the soil. Unless composition is made with them, they return annually at a certain season, when they carry off the grain, seize the cattle and other property; and even life itself is in jeopardy from the attacks of those prowling marauders. The vast horde of Midianites that overran Canaan made them the greatest scourge which had ever afflicted the Israelites. **made . . . dens . . . in the mountains and caves**—not, of course, excavating them, for they were there already, but making them fit for habitation.

7-10. A PROPHET REBUKES THEM. **the Lord sent a prophet unto the children of Israel**—The curse of the national calamity is authoritatively traced to their infidelity as the cause.

ADAM CLARKE

eastern borders of the Dead Sea, and their capital was Arnon.

2. *Made them the dens which are in the mountains.* Nothing can give a more distressing description of the state of the Israelites than what is here related. They durst not reside in the plain country, but were obliged to betake themselves to dens and caves of the mountains, and live like wild beasts, and were hunted like them by their adversaries.

3. *Children of the east.* Probably those who inhabited Arabia Deserta, Ishmaelites.

4. *Encamped against them.* Wandering hordes of Midianites, Amalekites, and Ishmaelites came, in the times of harvest and autumn, and carried away their crops, their fruit, and their cattle. And they appear to have come early, encamped in the plains, and watched the crops till they were ready to be carried off. This is frequently the case even to the present day. *Till thou come unto Gaza.* That is, the whole breadth of the land, from Jordan to the coast of the Mediterranean Sea.

5. *They came up with their cattle and their tents.* All this proves that they were different tribes of wanderers who had no fixed residence; but, like their descendants the Bedouins or wandering Arabs, removed from place to place to get prey for themselves and forage for their cattle.

8. *The Lord sent a prophet.* The Jews say that this was Phinehas; but it is more likely that it was some prophet or teacher raised up by the Lord to warn and instruct them.

JOSEPH PARKER:

Israel cried unto the Lord. What was the divine answer to that cry? It was a prophet. Jewish legend says it was Phinehas, son of Eleazar. The prayer was answered by a man: "The Lord sent a prophet unto the children of Israel." A "prophet" is a teacher, a man who sees the largest relations of things, one who lives above the cloud and can see what is going on underneath it; a seer, a man of penetrating vision, a man whose eyes are within, and from whom God has hidden nothing of wisdom, grace, purpose, and issue. The age must be prepared for its prophets. When the age is haughty, self-contented, self-idolatrous, prophets go for nothing; they are the object of sneering remark; they may be caricatured, they may be turned into food for merriment; but when the age becomes like a door swinging on broken hinges, or like a sear and yellow leaf when all hope has died out of it, then men ask if there be not a prophet, or one who can pray—a seer who can penetrate beyond appearances and discover germs of life or hints of hope? It was so now. The prophet came, and delivered a judicial speech.

Here you find a reminder, a reference to history. Memory was awakened and turned upon the days that had gone. God works through recollection. Marvellous are the miracles which God works by the power of memory: memory goes back, and brings to mind things forgotten, uses them in the light of today, observes their action upon the circumstances which make up the immediate present; and oftentimes a man needs no hotter hell than an awakened and stimulated memory. The recollection was followed by a reproof: "But ye have not obeyed my voice," saying in effect: I have not changed; I was continuing the line; my purpose was one of deliverance and success and honor for Israel, but ye failed in obedience: first you became reluctant, hesitant, then weary, then you complained of monotony, then you said the yoke galled your shoulders, then you fell clean away, then you built Asherah and worshipped Baal; this is the reason of all that has come upon you; blame yourselves: for men who fall away from the road of obedience fail of the heaven of blessedness.—*The People's Bible*

MATTHEW HENRY

II. The person that gave him the commission was an *angel of the Lord*. This angel is here called *Jehovah*, the incommunicable name of God (*v.* 14, 16), and he said, *I will be with thee*.

1. This divine person appeared here to Gideon, and it is observable how he found him, (1) Retired—all alone. God often manifests himself to his people when they are out of the noise and hurry of this world. (2) Employed in threshing wheat, with a *staff* or *rod*, probably because he had but little to thresh, he needed not the oxen to tread it out. The work he was about was an emblem of that greater work to which he was now to be called, as the disciples' fishing was. From threshing corn he is fetched to thresh the Midianites, Isa. xli. 15. (3) Distressed; he was threshing his wheat, not in the threshing-floor, the proper place, but *by the wine-press*, in some private unsuspected corner, for fear of the Midianites.

2. Let us now see what passed between the angel and Gideon, who knew not with certainty, till after he was gone, that he was an angel, but supposed he was a prophet.

(1) The angel accosted him with respect, and assured him of the presence of God with him, *v.* 12. By this word, [1] He gives him his commission. [2] He inspires him with all necessary qualifications for the execution of his commission. [3] He assures him of success; for, *if God be for us, who can prevail against us?*

(2) Gideon gave a very melancholy answer to this joyful salutation (*v.* 13 : *O my Lord! if the Lord be with us why then has all this befallen us?* Gideon, as if not conscious to himself of anything great or encouraging in his own spirit, fastens only on the assurance the angel had given him of God's presence. The angel spoke in particular to him: *The Lord is with thee*; but he expostulates for all: *If the Lord be with us*, herding himself with the thousands of Israel, and admitting no comfort but what they might be sharers in, so far is he from the thoughts of monopolising it, though he had so fair an occasion given him. Gideon was a mighty man of valour, but as yet weak in faith. This was his weakness. We must not expect that the miracles which were wrought when a church was in the forming, and some great truth in the settling, should be continued and repeated when the formation and settlement are completed: no, nor that the mercies God showed to our fathers that served him, and kept close to him, should be renewed to us, if we degenerate and revolt from him.

(3) The angel gave him a very effectual answer to his objections, by giving him a commission to deliver Israel out of the hands of the Midianites, and assuring him of success therein, *v.* 14. Now the angel is called *Jehovah*, for he speaks as one having authority, and not as a messenger. [1] There was something extraordinary in the look he now gave to Gideon. He looked upon him, and smiled at the objections he made, but girded and clothed him with such power as would shortly enable him to answer them himself, and make him ashamed that ever he had made them. It was a speaking look, like Christ's upon Peter (Luke xxii. 61), a powerful look, a look that strangely darted new light and life into Gideon's breast. [2] But there was much more in what he said to him. *First*, He commissioned him to appear and act as Israel's deliverer. Such a one the few thinking people in the nation, and Gideon among the rest, were now expecting to be raised up, and now Gideon is told, "Thou art the man: *Go in this thy might*, this might wherewith thou art now threshing wheat; go and employ it to a nobler purpose; *I will make thee a thresher of men*." "Go, not in thy might, but go in *this* thy might, this which thou hast now received, *go in the strength of the Lord God*, that is, the strength with which thou must strengthen thyself." *Secondly*, He assured him of success. *Thou shalt save Israel from the hand of the Midianites*, and so shalt not only be an eye-witness, but a glorious instrument, of such wonders as thy *fathers told thee of*. Gideon, we may suppose, looked as one astonished at this strange and surprising power conferred upon him.

(4) Gideon made a very modest objection against this commission (*v.* 15): *O my Lord! wherewith shall I save Israel?* This question bespeaks him either, [1] Distrustful of God and his power. Or, [2] Inquisitive concerning the methods he must take: "Lord, I labour under all imaginable disadvantages for it; if I must do it, thou must put me in the way." Or rather, [3] Humble, self-diffident, and self-denying. The angel had honoured him, but see how meanly he speaks of himself: "My family is comparatively poor in Manasseh and I am the least, that have the least honour and interest, *in my father's house*; what can I pretend to do? I am utterly unfit for the service, and unworthy of the honour." God delights

JAMIESON, FAUSSET, BROWN

11-16. AN ANGEL SENDS GIDEON TO DELIVER THEM. **there came an angel of the Lord**—He appeared in the character and equipments of a traveller (vs. 21), who sat down in the shade to enjoy a little refreshment and repose. Entering into conversation on the engrossing topic of the times, the grievous oppression of the Midianites, he began urging Gideon to exert his well-known prowess on behalf of his country. Gideon, in replying, addresses him at first in a style equivalent (in *Hebrew*) to "sir," but afterwards gives to him the name usually applied to God. **an oak**—*Hebrew*, "the oak"—as famous in after-times. **Ophrah**—a city in the tribe of Manasseh, about sixteen miles north of Jericho, in the district belonging to the family of Abiezer (Josh. 17:2). **his son Gideon threshed wheat by the wine press**—This incident tells emphatically the tale of public distress. The small quantity of grain he was threshing, indicated by his using a flail instead of the customary treading of cattle—the unusual place, near a wine press, under a tree, and on the bare ground, not a wooden floor, for the prevention of noise—all these circumstances reveal the extreme dread in which the people were living.

13. if the Lord be with us, why then is all this befallen us?—Gideon's language betrays want of reflection, for the very chastisements God had brought on His people showed His presence with, and His interest in, them.

14. the Lord looked upon him, and said, Go in this thy might . . . have not I sent thee?—The command and the promise made Gideon aware of the real character of his visitor; and yet like Moses, from a sense of humility, or a shrinking at the magnitude of the undertaking, he excused himself from entering on the enterprise. And even though assured that, with the divine aid, he would overcome the Midianites as easily as if they were but one man, he still hesitates and wishes to be better assured that the mission was really from God. He resembles Moses also in the desire for a sign; and in both cases it was the rarity of revelations in such periods of general corruption that made them so desirous of having the fullest conviction of being addressed by a heavenly messenger. The request was reasonable, and it was graciously granted.

ADAM CLARKE

11. *There came an angel of the Lord.* The prophet came to teach and exhort; the angel comes to confirm the word of the prophet, to call and commission him who was intended to be their deliverer, and to work miracles, in order to inspire him with supernatural courage and a confidence of success. *Ophrah.* Or Ephra, was a city, or village rather, in the half-tribe of Manasseh, beyond Jordan.

His son Gideon threshed wheat. This is not the only instance in which a man taken from agricultural employments was made general of an army, and the deliverer of his country. Shamgar was evidently a ploughman, and with his oxgoad he slew many Philistines, and became one of the deliverers of Israel. *Threshed wheat by the winepress.* This was a place of privacy; he could not make a threshing floor in open day as the custom was, for fear of the Midianites, who were accustomed to come and take it away as soon as threshed. He got a few sheaves from the field and brought them home to have them privately threshed for the support of the family. As there could be no vintage among the Israelites in their present distressed circumstances, the winepress would never be suspected by the Midianites to be the place of threshing corn.

13. *And Gideon said unto him.* This speech is remarkable for its energy and simplicity; it shows indeed a measure of despondency, but not more than the circumstances of the case justified.

14. *Go in this thy might.* What does the angel mean? He had just stated that Jehovah was with Gideon; and he now says, *Go in this thy might*, i.e., in the might of Jehovah, who is with thee.

15. *Wherewith shall I save Israel?* I have neither men nor money. *Behold, my family is poor in Manasseh.* "Behold, my thousand is impoverished." Tribes were anciently divided into tens, and fifties, and hundreds, and thousands; the thousands therefore marked grand divisions, and consequently numerous families; Gideon here intimates that the families of which he made a part were very much diminished.

F. B. MEYER:

The strength-giving power of a look from the eyes of Christ? Gideon was weak enough. He said, quite naturally, "My family is the poorest in Manasseh, and I am the least in my father's house." But from the moment of that look, accompanied by that summons, he arose in a strength that never afterwards faltered. How truly "God hath chosen the foolish things of the world to confound the wise; and the weak things of the world to confound the things which are mighty."

It was a look of expectation. Gideon felt that the angel expected him to save Israel. It is a great matter to excite hope in a man. Tell him that you are anticipating some noble deed from him, and you may light a spark that will set his whole soul aglow. It is of immense importance to stir the timid and retiring with fresh conceptions of the possibilities of their lives.

It was a look of encouragement. Those gentle, loving eyes said, as though they spoke, "I will be with thee; do not hesitate to look for Me in every hour of need." Such looks Christ still gives us across the battlefields of life; and if our eyes are fixed upon Him, we shall surely hear Him saying to us, "My grace is sufficient for thee: go in this thy might!"

It was a look of strength-giving might. It carried help with it. On its beam new spiritual force sped from the speaker to the listener; from captain to cadet. So from the excellent glory one look from Jesus will bring reinforcement. As He looks on us He imparts his strength to us, and says, Go in this thy might. "Be strong in the Lord, and in the power of his might."

—*Great Verses Through the Bible*

MATTHEW HENRY

to advance the humble.

(5) This objection was soon answered by a repetition of the promise that God would be with him, *v.* 16. "*Surely I will be with thee*, to direct and strengthen thee, and be assured *thou shalt smite the Midianites as one man*, as easily as if they were but one man and as effectually. All the thousands of Midian shall be as if they had but one neck, and thou shalt have the cutting of it off."

(6) Gideon desires to have his faith confirmed touching this commission. He therefore humbly begs of this divine person, whoever he was, [1] That he would give him a sign, *v.* 17. Now, under the dispensation of the Spirit, we are not to expect signs before our eyes, such as Gideon here desired, but must earnestly pray to God that, if *we have found grace in his sight*, he would show us a sign in our heart, by the powerful operations of his Spirit there, *fulfilling the work of faith.* [2] That he would give him a further and longer opportunity of conversation with him, *v.* 18. Upon the angel's promise to stay to dinner with him, he intended, *First*, To testify his grateful and generous respects to this stranger, and, in him, to God who sent him. Out of the little which the Midianites had left him he would gladly spare enough to entertain a friend, especially a messenger from heaven. *Secondly*, To try who and what this extraordinary person was. What he brought out is called his *present*, *v.* 18. It is the same word that is used for a meat-offering. If he ate of it as common meat, he would suppose him to be a man, a prophet; if otherwise, as it proved, he should know him to be an angel.

(7) The angel ordered him to take the flesh and bread out of the basket, and lay it upon a hard and cold rock, and to pour out the broth upon it, which, if he brought it hot, would soon be cold there; and *Gideon did so* (*v.* 20), believing that the angel appointed it with an intention to give him a sign. [1] He turned the *meat into an offering made by fire, of a sweet savour.* [2] He brought fire *out of the rock*, to consume this sacrifice. Hereby he gave him a sign that he had *found grace in his sight*. This acceptance of his sacrifice evidenced the acceptance of his person, and confirmed his commission. [3] He *departed out of his sight* immediately.

(8) Gideon, though no doubt he was confirmed in his faith by the indications was put into a great fright till God removed his fears. [1] Gideon speaks peril to himself (*v.* 22): *When he perceived that he was an angel* he cried out, *Alas! O Lord! God* be merciful to me, I am undone, for *I have seen an angel.* In this world of sense, it is a very awful thing to have any sensible conversation with that world of spirits to which we are so much strangers. Gideon's courage failed him now. [2] God speaks peace to him, *v.* 23. The Lord had *departed out of his sight*, *v.* 21. But though he must no longer walk by sight he might still live by faith. For the Lord said to him, "*Peace be unto thee, thou shalt not die.*"

3. The memorial of this vision which Gideon set up was a monument in the form of an altar, of use to preserve the remembrance of the vision, which was known by the name *Jehovah-shalom* (*v.* 24)—*The Lord peace.* This is, (1) The title of the Lord that spoke to him. Or, (2) The substance of what he said to him: "*The Lord spoke peace.*" Or, (3) A prayer grounded upon what he had said, so the margin understands it, *The Lord send peace*, that is, rest from the present trouble, for still the public welfare lay nearest his heart.

Verses 25-32

I. Orders are given to Gideon to begin his government with the reformation of his father's house, *v.* 25, 26. The same night after he had seen God, when he was full of thoughts concerning what had passed, *the Lord said unto him* in a dream, *Do so and so.* Bid God welcome, and he will come again. Gideon is appointed, 1. To throw down Baal's altar, which it seems his father had, either for his own house or perhaps for the whole town. He must likewise *cut down the grove that was by it.* 2. To erect an altar to God, *to Jehovah his God.* God directs him to the place where he should build it, on the *top of the rock.* The word here used for the rock on which the altar was to be built signifies a fortress, or stronghold, erected, some think, to secure them from the Midianites. On this altar, (1) He was to offer sacrifice. Two bullocks he must offer: his father's *young bullock, and the second bullock of seven years old.* The former, we may suppose, he was to offer for himself, the latter *for the sins of the people* whom he was to deliver. (2) Baal's grove, or image, or whatever it was that was the sanctity or beauty of his altar, must not only be burnt, but must be used as fuel for God's altar. God ordered Gideon

JAMIESON, FAUSSET, BROWN

17-32. GIDEON'S PRESENT CONSUMED BY FIRE. **18. Depart not hence, I pray thee, until I . . . bring forth my present**—*Hebrew*, my *mincha*, or meat offering; and his idea probably was to prove, by his visitor's partaking of the entertainment, whether or not he was more than man.

19. Gideon went in, and made ready a kid; . . . the flesh he put in a basket, and he put the broth in a pot—(See on Gen. 18). The flesh seems to have been roasted, which is done by cutting it into kobab, i.e., into small pieces, fixed on a skewer, and put before the fire. The broth was for immediate use; the other, brought in a hand-basket was intended to be a future supply to the traveller.

The miraculous fire that consumed it and the vanishing of the stranger, not by walking, but as a spirit in the fire, filled Gideon with awe. A consciousness of demerit fills the heart of every fallen man at the thought of God, with fear of His wrath; and this feeling was increased by a belief prevalent in ancient times, that whoever saw an angel would forthwith die. The acceptance of Gideon's sacrifice betokened the acceptance of his person; but it required an express assurance of the divine blessing, given in some unknown manner, to restore his comfort and peace of mind. **24-32. it came to pass the same night, that the Lord said unto him**—The transaction in which Gideon is here described as engaged was not entered on till the night after the vision.

Take thy father's . . . second bullock—The Midianites had probably reduced the family herd; or, as Gideon's father was addicted to idolatry, the best may have been fattened for the service of Baal; so that the second was the only remaining one fit for sacrifice to God. **throw down the altar of Baal that thy father hath**—standing upon his ground, though kept for the common use of the townsmen. **cut down the grove that is by it**—dedicated to Ashtaroth. With the aid of ten confidential servants he demolished the one altar and raised on the appointed spot the altar of the Lord; but, for fear of opposition, the work had to be done under cover of night.

ADAM CLARKE

16. *Thou shalt smite the Midianites as one man.* You shall as surely conquer all their host as if you had but one man to contend with; or, You shall destroy them to a man.

17. *Shew me a sign.* Work a miracle, that I may know that you have wisdom and power sufficient to authorize and qualify me for the work.

18. *And bring forth my present.* My *minchah;* generally an offering of bread, wine, oil, flour, and suchlike. It seems from this that Gideon supposed the person to whom he spoke to be a divine person. Nevertheless, what he prepared and brought out appears to be intended simply as an entertainment to refresh a respectable stranger.

20. *Take the flesh.* The angel intended to make the flesh and bread an offering to God, and the broth a libation.

21. *The angel . . . put forth the end of the staff.* He appeared like a traveller with a staff in his hand; this he put forth, and having touched the flesh, fire rose out of the rock and consumed it. Here was the most evident proof of supernatural agency. *Then the angel . . . departed out of his sight.* Though the angel vanished out of his sight, yet God continued to converse with him either by secret inspiration in his own heart or by an audible voice.

22. *Alas, O Lord God! for because I have seen.* This is an elliptical sentence, a natural expression of the distressed state of Gideon's mind; as if he had said, Have mercy on me, O Lord God! else I shall die; because I have seen an angel of Jehovah face-to-face. We have frequently seen that it was a prevalent sentiment, as well before as under the law, that if any man saw God, or His representative angel, he must surely die.

23. *Fear not: thou shalt not die.* Here the discovery is made by God himself; Gideon is not curiously prying into forbidden mysteries, therefore he shall not die.

24. *Gideon built an altar . . . and called it Jehovah-shalom.* The words *Yehovah shalom* signify, "The Lord is my peace," or, "The peace of Jehovah"; and this name he gave the altar in reference to what God had said, v. 23, "Peace be unto thee."

25. *Take thy father's young bullock, even the second bullock.* There is some difficulty in this verse, for, according to the Hebrew text, two bullocks are mentioned here; but there is only one mentioned in verses 26 and 28. But what was this second bullock? Some think that it was a bullock that was fattened in order to be offered in sacrifice to Baal. This is very probable, as the *second bullock* is so particularly distinguished from another which belonged to Gideon's father. As the altar was built upon the ground of Joash, yet appears to have been public property (see vv. 29-30), so this second ox was probably reared and fattened at the expense of the men of that village; else why should they so particularly resent its being offered to Jehovah?

26. *With the wood of the grove.* It is probable that *Asherah* here signifies *Astarte;* and that there was a wooden image of this goddess on the altar of Baal.

MATTHEW HENRY

to do this, [1] To try his zeal for religion, which it was necessary he should give proofs of before he took the field. [2] That some steps might hereby be taken towards Israel's reformation, which must prepare the way for their deliverance. Sin, the cause, must be taken away, else how should the trouble, which was but the effect, come to an end?

II. Gideon was *obedient to the heavenly vision, v.* 27. He that was to command the Israel of God must first *save his people from their sins,* and then save them from their enemies. 1. He had servants of his own, whom he could confide in. 2. He did not scruple taking his father's bullock and offering it to God without his father's consent, because God, who expressly commanded him to do so, had a better title to it than his father had, and it was the greatest real kindness he could do to his father to prevent his sin. 3. He expected to incur the displeasure of his father's household by it; while he was sure of the favour of God, he feared not the anger of men. Yet, 4. To prevent their resistance in the doing of it he prudently chose to do it by night.

III. He was brought into peril of his life for doing it, *v.* 28–30. 1. It was soon discovered what was done, for the men of the city *rose early in the morning* to say their matins at Baal's altar. 2. It was soon discovered who had done it. 3. Gideon being found guilty of the fact, these degenerate Israelites require his own father to deliver him up: *Bring out thy son, that he may die.*

IV. He was rescued out of the hands of his persecutors by his own father, *v.* 31.

1. There were those that stood against Gideon, that would have him put to death. Notwithstanding the heavy judgments they were at this time under for their idolatry, yet they hated to be reformed.

2. Yet then *Joash stood for him*; he was one of the chief men of the city.

(1) This Joash had patronised Baal's altar, yet now protects him that had destroyed it, [1] Out of natural affection to his son. If Joash had a kindness for Baal, yet he had a greater kindness for his son. Or, [2] Out of a care for the public peace. The mob grew riotous, and, he feared, would grow more so, and therefore, as some think, he bestirred himself to repress the tumult. Or, [3] Out of a conviction that Gideon had done well. Let us do our duty, and then trust God with our safety.

(2) Two things Joash urges:—[1] That it was absurd for them to plead for Baal. It is bad to commit sin, but it is great wickedness indeed to plead for it, especially to plead for Baal, that idol, whatever it is, which possesses that room in the heart which God should have. [2] That it was needless for them to plead for Baal. If he were not a god, as was pretended, they could have nothing to say for him; if he were, he was able to plead for himself.

(3) Gideon's father hereupon gave him a new name (*v.* 32); he called him *Jerubaal*: "Let Baal plead; let him plead against him if he can; if he have anything to say for himself against his destroyer, let him say it."

Verses 33–40

I. The descent which the enemies of Israel made upon them, *v.* 33. A vast number of Midianites, Amalekites, and Arabians, made their headquarters in the valley of Jezreel, in the heart of Manasseh's tribe, not far from Gideon's city. But it proved that *the measure of their iniquity was full* and the year of recompence had come; they must now *make an end to spoil* and *must be spoiled,* and they are *gathered as sheaves to the floor* (Mic. iv. 12, 13), for Gideon to thresh.

II. The preparation which Gideon makes to attack them in their camp, *v.* 34, 35. 1. God by his Spirit put life into Gideon: *The Spirit of the Lord clothed Gideon* (so the word is), clothed him as a robe, to put honour upon him, clothed him as a coat of mail, to put defence upon him. Whom God calls to his work he will qualify and animate for it. 2. Gideon with his trumpet put life into his neighbours, God working with him. (1) The men of Abiezer, though lately enraged against him for throwing down the altar of Baal, and though they had condemned him to death as a criminal, were now convinced of their error, and bravely came in to his assistance. (2) Distant tribes, even Asher and Naphtali, which lay most remote, though strangers to him, obeyed his summons, *v.* 35.

III. The signs which God gratified him with, for the confirming both of his own faith and that of his followers. Observe, 1. His request for a sign (*v.* 36, 37): "Let me by this *know that thou wilt save Israel by my hand,* let *a fleece of wool,* spread in the open air, be *wet with the dew,* and let the ground about it be dry." The purport of this is, *Lord, I believe, help thou my unbelief.* When he repeated his request for a second sign, the reverse of the

JAMIESON, FAUSSET, BROWN

A violent commotion was excited next day, and vengeance vowed against Gideon as the perpetrator.

"Joash, his father, quieted the mob in a manner similar to that of the town clerk of Ephesus. It was not for them to take the matter into their own hands. The one, however, made an appeal to the magistrate; the other to the idolatrous god himself" [CHALMERS].

33-39. THE SIGNS. **33. all the Midianites . . . pitched in Jezreel**—The confederated troops of Midian, Amalek, and their neighbors, crossing the Jordan to make a fresh inroad on Canaan, encamped in the plains of Esdraelon (anciently Jezreel). The southern part of the Ghor lies in a very low level, so that there is a steep and difficult descent into Canaan by the southern wadies. Keeping this in view, we see the reason why the Midianite army, from the east of Jordan, entered Canaan by the northern wadies of the Ghor, opposite Jezreel. **34. the Spirit of the Lord came upon Gideon**—Called in this sudden emergency into the public service of his country, he was supernaturally endowed with wisdom and energy commensurate with the magnitude of the danger and the difficulties of his position. His summons to war was enthusiastically obeyed by all the neighboring tribes.

On the eve of a perilous enterprise, he sought to fortify his mind with a fresh assurance of a divine call to the responsible office. The miracle of the fleece was a very remarkable one—especially, considering the copious dews that fall in his country. The divine patience and condescension were wonderfully manifested in reversing the form of the miracle. Gideon himself seems to have been

ADAM CLARKE

27. *He feared his father's household.* So it appears that his father was an idolater; but as Gideon had ten men of his own servants whom he could trust in this matter, it is probable that he had preserved the true faith, and had not bowed his knee to the image of Baal.

28. *The second bullock was offered.* It appears that the second bullock was offered because it was just seven years old, v. 25, being calved about the time that the Midianitish oppression began; and it was now to be slain to indicate that their slavery should end with its life. The young bullock, v. 25, is supposed to have been offered for a peace offering; the bullock of seven years old, for a burnt offering.

29. *Gideon the son of Joash hath done this thing.* They fixed on him the more readily because they knew he had not joined with them in their idolatrous worship.

30. *The men of the city said.* They all felt an interest in the continuance of rites in which they had often many sensual gratifications. Baal and Ashtaroth would have more worshippers than the true God, because their rites were more adapted to the fallen nature of man.

31. *Will ye plead for Baal?* The words are very emphatic: "Will ye plead in earnest for Baal? Will ye really save *him*? If *he* be God, *Elohim,* let him contend for himself, seeing his altar is thrown down."

32. *He called him Jerubbaal.* That is, "Let Baal contend"; changed, 2 Sam. xi. 21, into *Jerubbesheth,* "He shall contend against confusion or shame"; thus changing *baal,* "lord," into *bosheth,* "confusion or ignominy."

33. *Then all the Midianites.* Hearing of what Gideon had done, and apprehending that this might be a forerunner of attempts to regain their liberty, they formed a general association against Israel.

34. *The Spirit of the Lord came upon Gideon.* He was endued with preternatural courage and wisdom.

36. *If thou wilt save Israel.* Gideon was very bold, and God was very condescending. But probably the request itself was suggested by the Divine Spirit.

MATTHEW HENRY

former, he did it with a very humble apology, deprecating God's displeasure, because it looked so like a peevish humoursome distrust of God. God's favour must be sought with great reverence, a due sense of our distance, and a religious fear. 2. God's gracious grant of his request. See how tender God is of true believers though they be weak. Gideon would have *the fleece wet* and the *ground dry*; but then, lest any should object, "It is natural for wool, if ever so little moisture fall, to drink it in and retain it, and therefore there was nothing extraordinary in this," though the quantity wrung out was sufficient to obviate such an objection, yet he desires that next night the ground might be wet and the fleece dry, and it is done, so willing is God to *give to the heirs of promise strong consolation* (Heb. vi. 17, 18), even by two immutable things. He suffers himself, not only to be prevailed with by their importunities, but even to be prescribed to by their doubts and dissatisfactions. Is Gideon desirous that the dew of divine grace might descend upon himself in particular? He sees the fleece wet with dew to assure him of it. Does he desire that God will be as the dew to all Israel? Behold, all the ground is wet.

CHAPTER 7

Verses 1–8

I. Gideon applies himself to do the part of a good general. He pitched near a famous well, that his army might not be distressed for want of water, and gained the higher ground, which possibly might be some advantage to him, for the Midianites *were beneath him in the valley*. Note, Faith in God's promises must not slacken, but rather quicken, our endeavours.

II. The army consisted of 32,000 men, a small army in comparison with what Israel might have raised, and a very small one in comparison with what the Midianites had now brought into the field; Gideon was ready to think them too few, but God tells him they are *too many*, *v.* 2. He would hereby silence and exclude boasting. This is the reason here given by him who knows the pride that is in men's hearts: *Lest Israel vaunt themselves against me*.

Two ways God took to lessen their numbers:—1. He ordered all that would own themselves timorous and faint-hearted to be dismissed, *v.* 3. One would have thought there would be scarcely one Israelite to be found that against such an enemy as the Midianites, and under such a leader as Gideon, would own himself fearful; yet above two parts of three took advantage of this proclamation, and filed off. Some think the oppression they had been under so long had broken their spirits, others, more probably, that consciousness of their own guilt had deprived them of their courage. Sin stared them in the face, and therefore they durst not look death in the face. 2. He directed the cashiering of all that remained except 300 men, and he did it by a sign: *The people are yet too many* for me to make use of, *v.* 4. But God saith they are yet *too many*, which may help us to understand those providences which sometimes seem to weaken the church and its interests. Gideon is ordered to bring his soldiers to the watering, probably to the well of Harod (*v.* 1) and the stream that ran from it. Now some, and no doubt the most, would kneel down on their knees to drink, and put their mouths to the water as horses do. Others, it may be, would not make such a formal business of it, but as a dog laps with his tongue, a lap and away, so they would hastily take up a little water in their hands, and cool their mouths with that, and be gone. Three hundred and no more there were of this latter sort, that drank in haste, and by those God tells Gideon he would rout the Midianites, *v.* 7. (1) Men that were hardy, that could endure long fatigue, without complaining of thirst or weariness. (2) Men that were hasty, that thought it long till they were engaged with the enemy, preferring the service of God and their country before their necessary refreshment. It was a great trial to the faith and courage of Gideon, when God bade him let all the rest of the people but these 300 *go every man to his place*. Thus strangely was Gideon's army purged, and modelled, and reduced instead of being recruited. Let us see how this little despicable regiment, on which the stress of the action must lie, was accoutred and fitted out. Every soldier turns sutler: They *took victuals in their hands* (*v.* 8), left their bag and baggage behind, and every man burdened himself with his own provision, which was a trial of their faith, whether they could trust God when they had no more provisions with them than they could carry, and a trial of their diligence, whether they could carry as

JAMIESON, FAUSSET, BROWN

conscious of incurring the displeasure of God by his hesitancy and doubts; but He bears with the infirmities of His people.

CHAPTER 7

Vss. 1-8. GIDEON'S ARMY. **1. Jerubbaal**—This had now become Gideon's honorable surname, "the enemy of Baal." **well**—rather "spring of Harod," i.e., "fear, trembling"—probably the same as the fountain in Jezreel (I Sam. 29:1). It was situated not far from Gilboa, on the confines of Manasseh, **and the name "Harod"** was bestowed on it with evident reference to the panic which seized the majority of Gideon's troops. The host of the Midianites were on the northern side of the valley, seemingly deeper down in the descent towards the Jordan, near a little eminence. **2. the Lord said unto Gideon, The people ... are too many**—Although the Israelitish army mustered only 32,000—or one-sixth of the Midianitish host—the number was too great, for it was the Lord's purpose to teach Israel a memorable lesson of dependence on Him. **3. Now therefore ..., proclaim in the ears of the people, saying, Whosoever is fearful ..., let him return**—This proclamation was in terms of an established law (Deut. 20:8).

4. too many—Two reductions were ordered, the last by the application of a test which was made known to Gideon alone. **bring them down unto the water**—When the wandering people in Asia, on a journey or in haste, come to water, they do not stoop down with deliberation on their knees, but only bend forward as much as is necessary to bring their hand in contact with the stream, and throw it up with rapidity, and at the same time such address, that they do not drop a particle. The Israelites, it seems, were acquainted with the practice; and those who adopted it on this occasion were selected as fit for a work that required expedition. The rest were dismissed according to the divine direction. **7. the Lord said, By the three hundred men that lapped will I save you**—It is scarcely possible to conceive a more severe trial than the command to attack the overwhelming forces of the enemy with such a handful of followers. But Gideon's faith in the divine assurance of victory was steadfast, and it is for this he is so highly commended (Heb. 11:32).

ADAM CLARKE

CHAPTER 7

1. *Then Jerubbaal, who is Gideon*. It appears that Jerubbaal was now a surname of Gideon, from the circumstance mentioned chap. vi. 32. See chap. viii. 35. *The well of Harod*. If this was a town or village, it is nowhere else mentioned. Probably, as *charad* signifies to "shake or tremble through fear," the fountain in question may have had its name from the terror and panic with which the Midianitish host was seized at this place.

2. *The people that are with thee are too many*. Had he led up a numerous host against his enemies, the excellence of the power by which they were discomfited might have appeared to be of man and not of God. By the manner in which this whole transaction was conducted, both the Israelites and Midianites must see that the thing was of God. This would inspire the Israelites with confidence, and the Midianites with fear.

3. *Whosoever is fearful and afraid, let him return . . . from mount Gilead*. Gideon is certainly not at Mount Gilead at this time, but rather near Mount Gilboa. Gilead was on the other side of Jordan. Calmet thinks there must either have been two Gileads, which does not from the Scripture appear to be the case, or that the Hebrew text is here corrupted, and that for Gilead we should read Gilboa. This reading, though adopted by Houbigant, is not countenanced by any MS., nor by any of the versions.

Dr. Hales endeavors to reconcile the whole by the supposition that there were in Gideon's army many of the eastern Manassites, who came from Mount Gilead; and that these probably were more afraid of their neighbors, the Midianites, than were the western tribes; and therefore proposes to read the text thus: "Whosoever from Mount Gilead is fearful and afraid, let him return (home) and depart early. So there returned (home) twenty-two thousand of the people." Perhaps this is on the whole the best method of solving this difficulty.

5. *Every one that lappeth of the water . . . as a dog*. The original word *yalok* is precisely the sound which a dog makes when he is drinking.

6. *The number of them that lapped*. From this account it appears that some of the people went down on their knees, and putting their mouths to the water, sucked up what they needed; the others stooped down, and taking up water in the hollow of their hands, applied it to their mouth.

8. *So the people took victuals*. The 300 men that he reserved took the victuals necessary for the day's expenditure, while the others were dismissed to their tent and their houses as they thought proper.

MATTHEW HENRY

much as they had occasion for. This was indeed living from hand to mouth. Every soldier turns trumpeter as if they had been going rather to a game than to a battle.

Verse 9–15

Gideon's army being diminished as we have found it was, he must either fight by faith or not at all; God therefore here provides recruits for his faith, instead of recruits for his forces.

I. He furnishes him with a good foundation to build his faith upon. Nothing but a word from God will be a footing for faith. 1. A word of command to warrant the action. *Arise, get thee down* with this handful of men *unto the host.* 2. A word of promise to assure him of the success. *I have delivered it into thy hand*; it is all thy own. This *word of the Lord* came to him the same night, when he was greatly agitated and full of care how he should come off; *in the multitude of his thoughts within him these comforts did delight his soul.*

II. He furnishes him with a good prop to support his faith with. 1. He orders him to be his own spy, and now in the dead of the night to go down privately into the host of Midian, and see what intelligence he could gain: "*If thou fear to go down* to fight, go first only with thy own servant (*v.* 10) and *hear what they say*" (*v.* 11); and it is intimated to him that he should hear that which would greatly strengthen his faith. He must take with him *Phurah his servant*, probably one of the ten that had helped him to break down the altar of Baal. 2. Being so, he orders him the sight of something that was discouraging. It was enough to frighten him to discern, perhaps by moonlight, the vast numbers of the enemy (*v.* 12), the men like grasshoppers for multitude, and they proved no better than grasshoppers for strength and courage; the camels one could not count, any more than the sand. But, 3. He causes him to hear that which was to him a very good omen. He overheard two soldiers of the enemy, that were comrades, talking. (1) One of them tells his dream: He saw a barley-cake come rolling down the hill into the camp of the Midianites, and "methought this rolling cake struck one of our tents with such violence that it overturned the tent, forced down the stakes, and broke the cords at one blow, and buried its inhabitants," *v.* 13. (2) The other undertakes to interpret this dream, *This is nothing else save the sword of Gideon*, *v.* 14. Gideon, who had threshed corn for his family, and made cakes for his friend (*ch.* vi. 11–19), was fitly represented by a cake,—that he and his army were as inconsiderable as a cake made of a little flour, as contemptible as a barley-cake, hastily got together as a cake suddenly baked upon the coals, and as unlikely to conquer this great army as a cake to overthrow a tent. It was an evidence that the enemy was quite dispirited, and that the name of Gideon had become so formidable to them that it disturbed their sleep.

Lastly, Gideon was exceedingly encouraged. He was very well pleased to hear himself compared to a barley-cake, when it proved to effect such great things. He gave God the glory of it; and in a short ejaculation thanked God for the victory he was now sure of, and for this encouragement to expect it. He gave his friends a share in the encouragements he had received: *Arise*, prepare to march presently; *the Lord has delivered Midian into your hand.*

Verses 16–22

I. The alarm which Gideon gave to the hosts of Midian in the dead time of the night; for it was intended that those who had so long been a terror to Israel should themselves be routed and ruined purely by terror.

Gideon, 1. Divided his army, small as it was, into three battalions (*v.* 16), one of which he himself commanded (*v.* 19). 2. He ordered them all to do as he did, *v.* 17. Such is the word of command which our Lord Jesus, the captain of our salvation, gives his soldiers; for he has *left us an example*, with a charge to follow it: *As I do, so shall you do.* 3. He made his descent in the night, when they were secure and least expected it, and when the smallness of his army would not be discovered. In the night all frights are most frightful. He accoutred his army with every man a trumpet in his right hand, and an earthen pitcher, with a torch in it, in his left. The fewness of his men favoured his design. Three ways Gideon contrived to strike a terror upon this army, (1) With a great noise. Every man must blow his trumpet in the most terrible manner he could and clatter an earthen pitcher to pieces at the same time. (2) With a great blaze. The lighted torches were hid in the pitchers, and then, being taken out all together of a sudden, would make a glaring show. Perhaps with these they set some of the tents on the outside of the

JAMIESON, FAUSSET, BROWN

8. the host of Midian was beneath him in the valley—Attention to the relative position of the parties is of the greatest importance to an understanding of what follows.

9-15. HE IS ENCOURAGED BY THE DREAM AND THE INTERPRETATION OF THE BARLEY CAKE. **9-10. Arise, get thee down unto the host . . . But if thou fear to go down, go thou with Phurah thy servant**—In ancient times it was reckoned no degradation for persons of the highest rank and character to act as spies on an enemy's camp; and so Gideon did on this occasion. But the secret errand was directed by God, who intended that he should hear something which might animate his own valor and that of his troops. **11. the outside of the armed men that were in the host**—"Armed," means embodied under the five officers established by the ordinary laws and usages of encampments. The camp seems to have been unprotected by any rampart, since Gideon had no difficulty in reaching and overhearing a conversation, so important to him. **12. the valley like grasshoppers for multitude; and the Midianites and the Amalekites . . . lay along in their camels without number**—a most graphic description of an Arab encampment. They lay wrapt in sleep, or resting from their day's plunder, while their innumerable camels were stretched round about them. **13. I dreamed a dream, and, lo, a cake of barley bread tumbled into the host of Midian**—This was a characteristic and very expressive dream for an Arab in the circumstances. The rolling down the hill, striking against the tents, and overturning them, naturally enough connected it in his mind with the position and meditated attack of the Israelitish leader. The circumstance of the cake, too, was very significant. Barley was usually the food of the poor, and of beasts; but most probably, from the widespread destruction of the crops by the invaders, multitudes must have been reduced to poor and scanty fare.

15. when Gideon heard the telling of the dream, and the interpretation . . . he worshipped—The incident originated in the secret overruling providence of God, and Gideon, from his expression of pious gratitude, regarded it as such. On his mind, as well as that of his followers, it produced the intended effect—that of imparting new animation and impulse to their patriotism.

16-24. HIS STRATAGEM AGAINST MIDIAN. **16. he divided the three hunderd men into three companies**—The object of dividing his forces was, that they might seem to be surrounding the enemy.

The pitchers were empty to conceal the torches, and made of earthenware, so as to be easily broken; and the sudden blaze of the held-up lights—the loud echo of the trumpets, and the shouts of Israel, always terrifying (Num. 23:21), and now more terrible than ever by the use of such striking words, broke through the stillness of the midnight air.

ADAM CLARKE

9. *I have delivered it into thine hand.* I have determined to do it, and it is as sure as if it were done.

13. *Told a dream.* Both the dream and the interpretation were inspired by God for the purpose of increasing the confidence of Gideon, and appalling his enemies.

14. *Into his hand hath God delivered Midian.* This is a full proof that God had inspired both the dream and its interpretation.

16. *He divided the three hundred men.* Though the victory was to be from the Lord, yet he knew that he ought to use prudential means; and those which he employed on this occasion were the best calculated to answer the end.

MATTHEW HENRY

camp on fire. (3) With a great shout. Every man must cry, *For the Lord and for Gideon*, so some think it should be read in *v.* 18, for there the sword is not in the original, but it is in *v.* 20, *The sword of the Lord and of Gideon.* The sword of the Lord is all in all to the success of the sword of Gideon, yet the sword of Gideon must be employed always in subserviency and subordination to God.

This method here taken of defeating the Midianites may be alluded to, as typifying the destruction of the devil's kingdom in the world by the preaching of the everlasting gospel, the sounding of that trumpet, and the holding forth of that light out of earthen vessels, 2 Cor. iv. 6, 7. Thus God chose the *foolish things of the world to confound the wise*, a barley-cake to overthrow the tents of Midian, that the *excellency of the power might be of God only*; the gospel is a sword, not in the hand, but in the mouth.

II. The wonderful success of this alarm. Gideon's soldiers observed their orders, and *stood every man in his place round about the camp* (*v.* 21), sounding his trumpet to excite them to fight one another, and holding out his torch to light them to their ruin. Observe how the design took effect. 1. They feared the Israelites. *All the host* immediately took the alarm; they had reason to suspect that it was a very great army which was to be ushered in with all those trumpeters and torch-bearers. But there was more of a supernatural power impressing this terror upon them. God himself gave it the setting on. See the power of imagination, and how much it may become a terror at some times, as at other times it is a pleasure. 2. They fell foul upon one another: *The Lord set every man's sword against his fellow*, *v.* 22. God often makes the enemies of his church instruments to destroy one another. 3. They fled for their lives.

Verses 23–25

We have here the prosecution of this glorious victory. 1. Gideon's soldiers that had been dismissed got together again, and vigorously pursued those whom they had not courage to face. Those who were fearful and afraid to fight (*v.* 3) now took heart, when the worst was over, and were ready enough to divide the spoil, though backward to make the onset. 2. The Ephraimites, upon a summons from Gideon, came in unanimously, and secured the passes over Jordan, by the several fords, to cut off the enemies' retreat into their own country. 3. Two of the chief commanders of the host of Midian were taken and slain by the Ephraimites on this side Jordan, *v.* 25. Their names perhaps signified their nature, *Oreb* signifies a *raven*, and *Zeeb* a *wolf* (*corvus* and *lupus*).

JAMIESON, FAUSSET, BROWN

The sleepers started from their rest; not a blow was dealt by the Israelites; but the enemy ran tumultuously, uttering the wild, discordant cries peculiar to the Arab race. They fought indiscriminately, not knowing friend from foe. The panic being universal, they soon precipitately fled, directing their flight down to the Jordan, by the foot of the mountains of Ephraim, to places known as the "house of the acacia," and "the meadow of the dance."

23. the men of Israel gathered themselves together—These were evidently the parties dismissed, who having lingered at a little distance from the scene of contest, now eagerly joined in the pursuit southwestward through the valley. **24. Gideon sent messengers throughout all mount Ephraim**—The Ephraimites lay on the south and could render seasonable aid. **Come . . . , take before them the waters unto Beth-barah** (See on ch. 3:28)—These were the northern fords of the Jordan, to the east-northeast of wady Maleh. **the men of Ephraim gathered themselves together . . . unto Beth-barah**—A new conflict ensued, in which two secondary chiefs were seized and slain on the spots where they were respectively taken. The spots were named after these chiefs, Oreb, "the Raven," and Zeeb, "the Wolf"—appropriate designations of Arab leaders.

ADAM CLARKE

18. *The sword of the Lord, and of Gideon.* The word *chereb, sword*, is not found in this verse, though it is necessarily implied, and is found in v. 20.

20. *Blew the trumpets, and brake the pitchers.* How astonishing must the effect be, in a dark night, of the sudden glare of 300 torches, darting their splendor, in the same instant, on the half-awakened eyes of the terrified Midianites, accompanied with the clangor of 300 trumpets, alternately mingled with the thundering shout of "A sword for the Lord and for Gideon!"

21. *They stood every man in his place.* Each of the three companies kept their station, and continued to sound their trumpets. The Midianites seeing this, and believing that they were the trumpets of a numerous army which had then penetrated their camp, were thrown instantly into confusion; and supposing that their enemies were in the midst of them, they turned their swords against every man they met, while at the same time they endeavored to escape for their lives. No stratagem was ever better imagined, better executed, or more completely successful.

22. *Fled to Beth-shittah.* This is nowhere else mentioned in Scripture. *Zererath.* This and *Tabbath* are nowhere else to be found. *Abel-meholah.* This was the birthplace of the prophet Elisha, 1 Kings xix. 16. It was beyond Jordan, in the tribe of Manasseh, 1 Kings iv. 12.

23. *The men of Israel gathered.* It is very likely that these were some persons whom Gideon had sent home the day before, who, now hearing that the Midianites were routed, went immediately in pursuit.

24. *Take before them the waters unto Beth-barah.* This is probably the same place as that mentioned John i. 28, where the Hebrews forded Jordan under the direction of Joshua. To this place the Midianites directed their flight, that they might escape into their own country; and here, being met by the Ephraimites, they appear to have been totally overthrown, and their two generals taken.

25. *They slew Oreb upon the rock Oreb.* These two generals had taken shelter, one in the cavern of the rock, the other in the vat of a winepress; both of which places were, from this circumstance, afterwards called by their names. *Brought the heads of Oreb and Zeeb to Gideon. Oreb* signifies a "raven," and *Zeeb* a "wolf." In all ancient nations we find generals and princes taking their names from both birds and beasts.

MATTHEW HENRY

CHAPTER 8

Verses 1–3

No sooner were the Midianites, the common enemy, subdued, than the children of Israel were ready to quarrel among themselves. The Ephraimites, when they brought the heads of Oreb and Zeeb to Gideon as general, picked a quarrel with him and grew very hot upon it.

I. Their accusation was very peevish and unreasonable: *Why didst thou not call us when thou wentest to fight with the Midianites? v.* 1. Ephraim was very jealous of Manasseh, lest that tribe should at any time eclipse the honour of theirs. How unjust was their quarrel with Gideon! But, 1. Gideon was called of God, and neither took the honour to himself nor did he himself dispose of honours, but left it to God to do all. So that the Ephraimites in this quarrel, reflected upon the divine conduct. 2. Why did not the Ephraimites offer themselves willingly to the service? The case itself called them, they needed not wait for a call from Gideon. Cowards will seem valiant when the danger is over, but those consult their reputation who try not their courage when danger is near.

II. Gideon's answer was intended not so much to justify himself as to please and pacify them, *v.* 2, 3. He answers them, 1. With a great deal of meekness, and he won as true honour by this command which he had over his own passion as by his victory over the Midianites. 2. With a great deal of modesty, magnifying their performances above his own: *Is not the gleaning of the grapes of Ephraim*, who picked up the stragglers of the enemy, and cut off those of them that escaped, *better than the vintage of Abiezer*—a greater honour to them, and better service to the country, than the first attack Gideon made upon them? The improving of a victory is often more

JAMIESON, FAUSSET, BROWN

CHAPTER 8

VSS. 1-9. THE EPHRAIMITES OFFENDED, BUT PACIFIED. **1. the men of Ephraim said, Why hast thou served us thus?**—Where this complaint was made, whether before or after the crossing of the Jordan, cannot be determined. By the overthrow of the national enemy, the Ephraimites were benefited as largely as any of the other neighboring tribes. But, piqued at not having been sharers in the glory of the victory, their leading men could not repress their wounded pride; and the occasion only served to bring out an old and deep-seated feeling of jealous rivalry that subsisted between the tribes (Isa. 9:21). The discontent was groundless, for Gideon acted according to divine directions. Besides, as their tribe was conterminous with that of Gideon, they might, had they been really fired with the flame of patriotic zeal, have volunteered their services in a movement against the common enemy.

2, 3. he said, What have I done now in comparison of you?—His mild and truly modest answer breathes the spirit of a great as well as good man, who was calm, collected, and self-possessed in the midst of most exciting scenes. It succeeded in throwing oil on the troubled waters (Prov. 16:1), and no wonder, for in the height of generous self-denial, it ascribes to his querulous brethren a greater share of merit and glory than belonged to himself (I Cor. 13:4; Philemon 2:3).

ADAM CLARKE

CHAPTER 8

1. *The men of Ephraim said.* This account is no doubt displaced; for what is mentioned here could not have taken place till the return of Gideon from the pursuit of the Midianites, for he had not yet passed Jordan, v. 4. And it was when he was beyond that river that the Ephraimites brought the heads of Oreb and Zeeb to him, chap. vii. 25.

2. *Is not the gleaning?* That is, The Ephraimites have performed more important services than Gideon and his men; and he supports the assertion by observing that it was they who took the two Midianitish generals, having discomfited their hosts at the passes of Jordan.

3. *Then their anger was abated.* "A soft answer turneth away wrath." He might have said that he could place but little dependence on his brethren when, through faintheartedness, 22,000 left him at one time; but he passed this by, and took a more excellent way.

MATTHEW HENRY

honourable, and of greater consequence, than the winning of it. Gideon shows us, (1) That humility of deportment is the best way to remove envy. (2) It is likewise the surest method of ending strife.

Now what was the issue of this controversy? The Ephraimites had *chidden with him sharply* (*v.* 1), but Gideon's *soft answer turned away their wrath*, Prov. xv. 1.

Verses 4–17

I. Gideon, as a valiant general, pursuing the remaining Midianites, and, it seems, the two kings of Midian, being better provided than the rest for an escape, with 15,000 men got over Jordan before the passes could be secured by the Ephraimites, and made towards their own country. Gideon thinks he does not fully execute his commission to save Israel if he lets them escape.

1. His firmness was very exemplary under the greatest disadvantages and discouragements. (1) He took none with him but his 300 men. He expected more from 300 men, supported by a particular promise, than from so many thousands supported only by their own valour. (2) They were *faint, and yet pursuing*. (3) Though he met with discouragement from those of his own people. If those that should be our helpers in the way of our duty prove hindrances to us, let not this drive us off from it. (4) He made a very long march by *the way of those that dwelt in tents* (*v.* 11). Now he found it an advantage to have his 300 men such as could bear hunger, and thirst, and toil.

2. His success was very encouraging to resolution and industry in a good cause. He routed the army (*v.* 11), and took the two kings prisoners, *v.* 12.

II. Here is Gideon, as a righteous judge, chastising the insolence of the disaffected Israelites, the men of Succoth, and the men of Penuel.

1. Their crime was great. Gideon, with a handful of feeble folk was pursuing the common enemy, to complete the deliverance of Israel. His way led him through the city of Succoth first and afterwards of Penuel. He only begs some necessary food for his soldiers that were ready to faint for want, and he does it very humbly and importunately: *Give, I pray you, loaves of bread unto the people that follow me*, *v.* 5. The request would have been reasonable if they had been but poor travellers in distress. Nothing could be more just than that their brethren should furnish them with the best provisions their city afforded. But the princes of Succoth neither *feared God nor regarded man*. For, (1) In contempt of God, they refused to answer the just demands of him whom God had raised up to save them, and were very willing to believe that the remaining forces of Midian, which they had now seen march through their country, would be too hard for him. (2) The bowels of their compassion were shut up against their brethren; they were as destitute of love as they were of faith, and would not give morsels of bread (so some read it) to those that were ready to perish. The men of Penuel gave the same answer to the same request, defying *the sword of the Lord and of Gideon*, *v.* 8.

2. The warning he gave them of the punishment of their crime was very fair. (1) He did not punish it immediately because he would not seem to do it in a heat of passion. But, (2) He told them how he would punish it (*v.* 7, 9), to show the confidence he had of success in the strength of God, and that they might upon second thoughts repent of their folly, sending after him succours and supplies. God gives notice of danger, and space to repent, that sinners may *flee from the wrath to come*.

3. The warning being slighted, the punishment, though very severe, was really very just.

(1) The princes of Succoth were first made examples. And he punished them with thorns and briers, but, it should seem, not unto death. With these, [1] He tormented their bodies. [2] He instructed their minds: With these *he taught the men of Succoth*, *v.* 16. The correction he gave them was intended, not for destruction, but wholesome discipline, to make them wiser and better for the future. *He made them know* (so the word is), made them know themselves and their folly, God and their duty. Note, Many are taught with the briers and thorns of affliction that would not learn otherwise.

(2) The doom of the men of Penuel comes next. [1] He *beat down their tower*, in which they trusted, perhaps scornfully advising Gideon and his men rather to secure themselves in that than to pursue the Midianites. [2] He *slew the men of the city* that were most insolent and abusive, for terror to the rest, and *so he taught the men of Penuel*.

JAMIESON, FAUSSET, BROWN

4. Gideon came to Jordan, and passed over—much exhausted, but eager to continue the pursuit till the victory was consummated. **5. he said unto the men of Succoth**—i.e., a place of tents or booths. The name seems to have been applied to the whole part of the Jordan valley on the west, as well as on the east side of the river, all belonging to the tribe of Gad (cf. Gen. 33:17; I Kings 7:46; with Josh. 13:27). Being engaged in the common cause of all Israel, he had a right to expect support and encouragement from his countrymen everywhere. **6. the princes of Succoth said, Are the hands of Zebah and Zalmunna now in thine hand**—an insolent as well as a time-serving reply. It was insolent because it implied a bitter taunt that Gideon was counting with confidence on a victory which they believed he would not gain; and it was time-serving, because living in the near neighborhood of the Midianite sheiks, they dreaded the future vengeance of those roving chiefs. This contumelious manner of acting was heartless and disgraceful in people who were of Israelitish blood. **7. I will tear your flesh with the thorns of the wilderness and with briers**—a cruel torture, to which captives were often subjected in ancient times, by having thorns and briers placed on their naked bodies and pressed down by sledges, or heavy implements of husbandry being dragged over them. **8. he went up thence to Penuel, and spake unto them likewise**—a neighboring city, situated also in the territory of Gad, near the Jabbok, and honored with this name by Jacob (Gen. 32: 30, 31). **9. he spake . . . , When I come again in peace I will break down this tower**—Intent on the pursuit, and afraid of losing time, he postponed the merited vengeance till his return. His confident anticipation of a triumphant return evinces the strength of his faith; and his specific threat was probably provoked by some proud and presumptuous boast, that in their lofty watchtower the Penuelites would set him at defiance.

10-27. ZEBAH AND ZALMUNNA TAKEN. **10. Now Zebah und Zalmunna were in Karkor**—a town on the eastern confines of Gad. The wreck of the Midianite army halted there. **11. Gideon went up by the way of them that dwelt in tents on the east**—He tracked the fugitives across the mountain range of Gilead to the northeast of the Jabbok, and there came upon them unexpectedly while they were resting secure among their own nomadic tribes. Jogbehah is supposed to be Ramoth-gilead; and, therefore, the Midianites must have found refuge at or near Abela, "Abel-cheramim," the plain of the vineyards. **12. when Zebah and Zalmunna fled, he pursued after them**—A third conflict took place. His arrival at their last quarters, which was by an unwonted path, took the fugitives by surprise, and the conquest of the Midianite horde was there completed. **13. Gideon returned from battle before the sun was up**—He seems to have returned by a nearer route to Succoth, for what is rendered in our version "before the sun was up," means "the heights of Heres, the sun-hills." **14. he described**—wrote the names of the seventy princes or elders. It was from them he had received so inhospitable a treatment.

16. he took . . . the thorns of the wilderness and briers, and with them he taught the men of Succoth—By refusing his soldiers refreshment, they had committed a public crime, as well as an act of inhumanity, and were subjected to a horrible punishment, which the great abundance and remarkable size of the thorn bushes, together with the thinness of clothing in the East, has probably suggested.

ADAM CLARKE

5. *Give, I pray you, loaves of bread.* As Gideon was engaged in the common cause of Israel, he had a right to expect succor from the people at large. His request to the men of Succoth and Penuel was both just and reasonable.

6. *Are the hands of Zebah and Zalmunna now in thine hand?* They feared to help Gideon, lest, if he should be overpowered, the Midianites would revenge it upon them; and they dared not trust God.

7. *I will tear your flesh.* What this punishment consisted in I cannot say. It must mean a severe punishment; as if he had said, I will thresh your flesh with briers and thorns, as corn is threshed out with threshing instruments; or, You shall be trodden down under the feet of my victorious army, as the corn is trodden out with the feet of the ox.

8. *Succoth* was beyond Jordan, in the tribe of Gad. *Penuel* was also in the same tribe, and not far distant from Succoth.

9. *I will break down this tower.* Probably they had not only denied him, but insultingly pointed to a tower in which their chief defense lay; and intimated to him that he might do his worst, for they could amply defend themselves.

10. *Zebah and Zalmunna were in Karkor.* If this were a place, it is nowhere else mentioned in Scripture. Some contend that *karkor* signifies "rest"; and thus the Vulgate understood it: Zebah and Zalmunna "rested," with all their army. And this seems the most likely, for it is said, v. 11, that Gideon smote the host, for the host was "secure."

13. *Returned from battle before the sun was up.* This does not appear to be a proper translation. It should be rendered "from the ascent of Chares"; this is the reading of the Septuagint, the Syriac, and the Arabic.

14. *He described unto him the princes of Succoth.* The young man probably gave him the names of seventy persons, the chief men of Succoth, who were those who were most concerned in refusing him and his men the refreshment he requested.

16. *He taught the men of Succoth.* Instead of *he taught,* Houbigant reads "he tore"; and this is not only agreeable to what Gideon had threatened, v. 7, but is supported by the Vulgate, Septuagint, Chaldee, Syriac, and Arabic. The Hebrew text might have been easily corrupted in this place by the change of *shin* into *ain,* letters very similar to each other.

MATTHEW HENRY

Verses 18–21

The kings of Midian must now be reckoned with. 1. They are indicted for the murder of Gideon's brethren some time ago at Mount Tabor. When the children of Israel, for fear of the Midianites, made themselves *dens in the mountains* (*ch.* vi. 2), those young men, it is likely, took shelter in that mountain, where they were found by these two kings, and most basely and barbarously slain in cold blood. 2. Being found guilty of this murder by their own confession by him must *their blood be shed*, though they were kings. 3. The execution is done by Gideon himself with his own hand, because he was the *avenger of blood*; he bade his son slay them. But, (1) The young man himself desired to be excused *because he was yet a youth.* (2) The prisoners themselves desired that Gideon would excuse it (*v.* 21), "Thou art at thy full strength; he has not yet come to it; therefore be thou the executioner."

Verses 22–28

I. Gideon's laudable modesty, after his great victory, in refusing the government which the people offered him. 1. It was honest in them to offer it: *Rule thou over us, for thou hast delivered us, v.* 22. 2. It was honourable in him to refuse it: *I will not rule over you, v.* 23. What he did was with a design to serve them, not to rule them—to make them safe, easy, and happy, not to make himself great or honourable. "*The Lord shall* still *rule over you*, and constitute your judges by the special designation of his own Spirit, as he has done." This intimates, (1) His modesty, and the mean opinion he had of himself and his own merits. (2) His piety, and the great opinion he had of God's government.

II. Gideon's irregular zeal to perpetuate the remembrance of this victory by an ephod made of the choicest of the spoils. 1. He asked the men of Israel to give him the ear-rings of their prey. 2. He himself added the spoil he took from the kings of Midian. 3. Of this he made an ephod, *v.* 27. (1) It was plausible enough, and might be well intended to preserve a memorial of so divine a victory in the judge's own city. But it was a very unadvised thing to make that memorial to be an ephod, a sacred garment. I would gladly put the best construction that can be upon the actions of good men, and such a one we are sure Gideon was. But we have reason to suspect that this ephod had, as usual, a teraphim annexed to it (Hos. iii. 4), and that, having an altar already built by divine appointment (*ch.* vi. 26), which he erroneously imagined he might still use for sacrifice, he intended this for an oracle, to be consulted in doubtful cases. So the learned Dr. Spencer supposes. Each tribe having now very much its government within itself, they were too apt to covet their religion among themselves. We read very little of Shiloh, and the ark there, in all the story of the Judges. Note, Many are led into false ways by one false step of a good man. The beginning of sin, particularly of idolatry and will-worship, *is as the letting forth of water*, so it has been found in the fatal corruptions of the church of Rome; therefore *leave it off before it be meddled with.* (2) It became a snare to Gideon himself, abating his zeal for the house of God in his old age, and much more to his house, who were drawn by it into sin, and it proved the ruin of the family.

III. Gideon's happy agency for the repose of Israel, *v.* 28. Gideon, though he would not assume the honour and power of a king, governed as a judge, and did all the good offices he could for his people; so that *the country was in quietness forty years.* Hitherto the times of Israel had been reckoned by forties. Othniel judged forty years, Ehud eighty—just two forties, Barak forty, and now Gideon forty, providence so ordering it to bring in mind the forty years of their wandering in the wilderness. After these, Eli ruled forty years (1 Sam. iv. 18), Samuel and Saul forty (Acts xiii. 21), David forty, and Solomon forty. Forty years is about an age.

Verses 29–35

The conclusion of the story of Gideon. 1. He lived privately, but retired to the house he had lived in before his elevation. Thus that brave Roman who was called from the plough upon a sudden occasion to command the army when the action was over returned to his plough again. 2. His family was multiplied. 3. He died in honour, in a good old age.

JAMIESON, FAUSSET, BROWN

18. Then said he unto Zebah and Zalmunna, What manner of men were they whom ye slew at Tabor?—This was one of the countless atrocities which the Midianite chiefs had perpetrated during their seven years' lawless occupancy. It is noticed now for the first time when their fate was about to be determined. **each one resembled the children of a king**—An Orientalism for great beauty, majesty of appearance, uncommon strength, and grandeur of form. **19. They were my brethren, even the sons of my mother**—That is, uterine brothers; but, in all countries where polygamy prevails, "the son of my mother" implies a closeness of relationship and a warmth of affection never awakened by the looser term, "brother." **20. he said unto Jether his first-born, Up, and slay them**—The nearest of kin was the blood avenger; but a magistrate might order any one to do the work of the executioner; and the person selected was always of a rank equal or proportioned to that of the party doomed to suffer (I Kings 2:29). Gideon intended, then, by the order to Jether, to put an honor on his son, by employing him to slay two enemies of his country; and on the youth declining, he performed the bloody deed himself.

22, 23. the men of Israel said unto Gideon, Rule thou over us . . . Gideon said unto them, the Lord shall rule over you—Their unbounded admiration and gratitude prompted them, in the enthusiasm of the moment, to raise their deliverer to a throne, and to establish a royal dynasty in his house. But Gideon knew too well, and revered too piously the principles of the theocracy, to entertain the proposal for a moment. Personal and family ambition was cheerfully sacrificed to a sense of duty, and every worldly motive was kept in check by a supreme regard to the divine honor. He would willingly act as judge, but the Lord alone was King of Israel.

24-26. Gideon said unto them, I would desire a request of you—This was the contribution of an earring (sing.). As the ancient Arabians (Ishmaelites and Midianites being synonymous terms, Gen. 37:25, 28) were gorgeously adorned with barbaric pearl and gold, an immense amount of such valuable booty had fallen into the hands of the Israelitish soldiers. The contribution was liberally made, and the quantity of gold given to him equalled about $25,000.00 in today's measure. **ornaments**—crescent-like plates of gold suspended from the necks, or placed on the breasts of the camels. **collars**—rather earrings, or drops of gold or pearl. **purple**—a royal color. The ancient, as well as modern Arabs, adorned the necks, breasts, and legs, of their riding animals with sumptuous housing. **27. Gideon made an ephod thereof, and put it in his city, . . . Ophrah**—That no idolatrous use was in view, nor any divisive course from Shiloh contemplated, is manifest from verse 33. Gideon proposed, with the gold he received, to make an ephod for his use *only* as a civil magistrate or ruler, as David did (I Chron. 15:27), and a magnificent pectoral or breastplate also. It would seem, from the history, that he was not blamable in making this ephod, as a civil robe or ornament merely, but that it *afterward* became an object to which religious ideas were attached; whereby it proved a snare, and consequently an evil, by *perversion*, to Gideon and his house [TAYLOR'S FRAGMENT].

28. MIDIAN SUBDUED. **28. Thus was Midian subdued before the children of Israel**—This invasion of the Arab hordes into Canaan was as alarming and desolating as the irruption of the Huns into Europe. It was the severest scourge ever inflicted upon Israel; and both it and the deliverance under Gideon lived for centuries in the minds of the people (Ps. 83:11).

ADAM CLARKE

18. *What manner of men were they whom ye slew at Tabor?* We have no antecedent to this question, and are obliged to conjecture one. It seems as if Zebah and Zalmunna had massacred the family of Gideon while he was absent on this expedition. Gideon had heard some confused account of it, and now questions them concerning the fact. They boldly acknowledge it, and describe the persons whom they slew, by which he found they were his own brethren. This determines him to avenge their death by slaying the Midianitish kings, whom he otherwise was inclined to save.

20. *He said unto Jether his firstborn.* By the ancient laws of war, prisoners taken in war might be either slain, sold, or kept for slaves. To put a captive enemy to death no executioner was required. Gideon slays Zebah and Zalmunna with his own hand. So Samuel is said to have hewn Agag in pieces, 1 Sam. xv. 33.

21. *The ornaments that were on their camels' necks.* The heads, necks, bodies, and legs of camels, horses, and elephants are highly ornamented in the Eastern countries; and indeed this was common, from the remotest antiquity, in all countries. Instead of *ornaments*, the Septuagint translate "the crescents" or "half-moons"; and this is followed by the Syriac and Arabic. We learn from v. 24 that the Ishmaelites, or Arabs, as they are termed by the Targum, Syriac, and Arabic, had golden earrings, and probably a crescent in each; for it is well known that the Ishmaelites, and the Arabs who descended from them, were addicted very early to the worship of the moon; and so attached were they to this superstition that, although Mohammed destroyed the idolatrous use of the crescent, yet it was universally borne in their ensigns, and on the tops of their mosques.

22. *Rule thou over us, both thou, and thy son, and thy son's son.* That is, Become our king, and let the crown be hereditary in your family. What a weak, foolish, and inconstant people were these! As yet their government was a theocracy; and now, dazzled with the success of a man who was only an instrument in the hands of God to deliver them from their enemies, they wish to throw off the divine yoke, and shackle themselves with an unlimited hereditary monarchy!

23. *The Lord shall rule over you.* Few with such power at their command would have acted as Gideon. His speech calls them back to their first principles, and should have excited in them both shame and contrition.

24. *Give me every man the earrings of his prey.* The spoils taken from their enemies in this warfare. This is a transaction very like to that of the Israelites and Aaron when they brought him their golden earrings, out of which he made the molten calf, Exod. xxxii. 2, etc. Whether Gideon designed this ephod for an instrument of worship or merely as a trophy is not very clear. It is most likely that he had intended to establish a place of worship at Ophrah, and he took this occasion to provide the proper sacerdotal vestments.

27. *Gideon made an ephod thereof.* That is, he made an ephod out of this mass of gold; but he could not employ it all in making this one garment, for it is not likely that any man could wear a coat of nearly one hundred pounds' weight. It is likely that he made a whole Tabernacle service in miniature out of this gold. *All Israel went thither a whoring after it.* This form of speech often occurs, and has been often explained. The whole Jewish nation is represented as being united to God as a wife is to her husband. Any act of idolatry is considered as a breach of their covenant with God, as an act of whoredom is the breach of the marriage agreement between man and wife.

28. *Forty years in the days of Gideon.* The Midianites were so completely humbled that they could make head no more against Israel during the forty years in which the government of Gideon lasted.

31. *His concubine.* A lawful but secondary wife, whose children could not inherit. *Whose name he called Abimelech.* That is, "my father is king" or "my father hath reigned." This name was doubtless given by the mother, and so

MATTHEW HENRY

4. After his death the people corrupted themselves, and went all to naught. As soon as ever Gideon was dead they *went a whoring after Baalim, v.* 33. False worships made way for false deities. They now chose a new god (*ch.* v. 8), a god of a new name, *Baalberith* (a goddess, say some); Berith, some think, was Berytus, the place where the Phoenicians worshipped this idol. The name signifies *the Lord of a covenant*. Perhaps he was so called because his worshippers joined themselves by covenant to him, in imitation of Israel's covenanting with God; for the devil is God's ape. In this revolt of Israel to idolatry they showed, (1) Great ingratitude to God (*v.* 34): *They remembered not the Lord.* (2) Great ingratitude to Gideon, *v.* 35. Israel showed not kindness to Gideon's family. No wonder if those who forget their God forget their friends.

JAMIESON, FAUSSET, BROWN

ADAM CLARKE

it should be understood here; she wished to raise her son to the supreme government, and therefore gave him a name which might serve to stimulate him to seek that which she hoped he should enjoy in his father's right.

33. *A whoring after Baalim.* This term has probably a different meaning here from what it has v. 7; for it is very likely that in most parts of the pagan worship there were many impure rites, so that going *a whoring after Baalim* may be taken in a literal sense. *Baal-berith.* Literally, "the lord of the covenant."

34. *Remembered not the Lord their God.* They attributed their deliverance to some other cause, and did not give Him the glory of their salvation.

35. *Neither shewed they kindness to the house of . . . Gideon.* They were both unthankful and unholy. Though they had the clearest proofs of God's power and goodness before their eyes, yet they forgot Him. And although they were under greatest obligations to Gideon, and were once so sensible of them that they offered to settle the kingdom on him and his family, yet they forgot him also.

Jerubbaal, namely, Gideon. This is improper; it should be "Jerubbaal Gideon," as we say "Simon Peter," or call any man by his Christian name and surname.

MATTHEW HENRY — CHAPTER 9

Verses 1–6

We are here told by what arts Abimelech got into authority, and made himself great. His mother perhaps had instilled into his mind some towering ambitious thoughts, and the name his father gave him, carrying royalty in it, might help to blow up these sparks. He had no call from God to this honour as his father had, nor was there any present occasion for a judge to deliver Israel as there was when his father was advanced.

I. How craftily he got his mother's relations into his interests. Shechem was a city in the tribe of Ephraim, of great note. Joshua had held his last assembly there. If that city would but appear for him, and set him up, he thought it would go far in his favour. None would have dreamed of making such a one king, if he had not dreamed of it himself. And see here, 1. How he wheedled them into the choice, *v.* 2, 3. He basely suggested that Gideon having left seventy sons, they were designing to keep the power which their father had in their hands. "Now," says he, "you had better have one king than more." *Remember that I am your bone and your flesh.* The plot took wonderfully. The magistrates of Shechem were pleased to think of their city being a royal city and the metropolis of Israel, and therefore they *inclined to follow him; for they said,* "*He is our brother*, and his advancement will be our advantage." 2. How he got money from them to bear the charges of his pretensions (*v.* 4): *They gave him seventy pieces of silver;* money out of the house of Baal-berith, that is, out of the public treasury, which, out of respect to their idol, they deposited in his temple to be protected by him. How unfit was he to reign over Israel, because unlikely to defend them, who, instead of restraining and punishing idolatry, thus early made himself a pensioner to an idol! 3. What soldiers he enlisted. He hired into his service vain and light persons, the scum and scoundrels of the country, men of broken fortunes, giddy heads, and profligate lives.

II. How cruelly he got his father's sons out of the way.

1. The first thing he did with the rabble he headed was to kill all his brethren at once, publicly, and in cold blood, threescore and ten men, one only escaping, all slain upon one stone. (1) The power of ambition what beasts it will turn men into! (2) The peril of honour and high birth.

2. Way being thus made for Abimelech's election, the men of Shechem proceeded to choose him king, *v.* 6. God was not consulted whether they should have any king at all, much less who it should be. But, (1) The Shechemites aided and abetted him in the murder of his brethren (*v.* 24), and then they *made him king. Pretium sceleris tulit hic diadema—His wickedness was rewarded with a diadem.* (2) The rest of the Israelites were so very sottish as to sit by unconcerned. It is for this that they are charged with ingratitude (*ch.* viii. 35): *Neither showed they kindness to the house of Jerubbaal.*

JAMIESON, FAUSSET, BROWN — CHAPTER 9

VSS. 1-6. ABIMELECH IS MADE KING BY THE SHECHEMITES. **1. Abimelech the son of Jerubbaal went to Shechem**—The idolatry which had been stealthily creeping into Israel during the latter years of Gideon was now openly professed; Shechem was wholly inhabited by its adherents; at least, idolaters had the ascendency. Abimelech, one of Gideon's numerous sons, was connected with that place. Ambitious of sovereign power, and having plied successfully the arts of a demagogue with his maternal relatives and friends, he acquired both the influence and money by which he raised himself to a throne. **communed . . . with all the family of the house of his mother's father**—Here is a striking instance of the evils of polygamy—one son has connections and interests totally alien to those of his brothers. **2. Whether is better for you, either that all the sons of Jerubbaal, . . . or that one reign over you**—a false insinuation, artfully contrived to stir up jealousy and alarm. Gideon had rejected, with abhorrence, the proposal to make himself or any of his family king, and there is no evidence that any of his other sons coveted the title.

4. the house of Baal-berith—either the temple, or the place where this idol was worshipped; Baal-berith, "god of the covenant," by invocation of whom the league of cities was formed. **Abimelech hired vain and light persons, which followed him**—idle, worthless vagabonds, the scum of society, who had nothing to lose, but much to gain from the success of a revolutionary movement. **5. went unto . . . Ophrah, and slew his brethren . . . upon one stone**—This is the first mention of a barbarous atrocity which has, with appalling frequency, been perpetrated in the despotic countries of the East—that of one son of the deceased monarch usurping the throne and hastening to confirm himself in the possession by the massacre of all the natural or legitimate competitors. Abimelech slew his brethren *on one stone*, either by dashing them from one rock, or sacrificing them on one stone altar, in revenge for the demolition of Baal's altar by their father. This latter view is the more probable, from the Shechemites (vs. 24) aiding in it. **threescore and ten persons**—A round number is used, but it is evident that two are wanting to complete that number. **6. all the men of Shechem . . . , and all the house of Millo**—i.e., a mound or rampart, so that the meaning is, all the men in the house or temple; namely, the priests of Baal. **made Abimelech king, by the plain of the pillar**—rather, by the oak near a raised mound—so that the ceremony of coronation might be conspicuous to a crowd.

ADAM CLARKE — CHAPTER 9

1. *Abimelech . . . went to Shechem.* We have already seen that Abimelech was the son of Gideon by his concubine at Shechem. His going thither immediately after his father's death was to induce his townsmen to proclaim him governor in the place of his father. Shechem was the residence of his mother, and of all her relatives.

2. *Whether is better for you, either that all the sons?* This was a powerful argument: Whether will you have seventy tyrants or only one? For, as he had no right to the government, and God alone was King at that time in Israel, so he must support his usurped rule by whatever means were most likely to effect it: a usurped government is generally supported by oppression and the sword.

3. *He is our brother.* We shall be raised to places of trust under him, and our city will be the capital of the kingdom.

4. *Threescore and ten pieces of silver.* Probably shekels; and this was the whole of his exchequer. As he was now usurping the government of God, he began with a contribution from the idol temple. A work begun under the name and influence of the devil is not likely to end to the glory of God or to the welfare of man. *Hired vain and light persons.* "Worthless and dissolute men"; persons who were living on the public, and had nothing to lose. Such was the foundation of his Babel government. By a cunning management of such rascals most revolutions have been brought about.

5. *Slew his brethren.* His brothers by the father's side, chap. viii. 30. This was a usual way of securing an ill-gotten throne, the person who had no right destroying all those that had right, that he might have no competitors. *Yet Jotham . . . was left.* That is, all the seventy were killed except Jotham, if there were not seventy besides Jotham.

6. *And all the house of Millo.* If *Millo* be the name of a place, it is nowhere else mentioned in the sacred writings. But it is probably the name of a person of note and influence in the city of Shechem—"the men of Shechem and the family of Millo."

MATTHEW HENRY

Verses 7–21

Only Jotham, the youngest son of Gideon, who by a special providence escaped the common ruin of his family (*v.* 5), dealt plainly with the Shechemites. Jotham did not go about to raise an army out of the other cities of Israel but he contents himself with giving a faithful reproof to the Shechemites, and fair warning of the fatal consequences.

I. His preface is very serious: "*Hearken unto me, you men of Shechem, that God may hearken unto you*", *v.* 7.

II. His parable is very ingenious—that when the trees were disposed to choose a king the government was offered to those valuable trees the olive, the fig tree, and the vine, but they refused it, choosing rather to serve than rule, to do good than bear sway. But the same tender being made to the bramble he accepted it with vain-glorious exultation.

1. He hereby applauds the generous modesty of Gideon, and the other judges who were before him, and perhaps of the sons of Gideon, who had declined accepting the state and power of kings when they might have had them, and likewise shows that it is in general the temper of all wise and good men to decline preferment and to choose rather to be useful than to be great. (1) There was no occasion at all for the trees to choose a king. Nor was there any occasion for Israel to talk of setting a king over them; for *the Lord was their king.* (2) When they had it in their thoughts to choose a king they did not offer the government to the stately cedar, or the lofty pine, which are only for show and shade, and not otherwise useful till they are cut down, but to the fruit trees, the vine and the olive. Those that bear fruit for the public good are justly respected and honoured. (3) The reason which all these fruit trees gave for their refusal was much the same. The olive pleads (*v.* 9), *Should I leave my fatness?* And the vine (*v.* 13), *Should I leave my wine,* wherewith both God and man are served and honoured? for oil and wine were used both at God's altars and at men's tables. And *shall I leave my sweetness, saith the fig tree, and my good fruit* (*v.* 11), *and go to be promoted over the trees?* or, as the margin reads it, *go up and down for the trees?* It is intimated, [1] That government involves a man in a great deal both of toil and care. [2] That those who are preferred to places of public trust and power must resolve to forego all their private interests and advantages, and sacrifice them to the good of the community. [3] That those who are advanced to honour and dignity are in great danger of losing their fatness and fruitfulness. Preferment is apt to make men proud and slothful, and thus spoil their usefulness, for which reason those that desire to do good are afraid of being too great.

2. He hereby exposes the ridiculous ambition of Abimelech, whom he compares to the bramble or thistle, *v.* 14. The bramble is a worthless plant, not to be numbered among the trees, useless and fruitless, nay, hurtful and vexatious, scratching and tearing, and doing mischief; it began with the curse, and its end is to be burned. Such a one was Abimelech, and yet chosen to the government *by the trees, by all the trees.* Let us not think it strange if we see *folly set in great dignity* (Eccles. x. 6), and the *vilest men exalted* (Ps. xii. 8), and men blind to their own interest in the choice of their guides.

III. His application is very close and plain. In it, 1. He reminds them of the many good services his father had done for them, *v.* 17. 2. He aggravates their unkindness to his father's family. They had not *done to him according to the deserving of his hands, v.* 16. Gideon had left many sons that were an honour to his name and family, and these they had barbarously murdered; one son he had left was *the son of his maid-servant,* whom all that had any respect to Gideon's honour would endeavour to conceal, yet him they made their king. 3. He leaves it to the event to determine whether they had done well. (1) If they prospered long in this villainy, he would give them leave to say they had done well, *v.* 19. But, (2) If they had, as he was sure they had, dealt basely and wickedly in this matter, let them never expect to prosper, *v.* 20.

Jotham, having given them this admonition, made a shift to escape with his life, *v.* 21. But, for fear of Abimelech, he lived in exile, in some remote obscure place.

Verses 22–49

Three years Abimelech reigned, after a sort, without any disturbance; it is not said, He judged Israel, or did any service at all to his country, but so long he enjoyed the title and dignity of a king. But the triumphing of the wicked is short. The ruin of these confederates in wickedness was from the righteous hand of the God. *He sent an evil spirit between Abimelech and the Shechemites* (*v.* 23), that is, they

JAMIESON, FAUSSET, BROWN

7-21. JOTHAM BY A PARABLE REPROACHES THEM. **7. he . . . stood in the top of mount Gerizim, and lifted up his voice**—The spot he chose was, like the housetops, the public place of Shechem; and the parable drawn from the rivalry of the various trees was appropriate to the diversified foliage of the valley below. Eastern people are exceedingly fond of parables and use them for conveying reproofs—which they could not give in any other way. The top of Gerizim is not so high in the rear of the town, as it is nearer to the plain. With a little exertion of voice, he could easily have been heard by the people of the city; for the hill so overhangs the valley, that a person from the side or summit would have no difficulty in speaking to listeners at the base. Modern history records a case, in which soldiers on the hill shouted to the people in the city and endeavored to instigate them to an insurrection. There is something about the elastic atmosphere of an Eastern clime which causes it to transmit sound with wonderful celerity and distinctness [HACKETT].

13. wine, which cheereth God and man—not certainly in the same manner. God might be said to be "cheered" by it, when the sacrifices were accepted, as He is said also to be honored by oil (vs. 9).

21. Jotham . . . went to Beer—the modern village El-Bireh, on the ridge which bounds the northern prospect of Jerusalem.

22-49. GAAL'S CONSPIRACY. **22. When Abimelech had reigned three years**—His reign did not, probably at first, extend beyond Shechem; but by stealthy and progressive encroachments he subjected some of the neighboring towns to his sway. None could "reign" in Israel, except by rebellious usurpation; and hence the reign of Abimelech is expressed in the original by a word signifying "despotism," not that which describes the mild and divinely authorized rule of the judge.

ADAM CLARKE

7. *Stood in the top of mount Gerizim.* Gerizim and Ebal were mounts very near to each other; the former lying to the north, the latter to the south, and at the foot of them Shechem.

That God may hearken unto you. It appears that Jotham received this message from God, and that he spoke on this occasion by divine inspiration.

8. *The trees went forth on a time.* This is the oldest, and without exception the best, fable in the world. It is not to be supposed that a fable, if well-formed, requires much illustration; every part of this, a few expressions excepted, illustrates itself, and tells its own meaning. *To anoint a king.* Hence it appears that anointing was usual in the installation of kings long before there was any king in Israel; for there is much evidence that the Book of Judges was written before the days of Saul and David. *The olive tree.* The olive was the most useful of all the trees in the field or forest, as the bramble was the meanest and the most worthless.

9. *Wherewith . . . they honor God and man.* I believe the word *elohim* here should be translated "gods," for the parable seems to be accommodated to the idolatrous state of the Shechemites. Thus it was understood by the Vulgate, Arabic, and others.

11. *But the fig tree said . . . Should I forsake my sweetness?* The fruit of the fig tree is the sweetest or most luscious of all fruits.

13. *Which cheereth God and man.* I believe *elohim* here is to be taken in the same sense proposed on v. 9. Vast libations of wine, as well as much oil, were used in heathenish sacrifices and offerings; and it was their opinion that the gods actually partook of, and were delighted with, both the wine and oil.

14. *Then said all the trees unto the bramble.* The word *atad,* which we translate *bramble,* is supposed to mean the *rhamnus,* which is the largest of thorns, producing dreadful spikes, similar to darts.

15. *Come and put your trust in my shadow.* The vain boast of the would-be sovereign, and of the man who is seeking to be put into power by the suffrages of the people. All promise, no performance. *Let fire come out of the bramble.* The bramble was too low to give shelter to any tree, and so far from being able to consume others that the smallest fire will reduce it to ashes, and that in the shortest time. Hence the very transitory mirth of fools is said to be like the cracking of thorns under a pot. Abimelech was the *bramble;* and the *cedars of Lebanon,* all the nobles and people of Israel. Could they therefore suppose that such a lowborn, uneducated, cruel, and murderous man could be a proper protector or a humane governor? He who could imbrue his hands in the blood of his brethren in order to get into power was not likely to stop at any means to retain that power when possessed. If therefore they took him for their king, they might rest assured that desolation and blood would mark the whole of his reign. The condensed moral of the whole fable is this: Weak, worthless, and wicked men will ever be foremost to thrust themselves into power; and, in the end, to bring ruin upon themselves, and on the unhappy people over whom they preside.

20. *Let fire come out from Abimelech.* As the thorn or bramble may be the means of kindling other wood, because it may be easily ignited, so shall Abimelech be the cause of kindling a fire of civil discord among you that shall consume the rulers and great men of your country. A prophetic declaration of what would take place.

MATTHEW HENRY

grew jealous one of another and ill-affected one to another. This was from God. He permitted the devil, that great mischief-maker, to sow discord between them, and he is *an evil spirit*, whom God not only keeps under his check, but sometimes serves his own purposes by. Their own lusts were evil spirits; they are devils in men's own hearts; from them come wars and fightings. These God gave them up to, and so might be said to *send the evil spirits between them.* When men's sin is made their punishment, though God is not the author of the sin, yet the punishment is from him. The Shechemites that countenanced Abimelech's pretensions, aided and abetted him in his bloody project, and avowed the fact by making him king after he had done it, must fall with him, fall by him, and fall first.

I. The Shechemites began to affront Abimelech. 1. They *dealt treacherously with him, v.* 23. It is not said, They repented of their sin in owning him. 2. They aimed to seize him when he was at Arumah (*v.* 41), his country seat. Expecting him to come to town, they *set liers in wait for him* (*v.* 25). Those who were thus posted, he not coming, took the opportunity of robbing travellers. 3. They entertained one Gaal, and set him up as their head in opposition to Abimelech, *v.* 26. This Gaal is said to be the son of *Ebed*, which signifies *a servant*. As Abimelech was by the mother's side, so he by the father's, the son of a servant. Here was one bramble contesting with another. He was a bold ambitious man, so he went over to them to blow the coals, and they *put their confidence in him.* 4. They did all the despite they could to Abimelech's name, *v.* 27. They *went into the house of their god*, to solemnize their feast of ingathering, and there *they did eat, and drink, and cursed Abimelech*, praying to their idol to destroy him. That very temple whence they had fetched money to set him up with did they now meet in to curse him and contrive his ruin. 5. They pleased themselves with Gaal's vaunted defiance of Abimelech, *v.* 28, 29. They loved to hear that impudent upstart speak scornfully, (1) Of Abimelech. (2) Of his good father likewise, Gideon: *Is not he the son of Jerubbaal?* (3) Of his prime minister of state, *Zebul his officer, and ruler of the city.* Gaal aimed not to recover Shechem's liberty, only to change their tyrant: "*O that this people were under my hand!*" This pleased the Shechemites, who were now as sick of Abimelech as ever they had been fond of him. Men of no conscience will be men of no constancy.

II. Abimelech turned all his force upon them, and, in a little time, quite ruined them. Observe the steps of their overthrow.

1. The Shechemites' counsels were betrayed to Abimelech by Zebul his confidant, the ruler of the city, who continued hearty for him. *His anger was kindled*, (*v.* 30). He thinks it best that he should march his forces by night into the neighbourhood. How could the Shechemites hope to speed in their attempt when the ruler of their city was in the interests of their enemy?

2. Gaal, that headed their faction, having been betrayed by Zebul, Abimelech's confidant, was most wretchedly bantered by him. "It is but *the shadow of the mountains* which thou takest to be an army." By this he intended, (1) To ridicule him. (2) To detain him, while the forces of Abimelech were coming up. Then Zebul took another way to banter him, upbraiding him with what he had said but a day or two before, in contempt of Abimelech (*v.* 38). Now Zebul, in Abimelech's name, challenges him: *Go out, and fight with them*, if thou darest.

3. Abimelech routed Gaal's forces that sallied out of the town, *v.* 39, 40.

4. Zebul that night expelled Gaal, and the party he had brought with him into Shechem, out of the city (*v.* 41), sending him to the place whence he came.

5. Abimelech, the next day, set upon the city, and quite destroyed it, for their treacherous dealings with him. He resolved to follow his blow, and effectually to chastise their treachery. (1) He had intelligence brought him that the people of Shechem had come out *into the field*, *v.* 42, to plough and sow. Others think they went out into the field of battle; though Gaal was driven out, they would not lay down their arms. (2) He himself, with a strong detachment, cut off the communication between them and the city, and then sent two companies of his men, who were too strong for them, and they put them all to the sword, and *ran upon those that were in the fields and slew them.* (3) He then fell upon the city itself, and sowed it with salt, that it might remain a lasting monument of the punishment of perfidiousness. Yet Abimelech prevailed not to make its desolations perpetual; for it was afterwards rebuilt, and became so considerable a place that all Israel came thither to make Rehoboam king, 1 Kings xii. 1.

JAMIESON, FAUSSET, BROWN

23. Then God sent an evil spirit between Abimelech and the men of Shechem—In the course of providence, jealousy, distrust, secret disaffection, and smothered rebellion appeared among his subjects disappointed and disgusted with his tyranny; and God permitted those disorders to punish the complicated crimes of the royal fratricide and idolatrous usurper.

26. Gaal . . . came with his brethren . . . , and the men of Shechem put their confidence in him—An insurrection of the original Canaanites, headed by this man, at last broke out in Shechem.

28-45. would to God this people were under my hand—He seems to have been a boastful, impudent, and cowardly person, totally unfit to be a leader in a revolutionary crisis.

The consequence was that he allowed himself to be drawn into an ambush—was defeated—the city of Shechem destroyed and strewn with salt. The people took refuge in the stronghold, which was set on fire, and all in it perished.

ADAM CLARKE

23. *God sent an evil spirit.* He permitted jealousies to take place which produced factions; and these factions produced insurrections, civil contentions, and slaughter.

25. *The men of Shechem set liers in wait.* It pleased God to punish this bad man by the very persons who had contributed to his iniquitous elevation. So God often makes the instruments of men's sins the means of their punishment. It is likely that although Abimelech had his chief residence at Shechem, yet he frequently went to Ophrah, the city of his father, his claim to which there was none to oppose, as he had slain all his brethren. It was probably in his passage between those two places that the Shechemites had posted cutthroats, in order to assassinate him; as such men had no moral principle, they robbed and plundered all who came that way.

26. *Gaal the son of Ebed.* Of this person we know no more than is here told. He was probably one of the descendants of the Canaanites, who hoped from the state of the public mind, and their disaffection to Abimelech, to cause a revolution, and thus to restore the ancient government as it was under Hamor, the father of Shechem.

28. *Zebal his officer. Pekido*, "his overseer"; probably governor of Shechem in his absence.

29. *Would to God this people were under my hand!* The very words and conduct of a sly, hypocritical demagogue. *Increase thine army, and come out.* When he found his party strong, and the public feeling warped to his side, then he appears to have sent a challenge to Abimelech to come out and fight him.

31. *They fortify the city against thee.* Under pretense of repairing the walls and towers, they were actually putting the place in a state of defense, intending to seize on the government as soon as they should find Abimelech coming against them.

35. *Stood in the entering of the gate.* Having probably got some intimation of the designs of Zebul and Abimelech.

37. *By the plain of Meonenim.* Some translate, "by the way of the oaks," or oaken groves; others, "by the way of the magicians," or "regarders of the times," as in our margin. Probably it was a place in which augurs and soothsayers dwelt.

45. *And sowed it with salt.* Intending that the destruction of this city should be a perpetual memorial of his achievements. The salt was not designed to render it barren, as some have imagined; for who would think of cultivating a city? But as salt is an emblem of incorruption and perpetuity, it was no doubt designed to perpetuate the memorial of this transaction, and as a token that he wished this desolation to be eternal. This sowing a place with salt was a custom in different nations to express permanent desolation and abhorrence.

MATTHEW HENRY | JAMIESON, FAUSSET, BROWN | ADAM CLARKE

6. Those that retired into a stronghold of their idol-temple were all destroyed there. These are called *the men of the tower of Shechem* (*v.* 46, 47), some castle that belonged to the city, but lay at some distance from it. But that which they hoped would be for their welfare proved to them a snare and a trap, as those will certainly find that run to idols for shelter. All that were in it were either burnt or stifled with the smoke. What inventions men have to destroy one another! Whence come these cruel wars and fightings but from their lusts? About 1000 men and women perished in these flames, many of whom, it is probable, were no way concerned in the quarrel between Abimelech and the Shechemites, yet, in this civil war, they came to this miserable end; for men of factious turbulent spirits *perish not alone in their iniquity*, but involve many more, that follow them in their simplicity, in the same calamity with them.

Verses 50–57

Thebez was a small city, probably not far from Shechem, dependent upon it, and in confederacy with it.

I. Abimelech attempted the destruction of this city (*v.* 50), and drove all the inhabitants of the town into the castle, or citadel, *v.* 51.

II. In the attempt he was himself destroyed, having his brains knocked out with a piece of a millstone, *v.* 57. Three circumstances are worthy of observation in the death of Abimelech:—1. That he was slain with a stone, as he had slain his brethren all *upon one stone*. 2. That he had his skull broken. Vengeance aimed at that guilty head which had worn the usurped crown. 3. That the stone was cast upon him by a woman, *v.* 53. Nothing troubled him so much as this, that it should be said, A woman slew him. See, (1) His foolish pride, in laying so much to heart this little circumstance of his disgrace. Here was no care taken about his precious soul, no concern what would become of that, no prayer to God for his mercy; but very solicitous he is to patch up his shattered credit, when there is no patching his shattered skull. "O let it never be said that such a mighty man as Abimelech was killed by a woman!" (2) His foolish project to avoid this disgrace; nothing could be more ridiculous; his own servant must run him through, not to rid him the sooner out of his pain, but *that men say not, A woman slew him.*

III. The issue of all is that Abimelech being slain, 1. Israel's peace was restored, and an end was put to this civil war. 2. God's justice was glorified (*v* 56, 57). Though wickedness may prosper awhile, it will not prosper always.

50-57. ABIMELECH SLAIN. **50. Then went Abimelech to Thebez, and encamped against Thebez**—now Tubas—not far from Shechem. **51. all the men and women . . . gat them up to the top of the tower**—The Canaanite forts were generally mountain fastnesses or keeps, and they often had a strong tower which served as a last refuge. The Assyrian bas-reliefs afford counterparts of the scene here described so vivid and exact, that we might almost suppose them to be representations of the same historic events. The besieged city—the strong tower within—the men and *women* crowding its battlements—the fire applied to the doors, and even the huge fragments of stone dropping from the hands of one of the garrison on the heads of the assailants—are all well represented to the life—just as they are here described in the narrative of inspired truth [Goss].

46. *An hold of the house of the god Berith.* This must mean the precincts of the temple, as we find there were a thousand men and women together in that place.

53. *A piece of a millstone.* "A piece of a chariot wheel"; but the word is used in other places for upper millstones, and is so understood here by the Vulgate, Septuagint, Syriac, and Arabic. *And all to break his skull.* A most nonsensical version of *vattarits eth gulgolto*, which is literally, "And she brake (or fractured) his skull." Plutarch, in his life of Pyrrhus, observes that this king was killed at the siege of Thebes by a piece of a tile, which a woman threw upon his head.

54. *Draw thy sword, and slay me.* It was a disgrace to be killed by a woman. Abimelech was also afraid that, if he fell thus mortally wounded into the hands of his enemies, they might treat him with cruelty and insult.

56. *Thus God rendered.* Both fratricide Abimelech and the unprincipled men of Shechem had the iniquity visited upon them of which they had been guilty. Man's judgment may be avoided, but there is no escape from the judgments of God.

CHAPTER 10

Verses 1–5

Quiet and peaceable were the reigns of these two judges, Tola and Jair, who make but a small figure and take up but a very little room in this history. But no doubt they were both *raised up of God* to serve their country in the quality of judges, not pretending, as Abimelech had done, to the grandeur of kings, nor, like him, taking the honour they had to themselves, but being called of God to it. 1. Concerning Tola it is said that he arose after Abimelech to defend Israel, *v.* 1. God animated this good man to appear for the reforming of abuses, the putting down of idolatry, the appeasing of tumults, and the healing of the wounds given to the state by Abimelech's usurpation. 2. Jair was a Gileadite, so was his next successor Jephthah, both of that half tribe of Manasseh which lay on the other side of Jordan. That which is chiefly remarkable concerning this Jair is the increase and honour of his family: *He had thirty sons*, *v.* 4. And, (1) They had good preferments, for they *rode on thirty ass colts*; that is, they were judges itinerant, who, as deputies to their father, rode from place to place in their several circuits to administer justice. (2) They had good possessions, every one a city, out of those that were called, from their ancestor of the same name with their father, *Havoth-jair—the villages of Jair*; yet they are called *cities*. Villages are cities to a contented mind.

Verses 6–9

While those two judges, Tola and Jair, presided in the affairs of Israel, things went well, but afterwards,

I. Israel returned to their idolatry. 1. They worshipped many gods; not only their old demons Baalim and Ashtaroth, which the Canaanites had worshipped, but, as if they would proclaim their folly to all their neighbours, they served the gods of Syria, Zidon, Moab, Ammon, and the Philistines. It looks as if

CHAPTER 10

VSS. 1-5. TOLA JUDGES ISRAEL IN SHAMIR. **1. after Abimelech there arose to defend Israel, Tola**—i.e., to save. Deliverance was necessary as well from intestine usurpation as from foreign aggression. **the son of Puah**—He was uncle to Abimelech by the father's side, and consequently brother of Gideon; yet the former was of the tribe of Issachar, while the latter was of Manasseh. They were, most probably, uterine brothers. **dwelt in Shamir in mount Ephraim**—As a central place, he made it the seat of government.

3. Jair, a Gileadite—This judge was a different person from the conqueror of that northeastern territory, and founder of Havoth-jair, or "Jair's villages." (Num. 32:41; Deut. 3:14; Josh. 13:3; I Chron. 2:22.) **4. he had thirty sons that rode on thirty ass colts**—This is a characteristic trait of Eastern manners in those early times; and the grant of a village to each of his thirty sons was a striking proof of his extensive possessions. His having thirty sons is no conclusive evidence that he had more than one wife, much less that he had more than one at a time. There are instances, in this country, of men having as many children by two successive wives.

6-9. ISRAEL OPPRESSED BY THE PHILISTINES AND AMMONITES. **6. the children of Israel did evil again in the sight of the Lord**—This apostasy seems to have exceeded every former one in the grossness and universality of the idolatry practised. **7. Philistines, and . . . the children of Ammon**—The

CHAPTER 10

1. *Tola the son of Puah.* As this Tola continued twenty-three years a judge of Israel after the troubles of Abimelech's reign, it is likely that the land had rest, and that the enemies of the Israelites had made no hostile incursions into the land during his presidency and that of Jair, which together continued forty-five years.

4. *He had thirty sons.* It appears that there were both peace and prosperity during the time that Jair governed Israel. He had, it seems, provided for his family, and given a village to each of his thirty sons; which were, in consequence, called *Havoth Jair* or the "villages of Jair." Their riding *on thirty ass colts* seems to intimate that they were persons of consideration, and kept up a certain dignity in their different departments.

6. *And served Baalim.* They became universal idolaters, adopting every god of the surrounding nations. *Baalim and Ashtaroth* may signify "gods" and "goddesses" in general.

MATTHEW HENRY

the chief trade of Israel had been to import deities from all countries. It is hard to say whether it was more impious or impolitic to do this. Those nations which by their wicked arts they sought to make their friends by the righteous judgments of God became their enemies and oppressors. 2. They did not so much as admit the God of Israel to be one of those many deities they worshipped, but quite cast him off. Those that think to serve both God and Mammon will soon come entirely to forsake God, and to serve Mammon only. If God have not all the heart, he will soon have none of it.

II. God renewed his judgments upon them, bringing them under the power of oppressing enemies. God had appointed that, if any of the cities of Israel should revolt to idolatry, the rest should make war upon them and cut them off, Deut. xiii. 12, &c. God brought the neighbouring nations upon them, to chastise them for their apostasy. The oppression of Israel by the Ammonites, the posterity of Lot, was, 1. Very long. It continued eighteen years. 2. Very grievous. They began with those tribes that lay next them on the other side Jordan, here called *the land of the Amorites* (*v.* 8) because the Israelites had so wretchedly degenerated, and had made themselves so like the heathen, that they had become, in a manner, perfect Amorites (Ezek. xvi. 3). But by degrees they pushed forward, came over Jordan, and invaded Judah, and Benjamin, and Ephraim (*v.* 9), three of the most famous tribes of Israel, yet thus insulted when they had forsaken God, and unable to make head against the invader.

Verses 10–18

I. A humble confession which Israel make to God in their distress, *v.* 10. They confess their omissions, for in them their sin began— "We have forsaken our God," and their commissions—"We have served Baalim, and herein have done foolishly, treacherously, and very wickedly."

II. A humbling message which God thereupon sends to Israel, whether by an angel (as *ch.* ii. 1) or by a prophet (as *ch.* vi. 8) is not certain. Now in this message, 1. He upbraids them with their great ingratitude, reminds them of the great things he had done for them. God had in justice corrected them, and in mercy delivered them, and therefore might reasonably expect that either through fear or through love they would adhere to him and his service. 2. He shows them how justly he might now abandon them to ruin, by abandoning them to the *gods that they had served.* To awaken them to a thorough repentance and reformation, he lets them see, (1) Their folly in serving Baalim. "*Go, and cry unto the gods which you have chosen*" (*v.* 14), try what they can do for you now. It is necessary, in true repentance, that there be a full conviction of the utter insufficiency of all those things to help us. We must be convinced that the pleasures of sense on which we have doted cannot be our satisfaction, nor the wealth of the world which we have coveted be our portion, that we cannot be happy or easy anywhere but in God. (2) Their misery and danger in forsaking God.

III. A humble submission which Israel hereupon made to God's justice, with a humble application to his mercy, *v.* 15. They not only repeat their confession, *We have sinned,* but, 1. They surrender themselves to God's justice: *Do thou unto us whatsoever seemeth good unto thee.* 2. They supplicate for God's mercy.

IV. A blessed reformation set on foot hereupon. They brought forth fruits meet for repentance (*v.* 16): *They put away the gods of strangers* (as the word is), strange gods, and they *served the Lord.* This is true repentance not only for sin, but from sin.

V. God's gracious return in mercy to them, which is expressed here very tenderly (*v.* 16): *His soul was grieved for the misery of Israel.* As he is pleased to put himself into the relation of a father to his people that are in covenant with him, so he is pleased to represent his goodness to them by the compassions of a father towards his children; for, as he is the Father of lights, so he is the Father of mercies.

VI. Things are now working towards their deliverance from the Ammonites' oppression, *v.* 17, 18. God had said, "I will deliver you no more"; but now they are not what they were, they are other men, they are new men, and now he will deliver them. 1. The Ammonites are hardened to their own ruin. They gathered together in one body, that they might be destroyed at one blow, Rev. xvi. 16. 2. The Israelites are animated to their own rescue. They assembled likewise, *v.* 17. During their eighteen years' oppression, as in their former servitudes, they were run down by their enemies, because they would not incorporate; each family, city, or tribe, would stand by itself, and act independently, and so they all became an easy prey to the oppressors, for want

JAMIESON, FAUSSET, BROWN

predatory incursions of these two hostile neighbors were made naturally on the parts of the land respectively contiguous to them. But the Ammonites, animated with the spirit of conquest, carried their arms across the Jordan; so that the central and southern provinces of Canaan were extensively desolated.

10-15. THEY CRY TO GOD. **10. The children of Israel cried unto the Lord, We have sinned against thee**—The first step of repentance is confession of sin, and the best proof of its sincerity is given by the transgressor, when he mourns not only over the painful consequences which have resulted from his offenses to himself, but over the heinous evil committed against God. **11. the Lord said . . . , Did I not deliver you from the Egyptians**—The circumstances recorded in this and the following verses were not probably made through the high priest, whose duty it was to interpret the will of God. **12. Maonites**—i.e., Midianites.

16-18. THEY REPENT; GOD PITIES THEM. **they put away the strange gods . . . and served the Lord; and his soul was grieved for the misery of Israel**—On their abandonment of idolatry and return to purity of worship, God graciously abridged the term of national affliction and restored times of peace.

17, 18. the children of Ammon were gathered together—From carrying on guerrilla warfare, the Ammonites proceeded to a continued campaign. Their settled aim was to wrest the whole of the trans-jordanic territory from its actual occupiers. In this great crisis, a general meeting of the Israelitish tribes was held at Mizpeh. This Mizpeh was in eastern Manasseh (Josh. 11:3).

ADAM CLARKE

7. *The anger of the Lord was hot.* This divine displeasure was manifested in delivering them into the hands of the Philistines and the Ammonites. The former dwelt on the western side of Jordan, the latter on the eastern; and it appears that they joined their forces on this occasion to distress and ruin the Israelites, though the Ammonites were the most active.

11. *And the Lord said.* By what means these reproofs were conveyed to the Israelites, we know not; it must have been by an angel, a prophet, or some holy man inspired for the occasion.

15. *We have sinned.* The reprehension of this people was kind, pointed, and solemn; and their repentance, deep. And they gave proofs that their repentance was genuine by putting away all their idols, but they were ever fickle and uncertain.

17. *The children of Ammon were gathered together.* Literally, "They cried against Israel"—they sent out criers in different directions to stir up all the enemies of Israel; and when they had made a mighty collection, they encamped in Gilead.

18. *What man is he that will begin to fight?* It appears that, although the spirit of patriotism had excited the people at large to come forward against their enemies, yet they had no general, none to lead them forth to battle. God, however, who had accepted their sincere repentance, raised them up an able captain in the person of Jephthah; and in him the suffrages of the people were concentrated, as we shall see in the following chapter. In those ancient times much depended on the onset; a war was generally terminated in one battle. The first impression was therefore of great consequence, and it re-

MATTHEW HENRY

of a due sense of a common interest to cement them: but, whenever they got together, they did well; so they did here. When God's Israel become as one man to advance a common good and oppose a common enemy what difficulty can stand before them?

CHAPTER 11

Verses 1–3

The princes and people of Gilead we left, in the close of the foregoing chapter, consulting about the choice of a general. Now all agreed that Jephthah, the Gileadite, was a mighty man of valour, and very fit for that purpose, none so fit as he, but he lay under three disadvantages:—1. He was *the son of a harlot* (*v.* 1), of *a strange woman* (*v.* 2), an Ishmaelite, say the Jews. If his mother was a harlot, that was not his fault, however, it was his disgrace. Men ought not to be reproached with any of the infelicities of their parentage or extraction. The son of a harlot, if born again, born from above, shall be accepted of God, and be as welcome as any other to the glorious liberties of his children. 2. He had been driven from his country by his brethren. His father's legitimate children, insisting upon the rigour of the law, thrust him out from having any inheritance with them, without any consideration of his extraordinary qualifications, which merited a dispensation, and would have made him a mighty strength and ornament of their family. God often humbles those whom he designs to exalt, and makes that *stone the head of the corner which the builders refused*; so Joseph, Moses, and David, the three most eminent of the shepherds of Israel, were all thrust out by men, before they were called of God to their great offices. 3. He had, in his exile, headed a rabble, *v.* 3. Being driven out by his brethren, his great soul would not suffer him either to dig or beg, but by his sword he must live; those that were reduced to such straits, and animated by such a spirit, enlisted themselves under him. *Vain men* they are here called, that is, men that had run through their estates and had to seek for a livelihood. These went out with him, not to rob or plunder, but to hunt wild beasts. This is the man that must save Israel.

Verses 4–11

I. The distress which the children of Israel were in upon the Ammonites' invasion of their country, *v.* 4.

II. The court which the elders made to Jephthah hereupon to come and help them. They did not write or send a messenger to him, but went themselves to fetch him. They know him to be a bold man, and inured to the sword, and therefore he must be the man. See how God prepares men for the service he designs them for, and makes their troubles work for their advancement. If Jephthah had not been put to his shifts by his brethren's unkindness, he would not have had such occasion as this gave him to exercise and improve his martial genius, and so to signalize himself and become famous. An army without a general is like a body without a head. Any community would humbly beg the favour of being commanded rather than that every man should be his own master. Blessed be God for government, for a good government.

III. The objections Jephthah makes against accepting their offer: *Did you not hate me, and expel me? v.* 7. Jephthah was very willing to serve his country, but he thought fit to give them a hint of their former unkindness to him, that they might repent of their sin in using him so ill. Thus Joseph humbled his brethren before he made himself known to them. Many slight God and good men till they come to be in distress, and then they are desirous of God's mercy and good men's prayers.

IV. Their urgency with him to accept the government they offer him, *v.* 8. Let this instance be, 1. A caution to us not to despise or trample upon any because they are mean. Make no man our enemy, because we know not how soon our distresses may be such as that we may be highly concerned to make him our friend. 2. An encouragement to men of worth that are slighted or ill-treated. Let them bear it with meekness and cheerfulness, and leave it to God to make their light shine out of obscurity.

V. The bargain he makes with them. God had forgiven Israel the affronts they had put upon him (*ch.* x. 16), and therefore Jephthah will forgive. 1. He puts to them a fair question, *v.* 9. "Now if, by the blessing of God, I come home a conqueror, tell me plainly *shall I be your head?* If I deliver you, under God, shall I, under him, reform you?" The

JAMIESON, FAUSSET, BROWN

CHAPTER 11

Vss. 1-3. JEPHTHAH. **1. Jephthah**—"opener." **son of an harlot**—a concubine, or foreigner; implying an inferior sort of marriage prevalent in Eastern countries. Whatever dishonor might attach to his birth, his own high and energetic character rendered him early a person of note. **Gilead begat Jephthah**—His father seems to have belonged to the tribe of Manasseh (I Chron. 7:14, 17).

2. Thou shalt not inherit in our father's house—As there were children by the legitimate wife, the son of the secondary one was not entitled to any share of the patrimony, and the prior claim of the others was indisputable. Hence, as the brothers of Jephthah seem to have resorted to rude and violent treatment, they must have been influenced by some secret ill-will. **3. Jephthah . . . dwelt in the land of Tob**—on the north of Gilead, beyond the frontier of the Hebrew territories (II Sam. 10:6, 8). **there were gathered vain men to Jephthah**—idle, daring, or desperate. **and went out with him**—followed him as a military chief. They led a freebooting life, sustaining themselves by frequent incursions on the Ammonites and other neighboring people, in the style of Robin Hood. The same kind of life is led by many an Arab or Tartar still, who as the leader of a band, acquires fame by his stirring or gallant adventures. It is not deemed dishonorable when the expeditions are directed against those out of his own tribe or nation. Jephthah's mode of life was similar to that of David when driven from the court of Saul.

4-11. THE GILEADITES COVENANT WITH JEPHTHAH. **4. in process of time**—on the return of the season. **the children of Ammon made war against Israel**—Having prepared the way by the introduction of Jephthah, the sacred historian here resumes the thread of his narrative from ch. 10:17. The Ammonites seem to have invaded the country, and active hostilities were inevitable. **5, 6. the elders of Gilead went to fetch Jephthah**—All eyes were directed towards him as the only person possessed of the qualities requisite for the preservation of the country in this time of imminent danger; and a deputation of the chief men was despatched from the Hebrew camp at Mizpeh to solicit his services.

7-9. Jephthah said, Did not ye hate me?—He gave them at first a haughty and cold reception. It is probable that he saw some of his brothers among the deputies. Jephthah was now in circumstances to make his own terms. With his former experience, he would have shown little wisdom or prudence without binding them to a clear and specific engagement to invest him with unlimited authority, the more especially as he was about to imperil his life in their cause. Although ambition might, to a certain degree, have stimulated his ready compliance, it is impossible to overlook the piety of his language, which creates a favorable impression that his roving life, in a state of social manners so different from ours, was not incompatible with habits of personal religion.

ADAM CLARKE

quired a person skillful, valorous, and strong, to head the attack. Jephthah was a person in whom all these qualifications appear to have met. When God purposes to deliver, He, in the course of His providence, will find out, employ, and direct the proper means.

CHAPTER 11

1. *Now Jephthah . . . was the son of an harlot.* I think the word *zonah,* which we here render *harlot,* should be translated, as is contended for on Josh. ii. 1, viz., a "hostess," keeper of an inn or tavern for the accommodation of travellers; and thus it is understood by the Targum of Jonathan on this place: "and he was the son of a woman, a tavern keeper." See the note referred to above. She was very probably a Canaanite, as she is called, v. 2, a *strange woman,* a "woman of another race"; and on this account his brethren drove him from the family, as he could not have a full right to the inheritance, his mother not being an Israelite.

3. *There were gathered vain men to Jephthah. Reykim,* "empty men"—persons destitute of good sense, and profligate in their manners. The word may, however, mean in this place "poor persons," without property, and without employment. The versions in general consider them as plunderers.

4. *The children of Ammon made war.* They had invaded the land of Israel, and were now encamped in Gilead. See chap. x. 17.

6. *Come, and be our captain.* The Israelites were assembled in Mizpeh, but were without a captain to lead them against the Ammonites. And we find, from the conclusion of the preceding chapter, that they offered the command to any that would accept it.

8. *Therefore we turn again to thee now.* **We are convinced that we have dealt unjustly by thee, and we wish now to repair our fault, and give thee this sincere proof of our regret for having acted unjustly, and of our confidence in thee.**

MATTHEW HENRY

same question is put to those who desire salvation by Christ. "If he save you, will you be willing that he shall rule you? for on no other terms will he save you. If he make you happy, shall he make you holy? If he be your helper, shall he be your head?" 2. They immediately give him a positive answer (*v.* 10): "We will *do according to thy words*; command us in war, and thou shalt command us in peace." Thus was the original contract ratified between Jephthah and the Gileadites, which all Israel, it should seem, agreed to afterwards, for it is said (*ch.* xii. 7), *he judged Israel.* He hereupon went with them (*v.* 11) to the place where they were all assembled (*ch.* x. 17), and there by common consent they *made him head and captain.* Jephthah, to obtain this little honour, was willing to expose his life for them (*ch.* xii. 3), and shall we be discouraged in our Christian warfare by any of the difficulties we may meet with in it, when Christ himself has promised *a crown of life to him that overcometh*?

VI. Jephthah's pious acknowledgment of God in this great affair (*v.* 11): *He uttered all his words before the Lord in Mizpeh,* that is, upon his elevation, he immediately retired to his devotions, and in prayer spread the whole matter before God. He utters before God all his thoughts and cares in this matter; for God gives us leave to be free with him. 1. "Lord, the people have made me their head; wilt thou confirm the choice, and own me as thy people's head under thee and for thee?" "Lord," said Jephthah, "I will not accept the government unless thou give me leave." 2. Thus Jephthah opened the campaign with prayer. That was likely to end gloriously which began thus piously.

Verses 12–28

The treaty between Jephthah, now judge of Israel, and the king of the Ammonites.

I. Jephthah, as one having authority, sent to the king of Ammon, who in this war was the aggressor, to demand his reasons for invading the land of Israel. Now this fair demand shows, 1. That Jephthah did not delight in war, though he was a mighty man of valour, but was willing to prevent it by a peaceable accommodation. War should be the last remedy, not to be used till all other methods of ending matters in variance have been tried. This rule should be observed in going to law. The sword of justice, as well as the sword of war, must not be appealed to till the contending parties have first endeavoured by gentler means to understand one another, and to accommodate matters in variance, 1. Cor. vi. 1. 2. That Jephthah did delight in equity, and designed no other than to do justice.

II. The king of the Ammonites now gives in his demand, which he should have published before he had invaded Israel, *v.* 13. His pretence is, "Israel took away my lands long since; now therefore restore those lands."

III. Jephthah gives a very full and satisfactory answer to this demand, showing that the Ammonites had no title to this country that lay between the rivers Arnon and Jabbok, now in the possession of the tribes of Reuben and Gad.

1. That Israel never took any land away either from the Moabites or Ammonites. He puts them together because they were brethren, the children of Lot, near neighbours, and of united interests, having the same god, Chemosh, and perhaps sometimes the same king. The lands in question Israel took away from Sihon king of the Amorites. If the Amorites, before Israel came into that country, had taken these lands from the Moabites or Ammonites, as it should seem they had (Num. xxi. 26; Josh. xiii. 25), Israel was not concerned to enquire into that or answer for it.

2. That they were so far from invading the property of any other nations than the devoted posterity of cursed Canaan (one of the branches of which the Amorites were, Gen. x. 16) that they would not so much as force a passage through the country either of the Edomites, the seed of Esau, or of the Moabites, the seed of Lot.

3. That in that war in which they took this land out of the hands of Sihon king of the Amorites he was the aggressor, and not they, *v.* 19, 20. They sent a humble petition to him for leave to go through his land, willing to give him any security for their good behaviour in their march. But Sihon not only denied them this courtesy, but he mustered all his forces, and fought against Israel (*v.* 20). Israel therefore, in their war with him, stood in their own just and necessary defence, and therefore, having routed his army, might justly, in further revenge of the injury, seize his country as forfeited. Thus Israel came to the possession of this country and it is very unreasonable for the Ammonites to question their title.

JAMIESON, FAUSSET, BROWN

10, 11. the elders of Israel said unto Jephthah, The Lord be witness between us—Their offer being accompanied by the most solemn oath, Jephthah intimated his acceptance of the mission, and his willingness to accompany them.

But to make "assurance doubly sure," he took care that the pledge given by the deputies in Tob should be ratified in a general assembly of the people at Mizpeh—and the language of the historian, "Jephthah uttered all his words before the Lord," seems to imply that his inauguration with the character and extraordinary office of judge was solemnized by prayer for the divine blessing, or some religious ceremonial.

12-28. HIS EMBASSY TO THE KING OF AMMON. **12-28. Jephthah sent messengers unto the king of the children of Ammon**—This first act in his judicial capacity reflects the highest credit on his character for prudence and moderation, justice and humanity. The bravest officers have always been averse to war; so Jephthah, whose courage was indisputable, resolved not only to make it clearly appear that hostilities were forced upon him, but to try measures for avoiding, if possible, an appeal to arms: and in pursuing such a course he was acting as became a leader in Israel (Deut. 20:10-18).

13. the king of Ammon answered . . . , Because Israel took away my land—(See on Deut. 2:19-37). The subject of quarrel was a claim of right advanced by the Ammonite monarch to the lands which the Israelites were occupying. Jephthah's reply was clear, decisive, and unanswerable;—first, those lands were not in the possession of the Ammonites when his countrymen got them, and that they had been acquired by right of conquest from the Amorites;

ADAM CLARKE

11. *Jephthah went with the elders.* The elders had chosen him for their head; but, to be valid, this choice must be confirmed by the people; therefore it is said, *The people made him head.* But even this did not complete the business; God must be brought in as a Party to this transaction; and therefore *Jephthah uttered all his words before the Lord*—the terms made with the elders and the people on which he had accepted the command of the army; and, being sure of the divine approbation, he entered on the work with confidence.

12. *Jephthah sent messengers.* He wished the Ammonites to explain their own motives for undertaking a war against Israel, as then the justice of his cause would appear more forcibly to the people.

13. *From Arnon even unto Jabbok, and unto Jordan.* That is, all the land that had formerly belonged to the Amorites, and to the Moabites, who it seems were confederates on this occasion.

22. *From the wilderness even unto Jordan.* From Arabia Deserta on the east to Jordan on the west.

MATTHEW HENRY

4. He pleads a grant from the crown, and claims under that, *v.* 23, 24. God gave them the land by an express and particular conveyance, such as vested the title in them, which they might make good against all the world. Deut. ii. 24, *I have given into thy hand Sihon and his land.* To corroborate this plea, he urges an argument *ad hominem—directed to the man*: *Wilt thou possess that which Chemosh thy god giveth thee?* Not that Jephthah thought Chemosh a god, only he is *thy god*, and the worshippers even of those dunghill deities that could do neither good nor evil yet thought themselves beholden to them for all they had (Hos. ii. 12). "Now," says Jephthah, "we have as good a title to our country as you have to yours."

5. He pleads prescription. (1) Their title had not been disputed when they first entered upon it, *v.* 25. (2) Their possession had never yet been disturbed, *v.* 26. He pleads that they had kept this country as their own now about 300 years, and the Ammonites in all that time had never attempted to take it from them. So that, supposing their title had not been clear at the first, yet, no claim having been made for so many generations, the entry of the children of Ammon, without doubt, was barred for ever. A title so long unquestioned shall be presumed unquestionable.

6. By these arguments Jephthah justifies himself and his own cause and condemns the Ammonites: "*Thou doest me wrong to war against me*, and must expect to speed accordingly," *v.* 27. The children of Israel, in the days of their prosperity and power (for some such days they had in the times of the judges) had conducted themselves very inoffensively to all their neighbours. The king of the Ammonites, when he would seek an occasion of quarrelling with them, was forced to look 300 years back for a pretence.

7. For the deciding of the controversy, he puts himself upon God and his sword, and the king of Ammon joins issue with him (*v.* 27, 28): *The Lord the Judge be judge this day.*

Neither Jephthah's apology, nor his appeal, wrought upon the king of the children of Ammon; they had found the sweets of the spoil of Israel, in the eighteen years wherein they had oppressed them (*ch.* x. 8), and hoped now to make themselves masters of the tree with the fruit of which they had so often enriched themselves.

Verses 29–40

We have here Jephthah triumphing, but troubled and distressed by an unadvised vow.

I. Jephthah's victory was clear. 1. God gave him an excellent spirit, and he improved it bravely, *v.* 29. The Spirit of the Lord came upon him, and very much advanced his natural faculties, enduing him with power from on high. Hereby God confirmed him in his office, and assured him of success in his undertaking. Thus animated, he loses no time, but with an undaunted resolution takes the field. 2. God gave him eminent success, and he bravely improved that too (*v.* 32). Having routed their forces in the field, he pursued them to their cities. But it does not appear that he utterly destroyed the people, nor that he offered to make himself master of the country. Though others' attempting wrong to us will justify us in the defence of our own right, yet it will not authorize us to do them wrong.

II. Jephthah's vow is dark, and much in the clouds. When he was going out from his own house upon this hazardous undertaking, in prayer to God for his presence with him he makes a secret but solemn vow or religious promise to God, that, if God would graciously bring him back a conqueror, whosoever or whatsoever should first come out of his house to meet him it should be devoted to God, and offered up for a burnt-offering. At his return, tidings of his victory coming home before him, his own and only daughter meets him with the seasonable expressions of joy. This puts him into a great confusion; but there was no remedy: after she had taken some time to lament her own infelicity, she cheerfully submitted to the performance of his vow. Now,

1. There are several good lessons to be learnt out of this story. (1) That there may be remainders of distrust and doubting even in the hearts of true and great believers. A fond conceit he had that he could not promise himself a victory unless he proffered something considerable to be given to God in lieu of it. (2) That yet it is very good, when we are in the pursuit or expectation of any mercy, to make vows to God of some instance of acceptable service to him, not as a purchase of the favour we desire, but as an expression of our gratitude to him and the deep sense we have of our obligations to render according to the benefit done to us. (3) That we have great need to be very cautious and well advised in the making of such

JAMIESON, FAUSSET, BROWN

secondly, the Israelites had now, by a lapse of 300 years of undisputed possession, established a prescriptive right to the occupation; and thirdly, having received a grant of them from the Lord, his people were entitled to maintain their right on the same principle that guided the Ammonites in receiving, from their god Chemosh, the territory they now occupied.

This diplomatic statement, so admirable for the clearness and force of its arguments, concluded with a solemn appeal to God to maintain, by the issue of events, the cause of right and justice. **28. Howbeit the king of Ammon hearkened not unto the words of Jephthah**—His remonstrances to the aggressor were disregarded, and war being inevitable, preparations were made for a determined resistance.

29-31. His Vow. **29. Then the Spirit of the Lord came upon Jephthah**—The calm wisdom, sagacious forethought, and indomitable energy which he was enabled to display, were a pledge to himself and a convincing evidence to his countrymen, that he was qualified by higher resources than his own for the momentous duties of his office. **he passed over Gilead, and Manasseh**—the provinces most exposed and in danger, for the purpose of levying troops, and exciting by his presence a widespread interest in the national cause. Returning to the camp at Mizpeh, he then began his march against the enemy. There he made his celebrated vow, in accordance with an ancient custom for generals at the outbreak of a war, or on the eve of a battle, to promise the god of their worship a costly oblation, or dedication of some valuable booty, in the event of victory. Vows were in common practice also among the Israelites. They were encouraged by the divine approval as emanating from a spirit of piety and gratitude; and rules were laid down in the law for regulating the performance. But it is difficult to bring Jephthah's vow within the legitimate range (see on Lev. 27:28). **31. whatsoever cometh forth of the doors of my house to meet me**—This evidently points not to an animal, for that might have been a dog; which, being unclean, was unfit to be offered; but to a person, and it looks extremely as if he, from the first, contemplated a human sacrifice. Bred up as he had been, beyond the Jordan, where the Israelitish tribes, far from the tabernacle, were looser in their religious sentiments, and living latterly on the borders of a heathen country where such sacrifices were common, it is not improbable that he may have been so ignorant as to imagine that a similar immolation would be acceptable to God. His mind, engrossed with the prospect of a contest, on the issue of which the fate of his country depended, might, through the influence of superstition, consider the dedication of the object dearest to him the most likely to ensure success. **shall surely be the Lord's; and** [or] **I will offer it up for a burnt offering**—The adoption of the latter particle, which many interpreters suggest, introduces the important alternative, that if it were a person, the dedication would be made to the service of the sanctuary; if a proper animal or thing, it would be offered on the altar.

32, 33. He Overcomes the Ammonites. **32. Jephthah passed over unto the children of Am-**

ADAM CLARKE

23. *The Lord God of Israel hath dispossessed the Amorites.* Jephthah shows that the Israelites did not take the land of the Moabites or Ammonites, but that of the Amorites, which they had conquered from Sihon, their king, who had without cause or provocation attacked them; and although the Amorites had taken the lands in question from the Ammonites, yet the title by which Israel held them was good, because they took them not from the Ammonites, but conquered them from the Amorites.

So now the Lord . . . hath dispossessed the Amorites. The circumstances in which the Israelites were when they were attacked by the Amorites plainly proved that, unless Jehovah had helped them, they must have been overcome. God defeated the Amorites and made a grant of their lands to the Israelites; and they had, in consequence, possessed them for three hundred years, v. 26.

24. *Wilt not thou possess that which Chemosh thy god giveth thee?* As if he had said: "It is a maxim with you, as it is among all nations, that the lands which they conceive to be given them by their gods, they have an absolute right to, and should not relinquish them to any kind of claimant. You suppose that the land which you possess was given you by your god Chemosh; and therefore you will not relinquish what you believe you hold by a divine right. Now we know that Jehovah, our God, who is the Lord of heaven and earth, has given the Israelites the land of the Amorites; and therefore we will not give it up."

27. *The Lord the Judge be judge . . . between the children of Israel.* If you be right, and we be wrong, then Jehovah, who is the sovereign and incorruptible Judge, shall determine in your favor; and to Him I submit the righteousness of my cause.

29. *Then the Spirit of the Lord came upon Jephthah.* The Lord qualified him for the work He had called him to do, and thus gave him the most convincing testimony that his cause was good.

31. *Shall surely be the Lord's, and I will offer it up for a burnt offering.* The translation, according to the most accurate Hebrew scholars, is this: "I will consecrate it to the Lord, or I will offer it for a burnt offering"; that is, "If it be a thing fit for a burnt offering, it shall be made one; if fit for the service of God, it shall be consecrated to Him." That conditions of this kind must have been implied in the vow is evident enough. If a dog had met him, this could not have been made a burnt offering; and if his neighbor or friend's wife, son, or daughter had been returning from a visit to his family, his vow gave him no right over them. Besides, human sacrifices were ever an abomination to the Lord, and this was one of the grand reasons why God drove out the Canaanites.

From v. 39 it appears evident that Jephthah's daughter was not sacrificed to God, but consecrated to Him in a state of perpetual virginity; for the text says, "She knew no man, for this was a statute in Israel"; viz., that persons thus dedicated or consecrated to God should live in a state of unchangeable celibacy. Thus this celebrated place is, without violence to any part of the text, or to any proper rule of construction, cleared of all difficulty, and caused to speak a language consistent with itself, and with the nature of God.

The Targumist refers here to the law, Lev. xxvii. 1-5, where the Lord prescribes the price at which either males or females, who had been vowed to the Lord, might be redeemed. "When a man shall make a singular vow, the persons shall be for the Lord by thy estimation . . . the male from twenty years old even unto sixty . . . shall be fifty shekels of silver . . . And if it be a female, then thy estimation shall be thirty shekels. And if it be from five years old even unto twenty years . . . the male twenty shekels, and for the female ten." This also is an argument that the daughter of Jephthah was not sacrificed, as the father had it in his power, at a very moderate price, to have redeemed her; and surely the blood of his daughter must have been of more value in his sight than thirty shekels of silver!

33. *Twenty cities.* That is, he either took or destroyed twenty cities of the Ammonites, and

MATTHEW HENRY

vows, lest, by indulging a present emotion even of pious zeal, we entangle our own consciences. (4) That what we have solemnly vowed to God we must conscientiously perform, if it be possible and lawful, though it be ever so difficult and grievous to us. (5) That it well becomes children obediently and cheerfully to submit to their parents in the Lord, and particularly to comply with their pious resolutions for the honour of God and the keeping up of religion in their families, though they be harsh and severe, as the Rechabites, who for many generations religiously observed the commands of Jonadab their father in forbearing wine, and Jephthah's daughter here, who, for the satisfying of her father's conscience, and for the honour of God and her country, yielded herself as one devoted (*v.* 36). (6) That our friends' grievances should be our griefs. Where she went to bewail her hard fate the virgins, her companions, joined with her in her lamentations, *v.* 38. Those are unworthy the name of friends that will only rejoice with us, and not weep with us. (7) That heroic zeal for the honour of God and Israel, though alloyed with infirmity and indiscretion, is worthy to be had in perpetual remembrance. It well became the daughters of Israel by an annual solemnity to preserve the honourable memory of Jephthah's daughter, who made light even of her own life.

2. Yet there are some difficult questions that do arise upon this story.

(1) It is hard to say what Jephthah did to his daughter in performance of his vow. [1] Some think he only shut her up totally to sequester her from all the affairs of this life, and consequently from marriage, and to employ her wholly in the acts of devotion all her days. That which countenances this opinion is that she is *said to bewail her virginity* (*v.* 37, 38) and that *she knew no man, v.* 39. [2] It seems more probable that he offered her up for a sacrifice, according to the letter of his vow, misunderstanding that law which spoke of persons devoted by the curse of God as if it were to be applied to such as were devoted by men's vows (Lev. xxvii. 29, *None devoted shall be redeemed, but shall surely be put to death*). Since he had made such a vow, he thought better to kill his daughter than break his vow, and let Providence bear the blame, that brought her forth to meet him.

(2) But, supposing that Jephthah did sacrifice his daughter, the question is whether he did well. [1] Some justify him in it, and think he did well, and as became one that preferred the honour of God before that which was dearest to him in this world. But, [2] Most condemn Jephthah; he did ill to make so rash a vow, and worse to perform it. He could not be bound by his vow to that which God had forbidden by the letter of the sixth commandment: *Thou shalt not kill.* God had forbidden human sacrifices, so that it was (says Dr. Lightfoot) in effect a sacrifice to Moloch.

JAMIESON, FAUSSET, BROWN

mon . . . , and the Lord delivered them into his hands—He met and engaged them at Aroer, a town in the tribe of Gad, upon the Arnon. A decisive victory crowned the arms of Israel, and the pursuit was continued to Abel (plain of the vineyards), from south to north, over an extent of about sixty miles. **34. Jephthah came to Mizpeh unto his house, and, behold, his daughter came out to meet him with timbrels and with dances**—The return of the victors was hailed, as usual, by the joyous acclaim of a female band (I Sam. 18:6), the leader of whom was Jephthah's daughter. The vow was full in his mind, and it is evident that it had not been communicated to anyone, otherwise precautions would doubtless have been taken to place another object at his door. The shriek, and other accompaniments of irrepressible grief, seem to indicate that her life was to be forfeited as a sacrifice; the nature of the sacrifice (which was abhorrent to the character of God) and distance from the tabernacle does not suffice to overturn this view, which the language and whole strain of the narrative plainly support; and although the lapse of two months might be supposed to have afforded time for reflection, and a better sense of his duty, there is but too much reason to conclude that he was impelled to the fulfilment by the dictates of a pious but unenlightened conscience.

ADAM CLARKE

completely routed their whole army.

34. *With timbrels and with dances.* From this instance we find it was an ancient custom for women to go out to meet returning conquerors with musical instruments, songs, and dances; and that it was continued afterwards is evident from the instance given 1 Sam. xviii. 6.

35. *Thou hast brought me very low.* He was greatly distressed to think that his daughter, who was his only child, should be, in consequence of his vow, prevented from continuing his family in Israel; for it is evident that he had not any other child, for *beside her,* says the text, *he had neither son nor daughter,* v. 34. He might, therefore, well be grieved that thus his family was to become extinct in Israel.

36. *And she said unto him.* What a pattern of filial piety and obedience! She was at once obedient, pious, and patriotic. A woman to have no offspring was considered to be in a state of the utmost degradation among the Hebrews; but she is regardless of all this, seeing her father is in safety, and her country delivered.

37. *I and my fellows.* Whether she meant the young women of her own acquaintance or those who had been consecrated to God in the same way, though on different accounts, is not quite clear; but it is likely she means her own companions. And her going up and down upon the mountains may signify no more than her paying each of them a visit at their own houses, previously to her being shut up at the Tabernacle; and this visiting of each at their own homes might require the space of two months. This I am inclined to think is the meaning of this difficult clause.

39. *And she knew no man.* She continued a virgin all the days of her life.

40. *To lament the daughter of Jephthah.* I am satisfied that this is not a correct translation of the original. Houbigant translates the whole verse thus: "But this custom prevailed in Israel, that the virgins of Israel went at different times, four days in the year, to the daughter of Jephthah that they might comfort her." This verse also gives evidence that the daughter of Jephathah was not sacrificed; nor does it appear that the custom or statute referred to here lasted after the death of Jephthah's daughter.

MATTHEW HENRY

CHAPTER 12

Verses 1–7

I. The unreasonable displeasure of the men of Ephraim against Jephthah, because he had not called them in to his assistance against the Ammonites, that they might share in the triumphs and spoils, *v.* 1. Pride was at the bottom of the quarrel. Proud men think all the honours lost that go beside themselves, and then *who can stand before envy*? The anger of the Ephraimites at Jephthah was, 1. Causeless and unjust. Why *didst thou not call us to go with thee?* For a good reason. Because it was the men of Gilead that had made him their captain, not the men of Ephraim, so that he had no authority to call them. 2. It was cruel and outrageous. They get together in a tumultuous manner, pass over Jordan as far as Mizpeh in Gilead, where Jephthah lived, and no less will satisfy their fury but they will burn his house and him in it. Those resentments that have the least reason for them have commonly the most rage in them. Barbarous men take a pleasure in adding affliction to the afflicted.

II. Jephthah's warm vindication of himself. Whether they would be pacified or no, Jephthah takes care.

1. To justify himself, *v.* 2, 3. He makes it out that they had no cause at all to quarrel with him, for, (1) It was not in pursuit of glory that he had engaged in this war, but for the necessary defence of his country. (2) He had invited the Ephraimites to come and join with him, but they had declined the service. He had more cause to quarrel with them for deserting the common interests of Israel in a time of need. It is no new thing for those who are themselves most culpable to be most clamorous in accusing the

JAMIESON, FAUSSET, BROWN

CHAPTER 12

Vss. 1-3. The Ephraimites Quarrelling with Jephthah. **1. the men of Ephraim gathered themselves together**—*Heb.*, "were summoned." **and went northward**—After crossing the Jordan, their route from Ephraim was, strictly speaking, in a north-easterly direction, toward Mizpeh. **the men of Ephraim . . . said unto Jephthah, Wherefore . . . didst** [thou] **not call us?**—This is a fresh development of the jealous, rash, and irritable temper of the Ephraimites. The ground of their offense now was their desire of enjoying the credit of patriotism although they had not shared in the glory of victory.

2. when I called you, ye delivered me not out of their hands—The straightforward answer of Jephthah shows that their charge was false; their complaint of not being treated as confederates and allies entirely without foundation; and their boast of a ready contribution of their services came with an ill grace from people who had purposely delayed appearing till the crisis was past. **3. when I saw that ye delivered me not, I put my life in my hands**—A common form of speech in the East for under-

ADAM CLARKE

CHAPTER 12

1. *The men of Ephraim gathered themselves together.* "They called each other to arms," summoning all their tribe and friends to arm themselves to destroy Jephthah and the Gileadites, being jealous lest they should acquire too much power.

MATTHEW HENRY

innocent. (3) The enterprise was very hazardous. The honour they envied was bought dearly enough; they needed not to grudge it to him; few of them would have ventured so far for it. (4) He does not take the glory of the success to himself but gives it all to God: "*The Lord delivered them into my hands.* If God was pleased so far to make use of me for his glory, why should you be offended at that?"

2. When this just answer (though not so soft an answer as Gideon's) did not prevail to turn away their wrath, he took care both to defend himself from their fury and to chastise their insolence with the sword, by virtue of his authority as Israel's judge. (1) The Ephraimites had not only quarrelled with Jephthah, but, when his neighbours and friends appeared to take his part, they had abused them. "Who cares for you? All your neighbours know what you are, no better than fugitives and vagabonds, separated from your brethren, and driven hither into a corner." It is an ill thing to fasten names or characters of reproach upon persons or countries, as is common, especially upon those that lie under outward disadvantages: it often occasions quarrels that prove of ill consequence, as it did here. (2) This affront raises the Gileadites' blood, and the indignity done to themselves, as well as to their captain, must be revenged. [1] They routed them in the field, *v.* 4. [2] The Gileadites, who perhaps were better acquainted with the passages of Jordan than the Ephraimites were, secured them with strong guards, who were ordered to slay every Ephraimite that offered to pass the river. Here was, *First,* Cruelty. There needed not this severity to cut off all that escaped. Shall the sword devour for ever? *Secondly,* Cunning enough in the discovery of them. It seems the Ephraimites, though they spoke the same language with other Israelites, yet had got a custom in the dialect of their country to pronounce the Hebrew letter *Shin* like *Samech.* Those that first used *s* for *sh,* did it either because it was shorter or because it was finer, and their children learnt to speak like them, so that you might know an Ephraimite by it; as in England we know a west-country man or a north-country man, nay, perhaps a Shropshire man, and a Cheshire man, by his pronunciation. *Thou art a Galilean, and thy speech betrays thee.* If they took a man that they suspected to be an Ephraimite, but he denied it, they bade him say *Shibboleth;* but either he *could not,* or he did not, pronounce it aright, but said *Sibboleth,* and so was known to be an Ephraimite, and was slain immediately. *Shibboleth* signifies a *river or stream*: "Ask leave to go over Shibboleth, the river."

3. The punishment of these proud and passionate Ephraimites, which in several instances answered to their sin. (1) They were proud of the honour of their tribe, but how soon were they brought to be ashamed or afraid to own their country! *Art thou an Ephraimite?* No, now rather of any tribe than that. (2) They had gone in a rage over Jordan to burn Jephthah's house with fire, but now they came back to Jordan as sneakingly as they had passed it furiously, and were cut off from ever returning to their own houses. (3) They had upbraided the Gileadites with the infelicity of their country, lying at such a distance, and now they suffered by an infirmity peculiar to their own country, in not being able to pronounce *Shibboleth.* (4) They had called the Gileadites, unjustly, fugitives, and now they really and in good earnest became fugitives themselves. He that rolls the stone of reproach unjustly upon another, let him expect that it will justly return upon himself.

III. The end of Jephthah's government. He judged Israel but six years, and then died, *v.* 7. Perhaps the death of his daughter sunk him so that he never looked up afterwards, but it shortened his days, and he went to his grave mourning.

Verses 8–15

We have here a short account of the short reigns of three more of the judges of Israel, the first of whom governed but seven years, the second ten, and the third eight.

I. Ibzan of Bethlehem, most probably Bethlehem of Judah, David's city, not that in Zebulun, which is only mentioned once, Josh. xix. 15. He ruled but seven years, but by the number of his children, and his disposing of them all in marriage himself it appears that he lived long. That which is remarkable concerning him is, 1. That he had many children, sixty in all. 2. That he had an equal number of each sex, thirty sons and thirty daughters, a thing which does not often happen in the same family, yet, in the great family of mankind, he that at first made two, male and female, by his wise providence preserves a succession of both in some sort of equality as far as is requisite to the keeping up of the generations of

JAMIESON, FAUSSET, BROWN

taking a duty of imminent peril. This Jephthah had done, having encountered and routed the Ammonites with the aid of his Gileadite volunteers alone; and since the Lord had enabled him to conquer without requiring assistance from any other tribe, why should the Ephraimites take offense? They ought rather to have been delighted and thankful that the war had terminated without their incurring any labor and danger.

4-15. DISCERNED BY THE WORD SIBBOLETH, ARE SLAIN BY THE GILEADITES. **4. the men of Gilead smote Ephraim, because they said, Ye Gileadites are fugitives of Ephraim**—The remonstrances of Jephthah, though reasonable and temperate, were not only ineffectual, but followed by insulting sneers that the Gileadites were reckoned both by the western Manassites and Ephraimites as outcasts—the scum and refuse of their common stock. This was addressed to a peculiarly sensitive people. A feud immediately ensued. The Gileadites, determined to chastise this public affront, gave them battle; and having defeated the Ephraimites, they chased their foul-mouthed but cowardly assailants out of the territory. Then rushing to the fords of the Jordan, they intercepted and slew every fugitive.

The method adopted for discovering an Ephraimite was by the pronunciation of a word naturally suggested by the place where they stood. "Shibboleth," means a stream; "Sibboleth," a burden. The Eastern tribe had, it seems, a dialectical provincialism in the sound of Shibboleth; and the Ephraimites could not bring their organs to pronounce it.

7. Jephthah died—After a government of six years, this mighty man of valor died; and however difficult it may be for us to understand some passages in his history, he has been ranked by apostolic authority among the worthies of the ancient church.

He was followed by a succession of minor judges, of whom the only memorials preserved relate to the number of their families and their state.

ADAM CLARKE

3. *I put my life in my hands.* I exposed myself to the greatest difficulties and dangers. But whence did this form of speech arise? Probably from a man's laying hold of his sword, spear, or bow. "This is the defender of my life; on this, and my proper use of it, my life depends."

4. *And fought with Ephraim.* Some commentators suppose that there were two battles in which the Ephraimites were defeated: the first mentioned in the above clause, and the second occasioned by the taunting language mentioned in the conclusion of the verse, "Ye Gileadites are fugitives of Ephraim." Where the point of this reproach lies, or what is the reason of it, cannot be easily ascertained.

6. *Say now Shibboleth: and he said Sibboleth.* The original differs only in the first letter *samech,* instead of *sheen.* But there must have been a very remarkable difference in the pronunciation of the Ephraimites, when instead of *shibboleth,* an "ear of corn" (see Job xxiv. 24), they said *sibboleth,* which signifies "a burden," Exod. vi. 6; and a heavy burden were they obliged to bear who could not pronounce this test letter. The sound of *th* cannot be pronounced by the Persians in general; and yet it is a common sound among the Arabians. *For he could not frame to pronounce it right.* This is not a bad rendering of the original; "and they did not direct to speak it thus."

8. *And after him Ibzan.* It appears that during the administration of *Jephthah,* six years—*Ibzan,* seven years—*Elon,* ten years—and *Abdon,* eight years (in the whole thirty-one years), the Israelites had peace in all their borders; and we shall find by the following chapter that in this time of rest they corrupted themselves, and were afterwards delivered into the power of the Philistines.

MATTHEW HENRY

men upon earth. 3. That he took care to marry them all. The Jews say, Every father owes three things to his son: to teach him to read the law, give him a trade, and get him a wife.

II. Elon of Zebulun, in the north of Canaan, was next raised up to preside in public affairs, to administer justice, and to reform abuses. Ten years he continued a blessing to Israel, and then died, *v.* 11, 12. Dr. Lightfoot computes that in the beginning of his time the forty years' oppression by the Philistines began (spoken of *ch.* xiii. 1), and about that time Samson was born.

III. Abdon, of the tribe of Ephraim, succeeded, and in him that illustrious tribe begins to recover its reputation. This Abdon was famous for the multitude of his offspring (*v.* 14): he had forty sons and thirty grandsons, all of whom he lived to see grown up. It was a satisfaction to him thus to see his children's children, but he did not see peace upon Israel, for by this time the Philistines had begun to break in upon them.

It is very strange that in the history of all these judges, some of whose actions are very particularly related, there is not so much as once mention made of the high priest, or any other priest or Levite, appearing either for counsel or action in any public affair, from Phinehas (Judges xx. 28) to Eli, which may well be computed 250 years; only the names of the high priests at that time are preserved, 1 Chron. vi. 4-7; and Ezra vii. 3-5. How can this strange obscurity of that priesthood for so long a time, now in the beginning of its days, agree with that mighty splendour with which it was introduced and the figure which the institution of it makes in the law of Moses? Surely it intimates that the institution was chiefly intended to be typical, and that the great benefits that seemed to be promised by it were to be chiefly looked for in its antitype, the everlasting priesthood of our Lord Jesus, in comparison of the superior glory of which that priesthood had no glory, 2 Cor. iii. 10.

JAMIESON, FAUSSET, BROWN

ADAM CLARKE

KEIL–DELITZSCH:

Verses 8, 9. *Ibzan* sprang from *Bethlehem*—hardly, however, the town of that name in the tribe of Judah, as *Josephus* affirms (Ant. vv. 7, 13), for that is generally distinguished either as Bethlehem "of Judah" (Judg. 17:7, 9; Ruth 1:2; 1 Sam. 17:12), or Bethlehem *Ephratah* (Mic. 5:1), but probably Bethlehem in the tribe of Zebulun (Josh. 9:15). He had thirty sons and thirty daughters, the latter of whom he sent away (out of his house), i.e., gave them in marriage, and brought home thirty women in their places from abroad as wives for his sons. He judged Israel seven years, and was buried in Bethlehem.

Verses 11, 12. His successor was *Elon* the Zebulunite, who died after filling the office of judge for ten years, and was buried at *Aijalon*, in the land of Zebulun. This *Aijalon* has probably been preserved in the ruins of *Jalûn*, about four hours' journey to the east of Akka, and half an hour to the s.s.w. of Mejdel Kerun.

Verses. 13–15. He was followed by the judge *Abdon*, the son of Hillel of *Pirathon*. This place, where Abdon died and was buried after holding the office of judge for eight years, was in the land of Ephraim, on the mountains of the Amalekites (v. 15). It is mentioned in 2 Sam. 23:30 and 1 Chron. 11:31 as the home of Benaiah the hero; has been preserved in the village of *Feráta*, about two hours and a half to the s.s.w. of Nabulus.—*Commentary on the Old Testament*

CHAPTER 13 (Matthew Henry)

Verses 1–7

The first verse gives us a short account of the great distress that Israel was in, which gave occasion for the raising up of a deliverer. They did evil, as they had done, *in the sight of the Lord.* The enemies God now sold them to were the Philistines, their next neighbours, an inconsiderable people in comparison with Israel (they had but five cities of any note), and yet, when God made use of them as the staff in his hand, they were very oppressive and vexatious. And this trouble lasted longer than any yet: it continued forty years, though probably not always alike violent. When Israel was in this distress Samson was born; and here we have his birth foretold by an angel. Observe,

I. His extraction. He was of the tribe of Dan, *v.* 2. *Dan* signifies a *judge* or *judgment*, Gen. xxx. 6. The lot of the tribe of Dan lay next to the country of the Philistines, and therefore one of that tribe was most fit to be made a bridle upon them. His parents had been long childless. Many eminent persons were born of mothers that had been kept a great while in the want of the blessing of children, as Isaac, Joseph, Samuel, and John Baptist, that the mercy might be the more acceptable when it did come.

II. The glad tidings brought to his mother, that she should have a son. The messenger was an *angel of the Lord* (*v.* 3), yet appearing as a man, with the aspect and garb of a prophet, or man of God. It was not so much for the sake of Manoah and his wife, obscure Danites, that this extraordinary message was sent, but for Israel's sake, whose deliverer he was to be, and not only so but for the Messiah's sake, whose type he was to be, and whose birth must be foretold by an angel, as his was. The angel, in the message he delivers, 1. Takes notice of her affliction: *Behold now, thou art barren and bearest not.* "*Now* thou art barren, but thou shalt not be always so," as she feared, "not long so." 2. He assures her that she should *conceive and bear a son* (*v.* 3) and repeats the assurance, *v.* 5. To show the power of a divine word, the strongest man that ever was was a child of promise. 3. He appoints that the child should be a Nazarite from his birth, and therefore that the mother should be subject to the law of the Nazarites (though not under the vow of a Nazarite) and should *drink no wine or strong drink* so long as this child was to have its nourishment from her, either in the womb or at the breast, *v.* 4, 5. Other judges had corrected their apostasies from God, but Samson must appear as one, more than any of them,

CHAPTER 13 (Jamieson, Fausset, Brown)

Vs. 1. Israel Serves the Philistines Forty Years. **1. the Lord delivered them into the hand of the Philistines forty years**—The Israelites were represented (ch. 10:6, 7) as having fallen universally into a state of gross and confirmed idolatry, and in chastisement of this great apostasy, the Lord raised up enemies that harassed them in various quarters, especially the Ammonites and Philistines. The invasions and defeat of the former were narrated in the two chapters immediately preceding this; and now the sacred historian proceeds to describe the inroads of the latter people. The period of Philistine ascendency comprised forty years, reckoning from the time of Elon till the death of Samson.

2-10. An Angel Appears to Manoah's Wife. **2. Zorah**—a Danite town (Josh. 15:33) lying on the common boundary of Judah and Dan, so that it was near the Philistine border.

3. the angel of the Lord—The messenger of the covenant, the divine personage who made so many remarkable appearances of a similar kind already described.

5. thou shalt conceive, and bear a son—This predicted child was to be a Nazarite. The mother was, therefore, for the sake of her promised offspring, required to practice the rigid abstinence of the Nazarite law (see on Num. 6:3).

CHAPTER 13 (Adam Clarke)

1. *Delivered them into the hand of the Philistines.* It does not appear that after Shamgar, to the present time, the Philistines were in a condition to oppress Israel, or God had not permitted them to do it; but now they have a commission, the Israelites having departed from the Lord. Nor is it evident that the Philistines had entirely subjected the Israelites, as there still appears to have been a sort of commerce between the two people. They had often vexed and made inroads upon them, but they had them not in entire subjection; see chap. xv. 11.

2. *A certain man of Zorah.* A town in the tribe of Judah, but afterwards given to Dan.

3. *The angel of the Lord.* Generally supposed to have been the same that appeared to Moses, Joshua, Gideon, etc., and no other than the Second Person of the ever-blessed Trinity.

4. *Beware . . . drink not wine.* As Samson was designed to be a Nazarite from the womb, it was necessary that, while his mother carried and nursed him, she should live the life of a Nazarite, neither drinking wine nor any inebriating liquor, nor eating any kind of forbidden meat. See the account of the Nazarite and his vow in the notes on Num. vi. 2, etc.

MATTHEW HENRY

consecrated to God; and, notwithstanding what we read of his faults, we have reason to think that being a Nazarite of God's making he did exemplify, not only the ceremony, but the substance of that *separation to the Lord* in which the Nazariteship did consist, Num. vi. 2. The mother of this deliverer must therefore deny herself, and not eat any unclean thing; what was lawful at another time was now to be forborne. Women with child ought conscientiously to avoid whatever they have reason to think will be any way prejudicial to the health or good constitution of the fruit of their body. And perhaps Samson's mother was to refrain from wine and strong drink, not only because he was designed for a Nazarite, but because he was designed for a man of great strength, which his mother's temperance would contribute to. 4. He foretells the service which this child should do to his country: *He shall begin to deliver Israel.* Observe, *He shall begin* to deliver Israel. This intimated that the oppression of the Philistines should last long. He shall only *begin* to deliver Israel, which intimates that the trouble should still be prolonged. Now herein Samson was a type of Christ, (1) As a Nazarite to God, a Nazarite from the womb. For, though our Lord Jesus was not a Nazarite himself, yet he was typified by the Nazarites, as being perfectly pure from all sin, not so much as conceived in it, and entirely devoted to his Father's honour. (2) As a deliverer of Israel; for he is Jesus a Saviour, who saves his people from their sins. But with this difference: Samson did only begin to deliver Israel (David was afterwards raised up to complete the destruction of the Philistines), but our Lord Jesus is both Samson and David too, both the *author and finisher of our faith.*

III. The report which Manoah's wife, in a transport of joy, brings in all haste to her husband, of this surprising message, *v.* 6, 7. 1. Of the messenger. It was a man of God, *v.* 6. His countenance she could describe; it was very awful: he had such a majesty in his looks, that according to the idea she had of an angel he had the very countenance of one. But his name she can give no account of, nor to what tribe or city of Israel he belonged. She was abundantly satisfied that he was a servant of God; his person and message she thought carried their own evidence along with them, and she enquired no further. 2. Of the message. She gives him a particular account both of the promise and of the precept (*v.* 7), that he also might believe the promise. Thus should yoke-fellows communicate to each other their experiences of communion with God, that they may be helpful to each other in *the way that is called holy.*

Verses 8–14

An account of a second visit which the angel of God made to Manoah and his wife.

I. Manoah earnestly prayed for it, *v.* 8. 1. He takes it for granted that this child of promise shall in due time be given them, and speaks without hesitation of *the child that shall be born. Blessed are those that have not seen and yet,* as Manoah here, *have believed.* 2. All his care is *what they should do to the child* that should be born. Note, Good men are more solicitous and desirous to know the duty that is to be done by them than to know the events that shall occur concerning them; for duty is ours, events are God's. 3. He therefore prays to God to send the same blessed messenger again, to give them further instructions concerning the management of this Nazarite, fearing lest his wife's joy for the promise might have made her forget some part of the precept, in which he was desirous to be fully informed, and lie under no mistake. Would we have God's messengers, the ministers of his gospel, to bring a word proper for us, and for our instruction? *Entreat the Lord* to send them to us, to teach us, Rom. xv. 30, 32.

II. God graciously granted it: *God hearkened to the voice of Manoah, v.* 9.

1. The angel appears the second time also to the wife, when she is sitting alone, probably tending the flocks. Solitude is often a good opportunity of communion with God; good people have thought themselves never less alone than when alone, if God be with them.

2. She goes in all haste to call her husband, doubtless humbly beseeching the stay of this blessed messenger till she should return and her husband with her, *v.* 10, 11. The man of God is very willing she should call her husband, John iv. 16. Manoah is not disgusted that the angel did not this second time appear to him, but very willingly goes after his wife to the man of God. If the wife will lead, let not the husband think it any disparagement to him to follow her in that which is virtuous and praiseworthy.

3. Manoah having come to the angel, and being satisfied by him that he was the same that had ap-

JAMIESON, FAUSSET, BROWN

he shall begin to deliver Israel out of the hands of the Philistines—a prophecy encouraging to a patriotic man; the terms of it, however, indicated that the period of deliverance was still to be distant.

6-8. then Manoah entreated the Lord—On being informed by his wife of the welcome intimation, the husband made it the subject of earnest prayer to God. This is a remarkable instance, indicative of the connection which God has established between prayer and the fulfilment of His promises.

11-14. THE ANGEL APPEARS TO MANOAH. **11. Art thou the man that spakest unto the woman?**—Manoah's intense desire for the repetition of the angel's visit was prompted not by doubts or anxieties of any kind, but was the fruit of lively faith, and of his great anxiety to follow out the instructions given. Blessed was he who had not seen, yet had believed.

ADAM CLARKE

5. *He shall begin to deliver Israel.* Samson only began this deliverance, for it was not till the days of David that the Israelites were completely redeemed from the power of the Philistines.

6. *But I asked him not whence he was, neither told he me his name.* This clause is rendered very differently by the Vulgate, the negative not being omitted: "Who, when I asked who he was and whence he came, and by what name he was called, would not tell me; but this he said."

The negative is also wanting in the Septuagint, as it stands in the Complutensian Polyglot: "And I asked him whence he was, and his name, but he did not tell me." This is also the reading of the Codex Alexandrinus; but the Septuagint, in the London Polyglot, together with the Chaldee, Syriac, and Arabic, read the negative particle with the Hebrew text, "I asked not his name."

9. *The angel of God came again.* This second appearance of the angel was probably essential to the peace of Manoah, who might have been jealous of his wife had he not had this proof that the thing was of the Lord.

MATTHEW HENRY

peared to his wife, does, with all humility, (1) Welcome the promise (*v.* 12): *Now let thy words come to pass;* this was the language, not only of his desire, but of his faith, like that of the blessed Virgin, Luke i. 38. "*Be it according to thy word.* Lord, I lay hold on what thou hast said, and depend upon it; *let it come to pass.*" (2) Beg that the prescriptions given might be repeated: *How shall we order the child?* The directions were given to his wife, but he looks upon himself as concerned to assist her in the careful management of this promised seed, according to order; for the utmost care of both the parents, and their constant joint endeavour, are little enough to be engaged for the good ordering of children that are devoted to God and to be brought up for him. Let not one devolve it on the other, but both do their best. Those to whom God has given children must be very careful how they order them, and what they do unto them, that they may drive out the foolishness that is *bound up in their hearts,* form their minds and manners well betimes, and *train them in the way wherein they should go.* Herein pious parents will beg divine assistance. "Lord, teach us how we may order our children, that they may be Nazarites, and living sacrifices to thee."

4. The angel repeats the directions he had before given (*v.* 13, 14). There is need of a good deal both of caution and observation, for the right ordering both of ourselves and of our children. Those that would preserve themselves pure must keep at a distance from that which borders upon sin or leads to it. When she was with child of a Nazarite, she must not eat *any unclean thing*; so those *in whom Christ is formed* must carefully *cleanse themselves from all filthiness of flesh and spirit,* and do nothing to the prejudice of that new man.

Verses 15–23

I. What further passed between Manoah and the angel at this interview. It was in kindness to him that while the angel was with him it was concealed from him that he was an angel. We could not bear the sight of the divine glory unveiled. God having determined to speak to us by men like ourselves, prophets and ministers, even when he spoke by his angels, or by his Son, they appeared in the likeness of men, and were taken but for men of God. Now,

1. The angel declined to accept his treat, and appointed him to turn it into a sacrifice. Manoah begged he would take some refreshment with him (*v.* 15), but the angel told him (*v.* 16) he would *not eat of his bread,* any more than he would of Gideon's, but directed him to offer it to God, *ch.* vi. 20, 21. Though we cannot live without meat and drink, yet we eat and drink to the glory of God, and so turn even our common meals into sacrifices.

2. The angel declined telling him his name. Manoah desired to know his name (*v.* 17), and of what tribe he was, "*That when thy sayings come to pass, we may do thee honour.*" What Manoah asked for instruction in his duty he was readily told (*v.* 12, 13), but what he asked to gratify his curiosity was denied. God has in his word given us full directions concerning our duty, but he never designed to answer all the enquiries of a speculative head. We must never indulge a vain curiosity in our enquiries concerning these things, Col. ii. 18. *Nescire velle quæ Magister maximus docere non vult erudita inscitia est—To be willingly ignorant of those things which our great Master refuses to teach us is to be at once ignorant and wise.*

3. The angel assisted and owned their sacrifice. Thus we must bring our hearts to God as living sacrifices, and submit them to the operation of his Spirit. Prayer is the ascent of the soul to God. But it is Christ in the heart by faith that makes it an offering of a sweet-smelling savour: without him our services are offensive smoke, but, in him, acceptable flame. We may apply it to Christ's sacrifice of himself for us; he ascended in the flame of his own offering, for *by his own blood he entered in once into the holy place,* Heb. ix. 12.

II. An account of the impressions which this vision made upon Manoah and his wife. 1. In Manoah's reflection upon it there is *great fear, v.* 22. He had spoken with great assurance of the son they should shortly be the joyful parents of (*v.* 8, 12), and yet is now put into confusion. *We shall surely die.* It was a vulgar opinion generally received among the ancient Jews that it was present death to see God or an angel; and this notion quite overcame his faith for the present, as it did Gideon's, *ch.* vi. 22. 2. In his wife's reflection upon it there is great faith, *v.* 23. Here the weaker vessel was the stronger believer, which perhaps was the reason why the angel chose once and again to appear to her. Yoke-fellows should piously assist each other's faith and joy as there is occasion.

JAMIESON, FAUSSET, BROWN

CHARLES H. SPURGEON:

The first remark arising out of the story of Manoah and his wife is this—that oftentimes we pray for blessings which will make us tremble when we receive them. Manoah had asked that he might see an angel, and he saw him: in answer to his request the wonderful One condescended to reveal himself a second time, but the consequence was that the good man was filled with astonishment and dismay, and turning to his wife, he exclaimed, "We shall surely die, because we have seen God." Brethren, do we always know what we are asking for when we pray? We are imploring an undoubted blessing, and yet if we knew the way in which such blessing must necessarily come, we should, perhaps, hesitate before we pressed our suit.

You have been entreating very much for growth in holiness. Do you know, brother, that in almost every case that means increased affliction? For we do not make much progress in the divine life except when the Lord is pleased to try us in the furnace and purge us with many fires. Do you desire the mercy on that condition? Are you willing to take it as God pleases to send it, and to say, "Lord, if spiritual growth implies trial, if it signifies a long sickness of body, if it means deep depression of soul, if it entails the loss of property, if it involves the taking away of my dearest friend, yet I make no reserve, but include in the prayer all that is needful to the good end. When I say, sanctify me wholly—spirit, soul, and body—I leave the process to Thy discretion." Suppose you really knew all that it would bring upon you, would you not pray, at any rate, with more solemn tones? I hope you would not hesitate, but, counting all the cost, would still desire to be delivered from sin; but, at any rate, you would put up your petition with deliberation, weighing every syllable, and then when the answer came you would not be so astonished at its peculiar form. Often and often the blessing which we used so eagerly to implore is the occasion of the suffering which we deplore. We do not know God's methods. We set Him ways which He does not choose to follow.

—The Treasury of the Old Testament

15-23. MANOAH'S SACRIFICE. **15. Manoah said unto the angel . . . , I pray thee, let us detain thee, until we shall have made ready a kid**—The stranger declined the intended hospitality and intimated that if the meat were to be an offering, it must be presented to the Lord. Manoah needed this instruction, for his purpose was to offer the prepared viands to him, not as the Lord, but as what he imagined him to be, not even an angel (vs. 16), but a prophet or merely human messenger. It was on this account, and not as rejecting divine honors, that he spoke in this manner to Manoah. The angel's language was exactly similar to that of our Lord (Matt. 19:17).

17. Manoah said unto the angel . . . , What is thy name?—Manoah's request elicited the most unequivocal proofs of the divinity of his supernatural visitor—in his name "secret" (in the *Marg.* wonderful), and in the miraculous flame that betokened the acceptance of the sacrifice.

ADAM CLARKE

15. *Until we shall have made ready a kid.* Not knowing his quality, Manoah wished to do this as an act of hospitality.

16. *I will not eat of thy bread.* As I am a spiritual being, I subsist not by earthly food. *And if thou wilt offer a burnt offering.* Neither shall I receive that homage which belongs to God; you must therefore offer your burnt offering to Jehovah.

18. *Seeing it is secret.* It was because it was *secret* that they wished to know it. The angel does not say that it was *secret,* but *hy peli,* "It is wonderful"; the very character that is given to Jesus Christ, Isa. ix. 6: "His name shall be called Wonderful"; and it is supposed by some that the angel gives this as his name, and consequently that he was our blessed Lord.

19. *The angel did wonderously.* He acted according to his name; he, being "wonderful," performed wonderful things, probably causing fire to arise out of the rock and consume the sacrifice, and then ascending in the flame.

22. *We shall surely die, because we have seen God.* See the note on chap. vi. 22.

MATTHEW HENRY

None could argue better than Manoah's wife does here: *We shall surely die,* said her husband; "Nay," said she, "the tokens of his favour which we have received forbid us to think that he designs our destruction. Had he thought fit to kill us, (1) He would not have accepted our sacrifice. (2) He would not have shown us all these things, nor would he have given these exceedingly great and precious promises of a son that shall be a Nazarite and a deliverer of Israel." Note, Hereby it appears that God designs not the death of sinners that he has accepted the great sacrifice which Christ offered up for their salvation. And let those good Christians who have had communion with God in the word and prayer, to whom he has graciously manifested himself, take encouragement thence in a cloudy and dark day. "God would not have done what he has done for my soul if he had designed to forsake me, and leave me to perish at last; for his work is perfect, nor will he mock his people with his favours." Learn to reason as Manoah's wife did.

Verses 24–25

1. Samson's birth. The woman that had been long barren bore a son, according to the promise. 2. His name, *Samson,* has been derived, by some, from *Shemesh, the sun,* turned into a diminutive, *sol exiguus —the sun in miniature,* perhaps because, being born like Moses to be a deliverer, he was like him exceedingly fair, his face shone like a little sun, because of his great strength. The sun is compared to a *strong man* (Ps. xix. 5). A little sun, because the glory of, and a light to, his people Israel, a type of Christ, the Sun of righteousness. 3. His childhood. He far outgrew other children of his age; it appeared that the Lord blessed him, qualified him, both in body and mind, for something great and extraordinary. 4. His youth. When he grew up a little *the Spirit of the Lord began to move him, v.* 25. The Spirit of God moved Samson in the camp of Dan to oppose the incursions of the Philistines; there Samson, when a child, appeared among them, and signalized himself by some very brave actions, excelling them all in manly exercises and trials of strength: and probably he showed himself more than ordinarily zealous against the enemies of his country.

JAMIESON, FAUSSET, BROWN

24, 25. SAMSON BORN. **24. the woman bare a son, and called his name Samson**—The birth of this child of promise, and the report of the important national services he was to render, must, from the first, have made him an object of peculiar interest and careful instruction.

25. the Spirit of the Lord began to move him at times—not, probably, as it moved the prophets, who were charged with an inspired message, but kindling in his youthful bosom a spirit of high and devoted patriotism. **Eshtaol**—the free city. It, as well as Zorah, stood on the border between Judah and Dan.

ADAM CLARKE

23. *If the lord were pleased to kill us.* This is excellent reasoning, and may be of great use to every truly religious mind, in cloudy and dark dispensations of divine providence. It is not likely that God, who has preserved you so long, borne with you so long, and fed and supported you all your life long, girding you when you knew Him not, is less willing to save and provide for you and yours now than He was when, probably, you trusted less in Him. He who freely gave His Son to redeem you can never be indifferent to your welfare; and if He gave you power to pray to and trust in Him, is it at all likely that He is now seeking an occasion against you, in order to destroy you? Nor would He have told you such things of His love, mercy, and kindness, and unwillingness to destroy sinners, as He has told you in His sacred Word if He had been determined not to extend His mercy to you.

24. *And called his name Samson.* The original, *shimshon,* which is from the root *shamash,* "to serve" (whence *shemesh,* "the sun"), probably means either a "little sun" or a "little servant"; and this latter is so likely a name to be imposed on an only son, by maternal fondness, that it leaves but little doubt of the propriety of the etymology. *And the Lord blessed him.* Gave evident proofs that the child was under the peculiar protection of the Most High, causing him to increase daily in stature and extraordinary strength.

25. *The Spirit of the Lord began to move him.* He felt the degrading bondage of his countrymen, and a strong desire to accomplish something for their deliverance. These feelings and motions he had from the Divine Spirit. *Camp of Dan.* Probably the place where his parents dwelt; for they were Danites, and the place is supposed to have its name from its being the spot where the Danites stopped when they sent some men of their company to rob Micah of his teraphim (see chap. xviii). As he had these influences *between Zorah and Eshtaol,* it is evident that this was while he dwelt at home with his parents, for Zorah was the place where his father dwelt; see v. 2. Thus God began, from Samson's infancy, to qualify him for the work to which He had called him.

MATTHEW HENRY

CHAPTER 14

Verses 1–9

I. Samson, under the extraordinary guidance of Providence, seeks an occasion of quarrelling with the Philistines, by joining in affinity with them—a strange method, but the truth is Samson was himself a riddle, a paradox of a man, and did that which was really great and good, by that which was seemingly weak and evil.

1. As the negotiation of Samson's marriage was a common case, we may observe, (1) That it was foolish to set his affections upon a daughter of the Philistines. Shall one that is not only an Israelite, but a Nazarite, devoted to the Lord, covet to become one with a worshipper of Dagon? Shall one marked for a patriot of his country match among those that are its sworn enemies? His parents did well to dissuade him from yoking himself thus unequally with unbelievers. "*Is there never a woman among the daughters of thy brethren,* or, if none of our tribe, *never a one among all thy people,* never an Israelite, that pleases thee, or that thou canst think worthy of thy affection, that thou shouldest marry a Philistine?" (2) If there had not been a special reason for it, it certainly would have been improper in him to insist upon his choice, and in them to agree to it at last. This Nazarite, in his subjection to his parents, asking their consent, and not proceeding till he had it, was an example to all children.

2. But this treaty of marriage is expressly said to be *of the Lord, v.* 4. Not only that God afterwards overruled it to serve his designs against the Philistines, but that he put it into Samson's heart to make this choice, that he *might have occasion against the Philistines.* It should seem, the way in which the Philistines oppressed Israel was, not by great armies, but by the clandestine incursions of their giants and small parties of their plunderers. In the same way therefore Samson must deal with them; let him but by this marriage get among them, and he would be a *thorn in their sides.*

II. Samson, by a special providence, is animated and encouraged to attack the Philistines. God prepared him for it by two occurrences:—

JAMIESON, FAUSSET, BROWN

CHAPTER 14

VSS. 1-5. SAMSON DESIRES A WIFE OF THE PHILISTINES. **1, 2. Timnath**—now Tibna, about three miles from Zorah, his birthplace. **saw a woman . . . of the Philistines; and told his father and his mother, and said, . . . get her for me to wife**—In the East parents did, and do in many cases still, negotiate the marriage alliances for their sons. During their period of ascendency, the Philistine invaders had settled in the towns; and the intercourse between them and the Israelites was often of such a friendly and familiar character as to issue in matrimonial relations. Moreover, the Philistines were not in the number of the seven devoted nations of Canaan—with whom the law forbade them to marry. **3. Is there never a woman among the daughters of thy brethren**—i.e., of thine own tribe—a Danite woman. **Samson said . . . , Get her for me, for she pleaseth me well**—lit., "she is right in mine eyes"—not by her beautiful countenance or handsome figure, but *right or fit for his purpose.* And this throws light on the historian's remark in reference to the resistance of his parents: they "knew not that it was of the Lord, that he sought an occasion against the Phillistines"—rather *from* the Philistines—originating on their side. The Lord, by a course of retributive proceedings, was about to destroy the Philistine power, and the means which He meant to employ was not the forces of a numerous army, as in the case of the preceding judges, but the miraculous prowess of the single-handed champion of Israel. In these circumstances, the provocation to hostilities could only spring out of a *private* quarrel, and this marriage scheme was doubtless suggested by the secret influence of the Spirit as the best way of accomplishing the intended result.

ADAM CLARKE

CHAPTER 14

1. *Went down to Timnath.* A frontier town of the Philistines, at the beginning of the lands belonging to the tribe of Judah, Josh. xv. 57; but afterwards given up to Dan, Josh. xix. 43. David took this place from the Philistines, but they again got possession of it in the reign of Ahaz, 2 Chron. xxviii. 18.

3. *Is there never a woman?* To marry with any that did not belong to the Israelitish stock was contrary to the law, Exod. xxxiv. 16; Deut. vii. 3. But this marriage of Samson was said to be "of the Lord," v. 4; that is, God permitted it (for in no other sense can we understand the phrase) that it might be a means of bringing about the deliverance of Israel. *For she pleaseth me well.* "For she is right in my eyes."

MATTHEW HENRY

1. By enabling him, in one journey to Timnath, to *kill a lion, v.* 5, 6. (1) Samson's encounter with the lion was hazardous. It was a young lion, one of the fiercest sort, that set upon him, roaring for his prey. He was all alone in the vineyards, whither he had rambled from his father and mother, probably to eat grapes. Had Samson met with this lion in the way, he might have had more reason to expect help both from God and man than here in the solitary vineyards, out of his road. But there was a special providence in it, and the more hazardous the encounter was, (2) The victory was so much the more illustrious. It was obtained without any difficulty: he strangled the lion, and tore his throat as easily as he would have strangled a kid. Christ engaged the roaring lion, and conquered him in the beginning of his public work (Matt. iv. 1, &c.), and afterwards spoiled principalities and powers, triumphing over them *in himself.* He was *exalted in his own strength.* He did not boast of it, did *not so much as tell his father nor mother* that which many a one would soon have published through the whole country. Modesty and humility make up the brightest crown of great performances.

2. By providing him, the next journey, with honey in the carcase of this lion, *v.* 8, 9. When he came down the next time he found the carcase of the lion; the birds or beasts of prey, it is likely, had eaten the flesh, and in the skeleton a swarm of bees had knit, and made a hive of it, and had not been idle, but had there laid up a good stock of honey, which was one of the staple commodities of Canaan. Samson, having a better title than any man to the hive, seizes the honey with his hands. This supposes an encounter with the bees; but he that dreaded not the lion's paws had no reason to fear *their* stings. By dislodging the bees he was taught not to fear the multitude of the Philistines; though they *compassed him about like bees.* Of the honey he here found, (1) He ate himself, asking no questions for conscience's sake. John Baptist, that Nazarite of the New Testament, lived upon wild honey. (2) He gave to his parents, and they did eat; he did not eat all himself. He let his parents share with him. Let those that by the grace of God have found sweetness in religion themselves communicate their experience to their friends and relations, and invite them to come and share with them. He told not his parents whence he had it, lest they should scruple eating it. Honey is honey still, though in a dead lion.

Verses 10–20

An account of Samson's wedding feast and the occasion it gave him to fall foul upon the Philistines.

I. Samson conformed to the custom of the country in making a festival of his nuptial solemnities, which continued seven days, *v.* 10. It is no part of religion to go contrary to the innocent usages of the places where we live: nay, it is a reproach to religion when those who profess it give just occasion to others to call them covetous, sneaking, and morose. A good man should strive to make himself, in the best sense, a good companion.

II. His wife's relations paid him the accustomed respect of the place upon that occasion, and brought him thirty young men to keep him company during the solemnity, and to attend him as his grooms-men (*v.* 11): *When they saw him,* they brought these, seemingly to be his companions, but really to be a guard upon him, or spies to observe him.

III. Samson, to entertain the company, propounds a riddle to them, and lays a wager with them that they cannot find it out in seven days, *v.* 12–14. The usage, it seems, was very ancient upon such occasions. Now, 1. Samson's riddle was his own invention, for it was his own achievement that gave occasion for it: *Out of the eater came forth meat, and out of the strong came forth sweetness.* Read my riddle, what is this? This riddle is applicable to many of the methods of divine providence and grace. When God, by an overruling providence, brings good out of evil to his church and people,—when that which threatened their ruin turns to their advantage,—when their enemies are made serviceable to them, and the wrath of men turns to God's praise,—then comes *meat out of the eater* and *sweetness out of the strong.* See Phil. i. 12.

IV. His companions, when they could not expound the riddle themselves, obliged his wife to get from him the exposition of it, *v.* 15. If she would not use means with the bridegroom to let them into the meaning of it, they would *burn her and her father's house with fire.* Could anything be more brutish?

V. His wife, by unreasonable importunity, obtains from him a key to his riddle. It was *on the seventh day,* that is, the seventh day of the week (as Dr.

JAMIESON, FAUSSET, BROWN

6-9. HE KILLS A LION. **5-9. a young lion**—*Heb.*, a lion in the pride of his youthful prime. The wild mountain passes of Judah were the lairs of savage beasts; and most or all the "lions" of Scripture occur in that wild country. His rending and killing the shaggy monster, without any weapon in his hand, were accomplished by that superhuman courage and strength which the *occasional* influences of the Spirit enabled him to put forth, and by the exertion of which, in such private incidental circumstances, he was gradually trained to confide in them for the more public work to which he was destined. **7. he went down, and talked with the woman**—The social intercourse between the youth of different sexes is extremely rare and limited in the East, and generally so after they are betrothed.

8. after a time he returned to take her—probably after the lapse of a year—the usual interval between the ceremonies of betrothal and marriage. It was spent by the bride elect with her parents in preparation for the nuptials—and at the proper time the bridegroom returned to take her home. **he turned aside to see the carcass of the lion; and, behold, there was a swarm of bees and honey in the carcass of the lion**—In such a climate, the myriads of insects and the ravages of birds of prey, together with the influences of the solar rays, would, in a few months, put the carcass in a state inviting to such cleanly animals as bees.

10, 11. HIS MARRIAGE FEAST. **10. his father went down**—The father is mentioned as the head and representative of Samson's relatives. **Samson made there a feast**—The wedding festivity lasted a week. The men and women were probably entertained in separate apartments—the bride, with her female relatives, at her parents' house; Samson, in some place obtained for the occasion, as he was a stranger. A large number of paranymphs, or "friends of the bridegroom," furnished, no doubt, by the bride's family, attended his party, ostensibly to honor the nuptials, but really as spies on his proceedings.

12-18. HIS RIDDLE. **12-18. I will now put forth a riddle**—Riddles are a favorite Oriental amusement at festive entertainments of this nature, and rewards are offered to those who give the solution. Samson's riddle related to honey in the lion's carcass. The prize he offered was thirty *sindinim,* or shirts, and thirty changes of garments, probably woolen.

ADAM CLARKE

5. *A young lion roared against him.* Came fiercely out upon him, ready to tear him to pieces.

6. *He rent him as he would have rent a kid.* Now it is not intimated that he did this by his own natural strength, but by the Spirit of the Lord coming mightily upon him; so that his strength does not appear to be his own, nor to be at his command. His might was, by the will of God, attached to his hair and to his being a Nazarite.

7. *And talked with the woman.* That is, concerning marriage; thus forming the espousals.

8. *After a time.* Probably about one year, as this was the time that generally elapsed between espousing and wedding. *A swarm of bees and honey in the carcase.* By length of time the flesh had been entirely consumed off the bones, and a swarm of bees had formed their combs within the region of the thorax, nor was it an improper place; nor was the thing unfrequent, if we may credit ancient writers, the carcasses of slain beasts becoming a receptacle for wild bees.

10. *Samson made there a feast.* The marriage feast, when he went to marry his espoused wife.

11. *They brought thirty companions.* These are called in Scripture "children of the bride-chamber," and friends of the bridegroom.

12. *I will now put forth a riddle.* Probably this was one part of the amusements at a marriage feast, each in his turn proposing a riddle, to be solved by any of the rest on a particular forfeit; the proposer forfeiting, if solved, the same which the company must forfeit if they could not solve it. *Thirty sheets.* I have no doubt that the Arab *hyke* is here meant, a dress in which the natives of the East wrap themselves, as a Scottish Highlander does in his plaid.

MATTHEW HENRY

Lightfoot conjectures), but the fourth day of the feast, that they solicited her to entice her husband (*v.* 15), and she did it, 1. With great art and management (*v.* 16). 2. With great success. At last, being quite wearied with her importunity, he told her what was the meaning of his riddle, and though we may suppose she promised secrecy, and that if he would but let her know she would tell nobody, she immediately told it to the *children of her people*; nor could he expect better from a Philistine. The riddle is at length *unriddled* (*v.* 18): *What is sweeter than honey*, or a better meat? Prov. xxiv. 13. *What is stronger than a lion*, or a greater devourer? Samson generously owns they had won the wager. But he thought fit to tell them: *If you had not ploughed with my heifer*, made use of your interest with my wife, *you would not have found out my riddle*. Satan, in his temptations, could not do us the mischief he does if he did not plough with the heifer of our own corrupt nature.

VI. Samson pays his wager to these Philistines with the spoils of others of their countrymen, *v.* 19.

VII. This proves a good occasion of weaning Samson from his new relations. He found how his companions had abused him and how his wife had betrayed him, and therefore *his anger was kindled*, *v.* 19. And, meeting with this ill usage among them, he *went up to his father's house*. It were well for us if the unkindnesses we meet with from the world, and our disappointments in it, had but this good effect upon us, to oblige us by faith and prayer to return to our heavenly Father's house and rest there. The inconveniences that occur in our way should make us love home and long to be there.

JAMIESON, FAUSSET, BROWN

Three days were passed in vain attempts to unravel the enigma. The festive week was fast drawing to a close when they secretly enlisted the services of the newly married wife, who having got the secret, revealed it to her friends. **18. If ye had not ploughed with my heifer, ye had not found out my riddle**—a metaphor borrowed from agricultural pursuits, in which not only oxen but cows and heifers were, and continue to be, employed in dragging the plough. Divested of metaphor, the meaning is taken by some in a criminal sense, but probably means no more than that they had resorted to the aid of his wife—an unworthy expedient, which might have been deemed by a man of less noble spirit and generosity as releasing him from the obligation to fulfil his bargain.

19, 20. HE SLAYS THIRTY PHILISTINES. **19, 20. went down to Askelon, and slew thirty men**—This town was about twenty-four miles west by southwest from Timnah; and his selection of this place, which was dictated by the Divine Spirit, was probably owing to its bitter hostility to Israel. **took their spoil**—The custom of stripping a slain enemy was unknown in Hebrew warfare. **20. Samson's wife was given to his companion, whom he had used as his friend**—i.e., "the friend of the bridegroom," who was the medium of communicating during the festivities between him and his bride. The acceptance of her hand, therefore, was an act of base treachery, that could not fail to provoke the just resentment of Samson.

ADAM CLARKE

17. *And she wept before him.* Not through any love to him, for it appears she had none, but to oblige her paramours; and of this he soon had ample proof.

18. *If ye had not plowed with my heifer.* If my wife had not been unfaithful to my bed, she would not have been unfaithful to my secret; and, you being her paramours, your interest was more precious to her than that of her husband. She has betrayed me through her attachment to you.

19. *The Spirit of the Lord came upon him.* "The spirit of fortitude from before the Lord."—Targum. He was inspired with unusual courage, and he felt strength proportioned to his wishes. *He . . . slew thirty men . . . and took their spoil.* He took their *hayks*, their *kumjas*, and *caftans*, and gave them to the thirty persons who, by unfair means, had solved his riddle; thus they had what our version calls "thirty sheets, and thirty changes of raiment."

20. *But Samson's wife was given to his companion.* This was the same kind of person who is called "the friend of the bridegroom," John iii. 29. And it is very likely that she loved this person better than she loved her husband, and went to him as soon as Samson had gone to his father's house at Zorah. She might, however, have thought herself abandoned by him, and therefore took another; this appears to have been the persuasion of her father, chap. xv. 2. But her betraying his secret and his interests to his enemies was a full proof he was not very dear to her; though, to persuade him to the contrary, she shed many crocodile tears; see v. 16.

MATTHEW HENRY — CHAPTER 15

Verses 1–8

I. Samson's return to his wife, whom he had left in displeasure; when time had a little cooled his resentments, he came back to her, *visited her with a kid*, *v.* 1. It was intended as a token of reconciliation, and perhaps was then so used. When differences happen between near relations, let those be ever reckoned the wisest that are most forward to forgive and forget injuries.

II. The repulse he met with. Her father forbade him to come near her; for truly he had married her to another, *v.* 2. He endeavours, 1. To justify himself in this wrong: *I verily thought that thou hadst utterly hated her*. 2. He endeavours to pacify Samson by offering him his younger daughter. Samson scorned his proposal; he knew better things than *to take a wife to her sister*, Lev. xviii. 18.

III. The revenge Samson took upon the Philistines for this abuse. He looks upon himself as a public person, and the affront as done to the whole nation of Israel. Now the way Samson took to be revenged on them was by setting their cornfields on fire, which would be a great weakening and impoverishing to the country, *v.* 4, 5. 1. The method he took to do it was very strange. He sent 150 couple of foxes, tied tail to tail, into the cornfields; every couple had a stick of fire between their tails, with which, being terrified, they ran into the corn for shelter, and so set fire to it; thus the fire would break out in many places at the same time. We never find Samson, in any of his exploits, making use of any person whatsoever, either servant or soldier. By the meanness and weakness of the animals he employed, he designed to put contempt upon the enemies he fought against. This stratagem is often alluded to to show how the church's adversaries have often united in a fire-brand, some cursed project or other, to waste the church of God, and particularly to kindle the fire of division in it. 2. The mischief he hereby did to the Philistines was very great. It was in the time of wheat harvest (*v.* 1), so that the straw being dry it soon burnt the shocks of corn that were cut, and *the standing corn, and the vineyards and olives*.

IV. The Philistines' outrage against Samson's treacherous wife and her father. Understanding that they had provoked Samson to do this mischief to the country, the rabble set upon them and burnt them with fire, perhaps in their own house, *v.* 6. The Philistines had threatened Samson's wife that, if she would not get the riddle out of him, they would *burn her and her father's house with fire, ch.* xiv. 15. She, to save herself and oblige her countrymen, betrayed her husband. The very thing that she feared, and sought by sin to avoid, came upon her; she and her father's house were burnt with fire. The mischief

JAMIESON, FAUSSET, BROWN — CHAPTER 15

Vss. 1, 2. SAMSON IS DENIED HIS WIFE. **1. in the time of wheat harvest**—i.e., about the end of our April, or the beginning of our May. The shocks of grain were then gathered into heaps, and lying on the field or on the threshing-floors. It was the dry season, dry far beyond our experience, and the grain in a most combustible state. **Samson visited his wife with a kid**—It is usual for a visitor in the East to carry some present; in this case, it might be not only as a token of civility, but of reconciliation. **he said**—i.e., to himself. It was his secret purpose. **into the chamber**—the female apartments or harem. **2. her father said, I verily thought that thou hadst utterly hated her**—This allegation was a mere sham—a flimsy pretext to excuse his refusal of admittance. The proposal he made of a marriage with her younger sister was but an insult to Samson, and one which it was unlawful for an Israelite to accept (Lev. 18:18).

3-8. HE BURNS THE PHILISTINES' CORN. **3. Samson said . . . , Now shall I be more blameless than the Philistines**—This nefarious conduct provoked the hero's just indignation, and he resolved to take signal vengeance. **4. went and caught three hundred foxes**—rather jackals; an animal between a wolf and a fox, which, unlike our fox, a solitary creature, prowls in large packs or herds and abounds in the mountains of Palestine. The collection of so great a number would require both time and assistance. **took firebrands**—torches or matches, which would burn slowly, retaining the fire, and blaze fiercely when blown by the wind. He put two jackals together, tail by tail, and fastened tightly a fire-match between them. At nightfall he lighted the firebrand and sent each pair successively down from the hills, into the "Shefala," or plain of Philistia, lying on the borders of Dan and Judah, a rich and extensive corn district. The pain caused by the fire would make the animals toss about to a wide extent, kindling one great conflagration. But no one could render assistance to his neighbor: the devastation was so general, the panic would be so great. **6. Who hath done this**—The author of this outrage, and the cause that provoked such an extraordinary retaliation, soon became known; and the sufferers, enraged by the destruction of their crops, rushing with tumultuous fury to the house of Samson's wife, "burnt her and her father with fire." This was a remarkable retribution. To avoid this menace, she had betrayed her husband; and by that unprincipled conduct, eventually exposed herself to the horrid doom which, at the sacrifice of conjugal fidelity, she had sought to escape.

ADAM CLARKE — CHAPTER 15

1. *Visited his wife with a kid.* On her betraying him, he had, no doubt, left her in great disgust. After some time his affection appears to have returned; and, taking a kid, or perhaps a fawn, as a present, he goes to make reconciliation, and finds her given to his brideman, probably the person to whom she betrayed his riddle.

2. *Thou hadst utterly hated her.* As he was conscious she had given him great cause so to do. *Her younger sister.* The father appears to have been perfectly sincere in this offer.

4. *Went and caught three hundred foxes.* There has been much controversy concerning the meaning of the term *shualim*, some supposing it to mean "foxes" or "jackals," and others "handfuls or sheaves of corn." Much of the force of the objections against the common version will be diminished by the following considerations: (1) Foxes, or jackals, are common and gregarious in that country. (2) It is not hinted that Samson collected them alone; he might have employed several hands in this work. (3) It is not said he collected them all in one day; he might have employed several days, as well as many persons, to furnish him with these means of vengeance.

MATTHEW HENRY

we seek to escape by any unlawful practices we often pull upon our own heads.

V. The occasion Samson took hence to do them a yet greater mischief, which touched their bone and their flesh, *v.* 7, 8. "I have Israel's cause to plead as a public person, and for the wrongs done to them *I will be avenged on you*." So he *smote them hip and thigh with a great stroke*, so the word is. And, when he had done, he retired, to a natural fortress in the top of the rock Etam, where he waited to see whether the Philistines would be tamed by the correction he had given them.

Verses 9–17

I. Samson violently pursued by the Philistines. They pitched in Judah, and spread themselves up and down the country, to find out Samson, whom they heard had come this way, *v.* 9. Here was an army sent against one man, for indeed he was himself an army. Thus a whole band of men was sent to seize our Lord Jesus, that blessed Samson, though a tenth part would have served now that his hour had come, and ten times as many would have done nothing if he had not yielded.

II. Samson basely betrayed and delivered up by the men of Judah, *v.* 11. Of Judah were they? Degenerate branches of that valiant tribe! Perhaps they were disaffected to Samson because he was not of their tribe. Out of a foolish fondness for their forfeited precedency, they would rather be oppressed by Philistines than rescued by a Danite. Often has the church's deliverance been obstructed by such jealousies and pretended points of honour. Sin dispirits men, nay, it infatuates them, and hides from their eyes the things that belong to their peace. Probably Samson went into the border of that country to offer his service, *supposing his brethren would have understood how that God by his hand would deliver them*, as Moses did, Acts vii. 25. They begged of him that he would suffer them to bind him, and deliver him up to the Philistines. Cowardly unthankful wretches!

III. Samson tamely yielding to be bound by his countrymen, and delivered into the hands of his enraged enemies, *v.* 12, 13. He patiently submitted, 1. That he might give an example of great meekness, mixed with great strength and courage; as one that had rule over his own spirit, he knew how to yield as well as how to conquer. 2. That, by being delivered up to the Philistines, he might have an opportunity of making a slaughter among them. Justly is their misery prolonged who, to oblige their worst enemies, thus abuse their best friend. Never were men so infatuated except those who thus treated our blessed Saviour.

IV. Samson making his part good even when he was delivered fast pinioned with two new cords. The Philistines, when they had him among them, *shouted against him* (*v.* 14), so triumphing in their success, and insulting over him. When they shouted against him as a man run down, confident that all was their own, then the *Spirit of the Lord came upon him*. Thus fired, 1. He presently got clear of his bonds. The two new cords, upon the first struggle he gave, broke, and were *melted* (as the original word is) from off his hands, no doubt to the great amazement and terror of those that shouted against him, whose shouts were hereby turned into shrieks. Observe, *Where the Spirit of the Lord is there is liberty*, and those are free indeed who are thus freed. This typified the resurrection of Christ by the power of the Spirit of holiness. In it he loosed the bands of death, and its cords, the graveclothes, fell from his hands without being loosed, as Lazarus's were, because it was impossible that the mighty Saviour should be holden of them; and thus he triumphed over the powers of darkness that shouted against him, as if they had him sure. 2. He made a great destruction among the Philistines, who all gathered about him to make sport with him, *v.* 15. See how poorly he was armed: he had no better weapon than the jaw-bone of an ass, and yet what execution he did with it! he never laid it out of his hand till he had with it laid 1,000 Philistines dead upon the spot. Had it been the jaw-bone of a lion, especially that which he himself had slain, it might have helped to heighten his fancy and to make him think himself the more formidable; but to take the bone of that despicable animal was to do wonders by *the foolish things of the world*, that the *excellency of the power might be of God and not of man*.

V. Samson celebrating his own victory, since the men of Judah would not do even that for him. He composed a short song, which he sang to himself. The burden of this song was, *With the jaw-bone of an ass, heaps upon heaps, have I slain a thousand men*, *v.* 16. The same word in Hebrew (*chamor*) signifies

JAMIESON, FAUSSET, BROWN

7. Samson said . . . , Though ye have done this, yet will I be avenged of you—By that act the husbandmen had been the instruments in avenging his private and personal wrongs. But as a judge, divinely appointed to deliver Israel, his work of retribution was not yet accomplished. **8. smote them hip and thigh**—a proverbial expression for a merciless slaughter.

9-13. HE IS BOUND BY THE MEN OF JUDAH, AND DELIVERED TO THE PHILISTINES. **8. he went down and dwelt in the top of the rock Etam**—rather went down and dwelt in the cleft—i.e., the cave or cavern of the cliff Etam. **9. Then the Philistines went up**—to the high land of Judah. **and spread themselves in Lehi**—now El-Lekieh, abounding with limestone cliffs; the sides of which are perforated with caves. The object of the Philistines in this expedition was to apprehend Samson, in revenge for the great slaughter he had committed on their people.

With a view of freeing his own countrymen from all danger from the infuriated Philistines, he allowed himself to be bound and surrendered a fettered prisoner into their power. Exulting with joy at the near prospect of riddance from so formidable an enemy, they went to meet him.

But he exerted his superhuman strength, and finding a new (or moist) jawbone of an ass, he laid hold of it, and with no other weapon, slew a thousand men at a place which he called Ramath-lehi—i.e., the hill of the jawbone.

16. With the jawbone of an ass, heaps upon heaps, with the jaw of an ass have I slain a thousand men—The inadequacy of the weapon plainly shows this to have been a miraculous feat, "a case of supernatural strength," just as the gift of prophecy is a case of supernatural knowledge [CHALMERS].

ADAM CLARKE

8. *He smote them hip and thigh.* This also is variously understood, but the general meaning seems plain. He appears to have had no kind of defensive weapon; therefore he was obliged to grapple with them and, according to the custom of wrestlers, trip up their feet, and then bruise them to death. *The top of the rock Etam.* It is very likely that this is the same place as that mentioned in 1 Chron. iv. 32; it was in the tribe of Simeon, and on the borders of Dan, and probably a fortified place.

10. *To bind Samson are we come up.* It seems they did not wish to come to an open rupture with the Israelites, provided they would deliver up him who was the cause of their disasters.

11. *Three thousand men of Judah went.* It appears evidently from this that Samson was strongly posted, and they thought that no less than three thousand men were necessary to reduce him.

12. *That ye will not fall upon me yourselves.* He could not bear the thought of contending with and slaying his own countrymen, for there is no doubt that he could have as easily rescued himself from their hands as from those of the Philistines.

13. *They bound him with two new cords.* Probably his hands with one and his legs with the other.

14. *When he came unto Lehi.* This was the name of the place to which they brought him, either to put him to death, or keep him in perpetual confinement. *Shouted against him.* His capture was a matter of public rejoicing.

15. *He found a new jawbone of an ass.* I rather think that the word *teriyah*, which we translate *new*, and the margin "moist," should be understood as signifying the *tabia* or putrid state of the ass from which this jawbone was taken.

16. *With the jawbone of an ass, heaps upon heaps.* I cannot see the propriety of this rendering of the Hebrew words *bilchi hachamor, chamor chamorathayim;* I believe they should be translated thus:

"With the jawbone of this ass, an ass [the

MATTHEW HENRY

both an *ass* and a *heap*, so that this is an elegant paronomasia, and represents the Philistines falling as tamely as asses. He also gave a name to the place, to perpetuate the Philistines' disgrace, *v.* 17. *Ramath-lehi*, the *lifting up of the jaw-bone*.

Verses 18–20

I. The distress which Samson was in after this great performance (*v.* 18). He found himself reduced to the last extremity for want of water and ready to faint. Josephus says, It was designed to chastise him for not making mention of God and his hand in his memorial of the victory he had obtained, but taking all the praise to himself: *I have slain a thousand men.*

II. His prayer to God in this distress. Those that forget to attend God with their praises may perhaps be compelled to attend him with their prayers. Afflictions are often sent to bring unthankful people to God. Two things he pleads with God in this prayer, 1. He owns himself God's servant in what he had been doing: He calls his victory a *deliverance*, a *great* deliverance; for, if God had not helped him, he had not only not conquered the Philistines, but had been swallowed up by them. Note, Past experiences of God's power and goodness are excellent pleas in prayer for further mercy. 2. His being now exposed to his enemies: *Lest I fall into the hands of the uncircumcised*, and then they will triumph, will *tell it in Gath, and in the streets of Ashkelon.*

III. The seasonable relief God sent him. God heard his prayer, and sent him water. I rather incline to our marginal reading: *God clave a hollow place that was in Lehi:* the place of his action was, from the jaw-bone, called *Lehi*; even before the action we find it so called, *v.* 9, 14. And there God caused water to spring up in abundance. Of this fair water he drank, and his spirits revived. We should be more thankful for the mercy of water did we consider how ill we can spare it.

IV. The memorial of this, in the name Samson gave to this upstart fountain, *Enhakkore, the well of him that cried*, thereby keeping in remembrance both his own distress and God's favour to him. Many a spring of comfort God opens to his people, which may fitly be called by this name; it is *the well of him that cried.* Samson had given a name to the place which denoted him great and triumphant—*Ramath-lehi*, the *lifting up of the jaw-bone*; but here he gives it another name, which denotes him needy and dependent.

V. The continuance of Samson's government after these achievements, *v.* 20. At length Israel submitted to him whom they had betrayed. It was a mercy to Israel that, though they were oppressed by a foreign enemy, yet they had a judge that preserved order and kept them from ruining one another. Twenty years his government continued, but of the particulars we have no account, save of the beginning of his government in this chapter and the end of it in the next.

JAMIESON, FAUSSET, BROWN

a hollow place . . . in the jaw—in Lehi—taking the word as a proper noun, marking the place. **there came water thereout; and when he had drunk, his spirit came again**—His strength, exhausted by the violent and long-continued exertion, was recruited by the refreshing draft from the spring; and it was called En-hakkore, the "supplication well," a name which records the piety of this heroic champion.

ADAM CLARKE

foal] of two asses;
With the jawbone of this ass I have slain a thousand men."

This appears to have been a triumphal song on the occasion; and the words are variously rendered both by the versions and by expositors.

17. *Ramath-lehi.* The "lifing up (or casting away) of the jawbone." Lehi was the name of the place before, Ramath was now added to it here; he lifted up the jawbone against his enemies, and slew them.

18. *I die for thirst.* The natural consequence of the excessive fatigue he had gone through in this encounter.

19. *God clave an hollow place that was in the jaw.* "That was in Lehi"; that is, there was a hollow place in this Lehi, and God caused a fountain to spring up in it. *En-hakkore.* "The well of the implorer"; this name he gave to the spot where the water rose, in order to perpetuate the bounty of God in affording him this miraculous supply. *Which is in Lehi unto this day.* Consequently not "in the jawbone of the ass," a most unfortunate rendering.

20. *He judged Israel . . . twenty years.* In the margin it is said, "He seems to have judged southwest Israel during twenty years of their servitude of the Philistines," chap. xiii. 1. Instead of *twenty years,* the Jerusalem Talmud has "forty years"; but this reading is not acknowledged by any MS. or version.

MATTHEW HENRY — CHAPTER 16

Verses 1–3

1. Samson's sin, *v.* 1. His taking a Philistine to wife, in the beginning of his time, was in some degree excusable, but to join himself to a harlot that he accidentally saw among them was a profanation of his honour as an Israelite, as a Nazarite. *Tell it not in Gath.* 2. Samson's danger. Notice was sent to the magistrates of Gaza, perhaps by the treacherous harlot herself, that Samson was in the town, *v.* 2. The gates of the city were thereupon shut, guards set, all kept quiet, that Samson might suspect no danger. Now they thought they had him in prison, and doubted not but to be the death of him the next morning. O that all those who indulge their sensual appetites in drunkenness, uncleanness, or any fleshly lusts, would see themselves thus surrounded by their spiritual enemies! 3. Samson's escape, *v.* 3. He rose at midnight, perhaps roused by the checks of his own conscience. He arose with a penitent abhorrence (we hope) of the sin he was now committing, and of himself because of it, and with a pious resolution not to return to it. It was bad that he lay down without such checks; but it would have been worse if he had lain still under them. He makes immediately towards the gate of the city, stays not to break open the gates, but plucks up the posts, takes them, gates and bar and all, *up to the top of a hill*, in disdain of their attempt to secure him with gates and bars, proof of the great strength God had given him and a type of Christ's victory over death and the grave. He not only rolled away the stone from the door of the sepulchre, and so came forth himself, but carried

JAMIESON, FAUSSET, BROWN — CHAPTER 16

Vss. 1-3. **1. Samson Carries Away the Gates of Gaza. Gaza**—now Guzzah, the capital of the largest of the five Philistine principal cities, about fifteen miles southwest of Ashkelon. The object of this visit to this city is not recorded, and unless he had gone in disguise, it was a perilous exposure of his life in one of the enemy's strongholds. It soon became known that he was there; and it was immediately resolved to secure him; but deeming themselves certain of their prey, the Gazites deferred the execution of their measure till the morning. **3. Samson . . . arose at midnight, and took the doors of the gate of the city**—A ruinous pile of masonry is still pointed out as the site of the gate. It was probably a part of the town wall, and as this ruin is "toward Hebron," there is no improbability in the tradition. **carried them up to the top of an hill, that is before Hebron**—That hill is El-Montar; but by Hebron in this passage is meant "the mountains of Hebron"; for otherwise Samson, had he run night and day from the time of his flight from Gaza, could only have come on the evening of the following day within sight of the city of Hebron. The city of Gaza was, in those days, probably not less than three-quarters of an hour distant from El-Montar. To have climbed to the top of this hill with the ponderous doors and their bolts on his shoulders, through a road of thick sand, was a feat which none but a Samson could have accomplished [Van de Velde].

ADAM CLARKE — CHAPTER 16

1. *Then went Samson to Gaza, and saw there an harlot.* The Chaldee, as in the former case, renders the clause thus: "Samson saw there a woman, an inn-keeper." Perhaps the word *zonah* is to be taken here in its double sense: one who keeps a house for the entertainment of travellers, and who also prostitutes her person. Gaza was situated near the Mediterranean Sea, and was one of the most southern cities of Palestine. It has been supposed by some to have derived its name from the treasures deposited there by Cambyses, king of the Persians, because they say *Gaza*, in Persian, signifies "treasure"; so Pomponius Mela, and others. But it is more likely to be a Hebrew word, and that this city derived its name, *azzah*, from *azaz*, "to be strong," it being a strong or well-fortified place.

2. *They compassed him in.* They shut up all the avenues, secured the gates, and set persons in ambush near them, that they might attack him on his leaving the city early the next morning.

3. *An hill . . . before Hebron.* Possibly there were two Hebrons; it could not be the city generally understood by the word Hebron, as that was about twenty miles distant from Gaza; unless we suppose that *al peney Chebron* is to be understood of the road "leading to Hebron": he carried all to the top of that hill which was on the road leading to Hebron.

MATTHEW HENRY

away the gates of the grave, bar and all, and so left it, ever after, an open prison to all that are his.

Verses 4–17

The burnt child dreads the fire; yet Samson, that has more than the strength of a man, in this comes short of the wisdom of a child; for, though he had been more than once brought into the highest degree of mischief and danger by the love of women and lusting after them, yet he would not take warning, but is here again taken in the same snare, and this third time pays for all. This bad woman, that brought Samson to ruin, is here named *Delilah*, an infamous name, fitly used to express the person that by flattery or falsehood brings destruction on those to whom kindness is pretended.

I. The affection Samson had for Delilah: he loved her, *v.* 4. Whether she was an Israelite or a Philistine is not certain. If an Israelite, which is scarcely probable, yet she had the heart of a Philistine.

II. The interest which the lords of the Philistines made with her to betray Samson, *v.* 5. 1. That which they told her they designed was to humble him, or afflict him; they would promise not to do him any hurt, only they would disable him not to do them any. 2. That which they desired was to know where his great strength lay, and by what means he might be bound. They engaged Delilah to get it out of him, telling her what a kindness it would be to them, and perhaps assuring her it should not be improved to any real mischief, either to him or her. 3. For this they bid high, promised to give her each of them 1,100 pieces of silver, 5,500 in all. With this she was hired to betray one she pretended to love.

III. The arts by which he put her off from time to time. She asked him *where his great strength lay*, and whether it were possible for him to be bound and afflicted (*v.* 6), pretending that she thought it was impossible he should be bound otherwise than by her charms.

1. When she urged him very much, he told her, (1) That he might be bound with *seven green withs*, *v.* 7. The experiment was tried (*v.* 8), but he *broke the withs* as easily *as a thread of tow is broken when it toucheth the fire*, *v.* 9. (2) When she still continued her importunity (*v.* 10) he told her that with two new ropes he might be so cramped and hampered that he might be as easily dealt with as any other man, *v.* 11. This experiment failed: the *new ropes* broke from off his arm *like a thread*, *v.* 12. (3) He then told her that the weaving of the seven locks of his head would make a great alteration in him, *v.* 13. This came nearer the matter than any thing he had yet said. His strength appeared to be very much in his hair, when, upon the trial of this, purely by the strength of his hair, he carried away the *pin of the beam* and *the web*.

2. In the making of all these experiments, it is hard to say whether there appears more of Samson's weakness or Delilah's wickedness. (1) Could anything be more wicked than her restless and unreasonable importunity with him to discover a secret which she knew would endanger his life. What could be more base and disingenuous, more false and treacherous, than to lay his head in her lap, as one whom she loved, and at the same time to design the betraying of him to those by whom he was mortally hated? (2) Could anything be more weak than for him to continue a parley with one who, he so plainly saw, was aiming to do him a mischief?

IV. The disclosure he at last made of this great secret; and, if the disclosure proved fatal to him, he must thank himself, who had not power to keep his own counsel from one that manifestly sought his ruin. Delilah signifies a *consumer*; she was so to him. Observe, 1. How she teased him, telling him she would not believe he loved her, unless he would gratify her in this matter (*v.* 15): *How canst thou say, I love thee, when thy heart is not with me?* She continued many days vexatious to him with her importunity, so that he had no pleasure of his life with her (*v.* 16). 2. How she conquered him (*v.* 17): He *told her all his heart*. God left him to himself to do this foolish thing, to punish him for indulging himself in the lusts of uncleanness. *No razor should come upon his head, ch.* xiii. 5. His consecration to God was to be his strength. Therefore the badge of his consecration was the pledge of his strength; if he lose the former, he knows he forfeits the latter. "If I be shaven, I shall no longer be a Nazarite, and then my strength will be lost." The making of his bodily strength to depend so much on his hair, which could have no natural influence upon it either one way or other, teaches us to magnify divine institutions, and to expect God's grace, and the continuance of it, only in the use of those means of grace wherein he has appointed us to attend upon him, the word,

JAMIESON, FAUSSET, BROWN

4-14. Delilah Corrupted by the Philistines. **4. he loved a woman in the valley of Sorek**—The location of this place is not known, nor can the character of Delilah be clearly ascertained. Her abode, her mercenary character, and her heartless blandishments afford too much reason to believe she was a profligate woman. **5. the lords of the Philistines**—The five rulers deemed no means beneath their dignity to overcome this national enemy. **Entice him, and see wherein his great strength lieth**—They probably imagined that he carried some amulet about his person, or was in the possession of some important secret by which he had acquired such herculean strength; and they bribed Delilah, doubtless by a large reward, to discover it for them. She undertook the service and made several attempts, plying all her arts of persuasion or blandishment in his soft and communicative moods, to extract his secret.

7. Samson said . . . , If they bind me with seven green withs—Vine tendrils, pliant twigs, or twists made of crude vegetable stalks are used in many Eastern countries for ropes at the present day. **8. she bound him with them**—probably in a sportive manner, to try whether he was jesting or in earnest. **9. there were men lying in wait, abiding . . . in the chamber**—The *Heb.*, literally rendered, is, "in the inner or most secret part of the house." **10. And Delilah said**—To avoid exciting suspicion, she must have allowed some time to elapse before making this renewed attempt. **12. new ropes**—It is not said of what material they were formed; but from their being dried, it is probable they were of twigs, like the former. The *Hebrew* intimates that they were twisted, and of a thick, strong description. **13. If thou weavest the seven locks of my head**—braids or tresses, into which, like many in the East, he chose to plait his hair. Working at the loom was a female employment; and Delilah's appears to have been close at hand. It was of a very simple construction; the woof was driven into the warp, not by a reed, but by a wooden spatula. **The extremity of the web was fastened to a pin or stake fixed in the wall or ground; and while Delilah sat squatting at her loom, Samson lay stretched on the floor, with his head reclining on her lap—a position very common in the East. went away with the pin of the beam, and with the web—i.e., the whole weaving apparatus.**

15-20. He Is Overcome. **15-20. she pressed him daily with her words**—Though disappointed and mortified, this vile woman resolved to persevere; and conscious how completely he was enslaved by his passion for her, she assailed him with a succession of blandishing arts, till she at length discovered the coveted secret.

17. if I be shaven, then my strength will go from me—His herculean powers did not arise from his hair, but from his peculiar relation to God as a Nazarite. His unshorn locks were a sign of his Nazaritism, and a pledge on the part of God that his supernatural strength would be continued.

ADAM CLARKE

4. *He loved a woman in the valley of Sorek*. Some think Samson took this woman for his wife; others, that he had her as a concubine. It appears she was a Philistine; and however strong his love was for her, she seems to have had none for him. He always matched improperly, and he was cursed in all his matches. Where the *valley* or "brook" *of Sorek* was is not easy to be ascertained.

5. *See wherein his great strength lieth*. They saw that his stature was not remarkable and that, nevertheless, he had most extraordinary strength; therefore they supposed that it was the effect of some charm or amulet.

7. *Seven green withs*. That is, any kind of pliant, tough wood, twisted in the form of a cord or rope.

9. *Men lying in wait*. They probably did not appear, as Samson immediately broke his bonds when this bad woman said, *The Philistines be upon thee*.

11. *If they bind me fast with new ropes*. Samson wishes to keep up the opinion which the Philistines held, viz., that his mighty strength was the effect of some charm; and therefore he says, "Seven green withs which had not been dried; new ropes that were never occupied; weave the seven locks of my hair with the web." The *green* withs, the *new* ropes, and the number *seven* are such matters as would naturally be expected in a charm or spell.

13. *The seven locks of my head*. Probably Samson had his long hair plaited into seven divisions. Every person must see that this verse ends abruptly, and does not contain a full sense. Houbigant has particularly noticed this, and corrected the text from the Septuagint, the reading of which I shall here subjoin: "If thou shalt weave the seven locks of my head with the web, and shalt fasten them with the pin in the wall, I shall become weak like other men. And so it was that, when he slept, Dalida took the seven locks of his head, and wove them with the web, and fastened it with the pin to the wall and said unto him."

16. *His soul was vexed unto death*. What a consummate fool was this strong man! Might he not have seen, from what already took place, that Delilah intended his ruin? After trifling with her, and lying thrice, he at last commits to her his fatal secret, and thus becomes a traitor to himself and to his God.

17. *If I be shaven, then my strength will go from me*. The miraculous strength of Samson must not be supposed to reside either in his hair or in his muscles, but in that relation in which he stood to God as a Nazarite, such a person being bound by a solemn vow to walk in a strict conformity to the laws of his Maker. It was a part of the Nazarite's vow to permit no razor to pass on his head; and his long hair was the mark of his being a Nazarite, and of his vow to God. When Samson permitted his hair to be shorn off, he renounced and broke his Nazarite vow, in consequence of which God abandoned him; and therefore we are told, in v. 20, that "the Lord was departed from him."

MATTHEW HENRY	JAMIESON, FAUSSET, BROWN	ADAM CLARKE

sacraments, and prayer.

Verses 18–21

The fatal consequences of Samson's folly in betraying his own strength. Observe, 1. What care Delilah took to make sure of the money for herself. It would have grieved one's heart to have seen one of the bravest men in the world sold and bought, as a *sheep for the slaughter*. 2. What course she took to deliver him up to them according to the bargain. See what a treacherous method she took (*v*. 19): She *made him sleep upon her knees*. See the fatal consequences of security. Satan ruins men by rocking them asleep, flattering them into a good opinion of their own safety, and so bringing them to mind nothing and fear nothing, and then he robs them of their strength and honour and leads them captive at his will. When he was asleep she had a person ready to cut off his hair, which he did so silently and so quickly that it did not awake him. 3. What little concern he himself was in at it, *v*. 20. He could not but miss his hair as soon as he awoke, and yet said, "*I will shake myself as at other times* after sleep." He soon found in himself some change, and yet *wist not that the Lord had departed from him*: he did not consider that this was the reason of the change. Note, Many have lost the favourable presence of God and are not aware of it; they have provoked God to withdraw from them, but are not sensible of their loss. 4. What improvement the Philistines soon made of their advantages against him, *v*. 21. The Philistines took him when God had departed from him. If we sleep in the lap of our lusts, we shall certainly wake in the hands of the Philistines. It is probable they had promised Delilah not to kill him, but they took an effectual course to disable him. The first thing they did, when they had him in their hands and found they could manage him, was to *put out his eyes*, by *applying fire to them*, says the Arabic version. They considered that his eyes would never come again, as perhaps his hair might, and that the strongest arms could do little without eyes to guide them, and therefore, if now they blind him, they for ever blind him. His eyes were the inlets of his sin: he saw the harlot at Gaza, and went in unto her (*v*. 1), and now his punishment began there, *They brought him down to Gaza*, that there he might appear in weakness where he had lately given such proofs of his strength (*v*. 3). They *bound him with fetters of brass* who had before been held in the cords of his own iniquity, and he did *grind in the prison*. Poor Samson, how hast thou fallen! How is thy honour laid in the dust!

Verses 22–31

Though the last stage of Samson's life was inglorious there was honour in his death. No doubt he greatly repented of his sin, for that God was reconciled to him appears, 1. By the return of the sign of his Nazariteship (*v*. 22): *His hair began to grow again, as when he was shaven*, that is, to be as thick and as long as when it was cut off. It seems to have been extraordinary, and designed for a special indication of the return of God's favour to him upon his repentance. 2. By the use God made of him for the destruction of the enemies of his people, and that at a time when it would be most for the vindication of the honour of God, and not immediately for the defence and deliverance of Israel. Observe,

I. How insolently the Philistines affronted the God of Israel, 1. By the sacrifices they offered to Dagon, his rival. This Dagon they call their *god*, a god of their own making, represented by an image, the upper part of which was in the shape of a man, the lower part of a fish, purely the creature of fancy; yet it served them to set up in opposition to the true and living God. It was only such a dunghill-deity as Dagon that was fit to be made a patron of the villainy. 2. By the sport they made with Samson, God's champion, they reflected on God himself. They made one another laugh to see how, being blind, he stumbled and blundered. They said, *Where is now thy God?* Being a penitent, his godly sorrow makes him patient, and he accepts the indignity as the punishment of his iniquity.

II. How justly the God of Israel brought sudden destruction upon them by the hands of Samson. Thousands of the Philistines had got together, to attend their lords in the sacrifices and joys of this day, and to be the spectators of this comedy. They were all slain. Observe,

1. Who were destroyed: All the *lords of the Philistines* (*v*. 27), who had by bribes corrupted Delilah to betray Samson to them. Samson had been drawn into sin by the Philistine women, and now a great slaughter is made among them.

2. When they were destroyed. (1) When they were merry, secure, and jovial, and far from apprehending

19. she called for a man, and she caused him to shave off the seven locks of his head—It is uncertain, however, whether the ancient Hebrews cut off the hair to the same extent as Orientals now. The word employed is sometimes the same as that for shearing sheep, and therefore the instrument might be only scissors. **20. he wist not that the Lord was departed from him**—What a humiliating and painful spectacle! Deprived of the divine influences—degraded in his character—and yet, through the infatuation of a guilty passion, scarcely awake to the wretchedness of his fallen condition!

21, 22. THE PHILISTINES TOOK HIM AND PUT OUT HIS EYES. **21. the Philistines took him, and put out his eyes**—To this cruel privation prisoners of rank and consequence have commonly been subjected in the East. The punishment is inflicted in various ways, by scooping out the eyeballs, by piercing the eye, or destroying the sight by holding a red-hot iron before the eyes. His security was made doubly sure by his being bound with fetters of brass (copper), not of leather, like other captives. **he did grind in the prison-house**—This grinding with hand millstones being the employment of menials, he was set to it as the deepest degradation.

Howbeit the hair on his head began to grow again—It is probable that he had now reflected on his folly; and becoming a sincere penitent, renewed his Nazarite vow. "His hair grew together with his repentance, and his strength with his hairs" [BISHOP HALL].

23-25. THEIR FEAST TO DAGON. **23. the lords of the Philistines gathered to offer a great sacrifice unto Dagon**—It was a common practice in heathen nations, on the return of their solemn religious festivals, to bring forth their war prisoners from their places of confinement or slavery; and, in heaping on them every species of indignity, they would offer their grateful tribute to the gods by whose aid they had triumphed over their enemies. Dagon was a sea-idol, usually represented as having the head and upper parts human, while the rest of the body resembled a fish.

26-31. HIS DEATH. **27. there were upon the roof about three thousand men and women, that beheld while Samson made sport**—This building seems to have been similar to the spacious and open amphitheaters well known among the Romans and still found in many countries of the East. They are built wholly of wood. The standing-place for

19. *She began to afflict him.* She had probably tied his hands slyly, while he was asleep, and after having cut off his hair, she began to insult him before she called the Philistines, to try whether he were really reduced to a state of weakness. Finding he could not disengage himself, she called the Philistines, and he, being alarmed, rose up, thinking he could exert himself as before, and shake himself, i.e., disengage himself from his bonds and his enemies. But *he wist not that the Lord was departed from him;* for as Delilah had cut off his locks while he was asleep, he had not yet perceived that they were gone.

21. *Put out his eyes.* Thus was the lust of the eye, in looking after and gazing on strange women, punished. As the Philistines did not know that his strength might not return, they put out his eyes, that he might never be able to plan any enterprise against them. *He did grind in the prison house.* Before the invention of wind and water mills, the grain was at first bruised between two stones, afterwards ground in hand mills.

22. *The hair of his head began to grow again.* And may we not suppose that, sensible of his sin and folly, he renewed his Nazarite vow to the Lord, in consequence of which his supernatural strength was again restored?

23. *Unto Dagon their god.* Diodorus Siculus describes their god thus: "It had the head of a woman, but all the rest of the body resembled a fish."

25. *Call for Samson, that he may make us sport.* What the sport was we cannot tell; probably it was an exhibition of his prodigious strength.

27. *Now the house was full of men.* It was either the prison house, house of assembly, or a temple of Dagon, raised on pillars, open on all sides, and flat-roofed, so that it could accommodate a multitude of people on the top.

MATTHEW HENRY

themselves in any danger. (2) It was when they were praising Dagon their god. (3) It was when they were making sport with an Israelite, a Nazarite, and insulting over him, persecuting him whom God had smitten. Those know not what they do, nor whom they affront, that make sport with a good man.

3. How they were destroyed. Samson pulled the house down upon them. (1) He gained strength to do it by prayer, *v.* 28. That strength which he had lost by sin he, like a true penitent, recovers by prayer. He prayed to God to remember him and strengthen him this once, thereby owning that his strength for what he had already done he had from God, and begged it might be afforded to him once more, to give them a parting blow. Samson died praying, so did our blessed Saviour; but Samson prayed for vengeance, Christ for forgiveness. (2) He gained opportunity to do it by leaning on the two pillars which were the chief supports of the building. The vast concourse of people that were upon the roof contributed to the fall of it. Few could escape being either stifled or crushed to death. Now in this, [1] The Philistines were greatly mortified. All their lords and great men were killed; the temple of Dagon (as many think the house was) was pulled down, and Dagon buried in it. [2] Samson may very well be justified, and brought in not guilty of any sinful murder either of himself or the Philistines. Nor was he *felo de se*, or *a self-murderer*, in it; for it was not his own life that he aimed at. [3] God was glorified in pardoning Samson's great transgressions, of which this was an evidence. [4] Christ was plainly typified. He pulled down the devil's kingdom, as Samson did Dagon's temple; and, when he died, he obtained the most glorious victory over the powers of darkness. Then when his arms were stretched out upon the cross, as Samson's to the two pillars, he gave a fatal shake to the gates of hell, and, *through death, destroyed him that had the power of death, that is, the devil* (Heb. ii. 14, 15), and herein exceeded Samson, that he not only died with the Philistines, but rose again to triumph over them.

Lastly, The story of Samson concludes, 1. With an account of his burial. 2. With the repetition of the account we had before of the continuance of his government: *He judged Israel twenty years.*

JAMIESON, FAUSSET, BROWN

the spectators is a wooden floor resting upon two pillars and rising on an inclined plane, so as to enable all to have a view of the area in the center. In the middle there are two large beams, on which the whole weight of the structure lies, and these beams are supported by two pillars placed almost close to each other, so that when these are unsettled or displaced, the whole pile must tumble to the ground. **28. Samson called unto the Lord**—His penitent and prayerful spirit seems clearly to indicate that this meditated act was not that of a vindictive suicide, and that he regarded himself as putting forth his strength in his capacity of a public magistrate. He must be considered, in fact, as dying for his country's cause. His death was not designed or sought, except as it might be the inevitable consequence of his great effort. His prayer must have been a silent ejaculation, and, from its being revealed to the historian, approved and accepted of God.

31. Then his brethren and all the house of his father came down and took him, and brought him up, and buried him—This awful catastrophe seems to have so completely paralyzed the Philistines, that they neither attempted to prevent the removal of Samson's corpse, nor to molest the Israelites for a long time after. Thus the Israelitish hero rendered by his strength and courage signal services to his country, and was always regarded as the greatest of its champions. But his slavish subjection to the domination of his passions was unworthy of so great a man and lessens our respect for his character. Yet he is ranked among the ancient worthies who maintained a firm faith in God (Heb. 11:32).

ADAM CLARKE

28. *Samson called unto the Lord.* It was in consequence of his faith in God that he should be strengthened to overthrow his enemies and the enemies of his country that he is mentioned, Hebrews xi., among those who were remarkable for their faith.

29. *The two middle pillars upon which the house stood.* Much learned labor has been lost on the attempt to prove that a building like this might stand on two pillars. But what need of this? There might have been as many pillars here as were in the temple of Diana at Ephesus, and yet the two center pillars be the key of the building; these being once pulled down, the whole house would necessarily fall.

30. *So the dead which he slew.* We are informed that the house was full of men and women, with about three thousand of both sexes on the top; now as the whole house was pulled down, consequently the principal part of all these were slain; and among them we find there were the lords of the Philistines. The death of these, with so many of the inferior chiefs of the people, was such a crush to the Philistine ascendancy that they troubled Israel no more for several years, and did not even attempt to hinder Samson's relatives from taking away and burying his dead body.

31. *He judged Israel twenty years.* It is difficult to ascertain the time of Samson's magistracy, and the extent of country over which he presided. His jurisdiction seems to have been very limited, and to have extended no farther than over those parts of the tribe of Dan contiguous to the land of the Philistines. This is what our margin intimates on v. 20 of chap. xv. Many suppose that he and Eli were contemporaries, Samson being rather an executor of the divine justice upon the enemies of his people than an administrator of the civil and religious laws of the Hebrews. Allowing Eli and Samson to have been contemporaries, this latter part might have been entirely committed to the care of Eli.

MATTHEW HENRY — CHAPTER 17

Verses 1–6

I. Micah and his mother quarrelling. 1. The son robs the mother. The old woman had hoarded, with long scraping and saving, a great sum of money, 1,100 pieces of silver. It is likely she intended, when she died, to leave it to her son. 2. The mother curses the son, or whoever had taken her money. See what mischief the love of money makes, how it destroys the duty and comfort of every relation. Outward losses drive good people to their prayers, but bad people to their curses.

II. Micah and his mother reconciled. 1. The son was so terrified with his mother's curses that he restored the money. 2. The mother was so pleased with her son's repentance that she recalled her curses, and turned them into prayers for her son's welfare: *Blessed be thou of the Lord, my son.*

III. Micah and his mother agreeing to turn their money into a god, and set up idolatry in their family. And though this was only the worship of the true God by an image, against the *second* commandment, yet this opened the door to the worship of other gods, Baalim and the groves, against the *first and great* commandment. Observe,

1. The mother's contrivance of this matter. When the silver was restored she pretended she had *dedicated it to the Lord* (*v.* 3) before it was stolen. "Come," said she to her son, "the money is mine, but thou hast a mind to it; let it be neither mine nor thine, but let us both agree to make it into an image for a religious use." Probably this old woman was one of those that came out of Egypt, and would have such images made as she had seen there; and perhaps told her son that this way of worshipping God by images was, to her knowledge, the old religion.

2. The son's compliance with her. It should seem, when she first proposed the thing he stumbled at it, knowing what the second commandment was. But, when the images were made, Micah, by his mother's persuasion, was not only well reconciled to them, but greatly pleased. But observe how the old woman's covetousness prevailed, in part, above her superstition. She had wholly dedicated the silver to make the graven and molten images (*v.* 3), but, when it came to be done, she made less than a fifth part serve, even 200 *shekels*, *v.* 4. Now observe,

(1) What was the corruption here introduced, *v.* 5.

JAMIESON, FAUSSET, BROWN — CHAPTER 17

VSS. 1-4. MICAH RESTORING THE STOLEN MONEY TO HIS MOTHER, SHE MAKES IMAGES. **1. a man of mount Ephraim**—i.e., the mountainous parts of Ephraim. This and the other narratives that follow form a miscellaneous collection, or appendix to the Book of Judges. It belongs to a period when the Hebrew nation was in a greatly disordered and corrupt state. This episode of Micah is connected with chapter 1:34. It relates to his foundation of a small sanctuary of his own—a miniature representation of the Shiloh tabernacle—which he stocked with images modelled probably in imitation of the ark and cherubim.

Micah and his mother were sincere in their intention to honor God. But their faith was blended with a sad amount of ignorance and delusion. The divisive course they pursued, as well as the will-worship they practised, subjected the perpetrators to the penalty of death.

3. a graven image and a molten image—The one carved from a block of wood or stone, to be plated over with silver; the other, a figure formed of the solid metal cast into a mould. It is observable, however, that only 200 shekels were given to the founder. Probably the expense of making two such figures of silver, with their appurtenances (pedestals, bases, etc.), might easily cost, in those days, 200 shekels, which would be a sum not adequate to the formation of large statues [TAYLOR'S FRAGMENT].

ADAM CLARKE — CHAPTER 17

1. *And there was a man of mount Ephraim.* It is extremely difficult to fix the chronology of this and the following transactions. Some think them to be here in their natural order; others, that they happened in the time of Joshua, or immediately after the ancients who outlived Joshua. All that can be said with certainty is this, that they happened when there was no king in Israel; i.e., about the time of the judges, or in some time of the anarchy, v. 6.

2. *About which thou cursedst.* Houbigant and others understand this of putting the young man to his oath. It is likely that when the mother of Micah missed the money, she poured imprecations on the thief; and that Micah, who had secreted it, hearing this, was alarmed, and restored the money lest the curses should fall on him.

3. *I had wholly dedicated.* From this it appears that Micah's mother, though she made a superstitious use of the money, had no idolatrous design, for she expressly says she had dedicated it "to Jehovah"; and this appears to have been the reason why she poured imprecations on him who had taken it.

4. *A graven image and a molten image.* What these images were we cannot positively say; they were most probably some resemblance of matters belonging to the Tabernacle.

MATTHEW HENRY

The man Micah had *a house of gods, a house of God*, so the LXX, for so he thought it, as good as that at Shiloh, and better, because his own, for people love to have their religion under their girdle, to manage it as they please. *A house of error*, so the Chaldee, for really it was so, a deviation from the way of truth and an inlet to all deceit. He made *teraphim*, little images which he might advise with as there was occasion, and receive informations, directions, and predictions from. Thus, while the honour of Jehovah was pretended (*v.* 3), yet, his institution being relinquished, these Israelites unavoidably lapsed into downright idolatry and demon-worship. Some room or apartment in the house of Micah was appointed for the temple or house of God; an ephod, or holy garment, was provided for his priest to officiate in, in imitation of those used at the tabernacle of God, and one of his sons he consecrated, probably the eldest, to be his priest. Here idolatry began, and it spread like a fretting leprosy. Dr. Lightfoot would have us observe that as 1,100 pieces of silver were here devoted to the making of an idol, which ruined religion, especially in the tribe of Dan, so 1,100 pieces of silver were given by each Philistine lord for the ruin of Samson.

(2) What was the cause of this corruption (*v.* 6): *There was no king in Israel*, no judge or sovereign prince to take cognizance of the setting up of these images. Every man did that which was *right in his own eyes*, and then they soon did that which was *evil in the sight of the Lord*. See what a mercy government is, and what reason there is that not only *prayers and intercessions, but giving of thanks*, should *be made for kings and all in authority*, 1. Tim. ii. 1, 2. Nothing contributes more, under God, to the support of religion in the world, than the due administration of those two great ordinances, magistracy and ministry.

Verses 7–13

An account of Micah's furnishing himself with a Levite for his chaplain. I. By his mother's side he was of the family of Judah, and lived at Bethlehem. Thence he went to *sojourn where he could find a place*, and in his travels came to the house of Micah in Mount Ephraim, *v.* 8. Some think it was his unhappiness that he was under a necessity of removing, because he was neglected and starved, at Bethlehem. Israel's forsaking God began with forsaking the Levites. It is a sign religion is going to decay when good ministers are neglected and at a loss for a livelihood.

II. What bargain Micah made with him. Micah courts him into his family (*v.* 10), and promises him, 1. Good preferment: *Be unto me a father and a priest*. He asks not for his credentials. He might serve for a priest to a graven image, like Jeroboam's priest of the *lowest of the people*, 1 Kings xii. 31. No marvel if those who can make any thing serve for a god can also make any thing serve for a priest. 2. A tolerable maintenance. He will allow him *meat, and drink, and clothes, a double suit*, so the word is in the margin, a better and a worse, one for every day's wear and one for holy days, and ten shekels, about twenty-five shillings, a year for spending money—a poor salary in comparison of what God provided for the Levites that behaved well; but those that forsake God's service will never better themselves, nor find a better master. The ministry is the best calling but the worst trade in the world.

III. The Levite's settlement with him (*v.* 11): He was *content to dwell with the man*; though his work was superstitious and his wages were scandalous. Micah, thinking himself holier than any of his neighbours, presumed to consecrate this Levite, *v.* 12.

IV. Micah's satisfaction in this (*v.* 13): *Now know I that the Lord will do me good*. 1. He thought it was a sign of God's favour to him and his images that he had so opportunely sent a Levite to his door. 2. He thought now that the error of his priesthood was amended all was well, though he still retained his graven and molten image. Note, Many deceive themselves into a good opinion of their state by a partial reformation. They think they are as good as they should be, because, in some one particular instance, they are not so bad as they have been. 3. He thought the making of a Levite into a priest was a very meritorious act, which really was a presumptuous usurpation. 4. He thought that having a Levite in the house with him would of course entitle him to the divine favour. Having a Levite to be their priest, amounts to no security at all that God will do them good, unless they be good themselves, and make a good use of these advantages.

JAMIESON, FAUSSET, BROWN

5. the man Micah had a house of gods—*Hebrew*, "a house of God"—a domestic chapel, a private religious establishment of his own. **an ephod**—(see on Exod. 28:4). **teraphim**—tutelary gods of the household (see on Gen. 31:19, 30). **consecrated one of his sons, who became his priest**—The assumption of the priestly office by any one out of the family of Aaron was a direct violation of the divine law (Num. 3:10; 16:17; Deut. 21:5; Heb. 5:4).

6. every man did that which was right in his own eyes—From want of a settled government, there was no one to call him to account. No punishment followed any crime.

7. Bethlehem-judah—so called in contradistinction to a town of the same name in Zebulun (Josh. 19:15). **of the family** [i.e., tribe] **of Judah**—Men of the tribe of Levi might connect themselves, as Aaron did (Exod. 6:23), by marriage with another tribe; and this young Levite belonged to the tribe of Judah, by his mother's side, which accounts for his being in Bethlehem, not one of the Levitical cities. **8. the man departed . . . to sojourn where he could find a place**—A competent provision being secured for every member of the Levitical order, his wandering about showed him to have been a person of a roving disposition or unsettled habits. In the course of his journeying he came to the house of Micah, who, on learning what he was, engaged his permanent services. **10. Micah said unto him, Dwell with me, be unto me a father**—a spiritual father, to conduct the religious services of my establishment. He was to receive, in addition to his board, a salary of ten shekels of silver. **a suit of apparel**—not only dress for ordinary use, but vestments suitable for the discharge of his priestly functions.

12. Micah consecrated the Levite—*Hebrew*, "filled his hand." This act of consecration was not less unlawful for Micah to perform than for this Levite to receive (see on ch. 18:30). **13. Now know I that the Lord will do me good**—The removal of his son, followed by the installation of this Levite into the priestly office, seems to have satisfied his conscience, that by what he deemed the orderly ministrations of religion he would prosper. This expression of his hope evinces the united influence of ignorance and superstition.

ADAM CLARKE

5. *The man Micah had an house of gods. Beith Elohim* should, I think, be translated "house (or temple) of God"; for it is very likely that both the mother and the son intended no more than a private or domestic chapel, in which they proposed to set up the worship of the true God.

Made an ephod. Perhaps the whole of this case may be stated thus: Micah built a house of God—a chapel in imitation of the sanctuary; he made a graven image representing the ark, a molten image to represent the mercy seat, teraphim to represent the cherubim above the mercy seat, and an ephod in imitation of the sacerdotal garments; and he consecrated one of his sons to be priest. Thus gross idolatry was not the crime of Micah; he only set up in his own house an epitome of the divine worship as performed at Shiloh. What the *teraphim* were, see the note on Gen. xxxi. 19; for the *ephod*, see the note on Exod. xxv. 7; and for the sacerdotal vestments in general, see the note on Exod. xxviii. 5, etc.

6. *There was no king in Israel.* The word *melech*, which generally means *king*, is sometimes taken for a supreme governor, judge, magistrate, or ruler of any kind (see Gen. xxxvi. 31 and Deut. xxxiii. 5), and it is likely it should be so understood here. *Every man did that which was right in his own eyes.* He was his own governor, and what he did he said was right; and, by his cunning and strength, defended his conduct. When a man's own will, passions, and caprice are to be made the rule of law, society is in a most perilous and ruinous state.

7. *Of the family of Judah.* The word *family* may be taken here for "tribe"; or the young man might have been of the tribe of Judah by his mother, and of the tribe of Levi by his father, for he is called here a Levite; and it is probable that he might have officiated at Shiloh, in the Levitical office. A Levite might marry into any other tribe, providing the woman was not an heiress.

8. *To sojourn where he could find.* He went about the country seeking for some employment, for the Levites had no inheritance.

10. *Be unto me a father and a priest.* You shall be master of my house, as if you were my father; and, as priest, you shall appear in the presence of God for me. The term *father* is often used to express honor and reverence. *Ten shekels of silver.* About thirty shillings per annum, with board, lodging, and clothes. Very good wages in those early times.

11. *The Levite was content.* He thought the place a good one, and the wages respectable.

12. *Micah consecrated the Levite.* "He filled his hands"; i.e., he gave him an offering to present before the Lord, that he might be accepted by Him.

13. *Now know I that the Lord will do me good.* As he had already provided an epitome of the Tabernacle, a model of the ark, mercy seat, and cherubim, and had got proper sacerdotal vestments, and a Levite to officiate, he took for granted that all was right, and that he should now have the benediction of God.

MATTHEW HENRY

CHAPTER 18

Verses 1–6

1. The eye which these Danites had upon Laish, not the whole tribe of Dan, but one family of them, to whose lot, in the subdivision of Canaan, that city fell. Hitherto this family had sojourned with their brethren, who had taken possession of their lot, which lay between Judah and the Philistines, and had declined going to their own city, because there was *no king in Israel* to rule over them, *v.* 1. But at length necessity forced them to arouse themselves, and they began to think of an inheritance to dwell in. 2. They sent *five men to search the land* (*v.* 2). The men they sent were men of valour, who, if they fell into their enemies' hands, knew how to look danger in the face. 3. The acquaintance which their spies got with Micah's priest. It seems, they had known this Levite formerly, he having in his rambles been sometimes in their country. They knew him again by his voice, *v.* 3. They, understanding that he had an oracle in his custody, desired he would tell them whether they should prosper in their present undertaking, *v.* 5. They seem to have had a greater opinion of Micah's teraphim than of God's urim; for they had passed by Shiloh, and, for aught that appears, had not enquired there of God's high priest, but Micah's shabby Levite shall be an oracle to them. He made them believe he had an answer from God encouraging them to go on, and assuring them of good success (*v.* 6).

Verses 7–13

I. The observation which the spies made upon the city of Laish, *v.* 7. Never was place so ill governed and so ill guarded, which would make it a very easy prey to the invader.

1. It was ill governed, for every man might be as bad as he would, and there was no magistrate, no *heir of restraint* (as the word is), so that by the most impudent immoralities they provoked God's wrath, and by all manner of mutual mischiefs weakened and consumed one another. See here, (1) What the office of magistrate is. They are to be *heirs of restraint*, for the restraining of that which is evil. They are *possessors of restraint*, entrusted with their authority for this end, that they may check and suppress every thing that is vicious and be *a terror to evil doers.* It is only God's grace that can renew men's depraved minds and turn their hearts; but the magistrate's power may restrain their bad practices and tie their hands, so that the wickedness of the wicked may not be either so injurious or so infectious as otherwise it would be. (2) See what method must be used for the restraint of wickedness. Sinners must be put to shame, that those who will not be restrained by the shamefulness of the sin before God and their own consciences may be restrained by the shamefulness of the punishment before men. All ways must be tried to dash sin out of countenance and cover it with contempt, to make people ashamed of their idleness, drunkenness, cheating, lying, and other sins, by making reputation always appear on virtue's side. (3) See how miserable, and how near to ruin, those places are that either have no magistrates or none that bear the sword to any purpose.

2. It was ill guarded. The people of Laish were careless, quiet, and secure, their gates left open, their walls out of repair, because under no apprehension of danger in any way. It was a sign that the Israelites, through their sloth and cowardice, were not now such a terror to the Canaanites as they were when they first came among them, else the city of Laish, which probably knew itself to be assigned to them, would not have been so very secure. And, *lastly*, they had *no business with any man*, which bespeaks either the idleness or the independency they affected: they scorned to be either in subjection to or alliance with any of their neighbours. They cared for nobody and therefore nobody cared for them. Such as these were the men of Laish.

II. The encouragement which they consequently gave to their countrymen that sent them to prosecute their design upon this city, *v.* 8–10. 1. They represent the place as desirable (*v.* 9), better than the mountainous country into which they were crowded by the Philistines. 2. They represent it as attainable. They do not at all question but, with God's blessing, they may soon get possession of it; for *the people are secure*, *v.* 10.

III. The Danites' expedition against Laish. This particular family of them, to whose lot that city fell, now at length make towards it, *v.* 11–13. The military men were but 600 in all. It was strange that none of their brethren of their own tribe came in to their assistance; but it was long after Israel came to Canaan before there appeared among them anything of a

JAMIESON, FAUSSET, BROWN

CHAPTER 18

Vss. 1-26. THE DANITES SEEK OUT AN INHERITANCE. **1-6. In those days . . . the Danites sought them an inheritance to dwell in**—The Danites had a territory assigned them as well as the other tribes. But either through indolence, or a lack of energy, they did not acquire the full possession of their allotment, but suffered a considerable portion of it to be wrested out of their hands by the encroachments of their powerful neighbors, the Philistines. In consequence, being straitened for room, a considerable number resolved on trying to effect a new and additional settlement in a remote part of the land. A small deputation, being despatched to reconnoitre the country, arrived on their progress northward at the residence of Micah. Recognizing his priest as one of their former acquaintances, or perhaps by his provincial dialect, they eagerly enlisted his services in ascertaining the result of their present expedition. His answer, though apparently promising, was delusive, and really as ambiguous as those of the heathen oracles. This application brings out still more clearly and fully than the schism of Micah the woeful degeneracy of the times. The Danites expressed no emotions either of surprise or of indignation at a Levite daring to assume the priestly functions, and at the existence of a rival establishment to that of Shiloh. They were ready to seek, through means of the teraphim, the information that could only be lawfully applied for through the high priest's Urim. Being thus equally erroneous in their views and habits as Micah, they show the low state of religion, and how much superstition prevailed in all parts of the land. **7-10. the five men departed, and came to Laish**—or Leshem (Josh. 19:47). supposed to have been peopled by a colony of Zidonians.

The place was very secluded—the soil rich in the abundance and variety of its produce, and the inhabitants, following the peaceful pursuits of agriculture, lived in their fertile and sequestered valley, according to the Zidonian style of ease and security, happy among themselves, and maintaining little or no communication with the rest of the world. The discovery of this northern paradise seemed, to the delight of the Danite spies, an accomplishment of the priest's prediction.

They hastened back to inform their brethren in the south both of the value of their prize, and how easily it could be made their prey.

11. there went from thence of the family of the Danites . . . six hundred men—This was the collective number of the men who were equipped with arms to carry out this expeditionary enterprise, without including the families and furniture of the emigrants (vs. 21). Their journey led them through the territory of Judah, and their first halt-

ADAM CLARKE

CHAPTER 18

1. *There was no king in Israel.* See chap. xvii. 6. The circumstances related here show that this must have happened about the time of the preceding transactions. *The tribe of the Danites.* That is, a part of this tribe; some families of it. *All their inheritance.* That is, they had not received an extent of country sufficient for them. Some families were still unprovided for, or had not sufficient territory; for we find from Josh. chap. xix. 40, etc., that, although the tribe of Dan did receive their inheritance with the rest of the tribes of Israel, yet their coasts "went out too little for them," and they went and fought "against Leshem [called here Laish], and took it." This circumstance is marked here more particularly than in the Book of Joshua. See on Josh. xix. 47.

2. *Five men . . . men of valour.* The Hebrew word *chayil* has been applied to personal prowess, to mental energy, and to earthly possessions. They sent those in whose courage, judgment, and prudence they could safely confide.

3. *They knew the voice of the young man.* They knew by his dialect or mode of pronunciation that he was not an Ephraimite. We have already seen (chap. xii. 6) that the Ephraimites could not pronounce certain letters.

5. *Ask counsel . . . of God.* As the Danites use the word *Elohim* here for *God*, we are necessarily led to believe that they meant the true God; especially as the Levite answers, v. 6, "Before the Lord [*Yehovah*] is your way." Though the former word sometimes may be applied to idols, whom their votaries clothed with the attributes of God, yet the latter is never applied but to the true *God* alone. As the Danites succeeded according to the oracle delivered by the Levite, it is a strong presumption that the worship established by Micah was not of an idolatrous kind.

7. *After the manner of the Zidonians.* Probably the people of *Laish* or Leshem were originally a colony of the *Sidonians,* who, it appears, were an opulent people; and, being in possession of a strong city, lived in a state of security, not being afraid of their neighbors. In this the Leshemites imitated them, though the sequel proves they had not the same reason for their confidence.

They were far from the Zidonians. Being, as above supposed, a Sidonian colony, they might naturally expect help from their countrymen; but, as they dwelt a considerable distance from Sidon, the Danites saw that they could strike the blow before the news of invasion could reach Sidon.

And had no business with any man. In the most correct copies of the Septuagint, this clause is thus translated: "And they had no transactions with Syria." Now it is most evident that, instead of *adam,* "man," they read *aram,* "Syria"; words which are so nearly similar that the difference which exists is only between the *resh* and *daleth,* and this, both in MSS. and in printed books, is often indiscernible. It may be proper to observe that *Laish* was on the frontiers of Syria; but as they had no intercourse with the Syrians, from whom they might have received the promptest assistance, this was an additional reason why the Danites might expect success.

9. *Arise.* This is a very plain address, full of good sense, and well adapted to the purpose. It seems to have produced an instantaneous effect.

11. *Six hundred men.* These were not the whole, for we find they had children, v. 21; but these appear to have been 600 armed men.

MATTHEW HENRY

public spirit. It appears (by *v.* 21) that these 600 were the whole number that went to settle there, for they had their families and effects with them, their *little ones and cattle.* The second day's march brought them to Mount Ephraim, near Micah's house (*v.* 13), and there we must pause awhile.

Verses 14–26

The Danites had sent out their spies to find out a country for them. Now that they came to the place they oblige them with a further discovery—they can tell them where there are gods: "Here, *in these houses,* there are an ephod, and teraphim, and a great many fine things for devotion, such as we have not the like in our country; *now therefore consider what you have to do, v.* 14. We consulted them, and had a good answer from them; they are worth having, and, if we can but make ourselves masters of these gods, we may the better hope to prosper, and make ourselves masters of Laish." So far they were in the right, that it was desirable to have God's presence with them, but wretchedly mistaken when they took these images (which were fitter to be used in a puppet-play than in acts of devotion) for tokens of God's presence. The place they were going to settle in being so far from Shiloh, they thought they had more need of a *house of gods* among themselves than Micah had that lived so near to it. Being determined to take these gods along with them, we are here told how they stole the images, cajoled the priest, and frightened Micah from attempting to rescue them.

I. The five men that knew the house and the avenues to it, and particularly the chapel, went in and fetched out the images, with the ephod, and teraphim, and all the appurtenances, while the 600 kept the priest in talk at the gate, *v.* 16–18. See what little care this sorry priest took of his gods. See how impotent these sorry gods were, that could not keep themselves from being stolen. O the sottishness of these Danites! They must have *gods to go before them,* not of their own making indeed, but, which was as bad, of their own stealing. Their idolatry began in theft, a proper prologue for such an opera. In order to the breaking of the second commandment, they begin with the eighth, and take their neighbour's goods to make them their gods.

II. They set upon the priest, and flattered him into a good humour, not only to let the gods go, but to go himself along with them; for without him they knew not well how to make use of the gods. Observe, 1. How they tempted him, *v.* 19. They assured him of better preferment with them than what he now had. 2. How they won him. A little persuasion served: *His heart was glad, v.* 20. He takes the images with him, and carries the infection of the idolatry into a whole city. If ten shekels won him (as Bishop Hall expresses it), eleven would lose him; for what can hold those that have made shipwreck of a good conscience? *The hireling flees because he is a hireling.*

III. They frightened Micah back when he pursued them to recover his gods. His neighbours got together, and pursued the robbers, who, having their children and cattle before them (*v.* 21), could make no great haste. The pursuers called after them, desiring to speak a word with them; those in the rear turned about and asked Micah what he would have, *v.* 23. He argues with them, and pleads his right, which he thought should prevail; but they, in answer, plead their might, which, it proved, did prevail.

1. He insists upon the wrong they had certainly done him (*v.* 24): "*You have taken away my gods,* my images of God. I made them myself." What a folly was it for him to call those his *gods* which he had made, when he only that made us is to be worshipped by us as a God!

2. They insist upon the mischief they would certainly do him if he prosecuted his demand. They would not hear reason, nor do justice, nor so much as offer to pay him the prime cost he had been at upon those images. They would not so much as give him good words, but resolved to justify their robbery with murder if he did not immediately let fall his claims, *v.* 25. Micah has not courage enough to venture his life for the rescue of his gods, so little opinion has he of their being able to protect him and bear him out, and therefore tamely gives them up (*v.* 26). If the loss of our idols cure us of the love of them, and make us say, *What have we to do any more with idols?* the loss will be unspeakable again. See Isa. ii. 20; xxx. 22.

Verses 27–31

I. Laish conquered by the Danites. They proceeded on their march, and, because they met with no disaster, perhaps concluded they had not done amiss in robbing Micah. Many justify themselves in their impiety by their prosperity. Observe, 1. The

JAMIESON, FAUSSET, BROWN

ing-place was "behind," that is, on the west of Kirjath-jearim, on a spot called afterwards "the camp of Dan." Prosecuting the northern route, they skirted the base of the Ephraimite hills.

On approaching the neighborhood of Micah's residence, the spies having given information that a private sanctuary was kept there, the priest of which had rendered them important service when on their exploring expedition, it was unanimously agreed that both he and the furniture of the establishment would be a valuable acquisition to their proposed settlement. A plan of spoliation was immediately formed.

While the armed men stood sentinels at the gates, the five spies broke into the chapel, pillaged the images and vestments, and succeeded in bribing the priest also by a tempting offer to transfer his services to their new colony. Taking charge of the ephod, the teraphim, and the graven image, he "went in the midst of the people"—a central position assigned him in the march, perhaps for his personal security; but more probably in imitation of the place appointed for the priests and the ark, in the middle of the congregated tribes, on the marches through the wilderness. This theft presents a curious medley of low morality and strong religious feeling. The Danites exemplified a deep-seated principle of our nature—that men have religious affections, which must have an object on which these may be exercised, while they are often not very discriminating in the choice of the objects. In proportion to the slender influence religion wields over the heart, the greater is the importance attached to external rites; and in the exact observance of these, the conscience is fully satisfied, and seldom or never molested by reflections on the breach of minor morals. **22-26. the men that were in the houses near to Micah's house were gathered together**—The robbers of the chapel being soon detected, a hot pursuit was forthwith commenced by Micah, at the head of a considerable body of followers. The readiness with which they joined in the attempt to recover the stolen articles affords a presumption that the advantages of the chapel had been open to all in the neighborhood; and the importance which Micah, like Laban, attached to his teraphim, is seen by the urgency with which he pursued the thieves, and the risk of his life in attempting to procure their restoration. Finding his party, however, not a match for the Danites, he thought it prudent to desist, well knowing the rule which was then prevalent in the land, that

They should take who had the power,
And they should keep who could.

ADAM CLARKE

12. *Mahaneh-dan.* "The camp of Dan"; so called from the circumstance of this armament encamping there. See chap. xiii. 25, which affords some proof that this transaction was previous to the days of Samson.

14. *Consider what ye have to do.* They probably had formed the design to carry off the priest and his sacred utensils.

18. *These went into Micah's house.* The 5 men went in, while the 600 armed men stood at the gate.

19. *Lay thine hand upon thy mouth.* This was the token of silence. The god of silence, Harpocrates, is represented on ancient statues with his finger pressed on his lips.

20. *Went in the midst of the people.* He was glad to be employed by the Danites; and went into the crowd, that he might not be discovered by Micah or his family.

21. *The little ones and the cattle.* These men were so confident of success that they removed their whole families, household goods, cattle, and all. *And the carriage.* Their "substance, precious things, or valuables"; or rather the "luggage" or "baggage."

24. *Ye have taken away my gods.* As Micah was a worshipper of the true God, as we have seen, he cannot mean any kind of idols by the word *elohai* here used. He undoubtedly means those representations of divine things and symbols of the divine presence such as the teraphim, ephod, etc.; for they are all evidently included under the word *elohai,* which we translate *my gods.*

MATTHEW HENRY

people of Laish were quiet and secure, which made them a very easy prey to this little handful of men that came upon them, *v.* 27. 2. What a complete victory they obtained over them: They *put all the people to the sword,* and burnt down so much of the city as they thought fit to rebuild (*v.* 27, 28).

3. How the conquerors settled themselves in their room, *v.* 28, 29. They built the city, or much of it, anew and *called the name of it Dan,* to be a witness for them that, though separated so far off from their brethren, they were nevertheless Danites by birth.

II. Idolatry immediately set up there. God had graciously performed his promise, in putting them in possession of that which fell to their lot. But the first thing they do after they are settled is to break his statutes. As soon as they began to settle themselves they *set up the graven image* (*v.* 30), perversely attributing their success to that idol. Their Levite, who officiated as priest, is at length *named* here—*Jonathan, the son of Gershom, the son of Manasseh.* The word *Manasseh,* in the original, has the letter נ, *n,* set over the head, which, some of the Jewish rabbis say, is an intimation that it should be left out, and then *Manasseh* will be *Moses,* and this Levite, they say, was grandson to the famous Moses, who indeed had a son named Gershom. The vulgar Latin reads it *Moses.* And if indeed Moses had a grandson that was rakish, and was picked up as a fit tool to be made use of in the setting up of idolatry, it is not the only instance of the unhappy degenerating of the posterity of great and good men. Children's children are not always the crown of old men. But the learned Bishop Patrick takes this to be an idle conceit of the rabbis, and supposes this Jonathan to be of some other family of the Levites. How long these corruptions continued we are told in the close. The posterity of this Jonathan continued to act as priests to this family of Dan that was seated as Laish. These images continued till Samuel's time, for so long *the ark of God was at Shiloh*; and it is probable that in his time effectual care was taken to suppress and abolish this idolatry. See how dangerous it is to admit an infection, for spiritual distempers are not so soon cured as caught.

JAMIESON, FAUSSET, BROWN

THEY WIN LAISH. 27-29. **27. they . . . came unto Laish . . . smote them** [the inhabitants] **. . . and burnt the city**—"We are revolted by this inroad and massacre of a quiet and secure people. Nevertheless, if the original grant of Canaan to the Israelites gave them the warrant of a divine commission and command for this enterprise, that sanctifies all and legalizes all" [CHALMERS]. This place seems to have been a dependency of Zidon, the distance of which, however, rendered it impossible to obtain aid thence in the sudden emergency. **28-29. they built a city, and . . . called the name of that city Dan**—It was in the northern extremity of the land, and hence the origin of the phrase, "from Dan to Beersheba."

30, 31. THEY SET UP IDOLATRY. **30. the children of Dan set up the graven image**—Their distance secluded them from the rest of the Israelites, aud doubtless this, which was their apology for not going to Shiloh, was the cause of perpetuating idolatry among them for many generations.

ADAM CLARKE

27. *Unto a people . . . at quiet and secure.* They found the report given by the spies to be correct. The people were apprehensive of no danger, and were unprepared for resistance; hence they were all put to the sword, and their city burned up.

28. *There was no deliverer.* They had no succor; because the Sidonians, from whom they might have expected it, were at too great a distance.

29. *Called the name of the city Dan.* This city was afterwards very remarkable as one of the extremities of the Promised Land. The extent of the Jewish territories was generally expressed by the phrase, "From Dan to Beersheba"; that is, "From the most northern to the southern extremity."

30. *The children of Dan set up the graven image.* They erected a chapel, or temple, among themselves, as Micah had done before, having the same implements and the same priest. *And Jonathan the son of Gershom.* Either this was the name of the young Levite or they had turned him off and got this Jonathan in his place. *The son of Manasseh.* Who this Manasseh was, none can tell; nor does the reading appear to be genuine. Instead of *Manasseh,* the word should be read *Mosheh,* "Moses," as it is found in some MSS., in the Vulgate, and in the concessions of the most intelligent Jews. The Jews, as R. D. Kimchi acknowledges, have suspended the letter *nun* over the word *Mosheh,* which, by the addition of the points, they have changed into *Manasseh,* because they think it would be a great reproach to their legislator to have had a grandson who was an idolater. That Gershom the son of Moses is here intended is very probable.

Until the day of the captivity of the land. Calmet observes, "The posterity of this Jonathan executed the office of priest in the city of Dan, all the time that the idol of Micah (the teraphim, ephod, etc.) was there. But this was only while the house of the Lord was at Shiloh; and, consequently, the sons of Jonathan were priests at Dan only till the time in which the ark was taken by the Philistines, which was the last year of Eli, the high priest; for after that the ark no more returned to Shiloh." This is evident; and on this very ground Houbigant contends that, instead of *haarets,* "the land," we should read *haaron,* "the ark"; for nothing is easier than the *vau* and *final nun* to be mistaken for the *final tsade,* which is the only difference between "the captivity of the land" and "the captivity of the ark." And this conjecture is the more likely, because the next verse tells us that Micah's graven image continued at Dan "all the time that the house of God was in Shiloh," which was till the ark was taken by the Philistines.

MATTHEW HENRY — CHAPTER 19

Verses 1–15

This Levite was of Mount Ephraim, *v.* 1. He married a wife of Bethlehem-Judah. It does not appear that he had any other wife, and the margin calls her *a wife, a concubine, v.* 1.

I. This Levite's concubine played the whore and eloped from her husband, *v.* 2. The Chaldee reads it only that she *carried herself insolently to him,* or *despised him,* and, he being displeased at it, *she went away from him,* and was received and entertained at her father's house. When she treacherously departed from her husband to embrace the bosom of a stranger, her father ought not to have countenanced her sin. Children's ruin is often owing very much to parents' indulgence.

II. The Levite went himself to court her return. She is addressed in the kindest manner by her injured husband, who takes a long journey on purpose to beseech her to be reconciled, *v.* 3. It is part of the character of the wisdom from above that it is gentle and easy to be entreated. He spoke *friendly* to her, or *comfortably* (for so the Hebrew phrase of *speaking to the heart* commonly signifies), which intimates that she was in sorrow, penitent for what she had done amiss.

III. Her father made him very welcome. 1. He entertains him kindly, *rejoices to see him* (*v.* 3), treats him generously for three days, *v.* 4. And the Levite, to show that he was perfectly reconciled, accepted his kindness, and we do not find that he upbraided him or his daughter with what had been amiss. It

JAMIESON, FAUSSET, BROWN — CHAPTER 19

VSS. 1-15. A LEVITE GOING TO BETHLEHEM TO FETCH HIS WIFE. **1. it came to pass in those days**—The painfully interesting episode that follows, together with the intestine commotion the report of it produced throughout the country, belongs to the same early period of anarchy and prevailing disorder. **a certain Levite . . . took a concubine**—The priests under the Mosaic law enjoyed the privilege of marrying as well as other classes of the people. It was no disreputable connection this Levite had formed; for a nuptial engagement with a concubine-wife (though, as wanting in some outward ceremonies, it was reckoned a secondary or inferior relationship) possessed the true essence of marriage; it was not only lawful, but sanctioned by the example of many good men. **2. his concubine . . . went away from him unto her father's house**—The cause of the separation assigned in our version rendered it unlawful for her husband to take her back (Deut. 24:4); and according to the uniform style of sentiment and practice in the East, she would have been put to death, had she gone to her father's family. Other versions concur with Josephus, in representing the reason for the flight from her husband's house to be, that she was disgusted with him, through frequent brawls. **3. And her husband arose, and went after her to speak friendly unto her**—*Hebrew,* speak to her heart, in a kindly and affectionate manner, so as to rekindle her affection. Accompanied by a servant, he ar-

ADAM CLARKE — CHAPTER 19

1. *There was no king in Israel.* All sorts of disorders are attributed to the want of civil government; justice, right, truth, and humanity had fallen in the streets. *Took to him a concubine.* We have already seen that the *concubine* was a sort of secondary wife; and that such connections were not disreputable, being according to the general custom of those times.

2. *Played the whore.* Neither the Vulgate, Septuagint, Targum, nor Josephus understand this word as implying any act of conjugal infidelity on the woman's part. They merely state that the parties disagreed, and the woman returned to her father's house. Indeed all the circumstances of the case vindicate this view of the subject. If she had been a *whore,* or adulteress, it is not very likely that her husband would have gone after her to *speak friendly,* literally, "to speak to her heart," and entreat her to return. The Vulgate simply states that she "left him"; the Septuagint, that she "was angry with" him; the Targum, that she "despised him"; Josephus, that she "was alienated," or separated herself, from him. Houbigant translates the clause: "Who when she was alienated from him or angry with him, left him." I think the true meaning to be among the above interpretations.

3. *He rejoiced to meet him.* He hoped to be able completely to reconcile his daughter and

MATTHEW HENRY

becomes all, but especially Levites, to forgive as God does. Every thing among them gave a hopeful prospect of their living comfortably together for the future. 2. He is very earnest for his stay, as a further demonstration of his hearty welcome. The affection he had for him, and the pleasure he took in his company, proceeded, (1) From a civil regard to him as his son-in-law and an ingrafted branch of his own house. Note, Love and duty are due to those to whom we are related by marriage as well as to those who are bone of our bone. (2) From a pious respect to him as a Levite, a servant of God's house. [1] He engages him to stay as long as he possibly could. The Levite, though nobly treated, was very urgent to be gone. A good man's heart is where his business is. It is a sign a man has either little to do at home, or little heart to do what he has to do, when he can take pleasure in being long abroad where he has nothing to do. [2] He forces him to stay till the afternoon of the fifth day, and this, as it proved, was unkind, *v.* 8, 9. Had they set out early, they might have reached some better lodging-place than that which they were now constrained to take up with, nay, they might have got to Shiloh.

IV. In his return home he was forced to lodge at Gibeah, a city in the tribe of Benjamin, afterwards called *Gibeah of Saul,* which lay on his road towards Shiloh and Mount Ephraim. When night came they could not pursue their journey. 1. The servant proposed that they should lodge in Jebus, afterwards Jerusalem, but as yet in the possession of Jebusites. If they had done so, it is probable they would have had much better usage than they met with in Gibeah of Benjamin. Debauched and profligate Israelites are worse and much more dangerous than Canaanites themselves. 2. Having passed by Jebus they stopped at Gibeah (*v.* 13–15); there they sat down in the street, nobody offering them a lodging. This traveller, though a Levite (and to those of that tribe God had particularly commanded his people to be kind upon all occasions), met with very cold entertainment at Gibeah: *No man took them into his house.*

Verses 16–21

When the Levite, and his wife, and servant, were beginning to fear that they must lie in the street all night (and as good have laid in a den of lions) they were at length invited into a house, and we are here told,

I. Who that kind man was that invited them. 1. He was a man of Mount Ephraim, and only sojourned in Gibeah, *v.* 16. Of all the tribes of Israel, the Benjamites had most reason to be kind to poor travellers, for their ancestor, Benjamin, was born upon the road, his mother being then upon a journey, and very near to this place, Gen. xxxv. 16, 17. Yet they were hard-hearted to a traveller in distress, while an honest Ephraimite had compassion on him, and, no doubt, was the more kind to him, when, upon enquiry, he found that he was his countryman, of Mount Ephraim likewise. 2. He was an old man, one that retained some of the expiring virtue of an Israelite. The rising generation was entirely corrupted; if there was any good remaining among them, it was only with those that were old and going off. 3. He was coming home from his work out of the field at eventide. The rest had given themselves up to sloth and luxury, and no marvel there was among them, as in Sodom, abundance of uncleanness, when there was among them, as in Sodom, abundance of idleness, Ezek. xvi. 49.

II. How free and generous he was in his invitation. He did not stay till they applied to him to beg for a night's lodging. Thus our good God answers before we call. Note, A charitable disposition expects only opportunity, not importunity, to do good, and will succour upon sight, unsought unto. Charity is not apt to distrust, but *hopeth all things* (1 Cor. xiii. 7).

Verses 22–30

I. The great wickedness of the men of Gibeah. The sinners are here called *sons of Belial,* that is, ungovernable men, men that would endure no yoke, children of the devil (for he is Belial), resembling him, and joining with him in rebellion against God and his government.

1. They made a rude and insolent assault, in the night, upon the habitation of an honest man, that not only lived peaceably among them, but kept a good house and was a blessing and ornament to their city.

2. They had a particular spite at the strangers that were within their gates, that only desired a night's lodging among them, contrary to the laws of hospitality, which all civilized nations have accounted sacred, and which the master of the house pleaded with them (*v.* 23).

3. They designed in the most filthy and abominable manner (not to be thought of without horror and detestation) to abuse the Levite. *Bring him forth*

JAMIESON, FAUSSET, BROWN

rived at the house of his father-in-law, who rejoiced to meet him, in the hope that a complete reconciliation would be brought about between his daughter and her husband. The Levite, yielding to the hospitable importunities of his father-in-law, prolonged his stay for days. **8. tarried** [with reluctance] **until afternoon**—lit., "the decline of the day." People in the East, who take little or nothing to eat in the morning, do not breakfast till from 10 to 12 A.M., and this meal the hospitable relative had purposely protracted to so late a period as to afford an argument for urging a further stay. **9. the day draweth toward evening**—*Hebrew,* "the pitching time of day." Travellers who set out at daybreak usually halt about the middle of the afternoon the first day, to enjoy rest and refreshment. It was, then, too late a time to commence a journey. But duty, perhaps, obliged the Levite to indulge no further delay. **10. the man . . . departed, and came over against Jebus**—The note, "which is Jerusalem," must have been inserted by Ezra or some later hand. Jebus being still, though not entirely (ch. 1:8) in the possession of the old inhabitants, the Levite resisted the advice of his attendant to enter it and determined rather to press forward to pass the night in Gibeah, which he knew was occupied by Israelites. The distance from Bethlehem to Jerusalem is about six miles. The event showed that it would have been better to have followed the advice of his attendant—to have trusted themselves among aliens than among their own countrymen. **13. in Gibeah, or in Ramah**—The first of these places was five miles northeast, the other from four to five north of Jerusalem. **15. when he went in he sat him down in a street of the city**—The towns of Palestine at this remote period could not, it seems, furnish any establishment in the shape of an inn or public lodging-house. Hence we conclude that the custom, which is still frequently witnessed in the cities of the East, was then not uncommon, for travellers who were late in arriving and who had no introduction to a private family, to spread their bedding in the streets, or wrapping themselves up in their cloaks, pass the night in the open air. In the Arab towns and villages, however, the sheik, or some other person, usually comes out and urgently invites the strangers to his house. This was done also in ancient Palestine (Gen. 18:4; 19:2). That the same hospitality was not shown in Gibeah seems to have been owing to the bad character of the people.

16-21. AN OLD MAN ENTERTAINS HIM AT GIBEAH. **16. there came an old man from his work out of the field at even, which was also of mount Ephraim**—Perhaps his hospitality was quickened by learning the stranger's occupation, and that he was on his return to his duties at Shiloh. **19. there is no want of anything**—In answering the kindly inquiries of the old man, the Levite deemed it right to state that he was under no necessity of being burdensome on anyone, for he possessed all that was required to relieve his wants. Oriental travellers always carry a stock of provisions with them; and knowing that even the khans or lodging-houses they may find on their way afford nothing beyond rest and shelter, they are careful to lay in a supply of food both for themselves and their beasts. Instead of hay, which is seldom met with, they used chopped straw, which, with a mixture of barley, beans, or the like, forms the provender for cattle. The old man, however, in the warmth of a generous heart, refused to listen to any explanation, and bidding the Levite keep his stocks for any emergency that might occur in the remainder of his journey, invited them to accept of the hospitalities of his house for the night. **20. only lodge not in the street**—As this is no rare or singular circumstance in the East, the probability is that the old man's earnest dissuasive from such a procedure arose from his acquaintance with the infamous practices of the place.

22-28. THE GIBEAHITES ABUSE HIS CONCUBINE TO DEATH. **22. certain sons of Belial beset the house**—The narrative of the horrid outrage that was committed—of the proposal of the old man—the unfeeling, careless, and in many respects, inexplicable conduct of the Levite towards his wife, disclose a state of morality that would have appeared incredible, did it not rest on the testimony of the sacred historian.

ADAM CLARKE

her husband.

8. *And they tarried until afternoon.* Merely that they might avoid the heat of the day, which would have been very inconvenient in travelling.

9. *The day groweth to an end.* "The day is about to pitch its tent"; that is, it was near the time in which travellers ordinarily pitched their tents, to take up their lodging for the night.

11. *When they were by Jebus.* This was Jerusalem, in which, though after the death of Joshua it appears to have been partly conquered by the tribe of Judah, yet the Jebusites kept the stronghold of Zion till the days of David, by whom they were finally expelled.

15. *No man . . . took them into his house to lodging.* There was probably no inn in this place, and therefore they could not have a lodging unless furnished by mere hospitality.

20. *All thy wants lie upon me.* Here was genuine hospitality: "Keep your bread and wine for yourselves, and your straw and provender for your asses; you may need them before you finish your journey; I will supply all your wants for this night, therefore do not lodge in the street."

22. *Sons of Belial.* Profligate fellows. *That we may know him.* See Genesis xix. These were genuine sodomites as to their practice; sons of Belial, rascals and miscreants of the deepest dye; worse than brutes, being a compound of beast and devil inseparably blended.

MATTHEW HENRY

that we may know him. Now, (1) This was the sin of Sodom, and is thence called *Sodomy.* What did it avail them that they had the ark of God in Shiloh when they had Sodom in their streets—God's law in their fringes, but the devil in their hearts? (2) This was the punishment of their idolatry, that sin to which they were, above all others, most addicted. He gave them up to these vile affections, by which they dishonoured themselves as they had by their idolatry dishonoured him and turned his glory into shame, Rom. i. 24, 28.

4. They were deaf to the reproofs and reasonings of the good man of the house, who, being well acquainted (we may suppose) with the story of Lot and the Sodomites, set himself to imitate Lot, *v.* 23, 24. Compare Gen. xix. 6–8. But in one thing he conformed too far to Lot's example in offering them his daughter to do what they would with. He had not power thus to prostitute his daughter, nor ought he to have done this evil that good might come. But *they would not hearken to him, v.* 25. Headstrong lusts are like the deaf adder that stoppeth her ear; they sear the conscience and make it insensible.

5. They got the Levite's wife among them, and abused her to death, *v.* 25. They slighted the old man's offer of his daughter to their lust.

II. The notice that was sent of this wickedness to all the tribes of Israel. The poor abused woman made towards her husband's lodgings as soon as ever the approach of the daylight obliged these sons of Belial to let her go (for these works of darkness hate and dread the light), *v.* 25. Down she fell at the door, with her hands on the threshold, and in that posture of a penitent, with her mouth in the dust, she expired. There he found her (*v.* 26, 27), soon perceived she was dead (*v.* 28), took up her dead body, waived his purpose of going to Shiloh, and went directly home. There was no king in Israel to appeal to, and demand justice from. He has therefore no other way left him than to appeal to the people: let the community be judge. To each of the tribes, in their respective meetings, he sent by special messengers a remonstrance of the wrong that was done him, in all its aggravating circumstances, and with it a piece of his wife's dead body (*v.* 29), to represent their barbarous usage of his wife. All that saw the pieces of the dead body, and were told how the matter was, expressed the same sentiments upon it. 1. That the men of Gibeah had been guilty of a very heinous piece of wickedness, the like to which had never been known before in Israel, *v.* 30. 2. That a general assembly of all Israel should be called, to debate what was fit to be done for the punishment of this wickedness, that a stop might be put to this threatening inundation of debauchery, and the wrath of God might not be poured upon the whole nation for it. We have here the three great rules by which those that sit in council ought to go in every arduous affair. (1) Let every man retire into himself, and weigh the matter impartially and fully in his own thoughts, and seriously and calmly consider it, without prejudice on either side, before he speaks upon it. (2) Let them freely talk it over, and every man take advice of his friend, know his opinion and his reasons, and weigh them. (3) Then let every man speak his mind, and give his vote according to his conscience. In the multitude of such counsellors there is safety.

JAMIESON, FAUSSET, BROWN

Both men ought to have protected the women in the house, even though at the expense of their lives, or thrown themselves on God's providence. It should be noted, however, that the guilt of such a foul outrage is not fastened on the general population of Gibeah.

29. divided her . . . into twelve pieces—The want of a regular government warranted an extraordinary step; and certainly no method could have been imagined more certain of rousing universal horror and indignation than this terrible summons of the Levite.

ADAM CLARKE

24. *Here is my daughter a maiden.* Such a proposal was made by Lot to the men of Sodom, Genesis xix, but nothing can excuse either. That the rights of hospitality were sacred in the East, the most highly regarded, we know; and that a man would defend, at the expense of his life, the stranger whom he had admitted under his roof, is true; but how a father could make such a proposal relative to his virgin daughter must remain among those things which are incomprehensible.

25. *So the man took his concubine.* The word *yachazek*, which we here translate simply *took*, signifies rather to "take or seize by violence." The woman would not go out to them; but her graceless husband forced her to go, in order that he might save his own body. He could have had but little love for her, and this was the cause of their separation before. The men of Gibeah who wished to abuse the body of the Levite; the Levite who wished to save his body at the expense of the modesty, reputation, and life of his wife; and the old man who wished to save his guest at the expense of the violation of his daughter are all characters that humanity and modesty wish to be buried in everlasting oblivion. *When the day began to spring.* Their turpitude could not bear the full light of the day, and they dismissed the poor woman when the day began to break.

26. *Fell down at the door.* She had strength to reach the door, but not to knock for admittance; when she reached the door she fell down dead!

29. *Divided her . . . into twelve pieces.* There is no doubt that with the pieces he sent to each tribe a circumstantial account of the barbarity of the men of Gibeah; and it is very likely that they considered each of the pieces as expressing an execration, "If ye will not come and avenge my wrongs, may ye be hewn in pieces like this abused and murdered woman!"

30. *There was no such deed done nor seen.* They were all struck with the enormity of the crime, and considered it a sovereign disgrace to all the tribes of Israel. *Consider of it.* Literally, "Put it to yourselves; take counsel upon it; and speak." This was the prelude to the council held, and the subsequent operations, which are mentioned in the following chapter.

MATTHEW HENRY — CHAPTER 20

Verses 1–11

I. A general meeting of all the congregation of Israel to examine the matter concerning the Levite's concubine, and to consider what was to be done upon it, *v.* 1, 2. They came together by the consent and agreement, as it were, of one common heart, fired with a holy zeal for the honour of God and Israel. 1. The place of their meeting was *Mizpeh*; they gathered together unto the Lord there, for Mizpeh was so very near to Shiloh that their encampment might very well be supposed to reach from Mizpeh to Shiloh. Shiloh was a small town, and therefore, when there was a general meeting of the people to present themselves before God, they chose Mizpeh for their headquarters. 2. The persons that met were all Israel, from Dan in the north to Beersheba in the south, with the land of Gilead (that is, the tribes on the other side Jordan), all *as one man*, so unanimous were they in their concern for the public good. In this assembly of all Israel, the chief (or corners) of the people (for rulers are the cornerstones of the people, that keep all together) presented themselves as the representatives of the rest. They rendered themselves at their respective posts, at the head of the thousands and hundreds, the fifties and

JAMIESON, FAUSSET, BROWN — CHAPTER 20

VSS. 1-7. THE LEVITE, IN A GENERAL ASSEMBLY, DECLARES HIS WRONG. **1. all . . . the congregation was gathered as one man**—In consequence of the immense sensation the horrid tragedy of Gibeah had produced, a national assembly was convened, at which "the chief of all the people" from all parts of the land, including the eastern tribes, appeared as delegates. **Mizpeh**—the place of convention (for there were other Mizpehs), was in a town situated on the confines of Judah and Benjamin (Josh. 15: 38; 18:26). Assemblies were frequently held there afterwards (I Samuel 7:11; 10:17); and it was but a short distance from Shiloh. The phrase, "unto the Lord," may be taken in its usual sense, as denoting consultation of the oracle. This circumstance, together with the convention being called "the assembly of the people of God," seems to indicate, that amid the excited passions of the nation, those present felt the profound gravity of the occasion and adopted the best means of maintaining a becoming deportment.

ADAM CLARKE — CHAPTER 20

1. *Unto the Lord in Mizpeh.* This city was situated on the confines of Judah and Benjamin, and is sometimes attributed to the one, sometimes to the other. It seems that there was a place here in which the Lord was consulted, as well as at Shiloh; in 1 Mac. iii. 46 we read. "In Maspha was the place where they prayed aforetime in Israel." These two passages cast light on each other.

2. *The chief of all the people.* The "corners," *pinnoth*; for as the cornerstones are the strength of the walls, so are the chiefs the strength of the people. Hence Christ is called the "chief cornerstone." *In the assembly of the people of God.* The Septuagint translate, "And all the tribes of Israel stood up before the face of the Lord, in the Church of the people of God."

MATTHEW HENRY

tens, over which they presided; for so much order and government, we may suppose, at least, they had among them, though they had no general or commander-in-chief. So that here was, (1) A general congress of the states for counsel. (2) A general rendezvous of the militia for action, all that drew sword and were men of war (*v.* 17).

II. Notice given to the tribe of Benjamin of this meeting (*v.* 3): *They heard that the children of Israel had gone up to Mizpeh.* But the notice they had of this meeting rather hardened and exasperated them than awakened them to think of the things that belonged to their peace and honour.

III. A solemn examination of the crime charged upon the men of Gibeah. The Levite gives a particular account of the matter. He concludes his declaration with an appeal to the judgment of the court (*v.* 7): *You are all children of Israel,* and therefore you *know law and judgment,* Esther i. 13, therefore give your advice and counsel what is to be done.

IV. The resolution they came to hereupon, which was that, being now together, they would not disperse till they had seen vengeance taken upon this wicked city, which was the reproach and scandal of their nation. Observe, 1. Their zeal against the lewdness that was committed. They would not return to their houses, how much soever their families and their affairs at home wanted them, till they had vindicated the honour of God and Israel. 2. Their prudence in sending out a considerable body of their forces to fetch provisions for the rest, *v.* 9, 10. 3. Their unanimity in these counsels, and the execution of them. The resolution was voted, *Nemine contradicente—Without a dissenting voice* (*v.* 8). This was their glory and strength, that the several tribes had no separate interests when the common good was concerned.

Verses 12–17

I. The fair and just demand which the tribes of Israel, now encamped, sent to the tribe of Benjamin, to deliver up the malefactors of Gibeah to justice, *v.* 12, 13. The Israelites were zealous against the wickedness that was committed, yet they were discreet in their zeal, and did not think it would justify them in falling upon the whole tribe of Benjamin unless they, by refusing to give up the criminals, and protecting them against justice, should make themselves guilty, *ex post facto—as accessories after the fact.*

II. The wretched obstinacy and perverseness of the men of Benjamin, who seem to have been as unanimous and zealous in their resolutions to stand by the criminals as the rest of the tribes were to punish them, so little sense had they of their honour, duty, and interest. They took it ill that the other tribes should meddle with their concerns; they would not do that which they knew was their duty because they were reminded of it by their brethren, by whom they scorned to be taught and controlled.

2. They were so prodigiously vain and presumptuous as to make head against the united force of all Israel. How could they expect to prosper when they fought against justice, and consequently against the just God himself, against those that had the high priest and the divine oracle on their side, and so acted in downright rebellion against the sacred and supreme authority of the nation. It should seem they depended upon the skill of their men to make up what was wanting in numbers, especially a regiment of slingers, 700 men, who, though left-handed, were so dexterous at slinging stones that they would not be a hair's breadth beside their mark, *v.* 16. But these good marksmen were very much out in their aim when they espoused this bad cause.

Verses 18–25

The defeat of the men of Israel in their first and second battle with the Benjamites.

I. Before their first engagement they asked counsel of God concerning the order of their battle and were directed, and yet they were sorely beaten. The whole army lay siege to Gibeah, *v.* 19. The Benjamites advance to raise the siege, the army prepares to give them a warm reception (*v.* 20), and turns upon them to fight them, *v.* 20. But between the Benjamites that attacked them in the front with incredible fury, and the men of Gibeah that sallied out upon their rear, they were put into confusion and lost 22,000 men, *v.* 21.

II. Before their second engagement they again *asked counsel of God,* and more solemnly than before; for they *wept before the Lord until evening* (*v.* 23). Also at this time they did not ask who should go up first, but whether they should go up at all. God bade them go up; he allowed the attempt for, though Benjamin was their brother, he was a gangrened member of their body and must be cut off. Upon this they encouraged themselves, perhaps more in

JAMIESON, FAUSSET, BROWN

3. Now the children of Benjamin heard that the children of Israel were gone up to Mizpeh—Some suppose that Benjamin had been passed over, the crime having been perpetrated within the territory of that tribe; and that, as the concubine's corpse had been divided into twelve pieces—two had been sent to Manasseh, one respectively to the western and eastern divisions. It is more probable that Benjamin had received a formal summons like the other tribes, but chose to treat it with indifference, or haughty disdain. **4-7. the Levite, the husband of the woman that was slain, answered and said**—The injured husband gave a brief and unvarnished recital of the tragic outrage, from which it appears that force was used, which he could not resist. His testimony was doubtless corroborated by those of his servant and the old Ephraimite. There was no need of strong or highly colored description to work upon the feelings of the audience. The facts spoke for themselves and produced one common sentiment of detestation and vengeance.

8. Their Decree. **8. all the people arose as one man**—The extraordinary unanimity that prevailed shows, that notwithstanding great disorders had broken out in many parts, the people were sound at the core; and remembering their national covenant with God, they now felt the necessity of wiping out so foul a stain on their character as a people. It was resolved that the inhabitants of Gibeah should be subjected to condign punishment. But the resolutions were conditional. For as the common law of nature and nations requires that an inquiry should be made and satisfaction demanded, before committing an act of hostility or vengeance, messengers were despatched through the whole territory of Benjamin, demanding the immediate surrender or execution of the delinquents. The request was just and reasonable; and by refusing it the Benjamites virtually made themselves a party in the quarrel. It must not be supposed that the people of this tribe were insensible or indifferent to the atrocious character of the crime that had been committed on their soil. But their patriotism or their pride was offended by the hostile demonstration of the other tribes. The passions were inflamed on both sides; but certainly the Benjamites incurred an awful responsibility by the attitude of resistance they assumed. **14-17. the children of Benjamin gathered themselves out of the cities unto Gibeah**—Allowing their valor to be ever so great, nothing but blind passion and unbending obstinacy could have impelled them to take the field against their brethren with such a disparity of numbers. **16. left-handed: every one could sling stones at an hair-breadth, and not miss**—The sling was one of the earliest weapons used in war. The Hebrew sling was probably similar to that of the Egyptian, consisting of a leather thong, broad in the middle, with a loop at one end, by which it was firmly held with the hand; the other end terminated in a lash, which was let slip when the stone was thrown. Those skilled in the use of it, as the Benjamites were, could hit the mark with unerring certainty. A good sling could carry its full force to the distance of 200 yards.

18-28. The Israelites Lose Forty Thousand. **18-28. the children of Israel arose, and went up to the house of God**—This consultation at Shiloh was right. But they ought to have done it at the commencement of their proceedings. Instead of this, all their plans were formed, and never doubting, it would seem, that the war was just and inevitable, the only subject of their inquiry related to the precedency of the tribes—a point which it is likely was discussed in the assembly. Had they asked counsel of God sooner, their expedition would have been conducted on a different principle—most probably by reducing the number of fighting men, as in the case of Gideon's army. As it was, the vast number of volunteers formed an excessive and unwieldy force, unfit for strenuous and united action against a small, compact, and well-directed army. A panic ensued, and the confederate tribes, in two successive engagements, sustained great losses. These repeated disasters (notwithstanding their attack on Benjamin had been divinely authorized) overwhelmed them with shame and sorrow.

ADAM CLARKE

3. *Tell us, how was this wickedness?* They had heard before, by the messengers he sent with the fragments of his wife's body; but they wish to hear it, in full council, from himself.

10. *Ten men of an hundred.* Expecting that they might have a long contest, they provide sutlers for the camp; and it is probable that they chose these tenths by lot.

13. *Deliver us the men.* Nothing could be fairer than this. They wish only to make the murderers answerable for their guilt. *Benjamin would not hearken.* Thus making their whole tribe partakers of the guilt of the men of Gibeah. By not delivering up those bad men, they in effect said: "We will stand by them in what they have done, and would have acted the same part had we been present." This proves that the whole tribe was excessively depraved.

15. *Twenty and six thousand.* Some copies of the Septuagint have 23,000, others 25,000. The Vulgate has this latter number; the Complutensian Polyglot and Josephus have the same.

16. *Left-handed.* They were ambidexters—could use the right hand and the left with equal ease and effect. See the note on chap. iii. 15. *Could sling stones at a hair . . . and not miss. Velo yachati,* "and not sin." Here we have the true import of the term "sin"; it signifies simply to "miss the mark." Men miss the mark of true happiness in aiming at sensual gratifications; which happiness is to be found only in the possession and enjoyment of the favor of God, from whom their passions continually lead them. He alone hits the mark, and ceases from sin, who attains to God through Christ Jesus.

18. *Went up to the house of God.* Some think that a deputation was sent from Shiloh, where Phinehas, the high priest, was, to inquire, not concerning the expediency of the war, nor of its success, but which of the tribes should begin the attack. Having so much right on their side, they had no doubt of the justice of their cause. Having such a superiority of numbers, they had no doubt of success. *And the Lord said, Judah.* But He did not say that they should conquer.

[illegible] *Destroyed down to the ground . . . twenty and two thousand men.* That is, so many were left dead on the field of battle.

23. *Go up against him.* It appears most evident that the Israelites did not seek the protection of God. They trusted in the goodness of their cause and in the multitude of their army. God humbled them, and delivered them into the hands of their enemies, and showed them that the race was not to the swift, nor the battle to the strong.

MATTHEW HENRY

their own strength than in the divine commission, and made a second attempt upon the forces of the rebels, in the same place where the former battle was fought (*v.* 22). But they were this second time repulsed, with the loss of 18,000 men, *v.* 25. But what shall we say to these things, that so just and honourable a cause should thus be put to the worst once and again? Were they not fighting God's battles against sin? 1. God's judgments are a great deep, and his way is in the sea. We may be sure of the righteousness, when we cannot see the reasons, of God's proceedings. 2. God would hereby show them, and us in them, that *the race is not to the swift nor the battle to the strong*, that we are not to confide in numbers, which perhaps the Israelites did with too much assurance. We must never lay the weight on an arm of flesh, which only the Rock of ages will bear. 3. God designed hereby to correct Israel for their sins. They did well to show such a zeal against the wickedness of Gibeah: but *were there not with them, even with them, sins against the Lord their God?* Some think it was a rebuke to them for not witnessing against the idolatry of Micah and the Danites. 4. God would hereby teach us not to think it strange if a good cause should suffer defeat for a while, nor to judge of the merits of it by the success of it. The interest of grace in the heart, and of religion in the world, may be foiled, and suffer great loss, and seem to be quite run down, but judgment will be brought forth to victory at last. *Vincimur in praelio, sed non in bello—We are foiled in a battle, but not in the whole campaign.* Right may fall, but it shall arise.

Verses 26–48

A full account of the complete victory which the Israelites obtained over the Benjamites in the third engagement: the righteous cause was victorious at last.

I. How the victory was obtained. Two things they had trusted too much to in the former engagements—the goodness of their cause and the superiority of their numbers. It was true that they had both right and strength on their side, which were great advantages; but they depended too much upon them, to the neglect of those duties to which now, this third time, when they see their error, they apply themselves.

1. They were previously so confident of the goodness of their cause that they thought it needless to address themselves to God for his presence and blessing. They took it for granted that God would bless them, nay, perhaps they concluded that he owed them his favour. Before they only consulted God's oracle, *Who shall go up first?* And, *Shall we go up?* But now they implored his favour, fasted and prayed, and *offered burnt-offerings and peace-offerings* (*v.* 26), to make an atonement for sin and an acknowledgment of their dependence upon God. And when they were in this frame, and thus sought the Lord, then he not only ordered them to go up against the Benjamites the third time, but gave them a promise of victory: *Tomorrow I will deliver them into thy hand*, *v.* 28.

2. They were previously so confident of the greatness of their strength that they thought it needless to use any art, to lay any ambush, or form a stratagem, not doubting but to conquer purely by a strong hand; but now they saw it was requisite to use some policy, as if they had an enemy to deal with them that had been superior in number; accordingly, they set *liers in wait* (*v.* 29), and gained their point, as their fathers did before Ai (Josh. viii).

(1) Observe the method they took. The body of the army faced the city of Gibeah, as they had done before, advancing towards the gates, *v.* 30. The Benjamites, the body of whose army was now quartered at Gibeah, sallied out upon them, and charged them with great bravery. The besiegers gave back, retired with precipitation, as if their hearts failed them upon the sight of the Benjamites. But, when the Benjamites were all drawn out of the city, the ambush seized the city (*v.* 37), gave a signal to the body of the army (*v.* 38, 40), which immediately turned upon them (*v.* 41), and, it should seem, another considerable party that was posted at Baal-tamar came upon them at the same time (*v.* 33); so that the Benjamites were quite surrounded, which put them into the greatest consternation that could be. A sense of guilt now disheartened them. Every man's hand was against them.

(2) Observe in this story, [1] That the Benjamites, in the beginning of the battle, were confident that the day was their own. Sometimes God suffers wicked men to be lifted up in successes and hopes, that their fall may be the sorer. See how short their joy is, and their triumphing but for a moment. [2] Evil was near them and they did not know it, *v.* 34. [3] Though the men of Israel played their parts so well in this engagement, yet the victory is ascribed to

JAMIESON, FAUSSET, BROWN

KEIL–DELITZSCH:

Verse 26. After this second terrible overthrow, "the children of Israel" (those who were engaged in the war), and "all the people," i.e., the rest of the people, those members of the congregation who were not capable of bearing arms, old men and women, came to Bethel to complain to the Lord of their misfortune and secure His favor by fasting and sacrifices. The congregation now discovered from this repeated defeat that the Lord had withdrawn His grace and was punishing them. Their sin, however, did not consist in the fact that they had begun the war itself—for the law in Deut. 22:22, to which they themselves had referred in verse 13, really required this—but rather in the state of mind with which they had entered upon the war, their strong self-consciousness and great confidence in their own might and power. They had indeed inquired of God (*Elohim*) who should open the conflict; but they had neglected to humble themselves before Jehovah the covenant God, in the consciousness not only of their own weakness and sinfulness, but also of grief at the moral corruption of their brother-tribe. It is certainly not without significance that in verse 18 it is stated that "they asked God," i.e., they simply desired a supreme or divine decision as to the question who should lead the van in the war; whereas, after the first defeat, they wept before *Jehovah*, and inquired of *Jehovah* (v. 23), the covenant God, for whose law and right they were about to contend. But even then there were still wanting the humility and penitence, without which the congregation of the Lord could not successfully carry on the conflict against the ungodly.

—Commentary on the Old Testament

Led to reflection, they became sensible of their guilt in not repressing their national idolatries, as well as in too proudly relying on their superior numbers and the precipitate rashness of this expedition. Having humbled themselves by prayer and fasting, as well as observed the appointed method of expiating their sins, they were assured of acceptance as well as of victory. The presence and services of Phinehas on this occasion help us to ascertain the chronology thus far, that the date of the occurrence must be fixed shortly after the death of Joshua.

29-48. THEY DESTROY ALL THE BENJAMITES, EXCEPT SIX HUNDRED. **29-48. Israel set liers in wait round about Gibeah**—A plan was formed of taking that city by stratagem, similar to that employed in the capture of Ai.

33. Baal-tamar—a palm grove, where Baal was worshipped. The main army of the confederate tribes was drawn up there. **out of the meadows of Gibeah**—*Heb.*, "the caves of Gibeah."

34. there came against Gibeah ten thousand chosen men—This was a third division, different both from the ambuscade and the army, who were fighting at Baal-tamar. The general account stated in verse 35 is followed by a detailed narrative of the battle, which is continued to the end of the chapter.

ADAM CLARKE

26. *And wept.* Had they humbled themselves, fasted and prayed, and offered sacrifices at first, they had not been discomfited. *And fasted that day until even.* This is the first place where fasting is mentioned as a religious ceremony, or as a means of obtaining help from God. And in this case, and many since, it has been powerfully effectual. At present it is but little used—a strong proof that self-denial is wearing out of fashion.

28. *Phinehas, the son of Eleazar.* This was the same Phinehas who is mentioned Numbers xxv, and consequently these transactions must have taken place shortly after the death of Joshua.

29. *Israel set liers in wait.* Though God had promised them success, they knew they could expect it only in the use of the proper means. They used all prudent precaution, and employed all their military skill.

32. *Let us . . . draw them from the city.* They had two reasons for this: (1) They had placed an ambuscade behind Gibeah, which was to enter and burn the city as soon as the Benjamites had left it. (2) It would seem that the slingers, by being within the city and its fortifications, had great advantage against the Israelites by their slings, whom they could not annoy with their swords, unless they got them to the plain country.

33. *Put themselves in array at Baal-tamar.* The Israelites seem to have divided their army into three divisions: one was at Baal-tamar, a second behind the city in ambush, and the third skirmished with the Benjamites before Gibeah.

MATTHEW HENRY

God (*v.* 35). They *trode down the men of Benjamin with ease* when God fought against them, *v.* 43.

II. How the victory was prosecuted and improved in a military execution done upon these sinners against their own souls. 1. Gibeah itself, that nest of lewdness, was destroyed in the first place. 2. The army in the field was quite routed and cut off. 3. Those that escaped from the field were pursued, and cut off in their flight. 4. Even those that tarried at home were involved in the ruin. So that of all the tribe of Benjamin, for aught that appears, there remained none alive but 600 men that took shelter in the rock Rimmon, and lay close there four months, *v.* 47.

This affair of Gibeah is twice spoken of by the prophet Hosea as the beginning of the corruption of Israel and a pattern to all that followed (Hos. ix. 9): *They have deeply corrupted themselves as in the days of Gibeah;* and (Hos. x. 9), *Thou hast sinned from the days of Gibeah*; and it is added that *the battle in Gibeah against the children of iniquity did not* (that is, did not *at first*) overtake them.

JAMIESON, FAUSSET, BROWN

45. they turned and fled towards the wilderness unto the rock of Rimmon—Many of the fugitives found refuge in the caves of this rocky mountain, which is situated to the northeast of Beth-el. Such places are still sought as secure retreats in times of danger; and until the method of blowing up rocks by gunpowder became known, a few men could in such caves sustain a siege for months. **46. all which fell that day of Benjamin were twenty and five thousand men**—On comparing this with verse 35, it will be seen that the loss is stated here in round numbers and is confined only to that of the third day. We must conclude that 1000 had fallen during the two previous engagements, in order to make the aggregate amount given (vs. 15). **48. the men of Israel turned again upon the children of Benjamin, and smote them with the edge of the sword**—This frightful vengeance, extending from Gibeah to the whole territory of Benjamin, was executed under the impetuous impulse of highly excited passions. But doubtless the Israelites were only the agents of inflicting the righteous retributions of God; and the memory of this terrible crisis, which led almost to the extermination of a whole tribe, was conducive to the future good of the whole nation.

ADAM CLARKE

35. *Twenty and five thousand and an hundred.* As the Benjamites consisted only of 26,700 slingers; or, as the Vulgate, Septuagint, and others read, 25,000, which is most probably the true reading, then the whole of the Benjamites were cut to pieces, except 600 men, who we are informed fled to the rock Rimmon, where they fortified themselves.

38. *Now there was an appointed sign.* From this verse to the end of the chapter we have the details of the same operations which are mentioned, in a general way, in the preceding part of the chapter.

45. *Unto the rock of Rimmon.* This was some strong place, but where situated is not known. Here they maintained themselves four months, and it was by these alone that the tribe of Benjamin was preserved from utter extermination. See the following chapter.

MATTHEW HENRY — CHAPTER 21

Verses 1–15

I. The ardent zeal which the Israelites had expressed against the wickedness of the men of Gibeah, as it was countenanced by the tribe of Benjamin. 1. While the general convention of the states was gathering together, they bound themselves with the great execration, which they called the *Cherum*, utterly to destroy all those cities that should not send in their representatives, for they would look upon such refusers as having no indignation at the crime committed, no concern for the securing of the nation from God's judgments by the administration of justice, nor any regard to the authority of a common consent, by which they were summoned to meet. 2. When they had met and heard the cause they made another solemn oath that none of all the thousands of Israel then present, nor any of those whom they represented (not intending to bind their posterity), should, if they could help it, *marry a daughter* to a Benjamite, *v.* 1. This was made an article of the war, not with any design to extirpate the tribe, but because in general they would treat those who were then actors and abettors of this villainy in all respects as they treated the devoted nations of Canaan, whom they were not only obliged to destroy, but with whom they were forbidden to marry.

II. The deep concern which the Israelites did express for the destruction of the tribe of Benjamin when it was accomplished. Observe,

1. The tide of their anger at Benjamin's crime did not run so high and so strong before but the tide of their grief for Benjamin's destruction ran as high and as strong after: *They repented for Benjamin their brother*, *v.* 6, 15. They did not repent of their zeal against the sin. But they repented of the sad consequences of what they had done, that they had carried the matter further than was either just or necessary. It would have been enough to destroy all they found in arms; they needed not to have cut off the husbandman and shepherds, the women and children. Note, (1) There may be over-doing in well-doing. Great care must be taken in the government of our zeal, lest that which seemed supernatural in its causes prove unnatural in its effects. That is no good divinity which swallows up humanity. Many a war is ill ended which was well begun. (2) Even necessary justice is to be done with compassion. God does not punish with delight, nor should men. (3) Strong passions make work for repentance. What we say and do in a heat our calmer thoughts commonly wish undone again. Now,

2. How did they express their concern? (1) By their grief for the breach that was made. They came to the house of God, for thither they brought all their doubts, all their counsels, all their cares, and all their sorrows. *There is one tribe lacking*. Benjamin become a Benoni, the son of the right hand a son of sorrow! In this trouble they built an altar, to atone for their folly in the pursuit of victory, and to implore the divine favour in their present strait. Every thing that grieves us should bring us to God. (2) By their amicable treaty with the poor distressed refugees that were hidden in the rock Rimmon, to whom they sent an act of indemnity, assuring them, upon the public faith, that they would now no longer treat them as enemies, but receive them as brethren,

JAMIESON, FAUSSET, BROWN — CHAPTER 21

Vss. 1-15. THE PEOPLE BEWAIL THE DESOLATION OF ISRAEL. **2. the people came to the house of God, . . . and lifted up their voices, and wept**—The characteristic fickleness of the Israelites was not long in being displayed; for scarcely had they cooled from the fierceness of their sanguinary vengeance, than they began to relent and rushed to the opposite extreme of self-accusation and grief at the desolation which their impetuous zeal had produced. Their victory saddened and humbled them. Their feelings on the occasion were expressed by a public and solemn service of expiation at the house of God. And yet this extraordinary observance, though it enabled them to find vent for their painful emotions, did not afford them full relief, for they were fettered by the obligation of a religious vow, heightened by the addition of a solemn anathema on every violator of the oath. There is no previous record of this oath; but the purport of it was, that they would treat the perpetrators of this Gibeah atrocity in the same way as the Canaanites, who were doomed to destruction; and the entering into this solemn league was of a piece with the rest of their inconsiderate conduct in this whole affair.

6. There is one tribe cut off from Israel this day—i.e., in danger of becoming extinct; for, as it appears from verse 7, they had massacred all the women and children of Benjamin, and 600 men alone survived of the whole tribe. The prospect of such a blank in the catalogue of the twelve tribes, such a gap in the national arrangements, was too painful to contemplate, and immediate measures must be taken to prevent this great catastrophe. **8. there came none to the camp from Jabesh-gilead to the assembly**—This city lay within the territory of eastern Manasseh, about fifteen miles east of the Jordan, and was, according to Josephus, the capital of Gilead. The ban which the assembled tribes had pronounced at Mizpeh seemed to impose on them the necessity of punishing its inhabitants for not joining the crusade against Benjamin; and thus, with a view of repairing the consequences of one rash proceeding, they hurriedly rushed to the perpetration of another, though a smaller tragedy. But it appears (vs. 11) that, besides acting in fulfilment of their oath, the Israelites had the additional object by this raid of supplying wives to the Benjamite remnant. This shows the intemperate fury of the Israelites in the indiscriminate slaughter of the women and children.

ADAM CLARKE — CHAPTER 21

1. *Now the men of Israel had sworn.* Of this oath we had not heard before; but it appears they had commenced this war with a determination to destroy the Benjamites utterly, and that if any of them escaped the sword, no man should be permitted to give him his daughter to wife. By these means the remnant of the tribe must soon have been annihilated.

2. *The people came to the house of God.* Literally, "the people came to Bethel"; this is considered as the name of a place by the Chaldee, Syriac, Arabic, and Septuagint. *And wept sore.* Their revenge was satisfied, and now reflection brought them to contrition for what they had done.

3. *Why is this come to pass?* This was a very impertinent question. They knew well enough how it came to pass. It was right that the men of Gibeah should be punished, and it was right that they who vindicated them should share in that punishment; but they carried their revenge too far. They endeavored to exterminate both man and beast, chap. xx. 48.

4. *Built there an altar.* This affords some evidence that this was not a regular place of worship, else an altar would have been found in the place; and their act was not according to the law, as may be seen in several places of the Pentateuch. But there was neither king nor law among them, and they did whatever appeared right in their own eyes.

7. *How shall we do for wives for them?* From this it appears that they had destroyed all the Benjamitish women and children! They had set out with the purpose of exterminating the whole tribe, and therefore they massacred the women, that if any of the men escaped, they might find neither wife nor daughter; and they bound themselves under an oath not to give any of their females to any of the remnant of this tribe, that thus the whole tribe might utterly perish.

8. *There came none to the camp from Jabesh-gilead.* As they had sworn to destroy those who would not assist in this war, v. 5, they determined to destroy the men of Jabesh, and to leave none alive except the virgins, and to give these to the 600 Benjamites that had escaped to the rock Rimmon. So 12,000 men went, smote the city, and killed all the males and all the married women. The whole account is dreadful; and none could have been guilty of all these enormities but those who were abandoned of God. The crime of the men of Gibeah was of the deepest dye; the punishment, involving both the guilty and the innocent, was extended to the most criminal excess; and their mode of redressing the evil which they had occasioned was equally abominable.

13. *And to call peaceably unto them.* To proclaim peace to them; to assure them that the enmity was all over, and that they might with safety leave their stronghold.

MATTHEW HENRY

v. 13. (3) By the care they took to provide wives for them, that their tribe might be built up again, and the ruins of it repaired. All heads were at work to find out ways and means for the rebuilding of this tribe. While the poor distressed Benjamites that were hidden in the rock feared their brethren were contriving to ruin them, they were at the same time upon a project to prefer them. Four hundred virgins that were marriageable were found in Jabesh-Gilead, and these were married to so many of the surviving Benjamites, *v.* 14. Perhaps the alliance now contracted between Benjamin and Jabesh-Gilead made Saul, who was a Benjamite, the more concerned for that place (1 Sam. xi. 4), though then inhabited by new families.

Verses 16–25

We have here the method that was taken to provide the 200 Benjamites that remained with wives.

I. At Shiloh, in the fields, all the young ladies of that city met to dance, in honour of a *feast of the Lord*, probably the feast of tabernacles (*v.* 19), for that feast was the only season wherein the Jewish virgins were allowed to dance, and that not so much for their own recreation as to express their holy joy, as David when he danced before the ark. The dancing was very modest and chaste. However their dancing thus in public made them an easy prey to those that had a design upon them.

II. The elders of Israel gave authority to the Benjamites to *lie in wait in the vineyards* and catch every man a wife for himself, and carry them straight away to their own country, *v.* 20, 21. Here was a very preposterous way of match-making, when both the mutual affection of the young people and the consent of the parents must be presumed to come after; the case was extraordinary, and may by no means be drawn into a precedent. Overhasty marriages often occasion a leisurely repentance; and what comfort can be expected from a match made either by force or fraud?

III. They undertook to pacify the fathers of these young women. The oath they were bound by, not to give their daughters to Benjamites, might perhaps stick with some of them, whose consciences were tender. The necessity was urgent (*v.* 22): *We reserved not to each man his wife*, owning now that they did ill to destroy all the women, and desiring to atone for their too rigorous construction of their vow to destroy them by the most favourable construction of their vow not to match with them.

Lastly, In the close of all we have, 1. The settling of the tribe of Benjamin again. The few that remained returned to the inheritance of that tribe, *v.* 23. And soon after from among them sprang Ehud, who was famous in his generation, the second judge of Israel, *ch.* iii. 15. 2. The disbanding and dispersing of the army of Israel, *v.* 24. They did not set up for a standing army, nor pretend to make any alterations or establishments in the government; but, when the affair was over for which they were called together, they quietly departed in God's peace, every man to his family.

JAMIESON, FAUSSET, BROWN

16-21. The Elders Consult How to Find Wives for Those That Were Left. **16. the elders of the congregation said, How shall we do for wives for them that remain**—Though the young women of Jabesh-gilead had been carefully spared, the supply was found inadequate, and some other expedient must be resorted to. **17. There must be an inheritance for them that are escaped of Benjamin**—As they were the only rightful owners of the territory, provision must be made for transmitting it to their legitimate heirs, and a new act of violence was meditated (vs. 19); the opportunity for which was afforded by the approaching festival—a feast generally supposed to be the feast of tabernacles. This, like the other annual feasts, was held in Shiloh, and its celebration was attended with more social hilarity and holiday rejoicings than the other feasts. **19. on the east side of the highway that goeth up from Bethel to Shechem**—The exact site of the place was described evidently for the direction of the Benjamites. **21. daughters of Shiloh come out to dance in dances**—The dance was anciently a part of the religious observance. It was done on festive occasions, as it is still in the East, not in town, but in the open air, in some adjoining field, the women being by themselves. The young women being alone indulging their light and buoyant spirits, and apprehensive of no danger, facilitated the execution of the scheme of seizing them, which closely resembles the Sabine rape in Roman history. The elders undertook to reconcile the families to the forced abduction of their daughters. And thus the expression of their public sanction to this deed of violence afforded a new evidence of the evils and difficulties into which the unhappy precipitancy of the Israelites in this crisis had involved them.

ADAM CLARKE

14. *Yet so they sufficed them not.* There were 600 men at Rimmon, and all the young women they saved from Jabesh were only 400; therefore there were 200 still wanting.

19. *There is a feast of the Lord.* What this feast was is not known; it might be either the Passover, Pentecost, or the Feast of Tabernacles, or indeed some other peculiar to this place. All the above feasts were celebrated at that time of the year when the vines were in full leaf; therefore the Benjamites might easily conceal themselves in the vineyards; and the circumstances will answer to any of those feasts.

On the east side of the highway. I can see no reason for this minute description, unless it intimates that this feast was to be held this year in rather a different place to that which was usual; and, as the Benjamites had been shut up in their stronghold in Rimmon, they might not have heard of this alteration; and it was necessary, in such a case, to give them the most circumstantial information, that they might succeed in their enterprise without being discovered.

21. *And catch you every man his wife.* That is, Let each man of the 200 Benjamites seize and carry off a woman, whom he is, from that hour, to consider as his *wife*.

22. *Be favourable unto them.* They promise to use their influence with the men of Shiloh to induce them to consent to a connection thus fraudulently obtained, and which the necessity of the case appeared to them to justify.

We reserved not to each man his wife in the war. The reading of the Vulgate is very remarkable: "Pardon them, for they have not taken them as victors take captives in war; but when they requested you to give them you did not; therefore the fault is your own." Here it is intimated that application had been made to the people of Shiloh to furnish these 200 Benjamites with wives, and that they had refused; and it was this refusal that induced the Benjamites to seize and carry them off. Houbigant translates the Hebrew thus: "Pardon them, I beseech you, for they have not each taken his wife to the war; and unless you now give these to them, you will sin."

23. *They went and returned unto their inheritance.* It appears that the Benjamites acted in the most honorable way by the women whom they had thus violently carried off; and we may rest assured they took them to an inheritance at least equal to their own, for it does not appear that any part of the lands of the Benjamites was alienated from them, and the 600 men in question shared, for the present, the inheritance of many thousands.

24. *Every man to his tribe.* Though this must have been four months after the war with Benjamin, chap. xx. 47, yet it appears the armies did not disband till they had got the remnant of Benjamin settled, as is here related.

25. *In those days there was no king in Israel.* Let no one suppose that the sacred writer, by relating the atrocities in this and the preceding chapters, justifies the actions themselves; by no means. Indeed, they cannot be justified; and the writer by relating them gives the strongest proof of the authenticity of the whole, by such an impartial relation of facts that were highly to the discredit of his country.

THE BOOK OF RUTH

I. The choice of faith (1:1-2:23)
A. Naomi's sorrows (1:1-13)
1. Elimelech to Moab (1:1-2)
2. The sorrows (1:3-13)
B. Ruth's choice (1:14-22)
1. Orpah (1:14)
2. Ruth (1:15-18)
3. The homecoming of bitterness (1:19-22)
C. Boaz's field (2:1-23)
1. Ruth's purpose (2:1-3)
2. Boaz (2:4-16)
3. The means of support (2:17-23)

II. The venture of faith (3:1-18)
A. Naomi—doubtful yet in light of times (3:1-5)
B. Ruth—the claims of kinsman rights (3:6-9)
C. Boaz (3:10-18)
1. The appeal to next of kin (3:10-13)
2. The tender love (3:14-18)

III. The reward of faith (4:1-22)
A. The redemption (4:1-12)
B. The marriage (4:13a)
C. The issue (4:13b-22)

This short history of the domestic affairs of one particular family properly follows the book of Judges (the events related here happening in the days of the judges) and goes before the books of Samuel, because in the close it introduces David. It relates not miracles nor laws, wars nor victories, nor the revolutions of states, but the affliction first and afterwards the comfort of Naomi, the conversion first and afterwards the promotion of Ruth.

The design of this book is to lead to providence, to show us how familiar it is about our private concerns (1 Sam. 2:7, 8; Ps. 113:7–9). It is also designed to lead to Christ who descended from Ruth, and part of whose genealogy concludes the book, whence it is fetched into Matthew 1.

MATTHEW HENRY

CHAPTER 1

Verses 1–5

The first words give all the date we have of this story. It was *in the days when the judges ruled* (*v.* 1). It must have been towards the beginning of the judges' time, for Boaz, who married Ruth, was born of Rahab, who received the spies in Joshua's time. Some think it was in the days of Ehud, others of Deborah; the learned Bishop Patrick inclines to think it was in the days of Gideon, because in his days only we read of a famine by the Midianites' invasion, Judges vi. 3, 4.

I. A famine in the land, in the land of Canaan, that land *flowing with milk and honey*. This was one of the judgments which God had threatened to bring upon them for their sins, Lev. xxvi. 19, 20. When the land had rest, yet it had not plenty; even in Bethlehem, which signifies *the house of bread*, there was scarcity. A *fruitful land is turned into barrenness*, to correct and restrain the luxury and wantonness of those that dwell therein.

II. An account of one particular family distressed in the famine; it is that of *Elimelech*. His name signifies *my God a king*. His wife was *Naomi*, which signifies my *amiable* or *pleasant one*. But his son's names were *Mahlon* and *Chilion*, *sickness* and *consumption*, perhaps because weakly children.

III. The removal of this family from Bethlehem into the country of Moab on the other side Jordan, for subsistence, because of the famine, *v.* 1, 2. It seems there was plenty in the country of Moab when there was scarcity of bread in the land of Israel. Thither Elimelech goes, to sojourn for a time, during the dearth, as Abraham, on a similar occasion, went into Egypt, and Isaac into the land of the Philistines. Now here, 1. Elimelech's care to provide for his family, and his taking his wife and children with him, were without doubt commendable. But, 2. I see not how his removal into the country of Moab, upon this occasion, could be justified. The seed of Israel were now fixed, and ought not to remove into the territories of the heathen. What reason had Elimelech to go more than any of his neighbours? If he could not be content with the short allowance that his neighbours took up with, if he could not live in hope that there would come years of plenty again in due time, or could not with patience wait for those years, it was his fault, and he did by it dishonour God and the good land he had given them, *weaken the hands of his brethren*, with whom he should have been willing to take his lot, and set an ill example to others. It is an evidence of a discontented, distrustful, unstable spirit, to be weary of the place in which God hath set us, and to be for leaving it immediately whenever we meet with any uneasiness or inconvenience in it. Or, if he would remove, why to the country of Moab? If he had made enquiry, it is probable he would have found plenty in some of the tribes of Israel, those, for instance, on the other side Jordan, that bordered on the land of Moab; if he had had that zeal for God and that affection for his brethren which became an Israelite, he would not have persuaded himself so easily to go and sojourn among Moabites.

IV. The marriage of his two sons to two of the daughters of Moab after his death, *v.* 4. All agree that this was ill done. The Chaldee says, *They transgressed the decree of the word of the Lord in taking strange wives.* It does not appear that the women they married were proselyted to the Jewish religion, for Orpah is said to return to her gods (*v.* 15). It is a groundless tradition of the Jews that Ruth was the

JAMIESON, FAUSSET, BROWN

CHAPTER 1

Vss. 1-5. Elimelech, Driven by Famine into Moab, Dies There. **1. in the days when the judges ruled**—The beautiful and interesting story which this book relates belongs to the early times of the judges. The precise date cannot be ascertained.

2. Elimelech—signifies "My God is king." **Naomi**—"fair or pleasant"; and their two sons, Mahlon and Chilion, are supposed to be the same as Joash and Saraph (I Chron. 4:22). **Ephrathites**—The ancient name of Bethlehem was Ephrath (Gen. 35:19; 48:7), which was continued after the occupation of the land by the Hebrews, even down to the time of the prophet Micah (Micah 5:2). **Bethlehem-judah**—so called to distinguish it from a town of the same name in Zebulun. The family, compelled to emigrate to Moab through pressure of a famine, settled for several years in that country.

After the death of their father, the two sons married Moabite women. This was a violation of the Mosaic law (Deut. 7:3; 23:3; Ezra 9:2; Neh. 13:23); and Jewish writers say that the early deaths of both the young men were divine judgments inflicted on them for those unlawful connections.

ADAM CLARKE

CHAPTER 1

1. *When the judges ruled.* We know not under what judge this happened. *There was a famine.* Probably occasioned by the depredations of the Philistines, Ammonites, etc., carrying off the corn as soon as it was ripe, or destroying it on the field.

2. *Elimelech.* That is, "God is my king." *Naomi.* "Beautiful" or "amiable." *Mahlon.* "Infirmity." *Chilion.* "Finished, completed."

3. *Elimelech . . . died.* Probably a short time after his arrival in Moab.

4. *And they took them wives.* The Targum very properly observes that "they transgressed the decree of the word of the Lord, and took to themselves strange women."

MATTHEW HENRY

daughter of Eglon king of Moab.

V. The death of Elimelech and his two sons, and the disconsolate condition Naomi was thereby reduced to. Her husband died (*v.* 3) and her two sons (*v.* 5) soon after their marriage, and the Chaldee says, *Their days were shortened,* because they transgressed the law in marrying strange wives. When Naomi had lost her husband she put so much the more confidence in her sons. How disconsolate the spirit of poor Naomi, when the woman was *left of her two sons and her husband;* When *these two things, loss of children and widowhood, come upon her in a moment, by whom shall she be comforted?* Isa. xlvii. 9; li. 19. It is God alone who has wherewithal to comfort those who are thus cast down.

Verses 6–18

I. The good affection Naomi bore to the land of Israel, *v.* 6. Though the country of Moab had afforded her shelter and supply in a time of need, yet she did not intend it should be her rest for ever; no land should be that but the holy land, in which the sanctuary of God was.

1. God, at last, returned in mercy to his people. At length God graciously *visited his people in giving them bread.* Plenty is God's gift, and it is his visitation which by bread, the staff of life, *holds our souls in life.* Though this mercy be the more striking when it come after famine, yet if we have constantly enjoyed it, and never known what famine meant, we are not to think it the less valuable.

2. Naomi at last has good news brought her of plenty in Bethlehem, and then she can think of no other than returning thither again. Though there be a reason for our being in bad places, yet, when the reason ceases, we must by no means continue in them. Forced absence from God's ordinances, and forced presence with wicked people, are great afflictions; but when the force ceases, and such a situation is continued of choice, then it becomes a great sin. The land of Moab had now become a melancholy place to her. Now she will go to Canaan again. Earth is embittered to us, that heaven may be endeared.

II. The good affection which her daughters-in-law, and one of them especially, bore to her, and her generous return of their good affection.

1. They were both so kind as to accompany her, some part of the way at least, when she returned towards the land of Judah. By this we see both that Naomi, as became an Israelite, had been very kind to them and had won their love, and that Orpah and Ruth had a just sense of her kindness. They had dwelt together in unity, though *those* were dead by whom the relation between them came. Though they retained an affection for the gods of Moab (*v.* 15), and Naomi was still faithful to the God of Israel, yet that was no hindrance to either side from love and kindness, and all the good offices that the relation required. Mothers-in-law and daughters-in-law are too often at variance (Matt. x. 35), and therefore it is the more commendable if they live in love.

2. When they had gone a little way with her, Naomi, with a great deal of affection, urged them to go back (*v.* 8, 9): *Return each to her mother's house.* Naomi suggests that their own mothers would be more agreeable to them than a mother-in-law, especially when their own mothers had houses and their mother-in-law was not sure she had a place to lay her head in which she could call her own. She dismisses them,

(1) With commendation.

(2) With prayer. It is very proper for friends, when they part, to part with prayer. She sends them home with her blessing; and the blessing of a mother-in-law is not to be slighted. In this blessing she twice mentions the name *Jehovah,* Israel's God, and the only true God, that she might direct her daughters to look up to him as the only fountain of all good. That they might be happy in marrying again: *The Lord grant that you may find rest, each of you in the house of her husband.*

(3) She dismissed them with great affection: *She kissed them,* wished she had somewhat better to give them, but silver and gold she had none. However, this parting kiss shall be the seal of a true friendship.

3. The two young widows could not think of parting with their good mother-in-law, so much had the good conversation of that pious Israelite won upon them. "*Surely we will return with thee unto thy people,* and take our lot with thee." It is a rare instance of affection to a mother-in-law and an evidence that they had, for her sake, conceived a good opinion of the people of Israel. Even Orpah, who afterwards went back to her gods, now seemed resolved to go forward with Naomi.

4. Naomi sets herself to dissuade them from going along with her, *v.* 11–13.

(1) Naomi urged her afflicted condition. If she

JAMIESON, FAUSSET, BROWN

6-18. Naomi, Returning Home, Ruth Accompanies Her. **6, 7. Then she arose with her daughters-in-law, that she might return from the country of Moab**–The aged widow, longing to enjoy the privileges of Israel, resolved to return to her native land as soon as she was assured that the famine had ceased, and made the necessary arrangements with her daughters-in-law.

8. Naomi said unto her two daughters-in-law, Go, return each to her mother's house–In Eastern countries women occupy apartments separate from those of men, and daughters are most frequently in those of their mother. **the Lord deal kindly with you, as ye have dealt with the dead**–i.e., with my sons, your husbands, while they lived.

9. The Lord grant that ye may find rest–enjoy a life of tranquillity, undisturbed by the cares, incumbrances, and vexatious troubles to which a state of widowhood is peculiarly exposed. **Then she kissed them**–the Oriental manner when friends are parting.

ADAM CLARKE

5. *And Mahlon and Chilion died.* The Targum adds, "And because they transgressed the decree of the word of the Lord, and joined affinity with strange people, therefore their days were cut off."

JOSEPH PARKER:

What a speech!—to be worthy of such a testimony; to have so lived at home as to elicit this benediction. What a glimpse into home life! What a quiet sabbatic house—a house sacred as an altar, secure against evil as a fortress! Is there aught so lovely, so attractive, so invaluable as a real, sunny, happy, gladsome home, where the opening of every door is an enlargement of hospitality, where the windows are all too small to receive heaven's benison of light, where every life considers every other life, and the whole household economy is as a concerted piece of music? In this direction all men, women, and children should move. Home should be the sweetest, happiest place on earth. On closing the household gate, the one who enters in should be able to sigh relief—release from pursuing anxieties; and the whole house should be beautiful and sacred as a church dedicated to God. In words such as we find in the eighth verse we have family life embodied in a sentence: "The Lord deal kindly with you, as ye have dealt with the dead, and with me." Her throat swelled with a great sob as she referred to the dead. Oh, to have no cruel reflections concerning the dead—to know that while they were living we did the best we could for them: we spared no trouble to lighten their burdens; we never said we were tired; we seemed rather to invite the labor than to evade it, if we could make their pillow easier and could add to their day's outlook one brighter beam of light—then the very death sanctifies the memory, and throws a singular charm upon all the future—akin to a happy expectancy, akin to the possibility of a sudden surprise by reappearance and rejunction. Do not mourn the dead, for you can do nothing to repair the injury which was inflicted upon them in their lifetime; they are beyond the reach of reparation. The only thing possible now is to do good twice over to those who are living with you, to set up—not stones, but living tablets, sacred to the memory of the misunderstood and the ill-used, the neglected and the distressed.

"Then she kissed them; and they lifted up their voice, and wept" (v. 9). Not a word was said. There are times when words are simply useless; there are sacred hours when the best-chosen words fall upon our ear with a sense of irritation. "They lifted up their voice, and wept"; they kissed to one another all their meaning. A lifetime was in that pressure, memories not to be spoken in detailed expressions consecrated that kiss of love. Who can without tears cut the associations of memory and of happy and sacred life? The heart that can do so is a heart no more; it is but a piece of stone.

—The People's Bible

MATTHEW HENRY

had had any sons in Canaan, or any near kinsmen, whom she could have expected to marry the widows it might have been some encouragement to them to hope for a comfortable settlement at Bethlehem. The greatest grievance of that poor condition to which she was reduced was that she was not in a capacity to do for them as she would. She laments most the trouble that redounded to them from it. A gracious generous spirit can better bear its own burden than it can bear to see it a grievance to others, or others in any way drawn into trouble by it. Naomi could more easily want herself than see her daughters want.

(2) Did Naomi do well thus to discourage her daughters from going with her, when, by taking them with her, she might save them from the idolatry of Moab and bring them to the faith and worship of the God of Israel? Naomi, no doubt, desired to do so. But, [1] If they did come with her, she would not have them to come upon her account. Those that take upon them a profession of religion only in complaisance to their relations, to oblige their friends, or for the sake of company, will be converts of small value and of short continuance. [2] If they did come with her, she would have them to make it their deliberate choice, and to sit down first and count the cost, as it concerns those to do that may take up a profession of religion. It is good for us to be told the worst. Our Saviour took this course with him who, in the heart of zeal, spoke that bold word, *Master, I will follow thee whithersoever thou goest.* "Come, come," says Christ, "canst thou fare as I fare? *The Son of man has not where to lay his head;* know this, and then consider whether thou canst find in thy heart to take thy lot with him," Matt. viii. 19, 20. Thus Naomi deals with her daughters-in-law. Thoughts ripened into resolves by serious consideration are likely to be kept always in the imagination of the heart, whereas what is soon ripe is soon rotten.

5. Orpah was easily persuaded to yield to her own corrupt inclination, and to go back to her country, her kindred, and her father's house, now when she stood fair for an effectual call from it. They both *lifted up their voice and wept again* (*v.* 14), being much affected with the tender things that Naomi had said. But it had a different effect upon them: to Orpah the representation Naomi had made of the inconveniences they must count upon if they went forward to Canaan sent her back to the country of Moab, but, on the contrary, it strengthened Ruth's resolution. (1) *Orpah kissed her mother-in-law,* that is, took an affectionate leave of her, bade her farewell for ever. Orpah's kiss showed she had an affection for Naomi and was loth to part from her; yet she did not love her well enough to leave her country for her sake. Thus many have a value and affection for Christ, and yet come short of salvation by him, because they cannot find in their hearts to forsake other things for him. They love him and yet leave him, because they do not love him enough, but love other things better. Thus the young man that went away from Christ went away sorrowful, Matt. xix. 22. But, (2) *Ruth clave unto her.* Whether, when she came from home, she was resolved to go forward with her or no does not appear.

6. Naomi persuades Ruth to go back, urging, as a further inducement, her sister's example: Now, *return thou after thy sister,* that is, "If ever thou wilt return, return now. This is the greatest trial of thy constancy; stand this trial, and thou art mine for ever."

7. Ruth puts an end to the debate by a most solemn profession of her immovable resolution never to forsake her, nor to return to her own country, and her old relations again, *v.* 16, 17.

(1) Nothing could be said more fine, more brave, than this. She seems to have had another spirit, and another speech, now that her sister had gone, and it is an instance of the grace of God inclining the soul to the resolute choice of the better part. [1] She begs of her mother-in-law to say no more against her going: *Entreat me not to leave thee, or to return from following after thee.* [2] She is very particular in her resolution to cleave to her and never to forsake her; and she speaks the language of one resolved for God and heaven. *First,* She will travel with her: *Whither thou goest I will go,* though to a country I never saw, though far from my own country, yet with thee every road shall be pleasant. *Secondly,* She will dwell with her: "*Where thou lodgest I will lodge,* though it be in a cottage, nay, though it be no better a lodging than Jacob had when he had the stones for his pillow. *Thirdly,* She will twist interests with her: *Thy people shall be my people. Fourthly,* She will join in religion with her. Thus she determined to be hers—*usque ad aras*—*to the very altars*: "*Thy God shall be my God.*" *Fifthly,* She will gladly die in the same bed: *Where thou diest will I die. Sixthly,* She will desire to be buried in the same grave, and to lay her bones by hers: *There will I be buried,*

JAMIESON, FAUSSET, BROWN

11. are there yet any more sons in my womb, that they may be your husbands?—This alludes to the ancient custom (Gen. 38:26) afterwards expressly sanctioned by the law of Moses (Deut. 25:5), which required a younger son to marry the widow of his deceased brother.

12, 13. Turn again, my daughters, go your way—That Naomi should dissuade her daughters-in-law so strongly from accompanying her to the land of Israel may appear strange. But it was the wisest and most prudent course for her to adopt: first, because they might be influenced by hopes which could not be realized; second, because they might be led, under temporary excitement, to take a step they might afterwards regret; and, third, because the sincerity and strength of their conversion to the true religion, which she had taught them, would be thoroughly tested. **13. the hand of the Lord is gone out against me**—i.e., I am not only not in a condition to provide you with other husbands, but so reduced in circumstances that I cannot think of your being subjected to privations with me.

The arguments of Naomi prevailed with Orpah, who returned to her people and her gods.

But Ruth clave unto her; and even in the pages of Sterne, that great master of pathos, there is nothing which so calls forth the sensibilities of the reader as the simple effusion he has borrowed from Scripture—of Ruth to her mother-in-law [CHALMERS].

ADAM CLARKE

11. *Are there yet any more sons.* This was spoken in allusion to the custom that, when a married brother died without leaving posterity, his brother should take his widow; and the children of such a marriage were accounted the children of the deceased brother.

14. *And Orpah kissed her mother in law.* The Septuagint adds, "And returned to her own people." The Vulgate, Syriac, and Arabic are to the same purpose.

15. *Gone back . . . unto her gods.* They were probably both idolaters; their having been proselytes is an unfounded conjecture. Chemosh was the grand idol of the Moabites. The conversion of Ruth probably commenced at this time.

16. *And Ruth said.* A more perfect surrender was never made of friendly feelings to a friend: "I will not leave you—I will follow you; I will lodge where you lodge—take the same fare with which you meet.

Thy people shall be my people—I most cheerfully abandon my own country, and determine to end my days in yours. I will also henceforth have no god but thy God—and be joined with you in worship, as I am in affection and consanguinity. I will cleave unto you even unto death; die where you die; and be buried, if possible, in the same grave. This was a most extraordinary attachment, and evidently without any secular motive.

MATTHEW HENRY

not desiring to have so much as her dead body carried back to the country of Moab, in token of any remaining kindness for it; but, Naomi and she having joined souls, she desires they may mingle dust, in hopes of rising together, and being together for ever in the other world. [3] She backs her resolution to adhere to Naomi with a solemn oath: *The Lord do so to me, and more also* (which was an ancient form of imprecation), *if aught but death part thee and me.*

(2) This is a pattern of a resolute convert to God and religion. Thus must we be at a point. [1] We must take the Lord for our God. "This God is *my God for ever and ever*; I have avouched him for mine." [2] When we take God for our God we must take his people for our people in all conditions; though they be a poor despised people, yet, if they be his, they must be ours. [3] Having cast in our lot among them, we must be willing to take our lot with them and to fare as they fare.

8. Naomi is hereby silenced (*v.* 18): *When she saw that Ruth was steadfastly minded to go with her* (which was the very thing she aimed at in all that she had said, to make her of a steadfast mind in going with her), when she saw that she had gained her point, she was well satisfied, and *left off speaking to her*.

Verses 19–22

Naomi and Ruth, after many a weary step, came at last to Bethlehem. And they came very seasonably, *in the beginning of the barley-harvest*, which was the first of their harvests, that of wheat following after. And now they had opportunity to provide for winter.

I. The discomposure of the neighbours upon this occasion (*v.* 19): *All the city was moved about them.* Her old acquaintance gathered about her, to enquire concerning her state, and to bid her welcome to Bethlehem again. Or perhaps they were *moved about her*, lest she should be a charge to the town, she looked so bare. And they said, *Is this Naomi?* Those with whom she had formerly been intimate were surprised to see her in this condition; she was so much broken and altered with her afflictions. *Is this Naomi?* The generality asked it in compassion and commiseration: "Is this she that lived so plentifully, and kept so good a house, and was so charitable to the poor? Afflictions will make great and surprising changes in a little time. When we see how sickness and old age alter people, change their countenance and temper, we may think of what the Bethlehemites said: "*Is this Naomi?*" God, by his grace, fit us for all such changes, especially the great change!

II. The composure of Naomi's spirit. If some upbraided her with her poverty, she was not moved against them, as she would have been if she had been poor and proud: *Call me not Naomi, call me Mara,* &c. "*Naomi* signifies *pleasant* or *amiable*; but all my pleasant things are laid waste; call me *Mara*, *bitter* or *bitterness*, for I am now a woman of a sorrowful spirit."

1. The change of her state, and how it is described, with a pious regard to the divine providence, and without any passionate murmurings or complaints. She now *came home again empty*, a widow and childless, and probably had sold her goods, and of all the effects she took with her brought home no more than the clothes on her back. (2) She acknowledges the hand of God, his mighty hand, in the affliction. "It is the Lord that has *brought me home again empty*; it is the Almighty that has afflicted me." Note, Nothing conduces more to satisfy a gracious soul under an affliction than the consideration of the hand of God in it. He that empties us of the creature knows how to fill us with himself.

2. The compliance of her spirit with this change: "*Call me not Naomi*, for I am no more pleasant, either to myself or to my friends; *but call me Mara*, a name more agreeable to my present state." If God deal bitterly with her, she will accommodate herself to the dispensation, and is willing to be called *Mara*, *bitter*. An affliction rightly borne does us good. *Tribulation works patience.*

CHAPTER 2

Verses 1–3

Naomi had now gained a settlement in Bethlehem among her old friends; and here we have an account,

I. Of her rich kinsman, Boaz, *a mighty man of wealth*, *v.* 1. The Chaldee reads it, *mighty in the law*. He carries might in his name, *Boaz—in him is strength*; and he was of the family of Elimelech, that family which was now reduced and brought so low.

II. Of her poor daughter-in-law, Ruth. 1. Her condition was very low and poor, which was a great trial to the faith and constancy of a young proselyte.

JAMIESON, FAUSSET, BROWN

19-22. **They Come to Bethlehem.** **19-22. all the city was moved about them**—The present condition of Naomi, a forlorn and desolate widow, presented so painful a contrast to the flourishing state of prosperity and domestic bliss in which she had been at her departure. **in the beginning of barley harvest**—corresponding to the end of our March.

CHAPTER 2

Vss. 1-3. **Ruth Gleans in the Field of Boaz.**

ADAM CLARKE

17. *The Lord do so to me, and more.* May He inflict any of those punishments on me, and any worse punishment, if I part from you till death. And it appears that she was true to her engagement; for Naomi was nourished in the house of Boaz in her old age, and became the fosterer and nurse of their son Obed, chap. iv. 15-16.

19. *All the city was moved about them.* It appears that Naomi was not only well-known, but highly respected also, at Bethlehem—a proof that Elimelech was of high consideration in that place.

20. *Call me not Naomi.* That is, "beautiful" or "pleasant." *Call me Mara.* That is, "bitter"; one whose life is grievous to her. *The Almighty. Shaddai*, He who is self-sufficient, has taken the props and supports of my life.

21. *I went out full.* Having a husband and two sons. *The Lord hath brought me home again empty.* Having lost all three by death. It is also likely that Elimelech took considerable property with him into the land of Moab; for as he fled from the face of the famine, he would naturally take his property with him; and on this Naomi subsisted till her return to Bethlehem, which she might not have thought of till all was spent.

22. *In the beginning of barley harvest.* This was in the beginning of spring, for the barley harvest began immediately after the Passover, and that feast was held on the fifteenth of the month Nisan, which corresponds nearly with our March.

CHAPTER 2

1. *A mighty man of wealth.* Some suppose Boaz to have been one of the judges of Israel; he was no doubt a man of considerable property.

MATTHEW HENRY

Naomi and her daughter-in-law have no way of getting necessary food but by gleaning corn. 2. Her character, in this condition, was very good (*v.* 2). She is *not mindful of the country from which she came out*, otherwise she had now a fair occasion to return. The God of Israel shall be her God, and, though he slay her, yet will she trust in him and never forsake him. *Let me go to the field, and glean ears of corn.* Let Ruth be remembered, who is a great example, (1) Of humility. When Providence had made her poor she did not say, "To glean, which is in effect to beg, I am ashamed." She does not tell her mother she was never brought up to live upon crumbs. Though she was not brought up to it, she is brought down to it, and is not uneasy at it. (2) Of industry. "*Let me go and glean ears of corn*, which will turn to some good account." A disposition to diligence bodes well both for this world and the other. We must not be shy of any honest employment, though it be mean, *ἐργον ουδεν ὀνεῖδος—No labour is a reproach.* (3) Of regard to her mother. Though she was but her mother-in-law, she is dutifully observant of her. (4) Of dependence upon Providence, intimated in that, I will *glean after him in whose sight I shall find grace.* She knows not which way to go, nor whom to enquire for, but will trust Providence to raise her up some friend or other that will be kind to her. And it did well for Ruth; for when she went out alone, without guide or companion, to glean, *her hap was to light on the field of Boaz, v.* 3. To her it seemed casual but Providence directed her steps to this field. Many a great affair is brought about by a little turn, which seemed fortuitous to us, but was directed by Providence with design.

Verses 4–16

Now Boaz himself appears, and a great deal of decency appears in his carriage:

I. Towards his own servants, and those that were employed for him in reaping and gathering in his corn. Harvest-time is busy time, many hands must then be at work. Boaz is here an example of a good master.

1. He had a servant that was set over the reapers, *v.* 6.

2. Yet he came himself to his reapers, to see how the work went forward. It was for the encouragement of his servants, who would go on the more cheerfully in their work when their master countenanced them so far as to make them a visit.

3. Kind and pious salutations were interchanged between Boaz and his reapers.

(1) He said to them, *The Lord be with you*; and they replied, *The Lord bless thee, v.* 4. Hereby they expressed, [1] Their mutual respect to each other. Things are likely to go on well in a house where there is such goodwill as this between master and servants. [2] Their joint-dependence upon the divine providence. They express their kindness to each other by praying one for another.

(2) Let us hence learn to use, [1] Courteous salutations, as expressions of a sincere goodwill to our friends. [2] Pious ejaculations, lifting up our hearts to God for his favour, in such short prayers as these. Only we must take heed that they do not degenerate into formality.

4. He took an account from his rearers concerning a stranger he met with in the field, and gave necessary orders concerning her, that they should not touch her (*v.* 9) nor reproach her, *v.* 15. He also ordered them to be kind to her, and *let fall some of the handfuls on purpose for her.*

II. Boaz was very kind to Ruth, and showed her a great deal of favour, induced to it by the account he had of her, and what he observed concerning her.

1. The steward gave to Boaz a very fair account of her, proper to recommend her to his favour, *v.* 6, 7. (1) That she was a stranger, and therefore one of those that by the law of God were to *gather the gleanings of the harvest*, Lev. xix. 9, 10. (2) That she was allied to his family; she came back with Naomi, the wife of Elimelech, a kinsman of Boaz. (3) That she was a proselyte, for she came out of the country of Moab to settle in the land of Israel. (4) That she was very modest, and had not gleaned till she had asked leave. (5) That she was very industrious, and had continued close to her work from morning even until now. Now, in the heat of the day, she tarried a little in the booth that was set up in the field for shelter.

2. Boaz was hereupon extremely civil to her. (1) He ordered her to attend his reapers in every field they gathered in and not to glean in the field of another, for she should not need to go anywhere else to better herself (*v.* 8). (2) He charged all his servants to be very tender of her and respectful to her. She was a stranger, and it is probable her language, dress, and mien differed much from theirs. (3) He bade her welcome to the entertainment he had provided for his own servants. He ordered her, not

JAMIESON, FAUSSET, BROWN

2. Ruth . . . said unto Naomi, Let me now go to the field, and glean—The right of gleaning was conferred by a positive law on the widow, the poor, and the stranger (see on Lev. 19:9, 10; Deut. 24:19, 21). But liberty to glean *behind the reapers* was not a right that could be claimed; it was a privilege granted or refused according to the good will or favor of the owner.

3. her hap was to light on a part of the field belonging unto Boaz—Fields in Palestine being unenclosed, the phrase signifies that portion of the open ground which lay within the landmarks of Boaz.

4-23. He Takes Knowledge of Her, and Shows Her Favor. **4. Boaz came from Bethlehem, and said unto the reapers, The Lord be with you**—This pious salutation between the master and his laborers strongly indicates the state of religious feeling among the rural population of Israel at that time, as well as the artless, happy, and unsuspecting simplicity which characterized the manners of the people. The same patriarchal style of speaking is still preserved in the East. **5. his servant that was set over the reapers**—an overseer whose special duty was to superintend the operations in the field, to supply provision to the reapers, and pay them for their labor in the evening.

7. she said, . . . Let me glean and gather after the reapers among the sheaves—Various modes of reaping are practised in the East. Where the crop is thin and short, it is plucked up by the roots. Sometimes it is cut with the sickle. Whether reaped in the one way or the other, the grain is cast into sheaves loosely thrown together, to be subjected to the process of threshing, which takes place, for the most part, immediately after the reaping. Field labors were begun early in the morning—before the day became oppressively hot. **she tarried a little in the house**—i.e., the field tent, erected for the occasional rest and refreshment of the laborers. **8, 9. said Boaz unto Ruth, . . . bide here fast by my maidens**—The reaping was performed by women while the assortment of sheaves was the duty of menservants. The same division of harvest labor obtains in Syria still. Boaz not only granted to Ruth the full privilege of gleaning after his reapers, but provided for her personal comfort. **go unto the vessels, and drink of that which the young men have drawn**—Gleaners were sometimes allowed, by kind and charitable masters, to partake of the refreshments provided for the reapers. The vessels alluded to were skin bottles, filled with water—and the bread was soaked in vinegar (vs. 14); a kind of poor, weak wine, sometimes mingled with a little olive oil—very cooling, as would be required in harvest-time. This grateful refection is still used in the harvest-field.

ADAM CLARKE

2. *Glean ears of corn.* The word *glean* comes from the French *glaner*, to gather ears or grains of corn. This was formerly a general custom in England and Ireland; the poor went into the fields and collected the straggling ears of corn after the reapers. *After him in whose sight I shall find grace.* She did not mean Boaz; but she purposed to go out where they were now reaping, and glean after any person who might permit her, or use her in a friendly manner. The words seem to intimate that, notwithstanding the law of Moses, the gleaners might be prevented by the owner of the field.

3. *And her hap was.* So she was accidentally or providentially led to that part of the cultivated country which belonged to Boaz.

4. *Boaz came from Beth-lehem.* This salutation between Boaz and his reapers is worthy of particular regard; he said, "Jehovah be with you!" They said, "May Jehovah bless thee!" Can a pious mind read these godly salutations without wishing for a return of those simple primitive times?

7. *That she tarried a little in the house.* It seems as if the reapers were now resting in their tent, and that Ruth had just gone in with them to take her rest also.

8. *Abide here fast by my maidens.* These were probably employed in making bands, and laying on them enough to form a sheaf, which the binders would tie and form into shocks. When the maidens had gathered up the scattered handfuls thrown down by the reapers, Ruth picked up any straggling heads or ears which they had left.

9. *The young men that they shall not touch thee.* This was peculiarly necessary, as she was a stranger and unprotected.

MATTHEW HENRY

only to drink of the water which was drawn for them, but at *meal-time to come and eat of their bread* (*v.* 14), yea, and she should be welcome to their sauce too: *Come, dip thy morsel in the vinegar*, to make it savoury. And he himself, happening to be present when the reapers sat down to meat, *reached her parched corn* to eat. (4) He commended her for her dutiful respect to her mother-in-law, whom, though he did not know her by sight, yet he had heard of (*v.* 11). But that which especially he commended her for was that she had left her own country, and had become a proselyte to the Jewish religion. (5) He prayed for her (*v.* 12): *The Lord recompense thy work*. Those that by faith come under the wings of the divine grace may be sure of a full recompence of reward for their so doing. The Jews describe a proselyte to be one that is *gathered under the wings of the divine majesty*. (6) He encouraged her to go on in her gleaning. Boaz ordered his servants to let her glean among the sheaves and not to reproach her.

3. Ruth received his favours with a great deal of humility and gratitude. She paid all possible respect to him, and gave him honour, according to the usage of the country (*v.* 10): *She fell on her face, and bowed herself to the ground*. She humbly owned herself unworthy of his favours: "*I am a stranger*" (*v.* 10) and *not like one of thy handmaids* (*v.* 13). She begs the continuance of his good-will. When Boaz gave her her dinner with his reapers she only ate so much as would suffice her, and immediately rose up to glean, *v.* 14, 15.

Verses 17–23

I. Ruth finishes her day's work, *v.* 17. 1. She took care not to lose time, for she gleaned until evening. 2. She took care not to lose what she had gathered, but threshed it herself, that she might the more easily carry it home, and might have it ready for use. Ruth had gathered it ear by ear, but, when she had put it all together, it was an ephah of barley, about four pecks.

II. She paid her respects to her mother-in-law and *showed her what she had gleaned*, that she might see she had not been idle. She gave her an account of her day's work, and how a kind providence had favoured her in it. Naomi asked her where she had been: *Where hast thou gleaned to-day?* Ruth gave her a particular account of the kindness she had received from Boaz (*v.* 19) and the hopes she had of further kindness from him, he having ordered her to attend his servants throughout all the harvest, *v.* 21. Naomi prayed heartily for him that had been her daughter's benefactor, even before she knew who it was (*v.* 19), *Blessed be he*, whoever he was, *that did take knowledge of thee*, shooting the arrow of prayer at a venture. She now remembered the former kindnesses Boaz had shown to her husband and sons, and joins those to this: he has not *left off his kindness to the living and to the dead*. She acquainted Ruth with the relation their family was in to Boaz: *The man is near of kin to us*. Observe the chain of thought here, and in it a chain of providences, bringing about what was designed concerning Ruth. Ruth names Boaz as one that had been kind to her. Naomi bethinks herself who that should be, and presently recollects herself: "*The man is near of kin to us;* now that I hear his name, I remember him very well." She appointed Ruth to continue her attendance in the fields of Boaz (*v.* 22): "*Let them not meet thee in any other field*, for that will be construed a contempt of his courtesy." Has the Lord dealt bountifully with us? Let us not be found in any other field, nor seek for happiness and satisfaction in the creature. Ruth dutifully observed her mother's directions; she continued to glean, to the end, not only of barley-harvest, but of the wheat-harvest, which followed it, that she might gather food in harvest to serve for winter, Prov. vi. 6–8.

JAMIESON, FAUSSET, BROWN

14. he reached her parched corn, and she did eat, and was sufficed, and left—some of the new grain, roasted on the spot, and fit for use after being rubbed in the hands—a favorite viand in the East. He gave her so much, that after satisfying her own wants, she had some (vs. 18) in reserve for her mother-in-law.

16. let fall also some of the handfuls on purpose for her—The gleaners in the East glean with much success; for a great quantity of corn is scattered in the reaping, as well as in their manner of carrying it. One may judge, then, of the large quantity which Ruth would gather in consequence of the liberal orders given to the servants. These extraordinary marks of favor were not only given from a kindly disposition, but from regard to her good character and devoted attachment to her venerable relative. **17. and beat out that she had gleaned**—When the quantity of grain was small, it was beat out by means of a stick. **an ephah**—supposed to contain about a bushel.

21. all my harvest—both barley and wheat harvests. The latter was at the end of May or the beginning of June.

20. the man is . . . one of our next kinsmen—*Heb.*, "one of our redeemers"—on whom it devolves to protect us, to purchase our lands, and marry you, the widow of his next kinsman. She said, "one of them," not that there were many in the same close relationship, but that he was a very near kinsman, one other individual only having the precedence.

22. Naomi said unto Ruth . . . , It is good . . . that thou go out with his maidens—a prudent recommendation to Ruth to accept the generous invitation of Boaz, lest, if she were seen straying into other fields, she might not only run the risk of rude treatment, but displease him by seeming indifferent to his kind liberality. Moreover, the observant mind of the old matron had already discerned, in all Boaz' attentions to Ruth, the germs of a stronger affection, which she wished to increase.

ADAM CLARKE

12. *The Lord recompense thy work.* The dutiful respect which you have paid to your husband, and your tender and affectionate attachment to your aged mother-in-law. *And a full reward be given thee.* This is spoken with great modesty and piety: The kindness I show you is little in comparison of your desert; God alone can give you a *full reward* for your kindness to your husband and mother-in-law; and He will do it, because you are come to trust under His wings—to become a proselyte to His religion. It is evident from this that Ruth had already attached herself to the Jewish religion.

13. *Not like unto one of thine handmaidens.* I am as unworthy of your regards as any of your own maidservants, and yet you show me distinguished kindness.

14. *Dip thy morsel in the vinegar.* The *chomets,* which we here translate *vinegar,* seems to have been some refreshing kind of acid sauce used by the reapers to dip their bread in, which both cooled and refreshed them. *Parched corn.* This was a frequent repast among the ancients in almost countries.

15. *Let her glean even among the sheaves.* This was a privilege; for no person should glean till the sheaves were all bound, and the shocks set up.

10. *Then she fell on her face.* Prostrated herself, as was the custom in the East when inferiors approached those of superior rank.

17. *An ephah of barley.* Not less than seven gallons and a half; a good day's work.

18. *And gave to her that she had reserved.* As Ruth had received a distinct portion at dinnertime, of which she had more than she could eat, v. 14; it appears she brought the rest home to her mother-in-law, as is here related.

20. *To the living and to the dead.* Naomi and Ruth were the living; and they were also the representatives of Elimelech and Mahlon, who were dead. *One of our next kinsmen. Miggoaleynu,* or our "redeemers"; one who has the right to redeem the forfeited inheritance of the family. The word *goel* signifies a "near kinsman"—one who by the Mosaic law had a right to redeem an inheritance.

21. *Keep fast by my young men.* The word *hannearim* should be translated "servants," both the male and female being included in it; the latter especially, as we see in vv. 22-23.

23. *And of wheat harvest.* That is, she was to continue gleaning in the farm of Boaz to the end of the barley harvest; and then, when the wheat harvest began, to continue to its conclusion in the same way. In the interim, as well as each night, she lodged with her mother-in-law.

CHAPTER 3

Verses 1–5

I. Naomi's care for her daughter's comfort is without doubt very commendable. She is full of contrivance how to get her well married. Her wisdom projected that for her daughter which her daughter's modesty forbade her to project for herself, *v.* 1. This she did, 1. In justice to the dead, to raise up seed to those that were gone, and so to preserve the family from being extinct. 2. In kindness and gratitude to her daughter-in-law, who had conducted herself very dutifully and respectfully to her. "*My daughter*" (said she, looking upon her in all respects as her own), "*shall I not seek rest for thee,*" that is, a settlement in the married state. A married state is,

CHAPTER 3

VSS. 1-13. BY NAOMI'S INSTRUCTIONS, RUTH LIES AT BOAZ'S FEET, WHO ACKNOWLEDGES THE DUTY OF A KINSMAN.

CHAPTER 3

1. *Shall I not seek rest for thee?* That is, Shall I not endeavor to procure you a proper husband?

MATTHEW HENRY

or should be, a state of rest to young people. Wandering affections are then fixed, and the heart must be at rest. It is at rest in the house of a husband, and in his heart, *ch.* i. 9. Those are giddy indeed that marriage does not compose.

II. The course she took in order to her daughter's preferment was very extraordinary and looks suspicious. If there was any thing improper in it, the fault must lie upon Naomi, who put her daughter upon it, and who knew, or should know, the laws and usages of Israel better than Ruth. 1. It was true that Boaz, being near of kin to the deceased, and (for aught that Naomi knew to the contrary) the nearest of all now alive, was obliged by the divine law to marry the widow of Mahlon, who was the eldest son of Elimelech, and was dead without issue (*v.* 2). "Why should we not remind him of his duty?" 2. It was a convenient time to remind him of it, now that he had got so much acquaintance with Ruth by her constant attendance on his reapers during the whole harvest, which was now ended. It was a good opportunity to apply to him when he made a winnowing-feast at his threshing-floor (*v.* 2). 3. Naomi thought Ruth the most proper person to do it herself; and perhaps it was the usage in that country that in this case the woman should make the demand; so much is intimated by the law, Deut. xxv. 7–9. "*Wash thyself and anoint thee*, put on thy raiment, and go down to the floor," whither, it is probable, she was invited to the supper there made; but she must not make herself known, that is, not make her errand known till the company had dispersed and Boaz had retired. But, 4. Her coming to lie down at his feet, when he was asleep in his bed, had such an appearance of evil, that we know not well how to justify it. All agree that it is not to be drawn into a precedent; neither our laws nor our times are the same that were then; yet I am willing to make the best of it. If Boaz was, as they presumed, the next kinsman, she was his wife before God (as we say), and there needed but little ceremony to complete the nuptials; and Naomi did not intend that Ruth should approach to him any otherwise than as his wife. She knew Boaz to be a grave sober man, a virtuous and religious man, and one that feared God. She knew Ruth to be a modest woman, *chaste, and a keeper at home*, Tit. ii. 5. Naomi herself designed nothing but what was honest and honourable. If what she advised had been then as indecent and immodest (according to the usage of the country), as it seems now to us, we cannot think that Naomi would have had so little wisdom as to put her daughter upon it, and have alienated the affections of so grave and good a man as Boaz from her. We must therefore think that the thing did not look so ill then as it does now. We may be sure, if Ruth had apprehended any evil in that which her mother advised her to, she was a woman of too much virtue and too much sense to promise as she did (*v.* 5): *All that thou sayest unto me I will do.*

Verses 6–13

I. Boaz's good management of his common affairs. It is probable, according to the common usage, 1. When his servants winnowed, he was with them to prevent carelessness in the winnowing. 2. When he had more than ordinary work to be done, he treated his servants with extraordinary entertainments, and, for their encouragement, did *eat and drink with them.* 3. When Boaz had supped with his workmen, and been awhile pleasant with them, he *went to bed in due time*, so early that by midnight he had his first sleep (*v.* 8). 4. He had his bed or couch laid *at the end of the heap of corn*; he was like his father Jacob, a plain man, that, when there was occasion, could make his bed in a barn, and, if need were, sleep contentedly in the straw.

II. Ruth's good assurance in the management of her affair. When he awaked in the night, and perceived there was somebody at his feet, and enquired who it was, she told him her name and then her errand (*v.* 9), that she came to put herself under his protection, as the person appointed by the divine law to be her protector: "*Thou art he that has a right to redeem* a family and an estate from perishing, and therefore *let this ruin be under thy hand*: and *spread thy skirt over me*—be pleased to espouse me and my cause."

III. The good acceptance Ruth gained with Boaz. He knew her demand was just and honourable, and treated her accordingly. Boaz knew it was not any sinful lust that brought her thither, and therefore bravely maintained both his own honour and hers.

(1) He commended her, spoke kindly to her, called her his *daughter*, and spoke honourably of her, as a woman of eminent virtue. It was very kind to leave her own country and come along with her mother to the land of Israel, to dwell with her, and help to maintain her. For this he had blessed her (*ch.* ii. 12);

JAMIESON, FAUSSET, BROWN

F. B. MEYER:

"The part of a kinsman." According to the old Hebrew law, Ruth was already married to Boaz, on the supposition that he was next of kin. Naomi apparently had no knowledge of a nearer kinsman than he (cf. 2:20; 3:12; Deut. 25:5–10). There was therefore no immodesty in Naomi's proposals, though they are foreign to our modern practice. But clearly Boaz acted with admirable self-restraint. His earnest concern was for the good name of the young girl who had thrown herself on his protection (vv. 11, 14). Next to God's grace, the one thought which helps us in the hour of testing is to put the interests of another before our own. Love to our neighbor is ultimately love to ourselves.—*Bible Commentary*

2. he winnoweth barley to-night in the threshing-floor—The winnowing process is performed by throwing up the grain, after being trodden down, against the wind with a shovel. The threshing-floor, which was commonly on the harvest-field, was carefully leveled with a large cylindric roller and consolidated with chalk, that weeds might not spring up, and that it might not chop with drought. The farmer usually remained all night in harvest-time on the threshing-floor, not only for the protection of his valuable grain, but for the winnowing. That operation was performed in the evening to catch the breezes which blow after the close of a hot day, and which continue for the most part of the night. This duty at so important a season the master undertakes himself; and, accordingly, in the simplicity of ancient manners, Boaz, a person of considerable wealth and high rank, laid himself down to sleep on the barn floor, at the end of the heap of barley he had been winnowing. **4. go in, and uncover his feet, and lay thee down**—Singular as these directions may appear to us, there was no impropriety in them, according to the simplicity of rural manners in Bethlehem. In ordinary circumstances these would have seemed indecorous to the world; but in the case of Ruth, it was a method, doubtless conformable to prevailing usage, of reminding Boaz of the duty which devolved on him as the kinsman of her deceased husband.

Boaz probably slept upon a mat or skin; Ruth lay crosswise at his feet—a position in which Eastern servants frequently sleep in the same chamber or tent with their master; and if they want a covering, custom allows them that benefit from part of the covering on their master's bed. Resting, as the Orientals do at night, in the same clothes they wear during the day, there was no indelicacy in a stranger, or even a woman, putting the extremity of this cover over her. **9. I am Ruth thine handmaid: spread therefore thy skirt over thine handmaid; for thou art a near kinsman**—She had already drawn part of the mantle over her; and she asked him now to do it, that the act might become his own. To spread a skirt over one is, in the East, a symbolical action denoting protection. To this day in many parts of the East, to say of anyone that he put his skirt over a woman, is synonymous with saying that he married her; and at all the marriages of the modern Jews and Hindoos, one part of the cere-

ADAM CLARKE

2. *He winnoweth barley to night.* It is very likely that the winnowing of grain was effected by taking up, in a broad, thin vessel or sieve, a portion of the corn, and letting it down slowly in the wind. It is said here that this was done at night; probably what was threshed out in the day was winnowed in the evening, when the sea breeze set in, which was common in Palestine.

3. *Wash thyself therefore.* She made Ruth put on her best dress, that Boaz might, in the course of the day, be the more attracted by her person, and be the better disposed to receive her as Naomi wished.

4. *Uncover his feet, and lay thee down.* It is said that women in the East, when going to the bed of their lawful husbands, through modesty, and in token of subjection, go to the bed's foot, and gently raising the clothes, creep under them up to their place.

7. *Went to lie down.* As the threshing floors of the Eastern nations are in general in the open air, it is very likely that the owner continued in the fields till the grain was secured, having a tent in the place where the corn was threshed and winnowed. Boaz seems to have acted thus.

9. *Spread therefore thy skirt over thine handmaid.* Hebrew, "Spread thy wing." The wing is the emblem of protection, and is a metaphor taken from the young of fowls, which run under the wings of their mothers, that they may be saved from birds of prey. The meaning here is, "Take me to thee for wife."

MATTHEW HENRY

but now he says, Thou hast *shown more kindness in the latter end than at the beginning* (*v.* 10), in that she consulted not her own fancy, but her husband's family, in marrying again.

(2) He promised her marriage (*v.* 11): "*Fear not* that I will slight thee, or expose thee; no, *I will do all that thou requirest*, for it is the same that the law requires, from the next of kin, and I have no reason to decline it, *for all the city of my people doth know that thou art a virtuous woman*," *v.* 11.

(3) He made his promise conditional, and could not do otherwise, for it seems there was a kinsman that was nearer than he, to whom the right of redemption did belong, *v.* 12. He would himself propose it to the other kinsman, and know his mind. If the other kinsman refused to do the kinsman's part, he would do it, would marry the widow, redeem the land, and so repair the family. Bishop Hall thus sums up this matter: "Boaz, instead of touching her as a wanton, blesseth her as a father, encourageth her as a friend, promiseth her as a kinsman, rewards her as a patron, and sends her away laden with hopes and gifts, no less chaste, more happy, than she came."

Verses 14–18

I. How Ruth was dismissed by Boaz. 1. With a charge to keep counsel (*v.* 14): *Let it not be known that a woman came into the floor*, and lay all night so near to Boaz. 2. He dismissed her with a good present of corn, which would be very acceptable to her poor mother at home, and an evidence for her that he had not sent her away in dislike, which Naomi might have suspected if he had sent her away empty. He gave it to her in her *veil*, or *apron*, or *mantle*, gave it to her by measure.

II. How she was welcomed by her mother-in-law. She asked her, "*Who art thou, my daughter?* Art thou a bride or no? Must I give thee joy?" So Ruth told her how the matter stood (*v.* 17), whereupon her mother, 1. Advised her to be satisfied in what was done: *Sit still, my daughter, till thou know how the matter will fall* (*v.* 18). 2. She assured her that Boaz, having undertaken this matter, would approve himself a faithful careful friend: *He will not be at rest till he have finished the matter.*

JAMIESON, FAUSSET, BROWN

mony is for the bridegroom to put a silken or cotton cloak around his bride.

15. Bring the veil that thou hast upon thee, and hold it—Eastern veils are large sheets—those of ladies being of red silk; but the poorer or common class of women wear them of blue, or blue and white striped linen or cotton. They are wrapped round the head, so as to conceal the whole face except one eye. **17. six measures of barley**—*Heb.*, "six *seahs*," a *seah* contained about two gallons and a half, six of which must have been rather a heavy load for a woman.

ADAM CLARKE

10. *In the latter end than at the beginning.* It is not easy to find out what Boaz means. Perhaps *chesed*, which we translate *kindness*, means "piety"; as if he had said: You have given great proof of your piety in this latter instance, when you have avoided the young, and those of your own age, to associate yourself with an elderly man, merely for the purpose of having the divine injunction fulfilled, viz., that the brother, or next akin, might take the wife of the deceased, and raise a family to him who had died childless, that his name might not become extinct in Israel. *Whether poor or rich.* So it appears from this that it was not to mend her condition in life that Ruth endeavored to get Boaz for her husband, for she might have had a rich young man, but she preferred the building up the house of her deceased husband.

12. *There is a kinsman nearer than I.* It is very likely that Naomi was not acquainted with this circumstance.

13. *As the Lord liveth.* Thus he bound himself by an oath to take her to wife if the other should refuse.

15. *Bring the veil.* This seems to have been a cloak. *Six measures of barley.* We supply the word *measures*, for the Hebrew mentions no quantity. If the omer be meant, which is about six pints, this would amount to but about four gallons and a half.

MATTHEW HENRY — CHAPTER 4

Verses 1–8

1. Boaz calls a court immediately. It is probable he was himself one of the elders (or aldermen) of the city. But why was Boaz so hasty, why so fond of the match? Ruth was not rich, but a poor stranger. But that which made Boaz in love with her, and solicitous to expedite the affair, was that all her neighbours agreed she was a virtuous woman. He will therefore bring it to a conclusion immediately. It was not court-day, but he got ten men of the elders of the city to meet him in the town hall over the gate, where public business used to be transacted, *v.* 2. So many, it is probable, by the custom of the city, made a full court. 2. He summons his rival to come and hear the matter that was to be proposed to him (*v.* 1). 3. He proposes to the other kinsman the redemption of Naomi's land, which, it is probable, had been mortgaged for money to buy bread with when the famine was in the land (*v.* 3): "*Naomi has a parcel of land to sell.*" This he gives the kinsman legal notice of (*v.* 4), that he might have the refusal of it. 4. The kinsman seemed forward to redeem the land till he was told that, if he did that, he must marry the widow, and then he flew off. "*I cannot redeem it for myself.* I will not meddle with it upon these terms, lest I mar my own inheritance." The land, he thought, would be an improvement of his inheritance, but not the land with the woman; that would mar it. 5. The right of redemption is fairly resigned to Boaz. If this nameless kinsman lost a good bargain, a good estate, and a good wife too, he may thank himself for not considering it better, and Boaz will thank him for making his way clear to that which he valued and desired above any thing. In those ancient times it was not the usage to pass estates by writings, as afterwards (Jer. xxxii. 10, &c.), but by some sign or ceremony, as with us by livery and seisin, as we commonly call it, that is, the delivery of seisin, seisin of a house by giving the key, of land by giving turf and a twig. The ceremony here used was, he that surrendered *plucked off his shoe* and gave it to him to whom he made the surrender, intimating thereby that, whatever right he had to tread or go upon the land, he conveyed and transferred it, upon a valuable consideration, to the purchaser: this was a *testimony in Israel*, *v.* 7. And it was done in this case, *v.* 8.

JAMIESON, FAUSSET, BROWN — CHAPTER 4

VSS. 1-5. BOAZ CALLS INTO JUDGMENT THE NEXT KINSMAN. **1. Then went Boaz up to the gate of the city**—a roofed building, unenclosed by walls; the place where, in ancient times, and in many Eastern towns still, all business transactions are made, and where, therefore, the kinsman was most likely to be found. No preliminaries were necessary in summoning one before the public assemblage; no writings and no delay were required. In a short conversation the matter was stated and arranged—probably in the morning as people went out, or at noon when they returned from the field. **2. he took ten men of the elders of the city**—as witnesses. In ordinary circumstances, two or three were sufficient to attest a bargain; but in cases of importance, such as matrimony, divorce, conveyancing of property, it was the Jewish practice to have ten (I Kings 21: 8). **3. Naomi . . . selleth a parcel of land**—i.e., entertains the idea of selling. In her circumstances she was at liberty to part with it (Lev. 25:25). Both Naomi and Ruth had an interest in the land during their lives; but Naomi alone was mentioned, not only because she directed all the negotiations, but because the introduction of Ruth's name would awaken a suspicion of the necessity of marrying her, before the first proposition was answered. **4. there is none to redeem it beside thee; and I am after thee**—(See on Deut. 25:5-10). The redemption of the land of course involved a marriage with Ruth, the widow of the former owner.

6-8. HE REFUSES THE REDEMPTION. **6. The kinsman said, I cannot redeem it . . . , lest I mar mine own inheritance**—This consequence would follow, either, first, from his having a son by Ruth, who, though heir to the property, would not bear his name; his name would be extinguished in that of her former husband; or, secondly, from its having to be subdivided among his other children, which he had probably by a previous marriage. This right, therefore, was renounced and assigned in favor of Boaz, in the way of whose marriage with Ruth the only existing obstacle was now removed. **7, 8. a man plucked off his shoe**—Where the kinsman refused to perform his duty to the family of his deceased relation, the widow was directed to pull off the shoe with some attendant circumstances of

ADAM CLARKE — CHAPTER 4

1. *Then went Boaz up to the gate.* We have often had occasion to remark that the *gate* or entrance to any city or town was the place where the court of justice was ordinarily kept. *Ho, such a one! . . . sit down here.* This familiar mode of compellation is first used here. The original is *shebah poh, peloni almoni!* "Hark ye, Mr. Such-a-one of such a place! come and sit down here." This is used when the person of the individual is known, and his name and residence unknown. *Almoni* comes from *alam*, "to be silent or hidden"; hence the Septuagint render it by "thou unknown person": *peloni* comes from *palah*, "to sever or distinguish"; you of such a particular place.

2. *He took ten men.* Probably it required this number to constitute a court. How simple and how rational was this proceeding!

4. *I thought to advertise thee.* Both Kennicott and Houbigant have noticed several corruptions in the pronouns of this and the following verses; and their criticisms have been confirmed by a great number of MSS. since collated. The text corrected reads thus: "And I said I will reveal this to thy ear, saying, Buy it before the inhabitants, and before the elders of my people. If thou wilt redeem it, redeem it; but if thou wilt not redeem it, tell me, that I may know; for there is none to redeem it but thou, and I who am next to thee. And he said, I will redeem it. And Boaz said, In the day that thou redeemest the land from the hand of Naomi, thou wilt also acquire Ruth, the wife of the dead, that thou mayest raise up the name of the dead upon his inheritance," vv. 4-5.

I will redeem it. I will pay down the money which it is worth. He knew not of the following condition.

5. *Thou must buy it also of Ruth.* More properly, "Thou wilt also acquire Ruth." You cannot get the land without taking the wife of the deceased; and then the children which you may have shall be reputed the children of Mahlon, your deceased kinsman.

6. *I cannot redeem it for myself.* The Targum

MATTHEW HENRY

Boaz now sees his way clear to perform his promise made to Ruth that he would do the kinsman's part, but in the gate of his city, before the elders and all the people, publishes a marriage-contract between himself and Ruth the Moabitess, and therewith the purchase of all the estate that belonged to the family of Elimelech. Now concerning this marriage it appears,

I. That it was solemnized, or at least published, before many witnesses, *v.* 9, 10. 1. "That I have bought the estate. Whoever has it, or any part of it, mortgaged to him, let him come to me and he shall have his money." 2. "That I have purchased the widow to be my wife." He had no portion with her; what jointure she had was encumbered, and he could not have it without giving as much for it as it was worth, and therefore he might well say he purchased her. He designed, in marrying her, to preserve the memory of the dead, that the name of Mahlon, though he left no son to bear it up, by this means might be preserved. And observe that because Boaz did this honour to the dead, as well as this kindness to the living, God did him the honour to bring him into the genealogy of the Messiah, by which his family was dignified above all the families of Israel; while the other kinsman, that was so much afraid of diminishing himself, and marring his inheritance, by marrying the widow, has his name, family, and inheritance, buried in oblivion and disgrace. Our Lord Jesus is our *Goel*, our *Redeemer*, our everlasting Redeemer. He looked, like Boaz, with compassion on the deplorable state of fallen mankind. At a vast expense he redeemed the heavenly inheritance for us, which by sin was mortgaged, and forfeited into the hands of divine justice, and which we should never have been able to redeem.

II. That it was attended with many prayers. The elders and all the people, when they witnessed to it, wished well to it, and blessed it, *v.* 11, 12.

1. The senior elder, it is likely, made this prayer, and the rest of the elders, with the people, joining in it, and therefore it is spoken of as made by them all; for in public prayers, though but one speaks, we must all pray. Marriages ought to be blessed, and accompanied with prayer. We ought to desire and pray for the welfare and prosperity one of another.

2. Now here, (1) They prayed for Ruth, *The Lord make the woman that has come into thy house like Rachel and Leah*, that is, "God make her a good wife and a fruitful mother." (2) They prayed for Boaz. They desired that the wife might be a blessing in the private affairs of the house, and the husband a blessing in the public business of the town, that she in her place, and he in his, might be wise, virtuous, and successful. (3) They prayed for the family: "*Let thy house be like the house of Pharez*," that is, "let it be very numerous, let it greatly increase and multiply as the house of Pharez did." The Bethlehemites were of the house of Pharez. Now they prayed that the family of Boaz, which was one branch of that stock, might in process of time become as numerous and great as the whole stock now was.

I. Ruth a wife. Boaz took her, with the usual solemnities, to his house, and *she became his wife* (*v.* 13). Boaz had prayed that this pious proselyte might receive a full reward of her courage and constancy from the God of Israel, *under whose wings she had come to trust*; and now he became an instrument of that kindness, which was an answer to his prayer, and helped to make his own words good.

II. Ruth a mother: *The Lord gave her conception*; for *the fruit of the womb is his reward*, Ps. cxxvii. 3.

III. Ruth still a daughter-in-law, and the same that she always was, to Naomi, who was so far from being forgotten that she was a principal sharer in these new joys. Prayer to God attended the marriage (*v.* 11), and praise to him attended the birth of the child. What a pity it is that such pious language should either be disused among Christians or degenerate into a formality. "*Blessed be the Lord* that has sent thee this grandson," *v.* 14, 15. They say of Ruth that she loved Naomi, and therefore was better to her than seven sons. The bonds of love prove stronger than those of nature, so here there was a daughter-in-law better than an own child. (1) The child is named by the neighbours, *v.* 17. The good women would have it called *Obed, a servant*, either in remembrance of the meanness and poverty of the mother or in prospect of his being hereafter a servant, and very serviceable, to his grandmother. (2) The child is nursed by the grandmother. Grandmothers are often the most fond.

IV. Ruth is hereby brought in among the ancestors of David and Christ, which was the greatest honour. The genealogy is here drawn from Pharez, through Boaz and Obed, to David and so leads towards the Messiah.

JAMIESON, FAUSSET, BROWN

contemptuous disdain. But, as in this case, there was no refusal, the usual ignominy was spared; and the plucking off the shoe, the only ceremony observed, was a pledge of the transaction being completed.

9-12. HE MARRIES RUTH. **9. Boaz said unto the elders, Ye are witnesses this day that I have bought all that was . . . Chilion's and Mahlon's, of the hand of Naomi**—Although the widow of Chilion was still living, no regard was paid to her in the disposal of her husband's property. From her remaining in Moab, she was considered to have either been married again, or to have renounced all right to an inheritance with the family of Elimelech. **10. Ruth the Moabitess . . . have I purchased to be my wife**—This connection Boaz not only might form, since Ruth had embraced the true religion, but he was under a legal necessity of forming it.

11. all the people and the elders said, We are witnesses—A multitude, doubtless from curiosity or interest, were present on the occasion. There was no signing of deeds; yet was the transfer made, and complete security given, by the public manner in which the whole matter was carried on and concluded. **the Lord make the woman that is come into thine house like Rachel and Leah**—This was the usual bridal benediction.

12. let thy house be like the house of Pharez—i.e., as honorable and numerous as his. He was the ancestor of the Bethlehem people, and his family one of the five from which the tribe of Judah sprang.

13-18. SHE BEARS OBED. **17. Obed**—means "servant." **18-22. these are the generations of Pharez**—i.e., his descendants. This appendix shows that the special object contemplated by the inspired author of this little book was to preserve the memory of an interesting domestic episode, and to trace the genealogy of David. There was an interval of 380 years between Salmon and David. It is evident that whole generations are omitted; the leading personages only are named, and grandfathers are said, in Scripture language, to beget their grandchildren, without specifying the intermediate links.

ADAM CLARKE

gives the proper sense of this passage: "And the kinsman said, On this ground I cannot redeem it because I have a wife already; and I have no desire to take another, lest there should be contention in my house, and I should become a corrupter of my inheritance. Do thou redeem it, for thou hast no wife; for I cannot redeem it."

7. *A man plucked off his shoe.* The law of such a case is given at large in Deut. xxv. 5-9. It was simply this: If a brother, who had married a wife, died without children, the eldest brother was to take the widow, and raise up a family to the brother deceased; and he had a right to redeem the inheritance, if it had been alienated. But if the person who had the right of redemption would not take the woman, she was to pull off his shoe and spit in his face; and he was ever after considered as a disgraced man. In the present case the shoe only is taken off, probably because the circumstances of the man were such as to render it improper for him to redeem the ground and take Ruth to his wife; and because of this reasonable excuse, the contemptuous part of the ceremony is omitted.

11. *We are witnesses.* It is not very likely that any writing was drawn up. There was an appeal made to the people then present, whether they had seen and understood the transaction; who answered, "We have witnessed it." *The Lord make the woman . . . like Rachel and like Leah.* May your family be increased by her means, as the tribes were formed by means of Rachel and Leah, wives of the patriarch Jacob! *Which two did build the house of Israel.* We have already seen that *ben*, a "son," comes from the root *banah*, "he built"; and hence *eben*, a "stone," because as a house is built of stones, so is a family of children.

12. *Like the house of Pharez.* This was very appropriate; for from Pharez, the son of Judah, by Tamar, came the family of the Bethlehemites and that of Elimelech.

13. *So Boaz took Ruth.* The law of Moses had prohibited the Moabites, even to the tenth generation, from entering into the congregation of the Lord; but this law, the Jews think, did not extend to women; and even if it had, Ruth's might be considered an exempt case, as she already had been incorporated into the family by marriage; and left her own country, people, and gods, to become a proselyte to the true God in the land of Israel.

15. *Better to thee than seven sons.* If Naomi had had even a numerous family of sons, it is most likely that they would have been scattered to different quarters from her, and settled in life; whereas Ruth cleaved to her, and it was by her affectionate services that Naomi was preserved alive.

17. *Her neighbours gave it a name.* That is, they recommended a name suitable to the circumstances of the case; and the parents and grandmother adopted it. *They called his name Obed.* "Serving," from *abad*, "he served." Why was this name given? Because he was to be the "nourisher of her old age," v. 15. *He is the father of Jesse, the father of David.* And for the sake of this conclusion, to ascertain the line of David, and in the counsel of God to fix and ascertain the line of the Messiah, was this instructive little book written.

19. *Hezron begat Ram.* He is called Aram here by the Septuagint, and also by Matthew, chap. i. 3.

20. *Amminadab begat Nahshon.* The Targum adds, "And Nahshon was chief of the house of his father in the tribe of Judah."

The ten persons whose genealogy is recorded in the last five verses may be found, with a trifling change of name, in the genealogical list in Matt. i. 3-6, as forming important links in the line of the Messiah. To introduce this appears to have been the principal object of the writer, as introductory to the following books, where the history of David, the regal progenitor and type of the Messiah, is so particularly detailed.

THE BOOK OF FIRST SAMUEL

I. Samuel (1:1-7:17)
A. Preparation (1:1-4:1a)
1. Birth and childhood (1:1-2:11)
2. Life at Shiloh (2:12-36)
3. Call (3:1-4:1a)
B. Crisis (4:1b-7:1)
1. Eli (4:1b-22)
2. The Ark (5:1-7:1)
C. Judgeship (7:2-17)
1. Twenty years (7:2)
2. Ebenezer (7:3-12)
3. Samuel, governing on circuit (7:13-17)
II. Saul (8:1-15:35)
A. Appointment (8:1-10:27)
1. The people's demand (8:1-22)
2. Samuel's search (9:1-27)
3. Anointing and coronation (10:1-27)
B. Reign (11:1-14:52)
1. Kingdom established (11:1-12:25)
2. Wars (13:1-14:52)
C. Rejection (15:1-35)
1. War with Amalek (15:1-8)
2. Disobedience (15:9-15)
3. Rejection (15:16-34)
4. Samuel mourned for Saul (15:35)
III. David (16:1-31:13)
A. Preparation (16:1-20:42)
1. Anointed (16:1-23)
2. Progress (17:1-18:5)
3. Difficulties (18:6-20:42)
B. In exile (21:1-27:12)
1. Flight (21:1-15)
2. Varied experiences (22:1-27:12)
C. Returning (28:1-31:13)
1. Saul and the witch (28:1-25)
2. David (29:1-30:31)
3. Death of Saul (31:1-13)

This book, and that which follows it, bear the name of Samuel in the title—not because he was the penman of them, but because the first book begins with a large account of him (his birth and childhood, his life and government). The rest of these two volumes that are denominated from him contains the history of the reigns of Saul and David, who were both anointed by him. And, because the history of these two kings takes up the greatest part of these books, the Vulgar Latin calls them the *First* and *Second Books of the Kings,* and the two that follow the *Third* and *Fourth,* which the titles in our English Bibles take notice of with an *alias: otherwise called the First Book of the Kings, etc.* The LXX calls them the first and second Book *of the Kingdoms.*

MATTHEW HENRY

CHAPTER 1

Verses 1-8

We have here an account of the state of the family into which Samuel the prophet was born. His father's name was Elkanah, a Levite, and of the family of the Kohathites (the most honourable house of that tribe) as appears, 1 Chron. vi. 33, 34. His ancestor Zuph was an Ephrathite, that is, of Bethlehem-Judah, which was called *Ephrathah,* Ruth i. 2. There this family of the Levites was first seated, but one branch of it, in process of time, removed to Mount Ephraim, from which Elkanah descended. This Elkanah lived at Ramah, or Ramathaim, which signifies *the double Ramah,* the higher and lower town.

I. It was a devout family. All the families of Israel should be so, but Levites' families in a particular manner. Ministers should be patterns of family religion. Elkanah went up at the solemn feasts to the tabernacle at Shiloh, to *worship and to sacrifice to the Lord of hosts.* Probably Samuel the prophet was the first that used this title of God, for the comfort of Israel, when in his time their hosts were few and feeble and those of their enemies many and mighty; then it would be a support to them to think that the God they served was Lord of hosts, of all the hosts both of heaven and earth. Elkanah was a country Levite, and, for aught that appears, had not any place or office which required his attendance at the tabernacle, but he went up as a common Israelite, with his own sacrifices, to encourage his neighbours and set them a good example. And that which made it the more commendable in him was, 1. That there was a general decay and neglect of religion in the nation. 2. That Hophni and Phinehas, the sons of Eli, were the men that were now chiefly employed in the service of the house of God; and they were men that conducted themselves very ill in their place, yet Elkanah went up to sacrifice. If the priests did not do their duty, he would do his.

II. Yet it was a divided family, and the division of it carried with them both guilt and grief.

1. The original cause of this division was Elkanah's marrying two wives, which was a transgression of the original institution of marriage, to which our Saviour reduces it. Matt. xix. 5, 8, *From the beginning it was not so.* It made mischief in Abraham's family, and Jacob's, and here in Elkanah's.

2. That which followed upon this error was that the two wives could not agree. They had different blessings: Peninnah, like Leah, was fruitful and had many children, which should have made her easy and thankful, though she was but a second wife, and was less beloved; Hannah, like Rachel, was childless indeed, but she was very dear to her husband. But they were of different tempers: Peninnah could not bear the blessing of fruitfulness, but she grew haughty and insolent; Hannah could not bear the affliction of barrenness, but she grew melancholy and discon-

JAMIESON, FAUSSET, BROWN

CHAPTER 1

Vss. 1-8. Of Elkanah and His Two Wives. **1. a certain man of Ramathaim-zophim**—The first word being in the dual number, signifies the double city—the old and new town of Ramah (vs. 19). There were five cities of this name, all on high ground. This city had the addition of Zophim attached to it, because it was founded by Zuph, "an Ephrathite," that is a native of Ephratha. Bethlehem, and the expression of Ramathaim-zophim must, therefore, be understood as Ramah in the land of Zuph in the hill country of Ephratha. Others, considering "mount Ephraim" as pointing to the locality in Joseph's territory, regard "Zophim" not as a proper but a common noun, signifying watchtowers, or watchmen, with reference either to the height of its situation, or its being the residence of prophets who were watchmen (Ezek. 3:17). Though a native of Ephratha or Bethlehem-judah, Elkanah was a Levite (I Chron. 6:33, 34). Though of this order, and a good man, he practised polygamy. This was contrary to the original law, but it seems to have been prevalent among the Hebrews in those days, when there was no king in Israel, and every man did what seemed right in his own eyes. **3. this man went up out of his city yearly to worship in Shiloh**—In that place was the "earth's one sanctuary," and thither he repaired at the three solemn feasts, accompanied by his family at one of them—probably the passover. Although a Levite, he could not personally offer a sacrifice—that was exclusively the office of the priests; and his piety in maintaining a regular attendance on the divine ordinances is the more worthy of notice because the character of the two priests who administered them was notoriously bad. But doubtless he believed, and acted on the belief, that the ordinances were "effectual means of salvation, not from any virtue in them, or in those who administered them, but from the grace of God being communicated through them."

ADAM CLARKE

CHAPTER 1

1. *Ramathaim-zophim.* Literally, "the two high places of the watchman"; these were, no doubt, two contiguous hills, on which watchtowers were built, and in which watchmen kept continual guard for the safety of the country, and which afterwards gave name to the place.

2. *He had two wives.* The custom of those times permitted polygamy; but wherever there was more than one wife, we find the peace of the family greatly disturbed by it. *The name of the one was Hannah.* Channah, which signifies "fixed" or "settled"; and *the other Peninnah,* which signifies a "jewel" or "pearl."

3. *Went up out of his city yearly to worship.* As the ark was at Shiloh, there was the temple of God, and thither all the males were bound by the law to go once a year, on each of the great national festivals: viz., the Passover, Pentecost, and Feast of Tabernacles.

The Lord of hosts. Yehovah tsebaoth, "Jehovah of armies." As all the heavenly bodies were called the "hosts of heaven," *tseba hashshamayim,* Jehovah being called Lord of this host showed that He was their Maker and Governor; and consequently He, not they, was the proper object of religious worship. The sun, moon, planets, and stars were the highest objects of religious worship to the heathen in general. The Jewish religion, teaching the knowlegde of a Being who was the Lord of all these, showed at once its superiority to all that heathenism could boast. This is the first place where *Lord of hosts* is mentioned in the Bible; and this is so much in the style of the prophets Isaiah, Jeremiah, that it gives some weight to the supposition that this book was written by a person who lived in or after the times of these prophets.

MATTHEW HENRY

tented: and Elkanah had a difficult part to act between them.

(1) Elkanah kept up his attendance at God's altar notwithstanding this unhappy difference in his family, and took his wives and children with him, that, if they could not agree in other things, they might agree to worship God together. If the devotions of a family prevail not to put an end to its divisions, yet let not the divisions put a stop to the devotions.

(2) He did all he could to encourage Hannah, and to keep up her spirits under her affliction, *v.* 4, 5. At the feast he offered peace-offerings, to supplicate for peace in his family. [1] He studied to show his love so much the more because she was afflicted, insulted, and low-spirited. [2] He showed his great love to her by the share he gave her of his peace-offerings. Thus we should testify our affection to our friends and relations, by abounding in prayer for them.

(3) Peninnah was extremely peevish and provoking. [1] She upbraided Hannah with her affliction, despised her because she was barren, and gave her taunting language, as one whom Heaven did not favour. [2] She envied the interest she had in the love of Elkanah. [3] She did this most when they *went up to the house of the Lord,* perhaps because then they were more together than at other times, or because then Elkanah showed his affection most to Hannah. That which she designed was to make her fret, perhaps in hopes to break her heart, that she might possess her husband's heart solely.

(4) Hannah (poor woman) could not bear the provocation: *She wept, and did not eat, v.* 7. Yet it was her infirmity so far to give way to the sorrow of the world as to unfit herself for holy joy in God. Those that are of a fretful spirit, and are apt to lay provocations too much to heart, are enemies to themselves, and strip themselves very much of the comforts both of life and godliness.

(5) Elkanah said what he could to her to comfort her. *Hannah, why weepest thou?* Those that by marriage are made one flesh ought thus far to be of one spirit, too, to share in each other's troubles, so that one cannot be easy while the other is uneasy. He intimates that nothing should be wanting on his part to balance her grief: "*Am not I better to thee than ten sons?* Thou knowest thou hast my entire affection, and let that comfort thee." Note, We ought to take notice of our comforts, to keep us from grieving excessively for our crosses; for our crosses we deserve, but our comforts we have forfeited. If we would keep the balance even, we must look at that which is for us, as well as at that which is against us, else we are unjust to Providence and unkind to ourselves.

Verses 9–18

Elkanah had gently reproved Hannah for her inordinate grief, and here we find the good effect of the reproof.

I. It brought her to her meat. She ate and drank, *v.* 9. She did not harden herself in sorrow, nor grow sullen when she was reproved for it. It is as great a piece of self-denial to control our passions as it is to control our appetites.

II. It brought her to her prayers. "Instead of binding the burden thus upon my own shoulders, had I not better ease myself of it, and cast it upon the Lord by prayer?" If ever she will make a more solemn address than ordinary to the throne of grace upon this errand, now is the time. They are at Shiloh, at the door of the tabernacle, where God had promised to meet his people, and which was the *house of prayer.* They had recently offered their peace-offerings. Now concerning Hannah's prayer,

1. The warm and lively devotion there was in it, which appeared in several instances, for our direction in prayer. (1) She improved the present grief and trouble of her spirit for the exciting and quickening of her pious affections in prayer: *Being in bitterness of soul, she prayed, v.* 10. This good use we should made of our afflictions, they should make us the more lively in our addresses to God. Our blessed Saviour himself, *being in an agony, prayed more earnestly,* Luke xxii. 44. (2) She mingled tears with her prayers. It was not a dry prayer: she wept sore. (3) She was very particular, and yet very modest, in her petition. She begged a child, a man-child, that it might be fit to serve in the tabernacle. (4) She made a solemn vow, or promise, that if God would give her a son she would *give him up to God, v.* 11. He would be by birth a Levite, and so devoted to the service of God, but he should be by her vow a Nazarite, and his very childhood should be sacred. Note further, it is very proper, when we are in pursuit of any mercy, to bind our own souls with a bond. Not that hereby we can pretend to merit the gift, but thus we are qualified for it and for the comfort of it. In hope of mercy,

JAMIESON, FAUSSET, BROWN

4. when . . . Elkanah offered, he gave to Peninnah . . . portions—The offerer received back the greater part of the peace offerings, which he and his family or friends were accustomed to eat at a social feast before the Lord. (See on Lev. 3: 7; Deut. 12:12.) It was out of these consecrated viands Elkanah gave portions to all the members of his family; but "unto Hannah he gave a worthy portion"; i.e., a larger choice, according to the Eastern fashion of showing regard to beloved or distinguished guests. (See on ch. 9:23, 24; also Gen. 43:45.) **6. her adversary provoked her sore**—The conduct of Peninnah was most unbecoming. But domestic broils in the houses of polygamists are of frequent occurrence, and the most fruitful cause of them has always been jealousy of the husband's superior affection, as in this case of Hannah.

9-18. HANNAH'S PRAYER. **9-11. she prayed . . . and vowed a vow**—Here is a specimen of the intense desire that reigned in the bosoms of the Hebrew women for children. This was the burden of Hannah's prayer; and the strong preference she expressed for a male child originated in her purpose of dedicating him to the tabernacle service. The circumstance of his birth bound him to this; but his residence within the precincts of the sanctuary would have to commence at an earlier age than usual, in consequence of the Nazarite vow.

ADAM CLARKE

4. *He gave . . . portions.* The sacrifices which were made were probably peace offerings, of which the blood was poured out at the foot of the altar; the fat was burnt on the fire; the breast and right shoulder were the portion of the priest; and the rest belonged to him who made the offering; on it he and his family feasted, each receiving his portion; and to these feasts God commands them to invite the Levite, the poor, the widow, and the orphan, Deut. xvi. 11.

5. *Unto Hannah he gave a worthy portion.* The Hebrew here is very obscure; "He gave her one portion of two faces." As the showbread that was presented to the Lord was called the "bread of faces," because it was placed before the face or appearances of the Lord; probably this was called *manah appayim,* because it was the portion that belonged to, or was placed before, the person who had offered the sacrifice. On this ground it might be said that Elkanah gave Hannah his own portion, or a part of that which was placed before himself. Whatever it was, it was intended as a proof of his especial love to her.

6. *And her adversary.* That is, Peninnah. *Provoked her sore.* Was constantly striving to irritate and vex her, *to make her fret*—to make her discontented with her lot, because the Lord had denied her children.

7. *And as he did so year by year.* As the whole family went up to Shiloh to the annual festivals, Peninnah had both sons and daughters to accompany her, v. 4, but Hannah had none; and Peninnah took this opportunity particularly to twit Hannah with her barrenness, by making an ostentatious exhibition of her children. *Therefore she wept.* She was greatly distressed, because it was a great reproach to a woman among the Jews to be barren; because, say some, everyone hoped that the Messiah should spring from her line.

8. *Am not I better to thee than ten sons?* Ten, a certain for an uncertain number. Is not my especial affection for you better than all the comfort you could gain, even from a numerous family?

11. *I will give him unto the Lord.* Samuel, as a descendant of the house of Levi, was the Lord's property from twenty-five years of age till fifty; but the vow here implies that he should be consecrated to the Lord from his infancy to his death, and that he should act not only as a Levite, but as a Nazarite, on whose head no razor should pass.

MATTHEW HENRY

let us promise duty. (5) She spoke all this so softly that none could hear her. Her lips moved, but *her voice was not heard, v.* 13. She trusted God's knowledge of the heart. Thoughts are words to him.

2. The hard censure she fell under for it. Eli was now high priest, and judge in Israel; he sat upon a seat in the temple, to oversee what was done there, *v.* 9. The tabernacle is here called the *temple*, because it was now fixed, and served all the purposes of a temple. There Eli sat to receive addresses and give direction, and somewhere (it is probable in a private corner) he espied Hannah at her prayers, and by her unusual manner fancied she was drunken, and spoke to her accordingly (*v.* 14): *How long wilt thou be drunken?*—the very imputation that Peter and the apostles fell under when the Holy Ghost *gave them utterance*, Acts ii. 13. Perhaps in this degenerate age it was no strange thing to see drunken women at the door of the tabernacle. When a disease is epidemical every one is suspected to be tainted with it. She had been reproved by Elkanah because she would not eat and drink, and now to be reproached by Eli as if she had eaten and drunk too much was very hard.

3. Hannah's humble vindication of herself from this crime with which she was charged. (1) In justice to herself she expressly denies the charge. "No, my lord, it is not as you suspect; I have drunk neither wine nor strong drink, not any at all, *count not thy handmaid for a daughter of Belial.*" Note, The very manner of her speaking in her own defence was sufficient to demonstrate that she was not drunk. (2) In justice to him, she gives an account of her present behaviour. She had been more than ordinarily fervent in prayer to God, and this, she tells him, was the true reason of the transport and disorder she seemed to be in.

4. The atonement Eli made for his rash unfriendly censure, by a kind and fatherly benediction, *v.* 17. He now encouraged Hannah's devotions as much as before he had discountenanced them; and intimated that he was satisfied of her innocency by those words, *Go in peace. The God of Israel grant thee thy petition*, whatever it is, *that thou hast asked of him.*

5. The great satisfaction of mind with which Hannah now went away, *v.* 18. She went her way and did eat of what remained of the peace-offerings *and her countenance was no more sad.* Whence came this sudden happy change? She had by prayer committed her case to God and left it with him, and now she was no more perplexed about it. She had prayed for herself, and Eli had prayed for her; and she believed that God would either give her the mercy she had prayed for or make up the want of it to her some other way. Prayer is heart's ease to a gracious soul.

Verses 19–28

I. The return of Elkanah and his family to their own habitation, when the days appointed for the feast were over, *v.* 19. They had a journey before them, and a family of children to take with them, and yet they would not stir till they had worshipped God together. Prayer and provender do not hinder a journey.

II. The birth and name of this desired son. At length the Lord remembered Hannah, for she conceived and bore a son. This son the mother called *Samuel, v.* 20. Some make the etymology of this name to be much the same with that of *Ishmael—heard of God*, because the mother's prayers were remarkably heard, and he was an answer to them. Others, because of the reason she gives for the name, make it to signify *asked of God.* Mercies in answer to prayer are to be remembered with peculiar expressions of thankfulness, as Ps. cxvi. 1, 2. How many seasonable deliverances and supplies may we call *Samuels, asked of God*! He was asked of God and was at the same time dedicated to him.

III. The close attendance Hannah gave to the nursing of him, not only because he was dear to her, but because he was devoted to God. Hannah, though she felt a warm regard for the courts of God's house, begged leave of her husband to stay at home; for the women were not under any obligation to go up to the three yearly feasts, as the men were. However Hannah had been accustomed to go, but now desired to be excused, 1. Because she would not be so long absent from her nursery. God will have mercy and not sacrifice. Those that are detained from public ordinances by the nursing and tending of little children may take comfort from this instance, and believe that, if they do that with an eye to God, he will graciously accept them therein. 2. Because she would not go up to Shiloh till her son was big enough, not only to be taken thither, but to be left there; for, if once she took him thither, she thought she could

JAMIESON, FAUSSET, BROWN

12-18. Eli marked her mouth—The suspicion of the aged priest seems to indicate that the vice of intemperance was neither uncommon nor confined to one sex in those times of disorder.

This mistaken impression was immediately removed, and, in the words, "God grant," or rather, "will grant," was followed by an invocation which, as Hannah regarded it in the light of a prophecy pointing to the accomplishment of her earnest desire, dispelled her sadness, and filled her with confident hope. The character and services of the expected child were sufficiently important to make his birth a fit subject for prophecy.

20. SAMUEL BORN. **20. called his name Samuel**—doubtless with her husband's consent. The names of children were given sometimes by the fathers, and sometimes by the mothers (see on Gen. 4:1, 26; 5:29; 19:37; 21:3); and among the early Hebrews, they were commonly compound names, one part including the name of God.

21. the man Elkanah . . . went up to offer . . . his vow—The solemn expression of his concurrence in Hannah's vow was necessary to make it obligatory. (See on Num. 30.) **22. But Hannah went not up**—Men only were obliged to attend the solemn feasts (Exod. 23: 17). But Hannah, like other pious women, was in the habit of going, only she deemed it more prudent and becoming to defer her next journey till her son's age would enable her to fulfil her vow.

ADAM CLARKE

9. *Eli . . . sat upon a seat. Al hakkisse*, upon the throne, i.e., of judgment; for he was then judge of Israel. *By a post of the temple of the Lord.* I think this is the first place where *heychal Yehovah*, "temple of Jehovah," is mentioned. This gives room for a strong suspicion that the Books of Samuel were not compiled till the first Temple was built, or after the days of Solomon. After this the word *temple* is frequent in the books of Kings, Chronicles, and in the prophets.

13. *Spake in her heart; only her lips moved.* She prayed; her whole heart was engaged. And though she spake not with an audible voice, yet her lips formed themselves according to the pronunciation of the words which her *heart* uttered.

15. *I have drunk neither wine nor strong drink.* "Neither wine nor inebriating drink has been *poured out unto me;* but I have poured out my soul unto the Lord." There is a great deal of delicacy and point in this vindication.

16. *Count not thine handmaid for a daughter of Belial.* "Put not thy handmaiden before the faces of a daughter of Belial." "If I am a drunkard, and strive by the most execrable hypocrisy (praying in the house of God) to cover my iniquity, then I am the chief of the daughters of Belial." Or, "Give not thy handmaid (to reproach) before the faces of the daughters of Belial."

17. *Grant thee thy petition.* He was satisfied he had formed a wrong judgment, and by it had added to the distress of one already sufficiently distressed. The fact that Eli supposed her to be *drunken*, and the other of the conduct of Eli's sons, prove that religion was at this time at a very low ebb in Shiloh; for it seems drunken women did come to the place, and lewd women were to be found there.

18. *Let thine handmaid find grace.* Continue to think favorably of me, and to pray for me.

20. *Called his name Samuel.* As she gave this name to her son because she had *asked him of the Lord*, the word *Shemuel* must be here considerably contracted; if it express this sentiment, the component parts of it are the following: *shaul meEl*, "asked of God." This name would put both the mother and the son in continual remembrance of the divine interposition at his birth (see on v. 28).

21. *The man Elkanah, and all his house.* He and the whole of his family, Hannah and her child excepted, who purposed not to go up to Shiloh till her son was old enough to be employed in the divine service. *And his vow.* Probably he had also made some vow to the Lord on the occasion of his wife's prayer and vow; in which, from his love to her, he could not be less interested than herself.

MATTHEW HENRY

never find in her heart to bring him back again.

IV. The solemn entering of this child into the service of the sanctuary. Some think it was as soon as he was weaned from the breast, which, the Jews say, was not till he was three years old. Others think it was not till he was weaned from childish things, at eight or ten years old. It is said (*v.* 24), *The child was young.* Observe how she presented her child, 1. With a sacrifice; no less than three bullocks, with a meat-offering for each, *v.* 24. A bullock, perhaps, for each year of the child's life. Or one for a burnt-offering, another for a sin-offering, and the third for a peace-offering. 2. With a grateful acknowledgment of God's goodness in answer to prayer. This she makes to Eli, because he had encouraged her to hope for an answer of peace (*v.* 26, 27): *"For this child I prayed."* 3. With a full surrender of all her interest in this child unto the Lord (*v.* 28): *I have lent him to the Lord as long as he liveth.* (1) Whatever we give to God, it is what we have first asked and received from him. *Of thy own, Lord, have we given thee,* 1 Chron. xxix. 14, 16. (2) Whatever we give to God may upon this account be said to be *lent* to him. When by baptism we dedicate our children to God, let us remember that they were his before by a sovereign right, and that they are ours still so much the more to our comfort.

Lastly, The child Samuel did his part beyond what could have been expected from one of his years; for of him that seems to be spoken, *He worshipped the Lord there,* that is, *he said his prayers.* Little children should learn betimes to worship God. Their parents should instruct them in his worship and bring them to it, put them upon engaging in it as well as they can, and God will graciously accept them and teach them to do better.

JAMIESON, FAUSSET, BROWN

24. three bullocks—*Sept.* renders it "a bullock of three years old"; which is probably the true rendering.

JOHN LANGE:

Verse 28. "And also I" refers back to the words "and the Lord hath given me," and implies a requital, "and I in my turn." It cannot be shown that it means "lend," as is generally assumed; it occurs in 1 Sam. 1:28, in the sense of "grant," "give." Further, the signification "lend" is here inappropriate, because the "I also" expressly brings out the correspondence to the "gave" of verse 27. It means "cause to ask or demand," "grant what is demanded," "give." The sense is: the Lord gave him to me, and so have I given him to the Lord, as one asked or demanded. Calvin: "The sense is plain enough—namely, that she gave, dedicated to God the child obtained from Him by prayer." The short concluding sentence "he is asked for the Lord" expresses her determination to give him to the Lord for His service.

—*Commentary on the Holy Scriptures*

ADAM CLARKE

24. *With three bullocks.* The Septuagint, the Syriac, and the Arabic read, "a bullock of three years old"; and this is probably correct, because we read, v. 25, that they slew "the bullock." We hear of no more, and we know that a bullock or heifer of three years old was ordinarily used; see Gen. xv. 9. *One ephah of flour.* Seven gallons and a half. *A bottle of wine.* "A skin full of wine." Their bottles for wine and fluids in general were made out of skins of goats, stripped off without being cut up; the places whence the legs were extracted sewed up, as also the lower part; and the top tied. These three things, the ox, the flour, and the wine, probably constituted the consecration offering.

26. *As thy soul liveth.* As sure as you are a living soul, so surely am I the person who stood by you here praying.

28. *Therefore also I have lent him to the Lord.* There is here a continual reference to her vow, and to the words which she used in making that vow. The word "Samuel," as we have already seen, is a contraction of the words *Shaul meEl,* that is, "asked or lent of God"; for his mother said, v. 27, "The Lord hath given me my petition, which [*shaalti*] I asked of him." In v. 28 she says: *hu shaul layhovah,* "He shall be lent unto the Lord." Here we find the verb is the same; and it is remarked by grammarians that *shaal,* "he asked," making in the participle *pahul shaul,* "asked," in the conjugation *hiphil* signifies to "lend"; therefore, says his mother, v. 28, *hishiltihu layhovah,* "I have lent him to the Lord." This twofold meaning of the Hebrew root is not only followed by our translators, but also by the Vulgate, Septuagint, and Syriac.

And he worshipped the Lord there. Instead of *he worshipped,* "they worshipped" is the reading of six of Kennicott's and De Rossi's MSS., of some copies of the Septuagint, and of the Vulgate, Syriac, and Arabic.

MATTHEW HENRY — CHAPTER 2

Verses 1–10

We have here Hannah's thanksgiving, dictated, not only by the spirit of prayer, but by the spirit of prophecy. Observe in general, 1. When she had received mercy from God she owned it, with thankfulness to his praise. Praise is our rent, our tribute. We are unjust if we do not pay it. 2. The mercy she had received was an answer to prayer, and therefore she thought herself especially obliged to give thanks for it. 3. Her thanksgiving is here called a prayer: *Hannah prayed*; for thanksgiving is an essential part of prayer. *Her voice was not heard;* but in her thanksgiving she spoke, that all might hear her. She made her supplication *with groanings that could not be uttered,* but now her lips were opened to *show forth God's praise.* Three things we have in this thanksgiving:

I. Hannah's triumph in God, in his glorious perfections, and the great things he had done for her, *v.* 1–3.

1. What great things she says of God. She takes little notice of the particular mercy she was now rejoicing in. She overlooks the gift, and praises the giver; whereas most forget the giver and fasten only on the gift. Four of God's glorious attributes Hannah here celebrates, (1) His unspotted purity. *There is none holy as the Lord.* (2) His almighty power: *Neither is there any rock like our God.* (3) His unsearchable wisdom: *The Lord,* the Judge of all, *is a God of knowledge.* (4) His unerring justice: *By him actions are weighed.*

2. How she solaces herself in these things. What we give God the glory of we may take the comfort of. Hannah does so, (1) In holy joy: *My heart rejoiceth in the Lord*; not so much in her son as in her God. (2) In holy triumph: *"My horn is exalted*; not only is my reputation saved by my having a son, but greatly raised by having such a son." *My horn is exalted* means this, "My praises are very much elevated to an unusual strain." *My mouth is enlarged,* that is, "Now I have wherewith to answer those that reproached me."

3. How she herewith silences those that set up themselves as rivals with God and rebels against him (*v.* 3): *Talk no more so exceedingly proudly.*

II. The notice she takes of the wisdom and sovereignty of the divine providence, in its disposals of the affairs of the children of men.

1. The strong are soon weakened and the weak are soon strengthened, when God pleases, *v.* 4. On

JAMIESON, FAUSSET, BROWN — CHAPTER 2

VSS. 1-11. HANNAH'S SONG IN THANKFULNESS TO GOD. **1. Hannah prayed, and said**—Praise and prayer are inseparably conjoined in Scripture (Col. 4:2; I Tim. 2:1). This beautiful song was her tribute of thanks for the divine goodness in answering her petition.

mine horn is exalted in the Lord—Allusion is here made to a peculiarity in the dress of Eastern women about Lebanon, which seems to have obtained anciently among the Israelite women, that of wearing a tin or silver horn on the forehead, on which their veil is suspended. Wives, who have no children, wear it projecting in an oblique direction, while those who become mothers forthwith raise it a few inches higher, inclining towards the perpendicular, and by this slight but observable change in their headdress, make known, wherever they go, the maternal character which they now bear.

ADAM CLARKE — CHAPTER 2

1. *And Hannah prayed, and said.* The Chaldee very properly says, "And Hannah prayed in the spirit of prophecy"; for indeed the whole of this prayer, or as it may be properly called "oracular declaration," is a piece of regular prophecy, every part of it having respect to the future, and perhaps not a little of it declaratory of the Messiah's kingdom. In the best MSS. the whole of this hymn is written in hemistich or poetic lines. I shall here produce it in this order, following the plan as exhibited in Kennicott's Bible, with some trifling alterations of our present version:

1. *My heart exulteth in Jehovah;*
My horn is exalted in Jehovah.
My mouth is incited over mine enemies,
For I have rejoiced in thy salvation.
2. *There is none holy like Jehovah,*
For there is none besides thee;
There is no rock like our God.
3. *Do not magnify yourselves, speak not proudly, proudly.*
Let not prevarication come out of your mouth;
For the God of knowledge is Jehovah,
And by him actions are directed.
4. *The bows of the heroes are broken,*
And the tottering are girded with strength.
5. *The full have hired out themselves for bread,*
And the famished cease for ever.
The barren hath borne seven,
And she who had many children is greatly enfeebled.
6. *Jehovah killeth, and maketh alive;*
He bringeth down to the grave, and bringeth up.
7. *Jehovah maketh poor, and maketh rich;*
He bringeth down, and he even exalteth.
8. *He lifteth up the poor from the dust;*
From the dunghill he exalteth the beggar,
To make him sit with the nobles,
And inherit the throne of glory.
For to Jehovah belong the pillars of the earth,
And upon them he hath placed the globe.

MATTHEW HENRY

the one hand, if he speak the word, *the bows of the mighty men are broken*; they are disarmed, disabled to do as they have before done and as they have designed to do. On the other hand, if the Lord speak the word, those who stumble through weakness, who were so feeble that they could not go straight or steady, are *girded with strength*, in body and mind, and are able to bring great things to pass.

2. The rich are soon impoverished, and the poor strangely enriched on a sudden, *v.* 5. *Riches flee away* (Prov. xxiii. 5), and leave those miserable who, when they had them, placed their happiness in them. To those that have been full and free poverty and slavery must needs be doubly grievous. But, on the other hand, sometimes Providence so orders it that *those who are hungry cease*, that is, cease to hire out themselves for bread as they have done. It may be understood of the same person; those that were rich God makes poor. and after awhile makes rich again, as Job; he gave, he takes away, and then gives again, Let not the rich be proud and secure, for God can soon make them poor; let not the poor despond and despair, for God can in due time enrich them again.

3. Empty families are replenished and numerous families diminished and made few. *The barren hath borne seven*, meaning herself, for, though at present she had but one son, yet that one being a Nazarite, devoted to God and employed in his immediate service, he was to her as good as seven. Or it is the language of her faith. Now that she had one she hoped for more, and was not disappointed.

4. God is the sovereign Lord of life and death (*v.* 6): *The Lord killeth and maketh alive*. Nothing is too hard for God to do, no, not the quickening of the dead, and putting life into dry bones.

5. Advancement and abasement are both from him. He brings some low and lifts up others (*v.* 7), humbles the proud and gives grace and honour to the lowly, lays those in the dust that would vie with the God above them and trample upon all about them (Job xl. 12, 13), but lifts up those with his salvation that humble themselves before him, Jam. iv. 10. Joseph, and Daniel, Moses and David, were thus strangely advanced, from a prison to a palace, from a sheep-hook to a sceptre.

6. A reason is given for all these dispensations which obliges us to acquiesce in them, how surprising soever they are: *For the pillars of the earth are the Lord's*. (1) If we understand this literally, it intimates God's almighty power, which cannot be controlled. He upholds the whole creation, founded the earth, and still sustains it by the word of his power. What cannot he do in the affairs of families and kingdoms, far beyond our conception and expectation, *who hangs the earth upon nothing*? Job xxvi. 7. But, (2) If we understand it figuratively, it intimates his incontestable sovereignty, which cannot be disputed. The princes and great ones of the earth, the directors of states and governments, are the *pillars of the earth*, Ps. lxxv. 3. On these hinges the affairs of the world seem to turn, but they are the Lord's, Ps. xlvii. 9. From him they have their power, and therefore he may advance whom he pleases; and who may say, *What doest thou*?

III. A prediction of the preservation and advancement of all God's faithful friends, and the destruction of all his and their enemies. Having testified her joyful triumph in what God had done, and is doing, she concludes with joyful hopes of what he would do, *v.* 9, 10. Pious affections in those days rose many times to the height of prophecy. This prophecy may refer, 1. More immediately to the government of Israel by Samuel, and by David whom he was employed to anoint. Israel (that in the time of the judges had made so small a figure and had much ado to subsist) should now shortly become great and considerable, and give law to all its neighbours. An extraordinary change that was; and the birth of Samuel was, as it were, the dawning of that day. But, 2. We have reason to think that this prophecy looks further, to the kingdom of Christ, and the administration of that kingdom of grace, of which she now comes to speak, having spoken so largely of the kingdom of providence. And here is the first time that we meet with the name *Messiah*, or *his Anointed*. The ancient expositors, both Jewish and Christian, make it to look beyond David, to the Son of David. Glorious things are here spoken of the kingdom of the Mediator. Concerning that kingdom we are here assured, (1) That all the loyal subjects of it shall be carefully and powerfully protected (*v.* 9): *He will keep the feet of his saints*. If he will keep their feet, much more their head and hearts. Or he will keep their feet, that is, he will secure the ground they stand on, and establish their goings; he will set a guard of grace upon their affections and

JAMIESON, FAUSSET, BROWN

5. they that were hungry ceased—i.e., to hunger.

the barren hath born seven—i.e., many children.

6. he bringeth down to the grave, and bringeth up—i.e., He reduces to the lowest state of degradation and misery, and restores to prosperity and happiness.

8. He raiseth up the poor out of the dust, and lifteth up the beggar from the dunghill—The dunghill, a pile of horse, cow, or camel offal, heaped up to dry in the sun, and used as fuel, was, and is, one of the common haunts of the poorest mendicants; and the change that had been made in the social position of Hannah, appeared to her grateful heart as auspicious and as great as the elevation of a poor despised beggar to the highest and most dignified rank. **inherit the throne of glory**—i.e., possesses seats of honor.

ADAM CLARKE

9. *The foot of his saints he shall keep*
And the wicked shall be silent in darkness;
For by strength shall no man prevail.
10. *Jehovah shall bruise them who contend with him;*
Upon them shall be thunder in the earth;
And he shall give strength to his King,
And shall exalt the horn of his Messiah.

It is not particularly stated here when Hannah composed or delivered this hymn; it appears from the connection to have been at the very time in which she dedicated her son to God at the Tabernacle, though some think that she composed it immediately on the birth of Samuel. The former sentiment is probably the most correct.

Mine horn is exalted in the Lord. We have often seen that *horn* signifies power, might, and dominion. It is thus constantly used in the Bible, and was so used among the heathens. *My mouth is enlarged*. My faculty of speech is "incited, stirred up," to express God's disapprobation against my adversaries.

2. *None holy*. Holiness is peculiar to the God of Israel; no false god ever pretended to holiness. It was no attribute of heathenism, nor of any religion ever professed in the world before or since the true revelation of the true God. *There is none beside thee*. There can be but one unoriginated, infinite, and eternal Being; that Being is Jehovah. *Any rock like our God*. Rabbi Maimon has observed that the word *tsur*, which we translate *rock*, signifies, when applied to Jehovah, "fountain, source, spring." There is no source whence continual help and salvation can arise but our God.

3. *A God of knowledge*. He is the most wise, teaching all good, and knowing all things. *Actions are weighed*. *Nithkenu*, they are "directed"; it is by His counsel alone that we can successfully begin, continue, or end, any work.

5. *They that were full*. All the things mentioned in these verses frequently happen in the course of the divine providence; and indeed it is the particular providence of God that Hannah seems more especially to celebrate through the whole of this simple yet sublime ode.

6. *The Lord killeth*. God is the Arbiter of life and death; He only can give life, and He only has a right to take it away. *He bringeth down to the grave*. The Hebrew word *sheol*, which we translate *grave*, seems to have the same meaning in the Old Testament with *hades* in the New, which is the word generally used by the Septuagint for the other. It means the grave, the state of the dead, and the invisible place, or place of separate spirits. Sometimes we translate it "hell," which now means the state of perdition, or place of eternal torments. The Targum seems to understand it of death and the resurrection. "He kills and commands to give life; he causes to descend into Sheol, that in the time to come he may bring them into the lives of eternity," i.e., the life of shame and everlasting contempt, and the life of glory.

7. *The Lord maketh poor*. For many cannot bear affluence, and if God should continue to trust them with riches, they would be their ruin. *Maketh rich*. Some He can trust, and therefore makes them stewards of His secular bounty.

8. *To set them among princes*. There have been many cases where, in the course of God's providence, a person has been raised from the lowest and most abject estate to the highest; from the plough to the imperial dignity; from the dungeon to the throne; from the dunghill to nobility. The story is well-known of the patriarch Joseph. *For the pillars of the earth are the Lord's*. He is almighty, and upholds all things by the word of His power.

9. *He will keep the feet of his saints*. He will order and direct all their goings, and keep them from every evil way. The wicked shall be silent in darkness. The Targum understands this of their being sent to the darkness of hell; they shall be slain. *By strength shall no man prevail*. Because God is omnipotent, and no power can be successfully exerted against Him.

MATTHEW HENRY

actions, that their feet may neither wander out of the way nor stumble in the way. (2) That all the powers engaged against it shall not be able to effect the ruin of it. (3) That all the enemies of it will certainly be broken and brought down: *The wicked shall be silent in darkness, v.* 9. (4) That the conquests of this kingdom shall extend themselves to distant regions: *The Lord shall judge the ends of the earth.* David's victories and dominions reached far, but the *uttermost parts of the earth* are promised to the Messiah for his *possession* (Ps. ii. 8). (5) That the power and honour of Messiah the prince shall grow and increase more and more: *He shall give strength unto his king,* for the accomplishing of his great undertaking (Ps. lxxxix. 21, and see Luke xxii. 43), strengthen him to go through the difficulties of his humiliation, and in his exaltation he will *lift up the head* (Ps. cx. 7), lift up the horn, the power and honour, of his *anointed,* and *make him higher than the kings of the earth,* Ps. lxxxix. 27.

Verses 11–26

In these verses we have the good character of Elkanah's family, and the bad character of Eli's family.

I. Let us see how well things went in Elkanah's family and how much better than formerly. 1. Eli dismissed them from the house of the Lord, when they had entered their little son there, with a blessing, *v.* 20. If Hannah had then had many children, it would not have been such a generous piece of piety to part with one out of many for the service of the tabernacle; but when she had but one, to present him to the Lord was such an act of heroic piety as should by no means lose its reward. As when Abraham had offered Isaac he received the promise of a numerous issue (Gen. xxii. 16, 17), so did Hannah, when she had presented Samuel unto the Lord a living sacrifice. 2. They returned to their own habitation. This is twice mentioned, *v.* 11, and again *v.* 20. 3. They kept up their constant attendance at the house of God with their *yearly sacrifice, v.* 19. They did not think that their son's ministering there would excuse them. We may suppose they went thither to see their child oftener than once a year, for it was not ten miles from Ramah; but their annual visit is taken notice of because then they brought their yearly sacrifice, and then Hannah fitted up her son (and some think oftener than once a year) with a new suit of clothes, *a little coat* (*v.* 19) and everything belonging to it. 4. The child Samuel did very well. Four separate times he is mentioned in these verses, and two things we are told of:—(1) The service he did to the Lord. He did well indeed, for he *ministered to the Lord* (*v.* 11, 18). Perhaps he attended immediately on Eli's person. He could light a candle, or hold a dish, or run on an errand, or shut a door; and, because he did this with a pious disposition of mind it is called *ministering to the Lord.* (2) The blessing he received from the Lord. He *grew before the Lord,* as a tender plant (*v.* 21), *grew on* (*v.* 26) in strength and stature, and especially in wisdom and understanding. *He was in favour with the Lord and with man.* What is here said of Samuel is said of our blessed Saviour, that great example, Luke ii. 52.

II. Let us now see how ill things went in Eli's family, though seated at the very door of the tabernacle. The nearer the church the further from God. 1. The abominable wickedness of Eli's sons (*v.* 12): *The sons of Eli were sons of Belial.* It is emphatically expressed. *They knew not the Lord.* They were resident at the fountain-head both of magistracy and ministry, and yet they were *sons of Belial,* and their honour, power, and learning, made them so much the worse. It is hard to say which dishonours God more, idolatry or profaneness, especially the profaneness of the priests.

(1) They profaned the offerings of the Lord, and made a gain to themselves, or rather a gratification of their own luxury, out of them. [1] They robbed the offerers, and seized for themselves some of their part of the sacrifice of the peace-offerings. The priests had for their share the *wave-breast* and the *heave shoulder* (Lev. vii. 34), but these did not content them. [2] They stepped in before God himself, and encroached upon his right too. *As if it were a small thing to weary men, they wearied my God also,* Isa. vii. 13. The effect was, *First,* That God was displeased: *The sin of the young men was very great before the Lord, v.* 17. *Secondly,* That religion suffered by it: *Men abhorred the offerings of the Lord.* In the midst of this sad story comes in the repeated mention of Samuel's devotion. *But Samuel ministered before the Lord,* as an instance of the power of God's grace, in preserving him pure and pious in the midst of this wicked crew; and this helped to keep up the

JAMIESON, FAUSSET, BROWN

10. the Lord shall judge the ends of the earth . . . exalt the horn of his anointed—This is the first place in Scripture where the word "anointed," or Messiah, occurs; and as there was no king in Israel at the time, it seems the best interpretation to refer it to Christ. There is, indeed, a remarkable resemblance between the song of Hannah and that of Mary (Luke 1:46).

20. Eli blessed Elkanah and his wife—This blessing, like that which he had formerly pronounced, had a prophetic virtue; which, before long, appeared in the increase of Hannah's family (vs. 21), and the growing qualifications of Samuel for the service of the sanctuary.

11. the child did minister unto the Lord before Eli the priest—He must have been engaged in some occupation suited to his tender age, as in playing upon the cymbals, or other instruments of music; in lighting the lamps, or similar easy and interesting services. **19. his mother made him a little coat, and brought it to him from year to year**—Aware that he could not yet render any useful service to the tabernacle, she undertook the expense of supplying him with wearing apparel. All weaving stuffs, manufacture of cloth, and making of suits were anciently the employment of women.

12-17. The Sin of Eli's Sons. **12. Now the sons of Eli were sons of Belial**—not only careless and irreligious, but men loose in their actions, and vicious and scandalous in their habits. Though professionally engaged in sacred duties, they were not only strangers to the power of religion in the heart, but they had thrown off its restraints, and even ran, as is sometimes done in similar cases by the sons of eminent ministers, to the opposite extreme of reckless and open profligacy. **13. the priest's custom with the people**—When persons wished to present a sacrifice of peace offering on the altar, the offering was brought in the first instance to the priest, and as the Lord's part was burnt, the parts appropriated respectively to the priests and offerers were to be sodden. But Eli's sons, unsatisfied with the breast and shoulder, which were the perquisites appointed to them by the divine law (Exod. 29:27; Lev. 7:31, 32), not only claimed part of the offerer's share, but rapaciously seized them previous to the sacred ceremony of heaving or waving (see on Lev. 7:34); and moreover they committed the additional injustice of taking up with their fork those portions which they preferred, while still raw. Pious people revolted at such rapacious and profane encroachments on the dues of the altar, as well as what should have gone to constitute the family and social feast of the offerer. The truth is, the priests having become haughty and unwilling in many instances to accept invitations to those feasts, presents of meat were sent to them; and this, though done in courtesy at first, being, in course of time, established into a right, gave rise to all the rapacious keenness of Eli's sons.

18-26. Samuel's Ministry. **18. But Samuel ministered before the Lord, being a child**—This notice of his early services in the outer courts of the tabernacle was made to pave the way for the remarkable prophecy regarding the high priest's family. **girded with a linen ephod**—A small shoulder-garment or apron, used in the sacred service by the inferior priests and Levites; sometimes also by judges or eminent persons, and hence allowed to Samuel, who, though not a Levite, was devoted to God from his birth.

ADAM CLARKE

10. *The adversaries of the Lord shall be broken.* Those who "contend with him" by sinning against His laws, opposing the progress of His word, or persecuting His people. *Shall judge the ends of the earth.* His empire shall be extended over all mankind by the preaching of the everlasting gospel, for to this the afterpart of the verse seems to apply: "He shall give strength unto his king, and shall exalt the horn of his anointed [Christ]," or, as the Targum says, "He shall multiply the kingdom of the Messiah." Here *the horn* means spiritual as well as secular dominion.

20. *Eli blessed Elkanah.* The natural place of this verse seems to be before the eleventh; after which the twenty-first should come in; after the twenty-first, perhaps the twenty-sixth should come in. The subjects in this chapter seem very much entangled and confused by the wrong position of the verses.

19. *Made him a little coat.* "A little cloak," an upper garment; probably intended to keep him from the cold, and to save his other clothes from being abused in his meaner services. It is probable that she furnished him with a new one each year, when she came up to one of the annual sacrifices.

12. *The sons of Eli were sons of Belial.* They were perverse, wicked, profligate men.

13. *When any man offered sacrifice.* That is, when a peace offering was brought, the right shoulder and the breast belonged to the priest, the fat was burnt upon the altar, and the blood was poured at the bottom of the altar; the rest of the flesh belonged to the offerer. Under pretense of taking only their own part, they took the best of all they chose, and as much as they chose.

15. *Before they burnt the fat.* They would serve themselves before God was served! This was iniquity and arrogance of the first magnitude. *He will not have sodden flesh.* He chooses roast meat, not boiled; and if they had it in the pot before the servant came, he took it out that it might be roasted.

17. *Wherefore the sin of the young men was very great.* That is, Hophni and Phinehas, the sons of Eli. *Men abhorred the offering.* As the people saw that the priests had no piety, and that they acted as if there was no God, they despised God's service, and became infidels.

MATTHEW HENRY

sinking credit of the sanctuary in the minds of the people.

(2) They debauched the women that came to worship at the door of the tabernacle, *v.* 22.

2. The reproof which Eli gave his sons for this their wickedness: *Eli was very old* (*v.* 22) and could not himself inspect the service of the tabernacle as he had done, but left all to his sons, who, because of the infirmities of his age, slighted him, and did what they would. It should seem he did not so much as reprove them till he heard of their debauching the women, and then he thought fit to give them a check. Now concerning the reproof he gave them observe,

(1) That it was very just and rational. That which he said was very proper. [1] He tells them that the matter of fact was too plain to be denied and too public to be concealed: "*I hear of your evil dealings by all this people,*" *v.* 23. [2] He shows them the bad consequences of it, that they not only sinned, but made Israel to sin, and would have the people's sin to answer for as well as their own. [3] He warns them of the danger they brought themselves into by it, *v.* 25. He intimates to them what God afterwards told him, that the *iniquity* would not be *purged with sacrifice nor offering, ch.* iii. 14.

(2) It was too mild and gentle. He should have rebuked them sharply. Their crimes deserved sharpness; their temper needed it; the softness of his dealing with them would but harden them the more. What he said was right, but it was not enough.

3. Their obstinacy against this reproof. They *hearkened not to their father*, though he was also a judge. Samuel's tractableness is again mentioned (*v.* 26), to shame their obstinacy: *The child Samuel grew.* God's grace is his own; he denied it to the sons of the high priest and gave it to the child of an obscure country Levite.

Verses 27–36

Eli reproved his sons too gently, and did not threaten them as he should, and therefore God sent a prophet to him to reprove him sharply. The message is sent to Eli himself, because God would bring him to repentance and save him; not to his sons, whom he had determined to destroy.

I. He reminds him of the great things God had done for the house of his fathers and for his family. He appeared to Aaron in Egypt (Exod. iv. 27), in the house of bondage, as a token of further favour which he designed for him, *v.* 27. He advanced him to the priesthood, entailed it upon his family, and thereby dignified it above any of the families of Israel.

II. He exhibits a high charge against him and his family. His children did wickedly, and he connived at it, and thereby involved himself in the guilt; the indictment therefore runs against them all, *v.* 29. 1. His sons had impiously profaned the holy things of God: "*You kick at my sacrifice which I have commanded.*" 2. Eli had bolstered them up in it, by not punishing their insolence and impiety: "Thou for thy part *honourest thy sons above me.*" 3. They had all shared in the gains of the sacrilege. It is to be feared that Eli himself, though he disliked and reproved the abuses they committed, yet did not forbear to eat of the roast meat they sacrilegiously got, *v.* 15.

III. He declares the cutting off of the entail of the high priesthood from his family (*v.* 30): *I said, indeed, that thy house, and the house of thy father* Ithamar (for from that younger son of Aaron Eli descended), *should walk before me for ever.* Upon what occasion the dignity of the high priesthood was transferred from the family of Eleazar to that of Ithamar does not appear; but it seems this had been done, and Eli stood fair to have that honour perpetuated to his posterity. But observe, the promise carried its own condition along with it: *They shall walk before me for ever*, that is, "they shall have the honour, provided they faithfully do the service." *Walking before God* is the great condition of the covenant, Gen. xvii. 1. Let them set me before their face, and I will set them before my face continually (Ps. xli. 12), otherwise not. But now the Lord says, *Be it far from me.* "Now that you cast me off you can expect no other than that I should cast you off; you will not walk before me as you should, and therefore you shall not."

IV. He gives a good reason for this revocation, taken from a settled and standing rule of God's government, according to which all must expect to be dealt with (like that by which Cain was tried, Gen. iv. 7): *Those that honour me I will honour, and those that despise me shall be lightly esteemed.* The way to be truly great is to be truly good. If we humble and deny ourselves in anything to honour

JAMIESON, FAUSSET, BROWN

22. the women that assembled at the door of the tabernacle—This was an institution of holy women of a strictly ascetic order, who had relinquished worldly cares and devoted themselves to the Lord; an institution which continued down to the time of Christ (Luke 2:37).

Eli was, on the whole, a good man, but lacking in the moral and religious training of his family. He erred on the side of parental indulgence; and though he reprimanded them (see on Deut. 21:18-21), yet, from fear or indolence, he shrank from laying on them the restraints, or subjecting them to the discipline, their gross delinquencies called for. In his judicial capacity, he winked at their flagrant acts of maladministration and suffered them to make reckless encroachments on the constitution, by which the most serious injuries were inflicted both on the rights of the people and the laws of God.

25. they hearkened not unto the voice of their father, *because* [it should be *therefore*] **the Lord would slay them**—It was not God's preordination, but their own wilful and impenitent disobedience which was the cause of their destruction.

27-35. A PROPHECY AGAINST ELI'S HOUSE. **27. there came a man of God unto Eli, and said . . . there shall not be an old man in thine house**—So much importance has always, in the East, been attached to old age, that it would be felt to be a great calamity, and sensibly to lower the respectability of any family which could boast of few or no old men. The prediction of this prophet was fully confirmed by the afflictions, degradation, poverty, and many untimely deaths with which the house of Eli was visited after its announcement (see on ch. 4:11; 14:3; 22:18-23; I Kings 2:27).

KEIL–DELITZSCH:

Verse 27. Before the Lord interposed in judgment, He sent a prophet (a "man of God," as in Judg. 13:6) to the aged Eli, to announce as a warning for all ages the judgment which was about to fall upon the worthless priests of his house. In order to arouse Eli's own conscience, he had pointed out to him, on the one hand, the grace manifested in the choice of his father's house, i.e., the house of Aaron, to keep His sanctuary (vv. 27b, 28), and, on the other hand, the desecration of the sanctuary by the wickedness of his sons (v. 29). Then follows the sentence: The choice of the family of Aaron still stood fast, but the deepest disgrace would come upon the despisers of the Lord (v. 30): the strength of his house would be broken; all the members of his house were to die early deaths. They were not, however, to be removed entirely from service at the altar, but to their sorrow were to survive the fall of the sanctuary (v. 31–34).

—*Commentary on the Old Testament*

ADAM CLARKE

22. *They lay with the women that assembled.* It is probable that these were persons who had some employment about the Tabernacle. See the note on Exod. xxxviii. 8, where the Hebrew text is similar to that in this place.

23. *Why do ye such things?* Eli appears to have been a fondly affectionate, easy father, who wished his sons to do well, but did not bring them under proper discipline, and did not use his authority to restrain them. As judge, he had power to cast them immediately out of the vineyard, as wicked and unprofitable servants; this he did not, and his and their ruin was the consequence.

25. *If one man sin against another.* All differences between man and man may be settled by the proper judge; but if a man sin against the Supreme Judge, God himself, who shall reconcile him to his Maker? Your sin is immediately against God himself, and is the highest insult that can be offered, because it is in the matter of His own worship; therefore you may expect His heaviest judgments. *Because the Lord would slay them.* The particle *ki*, which we translate *because*, and thus make their continuance in sin the effect of God's determination to destroy them, should be translated "therefore," as it means in many parts of the sacred writings.

27. *There came a man of God.* Who this was we know not, but the Chaldee terms him *nebiya daya*, "a prophet of Jehovah." Unto the *house of thy father.* That is, to Aaron; he was the first high priest; the priesthood descended from him to his eldest son, Eleazar, then to Phinehas. Afterwards it became established in the younger branch of the family of Aaron; for Eli was a descendant of Ithamar, Aaron's youngest son. From Eli it was transferred back again to the family of Eleazar, because of the profligacy of Eli's sons.

28. *And did I choose him?* The high priesthood was a place of the greatest honor that could be conferred on man, and a place of considerable emolument; for from their part of the sacrifices they derived a most comfortable livelihood.

29. *Wherefore kick ye at my sacrifice?* They disdained to take the part allowed by law, and would take for themselves what part they pleased, and as much as they pleased, vv. 13-16; thus they kicked at the sacrifices. *Honourest thy sons above me.* Permitting them to deal, as above, with the offerings and sacrifices, and take their part before the fat, etc., was burned unto the Lord; thus they were first served. At this Eli connived, and thus honored his sons above God.

30. *Should walk before me for ever.* See Exod. xxix. 9; xl. 15; Num. xxv. 10-13, where it is positively promised that the priesthood should be continued in the family of Aaron forever. But although this promise appears to be absolute, yet we plainly see that, like all other apparently absolute promises of God, it is conditional, i.e., a condition is implied though not expressed. *But now . . . be it far from me.* You have walked unworthily; I shall annul My promise, and reverse My ordinance (see Jer. xviii. 8, 10).

For them that honour me. This is a plan from which God will never depart; this can have no alteration; every promise is made in reference to it: They who honor God shall be honored; they who despise Him "shall be lightly esteemed."

MATTHEW HENRY

God, and have a single eye to him in it, we may depend upon this promise, he will put the best honour upon us. See John xii. 26.

V. He foretells the particular judgments which should come upon his family, to its perpetual ignominy.

1. That their power should be broken (*v.* 31): *I will cut off thy arm, and the arm of thy father's house*. They should be stripped of all their authority, should be deposed, and have no influence upon the people as they had had.

2. That their lives should be shortened. It is twice spoken: "*There shall not be an old man in thy house for ever*"; and again (*v.* 33), "*All the increase of thy house*, from generation to generation, *shall die in the flower of their age*."

3. That all their comforts should be embittered. (1) The comfort they had in the sanctuary, in its wealth and prosperity: *Thou shalt see an enemy in my habitation*. This was fulfilled in the Philistines' invasions and the mischiefs they did to Israel (*ch.* xiii. 19). (2) The comfort of their children: "*The man of thine whom I shall not cut off by an untimely death*" shall live to be a blot and burden to the family. Grief for a dead child is great, but for a bad child often greater.

4. That their substance should be wasted and they should be reduced to extreme poverty (*v.* 26): "*He that is left* alive *in thy house* shall have little joy of his life, for want of a livelihood; he shall come and crouch to the succeeding family for a subsistence." (1) He shall beg for the smallest alms—*a piece of silver* (and the word signifies the *least* piece) and *a morsel of bread*. Want is the just punishment of wantonness. Those who could not be content without dainties and varieties are brought, they or theirs, to want necessaries. (2) He shall beg for the meanest office: *Put me into somewhat belonging to the priesthood* (as it is in the original); *make me as one of the hired servants*, the fittest place for a prodigal. Plenty and power are forfeited when they are abused. This, it is probable, was fully accomplished when Abiathar, who was of Eli's race, was deposed by Solomon for treason, and he and his turned out of office in the temple (1 Kings ii. 26, 27).

5. That God would shortly begin to execute these judgments in the death of Hophni and Phinehas, the sad tidings of which Eli himself should live to hear: *This shall be a sign to thee*, *v.* 34.

VI. In the midst of all these threatenings against the house of Eli, here is mercy promised to Israel (*v.* 35): *I will raise me up a faithful priest*. 1. This was fulfilled in Zadoc, of the family of Eleazar, who came into Abiathar's place in the beginning of Solomon's reign, and was faithful to his trust. If some betray their trust, yet others shall be raised up that will be true to it. God's work shall never fall to the ground for want of hands to carry it on. 2. It has its full accomplishment in the priesthood of Christ.

JAMIESON, FAUSSET, BROWN

31. I will cut off thine arm, and the arm of thy father's house—By the withdrawal of the high priesthood from Eleazar, the elder of Aaron's two sons (after Nadab and Abihu were destroyed), that dignity had been conferred on the family of Ithamar, to which Eli belonged, and now that his descendants had forfeited the honor, it was to be taken from them and restored to the elder branch.

32. thou shalt see an enemy in my habitation—A successful rival for the office of high priest shall rise out of another family (II Sam. 15: 35; I Chron. 24:3; 29:22). But the marginal reading, "thou shalt see the affliction of the tabernacle," seems to be a preferable translation.

ADAM CLARKE

31. *I will cut off thine arm.* I will destroy the strength, power, and influence of your family.

32. *Thou shalt see an enemy in my habitation.* Every version and almost every commentator understands this clause differently. The word *tsar*, which we translate an *enemy*, and the Vulgate a "rival," signifies "calamity"; and this is the best sense to understand it in here. The calamity which he saw was the defeat of the Israelites, the capture of the ark, the death of his wicked sons, and the triumph of the Philistines. All this he saw, that is, knew to have taken place, before he met with his own tragical death. *In all the wealth which God shall give Israel.* This also is dark. The meaning may be this: God has spoken good concerning Israel; He will, in the end, make the triumph of the Philistines their own confusion; and the capture of the ark shall be the desolation of their gods; but the Israelites shall first be sorely pressed with calamity. *There shall not be an old man.* This is repeated from the preceding verse; all the family shall die in the flower of their years, as is said in the following verse.

34. *They shall die both of them.* Hophni and Phinehas were both killed very shortly after in the great battle with the Philistines in which the Israelites were completely routed, and the ark taken (see chap. iv).

35. *A faithful priest.* This seems to have been spoken of Zadok, who was anointed high priest in the room of Abiathar, the last descendant of the house of Eli (see 1 Kings ii. 26-27). Abiathar was removed because he had joined with Adonijah, who had got himself proclaimed king (see 1 Kings i. 7). *I will build him a sure house.* I will continue the priesthood in his family. *He shall walk before mine anointed.* He shall minister before Solomon, and the kings which shall reign in the land. The Targum says, "He shall walk before my Messiah," and the Septuagint expresses it, "before my Christ."

36. *Shall come and crouch to him.* Shall prostrate himself before him in the most abject manner, begging to be employed even in the meanest offices about the Tabernacle, in order to get even the most scanty means of support. *A morsel of bread.* A mouthful; what might be sufficient to keep body and soul together. See the sin and its punishment. They formerly pampered themselves, and fed to the full on the Lord's sacrifices; and now they are reduced to a *morsel of bread.*

MATTHEW HENRY — CHAPTER 3

Verses 1–10

We are here told, 1. How industrious Samuel was in serving God. It was an aggravation of the wickedness of Eli's sons that the child Samuel shamed them. They rebelled against the Lord, but Samuel ministered to him; they slighted their father's admonitions, but Samuel was observant of them; he ministered before Eli, under his eye and direction. Those are fittest to rule who have learnt to obey. 2. How scarce a thing prophecy then was, which made the call of Samuel to be the greater surprise to himself and the greater favour to Israel: *The word of the Lord was precious in those days*. It was precious, for what there was (it seems) was private: *There was no open vision*. Perhaps the impiety and impurity that prevailed in the tabernacle, and no doubt corrupted the whole nation, had provoked God, as a token of his displeasure, to withdraw the Spirit of prophecy.

The manner of God's revealing himself to Samuel is here related very particularly, for it was uncommon.

I. Eli had retired. Samuel had waited on him to his bed (*v.* 2): *Eli had laid down in his place*.

II. Samuel had laid down to sleep, in some closet near to Eli's room, ready within call if the old man should want any thing in the night. When his own sons were a grief to him, his little servitor was his joy. *Samuel had laid down ere the lamp of God went out*, *v.* 3.

III. God called him by name, and he took it for Eli's call, and ran to him, *v.* 4, 5. Here we have an instance, 1. Of Samuel's industry, and readiness to wait on Eli. "Here am I," said he—a good example to servants, to come when they are called; and to the

JAMIESON, FAUSSET, BROWN — CHAPTER 3

Vss. 1-10. THE LORD APPEARS TO SAMUEL IN A VISION. **1. the child Samuel ministered unto the Lord before Eli**—His ministry consisted, of course, of such duties in or about the sanctuary as were suited to his age, which is supposed now to have been about twelve years. Whether the office had been specially assigned him, or it arose from the interest inspired by the story of his birth, Eli kept him as his immediate attendant; and he resided not *in* the sanctuary, but in one of the tents or apartments around it, assigned for the accommodation of the priests and Levites, *his* being near to that of the high priest. **the word of the Lord was precious in those days**—It was very rarely known to the Israelites; and in point of fact only two prophets are mentioned as having appeared during the whole administration of the judges (Judg. 4:4; 6:8). **there was no open vision**—no publicly recognized prophet whom the people could consult, and from whom they might learn the will of God. There must have been certain indubitable evidences by which a communication from heaven could be distinguished. Eli knew them, for he may have received them, though not so frequently as is implied in the idea of an "open vision." **3. ere the lamp of God went out in the temple of the Lord**—The "temple" seems to have become the established designation of the tabernacle, and the time indicated was towards the morning twilight, as the lamps were extinguished at sunrise (see on Lev. 6:12, 13). **5. he ran unto Eli, and said, Here am I, for thou calledst me**—It is evident that his sleeping chamber was close to that of

ADAM CLARKE — CHAPTER 3

1. *Samuel ministered unto the Lord.* He performed minor services in the Tabernacle, under the direction of Eli, such as opening the doors, etc. (see v. 15). *The word of the Lord was precious.* There were but few revelations from God; and because the word was scarce, therefore it was valuable. The author of this book probably lived at a time when prophecy was frequent. *There was no open vision.* There was no public accredited prophet; one with whom the secret of the Lord was known to dwell, and to whom all might have recourse in cases of doubt or public emergency.

2. *Eli was laid down in his place.* It is very likely that, as the ark was a long time at Shiloh, they had built near to it certain apartments for the high priest and others more immediately employed about the Tabernacle. In one of these, near to that of Eli, perhaps under the same roof, Samuel lay when he was called by the Lord.

3. *Ere the lamp of God went out.* Before sunrise; for it is likely that the lamps were extinguished before the rising of the sun (see Exod. xxvii. 21; Lev. xxiv. 3).

4. *The Lord called Samuel.* The voice probably came from the holy place, near to which Eli and Samuel were both lying.

MATTHEW HENRY

younger, not only to submit to the elder, but to be careful and tender of them. 2. Of his unacquaintedness with the visions of the Almighty, that he took that to be only Eli's call which was really the call of God. Such mistakes as these we make oftener than we think. God calls to us by his word, and we take it to be only the call of the minister, and answer it accordingly; he calls to us by his providences, and we look only at the instruments. Eli assured him he did not call him, but mildly bade him lie down again. So *Samuel went and lay down.*

IV. The same call was repeated, and the same mistake made, a second and third time, *v.* 6–9. 1. God continued to call the child *yet again* (*v.* 6), and *again the third time*, *v.* 8. 2. Samuel was still ignorant that it was the Lord that called him (*v.* 7): *Samuel did not yet know the Lord.* The witness of the Spirit in the hearts of the faithful is often thus mistaken, by which means they lose the comfort of it; and the strivings of the Spirit with the consciences of sinners are likewise often mistaken, and so the benefit of their convictions is lost. Samuel went to Eli this second and third time, and he tells Eli, with great assurance, *"Thou didst call me* (*v.* 6–8), it could be no one else." But there was a special providence in it, that he should go thus often to Eli; for hereby, at length, *Eli perceived that the Lord had called the child*, *v.* 8. This would be a mortification to him, and he would apprehend it to be a step towards his family's being degraded, that when God had something to say he should choose to say it to the child Samuel, his servant that waited on him, and not to him.

V. At length Samuel was put into a posture to receive a message from God. 1. Eli, perceiving that it was the voice of God that Samuel heard, gave him instructions what to say, *v.* 9. The instruction was, when God called the next time, to say, *Speak, Lord, for thy servant heareth.* We may expect that God will speak to us, when we set ourselves to hearken to what he says, Ps. lxxxv. 8; Hab. ii. 1. When we come to read the word of God, and to attend on the preaching of it, we should come thus disposed, submitting ourselves to the commanding light and power of it: *Speak, Lord, for thy servant heareth.* 2. It should seem that God spoke the fourth time in a way somewhat different from the other; now *he stood and called*, which intimates that there was now some visible appearance of the divine glory to Samuel. This satisfied him that it was not Eli that called. Now also the call was doubled—*Samuel, Samuel*, as if God delighted in the mention of his name. 3. Samuel said, as he was taught, *Speak, for thy servant heareth.* Samuel did not now rise and run as before when he thought Eli called, but lay still and listened. The more sedate and composed our spirits are the better prepared they are for divine discoveries. All must be silent when he speaks. But observe, Samuel left out one word; he did not say, *Speak, Lord*, but only, *Speak, for thy servant heareth*, perhaps, as Bishop Patrick suggests, out of uncertainty whether it was God that spoke to him or no.

Verses 11–18

I. The message which, after all this introduction, God delivered to Samuel concerning Eli's house. The message is short, not nearly so long as that which the man of God brought, *ch.* ii. 27. But it is a sad message, to ratify the message in the former chapter, and to bind on the sentence there pronounced.

1. Concerning the sin: it is the *iniquity that he knoweth*, *v.* 13. The man of God told him of it, and many a time his own conscience had told him of it. *His sons made themselves vile, and he restrained them not.* Or, as it is in the Hebrew, he *frowned not upon them.*

2. Concerning the punishment: it is *that which I have spoken concerning his house*, *v.* 12 and 13. When that sentence began to be executed it would be very dreadful and amazing to all Israel (*v.* 11): *Both the ears of every one that heareth it shall tingle.* Every Israelite would be struck with terror and astonishment to hear of the slaying of Eli's sons, the breaking of Eli's neck, and the dispersion of Eli's family. "The *iniquity of Eli's house shall not be purged with sacrifice nor offering for ever.* No atonement shall be made for the sin, nor any abatement of the punishment." This was the imperfection of the legal sacrifices, that there were iniquities which they did not reach, which they would not purge; *but the blood of Christ cleanseth from all sin*, and secured all those that by faith are interested in it from that eternal death which is the wages of sin.

II. The delivery of this message to Eli.

1. Samuel's modest concealment of it, *v.* 15. (1) He *lay till the morning*, and we may well suppose he lay awake pondering on what he had heard. (2) *He*

JAMIESON, FAUSSET, BROWN

the aged high priest and that he was accustomed to be called during the night.

The three successive calls addressed to the boy convinced Eli of the divine character of the speaker, and he therefore exhorted the child to give a reverential attention to the message.

F. B. MEYER:

"And the Lord came, and stood, and called as at other times, Samuel, Samuel!" See the urgency of God! Four times He came and stood, and called. Mark how He stands at the door to knock. At first He was content to call the lad once by name: but after three unsuccessful attempts to attract him to himself, He uttered the name twice, with strong urgency in the appeal, Samuel! Samuel! This has been called God's double knock. There are seven or eight of these double knocks in Scripture: Simon, Simon; Saul, Saul; Abraham, Abraham.

How may we be sure of a divine call?

We may know God's call when it grows in intensity. If an impression comes into your soul, and you are not quite sure of its origin, pray over it; above all, act on it so far as possible, follow in the direction in which it leads—and as you lift up your soul before God, it will wax or wane. If it wanes at all, abandon it. If it waxes follow it, though all hell attempt to stay you.

We may test God's call by the assistance of godly friends. The aged Eli perceived that the Lord had called the child, and gave him good advice as to the manner in which he should respond to it. Our special gifts and the drift of our circumstances will also assuredly concur in one of God's calls.

We may test God's call by its effect on us. Does it lead to self-denial? Does it induce us to leave the comfortable bed and step into the cold? Does it drive us forth to minister to others? Does it make us more unselfish, loving, tender, modest, humble? Whatever is to the humbling of our pride, and the glory of God, may be truly deemed God's call. Be quick to respond, and fearlessly deliver the message the Lord has given you.—*Great Verses Through the Bible*

ADAM CLARKE

7. *Samuel did not yet know the Lord.* He had not been accustomed to receive any revelation from Him. He knew and worshipped the God of Israel; but he did not know Him as communicating especial revelation of His will.

9. *Speak, Lord; for thy servant heareth.* This was the usual way in which the prophets spoke when they had intimations that the Lord was about to make some especial revelation.

10. *The Lord came, and stood.* He heard the voice as if it was approaching nearer and nearer, till at last, from the sameness of the tone, he could imagine that it ceased to approach; and this is what appears to be represented under the notion of God standing and calling.

11. *The Lord said to Samuel.* He probably saw nothing, and only heard the voice; for it was not likely that any extraordinary representation could have been made to the eyes of a person so young. *The ears . . . shall tingle.* It shall be a piercing word to all Israel; it shall astound them all; and, after having heard it, it will still continue to resound in their ears.

12. *I will perform . . . all things which I have spoken.* That is, what He had declared by the prophet, whose message is related in chap. ii. 27, etc. *When I begin, I will also make an end.* I will not delay the execution of My purpose: when I begin, nothing shall deter Me from bringing all My judgments to a conclusion.

13. *I will judge his house for ever.* I will continue to execute judgments upon it till it is destroyed. *His sons made themselves vile* (see chap. ii. 12-17, 22-25). *He restrained them not.* He did not use his parental and juridical authority to curb them, and prevent the disorders which they committed.

14. *Shall not be purged with sacrifice nor offering.* That is, God was determined that they should be removed by a violent death. They had committed the sin unto death; and no offering or sacrifice could prevent this. What is spoken here relates to their temporal death only.

MATTHEW HENRY

opened the doors of the house of the Lord, in the morning, as he used to do, being up first in the tabernacle. That he should do so at other times was an instance of extraordinary towardliness in a child, but that he should do so this morning was an instance of great humility. God had highly honoured him above all the children of his people, yet he was not proud of the honour, but, as cheerfully as ever, went and opened the doors of the tabernacle. (3) *He feared to show Eli the vision*, because he was afraid to grieve and trouble the good old man.

2. Eli's careful enquiry into it, *v.* 16, 17. As soon as ever he heard Samuel's stirring he called for him, probably to his bedside. He had reason enough to fear that the message prophesied no good concerning him, but evil; and yet, because it was a message from God, he could not contentedly be ignorant of it. A good man desires to be acquainted with all the will of God, whether it make for him or against him.

3. Samuel's faithful delivery of his message at last (*v.* 18); *He told him every whit.*

4. Eli's pious acquiescence in it. He did not question Samuel's integrity, was not cross with him, nor had he any thing to object against the equity of the sentence. *It is the Lord, let him do what seemeth him good. It is the Lord*, with whom there is no unrighteousness, who never did nor ever will do any wrong to any of his creatures, nor exact more than their iniquity deserves. "*Let him do what seemeth him good.* I have nothing to say against his proceedings."

Verses 19–21

Samuel being thus brought acquainted with the visions of God,

I. God did him honour. Having begun to favour him, he carried on and crowned his own work in him: *Samuel grew, for the Lord was with him*, *v.* 19. God honoured Samuel; 1. By further manifestations of himself to him: *The Lord revealed himself again to Samuel in Shiloh*, *v.* 21. 2. By fulfilling what he spoke by him: *God did let none of his words fall to the ground*, *v.* 19. Whatever Samuel said, as a prophet, it proved true, and was accomplished in its season.

II. Israel did him honour. They all knew and owned *that Samuel was established to be a prophet*, *v.* 20. 1. He grew famous. 2. He grew useful and very serviceable to his generation. He that began betimes to *be* good soon came to *do* good.

JAMIESON, FAUSSET, BROWN

The burden of it was an extraordinary premonition of the judgments that impended over Eli's house; and the aged priest, having drawn the painful secret from the child, exclaimed, "It is the Lord; let him do what seemeth him good." Such is the spirit of meek and unmurmuring submission in which we ought to receive the dispensations of God, however severe and afflictive. But, in order to form a right estimate of Eli's language and conduct on this occasion, we must consider the overwhelming accumulation of judgments denounced against his person, his sons, his descendants—his altar, and nation. With such a threatening prospect before him, his piety and meekness were wonderful. In his personal character he seems to have been a good man, but his sons' conduct was flagrantly bad; and though his misfortunes claim our sympathy, it is impossible to approve or defend the weak and unfaithful course which, in the retributive justice of God, brought these adversities upon him.

ADAM CLARKE

15. *Samuel feared to show Eli.* He reverenced him as a father, and he feared to distress him by showing what the Lord had purposed to do.

17. *God do so to thee, and more also.* This was a very solemn adjuration; he suspected that God had threatened severe judgments, for he knew that his house was very criminal; and he wished to know what God had spoken. The words imply thus much: If thou do not tell me fully what God has threatened, may the same and greater curses fall on thyself.

18. *Samuel told him every whit.* "Everything." The Hebrew, "all these words." *It is the Lord.* He is sovereign, and will do what He pleases; He is righteous, and will do nothing but what is just. *Let him do what seemeth him good.* There is much of a godly submission, as well as a deep sense of his own unworthiness, found in these words. He also had sinned, so as to be punished with temporal death; but surely there is no evidence that the displeasure of the Lord against him was extended to a future state.

20. *All Israel from Dan even to Beer-sheba.* Through the whole extent of Palestine; Dan being at the northern, Beer-sheba at the southern extremity. *Was established to be a prophet.* The word *neeman*, which we translate *established*, signifies "faithful": "The faithful Samuel was a prophet of the Lord."

21. *The Lord appeared again.* "And Jehovah added to appear"; that is, He continued to reveal himself to Samuel at Shiloh. *By the word of the Lord.* By the spirit and word of prophecy.

MATTHEW HENRY

CHAPTER 4

Verses 1–9

I. A war entered into with the Philistines, *v.* 1. It was an attempt to throw off the yoke of their oppression, and would have succeeded better if they had first repented and reformed, and so begun their work at the right end.

II. The defeat of Israel in that war, *v.* 2. Israel, who were the aggressors, were smitten, and had 4,000 men killed upon the spot. Sin, the accursed thing, was in the camp, and gave their enemies all the advantage against them they could wish for.

III. The measures they concerted for another engagement. 1. They quarrelled with God for appearing against them (*v.* 3): *Wherefore has the Lord smitten us?* They expostulate boldly with God about it, are displeased at what God has done, and dispute the matter with him. 2. They imagined that they could oblige him to appear for them the next time by bringing the ark into their camp. They sent to Shiloh for the ark, and Eli had not courage enough to detain it, but sent his ungodly sons, Hophni and Phinehas, along with it, or at least permitted them to go. See here, (1) The profound veneration the people had for the ark. "O send for that, and it will do wonders for us." The ark was, by institution, a visible token of God's presence. They thought that, by paying a great respect to this sacred chest, they should prove themselves to be Israelites and engage God Almighty to appear in their favour. It is common for those that have estranged themselves from the vitals of religion to discover a great fondness for the rituals and external observances of it. And yet indeed they did but make an idol of the ark, and looked upon it to be as much an image of the God of Israel as those idols which the heathen worshipped were of their gods. (2) Their egregious folly in thinking that the ark, if they had it in their camp, would certainly *save them out of the hand of their enemies*, and bring victory back to their side. What good would the ark do them, the shell without the kernel? Instead of honouring God by what they did, they really affronted him. If there had been nothing else to invalidate their expectations from the ark, how could they expect it should bring a blessing when Hophni and Phinehas were the men that carried it?

JAMIESON, FAUSSET, BROWN

CHAPTER 4

Vss. 1-11. ISRAEL OVERCOME BY THE PHILISTINES. **1. the word of Samuel came to all Israel**—The character of Samuel as a prophet was now fully established. The want of an "open vision" was supplied by him, for "none of his words were let fall to the ground" (ch. 3:19); and to his residence in Shiloh all the people of Israel repaired to consult him as an oracle, who, as the medium of receiving the divine command, or by his gift of a prophet, could inform them what was the mind of God. It is not improbable that the rising influence of the young prophet had alarmed the jealous fears of the Philistines. They had kept the Israelites in some degree of subjection ever since the death of Samson and were determined, by further crushing, to prevent the possibility of their being trained by the counsels, and under the leadership, of Samuel, to reassert their national independence. At all events, the Philistines were the aggressors (vs. 2). But, on the other hand, the Israelites were rash and inconsiderate in rushing to the field without obtaining the sanction of Samuel as to the war, or having consulted him as to the subsequent measures they took. **Israel went out against the Philistines to battle**—i.e., to resist this new incursion. **Eben-ezer . . . Aphek**—Aphek, which means "strength," is a name applied to any fort or fastness. There were several Apheks in Palestine; but the mention of Eben-ezer determines this "Aphek" to be in the south, among the mountains of Judah, near the western entrance of the pass of Beth-horon, and consequently on the borders of the Philistine territory. The first encounter at Aphek being unsuccessful, the Israelites determined to renew the engagement in better circumstances. **3-9. Let us fetch the ark of the covenant of the Lord out of Shiloh unto us**—Strange that they were so blind to the real cause of the disaster and that they did not discern, in the great and general corruption of religion and morals (ch. 2 and 7:3; Ps. 78:58), the reason why the presence and aid of God were not extended to them. Their first measure for restoring the national spirit and energy ought to have been a complete reformation—a universal return to purity of

ADAM CLARKE

CHAPTER 4

1. *The word of Samuel came to all Israel.* This clause certainly belongs to the preceding chapter, and is so placed by the Vulgate, Septuagint, Syriac, and Arabic. *Pitched beside Eben-ezer.* This name was not given to this place till more than twenty years after this battle (see chap. vii. 12; for the monument called the "Stone of Help" was erected by Samuel in the place which was afterwards, from this circumstance, called Ebenezer when the Lord had given the Israelites a signal victory over the Philistines. It was situated in the tribe of Judah, between Mizpeh and Shen, and not far from the Aphek here mentioned. This is another proof that this book was compiled after the times and transactions which it records, and probably from memoranda which had been made by a contemporary writer.

3. *Let us fetch the ark.* They vainly supposed that the ark could save them when the God of it had departed from them because of their wickedness. They knew that in former times their fathers had been beaten by their enemies when they took not the ark with them to battle, as in the case of their wars with the Canaanites, Num. xiv. 44-45; and that they had conquered when they took this with them, as in the case of the destruction of Jericho, Josh. vi. 4. It was customary with all the nations of the earth to take their gods and sacred ensigns with them to war.

4. *The Lord of hosts.* See on chap. i. 3. *Dwelleth between the cherubims.* Of what shape the cherubim were, we know not; but there was one of these representative figures placed at each end of the ark of the covenant; and between them, on the lid or cover of that ark, which was called the "propitiatory" or "mercy seat," the *shechinah*, or symbol of the Divine Presence, was said to dwell. They thought, therefore, if they had the ark, they must necessarily have the presence and influence of Jehovah.

MATTHEW HENRY

IV. The great joy there was in the camp of Israel when the ark was brought into it (*v.* 5): *They shouted, so that the earth rang again.* Now they thought themselves sure of victory.

V. The consternation into which the bringing of the ark into the camp of Israel put the Philistines. The two armies lay so near encamped that the Philistines heard the shout the Israelites gave on this great occasion. They soon understood what it was they triumphed in (*v.* 6), and were afraid of the consequences. For, 1. It had never been done before in their days: *God has come into their camp*, and therefore *woe unto us* (*v.* 7), and again, *woe unto us, v.* 8. See what gross notions they had of the divine presence, as if the God of Israel were not as much in the camp before the ark came thither, which may very well be excused in them, since the notions the Israelites themselves had of that presence were no better. 2. When it had been done in the days of old, it had wrought wonders: *These are the gods that smote the Egyptians with all the plagues in the wilderness*, 4. 8. Here they were as much out in their history as in their divinity: the plagues of Egypt were inflicted before the ark was made and before Israel came into the wilderness. Yet, it should seem, they scarcely believed themselves when they spoke thus formidably of *these mighty gods*, but only bantered; they stirred up one another to fight so much the more stoutly.

Verses 10–11

Here is a short account of the issue of this battle.

I. Israel was smitten, the army dispersed and totally routed. 1. Though they had the better cause, were the people of God, yet they failed of success, for *their rock had sold them.* A good cause often suffers for the sake of the bad men that undertake it. 2. Though they had the greater confidence, and were the more courageous. The ark in the camp will add nothing to its strength when there is an Achan in it.

II. The ark itself was taken by the Philistines; and Hophni and Phinehas were *both slain, v.* 11. 1. The slaughter of the priests, considering their bad character, was no great loss to Israel, but it was a dreadful judgment upon the house of Eli. The word which God had spoken was fulfilled in it (*ch.* ii. 34). But, 2. The taking of the ark, was a very great judgment upon Israel, and a certain token of God's hot displeasure against them. Now they are made to see their folly in trusting to their external privileges when they had by their wickedness forfeited them, and fancying that the ark would save them when God had departed from them.

Verses 12–18

Tidings are here brought to Shiloh of the fatal issue of their battle with the Philistines. Bad news flies fast. Thither therefore an express posted away immediately; it was a man of Benjamin; the Jews fancy it was Saul. *He rent his clothes, and put earth upon his head*, by these signs to proclaim the sorrowful news. He went straight to Shiloh with it.

I. How the city received it. *Eli sat in the gate* (*v.* 13, 18), but the messenger passed him by, and told it in the city, with all the aggravating circumstances; and now *both the ears of every one that heard it tingled*, as was foretold, *ch.* iii. 11. Their hearts trembled, and every face gathered blackness. *All the city cried out* (*v.* 13), and well they might, for it was a particular loss to Shiloh, and the ruin of that place; for, though the ark was soon rescued out of the hands of the Philistines, yet it never returned to Shiloh again. This abandoning of Shiloh Jerusalem is long afterwards reminded of, and told to take warning by. Jer. vii. 12, "*Go see what I did to Shiloh.*"

II. What a fatal blow it was to old Eli. 1. With what fear he expected the tidings. Though old, and blind, and heavy, yet he could not keep his chamber when he was sensible the glory of Israel lay at stake, but placed himself by the way side, to receive the first intelligence; for *his heart trembled for the ark of God, v.* 13. He also apprehended imminent danger. Israel had forfeited the ark (his own sons especially) and now the threatening comes to his mind, that he should *see an enemy in God's habitation* (*ch.* ii. 32); and perhaps his own heart reproached him for not using his authority to prevent the carrying of the ark into the camp. All good men lay the interests of God's church nearer their hearts than any secular interest or concern of their own. How can we be easy if the ark be not safe? 2. With what grief he received the tidings. Though he could not see, he could hear the *tumult* and *crying of the city*, and perceived it to be the voice of lamentation. He is told there is an express come from the army, who relates the story to him very distinctly, having himself been an eye-witness of it, *v.* 16, 17. The account of the defeat of the army, and the slaughter of a great number of the soldiers,

JAMIESON, FAUSSET, BROWN

worship and morals. But, instead of cherishing a spirit of deep humiliation and sincere repentance, instead of resolving on the abolition of existing abuses, and the re-establishing of the pure faith, they adopted what appeared an easier and speedier course—they put their trust in ceremonial observances, and doubted not but that the introduction of the ark into the battlefield would ensure their victory. In recommending this extraordinary step, the elders might recollect the confidence it imparted to their ancestors (Num. 10:35; 14:44), as well as what had been done at Jericho. But it is more probable that they were influenced by the heathenish ideas of their idolatrous neighbors, who carried their idol Dagon, or his sacred symbols, to their wars, believing that the power of their divinities was inseparably associated with, or residing in, their images. In short, the shout raised in the Hebrew camp, on the arrival of the ark, indicated very plainly the prevalence among the Israelites at this time of a belief in national deities—whose influence was local, and whose interest was especially exerted in behalf of the people who adored them.

The joy **of the Israelites was an emotion springing out of the same superstitious sentiments as the corresponding dismay of their enemies; and to afford them a convincing, though painful proof of their error, was the ulterior object of the discipline to which they were now subjected—a discipline by which God, while punishing them for their apostasy by allowing the capture of the ark, had another end in view—that of signally vindicating His supremacy over all the gods of the nations.**

12-22. ELI HEARING THE TIDINGS. **13. Eli sat upon a seat by the wayside—The aged priest, as a public magistrate, used, in dispensing justice, to seat himself daily in a spacious recess at the entrance gate of the city. In his intense anxiety to learn the issue of the battle, he took up his usual place as the most convenient for meeting with passers-by. His seat was an official chair, similar to those of the ancient Egyptian judges, richly carved, superbly ornamented, high, and *without a back*.**

ADAM CLARKE

5. *All Israel shouted.* Had they humbled themselves, and prayed devoutly and fervently for success, they would have been heard and saved.

7. *God is come into the camp.* They took for granted, as did the Israelites, that His presence was inseparable from His ark or shrine.

8. *These mighty Gods.* "From the hand of these illustrious Gods." Probably this should be translated in the singular, and not in the plural: "Who shall deliver us from the hand of this illustrious God?"

9. *Be strong.* This was the address to the whole army, and very forcible it was. "If ye do not fight, and acquit yourselves like men, ye will be servants to the Hebrews, as they have been to you; and you may expect that they will avenge themselves of you for all the cruelty you have exercised towards them."

11. *Hophni and Phinehas were slain.* They probably attempted to defend the ark, and lost their lives in the attempt.

12. *Came to Shiloh the same day.* The field of battle could not have been at any great distance, for this young man reached Shiloh the same evening after the defeat. *With his clothes rent, and with earth upon his head.* These were signs of sorrow and distress among all nations. The *clothes rent* signified the rending, dividing, and scattering of the people; the *earth*, or "ashes," on the head signified their humiliation: "We are brought down to the dust of the earth; we are near to our graves."

13. *His heart trembled for the ark of God.* He was a most mild and affectionate father, and yet the safety of the ark lay nearer to his heart than the safety of his two sons. Who can help feeling for this aged, venerable man?

MATTHEW HENRY

was very grievous to him as a judge; the tidings of the death of his two sons, who, he had reason to fear, died impenitent, touched him in a tender part as a father. He does not interrupt the narrative with any passionate lamentations for his sons, like David for Absalom, but waits for the end of the story, not doubting but that the messenger, being an Israelite, would, without being asked, say something of the ark; and if he could but have said, "Yet the ark of God is safe, and we are bringing that home," his joy for that would have overcome his grief for all the other disasters. When the messenger concludes his story with, *The ark of God is taken*, he is struck to the heart, and, it should seem, he swooned away, and died immediately. His heart was broken first, and then his neck. Thus were the folly and wickedness of those sons of his, whom he had indulged, his ruin at last. Yet we must observe, to Eli's praise, that it was the loss of the ark that was his death, not the slaughter of his sons.

Verses 19–22

Another melancholy story, that carries on the desolations of Eli's house, and the sorrowful feeling which the tidings of the ark's captivity excited. It is concerning the wife of Phinehas, one of those ungracious sons of Eli that had brought all this mischief on Israel.

I. She was a woman of a very tender spirit. She was near her time. When she heard of the death of her father-in-law whom she reverenced, and her husband whom, bad as he was, she loved, but especially of the loss of the ark, *she travailed, for her pains came* thickly *upon her* (*v.* 19), and though she had strength to bear the child, she, soon after, fainted and died, being very willing to let life go when she had lost the greatest comforts of her life.

II. She was a woman of a very gracious spirit. Her concern for the death of her husband and father-in-law was an evidence of her natural affection; but her much greater concern for the loss of the ark was an evidence of her pious and devout affection to God and sacred things. *She said, The glory has departed from Israel.*

1. The women that attended her *said unto her, Fear not*, now the worst is past, *for thou hast borne a son* (and perhaps it was her first-born), *but she answered not, neither did she regard it*. What is it to one that is lamenting the loss of the ark? Small comfort could she have of a child born in Israel, in Shiloh, when the ark is lost, and is a prisoner in the land of the Philistines.

2. This made her give her child a name which should perpetuate the remembrance of the calamity and her sense of it. She orders them to call it *I-chabod*, that is, *Where is the glory*? Or, *Alas for the glory*! or, *There is no glory* (*v.* 21), which she thus explains with her dying lips (*v.* 22): "*The glory has departed from Israel; for the ark of God is taken.*" If God go, the glory goes, and all good goes.

JAMIESON, FAUSSET, BROWN

The calamities announced to Samuel as about to fall upon the family of Eli were now inflicted in the death of his two sons, and after his death, by that of his daughter-in-law, whose infant son received a name that perpetuated the fallen glory of the church and nation. The public disaster was completed by the capture of the ark. Poor Eli! He was a good man, in spite of his unhappy weaknesses. So strongly were his sensibilities enlisted on the side of religion, that the news of the capture of the ark proved to him a knell of death; and yet his overindulgence, or sad neglect of his family—the main cause of all the evils that led to its fall—has been recorded, as a beacon to warn all heads of Christian families against making shipwreck on the same rock.

ADAM CLARKE

17. *And the messenger answered.* Never was a more afflictive message, containing such a variety of woes, each rising above the preceding, delivered in so few words. (1) *Israel is fled before the Philistines.* (2) *There hath also been a great slaughter among the people.* (3) *Thy two sons also, Hophni and Phinehas, are dead.* (4) *The ark of God is taken.*

This was the most dreadful of the whole; now Israel is dishonored in the sight of the heathen, and the name of the Lord will be blasphemed by them. Besides, the capture of the ark shows that God is departed from Israel; and now there is no further hope of restoration for the people, but every prospect of the destruction of the nation, and the final ruin of all religion!

18. *When he made mention of the ark of God.* Eli bore all the relation till the messenger came to this solemn word; he had trembled before for the ark, and now, hearing that it was captured, he was transfixed with grief, fell down from his seat, and dislocated his neck! Behold the judgments of God! But shall we say that this man, however remiss in the education of his children, and criminal in his indulgence towards his profligate sons, which arose more from the easiness of his disposition than from a desire to encourage vice, is gone to perdition? God forbid! *He had judged Israel forty years.* Instead of *forty years*, the Septuagint was here "twenty years." All the other versions, as well as the Hebrew text, have forty years.

19. *And his daughter in law.* This is another very affecting story; the defeat of Israel, the capture of the ark, the death of her father-in-law, and the slaughter of her husband were more than a woman in her circumstances, near the time of her delivery, could bear. *She bowed*, travailed, was delivered of a son, gave the child a name indicative of the ruined state of Israel, and expired!

21. *She named the child I-chabod.* The versions are various on the original words. It is pretty evident they did not know well what signification to give the name; and we are left to collect its meaning from what she says afterwards, *The glory is departed from Israel;* the words literally mean, "Where is the glory?" And indeed where was it, when the armies of Israel were defeated by the Philistines, the priests slain, the supreme magistrate dead, and the ark of the Lord taken?

MATTHEW HENRY

CHAPTER 5

Verses 1–5

I. The Philistines' triumph over the ark, which they were the more pleased to be now masters of because before the battle they were possessed with a great fear of it, *ch.* iv. 7. When they had it in their hands God restrained them, that they did not offer any violence to it, but carefully carried it to a place of safety. They carried it to Ashdod, one of their five cities, and that in which Dagon's temple was; there they placed the ark of God, *by Dagon* (*v.* 2), either, 1. As a sacred thing, which they designed to pay some religious respect to, in conjunction with Dagon; for the gods of the heathen were never looked upon as averse to partners. Though the nations would not change their gods, yet they would multiply them and add to them. But they were mistaken in the God of Israel when, in putting his ark by Dagon's image, they intended to do him honour; for he is not worshipped at all if he is not worshipped alone. Or rather, 2. They placed it there as a trophy of victory, in honour of Dagon their god. (1) God will show of how little account the ark of the covenant is if the covenant itself be broken and neglected; even sacred signs are not things that either he is tied to or we can trust to. (2) For a time, God may have so much the more glory, in reckoning with those that thus affront him, and get him honour upon them. Having punished Israel, that betrayed the ark, by giving it into the hands of the Philistines, he will next deal with those that abused it, and will fetch it out of their hands again.

II. The ark's triumph over Dagon. Once and again Dagon was made to fall before it. The next morning,

JAMIESON, FAUSSET, BROWN

CHAPTER 5

Vss. 1, 2. THE PHILISTINES BRING THE ARK INTO THE HOUSE OF DAGON. 1. Ashdod—**or Azotus, one of the five Philistine satrapies, and a place of great strength. It was an inland town, thirty-four miles north of Gaza, now called Esdud.**

2. the house of Dagon—**Stately temples were erected in honor of this idol, which was the principal deity of the Philistines, but whose worship extended over all Syria, as well as Mesopotamia and Chaldea; its name being found among the Assyrian gods on the cuneiform inscriptions [RAWLINSON]. It was represented under a monstrous combination of a human head, breast, and arms, joined to the belly and tail of a fish. The captured ark was placed in the temple of Dagon, right before this image of the idol.**

ADAM CLARKE

CHAPTER 5

1. *Brought it from Eben-ezer unto Ashdod.* Ashdod or Azotus was one of the five satrapies or lordships of the Philistines.

2. *The house of Dagon.* On this idol, which was supposed to be partly in a human form and partly in that of a fish, see the note on Judg. xvi. 23.

The motive which induced the Philistines to set up the ark in the temple of Dagon may be easily ascertained. It was customary in all nations to dedicate the spoils taken from an enemy to their gods: (1) as a gratitude offering for the help which they supposed them to have furnished; and (2) as a proof that their gods, i.e., the gods of the conquerors, were more powerful than those of the conquered. It was, no doubt, to insult the God of Israel, and to insult and terrify His people, that they placed His ark in the temple of Dagon.

MATTHEW HENRY

when the worshippers of Dagon came to pay their devotions to his shrine, they found their triumphing short, Job xx. 5.

1. Dagon had *fallen upon his face to the earth before the ark*, *v.* 3. Great care was taken, in setting up the images of their gods, to fix them. The prophet takes notice of it, Isa. xli. 7, *He fastened it with nails that it should not be moved*; and again, Isa. xlvi. 7. And yet Dagon's fastenings stood him in no stead. The kingdom of Satan will certainly fall before the kingdom of Christ, error before truth, profaneness before godliness, and corruption before grace in the hearts of the faithful. When the interests of religion seem to be run down and ready to sink, yet even then we may be confident that the day of their triumph will come.

2. The priests, finding their idol on the floor, make all the haste they can, before it be known, to set him in his place again. A sorry silly thing it was to make a god of, which, when it was down, wanted help to get up again; and sottish wretches those were that could pray for help from that idol that needed, and in effect implored, their help. How could they attribute their victory to the power of Dagon when Dagon himself could not keep his own ground before the ark? But they are resolved Dagon shall be their god still, and therefore set him in his place.

3. The next night Dagon fell the second time, *v.* 4. The head and hands were *cut off upon the threshold*, so that nothing remained but the stump, or, as the margin reads it, *the fishy part of* Dagon; for (as many learned men conjecture) the upper part of this image was in a human shape, the lower in the shape of a fish, as mermaids are painted. The misshapen monster is by this fall made to appear, (1) Very ridiculous, and worthy to be despised. A pretty figure Dagon made now, when the fall had anatomized him, and shown how the human part and the fishy part were artificially put together. (2) Very impotent, and unworthy to be prayed to or trusted in; for his losing his head and hands proved him utterly destitute both of wisdom and power, and for ever disabled either to advise or act for his worshippers.

4. The threshold of Dagon's temple was ever looked upon as sacred, and not to be trodden on, *v.* 5. Some think that reference is had to this superstitious usage of Dagon's worshippers in Zeph. i. 9, where God threatens to punish those who, in imitation of them, leaped over the threshold. Instead of despising Dagon, for the threshold's sake that beheaded him, they were almost ready to worship the threshold because it was the block on which he was beheaded.

Verses 6–12

The downfall of Dagon (if the people had made a good use of it, and had been brought by it to repent of their idolatries and to humble themselves before the God of Israel and seek his face) might have prevented the vengeance which God here proceeds to take upon them for the indignities done to his ark. *He destroyed them.* At Gath it is called *a great destruction* (*v.* 9), *a deadly destruction*, *v.* 11. And it is expressly said (*v.* 12) that those who were *smitten with the emerods were the men that died not* by the other *destruction*, which probably was the pestilence. Those that were not destroyed *he smote with emerods* (*v.* 6), *in their secret parts* (*v.* 9), so grievous that (*v.* 12) the *cry went up to heaven*, that is, it might be heard a great way off, and perhaps, in the extremity of their pain and misery, they cried, not to Dagon, but to the God of heaven. The emerods was both a painful and shameful disease. By it God would humble their pride, and put contempt upon them, as they had done upon his ark. The disease was epidemical, and perhaps, among them, a new disease. *Ashdod was smitten, and the coasts thereof*, the country round. The men of Ashdod were soon aware that it was *the hand of God, the God of Israel*, *v.* 7. Thus they were constrained to acknowledge his power and dominion, and confess themselves within his jurisdiction, and yet they would not renounce Dagon and submit to Jehovah; but rather, now that he touched their bone and their flesh, they were ready to curse him to his face, and instead of making their peace with him, and courting the stay of his ark upon better terms, they desired to get clear of it. Carnal hearts, when they smart under the judgments of God, would rather, if it were possible, put him far from them than enter into covenant and communion with him, and make him their friend. Thus the men of Ashdod resolve, *The ark of the God of Israel shall not abide with us.* It is resolved to change the place of its imprisonment. It was agreed that it should be carried to Gath, *v.* 8. Some superstitious conceit they had that the fault was in the place, and that the ark would be better pleased

JAMIESON, FAUSSET, BROWN

3-5. DAGON FALLS DOWN. 3. they of Ashdod arose early—They were filled with consternation when they found the object of their stupid veneration prostrate before the symbol of the divine presence.

Though set up, it fell again, and lay in a state of complete mutilation; its head and arms, severed from the trunk, were lying in distant and separate places, as if violently cast off, and only the fishy part remained. The degradation of their idol, though concealed by the priests on the former occasion, was now more manifest and infamous. It lay in the attitude of a vanquished enemy and a suppliant, and this picture of humiliation significantly declared the superiority of the God of Israel.

5. Therefore neither the priests . . . nor any . . . tread on the threshold of Dagon—A superstitious ceremony crept in, and in the providence of God was continued, by which the Philistines contributed to publish this proof of the helplessness of their god. **unto this day**—The usage continued in practice at the time when this history was written—probably in the later years of Samuel's life.

6-12. THE PHILISTINES ARE SMITTEN WITH EMERODS. 6. the hand of the Lord was heavy upon them of Ashdod—The presumption of the Ashdodites was punished by a severe judgment that overtook them in the form of a pestilence. **smote them with emerods**—bleeding piles, hemorrhoids (Ps. 78:66), in a very aggravated form. As the heathens generally regarded diseases affecting the secret parts of the body as punishments from the gods for trespasses committed against themselves, the Ashdodites would be the more ready to look upon the prevailing epidemic as demonstrating the anger of God, already shown against their idol.

7. the ark of God shall not abide with us—It was removed successively to several of the large towns of the country, but the same pestilence broke out in every place and raged so fiercely and fatally that the authorities were forced to send the ark back into the land of Israel.

ADAM CLARKE

3. *They of Ashdod arose early on the morrow.* Probably to perform some act of their superstition in the temple of their idol. *Dagon was fallen upon his face.* This was one proof, which they little expected, of the superiority of the God of Israel. *Set him in his place again.* Supposing his fall might have been merely accidental.

4. *Only the stump of Dagon was left.* Literally, Only *dagon* (i.e., the "little fish") was left. Dagon had the head, arms, and hands of a man or woman, and the rest of the idol was in the form of a fish, to which Horace is supposed to make allusion in the following words: "The upper part resembling a beautiful woman; the lower, a fish." All that was human in his form was broken off from what resembled a fish. Here was a proof that the affair was not accidental; and these proofs of God's power and authority prepared the way for His judgments.

5. *Tread on the threshold.* Because the arms of Dagon were broken off by his fall on the threshold, the threshold became sacred, and neither his priests nor worshippers ever tread on the threshold. Thus it was ordered in the divine providence that, by a religious custom of their own, they should perpetuate their disgrace, the insufficiency of their worship, and the superiority of the God of Israel.

It is supposed that the idolatrous Israelites, in the time of Zephaniah, had adopted the worship of Dagon: and that in this sense chap. i. 9 is to be understood: "In the same day also will I punish all those that leap on the threshold." In order to go into such temples, and not tread on the threshold, the people must step or leap over them; and in this way the above passage may be understood.

6. *Smote them with emerods.* The word *apholim*, from *aphal*, to be "elevated," probably means the disease called the bleeding piles, which appears to have been accompanied with dysentery, bloody flux, and ulcerated anus.

7. *His hand is sore upon us, and upon Dagon our god.* Here the end was completely answered: they now saw that they had not prevailed against Israel on account of their god being more powerful than Jehovah; and they now felt how easily this God can confound and destroy their whole nation.

8. *The lords of the Philistines.* The word *sarney*, which we translate *lords*, is rendered by the Chaldee "tyrants." The Syriac is the same. By the Vulgate and Septuagint, "satraps." Palestine was divided into five satrapies: Ashdod, Ekron, Askelon, Gath, and Gaza (see Josh. xiii. 8). But these were all federates, and acted under one general government, for which they assembled in council.

Let the ark . . . be carried about. They

MATTHEW HENRY

with another lodging, further off from Dagon's temple; and therefore, instead of returning it, as they should have done, to its own place, they contrive to send it to another place. *Gath* is pitched upon, a place famed for a race of giants, but their strength and stature are no fence against the pestilence and the emerods: the men of that city were smitten, *both great and small* (*v.* 9), both dwarfs and giants, all alike to God's judgments. They were all at last weary of the ark, and very willing to get rid of it. It was sent from Gath to Ekron, and, coming by order of council, the Ekronites could not refuse it, but were much exasperated against their great men for sending them such a fatal present (*v.* 10): *They have sent it to us to slay us and our people.* A general assembly is instantly called, to advise about *sending the ark again to its place*, *v.* 11. While they are consulting about it, the hand of God is doing execution; and their contrivances to evade the judgment do but spread it. Many drop down dead among them. Many more are raging ill of the emerods, *v.* 12. What shall they do?

JAMIESON, FAUSSET, BROWN

11. they sent—i.e., the magistrates of Ekron. **12. the cry of the city went up to heaven**—The disease is attended with acute pain, and it is far from being a rare phenomenon in the Philistian plain [VAN DE VELDE].

ADAM CLARKE

probably thought that their affliction rose from some natural cause; and therefore they wished the ark to be carried about from place to place, to see what the effects might be. If they found the same evil produced wherever it came, then they must conclude that it was a judgment from the God of Israel.

9. *The hand of the Lord was against the city.* As it was at Ashdod, so it was at Gath.

12. *The men that died not.* Some it seems were smitten with instant death; others, with the hemorrhoids; and there was a universal consternation; *and the cry of the city went up to heaven*—it was an exceeding great cry.

MATTHEW HENRY

CHAPTER 6

Verses 1–9

The ark was *in the country of the Philistines seven months.* So long as they carried it captive, they should find it a curse to them. 1. Seven months Israel was punished with the absence of the ark, that special token of God's presence. A melancholy time no doubt, but they had this to comfort themselves with, that, wherever the ark is, *the Lord is in his holy temple*, and by faith and prayer we may have access with boldness to him there. We may have God nigh unto us when the ark is at a distance. 2. Seven months the Philistines were punished with the presence of the ark; so long it was a plague to them, because they would not send it home sooner. Note, Sinners lengthen out their own miseries by obstinately refusing to part with their sins. But at length it is determined that the ark must be sent back.

I. The priests and the diviners are consulted about it, *v.* 2. They were supposed to be best acquainted both with the rules of wisdom and with the rites of worship and atonement, and therefore it was proper to ask them, *What shall we do to the ark of Jehovah*?

II. They give their advice very fully, and seem to be very unanimous in it. 1. They urge it upon them that it was absolutely necessary to send the ark back, from the example of Pharaoh and the Egyptians, *v.* 6. 2. They advise that, when they sent it back, they should send a trespass-offering with it, *v.* 3. They knew the God of Israel was a jealous God, and those with whom he had such a quarrel must *in any wise return him a trespass-offering*, and they could not expect to be healed upon any other terms. But when they began to contrive what that satisfaction should be, they became wretchedly vain in their imaginations. 3. They direct that this trespass-offering should be an acknowledgment of the punishment of their iniquity. They must make images of the *emerods*, that is, of the swellings and sores with which they had been afflicted, so making the reproach of that shameful disease perpetual by their own act and deed (Ps. lxxviii. 66), also images of the *mice that had marred the land*, owning thereby the almighty power of the God of Israel, who could chastise and humble them, even in the day of their triumph, by such small and despicable animals. These images must be made of gold, the most precious metal, to intimate that they would gladly purchase their peace with the God of Israel at any rate. The *golden emerods* must be, in number, five, according to the *number of the lords*, who, it is likely, were all afflicted with them, and were content thus to own it; it was advised that the *golden mice* should be five too. 4. They encourage them to hope that hereby they would take an effectual course to get rid of the plague: *You shall be healed*, *v.* 3. "Let them therefore send back the ark, and then," say they, "*It shall be known to you why his hand is not removed from you*, that is, by this it will appear whether it is for your detaining the ark that you are thus plagued; for, if it be, upon your delivering it up the plague will cease." 5. Yet they put them in a way to make a further trial whether it was the hand of the God of Israel that had smitten them with these plagues or no. They must, in honour of the ark, put it on a new cart or carriage, to be drawn by two milch-cows (*v.* 7), unused to draw, and inclined to home. They must have no one to lead or drive them, but must take their own way, which, in all reason, one might expect, would be home again; and yet, unless the God of Israel, after

JAMIESON, FAUSSET, BROWN

CHAPTER 6

Vss. 1-9. THE PHILISTINES COUNSEL HOW TO SEND BACK THE ARK. **1. the ark . . . was in the country of the Philistines seven months**—Notwithstanding the calamities which its presence had brought on the country and the people, the Philistine lords were unwilling to relinquish such a prize, and tried every means to retain it with peace and safety, but in vain.

2. the Philistines called for the priests and the diviners—The designed restoration of the ark was not, it seems, universally approved of, and many doubts were expressed whether the prevailing pestilence was really a judgment of Heaven. The priests and diviners united all parties by recommending a course which would enable them easily to discriminate the true character of the calamities, and at the same time to propitiate the incensed Deity for any acts of disrespect which might have been shown to His ark. **4. Five golden emerods**—Votive or thank offerings were commonly made by the heathen in prayer for, or gratitude after, deliverance from lingering or dangerous disorders, in the form of metallic (generally silver) models or images of the diseased parts of the body. This is common still in Roman Catholic countries, as well as in the temples of the Hindoos and other modern heathen. **five golden mice**—This animal is supposed by some to be the jerboa or jumping-mouse of Syria and Egypt [BOCHART]; by others, to be the short-tailed field mouse, which often swarms in prodigious numbers and commits great ravages in the cultivated fields of Palestine. **5. give glory unto the God of Israel**—By these propitiatory presents, the Philistines would acknowledge His power and make reparation for the injury done to His ark. **lighten his hand . . . from off your gods**—Elohim for god. **6. Wherefore then do ye harden your hearts, as the Egyptians and Pharaoh hardened their hearts**—The memory of the appalling judgments that had been inflicted on Egypt was not yet obliterated. Whether preserved in written records, or in floating tradition, they were still fresh in the minds of men, and being extensively spread, were doubtless the means of diffusing the knowledge and fear of the true God. **7. make a new cart**—Their object in making a new one for the purpose seems to have been not only for cleanliness and neatness, but from an impression that there would have been an impropriety in using one that had been applied to meaner or more common services. It appears to have been a covered wagon (see on II Sam. 6:3). **two milch kine**—Such untrained heifers, wanton and vagrant, would pursue no certain and regular path, like those accustomed to the yoke, and therefore were most unlikely of their own spontaneous motion to prosecute the direct road to the land of Israel. **bring their calves home from them**—The strong natural affection of the dams might be supposed to stimulate their return homewards, rather than direct their steps in a foreign country.

ADAM CLARKE

CHAPTER 6

2. *The diviners. Kosemim*, from *kasam*, "to presage or prognosticate" (see Deut. xviii. 10). In what their pretended art consisted, we know not.

3. *Send it not empty.* As it appears you have trespassed against Him, send Him an offering for this trespass. *Why his hand is not removed.* The sense is, If you send Him a trespass offering, and you be cured, then you shall know why His judgments have not been taken away from you previously to this offering.

4. *Five golden emerods, and five golden mice.* One for each satrapy. The emerods had afflicted their bodies; the mice had marred their land. Both they considered as sent by God; and, making an image of each, and sending them as a trespass offering, they acknowledged this.

6. *Wherefore then do ye harden your hearts?* They had heard how God punished the Egyptians, and they are afraid of similar plagues. *Did they not let the people go?* And has He not wrought wonderfully among us? And should we not send back His ark?

7. *Make a new cart.* It was indecent and improper to employ in any part of the worship of God anything that had before served for a common purpose. When David removed the ark from the house of Abinadab, he put it on a new cart, 2 Sam. vi. 3. *Bring their calves home from them.* So it appears that their calves had been with them in the fields. This was a complete trial: unless they were supernaturally influenced, they would not leave their calves: unless supernaturally directed, they would not leave their home, and take a way unguided, which they had never gone before.

8. *The jewels of gold.* The word *keley*, which our translators so often render *jewels*, signifies "vessels, implements, ornaments."

MATTHEW HENRY

all the other miracles he has wrought, will work one more, and by an invisible power lead these cows, contrary to their mutual instinct and inclination, to the land of Israel, and particularly to Beth-shemesh, they will retract their former opinion, and will believe it was not the hand of God that smote them, but it was a chance that *happened to them, v.* 8, 9.

Verses 10–18

I. How the Philistines dismissed the ark, *v.* 10, 11. They were made as glad to part with it as ever they had been to take it. 1. They received no money or price for the ransom of it, as they hoped to do, even beyond a king's ransom. 2. They gave jewels of gold, as the Egyptians did to the Israelites, to be rid of it.

II. How the kine brought it to the land of Israel, *v.* 12. They *took the straight way to Beth-shemesh,* the next city of the land of Israel, and a priests' city, *and turned not aside.* This was a wonderful instance of the power of God over the brute-creatures that cattle unaccustomed to the yoke should go the straight road to Beth-shemesh, a city eight or ten miles off, never miss the way, never turn aside into the fields to feed themselves, nor turn back home to feed their calves.

III. How it was welcomed to the land of Israel: *The men of Beth-shemesh were reaping their wheat-harvest, v.* 13. They were going on with their worldly business, and were in no care about the ark. God will in his own time effect the deliverance of his church, not only though it be fought against by its enemies, but though it be neglected by its friends. The same invisible hand that directed the kine to the land of Israel brought them into the field of Joshua, for the sake of the great stone in that field, which was convenient to put the ark upon, and which is spoken of, *v.* 14, 15, 18. 1. When the reapers *saw the ark, they rejoiced* (*v.* 13). Though they had not zeal and courage enough to attempt the rescue or ransom of it, yet, when it did come, they bade it heartily welcome. 2. They offered up the kine for a burnt-offering, to the honour of God, and made use of the wood of the cart for fuel, *v.* 14. Probably the Philistines intended these, when they sent them, to be a part of their trespass-offering, to make atonement, *v.* 3, 7. 3. They deposited the ark, with a chest of jewels that the Philistines presented, upon the great stone in the open field, a cold lodging for the ark of the Lord and a very mean one; yet better so than in Dagon's temple, or in the hands of the Philistines. As the burning of the cart and cows that brought home the ark might be construed to signify their hopes that it should never be carried away again out of the land of Israel, so the setting of it upon a great stone might signify their hopes that it should be established again upon a firm foundation. The church is built upon a rock. 4. They offered the sacrifices of thanksgiving to God, some think upon the great stone, more probably upon an altar of earth made for the purpose, *v.* 15. This accidental bringing of the ark hither was an indication of its designed settlement there, in process of time. It was one of those cities which were assigned out of the lot of Judah to the *sons of Aaron* Josh. xxi. 16. Whither should the ark go but to a priests' city? And it was well they had those of that sacred order ready to take down the ark and to offer the sacrifices. 5. The lords of the Philistines returned to Ekron, much affected, we may suppose, with what they had seen of the glory of God and the zeal of the Israelites, and yet not reclaimed from the worship of Dagon.

Verses 19–21

1. The sin of the men of Beth-shemesh: *They looked into the ark of the Lord, v.* 19. We were all ruined by an ambition of forbidden knowledge. That which made this looking into the ark a great sin was that it proceeded from a very low and mean opinion of the ark. It may be they presumed upon the present mean circumstances the ark was in, newly come out of captivity, and unsettled. It is an offence to God if we think meanly of his ordinances because of the meanness of the manner of their administration. Had they looked with an understanding eye upon the ark, and not judged purely by outward appearance, they would have thought that the ark never shone with greater majesty than it did now. 2. Their punishment for this sin: *He smote the men of Beth-shemesh, many of them, with a great slaughter.* Josephus says only seventy were smitten. 3. The terror that was struck upon the men of Beth-shemesh by this severe stroke. They said, as well they might, *Who is able to stand before this holy Lord God? v.* 20. To stand before God to worship him (blessed be his name) is not impossible; we are through Christ invited, encouraged, and enabled to do it, but to stand before

JAMIESON, FAUSSET, BROWN

8. take the ark of the Lord, and lay it upon the cart—This mode of carrying the sacred symbol was forbidden; but the ignorance of the Philistines made the indignity excusable (see on II Sam. 6:6). **put the jewels . . . in a coffer by the side thereof**—The way of securing treasure in the East is still in a chest, chained to the house wall or some solid part of the furniture. **9. Beth-shemesh**—i.e., "house of the sun," now Ain Shems [ROBINSON], a city of priests in Judah, in the southeast border of Dan, lying in a beautiful and extensive valley. Josephus says they were set agoing near a place where the road divided into two—the one leading back to Ekron, where were their calves, and the other to Beth-shemesh. Their frequent lowings attested their ardent longing for their young, and at the same time the supernatural influence that controlled their movements in a contrary direction. **12. the lords of the Philistines went after them**—to give their tribute of homage, to prevent imposture, and to obtain the most reliable evidence of the truth. The result of this journey tended to their own deeper humiliation, and the greater illustration of God's glory. **14. they clave**—i.e., the Beth-shemites, in an irrepressible outburst of joy. **offered the kine**—Though contrary to the requirements of the law (Lev. 1:3; 22:19), these animals might properly be offered, as consecrated by God Himself; and though not beside the tabernacle, there were many instances of sacrifices offered by prophets and holy men on extraordinary occasions in other places. **17-18. these are the golden emerods . . . and the mice**—There were five representative images of the emerods, corresponding to the five principal cities of the Philistines. But the number of the golden mice must have been greater, for they were sent from the walled towns as well as the country villages. **unto the great stone of Abel**—*Abel* or Aben means "stone," so that without resorting to *italics,* the reading should be, "the great stone."

19. he smote the men of Beth-shemesh, because they had looked into the ark—In the ecstasy of delight at seeing the return of the ark, the Beth-shemesh reapers pried into it beneath the wagon cover; and instead of covering it up again, as a sacred utensil, they let it remain exposed to common inspection, wishing it to be seen, in order that all might enjoy the triumph of seeing the votive offerings presented to it, and gratify curiosity with the sight of the sacred shrine. This was the offense of those Israelites (Levites, as well as common people), who had treated the ark with less reverence than the Philistines themselves. **he smote of the people fifty thousand and threescore and ten men**—Beth-shemesh being only a village, this translation *must* be erroneous, and should be, "he smote fifty out of a thousand," being only 1400 in all who indulged this curiosity. God, instead of decimating, according to an ancient usage, slew only a twentieth part; i.e., according to Josephus, 70 out of 1400 (see on Num. 4:18-22).

ADAM CLARKE

9. *A chance that happened to us.* The word *mikreh,* from *karah,* to "meet or coalesce," signifies an event that naturally arises from such concurring causes as, in the order and nature of things, must produce it.

12. *Lowing as they went.* Calling for their calves. *To the right hand or to the left.* Some think they were placed where two roads met: one going to Ekron, the other to Beth-shemesh. It is possible that they were put in such circumstances as these for the greater certainty of the affair: to have turned from their own homes, from their calves and known pasture, and to have taken the road to a strange country, must argue supernatural influence. *The lords of the Philistines went after.* They were so jealous in this business that they would trust no eyes but their own. All this was wisely ordered, that there might be the fullest conviction of the being and interposition of God.

14. *They clave the wood of the cart.* Both the cart and the cattle, having been thus employed, could no longer be devoted to any secular services; therefore the cattle were sacrificed, and the cart was broken up for fuel to consume the sacrifice.

15. *The Levites took down.* It appears there were some of the tribe of Levi among the people of Beth-shemesh; to them appertained the service of the Tabernacle.

17. *These are the golden emerods.* Each of these cities, in what may be called its corporate capacity, sent a golden emerod.

19. *He smote of the people fifty thousand and threescore and ten men.* The present Hebrew text of this most extraordinary reading stands thus: "And he smote among the men of Beth-shemesh, (because they looked into the ark of Jehovah,) and he smote among the people seventy men, fifty thousand men."

From the manner in which the text stands, and from the great improbability of the thing, it is most likely that there is a corruption in this text, or that some explanatory word is lost, or that the number *fifty thousand* has been added by ignorance or design; it being very improbable that such a small village as Beth-shemesh should contain or be capable of employing fifty thousand and seventy men in the fields at wheat harvest, much less that they could all peep into the ark on the stone of Abel, in the cornfield of Joshua.

That the words are not naturally connected in the Hebrew text is evident; and they do not stand better in the versions. (1) The Vulgate renders it thus: "And he smote of the [chief] people seventy men, and fifty thousand of the [common] people." (2) The Targum of Jonathan is something similar to the Vulgate: "And he smote of the elders of the people seventy men; and of the congregation fifty thousand men." (3) The Septuagint follow the Hebrew text: "And he smote of them seventy men; and fifty thousand men." (4) The Syriac is as follows: "And the Lord smote among the people five thousand and seventy men." (5) The Arabic is nearly similar: "And the Lord smote among the people; and there died of them five thousand and seventy men." (6) Josephus is different from all the rest, for he renders the place thus, *Antiq. Jud.,* lib. vi, cap. i, sect. 4: "But the displeasure and wrath of God pursued them so, that seventy men of the village of Beth-shemesh, approaching the ark, which they were not worthy to touch (not being priests), were struck with lightning." Here we find the whole *fifty thousand* is omitted.

The common reading may be defended if we only suppose the omission of a single letter, the particle of comparison *ke,* "like, as, or equal to." The passage would then read: "And he smote of the people seventy men, equal to fifty thousand men"; that is, they were the elders or governors of the people. Some solve the difficulty by translating, "He slew seventy men out of fifty thousand men." There are various other methods invented by learned men to remove this difficulty, which I shall not stop to examine; all, however, issue in this point, that only seventy men were slain; and this is without doubt the most probable.

With a great slaughter. Seventy men slain, out of an inconsiderable village in a harvest

MATTHEW HENRY

God to contend with him we are not able. 4. Their desire, hereupon, to be rid of the ark. They asked, *To whom shall he go up from us? v.* 20.

They sent messengers to the elders of Kirjath-jearim, a strong city further up in the country, and begged of them to come and fetch the ark up thither, *v.* 21. It lay in the way from Beth-shemesh to Shiloh, so that when they sent to them to fetch it, we may suppose, they intended that the elders of Shiloh should fetch it thence, but God intended otherwise. Thus was it sent from town to town, and no care taken of it by the public, a sign that there was no king in Israel.

JAMIESON, FAUSSET, BROWN

21. Kirjath-jearim—"the city of woods," also called Kirjath-baal (Josh. 15:60; 18:14; I Chron. 13:6, 7). This was the nearest town to Beth-shemesh; and being a place of strength, it was a more fitting place for the residence of the ark. Beth-shemesh being in a low plain, and Kirjath-jearim on a hill, explains the message, "Come ye down, and fetch it up to you."

ADAM CLARKE

day, was certainly a great slaughter.

20. *Who is able to stand?* Why this exclamation? They knew that God had forbidden any to touch His ark but the priests and Levites; but they endeavored to throw that blame on God, as a Being hard to be pleased, which belonged solely to themselves.

21. *To the inhabitants of Kirjath-jearim.* They wished the ark away out of their village, but why they sent to this city instead of sending to Shiloh does not appear. Probably Shiloh had been destroyed by the Philistines, after the late defeat of Israel. This is most likely, as the ark was never more taken back to that place.

MATTHEW HENRY — CHAPTER 7

Verses 1–2

Here we must attend the ark to Kirjath-jearim, to hear not a word more of it except once (*ch.* xiv. 18), till David fetched it thence, about forty years after, 1 Chron. xiii. 6.

I. The men of Beth-shemesh have by their own folly made that a burden which might have been a blessing.

1. The men of Kirjath-jearim cheerfully bring it among them, *v.* 1. Their neighbours the Beth-shemites, were not more glad to get rid of it than they were to receive it, knowing very well that what slaughter the ark had made at Beth-shemesh was not an act of arbitrary power, but of necessary justice, and those that suffered by it must blame themselves, not the ark.

2. They carefully provided for its decent entertainment among them, with true affection, with respect and reverence.

(1) They provided a proper place to receive it, in the house of Abinadab, which stood upon the highest ground, and, probably, was the best house in their city. The men of Beth-shemesh left it exposed upon a stone in the open field, but the men of Kirjath-jearim gave it house-room. God will find out a resting-place for his ark; if some thrust it from them, yet the hearts of others shall be inclined to receive it. It is no new thing for God's ark to be thrust into a private house.

(2) They provided a proper person to attend it: *They sanctified Eleazar his son to keep it*; not the father, because he was aged and infirm. His business was to keep the ark, not only from being seized by malicious Philistines, but from being touched or looked into by too curious Israelites. He was to keep the room clean and decent in which the ark was, that it might not look like a neglected thing. It does not appear that this Eleazar was of the tribe of Levi, much less of the house of Aaron. We may suppose that some devout Israelites would come and pray before the ark, and those that did so he was there ready to attend and assist. For this purpose they set him apart for it in the name of all their citizens. This was irregular, but was excusable because of the present distress.

II. Yet we are very loth to leave it here, wishing it well at Shiloh again, but that is made desolate (Jer. vii. 14), it must lie by the way for want of some public-spirited men to bring it to its proper place. 1. The time of its continuance here was long. Above forty years it lay in a remote, obscure, private place, unfrequented and almost unregarded (*v.* 2). It was very strange that all the time that Samuel governed, the ark was never brought to its place in the holy of holies, an evidence of the decay of holy zeal among them. God suffered it to be so, to punish them for their neglect when it was in its place. 2. Twenty years of this time had passed before the house of Israel was sensible of the want of the ark. The Septuagint read it somewhat more clearly than we do; *and it was twenty years, and* (that is, when) *the whole house of Israel looked up again after the Lord.* While it was absent from the tabernacle, the token of God's special presence was wanting, nor could they keep the day of atonement as it should be kept. They were content with the altars without the ark; so easily can formal professors rest satisfied in a round of external performances, without any tokens of God's presence or acceptance. But at length they bethought themselves, and began to lament after the Lord, stirred up to it, it is probable, by the preaching of Samuel, with which an extraordinary working of the Spirit of God set in. A general disposition to repentance and reformation now appears throughout all Israel. True repentance and conversion begin in lamenting after the Lord. It was better with the Israelites when they wanted the ark, and were lament-

JAMIESON, FAUSSET, BROWN — CHAPTER 7

Vss. 1-2. THE ARK AT KIRJATH-JEARIM. **1. the men of Kirjath-jearim**—"the city of woods," also Kirjath-baal (Josh. 15:60; 18:14; I Chron. 13:5, 6). It was the nearest town to Beth-shemesh and stood on a hill. This was the reason of the message (ch. 6:21), and why this was chosen for the convenience of people turning their faces to the ark (I Kings 8: 29-35; Ps. 28:2; Dan. 6:10).

brought it into the house of Abinadab—Why it was not transported at once to Shiloh where the tabernacle and sacred vessels were remaining, is difficult to conjecture.

sanctified . . . his son—He was not a Levite, and was therefore only set apart or appointed to be keeper of the place.

2. the ark abode in Kirjath-jearim . . . twenty years—It appears, in the subsequent history, that a much longer period elapsed before its final removal from Kirjath-jearim (II Sam. 6; I Chron. 13). But that length of time had passed when the Israelites began to revive from their sad state of religious decline. The capture of the ark had produced a general indifference either as to its loss or its recovery. **all the house of Israel lamented after the Lord**—They were then brought, doubtless by the influence of Samuel's exhortations, to renounce idolatry, and to return to the national worship of the true God.

ADAM CLARKE — CHAPTER 7

1. *Fetched up the ark.* When these people received the message of the Beth-shemites, they probably consulted Samuel, with whom was the counsel of the Lord, and he encouraged them to go and bring it up, else they might have expected such destruction as happened to the Beth-shemites.

Sanctified Eleazar. Perhaps this sanctifying signifies no more than setting this man apart, simply to take care of the ark.

2. *It was twenty years.* This chapter contains the transactions of at least twenty years, but we know not the date of each event.

MATTHEW HENRY

ng after it, than when they had the ark, and were rying into it, or priding themselves in it.

Verses 3–6

We may well wonder where Samuel was and what e was doing all this while, but his labours among is people are not mentioned till there appears the ruit of them. When he perceived that they began o *lament after the Lord* he struck while the iron was ot, and two things he endeavoured to do for them,

I. He endeavoured to separate between them and heir idols, for *there* reformation must begin. He *poke to all the house of Israel* (*v.* 3), going, as it hould seem, from place to place, an itinerant preacher for we find not that they were gathered together till . 5), and wherever he came this was his exhortation, "*If you do indeed return to the Lord*, then know, . That you must renounce and abandon your idols. Put away Baalim, the strange gods, and Ashtaroth, he strange goddess," for such also they had. Ashtaoth is particularly named because it was the bestbeloved idol. True repentance strikes at the darling in, and will with a peculiar zeal and resolution put away that, the sin which most *easily besets us*. 2. That ou must make a solemn business of returning to God, and do it with a serious consideration and a steadfast esolution, for both are included in *preparing the heart*, directing, disposing, establishing, the heart unto the Lord. 3. That you must be wholly for God, or him and no other, *serve him only*, else you do not serve him at all so as to please him. Take this course, and *he will deliver you out of the hand of the Philistines*. This was the purport of Samuel's preaching, and it had a wonderfully good effect (*v.* 4): *They put away Baalim and Ashtaroth*, not only quitted the worship of them, but destroyed their images, demolished their altars, and quite abandoned them.

II. He endeavoured to engage them for ever to God and his service.

1. He summons all Israel, at least by their elders, as their representatives, to meet him at Mizpeh (*v.* 5), and there he promises to pray for them. When we come together in religious assemblies, we must remember that it is as much our business there to join in public prayers as it is to hear a sermon.

2. They obey his summons, and not only come to the meeting, but conform to the intentions of it, and appear there very well disposed, *v.* 6.

(1) *They drew water and poured it out before the Lord*, signifying, [1] Their humiliation and contrition for sin, owning themselves as water spilt upon the ground, which cannot be gathered up again (2 Sam. xiv. 14). The Chaldee reads it, *They poured out their hearts in repentance before the Lord.* [2] Their earnest prayers and supplications to God for mercy. [3] Their universal reformation; they thus expressed their willingness to part with all their sins, and to retain no more of the relish or savour of them than the vessel does of the water that is poured out of it. [4] Some think it signifies their joy in the hope of God's mercy, which Samuel had assured them of.

(2) *They fasted*, abstained from food, afflicted their souls, so expressing repentance.

(3) They made a public confession: *We have sinned against the Lord*, so giving glory to God and taking shame to themselves.

3. Samuel judged them at that time in Mizpeh, that is, he assured them, in God's name, of the pardon of their sins, upon their repentance, and that God was reconciled to them. It was a judgment of absolution. Whereas before he acted only as a prophet, now he began to act as a magistrate, to prevent their relapsing into those sins which now they seemed to have renounced.

Verses 7–12

I. The Philistines invade Israel (*v.* 7), taking umbrage from that general meeting for repentance and prayer as if it had been a rendezvous for war. 1. How evil sometimes seems to come out of good! The religious meeting of the Israelites at Mizpeh brought trouble upon them from the Philistines. When sinners begin to repent and reform, they must expect that Satan will muster all his force against them, and set his instruments on work to the utmost to oppose and discourage them. But, 2. How good is, at length, brought out of that evil. Israel could never be threatened more seasonably than at this time, when they were repenting and praying, nor could they have been better prepared to receive the enemy.

II. Israel cleaves closely to Samuel, as their best friend, under God, in this distress; though he was no military man, nor ever celebrated as a mighty man of valour, yet, they engaged Samuel's prayers for them: *Cease not to cry unto the Lord our God for us*, *v.* 8. They were here unarmed, unprepared for war, come together to fast and pray, not to fight; prayers

JAMIESON, FAUSSET, BROWN

3-6. THE ISRAELITES, THROUGH SAMUEL'S INFLUENCE, SOLEMNLY REPENT AT MIZPEH. **3-6. Samuel spake unto all the house of Israel**—A great national reformation was effected through the influence of Samuel. Disgusted with their foreign servitude, and panting for the restoration of liberty and independence, they were open to salutary impressions; and convinced of their errors, they renounced idolatry. The re-establishment of the faith of their fathers was inaugurated at a great public meeting, held at Mizpeh in Judah, and hallowed by the observance of impressive religious solemnities.

Samuel judged . . . Israel in Mizpeh—At the time of Eli's death he could not have much exceeded twenty years of age; and although his character and position must have given him great influence, it does not appear that hitherto he had done more than prophets were wont to do. Now he entered on the duties of a civil magistrate.

The drawing water, and pouring it out before the Lord, seems to have been a symbolical act by which, in the people's name, Samuel testified their sense of national corruption, their need of that moral purification of which water is the emblem, and their sincere desire to pour out their hearts in repentance before God.

7-14. WHILE SAMUEL PRAYS, THE PHILISTINES ARE DISCOMFITED. **7-11. when the Philistines heard . . .**—The character and importance of the national convention at Mizpeh were fully appreciated by the Philistines. They discerned in it the rising spirit of religious patriotism among the Israelites that was prepared to throw off the yoke of their domination. Anxious to crush it at the first, they made a sudden incursion while the Israelites were in the midst of their solemn celebration.

Unprepared for resistance, they besought Samuel to supplicate the divine interposition to save them from their enemies.

ADAM CLARKE

3. *And Samuel spake.* We have heard nothing of this judge since he served in the Tabernacle. He was now grown up, and established for a prophet in the land of Israel. *If ye do return.* From your backsliding and idolatry. *With all your hearts.* For outward services and professions will avail nothing.

4. *Put away Baalim and Ashtaroth.* These were not two particular deities, but two *genera* of idols: the one masculine, Baalim; the other feminine, Ashtaroth; both the words are in the plural number, and signify all their "gods" and "goddesses."

5. *Gather all Israel to Mizpeh.* This appears to have been an armed assembly, though probably collected principally for religious and political purposes; but Samuel knew that an unarmed multitude could not safely be convened in the vicinity of the Philistines.

6. *Drew water, and poured it out.* It is not easy to know what is meant by this; it is true that pouring out water, in the way of libation, was a religious ordinance among the Hebrews (Isa. xii. 3), and among most other nations, particularly the Greeks and Romans, who used, not only water, but wine, milk, honey, and blood. The Chaldee paraphrast understands the place differently, for he translates: "And they poured out their hearts in penitence, as waters, before the Lord." That deep penitential sorrow was represented under the notion of pouring out water. We have a direct proof in the case of David, who says, Ps. xxii. 14, "I am poured out like water . . . my heart is like wax; it is melted in the midst of my bowels." And to repentance, under this very similitude, the prophet exhorts fallen Jerusalem: "Arise, cry out in the night: in the beginning of the watches pour out thine heart like water before the face of the Lord," Lam. ii. 19.

And Samuel judged. He gave them ordinances, heard and redressed grievances, and taught them how to get reconciled to God. The assembly, therefore, was held for religio-politico-military purposes.

7. *The Philistines went up against Israel.* They went to give them battle before that, by continual accessions of numbers, they should become too powerful.

8. *Cease not to cry unto the Lord.* They had strong confidence in the intercession of Samuel, because they knew he was a holy man of God.

MATTHEW HENRY

and tears therefore being all the weapons many of them are now furnished with, to these they have recourse.

III. Samuel intercedes with God for them, and does it *by sacrifice*, *v.* 9. Samuel's sacrifice without his prayer would have been an empty shadow, his prayer without the sacrifice would not have been so prevalent, but both together teach us what great things we may expect from God in answer to those prayers which are made with faith in Christ's sacrifice. It was a burnt-offering, which was offered purely for the glory of God. It was but one sucking lamb that he offered; for it is the integrity and intention of the heart that God looks at, more than the bulk or number of the offerings. Samuel was no priest, but he was a Levite and a prophet; the case was extraordinary, and what he did was by special direction, and therefore accepted of God.

IV. God gave a gracious answer to Samuel's prayer (*v.* 9): *The Lord heard him.* He was himself a *Samuel, asked of God*, and many a Samuel, many a mercy in answer to prayer, God gave him. The prayer of Samuel was honoured; for at the very time when he was offering up his sacrifice, and his prayer with it, the battle began, and turned immediately against the Philistines. As in a former engagement with the Philistines God had justly chastised their presumptuous confidence in the presence of the ark, on the shoulders of two profane priests, so now he graciously accepted their humble dependence upon the prayer of faith from the mouth and heart of a pious prophet.

V. Samuel erected a thankful memorial of this victory, to the glory of God and for the encouragement of Israel, *v.* 12. He set up an *Eben-ezer, the stone of help*. The place where this memorial was set up was the same where, twenty years before, the Israelites were smitten before the Philistines, for that was beside Eben-ezer, *ch.* iv. 1. The reason he gives for the name is, *Hitherto the Lord hath helped us*, in which he speaks thankfully of what was past, and yet he speaks somewhat doubtfully for the future: "Hitherto things have done well, but what God may yet do with us we know not, *that* we refer to him; but let us praise him for what he has done." *Having obtained help from God. I continue hitherto*, says blessed Paul, Acts xxvi. 22.

Verses 13–17

It appears (2 Chron. xxxv. 18) that in the days of Samuel the prophet the people of Israel kept the ordinance of the passover with more than ordinary devotion, notwithstanding the distance of the ark and the desolations of Shiloh. Here we are only told how instrumental he was, 1. In securing the public peace (*v.* 13): *In his days the Philistines came no more into the coast of Israel.* Samuel was a protector and deliverer to Israel, not by dint of sword, as Gideon, nor by strength of arm, as Samson, but by the power of prayer to God and carrying on a work of reformation among the people. Religion and piety are the best securities of a nation. 2. In recovering the public rights, *v.* 14. By his influence Israel had the courage to demand the cities which the Philistines had unjustly taken from them. It is added, *There was peace between Israel and the Amorites*, that is, the Canaanites, the remains of the natives. 3. In administering public justice (*v.* 15, 16): *He judged Israel.* Even after Saul was made king he promised them (*ch.* xii. 23), *I will* not cease to *teach you the good and the right way.* He kept courts at Beth-el, Gilgal, and Mizpeh, all in the tribe of Benjamin; but his constant residence was at Ramah, his father's city, and there he judged Israel. 4. In keeping up the public exercises of religion; for there, where he lived, he built an altar to the Lord, not in contempt of the altar that was at Nob, or Gibeon. He did as the patriarchs did, he built an altar where he lived, both for the use of his own family and for the good of the country that resorted to it.

JAMIESON, FAUSSET, BROWN

The prophet's prayers and sacrifice were answered by such a tremendous storm of thunder and lightning that the assailants, panic-struck, were disordered and fied. The Israelites, recognizing the hand of God, rushed courageously on the foe they had so much dreaded and committed such immense havoc, that the Philistines did not for long recover from this disastrous blow. This brilliant victory secured peace and independence to Israel for twenty years, as well as the restitution of the usurped territory.

12. Samuel took a stone, and set it between Mizpeh and Shen—on an open spot between the town and "the crag" (some well-known rock in the neighborhood). A huge stone pillar was erected as a monument of their victory (Lev. 26:1). The name—Eben-ezer—is thought to have been written on the face of it.

ADAM CLARKE

9. *Samuel took a sucking lamb.* This sucking lamb must have been eight days under its mother before it could be offered, as the law says, Lev. xxii. 27.

10. *The Lord thundered with a great thunder.* Literally, "The Lord thundered with a great voice"—He confounded them with a mighty tempest of thunder and lightning, and no doubt slew many by the lightning.

11. *Under Beth-car.* We know not where this place was; the Septuagint have Beth-chor; the Targum, Beth-saron; and the Syriac and Arabic, Beth-jasan.

12. *Called the name of it Eben-ezer. Eben haezer*, "The Stone of Help"; perhaps a pillar is meant by the word *stone*.

13. *They came no more into the coast of Israel.* Perhaps a more signal victory was never gained by Israel; the Lord had brought them low, almost to extermination; and now, by His miraculous interference, He lifts them completely up, and humbles to the dust their proud oppressors. God often suffers nations and individuals to be brought to the lowest extremity, that He may show His mercy and goodness by suddenly rescuing them from destruction, when all human help has most evidently failed.

14. *The cities which the Philistines had taken.* We are not informed of the particulars of these reprisals, but we may rest assured all this was not done in one day; perhaps the retaking of the cities was by slow degrees, through the space of several years. *There was peace between Israel and the Amorites.* That is, all the remaining Canaanites kept quiet, and did not attempt to molest the Israelites, when they found the Philistines, the most powerful of the ancient inhabitants of the land, broken and subdued before them.

16-17. *He went from year to year in circuit.* When he was at Bethel, the tribe of Ephraim, and all the northern parts of the country, could attend him; when at Gilgal, the tribe of Benjamin, and those beyond Jordan, might have easy access to him; and when at Mizpeh, he was within reach of Judah, Simeon, and Gad. But *Ramah* was the place of his ordinary abode; and there he held his court, for *there he judged Israel;* and, as it is probable that Shiloh was destroyed, it is said that *there* (viz., at Ramah) *he built an altar unto the Lord.* This altar, being duly consecrated, the worship performed at it was strictly legal. *Ramah,* which is said to be about six miles from Jerusalem, was the seat of prophecy during the life of Samuel; and there it is probable all Israel came to consult him on matters of a spiritual nature, as there was the only altar of God in the land of Israel.

MATTHEW HENRY

CHAPTER 8

Verses 1–3

Two sad things we find here, but not strange things:—1. A good and useful man growing old and unfit for service (*v.* 1): *Samuel was old*, and could not judge Israel, as he had done. He is not reckoned to be past sixty years of age now, perhaps not so much; but he was a man betimes, was full of thoughts and cares when he was a child. The fruits that are the first ripe keep the worst. He had spent his strength and spirits in the fatigue of public business, and now, if he think to shake himself as at other times, he finds he is mistaken, old age has cut his hair. Those that are in the prime of their time ought to be busy

JAMIESON, FAUSSET, BROWN

CHAPTER 8

VSS. 1-18. OCCASIONED BY THE ILL-GOVERNMENT OF SAMUEL'S SONS, THE ISRAELITES ASK A KING. **1. when Samuel was old**—He was now about fifty-four years of age, having discharged the office of sole judge for twelve years.

ADAM CLARKE

CHAPTER 8

1. *When Samuel was old.* Supposed to be about sixty.

MATTHEW HENRY

in doing the work of life. 2. The children of a good man turning aside, and not treading in his steps. We have reason to think that Samuel gave them their commissions, not because they were his sons, but because, for aught that yet appeared, they were men very fit for the trust. But, alas! *his sons walked not in his ways* (*v.* 3), and, when their character was the reverse of his, their relation to so good a man, which otherwise would have been their honour, was really their disgrace. When Samuel's sons were made judges, and settled at a distance from him, then they discovered themselves. Many that have done well in a state of subjection have been spoiled by preferment and power. Honours change men's minds, and too often for the worse. It does not appear that Samuel's sons were so profane and vicious as Eli's sons; but, whatever they were in other respects, they were corrupt judges, they *turned aside after lucre*, after *the mammon of unrighteousness*, so the Chaldee reads it. In determining controversies, they had an eye to the bribe, not to the law, and enquired who bid highest, not who had right on his side.

Verses 4–22

We have here the starting of a matter perfectly new and surprising, which was the setting up of kingly government in Israel.

I. The address of the elders to Samuel in this matter (*v.* 4, 5). They came to him to his house at Ramah with their address, which contained,

1. A remonstrance of their grievances: in short, *Thou art old, and thy sons walk not in thy ways.* (1) It was true that Samuel was old; yet it made him the more wise and experienced, and, upon that account, the fitter to rule. (2) It was true that his sons did not walk in his ways; the more was his grief, but they could not say it was his fault: he had not, like Eli, indulged them in their badness, but was ready to receive complaints against them.

2. A petition for the redress of these grievances, by setting a king over them: *Make us a king to judge us like all the nations.* Thus far it was well, that they did not rise up in rebellion against Samuel and set up a king for themselves. But it appears by what followed that it was an evil proposal and ill made, and was displeasing to God. They must have a king to judge them with external pomp and power, like *all the nations.* A poor prophet in a mantle, though conversant in the visions of the Almighty, looked mean in the eyes of those who judged by outward appearance; but a king in a purple robe, with his guards and officers of state, would look great: and such a one they must have.

II. Samuel's resentment of this address, *v.* 6. 1. It cut him to the heart. Probably it was a surprise to him. It *displeased him when they said, Give us a king to judge us,* because that reflected upon God and his honour. 2. It drove him to his knees; he gave them no answer for the present, but took time to consider of what they proposed, and prayed unto the Lord for direction what to do.

III. The instruction God gave him concerning this matter. He tells him,

1. That which would be an allay to his displeasure. Samuel was much disturbed at the proposal: but God tells him he must not think it either hard or strange. (1) He must not think it hard that they had put this slight upon him, for they had herein put a slight upon God himself. If God interest himself in the indignities that are done us, we may well afford to bear them patiently. Samuel must not complain that they were weary of his government, for really they were weary of God's government. The government of Israel had hitherto been a Theocracy, a divine government; their judges had their call and commission immediately from God; the affairs of their nation were under his peculiar direction. (2) He must not think it strange for they do as they always have done. They had always been rude to their governors, witness Moses and Aaron.

2. He tells him that which would be an answer to their demand. Samuel would not have known what to say if God had not instructed him, but he gives them, with assurance, the answer God sent them.

(1) He must tell them that *they shall have a king. Hearken to the voice of the people*, *v.* 7, and again, *v.* 9. God bade Samuel humour them in this matter, [1] That they might be beaten with their own rod, and might feel, to their cost, the difference between his government and the government of a king. [2] To prevent something worse. If they were not gratified, they would either rise in rebellion against Samuel or universally revolt from their religion and admit the gods of the nations, that they might have kings like them.

(2) But he must tell them, withal, that when they have a king they will soon have enough of him, and

JAMIESON, FAUSSET, BROWN

Unable, from growing infirmities, to prosecute his circuit journeys through the country, he at length confined his magisterial duties to Ramah and its neighborhood, delegating to his sons as his deputies (ch. 7:15) the administration of justice in the southern districts of Palestine, their provincial court being held at Beersheba. The young men, however, did not inherit the high qualities of their father.

Having corrupted the fountains of justice for their own private aggrandizement, a deputation of the leading men in the country lodged a complaint against them in headquarters, accompanied with a formal demand for a change in the government. The limited and occasional authority of the judges, the disunion and jealousy of the tribes under the administration of those rulers, had been creating a desire for a united and permanent form of government; while the advanced age of Samuel, together with the risk of his death happening in the then unsettled state of the people, was the occasion of calling forth an expression of this desire now.

6. the thing displeased Samuel when they said, Give us a king to judge us— Personal and family feelings might affect his views of this public movement. But his dissatisfaction arose principally from the proposed change being revolutionary in its character.

Though it would not entirely subvert their theocratic government, the appointment of a visible monarch would necessarily tend to throw out of view their unseen King and Head.

God intimated, through Samuel, that their request would, in anger, be granted, while at the same time he apprised them of some of the evils that would result from their choice.

ADAM CLARKE

He made his sons judges. He appointed them as his lieutenants to superintend certain affairs in Beersheba, which he could not conveniently attend to himself. But they were never *judges* in the proper sense of the word; Samuel was the last judge in Israel, and he judged it to the day of his death. See chap. vii. 15.

3. *His sons walked not in his ways.* Their iniquity is pointed out in three words: (1) they *turned aside after lucre;* the original (*batsa*) signifies to "cut, clip, break off." It expresses here the idea of avarice, of getting money by hook or by crook. (2) They *took bribes;* "gifts or presents" blind their eyes. (3) They *perverted judgment*—they turned judgment aside; they put it out of its regular path; they sold it to the highest bidder. Thus the wicked rich man had his cause, and the poor man was oppressed and deprived of his right.

5. *Make us a king.* Hitherto, from the time in which they were a people, the Israelites were under a theocracy; they had no other king but God. Now they desire to have a king like the other nations around them, who may be their general in battle; for this is the point at which they principally aim.

6. *The thing displeased Samuel.* Because he saw that this amounted to a formal renunciation of the divine government. *Samuel prayed unto the Lord.* He begged to know His mind in this important business.

7. *They have rejected me.* They wish to put that government in the hands of a mortal which was always in the hands of their God. But *hearken unto the voice of the people*—grant them what they request. So we find God grants that in His displeasure which He withholds in His mercy.

9. *Shew them the manner of the king.* The word *mishpat*, which we here render *manner*, signifies simply what the king would and might require, according to the *manner* in which kings in general ruled; all of whom, in those times, were absolute and despotic.

MATTHEW HENRY

will, when it is too late, repent of their choice.

IV. Samuel's faithful delivery of God's mind to them, *v.* 10. He *told them all the words of the Lord,* how ill he resented it, that he construed it a rejecting of him, and compared it with their serving other gods. He lays before them, very particularly, what would be, not the right of a king in general, but *the manner of the king that should reign over them,* according to the pattern of the nations, *v.* 11.

1. If they will have such a king as the nations have, let them consider, (1) That a king must have a great retinue, a multitude of attendants. And whence must he have these? "Why, he will take your sons, and will *appoint them for himself,*" *v.* 11. They must wait upon him, *ear his ground, and reap his harvest* (*v.* 12), and count it their preferment too, *v.* 16. (2) He must keep a great table. (3) He must needs have a standing army, for guards and garrisons. (4) "You may expect that he will have great favourites, whom, having dignified and ennobled, he must enrich out of your inheritances (*v.* 14). How will you like that?" (5) "He must have great revenues to maintain his grandeur and power. He will take the tenth of the fruits of your ground (*v.* 15), and your cattle," *v.* 17.

2. These would be their grievances. When they complained to God he *would not hear them, v.* 18.

V. The people's obstinacy in their demand, *v.* 19, 20. "*We will have a king over us,* whatever God or Samuel say to the contrary; we will have a king, whatever it cost us, and whatever inconvenience we bring upon ourselves or our posterity by it." They were quite deaf to reason and blind to their own interest. They could not stay God's time. God had intimated to them in the law that, in due time, Israel should have a king (Deut. xvii. 14, 15). Could they but have waited ten or twelve years longer they would have had David, a king of God's giving in mercy, and all the calamities that attended the setting up of Saul would have been prevented.

VI. The dismissing of them with an intimation that very shortly they should have what they asked. 1. *Samuel rehearsed all their words in the ears of the Lord, v.* 21. It bespeaks a holy familiarity, to which God graciously admits his people: they speak in the ears of the Lord, as one friend whispers with another. 2. God gave direction that they should have a king, since they were so inordinately set upon it (*v.* 22): "*Make them a king,* and let them make their best of him." *So he gave them up to their own hearts' lusts.* Samuel sent them home for the present, *every man to his city;* for the designation of the person must be left to God; they had now no more to do.

JAMIESON, FAUSSET, BROWN

11. This will be the manner of the king—The following is a very just and graphic picture of the despotic governments which anciently and still are found in the East, and into conformity with which the Hebrew monarchy, notwithstanding the restrictions prescribed by the law, gradually slid. **He will take your sons, and appoint them for himself**—Oriental sovereigns claim a right to the services of any of their subjects at pleasure. **some shall run before his chariots**—The royal equipages were, generally throughout the East (as in Persia they still are), preceded and accompanied by a number of attendants who ran on foot. **12. he will appoint him captains**—In the East, a person must accept any office to which he may be nominated by the king, however irksome it may be to his taste or ruinous to his interests. **13. he will take your daughters to be confectionaries**—Cookery, baking, and the kindred works are, in Eastern countries, female employment, and thousands of young women are occupied with these offices in the palaces even of petty princes. **14-18. he will take your fields . . .**—The circumstances mentioned here might be illustrated by exact analogies in the conduct of many Oriental monarchs in the present day. **19-22. Nevertheless the people refused to obey the voice of Samuel**—They sneered at Samuel's description as a bugbear to frighten them. Determined, at all hazards, to gain their object, they insisted on being made like all the other nations, though it was their glory and happiness to be unlike other nations in having the Lord for their King and Lawgiver (Num. 23:9; Deut. 33:28).

Their demand was conceded, for the government of a king had been provided for in the law; and they were dismissed to wait the appointment, which God had reserved to Himself (Deut. 17:14-20).

ADAM CLARKE

ALEXANDER MACLAREN:

Samuel is bidden to "show them the manner of the king that shall reign over them." He sketches, in somber outline, the picture of an Eastern despot, the only kind of king which the world then knew. The darker features of these monarchies are not included. There is no harem, nor cruelty, nor monstrous vice, in the picture; but the diversion of labor to minister to royal pomp, the establishment of a standing army, the alienation of land to officals, heavy taxation and forced labor make up the items. To these is added (v. 18) that the royalty, now so eagerly desired, would sooner or later become a burden, and that then they or their sons would find it was easier to put on than to put off the yoke; for "the Lord will not hear you in that day," in reference, that is, to the removal of the king. They were exchanging an unseen King who gave all things for one who would take and not give.—*Expositions of Holy Scripture*

19. *The people refused to obey.* They would have the king, his manner and all, notwithstanding the solemn warning which they here receive.

20. *May judge us.* This appears to be a rejection of Samuel. *Go out before us.* Be in every respect our head and governor. And *fight our battles.* Be the general of our armies.

21. *Rehearsed them in the ears of the Lord.* He went to the altar, and in his secret devotion laid the whole business before God.

22. *Hearken unto their voice.* Let them have what they desire, and let them abide the consequences. *Go ye every man unto his city.* It seems the elders of the people had tarried all this time with Samuel, and when he had received his ultimate answer from God, he told them of it and dismissed them.

MATTHEW HENRY — CHAPTER 9

Verses 1–2

We are here told, 1. What a good family Saul was of, *v.* 1. He was of the tribe of Benjamin; so was the New Testament Saul, who also was called *Paul,* and he mentions it as his honour, for Benjamin was a favourite, Rom. xi. 1; Phil. iii. 5. That tribe, though fewest in number, was first in dignity. His father was *Kish, a mighty man of power,* or, as the margin reads it, *in substance;* in spirit bold, in body strong, in estate wealthy. 2. What a good figure Saul made, *v.* 2. No mention is here made of his wisdom or virtue, his learning or piety, or any of the accomplishments of his mind, but that he was a tall, proper, handsome man, that had a good face, a good shape, and a good presence, graceful and well proportioned: *Among all the children of Israel there was not a goodlier person than he.* He was taller by the head and shoulders than any of the people. When God chose a king after his own heart he pitched upon one that was not at all remarkable for the height of his stature, nor any thing in his countenance but the innocence and sweetness that appeared there, *ch.* xvi. 7, 12. But when he chose a king after the people's heart, who aimed at nothing so much as stateliness and grandeur, he pitched upon this huge tall man, who, if he had no other good qualities, yet would look great.

Verses 3–10

I. A great man rising from small beginnings. It does not appear that Saul had any preferment at all, or was in any post of honour or trust, till he was chosen king of Israel.

II. A great event arising from small occurrences. How low does the history begin! Having to trace Saul to the crown, we find him first employed as meanly as any we meet with called out to preferment.

1. Saul's father sends him with one of his servants to seek some asses that he had lost. Saul and his servants travelled far (probably on foot) in quest of the asses, but in vain: they found them not. He missed

JAMIESON, FAUSSET, BROWN — CHAPTER 9

Vss. 1-14. Saul, Despairing to Find His Father's Asses, Comes to Samuel. **1. a mighty man of power**—i.e., of great wealth and substance. The family was of high consideration in the tribe of Benjamin, and therefore Saul's words must be set down among the common forms of affected/humility, which Oriental people are wont to use.

2. Saul, a choice young man, and a goodly—He had a fine appearance; for it is evident that he must have been only a little under seven feet tall. A gigantic stature and an athletic frame must have been a popular recommendation at that time in that country.

3. the asses of Kish Saul's father were lost. And Kish said to Saul . . . , arise, go seek the asses—The probability is that the family of Kish, according to the immemorial usage of Oriental shepherds in the purely pastoral regions, had let the animals roam at large during the grazing season, at the close of which messengers were despatched in search of them. Such travelling searches are common; and, as each owner has his own stamp marked on his cattle, the mention of it to the shepherds he meets gradually leads to the discovery of the strayed animals. This ramble of Saul's had nothing extra-

ADAM CLARKE — CHAPTER 9

1. *A mighty man of power.* Literally, a "strong man"; this appears to be the only power he possessed; and the physical strength of the father may account for the extraordinary size of the son. See v. 2.

2. *From his shoulders and upward.* It was probably from this very circumstance that he was chosen for king; for, where kings were elective, in all ancient times great respect was paid to personal appearance.

3. *The asses of Kish . . . were lost.* What a wonderful train of occurrences were connected in order to bring Saul to the throne of Israel! Everything seemed to go on according to the common course of events, and yet all conspired to favor the election of a man to the kingdom who certainly did not come there by the approbation of God.

MATTHEW HENRY

what he sought, but he met with the kingdom, of which he never dreamed.

2. When he could not find them, he determined to return to his father (*v.* 5), in consideration of his father's tender concern for him.

3. His servant proposed that, since they were now at Ramah, they should call on Samuel, and take his advice in this important affair. They were close by the city where Samuel lived, and that put it into their heads to consult him (*v.* 6). *He is a man of God, and an honourable man.* This was the honour of Samuel, as a man of God, that *all he saith comes surely to pass.* They agreed to consult him concerning *the way that they should go*; *peradventure he can show us.* Most people would rather be told their fortune than told their duty, how to be rich than how to be saved. If it were the business of the men of God to direct for the recovery of lost asses, they would be consulted much more than they are now that it is their business to direct for the recovery of lost souls. Saul was thoughtful what present they should bring to the man of God. They could not present him with loaves and cakes (1 Kings xiv. 3), for their bread was spent; but the servant bethought himself that he had in his pocket the fourth part of a shekel. "That will do," says Saul; "*let us go,*" *v.* 10. He came to him as a fortune-teller, rather than as a prophet, and therefore thought the fourth part of a shekel was enough to give him. Most people love a cheap religion, and like it best when they can devolve the expense of it on others. The historian here takes notice of the name then given to the prophets: they called them *Seers*, or *seeing men* (*v.* 9), not but that the name *prophet* was then used, and applied to such persons, but that of seers was more in use. Those that are prophets must first be seers; those who undertake to speak to others of the things of God must have an insight into those things themselves.

Verses 11–17

I. Saul, by an ordinary enquiry, is directed to Samuel, *v.* 11–14. Gibeah of Saul was not twenty miles from Ramah where Samuel dwelt, and was near to Mizpeh where he often judged Israel.

1. The maid-servants of Ramah, whom they met with at the places of drawing water, could give him and his servant intelligence concerning Samuel. (1) That there was a sacrifice that day in the high place. Samuel had built an altar at Ramah (*ch.* vii. 17), and here we have him making use of that altar. (2) That Samuel came that day to the city. (3) That this was just the time of their meeting to feast before the Lord upon the sacrifice. (4) That the people would not eat till Samuel came, because *he* must bless the sacrifice. [1] As a common meal. Or, [2] As a religious assembly. When the sacrifice was offered it was requisite that it should in a particular manner be blessed, as is the Christian eucharist.

2. Saul and his servant followed the directions given them, and very opportunely met Samuel going to the high place, the synagogue of the city, *v.* 14.

II. Samuel, by an extraordinary revelation, is informed concerning Saul. He was a seer, and therefore must see this in a way peculiar to himself.

1. God had told him, the day before, that he would, at this time, send him the man that should serve the people of Israel for such a king as they wished to have. He *told him in his ear,* that is, privately, by a secret whisper to his mind, or perhaps by a still small voice. The Hebrew phrase is, *He uncovered the ear of Samuel.* When God will manifest himself to a soul, he uncovers the ear, says, *Ephphatha, Be opened*; he takes *the veil from off the heart,* 2 Cor. iii. 16. Though God had, in displeasure, granted their request for a king, yet here he speaks tenderly of Israel. (1) He calls them again and again his people; though a peevish and provoking people, yet mine still. (2) He sends them a man to be captain over them. (3) He does it with a gracious respect to them and to their cry: *I have looked upon my people,* and *their cry has come unto me.*

2. When Saul came up towards him in the street God again whispered Samuel in the ear (*v.* 17): *Behold the man whom I spoke to thee of*; That he might be fully satisfied, God told him expressly, *That is the man* that shall *restrain* (for magistrates are heirs of restraint) *my people Israel.*

Verses 18–27

Providence having at length brought Samuel and Saul together, we have here an account of what passed between them in the gate, at the feast, and in private.

I. In the gate of the city; passing through that, Saul found him (*v.* 18), and, asked him the way to Samuel's house. Samuel answered him, "*I am the seer*, the person you enquire for," *v.* 19. Samuel

JAMIESON, FAUSSET, BROWN

ordinary in it, except its *superior* directions and issue, which turned its uncertainty into certainty. **4, 5. he passed through mount Ephraim**—This being situated on the north of Benjamin, indicates the direction of Saul's journey. The district explored means the whole of the mountainous region, with its valleys and defiles, which belonged to Ephraim. Turning apparently southwards—probably through the verdant hills between Shiloh and the vales of Jordan (Shalisha and Shalim)—he approached again the borders of Benjamin, scoured the land of Zuph, and was proposing to return, when his servant recollected that they were in the immediate neighborhood of the man of God, who would give them counsel. **6. there is in this city a man of God**—Ramah was the usual residence of Samuel, but several circumstances, especially the mention of Rachel's sepulchre, which lay in Saul's way homeward, lead to the conclusion that "this city" was not the Ramah where Samuel dwelt. **peradventure he can show us our way that we should go**—It seems strange that a dignified prophet should be consulted in such an affair. But it is probable that at the introduction of the prophetic office, the seers had discovered things lost or stolen, and thus their power for higher revelations was gradually established. **7. Saul said to his servant, But behold, if we go, what shall we bring the man?**—According to Eastern notions, it would be considered a want of respect for any person to go into the presence of a superior man of rank or of official station without a present of some kind in his hand, however trifling in value. **the bread is spent in our vessels**—Shepherds, going in quest of their cattle, put up in a bag as much flour for making bread as will last sometimes for thirty days. It appears that Saul thought of giving the man of God a cake from his travelling bag, and this would have been sufficient to render the indispensable act of civility—the customary tribute to official dignity. **8. the fourth part of a shekel of silver**—rather more than quarter. Contrary to our Western notions, money is in the East the most acceptable form in which a present can be made to a man of rank. **9. seer . . . Prophet**—The recognized distinction in latter times was, that a seer was one who was favored with visions of God—a view of things invisible to mortal sight; and a prophet foretold future events. **11. as they went up the hill**—The modern village, Er-Rameh, lies on an eminence; and on their way they met a band of young maidens going out to the well, which, like all similar places in Palestine, was beyond the precincts of the town. From these damsels they learned that the day was devoted to a festival occasion, in honor of which Samuel had arrived in the city; that a sacrifice had been offered, which was done by prophets in extraordinary circumstances at a distance from the tabernacle, and that a feast was to follow—implying that it had been a peace offering, and that, according to the venerable practice of the Israelites, the man of God was expected to ask a special blessing on the food in a manner becoming the high occasion. **14. Samuel came out against them for to go up to the high place**—Such were the simple manners of the times that this prophet, the chief man in Israel, was seen going to preside at a high festival undistinguished either by his dress or equipage from any ordinary citizen.

15-27. God Reveals to Samuel Saul's Coming, and His Appointment to the Kingdom. **15. Now the Lord had told Samuel in his ear a day before**—The description of Saul, the time of his arrival, and the high office to which he was destined, had been secretly intimated to Samuel from heaven. The future king of Israel was to fight the battles of the Lord and protect His people. It would appear that they were at this time suffering great molestation from the Philistines, and that this was an additional reason of their urgent demands for the appointment of a king (see on ch. 10:5; 13:3).

18. Tell me, I pray thee, where the seer's house is—Satisfying the stranger's inquiry, Samuel invited him to the feast, as well as to sojourn till the morrow; and, in order to reconcile him to the delay, he assured him that the strayed asses had been recovered.

ADAM CLARKE

7. *There is not a present to bring to the man of God.* We are not to suppose from this that the prophets took money to predict future events; Saul only refers to an invariable custom, that no man approached a superior without a present of some kind or other. We have often seen this before; even God, who needs nothing, would not that His people should approach Him with empty hands.

9. *Beforetime in Israel.* This passage could not have been a part of this book originally; but we have already conjectured that Samuel, or some contemporary author, wrote the memoranda out of which a later author compiled this book. This hypothesis, sufficiently reasonable in itself, solves all difficulties of this kind. *Was beforetime called a Seer.* The word *seer, roeh*, occurs for the first time in this place; it literally signifies a "person who sees." A "seer" and a "prophet" were the same in most cases; only with this difference, the seer was always a prophet, but the prophet was not always a seer. I think the ninth verse comes more naturally in after the eleventh.

11. *Young maidens going out to draw water.* So far is it from being true that young women were always kept closely shut up at home, that we find them often in the field, drawing and carrying water, as here.

12. *He came to day to the city.* Though Samuel lived chiefly in Ramah, yet he had a dwelling in the country, at a place called Naioth, where it is probable there was a school of the prophets (see chap. xix. 18-24). *A sacrifice of the people.* A great feast. The animals used were first sacrificed to the Lord; that is, their blood was poured out before Him; and then all the people fed on the flesh. By *high place* probably Samuel's altar is alone meant, which no doubt was raised on an eminence.

13. *He doth bless the sacrifice.* He alone can perform the religious rites which are used on this occasion.

14. *Came out against them.* Met them.

15. *Now the Lord had told Samuel.* How this communication was made we cannot tell.

16. *Thou shalt anoint him to be captain.* Not to be "king," but to be *nagid* or captain of the Lord's host. But in ancient times no king was esteemed who was not an able warrior.

17. *Behold the man whom I spake to thee of!* What an intimate communion must Samuel have held with his God! A constant familiarity seems to have existed between them.

19. *I am the seer.* This declaration would prepare Saul for the communications afterwards made.

MATTHEW HENRY

knew him before he knew Samuel. 1. Samuel obliges him to stay with him till the next day. Saul had nothing in his mind but to find his asses, but Samuel would take him off from that care, and dispose him to the exercises of piety; and therefore bids him *go to the high place.* 2. He satisfies him about his asses (*v.* 20): *Set not thy mind on them,* be not in further care about them; *they are found.* By this Saul might perceive that he was a prophet. 3. He surprises him with an intimation of preferment before him: "*On whom is all the desire of Israel?* Is it not a king that they are set upon, and there is never a man in Israel that will suit them as thou wilt." 4. To this strange intimation Saul returns a very modest answer, *v.* 21. Samuel, he thought, did but banter him, because he was a tall man, but a very unlikely man to be a king, *I am a Benjamite, my family the least,* probably a younger house, not in any place of honour, or trust, no, not in their own tribe.

II. At the public feast; thither Samuel took him and his servant. Samuel treats him not as a common person, but a person of quality and distinction, to prepare both him and the people for what was to follow. Two marks of honour he put upon him:—1. He set him *in the best place.* 2. He presented him with the *best dish.* And what should this precious dish be for the king-elect? It was a plain shoulder of mutton (*v.* 23, 24). The right shoulder of the peace-offerings was to be given to the priests, who were God's receivers (Lev. vii. 32); the next in honour to that was the left shoulder, which probably was always allotted to those that sat at the upper end of the table, and was wont to be Samuel's mess at other times; so that his giving it to Saul now was an implicit resignation of his place to him.

III. What passed between them in private. Both that evening and early the next morning Samuel communed with Saul upon the flat roof of the house, *v.* 25, 26. We may suppose Samuel now told him the whole story of the people's desire of a king, the grounds of their desire, and God's grant of it. Early in the morning he sent him towards home, brought him part of the way, bade him send his servant before, that they might be private (*v.* 27), and there, as we find in the beginning of the next chapter, he anointed him, and therein showed him the *word of the Lord.*

JAMIESON, FAUSSET, BROWN

20. on whom is all the desire of Israel? Is it not on thee, and on thy father's house?—This was a covert and indirect premonition of the royal dignity that awaited him; and, though Saul's answer shows that he fully understood it, he affected to doubt that the prophet was in earnest. **21. And Saul answered and said, Am not I a Benjamite, of the smallest of the tribes of Israel . . .**—By selecting a king from this least and nearly extinct tribe (Judg. 20), divine wisdom designed to remove all grounds of jealousy among the other tribes. **22. Samuel took Saul and his servant and brought them into the parlour**—The toil-worn but noble-looking traveller found himself suddenly seated among the principal men of the place and treated as the most distinguished guest.

24. the cook took up the shoulder . . . , and set it before Saul. And Samuel said, Behold that which is left; set it before thee, and eat—i.e., reserved (see on Gen. 18:6; 43:34). This was, most probably, the right shoulder; which, as the perquisite of the sacrifice, belonged to Samuel, and which he had set aside for his expected guest. In the sculptures of the Egyptian shambles, also, the first joint taken off was always the right shoulder for the priest. The meaning of those distinguished attentions must have been understood by the other guests. **25. Samuel communed with Saul upon the top of the house**—Saul was taken to lodge with the prophet for that night. Before retiring to rest, they communed on the flat roof of the house, the couch being laid there (Josh. 2:6), when, doubtless, Samuel revealed the secret and described the peculiar duties of a monarch in a nation so related to the Divine King as Israel. Next morning early, Samuel roused his guest, and conveying him on his way towards the skirts of the city, sought, before parting, a *private* interview—the object of which is narrated in the next chapter.

ADAM CLARKE

20. *As for thine asses.* Thus he shows him that he knows what is in his heart, God having previously revealed these things to Samuel. *And on whom is all the desire of Israel?* Saul understood this as implying that he was chosen to be king.

21. *Am not I a Benjamite?* This speech of Saul is exceedingly modest; he was now becomingly humble; but who can bear elevation and prosperity? The tribe of Benjamin had not yet recovered its strength after the ruinous war it had with the other tribes, Judges xx.

22. *Brought them into the parlour.* It might as well be called "kitchen"; it was the place where they sat down to feast.

23. *Said unto the cook. Tabbach,* here rendered *cook;* the singular of *tabbachoth,* "female cooks," chap. viii. 13, from the root *tabach,* "to slay or butcher." Probably the butcher is here meant.

24. *The shoulder, and that which was upon it.* Probably the shoulder was covered with a part of the caul, that it might be the better roasted. Why was the shoulder set before Saul? Not because it was the best part, but because it was an emblem of the government to which he was now called. See Isa. ix. 6: "And the government shall be upon his shoulder."

25. *Upon the top of the house.* All the houses in the East were flat-roofed; on these people walked, talked, and frequently slept, for the sake of fresh and cooling air.

26. *Called Saul to the top of the house.* Saul had no doubt slept there all night; and now, it being the "break of day," "Samuel called to Saul on the top of the house, saying, Up, that I may send thee away." There was no calling him to the housetop a second time; he was sleeping there, and Samuel called him up.

27. *As they were going down.* So it appears that Saul arose immediately, and Samuel accompanied him out of the town, and sent the servant on, that he might show Saul the *word*—the "counsel" or "design," of the Lord. What this was we shall see in the following chapter.

CHAPTER 10 (MATTHEW HENRY)

Verses 1–8

Samuel is here executing the office of a prophet, giving Saul full assurance from God that he should be king.

I. He *anointed him* and *kissed him, v.* 1. This was not done in a solemn assembly, but it was done by divine appointment, which made up the want of all external solemnities. 1. Samuel, by anointing Saul, assured him that it was God's act to make him king: *Is it not because the Lord hath anointed thee?* 2. By kissing him, he assured him of his own approbation of the choice, though it abridged his power and eclipsed his glory and the glory of his family. It was likewise a kiss of homage and allegiance; hereby he not only owns him to be king, but his king, and in this sense we are commanded to *kiss the Son,* Ps. ii. 12. He reminds him, (1) Of the nature of the government to which he is called. He was anointed to be a captain, a commander in war, which bespeaks care, and toil, and danger. (2) Of the origin of it: *The Lord hath anointed thee.* By him he ruled, and therefore must rule for him, in dependence on him, and with an eye to his glory. (3) Of the end of it. It is over his inheritance, to take care of that, protect it, and order all the affairs of it for the best, as a steward whom a great man sets over his estate.

II. For his further satisfaction he gives him some signs, which should come to pass immediately this very day. 1. He should presently meet with some that would bring him intelligence from home of the care his father's house was in concerning him, *v.* 2. These he would meet hard by Rachel's sepulchre. Here two men would meet him, and would tell him the asses were found. 2. He should next meet with others going to Bethel, where, it should seem, there was a high place for religious worship, and these men were bringing their sacrifices thither, *v.* 3, 4. It is supposed that those kids and loaves, and the bottle of wine which the three men had with them, were designed for sacrifice, with the meat-offerings and drink-offerings that were to attend the sacrifice; yet Samuel tells Saul that they will give him two of their loaves, and he must take them. It would be construed a fit present for a prince; and, as such, Saul must receive it the first present that was brought to him, by such

CHAPTER 10 (JAMIESON, FAUSSET, BROWN)

Vss. 1-27. SAMUEL ANOINTS SAUL, AND CONFIRMS HIM BY THE PREDICTION OF THREE SIGNS. **1. Then Samuel took a vial of oil**—This was the ancient (Judg. 9:8) ceremony of investiture with the royal office among the Hebrews and other Eastern nations. But there were two unctions to the kingly office; the one in private, by a prophet (ch. 16:13), which was meant to be only a prophetic intimation of the person attaining that high dignity—the more public and formal inauguration (II Sam. 2:4; 5:3) was performed by the high priest, and perhaps with the holy oil, but that is not certain. The first of a dynasty was thus anointed, but not his heirs, unless the succession was disputed (I Kings 1:39; II Kings 11:12; 23:30; II Chron. 23:11). **kissed him**—This salutation, as explained by the words that accompanied it, was an act of respectful homage, a token of congratulation to the new king (Ps. 2:12).

2. When thou art departed from me to-day—The design of these specific predictions of what should be met with on the way, and the number and minuteness of which would arrest attention, was to confirm Saul's reliance on the prophetic character of Samuel, and lead him to give full credence to what had been revealed to him as the word of God. **Rachel's sepulchre**—near Bethlehem (see on Gen. 35:16). **Zelzah**—or Zelah, now *Bet-jalah,* in the neighborhood of that town. **3. the plain—or the oak of Tabor, not the celebrated mount, for that was far distant. three men going up to God to Bethel—apparently to offer sacrifices there at a time when the ark and the tabernacle were not in a settled abode, and God had not yet declared the permanent place which He should choose. The kids were for sacrifice, the loaves for the offering, and the wine for the libations.**

CHAPTER 10 (ADAM CLARKE)

1. *Took a vial of oil.* The reasons of this rite the reader will find largely stated in the note on Exod. xxix. 7. The anointing mentioned here took place in the open field. See the preceding chapter, vv. 26-27. How simple was the ancient ceremony of consecrating a king! A prophet or priest poured oil upon his head, and kissed him; and said, "Thus the Lord hath anointed thee to be captain over his inheritance." This was the whole of the ceremony. Even in this anointing, Saul is not acknowledged as king, but simply *nagid,* "a captain"—one who goes before and leads the people.

2. *Rachel's sepulchre.* This was nigh to Bethlehem (see Gen. xxxv. 19). *At Zelzah.* If this be the name of a place, nothing is known of it. The Hebrew *betseltsach* is translated by the Septuagint "dancing greatly"; now this may refer to the joy they felt and expressed on finding the asses, or it may refer to those religious exultations, or playing on instruments of music, mentioned in the succeeding verses.

3. *Three men going up to God to Beth-el.* Jacob's altar was probably still there, Gen. xxviii. 19. However this might be, it was still considered, as its name implies, "the house of God"; and to it they were now going, to offer sacrifice. The *three kids* were for sacrifice; the *three loaves of bread,* to be offered probably as a thank offering; and the *bottle* or skin full of *wine,* for a libation. When the blood was

MATTHEW HENRY

as knew not what they did, nor why they did it, but God put it into their hearts, which made it the more fit to be a sign to him. 3. The most remarkable sign of all would be his joining with a company of prophets that he should meet with, under the influence of a spirit of prophecy, which should at that time come upon him. What God works in us by his Spirit serves much more for the confirming of faith than any thing wrought for us by his providence. He here (*v.* 5, 6) tells him, (1) Where this would happen: *At the hill of God,* where there was a *garrison of the Philistines.* After they were subdued in the beginning of his time they got ground again, so far as to force this garrison into that place, and thence God raised up the man that should chastise them. There was a place that was called the *hill of God,* because of one of the schools of the prophets built upon it; and such respect did even Philistines themselves pay to religion that a garrison of their soldiers suffered a school of God's prophets to live peaceably by them, and did not disturb the public exercises of their devotion. (2) Upon what occasion; he should meet *a company of prophets with music before them, prophesying,* and with them he should join himself. These prophets employed themselves in the study of the law, in instructing their neighbours, and in the acts of piety, especially in praising God. What a pity was it that Israel should be weary of the government of such a man, who had, as a man of God, settled the schools of the prophets! These prophets had been at the high place, probably offering sacrifice, and now they came back singing psalms. Saul should find himself strongly moved to join with them, and should be turned thereby *into another man* from what he had been while he lived in a private capacity.

III. He directs him to proceed in the administration of his government as Providence should lead him, and as Samuel should advise him. 1. He must follow Providence in ordinary cases (*v.* 7): "*Do as occasion shall serve thee.* Take such measures as thy own prudence shall direct thee." But, 2. In an extraordinary strait that would hereafter befall him at Gilgal, and would be the most critical juncture of all, when he would have special need of divine aids, he must wait for Samuel to come to him, and must tarry *seven days* in expectation of him, *v.* 8. How his failing in this matter proved his fall we find afterwards, *ch.* xiii. 11.

Verses 9–16

Saul has now taken his leave of Samuel, much amazed.

I. What occurred by the way, *v.* 9. Those signs which Samuel had given him came to pass very punctually; but that which gave him the greatest satisfaction of all was this, he found immediately that God had given him *another heart.* A new fire was kindled in his breast. Seeking the asses is quite out of his mind, and he thinks of nothing but fighting the Philistines, redressing the grievances of Israel, making laws, administering justice, and providing for the public safety; these are the things that now fill his head. He has no longer the heart of a husbandman, which is low, and mean, and narrow, and concerned only about his corn and cattle; but the heart of a statesman, a general, a prince. Whom God calls to any service he will make fit for it.

II. What occurred when he came near home. They came to *the hill* (*v.* 10), that is, to *Gibeah,* or *Geba,* which signifies *a hill.* He met with the prophets as Samuel had told him, and the Spirit of God came upon him, strongly and suddenly (so the word signifies), but not so as to rest and abide upon him. However, for the present, it had a strange effect upon him; for he immediately joined with the prophets in their devotion. *He prophesied among them.*

1. His prophesying was publicly taken notice of, *v.* 11, 12. He was now among his acquaintance, who, when they saw him among the prophets, called one another to come and see a strange sight. This would prepare them to accept him as a king. Now, (1) They all wondered to see Saul among the prophets: *What is this that has come to the son of Kish;* Though this school of the prophets was near his father's house, yet he had never associated with them. Now to see him prophesying among them was a surprise to them, as it was long after when his namesake, in the New Testament, preached that gospel which he had before persecuted, Acts ix. 21. Where God gives another heart it will soon show itself. (2) One of them, that was wiser than the rest, asked, "*Who is their father,* or instructor? Is it not God? Are they not all taught of him? Do they not all owe their gifts to him? And is he limited? Cannot he make Saul a prophet, as well as any of them, if he please?" Or, "Is not Samuel their father?" (3) It became a proverb, commonly used in Israel, when they would express

JAMIESON, FAUSSET, BROWN

5. the hill of God—probably Geba (ch. 13:3), so called from a school of the prophets being established there. The company of prophets were, doubtless, the pupils at this seminary, which had probably been instituted by Samuel, and in which the chief branches of education taught were a knowledge of the law, and of psalmody with instrumental music, which is called "prophesying" (here and in I Chron. 25:1, 7). **6. the Spirit of the Lord will come upon thee**—lit., rush upon thee, suddenly endowing thee with a capacity and disposition to act in a manner far superior to thy previous character and habits; and instead of the simplicity, ignorance, and sheepishness of a peasant, thou wilt display an energy, wisdom, and magnanimity worthy of a prince.

8. thou shalt go down before me to Gilgal—This, according to Josephus, was to be a standing rule for the observance of Saul while the prophet and he lived; that in every great crisis, such as a hostile incursion on the country, he should repair to Gilgal, where he was to remain seven days, to afford time for the tribes on both sides Jordan to assemble, and Samuel to reach it.

9. when he had turned his back to go from Samuel, God gave him another heart—Influenced by the words of Samuel, as well as by the accomplishment of these signs, Saul's reluctance to undertake the onerous office was overcome. The fulfilment of the two first signs is passed over, but the third is specially described. The spectacle of a man, though more fit to look after his father's cattle than to take part in the sacred exercises of the young prophets—a man without any previous instruction, or any known taste, entering with ardor into the spirit, and skilfully accompanying the melodies of the sacred band, was so extraordinary a phenomenon, that it gave rise to the proverb, "Is Saul also among the prophets?" (see on ch. 19:24). The prophetic spirit had come upon him; and to Saul it was as personal and experimental an evidence of the truth of God's word that had been spoken to him, as converts to Christianity have in themselves from the sanctifying power of the Gospel.

12. But who is their father?—The *Sept.* reads, "Who is his father?" referring to Saul the son of Kish.

ADAM CLARKE

poured out before the Lord, they feasted on the flesh and on the bread; and probably had a sufficiency of the wine left for their own drinking.

4. *And they will salute thee.* "And they will inquire of thee concerning peace," i.e., welfare. In the East, if this salutation be given, then the person or persons giving it may be reckoned friends; if the others return it, then there is friendship on both sides.

5. *The hill of God.* The Targum says, "The hill on which the ark of the Lord was." Calmet supposes it to be a height near Gibeah. *The garrison of the Philistines.* Probably they kept a watch on the top of this hill, with a company of soldiers to keep the country in check. *A company of prophets.* A company of scribes, says the Targum. Probably the scholars of the prophets; for the prophets seem to have been the only accredited teachers, at particular times, in Israel; and at this time there does not appear to have been any other prophet besides Samuel in this quarter.

A psaltery. Nebel. As the word signifies in other places a "bottle or flagon," it was probably something like the bagpipe. *A tabret. Toph;* a sort of drum or cymbal. *A pipe. Chalile,* from *chal,* "to make a hole or opening"; a sort of pipe, flute, clarinet, or the like. *A harp. Kinnor;* a stringed instrument similar to our harp, or that on the model of which a harp was formed.

7. *Thou do as occasion serve thee.* After God has shown you all these signs that you are under His especial guidance, fear not to undertake anything that belongs to your office, for God is with you.

8. *Seven days shalt thou tarry.* I will come to you within seven days, offer sacrifices, receive directions from the Lord, and deliver them to you. It is likely that these seven days referred to the time in which Samuel came to Saul to Gilgal, offered sacrifices, and confirmed the kingdom to him, after he had defeated the Ammonites (see chap. xi. 14-15).

10. *Behold, a company of prophets.* See on v. 5.

12. *But who is their father?* The Septuagint, in its principal editions, adds, "Is it not Kish?" This makes the sense more complete.

MATTHEW HENRY

their wonder at a bad man's either becoming good, or at least being found in good company, *Is Saul among the prophets?*

2. His being anointed was kept private. When he had done prophesying, (1) He went straight *to the high place* (*v.* 13), to give God thanks for his mercies to him and to pray for the continuance of those mercies. But, (2) He industriously concealed from his relations what had passed. His uncle, who met with him either at the high place or as soon as he came home, examined him, *v.* 14. Saul owned, for his servant knew it, that they had been with Samuel, and that he told them the asses were found, but said not a word of *the kingdom*, *v.* 14, 15. This was an instance, [1] Of his humility. [2] Of his prudence. Had he been forward to proclaim it, he would have been envied, and he knew not what difficulty that might have created him.

Verses 17–27

Saul's nomination to the throne is here made public, in a general assembly of the elders of Israel, the representatives of their respective tribes at Mizpeh. The people having met in a solemn assembly, in which God was in a peculiar manner present (and therefore, it is said they were *called together unto the Lord*, *v.* 17), Samuel acts for God among them.

I. He reproves them for casting off the government of a prophet, and desiring that of a captain. 1. He shows them (*v.* 18) how happy they had been under the divine government; when God ruled them, he *delivered them out of the hand of those that oppressed them*, and what would they desire more? 2. He likewise shows them (*v.* 19) what an affront they had put upon God. "*You have this day rejected your God*; you have in effect done it: so he construes it, and he might justly, for your so doing, reject you."

II. He puts them upon choosing their king by lot. Benjamin is taken out of all the tribes (*v.* 20), and out of that tribe Saul the son of Kish, *v.* 21. By this method it would appear to the people, as it already appeared to Samuel, that Saul was appointed of God to be king; for *the disposal of the lot is of the Lord.*

III. It is with much ado, and not without further enquiries of the Lord, that Saul is at length produced. When the lot fell upon him, every one expected he should answer to his name at the first call, but, instead of that, none of his friends could find him (*v.* 21), he had *hidden himself among the stuff* (*v.* 22). 1. He withdrew, in hopes that, upon his not appearing, they would proceed to another choice. We may suppose he was at this time really averse to take upon him the government, (1) Because he was conscious to himself of unfitness for so great a trust. (2) Because it would expose him to the envy of his neighbours. (3) Because he understood, by what Samuel had said, that the people sinned in asking a king. (4) Because the affairs of Israel were at this time in a bad posture; the Philistines were strong, the Ammonites threatening: and he must be bold indeed that will set sail in a storm.

2. But the congregation, believing that choice well made which God himself made, would leave no way untried to find him out on whom the lot fell.

IV. Samuel presents him to the people, and they accept him. He needed not to mount the bench, or scaffold, to be seen; for he was taller than any of them by *head and shoulders*, *v.* 23. "Look you," said Samuel, "what a king God has chosen for you, just such a one as you wished for; *there is none like him among all the people*, that has so much majesty in his countenance and such a graceful stateliness in his mien; he is in the crowd like a cedar among the shrubs." The people hereupon signified their approbation of the choice, and their acceptance of him; they *shouted and said, Let the king live*, that is, "Let him long reign over us in health and prosperity."

V. Samuel settles the original contract between them, and leaves it upon record, *v.* 25. He fixed the land marks between them, that neither might encroach upon the other. Let them rightly understand one another at first, and let the agreement remain in black and white, which will tend to preserve a good understanding between them ever after.

VI. The convention was dissolved when the solemnity was over: *Samuel sent every man to his house. Saul also went home to Gibeah*, to his father's house, not puffed up with the name of a kingdom under him. At Gibeah ha had no palace, no throne, no court, yet thither he goes. If he must be a king, as one mindful of the rock out of which he was hewn, he will make his own city the royal city, nor will he be ashamed (as too many are when they are preferred) of his mean relations.

1. How did the people stand affected to their new king? The generality of them, it should seem, did

JAMIESON, FAUSSET, BROWN

17. Samuel called the people together . . . at Mizpeh—a shaft-like hill near Hebron, 500 feet in height. The national assemblies of the Israelites were held there. A day having been appointed for the election of a king, Samuel, after having charged the people with a rejection of God's institution and a superseding of it by one of their own, proceeded to the nomination of the new monarch. As it was of the utmost importance that the appointment should be under the divine direction and control, the determination was made by the miraculous lot, tribes, families, and individuals being successively passed until Saul was found.

His concealment of himself must have been the result either of innate modesty, or a sudden nervous excitement under the circumstances. When dragged into view, he was seen to possess all those corporeal advantages which a rude people desiderate in their sovereigns; and the exhibition of which gained for the prince the favorable opinion of Samuel also.

In the midst of the national enthusiasm, however, the prophet's deep piety and genuine patriotism took care to explain "the manner of the kingdom," i.e., the royal rights and privileges, together with the limitations to which they were to be subjected; and in order that the constitution might be ratified with all due solemnity, the charter of this constitutional monarchy was recorded and laid up "before the Lord," i.e., deposited in the custody of the priests, along with the most sacred archives of the nation. **26. Saul also went home to Gibeah**—near Geba. This was his place of residence (see on Judg. 20), about five miles north of Jerusalem.

ADAM CLARKE

13. *He came to the high place.* I suppose this to mean the place where Saul's father lived, as it is evident the next verse shows him to be at *home.*

14. *Saul's uncle.* The word *dod* signifies a "beloved one, love, a lover, friend," and is the same as "David." It is supposed to mean *uncle* here, but I think it means some familiar friend

18. *I brought up Israel out of Egypt.* These are similar to the upbraidings in chap. vii. 7, etc.

19. *Present yourselves . . . by your tribes.* It appears that, in order to find out the proper person who should be made their king, they must determine by lot: (1) the tribe, (2) the thousands or grand divisions by families, (3) the smaller divisions by families, and (4) the individual.

21. *When they sought him, he could not be found.* Through modesty or fear he had secreted himself.

22. *The Lord answered.* What a continual access to God! and what condescension in His attention to all their requests! The *stuff* among which he had secreted himself may mean the carts, baggage, etc., brought by the people to Mizpeh.

24. *God save the king.* There is no such word here; no, nor in the whole Bible; nor is it countenanced by any of the versions. The words which we thus translate here and elsewhere are simply *yechi hammelech*, "May the king live"; and so all the versions, the Targum excepted, which says, "May the king prosper!"

25. *The manner of the kingdom.* It is the same word as in chap. viii. 9; and doubtless the same thing is implied as is there related. But possibly there was some kind of compact or covenant between them and Saul; and this was the thing that was written in a book, and laid up before the Lord, probably near the ark.

MATTHEW HENRY

not show themselves much concerned: They *went every man to his own house*. But, (1) There were some so faithful as to attend him: *A band of men whose hearts God had touched*, *v.* 26. A small company went with him to Gibeah, as his life-guard. They were those *whose hearts God had touched*, in this instance, to do their duty. (2) There were others so spiteful as to affront him; children of Belial, men that would endure no yoke. Thus differently are men affected to our exalted Redeemer. God hath set him king upon the holy hill of Sion. There is a remnant *whose hearts God has touched*, whom he has *made willing in the day of his power*. But there are others who despise him, who ask, *How shall this man save us?*

2. How did Saul resent the bad conduct of those that were disaffected to his government? *He held his peace*. Margin, *He was as though he had been deaf*.

JAMIESON, FAUSSET, BROWN

there went . . . a band of men, whose hearts God had touched—who feared God and regarded allegiance to their king as a conscientious duty. They are opposed to "the children of Belial." **27. the children of Belial said, How shall this man save us? And they despised him, and brought him no presents**—In Eastern countries, the honor of the sovereign and the splendor of the royal household are upheld, not by a fixed rate of taxation, but by presents brought at certain seasons by officials, and men of wealth, from all parts of the kingdom, according to the means of the individual, and of a customary registered value. Such was the tribute which Saul's opponents withheld, and for want of which he was unable to set up a kingly establishment for a while. But "biding his time," he bore the insult with a prudence and magnanimity which were of great use in the beginning of his government.

ADAM CLARKE

26. *A band of men.* Not a military band, as I imagine, but some secret friends, or companions, who were personally attached to him.

27. *Brought him no presents.* They gave him no proofs that they acknowledged either the divine appointment or his authority. Saul was now a public character, and had a right to support from the public. These sons of Belial refused to bear their part; they brought him no presents. He marked it, but at present held his peace; "he was as if he were deaf."

CHAPTER 11

Verses 1–4

The Ammonites were bad neighbours to those tribes of Israel that lay next them, though descendants from just Lot, and, for that reason, dealt civilly with by Israel. See Deut. ii. 19. The city of Jabesh-Gilead had been, some ages ago, destroyed by Israel's sword of justice, for not appearing against the wickedness of Gibeah (Judges xxi. 10); and now being replenished again, probably by the posterity of those that then escaped the sword, it is in danger of being destroyed by the Ammonites, as if some bad fate attended the place. Nahash, king of Ammon (1 Chron. xix. 1), laid siege to it.

I. The besieged beat a parley (*v.* 1): "*Make a covenant with us, and we will* surrender upon terms, and *serve thee*." They had lost the virtue of Israelites, else they would not have thus lost the valour of Israelites, nor tamely yielded to serve an Ammonite.

II. The besiegers offer them base and barbarous conditions; they will spare their lives, and take them to be their servants, upon condition that they shall *put out their right eyes*, *v.* 2. The Gileadites were content to part with their liberty and estates. But their abject concessions make the Ammonites more insolent in their demands. 1. They must torment them, and put them to pain, exquisite pain, for so the thrusting out of an eye would do. 2. They must disable them for war, for in those times they fought with shields in their left hands, which covered their left eye, so that a soldier without his right eye was in effect blind.

III. The besieged desire, and obtain, seven days' time to consider of this proposal, *v.* 3. Nahash, not imagining it possible that, in so short a time, they should have relief, and being very secure of the advantages he thought he had against them, in a bravado gave them seven days, that the reproach upon Israel, for not rescuing them, might be greater, and his triumphs the more illustrious.

IV. Notice is sent of this to Gibeah. They said they would send messengers *to all the coasts of Israel* (*v.* 3), which made Nahash the more secure, for that, he thought, would be a work of time. But the messengers, either of their own accord or by order from their masters, went straight to Gibeah, and, not finding Saul within, told their news to the people, who fell a-weeping upon hearing it, *v.* 4.

Verses 5–11

What is here related turns very much to the honour of Saul, and shows the happy fruits of that other spirit with which he was endued.

I. His humility. Though he was anointed king, and accepted by his people, yet he did not think it below him to know the state of his own flocks, but went himself to see them, and came in the evening, with his servants, *after the herd out of the field*, *v.* 5. Like Paul, he worked with his hands; for, if he neglect his domestic affairs, how must he maintain himself and his family?

II. His concern for his neighbours. When he perceived them in tears, he asked, "*What ails the people that they weep?* Let me know, that, if it be a grievance which can be redressed, I may help them, and that, if not, I may weep with them."

III. His zeal for the safety and honour of Israel. When he heard of the insolence of the Ammonites, and the distress of a city, a mother in Israel, *the Spirit of God came upon him*, and put great thoughts into his mind, *and his anger was kindled greatly*, *v.* 6. He was angry at the insolence of the Ammonites, angry at the mean and sneaking spirit of the men of Jabesh-Gilead, angry to see his neighbours weep-

CHAPTER 11

Vss. 1-4. Nahash Offers Them of Jabesh-gilead a Reproachful Condition. **1. Then Nahash the Ammonite came up**—Nahash (serpent); (see on Judg. 8:3). The Ammonites had long claimed the right of original possession in Gilead. Though repressed by Jephthah (Judg. 11:33), they now, after ninety years, renew their pretensions; and it was the report of their threatened invasion that hastened the appointment of a king (ch. 12:12).

Make a covenant with us, and we will serve thee—They saw no prospect of aid from the western Israelites, who were not only remote, but scarcely able to repel the incursions of the Philistines from themselves. **2. thrust out all your right eyes**—lit., scoop or hollow out the ball. This barbarous mutilation is the usual punishment of usurpers in the East—inflicted on chiefs; sometimes, also, even in modern history, on the whole male population of a town. Nahash meant to keep the Jabeshites useful as tributaries, whence he did not wish to render them wholly blind, but only to deprive them of their right eye, which would disqualify them for war. Besides, his object was, through the people of Jabesh-gilead, to insult the Israelitish nation.

3, 4. send messengers unto all the coasts of Israel—a curious proof of the general dissatisfaction that prevailed as to the appointment of Saul. Those Gileadites deemed him capable neither of advising nor succoring them; and even in his own town the appeal was made to the people—not to the prince.

CHAPTER 11

2. *I may thrust out all your right eyes.* This cruel condition would serve at once as a badge of their slavery, and a means of incapacitating them from being effective warriors.

3. *Give us seven days' respite.* Such promises are frequently made by besieged places: "We will surrender if not relieved in so many days"; and such conditions are generally received by the besiegers.

5. *Saul came after the herd.* He had been bred up to an agricultural life, and after his consecration he returned to it, waiting for a call of divine providence, which he considered he had now received in the message from Jabesh-gilead.

6. *The Spirit of God came upon Saul.* He felt himself strongly excited to attempt the relief of his brethren. *And his anger was kindled greatly.* I believe this means no more than that "his courage was greatly excited"—he felt himself strong for fight, and confident of success.

MATTHEW HENRY

ing, when it was fitter for them to be preparing for war.

IV. The authority and power he exerted upon this important occasion. He soon let Israel know that he had a care for the public, and knew how to command men into the field, as well as how to drive cattle out of the field, *v.* 5, 7. He sent a summons to all the coasts of Israel, and ordered all the military men forthwith to appear in arms at a general rendezvous in Bezek. Observe, 1. His modesty, in joining Samuel in commission with himself. He would not execute the office of a king without a due regard to that of a prophet. 2. His mildness in the penalty threatened against those that should disobey his orders. He hews a yoke of oxen in pieces, and sends the pieces to the several cities of Israel, threatening, with respect to him who should decline the public service, not, "Thus shall it be done to *him*," but, "Thus shall it be done to his *oxen*." The effect of this summons was that the militia, or trained bands, of the nation, *came out as one man*, and the reason given is, because *the fear of the Lord fell upon them.* Those that fear God will make conscience of their duty to all men, particularly to their rulers.

V. His prudent proceedings in this great affair, *v.* 8. He numbered those that came in to him, that he might know his own strength, and how to distribute his forces in the best manner. In this muster, it seems, Judah, though numbered by itself, made no great figure; for it was but an eleventh part of the whole number, 30,330, though the rendezvous was at Bezek, in that tribe.

VI. His faith and confidence and his courage and resolution, in this enterprise. He now sends back this assurance (in which, it is probable, Samuel encouraged him): "*To-morrow*, by such an hour, before the enemy can pretend that the seven days have expired, *you shall have deliverance*, *v.* 9. Be you ready to do your part, and we will not fail to do ours. Do you sally out upon the besiegers, while we surround them." Saul knew he had a just cause, a clear call, and God on his side, and therefore doubted not of success. This was good news to the besieged Gileadites. When they heard it they were glad, relying on the assurances that were sent to them. And they sent into the enemies' camp (*v.* 10) to tell them that next day they would be ready to meet them, which the enemies understood as an intimation that they despaired of relief, and so were made the more secure by it.

VII. His industry and close application to this business. When the Spirit of the Lord comes upon men it will make them expert even without experience. A vast army (especially in comparison with the present usage) Saul had now at his foot, and a long march before him, nearly sixty miles, and over Jordan too. No cavalry in his army, but all infantry, which he divides into three battalions, *v.* 11. With what incredible swiftness he flew to the enemy. He was better than his word, for he promised help next day, *by that time the sun was hot* (*v.* 9), but brought it before day, *in the morning-watch*, *v.* 11. With what incredible bravery he flew upon the enemy. Betimes in the morning he was in the midst of their host; and his men, being marched against them in three columns, surrounded them on every side, so that they could have neither heart nor time to make head against them

Lastly, To complete his honour, God crowned all these virtues with success. Jabesh-Gilead was rescued, and the Ammonites were totally routed.

Verses 12–15

We have here the improvement of the glorious victory which Saul had obtained.

I. The people took this occasion to show their jealousy for the honour of Saul, and their resentment of the indignities done him. The sons of Belial that would not have him to reign over them should be brought forth and slain, *v.* 12. They had not courage thus to move for the prosecution of those that opposed him when he himself looked mean, but, now that his victory made him look great, nothing would serve but they must be put to death.

II. Saul took this occasion to give further proofs of his clemency, for, without waiting for Samuel's answer, he himself quashed the motion (*v.* 13): *There shall not a man be put to death this day.* 1. Because it was a day of joy and triumph: *To-day the Lord has wrought salvation in Israel*; and, since God has been so good to us all, let us not be harsh to one another. 2. Because he hoped they were by this day's work brought to a better temper, were now convinced that this man, under God, could save them, now honoured him whom before they had despised; and, if they are but reclaimed, he is secured from receiving any disturbance by them, and therefore his

JAMIESON, FAUSSET, BROWN

5-11. THEY SEND TO SAUL, AND ARE DELIVERED. 7. he took a yoke of oxen, and hewed them in pieces—(see on Judg. 19.) This particular form of war-summons was suited to the character and habits of an agricultural and pastoral people. Solemn in itself, the denunciation that accompanied it carried a terrible threat to those that neglected to obey it. Saul conjoins the name of Samuel with his own, to lend the greater influence to the measure, and to strike greater terror unto all contemners of the order. The small contingent furnished by Judah suggests that the disaffection to Saul was strongest in that tribe. **8. Bezek**—This place of general muster was not far from Shechem, on the road to Beth-shan, and nearly opposite the ford for crossing to Jabesh-gilead. The great number on the muster roll showed the effect of Saul's wisdom and promptitude.

11. on the morrow Saul put the people in three companies—Crossing the Jordan in the evening, Saul marched his army all night, and came at daybreak on the camp of the Ammonites, who were surprised in three different parts, and totally routed. This happened before the seven days' truce expired.

12-15. SAUL CONFIRMED KING. **12, 13. the people said . . . , Who is he that said, Shall Saul reign over us?**—The enthusiastic admiration of the people, under the impulse of grateful and generous feelings, would have dealt summary vengeance on the minority who opposed Saul, had not he, either from principle or policy, shown himself as great in clemency as in valor.

ADAM CLARKE

7. *He took a yoke of oxen.* The sending the pieces of the oxen was an act similar to that of the Levite, Judg. xix. 29.

10. *To morrow we will come out unto you.* They concealed the information they had received of Saul's promised assistance. They did come out unto them; but it was in a different manner to what the Ammonites expected.

11. *Put the people in three companies.* Intending to attack the Ammonites in three different points, and to give his own men more room to act. *In the morning watch.* He probably began his march in the evening, passed Jordan in the night, and reached the camp of the Ammonites by daybreak. *That two of them were not left together.* This proves that the rout was complete.

12. *Who is he that said, Shall Saul reign?* Now, flushed with victory and proud of their leader, they wished to give him a proof of their attachment by slaying, even in cold blood, the persons who were at first averse from his being entrusted with the supreme power!

13. *There shall not a man be put to death.* This was as much to Saul's credit as the lately proposed measure was to the discredit of his soldiers.

MATTHEW HENRY

point is gained. If an enemy be made a friend, that will be more to our advantage than to have him slain.

III. Samuel took this occasion to call the people together *before the Lord in Gilgal, v.* 14, 15. 1. That they might publicly give God thanks for their late victory. 2. That they might confirm Saul in the government, more solemnly than had been yet done, that he might not retire again to his obscurity.

CHAPTER 12

Verses 1–5

I. Samuel gives them a short account of the late revolution, and of the present posture of their government, by way of preface to what he had further to say to them, *v.* 1, 2. 1. For his own part, he had spent his days in their service: "*I have walked before you,* as a guide to direct you, as a shepherd that leads his flock (Ps. lxxx. 1), *from my childhood unto this day.*" "And now my best days are done: *I am old and grey-headed*"; therefore they were the more unkind to cast him off, yet therefore he was the more willing to resign. 2. As for his sons, "*Behold*" (says he), "*they are with you*", you may, if you please, call them to an account for any thing they have done amiss. 3. As for their new king, Samuel had gratified them in setting him over them (*v.* 1). Now that you have made yourselves like the nations in your civil government, and have cast off the divine administration in that, take heed lest you make yourselves like the nations in religion and cast off the worship of God.

II. He solemnly appeals to them concerning his own integrity in the administration of the government (*v.* 3): *Witness against me, whose ox have I taken?*

1. His design in this appeal. By this he intended, (1) To convince them of the injury they had done him in setting him aside. (2) To preserve his own reputation. Those that heard of Samuel's being rejected as he was, would be ready to suspect that certainly he had done some evil thing, or he would never have been so ill treated. (3) As he designed hereby to leave a good name behind him, so he designed to leave his successor a good example before him; let him write after his copy, and he will write fair.

2. In the appeal itself observe,

(1) What it is that Samuel here acquits himself from. [1] He had never taken that which was not his own, ox or ass, had never distrained their cattle for tribute, fines, or forfeitures, nor used their service without paying for it. [2] He had never defrauded those with whom he dealt, nor oppressed those that were under his power. [3] He had never taken bribes to pervert justice.

(2) How he calls upon those that had slighted him to bear witness concerning his conduct: "*Here I am; witness against me.*

III. Upon this appeal he is honourably acquitted. All he desired was that they should do him justice, and that they did (*v.* 4).

IV. This honourable testimony borne to Samuel's integrity is left upon record to his honour (*v.* 5): "*The Lord is witness,* who searcheth the heart, *and his anointed is witness,* who trieth overt acts"; and the people agree to it: "*He is witness.*"

Verses 6–15

Samuel, having sufficiently secured his own reputation, instead of upbraiding the people upon it with their unkindness to him, sets himself to instruct them in the way of their duty.

I. He reminds them of the great goodness of God to them and to their fathers, gives them an abstract of the history of their nation, that, by the consideration of the great things God had done for them, they might be for ever engaged to love him and serve him. He not only puts them in mind of what God had done for them in their days, but of what he had done of old, in the days of their fathers, because the present age had the benefit of God's former favours. 1. He reminds them of their deliverance out of Egypt. 2. He reminds them of the miseries and calamities which their fathers brought themselves into by forgetting God and serving other gods, *v.* 9. 3. He reminds them of their fathers' repentance and humiliation before God for their idolatries: *They said, We have sinned, v.* 10. 4. He reminds them of the glorious deliverances God had wrought for them, the victories he had blessed them with, and their happy settle-

JAMIESON, FAUSSET, BROWN

The calm and sagacious counsel of Samuel directed the popular feelings into a right channel, by appointing a general assembly of the militia, the really effective force of the nation, at Gilgal, where, amid great pomp and religious solemnities, the victorious leader was confirmed in his kingdom.

CHAPTER 12

Vss. 1-5. Samuel Testifies His Integrity. 1. Samuel said unto all Israel—**This public address was made after the solemn re-instalment of Saul, and before the convention at Gilgal separated. Samuel, having challenged a review of his public life, received a unanimous testimony to the unsullied honor of his personal character, as well as the justice and integrity of his public administration.**

5. the Lord is witness against you, and his anointed is witness—**that, by their own acknowledgment, he had given them no cause to weary of the divine government by judges, and that, therefore, the blame of desiring a change of government rested with themselves. This was only insinuated, and they did not fully perceive his drift.**

6-16. He Reproves the People for Ingratitude. 7. Now therefore stand still, that I may reason with you—**The burden of this faithful and uncompromising address was to show them, that though they had obtained the change of government they had so importunely desired, their conduct was highly displeasing to their heavenly King; nevertheless, if they remained faithful to Him and to the principles of the theocracy, they might be delivered from many of the evils to which the new state of things would expose them. And in confirmation of those statements, no less than in evidence of the divine displeasure, a remarkable phenomenon, on the invocation of the prophet, and of which he gave due premonition, took place.**

ADAM CLARKE

14. *Renew the kingdom.* The unction of Saul, in the first instance, was a very private act; and his being appointed to be king was not known to the people in general. He had now shown himself worthy to command the people; and Samuel takes advantage of this circumstance to gain the general consent in his favor.

15. *There they made Saul king.* It is likely, from these words, that Saul was anointed a second time; he was now publicly acknowledged, and there was no gainsayer. Thus far Saul acted well, and the kingdom seemed to be confirmed in his hand; but soon through imprudence he lost it.

CHAPTER 12

1. *And Samuel said.* It is very likely that it was at this public meeting Samuel delivered the following address; no other time seems to be given for it, and this is the most proper that could be chosen.

2. *My sons are with you.* It is generally agreed that these words intimate that Samuel had deprived them of their public employ, and reduced them to a level with the common people. *Have walked before you from my childhood.* He had been a long, steady, and immaculate servant of the public.

3. *Witness against me.* Did ever a minister of state, in any part of the world, resign his office with so much self-consciousness of integrity, backed with the universal approbation of the public?

7. *Now therefore stand still.* I have arraigned myself before God and you; I now arraign you before God.

8. *The Lord sent Moses and Aaron.* He shows them that through all their history God had ever raised them up deliverers, when their necessities required such interference.

ments, many a time, after days of trouble and distress, *v.* 11. He specifies some of their judges, Gideon and Jephthah, great conquerors in their time. 5. At last he puts them in mind of God's late favour to the present generation, in gratifying them with a king, when they would prescribe to God by such a one to save them out of the hand of Nahash king of Ammon, *v.* 12, 13. Now it appears that this was the immediate occasion of their desiring a king: Nahash threatened them; they desired Samuel to nominate a general; he told them that God was commander-in-chief in all their wars and they needed no other, that what was wanting in them should be made up by his power: *The Lord is your king.* But they insisted on it, *Nay, but a king shall reign over us.* "And now," said he, "you have a king, a king of your own asking—let that be spoken to your shame; but a king of God's making—let that be spoken to his honour and the glory of his grace."

II. He shows them that they are now upon their good behaviour, they and their king. Let them not think that they had now cut themselves off from all dependence upon God.

1. Their obedience to God would certainly be their happiness, *v.* 14. If they would not revolt from God to idols, but would persevere in their allegiance to him, then they and their king should certainly be happy. (1) "You shall continue in the way of your duty to God, which will be your honour and comfort." (2) "You shall continue under the divine guidance and protection": *You shall be after the Lord,* so it is in the original, that is, "he will go before you to lead and prosper you, and make your way plain. *The Lord is with you while you are with him.*"

2. Their disobedience would as certainly be their ruin (*v.* 15).

Verses 16–25

Two things Samuel here aims at:—

I. To convince the people of their sin in desiring a king. They were now rejoicing before God in and with their king (*ch.* xi. 15), and offering to God the sacrifices of praise, which they hoped God would accept; and this perhaps made them think that there was no harm in their asking a king.

1. The expression of God's displeasure against them for asking a king. At Samuel's word, God sent prodigious thunder and rain upon them, at a season of the year when, in that country, the like was never seen or known before, *v.* 16–18. Thunder and rain have natural causes and sometimes terrible effects. But Samuel made it to appear that this was designed by the almighty power of God on purpose to convince them that they had done very *wickedly in asking a king.* He spoke to them of it (*v.* 16, 17): *Stand and see this great thing.* If what he said in a *still small voice* did not reach their hearts, nor his doctrine which dropped as the dew, they shall hear God speaking to them in dreadful claps of thunder and the great rain of his strength. Samuel, that son of prayer, was still famous for success in prayer. He intimated to them that how serene and prosperous soever their condition seemed to be now that they had a king, like the weather in wheat-harvest, yet, if God pleased, he could soon change the face of their heavens.

2. The impressions which this made upon the people. It startled them very much, as well it might. (1) *They greatly feared the Lord and Samuel.* (2) They owned their sin and folly in desiring a king: *We have added to all our sins this evil, v.* 19. (3) They earnestly begged Samuel's prayers (*v.* 19): *Pray for thy servants, that we die not.* They were apprehensive of their danger from the wrath of God, and could not expect that he should hear their prayers for themselves, and therefore they entreat Samuel to pray for them. Now they see their need of him whom awhile ago they slighted.

II. To confirm the people in their religion, and engage them for ever to cleave unto the Lord. The design of his discourse is much the same with Joshua's, *ch.* xxiii. and xxiv.

1. He would not that the terrors of the Lord should frighten them from him, for they were intended to frighten them to him (*v.* 20): *"Fear not; though you have done all this wickedness,* and though God is angry with you for it, yet do not therefore abandon his service, nor *turn from following him." Fear not,* that is, "despair not, fear not with amazement, the weather will clear up after the storm. Fear not; for, though God will frown upon his people, yet he will not forsake them (*v.* 22) *for his great name's sake;* do not you forsake him then."

2. He cautions them against idolatry: *"Turn not aside* from God and the worship of him" (*v.* 20 and again *v.* 21); "for if you turn aside from God, whatever

11. Bedan—The *Sept.* reads "Barak"; and for "Samuel," some versions read "Samson," which seems more natural than that the prophet should mention himself to the total omission of the greatest of the judges. (Cf. Heb. 11:32).

17-25. HE TERRIFIES THEM WITH THUNDER IN HARVEST-TIME. **17. Is it not wheat harvest to-day?** That season in Palestine occurs at the end of June or beginning of July, when it seldom or never rains, and the sky is serene and cloudless. There could not, therefore, have been a stronger or more appropriate proof of a divine mission than the phenomenon of rain and thunder happening, without any prognostics of its approach, upon the prediction of a person professing himself to be a prophet of the Lord, and giving it as an attestation of his words being true.

The people regarded it as a miraculous display of divine power, and, panic-struck, implored the prophet to pray for them.

Promising to do so, he dispelled their fears. The conduct of Samuel, in this whole affair of the king's appointment, shows him to have been a great and good man who sank all private and personal considerations in disinterested zeal for his country's good and whose last words in public were to warn the people, and their king, of the danger of apostasy and disobedience to God.

11. *Jerubbaal.* That is, Gideon. *And Bedan:* instead of *Bedan,* whose name occurs nowhere else as a judge or deliverer of Israel, the Septuagint have "Barak"; the same reading is found in the Syriac and Arabic. The Targum has Samson. Instead of *Samuel,* the Syriac and Arabic have "Samson"; and it is most natural to suppose that Samuel does not mention himself in this place.

12. *When ye saw that Nahash.* This was not the first time they had demanded a king; see before, chap. viii. 5. But at the crisis mentioned here they became more importunate; and it was in consequence of this that the kingdom was a second time confirmed to Saul. Saul was elected at Mizpeh, he was confirmed at Gilgal.

14. *If ye will fear the Lord.* On condition that you rebel no more, God will take you and your king under His merciful protection, and He and His kingdom shall be confirmed and continued.

17. *Is it not wheat harvest to day?* That is, This is the time of wheat harvest. According to Jerome, who spent several years in the Promised Land, this harvest commenced about the end of June or beginning of July, in which he says he never saw rain in Judea.

18. *The Lord sent thunder and rain that day.* This was totally unusual; and, as it came at the call of Samuel, was a most evident miracle. *Greatly feared the Lord.* They dreaded His terrible majesty; and they feared Samuel, perceiving that he had so much power with God.

19. *Pray for thy servants . . . that we die not.* As they knew they had rebelled against God, they saw that they had everything to fear from His justice and power.

20. *Ye have done all this wickedness.* That is, although you have done all this wickedness: what was past God would pass by, provided they would be obedient in the future.

21. *After vain things.* That is, idols; which he calls here *hattohu,* the same expression found in Gen. i. 2. The earth was *tohu;* it was waste, empty, and formless; so idols—they are confusion, and things of naught.

MATTHEW HENRY

you turn aside to, you will find it is a vain thing, that can never answer your expectations, but will certainly deceive you if you trust to it; it is a broken reed, a broken cistern."

3. He comforts them with an assurance that he would continue his care and concern for them, *v.* 23. They asked him only to pray for them, but he promised to do more for them, not only to pray for them, but to teach them; though they were not willing to be under his government as a judge, he would not therefore deny them his instructions as a prophet.

4. He concludes with an earnest exhortation to practical religion and serious godliness, *v.* 24, 25.

CHAPTER 13

Verses 1–7

The people of Israel offended God else he would not have left them, as here it appears he did; for,

I. Saul was very weak and impolitic, and did not order his affairs with discretion. *Saul reigned one year*, and nothing happened that was considerable, it was a year of no action; but in his second year he did as follows:—1. He chose a band of 3,000 men, of whom he himself commanded 2,000, and his son Jonathan 1,000, *v.* 2. The rest of the people he dismissed to their tents. If he intended these only for the guard of his person and his honorary attendants, it was impolitic to have so many, if for a standing army, in apprehension of danger from the Philistines, it was no less impolitic to have so few; and perhaps the confidence he put in this select number, and his disbanding the rest of that brave army with which he had lately beaten the Ammonites (*ch.* xi. 8–11), was looked upon as an affront to the kingdom, excited general disgust, and was the reason he had so few at his call when he had occasion for them. 2. He ordered his son Jonathan to surprise and destroy the garrison of the Philistines that lay near him in Geba, *v.* 3. 3. When he had thus exasperated the Philistines, then he began to raise forces, which, if he had acted wisely, he would have done before. As many as thought fit came to Saul to Gilgal, *v.* 4. But now the generality, we may suppose, drew back (either in dislike of Saul's politics or in dread of the Philistines' power).

II. Never did the Philistines appear in such a formidable body as they did now, upon this provocation which Saul gave them. If Saul had asked counsel of God before he had given the Philistines this provocation, he and his people might the better have borne this threatening trouble which they had now brought on themselves by their own folly.

III. Never were the people of Israel so faint-hearted, so sneaking, so very cowardly, as they were now. Some considerable numbers, it may be, came to Saul to Gilgal; but, hearing of the Philistines' numbers and preparations, their spirits sunk within them, some think because they did not find Samuel there with Saul. Now that they saw the Philistines making war upon them, and Samuel not coming in to help them, they knew not what to do; *men's hearts failed them for fear*. And, 1. Some absconded. Thousands of degenerate Israelites tremble at the approach of a great crowd of Philistines. Guilt makes men cowards. 2. Others fled (*v.* 7): They *went over Jordan to the land of Gilead*, as far as they could from the danger, and to a place where they had lately been victorious over the Ammonites. 3. Those that stayed with Saul *followed him trembling*, expecting no other than to be cut off, and having their hands and hearts very much weakened by the desertion of so many of their troops.

JAMIESON, FAUSSET, BROWN

CHAPTER 13

Vss. 1, 2. SAUL'S SELECTED BAND. **1. Saul reigned one year**—(*see Marg*). The transactions recorded in the eleventh and twelfth chapters were the principal incidents comprising the first year of Saul's reign; and the events about to be described in this happened in the second year.

2. Saul chose him three thousand men of Israel—This band of picked men was a bodyguard, who were kept constantly on duty, while the rest of the people were dismissed till their services might be needed. It seems to have been his tactics to attack the Philistine garrisons in the country by different detachments, rather than by risking a general engagement; and his first operations were directed to rid his native territory of Benjamin of these enemies.

3, 4. HE CALLS THE HEBREWS TO GILGAL AGAINST THE PHILISTINES. **3. Jonathan** [God-given] **smote the garrison of the Philistines . . . in Geba**—Geba and Gibeah were towns in Benjamin, very close to each other (Josh. 18:24, 28). The word rendered "garrison" is different from that of verse 23; ch. 14:1, and signifies, lit., something erected; probably a pillar or flagstaff, indicative of Philistine ascendency. That the secret demolition of this standard, so obnoxious to a young and noble-hearted patriot, was the feat of Jonathan referred to, is evident from the words, "the Philistines heard of it," which is not the way we should expect an attack on a fortress to be noticed. **Saul blew the trumpet throughout all the land**—This, a well-known sound, was the usual Hebrew war-summons; the first blast was answered by the beacon fire in the neighboring places. A second blast was blown—then answered by a fire in a more distant locality, whence the proclamation was speedily diffused over the whole country. As the Philistines resented what Jonathan had done as an overt attempt to throw off their yoke, a levy, en masse, of the people was immediately ordered, the rendezvous to be the old camping-ground at Gilgal.

5. THE PHILISTINES' GREAT HOST. **5. The Philistines gathered themselves together to fight with Israel, thirty thousand chariots, and six thousand horsemen**—Either this number must include chariots of every kind—or the word "chariots" must mean the men fighting in them (II Sam. 10:18; I Kings 20:21; I Chron. 19:18); or, as some eminent critics maintain, *Sheloshim*, thirty, has crept into the text, instead of *Shelosh*, three. The gathering of the chariots and horsemen must be understood to be on the Philistine plain, before they ascended the western passes and pitched in the heart of the Benjamite hills, in "Michmash," (now Mukmas), a "steep precipitous valley" [ROBINSON], eastward from Bethaven (Beth-el).

6, 8. THE ISRAELITES' DISTRESS. **6. When the men of Israel saw that they were in a strait**—Though Saul's gallantry was unabated, his subjects displayed no degree of zeal and energy. Instead of venturing an encounter, they fled in all directions. Some, in their panic, left the country (vs. 7), but most took refuge in the hiding-places which the broken ridges of the neighborhood abundantly afford. The rocks are perforated in every direction with "caves," and "holes," and "pits"—crevices and fissures sunk deep in the rocky soil, subterranean granaries or dry wells in the adjoining fields. The name of Michmash (hidden treasure) seems to be derived from this natural peculiarity [STANLEY].

ADAM CLARKE

24. *Only fear the Lord.* Know, respect, and reverence Him. *Serve him.* Consider Him your Lord and Master; consider yourselves His servants. *In truth.* Be ever honest, ever sincere; *with all your heart*—have every affection engaged in the work of obedience; act not merely from a principle of duty, but also from a pious, affectionate sense of obligation. Act towards your God as an affectionate child should act towards a tender and loving parent.

25. *Ye shall be consumed.* If you do wickedly you shall be destroyed, your kingdom destroyed, and your king destroyed.

CHAPTER 13

1. *Saul reigned one year.* A great deal of learned labor has been employed and lost on this verse, to reconcile it with propriety and common sense. I shall not recount the meanings put on it. I think this clause belongs to the preceding chapter, either as a part of the whole or a chronological note added afterwards; as if the writer had said, "These things [related in chap. xii] took place in the first year of Saul's reign"; and then he proceeds in the next place to tell us what took place in the second year, the two most remarkable years of Saul's reign. In the first he is appointed, anointed, and twice confirmed, viz., at Mizpeh and at Gilgal; in the second, Israel is brought into the lowest state of degradation by the Philistines, Saul acts unconstitutionally, and is rejected from being king. These things were worthy of an especial chronological note.

And when he had reigned. This should begin the chapter, and be read thus: "And when Saul had reigned two years over Israel, he chose him three thousand." The Septuagint has left the clause out of the text entirely, and begins the chapter thus: "And Saul chose to himself three thousand men out of the men of Israel."

2. *Two thousand were with Saul.* Saul, no doubt, meditated the redemption of his country from the Philistines; and having chosen 3,000 men, he thought best to divide them into companies, and send one against the Philistine garrison at *Michmash*, another against that at *Beth-el*, and the third against that at *Gibeah.* He perhaps hoped, by surprising these garrisons, to get swords and spears for his men, of which we find (v. 22) they were entirely destitute.

3. *Jonathan smote.* He appears to have taken this garrison by surprise, for his men had no arms for a regular battle, or taking the place by storm. This is the first place in which this brave and excellent man appears, a man who bears one of the most amiable characters in the Bible. *Let the Hebrews hear.* Probably this means the people who dwelt beyond Jordan, who might very naturally be termed here *haibrim*, from *abar*, "he passed over"; those who are beyond the river Jordan, as Abraham was called *Ibri* because he dwelt beyond the river Euphrates.

4. *The people were called together.* The smiting of this garrison was the commencement of a war, and in effect the shaking off of the Philistine yoke; and now the people found that they must stand together, and fight for their lives.

5. *Thirty thousand chariots, and six thousand horsemen.* There is no proportion here between the chariots and the cavalry. The largest armies ever brought into the field, even by mighty emperors, never were furnished with *thirty thousand* chariots. I think *sheloshim*, "thirty," is a false reading for *shalosh*, "three." The Syriac and the Arabic both signify "three thousand"; and this was a fair proportion to the horsemen. This is most likely to be the true reading.

6. *The people did hide themselves.* They, being few in number, and totally unarmed as to swords and spears, were terrified at the very numerous and well-appointed army of the Philistines. Judea was full of rocks, caves, thickets, where people might shelter themselves from their enemies.

7. While some hid themselves others fled beyond *Jordan;* and those who did cleave to Saul *followed him trembling.*

MATTHEW HENRY

Verses 8–14

I. Saul's offence in offering sacrifice before Samuel came. Samuel, when he anointed him, had ordered him to tarry for him seven days in Gilgal, *ch.* x. 8. Perhaps that order was lately repeated with reference to this particular occasion.

This order Saul broke. 1. He presumed to offer sacrifice without Samuel. 2. He determined to engage the Philistines without Samuel's directions. So self-sufficient Saul was that he thought it not worth while to stay for a prophet of the Lord either to pray for him or to advise him. (1) He did not send any messenger to Samuel, to know his mind. (2) When Samuel came he rather seemed to boast of what he had done than to repent of it; for he *went forth to salute him*, as his brother-sacrificer. He went out to *bless him*, so the word is, as if he now thought himself a complete priest. (3) He charged Samuel with breach of promise: *Thou camest not within the days appointed* (*v.* 11). (4) When he was charged with disobedience he justified himself in what he had done, and gave no sign at all of repentance for it. See what excuses he made, *v.* 11, 12. He would have this act of disobedience pass, [1] For an instance of his prudence. [2] For an instance of his piety. He would be thought very devout, and in great care not to engage the Philistines till he had by prayer and sacrifice engaged God on his side: "*The Philistines*," said he, "*will come down upon me, before I have made my supplication to the Lord*, and then I am undone." And yet, lastly, He owns it went against his conscience to do it: *I forced myself and offered a burnt-offering.*

II. The sentence passed upon Saul for this offence. 1. He shows him the aggravations of his crime, and charges him with being an enemy to himself, and his interest—*Thou hast done foolishly*, and a rebel to God and his government—"*Thou hast not kept the commandment of the Lord thy God*, that commandment wherewith he intended to try thy obedience." Sin is folly, and sinners are the greatest fools. 2. He reads his doom (*v.* 14): He shows that there is no sin little, because no little god to sin against; but that every sin is a forfeiture of the heavenly kingdom, for which we stood fair. Saul lost his kingdom for want of two or three hours' patience.

Verses 15–23

1. Samuel departs in displeasure. Saul has set up for himself, and now he is left to himself: *Samuel gat him from Gilgal* (*v.* 15). Yet in going up to Gibeah of Benjamin, which was Saul's city, he intimated that he had not quite abandoned him. 2. Saul goes after him to Gibeah, and there musters his army, and finds his whole number to be but 600 men, *v.* 15, 16. 3. The Philistines ravage the country. The body of their army lay in an advantageous pass at Michmash, but thence they sent out three separate parties or detachments that took several ways, to plunder the country. By these the land of Israel was both terrified and impoverished, and the Philistines were animated and enriched. 4. The Israelites that take the field with Saul are unarmed, having only slings and clubs, not a sword or spear among them all, except what Saul and Jonathan themselves have, *v.* 19, 22. (1) How politic the Philistines were! They put down all the smiths' shops, transplanted the smiths into their own country, and forbade any Israelite, under severe penalties, to exercise the trade or mystery

JAMIESON, FAUSSET, BROWN

8. he [Saul] **tarried seven days**—He was still in the eastern borders of his kingdom, in the valley of Jordan. Some bolder spirits had ventured to join the camp at Gilgal; but even the courage of those stout-hearted men gave way in prospect of this terrible visitation; and as many of them were stealing away, he thought some immediate and decided step must be taken.

9-16. SAUL, WEARY OF WAITING FOR SAMUEL, SACRIFICES. **9. Saul said, Bring hither a burnt offering to me, and peace offerings**—Saul, though patriotic enough in his own way, was more ambitious of gaining the glory of a triumph to himself than ascribing it to God. He did not understand his proper position as king of Israel; and although aware of the restrictions under which he held the sovereignty, he wished to rule as an autocrat, who possessed absolute power both in civil and sacred things. This occasion was his first trial. Samuel waited till the last day of the seven, in order to put the constitutional character of the king to the test; and, as Saul, in his impatient and passionate haste knowingly transgressed (vs. 12) by invading the priest's office and thus showing his unfitness for his high office (as he showed nothing of the faith of Gideon and other Hebrew generals), he incurred a threat of the rejection which his subsequent waywardness confirmed.

15, 16. Samuel . . . gat him . . . unto Gibeah . . . and Saul, and Jonathan his son, and the people that were present with them, abode in Gibeah—Saul removed his camp thither, either in the hope that, it being his native town, he would gain an increase of followers or that he might enjoy the counsels and influence of the prophet.

17. the spoilers came out of the camp of the Philistines in three companies—ravaging through the three valleys which radiate from the uplands of Michmash to Ophrah on the north, through the pass of Beth-horon on the west, and down the ravines of Zeboim (the hyænas), towards the Ghor or Jordan valley on the east. **19. Now there was no smith found throughout . . . Israel**—The country was in the lowest state of depression and degradation. The Philistines, after the great victory over the sons of Eli, had become the virtual masters of the land. Their policy in disarming the natives has been often fol-

ADAM CLARKE

8. *He tarried seven days, according to the set time.* Samuel in the beginning had told Saul to wait seven days, and he would come to him, and show him what to do, chap. x. 8. What is here said cannot be understood of that appointment, but of a different one. Samuel had at this time promised to come to him within seven days, and he kept his word, for we find him there before the day was ended; but as Saul found he did not come at the beginning of the seventh day, he became impatient, took the whole business into his own hand, and acted the parts of prophet, priest, and king; and thus he attempted a most essential change in the Israelitish constitution. In it the king, the prophet, and the priest are in their nature perfectly distinct. What such a rash person might have done, if he had not been deprived of his authority, who can tell? But his conduct on this occasion sufficiently justifies that deprivation. That he was a rash and headstrong man is also proved by his senseless adjuration of the people about "food," chap. xiv. 24, and his unfeeling resolution to put the brave Jonathan, his own son, to death, because he had unwittingly acted contrary to this adjuration, v. 44. Saul appears to have been a brave and honest man, but he had few of those qualities which are proper for a king.

9. *And he offered the burnt offering.* This was most perfectly unconstitutional; he had no authority to offer, or cause to be offered, any of the Lord's sacrifices.

10. *Behold, Samuel came.* Samuel was punctual to his appointment; one hour longer of delay would have prevented every evil, and by it no good would have been lost.

11. *And Saul said.* Here he offers three excuses for his conduct: (1) the people were fast leaving his standard; (2) Samuel did not come "at the time"; at the very commencement of the time he did not come, but within that time he did come; (3) the Philistines were coming fast upon him. Saul should have waited out the time; and at all events he should not have gone contrary to the counsel of the Lord.

12. *I forced myself.* It was with great reluctance that I did what I did. In all this Saul was sincere, but he was rash, and regardless of the precept of the Lord, which precept or command he most evidently had received, v. 13. And one part of this precept was, that the Lord should tell him what he should do. Without this information, in an affair under the immediate cognizance of God, he should have taken no step.

14. *The Lord hath sought him a man after his own heart.* That this man was David is sufficiently clear from the sequel. But in what sense was he a man after God's own heart? Answer: (1) in his strict attention to the law and worship of God; (2) in his admitting. in the whole of his conduct, that God was King in Israel, and that he himself was but His vicegerent; (3) in never attempting to alter any of those laws, or in the least change the Israelitish constitution; (4) in all his public official conduct he acted according to the divine mind, and fulfilled the will of his Maker; thus was he a man after God's own heart. In reference to his private or personal moral conduct, the word is never used.

15. *And Samuel arose.* Though David, in the divine purpose, is appointed to be captain over the people, yet Saul is not to be removed from the government during his life; Samuel therefore accompanies him to Gibeah, to give him the requisite help in this conjuncture. *About six hundred men.* The whole of the Israelitish army at this time, and not one sword or spear among them!

17. *The spoilers came out.* The Philistines, finding that the Israelites durst not hazard a battle, divided their army into three bands, and sent them in three different directions to pillage and destroy the country. Jonathan profited by this circumstance, and attacked the remains of the army at Michmash, as we shall see in the succeeding chapter.

19. *Now there was no smith found.* It is very likely that in the former wars the Philistines carried away all the smiths from Israel.

21. *Yet they had a file.* The Hebrew *petsirah*,

MATTHEW HENRY

of working in brass or iron. They must go to some or other of their garrisons, to have all their iron-work done, and no more might an Israelite do than use a file (*v.* 20, 21). (2) How impolitic Saul was, that did not, in the beginning of his reign, set himself to redress this grievance. (3) How slothful and mean-spirited the Israelites were, that suffered the Philistines thus to impose upon them and had no thought nor spirit to help themselves. If they had not been dispirited, they could not have been disarmed, but it was sin that made them naked to their shame.

JAMIESON, FAUSSET, BROWN

lowed in the East. For repairing any serious damage to their agricultural implements, they had to apply to the neighboring forts. "Yet they had a file," as a kind of privilege, for the purpose of sharpening sundry smaller utensils of husbandry.

ADAM CLARKE

from *patsar*, "to rub hard," is translated very differently by the versions and by critics. Our translation may be as likely as any: they permitted them the use of *a file* (I believe the word means grindstone) to restore the blunted edges of their *axes* and *goads*.

22. *In the day of battle . . . there was neither sword nor spear.* But if the Israelites enjoyed such profound peace and undisturbed dominion under Samuel, how is it that they were totally destitute of arms, a state which argues the lowest circumstances of oppression and vassalage? In answer to this we may observe, that the bow and the sling were the principal arms of the Israelites; for these they needed no smith. The most barbarous nations, who have never seen iron, have nevertheless bows and arrows; the arrowheads generally made of flint.

MATTHEW HENRY

CHAPTER 14

Verses 1-15

I. Of the goodness of God in restraining the Philistines, who had a vast army of valiant men in the field, from falling upon that little handful of timorous trembling people that Saul had with him.

II. Of the weakness of Saul, who seems here to have been quite at a loss, and unable to help himself. 1. He pitched his tent under a tree, and had but 600 men with him, *v.* 2. He durst not stay in Gibeah, but got into some obscure place, in the uttermost part of the city, under a pomegranate-tree, under *Rimmon.* 2. Now he sent for a priest, and the ark, a priest from Shiloh, and the ark from Kirjath-jearim, *v.* 3, 18. Samuel, the Lord's prophet, had forsaken him, but he thinks he can make up that loss by commanding Ahiah, the Lord's priest, to attend him. He will also have the ark brought in hopes that this would make up the deficiency of his forces; one would have supposed that they would never bring the ark into the camp again, since, the last time, it not only did not save them, but did itself fall into the Philistines' hands. But it is common for those that have lost the substance of religion to be most fond of the shadows of it, as here is a deserted prince courting a deserted priest.

III. Of the bravery and piety of Jonathan, the son of Saul, who was much fitter than the father to wear the crown. "A sweet imp (says Bishop Hall) out of a crab-stock."

1. He resolved to go *incognito—unknown to any one,* into the camp of the Philistines. The way of access to the enemies' camp is described (*v.* 4, 5) as being peculiarly difficult, and their natural entrenchments impregnable, yet this does not discourage him; the strength and sharpness of the rocks do but harden and whet his resolution. Great and generous souls are animated by opposition and take a pleasure in breaking through it.

2. He encouraged his armour-bearer, a young man that attended him, to go along with him in this daring enterprise, (*v.* 6): "*Come, and let us* put our lives in our hands, *and go over to the* enemies' *garrison,* and try what we can do to put them into confusion." (1) They are uncircumcised. Fear not, we shall do well enough with them, for they are not under the protection of God's covenant as we are. If such as are enemies to us are also strangers to God, we need not fear them. (2) "God is able to make us two victorious over their unnumbered regiments. *There is no restraint in the Lord to save by many or by few.*" This is a truth easily granted in general, and yet it is not so easy to apply it to a particular case; when we are but few to believe that God can not only save us, but save by us, this is an instance of faith, which, wherever it is, shall obtain a good report. (3) Who knows but he that can use us for his glory will do it? *It may be the Lord will work for us.* An active faith will venture far in God's cause upon an *it may be.* Jonathan's armour-bearer, or esquire, as if he had learned to carry, not his arms only, but his heart, promised to stand by him and to follow him whithersoever he went, *v.* 7.

3. How bold soever his resolution was, he resolved to follow Providence in the execution of it. "Come" (says he to his confidant), "we will discover ourselves to the enemy, as those that are not afraid to look them in the face (*v.* 8), and then, if they be so cautious as to bid us stand, we will advance no further, taking it for an intimation of Providence that God would have us act defensively (*v.* 9); but if they challenge us, and the first sentinel we meet bid us march on, we will push forward, and make as brisk an onset, assuredly gathering thence that it is the will of God we should act offensively, and then not doubting

JAMIESON, FAUSSET, BROWN

CHAPTER 14

Vss. 1-14. JONATHAN MIRACULOUSLY SMITES THE PHILISTINES' GARRISON. **1. the Philistines' garrison**—*Marg.,* the standing camp "in the passage of Michmash" (ch. 13:16, 23), now Wady Es-Suweinit. "It begins in the neighborhood of Betin (Beth-el) and El-Bireh (Beetroth), and as it breaks through the ridge below these places, its sides form precipitous walls. On the right, about a quarter of an acre below, it again breaks off, and passes between high perpendicular precipices" [ROBINSON]. **2. Saul tarried in the uttermost part or Gibeah**—*Heb.,* Geba, entrenched, along with Samuel and Ahiah the high priest, on the top of one of the conical or spherical hills which abound in the Benjamite territory, and favorable for an encampment, called Migron (a precipice).

4. between the passages—i.e., the deep and great ravine of Suweinit. **Jonathan sought to go over unto the Philistines' garrison**—a distance of about three miles running between two jagged points; *Heb.,* "teeth of the cliff." **there was a sharp rock on the one side, and a sharp rock on the other side . . . Bozez**—(shining) from the aspect of the chalky rock. **Seneh**—(the thorn) probably from a solitary acacia on its top. They are the only rocks of the kind in this vicinity; and the top of the crag towards Michmash was occupied as the post of the Philistines. The two camps were in sight of each other; and it was up the steep rocky sides of this isolated eminence that Jonathan and his armorbearer (vs. 6) made their adventurous approach. This enterprise is one of the most gallant that history or romance records. The action, viewed in itself, was rash and contrary to all established rules of military discipline, which do not permit soldiers to fight or to undertake any enterprise that may involve important consequences without the order of the generals.

6. it may be that the Lord will work for us—This expression did not imply a doubt; it signified simply that the object he aimed at was not in his own power—but it depended upon God—and that he expected success neither from his own strength nor his own merit.

9, 10. if they say, Come up unto us; then we will go up: for the Lord hath delivered them into our hand—When Jonathan appears here to prescribe a sign or token of God's will, we may infer that the same spirit which inspired this enterprise suggested the means of its execution, and put into his heart what to ask of God. (See on Gen. 24:12-14.)

ADAM CLARKE

CHAPTER 14

1. *Come, and let us go over.* This action of Jonathan was totally contrary to the laws of war; no military operation should be undertaken without the knowledge and command of the general. But it is likely that he was led to this by a divine influence.

2. *Under a pomegranate tree.* Under *Rimmon,* which not only signifies a *pomegranate tree,* but also a strong rock, in which 600 Benjamites took shelter, Judg. xx. 45. Probably it was in this very rock that Saul and his 600 men now lay hidden.

3. *Ahiah, the son of Ahitub.* Phinehas, son of Eli, the high priest, had two sons, Ahitub and Ichabod; the latter was born when the ark was taken, and his mother died immediately after. Ahiah is also called Ahimelech, chap. xxii. 9. *Wearing an ephod.* That is, performing the functions of the high priest. This man does not appear to have been with Saul when he offered the sacrifices, chap. xiii. 9, etc.

4. *The name of the one was Bozez.* "Slippery"; *and the name of the other Seneh,* "treading down."—Targum.

6. *Let us go over.* Moved, doubtless, by a divine impulse. *There is no restraint to the Lord.* This is a fine sentiment; and where there is a promise of defense and support, the weakest, in the face of the strongest enemy, may rely on it with the utmost confidence.

9. *If they say thus unto us.* Jonathan had no doubt asked this as a sign from God; exactly as Eliezer, the servant of Abraham, did, Gen. xxiv. 12.

MATTHEW HENRY	JAMIESON, FAUSSET, BROWN	ADAM CLARKE

but he will *stand by us*," *v.* 10. And upon this issue he puts it, firmly believing, (1) That God has the governing of the hearts and tongues of all men. Jonathan knew God could discover his mind to him as surely by the mouth of a Philistine as by the mouth of a priest. (2) That God will, some way or other, direct the steps of those that *acknowledge him in all their ways*.

4. Providence gave him the sign he expected, and he answered the signal. He and his armour-bearer did not surprise the Philistines when they were asleep, but discovered themselves to them by day light, *v.* 11. The guards of the Philistines, (1) Disdained them, *Behold, the Hebrews come forth out of their holes.* (2) They defied them (*v.* 12): *Come, and we will show you a thing.* They bantered them. This greatly emboldened Jonathan. With it he encouraged his servant; he had spoken with uncertainty (*v.* 6): *It may be the Lord will work for us*; but now he speaks with assurance (*v.* 12). *The Lord has delivered them into the hand of Israel.* His faith being thus strengthened, no difficulty can stand before him; he climbs up the rock upon all fours (*v.* 13), though he has nothing to cover him, nor any but his own servant to second him, nor any human probability of any thing but death before him.

5. The wonderful success of this daring enterprise. The Philistines, instead of falling upon Jonathan, to slay him, or take him prisoner, fell before him (*v.* 13) unaccountably, upon the first blow he gave. They fall, that is, (1) They were many of them slain by him and his armour-bearer, *v.* 14. It was God's right hand and his arm that got him this victory. (2) The rest were put to flight, and fell foul upon one another (*v.* 15): *There was trembling in the host.* It is called *a trembling of God.* He that made the heart knows how to make it tremble. To complete the confusion, even the earth quaked, and made them ready to fear that it would sink under them.

Verses 16–23

I. The Philistines were, by the power of God, set against one another. They melted away like snow before the sun, and *went on beating down one another* (*v.* 16), for (*v.* 20) *every man's sword was against his fellow.* Now, God showed them the folly of their confidence, by making their own swords and spears the instruments of their destruction, and more fatal in their own hands than if they had been in the hands of Israel.

II. The Israelites were hereby animated against them.

1. Notice was soon taken of it by the watchmen of Saul, those that stood sentinel at Gibeah, *v.* 16.

2. Saul began to enquire of God, but soon desisted. He called for the ark (*v.* 18), desiring to know whether it would be safe for him to attack the Philistines, upon the disorder they perceived them to be in. Many will consult God about their safety that would never consult him about their duty. But, perceiving by his scouts that the noise in the enemy's camp increased, he commanded the priest that officiated to break off abruptly: "*Withdraw thy hand* (*v.* 19), consult no more, wait no longer for an answer. It is rather a prohibition to his enquiring of the Lord, either, (1) Because now he thought he did not need an answer, the case was plain enough. Or, (2) Because he was in such haste to fight a falling enemy that he would not stay to make an end of his devotions.

3. He, and all the little force he had, made a vigorous attack upon the enemy; and all the people *were cried together* (so the word is, *v.* 20), for want of the silver trumpets wherewith God appointed them to sound an alarm in the day of battle, Num. x. 9. They summoned them by shouting, and their number was not so great but that they might soon be got together.

4. Every Hebrew, even those from whom one would least have expected it, now turned his hand against the Philistines. (1) Those that had deserted and gone over to the enemy, and were among them, now fought against them, *v.* 21. Such as had been taken prisoners by them, were as goads in their sides. (2) Those that had fled their colours, and hid themselves in the mountains, returned to their posts, and joined in with the pursuers (*v.* 22). It was not much to their praise to appear now, but it would have been more their reproach if they had not appeared. Thus all hands were at work against the Philistines, yet it is said (*v.* 23), it was *the Lord that saved Israel that day*. He did it by them, for without him they could do nothing.

Verses 24–35

An account of the distress of the children of Israel, even in the day of their triumphs.

I. Saul forbade the people, under the penalty of

11. Behold, the Hebrews come forth out of their holes—As it could not occur to the sentries that two men had come with hostile designs, it was a natural conclusion that they were Israelite deserters. And hence no attempt was made to hinder their ascent, or stone them.

14. that first slaughter, which Jonathan and his armourbearer made, was about twenty men, within as it were an half acre of land, which a yoke of oxen might plough—This was a very ancient mode of measurement, and it still subsists in the East. The men who saw them scrambling up the rock had been surprised and killed, and the spectacle of twenty corpses would suggest to others that they were attacked by a numerous force. The success of the adventure was aided by a panic that struck the enemy, produced both by the sudden surprise and the shock of an earthquake. The feat was begun and achieved by the faith of Jonathan, and the issue was of God.

16. the watchmen of Saul . . . looked—The wild disorder in the enemies' camp was described and the noise of dismay heard on the heights of Gibeah. **17-19. Then said Saul unto the people that were with him, Number now, and see who is gone from us**—The idea occurred to him that it might be some daring adventurer belonging to his own little troop, and it would be easy to discover him. **Saul said unto Ahiah, Bring hither the ark of God**—There is no evidence that the ark had been brought from Kirjath-jearim. The *Sept.* version is preferable; which, by a slight variation of the text, reads, "the ephod;" i.e., the priestly cape, which the high priest put on when consulting the oracle. That this should be at hand is natural, from the presence of Ahiah himself, as well as the nearness of Nob, where the tabernacle was then situated. **Withdraw thine hand**—The priest, invested with the ephod, prayed with raised and extended hands. Saul, perceiving that the opportunity was inviting, and that God appeared to have sufficiently declared in favor of His people, requested the priest to cease, that they might immediately join in the contest. The season for consultation was past—the time for prompt action was come. **20-22. Saul and all the people**—All the warriors in the garrison at Gibeah, the Israelite deserters in the camp of the Philistines, and the fugitives among the mountains of Ephraim, now all rushed to the pursuit, which was hot and sanguinary.

23. So the Lord saved Israel that day; and the battle passed over unto Beth-aven—i.e., Beth-el. It passed over the forest, now destroyed, on the central ridge of Palestine, then over to the other side from the eastern pass of Michmash (vs. 31), to the western pass of Aijalon, through which they escaped into their own plains.

12. *Come up to us, and we will shew you a thing.* This was the favorable sign which Jonathan had requested. The Philistines seem to have meant, Come, and we will show you how well fortified we are, and how able to quell all the attacks of your countrymen.

13. *Jonathan climbed up.* It seems he had a part of the rock still to get over. When he got over, he began to slay the guards, which were about twenty in number; these were a sort of outpost or advanced guard to the garrison. *Slew after him.* Jonathan knocked them down, and the armor-bearer dispatched them. This seems to be the meaning.

14. *An half acre of land.* The ancients measured land by the quantum which a yoke of oxen could plough in a day. The original is obscure, and is variously understood. It is probably a proverbial expression for a "very small space."

16. *The watchmen of Saul.* Those who were sent out as scouts to observe the motions of the army. *Melted away.* There was no order in the Philistine camp, and the people were dispersing in all directions. The Vulgate has, "And behold the multitude were prostrate"; many lay dead upon the field, partly by the sword of Jonathan and his armor-bearer, and partly by the swords of each other, v. 20.

17. *Number now.* Saul perceived that the Philistines were routed, but could not tell by what means; supposing that it must be by some of his own troops, he called a muster to see who and how many were absent.

18. *Bring hither the ark of God.* He wished to inquire what use he should make of the present favorable circumstances, and to proceed in the business as God should direct.

19. *While Saul talked unto the priest.* Before he had made an end of consulting him, the increasing noise of the panic-struck Philistines called his attention; and finding there was no time to lose, he immediately collected his men and fell on them.

21. *The Hebrews that were with the Philistines.* We may understand such as they held in bondage, or who were their servants. Instead of *Hebrews* the Septuagint read, "the slaves"; from which it is evident that, instead of *Ibrim*, "Hebrews," they found in their text *abadim*, "servants."

MATTHEW HENRY

a curse, to taste any food that day, *v.* 24. He did it with a good intention, lest the people, who perhaps had been kept for some time at short allowance, when they found plenty of victuals in the deserted camp of the Philistines, should fall greedily upon that, and so lose time in pursuing the enemy. And yet his making this severe order was unwise; for, if it gained time, it lost strength, for the pursuit. It was impious to enforce the prohibition with a curse and an oath. Had he no penalty less than an anathema wherewith to support his military discipline?

II. The people observed his order. 1. The soldiers were tantalized; for, in their pursuit of the enemy, it happened that they went through a wood so full of wild honey that it dropped from the trees upon the ground, yet, for fear of the curse, they did not so much as taste the honey, *v.* 25, 26. 2. Jonathan fell under the curse through ignorance. He heard not of the charge his father had given; for, having bravely forced the lines, he was then following the chase. He, not knowing any peril in it, took up a piece of honey-comb upon the end of his staff, and sucked it (*v.* 27), and was sensibly refreshed by it. He thought no harm, nor feared any, till one of the people acquainted him with the order, and then he found himself in a snare. Many a good son has been distressed by the rashness of an inconsiderate father. Jonathan, for his part, lost the crown he was heir to by his father's folly. 3. The soldiers were faint, and grew feeble, in the pursuit of the Philistines. Jonathan foresaw this would be the effect of it; their spirits would flag, and their strength would fail, for want of sustenance. 4. The worst effect of all was that at evening, when the restraint was taken off and they returned to their food again, they were so greedy and eager upon it that they ate the flesh with the blood, expressly contrary to the law of God, *v.* 32. Two hungry meals, we say, make the third a glutton; it was so here. Saul, being informed of it, reproved them for the sin (*v.* 33). To put a stop to this irregularity, Saul ordered them to set up a great stone before him, and let all that had cattle to kill, for their present use, bring them thither, and kill them under his eye upon that stone (*v.* 33), and the people did so (*v.* 34), so easily were they restrained and reformed when their prince took care to do his part.

III. On this occasion Saul built an altar (*v.* 35), that he might offer sacrifice, either by way of acknowledgment of the victory or by way of atonement for the sin. *The same was the first altar that he built.* Saul was turning aside from God, and yet now he began to build altars, being most zealous (as many are) for the form of godliness when he was denying the power of it. See Hos. viii. 14, *Israel has forgotten his Maker, and buildeth temples.*

Verses 36–46

I. Saul's boasting against the Philistines. He proposed to pursue them all night, and *not leave a man of them, v.* 36. Here he showed much zeal, but little discretion; for his army, thus fatigued, could as ill spare a night's sleep as a meal's meat. Only the priest thought it convenient to go on with the devotions that were broken off abruptly (*v.* 19), and to consult the oracle: *Let us draw near hither unto God.* Princes and great men have need of such about them as will thus be their remembrancers, wherever they go, to take God along with them. And, when the priest proposed it, Saul could not for shame reject the proposal, but *asked counsel of God* (*v.* 37).

II. His falling foul on his son Jonathan: for, while he is prosecuted, the Philistines make their escape.

1. God, by giving an intimation of his displeasure, put Saul upon searching for an accursed thing. Saul swears by his Maker that whoever was the Achan that troubled the camp, by eating the forbidden fruit, should certainly die, though it were Jonathan himself. (*v.* 39).

2. Jonathan was discovered by lot to be the offender. Saul would have lots cast between himself and Jonathan on the one side, and the people on the other, perhaps because he was as confident of Jonathan's innocency in this matter as of his own, *v.* 40. Jonathan at length was taken (*v.* 42), Providence designing hereby to countenance and support a lawful authority, reserving another way to bring off one that had done nothing worthy of death.

3. Jonathan ingenuously confesses the fact, and Saul, with an angry curse, passes sentence upon him. Jonathan denies not the truth, only he thinks it hard that he must *die for it, v.* 43. He might very fairly have pleaded his ignorance of the law, but he submitted to the necessity with a great and generous mind: "God's and my father's will be done". It is as brave to yield in some cases as it is in other cases to fight. Saul is not mollified by his filial submission nor the hardness of his case; but with another im-

JAMIESON, FAUSSET, BROWN

24. Saul had adjured the people—Afraid lest so precious an opportunity of effectually humbling the Philistine power might be lost, the impetuous king laid an anathema on any one who should taste food until the evening. This rash and foolish denunciation distressed the people, by preventing them taking such refreshments as they might get on the march, and materially hindered the successful attainment of his own patriotic object.

25. all they of the land came to a wood; and there was honey—The honey is described as "upon the ground," "dropping" from the trees, and in honeycombs—indicating it to be bees' honey. "Bees in the East are not, as in England, kept in hives; they are all in a wild state. The forests literally flow with honey; large combs may be seen hanging on the trees as you pass along, full of honey" [ROBERTS].

31-34. the people were very faint. And the people flew upon the spoil—at evening, when the time fixed by Saul had expired. Faint and famishing, the pursuers fell voraciously upon the cattle they had taken, and threw them on the ground to cut off their flesh and eat them raw, so that the army, by Saul's rashness, were defiled by eating blood, or living animals; probably, as the Abyssinians do, who cut a part of the animal's rump, but close the hide upon it, and nothing mortal follows from that wound. They were painfully conscientious in keeping the king's order for fear of the curse, but had no scruple in transgressing God's command. To prevent this violation of the law, Saul ordered a large stone to be rolled, and those that slaughtered the oxen to cut their throats on that stone. By laying the animal's head on the high stone, the blood oozed out on the ground, and sufficient evidence was afforded that the ox or sheep was dead before it was attempted to eat it.

KEIL–DELITZSCH:

Verse 35. As a thanksgiving for this victory, Saul built an altar to the Lord. "He began to build it," i.e., he built this altar at the beginning, or as the first altar. This altar was probably not intended to serve as a place of sacrifice, but simply to be a memorial of the presence of God, or the revelation of God which Saul had received in the marvellous victory.

Verse 36. After the people had strengthened themselves in the evening with food, Saul wanted to pursue the Philistines still farther during the night, and to plunder them until the light (i.e. till break of day), and utterly destory them. The people assented to this proposal, but the priest (Ahiah) wished first of all to obtain the decision of God upon the matter. "We will draw near to God here" (before the altar which has just been built).

Verse 37. But when Saul inquired of God (through the Urim and Thummim of the high priest), "Shall I go down after the Philistines? wilt thou deliver them into the hand of Israel?" God did not answer him. Saul was to perceive from this that the guilt of some sin was resting upon the people, on account of which the Lord had turned away His countenance and was withdrawing His help.

—*Commentary on the Old Testament*

ADAM CLARKE

24. *Saul had adjured the people.* He was afraid if they waited to refresh themselves the Philistines would escape out of their hands, and therefore he made the taking any food till sunset a capital crime. This was the very means of defeating his own intention; for as the people were exhausted for want of food, they could not continue the pursuit of their enemies. Had it not been for this foolish adjuration, there had been a greater slaughter of the Philistines, v. 30.

25. *There was honey upon the ground.* There were many wild bees in that country, and Judea is expressly said to be a land flowing with milk and *honey.*

26. *The honey dropped.* It seems to have dropped from the trees on the ground. Honey dews, as they are called, are not uncommon in most countries; and this appears to have been something of this kind.

27. *His eyes were enlightened.* Hunger and fatigue affect and dim the sight; on taking food, this affection is immediately removed.

33. *Roll a great stone unto me.* Probably this means that they should set up an altar to the Lord, on which the animals might be properly slain, and the blood poured out upon the earth; and a large stone was erected for an altar.

35. *Saul built an altar.* And this we are informed was *the first* he had built; Samuel, as prophet, had hitherto erected the altars, and Saul thought he had sufficient authority to erect one himself without the prophet, as he once offered sacrifice without him.

36. *Then said the priest.* It is evident that Ahiah doubted the propriety of pursuing the Philistines that night; and as a reverse of fortune might be ruinous after such a victory, he wished to have specific directions from the Lord.

37. *He answered him not that day.* Why was this answer delayed? Surely Jonathan's eating the honey was no sin. This could not have excited God's displeasure. And yet the lot found out Jonathan! But did this argue that he had incurred guilt in the sight of God? I answer: It did not; for Jonathan was delivered, by the authority of the people, from his father's rash curse; no propitiation is offered for his supposed transgression to induce God to pardon it; nor do we find any displeasure of God manifested on the occasion.

41. *Lord God of Israel, Give a perfect lot.* Both the Vulgate and Septuagint add much to this verse: "And Saul said to the Lord God of Israel, Lord God of Israel, give judgment. Why is it that thou hast not answered thy servant to-day? If the iniquity be in me, or Jonathan my son, make it manifest. Or if this iniquity be in thy people, give sanctification."

42. *And Jonathan was taken.* The object of the inquiry most evidently was, Who has gone contrary to the king's adjuration today? The answer to that must be Jonathan.

MATTHEW HENRY

precation he gives judgment upon Jonathan (*v.* 44): "*God do so and more also* to me if I do not execute the law upon thee, *for thou shalt surely die, Jonathan.*" (1) He passed this sentence too hastily, without consulting the oracle. Jonathan had a very good plea in arrest of the judgment. What he had done was not *malum in se—bad in itself*; and, as for the prohibition of it, he was ignorant of that, so that he could not be charged with rebellion or disobedience. (2) He did it in fury. Had Jonathan been worthy to die, yet it would have become a judge, much more a father, to pass sentence with tenderness and compassion. Justice is debased when it is administered with wrath and bitterness. (3) He backed it with a curse upon himself if he did not see the sentence executed; and this curse did return upon his own head. Jonathan escaped, but God did so to Saul, and more also; for he was rejected of God and made anathema. Let none upon any occasion dare to use such imprecations as these, lest God say Amen to them, and *make their own tongues to fall upon them*, Ps. lxiv. 8. Yet we have reason to think that Saul's bowels yearned towards Jonathan, so that he really punished himself, and very justly, when he seemed so severe upon Jonathan. By all these vexatious accidents God did likewise correct him for his presumption in offering sacrifice without Samuel.

4. The people rescued Jonathan out of his father's hands, *v.* 45. Hitherto they had expressed themselves very observant of Saul. What seemed good to him they acquiesced in, *v.* 36, 40. But, when Jonathan is in danger, Saul's word is no longer a law to them, but with the utmost zeal they oppose the execution of his sentence: "*Shall Jonathan die*—that blessing, that darling, of his country? Shall that life be sacrificed to a punctilio of law and honour which was so bravely exposed for the public service, and to which we owe our lives and triumphs? No, we will never stand by and see him thus treated whom God delights to honour." It is good to see Israelites zealous for the protection of those whom God has made instruments of public good. "*As the Lord liveth there shall not* only not his head, but not *a hair of his head fall to the ground*"; they did not rescue him by violence, but by reason and resolution; and Josephus says they made their prayer to God that he might be loosed from the curse. They plead for him that *he has wrought with God this day*; that is, "he has owned God's cause, and God has owned his endeavours, and therefore his life is too precious to be thrown away upon a nicety."

5. The design against the Philistines is quashed by this incident (*v.* 46): *Saul went up from following them*, and so an opportunity was lost of completing the victory.

Verses 47–52

A general account of Saul's court and camp. 1. Of his court and family, the names of his sons and daughters (*v.* 49), and of his wife and his cousin-german that was general of his army, *v.* 50. There is mention of another wife of Saul's (2 Sam. xxi. 8), Rizpah, a secondary wife, and of the children he had by her. 2. Of his camp and military actions. (1) How he levied his army: *When he saw any strong valiant man*, that was remarkably fit for service, *he took him unto him* (*v.* 52), as Samuel had told them the manner of the king would be (*ch.* viii. 11). (2) How he employed his army. He guarded his country against the insults of its enemies on every side, and prevented their incursions, *v.* 47, 48. But the enemies he struggled most with were the Philistines, with whom he had *sore war all his days*, *v.* 52.

JAMIESON, FAUSSET, BROWN

ADAM CLARKE

F. B. MEYER:

The man who wrought with God rescued. In this case the voice of the people was the voice of God. If a man dares to stand alone with God, he cannot be put to shame. If he says of the Lord, "He is my refuge and my fortress; my God, in whom I trust," ten thousand voices answer: "He shall cover thee with his feathers, and under his wings shalt thou trust. . . . Thou shalt not be afraid." "No weapon that is formed against thee shall prosper; and every tongue that shall rise against thee in judgment thou shalt condemn." One with God is always on the stronger side.

How safe are they who do God's commandments, hearkening to the voice of his word! When our Lord was arrested, he stood boldly before his captors and, interposing between them and his timid disciples, said, "If ye seek me, let these go their way." This is his invariable method. As the mother bird interposes for her helpless young; as the ring of fire intercepts the night attack of the wild beast; as the broad river and its streams bar the progress of the foe, so the Lord is round about his people forever!—*Bible Commentary*

36-46. the people rescued Jonathan, that he died not—When Saul became aware of Jonathan's transgression in regard to the honey, albeit it was done in ignorance and involved no guilt, he was, like Jephthah, about to put his son to death, in conformity with his vow. But the more enlightened conscience of the army prevented the tarnishing the glory of the day by the blood of the young hero, to whose faith and valor it was chiefly due.

47, 48. So Saul . . . fought against all his enemies on every side—This signal triumph over the Philistines was followed, not only by their expulsion from the land of Israel, but by successful incursions against various hostile neighbors, whom he harassed though he did not subdue them.

45. *And the people said . . . Shall Jonathan die, who hath wrought this great salvation in Israel? God forbid: as the Lord liveth, there shall not one hair of his head fall to the ground.* Here was a righteous and impartial jury, who brought in a verdict according to the evidence: No man should die but for a breach of the law of God; but Jonathan hath not broken any law of God; therefore Jonathan should not die. *He hath wrought with God this day.* God has been Commander in chief; Jonathan has acted under His directions. *So the people rescued Jonathan.* And God testified no displeasure; and perhaps He permitted all this that He might correct Saul's propensity to rashness.

47. *So Saul took the kingdom.* The Targum appears to give the meaning of this expression: "Saul prospered in his government over Israel." And the proofs of his prosperity are immediately subjoined. *Fought against all his enemies.* Of the wars which are mentioned here we have no particulars; they must have endured a long time, and have been, at least in general, successful.

48. *Smote the Amalekites.* This war is mentioned in the following chapter.

49. *Now the sons of Saul.* We do not find Ishbosheth here.

52. *When Saul saw any strong man.* This was very politic. He thus continued to recruit his army with strong and effective men.

CHAPTER 15

Verses 1–9

I. Samuel, in God's name, solemnly requires Saul to be obedient to the command of God, and plainly intimates that he was now about to put him upon a trial, in one particular instance, whether he would be obedient, or no, *v.* 1. 1. He reminds him of what God had done for him: "*The Lord sent me to anoint thee to be a king.*" God gave thee thy power, and therefore he expects thou shouldst use thy power for him. Men's preferment, instead of releasing them from their obedience to God, obliges them so much the more to it. 2. He tells him, in general, that, in consideration of this, whatever God commanded him to do he was bound to do it: *Now therefore hearken to the voice of the Lord.*

II. He appoints him a particular piece of service, in which he must now show his obedience to God more than in any thing he had done yet. He also gives him a reason for the command, that the severity

CHAPTER 15

Vss. 1-6. SAUL SENT TO DESTROY AMALEK. **1. Samuel also said unto Saul, The Lord sent me to anoint thee . . . : now therefore hearken unto . . . the Lord**—Several years had been passed in successful military operations against troublesome neighbors. During these Saul had been left to act in a great measure at his own discretion as an independent prince. Now a second test is proposed of his possessing the character of a theocratic monarch in Israel; and in announcing the duty required of him, Samuel brought before him his official station as the Lord's vicegerent, and the peculiar obligation under which he was laid to act in that capacity. He had formerly done wrong, for which a severe rebuke and threatening were administered to him (ch. 13:13, 14). Now an opportunity was afforded him of retrieving that error by an exact obedience to the divine command.

CHAPTER 15

1. *The Lord sent me to anoint thee.* This gave him a right to say what immediately follows.

MATTHEW HENRY

he must use might not seem hard: *I remember that which Amalek did to Israel, v.* 2. God had an ancient quarrel with the Amalekites, for the injuries they did to his people Israel, Exod. xvii. 8, &c., and the crime is aggravated, Deut. xxv. 18. This is the work that Saul is now appointed to do (*v.* 3): "*Go and smite Amalek*. Israel is now strong, now go and make a full riddance of that nation."

III. Saul hereupon musters his forces, and makes a descent upon the country of Amalek. Saul numbered them in *Telaim*, which signifies *lambs*. He numbered them *like lambs* (so the vulgar Latin), numbered them *by the paschal lambs* (so the Chaldee), allowing ten to a lamb, a way of numbering used by the Jews in the later times of their nation. Saul drew all his forces to the *city of Amalek*.

IV. He gave friendly advice to the Kenites to separate themselves from the Amalekites among whom they dwelt. The Kenites were of the family and kindred of Jethro, Moses's father-in-law, a people that dwelt in tents, which made it easy for them, upon every occasion, to remove to other lands not appropriated. Many of them, at this time, dwelt among the Amalekites, fortified by nature, for *they put their nest in a rock*, being hardy people that could live any where, and affected fastnesses. Num. xxiv. 21. Saul must not waste them. 1. He acknowledges the kindness of their ancestors to Israel, when they came out of Egypt. Jethro and his family had been very helpful and serviceable to them in their passage through the wilderness, had been to them instead of eyes, and this is remembered to their posterity many ages after. Thus a good man leaves the divine blessing for an inheritance to his children's children; those that come after us may be reaping the benefit of our good works when we are in our graves. 2. He desires them to remove their tents from among the Amalekites.

V. Saul prevailed against the Amalekites, for it was rather an execution of condemned malefactors than a war with contending enemies. They were idolaters, and were guilty of many other sins, for which they deserved to fall under the wrath of God; yet, when God would reckon with them, he fastened upon the sin of their ancestors in abusing his Israel as the ground of his quarrel.

VI. Yet he did his work by halves, *v.* 9. 1. He *spared Agag*, because he was a king like himself, and perhaps in hope to get a great ransom for him. 2. He spared the best of the cattle, and destroyed only the refuse, that was good for little. Many of the people, we may suppose, made their escape, and took their effects with them into other countries, and therefore we read of Amalekites after this.

Verses 10–23

Saul is here called to account by Samuel concerning the execution of his commission against the Amalekites.

I. What passed between God and Samuel, in secret, upon this occasion, *v.* 10, 11. 1. God determines Saul's rejection, and acquaints Samuel with it: *It repenteth me that I have set up Saul to be king*. Repentance in God is not, as it is in us, a change of his mind, but a change of his method or dispensation. He does not alter his will, but wills an alteration. The change was in Saul: *He has turned back from following me*; this construction God put upon the partiality of his obedience, and the prevalency of his covetousness. And hereby he did himself make God his enemy. 2. Samuel laments and deprecates it. *It grieved Samuel* that Saul had forfeited God's favour, and that God had resolved to cast him off; and he *cried unto the Lord all night*. The rejection of sinners is the grief of good people; God delights not in their death, nor should we.

II. What passed between Samuel and Saul in public. Samuel, being sent of God to him with these heavy tidings, went, as Ezekiel, in *bitterness of soul*, to meet him. But Samuel was informed that Saul had set up a triumphal arch, or some monument of his victory, at Carmel, a city in the mountains of Judah, seeking his own honour more than the honour of God, and also that he had marched in great state to Gilgal, for this seems to be intimated in the manner of expression: *He has gone about, and passed on, and gone down*, with a great deal of pomp and parade. There Samuel gave him the meeting, and,

1. Saul makes his boast to Samuel of his obedience: "*Blessed be thou of the Lord*, for thou sentest me upon a good errand, in which I have had great success, and *I have performed the commandment of the Lord*." It is very likely, if his conscience had not charged him with disobedience, he would not have been so forward to proclaim his obedience; for by this he hoped to prevent Samuel's reproving him. Thus sinners think, by justifying themselves, to escape

JAMIESON, FAUSSET, BROWN

2, 3. Amalek—the powerful tribe which inhabited the country immediately to the eastward of the northern Cushites. Their territory extended over the whole of the eastern portion of the desert of Sinai to Rephidim—the earliest opponent (Deut. 25:18; Exod. 17:8-16)—the hereditary and restless enemy of Israel (Num. 14:45; Judg. 3:13; 6:3), and who had not repented (ch. 14:48) of their bitter and sleepless hatred during the 500 years that had elapsed since their doom was pronounced. Being a people of nomadic habits, they were as plundering and dangerous as the Bedouin Arabs, particularly to the southern tribes. The national interest required, and God, as King of Israel, decreed that this public enemy should be removed. Their destruction was to be without reservation or exception. **I remember**—I am reminded of what Amalek did—perhaps by the still remaining trophy or memorial erected by Moses (Exod. 17:15, 16). **4. Saul gathered the people together**—The alacrity with which he entered on the necessary preparations for the expedition gave a fair, but delusive promise of faithfulness in its execution. **Telaim**—or Telem, among the uttermost cities of the tribe of Judah towards the coast of Edom (Josh. 15:21, 24). **5. Saul came to a city of Amalek**—probably their capital. **laid wait in the valley**—following the strategic policy of Joshua at Ai (Josh. 6). **6. Kenites**—(See on Judg. 1:16). In consequence, probably, of the unsettled state of Judah, they seem to have returned to their old desert tracts. Though now intermingled with the Amalekites, they were not implicated in the offenses of that wicked race; but for the sake of their ancestors, between whom and those of Israel there had been a league of amity, a timely warning was afforded them to remove from the scene of danger.

7-9. He Spares Agag and the Best of the Spoil. **7-9. Saul smote the Amalekites**—His own view of the proper and expedient course to follow was his rule, not the command of God. **8. he took Agag . . . alive**—This was the common title of the Amalekite kings. He had no scruple about the apparent cruelty of it, for he made fierce and indiscriminate havoc of the people. But he spared Agag, probably to enjoy the glory of displaying so distinguished a captive, and, in like manner, the most valuable portions of the booty, as the cattle. By this wilful and partial obedience to a positive command, complying with it in some parts and violating it in others, as suited his own taste and humor, Saul showed his selfish, arbitrary temper, and his love of despotic power, and his utter unfitness to perform the duties of a delegated king in Israel.

10, 11. God Rejects Him for Disobedience. **10, 11. Then came the word of the Lord unto Samuel, saying, It repenteth me that I have set up Saul**—Repentance is attributed in Scripture to Him when bad men give Him cause to alter His course and method of procedure, and to treat them as if He did "repent" of kindness shown. To the heart of a man like Samuel, who was above all envious considerations, and really attached to the king, so painful an announcement moved all his pity and led him to pass a sleepless night of earnest intercession.

12. Saul came to Carmel—in the south of Judah (Josh. 15:55; ch. 25:2). **12. he set him up a place**—i.e., a pillar (II Samuel 18:18); lit., a *hand*—indicating that whatever was the form of the monument, it was surmounted, according to the ancient fashion, by the figure of a hand, the symbol of power and energy. The erection of this vainglorious trophy was an additional act of disobedience. His pride had overborne his sense of duty in first raising this monument to his own honor, and then going to Gilgal to offer sacrifice to God. **13. Saul said unto him, Blessed be thou of the Lord; I have performed the commandment of the Lord**—Saul was either blinded by a partial and delusive self-love, or he was, in his declaration to Samuel, acting the part of a bold and artful hypocrite. He professed to have fulfilled the divine command, and that the blame of any defects in the execution lay with the people.

ADAM CLARKE

2. *I remember that which Amalek did*. The Amalekites were a people of Arabia Patraea, who had occupied a tract of country on the frontiers of Egypt and Palestine. They had acted with great cruelty towards the Israelites on their coming out of Egypt (Exod. xvii. 8). They came upon them when they were "faint and weary," and "smote the hindmost of the people"—those who were too weak to keep up with the rest (see Deut. xxv. 18). And God then purposed that Amalek, as a nation, should be blotted out from under heaven, which purpose was now fulfilled by Saul upwards of four hundred years afterwards!

3. *Slay both man and woman*. Nothing could justify such an exterminating decree but the absolute authority of God. This was given. All the reasons of it we do not know; but this we know well, the Judge of all the earth doth right. This war was not for plunder, for God commanded that all the property as well as all the people should be destroyed.

5. *Saul came to a city of Amalek*. I believe the original should be translated, "And Saul came to the city Amalek," their capital being called by the name of their tribe.

6. *Said unto the Kenites*. The Kenites were an ancient people. Jethro, the father-in-law of Moses, was a Kenite. Hobab, his son (if the same person be not meant), was guide to the Hebrews through the wilderness. They had a portion of the Promised Land, near to the city Arad (see Judg. i. 16); and for more particulars concerning them and the Amalekites see the notes on Num. xxvi. 20-21.

11. *It repenteth me that I have set up Saul*. That is, I placed him on the throne; I intended, if he had been obedient, to establish his kingdom. He has been disobedient; I change My purpose, and the kingdom shall not be established in his family. This is what is meant by God's repenting—"changing a purpose" according to conditions already laid down or mentally determined.

12. *He set him up a place*. Literally, a "hand," *yad*. Some say it was a monument; others, a triumphal arch. Probably it was no more than a hand, pointing out the place where Saul had gained the victory. Absalom's pillar is called "the hand of Absalom," 2 Sam. xviii. 18.

MATTHEW HENRY

being *judged of the Lord*; whereas the only way to do that is by *judging ourselves*.

2. Samuel convicts him by a plain demonstration of his disobedience. "Hast thou performed the commandment of the Lord? *What means then the bleating of the sheep?*" *v.* 14. Samuel appeals to them as witnesses against him. The noise the cattle made would be a *witness against him*.

3. Saul insists upon his own justification against this charge, *v.* 15. The fact he cannot deny; the sheep and oxen were brought from the Amalekites. But, (1) It was not his fault, for *the people spared them*; as if they durst have done it without the express orders of Saul, when they knew it was against the express orders of Samuel. Sin is a brat that nobody cares to have laid at his doors. It is the sorry subterfuge of an impenitent heart, that will not confess its guilt, to lay the blame on those that were tempters, or partners, or only followers in it. (2) It was with a good intention: "It was *to sacrifice to the Lord thy God*." This was a false plea, for both Saul and the people designed their own profit in sparing the cattle. But, if it had been true, it would still have been frivolous, for God hates robbery for burnt-offering.

4. Samuel overrules, or rather overlooks, his plea, and proceeds, in God's name, to give judgment against him. (1) He reminds Saul of the honour God had done him in making him king (*v.* 17), *when he was little in his own sight*. Those that are advanced to honour and wealth ought often to remember their mean beginnings, that they may never think highly of themselves, but always study to do great things for the God that has advanced them. (2) He lays before him the plainness of the orders he was to execute (*v.* 18): *The Lord sent thee on a journey*; so easy was the service, and so certain the success, that it was rather to be called a *journey* than a *war*. Had he denied himself, and set aside the consideration of his own profit so far as to have destroyed all that belonged to Amalek, he would have been no loser by it at last, nor have gone this *warfare on his own charges*. And therefore, (3) He shows him how inexcusable he was in aiming to make a profit of this expedition, and to enrich himself by it (*v.* 19): "*Wherefore then didst thou fly upon the spoil*, and convert that to thy own use which was to have been destroyed for God's honour?" *Thou didst not obey the voice of the Lord*.

5. Saul repeats his vindication of himself, as that which, in defiance of conviction, he resolved to abide by, *v.* 20, 21. He denies the charge (*v.* 20): "*Yea, I have obeyed*, I have done all I should do"; for he had done all which he thought he needed to do, so much wiser was he in his own eyes than God himself. As to the spoil, he owns it should have been *utterly destroyed*. But he thought that would be wilful waste; the cattle of the Midianites were taken for a prey in Moses's time (Num. xxxi. 32, &c.), and why not the cattle of the Amalekites now? Better they should be a prey to the Israelites than to the fowls of the air and the wild beasts; and therefore he connived at the people's carrying it away for *sacrifice to the Lord* here at Gilgal, whither they were now bringing them.

6. Samuel gives a full answer to his apology, since he did insist upon it, *v.* 22, 23. He appeals to his own conscience: *Has the Lord as great delight in sacrifices as in obedience?* Here we are plainly told. (1) That humble, sincere, and conscientious obedience to the will of God is more pleasing and acceptable to him than *all burnt-offerings and sacrifices*. A careful conformity to moral precepts recommends us to God more than all ceremonial observances, Mic. vi. 6–8; Hos. vi. 6. Obedience was the law of innocency, but sacrifice supposes sin come into the world and is but a feeble attempt to take that away which obedience would have prevented. It is much easier to bring a bullock or lamb to be burnt upon the altar than to bring *every high thought into obedience* to God and the will subject to his will. (2) That nothing is so provoking to God as disobedience, setting up our wills in competition with his. This is here called *rebellion* and *stubbornness*, and is said to be as bad as *witchcraft* and *idolatry*, *v.* 23. It is as bad to set up other gods as to live in disobedience to the true God. It was disobedience that made us all sinners (Rom. v. 19), and this is the malignity of sin, that it is the *transgression of the law*, and consequently it is *enmity to God*, Rom. viii. 7.

7. He reads his doom: in short, "*Because thou hast rejected the word of the Lord*, hast *despised it* (so the Chaldee), hast *made nothing of it* (so the LXX.), therefore he has *rejected thee*, despised and made nothing of thee, but cast thee off *from being king*." Those are unfit and unworthy to rule over men who are not willing that God should rule over them.

JAMIESON, FAUSSET, BROWN

Samuel saw the real state of the case, and in discharge of the commission he had received before setting out, proceeded to denounce his conduct as characterized by pride, rebellion, and obstinate disobedience.

When Saul persisted in declaring that he had obeyed, alleging that the animals, whose bleating was heard, had been reserved for a liberal sacrifice of thanksgiving to God, his shuffling, prevaricating answer called forth a stern rebuke from the prophet. It well deserved it—for the destination of the spoil to the altar was a flimsy pretext—a gross deception, an attempt to conceal the selfishness of the original motive under the cloak of religious zeal and gratitude.

ADAM CLARKE

15. ***The people spared the best of the sheep.*** **It is very likely that the people did spare the best of the prey; and it is as likely that Saul might have restrained them if he would. That they might not love war, God had interdicted spoil and plunder; so the war was undertaken merely from a sense of duty, without any hope of enriching themselves by it.**

21. ***To sacrifice unto the Lord.*** **Thus he endeavors to excuse the people. They did not take the spoil in order to enrich themselves by it, but to** ***sacrifice unto the Lord;*** **and did not this motive justify their conduct?**

22. ***Hath the Lord as great delight?*** **This was a very proper answer to and refutation of Saul's excuse. Is not obedience to the will of God the end of all religion, of its rites, ceremonies, and sacrifices?**

23. ***For rebellion is as the sin of witchcraft, and stubbornness is as iniquity and idolatry.*** **This is no translation of those difficult words. It appears to me that the three nouns which occur first in the text refer each to the three last in order. Thus,** ***chattah,*** **"transgression," refers to** ***aven,*** **"iniquity," which is the principle whence transgression springs.** ***Kesem,*** **"divination," refers to** ***teraphim,*** **consecrated images used in incantations. And** ***meri,*** **"rebellion," refers evidently to** ***haphstar,*** **"stubbornness," whence rebellion springs. The meaning therefore of this difficult place may be the following: As transgression comes from iniquity, divination from teraphim, and rebellion from stubbornness, so, because you have rejected the word of the Lord, He has also rejected you from being king.**

ALEXANDER MACLAREN:

Note the disobedience. Partial obedience is complete disobedience. Saul and his men obeyed as far as suited them; that is to say, they did not obey God at all, but their own inclinations, both in sparing the good and in destroying the worthless. What was not worth carrying off they destroyed—not because of the command but to save trouble. This one fault seems only a small thing to entail the loss of a kingdom. But is it so? It was obviously not an isolated act on Saul's part, but indicated his growing impatience of the divine control, exercised on him through Samuel. He was in a difficult position. He owed his kingdom to the prophet; and the very condition on which he held it was that of submission to Samuel's authority. No wonder that his elevation quickened the growth of his masterfulness and gloomy, impetuous self-will—traits in his character which showed themselves very early in his reign! No wonder either that such a king, held in leading-strings by a prophet, should chafe!

The more insignificant the act in itself, the more significant it may be as a flag of revolt. Disobedience which will not do a little thing is great disobedience. Nor was this the first time that Saul had "kicked," like another Saul, "against the pricks." Gilgal had seen a previous instance of his impetuous self-assertion, masked by apparent deference; and the inference is fair that the interval between the two pieces of rebellion had been of a piece with them. Trivial acts, especially when repeated, show deep-seated evil. There may be only a coil of the snake visible, but that betrays the presence of the slimy folds, though they are covered from sight among the leaves. The tiny shoot of a plant, peeping above the ground, does not mean that the roots are short; they may run for yards. Nor can any act be called small, of which the motive is disregard of God's plain command: "He that is unjust in the least is unjust also in much." Saul never had much religion. He had never heard of Samuel till that day when he came to consult him about the asses. It was a wonder to his acquaintances to find him "among the prophets"; and all his acts of worship have about them a smack of self, and an exclusive regard to the mere externals of sacrifice, which imply a shallow notion of religion and a spirit unsubdued by its deeper influences.—*Expositions of Holy Scripture*

MATTHEW HENRY

Verses 24–31

Saul is at length brought to put himself into the dress of a penitent; but it is too evident that he only acts the part of a penitent, and is not one in deed.

I. How poorly he expressed his repentance. It was with much ado that he was made sensible of his fault, and not till he was threatened with being deposed. This touched him in a tender part. Then he began to relent, and not till then. 1. He made his application to Samuel only, and seemed most solicitous to stand right in his opinion only to preserve his reputation with the people, because they all knew Samuel to be a prophet, and the man that had been the instrument of his preferment. Thinking it would please Samuel, and be a sort of bribe to him, he puts it into his confession: *I have transgressed the commandment of the Lord and thy word*; as if he had been in God's stead, *v.* 24. He also applies to Samuel for forgiveness (*v.* 25): *I pray thee, pardon my sin*; as if any could forgive sin but God only. The most charitable construction we can put upon this of Saul is to suppose that he looked upon Samuel as a sort of mediator between him and God, and intended an address to God in his application to him. 2. He excused his fault even in the confession of it, and that is never the fashion of a true penitent (*v.* 24): I did it *because I feared the people, and obeyed their voice*. 3. All his care was to save his credit, and preserve his interest in the people, lest they should revolt from him, or at least despise him. Therefore he courts Samuel with so much earnestness (*v.* 25); he feared that if Samuel forsook him the people would do so too.

II. How little he got by these thin shows of repentance. 1. Samuel repeated the sentence passed upon him, so far was he from giving any hopes of the repeal of it, *v.* 26, the same with *v.* 23. 2. He illustrates the sentence by a sign. When Samuel was turning from him he tore his clothes to detain him (*v.* 27). Samuel put a construction upon this accident which none but a prophet could do. He made it to signify the *rending of the kingdom* from him (*v.* 28), and that, like this, was his own doing. "He hath rent it from thee, and *given it to a neighbour better than thou*," namely, to David, who afterwards, upon occasion, cut off the skirt of Saul's robe (1 Sam. xxiv. 4), upon which Saul said (1 Sam. xxiv. 20), *I know that thou shalt surely be king*, perhaps remembering this sign, the tearing of the skirt of Samuel's mantle. 3. He ratified it by a solemn declaration of its being irreversible (*v.* 29): *The Strength of Israel will not lie.*

Verses 32–35

Samuel, as a prophet, is here set over kings, Jer. i. 10.

I. He destroys king Agag.

1. How Agag's present vain hopes were frustrated: He *came delicately*, in a stately manner, to show that he was a king. Having escaped the sword of Saul, that man of war, he thought he was in no danger from Samuel, an old prophet, a man of peace.

2. How his former wicked practices were now punished. Samuel calls him to account, not only for the sins of his ancestors, but his own sins: *Thy sword has made women childless*, *v.* 33.

II. He deserts king Saul, takes leave of him (*v.* 34), and *never came any more to see him* (*v.* 35). He looked upon him as rejected of God, and therefore he forsook him. Yet he *mourned for Saul*, thinking it a very lamentable thing that a man who stood so fair for great things should ruin himself so foolishly.

JAMIESON, FAUSSET, BROWN

24. I feared the people, and obeyed their voice—This was a different reason from the former he had assigned. It was the language of a man driven to extremities, and even had it been true, the principles expounded by Samuel showed that it could have been no extenuation of the offense. The prophet then pronounced the irreversible sentence of the rejection of Saul and his family. He was judicially cut off for his disobedience. **24. 25. I have sinned . . . turn again with me, that I may worship the Lord**—The erring, but proud and obstinate monarch was now humbled. He was conscience-smitten for the moment, but his confession proceeded not from sincere repentance, but from a sense of danger and desire of averting the sentence denounced against him. For the sake of public appearance, he besought Samuel not to allow their serious differences to transpire, but to join with him in a public act of worship. Under the influence of his painfully agitated feelings, he designed to offer sacrifice, partly to express his gratitude for the recent victory, and partly to implore mercy and a reversal of his doom. It was, from another angle, a politic scheme, that Samuel might be betrayed into a countenancing of his design in reserving the cattle for sacrificing. Samuel declined to accompany him. **27. he laid hold upon the skirt of his mantle**—the *moil*, upper tunic, official robe. In an agony of mental excitement, he took hold of the prophet's dress to detain him; the rending of the mantle was adroitly pointed to as a significant and mystical representation of his severance from the throne. **29. the Strength of Israel will not lie**—*Heb.*, "He that gives a victory to Israel," a further rebuke of his pride in rearing the Carmel trophy, and an intimation that no loss would be sustained in Israel by his rejection. **31. Samuel turned again after Saul**—not to worship along with him; but first, that the people might have no ground, on pretense of Saul's rejection, to withdraw their allegiance from him; and secondly, to compensate for Saul's error, by executing God's judgment upon Agag. **32. Agag came unto him delicately**—or cheerfully, since he had gained the favor and protection of the king. **33. Samuel hewed Agag**—This cruel tyrant met the retribution of a righteous Providence. Never has it been unusual for great or official personages in the East to perform executions with their own hands. Samuel did it "before the Lord" in Gilgal, appointing that same mode of punishment (hitherto unknown in Israel) to be used towards him, which he had formerly used towards others.

ADAM CLARKE

24. *I have sinned . . . because I feared the people.* This was the best excuse he could make for himself; but had he feared God more, he need have feared the people less.

25. *Pardon my sin.* Literally, "bear my sin"; take it away; forgive what I have done against thee, and be my intercessor with God, that He may forgive my offense against Him.

26. *I will not return with thee.* I cannot acknowledge you as king, seeing the Lord has rejected you.

29. *The Strength of Israel will not lie.* What God has purposed He will bring to pass, for He has all power in the heavens and in the earth; and He will not *repent*—change His purpose—concerning you.

32. *Agag came unto him delicately.* The Septuagint have "trembling"; the original, "delicacies"; probably *ish,* "man," understood; "a man of delights, a pleasure-taker"; the Vulgate, "very fat and trembling." *Surely the bitterness of death is past.* Almost all the versions render this differently from ours. "Surely death is bitter," is their general sense; and this seems to be the true meaning.

33. *As thy sword hath made women childless.* It appears that Agag had forfeited his life by his own personal transgressions, and that his death now was the retribution of his cruelties.

35. *And Samuel came no more to see Saul.* But we read, chap. xix. 22-24, that Saul went to see Samuel at Naioth, but this does not affect what is said here. From this time Samuel had no connection with Saul; he never more acknowledged him as king; he mourned and prayed for him, and continued to perform his prophetic functions at Ramah, and at Naioth, superintending the school of the prophets in that place.

MATTHEW HENRY — CHAPTER 16

Verses 1–5

Samuel had retired to his own house in Ramah, with a resolution not to appear any more in public business, but to addict himself wholly to the instructing and training up of the sons of the prophets, over whom he presided, as we find, *ch.* xix. 20.

I. God reproves him for continuing so long to mourn for the rejection of Saul. "Mourn not for Saul, for I *have provided me a king*. The people provided themselves a king and he proved bad, now I will provide myself one, *a man after my own heart*."

II. He sends him to Bethlehem, to anoint one of the sons of Jesse, a person probably not unknown to Samuel. *Fill thy horn with oil.*

III. Samuel objects the peril of going on this errand (*v.* 2): *If Saul hear it, he will kill me.* By this it appears, 1. That Saul had grown very wicked and outrageous since his rejection, else Samuel would not have mentioned this. What impiety would he not be guilty of who durst kill Samuel? 2. That Samuel's faith was not so strong as one would have expected, else he would not have thus feared the rage of Saul.

JAMIESON, FAUSSET, BROWN — CHAPTER 16

Vss. 1-10. SAMUEL SENT BY GOD TO BETHLEHEM. **1. the Lord said unto Samuel, How long wilt thou mourn for Saul**—Samuel's grief on account of Saul's rejection, accompanied, doubtless, by earnest prayers for his restitution, showed the amiable feelings of the man; but they were at variance with his public duty as a prophet. The declared purpose of God to transfer the kingdom of Israel into other hands than Saul's was not an angry menace, but a fixed and immutable decree; so that Samuel ought to have sooner submitted to the peremptory manifestation of the divine will. But to leave him no longer room to doubt of its being unalterable, he was sent on a private mission to anoint a successor to Saul (see on ch. 10:1). The immediate designation of a king was of the greatest importance for the interests of the nation in the event of Saul's death, which, to this time, was dreaded; it would establish David's title and comfort the minds of Samuel and other good men with a right settlement, whatever contingency might happen. **I have provided me a king**—The language is remarkable, and

ADAM CLARKE — CHAPTER 16

1. *Fill thine horn with oil.* Horns appear to have been the ancient drinking vessels of all nations; and we may suppose that most persons who had to travel much always carried one with them, for the purpose of taking up water from the fountains to quench their thirst.

MATTHEW HENRY

IV. God orders him to cover his design with a sacrifice: *Say, I have come to sacrifice*; and it was true he did, and it was proper that he should, when he came to anoint a king, *ch.* xi. 15. Let him give notice of a sacrifice, and invite Jesse (who, it is probable, was the principal man of the city) and his family to come to the feast upon the sacrifice; and, says God, *I will show thee what thou shalt do*. Those that go about God's work in God's way shall be directed step by step.

V. Samuel went accordingly to Bethlehem, not in pomp, or with any retinue, only a servant to lead the heifer which he was to sacrifice; yet *the elders of Bethlehem trembled at his coming*, fearing it was an indication of God's displeasure against them and that he came to denounce some judgment for the iniquities of the place. They asked him, "*Comest thou peaceably?*" "*I come peaceably*, for *I come to sacrifice*, not with a message of wrath against you, but with the methods of peace and reconciliation; and therefore you may bid me welcome and need not fear my coming; therefore *sanctify yourselves*, and prepare to join with me in the sacrifice, that you may have the benefit of it."

VI. He had a particular regard to Jesse and his sons, for with them his private business lay, with which, it is likely, he acquainted Jesse at his first coming, and took up his lodging at his house. Samuel assisted them in their family preparations for the public sacrifice, and, it is probable, chose out David, and anointed him, at the family-solemnities, before the sacrifice was offered or the holy feast solemnized. Perhaps he offered private sacrifices, like Job, *according to the number of them all* (Job i. 5), and, under colour of that, called for them all to appear before him.

Verses 6–13

I. How all the elder sons, who stood fairest for the preferment, were passed by.

1. Eliab, the eldest, was privately presented first to Samuel, probably none being present but Jesse only, and Samuel thought he must needs be the man: *Surely this is the Lord's anointed, v.* 6. When God would please the people with a king he chose a comely man; but, when he would have one after his own heart, he should not be chosen by the outside. *The Lord looks on the heart*, that is, (1) He knows it. We can tell how men look, but he can tell what they are. God looks on the heart, and sees the thoughts and intents. (2) He judges men by it. Let us reckon that to be true beauty which is within, and judge of men, as far as we are capable, by their minds, not their mien.

2. When Eliab was set aside, Abinadad and Shammah, and, after them, four more of the sons of Jesse, seven in all, were presented to Samuel, as likely for his purpose; but Samuel, who now attended more carefully than he did at first to the divine direction, rejected them all: *The Lord has not chosen these, v.* 8, 10.

II. How David at length was pitched upon. He was the youngest of all the sons of Jesse; his name signifies *beloved*, for he was a type of the beloved Son. Observe, 1 How he was in the fields, *keeping the sheep* (*v.* 11), and was left there, though there was a sacrifice and a feast at his father's house. David was taken *from following the ewes to feed Jacob* (Ps. lxxviii. 71), as Moses from keeping the flock of Jethro. We should think a military life, but God saw a pastoral life (which gives advantage for contemplation and communion with heaven), the best preparative for kingly power, at least for those graces of the Spirit which are necessary to the due discharge of that trust which attends it. 2. How earnest Samuel was to have him sent for: "*We will not sit down* to meat *till he come hither*; for, if all the rest be rejected, this must be he." 3. What appearance he made when he did come. No notice is taken of his clothing. No doubt that was according to his employment, mean and coarse, as shepherds' coats commonly are, but he had a very honest look, not stately, as Saul's, but sweet and lovely: *He was ruddy, of a beautiful countenance, and goodly to look to* (*v.* 12). Though he was so far from using any art to help his beauty, that his employment exposed it to the sun and wind, his modest blush, when he was brought before Samuel made him look much the handsomer. 4. The anointing of him. The Lord told Samuel in his ear (as he had done, *ch.* ix. 15) that this was he whom he must anoint, signifying thereby, (1) A divine designation to the government entailed upon him, to come to him in due time. (2) A divine communication of gifts and graces, to fit him for the government, and make him a type of him who was to be the Messiah, the anointed One, who received the Spirit, not by measure, but without measure. He is said to be anointed *in the midst of his brethren*. Bishop Patrick reads it, *He anointed him from the*

JAMIESON, FAUSSET, BROWN

intimates a difference between this and the former king. Saul was the people's choice—the fruit of their wayward and sinful desires for their own honor and aggrandizement. The next was to be a king who would consult the divine glory, and selected from that tribe to which the pre-eminence had been early promised (Gen. 49:10). **2. How can I go?**—This is another instance of human infirmity in Samuel. Since God had sent him on this mission, He would protect him in the execution. **I am come to sacrifice**—It seems to have been customary with Samuel to do this in the different circuits to which he went, that he might encourage the worship of God. **3. call Jesse to the sacrifice**—i.e., the social feast that followed the peace offering. Samuel, being the offerer, had a right to invite any guest he pleased. **4. the elders of the town trembled at his coming**—Bethlehem was an obscure town, and not within the usual circuit of the judge. The elders were naturally apprehensive, therefore, that his arrival was occasioned by some extraordinary reason, and that it might entail evil upon their town, in consequence of the estrangement between Samuel and the king. **5. sanctify yourselves**—by the preparations described (Exod. 19:14, 15). The elders were to sanctify themselves. Samuel himself took the greatest care in the sanctification of Jesse's family. Some, however, think that the former were invited only to join in the sacrifice, while the family of Jesse were invited by themselves to the subsequent feast.

6-10. Samuel said, Surely the Lord's anointed is before him—Here Samuel, in consequence of taking his impressions from the external appearance, falls into the same error as formerly (ch. 10:24).

11-14. HE ANOINTS DAVID. **11. There remaineth yet the youngest, and, behold, he keepeth the sheep**—Jesse having evidently no idea of David's wisdom and bravery, spoke of him as the most unfit. God, in His providence, so ordered it, that the appointment of David might the more clearly appear to be a divine purpose, and not the design either of Samuel or Jesse. David having not been sanctified with the rest of his family, it is probable that he returned to his pastoral duties the moment the special business on which he had been summoned was done.

12. he was ruddy, . . .—Josephus says that David was ten, while most modern commentators are of the opinion that he must have been fifteen years of age.

13. Then Samuel took the horn of oil, and anointed him—This transaction must have been strictly private.

ADAM CLARKE

2. *Take an heifer with thee, and say, I am come to sacrifice.* This was strictly true; Samuel did offer a sacrifice; and it does not appear that he could have done the work which God designed unless he had offered this sacrifice, and called the elders of the people together, and thus collected Jesse's sons. But he did not tell the principal design of his coming. Had he done so, it would have produced evil and no good; and though no man, in any circumstances, should ever tell a lie, yet in all circumstances he is not obliged to tell the whole truth, though in every circumstance he must tell nothing but the truth, and in every case so tell the truth that the hearer shall not believe a lie by it.

3. *Call Jesse to the sacrifice.* The common custom was, after the blood of the victim had been poured out to God, and the fat burned, to feast on the flesh of the sacrifice. This appears to have been the case in all except in the whole burnt offering; this was entirely consumed.

4. *The elders of the town trembled at his coming.* They knew he was a prophet of the Lord, and they were afraid that he was now come to denounce some judgments of the Most High against their city.

5. *Sanctify yourselves.* Change your clothes, and wash your bodies in pure water, and prepare your minds by meditation, reflection, and prayer; that, being in the spirit of sacrifice, you may offer acceptably to the Lord.

7. *Man looketh on the outward appearance.* And it is well he should, and confine his looks to that; for when he pretends to sound the heart, he usurps the prerogative of God.

10. *Seven of his sons.* This certainly was not done publicly; Samuel, Jesse, and his children must have been in a private apartment, previously to the public feast on the sacrifice; for Samuel says, v. 11, "We will not sit down till he [David] come."

12. *He was ruddy.* I believe the word here means "red-haired."

MATTHEW HENRY

midst of his brethren, that is, he singled him out from the rest, and privately anointed him, but with a charge to keep his own counsel, and not to let his own brethren know it, as by what we find (*ch.* xvii. 28), it should seem, Eliab did not. Dr. Lightfoot reckons that he was about twenty-five, and that his troubles lasted but five years. 5. The happy effects of this anointing: The *Spirit of the Lord came upon David from that day forward, v.* 13. The anointing of him was not an empty ceremony, but a divine power went along with that instituted sign, and he found himself inwardly advanced in wisdom, and courage, and concern for the public, though not at all advanced in his outward circumstances. Some think that his courage, by which he slew the lion and the bear, and his extraordinary skill in music, were the effects and evidences of the Spirit's coming upon him. Samuel, having done this, went to Ramah in safety, and we never read of him again but once (*ch.* xix. 18), till we read of his death; now he retired to die in peace, since his eyes had seen the sceptre brought into the tribe of Judah.

Verses 14–23

Saul falling and David rising.

I. Here is Saul made a terror to himself (*v.* 14): *The Spirit of the Lord departed from him.* He lost all his good qualities. This was the effect of his rejecting God, and an evidence of his being rejected by him. The consequence of this was that *an evil spirit from God troubled him.* Those that drive the good Spirit away from them do of course become a prey to the evil spirit. He grew fretful, and peevish, and discontented, timorous and suspicious, ever and anon starting and trembling.

II. Here is David made a physician to Saul, and by this means brought to court, a physician that helped him against the worst of diseases, when none else could. 1. The means they all advised him to for his relief was music (*v.* 16): "Let us have a *cunning player on the harp* to attend thee." Saul's servants did not amiss to send for music as a help to cheer up the spirits, if they had but withal sent for a prophet to give him good counsel. 2. One of his servants recommended David to him, as a fit person to be employed in the use of these means, little imagining that he was the man whom Samuel meant when he told Saul of a neighbour of his, better than he, who should have the kingdom, *ch.* xv. 28. Though David, after he was anointed, returned to his country business, yet the workings of the Spirit signified by the oil could not be hid, but made him shine in obscurity so that all his neighbours observed with wonder the great improvements of his mind on a sudden. David, even in his shepherd's garb, has become an oracle, a champion, and every thing that is great. His fame reached the court soon, for Saul was inquisitive after such young men, *ch.* xiv. 52. When the Spirit of God comes upon a man he will make his face to shine. 3. David is hereupon sent for to court. (1) His father was very willing to part with him, sent him very readily, and a present with him to Saul, *v.* 20. The present was, according to the usage of those times, bread and wine (compare, *ch.* x. 3, 4.) therefore acceptable because expressive of the homage and allegiance of him that sent it. (2) Saul became very kind to him (*v.* 21), *loved him greatly*, and designed to *make him his armour-bearer*, and asked his father's leave to keep him in his service (*v.* 22): *Let David, I pray thee, stand before me.* David's music was Saul's physic. Music has a natural tendency to compose and exhilarate the mind, when it is disturbed and saddened. On some it has a greater influence and effect than on others, and, probably, Saul was one of those. It made his spirit sedate, and allayed those tumults by which the devil had advantage against him. Music cannot work upon the devil, but it may shut up the passages by which he had access to the mind. Saul found, even after he had conceived an enmity to David, that no one else could do him the same service (*ch.* xix. 9, 10).

JAMIESON, FAUSSET, BROWN

14-18. The Spirit of the Lord departed from Saul, and an evil spirit from the Lord troubled him—His own gloomy reflections, the consciousness that he had not acted up to the character of an Israelitish king, the loss of his throne, and the extinction of his royal house, made him jealous, irritable, vindictive, and subject to fits of morbid melancholy.

19. Saul sent messengers unto Jesse, and said, Send me David—In the East the command of a king is imperative; and Jesse, however reluctant and alarmed, had no alternative but to comply. **20. Jesse took an ass laden with bread, and a bottle of wine, and a kid, and sent them . . . unto Saul**—as a token of homage and respect. **21. David came to Saul**—Providence thus prepared David for his destiny, by placing him in a way to become acquainted with the manners of the court, the business of government, and the general state of the kingdom. **became his armourbearer**—This choice, as being an expression of the king's partiality, shows how honorable the office was held to be. **23. David took an harp, and played with his hand: so Saul was refreshed, and was well**—The ancients believed that music had a mysterious influence in healing mental disorders.

ADAM CLARKE

13. *The Spirit of the Lord came upon David.* God qualified him to be governor of his people, by infusing such graces as wisdom, prudence, counsel, courage, liberality, and magnanimity.

14. *The Spirit of the Lord departed from Saul.* He was thrown into such a state of mind by the judgments of God as to be deprived of any regal qualities which he before possessed. God seems to have taken what gifts he had and given them to David; and then the evil spirit came upon Saul; for what God fills not, the devil will. *An evil spirit from the Lord.* The evil spirit was either immediately sent from the Lord or permitted to come. Whether this was a diabolic possession or a mere mental malady, the learned are not agreed; it seems to have partaken of both. That Saul had fallen into a deep melancholy, there is little doubt.

23. *The evil spirit from God.* The word *evil* is not in the common Hebrew text, but it is in the Vulgate, Septuagint, Targum, Syriac, and Arabic. The Septuagint leave out "of God," and have "the evil spirit." The Targum says, "The evil spirit from before the Lord"; and the Arabic has it, "The evil spirit by the permission of God"; this is at least the sense.

MATTHEW HENRY

CHAPTER 17

Verses 1–11

It was not long ago that the Philistines were soundly beaten, but here we have them making head again.

I. How they *defied Israel with their armies, v.* 1. They made a descent upon the Israelites' country, and possessed themselves, as it should seem, of some part of it, for they encamped in a place *which belonged to Judah.* The Philistines (it is probable) had heard that Samuel had fallen out with Saul and forsaken him, and that Saul had grown melancholy and unfit. Saul mustered his forces, and faced them,

JAMIESON, FAUSSET, BROWN

CHAPTER 17

VSS. 1-3. THE ISRAELITES AND PHILISTINES BEING READY TO BATTLE. **1. the Philistines gathered together their armies**—twenty-seven years after their overthrow at Michmash. Having now recovered their spirits and strength, they sought an opportunity of wiping out the infamy of that national disaster, as well as to regain their lost ascendency over Israel. **Shochoh**—now Shuweikeh, a town in the western plains of Judah (Josh. 15:35), nine Roman miles from Eleutheropolis, toward Jerusalem [ROBINSON]. **Azekah**—a small place in the neigh-

ADAM CLARKE

CHAPTER 17

1. *Now the Philistines gathered together.* We have already seen that there was war between Saul and the Philistines all his days (see chap. xiv. 52).

Shochoh and Azekah. Places which lay to the south of Jerusalem and to the west of Bethlehem.

MATTHEW HENRY

v. 2, 3. The evil spirit, for the present, had left Saul, *ch.* xvi. 23. David's harp having given him some relief, perhaps the alarms and affairs of the war prevented the return of the distemper. Business is a good antidote against melancholy. David had returned to Bethlehem to keep his father's sheep; this was a rare instance, in a young man that stood so fair for preferment, of humility and affection to his parents.

II. How they defied Israel with their champion Goliath, hoping by him to recover their reputation and dominion. Perhaps the army of the Israelites was superior in number and strength to that of the Philistines, which made the Philistines decline a battle, and stand at bay with them, desiring rather to put the issue upon a single combat, in which, having such a champion, they hoped to gain the victory. Now concerning this champion,

1. His prodigious size. He was of the sons of Anak, who at Gath kept their ground in Joshua's time (Josh. xi. 22). He was in height *six cubits and a span, v.* 4. The learned Bishop Cumberland has made it out that the scripture-cubit was above twenty-one inches and a span was half a cubit, by which computation Goliath wanted but eight inches of four yards in height, eleven feet and four inches, a monstrous stature.

2. His armour. *A helmet of brass on his head, a coat of mail,* made of brass plates laid over one another, like the scales of a fish; and, because his legs would lie most within the reach of an ordinary man, he wore brass boots, and had a large corselet of brass about his neck. The coat is said to weigh 5,000 shekels. But some think it should be translated, not the *weight* of the coat, but the *value* of it, was 5,000 shekels. His offensive weapons were extraordinary, of which his spear only is here described, *v.* 7. It was like a weaver's beam. His arm could manage that which an ordinary man could scarcely heave. His shield only, was carried before him by his esquire, probably for state; for he that was clad in brass little needed a shield.

3. His challenge. The Philistines having chosen him for their champion, to save themselves from the hazard of a battle, he here throws down the gauntlet, and bids defiance to the armies of Israel, *v.* 8–10. He came into the valley that lay between the camps, and, his voice probably being as much stronger than other people's as his arm was, he cried so as to make them all hear him, *Give me a man, that we may fight together.* He looked upon Israel with disdain and defies them to find a man among them bold enough to enter the list with him. (1) He upbraids them with their folly in drawing an army together. (2) He offers to put the war entirely upon the issue of the duel he proposes: "If your champion kill me, we will be your servants; if I kill him, you shall be ours." This, says Bishop Patrick, was only a bravado. The Chaldee paraphrase brings him in boasting that he was the man that had killed Hophni and Phinehas and taken the ark prisoner.

4. The terror this struck upon Israel: *Saul and all his army were greatly afraid, v.* 11. The people would not have been dismayed but that they observed Saul's courage failed him; and it is not to be expected that, if the leader be a coward, the followers should be bold. Jonathan must sit still, because the honour of engaging Goliath is reserved for David.

Verses 12–30

Forty days the two armies lay encamped facing one another, and perhaps there were frequent skirmishes between small detached parties. All this while, morning and evening, did the insulting champion appear in the field and repeat his challenge. All this while David is keeping his father's sheep, but at the end of forty days Providence brings him to the field to win and wear the laurel which no other Israelite dares venture for.

I. The state of his family. His father was old (*v.* 12). David's three elder brethren, who perhaps envied his place at the court, got their father to send for him home, and let them go to the camp, where they hoped to signalize themselves and eclipse him (*v.* 13, 14), while David himself returned to the care, and toil, and (as it proved, *v.* 34) the peril, of *keeping his father's sheep.*

II. The orders his father gave him to go and visit his brethren in the camp. He must carry some bread and cheese to his brethren, ten loaves with some parched corn for themselves (*v.* 17) and ten cheeses for a present to their colonel, *v.* 18. David must still be the drudge of the family, though he was to be the greatest ornament of it. He had not so much as an ass at command to carry his load, but must take it on his back, and yet run to the camp. He must observe how his brethren fared, whether they were not reduced to short allowance, whom they associate

JAMIESON, FAUSSET, BROWN

borhood. **Ephes-dammim**—or Pas-dammim (I Chron. 11:13), "the portion or effusion of blood," situated between the other two. **2. valley of Elah**—i.e., the Terebinth, now Wady Er-Sumt [ROBINSON]. Another valley somewhat to the north, now called Wady Beit Hanina, has been fixed on by the tradition of ages.

4-11. GOLIATH CHALLENGES A COMBAT. **4-11. a champion**—*Heb.*, a "man between two"; i.e., a person who, on the part of his own people, undertook to determine the national quarrel by engaging in single combat with a chosen warrior in the hostile army.

5. helmet of brass—The Philistine helmet had the appearance of a row of feathers set in a tiara, or metal band, to which were attached scales of the same material, for the defense of the neck and the sides of the face [OSBORN]. **a coat of mail**—a kind of corslet, quilted with leather or plates of metal, reaching only to the chest, and supported by shoulder straps, leaving the shoulders and arms at full liberty. **6. greaves of brass**—boots, terminating at the ankle, made in one plate of metal, but round to the shape of the leg, and often lined with felt or sponge. They were useful in guarding the legs, not only against the spikes of the enemy, but in making way among thorns and briers. **a target of brass**—a circular frame, carried at the back, suspended by a long belt which crossed the breast from the shoulders to the loins. **7. staff of his spear**—rather under five feet long, and capable of being used as a javelin (ch. 19:10). It had an iron head. **one bearing a shield**—In consequence of their great size and weight, the Oriental warrior had a trusty and skilful friend, whose office it was to bear the large shield behind which he avoided the missile weapons of the enemy. He was covered, cap-a-pie, with defensive armor, while he had only two offensive weapons—a sword by his side and a spear in his hand. **8-11. I defy the armies of Israel . . . ; give me a man, that we may fight together**—In cases of single combat, a warrior used to go out in front of his party, and advancing towards the opposite ranks, challenge someone to fight with him. If his formidable appearance, or great reputation for physical strength and heroism, deterred any from accepting the challenge, he used to parade himself within hearing of the enemy's lines, specify in a loud, boastful, bravado style, defying them, and pouring out torrents of abuse and insolence to provoke their resentment.

12-58. DAVID ACCEPTS THE CHALLENGE, AND SLAYS HIM. **17. Take now for thy brethren an ephah of this parched corn, and these ten loaves**—In those times campaigns seldom lasted above a few days at a time. The soldiers were volunteers or militia, who were supplied with provisions from time to time by their friends at home. **18. carry these ten cheeses to the captain**—to enlist his kind attention. Oriental cheeses are very small; and although they are frequently made of so soft a consistence as to resemble curds, those which David carried seem to have been fully formed, pressed, and sufficiently dried to admit of their being carried. **take their pledge**—Tokens of the soldiers' health and safety were sent home in the convenient form of a lock of their hair, or piece of their nail, or such like. **20. David left the sheep with a keeper**—This is the only instance in which the hired shepherd is distinguished from the master or one of his family. **trench**—some feeble attempt at a rampart. It appears (see *Marg.*) to have been formed by a line of carts or chariots, which, from the earliest times, was the practice of nomad people.

ADAM CLARKE

2. *The valley of Elah.* Some translate this the "turpentine valley" or "the valley of the terebinth trees"; and others, "the valley of oaks."

3. *The Philistines stood on a mountain.* These were two eminences or hills from which they could see and talk with each other.

4. *There went out a champion.* Our word *champion* comes from *campus,* "the field." "Champion is he, properly, who fights in the field; i.e., in camps." But is this the meaning of the original *ish habbenayim,* a "middle man," the "man between two"; that is, as here, the man who undertakes to settle the disputes between two armies or nations? So our ancient champions settled disputes between contending parties by what was termed camp fight; hence the *campio* or "champion."

Whose height was six cubits and a span. The word *cubit* signifies the length from *cubitus,* the elbow, to the top of the middle finger, which is generally rated at eighteen inches. The *span* is the distance from the top of the middle finger to the end of the thumb, when extended as far as they can stretch on a plain; this is ordinarily nine inches. The height of this Philistine would then be nine feet nine inches, which is a tremendous height for a man. But the versions are not all agreed in his height. The Septuagint read "four cubits and a span"; and Josephus reads the same. It is necessary however to observe that the Septuagint, in the Codex Alexandrinus, read with the Hebrew text.

5. *He was armed with a coat of mail.* The words in the original mean "a coat of mail" formed of plates of brass overlapping each other, like the scales of a fish, or tiles of a house. *The weight . . . five thousand shekels.* Goliath's coat of mail, weighing *five thousand shekels,* was exactly 156 pounds 4 ounces avoirdupois. A vast weight for a coat of mail, but not all out of proportion to the man!

6. *Greaves of brass upon his legs.* This species of armor may be seen on many ancient monuments. It was a plate of brass which covered the shin or forepart of the leg, from the knee down to the instep, and was buckled with straps behind the leg.

A target of brass between his shoulders. There are different opinions concerning this piece of armor, called here *kidon.* Some think it was a covering for the shoulders; others, that it was a javelin or dart; others, that it was a lance; some, a club; and others, a sword. It is certainly distinguished from the shield, v. 41, and is translated a "spear," Josh. viii. 18.

7. *His spear's head weighed six hundred shekels of iron.* That is, his spear's head was of iron, and it weighed *six hundred shekels;* this, according to the former computation, would amount to eighteen pounds twelve ounces. *And one bearing a shield. Hatstsinnah,* from *tsan,* "pointed or penetrating," if it does not mean some kind of lance, must mean a *shield* with what is called the *umbo,* a sharp protuberance in the middle, with which they could as effectually annoy their enemies as defend themselves.

10. *I defy.* "I strip and make bare" the armies of Israel, for none dared to fight him.

11. *Saul and all Israel . . . were dismayed.* They saw no man able to accept the challenge.

12. Verses 12 to 31 inclusive are wanting in the Septuagint; as also v. 41; and from v. 54 to the end; with the first five verses of chap. xviii, and verses 9-11, 17-19 of the same.

18. *Carry these ten cheeses.* "Cheeses of milk," says the margin. In the East they do not make what we call cheese; they press the milk but slightly, and carry it in rush baskets. It is highly salted, and little different from curds.

MATTHEW HENRY

with, and what sort of life they lead.

III. David's dutiful obedience, so well had he learnt to obey before he pretended to command. God's providence brought him to the camp very seasonably, when both sides had set the battle in array, *v.* 21. Both sides were now preparing to fight.

1. How brisk and lively David was, *v.* 22. Though he had come a long journey with a great load, he *ran into the army*, to see what was doing there, and to pay his respects to his brethren.

2. How bold and daring the Philistine was, *v.* 23. Now that the armies were drawn out into a line of battle he appeared first to renew his challenge.

3. How timorous and faint-hearted the men of Israel were. Upon his approach, they *fled from him and were greatly afraid*, *v.* 24.

4. How high Saul bid for a champion. Whoever will do it shall have as good preferment as he can give him, *v.* 25.

5. How much concerned David was to assert the honour of God and Israel against the impudent challenges of this champion. Two considerations, it seems, fired David with a holy indignation:—(1) That the challenger was one that was uncircumcised, a stranger to God and out of covenant with him. (2) That the challenged were the armies of the living God, devoted to him, employed by him and for him, so that the affronts offered to them reflected upon the living God himself, and *that* he could not bear. When therefore some had told him what was the reward proposed for killing the Philistine (*v.* 27) he asked others (*v.* 30), with the same resentment, which he expected would at length come to Saul's ear.

6. How he was browbeaten and discouraged by his eldest brother Eliab, *v.* 28. (1) As the fruit of Eliab's jealousy. He was the eldest brother, and David the youngest. Eliab was now vexed that his younger brother should speak those bold words against the Philistine which he himself durst not say. He would rather that Goliath should triumph over Israel than that David should be the man that should triumph over him. Eliab intended, in what he said, to represent him to those about him as an idle proud lad. He gives them to understand that his business was only to keep sheep, and falsely insinuates that he was a careless unfaithful shepherd. David could not escape this hard character from his own brother. (2) As a trial of David's meekness, patience, and constancy. A short trial it was, and he approved himself well in it; for, [1] He bore the provocation with admirable temper (*v.* 29): "*What have I now done?*" He had right and reason on his side, and knew it, and therefore with a soft answer turned away his brother's wrath. This conquest of his own passion was in some respects more honourable than his conquest of Goliath. [2] He broke through the discouragement with admirable resolution. He would not be driven off from his thoughts of engaging the Philistine by the ill-will of his brother.

Verses 31–39

David is at length presented to Saul for his champion (*v.* 31) and he bravely undertakes to fight the Philistine (*v.* 32). A little shepherd, come but this morning from keeping sheep, has more courage than all the mighty men of Israel, and encourages them. Two things David had to do with Saul:—

I. To get clear of the objection Saul made against his undertaking. "Alas!" says Saul, "thou hast a good heart to it, but art by no means an equal match for this Philistine." David, in reasoning with him, argues from experience; though he was but a youth, and never in the wars, yet perhaps he had done as much as the killing of Goliath came to, for he had had, by divine assistance, spirit enough to subdue a lion once and another time a bear that robbed him of his lambs, *v.* 34–36. To these he compares this uncircumcised Philistine, looks upon him to be as much a ravenous beast as either of them, and therefore doubts not but to deal as easily with him; and hereby he gives Saul to understand that he was not so inexperienced in hazardous combats as he took him to be.

1. He tells his story like a man of spirit. When David kept sheep, (1) He approved himself very careful and tender of his flock. He could not see a lamb in distress but he would venture his life to rescue it. This temper made him fit to be a king, to whom the lives of subjects should be dear and their blood precious (Ps. lxxii. 14), and fit to be a type of Christ, the good Shepherd, who *gathers the lambs in his arms and carries them in his bosom* (Isa. xl. 11), and who not only ventured, but *laid down his life for his sheep.* (2) He approved himself very bold and brave in the defence of his flock. "Thy servant *slew both the lion and the bear.*"

JAMIESON, FAUSSET, BROWN

22. left his carriage in the hand of the keeper of the carriage—to make his way to the standard of Judah.

25. make his father's house free in Israel—His family should be exempted from the impositions and services to which the general body of the Israelites were subjected.

34-36. a lion, and a bear—There were two different rencontres, for those animals prowl alone. The bear must have been a Syrian bear, which is believed to be a distinct species, or perhaps a variety, of the brown bear. The beard applies to the lion alone. Those feats seem to have been performed with no weapons more effective than the rude staves and stones of the field, or his shepherd's crook.

F. B. MEYER:

The armies of the living God (1 Sam. 17:26, 36). This made all the difference between David and the rest of the camp. To Saul and his soldiers God was an absentee—a name, but little else. They believed that He had done great things for his people in the past, and that at some future time, in the days of the Messiah, He might be expected to do great things again; but no one thought of Him as present. Keenly sensitive to the defiance of the Philistine, and grieved by the apathy of his people, David, on the other hand, felt that God was alive. He had lived alone with Him in the solitude of the hills till God had become one of the greatest and most real facts of his young existence; and as the lad went to and fro among the armed warriors, he was sublimely conscious of the presence of the living God amid the clang of the camp.

This is what we need. To live so much with God that when we come among men, whether in the bazaars of India or the marketplace of an English town, we may be more aware of His overshadowing presence than of the presence or absence of anyone. Lo, God is here! This place is hallowed ground! But none can realize this by the act of the will. We can only find God everywhere when we carry Him everywhere. The miner sees by the light he carries on his forehead.

Each of us is opposed by difficulties, privations, and trials of different sorts. But the one answer to them all is faith's vision of the living God. We can face the mightiest foe in His name. If our faith can but make Him a passage, along which He shall come, there is no Goliath He will not quell; no question He will not answer; no need He will not meet.—*Great Verses Through the Bible*

ADAM CLARKE

29. *Is there not a cause? Halo dabar hu.* I believe the meaning is what several of the versions express: "I have spoken but a word."

32. *And David said.* This properly connects with the eleventh verse.

33. *Thou art but a youth.* Supposed to be about twenty-two or twenty-three years of age.

34. *Thy servant kept his father's sheep.* He found it necessary to give Saul the reasons why he undertook this combat, and why he expected to be victorious.

35. *The slaying of the lion and the bear* mentioned here must have taken place at two different times; perhaps the verse should be read thus: "I went out after him [the lion] and smote him, etc. And when he [the bear] rose up against me, I caught him by the beard and slew him."

MATTHEW HENRY

2. He applies his story like a man of faith. He owns (*v.* 37) it was *the Lord that delivered him from the lion and the bear*; to him he gives the praise of that great achievement, and thence he infers, *He will deliver me out of the hand of this Philistine*. Thus David took off Saul's objection against his undertaking, and gained a commission to fight the Philistine.

II. To get clear of the armour wherewith Saul would, by all means, have him dressed up when he went upon this great action (*v.* 38). David, being not yet resolved which way to attack his enemy, *girded on his sword*, but he found the armour would but encumber him, and would be rather his burden than his defence, and therefore he desires leave of Saul to put them off again. "I have never been accustomed to such accoutrements as these."

Verses 40–47

I. The preparations made on both sides for the encounter. The Philistine was already fixed, as he had been daily for the last forty days. Well might he go with his armour, for he had sufficiently proved it. But what arms and ammunition is David furnished with? Truly none but what he brought with him as a shepherd; no breastplate, nor corselet, but his plain shepherd's coat; no spear, but his staff; no sword nor bow, but his sling; no quiver, but his scrip; nor any arrows, but, instead of them, five smooth stones picked up out of the brook, *v.* 40. By this it appeared that his confidence was purely in the power of God.

II. The conference which precedes the encounter,

1. How very proud Goliath was, (1) With what scorn he looked upon his adversary, *v.* 42. He took notice of his person, that he was but a youth, not come to his strength, *ruddy and of a fair countenance*, fitter to accompany the virgins of Israel in their dances than to lead on the men of Israel in their battles. He took notice of his array with great indignation (*v.* 43), "*Am I a dog, that thou comest to me with staves?*" (2) With what confidence he presumed upon his success. He cursed David by his gods. "*Come unto me, and I will give thy flesh to the fowls of the air*, it will be a tender and delicate feast for them."

2. How very pious David was. His speech savours nothing of ostentation, but God is all in all in it, *v.* 45–47. (1) He derives his authority from God: "*I come to thee in the name of the Lord*, by the special grace of his covenant," *the God of the armies of Israel*. The name of God David relied on, as Goliath did on his sword and spear. (2) He depends for success upon God, *v.* 46. David speaks with as much assurance as Goliath had done, but upon better ground; it is his faith that says, "*This day will the Lord deliver thee into my hand*, and not only thy carcase, but the carcases of the host of the Philistines, shall be given to the birds and beasts of prey." (3) He devotes the praise and glory of all to God. [1] All the world should be made to know that there is a God, and that the God of Israel is the one only living and true God, and all other pretended deities are vanity and a lie. [2] All Israel shall *know that the Lord saveth not with sword and spear* (*v.* 47), but can, when he pleases, save without either and against both, Ps. xlvi. 9. David addresses himself to this combat rather as a priest that was going to offer a sacrifice to the justice of God than as a soldier that was going to engage an enemy of his country.

Verses 48–58

1. The engagement between the two champions, *v.* 48. To this engagement the Philistine advanced with a great deal of state and gravity; if he must encounter a pigmy, yet it shall be like a stalking mountain, overlaid with brass and iron, *to meet David*. David advanced with no less activity and cheerfulness, as one that aimed more to do execution than to make a figure: He *hasted, and ran*, being lightly clad, to *meet the Philistine*. We may imagine with what tenderness and compassion the Israelites saw such a pleasing youth as this throwing himself into the mouth of destruction, but he knew whom he had believed and for whom he acted. 2. The fall of Goliath in this engagement. He was in no haste, because in no fear, but confident that he should soon at one stroke cleave his adversary's head; but, while he was preparing to do it solemnly, David did his business effectually, without any parade: he slang a stone which hit him in the forehead, and, in the twinkling of an eye, fetched him to the ground, *v.* 49. Goliath knew there were famous slingers in Israel (Judges xx. 16), yet was either so forgetful or presumptuous as to go with the beaver of his helmet open. To complete the execution, David drew Goliath's own sword, a two-handed weapon for David, and with it *cut off his head*, *v.* 51. David's victory over Goliath was typical of the triumphs of the son of David over

JAMIESON, FAUSSET, BROWN

37. The Lord that delivered me—It would have been natural for a youth, and especially an Oriental youth, to make a parade of his gallantry. But David's piety sank all consideration of his own prowess and ascribed the success of those achievements to the divine aid, which he felt assured would not be withheld from him in a cause which so intimately concerned the safety and honor of His people. **Saul said unto David, Go, and the Lord be with thee**—The pious language of the modest but valiant youth impressed the monarch's heart. He felt that it indicated the true military confidence for Israel, and, therefore, made up his mind, without any demur, to sanction a combat on which the fate of his kingdom depended, and with a champion supporting his interests apparently so unequal to the task. **38, 39. Saul armed David with his armour**—The ancient Hebrews were particularly attentive to the personal safety of their warriors, and hence Saul equipped the youthful champion with his own defensive accoutrements, which would be of the best style. It is probable that Saul's coat of mail, or corslet, was a loose shirt, otherwise it could not have fitted both a stripling and a man of the colossal stature of the king. **40. brook**—wady. **bag**—or scrip for containing his daily food. **sling**—The sling consisted of a double rope with a thong, probably of leather, to receive the stone. The slinger held a second stone in his left hand. David chose five stones, as a reserve, in case the first should fail. Shepherds in the East carry a sling and stones still, for the purpose of driving away, or killing, the enemies that prowl about the flock. **42-47. the Philistine said . . . said David to the Philistine**—When the two champions met, they generally made each of them a speech, and sometimes recited some verses, filled with allusions and epithets of the most opprobrious kind, hurling contempt and defiance at one another. This kind of abusive dialogue is common among the Arab combatants still.

David's speech, however, presents a striking contrast to the usual strain of these invectives. It was full of pious trust, and to God he ascribed all the glory of the triumph he anticipated.

49. smote the Philistine in his forehead—At the opening for the eyes—that was the only exposed part of his body. **51. cut off his head**—not as an evidence of the giant's death, for his slaughter had been effected in presence of the whole army, but as a trophy to be borne to Saul. The heads of slain enemies are always regarded in the East as the most welcome tokens of victory.

ADAM CLARKE

37. *Go, and the Lord be with thee.* Saul saw that these were reasonable grounds of confidence, and therefore wished him success.

39. *I cannot go with these.* In ancient times it required considerable exercise and training to make a man expert in the use of such heavy armor. *I have not proved them*, says David; I am wholly unaccustomed to such armor and it would be an encumbrance to me.

40. *He took his staff.* What we would call his crook. *A shepherd's bag.* That in which he generally carried his provisions while keeping the sheep in the open country. *And his sling.* The sling, among both the Greeks and Hebrews, has been a powerful offensive weapon. See what has been said on **Judg. xx. 16. It is** composed of two strings and a leathern strap; the strap is in the middle, and is the place where the stone lies. The string on the right end of the strap is firmly fastened to the hand; that on the left is held between the thumb and middle joint of the forefinger. It is then whirled two or three times round the head; and when discharged, the finger and thumb let go their hold of the left-end string. The velocity and force of the sling are in proportion to the distance of the strap from the shoulder joint.

42. *He disdained him.* He held him in contempt; he saw that he was young, and from his ruddy complexion supposed him to be effeminate.

43. *Am I a dog, that thou comest to me with staves?* It is very likely that Goliath did not perceive the sling, which David might have kept coiled up within his hand. *Cursed David by his gods.* Prayed his gods to curse him. This long parley between David and Goliath is quite in the style of those times.

44. *Come to me, and I will give thy flesh.* He intended, as soon as he could lay hold on him, to pull him to pieces.

45. *Thou comest to me with a sword.* "I come to thee with the name [*beshem*] of Jehovah of hosts, the God of the armies of Israel." What Goliath expected from his arms, David expected from the ineffable name.

46. *This day will the Lord deliver thee into mine hand.* This was a direct and circumstantial prophecy of what did take place.

47. *For the battle is the Lord's.* It is the Lord's war. You are fighting against Him and His religion, as the champion of your party; I am fighting for God, as the champion of His cause.

49. *Smote the Philistine in his forehead.* Except his face, Goliath was everywhere covered over with strong armor. Either he had no beaver to his helmet, or it was lifted up so as to expose his forehead; but it does not appear that the ancient helmets had any covering for the face.

MATTHEW HENRY

Satan and all the powers of darkness, whom he *spoiled, and made a show of them openly* (Col. ii. 15), and we through him are *more than conquerors*. 3. The defeat of the Philistines' army hereupon. They relied wholly upon the strength of their champion, and therefore, when they saw him slain, they did not, as Goliath had offered, throw down their arms and surrender themselves servants to Israel (*v.* 9), but took to their heels, being wholly dispirited, and thinking it to no purpose to oppose one before whom such a mighty man had fallen: *They fled* (*v.* 51), and this put life into the Israelites, who *shouted and pursued them*. They seized all the baggage, plundered the tents (*v.* 53), and enriched themselves with the spoil. 4. David's disposal of his trophies, *v.* 54. He brought the head of the Philistine to Jerusalem, to be a terror to the Jebusites, who held the strong-hold of Sion. *His armour he laid up in his tent*; only the sword was preserved behind the ephod in the tabernacle, as consecrated to God, *ch.* xxi. 9. 5. The notice that was taken of David. Saul had forgotten him, being melancholy and mindless, and little thinking that his musician would have spirit enough to be his champion. Abner was a stranger to him, but brought him to Saul (*v.* 57), and he gave a modest account of himself, *v.* 58. And now he was introduced to the court with much greater advantages than before, in which he owned God's hand performing all things for him.

JAMIESON, FAUSSET, BROWN

52 Shaaraim—(See Josh. 15:36). **54. tent**—the sacred tabernacle. David dedicated the sword of Goliath as a votive offering to the Lord. **55-58. Saul . . . said unto Abner . . . whose son is this youth?**—A young man is more spoken of in many Eastern countries by his father's name than his own. The growth of the beard, and other changes on a now full-grown youth, prevented the king from recognizing his former favorite minstrel.

ADAM CLARKE

MATTHEW HENRY — CHAPTER 18

Verses 1-5

David was anointed to the crown to take it out of Saul's hand, and over Jonathan's head, and yet here we find,

I. That Saul, who was now in possession of the crown, reposed a confidence in him, God so ordering it, that he might by his preferment at court be prepared for future service. Saul now took David home with him, and would not suffer him to return again to his retirement, *v.* 2. *Saul set him over the men of war* (*v.* 5), not that he made him general (Abner was in that post), but perhaps captain of the lifeguard. He employed him in the affairs of government; and *David went out whithersoever Saul sent him*. Those that hope to rule must first learn to obey.

II. That Jonathan, who was heir to the crown, entered into covenant with him, God so ordering it, that David's way might be the clearer when his rival was his friend. 1. Jonathan conceived an extraordinary kindness and affection for him (*v.* 1): *The soul of Jonathan was* immediately *knit* unto *the soul of David*. Jonathan had formerly set upon a Philistine army with the same faith and bravery with which David had now attacked a Philistine giant; so that there was between them a very near resemblance. None had so much reason to dislike David as Jonathan had, because he was to put him by the crown, yet none regards him more. 2. He testified his love to David by a generous present he made him, *v.* 4. He takes care to put him speedily into the habit of a courtier (for he gave him a robe) and of a soldier, for he gave him, instead of his staff and sling, a sword and bow, and, instead of his shepherd's scrip, a girdle, either a belt or a sash; the same that he himself had worn and he stripped himself of them to dress David in them. Saul's would not fit him, but Jonathan's did. Their bodies were of a size, a circumstance which well agreed with the suitableness of their minds. David is seen in Jonathan's clothes, that all may take notice he is a Jonathan's second self. Our Lord Jesus has thus shown his love to us, that he stripped himself to clothe us, emptied himself to enrich us; nay, he did more than Jonathan, he clothed himself with our rags, whereas Jonathan did not put on David's. 3. He endeavoured to perpetuate this friendship. They made a covenant with each other, *v.* 3.

III. That both court and country agree to bless him. And it was certainly a great instance of the power of God's grace in David that he was able to bear all this respect and honour flowing in upon him on a sudden without being lifted up above measure. Those that climb so fast have need of good heads and good hearts.

Verses 6-11

Now begin David's troubles, and they not only tread on the heels of his triumphs, but take rise from them.

I. He was too much magnified by the common people. Some time after the victory Saul went on a triumphant progress through the cities of Israel. And, when he made his public entry into any place, the women had got a song which they sang, the burden of which was, *Saul has slain his thousands, and*

JAMIESON, FAUSSET, BROWN — CHAPTER 18

2. Saul would let him go no more home—He was established as a permanent resident at court.

Vss. 1-4. Jonathan Loves David. **1. the soul of Jonathan was knit with the soul of David**—They were nearly of an age. The prince had taken little interest in David as a minstrel; but his heroism and modest, manly bearing, his piety and high endowments, kindled the flame not of admiration only, but of affection, in the congenial mind of Jonathan. **3. Then Jonathan and David made a covenant**—Such covenants of brotherhood are frequent in the East. They are ratified by certain ceremonies, and in presence of witnesses, that the persons covenanting will be sworn brothers for life. **4. Jonathan stripped himself of the robe that was upon him, and gave it to David**—To receive any part of the dress which had been *worn* by a sovereign, or his eldest son and heir, is deemed, in the East, the *highest* honor which can be conferred on a subject (see on Esther 6:8). The girdle, being connected with the sword and the bow, may be considered as being part of the military dress, and great value is attached to it in the East.

5-9. Saul Envies His Praise. **6. the women came out of all the cities of Israel**—in the homeward march from the pursuit of the Philistines. This is a characteristic trait of Oriental manners. On the return of friends long absent, and particularly on the return of a victorious army, bands of women and children issue from the towns and villages, to form a triumphal procession, to celebrate the victory, and, as they go along, to gratify the soldiers with dancing, instrumental music, and extempore songs, in honor of the generals who have earned the highest distinction by feats of gallantry. The Hebrew women, therefore, were merely paying the customary gratulations to David as the deliverer of their country, but they committed a great indiscretion by praising a subject at the expense of their sovereign.

ADAM CLARKE — CHAPTER 18

A. B. SIMPSON:

We see the picture of a holy friendship. The attachment of David and Jonathan is spoken of in the highest terms. "The soul of Jonathan was knit with the soul of David, and Jonathan loved him as his own soul." And in the pledge of his affection he made a covenant with his friend and stripped himself of his princely robe, and even of his personal and inner garments, bearing, no doubt, the monogram of his royal name, and even the very sword, which was to a warrior the badge of his highest honor, and his bow and his very girdle, which was the most sacred article of personal apparel in an Oriental wardrobe, for it was his purse and the repository of all his secrets and sacred treasures—all these Jonathan gave to David as the expression of his unreserved oneness with the friend of his inmost heart.—*Christ in the Bible*

6. *The women came out*. It was the principal business of certain women to celebrate victories, sing at funerals, etc. *With instruments of musick*. The original word (*shalishim*) signifies instruments with three strings.

7. *Saul hath slain his thousands*. As it cannot literally be true that Saul had slain thousands, and David ten thousands, it would be well to translate the passage thus: "Saul hath smitten or fought against thousands; David, against tens of thousands."

MATTHEW HENRY

David his ten thousands.

II. This mightily displeased Saul, and made him envy David, *v.* 8, 9. He ought to have considered that they referred only to this late action, and intended not to diminish any of Saul's former exploits. David, in killing Goliath, did in effect slay all the Philistines that were slain that day and defeated the whole army; so that they did but give David his due. But Saul was very wroth, and presently suspected some treasonable design at the bottom of it, *What can he have more but the kingdom?*

III. In his fury he aimed to kill David, *v.* 10, 11. 1. His fits of frenzy returned upon him. Those that indulge themselves in envy and uncharitableness *give place to the devil*, and prepare for the re-entry of the unclean spirit, with seven others more wicked. Saul pretended a religious ecstasy: *He prophesied in the midst of the house*, that is, he had the gestures and motions of a prophet, and humoured the thing well enough to decoy David, that he might be off his guard; and perhaps designing, if he could but kill him, to impute it to a divine impulse but really it was a hellish fury that actuated him. 2. David returns to his harp: *He played with his hand as at other times.* 3. He took this opportunity to aim at the death of David. He had a javelin or dart in his hand, which he projected, endeavouring to slay David, not in a sudden passion, but deliberately. One would think he should have allowed himself to consider the kindness David was now doing him, in relieving him, as no one else could, against the worst of troubles. Compare David, with his harp in his hand, aiming to serve Saul, and Saul, with his javelin in his hand, aiming to slay David; and observe the meekness and usefulness of God's persecuted people and the brutishness and barbarity of their persecutors. 4. David happily avoided the blow twice. He did not throw the javelin at Saul again, though he had both strength and courage enough, and colour of right, to make resistance, yet he did no more than secure himself, by getting out of the way of it.

Verses 12–30

Saul began in open hostility when he threw the javelin at him. His enmity proceeded, and David received the attacks.

I. How Saul expressed his malice against David. 1. He was *afraid of him, v.* 12. He really stood in awe of him, as Herod feared John, Mark vi. 20. Saul was sensible that he had lost the favourable presence of God himself, and that David had it, and for this reason he feared him. The way to be both feared and loved, feared by those to whom we would wish to be a terror and loved by those to whom we would wish to be a delight, is to *behave ourselves wisely*. 2. He removed him from court, and gave him a regiment in the country, *v.* 13, that he might not secure the interest of the courtiers. Yet herein he did impoliticly; for it gave David an opportunity of ingratiating himself with the people, who therefore *loved him* (*v.* 16) because he *went out and came in before them*. 3. He stirred him up to take all occasions of quarrelling with the Philistines (*v.* 17), insinuating to him that he would do good service to his prince and good service to his God, and would qualify himself for the honour he designed him, which was to marry his eldest daughter to him. 4. He did what he could to provoke him by breaking his promise with him, and giving his daughter to another. 5. When he was disappointed in this, he proffered him his other daughter. (1) Perhaps he hoped that she would, even after her marriage to David, take part with her father against her husband. (2) The conditions of the marriage must be that he killed 100 Philistines, and, as proofs that those he had slain were uncircumcised, he must bring in their foreskins. David, in doing this, would make them seek to be revenged on him, which was the thing that Saul desired and designed. *For Saul thought to make David fall by the Philistines, v.* 25. [1] Saul's conscience would not suffer him to aim at David's life himself, but he thought that to expose him designedly to the Philistines had nothing bad in it (*Let not my hand be upon him, but the hand of the Philistines*). [2] Saul pretended extraordinary kindness for David even when he aimed at his ruin: *Thou shalt be my son-in-law*, says he (*v.* 21).

II. How David conducted himself when the tide of Saul's displeasure ran thus high against him.

1. *He behaved himself wisely in all his ways.* He did not complain of hard measure nor make himself the head of a party, but managed all the affairs he was entrusted with as one that made it his business to do real service to his king and country. And then *the Lord was with him* to give him success in all his undertakings.

2. When it was proposed to him to be son-in-law

JAMIESON, FAUSSET, BROWN

9. Saul eyed David—i.e., invidiously, with secret and malignant hatred.

10-12. Seeks to Kill Him. **10. on the morrow the evil spirit from God came upon Saul**—This rankling thought brought on a sudden paroxysm of his mental malady. **he prophesied**—The term denotes one under the influence either of a good or a bad spirit. In the present it is used to express that Saul was in a frenzy.

David, perceiving the symptoms, hastened, by the soothing strains of his harp, to allay the stormy agitation of the royal mind. But before its mollifying influence could be felt, Saul hurled a javelin at the head of the young musician. **there was a javelin in Saul's hand**—Had it been followed by a fatal result, the deed would have been considered the act of an irresponsible maniac. It was repeated more than once ineffectually, and Saul became impressed with a dread of David as under the special protection of Providence.

13-16. Fears Him for His Good Success. **13. Therefore Saul removed him from him**—sent him away from the court, where the principal persons, including his own son, were spellbound with admiration of the young and pious warrior. **and made him captain over a thousand**—gave him a military commission, which was intended to be an honorable exile. But this post of duty served only to draw out before the public the extraordinary and varied qualities of his character, and to give him a stronger hold of the people's affections.

17-21. He Offers Him His Daughter for a Snare. **17. Saul said to David, Behold my elder daughter Merab, her will I give thee to wife**—Though bound to this already, he had found it convenient to forget his former promise. He now holds it out as a new offer, which would tempt David to give additional proofs of his valor. But the fickle and perfidious monarch broke his pledge at the time when the marriage was on the eve of being celebrated, and bestowed Merab on another man (see on II Sam. 21:8); an indignity as well as a wrong, which was calculated deeply to wound the feelings and provoke the resentment of David. Perhaps it was intended to do so, that advantage might be taken of his indiscretion. But David was preserved from this snare. **20. Michal, Saul's daughter, loved David**—This must have happened some time after. **they told Saul, and the thing pleased him**—Not from any favor to David, but he saw that it would be turned to the advancement of his malicious purposes, and the more so when, by the artful intrigues and flattery of his spies, the loyal sentiments of David were discovered.

ADAM CLARKE

10. *The evil spirit from God.* See on chap. xvi. 14, etc. *He prophesied in the midst of the house.* He was beside himself; made prayers, supplications, and incoherent imprecations. But let us examine the original more closely: it is said that Saul prophesied in the midst of his house, that is, he prayed in his family, while David was playing on the harp; and then suddenly threw his javelin, intending to have killed David. Let it be observed that the word *vaiyithnabbe* is the third person singular of the future *hithpael*, the sign of which is not only to do an action on or for oneself, but also to feign or pretend to do it. The meaning seems to be, Saul pretended to be praying in his family, the better to conceal his murderous intentions, and render David unsuspicious; who was, probably, at this time performing the musical part of the family worship. This view of the subject makes the whole case natural and plain.

11. *Saul cast the javelin.* The *javelin* or "spear" was the emblem of regal authority; kings always had it at hand, and in ancient monuments they are always represented with it.

13. *Made him his captain.* This was under pretense of doing him honor, when it was in effect only to rid himself of the object of his envy.

15. *He was afraid of him.* He saw that, by his prudent conduct, he was every day gaining increasing influence.

21. *That she may be a snare to him.* Saul had already determined the condition on which he would give his daughter to David; viz., that he should slay 100 Philistines. This he supposed David would undertake for the love of Michal, and that he must necessarily perish in the attempt; and thus Michal would become a snare to him.

MATTHEW HENRY

to the king he once and again received the proposal with all possible modesty and humility. (1) How highly he speaks of the honour offered him: *To be son-in-law to the king*. Religion is so far from teaching us to be rude and unmannerly that it does not allow us to be so. We must *render honour to whom honour is due*. (2) How humbly he speaks of himself: *Who am I? Who am I, a poor man, and lightly esteemed?* It well becomes us, however God has advanced us, always to have low thoughts of ourselves.

3. When the slaying of 100 Philistines was made the condition of David's marrying Saul's daughter he readily closed with it (*v.* 26). He would not seem to suspect that Saul designed his hurt by it. He knew God was with him, and therefore, whatever Saul hoped, David did not fear falling by the Philistines, though he must needs expose himself much by such an undertaking as this.

Even after he was married he continued his good services to Israel. When the princes of the Philistines began to move towards another war David was ready to oppose them, and *behaved himself more wisely than all the servants of Saul*, *v.* 30. The law dispensed with men from going to war the first year after they were married (Deut. xxiv. 5), but David loved his country too well to make use of that dispensation.

III. How God brought good to David out of Saul's project against him. 1. Saul gave him his daughter to be a snare to him, but in this respect that marriage was a kindness to him. 2. Saul thought, by putting him upon dangerous services, to have him taken off, but the more he did against the Philistines the better they loved him, so that *his name was much set by* (*v.* 30), which would make his coming to the crown the more easy.

CHAPTER 19

Verses 1–7

Saul and Jonathan appear here in their different characters, with reference to David.

I. Never was enemy so unreasonably cruel as Saul. His projects to take him off had failed, and therefore he proclaims him an outlaw, and charges all about him, upon their allegiance, to take the first opportunity to kill David. It was strange that he who knew how well Jonathan loved him should expect him to kill him; but he thought that because he was heir to the crown he must needs be as envious at David as himself was.

II. Never was friend so surprisingly kind as Jonathan. He not only continued to delight much in him, though David's glory eclipsed his, but bravely appeared for him now that the stream ran so strongly against him.

1. He took care for his present security by letting him know his danger (*v.* 2).

2. He took pains to pacify his father and reconcile him to David. The next morning he ventured to commune with him concerning David (*v.* 3).

(1) His intercession for David was very prudent. He pleads, [1] The good services David had done to the public, and particularly to Saul. Witness the relief he had given him against his distemper with his harp, and his bold encounter with Goliath, that memorable action, which did, in effect, save Saul's life and kingdom. [2] He pleads his innocency. If he be slain, it is without cause. Jonathan could not entail anything upon his family more pernicious than the guilt of innocent blood.

(2) His intercession, being thus prudent, was prevalent. God inclined the heart of Saul to hearken to the voice of Jonathan. [1] He recalled the bloody warrant for his execution (*v.* 6): *As the Lord liveth, he shall not be slain*. We suppose that he spoke as he thought for the present, but the convictions soon wore off and his corruptions prevailed and triumphed over them. [2] He renewed the grant of his place at court. Jonathan brought him to Saul, and *he was in his presence as in times past* (*v.* 7), hoping that now the storm was over.

Verses 8–10

I. David continues his good services to his king and country. 1. As bold as ever in using his sword for the service of his country, *v.* 8. The war broke out again with the Philistines, which gave David occasion again to signalize himself. 2. As cheerful as ever in using his harp for the service of the prince. When Saul was disturbed with his former fits of melancholy *David played with his hand*, *v.* 9. He had learned to render good for evil, and to trust God with his safety in the way of his duty.

II. Saul continues his malice against David. He that but the other day had sworn by his Maker that David *should not be slain* now endeavours to slay

JAMIESON, FAUSSET, BROWN

25. The king desireth not any dowry—In Eastern countries the husband *purchases* his wife either by gifts or services. As neither David nor his family were in circumstances to give a suitable dowry for a princess, the king intimated that he would be graciously pleased to accept some gallant deed in the public service. **a hundred foreskins of the Philistines**—Such mutilations on the bodies of their slain enemies were commonly practised in ancient war, and the number told indicated the glory of the victory. Saul's willingness to accept a public service had an air of liberality, while his choice of so difficult and hazardous a service seemed only putting a proper value on gaining the hand of a king's daughter. But he covered unprincipled malice against David under this proposal, which exhibited a zeal for God and the covenant of circumcision. **26. the days were not expired**—The period within which this exploit was to be achieved was not exhausted. **27. David . . . slew of the Philistines two hundred men**—The number was doubled, partly to show his respect and attachment to the princess, and partly to oblige Saul to the fulfilment of his pledge. **29. Saul was yet the more afraid of David**—because Providence had visibly favored him, by not only defeating the conspiracy against his life, but through his royal alliance paving his way to the throne.

CHAPTER 19

VSS. 1-7. JONATHAN DISCLOSES HIS FATHER'S PURPOSE TO KILL DAVID. **1. Saul spake to Jonathan his son, and to all his servants, that they should kill David**—The murderous design he had secretly cherished he now reveals to a few of his intimate friends. Jonathan was among the number. He prudently said nothing at the time, but secretly apprised David of his danger; and waiting till the morning, when his father's excited temper would be cooled, he stationed his friend in a place of concealment, where, overhearing the conversation, he might learn how matters really stood and take immediate flight, if necessary. **4-7. Jonathan spake good of David**—He told his father he was committing a great sin to plot against the life of a man who had rendered the most invaluable services to his country and whose loyalty had been uniformly steady and devoted. The strong remonstrances of Jonathan produced an effect on the impulsive mind of his father. As he was still susceptible of good and honest impressions, he bound himself by an oath to relinquish his hostile purpose; and thus, through the intervention of the noble-minded prince, a temporary reconciliation was effected, in consequence of which David was again employed in the public service.

8-17. SAUL'S MALICIOUS RAGE BREAKS OUT AGAINST DAVID. **8-10. David went out, and fought with the Philistines, and slew them with a great slaughter**—A brilliant victory was gained over the public enemy. But these fresh laurels of David reawakened in the moody breast of Saul the former spirit of envy and melancholy.

ADAM CLARKE

25. *But an hundred foreskins*. That is, You shall slay 100 Philistines, and you shall produce their foreskins as a proof not only that you have killed 100 men but that these are of the uncircumcised.

27. *Slew . . . two hundred men*. The Septuagint has only "one hundred men." Saul covenanted with David for a hundred; and David himself says, 2 Sam. iii. 14, that he espoused Michal for a hundred; hence it is likely that "one hundred" is the true reading.

30. *Then the princes of the Philistines went forth*. Probably to avenge themselves on David and the Israelites; but of this war we know no more than that David was more skillful and successful in it than any of the other officers of Saul. His military skill was greater, and his success was proportionate to his skill and courage; hence it is said he *behaved himself more wisely than all the servants of Saul*.

CHAPTER 19

1. *That they should kill David*. Nothing less than the especial interposition of God could have saved David's life, when every officer about the king's person, and every soldier, had got positive orders to dispatch him.

2. *Take heed to thyself until the morning*. Perhaps the order was given to slay him the next day; and therefore Jonathan charges him to be particularly on his guard at that time, and to hide himself.

5. *For he did put his life in his hand*. The pleadings in this verse, though short, are exceedingly cogent; and the argument is such as could not be resisted.

6. *He shall not be slain*. In consequence of this oath, we may suppose he issued orders contrary to those which he had given the preceding day.

7. *He was in his presence, as in times past*. By Jonathan's advice he had secreted himself on that day on which he was to have been assassinated; the king having sworn that he should not be slain, David resumes his place in the palace of Saul.

9. *And the evil spirit from the Lord*. His envy and jealousy again returned, producing distraction of mind, which was exacerbated by diabolic influence (see on chap. xvi. 14).

MATTHEW HENRY

him himself. Saul's fear and jealousy made him a torment to himself, so that he could not sit in his house without a javelin in his hand, pretending it was for his preservation, but designing it for David's destruction; for he endeavoured to nail him to the wall, running at him so violently that he struck the *javelin into the wall* (*v.* 10).

III. God continues his care of David and still watches over him for good. Saul missed his blow. David was too quick for him and fled, and by a kind providence escaped that night. To these preservations among others, David often refers in his Psalms, when he speaks of God's being his shield and buckler, his rock and fortress, and delivering his *soul from death.*

Verses 11–17

I. Saul's further design of mischief to David. When David had escaped the javelin, Saul sent some of his guards after him to lay wait at the door of his house, and to assassinate him in the morning as soon as he stirred out, *v.* 11.

II. David's wonderful deliverance out of this danger. Michal was the instrument of it, whom Saul gave him to be a snare to him, but she proved his protector and helper. She, knowing her father's great indignation at David, soon suspected the design, and bestirred herself for her husband's safety. 1. She got David out of the danger. She told him how imminent the peril was (*v.* 11): *Tomorrow thou wilt be slain.* David himself was better versed in the art of fighting than of flying, but *Michal let him down through a window* (*v.* 2), and so he *fled and escaped.* 2. She practised a deception upon Saul and those whom he employed to be the instruments of his cruelty. When the doors of the house were opened in the morning, and David did not appear, the messengers would search the house for him, and did so. But Michal told them he was sick in bed (*v.* 14), and, if they would not believe her, they might see, for (*v.* 13) she had put a wooden image in the bed, and wrapped it up close and warm as if it had been David asleep, not in a condition to be spoken to; the goats' hair about the image was to resemble David's hair, the better to impose upon them. Saul, when he heard it, gave positive orders: *Bring him to me in the bed, that I may slay him, v.* 15. When the messengers were sent again, the cheat was discovered, *v.* 16. But by this time David was safe, and Michal was not then much concerned at the discovery. Saul chid her for helping David to escape (*v.* 17).

Verses 18–24

I. David's place of refuge. Having got away in the night from his own house, he fled not to Bethlehem but ran straight to Samuel and *told him all that Saul had done to him, v.* 18. 1. Because Samuel was the man that had given him assurance of the crown. In flying to Samuel he made God his refuge, trusting in the *shadow of his wings*; where else can a good man think himself safe? 2. Because Samuel, as a prophet, was best able to advise him what to do in this day of his distress. 3. Because with Samuel there was a college of prophets with whom he might join in praising God, and this would be the greatest relief imaginable to him in his present distress. He met with little rest or satisfaction in Saul's court, and therefore went to seek it in Samuel's church.

II. David's protection in this place: *He and Samuel went and dwelt* (*or lodged*) *in Naioth,* where the school of the prophets was, in Ramath. But Saul, having notice of it by some of his spies (*v.* 19), sent officers to seize David, *v.* 20. When they did not bring him he sent more; when they returned not he sent the third time (*v.* 21), and, hearing no tidings of these, he went himself, *v.* 22. How was David delivered, now that he was just ready to fall (like his own lamb formerly) into the mouth of the lions? Not as he delivered his lamb, by slaying the lion, or, as Elijah was delivered, by consuming the messengers with *fire from heaven,* but by turning the lions for the present into lambs.

1. When the messengers came into the congregation where David was among the prophets *the Spirit of God* came upon them, and they joined with the priest in praising God. Instead of seizing David, they themselves were seized. And thus, (1) God secured David; for either they were put into such an ecstasy by the spirit of prophecy, that they could not think of anything else, and so forgot their errand and never minded David, or they were by it put, for the present, into so good a frame that they could not entertain the thought of doing so bad a thing. (2) He put an honour upon the sons of the prophets and the communion of saints, and showed how he can strike an awe upon the worst of men, by the tokens of his presence in the assemblies. See also the benefit of religious societies. (3) He magnified his power

JAMIESON, FAUSSET, BROWN

On David's return to court, the temper of Saul became more fiendish than ever; the melodious strains of the harp had lost all their power to charm; and in a paroxysm of uncontrollable frenzy he aimed a javelin at the person of David—the missile having been thrown with such force that it pierced the chamber wall. David providentially escaped; but the king, having now thrown off the mask and being bent on aggressive measures, made his son-in-law's situation everywhere perilous.

11, 12. Saul sent messengers unto David's house, to watch him, and to slay him—The fear of causing a commotion in the town, or favoring his escape in the darkness, seemed to have influenced the king in ordering them to patrol till the morning.

This infatuation was overruled by Providence to favor David's escape; for his wife, secretly apprised by Jonathan, who was aware of the design, or by spying persons in court livery watching the gate, let him down through a window (see on Josh. 2:15). **13, 14. Michal took an image, and laid it in the bed**—"an image," lit., "the teraphim," and laid, not in the bed, but literally on the "divan"; and "the pillows," i.e., the cushion, which usually lay at the back of the divan and was stuffed with "goat's hair," she took from its bolster or heading at the upper part of the divan. This she placed lower down, and covered with a mantle, as if to foster a proper warmth in a patient; at the same time spreading the goat's hair skin so as to resemble human hair in a dishevelled state. The pretext was that David lay there sick. The first messengers of Saul, keeping at a respectable distance, were deceived; but the imposition was detected on a closer inspection. **15. Bring him to me in the bed**—a portable couch or mattress.

18-23. DAVID FLEES TO SAMUEL. **18-21. David fled, . . . and came to Samuel to Ramah**—Samuel was living in great retirement, superintending the school of the prophets, established in the little hamlet of Naioth, in the neighborhood of Ramah. It was a retreat congenial to the mind of David; but Saul, having found out his asylum, sent three successive bodies of men to apprehend him.

The character of the place and the influence of the sacred exercises produced such an effect on them that they were incapable of discharging their commission, and were led, by a resistless impulse, to join in singing the praises of God.

ADAM CLARKE

10. *But he slipped away.* He found he could not trust Saul, and therefore was continually on his watch. His agility of body was the means of his preservation at this time.

11. *To slay him in the morning.* When they might be able to distinguish between him and Michal, his wife; for had they attempted his life in the night season, there would have been some danger to Michal's life. Besides, Saul wished to represent him as a traitor; and consequently an attack upon him was justifiable at any time, even in the fullest daylight.

12. *Let David down through a window.* As Saul's messengers were sent to David's house to watch him, they would naturally guard the gate, or lie in wait in that place by which David would come out. Michal, seeing this, let him down to the ground through a window, probably at the back part of the house.

13. *Michal took an image. Eth hatteraphim,* "the teraphim." The Hebrew word appears to mean any kind of image, in any kind of form, as a representative of some reality. Here it must have been something in the human form, because it was intended to represent a man lying in bed, indisposed. *A pillow of goats' hair.* Perhaps she formed the appearance of a sick man's head muffled up by this pillow or bag of goats' hair. So I think the original might be understood. The goats' hair was merely accidental, unless we could suppose that it was designed to represent the hair of David's head, which is not improbable.

17. *Let me go; why should I kill thee?* That is, If you do not let me go, I will kill you. This she said to excuse herself to her father; as a wife she could do not less than favor the escape of her husband, being perfectly satisfied that there was no guilt in him. It is supposed that it was on this occasion that David wrote the fifty-ninth psalm, "Deliver me from mine enemies."

18. *David fled, and escaped . . . to Samuel.* He, no doubt, came to this holy man to ask advice; and Samuel thought it best to retain him for the present, with himself at Naioth, where it is supposed he had a school of prophets.

20. *The company of the prophets prophesying.* Employed in religious exercises. *Samuel . . . appointed over them.* Being head or president of the school at this place. *The Spirit of God was upon the messengers.* They partook of the same influence, and joined in the same exercise, and thus were prevented from seizing David.

MATTHEW HENRY

over the spirits of men.

2. Saul himself was likewise seized with the spirit of prophecy. One would have thought that so bad a man as he was in no danger of being turned into a prophet, yet he prophesies, as his messengers did, *v.* 23. He stripped off his royal robe and warlike habiliments, because they were either too fine or too heavy for this service, and fell into a trance as it should seem, or into a rapture, which continued all that day and night. Now the proverb recurs, *Is Saul among the prophets?* See *ch.* x. 12.

JAMIESON, FAUSSET, BROWN

Saul, in a fit of rage and disappointment, determined to go himself. But, before reaching the spot, his mental susceptibilities were roused even more than his messengers, and he was found, before long, swelling the ranks of the young prophets. This singular change can be ascribed only to the power of Him who can turn the hearts of men even as the rivers of water.

24. Saul Prophesies. **24. lay down naked**—i.e., divested of his armor and outer robes—in a state of trance. Thus God, in making the wrath of man to praise Him, preserved the lives of all the prophets, frustrated all the purposes of Saul, and preserved the life of His servant.

ADAM CLARKE

23. *He went on, and prophesied.* The Divine Spirit seemed to have seized him at the well of Sechu; and he went on from that prophesying—praying, singing praises—till he came to Naioth.

24. *He stripped off his clothes.* Threw off his royal robes or military dress, retaining only his tunic; and continued so all that day and all that night, uniting with the sons of the prophets in prayers, singing praises, and other religious exercises, which were unusual to kings and warriors; and this gave rise to the saying, *Is Saul also among the prophets?* By bringing both him and his men thus under a divine influence, God prevented them from injuring the person of David.

MATTHEW HENRY — CHAPTER 20

Verses 1–8

I. While Saul lay bound by his trance at Naioth David escaped to the court, and got to speak with Jonathan. It was happy for him that he had such a friend at court, when he had such an enemy on the throne. If there be those that hate and despise us, let us not be disturbed at that, for there are those also that love and respect us. 1. David appeals to Jonathan himself concerning his innocency, *What have I done? v.* 1. 2. He endeavours to convince him that, notwithstanding his innocency, Saul sought his life. Jonathan, as became a dutiful son, endeavoured to cover his father's shame, as far as was consistent with justice and fidelity to David. David therefore gives him the assurance of an oath concerning his own danger, "*As the Lord liveth,* and as *thy soul liveth, there is but a step between me and death,*" *v.* 3.

II. Jonathan generously offers him his service (*v.* 4): *Whatsoever thou desirest I will even do it for thee.*

III. David only desires him to satisfy himself, and then to satisfy him whether Saul did really design his death or no. 1. The method of trial he proposed was very natural. The two next days Saul was to dine publicly, upon occasion of the solemnities of the new moon, when extraordinary sacrifices were offered and feasts made upon the sacrifices. At these solemn feasts Saul had either all his children to sit with him, and David had a seat as one of them, or all his great officers, and David had a seat as one of *them.* However it was, David resolved his seat should be empty. If Saul admitted an excuse for his absence, he would conclude he had changed his mind and was reconciled to him; but if he resented it, and was put into a passion by it, it was easy to conclude he designed him a mischief. 2. The excuse he desired Jonathan to make for his absence, was that he was invited by his elder brother to Bethlehem, his own city, to celebrate with his relations there, because, they had now a yearly sacrifice, and a holy feast upon it, for *all the family, v.* 6. They kept a day of thanksgiving in their family for the comforts they enjoyed, and of prayer for the continuance of them. 3. The arguments he used with Jonathan to persuade him to do this kindness for him were very pressing, *v.* 8. (1) That he had entered into a league of friendship with him. (2) That he would by no means urge him to espouse his cause if he was not sure that it was a righteous cause. No honest man will urge his friend to do a dishonest thing for his sake.

Verses 9–23

I. Jonathan protests his fidelity to David in his distress. He faithfully promised him that he would let him know how, upon trial, he found his father affected towards him, "If there be *good towards thee,* I will *show it thee,* that thou mayest be easy (*v.* 12), if evil, I will *send thee away,* that thou mayest be safe" (*v.* 13); and thus he would help to deliver him from the evil if it were real and from the fear of evil if it were but imaginary. Jonathan adds to his protestations his hearty prayers: "*The Lord be with thee,* to protect and prosper thee, *as he has been* formerly *with my father,* though now he has withdrawn."

II. He provides for the entail of the covenant of friendship with David upon his posterity, *v.* 14–16. He engages David to be a friend to his family when he was gone (*v.* 15). The house of David must likewise be bound to the house of Jonathan from generation to generation; he *made a covenant* (*v.* 16) *with the house of David.* This kindness, 1. He calls *the kindness of the Lord,* because it is such kindness as God shows. 2. He secures it by an imprecation (*v.* 16): *The Lord require it at the hand of David's seed* if they prove so far David's enemies as to deal wrongfully with the posterity of Jonathan, David's friend. Having him-

JAMIESON, FAUSSET, BROWN — CHAPTER 20

Vss. 1-10. David Consults with Jonathan for His Safety. **1. David fled from Naioth in Ramah, and came and said before Jonathan**—He could not remain in Naioth, for he had strong reason to fear that when the religious fit, if we may so call it, was over, Saul would relapse into his usual fell and sanguinary temper. It may be thought that David acted imprudently in directing his flight to Gibeah. But he was evidently prompted to go thither by the most generous feelings—to inform his friend of what had recently occurred, and to obtain that friend's sanction to the course he was compelled to adopt. Jonathan could not be persuaded there was any real danger after the oath his father had taken; at all events, he felt assured his father would do nothing without telling him. Filial attachment naturally blinded the prince to defects in the parental character and made him reluctant to believe his father capable of such atrocity. David repeated his unshaken convictions of Saul's murderous purpose, but in terms delicately chosen (vs. 3), not to wound the filial feelings of his friend; while Jonathan, clinging, it would seem, to a hope that the extraordinary scene enacted at Naioth might have wrought a sanctified improvement on Saul's temper and feelings, undertook to inform David of the result of his observations at home. **5. David said to Jonathan, Behold tomorrow is the new moon, and I should not fail to sit with the king at meat**—The beginning of a new month or moon was always celebrated by special sacrifices, followed by feasting, at which the head of a family expected all its members to be present. David, both as the king's son-in-law and a distinguished courtier, dined on such occasions at the royal table, and from its being generally known that David had returned to Gibeah, his presence in the palace would be naturally expected. This occasion was chosen by the two friends for testing the king's state of feeling. As a suitable pretext for David's absence, it was arranged that he should visit his family at Bethlehem, and thus create an opportunity of ascertaining how his non-appearance would be viewed. The time and place were fixed for Jonathan reporting to David; but as circumstances might render another interview unsafe, it was deemed expedient to communicate by a concerted signal.

11-23. Their Covenant Renewed by Oath. **11. Jonathan said to David, Come, let us go into the field**—The private dialogue, which is here detailed at full length, presents a most beautiful exhibition of these two amiable and noble-minded friends. Jonathan was led, in the circumstances, to be the chief speaker. The strength of his attachment, his pure disinterestedness, his warm piety, his invocation to God (consisting of a prayer and a solemn oath combined), the calm and full expression he gave of his conviction that his own family were, by the divine will, to be disinherited, and David elevated to the possession of the throne, the covenant entered into with David on behalf of his descendants, and the imprecation (vs. 16) denounced on any of them who should violate his part of the conditions, the reiteration of this covenant on both sides (vs. 17) to make it indissoluble—all this indicates such a power of mutual affection, such magnetic attractiveness in the character of David, such susceptibility and elevation of feeling in the heart of Jonathan, that this interview for dramatic interest and moral beauty stands unrivalled in the records of human friendship.

ADAM CLARKE — CHAPTER 20

1. *David fled from Naioth.* On hearing that Saul had come to that place, knowing that he was no longer in safety, he fled for his life.

2. *My father will do nothing.* Jonathan thought that his father could have no evil design against David, because of the oath which he had sworn to himself, chap. xix. 6; and at any rate, that he would do nothing against David without informing him.

3. *There is but a step between me and death.* My life is in the most imminent danger. Your father has, most assuredly, determined to destroy me.

5. *To morrow is the new moon.* The months of the Hebrews were lunar months, and they reckoned from new moon to new moon. And as their other feasts, particularly the Passover, were reckoned according to this, they were very scrupulous in observing the first appearance of each new moon. On these new moons they offered sacrifices, and had a feast; as we learn from Num. x. 10; xxviii. 11. And we may suppose that the families, on such occasions, sacrificed and feasted together.

12. *Jonathan said . . . O Lord God of Israel.* There is, most evidently, something wanting in this verse. The Septuagint has, "The Lord God of Israel doth know." The Syriac and Arabic, "The Lord God of Israel is witness." Either of these makes a good sense. But two of Dr. Kennicott's MSS. supply the word *chai,* "liveth"; and the text reads thus, "As the Lord God of Israel liveth, when I have sounded my father—if there be good, and I then send not unto thee, and show it thee, the Lord do so and much more to Jonathan." This makes a still better sense.

13. *The Lord be with thee, as he hath been with my father.* From this and other passages here it is evident that Jonathan knew that the Lord had appointed David to the kingdom.

14. *Shew me the kindness of the Lord.* When you come to the kingdom, if I am alive, you shall show kindness to me, and you shall continue that kindness to my family after me.

MATTHEW HENRY

self sworn to David, he caused David to swear to him, which David consented to swear by his love to him, which he looked upon as a sacred thing. Jonathan's heart was so much upon it that, when they parted this time, he concluded with a solemn appeal to God: *The Lord be between me and thee for ever* (*v.* 23). It was in remembrance of this covenant that David was kind to Mephibosheth, 2 Sam. ix. 7; xxi. 7.

III. He settled by what signs and tokens he would give him notice how his father stood affected towards him. David would be missed and would be enquired after, *v.* 18. On the third day, by which time he would have returned from Bethlehem, he must be at such a place (*v.* 19), and Jonathan would come towards that place with his bow and arrows to shoot for diversion (*v.* 20), would send his lad to fetch his arrows, and, if they were shot short of the lad, David must take it for a signal of safety, and not be afraid to show his head (*v.* 21); but, if he shot beyond the lad, it was a signal of danger, and he must shift for his safety, *v.* 22.

Verses 24–34

Jonathan is here effectually convinced of that which he was so loth to believe, that his father had an implacable enmity to David, and would certainly be the death of him if it were in his power.

I. David is missed from the feast on the first day, but nothing is said of him. *The king sat upon his seat as at other times* (*v.* 25), and yet had his heart full of envy and malice against David. When the king came to take his seat Jonathan arose, in reverence to him both as a father and as his sovereign; everyone knew his place, but David's was empty. But that day Saul took no notice that he missed David, but said within himself, "*Surely he is not clean, v.* 26. Some ceremonial pollution has befallen him."

II. He is enquired for the second day, *v.* 27. Saul asked Jonathan, who he knew was his confidant, *Wherefore cometh not the son of Jesse to meat?*

III. Jonathan makes his excuse, *v.* 28, 29. 1. That he was keeping the feast in another place, and that he had gone to pay his respects to his relations. He pleads, 2. That he did not go without leave humbly asked and obtained from Jonathan, as his superior officer.

IV. Saul hereupon breaks out into a most extravagant passion, and rages like a lion disappointed of his prey. David was out of his reach, but he falls upon Jonathan for his sake (*v.* 30, 31). He does in effect call him, 1. A bastard: *Thou son of the perverse rebellious woman.* 2. A traitor: *Thou son of perverse rebellion* (so the word is), that is, "thou perverse rebel." 3. A fool: *Thou hast chosen the son of Jesse* for thy friend *to thy own confusion*, for while he lives *thou shalt never be established.*

V. Jonathan is sorely grieved and put into disorder by his father's barbarous passion, and the more because he had hoped better things, *v.* 2. His father's reflections upon himself he made no return to. *When thou art the anvil lie thou still.* But his dooming David to die he could not bear: to that he replied with some heart (*v.* 32), *Wherefore shall he be slain? What has he done?* Generous spirits can much more easily bear to be abused themselves than to hear their friends abused. Saul was now so outrageous that he threw his javelin at Jonathan, *v.* 33. Jonathan *rose from table*, thinking it high time when his life was struck at, and *would eat no meat.*

Verses 35–42

1. He went at the time and to the place appointed (*v.* 35), within sight of which he knew David lay hid, sent his footboy to fetch his arrows, which he would shoot at random (*v.* 36), and gave David the fatal signal by shooting an arrow beyond the lad (*v.* 37). Finding the coast clear and no danger of a discovery, he presumed upon one minute's personal conversation with David after he had bidden him flee for his life. 2. The most sorrowful parting of these two friends, who, for aught that appears, never came together again but once, and that was by stealth *in a wood, ch.* xxiii. 16. They took leave of each other with the greatest affection imaginable, with kisses and tears. The separation of two such faithful friends was equally grievous to them both, but David's case was the more deplorable; for, when Jonathan was returning to his family and friends, David was leaving all his comforts, even those of God's sanctuary.

JAMIESON, FAUSSET, BROWN

19. when thou hast stayed three days—either with your family at Bethlehem, or wherever you find it convenient. **come to the place where thou didst hide thyself when the business was in hand**—*Heb.*, "in the day or time of the business," when the same matter was under inquiry formerly (ch. 19:22). **remain by the stone Ezel**—*Heb.*, "the stone of the way"; a sort of milestone which directed travellers. He was to conceal himself in some cave or hiding-place near that spot. **23. as touching the matter which thou and I have spoken of**—The plan being concerted, the friends separated for a time, and the amiable character of Jonathan again peers out in his parting allusion to their covenant of friendship.

24-40. SAUL, MISSING DAVID, SEEKS TO KILL JONATHAN. **25. the king sat upon his seat, as at other times . . . by the wall**—The left-hand corner at the upper end of a room was and still is in the East, the most honorable place. The person seated there has his left arm confined by the wall, but his right hand is at full liberty. From Abner's position next the king, and David's seat being left empty, it would seem that a state etiquette was observed at the royal table, each of the courtiers and ministers having places assigned them according to their respective gradations of rank. **Jonathan arose**—either as a mark of respect on the entrance of the king, or in conformity with the usual Oriental custom for a son to stand in presence of his father. **26. he is not clean**—No notice was taken of David's absence, as he might be laboring under some ceremonial defilement. **27. on the morrow, which was the second day of the month**—The time of the moon's appearance being uncertain—whether at midday, in the evening, or at midnight, the festival was extended over two days. Custom, not the law, had introduced this. **Saul said unto Jonathan his son, Wherefore cometh not the son of Jesse**—The question was asked, as it were, casually, and with as great an air of indifference as he could assume. And Jonathan having replied that David had asked and obtained his permission to attend a family anniversary at Bethlehem, the pent-up passions of the king burst out in a most violent storm of rage and invective against his son. **30. Thou son of the perverse rebellious woman**—This is a striking Oriental form of abuse. Saul was not angry with his wife; it was the son alone, upon whom he meant, by this style of address, to discharge his resentment. The principle on which it is founded seems to be, that to a genuine filial instinct it is a more inexpiable offense to hear the name or character of a parent traduced, than any personal reproach. This was, undoubtedly, one cause of "the fierce anger" in which the high-minded prince left the table without tasting a morsel. **33. Saul cast a javelin at him**—This is a sad proof of the maniacal frenzy into which the unhappy monarch was transported.

35. Jonathan went out into the field at the time appointed—or, "at the place appointed." **36. he said unto his lad, Run, find out now the arrows which I shoot**—The direction given aloud to the attendant was the signal preconcerted with David. It implied danger. **40. Jonathan gave his artillery unto his lad**—i.e., his missive weapons. The French word *artillerie*, signifies "archery." The term is still used in England, in the designation of the "artillery company of London," the association of archers, though they have long disused bows and arrows. Jonathan's boy being despatched out of the way, the friends enjoyed the satisfaction of a final meeting.

41, 42. JONATHAN AND DAVID LOVINGLY PART. **41, 42. David . . . fell on his face and bowed three times**—a token of homage to the prince's rank; but on a close approach, every other consideration was sunk in the full flow of the purest brotherly affection. **42. Jonathan said to David, Go in peace**—The interview being a stolen one, and every moment precious, it was kindness in Jonathan to hasten his friend's departure.

ADAM CLARKE

25. *The king sat upon his seat.* It seems that there was one table for Saul, Jonathan, David, and Abner—Saul having the chief seat, that next to the wall. As only four sat at this table, the absence of any one would soon be noticed.

29. *Our family hath a sacrifice.* Such sacrifices were undoubtedly festal ones; the beasts slain for the occasion were first offered to God, and their blood poured out before Him; afterwards all that were bidden to the feast ate of the flesh. This was a family entertainment, at the commencement of which God was peculiarly honored.

30. *Thou son of the perverse rebellious woman.* The Hebrew might be translated, "Son of an unjust rebellion"; that is, "Thou art a rebel against thy own father."

34. *Jonathan arose . . . in fierce anger.* We should probably understand this rather of Jonathan's grief than of his *anger*, the latter clause explaining the former: *for he was grieved for David.*

38. *Make speed, haste, stay not.* Though these words appear to be addressed to the lad, yet they were spoken to David, indicating that his life was at stake, and only a prompt flight could save him.

40. *Jonathan gave his artillery.* I believe this to be the only place in our language where the word *artillery* is not applied to cannon or ordnance. The original (*keley*) signifies simply "instruments," and here means the bow, quiver, and arrows.

41. *Until David exceeded.* David's distress must, in the nature of things, be the greatest. Besides his friend Jonathan, whom he was now about to lose forever, he lost his wife, relatives, country; and, what was most afflictive, the altars of his God, and the ordinances of religion.

MATTHEW HENRY

CHAPTER 21

Verses 1–9

I. David, in distress, flies to the tabernacle of God, now pitched at Nob, supposed to be a city in the tribe of Benjamin. Since Shiloh was forsaken, the tabernacle was often removed, though the ark still remained at Kirjath-jearim. Hither David came in his flight from Saul's fury (*v.* 1), and applied to Ahimelech the priest. Samuel the prophet could not protect him, Jonathan the prince could not. He therefore has recourse next to Ahimelech the priest. He foresees he must not be an exile, and therefore comes to the tabernacle, 1. To take an affecting leave of it, for he knows now when he shall see it again. 2. To enquire of the Lord there, and to beg direction from him in the way both of duty and safety.

II. Ahimelech the priest, having heard that he had fallen into disgrace at court, looked shy upon him, as most are apt to do upon their friends when the world frowns upon them. He was afraid of incurring Saul's displeasure by entertaining him. *Why art thou alone?* He that was suddenly advanced from the solitude of a shepherd's life to the crowds and hurries of the camp is now as soon reduced to the desolate condition of an exile.

III. David, under pretence of being sent by Saul upon public services, solicits Ahimelech to supply his present wants, *v.* 2, 3.

1. David did not behave like himself. He told Ahimelech a gross untruth, that Saul had ordered him business to despatch, that his attendants were dismissed to such a place, and that he was charged to observe secrecy. This was all false. It was ill done, and proved of bad consequence; for it *occasioned the death of the priests of the Lord*, as David reflected upon it afterwards with regret, *ch.* xxii. 22. David was a man of great faith and courage, and yet now both failed him, and he fell thus foully through fear and cowardice, and both owing to the weakness of his faith.

2. Two things David begged of Ahimelech, *bread* and a *sword.*

(1) He wanted bread: *Five loaves, v.* 3. The priest objected that he had none but hallowed bread, *show-bread*, which had stood a week on the golden table in the sanctuary, and was taken thence for the use of the priests and their families, *v.* 4. David pleads that he and those that were with him, in this case of necessity, might lawfully eat of the hallowed bread, for they were not only able to answer his terms of keeping from women for three days past, but *the vessels* (that is, the bodies) *of the young men were holy*, being *possessed in sanctification and honour at all times.* He pleads that the bread is in a manner common now that what was primarily the religious use of it is over; especially (as our margin reads it) *when there is other bread* (*hot, v.* 6) *sanctified this day in the vessel*, and put in the room of it upon the table. This was David's plea, and the Son of David approves it, and shows from it that mercy is to be preferred to sacrifice, that ritual observances must give way to moral duties, and that that may be done in a case of an urgent providential necessity which may not otherwise be done. He brings it to justify his disciples in plucking the ears of corn on the sabbath day, for which the Pharisees censured them, Matt. xii. 3, 4. Ahimelech hereupon supplies him: *He gave him hallowed bread* (*v.* 6). The show-bread was but twelve loaves in all, yet out of these he gave David five (*v.* 3), though they had no more in the house; but he trusted Providence.

(2) He wanted a sword. It happened that he had now no weapons with him, the reason of which he pretends to be because he came away in haste, *v.* 8. There was not a sword to be found about the tabernacle but the sword of Goliath, which was laid up behind the ephod. Probably David had an eye to that when he asked the priest to help him with a sword; for, that being mentioned, O! says he, *there is none like that, give it to me, v.* 9. Two things we may observe concerning this sword: Whenever he looked upon it, it would be a great support to his faith, by bringing to mind that great instance of the particular care and countenance of the divine providence respecting him. Experiences are great encouragements. He had gratefully given it back to God, dedicating it to him and to his honour as a token of his thankfulness; and now in his distress it stood him greatly in stead.

Thus was David well furnished with arms and victuals; but it fell out very unhappily that there was one of Saul's servants then attending before the Lord, *Doeg* by name, that proved a base traitor both to David and to Ahimelech. He was by birth an Edomite (*v.* 7), and though proselyted to the Jewish religion under Saul, yet he retained the ancient and

JAMIESON, FAUSSET, BROWN

CHAPTER 21

Vss. 1-7. DAVID, AT NOB, OBTAINS OF AHIMELECH HALLOWED BREAD. **1. Then came David to Nob to Ahimelech**—Nob, a city of the priests (ch. 22:19), was in the neighborhood of Jerusalem, on the Mount of Olives—a little north of the top, and on the northeast of the city. It is computed to have been about five miles distant from Gibeah. Ahimelech, the same as Ahiah, or perhaps his brother, both being sons of Ahitub (cf. ch. 14:3, with ch. 22: 4-11, 20). His object in fleeing to this place was partly for the supply of his necessities, and partly for comfort and counsel, in the prospect of leaving the kingdom.

Ahimelech was afraid at the meeting of David—suspecting some extraordinary occurrence by his appearing so suddenly, and in such a style, for his attendants were left at a little distance.

2. The king hath commanded me a business, and hath said unto me, Let no man know—This was a direct falsehood, extorted through fear. David probably supposed, like many other persons, that a lie is quite excusable which is told for the sole purpose of saving the speaker's life. But what is essentially sinful, can never, from circumstances, change its immoral character; and David had to repent of this vice of lying (Ps. 119:29).

4. there is hallowed bread—There would be plenty of bread in his house; but there was no time to wait for it. "The hallowed bread" was the old shew-bread, which had been removed the previous day, and which was reserved for the use of the priests alone (Lev. 24:9). Before entertaining the idea that this bread could be lawfully given to David and his men, the high priest seems to have consulted the oracle (ch. 22:10) as to the course to be followed in this emergency. A dispensation to use the hallowed bread was specially granted by God Himself. **5. these three days**—as required by law (Exod. 19:15). David and his attendants seem to have been lurking in some of the adjoining caves, to elude pursuit, and to have been, consequently, reduced to great extremities of hunger. **the bread is in a manner common**—i.e., now that it is no longer standing on the Lord's table. It is eaten by the priests, and may also, in our circumstances, be eaten by us. **yea, though it were sanctified this day in the vessel**—i.e., though the hallowed bread had been but newly placed on the vessel, the ritual ordinance would have to yield to the great law of necessity and mercy (see on Matt. 12:3; Mark 2:25; Luke 6:3). **6. there was no bread there—in the tabernacle.** The removal of the old and the substitution of the new bread was done on the Sabbath (Lev. 24:8), the loaves being kept warm in an oven heated the previous day.

9. HE TAKES GOLIATH'S SWORD. **9. sword of Goliath**—(See on ch. 18:54). **behind the ephod**—in the place allowed for keeping the sacred vestments, of which the ephod is mentioned as the chief. The giant's sword was deposited in that safe custody as a memorial of the divine goodness in delivering Israel. **There is none like that**—not only for its size and superior temper, but for its being a pledge of the divine favor to him, and a constant stimulus to his faith.

ADAM CLARKE

CHAPTER 21

1. *Then came David to Nob.* There were two places of this name, one on this side, the second on the other side of Jordan. But it is generally supposed that Nob, near Gibeah of Benjamin, is the place here intended; it was about twelve miles from Jerusalem. *Why art thou alone?* Ahimelech probably knew nothing of the difference between Saul and David; and as he knew him to be the king's son-in-law, he wondered to see him come without any attendants.

2. *The king hath commanded me a business.* All said here is an untruth, and could not be dictated by the Spirit of the Lord; but there is no reason to believe that David was under the influence of divine inspiration at this time.

6. *So the priest gave him hallowed bread.* To this history our Lord alludes, Mark ii. 25, in order to show that in cases of absolute necessity a breach of the ritual law was no sin. It was lawful for the priests only to eat the shewbread; but David and his companions were starving, no other bread could be had at the time, and therefore he and his companions ate of it without sin.

9. *The sword of Goliath.* It has already been conjectured (see chap. xvii) that the sword of Goliath was laid up as a trophy in the Tabernacle.

MATTHEW HENRY

hereditary enmity of Edom to Israel. He was master of the herds. Some occasion or other he had at this time to wait on the priest, it is said, he was *detained before the Lord.* He would rather have been any where else than before the Lord, and therefore, instead of minding the business he came about, was plotting to do David a mischief and to be revenged on Ahimelech for detaining him.

Verses 10–15

David, though king elect, is here an exile. Thus do God's providences sometimes seem to run counter to his promises. 1. David's flight into the land of the Philistines, where he hoped to remain undiscovered in the camp of Achish king of Gath, *v.* 10. To him David now went directly, as to one he could confide in, as afterwards (*ch.* xxvii. 2, 3). God's persecuted people have often found better usage from Philistines than from Israelites, in the Gentile theatres than in the Jewish synagogues. The king of Judah imprisoned Jeremiah, and the king of Babylon set him at liberty. 2. The disgust which the servants of Achish took at his being there, and their complaint of it to Achish (*v.* 11): "*Is not this David?* Is not this he that has triumphed over the Philistines?" As such, he must be an enemy to our country; and is it safe or honourable for us to protect or entertain such a man? Achish perhaps had intimated to them that it would be policy to entertain David, because he was now an enemy to Saul, and he might be hereafter a friend to them. It is common for the outlaws of a nation to be sheltered by the enemies of that nation. 3. The fright which this put David into. Though he had some reason to put confidence in Achish, yet, when he perceived the servants of Achish jealous of him, he began to be afraid that Achish would be obliged to deliver him up to them, and he was *sorely afraid* (*v.* 12). 4. The course he took to get out of their hands: *He feigned himself mad, v.* 13. It may in some degree be excused, for it was like a stratagem in war, by which he imposed upon his enemies for the preservation of his own life. 5. His escape by this means, *v.* 14, 15. I am apt to think Achish was aware that the delirium was but counterfeit, but, being desirous to protect David (as we find afterwards he was very kind to him, even when the lords of the Philistines favoured him not, *ch.* xxviii. 1, 2; xxix. 6), he pretended to his servants that he really thought he was mad. "I will show him no kindness, but then you shall do him no hurt, for, if he be a madman, he is to be pitied." He therefore *drove him away*, as it is in the title of Ps. xxxiv.

JAMIESON, FAUSSET, BROWN

7. Doeg, an Edomite—who had embraced the Hebrew religion. **detained before the Lord**—at the tabernacle, perhaps, in the performance of a vow, or from its being the Sabbath, which rendered it unlawful for him to prosecute his journey. **the chiefest of the herdsmen that belonged to Saul**—Eastern monarchs anciently had large possessions in flocks and herds; and the office of the chief shepherd was an important one.

10-15. At Gath He Feigns Himself Mad. **10. David . . . fled . . . to Achish the king of Gath**—which was one of the five principalities of the Philistines. In this place his person must have been known, and to venture into that country, he their greatest enemy, and with the sword of Goliath in his hand, would seem to have been a perilous experiment; but, doubtless, the protection he received implies that he had been directed by the divine oracle. Achish was generous (ch. 27:6). He might wish to weaken the resources of Saul, and it was common in ancient times for great men to be harbored by neighboring princes.

13. feigned himself mad—It is supposed to have been an attack of epilepsy, real or perhaps only pretended. This disease is relieved by foaming at the mouth. **let his spittle fall down upon his beard**—No wonder that Achish supposed him insane, as such an indignity, whether done by another, or one's self, to the beard, is considered in the East an intolerable insult.

ADAM CLARKE

7. *Detained before the Lord.* Probably fulfilling some vow to the Lord, and therefore for a time resident at the Tabernacle. *And his name was Doeg.* From chap. xxii. 9 we learn that this man betrayed David's secret to Saul, which caused him to destroy the city, and slay eighty-five priests. We learn from its title that the fifty-second psalm was made on this occasion; but titles are not to be implicitly trusted.

10. *Went to Achish the king of Gath.* This was the worst place to which he could have gone; it was the very city of Goliath, whom he had slain, and whose sword he now wore; and he soon found, from the conversation of the servants of Achish, that his life was in the most imminent danger in this place.

13. *And he changed his behaviour.* Some imagine David was so terrified at the danger to which he was now exposed that he was thrown into a kind of frenzy, accompanied with epileptic fits. This opinion is countenanced by the Septuagint, who render the passage thus: "Behold, ye see an epileptic man. Why have ye introduced him to me? Have I any need of epileptics, that ye have brought him to have his fits before me?" It is worthy of remark that the spittle falling upon the beard, i.e., frothing at the mouth, is a genuine concomitant of an epileptic fit.

If this translation be allowed, it will set the conduct of David in a clearer point of view than the present translation does. But others think the whole was a feigned conduct, and that he acted the part of a lunatic or madman in order to get out of the hands of Achish and his courtiers.

MATTHEW HENRY — CHAPTER 22

Verses 1–5

I. David shelters himself in the cave of Adullam, *v.* 1. Whether it was a natural or artificial fastness does not appear; it is probable that the access to it was so difficult that David thought himself able, with Goliath's sword, to keep it against all the forces of Saul, while he was waiting to see (as he says here, *v.* 3) what God would do with him. The promise of the kingdom implied a promise of preservation to it, and yet David used proper means for his own safety, otherwise he would have tempted God. He did not do anything that aimed to destroy Saul, but only to secure himself. It was at this time that David penned Psalm cxlii, which is entitled, *A prayer when David was in the cave.*

II. Thither his relations flocked to him, *his brethren and all his father's house*, to be protected by him, to give assistance to him, and to take their lot with him. Now Joab, and Abishai, and the rest of his relations, came to him, to suffer and venture with him.

III. Here he began to raise forces in his own defence, *v.* 2. He found by the late experiments he had made that he could not save himself by flight, and therefore was necessitated to do it by force, wherein he never acted offensively, never offered any violence to his prince nor gave any disturbance to the peace of the kingdom but only used his forces as a guard to his own person. The regiment he had was made up not of great men, nor rich men, nor stout men, no, nor good men, but men *in distress, in debt, and discontented*, men of broken fortunes and restless spirits, that were put to their shifts, and knew not well what to do with themselves. When David had fixed his headquarters in the cave of Adullam, they came and enlisted themselves under him to the number of about 400.

IV. He took care to settle his parents in a place of safety. No such place could he find in all the land of Israel while Saul was so bitterly enraged against him and all that belonged to him for his sake; he therefore goes with them to the king of Moab,

JAMIESON, FAUSSET, BROWN — CHAPTER 22

Vss. 1-8. David's Kindred and Others Resort to Him at Adullam. **1. David . . . escaped to the cave Adullam**—supposed to be that now called Deir-Dubban, a number of pits or underground vaults, some nearly square, and all about fifteen or twenty feet deep, with perpendicular sides, in the soft limestone or chalky rocks. They are on the borders of the Philistine plain at the base of the Judea mountains, six miles southwest from Bethlehem, and well adapted for concealing a number of refugees.

his brethren and all his father's house . . . went down—to escape the effects of Saul's rage, which seems to have extended to all David's family. From Bethlehem to Deir-Dubban it is, indeed, a descent all the way.

2. every one that was in distress—(See on Judg. 11:3).

3. David went thence to Mizpeh of Moab—Mizpeh signifies a watchtower, and it is evident that it must be taken in this sense here, for (vs. 4) it is called "the hold" or fort. The king of Moab was an enemy of Saul (ch. 14:47), and

ADAM CLARKE — CHAPTER 22

1. *The cave Adullam.* This was in the tribe of Judah, and, according to Eusebius and Jerome, ten miles eastward of what they call Eleutheropolis.

2. *And every one that was in distress . . . debt . . . discontented.* It is very possible that these several disaffected and exceptionable characters might at first have supposed that David, unjustly persecuted, would be glad to avail himself of their assistance that he might revenge himself upon Saul, and so they in the meantime might profit by plunder. But if this were their design they were greatly disappointed, for David never made any improper use of them. Whatever they were before they came to David, we find that he succeeded in civilizing them, and making profitable to the state those who were before unprofitable.

3. *He said unto the king of Moab.* David

MATTHEW HENRY

and puts them under his protection, *v.* 3, 4. The first thing he does is to find them a quiet habitation, whatever became of himself. With what a humble faith he expects the issue of his present distresses: *Till I know what God will do for me.*

V. He had the advice and assistance of the prophet Gad, who probably was one of the sons of the prophets that were brought up under Samuel, and was by him recommended to David for his chaplain or spiritual guide. He advised him to go into the land of Judah (*v.* 5), as one that was confident of his own innocency, and was well assured of the divine protection, and was desirous, even in his present hard circumstances, to do some service to his tribe and country.

Verses 6–19

The progress of Saul's wickedness. He seems to have laid aside the thoughts of all other business and to have devoted himself wholly to the pursuit of David. He heard at length, by the common fame of the country, that David *was discovered.* Hereupon he called all his servants about him, and sat down under a tree, or grove, in the high place at Gibeah, with his spear in his hand for a sceptre, intimating the present temper of his spirit, or its distemper rather, which was to kill all that stood in his way. In this bloody court of inquisition,

I. Saul seeks for information against David and Jonathan, *v.* 7, 8. Two things he was willing to suspect. 1. That his servant David did *lie in wait* for him and seek his life, which was utterly false. He really sought David's life. 2. That his son Jonathan stirred him up to do so, and was confederate with him in compassing and imagining the death of the king. This also was notoriously false. Saul took it for granted that Jonathan and David were in a plot against him, his crown and dignity and was displeased with his servants that they did not give him information of it, and told them, (1) That they were very unwise, for David would never be able to give them such rewards as he had for them. (2) That they were unfaithful: *You have conspired against me.* (3) That they were very unkind. He thought to work upon their good nature with that word: *There is none of you that is* so much as *sorry for me,* or *solicitous for me,* as some read it.

II. Though he could not learn anything from his servants against David or Jonathan, yet he got information from Doeg against Ahimelech the priest.

1. An indictment is brought against Ahimelech by Doeg, and he himself is evidence against him, *v.* 9, 10, and therefore tells Saul what kindness Ahimelech had shown to David. He had *enquired of God for him* (which the priest used not to do but for public persons and about public affairs) and he had furnished him with *bread and a sword.* All this was true; but it was not the whole truth. He ought to have told Saul further that David had made Ahimelech believe he was then going upon the king's business; so that what service he did to David, however it proved, was designed in honour to Saul, and this would have cleared Ahimelech.

2. Ahimelech is summoned to appear before the king, and upon this indictment he is arraigned. The king sent for him and all the priests who then attended the sanctuary, whom he supposed to be aiding and abetting. Saul arraigns Ahimelech himself with the utmost disdain and indignation (*v.* 12): *Hear now, thou son of Ahitub*; not so much as calling him by his name, much less giving him his title of distinction. Ahimelech holds up his hand at the bar in these words: "*Here I am, my lord,* ready to hear my charge, knowing I have done no wrong."

3. His indictment is read to him (*v.* 13), that he, as a false traitor, had joined himself with the son of Jesse in a plot to depose and murder the king. "His design" (says Saul) "was to *rise up against me,* and thou didst assist him with victuals and arms." See what bad constructions the most innocent actions are liable to, how unsafe those are that live under a tyrannical government, and what reason we have to be thankful for the happy constitution and administration of the government we are under.

4. To this indictment he pleads, Not guilty, *v.* 14, 15. He owns the fact, but denies that he did it traitorously or maliciously, or with any design against the king. He insists upon the settled reputation David had, as the most faithful of all the servants of Saul, the honour the king had put upon him in marrying his daughter to him, the use the king had often made of him, and the trust he had reposed in him. He pleads that he had been wont to *enquire of God for him* when he was sent by Saul upon any expedition, and did it now as innocently as ever he had done it.

JAMIESON, FAUSSET, BROWN

the great-grandson of Ruth, of course, was related to the family of Jesse. David, therefore, had less anxiety in seeking an aylum within the dominions of this prince than those of Achish, because the Moabites had no grounds for entertaining vindictive feelings against him, and their enmity to Saul rendered them the more willing to receive so illustrious a refugee from his court. **5. the prophet Gad said unto David, Abide not in the hold**—This sound advice, no doubt, came from a higher source than Gad's own sagacity. It was right to appear publicly among the people of his own tribe, as one conscious of innocence and trusting in God; and it was expedient that, on the death of Saul, his friends might be encouraged to support his interest. **forest of Harath**—southwest of Jerusalem.

6. Saul abode . . . under a tree in Ramah—lit., "under a grove on a hill." Oriental princes frequently sit with their court under some shady canopy in the open air. A spear was the early scepter. **7. Hear now, ye Benjamites**—This was an appeal to stimulate the patriotism or jealousy of his own tribe, from which he insinuated it was the design of David to transfer the kingdom to another. This address seems to have been made on hearing of David's return with his four hundred men to Judah. A dark suspicion had risen in the jealous mind of the king that Jonathan was aware of this movement, which he dreaded as a conspiracy against the crown.

9-16. DOEG ACCUSES AHIMELECH. **9. Doeg . . . set over the servants**—*Sept.*, the mules of Saul. **10. he inquired of the Lord for him**—Some suppose that this was a malicious fiction of Doeg to curry favor with the king, but Ahimelech seems to acknowledge the fact. The poor simple-minded high priest knew nothing of the existing family feud between Saul and David. The informer, if he knew it, said nothing of the cunning artifice by which David obtained the aid of Ahimelech.

ADAM CLARKE

could not trust his parents within the reach of Saul, and he found it very inconvenient to them to be obliged to go through all the fatigues of a military life, and therefore begs the king of Moab to give them shelter.

5. *Get thee into the land of Judah.* Gad saw that in this place alone he could find safety.

6. *Saul abode in Gibeah.* Saul and his men were in pursuit of David, and had here, as in the general custom in the East, encamped on a "height," for so *Ramah* should be translated, as in the margin. His *spear,* the ensign of power (see on chap. xviii. 11) was at hand, that is, stuck in the ground where he rested, which was the mark to the soldiers that there was their general's tent. *And all his servants were standing about him.* That is, they were encamped around him, or perhaps here there is a reference to a sort of council of war called by Saul for the purpose of delivering the speech recorded in the following verses.

9. *Doeg the Edomite, which was set over the servants of Saul.* In chap. xxi. 7 he is said to be "the chiefest of the herdmen that belonged to Saul," and the Septuagint intimate that he was over the mules of Saul.

14. *And who is so faithful?* The word *neeman,* which we here translate *faithful,* is probably the name of an officer.

15. *Did I then begin to enquire of God?* He probably means that his inquiring now for David was no new thing, having often done so before, and without ever being informed it was either wrong in itself or displeasing to the king. Nor is it likely that Ahimelech knew of any disagreement between Saul and David. He knew him to be the king's son-in-law, and he treated him as such.

MATTHEW HENRY

5. Saul himself gives judgment against him (*v.* 16): *Thou shalt surely die, Ahimelech,* as a rebel, *thou and all thy father's house.* What could be more unjust? (1) It was unjust that Saul should himself, himself alone, give judgment in his own cause. (2) That so fair a plea should be overruled and rejected without any reason given. (3) That sentence should be passed so hastily. (4) That the sentences should be passed not only on Ahimelech himself, who was the only person accused by Doeg, but on *all his father's house,* against whom nothing was alleged. (5) That the sentence should be pronounced not for the support of justice, but for the gratification of his brutish rage.

6. He issues a warrant for the immediate execution of this bloody sentence.

(1) He ordered his footmen to be the executioners of this sentence, but they refused, *v.* 17. [1] Never was the command of a prince more barbarously given: *Turn and slay the priests of the Lord.* He seems well pleased with this opportunity of being revenged on the priests of the Lord, since God himself was out of his reach. [2] Never was the command of a prince more honourably disobeyed. The footmen had more sense and grace than their master. They would not offer to fall upon the priests of the Lord, such a reverence had they for their office, and such a conviction of their innocence.

(2) He ordered Doeg (the accuser) to be the executioner, and he obeyed. The most bloody tyrants have found out instruments of their cruelty as barbarous as themselves. Doeg is no sooner commanded to fall upon the priests than he does it willingly enough, and, meeting with no resistance, slays with his own hand (for aught that appears) on that same day eighty-five priests that were of the age of ministration, between twenty and fifty, for they *wore a linen ephod* (*v.* 18), and perhaps appeared at this time before Saul in their habits, and were slain in them. Doeg, by Saul's order no doubt, having murdered the priests, went to their city Nob, and put all to the sword there (*v.* 19), *men, women, and children,* and the cattle too. How deplorable was the state of religion at this time in Israel! To see their priests weltering in their own blood, and the heirs of the priesthood too, and the city of the priests made a desolation, so that the altar of God must needs be neglected for want of attendants, and this by the unjust and cruel order of their own king to satisfy his brutish rage—this could not but go to the heart of all pious Israelites, and make them wish a thousand times they had been satisfied with the government of Samuel and his sons.

Verses 20–23

1. The escape of Abiathar, the son of Ahimelech, out of the desolations of the priests' city. Probably when his father went to appear, upon Saul's summons, he was left at home to attend the altar, by which means he escaped the first execution, and, before Doeg and his bloodhounds came to Nob, he had intelligence of the danger, and had time to shift for his own safety. And whither should he go but to David? *v.* 20. 2. David's resentment of the melancholy tidings he brought. David greatly lamented the calamity itself, but especially his being accessory to it: *I have occasioned the death of all the persons of thy father's house, v.* 22. 3. The protection he granted to Abiathar. *With me thou shalt be in safeguard, v.* 23. David, having now time to recollect himself, speaks with assurance of his own safety, and promises that Abiathar shall have the full benefit of his protection. David had now not only a prophet, but a priest, a high-priest, with him, to whom he was a blessing and they to him, and both a happy omen of his success. Yet it appears (by *ch.* xxviii. 6) that Saul had a high priest too, for he preferred Ahitub the father of Zadok, of the family of Eleazar (1 Chron. vi. 8), even those that hate the power of godliness yet will not be without the form.

JAMIESON, FAUSSET, BROWN

The *facts looked* against him, and the whole priesthood along with him were declared abettors of conspiracy.

17-19. SAUL COMMANDS TO KILL THE PRIESTS. **17. the footmen that stood about him**—his bodyguard, or his runners (ch. 8:11; II Sam. 15:1; I Kings 1:5; I Kings 14:28), who held an important place at court (II Chronicles 12:10). But they chose rather to disobey the king than to offend God by imbruing their hands in the blood of his ministering servants.

A foreigner alone (Ps. 52:1-3) could be found willing to be the executioner of this bloody and sacrilegious sentence. Thus was the doom of the house of Eli fulfilled.

19. Nob, the city of the priests, smote he with the edge of the sword—The barbarous atrocities perpetrated against this city seem to have been designed to terrify all the subjects of Saul from affording either aid or an asylum to David. But they proved ruinous to Saul's own interest, as they alienated the priesthood and disgusted all good men in the kingdom.

20-23. ABIATHAR ESCAPES AND FLEES AFTER DAVID. **20. one of the sons of Ahimelech . . . escaped**—This was Abiathar, who repaired to David in the forest of Hareth, rescuing, with his own life, the high priest's vestments (ch. 23:6, 9).

On hearing his sad tale, David declared that he had dreaded such a fatal result from the malice and intriguing ambition of Doeg; and, accusing himself as having been the occasion of all the disaster to Abiathar's family, David invited him to remain, because, firmly trusting himself in the accomplishment of the divine promise, David could guarantee protection to him.

ADAM CLARKE

17. *But the servants of the king would not.* They dared to disobey the commands of the king in a case of such injustice, inhumanity, and irreligion.

18. *And Doeg . . . fell upon the priests.* A ruthless Edomite, capable of any species of iniquity.

19. *And Nob . . . smote he with the edge of the sword.* This is one of the worst acts in the life of Saul; his malice was implacable, and his wrath was cruel, and there is no motive of justice or policy by which such a barbarous act can be justified.

20. *Abiathar, escaped.* This man carried with him his sacerdotal garments, as we find from chap. xxiii. 6, 9.

MATTHEW HENRY — CHAPTER 23

Verses 1–6

The prophet Gad ordered David to go into the land of Judah, *ch.* xxii. 5. Since Saul neglected the public safety, he might take care of it, notwithstanding the ill treatment that was given him.

I. Tidings are brought to David that the Philistines had made a descent upon the city of Keilah and plundered the country thereabouts, *v.* 1. The way for any country to be quiet is to let God's church be quiet in it. If Saul fight against David, the Philistines shall fight against his country.

II. David is forward enough to come in for their relief. 1. David's generosity and public-spiritedness.

JAMIESON, FAUSSET, BROWN — CHAPTER 23

Vss. 1-6. DAVID RESCUES KEILAH. **1. Then they told David**—rather, "now they had told"; for this information had reached him previous to his hearing (vs. 6) of the Nob tragedy. **Keilah**—a city in the west of Judah (Josh. 15:44), not far from the forest of Hareth. **and they rob the threshing-floors**—These were commonly situated on the fields and were open to the wind (Judg. 6:11; Ruth 3:2).

ADAM CLARKE — CHAPTER 23

1. *The Philistines fight against Keilah.* Keilah was a fortified town in the tribe of Judah near to Eleutheropolis, on the road to Hebron. *Rob the threshingfloors.* This was an ancient custom of the Philistines, Midianites, and others (see Judg. vi. 4). When the corn was ripe and fit to be threshed, and they had collected it at the threshing floors, which were always in the open field, their enemies came upon them and spoiled them of the fruits of their harvest.

MATTHEW HENRY

He was concerned for the safety of his country and could not sit still to see that ravaged: though Saul, whose business it was to guard the borders of his land, hated him and sought his life. 2. David's piety and regard to God. He enquired of the Lord by the prophet Gad: *Shall I go and smite these Philistines?*

III. God appointed him once and again to go against the Philistines, and promised him success: *Go, and smite the Philistines*, *v.* 2. His men opposed it, *v.* 3. To satisfy them, therefore, he *enquired of the Lord again*, and now received, not only a full commission, which would warrant him to fight though he had no orders from Saul (*Arise, go down to Keilah*), but also a full assurance of victory: *I will deliver the Philistines into thy hand*, *v.* 4.

IV. He went accordingly against the Philistines, routed them, and rescued Keilah, (*v.* 5), and it should seem he made a sally into the country of the Philistines, for he carried off their cattle by way of reprisal for the wrong they did to the men of Keilah in robbing their threshing-floors.

I. Saul contriving within himself the destruction of David (*v.* 7, 8). Was it not told him that he had bravely relieved Keilah and delivered it out of the hands of the Philistines? This should have put Saul upon considering what honour should be done to David. But, instead of that, he catches at it as an opportunity of doing David a mischief. 1. How Saul abused the *God of Israel*. *God hath delivered him into my hand*; as if he who was rejected of God were in this instance favoured by him. He impiously connects God with his cause, because he thought he had gained one point. 2. How Saul abused the Israel of God, in making them the servants of his malice against David. He called all the people together to march to Keilah, pretending to oppose the Philistines, but intending to besiege David and his men.

II. David consulting with God concerning his own preservation. No sooner is the ephod brought to him than he makes use of it: *Bring hither the ephod*. We have the scriptures, those lively oracles, in our hands; let us take advice from them in doubtful cases. "Bring hither the Bible."

1. David's address to God upon this occasion is, (1) Very solemn and reverent. Twice he calls God the *Lord God of Israel*, and thrice calls himself his *servant*, *v.* 10, 11. "Lord, direct me in this matter, about which I am now at a loss." If he had asked the men (the magistrates or elders) of Keilah themselves what they would do in that case, they could not have told him, not knowing their own minds, or they might have told him they would protect him, and yet afterwards have betrayed him; but God could tell him infallibly: "When Saul besieges their city, and demands of them that they surrender thee into his hands, they will deliver thee up rather than stand the shock of Saul's fury."

2. David, having thus far notice given him of his danger, quitted Keilah, *v.* 13. His followers had now increased in number to 600; with these he went out, not knowing whither he went, but resolving to follow Providence. This broke Saul's measures. He thought God had delivered David into his hand, but it proved that God delivered him out of his hand, as a bird out of the snare of the fowler.

Verses 14–18

I. David abode in a *wilderness, in a mountain* (*v.* 14), *in a wood*, *v.* 15. He did not draw up his forces against Saul, surprise him by some stratagem or other, and so avenge his own quarrel and put an end to the calamities of the country under Saul's tyrannical government. He keeps God's way, waits God's time, and is content to secure himself in woods and wilderness. What shall we say to this? Let it reconcile even great and active men to privacy and restraint, and let it make us long for that kingdom where goodness shall for ever be in glory and holiness in honour.

II. Saul hunting him, as his implacable enemy. He sought him every day, so restless was his malice, *v.* 14.

III. God defending him, as his powerful protector. God delivered him not into Saul's hand, as Saul hoped (*v.* 7).

IV. Jonathan comforting him as his faithful and constant friend. True friendship will not shrink from danger, but can easily venture, will not shrink from condescension, but can easily stoop, and exchange a palace for a wood, to serve a friend. The very sight of Jonathan was reviving to David. 1. As a pious friend he *strengthened his hand in God*. David, though a strong believer, needed the help of his friends for the perfecting of what was lacking in his faith; and herein Jonathan was helpful to him, by reminding him of the promise of God. Jonathan

JAMIESON, FAUSSET, BROWN

David inquired of the Lord—most probably through Gad (II Sam. 24; I Chron. 21:9), who was present in David's camp (ch. 22:5), probably by the recommendation of Samuel. To repel unprovoked assaults on unoffending people who were engaged in their harvest operations, was a humane and benevolent service. But it was doubtful how far it was David's duty to go against a public enemy without the royal commission; and on that account he asked, and obtained, the divine counsel. A demur on the part of his men led David to renew the consultation for their satisfaction; after which, being fully assured of his duty, he encountered the aggressors and, by a signal victory, delivered the people of Keilah from further molestation. **6. an ephod**—in which was the Urim and Thummim (Exod. 28:30). It had, probably, been committed to his care, while Ahimelech and the other priests repaired to Gibeah, in obedience to the summons of Saul.

7-13. SAUL'S COMING, AND TREACHERY OF THE KEILITES. **7. it was told Saul that David was come to Keilah**—Saul imagined himself now certain of his victim, who would be hemmed within a fortified town. The wish was father to the thought. How wonderfully slow and unwilling to be convinced by all his experience, that the special protection of Providence shielded David from all his snares! **8. Saul called all the people together to war**—not the united tribes of Israel, but the inhabitants of the adjoining districts. This force was raised, probably, on the ostensible pretext of opposing the Philistines, while, in reality, it was secretly to arouse mischief against David.

9. he said to Abiathar the priest, Bring hither the ephod—The consultation was made, and the prayer uttered, by means of the priest. The alternative conditions here described have often been referred to as illustrating the doctrine of God's foreknowledge and preordination of events.

14-18. DAVID ESCAPES TO ZIPH. **14, 15. David abode in the wilderness . . . of Ziph**—A mountainous and sequestered region was generally called a wilderness, and took its name from some large town in the district. Two miles southeast of Hebron, and in the midst of a level plain, is Tell-ziph, an isolated and conical hillock, about 100 feet high, probably the acropolis [VAN DE VELDE], or the ruins [ROBINSON] of the ancient city of Ziph, from which the surrounding wilderness was called. It seems, anciently, to have been covered by an extensive woods. The country has for centuries lost its woods and forests, owing to the devastations caused by man.

16. Jonathan went to David into the wood, and strengthened his hand in God—by the recollection of their mutual covenant. What a victory over natural feelings and lower considerations must the faith of Jonathan have won, before he could seek such an interview and give utterance to such sentiments!

ADAM CLARKE

2. *Therefore David enquired of the Lord*. In what way David made this inquiry we are not told, but it was proably by means of Abiathar; and therefore I think, with Houbigant, that the sixth verse should be read immediately after the first. *The Lord said . . . Go, and smite*. He might now go with confidence, being assured of success.

4. *David enquired of the Lord yet again*. This was to satisfy his men, who made the strong objections mentioned in the preceding verse.

5. *Brought away their cattle*. The forage and spoil which the Philistines had taken, driving the country before them round about Keilah.

8. *Saul called all the people together*. That is, all the people of that region or district, that they might scour the country, and hunt out David from all his haunts.

9. *Bring hither the ephod*. It seems as if David himself, clothed with the ephod, had consulted the Lord; vv. 10-12 contain the words of the consultation and the Lord's answer.

14. *Wilderness of Ziph*. Ziph was a city in the southern part of Judea, not far from Carmel.

MATTHEW HENRY

was not in a capacity of doing anything to strengthen him, but he assured him God would. 2. As a self-denying friend, he took a pleasure in the prospect of David's advancement to that honour which was his own birthright, *v.* 17. "Thou shalt live to be king, and I shall think it preferment enough to be next thee, near thee, though under thee, and will never pretend to be a rival with thee." 3. As a constant friend, he renewed his league of friendship with him, *v.* 18. True love takes delight in repeating its engagements. Our covenant with God should be often renewed, and therein our communion with him kept up. David and Jonathan now parted, and never came together again in this world.

Verses 19–29

1. The Ziphites offer their service to Saul, to betray David to him, *v.* 19, 20. He was sheltering himself in the wilderness of Ziph (*v.* 14, 15), putting the more confidence in the people of that country because they were of his own tribe. But, to ingratiate themselves with Saul, they went to him, and not only informed him where David quartered (*v.* 19), but invited him to come into their country and promised to deliver him into his hand, *v.* 20. 2. Saul thankfully receives their information, and gladly lays hold of the opportunity of hunting David in their wilderness. He likewise insinuates the little concern that the generality of his people showed for him. "You have compassion on me, which others have not." It was strange that Saul did not go down with them immediately, but the Ziphites had laid their spies upon all the places where he was likely to be discovered, and therefore Saul thought himself sure of his prey. 3. The imminent peril that David was now brought into. Upon intelligence that the Ziphites had betrayed him, he retired from the hill of Hachilah to the wilderness of Maon (*v.* 24), and at this time he penned the 54th Psalm, as appears by the title, wherein he calls the Ziphites *strangers*, though they were Israelites, because they used him barbarously; but he puts himself under the divine protection: "*Behold, God is my helper*, and then all shall be well." Saul pursued him closely (*v.* 25), till he came so near him that there was but a mountain between them (*v.* 26), David and his men on one side of the mountain flying and Saul and his men on the other side pursuing. But this mountain was an emblem of the divine Providence coming between David and the destroyer, like the pillar of cloud between the Israelites and the Egyptians. David was concealed by this mountain and Saul confounded by it. Saul hoped with his numerous forces to enclose David, but the ground did not prove convenient for his design, and so it failed. A new name was given to the place in remembrance of this (*v.* 28): *Selah-hammahlekoth—the rock of division*, because it divided between Saul and David. 4. The deliverance of David out of this danger. Providence gave Saul a diversion, when he was just ready to lay hold of David; notice was brought him that the Philistines were *invading the land* (*v.* 27). He found himself under a necessity of *going against the Philistines* (*v.* 28), and by this means David was delivered. As this Saul was diverted, so another Saul was converted, just then when he was *breathing out threatenings and slaughter against the saints of the Lord*, Acts. ix. 1. 5. David having thus escaped, took shelter in some natural fortresses, which he found in the wilderness of En-gedi, *v.* 29.

JAMIESON, FAUSSET, BROWN

To talk with calm and assured confidence of himself and family being superseded by the man who was his friend by the bonds of a holy and solemn covenant, could only have been done by one who, superior to all views of worldly policy, looked at the course of things in the spirit and through the principles of that theocracy which acknowledged God as the only and supreme Sovereign of Israel. Neither history nor fiction depicts the movements of a friendship purer, nobler, and more self-denying than Jonathan's!

19-29. SAUL PURSUES HIM. **19-23. Then came up the Ziphites to Saul, saying, Doth not David hide himself with us?**—From the tell of Ziph a panorama of the whole surrounding district is to be seen. No wonder, then, that the Ziphites saw David and his men passing to and fro in the mountains of the wilderness. Spying him at a distance when he ventured to show himself on the hill of Hachilah, "on the right hand of the wilderness," i.e., the south side of Ziph, they sent in haste to Saul, to tell him of the lurking place of his enemy [VAN DE VELDE].

25. David . . . came down into a rock, and abode in the wilderness of Maon—Tell Main, the hillock on which was situated the ancient Maon (Josh. 15:55), and from which the adjoining wilderness took its name, is one mile north, ten east from Carmel. The mountain plateau seems here to end. It is true the summit ridge of the southern hills runs out a long way further towards the southwest; but towards the southeast the ground sinks more and more down to a tableland of a lower level, which is called "the plain to the right hand [i.e., to the south] of the wilderness" [VAN DE VELDE].

29. David went up from thence, and dwelt in strongholds at En-gedi—i.e., "the spring of the wild goats or gazelles"—a name given to it from the vast number of ibexes or Syrian chamois which inhabit these cliffs on the western shore of the Dead Sea (Josh. 15:62). It is now called Ain Jiddy. On all sides the country is full of caverns, which might then serve as lurking places for David and his men, as they do for outlaws at the present day [ROBINSON].

ADAM CLARKE

KEIL–DELITZSCH:

The *treachery of the Ziphites* forms a striking contrast to Jonathan's treatment of David. They went up to Gibeah to betray to Saul the fact that David was concealed in the wood upon their mountain heights, and indeed "upon the hill Hachilah, which lies to the south of the waste." The hill of *Ziph* is a flattened hill standing by itself, of about a hundred feet in height. "There is no spot from which you can obtain a better view of David's wanderings backwards and forwards in the desert than from the hill of *Ziph*, which affords a true panorama. The Ziphites could see David and his men moving to and fro in mountains of the desert of *Ziph*, and could also perceive how he showed himself in the distance upon the hill *Hachilah* on the south side of *Ziph* (which lies to the right by the desert); whereupon they sent as quickly as possible to Saul, and betrayed to him the hiding-place of his enemy."

—Commentary on the Old Testament

25. *The wilderness of Maon.* Maon was a mountainous district in the most southern parts of Judah.

28. *They called that place Sela-hammahlekoth.* That is, "the rock of divisions"; because, says the Targum, "the heart of the king was divided to go hither and thither." Here Saul was obliged to separate himself from David, in order to go and oppose the invading Philistines.

29. *Strong holds at En-gedi.* En-gedi was situated near to the western coast of the Dead Sea, not far from Jeshimon. It literally signifies the "kid's well," and was celebrated for its vineyards, Cant. i. 14. It was also celebrated for its balm. It is reported to be a mountainous territory, filled with caverns; and consequently proper for David in his present circumstances.

MATTHEW HENRY — CHAPTER 24

Verses 1–8

I. Saul renews his pursuit of David, *v.* 1, 2. Hearing that he is *in the wilderness of En-gedi*, he draws out 3,000 choice men, and goes in pursuit of him *upon the rocks of the wild goats*.

II. Providence brings Saul alone into the same cave wherein David and his men had hidden themselves, *v.* 3. In those countries there were very large caves in the sides of the rocks or mountains, partly natural, but probably much enlarged by art for the sheltering of sheep from the heat of the sun; hence we read of places where the flocks did rest at noon (Cant. i. 7), and this cave seems to be spoken of as one of the sheep-cotes. Saul, passing by, turned in himself alone. He turned aside to *cover his feet*, that is, to sleep awhile.

III. David's servants stir him up to kill Saul now that he has so fair an opportunity to do it, *v.* 4. Saul now lay at his mercy. How apt we are to misunderstand, 1. The promises of God. God had assured David that he would deliver him from Saul, and his men interpret this as a warrant to destroy Saul. 2. The providences of God. Because it was now in his power to kill him, they concluded he might lawfully do it.

JAMIESON, FAUSSET, BROWN — CHAPTER 24

Vss. 1-7. DAVID IN A CAVE AT EN-GEDI CUTS OFF SAUL'S SKIRT, BUT SPARES HIS LIFE. **2. Saul . . . went . . . to seek David . . . upon the rocks of the wild goats**—Nothing but the blind infatuation of fiendish rage could have led the king to pursue his outlawed son-in-law among those craggy and perpendicular precipices, where were inaccessible hiding places. The large force he took with him seemed to give him every prospect of success. But the overruling providence of God frustrated all his vigilance. **3. he came to the sheepcotes**—most probably in the upper ridge of Wady Chareitun. There a large cave—I am quite disposed to say the cave—lies hardly five minutes to the east of the village ruin, on the south side of the wady. It is high upon the side of the calcareous rock, and it has undergone no change since David's time. The same narrow natural vaulting at the entrance; the same huge natural chamber in the rock, probably the place where Saul lay down to rest in the heat of the day; the same side vaults, too, where David and his men were concealed. There, accustomed to the obscurity of the cavern, they saw Saul enter, while,

ADAM CLARKE — CHAPTER 24

1. *Saul was returned.* It is very probable that it was only a small marauding party that had made an excursion in the Israelitish borders, and this invasion was soon suppressed.

2. *Rocks of the wild goats.* The original is variously understood. The Vulgate makes a paraphrase: "On the most precipitous rocks over which the ibexes alone can travel." The Targum: "the caverns of the rocks." The Septuagint make the original a proper name.

3. *The sheepcotes.* Caves in the rocks, in which it is common, even to the present time, for shepherds and their flocks to lodge. According to Strabo there are caverns in Syria one of which is capable of containing 4,000 men.

MATTHEW HENRY

IV. David *cut off the skirt of his robe*, but soon repented that he had done this because it was an affront to Saul's royal dignity.

V. He reasons strongly both with himself and with his servants against doing Saul any hurt. 1. He reasons with himself (*v.* 6): *The Lord forbid that I should do this thing.* He considered Saul now, not as his enemy but as God's anointed (that is, the person whom God had appointed to reign as long as he lived, and who, as such, was under the particular protection of the divine law). 2. He reasons with his servants: *He suffered them not to rise against Saul, v.* 7. Thus did he render good for evil and was herein both a type of Christ, who saved his persecutors, and an example to all Christians.

VI. He followed Saul out of the cave, and, though he would not take the opportunity to slay him, yet he wisely took the opportunity, if possible, to slay his enmity, by convincing him that he was not such a man as he took him for. 1. Even in showing his head now he testified that he had an honourable opinion of Saul. 2. His behaviour was very respectful: He *stooped with his face to the earth, and bowed himself.*

Verses 9–15

David's warm and pathetic speech to Saul to persuade him to be reconciled.

I. He calls him *father* (*v.* 11), for he was not only, as king, the father of his country, but he was, in particular, his father-in-law.

II. He lays the blame of his rage against him upon his evil counsellors: *Wherefore hearest thou men's words? v.* 9.

III. He solemnly protests his own innocence, and that he is far from designing any hurt or mischief to Saul: "*There is neither evil nor transgression in my hand, v.* 11. Perhaps it was about this time that David penned the seventh psalm, concerning the affair of Cush the Benjamite (that is, Saul, as some think).

IV. He produces undeniable evidence to prove the falsehood of the suggestion upon which Saul's malice against him was grounded. David was charged with seeking Saul's hurt: "*See*," says he, "*yea, see the skirt of thy robe, v.* 11. Had that been true of which I am accused, I should now have had thy head in my hand." *The Lord delivered thee*, very surprisingly, *to-day into my hand. Some bade me kill thee.* It was upon a good principle that he refused to do it; by the fear of God he was restrained from it. Such a happy command he had of himself that his nature, in the midst of the greatest provocation, was not suffered to rebel against his principles.

V. He declares it to be his fixed resolution never to be his own avenger: "*The Lord avenge me of thee*, that is, deliver me out of thy hand; but, whatever comes of it, *my hand shall not be upon thee*" (*v.* 12). Bad men will do bad things; according as men's principles and dispositions are, so will their actions be.

VI. He endeavours to convince Saul that as it was a bad thing, so it was a mean thing, for him to give chase to such an inconsiderable person as he was (*v.* 14): *Whom does the king of Israel pursue* with all this care and force? *A dead dog; a flea; one flea*, so it is in the Hebrew. It is below so great a king to enter the lists with one that is so unequal a match for him, one of his own servants, bred a poor shepherd, now an exile, neither able nor willing to make any resistance. What credit would it be to Saul to trample upon a dead dog? What pleasure could it be to him to hunt a flea, a single flea, which (as some have observed), if it be sought, is not easily found, if it be found, is not easily caught, and, if it be caught, is a poor prize, especially for a prince.

VII. He once and again appeals to God as the righteous Judge (*v.* 12 and *v.* 15): *The Lord judge between me and thee.*

Verses 16–22

I. Saul's penitent reply to David's speech. 1. He melted into tears. He speaks as one quite overcome with David's kindness: *Is this thy voice, my son David?* He *lifted up his voice and wept, v.* 16. 2. He ingenuously acknowledges David's integrity and his own iniquity (*v.* 17): *Thou art more righteous than I.* This fair confession was enough to prove David innocent (even his enemy himself being judge), but not enough to prove Saul himself a true penitent. 3. He prays God to recompense David for this his generous kindness to him. *The Lord reward thee good, v.* 19. 4. He prophesies his advancement to the throne (*v.* 20): I *know well that thou shalt surely be king.* He knew it before, by the promise Samuel had made him of it compared with the excellent spirit that appeared in David, which highly aggravated his sin and folly in persecuting him as he did. This acknow-

JAMIESON, FAUSSET, BROWN

blinded by the glare of the light outside, he saw nothing of him whom he so bitterly persecuted. **4-7. the men of David said . . . Behold the day of which the Lord said unto thee, Behold, I will deliver thine enemy into thine hand**—God had never made any promise of delivering Saul into David's hand; but, from the general and repeated promises of the kingdom to him, they concluded that the king's death was to be effected by taking advantage of some such opportunity as the present. David steadily opposed the urgent instigations of his followers to put an end to his and their troubles by the death of their persecutor (a revengeful heart would have followed their advice, but David rather wished to overcome evil with good, and heap coals of fire upon his head); he, however, cut off a fragment from the skirt of the royal robe. It is easy to imagine how this dialogue could be carried on and David's approach to the king's person could have been effected without arousing suspicion. The bustle and noise of Saul's military men and their beasts, the number of cells or divisions in these immense caverns (and some of them far interior) being enveloped in darkness, while every movement could be seen at the cave's mouth—the probability that the garment David cut from might have been a loose or upper cloak lying on the ground, and that Saul might have been asleep—these facts and presumptions will be sufficient to account for the incidents detailed.

8-15. He Urges Thereby His Innocency. **8. David also arose . . . and went out of the cave, and cried after Saul**—The closeness of the precipitous cliffs, though divided by deep wadies, and the transparent purity of the air enable a person standing on one rock to hear distinctly the words uttered by a speaker standing on another (Judg. 9:7).

The expostulation of David, followed by the visible tokens he furnished of his cherishing no evil design against either the person or the government of the king, even when he had the monarch in his power, smote the heart of Saul in a moment and disarmed him of his fell purpose of revenge.

He owned the justice of what David said, acknowledged his own guilt, and begged kindness to his house. He seems to have been naturally susceptible of strong, and, as in this instance, of good and grateful impressions. The improvement of his temper, indeed, was but transient—his language that of a man overwhelmed by the force of impetuous emotions and constrained to admire the conduct, and esteem the character, of one whom he hated and dreaded. But God overruled it for ensuring the present escape of David. Consider his language and behavior. This language —"a dead dog," "a flea," terms by which, like Eastern people, he strongly expressed a sense of his lowliness and the entire committal of his cause to Him who alone is the judge of human actions, and to whom vengeance belongs, his steady repulse of the vindictive counsels of his followers; the relentings of heart which he felt even for the apparent indignity he had done to the person of the Lord's anointed; and the respectful homage he paid the jealous tyrant who had set a price on his head—evince the magnanimity of a great and good man, and strikingly illustrate the spirit and energy of his prayer "when he was in the cave" (Ps. 142).

ADAM CLARKE

ALEXANDER MACLAREN:

We have the scene in the cave. The interior would be black as night to one looking inward with eyes fresh from the blinding glare of such sunlight upon limestone, but it would hold a glimmering twilight for one looking outward, with eyes accustomed to the gloom. David and his men, keeping close to the walls and hiding behind angles, might well be unobserved by Saul at the mouth, and probably never looking in at all. How vividly the whispered eagerness of the outcasts round David is reproduced! They think it would be "tempting Providence" to let such a chance slip. They put a religious varnish on their advice. It would be almost impious not to kill Saul, for here was the hand of God evidently fulfilling a prophecy! There may have been some unrecorded prediction of the sort which they seem to quote; but more probably they are only referring to David's designation to the crown, which they had come to know.

It never struck them as possible that it could "seem good" to a wise man not to cut his enemy's throat when he could do it without danger to himself. So they would watch David stealing down quietly to the place where the unconscious king was crouching, and getting close behind him, knife in hand. How disgusted they must have been when the blade, that flashed for a moment in the light at the cave's mouth, was not buried in Saul's great back, but only hacked off the end of his robe spread out behind him! No personal animosity was in David. However he had been driven to consort with outlaws, and to live a kind of freebooter's life, his natural sweetness was unspoiled, and was reinforced by solemn veneration for the sanctity of the Lord's anointing, which he reverenced all the more because he himself had received it.

—*Expositions of Holy Scripture*

13. *Wickedness proceedeth from the wicked.* This proverb may be thus understood: He that does a wicked act gives proof thereby that he is a wicked man.

14. *After a dead dog.* A term used among the Hebrews to signify the most sovereign contempt (see 2 Sam. xvi. 9). One utterly incapable of making the least resistance against Saul, and the troops of Israel. The same idea is expressed in the term *flea*. The Targum properly expresses both thus: "one who is weak, one who is contemptible."

19. *If a man find his enemy, will he let him go well away?* Or rather, "Will he send him in a good way?" But Houbigant translates the whole clause thus: "If a man, finding his enemy, send him by a good way, *the Lord will give him his reward.*" The words which are here put in italic are not in the Hebrew text, but they are found, at least in the sense, in the Septuagint, Syriac, and Arabic, and seem necessary to complete the sense. "Therefore," adds Saul, "the Lord will reward thee good for what thou hast done unto me."

20. *I know well that thou shalt surely be king.* Hebrew, "Reigning, thou shalt reign."

MATTHEW HENRY

ledgment which Saul made of David's incontestable title to the crown was a great encouragement to David himself and a support to his faith and hope. 5. He binds David with an oath hereafter to show the same tenderness of his seed and of his name as he had now shown of his person, *v.* 21. This oath he afterwards religiously observed: he supported Mephibosheth, and executed those as traitors that slew Ish-bosheth.

II. Their parting in peace. 1. Saul, for the present, desisted from the persecution. He went home convinced, but not converted; ashamed of his envy of David, yet retaining in his breast that root of bitterness; vexed that, when at last he had found David, he could not at that time find in his heart to destroy him, as he had designed. 2. David continued to shift for his own safety. He knew Saul too well to trust him, and therefore *got him up into the hold.*

CHAPTER 25

Verse 1

A short account of Samuel's death and burial. 1. Though he was a great man he spent the latter end of his days in retirement and obscurity because Israel had rejected him, for which God thus justly chastised them. 2. Though he was a firm friend to David, for which Saul hated him, yet he died in peace even in the worst of the days of the tyranny of Saul. Though Saul loved him not, yet he feared him, as Herod did John, and feared the people, for all knew him to be a prophet. 3. All Israel lamented him. His personal merits commanded this honour to be done him at his death. His former services to the public, when he judged Israel, made this respect to his name and memory a just debt. The sons of the prophets had lost the founder of their colleges. But Samuel was a constant intercessor for Israel, *ch.* xii. 23. If he go, they part with the best friend they have. 4. They buried him, not in the school of the prophets at Naioth, but in his own house at Ramah, where he was born. 5. David, hereupon, went down to the wilderness of Paran, retiring perhaps to mourn for the death of Samuel. Now that he had lost so good a friend, he apprehended his danger to be greater than ever, and therefore withdrew to a wilderness out of the limits of the land of Israel; and now it was that he *dwelt in the tents of Kedar*, Ps. cxx. 5.

Verses 2–11

The story of Nabal.

I. A short account of a man we should never have heard of if there had not happened some communication between him and David. 1. His name: *Nabal—a fool*; so it signifies. 2. His family: He was of the house of Caleb and inherited Caleb's estate; for Maon and Carmel lay near Hebron, which was given to Caleb (Josh. xv. 54, 55; xiv. 14), but he was far from inheriting his virtues. The LXX, and some other ancient versions, read it: He was a dogged man, of a currish disposition, surly and snappish, and always snarling. 3. His wealth: He was very great, that is, very rich (for riches make men look great in the eye of the world), otherwise, to one that takes his measures aright, he really looked very mean. 4. His wife—Abigail, a woman of great understanding. Her name signifies, *the joy of her father*; yet he could not promise himself much joy of her when he married her to such a husband, enquiring more after his wealth than after his wisdom. Many a child is thrown away upon a heap of worldly wealth, married to that, and to nothing else that is desirable. Many an Abigail is tied to a Nabal. 5. His character. He had no sense either of honour or honesty; not of honour, for he was churlish, cross, and ill-humoured; not of honesty, for he was evil in his doings, hard and oppressive.

II. David's humble request to him, that he would send him some victuals for himself and his men.

1. David, it seems, was in such distress that he would be glad to be beholden to him, and did in effect come a begging to his door.

2. He chose a good time to send to Nabal, when he had many hands employed about him in shearing his sheep, for whom he was to make a plentiful entertainment, so that good cheer was stirring. It was usual to make feasts at their sheep-shearings, as appears by Absalom's feast on that occasion (2 Sam. xiii. 24).

3. David ordered his men to deliver their message to him with a great deal of courtesy and respect: "*Go to Nabal, and greet him in my name*", *v.* 5. *Thus shall you say to him that liveth*: "*Peace be to thee*, all good both to soul and body. *Peace be to thy house and to all that thou hast*." He bids them call him his *son David* (*v.* 8), intimating that David honoured him as a father.

4. He pleaded the kindness which Nabal's shep-

JAMIESON, FAUSSET, BROWN

CHAPTER 25

Vss. 1-9. Samuel Dies. **1. Samuel died**—After a long life of piety and public usefulness, he left behind him a reputation which ranks him among the greatest of Scripture worthies. **buried him in his house at Ramah**—i.e., his own mausoleum. The Hebrews took as great care to provide sepulchers anciently as people do in the East still, where every respectable family has its own house of the dead. Often this is in a little detached garden, containing a small stone building (where there is no rock), resembling a house, which is called the sepulcher of the family—it has neither door nor window. **David arose, and went down to the wilderness of Paran**—This removal had probably no connection with the prophet's death; but was probably occasioned by the necessity of seeking provision for his numerous followers. **the wilderness of Paran**—stretching from Sinai to the borders of Palestine in the southern territories of Judea. Like other wildernesses, it presented large tracts of natural pasture, to which the people sent their cattle at the grazing season, but where they were liable to constant and heavy depredations by prowling Arabs. David and his men earned their subsistence by making reprisals on the cattle of these freebooting Ishmaelites; and, frequently for their useful services, they obtained voluntary tokens of acknowledgment from the peaceful inhabitants.

2. in Carmel—now **Kurmul.** The district takes its name from this town, now a mass of ruins; and about a mile from it is Tell Main, the hillock on which stood ancient Maon. **the man was very great**—His property consisted in cattle, and he was considered wealthy, according to the ideas of that age. **3. he was of the house of Caleb**—of course, of the same tribe with David himself; but many versions consider Caleb (dog) not as a proper, but a common noun, and render it, "he was snappish as a dog."

4-9. Nabal did shear his sheep, and David sent out ten young men . . .—David and his men lurked in these deserts. associating with the herdsmen and shepherds of Nabal and others and doing them good offices, probably in return for information and supplies obtained through them. Hence when Nabal held his annual sheepshearing in Carmel, David felt himself entitled to share in the festival and sent a message, recounting his own services and asking for a present. "In all these particulars we were deeply struck with the truth and strength of the biblical description of manners and customs almost identically the same as they exist at the present day. On such a festive occasion, near a town or village, even in our own time, an Arab sheik of the neighboring desert would hardly fail to put in a word either in person or by message; and his message, both in

ADAM CLARKE

He knew this before, and yet he continued to pursue David with the most deadly hatred.

21. *Swear now.* Saul knew that an oath would bind David, though it was insufficient to bind himself (see chap. xix. 6). He had sworn to his son Jonathan that David should not be slain, and yet sought by all means in his power to destroy him!

22. *David and his men gat them up unto the hold.* "Went up to Mizpeh," according to the Syriac and Arabic. David could not trust Saul with his life.

CHAPTER 25

1. *And Samuel died.* Samuel lived, as is supposed, about ninety-eight years. *Buried him in his house.* Probably this means, not his dwelling house, but the house or tomb he had made for his sepulchure; and thus the Syriac and Arabic seem to have understood it.

David . . . went down to the wilderness of Paran. This was either on the confines of Judea or in the Arabia Petraea, between the mountains of Judah and Mount Sinai; it is evident from the history that it was not far from Carmel, on the south confines of Judah.

3. *The name of the man was Nabal.* The word *nabal* signifies to be "foolish, base, or villainous." *The name of his wife Abigail.* The "joy or exultation of my father." *Of the house of Caleb. Vehu Chalibi*, "He was a Calebite." But as the word *caleb* signifies "a dog," the Septuagint have understood it as implying a man of a canine disposition, and translate it thus, "He was a doggish man." It is understood in the same way by the Syriac and Arabic.

6. *Peace be both to thee.* This is the ancient form of sending greetings to a friend: "Peace to thee, peace to thy household, and peace to all that thou hast." That is, "May both thyself, thy family, and all that pertain unto thee, be in continual prosperity!"

MATTHEW HENRY

herds had received from David and his men. (1) They did not hurt them themselves, were not a terror to them, nor took any of the lambs out of the flock. Yet, considering the character of David's men, men in distress, and debt, and discontented, and the scarcity of provisions in his camp, it was not without a great deal of care and good management that they were kept from plundering. (2) They protected them from being hurt by others. Nabal's servants, to whom he appealed, went further (*v.* 16): *They were a wall unto us, both by night and day.* David's soldiers were a guard to Nabal's shepherds when the bands of the *Philistines robbed the threshing-floors* (*ch.* xxiii. 1) and would have robbed the sheepfolds. From those plunderers Nabal's flocks were protected by David's care, and therefore he says, *Let us find favour in thy eyes.*

5. He was very modest in his request. "Give whatsoever comes to thy hand, and we will be thankful for it." David demands not what he wanted as a debt, either by way of tribute as he was a king, or by way of contribution as he was a general, but asks it as a boon to a friend, that was his humble servant.

III. Nabal's churlish answer to this modest petition, *v.* 10, 11. Nabal not only denied him, but abused him. 1. He speaks scornfully of David as an insignificant man, not worth taking notice of. The Philistines could say of him, *This is* David *the king of the land,* that *slew his ten thousands* (*ch.* xxi. 11), yet Nabal his near neighbour, and one of the same tribe, affects not to know him, or not to know him to be a man of any merit or distinction: *Who is David? And who is the son of Jesse?* 2. He upbraids him with his present distress, and takes occasion from it to represent him as a bad man, that was fitter to be set in the stocks for a vagrant than to have any kindness shown him. How naturally does he speak the churlish clownish language of those that hate to give alms! David was reduced to this distress, not by any fault but purely by the good services he had done to his country and the honours which his God had put upon him; and yet he was represented as a fugitive and runagate. 3. He insists much upon the property he had in the provisions of his table, and will by no means admit anybody to share in them. We mistake if we think we are absolute lords of what we have and may do what we please with it. No, we are but stewards, and must use it as we are directed, remembering it is not our own, but his that entrusted us with it.

Verses 12–17

I. The report made to David of the abuse Nabal had given to his messengers (*v.* 12): *They turned their way.* They showed their displeasure by breaking off abruptly from such a churl. Christ's servants, when they are thus abused, must leave it to him to plead his own cause and wait till he appear in it.

II. David's hasty resolution hereupon. He girded on his sword, and ordered his men to do so too. 1. He repented of the kindness he had done to Nabal, and looked upon it as thrown away upon him. He said, "*Surely in vain have I kept all that this fellow hath in the wilderness.*" 2. He determined to destroy Nabal and all that belonged to him, *v.* 22. Here David did not act like himself. His resolution was bloody, to cut off all the males of Nabal's house. The ratification of his resolution was passionate: *So, and more also do God to the enemies of David. Is this thy voice, O David?* Is this he who but the other day spared him who sought his life, and yet now will not spare anything that belongs to him who has only put an affront upon his messengers? He who at other times used to be calm and considerate is now put into such a heat by a few hard words that nothing will atone for them but the blood of a whole family. What are the best of men, when God leaves them to themselves? From Nabal he expected kindness, and therefore the affront he gave him was a surprise to him, found him off his guard, and, by a sudden and unexpected attack, put him for the present into disorder. What need have we to pray, *Lord, lead us not into temptation!*

III. The account given of this matter to Abigail by one of the servants, who was more considerate than the rest, *v.* 14. Abigail, being a woman of good understanding, took cognizance of the matter, even from her servant, who, 1. Did David justice in commending him and his men for their civility to Nabal's shepherds, *v.* 15, 16. "The men were very good to us, and, though they were themselves exposed, yet they protected us and were a wall unto us." 2. He did Nabal no wrong in condemning him for his rudeness to David's messengers: *He railed on them* (*v.* 14), *he flew upon them* (so the word is) with an intolerable rage; "for," say they, "it is his usual practice," *v.* 17. 3. He did Abigail and the whole

JAMIESON, FAUSSET, BROWN

form and substance, would be only a transcript of that of David" [ROBINSON].

10-13. THE CHURLISH ANSWER PROVOKES HIM. **10-12. Nabal answered David's servants . . . Who is David? . . .**—Nabal's answer seems to indicate that the country was at the time in a loose and disorderly state. David's own good conduct, however, as well as the important services rendered by him and his men, were readily attested by Nabal's servants.

The preparations of David to chastise his insolent language and ungrateful requital are exactly what would be done in the present day by Arab chiefs, who protect the cattle of the large and wealthy sheep-masters from the attacks of the marauding border tribes or wild beasts. Their protection creates a claim for some kind of tribute, in the shape of supplies of food and necessaries, which is usually given with great good-will and gratitude; but when withheld, is enforced as a right. Nabal's refusal, therefore, was a violation of the established usages of the place. **13. two hundred men abode by the stuff**—This addition to his followers was made after his return into Judah (see on ch. 22:2).

14-35. ABIGAIL PACIFIES HIM. **14-18. Then Abigail made haste**—The prudence and address of Nabal's wife were the means of saving him and family from utter destruction.

ADAM CLARKE

7. *Thy shepherds which were with us, we hurt them not.* It is most evident that David had a claim upon Nabal, for very essential services performed to his herdmen at Carmel. He not only did them no hurt, and took none of their flocks for the supply of his necessities, but he protected them from the rapacity of others. "They were a wall unto us," said Nabal's servants, "both by night and day."

8. *Whatsoever cometh to thine hand.* As you are making a great feast for your servants, and I and my men, as having essentially served you, would naturally come in for a share were we present, send a portion by my ten young men for me and my men, that we also may rejoice with you. Certainly this was a very reasonable and a very modest request.

10. *Who is David?* Nabal's answer shows the surliness of his disposition. It was unjust to refuse so reasonable a request, and the manner of the refusal was highly insulting. It is true what his own servants said of him, "He is such a son of Belial, that a man cannot speak to him," v. 17.

F. B. MEYER:

A rich man's churlishness. This Carmel was a city in the mountains of Judah, ten miles south of Hebron (Josh. 15:55). Though a descendant of Caleb, Nebal had none of that hero's spirit. He had great wealth, but little wit. Today the Arab tribe which guards the shepherd or caravan, or restrains itself from plundering, expects some acknowledgment. It was unfair that the rich sheep master should take all the advantage and make no return and worse, cap injustice with a coarse jest. Nabal's shepherds were quite explicit in their testimony to the benefits they had received (vv. 7, 15, 16). His jibes and churlishness justified the general estimate entertained by those who knew him best.

For David to take the sword to avenge the insult stands out in striking contrast to him who "when he was reviled, reviled not again." Revenge for an insult where one has personally suffered has no place in Christ's teaching, and is separated by a whole heaven from the magisterial use of the sword referred to in Rom. 13:4. In later years David must have been very thankful for the interposition, through Abigail, of God's grace that arrested his hand.

—*Bible Commentary*

MATTHEW HENRY

family a kindness in making her sensible what was likely to be the consequence. Something therefore must be done to pacify David.

Verses 18–31

An account of Abigail's prudent management for the preserving of her husband and family from the destruction that was just coming upon them. Wisdom in such a case as this was better than weapons of war. 1. It was her wisdom that what she did she did quickly, and without delay. Those that desire conditions of peace must send when the enemy is yet a great way off, Luke xiv. 32. 2. It was her wisdom that what she did she did herself, being a woman of great prudence and very happy address.

Abigail must endeavour to atone for Nabal's faults.

I. By a most generous present, Abigail atones for his denial of their request. Abigail prepares the very best the house afforded and abundance of it (*v.* 18), not only *bread* and *flesh*, but *raisins* and *figs*. Nabal grudged them *water*, but she took *two bottles* (*casks* or *rundlets*) *of wine*, loaded her asses with these provisions, and sent them before. Abigail not only lawfully, but laudably, disposed of all these goods of her husband's without his knowledge, because it was for the necessary defence of him and his family, which otherwise would have been inevitably ruined. Husbands and wives, for their common good and benefit, have a joint-interest in their worldly possessions; but if either waste, or unduly spend in any way, it is a robbing of the other.

II. By a most obliging demeanour, and charming speech, she atones for the abusive language which Nabal had given them. She met David upon the march, big with resentment, and meditating the destruction of Nabal (*v.* 20); but with all possible expressions of complaisance and respect she humbly begs his favour, and solicits him to pass by the offence.

1. She speaks to him all along with deference and respect. She does not upbraid him with the heat of his passion, but endeavours to bring him to a better temper.

2. She takes the blame of the ill-treatment of his messengers upon herself: "*Upon me, my lord, upon me, let this iniquity be*," *v.* 24. Abigail here discovered the sincerity and strength of her conjugal affection and concern for her family: whatever Nabal was, he was her husband.

3. She excuses her husband's fault by imputing it to his natural weakness and want of understanding (*v.* 25). He is simple, but not spiteful. Forgive him, for he knows not what he does.

4. She pleads her own ignorance of the matter: "*I saw not the young men*, else they should have had a better answer."

The very mentioning of what he was about to do, to shed blood and to avenge himself, was enough to work upon such a tender gracious spirit as David had; and it should seem, by his reply (*v.* 33), that it affected him. She applauds David for the good services he had done against the common enemies of his country. "*My lord fighteth the battles of the Lord* against the Philistines, and therefore he will leave it to God to fight his battles against those that affront him," *v.* 28. She foretells the glorious issue of his present troubles. She speaks with assurance, (1) That God would keep him safe: *The soul of my lord shall be bound in the bundle of life with the Lord thy God*, that is, God shall *hold thy soul in life* (as the expression is, Ps. lxvi. 9) as we hold those things which are bundled up or which are precious to us, Ps. cxvi. 15. The Jews understand this not only of the *life that now is*, but of that *which is to come*, and therefore use it commonly as an inscription on their gravestones. "Here we have laid the body, but trust that *the soul is bound up in the bundle of life, with the Lord our God*." (2) That God would make him victorious over his enemies. "*The Lord will certainly make my lord a sure house*, therefore *forgive this trespass*." She is confident that if he pass by the offence it will afterwards be no grief to him; but, on the contrary, it would yield him unspeakable satisfaction that his wisdom and grace had got the better of his passion.

Verses 32–35

As an ear-ring of gold, and an ornament of fine gold, so is a wise reprover upon an obedient ear, Prov. xxv. 12. Abigail was a wise reprover of David's passion, and he gave an obedient ear to the reproof, according to his own principle (Ps. cxli. 5): *Let the righteous smite me, it shall be a kindness*.

I. David gives God thanks for sending him this happy check to a sinful way (*v.* 32): *Blessed be the Lord God of Israel, who sent thee this day to meet me*. God is to be acknowledged in all the kindnesses that our friends do us either for soul or body.

JAMIESON, FAUSSET, BROWN

She acknowledged the demand of her formidable neighbors; but justly considering, that to atone for the insolence of her husband, a greater degree of liberality had become necessary, she collected a large amount of food, accompanying it with the most valued products of the country. **bottles**—goatskins, capable of holding a great quantity. **parched corn**—It was customary to eat parched corn when it was fully grown, but not ripe. **19. she said unto her servants, Go on before me; behold, I come after you**—People in the East always try to produce an effect by their presents, loading on several beasts what might be easily carried by one, and bringing them forward, article by article, in succession. Abigail not only sent her servants in this way, but resolved to go in person, following her present, as is commonly done, to watch the impression which her munificence would produce. **23. she hasted, and lighted off the ass, and fell before David on her face**—Dismounting in presence of a superior is the highest token of respect that can be given; and it is still an essential act of homage to the great. Accompanying this act of courtesy with the lowest form of prostration, she not only by her attitude, but her language, made the fullest amends for the disrespect shown by her husband, as well as paid the fullest tribute of respect to the character and claims of David.

25. Nabal—signifying *fool*, gave pertinence to his wife's remark. **26. let thine enemies . . . be as Nabal**—be as foolish and contemptible as he.

29. the soul of my lord shall be bound in the bundle of life with the Lord thy God—An Orientalism, expressing the perfect security of David's life from all the assaults of his enemies, under the protecting shield of Providence, who had destined him for high things.

32-35. David said to Abigail, Blessed be the Lord—Transported by passion and blinded by revenge, he was on the eve of perpetrating a great injury.

ADAM CLARKE

18. *Took two hundred loaves*. The Eastern bread is ordinarily both thin and small, and answers to our cakes. *Two bottles of wine*. That is, two goatskins full. The hide is pulled off the animal without ripping up; the places where the legs, etc., were are sewed up, and then the skin appears one large bag. This is properly the Scripture and Eastern "bottle." *Five sheep*. Not one sheep to one hundred men. *Clusters of raisins*. Raisins dried in the sun. *Cakes of figs*. Figs cured, and then pressed together.

Now all this provision was a matter of little worth, and, had it been granted in the first instance, it would have perfectly satisfied David, and secured the good offices of him and his men. Abigail showed both her wisdom and prudence in making this provision. Out of 3,000 sheep Nabal could not have missed 5; and as this claim was made only in the time of sheep-shearing, it could not have been made more than once in the year; and it certainly was a small price for such important services.

20. *She came down . . . and . . . David . . . came down*. David was coming down Mount Paran; Abigail was coming down from Carmel.

22. *So and more also do God*. Nothing can justify this part of David's conduct. Whatever his provocation might have been, he had suffered, properly speaking, no wrongs; and his resolution to cut off a whole innocent family, because Nabal had acted ungenerously towards him, was abominable and cruel, not to say diabolic. *Any that pisseth against the wall*. This expression certainly means either men or dogs, and should be thus translated, "if I leave any male."

29. *Shall be bound in the bundle of life*. Thy life shall be precious in the sight of the Lord. *Them shall he sling out*. Far from being bound and kept together in union with the Fountain of life, He will cast them off from himself as a stone is cast out from a sling. This betokens both force and violence.

MATTHEW HENRY

II. He gives Abigail thanks for interposing so opportunely between him and the mischief he was about to do: *Blessed be thy advice, and blessed be thou, v.* 33.

III. He seems very apprehensive of the great danger he was in, which magnified the mercy of his deliverance. He speaks of the sin as very great. He was coming to shed blood, a sin of which when in his right mind he had a great horror, witness his prayer, *Deliver me from blood-guiltiness*.

IV. He dismissed her with an answer of peace, *v.* 35. He does, in effect, own himself overcome by her eloquence: "*I have hearkened to thy voice*, and will not prosecute the intended revenge, for I *have accepted thy person*, am well pleased with thee and what thou hast said."

Verses 36–44

We are now to attend Nabal's funeral and Abigail's wedding.

I. Nabal's funeral.

1. *Nabal dead drunk, v.* 36. Abigail came home, and, it should seem, he had so many people and so much plenty about him that he neither missed her nor the provisions she took to David. *He was very drunk*, a sign he was *Nabal, a fool*, that could not use his plenty without abusing it, could not be pleasant with his friends without making a beast of himself. There is not a surer sign that a man has but little wisdom, not a surer way to ruin the little he has, than drinking to excess. Nabal, that never thought he could bestow too little in charity, never thought he could bestow too much in luxury.

2. Nabal again dead with melancholy, *v.* 37. Next morning, when he had come to himself a little, his wife told him how near to destruction he had brought himself and his family by his own rudeness, and with what difficulty she had interposed to prevent it; and, upon this *his heart died within him and he became as a stone*. He grew sullen, and said little, ashamed of his own folly.

3. Nabal, at last, dead indeed: *About ten days after*, when he had been kept so long under this pressure and pain, *the Lord smote him that he died* (*v.* 38).

II. Abigail's wedding. David was charmed with the beauty of her person, and the uncommon prudence of her conduct and address. He courted by proxy, his affairs, perhaps, not permitting him to come himself. She received the address with great modesty and humility (*v.* 41), reckoning herself unworthy of the honour. She agreed to the proposal, went with his messengers, took a retinue with her agreeable to her quality, and *she became his wife, v.* 42. She married him in faith, not questioning but that, though now he had not a house of his own, yet God's promise to him would at length be fulfilled.

Lastly, On this occasion we have some account of David's wives. 1. One that he had lost before he married Abigail, Michal, Saul's daughter, his first, and the wife of his youth, to whom he would have been constant if she would have been so to him, but Saul had given her to another (*v.* 44), in token of his displeasure against him and disclaiming the relation of a father-in-law to him. 2. Another that he married besides Abigail (*v.* 43), and, as should seem, before her. for she is named first, *ch.* xxvii. 3. David was carried away by the corrupt custom of those times. When David could not keep his first wife he thought that would excuse him if he did not keep to his second. But we deceive ourselves if we think to make others' faults a cloak for our own.

JAMIESON, FAUSSET, BROWN

Doubtless, the timely appearance and prudent address of Abigail were greatly instrumental in changing his purpose. At all events, it was the means of opening his eyes to the moral character of the course on which he had been impetuously rushing; and in accepting her present, he speaks with lively satisfaction as well as gratitude to Abigail, for having relieved him from bloodshed.

36-44. NABAL'S DEATH. **36. he held a feast in his house, like the feast of a king**—The sheepshearing season was always a very joyous occasion. Masters usually entertained their shepherds; and even Nabal, though of a most niggardly disposition, prepared festivities on a scale of sumptuous liberality. The modern Arabs celebrate the season with similar hilarity.

37, 38. in the morning . . . his wife had told him these things, that his heart died within him—He probably fainted from horror at the perilous situation in which he had unconsciously placed himself; and such a shock had been given him by the fright to his whole system, that he rapidly pined and died.

39-42. the Lord hath returned the wickedness of Nabal upon his own head—If this was an expression of pleasure, and David's vindictive feelings were gratified by the intelligence of Nabal's death, it was an instance of human infirmity which we may lament; but perhaps he referred to the unmerited reproach (vss. 10, 11), and the contempt of God implied in it. **David sent and communed with Abigail, to take her to wife**—This unceremonious proceeding was quite in the style of Eastern monarchs, who no sooner take a fancy for a lady than they despatch a messenger to intimate their royal wishes that she should henceforth reside in the palace; and her duty is implicitly to obey. David's conduct shows that the manners of the Eastern nations were already imitated by the great men in Israel; and that the morality of the times which God permitted, gave its sanction to the practice of polygamy. His marriage with Abigail brought him a rich estate. **44. Michal**—By the unchallengeable will of her father, she who was David's wife was given to another. But she returned and sustained the character of his wife when he ascended the throne.

ADAM CLARKE

KEIL–DELITZSCH:

Verse 37. Then, "when the wine had gone from Nabal," i.e., when he had become sober, she related the matter to him; whereat he was so terrified that he was smitten with a stroke. This is the meaning of the words, "his heart died within him, and it became as stone." The cause of it was not his anger at the loss he had sustained, or merely his alarm at the danger to which he had been exposed, and which he did not believe to be over yet, but also his vexation that his wife should have made him humble himself in such a manner; for he is described as a hard, i.e., an unbending, self-willed man.

Verse 38. About ten days later "the Lord smote him so that he died," i.e., the Lord put an end to his life by a second stroke.

—*Commentary on the Old Testament*

37. *His heart died within him, and he became as a stone.* He was thunderstruck, and was so terrified at the apprehension of what he had escaped that the fear overcame his mind, he became insensible to all things around him, probably refused all kinds of nourishment, and died in ten days.

39. *To take her to him to wife.* It is likely that he had heard before this that Saul, to cut off all his pretensions to the throne, had married Michal to Phalti; and this justified David in taking Abigail or any other woman; and, according to the then custom, it was not unlawful for David to take several wives. By his marriage with Abigail it is probable he became possessed of all Nabal's property in Carmel and Maon.

43. *David also took Ahinoam.* Many think that this was his wife before he took Abigail; she is always mentioned first in the list of his wives and she was the mother of his eldest son, Ammon.

44. *Phalti.* Called also Phaltiel, 2 Sam. iii. 15. *Of Gallim.* Probably a city or town in the tribe of Benjamin; see Isa. x. 30. It is likely therefore that Saul chose this man because he was of his own tribe.

MATTHEW HENRY — CHAPTER 26

Verses 1–5

1. Saul gets information of David's movements and acts offensively. The Ziphites came to him and told him where David now was, in the same place where he was when they formerly betrayed him, *ch.* xxiii. 19. For aught we know, Saul would have continued in the same good mind that he was in (*ch.* xxiv. 17), and would not have given David this fresh trouble, if the Ziphites had not put him on. Saul readily caught at the information, and went down with an army to the place where David hid himself, *v.* 2.

2. David gets information of Saul's movements and acts defensively. He sought only his own safety, not Saul's ruin; therefore he *abode in the wilderness* (*v.* 3), curbing the bravery of his own spirit by a silent retirement, showing more true valour than he could have done by an irregular resistance. (1) He had spies who informed him of Saul's descent, for he would not believe that Saul would deal so basely with him till he had the utmost evidence of it. (2) He

JAMIESON, FAUSSET, BROWN — CHAPTER 26

VSS. 1-4. SAUL COMES TO THE HILL OF HACHILAH AGAINST DAVID. **1. the Ziphites came unto Saul to Gibeah**—This people seem to have thought it impossible for David to escape, and therefore recommended themselves to Saul, by giving him secret information (see on ch. 23:19). The knowledge of their treachery makes it appear strange that David should return to his former haunt in their neighborhood; but, perhaps he did it to be near Abigail's possessions, and under the impression that Saul had become mollified. But the king had relapsed into his old enmity. Though Gibeah, as its name imports, stood on an elevated position, and the desert of Ziph, which was in the hilly region of Judea, may have been higher than Gibeah, it was still necessary to descend in leaving the latter place; thence Saul (vss. 2) " went down to the wilderness of Ziph." **4-5. David . . . sent out spies . . . and David arose and came to the place where Saul had pitched**—Having obtained certain information of the locality, he

ADAM CLARKE — CHAPTER 26

1. *The Ziphites came.* This is the second time that these enemies of David endeavored to throw him into the hands of Saul (see chap. xxiii. 19).

2. *Three thousand chosen men.* Though they knew that David was but 600 strong, yet Saul thought it was not safe to pursue such an able general with a less force than that mentioned in the text; and, that he might the better depend on them, they were all elect or picked men out of the whole of his army.

5. *David arose.* As David and his men knew the country, they had many advantages over Saul and his men, and no doubt could often

MATTHEW HENRY

observed with his own eyes how Saul was encamped, *v.* 5.

Verses 6–12

I. David's bold adventure into Saul's camp in the night, accompanied only by his kinsman, Abishai, the son of Zeruiah. Like Gideon, he ventured through the guards, with a special assurance of the divine protection.

II. The posture he found the camp in: *Saul lay sleeping in the trench*, or, as some read it, *in his chariot, and in the midst of his carriages*, with *his spear stuck in the ground* by him, and all the soldiers, even those that were appointed to stand sentinel, were *fast asleep, v.* 12. Something extraordinary there was in it that they should all be asleep together, and so fast asleep that David and Abishai walked and talked among them, and yet none of them stirred. How helpless do Saul and all his forces lie, all, in effect, disarmed and chained! and yet nothing is done to them; they are only rocked asleep.

III. Abishai's request to David for a commission to dispatch Saul with the spear that stuck at his bolster. It was a special providence which gave him this opportunity; he ought not therefore to let it slip.

IV. David's generous refusal to suffer any harm to be done to Saul, and in it a resolute adherence to his principles of loyalty, *v.* 9. No man could do it and be guiltless. The thing he feared was guilt and his concern respected his innocence more than his safety. He resolved to wait till God shall think fit to avenge him on Saul, and he will by no means *avenge himself* (*v.* 10). Thus bravely does he prefer his conscience to his interest and trusts God with the issue.

He and Abishai carried away the spear and cruse of water which Saul had by his bedside (*v.* 12).

Verses 13–20

David having got safely from Saul's camp himself, and having brought with him proofs sufficient that he had been there, posts himself conveniently, so that they might hear him and yet not reach him (*v.* 13), and then begins to reason with them upon what had passed.

I. He reasons ironically with Abner, and keenly banters him. Abner got up and enquired who called, and disturbed the king's repose. "It is I," said David, and then he upbraids him with his sleeping when he should have been upon his guard. David, to put him into confusion, told him, 1. That he had lost his honour (*v.* 15). 2. That he deserved to lose his head (*v.* 16): "*You are all worthy to die*, by martial law, for being off your guard, when you had the king himself asleep in the midst of you. *Ecce signum—Behold this token.* See where the king's spear is, in the hand of him whom the king himself is pleased to count his enemy. Those that took away this might as easily and safely have taken away his life. Now see who are the king's best friends, you that neglected him and left him exposed or I that protected him when he was exposed.

II. He reasons seriously and affectionately with Saul. By this time he was so well awake as to hear what was said, and to discern who said it (*v.* 17): *Is this thy voice, my son David?* He had given his wife to another and yet calls him *son*, thirsted after his blood and yet is glad to hear his voice. And now David has as fair an opportunity of reaching Saul's conscience as he had just now of taking away his life.

1. He complains of the very melancholy condition he was brought into by the enmity of Saul against him. Two things he laments: —(1) That he was driven from his master and from his business: "*My lord pursues after his servant, v.* 18. Instead of being owned as a servant, I am pursued as a rebel. (2) That he was driven from his God and from his religion; he was constrained to live among the worshippers of strange gods and was thereby thrust into temptation to join with them in their idolatrous worship. If David had not been a man of extraordinary grace, and firmness to his religion, the ill usage he met with from his own prince and people, who were Israelites and worshippers of the true God, would have prejudiced him against the religion they professed and have driven him to communicate with idolators.

2. He insists upon his own innocency: *What have I done or what evil is in my hand? v.* 18.

3. He endeavours to convince Saul that his pursuit of him is not only wrong, but mean, and much below him. He compares himself to a partridge, a very innocent harmless bird, which, when attempts are made upon its life, flies if it can, but makes no resistance. And would Saul bring the flower of his army into the field only to hunt one poor partridge? "Let us join in making our peace with God, reconciling ourselves to him, which may be done, by sacrifice;

JAMIESON, FAUSSET, BROWN

seems, accompanied by his nephew (vs. 6), to have hid himself, perhaps disguised, in a neighboring wood, or hill, on the skirts of the royal camp towards night, and waited to approach it under covert of the darkness.

5-25. DAVID STAYS ABISHAI FROM KILLING SAUL, BUT TAKES HIS SPEAR AND CRUSE. **5. Saul lay in the trench, and the people pitched round about him**—Among the nomad people of the East, the encampments are usually made in a circular form. The circumference is lined by the baggage and the men, while the chief's station is in the center, whether he occupy a tent or not. His spear, stuck in the ground, indicates his position. Similar was the disposition of Saul's camp—in this hasty expedition he seems to have carried no tent, but to have slept on the ground. The whole troop was sunk in sleep around him. **8-12. Then said Abishai to David, God hath delivered thine enemy into thine hand**—This midnight stratagem shows the activity and heroic enterprise of David's mind, and it was in unison with the style of warfare in ancient times. **let me smite him . . . even to the earth at once**—The ferocious vehemence of the speaker is sufficiently apparent from his language, but David's magnanimity soared far above the notions of his followers. Though Saul's cruelty and perfidy and general want of right principle had sunk him to a low pitch of degradation, yet that was no reason for David's imitating him in doing wrong. Besides, he was the sovereign; David was a subject. Though God had rejected him from the kingdom, it was in every way the best and most dutiful course, instead of precipitating his fall by imbruing their hands in his blood and thereby contracting the guilt of a great crime, to wait the awards of that retributive providence which sooner or later would take him off by some sudden and mortal blow. He who, with impetuous haste was going to exterminate Nabal, meekly spared Saul. But Nabal refused to give a tribute to which justice and gratitude, no less than custom, entitled David. Saul was under the judicial infatuation of heaven. Thus David withheld the hand of Abishai; but, at the same time, he directed him to carry off some things which would show where they had been, and what they had done. Thus he obtained the best of victories over him, by heaping coals of fire on his head. **11. the spear that is at his bolster, and the cruse of water**—The Oriental spear had, and still has, a spike at the lower extremity, intended for the purpose of sticking the spear into the ground when the warrior is at rest. This common custom of Arab sheiks was also the practice of the Hebrew chiefs. **at his bolster**—lit., "at his head"; perhaps, Saul as a sovereign had the distinguished luxury of a bolster carried for him. A "cruse of water" is usually, in warm climates, kept near a person's couch, as a drink in the nighttime is found very refreshing. Saul's cruse would probably be of superior materials, or more richly ornamented than common ones, and therefore by its size or form be easily distinguished. **13-20. Then David . . . stood on the top of a hill afar off . . . and cried to the people**—(See on Judg. 9:7). The extraordinary purity and elasticity of the air in Palestine enable words to be distinctly heard that are addressed by a speaker from the top of one hill to people on that of another, from which it is separated by a deep intervening ravine. Hostile parties can thus speak to each other, while completely beyond the reach of each other's attack. It results from the peculiar features of the country in many of the mountain districts. **15. David said to Abner, Art not thou a valiant man: . . . wherefore then hast thou not kept thy lord the king?**—The circumstance of David having penetrated to the center of the encampment, through the circular rows of the sleeping soldiers, constituted the point of this sarcastic taunt. This new evidence of David's moderation and magnanimous forbearance, together with his earnest and kindly expostulation, softened the obduracy of Saul's heart. **19. If the Lord have stirred thee up against me**—By the evil spirit He had sent, or by any spiritual offenses by which we have mutually displeased Him. **let him accept an offering**—i.e., let us conjointly offer a sacrifice for appeasing His wrath against us. **if they be the children of men**—The prudence, meekness, and address of David in ascribing the king's enmity to the instigations of some malicious traducers, and not to the jealousy of Saul himself, is worthy of notice. **saying, Go, serve other gods**—This was the drift of their conduct. By driving him from the land and ordinances of the true worship, into foreign and heathen countries, they were exposing him to all the seductions of idolatry. **20. as when one doth hunt a partridge**—People in the East, in hunting the

ADAM CLARKE

watch them without being discovered. *Saul lay in the trench.* The word *bammaegal*, which we translate *in the trench*, and in the margin "in the midst of his carriages," is rendered by some "in a ring of carriages," and by others "in the circle," i.e., which was formed by his troops. As *agal* signifies anything "round," it may here refer to a round pavilion or tent made for Saul, or else to the form of his camp.

6. *Abishai the son of Zeruiah.* She was David's sister, and therefore Abishai and Joab were nephews to David.

8. *God hath delivered thine enemy into thine hand.* Here Abishai uses the same language as did David's men when Saul came into the cave at En-gedi (see chap. xxiv. 4, etc.), and David uses the same language in reply.

10. *The Lord shall smite him*—he shall die by a stroke of the divine judgment; *or his day shall come to die*—he shall die a natural death, which in the course of things must be before mine, and thus I shall get rid of mine enemy; *or he shall descend into the battle, and perish*—he shall fall by the enemies of his country. These are the three ordinary ways by which man accomplishes his day. Murder David could not consider to be lawful; this would have been taking the matter out of God's hand, and this David would not do.

12. *David took the spear and the cruse.* The *spear*, we have already seen, was the emblem of power and regal dignity. But it is usual, in Arab camps, for every man to have his lance stuck in the ground beside him, that he may be ready for action in a moment. The cruse of water resembled, in some measure, the canteens of our soldiers. In such a climate, where water was always scarce, it was necessary for each man to carry a little with him, to refresh him on his march.

15. *Art not thou a valiant man?* This is a strong irony. "Ye are worthy to die; ye are sons of death"—You deserve death for this neglect of your king.

19. *Let him accept an offering.* If God have stirred you up against me, why, then, let Him deliver my life into your hand, and accept it as a sacrifice. But as the word is *minchah*, a gratitude offering, perhaps the sense may be this: Let God accept a gratitude offering from you, for having purged the land of a worker of iniquity.

Saying, Go, serve other gods. His being obliged to leave the Tabernacle, and the place where the true worship of God was performed, and take refuge among idolaters, said in effect, *Go, serve other gods.*

20. *As when one doth hunt a partridge.* It is worthy of remark that the Arabs, observing

MATTHEW HENRY

and then I hope the sin will be pardoned, whatever it is, and the trouble, which is so great a vexation both to thee and me, will come to an end." See the right method of peace-making; let us first make God our friend by Christ the great Sacrifice, and then all other enmities shall be slain, Eph. ii. 16; Prov. xvi. 7. He decently lays the blame upon the evil counsellors who advised the king to that which was dishonourable and dishonest, and insists upon it that they be removed from about him and forbidden his presence, as men cursed before the Lord.

Verses 21–25

I. Saul's penitent confession of his fault and folly in persecuting David and his promise to do so no more. He acknowledges he has done very wrong to persecute him, that he has therein acted against God's law (*I have sinned*), and against his own interest (*I have played the fool*), in pursuing him as an enemy who would have been one of his best friends. He invites him to court again: *Return, my son David.* He promises him that he will not persecute him as he has done, but protect him: *I will no more do thee harm.*

II. David's improvement of Saul's convictions and confessions and the evidence he had to produce of his own sincerity. He desired that one of the footmen might fetch the spear (*v.* 22), and then (*v.* 23), 1. He appeals to God as judge of the controversy: *The Lord render to every man his righteousness.* 2. He reminds Saul again of the proof he had now given of his respect to him from a principle of loyalty: *I would not stretch forth my hand against the Lord's anointed,* intimating to Saul that the anointing oil was his protection, for which he was indebted to the Lord and ought to express his gratitude to him. 3. Not relying much upon Saul's promises, he puts himself under God's protection, and begs his favour (*v.* 24): "*Let my life be much set by in the eyes of the Lord,* how light soever thou makest of it."

III. Saul's prediction of David's advancement. He commends him (*v.* 25): *Blessed be thou, my son David.* He foretells his victories, and his elevation at last: *Thou shalt do great things.* The princely qualities which appeared in David—his generosity in sparing Saul, his military authority in reprimanding Abner for sleeping, his care of the public good, and the signal tokens of God's presence with him—convinced Saul that he would certainly be advanced to the throne at last, according to the prophecies concerning him.

Lastly, A palliative cure being thus made of the wound, they parted friends. Saul returned to Gibeah. *David went on his way.* And, after this parting, it does not appear that ever Saul and David saw one another again.

JAMIESON, FAUSSET, BROWN

partridge and other game birds, pursue them, till observing them becoming languid and fatigued after they have been put up two or three times, they rush upon the birds stealthily and knock them down with bludgeons [SHAW'S TRAVELS]. It was exactly in this manner that Saul was pursuing David. He drove him from time to time from his hiding-place, hoping to render him weary of his life, or obtain an opportunity of accomplishing his destruction.

25. So David went on his way—Notwithstanding this sudden relenting of Saul, David placed no confidence in his professions or promises, but wisely kept at a distance and awaited the course of Providence.

ADAM CLARKE

that partridges, being put up several times, soon become so weary as not to be able to fly; they in this manner hunt them upon the mountains, till at last they can knock them down with their clubs. It was in this manner that Saul hunted David, coming hastily upon him, and putting him up from time to time, in hopes that he should at length, by frequent repetitions of it, be able to destroy him.

21. *I have sinned.* Perhaps the word *chatathi,* "I have sinned," should be read, "I have erred, or, have been mistaken."

25. *Thou shalt both do great things, and also shalt still prevail.* The Hebrew is, "Also in doing thou shalt do, and being able thou shalt be able"; which the Targum translates, "Also in reigning thou shalt reign, and in prospering thou shalt prosper"—which in all probability is the meaning.

MATTHEW HENRY

CHAPTER 27

Verses 1–7

I. The prevalence of David's fear, which was the effect of the weakness of his faith (*v.* 1). In a melancholy mood, he draws this dark conclusion: *I shall one day perish by the hand of Saul.* But, *O thou of little faith: wherefore dost thou doubt?* Though he had no reason to trust Saul's promises, had he not all the reason in the world to trust the promises of God? Unbelief is a sin that easily besets even good men. *Lord, increase our faith.*

II. The resolution he came to hereupon. Now that Saul had, for this time, returned to his place, he determined to take this opportunity of retiring into the Philistines' country. David was no friend to himself in taking this course. God had appointed him to set up his standard *in the land of Judah, ch.* xxii. 5. How could he expect the protection of the God of Israel if he went out of the borders of the land of Israel?

III. The kind reception he had at Gath. Achish bade him welcome, partly out of generosity, being proud of entertaining so brave a man, partly out of policy, hoping to engage him for ever to his service, and that his example would invite many more to desert and come over to him. No doubt he gave David a solemn promise of protection, which he could rely upon when he could not trust Saul's promises.

IV. Saul's desisting from the further prosecution of him (*v.* 4). Saul sought no more for him, contenting himself with his banishment.

V. David's removal from Gath to Ziklag.

1. David's request for leave to remove was prudent and very modest, *v.* 5. (1) It was really prudent. David knew what it was to be envied in the court of Saul, and had much more reason to fear in the court of Achish, and therefore declines preferment there. In a town of his own he might have the more free

JAMIESON, FAUSSET, BROWN

CHAPTER 27

VSS. 1-4. SAUL HEARING THAT DAVID WAS FLED TO GATH, SEEKS NO MORE FOR HIM. **1. David said in his heart, . . . there is nothing better for me than that I should speedily escape into the land of the Philistines**—This resolution of David's was, in every respect, wrong: (1) It was removing him from the place where the divine oracle intimated him to remain (ch. 22:5); (2) It was rushing into the idolatrous land, for driving him into which he had denounced an imprecation on his enemies (ch. 26:19); (3) It was a withdrawal of his counsel and aid from God's people. It was a movement, however, overruled by Providence to detach him from his country and to let the disasters impending over Saul and his followers be brought on by the Philistines. **2. Achish, the son of Maoch, king of Gath**—The popular description of this king's family creates a presumption that he was a different king from the reigning sovereign on David's first visit to Gath. Whether David had received a special invitation from him or a mere permission to enter his territories, cannot be determined. It is probable that the former was the case. From the universal notoriety given to the feud between Saul and David, which had now become irreconcilable, it might appear to Achish good policy to harbor him as a guest, and so the better pave the way for the hostile measures against Israel which the Philistines were at this time meditating.

5-12. DAVID BEGS ZIKLAG OF ACHISH. **5. let them give me a place in some town in the country**—It was a prudent arrangement on the part of David; for it would prevent him being an object of jealous suspicion, or of mischievous plots among the Philistines. It would place his followers more beyond the risk of contamination by the idolatries of the court and capital; and it would give him an op-

ADAM CLARKE

CHAPTER 27

1. *I shall now perish one day by the hand of Saul.* This was a very hasty conclusion; God had so often interposed in behalf of his life that he was authorized to believe the reverse.

2. *David arose, and he passed over . . . unto Achish.* There is not one circumstance in this transaction that is not blameable. David joins the enemies of his God and of his country, acts a most inhuman part against the Geshurites and Amalekites, without even the pretense of a divine authority; tells a most deliberate falsehood to Achish, his protector, relative to the people against whom he had perpetrated this cruel act, giving him to understand that he had been destroying the Israelites, his enemies. I undertake no defense of this conduct of David; it is all bad, all defenseless; God vindicates him not.

3. *Every man with his household.* So it appears that the men who consorted with David had wives and families. David and his company resembled a tribe of the wandering Arabs.

MATTHEW HENRY

exercise of his religion, and keep his men better to it, and not have his righteous soul vexed, as it was at Gath, with the idolatries of the Philistines. (2) As it was presented to Achish it was very modest. He does not prescribe to him what place he should assign him. "*Why should thy servant dwell in the royal city*, to crowd thee, and disoblige those about thee?"

2. The grant which Achish made to him, upon that request, was very generous and kind (*v.* 6, 7): *Achish gave him Ziklag.* Hereby, (1) Israel recovered their ancient right; for Ziklag was in the lot of the tribe of Judah (Josh. xv. 31), and afterwards, out of that lot, was assigned, with some other cities, to Simeon, Josh. xix. 5. But either it was never subdued, or the Philistines had, in some struggle with Israel, made themselves masters of it. (2) David gained a commodious settlement, not only at a distance from Gath, but bordering upon Israel. Though we do not find that he augmented his forces at all while Saul lived (for, *ch.* xxx. 10, he had but his *six hundred* men), yet, immediately after Saul's death, that was the rendezvous of his friends.

Verses 8–12

An account of David's actions while he was in the land of the Philistines, a fierce attack he made, his success in it, and the representation he gave of it to Achish. 1. We may acquit him of injustice and cruelty in this action because those people whom he cut off were such as heaven had long since doomed to destruction. The Amalekites were to be all cut off. Probably the Geshurites and Gezrites were branches of Amalek. Saul was rejected for sparing them, David makes up the deficiency of his obedience before he succeeds him. 2. Yet we cannot acquit him of dissimulation with Achish in the account he gave him of this expedition. (1) David, it seems, was not willing that he should know the truth, and therefore spared none to carry tidings to Gath (*v.* 11), not because he was ashamed of what he had done as a bad thing, but because he was afraid, if the Philistines knew it, they would be apprehensive of danger to themselves or their allies by harbouring him among them and would expel him from their coasts. (2) He hid it from Achish with an equivocation not at all becoming his character. Being asked which way he had made his sally, he answered, *Against the south of Judah*, *v.* 13. It was true he had invaded those countries that lay south of Judah, but he made Achish believe he had invaded those that lay south in Judah, the Ziphites for example, that had once and again betrayed him; so Achish understood him, and thence inferred that he *had made his people Israel to abhor him*, and so rivetted himself in the interest of Achish.

JAMIESON, FAUSSET, BROWN

portunity of making reprisals on the freebooting tribes that infested the common border of Israel and the Philistines.

6. Ziklag—Though originally assigned to Judah (Josh. 15:31), and subsequently to Simeon (Josh. 19:5), this town had never been possessed by the Israelites. It belonged to the Philistines, who gave it to David.

8. David . . . went up, and invaded the Geshurites—(See Josh. 13:2). **and the Girzites**—or the Gerizi [GESENIUS], (Josh. 12:12), some Arab horde which had once encamped there. **and the Amalekites**—Part of the district occupied by them lay on the south of the land of Israel (Judg. 5:14; 12:15). **10. Achish said, Whither have ye made a road to-day?**—i.e., *raid*, a hostile excursion for seizing cattle and other booty. **David said, Against the south of Judah, and against the south of the Jerahmeelites**—Jerahmeel was the great-grandson of Judah, and his posterity occupied the southern portion of that tribal domain. **the south of the Kenites**—the posterity of Jethro, who occupied the south of Judah (Judg. 1:16; Num. 24:21). The deceit practised upon his royal host and the indiscriminate slaughter committed, lest any one should escape to tell the tale, exhibit an unfavorable view of this part of David's history.

ADAM CLARKE

5. *Why should thy servant dwell in the royal city?* He seemed to intimate that two princely establishments in the same city were too many. Achish appears to have felt the propriety of his proposal, and therefore appoints him Ziklag.

6. *Achish gave him Ziklag.* Ziklag was at first given to the tribe of Judah, but afterwards it was ceded to that of Simeon, Josh. xv. 31; xix. 5. The Philistines had, however, made themselves masters of it, and held it to the time here mentioned; it then fell into the tribe of Judah again, and continued to be the property of the kings of Judah. This verse is a proof that this book was written long after the days of Samuel, and that it was formed by a later hand, out of materials which had been collected by a contemporary author.

9. *David smote the land.* Here was a complete extirpation of all these people, not one being left alive, lest he should carry tidings of the disasters of his country! The spoil which David took consisted of sheep, oxen, asses, camels, and apparel.

10. *Whither have ye made a road to day?* He had probably been in the habit of making predatory excursions. This seems to be implied in the question of Achish.

MATTHEW HENRY

CHAPTER 28

Verses 1–6

I. The design of the Philistines against Israel. They resolved to *fight them.*

II. The expectation Achish had of assistance from David in this war. "If I protect thee, I may demand service from thee"; and he will think himself happy if he may have such a man as David on his side. David gave him an ambiguous answer: "We will see what will be done; it will be time enough to talk of that hereafter; but *surely thou shalt know what thy servant can do*" (*v.* 2). Thus he keeps himself free from a promise to serve him and yet keeps up his expectation of it.

III. The drawing of the armies, on both sides, into the field (*v.* 4): *The Philistines pitched in Shunem*, which was in the tribe of Issachar, a great way north from their country. On some of the adjacent mountains of Gilboa Saul mustered his forces, and prepared to engage the Philistines.

IV. The terror Saul was in: He *saw the host of the Philistines*, more numerous, better armed, and in better heart, than his own were. Had he kept close to God, he needed not have been afraid at the sight of an army of Philistines; now his interest failed, his armies dwindled and looked mean, and, which was worse, his spirits failed him. Now he remembered the guilty blood of the Amalekites which he had spared, and the innocent blood of the priests which he had spilt. His sins were set in order before his eyes, which robbed him of all his courage. In this distress *Saul enquired of the Lord*, *v.* 6. He enquired in such a manner that it was as if he had *not enquired at all.* Therefore it is said (1 Chron. x. 14), *He enquired not of the Lord*; for he did it faintly and coldly, and with a secret design, if God did not answer him, to consult the devil. He did not enquire in faith, but with a double unstable mind. Could he that hated and persecuted Samuel and David, who were both

JAMIESON, FAUSSET, BROWN

CHAPTER 28

VSS. 1-6. ACHISH'S CONFIDENCE IN DAVID. **1. The Philistines gathered their armies together for warfare, to fight with Israel**—The death of Samuel, the general dissatisfaction with Saul, and the absence of David, instigated the cupidity of those restless enemies of Israel. **Achish said to David, Know thou assuredly that thou shalt go out with me to battle**—This was evidently to try him. Achish, however, seems to have thought he had gained the confidence of David and had a claim on his services. **2. Surely thou shalt know what thy servant can do**—This answer, while it seemed to express an apparent cheerfulness in agreeing to the proposal, contained a studied ambiguity—a wary and politic generality. **Therefore will I make thee keeper of mine head**—or my life; i.e., captain of my body-guard—an office of great trust and high honor.

4. the Philistines . . . pitched in Shunem—Having collected their forces for a last grand effort, they marched up from the seacoast and encamped in the "valley of Jezreel." The spot on which their encampment was fixed was Shunem (Josh. 19:18), now Sulem, a village which still exists on the slope of a range called "Little Hermon." On the opposite side, on the rise of Mount Gilboa, hard by "the spring of Jezreel," was Saul's army—the Israelites, according to their wont, keeping to the heights, while their enemies clung to the plain.

ADAM CLARKE

CHAPTER 28

2. *Surely thou shalt know what thy servant can do.* This was another equivocal answer, and could be understood only by his succeeding conduct. It might imply what he could do in favor of the Philistines against Israel, or in favor of Israel against the Philistines. Achish understood it in the former sense, and therefore he said to David, *I will make thee keeper of mine head for ever;* i.e., You shall be captain of my lifeguards.

5. *When Saul saw.* He saw from the superiority of his enemies, from the state of his army, and especially from his own state towards God, that he had everything to fear.

6. *The Lord answered him not.* He used the three methods by which supernatural intelligence was ordinarily given: (1) *Dreams.* The person prayed for instruction, and begged that

MATTHEW HENRY

prophets, expect to be answered by prophets? Could he that had slain the high priest, expect to be answered by Urim? Or could he that had sinned away the Spirit of grace, expect to be answered by dreams?

V. The mention of some things that had happened a good while ago, to introduce the following story, *v.* 3. 1. The death of Samuel. Samuel was dead, which made the Philistines the more bold and Saul the more afraid. 2. Saul's edict against witchcraft. He had put the laws in execution against *those that had familiar spirits,* who must not be *suffered to live,* Exod. xxii. 18. Some think that he did this while he was under Samuel's influence. Perhaps when Saul was himself troubled with an evil spirit he suspected that he was bewitched, and, for that reason, cut off all that had familiar spirits. Many seem zealous against sin, when they themselves are any way hurt by it (they will inform against swearers if they swear at them, or against drunkards if in their drink they abuse them), who otherwise have no concern for the glory of God, nor any dislike of sin as sin.

Verses 7–14

I. Saul seeks for a witch, *v.* 7. When God *answered him not,* if he had humbled himself by repentance and persevered in seeking God, who knows but that at length he might have been entreated for him? but, since he can discern no comfort either from heaven or earth (Isa. viii. 21, 22), he resolves to knock at the gates of hell, and to see if any there will befriend him and give him advice: *Seek me a woman that has a familiar spirit, v.* 7. His servants presently recommended one to him at Endor. To her he resolves to apply. Herein he is chargeable, 1. With contempt of the God of Israel. 2. With contradiction to himself.

II. He hastens to her, but goes by night, and in disguise, only with two servants, and probably on foot, *v.* 8. Those that are led captive by Satan are forced, 1. To disparage themselves. Never did Saul look so mean as when he went sneaking to a sorry witch to know his fortune. 2. To dissemble. Such is the power of natural conscience that even those who do evil blush and are ashamed to do it.

III. He tells her his errand and promises her impunity. 1. All he desires of her is to bring up one from the dead. It was necromancy, or divination by the dead, that he hoped to serve his purpose by. This was expressly forbidden by the law (Deut. xviii. 11). *Bring me up him whom I shall name, v.* 8. It was generally taken for granted that souls exist after death, and that great knowledge was attributed to separate souls. But to think that any good souls would come up at the beck of an evil spirit, or that God would suffer him to reap any real advantage by a cursed diabolical invention, was very absurd. 2. She signifies her fear of the law, and her suspicion that this stranger came to draw her into a snare (*v.* 9): *Thou knowest what Saul has done.* How sensible she is of danger from the edict of Saul, and what care she is in to guard against it; but not at all apprehensive of the obligations of God's law and the terrors of his wrath. She considered what *Saul* had done, not what *God* had done, against such practices, and feared a snare laid for her life more than a snare laid for her soul. 3. Saul promises with an oath not to betray her, *v.* 10. But he promised more than he could perform when he said, *There shall no punishment happen to thee;* for he that could not secure himself could much less secure her from divine vengeance.

IV. Samuel, who was lately dead, is the person whom Saul desired to have some talk with. 1. As soon as Saul had given the witch the assurance she desired she applied to her witchcrafts, and asked, *Whom shall I bring up to thee? v.* 11. 2. Saul desires to speak with Samuel: *Bring me up Samuel.* Samuel had anointed him to the kingdom and had formerly been his faithful friend and counsellor. While Samuel was living at Ramah, not far from Gibeah of Saul, and presided there in the school of the prophets, we never read of Saul's going to him to consult him (it would have been well for him if he had)! Saul said, *Bring me up Samuel,* and the very next words are, *When the woman saw Samuel* (*v.* 12). The witch, upon sight of the apparition, was aware that her client was Saul (*v.* 12): "*Why hast thou deceived me* with a disguise; for thou art Saul, the very man that I am afraid of above any man?" Had she believed that it was really Samuel whom she saw, she would have had more reason to be afraid of him, who was a good prophet, than of Saul, who was a wicked king. Saul bade her not to be afraid of him and enquired *what she saw? v.* 13. *O,* says the woman, *I saw gods* (that is, a spirit) *ascending out of the earth.* Poor gods that ascend *out of the earth;* But she speaks the language of the heathen, who had their

JAMIESON, FAUSSET, BROWN

3. **Now Samuel was dead . . .**—This event is here alluded to as affording an explanation of the secret and improper methods by which Saul sought information and direction in the present crisis of his affairs. Overwhelmed in perplexity and fear, he yet found the common and legitimate channels of communication with Heaven shut against him. And so, under the impulse of that dark, distempered, superstitious spirit which had overmastered him, he resolved, in desperation, to seek the aid of one of those fortune-telling impostors whom, in accordance with the divine command (Lev. 19:31; 20:6, 27; Deut. 18:11), he had set himself formerly to exterminate from his kingdom.

7-25. SAUL SEEKS A WITCH, WHO, BEING ENCOURAGED BY HIM, RAISES UP SAMUEL. **7. Then said Saul unto his servants, Seek me a woman that hath a familiar spirit**—From the energetic measures which he himself had taken for extirpating the dealers in magical arts (the profession having been declared a capital offense), his most attached courtiers might have had reason to doubt the possibility of gratifying their master's wish. Anxious inquiries, however, led to the discovery of a woman living very secluded in the neighborhood, who had the credit of possessing the forbidden powers. To her house he repaired by night in disguise, accompanied by two faithful servants. **En-dor**—"the fountain of the circle"—that figure being constantly affected by magicians—was situated directly on the other side of the Gilboa range, opposite Tabor; so that, in this midnight adventure, Saul had to pass over the shoulder of the ridge on which the Philistines were encamped.

8. bring me him up, whom I shall name unto thee—This pythoness united to the arts of divination a claim to be a necromancer (Deut. 18:11); and it was her supposed power in calling back the dead of which Saul was desirous to avail himself. Though she at first refused to listen to his request, she accepted his pledge that no risk would be incurred by her compliance. It is probable that his extraordinary stature, the deference paid him by his attendants, the easy distance of his camp from En-dor, and the proposal to call up the great prophet and first magistrate in Israel (a proposal which no private individual would venture to make), had awakened her suspicions as to the true character and rank of her visitor.

ADAM CLARKE

God would answer by a significant dream. (2) *Urim.* This was a kind of oracular answer given to the high priest when clothed with the ephod, on which were the Urim and Thummim. How these communicated the answer is not well-known. (3) *Prophets.* Who were requested by the party concerned to consult the Lord on the subject in question, and to report his answer. The prophets at that time could only be those in the schools of the prophets, which Samuel had established at Naioth and Gibeah.

3. *Samuel was dead.* And there was no longer a public accredited prophet to consult. *Those that had familiar spirits, and the wizards.* See the note on Lev. xix. 31, and Exod. xxii. 18.

7. *At En-dor.* This was a city in the valley of Jezreel, at the foot of Mount Gilboa, where the army of Saul had now encamped.

8. *Saul disguised himself.* That he might not be known by the woman, lest she, being terrified, should refuse to use her art.

13. *I saw gods ascending out of the earth.* The word *elohim,* which we translate *gods,* is the word which is used for the Supreme Being throughout the Bible; but all the versions, the Chaldee excepted, translate it in the plural number, as we do. The Chaldee has, "I see an angel of the Lord ascending from the earth."

MATTHEW HENRY

infernal deities and had them in veneration. If Saul had thought it necessary to his conversation with Samuel that the body of Samuel should be called out of the grave, he would have taken the witch with him to Ramah, where his sepulchre was; but the design was wholly upon his soul, which yet, if it became visible, was expected to appear in the usual resemblance of the body; and God permitted the devil, to answer the design that those who would not *receive the love of the truth* might be *given up to strong delusions and believe a lie*. Saul, it seems, was not permitted to see any manner of similitude himself, but he must take the woman's word for it, that she saw *an old man covered with a mantle, or robe*, the habit of a judge, which Samuel had sometimes worn. Saul, perceiving, by the woman's description, that it was Samuel, *stooped with his face to the ground* in reverence to Samuel, though he saw him not.

Verses 15–19.

The conference between Saul and Satan. Saul came in disguise (*v*. 8), but Satan soon discovered him, *v*. 12. Satan comes in disguise, in the disguise of Samuel's mantle, and Saul cannot discover him. Such is the disadvantage we labour under, in wrestling with *the rulers of the darkness of this world*, that they know us, while we are ignorant of their wiles and devices.

I. The spectre, or apparition, personating Samuel, asks why he is sent for (*v*. 15): *Why hast thou disquieted me to bring me up?*

II. Saul makes his complaint to this counterfeit Samuel, mistaking him for the true; and a most doleful complaint it is: "*I am sorely distressed*, and know not what to do, *for the Philistines make war against me*. But, alas! *God has departed from me*." He does not, like a penitent, own the righteousness of God in this; but, like a man enraged, flies out against God as unkind and flies off from him: *Therefore I have called thee*; as if Samuel, a servant of God, would favour those whom God frowned upon, or as if a dead prophet could do him more service than the living ones.

III. It is cold comfort which this evil spirit in Samuel's mantle gives to Saul, and is manifestly intended to drive him to despair and self-murder. Had it been the true Samuel he would have told him to repent and make his peace with God, and recall David from his banishment, that he might hope in this way to find mercy with God; but, instead of that, he represents his case as helpless and hopeless, serving him as he did Judas, to whom he was first a tempter and then a tormentor, persuading him first to sell his master and then to hang himself. 1. He upbraids him with his present distress (*v*. 16). 2. He upbraids him with the anointing of David to the kingdom, *v*. 17. Yet, to make him believe that he was Samuel, the apparition affirmed that it was God who spoke by him. The devil knows how to speak with an air of religion, and can teach *false apostles to transform themselves into the apostles of Christ* and imitate their language. 3. He upbraids him with his disobedience to the command of God in not destroying the Amalekites, *v*. 18. Satan had helped him to palliate and excuse that sin when Samuel was dealing with him to bring him to repentance, but now he aggravates it, to make him despair of God's mercy.

4. He foretells his approaching ruin, *v*. 19. (1) That his army should be routed by the Philistines. (2) That he and his sons should be slain in the battle: *Tomorrow thou and thy sons shall be with me*, that is, in the state of the dead, separate from the body.

Verses 20–25

How Saul received this terrible message from the ghost he consulted. He desired to be told *what he should do* (*v*. 15), but was only told what he had not done and what should be done to him.

I. How he sunk under the load, *v*. 20. He was indeed unfit to bear it, having *eaten nothing all the day before*, nor *that night*. He came fasting from the camp, and continued fasting; not for want of food, but for want of an appetite. *He fell all along on the earth*, as if the archers of the Philistines had already hit him, *and there was no strength in him* to bear up against these heavy tidings. Now he had enough of consulting witches, and found them miserable comforters.

II. With what difficulty he was persuaded to take so much relief as was necessary to carry him back to his post in the camp. The witch was very importunate with him to take some refreshment, that he might be able to get clear from her house, fearing that if he should be ill, especially if he should die there, she should be punished for it as a traitor, though she had escaped punishment as a witch. 1. She showed herself very importunate with him to take some refreshment. She had a fat calf at hand (and

JAMIESON, FAUSSET, BROWN

The story has led to much discussion whether there was a real appearance of Samuel or not. On the one hand, the woman's profession, which was forbidden by the divine law, the refusal of God to answer Saul by any divinely constituted means, the well-known age, figure, and dress of Samuel, which she could easily represent herself, or by an accomplice—his apparition being evidently at some distance, being muffled, and not actually seen by Saul, whose attitude of prostrate homage, moreover, must have prevented him distinguishing the person though he had been near, and the voice seemingly issuing out of the ground, and coming along to Saul—and the vagueness of the information, imparted much which might have been reached by natural conjecture as to the probable result of the approaching conflict—the woman's representation—all of this has led many to think that this was a mere deception. On the other hand, many eminent writers (considering that the apparition came before her arts were put in practice; that she herself was surprised and alarmed; that the prediction of Saul's own death and the defeat of his forces was confidently made), are of opinion that Samuel really appeared.

ALEXANDER MACLAREN:

The scene at Endor makes one's flesh creep. No more tragic picture of failure and despair was ever painted. The greatest dramatists, whose creations move the terror and pity of the world, have imagined no more heart-touching figure.

It matters very little—nothing at all in fact—either for the dramatic force or for the religious impressiveness of the scene, whether the woman "brought up" Samuel, or whether she was as much awed as Saul was, by the coming up of "an old man" covered with the well-known "mantel." The boding prophecy of tomorrow's defeat and death filled yet fuller the cup that had seemed to be already full of all misery. And that collapse of strength in the huddled figure, prostrate in the witch's den, may well stand for a prophecy of what will be the upshot at the last of a self-will that boasts of its own power, and tries to shake off dependence on God.

—*Expositions of Holy Scripture*

ADAM CLARKE

ALEXANDER MACLAREN:

Among all the persons of Scripture who are represented as having fallen away from God and wrecked their lives, perhaps there is none so impressive as the giant form of the first king of Israel. Huge and black, seamed and scarred with lightning marks of passions, moody and suspicious, devil-ridden and lonely, doubting his truest friends, and even his son, striking blindly in his fury at the gracious, sunny poet-warrior who shows so bright, so full of resource, so nimble, so generous, by contrast with the heavy strength of the moody giant, and ever escapes the javelin that quivers harmlessly in the wall, with an inevitable destiny hanging over his head, and at last creeping to "wizards that peep and mutter," and dying a suicide, with his army in full flight and his son dead at his feet—what a course and what an end for the chosen of the Lord, on whom the Spirit of Lord came with the anointing oil and gave him a new heart for his kingly office.

I know not anywhere a sadder story: and I know not where human lips ever poured out a more awful wail—like a Titan in his rage of pain—than these words of our text. Bright hopes and fair promise, and much that was good and true in performance—all came to this.

—*Expositions of Holy Scripture*

17. *The Lord hath done to him*. I believe these words are spoken of Saul; and as they are spoken to him, it seems evident that *him* should be "thee." The Septuagint, "to thee."

20. *Then Saul fell straightway all along the earth*. Literally, "He fell with his own length," or "with the fulness of his stature." He was so overwhelmed with this most dreadful message that he swooned away, and thus fell at his own length upon the ground.

MATTHEW HENRY

the word signifies one that was made use of in treading out the corn, and therefore could the worse be spared); this she prepared for his entertainment, *v.* 24. 2. He showed himself very averse to it: *He refused, and said, I will not eat* (*v.* 23). Had he laboured only under a defect of animal spirits, food might have helped him; but, alas! his case was out of the reach of such succours. What are dainty meats to a wounded conscience? 3. The woman at length, with the help of his servants, overpersuaded him, against his inclination and resolution, to take some refreshment. Saul was somewhat revived so that he and his servants *rose up and went away* before it was light (*v.* 25), that they might hasten to their business. Josephus here much admires the bravery and magnanimity of Saul, that, though he was assured he should lose both his life and honour, yet he would not desert his army, but resolutely returned to the camp, and stood ready for an engagement.

CHAPTER 29

Verses 1–5

I. The great strait that David was in. The two armies of the Philistines and the Israelites were encamped and ready to engage, *v.* 1. Achish, who had been kind to David, had obliged him to come himself and bring the forces he had into his service. David came accordingly, and, upon a review of the army, was found with Achish, in the post assigned him in the rear, *v.* 2. 1. If, when the armies engaged, he should retire, he would fall under the indelible reproach, not only of cowardice and treachery, but of base ingratitude to Achish. 2. If he should, as was expected from him, fight for the Philistines against Israel, he would incur the imputation of being an enemy to the Israel of God and a traitor to his country, would make his own people hate him, and unanimously oppose his coming to the crown. If Saul should be killed (as it proved he was) in this engagement, the fault would be laid at David's door, as if he had killed him. So that on each side there seemed to be both sin and scandal. Into this strait he brought himself by his own unadvisedness, in quitting the land of Judah. Therefore, though God might justly have left him in this difficulty, to chastise him for his folly, yet, because his heart was upright with him, he would *not suffer him to be tempted above what he was able, but with the temptation made a way for him to escape*, 1 Cor. x. 13.

II. A door opened for his deliverance out of this strait. God inclined the hearts of the princes of the Philistines to oppose his being employed in the battle, and to insist upon his being dismissed. 1. It was a proper question which they asked, upon the mustering of the forces, "*What do these Hebrews here? v.* 3. It was an honourable testimony which Achish, on this occasion gave to David. He looked upon him as a refugee, that fled from a wrongful prosecution in his own country, and had put himself under his protection, whom therefore he was obliged, in justice, to take care of, and thought he might in prudence employ. 2. Yet the princes are peremptory in it, that he must be sent home. (1) Because he had been an old enemy to the Philistines; witness what was sung in honour of his triumphs over them: *Saul slew his thousands, and David his ten thousands, v.* 5. (2) Because he might be a most dangerous enemy to them, and do them more mischief than all Saul's army could (*v.* 4): "He may *in the battle be an adversary to us*, and surprise us with an attack in the rear."

Verses 6–11

Achish was but one of five, though the chief, and the only one that had the title of king; accordingly, in a council of war held on this occasion, he was over-voted, and obliged to dismiss David, though he was extremely fond of him.

I. The discharge Achish gives him is very honourable, and not a final discharge, but only from the present service. 1. He signifies the great pleasure and satisfaction he had taken in him and in his conversation: *Thou art good in my sight as an angel of God, v.* 9. 2. He gives him a testimonial of his good behaviour, *v.* 6. It is very full and in obliging terms: "*Thou hast been upright*, and thy whole conduct has been *good in my sight*, and *I have not found evil in thee*." 3. He lays all the blame of his dismission upon the princes, who would by no means suffer him to continue in the camp. 4. He orders him to be gone early, as soon as it was light (*v.* 10).

II. His reception of this discourse is very complimental; but, I fear, not without some degree of dissimulation. He seemed anxious to serve him when he was at this juncture really anxious to leave him.

III. God's providence ordered it wisely and graci-

JAMIESON, FAUSSET, BROWN

24. the woman had a fat calf . . . and she hasted, and killed it . . .—(See on Gen. 18:1-8).

25. Then they rose up, and went away that night—Exhausted by long abstinence, overwhelmed with mental distress, and now driven to despair, the cold sweat broke on his anxious brow, and he sank helpless on the ground. But the kind attentions of the woman and his servants having revived him, he returned to the camp to await his doom.

CHAPTER 29

VSS. 1-5. DAVID MARCHING WITH THE PHILISTINES TO FIGHT WITH ISRAEL. **1. Aphek**—(Josh. 12:8), in the tribe of Issachar, and in the plain of Esdraelon. A person who compares the Bible account of Saul's last battle with the Philistines, with the region around Gilboa, has the same sort of evidence that the account relates what is true, that a person would have that such a battle as Waterloo really took place. Gilboa, Jezreel, Shunem, En-dor, are all found, still bearing the same names. They lie within sight of each other. Aphek is the only one of the cluster not yet identified. Jezreel on the northern slope of Gilboa, and at the distance of twenty minutes to the east, is a large fountain, and a smaller one still nearer; just the position which a chieftain would select, both on account of its elevation and the supply of water needed for his troops [HACKETT'S SCRIPTURE ILLUSTRATED]. **2. David and his men passed on in the rereward with Achish**—as the commander of the lifeguards of Achish, who was general of this invading army of the Philistines.

3. these days, or these years—He had now been with the Philistines a full year and four months (ch. 27:7), and also some years before. It has been thought that David kept up a private correspondence with this Philistine prince, either on account of his native generosity, or in the anticipation that an asylum in his territories would sooner or later be needed.

4. the princes of the Philistines were wroth with him—It must be considered a happy circumstance in the overruling providence of God to rescue David out of the dangerous dilemma in which he was now placed. But David is not free from censure in his professions to Achish (vs. 8), to do what he probably had not the smallest purpose of doing—of fighting with Achish against his enemies. It is just an instance of the unhappy consequences into which a false step—a departure from the straight course of duty—will betray everyone who commits it. **9. notwithstanding the princes of the Philistines have said**—The Philistine government had constitutional checks—or at least the king was not an absolute sovereign; but his authority was limited—his proceedings liable to be controlled by "the powerful barons of that rude and early period—much as the kings of Europe in the Middle Ages were by the proud and lawless aristocracy which surrounded them" [CHALMERS].

ADAM CLARKE

23. *I will not eat.* It is no wonder that not only his strength, but also his appetite, had departed from him. *And sat upon the bed.* Beds or couches were the common places on which the ancients sat to take their repasts.

24. *The woman had a fat calf.* In hot countries they could not keep flesh meat by them any length of time; hence they generally kept young animals, such as calves, lambs, and kids, ready for slaughter; and when there was occasion, one of them was killed, and dressed immediately. *Unleavened bread.* There was not time to bake leavened bread; that would have taken considerable time, in order that the leaven might leaven the whole lump.

CHAPTER 29

1. *To Aphek.* This was a place in the valley of Jezreel between Mounts Tabor and Gilboa. *Pitched by a fountain.* To be near a *fountain*, or "copious spring of water," was a point of great importance to an army in countries such as these, where water was so very scarce.

3. *These days, or these years.* I suppose these words to mark no definite time, and may be understood thus: "Is not this David, who has been with me for a considerable time?"

4. *The princes of the Philistines were wroth.* It is strange that they had not yet heard of David's destruction of a village of the Geshurites, Gezrites, and Amalekites, chap. xxvii. Had they heard of this, they would have seen much more cause for suspicion.

6. *Thou hast been upright.* So he thought, for as yet he had not heard of the above transaction, David having given him to understand that he had been fighting against Israel.

8. *David said . . . what have I done?* It was in the order of God's gracious providence that the Philistine lords refused to let David go with them to this battle. Had he gone, he had his choice of two sins: (1) If he had fought for the Philistines, he would have fought against God and his country. (2) If he had in the battle gone over to the Israelites, he would have deceived and become a traitor to the hospitable Achish.

MATTHEW HENRY

ously for him. For, besides that the snare was broken it proved a happy hastening of him to the relief of his own city, which sorely wanted him, though he did not know it. Thus the disgrace which the lords of the Philistines put upon him proved, in more ways than one, an advantage to him. *The steps of a good man are ordered by the Lord, and he delighteth in his way.* What he does with us we know not now, but we shall know hereafter, and shall see it was all for good.

CHAPTER 30

Verses 1–6

I. The descent which the Amalekites made upon Ziklag in David's absence. They surprised the city when it was left unguarded, plundered it, burnt it, and carried all the women and children captives, *v.* 1, 2. They intended, by this, to revenge the like havoc that David had lately made of them and their country, *ch.* xxvii. 8. 1. How wonderfully God inclined the hearts of these Amalekites to carry the women and children away captives, and not to kill them.

II. The confusion and consternation that David and his men were in when they found their houses in ashes and their wives and children gone into captivity. Three days' march they had from the camp of the Philistines to Ziklag, and now that they came thither weary, but hoping to find rest in their houses and joy in their families, behold a black and dismal scene was presented to them (*v.* 3), which made them all weep (David himself not excepted), though they were men of war, *till they had no more power to weep, v.* 4.

III. The mutiny and murmuring of David's men against him (*v.* 6): *David was greatly distressed*, for, in the midst of all his losses, his own people spoke of stoning him, 1. Because they looked upon him as the occasion of their calamities, by the provocation he had given the Amalekites, and his indiscretion in leaving Ziklag without a garrison in it. 2. Because now they began to despair of that preferment which they had promised themselves in following David. They hoped ere this to have been all princes; and now find themselves all beggars. Saul had driven him from his country, the Philistines had driven him from their camp, the Amalekites had plundered his city, his wives were taken prisoners, and now, to complete his woe, his own familiar friends, in whom he trusted, whom he had sheltered, and who did eat of his bread, instead of sympathising with him, *lifted up the heel against him*, and threatened to stone him. Great faith must expect such severe exercises. Things are sometimes at the worst with the church and people of God just before they begin to mend.

IV. David's pious dependence upon the divine providence and grace in this distress: *But David encouraged himself in the Lord his God.* His men fretted at their loss. *The soul of the people was bitter*, so the word is. Their own discontent and impatience added *wormwood and gall* to the affliction and misery, and made their case doubly grievous. But David bore in better, though he had more reason than any of them to lament it; they gave liberty to their passions, but he set his graces on work, and by encouraging himself in God, while they dispirited each other, he kept his spirit calm and sedate. It was David's practice, and he had the comfort of it, *What time I am afraid I will trust in thee.* When he was at his wits' end he was not at his faith's end.

Verses 7–20

I. He enquired of the Lord both concerning his duty—*Shall I pursue after this troop?* and concerning the event—*Shall I overtake them? v.* 8. David had no room to doubt but that his war against these Amalekites was just, and he had an inclination strong enough to set upon them when it was for the recovery of that which was dearest to him in this world; and yet he would not go about it without asking counsel of God, thereby owning his dependence upon God and submission to him.

II. He went himself in person, and took with him all the force he had in pursuit of the Amalekites, *v.* 9, 10. See how quickly the mutiny among the soldiers was quelled by his patience and faith. When they *spoke of stoning him* (*v.* 6), if he had spoken of hanging them, or had ordered that the ringleaders of the faction should immediately have their heads struck off, though it would have been just, yet it might have been of pernicious consequence to his interest in this critical juncture. All his men were willing to go along with him in pursuit of the Amalekites, and he needed them all; but he was forced to drop a third part of them by the way; 200 out of

JAMIESON, FAUSSET, BROWN

CHAPTER 30

VSS. 1-5. THE AMALEKITES SPOIL ZIKLAG. **1. Amalekites had invaded the south, and Ziklag**—While the strength of the Philistine forces was poured out of their country into the plain of Esdraelon, the Amalekite marauders seized the opportunity of the defenseless state of Philistia to invade the southern territory. Of course, David's town suffered from the ravages of these nomad plunderers, in revenge for his recent raid upon their territory. **2. they slew not any, either great or small, but carried them away**—Their conduct seems to stand in favorable contrast to that of David (ch. 27:11). But their apparent clemency did not arise from humane considerations. It is traceable to the ancient war usages of the East, where the men of war, on the capture of a city, were unsparingly put to death, but there were no warriors in Ziklag at the time. The women and boys were reserved for slaves, and the old people were spared out of respect to age. **3. David and his men came to the city, and, behold, it was burned with fire**—The language implies that the smoke of the conflagration was still visible, and the sacking very recent.

6-15. BUT DAVID, ENCOURAGED BY GOD, PURSUES THEM. **6. David was greatly distressed**—He had reason, not only on his own personal account (vs. 5), but on account of the vehement outcry and insurrectionary threats against him for having left the place so defenseless that the families of his men fell an unresisting prey to the enemy.

Under the pressure of so unexpected and widespread a calamity, of which he was upbraided as the indirect occasion, the spirit of any other leader guided by ordinary motives would have sunk; "but David encouraged himself in the LORD his God."

His faith supplied him with inward resources of comfort and energy, and through the seasonable inquiries he made by Urim, he inspired confidence by ordering an immediate pursuit of the plunderers.

ADAM CLARKE

CHAPTER 30

F. B. MEYER:

"David encouraged himself in the Lord his God." His God! Doubtless the chronicler heard him say repeatedly, as he was so fond of saying, "My God, my God." "I will say unto God, my rock, why hast thou forsaken me?" Though he had seriously compromised God's cause, by the failure of his faith, by consorting with Achish and the Philistines, by a tortuous and treacherous policy, yet God was still his God; and, in the supreme crisis which had overtaken him, he naturally betook himself to the covert of those loving wings.

He encouraged himself. He would go back on promises of forgiveness and help which had so often cheered him in similar straits. He would recall his songs in former nights as black as this, and therefore would have hope. He would remember that he had been brought through worse trials; and surely He who had helped him against Goliath and Saul would not fail him against the Amalekites. Besides, he had probably left his dear ones in the protection of the encamping angel; and though his faith might be tried, it could not be entirely disappointed. In this way he encouraged himself. All around was tumult and fear; but in God peace and rest brooded, as swans on a tranquil lake. His men might speak of stoning him; his heart be greatly distressed for wives and children; his life be in jeopardy: but God was a very present help. "Why art thou cast down, and disquieted, O my soul? Hope thou in God."

In similar circumstances, let us have resort to similar sources of comfort; hide in God, and encourage ourselves in Him. It was in this spirit that John Knox, when about to face death, said to his wife, "Read to me where I first cast anchor."—*Great Verses Through the Bible*

7. *Bring me hither the ephod.* **It seems as if David had put on the ephod, and inquired of the Lord for himself; but it is more likely that he caused Abiathar to do it.**

MATTHEW HENRY

600 were so fatigued with their long march, that they could not pass the brook Besor. 1. A great trial of David's faith, whether he could go on, in dependence upon the word of God, when so many of his men failed him. When we are disappointed and discouraged in our expectations from second causes, then to go on with cheerfulness, confiding in the divine power, this is giving glory to God, by believing against hope, in hope. 2. A great instance of David's tenderness to his men, that he would by no means urge them beyond their strength, though the case itself was so very urgent. The son of David thus considers the frame of his followers, who are not all alike strong and vigorous in their spiritual pursuits and conflicts; but, where we are weak, there he is kind; nay, more, there he is strong, 2 Cor. xii. 9, 10.

III. Providence threw one in their way that gave them intelligence of the enemy's motions, and guided theirs; a poor Egyptian lad, scarcely alive. 1. His master's cruelty to him. He had got out of him all the service he could, and when the lad fell sick he barbarously left him to perish in the field. Justly did Providence make this poor servant, that was thus basely abused, instrumental towards the destruction of a whole army of Amalekites and his master among the rest. 2. David's compassion to him. Though he had reason to think he was one of those that had helped to destroy Ziklag, yet, finding him in distress, be generously relieved him, not only with *bread and water* (*v.* 11), but with *figs and raisins*, *v.* 12. Though the Israelites were in haste, and had no great plenty for themselves, yet they would not *forbear to deliver one that was drawn unto death*, nor say, *Behold, we knew it not*, Prov. xxiv. 11, 12. 3. The intelligence David received from this poor Egyptian when he had come to himself. He gave an account concerning his party. (1) What they had done (*v.* 14): *We made an invasion*, &c. (2) Whither they had gone, *v.* 15. This he promised David to inform him of upon condition he would spare his life and protect him from his master, who, if he could hear of him again (he thought), would add cruelty to cruelty. Such an opinion this poor Egyptian had of the obligation of an oath that he desired no greater security for his life than this: *Swear unto me by God*, not by the gods of Egypt or Amalek, but by the one supreme God.

IV. David, being directed to the place where they lay, securely celebrating their triumphs, fell upon them, and, as he used to pray, *saw his desire upon his enemies*. 1. The spoilers were cut off. The Amalekites, finding the booty was rich were making themselves very merry with it, *v.* 16. In this posture David surprised them, which made the conquest of them, and the blow he gave them, the more easy. 2. The spoil was recovered and brought off, and nothing was lost, but a great deal gotten. (1) They retrieved all their own (*v.* 18, 19): *David rescued his two wives*; this is mentioned particularly, because this pleased David more than all the rest of his achievements. (2) They took all that belonged to the Amalekites besides (*v.* 20): *Flocks and herds*. Those who lately spoke of stoning him now cried him up, because they got by him more than they had then lost. Thus are the world and its sentiments governed by interest.

Verses 21–31

An account of the distribution of the spoil which was taken from the Amalekites. David disposed of the spoil as one that knew that justice and charity must govern us in the use we make of whatever we have in this world.

I. David was just and kind to those who abode by the stuff. He saluted them; *he asked them of peace* (so the word is), bade them be of good cheer, they should lose nothing by staying behind; for of this they seemed afraid, as perhaps David saw by their countenances.

1. There were those that opposed their coming in to share in the spoil; some of David's soldiers, probably the same that spoke of stoning him, spoke now of defrauding their brethren; they are called wicked men and *men of Belial*, *v.* 22. These made a motion that the 200 men who abode by the stuff should only have their wives and children given them, but none of their goods.

2. David would by no means admit this, but ordered that those who tarried behind should come in for an equal share in the spoils with those that went to the battle, *v.* 23, 24. God's mercy to us should make us merciful to one another. It was true they tarried behind; but, [1] It was not for want of goodwill to the cause or to their brethren, but because they had not strength to keep up with them. [2] Though they tarried behind now, they had formerly engaged many times in battle and done their part as well as the best of their brethren. [3] Even now they did good service, for they abode by the stuff, to guard

JAMIESON, FAUSSET, BROWN

9. came to the brook Besor—now Wady Gaza, a winter torrent, a little to the south of Gaza. The bank of a stream naturally offered a convenient rest to the soldiers, who, through fatigue, were unable to continue the pursuit.

11-15. they found an Egyptian in the field, and brought him to David—Old and home-born slaves are usually treated with great kindness. But a purchased or captured slave must look to himself; for, if feeble or sick, his master will leave him to perish rather than encumber himself with any additional burden. This Egyptian seems to have recently fallen into the hands of an Amalekite, and his master having belonged to the marauding party that had made the attack on Ziklag, he could give useful information as to the course taken by them on their return.

14. the Cherethites—i.e., the Philistines (Ezek. 25:16; Zeph. 2:5).

15. Swear unto me by God—Whether there was still among these idolatrous tribes a lingering belief in one God, or this Egyptian wished to bind David by the God whom the Hebrews worshipped, the solemn sanction of an oath was mutually recognized.

16-31. AND RECOVERS HIS TWO WIVES AND ALL THE SPOIL. **16. they were spread abroad upon all the earth**—Believing that David and all his men of war were far away, engaged with the Philistine expedition, they deemed themselves perfectly secure and abandoned themselves to all manner of barbaric revelry. The promise made in answer to the devout inquiries of David (vs. 8) was fulfilled. The marauders were surprised and panic-stricken. A great slaughter ensued—the people as well as the booty taken from Ziklag was recovered, besides a great amount of spoil which they had collected in a wide, freebooting excursion.

21. David came to the two hundred men, which were so faint that they could not follow—This unexpected accession of spoil was nearly proving an occasion of quarrel through the selfish cupidity of some of his followers, and serious consequences might have ensued had they not been prevented by the prudence of the leader, who enacted it as a standing ordinance—the equitable rule—that all the soldiers should share alike (see on Num. 31:11, 27).

ADAM CLARKE

9. *The brook Besor*. This had its source in the mountain of Idumea, and fell into the Mediterranean Sea beyond Gaza.

14. *Upon the south of the Cherethites*. In 2 Sam. xv. 18 we find that the Cherethites formed a part of David's guards. *South of Caleb*. Somewhere about Kirjath-arba, or Hebron, and Kirjath-sepher, these being in the possession of Caleb and his descendants.

15. *Swear unto me*. At the conclusion of this verse the Vulgate, Syriac, and Arabic add that "David swore to him." This is not expressed in the Hebrew, but is necessarily implied.

16. *Out of the land of the Philistines*. That these Amalekites were enemies to the Philistines is evident, but it certainly does not follow from this that those whom David destroyed were enemies also.

17. *There escaped not a man of them*. It is well-known to every careful reader of the Bible that the Amalekites were a proscribed people, even by God himself.

20. *And David took all the flocks*. He and his men not only recovered all their own property, but they recovered all the spoil which these Amalekites had taken from the south of Judah, the Cherethites, and the south of Caleb. When this was separated from the rest, it was given to David, and called "David's spoil."

22. *Men of Belial*. This is a common expression to denote the sour, the rugged, the severe, the idle, and the profane.

23. *That which the Lord hath given us*. He very properly attributes this victory to God, the numbers of the Amalekites being so much greater than his own. Indeed, as many fled away on camels as were in the whole host of David.

MATTHEW HENRY

that which somebody must take care of, else that might have fallen into the hands of some other enemy. Every post of service is not alike a post of honour, yet those that are in any way serviceable to the common interest, though in a meaner station, ought to share in the common advantages, as in the natural body every member has its use and therefore has its share of the nourishment. Thus he settled the matter for the time to come, made it a statute of his kingdom (a statute of distributions, *primo Davidus—in the first year of David's reign*), an ordinance of war (*v.* 25), that *as his part is that goes down to the battle*, and hazards his life in the high places of the field, so shall his be that guards the carriages.

II. David was generous and kind to all his friends. When he had given every one his own with interest there was a considerable overplus; probably the spoil of the tents of the Amalekites consisted much in plate and jewels (Judges viii. 24, 26), and these he thought fit to make presents of to his friends, even the *elders of Judah, v.* 26. Several places are here named to which he sent of these presents, all of them in or near the tribe of Judah. The first place named is *Bethel*. Thither David sent the first and best, to those that attended there, for his sake who is the first and best. *Hebron* is named last (*v.* 31), the largest share, having an eye upon that place as fittest for his headquarters, 2 Sam. ii. 1. In David's sending these presents observe, 1. His generosity. He aimed not to enrich himself, but to serve his country. It becomes gracious souls to be generous. 2. His gratitude. He sent presents to *all the places where he and his men were wont to haunt* (*v.* 31), that is, to all that he had received kindness from, that had sheltered him and sent him intelligence or provisions. 3. His piety. He calls his present *a blessing*; for no present we give to our friends will be a comfort to them but as it is made so by the blessing of God: it intimates that his prayers for them accompanied his present. 4. His policy. He sent these presents among his countrymen to engage them to be ready to appear for him upon his accession to the throne, which he now saw at hand.

JAMIESON, FAUSSET, BROWN

26. when David came to Ziklag, he sent of the spoil to the elders of Judah—This was intended as an acknowledgment to the leading men in those towns and villages of Judah which had ministered to his necessities in the course of his various wanderings. It was the dictate of an amiable and grateful heart; and the effect of this well-timed liberality was to bring a large accession of numbers to his camp (I Chron. 12:22). The enumeration of these places shows what a numerous and influential party of adherents to his cause he could count within his own tribe.

ADAM CLARKE

25. *He made it a statute and an ordinance for Israel.* Nothing could be more just and proper than this law; he who stays at home to defend house and property has an equal right to the booty taken by those who go out to the war. There was a practice of this kind among the Israelites long before this time; see Num. xxxi. 27; Josh. xxii. 8; and the note on this latter verse. *Unto this day.* This is another indication that this book was composed long after the facts it commemorates.

26. *Unto the elders of Judah.* These were the persons among whom he sojourned during his exile, and who had given him shelter and protection. Gratitude required these presents.

27. *To them which were in Beth-el.* This was in the tribe of Ephraim. *South Ramoth.* So called to distinguish it from Ramoth-gilead, beyond Jordan. This Ramoth belonged to the tribe of Simeon, Josh. xix. 8. *In Jattir.* It was situated in the mountains, and belonged to Judah.

28. *In Aroer.* Situated beyond Jordan, on the banks of the river Arnon, in the tribe of Gad.

29. *And . . . the cities of the Kenites.* A very small tract on the southern coast of the Dead Sea.

30. *Hormah.* The general name of those cities which belonged to Arad, king of Canaan, and were devoted to destruction by the Hebrews, and thence called Hormah (see Num. xxi. 1-3). *In Chor-ashan.* Probably the same as Ashan in the tribe of Judah (see Josh. xv. 42). It was afterwards ceded to Simeon, Josh. xix. 7.

31. *To them which were in Hebron.* This was a place strongly attached to David, and David to it, and the place where he was proclaimed king, and where he reigned more than seven years previously to the death of Ish-bosheth, Saul's son, who was, for that time, his competitor in the kingdom.

MATTHEW HENRY

CHAPTER 31

Verses 1–7

The day of recompense has now come, in which Saul should descend into battle and perish, *ch.* xxvi. 10.

I. He sees his soldiers fall about him, *v.* 1. The best of the troops were put into disorder, and multitudes slain.

II. He sees his sons fall before him. The victorious Philistines pressed most forcibly upon the king of Israel and those about him. His sons were next him, and they were all three slain before his face. Jonathan, that wise, valiant, good man, who was as much David's friend as Saul was his enemy, yet falls with the rest. Duty to his father would not permit him to stay at home, or to retire when the armies engaged. If the family must fall, Jonathan, that is one of it, must fall with it. He would hereby make David's way to the crown the more clear and open. For, though Jonathan himself would have cheerfully resigned all his title yet it is very probable that many of the people would have made use of his name for the support of the house of Saul, or at least would have come in but slowly to David. If Ish-bosheth (who was now left at home as one unfit for action, and so escaped) had so many friends, what would Jonathan have had, who had been the darling of the people and had never forfeited their favour? This would have embarrassed David.

III. Saul is sorely wounded by the Philistines and then slain by his own hand. The archers hit him (*v.* 3), so that he could neither fight nor fly, and therefore must inevitably fall into their hands. 1. He was desirous to die by the hand of his own servant rather than by the hand of the Philistines, lest they should abuse him as they had abused Samson. As he lived, so he died, proud and jealous, and a terror to himself and all about him. Those are in a deplorable condition indeed who leap into a hell before them, to escape a hell within them. 2. When he could not obtain that favour he became his own executioner. His armour-bearer would not run him through, for, having a profound reverence for the king his master, he could not do him any hurt

IV. His armour-bearer who refused to kill him refused not to die with him, but *fell likewise upon his sword, v.* 5. The Jews say that Saul's armour-bearer

JAMIESON, FAUSSET, BROWN

CHAPTER 31

Vss. 1-7. SAUL HAVING LOST HIS ARMY AT GILBOA, AND HIS SONS BEING SLAIN, HE AND HIS ARMORBEARER KILL THEMSELVES. **1. Now the Philistines fought against Israel**—In a regular engagement, in which the two armies met (ch. 28:1-4), the Israelites were forced to give way, being annoyed by the arrows of the enemy, which, destroying them at a distance before they came to close combat, threw them into panic and disorder. Taking advantage of the heights of Mount Gilboa, they attempted to rally, but in vain. Saul and his sons fought like heroes; but the onset of the Philistines being at length mainly directed against the quarter where they were, Jonathan and two brothers, Abinadab or Ishui (ch. 14:49) and Melchishua, overpowered by numbers, were killed on the spot.

3. the battle went sore against Saul . . .—He seems to have bravely maintained his ground for some time longer; but exhausted with fatigue and loss of blood, and dreading that if he fell alive into the enemy's hands, they would insolently maltreat him (Josh. 8:29; 10:24; Judg. 8:21), he requested his armorbearer to despatch him. However, that officer refused to do so. Saul then falling on the point of his sword killed himself; and the armorbearer, who, according to Jewish writers, was Doeg, following the example of his master, put an end to his life also. They died by one and the same sword—the very weapon with which they had massacred the Lord's servants at Nob. **6. So Saul died** [see on I Chron. 10:13, 14; Hos. 13:11], **and his three sons**—The influence of a directing Providence is evidently to be traced in permitting the death of Saul's three eldest and most

ADAM CLARKE

CHAPTER 31

1. *Now the Philistines fought.* This is the continuation of the account given in chap. xxix. *The men of Israel fled.* It seems as if they were thrown into confusion at the first onset, and turned their backs upon their enemies.

2. *Followed hard upon Saul and upon his sons.* They, seeing the discomfiture of their troops, were determined to sell their lives as dear as possible, and therefore maintained the battle till the three brothers were slain.

3. *He was sore wounded of the archers.* It is likely that Saul's sons were slain by the archers, and that Saul was now mortally wounded by the same. Houbigant translates, "The archers rushed upon him, from whom he received a grievous wound."

MATTHEW HENRY

was Doeg.

V. The country was put into such confusion by the rout of Saul's army that the inhabitants of the neighbouring cities (*on that side Jordan*, as it might be read) quitted them, and the Philistines, for a time, had possession of them, till things were settled in Israel (*v.* 7).

Verses 8–13

The scripture makes no mention of the souls of Saul and his sons, but of their bodies only.

I. How they were basely abused by the Philistines. The day after the battle, when they had recovered their fatigue, they came to strip the slain, and, among the rest, found the bodies of Saul and his three sons, *v.* 8. Saul might have saved himself the fatal thrust and have made his escape; for the pursuers (in fear of whom he slew himself) came not to the place where he was till the next day. Finding Saul's body, 1. They cut off his head. They intended it in general, for a reproach to Israel, who promised themselves that a crowned and an anointed head would save them from the Philistines, and a particular reproach to Saul, who was taller by the head than other men (which perhaps he was wont to boast of), but was now shorter by the head. 2. They stripped him of his armour (*v.* 9), and sent that to be set up as a trophy of their victory, in the house of Ashtaroth their goddess (*v.* 10); and we are told, 1 Chron. x. 10, that they fastened his head in the temple of Dagon. 3. They sent expresses throughout their country, and ordered public notice to be given in the houses of their gods of the victory they had obtained (*v.* 9), that public rejoicings might be made and thanks given to their gods. 4. They fastened his body and the bodies of his sons (as appears, *v.* 12) to the wall of *Beth-shan*, a city that lay not far from Gilboa and very near to the river Jordan. Hither the dead bodies were dragged and here hung up in chains, to be devoured by the birds of prey.

II. How they were bravely rescued by the men of Jabesh-Gilead. Little more than the river Jordan lay between Beth-shan and Jabesh-Gilead, and Jordan was in that place passable by its fords; a bold adventure was therefore made by the valiant men of that city, who in the night passed the river, took down the dead bodies, and gave them decent burial, *v.* 11, 13. This they did, 1. Out of a common concern for the honour of Israel, or the land of Israel, which ought not to be defiled by the exposing of any dead bodies, and especially of the crown of Israel, which was thus profaned by the uncircumcised. 2. Out of a particular sense of gratitude to Saul, for his zeal and forwardness to rescue them from the Ammonites when he first came to the throne, *ch.* xi. They buried the bodies, when, by burning over them, they had sweetened them (or, if they burnt them, they buried the bones and ashes), under a tree, which serves for a gravestone and monument. They *fasted seven days*; thus they lamented the death of Saul and the present distracted state of Israel, and perhaps joined prayers with their fasting for the re-establishment of their shattered state.

This book began with the birth of Samuel, but now it ends with the burial of Saul, the comparing of which two together will teach us to prefer the honour that comes from God before any of the honours which this world pretends to have the disposal of.

JAMIESON, FAUSSET, BROWN

energetic sons, particularly that of Jonathan, for whom, had he survived his father, a strong party would undoubtedly have risen and thus obstructed the path of David to the throne. **and all his men, that same day together**—his servants or bodyguard (I Chron. 10:6). **7. the men of Israel that were on the other side of the valley**—probably the valley of Jezreel—the largest and southernmost of the valleys that run between Little Hermon and the ridges of the Gilboa range direct into the Jordan valley. It was very natural for the people in the towns and villages there to take fright and flee, for had they waited the arrival of the victors, they must, according to the war usages of the time, have been deprived either of their liberty or their lives.

8-10. THE PHILISTINES TRIUMPH OVER THEIR DEAD BODIES. **8. on the morrow, when the Philistines came to strip the slain, that they found Saul and his three sons fallen**—On discovering the corpses of the slaughtered princes on the battlefield, the enemy reserved them for special indignities. They consecrated the armor of the king and his sons to the temple of Ashtaroth, fastened their bodies on the temple of Shen, while they fixed the royal heads ignominiously in the temple of Dagon (I Chron. 10: 10); thus dividing the glory among their several deities. **10. to the wall**—(II Sam. 21:12)—"the street" of Beth-shan. The street was called from the temple which stood in it. And they had to go along it to the wall of the city (see Josh. 17:11).

11-13. THE MEN OF JABESH-GILEAD RECOVER THE BODIES AND BURY THEM AT JABESH. **11-13. the inhabitants of Jabesh-gilead heard of that which the Philistines had done**—Mindful of the important and timely services Saul had rendered them, they gratefully and heroically resolved not to suffer such indignities to be inflicted on the remains of the royal family. **12. valiant men arose, and went all night, and took the body of Saul and the bodies of his sons**—Considering that Beth-shan is an hour and a half's distance, and by a narrow upland passage, to the west of the Jordan—the whole being a journey from Jabesh-gilead of about ten miles, they must have made all haste to travel thither to carry off the headless bodies and return to their own side of the Jordan in the course of a single night. **burnt them**—This was not a Hebrew custom. It was probably resorted to on this occasion to prevent all risk of the Beth-shanites coming to disinter the royal remains for further insult.

ADAM CLARKE

6. *And all his men.* Probably meaning those of his troops which were his life or body guards: as to the bulk of the army, it fled at the commencement of the battle, v. 1.

7. *The men of Israel that were on the other side of the valley.* They appear to have been panic-struck, and therefore fled as far as they could out of the reach of the Philistines. As the Philistines possessed Beth-shan, situated near to Jordan, the people on the other side of that river, fearing for their safety, fled also.

8. *On the morrow.* It is very likely that the battle and pursuit continued till the night, so that there was no time till the next day to strip and plunder the slain.

9. *And they cut off his head.* It is possible that they cut off the heads of his three sons likewise; for although only his head is said to be cut off, and his body only to be fastened to the walls of Beth-shan, yet we find that the men of Jabesh-gilead found both his body and the bodies of his three sons fastened to the walls, v. 12.

10. *They put his armour in the house of Ashtaroth.* As David had done in placing the sword of Goliath in the Tabernacle. We have already seen that it was common for the conquerors to consecrate armor and spoils taken in war to those who were the objects of religious worship. *They fastened his body to the wall.* Probably by means of iron hooks; but it is said, 2 Sam. xxi. 12, that these bodies were fastened "in the street of Beth-shan." This may mean that the place where they were fastened to the wall was the main street or entrance into the city.

11. *When the inhabitants of Jabesh-gilead heard.* This act of the men of Jabesh-gilead was an act of gratitude due to Saul, who, at the very commencement of his reign, rescued them from Nahash, king of the Ammonites (see chap. xi. 1, etc.) and by his timely succors saved them from the deepest degradation and the most oppressive tyranny.

12. *And burnt them there.* It has been denied that the Hebrews burned the bodies of the dead, but that they buried them in the earth, or embalmed them, and often burned spices around them. These, no doubt, were the common forms of sepulture, but neither of these could be conveniently practiced in the present case. They could not have buried them about Beth-shan without being discovered; and as to embalming, that was most likely out of all question, as doubtless the bodies were now too putrid to bear it. They therefore burned them, because there was no other way of disposing of them at that time so as to do them honor; and the bones and ashes they collected, and buried under a tree or in a grove at Jabesh.

13. *And fasted seven days.* To testify their sincere regret for his unfortunate death, and the public calamity that had fallen upon the land.

THE BOOK OF SECOND SAMUEL

I. David's rise (1:1-10:19)
A. The reign over Judah (1:1-4:12)
1. His lamentation for Saul and Jonathan (1:1-27)
2. His anointing as king of Judah (2:1-4)
3. War between Judah and Israel (2:5-4:12)

B. The reign over the whole nation (5:1-10:19)
1. Crowning (5:1-5)
2. First victories (5:6-25)
3. The provision for the Ark (6:1-23)
4. Concerning the Temple (7:1-29)
5. Conquests (8:1-14)
6. The appointment of officers (8:15-18)
7. Kingly kindness to Mephibosheth (9:1-13)
8. Victories over Ammon and Syria (10:1-19)

II. David's fall (11:1-20:26)
A. The sin (11:1-12:31)
1. War (11:1)
2. Sin (11:2-27)
3. Repentance (12:1-31)

B. The punishment (13:1-18:39)
1. In the family (13:1-14:24)
   a. Amnon and Tamar (13:1-22)
   b. Absalom (13:23-14:24)
2. In the kingdom—Absalom (14:25-18:39)

C. The restoration (19:1-20:26)
1. The king's return (19:1-43)
2. Insurrection quelled (20:1-26)

III. Appendix (21:1-24:25)
A. The government of God (21:1-22 & 24:1-25)
1. Famine (21:1-22)
2. The census (24:1-25)

B. The character of David (22:1-23:7)
1. Psalm—God's government (22:1-51)
2. Psalm—failure and God's faithfulness (23:1-7)

C. The heroic age—the mighty men (23:8-39)

This book is the history of the reign of king David. We had in the preceding book an account of his designation to the government and his struggles with Saul, which ended at length in the death of his persecutor. This book begins with his accession to the throne and is entirely taken up with the affairs of the government during the forty years he reigned, and therefore is entitled by the LXX *The Third Book of the Kings.*

It gives us an account of David's triumphs and his troubles. His triumphs over the house of Saul (chs. 1–4), over the Jebusites and Philistines (ch. 5), at the bringing up of the ark (chs. 6, 7), over the neighboring nations that opposed him (chs. 8–10); and so far the history is what we might expect from David's character. But his cloud has a dark side. Many things in his history are very instructive, but for the hero it must be confessed that his honor shines brighter in his psalms than in his annals.

MATTHEW HENRY

CHAPTER 1

Verses 1–10

I. David settling again in Ziklag, his own city, after he had rescued his family and friends out of the hands of the Amalekites (*v.* 1): He *abode in Ziklag.* There he was ready to receive those that came into his interests; not men in distress and debt, as his first followers were, but persons of quality in their country, *mighty men, men of war,* and *captains of thousands* (as we find, 1 Chron. xii. 1, 8, 20); such came day by day to him.

II. Intelligence brought him thither of the death of Saul. It was strange that he did not leave some spies about the camp, to bring him early notice of the issue of the engagement, a sign that he desired not Saul's woeful day, nor was impatient to come to the throne. 1. The messenger presents himself to David as an express, in the posture of a mourner for the deceased prince and a subject to the succeeding one. He came with his clothes rent, and made obeisance to David (*v.* 2), pleasing himself with the fancy that he had the honour to be the first that did him homage as his sovereign, but it proved he was the first that received from him sentence of death as his judge. 2. He gives him a general account of the issue of the battle and he told him very distinctly that the army of Israel was routed, many slain, and, among the rest, Saul and Jonathan, *v.* 4. He named only Saul and Jonathan, because he knew David would be most solicitous to know their fate; for Saul was the man whom he most feared and Jonathan the man whom he most loved. 3. He gives him a more particular account of the death of Saul. He therefore asks, *How knowest thou that Saul and Jonathan are dead?* in answer to which the young man tells him a very ready story, putting it past doubt that Saul was dead, for he himself had been not only an eye-witness of his death, but an instrument of it. He says nothing, in his narrative, of the death of Jonathan, but accounts only for Saul, thinking (as David understood it well enough, *ch.* iv. 10) that he should be welcome for that, and rewarded as one that brought good tidings. The account he gives of this matter is, (1) Very particular. That he happened to go to the place where Saul was (*v.* 6), that he found Saul endeavouring to run himself through with his own spear, none of his attendants being willing to do it for him. He therefore called this stranger to him (*v.* 7). Understanding that he was an Amalekite (neither one of his subjects nor one of his enemies), he begs this favour from him (*v.* 9): *Stand upon me, and slay me.* "Hereupon," saith our young man, "*I stood upon him, and slew him*" (*v.* 10) at which word, perhaps, he observed David look upon him with some show of displeasure, and therefore he excuses himself in the next words: "*For I was sure he could not live.*" (2) It is doubtful whether this story be true. But most interpreters think that it was false, and that, though he might happen to be present, yet he was not assisting in the

JAMIESON, FAUSSET, BROWN

CHAPTER 1

VSS. 1-16. AN AMALEKITE BRINGS TIDINGS OF SAUL'S DEATH. **1. David had abode two days in Ziklag**—Though greatly reduced by the Amalekite incendiaries, that town was not so completely sacked and destroyed, but David and his 600 followers, with their families, could still find some accommodation.

2-12. a man came out of the camp from Saul—As the narrative of Saul's death, given in the last chapter, is inspired, it must be considered the true account, and the Amalekite's story a fiction of his own, invented to ingratiate himself with David, the presumptive successor to the throne. David's question, "How went the matter?" evinces the deep interest he took in the war—an interest that sprang from feelings of high and generous patriotism—not from views of ambition. The Amalekite, however, judging him to be actuated by a selfish principle, fabricated a story improbable and inconsistent, which he thought would procure him a reward. Having probably witnessed the suicidal act of Saul, he thought of turning it to his own account, and suffered the penalty of his grievously mistaken calculation (cf. vs. 9 with I Sam. 31:4, 5).

ADAM CLARKE

CHAPTER 1

2. *A man came out of the camp.* The whole account which this young man gives is a fabrication; in many of the particulars it is grossly self-contradictory. There is no fact in the case but the bringing of the crown, or diadem, and bracelets of Saul, which, as he appears to have been a plunderer of the slain, he found on the field of battle; and he brought them to David, and told the lie of having dispatched Saul, merely to ingratiate himself with David.

MATTHEW HENRY

death of Saul, but told David so in expectation that he would reward him for it, as having done him a piece of good service. (3) However he produced that which was proof sufficient of the death of Saul, the crown that was upon his head and the bracelet that was on his arm. These fell into the hands of this Amalekite. The tradition of the Jews is that this Amalekite was the son of Doeg, and that Doeg, who they suppose was Saul's armour-bearer, before he slew himself gave Saul's crown and bracelet (the ensigns of his royalty) to his son, and bade him carry them to David, to curry favour with him.

Verses 11–16

I. David's reception of these tidings. So far was he from falling into a transport of joy, as the Amalekite expected, that he fell into a passion of weeping, *rent his clothes* (*v.* 11), *mourned and fasted* (*v.* 12), not only for his people Israel and Jonathan his friend, but for Saul his enemy. This he did, not only as a man of honour, but as a good man and a man of conscience, that had forgiven the injuries Saul had done him and bore him no malice. He knew it, before his son wrote it (Prov. xxiv. 17, 18), that if we *rejoice when our enemy falls the Lord sees it, and it displeases him;* and that *he who is glad at calamities shall not go unpunished*, Prov. xvii. 5. By what he did when he heard of Saul's death, we may perceive that his natural temper was very tender, and that he was kindly affected even to those that hated him.

II. The reward he gave to him that brought him the tidings. Instead of preferring him, he put him to death, judged him out of his own mouth, as a murderer of his prince, and ordered him to be forthwith executed for the same. David herein did not do unjustly. The man was an Amalekite. This, lest he should have mistaken it in his narrative, he made him own a second time, *v.* 13. He did himself confess the crime, so that the evidence was, by the consent of all laws, sufficient to convict him; for every man is presumed to make the best of himself. If he did as he said, he deserved to die for treason (*v.* 14), doing that which, it is probable, he heard Saul's own armour-bearer refuse to do; if not, yet by boasting of it to David, he showed what opinion he had of him, that he would rejoice in it, as one altogether like himself, which was an intolerable affront to him who had himself once and again refused to *stretch forth his hand against the Lord's anointed.*

Verses 17–27

When David had rent his clothes, mourned, and wept, and fasted, for the death of Saul, one would think he had made full payment of the debt of honour he owed to his memory; yet this is not all: we have here a poem he wrote on that occasion. By this elegy he designed both to express his own sorrow for this great calamity and to impress the like on the minds of others, who ought to lay it to heart. Those might gain information by poems that would not read history.

I. The orders David gave with this elegy (*v.* 18): *He bade them teach the children of Judah the use of the bow*, either, 1. The bow used in war. David hereby showed his authority over and concern for the armies of Israel, and set himself to rectify the errors of the former reign. But we find that the companies which had now come to David to Ziklag were armed with bows (1 Chron. xii. 2); therefore, 2. Some understand it either of some musical instrument called *a bow* (to which he would have the mournful ditties sung) or of the elegy itself. *He bade them teach the children of Judah Kesheth, the bow*, that is, this song, which was so entitled for the sake of Jonathan's bow, the achievements of which are here celebrated. It is *written in the book of Jasher*, there it was kept upon record, and thence transcribed into this history. That book was probably a collection of state-poems; what is said to be written in that book (Josh. x. 13) is also poetical, a fragment of an historical poem.

II. The elegy itself. It is not a divine hymn, nor given by inspiration of God to be used in divine service, nor is there any mention of God in it; but it is a human composition, and therefore was inserted, not in the book of Psalms but in the book of Jasher, which, being only a collection of common poems, is long since lost. This elegy proves David to have been,

1. A man of an excellent spirit, in four things:—

(1) He was very generous to Saul, his sworn enemy. [1] He conceals his faults; and, though there was no preventing their appearance in his history, yet they should not appear in this elegy. Charity teaches us to make the best we can of everybody and to say nothing of those of whom we can say no good, especially when they are gone. *De mortuis nil nisi bonum—Say nothing but good concerning the dead.*

JAMIESON, FAUSSET, BROWN

10. the crown—a small metallic cap or wreath, which encircled the temples, serving the purpose of a helmet, with a very small horn projecting in front, as the emblem of power. **the bracelet that was on his arm**—the armlet worn above the elbow; an ancient mark of royal dignity. It is still worn by kings in some Eastern countries.

13-15. David said unto the young man . . . , Whence art thou?—The man had at the outset stated who he was. But the question was now formally and judicially put. The punishment inflicted on the Amalekite may seem too severe, but the respect paid to kings in the West must not be regarded as the standard for that which the East may think due to royal station. David's reverence for Saul, as the Lord's anointed, was in his mind a principle on which he had faithfully acted on several occasions of great temptation. In present circumstances it was especially important that his principle should be publicly known; and to free himself from the imputation of being in any way accessory to the execrable crime of regicide was the part of a righteous judge, no less than of a good politician.

17-27. David Laments Saul and Jonathan. **17. David lamented with this lamentation**—It has always been customary for Eastern people, on the death of great kings and warriors, to celebrate their qualities and deeds in funeral songs.

This inimitable pathetic elegy is supposed by many writers to have become a national war-song, and to have been taught to the young Israelites under the name of "The Bow," in conformity with the practice of Hebrew and many classical writers in giving titles to their songs from the principal theme (Ps. 22; 56; 60; 80; 100). Although the words "use of" are a supplement by our translators, they may be rightly introduced, for the natural sense of this parenthetical verse is, that David took immediate measures for instructing the people in the knowledge and practice of archery, their great inferiority to the enemy in this military arm having been the main cause of the late national disaster.

ADAM CLARKE

JOHN LANGE:

Verse 11. "Weeping and mourning aloud" and rending the garments on the breast were signs of grief and sorrow for the dead (Gen. 37:34, 35; 50:1; 2 Sam. 3:32, 34; Judg. 11:35). The whole body of soldiers took part in David's deep grief. The Sept. adds at the end: "rent their clothes" as explanatory of the terse Hebrew text. The numerous signs of sorrow here mentioned, rending the garments, mourning, weeping, fasting ("till evening") exhibit the greatness of David's sincere grief. The order of mention of the objects of the lamentation is the inverse of that in verse 4: Saul, Jonathan, the people. His grief for *Saul* shows his heart to be free from bitterness, revenge and malignant joy; he mourns the fall of the *anointed* of the Lord. His heart must have been filled with deep sorrow for the death of Jonathan, whom he had not seen since the incident recorded in 1 Sam. 23:18. He laments over the slain and scattered *people* for the misery and ignominy that had befallen them through defeat by the uncircumcised heathen. He calls them "people of the Lord" with special reference to their position as a people chosen by the Lord from all nations, thus His special property by a holy covenant, whose wars against foreign nations, out of whom he had separated them, are *the Lord's wars*. The *house of Israel* denotes the people as a unit, with reference to their common descent. The people of *the Lord* was in this battle abandoned by the Lord; the *house* of Israel as a whole and in all its parts was cast down.

—*Commentary on the Holy Scriptures*

16. *Thy blood be upon thy head.* If he killed Saul, as he said he did, then he deserved death; at that time it was not known to the contrary, and this man was executed on his own confession.

18. *The use of the bow. The use of* is not in the Hebrew; it is simply *the bow*, that is, a song thus entitled. This lamentation is justly admired as a picture of distress the most tender and most striking; unequally divided by g[illegible] into longer and shorter breaks, as nature could pour them forth from a mind interrupted by the alternate recurrence of the most lively images of love and greatness.

MATTHEW HENRY

[2] He celebrates that which was praiseworthy in him. That he was *anointed with oil* (*v.* 21), the sacred oil, which signified his elevation to, and qualification for, the government. That he was a man of war, a *mighty man* (*v.* 19–21), that he had often been victorious over the enemies of Israel and *vexed them whithersoever he turned*, 1 Sam. xiv. 47. Though his sun set under a cloud, time was when it shone brightly. That take him with Jonathan he was a man of a very agreeable temper, that recommended himself to the affections of his subjects (*v.* 23): *Saul and Jonathan were lovely and pleasant.* Jonathan was always so, and Saul was so as long as he concurred with him. Take them together, and in the pursuit of the enemy, never were men more bold, more brave; they were *swifter than eagles and stronger than lions.* They were lovely and pleasant one to another, Jonathan a dutiful son, Saul an affectionate father; and therefore dear to each other in their lives, and *in their death they were not divided*, but kept close together in the stand they made against the Philistines, and fell together in the same cause.

(2) He was very grateful to Jonathan. He lamented him for what he had been: "*Very pleasant hast thou been unto me*; but that pleasantness is now over, and *I am distressed for thee.*" He had reason to say that Jonathan's love to him was wonderful; surely never was the like, for a man to love one who he knew was to take the crown over his head, and to be so faithful to his rival. [1] That nothing is more delightful in this world than a true friend, that is wise and good, that kindly receives and returns our affection, and is faithful to us in all our true interests. [2] That nothing is more distressful than the loss of such a friend; it is parting with a piece of one's self. The more we love the more we grieve.

(3) He was deeply concerned for the honour of God; for this is what he has an eye to when he fears lest *the daughters of the uncircumcised*, that are out of covenant with God, should triumph over Israel, and the God of Israel, *v.* 20. Good men are touched in a very sensible part by the reproaches of those that reproach God.

(4) He was deeply concerned for the public welfare. It was the beauty of Israel that was slain (*v.* 19) and the honour of the public that was disgraced. David hoped God would make him instrumental to repair those losses and yet laments them.

2. A man of a fine imagination, as well as a wise and holy man. (1) The embargo he would fain lay upon fame is elegant (*v.* 20): *Tell it not in Gath.* It grieved him to the heart to think that it would be proclaimed in the cities of the Philistines. (2) The curse he entails on the mountains of Gilboa, the theatre on which this tragedy was acted: *Let there be no dew upon you, nor fields of offerings, v.* 21. This is the reproach David fastens upon the mountains of Gilboa, which, having been stained with royal blood, thereby forfeited celestial dews.

JAMIESON, FAUSSET, BROWN

19. The beauty of Israel—lit., the gazelle or antelope of Israel. In Eastern countries, that animal is the chosen type of beauty and symmetrical elegance of form. **how are the mighty fallen!**—This forms the chorus. **21. let there be no dew, neither let there be rain**—To be deprived of the genial atmospheric influences which, in those anciently cultivated hills, seem to have reared plenty of first fruits in the corn harvests, was specified as the greatest calamity the lacerated feelings of the poet could imagine. The curse seems still to lie upon them; for the mountains of Gilboa are naked and sterile. **the shield of the mighty is vilely cast away**—To cast away the shield was counted a national disgrace. Yet, on that fatal battle of Gilboa, many of the Jewish soldiers, who had displayed unflinching valor in former battles, forgetful of their own reputation and their country's honor, threw away their shields and fled from the field. This dishonorable and cowardly conduct is alluded to with exquisitely touching pathos. **24. Ye daughters of Israel, weep over Saul, who clothed you in scarlet, with other delights . . .**—The fondness for dress, which anciently distinguished Oriental women, is their characteristic still. It appears in their love of bright, gay, and divers colors, in profuse display of ornaments, and in various other forms. The inmost depths of the poet's feeling are stirred, and his amiable disposition appears in the strong desire to celebrate the good qualities of Saul, as well as Jonathan. But the praises of the latter form the burden of the poem, which begins and ends with that excellent prince.

ADAM CLARKE

His reverence for Saul and his love for Jonathan have their strongest colorings; but their greatness and bravery come full upon him, and are expressed with peculiar energy.

Being himself a warrior, it is in that character he sees their greatest excellence; and though his imagination hurries from one point of recollection to another, yet we hear him—at first, at last, everywhere—lamenting, "How are the mighty fallen!" It is almost impossible to read the noble original without finding every word swollen with a sign or broken with a sob. A heart pregnant with distress, and striving to utter expressions descriptive of its feelings, which are repeatedly interrupted by an excess of grief, is most sensibly painted throughout the whole.

MATTHEW HENRY — CHAPTER 2

Verses 1–7

When Saul and Jonathan were dead, though David knew himself anointed to be king, yet he did not immediately send messengers through all the coasts of Israel to summon all people to come in and swear allegiance to him. Many had come in to his assistance from several tribes while he continued at Ziklag, as we find (1 Chron. xii. 1–22), and with such a force he might have come in by conquest. But he that will rule with meekness will not rise with violence.

I. The direction he sought and had from God in this critical juncture, *v.* 1. He doubted not of success, yet he used proper means, both divine and human. 1. David, according to the precept, *acknowledged God in his way.* He enquired of the Lord by the breastplate of judgment, which Abiathar brought to him. We must apply to God not only when we are in distress, but even when the world smiles upon us and second causes work in favour of us. His enquiry was, *Shall I go up to any of the cities of Judah?* Though Ziklag be in ruins, he will not quit it without direction from God. "If I stir hence, *Shall I go to one of the cities of Judah?*" 2. God, according to the promise, directed his path, bade him go up, told him whither, unto Hebron, a priests' city, one of the cities of refuge, so it was to David, and an intimation that God himself would be to him a little sanctuary.

II. The care he took of his family and friends in his removal to Hebron. 1. He took his wives with him (*v.* 2), that, as they had been companions with him in tribulation, they might be so in the kingdom. It does not appear that as yet he had any children; his first was born in Hebron, *ch.* iii. 2. 2. He took

JAMIESON, FAUSSET, BROWN — CHAPTER 2

Vss. 1-7. DAVID, BY GOD'S DIRECTION, GOES UP TO HEBRON, AND IS MADE KING OVER JUDAH. **1. David inquired of the Lord**—By Urim (I Sam. 23:6, 9; 30:7, 8). He knew his destination, but he knew also that the providence of God would pave the way. Therefore he would take no step in such a crisis of his own and the nation's history, without asking and obtaining the divine direction.

He was told to go into Judah, and fix his headquarters in Hebron, whither he accordingly repaired with his now considerable force. There his interests were very powerful; for he was not only within his own tribe, and near chiefs with whom he had been long in friendly relations (see on I Sam. 30:26-31), but Hebron was the capital and center of Judah, and one of the Levitical cities; the inhabitants of which were strongly attached to him, both from sympathy with his cause ever since the massacre at Nob, and from the prospect of realizing in his person their promised pre-eminence among the tribes.

ADAM CLARKE — CHAPTER 2

1. *David enquired of the Lord.* By means of Abiathar, the priest; for he did not know whether the different tribes were willing to receive him, though he was fully persuaded that God had appointed him king over Israel.

Unto Hebron. The metropolis of the tribe of Judah, one of the richest regions in Judea.

MATTHEW HENRY

his friends and followers with him, v. 3. They had accompanied him in his wanderings, and therefore, when he gained a settlement, they settled with him.

III. The honour done him by the men of Judah: They *anointed him king over the house of Judah*, v. 4. The tribe of Judah had often stood by itself more than any other of the tribes. In Saul's time it was numbered by itself as a distinct body (1 Sam. xv. 4) and those of this tribe had been accustomed to act separately. They did so now; yet they did it for themselves only; they did not pretend to anoint him king *over all Israel* (as Judg. ix. 22), but only *over the house of Judah*. He was first anointed king in *reversion*, then *in possession* of one tribe only, and at last of all the tribes. Thus the kingdom of the Messiah, the Son of David, is set up by degrees; he is Lord of all by divine designation, but *we see not yet all things put under him*, Heb. ii. 8.

IV. The respectful message he sent to the men of Jabesh-Gilead, to return them thanks for their kindness to Saul. Still he studies to honour the memory of his predecessor, and thereby to show that he was far from aiming at the crown from any principle of ambition or enmity to Saul, but purely because he was called of God to it. "Saul was your lord," says David, "and therefore you did well to show him this kindness and do him this honour." He prays to God to bless them for it, and to recompense it to them: *Blessed are you. The Lord show kindness and truth to you* (v. 6). He promises to make them amends for it: *I also will requite you*. He does not turn them over to God for a recompense that he may excuse himself from rewarding them. Good wishes are good things, and instances of gratitude, but they are too cheap to be rested in where there is an ability to do more.

Verses 8-17

I. A rivalship between two kings—David, whom God made king, and Ish-bosheth, whom Abner made king. One would have thought David would come to the throne without any opposition, since all Israel knew how manifestly God had designated him to it; but such a spirit of contradiction is there, in the devices of men, to the counsels of God, that such a weak and silly thing as Ish-bosheth, who was not thought fit to go with his father to the battle, shall yet be thought fit to succeed him in the government, rather than David shall come peaceably to it. 1. Abner was the person who set up Ish-bosheth in competition with David, perhaps in his zeal for the lineal succession, or rather in his affection to his own family and relations (for he was Saul's uncle), and because he had no other way to secure to himself the post of honour he was in, as captain of the host. Ish-bosheth would never have set up himself if Abner had not set him up, and made a tool of him to serve his own purposes. 2. Mahanaim, the place where he first made his claim, was on the other side Jordan, where it was thought David had the least interest, and being at a distance from his forces they might have time to strengthen themselves. But, having set up his standard there, the unthinking people of all the tribes of Israel (that is, the generality of them) submitted to him (v. 9), and Judah only was entirely for David.

II. An encounter between their two armies.

1. It does not appear that either side brought their whole force into the field, for the slaughter was but small, v. 30, 31. It is likely, David would not suffer them to act offensively, choosing rather to wait till the thing would do itself or rather till God would do it for him, without the effusion of Israelitish blood. The men of Israel stand neuter, and sit down tamely under Ish-bosheth, for so many years. *Wise men, mighty men, men of valour, expert in war*, and not of double heart, and yet for seven years together, most of them seemed indifferent in whose hand the public administration was.

2. In this battle Abner was the aggressor. David sat still to see how the matter would fall, but the house of Saul, and Abner at the head of it, gave the challenge.

The seat of the war was Gibeon. Abner chose it because it was in the lot of Benjamin, where Saul had the most friends; yet, since he offered battle, Joab, David's general, would not decline it, but there joined issue with him, and met him *by the pool of Gibeon*, v. 13. David's cause, being built upon God's promise, feared not the disadvantages of the ground. The pool between gave both sides time to deliberate. The engagement was at first proposed by Abner, and accepted by Joab, to be between twelve and twelve of a side. (1) It should seem this trial of skill began in sport. Abner made the motion (v. 14): *Let the young men arise and play before us*, as gladiators. He meant, "Let them *fight* before us," when he said, "Let them *play* before us." Joab, having been bred up under David, had so much wisdom as not to

JAMIESON, FAUSSET, BROWN

The princes of Judah, therefore, offered him the crown over their tribe, and it was accepted. More could not, with prudence, be done in the circumstances of the country (I Chron. 11:3).

5-7. David sent messengers unto the men of Jabesh-gilead—There can be no doubt that this message of thanks for their bold and dangerous enterprise in rescuing the bodies of Saul and his sons was an expression of David's personal and genuine feeling of satisfaction. At the same time, it was a stroke of sound and timely policy. In this view the announcement of his royal power in Judah, accompanied by the pledge of his protection of the men of Jabesh-gilead, should they be exposed to danger for their adventure at Beth-shan, would bear an important significance in all parts of the country and hold out an assurance that he would render them the same timely and energetic succor that Saul had done at the beginning of his reign.

8-17. ABNER MAKES ISH-BOSHETH KING OVER ISRAEL. **8-17. Abner, son of Ner, captain of Saul's host, took Ish-bosheth**—Here was the establishment of a rival kingdom, which, however, would probably have had no existence but for Abner. **Ish-bosheth**—or Esh-baal (I Chron. 8:33; 9:39). The Hebrews usually changed names ending with Baal into Bosheth (shame) (cf. Judg. 9:53 with ch. 11:21). This prince was so called from his imbecility. **Abner**—was first cousin of Saul, commander of the forces, and held in high respect throughout the country. Loyalty to the house of his late master was mixed up with opposition to David and views of personal ambition in his originating this factious movement. He, too, was alive to the importance of securing the eastern tribes; so, taking Ish-bosheth across the Jordan, he proclaimed him king at Mahanaim, a town on the north bank of the Jabbok, hallowed in patriarchal times by the divine presence (Gen. 32:2). There he rallied the tribes around the standard of the unfortunate son of Saul. **9. over Gilead**—used in a loose sense for the land beyond Jordan. **Ashurites**—the tribe of Asher in the extreme north. **Jezreel**—the extensive valley bordering on the central tribes. **over all Israel . . . 10. But Judah**—David neither could nor would force matters. He was content to wait God's time and studiously avoided any collision with the rival king, till, at the lapse of two years, hostilities were threatened from that quarter.

12. Abner . . . and the servants of Ish-bosheth . . . went out from Mahanaim to Gibeon—This town was near the confines of Judah, and as the force with which Abner encamped there seemed to have some aggressive design, David sent an army of observation, under the command of Joab, to watch his movements.

14. Abner said to Joab, Let the young men now arise, and play before us—Some think that the proposal was only for an exhibition of a little tilting match for diversion. Others suppose

ADAM CLARKE

4. *Anointed David king.* He was anointed before by Samuel, by which he acquired a right to the kingdom; by the present anointing he had authority over the kingdom. The other parts of the kingdom were, as yet, attached to the family of Saul.

5. *David sent messengers unto . . . Jabesh-gilead.* This was a generous and noble act, highly indicative of the grandeur of David's mind. He respected Saul as his once legitimate sovereign; he loved Jonathan as his most intimate friend.

8. *Abner the son of Ner.* This man had long been one of the chief captains of Saul's army, and commander in chief on several occasions; he was probably envious of David's power, by whom he had often been outgeneraled in the field.

9. *Made him king over Gilead.* These were places beyond Jordan; for as the Philistines had lately routed the Israelites, they were no doubt in possession of some of the principal towns. Abner was therefore afraid to bring the new king to any place where he was likely to meet with much resistance, till he had got his army well-recruited.

10. *Ish-bosheth . . . reigned two years.* It is well observed that Ish-bosheth reigned all the time that David reigned in Hebron, which was seven years and six months. Some think that Abner in effect reigned the last five years of Ish-bosheth, who had only the name of king after the first two years. Or the text may be understood thus: "When Ish-bosheth had reigned two years over Israel, he was forty years of age."

MATTHEW HENRY

make such a proposal, yet had not resolution enough to resist and gainsay it when another made it; for he stood upon a point of honour, and thought it a blemish to his reputation to refuse a challenge, and therefore said, *Let them arise.* Twelve of each side were accordingly called out as champions to enter the lists, a double jury of life and death, and the champions on Abner's side seem to have been most forward, for they took the field first (*v.* 15). But, (2) However it began, it ended in blood (*v.* 16): They thrust *every man his sword into his fellow's side* (spurred on by honour, not by enmity); so they *fell down together*, that is, all the twenty-four were slain. The wonderful obstinacy of both sides was remembered in the name given to the place: *Helkath-hazzurim—the field of rocky men*, men that were not only strong in body, but of firm and unshaken constancy, that stirred not at the sight of death. The whole army at length engaged, and Abner's forces were routed, *v.* 17.

Verses 18–24

The contest between Abner and Asahel. Asahel, the brother of Joab and cousin-german to David, was one of the principal commanders of David's forces, and was famous for swiftness in running: he was *as light of foot as a wild roe* (*v.* 18); this he got the name of by swift pursuing, not swift flying. He was not comparable to Abner as a skilful experienced soldier.

I. How rash he was in aiming to make Abner his prisoner. He pursued after him, and no other, *v.* 19. Proud of his relation to David and Joab, his own swiftness, and the success of his party, no less a trophy of victory would now serve the young warrior than Abner himself, either slain or bound, which he thought would put an end to the war and effectually open David's way to the throne.

II. How generous Abner was in giving him notice of the danger he exposed himself to, and advising him not to *meddle to his own hurt*, 2 Chron. xxv. 19. 1. He bade him content himself with a less prey (*v.* 21). 2. He begged of him not to put him upon the necessity of slaying him in his own defence, which he was very loth to do, but must do rather than be slain by him, *v.* 22.

III. How fatal Asahel's rashness was to him. He refused to turn aside, thinking that Abner spoke so courteously because he feared him; but what came of it? Abner, as soon as he came up to him, gave him his death's wound with a back stroke (*v.* 23): *He smote him with the hinder end of his spear*, from which he feared no danger. Joab and Abishai, instead of being disheartened were exasperated by it, pursued Abner with so much the more fury (*v.* 24), and overtook him at last about sunset, when the approaching night would oblige them to retire.

Verses 25–32

I. Abner, being conquered, meanly begs for a cessation of arms. He rallied the remains of his forces on the top of a hill (*v.* 25), as if he would have made head again, but becomes a humble supplicant to Joab for a little breathing-time, *v.* 26. He that was most forward to fight was the first that had enough of it. He that made a jest of bloodshed (*Let the young men arise and play before us*, *v.* 14) is now shocked at it, when he finds himself on the losing side. Then it was but playing with the sword; now, *Shall the sword devour for ever?* Now he can appeal to Joab himself concerning the miserable consequences of a civil war: *Knowest thou not that it will be bitterness in the latter end?* Now he begs of Joab to sound a retreat, and pleads that they were brethren, who ought not thus to bite and devour one another. How easy it is for men to use reason when it makes for them who would not use it if it made against them. If Abner had been the conqueror, we should not have had him complaining of the voraciousness of the sword and the miseries of a civil war, nor pleading that both sides were brethren.

II. Joab, though a conqueror, generously grants it, and sounds a retreat, knowing very well his master's mind and how averse he was to the shedding of blood.

III. The armies being separated, both retired to the places whence they came, and both marched in the night, Abner to Mahanaim, on the other side Jordan (*v.* 29), and Joab to Hebron, where David was, *v.* 32. Asahel's funeral is here mentioned; the rest they buried in the field of battle, but he was carried to Bethlehem, and buried in the sepulchre of his father, *v.* 32.

JAMIESON, FAUSSET, BROWN

that, both parties being reluctant to commence a civil war, Abner proposed to leave the contest to the decision of twelve picked men on either side. This fight by championship instead of terminating the matter, inflamed the fiercest passions of the two rival parties; a general engagement ensued, in which Abner and his forces were defeated and put to flight.

19-22. ASAHEL SLAIN. **19. Asahel pursued after Abner**—To gain the general's armor was deemed the **grandest trophy. Asahel, ambitious of securing Abner's**, had outstripped all other pursuers, and was fast gaining on the retreating commander. Abner, conscious of possessing more physical power, and unwilling that there should be "blood" between himself and Joab, Asahel's brother, twice urged him to desist.

The impetuous young soldier being deaf **to the generous remonstrance, the veteran** raised the pointed butt of his lance, as the modern Arabs do when pursued, and, with a sudden back-thrust, transfixed him on the spot, so that he fell, and lay weltering in his blood. But Joab and Abishai continued the pursuit by another route till sunset.

On reaching a rising ground, and receiving a fresh reinforcement of some Benjamites, Abner rallied his scattered troops and earnestly appealed to Joab's better feelings to stop the further effusion of blood, which, if continued, would lead to more serious consequences—a destructive civil war.

Joab, while upbraiding his opponent as the sole cause of the fray, felt the force of the appeal and led off his men; while Abner probably dreading a renewal of the attack when Joab should learn his brother's fate, and vow fierce revenge, endeavored, by a forced march, to cross the Jordan that night. On David's side the loss was only nineteen men, besides Asahel. But of Ish-bosheth's party there fell three hundred and sixty. This skirmish is exactly similar to the battles of the Homeric warriors, among whom, in the flight of one, the pursuit by another, and the dialogue held between them, there is vividly represented the style of ancient warfare.

ADAM CLARKE

14. *Let the young men . . . play before us.* This was diabolical play, where each man thrust his sword into the body of the other, so that the twenty-four (twelve on each side) fell down dead together!

16. *Caught every one his fellow by the head.* Probably by the beard, if these persons were not too young to have one, or by the hair of the head. Alexander ordered all the Macedonians to shave their beards; and being asked by Parmenion why they should do so, answered, "Dost thou not know that in battle there is no better hold than the beard?"

18. *Asahel was as light of foot as a wild roe.* To be swift of foot was deemed a great accomplishment in the heroes of antiquity; "the swift-footed Achilles" is an epithet which Homer gives to that hero no less than thirty times in the course of the *Iliad*.

F. GARDINER:

"Asahel pursued after Abner." Asahel, the youngest of the three nephews of David, took part in the battle with his elder brothers, and well knowing how completely the cause of Ishbosheth depended upon Abner, pertinaciously sought him out in the pursuit. His great fleetness enabled him to overtake Abner and, coming behind him, endanger his life. Abner was unwilling to injure him, and only after remonstrating with him, and urging him to seek the spoil of some warrior more nearly his equal (vv. 20–22), did he unwillingly slay him "with the hinder end of his spear." The spears were sharpened at the "hinder end" for the purpose of sticking them into the ground (1 Sam. 26:7). Abner's reluctance to kill Asahel may have been partly on account of his extreme youth, but was chiefly through dread of the vengeance of Joab (v. 22). "The fifth rib" here, and wherever else it occurs, should be translated *abdomen*.

—*Ellicott's Commentary on the Whole Bible*

27. *And Joab said.* The meaning of this verse appears to be this: If Abner had not provoked the battle (see v. 14) Joab would not have attacked the Israelites that day, as his orders were probably to act on the defensive. Therefore the blame fell upon Israel.

29. *They came to Mahanaim.* So they returned to the place whence they set out (see v. 12). This was the commencement of the civil wars between Israel and Judah, and properly the commencement of the division of the two kingdoms, through which both nations were deluged with blood.

MATTHEW HENRY

CHAPTER 3

Verses 1–6

I. The struggle that David had with the house of Saul before his settlement in the throne was completed, *v.* 1. The length of this war tried the faith and patience of David. The house of Saul waxed weaker and weaker, lost places, lost men, sunk in its reputation, and was foiled in every engagement. But the house of David grew stronger. Many deserted the declining cause of Saul's house. The contest between grace and corruption in the hearts of believers, who are sanctified but in part, may fitly be compared to this recorded here. There is a long war between them, the flesh lusting against the spirit and the spirit against the flesh; but, as the work of sanctification is carried on, corruption, like the house of Saul, grows weaker and weaker; while grace, like the house of David, grows stronger and stronger, till it come to a perfect man, and judgment be brought forth unto victory.

II. The increase of his own house. Here is an account of six sons he had by six several wives, in the seven years he reigned in Hebron. It was David's fault thus to multiply wives, contrary to the law (Deut. xvii. 17), and it was a bad example to his successors. We read not that any of these sons came to be famous (three of them were infamous, Amnon, Absalom, and Adonijah). His son by Abigail is called *Chileab* (*v.* 3), whereas (1 Chron. iii. 1) he is called *Daniel*. His first name was *Daniel—God has judged me* (namely, against Nabal), but David's enemies reproached him, and said, "It is Nabal's son, and not David's," as he grew up, he became, in his countenance and features, extremely like David, upon which he gave him the name of *Chileab*, which signifies, *like his father*, or the father's picture. Absalom's mother is said to be the daughter of Talmai, king of Geshur, a heathen prince. Perhaps David thereby hoped to strengthen his interest, but the issue of the marriage was one that proved his grief and shame. The last is called *David's wife*, which therefore, some think, was Michal, his first and most rightful wife, called here by another name: and, though she had no child after she mocked David, she might have had before.

Verses 7–21

I. Abner breaks with Ish-bosheth, upon a little provocation which Ish-bosheth unadvisedly gave him. 1. Ish-bosheth accused Abner of no less a crime than debauching one of his father's concubines, *v.* 7. 2. Abner resented the charge very strongly. He lets Ish-bosheth know, (1) That he scorned to be reproached with it by him, and would not take reproof at his hands. Proud men will not bear to be reproved, especially by those whom they think they have obliged. (2) That he would certainly be revenged on him, *v.* 9, 10. With the utmost degree of arrogance and insolence he lets him know that, as he had raised him up, so he could pull him down again and would do it. Abner's ambition made him zealous for Ish-bosheth, and now his revenge made him as zealous for David. If he had sincerely regarded God's promise to David, and acted with an eye to that, he would have been steady and uniform in his counsels. If Ish-bosheth had had the spirit of a man, especially of a prince, he might have answered him that his merits were the aggravation of his crimes, that he would not be served by so base a man. But he was conscious to himself of his own weakness, and therefore said not a word.

II. Abner treats with David. We must suppose that he began to grow weary of Ish-bosheth's cause, and sought an opportunity to desert it. He *sent messengers to David*, to tell him that he was at his service. Note, God can find out ways to make those serviceable to the kingdom of Christ who yet have no sincere affection for it and who have vigorously set themselves against it. Enemies are sometimes made a footstool, not only to be trodden upon, but to ascend by. The earth helped the woman.

III. David enters into a treaty with Abner, but upon condition that he shall procure him the restitution of Michal his wife, *v.* 13. 1. David showed the sincerity of his conjugal affection to his first and most rightful wife; neither her marrying another, nor his, had alienated him from her. Many waters could not quench that love. 2. He testified his respect to the house of Saul. He cannot be pleased with the honours of the throne unless he have Michal, Saul's daughter, to share with him in them, so far is he from bearing any malice to the family of his enemy. Abner sent him word that he must apply to Ish-bosheth, which he did (*v.* 14), pleading that he had purchased her at a dear rate, and she was wrongfully taken from him. Ish-bosheth durst not deny his

JAMIESON, FAUSSET, BROWN

CHAPTER 3

Vss. 1-5. SIX SONS BORN TO DAVID. **1. there was long war between the house of Saul and the house of David**—The rival parties had varying success, but David's interest steadily increased; less, however, by the fortunes of war, than a growing adherence to him as the divinely designated king.

2. unto David were sons born in Hebron—The six sons mentioned had all different mothers.

3. Chileab—(his father's picture)—called also Daniel (I Chron. 3:1). **Maacah, the daughter of Talmai king of Geshur**—a region in Syria, north of Israel. This marriage seems to have been a political match, made by David, with a view to strengthen himself against Ish-bosheth's party, by the aid of a powerful friend and ally in the north. Piety was made to yield to policy, and the bitter fruits of this alliance with a heathen prince he reaped in the life of the turbulent Absalom. **5. Eglah, David's wife**—This addition has led many to think that Eglah was another name for Michal, the *first* and *proper* wife, who, though she had no family after her insolent ridicule of David (ch. 6:23), might have had a child before.

6-12. ABNER REVOLTS TO DAVID. **6-11. Abner made himself strong for the house of Saul**—In the East, the wives and concubines of a king are the property of his successor to this extent, that for a private person to aspire to marry one of them would be considered a virtual advance of pretensions to the crown (see on I Kings 2:17). It is not clear whether the accusation against Abner was well or ill founded. But he resented the charge as an indignity, and, impelled by revenge, determined to transfer all the weight of his influence to the opposite party. He evidently set a full value on his services, and seems to have lorded it over his weak nephew in a haughty, overbearing manner.

12. Abner sent messengers to David—Though his language implied a secret conviction, that in supporting Ish-bosheth he had been laboring to frustrate the divine purpose of conferring the sovereignty of the kingdom on David, this acknowledgment was no justification either of the measure he was now adopting, or of the motives that prompted it. Nor does it seem possible to uphold the full integrity and honor of David's conduct in entertaining his secret overtures for undermining Ish-bosheth, except we take into account the divine promise of the kingdom, and his belief that the secession of Abner was a means designed by Providence for accomplishing it. The demand for the restoration of his wife Michal was perfectly fair; but David's insisting on it at that particular moment, as an indispensable condition of his entering into any treaty with Abner, seems to have proceeded not so much from a lingering attachment as from an expectation that his possession of her would incline some adherents of the house of Saul to be favorable to his cause.

ADAM CLARKE

CHAPTER 3

1. *There was long war.* Frequent battles and skirmishes took place between the followers of David and the followers of Ish-bosheth, after the two years mentioned above, to the end of the fifth year, in which Ish-bosheth was slain by Rechab and Baanah.

6. *Abner made himself strong.* This strengthening of himself, and going in to the late king's concubine, were most evident proofs that he wished to seize upon the government (see 1 Kings ii. 21-22; xii. 8; xvi. 21).

8. *Am I a dog's head?* Do you treat a man with indignity who has been the only prop of your tottering kingdom, and the only person who could make head against the house of David?

9. *Except, as the Lord hath sworn to David.* And why did he not do this before, when he knew that God had given the kingdom to David? Was he not now, according to his own concession, fighting against God?

13. *Except thou first bring Michal.* David had already six wives at Hebron; and none of them could have such pretensions to legitimacy as Michal, who had been taken away from him and married to Phaltiel. However distressing it was to take her from a husband who loved her most tenderly (see v. 16), yet prudence and policy required that he should strengthen his own interest in the kingdom as much as possible; and that he should not leave a princess in the possession of a man who might, in her right, have made pretensions to the throne. Besides, she was his own lawful wife, and he had a right to demand her when he pleased.

MATTHEW HENRY

demand, but took her from Phaltiel, to whom Saul had married her (*v.* 15), and Abner conducted her to David, not doubting but that then he should be doubly welcome when he brought him a wife in one hand and a crown in the other. Her latter husband was loth to part with her, but there was no remedy: he must thank himself: for when he took her he knew that another had a right to her. If any disagreement has separated husband and wife, as they expect the blessing of God let them be reconciled, and come together again; let all former quarrels be forgotten, and let them live together in love, according to God's holy ordinance.

IV. Abner uses his interest with the elders of Israel to bring them over to David, knowing that whichever way they went the common people would follow of course. No man can pretend to greater personal merit than David nor to less than Ish-bosheth. You have tried them both, *Detir digniori—Give the crown to him that best deserves it.* Let David be your king. God, having promised, by David's hand, to save Israel, it is both your duty, in compliance with God's will, and your interest, in order to your victories over your enemies, to submit to him; and it is the greatest folly in the world to oppose him.

V. David concludes the treaty with Abner. Abner reported to David the sense of the people and the success of his communications with them, *v.* 19. He came now with a retinue of twenty men, and David entertained them with a *feast* (*v.* 20) in token of reconciliation and joy and as a pledge of the agreement between them: it was a feast upon a covenant, like that, Gen. xxvi. 30.

Verses 22–39

The murder of Abner by Joab, and David's deep resentment of it.

I. Joab very insolently fell foul upon David for treating with Abner. He was informed that Abner was just gone (*v.* 22, 23), and that a great many kind things had passed between David and him. He chides David, and reproaches him to his face (*v.* 24, 25): *What hast thou done?* As if David were accountable to him for what he did: "*Why hast thou sent him away,* when thou mightest have made him a prisoner? He came as a spy, and will certainly betray thee." We find no answer that David gave him, not because he feared him, as Ish-bosheth did Abner (*v.* 11), but because he despised him.

II. Joab very treacherously sent for Abner back, and, under colour of a private conference with him, barbarously killed him with his own hand. That he made use of David's name, under pretence of giving him some further instructions, is intimated in that, *but David knew it not, v.* 26. Abner very innocently returned to Hebron, and, when he found Joab waiting for him at the gate, turned aside with him to speak with him, and there Joab murdered him (*v.* 27), and it is intimated (*v.* 30) that Abishai was privy to the design, and was aiding and abetting. Abner had maliciously, and against the convictions of his conscience, opposed David. He had now basely deserted Ish-bosheth and betrayed him, under pretence of regard to God and Israel, but really from a principle of pride, and revenge, and impatience of control. It is as certain that Joab was unrighteous, and, in what he did, did wickedly. Abner had indeed slain his brother Asahel, and Joab and Abishai pretended herein to be the avengers of his blood (*v.* 27, 30); but Abner slew Asahel in an open war. He did it likewise, in his own defence, and not till he had given him fair warning but Joab here shed *the blood of war in peace,* 1 Kings ii. 5. That which was at the bottom of Joab's enmity to Abner made it much worse. Joab was now general of David's forces; but, if Abner should come into his interest, he would possibly be preferred before him, being a senior officer, and more experienced in the art of war. He did it treacherously, and under pretence of speaking peaceably to him, Deut. xxvii. 24. Had he challenged him, he would have done like a soldier; but to assassinate him was done villainously and like a coward. Abner was now actually in his master's service, so that, through his side, he struck at David himself. It was a great aggravation of the murder that he did it in the gate, openly and avowedly, as one that was not ashamed.

III. David laid deeply to heart and in many ways expressed his detestation of this execrable villainy.

1. He washed his hands from the guilt of Abner's blood. *I and my kingdom are guiltless before the Lord for ever, v.* 28.

2. He entailed the curse for it upon Joab and his family (*v.* 29): "*Let it rest on the head of Joab.*" A resolute punishment of the murderer himself would better have become David than this passionate imprecation of God's judgments upon his posterity.

JAMIESON, FAUSSET, BROWN

17-21. Abner had communication with the elders of Israel—He spoke the truth in impressing their minds with the well-known fact of David's divine designation to the kingdom. But he acted a base and hypocritical part in pretending that his present movement was prompted by religious motives, when it sprang entirely from malice and revenge against Ish-bosheth. The particular appeal of the Benjamites was a necessary policy; their tribe enjoyed the honor of giving birth to the royal dynasty of Saul; they would naturally be disinclined to lose that *prestige.* They were, besides, a determined people, whose contiguity to Judah might render them troublesome and dangerous. The enlistment of their interest, therefore, in the scheme, would smooth the way for the adhesion of the other tribes; and Abner enjoyed the most convenient opportunity of using his great influence in gaining over that tribe while escorting Michal to David with a suitable equipage. The mission enabled him to cover his treacherous designs against his master—to draw the attention of the elders and people to David as uniting in himself the double recommendation of being the nominee of Jehovah, no less than a connection of the royal house of Saul, and, without suspicion of any dishonorable motives, to advocate policy of terminating the civil discord, by bestowing the sovereignty on the husband of Michal. In the same character of public ambassador, he was received and feted by David; and while, ostensibly, the restoration of Michal was the sole object of his visit, he busily employed himself in making private overtures to David for bringing over to his cause those tribes which he had artfully seduced. Abner pursued a course unworthy of an honorable man and though his offer was accepted by David, the guilt and infamy of the transaction were exclusively his.

22-30. Joab Kills Abner. **24. Joab came to the king and said, What hast thou done?**—Joab's knowledge of Abner's wily character might have led him to doubt the sincerity of that person's proposals and to disapprove the policy of relying on his fidelity. But undoubtedly there were other reasons of a private and personal nature which made Joab displeased and alarmed by the reception given to Abner. The military talents of that general, his popularity with the army, his influence throughout the nation, rendered him a formidable rival. In the event of his overtures being carried out, the important service of bringing over all the other tribes to the king of Judah would establish so strong a claim on the gratitude of David, that his accession would inevitably raise a serious obstacle to the ambition of Joab. To these considerations was added the remembrance of the blood-feud that existed between them since the death of his brother Asahel (ch. 2:23). Determined, therefore, to get Abner out of the way, Joab feigned some reason, probably in the king's name, for recalling him, and, going out to meet him, stabbed him unawares; not within Hebron, for it was a city of refuge, but at a noted well in the neighborhood.

ADAM CLARKE

16. *Weeping behind her.* If genuine affection did not still subsist between David and Michal, it was a pity to have taken her from Phaltiel, who had her to wife from the conjoint authority of her father and her king. Nevertheless David had a legal right to her, as she had never been divorced, for she was taken from him by the hand of violence.

18. *The Lord hath spoken of David.* Where is this spoken? Such a promise is not extant. Perhaps it means no more than, "Thus, it may be presumed, God hath determined."

21. *He went in peace.* David dismissed him in good faith, having no sinister design in reference to him.

27. *And smote him there.* Joab feared that, after having rendered such essential services to David, Abner would be made captain of the host. He therefore determined to prevent it by murdering the man, under pretense of avenging the death of his brother Asahel. The murder, however, was one of the most unprovoked and wicked; and such was the power and influence of this nefarious general that the king dared not bring him to justice for his crime. In the same way he murdered Amasa a little time afterwards (see chap. xx. 10).

29. *Let it rest on the head.* All these verbs may be rendered in the future tense: it will rest on the head of Joab, etc. This was a prophetic declaration which sufficiently showed the displeasure of God against this execrable man.

MATTHEW HENRY

3. He called upon all about him, even Joab himself, to lament the death of Abner (*v.* 31). When he could not call him a saint or a good man, he said nothing of that, but what was true he gave him the praise of, though he had been his enemy, that he was *a prince and a great man.* (1) Let them all lament it. A public loss must be every man's grief, for every man shares in it. Thus David took care that honour should be done to the memory of a man of merit, to animate others. (2) Let Joab, in a particular manner, lament it, which he has less heart but more reason to do than any of them.

4. David himself followed the corpse as chief mourner, and made a funeral oration at the grave. He attended the bier (*v.* 31) *and wept at the grave, v.* 32. Because he had been a man of bravery in the field, and might have done great service in the public counsels at this critical juncture, all former quarrels are forgotten and David is a true mourner for his fall. What he said over the grave fetched tears from the eyes of all that were present: *Died Abner as a fool dieth?* (1) He speaks as one vexed that Abner was fooled out of his life, imposed upon by a colour of friendship, slain by surprise. The wisest and stoutest of men have no fence against treachery. To see Abner, who thought himself the main hinge on which the great affairs of Israel turned, made a fool of by a base rival, and falling on a sudden a sacrifice to his ambition and jealousy—this stains the pride of all glory, and should put one out of conceit with worldly grandeur. Or, (2) He speaks as one boasting that Abner did not fool himself out of his life: "*Died Abner as a fool dies?* No, he did not, not as a criminal, a traitor or felon." *Died Abner as Nabal died?* so the LXX read it. Nabal died as he lived, like himself, like a sot: but Abner's fate was such as might have been the fate of the wisest and best man in the world.

5. He fasted all that day, and would by no means be persuaded to eat any thing till night, *v.* 34.

6. He bewailed it that he could not with safety do justice on the murderers, *v.* 30. He was weak, his kingdom was newly planted, and a little shake would overthrow it. Joab's family had a great interest, were bold and daring, and to make them his enemies now might be of bad consequence. David contents himself as a private person, to leave them to the judgment of God: *The Lord shall reward the doer of evil according to his wickedness.* Now this is a diminution, (1) To David's greatness. (2) To David's goodness. He ought to have done his duty, and trusted God with the issue. *Fiat justitia, ruat coelum—Let justice be done, though the heavens should fall asunder.* If the law had had its course against Joab, perhaps the murder of Ish-bosheth, Amnon, and others, would have been prevented. It was carnal policy and cruel pity that spared Joab.

JAMIESON, FAUSSET, BROWN

31. David said to Joab, and to all the people that were with him, Rend your clothes; gird you with sackcloth—David's sorrow was sincere and profound, and he took occasion to give it public expression by the funeral honors he appointed for Abner.

King David himself followed the bier—a sort of wooden frame, partly resembling a coffin, and partly a hand-barrow.

33, 34. the king lamented over Abner—This brief elegy is an effusion of indignation as much as of sorrow. As Abner had stabbed Asahel in open war, Joab had not the right of the Goel. Besides, he had adopted a lawless and execrable method of obtaining satisfaction (see on I Kings 2:5).

The deed was an insult to the authority, as well as most damaging to the prospects of the king. But David's feelings and conduct on hearing of the death, together with the whole character and accompaniments of the funeral solemnity, tended not only to remove all suspicion of guilt from him, but even to turn the tide of popular opinion in his favor, and to pave the way for his reigning over all the tribes more honorably than by the treacherous negotiations of Abner.

ADAM CLARKE

31. *David said to Joab.* He commanded him to take on him the part of a principal mourner.

33. *The king lamented over Abner.* This lamentation, though short, is very pathetic. It is a high strain of poetry; but the measure cannot be easily ascertained. Our own translation may be measured thus:

Died Abner as a fool dieth?
Thy hands were not bound,
Nor thy feet put into fetters.
As a man falleth before the wicked,
So hast thou fallen!

Or thus:

Shall Abner die
A death like to a villain's?
Thy hands not bound,
Nor were the fetters to thy feet applied.
Like as one falls before the sons of guilt,
So hast thou fallen!

36. *The people took notice.* They saw that the king's grief was sincere, and that he had no part nor device in the murder of Abner; see v. 37.

39. *I am this day weak.* Had Abner lived, all the tribes of Israel would have been brought under my government. *Though anointed king.* I have little else than the title: first, having only one tribe under my government; and secondly, the sons of Zeruiah, Joab and his brethren, having usurped all the power, and reduced me to the shadow of royalty. *The Lord shall reward the doer of evil.* That is, Joab, whom he appears afraid to name.

MATTHEW HENRY — CHAPTER 4

Verses 1–8

I. The weakness of Saul's house. 1. As for Ish-bosheth, his hands were feeble, *v.* 1. All the strength they ever had was from Abner's support, and now that he was dead he had no spirit left in him. He sees himself forsaken by his friends and at the mercy of his enemies. 2. As for Mephibosheth, who in the right of his father Jonathan had a prior title, his feet were lame, and he was unfit for any service, *v.* 4. He was but five years old when his father and grandfather were killed. His nurse, hearing of the Philistines' victory, was apprehensive that they would immediately aim at her young master, who was now next heir to the crown. She fled with the child in her arms, and, making more haste than good speed, she fell with the child, and by the fall some bone was broken or put out, and not well set, so that he was lame of it as long as he lived.

II. The murder of Saul's son.

1. Who were the murderers: *Baanah and Rechab, v.* 2, 3. They were brothers, Ish-bosheth's own servants, employed under him, so much the more base and treacherous was it in them to do him a mischief. They were Benjamites, of his own tribe. They were of the city of Beeroth; the inhabitants, upon some occasion or other, perhaps upon the death of Saul, retired to Gittaim. There the Beerothites were when this was written.

2. How the murder was committed, *v.* 5–7. Ish-bosheth was a sluggish man, loved his ease and hated business: and when he should have been, at this critical juncture, at the head of his forces in the field, or at the head of his counsels in a treaty with David, he was lying upon his bed and sleeping, for his hands were feeble (*v.* 1), and so were his head and heart. The treachery of Baanah and Rechab. They came

JAMIESON, FAUSSET, BROWN — CHAPTER 4

VSS. 1-2. BAANAH AND RECHAB SLAY ISH-BOSHETH, AND BRING HIS HEAD TO HEBRON.

4. Jonathan, Saul's son, had a son that was lame of his feet—This is mentioned as a reason why, according to Oriental notions, he was considered unfit for exercising the duties of sovereignty.

5. Rechab and Baanah went and came about the heat of the day to the house of Ish-bosheth . . .—It is still a custom in the East to allow their soldiers a certain quantity of corn, together with some pay; and these two captains very naturally went to the palace the day before to fetch wheat, in order to distribute it to the soldiers, that it might be sent to the mill at the accustomed hour in the morning.

ADAM CLARKE — CHAPTER 4

1. *All the Israelites were troubled.* Abner was their great support, and on him they depended; for it appears that Ish-bosheth was a feeble prince, and had few of those qualities requisite for a sovereign.

4. *He fell, and became lame.* Dislocated his ankle, knee, or thigh, which was never after reduced, and thus he became lame.

2. *Captains of bands.* Whether Ish-bosheth kept bands of marauders, whose business it was to make sudden incursions into the country places, and carry off grain, provisions, cattle, etc., we know not; but such persons would be well-qualified for the bloody work in which these two men were afterwards employed.

3. *The Beerothites fled to Gittaim.* Probably the same as Gath, as Ramathaim is the same as Ramah.

5. *Lay on a bed at noon.* It is a custom in all hot countries to travel or work very early and very late, and rest at noonday, in which the heat chiefly prevails.

MATTHEW HENRY

into the house, under pretence of fetching wheat for the victualling of their regiments. The king's corn-chamber and his bed-chamber lay near together, which gave them an opportunity, when they were fetching wheat, to murder him as he lay on the bed.

3. The murderers triumphed in what they had done. As if they had performed some very glorious action they made a present of Ish-bosheth's head to David (*v.* 8). Not that they had any regard either to God or to David's honour; they aimed at nothing but to make their own fortunes and to get preferment in David's court.

Verses 9–12

Justice done upon the murderers of Ish-bosheth.

I. Sentence passed upon them. There needed no evidence, their own tongues witnessed against them; they were so far from denying the fact that they gloried in it. David therefore shows them the heinousness of the crime. Ish-bosheth was a righteous person, he had done them no wrong, nor designed them any. David owns Ish-bosheth an honest man, though he had created him a great deal of trouble unjustly. The manner of it much aggravated the crime. To slay him in his own house and upon his bed, when he was in no capacity of making any opposition, this is treacherous and barbarous. He quotes a precedent (*v.* 10): he had put him to death who had brought him the tidings of the death of Saul, because he thought it would be good tidings to David. He ratifies the sentence with an oath (*v.* 9): *As the Lord liveth, who hath redeemed my soul out of all adversity.* He expresses himself thus resolutely, to prevent the making of any intercession for the criminals by those about him, and thus piously to intimate that his dependence was upon God for the putting of him in possession of the promised throne, and that he would not be beholden to any man to help him to it by any indirect or unlawful practices. Hereupon he signs a warrant for the execution of these men, *v.* 12. If wicked men smite Ish-bosheth, they deserve to die for taking God's work out of his hand.

II. Execution done. The murderers were put to death according to law, to be monuments of David's justice. But what a confusion was this to the two murderers! What a horrid disappointment! And such those will meet with who think to serve the interests of the Son of David by any immoral practices, by war and persecution, fraud and rapine, who, under colour of religion, murder princes, break solemn contracts, lay countries waste, *hate their brethren, and cast them out, and say, Let the Lord be glorified, kill them, and think they do God good service.* However men may canonize such methods of serving the church and the catholic cause, Christ will let them know, another day, that Christianity was not intended to destroy humanity; and those who thus think to merit heaven shall not escape the damnation of hell.

JAMIESON, FAUSSET, BROWN

7. when they came into the house, he lay on his bed—Rechab and Baanah came in the heat of the day, when they knew that Ish-bosheth, their master, would be resting on his divan; and as it was necessary, for the reason just given, to have the corn the day before it was needed, their coming at that time, though it might be a little earlier than usual, created no suspicion, and attracted no notice [HARMER]. **gat them away through the plain all night**—i.e., the valley of the Jordan, through which their way lay from Mahanaim to Hebron. **8. They brought the head of Ish-bosheth unto David . . . , and said, Behold the head of Ish-bosheth**—Such bloody trophies of rebels and conspirators have always been acceptable to princes in the East, and the carriers have been liberally rewarded. Ish-bosheth being a usurper, the two assassins thought they were doing a meritorious service to David by removing the only existing obstacle to the union of the two kingdoms.

10-12. DAVID CAUSES THEM TO BE PUT TO DEATH. **12. slew them, and cut off their hands and their feet**—as the instruments in perpetrating their crime. The exposure of the mutilated remains was intended as not only a punishment of their crime, but also the attestation of David's abhorrence.

ADAM CLARKE

6. *As though they would have fetched wheat.* As these men were accustomed to bring wheat from these stores, from which it appears there was an easy passage to the king's chamber, no man would suspect their present errand, as they were in the habit of going frequently to that place.

8. *They brought the head . . . unto David.* They thought, as did the poor lying Amalekite, to ingratiate themselves with David by this abominable act.

9. *Who hath redeemed my soul out of all adversity.* This was, in David's case, a very proper view of the goodness and watchful providence of God towards him.

10. *A reward for his tidings. Euangelia,* Septuagint. Here is a proof that *evangelium,* or "gospel," signifies the *reward* which the bringer of good tidings is entitled to receive.

11. *How much more?* Here are several things which aggravated the guilt of those wicked men. (1) Ish-bosheth was an innocent man, and therefore none could have any ground of quarrel against him. (2) He was in his own house, which was his sanctuary, and none but the worst of men would disturb him there. (3) He was upon his bed, resting in the heat of the day, and so free from suspicion that he was not even attended by his guards, nor had he his doors secured. To take away the life of such a man in such circumstances, whom also they professed to hold as their sovereign, was the most abandoned treachery.

12. *And they slew them.* None ever more richly deserved death; and by this act of justice David showed to all Israel that he was a decided enemy to the destruction of Saul's family, and that none could lift up their hands against any of them without meeting with condign punishment. In all these cases I know not that it was possible for David to show more sincerity or a stricter regard for justice.

MATTHEW HENRY

CHAPTER 5

Verses 1–5

I. The humble address of all the tribes to David, beseeching him to take upon him the government and owning him for their king. Judah had submitted to David as their king above seven years ago, and their ease and happiness, under his administration, encouraged the rest of the tribes to make their court to him. What numbers came from each tribe, with what zeal and sincerity they came, and how they were entertained for three days at Hebron, when they were all of one heart to make David king, we have a full account, 1 Chron. xii. 23–40. Here we have the grounds they went upon in making David king. 1. Their relation to him was some inducement: "*We are thy bone and thy flesh*" (*v.* 1), not only thou art our bone and our flesh, not a stranger, unqualified by the law to be king (Deut. xvii. 15), but we are thine. Thou wilt be as glad as we shall be to put an end to this long civil war; and thou wilt take pity on us, protect us, and do thy utmost for our welfare." Those who take Christ for their king may thus plead with him: *We are thy bone and thy flesh,* thou hast made thyself in all things *like unto thy brethren* (Heb. ii. 17); therefore be thou our ruler, and let this ruin be under thy hand," Isa. iii. 6. 2. His former good services to the public were a further inducement (*v.* 2). 3. The divine appointment was the greatest inducement of all.

II. The public and solemn inauguration of David, *v.* 3. A convention of the states was called; all the elders of Israel came to him; the contract was settled, the *pacta conventa—covenants,* sworn to, and subscribed on both sides. He obliged himself to protect

JAMIESON, FAUSSET, BROWN

CHAPTER 5

VSS. 1-5. THE TRIBES ANOINT DAVID KING OVER ISRAEL. **1. Then came all the tribes of Israel**—a combined deputation of the leading authorities in every tribe.

David possessed the first and indispensable qualification for the throne; viz., that of being an Israelite (Deut. 17:15). Of his military talent he had furnished ample proof, and the people's desire for his assumption of the government of Israel was further increased by their knowledge of the will and purpose of God, as declared by Samuel (I Sam. 16: 11-13).

3. King David made a league with them in Hebron before the Lord—(see on I Sam. 10:25). This formal declaration of the constitution was chiefly made at the commencement of a new dynasty, or at the restoration of the royal family after a

ADAM CLARKE

CHAPTER 5

1. *Then came all the tribes of Israel.* Ish-bosheth, the king, and Abner, the general, being dead, they had no hope of maintaining a separate kingdom, and therefore thought it better to submit to David's authority. And they founded their resolution on three good arguments:

(1) David was their own countryman; *We are thy bone and thy flesh.* (2) Even in Saul's time David had been their general, and had always led them to victory; *Thou wast he that leddest out and broughtest in Israel.* (3) God had appointed him to the kingdom, to govern and protect the people; *The Lord said to thee, Thou shalt feed my people Israel, and . . . be a captain over Israel.*

MATTHEW HENRY

them as their judge in peace and captain in war; and they obliged themselves to obey him. He *made a league* with them to which God was a witness: it was *before the Lord*. Hereupon he was, for the third time, anointed king. His advances were gradual, that his faith might be tried and that he might gain experience. And thus his kingdom typified that of the Messiah, which was to come to its height by degrees; for *we see not yet all things put under him* (Heb. ii. 8), but we shall see it, 1 Cor. xv. 25.

III. A general account of his reign and age. He was thirty years old when he began to reign, upon the death of Saul, *v.* 4. At that age the Levites were at first appointed to begin their administration, Num. iv. 3. About that age the Son of David entered upon his public ministry, Luke iii. 23. Then men come to their full maturity of strength and judgment. He reigned, in all, forty years and six months, of which seven years and a half in Hebron and thirty-three years in Jerusalem, *v.* 5. Hebron had been famous, Josh. xiv. 15. It was a priest's city. But Jerusalem was to be more so, and to be the holy city.

Verses 6–10

If Salem, the place of which Melchizedec was king, was Jerusalem (as seems probable from Ps. lxxvi. 2), it was famous in Abraham's time. Joshua, in his time, found it the chief city of the south part of Canaan, Joshua x. 1–3. It fell to Benjamin's lot (Joshua xviii. 28), but joined close to Judah's, Joshua xv. 8. The children of Judah had taken it (Judges i. 8), but the children of Benjamin suffered the Jebusites to dwell among them (Judges i. 21), and they grew so upon them that it became a *city of Jebusites*, Judges xix. 11. Now the very first exploit David did, after he was anointed king over all Israel, was to gain Jerusalem out of the hand of the Jebusites, which, because it belonged to Benjamin, he could not well attempt till that tribe, which long adhered to Saul's house (1 Chron. xii. 29), submitted to him.

I. The Jebusites' defiance of David and his forces. They said, *Except thou take away the blind and the lame, thou shalt not come in hither*, *v.* 6. They sent David this provoking message, because they could not believe that *ever an enemy would enter into the gates of Jerusalem*, Lam. iv. 12. They confided either, 1. In the protection of their gods, which David, in contempt, had called *the blind and the lame*, for *they have eyes and see not, feet and walk not*. Or, 2. In the strength of their fortifications, which they thought were made so impregnable by nature or art, or both, that the blind and the lame were sufficient to defend them against the most powerful assailant. The stronghold of Zion they especially depended on, as that which could not be forced.

II. David's success against the Jebusites. Their pride and insolence, instead of daunting him, animated him, and when he made a general assault he gave this order to his men: "*He that smiteth the Jebusites, let him also throw down into the ditch*, or gutter, *the lame and the blind*, which are set upon the wall to affront us and our God." David, having gained the fort, said that these images, which could not protect their worshippers, should never have any place there more.

III. His fixing his royal seat in Sion. He himself dwelt in the fort and he built houses round about for his attendants and guards (*v.* 9) from Millo (the townhall, or state-house) and inward. He proceeded and prospered in all he set his hand to, grew great in honour, strength, and wealth, more and more honourable in the eyes of his subjects and formidable in the eyes of his enemies; for *the Lord God of hosts was with him.*

Verses 11–15

I. David's house built, a royal palace, fit for the reception of the court he kept and the homage that was paid to him, *v.* 11. Hiram, king of Tyre, a wealthy prince, when he sent to congratulate David on his accession to the throne, offered him workmen to build him a house. David thankfully accepted the offer, and Hiram's workmen built David a house to his mind. Many have excelled in arts and sciences who were strangers to the covenants of promise. Yet David's house was never the worse, nor the less fit to be dedicated to God, for being built by the sons of the stranger. It is prophesied of the gospel church, *The sons of the strangers shall build up thy walls, and their kings shall minister unto thee*, Isa. lx. 10.

II. David's government settled and built up, *v.* 12. 1. His kingdom was established, there was nothing to shake it. He that made him king established him, because he was to be a type of Christ, with whom God's hand should be established. 2. It was exalted in the eyes both of its friends and enemies. Never had the nation of Israel looked so great or made such a figure as it began now to do. God did not make

JAMIESON, FAUSSET, BROWN

usurpation (II Kings 11:17), though circumstances sometimes led to its being renewed on the accession of any new sovereign (I Kings 12:4). It seems to have been accompanied by religious solemnities.

6-12. HE TAKES ZION FROM THE JEBUSITES. **6. the king and his men went to Jerusalem unto the Jebusites**—The first expedition of David, as king of the whole country, was directed against this place, which had hitherto remained in the hands of the natives.

It was strongly fortified and deemed so impregnable that the blind and lame were sent to man the battlements, in derisive mockery of the Hebrew king's attack, and to shout, "David cannot come in hither." To understand the full meaning and force of this insulting taunt, it is necessary to bear in mind the depth and steepness of the valley of Gihon, and the lofty walls of the ancient Canaanitish fortress. **7. stronghold of Zion**—Whether Zion be the southwestern hill commonly so called, or the peak now level on the north of the temple mount, it is the towering height which catches the eye from every quarter—"the hill fort," "the rocky hold" of Jerusalem. **8. Whosoever getteth up to the gutter**—This is thought by some to mean a subterranean passage; by others a spout through which water was poured upon the fire which the besiegers often applied to the woodwork at the gateways, and by the projections of which a skilful climber might make his ascent good; a third class render the words, "whosoever dasheth them against the precipice" (I Chron. 11:6). **9. David dwelt in the fort . . .**—Having taken it by storm, he changed its name to "the city of David," to signify the importance of the conquest, and to perpetuate the memory of the event. **David built round about from Millo and inward**—probably a row of stone bastions placed on the northern side of Mount Zion, and built by David to secure himself on that side from the Jebusites, who still lived in the lower part of the city. The house of Millo was perhaps the principal corner tower of that fortified wall.

11, 12. Hiram . . . sent carpenters and masons—The influx of Tyrian architects and mechanics affords a clear evidence of the low state to which, through the disorders of long-continued war, the better class of artisans had declined in Israel.

ADAM CLARKE

3. *They anointed David king.* This was the third time that David was anointed, having now taken possession of the whole kingdom.

6. *The king and his men went to Jerusalem.* This city was now in the hands of the Jebusites, but how they got possession of it is not known; probably they took it during the wars between Ish-bosheth and David. After Joshua's death, what is called the lower city was taken by the Israelites; and it is evident that the whole city was in their possession in the time of Saul, for David brought the head of Goliath thither, 1 Sam. xvii. 54. It appears to have been a very strong fortress and, from what follows, deemed impregnable by the Jebusites. It was right that the Israelites should repossess it, and David very properly began his reign over the whole country by the siege of this city.

Except thou take away the blind and the lame. It appears that the Jebusites, vainly confiding in the strength of their fortress, placed lame and blind men upon the walls, and thus endeavored to turn into ridicule David's attempt to take the place.

11. *Hiram king of Tyre.* He was a very friendly man, and no doubt a believer in the true God. He was not only a friend to David, but also of his son Solomon, to whom, in building the Temple, he afforded the most important assistance.

MATTHEW HENRY

Israel his subjects for his sake, that he might be great, and rich, and absolute: but he made him their king for their sake, that he might lead, and guide, and protect them.

III. David's family multiplied and increased. All the sons that were born to him after he came to Jerusalem are here mentioned together, eleven in all, besides the six that were born to him before in Hebron, *ch.* iii. 2, 5. It is said that he *took more concubines and wives, v.* 13. Shall we praise him for this? We praise him not; we justify him not; nor can we scarcely excuse him. The bad example of the patriarchs might make him think there was no harm in it, and he might hope it would strengthen his interest, by multiplying his alliances, and increasing the royal family. But one vine by the side of the house, with the blessing of God, may send boughs to the sea and branches to the rivers. David had many wives, and yet that did not keep him from coveting his neighbour's wife and defiling her; for men that have once broken the fence will wander endlessly.

Verses 17–25

The particular service for which David was raised up was to *save Israel out of the hand of the Philistines, ch.* iii. 18. Two great victories obtained over the Philistines we have here an account of, by which David not only balanced the disgrace and retrieved the loss Israel had sustained in the battle wherein Saul was slain, but went far towards the total subduing of those vexatious neighbours.

I. In both these actions the Philistines were the aggressors. 1. In the former they *came up to seek David* (*v.* 17), because they *heard that he was anointed king over Israel.* They therefore try to crush his government in its infancy, before it was well settled. They took counsel together, but were *broken in pieces,* Isa. viii. 9, 10. 2. In the latter they *came up yet again,* hoping to recover what they had lost in the former engagement, their hearts being hardened to their destruction, *v.* 22. 3. In both they *spread themselves in the valley of Rephaim,* which lay very near Jerusalem. That city they hoped to make themselves masters of before David had completed the fortifications. Their spreading themselves intimates that they were very numerous.

II. In both, David, though forward enough to go forth against them yet entered not upon action till he had *enquired of the Lord* by the breast-plate of judgment, *v.* 19, and again, *v.* 23. His enquiry was twofold:—1. Concerning his duty: "*Shall I go up?*" Achish had been kind to him in his distress, and had protected him. "Now," says David, "ought not I, in remembrance of that, rather to make peace with them than to make war with them?" "No," says God, "they are Israel's enemies, *go up.*" 2. Concerning his success. His conscience asked the former question, *Shall I go up?* His prudence asked this, *Wilt thou deliver them into my hand?* Hereby he owns his dependence on God for victory. Yea, says God, *I will doubtless do it.* If God send us, he will bear us out and stand by us. The assurance God has given us of victory over our spiritual enemies, that he will tread Satan under our feet shortly, should animate us in our spiritual conflicts. David had now a great army at command and in good heart, yet he relied more on God's promise than his own force.

III. In the former of these engagements David routed the army of the Philistines by dint of sword (*v.* 20): he *smote them*; and when he had done, 1. He gave his God the glory. He called the place *Baal-perazim, the master of the breaches,* because, God having broken in upon their forces, he soon had the mastery of them. 2. He put their gods to shame. They brought the images of their gods into the field as their protectors, in imitation of the Israelites bringing the ark into their camp; but, being put to flight, they could not stay to carry off their images, for they were a *burden to the weary beasts* (Isa. xlvi. 1), and therefore they left them to fall with the rest of their baggage into the hands of the conqueror. David and his men converted to their own use the rest of the plunder, but the images they burnt, as God had appointed (Deut. vii. 5). Bishop Patrick well observes here that when the ark fell into the Philistines' hands it consumed them, but when these images fell into the hands of Israel, they could not save themselves from being consumed.

IV. In the latter of these engagements God gave David some sensible tokens of his presence with him, bade him not fall upon them directly, as he had done before, but *fetch a compass behind them, v.* 23. 1. God appoints him to draw back, as *Israel stood still to see the salvation of the Lord.* 2. He promised him to charge the enemy himself, by an invisible host of angels, *v.* 24. "Thou shalt hear the *sound of a going,* like the march of an army in the air, *upon the*

JAMIESON, FAUSSET, BROWN

13-16. Eleven Sons Born to Him. **13. David took him more concubines and wives**—In this conduct David transgressed an express law, which forbade the king of Israel to multiply wives unto himself (Deut. 17:17).

17-25. He Smites the Philistines. **17. when the Philistines heard that they had anointed David king over Israel**—During the civil war between the house of Saul and David, those restless neighbors had remained quiet spectators of the contest. But now, jealous of David, they resolved to attack him before his government was fully established. **18. valley of Rephaim**—i.e., of giants, a broad and fertile plain, which descends gradually from the central mountains towards the northwest. It was the route by which they marched against Jerusalem. The "hold" to which David went down "was some fortified place where he might oppose the progress of the invaders," and where he signally defeated them.

21. there they left their images—probably their lares or household deities, which they had brought into the field to fight for them. They were burnt as ordained by law (Deut. 7:5).

22. the Philistines came up yet again—The next year they renewed their hostile attempt with a larger force, but God manifestly interposed in David's favor.

ADAM CLARKE

13. *David took him more concubines.* He had, in all conscience, enough before; he had, in the whole, eight wives and ten concubines.

14. *These be the names.* Eleven children are here enumerated in the Hebrew text, but the Septuagint has no less than twenty-four.

17. *The Philistines came up to seek David.* Ever since the defeat of the Israelites and the fall of Saul and his sons, the Philistines seem to have been in undisturbed possession of the principal places in the land of Israel; now, finding that David was chosen king by the whole nation, they thought best to attack him before his army got too numerous, and the affairs of the kingdom were properly settled.

19. *David enquired of the Lord.* He considered himself only the captain of the Lord's host, and therefore would not strike a stroke without the command of his Superior.

20. *The Lord hath broken forth.* He very properly attributes the victory of Jehovah, without whose strength and counsel he could have done nothing. *Baal-perazim.* The "plain or chief of breaches," because of the breach which God made in the Philistine army.

21. *They left their images.* It was the custom of most nations to carry their gods with them to battle.

23. *Fetch a compass behind them.* When they may be had, God will not work without using human means. By this He taught David caution, prudence, and dependence on the divine strength.

MATTHEW HENRY

tops of the mulberry trees." God's grace must quicken our endeavours. The sound of the going was, (1) A signal to David when to move; it is comfortable going out when God goes before us. And, (2) Perhaps it was an alarm to the enemy, and put them into confusion. Hearing the march of an army against their front, they retreated with precipitation, and fell into David's army which lay behind them in their rear. (3) The success of this is briefly set down, *v.* 25. David observed his orders, waited till God moved, and stirred then, but not till then. He smote the Philistines, even to the borders of their own country. When the kingdom of the Messiah was to be set up, the apostles that were to beat down the devil's kingdom must not attempt anything till they received the promise of the Spirit, who *came with a sound from heaven as of a rushing mighty wind* (Acts ii. 2), which was typified by this sound of the going on the tops of the mulberry trees; and, when they heard that, they must bestir themselves, and did so; they went forth conquering and to conquer.

CHAPTER 6

Verses 1–5

The ark was lodged in Kirjath-jearim, immediately after its return out of its captivity among the Philistines (1 Sam. vii. 1, 2). Once Saul called for it, 1 Sam. xiv. 18. That which in former days had made so great a figure is as a neglected thing for many years. Perpetual visibility is no mark of the true church. God is graciously present with the souls of his people even when they want the external tokens of his presence. But now that David is settled in the throne the honour of the ark begins to revive.

I. Here is honourable mention made of the ark. Because it had not been spoken of a great while, now it is described (*v.* 2): *the ark of God whose name is called by the name of the Lord of hosts that dwelleth between the cherubim.* Let us learn hence, 1. To think and speak highly of God. He is the name above every name, *the Lord of hosts,* that has all the creatures in heaven and earth, at his command, and yet is pleased to dwell between the cherubim, over the propitiatory or mercy-seat, graciously manifesting himself to his people, reconciled in a Mediator, and ready to do them good. 2. To think and speak honourably of holy ordinances, which are to us, as the ark was to Israel, the token of God's presence (Matt. xxviii. 20), and the means of our communion with him, Ps. xxvii. 4. Christ is our ark.

II. Here is an honourable attendance given to the ark upon the removal of it. David made the motion (1 Chron. xiii. 1–3). All the chosen men of Israel are called together to grace the solemnity, to pay their respect to the ark, and to testify their joy in its restoration. This would help to inspire the young people of the nation, who perhaps had scarcely heard of the ark, with a great veneration for it.

III. Here are great expressions of joy upon the removal of the ark, *v.* 5. As secret worship is better the more secret it is, so public worship is better the more public it is; and we have reason to rejoice when restraints are taken off, and the ark of God finds welcome in the city of David, and has not only the protection and support, but the countenance and encouragement, of the civil powers; for joy of this they *played before the Lord.* Dr. Lightfoot supposes that, upon this occasion, David penned the 68th Psalm, because it begins with that ancient prayer of Moses at the removing of the ark, *Let God arise, and let his enemies be scattered*; and notice is taken there (*v.* 25) of the *singers and players on instruments* that attended, and (*v.* 27) of the princes of several of the tribes; and perhaps those words in the last verse, *O God, thou art terrible out of thy holy places,* were added upon occasion of the death of Uzzah.

IV. Here is an error that they were guilty of in this matter, that they carried the ark in a cart or carriage, whereas the priests should have carried it upon their shoulders, *v.* 3. The Kohathites that had the charge of the ark had no waggons assigned them, because *their service was to bear it upon their shoulders,* Num. vii. 9. The ark was no such heavy burden but that they might, among them, have carried it as far as Mount Sion upon their shoulders, they needed not to put it in a cart like a common thing. It was no excuse for them that the Philistines had done so and were not punished for it; they knew no better. Philistines may cart the ark with impunity; but, if Israelites do so, they do it at their peril. And it mended the matter very little that it was a new cart; old or new, it was not what God had appointed.

Verses 6–11

Uzzah struck dead for touching the ark, when it

JAMIESON, FAUSSET, BROWN

24. the sound of a going in the tops of the mulberry trees—now generally thought not to be mulberry trees, but some other tree, most probably the poplar, which delights in moist situations, and the leaves of which are rustled by the slightest movement of the air (ROYLE).

CHAPTER 6

VSS. 1-5. DAVID FETCHES THE ARK FROM KIRJATH-JEARIM ON A NEW CART. **1. Again David gathered together all the chosen men of Israel**—(See ch. 5:1). The object of this second assembly was to commence a national movement for establishing the ark in Jerusalem, after it had continued nearly fifty years in the house of Abinadab (see on I Chron. 13:1-5).

2. from Baale of Judah—A very large force of picked men were selected for this important work lest the undertaking might be opposed or obstructed by the Philistines. Besides, a great concourse of people accompanied them out of veneration for the sacred article. The journey *to* Baale, which is related (I Chron. 13:6), is here presupposed, and the historian describes the course of the procession *from* that place to the capital.

3. they set the ark of God upon a new cart—or covered wagon (see on I Sam. 6:7). This was a hasty and inconsiderate procedure, in violation of an express statute (see on Num. 4:14, 15; 7:9; 18:3).

ADAM CLARKE

24. *When thou hearest the sound of a going.* If there had not been an evident supernatural interference, David might have thought that the sleight which he had used was the cause of his victory. By the going in the tops of the mulberry trees, probably only a rustling among the leaves is intended.

25. *And David did so.* He punctually obeyed the directions of the Lord, and then everything succeeded to his wish.

CHAPTER 6

1. *Thirty thousand.* This is supposed to have been a new levy; and thus he augmented his army by 30,000 fresh troops. The Septuagint has 70,000.

2. *From Baale of Judah.* This is supposed to be the same city which, in Josh. xv. 60, is called Kirjath-baal or Kirjath-jearim (see 1 Chron. xiii. 6); or Baalah, Josh. xv. 9. *Whose name is called by the name of the Lord.* That is, "The ark is called the ark of the Lord of hosts." But this is not a literal version. The word *shem,* "name," occurs twice together; probably one of them should be read *sham,* "there." There the name of the Lord of hosts was invoked.

5. *On all manner of instruments made of fir wood.* This place should be corrected from the parallel place, 1 Chron. xiii. 8: "All Israel played before God, with all their might, and with singing, and with harps, and with psalteries." Instead of *bechol atsey,* "with all woods" or "trees," the parallel place is *bechol oz,* "with all their strength." This makes a good sense; the first makes none. The Septuagint, in this place, has the same reading: "with might."

3. *A new cart.* Everything used in the worship of God was hallowed or set apart for that purpose; a new cart was used through respect, as that had never been applied to any profane or common purpose. But this is not sufficient, for the ark should have been carried on the shoulders of the priests; and the neglect of this ceremony was the cause of the death of Uzzah.

MATTHEW HENRY

was upon its journey towards the city of David, a sad providence, which damped their mirth, stopped the progress of the ark, and, for the present, dispersed this great assembly, which had come together to attend it, and sent them home in a fright.

I. Uzzah's offence seems very small. He and his brother Ahio, the sons of Abinadab, in whose house the ark had long been lodged, having been used to attend it, undertook to drive the cart in which the ark was carried, this being perhaps the last service they were likely to do it; for others would be employed about it when it came to the city of David. Ahio went before, to clear the way, and, if need were, to lead the oxen. Uzzah followed close to the side of the cart. It happened that the oxen shook it, *v.* 6. The critics are not agreed about the signification of the original word: *They stumbled* (so our margin); *they kicked* (so some), perhaps against the goad with which Uzzah drove them; *they stuck in the mire*, so some. By some accident or other the ark was in danger of being overthrown. Uzzah thereupon laid hold of it, to save it from falling. Uzzah was a Levite, but priests only might touch the ark. The law was express concerning the Kohathites, that, though they were to carry the ark by the staves, yet *they must not touch any holy thing, lest they die*, Num. iv. 15.

II. His punishment for this offence seems very great (*v.* 7). There he sinned, and there he died, *by the ark of God*; even the mercy-seat would not save him. Why was God thus severe with him? 1. The touching of the ark was forbidden to the Levites expressly under pain of death—*lest they die*. 2. God saw the presumption and irreverence of Uzzah's heart. Perhaps he affected to show, before this great assembly, how bold he could make with the ark, having been so long acquainted with it. 3. David afterwards owned that Uzzah died for an error they were all guilty of, which was carrying the ark in a cart. But Uzzah was singled out to be made an example, perhaps because he had been most forward in advising that way of conveyance. 4. God would hereby strike an awe upon the thousands of Israel, would convince them that the ark was never the less venerable for its having been so long in mean circumstances, and thus he would teach them to rejoice with trembling, and always to treat holy things with reverence and holy fear.

III. David's feelings on the infliction of this stroke were keen, and perhaps not altogether as they should have been. 1. He was displeased. *David's anger was kindled.* It is the same word that is used for God's displeasure, *v.* 7. Because God was angry, David was angry and out of humour. The death of Uzzah was indeed an eclipse to the glory of a solemnity, but he ought nevertheless to have subscribed to the righteousness and wisdom of God in it, and not to have been displeased at it. When we lie under God's anger we must keep under our own. 2. He was afraid, *v.* 9. It should seem he was afraid with amazement; for he said, *How shall the ark of the Lord come to me?* As if God was so extremely tender of his ark that there was no dealing with it; and therefore better for him to keep it at a distance. He should rather have said, "Let the ark come to me, and I will take warning by this to treat it with more reverence." David therefore will not bring the ark into his own city (*v.* 10) till he is better prepared for its reception. 3. He took care to perpetuate the remembrance of this stroke by a new name he gave to the place: *Perez-uzzah, the breach of Uzzah*, *v.* 8. He had been lately triumphing in the breach made upon his enemies, and called the place *Baal-perazim, a place of breaches.* But here is a breach upon his friends. The memorial of this stroke would be a warning to posterity to take heed of all rashness and irreverence in dealing about holy things. 4. He lodged the ark in a good house, the house of Obed-edom a Levite, which happened to be near the place where this disaster happened, and there, (1) It was kindly entertained and welcomed, and continued there *three months*, *v.* 10, 11. Obed-edom knew what slaughter the ark had made among the Philistines and the Bethshemites. He saw Uzzah struck dead for touching it, and perceived that David himself was afraid of meddling with it; yet he opens his doors to it without fear, knowing it was a *savour of death unto death* only to those that treated it ill. (2) It paid well for its entertainment: *The Lord blessed Obed-edom and all his household.* The same hand that punished Uzzah's proud presumption rewarded Obed-edom's humble boldness, and made the ark to him a *savour of life unto life*. The ark is a guest which none shall lose by that bid it welcome. It is good living in a family that entertains the ark, for all about it will fare the better for it.

Verses 12–19

The second attempt to bring the ark home to the

JAMIESON, FAUSSET, BROWN

6-11. UZZAH SMITTEN. **6. they came to Nachon's threshing-floor**—or Chidon's (I Chron. 13:9). The Chaldee version renders the words, "came to the place prepared for the reception of the ark," i.e., near the city of David (vs. 13). **the oxen shook it**—or stumbled (I Chron. 13:9). Fearing that the ark was in danger of being overturned, Uzzah, under the impulse of momentary feeling, laid hold of it to keep it steady.

Whether it fell and crushed him, or some sudden disease attacked him, he fell dead upon the spot. This melancholy occurrence not only threw a cloud over the joyous scene, but entirely stopped the procession; for the ark was left where it then was, in the near neighborhood of the capital. It is of importance to observe the proportionate severity of the punishments attending the profanation of the ark. The Philistines suffered by diseases, from which they were relieved by their oblations, because the law had not been given to them; the Beth-shemites also suffered, but not fatally; their error proceeded from ignorance or inadvertency. But Uzzah, who was a Levite, and well instructed, suffered death for his breach of the law. The severity of Uzzah's fate may seem to us too great for the nature and degree of the offense. But it does not become us to sit in judgment on the dispensations of God; and, besides, it is apparent that the divine purpose was to inspire awe of His majesty, a submission to His law, and a profound veneration for the symbols and ordinances of His worship.

9. David was afraid of the Lord that day . . .—His feelings on this alarming judgment were greatly excited on various accounts, dreading that the displeasure of God had been provoked by the removal of the ark, that the punishment would be extended to himself and people, and that they might fall into some error or neglect during the further conveyance of the ark. He resolved, therefore, to wait for more light and direction as to the path of duty. An earlier consultation by Urim would have led him right at the first, whereas in this perplexity and distress, he was reaping the fruits of inconsideration and neglect.

11. Obed-edom the Gittite—a Levite (I Chron. 15:18, 21, 24; 16:5; 26:4). He is called a Gittite, either from his residence at Gath, or more probably from Gath-rimmon, one of the Levitical cities (Josh. 21:24, 25).

ADAM CLARKE

6. *Uzzah put forth his hand.* In Num. iv. 15-20, the Levites are forbidden to touch the ark on pain of death; this penalty was inflicted upon Uzzah, and he was the first that suffered for a breach of this law.

7. *Smote him there for his error.* Uzzah sinned through ignorance and precipitancy; he had not time to reflect. The oxen suddenly stumbled; and, fearing lest the ark should fall, he suddenly stretched out his hand to prevent it. Had he touched the ark with impunity, the populace might have lost their respect for it and its sacred service; the example of Uzzah must have filled them with fear and sacred reverence; and, as to Uzzah, no man can doubt of his eternal safety.

10. *But David carried it aside.* The house of Obed-edom appears to have been very near the city which they were about to enter.

11. *The Lord blessed Obed-edom.* And why? Because he had the ark of the Lord in his house. Whoever entertains God's messengers or consecrates his house to the service of God will infallibly receive God's blessing.

MATTHEW HENRY

city of David; and this succeeded, though the former miscarried.

I. The blessing with which the house of Obed-edom was blessed was an evidence that God was reconciled to them, and his anger was turned away. If God be at peace with them, they can cheerfully go on with their design. 1. It was an evidence that the ark was not such a burdensome stone as it was taken to be, but, on the contrary, happy was the man that had it near him. Christ is indeed a *stone of stumbling, and a rock of offence*, to those that are disobedient; but to those who believe he is a *corner-stone, elect, precious*, 1 Pet. ii. 6–8.

II. How David managed the matter now. 1. He ordered those whose business it was to carry it on their shoulders. This is implied here (*v.* 13) and expressed 1 Chron. xv. 15. 2. At their first setting out he offered sacrifices to God (*v.* 13) by way of atonement for their former errors. 3. He himself attended the solemnity with the highest expressions of joy that could be (*v.* 14): *He danced before the Lord with all his might*; he leaped for joy. His dancing was not artificial, by any certain rule or measure, but was a natural expression of his great joy and exultation of mind. 4. All the people triumphed in this advancement of the ark (*v.* 15): *They brought it up* into the royal city *with shouting*, and *with sound of trumpet*. 5. The ark was safely brought to, and honourably deposited in, the place prepared for it, *v.* 17. They set it in *the midst of the tabernacle*, or tent, *which David had pitched for it*. As soon as ever it was lodged, he offered burnt-offerings and peace-offerings, in thankfulness to God and in supplication to God for the continuance of his favour. 6. The people were then dismissed with great satisfaction. He sent them away, (1) With a gracious prayer: *He blessed them in the name of the Lord of hosts* (*v.* 18). He testified his desire for their welfare by this prayer, and let them know they had a king that loved them. (2) With a generous treat; for so it was, rather than a distribution of alms.

Verses 20–23

David, having dismissed the congregation with a blessing, *returned to bless his household* (*v.* 20), to offer up his family thanksgiving for this national mercy.

Never did David return to his house with so much pleasure and satisfaction as he did now that he had got the ark into his neighbourhood; and yet even this joyful day concluded with some uneasiness, occasioned by his wife. Michal was not pleased with his dancing before the ark. When he came home she scolded him. She thought he degraded himself in dancing before the ark.

I. When she saw David in the street dancing before the Lord she *despised him in her heart*, *v.* 16. She thought this mighty zeal of his for the ark of God, and the transport of joy he was in upon its coming home, was unbecoming so great a soldier, and statesman, and monarch.

II. When he came home in the very best disposition she went out to meet him with her reproaches.

1. How she taunted him (*v.* 20): "*How glorious was the king of Israel to-day*. What a figure didst thou make to-day in the midst of the mob!" That which displeased her was his affection to the ark, but she basely represents his conduct, in dancing before the ark, as lewd and immodest. We have no reason to think that this was true in fact. David, no doubt, observed decorum, and governed his zeal with discretion. To disparage one who had shown such affection for her that he would not accept a crown unless he might have her restored to him (*ch.* iii. 13), was a most base and wicked thing, and showed her to have more of Saul's daughter in her than of David's wife or Jonathan's sister.

2. How he replied to her reproach.

(1) He designed to honour God (*v.* 21): *It was before the Lord*, and with an eye to him. Whatever invidious construction she was pleased to put upon it, he had the testimony of his conscience for him that he sincerely aimed at the glory of God. Here he reminds her indeed of the setting aside of her father's house, to make way for him to the throne, that she might not think herself the most proper judge of propriety: "*God chose me before thy father, and appointed me to be ruler over Israel*, and, if the expressions of a warm devotion to God were looked upon as mean and unfashionable in thy father's court, yet *I will play before the Lord*, and thereby bring them into reputation again. [1] If we can approve ourselves to God in what we do in religion, and do it as before the Lord, we need not value the censures and reproaches of men. [2] The more we are vilified for well-doing the more resolute we should be in it, and hold our religion the faster.

JAMIESON, FAUSSET, BROWN

12-19. David Afterwards Brings the Ark to Zion. **12. it was told King David, saying, The Lord hath blessed the house of Obed-edom and all that pertaineth unto him, because of the ark of God**—The lapse of three months not only restored the agitated mind of the monarch to a tranquil and settled tone, but led him to a discovery of his former error. Having learned that the ark was kept in its temporary resting-place not only without inconvenience or danger, but with great advantage, he resolved forthwith to remove it to the capital, with the observance of all due form and solemnity (I Chron. 15:1-13). It was transported now on the shoulders of the priests, who had been carefully prepared for the work, and the procession was distinguished by extraordinary solemnities and demonstrations of joy. **13. when they that bare the ark . . . had gone six paces**—Some think that four altars were hastily raised for the offering of sacrifices at the distance of every six paces (but see I Chron. 15:26). **14. David danced before the Lord**—The Hebrews, like other ancient people, had their sacred dances, which were performed on their solemn anniversaries and other great occasions of commemorating some special token of the divine goodness and favor. **with all his might**—intimating violent efforts of leaping, and divested of his royal mantle—in a state of undress—conduct apparently unsuitable to the gravity of age or the dignity of a king. But it was unquestionably done as an act of religious homage, his attitudes and dress being symbolic, as they have always been in Oriental countries, of penitence, joy, thankfulness, and devotion. **17. they brought in the ark of the Lord, and set it in his place in the midst of the tabernacle that David had pitched for it**—The old tabernacle remained at Gibeon (I Chron. 16:39; 21:29; II Chron. 1:3). Probably it was not removed because it was too large for the temporary place the king had appropriated, and because he contemplated the building of a temple. **18. he blessed the people**—in the double character of prophet and king (see on I Kings 8:55, 56). **19. cake of bread**—unleavened and slender. **a good piece of flesh**—roast beef.

20-23. Michal's Barrenness. **Michal . . . came out to meet David . . .**—Proud of her royal extraction, she upbraided her husband for lowering the dignity of the crown and acting more like a buffoon than a king. But her taunting sarcasm was repelled in a manner that could not be agreeable to her feelings while it indicated the warm piety and gratitude of David.

ADAM CLARKE

KEIL–DELITZSCH:

After sacrificing the cart, with the cows, as a burnt offering to the Lord, the inhabitants of Bethshemesh gave a further practical expression to their joy at the return of the ark, by offering burnt offerings and slain offerings in praise of God. In the burnt offerings they consecrated themselves afresh, with all their members, to the service of the Lord; and in the slain offerings, which culminated in the sacrifical meals, they sealed anew their living fellowship with the Lord. The offering of these sacrifices at Bethshemesh was no offence against the commandment, to sacrifice to the Lord at the place of His sanctuary alone. The ark of the covenant was the throne of the gracious presence of God, before which the sacrifices were really offered at the tabernacle. The Lord had sanctified the ark afresh as the throne of His presence, by the miracle which He had wrought in bringing it back again.

—*Commentary on the Old Testament*

19. *A cake of bread*. Such as those which are baked without leaven, and are made very thin. *A good piece of flesh, and a flagon of wine*. The words *of flesh* and *of wine* we add; they are not in the Hebrew.

20. *To bless his household*. This was according to the custom of the patriarchs, who were priests in their own families. It is worthy of remark that David is called "patriarch" by Stephen, Acts ii. 29, though living upwards of four hundred years after the termination of the patriarchal age.

How glorious was the king of Israel! This is a strong irony. From what Michal says, it is probable that David used some violent gesticulations, by means of which some parts of his body became uncovered.

21. *It was before the Lord, which chose me*. David felt the reproach, and was strongly irritated, and seems to have spoken to Michal with sufficient asperity.

MATTHEW HENRY

(2) He designed thereby to humble himself: "*I will be base in my own sight*, and will think nothing too mean to stoop to for the honour of God."

(3) He doubted not but even this would turn to his reputation among those whose reproach Michal pretended to fear: *Of the maid-servants shall I be had in honour*. She unjustly reproached David for his devotion. *Those that honour God he will honour*; but those that despise him, and his servants and service, *shall be lightly esteemed*.

CHAPTER 7

Verses 1–3

I. David at rest. *He sat in his house* (*v.* 1), quiet and undisturbed, having no occasion to take the field. He had not been long at rest, nor was it long before he was again engaged in war; but at present he enjoyed a calm, and he was in his element when he was sitting in his house, meditating in the law of God.

II. David's thought of building a temple for the honour of God. He had built a palace for himself and a city for his servants; and now he thinks of building a habitation for the ark. 1. Thus he would make a grateful return for the honours God put upon him. *What shall I render unto the Lord?* 2. Thus he would improve the present calm, and make a good use of the rest God had given him. David considered (*v.* 2) the stateliness of his own habitation (*I dwell in a house of cedar*), and compared with that the meanness of the habitation of the ark (*the ark dwells within curtains*), and thought this incongruous, that he should dwell in a palace and the ark in a tent. David had been uneasy till he found out *a place for the ark* (Ps. cxxxii. 4, 5), and now he is uneasy till he finds out a better place. Gracious grateful souls cannot enjoy their own accommodations while they see the church of God in distress and under a cloud. David can take little pleasure in a house of cedar for himself, unless the ark have one.

III. His communicating this thought to Nathan the prophet. David told him, that by him he might know the mind of God. It was certainly a good work, but it was uncertain whether it was the will of God that David should have the doing of it.

IV. Nathan's approbation of it: *Go, do all that is in thy heart; for the Lord is with thee*, *v.* 3. Nathan easily gathered what was in his heart, and bade him go on and prosper. We ought to do all we can to encourage and promote the good purposes and designs of others, and put in a good word, as we have opportunity, to forward a good work. Nathan spoke this, not in God's name, but as from himself; not as a prophet, but as a wise and good man.

Verses 4–17

A full revelation of God's favour to David, the notices and assurances of which God sent him by Nathan the prophet. The design of it is to take him off from his purpose of building the temple and it was therefore sent, 1. By the same hand that had given him encouragement to do it, lest, if it had been sent by any other, Nathan should be despised and insulted and David should be perplexed. 2. The same night, that Nathan might not continue long in an error nor David have his head any further filled with thoughts of that which he must never bring to pass.

I. David's purpose to build God a house is superseded. God took notice of that purpose, for he knows what is in man; and he was well pleased with it, as appears 1 Kings viii. 18, *Thou didst well that it was in thy heart*; yet he forbade him to go on with his purpose (*v.* 5): "*Shalt thou build me a house?* No, *thou shalt not* (as it is explained in the parallel place, 1 Chron. xvii. 4); there is other work appointed for thee to do, which must be done first." David is a man of war, and he must enlarge the borders of Israel, by carrying on their conquests. David is a sweet psalmist, and he must prepare psalms for the use of the temple when it is built, and settle the courses of the Levites; but his son's genius will better suit for building the house, and he will have a better treasure to bear the charge of it, and therefore let it be reserved for him to do. *As every man hath received the gift, so let him minister*. The building of a temple was to be a work of time, and preparation made for it; but it was a thing that had never been spoken of till now. God tells him, 1. That hitherto he had never had a house built for him (*v.* 6), a tabernacle had served hitherto, and it might serve awhile longer. God regards not outward pomp in his service; his presence was as surely with his people when the ark was in a tent as when it was in a temple. Christ, like the ark, when here on earth walked in a tent or tabernacle,

JAMIESON, FAUSSET, BROWN

CHAPTER 7

VSS. 1-3. NATHAN APPROVES THE PURPOSE OF DAVID TO BUILD GOD A HOUSE.

2. the king said unto Nathan the prophet, See now, I dwell in an house of cedar—The palace which Hiram had sent men and materials to build in Jerusalem had been finished. It was magnificent for that age, though made wholly of wood: houses in warm countries not being required to possess the solidity and thickness of walls which are requisite for dwellings in regions exposed to rain and cold. Cedar was the rarest and most valuable timber. The elegance and splendor of his own royal mansion, contrasted with the mean and temporary tabernacle in which the ark of God was placed, distressed the pious mind of David.

Nathan said to the king, Go, do all that is in thine heart—The piety of the design commended it to the prophet's mind, and he gave his hasty approval and encouragement to the royal plans. The prophets, when following the impulse of their own feelings, or forming conjectural opinions, fell into frequent mistakes. (See on I Sam. 16:6; II Kings 4:27.)

4-17. GOD APPOINTS HIS SUCCESSOR TO BUILD IT.

4-17. it came to pass that night, that the word of the Lord came unto Nathan—The command was given to the prophet on the night immediately following; i.e., before David could either take any measures or incur any expenses.

ADAM CLARKE

22. *I will yet be more vile*. The plain meaning of these words appears to be this: "I am not ashamed of humbling myself before that God who rejected thy father because of his obstinacy and pride, and chose me in his stead to rule his people; and even those maidservants, when they come to know the motive of my conduct, shall acknowledge its propriety, and treat me with additional respect; and as for thee, thou shalt find that thy conduct is as little pleasing to God as it is to me."

CHAPTER 7

1. *When the king sat in his house*. That is, when he became resident in the palace which Hiram, king of Tyre, had built for him. *And the Lord had given him rest*. This was after he had defeated the Philistines, and cast them out of all the strong places in Israel which they had possessed after the overthrow of Saul.

3. *Nathan said to the king*. In this case he gave his judgment as a pious and prudent man, not as a prophet; for the prophets were not always under a divine afflatus; it was only at select times they were thus honored.

5. *Shalt thou build me an house?* That is, You shall not; this is the force of the interrogative in such a case.

MATTHEW HENRY

for he *went about doing good*, and dwelt not in any house of his own, till he ascended on high, to the mansions above, in his Father's house, and there he sat down. The church, like the ark, in this world is ambulatory, dwells in a tent, because its present state is both pastoral and military; its continuing city is to come. David, in his psalms, often calls the tabernacle a temple (as Ps. v. 7; xxvii. 4; xxix. 9; lxv. 4; cxxxviii. 2), because it answered the intention of a temple, though it was made but of curtains. 2. That he had never given any orders or directions, or the least intimation, to any of the sceptres of Israel, that is, to any of the judges, 1 Chron. xvii. 6 (for rulers are called *sceptres*, Ezek. xix. 14, the great Ruler is called so, Num. xxiv. 17), concerning the building of the temple, *v.* 7.

II. David is reminded of the great things God had done for him. 1. He had raised him from a very mean and low condition: *He took him from the sheep-cote*. 2. He had given him success and victory over his enemies (*v.* 9): "*I was with thee whithersoever thou wentest*, to protect thee when pursued, to prosper thee when pursuing." 3. He had crowned him not only with power and dominion in Israel, but with honour and reputation among the nations about: *I have made thee a great name*.

III. A happy establishment is promised to God's Israel, *v.* 10, 11. This comes in in a parenthesis, before the promises made to David himself, to let him understand that what God designed to do for him was for Israel's sake, that they might be happy under his administration, and to give him the satisfaction of foreseeing peace upon Israel, when it was promised him that he should *see his children's children*, Ps. cxxviii. 6. Two things are promised:—1. A quiet place: Canaan should be clearly their own without any ejection or molestation. 2. A quiet enjoyment of that place: *The children of wickedness* (meaning especially the Philistines, who had been so long a plague to them) *shall not afflict them any more*.

IV. Blessings are entailed upon the family and posterity of David. David had purposed to build God a house, and, in requital, God promises to *build him a house*, *v.* 11.

1. Some of these promises relate to Solomon, his immediate successor, and to the royal line of Judah. (1) That God would advance him to the throne. (2) That he would settle him in the throne: *I will establish his kingdom* (*v.* 12), *the throne of his kingdom*, *v.* 13. (3) That he would employ him in that good work of building the temple, which David had only the satisfaction of designing: *He shall build a house for my name*, *v.* 13. (4) That he would take him into the covenant of adoption (*v.* 14, 15): *I will be his father, and he shall be my son*. We need no more to make us and ours happy than to have God to be a Father to us and them. The promise here speaks *as unto sons*. [1] That his Father would correct him when there was occasion; for *what son is he whom the Father chasteneth not?* Not a stroke, or wound, but a gentle touch. [2] That yet he would not disinherit him (*v.* 15): The revolt of the ten tribes from the house of David was their correction for iniquity, but the constant adherence of the other two to that family, perpetuated the mercy of God to the seed of David, though that family was cut short, yet it was not cut off, as the house of Saul was.

2. Others of them relate to Christ, who is often called *David* and the *Son of David*, that Son of David to whom these promises pointed and in whom they had their full accomplishment. He was of the *seed of David*, Acts. xiii. 23. That promise, *I will be his Father, and he shall be my Son*, is expressly applied to Christ by the apostle, Heb. i. 5. But the establishing of his house, and his throne, and his *kingdom, for ever* (*v.* 13, and again, and a third time, *v.* 16, *for ever*), can be applied to no other than Christ and his kingdom. David's house and kingdom have long since come to an end; it is only the Messiah's kingdom that is everlasting, and *of the increase of his government and peace there shall be no end*. Now, (1) This message Nathan faithfully delivered to David (*v.* 17); though, in forbidding him to build the temple, he contradicted his own words. (2) These promises God faithfully performed to David and his seed in due time.

Verses 18–29

The solemn address David made to God, in answer to the gracious message God had sent him.

I. The place he retired to: He *went in before the Lord*, that is, into the tabernacle where the ark was, which was the token of God's presence; before *that* he presented himself.

II. The posture he put himself into: He *sat before the Lord*. 1. It denotes the posture of his body. Kneeling or standing is certainly the most proper gesture to be used in prayer. *David went in, and took his place before the Lord*, so it may be read; but,

JAMIESON, FAUSSET, BROWN

JOSEPH PARKER:

Nathan and David settled the matter according to their own will. Nathan was a man who might perhaps not be indisposed to agree with the king whatever he said. He may come to another temper under divine ministry; for that we must wait. The idea struck Nathan as a good one. Nathan had no objection. He said: The idea is beautiful: carry it out instantaneously; the Lord is evidently with thee; this is a thought the image and superscription of which cannot be mistaken; and Nathan went home to sleep. There are some things that appear to need no judgment. There are some proposals that are so beautiful and precious that we at once accept them, endorse them, and pass them on to fulfillment, and then retire to rest. The Lord taught David another lesson. He said: This thing is all wrong; it is out of season; there is much more to be done before this man can advance in the direction he has proposed: my house must not be built by his hands; I have an interest in my house: I care for the masonry as well as for the sanctuary.—*The People's Bible*

11. Also the Lord telleth thee that he will make thee an house—As a reward for his pious purpose, God would increase and maintain the family of David and secure the succession of the throne to his dynasty. **12. I will set up thy seed after thee . . .**—It is customary for the *oldest son born after the father's succession to the throne* to succeed him in his dignity as king. David had several sons by Bath-sheba born after his removal to Jerusalem (ch. 5:14-16; cf. I Chron. 3:5). But by a special ordinance and promise of God, his successor was to be a son born after this time; and the departure from the established usage of the East in fixing the succession, can be accounted for on no other known ground, except the fulfilment of the divine promise.

13. He shall build an house for my name, and I will establish the throne of his kingdom for ever—This declaration referred, in its primary application, to Solomon, and to the temporal kingdom of David's family. But in a larger and sublimer sense, it was meant of David's Son of another nature (Heb. 1:8).

18-29. DAVID'S PRAYER AND THANKSGIVING. **18. Then went King David in, and sat before the Lord**—Sitting was anciently an attitude for worship (Exod. 17:12; I Sam. 4:13; I Kings 19:4). As to the particular attitude David sat, most probably, *upon*

ADAM CLARKE

7. *With any of the tribes*. "Spake I a word to any of the judges?" is the reading in the parallel place, 1 Chron. xvii. 6; and this is probably the true reading. Indeed, there is but one letter of difference between them, and letters which might be easily mistaken for each other.

10. *I will appoint a place*. I "have" appointed a place, and "have" planted them.

11. *The Lord . . . will make thee an house*. You have in your heart to make Me a house; I have it in My heart to make you a house.

13. *He shall build*. That is, Solomon shall build My temple, not you, because you have shed blood abundantly, and have made great wars (see 1 Chron. xxii. 8).

14. *If he commit iniquity*—depart from the holy commandment delivered to him, *I will chasten him with the road of men*—he shall have affliction, but his government shall not be utterly subverted.

***The throne of his kingdom for ever*. This is a reference to the government of the spiritual Kingdom, the kingdom of the Messiah, agreeably to the predictions of the prophet long after, and by which this passage is illustrated: "Of the increase of his government and peace there shall be no end, upon the throne of David, and upon his kingdom, to order it, and to establish it with judgment and with justice from henceforth even for ever," Isa. ix. 7.**

MATTHEW HENRY

when he prayed, he stood up as the manner was. Or he *went in and continued before the Lord*, stayed some time silently meditating, before he began his prayer, and then remained longer than usual in the tabernacle. Or, 2. It may denote the frame of his spirit at this time.

III. The prayer itself, which is full of the breathings of pious and devout affection towards God.

1. He speaks very humbly of himself and his own merits. So he begins as one astonished: *Who am I, O Lord God; and what is my house? v.* 18. He had low thoughts (1) Of his personal merits: *Who am I?* He was upon all accounts a very considerable and valuable man. His endowments both of body and mind were extraordinary. Yet, when he comes to speak of himself before God, he says, "*Who am I?* A man not worth taking notice of." (2) Of the merits of his family: *What is my house?* His house was of the royal tribe, and descended from the prince of that tribe; and yet, like Gideon, he thinks his family poor in Judah and himself *the least in his father's house*, Judges vi. 15. All our attainments must be looked upon as God's vouchsafements.

2. He speaks very highly and honourably of God's favours to him. (1) In what he had done for him: "*Thou hast brought me hitherto*, to this great dignity and dominion. Hitherto thou hast helped me." (2) In what he had yet further promised him. God had done great things for him already, and yet, as if those had been nothing, he had promised to do much more, *v.* 19. We must own, as David here, [1] That it is far beyond what we could expect: *Is this the manner of men?* that is, *First*, Can man expect to be so dealt with by his Maker? He is brought near to God, purchased at a high rate, taken into covenant and communion with God; could this ever have been thought of? *Secondly*, Do men usually deal thus with one another? No, the way of our God is far above the manner of men. Though he be high, he has respect to the lowly; and is this the manner of men? Though he is offended by us, he beseeches us to be reconciled, waits to be gracious, multiplies his pardons: and is this the manner of men? [2] That beyond this there is nothing we can desire: "*And what can David say more unto thee? v.* 20. What can I ask or wish for more? *Thou, Lord, knowest thy servant*; knowest what will make me happy, and what thou hast promised is enough to do so." The promise of Christ includes all. What can we say more for ourselves in our prayers than he has said for us in his promises?

3. He ascribes all to the free grace of God (*v.* 21), both the great things he had done for him and the great things he had made known to him.

4. He adores the greatness and glory of God (*v.* 22): *Thou art great, O Lord God! for there is none like thee.* God's gracious condescension to him, and the honour he had put upon him, did not at all abate his awful veneration for the divine Majesty; for the nearer any are brought to God the more they see of his glory, and the dearer we are in his eyes the greater he should be in ours.

5. He expresses a great esteem for the Israel of God, *v.* 23, 24. As there was none among the gods to be compared with Jehovah, so none among the nations to be compared with Israel, considering,

(1) The works he had done for them. He went to redeem them, applied himself to it as a great work, went about it with solemnity. The redemption of Israel, as described here, was typical of our redemption by Christ in that, [1] They were redeemed from the nations and their gods; so are we from all iniquity and all conformity to this present world. Christ came to save his people from their sins. [2] They were redeemed to be a peculiar people unto God, purified and appropriated to himself, that he might make himself a great name and do for them great things.

(2) The covenant he had made with them, *v.* 24. It was, [1] Mutual: "They to be a people to thee, and thou to be a God to them; all their interests consecrated to thee, and all thy attributes engaged for them." [2] Immutable: "Thou hast confirmed them." He that makes the covenant makes it sure and will make it good.

6. He concludes with humble petitions to God. (1) He grounds his petitions upon the message which God had sent him (*v.* 27): "Thou hast of thy own good will given me the promise that thou wilt build me a house, else I could never have found in my heart to pray such a prayer as this," too great for me to beg, but not too great for thee to give. (2) He builds his faith and hopes to speed upon the fidelity of God's promise (*v.* 25): "*Thou art that God* (thou art *he*, even *that God*, the *Lord of hosts*, and *God of Israel*, or *that God whose words are true*, that God whom one may depend upon); and *thou hast promised this goodness unto thy servant*, which I am therefore bold

JAMIESON, FAUSSET, BROWN

his heels. It was the posture of the ancient Egyptians before the shrines; it is the posture of deepest respect before a superior in the East. Persons of highest dignity sit thus when they do sit in the presence of kings and it is the only sitting attitude assumed by the modern Mohammedans in their places and rites of devotion.

19. is this the manner of man, O Lord God?—i.e., is it customary for men to show such condescension to persons so humble as I am? (See on I Chron. 17:17).

20. what can David say more unto thee?—i.e., my obligations are greater than I can express.

ADAM CLARKE

19. *And is this the manner of man?* Literally: "And this, O Lord God, is the law of Adam." Does he refer to the promise made to Adam, "The seed of the woman shall bruise the head of the serpent"? From my line shall the Messiah spring and be the spiritual and triumphant King for ever and ever.

20. *What can David say more?* How can I express my endless obligation to Thee?

CHARLES H. SPURGEON:

David had first found it in his heart to build a house for God. Sitting in his house of cedar he resolved that the ark of God should no longer abide under curtains, but should be more suitably housed. The Lord, however, did not design that David should build his temple, though He accepted his pious intentions and declared that it was well that it was in his heart. From which we may learn that our intentions to serve the Lord in a certain manner may be thoroughly good and acceptable, and yet we may not be permitted to carry them out. We may have the will but not the power: the aspiration but not the qualification. We may have to stand aside and see another do the task which we had chosen for ourselves, and yet we may be nonetheless pleasing to the Lord, who in His great love accepts the will for the deed. It is a holy self-denial which in such cases rejoices to see the Lord glorified by others, and at the Captain's bidding cheerfully stands back in the rear when zeal had urged it to rush to the front. It is as true service not to do as to do when the Lord's word prescribes it.

The reason why David was not to build the house is not stated here, but you will find it in 1 Chron. 28:2, 3: "Then David the king stood up upon his feet, and said, Hear me, my brethren, and my people: As for me, I had in mine heart to build an house of rest for the ark of the covenant of the Lord, and for the footstool of our God, and had made ready for the buidling: but God said unto me, Thou shalt not build an house for my name, because thou hast been a man of war, and hast shed blood." David's wars had been necessary and justifiable, and by them the people of the Lord had been delivered; but the ever merciful One did not delight in them, and would not use for building His temple an instrument which had been stained with blood. The great Prince of Peace would not have a warriors's hand to build the palace of His worship, choosing rather that a man whose mind had exercised itself in quieter pursuits should be the founder of the place of rest for the ark of His covenant of peace. He is not so short of instruments as to use a sword for a trowel, or a spear for a measuring rod, especially when these have been dyed in the blood of His creatures. In your own household affairs you do use the same implement or utensil for opposite purposes; if David, therefore, is used to smite Philistines, he is not to be employed in erecting a temple; Solomon, his son, a man of peace, is called to do that holy work.—*The Treasury of the Old Testament*

MATTHEW HENRY

to pray for." (3) Thence he fetches the matter of his prayer, and refers to that as the guide of his prayers. [1] He prays for the performance of God's promise (*v.* 25): "I desire no more, and I expect no less." Thus we must turn God's promises into prayers, and then they shall be turned into performances; for, with God, saying and doing are not two things, as they often are with men. [2] He prays for the glorifying of God's name (*v.* 26): *Let thy name be magnified for ever.* This ought to be the summary and centre of all our prayers, the Alpha and the Omega of them. Begin with *Hallowed be thy name,* and end with *Thine is the glory for ever.* "Whether I be magnified or no, *let thy name be magnified.*" [3] He prays for his house, for to that the promise has special reference, *First,* That it might be happy (*v.* 29): *Let it please thee to bless the house of thy servant. Secondly,* That the happiness of it might remain: "Let it be *established before thee* (*v.* 26); let it *continue for ever before thee,*" *v.* 29. He longs 1. That none of his might ever forfeit it, but that they might walk before God, which would be their establishment. 2. That his kingdom might have its perfection and perpetuity in the kingdom of the Messiah. When Christ for ever sat down on the right hand of God (Heb. x. 12), and received all possible assurance that his seed and throne shall be as the days of heaven, this prayer of David the son of Jesse for his seed was abundantly answered, that it might *continue before God for ever.*

JAMIESON, FAUSSET, BROWN

ADAM CLARKE

25. *And do as thou hast said.* David well knew that all the promises made to himself and family were conditional, and therefore he prayed that they might be fulfilled. His posterity did not walk with God, and therefore they were driven from the throne. All the promises have failed to David and his natural posterity, and to Christ and His spiritual seed alone are they fulfilled.

MATTHEW HENRY

CHAPTER 8

Verses 1–8

David has now commission given him to make war for the avenging of Israel's quarrels and the recovery of their rights; for as yet they were not in full possession of that country to which by the promise of God they were entitled.

I. He quite subdued the Philistines, *v.* 1. They had long been vexatious and oppressive to Israel. Saul got no ground against them; but David completed Israel's deliverance out of their hands, which Samson had begun long before, Judges xiii. 5. *Metheg-ammah* was *Gath* (the chief and royal city of the Philistines) and the towns belonging to it, among which there was a constant garrison kept by the Philistines on the hill Ammah (2 Sam. ii. 24), which was *Metheg,* a *bridle* (so it signifies) or *curb* upon the people of Israel; this David took out of their hand and used it as a curb upon them.

II. He smote the Moabites, and made them tributaries to Israel, *v.* 2. He divided the country into three parts, two of which he destroyed, the third part he spared, to till the ground and be servants to Israel. Now Balaam's prophecy was fulfilled, *A sceptre shall arise out of Israel, and shall smite the corners of Moab.* The Moabites continued tributaries to Israel till after the death of Ahab, 2 Kings iii. 4, 5. Then they rebelled and were never reduced.

III. He smote the Syrians or Aramites. Of them there were two distinct kingdoms, as we find them spoken of in the title of the 60th Psalm: *Aram Naharaim,—Syria of the rivers,* whose head city was Damascus (famed for its rivers, 2 Kings v. 12), and *Aram Zobah,* which joined to it, but extended to Euphrates. These were the two northern crowns. 1. David began with the Syrians of Zobah, *v.* 3, 4. As he went to settle his border at the river Euphrates (for so far the land conveyed by the divine grant to Abraham and his seed did extend, Gen. xv. 18), the king of Zobah opposed him, being himself possessed of those countries which belonged to Israel; but David routed his forces, and took his chariots and horsemen.

IV. In all these wars, 1. David was protected: *The Lord preserved him whithersoever he went.* 2. He was enriched. He took the shields of gold which the servants of Hadadezer had in their custody (*v.* 7) and much brass from several cities of Syria (*v.* 8), which he was entitled to by the ancient entail of these countries on the seed of Abraham.

Verses 9–14

1. The court made to David by the king of Hamath, who, it seems was at this time at war with the king of Zobah. He, hearing of David's success against his enemy, sent his own son ambassador to him (*v.* 9, 10) to beg his friendship. And David lost nothing by taking this little prince under his protection; for the wealth he had from the countries he conquered by way of spoil he had from this by way of present or gratuity: *Vessels of silver and gold.* Better get by composition than by compulsion. 2. The offering David made to God of the spoils of the nations. He dedicated all to the Lord, *v.* 11, 12. This crowned

JAMIESON, FAUSSET, BROWN

CHAPTER 8

VSS. 1, 2. DAVID SUBDUES THE PHILISTINES, AND MAKES THE MOABITES TRIBUTARY. **1. David took Metheg-ammah out of the hand of the Philistines**—that is, Gath and her suburban towns (I Chron. 18:1). That town had been "a bridle" by which the Philistines kept the people of Judah in check. David used it now as a barrier to repress that restless enemy. **2. he smote Moab and measured them with a line**—This refers to a well-known practice of Eastern kings, to command their prisoners of war, particularly those who, notorious for the atrocity of their crimes or distinguished by the indomitable spirit of their resistance, had greatly incensed the victors, to lie down on the ground. Then a certain portion of them, which was determined by lot, but most commonly by a measuring line, were put to death. Our version makes him put two-thirds to death, and spare one-third. The *Septuagint* and *Vulgate* make one-half. This war usage was not, perhaps, usually practised by the people of God; but Jewish writers assert that the cause of this particular severity against this people was their having massacred David's parents and family, whom he had, during his exile, committed to the king of Moab.

3-14. HE SMITES HADADEZER AND THE SYRIANS. **3. Zobah**—(I Chron. 18:3). This kingdom was bounded on the east by the Euphrates, and it extended westward from that river, perhaps as far north as Aleppo. It was long the chief among the petty kingdoms of Syria, and its king bore the hereditary title of Hadadezer or Hadarezer (Hadad—helped). **as he went to recover his border at the river Euphrates**—in accordance with the promises God made to Israel that He would give them all the country as far as the Euphrates (Gen. 15:18; Num. 24:17). In the first compaign David signally defeated Hadadezer. Besides a great number of foot-prisoners, he took from him an immense amount of booty in chariots and horses. Reserving only a small number of the latter, he hamstrung the rest. The horses were thus mutilated because they were forbidden to the Hebrews, both in war and agriculture. So it was of no use to keep them. Besides, their neighbors placed much dependence on cavalry, but having, for want of a native breed, to procure them by purchase, the greatest damage that could be done to such enemies was to render their horses unserviceable in war. (See also Gen. 46:6; Josh. 11:6, 9.) A king of Damascene-Syria came to Hadadezer's succor; but David routed those auxiliary forces also, took possession of their country, put garrisons into their fortified towns, and made them tributary. **9. Toi king of Hamath**—Cœle-Syria; northwards, it extended to the city Hamath on the Orontes, which was the capital of the country. The Syrian prince, being delivered from the dread of a dangerous neighbor, sent his son with valuable presents to David to congratulate him on his victories, and solicit his alliance and protection. **10. Joram**—or Hadoram (I Chron. 18:10). **11. Which also King David did dedicate unto the Lord**—Eastern princes have always been accustomed to hoard up vast quantities of gold.

ADAM CLARKE

CHAPTER 8

1. *David took Metheg-ammah.* This is variously translated. The Vulgate has, "David removed the bondage of the tribute," which the Israelites paid to the Philistines. Some think it means a fortress, city, or strong town; but no such place as Metheg-ammah is known. Probably the Vulgate is nearest the truth.

2. *And measured them with a line . . . even with two lines.* It has been generally conjectured that David, after he had conquered Moab, consigned two-thirds of the inhabitants to the sword; but I think the text will bear a meaning much more reputable to that king. The first clause of the verse seems to determine the sense: *he measured them with a line, casting them down to the ground*—to put to death, and with one line to keep alive. Death seems here to be referred to the cities by way of metaphor; and from this view of the subject we may conclude that two-thirds of the cities, that is, the strong places of Moab, were erased; and not having strong places to trust to, the text adds, *So the Moabites became David's servants, and brought gifts,* i.e., were obliged to pay tribute. The word *line* may mean the same here as our rod, i.e., the instrument by which land is measured.

3. *David smote . . . Hadadezer.* He is supposed to have been king of all Syria, except Phoenicia, and, wishing to extend his dominions to the Euphrates, invaded a part of David's dominions which lay contiguous to it; but being attacked by David, he was totally routed.

4. *A thousand chariots.* It is strange that there were 1,000 chariots, and only 700 horsemen taken, and 20,000 footmen. But as the discomfiture appears complete, we may suppose that the chariots, being less manageable, might be more easily taken, while the horsemen might, in general, make their escape. The infantry also seem to have been surrounded, when 20,000 of them were taken prisoners. *David houghed all the chariot horses.* "And David disjointed all the chariots," except a hundred chariots which he reserved for himself.

6. *Brought gifts.* Paid tribute.

7. *David took the shields of gold.* We know not what these were. Some translate "arms," others "quivers," others "bracelets," others "collars," and others "shields." They were probably costly ornaments by which the Syrian soldiers were decked and distinguished. And those who are called *servants* here were probably the choice troops or bodyguard of Hadadezer.

MATTHEW HENRY

all his victories, and made them far to outshine Alexander's or Cæsar's, that they sought their own glory, but he aimed at the glory of God. All the precious things he was master of were dedicated things, that is, they were designed for the building of the temple. Their gods of gold David burnt (2 Sam. v. 21), but their vessels of gold he dedicated. Thus in the conquest of a soul, by the grace of the Son of David, what stands in opposition to God must be destroyed, every lust mortified and crucified, but what may glorify him must be dedicated and the property of it altered. 3. The reputation he got, in a particular manner, by his victory over the Syrians and their allies the Edomites. *He got himself a name.* Something extraordinary there was in that action, which turned very much to his honour, yet he is careful to transfer the honour to God. 4. His success against the Edomites. They all became David's servants, *v.* 13. The Edomites continued long tributary to the kings of Judah, as the Moabites were to the kings of Israel, till, in Joram's time, they revolted (2 Chron. xxi. 8) as Isaac had there foretold that Esau should, in process of time, break the yoke from off his neck. Thus David by his conquests, (1) Secured peace to his son, that he might have time to build the temple. And, (2) Procured wealth for his son, that he might have wherewith to build it. God employs his servants variously, some in the spiritual battles, others in the spiritual buildings; and one prepares work for the other, that God may have the glory of all. All David's victories were typical of the success of the gospel against the kingdom of Satan, in which the Son of David rode forth, conquering and to conquer.

Verses 15–18

David was not so engaged in his wars abroad as to neglect the administration of the government at home.

I. His care extended itself to all the parts of his dominion: *He reigned over all Israel* (*v.* 15).

II. He did justice with an unbiassed unshaken hand: *He executed judgment unto all his people.* This intimates, 1. His industry and close application to business, his easiness of access and readiness to admit all addresses and appeals made to him. 2. His impartiality and the equity of his proceedings, in administering justice. See Ps. lxxii. 1, 2.

III. He kept good order and good officers in his court. David being the first king that had an established government (for Saul's reign was short and unsettled) he had the modelling of the administration. In Saul's time we read of no other great officer than Abner, that was captain of the host. But David appointed more officers. 1. Two military officers: Joab that was general of the forces in the field, and Banaiah that was over the Cherethites and Pelethites, who were either the city train-bands (*archers and slingers*, so the Chaldee), or rather the life-guards, or standing force, that attended the king's person, the prætorian band, the militia. They were ready to do service at home, to assist in the administering of justice, and to preserve the public peace. 2. Two ecclesiastical officers: *Zadok and Ahimelech were priests*, that is, they were most employed in the priests' work under Abiathar, the high priest. 3. Two civil officers: one that was recorder, or remembrancer, to put the king in mind of business in its season (he was prime minister of state, yet not entrusted with the custody of the king's conscience, as they say of our lord chancellor, but only of the king's memory); another that was scribe, or secretary of state, that drew up public orders and despatches, and recorded judgments given. 4. David's sons, as they grew up to be fit for business, were made chief rulers. They were chief about the king (so it is explained, 1 Chron. xviii. 17), employed near him, that they might be under his eye. David made his sons chief rulers; but all believers, Christ's spiritual seed, are better preferred, for they are *made to our God kings and priests*, Rev. i. 6.

CHAPTER 9

Verses 1–8

I. David's enquiry after the remains of the ruined house of Saul, *v.* 1. This was a great while after his accession to the throne, for it should seem that Mephibosheth, who was but five years old when Saul died, had now a son born, *v.* 12. David had too long forgotten his obligations to Jonathan, but now, at length, they are brought to his mind.

1. He sought an opportunity to do good. *Is there any yet left of the house of Saul, that I may show him kindness? v.* 3. "Is there any, not only to whom I may do justice (Num. v. 8), but to whom I may

JAMIESON, FAUSSET, BROWN

This is the first instance of a practice uniformly followed by David of reserving, after defraying expenses and bestowing suitable rewards upon his soldiers, the remainder of the spoil taken in war, to accumulate for the grand project of his life—the erection of a national temple at Jerusalem.

David gat him a name when he returned from smiting of the Syrians—Instead of Syrians, the *Sept.* version reads Edomites, which is the true reading, as is evident from verse 14. This conquest, made by the army of David, was due to the skilful generalship and gallantry of Abishai and Joab. (I Chron. 18:12; cf. Ps. 60, title.) The valley was the ravine of salt (the Ghor), adjoining the Salt Mountain, at the southwestern extremity of the Dead Sea, separating the ancient territories of Judah and Edom [ROBINSON].

15-18. HIS REIGN. **15. David executed judgment and justice unto all his people**—Though involved in foreign wars, he maintained an excellent system of government at home, the most eminent men of the age composing his cabinet of ministers.

16. Joab . . . was over the host—by virtue of a special promise (ch. 5:8). **recorder**—historiographer or daily annalist, an office of great trust and importance in Eastern countries.

17. Zadok . . . and Ahimelech . . . were the priests—On the massacre of the priests at Nob, Saul conferred the priesthood on Zadok, of the family of Eleazar (I Chron. 6:50), while David acknowledged Ahimelech, of Ithamar's family, who fled to him. The two high priests exercised their office under the respective princes to whom they were attached. But, on David's obtaining the kingdom over all Israel, they both retained their dignity; Ahimelech officiating at Jerusalem, and Zadok at Gibeon (I Chron. 16:39). **18. Cherethites**—i.e., Philistines (Zeph. 2:5). **Pelethites**—from Pelet (I Chron. 12:3). They were the valiant men who, having accompanied David during his exile among the Philistines, were made his bodyguard.

CHAPTER 9

VSS. 1-12. DAVID SENDS FOR MEPHIBOSHETH. **1. David said, Is there yet any that is left of the house of Saul**—

ADAM CLARKE

13. *David gat him a name.* Became a very celebrated and eminent man. The Targum has it, "David collected troops"; namely, to recruit his army when he returned from smiting the Syrians. His many battles had no doubt greatly thinned his army.

14. *He put garrisons in Edom.* He repaired the strong cities which he had taken, and put garrisons in them to keep the country in awe.

16. *Joab . . . was over the host.* General and commander in chief over all the army. *Ahilud . . . recorder. Mazkir*, "remembrancer"; one who kept a strict journal of all the proceedings of the king and operations of his army; a chronicler.

17. *Seraiah . . . the scribe.* Most likely the king's private secretary.

18. *Benaiah.* The chief of the second class of David's worthies. We shall meet with him again. *The Cherethites and the Pelethites.* The former supposed to be those who accompanied David when he fled from Saul; the latter, those who came to him at Ziklag. But the Targum translates these two names thus, "the archers and the slingers"; and this is by far the most likely.

CHAPTER 9

1. *Is there yet any that is left?* David, recollecting the covenant made with his friend Jonathan, now inquires after his family. It is supposed that political considerations prevented him from doing this sooner.

3. *That I may shew the kindness of God unto him?* That is, the utmost, the highest degrees of kindness.

MATTHEW HENRY | JAMIESON, FAUSSET, BROWN | ADAM CLARKE

show kindness?" The most necessitous are the least clamorous.

2. Those he enquired after were the remains of the house of Saul, to whom he would show kindness for Jonathan's sake. He was desirous to show kindness to the house of Saul, not only because he trusted in God and feared not what they could do unto him, but because he was of a charitable disposition, and forgave what they had done to him. We must not be backward to do any office of love and goodwill to those that have done us many an injury. 1 Pet. iii. 9,—*but, contrariwise, blessing*. This is the way to overcome evil, and to find mercy for ourselves and ours, when we or they need it. Jonathan was David's sworn friend, and therefore he would show kindness to his house. The kindness we have promised we must conscientiously perform, though it should not be claimed. God is faithful to us; let us not be unfaithful to one another. Though there be not a solemn league of friendship tying us to this constancy of love, yet there is a sacred law of friendship no less obliging, that to him that is in misery pity should be shown by his friend, Job. vi. 14. *A brother is born for adversity*. Friendship obliges us to take cognizance of the families and surviving relations of those we have loved.

3. The kindness he promised to show them he calls the *kindness of God*; not only great kindness, but, (1) Kindness in pursuance of the covenant that was between him and Jonathan, to which God was a witness. See 1 Sam. xx. 42. (2) Kindness after God's example; for we must be merciful as he is. Jonathan's request to David was (1 Sam. xx. 14, 15), "*Show me the kindness of the Lord, that I die not*, and the same to my seed."

II. Information given him concerning Mephibosheth, the son of Jonathan. Ziba was an old retainer to Saul's family, and knew the state of it. He informed the king that Jonathan's son was living, but *lame* (how he came to be so we read before, *ch.* iv. 4), and that he lived in obscurity, probably among his mother's relations in Lo-debar, in Gilead, on the other side Jordan, where he was *forgotten, as a dead man out of mind*.

III. The bringing of him to court. The king sent (Ziba, it is likely) to bring him up to Jerusalem with all convenient speed, *v.* 5. Thus he eased Machir of his trouble, and perhaps recompensed him for what he had laid out on Mephibosheth's account. This Machir appears to have been a very generous free-hearted man, and to have entertained Mephibosheth, not out of any disaffection to David or his government, but in compassion to the reduced son of a prince, for afterwards we find him kind to David himself when he fled from Absalom. He is named (*ch.* xvii. 27) among those that furnished the king with what he wanted at Mahanaim.

1. Mephibosheth presented himself to David. Lame as he was, *he fell on his face, and did homage*, *v.* 6. David had thus made his honours to Mephibosheth's father, Jonathan, when he was next to the throne (1 Sam. xx. 41, *he bowed himself to him three times*), and now Mephibosheth, in like manner, addresses him, when affairs are so completely reversed.

2. David received him with all the kindness that could be. (1) He spoke to him as one surprised, but pleased to see him. (2) He bade him not be afraid: *Fear not*, *v.* 7. He assures him that he sent for him, not with any bad design upon him, but to show him kindness. (3) He gives him, by grant from the crown, *all the land of Saul his father*, that is, his paternal estate, which was forfeited by Ish-bosheth's rebellion and added to his own revenue. True friendship will be generous. (4) Though he had thus given him a good estate, sufficient to maintain him, yet for Jonathan's sake (whom perhaps he saw some resemblance of in Mephibosheth's face), he will take him to be a constant guest at his own table, where he will be comfortably fed. Though Mephibosheth was lame and unsightly, and does not appear to have had any great fitness for business, yet, for his good father's sake, David took him to be one of his family.

3. Mephibosheth accepts this kindness with great humility and self-abasement. How does he magnify David's kindness! It would have been easy to lessen it if he had been so disposed.

Verses 9–13

The matter is here settled concerning Mephibosheth. 1. This grant of his father's estate is confirmed to him, and Ziba called to be a witness to it (*v.* 9); and, it should seem, Saul had a very good estate, fields and vineyards to bestow, 1 Sam. xxii. 7. Be it ever so much, Mephibosheth is now master of it all. 2. The management of the estate is committed to Ziba. How unfaithful Ziba was to him we shall

F. B. MEYER:

"Thou shalt eat bread at my table continually" (2 Sam. 9:7). Four times in this chapter we are told of the lame man eating bread at the royal table. But what are these facts recorded and repeated for, save to accentuate the infinite blessings which come to us through the divine love?

Mephibosheth had done nothing to merit the royal favor. Not a word is said of his being well-favored and attractive. So far from that, he was lame on both his feet, and probably a sickly invalid. In his own judgment he was worthless as a dead dog. His state was impoverished; no deed of prowess could win David's notice; he was almost entirely at the mercy of his servant, Ziba. In these respects there are many analogies to our own condition in the sight of God. We are lame indeed; and, so far as we are concerned, it is quite impossible that we should ever win the divine regard, or sit at his table among his sons.

But between David and Jonathan a covenant had been struck, which had provided for the children of the ill-fated Jonathan (1 Sam. 20:14–16). It was because of this sacred obligation that Mephibosheth fared as he did. Look away, child of God, to the covenant struck between God and thy representative, the Son of His love. It is idle of thee to seek to propitiate the divine favor, or earn a seat at His table; but if you are willing to identify yourself with your Lord, and to shelter yourself in Him by the living union of faith; if you can base your plea on the blood of the everlasting covenant—then the provisions of that covenant between Father and Son shall be extended to you: and because of God's love to Jesus you will sit at the divine table and be regarded as one of the heirs of the great King.—*Great Verses Through the Bible*

On inquiry, Saul's land steward was found, who gave information that there still survived Mephibosheth, a son of Jonathan, who was five years old at his father's death, and whom David, then wandering in exile, had never seen. His lameness (ch. 4:4) had prevented him from taking any part in the public contests of the time. Besides, according to Oriental notions, the younger son of a crowned monarch has a preferable claim to the succession over the son of a mere heir-apparent; and hence his name was never heard of as the rival of his uncle Ish-bosheth. His insignificance had led to his being lost sight of, and it was only through Ziba that David learned of his existence, and the retired life he passed with one of the great families in transjordanic Canaan who remained attached to the fallen dynasty. Mephibosheth was invited to court, and a place at the royal table on public days was assigned him, as is still the custom with Eastern monarchs.

Saul's family estate, which had fallen to David in right of his wife (Num. 27:8), or been forfeited to the crown by Ish-bosheth's rebellion (ch. 12:8), was provided (vs. 11; also ch. 19:28), for enabling Mephibosheth to maintain an establishment suitable to his rank, and Ziba appointed steward to manage it, on the condition of receiving one-half of the pro-

7. *Will restore thee all the land*. I believe this means the mere family estate of the house of Kish, which David as king might have retained, but which most certainly belonged, according to the Israelitish law, to the descendants of the family. *And thou shalt eat bread at my table*. This was kindness (the giving up the land was justice), and it was the highest honor that any subject could enjoy, as we may see from the reference made to it by our Lord, Luke xxii. 30: "That ye may eat and drink at my table in my kingdom." For such a person David could do no more. His lameness rendered him unfit for any public employment.

MATTHEW HENRY

find afterwards, *ch.* xvi. 3. Now because David was a type of Christ, his Lord and son, his root and offspring, let his kindness to Mephibosheth serve to illustrate the kindness and love of God our Saviour towards fallen man, which yet he was under no obligation to, as David was to Jonathan. Man was convicted of rebellion against God, and, like Saul's house, under a sentence of rejection from him, was not only brought low and impoverished, but lame and impotent, made so by the fall. The Son of God enquires after this degenerate race, and comes to seek and save them. To those of them that humble themselves before him, and commit themselves to him, he restores the forfeited inheritance, he entitles them to a better paradise than that which Adam lost, and takes them into communion with himself, sets them with his children at his table, and feasts them with the dainties of heaven.

CHAPTER 10

Verses 1–5

I. The great respect David paid to his neighbour, the king of the Ammonites, *v.* 1, 2. 1. The inducement to it was some kindness he had formerly received from Nahash the deceased king. He *showed kindness to me*, says David (*v.* 2). If David received kindness, he resolves gratefully to return it. 2. The particular instance was sending an embassy to condole with him on his father's death. *David sent to comfort him.* It is a comfort to children, when their parents are dead, to find that their parents' friends are theirs, and that they intend to keep up an acquaintance with them.

II. The great affront which Hanun the king of the Ammonites put upon David in his ambassadors. 1. He hearkened to the spiteful suggestions of his princes, who insinuated that David's ambassadors, under pretence of being comforters, were sent as spies, *v.* 3. False men are ready to think others as false as themselves. Bishop Patrick's note on this is that "there is nothing so well meant but it may be ill interpreted, and is wont to be so by men who love nobody but themselves." 2. Entertaining this vile suggestion, he basely abused David's ambassadors, like a man of a sordid villainous spirit, that was fitter to rake a kennel than to wear a crown. They and their reputation were under the special protection of the law of nations; they put a confidence in the Ammonites, and came among them unarmed; yet Hanun used them like rogues and vagabonds, and worse, *shaved off the one half of their beards, and cut off their garments in the midst*, to expose them to the contempt and ridicule of his servants.

III. David's tender concern for his servants that were thus abused. He sent to meet them and directed them to stay at Jericho, a private place, where they would not have occasion to come into company, till that half of their beards which was shaved off had grown to such a length that the other half might be decently cut to it, *v.* 5. The Jews wore their beards long, reckoning it an honour to appear aged and grave. Let us learn not to lay too much to heart unjust reproaches; after awhile they will wear off themselves, and turn only to the shame of their authors, while the injured reputation in a little time grows again, as these beards did. God will *bring forth thy righteousness as the light*, therefore *wait patiently for him*, Ps. xxxvii. 6, 7.

Verses 6–14

I. The preparation which the Ammonites made for war, *v.* 6. They found themselves an unequal match, and were forced to hire forces of other nations into their service.

II. The speedy descent which David's forces made upon them, *v.* 7. When David heard of their military preparations, he sent Joab with a great army to attack them, *v.* 7. It was David's prudence to carry the war into their country, and fight them at the entering in of the gate of their capital city, *Rabbah*, as some think, or *Medeba*, a city in their borders, before which they pitched to guard their coast, 1 Chron. xix. 7.

III. Preparations made on both sides for an engagement. 1. The enemy disposed themselves into two bodies, one of Ammonites, which, being their own, were posted at the gate of the city; the other of Syrians, whom they had taken into their pay, and who were therefore posted at a distance in the field, to charge the forces of Israel in the flank or rear, while the Ammonites charged them in the front, *v.* 8. 2. Joab, like a wise general, accordingly divided his forces: the choicest men he took under his own command, to fight the Syrians. The rest of the forces he put under the command of Abishai his brother, to engage the Ammonites, *v.* 10.

JAMIESON, FAUSSET, BROWN

duce in remuneration for his labor and expense, while the other moiety was to be paid as rent to the owner of the land (ch. 19:29). **10. Ziba had fifteen sons and twenty servants**—The mention of his sons and the slaves in his house was to show that Mephibosheth would be honored with an equipage "as one of the king's sons." **12. Mephibosheth had a young son, whose name was Micah**—Whether born before or after his residence in Jerusalem, cannot be ascertained. But through him the name and memory of the excellent Jonathan was preserved (see on I Chron. 8:34, 35; 9:40, 41).

CHAPTER 10

VSS. 1-5. DAVID'S MESSENGERS, SENT TO COMFORT HANUN, ARE DISGRACEFULLY TREATED. **2. Then said David, I will show kindness unto Hanun, the son of Nahash, as his father showed kindness unto me**—It is probable that this was the Nahash against whom Saul waged war at Jabesh-gilead (I Sam. 11:11). David, on leaving Gath, where his life was exposed to danger, found an asylum with the king of Moab; and as Nahash, king of the Ammonites, was his nearest neighbor, it may be that during the feud between Saul and David, he, through enmity to the former, was kind and hospitable to David. **3. the princes of the children of Ammon said unto Hanun**—Their suspicion was not warranted either by any overt act or by any cherished design of David: it must have originated in their knowledge of the denunciations of God's law against them (Deut. 23:3-6), and of David's policy in steadfastly adhering to it.

4. Hanun took David's servants and shaved off the one-half of their beards—From the long flowing dress of the Hebrews and other Orientals, the curtailment of their garments must have given them an aspect of gross indelicacy and ludicrousness. Besides, a knowledge of the extraordinary respect and value which has always been attached, and the gross insult that is implied in any indignity offered, to the beard in the East, will account for the shame which the deputies felt, and the determined spirit of revenge which burst out in all Israel on learning the outrage. Two instances are related in the modern history of Persia, of similar insults by kings of haughty and imperious temper, involving the nation in war; and we need not, therefore, be surprised that David vowed revenge for this wanton and public outrage. **5. Tarry at Jericho**—or in the neighborhood, after crossing the fords of the Jordan.

6-14. THE AMMONITES OVERCOME. **6. when the children of Ammon saw that they stank before David**—To chastise those insolent and inhospitable Ammonites, who had violated the common law of nations, David sent a large army under the command of Joab, while they, informed of the impending attack, made energetic preparations to repel it by engaging the services of an immense number of Syrian mercenaries. **Beth-rehob**—the capital of the low-lying region between Lebanon and Anti-Lebanon. **Zoba**—(see on ch: 8. 3). **of King Maachah**—His territories lay on the other side of Jordan, near Gilead (Deut. 3:14). **Ish-tob**—i.e., the men of Tob—the place of Jephthah's marauding adventures (see also I Chron. 19:6; Ps. 60, title).

ADAM CLARKE

10. *Thou therefore, and thy sons . . . shall till the land.* It seems that Ziba and his family had the care of the whole estate, and cultivated it at their own expense, yielding the half of the produce to the family of Mephibosheth.

11. *So shall thy servant do.* The promises of Ziba were fair and specious, but he was a traitor in his heart, as we shall see in the rebellion of Absalom.

CHAPTER 10

2. *I will shew kindness unto Hanun the son of Nahash.* We do not know exactly the nature or extent of the obligation which David was under to the king of the Ammonites.

4. *Shaved off the one half of their beards.* The beard is held in high respect in the East; the possessor considers it his greatest ornament, often swears by it, and in matters of great importance *pledges* it. Nothing can be more secure than a pledge of this kind; its owner will redeem it at the hazard of his life. The beard was never cut off but in mourning, or as a sign of slavery. Cutting off half of the beard and the clothes rendered the men ridiculous, and made them look like slaves; what was done to these men was an accumulation of insult.

6. *The children of Ammon saw that they stank.* That is, that their conduct rendered them abominable. This is the Hebrew mode of expressing such a feeling. *The Syrians of Beth-rehob.* This place was situated at the extremity of the valley between Libanus and Anti-libanus. The Syrians of Zoba were subject to Hadadezer. *Maacah* was in the vicinity of Mount Hermon, beyond Jordan, in the Trachonitis. *Ish-tob.* This was probably the same with Tob, to which Jephthah fled from the cruelty of his brethren. It was situated in the land of Gilead.

7. *All the host of the mighty.* All his worthies, and the flower of his army.

8. *At the entering in of the gate.* This was the city of Medeba, as we learn from 1 Chron. xix. 7.

9. *Before and behind.* It is probable that one of the armies was in the field, and the other in the city, when Joab arrived. When he fronted this army, the other appears to have issued from the city, and to have taken him in the rear. He was therefore obliged to divide his army as here mentioned, one part to face

MATTHEW HENRY

IV. Joab's speech before the battle, *v.* 11, 12. 1. He prudently concerts the matter with Abishai his brother. He supposes the worst, that one of them should be obliged to give back; and in that case, upon a signal given, the other should send a detachment to receive it. Christ's soldiers should thus strengthen one another's hands in their spiritual warfare. The strong must succour and help the weak. Those that through grace are conquerors over temptation must counsel, and comfort, and pray for, those that are tempted. *When thou art converted, strengthen thy brethren,* Luke xxii. 32. 2. He bravely encourages himself, and his brother, and the rest of the officers and soldiers. When Joab saw the front of the battle was against him, both before and behind, instead of giving orders to make an honourable retreat, he animated his men to charge so much more furiously: *Be of good courage and let us play the men,* not for pay and preferment, for honour and fame, but *for our people, and for the cities of our God,* for the public safety and welfare, in which the glory of God is so much interested. *God and our country* was the word. 3. He piously leaves the issue with God. When we make conscience of doing our duty we may, with the greatest satisfaction, leave the event with God.

V. The victory Joab obtained over the confederate forces of Syria and Ammon, *v.* 13, 14. The Syrians were first routed by Joab, and then the Ammonites by Abishai; the Ammonites seem not to have fought at all, but, upon the retreat of the Syrians, to have fled into the city.

Verses 15–19

1. A new attempt of the Syrians to recover their lost honour and to check the progress of David's victorious arms. 2. The defeat of this attempt by the vigilance and valour of David, who, in a pitched battle, routed the Syrians (*v.* 18). Their general was killed in the battle, and David came home in triumph. 3. The consequence of this victory over the Syrians. (1) David gained several tributaries, *v.* 19. *The kings,* or petty princes, that had been subject to Hadarezer, when they saw how powerful David was, very wisely *made peace with Israel,* whom they found they could not make war with, *and served them,* since they were able to give them protection. Thus the promise made to Abraham (Gen. xv. 18), and repeated to Joshua (*ch.* i. 4), that the borders of Israel should extend to the river Euphrates, was performed, at length. (2) The Ammonites lost their old allies: *The Syrians feared to help the children of Ammon.*

JAMIESON, FAUSSET, BROWN

As the Israelite soldiers poured into the Ammonite territory, that people met them at the frontier town of Medeba (I Chron. 19:7-9), the native troops covering the city, while the Syrian mercenaries lay at some distance encamped in the fields. In making the attack, Joab divided his forces into two separate detachments—the one of which, under the command of his brother, Abishai, was to concentrate its attack upon the city, while he himself marched against the overwhelming host of mercenary auxiliaries. It was a just and necessary war that had been forced on Israel, and they could hope for the blessing of God upon their arms. With great judgment the battle opened against the mercenaries, who could not stand against the furious onset of Joab, and not feeling the cause their own, consulted their safety by flight. The Ammonites, who had placed their chief dependence upon a foreign aid, then retreated to entrench themselves within the walls of the town.—**14. So Joab returned and came to Jerusalem**—Probably the season was too far advanced for entering on a siege.

15-19. THE SYRIANS DEFEATED. **16. Hadadezer sent and brought out the Syrians that were beyond the river**—This prince had enjoyed a breathing-time after his defeat (ch. 8:3). But alarmed at the increasing power and greatness of David, as well as being an ally of the Ammonites, he levied a vast army not only in Syria, but in Mesopotamia, to invade the Hebrew kingdom. Shobach, his general, in pursuance of this design, had marched his troops as far as Kelam, a border town of eastern Manasseh, when David, crossing the Jordan by forced marches, suddenly surprised, defeated, and dispersed them. As a result of this great and decisive victory, all the petty kingdoms of Syria submitted and became his tributaries (see on I Chron. 19).

ADAM CLARKE

the Syrians commanded by himself, and the other to face the Ammonites commanded by his brother Abishai.

12. *Be of good courage.* This is a very fine military address, and is equal to anything in ancient or modern times.

14. *The Syrians were fled.* They betook themselves to their own confines, while the Ammonites escaped into their own city.

16. *The Syrians that were beyond the river.* That is, the Euphrates. *Hadarezer.* This is the same that was overthrown by David, chap. viii, and there called Hadadezer, which is the reading here of about thirty of Kennicott's and De Rossi's MSS. But the *resh* and *daleth* are easily interchanged.

17. *David . . . gathered all Israel together.* He thought that such a war required his own presence.

18. *Seven hundred chariots . . . and forty thousand horsemen.* In the parallel place, 1 Chron. xix. 18, it is said, "David slew of the Syrians seven thousand men which fought in chariots." It is difficult to ascertain the right number in this and similar places. The Jews expressed their numbers, not by words at full length, but by numeral letters; and, as many of the letters bear a great similarity to each other, mistakes might easily creep in when the numeral letters came to be expressed by words at full length. This alone will account for the many mistakes which we find in the numbers in these books, and renders a mistake here very probable. The letter *zain,* with a dot above, stands for 7,000; *nun,* for 700. The great similarity of these letters might easily cause the one to be mistaken for the other, and so produce an error in this place.

19. *Made peace with Israel.* They made this peace separately, and were obliged to pay tribute to the Israelites.

We have now done with the first part of this book, in which we find David great, glorious, and pious. We come to the second part, in which we shall have the pain to observe him fallen from God, and his horn defiled in the dust by crimes of the most flagitious nature. Let him that most assuredly standeth take heed lest he fall.

MATTHEW HENRY — CHAPTER 11

Verses 1–5

I. David's glory, in pursuing the war against the Ammonites, *v.* 1. Rabbah, their metropolis, made a stand, and held out a great while. To this city Joab laid close siege, and it was at the time of this siege that David fell into sin.

II. David's shame, in being himself conquered, and led captive by his own lust. The sin he was guilty of was adultery, against the letter of the seventh commandment.

1. Observe the occasions which led to this sin. (1) Neglect of his business. When he should have been abroad with his army in the field, fighting the battles of the Lord, he devolved the care upon others, and he himself *tarried still at Jerusalem, v.* 1. Had he been now at his post at the head of his forces, he would have been out of the way of this temptation. When we are out of the way of our duty we are in the way of temptation. (2) Love of ease, and the indulgence of a slothful temper: *He came off his bed at evening-tide, v.* 2. Idleness gives great advantage to the tempter. Standing waters gather filth. The bed of sloth often proves the bed of lust. (3) A wandering eye: *He saw a woman washing herself,* probably from some ceremonial pollution, according to the law.

2. The steps of the sin. When he saw her, lust immediately conceived, and, (1) He enquired who she was (*v.* 3), perhaps intending only, if she were unmarried, to take her to wife. (2) The corrupt desire growing more violent, though he was told she was a wife, and whose wife she was, yet he sent messengers for her, and then, it may be, intended only to please himself with her company and conversation. But, (3) When she came *he lay with her,* she too easily consenting, because he was a great man, and famed for his goodness too.

3. The aggravations of the sin. (1) He was now in years, fifty at least. (2) He had many wives and concubines of his own. (3) Uriah, whom he wronged, was one of his own worthies, hazarding his life in

JAMIESON, FAUSSET, BROWN — CHAPTER 11

Vss. 1. JOAB BESIEGES RABBAH. **1. at the time when kings go forth to battle**—The return of spring was the usual time of commencing military operations. This expedition took place the year following the war against the Syrians; and it was entered upon because the disaster of the former campaign having fallen chiefly upon the Syrian mercenaries, the Ammonites had not been punished for their insult to the ambassadors. **David sent Joab and his servants . . . they destroyed the children of Ammon**—The powerful army that Joab commanded ravaged the Ammonite country and committed great havoc both on the people and their property, until having reached the capital, they besieged Rabbah—"Rabbah" denotes a great city. This metropolis of the Ammonites was situated in the mountainous tract of Gilead, not far from the source of the Arnon. Extensive ruins are still found on its site.

2-12. DAVID COMMITS ADULTERY WITH BATH-SHEBA. **2. it came to pass in an eventide, that David arose from off his bed**—The Hebrews, like other Orientals, rose at daybreak, and always took a nap during the heat of the day. Afterwards they lounged in the cool of the evening on their flat-roofed terraces. It is probable that David had ascended to enjoy the open-air refreshment earlier than usual. **3. one said**—lit., he said to himself, **"Is not this Bath-sheba?"** etc. She seems to have been a celebrated beauty, whose renown had already reached the ears of David, as happens in the East, from reports carried by the women from harem to harem. **Bath-sheba, the daughter of Eliam**—or Ammiel (I Chron. 3:5), one of David's worthies (ch. 23: 34), and son of Ahithophel. **4. David sent messengers, and took her**—The despotic kings of the East, when they take a fancy for a woman, send an officer to the house were she lives, who announces it to be the royal pleasure she should remove to the palace. An apartment is there assigned to her; and if she is made queen, the monarch orders the announce-

ADAM CLARKE — CHAPTER 11

1. *When kings go forth.* This was about a year after the war with the Syrians spoken of before, and about the spring of the year, as the most proper season for military operations.

2. *In an eveningtide . . . David arose.* He had been reposing on the roof of his house, to enjoy the breeze, as the noonday was too hot for the performance of business. This is still a constant custom on the flat-roofed houses in the East. *He saw a woman washing herself.* How could any woman of delicacy expose herself where she could be so fully and openly viewed? Did she not know that she was at least in view of the king's terrace? Was there no design in all this?

3. *The daughter of Eliam.* Called, 1 Chron. iii. 5, Ammiel; a word of the same meaning; "The people of my God, The God of my people." This name expressed the covenant—"I will be your God; we will be Thy people."

4. *And she came in unto him.* We hear nothing of her reluctance, and there is no evidence that she was taken by force.

MATTHEW HENRY

the high places of the field for the honour and safety of him and his kingdom, where he himself should have been. (4) Bath-sheba, whom he debauched, was a lady of good reputation. The adulterer not only wrongs and ruins his own soul, but, as much as he can, another's soul too. (5) David was a king, whom God had entrusted with the sword of justice and the execution of the law upon other criminals, particularly upon adulterers. I can think but of one excuse for it, which is that it was done but once; it was far from being his practice; it was by the surprise of a temptation that he was drawn into it. He was not one of those of whom the prophet complains that *they were as fed horses, neighing every one after his neighbour's wife* (Jer. v. 8); but this once God left him to himself. But by this instance we are taught what need we have to pray every day, *Father, in heaven, lead us not into temptation*, and to watch, that we enter not into it.

Verses 6–13

Uriah, we may suppose, had now been absent from his wife some weeks. The situation of his wife would *bring to light the hidden works of darkness*; and when Uriah, at his return, should find how he had been abused, and by whom, it might well be expected, 1. That he would prosecute his wife, according to law, and have her stoned to death. This Bath-sheba was apprehensive of when she sent to let David know she was with child, intimating that he was concerned to protect her. 2. It might also be expected that since he could not prosecute David by law for an offence of this nature he would take his revenge another way, and raise a rebellion against him. To prevent this double mischief, David endeavours to father the child which should be born upon Uriah himself, and therefore sends for him home to stay a night or two with his wife.

I. How the plot was laid. Uriah must come home from the army under pretence of bringing David an account *how the war prospered*, and how they went on with the siege of Rabbah, *v.* 7. David, having had as much conference with Uriah as he thought requisite to cover the design, sent him to his house. When that project failed the first night, and Uriah, being weary of his journey and more desirous of sleep than meat, lay all night in the guard-chamber, the next night *he made him drunk* (*v.* 13). It is a very wicked thing, upon any design whatsoever, to make a person drunk. Robbing a man of his reason is worse than robbing him of his money.

II. How this plot was defeated by Uriah's firm resolution not to lie in his own bed. "Joab, and all the mighty men of Israel, lie hard and uneasy, and much exposed to the weather and to the enemy; and shall I go and take my ease and pleasure at my own house?" No, he protests he will not do it. Now, (1) This was in itself a generous resolution, and showed Uriah to be a man of a public spirit, bold and hardy, and mortified to the delights of sense. (2) It might have been of use to awaken David's conscience, and make his heart to smite him for what he had done.

Verses 14–27

When David's project of fathering the child upon Uriah himself failed, so that, in process of time, Uriah would certainly know the wrong that had been done him, the devil put it into David's heart to take him off. That innocent, valiant, gallant man, who was ready to die for his prince's honour, must die by his prince's hand. See how fleshly lusts war against the soul, and what devastations they make in that war; how they blind the eyes, harden the heart, sear the conscience, and deprive men of all sense of honour and justice. The devil, having, as a poisonous serpent, put it into David's heart to murder Uriah, as a subtle serpent he puts it into his head how to do it.

I. Orders are sent to Joab to set Uriah in the front of the hottest battle, and then to desert him, and abandon him to the enemy, *v.* 14, 15. 1. It was deliberate. 2. He sent the letter by Uriah himself, than which nothing could be more base and barbarous, to make him accessory to his own death. 3. Advantage must be taken of Uriah's own courage and zeal for his king and country, which deserve the greatest praise and recompence, to betray him the more easily to his fate. 4. Many must be involved in the guilt. Joab, the general, and all that retire from Uriah when they ought in conscience to support and second him, became guilty of his death. 5. Uriah cannot thus die alone: the party he commands is in danger of being cut off with him. 6. It will be the triumph and joy of the Ammonites, the sworn enemies of God and Israel.

II. Joab executes these orders. In the next assault

JAMIESON, FAUSSET, BROWN

ment to be made that he has made choice of her to be queen. Many instances in modern Oriental history show the ease and despatch with which such secondary marriages are contracted, and a new beauty added to the royal seraglio. But David had to make a promise, or rather an express stipulation, to Bath-sheba, before she complied with the royal will (I Kings 1:13, 15, 17, 28); for in addition to her transcendent beauty, she appears to have been a woman of superior talents and address in obtaining the object of her ambition; in her securing that her son should succeed on the throne; in her promptitude to give notice of her pregnancy; in her activity in defeating Adonijah's natural expectation of succeeding to the crown; in her dignity as the king's mother—in all this we see very strong indications of the ascendency she gained and maintained over David, who, perhaps, had ample leisure and opportunity to discover the punishment of this unhappy connection in more ways than one [TAYLOR'S CALMET]. **5. the woman conceived, and sent and told David**—Some immediate measures of concealing their sin were necessary, as well for the king's honor as for her safety, for death was the punishment of an adulteress (Lev. 20:10).

8. David said to Uriah, Go down to thy house—This sudden recall, the manner of the king, his frivolous questions (vs. 7), and his urgency for Uriah to sleep in his own house, probably awakened suspicions of the cause of this procedure. **there followed him a mess of meat from the king**—A portion of meat from the royal table, sent to one's own house or lodgings, is one of the greatest compliments which an Eastern prince can pay. **9. But Uriah slept at the door of the king's house**—It is customary for servants to sleep in the porch or long gallery; and the guards of the Hebrew king did the same. Whatever his secret suspicions might have been, Uriah's refusal to indulge in the enjoyment of domestic pleasure, and his determination to sleep "at the door of the king's house," arose (vs. 11) from a high and honorable sense of military duty and propriety. But, doubtless, the resolution of Uriah was overruled by that Providence which brings good out of evil, and which has recorded this sad episode for the warning of the church.

14-27. URIAH SLAIN. **14, 15. David wrote a letter to Joab, and sent it by the hand of Uriah . . . Set ye Uriah in the forefront of the hottest battle**—The various arts and stratagems by which the king tried to cajole Uriah, till at last he resorted to the horrid crime of murder—the cold-blooded cruelty of despatching the letter by the hands of the gallant but much-wronged soldier himself, the enlistment of Joab to be a partaker of his sin, the heartless affectation of mourning, and the indecent haste of his marriage with Bath-sheba—have left an indelible stain upon the character of David, and exhibit a painfully humiliating proof of the awful lengths to which the best of men may go when they forfeit the restraining grace of God.

ADAM CLARKE

F. B. MEYER:

Giving rein to self-indulgence. This was not an isolated sin. For some time, backsliding had been eating out David's heart. The cankerworm takes its toll before the noble tree crashes to the ground. Joab and his brave soldiers were in the thick of a great conflict. Rabbah was being besieged and had not fallen. It was a time when kings went out to battle, but David tarried at home. It was a fatal lethargy. If the king had been in his place, this sin would never have besmirched his character.

A look, as in Eve's case, opened the door to the devil. "Turn away mine eyes from beholding vanity." However great our attainments and however high our standing, we are all liable to attack and failure; but when we abide in Christ, no weapon that hell can forge can hurt us. When we have sinned, our only safety is in instant confession. This David delayed for a year and till forced to it. He was more eager to evade the consequences than to deal with his transgression. Sober David was far worse, here, than drunken Uriah. The singular self-restraint of the soldier threw the sin of the king into terrible and disgraceful prominence.—*Bible Commentary*

8. *Go down to thy house, and wash thy feet.* Uriah had come off a journey, and needed this refreshment; but David's design was that he should go and lie with his wife, that the child now conceived should pass for his, the honor of Bath-sheba be screened, and his own crime concealed. *A mess of meat from the king.* All this was artfully contrived.

9. *Slept at the door.* That is, in one of the apartments or niches in the court of the king's house.

10. *Camest thou not from thy journey?* It is not your duty to keep watch or guard; you are come from a journey, and need rest and refreshment.

11. *The ark, and Israel . . . abide in tents.* It appears therefore that they had taken the ark with them to battle. This was the answer of a brave, generous, and disinterested man. I will not indulge myself while all my fellow soldiers are exposed to hardships, and even the ark of the Lord in danger.

13. *He made him drunk.* Supposing that in this state he would have been off his guard, and hasten down to his house.

14. *David wrote a letter.* This was the sum of treachery and villainy. He made this most noble man the carrier of letters which prescribed the mode in which he was to be murdered.

MATTHEW HENRY

that is made upon the city Uriah has the most dangerous post assigned him, and he is slain in it, *v.* 16, 17. It was strange that Joab would do such a thing merely upon a letter, without knowing the reason. But, 1. Perhaps he supposed Uriah had been guilty of some great crime. 2. Joab had been guilty of blood, and we may suppose it pleased him very well to see David himself falling into the same guilt.

III. He sends an account of it to David. An express is despatched away immediately with a report of this last disgrace and loss which they had sustained, *v.* 18. He slyly orders the messenger to soothe it with telling him that Uriah the Hittite was dead also. The messenger delivered this message agreeably to orders, *v.* 22–24. He makes the besieged to sally out first upon the besiegers (*they came out unto us into the field*), represents the besiegers as doing their part with great bravery (*we were upon them even to the entering of the gate*—we forced them to retire into the city with precipitation), and so concludes with a slight mention of the slaughter made among them by some shot from the wall: *Some of the king's servants are dead*, and particularly *Uriah the Hittite*, an officer of note, stood first in the list of the slain.

IV. David receives the account with a secret satisfaction, *v.* 25.

V. He marries the widow in a little time. She submitted to the ceremony of mourning for her husband as short a time as custom would admit (*v.* 26), and then David took her to his house as his wife, and she bore him a son. The whole *matter of Uriah* (as it is called, 1 Kings xv. 5), the adultery, falsehood, murder, and this marriage at last, it was all displeasing to the Lord. God sees and hates sin in his own people. Nay, the nearer any are to God in profession the more displeasing to him their sins are. Let none therefore encourage themselves in sin by the example of David; for those that sin as he did will fall under the displeasure of God as he did.

JAMIESON, FAUSSET, BROWN

KEIL–DELITZSCH:

David's deep fall forms a turning point not only in the inner life of the great king, but also in the history of his reign. Hitherto David had kept free from the grosser sins, and had only exhibited such infirmities and failings as simulation, prevarication, etc., which clung to all the saints of the Old Covenant, and were hardly regarded as sins in the existing stage of religious culture at that time (although God never left them unpunished, but invariably visited them upon His servants with humiliations and chastisements of various kinds). Among the unacknowledged sins which God tolerated because of the hardness of Israel's heart was polygamy, which encouraged licentiousness and the tendency to sensual excesses, and to which but a weak barrier had been presented by the warning that had been given for the Israelitish kings against taking many wives (Deut. 17:17), opposed as such a warning was to the notion so prevalent in the East both in ancient and modern times, that a well-filled harem is essential to the splendor of a princely court. The custom to which this notion gave rise opened a dangerous precipice in David's way, and led to a most grievous fall, that can only be explained, as O.V. Gerlach has said, from the intoxication consequent upon undisturbed prosperity and power, which grew with every year of his reign, and occasioned a long series of most severe humiliations and divine chastisements that marred the splendor of his reign, notwithstanding the fact that the great sin was followed by deep and sincere repentance.
—*Commentary on the Old Testament*

ADAM CLARKE

27. ***When the mourning was past.*** Probably it lasted only seven days. ***She became his wife.*** This hurried marriage was no doubt intended on both sides to cover the pregnancy. ***But the thing that David had done displeased the Lord.*** It was necessary to add this, lest the splendor of David's former virtues should induce any to suppose his crimes were passed over, or looked on with an indulgent eye, by the God of purity and justice. Sorely he sinned, and sorely did he suffer for it; he sowed one grain of sweet, and reaped a long harvest of calamity and woe.

MATTHEW HENRY

CHAPTER 12

Verses 1–14

It seems to have been a great while after David had been guilty of adultery with Bath-sheba before he was brought to repentance for it. For, when Nathan was sent to him, the child was born (*v.* 14). What shall we think of David's state all this while? We may well suppose his comforts and the exercises of his graces suspended, and his communion with God interrupted; during all that time, it is certain, he penned no psalms, his harp was out of tune, and his soul like a tree in winter, that has life in the root only.

I. The messenger God sent to him. He sent a prophet — Nathan, his faithful friend and confidant, to instruct and counsel him, *v.* 1. Though God may suffer his people to fall into sin, he will not suffer them to lie still in it. He sends after us before we seek after him, else we should certainly be lost. Nathan was the prophet by whom God had sent him notice of his kind intentions towards him (*ch.* vii. 4), and now, by the same hand, he sends him this message of wrath.

II. The message Nathan delivered to him.

1. He fetched a compass with a parable, which seemed to David as a complaint made to him against one of his subjects that had wronged his poor neighbour. (1) Nathan represented to David a grievous injury which a rich man had done to an honest neighbour that was not able to contend with him: *The rich man had many flocks and herds* (*v.* 2); the poor man had one lamb only. This poor man had but one lamb, a ewe-lamb, a little ewe-lamb, having not wherewithal to buy or keep more. But it was a *cade*-lamb (as we call it); *it grew up with his children*, *v.* 3. He was fond of it, and it was familiar with him at all times. The rich man, having occasion for a lamb to entertain a friend with, took the poor man's lamb from him by violence and made use of that (*v.* 4), either out of covetousness, because he grudged to make use of his own, or rather out of luxury, because he fancied the lamb that was thus tenderly kept, and ate and drank like a child, must needs be more delicate food than any of his own and have a better relish. (2) In this he showed him the evil of the sin he had been guilty of in defiling Bath-sheba. He had many wives and concubines, whom he kept at a distance, as rich men keep their flocks in their fields. Marriage is a remedy against fornication, but marrying many is not; for, when once the law of unity is transgressed, the indulged lust will hardly stint itself. Observe that this evil disposition is called a traveller, for in the beginning it is only so, but,

JAMIESON, FAUSSET, BROWN

CHAPTER 12

Vss. 1-6. NATHAN'S PARABLE. **1. the Lord sent Nathan unto David**—The use of parables is a favorite style of speaking among Oriental people, especially in the conveyance of unwelcome truth. This exquisitely pathetic parable was founded on a common custom of pastoral people who have pet lambs, which they bring up with their children, and which they address in terms of endearment. The atrocity of the real, however, far exceeded that of the fictitious offense.

ADAM CLARKE

CHAPTER 12

1. ***There were two men in one city.*** There is nothing in this parable that requires illustration; its bent is evident; and it was constructed to make David, unwittingly, pass sentence on himself. It was in David's hand what his own letters were in the hands of the brave but unfortunate Uriah.

JOSEPH PARKER:

In reading the opening words of this chapter we can have no doubt as to their authenticity. The words are these, "And the Lord sent Nathan unto David." We cannot mistake the *heaven-sent man*. Wherever he is sent he carries his credentials along with him, not written with pen and ink, but so written in his face or tone or manner as to leave no doubt as to the divinity of his mission and the heavenliness of his inspiration. "Pray ye therefore the Lord of the harvest, that he will send forth laborers into his harvest." It is in vain for men to send themselves, or to imagine that they can confer any advantage upon the Christian cause on account of their own dignity, or personal renown, or social recognition in any direction. God himself must send, in his own way. The man is exalted by his mission. Though a dumb man to begin with, he waxes eloquent in God's cause; though a stammerer at the outset, he is no stammerer at the end. Is there a greater blessing known among us than to be brought now and again into vital association with a heaven-sent man, whether he come as speaker or writer or private friend—a man who has in very deed a gift in prayer, a genius of sympathy, an inspiration of method and of tone, so that his gracious appeal is thrown over us ere yet we have given him full consent?—*The People's Bible*

MATTHEW HENRY

in time, it becomes a guest, and, in conclusion, is master of the house. (3) By this parable he drew from David a sentence against himself. For David supposing it to be a case in fact, and not doubting the truth of it when he had it from Nathan himself, gave judgment immediately against the offender, and confirmed it with an oath, *v.* 5, 6. [1] That, for his injustice in taking away the lamb, he should restore fourfold, according to the law (Exod. xxii. 1), *four sheep for a sheep.* [2] That for his tyranny and cruelty, and the pleasure he took in abusing a poor man, he should be put to death.

2. He closed in with him, at length, in the application of the parable. In plain terms, "*Thou art the man* who hast done this wrong, and a much greater, to thy neighbour." Did he deserve to die who took his neighbour's lamb? and dost not thou who hast taken thy neighbour's wife? Now he speaks immediately from God, not as a petitioner for a poor man, but as an ambassador from the great God, with whom is no respect of persons.

(1) God, by Nathan, reminds David of the great things he had done and designed for him, anointing him to be king, and preserving him to the kingdom (*v.* 7). He had given him the house of Israel and Judah. The wealth of the kingdom was at his service and everybody was willing to oblige him.

(2) He charges him with a high contempt of the divine authority, in the sins he had been guilty of: *Wherefore hast thou* (presuming upon thy royal dignity and power) *despised the commandment of the Lord? v.* 9. [1] The murder of Uriah is twice mentioned: "*Thou hast killed Uriah with the sword. Thou hast slain him with the sword of the children of Ammon,* those uncircumcised enemies of God and Israel." [2] The marrying of Bath-sheba is likewise twice mentioned, because he thought there was no harm in that (*v.* 9): *Thou hast taken his wife to be thy wife,* and again, *v.* 10. To marry her whom he had before defiled, and whose husband he had slain, was an affront upon the ordinance of marriage, making that not only to palliate, but in a manner to consecrate, such villainies.

(3) He threatens an entail of judgments upon his family for this sin (*v.* 10): "*The sword shall never depart from thy house,* not in thy time nor afterwards, but, for the most part, thou and thy posterity shall be engaged in war." Can the mercy and the sword consist with each other? Yes, those may lie under great and long afflictions who yet shall not be excluded from the grace of the covenant. The reason given is, *Because thou hast despised me.* It is particularly threatened, [1] That his children should be his grief: *I will raise up evil against thee out of thy own house.* [2] That his wives should be his shame, that by an unparalleled piece of villainy they should be publicly debauched before all Israel, *v.* 11, 12.

3. David's penitent confession of his sin hereupon. *I have sinned against the Lord, v.* 13.

4. His pardon declared, upon this penitent confession, but with a proviso. When David said *I have sinned,* and Nathan perceived that he was a true penitent,

(1) He did, in God's name, assure him that his sin was forgiven: "*The Lord also has put away thy sin* out of the sight of his avenging eye; *thou shalt not die,*" that is, "not die eternally, nor be for ever put away from God, as thou wouldest have been if he had not put away the sin." "*The sword shall not depart from thy house,* but, [1] It shall not cut thee off, thou shalt come to thy grave in peace." [2] "Though thou shalt all thy days be *chastened of the Lord,* yet thou *shalt not be condemned with the world.*"

(2) Yet he pronounces a sentence of death upon the child, *v.* 14. Behold the sovereignty of God! The guilty parent lives, and the guiltless infant dies. [1] David had, by his sin, wronged God in his honour; he had *given occasion to the enemies of the Lord to blaspheme.* There is this great evil in the scandalous sins of those that profess religion, and relation to God, that they furnish the enemies of God and religion with matter for reproach and blasphemy, Rom. ii. 24. [2] God will therefore vindicate his honour by showing his displeasure against David for this sin, and letting the world see that though he loves David he hates his sin; and he chooses to do it by the *death of the child.*

Verses 15–25

Nathan, having delivered his message, stayed not at court, but went home, probably to pray for David, to whom he had been preaching. David named one of his sons by Bath-sheba *Nathan,* in honour of this prophet (1 Chron. iii. 5), and it was that son of whom Christ, the great prophet, lineally descended, Luke iii. 31. When Nathan retired, David, it is probable,

JAMIESON, FAUSSET, BROWN

5. the man that hath done this thing shall surely die—This punishment was more severe than the case deserved, or than was warranted by the divine statute (Exod. 22:1 . The sympathies of the king had been deeply enlisted, his indignation aroused, but his conscience was still asleep; and at the time when he was most fatally indulgent to his own sins, he was most ready to condemn the delinquencies and errors of others.

7-23. HE APPLIES IT TO DAVID, WHO CONFESSES HIS SIN, AND IS PARDONED. **7. Nathan said to David, Thou art the man**—These awful words pierced his heart, aroused his conscience, and brought him to his knees. The sincerity and depth of his penitent sorrow are evinced by the Psalms he composed [32; 51; 103]. He was pardoned, so far as related to the restoration of the divine favor. But as from his high character for piety, and his eminent rank in society, his deplorable fall was calculated to do great injury to the cause of religion, it was necessary that God should testify His abhorrence of sin by leaving even His own servant to reap the bitter temporal fruits. David was not himself doomed, according to his own view of what justice demanded (vs. 5); but he had to suffer a quadruple expiation in the successive deaths of four sons, besides a lengthened train of other evils. **8. I gave thee thy master's house, and thy master's wives**—The phraseology means nothing more than that God in His providence had given David, as king of Israel, everything that was Saul's. The history furnishes conclusive evidence that he never actually married any of the wives of Saul. But the harem of the preceding king belongs, according to Oriental notions, as a part of the regalia to his successor.

11. I will raise up evil against thee out of thine own house,... The prophet speaks of God threatening to do what He only permitted to be done. The fact is, that David's loss of character by the discovery of his crimes, tended, in the natural course of things, to diminish the respect of his family, to weaken the authority of his government, and to encourage the prevalence of many disorders throughout his kingdom.

ADAM CLARKE

5. *The man . . . shall surely die.* Literally, "He is a son of death," a very bad man, and one who deserves to die. But the law did not sentence a sheep-stealer to death. Let us hear it: "If a man steal an ox, or a sheep . . . he shall restore five oxen for an ox, and four sheep for a sheep," Exod. xxii. 1; and hence David immediately says, "He shall restore the lamb fourfold."

7. *Thou art the man.* What a terrible word! And by it David appears to have been transfixed, and brought into the dust before the messenger of God.

8. *Thy master's wives into thy bosom.* Perhaps this means no more than that he had given him absolute power over everything possessed by Saul; and as it was the custom for the new king to succeed even to the wives and concubines, the whole harem of the deceased king, so it was in this case; and the possession of the wives was a sure proof that he had got all regal rights.

9. *Thou hast killed Uriah.* You are the murderer, as having planned his death; the sword of the Ammonites was your instrument only.

11. *I will take thy wives.* That is, In the course of My providence I will permit all this to be done. Had David been faithful, God, by His providence, would have turned all this aside; but now, by his sin, he has made that providence his enemy which before was his friend.

13. *The Lord . . . hath put away thy sin.* Many have supposed that David's sin was now actually pardoned, but this is perfectly erroneous. David, as an adulterer, was condemned to death by the law of God, and he had according to that law passed sentence of death upon himself. God alone, whose law that was, could revoke that sentence, or dispense with its execution. Therefore Nathan, who had charged the guilt home upon his conscience, is authorized to give him the assurance that he should not die a temporal death for it: *The Lord also hath put away thy sin; thou shalt not die.* There is something very remarkable in the words of Nathan: *The Lord also hath put away thy sin; thou shalt not die.* "Also Jehovah hath caused thy sin to pass over, or transferred thy sin; thou shalt not die." God has transferred the legal punishment of this sin to the child; he shall die, you shall not die. And this is the very point on which the prophet gives him the most direct information: The child that is born unto you shall surely die—"dying he shall die."

MATTHEW HENRY

retired likewise, and penned the 51st Psalm, in which (though he had been assured that his sin was pardoned) he prays earnestly for pardon, and greatly laments his sin; for then will true penitents be ashamed of what they have done when God is *pacified towards them*, Ezek. xvi. 63.

I. The child's illness: *The Lord struck* it, *and it was very sick*.

II. David's humiliation under this token of God's displeasure, and the intercession he made with God for the life of the child (*v.* 16, 17): *He fasted, and lay all night upon the earth.* This was an evidence of the truth of his repentance. For, 1. Hereby it appeared that he was willing to bear the shame of his sin, for this child would be a continual memorandum of it, therefore he was so far from desiring its death, as most in such circumstances do, that he prayed earnestly for its life. 2. A very tender compassionate spirit appeared in this towards little children, even their own; and this was another sign of a broken contrite spirit. Those that are penitent will be pitiful. 3. He discovered, in this, a great concern for another world, which is an evidence of repentance. Nathan had told him that certainly the child should die; yet, while it is in the reach of prayer, he earnestly intercedes with God for it, chiefly (as we may suppose) that its soul might be safe and happy in another world, and that his sin might not come against the child, and that it might not fare the worse for that in the future state.

III. The death of the child: It *died on the seventh day* (*v.* 18), when it was seven days old, and therefore not circumcised, which David might perhaps interpret as a further token of God's displeasure, that it died before it was brought under the seal of the covenant; yet he does not therefore doubt of its being happy, for the benefits of the covenant do not depend upon the seals.

IV. David's wonderful calmness and composure of mind when he understood the child was dead.

1. What he did. (1) He laid aside the expressions of his sorrow, washed and anointed himself, and called for clean linen, that he might decently appear before God in his house. (2) *He went up to the tabernacle and worshipped,* like Job when he heard of the death of his children. (3) *Then he went to his own house* and refreshed himself, as one who found benefit by his religion in the day of his affliction.

2. The reason he gave for what he did. His servants thought it strange that he should afflict himself so for the sickness of the child and yet take the death of it so easily, and asked him the reason of it (*v.* 21), in answer to which he gives this plain account of his conduct, (1) That while the child was alive he thought it his duty to importune the divine favour towards it, *v.* 22. When our relations and friends have fallen sick, the prayer of faith has prevailed much; while there is life there is hope, and, while there is hope, there is room for prayer. (2) That now the child was dead he thought it as much his duty to be satisfied in the divine disposal concerning it (*v.* 23): *Now, wherefore should I fast?* Two things checked his grief:—[1] *I cannot bring him back again*; and again, *He shall not return to me.* Those that are dead are out of the reach of prayer; nor can our tears profit them. [2] *I shall go to him. First,* To him to the grave. Note, The consideration of our own death should moderate our sorrow at the death of our relations. *Secondly,* To him to heaven, to a state of blessedness, which even the Old Testament saints had some expectation of. This may comfort us when our children are removed from us by death, they are better provided for, both in work and wealth, than they could have been in this world. We shall be with them shortly, to part no more.

V. The birth of Solomon. Though David's marrying Bath-sheba had displeased the Lord, yet he was not therefore commanded to divorce her. Bath-sheba, no doubt, was greatly afflicted with the sense of her sin, and the tokens of God's displeasure. But, God having restored to David the joys of his salvation, he comforted her with the same comforts with which he himself was comforted of God (*v.* 24). 1. Inasmuch as, by his providence, he gave them a son. They called him *Solomon—peaceful,* because his birth was a token of God's being at peace with them, because of the prosperity which was entailed upon him, and because he was to be a type of Christ, the prince of peace. David had very patiently submitted to the will of God in the death of the other child, and now God made up the loss of that, abundantly to his advantage, in the birth of this. 2. Inasmuch as, by his grace, he particularly owned and favoured that son: *The Lord loved him* (*v.* 24 and 25), ordered him, by the prophet Nathan, to be called *Jedidiah—Beloved of the Lord.*

JAMIESON, FAUSSET, BROWN

15-23. the Lord struck the child . . . and it was very sick—The first visible chastisement inflicted on David appeared on the person of that child which was the evidence and monument of his guilt.

His domestics were surprised at his conduct, and in explanation of its singularity, it is necessary to remark that the custom in the East is to leave the nearest relative of a deceased person to the full and undisturbed indulgence of his grief, till on the third or fourth day at farthest (John 11:17). Then the other relatives and friends visit him, invite him to eat, lead him to a bath, and bring him a change of dress, which is necessary from his having sat or lain on the ground. The surprise of David's servants, then, who had seen his bitter anguish while the child was sick, arose apparently from this, that when he found it was dead, he who had so deeply lamented arose of himself from the earth, without waiting for their coming to him, immediately bathed and anointed himself, instead of appearing as a mourner, and after worshiping God with solemnity, returned to his wonted repast, without any interposition of others.

24, 25. SOLOMON IS BORN. **24. Bath-sheba . . . bare a son, and he called his name Solomon**—i.e., peaceable. But Nathan gave him the name of Jedediah, by command of God, or perhaps only as an expression of God's love. This love and the noble gifts with which he was endowed, considering the criminality of the marriage from which he sprang, is a remarkable instance of divine goodness and grace.

ADAM CLARKE

16. *David . . . besought God for the child.* How could he do so after the solemn assurance that he had from God that the child should die? The justice of God absolutely required that the penalty of the law should be exacted; either the father or the son shall die. This could not be reversed.

22. *Who can tell?* David, and indeed all others under the Mosaic dispensation, were so satisfied that all God's threatenings and promises were conditional that even in the most positive assertions relative to judgments, etc., they sought for a change of purpose. And notwithstanding the positive declaration of Nathan relative to the death of the child, David sought for its life, not knowing but that might depend on some unexpressed condition, such as earnest prayer, fasting, humiliation, and in these he continued while there was hope.

23. *I shall go to him, but he shall not return to me.* It is not clear whether David by this expressed his faith in the immortality of the soul; going to him may only mean, "I also shall die, and be gathered to my fathers, as he is."

24. *David comforted Bath-sheba.* His extraordinary attachment to this beautiful woman was the cause of all his misfortunes. *He called his name Solomon.* This name seems to have been given prophetically, for *sholomah* signifies "peaceable," and there was almost uninterrupted peace during his reign.

25. *Called . . . Jedidiah.* Literally, "the beloved of the Lord."

MATTHEW HENRY

Verses 26–31

An account of the conquest of Rabbah, and other cities of the Ammonites. Though this comes in here after the birth of David's child, yet it is most probable that it was effected a good while before, and soon after the death of Uriah, perhaps during the days of Bath-sheba's mourning for him. Observe, 1. That God was very gracious in giving David this great success against his enemies. Justly might he have made his sword, thenceforward, a plague to David and his kingdom; yet he breaks it and makes David's sword victorious, even before he repents, that this *goodness of God might lead him to repentance*. 2. That Joab acted very honestly and honourably; for when he had taken *the city of waters*, the royal city, where the palace was, and from which the rest of the city was supplied with water (and therefore, upon the cutting off of that, would be obliged speedily to surrender), he sent to David to come in person to complete this great action, that he might have the praise of it, *v.* 26–28. 3

That David was both too haughty and too severe upon this occasion, and neither so humble nor so tender as he should have been. (1) He seems to have been too fond of the crown of the king of Ammon, *v.* 30. Because it was of extraordinary value, by reason of the precious stones with which it was set, David would have it set upon his head, though it would have been better to have cast it at God's feet, and at this time to have put his own mouth in the dust, under guilt. (2) He seems to have been too harsh with his prisoners of war, *v.* 31. Taking the city by storm, after it had obstinately held out against a long and expensive siege, if he had put all whom he found in arms to the sword in the heat of battle, it would have been severe enough; but to kill them afterwards in cold blood, and by cruel tortures, with saws and harrows, tearing them to pieces, did not become him who, when he entered upon the government, promised to sing of mercy as well as judgment, Ps. ci. 1.

JAMIESON, FAUSSET, BROWN

26-31. RABBAH IS TAKEN. **26. Joab fought against Rabbah**—The time during which this siege lasted, since the intercourse with Bath-sheba, and the birth of at least one child, if not two, occurred during the progress of it, probably extended over two years.

27. the city of waters—Rabbah, like Aroer, was divided into two parts—one the lower town, insulated by the winding course of the Jabbok, which flowed almost round it, and the upper and stronger town, called the royal city. "The first was taken by Joab, but the honor of capturing so strongly a fortified place as the other was an honor reserved for the king himself." **28. encamp against the city, and take it**—It has always been characteristic of Oriental despots to monopolize military honors; and as the ancient world knew nothing of the modern refinement of kings gaining victories by their generals, so Joab sent for David to command the final assault in person. A large force was levied for the purpose. David without much difficulty captured the royal city and obtained possession of its immense wealth. **lest I take the city, and it be called after my name**—The circumstance of a city receiving a new name after some great person, as Alexandria, Constantinople, Hyderabad, is of frequent occurrence in the ancient and modern history of the East. **30. he took the king's crown from off his head**—While the treasures of the city were given as plunder to his soldiers, David reserved to himself the crown, which was of rarest value. Its great weight makes it probable that it was like many ancient crowns, not worn, but suspended over the head, or fixed on a canopy on the top of the throne. **the precious stones**—*Hebrew*, "stone" was a round ball composed of pearls and other jewels, which was in the crown, and probably taken out of it to be inserted in David's own crown. **31. he brought forth the people . . . and put them under saws . . .** This excessive severity and employment of tortures, which the Hebrews on no other occasion are recorded to have practised, was an act of retributive justice on a people who were infamous for their cruelties (I Sam. 11:2; Amos 1:13).

ADAM CLARKE

26. *And took the royal city.* How can this be, when Joab sent to David to come to take the city, in consequence of which David did come and take that city? The explanation seems to be this: Rabbah was composed of a city and citadel; the former, in which was the king's residence, Joab had taken, and supposed he could soon render himself master of the latter, and therefore sends to David to come and take it, lest, he taking the whole, the city should be called after his name.

27. *And have taken the city of waters.* The city where the tank or reservoir was that supplied the city and suburbs with water. Some think that the original should be translated, "I have intercepted, or cut off, the waters of the city"; and Houbigant translates the place, "And I have already drawn off the waters from the city." This perfectly agrees with the account in Josephus, who says, "Having cut off their waters," *Antiq.*, lib. vii, cap. 7. This was the reason why David should come speedily, as the citadel, deprived of water, could not long hold out.

30. *The weight whereof was a talent of gold.* If this talent was only seven pounds, as Whiston says, David might have carried it on his head with little difficulty; but this weight, according to common computation, would amount to more than one hundred pounds! If, however, *mishkalah* be taken for the value, not the weight, then all is plain. Now this seems to be the true sense, because of the added words *with the precious stones;* i.e., the gold of the crown, and the jewels with which it was adorned, were equal in value to a talent of gold.

31. *He brought forth the people . . . and put them under saws.* From this representation a great cry has been raised against "David's unparalleled, if not diabolic, cruelty." I believe this interpretation was chiefly taken from the parallel place, 1 Chron. xx. 3, where it is said he "cut them with saws . . . and with axes." Instead of *vaiyasar*, "he sawed," we have here (in Samuel) *vaiyasem*, "he put them"; and these two words differ from each other only in a part of a single letter, *resh* for *mem*. And it is worthy of remark that, instead of *vaiyasar*, "he sawed," in 1 Chron. xx. 3, six or seven MSS. collated by Dr. Kennicott have *vaiyasem*, "he put them"; nor is there found any various reading in all the MSS. yet collated for the text in this chapter that favors the common reading in Chronicles. The meaning therefore is, He made the people slaves, and employed them in sawing, making iron harrows, or mining (for the word means both), and in hewing of wood, and making of brick.

CHAPTER 13

MATTHEW HENRY

Verses 1–20

A particular account of the abominable wickedness of Amnon in ravishing his sister. Amnon's character, we have reason to think, was bad in other things; if he had not forsaken God, he would never have been given up to these vile affections.

I. The devil, as an unclean spirit, put it into his heart to lust after his sister Tamar. Beauty is a snare to many; it was so to her. Amnon's lust was, 1. Unnatural in itself. Such a spirit of contradiction there is in man's corrupt nature that still it desires forbidden fruit, and the more strongly it is forbidden the more greedily it is desired. 2. It was very uneasy to him. He was so vexed that he could not gain an opportunity to solicit her chastity that he *fell sick*, *v.* 2.

II. The devil, as a subtle serpent, put it into his head how to compass this wicked design. Amnon had a friend, a subtle man, cunning to carry on an intrigue of this nature, *v.* 3.

1. He took notice that Amnon looked ill, and, being a subtle man, concluded that he was love-sick (*v.* 4). *Being the king's son*, "Thou hast the power of a prince to command what thou wantest and wishest for: use that power, therefore, and gratify thyself."

2. Amnon having the impudence to own his wicked lust, miscalling it *love* (*I love Tamar*), Jonadab put him in a way to compass his design, *v.* 5. Amnon is already sick, but goes about; he must take upon him to be so ill as not to be able to get up. The best dish from the king's table cannot please him; but, if he can eat anything, it must be from his sister

JAMIESON, FAUSSET, BROWN

VSS. 1-5. AMNON LOVES TAMAR. **1. Tamar**—daughter of David by Maachah (ch. 3:3). **2. for she was a virgin**—Unmarried daughters were kept in close seclusion from the company of men; no strangers, nor even their relatives of the other sex, being permitted to see them without the presence of witnesses. Of course, Amnon must have seen Tamar, for he had conceived a violent passion for her, which, though forbidden by the law (Lev. 18:11), yet with the sanction of Abraham's example (Gen. 20:12), and the common practice in neighboring countries for princes to marry their half sisters, he seems not to have considered an improper connection. But he had no means of making it known to her, and the pain of that disappointment preying upon his mind produced a visible change in his appearance and health. **3. Jonadab, the son of Shimeah**—or Shammah (I Sam. 16:9). By the counsel and contrivance of this scheming cousin a plan was devised for obtaining an unrestricted interview with the object of his attachment. **4. my brother Absalom's sister**—In Eastern countries, where polygamy prevails, the girls are considered to be under the special care and protection of their uterine brother, who is the guardian of their interests and their honor, even more than their father himself (see on Gen. 34:6-25).

ADAM CLARKE

1. *Whose name was Tamar.* Tamar was the daughter of David and Maacah, daughter of the king of Geshur, and the sister of Absalom. Amnon was David's eldest son by Ahinoam. She was therefore sister to Amnon only by the father's side, i.e., half sister; but whole sister to Absalom.

2. *Amnon was so vexed . . . for she was a virgin.* It has been well remarked that "the passion of love is nowhere so wasting and vexatious as where it is unlawful."

MATTHEW HENRY

Tamar's fair hand.

3. Amnon followed these directions, and thus got Tamar within his reach. David was always fond of his children, and concerned if anything ailed them; he no sooner hears that Amnon is sick than he comes himself to visit him. At parting, the indulgent father asks, "Is there anything thou hast a mind to, that I can procure for thee?" "Yes, Sir," says the dissembling son, "my stomach is weak, and I know not of any thing I can eat, unless it be a cake of my sister Tamar's making, and I cannot be satisfied that it is so unless I see her make it, and it will do me the more good if I eat it at her hand." David saw no reason to suspect any mischief intended. He therefore immediately orders Tamar to go and attend her sick brother, *v.* 7.

4. Having got her to him, he contrives to have her alone. Tamar has not the least thought of that which his polluted breast is full of; and therefore she makes no scruple of being alone with him *in the inner chamber, v.* 10. And now the mask is thrown off, the meat is thrown by, and the wicked wretch calls her *sister*, and yet impudently courts her to *come and lie with him, v.* 11.

III. The devil, as a strong tempter, deafens his ear to all the reasonings with which she resisted his assaults and would have persuaded him to desist. 1. She calls him *brother*, reminding him of the nearness of the relation, which made it unlawful for him to marry her, much less to debauch her. It was expressly forbidden (Lev. xviii. 9) under a severe penalty, Lev. xx. 17. 2. She entreats him not to force her, which intimates that she would never consent to it in any degree. 3. She lays before him the great wickedness of it. 4. She represents to him the shame of it. 5. To divert him from his wicked purpose she intimates to him that probably the king, rather than he should die for love of her, would dispense with the divine law and let him marry her: not as if she thought he had such a dispensing power, or would pretend to it; but she was confident that, upon notice given to the king by himself of this wicked desire, he would take an effectual course to protect her from him. But all her arts and all her arguments availed not. His proud spirit cannot bear a denial; but her honour, and all that was dear to her, must be sacrificed to his outrageous lust, *v.* 14. It is to be feared that Amnon, though young, had long lived a lewd life, for a man could not of a sudden arrive at such a pitch of wickedness.

IV. The devil, as a tormentor and betrayer, immediately turns his love of her into hatred (*v.* 15).

1. He basely turned her out of doors by force. To dismiss her thus as if she had done some wicked thing, obliged her, in her own defence, to proclaim the wrong. We may learn from it the mischievous consequences of sin (at last, it bites like a serpent); sins, sweet in the commission, afterwards become odious and painful, and the sinner's own conscience makes them so to himself. But to hate the person he had abused showed that his conscience was terrified, but his heart not at all humbled.

2. What becomes of the poor victim? (1) She bitterly lamented the injury she had received, as it was a stain to her honour, though no real blemish to her virtue. She tore her fine clothes in token of her grief, and put ashes upon her head, loathing her own beauty and ornaments, because they had occasioned Amnon's unlawful love; and she went on crying for another's sin, *v.* 19. (2) She retired to her brother Absalom's house, because he was her own brother, and there she lived in solitude and sorrow, in token of her modesty and detestation of uncleanness. Absalom spoke kindly to her, bade her pass by the injury for the present, designing himself to revenge it, *v.* 20.

Verses 21–29

What Solomon says of the beginning of strife is as true of the beginning of all sin, it is as the letting forth of water. One mischief begets another.

I. How David resented the tidings of Amnon's sin. But was it enough for him to be angry? He ought to have punished his son for it, and have put him to open shame.

II. How Absalom resented it. He resolves already to do the part of a judge in Israel; and, since his father will not punish Amnon, he will, from a principle, not of justice or zeal for virtue, but of revenge, because he reckons himself affronted in the abuse done to his sister.

1. The design conceived: *Absalom hated Amnon* (*v.* 22). Absalom's hatred of his brother's crime would have been commendable, and he might justly have prosecuted him for it by a due course of law, for example to others, and the making of some compensation to his injured sister; but to hate his person,

JAMIESON, FAUSSET, BROWN

6-27. HE DEFILES HER. **6. Amnon lay down, and made himself sick**—The Orientals are great adepts in feigning sickness, whenever they have any object to accomplish. **let Tamar my sister come and make me a couple of cakes**—To the king Amnon spoke of Tamar as "his sister," a term artfully designed to hoodwink his father; and the request appeared so natural, the delicate appetite of a sick man requiring to be humored, that the king promised to send her. The cakes seem to have been a kind of fancy bread, in the preparation of which Oriental ladies take great delight. Tamar, flattered by the invitation, lost no time in rendering the required service in the house of her sick brother.

12-14. do not force me—The remonstrances and arguments of Tamar were so affecting and so strong, that had not Amnon been violently goaded on by the lustful passion of which he had become the slave, they must have prevailed with him to desist from his infamous purpose. In bidding him, however, "speak to the king, for he will not withhold me from thee," it is probable that she urged this as her last resource, saying anything she thought would please him, in order to escape for the present out of his hands. **15. Then Amnon hated her exceedingly**—It is not unusual for persons instigated by violent and irregular passions to go from one extreme to another. In Amnon's case the sudden revulsion is easily accounted for; the atrocity of his conduct, with all the feelings of shame, remorse, and dread of exposure and punishment, now burst upon his mind, rendering the presence of Tamar intolerably painful to him. **17. bolt the door after her**—The street door of houses in the East is always kept barred—the bolts being of wood. In the great mansions, where a porter stands at the outside, this precaution is dispensed with; and the circumstance, therefore, of a prince giving an order so unusual shows the vehement perturbation of Ammon's mind. **18. garment of divers colours**—As embroidery in ancient times was the occupation or pastime of ladies of the highest rank, the possession of these parti-colored garments was a mark of distinction; they were worn exclusively by young women of royal condition. Since the art of manufacturing cloth stuffs has made so great progress, dresses of this variegated description are now more common in the East. **19. Tamar put ashes on her head, and rent her garment of divers colours . . . laid her hand on her head, and went on crying**—i.e., sobbing. Oriental manners would probably see nothing beyond a strong sense of the injury she had sustained, if Tamar actually rent her garments. But, as her veil is not mentioned, it is probable that Amnon had turned her out of doors without it, and she raised her hand with the design to conceal her face. By these signs, especially the rending of her distinguishing robe, Absalom at once conjectured what had taken place. Recommending her to be silent about it and not publish her own and her family's dishonor, he gave no inkling of his angry feelings to Amnon. But all the while he was in secret "nursing his wrath to keep it warm," and only "biding his time" to avenge his sister's wrongs, and by the removal of the heir-apparent perhaps further also his ambitious designs. **20. So Tamar remained desolate in her brother Absalom's house**—He was her natural protector, and the children of polygamists lived by themselves, as if they constituted different families.

ADAM CLARKE

12. *Nay, my brother.* There is something exceedingly tender and persuasive in this speech of Tamar; but Amnon was a mere brute, and it was all lost on him.

JOHN LANGE:

"Such things are not done in Israel," it is against the law and custom of the people of God (as contrasted with the heathen). Compare Lev. 20:17 with verses 7 and 26. Tamar repels the wickedness from the highest moral point of view, which is determined by the theocratic-national position and significance of Israel. The word "folly" is here used of unchastity as in 34:7. The same sense is given substantially by the rendering of Eng. A.V.: "not so should it be done in Israel" (as Philippson). Keil remarks that the expression recalls Gen. 34:7 (where it is a commentary on Shechem's conduct to Dinah), the words being the same; and *Bib. Com.* adds that Tamar probably knew the passage in Genesis, and wished to profit by it. But, as this passage is a remark of the editor of the Pentateuch (as the phrase "in Israel" shows), and it is doubtful whether the Pentateuch in its present shape existed in David's time, the resemblance between the two passages must be otherwise explained. The phrase in question may have been a common one, or the editor of Genesis may have taken it from our narrative, as a remark appropriate in his narrative.

—*Commentary on the Holy Scriptures*

21. *But when King David heard.* To this verse the Septuagint add the following words: "But he would not grieve the soul of Amnon his son, for he loved him, because he was his firstborn." The same addition is found in the Vulgate and in Josephus, and it is possible that this once made a part of the Hebrew text.

MATTHEW HENRY

and design his death by assassination, was to put a great affront upon God, by offering to repair the breach of his seventh commandment by the violation of his sixth, as if they were not all alike sacred. *But he that said, Do not commit adultery, said also, Do not kill*, James ii. 11.

2. The design concealed. He said nothing to Amnon. If Absalom had reasoned the matter with Amnon, he might have convinced him of his sin and brought him to repentance. Two full years Absalom nursed this root of bitterness, *v.* 24. It may be, at first, he did not intend to kill his brother, and only waited for an occasion to disgrace him or do him some other mischief; but in time his hatred ripened to this, that he would be no less than the death of him.

3. The design laid. (1) Absalom has a feast at his house in the country, as Nabal had, on occasion of his sheep-shearing, *v.* 23. (2) To this feast he invites the king his father, and all the princes of the blood (*v.* 24), that he might make himself the more respected among his neighbours. The king would not go himself, because he would not put him to the expense of his entertainment, *v.* 25. Absalom got leave for Amnon, and all the rest of the king's sons, to come and grace his table in the country, *v.* 26, 27. Absalom had so effectually concealed his enmity to Amnon that David saw no reason to suspect any design upon him in that particular invitation.

4. The design executed, *v.* 28, 29. (1) Absalom's entertainment was very plentiful; for he resolves that they shall all be merry with wine. But, (2) The orders he gave to his servants concerning Amnon, that they should mingle his blood with his wine, were very barbarous. He would have Amnon slain *when his heart was merry with wine*, not giving him time to say, *Lord, have mercy upon me*. His servants must be employed to do it, and so be involved in the guilt. He was to give the word of command—*Smite Amnon*; and then they must *kill him*. He did it in the presence of *all the king's sons*, of whom it is said (*ch.* viii. 18) that they were *chief rulers*; so that it was an affront to public justice and to the king his father, whom they represented. There is reason to suspect that Absalom did this, not only to revenge his sister's quarrel, but to make way for himself to the throne, which he was ambitious of, and which he would stand fair for if Amnon the eldest son was taken off. When the word of command was given Absalom's servants failed not to execute it, being buoyed up with an opinion that their master, being now next heir to the crown, would save them from harm. Now the threatened sword is drawn in David's house which should not depart from it. *First*, His eldest son falls by it. *Secondly*, All his sons flee from it, and come home in terror, not knowing how far their brother Absalom's bloody design might extend.

Verses 30–39

I. The fright that David was put into by a false report brought to Jerusalem that Absalom had *slain all the king's sons*, *v.* 30. This false news gave as much affliction to David, for the present, as if it had been true, *v.* 31.

II. The rectifying of the mistake in two ways:— 1. By the sly suggestions of Jonadab, David's nephew, who could tell him, *Amnon only is dead*, and not all the king's sons (*v.* 32, 33), and could tell him too that it was done by the appointment of Absalom, and designed from the day Amnon forced his sister Tamar. It is well if Jonadab was not as guilty of Amnon's death as he was of his sin; such friends do those prove who are hearkened to as counsellors to do wickedly: he that would not be so kind as to prevent Amnon's sin would not be so kind as to prevent his ruin, when, it should seem, he might have done both. 2. By the safe return of all the king's sons except Amnon. They bring the certain sad news that Absalom had murdered their brother Amnon. That Amnon was dead, and slain by his own brother in such a treacherous barbarous manner, was enough to put the king and court, the king and kingdom, into real mourning. Sorrow is never more reasonable than when there is sin in the case.

III. Absalom's flight from justice. He was now as much afraid of the king's sons as they were of him; they fled from his malice, he from their justice. No part of the land of Israel would shelter him. He therefore made the best of his way to his mother's relations, and was entertained by his grandfather *Talmai, king of Geshur* (*v.* 37), and there he was protected *three years* (*v.* 38).

IV. David's uneasiness for his absence. He mourned for Amnon a good while (*v.* 37), but time wore off his detestation of Absalom's sin; instead of loathing him as a murderer, he *longs to go forth to him*, *v.* 39.

JAMIESON, FAUSSET, BROWN

23. **Absalom had sheepshearers in Baal-hazor, which is beside Ephraim**—A sheepshearing feast is a grand occasion in the East. Absalom proposed to give such an entertainment at his estate in Baal-hazor, about eight miles northeast of Jerusalem near a town called Ephraim (Josh. 11:10). He first invited the king and his court; but the king declining, on account of the heavy expense to which the reception of royalty would subject him, Absalom then limited the invitation to the king's sons, which David the more readily agreed to, in the hope that it might tend to the promotion of brotherly harmony and union.

28-36. AMNON IS SLAIN. **28. Absalom had commanded his servants, saying . . . when Amnon's heart is merry with wine . . . kill him, fear not**—On a preconcerted signal from their master, the servants, rushing upon Amnon, slew him at the table, while the rest of the brothers, horror-struck, and apprehending a general massacre, fled in affrighted haste to Jerusalem. **29. every man gat him upon his mule**—This had become the favorite equipage of the great. King David himself had a state mule (I Kings 1:33). The Syrian mules are, in activity, strength, and capabilities, still far superior to ours.

30. tidings came to David, saying, Absalom hath slain all the king's sons—It was natural that in the consternation and tumult caused by so atrocious a deed, an exaggerated report should reach the court, which was at once plunged into the depths of grief and despair. But the information of Jonadab, who seems to have been aware of the plan, and the arrival of the other princes, made known the real extent of the catastrophe.

37-39. ABSALOM FLEES TO TALMAI. **37. Absalom fled, and went to Talmai**—The law as to premeditated murder (Num. 35:21) gave him no hope of remaining with impunity in his own country. The cities of refuge could afford him no sanctuary, and he was compelled to leave the kingdom, taking refuge at the court of Geshur, with his maternal grandfather, who would, doubtless, approve of his conduct.

ADAM CLARKE

23. *Absalom had sheepshearers*. These were times in which feasts were made, to which the neighbors and relatives of the family were invited.

26. *Let my brother Amnon go*. He urged this with the more plausibility because Amnon was the firstborn, and presumptive heir to the kingdom; and he had disguised his resentment so well before that he was not suspected.

30. *Absalom hath slain all the king's sons*. Fame never lessens but always magnifies a fact. Report, contrary to the nature of all other things, gains strength by going.

32. *And Jonadab . . . said . . . Amnon only is dead*. This was a very bad man, and here speaks coolly of a most bloody tragedy, which himself had contrived.

37. *Absalom fled*. As he had committed willful murder, he could not avail himself of a city of refuge, and was therefore obliged to leave the land of Israel and take refuge with Talmai, king of Geshur, his grandfather by his mother's side.

39. *David longed to go forth unto Absalom*. We find that he had a very strong paternal affection for this young man, who appears to have had little to commend him but the beauty of his person. David wished either to go to him or to bring him back, for the hand of time had now wiped off his tears for the death of his son Amnon. Joab had marked this disposition, and took care to work on it, in order to procure the return of Absalom. It would have been well for all parties had Absalom ended his days at Geshur. His return brought increasing wretchedness to his unfortunate father. And it may be generally observed that those undue, unreasonable paternal attachments are thus rewarded.

MATTHEW HENRY

CHAPTER 14

Verses 1–20

I. Joab's design to get Absalom recalled out of banishment, *v.* 1. 1. As a courtier. Joab, finding how David stood affected, undertook this good office. 2. As a friend to Absalom. He plainly foresaw that his father would at length be reconciled to him, and therefore thought he should make both his friends if he were instrumental to bring it about. 3. As a statesman, and one concerned for the public welfare. He knew how much Absalom was the darling of the people, and, if David should die while he was in banishment, it might occasion a civil war, for it is probable that though all Israel loved his person, yet they were much divided upon his case. 4. As one who was himself a delinquent, by the murder of Abner. Whatever favour he could procure to be shown to Absalom would corroborate his reprieve.

II. His contrivance to do it by laying somewhat of a parallel case before the king so dexterously that the king took it for a real case, and gave judgment upon it, as he had done upon Nathan's parable.

1. The person he employed is not named, but she is said to be *a woman of Tekoah*. It is said, She was *a wise woman*, one that had a quicker wit and a readier tongue than most of her neighbours, *v.* 2. The truth of the story would be the less suspected when it came, as was supposed, from the person's own mouth.

2. The character she put on was that of a disconsolate widow, *v.* 2. Joab knew such a one would have an easy access to the king, who was always ready to comfort the mourners.

3. It was a case of compassion which she had to represent to the king, the judgment of all the inferior courts being against her. She tells the king that she had buried her husband (*v.* 5),—that she had two sons that were the support and comfort of her widowed state,—that these two fell out and fought, and one of them unhappily killed the other (*v.* 6),—that, for her part, she was desirous to protect the manslayer, yet the other relations insisted upon it that the surviving brother should be put to death according to law, that, by destroying the heir the inheritance might be theirs: and thus they would cut off, (1) Her comfort: "*They shall quench my coal*, deprive me of the only support of my old age, and put a period to all my joy in this world, which is reduced to this one coal." (2) Her husband's memory: "His family will be quite extinct, and they will *leave* him *neither name nor remainder*," *v.* 7.

4. The king promised her his favour and a protection for her son. (1) Upon the representation of her case he promised to consider of it and to give orders about it, *v.* 8. (2) The woman was not content with this, but begged that he would immediately give judgment in her favour. (3) Being thus pressed, he made a further promise that she should not be injured nor insulted by her adversaries, but he would protect her from all molestation, *v.* 10. (4) Yet this does not content her, unless she can get her son's pardon, and protection for him too. Parents are not easy, unless their children be safe, safe for both worlds: "*Let not the avenger of blood destroy my son* (*v.* 11), for I am undone if I lose him; as good take my life as his." "*Remember* how *the Lord thy God* spared Cain, forgave thee the blood of Uriah, and let the king, that has found mercy, show mercy." (5) This importunate widow, by pressing the matter thus closely, obtains at last a full pardon for her son, ratified with an oath as she desired. Whether David did well thus to undertake the protection of a murderer, whom the cities of refuge would not protect, I cannot say. But there was room enough for a favourable judgment: he had slain his brother, but he *hated him not in time past*; it was upon a sudden provocation, and, for aught that appeared, it might be done in his own defence.

5. The case being thus adjudged in favour of her son, it is now time to apply it to the king's son, Absalom. The mask here begins to be thrown off, and another scene opened. The king is surprised, but not at all displeased, to find his humble petitioner become an advocate for the prince his son. She begs his pardon, and his patience, for what she had further to say (*v.* 12). (1) She supposes Absalom's case to be, in effect, the same with that which she had put as her son's; and therefore, if the king would protect her son, though he had slain his brother, much more ought he to protect his own, and to *fetch home his banished*, *v.* 13. It is true, Absalom's case differed very much from that which she had put. Absalom did not slay his brother upon a hasty passion. Absalom was not an only son, as hers was; David had many more. But David was himself too well affected to the cause to be critical, and was more desirous than

JAMIESON, FAUSSET, BROWN

CHAPTER 14

VSS. 1-21. JOAB INSTRUCTS A WOMAN OF TEKOAH.

2. Joab sent to Tekoah, and fetched thence a wise woman—The king was strongly attached to Absalom; and having now got over his sorrow for the violent death of Amnon, he was desirous of again enjoying the society of his favorite son, who had now been three long years absent. But a dread of public opinion and a regard to the public interests made him hesitate about recalling or pardoning his guilty son; and Joab, whose discerning mind perceived this struggle between parental affection and royal duty, devised a plan for relieving the scruples, and, at the same time, gratifying the wishes, of his master. Having procured a countrywoman of superior intelligence and address, he directed her to seek an audience of the king, and by soliciting his royal interposition in the settlement of a domestic grievance, convinced him that the life of a murderer might in some cases be saved. Tekoah was about twelve miles south of Jerusalem, and six south of Bethlehem; and the design of bringing a woman from such a distance was to prevent either the petitioner being known, or the truth of her story easily investigated. Her speech was in the form of a parable—the circumstances—the language—the manner—well suited to the occasion, represented a case as like David's as it was policy to make it, so as not to be prematurely discovered. Having got the king pledged, she avowed it to be her design to satisfy the royal conscience, that in pardoning Absalom he was doing nothing more than he would have done in the case of a stranger, where there could be no imputation of partiality. The device succeeded; David traced its origin to Joab; and, secretly pleased at obtaining the judgment of that rough, but generally sound-thinking soldier, he commissioned him to repair to Geshur and bring home his exiled son.
7. they shall quench my coal which is left—The life of man is compared in Scripture to a light. To quench the light of Israel (ch. 21:17) is to destroy the king's life; to ordain a lamp for any one (Ps. 132:17) is to grant him posterity; to quench a coal signifies here the extinction of this woman's only remaining hope that the name and family of her husband would be preserved. The figure is a beautiful one; a coal live, but lying under a heap of embers—all that she had to rekindle her fire—to light her lamp in Israel.
9. the woman said . . . O king, the iniquity be on me—i.e., the iniquity of arresting the course of justice and pardoning a homicide, whom the Goel was bound to slay wherever he might find him, unless in a city of refuge. This was exceeding the royal prerogative, and acting in the character of an absolute monarch. The woman's language refers to a common precaution taken by the Hebrew judges and magistrates, solemnly to transfer from themselves the responsibility of the blood they doomed to be shed, either to the accusers or the criminals (ch. 1:16; 3:28); and sometimes the accusers took it upon themselves (Matt. 27:25).

13-17. Wherefore, then, hast thou thought such a thing against the people of God . . .—Her argument may be made clear in the following paraphrase:—You have granted me the pardon of a son who had slain his brother, and yet you will not grant to your subjects the restoration of Absalom, whose criminality is not greater than my son's, since he killed his brother in similar circumstances of provocation.

ADAM CLARKE

CHAPTER 14

2. *Joab sent to Tekoah.* Tekoah, according to Jerome, was a little city in the tribe of Judah, about twelve miles from Jerusalem.

5. *I am indeed a widow woman.* It is very possible that the principal facts mentioned here were real, and that Joab found out a person whose circumstances bore a near resemblance to that which he wished to represent.

7. *The whole family is risen.* They took on them the part of the avenger of blood, the nearest akin to the murdered person having a right to slay the murderer. *They shall quench my coal which is left.* A man and his descendants or successors are often termed in Scripture a lamp or light. Thus, *quench my coal that is left* means destroying all hope of posterity, and extinguishing the family from among the people.

9. *The iniquity be on me.* She intimates that, if the king should suppose that the not bringing the offender to the assigned punishment might reflect on the administration of justice in the land, she was willing that all blame should attach to her and her family, *and the king and his throne be guiltless.*

10. *Whosoever saith ought unto thee.* Neither did this bring the matter to such a bearing that she could come to her conclusion, which was to get the king pledged by a solemn promise that all proceedings relative to the case should be stopped.

11. *Let the king remember the Lord thy God.* Consider that when God is earnestly requested to show mercy He does it in the promptest manner; He does not wait till the case is hopeless. The danger to which my son is exposed is imminent; if the king do not decide the business instantly, it may be too late. *And he said, As the Lord liveth.* Thus he binds himself by a most solemn promise and oath, and this is what the woman wanted to extort.

13. *Wherefore then hast thou thought such a thing?* The woman, having now received the king's promise confirmed by an oath, that her son should not suffer for the murder of his brother, comes immediately to her conclusion: Is not the king to blame? Does he now act a consistent part? He is willing to pardon the meanest of his subjects the murder of a brother at the instance of a poor widow, and he is not willing to pardon his son Absalom, whose restoration to favor is the desire of the whole nation.

MATTHEW HENRY

she could be to bring that favourable judgment to his own son which he had given concerning hers. (2) She reasons with the king, to persuade him to recall Absalom out of banishment, give him his pardon, and take him into his favour again. [1] She pleads the interest which the people of Israel had in him. [2] She pleads man's mortality (*v.* 14): "*We must needs die.* Amnon must have died, some time, if Absalom had not killed him; and, if Absalom be now put to death for killing him, that will not bring him to life again." [3] She pleads God's mercy and his clemency towards poor guilty sinners, *v.* 14. Here are two great instances of the mercy of God to sinners: *First,* The patience he exercises towards them. His law is broken, yet he does not immediately take away the life of those that break it. *Secondly,* The provision he has made for their restoration to his favour, that though by sin they have banished themselves from him, yet they might not be expelled, or cast off, for ever. Poor banished sinners are likely to be for ever expelled from God if some course be not taken to prevent it. It is against the mind of God that they should be so, for he is not willing that any should perish.

6. She concludes her address with high compliments to the king, and strong expressions of her assurance that he would do what was just and kind both in the one case and in the other (*v.* 15–17). (1) She would not have troubled the king thus, but that the people made her afraid. Understanding it of Absalom's case, she gives the king to understand, what he did not know before, that the nation was disgusted at his severity towards Absalom to such a degree that she was really afraid it would occasion a general mutiny or insurrection. (2) She applied to him with a great confidence in his wisdom and clemency. What this woman says by way of compliment the prophet says by way of promise (Zech. xii. 8), that, when *the weak shall be as David, the house of David shall be as the angel of the Lord.*

7. The hand of Joab is suspected by the king, and acknowledged by the woman, to be in all this, *v.* 18–20. (1) The king soon suspected it. (2) The woman very honestly owned it: "*Thy servant Joab bade me.* She speaks the truth as it was, and gives us an example to do likewise, and never to tell a lie for the concealing of a well-managed scheme. *Dare to be true; nothing can need a lie.*

Verses 21–27

I. Orders given for the bringing back of Absalom. Joab, having received these orders, 1. Returns thanks to the king for doing him the honour to employ him in an affair so universally grateful, *v.* 22. 2. Delays not to execute David's orders; he brought Absalom to Jerusalem, *v.* 23. I see not how David can be justified in suspending the execution of the ancient law (Gen. ix. 6), *Whoso sheds man's blood, by man shall his blood be shed.* God's laws were never designed to be like cobwebs, which catch the little flies, but suffer the great ones to break through. But, though he allowed him to return to his own house, he forbade him the court, and would not see him himself, *v.* 24. He put him under this interdict, (1) For his own honour, that he might not seem to forgive him too easily. (2) For Absalom's greater humiliation.

II. Occasion taken hence to give an account of Absalom. Nothing is said of his wisdom and piety, nothing of his devotion. All that is here said of him is, 1. That he was a very handsome man (*v.* 25), a poor commendation for a man that had nothing else in him valuable. Handsome are those that handsome do. Many a polluted deformed soul dwells in a fair and comely body; witness Absalom's, that was polluted with blood, and deformed with unnatural disaffection to his father and prince. In his body there was no blemish, but in his mind nothing but wounds and bruises. 2. That he had a very fine head of hair, not as the hair of a Nazarite (he was far from that strictness), but as the hair of a beau. He let it grow till it was a burden to him, and was heavy on him, nor would he cut it as long as ever he could bear it; as pride feels no cold, so it feels no heat, and that which feeds and gratifies it is not complained of, though very uneasy. He did poll it at certain times, that it might be seen how much it excelled other men's, and it weighed 200 shekels, which some reckon to be three pounds and two ounces of our weight; and with the oil and powder, especially if powdered (as Josephus says the fashion then was) with gold dust, it is not at all incredible that it should weigh so much. This fine hair proved his halter, *ch.* xviii. 9. 3. That his family began to be built up. It is probable that it was a good while before he had a child; and then it was that, despairing of having one, he set up that pillar which

JAMIESON, FAUSSET, BROWN

Absalom has reason to complain that he is treated by his own father more sternly and severely than the meanest subject in the realm; and the whole nation will have cause for saying that the king shows more attention to the petition of a humble woman than to the wishes and desires of a whole kingdom. The death of my son is a private loss to my family, while the preservation of Absalom is the common interest of all Israel, who now look to him as your successor on the throne.

22-33. JOAB BRINGS ABSALOM TO JERUSALEM. **22. To-day thy servant knoweth that I have found grace in thy sight**—Joab betrayed not a little selfishness amid his professions of joy at this act of grace to Absalom, and flattered himself that he now brought both father and son under lasting obligations. In considering this act of David, many extenuating circumstances may be urged in favor of it; the provocation given to Absalom; his being now in a country where justice could not overtake him; the risk of his imbibing a love for heathen principles and worship; the safety and interests of the Hebrew kingdom; together with the strong predilection of the Hebrew people for Absalom, as represented by the stratagem of Joab—these considerations form a plausible apology for David's grant of pardon to his bloodstained son. But, in granting this pardon, he was acting in the character of an Oriental despot rather than a constitutional king of Israel. The feelings of the father triumphed over the duty of the king, who, as the supreme magistrate, was bound to execute impartial justice on every murderer, by the express law of God (Gen. 9:6; Num. 35:30, 31), which he had no power to dispense with (Deut. 18: 18; Josh. 1:8; I Sam. 10:25). **25. But in all Israel there was none to be so much praised as Absalom for his beauty**—This extraordinary popularity arose not only from his high spirit and courtly manners, but from his uncommonly handsome appearance. One distinguishing feature, seemingly an object of great admiration, was a profusion of beautiful hair. Its extraordinary luxuriance compelled him to cut it "at every year's end"; lit., "at times," "from time to time," when it was found to weigh 200 shekels—equal to 112 oz. troy; but as "the weight was after the king's shekel," which was less than the common shekel, the rate has been reduced as low as 3 lbs. 2 oz. [BOCHART], and even less by others.

ADAM CLARKE

14. *For we must needs die.* Whatever is done must be done quickly; all must die; God has not exempted any person from this common lot. Though Amnon be dead, yet the death of Absalom cannot bring him to life nor repair this loss. The argument contained in v. 14 is very elegant, and powerfully persuasive; but one clause of it has been variously understood, *Neither doth God respect any person.* The Hebrew is, "And God doth not take away the soul." The Septuagint has it, "And God will receive the soul." This intimates that, after human life is ended, the soul has a state of separate existence with God. This was certainly the opinion of these translators, and was the opinion of the ancient Jews.

20. *According to the wisdom of an angel of God.* This is quite in the style of Asiatic flattery.

21. *And the king said unto Joab.* It appears that Joab was present at the time when the woman was in conference with the king, and no doubt others of David's courtiers or officers were there also.

24. *Let him not see my face.* He would not at once restore him to favor, though he had now remitted his crime, so that he should not die for it.

25. *None to be so much praised as Absalom.* It was probably his personal beauty that caused the people to interest themselves so much in his behalf.

MATTHEW HENRY

is mentioned, *ch.* xviii. 18, to bear up his name; but afterwards he had three sons and one daughter, *v.* 27.

Verses 28–33

Three years Absalom had been an exile from his father-in-law, and now two years a prisoner at large in his own house, and, in both, better dealt with than he deserved; yet his spirit was still unhumbled. He thinks himself sorely wronged that he is not restored to all his places at court. He longed to see the king's face, pretending it was because he loved him, but really because he wanted an opportunity to supplant him. He cannot do his father a mischief till he is reconciled to him; this therefore is the first branch of his plot; this snake cannot sting again till he be warmed in his father's bosom. He gained this point, not by promises of reformation, but by insults and injuries. 1. By his insolent carriage towards Joab, he brought him to mediate for him. A person in Absalom's circumstances should have sent to Joab a kindly message, but instead of this, he bids his servants set Joab's cornfields on fire (*v.* 30). Strange that Absalom should think, by doing Joab a mischief, to prevail with him to do him a kindness. Yet by this means he brings Joab to him, *v.* 31. And now Joab (perhaps frightened at the surprising boldness and fury of Absalom, and apprehensive that he had made an interest in the people strong enough to bear him out, not only puts up with this injury, but goes on his errand to the king. 2. By his insolent message to the king, he recovered his place at court, to see the king's face, that is, to become a privy counsellor, Esther i. 14. (1) His message was haughty and imperious, and very unbecoming either a son or a subject, *v.* 32. He undervalued the favour that had been shown him in recalling him from banishment, and restoring him to his own house, and that in Jerusalem. He defies the king's justice: "Let him kill me, if he can find it in his heart." (2) Yet with this message he carried his point, *v.* 33. David's strong affection for him construed all this to be the language of a great respect to his father, and an earnest desire of his favour, when, alas! it was far otherwise. Absalom, by the posture of his body, testified his submission to his father: *He bowed himself on his face to the ground*; and David, with a kiss, sealed his pardon.

CHAPTER 15

Verses 1–6

Absalom is no sooner restored to his place at court than he aims to be on the throne. If he had had any sense of gratitude he would have studied how to oblige his father, and make him easy; but, on the contrary, he meditates how to undermine him, by stealing the hearts of the people from him. Two things recommend a man to popular esteem—greatness and goodness.

I. Absalom looks great, *v.* 1. He had learned of the king of Geshur (what was not allowed to the kings of Israel) to multiply horses, which made him look desirable, while his father, on his mule, looked despicable. The people desired a king like the nations. Samuel had foretold that this would be *the manner of the king*: He shall *have chariots and horsemen, and some shall run before his chariots* (1 Sam. viii. 11); and this is Absalom's manner. Fifty footmen running before him would highly gratify his pride and the people's foolish fancy. David thinks that this parade is designed only to grace his court, and connives at it.

II. Absalom will seem very good too, but with a very bad design. Had he proved himself a good son and a good subject he would have shown himself worthy of future honours, after his father's death. Those that know how to obey well know how to rule. Those are good indeed that are good in their own place, not that pretend how good they would be in other people's places.

1. He wishes that he were a judge in Israel, *v.* 4. He that should himself have been judged to death for murder has the impudence to aim at being a judge of others. We read not of Absalom's wisdom, virtue, or learning in the laws, yet he wishes he were judge. Those are commonly most ambitious of preferment that are least fit for it; the best qualified are the most modest and self-diffident.

2. He takes a very bad course for the accomplishing of his wish. He wants to be such a judge that every man who has any cause shall come to him: in all causes he must preside. To gain the power he aims at, he endeavours to instil into the people's minds,

(1) A bad opinion of the present administration,

JAMIESON, FAUSSET, BROWN

28. So Absalom dwelt two full years in Jerusalem, and saw not the king's face—Whatever error David committed in authorizing the recall of Absalom, he displayed great prudence and command over his feelings afterwards—for his son was not admitted into his father's presence but was confined to his own house and the society of his own family. This slight severity was designed to bring him to sincere repentance, on perceiving that his father had not fully pardoned him, as well as to convince the people of David's abhorrence of his crime. Not being allowed to appear at court, or to adopt any state, the courtiers kept aloof; even his cousin did not deem it prudent to go into his society. For two full years his liberty was more restricted, and his life more apart from his countrymen while living in Jerusalem, than in Geshur; and he might have continued in this disgrace longer, had he not, by a violent expedient, determined (vs. 30) to force his case on the attention of Joab, through whose kind and powerful influence a full reconciliation was effected between him and his father.

CHAPTER 15

Vss. 1-9. ABSALOM STEALS THE HEARTS OF ISRAEL. **1. Absalom prepared him chariots and horses, and fifty men to run before him**—This was assuming the state and equipage of a prince. The royal guards, called runners, avant-couriers, amounted to fifty (I Kings 1:5). The chariot, as the Hebrew indicates, was of a magnificent style; and the horses, a novelty among the Hebrew people, only introduced in that age as an appendage of royalty (Ps. 32:9; 66:12), formed a splendid retinue, which would make him "the observed of all observers."

2. Absalom rose up early, and stood beside the way of the gate—Public business in the East is always transacted early in the morning—the kings sitting an hour or more to hear causes or receive petitions, in a court held anciently, and in many places still, in the open air at the city gateway; so that, as those whose circumstances led them to wait on King David required to be in attendance on his morning levees, Absalom had to rise up early and stand beside the way of the gate. Through the growing infirmities of age, or the occupation of his government with foreign wars, many private causes had long lain undecided, and a deep feeling of discontent prevailed among the people. This dissatisfaction was artfully fomented by Absalom, who addressed himself to the various suitors; and after briefly hearing their tale, he gratified everyone with a favorable opinion of his case. Studiously concealing his ambitious designs, he expressed a wish to be invested with official power, only that he might accelerate the course of justice and advance the public interests.

ADAM CLARKE

27. *Unto Absalom there were born.* These children did not survive him (see chap. xviii. 18). *Tamar.* The Septuagint adds, "And she became the wife of Roboam, the son of Solomon, and bare to him Abia" (see Matt. i. 7). Josephus says the same. This addition is not found in the other versions.

30. *Go and set it on fire.* This was strange conduct, but it had the desired effect. He had not used his influence to get Absalom to court; now he uses it, and succeeds.

CHAPTER 15

1. *Absalom prepared him chariots and horses.* After all that has been said to prove that *horses* here mean "horsemen," I think it most likely that the writer would have us to understand *chariots* drawn by *horses. Fifty men to run before him.* Affecting in every respect the regal state by this establishment.

MATTHEW HENRY

as if the affairs of the kingdom were altogether neglected, and no care taken about them. "*There is no man deputed of the king to hear thee.* The king is himself old, and past business, or so taken up with his devotions that he never minds business; his sons are so addicted to their pleasures that, though they have the name of chief rulers, they take no care of the affairs committed to them." Every appellant shall be made to believe that he will never have justice done him, unless Absalom be viceroy or lord-justice. It is the way of turbulent, factious, aspiring men, to reproach the government they are under.

(2) A good opinion of his own fitness to rule. That the people might say, "O that Absalom were a judge!" he recommends himself to them, [1] As very diligent. [2] As very inquisitive and prying, and desirous to be acquainted with everyone's case. [3] As very familiar and humble. If any Israelite offered to do obeisance to him he took him and embraced him as a friend. No man's conduct could be more condescending, while his heart was as proud as Lucifer's.

Verses 7–12

The breaking out of Absalom's rebellion, which he had long been contriving. The same restless spirit was still working, and still they were given to change: as fond now of a new man as then of a new model. Absalom's plot being now ripe for execution,

I. The place he chose for the rendezvous of his party was Hebron, where he was born, and where his father began his reign and continued it several years. Everyone knew Hebron to be a royal city; and it lay in the heart of Judah's lot, in which tribe, probably, he thought his interest strong.

II. The pretence he had both to go thither and to invite his friends to him there was to offer a sacrifice to God, in performance of a vow he had made during his banishment, *v.* 7, 8. Under this pretence, 1. He got leave of his father to go to Hebron. David would be well pleased to hear that his son, being brought back, remembered his vow, and resolved to perform it. David was overjoyed to hear that Absalom inclined to *serve the Lord,* and therefore readily gave him leave to go to Hebron, and to go thither with solemnity. 2. He got a good number of sober substantial citizens to go along with him, *v.* 11. He knew that it was to no purpose to tempt them into his plot: they were inviolably firm to David. But he drew them in to accompany him, that the common people might think that they were in his interest, and that David was deserted by some of his best friends. When religion is made a stalking-horse, and sacrifice a shoeing-horn, to sedition and usurpation it is not to be wondered at if some that were well affected to religion, as these followers of Absalom here, are imposed upon by the fallacy, and drawn in to give countenance to that, with their names, which in their heart they abhor, not having known the depths of Satan.

III. The project he laid was to get himself proclaimed king throughout all the tribes of Israel upon a signal given, *v.* 10. Spies were sent abroad, to be ready in every country to receive the notice with satisfaction and acclamations of joy. Some would conclude that David was dead, others that he had resigned: many, if they had rightly understood the matter, would have abhorred the thought of it.

IV. The person he especially courted and relied upon in this affair was Ahithophel, a politic thinking man that had been David's counsellor. But, upon some disgust of David's against him, or his against David, he was banished and lived privately in the country. A fitter tool Absalom could not find in all the kingdom than one that was so great a statesman, and yet was disaffected to the present ministry. While Absalom was offering his sacrifices, in performance of his pretended vow, he sent for this man.

V. The party that joined with him proved at last very considerable. The people increased continually with Absalom, which made the conspiracy strong and formidable. Everyone whom he had complimented and caressed not only came himself, but made all the interest he could for him, so that he wanted not for numbers.

Verses 13–23

I. The notice brought to David of Absalom's rebellion, *v.* 13. The matter was bad enough, and yet it seems to have been made worse to him, for he was told that *the hearts of the men of Israel* (that is, the generality of them, at least the leading men) were *after Absalom.* It is the wisdom of princes to make sure of the hearts of their subjects; for, if they have them, they have their purses, and arms, and all, at their service.

II. The alarm this gave to David, and the resolu-

JAMIESON, FAUSSET, BROWN

His professions had an air of extraordinary generosity and disinterestedness, which, together with his fawning arts in lavishing civilities on all, made him a popular favorite. Thus, by forcing a contrast between his own display of public spirit and the dilatory proceedings of the court, he created a growing disgust with his father's government, as weak, careless, or corrupt, and seduced the affections of the multitude, who neither penetrated the motive nor foresaw the tendency of his conduct.

7. after forty years—It is generally admitted that an error has here crept into the text, and that instead of forty, we should read with the Syriac and Arabic versions, and Josephus, "four years"—i.e., after Absalom's return to Jerusalem, and his beginning to practice the base arts of gaining popularity. **my vow which I have vowed unto the Lord**—during his exile in Geshur. The purport of it was, that whenever God's providence should pave the way for his re-establishment in Jerusalem, he would offer a sacrifice of thanksgiving. Hebron was the spot selected for the performance of this vow, ostensibly as being his native place (ch. 3:3), and a famous high place, where sacrifices were frequently offered before the temple was built; but really as being in many respects the most suitable for the commencement of his rebellious enterprise. David, who always encouraged piety and desired to see religious engagements punctually performed, gave his consent and his blessing.

10-12. HE FORMS A CONSPIRACY. **10. Absalom sent spies throughout all the tribes of Israel**—These emissaries were to sound the inclination of the people, to further interests of Absalom, and exhort all the adherents of his party to be in readiness to join his standard as soon as they should hear that he had been proclaimed king. As the summons was to be made by the sound of trumpets, it is probable that care had been taken to have trumpeters stationed on the heights, and at convenient stations—a mode of announcement that would soon spread the news over all the country of his inauguration to the throne. **11. with Absalom went two hundred men . . . that were called**—From their quality, reputation, and high standing, such as would create the impression that the king patronized the movement and, being aged and infirm, was willing to adopt his oldest and noblest son to divide with him the cares and honors of government. **12. Absalom sent for Ahithophel**—who he knew was ready to join the revolt, through disgust and revenge, as Jewish writers assert, at David's conduct towards Bath-sheba, who was his granddaughter. **Giloh**—near Hebron. **the conspiracy was strong**—The rapid accession of one place after another in all parts of the kingdom to the party of the insurgents, shows that deep and general dissatisfaction existed at this time against the person and government of David. The remnant of Saul's partisans, the unhappy affair of Bath-sheba, the overbearing insolence and crimes of Joab, negligence and obstruction in the administration of justice—these were some of the principal causes that contributed to the success of this widespread insurrection.

ADAM CLARKE

6. *So Absalom stole the hearts.* His manner of doing this is circumstantially related above. He was thoroughly versed in the arts of the demagogue, and the common people heard him gladly. He used the patriot's arguments, and was everything of the kind, as far as promise could go. He found fault with men in power; and he only wanted their place, like all other pretended patriots, that he might act as they did, or worse.

7. *After forty years.* There is no doubt that this reading is corrupt, though supported by the commonly printed Vulgate, the Septuagint, and the Chaldee. But the Syriac has "four years," the Arabic the same, and Josephus has the same; so also the Sistine edition of the Vulgate and several MSS. of the same version. Theodoret also reads "four," not "forty"; and most learned men are of opinion that *arbaim,* "forty," is an error for *arba,* "four"; yet this reading is not supported by any Hebrew MS. yet discovered.

8. *While I abode at Geshur in Syria.* Geshur, the country of Talmai, was certainly not in Syria, but lay on the south of Canaan, in or near Edom, as is evident from Judg. i. 10; 1 Sam. xxvii. 8; chap. xiii. 37. Hence it is probable that *Aram,* "Syria," is a mistake for "Edom," *daleth* and *resh* being easily interchangeable. "Edom" is the reading of both the Syriac and Arabic.

10. *Absalom sent spies.* These persons were to go into every tribe; and the trumpet was to be blown as a signal for all to arise, and proclaim Absalom in every place. The trumpet was probably used as a kind of telegraph by the spies, trumpet exciting trumpet from place to place, so that in a few minutes all Israel would hear the proclamation.

11. *Went two hundred men.* These were probably soldiers, whom he supposed would be of considerable consequence to him. They had been seduced by his specious conduct, but knew nothing of his present design.

12. *Sent for Ahithophel.* When Absalom got him, he in effect got the prime minister of the kingdom to join him.

MATTHEW HENRY

tions he came to thereupon. We may well imagine him thunderstruck, when he heard that the son he loved so dearly, was so unnaturally and ungratefully in arms against him. David did not call a council, but, consulting only with God and his own heart, determined immediately to quit Jerusalem, *v.* 14. He took up this strange resolve, either, 1. As a penitent submitting to the rod, and lying down under God's correcting hand. Or, 2. As a politician. Jerusalem was a great city, but not tenable. It was too large to be garrisoned by so small a force as David had now with him. He had reason to fear that the generality of the inhabitants were too well affected to Absalom to be true to him. And he had such a kindness for Jerusalem that he was loth to make it the seat of war, and expose it to the calamities of a siege.

III. His hasty flight from Jerusalem. 1. He went out of Jerusalem himself on foot, while his son Absalom had chariots and horses. 2. He took his household with him, his wives and children, that he might protect them in this day of danger, and that they might be a comfort to him in this day of grief. 3. He took his life-guard with him, the Cherethites and Pelethites, who were under the command of Benaiah, and the Gittites, who were under the command of Ittai, *v.* 18. These Gittites seem to have been, by birth, Philistines, in David's service, having known him at Gath, and being greatly in love with him for his virtue and piety, and having embraced the Jews' religion. David made them *his bodyguard,* and they adhered to him in his distress. 4. As many as would, of the people of Jerusalem, he took with him, and made a halt at some distance from the city, to draw them up, *v.* 17. He compelled none. Christ enlists none but volunteers.

IV. His discourse with Ittai the Gittite, who commanded the Philistine-proselytes.

1. David dissuaded him from going along with him, *v.* 19, 20. (1) He would try whether he was hearty for him, and not inclined to Absalom. He therefore bids him return to his post in Jerusalem, and serve the new king. (2) If he was faithful to David, yet David would not have him exposed to the perils he now counted upon. "*Should I make thee go up and down with us?* No, return with thy brethren." Generous souls are more concerned at the share others have in their troubles than at their own. Ittai shall therefore be dismissed with a blessing: *Mercy and truth be with thee.* David's dependence was upon the mercy and truth of God for comfort and happiness, both for himself and his friends; see Ps. lxi. 7.

2. Ittai bravely resolved not to leave him, *v.* 21. Where David is, *whether in life or death,* safe or in peril, there will this faithful friend of his be; and he confirms this resolution with an oath, that he might not be tempted to break it. Thus should we cleave to the Son of David with full purpose of heart that *neither life nor death shall separate us from his love.*

V. The common people's sympathy with David in his affliction. When he and his attendants *passed over the brook Kidron* (the very same brook that Christ passed over when he entered upon his sufferings, John xviii. 1), *towards the way of the wilderness,* which lay between Jerusalem and Jericho, *all the country wept with a loud voice, v.* 23. To see a prince thus reduced, forced from his palace and in fear of his life, with a small retinue seeking shelter in a desert, to see the city of David, which he himself won, built, and fortified, made an unsafe abode for David himself.

Verses 24–30

I. The fidelity of the priests and Levites and their firm adherence to David and his interest. Zadok and Abiathar, and all the Levites, if he go, will accompany him, and take the ark with them, that, by it, they may ask counsel of God for him, *v.* 24.

II. David's dismission of them back into the city, *v.* 25, 26. Abiathar was high priest (1 Kings ii. 35), but Zadok was his assistant, and attended the ark most closely, while Abiathar was active in public business, *v.* 24. Therefore David directs his speech to Zadok. 1. He is very solicitous for the safety of the ark: "By all means *carry the ark back into the city,* surely Absalom, bad as he is, will do that no harm." 2. He is very desirous to return to the enjoyment of the privileges of God's house. 3. He is very submissive to the holy will of God concerning the issue of this dark dispensation. See him here patiently awaiting the event: "*Behold, here am I,* as a servant expecting orders"; and see him willing to commit himself to God concerning it: "*Let him do to me as seemeth good to him.* I have nothing to object. All is well that God does. *Let him do what he will.*" That we may not complain of what is, let us see God's hand in all events; and, that we may not be afraid of what shall be, let us see all events in God's hand.

JAMIESON, FAUSSET, BROWN

13-37. DAVID FLEES FROM JERUSALEM. **14. David said . . ., Arise, and let us flee**—David, anxious for the preservation of the city which he had beautified, and hopeful of a greater support throughout the country, wisely resolved on leaving Jerusalem.

18. all the Gittites, six hunderd men—These were a body of foreign guards, natives of Gath, whom David, when in the country of the Philistines, had enlisted in his service, and kept around his person.

Addressing their commander, Ittai, he made a searching trial of their fidelity in bidding them (vs. 19) abide with the new king.

23. the brook Kidron—a winter torrent that flows through the valley between the city and the eastern side of the Mount of Olives.

24. Zadok also and all the Levites . . ., bearing the ark—Knowing the strong religious feelings of the aged king, they brought it to accompany him in his distress. But as he could not doubt that both the ark and their sacred office would exempt them from the attacks of the rebels, he sent them back with it—not only that they might not be exposed to the perils of uncertain wandering—for he seems to place more confidence in the symbol of the divine presence than in God Himself—but that, by remaining in Jerusalem, they might render him greater service by watching the enemy's movements.

ADAM CLARKE

14. *David said . . . Arise . . . let us flee.* This, I believe, was the first time that David turned his back to his enemies. And why did he now flee? Jerusalem, far from not being in a state to sustain a siege, was so strong that even the blind and the lame were supposed to be a sufficient defense for the walls (see chap. v. 6).

And he had still with him his faithful Cherethites and Pelethites, besides 600 faithful Gittites, who were perfectly willing to follow his fortunes. There does not appear any reason why such a person, in such circumstances, should not act on the defensive, at least till he should be fully satisfied of the real complexion of affairs. But he appears to take all as coming from the hand of God; therefore he humbles himself, weeps, goes barefoot, and covers his head!

17. *And tarried in a place.* He probably waited till he saw all his friends safely out of the city.

19. *Thou art a stranger, and also an exile.* Some suppose that Ittai was the son of Achish, king of Gath, who was very much attached to David, and banished from his father's court on that account. He and his 600 men are generally supposed to have been proselytes to the Jewish religion.

23. *The brook Kidron.* This was an inconsiderable brook, and furnished with water only in winter, and in the rains (see John xviii. 1).

24. *Bearing the ark.* The priests knew that God had given the kingdom to David; they had no evidence that He had deposed him. They therefore chose to accompany him, and take the ark, the object of their charge, with them.

25. *Carry back the ark.* David shows here great confidence in God, and great humility. The ark was too precious to be exposed to the dangers of his migrations; he knew that God would restore him if He delighted in him, and he was not willing to carry off from the city of God that without which the public worship could not be carried on. He felt, therefore, more for this public worship and the honor of God than he did for his own personal safety.

MATTHEW HENRY

III. The confidence David put in the priests that they would serve his interest to the utmost of their power in his absence. He calls Zadok a *seer* (*v.* 27). One friend that is a seer, in such an exigency as this, was worth twenty that were not so quick-sighted. 1. Whom they should send to him—their two sons, Ahimaaz and Jonathan. 2. Whither they should send. He would encamp *in the plain of the wilderness* till he heard from them (*v.* 28), and then would move according to the information and advice they should send him.

IV. The melancholy posture that David and his men put themselves into, when, at the beginning of their march, they went up the *mount of Olives*, *v.* 30.

1. David himself went bare-foot, as a prisoner or a slave, for mortification, and went weeping. He could not but weep to think that one who came out of his bowels, and had so often lain in his arms, should thus lift up the heel against him. There was much of the displeasure of his God in it. His sin was *ever before him* (Ps. li. 3), but never so plain nor ever appearing so black as now. He never wept thus when Saul hunted him: but a wounded conscience makes troubles lie heavily, Ps. xxxviii. 4.

2. When David wept all his company wept likewise, being much affected with his grief and willing to share in it.

Verses 31–37

Nothing, it seems, appeared to David more threatening in Absalom's plot than that Ahithophel was in it; for one good head, in such a design, is worth a thousand good hands. Absalom was himself no politician, but he had got one entirely in his interest that was. If therefore he can be baffled, Absalom is as good as routed and the head of the conspiracy cut off. This David endeavours to do.

I. By prayer. When he heard that Ahithophel was in the plot he lifted up his heart to God in this short prayer: *Lord, turn the counsel of Ahithophel into foolishness*, *v.* 31. David prayed not against Ahithophel's person, but against his counsel.

II. By policy. We must second our prayer with our endeavours, else we tempt God. Now he penned the third Psalm, as appears by the title; and some think that his singing this was the worship he now paid to God. Just now Providence brought Hushai, the person that should be instrumental to befool Ahithophel. He came to condole with David on his present trouble, with his coat rent and earth upon his head; but David resolved to employ him as a spy upon Absalom, and sent him to Jerusalem, to wait for Absalom's arrival, as a deserter from David, and to offer him his service, *v.* 34. How this gross dissimulation, which David put Hushai upon, can be justified, as a stratagem in war, I do not see. The best that can be made of it is that Absalom, if he rebel against his father, must stand upon his guard against all mankind, and, if he will be deceived, let him be deceived. David recommended Hushai to Zadok, and Hushai, thus instructed, came to Jerusalem (*v.* 37), whither also Absalom soon after came with his forces.

CHAPTER 16

Verses 1–4

We read before how kind David was to Mephibosheth the son of Jonathan, how he prudently entrusted his servant Ziba with the management of his estate, while he generously entertained him at his own table, *ch.* ix. 10, but, it seems, Ziba is not content to be manager, he longs to be master, of Mephibosheth's estate. Now, he thinks, is his time to make himself so; if he can procure a grant of it from the crown, whether David or Absalom get the better it is all one to him, he hopes he shall secure his prey. 1. He made David a handsome present of provisions, which was the more welcome because it came seasonably (*v.* 1). David inferred from this that Ziba was a very discreet and generous man, and well affected to him, when, in all, he designed nothing but to make his own market and to get Mephibosheth's estate settled upon himself. Whatever Ziba intended in this present, God's providence sent it to David for his support very graciously. God makes use of bad men for good purposes to his people, and sends them meat by ravens. 2. Having by his present insinuated himself into David's affection, the next thing is to incense him against Mephibosheth, which he does by a false accusation, representing him as ungratefully designing to recover the crown to his own head, now that David and his son were contending for it. David enquires for him as one of his family, which gives Ziba occasion to tell this

JAMIESON, FAUSSET, BROWN

30. David went up by the ascent of mount Olivet—The same pathway over that mount has been followed ever since that memorable day. **had his head covered**—with a mourning wrapper. The humility and resignation of David marked strongly his sanctified spirit, induced by contrition for his transgressions. He had fallen, but it was the fall of the upright; and he rose again, submitting himself meekly in the meantime to the will of God [CHALMERS].

31. David said, Turn, O Lord, . . . the counsel of Ahithophel—this senator being the mainstay of the conspiracy.

32. when David was come to the top of the mount, where he worshipped—looking towards Jerusalem, where were the ark and tabernacle. **Hushai the Archite**—A native of Archi, on the frontiers of Benjamin and Ephraim (Josh. 16:2). Comparing the prayer against Ahithophel with the counsel to Hushai, we see how strongly a spirit of fervent piety was combined in his character with the devices of an active and far-seeing policy.

CHAPTER 16

VSS. 1-4. ZIBA, BY FALSE SUGGESTIONS, CLAIMS HIS MASTER'S INHERITANCE. **1. Ziba the servant of Mephibosheth met him**—This crafty man, anticipating the certain failure of Absalom's conspiracy, took steps to prepare for his future advancement on the restoration of the king.

a bottle of wine—a large goatskin vessel. Its size made the supply of wine proportioned to the rest of his present. **2. The asses be for the king's household to ride on**—The royal fugitives were moving on foot, not from inability to procure conveyances, but as being suitable to their present state of humiliation and penitence.

3. To-day shall the house of Israel restore me the kingdom of my father—Such a hope might not unnaturally arise at this period of civil distraction, that the family of David would destroy themselves by their mutual broils, and the people reinstate the old dynasty.

ADAM CLARKE

JOSEPH PARKER:

This comes of murdering Uriah! "The way of transgressors is hard." When we have wept our sympathetic tears over banished king David, let us go down to the grave of the valiant Uriah—the honest and ill-used soldier—and cry still more copiously over his dishonored body. It is right that David's harp should be broken, that David's throat should be choked, and that for songs he should have groaning and distress. God takes care of his law; man cannot sin against it without being made to feel the penalty of justice.

And David weeps as he goes up by mount Olivet. We cannot but pity David now and again. He was a noble soul—he was a poet. When the devil gave him breathing space, he said beautiful things, and purposed charitable actions. Perhaps we may never pity David more than when his punishment took the form of humiliation (16:5–14).—*The People's Bible*

31. *Turn the counsel of Ahithophel into foolishness.* Ahithophel was a wise man, and well versed in state affairs, and God alone could confound his devices.

32. *Where he worshipped God.* Though in danger of his life, he stops on the top of Mount Olivet for prayer! *Hushai the Archite.* He was the particular friend of David, and was now greatly affected by his calamity.

33. *Then thou shalt be a burden unto me.* It appears that Hushai was not a warrior, but was a wise, prudent, and discreet man, who could well serve David by gaining him intelligence of Absalom's conspiracy; and he directs him to form a strict confederacy with the priests Zadok and Abiathar, and to make use of their sons as couriers between Jerusalem and David's place of retreat.

37. *Absalom came into Jerusalem.* It is very probable that he and his partisans were not far from the city when David left it, and this was one reason which caused him to hurry his departure.

CHAPTER 16

1. *Two hundred loaves of bread.* The word *loaf* gives us a false idea of the ancient Jewish bread; it was thin cakes, not yeasted and raised like ours. *A bottle of wine.* A goat's skin full of wine.

2. *The asses be for the king's household.* This is the Eastern method of speaking when anything is presented to a great man: "This and this is for the slaves of the servants of Your Majesty," when at the same time the presents are intended for the sovereign himself, and are so understood. It is a high Eastern compliment: These presents are not worthy of your acceptance; they are fit only for the slaves of your slaves.

3. *To day shall the house of Israel.* What a base wretch was Ziba! and how unfounded was this accusation against the peaceable, loyal, and innocent Mephibosheth!

MATTHEW HENRY

false story of him, *v.* 3. David gives credit to the calumny, without further enquiry, convicts Mephibosheth of treason, seizes his lands as forfeited, and grants them to Ziba, a rash judgment, and which afterwards he was ashamed of, when the truth came to light, *ch.* xix. 29. Having by his wiles gained his point, Ziba secretly laughed at the king's credulity.

Verses 5–14

David bore Shimei's curses much better than he had borne Ziba's flatteries. By the latter he was brought to pass a wrong judgment on another, by the former to pass a right judgment on himself. The world's smiles are more dangerous than its frowns.

I. How insolent and furious Shimei was, and how his malice took occasion from David's present distress to be so much the more outrageous. David, in his flight, had come to Bahurim, a city of Benjamin in or near which this Shimei lived, who, being of the house of Saul (with the fall of which all his hopes of preferment fell), had an implacable enmity to David, unjustly looking upon him as the ruin of Saul and his family only because, by the divine appointment, he succeeded Saul, *v.* 5.

1. Why he took this opportunity to give vent to his malice. (1) Because now he thought he might do it safely. (2) Because now it would be most grievous to David, would add affliction to his grief, and pour vinegar into his wounds. (3) Because now he thought that Providence justified his reproaches, and that David's present afflictions proved him to be as bad a man as he was willing to represent him. Job's friends condemned him upon this false principle.

2. How his malice was expressed. (1) *He cast stones at David* (*v.* 6), as if his king had been a dog. *He cast dust* (*v.* 13), which, probably, would blow into his own eyes, like the curses he threw, which, being causeless, would return upon his own head. Thus, while his malice made him odious, the impotency of it made him ridiculous and contemptible. (2) What he said. With the stones he shot his arrows, even bitter words (*v.* 7, 8). What was done long since to the house of Saul was the only thing which he could recollect, and with this he upbraided David because it was the thing that he himself was a loser by. No man could be more innocent of the blood of the house of Saul than David was. Once and again he spared Saul's life, while Saul sought him. The blood of the house of Saul is here most unjustly charged upon David, [1] As that which gave him his character, and denominated him a bloody man and a man of Belial, *v.* 7. [2] As that which brought the present trouble upon him: *The Lord has returned upon thee the blood of the house of Saul.* See how forward malicious men are to press God's judgments into the service of their own passion and revenge. [3] As that which would now be his utter ruin; for he endeavours to make him despair of ever recovering his throne again.

II. See how patient and submissive David was under this abuse. The sons of Zeruiah, Abishai particularly, resented the affront keenly, as well they might: *Why should this dead dog* be suffered to *curse the king? v.* 9. If David will but give them leave, they will put these lying cursing lips to silence, and take off his head. But the king would by no means suffer it: *What have I to do with you? So let him curse.* Thus Christ rebuked the disciples who, in zeal for his honour, would have commanded fire from heaven on the town that affronted him, Luke ix. 55. Let us see with what considerations David quieted himself. 1. The chief thing that silenced him was that he had deserved this affliction. 2. He observes the hand of God in it: *The Lord hath said unto him, Curse David* (*v.* 10), and again, *So let him curse, for the Lord hath bidden him, v.* 11. As it was Shimei's sin, it was not from God, but from the devil and his own wicked heart. David looked above the instrument of his trouble to the supreme director, as Job, when the plunderers had stripped him, acknowledged, *The Lord hath taken away.* Nothing more proper to quiet a gracious soul under affliction than an eye to the hand of God in it. 3. He quiets himself under the less affliction with the consideration of the greater (*v.* 11): *My son seeks my life, much more may this Benjamite.* 4. He comforts himself with hopes that God would, in some way or other, bring good to him out of his affliction: *The Lord will requite me good for his cursing.* We may depend upon God as our paymaster, not only for our services, but for our sufferings. David, at length, is housed at Bahurim (*v.* 14), where he meets with refreshment and is hidden from this strife of tongues.

Verses 15–23

Absalom had notice sent him speedily by some of his friends at Jerusalem that David had withdrawn,

JAMIESON, FAUSSET, BROWN

There was an air of plausibility in Ziba's story. Many, on whom the king had conferred favors, were now deserting him. No wonder, therefore, that in the excitement of momentary feeling, believing, on the report of a slanderer, Mephibosheth to be among the number, he pronounced a rash and unrighteous judgment by which a great injury was inflicted on the character and interests of a devoted friend.

5-19. SHIMEI CURSES DAVID. **5. when King David came to Bahurim**—a city of Benjamin (ch. 3: 16; 19:16). It is, however, only the confines of the district that are here meant. **Shimei, a man of the family of Saul**—The misfortune of his family, and the occupation by David of what they considered their rightful possessions, afforded a natural, if not a justifiable cause for this ebullition of rude insults and violence. He upbraided David as an ambitious usurper, and charged him, as one whose misdeeds had recoiled upon his own head, to surrender a throne to which he was not entitled.

13. went along on the hill's side over against him—as he descended the rough road on the eastern side of the Mount of Olives, "went along the side"—lit., the rib of the hill. **threw stones at him**—as a mark of contempt and insult. **cast dust**—As if to add insult to injury, clouds of dust were thrown by this disloyal subject in the path of his unfortunate sovereign.

His language was that of a man incensed by the wrongs that he conceived had been done to his house. David was guiltless of the crime of which Shimei accused him; but his conscience reminded him of other flagrant iniquities; and he, therefore, regarded the cursing of this man as a chastisement from heaven. His answer to Abishai's proposal evinced the spirit of deep and humble resignation—the spirit of a man who watched the course of Providence, and acknowledged Shimei as the instrument of God's chastening hand. One thing is remarkable, that he acted more independently of the sons of Zeruiah in this season of great distress than he could often muster courage to do in the days of his prosperity and power.

14. refreshed themselves there—i.e., in the city of Bahurim.

ADAM CLARKE

4. *Thine are all.* This conduct of David was very rash; he spoiled an honorable man to reward a villain, not giving himself time to look into the circumstances of the case. But David was in heavy afflictions, and these sometimes make even a wise man mad.

5. *David came to Bahurim.* This place lay northward of Jerusalem, in the tribe of Benjamin. It is called Almon, Josh. xxi. 18; and Alemeth, 1 Chron. vi. 60. Bahurim signifies "youths," and Almuth "youth"; so the names are of the same import. *Cursed still as he came.* Used imprecations and execrations.

TODAY'S DICTIONARY OF THE BIBLE:

Shimei—*famous.* A Benjamite of the house of Saul, who stoned and cursed David when he reached Bahurim in his flight from Jerusalem on the occasion of the rebellion of Absalom (2 Sam. 16:5–13). After the defeat of Absalom he "came cringing to the king, humbly suing for pardon, bringing with him a thousand of his Benjamite tribesmen, and representing that he was heartily sorry for his crime, and had hurried the first of all the house of Israel to offer homage to the king" (19:16–23). David forgave him; but on his deathbed he gave Solomon special instructions regarding Shimei, of whose fidelity he seems to have been in doubt (1 Kings 2:8, 9). He was put to death at the command of Solomon because he had violated his word by leaving Jerusalem and going to Gath to recover two of his servants who had escaped (36–46).

10. *Because the Lord hath said.* The particle *vechi* should be translated "for if," not *because.* "For if the Lord hath said unto him, Curse David, who shall then say, Wherefore hast thou done so?"

11. *Let him curse; for the Lord hath bidden him.* No soul of man can suppose that God ever bade one man to curse another, much less that He commanded such a wretch as Shimei to curse such a man as David; but this is a peculiarity of the Hebrew language, which does not always distinguish between permission and commandment.

MATTHEW HENRY

and with what a small retinue he had gone; Absalom might take possession of Jerusalem when he pleased. Accordingly he came without delay (*v.* 15), extremely elevated, no doubt, with this success at first. The most celebrated politicians of that age were Ahithophel and Hushai. The former Absalom brings with him to Jerusalem (*v.* 15), the other meets him there (*v.* 16), so that he cannot but think himself sure of success. But miserable counsellors were they both; for,

I. Hushai would never counsel him to do wisely. He was really his enemy, and designed to betray him. 1. Hushai complimented him upon his accession to the throne, as if he had been abundantly satisfied in his title, and well pleased that he had come to the possession, *v.* 16. 2. Absalom was surprised to find *him* who was known to be David's intimate friend and confidant. 3. Hushai confirmed him in the belief that he was hearty for him. It was true, he loved his father; but he had had his day, and it was over; and why should he not love his successor as well? Thus he pretended to give reasons for a resolution he abhorred.

II. Ahithophel counselled him to do wickedly, and so did as effectually betray him as he did who was designedly false to him; for those that advise men to sin certainly advise them to their hurt; and that government which is founded in sin is founded in the sand.

1. It seems, Ahithophel was noted as a deep politician; his counsel was as if a man had enquired at the oracle of God, *v.* 23. Let us observe from this account of Ahithophel's fame for policy, (1) That many excel in worldly wisdom who are utterly destitute of heavenly grace, because those who set up for oracles themselves are apt to despise the oracles of God. (2) That frequently the greatest politicians act most foolishly for themselves.

2. His policy in this case defeated its own aim.

(1) The wicked counsel Ahithophel gave to Absalom. **Finding that David had left his concubines to keep the house, he advised him to *lie with them* (*v.* 21), because it would give assurance to all Israel,** [1] That he was in good earnest in his pretensions. No doubt he resolved to make himself master of all that belonged to his predecessor when he began with his concubines. [2] That he was resolved never to make peace with his father upon any terms. Having drawn the sword, he did, by this provocation, throw away the scabbard, which would strengthen the hands of his party and keep them firmly to him. This was Ahithophel's cursed policy, which bespoke him rather *an oracle of the devil than of God.*

(2) Absalom's compliance with this counsel. It entirely suited his lewd and wicked mind, and he delayed not to put it in execution, *v.* 22. Yet, in this, the word of God was fulfilled in the letter of it: God had threatened, by Nathan, that, for defiling Bathsheba, David should have his own wives publicly debauched (*ch.* xii. 11, 12), and some think that Ahithophel, in advising it, designed to be revenged on David for the injury done to Bath-sheba, who was his grand-daughter: for she was the daughter of Eliam (*ch.* xi. 3), who was the son of Ahithophel, *ch.* xxiii. 34.

JAMIESON, FAUSSET, BROWN

15-19. Hushai said unto Absalom, God save the king—Hushai's devotion to David was so well known, that his presence in the camp of the conspirators excited great surprise. Professing, however, with great address, to consider it his duty to support the cause which the course ot Providence and the national will had seemingly decreed should triumph, and urging his friendship for the father as a ground of confidence in his fidelity to the son, he persuaded Absalom of his sincerity, and was admitted among the councillors of the new king.

20-23. AHITHOPHEL'S COUNSEL. **20. Give counsel among you what we shall do**—This is the first cabinet council on record, although the deference paid to Ahithophel gave him the entire direction of the proceedings.

21 Ahithophel said unto Absalom—This councillor saw that now the die was cast; half measures would be inexpedient. To cut off all possibility of reconciliation between the king and his rebellious son, he gave this atrocious advice regarding the treatment of the royal women who had been left in charge of the palace. Women, being held sacred, are generally left inviolate in the casualties of war. The history of the East affords only one parallel to this infamous outrage of Absalom.

ADAM CLARKE

15. *The men of Israel.* These words are wanting in the Chaldee, Septuagint, Syriac, Vulgate, and Arabic.

18. *Whom the Lord, and this people . . . choose.* Here is an equivocation; Hushai meant in his heart that God and all the people of Israel had chosen David; but he spake so as to make Absalom believe that he spoke of him. For whatever of insincerity may appear in this, Hushai is alone answerable. What he says afterwards may be understood in the same way.

21. *Go in unto thy father's concubines.* It may be remembered that David left ten of them behind to take care of the house; see chap. xv. 16. Ahithophel advised this infernal measure in order to prevent the possibility of a reconciliation between David and his son; thus was the **prophecy to Nathan fulfilled, chap. xii. 11. And this was probably transacted in** the very same place where David's eye took the adulterous view of Bath-sheba (see chap. xi. 2). The wives of the conquered king were always the property of the conqueror; and in possessing these, he appeared to possess the right to the kingdom.

CHAPTER 17

Verses 1–14

Absalom is now in peaceable possession of Jerusalem; the palace-royal is his own. His good father reigned in Hebron, and only over the tribe of Judah, above seven years, and was not hasty to destroy his rival; his government was built upon a divine promise, and therefore he waited patiently in the meantime. But the young man, Absalom, not only hastens from Hebron to Jerusalem, but is impatient there till he has destroyed his father, and cannot be content with his throne till he has his life.

David and all that adhered to him must be cut off. None durst mention his personal merits, and the great services done to his country. None durst propose that his banishment should suffice. It is past dispute that David must be destroyed; all the question is how he may be destroyed.

I. Ahithophel advises that he be pursued immediately, this very night, with a flying army, that the king only be smitten and his forces dispersed, and then the people that were now for him would fall in with Absalom. Nothing could be more fatal to David than the taking of these measures. It was probable enough that upon a fierce attack, especially in the night, the small force he had would be put into confusion and disorder, and it would be an easy thing to *smite the king only.* Compare with this the plot of Caiaphas (that second Ahithophel) against the Son of David to crush his interest by destroying him. Let that *one man die for the people,* John xi. 50.

CHAPTER 17

Vss. 1-14. AHITHOPHEL'S COUNSEL OVERTHROWN BY HUSHAI. **1. Moreover Ahithophel said unto Absalom**—The recommendation to take prompt and decisive measures before the royalist forces could be collected and arranged, evinced the deep political sagacity of this councillor. The adoption of his advice would have extinguished the cause of David; and it affords a dreadful proof of the extremities to which the heartless prince was, to secure his ambitious objects, prepared to go, that the parricidal counsel "pleased Absalom well, and all the elders of Israel."

CHAPTER 17

1. *Let me now choose out twelve thousand men.* Had this counsel been followed, David and his little troop would soon have been destroyed; nothing but the miraculous interposition of God could have saved them.

3. *The man whom thou seekest is as if all returned.* Only secure David, and all Israel will be on your side. He is the soul of the whole; destroy him, and all the rest will submit.

MATTHEW HENRY

II. Hushai advises that they be not too hasty in pursuing David, but take time to draw up all their force against him, and to overpower him with numbers, as Ahithophel had advised to take him by surprise. Now Hushai, in giving this counsel, really intended to serve David and his interest, that he might have time to send him notice of his proceedings, and that David might gain time to gather an army and to remove into those countries beyond Jordan, in which, lying more remote, Absalom had probably least interest.

1. Absalom gave Hushai a fair invitation to advise him. All the elders of Israel approved of Ahithophel's counsel, yet God overruled the heart of Absalom not to proceed upon it, till he had consulted Hushai (*v.* 5): *Let us hear what he saith.*

2. Hushai gave very plausible reasons for what he said.

(1) He argued against Ahithophel's counsel, and undertook to show the danger of following his advice. [1] He insisted much upon it that David was a great soldier, a man of great conduct, courage, and experience, and not so weary and weak-handed as Ahithophel imagines. His retiring from Jerusalem must be imputed, not to his cowardice, but his prudence. [2] His attendants, though few, were mighty men (*v.* 8), valiant men (*v.* 10), men of celebrated bravery and versed in all the arts of war. [3] They were all exasperated against Absalom, who was the author of all this mischief, were chafed in their minds, and would fight with the utmost fury; there would be no standing before them, especially for such raw soldiers as Absalom's generally were. [4] He suggested that probably David and some of his men would lie in ambush, in some pit, or other close place, and fall upon Absalom's soldiers, and the defeat, though but of a small party, would dispirit all the rest, especially their own consciences at the same time accusing them of treason against one that, they were sure, was not only God's anointed, *but a man after his own heart, v.* 9.

(2) He offered his own advice, and gave his reasons; and, [1] He counselled that which he knew would gratify Absalom's proud vainglorious humour, though it would not be really serviceable to his interest. *First,* He advised that all Israel should be gathered together, that is, the militia of all the tribes. *Secondly,* He advised that Absalom go to battle in his own person, as if he looked upon him to be a better soldier than Ahithophel. [2] He counselled that which seemed to secure the success, at last, infallibly without running any hazard. For, if they could raise such vast numbers as they promised themselves, wherever they found David they could not fail to crush him. *First,* If in the field, they should cut off all his men with him, *v.* 12. Perhaps Absalom was better pleased with the design, of cutting off all the men that were with him, having a particular antipathy to some of David's friends. Thus Hushai gained his point by humouring his revenge, as well as his pride. *Secondly,* If in a city, they need not fear conquering him, for they should have hands enough, if occasion were, to draw the city itself into its river with ropes, *v.* 13.

(3) By all these arts, Hushai gained not only Absalom's approbation of his advice, but the unanimous concurrence of this great council of war; they all agreed that the counsel of Hushai was better than the counsel of Ahithophel, *v.* 14.

Verses 15–21

Hushai tells the priests what had passed in council, *v.* 15. But, it should seem, he was not sure but that yet Ahithophel's counsel might be followed, and was therefore jealous lest, if he made not the best of his way, the king would be *swallowed up, and all the people that were with him, v.* 16. Such strict guards did Absalom set upon all the avenues to Jerusalem that they had much ado to get this necessary intelligence to David. 1. The young priests that were to be the messengers were forced to retire secretly out of the city, by *En-rogel.* 2. Instructions were sent to them by a poor simple young woman, who probably went to that well under pretence of fetching water, *v.* 17. 3. Yet, by the vigilance of Absalom's spies, they were discovered, and information was brought to Absalom of their motions: *A lad saw them and told him, v.* 18. 4. They, being aware that they were discovered, sheltered themselves in a friend's house in Bahurim, where David had refreshed himself but just before, *ch.* xvi. 14. There they were happily hidden in a well, which now, in summer time, perhaps was dry, *v.* 18. The woman of the house very ingeniously covered the mouth of the well with a cloth, on which she spread corn to dry, so that the pursuers were not aware that there was a well; else they would have searched it, *v.* 19. Being thus pre-

JAMIESON, FAUSSET, BROWN

It was happily overruled, however, by the address of Hushai, who saw the imminent danger to which it would expose the king and the royal cause. He dwelt upon the warlike character and military experience of the old king—represented him and his adherents as mighty men, who would fight with desperation; and who, most probably, secure in some stronghold, would be beyond reach, while the smallest loss of Absalom's men at the outset might be fatal to the success of the conspiracy.

But his dexterity was chiefly displayed in that part of his counsel which recommended a general levy throughout the country; and that Absalom should take command of it in person—thereby flattering at once the pride and ambition of the usurper. The bait was caught by the vainglorious and wicked prince.

12. we will light upon him as the dew falleth upon the ground—No image could have symbolized the sudden onset of an enemy so graphically to an Oriental mind as the silent, irresistible, and rapid descent of this natural moisture on every field and blade of grass. **13. all Israel shall bring ropes to that city**—In besieging a town, hooks or cranes were often thrown upon the walls or turrets, by which, with ropes attached to them, the besiegers, uniting all their force, pulled down the fortifications in a mass of ruins. **14. The counsel of Hushai is better than the counsel of Ahithopel**—The reasons specified being extremely plausible, and expressed in the strong hyperbolical language suited to dazzle an Oriental imagination, the council declared in favor of Hushai's advice; and their resolution was the immediate cause of the discomfiture of the rebellion, although the council itself was only a link in the chain of causation held by the controlling hand of the Lord.

15-22. SECRET INTELLIGENCE SENT TO DAVID. **16. send quickly, and tell David**—Apparently doubting that his advice would be followed, Hushai ordered secret intelligence to be conveyed to David of all that transpired, with an urgent recommendation to cross the Jordan without a moment's delay, lest Ahithophel's address and influence might produce a change on the prince's mind, and an immediate pursuit be determined on. **17. by En-rogel**—the fuller's well in the neighborhood of Jerusalem, below the junction of the valley of Hinnom with that of Jehoshaphat. **18. and came to a man's house in Bahurim, which had a well in his court**—The court was that of the house, and the well an empty cistern. All the houses of the better class are furnished with such reservoirs. Nothing could more easily happen than that one of these wells, in consequence of a deficiency of water, should become dry and it would then answer as a place of retreat, such as David's friends found in the man's house at Bahurim. The spreading of a covering over the well's mouth for the drying of corn is a common practice.

ADAM CLARKE

TODAY'S DICTIONARY OF THE BIBLE:

Ahithophel—*brother of insipidity* or *impiety*—a man greatly renowned for his wisdom among the Jews. At the time of Absalom's revolt he deserted David (Ps. 41:9; 55:12–14) and espoused the cause of Absalom (2 Sam. 15:12). David sent his old friend Hushai back to Absolom to counteract the counsel of Ahithophel (2 Sam. 15:31–37). This end was so far gained that Ahithophel saw he no longer had any influence, and accordingly he at once left the camp of Absalom and returned to Giloh, his native place, where, after arranging his wordly affairs, he hanged himself, and was buried in the sepulchre of his fathers (2 Sam. 17:1–23). The possible reference to Ahithophel in Ps. 41:9 is quoted by Jesus in speaking of Judas (John 13:18).

13. *Shall all Israel bring ropes to that city.* The original word *chabalim,* which signifies *ropes,* and from which we have our word "cable," may have some peculiarity of meaning here; for it is not likely that any city could be pulled down with ropes. The Chaldee, which should be best judge in this case, translates the original word by "towers"; this gives an easy sense.

17. *En-rogel.* The "fullers' well," the place where they were accustomed to tread the clothes with their feet; hence the name *ein,* a "well," and *regel,* the "foot." *And a wench went and told them.* The word *wench* occurs nowhere else in the Holy Scriptures: and, indeed, has no business here, as the Hebrew word should have been translated "girl, maid, maidservant."

MATTHEW HENRY

served, they brought their intelligence very faithfully to David (*v.* 21), with this advice of his friends, that he should not delay to pass over Jordan, near to which, it seems, he now was.

Verses 22–29

I. The transporting of David and his forces over Jordan. He, and all that were with him, went over in the night, but none deserted him. Having got over Jordan, he marched many miles forward to Mahanaim, a Levites' city in the tribe of Gad. This city, which Ish-bosheth had made his royal city (*ch.* ii. 8), David now made his headquarters, *v.* 24. And now he had time to raise an army wherewith to oppose the rebels and give them a warm reception.

II. The death of Ahithophel, *v.* 23. He died by his own hands, *felo de se—a suicide.* He hanged himself for vexation that his counsel was not followed; for thereby, 1. He thought himself slighted, and an intolerable slur cast upon his reputation for wisdom. 2. He thought himself endangered and his life exposed. He concluded that, because his counsel was not followed, Absalom's cause would certainly miscarry, and then, whoever would find David's mercy, he concluded that he, who was the greatest criminal, and had particularly advised him to lie with his father's concubines, must be sacrificed to his justice. Now, as David had prayed, Ahithophel's counsel was *turned into foolishness to himself.*

III. Absalom's pursuit of his father. Not content that he had driven his good father to the utmost corner of his kingdom, he resolved to chase him out of the world. Absalom made one Amasa his general (*v.* 25), whose father was by birth Jether, an Ishmaelite (1 Chron. ii. 17), but by religion Ithra (as he is here called), an Israelite. Amasa was in the same relation to David that Joab was.

IV. The friends David met with in this distant country. Even Shobi, a younger brother of the royal family of the Ammonites, was kind to him, *v.* 27. We should, as we have opportunity, *do good to all men,* for *he that watereth shall be watered also himself,* when there is occasion. Machir, the son of Ammiel, was he that maintained Mephibosheth (*ch.* ix. 4), till David eased him of that charge, and is now repaid for it by that generous man, who, it seems, was the common patron of distressed princes. Barzillai we shall hear of again. These, compassionating David and his men, now that they were weary with a long march, brought him furniture for his house, *beds and basins,* and provision for his table, *wheat and barley,* &c., *v.* 28, 29. In token of their dutiful affection to him they brought in plenty of all that which he had occasion for. Let us learn hence to be generous and open-handed, according as our ability is, to all in distress. God sometimes makes up to his people that comfort from strangers which they are disappointed of in their own families.

CHAPTER 18

Verses 1–8

David raised an army here, and reinforcements were sent him from all the coasts of Israel, at least from the neighbouring tribes.

I. His army numbered and marshalled, *v.* 1, 2. Josephus says they were, in all, about 4,000. These he divided into regiments and companies, to each of which he appointed proper officers, and then disposed them, as is usual, into the right wing, the left wing, and the centre, two of which he committed to his two old experienced generals, Joab and Abishai, and the third to his new friend Ittai. Good order and good conduct may sometimes be as serviceable in an army as great numbers.

II. Himself over-persuaded not to go in person to the battle. David's true friends would not let him go, remembering what they had been told of Ahithophe'"s design to *smite the king only.* David showed his affection to them by being willing to venture with then (*v.* 2), and they showed theirs to him by opposing it. He might be more serviceable to them by tarrying in the city, with a reserve of his forces there, whence he might send them recruits. That may be a post of real service which yet is not a post of danger.

III. The charge he gave concerning Absalom, *v.* 5. When the army was drawn out, rank and file, Josephus says, he encouraged them, and prayed for them, but withal bade them all take heed of doing Absalom any hurt. Absalom would have David only smitten. David would have Absalom only spared. Each did his utmost, and showed how bad it is possible for a child to be to the best of fathers and how good it is possible for a father to be to the worst of children; as if it were designed to be a resemblance of man's

JAMIESON, FAUSSET, BROWN

23-29. AHITHOPHEL HANGS HIMSELF. **23. when Ahithophel saw that his counsel was not followed**—His vanity was wounded, his pride mortified on finding that his ascendency was gone; but that chagrin was aggravated by other feelings—a painful conviction that through the delay which had been resolved on, the cause of Absalom was lost. Hastening home, therefore, he arranged his private affairs, and knowing that the storm of retributive vengeance would fall chiefly upon him as the instigator and prop of the rebellion, he hanged himself. It may be remarked that the Israelites did not, at that time, refuse the rites of sepulture even to those who died by their own hands. He had an imitator in Judas, who resembled him in his treason, as well as in his infamous end. **24. Then David came to Mahanaim**—in the high eastern country of Gilead, the seat of Ish-bosheth's government. **Absalom passed over Jordan**—It is not said how long an interval elapsed, but there must have been sufficient time to make the intended levy throughout the kingdom. **25. Amasa**—By the genealogy it appears that this captain stood in the same relation to David as Joab, both being his nephews. Of course, Amasa was Absalom's cousin, and though himself an Israelite, his father was an Ishmaelite (I Chron. 2:17). Nahash is thought by some to be another name of Jesse, or according to others, the name of Jesse's wife. **27. when David was come to Mahanaim**—The necessities of the king and his followers were hospitably ministered to by three chiefs, whose generous loyalty is recorded with honor in the sacred narrative. **Shobi**—must have been a brother of Hanun. Disapproving, probably, of that young king's outrage upon the Israelite ambassadors, he had been made governor of Ammon by David on the conquest of that country. **Machir**—(See ch. 9: 4). Supposed by some to have been a brother of Bath-sheba, and Barzillai, a wealthy old grandee, whose great age and infirmities made his loyal devotion to the distressed monarch peculiarly affecting. The supplies they brought, which (besides beds for the weary) consisted of the staple produce of their rich lands and pastures, may be classified a follows: eatables—wheat, barley, flour, beans, lentils, sheep, and cheese; drinkables—"honey and butter" or cream. which, being mixed together, form a thin, diluted beverage, light, cool, and refreshing. Being considered a luxurious refreshment (Song of Sol. 4:11), the supply of it shows the high respect that was paid to David by his loyal and faithful subjects at Mahanaim. **29. in the wilderness**—spread out beyond the cultivated tablelands into the steppes of Hauran.

CHAPTER 18

VSS. 1-4. DAVID REVIEWING THE ARMIES. **1. David numbered the people that were with him**—The hardy mountaineers of Gilead came in great numbers at the call of their chieftains, so that, although without money to pay any troops, David soon found himself at the head of a considerable army. A pitched battle was now inevitable. But so much depending on the life of the king, he was not allowed to take the field in person; and he therefore divided his forces into three detachments under Joab, Abishai, and Ittai, the commander of the foreign guards.

5-13. GIVES THEM CHARGE OF ABSALOM. **5. Deal gently for my sake with the young man, even with Absalom**—This affecting charge, which the king gave to his generals, proceeded not only from his overwhelming affection for his children, but from his consciousness that this rebellion was the chastisement of his own crimes, Absalom being merely an instrument in the hand of retributive Providence;—and also from his piety, lest the unhappy prince should die with his sins unrepented of.

ADAM CLARKE

23. *Put his household in order.* This self-murder could not be called lunacy, as every step to it was deliberate. He foresaw Absalom's ruin; he did not choose to witness it, and share in the disgrace, and he could expect no mercy at the hands of David.

25. *Amasa captain of the host.* From the account in this verse it appears that Joab and Amasa were sisters' children, and both nephews to David.

28. *Brought beds.* These no doubt consisted in skins of beasts, mats, carpets, and suchlike things. *Basons.* Probably wooden bowls, such as the Arabs still use to eat out of, and to knead their bread in. *Earthen vessels.* Probably clay vessels, baked in the sun. These were perhaps used for lifting water, and boiling those articles which required to be cooked. *Wheat, and barley.* There is no direct mention of flesh-meat here; little was eaten in that country, and it would not keep. Whether the *sheep* mentioned were brought for their flesh or their milk, I cannot tell.

CHAPTER 18

1. *And set captains of thousands.* By this time David's small company was greatly recruited, but what its number was we cannot tell. Josephus says it amounted to 4,000 men. Others have supposed that they amounted to 10,000, for thus they understand a clause in v. 3, which they think should be read, "We are now ten thousand strong."

5. *Deal gently . . . with the young man.* David was the father of this worthless young man; and is it to be wondered at that he feels as a father? Who in his circumstances, that had such feelings as every man should have, would have felt or acted otherwise?

MATTHEW HENRY

wickedness towards God and God's mercy towards man. Deal gently with a traitor? Of all traitors, with a son? Must the cause of the quarrel be the motive of mercy? But was not this done in type of that immeasurable mercy of the true King and Redeemer of Israel, who prayed for his persecutors, for his murderers, *Father, forgive them. Deal gently with them for my sake.* When God sends an affliction to correct his children, it is with this charge, "Deal gently with them for my sake"; for he knows our frame.

IV. A complete victory gained over Absalom's forces. The battle was fought *in the wood of Ephraim* (*v.* 6), so called from some memorable action of the Ephraimites there, though it lay in the tribe of Gad. David thought fit to meet the enemy with his forces at some distance, before they came up to Mahanaim, lest he should bring that city into trouble which had so kindly sheltered him. The cause shall be decided by a pitched battle. Josephus represents the fight as very obstinate, but the rebels were at length totally routed and 20,000 of them slain, *v.* 7. Now they see what it is to take counsel *against the Lord and his anointed,* and to think of *breaking his bands asunder.* And that they might see that God fought against them, 1. They are conquered by a few, an army, in all probability, much inferior to theirs in number. 2. By that flight with which they hoped to save themselves they destroyed themselves. The pits and bogs, the stumps and thickets, and, as the Chaldee paraphrast understands it, the wild beasts of the wood, were probably the death of multitudes of the dispersed distracted Israelites.

Verses 9–18

Here is Absalom quite at a loss, at his wit's end first, and then at his life's end. Though they were forbidden to meddle with him, he durst not look them in the face; but, finding they were near him, he clapped spurs to his mule and made the best of his way, through thick and thin, and so rode headlong upon his own destruction.

I. He is hanged by the neck. Riding furiously, neck or nothing, *under the thick boughs of a great oak* which hung low and had never been cropped, either the twisted branches, or some one forked bough of the oak, caught hold of his head by his long hair, which had been so much his pride, and was now justly made a halter for him, and there he hung. His *mule went away* from *under him,* as if glad to get clear of such a burden. He hung *between heaven and earth,* as unworthy of either, as abandoned of both.

II. He is caught alive by one of the servants of David, who goes directly and tells Joab in what posture he found that arch-rebel, *v.* 10. Joab chides the man for not dispatching him (*v.* 11), the man, though zealous enough against Absalom, justified himself in not doing it. Those that love the treason hate the traitor. Joab could not deny this, nor blame the man for his caution.

III. He is so pitifully mangled as he hangs there, and receives his death in such a manner as to see all its terrors and feel all its pain. 1. Joab throws three darts into his body; while he broke the order of a too indulgent father, he did real service both to his king and country, and would have endangered the welfare of both if he had not done it. 2. Joab's young men, ten of them, smite him, before he is dispatched, *v.* 15. Joab hereupon sounds a retreat, *v.* 15. The danger is over, now that Absalom is slain; the people will soon return to their allegiance to David; and therefore no more blood shall be spilt.

IV. His body is disposed of disgracefully (*v.* 17, 18): They *cast it into a great pit in the wood*; they would not bring it to his father (for that circumstance would but have added to his grief), nor would they preserve it to be buried, but threw it into the next pit with indignation. Now where is the beauty he had been so proud of and for which he had been so much admired? Where are his aspiring projects, and the castles he had built in the air? His thoughts perish, and he with them. To aggravate the ignominy of Absalom's burial, the historian takes notice of a pillar he had erected in the valley of Kidron, near Jerusalem, to be a monument for himself (*v.* 18), at the foot of which, it is probable, he designed to be buried. What care do many people take about the disposal of their bodies, when they are dead, that have no care at all what shall become of their precious souls! Absalom had three sons (*ch.* xiv. 27), but, it seems, now he had none. His care was to have his name kept in remembrance, and it is so, to his everlasting dishonour.

Verses 19–33

I. How David was informed of it. He stayed behind at the city of Mahanaim. Absalom's scat-

JAMIESON, FAUSSET, BROWN

6. **wood of Ephraim**—This wood, of course, was on the east of Jordan. Its name was derived, according to some, from the slaughter of the Ephraimites by Jephthah—according to others, from the connection of blood with the transjordanic Manasseh. **7. the people of Israel were slain**—This designation, together with the immense slaughter mentioned later, shows the large extent to which the people were enlisted in this unhappy civil contest. **8. the wood devoured more people that the sword**—The thick forest of oaks and terebinths, by obstructing the flight, greatly aided the victors in the pursuit. **9. Absalom met the servants of David**—or was overtaken. "It is necessary to be continually on one's guard against the branches of trees; and when the hair is worn in large locks floating down the back, as was the case with a young man of the party to which I belonged, any thick boughs interposing in the path might easily dislodge a rider from his seat, and catch hold of his flowing hair" [HARTLEY]. Some, however, think that the sacred historian points not so much to the hair, as to the *head* of Absalom, which, being caught while running between two branches, was enclosed so firmly that he could not disengage himself from the hold, nor make use of his hands. **the mule that was under him went away**—The Orientals, not having saddles as we do, do not sit so firmly on the beasts they ride. Absalom quitting his hold of the bridle, apparently to release himself when caught in the oak, the mule escaped. **11. Joab said unto the man that told him, . . . I would have given thee ten shekels of silver and a girdle**—i.e., would have raised him from the ranks to the status of a commissioned officer. Besides a sum of money, a girdle, curiously and richly wrought, was among the ancient Hebrews a mark of honor, and sometimes bestowed as a reward of military merit. This soldier, however, who may be taken as a fair sample of David's faithful subjects, had so great a respect for the king's wishes, that no prospect of reward would have tempted him to lay violent hands on Absalom. But Joab's stern sense of public duty, which satisfied him that there could be neither safety to the king, nor peace to the kingdom, nor security to him and other loyal subjects, so long as that turbulent prince lived, overcame his sensibilities, and looking upon the charge given to the generals as more befitting a parent than a prince, he ventured to disobey it.

14-32. HE IS SLAIN BY JOAB. **14. he took three darts . . . and thrust them through the heart of Absalom**—The deed, partially done by Joab, was completed by his bodyguard. Being a violation of the expressed wish, as well as of all the fond paternal feelings of David, it must have been deeply offensive to the king, nor was it ever forgotten (I Kings 2:5); and yet there is the strongest reason for believing that Joab, in doing it, was actuated by a sincere regard to the interests of David, both as a man and a monarch. **16. Joab blew the trumpet . . . and held back the people**—Knowing that by the death of the usurper there was no occasion for further bloodshed, he put an end to the pursuit and thereby evinced the temperate policy of his conduct. However harsh and unfeeling to the king Joab may appear, there can be no doubt that he acted the part of a wise statesman in regarding the peace and welfare of the kingdom more than his master's private inclinations, which were opposed to strict justice as well as his own interests. Absalom deserved to die by the divine law (Deut. 21:18, 21), as well as being an enemy to his king and country; and no time was more fitting than when he met that death in open battle.

17. they took Absalom, and cast him into a great pit . . . and laid a very great heap of stones upon him—The people of the East indicate their detestation of the memory of an infamous person by throwing stones at the place where he is buried. The heap is increased by the gradual accumulation of stones which passers-by add to it. **18. Absalom in his lifetime had . . . reared for himself a pillar**—lit., *hand.* In the valley of Jehoshaphat, on the east of Jerusalem, is a tomb or cenotaph, said to be this "pillar" or monument: it is twenty-four feet square, dome-topped, and reaches forty feet in height. This may occupy the spot, but cannot itself be the work of Absalom, as it evidently bears the style of a later architecture.

ADAM CLARKE

7. *Twenty thousand men.* Whether these were slain on the field of battle or whether they were reckoned with those slain in the wood of Ephraim, we know not.

8. *The wood devoured more people.* It is generally supposed that, when the army was broken, they betook themselves to the wood, fell into pits, swamps, etc., and, being entangled, were hewn down by David's men.

9. *And his head caught hold of the oak.* It has been supposed that Absalom was caught by the hair, but no such thing is intimated in the text. Probably his neck was caught in the fork of a strong bough, and he was nearly dead when Joab found him; for it is said, v. 14, "He was yet alive," an expression which intimates he was nearly dead.

11. *And a girdle.* The military belt was the chief ornament of a soldier, and was highly prized in all ancient nations; it was also a rich present from one chieftain to another. Jonathan gave his to David, as the highest pledge of his esteem and perpetual friendship, 1 Sam. xvii. 4.

13. *Thou thyself wouldest have set thyself against me.* This is a strong appeal to Joab's loyalty, and respect for the orders of David; but he was proof against every fine feeling, and against every generous sentiment.

14. *I may not tarry thus with thee.* He had nothing to say in vindication of the purpose he had formed. *Thrust them through the heart of Absalom.* He was determined to make sure work, and therefore he pierced his heart.

15. *Ten young men . . . smote Absalom, and slew him.* That is, they all pierced the body; but there could be no life in it after three darts had been thrust through the heart.

16. *Joab blew the trumpet.* He knew that the rebellion was now extinguished by the death of Absalom, and was not willing that any further slaughter should be made of the deluded people.

17. *And laid a very great heap of stones.* This was the method of burying heroes, and even traitors, the heap of stones being designed to perpetuate the memory of the event, whether good or bad.

18. *Absalom's place.* Literally "Absalom's hand." See the note on 1 Sam. xv. 12.

MATTHEW HENRY

tered forces all made homeward towards Jordan, which was the contrary way from Mahanaim, so that his watchmen could not perceive how the battle went, till an express came on purpose to bring advice of the issue, which the king sat in the gate expecting to hear, *v.* 24.

1. Cushi was the man Joab ordered to carry the tidings (*v.* 21), an *Ethiopian*, so his name signifies, and some think that he was a black that waited on Joab.

2. Ahimaaz, the young priest (one of those who brought David intelligence of Absalom's motions, *ch.* xvii. 17), was very forward to be the messenger of these tidings. Thus he desired that he might have the pleasure and satisfaction of bringing the king, whom he loved, this good news. Joab knew David better than Ahimaaz did, and that the tidings of Absalom's death would spoil the acceptableness of all the rest; and he loves Ahimaaz too well to let **him be the messenger of those tidings (*v.* 20).** However, when Cushi was gone, Ahimaaz begged hard for leave to run after him, and with great importunity obtained it, *v.* 22, 23. Perhaps it was in tenderness to the king that he desired it. He knew he could get there before Cushi, and therefore was willing to prepare the king, by a vague and general report, for the plain truth which Cushi was ordered to tell him. If bad news must come, it is best that it come gradually, and will be the better borne.

3. They are both discovered by the watchman on the gate of Mahanaim, Ahimaaz first (*v.* 24), for, though Cushi had the lead, Ahimaaz soon outran him; but presently after Cushi appeared, *v.* 26. When he hears it is Ahimaaz he concludes he brings good news, *v.* 27. Ahimaaz, it seems, was so famous for running that he was known by it at a distance, and so eminently good that it is taken for granted, if he be the messenger, the news must needs be good.

4. Ahimaaz cries at a distance, "Peace, there is peace." And, when he comes near, he tells him the news more particularly, "They are all cut off *that lifted up their hand against the king*"; and, as became a priest, while he gives the king the joy of it, he gives God the glory of it. "*Blessed be the Lord thy God*, that has done this for thee, as thy God, pursuant to the promises made to uphold thy throne," *ch.* vii. 16. When he said this, *he fell down upon his face*, not only in reverence to the king, but in humble adoration of God, whose name he praised for this success. By directing David thus to give God thanks for his victory, he prepared him. The more our hearts are fixed and enlarged in thanksgiving to God for our mercies the better disposed we shall be to bear the afflictions mixed with them. Poor David is so much a father that he forgets he is a king, and therefore cannot rejoice in the news of a victory, till he know whether the *young man Absalom be safe*. Ahimaaz soon discerned, what Joab intimated to him, that the death of the king's son would make the tidings of the day very unwelcome. "When Joab sent the king's servant (namely, *Cushi*) *and me thy servant*, to bring the news, *I saw a great tumult*, but I have nothing to say about it. Cushi is better able to inform you than I am. I will not be the messenger of evil tidings; nor will I pretend to know that which I cannot give a perfect account of."

5. Cushi, the slow post, proves the sure one, and besides the confirmation of the news of the victory which Ahimaaz had brought—*The Lord has avenged thee of all those that rose up against thee* (*v.* 31)—he satisfied the king's enquiry concerning Absalom, *v.* 32. *Is he safe?* says David. "Yes," says Cushi, "he is safe in his grave"; but he tells the news so discreetly that, how unwelcome soever the message is, the messenger can have no blame. "*The enemies of my lord the king*, whoever they are, *and all that rise against thee to do thee hurt, be as that young man is.*"

II. How David received the intelligence. He forgets all the joy of his deliverance, and is quite overwhelmed with the sorrowful tidings of Absalom's death, *v.* 33. "*O my son Absalom! my son, my son Absalom! Would God I had died for thee. O Absalom! my son, my son!*"

JAMIESON, FAUSSET, BROWN

19. Then said Ahimaaz . . . Let me . . . run and bear the king tidings—The reasons why Joab declined to accept Ahimaaz' offer to bear intelligence of the victory to David, and afterwards let him go along with another, are variously stated by commentators—but they are of no importance. Yet the alacrity of the messengers, as well as the eager excitement of the expectants, is graphically described. **23. by the way of the plain**—or *ciccar*, circle. This word is only used elsewhere in connection with the valley of the Jordan. It is possible that there may have been a place or region so called on the tablelands of Gilead, as the *Septuagint* seems to indicate. Or Mahanaim may have been so situated, with the regard to the battlefield, as to be more easily accessible by a descent to the plain of the Jordan, than over the hills themselves. Or the word may signify (as EWALD explains) a manner of quick running [STANLEY]. **24. David sat between the two gates**—i.e., in the tower-house on the wall that overhung the gate of Mahanaim. Near it was a watchtower, on which a sentinel was posted, as in times of war, to notify every occurrence. The delicacy of Ahimaaz' communication was made up by the unmistakable plainness of Cushi's.

The death of Absalom was a heavy trial, and it is impossible not to sympathize with the outburst of feeling by which David showed that all thoughts of the victory he had won as a king were completely sunk in the painful loss he had sustained as a father. The extraordinary ardor and strength of his affection for this worthless son break out in the redundancy and vehemence of his mournful ejaculations.

ADAM CLARKE

21. *Tell the king what thou hast seen.* At this time the death of Absalom was not publicly known, but Joab had given Cushi private information of it. This Ahimaaz had not, for he could not tell the king whether Absalom was dead. To this Joab seems to refer, v. 22: "Thou hast no tidings ready."

24. *David sat between the two gates.* He was probably in the seat of justice.

25. *If he be alone, there is tidings.* That is, "good tidings." For if the battle had been lost, men would have been running in different directions through the country.

29. *I saw a great tumult.* It was very probable that Ahimaaz did not know of the death of Absalom; he had seen the rout of his army, but did not know of his death.

30. *Stand here.* He intended to confront two messengers, and compare their accounts.

32. *Is the young man Absalom safe?* This was the utmost of his solicitude, and it well merited the reproof which Joab gave him, chap. xix. 5.

MATTHEW HENRY — CHAPTER 19

Verses 1–8

Soon after the messengers had brought the news Joab and his victorious army followed.

I. What a disappointment it was to them to find the king in tears for Absalom's death, which they construed as a token of his displeasure against them for what they had done, whereas they expected him to have met them with joy and thanks for their good services: *It was told Joab*, *v.* 1. The report of it ran

JAMIESON, FAUSSET, BROWN — CHAPTER 19

VSS. 1-8. JOAB CAUSES THE KING TO CEASE MOURNING.

ADAM CLARKE — CHAPTER 19

MATTHEW HENRY

through the army (*v.* 2), *how the king was grieved for his son.* They were loth to blame the king, for *whatever he did used to please them* (*ch.* iii. 36), but they took it as a great mortification to them. *Their victory was turned into mourning, v.* 2. *They stole into the city as men ashamed, v.* 3. In compliment to their sovereign, they would not rejoice in that which they perceived so afflictive to him.

II. How plainly and vehemently Joab reproved David for this indiscreet management of himself in this critical juncture. David never more needed the hearts of his subjects than now. Joab magnifies the services of David's soldiers: "*This day they have saved thy life. Thou hast shamed their faces.*" What can be more absurd than to love thy enemies and to hate thy friends? He advises him to present himself immediately at the head of his troops, to smile upon them, welcome them home, congratulate their success, and return them thanks for their services.

III. How prudently and mildly David took the reproof and counsel given him, *v.* 8. He shook off his grief, anointed his head, and washed his face, that he might not appear unto men to mourn, and then made his appearance in public in the gate, which was as the guildhall of the city. Hither the people flocked to him to congratulate his and their safety, and all was well.

Verses 9–15

It is strange that David did not immediately march back to Jerusalem. Could not he himself go back with the victorious army he had with him in Gilead? He could, but he would go back as a prince, with the consent and unanimous approbation of the people, and not as a conqueror forcing his way. He would go back in honour, and like himself, not at the head of his forces, but in the arms of his subjects; for the prince that has wisdom and goodness enough to make himself his people's darling, without doubt, looks greater and makes a much better figure than the prince that has strength enough to make himself his people's terror.

I. The men of Israel (that is, the ten tribes) were the first that talked of it, *v.* 9, 10. David had formerly helped them, had fought their battles, subdued their enemies, and done them much service, and therefore it was a shame that he should continue banished from their country who had been so great a benefactor to it. Absalom had now disappointed them. "We were foolishly sick of the cedar, and chose the branch to reign over us; but we have had enough of him: he is consumed, and we narrowly escaped being consumed with him. Let us therefore return to our allegiance, and think of bringing the king back." Perhaps this was all the strife among them, not a dispute whether the king should be brought back, or no (all agreed it was to be done), but whose fault it was that it was not done.

II. The men of Judah were not so forward as the rest. David had intelligence of the good disposition of all the rest towards him, but nothing from Judah. David would not return till he knew the sense of his own tribe. That his way home might be the more clear, 1. He employed Zadok and Abiathar, the two chief priests, to treat with the elders of Judah, and to excite them to give the king an invitation back to his house, even to his house, which was the glory of their tribe, *v.* 11, 12. Perhaps they were so sensible of the greatness of the provocation they had given to David, by joining with Absalom, that they were afraid to bring him back, despairing of his favour; he therefore warrants his agents to assure them of it, with this reason: "*You are my brethren, my bone and my flesh,* and therefore I cannot be severe with you." 2. He particularly courted into his interest Amasa, who had been Absalom's general, but was his own nephew as well as Joab, *v.* 13. He owns him for his kinsman, and promises him that, if he will appear for him now, he will make him captain-general of all his forces in the room of Joab. But, if David did wisely for himself in designating Amasa for this post (Joab having now grown intolerably haughty), he did not do kindly by Amasa in letting his design be known, for it occasioned his death by Joab's hand, *ch.* xx. 10. 3. The point was hereby gained. He bowed the heart of the men of Judah to pass a vote for the recall of the king, *v.* 14. God's providence, by the priests' persuasions and Amasa's interest, brought them to this resolve. David stirred not till he received this invitation, and then he came as far back as Jordan, at which river they were to meet him, *v.* 15.

Verses 16–23

David, in his flight, remembered God particularly *from the land of Jordan* (Ps. xlii. 6), and now that land, more than any other, was graced with the glories

JAMIESON, FAUSSET, BROWN

3. the people gat them by stealth . . . to the city—The rumor of the king's disconsolate condition spread a universal and unseasonable gloom. His troops, instead of being welcomed back (as a victorious army always was) with music and other demonstrations of public joy, slunk secretly and silently into the city, as if ashamed after the commission of some crime. **4. the king covered his face**—one of the usual signs of mourning (see on ch. 15: 30). **7. Thou hast shamed . . . the faces of all thy servants**—by withdrawing thyself to indulge in grief, as if their services were disagreeable and their devotion irksome to thee. Instead of hailing their return with joy and gratitude, thou hast refused them the small gratification of seeing thee. Joab's remonstrance was right and necessary, but it was made with harshness. He was one of those persons who spoil their important services by the insolence of their manners, and who always awaken a feeling of obligation in those to whom they render any services. He spoke to David in a tone of hauteur that ill became a subject to show towards his king. **7. Now . . . arise, go forth, and speak comfortably unto thy servants**—The king felt the truth of Joab's reprimand; but the threat by which it was enforced, grounded as it was on the general's unbounded popularity with the army, showed him to be a dangerous person; and that circumstance, together with the violation of an express order to deal gently for his sake with Absalom, produced in David's mind a settled hatred, which was strongly manifested in his last directions to Solomon. **8. the king arose, and sat in the gate**—He appeared daily in the usual place for the hearing of causes. **all the people came before the king**—i.e., the loyal natives who had been faithful to his government, and fought in his cause. **Israel had fled**—i.e., the adherents of Absalom, who, on his defeat, had dispersed and saved themselves by flight.

9-43. THE ISRAELITES BRING THE KING BACK. **9. all the people were at strife throughout the tribes of Israel**—The kingdom was completely disorganized. The sentiments of three different parties are represented in verses 9 and 10: the royalists, the adherents of Absalom who had been very numerous, and those who were indifferent to the Davidic dynasty. In these circumstances the king was right in not hastening back, as a conqueror, to reascend his throne. A re-election was, in some measure, necessary. He remained for some time on the other side of Jordan, in expectation of being invited back.

That invitation was given without, however, the concurrence of Judah. David, disappointed and vexed by his own tribe's apparent lukewarmness, despatched the two high priests to rouse the Judahites to take a prominent interest in his cause. It was the act of a skilful politician. Hebron having been the seat of the rebellion, it was graceful on his part to encourage their return to allegiance and duty; it was an appeal to their honor not to be the last of the tribes. But this separate message, and the preference given to them, occasioned an outburst of jealousy among the other tribes that was nearly followed by fatal consequences.

13. And say ye to Amasa, etc.—This also was a dextrous stroke of policy. David was fully alive to the importance, for extinguishing the rebellion, of withdrawing from that cause the only leader who could keep it alive; and he, therefore, secretly intimated his intention to raise Amasa to the command of the army in the place of Joab, whose overbearing haughtiness had become intolerable. The king justly reckoned, that from natural temper as well as gratitude for the royal pardon, he would prove a more tractable servant; and David, doubtless, intended in all sincerity to fulfil this promise. But Joab managed to retain his high position (see on ch. 20). **14. he bowed the heart of all the men of Judah**—i.e., Amasa, who had been won over, used his great influence in re-attaching the whole tribe of Judah to the interest of David. **15. Judah came to Gilgal**—the most convenient place where preparations could be made for bringing the king and court over the Jordan.

ADAM CLARKE

2. *The victory . . . was turned into mourning.* Instead of rejoicing that a most unnatural and ruinous rebellion had been quashed, the people mourned over their own success, because they saw their king so immoderately afflicted for the loss of his worthless son.

4. *The king covered his face.* This was the custom of mourners.

5. *Thou hast shamed this day.* Joab's speech to David on his immoderate grief for the death of his rebellious son is not only remarkable for the insolence of office but also for good sense and firmness. Every man who candidly considers the state of the case must allow that David acted imprudently at least, and that Joab's firm reproof was necessary to arouse him to a sense of his duty to his people. But still, in his manner, Joab had far exceeded the bonds of that reverence which a servant owes to his master, or a subject to his prince. Joab was a good soldier, but in every respect a bad man, and a dangerous subject.

8. *The king . . . sat in the gate.* The place where justice was administered to the people.

11. *Speak unto the elders of Judah.* David was afraid to fall out with this tribe; they were in possession of Jerusalem, and this was a city of great importance to him. They had joined Absalom in his rebellion, and doubtless were now ashamed of their conduct. David appears to take no notice of their infidelity, but rather to place confidence in them, that their confidence in him might be naturally excited: and, to oblige them yet farther, purposes to make **Amasa captain of the host in the place of Joab.**

14. *And he bowed the heart of all the men of Judah.* The measures that he pursued were the best calculated that could be to accomplish this salutary end.

MATTHEW HENRY

of his return. David's soldiers furnished themselves with accommodations for their passage over this river, but, for his own family, *a ferry-boat* was sent on purpose, *v.* 18. Two remarkable persons met him on the banks of Jordan, both of whom had abused him wretchedly when he was in his flight.

I. Ziba, who by accusing his master had obtained from the king a grant of his estate, *ch.* xvi. 4, imposing upon his credulity, to draw him in to do a thing so unkind to the son of his friend Jonathan. He comes now to meet the king (*v.* 17), that he may obtain favour, and so come off the better when Mephibosheth shall shortly undeceive him, and clear himself, *v.* 26.

II. Shimei, who had railed at him, and cursed him, *ch.* xvi. 5, thinks it his interest to make his peace with him. Shimei, to recommend himself to the king, 1. Came with good company, with the men of Judah. 2. He brought a regiment of the men of Benjamin with him, offering his own and their service to the king. 3. What he did he hastened to do. He did it publicly. The offence was public, therefore the submission ought to be so. He owns his crime: *Thy servant doth know that I have sinned.* He begs the king's pardon: *Let not the king impute iniquity to thy servant*, that is, deal with me as I deserve. A motion made for judgment against him (*v.* 21) was made by Abishai, who would have ventured his life to have been the death of Shimei when he was cursing, *ch.* xvi. 9. David rejected Abishai's motion with displeasure: *What have I to do with you, you sons of Zeruiah?* The less we have to do with those who are of an angry revengeful spirit, and who put us upon doing what is harsh and rigorous, the better. It is the glory of kings to forgive those that humble and surrender themselves: *Satis est protrâsse leoni—It suffices the lion that he has laid his victim prostrate.* His joy inclined him to forgive. Yet this was not all; his experience of God's mercy in restoring him to his kingdom, his exclusion from which he attributed to his sin, inclined him to show mercy to Shimei. Shemei hereupon had his pardon signed and sealed with an oath.

Verses 24–30

The day of David's return was a day of bringing to remembrance. Among other things, after the case of Shimei, that of Mephibosheth comes to be enquired into, and he himself brings it on.

I. He went down in the crowd *to meet the king* (*v.* 24), and, as a proof of the sincerity of his joy in the king's return, we are here told what a true mourner he was for the king's banishment. He was never trimmed, nor put on clean linen, but wholly neglected himself, as one abandoned to grief for the king's affliction and the kingdom's misery.

II. When the king came to Jerusalem he made his appearance before him (*v.* 25); and when the king asked him why he, being one of his family, had stayed behind, and not accompanied him in his exile, he opened his case fully to the king. 1. He complained of Ziba, his servant, who should have been his friend, but had been in two ways his enemy; for, first, he had hindered him from going along with the king, by taking the ass himself which he was ordered to make ready for his master (*v.* 26), basely taking advantage of his lameness and his inability to help himself; and, secondly, he had accused him to David of a design to usurp the government, *v.* 27. 2. He gratefully acknowledged the king's great kindness to him when he and all his father's house lay at the king's mercy, *v.* 28. 3. He referred his cause to the king's pleasure, depending on the king's wisdom, and his ability to discern between truth and falsehood, and disclaiming all pretensions of his own merit.

III. David hereupon recalls the sequestration of Mephibosheth's estate; being deceived in his grant, he revokes it, and confirms his former settlement of it: "*I have said, Thou and Ziba divide the land* (*v.* 29), that is, Let it be as I first ordered it (*ch.* ix. 10); the property shall still be vested in thee, but Ziba shall have the occupancy: he shall till the land, paying thee a rent." Thus Mephibosheth is where he was; no harm is done, only Ziba goes away unpunished for his false and malicious information against his master.

IV. Mephibosheth drowns all his cares about his estate in his joy for the king's return (*v.* 30): "*Yea, let him take all*, the presence and favour of the king shall be to me instead of all."

Verses 31–39

Barzillai, the Gileadite, who had a noble seat at Rogelim, not far from Mahanaim, was the man who, of all the nobility and gentry of that country, had been most kind to David in his distress. If Absalom had prevailed, it is likely he would have suffered for his loyalty; but now he and his shall be no losers by it.

JAMIESON, FAUSSET, BROWN

18. ferry boat—probably rafts, which are still used on that part of the river.

17. Ziba, the servant of the house of Saul—He had deceived his master; and when ordered to make ready the ass for the lame prince to go and meet the king, he slipped away by himself to pay court first; so that Mephibosheth, being lame, had to remain in Jerusalem till the king's arrival.

16. Shimei . . . a thousand men of Benjamin with him—This display of his followers was to show what force he could raise against or in support of the king. Expressing the deepest regret for his former outrageous conduct, he was pardoned on the spot; and although the son of Zeruiah urged the expediency of making this chief a public example, his officiousness was repulsed by David with magnanimity, and with the greater confidence that he felt himself now re-established in the kingdom (see on I Kings 2:8,9).

20. I am come the first . . . of all the house of Joseph—i.e., before all the rest of *Israel* (Ps. 77:15; 80:1; 81:5; Zech. 10:6).

24-30. Mephibosheth . . . came down to meet the king. The reception given to Mephibosheth was less creditable to David. The sincerity of that prince's grief for the misfortunes of the king cannot be doubted. "He had neither dressed his feet"—not taken the bath, "nor trimmed his beard." The Hebrews cut off the hair on the upper lip (see on Lev. 13:45), and cheeks, but carefully cherished it on the chin from ear to ear. Besides dyeing it black or red colors, which, however, is the exception, and not the rule in the East, there are various modes of trimming it: they train it into a massy bushy form, swelling and round; or they terminate it like a pyramid, in a sharp point. Whatever the mode, it is always trimmed with the greatest care; and they usually carry a small comb for the purpose. The neglect of this attention to his beard was an undoubted proof of the depth of Mephibosheth's grief. The king seems to have received him upbraidingly, and not to have been altogether sure either of his guilt or innocence. It is impossible to commend the cavalier treatment, any more than to approve the partial award, of David in this case.

If he were too hurried and distracted by the pressure of circumstances to inquire fully into the matter, he should have postponed his decision; for if by "dividing the land" (vs. 29) he meant that the former arrangement should be continued by which Mephibosheth was acknowledged the proprietor, and Ziba the farmer, it was a hardship inflicted on the owner to fix him with a tenant who had so grossly slandered him. But if by "dividing the land," they were now to share alike, the injustice of the decision was greatly increased. In any view, the generous, disinterested spirit displayed by Mephibosheth was worthy a son of the noble-hearted Jonathan.

31-40. Barzillai the Gileadite—The rank, great age, and chivalrous devotion of this Gileadite chief wins our respect.

ADAM CLARKE

18. *There went over a ferry boat.* This is the first mention of anything of the kind. Some think a bridge or raft is what is here intended.

16. *Shimei the son of Gera.* It appears that Shimei was a powerful chieftain in the land; for he had here, in his retinue, no less than a thousand men.

20. *For thy servant doth know that I have sinned.* This was all he could do; his subsequent conduct alone could prove his sincerity. On such an avowal as this David could not but grant him his life.

24. *Neither dressed his feet.* He had given the fullest proof of his sincere attachment to David and his cause, and by what he had done, amply refuted the calumnies of his servant Ziba.

27. *The king is as an angel of God.* As if he had said, I state my case plainly and without guile; you are too wise not to penetrate the motives from which both myself and servant have acted. I shall make no appeal; with whatsoever you determine I shall rest contented.

29. *I have said, Thou and Ziba divide the land.* At first David gave the land of Saul to Mephibosheth; Ziba, his sons, and his servants were to work that land; and to Mephibosheth, as the lord, he was to give the half of the produce. Ziba met David in his distress with provisions, and calumniated Mephibosheth; David made him on the spot a grant of his master's land. Now he finds that he has acted too rashly, and therefore confirms the former grant; i.e., that Ziba should cultivate the ground, and still continue to give to Mephibosheth, as the lord, the half of the produce.

MATTHEW HENRY

I. Barzillai's great respect to David as his rightful sovereign: He *provided him with much sustenance*, for himself and his family, *while he lay at Mahanaim*, *v.* 32. God had given him a large estate, *for he was a very great man*, and, it seems, he had a large heart to do good with it: what else but that is a large estate good for?

II. The kind invitation David gave him to court (*v.* 33): *Come thou over with me*. He invited him, 1. That he might have the pleasure of his company and the benefit of his counsel. 2. That he might have an opportunity of returning his kindness: "*I will feed thee with me.*"

III. Barzillai's reply to this invitation, wherein, 1. He admires the king's generosity in making him this offer, lessening his service, and magnifying the king's return for it.

2. He declines accepting the invitation. He begs his majesty's pardon for refusing so generous an offer: but, (1) He is old, and unfit to remove at all, especially to court. (2) He is dying, and must begin to think of his long journey, his removal out of the world, *v.* 37.

3. He desires the king to be kind to his son Chimham: *Let him go over with my lord the king*, and have preferment at court. What favour is done to him Barzillai will take as done to himself.

IV. David's farewell to Barzillai. 1. He sends him back into his country with a kiss and a blessing (*v.* 39), signifying that in gratitude for his kindness he would love him and pray for him, and with a promise that whatever request he should at any time make to him he would be ready to oblige him (*v.* 38): *Whatsoever thou shalt think of*, when thou comest home to *ask of me*, that *will I do for thee*. 2. He takes Chimham forward with him, and leaves it to Barzillai to choose him his preferment: I will *do to him what shall seem good to thee*, *v.* 38. And, it should seem, Barzillai begged a country seat for him near Jerusalem, for, long after, we read of a place near Beth-lehem, David's city, which is called *the habitation of Chimham*, allotted to him, probably, not out of the crown-lands or the forfeited estates, but out of David's paternal estate.

Verses 40–43

David came over Jordan attended and assisted only by the men of Judah; but when he had advanced as far as Gilgal, the first stage on this side Jordan, *half the people of Israel* (that is, of their elders and great men) had come to kiss his hand, but found they came too late to witness the solemnity of his first entrance. This occasioned a quarrel between them and the men of Judah, and the beginning of further mischief. Here is, 1. The complaint which the men of Israel brought to the king against the men of Judah (*v.* 41), that they had performed the ceremony of bringing the king over Jordan, and not given them notice, as if they were not so well affected to the king, whereas the king himself knew that they had spoken of it before the men of Judah thought of it, *v.* 11. 2. The excuse which the men of Judah made for themselves, *v.* 42. (1) They plead relation to the king: "*He is near of kin to us*", and therefore in a matter of mere ceremony, as this was, we may claim precedency. (2) They deny the insinuated charge of self-seeking in what they had done: "*Have we eaten at all of the king's cost?* No, we have all borne our own charges. *Hath he given us any gift?* No, we have no design to engross the advantages of his return; you have come time enough to share in them." 3. The men of Israel's vindication of their charge, *v.* 43. They pleaded, "*We have ten parts in the king*" (Judah having Simeon only, whose lot lay within his, to join with him), "and therefore it is a slight upon us that our advice was not asked about *bringing back the king.*"

CHAPTER 20

Verses 1–3

David, in the midst of his triumphs, has to see his kingdom disturbed and his family disgraced.

I. His subjects revolting from him at the instigation of a *man of Belial*, whom they followed when they forsook the *man after God's own heart*. We must not think it strange, while we are in this world, if the end of one trouble be the beginning of another. A broken bone, when it is set, must have time to knit. **The ringleader of this rebellion was Sheba, a Benjamite by birth (*v.* 1), who had his habitation in Mount Ephraim, *v.* 21. Shimei and he** were both of Saul's tribe, and both retained the ancient grudge of that house. The occasion of it was that foolish quarrel, which we read of in the close of the foregoing chapter, between the elders of

JAMIESON, FAUSSET, BROWN

JOSEPH PARKER:

Chimham was the old man's son. Let us not forget the young. If we cannot take honors and high positions, we may introduce other people who may have some capability for high service, faculty for hard work, and hidden claim to just renown. Here is an old man who cares for the coming generation. Such a man, then, is not old in any sense of exhaustion and uselessness. Would that some people knew when their work was done, and that they would quietly step aside and let younger people have a chance in life! Is it not pitiable to see how some men cling on to the very last, while men of capability and fine spirit and good faculty are kept waiting, and are becoming discouraged and disheartened? Every man must answer such appeals for himself: no general judgment can be pronounced; but this can be said: blessed is the old man who knows there are young men behind him, and who is willing to stand aside and let other men have the opportunity which made him what he himself became.—*The People's Bible*

His declining to go to court, his recommendation of his son, his convoy across the Jordan, and his parting scene with the king, are interesting incidents. What mark of royal favor was bestowed on Chimham has not been recorded; but it is probable that David gave a great part of his personal patrimony in Bethlehem to Chimham and his heirs in perpetuity (Jer. 41:17).

35. the voice of singing men and singing women—Bands of professional musicians form a prominent appendage to the courts of Oriental princes. **37. buried by the grave of my father and my mother**—This is an instance of the strong affection of people in the East towards the places of sepulture appropriated to their families.

40-43. the king went on to Gilgal, ... and all the people of Judah conducted the king, and also half the people of Israel—Whether from impatience to move on or from some other cause, David did not wait till all the tribes had arrived to conduct him on his return to the capital. The procession began as soon as Amasa had brought the Judahite escort, and the preference given to this tribe produced a bitter jealousy, which was nearly kindling a civil war fiercer than that which had just ended.

A war of words ensued between the tribes—Israel resting their argument on their superior numbers; "they had ten parts in the king," whereas Judah had no more than one. Judah grounded their right to take the lead, on the ground of their nearer relationship to the king. This was a claim dangerous to the house of David; and it shows the seeds were already sown for that tribal dissension which, before long, led to the dismemberment of the kingdom.

CHAPTER 20

VSS. 1-9. SHEBA MAKES A PARTY IN ISRAEL. **1. Sheba ... a Benjamite**—Though nothing is known of this man, he must have been a person of considerable power and influence, before he could have raised so sudden and extensive a sedition. He belonged to the tribe of Benjamin, where the adherents of Saul's dynasty were still numerous; and perceiving the strong disgust of the other tribes with the part assumed by Judah in the restoration, his ill-designing heart resolved to turn it to the overthrow of David's authority in Israel. **every man to his tents**—This proverbial expression may have had its foundation in the fact, that many of the Israelite peasantry adhered to the custom of the patriarchs who tilled land, and yet lived in tents, as Syrian peasants often do

ADAM CLARKE

37. *Thy servant Chimham.* It is generally understood that this was Barzillai's son; and this is probable from 1 Kings ii. 7, where, when David was dying, he said, "Shew kindness unto the sons of Barzillai": and it is very probable that this Chimham was one of them. In Jer. xli. 17 mention is made of the "habitation of Chimham," which was near to Bethlehem; and it is reasonably conjectured that David had left that portion, which was probably a part of his paternal estate, to this son of Barzillai.

39. *The king kissed Barzillai, and blessed him.* The kiss was the token of friendship and farewell; the blessing was a prayer to God for his prosperity, probably a prophetical benediction.

42. *Wherefore then be ye angry for this matter?* We have not done this for our own advantage; we have gained nothing by it; we did it through loyal attachment to our king.

43. *We have ten parts in the king, and . . . more right.* We are ten tribes to one, or we are ten times so many as you, and consequently should have been consulted in this business. *The words of the men of Judah were fiercer than the words of the men of Israel.* They had more weight, for they had more reason on their side.

CHAPTER 20

1. *Sheba, the son of Bichri.* As this man was a Benjamite, he probably belonged to the family of Saul, and he seems to have had considerable influence in Israel to raise such an insurrection: but we know nothing further of him than what is related in this place. *We have no part in David.* We of Israel, we of the ten tribes, are under no obligation to the house of David. Leave him, and let every man fall into the ranks under his own leader.

MATTHEW HENRY

Israel and the elders of Judah, about bringing the king back. "If the king will suffer himself to be engrossed by the men of Judah, let him and them make their best of one another, and we will set up one for ourselves." This was proclaimed by Sheba (*v.* 1), who probably was a man of note, and had been active in Absalom's rebellion; the disgusted Israelites took the hint, and *went up from after David to follow Sheba* (*v.* 2). The perverting of words is the subverting of peace; and much mischief is made by forcing invidious constructions upon what is said and written and drawing consequences that were never intended. The men of Judah said, *The king is near of kin to us.* "By this," say the men of Israel, "you mean that *we have no part in him*"; whereas they meant no such thing.

II. His concubines imprisoned for life, and he himself under a necessity of putting them in confinement, because they had been defiled by Absalom, *v.* 3. Those whom he had loved must now be loathed.

Verses 4–13

We have here Amasa's fall just as he began to rise. He had been Absalom's general, and came over into David's interest, upon a promise that he should be general of his forces instead of Joab.

I. Amasa has a commission to raise forces for the suppressing of Sheba's rebellion, and is ordered to raise them with all possible expedition, *v.* 4. Amasa is sent to assemble the men of Judah within three days; but he finds them so backward and unready that he cannot do it within the time appointed (*v.* 5).

II. Upon Amasa's delay, Abishai, the brother of Joab, is ordered to take the guards and standing forces, and with them to pursue Sheba (*v.* 6, 7), for nothing could be of more dangerous consequence than to give him time. David gives these orders to Abishai, because he resolves to mortify Joab. Joab, without orders, though in disgrace, goes along with his brother.

III. Joab, near Gibeon, meets with Amasa, and barbarously murders him, *v.* 8–10. 1. He did subtilely, and with contrivance, and not upon a sudden provocation. He girded his coat about him, that it might not hang in his way, and girded his belt upon his coat, that his sword might be the readier to his hand; he also put his sword in a sheath too big for it, that, whenever he pleased, it might, upon a little shake, fall out, as if it fell by accident, and so he might take it into his hand, unsuspected, as if he were going to return it into the scabbard. 2. He did it treacherously, and under pretence of friendship, that Amasa might not be upon his guard. He called him *brother*. 3. He did it impudently, not in a corner, but at the head of his troops. He did it in contempt and defiance of David and the commission he had given to Amasa.

IV. Joab immediately resumes his general's place, and takes care to lead the army on in pursuit of Sheba. He knew how many favoured him rather than Amasa, who had been a traitor. What man of Judah would not be for his old king and his old general? But one would wonder with what face a murderer could pursue a traitor. Care is taken to remove the dead body out of the way, and to cover it with a cloth, *v.* 12, 13. Wicked men think themselves safe in their wickedness if they can but conceal it from the eye of the world: if it be hidden, it is with them as if it were never done.

Verses 14–22

I. The rebel, when he had rambled over all the tribes of Israel, and found them not so willing, upon second thoughts, to follow him, at length entered Abel-Beth-maacah, a strong city in the north. His adherents were mostly Berites, of Beeroth in Benjamin, *v.* 14.

II. Joab drew up all his force against the city, besieged it, battered the wall, and made it almost ready for a general storm, *v.* 15.

III. A discreet good woman of the city of Abel brings this matter to a good issue, so as to satisfy Joab and yet save the city.

1. Her treaty with Joab by which he is engaged to raise the siege, upon condition that Sheba be delivered up. It seems, none of all the men of Abel offered to treat with Joab. But this one woman with her wisdom saved the city. Souls know no difference of sex. Though the man be the head, it does not therefore follow that he has the monopoly of the brains, and therefore he ought not, by any salique law, to have the monopoly of the crown. Many a masculine heart, and more than masculine, has been found in a female breast; nor is the treasure of wisdom the less valuable for being lodged in the weaker vessel. In the treaty between this nameless heroine and Joab,

(1) She gains his audience and attention, *v.* 16, 17.
(2) She reasons with him on behalf of her city, and

JAMIESON, FAUSSET, BROWN

still. This was the usual watchword of national insurrection, and from the actual temper of the people, it was followed by effects beyond what he probably anticipated. **2. from Jordan even to Jerusalem**—The quarrel had broken out shortly after the crossing of the Jordan, between Judah and the other tribes, who withdrew; so that Judah was left nearly alone to conduct the king to the metropolis. **3. the king took the ten women his concubines**—Jewish writers say that the widowed queens of Hebrew monarchs were not allowed to marry again but were obliged to pass the rest of their lives in strict seclusion. David treated his concubines in the same manner after the outrage committed on them by Absalom. They were not divorced, for they were guiltless; but they were no longer publicly recognized as his wives; nor was their confinement to a sequestered life a very heavy doom, in a region where women have never been accustomed to go much abroad. **4. Then said the king to Amasa, Assemble me the men of Judah within three days**—Amasa is now installed in the command which David had promised him. The revolt of the ten tribes, probably, hastened the public declaration of this appointment, which he hoped would be popular with them, and Amasa was ordered within three days to levy a force from Judah sufficient to put down the insurrection. The appointment was a blunder, and the king soon perceived his error. The specified time passed, but Amasa could not muster the men. Dreading the loss of time, the king gave the commission to Abishai, and not to Joab—a new affront, which, no doubt, wounded the pride of the stern and haughty old general. But he hastened with his attached soldiers to go as second to his brother, determined to take the first opportunity of wreaking his vengeance on his successful rival. **8. Amasa went before them**—Having collected some forces, he by a rapid march overtook the expedition at Gibeon, and assumed the place of commander; in which capacity, he was saluted, among others, by Joab. **Joab's garment, that he had put on, was girded unto him**—in the fashion of travelers and soldiers. **a sword . . . and, as he went forth, it fell out**—i.e., out of the scabbard. According to Josephus, he let it drop on purpose as he was accosting Amasa, that stooping, as it were accidentally, to pick it up, he might salute the new general with the naked sword in his hand, without exciting any suspicion of his design. "He went forth" in a ceremonious manner to meet Amasa, now commander-in-chief, in order to seem to render to that officer, whom he considered as usurping his post, a conspicuous honor and homage. **9. took Amasa by the beard with the right hand to kiss him**—This act, common with two friends on meeting when one of them returns from a journey, indicates respect as well as kindliness, and the performance of it evinced the deep hypocrisy of Joab, who thereby put Amasa off his guard. No wonder, then, that while this act of friendly gratulation after long absence occupied Amasa's attention, he did not perceive the sword that was in Joab's *left* hand. The action of Joab was indeed a high compliment, but neither suspicious nor unusual and to this compliment, Amasa paying attention and no doubt returning it with suitable politeness, he could little expect the fatal event that Joab's perfidy produced.

10-13. Amasa Is Slain. **10. smote him . . . in the fifth rib**—the seat of the liver and bowels, where wounds are mortal. **struck him not again**—i.e., despatched him at the first blow. **11. He that favoureth Joab, and he that is for David, let him go after Joab**—It is a striking proof of Joab's unrivalled influence over the army, that with this villainous murder perpetrated before their eyes they unanimously followed him as their leader in pursuit of Sheba. A soldier conjoined his name with David's, and such a magic spell was in the word "Joab," that all the people "went on"—Amasa's men as well as the rest. The conjunction of these two names is very significant. It shows that the one could not afford to do without the other—neither Joab to rebel against David, nor David to get rid of Joab, though hating him.

14, 15. Joab Pursues Sheba unto Abel. **14. he went through all the tribes of Israel unto Abel**—beating up for recruits. But there the prompt marches of Joab overtook and hemmed him in by a close siege of the place. **15. Abel of Beth-maachah**—a verdant place—the addition of "Maachah" betokening that it belonged to the district Maachah, which lay far up the Jordan at the foot of Lebanon.

16-22. A Wise Woman Saves the City by Sheba's Head. **16. Then cried a wise woman**—The appeal of this woman, who, like Deborah, was probably a judge or governess of the place, was a strong one.

ADAM CLARKE

3. *The ten women.* He could not well divorce them; he could not punish them, as they were not in the transgression; he could no more be familiar with them, because they had been defiled by his son; and to have married them to other men might have been dangerous to the state. Therefore he shut them up and *fed them*—made them quite comfortable, and they continued as widows to their death.

4. *Then said the king to Amasa.* Thus he invests him with the command of the army, and sends him to collect the men of Judah, and to come back to receive his orders in relation to Sheba, in three days. It appears that Amasa found more difficulty in collecting his countrymen than was at first supposed; and this detaining him beyond the three days, David, fearing that Sheba's rebellion would get head, sent Abishai, who it appears was accompanied by Joab, to pursue after Sheba.

Amasa, it seems, caught up with them at Gibeon, v. 8, where he was treacherously murdered by the execrable Joab. 8. *Joab's garment.* It appears that this was not a military garment, and that Joab had no arms but a short sword, which he had concealed in his girdle; and this sword, or knife, was so loose in its sheath that it could be easily drawn out.

10. *In the fifth rib.* I believe *chomesh,* which we render here and elsewhere the *fifth rib,* means any part of the abdominal region. The Septuagint translate it "the groin"; the Targum, "the right side of the thigh." That it means some part of the abdominal region is evident from what follows, *and shed out his bowels to the ground.*

11. *He that favoreth Joab.* As if he had said, There is now no other commander besides Joab, and Joab is steadily attached to David; let those therefore who are loyal follow Joab.

14. *Unto Abel.* This is supposed to have been the capital of the district called Abilene in Luke's Gospel, chap. iii. 1. *Beth-maachah.* Is supposed to have been in the northern part of the Holy Land, on the confines of Syria, and probably in the tribe of Naphtali.

15. *They cast up a bank against the city.* The word which we render *bank* means most probably a "battering engine" of some kind, or a "tower" overlooking the walls, on which archers and slingers could stand and annoy the inhabitants, while others of the besiegers could proceed to sap the walls.

16. *A wise woman.* She was probably governess.

MATTHEW HENRY

very ingeniously. [1] That it was a city famous for wisdom (*v.* 18), as we translate it. [2] That the inhabitants were generally peaceable and faithful in Israel, *v.* 19. [3] That it was a mother in Israel, a guide and nurse to the towns and country about; and that it was a part of *the inheritance of the Lord.* [4] That they expected him to offer them peace before he made an attack upon them, according to that known law of war, Deut. xx. 10.

(3) Joab and Abel's advocate soon agree that Sheba's head shall be the ransom of the city. "Our quarrel is not with your city. Our quarrel is only with the traitor that is harboured among you; deliver him up, and we have done." A great deal of mischief would be prevented if contending parties would but understand one another. The single condition of peace is the surrender of the traitor. It is so in God's dealings with the soul, when it is besieged by conviction and distress: sin is the traitor; the beloved lust is the rebel; part with that, cast away the transgression, and all shall be well.

2. Her treaty with the citizens. She went to them in her wisdom and persuaded them to cut off Sheba's head. Joab hereupon raised the siege, and marched back to Jerusalem, with the trophies rather of peace than victory.

Verses 23–26

Here is an account of the state of David's court after his restoration. Joab retained the office of general. Benaiah, as before, was captain of the guards. Here is one new office erected, that of *treasurer* or one *over the tribute*, for it was not till towards the latter end of his time that David began to raise taxes.

JAMIESON, FAUSSET, BROWN

18. They were wont to speak in old time—The translation of the margin gives a better meaning, which is to this effect: When the people saw thee lay siege to Abel, they said, Surely he will ask if we will have peace, for the law (Deut. 20:10) prescribes that he should offer peace to strangers, much more then to Israelitish cities; and if he do this, we shall soon bring things to an amicable agreement, for we are a peaceable people. The answer of Joab brings out the character of that ruthless veteran as a patriot at heart, who, on securing the author of this insurrection, was ready to put a stop to further bloodshed and release the peaceable inhabitants from all molestation.

23-26. DAVID'S GREAT OFFICERS. **23. Now Joab was over all the host of Israel**—David, whatever his private wishes, found that he possessed not the power of removing Joab; so winking at the murder of Amasa, he re-established that officer in his former post of commander-in-chief. The enumeration of David's cabinet is here given to show that the government was re-established in its wonted course.

ADAM CLARKE

18. *They shall surely ask counsel at Abel.* Abel was probably famed for the wisdom of its inhabitants; and parties who had disputes appealed to their judgment, which appears to have been in such high reputation as to be final by consent of all parties.

19. *I . . . peaceable and faithful in Israel.* I am for peace, not contention of any kind; I am *faithful*—I adhere to David, and neither seek nor shall sanction any rebellion or anarchy in the land. Why then do you proceed in such a violent manner? Perhaps the woman speaks here in the name and on behalf of the city: "I am a peaceable city, and am faithful to the king." *A mother in Israel.* That is, a chief city of a district; for it is very likely that the woman speaks of the city, not of herself.

21. *His head shall be thrown to thee.* Thus it appears she had great sway in the counsels of the city; and that the punishment of a state rebel was then, what it is now in this kingdom, beheading.

23. *Joab was over all the host.* He had murdered Amasa and seized on the supreme command; and such was his power at present, and the service which he had rendered to the state by quelling the rebellion of Sheba, that David was obliged to continue him, and dared not to call him to account for his murders without endangering the safety of the state by a civil war. *Benaiah . . . over the Cherethites.* Benaiah was over the "archers and slingers." See the notes on chap. viii. 18.

24. *Adoram was over the tribute.* Probably the chief receiver of the taxes; or chancellor of the exchequer, as we term it. *Jehoshaphat . . . recorder.* The registrar of public events.

25. *Shevah was scribe.* The king's secretary.

26. *Ira . . . was a chief ruler about David.* The Hebrew is *cohen ledavid*, "a priest to David"; and so the Vulgate, Septuagint, Syriac, and Arabic. The Chaldee has *rab*, a "prince, or chief." He was probably a sort of domestic chaplain to the king. We know that the kings of Judah had their seers, which is nearly the same: Gad was David's seer, chap. xxiv. 11; and Jeduthun was the seer of King Josiah, 2 Chron. xxxv. 15.

MATTHEW HENRY — CHAPTER 21

Verses 1–9

I. The injury which Saul had, long before this, done to the Gibeonites. The Gibeonites were of the remnant of the Amorites (*v.* 2), who by a stratagem had made peace with Israel, and had the public faith pledged to them, Joshua ix., where it was agreed (*v.* 23) that they should have their lives secured, but be deprived of their lands and liberties, that they and theirs should be tenants in villainage to Israel. Saul, under colour of zeal for the honour of Israel, that it might not be said that they had any of the natives among them, aimed to root them out, and, in order to do that, slew many of them. It may be, he designed, by this severity towards the Gibeonites, to atone for his clemency towards the Amalekites. That which made this an exceedingly sinful sin was that he not only shed innocent blood, but therein violated the solemn oath by which the nation was bound to protect them.

II. We find the nation of Israel chastised with a sore famine, long after, for this sin of Saul. 1. Even in the land of Israel, that fruitful land, and in the reign of David, that glorious reign, there was a famine, great drought, and scarcity of provisions, the consequence of it, for three years together. 2. David enquired of God concerning it. Though he was himself a prophet, he must consult the oracle, and know God's mind in his own appointed way. 3. God was ready in his answer, though David was slow in his enquiries: *It is for Saul.* Time does not wear out the guilt of sin; nor can we build hopes of impunity upon the delay of judgments.

III. We have vengeance taken upon the house of Saul for the turning away of God's wrath from the land, which, at present, smarted for his sin.

1. David, probably by divine direction, referred it to the Gibeonites themselves to prescribe what satisfaction should be given them for the wrong that had been done them, *v.* 3.

2. They desired that seven of Saul's posterity might be put to death, and David granted their demand. (1) They required no *silver, nor gold, v.* 4. The

JAMIESON, FAUSSET, BROWN — CHAPTER 21

VSS. 1-9. THE THREE YEARS' FAMINE FOR THE GIBEONITES CEASE BY HANGING SEVEN OF SAUL'S SONS. **1. the Lord answered, It is for Saul, and for his bloody house, because he slew the Gibeonites**—The sacred history has not recorded either the time or the reason of this massacre. Some think that they were sufferers in the atrocity perpetrated by Saul at Nob (I Sam. 22:19), where many of them may have resided as attendants of the priests; while others suppose it more probable that the attempt was made afterwards, with a view to regain the popularity he had lost throughout the nation by that execrable outrage. **2. in his zeal to the children of Israel and Judah**—Under pretense of a rigorous and faithful execution of the divine law regarding the extermination of the Canaanites, he set himself to expel or destroy those whom Joshua had been deceived into sparing. His real object seems to have been, that the possessions of the Gibeonites, being forfeited to the crown, might be divided among his own people (cf. I Sam. 22:7). At all events, his proceeding against this people was in violation of a solemn oath, and involving *national* guilt. The famine was, in the wise and just retribution of Providence, made a *national* punishment, since the Hebrews either assisted in the massacre, or did not interpose to prevent it; since they neither endeavored to repair the wrong, nor expressed any horror of it; and since a general protracted chastisement might have been indispensable to inspire a proper respect and protection to the Gibeonite remnant that survived.

ADAM CLARKE — CHAPTER 21

1. *Then there was a famine.* Of this famine we know nothing; it is not mentioned in any part of the history of David. *Because he slew the Gibeonites.* No such fact is mentioned in the life and transactions of Saul, nor is there any reference to it in any other part of Scripture.

2. *The remnant of the Amorites.* The Gibeonites were Hivites, not Amorites, as appears from Josh. xi. 19: but *Amorites* is a name often given to the Canaanites in general, Gen. xv. 16; Amos ii. 8; and elsewhere.

3. *Wherewith shall I make the atonement?* It is very strange that a choice of this kind should be left to such a people. Why not ask this of God himself?

MATTHEW HENRY

Gibeonites had now a fair opportunity to get a discharge from their servitude. But they did not insist on this; though the covenant was broken on the other side, it should not be broken on theirs. They were *Nethinim*, given to God and his people Israel, and they would not seem weary of the service. (2) They required no lives but of Saul's family. (3) They would not impose it upon David to do this execution: *Thou shalt not for us kill any man* (*v.* 4), but we will do it ourselves, *we will hang them up unto the Lord* (*v.* 6), that, if there were any hardship in it, they might bear the blame, and not David or his house. (4) They did not require this out of malice against Saul or his family (had they been revengeful, they would have moved it themselves long before), but out of love to the people of Israel, whom they saw plagued for the injury done to them. (5) The nomination of the persons they left to David, who took care to secure Mephibosheth for Jonathan's sake, that, while he was avenging the breach of one oath, he might not himself break another (*v.* 7). (6) The place, time, and manner, of their execution, all added to the solemnity of their being sacrificed to divine justice. [1] They were hanged up, as anathemas, under a peculiar mark of God's displeasure; for the law had said, *He that is hanged is accursed of God*, Deut. xxi. 23; Gal. iii. 13. [2] They were hanged up in Gibeah of Saul (*v.* 6), to show that it was for his sin that they died.

Verses 10–14

I. Saul's sons not only hanged, but hanged in chains, their dead bodies left hanging, and exposed, till the judgment ceased, which their death was to turn away, by the sending of rain upon the land. They died as sacrifices, and thus they were, in a manner, offered up, not consumed all at once by fire, but gradually by the air.

II. Their dead bodies watched by Rizpah, the mother of two of them, *v.* 10. It was a great affliction to her, now in her old age, to see her two sons, who, we may suppose, had been a comfort to her, and were likely to be the support of her declining years, cut off in this dreadful manner. None know what sorrows they are reserved for. She may not see them decently interred, but they shall be decently attended. She attempts not to violate the sentence passed upon them, that they should hang there till God sent rain; she neither steals nor forces away their dead bodies, though the divine law might have been cited to bear her out; but she patiently submits, pitches a tent of sackcloth near the gibbets, where, with her servants and friends, she protects the dead bodies from birds and beasts of prey. Thus she let the world know that her sons died, not for any sin of their own, not as stubborn and rebellious sons. But they died for their father's sin, and therefore her mind could not be alienated from them by their hard fate. Though there is no remedy, but they must die, yet they shall die pitied and lamented.

III. The solemn interment of their dead bodies, with the bones of Saul and Jonathan, in the burying-place of their family. David was so far from being displeased at what Rizpah had done that he was himself stirred up by it to do honour to the house of Saul, and to these branches of it among the rest; thus it appeared that it was not out of any personal disgust to the family that he delivered them up, but that he was obliged to do it for the public good. 1. He now bethought himself of removing the bodies of Saul and Jonathan from the place where the men of Jabesh-Gilead had decently, but privately and obscurely, interred them, *under a tree*, 1 Sam. xxxi. 12, 13. 2. With them he buried the bodies *of those that were hanged*; for, when God's anger was turned away, they were no longer to be looked upon as a curse, *v.* 13, 14. When *water dropped upon them out of heaven* (*v.* 10), that is, when God sent rain to water the earth, they were taken down, for then it appeared *that God was entreated for the land.*

Verses 15–22

The story of some conflicts with the Philistines, which happened, as it should seem, in the latter end of David's reign. Though he had so subdued them that they could not bring any great numbers into the field, yet, as long as they had any giants among them to be their champions, they took all occasions to disturb the peace of Israel.

I. David himself was engaged with one of the giants. The Philistines began the war yet again, *v.* 15. David, though old, desired not a writ of ease from the public service, but he *went down* in person to fight *against the Philistines*. But he found age had cut his hair, and, after a little toil, he *waxed faint*. His body could not keep pace with his mind. The champion of the Philistines was soon aware of his

JAMIESON, FAUSSET, BROWN

6. Let seven men of his sons be delivered unto us, and we will hang them up unto the Lord—The practice of the Hebrews, as of most Oriental nations, was to slay first, and afterwards to suspend on a gibbet, the body not being left hanging after sunset. The king could not refuse this demand of the Gibeonites, who, in making it, were only exercising their right as blood-avengers; and, although through fear and a sense of weakness they had not hitherto claimed satisfaction, yet now that David had been apprised by the oracle of the cause of the long-prevailing calamity, he felt it his duty to give the Gibeonites full satisfaction—hence their specifying the number seven—which was reckoned full and complete. And if it should seem unjust to make the descendants suffer for a crime which, in all probability, originated with Saul himself, yet his sons and grandsons might be the instruments of his cruelty, the willing and zealous executors of this bloody *raid*. **the king said, I will give them**—David cannot be charged with doing this as an indirect way or ridding himself of rival competitors for the throne, for those delivered up were only collateral branches of Saul's family, and never set up any claim to the sovereignty. Moreover, David was only granting the request of the Gibeonites as God had bidden him do. **8. the five sons of Michal the daughter of Saul whom she brought up for Adriel**—Merab, Michal's sister, was the wife of Adriel; but Michal adopted and brought up the boys under her care. **9. they hanged them in the hill before the Lord**—Deeming themselves not bound by the criminal law of Israel (Deut. 21:22, 23), their intention was to let the bodies hang until God, propitiated by this offering, should send rain upon the land, for the want of it had occasioned the famine. It was a heathen practice to gibbet men with a view of appeasing the anger of the gods in seasons of famine, and the Gibeonites, who were a remnant of the Amorites (vs. 2), though brought to the knowledge of the true God, were not, it seems, free from this superstition. God, in His providence, suffered the Gibeonites to ask and inflict so barbarous a retaliation, in order that the oppressed Gibeonites might obtain justice and some reparation of their wrongs, especially that the scandal brought on the name of the true religion by the violation of a solemn national compact might be wiped away from Israel, and that a memorable lesson should be given to respect treaties and oaths.

10, 11. RIZPAH'S KINDNESS UNTO THE DEAD. **10. Rizpah . . . took sackcloth, and spread it for her upon the rock**—She erected a tent near the spot, in which she and her servants kept watch, as the relatives of executed persons were wont to do, day and night, to scare the birds and beasts of prey away from the remains exposed on the low-standing gibbets.

12-22. DAVID BURIES THE BONES OF SAUL AND JONATHAN IN THEIR FATHER'S SEPULCHER. **12. David went and took the bones of Saul and the bones of Jonathan his son,** etc.—Before long, the descent of copious showers, or perhaps an order of the king, gave Rizpah the satisfaction of releasing the corpses from their ignominious exposure; and, incited by her pious example, David ordered the remains of Saul and his sons to be transferred from their obscure grave in Jabesh-gilead to an honorable interment in the family vault at Zelah or Zelzah (I Sam. 10:2), now Beit-jala.

15-22. Moreover the Philistines had yet war again with Israel—Although the Philistines had completely succumbed to the army of David, yet the appearance of any gigantic champions among them revived their courage and stirred them up to renewed inroads on the Hebrew territory. Four successive contests they provoked during the latter period of David's reign, in the first of which

ADAM CLARKE

6. *Seven men of his sons.* Meaning sons, grandsons, or other near branches of his family.

8. *Five sons of Michal . . . whom she brought up.* Michal, Saul's daughter, was never married to Adriel, but to David, and afterwards to Phaltiel; though it is here said "she bore," *yaledah*, not *brought up*, as we falsely translate it. But we learn from 1 Sam. xviii. 19 that Merab, one of Saul's daughters, was married to Adriel.

9. *In the beginning of barley harvest.* This happened in Judea about the vernal equinox, or the twenty-first of March.

10. *Rizpah . . . took sackcloth.* Who can read the account of Rizpah's maternal affection for her sons that were now hanged without feeling his mind deeply impressed with sorrow? *Until water dropped upon them.* Until the time of the autumnal rains, which in that country commence about October.

12. *Took the bones of Saul.* The reader will recollect that the men of Jabesh-gilead burned the bodies of Saul and his sons, and buried the remaining bones under a tree at Jabesh (see 1 Sam. xxxi. 12-13). These David might have digged up again, in order to bury them in the family sepulchre.

15. *Moreover the Philistines had yet war.* There is no mention of this war in the parallel place, 1 Chron. xx. 4, etc. *David waxed faint.* This circumstance is nowhere else mentioned.

MATTHEW HENRY

advantage, perceived that David's strength failed him, and, being himself strong and well-armed, *he thought to slay David*; but God was not in his thoughts, and therefore in that very day they all perished. David was rescued by Abishai, who came seasonably in to his relief, *v.* 17. When *Abishai succoured him*, gave him a cordial, it may be, to relieve his fainting spirits, or appeared as his second, *he* (namely, David, so I understand it) *smote the Philistine and killed him*; for it is said (*v.* 22) that David had himself a hand in slaying the giants. David fainted, but he did not flee; though his strength failed him, he bravely kept his ground, and then God sent him this help in the time of need. Christ, in his agonies, was strengthened by an angel. In spiritual conflicts, even strong saints sometimes wax faint; then Satan attacks them furiously; but those that stand their ground and resist him shall be relieved, and made more than conquerors.

II. The rest of the giants fell by the hand of David's servants. 1. Saph was slain by Sibbechai, one of David's worthies, *v.* 18. 1 Chron. xi. 29. 2. Another, who was brother to Goliath, was slain by Elhanan, who is mentioned *ch.* xxiii. 24. 3. Another, who was of very unusual bulk, who had more fingers and toes than other people (*v.* 20), and such an unparalleled insolence that, though he had seen the fall of other giants, yet he defied Israel, was slain by *Jonathan the son of Shimea*. Shimea had one son named *Jonadab* (2 Sam. xiii. 3), whom I should have taken for the same with this Jonathan, but that the former was noted for subtlety, the latter for bravery. These giants were probably the remains of the sons of Anak, who, though long feared, fell at last. It is folly for the strong man to *glory in his strength*. David's servants were no bigger nor stronger than other men; yet thus, by divine assistance, they mastered one giant after another. The most powerful enemies are often reserved for the last conflict. David began his glory with the conquest of one giant, and here concludes it with the conquest of four. Death is a Christian's last enemy, and a son of Anak; but, through him that triumphed for us, we hope to be more than conquerors at last, even over that enemy.

JAMIESON, FAUSSET, BROWN

the king ran so imminent a risk of his life that he was no longer allowed to encounter the perils of the battlefield.

ADAM CLARKE

16. *Being girded with a new sword.* As the word *sword* is not in the original, we may apply the term *new* to his armor in general. He had got new arms, a new coat of mail, or something that defended him well, and rendered him very formidable; or it may mean a strong or sharp sword.

17. *That thou quench not the light of Israel.* David is here considered as the lamp by which all Israel was guided, and without whom all the nation must be involved in darkness. The lamp is the emblem of direction and support.

18. *A battle . . . at Gob.* Instead of *Gob*, several editions, and about forty of Kennicott's and De Rossi's MSS., have *nob;* but "Gezer" is the name in the parallel place, 1 Chron. xx. 4.

19. *Elhanan the son of Jaare-oregim . . . slew . . . Goliath the Gittite.* Here is a most manifest corruption of the text, or gross mistake of the transcriber; David, not *Elhanan,* slew *Goliath.* In 1 Chron. xx. 5, the parallel place, it stands thus: "Elhanan the son of Jair slew Lahmi the brother of Goliath the Gittite, whose spear staff was like a weaver's beam." This is plain, and our translators have borrowed some words from Chronicles to make both texts agree. The corruption may be easily accounted for by considering that *oregim,* which signifies "weavers," has slipped out of one line into the other; and that *beith hallachmi,* the Bethlehemite, is corrupted from *eth Lachmi;* then the reading will be the same as in Chronicles.

MATTHEW HENRY — CHAPTER 22

Verse 1

I. It has often been the lot of God's people to have many enemies, and to be in imminent danger of falling into their hands. David was a man after God's heart, but not after men's heart: many were those that hated him, and sought his ruin. Let not those whom God loves marvel if the world hate them.

II. Those that trust God in the way of duty shall find him a present help to them in their greatest dangers. We shall never be delivered from all our enemies till we get to heaven; and to that heavenly kingdom God will preserve all that are his, 2 Tim. iv. 18.

III. Those that have received many signal mercies from God ought to give him the glory of them. Every new mercy in our hand should put a new song into our mouth, even praises to our God.

IV. We ought to be speedy in our thankful returns to God: *In the day that God delivered him he sang this song*.

Verses 2–51

I. How David adores God, and gives him the glory of his infinite perfections. There is none like him, nor any to be compared with him (*v.* 32): *Who is God, save the Lord?* All others that are adored as deities are counterfeits and pretenders. *Who is a rock, save our God?* They are dead, but *the Lord liveth*, *v.* 47. God will finish his work, and his word is tried, and what we may trust.

II. How he triumphs in the interest he has in this God, and his relation to him, which he lays down as the foundation of all the benefits he has received from him: *He is my God*; as such he cries to him (*v.* 7), and cleaves to him (*v.* 22); "and, if *my God*, then *my rock*" (*v.* 2), that is "my strength and my power (*v.* 33), the rock under which I take shelter, the rock on which I build my hope," *v.* 3. Whatever is my strength and support, he is *the God of the rock of my salvation* (*v.* 47). David often hid himself in a rock (1 Sam. xxiv. 2), but God was his chief hiding-place. "He is my fortress, in which I am safe and think myself so—*my high tower*, or stronghold, in which I am out of the reach of real evils—the *tower of salvation* (*v.* 51), which can never be scaled, nor battered, nor undermined. Salvation itself saves me. Christ is spoken of as the *horn of salvation* in the house

JAMIESON, FAUSSET, BROWN — CHAPTER 22

VSS. 1-51. DAVID'S PSALM OF THANKSGIVING FOR GOD'S POWERFUL DELIVERANCE AND MANIFOLD BLESSINGS. The song contained in this chapter is the same as the eighteenth Psalm, where the full commentary will be given. It may be sufficient simply to remark that Jewish writers have noticed a great number of very minute variations in the language of the song as recorded here, from that embodied in the Book of Psalms—which may be accounted for by the fact that this, the first copy of the poem, was carefully revised and altered by David afterwards, when it was set to the music of the tabernacle. This inspired ode was manifestly the effusion of a mind glowing with the highest fervor of piety and gratitude, and it is full of the noblest imagery that is to be found within the range even of sacred poetry. It is David's grand tribute of thanksgiving for deliverance from his numerous and powerful enemies, and establishing him in the power and glory of the kingdom.

ADAM CLARKE — CHAPTER 22

1. *David spake unto the Lord the words of this song.* This is the same in substance, and almost in words, with Psalms xviii; and therefore the exposition of it must be reserved till it occurs in its course in that book, with the exception of a very few observations.

KEIL–DELITZSCH:

David calls God my rock and my castle in Ps. 31:4 as well (cf. Ps. 71:4). The two epithets are borrowed from the natural character of Palestine, where steep and almost inaccessible rocks afford protection to the fugitive, as David had often found at the time when Saul was pursuing him (1 Sam. 24:23; 22:5). But while David took refuge in rocks, he placed his hopes of safety not in their inaccessible character, but in God the Lord, the eternal spiritual rock, whom he could see in the earthly rock, so that he called Him his true castle. "My deliverer to me" gives the real explanation of the foregoing figures. The "to me" is omitted in Ps. 18:2, and only serves to strengthen the suffix, "my, yea *my* deliverer." "*My Rock-God,*" equivalent to God who is my Rock; this is formed after Deut. 32:4, where Moses calls the Lord the Rock of Israel because of His unchangeable faithfulness; for *zur*, a rock, is a figure used to represent immoveable firmness.

—*Commentary on the Old Testament*

MATTHEW HENRY

of David, Luke i. 69. "Am I burdened, and ready to sink? *The Lord is my stay* (*v.* 19), by whom I am supported. Am I in the dark, benighted, at a loss? *Thou art my lamp, O Lord!* to show me my way, and thou wilt dispel *my darkness*," *v.* 29. If we sincerely take the Lord for our God, all this, and much more, he will be to us, all we need and can desire.

III. What improvement he makes of his interest in God. If he be mine, 1. *In him will I trust* (*v.* 3). 2. *On him I will call* (*v.* 4), for *he is worthy to be praised.* 3. *To him will I give thanks* (*v.* 50), and that publicly.

IV. The full account he gives to others, of the great things God had done for him. This takes up most of the song. He gives God the glory both of his deliverances and of his successes.

1. He magnifies the great salvations God had wrought for him. To magnify the salvation, he observes,

(1) That the danger was very great and threatening out of which he was delivered. Men *rose up against him* (*v.* 40, 49) that *hated him* (*v.* 41), a *violent man* (*v.* 49), namely, Saul, who was malicious and vigorous in his pursuit. This is expressed figuratively, *v.* 5, 6. So violently did the waves of death beat upon him, so strongly did the cords and snares of death hold him, that he could not help himself, any more than a man in the grave can.

(2) That his deliverance was an answer to prayer, *v.* 7. He has here left us a good example, when we are in distress, to cry unto God with importunity, as children in a fright cry to their parents.

(3) That God appeared in a singular and extraordinary manner for him and against his enemies. The expressions are borrowed from the descent of the divine Majesty upon Mount Sinai, *v.* 8, 9, &c.

(4) That God manifested his particular favour and kindness to him in these deliverances (*v.* 20). *He delivered me, because he delighted in me.* The deliverance came not from common providence, but covenant-love. Herein he was a type of Christ, whom God upheld because he *delighted in him,* Isa. xlii. 1, 2.

2. He magnifies the great successes God had crowned him with. He had not only preserved but prospered him. He was blessed, (1) With liberty and enlargement. He was *brought into a large place* (*v.* 20). (2) With military skill, and strength, and swiftness. Though he was bred up to the crook, he was well instructed in the arts of war and qualified for the toils and perils of it. God, having called him to fight his battles, qualified him for the service. (3) With victory over his enemies, not only Saul and Absalom, but the Philistines, Moabites, Ammonites, Syrians, and other neighbouring nations, whom he subdued and made tributaries to Israel. His wonderful victories are here described, *v.* 38–43. (4) With advancement to honour and power. God *made his way perfect* (*v.* 33), gave him success in all his undertakings, *set him upon his high places* (*v.* 34), denoting both safety and dignity. God's gentleness, his grace and tender mercy, *made him great* (*v.* 36).

V. The comfortable reflections he makes upon his own integrity, which God, by those wonderful deliverances, had graciously owned and witnessed to, *v.* 21–25. He means especially his integrity with reference to Saul and Ish-bosheth, Absalom and Sheba, and those who either opposed his coming to the crown or endeavoured to dethrone him. They falsely accused him and misrepresented him, but he had the testimony of his conscience for him that he was not an ambitious aspiring man, a false and bloody man, as they called him. His conscience witnessed for him, 1. That he had made the word of God his rule, and had kept to it, *v.* 32. Wherever he was, God's judgments were before him as his guide; whithersoever he went, he took his religion along with him. 2. That he had carefully avoided the by-paths of sin. He had not wickedly departed from his God. He could not say but that he had taken some false steps, but he had not deserted God, nor forsaken his way. Sins of infirmity he could not acquit himself from, but the grace of God had kept him from presumptuous sins. David reflected with more comfort upon his victories over his own iniquity than upon his conquest of Goliath and all the hosts of the uncircumcised Philistines. If a great man be a good man, his goodness will be much more his satisfaction than his greatness.

VI. The comfortable prospects he has of God's further favour. As he looks back, so he looks forward, with pleasure, and assures himself of the kindness God has in store for all the saints, for himself, and also for his seed.

1. For all good people, *v.* 26–28. He takes occasion here to lay down God's procedure with the children of men:

JAMIESON, FAUSSET, BROWN

KEIL–DELITZSCH:

In verse 4, David sums up the contents of his psalm of thanksgiving in a general sentence of experience, which may be called the theme of the psalm, for it embraces "the result of the long life which lay behind him, so full of dangers and deliverances." "The praised one," an epithet applied to God, which occurs several times in the Psalms (48:2; 96:4; 113:3; 145:3). It is in apposition to Jehovah, and is placed first for the sake of emphasis: "I invoke Jehovah as the praised one." In verse 5 we have the commencement of the account of the deliverances out of great tribulations, which David had experienced at the hand of God.—*Commentary on the Old Testament*

F. B. MEYER:

"Thy gentleness hath made me great" (2 Sam. 22:36). The triumph of God's gentle goodness will be our song forever. In those far distant ages, when we look back on our earthly course, as a grown man on his boyhood, and when the words of this psalm shall express our glad emotions, we shall recognize that the hand which brought us thither was as gentle as our mother's; and that the things we craved, but failed to receive, were withheld by His gentle goodness. Our history tells what gentleness will do.

The Apostle besought the Corinthian converts by the gentleness of Christ (2 Cor. 10:1). Though there were abuses among them that seemed to call for stringent dealing, he felt that they could be best removed by the gentle love which he had learned from the heart of Christ. The wisdom which is from above is gentle as well as pure; and in dealing with the sin that chokes our growth, it is probable that gentleness will do more than severity. The gentleness of the nurse that cherishes her children; of the lover to her whom he cherishes above himself; of the infinite love which bears and endures to the uttermost—is the furnace before which the foul ingredients of our hearts are driven never to return. We might brave the lion; we are vanquished by the Lamb. We could withstand the scathing look of scorn; but when the gentle Lord casts on us the look of ineffable tenderness, we go out to weep bitterly.

That He had borne with us so lovingly; that He has filled our lives with mercy even when compelled to correct; that He has never altered in his tender behavior towards us; that He has returned our rebuffs and slights with meekness and forbearance; that He has never wearied of us—this is an everlasting tribute to the gentleness that makes great.—*Great Verses Through the Bible*

ADAM CLARKE

5. *When the waves of death compassed me.* Though in a primary sense many of these things belong to David, yet generally and fully they belong to the Messiah alone.

11. *He rode upon a cherub, and did fly . . . he was seen upon the wings of the wind.* In the original of this sublime passage, sense and sound are astonishingly well connected. The clap of the wing, the agitation and rush through the air are expressed here in a very extraordinary manner.

MATTHEW HENRY

(1) That he will do good to those that are upright in their hearts. [1] God's mercy and grace will be the joy of those that are merciful and gracious. [2] God's uprightness, his justice and faithfulness, will be the joy of those that are upright, just, and faithful, both towards God and man. [3] God's purity and holiness will be the joy of those that are pure and holy. On the other hand,

(2) That those who turn aside to crooked ways he will *lead forth with the workers of iniquity*, as he says in another psalm.

2. For himself. He foresaw that his conquests and kingdom would be yet further enlarged, *v.* 45, 46.

3. For his seed: He *showeth mercy to his Messiah* (*v.* 51), not only to David himself, but to that seed of his for evermore. David was himself anointed of God, therefore he doubted not but God would show mercy to him, that mercy which he had promised not to take from him nor from his posterity (*ch.* vii. 15, 16); on that promise he depends, with an eye to Christ, who alone is his *seed for evermore*, whose throne and kingdom still continue, and will to the end. Thus all his joys and all his hopes terminate, as ours should, in the great Redeemer.

JAMIESON, FAUSSET, BROWN

KEIL–DELITZSCH:

The grace which the Lord had shown to David was so great that the praise thereof could not be restricted to the narrow limits of Israel. With the dominion of David over the nations, there spread also the knowledge, and with this the praise, of the Lord who had given him the victory. Paul was therefore perfectly justified in quoting the verse before us (v. 50) in Rom. 16:9, along with Deut. 32:43 and Ps. 117:1, as a proof that the salvation of God was intended for the Gentiles also. The king whose salvation the Lord had magnified was not David as an individual, but David and his seed forever—that is to say, the royal family of David which culminated in Christ. David could thus sing praises upon the ground of the promise which he had received (7:12–16), and which is repeated almost verbatim in the last clause of verse 51.

—*Commentary on the Old Testament*

ADAM CLARKE

MATTHEW HENRY

CHAPTER 23

Verses 1–7

The last will and testament of king David, after he had settled the crown upon Solomon and his treasures upon the temple which was to be built.

I. He is described, 1. By the meanness of his origin: He was *the son of Jesse*. 2. The height of his elevation: He *was raised up on high*, as one favoured of God, and designed for something great, raised up as a prince, and as a prophet, to see further; for, (1) He was *the anointed of the God of Jacob*, and so was serviceable to the people of God in their civil interests, the protection of their country and the administration of justice among them. (2) He was *the sweet psalmist of Israel*, and so was serviceable to them in their religious exercises.

II. It is an account of his communion with God. 1. What God said to him both for his direction and for his encouragement as a king, and to be, in like manner, of use to his successors.

(1) Who spoke: *The Spirit of the Lord, the God of Israel*, and *the Rock of Israel*, which some think is an intimation of the Trinity of persons in the Godhead—the Father *the God of Israel*, the Son *the Rock of Israel*, and *the Spirit* proceeding from the Father and the Son, *who spoke by the prophets*, and particularly by David. David here avows his divine inspiration, that in his psalms, and in this composition, *The Spirit of God spoke by him*. This puts an honour upon the book of Psalms, and recommends them to our use in our devotions, that they are words which the Holy Ghost teaches.

(2) What was spoken. Here seems to be a distinction made between what the Spirit of God spoke *by* David, which includes all his psalms, and what the Rock of Israel spoke *to* David, which concerned himself and his family. Those whose office it is to teach others their duty must be sure to learn and do their own. Now that which is here said (*v.* 3, 4) may be considered, [1] With application to David, and his royal family. And so here is, *First*, The duty of magistrates enjoined them. When a king was spoken to from God he was not to be complimented with the height of his dignity and the extent of his power, but to be told his duty. *He must be just, ruling in the fear of God*; and so must all inferior magistrates in their places. Let rulers remember that they rule over men—not over beasts. They rule over men that have their follies and infirmities, and therefore must be borne with. It is not enough that they do no wrong, but they must not suffer wrong to be done. They must rule in the fear of God. They must also endeavour to promote the fear of God (that is, the practice of religion) among those over whom they rule. *He that* rules *in the fear of God shall be as the light of the morning*, *v.* 4. Light is sweet and pleasant, and he that does his duty shall have the comfort of it; his rejoicing will be the testimony of his conscience. Light is bright, and a good prince is illustrious; his justice and piety will be his honour. Light is a blessing, nor are there any greater and more extensive blessings to the public than princes that *rule in the fear of God*. As *the light of the morning*, which is most welcome after the darkness of the night. See Is. lxviii, 8, which were also some of the last words of David, and seem to refer to those recorded here. [2] With application to Christ, the Son of David, and then it must all be taken as a prophecy, and the original will bear it: *There shall be a ruler among men*, or over men, that *shall be just*, and *shall rule in the fear of*

JAMIESON, FAUSSET, BROWN

CHAPTER 23

VSS. 1-7. DAVID PROFESSES HIS FAITH IN GOD'S PROMISES. **1. Now these be the last words of David**—Various opinions are entertained as to the precise meaning of this statement, which, it is obvious, proceeded from the compiler or collector of the sacred canon. Some think that, as there is no division of chapters in the Hebrew Scriptures, this introduction was intended to show that what follows is no part of the king's poetical compositions; while still others consider it the last of his utterances as an inspired writer. **raised up on high**—from an obscure family and condition to a throne. **the anointed of the God of Jacob**—chosen to be king by the special appointment of that God, to whom, by virtue of an ancient covenant, the people or Israel owed all their peculiar destiny and distinguished privileges. **the sweet psalmist of Israel**—i.e., delightful, highly esteemed. **2. The Spirit of the Lord spake by me**—Nothing can more clearly show that all that is excellent in spirit, beautiful in language, or grand in prophetic imagery, which the Psalms of David contain, were owing, not to his superiority in natural talents or acquired knowledge, but to the suggestion and dictates of God's Spirit. **3. the Rock of Israel**—This metaphor, which is commonly applied by the sacred writers to the Almighty, was very expressive to the minds of the Hebrew people. Their national fortresses, in which they sought security in war, were built on high and inaccessible rocks.

spake to me—either preceptively, giving the following counsels respecting the character of an upright ruler in Israel, or prophetically, concerning David and his royal dynasty, and the great Messiah, of whom many think this is a prophecy, rendering the words, "he that ruleth"—"there shall be a ruler over men."

ADAM CLARKE

CHAPTER 23

1. *These be the last words of David.* I suppose the "last poetical composition" is here intended. He might have spoken many words after these in prose, but none in verse. The words of this song contain a glorious prediction of the Messiah's kingdom and conquests, in highly poetic language. *The sweet psalmist of Israel.* This character not only belonged to him as the finest poet in Israel, but as the finest and most divine poet of the whole Christian world. The *sweet psalmist of Israel* has been the sweet Psalmist of every part of the habitable world where religion and piety have been held in reverence.

2. *The Spirit of the Lord spake by me.* Hence the matter of his writing came by direct and immediate inspiration. *His word was in my tongue.* Hence the words of this writing were as directly inspired as the matter.

3. *The Rock of Israel.* The Fountain whence Israel was derived.

He that ruleth over men must be just. More literally, "He that ruleth in man is the just one"; or, "The just one is the ruler among men." *Ruling in the fear of God.* It is by God's fear that Jesus Christ rules the hearts of all His followers; and he who has not the fear of God before his eyes can never be a Christian.

MATTHEW HENRY

God, that is, shall order the affairs of religion and divine worship according to his Father's will; and he shall be as *the light of the morning*, &c., for he is the light of the world, and *as the tender grass*, for he is the *branch of the Lord*, and the *fruit of the earth*, Isa. iv. 2. God, by the Spirit, gave David the foresight of this, to comfort him under the many calamities of his family and the melancholy prospects he had of the degeneracy of his seed.

2. What comfortable use he made of this which God spoke to him, and what were his devout meditations on it, by way of reply, *v.* 5.

(1) Trouble supposed: *Although my house be not so with God*, and *although he make it not to grow.* David's family was not so with God as is described (*v.* 3, 4), and as he could wish, not so good, not so happy; it had not been so while he lived; he foresaw it would not be so when he was gone, that his house would be neither so pious nor so prosperous as one might have expected the offspring of such a father to be. This was what David's heart was upon concerning his children, that they might be right with God, faithful to him and zealous for him.

(2) Comfort ensured: *Yet he hath made with me an everlasting covenant.* Whatever trouble a child of God may have the prospect of, still he has some comfort or other to balance it (2. Cor. iv. 8, 9). God has made a covenant of grace with us in Jesus Christ, and we are here told, *First*, That it is an *everlasting* covenant, from everlasting in the contrivance and counsel of it, and to everlasting in the continuance and consequences of it. *Secondly*, That it is *ordered*, well ordered in all things, admirably well, to advance the glory of God and the honour of the Mediator, together with the holiness and comfort of believers. *Thirdly*, That the promised mercies are sure on the performance of the conditions. *Fourthly*, That it is *all our salvation.* Nothing but this will save us, and this is sufficient: it is this only upon which our salvation depends. *Fifthly*, That therefore it must be *all our desire.*

3. Here is the doom of the sons of Belial read, *v.* 6, 7. They shall be thrust away as thorns—rejected, abandoned. Now this is intended, [1] As a direction to magistrates to use their power for the punishing and suppressing of wickedness. Let them *thrust away the sons of Belial*; see Ps. ci. 8. Or, [2] As a caution to magistrates, and particularly to David's sons and successors, to see that they be not themselves sons of Belial (as too many of them were), for then neither the dignity of their place nor their relation to David would secure them from being thrust away by the righteous judgments of God.

Verses 8–38

I. The catalogue which his historian has here left upon record of the great soldiers that were in David's time is intended, 1. For the honour of David, who trained them up in the arts and exercises of war, and set them an example of conduct and courage. 2. For the honour of those worthies themselves, who were instrumental to bring David to the crown, settle and protect him in the throne, and enlarge his conquests. 3. To excite those that come after to a generous emulation. 4. To show how much religion contributes to the inspiring of men with true courage. David, both by his psalms and by his offerings for the service of the temple, greatly promoted piety among the grandees of the kingdom (1 Chron. xxix. 6), and, when they became famous for piety, they became famous for bravery.

II. Now these mighty men are here divided into three ranks:

1. The first three, who had done the greatest exploits and thereby gained the greatest reputation—Adino (*v.* 8), Eleazar (*v.* 9, 10), and Shammah (*v.* 11, 12). The exploits of this brave triumvirate are here recorded. They signalized themselves in the wars of Israel against their enemies, especially the Philistines. (1) Adino slew 800 at once with his spear. (2) Eleazar defied the Philistines, as they by Goliath, had defied Israel, but with better success and greater bravery: for when the men of Israel had gone away, he not only kept his ground, but *arose, and smote the Philistines*, on whom God struck a terror equal to the courage with which this great hero was inspired. His hand was weary, and yet it clave to his sword; as long as he had any strength remaining he held his weapon and followed his blow. Thus, in the service of God, we should keep up the willingness and resolution of the spirit, notwithstanding the weakness and weariness of the flesh—faint, yet pursuing (Judg. viii. 4), the hand weary, yet not quitting the sword. (3) Shammah met with a party of the enemy, that were foraging, and routed them, *v.* 11, 12. But observe, both concerning this exploit and the former, it is here said, *The Lord wrought a great*

JAMIESON, FAUSSET, BROWN

4. as the tender grass springing out of the earth by clear shining after rain—Little patches of grass are seen rapidly springing up in Palestine after rain; and even where the ground has been long parched and bare, within a few days or hours after the enriching showers begin to fall, the face of the earth is so renewed that it is covered over with a pure fresh mantle of green.

5. Although my house be not so with God, yet he hath made with me an everlasting covenant, ordered in all things and sure—"the light of the morning," i.e., the beginning of David's kingdom, was unlike the clear brilliant dawn of an Eastern day but was overcast by many black and threatening clouds; neither he nor his family had been like the tender grass springing up from the ground and flourishing by the united influences of the sun and rain; but rather like the grass that withereth and is prematurely cut down. The meaning is: although David's house had not flourished in an uninterrupted course of worldly prosperity and greatness, according to his hopes; although great crimes and calamities had beclouded his family history; some of the most promising branches of the royal tree had been cut down in his lifetime and many of his successors should suffer in like manner for their personal sins; although many reverses and revolutions may overtake his race and his kingdom, yet it was to him a subject of the highest joy and thankfulness that God will inviolably maintain His covenant with his family, until the advent of his greatest Son, the Messiah, who was the special object of his desire, and the author of his salvation.

6. But the sons of Belial shall be all of them as thorns—i.e., the wicked enemies and persecutors of this kingdom of righteousness. They resemble those prickly, thorny plants which are twisted together, whose spires point in every direction, and which are so sharp and strong that they cannot be touched or approached without danger; but hard instruments and violent means must be taken to destroy or uproot them. So God will remove or destroy all who are opposed to this kingdom.

8-39. A CATALOGUE OF HIS MIGHTY MEN. **8. These be the names of the mighty men whom David had**—This verse should be translated thus: He who sits in the seat of the Tachmonite (i.e., of Jashobeam the Hachmonite), who was chief among the captains, the same is Adino the Eznite; he lift up his spear against eight hundred, whom he slew at one time. The text is corrupt in this passage; the number eight hundred should be three hundred [DAVIDSON'S HERM.]. Under Joab he was chief or president of the council of war. The first or highest order was composed of him and his two colleagues, Eleazar and Shammah. Eleazar seems to have been left to fight the Philistines alone; and on his achieving the victory, they returned to the spoil.

In like manner Shammah was left to stand alone in his glory, when the Lord, by him, wrought a great victory. It is not very easy to determine whether the exploits that are afterwards described were performed by the first or the second three.

ADAM CLARKE

4. *He shall be as the light of the morning.* This verse is very obscure, for it does not appear from it who the person is of whom the prophet speaks. As the Messiah seems to be the whole subject of these last words of David, He is probably the Person intended. *As the tender grass.* The effects of this shining, and of the rays of His grace, shall be like the shining of the sun upon the young grass or corn, after a plentiful shower of rain.

5. *Although my house be not so with God.* Instead of *ken*, "so," read *kun*, "established"; and let the whole verse be considered as an interrogation, including a positive assertion, and the sense will be at once clear and consistent: "For is not my house (family) established with God; because He hath made with me an everlasting covenant, ordered in all, and preserved? For this (He) is all my salvation, and all my desire, although He make it (or him) not to spring up." All is sure relative to my spiritual successor, though he do not as yet appear; the covenant is firm, and it will spring forth in due time.

6. *But the sons of Belial shall be all of them as thorns.* There is no word in the text for *sons;* it is simply *Belial*, the "good-for-nothing man," and may here refer—first to Saul, and secondly to the enemies of our Lord.

8. *These be the names of the mighty men.* This chapter should be collated with the parallel place, 1 Chronicles xi. *The Tachmonite that sat in the seat.* Literally and properly, "Jashobeam the Hachmonite." See 1 Chron. xi. 11. *The same was Adino the Eznite.* This is a corruption for *he lift up his spear* (see 1 Chron. xi. 11). *Eight hundred, whom he slew at one time.* "Three hundred" is the reading in Chronicles, and seems to be the true one. The word *chalal*, which we translate "slain," should probably be translated "soldiers," as in the Septuagint; he withstood "three hundred soldiers" at one time.

9. *When they defied the Philistines that were there gathered.* This is supposed to refer to the war in which David slew Goliath.

11. *A piece of ground full of lentiles.* In 1 Chron. xi. 13 it is "a parcel of ground full of barley." There is probably a mistake of *adashim*, "lentiles," for *seorim*, "barley," or vice versa. Some think there were both *lentiles* and *barley* in the field, and that a marauding

MATTHEW HENRY

victory.

2. The next three were distinguished from, and dignified above, the thirty, but attained not to the first three, *v.* 23. Of this second triumvirate two only are named, Abishai and Benaiah, whom we have often met with in the story of David.

(1) A brave action of these three in conjunction. They attended David in his troubles in the cave of Adullam (*v.* 13), suffered with him, and therefore were afterwards preferred by him. When David and his brave men who attended him, who had acted so vigorously against the Philistines, were driven to shelter themselves in caves and strongholds, the Philistines put a garrison even in Bethlehem itself, *v.* 13, 14. [1] How earnestly David longed for the water of the well of Bethlehem. It was harvest-time; the weather was hot; he was thirsty; perhaps good water was scarce, and therefore he earnestly wished, "O that I could but have one draught of the water of the well of Bethlehem!" With the water of that well he had often refreshed himself when he was a youth. Other water might quench his thirst as well, but he had a fancy for that above any. [2] How bravely his three mighty men, Abishai, Benaiah, and another not named, ventured through the camp of the Philistines, upon the very mouth of danger, and fetched water from the well of Bethlehem, without David's knowledge, *v.* 16. How much they valued their prince, and with what pleasure they could run the greatest hazards and undergo the greatest hardships in his service! And shall not we covet to approve ourselves to our Lord Jesus by a ready compliance with every intimation of his will given us by his word, Spirit, and providence? How little they feared the Philistines! [3] How self-denyingly David, when he had this far-fetched dear-bought water, *poured it out before the Lord*, *v.* 17. Thus he would cross his own foolish fancy, and punish himself for entertaining and indulging it. Thus he would honour God and give glory to him. The water purchased at this rate he thought too precious for his own drinking and fit only to be poured out to God as a drink-offering. Bishop Patrick speaks of some who think that David hereby showed that it was not material water he longed for, but the Messiah, who had the water of life, who, he knew, should be born at Bethlehem, which the Philistines therefore should not be able to destroy.

(2) The brave actions of two of them on other occasions. Abishai slew 300 men at once, *v.* 18, 19. Benaiah did many great things. [1] He slew two Moabites that were lion-like men, so bold and strong, so fierce and furious. [2] He slew a lion in a pit, either in his own defence, as Samson, or perhaps in kindness to the country, a lion that had done mischief. It being in a time of snow, he was more stiff and the lion more fierce and ravenous, and yet he mastered him. [3] He slew an Egyptian, on what occasion it is not said; he was well armed, but Benaiah attacked him with no other weapon than a walking staff, dexterously wrested his spear out of his hand, and slew him with it, *v.* 21. For these and similar exploits David preferred him to be captain of the life-guard or standing forces, *v.* 23.

3. Inferior to the second three, but of great note, were the thirty-one here mentioned by name, *v.* 24, &c. The surnames here given them are taken, as it should seem, from the places of their birth or habitation, as many surnames with us originally were. From all parts of the nation, the most wise and valiant were picked up to serve the king. Several of those who are here named we find captains of the twelve courses which David appointed, one for each month in the year, 1 Chron. xxvii.

Christ, the Son of David, has his worthies too, who, like David's, are influenced by his example, fight his battles against the spiritual enemies of his kingdom, and in his strength are more than conquerors. Christ's apostles were his immediate attendants, did and suffered great things for him, and at length came to reign with him. They are mentioned with honour in the New Testament, as these in the Old, especially, Rev. xxi. 14. Nay, all the good soldiers of Jesus Christ have their names better preserved than even these worthies have; for they are written in heaven.

JAMIESON, FAUSSET, BROWN

15. the well of Bethlehem—An ancient cistern, with four or five holes in the solid rock, at about ten minutes' distance to the north of the eastern corner of the hill of Bethlehem, is pointed out by the natives as Bir-Daoud; that is, David's well. Dr. ROBINSON doubts the identity of the well; but others think that there are no good grounds for doing so. Certainly, considering this to be the ancient well, Bethlehem must have once extended ten minutes further to the north, and must have lain in times of old, not as now, on the summit, but on the northern rise of the hill; for the well is *by* or (I Chron. 11:7) *at* the gate. I find in the description of travellers, that the common opinion is, that David's captains had come from the southeast, in order to obtain, at the risk of their lives, the so-much-longed-for water; while it is supposed that David himself was then in the great cave that is not far to the southeast of Bethlehem; which cave is generally held to have been that of Adullam. But (Josh. 15:35) Adullam lay "in the valley"; that is, in the undulating plain at the western base of the mountains of Judea and consequently to the south-west of Bethlehem. Be this as it may, David's *men* had in any case to break through the host of the Philistines, in order to reach the well; and the position of Bir-Daoud agrees well with this [VAN DE VELDE].

19. the first three—The mighty men or champions in David's military staff were divided into three classes—the highest, Jashobeam, Eleazar, and Shammah; the second class, Abishai, Benaiah, and Asahel; and the third class, the thirty, of which Asahel was the chief.

There are thirty-one mentioned in the list, including Asahel; and these added to the two superior orders make thirty-seven. Two of them, we know, were already dead; viz., Asahel and Uriah; and if the dead, at the drawing up of the list, amounted to seven, then we might suppose a legion of honor, consisting of the definite number thirty, where the vacancies, when they occurred, were replaced by fresh appointments.

ADAM CLARKE

party of the Philistines came to destroy or carry them off, and these worthies defeated the whole, and saved the produce of the field. This is not unlikely.

13. *And three of the thirty.* The word *shalishim,* which we translate *thirty,* probably signifies an office or particular description of men. Of these *shalishim* we have here thirty-seven, and it can scarcely be said with propriety that we have thirty-seven out of thirty; and besides, in the parallel place, 1 Chronicles xi, there are sixteen added. The captains over Pharaoh's chariots are termed *shalishim,* Exod. xiv. 7. *The Philistines pitched in the valley of Rephaim.* This is the same war which is spoken of in chap. v. 17, etc.

16. *Poured it out unto the Lord.* To make libations, both of water and of wine, was a frequent custom among the heathen.

20. *Two lionlike men of Moab.* Some think that two real lions are meant; some that they were two savage, gigantic men; others, that two fortresses are meant. The words may signify, as the Targum has rendered it, "The two princes of Moab."

21. *He slew an Egyptian.* This man in 1 Chron. xi. 23 is stated to have been five cubits high, about seven feet six inches. *He went down to him with a staff.* I have known men who, with a staff only for their defense, could render the sword of the best-practiced soldier of no use to him.

23. *David set him over his guard.* The Vulgate renders this, "David made him his privy counsellor"; or according to the Hebrew, "He put him to his ears," i.e., confided his secrets to him.

24. *Asahel . . . was one of the thirty.* Asahel was one of those officers, or troops, called the *shalishim.* This Asahel, brother of Joab, was the same that was killed by Abner, chap. ii. 23.

25. *Shammah the Harodite.* There are several varieties in the names of the following *shalishim;* which may be seen by comparing these verses with 1 Chron. xi. 27.

39. *Uriah the Hittite: thirty and seven in all.* To these the author of 1 Chron. xi. 41 adds Zabad son of Ahlai.

MATTHEW HENRY

CHAPTER 24

Verses 1–9

I. The orders which David gave to Joab to number the people of Israel and Judah, *v.* 1, 2. Two things here seem strange:—1. The sinfulness of this. What harm was there in it? (1) Some think the fault was that he numbered those that were under twenty years old if they were but of stature and strength able to bear arms, and that this was the reason why this account was not enrolled, because it was illegal, 1 Chron. xxvii. 23, 24. (2) Others think the fault was that he did not require the half-shekel, which was to be paid for the service of the sanctuary whenever the people were numbered, as a *ransom for their souls,* Exod. xxx. 12. (3) Others think that he did it with a design to impose a tribute upon them for himself, to be put into his treasury. But nothing of this appears, nor was David ever a raiser of taxes. (4) This was the fault, that he had no orders from God to do it. (5) Some think that it was an affront to the ancient promise which God made to Abraham, that his seed should be innumerable as the dust of the earth; it savoured of distrust of that promise. (6) That which was the worst thing in numbering the people was that David did it in the pride of his heart, which was Hezekiah's sin in showing his treasures to the ambassadors. [1] It was a proud conceit of his own greatness in having the command of so numerous a people. [2] It was a proud confidence in his own strength. By publishing among the nations the number of his people, he thought to appear the more formidable.

2. The spring from which it is here said to arise is yet more strange, *v.* 1. It is not strange that *the anger of the Lord should be kindled against Israel.* But that, in this displeasure, he should move David to number the people is very strange. We are sure that God is not the author of sin; he tempts no man: we are told (1 Chron. xxi. 1) that *Satan provoked David to number Israel.* Satan, as an enemy, suggested it for a sin, as he put it into the heart of Judas to betray Christ. God, as righteous Judge, permitted it, with a design, from this sin of David, that princes may from these instances learn, when the judgments of God are abroad, to suspect that their sins are the ground of the controversy, and may therefore repent and reform themselves.

II. The opposition which Joab made to these orders. Even he was aware of David's folly and vain-glory in this design. There was no occasion to tax them, nor to enlist them, nor to make any distribution of them. They were all easy and happy; and Joab wished both that their number might increase and that the king, though old, might live to see their increase, and have the satisfaction of it. "*But why doth my lord the king delight in this thing?* What need is there of doing it?" *Pauperis est numerare pecus—Leave it to the poor to count their flocks.* Joab was aware of David's vanity herein, but he himself was not.

III. The orders executed notwithstanding. *The king's word prevailed, v.* 4. Joab, according to order, applied himself with some reluctancy to this unpleasing task, and took the captains of the host to help him. The sum total was, at length, brought to the king at Jerusalem, *v.* 9. Whether the numbers answered David's expectation or no we are not told, nor whether the account fed his pride or mortified it.

Verses 10–17

I. Here is David's penitent reflection upon and confession of his sin in numbering the people. When the account was finished and laid before him, that very night his conscience was awakened. 1. He was convinced of his sin: *His heart smote him* before the prophet came to him (I think it should not be read *for* (*v.* 11), but *and when David was up,* so it is in the original), his conscience showed him the evil of what he had done. 2. He confessed it to God and begged earnestly for the forgiveness of it. He owned that he had *done foolishly, very foolishly,* because he had done it in the pride of his heart.

II. The just and necessary correction which he suffered for this sin, David had been full of tossings to and fro all night under the sense of his sin, *and he arose in the morning* designing to speak with Gad his seer concerning it. God directed the prophet Gad what to say to him (*v.* 11),

1. Three things are taken for granted, (1) That David must be corrected for his fault. Of the seven things that God hates, pride is the first, Prov. vi. 17. (2) The punishment must answer to the sin. (3) It must be such a punishment as the people must have a large share in, *for God's anger was kindled against Israel, v.* 1. Though it was David's sin that immediately opened the sluice, the sins of the people all contributed to the deluge.

JAMIESON, FAUSSET, BROWN

CHAPTER 24

Vss. 1-9. David Numbers the People. **1. again the anger of the Lord was kindled against Israel, and he moved David against them to say, Go, number Israel and Judah**—"Again" carries us back to the former tokens of His wrath in the three years' famine. God, though He cannot tempt any man (Jas. 1:13), is frequently described in Scripture as doing what He merely permits to be done; and so, in this case, He permitted Satan to tempt David. Satan was the active mover, while God only withdrew His supporting grace, and the great tempter prevailed against the king. (See Exod. 7:13; I Sam. 26:19; ch. 16:10; Ps. 105:25; Isa. 7:17, etc.) **The** order was given to Joab, who, though not generally restrained by religious scruples, did not fail to present, in strong terms (see on I Chron. 21:3), the sin and danger of this measure. He used every argument to dissuade the king from his purpose. The sacred history has not mentioned the objections which he and other distinguished officers urged against it in the council of David. But it expressly states that they were all overruled by the inflexible resolution of the king. **5. they passed over Jordan**—This census was taken first in the eastern parts of the Hebrew kingdom; and it would seem that Joab was accompanied by a military force, either to aid in this troublesome work, or to overawe the people who might display reluctance or opposition. **the river of Gad**—"Wady" would be a better term. **It** extends over a course estimated at about sixty miles. which, though in summer almost constantly dry, exhibits very evident traces of being swept over by an impetuous torrent in winter (see on Deut. 2:36). **6. the land of Tahtim-hodshi**—i.e., the land lately acquired; viz., that of the Hagrites conquered by Saul (I Chron. 5-10). The progress was northward. Thence they crossed the country, and, proceeding along the western coast to the southern extremities of the country, they at length arrived in Jerusalem, having completed the enumeration of the whole kingdom in the space of nine months and twenty days. **9. Joab gave up the sum of the number of the people unto the king**—The amount here stated, compared with I Chron. 21:5, gives a difference of 300,000. The discrepancy is only apparent, and admits of an easy reconciliation; thus (see I Chron. 27), there were twelve divisions of generals, who commanded monthly, and whose duty was to keep guard on the royal person, each having a body of troops consisting of 24,000 men, which, together, formed an army of 288,000; and as a separate detachment of 12,000 was attendant on the twelve princes of the twelve tribes mentioned in the same chapter, so both are equal to 300,000. These were not reckoned in this book, because they were in the actual service of the king as a regular militia. But I Chronicles 21:5 joins them to the rest, saying, "all those of Israel were one million, one hundred thousand"; whereas the author of Samuel, who reckons only the eight hundred thousand, does not say, "all those of Israel," but barely "and Israel were," etc. It must also be observed that, exclusive of the troops before mentioned, there was an army of observation on the frontiers of the Philistines' country, composed of 30,000 men, as appears from chapter 6:1; which, it seems, were included in the number of 500,000 of the people of Judah by the author of Samuel. But the author of Chronicles, who mentions only 470,000, gives the number of that tribe exclusive of those thirty thousand men, because they were not all of the tribe of Judah, and therefore he does not say, "all those of Judah," as he had said, "all those of Israel," but only, "and those of Judah." Thus both accounts may be reconciled [Davidson].

10-14. He, Having Three Plagues Propounded by Gad, Repents, and Chooses Three Days' Pestilence. **10. David's heart smote him after that he had numbered the people. And David said unto the Lord, I have sinned**—The act of numbering the people was not in itself sinful; for Moses did it by the express authority of God. But David acted not only independently of such order of sanction, but from motives unworthy of the delegated king of Israel; from pride and vainglory; from self-confidence and distrust of God; and, above all, from ambitious designs of conquest, in furtherance of which he was determined to force the people into military service, and to ascertain whether he could muster an army sufficient for the magnitude of the enterprises he contemplated. It was a breach of the constitution, an infringement of the liberties of the people, and opposed to that divine policy which required that Israel should continue a separate peo-

ADAM CLARKE

CHAPTER 24

1. *He moved David against them.* God could not be angry with David for numbering the people if He moved him to do it; but in the parallel place (1 Chron. xxi. 1) it is expressly said, "Satan stood up against Israel, and provoked David to number Israel." David, in all probability, slackening in his piety and confidence toward God, and meditating some extension of his dominions without the divine counsel or command, was naturally curious to know whether the number of fighting men in his empire was sufficient for the work which he had projected. He therefore orders Joab and the captains to take an exact account of all the effective men in Israel and Judah. God is justly displeased with this conduct, and determines that the props of his vain ambition shall be taken away, by either famine, war, or pestilence.

3. *Joab said unto the king.* This very bad man saw that the measure now recommended by the king was a wrong one, and might be ruinous to the people, and therefore he remonstrated against it in a very sensible speech; but the king was infatuated, and would hear no reason.

5. *And pitched in Aroer.* This was beyond Jordan, on the river Arnon, in the tribe of Gad; hence it appears that they began their census with the most eastern parts of the country beyond Jordan.

6. *To Dan-jaan.* Or to "Dan of the woods." This is the place so frequently mentioned, situated at the foot of Mount Libanus, near to the source of the Jordan, the most northern city of all the possessions of the Israelites in what was called the Promised Land, as Beer-sheba was the most southern.

7. *The strong hold of Tyre.* This must have been the old city of Tyre, which was built on the mainland; the new city was built on a rock in the sea.

8. *Nine months and twenty days.* This was a considerable time; but they had much work to do, nor did they complete the work, as appears from 1 Chron. xxi. 6; xxvii. 24.

9. *In Israel eight hundred thousand . . . the men of Judah were five hundred thousand.* In the parallel place, 1 Chron. xxi. 5, the sums are widely different: in Israel 1,100,000, in Judah 470,000. Neither of these sums is too great, but they cannot both be correct, and which is the true number is difficult to say. The former seems the most likely; but more corruptions have taken place in the numbers of the historical books of the Old Testament than in any other part of the sacred records. To attempt to reconcile them in every part is lost labor; better at once acknowledge what cannot be successfully denied, that although the original writers of the Old Testament wrote under the influence of the Divine Spirit, yet we are not told that the same influence descended on all copiers of their words, so as absolutely to prevent them from making mistakes. They might mistake, and they did mistake; but a careful collation of the different historical books serves to correct all essential errors of the scribes.

10. *David said . . . I have sinned greatly.* We know not exactly in what this sin consisted. I have already hinted, that v. 1, that probably David now began to covet an extension of empire, and purposed to unite some of the neighboring states with his own; and having, through the suggestions of Satan or some other "adversary" (for so the word implies), given way to this covetous disposition, he could not well look to God for help, and therefore wished to know whether the thousands of Israel and Judah might be deemed equal to the conquests which he meditated. When God is offended and refuses assistance, vain is the help of man.

11. *For when David was up.* It is supposed that David's contrition arose from the reproof

MATTHEW HENRY

2. As to the punishment that must be inflicted,

(1) David is told to choose what rod he will be beaten with, *v.* 12, 13. His heavenly Father must correct him, but, to show that he does not do it willingly, he gives David leave to make choice whether it shall be by war, famine, or pestilence, that he might the more patiently bear the rod when it was a rod of his own choosing. The prophet bids him advise with himself, and then tell him what answer he should *return to him that sent him.*

(2) He objects only against the judgments of the sword, and, for the other two, he refers the matter to God, but intimates his choice of the pestilence (*v.* 14). [1] He begs that he may *not fall into the hand of man.* [2] He casts himself upon God: *Let us fall now into the hand of the Lord, for his mercies are great.* David refers it to God which of these shall be the scourge, and God chooses the shortest, that he may the sooner testify his being reconciled. But some think that David, by these words, intimates his choice of the pestilence. That is a judgment to which David himself, and his own family, lie as open as the meanest subject, but not so either to famine or sword, and therefore David, tenderly conscious of his guilt, chooses that. But David, a penitent, dares cast himself into God's hand, knowing he shall find that *his mercies are great.* Good men, even when they are under God's frowns, yet will entertain no other than good thoughts of him. *Though he slay me, yet will I trust in him.*

(3) A pestilence is accordingly sent (*v.* 15), which lasted from morning to the third day (so Mr. Poole), or only to the evening of the first day, the time appointed for the evening sacrifice, so Bishop Patrick and others.

III. God's gracious relaxation of the judgment, when it began to be inflicted upon Jerusalem (*v.* 16): *The angel stretched out his hand upon Jerusalem.* Perhaps there was more wickedness, especially more pride (and that was the sin now chastised), in Jerusalem than elsewhere, therefore the hand of the destroyer is stretched out upon that; but then *the Lord repented him of the evil,* and said to the destroying angel, *It is enough; stay now thy hand,* and *let mercy rejoice against judgment.* This was on Mount Moriah. Dr. Lightfoot observes that in the very place where Abraham, by a countermand from heaven, was stayed from slaying his son, this angel, by a like countermand, was stayed from destroying Jerusalem.

IV. David's renewed repentance for his sin upon this occasion, *v.* 17. He saw the angel (God opening his eyes for that purpose), saw his sword stretched out to destroy, a flaming sword, saw him ready to sheath it upon the orders given him to stay proceedings; seeing all this, he spoke to the *Lord, and said, Lo, I have sinned.* How he criminates himself, as if he could never speak ill enough of his own fault: "*I have sinned, and I have done wickedly;* mine is the crime, and therefore on me be the cross." How he intercedes for the people, whose bitter lamentations made his heart to ache, and his ears to tingle: *These sheep, what have they done?* Let this remind us of the grace of our Lord Jesus, who gave himself for our sins and was willing that God's hand should be against him, that we might escape. The shepherd was smitten that the sheep might be spared.

Verses 18–25

I. A command sent to David to erect an altar in the place where he saw the angel, *v.* 18. This was to intimate to David, 1. That God was now thoroughly reconciled to him; *for, if the Lord had been pleased to kill him, he would not have accepted an offering,* and therefore would not have ordered him to *build an altar.* God's encouraging us to offer to him spiritual sacrifices is evidence of his reconciling us to himself. 2. That peace is made between God and sinners by sacrifice, even by Christ the great propitiation, of whom all the legal sacrifices were types. 3. That when God's judgments are graciously stayed we ought to acknowledge it with thankfulness to his praise.

II. The purchase which David made of the ground. It seems the owner was a Jebusite, Araunah by name, proselyted no doubt to the Jewish religion, though by birth a Gentile, and therefore allowed, not only to dwell among the Israelites, but to have a possession of his own in a city, Lev. xxv. 29, 30. The piece of ground was a threshing-floor, a mean place, *yet* thus dignified—a place of labour, *therefore* thus dignified.

1. David went in person to the owner, to treat with him. See his justice, that he would not so much as use this place though the proprietor was an alien, though he himself was a king, and though he had express orders from God to rear an altar there, till he had bought it and paid for it. God *hates robbery for burnt-offering.* See his humility, though a

JAMIESON, FAUSSET, BROWN

ple. His eyes were not opened to the heinousness of his sin till God had spoken unto him by His commissioned prophet. **13. Shall seven years of famine come unto thee**—i.e., in addition to the three that had been already, with the current year included (see on I Chron. 21:11, 12).

14. David said, . . . Let us fall now into the hand of the Lord—His overwhelming sense of his sin led him to acquiesce in the punishment denounced, notwithstanding its apparent excess of severity. He proceeded on a good principle in choosing the pestilence. In pestilence he was equally exposed, as it was just and right he should be, to danger as his people, whereas, in war and famine, he possessed means of protection superior to them. Besides, he thereby showed his trust, founded on long experience, in the divine goodness.

15-25. HIS INTERCESSION TO GOD; THE PLAGUE CEASES. **15. from the morning**—rather *that* morning when Gad came, till the end of the three days. **there died of the people . . . seventy thousand men** Thus was the pride of the vainglorious monarch, confiding in the number of his population, deeply humbled. **16. the Lord repented him of the evil**—God is often described in Scripture as repenting when He ceased to pursue a course He had begun.

17. David . . . said [or had said], **I have sinned . . . but these sheep, what have they done?**—The guilt of numbering the people lay exclusively with David. But in the body politic as well as natural, when the head suffers, all the members suffer along with it; and, besides, although David's sin was the immediate cause, the great increase of national offenses at this time had (vs. 1) kindled the anger of the Lord.

18. Araunah—or Ornan (I Chron. 21:18), the Jebusite, one of the ancient inhabitants, who, having become a convert to the true religion, retained his house and possessions. He resided on Mount Moriah, the spot on which the temple was afterwards built (II Chron. 3:1); but that mount was not then enclosed in the town.

ADAM CLARKE

given by Gad, and that in the order of time the reproof came before the confession stated in the tenth verse. *David's seer.* A holy man of God, under the divine influence, whom David had as a domestic chaplain.

13. *Shall seven years of famine?* In 1 Chron. xxi. 12, the number is "three," not *seven;* and here the Septuagint has "three," the same as in Chronicles. This is no doubt the true reading, the letter *zain,* "seven," being mistaken for *gimel,* "three." A mistake of this kind might be easily made from the similarity of the letters.

14. *I am in a great strait: let us fall now into the hand of the Lord.* David acted nobly in this business. Had he chosen war, his own personal safety was in no danger, because there was already an ordinance preventing him from going to battle. Had he chosen famine, his own wealth would have secured his and his own family's support. But he showed the greatness of his mind in choosing the pestilence, to the ravages of which himself and household were exposed equally with the meanest of his subjects.

15. *From the morning . . . to the time appointed.* That is, from the morning of the day after David had made his election till the third day, according to the condition which God had proposed, and he had accepted. But it seems that the plague was terminated before the conclusion of the third day, for Jerusalem might have been destroyed, but it was not. Throughout the land, independently of the city, 70.000 persons were slain! This was a terrible mortality in the space of less than three days.

16. *The angel stretched out his hand upon Jerusalem.* By what means this destruction took place, we know not. It appears that an angel was employed in it, and that this minister of divine justice actually appeared as an object of sight; for it is said, v. 17, "When he [David] saw the angel that smote the people"; and both Ornan and his four sons saw him and were affrighted, 1 Chron. xxi. 20.

The threshingplace of Araunah. These threshing places, we have already seen, were made in the open air. In the parallel place, 1 Chron. xxi. 15, 20, etc., this person is called Ornan. The word that we render *Araunah* is written in this very chapter "Avarnah," v. 16; "Araniah," v. 18; "Araunah" or "Aravnah," v. 20 and the following; but in every place in 1 Chronicles xxi where it occurs it is written "Ornan." It is likely he had both names, "Araunah" and "Ornan"; but the varieties of spelling in 2 Samuel must arise from the blunders of transcribers.

17. *But these sheep, what have they done?* It seems that in the order of Providence there is no way of punishing kings in their regal capacity but by afflictions on their land, in which the people must necessarily suffer. If the king, therefore, by his own personal offenses, in which the people can have no part, bring down God's judgments upon his people (though they suffer innocently), grievous will be the account that he must give to God. *Against my father's house.* That is, against his own family; even to cut it off from the face of the earth.

18. *Go up, rear an altar unto the Lord.* This place is supposed to be Mount Moriah, where Abraham attempted to sacrifice Isaac, and where the temple of Solomon was afterwards built.

MATTHEW HENRY

king, he went himself (*v.* 19), and lost no honour by it. Araunah, when he saw him, *bowed himself to the ground before him, v.* 20. Great men will never be the less respected for their humility, but the more.

2. Araunah, when he understood his business (*v.* 21), generously offered him, not only the ground to build his altar on, but *oxen for sacrifices*, and other things that might be of use to him in the service (*v.* 22), and all this *gratis*, and a good prayer into the bargain: *The Lord thy God accept thee!* This he did, (1) Because he had a generous spirit with a great estate. *He gave as a king* (*v.* 23); though an ordinary subject, he had the spirit of a prince. In the Hebrew it is, *He gave, even the king to the king*, whence it is supposed that Araunah had been king of the Jebusites in that place. (2) Because he highly esteemed David, though his conqueror. (3) Because he had an affection for Israel, and earnestly desired that *the plague might be stayed*; and the honour of its being stayed at *his threshing-floor*, he would account a valuable consideration.

3. David resolved to pay the full value of it, and did so, *v.* 24. He will not offer that to God which costs him nothing. He thanked him, paid him *fifty shekels of silver* for the floor and the oxen for the present service, and afterwards 600 shekels of gold for the ground adjoining, to build the temple on.

III. The building of the altar, and the offering of the proper sacrifices upon it (*v.* 25), burnt-offerings to the glory of God's justice and peace-offerings to the glory of his mercy.

JAMIESON, FAUSSET, BROWN

21. to build an altar unto the Lord, that the plague may be stayed—It is evident that the plague was not stayed till after the altar was built, and the sacrifice offered, so that what is related (vs. 16) was by anticipation. Previous to the offering of this sacrifice, he had seen the destroying angel as well as offered the intercessory prayer (vs. 17). This was a sacrifice of expiation; and the reason why he was allowed to offer it on Mount Moriah was partly in gracious consideration to his fear of repairing to Gibeon (I Chron. 21:29, 30), and partly in anticipation of the removal of the tabernacle and the erection of the temple there (II Chron. 3:1). **23. All these things did Araunah, as a king, give**—Indicating, as the sense is, that this man had been anciently a heathen king or chief, but was now a proselyte who still retained great property and influence in Jerusalem, and whose piety was evinced by the liberality of his offers. The words, "as a king," are taken by some to signify simply, "he gave with royal munificence." **24. Nay; . . . I will . . . buy it of thee at a price**—The sum mentioned here, about fifty dollars, was paid for the floor, oxen and wood instruments only, whereas the large sum (I Chron. 21: 25) was paid afterwards for the whole hill, on which David made preparations for building the temple. **25. David offered burnt offerings and peace offerings**—There seem to have been two sacrifices; the first expiatory, the second a thanksgiving for the cessation of the pestilence (see on I Chron. 21:26).

ADAM CLARKE

22. *Here be oxen for burnt sacrifice.* He felt for the king, and showed his loyalty to him by this offer. He felt for the people, and was willing to make any sacrifice to get the plague stayed. He felt for his own personal safety, and therefore was willing to give up all to save his life. He felt for the honor of God, and therefore was glad that he had a sacrifice to offer, so that God might magnify both His justice and mercy.

23. *As a king, give unto the king.* Literally, "All these did King Araunah give unto the king." That there could not be a king of the Jebusites on Mount Moriah is sufficiently evident; and that there was no other king than David in the land is equally so. The word *hammelech*, "the king," given here to Araunah, is wanting in the Septuagint, Syriac, and Arabic; and, it is very probable, never made a part of the text. Perhaps it should be read, "All these did Araunah give unto the king."

THE BOOK OF FIRST KINGS

I. The passing of David (1:1-2:11)
- *A. The rebellion of Adonijah (1:1-37)*
- *B. The crowning of Solomon (1:38-53)*
- *C. The last charge and death of David (2:1-11)*

II. Solomon (2:12-11:43)
- *A. "In all his glory" (2:12-10:29)*
  1. Solomon and the traitors (2:12-46)
  2. The first divine appearing (3:1-15)
  3. The greatness of Solomon (3:16-4:34)
  4. His life work: the Temple (5:1-8:66)
  5. The second divine appearing (9:1-9)
  6. Material magnificence (9:10-10:29)
- *B. The passing of the glory (11:1-43)*
  1. Degeneracy and doom (11:1-13)
  2. Execution of judgment (11:14-43)

III. Division (12:1-16:34)
- *A. Rehoboam and Jeroboam (12:1-14:31)*
  1. The revolt of the ten tribes (12:1-33)
  2. Warning to Jeroboam (13:1-14:20)
  3. Rehoboam's reign (14:21-31)
- *B. Kings of Judah (15:1-24)*
  1. Abijam (15:1-8)
  2. Asa (15:9-24)
- *C. Kings of Israel (15:25-16:34)*
  1. Nadab (15:25-32)
  2. Baasha (15:33-16:7)
  3. Elah (16:8-14)
  4. Zimri (16:15-20)
  5. Omri (16:21-28)
  6. Ahab (16:29-34)

IV. Elijah (17:1-22:53)
- *A. The curse pronounced (17:1-24)*
- *B. The judgment of Carmel (18:1-46)*
- *C. Elijah in the wilderness (19:1-21)*
- *D. The downfall of Ahab (20:1-22:53)*
  1. Benhadad (20:1-43)
  2. Ahab and Naboth (21:1-16)
  3. Elijah pronouncing judgment (21:17-20)
  4. Micaiah's prediction and Ahab's death (22:1-40)
  5. The kings of Israel and Judah (22:41-53)

The Bible began with the story of patriarchs and prophets and judges—men whose converse with heaven was more immediate, the record of which strengthens our faith; but is not so easily accommodated to our case, now that we expect not visions, as the subsequent history of affairs like ours under the direction of common providence. Here also we find, though not many types and figures of the Messiah, yet great expectations of him; for not only prophets, but kings, desired to see the great mysteries of the gospel (Luke 10:24).

The two books of Samuel are introductions to the books of the Kings, as they relate the origin of the royal government in Saul and of the royal family in David. These two books give us an account of David's successor, Solomon, the division of his kingdom, and the succession of the several kings both of Judah and Israel, with an abstract of their history down to the captivity. And as from the book of Genesis we may collect excellent rules of economics for the good governing of families, so from these books we may collect rules of politics for the directing of public affairs.

There is in these books special regard to the house and lineage of David, from which Christ came. Some of his sons trod in his steps and others did not. The characters of the kings of Judah may be thus briefly given: David the devout, Solomon the wise, Rehoboam the simple, Abijah the valiant, Asa the upright, Jehoshaphat the religious, Jehoram the wicked, Ahaziah the profane, Joash the backslider, Amaziah the rash, Uzziah the mighty, Jotham the peaceable, Ahaz the idolater, Hezekiah the reformer, Manasseh the penitent, Amon the obscure, Josiah the tenderhearted, Jehoahaz, Jehoiakim, Jehoiachin, and Zedekiah, all wicked, and such as brought ruin quickly on themselves and their kingdom. The number of the good and bad is nearly equal, but the reigns of the good were generally long and those of the bad short.

MATTHEW HENRY

CHAPTER 1

Verses 1–4

David under the infirmities of old age. 1. It would have troubled one to see David so infirm. He was old, and his natural heat was so wasted that no clothes could keep him warm, *v.* 1. 2. It would have troubled one to see his physicians so weak and unskilful that they knew no other way of relieving him than by outward applications. *They covered him with clothes,* which where there is any inward heat, will keep it in, and so increase it; but, where it is not, they have none to communicate, no, not even royal clothing. They foolishly prescribed nuptials. His prophets should have been consulted as well as his physicians in an affair of this nature. That Abishag was married to David before she lay with him, and was his secondary wife, appears from his being imputed as a great crime to Adonijah that he desired to marry her (*ch.* ii. 22) after his father's death.

Verses 5–10

David had much affliction in his children. Amnon and Absalom had both been his grief; the one his first-born, the other his third, 2 Sam. iii. 2, 3. His second, whom he had by Abigail, we will suppose he had comfort in; his fourth was Adonijah (2 Sam. iii. 4) born in Hebron. He was a comely person, next in age, and (as it proved) next in temper, to Absalom, *v.* 6. In his father's eyes he had been a jewel, but was now a thorn.

I. His father had made a fondling of him, *v.* 6. He had not displeased him at any time. It was the son's fault that he was displeased at reproof whereby he lost the benefit of it; and it was the father's fault that, because he saw it displeased him, he did not reprove him; and now he justly smarted for indulging him.

II. He, in return, made a fool of his father. Because he was old, and confined to his bed, he *exalted himself,* and said, *I will be king, v.* 5. 1. He looked upon the days of mourning for his father to be at hand, and therefore he prepared to succeed him, though he knew that by the designation both of God and David Solomon was to be the man, 1 Chron. xxii. 9; xxiii. 1. 2. He looked upon his father as superannuated and good for nothing, and therefore he entered immediately upon the possession of the

JAMIESON, FAUSSET, BROWN

CHAPTER 1

Vss. 1-4. Abishag Cherishes David in His Extreme Age. **1. Now King David was old**—He was in the seventieth year of his age (II Samuel 5:4, 5). But the wear and tear of a military life, bodily fatigue, and mental care, had prematurely, if we may say it, exhausted the energies of David's strong constitution (I Sam. 16:12). In modern Palestine and Egypt the people, owing to the heat of the climate, sleep each in a *separate* bed. They only depart from this practice for medical reasons (Eccles. 4:11). The expedient recommended by David's physicians is the regimen still prescribed in similar cases in the East, particularly among the Arab population, not simply to give heat, but "to cherish," as they are aware that the inhalation of young breath will give new life and vigor to the worn-out frame. The fact of the health of the young and healthier person being, as it were, stolen to support that of the more aged and sickly is well established among the medical faculty. And hence the prescription for the aged king was made in a hygienic point of view for the prolongation of his valuable life, and not merely for the comfort to be derived from the natural warmth imparted to his withered frame [Tent and Khan]. The polygamy of the age and country may account for the introduction of this practice; and it is evident that Abishag was made a concubine or secondary wife to David (see on ch. 2:22). **3. a Shunammite**—Shunem, in the tribe of Issachar (Josh. 19:18), lay on an eminence in the plain of Esdraelon, five miles south of Tabor. It is now called Sulam.

5-31. Adonijah Usurps the Kingdom. **5. Then Adonijah the son of Haggith exalted himself**—Nothing is said as to the origin or rank of Haggith, so that it is probable she was not distinguished by family descent. Adonijah, though David's fourth son (II Sam. 3:4; I Chron. 3:2), was now the oldest alive; and his personal attractions and manners (I Sam. 9:2) not only recommended him to the leading men about court, but made him the favorite of his father, who, though seeing him assume an equipage becoming only the heir-presumptive to the throne (II Sam. 15:1), said nothing; and his silence was considered by many, as well as by Adonijah, to be equivalent to an expression of consent. The sinking

ADAM CLARKE

CHAPTER 1

1. *Now King David was old.* He was probably now about sixty-nine years of age. He was thirty years old when he began to reign, reigned forty, and died in the seventieth year of his age, 2 Sam. v. 4, and chap. ii. 11; and the transactions mentioned here are supposed to have taken place about a year before his death. *But he gat no heat.* Sixty-nine was not an advanced age; but David had been exhausted with various fatigues, and especially by family afflictions, so that he was much older in constitution than he was in years. Besides he seems to have labored under some wasting maladies, to which there is frequent reference in the Psalms.

2. *Let there be sought . . . a young virgin.* This was the best remedy which in his state could be prescribed. His nearly exhausted frame would infallibly absorb from her young and healthy body an additional portion of animal heat, and consequently trim and revive the flame of animal life.

5. *Adonijah the son of Haggith.* Who this woman was we know not; Adonijah was evidently David's eldest son now living, and one of whom his father was particularly fond; see v. 6.

MATTHEW HENRY

throne. His father is not fit to govern, for he is old and past ruling; nor Solomon, for he is young, and not yet able to rule; and therefore Adonijah will take the government upon him. 3. In pursuance of this ambitious project, (1) He got a great retinue (*v.* 5), *chariots and horsemen*, both for state and strength, to wait on him, and to fight for him. (2) He made great interest with no less than Joab, the general of the army, and Abiathar the high priest, *v.* 7. They were old men, who had been faithful to David in the most difficult and troublesome of his times, men of sense and experience, who, one would think, would not easily be wheedled. But God, in this matter, left them to themselves, perhaps to correct them for some former misconduct with a scourge of their own making. We are told (*v.* 8) who those were that were of such approved fidelity to David that Adonijah had not the confidence so much as to propose his project to them—Zadok, Benaiah, and Nathan. (3) He prepared a great entertainment (*v.* 9) at En-rogel, not far from Jerusalem; his guests were the king's sons, and the king's servants, whom he feasted and caressed to bring them over to his party; but Solomon was not invited, either because he despised him or because he despaired of him, *v.* 10. Some think that Adonijah slew these sheep and oxen, even fat ones, for sacrifice, and that it was a religious feast he made, beginning his usurpation with a show of devotion which he might do the more plausibly when he had the high priest himself on his side.

Verses 11–31

The effectual endeavours that were used by Nathan and Bath-sheba to obtain from David a ratification of Solomon's succession, for the crushing of Adonijah's usurpation. 1. David himself knew not what was doing. 2. Bath-sheba lived retired, and knew nothing of it either, till Nathan informed her. 3. Solomon, it is likely, knew of it, but was as a deaf man that heard not. Though he had years, and wisdom above his years, yet we do not find that he stirred to oppose Adonijah, but quietly composed himself and left it to God and his friends to order the matter. How then is the design brought about?

I. Nathan the prophet alarms Bath-sheba by acquainting her with the case, and puts her in a way to get an order from the king for the confirming of Solomon's title. He was concerned, because he knew God's mind, and David's and Israel's interest; it was by him that God had named Solomon *Jedidiah* (2 Sam. xii. 25), and therefore he could not sit still and see the throne usurped, which he knew was Solomon's right by the will of him from whom promotion cometh. Nathan applied to Bath-sheba, as one that had the greatest concern for Solomon, and could have the freest access to David. He informed her of Adonijah's attempt (*v.* 11), and that it was not with David's consent or knowledge. He suggested to her that not only Solomon was in danger of losing the crown, but that he and she too were in danger of losing their lives if Adonijah prevailed. Now, says Nathan, let me *give thee counsel how to save thy own life and the life of thy son*, *v.* 12. He directs her (*v.* 13) to go to the king, to remind him of his word and oath, that Solomon should be his successor; and to ask him in the most humble manner, *Why doth Adonijah reign?* He thought David was not so cold but this would warm him. Conscience, as well as a sense of honour, would put life into him upon such an occasion as this; and he promised (*v.* 14) that, while she was reasoning with the king upon this matter, he would come in and second her, as if he came accidentally.

II. Bath-sheba, according to Nathan's advice and direction, loses no time, but immediately makes her application to the king, to intercede for her life. She knew she should be welcome at any time. Her address to the king, on this occasion, is very discreet. 1. She reminded him of his promise made to her, and confirmed with a solemn oath, that Solomon should succeed him, *v.* 17. She knew how fast this would hold such a conscientious man as David was. 2. She informed him of Adonijah's attempt, which he was ignorant of (*v.* 18). She told him who were Adonijah's guests, and who were in his interest, and added, but "*Solomon thy servant has he not called,*" which plainly shows he looks upon him as his rival, and aims to undermine him, *v.* 19. 3. She pleads that it is very much in his power to obviate this mischief (*v.* 20): *The eyes of all Israel are upon thee,* not only as a *king*, but as a *prophet*. All Israel knew that David was not only himself *the anointed of the God of Jacob*, but that the *Spirit of the Lord spoke by him* (2 Sam. xxiii. 1, 2), and therefore waiting for and depending upon a divine designation, in a matter of such importance, David's word would be an oracle and a law to them. 4. She suggested the imminent

JAMIESON, FAUSSET, BROWN

health of the king prompted him to take a decisive step in furtherance of his ambitious designs. **7. he conferred with Joab**—The anxiety of Adonijah to secure the influence of a leader so bold, enterprising, and popular with the army was natural, and the accession of the hoary commander is easily accounted for from his recent grudge at the king (see on II Sam. 19:13). **and with Abiathar the priest**—His influence was as great over the priests and Levites—a powerful body in the kingdom—as that of Joab over the troops. It might be that both of them thought the crown belonged to Adonijah by right of primogeniture, from his mature age and the general expectations of the people (ch. 2:15). **8. But Zadok the priest**—He had been high priest in the tabernacle at Gibeon under Saul (I Chron. 16:39). David, on his accession, had conjoined him and Abiathar equal in the exercise of their high functions (II Sam. 8:17; 15:24; 29: 35). But it is extremely probable that some cause of jealousy or discord between them had arisen, and hence each lent his countenance and support to opposite parties. **Benaiah**—Distinguished for his bravery (I Sam. 23:20), he had been appointed captain of the king's bodyguard (II Sam. 8:18; 20:23; I Chron. 18:17), and was regarded by Joab as a rival. **Nathan the prophet**—He was held in high estimation by David, and stood on the most intimate relations with the royal family (II Sam. 12:25). **Shimei**—probably the person of this name who was afterwards enrolled among Solomon's great officers (ch. 4:18). **Rei**—supposed to be the same as Ira (II Sam. 20:26). **and the mighty men**—the select band of worthies. **9. En-rogel**—situated (Josh. 15:7-10) east of Jerusalem, in a level place, just below the junction of the valley of Hinnom with that of Jehoshaphat. It is a very deep well, measuring 125 feet in depth; the water is sweet, but not very cold, and it is at times quite full to overflowing. The Orientals are fond of enjoying festive repasts in the open air at places which command the advantage of shade, water, and verdure; and those *fêtes champêtres* are not cold collations, but magnificent entertainments, the animals being killed and dressed on the spot. Adonijah's feast at En-rogel was one of this Oriental description, and it was on a large scale (II Sam. 3:4, 5; 5:14-16; I Chron. 14:1-7). At the accession of a new king there were sacrifices offered (I Sam. 11:15). But on such an occasion it was no less customary to entertain the grandees of the kingdom and even the populace in a public manner (I Chron. 12:23-40). There is the strongest probability that Adonijah's feast was purely political, to court popularity and secure a party to support his claim to the crown. **11-27. Nathan spake unto Bath-sheba . . . let me . . . give thee counsel,** etc.—The revolt was defeated by this prophet, who, knowing the Lord's will (II Sam. 7:12; I Chron. 22:9), felt himself bound, in accordance with his character and office, to take the lead in seeing it executed. Hitherto the succession of the Hebrew monarchy had not been settled. The Lord had reserved to Himself the right of nomination (Deut. 17:15), which was acted upon in the appointments both of Saul and David; and in the case of the latter the rule was so far modified that his posterity were guaranteed the perpetual possession of the sovereignty (II Sam. 7:12). This divine purpose was known throughout the kingdom; but no intimation had been made as to whether the right of inheritance was to belong to the oldest son. Adonijah, in common with the people generally, expected that this natural arrangement should be followed in the Hebrew kingdom as in all others. Nathan, who was aware of the old king's solemn promise to Solomon, and, moreover, that this promise was sanctioned by the divine will, saw that no time was to be lost. Fearing the effects of too sudden excitement in the king's feeble state, he arranged that Bath-sheba should go first to inform him of what was being transacted without the walls, and that he himself should follow to confirm her statement. The narrative here not only exhibits the vivid picture of a scene within the interior of a palace, but gives the impression that a great deal of Oriental state ceremonial had been established in the Hebrew court.

20. the eyes of all Israel are upon thee, that thou shouldest tell them who shall sit on the throne—When the kings died without declaring their will, then their oldest son succeeded. But frequently they designated long before their death which of their sons should inherit the throne. The kings of Persia, as well as of other Eastern countries, have exercised the same right in modern and even recent times.

ADAM CLARKE

Prepared him chariots and horsemen. He copied the conduct of his brother Absalom in every respect. See 2 Sam. xv. 1.

7. *And he conferred with Joab.* Joab well knew if he made the new king he would necessarily be continued in the command of the army, and so govern him.

8. *And Nathan.* Some suppose that he was the preceptor of Solomon.

9. *Slew sheep and oxen.* Making a royal feast, in reference to his inauguration. As he had Abiathar the priest with him, no doubt these animals were offered sacrificially, and then the guests fed on the flesh of the victims.

11. *Hast thou not heard that Adonijah the son of Haggith doth reign?* He was now considered as being legally appointed to the regal office, and no doubt was about to begin to perform its functions.

12. *Save thine own life, and the life of thy son.* Nathan took for granted that Adonijah would put both Bath-sheba and Solomon to death as state criminals if he got established on the throne.

13. *Go and get thee in unto King David.* He knew that this woman had a sovereign influence over the king. *Didst not thou . . . swear?* It is very likely that David made such an oath, and that was known only to Bath-sheba and Nathan. It is nowhere else mentioned.

20. *That thou shouldest tell . . . who shall sit on the throne.* This was a monarchy neither hereditary nor elective; the king simply named his successor. This obtained less or more, anciently, in most countries.

MATTHEW HENRY

peril which she and her son would be in if this matter was not settled in David's lifetime, *v.* 21.

III. Nathan the prophet, according to his promise, seasonably stepped in, and seconded her, while she was speaking, before the king had given his answer. The king is told that Nathan the prophet has come, and he is sure to be always welcome to the king. He *bowed himself with his face to the ground, v.* 23. He deals a little more plainly with the king than Bath-sheba had done. 1. He makes the same representation of Adonijah's attempt as Bathsheba had made (*v.* 25, 26), adding that his party had already got to such a height of assurance as to shout, *God save king Adonijah*, as if king David were already dead. They had not invited him to their feast (*Me thy servant has he not called*), thereby intimating that they resolved not to consult either God or David in the matter. 2. He makes David sensible how much he was concerned to clear himself from having a hand in it: *Hast thou said, Adonijah shall reign after me?* (*v.* 24), and again (*v.* 27): *Is this thing done by my lord the king?* If it be, he is not so faithful either to God's word or to his own as we all took him to be; if it be not, it is high time that we witness against the usurpation, and declare Solomon his successor." Thus he endeavoured to incense David against them, that he might act the more vigorously for the support of Solomon's interest.

IV. David, hereupon, made a solemn declaration of his firm adherence to his former resolution, that Solomon should be his successor. Bath-sheba is called in (*v.* 28), and to her, as acting for and on behalf of her son, the king gives these fresh assurances. 1. He repeats his former promise and oath, owns that he had *sworn unto her by the Lord God of Israel that Solomon should reign after him, v.* 30. 2. He ratifies it with another, because the occasion called for it: *As the Lord liveth, that hath redeemed my soul out of all distress, even so will I certainly do this day*, without dispute, without delay. His form of swearing seems to be what he commonly used on solemn occasions, for we find it in 2 Sam. iv. 9. And it carries in it a grateful acknowledgment of the goodness of God to him. Perhaps he speaks thus, on this occasion, for the encouragement of his son and successor to trust in God in the distresses he also might meet with.

V. Bath-sheba receives these assurances (*v.* 31), with hearty good wishes for the king's health: *Let him live*. So far was she from thinking that he lived too long that she prayed he might live for ever, if it were possible, to adorn the crown he wore and to be a blessing to his people.

Verses 32–40

The effectual care David took both to secure Solomon's right and to preserve the public peace, by crushing Adonijah's project.

I. The express orders he gave for the proclaiming of Solomon. The persons he entrusted with this affair were Zadok, Nathan, and Benaiah, men of power and interest whom David had always found faithful to him. David orders them forthwith, with all possible solemnity, to proclaim Solomon. They must take with them *the servants of their lord*, the lifeguards, and all the servants of the household. They must set Solomon on the mule the king used to ride. 1. Zadok and Nathan, the two ecclesiastical persons, must, in God's name, anoint him king. 2. The great officers, civil and military, are ordered to give public notice of this, and to express the public joy upon this occasion by sound of trumpet, by which the law of Moses directed the gracing of great solemnities; to this must be added the acclamations of the people: "*Let king Solomon live.*" 3. They must then bring him in state to the city of David, and he must sit upon the throne of his father, as his viceroy, to despatch public business during his weakness and be his successor after his death: *He shall be king in my stead*. It would be a great satisfaction to David himself, and to all parties concerned, to have this done immediately, that upon the demise of the king there might be no dispute, or agitation, in the public affairs.

II. The great satisfaction which Benaiah, in the name of the rest, professed in these orders. The king said, "Solomon shall reign for me, and reign after me." "Amen" (says Benaiah heartily); "as the king says, so say we; and since we can bring nothing to pass without the concurrence of a propitious providence, *The Lord God of my lord the king say so too!*" *v.* 36. This is the language of his faith in that promise of God on which Solomon's government was founded. To this he adds a prayer for Solomon (*v.* 37), that God would be with him as he had been with David, and make his throne greater. He knew David was not one of those that envy their children's greatness, and that therefore he would not be disquieted at this prayer, nor take it as an affront, but would heartily

JAMIESON, FAUSSET, BROWN

21. I and my son . . . shall be counted offenders—i.e., slain, according to the barbarous usage of the East towards all who are rivals to the throne.

28-31. Then King David answered and said, Call me Bath-sheba—He renews to her the solemn pledge he had given, in terms of solemnity and impressiveness which show that the aged monarch had roused himself to the duty the emergency called for.

32-49. SOLOMON, BY DAVID'S APPOINTMENT, IS ANOINTED KING. **33. cause Solomon my son to ride upon mine own mule**—Directions were forthwith given for the immediate coronation of Solomon. A procession was to be formed by the "servants of their lord"—i.e., the king's bodyguard. Mules were then used by all the princes (II Sam. 13:29); but there was a state mule of which all subjects were forbidden, under pain of death, to make use, without special permission; so that its being granted to Solomon was a public declaration in his favor as the future king (see on Esther 6:8, 9). **bring him down to Gihon**—a pool or fountain on the west of Jerusalem (see on II Chron. 32:30), chosen as equally public for the counter proclamation. **34. anoint him**—done only in the case of a new dynasty or disputed succession (see on I Sam. 16:13; II Sam. 2:4). **35. Then ye shall come up after him, that he may come and sit upon my throne**—The public recognition of the successor to the throne, during the old king's lifetime, is accordant with the customs of the East.

ADAM CLARKE

21. *Shall be counted offenders.* When Adonijah and his party shall find that I and my son have had this promise from thee by oath, he will slay us both.

28. *Call me Bath-sheba.* She had gone out when Nathan came in, and he retired when she was readmitted. Each had a separate audience, but to Nathan the king did not express any will.

33. *Take with you the servants of your lord.* By these we may understand the king's guards, the guards of the city, the Cherethites and Pelethites, who were under the command of Benaiah; and in short, all the disposable force that was at hand. *Solomon . . . to ride upon mine own mule.* No subject could use anything that belonged to the prince without forfeiting his life. As David offered Solomon to ride on his own mule, this was full evidence that he had appointed him his successor.

34. *Blow ye with the trumpet.* After he has been anointed, make proclamation that he is king.

MATTHEW HENRY

say *Amen* to it.

III. The immediate execution of these orders, *v.* 38-40. No time was lost, but Solomon was brought in state to the place appointed, and there Zadok anointed him by the direction of Nathan the prophet and David the king, *v.* 39. In the tabernacle, where the ark was now lodged, was kept, among other sacred things, the holy oil for many religious services, thence Zadok took a *horn of oil*, which denotes both power and plenty and therewith anointed Solomon. The people, hereupon, express their great joy and satisfaction in the elevation of Solomon, surround him with their Hosannas—*God save king Solomon,* and attend him with their music and shouts of joy, *v.* 40.

Verses 41–53

I. The tidings of Solomon's inauguration brought to Adonijah and his party, in the midst of their jollity: *They had made an end of eating*, and, it should seem, it was a great while before they made an end, for all the affair of Solomon's anointing was ordered and finished while they were at dinner, glutting themselves. When *they made an end of eating*, and were preparing themselves to proclaim their king, and bring him in triumph into the city, they *heard the sound of the trumpet* (*v.* 41). Joab was an old man, and was alarmed at it, but Adonijah was very confident that the messenger, being a *worthy man, brought good tidings*, *v.* 42. "*Verily*, the best tidings I have to bring you is that *Solomon is made king*, so that your pretensions are all quashed." He relates to them, 1. With what great solemnity *Solomon* was *made king* (*v.* 44, 45), and that he was now *sitting on the throne of the kingdom*, *v.* 46. 2. With what general satisfaction Solomon was made king. The people were pleased. The courtiers were pleased: *The king's servants* attended him with an address of congratulation upon this occasion, *v.* 47. They *blessed king David.* They also prayed for Solomon, that God would make his name better than his father's, which it might well be when he had his father's foundation to build upon. A child, on a giant's shoulders, is higher than the giant himself. The king himself was pleased: He *bowed himself upon the bed*, not only to signify his acceptance of his servants' address, but to offer up his own address to God (*v.* 48).

II. The effectual crush which this gave to Adonijah's attempt. It spoiled the sport of his party, dispersed the company, and obliged every man to shift for his own safety.

III. The terror Adonijah himself was in and the course he took to secure himself. He had despised Solomon as not worthy to be his guest (*v.* 10), but now he dreads him as his judge: He *feared because of Solomon.* He *took hold on the horns of the altar,* which was always looked upon as a sanctuary or place of refuge (Exod. xxi. 14), intimating hereby that he durst not stand a trial, but threw himself upon the mercy of his prince, in suing for which he relied upon no other plea than the mercy of God, which was manifested in the institution and acceptance of the sacrifices that were offered on that altar and the remission of sin thereupon.

IV. His humble address to Solomon for mercy. By those who brought Solomon tidings where he was, he sent a request for his life (*v.* 15): *Let king Solomon swear to me that he will not slay his servant.*

V. The orders Solomon gave concerning him. He discharged him upon his good behaviour, *v.* 52, 53. He considered that Adonijah was his brother, and that it was the first offence. Thus the Son of David receives those to mercy that have been rebellious: if they will return to their allegiance, and be faithful to their Sovereign, their former crimes shall not be mentioned against them; but, if still they continue in the interests of the world and the flesh, this will be their ruin.

CHAPTER 2

Verses 1–11

David, that great and good man, is here a dying man (*v.* 1), and a dead man, *v.* 10. It is well there is another life after this, for death stains all the glory of this, and lays it in the dust.

I. The charge and instructions which David, when he was dying, gave to Solomon, his son and declared successor. He feels himself declining, and is not backward to own it, *I go the way of all the earth*, *v.* 2. Heb. *I am walking in it.* Death is a way; not only a period of this life, but a passage to a better. Even the sons and heirs of heaven must *go the way of all the earth*, they must needs die; but they walk with pleasure in this way, *through the valley of the shadow of death*, Ps. xxiii. 4. Prophets, and even kings, must go this way to brighter light and honour than

JAMIESON, FAUSSET, BROWN

39. an horn of oil out of the tabernacle—It was the sacred oil (Exod. 30:22) with which the kings were anointed.

40. all the people came up after him—i.e., from the valley to the citadel of Zion.

41. Adonijah, and all the guests that were with him, heard it as they had made an end of eating—The loud shouts raised by the populace at the joyous proclamation at Gihon, and echoed by assembled thousands, from Zion to En-rogel, were easily heard at that distance by Adonijah and his confederates. The arrival of a trusty messenger, who gave a full detail of the coronation ceremony, spread dismay in their camp. The wicked and ambitious plot they had assembled to execute was dissipated, and every one of the conspirators consulted his safety by flight.

50-53. ADONIJAH, FLEEING TO THE HORNS OF THE ALTAR, IS DISMISSED BY SOLOMON. **50. Adonijah . . . went and caught hold on the horns of the altar**—most probably the altar of burnt offering which had been erected on Mount Zion, where Abiathar, one of his partisans, presided as high priest. The horns or projections at the four corners of the altar, to which the sacrifices were bound, and which were tipped with the blood of the victim, were symbols of grace and salvation to the sinner. Hence the altar was regarded as a sanctuary (Exod. 21:14), but not to murderers, rebels, or deliberate perpetrators. Adonijah, having acted in opposition to the will of the reigning king, was guilty of rebellion, and stood self-condemned. Solomon spared his life on the express condition of his good behavior—living in strict privacy, leading a quiet, peaceable life, and meddling with the affairs of neither the court nor the kingdom. **53. they brought him down**—from the ledge around the altar on which he was standing. **he bowed himself**—i.e., did homage to Solomon as king.

CHAPTER 2

Vss. 1-11. DAVID DIES. **1. David . . . charged his son**—The charge recorded here was given to Solomon just before his death and is different from the farewell address delivered in public some time before (I Chron. 28:29). It is introduced with great solemnity. **2. I go the way of all the earth**—a beautiful and impressive periphrasis for death.

ADAM CLARKE

40. *The people piped with pipes.* They danced, sang, and played on what instruments of music they possessed. *The earth rent.* We use a similar expression in precisely the same sense: They rent the air with their cries.

43. *Jonathan answered.* He was properly a messenger about the court; we have met with him and Ahimaaz before, 2 Sam. xv. 36. He had now been an observer, if not a spy, on all that was doing, and relates the transactions to Adonijah, in the very order in which they took place.

50. *Adonijah feared.* He knew he had usurped the kingdom, and had not his father's consent; and, as he finds now that Solomon is appointed by David, he knows well that the people will immediately respect that appointment, and that his case is hopeless. He therefore took sanctuary, and, fleeing to the Tabernacle, laid hold on one of the horns of the altar, as if appealing to the protection of God against the violence of men. The altar was a privileged place, and it was deemed sacrilege to molest a man who had taken refuge there.

52. *If he will shew himself a worthy man.* If from henceforth he behave well, show himself to be contented, and not endeavor to make partisans, or stir up insurrections among the people, he shall be safe; *but if wickedness shall be found in him*—if he act at all contrary to this—*he shall die;* his blood shall be upon him.

53. *Go to thine house.* Intimating that he should have no place about the king's person nor under the government. Adonijah must have seen that he stood continually on his good behavior.

CHAPTER 2

2. *I go the way of all the earth.* I am dying. All the inhabitants of the earth must come to the dust. In life, some follow one occupation, some another; but all must, sooner or later, come to the grave.

MATTHEW HENRY

prophecy or sovereignty. David is going this way, and therefore gives Solomon directions what to do.

1. He charges him, in general, to keep God's commandments and to make conscience of his duty, *v.* 2–4. He prescribes to him, (1) A good rule to act by—the divine will: "Govern thyself by that." David's charge to him is to *keep the charge of the Lord* his *God.* (2) A good spirit to act with: *Be strong and show thyself a man,* though in years but a child. (3) Good reasons for all this. *That the Lord may continue* and so confirm *his word which he spoke concerning me.* Let each, in his own age, successively, keep God's charge, and then God will be sure to continue his word. We never let fall the promise till we let fall the precept. God had promised David that the Messiah should come from his loins, and that promise was absolute: but the promise that there should not fail him *a man on the throne of Israel* was conditional —if his seed behave themselves, as they should. If Solomon, in his day, fulfil the condition, he does his part towards the perpetuating of the promise. The condition is that he walk before God in all his institutions, in sincerity, with zeal and resolution.

2. He gives him directions concerning some particular persons, what to do with them. (1) Concerning Joab, *v.* 5. David was now conscious to himself that he had not done well to spare him, when he had made himself once and again obnoxious to the law, by the murder of Abner first and afterwards of Amasa, both of them great men, *captains of the hosts of Israel.* He slew them treacherously (*shed the blood of war in peace*), and injuriously to David: *Thou knowest what* he *did to me* therein. It aggravated Joab's crime that he was neither ashamed of the sin nor afraid of the punishment, but daringly wore the girdle and shoes that were stained with innocent blood, in defiance of the justice both of God and the king. David refers him to Solomon's wisdom (*v.* 6), with an intimation that he left him to his justice. (2) Concerning Barzillai's family, to whom he orders him to be kind for Barzillai's sake, who, we may suppose, by this time, was dead, *v.* 7. The kindnesses we have received from our friends must not be buried either in their graves or ours, but our children must return them to theirs. (3) Concerning Shimei, *v.* 8, 9. *He cursed me with a grievous curse;* the more grievous because he insulted him when he was in misery and poured vinegar into his wounds. His case is left with Solomon as one that knew what was fit to be done and would do as he found occasion. His turbulent spirit will soon give thee an occasion, which thou shouldst not fail to take, for the bringing of his *hoary head to the grave with blood.* This proceeded not from personal revenge, but a prudent zeal for the honour of the government and the covenant God had made with his family, the contempt of which ought not to be unpunished.

II. David's death and burial (*v.* 10): He *was buried in the city of David,* not in the burying place of his father, as Saul was, but in his own city, which he was the founder of. There were set the thrones, and there the tombs, of the house of David. His epitaph may be taken from 2 Sam. xxiii. 1. Here lies *David the son of Jesse, the man who was raised up on high, the anointed of the God of Jacob, and the sweet psalmist of Israel,* adding his own words (Ps. xvi. 9), *My flesh also shall rest in hope.*

Verses 12–25

I. Solomon's accession to the throne, *v.* 12. He came to it much more easily and peaceably than David did, and much sooner saw his government established. It is happy for a kingdom when the end of one good reign is the beginning of another, as it was here.

II. His just and necessary removal of Adonijah his rival, in order to the establishment of his throne.

1. Adonijah's treasonable project, which was to marry Abishag, David's concubine, not because he was in love with her, but because, by her, he hoped to renew his claim to the crown, which might stand him in stead. Absalom thought his pretensions much supported by lying with his father's concubines. Adonijah flatters himself that if he may succeed him in his bed, especially with the best of his wives, he may by that means step up to succeed him in his throne.

2. The means he used to compass this. He durst not make suit to Abishag immediately, but he engaged Bath-sheba to be his friend in this matter, who would be forward to believe it a matter of love, and not apt to suspect it a matter of policy. Bath-sheba was surprised to see Adonijah in her apartment, and asked him if he did not come with a design to do her a mischief, because she had been instrumental to crush his late attempt. "No," says he, "I come

JAMIESON, FAUSSET, BROWN

be thou strong, . . . and show thyself a man—This counsel is similar to the apostolic direction (I Cor. 16:13) and refers to the fortitude or strength of mind that was required to discharge the onerous functions of king. **3. keep the charge of the Lord thy God**—i.e., the divine law in all its ceremonial as well as moral requirements. But particular reference was intended to its political institutions, as it was only by strictly maintaining the conduct that became the Hebrew monarch (Deut. 17:10-20), that he would secure the blessing of peace and prosperity to his reign (see on Deut. 4:6; 29:10-21). **4. there shall not fail thee . . . a man on the throne of Israel**—a reference to the promise made to David of the sovereignty being vested perpetually in his lineage (II Sam. 7:11-16), which was confirmed to Solomon afterwards (see on ch. 9:5), and repeated with reference to its spiritual meaning long after (Jer. 33:17). **5, 6. thou knowest also what Joab . . . did**—The insolent and imperious conduct of that general had not only been deeply offensive to the feelings (II Sam. 18:5-15; 19:5-7), but calculated to bring reproach on the character, to injure the prospects, and endanger the throne of David. Passing over the injuries committed directly against himself, David dwelt with strong feelings on the base assassination of Abner and Amasa. **shed the blood of war in peace,** etc.—The obvious meaning is, that in peace he acted towards them as if they had been in a state of warfare; but perhaps these graphic expressions might be designed to impress Solomon's mind more strongly with a sense of the malice, treachery, and cruelty by which those murders were characterized. **6. Do . . . according to thy wisdom**—Joab's immense popularity with the army required that any proceedings instituted against him should be taken with great prudence and deliberation. **8. thou hast with thee Shimei**—Though David promised him a pardon, which being enforced by the presence of a thousand followers, could not have been well refused, he warned his son against Shimei as a turbulent and dangerous character. It must not be supposed that in these dying instructions David was evincing a fierce, vindictive spirit. He is rather to be considered as acting in the character of a king and magistrate, in noticing crimes which he had not been in a condition to punish, and pointing out persons of whom Solomon would be under a necessity to rid himself as dangerous to the state. The grateful mention of Barzillai's kindness was, however, a personal feeling that does honor to the warmth of his heart; and his silence as to Mephibosheth, the son of his beloved Jonathan, would imply the previous death of that prince. **9. for thou art a wise man**—Solomon had given early indications of wisdom before his miraculous endowment with the heavenly gift (see on ch. 3:11), and his own sagacity would dictate the course that should be followed in any new offense that Shimei might commit. **10. So David slept with his fathers**—about six months after the coronation of Solomon (cf. II Sam. 5:5, with I Chron. 29:27). The interval was spent in developing his ideas and plans for the future glory of the kingdom and providing for the permanent worship of God (see on I Chron. 22, et seq.). **was buried in the city of David**—Sepulchres were not allowed within the precincts of cities. Jerusalem, however, formed an exception; and yet, even there, the privilege was reserved chiefly for the royal family (Acts 2:29). Tradition says that the bones of David repose on Mount Zion, and the minaret of a small mosque points out the spot which tradition has fixed. His was a noble, a wondrous, and a humbling history. He was a good man, yet his life was deformed by various crimes of a very gross character. But there were many bright and noble traits in his character; he was an earnest lover of the divine law; his reign was signalized by many important services that contributed to the glory of God and the exaltation of His kingdom; and his name, as the sweet Psalmist of Israel, will be held in honor to the latest age of the Church.

12-24. SOLOMON SUCCEEDS HIM. **12. Then sat Solomon up on the throne of David his father**—His ascension to the royal dignity was made under the happiest auspices. Having been born after his father became monarch of the *whole* kingdom, his claim, according to the notions of Oriental people, was preferable to that of all, *even* his elder brothers. The Hebrew kingdom enjoyed internal prosperity; it was respected and renowned abroad, and Solomon well knew how to improve these advantages. **13-18. Adonijah . . . came to Bath-sheba**—Her question to him betrays an apprehension which his recent conduct might well warrant; but his pious acknowledgment of the divine will seemed apparently to indicate so entire an acquiescence in the settlement

ADAM CLARKE

Shew thyself a man. Act like a rational being, and not like a brute; and remember that he acts most like a man who is most devoted to his God.

3. *Keep the charge of the Lord.* Keep what God has given you to keep. (1) *Walk in his ways.* Not in your own, nor in the ways of a wicked, perishing world. (2) *Keep his statutes.* Consider all His appointments to be holy, just, and good; receive them as such and conscientiously observe them. (3) *Keep . . . his commandments.* Whatever He has bidden you to do, perform; what He has forbidden you to do, omit. (4) *Keep . . . his judgments.* What He has determined to be right is essentially and inherently right; what He has determined to be wrong or evil is inherently and essentially so. (5) *Keep . . . his testimonies.* Bear witness to all to which He has borne witness. His testimonies are true; there is no deceit or falsity in them.

4. *That the Lord may continue his word.* The prosperity which God has promised to grant to my family will depend on their faithfulness to the good they receive; if they live to God, they shall sit forever on the throne of Israel.

5. *Thou knowest . . . what Joab . . . did to me.* He did everything bad and dishonorable in itself, in the murder of Abner and Amasa, and indeed in the death of the profligate Absalom. *Shed the blood of war . . . upon his girdle . . . and in his shoes.* He stabbed them while he pretended to embrace them, so that their blood gushed out on his girdle, and fell into his shoes!

6. *Let not his hoar head go down to the grave in peace.* It would have been an insult to justice not to take the life of Joab. David was culpable in delaying it so long, but probably the circumstances of his government would not admit of his doing it sooner. According to the law of God, Joab, having murdered Abner and Amasa, should die.

7. *But shew kindness unto the sons of Barzillai.* See the notes on 2 Sam. xix. 31, etc.

8. *Thou hast with thee Shimei.* See on 2 Sam. xvi. 5, etc., and the notes on 2 Sam. xix. 18-23.

9. *Hold him not guiltless.* Do not consider him as an innocent man, though I have sworn to him that I would not put him to death by the sword. Yet as you are a wise man, and know how to treat such persons, treat him as he deserves. Only as I have sworn to him, and he is an aged man, let him not die a violent death; bring not down his hoary head to the grave with blood. So Solomon understood David, and so I think David should be understood; for the negative particle *lo* in the former clause, "hold him not guiltless," should be repeated in this latter clause, though not expressed, "his hoary head bring thou not down"—instances of which frequently occur in the Hebrew Bible.

MATTHEW HENRY

peaceably (*v.* 13), and to beg a favour" (*v.* 14), that she would use the great interest she had in her son to gain his consent, that he might marry Abishag (*v.* 16, 17). He would represent himself as an object of compassion, that had been deprived of a crown, and therefore might well be gratified in a wife. Thus he pretends to be well pleased with Solomon's accession to the throne, when he is doing all he can to give him disturbance. *His words were smoother than butter, but war was in his heart.*

3. Bath-sheba's address to Solomon on his behalf. She promised to speak to the king for him (*v.* 18) and did so, *v.* 19. Solomon received her with all the respect that was due to a mother, though he himself was a king: He *rose up to meet her, bowed himself to her*, and caused her *to sit on his right hand*, according to the law of the fifth commandment. She tells him her errand at last (*v.* 21): *Let Abishag be given to Adonijah thy brother.* It was strange that she did not suspect the treason, but more strange that she did not abhor the incest, that was in the proposal. But either she did not take Abishag to be David's wife, because the marriage was not consummated, or she thought it might be dispensed with to gratify Adonijah, in consideration of his tame submission to Solomon.

4. Solomon's just and judicious rejection of the request. Solomon convinces his mother of the unreasonableness of the request, and shows her the tendency of it, which, before, she was not aware of. His reply is somewhat sharp: "*Ask for him the kingdom also*, *v.* 22. To ask that he may succeed the king in his bed is, in effect, to ask that he may succeed him in his throne; for that is it he aims at." He convicts and condemns Adonijah for his pretensions, and both with an oath. He convicts him out of his own mouth, *v.* 23. He condemns him to die immediately: *He shall be put to death this day*, *v.* 24. It was plain enough that Adonijah aimed at the crown, and Solomon could not be safe while he lived. Ambitious turbulent spirits commonly prepare for themselves the instruments of death. Many a head has been lost by catching at a crown.

Verses 26–34

Abiathar and Joab were both aiding and abetting in Adonijah's rebellious attempt, and it is probable were at the bottom of this new motion made by Adonijah for Abishag, and it should seem Solomon knew it, *v.* 22. This was, in both, an intolerable affront both to God and to the government, and the worse because of their high station and the great influence their examples might have upon many. They are both equally guilty of the treason, but, in the judgment passed upon them, a difference is made and with good reason.

I. Abiathar, in consideration of his old services, is only degraded, *v.* 26, 27. 1. Solomon convicts him, and by his great wisdom finds him guilty. 2. He calls to mind the respect he had formerly shown to David his father, and that he had both ministered to him in holy things (*had borne before him the ark of the Lord*), and also had tenderly sympathized with him in his afflictions. 3. For this reason he spares Abiathar's life, but deposes him from his offices, and confines him to his country seat at Anathoth, forbids him the court, the city, the tabernacle, the altar, and all intermeddling in public business. 4. The depriving of Abiathar was the fulfilling of the threatening against the house of Eli (1 Sam. ii. 30), for he was the last high priest of that family.

II. Joab, in consideration of his old sins, is put to death.

1. His guilty conscience sent him to the horns of the altar. He heard that Adonijah was executed and Abiathar deposed, and therefore, fearing his turn would be next, he fled for refuge to the altar.

2. Solomon ordered him to be put to death there for the murder of Abner and Amasa; for these were the crimes upon which he thought fit to ground the sentence, rather than upon his treasonable adherence to Adonijah. On this he grounds the sentence that he *fell upon two men more righteous and better than he*, that had done him no wrong nor meant him any, and, had they lived, might probably have done David better service. For these crimes, (1) He must die, and die by the sword of public justice. (2) He must die at the altar, rather than escape. Joab resolved not to stir from the altar (*v.* 30). Benaiah made a scruple of either killing him there or dragging him thence; but Solomon knew the law, that the altar of God should give no protection to wilful murderers. In case of such sins as the blood of beasts would atone for the altar was a refuge, but not in Joab's case. He therefore orders him to be executed there.

JAMIESON, FAUSSET, BROWN

of the succession, that, in her womanly simplicity, she perceived not the deep cunning and evil design that was concealed under his request and readily undertook to promote his wishes. **19, 20. Bath-sheba . . . went unto King Solomon**—The filial reverence and the particular act of respect, which Solomon rendered, were quite in accordance with the sentiments and customs of the East. The right hand is the place of honor; and as it expressly said to have been assigned to "the king's mother," it is necessary to remark that, when a husband dies, his widow acquires a higher dignity and power, as a mother over her son, than she ever possessed before. Besides, the dignity of "king's mother" is a state office, to which certain revenues are attached. The holder has a separate palace or court, as well as possesses great influence in public affairs; and as the dignity is held for life, it sometimes happens, in consequence of deaths, that the person enjoying it may not be related to the reigning sovereign by natural maternity. Bath-sheba had evidently been invested with this honorable office. **22. why dost thou ask Abishag . . . ask for him the kingdom also**—(See on II Sam. 16:11; also on 12:8.) Solomon's indignation was roused; he in a moment penetrated the artful scheme, and from his associating the names of Abiathar and Joab, he seems to have suspected or known that those deep schemers had been the prompters of Adonijah. **23-25. God do so to me, and more also**—the common form of introducing a solemn oath. **if Adonijah have not spoken this word against his own life**—Whether there was a treasonable design to conceal under this request or not, the act, according to Eastern notions, was criminal, and of dangerous consequence to the state. There is no ground of censure upon Solomon for cruelty or precipitation in this instance. He had pardoned Adonijah's former conspiracy; but this new attempt was rebellion against the viceroy appointed by the divine King and called for condign punishment. The office of executioner was among the Hebrews, as in other ancient countries of the East, performed unceremoniously and privately—often without any previous warning—by the captain of the guard, or one of his officers (Matt. 14:10).

26, 27. unto Abiathar the priest said the king—This functionary, as the counsellor or accomplice of Adonijah, had deserved to share his fate. But partly from regard to his priestly dignity, and partly from his long associations with the late king, Solomon pronounced on him the mitigated sentence of banishment to his country estate at Anathoth, and thereby, as God's vicegerent, deprived him of his office and its emoluments. The sacred writer notices the remarkable fulfilment. Abiathar's degradation from the high priesthood (see on ch. 4:4), of the doom denounced against the house of Eli (I Sam. 2:30).

28-45. JOAB SLAIN. **28. Then tidings came to Joab**—The execution of these sentences respectively on Adonijah and Abiathar prepared Joab for his fate. Death, due to his great crimes (Num. 35:33), would long ago have been inflicted, had not his power and popularity with the army been too formidable for the old king. He now fled to the altar, which, though a recognized asylum, afforded no sanctuary to the rebel and murderer (Exod. 21:14). And, as he refused to leave it, he seems to have cherished some faint hope that a religious scruple would have been felt at the thought of violating the sanctity of the place by bloodshed. Benaiah, not liking to assume any responsibility, referred the matter to Solomon, who determined that the law should take its course (Deut. 19:13).

ADAM CLARKE

JOSEPH PARKER:

Adonijah the son of Haggith came to Bathsheba the mother of Solomon, desiring that she would speak to Solomon that he would give him Abishag the Shunammite to be his wife. Bathsheba, suspecting nothing, presented the petition to the king, but king Solomon, seeing the whole mean request, instantly determined upon the slaughter of Adonijah. To ask for the late king's concubine was in reality to commit an act of high treason. Solomon read, therefore, not merely the personal wish, but the hidden purpose of the former usurper, and by the hand of the chief of the bodyguard he brought Adonijah to his fate.

There is something moving about Solomon's treatment of Abiathar the priest. We have just seen that Abiathar was one with whom Adonijah took counsel at the time of his usurpation. Solomon remembered that he was a priest, and that he bore the ark of the Lord God before David, and therefore he restrained himself and would not at that time slay the priest. A singular sanctity seems at all times to have surrounded priestly men. Had Abiathar been a soldier, Solomon would have slain him instantly. But how can they be wholly bad who had borne the ark of the Lord God and have openly prayed for other men? It is hard to believe that any man who has been privileged to intercede with heaven on behalf of others should himself be rotten at the core. Abiathar had undoubtedly identified himself with the cause of David at one period of his life, and David had reposed confidence in the priest, saying, "Abide thou with me, fear not: for he that seeketh my life seeketh thy life: but with me thou shalt be in safe guard." But Abiathar was thrust out from being priest unto the Lord. Can any picture be more humiliating! There is no fall equal to that.

—*The People's Bible*

27. *So Solomon thrust out Abiathar.* This was for having taken part before with Adonijah, but by it a remarkable prophecy was fulfilled; see 1 Sam. ii. 13-35, and the notes there. God had told Eli that the priesthood should depart from his house; Abiathar was the last of the descendants of Ithamar, of which family was Eli, the high priest. Zadok, who was made priest in the stead of Abiathar, was of the family of Eliezer; and by this change the priesthood reverted to its ancient channel. Abiathar deserved this degradation; he supported Adonijah in his unnatural assumption of the royal dignity, even during the life of his father.

28. *Tidings came to Joab.* He heard that Adonijah had been slain and Abiathar banished, and probably he had heard of David's dying charge to Solomon. Fearing therefore for his personal safety, he takes refuge at the Tabernacle, as claiming divine protection, and desiring to have his case decided by God alone.

30. *Nay; but I will die here.* The altars were so sacred among all the people that, in general, even the vilest wretch found safety if he once reached the altar. This led to many abuses and the perversion of public justice; and at last it became a maxim that the guilty should be punished, should they even have taken refuge at the altars. God decreed that the presumptuous murderer who had taken refuge at the altar should be dragged thence and put to death; see Exod. xxi. 14.

MATTHEW HENRY

The holiness of any place should never countenance the wickedness of any person. Those who, by a lively faith, take hold on Christ and his righteousness, with a resolution, if they perish, to perish there, shall find in him a more powerful protection than Joab found at the horns of the altar. Benaiah slew him (*v.* 34), with the solemnity, no doubt, of a public execution.

3. Solomon pleased himself with this act of justice not as it gratified any personal revenge, but as it was the fulfilling of his father's orders and a real kindness to himself and his own government. Peace was hereby secured (*v.* 33) upon David. Upon *his seed, his house, and his throne*, shall there be *peace for ever from the Lord.* Now that such a turbulent man as Joab is removed there shall be peace. Solomon, in this blessing of peace upon his house and throne, piously looks upward to God as the author of it and forward to eternity as the perfection of it. "It shall be peace from the Lord, and peace for ever from the Lord." The Lord of peace himself give us that peace which is everlasting.

Verses 35–46

I. The preferment of Benaiah and Zadok, two faithful friends to Solomon and his government, *v.* 35. Joab being put to death, Benaiah was advanced to be general of the forces in his room, and, Abiathar being deposed, Zadok was made high priest in his room, and therein was fulfilled that word of God, when he threatened to cut off the house of Eli (1 Sam. ii. 35), *I will raise me up a faithful priest, and will build him a sure house.*

II. The course that was taken with Shimei. He is sent for, by a messenger, from his house at Bahurim, expecting perhaps no better than Adonijah's doom, being conscious of his enmity to the house of David; but Solomon knows how to make a difference of crimes and criminals. David had promised Shimei his life for his time. Solomon is not bound by that promise, yet he will not go directly contrary to it. 1. He confines him to Jerusalem, and forbids him, upon any pretence whatsoever, to go out of the city any further than the brook Kidron, *v.* 36, 37, lest he should make mischief among his neighbours, but took him to Jerusalem, where he kept him prisoner at large. He has his life upon easy terms: he shall live if he will but be content to live at Jerusalem. 2. Shimei submits to the confinement, and thankfully takes his life upon those terms. Two of his servants ran from him to the land of the Philistines, *v.* 39. Thither he pursued them, and thence brought them back to Jerusalem, *v.* 40. Solomon takes the forfeiture. Information is given him that Shimei has transgressed, *v.* 41. Had he represented to Solomon the urgency of the occasion, and begged leave to go, perhaps Solomon might have given him leave; but to presume either upon his ignorance or his connivance was to affront him in the highest degree. He condemns him for his former crime, cursing David, and throwing stones at him in the day of his affliction. He gives orders for the execution of Shimei immediately, *v.* 46.

JAMIESON, FAUSSET, BROWN

34. Benaiah . . . went up, and fell upon him—According to the terms of the statute (Exod. 21:14), and the practice in similar cases (II Kings 11:15), the criminal was to be dragged from the altar and slain elsewhere. But the truth is, that the sanctity of the altar was violated as much by the violence used in forcing the criminal from the place as in shedding his blood there; the express command of God authorized the former and therefore by implication permitted the latter. **was buried in his own house**—or family vault, at his property in the wilderness of Judah. His interment was included in the king's order, as enjoined in the divine law (Deut. 21: 23). **33. Their blood shall . . . return upon the head of Joab**, etc. —A reference is here made to the curse publicly and solemnly pronounced by King David (II Sam. 3:28, 29).

34-46. SHIMEI PUT TO DEATH. **36. the king sent and called for Shimei**—He was probably residing at Bahurim, his native place. But, as he was a suspicious character, Solomon condemned him henceforth to live in Jerusalem, on the penalty of death, for going without the gates. He submitted to this confinement for three years, when, violating his oath, he was arrested and put to death by Solomon for perjury, aggravated by his former crime of high treason against David.

46. the kingdom was established in the hand of Solomon—Now, by the death of Shimei, *all* the leaders of the rival factions had been cut off.

ADAM CLARKE

36. *Build thee an house.* Thus he gave him the whole city for a prison, and this certainly could have reduced him to no hardships.

37. *Thy blood shall be upon thine own head.* You know what to expect; if you disobey my orders you shall certainly be slain, and then you shall be considered as a self-murderer; you alone shall be answerable for your own death. Solomon knew that Shimei was a seditious man, and he chose to keep him under his own eye; for such a man at large, in favorable circumstances, might do much evil. His bitter revilings of David were a sufficient proof.

40. *And Shimei . . . went to Gath.* It is astonishing that with his eyes wide open he would thus run into the jaws of death.

45. *King Solomon shall be blessed.* He seems to think that, while such bad men remained unpunished, the nation could not prosper; that it was an act of justice which God required him to perform, in order to the establishment and perpetuity of his throne.

MATTHEW HENRY — CHAPTER 3

Verses 1–4

I Something that was unquestionably good, for which Solomon is to be praised and in which he is to be imitated. 1. He *loved the Lord*, *v.* 3. Particular notice was taken of God's love to him, 2 Sam. xii. 24. He had his name from it: *Jedidiah—beloved of the Lord.* And here we find he returned that love, as John, the beloved disciple, was most full of love. Solomon was a wise man, a rich man, a great man; yet the brightest encomium of him is that which is the character of all the saints, even the poorest, He *loved the Lord. He loved the worship of the Lord*, so the Chaldee; all that love God love his worship, love to hear from him and speak to him, and so to have communion with him. 2. He *walked in the statutes of David his father*, that is, in the statutes that David gave him, *ch.* ii. 2, 3; 1 Chron. xxviii. 9, 10, or in God's statutes, which David his father walked in before him; he kept close to God's ordinances. Those that truly *love God* will make conscience of *walking in his statutes.* 3. He was very free and generous in what he did for the honour of God. We must never think that wasted which is laid out in the service of God.

II. Here is something concerning which it may be doubted whether it was good or no. 1. His marrying Pharaoh's daughter, *v.* 1. We will suppose she was proselyted, otherwise the marriage would not have been lawful; yet, if so, surely it was not advisable. Some think that he did this with the advice of his

JAMIESON, FAUSSET, BROWN — CHAPTER 3

Vs. 1. SOLOMON MARRIES PHARAOH'S DAUGHTER. **1. Solomon made affinity with Pharaoh**—This was a royal title, equivalent to sultan, and the personal name of this monarch is said to have been Vaphres. The formation, on equal terms, of this matrimonial alliance with the royal family of Egypt, shows the high consideration to which the Hebrew kingdom had now arisen. Rosellini has given, from the Egyptian monuments, what is supposed to be a portrait of this princess. She was received in the land of her adoption with great éclat; for the Song of Solomon and the forty-fifth Psalm are supposed to have been composed in honor of this occasion, although they may both have a higher typical reference to the introduction of the Gentiles into the church. **brought her into the city of David**—i.e., Jerusalem. She was not admissible into the stronghold of Zion, the building where the ark was (Deut. 23:7, 8). She seems to have been lodged at first in his mother's apartments (Song of Sol. 3:4; 8:2), as a suitable residence was not yet provided for her in the new palace (ch. 7:8; 9:24; II Chron. 8:11). **building . . . the wall of Jerusalem**—Although David had begun (Ps. 51:18), it was, according to Josephus, reserved for Solomon to extend and complete the fortifications of the city. It has been questioned whether this marriage was in conformity with the law (see on Exod. 34:16; Deut. 7:3; Ezra 10:1-10; Neh. 13: 26). But it is nowhere censured in Scripture, as are

ADAM CLARKE — CHAPTER 3

1. *Solomon made affinity with Pharaoh.* This was no doubt a political measure in order to strengthen his kingdom, and on the same ground he continued his alliance with the king of Tyre; and these were among the most powerful of his neighbors. But should political considerations prevail over express laws of God? God had strictly forbidden His people to form alliances with heathenish women, lest they should lead their hearts away from Him into idolatry. Let us hear the law: "Neither shalt thou make marriages with them; thy daughter thou shalt not give unto his son, nor his daughter shalt thou take unto thy son. For they will turn away thy son from following me," Exod. xxxiv. 16; Deut. vii. 3-4. Now Solomon acted in direct opposition to these laws, and perhaps in this alliance were sown those seeds of apostasy from God and goodness in which he so long lived, and in which he so awfully died.

MATTHEW HENRY

friends, that she was a sincere convert (for the gods of the Egyptians are not reckoned among the strange gods which his strange wives drew him in to the worship of, *ch.* xi. 5, 6), and that the book of Canticles and the 45th Psalm were penned on this occasion, by which these nuptials were made typical of the mystical espousals of the church to Christ, especially the Gentile church. 2. His worshipping in the high places, and thereby tempting the people to do so too, *v.* 2, 3. Abraham built his altars on mountains (Gen. xii. 8; xxii. 2), and worshipped in a grove, Gen. xxi. 33. Thence the custom was derived, and was proper, till the divine law confined them to one place, Deut. xii. 5, 6. David kept to the ark, and did not care for the high places, but Solomon, though in other things he *walked in the statutes of his father*, in this came short of him. He showed thereby a great zeal for sacrificing, but to obey would have been better.

Verses 5–15

An account of a gracious visit which God paid to Solomon, and the communion he had with God.

I. The circumstances of this visit, *v.* 5. 1. The place. It was in Gibeon; that was the great high place, because there the tabernacle and the brazen altar were, 2 Chron. i. 3. There Solomon offered his great sacrifices, and there God owned him. The nearer we come to the rule in our worship the more reason we have to expect the tokens of God's presence. 2. The time. It was by night, the night after he had offered that generous sacrifice, *v.* 4. The more we abound in God's work the more comfort we may expect in him; if the day has been busy for him, the night will be easy in him. Silence and retirement befriend our communion with God. 3. The manner. It was in a dream, when he was asleep, his senses locked up, that God's access to his mind might be the more free and immediate. In this way God used to speak to the prophets (Num. xii. 6) and to private persons, for their own benefit, Job xxxiii. 15, 16. These divine dreams were plainly distinguishable from those in which there are divers vanities, Eccl. v. 7.

II. The gracious offer God made him, *v.* 5. He saw the glory of God shine about him, and heard a voice saying, *Ask what I shall give thee.*

III. The pious request Solomon hereupon made to God. He readily laid hold of this offer. Solomon prayed in his sleep, God's grace assisting him; yet it was a lively prayer. The grace of God wrought in him these gracious desires.

1. He acknowledges God's great goodness to his father David, *v.* 6. God's favours are doubly sweet when we observe them transmitted to us through the hands of those that have gone before us.

2. He owns his own insufficiency for the discharge of that great trust to which he is called, *v.* 7, 8. And here is a double plea to enforce his petition for wisdom:—(1) That his place required it, as he was successor to David. (2) That he wanted it. As one that had a humble sense of his own deficiency, he pleads, "*Lord, I am but a little child. I know not how to go out or come in* as I should, nor to do so much as the common daily business of the government." Paul's question (*Who is sufficient for these things?*) is much like Solomon's here, *Who is able to judge this thy so great a people? v.* 9. Absalom, who was a fool, wished himself a judge; Solomon, who was a wise man, trembles at the undertaking and suspects his own fitness for it.

3. He begs of God to give him wisdom (*v.* 9): *Give therefore thy servant an understanding heart.* Thus his good father prayed, and thus he pleaded. Ps. cxix. 125, *I am thy servant, give me understanding.* An understanding heart is God's gift, Prov. ii. 6. We must pray for it (James i. 5), and pray for it with application to our particular calling.

4. The favourable answer God gave to his request. It was a pleasing prayer (*v.* 10): *The speech pleased the Lord.* Those are accepted of God who prefer spiritual blessings to temporal. But that was not all; it was a prevailing prayer, and prevailed for more than he asked. (1) God gave him wisdom, *v.* 12. Such an insight, and such a foresight, never was prince so blessed with. (2) He gave him riches and honour over and above into the bargain (*v.* 13). These also are God's gift, and, as far as is good for them, are promised to all that *seek first the kingdom of God and the righteousness thereof,* Matt. vi. 33. Let young people learn to prefer grace to gold in all that they choose, because *godliness has the promise of the life that now is,* but *the life that now is* has not *the promise of godliness.* But, if we make sure of wisdom and grace, these will either bring outward prosperity with them or sweeten the want of it. God promised Solomon riches and honour absolutely, but long life

JAMIESON, FAUSSET, BROWN

the connections Solomon formed with other foreigners (ch. 11:1-3); whence it may be inferred that he had stipulated for her abandonment of idolatry, and conforming to the Jewish religion (Ps. 45:10, 11).

2-5. HIGH PLACES BEING IN USE HE SACRIFICES AT GIBEON. **3. Solomon loved the Lord**—This declaration, illustrated by what follows, affords undoubted evidence of the young king's piety; nor is the word "only," which prefaces the statement, to be understood as introducing a qualifying circumstance that reflected any degree of censure upon him. The intention of the sacred historian is to describe the generally prevailing mode of worship before the temple was built. The "high places" were altars erected on natural or artificial eminences, probably from the idea that men were brought nearer to the Deity. They had been used by the patriarchs, and had become so universal among the heathen that they were almost identified with idolatry. They were prohibited in the law (Lev. 17:3, 4; Deut. 12:13, 14; Jer. 7:31; Ezek. 6:3, 4; Hos. 10:8). But, so long as the tabernacle was migratory and the means for the national worship were merely provisional, the worship on those high places was tolerated. Hence, as accounting for their continuance, it is expressly stated (vs. 2) that God had not yet chosen a permanent and exclusive place for his worship. **4. the king went to Gibeon to sacrifice there**—The old tabernacle and the brazen altar which Moses had made in the wilderness were there (I Chron. 16:39; 21:29; II Chron. 1:3-6). The royal progress was of public importance. It was a season of national devotion. The king was accompanied by his principal nobility (II Chron. 1:2); and, as the occasion was most probably one of the great annual festivals which lasted seven days, the rank of the offerer and the succession of daily oblations may help in part to account for the immense magnitude of the sacrifices. **5. In Gibeon the Lord appeared to Solomon in a dream**—It was probably at the close of this season, when his mind had been elevated into a high state of religious fervor by the protracted services. Solomon felt an intense desire, and he had offered an earnest petition, for the gift of wisdom. In sleep his thoughts ran upon the subject of his prayer, and he dreamed that God appeared to him and gave him the option of every thing in the world—that he asked wisdom, and that God granted his request. His dream was but an imaginary repetition of his former desire, but God's grant of it was real.

6-15. HE CHOOSES WISDOM. **6. Solomon said**—i.e., had dreamed that he said.

7. I am but a little child—not in age, for he had reached manhood (ch. 2:9) and must have been at least twenty years old; but he was raw and inexperienced in matters of government.

10. the speech pleased the Lord—It was Solomon's waking prayers that God heard and requited, but the acceptance was signified in this vision.

ADAM CLARKE

F. B. MEYER:

The young king's wise choice. The chapter opens doubtfully. The affinity with Pharaoh and the two "onlys" of verses 2 and 3 are not promising (see Deut. 12:13, 14). Yet there were hopeful features in Solomon's love for God, and the devotion and obedience by which it was proved. It remained, however, to be seen which of these influences was to triumph in the outworking of his character. That is always the most urgent question in life. With too many the early dew and morning cloud pass away, leaving no trace (Hos. 6:4).

There is an inner wisdom which is of the heart rather than of the head, and which God's Spirit bestows on those who love him. Having this, we possess the key to all things in heaven and on earth (1 Cor.2:5ff). When a man seeks first the kingdom, all else is added (Matt. 6:33). Only the man who delights in God can be trusted with the gratification of his heart's desires (Ps. 37:4).

Live deep in God. Do not be dazzled or fascinated by outward things. Be concerned to know God's will and become the organ of his purpose. He will add to you all else that is needful for the fulfillment of your life-course.

—*Bible Commentary*

5. *The Lord appeared to Solomon in a dream.* This was the night after he had offered the sacrifices (see 2 Chron. i. 7), and probably after he had earnestly prayed for wisdom; see *Wisdom,* chap. vii. 7: "Wherefore I prayed, and understanding was given me: I called upon God, and the spirit of wisdom came to me." If this were the case, the dream might have been the consequence of his earnest prayer for wisdom. The images of those things which occupy the mind during the day are most likely to recur during the night; and this, indeed, is the origin of the greater part of our dreams. But this appears to have been supernatural.

7. *I know not how to go out or come in.* I am just like an infant learning to walk alone, and can neither go out nor come in without help.

9. *Give . . . an understanding heart to judge thy people.* He did not ask wisdom in general, but the true science of government. This wisdom he sought, and this wisdom he obtained.

12. *I have given thee a wise and an understanding heart.* I have given you a capacious mind, one capable of knowing much. Make a proper use of your powers, under the direction of My Spirit, and you shall excel in wisdom all that have gone before thee; neither after thee shall any arise like unto thee.

MATTHEW HENRY

upon condition (*v.* 14). *If thou wilt walk in my ways, as David did, then I will lengthen thy days.* He failed in the condition; and therefore, though he had riches and honour, he did not live so long to enjoy them as in the course of nature he might have done. [1] The way to obtain spiritual blessings is to be importunate for them, to wrestle with God in prayer for them, as Solomon did for wisdom, asking that only, as the *one thing needful.* [2] The way to obtain temporal blessings is to be indifferent to them and to refer ourselves to God concerning them. Solomon had wisdom given him because he did ask it and wealth because he did not ask it.

5. The grateful return Solomon made for the visit God was pleased to pay him, *v.* 15. He awoke, we may suppose in a transport of joy; being satisfied of God's favour, he began to think *what he should render to the Lord.* He had made his prayer at the high place at Gibeon, and there God had graciously met him; but he comes to Jerusalem to give thanks *before the ark of the covenant,* blaming himself, as it were, that he had not prayed there, the ark being the token of God's presence, and wondering that God had met him anywhere else. God's passing by our mistakes should persuade us to amend them. There he, (1) Offered a great sacrifice to God. (2) He made a great feast upon the sacrifice, that those about him might rejoice with him in the grace of God.

Verses 16–28

An instance is here given of Solomon's wisdom. The proof is fetched, not from the mysteries of state, though there no doubt he excelled, but from the trial of a cause between party and party.

I. The case opened, not by lawyers, but by the parties themselves, though they were women. These two women were harlots. It is probable the cause had been heard in the inferior courts, before it was brought before Solomon, the judges being unable to determine it. These two women, who lived in a house together, were each of them delivered of a son within three days of one another, *v.* 17, 18. One of them overlaid her child, and, in the night, exchanged it with the other (*v.* 19, 20), who was soon aware of the cheat put upon her, and appealed to public justice to be righted, *v.* 21.

II. The difficulty of the case. The question was, Who was the mother of this living child? Both mothers were vehement in their claim, and showed a deep concern about it. Neither will own the dead child, though it would be cheaper to bury that than to maintain the other: but it is the living one they strive for. The neighbours, though it is probable that some of them were present at the birth and circumcision of the children, yet had not taken so much notice of them as to be able to distinguish them.

III. The determination of it. Solomon, having patiently heard what both sides had to say, sums up the evidence, *v.* 23. Solomon calls for a sword, and gives orders to divide the living child between the two contenders. It proved an effectual discovery of the truth. Some think that Solomon did himself discern it, before he made this experiment, by the countenances of the women and their way of speaking. To find out the true mother, he could not try which the child loved best, and must therefore try which loved the child best; both pretended to a motherly affection, but their sincerity will be tried when the child is in danger. (1) She that knew the child was not her own, but in contending for it stood upon a point of honour, was well content to have it divided. (2) She that knew the child was her own, rather than the child should be butchered, gives it up to her adversary. How feelingly does she cry out, *O, my lord! give her the living child, v.* 26. "Let me see it hers, rather than not see it at all." By this tenderness towards the child it appeared that she was not the careless mother that had overlaid the dead child, but was the true mother of the living one, that could not endure to see its death, having compassion on the son of her womb.

IV. We are told what a great reputation Solomon got among his people by this and other instances of his wisdom, which would have a great influence upon the ease of his government: *They feared the king* (*v.* 28), *for they saw that the wisdom of God was in him,* that is, that wisdom with which God had promised to endue him.

JAMIESON, FAUSSET, BROWN

15. behold, it was a dream—The vivid impression, the indelible recollection he had of this dream, together with the new and increased energy communicated to his mind, and the flow of worldly prosperity that rushed upon him, gave him assurance that it came by divine inspiration and originated in the grace of God. The wisdom, however, that was asked and obtained was not so much of the heart as of the head—it was wisdom not for himself personally, but for his office, such as would qualify him for the administration of justice, the government of a kingdom, and for the attainment of general scientific knowledge.

16-28. HIS JUDGMENT BETWEEN TWO HARLOTS. **16. Then came there two women**—Eastern monarchs, who generally administer justice in person, at least in all cases of difficulty, often appeal to the principles of human nature when they are at a loss otherwise to find a clue to the truth or see clearly their way through a mass of conflicting testimony. The modern history of the East abounds with anecdotes of judicial cases, in which the decision given was the result of an experiment similar to this of Solomon upon the natural feelings of the contending parties.

ADAM CLARKE

But was not all this conditional? If he should walk in His ways, and keep His statutes and commandments, v. 14. Did not his unfaithfulness prevent the fulfillment of the divine purpose? No character in the sacred writings disappoints us more than the character of Solomon.

16. *Then came there two women . . . harlots.* The word *zonoth,* which we here, and in some other places, improperly translated *harlots,* is by the Chaldee (the best judge in this case) rendered "tavern keepers" (see on Josh. ii. 1). If these had been harlots, it is not likely they would have dared to appear before Solomon; and if they had been common women, it is not likely they would have had children; nor is it likely that such persons would have been permitted under the reign of David.

28. *They feared the king.* This decision proved that they could not impose upon him, and they were afraid to do those things which might bring them before his judgment seat. *They saw that the wisdom of God was in him.* They perceived that he was taught of God, judged impartially, and could not be deceived.

F. B. MEYER:

The incident gave convincing proof of the gift of wisdom. This is the most esteemed endowment of an Eastern potentate, who is called upon to arbitrate in cases that defy the labored processes of law and precedent. How could so difficult a case be decided? There were no witnesses on either side. But Solomon appealed to the instincts of a mother's love. The proposal to divide the child at once revealed the mother, who would rather expose herself to a life of anguish than see her child suffer or its life extinguished.

Bishop Hall, commenting on this incident, says, "Truth demands entireness; falsehood is satisfied with less. Satan, who has no right to the heart, is content with a piece of it; God, who made the heart, will have either all or none."

But surely there is a still deeper lesson. When we truly belong to Christ, sharing his nature and having fellowship in his kingdom, we shall live in quick sympathy with everything that touches his honor. The child of God instinctively winces whenever his Father's character is challenged, or a foul suggestion is made to his own soul. This is evidence of sonship.—*Bible Commentary*

MATTHEW HENRY

CHAPTER 4

Verses 1–19

I. Solomon upon his throne (*v.* 1): *So king Solomon was king*, that is, he was confirmed and established king *over all Israel.*

II. The great officers of his court. It is observable, 1. That several of them are the same that were in his father's time. Zadok and Abiathar were then priests (2 Sam. xx. 25), Jehoshaphat was then recorder, Benaiah, in his father's time, was a principal man in military affairs. 2. The rest were priests' sons. His prime-minister of state was *Azariah the son of Zadok the priest*. Two others of the first rank were the sons of Nathan the prophet, *v.* 5.

III. The purveyors for his household, whose business it was to send in provisions from several parts of the country, that thus, 1. His house might always be well furnished at the best hand. 2. That thus he himself, and those who immediately attended him, might the more closely apply themselves to the business of the state, not troubled about much serving. 3. That thus all the parts of the kingdom might be equally benefited by the taking off of the commodities that were the productions of their country and the circulating of the coin. Industry would hereby be encouraged, and consequently wealth increased, even in those tribes that lay most remote from the court. 4. The dividing of this trust into so many hands was prudent, that no man might be continually burdened with the care of it nor grow exorbitantly rich with the profit of it.

Verses 20–28

Such a kingdom, and such a court, surely never any prince had, as Solomon's.

I. Such a kingdom. The account here given of it is such as fully answers the prophecies which we have concerning it in Ps. lxxii., which is a psalm for Solomon, but with references to Christ. 1. The territories of his kingdom were large and its tributaries many; so it was foretold that he should *have dominion from sea to sea*, Ps. lxxii. 8–11. Solomon reigned over all the neighbouring kingdoms, who were his subjects by constraint. All the princes from the river Euphrates, north-east to the border of Egypt south-west, added to his wealth by serving him, and bringing him presents, *v.* 21. He had *peace on all sides*, *v.* 24. 2. The subjects of his kingdom, and its inhabitants, were many and cheerful. (1) They were numerous and the country was exceedingly populous (*v.* 20): *Judah and Israel were many*, and that good land was sufficient to maintain them all. (2) They were easy, they dwelt safely. They dwelt every man under *his vine and fig tree*. Solomon invaded no man's property, but what they had they could call their own: he protected every man in the possession and enjoyment of his property. (3) They were cheerful in the use of their plenty, *eating and drinking, and making merry*, *v.* 20. Go where you would, you might **see all the marks of plenty, peace, and satisfaction. The spiritual peace, and joy, and holy security,** of all the faithful subjects of the Lord Jesus were typified by this. *The kingdom of God is not*, as Solomon's was, *meat and drink*, but, what is infinitely better, *righteousness, and peace, and joy in the Holy Ghost*.

II. Such a court Solomon kept as can scarcely be paralleled. Ahasuerus, once in his reign, made a *great feast*, to *show the riches of his kingdom*, Esther i. 3, 4. But it was much more the honour of Solomon that he kept a constant table not of dainties but substantial food, for the entertainment of those who came to hear his wisdom. Thus Christ fed those whom he taught, 5,000 at a time, more than ever Solomon's table would entertain at once: and all believers have in him a continual feast. Herein he far outdoes Solomon, that he feeds all his subjects, not with the bread that perishes, but *with that which endures to eternal life*.

Verses 29–34

Solomon's wisdom was more his glory than his wealth.

I. The fountain of his wisdom: *God gave it him*, *v.* 29.

JAMIESON, FAUSSET, BROWN

CHAPTER 4

1-6. SOLOMON'S PRINCES. **1. So King Solomon was king over all Israel**—This chapter contains a general description of the state and glory of the Hebrew kingdom during the more flourishing or later years of his reign. **2. these were the princes**—or chief officers, as is evident from two of them marrying Solomon's daughters. **Azariah the son of Zadok the priest**—rather, the prince, as the *Hebrew* word frequently signifies (Gen. 41:45; Exod. 2:16; II Sam. 8:18); so that from the precedency given to his person in the list, he seems to have been prime minister, the highest in office next the king. **3. scribes**—i.e., secretaries of state. Under David, there had been only one. The employment of three functionaries in this department indicates either improved regulations by the division of labor, or a great increase of business, occasioned by the growing prosperity of the kingdom, or a more extensive correspondence with foreign countries. **recorder**—i.e., historiographer, or annalist—an office of great importance in Oriental courts, and the duties of which consisted in chronicling the occurrences of every day. **4. Benaiah . . . was over the host**—formerly captain of the guard. He had succeeded Joab as commander of the forces. **Zadok and Abiathar were the priests**—Only the first discharged the sacred functions; the latter had been banished to his country seat and retained nothing more than the name of high priest. **5. over the officers**—i.e., the provincial governors enumerated in vss. 17-19. **principal officer, and the king's friend**—perhaps president of the privy council, and Solomon's confidential friend or favorite. This high functionary had probably been reared along with Solomon. That he should heap those honors on the sons of Nathan was most natural, considering the close intimacy of the father with the late king, and the deep obligations under which Solomon personally lay to the prophet. **6. Ahishar was over the household**—steward or chamberlain of the palace. **Adoniram**—or Adoram (II Sam. 20:24; ch. 12:18), or Hadoram (II Chron. 10:18), **was over the tribute**—not the collection of money or goods, but the levy of compulsory laborers (cf. ch: 5:13, 14).

7-21. HIS TWELVE OFFICERS. **7. Solomon had twelve officers over all Israel.** The royal revenues were raised according to the ancient, and still, in many parts, existing usage of the East, not in money payments, but in the produce of the soil. There would be always a considerable difficulty in the collection and transmission of these tithes (I Sam. 8:15). Therefore, to facilitate the work, Solomon appointed twelve officers, who had each the charge of a tribe or particular district of country, from which, in monthly rotation, the supplies for the maintenance of the king's household were drawn, having first been deposited in "the store cities" which were erected for their reception (ch. 9:19; II Chron. 8:4, 6). **8. The son of Hur**—or, as the margin has it, *Benhur, Bendekar*. In the rural parts of Syria, and among the Arabs, it is still common to designate persons not by their own names, but as the sons of their fathers. **21. Solomon reigned over all kingdoms, from the river**—All the petty kingdoms between the Euphrates and the Mediterranean were tributary to him. Similar is the statement in vs. 24. **24. from Tiphsah**—i.e., Thapsacus, a large and flourishing town on the west bank of the Euphrates, the name of which was derived from a celebrated ford near it, the lowest on that river. **even to Azzah**—i.e., Gaza, on the southwestern extremity, not far from the Mediterranean. **22. Solomon's provision for one day**—not for the king's table only, but for all connected with the court, including, besides the royal establishment, those of his royal consorts, his principal officers, his bodyguards, his foreign visitors, etc. The quantity of fine floor used is estimated at 240 bushels: that of meal or common flour at 480. The number of cattle required for consumption, besides poultry and several kinds of game (which were abundant on the mountains) did not exceed in proportion what is needed in other courts of the East. **25. every man under his vine and . . . fig tree**—This is a common and beautiful metaphor for peace and security (Mic. 4:4; Zech. 3:10), founded on the practice, still common in modern Syria, of training these fruit trees up the walls and stairs of houses, so as to make a shady arbor, beneath which the people sit and relax. **26. forty thousand stalls**—for the royal mews (see on II Chron. 9:25). **28. Barley . . . and straw**—Straw is not used for litter, but barley mixed with chopped straw is the usual fodder of horses. **dromedaries**—one-humped camels, distinguished for their great fleetness.

29-34. HIS WISDOM. **29. God gave Solomon**

ADAM CLARKE

CHAPTER 4

2. *These were the princes which he had; Azariah the son of Zadok the priest.* These were his great, chief, or principal men. None of them were princes in the common acceptation of the word.

3. *Elihoreph and Ahiah . . . scribes.* "Secretaries" to the king. *Jehoshaphat . . . recorder.* Historiographer to the king, who chronicled the affairs of the kingdom. He was in this office under David (see 2 Sam. xx. 24).

5. *Azariah . . . was over the officers.* He had the superintendence of the twelve officers mentioned below (see v. 7). *Zabud . . . was principal officer.* Perhaps what we call "premier," or "prime minister." *The king's friend.* His chief favorite—his confidant.

6. *Ahishar was over the household.* The king's chamberlain. *Adoniram . . . was over the tribute.* What we call "chancellor of the exchequer." He received and brought into the treasury all the proceeds of taxes and tributes. He was in this office under David (see 2 Sam. xx. 24).

7. *Twelve officers.* The business of these twelve officers was to provide daily, each for a month, those provisions which were consumed in the king's household (see vv. 22-23). And the task for such a daily provision was not an easy one.

13. *Threescore great cities with walls and brazen bars.* These were fortified cities, their gates and bars covered with plates of brass.

20. *Eating and drinking, and making merry.* They were very comfortable, very rich, very merry, and very corrupt. And this full feeding and dissipation led to a total corruption of manners.

21. *Solomon reigned over all kingdoms.* The meaning of this verse appears to be that Solomon reigned over all the provinces from the river Euphrates to the land of the Philistines, even to the frontiers of Egypt. The Euphrates was on the east of Solomon's dominions; the Philistines were westward on the Mediterranean Sea; and Egypt was on the south. Solomon had, therefore, as tributaries the kingdoms of Syria, Damascus, Moab, and Ammon, which lay between the Euphrates and the Mediterranean. Thus he appears to have possessed all the land that God covenanted with Abraham to give to his posterity.

22. *Solomon's provision for one day*: Of fine flour—*thirty measures,* or "cors." The cor was the same as the homer, and contained nearly seventy-six gallons.

25. *Every man under his vine.* They were no longer obliged to dwell in fortified cities for fear of their enemies; they spread themselves over all the country, which they everywhere cultivated; and had always the privilege of eating the fruits of their own labors.

26. *Solomon had forty thousand stalls of horses . . . and twelve thousand horsemen.* In 2 Chron. ix. 25, instead of *forty thousand stalls,* we read "four thousand"; and even this number might be quite sufficient to hold horses for 12,000 horsemen; for stalls and stables may be here synonymous. In chap. x. 26 it is said he had "a thousand and four hundred chariots, and twelve thousand horsemen"; and this is the reading in 2 Chron. i. 14. In 2 Chron. ix. 25, already quoted, instead of *forty thousand stalls of horses,* the Septuagint has "four thousand mares." From this collation of parallel places we may rest satisfied that there is a corruption in the numbers somewhere; and as a sort of medium, we may take for the whole 4,000 stalls, 1,400 chariots, and 12,000 horsemen.

28. *And dromedaries.* The word *rechesh,* which we translate thus, is rendered "beasts," or "beasts of burden," by the Vulgate; "mares" by the Syriac and Arabic; "chariots" by the Septuagint; and "racehorses" by the Chaldee. The original word seems to signify a very swift kind of horse, and racehorse or post-horse is probably its true meaning. To communicate with so many distant provinces, Solomon had need of many animals of this kind.

29. *God gave Solomon wisdom.* He gave him a capacious mind, and furnished him with extra-

MATTHEW HENRY

II. The fulness of it: *He had wisdom and understanding, exceeding much.* It is called *largeness of heart*; for the heart is often put for the intellectual powers. He was very free and communicative, had the gift of utterance as well as wisdom, was as free of his learning as he was of his meat, and grudged neither to any that were about him. The greatness of Solomon's wisdom is illustrated by comparison. Chaldea and Egypt were nations famous for learning; thence the Greeks borrowed theirs; but the greatest scholars of these nations came short of Solomon, *v.* 30. *Solomon excelled them all* (*v.* 30), he outdid them and confounded them; his counsel was much more valuable.

III. The fame of it. It was talked of *in all nations round about.*

IV. The fruits of it; by these the tree is known: he did not bury his talent, but showed his wisdom,

1. In his compositions. It appears by what he spoke, or dictated to be written from him, (1) That he was a moralist, and a man of great prudence, for he spoke 3,000 *proverbs*, wise sayings, apophthegms, of admirable use for the conduct of human life. Whether those proverbs of Solomon that we have were any part of the 3,000 is uncertain. (2) That he was a poet and a man of great wit: *His songs were* 1,005, of which one only is extant, because that only was divinely inspired, which is therefore called his *Song of songs.* (3) That he was a natural philosopher, and a man of great learning and insight into the mysteries of nature. From his own and others' observations and experience, he wrote both of plants and animals (*v.* 33).

2. In his conversation. There came persons from all parts to *hear the wisdom of Solomon, v.* 34. But, *Lastly*, Solomon was, herein, a type of Christ, *in whom are hidden all the treasures of wisdom and knowledge*, and hidden for use; for he is *made of God to us wisdom.*

JAMIESON, FAUSSET, BROWN

wisdom and understanding exceeding much, and largeness of heart—i.e., high powers of mind, great capacity for receiving, as well as aptitude for communicating, knowledge. **30. Solomon's wisdom excelled the wisdom of all the children of the east country**—i.e., the Arabians, Chaldeans, and Persians (Gen. 25:6). **all the wisdom of Egypt**—Egypt was renowned as the seat of learning and sciences, and the existing monuments, which so clearly describe the ancient state of society and the arts, show the high culture of the Egyptian people. **31. wiser than all men**—i.e., all his contemporaries, either at home or abroad. **than Ethan**—or Jeduthun, of the family of Merari (I Chron. 6:44). **Heman**—(I Chron. 15: 17-19)—the chief of the temple musicians and the king's seers (I Chron. 25:5); the other two are not known. **the sons of Mahol**—either another name for Zerah (I Chron. 2:6); or taking it as a common noun, signifying a dance, a chorus, "the sons of Mahol" signify persons eminently skilled in poetry and music. **32. he spake three thousand proverbs**—embodying his moral sentiments and sage observations on human life and character. **songs . . . a thousand and five**—Psalm 72, 127, 132, and the Song of Songs are his.

33. he spake of trees, from the cedar . . . to the hyssop—all plants, from the greatest to the least. The Spirit of God has seen fit to preserve comparatively few memorials of the fruits of his gigantic mind. The greater part of those here ascribed to him have long since fallen a prey to the ravages of time, or perished in the Babylonish captivity, probably because they were not inspired.

ADAM CLARKE

ordinary assistance to cultivate it.

30. *The children of the east country.* That is the Chaldeans, Persians, and Arabians, who, with the Egyptians, were famed for wisdom and knowledge through all the world.

31. *He was wiser than all men.* He was wiser than any of those who were most celebrated in his time, among whom were the four after mentioned, viz., *Ethan, Heman, Chalcol,* and *Darda.* Ethan was probably the same as is mentioned in some of the psalms, particularly Psalms lxxxix, title; and among the singers in 1 Chron. vi. 42. There is a Heman mentioned in the title to Psalms lxxxviii. In 1 Chron. ii. 6 we have all the four names, but they are probably not the same persons, for they are there said to be the sons of Zerah, and he flourished long before Solomon's time.

32. *He spake three thousand proverbs.* The Book of Proverbs, attributed to Solomon, contains only about nine hundred or nine hundred and twenty-three distinct proverbs; and if we grant with some that the first nine chapters are not the work of Solomon, then all that can be attributed to him is only about six hundred and fifty. Of all his *thousand and five* songs or poems we have only one, the Book of Canticles, remaining, unless we include Psalms cxxvii, "Except the Lord build the house," etc., which in the title is said to be by or for him, though it appears more properly to be a psalm of direction, left him by his father, David, relative to the building of the Temple.

33. *He spake of trees . . . beasts . . . fowl . . . creeping things, and of fishes.* This is a complete system of natural history, as far as relates to the animal and vegetable kingdoms, and the first intimation we have of anything of the kind. Solomon was probably the first natural historian in the world.

MATTHEW HENRY

CHAPTER 5

Verses 1–9

The amicable correspondence between Solomon and Hiram. Tyre was a famous trading city, that lay close upon the sea, in the border of Israel. It is here said of Hiram the king that he was *ever a lover of David*; and we have reason to think he was a worshipper of the true God, and had himself renounced, though he could not reform, the idolatry of his city.

I. Hiram's embassy of compliment to Solomon, *v.* 1.

II. Solomon's embassy of business to Hiram, sent, it is likely, by messengers of his own. Solomon, in his letter to Hiram, acquaints him,

1. With his design to build a temple to the honour of God. Solomon tells Hiram, who was himself no stranger to the affair, (1) That David's wars were an obstruction to him, that he could not build this temple, though he designed it, *v.* 3. (2) That peace gave him an opportunity to build it, and therefore he resolved to set about it immediately: *God has given me rest* both at home and abroad, and there is no adversary (*v.* 4), no *Satan* (so the word is), no instrument of Satan to oppose it, or to divert us from it.

2. With his desire that Hiram would assist him herein. Lebanon was the place whence timber must be had, a noble forest in the north of Canaan, particularly expressed in the grant of that land to Israel—*all Lebanon*, Joshua xiii. 5, so that Solomon was proprietor of all its productions. But Solomon owned that though the trees were his the Israelites had not *skill to hew timber*, like the Sidonians, who were Hiram's subjects. Solomon courts Hiram to send him workmen, and promises (*v.* 6) both to *assist* them (*my servants shall be with thy servants*, to work under them), and to *pay* them (*unto thee will I give hire for thy servants*); for the labourer, even in church-work, though it be indeed its own wages, *is worthy of his hire.* The evangelical prophet seems to allude to this story, Isa. lx, where he prophesies, (1) That the *sons of strangers* (such were the Tyrians and Sidonians) shall *build up the wall* of the gospel temple, *v.* 10. (2) That *the glory of Lebanon* shall be brought to it to *beautify it, v.* 13.

3. Hiram's reception of, and return to, this message. (1) He received it with great satisfaction to himself: He *rejoiced greatly* (*v.* 7) that Solomon trod in his father's steps. In this Hiram's generous spirit rejoiced. With what pleasure Hiram speaks of Solomon's wisdom and the extent of his dominion.

JAMIESON, FAUSSET, BROWN

CHAPTER 5

VSS. 1-6. HIRAM SENDS TO CONGRATULATE SOLOMON. **1. Hiram . . . sent his servants unto Solomon**—the grandson of David's contemporary [KITTO]; or the same Hiram [WINER and others]. The friendly relations which the king of Tyre had cultivated with David are here seen renewed with his son and successor, by a message of condolence as well as of congratulation on his accession to the throne of Israel. The alliance between the two nations had been mutually beneficial by the encouragement of useful traffic. Israel, being agricultural, furnished corn and oil, while the Tyrians, who were a commercial people, gave in exchange their Phœnician manufactures, as well as the produce of foreign lands. A special treaty was now entered into in furtherance of that undertaking which was the great work of Solomon's splendid and peaceful reign. **6. command thou that they hew me cedar trees out of Lebanon**—Nowhere else could Solomon have procured materials for the woodwork of his contemplated building. The forests of Lebanon, adjoining the seas in Solomon's time, belonged to the Phœnicians, and the timber being a lucrative branch of their exports, immense numbers of workmen were constantly employed in the felling of trees as well as the transportation and preparation of the wood. Hiram stipulated to furnish Solomon with as large a quantity of cedars and cypresses as he might require and it was a great additional obligation that he engaged to render the important service of having it brought down, probably by the Dog river, to the seaside, and conveyed along the coast in floats; i.e., the logs being bound together, to the harbor of Joppa (II Chron. 2:16), whence they could easily find the means of transport to Jerusalem. **my servants shall be with thy servants**—The operations were to be on so extensive a scale that the Tyrians alone would be insufficient. A division of labor was necessary, and while the former would do the work that required skilful artisans, Solomon engaged to supply the laborers.

7-12. FURNISHES TIMBER TO BUILD THE TEMPLE. **7. Blessed be the Lord**—This language is no decisive evidence that Hiram was a worshipper of the true God, as he might use it only on the polytheistic principle of acknowledging Jehovah as the God of the Hebrews (see on II Chron. 2:12).

ADAM CLARKE

CHAPTER 5

6. *Any that can skill to hew timber.* An obsolete and barbarous expression for "any that know how to cut timber." They had neither carpenters nor builders among them, equal to the Sidonians. Sidon was a part of the territories of Hiram, and its inhabitants appear to have been the most expert workmen.

MATTHEW HENRY

Let us learn not to envy others either those secular advantages or those endowments of the mind wherein they excel us.

(2) He answered it with great satisfaction to Solomon, granting him what he desired, and showing himself very forward to assist him in this great and good work to which he was laying his hand. We have here his articles of agreement with Solomon. [1] He deliberated upon the proposal, before he returned an answer (*v.* 8). Those do not lose time who take time to consider. [2] He descended to particulars in the articles. Solomon had spoken of hewing the trees (*v.* 6), and Hiram agrees to what he desired concerning that (*v.* 8); but nothing had been said concerning carriage, he therefore undertakes to bring all the timber down from Lebanon by sea, a coasting voyage. Solomon must appoint the place where the timber shall be delivered, and thither Hiram will undertake to bring it and be responsible for its safety. As the Sidonians excelled the Israelites in timber-work, so they did in sailing; for Tyre and Sidon were *situate at the entry of the sea* (Ezek. xxvii. 3): they therefore were fittest to take care of the water-carriage. And, [3] If Hiram undertake for the work, he justly expects that Solomon shall undertake for the wages: "*Thou shalt accomplish my desire in giving food for my household* (*v.* 9), not only for the workmen, but for my own family." If Tyre supply Israel with craftsmen, Israel will supply Tyre with corn, Ezek. xxvii. 17. Thus, by the wise disposal of Providence, one country has need of another.

Verses 10–18

I. The performance of the agreement between Solomon and Hiram. 1. Hiram delivered Solomon the timber, according to his bargain, *v.* 10. 2. Solomon conveyed to Hiram the corn which he had promised him, *v.* 11.

II. The confirmation of the friendship that was between them hereby. It is wisdom to strengthen our friendship with those whom we find to be honest and fair, lest new friends prove not so firm and so kind as old ones.

III. The labourers whom Solomon employed in preparing materials for the temple. 1. Some were Israelites, who were employed felling trees and helping to square them, in conjunction with Hiram's servants; for this he appointed 30,000, but employed only 10,000 at a time, so that for one month's work they had two months' vacation, both for rest and for the despatch of their own affairs at home, *v.* 13, 14. It was temple service, yet Solomon takes care that they shall not be overworked. 2. Others were captives of other nations, who were to bear burdens and to hew stone (*v.* 15). 3. There were some employed as directors and overseers (*v.* 16), 3,300 that ruled over the people, for preparation was now to be made, not only for the temple, but for all the rest of Solomon's buildings, at Jerusalem, and here in the forest of Lebanon, and in other places of his dominion, of which see *ch.* ix. 17–19.

IV. The laying of the foundation of the temple; for that is the building his heart is chiefly upon, and therefore he begins with that, *v.* 17, 18. It should seem, Solomon was himself present, and president, at the founding of the temple, and that the first stone was laid with some solemnity. *Solomon commanded and they brought costly stones* for the foundation; though, being out of sight, worse might have served. That sincerity which is our gospel perfection obliges us to lay our foundation firm and to bestow most pains on that part of our religion which lies out of the sight of men.

JAMIESON, FAUSSET, BROWN

8. Hiram sent to Solomon, saying, I have considered the things . . . and I will do—The contract was drawn out formally in a written document (II Chron. 2:11), which, according to Josephus, was preserved both in the Jewish and Tyrian records.

10. fir trees—rather, the cypress. **11. food to his household**—This was an annual supply for the palace, different from that mentioned in II Chron. 2:10, which was for the workmen in the forests.

13-18. SOLOMON'S WORKMEN AND LABORERS. **13. Solomon raised a levy out of all Israel**—The renewed notice of Solomon's divine gift of wisdom (vs. 12) is evidently introduced to prepare for this record of the strong but prudent measures he took towards the accomplishment of his work. So great a stretch of arbitrary power as is implied in this compulsory levy would have raised great discontent, if not opposition, had not his wise arrangement of letting the laborers remain at home two months out of three, added to the sacredness of the work, reconciled the people to this forced labor. The carrying of burdens and the irksome work of excavating the quarries was assigned to the remnant of the Canaanites (ch. 9:20; II Chron. 8:7-9) and war prisoners made by David—amounting to 153,600. The employment of persons of that condition in Eastern countries for carrying on any public work, would make this part of the arrangements the less thought of. **17. brought great stones**—The stone of Lebanon is "hard, calcareous, whitish and sonorous, like free-stone" [SHAW]. The same white and beautiful stone can be obtained in every part of Syria and Palestine. **hewed stones**—or neatly polished, as the *Hebrew* word signifies (Exod. 20:25). Both Jewish and Tyrian builders were employed in hewing these great stones. **18. and the stone-squarers**—The margin, which renders it "the Giblites" (Josh. 13:5), has long been considered a preferable translation. This marginal translation also must yield to another which has lately been proposed, by a slight change in the *Hebrew* text, and which would be rendered thus: "Solomon's builders, and Hiram's builders, did hew them and bevel them" [THENIUS]. These great bevelled or grooved stones, measuring some twenty, others thirty feet in length, and from five to six feet in breadth, are still seen in the substructures about the ancient site of the temple; and, in the judgment of the most competent observers, were those originally employed "to lay the foundation of the house."

ADAM CLARKE

9. *Shall bring them down from Lebanon unto the sea.* As the river Adonis was in the vicinity of the forest of Lebanon, and emptied itself into the Mediterranean Sea, near Biblos, Hiram could transport the timber all squared, and cut so as to occupy the place it was intended for in the building, without any further need of axe or saw. It might be readily sent down the coast on rafts and landed at Joppa, or Jamnia, just opposite to Jerusalem, at the distance of about twenty-five miles. See 2 Chron. ii. 16.

11. *And Solomon gave Hiram.* The information in this verse of the annual stipend paid to Hiram is deficient, and must be supplied out of 2 Chron. ii. 10. Here *twenty thousand measures of wheat . . . and twenty measures of pure oil* is all that is promised. There, "twenty thousand measures of beaten wheat, and twenty thousand measures of barley, and twenty thousand baths of wine, and twenty thousand baths of oil" is the stipulation; unless we suppose the first to be for Hiram's own family, the latter for his workmen. Instead of *twenty* measures of oil, the Syriac, Arabic, and Septuagint, have "twenty thousand" measures, as in Chronicles. In 2 Chronicles, instead of *cors* of oil, it is *baths.* The *bath* was a measure much less than the *cor.*

13. *The levy was thirty thousand men.* We find from the following verse that only 10,000 were employed at once, and those only for one month at a time; and having rested two months, they again resumed their labor. These were the persons over whom Adoniram was superintendent, and were all Israelites.

15. *Threescore and ten thousand that bare burdens.* These were all strangers, or proselytes, dwelling among the Israelites, as we learn from the parallel place, 2 Chron. ii. 17-18.

16. *Besides . . . three thousand and three hundred which ruled over the people.* In the parallel place, 2 Chron. ii. 18, it is "three thousand and six hundred." The Septuagint has here the same number.

17. *Great stones.* Stones of very large dimensions. *Costly stones.* Stones that cost much labor and time to cut them out of the rock. *Hewed stones.* Everywhere squared and polished.

18. *And the stonesquarers.* Instead of *stone-squarers* the margin very properly reads "Giblites," *haggiblim,* and refers to Ezek. xxvii. 9, where we find the inhabitants of Gebal celebrated for their knowledge in shipbuilding. Some suppose that these Giblites were the inhabitants of Biblos, at the foot of Mount Libanus, northward of Sidon, on the coast of the Mediterranean Sea.

MATTHEW HENRY

CHAPTER 6

Verses 1–10

I. The temple is called *the house of the Lord* (*v.* 1), because it was, 1. Directed and modelled by him. Infinite Wisdom was the architect, and gave David the plan or pattern by the Spirit. 2. Dedicated and devoted to him and to his honour, to be employed in his service, for he manifested his glory in it in a way agreeable to that dispensation. This gave it its *beauty of holiness,* that it was *the house of the Lord,* which far transcended all its other beauties.

II. The time when it began to be built is exactly set down. 1. It was just 480 years after the bringing of the children of Israel out of Egypt. Allowing forty years to Moses, seventeen to Joshua, 299 to the Judges. forty to Eli, forty to Samuel and Saul, forty to David and four to Solomon before he began the work, we have just the sum of 480. David's tent, which was clean and convenient, though it was neither stately nor rich, is called the *house of the Lord* (2 Sam. xii.

JAMIESON, FAUSSET, BROWN

CHAPTER 6

VSS. 1-4. THE BUILDING OF SOLOMON'S TEMPLE. **2. the house which King Solomon built for the Lord**—The dimensions are given in cubits, which are to be reckoned according to the early standard (II Chron. 3:3), or holy cubit (Ezek. 40:5; 43:13), a handbreadth longer than the common or later one. It is probable that the internal elevation only is here stated.

ADAM CLARKE

CHAPTER 6

1. *The month Zif.* This answers to a part of our April and May; and was the second month of the sacred year, but the eighth month of the civil year. Before the time of Solomon, the Jews do not appear to have had any names for their months, but mentioned them in the order of their consecutive occurrence, first month, second month, third month, etc. In this chapter we find *Zif* and *Bul;* and in chap. viii. v. 2, we find another, *Ethanim;* and these are supposed to be borrowed from the Chaldeans; and consequently this book was written after the Babylonish captivity. Before this time we find only the word *Abib* mentioned as the name of a month, Exod. xiii. 4.

MATTHEW HENRY

20), and served as well as Solomon's temple; yet, when God gave Solomon great wealth, he put it into his heart thus to employ it, and graciously accepted him, chiefly because it was to be a shadow of good things to come, Heb. ix. 9. 2. It was in the fourth year of Solomon's reign, the first three years being taken up in settling the affairs of his kingdom, that he might not find any embarrassment from them in this work. It is not time lost which is spent in composing ourselves for the work of God, and disentangling ourselves from everything which might distract or divert us.

III. The materials are brought in, ready for their place (*v.* 7), so ready that there was *neither hammer nor axe heard in the house while it was in building.* It was to be the temple of the God of peace, and therefore no iron tool must be heard in it. Quietness and silence both become and befriend religious exercises: God's work should be done with as much care and as little noise as may be. The temple was thrown down with axes and hammers, and those that threw it down roared *in the midst of the congregation* (Ps. lxxiv. 4, 6); but it was built up in silence. Clamour and violence often hinder the work of God, but never further it.

IV. The dimensions are laid down (*v.* 2, 3) according to the rules of proportion. Some observe that the length and breadth were just double to that of the tabernacle.

V. An account of the windows (*v.* 4): They were *broad within, and narrow without,* Marg. Such should the eyes of our mind be, reflecting nearer on ourselves than on other people, looking much within, to judge ourselves, but little without, to censure our brethren.

VI. The chambers are described (*v.* 5, 6), which served as vestries, in which the utensils of the tabernacle were carefully laid up, and where the priests dressed. Care was taken that the beams should not be fastened in the walls to weaken them, *v.* 6. Let not the church's strength be impaired under pretence of adding to its beauty or convenience.

Verses 11–14

I. The word God sent to Solomon, when he was engaged in building the temple. He assured him that if he would proceed and persevere in obedience to the divine law, and keep in the way of duty and the true worship of God, the divine loving-kindness should be drawn out both to himself (*I will perform my word with thee*) and to his kingdom. This word God sent him probably by a prophet, 1. That by the promise he might be encouraged and comforted in his work. An eye to the promise will carry us cheerfully through our work; and those who wish well to the public will think nothing too much that they can do to secure and perpetuate to it the tokens of God's presence. 2. That, by the condition annexed, he might be awakened to consider that though he built the temple ever so strong the glory of it would soon depart, unless he and his people continued *to walk in God's statutes.*

II. The work Solomon did for God: *So he built the house* (*v.* 14), *so* animated by the message God had sent him, *so* admonished not to expect that God should own his building unless he were obedient to his laws. The strictness of God's government will never drive a good man from his service, but quicken him in it. Solomon built and finished, he went on with the work, and God went along with him till it was completed.

Verses 15–38

I. We have a particular account of the details of the building.

1. The wainscot of the temple. It was of cedar (*v.* 15), which was strong and durable, and of a very sweet smell. The wainscot was curiously carved with knops (like eggs or apples) and flowers, *v.* 18.

2. The gilding. It was not like ours, washed over, but *the whole house,* all the inside of the temple (*v.* 22), even the floor (*v.* 30), he *overlaid with gold,* and the most holy place with *pure gold, v.* 21.

3. The oracle, or *speaking-place, the holy of holies,* so called because thence God spoke to Moses, and perhaps to the high priest. In this place *the ark of the covenant was to be set, v.* 19. Solomon made everything new, except the ark, which was still the same that Moses made, with its mercy-seat and cherubim; that was the token of God's presence, which is always the same with his people whether they meet in tent or temple, and changes not with their condition.

4. The cherubim. Besides those at the ends of the mercy-seat, which covered the ark, (1) Solomon set up two more, very large ones, with wings made of olive-wood, and all overlaid with gold, *v.* 23, &c. (2) He carved cherubim upon all the walls of the

JAMIESON, FAUSSET, BROWN

ALEXANDER MACLAREN:

God's house is mostly built in silence. "The kingdom of God cometh not with observation." This can be seen in reference to its advance in the world. Destructive work is noisy; constructive work is silent. God was in "the still small voice," not in the wind or the earthquake or the fire. Christ's own career, how silent it was! Drums are loud and empty. The spread of the kingdom was unnoticed by the world's great ones—Caesars, philosophers, patricians, and it silently grew underground. Hence may flow—

1. An encouragement to those whose work is inconspicuous.
2. A lesson not to mistake noise and notoriety for spiritual progress.
3. Guidance as to our expectations of the advance of Christ's kingdom. It will transform society by slow, often unnoticed degrees, by radical change of individuals' habits. The elevation of humanity will be slow, like the imperceptible rise of the Norwegian coast. Sudden changes are short lived changes. "Lightly come, lightly go." What matures slowly will last long.

—*Expositions of Holy Scripture*

3. the porch—or portico, extended across the whole front (see on II Chron. 3:4). **windows of narrow lights**—i.e., windows with lattices, capable of being shut and opened at pleasure, partly to let out the vapor of the lamps, the smoke of the frankincense, and partly to give light [KEIL].

5-10. THE CHAMBERS THEREOF. **5. against the wall of the house he built chambers**—On three sides, there were chambers in three stories, each story wider than the one beneath it, as the walls were narrowed or made thinner as they ascended, by a rebate being made, on which the beams of the side floor rested, without penetrating the wall. These chambers were approached from the right-hand side, in the interior of the under story, by a winding staircase of stone, which led to the middle and upper stories. **7. there was neither hammer nor axe nor any tool of iron heard in the house while it was in building**—A subterranean quarry has been very recently discovered near Jerusalem, where the temple stones are supposed to have been hewn. There is unequivocal evidence in this quarry that the stones were dressed there; for there are blocks very similar in size, as well as of the same kind of stone, as those found in the ancient remains. Thence, probably, they would be moved on rollers down the Tyropean valley to the very side of the temple [TENT and KHAN]. **9, 10. built the house**—The temple is here distinguished from the wings or chambers attached to it—and its roofing was of cedar wood. **10. chambers . . . five cubits high**—The height of the whole three stories was therefore about fifteen cubits. **they rested on the house with timber of cedar**—i.e., because the beams of the side-stones rested on the ledges of the temple wall. The wing was attached to the house; it was connected with the temple, without, however, interfering injuriously with the sanctuary [KEIL].

11-14. GOD'S PROMISES UNTO IT. **11. the word of the Lord came to Solomon**—probably by a prophet. It was very seasonable, being designed: first, to encourage him to go on with the building, by confirming anew the promise made to his father David (II Sam. 7); and secondly, to warn him against the pride and presumption of supposing that after the erection of so magnificent a temple, he and his people would always be sure of the presence and favor of God. The condition on which that blessing could alone be expected was expressly stated. The dwelling of God among the children of Israel refers to those symbols of His presence in the temple, which were the visible tokens of His spiritual relation to that people.

15-22. THE CEILING AND ADORNING OF IT. **15. he built the walls of the house within**—The walls were wainscotted with cedar wood—the floor paved with cypress planks—the interior was divided (by a partition consisting of folding doors, which were opened and shut with golden chains) into two apartments—the back or inner room, i.e., the most holy place, was twenty cubits long and broad—the front, or outer room, i.e., the holy place, was forty cubits. The cedar wood was beautifully embellished with figures in relievo, representing clusters of foliage, open flowers, cherubims, and palm trees. The whole interior was overlaid with gold, so that neither wood nor stone was seen; nothing met the eye but pure gold, either plain or richly chased.

ADAM CLARKE

4. *Windows of narrow lights.* The Hebrew is "windows to look through, which shut." Probably latticed windows: windows through which a person within could see well; but a person without, nothing. "Windows," says the Targum, "which were open within and shut without."

7. *The house . . . was built of stone.* It appears that every stone was hewn and squared, and its place in the building ascertained, before it came to Jerusalem; the timbers were fitted in like manner. This greatly lessened the trouble and expense of carriage. On this account, that all was prepared at Mount Lebanon, *there was neither hammer nor ax nor any tool of iron heard in the building.* Nothing except mallets to drive the tenons into the mortices, and drive in the pins to fasten them, was necessary; therefore there was no noise.

9. *Covered the house with beams and boards of cedar.* The Eastern custom is very different from ours. We ceil with plaster, and make our floors of wood; they make their floors of plaster or painted tiles, and make their ceilings of wood.

11. *The word of the Lord came to Solomon.* Some think that this is the same revelation as that mentioned in chap. ix. 2, etc., which took place after the dedication of the Temple; but to me it appears different. It was a word to encourage him while building, to warn him against apostasy, and to assure him of God's continued protection of him and his family, if they continued faithful to the grace which God had given.

MATTHEW HENRY

house, *v.* 29. The heathen set up images of their gods and worshipped them; but these were designed to represent the servants and attendants of the God of Israel, the holy angels, not to be themselves worshipped.

5. The doors. The folding doors that led into the oracle were but a fifth part of the wall (*v.* 31), those into the temple were a fourth part (*v.* 33); but both were beautified with cherubim engraven on them, *v.* 32, 35.

6. The inner court, in which the brazen altar was at which the priests ministered. This was separated from the court where the people were by a low wall, three rows of hewn stone tipped with a cornice of cedar (*v.* 36), that over it the people might see what was done and hear what the priests said to them.

7. The time spent in this building. It was but seven years and a half from the founding to the finishing of it, *v.* 38.

II. Let us now see what was typified by this temple. 1. Christ is the true temple; he himself spoke of the temple of his body, John ii. 21. God himself prepared him his body, Heb. x. 5. *In him dwelt the fulness of the Godhead*, as the *Shechinah* in the temple. In him meet all God's spiritual Israel. Through him we have access with confidence to God. 2. Every believer is a living temple, in whom the Spirit of God dwells, 1 Cor. iii. 16. Even the body is such by virtue of its union with the soul, 1 Cor. vi. 19. We are not only wonderfully made by the divine providence, but more wonderfully made anew by the divine grace. This living temple is built upon Christ as its foundation and will be perfected in due time. 3. The gospel church is the mystical temple; it grows to a *holy temple in the Lord* (Eph. ii. 21), enriched and beautified with the gifts and graces of the Spirit, as Solomon's temple with gold and precious stones. Only Jews built the tabernacle, but Gentiles joined with them in building the temple. Even strangers and foreigners are built up *a habitation of God*, Eph. ii. 19, 22. The temple was divided into the holy place and the most holy, the courts of it into the outer and inner; so there are the visible and the invisible church. The door into the temple was wider than that into the oracle. Many enter into profession that come short of salvation. The top-stone of the gospel church will, at length, be brought forth with shoutings, and it is a pity that there should be the clashing of axes and hammers in the building of it. Angels are ministering spirits, attending the church on all sides and all the members of it. 4. Heaven is the everlasting temple. There the church will be fixed, and no longer movable. The streets of the new Jerusalem, in allusion to the flooring of the temple, are said to be *of pure gold*, Rev. xxi. 21. The cherubim there always attend the throne of glory. The temple was uniform, and in heaven there is the perfection of beauty and harmony. In Solomon's temple there was no noise of axes and hammers. Everything is quiet and serene in heaven; all that shall be stones in that building must in the present state of probation and preparation be fitted and made ready for it, hewn and squared by divine grace, and so made meet for a place there.

JAMIESON, FAUSSET, BROWN

31-35. **for the entering of the oracle**—The door of the most holy place was made of solid olive tree and adorned with figures. The door of the holy place was made of cypress wood, the sides being of olive wood. **36. the inner court**—was for the priests. Its wall, which had a coping of cedar, is said to have been so low that the people could see over it.

37, 38. THE TIME TAKEN TO BUILD IT. **37. In the fourth year was the foundation laid**—The building was begun in the second month of the fourth year and completed in the eighth month of the eleventh year of Solomon's reign, comprising a period of seven and a half years, which is reckoned here in round numbers. It was not a very large, but a very splendid building, requiring great care, and ingenuity, and division of labor. The immense number of workmen employed, together with the previous preparation of the materials, serves to account for the short time occupied in the process of building.

ADAM CLARKE

38. *In the eleventh year . . . was the house finished.* It is rather strange that this house required seven years and about six months to put all the stones and the timbers in their places, for we have already seen that they were all prepared before they came to Jerusalem; but the ornamenting, gilding, or overlaying with gold, making the carved work, cherubim, trees, flowers, etc., must have consumed a considerable time. The month *Bul* answers to a part of our October and November, as Zif, in which it was begun, answers to a part of April and May.

ALFRED BARRY:

"The inner court" (probably the "higher court" of Jer. 35:10) is described as built around the Temple proper, evidently corresponding to the outer court of the Tabernacle. As this was (see Ex. 28:9–13) 50 cubits by 100, it may be inferred, that by a duplication similar to that of all dimensions of the Temple itself, Solomon's Court was 100 cubits (or 150 feet) by 200 cubits (or 300 feet), covering a little more than an acre. The verse has been interpreted in two ways: either that the floor of the court was raised by three courses of stone, covered with a planking of cedar, or (as Josephus understands it) enclosed by a wall of three courses of stone, with a coping of cedar wood. The latter seems more probable. For in this court stood the altar of burnt offering and the laver, and all sacrifices went on, and this could hardly have been done on a wooden pavement; and besides this we observe that the whole arrangement is (chap. 7:12) compared with that of the great outer court of the palace where the wooden pavement would be still more unsuitable. It was what was called afterward the "Court of the Priests," and in it (see Ezek. 40:45) appear to have been chambers for the priests.

The mention of the "inner court" suggests that there was an outer court also. We have in 2 Kings 21:5; 23:12, a reference to the "two courts" of the Temple, and in Ezek. 40:17; 42:1, 8, a mention of the "outward" or "utter court." Josephus (*Antt.* viii. 3, § 3) declares that Solomon built beyond the inner court a great quadrangle, erected for it great and broad cloisters, and closed it with golden doors, into which all could enter, "being pure and observant of the laws." Even beyond this he indicates, though in rather vague and rhetorical language, an extension of the Temple area, as made by Solomon's great substructures, forming a court less perfectly enclosed, like the Court of the Gentiles in the later Temple. —*Ellicott's Commentary on the Whole Bible*

MATTHEW HENRY — CHAPTER 7

Verses 1–12

Never had any man so much of the spirit of building as Solomon had, nor to better purpose; he began with the temple, built for God first, and then all his other buildings were comfortable. 1. He built a house for himself (*v.* 1), *where he dwelt*, *v.* 8. His father had built a good house; but it was no reflection upon his father for him to build a better. Much of the comfort of this life is connected with an agreeable house. He was thirteen years building this house, whereas he built the temple in little more than seven years. He was in no haste for his own palace, but impatient till the temple was finished and fit for use. 2. He built *the house of the forest at Lebanon* (*v.* 2), supposed to be a country seat, so called from the trees that encompassed it. Express notice is taken of his buildings, not only in Jerusalem, but in Lebanon (*ch.* ix. 19), and we read of the tower of Lebanon, which looks towards Damascus (Cant. vii. 4), which probably was part of this house. A particular account is given of this house, that being built in Lebanon, a place famed for cedars, the pillars, and beams, and roof, were all cedar (*v.* 2, 3), and, being designed for pleasant prospects, there were three tiers of windows on each side, *light against light* (*v.* 4, 5), or, as it may be read, *prospect against prospect*. 3. He built piazzas before one of his houses, either that at Jerusalem or that in Lebanon, which were very famous—a porch of pillars (*v.* 6). He himself speaks of Wisdom's

JAMIESON, FAUSSET, BROWN — CHAPTER 7

Vs. 1. BUILDING OF SOLOMON'S HOUSE. **1. Solomon was building his own house thirteen years**—The time occupied in building his palace was nearly double that spent in the erection of the temple, because neither had there been the same previous preparations for it, nor was there the same urgency as in providing a place of worship, on which the national well-being so much depended.

2-7. OF THE HOUSE OF LEBANON. **2. He built also the house of the forest of Lebanon**—It is scarcely possible to determine whether this was a different edifice from the former, or whether his house, the house of the forest of Lebanon, and the one for Pharaoh's daughter, were not parts of one grand palace. As difficult is it to decide what was the origin of the name; some supposing it was so called because built on Lebanon; others, that it was in or near Jerusalem, but contained such a profuse supply of cedar columns as to have occasioned this peculiar designation. We have a similar peculiarity of name in the building called the East India house, though situated in London. The description is conformable to the arrangement of Eastern palaces. The building stood in the middle of a great oblong square, which was surrounded by an enclosing wall, against which the houses and offices of those attached to the court were built. The building itself was oblong, consisting of two square courts, flanking a large oblong hall which formed the center, and was

ADAM CLARKE — CHAPTER 7

1. *Building his own house.* This house is said to have been situated in Jerusalem, and probably was, what some call it, his winter's residence.

2. *The house of the forest of Lebanon.* It was not built in Lebanon, but is thought to have been on Mount Sion. It was probably called *the house of the forest of Lebanon* because it was built almost entirely of materials brought from that place.

MATTHEW HENRY

building her house, and *hewing out her seven pillars* (Prov. ix. 1). 4. At his house where he dwelt in Jerusalem he built a great hall, or porch of judgment, where was set the throne or king's bench, for the trial of causes, in which he himself was appealed to, and this was richly wainscoted with cedar, from the floor to the roof, *v.* 7. He had there also *another court within the porch*, nearer his house, of similar work, for his attendants to walk in, *v.* 8. 5. He built a house for his wife, where she kept her court, *v.* 8. It is said to be *like the porch*, because built of cedar like it.

Verses 13–47

We have here an account of the brasswork about the temple. There was no iron about the temple, though we find David preparing for the temple *iron for things of iron*, 1 Chron. xxix. 2.

I. The brazier whom Solomon employed to preside in this part of the work was Hiram, or Huram (2 Chron. iv. 11), who was by his mother's side an Israelite, of the tribe of Naphtali, by his father's side a man of Tyre, *v.* 14. If he had the ingenuity of a Tyrian, and the affection of an Israelite to the house of God, it was happy that the blood of the two nations mixed in him, for thereby he was qualified for the work to which he was designed. As the tabernacle was built with the wealth of Egypt, so the temple with the wit of Tyre.

II. All the brazen vessels were of *bright brass* (*v.* 45), *good* brass, so the Chaldee, that which was strongest and looked finest.

III. The place where all the brazen vessels were cast was the plain of Jordan, because the ground there was stiff and clayey, fit to make moulds of for the casting of the brass (*v.* 46), and Solomon would not have this dirty smoky work done in or near Jerusalem.

IV. The quantity was not accounted for. The vessels *were exceedingly numerous*, and it would have been an endless thing to keep the account of them; *neither was the weight of the brass*, when it was delivered to the workmen, searched or enquired into; so honest were the workmen, and such great plenty of brass they had, that there was no danger of wanting.

V. Some particulars of the brass-work are described.

1. Two brazen pillars were set up *in the porch of the temple* (*v.* 21), between the temple and the court of the priests, purely for ornament. (1) What an ornament they were we may gather from the account here given of the curious work that was about them, chequer-work, chain-work, net-work, lily-work, and pomegranates in rows, and all of bright brass. (2) Their significancy is intimated in the names given them (*v.* 21): *Jachin—he will establish*; and *Boaz—in him is strength.* Some think they were intended for memorials of the pillar of cloud and fire which led Israel through the wilderness: I rather think them designed for memorandums to the priests and others that came to worship at God's door, [1] To depend upon God for strength and establishment in all their religious exercises. When we come to wait upon God, and find our hearts wandering and unfixed, then by faith let us fetch in help from heaven: *Jachin—God will fix this roving mind. Boaz—in him is our strength*, who works in us both to will and to do. *I will go in the strength of the Lord God.* Spiritual strength and stability are to be had at the door of God's temple, where we must wait for the gifts of grace in the use of the means of grace. [2] It was a memorandum to them of the strength and establishment of the temple of God among them. But, with respect to this temple, when it was destroyed particular notice was taken of the destroying of these pillars (2 Kings xxv. 13, 17), which had been the tokens of its establishment, and would have been so if they had not forsaken God.

2. A brazen sea, a very large vessel, above five yards in diameter, and which contained above 500 barrels of water for the priests' use, in washing themselves and the sacrifices, and keeping the courts of the temple clean, *v.* 23, &c. It stood raised upon the figures of twelve oxen in brass. The Gibeonites,

JAMIESON, FAUSSET, BROWN

100 cubits long, by 50 broad. This was properly the house of the forest of Lebanon, being the part where were the cedar pillars of this hall. In front was the porch of judgment, which was appropriated to the transaction of public business. On the one side of this great hall was the king's house; and on the other the harem or royal apartments for Pharaoh's daughter (Esther 2:3,9). This arrangement of the palace accords with the Oriental style of building, according to which a great mansion always consists of three divisions, or separate houses—all connected by doors and passages—the men dwelling at one extremity, the women of the family at the other, while public rooms occupy the central part of the building. **10. the foundation was of costly stones, even great stones**—Enormous stones, corresponding exactly with the dimensions given, are found in Jerusalem at this day. Not only the walls from the foundation to the roof-beams were built of large hewn stones, but the spacious court around the palace was also paved with great square stones. **12. for the inner court of the house of the Lord**—should be, *as in* the inner court of the house of the Lord; the meaning is, that in this palace, as in the temple, rows of hewed stones and the cedar beams formed the enclosing wall.

13-51. HIRAM'S WORKS. **Solomon sent and fetched Hiram out of Tyre**—The Tyrians and other inhabitants on the Phœnician coast were the most renowned artists and workers in metal in the ancient world. **14. He was a widow's son of the tribe of Naphtali**—In II Chronicles 2:14 his mother is said to have been of the daughters of Dan. The apparent discrepancy may be reconciled thus: Hiram's mother, though belonging to the tribe of Dan, had been married to a Naphtalite, so that when married afterwards to a Tyrian, she might be described as a widow of the tribe of Naphtali. Or, if she was a native of the city Dan (Laish), she might be said to be of the daughters of Dan, as born in that place; and of the tribe of Naphtali, as really belonging to it. **a worker in brass**—This refers particularly to the works described in this chapter. But in II Chronicles 2:13 his artistic skill is represented as extending to a great variety of departments. In fact, he was appointed, from his great natural talents and acquired skill, to superintend the execution of all the works of art in the temple. **15-22. two pillars of brass of eighteen cubits high**—They were made of the brass (bronze) which was taken from the king of Zobah (I Chron. 18:8). In II Chronicles 3:15 they are said to have been thirty-five cubits high. There, however, their joint lengths are given; whereas here the length of the pillars is given separately. Each pillar was seventeen and a half cubits long, which is stated, in round numbers, as eighteen. Their dimensions in American measure are as follows: The pillars without the capitals measured thirty-two and a half feet long, and seven feet diameter; and if hollow, as WHISTON, in his translation of Josephus, thinks (Jer. 52:21), the metal would be about three and a half inches thick; so that the whole casting of one pillar must have been from sixteen to twenty tons. The height of the capitals was eight and three-fourths feet; and, at the same thickness of metal, would not weigh less than seven or eight tons each. The nature of the workmanship in the finishing of these capitals is described (vss. 17-22). The pillars, when set up, would stand forty feet in height [NAPIER'S METAL]. **17. nets of checker work**—i.e., branchwork, resembling the branches of palm trees, and *wreaths of chain-work*; i.e., plaited in the form of a chain, composing a sort of crown or garland. Seven of these were wound in festoons on one capital, and over and underneath them were fringes, one hundred in a row. Two rows of pomegranates strung on chains (II Chron. 3:16) ran round the capital (vs. 42; cf. II Chron. 4:12, 13; Jer. 52:23), which, itself, was of a bowl-like or globular form (vs. 41). These rows were designed to form a binding to the ornamental work—to keep it from falling asunder; and they were so placed as to be above the chain-work, and below the place where the branch-work was. **19. lily work**—beautiful ornaments, resembling the stalks, leaves, and blossoms of lilies—of large dimensions, as suited to the height of their position. **21. Jachin and . . . Boaz**—These names were symbolical, and indicated the strength and stability—not so much of the material temple, for they were destroyed along with it (Jer. 52:17), as of the spiritual kingdom of God, which was embodied in the temple. **23-26. he made a molten sea**—In the tabernacle was no such vessel; the laver served the double purpose of washing the hands and feet of the priests as well as the parts of the sacrifices. But in the temple there were separate vessels provided for these offices. (See on II Chron. 4:6.)

ADAM CLARKE

7. *A porch for the throne.* One porch appears to have been devoted to the purposes of administering judgment, which Solomon did in person.

8. *An house for Pharaoh's daughter.* This appears to have been a third house. Probably the whole three made but one building, and were in the same place, but distinguished from each other: the first as Solomon's palace; the second as a house of judgment, a courthouse; the third, the harem, or apartments for the women.

13. *Solomon sent and fetched Hiram out of Tyre.* This was not the Tyrian king, mentioned before, but a very intelligent coppersmith, of Jewish extraction by his mother's side, who was probably married to a Tyrian. In 2 Chron. ii. 14, this woman is said to be "of the daughters of Dan," but here "of the tribe of Naphtali." The king of Tyre, who gives the account as we have it in Chronicles, might have made the mistake, and confounded the two tribes; or she might have been of Naphtali by her father, and of Dan by her mother, and so be indifferently called of the tribe of Naphtali or of the daughters of Dan. This appears to be the best solution of the difficulty.

15. *A line of twelve cubits.* In circumference.

21. *The right pillar . . . Jachin.* That is, "He shall establish." *The left pillar . . . Boaz*, that is, "in strength." These were no doubt emblematical; for notwithstanding their names, they seem to have supported no part of the building.

MATTHEW HENRY

or Nethinim, who were to draw water for the house of God, had the care of filling it. Some think Solomon made the images of oxen to support this great cistern in contempt of the golden calf which Israel had worshipped, that (as Bishop Patrick expresses it) the people might see there was nothing worthy of adoration in those figures; they were fitter to make posts of than to make gods of.

3. Ten bases, or stands, or settles, of brass, on which were put ten lavers, to be filled with water for the service of the temple, because there would not be room at the molten sea for all that had occasion to wash there. The bases on which the lavers were fixed are very largely described here, *v.* 27, &c. They were curiously adorned and set upon wheels, that the lavers might be removed as there was occasion; but ordinarily they stood in two rows, five on one side of the court and five on the other, *v.* 39. Each laver contained forty baths, that is, about ten barrels, *v.* 38.

4. Besides these, there was a vast number of brass pots made to boil the flesh of the peace-offerings in, which the priests and offerers were to feast upon before the Lord (see 1 Sam. ii. 14); also shovels, wherewith they took out the ashes of the altar. Some think the word signifies *flesh-hooks*, with which they took meat out of the pot. The basins also were made of brass, to receive the blood of the sacrifices.

Verses 48–51

1. The making of the gold work of the temple, which it seems was done last, for with it the work of the house of God ended. All within doors was gold, and all made new (except the ark, with its mercy-seat and cherubim), the old being either melted down or laid by—the golden altar, table, and candlestick, with all their appurtenances. The altar of incense was still *one*, for Christ and his intercession are so: but he made ten golden tables, 2 Chron. iv. 8, and *ten golden candlesticks* (*v.* 49), intimating the much greater plenty both of spiritual food and heavenly light which the gospel blesses us with than the law of Moses did or could afford. Even the hinges of the door were of gold (*v.* 50). 2. The bringing in of the dedicated things, which David had devoted to the honour of God, *v.* 51. What was not expended in the building and furniture was laid up in the treasury, for repairs, exigencies, and the constant charge of the temple-service. What the parents have dedicated to God the children ought by no means to alienate or recall, but should cheerfully devote what was intended for pious and charitable uses, that they may, with their estates, inherit the blessing.

JAMIESON, FAUSSET, BROWN

The molten sea was an immense semicircular vase, measuring seventeen and a half feet in diameter, and being eight and three-fourths feet in depth. This, at three and a half inches in thickness, could not weigh less than from twenty-five to thirty tons in one solid casting—and held from 16,000 to 20,000 gallons of water. The brim was all carved with lilywork or flowers, and oxen were carved or cut on the outside all round, to the number of 300; and it stood on a pedestal of twelve oxen. These oxen must have been of considerable size, like the Assyrian bulls, so that their corresponding legs would give thickness or strength to support so great a weight for, when the vessel was filled with water, the whole weight would be about 100 tons [NAPIER]. (See on II Chron. 4:5.) **27-39. he made ten bases of brass**—These were trucks or four-wheeled carriages, for the support and conveyance of the lavers. The description of their structure shows that they were elegantly fitted up and skilfully adapted to their purpose. They stood, not on the axles, but on four rests attached to the axles, so that the figured sides were considerably raised above the wheels. They were all exactly alike in form and size. The lavers which were borne upon them were vessels capable each of holding 300 gallons of water, upwards of a ton weight. The whole, when full of water, would be no less than two tons [NAPIER]. **40-45. And Hiram made the lavers, and the shovels, and the basins**—These verses contain a general enumeration of Hiram's works, as well as those already mentioned as other minor things. The Tyrian artists are frequently mentioned by ancient authors as skilful artificers in fashioning and embossing metal cups and bowls; and we need not wonder, therefore, to find them employed by Solomon in making the golden and brazen utensils for his temple and palaces. **46. In the plain of Jordan did the king cast them**—Zarthan or Zaretan (Josh. 3:16), or Zartanah (ch. 4:12), or Zeredathah (II Chron. 4:17), was on the bank of the Jordan in the territories of western Manasseh. Succoth was situated on the eastern side of Jordan, at the ford of the river near the mouth of the Jabbok. One reason assigned by commentators for the castings being made there is, that at such a distance from Jerusalem that city would not be annoyed by the smoke and noxious vapors necessarily occasioned by the process. [Note in BAGSTER'S BIBLE.] But the true reason is to be found in the nature of the soil; *Marg.*, the thickness of the ground. That part of the Jordan valley abounds with marl. Clay and sand are the moulding material still used for bronze. Such large quantities of metal as one of these castings would contain could not be fused in one furnace, but would require a series of furnaces, especially for such a casting as the brazen sea—the whole series of furnaces being filled with metal, and fused at one time, and all tapped together, and the metal let run into the mould. Thus a national foundry was erected in the plain of Jordan [NAPIER]. **48. the altar of gold**—i.e., the altar of incense. **49. candlesticks of pure gold**—made, probably, according to the model of that in the tabernacle, which, along with the other articles of furniture, were deposited with due honor, as sacred relics, in the temple. But these seem not to have been used in the temple service; for Solomon made new lavers tables, and candlesticks, ten of each. (See further regarding the dimensions and furniture of the temple, in II Chron. 3:5.)

ADAM CLARKE

27. *He made ten bases.* That is, "pedestals," for the ten lavers to rest on.

38. *Then made he ten lavers.* These were set on the ten bases or pedestals, and were to hold water for the use of the priests in their sacred office, particularly to wash the victims that were to be offered as a burnt offering, as we learn from 2 Chron. iv. 6; but the brazen sea was for the priests to wash in. The whole was a building of vast art, labor, and expense.

KEIL–DELITZSCH:

The account of the vessels of the temple is brought to a close in verse 51: "So was ended all the work that King Solomon made in the house of the Lord; and Solomon brought all that was consecrated by his father, [namely] the silver and the gold [which were not wrought], and the vessels he placed in the treasuries of the house of Jehovah." As so much gold and brass had already been expended upon the building, it might appear strange that Solomon should not have used up all the treasures collected by his father, but should still be able to bring a large portion of it into the treasuries of the temple. But according to 1 Chron. 22:14, 16, and 29:2 sqq., David had collected together an almost incalculable amount of gold, silver, and brass, and had also added his own private treasure and the freewill offerings of the leading men of the nation (1 Chron. 29:7–9). Solomon was also able to devote to the building of the temple a considerable portion of his own very large revenues (cf. 10:14), so that a respectable remnant might still be left of the treasure of the sanctuary, which was not first established by David, but had been commenced by Samuel and Saul, and in which David's generals, Joab and others, had deposited a portion of the gold and silver that they had taken as booty (1 Chron. 26:20–28).

—Commentary on the Old Testament

MATTHEW HENRY

CHAPTER 8

Verses 1–11

The temple, though richly beautified, yet while it was without the ark was like a body without a soul, or a candlestick without a candle, or a house without an inhabitant. All the cost and pains bestowed on this stately structure are lost if God do not accept them. When therefore *all the work* is ended (*ch.* vii. 51), the *one thing needful* is the bringing in of the ark. This must crown the work.

I. Solomon presides in this service, as David did in the bringing up of the ark to Jerusalem. This great assembly he summons (*v.* 1), *at the feast in the seventh month* (*v.* 2), namely, the feast of tabernacles, which was appointed on the fifteenth day of that month, Lev. xxiii. 34. David, like a very *good* man, brings the ark to a *convenient* place, near him; Solomon, like a very *great* man, brings it to a *magnificent* place. Let children proceed in God's service where their parents left off.

II. All Israel attend the service, their judges and the chief of their tribes and families, all their officers, civil and military, and the heads of their clans.

JAMIESON, FAUSSET, BROWN

CHAPTER 8

Vss. 1-12. THE DEDICATION OF THE TEMPLE. **2. at the feast in the month Ethanim**—The public and formal inauguration of this national place of worship did not take place till eleven months after the completion of the edifice. The delay, most probably, originated in Solomon's wish to choose the most fitting opportunity when there should be a general rendezvous of the people in Jerusalem (vs. 2); and that was not till the next year. That was a jubilee year, and he resolved on commencing the solemn ceremonial a few days before the feast of tabernacles, which was the most appropriate of all seasons. That annual festival had been instituted in commemoration of the Israelites dwelling in booths during their stay in the winderness, as well as of the tabernacle, which was then erected, in which God promised to meet and dwell with His people, sanctifying it with His glory. As the tabernacle was to be superseded by the temple, there was admirable propriety in choosing the feast of tabernacles as the period for dedicating the new place of worship, and

ADAM CLARKE

CHAPTER 8

1. *Then Solomon assembled.* Solomon deferred the dedication of the Temple to the following year after it was finished, because that year, according to Archbishop Ussher, was a jubilee.

2. *At the feast in the month Ethanim.* The Feast of Tabernacles, which was celebrated in the seventh month of what is called the ecclesiastical year.

MATTHEW HENRY

These came together, on this occasion, 1. To do honour to Solomon, and to return him the thanks of the nation for all the good offices he had done. 2. To do honour to the ark. Public mercies call for public acknowledgments. Those that appeared before the Lord did not appear empty, for they all sacrificed sheep and oxen innumerable, *v.* 5.

III. The priests do their part of the service. In the wilderness, the Levites were to carry the ark, but here (it being the last time that the ark was to be carried) the priests themselves did it, as they were ordered to do when it surrounded Jericho. We are here told, 1. What was in the ark, nothing but the two tables of stone (*v.* 9), a treasure far exceeding all the dedicated things both of David and Solomon. The pot of manna and Aaron's rod were *by* the ark, but not *in* it. 2. What was brought up with the ark (*v.* 4): *The tabernacle of the congregation.* It is probable that both that which Moses set up in the wilderness, which was in Gibeon, and that which David pitched in Zion, were brought to the temple, to which they did, as it were, surrender all their holiness, merging it in that of the temple, which must henceforward be the place where God must be sought unto. Thus will all the church's holy things on earth, that are so much its joy and glory, be swallowed up in the perfection of holiness above. 3. Where it was fixed in its place, the place appointed for its rest after all its wanderings (*v.* 6): *In the oracle of the house*, whence they expected God to speak to them, even in the most holy place, which was made so by the presence of the ark, *under the wings of the* great *cherubim* which Solomon set up (*ch.* vi. 27), signifying the special protection of angels, under which God's ordinances and the assemblies of his people are taken.

IV. God graciously owns what is done and testifies his acceptance of it, *v.* 10, 11. The priests might come into the most holy place till God manifested his glory there; but, thenceforward, none might, at their peril, approach the ark, except the high priest, on the day of atonement. Therefore it was not till the priests had come out of it, of the oracle that the *Shechinah* took possession of it, in a cloud, which filled not only the most holy place, but the temple, so that the priests who burnt incense at the golden altar could not bear it. By this visible emanation of the divine glory, 1. God put an honour upon the ark, and owned it as a token of his presence. The glory of it had been long diminished and eclipsed by its frequent removes, the meanness of its lodging, and its being exposed too much to common view; but God will now show that it is as dear to him as ever, and he will have it looked upon with as much veneration as it was when Moses first brought it into his tabernacle. 2. He testified his acceptance of the building and furnishing of the temple as good service done to his name and his kingdom among men. 3. He struck an awe upon this great assembly; and, by what they saw, confirmed their belief of what they read in the books of Moses concerning the glory of God's appearances to their fathers. 4. He showed himself ready to hear the prayer Solomon was now about to make. But the glory of God appeared in a cloud, a dark cloud, to signify, (1) The darkness of that dispensation in comparison with the light of the gospel. (2) The darkness of our present state in comparison with the vision of God, which will be the happiness of heaven, where the divine glory is unveiled.

Verses 12–21

I. Solomon encourages the priests. The disciples of Christ *feared when they entered into the cloud*, though it was a *bright cloud* (Luke ix. 34), so did the priests when they found themselves wrapped in a thick cloud. To silence their fears, 1. He reminds them that this was a token of God's presence (*v.* 12). It is an indication of his favour; for he had said, *I will appear in a cloud*, Lev. xvi. 2. Where God dwells in light faith is swallowed up in vision and fear in love. 2. He himself bids it welcome, as worthy of all acceptation (*v.* 13): "*Surely I come,*" says God. "*Amen,*" says Solomon. "*Even so, come, Lord.* The house is thy own, entirely thy own, *I have surely built it for thee.*" It is Solomon's joy that God has taken possession; and it is his desire that he would keep possession. Let not the priests therefore dread that in which Solomon so much triumphs.

II. He instructs the people. He spoke briefly to the priests, but *turned his face about* (*v.* 14) from them *to the congregation* that stood in the outer court, and addressed himself to them largely.

1. He blessed them. When they saw the dark cloud enter the temple they blessed themselves, being astonished at it and afraid lest the thick darkness should be utter darkness to them. Solomon *blessed*

JAMIESON, FAUSSET, BROWN

praying that the same distinguished privileges might be continued to it in the manifestation of the divine presence and glory. At the time appointed for the inauguration, the king issued orders for all the heads and representatives of the nation to repair to Jerusalem and take part in the august procession. The lead was taken by the king and elders of the people, whose march must have been slow, as priests were stationed to offer an immense number of sacrifices at various points in the line of road through which the procession was to go. Then came the priests bearing the ark and the tabernacle—the old Mosaic tabernacle which was brought from Gibeon. Lastly, the Levites followed, carrying the vessels and ornaments belonging to the old, for lodgment in the new, house of the Lord. There was a slight deviation in this procedure from the order of march established in the wilderness (Num. 3:31; 4:15); but the spirit of the arrangement was duly observed.

The ark was deposited in the oracle; i.e., the most holy place, under the wings of the cherubim—not the Mosaic cherubim, which were firmly attached to the ark (Exod. 37:7, 8), but those made by Solomon, which were far larger and more expanded. **8. they drew out the staves**—a little way, so as to project (see on Exod. 25:15; Num. 4:6); and they were left in that position. The object was, that these projecting staves might serve as a guide to the high priest, in conducting him to that place where, once a year, he went to officiate before the ark; otherwise he might miss his way in the dark, the ark being wholly overshadowed by the wings of the cherubim. **9. There was nothing in the ark save the two tables of stone**—Nothing else was ever in the ark, the articles mentioned (Heb. 9:4) being not *in*, but *by* it, being laid in the most holy place before the testimony (Exod. 16:33; Num. 17:10). **10, 11. the cloud filled the house of the Lord**—The cloud was the visible symbol of the divine presence, and its occupation of the sanctuary was a testimony of God's gracious acceptance of the temple as of the tabernacle (Exod. 40:34). The dazzling brightness, or rather, perhaps, the dense portentous darkness of the cloud, struck the minds of the priests, as it formerly had done Moses, which such astonishment and terror (Lev. 16:2-13; Deut. 4:24; Exod. 40:35) that they could not remain. Thus the temple became the place where the divine glory was revealed, and the king of Israel established his royal residence.

12-21. SOLOMON'S BLESSING. **12. Then spake Solomon**—For the reassurance of the priests and people, the king reminded them that the cloud, instead of being a sign ominous of evil, was a token of approval. **The Lord said**—not in express terms, but by a continuous course of action (Exod. 13:21; 24:16; Num. 9:15).

13. I have surely built thee an house—This is an apostrophe to God, as perceiving His approach by the cloud, and welcoming Him to enter as guest or inhabitant of the fixed and permanent dwelling-place, which, at His command, had been prepared for His reception. **14. the king turned his face about**—From the temple, where he had been watching the movement of the mystic cloud, and while the people were standing, partly as the attitude of devotion, partly out of respect to royalty, the king gave a fervent expression of praise to God for the fulfilment of His promise (II Sam. 7:6-16).

ADAM CLARKE

8. *And there they are unto this day.* This proves that the book was written before the destruction of the first Temple, but how long before we cannot tell.

10. *When the priests were come out.* That is, after having carried the ark into the holy of holies, before any sacred service had yet commenced.

11. *The glory of the Lord had filled the house.* The cloud, the symbol of the divine glory and presence, appears to have filled not only the holy of holies, but the whole Temple, court and all, and to have become evident to the people; and by this Solomon knew that God had honored the place with His presence, and taken it for His habitation in reference to the people of Israel.

12. *The Lord said . . . he would dwell.* It was under the appearance of a cloud that God showed himself present with Israel in the wilderness (see Exod. xiv. 19-20). And at the dedication of the Tabernacle in the wilderness, God manifested himself in the same way that He did here at the dedication of the Temple; see Exod. xl. 34-35.

14. *Blessed all the congregation.* Though this blessing is not particularly stated, yet we may suppose that it was such as the high priest pronounced upon the people: "The Lord bless thee, and keep thee: the Lord make his face shine upon thee, and be gracious unto thee: the Lord lift up his countenance upon thee, and give thee peace" (see Num. vi. 24-26), for Solomon seems now to be acting the part of the high priest. But he may have in view more particularly the conduct of Moses, who, when he had seen that the people had done all the work of the Tabernacle, as the Lord had com-

MATTHEW HENRY

them, that is, he pacified them, and freed them from the consternation they were in.

2. He informed them concerning this house which he had built and was now dedicating.

(1) He began his account with a thankful acknowledgment of the good hand of his God upon him hitherto: *Blessed be the Lord God of Israel*, *v.* 15. What we have the pleasure of, God must have the praise of. He thus engaged the congregation to lift up their hearts in thanksgivings to God. Solomon here blessed God, [1] For his promise which he *spoke with his mouth to David.* [2] For the performance, that he had now *fulfilled it with his hand.* We have then the best sense of God's mercies, when we compare what God does with what he has said.

(2) Solomon is now making a solemn surrender or dedication of this house unto God. Here is a recital of the special causes and considerations moving Solomon to build this house. [1] He recites the want of such a place. *I chose no city to build a house in for my name;* therefore there is occasion for the building of this. [2] He recites David's purpose to build such a place. God chose the person first that should rule his people (*I chose David*, *v.* 16) and then put it into *his heart to build a house* for God's name, *v.* 17. [3] He recites God's promise concerning himself. God approved his father's purpose (*v.* 18): *Thou didst well, that it was in thy heart.* What he had done was not of his own head, nor for his own glory, but the work itself was according to his father's design and his doing it was according to God's designation. [4] He recites what he himself had done, and with what intention: *I have built a house*, not for my own name, but *for the name of the Lord God of Israel* (*v.* 20), and *set there a place for the ark*, *v.* 21. The more we do for God the more we are indebted to him; for our sufficiency is of him, and not of ourselves.

Verses 22–53

Solomon having made a general surrender of this house to God, which God had signified his acceptance of by taking possession, next followed Solomon's prayer, his request that this temple may be deemed and taken, not only for a house of sacrifice but a *house of prayer for all people*; and herein it was a type of the gospel church; see Isa. lvi. 7, compared with Matt. xxi. 13.

I. Solomon did not appoint one of the priests to do it, nor one of the prophets, but did it himself, *in the presence of all the congregation of Israel*, *v.* 22. 1. It was well that he was able to do it, a sign that he learnt to pray well, and knew how to express himself to God in a suitable manner, *pro re nata—on the spur of the occasion*, without a prescribed form. 2. It was well that he was not shy of performing divine service before so great a congregation. Solomon, in all his other glory, even on his ivory throne, looked not so great as he did now.

II. The posture in which he prayed was very reverent, and expressive of humility, seriousness, and fervency in prayer. 1. He *kneeled down*, as appears, *v.* 54, where he is said to *rise from his knees*; compare 2 Chron. vi. 13. Kneeling is the most proper posture for prayer, Eph. iii. 14. Mr. Herbert says, "Kneeling never spoiled silk stockings." 2. *He spread forth his hands towards heaven*, and (as it should seem by *v.* 54) continued so to the end of the prayer, hereby expressing his desire towards, and expectations from, God, as a *Father in heaven.* He spread forth his hands, as it were to offer up the prayer from an open enlarged heart and to present it to heaven, and also to receive thence, with both arms, the mercy which he prayed for.

III. The prayer itself was very long, and perhaps much longer than is here recorded. It is not making long prayers, but making them for a pretence, that Christ condemns. In this prayer Solomon does,

1. Give glory to God. This he begins with, as the most proper act of adoration. (1) He gives him the praise of what he is, the best of masters to his people: "*Who keepest covenant and mercy with thy servants;* doing that for them of which thou hast not given them an express promise, provided they *walk before thee with all their hearts.*" (2) He gives him thanks for what he had done, in particular, for his family (*v.* 24): "*Thou hast kept with thy servant David*, as with thy other servants, *that which thou promisedst him.*"

2. He sues for grace and favour from God.

(1) That God would perform to him and his the mercy which he had promised, *v.* 25, 26. Hitherto God has helped, 2. Cor. i. 10. Solomon repeats the promise (*v.* 25): *There shall not fail thee a man to sit on the throne*, not omitting the condition, *so that thy children take heed to their way*; for we cannot expect God's performance of the promise but upon

JAMIESON, FAUSSET, BROWN

JOSEPH PARKER:

Solomon's conception of the personality and dignity of God stands out quite conspicuously in the pages of history for its unrivalled sublimity. He speaks as one who was instructed in the mysteries of the kingdom. In this prayer of Solomon's there is what some persons often mistakenly call preaching even in the language of devotion. We are tempted to form too narrow a conception in prayer, and then to exclude from prayer much that in reality belongs to the very spirit and essence of communion. Solomon here tells God what he is, magnifies his attributes, adores his personality, as if giving God information regarding his own Deity; this would be the shallow criticism passed upon the prayer by those who do not understand what prayer is in all its scope and grandeur. Prayer is not request only, it is fellowship, communion, identification with God; it is the soul pouring itself out just as it will in all the tender compulsion of love, asking God for blessings, praising God for mercies, committing itself to God in view of all the mystery and peril of the future.—*The People's Bible*

22-61. HIS PRAYER. **22. Solomon stood before the altar**—This position was in the court of the people, on a brazen scaffold erected for the occasion (II Chron. 6:13), fronting the altar of burnt offering, and surrounded by a mighty concourse of people.

Assuming the attitude of a suppliant, kneeling (vs. 54, cf. II Chron. 6:24) and with uplifted hands, he performed the solemn act of consecration—an act remarkable, among other circumstances, for this, that it was done, not by the high priest or any member of the Aaronic family, but by the king in person, who might minister *about*, though not *in*, holy things.

This sublime prayer, which breathes sentiments of the loftiest piety blended with the deepest humility, naturally bore a reference to the national blessing and curse contained in the law—and the burden of it—after an ascription of praise to the Lord for the bestowment of the former, was an earnest supplication for deliverance from the latter.

ADAM CLARKE

manded them, blessed them, Exod. xxxix. 43; and the conduct of his father, David, who, when the ark had been brought into the city of David, and the burnt offerings and peace offerings completed, blessed the people in the name of the Lord, 2 Sam. vi. 18.

21. *Wherein is the covenant of the Lord.* As it is said, v. 9, that there was nothing in the ark but the two tables of stone, consequently these are called the covenant, i.e., a sign of the covenant, as our Lord calls the cup the new covenant in His blood, that is, the sign of the new covenant; for "This is my body" implies, "This is the *sign* or *emblem* of My body."

22. *Stood.* He ascended the brazen scaffold, five cubits long, and five cubits broad, and three cubits high, and then kneeled down upon his knees, with his hands spread up to heaven, and offered up the following prayer (see v. 54, and 2 Chron. v. 12-13).

And spread forth his hands toward heaven. This was a usual custom in all nations. In prayer the hands were stretched out to heaven, as if to invite and receive assistance from thence; while, humbly kneeling on their knees, they seemed to acknowledge at once their dependence and unworthiness.

24. *Who hast kept with thy servant David.* This is in reference to 2 Sam. vii. 13, where God promises to David that Solomon shall build a house for the name of the Lord. The Temple being now completed, this promise was literally fulfilled.

MATTHEW HENRY

our performance of the condition. And then he humbly begs this entail (*v.* 26): *Now, O God of Israel! let thy word be verified.*

(2) That God would have respect to this temple, that he would graciously own it. To this purpose,

[1] He premises, *First,* A humble admiration of God's gracious condescension (*v.* 27): "*But will God indeed dwell on the earth?* Can we imagine that a Being infinitely high, and holy, and happy, will stoop so low as to let it be said of him that he *dwells upon the earth*?" *Secondly,* A humble acknowledgment of the incapacity of the house he had built, though very capacious, to contain God: "*The heaven of heavens cannot contain thee,* this house is too little, too mean to be the residence of him that is infinite in being and glory."

[2] This premised, he prays in general, *First,* That God would graciously hear and answer the prayer he was now praying, *v.* 28. It was a humble prayer, an earnest prayer, a prayer made in faith: "Lord, *hearken to it, have respect to it,* not as the prayer of Israel's king but as the prayer of thy servant." *Secondly,* That God would in like manner hear and answer all the prayers that should, at any time hereafter, be made in or towards this house which he had now built, "*Hear it in heaven, that* is indeed *thy dwelling-place,* and, *when thou hearest, forgive.*" None but priests might come into that place; but when they worshipped in the courts of the temple, it must be with an eye towards it, as an instituted medium of their worship, helping the weakness of their faith, and typifying the mediation of Jesus Christ, who is the true temple.

[3] More particularly, he here puts divers cases: *First,* If God were appealed to by an oath for the determining of any controverted right between man and man, and the oath were taken before this altar, he prayed that God would, in some way or other, discover the truth, and judge between the contending parties, *v.* 31, 32. He prayed that, in difficult matters, this throne of grace might be a throne of judgment.

Secondly, If the people of Israel were groaning under any national calamity, or any particular Israelite under any personal calamity, he desired that the prayers they should make in or towards this house might be heard and answered.

a. In case of public judgments, he could not, he would not, ask that their prayer might be answered unless they did also *turn from their sin* (*v.* 35) and *turn again to God* (*v.* 33), that is, unless they did truly repent and reform. But if they did thus qualify for mercy he prays, (*a*) That God would hear from heaven. (*b*) That he would forgive their sin. (*c*) That he would *teach them the good way wherein they should walk,* by his Spirit, with his word and prophets; and thus they might be both profited by their trouble, and prepared for deliverance, which then comes in love when it finds us brought back to the good way of God and duty. (*d*) That he would then remove the judgment, and redress the grievance, in the mercy prayed for.

b. In case of personal afflictions, *v.* 38–40. He does not mention particulars, so numerous, so various, are the grievances of the children of men. He supposes that the complainants themselves would very sensibly feel their own burden. They *shall know every man the plague of his own heart,* and shall spread their hands, that is, spread their case, as Hezekiah spread the letter, in prayer, towards this house; whether the trouble be of body or mind, they shall represent it before God. He refers all cases of this kind, that should be brought hither, to God. (*a*) To his omniscience. (*b*) To his justice: *Give to every man according to his ways;* and he will not fail to do so, by the rules of grace, not the law, for then we should all be undone. (*c*) To his mercy: *Hear, and forgive, and do* (*v.* 39), *that they may fear thee all their days, v.* 40.

c. The case of the stranger that is not an Israelite is next mentioned, a proselyte that comes to the temple to pray to the God of Israel, being convinced of the folly and wickedness of worshipping the gods of his country. He begged that God would accept and answer the proselyte's prayer (*v.* 43): *Do according to all that the stranger calleth to thee for.* Thus early, thus ancient, were the indications of favour towards the *sinners of the Gentiles*: as there was then *one law for the native and for the stranger* (Exod. xii. 49), so there was one gospel for both.

d. The case of an army going forth to battle is next recommended by Solomon to the divine favour. It is supposed that the army is encamped at a distance, somewhere a great way off, sent by divine order *against the enemy, v.* 44.

e. The case of poor captives is the last that is here mentioned as a proper object of divine compassion. (*a*) He supposes that Israel will sin. He knew them,

JAMIESON, FAUSSET, BROWN

He specifies seven cases in which the merciful interposition of God would be required; and he earnestly bespeaks it on the condition of people praying towards that holy place.

CHARLES H. SPURGEON:

It is a dreadful mischief that there should be a plague in the heart, for a plague is a dreadful thing. A plague means, first, something which brings *pain*; and there is many a secret heartache in this world where we least suspect it. If you could take the roofs off houses, strange sights would be seen; but if once you could proceed to put a window into every heart, some of those whose faces look gladdest would appear to us to be among the most miserable of men. The plague of the heart means pain, care, worry, grief, and trouble of mind: but it means more than that, for the plague is a *disease.* Now, a diseased heart is something terrible. Often we see it reported that a man died suddenly of disease of the heart, which I suppose frequently means that that doctors do not know what he died of; but certainly anything that ails the heart is a disease in a most important organ. The hand may be cured, or we may even lose it and live; but when the heart is affected, the whole system gets out of gear, and life itself verges dangerously upon the edge of death. As it is with the heart of the body so it is with the soul's heart: its depravity, or, in other words, its moral disease, puts all the faculties out of order and ruins our whole nature. Nothing can be right with the immortal nature till the heart is cured of this plague. The worst point about the plague of the heart is the fact that if it be not removed it will ultimately *bring death* upon the soul. Plague at the heart is mortal, and I am much surprised if I have not in this great congregation some who have a present pain, a present disease of the heart, and who will, unless they adopt the cure we shall set before them, perish through this deadly plague. Oh, that while I am speaking to you the Holy Spirit may lead many a sin-sick soul to breathe out some such desire as that expressed by John Newton when he wrote,

"Physician of my sin-sick soul,
To Thee I bring my case;
My raging malady control,
And heal me by Thy grace."

—*The Treasury of the Old Testament*

ADAM CLARKE

27. *But will God indeed dwell on the earth?* This expression is full of astonishment, veneration, and delight. He is struck with the immensity, dignity, and grandeur of the Divine Being, but especially at His condescension to dwell with men; and though he sees, by His filling the place, that He has come now to make His abode with them, yet he cannot help asking the question, How can such a God dwell in such a place, and with such creatures?

Behold, the heaven. The words are all in the plural number in the Hebrew: *hashshamayim, ushemey hashshamayim;* "the heavens, and the heavens of heavens."

29. *My name shall be there.* I will there show forth My power and My glory by enlightening, quickening, pardoning, sanctifying, and saving all My sincere worshippers.

30. *Toward this place.* Both Tabernacle and Temple were types of our Lord Jesus, or of God manifested in the flesh; and He was and is the Mediator between God and man. All prayer, to be acceptable, and to be entitled to a hearing, must go to God through Him.

31. *If any man trespass against his neighbour.* Solomon puts here seven cases, in all of which the mercy and intervention of God would be indispensably requisite; and he earnestly bespeaks that mercy and intervention on condition that the people pray towards that holy place, and with a feeling heart make earnest supplication. The first case is one of doubtfulness; where a man has sustained an injury, and charges it on a suspected person, though not able to bring direct evidence of the fact, the accused is permitted to come before the altar of God and purge himself by his personal oath.

33. *When thy people Israel be smitten down.* The second case—when their enemies make inroads upon them, and defeat them in battle, and lead them into captivity.

35. *When heaven is shut up, and there is no rain.* The third case—when, because of their sin, and their ceasing to walk in the good way in which they should have walked, God refuses to send the early and latter rain, so that the appointed weeks of harvest come in vain, as there is no crop.

37. *If there be in the land famine . . . pestilence.* The fourth case includes several kinds of evils: (1) *Famine,* necessarily springing from the preceding clause, drought. (2) *Pestilence.* (3) *Blasting.* (4) *Mildew.* (5) *Locust.* (6) *Caterpillar.* The former refers to locusts brought by winds from other countries and settling on the land; the latter, to the young locusts bred in the land. (7) An *enemy,* having attacked their defensed cities. (8) Any other kind of *plague.* (9) *Sickness.*

41. *Moreoevr, concerning a stranger.* The fifth case relates to heathens coming from other countries with the design to become proselytes to the true religion; that they might be received, blessed, and protected as the true Israelites, that the name of Jehovah might be known over the face of the earth.

44. *If thy people go out to battle.* The sixth case refers to wars undertaken by divine appointment: *whithersoever thou shalt send them.*

MATTHEW HENRY

and himself, and the nature of man. (*b*) He supposes that, if Israel revolt from God, God will be *angry with them*, and *deliver them into the hand of their enemies*, to be carried captive into a strange country, *v.* 46. (*c*) He then supposes that they will bethink themselves, will repent and humble themselves, saying, *We have sinned and have done perversely* (*v.* 47), and *in the land of their enemies will return to God*, whom they had forsaken in their own land. (*d*) He supposes that in their prayers they will look towards their own land, the holy land, Jerusalem, the holy city, and the temple, the holy house, and directs them so to do (*v.* 48). (*e*) He prays that then God would *hear their prayers, forgive their sins, plead their cause*, and incline their enemies to *have compassion on them*, *v.* 49, 50.

Lastly, No place now, under the gospel, can be imagined to add any acceptableness to the prayers made in or towards it, as the temple then did. That was a shadow: the substance is Christ; whatever we ask in his name, it shall be given us.

Verses 54–61

Solomon, after his sermon in Ecclesiastes, gives us the conclusion of the whole matter; so he does here, after this long prayer; it is called his *blessing the people*, *v.* 55.

I. He gives God the glory of the great things he had done for Israel, *v.* 56. He stood up to *bless the congregation* (*v.* 55), but began with blessing God. He blesses God who has given, he does not say wealth, and honour, and power, and victory, to Israel, but *rest*, as if that were a blessing more valuable than any of those. 1. He refers to the *promises given by the hand of Moses*, as he did (*v.* 15, 24) to those which were made to David. There were promises given by Moses, as well as precepts. 2. He does, as it were, write a receipt in full on the back of these bonds: *There has not failed one word of all his good promises.*

II. He blesses himself and the congregation, expressing his earnest desire and hope of these four things: 1 The presence of God with them. This great congregation was now shortly to be scattered, and it was not likely that they would ever be all together again in this world. Solomon therefore dismisses them with this blessing: "*The Lord be present with us*, and that will be comfort enough when we are absent from each other. *The Lord our God be with us, as he was with our fathers* (*v.* 57); *let him not leave us*, let him be to us today, and to ours for ever, what he was to those that went before us." 2. The power of his grace upon them: "*Let him be with us*, and continue with us, not that he may enlarge our coasts and increase our wealth, but *that he may incline our hearts to himself, to walk in all his ways and to keep his commandments*," *v.* 58. 3. An answer to the prayer he had now made: "*Let these my words be nigh unto the Lord our God day and night*, *v.* 59. Let a gracious return be made to every prayer that shall be made here, and that will be a continual answer to this prayer." What Solomon asks here for his prayer is still granted in the intercession of Christ.

III. He solemnly charges his people to continue and persevere in their duty to God. Having spoken to God for them, he here speaks from God to them, and those only would fare the better for his prayers that were made better by his preaching.

Verses 62–66

We read before that Judah and Israel were very cheerful under their own vines and fig-trees; here we have them so in God's courts.

I. They had abundant joy and satisfaction while they attended at God's house, for there, 1. Solomon offered a great sacrifice, 22,000 oxen and 120,000 sheep, enough to have drained the country of cattle if it had not been a very fruitful land. All these sacrifices could not be offered in one day, but in the several days of the feast. 2. He kept a feast, the feast of tabernacles, as it should seem, after the feast of dedication, and both together lasted fourteen days (*v.* 65).

II. They carried this joy and satisfaction with them to their own houses. God's goodness was the matter of their joy, so it should be of ours at all times.

JAMIESON, FAUSSET, BROWN

The blessing addressed to the people at the close is substantially a brief recapitulation of the preceding prayer.

62-64. HIS SACRIFICE OF PEACE OFFERING. **62. the king, and all Israel . . . offered sacrifice before the Lord**—This was a burnt offering with its accompaniments, and being the first laid on the altar of the temple, was, as in the analogous case of the tabernacle, consumed by miraculous fire from heaven (see on II Chron. 7:12). On remarkable occasions, the heathens sacrificed hecatombs (a hundred animals), and even chiliombs (a thousand animals), but the public sacrifices offered by Solomon on this occasion surpassed all the other oblations on record, without taking into account those presented by private individuals, which, doubtless, amounted to a large additional number. The large proportion of the sacrifices were peace offerings, which afforded the people an opportunity of festive enjoyment. **63. So the king and all the children of Israel dedicated the house of the Lord**—The dedication was not a ceremony ordained by the law, but it was done in accordance with the sentiments of reverence naturally associated with edifices appropriated to divine worship. **64. The same day did the king hallow the middle of the court**—i.e., the whole extent of the priests' court—the altar of burnt offerings, though large (II Chron. 4:1), being totally inadequate for the vast number of sacrifices that distinguished this occasion. It was only a temporary erection to meet the demands of an extraordinary season, in aid of the established altar, and removed at the conclusion of the sacred festival.

65. THE PEOPLE JOYFUL. **65. from the entering in of Hamath unto the river of Egypt**—i.e., from one extremity of the kingdom to the other. The people flocked from all quarters. **seven days and seven days, even fourteen days**—The first seven were occupied with the dedication, and the other seven devoted to the feast of tabernacles (II Chron. 7:9). The particular form of expression indicates that the fourteen days were not continuous. Some interval occurred in consequence of the great day of atonement falling on the tenth of the seventh month (vs. 2), and the last day of the feast of tabernacles was on the twenty-third (II Chron. 7:10), when the people returned to their homes with feelings of the greatest joy and gratitude "for all the goodness that the LORD had done for David his servant, and for Israel his people."

ADAM CLARKE

46. *If they sin against thee.* This seventh case must refer to some general defection from truth, to some species of false worship, idolatry, or corruption of the truth and ordinances of the Most High.

In v. 46 we read, *If they sin against thee, (for there is no man that sinneth not)*. On this verse we may observe that the second clause, as it is here translated, renders the supposition in the first clause entirely nugatory; for if there be "no man that sinneth not," it is useless to say, "if they sin." But this contradiction is taken away by reference to the original, which should be translated, "If they shall sin against Thee, or should they sin against Thee; for there is no man that may not sin"; i.e., there is no man impeccable, none infallible, none that is not liable to transgress.

50. *And give them compassion before them who carried them captive.* He does not pray that they may be delivered out of that captivity, but that their enemies may use them well; and that they may, as formerly, be kept a separate and distinct people.

55. *He stood, and blessed all the congregation.* This blessing is contained in vv. 57 and 58.

59. *And let these my words.* This and the following verse is a sort of supplement to the prayer which ended in v. 53; but there is an important addition to this prayer in the parallel place, 2 Chron. vi. 41-42: "Now therefore arise, O Lord God, into thy resting place, thou, and the ark of thy strength: let thy priests, O Lord God, be clothed with salvation, and let thy saints rejoice in goodness. O Lord God, turn not away the face of thine anointed: remember the mercies of David thy servant."

61. *Let your heart therefore be perfect.* Be sincere in your faith; be irreproachable in your conduct.

63. *Two and twenty thousand oxen.* This was the whole amount of the victims that had been offered during the fourteen days; i.e., the seven days of the dedication, and the seven days of the Feast of Tabernacles.

64. *Did the king hallow the middle of the court.* The great altar of burnt offerings was not sufficient for the number of sacrifices which were then made; therefore the middle of the court was set apart, and an altar erected there for the same purpose.

65. *From . . . Hamath.* Supposed to be Antioch of Syria; *unto the river of Egypt*: i.e., from one extremity of the land to the other.

MATTHEW HENRY — CHAPTER 9

Verses 1–9

God had given a real answer to Solomon's prayer, and tokens of his acceptance of it, immediately, by the *fire from heaven* which consumed the sacrifices (as we find, 2 Chron. vii. 1); but here we have a more express and distinct answer to it.

I. In what way God gave him this answer. He appeared to him, as he had done at Gibeon, in the beginning of his reign, in a dream or vision, *v.* 2. The comparing of it with that intimates that it was the very night after he had finished the solemnities

JAMIESON, FAUSSET, BROWN — CHAPTER 9

VSS. 1-9. GOD'S COVENANT IN A SECOND VISION WITH SOLOMON. **1. And it came to pass, when Solomon had finished the building of the house**—This first verse is connected with the eleventh, all that is contained between verses 2-10 being parenthetical. **2. That** [rather, *for*] **the Lord appeared**—This appearance was, like the former one at Gibeon, most probably made in a supernatural vision, and on the night immediately following the dedication of the temple (II Chron. 7:12). The strain of it corre-

ADAM CLARKE — CHAPTER 9

2. *The Lord appeared to Solomon.* The design of this appearance, which was in a dream, as that was at Gibeon, was to assure Solomon that God had accepted his service, and had taken that house for His dwelling place, and

MATTHEW HENRY

of his festival, for so that was, 2 Chron. i. 6, 7.

II. The purport of this answer. 1. He assures him of his special presence in the temple he had built, in answer to the prayer he had made (*v.* 3): *I have hallowed this house.* Solomon had dedicated it, but it was God's prerogative to hallow it—to sanctify or consecrate it. 2. He shows him that he and his people were for the future *upon their good behaviour.* Let them not be secure now, as if they might live as they please now that they have the *temple of the Lord* among them, Jer. vii. 4. "*If thou wilt walk before me as David did, in integrity of heart and uprightness, then I will establish the throne of thy kingdom,* and not otherwise," for on that condition the promise was made, Ps. cxxxii. 12. "But know thou, and let thy family and kingdom know it, and be admonished by it, that *if you shall altogether turn from following me*" Israel, though a holy nation, will be cut off (*v.* 7), by one judgment after another. "The temple, though a holy house, which God himself has *hallowed for his name,* shall be abandoned and laid desolate (*v.* 8, 9): *This house which is high.*" Those that *now pass by it are astonished* at the bulk and beauty of it; but, if you forsake God, its height will make its fall the more amazing. God gave Solomon fair warning of this, now that he had newly built and dedicated it, that he and his people might not be high-minded, but fear.

Verses 10–14

Solomon and Hiram, their fair and friendly parting when the work was done. 1. Hiram made good his bargain to the utmost. So far was he from envying Solomon's growing greatness and reputation, that he helped to magnify him. 2. Solomon, no doubt, made good his bargain, and gave Hiram *food for his household,* as was agreed, *ch.* v. 9. But here we are told that he gave him twenty cities (small ones we may suppose, like those mentioned here, *v.* 19) *in the land of Galilee, v.* 11. Hiram came to see these cities, and did not like them (*v.* 12): *They pleased him not.* He called the country the land of *Cabul,* a Phœnician word (says Josephus) which signifies *displeasing, v.* 13. He therefore returned them to Solomon (as we find, 2 Chron. viii. 2), who repaired them, and then *caused the children of Israel to inhabit them.* The country was truly valuable, and so were the cities in it, but not agreeable to Hiram's genius. The Tyrians were merchants, trading men, that lived in fine houses, and became rich by navigation, but knew not how to value a country that was fit for corn and pasture. Hiram desired Solomon to gratify him by becoming his partner in trade, as we find he did, *v.* 27. Some take delight in husbandry, and wonder what pleasure sailors can take on a rough sea; others take as much delight in navigation, and wonder what pleasure husbandmen can take in a dirty country, like the land of Cabul.

Verses 15–28

A further account of Solomon's greatness.

I. His buildings. He raised a great levy both of men and money, because he projected a great deal of building, which would both employ many hands and put him to a vast expense, *v.* 15. He raised it, not for war (as other princes), which would spend the blood of his subjects, but for building, which would require only their labour and purses. Perhaps David observed Solomon's genius to lie towards building, and foresaw he would have his head and hands full of it, when he penned that song of degrees for Solomon, which begins, *Except the Lord build the house, those labour in vain that build it* (Ps. cxxvii. 1). And Solomon verily began his work at the right end, for he built God's house first, and finished that before he began his own; and then God blessed him, and he prospered in all his other buildings. The further order in Solomon's buildings is observable. God's house first for religion, then his own for his own convenience, then a house for his wife, to which she removed as soon as it was ready for her (*v.* 24), then Milo, the town-house or guild-hall, then the wall of Jerusalem, the royal city, then some cities of note and strength in the country, which were decayed and unfortified, Hazor, Megiddo, &c.

II. His workmen and servants. In doing such great works, he must needs employ abundance of workmen. 1. Solomon employed those who remained of the conquered nations in all the slavish work, *v.* 20, 21. 2. He employed Israelites in the more creditable services (*v.* 22, 23): *Of them he made no bondmen,* for they were God's freemen, and honoured their relation to God as a kingdom of priests.

III. His piety and devotion (*v.* 25): *Three times in a year* he offered burnt-offerings extraordinary (namely, at the three yearly feasts, the passover, pentecost, and feast of tabernacles) in honour of the divine

JAMIESON, FAUSSET, BROWN

sponds to this view, for it consists of direct answers to his solemn inaugural prayer (vs. 3 is in answer to ch. 8:29; vss. 4, 5 is in answer to ch. 8:25, 26; vss. 6-9 to ch. 8:33-46, see also Deut. 29:22-24).

8. this house, which is high—"high," either in point of situation, for it was built on a hill, and therefore conspicuous to every beholder; or "high" in respect to privilege, honor, and renown; or this "house of the Most High," notwithstanding all its beauty and magnificence, shall be destroyed, and remain in such a state of ruin and degradation as to be a striking monument of the just judgment of God. The record of this second vision, in which were rehearsed the conditions of God's covenant with Solomon and the consequences of breaking them, is inserted here as a proper introduction to the narrative about to be given of this king's commercial enterprises and ambitious desire for worldly glory; for this king, by encouraging an influx of foreign people and a taste for foreign luxuries, rapidly corrupted his own mind and that of this subjects, so that they turned from following God, they and their children (vs. 6).

10-23. THE MUTUAL PRESENTS OF SOLOMON AND HIRAM. **10. at the end of twenty years**—Seven and a half years were spent in building the temple, and twelve and a half or thirteen in the erection of his palace (ch. 7:1; II Chron. 8:1). This verse is only a recapitulation of the first, necessary to recover the thread of connection in the narrative. **11. Solomon gave Hiram twenty cities in the land of Galilee**—According to Josephus, they were situated on the northwest of it, adjacent to Tyre. Though lying within the boundaries of the promised land (Gen. 15:18; Josh. 1:4), they had never been conquered till then, and were inhabited by Canaanite heathens (Judg. 4:2-13, II Kings 15:29). They were probably given to Hiram, whose dominions were small, as a remuneration for his important services in furnishing workmen, materials, and an immense quantity of *wrought* gold (vs. 14) for the temple and other buildings [MICHAELIS]. The gold, however, as others think, may have been the amount of forfeits paid to Solomon by Hiram for not being able to answer the riddles and apothegms, with which, according to Josephus, in their private correspondence, the two sovereigns amused themselves. Hiram having refused these cities, probably on account of their inland situation making them unsuitable to his maritime and commercial people, Solomon satisfied his ally in some other way; and, taking these cities into his own hands, he first repaired their shattered walls, then filled them with a colony of Hebrews (II Chron. 8:2). **15-24. this is the reason of the levy**—A levy refers both to men and money, and the necessity for Solomon making it arose from the many gigantic works he undertook to erect. **Millo**—part of the fort of Jerusalem on Mount Zion (II Sam. 5:9; I Chron. 11:8), or a row of stone bastions around Mount Zion, Millo being the great corner tower of that fortified wall (ch. 11:27; II Chron. 32:5). **the wall of Jerusalem**—either repairing some breaches in it (ch. 11:27), or extending it so as to enclose Mount Zion. **Hazor**—fortified on account of its importance as a town in the northern boundary of the country. **Megiddo**—(now Leijun)—Lying in the great caravan road between Egypt and Damascus, it was the key to the north of Palestine by the western lowlands, and therefore fortified. **Gezer**—on the western confines of Ephraim, and, though a Levitical city, occupied by the Canaanites. Having fallen by right of conquest to the king of Egypt, who for some cause attacked it, it was given by him as a dowry to his daughter, and fortified by Solomon. **17. Beth-horon the nether**—situated on the way from Joppa to Jerusalem and Gibeon; it required, from so public a road, to be strongly garrisoned. **18. Baalath**—Baalbek. **Tadmor**—Palmyra, between Damascus and the Euphrates, was rebuilt and fortified as a security against invasion from northern Asia. In accomplishing these and various other works which were carried on throughout the kingdom, especially in the north, where Rezon of Damascus, his enemy, might prove dangerous, he employed vast numbers of the Canaanites as galley slaves (II Chron. 2:18), treating them as prisoners of war, who were compelled to do the drudgery and hard labor, while the Israelites were only engaged in honorable employment. **23. These were the chief of the officers**—(See on II Chron. 8:10).

24-28. SOLOMON'S YEARLY SACRIFICES. **24, 25. three times in a year**—viz., at the passover, pentecost, and feast of tabernacles (II Chron. 8:13; 31:3). The circumstances mentioned in these two verses form

ADAM CLARKE

would continue it, and establish him and his descendants upon the throne of Israel forever, provided they served Him with an upright heart; but, on the contrary, if they forsook Him, He would abandon both them and His temple.

10. *At the end of twenty years.* He employed seven years and a half in building the Temple, and twelve years and a half in building the king's house (see chap. vii. 1; 2 Chron. viii. 1).

11. *Solomon gave Hiram twenty cities.* It is very likely that Solomon did not give those cities to Hiram so that they should be annexed to his Tyrian dominions, but rather gave him the produce of them till the money was paid which he had advanced to Solomon for his buildings. It appears however that either Hiram did not accept them or that, having received the produce till he was paid, he then restored them to Solomon; for in the parallel place, 2 Chron. viii. 2, it is said, "The cities which Huram had restored to Solomon, Solomon built them, and caused the children of Israel to dwell there." Some think that they were heathen *cities* which Solomon had conquered, and therefore had a right to give them if he pleased, as they were not any part of the land given by promise to the Israelites.

14. *Sixscore talents of gold.* This was the sum which Hiram had lent, and in order to pay this Solomon had laid a tax upon his people, as we afterward learn.

15. *This is the reason of the levy.* That is, in order to pay Hiram the sixscore talents of gold which he had borrowed from him (Hiram not being willing to take the Galilean cities mentioned above; or, having taken them, soon restored them again), he was obliged to lay a tax upon the people; and that this was a grievous and oppressive tax we learn from chap. xii. 1-4, where the elders of Israel came to Rehoboam, complaining of their heavy state of taxation, and entreating that their yoke might be made lighter. *And Millo.* This is supposed to have been a deep valley between Mount Sion and what was called the city of Jebus, which Solomon filled up, and it was built on and became a sort of fortified place, and a place for public assemblies.

16. *Pharaoh . . . had gone up, and taken Gezer.* This city Joshua had taken from the Canaanites, Josh. x. 33 and xii. 12, and it was divided by lot to the tribe of Ephraim, and was intended to be one of the Levitical cities. But it appears that the Canaanites had retaken it, and kept possession till the days of Solomon, when his father-in-law, Pharaoh, king of Egypt, retook it, and gave it to Solomon in dowry with his daughter.

18. *And Tadmor in the wilderness.* This is almost universally allowed to be the same with the celebrated Palmyra, the ruins of which remain to the present day, and give us the highest idea of Solomon's splendor and magnificence. Palmyra stood upon a fertile plain surrounded by a barren desert, having the river Euphrates on the east.

19. *And all the cities of store.* Though by the multitude and splendor of his buildings Solomon must have added greatly to the magnificence of his reign; yet, however plenteous silver and gold were in his times, his subjects must have been greatly oppressed with the taxation necessary to defray such a vast public expenditure.

21. *A tribute of bondservice.* He made them do the most laborious part of the public works, the Israelites being generally exempt.

25. *Three times in a year did Solomon offer.* These three times were: (1) the *Passover,* (2) the Feast of *Pentecost,* (3) the Feast of *Tabernacles.*

MATTHEW HENRY

institution. It is said, He offered *on the altar which he* himself *built*. He took care to build it, and then, 1. He himself made use of it. Many will assist the devotions of others that neglect their own. 2. He himself had the benefit and comfort of it.

IV. His merchandise. He built a fleet of trading ships at Ezion-geber (*v.* 26), a port on the coast of the Red Sea, the furthest stage of the Israelites when they wandered in the wilderness, Num. xxxiii. 35. The fleet traded to Ophir in the East Indies, supposed to be that which is now called *Ceylon*. Gold was the commodity traded for, substantial wealth. It should seem, Solomon had before been Hiram's partner, or put a venture into his ships, which made him a rich return of 120 talents (*v.* 14), which encouraged him to build a fleet of his own. Solomon sent his own servants as factors, and merchants, and supercargoes, but hired Tyrians for sailors, for they had *knowledge of the sea*, *v.* 27. Thus one nation needs another, Providence so ordering it that there may be mutual commerce and assistance; for not only as Christians, but as men, we are members one of another. The fleet brought home to Solomon 420 *talents of gold*, *v.* 28. Solomon got much by his merchandise, but, it should seem, David got much more by his conquests. What were Solomon's 420 *talents* to David's 100,000 *talents of gold*? 1 Chron. xxii. 14; xxix. 4. Solomon got much by his merchandise, and yet he has directed us to a better trade, within reach of the poorest, having assured us from his own experience of both that the *merchandise of wisdom is better than the merchandise of silver and the gain thereof than fine gold*, Prov. iii. 14.

JAMIESON, FAUSSET, BROWN

a proper conclusion to the record of his buildings and show that his design in erecting those at Jerusalem was to remedy defects existing at the commencement of his reign (see on ch. 3:1-4). **26. Ezion-geber, which is beside Eloth**—These were neighboring ports at the head of the eastern or Elanitic branch of the Red Sea. Tyrian ship-carpenters and sailors were sent there for Solomon's vessels (see on II Chron. 8). **Ezion-geber**—i.e., the giant's backbone; so called from a reef of rocks at the entrance of the harbor. **Eloth**—Elim or Elath; i.e., "the trees"—a grove of terebinthes still exists at the head of the gulf.

28. Ophir—a general name, like the East or West Indies with us, for all the southern regions lying on the African, Arabian, or Indian seas, in so far as at that time known [HEEREN]. **gold, four hundred and twenty talents**—(See on II Chron. 8:18). At 125 pounds Troy, or 1500 ounces to the talent, and £4 to the ounce, this would make £2,604,000, or about $ 12,350,000.

ADAM CLARKE

26. *A navy of ships.* Literally, *oni*, "a ship." In the parallel place, 2 Chron. viii. 18, it is said that Hiram sent him *oniyoth*, "ships"; but it does not appear that Solomon in this case built more than one ship, and this was manned principally by the Tyrians.

MATTHEW HENRY — CHAPTER 10

Verses 1-13

An account of the visit which the queen of Sheba made to Solomon, no doubt when he was in the height of his piety and prosperity. Our Saviour calls her *the queen of the south*, for Sheba lay south of Canaan. The common opinion is that it was in Africa; and the Christians in Ethiopia, to this day, are confident that she came from their country, and that Candace was her successor, who is mentioned Acts viii. 27. But it is more probable that she came from the south part of Arabia.

I. On what errand the queen of Sheba came—not to treat of trade or commerce, but, 1. To satisfy her curiosity; for she had heard of his fame, especially for wisdom. 2. To receive instruction from him. She came to *hear his wisdom*, and thereby to improve her own (Matt. xii. 42), that she might be the better able to govern her own kingdom by his maxims of policy. But that which she chiefly aimed at was to be instructed in the things of God.

II. With what equipage she came, with a very great retinue, agreeable to her rank. Yet she came not as one begging, but brought enough abundantly to recompense Solomon for his attention to her, nothing mean or common, but gold, and precious stones, and spices, because she came to trade for wisdom.

III. What entertainment Solomon gave her. He despised not the weakness of her sex, but made her welcome and all her train, gave her liberty to put all her questions, to *commune with him of all that was in her heart* (*v.* 2) and gave her a satisfactory answer to *all her questions* (*v.* 3), whether natural, moral, political, or divine. But he informed her no doubt, with particular care, concerning God, and his law and instituted worship.

IV. How she was affected with what she saw and heard in Solomon's court. Divers things are here mentioned which she admired, the buildings and furniture of his palace, the provision that was made every day for his table, the orderly sitting of his servants, every one in his place, and the ready attendance of his ministers. But, above all these, the first thing mentioned is his wisdom (*v.* 4), and the last thing mentioned, which crowned all, is his piety, the *ascent by which he went up to the house of the Lord*.

V. How she expressed herself upon this occasion. 1. She owned her expectation far out-done, though it was highly raised by the report she heard, *v.* 6, 7. She is far from repenting her journey or calling herself a *fool* for undertaking it, but acknowledges it was well worth her while to come so far for the sight of that which she could not believe the report of. Those who, through grace, are brought to experience the delights of communion with God will say that the one-half was not told them of the pleasures of Wisdom's ways and the advantages of her gates. Glorified saints, much more, will say that it was a true report which they heard of the happiness of

JAMIESON, FAUSSET, BROWN — CHAPTER 10

Vss. 1-13. THE QUEEN OF SHEBA ADMIRES THE WISDOM OF SOLOMON. **1. the queen of Sheba**—Some think her country was the Sabean kingdom of Yemen, of which the capital was Saba, in Arabia Felix; others, that it was in African Ethiopia, i.e., Abyssinia, towards the south of the Red Sea. The opinions preponderate in favor of the former. This view harmonizes with the language of our Lord, as Yemen means "South"; and this country, extending to the shores of the Indian ocean, might in ancient times be considered "the uttermost parts of the earth." **heard of the fame of Solomon**—doubtless by the Ophir fleet. **concerning the name of the Lord**—meaning either his great knowledge of God, or the extraordinary things which God had done for him. **hard questions**—enigmas or riddles. The Orientals delight in this species of intellectual exercise and test wisdom by the power and readiness to solve them. **2. she came to Jerusalem with a very great train, with camels**—A long train of those beasts of burden forms the common way of travelling in Arabia; and the presents specified consist of the native produce of that country. Of course, a royal equipage would be larger and more imposing than an ordinary caravan.

6. It was a true report that I heard in mine own land of thy acts and of thy wisdom—The proofs she obtained of Solomon's wisdom—not from his conversation only, but also from his works; the splendor of his palace; the economy of his kitchen and table; the order of his court; the gradations and gorgeous costume of his servants; above all, the arched viaduct that led from his palace to the temple (II Kings 16:18), and the remains of which have been recently discovered [ROBINSON]—overwhelmed her with astonishment.

ADAM CLARKE — CHAPTER 10

1. *When the queen of Sheba heard.* As our Lord calls her "queen of the south" (Matt. xii. 42), it is likely the name should be written *Saba*, the "south." *With hard questions.* Septuagint, "riddles." With "parables and riddles," says the Arabic.

2. *She came to Jerusalem with . . . spices.* Those who contend that she was queen of the Sabaeans, a people of Arabia Felix, towards the southern extremity of the Red Sea, find several proofs of their opinion: (1) That the Sabaeans abounded in riches and spices. (2) All ancient authors speak, not only of their odoriferous woods, but of their rich gold and silver mines, and of their precious stones. (3) It is also well known that the Sabaeans had queens for their sovereigns, and not kings.

3. *Solomon told her all her questions.* Riddles, problems, fables, apologues formed the principal part of the wisdom of the East.

4. *Had seen all Solomon's wisdom.* By the answers which he gave to her subtle questions. *And the house that he had built.* Most probably his own house.

5. *The meat of his table.* The immense supply of all kinds of food daily necessary for the many thousands which were fed at and from his table. See chap. iv. 22-23. *And the sitting of his servants.* The various orders and distinctions of his officers. *The attendance of his ministers.* See the account of these and their attendance, chap. iv. 1, etc. *And their apparel.* The peculiarity of their robes, and their splendor and costliness. *And his cupbearers.* The original may as well be applied to his beverage, or to his drinking utensils, as to his cupbearers. *And his ascent by which he went up.* It seems very strange that the steps to the Temple should be such a separate matter of astonishment. All the versions have translated the original, "And the holocausts which he offered in the house of

MATTHEW HENRY

heaven, but that the thousandth part was not told them, 1 Cor. ii. 9. 2. She pronounced those happy that constantly attended him, and waited on him at table: "*Happy are thy men, happy are these thy servants* (*v.* 8); they may improve their own wisdom by hearing thine." 3. She blessed God, the giver of Solomon's wisdom and wealth, and the author of his advancement, who had made him king. "He has made thee king, not that thou mayest live in pomp and pleasure, and do what thou wilt, but *to do judgment and justice.*"

VI. How they parted. 1. She made a noble present to Solomon of *gold and spices*, *v.* 10. The present of gold and spices which the wise men of the east brought to Christ was signified by this, Matt. ii. 11. Thus she paid for the wisdom she had learned and did not think she bought it dearly. Let those that are taught of God give him their hearts, and the present will be more acceptable than this of gold and spices. The almug-trees are here spoken of (*v.* 11, 12) as extraordinary, because perhaps much admired by the queen of Sheba. 2. Solomon was not behind-hand with her: *He gave her whatsoever she asked*, patterns, we may suppose, of those things that were curious, by which she might make the like; or perhaps he gave her his precepts of wisdom and piety in writing, *besides that which he gave her of his royal bounty*, *v.* 13.

Verses 14–29

A further account of Solomon's prosperity.

I. How he increased his wealth. 1. Besides the gold that came from Ophir (*ch.* ix. 28), he brought so much into his country from other places that the whole amounted, every year, to 666 *talents* (*v.* 14). 2. He received a great deal in customs from the merchants, and in land-taxes from the countries his father had conquered and made tributaries to Israel, *v.* 15. 3. He was Hiram's partner in a Tharshish fleet, of Tyre, which imported once in three years, not only gold, and silver, and ivory, substantial goods and serviceable, but apes and peacocks, *v.* 22. 4. He had presents made him, every year, from the neighbouring princes and great men, because they had often occasion to consult him as an oracle, and sent him these presents by way of recompence for his advice in politics. 5. He traded to Egypt for horses and linen-yarn (or, as some read it, *linen-cloth*), the staple commodities of that country, and had his own merchants or factors whom he employed in this traffic and who were accountable to him, *v.* 28, 29.

II. What use he made of his wealth.

1. He laid out his gold in fine things for himself, which he might the better be allowed to do when he had before laid out so much in fine things for the house of God. (1) He made 200 targets, and 300 shields, of beaten gold (*v.* 16, 17), not for service, but for state, to be carried before him when he appeared in pomp. Solomon had *shields* and *targets* carried before him, to signify that he took more pleasure in using his power for the defence and protection of the good, to whom he would be a praise. (2) He made a stately throne, on which he sat, to give laws to his subjects, audience to ambassadors, and judgment upon appeals, *v.* 18–20. It was made of ivory, or elephants' teeth, which was very rich; and yet, as if he had so much gold that he knew not what to do with it, he *overlaid that with gold*, the best gold. (3) He made all his drinking vessels, and all the furniture of his table, even at his country seat, of pure gold, *v.* 21.

2. He made it circulate among his subjects, so that the kingdom was as rich as the king; for he had no separate interests of his own to consult, but sought the welfare of his people. Solomon was instrumental to bring so much gold into the country, and disperse it, that *silver was nothing accounted of*, *v.* 21. If *gold in abundance* would make silver to seem so despicable, shall not wisdom, and grace, and the foretastes of heaven, which are far better than gold, make earthly wealth seem much more despicable?

Now let us remember, 1. That this was he who, when he was *setting out in the world*, did not ask for the wealth and honour of it, but asked for *a wise and understanding heart*. 2. That this was he who, having tasted all these enjoyments, wrote a whole book to show the vanity of all worldly things and the folly of setting our hearts upon them, and to recommend to us the practice of serious godliness, which, through the grace of God, is within our reach, when the thousandth part of Solomon's greatness is a thousand times more than we can ever be so vain as to promise ourselves in this world.

JAMIESON, FAUSSET, BROWN

9. Blessed be the Lord thy God—(See on ch. 5:7.) It is quite possible, as Jewish writers say, that this queen was converted, through Solomon's influence, to the worship of the true God. But there is no record of her making any gift or offering in the temple. **10. she gave the king an hundred and twenty talents of gold**—$3,500,000. **11. almug trees**—Parenthetically, along with the valuable presents of the queen of Sheba, is mentioned a foreign wood, which was brought in the Ophir ships. It is thought by some to be the sandalwood; by others, to be the deodar—a species of fragrant fir, much used in India for sacred and important works. Solomon used it for stairs in his temple and palace (II Chron. 9:11), but chiefly for musical instruments. **13. King Solomon gave unto the queen of Sheba all her desire, whatsoever she asked, beside**—i.e., Solomon not only gave his illustrious guest all the insight and information she wanted; but, according to the Oriental fashion, he gave her ample remuneration for the presents she had brought.

14-29. His Riches. **14. Now the weight of gold that came to Solomon in one year**—666 talents, equal to about $20,000,000. The sources whence this was derived are not mentioned; nor was it the full amount of his revenue; for this was "Beside that he had of the merchantmen, and of the traffic of the spice merchants, and of all the kings of Arabia, and of the governors of the country." The great encouragement he gave to commerce was the means of enriching his royal treasury. By the fortifications which he erected in various parts of his kingdom, (particularly at such places as Thapsacus, one of the passages of Euphrates, and at Tadmor, in the Syrian desert), he gave complete security to the caravan trade from the depredations of the Arab marauders; and it was reasonable that, in return for this protection, he should exact a certain toll or duty for the importation of foreign goods. A considerable revenue, too, would arise from the use of the store cities and khans he built; and it is not improbable that those cities were emporia, where the caravan merchants unloaded their bales of spices and other commodities and sold them to the king's factors, who, according to the modern practice in the East, retailed them in the Western markets at a profit. "The revenue derived from the tributary kings and from the governors of the country" must have consisted in the tribute which all inferior magistrates periodically bring to their sovereigns in the East, in the shape of presents of the produce of their respective provinces. **16, 17. two hundred targets, six hundred shekels**—These defensive arms were anciently made of wood and covered with leather; those were covered with fine gold. $6,000 worth of gold was used in the gilding of each target—**$1800 for each shield.** They were intended for the state armory of the palace (see on ch. 14:26). **18-26. a great throne of ivory**—It seems to have been made not of solid ivory, but veneered. It was in the form of an armchair, with a carved back. The ascent to it was by six steps, on each of which stood lions, in place of a railing—while a lion, probably of gilt metal, stood at each side, which, we may suppose from the analogy of other Oriental thrones, supported a canopy. A golden footstool is mentioned (II Chron. 9:18) as attached to this throne, whose magnificence is described as unrivalled. **22. a navy of Tarshish**—Tartessus in Spain. There gold, and especially silver, was obtained, anciently, in so great abundance that it was nothing accounted of in the days of Solomon. But Tarshish came to be a general term for the West (Jonah 1). **at sea**—on the Mediterranean. **once in three years**—i.e., every third year. Without the mariner's compass they had to coast along the shore. The ivory, apes, and peacocks might have been purchased, on the outward or homeward voyage, on the north coast of Africa, where the animals were to be found. They were particularized, probably as being the rarest articles on board. **26-29.**—(See on II Chron. 1:14-17.)

ADAM CLARKE

the Lord." The Vulgate, Septuagint, Chaldee, Syriac, and Arabic, all express this sense; so does the German translation of Luther, from which, in this place, we have most pitifully departed: "And his burnt offering which he offered in the house of the Lord." *There was no more spirit in her.* She was overpowered with astonishment; she fainted.

8. *Happy are thy men.* All these are very natural expressions from a person in her state of mind.

10. *An hundred and twenty talents of gold.* After this verse the thirteenth should be read, which is here most evidently misplaced; and then the account of the queen of Sheba will be concluded, and that of Solomon's revenue will stand without interruption.

11. *Great plenty of almug trees.* In the parallel place, 2 Chron. ix. 10-11, these are called *algum trees.*

13. *All her desire, whatsoever she asked.* Some imagine she desired progeny from the wise king of Israel; and all the traditions concerning her state that she had a son by Solomon called Menilek, who was brought up at an Israelitish court, succeeded his mother in the kingdom of Saba, and introduced among his subjects the Jewish religion.

17. *He made three hundred shields.* The *magen* was a large shield by which the whole body was protected.

19. *The throne was round behind: and there were stays on either side.* This description seems to indicate that the throne was in the form of one of our ancient round-topped, two-armed chairs. This throne or chair of state was raised on a platform, the ascent to which consisted of six steps. What we call *stays* is in the Hebrew *yadoth*, "hands," which serves to confirm the conjecture above.

25. *They brought every man his present.* This means tribute; and it shows us of what sort that tribute was, viz., vessels of gold and silver, probably ingots; garments of very rich stuffs; armor, for little of this kind was ever made in Judea; spices, which doubtless sold well in that country; horses, which were very rare; and mules, the most necessary animal for all the purposes of life.

26. *He had a thousand and four hundred chariots.* See the note on chap. iv. 26.

27. *Made silver . . . as stones.* He destroyed its value by making it so exceedingly plenty. *As the sycomore trees.* He planted many cedars, and doubtless had much cedarwood imported; so that it became as common as the sycamore trees, which appear to have grown there in great abundance.

28. *Horses brought out of Egypt.* It is thought that the first people who used horses in war were the Egyptians; and it is well known that the nations who knew the use of this creature in battle had greatly the advantage of those who did not. God had absolutely prohibited horses to be imported or used, but in many things Solomon paid little attention to the divine command. *And linen yarn.* The original word, *mikveh*, is hard to be understood. The versions are all puzzled with it: the Vulgate and Septuagint make it a proper name: "And Solomon had horses brought out of Egypt, and from Coa, or Tekoa."

29. *A chariot came up . . . for six hundred shekels.* This was the ordinary price of a chariot, as 150 shekels were for a horse. *Kings of the Hittites.* These must have been the remains of the original inhabitants of Canaan, who had gone to some other country, probably Syria, and formed themselves into a principality there. It seems that neither horses nor chariots came out of Egypt but by means of Solomon's servants.

MATTHEW HENRY

CHAPTER 11

Verses 1–8

Solomon's defection and degeneracy.

I. Let us enquire into the occasions and particulars of it. *There was no king like Solomon who was beloved of his God, yet even him did outlandish women cause to sin.* There is the summary of his apostasy.

1. He doted on strange women, *many strange women.* (1) He gave himself to women, which his mother had particularly cautioned him against. Prov. xxxi. 3, *Give not thy strength unto women* (perhaps alluding to Samson, who lost his strength by giving information of it to a woman). His father David's fall began with the lusts of the flesh. The love of women has *cast down many wounded* (Prov. vii. 26) and *many* (says Bishop Hall) *have had their head broken by their own rib.* (2) He took many women, so many that, at last, they amounted to 700 wives and 300 concubines, 1,000 in all. Divine wisdom has appointed one woman for one man, and those who do not think one enough will not think two or three enough. (3) They were strange women, Moabites, Ammonites, &c., of the nations which God had particularly forbidden them to inter-marry with, *v.* 2. Some think it was in policy that he married these foreigners, by them to get intelligence of the state of those countries. (4) To complete the mischief, *Solomon clave unto these in love, v.* 2. Solomon was master of a great deal of knowledge, but to what purpose, when he had no better a government of his appetites?

2. He was drawn by them to the worship of strange gods, as Israel to Baal-peor by the daughters of Moab. *His wives turned away his heart after other gods, v.* 3, 4. (1) He grew cool and indifferent in his own religion and remiss in the service of the God of Israel: *His heart was not perfect with the Lord his God* (*v.* 4), nor did he *follow him fully* (*v.* 6), like David. *He was not perfect,* because he was not *constant.* (2) He tolerated and maintained his wives in their idolatry and made no scruple of joining with them in it. He built chapels for their gods (*v.* 7, 8), maintained their priests, and occasionally did himself attend their altars, making a jest of it, asking, "What harm is there in it? Are not all religions alike?" which (says Bishop Patrick) has been the *disease of some great wits.* These high places continued here, not utterly demolished, till Josiah's time, 2 Kings xxiii. 13. This is the account here given of Solomon's apostasy.

II. Let us now pause a while, and lament Solomon's fall; and we must justly stand and wonder at it.

1. How strange, (1) That Solomon, in his old age, should be ensnared with fleshly lusts, youthful lusts. (2) That so wise a man as Solomon was, so famed for a quick understanding and sound judgment, should suffer himself to be made such a fool of by these foolish women. (3) That one who had so often and so plainly warned others of the danger of the love of women should himself be so wretchedly bewitched with it; it is easier to see a mischief, and to show it to others, than to shun it ourselves. (4) That so good a man, so zealous for the worship of God, should do these sinful things.

2. What shall we say to all this? (1) Let him that thinks he stands take heed lest he fall. We see how weak we are of ourselves, without the grace of God; let us therefore live in a constant dependence on that grace. (2) See the danger of a prosperous condition, and how hard it is to overcome the temptations of it. Solomon, like Jeshurun, waxed fat and then kicked. (3) See what need those have to stand upon their guard who have made a great profession of religion, and shown themselves forward and zealous in devotion, because the devil will set upon them most violently, and, if they misbehave, the reproach is the greater. It is the evening that commends the day; let us therefore fear, lest, having run well, we seem to come short.

Verses 9–13

I. God's anger against Solomon for his sin. The thing he did *displeased the Lord* for there was in his sin, 1. The most base ingratitude that could be. God's appearing to Solomon was such a sensible confirmation of his faith as should have for ever prevented his worshipping *any other god.* 2. The most wilful disobedience. This was the very thing concerning which *God had commanded him—that he should not go after other gods,* yet he was not restrained by such an express admonition, *v.* 10.

II. The message he sent him hereupon (*v.* 11): *The Lord said unto Solomon* (it is likely by a prophet) that he must expect to smart for his apostasy. And here, 1. The sentence is just, that, since he had revolted from God, part of his kingdom should revolt from his family. Sin brings ruin upon families, cuts off entails, alienates estates, and lays men's honour in

JAMIESON, FAUSSET, BROWN

CHAPTER 11

Vss. 1-8. SOLOMON'S WIVES AND CONCUBINES IN HIS OLD AGE. **1. But King Solomon loved many strange women**—Solomon's extraordinary gift of wisdom was not sufficient to preserve him from falling into grievous and fatal errors. A fairer promise of true greatness, a more beautiful picture of juvenile piety, never was seen than that which he exhibited at the commencement of his reign. No sadder, more humiliating, or awful spectacle can be imagined than the besotted apostasy of his old age; and to him may be applied the words of Paul (Gal. 3:3), of John (Rev. 3:17), and of Isaiah (14:21). A love of the world, a ceaseless round of pleasure, had insensibly corrupted his heart, and produced, for a while at least, a state of mental darkness. The grace of God deserted him; and the son of the pious David—the religiously trained child of Bathsheba (Prov. 31:1-3), and pupil of Nathan, instead of showing the stability of sound principle and mature experience became at last an old and foolish king (Eccles. 4:13). His fall is traced to his "love of many strange women." Polygamy was tolerated among the ancient Hebrews; and, although in most countries of the East, the generality of men, from convenience and economy, confine themselves to one woman, yet a number of wives is reckoned as an indication of wealth and importance, just as a numerous stud of horses and a grand equipage are among us. The sovereign, of course, wishes to have a more numerous harem than any of his subjects; and the female establishments of many Oriental princes have, both in ancient and modern times, equalled or exceeded that of Solomon's. It is probable, therefore, that, in conformity with Oriental notions, he resorted to it as a piece of state magnificence. But in him it was unpardonable, as it was a direct and outrageous violation of the divine law (Deut. 17:17), and the very result which that statute was ordained to prevent was realized in him. His marriage with the daughter of Pharaoh is not censured either here or elsewhere (see on ch. 3:1). It was only his love for many strange women; for women, though in the East considered inferiors, exert often a silent but powerful seductive influence over their husbands in the harem, as elsewhere, and so it was exemplified in Solomon. **3. he had seven hundred wives, princesses**—They were, probably, according to an existing custom, the daughters of tributary chiefs, given as hostages for good conduct of their fathers. **concubines**—were legitimate, but lower or secondary wives. These the chief or first wife regards without the smallest jealousy or regret, as they look up to her with feelings of respectful submission. Solomon's wives became numerous, not all at once, but gradually. Even at an early period his taste for Oriental show seems to have led to the establishment of a considerable harem (Song of Sol. 6:8). **4. when Solomon was old**—He could not have been more than fifty. **his wives turned away his heart after other gods**—Some, considering the lapse of Solomon into idolatry as a thing incredible, regard him as merely humoring his wives in the practice of their superstition; and, in countenancing their respective rites by his presence, as giving only an outward homage—a sensible worship, in which neither his understanding nor his heart was engaged. The apology only makes matters worse, as it implies an adding of hypocrisy and contempt of God to an open breach of His law. There seems no possibility of explaining the language of the sacred historian, but as intimating that Solomon became an actual and open idolater, worshipping images of wood or stone in sight of the very temple which, in early life, he had erected to the true God. Hence that part of Olivet was called the high place of Tophet (Jer. 7:30-34), and the hill is still known as the Mount of Offense, of the Mount of Corruption (II Kings 23:13). **5-7. Ashtoreth** [Astarte], **Milcolm** [Molech], **and Chemosh**—He built altars for these three; but, although he is described (vs. 8) as doing the same for "all his strange wives," there is no evidence that they had idols distinct from these; and there is no trace whatever of Egyptian idolatry. **8. burnt incense and sacrificed unto their gods**—The first was considered a higher act of homage, and is often used as synonymous with worship (II Kings 22:17; 23:5).

9-13. GOD THREATENS HIM. **9. the Lord was angry with Solomon**—The divine appearance, first at Gibeon, and then at Jerusalem, after the dedication of the temple, with the warnings given him on both occasions, had left Solomon inexcusable; and it was proper and necessary that on one who had been so signally favored with the gifts of Heaven, but who had grossly abused them, a terrible judg-

ADAM CLARKE

CHAPTER 11

1. *Many strange women.* That is, idolaters; *together with the daughter of Pharaoh*—she was also one of those strange women and an idolater. But many think she became a proselyte to the Jewish religion: of this there is no evidence.

ALEXANDER MACLAREN:

Scripture never dims the defects of its heroes. Its portraits do not smooth out wrinkles, but, with absolute fidelity, give all faults. That pitiless truthfulness is no small proof of its inspiration. If these historical books were simply fragments of national records, owning no higher source than patriotism, they would never have blurted out the errors and sins of David and Solomon as they do. Where else are there national histories of which the very central idea is the laying bare of national sins and chastisements? or where else are there legends of the people's heroes which tell their sins without apology or reticence? The difference in tone augurs a different origin. The Old Testament histories are not written to tell Israel's glories, or even, we may say, to recount its history, but to tell God's dealings with Israel—a very different theme, and one which finds its material equally in the glories and in the miseries, which respectively follow its obedience and disobedience. So Solomon's fall is told in the same frank way as his wisdom and wealth; for what is of importance is not Solomon so much as God's dealings with Solomon, when his heart was turned away.

—*Expositions of Holy Scripture*

3. *He had seven hundred wives, princesses.* How he could get so many of the blood royal from the different surrounding nations is astonishing; but probably the daughters of noblemen, generals, etc., may be included. *And three hundred concubines.* These were wives of the second rank, who were taken according to the usages of those times; but their offspring could not inherit.

7. *The hill that is before Jerusalem.* This was the Mount of Olives.

9. *The Lord was angry with Solomon.* Had not this man's delinquency been strongly marked by the divine disapprobation, it would have had a fatal effect on the morals of mankind. Vice is vice, no matter who commits it. Solomon was wise; he knew better; his understanding showed him the vanity as well as the wickedness of idolatry. God *had appeared unto him twice,* and thus given him the most direct proof of His being and of His providence. The promises of God had been fulfilled to him in the most remarkable manner, and in such a way as to prove that they came by a divine counsel. All these were aggravations of Solomon's crimes, as to their demerit.

11. *Forasmuch as this is done of thee.* Was not this another warning from the Lord? And might not Solomon have yet recovered himself? Was there not mercy in this message which he might have sought and found?

MATTHEW HENRY

the dust. 2. Yet the mitigations of it are very kind, for David's sake (*v.* 12, 13), that is, for the sake of the promise made to David. The kingdom shall be rent from Solomon's house, but, (1) Not immediately. Solomon shall not live to see it done, but it shall be rent *out of the hand of his son*, a son that was born to him by one of his strange wives, for his mother was an Ammonitess (1 Kings xiv. 31). (2) Not wholly. One tribe, that of Judah, the strongest and most numerous, shall remain to the house of David (*v.* 13), for Jerusalem's sake, which David built, and for the sake of the temple there, which Solomon built; these shall not go into other hands.

Upon this message which God graciously sent to Solomon, to awaken his conscience and bring him to repentance, we have reason to hope that he humbled himself before God, confessed his sin, begged pardon, and returned to his duty, that he then published his repentance in the book of Ecclesiastes. That penitential sermon was as true an indication of a heart broken for sin and turned from it as David's penitential psalms were, though of another nature. God's grace in his people works variously. Thus, though Solomon fell, *he was not utterly cast down*; what God had said to David concerning him was fulfilled: *I will chasten him with the rod of men, but my mercy shall not depart from him*, 2 Sam. vii. 14, 15. Though God may suffer those whom he loves to fall into sin, he will not suffer them to lie still in it.

Verses 14–25

An account of two adversaries that appeared against him, inconsiderable, and that could not have done anything worth taking notice of if Solomon had not first made God his enemy. What hurt could Hadad or Rezon have done to so great and powerful a king as Solomon was if he had not, by sin, made himself mean and weak? And then those little people menace and insult him.

I. Both these adversaries God stirred up, *v.* 14, 23. Though they themselves were moved by principles of ambition or revenge, God made use of them to serve his design of correcting Solomon.

II. Both these adversaries had the origin of their enmity to Solomon and Israel laid in David's time, and in his conquests of their respective countries, *v.* 15, 24. Solomon had the benefit and advantage of his father's successes both in the enlargement of his dominion and the increase of his treasure, and would never have known anything but the benefit of them if he had kept closely to God; but now he finds evils to balance the advantages.

1. Hadad, an Edomite, was an adversary to Solomon. (1) What induced him to bear Solomon a grudge. David had conquered Edom, 2 Sam. viii. 14. Joab put all the males to the sword, *v.* 15, 16. A terrible execution he made, avenging on Edom their old enmity to Israel. From this general slaughter, while Joab was burying the slain, Hadad, a branch of the royal family, then a little child, was taken and preserved by some of the king's servants, and conveyed to Egypt, *v.* 17. They halted by the way, in Midian first, and then in Paran, where they furnished themselves with men to attend them, that their young master might go into Egypt with an equipage agreeable to his quality. There he was kindly sheltered by Pharaoh, as a distressed prince, and so recommended himself that he married the queen's sister (*v.* 19), and by her had a child, which the queen herself conceived such a kindness for that she brought him up in Pharaoh's house, among the king's children. (2) What enabled him to do Solomon a mischief. Upon the death of David and Joab, he returned to his own country, in which, it should seem, he settled and remained quiet while Solomon continued wise and watchful for the public good, but from which he had opportunity of making inroads upon Israel when Solomon, having sinned away his wisdom as Samson did his strength, forfeited the divine protection. What vexation Hadad gave to Solomon we are not here told, but only how loth Pharaoh was to part with him and how earnestly he solicited his stay (*v.* 22): *What hast thou lacked with me?* "Nothing," says Hadad; "but let me go to my own country, my native air, my native soil."

2. Rezon, a Syrian, was another adversary to Solomon. When David conquered the Syrians, he headed the remains, lived at large by spoil and rapine, till Solomon grew careless, and then he got possession of Damascus, reigned there (*v.* 24) and over the country about (*v.* 25), and he created troubles to Israel, probably in conjunction with Hadad, all the days of Solomon (namely, after his apostasy).

Verses 26–40

Here is the first mention of that infamous name *Jeroboam the son of Nebat, that made Israel to sin*,

JAMIESON, FAUSSET, BROWN

ment should fall. The divine sentence was announced to him probably by Ahijah; but there was mercy mingled with judgment, in the circumstance, that it should not be inflicted on Solomon personally—and that a remnant of the kingdom should be spared—"for David's sake, and for Jerusalem's sake, which had been chosen" to put God's name there; not from a partial bias in favor of either, but that the divine promise might stand (II Sam. 7). **13. I will give one tribe to thy son**—There were left to Rehoboam the tribes of Judah, Benjamin, and Levi (II Chron. 11:12, 13); and multitudes of Israelites, who, after the schism of the kingdom, established their residence within the territory of Judah to enjoy the privileges of the true religion (ch. 12:17). These are all reckoned as one tribe.

14-40. SOLOMON'S ADVERSARIES. **14. the Lord stirred up an adversary**—i.e., permitted him, through the impulse of his own ambition, or revenge, to attack Israel.

During the war of extermination, which Joab carried on in Edom (II Sam. 8:13), this Hadad, of the royal family, a mere boy when rescued from the sword of the ruthless conqueror, was carried into Egypt, hospitably entertained, and became allied with the house of the Egyptian king. In after years, the thought of his native land and his lost kingdom taking possession of his mind, he, on learning the death of David and Joab, renounced the ease, possessions, and glory of his Egyptian residence, to return to Edom and attempt the recovery of his ancestral throne.

The movements of this prince seem to have given much annoyance to the Hebrew government; but as he was defeated by the numerous and strong garrisons planted throughout the Edomite territory, Hadad seems to have offered his services to Rezon, another of Solomon's adversaries (vss. 23-25). This man, who had been general of Hadadezer and, on the defeat of that great king, had succesfully withdrawn a large force, went into the wilderness, led a predatory life, like Jephthah, David, and others, on the borders of the Syrian and Arabian deserts. Then, having acquired great power, he at length became king in Damascus, threw off the yoke, and was "the adversary of Israel all the days of Solomon." He was succeeded by Hadad, whose successors took the official title of Benhadad from him, the illustrious founder of the powerful kingdom of Damascene-Syria. These hostile neighbors, who had been long kept in check by the traditional fame of David's victories, took courage; and breaking out towards the latter end of Solomon's reign, they must have not only disturbed his kingdom by their inroads, but greatly crippled his revenue by stopping his lucrative traffic with Tadmor and the Euphrates. **26-40. Jeroboam**—This was an internal enemy of a still more formidable character.

ADAM CLARKE

13. *Will give one tribe . . . for David my servant's sake.* The line of the Messiah must be preserved.

14. *The Lord stirred up an adversary.* "A satan." When he sent to Hiram to assist him in building the temple of the Lord, he could say, "There was no satan," see chap. v. 4; and all his kingdom was in peace and security; "every man [dwelt] under his vine and under his fig tree," chap. iv. 25. But now that he had turned away from God, three satans rise up against him at once, Hadad, Rezon, and Jeroboam.

15. *Was gone up to bury the slain.* The slain Edomites; for Joab had in the course of six months exterminated all the males, except Hadad and his servants, who escaped to Egypt. Instead of *bury the slain*, the Targum has to "take the spoils of the slain."

17. *Hadad being yet a little child.* "A little boy"; one who was apprehensive of his danger, and could, with his father's servants, make his escape—not an infant.

18. *They arose out of Midian.* They at first retired to Midian, which lay to the southwest of the Dead Sea. Not supposing themselves in safety there, they went afterwards to Paran in the south of Idumea, and getting a number of persons to join them in Paran, they went straight to Egypt, where we find Hadad became a favorite with Pharaoh, who gave him his sister-in-law to wife, and incorporated him and his family with his own.

22. *Let me go in any wise.* It does not appear that he avowed his real intention to Pharaoh; for at this time there must have been peace between Israel and Egypt, Solomon having married the daughter of Pharaoh.

23. *Rezon the son of Eliadah.* Thus God fulfilled His threatening by the prophet Nathan: "If he commit iniquity, I will chasten him with the rod of men, and with the stripes of the children of men," 2 Sam. vii. 14.

24. *And reigned in Damascus.* Rezon was one of the captains of Hadadezer, whom David defeated. It seems that at this time Rezon escaped with his men; and having lived, as is supposed, some time by plunder, he seized on Damascus, and reigned there till David took Damascus, when he subdued Syria, and drove out Rezon. But after Solomon's defection from God, Rezon, finding that God had departed from Israel, recovered Damascus; and joining with Hadad, harassed Solomon during the remaining part of his reign. But some think that Hadad and Rezon were the same person.

26. *Jeroboam the son of Nebat.* From the context we learn that Jeroboam while a young

MATTHEW HENRY

an adversary to Solomon. God had expressly told (*v.* 11) that he would give the greatest part of his kingdom to his servant, and Jeroboam was the man.

I. Of his extraction, *v.* 26. He was of the tribe of Ephraim, the next in honour to Judah. His mother was a widow.

II. Of his elevation. It was Solomon's wisdom, when he had work to do, to employ proper persons in it. Jeroboam was ruler of the burden, or tribute, that is, either of the taxes or of the militia of the house of Joseph. Observe a difference between David, and both his predecessor and his successor: when Saul saw a *valiant man he took him to himself* (1 Sam. xiv. 52); when Solomon saw an *industrious* man he preferred him.

III. Of his designation to the government of the ten tribes after the death of Solomon. The Jews say that when he was employed by Solomon in building Millo he took opportunities of reflecting upon Solomon as oppressive to his people, and suggesting that which would alienate them from his government. Solomon made him ruler over the tribes of Joseph, and, as he was going to take possession of his government, he was told by a prophet in God's name that he should be king, which emboldened him to aim high, and in some instances to oppose the king. 1. The prophet by whom this message was sent was *Ahijah of Shiloh*; we shall read of him again, *ch.* xiv. 2. It seems, Shiloh was not so perfectly forsaken and forgotten of God but that, in remembrance of the former days, it was blessed with a prophet. 2. The sign by which it was represented to him was the rending of a garment into twelve pieces, and giving him ten, *v.* 30, 31. The prophets, both true and false, used such signs, even in the New Testament, as Agabus, Acts xxi. 10, 11. 3. The message itself, which is very particular. (1) He assures him that he shall be king over ten of the twelve tribes of Israel, *v.* 31. (2) He tells him the reason; not for his good character or deserts, but for the chastising of Solomon's apostasy: "Because he, and his family, and many of his people with him, *have forsaken me, and worshipped other gods*," *v.* 33. Jeroboam did not deserve so good a post, but Israel deserved so bad a prince. (3) He limits his expectations to the ten tribes only, and to them in reversion after the death of Solomon, lest he should aim at the whole and give immediate disturbance to Solomon's government. He is here told, [1] That two tribes (called here *one tribe*, because little Benjamin was in a manner lost in the thousands of Judah) should remain sure to the house of David, and he must never make any attempt upon them. He must not think that David was rejected, as Saul was. The house of David must be supported and kept in reputation, for all this, because out of it the Messiah must arise. *Destroy it not*, for that *blessing is in it*. [2] That Solomon must keep possession during his life, *v.* 34, 35. Jeroboam therefore must not offer to dethrone him, but wait with patience till his day shall come to fall. Children that do not tread in their parents' steps yet often fare the better in this world for their good parents' piety. (4) He gives him to understand that he will be upon his good behaviour. "If thou wilt *do what is right in my sight, I will build thee a sure house*, and not otherwise" (*v.* 38).

IV. Jeroboam's flight into Egypt, *v.* 40. In some way or other Solomon came to know of all this, probably from Jeroboam's own talk of it. 1. Solomon foolishly sought to kill his successor. 2. Jeroboam prudently withdrew into Egypt.

Verses 41–43

We have here the conclusion of Solomon's story, and in it, 1. Reference is had to another history then extant, but since lost, *the Book of the Acts of Solomon*, *v.* 41. Probably this book was written by a chronologer whom Solomon employed to write his annals, out of which the sacred writer extracted what God saw fit to transmit to the church. 2. A summary of the years of his reign (*v.* 42): His reign was as long as his father's, but not his life. Sin shortened his days. 3. His death and burial, and his successor, *v.* 43. (1) He followed his fathers to the grave, slept with them, and was buried in David's burying-place. (2) His son followed him in the throne.

JAMIESON, FAUSSET, BROWN

He was a young man of talent and energy, who, having been appointed by Solomon superintendent of the engineering works projected around Jerusalem, had risen into public notice, and on being informed by a very significant act of the prophet Ahijah of the royal destiny which, by divine appointment, awaited him, his mind took a new turn.

29. clad—rather wrapped up. The meaning is, "Ahijah, the Shilonite, the prophet, went and took a fit station *in the way*; and, in order that he might not be known, *he wrapped himself up*, so as closely to conceal himself, in a *new garment*, a *surtout*, which he afterwards tore in twelve pieces," Notwithstanding this privacy, the story, and the prediction connected with it, probably reached the king's ears; and Jeroboam became a marked man. His aspiring ambition, impatient for the death of Solomon, led him to form plots and conspiracies, in consequence of which he was compelled to flee to Egypt. Though chosen of God, he would not wait the course of God's providence, and therefore incurred the penalty of death by his criminal rebellion. The heavy exactions and compulsory labor (vs. 28) which Solomon latterly imposed upon his subjects, when his foreign resources began to fail, had prepared the greater part of the kingdom for a revolt under so popular a demagogue as Jeroboam.

40. Shishak—He harbored and encouraged the rebellious refugee, and was of a different dynasty from the father-in-law of Solomon.

ADAM CLARKE

man was employed by Solomon to superintend the improvements and buildings at Millo, and had so distinguished himself there by his industry and good conduct as to attract general notice, and to induce Solomon to set him over all the laborers employed in that work, belonging to the tribes of Ephraim and Manasseh, called here the "house of Joseph." At first it appears that Solomon employed none of the Israelites in any drudgery; but it is likely that as he grew profane, he grew tyrannical and oppressive; and at the works of Millo he changed his conduct; and there, in all probability, were the seeds of disaffection sown. And Jeroboam, being a clever and enterprising man, knew well how to avail himself of the general discontent.

29. *When Jeroboam went out of Jerusalem.* On what errand he was going out of Jerusalem, we know not. *Ahijah the Shilonite.* He was one of those who wrote the history of the reign of Solomon, as we find from 2 Chron. ix. 29, and it is supposed that it was by him God spake twice to Solomon; and particularly delivered the message which we find in this chapter, vv. 11-13.

31. *Take thee ten pieces. The garment* was the symbol of the kingdom of Israel; the *twelve pieces,* the symbol of the twelve tribes; the *ten pieces* given to Jeroboam, of the ten tribes which would be given to him, and afterwards form the kingdom of Israel, ruling in Samaria, to distinguish it from the kingdom of Judah, ruling in Jerusalem.

36. *That David my servant may have a light alway.* That his posterity may never fail, and the regal line never become extinct. This, as we have already seen, was in reference to the Messiah. He was not only David's Light, but he was a Light to enlighten the Gentiles.

37. *According to all that thy soul desireth.* It appears from this that Jeroboam had affected the kingdom, and was seeking for an opportunity to seize on the government. God now tells him, by His prophet, what he shall have, and what he shall not have, in order to prevent him from attempting to seize on the whole kingdom, to the prejudice of the spiritual seed of David.

38. *And build thee a sure house.* He would have continued his posterity on the throne of Israel had he not by his wickedness forfeited the promises of God, and thrown himself out of the protection of the Most High.

39. *But not for ever.* They shall be in affliction and distress till the Messiah come, who shall sit on the throne of David to order it and establish it in judgment and justice forever. Jarchi says, on this verse, "When the Messiah comes. the kingdom shall be restored to the house of David."

40. *Sought . . . to kill Jeroboam.* He thought by this means to prevent the punishment due to his crimes.

Unto Shishak king of Egypt. This is the first time we meet with the proper name of an Egyptian king, *Pharaoh* being the common name for all the sovereigns of that country.

41. *The book of the acts of Solomon.* These acts were written by "Nathan the prophet . . . Ahijah the Shilonite, and . . . Iddo the seer," as we learn from 2 Chron. ix. 29. Probably from these were the Books of Kings and Chronicles composed, but the original documents are long since lost.

42. *Solomon reigned . . . forty years.* Josephus says "fourscore years," which is sufficiently absurd.

43. *Solomon slept with his fathers.* He died in almost the flower of his age and, it appears, unregretted. His government was no blessing to Israel; and laid, by its exactions and oppressions, the foundation of that schism which was so fatal to the unhappy people of Israel and Judah.

CHAPTER 12 (MATTHEW HENRY)

Verses 1–15

Solomon had 1,000 wives and concubines, yet we read but of one son he had to bear up his name, and he a fool. Sin is a bad way of building up a family. Rehoboam was the son of the wisest of men,

CHAPTER 12 (JAMIESON, FAUSSET, BROWN)

CHAPTER 12 (ADAM CLARKE)

MATTHEW HENRY

yet did not inherit his father's wisdom. Neither wisdom nor grace runs in the blood. Solomon's court was a mart of wisdom and the rendezvous of learned men, and Rehoboam was the darling of the court; and yet all was not sufficient to make him a wise man.

I. The people desired a treaty with him at Shechem, and he condescended to meet them there. 1. Their pretence was to make him king, but the design was to unmake him. They would give him a public inauguration in another place than the city of David, that he might not seem to be king of Judah only. 2. The place was ominous: at *Shechem*, where Abimelech set up himself (Judges ix.); yet it had been famous for the convention of the states there, Joshua xxiv. 1. Rehoboam knew of the threatening, that the kingdom should be rent from him, and hoped by going to Shechem, and treating there with the ten tribes, to prevent it: yet it proved the most impolitic thing he could do, and hastened the rupture.

II. The representatives of the tribes addressed him, praying to be eased of the taxes they were burdened with. The meeting being appointed, they sent for Jeroboam out of Egypt to come and be their speaker. In their address, 1. They complain of the last reign: *Thy father made our yoke grievous*, *v.* 4. They complain not of his father's idolatry, so careless and indifferent were they in the matters of religion, as if God or Moloch were all one, so they might but live at ease and pay no taxes. Yet the complaint was groundless and unjust. Never did people live more at ease than they did, nor in greater plenty. Did they pay taxes? It was to advance the strength and magnificence of their kingdom. If Solomon's buildings cost them money, they cost them no blood, as war would do. Factious spirits will never want something to complain of. I know nothing in Solomon's administration that could make the people's yoke grievous, unless perhaps the women were connived at in oppressing them. 2. They demand relief from him, and on this condition will continue in their allegiance to the house of David.

III. Rehoboam consulted with those about him concerning the answer he should give to this address. 1. The grave experienced men of his council advised him by all means to give the petitioners a kind answer, and that he would redress all their grievances. The way to rule is to serve, to do good, and stoop to do it, to become all things to all men and so win their hearts. 2. The young men of his council were hot and haughty, and they advised him to return a severe and threatening answer to the people's demands. It was an instance of Rehoboam's weakness, (1) That he did not prefer aged counsellors, but had a better opinion of the young men that had grown up with him and with whom he was familiar, *v.* 8. It is of great consequence to young people, setting out in the world, on whom they depend upon for advice. If they reckon those that feed their pride, and further them in their pleasures, their best friends, they are already marked for ruin. (2) That he did not prefer moderate counsels, but was pleased with those that advised him to double the taxes. These young counsellors thought the old men expressed themselves but dully, *v.* 7. The old men did not undertake to put words into Rehoboam's mouth, but the young men will furnish him with very quaint and pretty phrases: *My little finger shall be thicker than my father's loins*, &c. That is not always the best sense that is best worded.

IV. He answered the people according to the counsel of the young men, *v.* 14, 15. He affected to be haughty and imperious, and fancied he could carry all before him with a high hand.

1. How Rehoboam was infatuated in his counsels. (1) He owned their reflections upon his father's government to be true: *My father made your yoke heavy;* and therein he was unjust to his father's memory. (2) He fancied himself better able to manage them, and impose upon them, than his father was. (3) He threatened not only to squeeze them by taxes, but to chastise them by cruel laws. (4) He gave this provocation to a people that by long ease and prosperity were made wealthy, and strong, and proud, to a people that were now disposed to revolt, and had one ready to head them.

2. How God's counsels were hereby fulfilled. It was *from the Lord*, *v.* 15. He left Rehoboam to his own folly, and *hid from his eyes* the *things which belonged to his peace*. Those that lose the kingdom of heaven throw it away, as Rehoboam did his, by their own wilfulness and folly.

Verses 16–24

The rending of the kingdom of the ten tribes from the house of David, to effect which,

I. The people were bold and resolute in their revolt. *What portion have we in David? v.* 16. Had they

JAMIESON, FAUSSET, BROWN

Vss. 1-5. Refusing the Old Men's Counsel. **1. Rehoboam went to Shechem**—He was the oldest, and perhaps the only son of Solomon, and had been, doubtless, designated by his father heir to the throne, as Solomon had been by David. The incident here related took place after the funeral obsequies of the late king and the period for public mourning had past. When all Israel came to make him king, it was not to exercise their old right of election (I Sam. 10:19-21), for, after God's promise of the perpetual sovereignty to David's posterity, their duty was submission to the authority of the rightful heir; but their object was, when making him king, to renew the conditions and stipulations to which their constitutional kings were subject (I Sam. 10:25). To the omission of such rehearsing which, under the peculiar circumstances in which Solomon was made king, they were disposed to ascribe the absolutism of his government. **Shechem**—This ancient, venerable, and central town was the place of convocation; and it is evident, if not from the appointment of that place, at least from the tenor of their language, and the concerted presence of Jeroboam, that the people were determined on revolt. **4. Thy father made our yoke grievous**—The splendor of Solomon's court and the magnitude of his undertakings being such, that neither the tribute of dependent states, nor the presents of foreign princes, nor the profits of his commercial enterprises, were adequate to carry them on, he had been obliged, for obtaining the necessary revenue, to begin a system of heavy taxation. The people looked only to the burdens, not to the benefits they derived from Solomon's peaceful and prosperous reign—and the evils from which they demanded deliverance were civil oppressions, not idolatry, to which they appear to have been indifferent or approving.

5. he said . . ., Depart yet for three days—It was prudent to take the people's demand into calm and deliberate consideration. Whether, had the advice of the sage and experienced counsellors been followed, any good result would have followed, it is impossible to say. It would at least have removed all pretext for the separation. But he preferred the counsel of his young companions (not in age, for they were all about forty-one, but inexperienced), who recommended prompt and decisive measures to quell the malcontents.

11. whips . . . scorpions—The latter, as contrasted with the former, are supposed to mean thongs thickly set with sharp iron points, used in the castigation of slaves. **15. the king hearkened not unto the people, for the cause was from the Lord**—That was the overruling cause. Rehoboam's weakness (Eccles. 2:18, 19) and inexperience in public affairs has given rise to the probable conjecture, that, like many other princes in the East, he had been kept secluded in the harem till the period of his accession (Eccles. 4:14), his father being either afraid of his aspiring to the sovereignty, like the two sons of David, or, which is more probable, afraid of prematurely exposing his imbecility. The king's haughty and violent answer to a people already filled with a spirit of discontent and exasperation, indicated so great an incapacity to appreciate the gravity of the crisis, so utter a want of common sense, as to create a belief that he was struck with judicial blindness. It was received with mingled scorn and derision. The revolt was accomplished, and yet so

ADAM CLARKE

1. *Rehoboam went to Shechem.* Rehoboam was probably the only son of Solomon; for although he had a thousand wives, he had not the blessing of a numerous offspring; and although he was the wisest of men himself. his son was a poor, unprincipled fool. Had Solomon kept himself within reasonable bounds in matrimonial affairs, he would probably have had more children; and such as would have had common sense enough to discern the delicacy of their situation, and rule according to reason and religion.

4. *The grievous service . . . and . . . heavy yoke.* They seem here to complain of two things—excessively laborious service and a heavy taxation.

7. *If thou wilt be a servant unto this people.* This is a constitutional idea of a king. He is the *servant*, but not the slave, of his people; every regal act of a just king is an act of service to the state. *They will be thy servants for ever.* The way to insure the obedience of the people is to hold the reins of empire with a steady and impartial hand; let the people see that the king lives for them and not for himself, and they will obey, love, and defend him.

10. *And the young men that were grown up with him.* It was a custom in different countries to educate with the heir to the throne young noblemen of nearly the same age.

11. *Chastise you with scorpions.* Should you rebel, or become disaffected, my father's *whip* shall be a *scorpion* in my hand. His was chastisement; mine shall be punishment. Isidore, and after him Calmet and others, assert that the scorpion was a sort of severe whip, the lashes of which were armed with iron points that sunk into and tore the flesh.

15. *The cause was from the Lord. Sibbah,* "the revolution, was from the Lord." God stirred up the people to revolt from a man who had neither skill nor humanity to govern them.

16. *So Israel departed unto their tents.* That is, the ten tribes withdrew their allegiance from Rehoboam; only Judah and Benjamin, frequently reckoned one tribe, remaining with him.

MATTHEW HENRY

enquired who gave Rehoboam this advice, and taken a course to remove those evil counsellors from about him, the rupture might have been prevented. Thus to rebel against the seed of David, whom God had advanced to the kingdom (entailing it on his seed), and to set up another king in opposition to that family, was a great sin; see 2 Chron. xiii. 5-8. (And it is here mentioned to the praise of the tribe of Judah that they *followed the house of David* (*v.* 17, 20), and found Rehoboam better than his word, nor did he rule with the rigour which at first he threatened.)

II. Rehoboam was imprudent in the further management of this affair. 1. He was very unadvised in sending Adoram, who was *over the tribute*, to treat with them, *v.* 18. The very sight of him, whose name was odious among them, exasperated them, and made them outrageous. 2. Some think he was also unadvised in quitting his ground, and making so much haste to Jerusalem, for thereby he deserted his friends and gave advantage to his enemies, who had gone to their tents indeed (*v.* 16) in disgust, but did not offer to make Jeroboam king till Rehoboam had gone, *v.* 20.

III. God forbade his attempt to recover by the sword what he had lost. The thing must rest as it is, and therefore God forbids the battle. 1. It was brave in Rehoboam to design the reducing of the revolters by force. His courage came to him when he had come to Jerusalem, *v.* 21. Judah and Benjamin (who feared the Lord and the king, and meddled not with those that were given to change) presently raised an army of 180,000 men, for the recovery of their king's right to the ten tribes, and were resolved to stand by him. 2. It was more brave in Rehoboam to desist when God, by a prophet, ordered him to lay down his arms. To proceed in this war would be not only to *fight against their brethren* (*v.* 24), whom they ought to love, but to fight against their God, to whom they ought to submit. Rehoboam and his people *hearkened to the word of the Lord*, disbanded the army, and acquiesced. (1) They regarded the command of God though sent by a poor prophet. (2) They consulted their own interest, concluding that though they had all the advantages, even that of right, on their side, yet they could not prosper if they fought in disobedience to God.

Verses 25–33

The beginning of the reign of Jeroboam. He built Shechem first and then Penuel—beautified and fortified them, but he formed another project for the establishing of his kingdom which was fatal to the interests of religion in it.

I. That which he designed was by some effectual means to secure those to himself who had now chosen him for their king, and to prevent their return to the house of David, *v.* 26, 27. 1. He was jealous of the people, afraid that, some time or other, they would kill him and go again to Rehoboam. Jeroboam could not put any confidence in the affections of his people, for what is got by usurpation cannot be enjoyed nor kept with any security. 2. He was distrustful of the promise of God, but he would contrive ways and means, and sinful ones too, for his own safety. A practical disbelief of God's all-sufficiency is at the bottom of all our treacherous departures from him.

II. The way he took to do this was by keeping the people from going up to Jerusalem to worship.

1. Jeroboam apprehended that, if the people continued to do this, they would in time return to the house of David, allured by the magnificence both of the court and of the temple. If they cleave to their old religion, they will go back to their old king.

2. He therefore dissuaded them from going up to Jerusalem, pretending to consult their ease: "*It is too much for you* to go so far to worship God, *v.* 28. Why should we now be tied to one place any more than in Samuel's time?"

3. He provided for the assistance of their devotion at home. Upon consultation with some of his politicians, he set up two golden calves, as tokens or signs of the divine presence, and some are so charitable as to think they were made to represent the mercy-seat and the cherubim over the ark; but more probably he adopted the idolatry of the Egyptians, in whose land he had sojourned for some time and who worshipped their god Apis under the similitude of a bull or calf. He intended, no doubt, by these to represent, or rather make present, not any false god, as Moloch or Chemosh, but the true God only, the God of Israel, the God that brought them up out of the land of Egypt, as he declares, *v.* 28. So that it was no violation of the first commandment, but the second. He set up two, by degrees to break people off from the belief of the unity of the godhead, which would pave the way to the polytheism of the

JAMIESON, FAUSSET, BROWN

quietly, that Rehoboam remained in Shechem, fancying himself the sovereign of a united kingdom, until his chief tax-gatherer, who had been most imprudently sent to treat with the people, had been stoned to death. This opened his eyes, and he fled for security to Jerusalem.

20-33. JEROBOAM MADE KING OVER THEM. **20. when all Israel heard that Jeroboam was come again**—This verse closes the parenthetical narrative begun at verse 2, and verses 21-24 resume the history from verse 1. Rehoboam determined to assert his authority by leading a large force into the disaffected provinces. But the revolt of the ten tribes was completed when the prophet Shemaiah ordered, in the Lord's name, an abandonment of any hostile measures against the revolutionists. The army, overawed by the divine prohibition, dispersed, and the king was obliged to submit.

25. Jeroboam built Shechem—destroyed by Abimelech (Judg. 9:1-49). It was rebuilt, and perhaps fortified, by Jeroboam, as a royal residence. **built Penuel**—a ruined city with a tower (Judg. 8:9), east of Jordan, on the north bank of the Jabbok. It was an object of importance to restore this fortress (as it lay on the caravan road from Gilead to Damascus and Palmyra) and to secure his frontier on that quarter. **26. Jeroboam said in his heart, Now shall the kingdom return to the house of David** Having received the kingdom from God, he should have relied on the divine protection. But he did not.

With a view to withdraw the people from the temple and destroy the sacred associations connected with Jerusalem, he made serious and unwarranted innovations on the religious observances of the country, on pretext of saving the people the trouble and expense of a distant journey. First, he erected two golden calves—the young bulls, Apis and Mnevis, as symbols (in the Egyptian fashion) of the true God, and the nearest, according to his fancy, to the figures of the cherubim.

ADAM CLARKE

18. *King Rehoboam sent Adoram.* As this was the person who was superintendent over the tribute, he was probably sent to collect the ordinary taxes; but the people, indignant at the master who had given them such a brutish answer, stoned the servant to death. The sending of Adoram to collect the taxes when the public mind was in such a state of fermentation was another proof of Rehoboam's folly and incapacity to govern.

20. *Made him king over all Israel.* What is called Israel here was ten-twelfths of the whole nation.

24. *For this thing is from me.* That is, the separation of the ten tribes from the house of David. *They . . . returned to depart.* This was great deference, in both Rehoboam and his officers, to relinquish, at the demand of the prophet, a war which they thought they had good grounds to undertake. The remnant of the people heard the divine command gratefully, for the mass of mankind are averse from war.

27. *And they shall kill me.* He found he had little cause to trust this fickle people; though they had declared for him it was more from caprice, desire of change, and novelty than from any regular and praiseworthy principle.

28. *Made two calves of gold.* It is strange that in pointing out his calves to the people he should use the same words that Aaron used when he made the golden calf in the wilderness, when they must have heard what terrible judgments fell upon their forefathers for this idolatry.

MATTHEW HENRY

Pagans.

4. The people complied with him herein, and were fond enough of the novelty: They *went to worship before the one, even unto Dan* (*v.* 30). Those that thought it much to go to Jerusalem, to worship God according to his institution, made no difficulty of going twice as far, to Dan, to worship him according to their own inventions. God had sometimes dispensed with the law concerning worshipping in one place, but never allowed the worship of him by images.

5. Having set up the gods, he fitted up accommodations for them. (1) He made a house of high-places, or of altars, one temple at Dan, we may suppose, and another at Beth-el (*v.* 31), and in each many altars. (2) He made priests of the lowest of the people; and the lowest of the people were good enough to be priests to his calves, and too good. He made priests out of every corner of the country. Thus were they dispersed as the Levites, but *were not of the sons of Levi.* But the priests of the high-places, or altars, he ordered to reside in Beth-el, as the priests at Jerusalem (*v.* 32), to attend the public service. (3) The feast of tabernacles, which God had appointed on the fifteenth day of the seventh month, he adjourned to the fifteenth day of the eighth month (*v.* 32), *the month which he devised of his own heart*, to show his power in ecclesiastical matters, *v.* 33. (4) He himself assuming a power to make priests, no marvel if he undertook to do the priests' work with his own hands: *He offered upon the altar.* He did it himself to get the reputation of a devout man. And thus, [1] Jeroboam sinned himself, yet perhaps excused himself that he did not do so ill as Solomon did, who worshipped other gods. [2] He *made Israel to sin*, drew them off from the worship of God and entailed idolatry upon their seed.

CHAPTER 13

Verses 1–10

I. A messenger sent to Jeroboam, to signify to him God's displeasure against his idolatry, *v.* 1. The army of Judah that aimed to ruin him was countermanded, and might not draw a sword against him (*ch.* xii. 24); but a prophet of Judah is sent to reclaim him from his evil way, and is sent in time, while he is but dedicating his altar, before his heart is hardened, for God delights not in the death of sinners, but would rather they would turn and live.

II. The message delivered in God's name, not whispered, but cried with a loud voice, denoting both the prophet's courage, and his earnestness. It was directed, not to Jeroboam nor to the people, but to the altar. Yet, in threatening the altar, God threatened the founder and worshippers, who might conclude, "If God's wrath fasten upon the lifeless guiltless altar, how shall we escape?" That which was foretold concerning the altar (*v.* 2) was that, in process of time, a prince of the house of David, Josiah by name, should pollute this altar by sacrificing the idolatrous priests themselves upon it, and burning the bones of dead men. Let Jeroboam know and be sure, 1. That the altar he now consecrated should be desecrated. 2. That the *priests of the high places* he now made should themselves be made sacrifices to the justice of God. 3. That this should be done by a branch *of the house of David.* It was about 356 years ere this prediction was fulfilled, yet it was spoken of as sure and nigh at hand, for a thousand years with God are but as one day.

III. A sign is given for the confirming of the truth of this prediction, that the altar should be shaken to pieces by an invisible power and the ashes of the sacrifice scattered (*v.* 3), which came to pass immediately, *v.* 5. This was, 1. A proof that the prophet was sent of God, *who confirmed the word with this sign following*, Mark xvi. 20. 2. A present indication of God's displeasure against these idolatrous sacrifices. 3. It was a reproach to the people, whose hearts were harder than these stones and rent not under the word of the Lord. 4. It was a specimen of what should be done to it in the accomplishment of this prophecy by Josiah; it was now rent, in token of its being then ruined.

IV. Jeroboam's hand withered, which he stretched out to seize or smite the man of God, *v.* 4. Jeroboam's inability to pull in his hand made him a spectacle to all about him, that they might see and fear. If God, in justice, harden the hearts of sinners, so that the hand they had stretched out in sin they cannot pull in again by repentance, that is a spiritual judgment, represented by this, and much more dreadful.

V. The sudden healing of the hand that was suddenly dried up, upon his submission, *v.* 6. That word of God which should have touched his conscience

JAMIESON, FAUSSET, BROWN

The one was placed at Dan, in the northern part of his kingdom; the other at Beth-el, the southern extremity, in sight of Jerusalem, and in which place he probably thought God was as likely to manifest Himself as at Jerusalem (Gen. 32; II Kings 2:2). The latter place was the most frequented—for the words (vs. 30) should be rendered, "the people even to Dan went to worship before the one" (Jer. 48:13; Amos 4:4, 5; 5:5; Hos. 5:8; 10: 8). The innovation was a sin because it was setting up the worship of God by symbols and images and departing from the place where He had chosen to put His name. Secondly, he changed the feast of tabernacles from the 15th of the seventh to the 15th of the eighth month. The ostensible reason might be, that the ingathering or harvest was later in the northern parts of the kingdom; but the real reason was to eradicate the old association with this, the most welcome and joyous festival of the year. **31. made priests of the lowest of the people**—lit., out of all the people, the Levites refusing to act. **He himself assumed to himself the functions of the high priest, at least, at the great festival, probably from seeing the king of Egypt conjoin the royal and sacred offices, and deeming the office of the high priest too great to be vested in a subject.**

CHAPTER 13

VSS. 1-22. JEROBOAM'S HAND WITHERS. **1. there came a man of God out of Judah**—Who this prophet was cannot be ascertained, He came by divine authoritiy. It could not be either Iddo or Ahijah, for both were alive after the events here related. **Jeroboam stood by the altar to burn incense**—It was at one of the annual festivals. The king, to give interest to the new ritual, was himself the officiating priest. The altar and its accompaniments would, of course, exhibit all the splendor of a new and gorgeously decorated temple. But the prophet foretold its utter destruction. **2. he cried against the altar**—which is put for the whole system of worship organized in Israel. **Behold, a child shall be born . . . Josiah by name**—This is one of the most remarkable prophecies recorded in the Scriptures; and, in its clearness, circumstantial minuteness, and exact prediction of an event that took place 360 years later, it stands in striking contrast to the obscure and ambiguous oracles of the heathen. Being publicly uttered, it must have been well known to the people; and every Jew who lived at the accomplishment of the event must have been convinced of the truth of a religion connected with such a prophecy as this. A present sign was given of the remote event predicted, in a visible fissure being miraculously made on the altar.

Incensed at the man's license of speech, Jeroboam stretched out his hand and ordered his attendants to seize the bold intruder. That moment the king's arm became stiff and motionless, and the altar split asunder, so that the fire and ashes fell on the floor. Overawed by the effects of his impiety, Jeroboam besought the prophet's prayer. His request was acceded to, and the hand was restored to its healthy state.

ADAM CLARKE

29. *One in Beth-el, and the other . . . in Dan.* One at the southern and the other at the northern extremity of the land. Solomon's idolatry had prepared the people for Jeroboam's abominations!

31. *An house of high places.* A temple of temples; he had many *high places* in the land, and to imitate the Temple at Jerusalem, he made one chief over all the rest, where he established a priesthood of his own ordination.

32. *Ordained a feast.* The Jews held their Feast of Tabernacles on the fifteenth day of the seventh month; Jeroboam, who would meet the prejudices of the people as far as he could, appointed a similar feast on the fifteenth of the eighth month, thus appearing to hold the thing while he subverted the ordinance.

CHAPTER 13

1. *There came a man of God.* Who this was we know not. The Chaldee, Syriac, and Arabic call him a "prophet." The Vulgate and Septuagint follow the Hebrew.

2. *He cried against the altar.* He denounced the destruction of this idolatrous system. *A child shall be born . . . Josiah by name.* This is one of the most remarkable and most singular prophecies of the Old Testament. It here most circumstantially foretells a fact which took place 340 years after the prediction, a fact which was attested by the two nations. The Jews, in whose behalf this prophecy was delivered, would guard it most sacredly; and it was the interest of the Israelites, against whom it was levelled, to impugn its authenticity and expose its falsehood, had this been possible. This prediction not only showed the knowledge of God, but His power. He gave, as it were, this warning to idolatry, that it might be on its guard, and defend itself against this Josiah whenever a person of that name should be found sitting on the throne of David. And no doubt it was on the alert, and took all prudent measures for its own defense; but all in vain, for Josiah, in the eighteenth year of his reign, literally accomplished this prophecy, as we may read in 2 Kings xxiii. 15-20.

3. *And he gave a sign.* A miracle to prove that the prophecy should be fulfilled in its season.

4. *Lay hold on him.* No doubt stretching out his own hand at the same time, through rage, pride, and haste, to execute his own orders. *And his hand . . . dried up.* The whole arm suddenly became rigid.

5. *The altar was also rent.* It split or clave of its own accord; and, as the split parts would decline at the top from the line of their perpendicular, so the ashes and coals would fall off, or be poured out.

6. *Intreat . . . the face of the Lord thy God.* The *face* of God is His favor, as we see in many parts of the sacred writings. He says, *thy God;* for Jeroboam knew that He was not his God, for he was now in the very act of acknowledg-

MATTHEW HENRY

humbled him not, but this which *touched his bone and his flesh* brings down his proud spirit. He looks for help now, 1. Not from his calves, but from God only, from his power and his favour. 2. Not by his own sacrifice or incense, but by the prayer and intercession of the prophet, whom he had just now threatened and aimed to destroy. But observe, He did not desire the prophet to pray that his sin might be pardoned, and his heart changed, only that *his hand might be restored.* The prophet immediately addresses himself to God for him. God put this further honour upon him, that at his word he recalled the judgment and by another miracle healed the withered hand, that by the goodness of God Jeroboam might be led to repentance, and, if he were not broken by the judgment, yet might be melted by the mercy. With both he seemed affected for the present, but the impressions wore off.

VI. The prophet's refusal of Jeroboam's kind invitation, in which observe, 1. That God forbade his messenger to eat or drink in Beth-el (*v.* 9), to show his detestation of their execrable idolatry and apostasy from God. 2. That Jeroboam was so affected with the cure of his hand that he was willing to express his gratitude to the prophet and pay him for his prayers, *v.* 7. 3. That the prophet, though hungry and weary, and perhaps poor, in obedience to the divine command refused both the entertainment and the reward proffered him.

Verses 11–22

The man of God had honestly and resolutely refused the king's invitation, though he promised him a reward; yet he was over-persuaded by an old prophet to come back with him, and dine in Beth-el, contrary to the command given him. Here we find how dearly his dinner cost him.

I. The old prophet's wickedness. I cannot but call him a false prophet. Perhaps he was trained up among the sons of the prophets, in one of Samuel's colleges not far off, whence he retained the name of a prophet, but, growing worldly and profane, the spirit of prophecy had departed from him. If he had been a good prophet he would have reproved Jeroboam's idolatry. 1. Whether he had any good design in fetching back the man of God is not certain. One may hope that he did it in compassion to him, concluding he wanted refreshment. I suppose it was done with a bad design, for false prophets have ever been the worst enemies to the true prophets, usually aiming to destroy them, but sometimes, as here, to debauch them and draw them from their duty. But, 2. It is certain that he took a very bad method to bring him back. When the man of God had told him, "I may not, and therefore I will not, return to eat bread with thee," he wickedly pretended that he had an order from heaven to fetch him back.

II. The good prophet's weakness, in suffering himself to be thus imposed upon: *He went back with him, v.* 19. He that had resolution enough to refuse the invitation of the king, who promised him a reward, could not resist the insinuations of one that pretended to be a prophet. The message delivered to the man of God was strange. Judgment is given upon it: "Thou shalt never reach thy own house, but shalt be a carcase quickly, nor shall thy dead body be brought to *the place of thy father's sepulchres,* to be interred." Yet it was more strange that the old prophet himself should be the messenger. The message could not but affect him the more when he himself had the delivering of it, and had so strong an impression made upon his spirit by it that he cried out, as one in an agony, *v.* 21. Perhaps it had a good effect upon him. Those who preach God's wrath to others have hard hearts indeed if they fear it not themselves.

Verses 23–34

I. The death of the deceived disobedient prophet. The old prophet that had deluded him, furnished him with an ass to ride home on; but by the way a lion set upon him, and killed him, *v.* 23, 24. Did he think this old prophet's house safer to eat in than other houses at Beth-el, when God had forbidden him to eat in any? That was to refine upon the command, and make himself wiser than God. Nothing is more provoking to him than disobedience to an express command. God is displeased at the sins of his own people, and no man shall be protected in disobedience by the sanctity of his profession, the dignity of his office, his nearness to God, or any good services he has done for him.

II. The wonderful preservation of his dead body, which was a token of God's mercy remembered in the midst of wrath. The lion that gently strangled him, or tore him, did not devour his dead body, nor so much as tear the ass, *v.* 24, 25, 28. Nay, what

JAMIESON, FAUSSET, BROWN

Jeroboam was artful, and invited the prophet to the royal table, not to do him honor or show his gratitude for the restoration of his hand, but to win, by his courtesy and liberal hospitality, a person whom he could not crush by his power. But the prophet informed him of a divine injunction expressly prohibiting him from all social intercourse with any in the place, as well as from returning the same way. The prohibition not to eat or drink in Beth-el was because all the people had become apostates from the true religion, and the reason he was not allowed to return the same way was lest he should be recognized by any whom he had seen in going.

11. Now there dwelt an old prophet in Beth-el—If this were a true prophet, he was a bad man.

18. an angel spake unto me by the word of the Lord—This circuitous mode of speaking, instead of simply saying, "the LORD spake to me," was adopted to hide an equivocation, to conceal a double meaning—an inferior sense given to the word angel—to offer a *seemingly superior* authority to persuade the prophet, while really the authority was secretly known to the speaker to be *inferior.* The "angel"—i.e., messenger, was his own sons, who were worshippers, perhaps priests, at Beth-el. As this man was governed by self-interest, and wished to curry favor with the king (whose purpose to adhere to his religious polity, he feared, might be shaken by the portents that had occurred), his hastening after the prophet of Judah, the deception he practised, and the urgent invitation by which, on the ground of a falsehood, he prevailed on the too facile man of God to accompany him back to his house in Beth-el, were to create an impression in the king's mind that he was an impostor, who acted in opposition to his own statement.

20-22. he cried unto the man of God that came from Judah—rather, "it cried," i.e., the word of the Lord.

23-32. THE DISOBEDIENT PROPHET SLAIN BY A LION. **24. a lion met him by the way, and slew him**—There was a wood near Beth-el infested with lions (II Kings 2:24). This sad catastrophe was a severe but necessary judgment of God, to attest the truth of the message with which the prophet had been charged. All the circumstances of this tragic occurrence (the undevoured carcass, the untouched ass, the unmolested passers-by the lion, though standing there) were calculated to produce an irresistible impression that the hand of God was in it.

ADAM CLARKE

ing other gods, and had no portion in the God of Jacob. *And the king's hand was restored.* Both miracles were wrought to show the truth of the Jewish religion, and to convince this bold innovator of his wickedness, and to reclaim him from the folly and ruinous tendency of his idolatry.

7. *Come home with me . . . and I will give thee a reward.* Come and be one of my priests, and I will give you a proper salary.

9. *For so it was charged me . . . Eat no bread.* That is, Have no kind of communication with those idolaters. He was charged also not to return by the way that he came; probably lest the account of what was done should have reached the ears of any of the people through whom he had passed, and he suffer inconveniences on the account, either by persecution from the idolaters or from curious people delaying him in order to cause him to give an account of the transactions which took place at Bethel.

11. *An old prophet.* Probably once a prophet of the Lord, who had fallen from his steadfastness, and yet not so deeply as to lose the knowledge of the true God and join with Jeroboam in his idolatries.

14. *And went after the man of God.* I can hardly think that this was with any evil design. His sons had given him such an account of the prediction, the power, and influence of this prophet that he wished to have a particular acquaintance with him, in order that he might get further information relative to the solemn import of the prophecy which he had denounced against the idolatry at Bethel.

18. *An angel spake unto me.* That he lied unto him is here expressly asserted and is amply proved by the event. But why should he deceive him? The simple principle of curiosity to know all about this prediction and the strange facts which had taken place, of which he had heard at second hand by means of his sons, was sufficient to induce such a person to get the intelligence he wished by any means.

19. *So he went back with him.* He permitted himself to be imposed on; he might have thought, as he had accomplished every purpose for which God sent him, and had actually begun to return by another way, God, who had given him the charge, had authority to say, "As thy purpose was to obey every injunction, even to the letter, I now permit thee to go with this old prophet, and take some refreshment."

20. *The word of the Lord came unto the prophet that brought him back.* "A great clamour," says Kennicott, "has been raised against this part of the history, on account of God's denouncing sentence on the true prophet by the mouth of the false prophet: but if we examine with attention the original words here, they will be found to signify either *he who brought him back;* or, *whom he had brought back;* for the very same words, *asher heshibo,* occur again in ver. 23, where they are now translated, *whom he had brought back;* and where they cannot be translated otherwise. This being the case, we are at liberty to consider the word of the Lord as delivered to the true prophet thus brought back; and then the sentence is pronounced by God himself, calling to him out of heaven, as in Gen. xxii. 11."

21. *And he.* That is, according to the above interpretation, the voice of God from heaven addressing the man of God, the old prophet having nothing to do in this business.

22. *Thy carcase shall not come.* This intimated to him that he was to die an untimely death, but probably did not specify by what means.

28. *The lion had not eaten the carcase, nor torn the ass.* All here was preternatural. The lion, though he had killed the man, does not devour him; the ass stands quietly by, not fearing the lion; and the lion does not attempt to tear the ass. Both stand as guardians of the fallen prophet. How evident is the hand of God in all!

MATTHEW HENRY

was more, he did not set upon the old prophet when he came to take up the corpse.

III. The care which the old prophet took of his burial. The case was indeed very lamentable that so good a man, a prophet so faithful, and so bold in God's cause, should, for one offence, die as a criminal, while an old lying prophet lives at ease and an idolatrous prince in pomp and power. We cannot judge of men by their sufferings, nor of sins by their present punishments; with some the flesh is destroyed that the spirit may be saved.

IV. The charge which the old prophet gave his sons concerning his own burial, that they should be sure to bury him in the same grave where the man of God was buried (*v.* 3): "*Lay my bones beside his bones.*" Though he was a lying prophet, yet he desired to *die the death of a* true prophet. "Gather not my soul with the sinners of Beth-el, but with the man of God." He does honour to the deceased prophet, as one whose *word* would not fall to the ground, though *he* did. It was foretold that men's bones should be burnt upon Jeroboam's altar: "Lay mine (says he) close to his, and then they will not be disturbed"; and it was, accordingly, their security, as we find, 2 Kings xxiii. 18. No mention is made here of the inscription on the prophet's tomb; but it is spoken of 2 Kings xxiii. 17, where Josiah asks, *What title is that?* and is told, *It is the sepulchre of the man of God that came from Judah, who proclaimed these things which thou hast done.*

V. The obstinacy of Jeroboam in his idolatry (*v.* 33): *He returned not from his evil way;* some hand was found that durst repair the altar God had rent, and then Jeroboam offered sacrifice on it again. Various methods had been used to reclaim him, but neither threats nor signs, neither judgments nor mercies, wrought upon him, so strangely was he wedded to his calves.

CHAPTER 14

Verses 1–6

Jeroboam persisted in his contempt of God and religion.

I. His child fell sick, *v.* 1. It is probable that he was his eldest son, and heir-apparent to the crown; for at his death all the kingdom went into mourning for him, *v.* 13. *At that time*, when Jeroboam prostituted and profaned the priesthood (*ch.* xiii. 33), his child sickened.

II. He sent his wife in disguise to enquire of Ahijah the prophet *what should become of the child*, *v.* 2, 3.

1. Jeroboam's great desire, under this affliction, is to know *what shall become of the child*, whether he will live or die. (1) It would have been more prudent if he had desired to know what means they should use for the recovery of the child, but by this instance, and those of Ahaziah (2 Kings i. 2) and Benhadad (2 Kings viii. 8), it should seem they had then such a foolish notion of fatality as took them off from all use of means; for, if they were sure the patient would live, they thought means needless; if he would die, they thought them useless. (2) It would have been more pious if he had begged the prophet's prayers, and cast away his idols from him; then the child might have been restored to him, as his hand was. But most people would rather be told their fortune than their faults or their duty.

2. That he might know the child's doom, he sent to Ahijah the prophet, who lived obscurely and neglected in Shiloh, blind through age, yet still blest with the visions of the Almighty, which need not bodily eyes, but are rather favoured by the want of them, the eyes of the mind being then most intent and least diverted. Jeroboam sent not to him for advice about the setting up of his calves, or the consecrating of his priests, but had recourse to him in his distress, when the gods he served could give him no relief. He sent to Ahijah, because he had *told him he should be king*, *v.* 2. "He was once the messenger of good tidings, surely he will be so again." Those that by sin disqualify themselves for comfort, and yet expect their ministers, because they are good men, should speak peace and comfort to them, greatly wrong both themselves and their ministers.

3. He sent his wife to enquire of the prophet, because she could best put the question without naming names, or making any other description than this, "Sir, I have a son ill; will he recover or not?" It would have been much fitter for her to have stayed at home to tend him than go to Shiloh to enquire what would become of him. If she go, she must go *incognito—in disguise*, not only to conceal herself from her own court and the country through which she passed, but also to conceal herself from the prophet himself, that he might only answer her

JAMIESON, FAUSSET, BROWN

31. bury me in the sepulchre wherein the man of God is buried—His motive in making this request was either that his remains might not be disturbed when the predicted events took place (see on II Kings 23:18), or he had some superstitious hope of being benefited at the resurrection by being in the same cave with a man of God.

CHAPTER 14

Vss. 1-20. Ahijah Denounces God's Judgments against Jeroboam. **1. At that time**—a phrase used often loosely and indefinitely in sacred history. This domestic incident in the family of Jeroboam probably occurred towards the end of his reign; his son Abijah was of age and considered by the people the heir to the throne.

2. Jeroboam said to his wife, Arise, I pray thee, and disguise thyself—His natural and intense anxiety as a parent is here seen, blended with the deep and artful policy of an apostate king. The reason of this extreme caution was an unwillingness to acknowledge that he looked for information as to the future, not to his idols, but to the true God; and a fear that this step, if publicly known, might endanger the stability of his whole political system; and a strong impression that Ahijah, who was greatly offended with him, would, if consulted openly by his queen, either insult or refuse to receive her. For these reasons he selected his wife, as, in every view, the most proper for such a secret and confidential errand, but recommended her to assume the garb and manner of a peasant woman. Strange infatuation, to suppose that the God who could reveal futurity could not penetrate a flimsy disguise! **3. And take with thee ten loaves, and cracknels, and a cruse of honey, and go to him**—This was a present in unison with the peasant character she assumed. Cracknels are a kind of sweet seed-cake. The prophet was blind, but having received divine premonition of the pretended countrywoman's coming, he addressed her the moment she appeared as the queen, apprised her of the calamities which, in consequence of the ingratitude of Jeroboam, his apostasy, and outrageous misgovernment of Israel,

ADAM CLARKE

30. *Alas, my brother!* This lamentation is very simple, very short, and very pathetic. Perhaps the old prophet said it as much in reference to himself, who had been the cause of his untimely death, as in reference to the man of God, whose corpse he now committed to the tomb.

31. *Lay my bones beside his bones.* This argues a strong conviction in the mind of the old prophet that the deceased was a good and holy man of God, and he is willing to have place with him in the general resurrection.

33. *Jeroboam returned not from his evil way.* There is something exceedingly obstinate and perverse, as well as blinding and infatuating, in idolatry. The prediction lately delivered at Bethel and the miracles wrought in confirmation of it were surely sufficient to have affected and alarmed any heart not wholly and incorrigibly hardened; and yet they had no effect on Jeroboam!

Made . . . the lowest of the people priests. So hardy was this bad man in his idolatry that he did not even attempt to form anything according to the model of God's true worship. *Whosoever would, he consecrated him.* He made no discrimination; any vagabond that offered was accepted even of those who had no character, who were too idle to work, and too stupid to learn.

34. *And this thing became sin.* These abominations were too glaring, and too insulting to the divine majesty, to be permitted to last; therefore his house was cut off, and destroyed from the face of the earth.

CHAPTER 14

1. *Abijah . . . fell sick.* This was but a prelude to the miseries which fell on the house of Jeroboam; but it was another merciful warning, intended to turn him from his idolatry and wickedness.

TODAY'S DICTIONARY OF THE BIBLE:

Abijah. The son of Rehoboam, whom he succeeded on the throne of Judah (1 Chron. 3:10). He is also called Abijam (1 Kings 14:31; 15:1–8). He began his three-year reign (913–911 B.C.) (2 Chron. 12:16; 13:1, 2) with a strenuous but unsuccessful effort to bring back the ten tribes " . . . to the House of David." His address to "Jeroboam and all Israel," before encountering them in battle, is worthy of being specially noticed (2 Chron. 13:5–12). It was a bloody battle, no fewer than 500,000 of the army of Israel dying on the field. He is described as having walked "in all the sins of his father" (1 Kings 15:3; 2 Chron. 11:20–22). It is said in 1 Kings 15:2 that "his mother's name was Maachah, the daughter of Abishalom"; but in 2 Chron. 13:2 we read, "his mother's name was Michaiah, the daughter of Uriel of Gibeah." The explanation is that Maachah is just a variation of the name Michaiah, and that Abishalom is probably the same as Absalom, the son of David. It is probable that "Uriel of Gibeah" married Tamar, the daughter of Absalom (2 Sam. 14:27), and by her had Maachah. The word "daughter" in 1 Kings 15:2 will thus, as it frequently elsewhere does, mean granddaughter.

3. *Ten loaves.* Probably common or household bread. *Cracknels.* "Spotted or perforated bread."

MATTHEW HENRY

question concerning her son, and not enter upon the unpleasing subject of her husband's defection.

III. God gave Ahijah notice of the approach of Jeroboam's wife, and that she came in disguise, and full instructions what to say to her (*v.* 5), which enabled him, as she came in at the door, to call her by her name, to her great surprise, and so to discover to all about him who she was (*v.* 6): *Come in, thou wife of Jeroboam, why feignest thou thyself to be another?*

Verses 7–20

I. The prophet anticipates the enquiry concerning the child, and foretells the ruin of Jeroboam's house for the wickedness of it.

1. God calls himself the *Lord God of Israel.* Though Israel had forsaken God, God had not cast them off. He is Israel's God, and therefore will take vengeance on him who did them the greatest mischief he could do them, debauched them and drew them away from God.

2. He upbraids Jeroboam with the great favour he had bestowed upon him, in making him king over God's chosen Israel, and taking the kingdom *from the house of David,* to bestow it upon him.

3. He charges him with his impiety and apostasy, and his idolatry particularly: *Thou hast done evil above all that were before thee, v.* 9. Jeroboam's calves, though pretended to be set up in honour of the God of Israel, yet are here called *other gods,* or *strange gods,* because by them he *changed the truth of God into a lie* and represented him as altogether different from what he is, and because many of the ignorant worshippers terminated their devotion in the image, and did not at all regard the God of Israel.

4. He foretells the utter ruin of Jeroboam's house, *v.* 10, 11. See this fulfilled, *ch.* xv. 29.

5. He foretells the immediate death of the sick child, *v.* 12, 13.

(1) In mercy to him, lest, if he live, he be infected with the sin, and so involved in the ruin, of his father's house. Observe the character given of him: *In him was found some good thing towards the Lord God of Israel, in the house of Jeroboam.* The divine image in miniature has a peculiar beauty and lustre in it. He only, of all Jeroboam's family, shall die in honour, shall be buried, and shall be lamented as one that lived desired. This hopeful child dies first of all the family, for God often *takes those soonest whom he loves best.* Heaven is the fittest place for them; this earth is not worthy of them.

(2) In wrath to the family. It was a sign the family would be ruined when *he* was taken by whom it might have been reformed.

6. He foretells the setting up of another family to rule over Israel, *v.* 14. This was fulfilled in Baasha of Issachar, who conspired against Nadab the son of Jeroboam, in the second year of his reign, and murdered him and all his family.

7. He foretells the judgments which should come upon the people of Israel for conforming to the worship which Jeroboam had established. It is here foretold, *v.* 15, (1) That they should never be easy, not rightly settled in their land, but continually *shaken like a reed in the water.* After they left the house of David, the government never continued long in one family, but one undermined and destroyed another. (2) That they should, ere long, be totally expelled out of their land. This was fulfilled in the captivity of the ten tribes by the king of Assyria.

II. Jeroboam's wife has nothing to say against the word of the Lord, but she goes home with a heavy heart to their house in *Tirzah,* a *sweet delightful place,* so the name signifies, famed for its beauty, Cant. vi. 4. 1. *The child died* (*v.* 17), and justly did all Israel mourn, for the loss of so hopeful a prince. 2. Jeroboam himself died soon after, *v.* 20, when he had reigned twenty-two years, and left his crown to a son who lost it, and his life, too, and all the lives of his family, within two years after.

Verses 21–31

Judah's story and Israel's are intermixed. Jeroboam out-lived Rehoboam, four or five years, yet his history is despatched first, that the account of Rehoboam's reign may be laid together; and a sad account it is.

I. Here is no good said of the king. All the account we have of him here is, 1. That he was forty-one years old when he began to reign. 2. That he reigned seventeen years in Jerusalem, *the city where God put his name,* where he had opportunity enough to know his duty, if he had but had a heart to do it. 3. That his mother was Naamah, an Ammonitess; this is twice mentioned, *v.* 21, 31. Probably she was daughter to Shobi the Ammonite, who was kind to David (2 Sam. xvii. 27), and David was too willing to requite him by matching his son into his family. 4. That he had

JAMIESON, FAUSSET, BROWN

impended over their house, as well as over the nation which too readily followed his idolatrous innovations.

8. thou hast not been as my servant David—David, though he fell into grievous sins, repented and always maintained the pure worship of God as enjoined by the law.

10. I will bring evil upon the house of Jeroboam—Strong expressions are here used to indicate the utter extirpation of his house; "him that is shut up and left in Israel," means those who were concealed with the greatest privacy, as the heirs of royalty often are where polygamy prevails; the other phrase, from the loose garments of the East having led to a different practice from what prevails in the West, cannot refer to men; it must signify either a very young boy, or rather, perhaps, a dog, so entire would be the destruction of Jeroboam's house that none, not even a dog, belonging to it should escape. This peculiar phrase occurs only in regard to the threatened extermination of a family (I Sam. 25:22-34). See the manner of extermination (ch. 16:4; 21:24). **12. the child shall die**—The death and general lamentation felt through the country at the loss of the prince were also predicted. The reason for the profound regret shown at his death arose, according to Jewish writers, from his being decidedly opposed to the erection of the golden calves, and using his influence with his father to allow his subjects the free privilege of going to worship in Jerusalem. **13. all Israel shall mourn for him, and bury him**—the only one of Jeroboam's family who should receive the rites of sepulture. **14. the Lord shall raise him up a king . . . but what? even now**—viz., Baasha (ch. 15:27); he was already raised—he was in being, though not in power.

17. Tirzah—a place of pre-eminent beauty (Song of Sol. 6:4), three hours' travelling east of Samaria, chosen when Israel became a separate kingdom, by the first monarch, and used during three short reigns as a residence of the royal house. The fertile plains and wooded hills in that part of the territory of Ephraim gave an opening to the formation of parks and pleasure grounds similar to those which were the "paradises" of Assyrian and Persian monarchs [STANLEY]. Its site is occupied by the large village of Taltise [ROBINSON]. As soon as the queen reached the gate of the palace, she received the intelligence that her son was dying, according to the prophet's prediction. **19. the rest of the acts of Jeroboam**—None of the threatenings denounced against this family produced any change in his policy or government.

21-24. REHOBOAM'S WICKED REIGN. **21. he reigned . . . in Jerusalem**—Its particular designation as "the city which the LORD did choose out of all the tribes of Israel, to put his name there, "seems given here, both as a reflection on the apostasy of the ten tribes, and as a proof of the aggravated wickedness of introducing idolatry and its attendant vices there. **his mother's name was Naamah, an Ammonitess**—Her heathen extraction and her influence as queen mother are stated to account for Rehoboam's tendency to depart from the true religion. Led by the warning of the prophet (ch. 12:23), as well as by the

ADAM CLARKE

5. *Feign herself to be another woman.* It would have been discreditable to Jeroboam's calves if it had been known that he had consulted a prophet of Jehovah.

8. *And rent the kingdom away from the house of David.* That is, permitted it to be rent, because of the folly and insolence of Rehoboam.

10. *Him that pisseth against the wall.* "Every male." The phrase should be thus rendered wherever it occurs.

11. *Shall the dogs eat.* They shall not have an honorable burial, and shall not come into the sepulchres of their fathers.

13. *In him there is found some good thing.* Far be it from God to destroy the righteous with the wicked; God respects even a little good, because it is a seed from himself.

15. *For the Lord shall smite Israel.* See this prophecy fulfilled, chap. xv. 28-30, when Baasha destroyed all the house and posterity of Jeroboam.

19. *The rest of the acts of Jeroboam . . . are written in the . . . chronicles.* For some important particulars relative to this reign, see 2 Chron. xiii. 1-20.

MATTHEW HENRY

continual war with Jeroboam (*v.* 30), which could not but be a perpetual uneasiness to him. 5. That when he had reigned but seventeen years he died, and left his throne to his son.

II. Here is much evil said of the subjects, both as to their character and their condition.

1. It is a most sad account that is here given of their apostasy from God, *v.* 22–24. Judah, the only professing people God had in the world, *did evil in his sight.* Their fathers had been bad enough, especially in the times of the judges, but they did abominable things, *above all that their fathers had done.* Nothing less than the *pouring out of the Spirit from on high* will keep God's Israel in their allegiance to him. (1) They became *vain in their imaginations* concerning God, and *changed his glory into an image,* for they built themselves *high places, images, and groves* (*v.* 23), profaning God's name by affixing to it their images, and God's ordinances by serving their idols with them. (2) They were given up to vile affections (as those idolaters Rom. i. 26, 27), for there were *sodomites in the land* (*v.* 24), *men with men working that which is unseemly,* and not to be thought of, much less mentioned, without abhorrence and indignation. They dishonoured God by one sin and then God left them to dishonour themselves by another.

2. See here how weak and poor they were; and this was the consequence of the former. Shishak, king of Egypt, came against them, and so far, either by force or surrender, made himself master of Jerusalem itself that he took away the treasures both of the temple and of the exchequer, of the house of the Lord and of the king's house, which David and Solomon had amassed, *v.* 25, 26. He also took away the golden shields that were made but in his father's time, *v.* 26. These the king of Egypt carried off as trophies of his victory; and, instead of them, Rehoboam made brazen shields. This was an emblem of the diminution of his glory. Sin makes the gold become dim, changes the most fine gold, and turns it into brass.

CHAPTER 15

Verses 1–8

A short account of the short reign of Abijam, the son of Rehoboam king of Judah. He makes a better figure, 2 Chron. xiii, where we have an account of his war with Jeroboam. There he is called *Abijah—My father is the Lord,* because no wickedness is there laid to his charge. But here, where we are told of his faults, *Jah,* the name of God, is taken away from his name, and he is called *Abijam.*

I. Few particulars are related concerning him. 1. Here began his reign in the beginning of Jeroboam's eighteenth year; for Rehoboam reigned but seventeen, *ch.* xiv. 21. Jeroboam indeed survived Rehoboam, but Rehoboam's Abijah lived to succeed him and to be a terror to Jeroboam, while Jeroboam's Abijah (whom we read of *ch.* xiv. 1) died before him. 2. He reigned scarcely three years, for he died before the end of Jeroboam's twentieth year, *v.* 9. Being made proud and secure by his great victory over Jeroboam (2 Chron. xiii. 21), God cut him off, to make way for his son Asa, who would be a better man. 3. *His mother's name was Maachah, the daughter of Abishalom,* that is, Absalom, David's son, as I am the rather inclined to think. 4. He carried on his father's wars with Jeroboam. As there was continual war between Rehoboam and Jeroboam, not set battles but frequent encounters, especially upon the borders, so there was between Abijam and Jeroboam (*v.* 7), till Jeroboam, with a great army, invaded him, and then Abijam, not being forbidden to act in his own defence, routed him, so that he compelled him to be quiet during the rest of his reign, 2 Chron. xiii. 20.

II. But, in general, we are told, 1. That he was not like David, had no hearty affection for the ordinances of God, though, to serve his purpose against Jeroboam, he pleaded his possession of the temple and priesthood, as that upon which he valued himself, 2 Chron. xiii. 10–12. He seemed to have zeal, but he wanted sincerity; he began pretty well, but he fell off, and *walked in all the sins of his father.* 2. That yet it was for David's sake that he was advanced, and continued upon the throne; it was *for his sake* (*v.* 4, 5) that God thus *set up his son after him*; not for his own sake, nor for the sake of his father, in whose steps he trod, *but for the sake of David,* whose example he would not follow. It aggravates the sin of a degenerate seed that they fare the better for the piety of their ancestors and owe their blessings to it, and yet will not imitate it.

Verses 9–24

A short account of the reign of Asa; we shall find

JAMIESON, FAUSSET, BROWN

large immigration of Israelites into his kingdom (ch. 12:17; II Chron. 11:16), he continued for the first three years of his reign a faithful patron of true religion (II Chron. 11:17). But afterwards he began and encouraged a general apostasy; idolatry became the prevailing form of worship, and the religious state of the kingdom in his reign is described by the high places, the idolatrous statues, the groves and impure rites that with unchecked license were observed in them. The description is suited to the character of the Canaanitish worship.

25-31. SHISHAK SPOILS JERUSALEM. **25, 26. Shishak king of Egypt came up**—He was the instrument in the hand of Providence for punishing the national defection. Even though this king had been Solomon's father-in-law, he was no relation of Rehoboam's; but there is a strong probability that he belonged to another dynasty (see on II Chron. 12). He was the Sheshonk of the Egyptian monuments, who is depicted on a bas-relief at Karnak, as dragging captives, who, from their peculiar physiognomy, are universally admitted to be Jews. **29. Now the rest of the acts of Rehoboam . . ., are they not written in the book of the chronicles?**—not the book so called and comprehended in the sacred canon, but the national archives of Judah. **30. there was war between Rehoboam and Jeroboam**—The former was prohibited from entering on an aggressive war; but as the two kingdoms kept up a jealous rivalry, he might be forced into vigilant measures of defense, and frequent skirmishes would take place on the borders.

CHAPTER 15

Vss. 1-8. ABIJAM'S WICKED REIGN OVER JUDAH. **1. Abijam**—His name was at first Abijah (II Chron. 12:16); "Jah," the name of God, according to an ancient fashion, being conjoined with it. But afterwards, when he was found "walking in all the sins of his father," that honorable addition was withdrawn, and his name in sacred history changed into Abijam [LIGHTFOOT].

2. Three years reigned he—(cf. vs. 1 with vs. 9). Parts of years are often counted in Scripture as whole years. The reign began in Jeroboam's eighteenth year, continued till the nineteenth, and ended in the course of the twentieth. **his mother's name was Maachah**—or Michaiah (II Chron. 13:2), probably altered from the one to the other on her becoming queen, as was very common under a change of circumstances. She is called the daughter of Abishalom, or Absalom (II Chron. 11:21), of Uriel (II Chron. 13:2). Hence, it has been thought probable that Tamar, the daughter of Absalom (II Sam. 14:27; 18:18), had been married to Uriel, and that Maachah was their daughter.

3. his heart was not perfect with the Lord . . . as the heart of David his father—(Cf. ch. 11:4; 14:22). He was not positively bad at first, for it appears (vs. 15) that he had done something to restore the pillaged treasures of the temple. This phrase contains a comparative reference to David's heart. His doing that which was right in the eyes of the Lord (vs. 5) is frequently used in speaking of the kings of Judah, and means only that they did or did not do that which, in the general course and tendency of their government, was acceptable to God. It furnishes no evidence as to the lawfulness or piety of one specific act. **4. for David's sake did the Lord . . . give him a lamp**—"A lamp" in one's house is an Oriental phrase for continuance of family name and prosperity. Abijam was not rejected only in consequence of the divine promise to David (see on ch. 11:13-36).

ADAM CLARKE

24. *There were also sodomites in the land. Kedeshim,* "consecrated persons"; persons who had devoted themselves in practices of the greatest impurity, to the service of the most impure idols.

26. *He took away the treasures.* All the treasures which Solomon had amassed, both in the Temple and in his own houses; a booty the most immense ever acquired in one place. *All the shields of gold which Solomon had made.* These were 300 in number, and were all made of beaten gold.

28. *The guard bare them.* The guard probably were just 300, answering to the number of the shields.

31. *Naamah an Ammonitess.* He was born of a heathen mother, and begotten of an apostate father. From such an impure fountain could sweet water possibly spring?

CHAPTER 15

1. *Reigned Abijam over Judah.* Of this son of Rehoboam, of his brethren, and of Rehoboam's family in general, see 2 Chronicles xii, where many particulars are added.

6. *There was war between Rehoboam and Jeroboam.* This was mentioned in the preceding chapter, v. 30, and it can mean no more than this: There was a continual spirit of hostility kept up between the two kingdoms, and no doubt frequent skirmishing between bordering parties; but it never broke out into open war, for this was particularly forbidden (see chap. xii. 24).

But why is this circumstance repeated, and the history of Abijam interrupted by the repetition? There is some reason to believe that *Rehoboam* is not the true reading, and that it should be "Abijam": "Now there was war between Abijam and Jeroboam all the days of his life." And this is the reading of *fourteen* of Kennicott's and De Rossi's MSS. The Syriac has "Abia the son of Rehoboam"; the Arabic has "Abijam." Some copies of the Targum have "Abijam" also. This is doubtless the true reading, as we know there was a very memorable war between Abijam and Jeroboam; see it particularly described in 2 Chron. xiii. 3, etc.

3. *His heart was not perfect.* He was an idolater, or did not support the worship of the true God. This appears to be the general meaning of the heart not being perfect with God.

4. *The Lord . . . give him a lamp.* That is, a son to succeed him (see chap. xi. 36).

5. *Save only in the matter of Uriah.* Properly speaking, this is the only flagrant fault or crime in the life of David. It was a horrible offense, or rather a whole system of offenses. See the notes on 2 Samuel xi and xii.

MATTHEW HENRY

a more copious history of it 2 Chron. xiv, xv and xvi.

I. The length of it: *He reigned forty-one years in Jerusalem, v.* 10. In the account we have of the kings of Judah we find the number of the good kings and the bad ones nearly equal; but then we may observe, to our comfort, that the reign of the good kings was generally long, but that of the bad kings short.

II. The general good character of it (*v.* 11): *Asa did that which was right in the eyes of the Lord,* and that is right indeed which is so in God's eyes. He did *as did David his father,* kept close to God, though he was not a prophet, or psalmist, as David was. If we come up to the graces of those that have gone before us it will be our praise with God, though we come short of their gifts.

III. The particular instances of Asa's piety. His times were times of reformation.

1. He removed that which was evil. Immorality he first struck at: *He took away the sodomites out of the land,* suppressed the brothels; for how can either prince or people prosper, while those cages of unclean and filthy birds, more dangerous than pest-houses, are suffered to remain? Then he proceeded against idolatry: *He removed all the idols,* even those *that his father had made, v.* 12. When it appeared that Maachah his mother, or rather his grandmother (but called his *mother* because she had the educating of him in his childhood), had an idol in a grove, he would by no means connive at her idolatry. Reformation must begin at home. Asa, in everything else, will honour and respect his mother; he loves her well, but he loves God better, and (like the Levite, Deut. xxxiii. 9) readily forgets the relation when it comes in competition with his duty. If she be an idolater, (1) Her idol shall be destroyed, publicly exposed to contempt, defaced, and burnt to ashes *by the brook Kidron.* (2) She shall be deposed. He removed her from being queen, or from the queen, that is, from conversing with his wife; he banished her from the court, and confined her to an obscure and private life.

2. He re-established that which was good (*v.* 15): He *brought into the house of God the dedicated things* which he himself had vowed out of the spoils of the Ethiopians he had conquered. When those who, in their infancy, were by baptism devoted to God, make it their own act and deed to join themselves to him and vigorously employ themselves in his service, this is bringing in the dedicated things which they and their fathers have dedicated.

IV. The policy of his reign. He built cities himself, to encourage the increase of his people (*v.* 23) and to invite others to him by the conveniences of habitation.

V. The faults of his reign. In both the things for which he was praised he was found defective. The fairest characters are not without some *but* or other in them. 1. Did he take away the idols? That was well; *but the high places were not removed* (*v.* 14); therein his reformation fell short. It was not well that Asa, when his hand was in, did not remove these. *Nevertheless his heart was perfect with the Lord.* This affords us a comfortable note, That those may be found honest and upright with God, and be accepted of him, who yet, in some instances, come short of doing the good they might and should do. The perfection which is made the indispensable condition of the new covenant is not to be understood of sinlessness (then we were all undone), but sincerity. 2. Did he bring in the dedicated things? That was well; but he afterwards alienated the dedicated things, when he took the gold and silver out of the house of God and sent them as a bribe to Benhadad, to hire him to break his league with Baasha, and, by making an inroad upon his country, to give him a diversion from the building of Ramah, *v.* 18, 19. Here he sinned, (1) In tempting Ben-hadad to break his league, and so to violate the public faith. If he did wrong in doing it, as certainly he did, Asa did wrong in persuading him to do it. (2) In that he could not trust God, who had done so much for him, to free him out of this strait, without using such indirect means to help himself. (3) In taking the gold out of the treasury of the temple, which was not to be made use of but on extraordinary occasions. The project succeeded. Ben-hadad made a descent upon the land of Israel, which obliged Baasha to retire with his whole force from Ramah (*v.* 20, 21), which gave Asa a fair opportunity to demolish his works there, and the timber and stones served him for the building of some cities of his own, *v.* 22. But, though the design prospered, we find it was displeasing to God; and though Asa valued himself upon the policy of it, and promised himself that it would effectually secure his peace, he was told by the prophet that he had done foolishly, and that *thenceforth he should have wars*; see 2 Chron. xvi. 7–9.

JAMIESON, FAUSSET, BROWN

9-22. ASA'S GOOD REIGN. **his mother's name was Maachah**—She was properly his grandmother, and she is here called "the king's mother," from the post of dignity which at the beginning of his reign she possessed. Asa, as a constitutional monarch, acted like the pious David, laboring to abolish the traces and polluting practices of idolatry, and in pursuance of his impartial conduct, he did not spare delinquents even of the highest rank.

13. also Maachah his mother, even her he removed from being queen—The sultana, or queen dowager, was not necessarily the king's natural mother (see ch. 2: 19), nor was Maachah. Her title, and the privileges connected with that honor and dignity which gave her precedency among the ladies of the royal family, and great influence in the kingdom, were taken away. She was degraded for her idolatry. **because she had made an idol in a grove**—A very obscene figure, and the grove was devoted to the grossest licentiousness. His plans of religious reformation, however, were not completely carried through, "the high places were not removed" (see on ch. 3:2). The suppression of this private worship on natural or artificial hills, though a forbidden service after the temple had been declared the exclusive place of worship, the most pious king's laws were not able to accomplish. **15. he brought in the things which his father had dedicated**—Probably the spoils which Abijam had taken from the vanquished army of Jeroboam (see on II Chron. 13:16). **and the things which himself had dedicated**—after his own victory over the Cushites (II Chron. 14:12). **16. there was war between Asa and Baasha king of Israel all their days**—Asa enjoyed a ten years' peace after Jeroboam's defeat by Abijam, and this interval was wisely and energetically spent in making internal reforms, as well as increasing the means of national defense (II Chron. 14:1-7). In the fifteenth year of his reign, however, the king of Israel commenced hostilities against him, and, invading his kingdom, erected a strong fortress at Ramah, which was near Gibeah, and only six Roman miles from Jerusalem. Afraid lest his subjects might quit his kingdom and return to the worship of their fathers, he wished to cut off all intercourse between the two nations. Ramah stood on an eminence overhanging a narrow ravine which separated Israel from Judah, and therefore he took up a hostile position in that place. **18-20. Then Asa took all the silver and the gold that were left in the . . . house of the Lord**—Asa's religious character is now seen to decline. He trusted not in the Lord (II Chron. 16:7). In this emergency Asa solicited the powerful aid of the king of Damascene-Syria; and to bribe him to break off his alliance with Baasha, he transmitted to him the treasure lying in the temple and palace. The Syrian mercenaries were gained. Instances are to be found, both in the ancient and modern history of the East, of the violation of treaties equally sudden and unscrupulous, through the presentation of some tempting bribe. Ben-hadad poured an army into the northern provinces of Israel, and having captured some cities in Galilee, on the borders of Syria, compelled Baasha to withdraw from Ramah back within his own territories. **18. Ben-hadad**—(See on ch. 11:24).

22. Then King Asa made a proclamation—The fortifications which Baasha had erected at Ramah were demolished, and with the materials were built other defenses, where Asa thought they were needed—at Geba (now Jeba) and Mizpeh (now Neby Samuil)—about two hours' travelling north of Jerusalem.

ADAM CLARKE

10. *His mother's name.* Our translators thought that "grandmother" was likely to be the meaning, and therefore have put it in the margin. *The daughter of Abishalom.* She is called, says Calmet, the "daughter of Absalom," according to the custom of the Scriptures, which give the name of "daughter" indifferently to the niece, the granddaughter, and great-granddaughter.

12. *The sodomites. Hakkedeshim;* literally, "the holy or consecrated ones" (see chap. xiv. 24).

14. *The high places were not removed.* He was not able to make a thorough reformation; this was reserved for his son Jehoshaphat. *Asa's heart was perfect.* He worshipped the true God, and zealously promoted His service (see on v. 3). And even the high places which he did not remove were probably those where the true God alone was worshipped.

15. *Which his father had dedicated.* On what account he and his father dedicated the things mentioned below, we know not; but it appears that Asa thought himself bound by the vow of his father.

16. *There was war.* That is, there was continual enmity (see on v. 6). But there was no open war till the thirty-sixth year of Asa, when Baasha, king of Israel, began to build Ramah, that he might prevent all communication between Israel and Judah (see 2 Chron. xv. 19 and xvi. 1). But this does not agree with what is said here, chap. xvi. 8-9, that Elah, the son and successor of Baasha, was killed by Zimri in the twenty-sixth year of the reign of Asa. Chronologers endeavor to reconcile this by saying that the years should be reckoned, not from the beginning of the reign of Asa, but from the separation of the kingdoms of Israel and Judah. It is most certain that Baasha could not make war upon Asa in the thirty-sixth year of his reign, when it is evident from this chapter that he was dead in the twenty-sixth year of that king. We must either adopt the mode of solution given by chronologists or grant that there is a mistake in some of the numbers; most likely in the parallel places in Chronicles, but which we have no direct means of correcting. But the reader may compare 2 Chron. xiv. 1 with xv. 10, 19 and xvi. 1.

17. *And Baasha . . . built Ramah.* As the word signifies a "high place," what is here termed *Ramah* was probably a hill (commanding a defile through which lay the principal road to Jerusalem) which Baasha fortified in order to prevent all intercourse with the kingdom of Judah, lest his subjects should cleave to the house of David.

18. *Asa took all the silver.* Shishak, king of Egypt, had not taken the whole; or there had been some treasures brought in since that time. *Ben-hadad.* This was the grandson of Rezon, called here Hezion, who founded the kingdom of Damascus (see chap. xi. 23-24).

19. *There is a league between me and thee.* Or, Let there be a league between me and thee, as there was *between my father and thy father.* There was no reason why Asa should have emptied his treasures at this time to procure the aid of the Syrian king, as it does not appear that there was any danger which himself could not have turned aside. He probably wished to destroy the kingdom of Israel; and to effect this purpose, even robbed the house of the Lord.

20. *Ijon, and Dan.* He appears to have attacked and taken those towns which constituted the principal strength of the kingdom of Israel.

21. *Dwelt in Tirzah.* This seems to have been the royal city (see v. 33 and chap. xiv. 17); and in this Baasha was probably obliged to shut himself up.

22. *None was exempted.* Every man was obliged to go and help to dismantle the fortress at Ramah which Baasha had built.

MATTHEW HENRY

VI. The troubles of his reign. For the most part he prospered; but, 1. Baasha king of Israel was a very troublesome neighbour to him. This was the effect of the division of the kingdoms, that they were continually vexing one another, which made them both an easier prey to the common enemy. 2. In his old age he was himself afflicted with the gout.

VII. The conclusion of his reign. He reigned long, but finished at last with honour, and left his throne to a successor no way inferior to him.

Verses 25–34

The miserable state of Israel, while the kingdom of Judah was happy under Asa's good government. It was threatened that they should be as *a reed shaken in the water* (*ch.* xiv. 15), and so they were, when, during the single reign of Asa, the government of their kingdom was in six or seven different hands. Jeroboam was upon the throne in the beginning of his reign and Ahab at the end of it, and between them were Nadab, Baasha, Elah, Zimri, Tibni, and Omri, undermining and destroying one another. This they got by deserting the house both of God and of David. 1. The ruin and extirpation of the family of Jeroboam, according to the word of the Lord by Ahijah. His son Nadab succeeded him. If the death of his brother Ahijah had had a due influence upon him to make him religious, and the honour done him at his death had engaged him to follow his good example, his reign might have been long and glorious; but he *walked in the way of his father* (*v.* 26), kept up the worship of his calves, and forbade his subjects to go up to Jerusalem to worship, *sinned and made Israel to sin*, and therefore God brought ruin upon him quickly, in the second year of his reign. He was besieging Gibbethon, a city which the Philistines had taken from the Danites, and there did Baasha, with others, conspire against him and kill him (*v.* 27), and so little interest had he in the affections of his people that his army chose his murderer for his successor. Baasha *slew him*, and *reigned in his stead*, *v.* 28. And the first thing he did when he came to the crown was to *cut off all the house of Jeroboam.* 2. The elevation of Baasha. He shall be tried awhile, as Jeroboam was. Twenty-four years he reigned (*v.* 33), but *walked in the way of Jeroboam* (*v.* 34), though he had seen the end of that way.

JAMIESON, FAUSSET, BROWN

23. in the time of his old age he was diseased in his feet—(See on II Chron. 16:10-12), where an additional proof is given of his religious degeneracy.

25-34. NADAB'S WICKED REIGN. **25. Nadab the son of Jeroboam began to reign**—No record is given of him, except his close adherence to the bad policy of his father.

27. Baasha smote him at Gibbethon—This town, within the tribe of Dan, was given to the Levites (Josh. 19:44). It lay on the Philistine borders, and having been seized by that people, Nadab laid siege to recover it.

29. when he reigned, he smote all the house of Jeroboam—It was according to a barbarous practice too common in the East, for a usurper to extirpate all rival candidates for the throne; but it was an accomplishment of Ahijah's prophecy concerning Jeroboam (ch. 14:10, 11).

ADAM CLARKE

23. *And the cities which he built.* Such as Geba and Mizpah, which he built out of the spoils of Ramah. *He was diseased in his feet.* Probably he had a strong rheumatic affection. This took place in the thirty-ninth year of his reign, three years before his death; and it is said that he sought to physicians rather than to the Lord, 2 Chron. xvi. 12-13.

24. *Asa slept with his fathers.* Of his splendid and costly funeral we read in 1 Chron. xvi. 14.

27. *Smote him at Gibbethon.* This was a city in the tribe of Dan, and generally in the possession of the Philistines.

29. *He smote all the house of Jeroboam.* This was according to Ahijah's prophetic declaration (see chap. xiv. 10, 14). Thus God made use of one wicked man to destroy another.

MATTHEW HENRY — CHAPTER 16

Verses 1–14

I. The ruin of the family of Baasha foretold. He was a man likely enough to have raised and established his family—active, politic, and daring; but he was an idolater, and this brought destruction upon his family.

1. God sent him warning of it before. (1) That, if he were thereby wrought upon to repent and reform, the ruin might be prevented. (2) That, if not, the destruction when it did come, whoever might be instruments of it, was the punishment of sin.

2. The warning was sent by *Jehu the son of Hanani.* The father was a seer, or prophet, at the same time (2 Chron. xvi. 7), and was sent to Asa king of Judah; but the son, who was young and more active, was sent on this longer and more dangerous expedition to Baasha king of Israel. This *Jehu* continued long in his usefulness, for we find him reproving Jehoshaphat (2 Chron. xix. 2) above forty years after, and writing the annals of that prince, 2 Chron. xx. 34.

(1) He reminds Baasha of the great things God had done for him (*v.* 2). God puts power into bad men's hands, which he makes to serve his good purposes, notwithstanding the bad use they make of it.

(2) He charges him with high crimes and misdemeanours. [1] That he had caused *Israel to sin* and brought them to pay to dunghill-deities the homage due to him only. [2] That he had himself *provoked God to anger with the work of his hands*, that is, by worshipping images, the *work of men's hands.* [3] That he had *destroyed the house of Jeroboam* (*v.* 7), *because he killed him*, namely, Jeroboam's son and all his, and is justly punished for the malice and ambition which actuated and governed him in all he did.

(3) He foretells the same destruction to come upon his family which he himself had been employed to bring upon the family of Jeroboam, *v.* 3, 4.

II. A reprieve granted for some time, so long that Baasha himself dies in peace, and is buried with honour in his own royal city (*v.* 6), so far is he from being a prey either to the dogs or to the fowls, which yet was threatened to his house, *v.* 4.

III. Execution done at last. Baasha's son Elah, like Jeroboam's son, Nadab, reigned two years, and then was slain by Zimri, one of his own soldiers, as

JAMIESON, FAUSSET, BROWN — CHAPTER 16

VSS. 1-8. JEHU'S PROPHECY AGAINST BAASHA. **1. Then the word of the Lord came to Jehu**—This is the only incident recorded in the life of this prophet. His father was also a prophet (II Chron. 16:7).

Forasmuch as I exalted thee—The doom he pronounced on Baasha was exactly the same as denounced against Jeroboam and his posterity. Though he had waded through slaughter to his throne, he owed his elevation to the appointment or permission of Him "by whom kings reign." **over my people Israel**—With all their errors and lapses into idolatry, they were not wholly abandoned by God. He still showed His interest in them by sending prophets and working miracles in their favor, and possessed a multitude of faithful worshippers in the kingdom of Israel. **7. also by the hand of the prophet Jehu**—This is not another prophecy, but merely an addition by the sacred historian, explanatory of the death of Baasha and the extinction of his family. The doom pronounced against Jeroboam (ch. 14:9), did not entitle him to take the execution of the sentence into his own hands; but from his following the same calf worship, he had evidently plotted the conspiracy and murder of that king in furtherance of his own ambitious designs; and hence, in his own assassination, he met the just reward of his deeds. The similitude to Jeroboam extends to their deaths as well as their lives—the reign of their sons, and the ruin of their families. **8. began Elah the son of Baasha to reign**—(cf. ch. 15:33). From this it will appear that Baasha died in the twenty-third year of his reign (see on ch. 15:2), and Elah, who was a prince of dissolute habits, reigned not fully two years.

ADAM CLARKE — CHAPTER 16

1. *Then the word of the Lord came to Jehu.* Of this prophet we know nothing but from this circumstance. It appears from 2 Chron. xvi. 7-10 that his father, Hanani, was also a prophet, and suffered imprisonment in consequence of the faithful discharge of his ministry to Asa.

2. *Made thee prince over my people.* That is, in the course of My providence, I suffered thee to become king; for it is impossible that God should make a rebel, a traitor, and a murderer, king over His people, or over any people. God is ever represented in Scripture as doing those things which, in the course of His providence, He permits to be done.

7. *And because he killed him.* This the Vulgate understands of Jehu, the prophet, put to death by Baasha: "On this account he killed him, that is, Jehu the prophet, the son of Hanani." Some think Baasha is intended, others Jeroboam, and others Nadab, the son of Jeroboam. The order is here confused, and the seventh verse should probably be placed between the fourth and fifth.

MATTHEW HENRY

Nadab was by Baasha; so like was his house made to that of Jeroboam, as was threatened, *v.* 3.

1. As then, so now, the king himself was first slain, but Elah fell more ingloriously than Nadab. Nadab was slain in the field of action and honour, he and his army then besieging Gibbethon (*ch.* xv. 27). Elah should have been with them to command in chief, but he loved his own ease and therefore stayed behind to take his pleasure; and, when he was *drinking himself drunk in his servant's house*, Zimri killed him, *v.* 9, 10. Death comes easily upon men when they are drunk. Besides the chronic diseases which men frequently bring themselves into by hard drinking, and which cut them off in the midst of their days, men in that condition are more easily overcome by an enemy, as Amnon by Absalom, and are liable to more bad accidents, being unable to help themselves.

2. As then, so now, the whole family was cut off, and rooted out. The first thing Zimri did was to *slay all the house of Baasha*; thus he held by cruelty what he got by treason.

Verses 15–28

Zimri, and Tibni, and Omri, are here striving for the crown. Proud aspiring men ruin one another, and involve others in the ruin. These confusions end in the settlement of Omri.

I. How he was chosen, as the Roman emperors often were, by the army in the field, now encamped before Gibbethon, that they might without delay avenge the death of Elah upon Zimri. The siege of Gibbethon is quitted (Philistines are sure to gain when Israelites quarrel) and Zimri is prosecuted.

II. How he conquered Zimri, who is said to have reigned seven days (*v.* 15), so long before Omri was proclaimed king and himself proclaimed traitor. Tirzah was a beautiful city, but not fortified, so that Omri soon made himself master of it (*v.* 17), forced Zimri into the palace, which being unable to defend, and yet unwilling to surrender, he burnt, and himself in it, *v.* 18.

III. How he struggled with Tibni, and at length got clear of him: *Half of the people followed this Tibni* (*v.* 21), probably those who were in Zimri's interest. The contest between these two lasted some years, and it was in the twenty-seventh year of Asa that Omri was first elected (*v.* 15), but it was not till the thirty-first year of Asa that he began to reign without a rival; then Tibni died, it is likely in battle, *and Omri reigned*, *v.* 22.

IV. How he reigned when he was at length settled on the throne. 1. He made himself famous by building Samaria, which, ever after, was the royal city of the kings of Israel. He bought the ground for *two talents of silver*. It was called *Samaria*, or *Shemeren* (as it is in the Hebrew), from Shemer, the former owner, *v.* 24. The kings of Israel changed their royal seats, Shechem first, then Tirzah, now Samaria; but the kings of Judah were constant to Jerusalem, the city of God.

2. He made himself infamous by his wickedness; for *he did worse than all that were before him*, *v.* 25. He went further than they had done in *establishing iniquity by a law*. Jeroboam caused Israel to sin by temptation, example, and allurement; but Omri did it by compulsion.

Verses 29–34

The beginning of the reign of Ahab, of whom we have more particulars recorded than of any of the kings of Israel.

I. He exceeded all his predecessors in wickedness, *did evil above all that were before him* (*v.* 30), and, as if it were done with a particular enmity both to God and Israel, to affront him and ruin them, it is said, *He did more to provoke the Lord God of Israel to anger than all the kings of Israel that were before him*, *v.* 33.

II. He married a wicked woman, *Jezebel* (*v.* 31), a zealous idolater, extremely imperious and malicious in her natural temper, addicted to witchcrafts and whoredoms (2. Kings ix. 22), and every way vicious. What mischiefs she did, and what mischief at last befell her (2 Kings ix. 33), we shall find in the following story.

III. He set up the worship of Baal and served the god of the Sidonians, Jupiter, a deified hero of the Phœnicians. In honour of this mock deity, whom they called *Baal—lord*, 1. Ahab built a temple in Samaria, the royal city, because the temple of God was in Jerusalem, the royal city of the other kingdom. 2. He reared an altar in that temple, on which to offer sacrifice to Baal. 3. He made a grove about his temple.

JAMIESON, FAUSSET, BROWN

9-22. ZIMRI'S CONSPIRACY. **9. Zimri . . . conspired against him**—During a carousal in the house of his chamberlain, Zimri slew him, and having seized the sovereignty, endeavored to consolidate his throne by the massacre of all the royal race. **15. did Zimri reign seven days**—The news of his conspiracy soon spread, and the army having proclaimed their general, Omri, king, that officer immediately raised the siege at Gibbethon and marched directly against the capital in which the usurper had established himself. Zimri soon saw that he was not in circumstances to hold out against all the forces of the kingdom; so, shutting himself up in the palace, he set it on fire, and, like Sardanapalus, chose to perish himself and reduce all to ruin, rather than that the palace and royal treasures should fall into the hands of his successful rival. The seven days' reign may refer either to the brief duration of his royal authority, or the period in which he enjoyed unmolested tranquillity in the palace. **19. For his sins which he sinned**—This violent end was a just retribution for his crimes. "His walking in the ways of Jeroboam" might have been manifested either by the previous course of his life, or by his decrees published on his ascension, when he made a strong effort to gain popularity by announcing his continued support of the calf worship. **21, 22. Then were the people divided into two parts**—The factions that ensued occasioned a four years' duration (cf. vs. 15 with vs. 23), of anarchy or civil war. Whatever might be the public opinion of Omri's merits a large body of the people disapproved of the mode of his election, and declared for Tibni. The army, however, as usual in such circumstances (and they had the will of Providence favoring them), prevailed over all opposition, and Omri became undisputed possessor of the throne. **Tibni died**—The *Heb.* does not enable us to determine whether his death was violent or natural.

23-28. OMRI BUILDS SAMARIA. **23. In the thirty and first year of Asa . . . began Omri to reign**—The twelve years of his reign are computed from the beginning of his reign, which was in the twenty-seventh year of Asa's reign. He held a contested reign for four years with Tibni; and then, at the date stated in this verse, entered on a sole and peaceful reign of eight years. **he bought the hill Samaria of Shemer**—The palace of Tirzah being in ruins, Omri, in selecting the site of his royal residence, was naturally influenced by considerations both of pleasure and advantage. In the center of a wide amphitheatre of mountains, about six miles from Shechem, rises an oblong hill with steep, yet accessible sides, and a long flat top extending east and west, and rising 500 or 600 feet above the valley. What Omri in all probability built as a mere palatial residence, became the capital of the kingdom instead of Shechem. It was as though Versailles had taken the place of Paris, or Windsor of London. The choice of Omri was admirable, in selecting a position which combined in a union not elsewhere found in Palestine: strength, beauty, and fertility [STANLEY]. **two talents of silver**—$4,250.00. Shemer had probably made it a condition of the sale, that the name should be retained. But as city and palace were built there by Omri, it was in accordance with Eastern custom to call it after the founder. The Assyrians did so, and on a tablet dug out of the ruins of Nineveh, an inscription was found relating to Samaria, which is called Beth-khumri—the house of Omri [LAYARD]. (See on II Kings 17:5.) **25-27. But Omri wrought evil**—The character of Omri's reign and his death are described in the stereotyped form used towards all the successors of Jeroboam in respect both to policy as well as time. **29-33. Ahab the son of Omri did evil in the sight of the Lord above all that were before him**—The worship of God by symbols had hitherto been the offensive form of apostasy in Israel, but now gross idolatry is openly patronized by the court. This was done through the influence of Jezebel, Ahab's queen. She was "the daughter of Eth-baal, king of the Zidonians." He was priest of Ashtaroth or Astarte, who, having murdered Philetes, king of Tyre, ascended the throne of that kingdom, being the eighth king since Hiram. Jezebel was the wicked daughter of this regicide and idol priest—and, on her marriage with Ahab, never rested till she had got all the forms of her native Tyrian worship introduced into her adopted country. **32. reared up an altar for Baal**—i.e., the sun, worshipped under various images. Ahab set up one (II Kings 3:2), probably as the Tyrian Hercules, in the temple in Samaria. No human sacrifices were offered—the fire was kept constantly burning—the priests officiated barefoot. Dancing and kissing the image (ch. 19:18) were

ADAM CLARKE

9. *Captain of half his chariots.* It is probable that Zimri, and some other who is not here named, were commanders of the cavalry.

11. *He slew all the house of Baasha.* He endeavored to exterminate his race, and blot out his memory.

13. *For all the sins of Baasha.* We see why it was that God permitted such judgments to fall on this family. Baasha was a grievous offender, and so also was his son Elah; they caused the people to sin, and they provoked God to anger by their idolatries.

15. *The people were encamped against Gibbethon.* It appears that, at this time, the Israelites had war with the Philistines, and were now besieging Gibbethon, one of their cities. This army, hearing that Zimri had rebelled and killed Elah, made Omri, their general, king, who immediately raised the siege of Gibbethon, and went to attack Zimri in the royal city of Tirzah; who, finding his affairs desperate, chose rather to consume himself in his palace than to fall into the hands of his enemies.

23. *In the thirty and first year of Asa.* There must be a mistake here in the number thirty-one; for, in vv. 10 and 15, it is said that Zimri slew his master, and began to reign in the twenty-seventh year of Asa; and as Zimri reigned only seven days, and Omri immediately succeeded him, this could not be in the thirty-first, but in the twenty-seventh, year of Asa. Jarchi reconciles the two places thus: "The division of the kingdom between Tibni and Omri began in the twenty-seventh year of Asa; this division lasted five years, during which Omri had but a share of the kingdom. Tibni dying, Omri came into the possession of the whole kingdom, which he held seven years; this was in the thirty-first year of Asa."

24. *He bought the hill Samaria of Shemer.* This should be read, "He bought the hill of Shomeron from Shomer, and called it Shomeron [i.e., Little Shomer], after the name of Shomer, owner of the hill." At first the kings of Israel dwelt at Shechem, and then at Tirzah; but this place having suffered much in the civil broils, and the place having been burned down by Zimri, Omri purposed to found a new city, to which he might transfer the seat of government. He fixed on a hill that belonged to a person of the name of *Shomer;* and bought it from him for *two talents of silver. Shomeron*, or, as it is corruptly written, *Samaria*, is situated in the midst of the tribe of Ephraim, not very far from the coast of the Mediterranean Sea, and about midway between Dan and Beersheba; thus Samaria became the capital of the ten tribes, the metropolis of the kingdom of Israel, and the residence of its kings. The kings of Israel adorned and fortified it; Ahab built a "house of ivory" in it, chap. xxii. 39; the kings of Syria had magazines or storehouses in it, for the purpose of commerce (see chap. xx. 34). And it appears to have been a place of considerable importance and great strength.

31. *He took to wife Jezebel.* This was the head and chief of his offending; he took to wife, not only a heathen, but one whose hostility to the true religion was well-known, and carried to the utmost extent.

33. *Ahab made a grove. Asherah,* Astarte, or Venus; what the Syriac calls an "idol."

MATTHEW HENRY

IV. One of his subjects, in imitation of his presumption, ventured to build Jericho, in defiance of the curse Joshua had long since pronounced on him that should attempt it, *v.* 34. He built for his children, but his eldest son died when he began, and youngest when he finished, and all the rest (it is supposed) between. None ever hardened his heart against God and prospered.

JAMIESON, FAUSSET, BROWN

among the principal rites.

34. JOSHUA'S CURSE FULFILLED UPON HIEL THE BUILDER OF JERICHO. **34. In his days did Hiel the Beth-elite build Jericho**—(see on Josh. 6:26). The curse took effect on the family of this reckless man but whether his oldest son died at the time of laying the foundation, and the youngest at the completion of the work, or whether he lost all his sons in rapid succession, till, at the end of the undertaking, he found himself childless, the poetical form of the ban does not enable us to determine. Some modern commentators think there is no reference either to the natural or violent deaths of Hiel's sons; but that he began in presence of his oldest son, but some unexpected difficulties, losses, or obstacles, delayed the completion till his old age, when the gates were set up in the presence of his youngest son. But the curse *was* fulfilled more than 500 years after it was uttered; and from Jericho being inhabited after Joshua's time (Judg. 3:13; II Sam. 10:5), it has been supposed that the act against which the curse was directed, was an attempt at the restoration of the walls—the very walls which had been miraculously cast down. It seems to have been within the territory of Israel; and the unresisted act of Hiel affords a painful evidence how far the people of Israel had lost all knowledge of, or respect for, the word of God.

ADAM CLARKE

34. *Did Hiel the Beth-elite build Jericho.* Joshua's curse is well-known: "Cursed be the man before the Lord, that riseth up and buildeth this city Jericho: he shall lay the foundation thereof in his firstborn, and in his youngest son shall he set up the gates of it," Josh. vi. 26. There are three opinions on the words, "lay the foundation . . . in his firstborn," and "set up the gates" in his youngest son. (1) It is thought that when he laid the foundation of the city his eldest son, the hope of his family, died by the hand and judgment of God, and that all his children died in succession; so that when the doors were ready to be hung, his youngest and last child died, and thus, instead of securing himself a name, his whole family became extinct. (2) These expressions signify only great delay in the building; that he who should undertake it should spend nearly his whole life in it. (3) That he who rebuilt this city should, in laying the foundation, slay or sacrifice his firstborn, in order to consecrate it, and secure the assistance of the objects of his idolatrous worship; and should slay his youngest at the completion of the work, as a gratitude offering for the assistance received. None of the versions, the Chaldee excepted, intimates that the children were either slain or died, which circumstance seems to strengthen the opinion that the passage is to be understood of delays and hindrances.

MATTHEW HENRY — CHAPTER 17

Verses 1–7

The history of Elijah begins somewhat abruptly. Elijah drops (so to speak) out of the clouds, as if, like Melchisedek, he were without father, without mother, and without descent, which made some of the Jews fancy that he was an angel sent from heaven; but the apostle has assured us that *he was a man subject to like passions as we are* (James v. 17). 1. The prophet's name: *Elijahu*—"*My God Jehovah is he*" (so it signifies), "is he who sends me and will own me and bear me out, is he to whom I would bring Israel back and who alone can effect that great work." 2. His country: He was *of the inhabitants of Gilead*, on the other side Jordan, either of the tribe of Gad or the half of Manasseh, for Gilead was divided between them. We need not enquire whence men are, but what they are: if it be a good thing, no matter though it come out of Nazareth. He is called a *Tishbite* from Thisbe. The beginning of his story:—

I. How he foretold a famine with which Israel should be punished for their sins. He proclaimed it to the king, in whose power it was to reform the land, and so to prevent the judgment. Unless he repented and reformed this judgment would be brought upon his land. There should be *neither dew nor rain for some years.* He prayed earnestly *that it might not rain*; and, according to his prayers, the heavens became as brass, till he *prayed again that it might rain.* Elijah lets Ahab know, 1. That *the Lord Jehovah* is the *God of Israel*, whom he had forsaken. 2. That he is a *living God*, and not like the gods he worshipped, which were dead dumb idols. 3. That he himself was God's servant in office, and a messenger sent from him. 4. That, notwithstanding the present peace and prosperity of the kingdom of Israel, God was displeased with them for their idolatry and would chastise them for it by the want of rain, which would effectually prove their impotency, and the folly of those who left the living God, to make their court to such as could do neither good nor evil. 5. He lets Ahab know what interest he had in heaven: It shall be *according to my word.*

II. How he was himself taken care of in that famine. 1. How he was hidden. God bade him go *and hide himself by the brook Cherith*, *v.* 3. For the present, in obedience to the divine command, he went and dwelt all alone in some obscure unfrequented place, probably among the reeds of the brook. If Providence calls us to solitude and retirement, it becomes us to acquiesce; when we cannot be useful we must be patient, and when we cannot work for God we must sit still quietly for him. 2. How he was fed. When the woman, the church, is *driven into the wilderness*, care is taken that she be fed and nourished there, time, times, and half a time, that is, three years and a half, which was just the time of Elijah's concealment. See Rev. xii. 6, 14. Elijah must drink of the brook, and the ravens were appointed to *bring him meat* (*v.* 4) and did so, *v.* 6. Here, (1) The provision was plentiful, and good, and constant, bread

JAMIESON, FAUSSET, BROWN — CHAPTER 17

VSS. 1-7. ELIJAH, PROPHESYING AGAINST AHAB, IS SENT TO CHERITH. **1. Elijah the Tishbite**—This prophet is introduced as abruptly as Melchisedek—his birth, parents, and call to the prophetic office being alike unrecorded. He is supposed to be called the Tishbite from Tisbeh, a place east of Jordan. **who was of the inhabitants**—or residents of Gilead, implying that he was not an Israelite, but an Ishmaelite, as MICHAELIS conjectures, for there were many of that race on the confines of Gilead. The employment of a Gentile as an extraordinary minister might be to rebuke and shame the apostate people of Israel. **said unto Ahab**—The prophet appears to have been warning this apostate king how fatal both to himself and people would be the reckless course he was pursuing. The failure of Elijah's efforts to make an impression on the obstinate heart of Ahab is shown by the penal prediction uttered at parting. **before whom I stand**—i.e., whom I serve (Deut. 18:5).

there shall not be dew nor rain these years—not absolutely; but the dew and the rain would not fall in the usual and necessary quantities. Such a suspension of moisture was sufficient to answer the corrective purposes of God, while an absolute drought would have converted the whole country into an uninhabitable waste.

but according to my word—not uttered in spite, vengeance, or caprice, but as the minister of God. The impending calamity was in answer to his earnest prayer, and a chastisement intended for the spiritual revival of Israel. Drought was the threatened punishment of national idolatry (Deut. 11:16, 17; 28:23). **2, 3. the word of the Lord came unto him, saying, Get thee hence, and turn thee eastward,** etc.—At first the king may have spurned the prediction as the utterance of a vain enthusiast; but when he found the drought did last and increase in severity, he sought Elijah, who, as it was necessary that he should be far removed from either the violence or the importunities of the king, was divinely directed to repair to a place of retreat, perhaps a cave on "the brook Cherith, that is, before [east of] Jordan." Tradition points it out in a small winter torrent, a little below the ford at Beth-shan. **6. the ravens brought him bread**—The idea of such unclean and voracious birds being employed to feed the prophet has ap-

ADAM CLARKE — CHAPTER 17

1. *Elijah the Tishbite.* The history of this great man is introduced very abruptly; his origin is enveloped in perfect obscurity. He is here said to be a *Tishbite.* Tishbeh, says Calmet, is a city beyond Jordan, in the tribe of Gad, and in the land of Gilead. Who was his father, or from what tribe he sprang, is not intimated; he seems to have been the prophet of Israel peculiarly, as we never find him prophesying in Judah. His Hebrew name, which we have corrupted into *Elijah* and "Elias," is *Alihu*, or, according to the vowel points, *Eliyahu;* and signifies "he is my God."

3. *Hide thyself by the brook Cherith.* This brook, and the valley through which it ran, are supposed to have been on the western side of Jordan, and not far from Samaria. Others suppose it to have been on the eastern side, because the prophet is commanded to go eastward, v. 3.

4. *I have commanded the ravens to feed thee.* You shall not lack the necessaries of life; you shall be supplied by an especial providence.

6. *And the ravens brought him bread and flesh.* This is the first account we have of flesh-meat breakfasts and flesh-meat suppers;

MATTHEW HENRY

and flesh twice a day, daily bread and food convenient. It ill becomes God's servants, especially his servants the prophets, to be nice and curious about their food and to affect dainties and varieties; instead of envying those who have daintier fare, we should think how many there are, better than we, who live comfortably upon coarser fare and would be glad of our leavings. (2) The caterers were very unlikely; the *ravens* brought it to him. Obadiah would gladly have entertained Elijah; but he was a man by himself, a figure of John the Baptist, whose meat was locusts and wild honey. If it be asked whence the ravens had this provision, how and where it was cooked, and whether they came honestly by it, we must answer, as Jacob did (Gen. xxvii. 20), *The Lord our God brought it to them.* But why ravens? [1] They are birds of prey, more likely to have taken his meat from him, or to have picked out his eyes (Prov. xxx. 17); but thus Samson's riddle is again unriddled, *Out of the eater comes forth meat.* [2] They are unclean creatures. *Every raven after his kind* was, by the law, forbidden to be eaten (Lev. xi. 15), yet Elijah did not think the meat they brought ever the worse for that, but ate and gave thanks, asking no question for conscience' sake. [3] Ravens feed on insects and carrion themselves, yet they brought the prophet man's meat and wholesome food. [4] Ravens could bring but a little, and broken meat, yet Elijah was thankful that he was fed, though not feasted. [5] Ravens neglect their own young ones, and do not feed them; yet when God pleases they shall feed his prophet. [6] Ravens are themselves fed by special providence (Job xxxviii. 41; Ps. cxlvii. 9), and now they fed the prophet.

Thus does Elijah, for a great while, *eat his morsels alone*, and his provision of water, which he has in an ordinary way from the brook, fails him before that which he has by miracle. The powers of nature are limited, but not the powers of the God of nature. Elijah's brook dried up (*v.* 7) *because there was no rain.*

Verses 8–16

An account of the further protection Elijah was taken under. When the brook was dried up Jordan was not; why did not God send him thither? Surely because he would show that he has a variety of ways to provide for his people and is not tied to any one.

I. The place he is sent to, to *Zarephath*, or *Sarepta*, a city of Sidon, out of the borders of the land of Israel, *v.* 9. Our Saviour takes notice of this as an early and ancient indication of the favour of God designed for the poor Gentiles, in the fulness of time, Luke iv. 25, 26. *Many widows were in Israel in the days of Elias*, yet he is sent to honour and bless with his presence a city of Sidon, a Gentile city, and so becomes (says Dr. Lightfoot) *the first prophet of the Gentiles.* Elijah was hated and driven out by his countrymen; therefore, lo, he turns to the Gentiles, as the apostles were afterwards ordered to do, Acts xviii. 6. But why to a city of Sidon? Perhaps because the worship of Baal came lately thence with Jezebel, who was a Sidonian (*ch.* xvi. 31). Jezebel was Elijah's greatest enemy; yet, to show her the impotency of her malice, God will find a hiding-place for him even in her country.

II. The person that is appointed to entertain him, a poor widow woman, destitute and desolate. It is God's way, and it is his glory, to make use of the *weak and foolish things of the world* and put honour upon them.

III. The provision made for him there. Providence brought the widow woman to meet him very opportunely at the gate of the city (*v.* 10).

1. Her case and character: (1) She had nothing to live upon but a handful of meal and a little oil. When she has eaten the little she has, for aught she yet sees, she must die for want, she and her son, *v.* 12. She had no fuel but the sticks she gathered in the streets. To her Elijah was sent, that he might still live upon Providence as much as he did when the ravens fed him. It was in compassion to the low estate of his handmaiden that God sent the prophet to her, not to beg of her, but to board with her, and he would pay well for his table. (2) She was very humble and industrious. He found her gathering sticks, and preparing to bake her own bread, *v.* 10, 12. (3) She was very charitable and generous. When this stranger desired her to go and fetch him some water to drink, she readily went, at the first word, *v.* 10, 11. She objected not to the present scarcity of it, nor asked him what he would give her, nor hinted that he was a stranger, an Israelite, but left off gathering the sticks for herself to fetch water for him. (4) It was a great trial for her faith and obedience when, having told the prophet how low her stock of meal and oil was and that she had but just enough for

JAMIESON, FAUSSET, BROWN

peared to many so strange that they have labored to make out the *Orebim*, which in our version has been rendered ravens, to be as the word is used (in Ezekiel 27:27) merchants; or Arabians (II Chron. 21:16; Neh. 4:7); or, the citizens of Arabah, near Beth-shan (Josh. 15:6; 18:18). But the common rendering (ch. 18:19) is, in our opinion, preferable to these conjectures. And, if Elijah was miraculously fed by ravens, it is idle to inquire where they found the bread and the flesh, for God would direct them.

After the lapse of a year, the brook dried up, and this was a new trial to Elijah's faith.

8-16. HE IS SENT TO A WIDOW OF ZAREPHATH. **8. the word of the Lord came to him**—Zarephath or Sarepta, now Surafend, whither he was directed to go, was far away on the western coast of Palestine, about nine miles south of Sidon, and within the dominions of Jezebel's impious father, where the famine also prevailed.

Meeting, at his entrance into the town, the very woman who was appointed by divine providence to support him, his faith was severely tested by learning from her that her supplies were exhausted and that she was preparing her last meal for herself and son.

ADAM CLARKE

and as this was the food appointed by the Lord for the sustenance of the prophet, we may naturally conjecture that it was the food of the people at large.

The subject in the fourth verse of this chapter deserves a more particular consideration. *I have commanded the ravens to feed thee.* It is contended that if we consider *orebim* to signify *ravens*, we shall find any interpretation on this ground to be clogged with difficulties. I need mention but a few. The raven is an unclean bird, "And these . . . ye shall have in abomination among the fowls . . . every raven after his kind," Lev. xi. 13-15. Is it therefore likely that God would employ this most unclean bird to feed His prophet? Besides, where could the ravens get any flesh that was not unclean?

The original word *orebim* has been considered by some as meaning "merchants," persons occasionally trading through that country, whom God directed, by inspiration, to supply the prophet with food. To get a constant supply from such hands in an extraordinary way was miracle enough; it showed the superintendence of God, and that the hearts of all men are in His hands.

7. *The brook dried up.* Because there had been no rain in the land for some time, God having sent this drought as a testimony against the idolatry of the people (see Deut. xi. 16-17).

9. *Get thee to Zarephath.* This was a town between Tyre and Sidon, but nearer to the latter, and is therefore called in the text *Zarephath, which belongeth to Sidon*; or, as the Vulgate and other versions express it, "Sarepta of the Sidonians." Sarepta is the name by which it goes in the New Testament.

12. *An handful of meal in a barrel.* The word *cad* is to be understood as implying an earthen jar; not a wooden vessel, or barrel of any kind. In the East they preserve their corn and meal in such vessels, without which precaution the insects would destroy them.

MATTHEW HENRY

herself and her son, he bade her *make a cake for him*, and make *his* first, and then *prepare for herself and her son*. Elijah, it is true, made mention of *the God of Israel* (*v.* 14), but what was that to a Sidonian? Or if she had a veneration for the name *Jehovah*, and valued the God of Israel as the true God, yet what assurance had she that this stranger was his prophet or had any warrant to speak in his name? It was easy for a hungry vagrant to impose upon her. But she gets over all these objections, and obeys the precept in dependence upon the promise. Those that deal with God must deal upon trust; seek first his kingdom, and then other things shall be added. But surely the increase of this widow's faith, to such a degree as to enable her thus to deny herself and to depend upon the divine promise, was as great a miracle in the kingdom of grace as the increase of her oil was in the kingdom of providence.

2. The care God took of her guest: *The barrel of meal wasted not*, *nor did the cruse of oil fail*, but still as they took from them more was added to them by the divine power, *v.* 16. Never did corn or olive so increase in the growing (says Bishop Hall) as these did in the using; but the *multiplying of the seed sown* (2 Cor. ix. 10) in the common course of providence is an instance of the power and goodness of God not to be overlooked because common. The meal and the oil multiplied, not in the hoarding, but in the spending. (1) This was a maintenance for the prophet. Still miracles shall be his daily bread. Hitherto he had been fed with bread and flesh, now he was fed with bread and oil, which they used as we do butter. (2) It was a maintenance for *the poor widow and her son*, and a recompence to her for entertaining the prophet. Christ has promised to those who open their doors to him that he will come in to them, and *sup with them*, and *they with him*, Rev. iii. 20. It is promised to those that trust in God that they *shall not be ashamed in the evil time, but in the days of famine they shall be satisfied*, Ps. xxxvii. 19.

Verses 17–24

A further recompence made to the widow for her kindness to the prophet; her son, when dead, is restored to life.

I. The sickness and death of the child. For aught that appears he was her only son, the comfort of her widowed estate. 1. She was nurse to a great prophet, was employed to sustain him, and had strong reason to think the Lord would do her good; yet now she loses her child. 2. She was herself nursed by miracle, and in the midst of all this satisfaction she was thus afflicted.

II. Her pathetic complaint to the prophet of this affliction. 1. She expresses herself passionately: *What have I to do with thee, O thou man of God?* The death of her child was now a surprise to her, and it is hard to keep our spirits composed when troubles come upon us suddenly and unexpectedly, and in the midst of our peace and prosperity. She calls him *a man of God*, and yet quarrels with him as if he had occasioned the death of her child. "Wherein have I offended thee, or been wanting in my duty? *Show me wherefore thou contendest with me*." 2. Yet she expresses herself penitently: "*Hast thou come to call my sin to* thy *remembrance*, as the cause of the affliction?" Perhaps she knew of Elijah's intercession against Israel, and, being conscious of her former worshipping of Baal the god of the Sidonians, she apprehends he had made intercession against her.

III. The prophet's address to God upon this occasion. He gave no answer to her expostulation, but brought it to God, and laid the case before him, not knowing what to say to it himself. He took the dead child from the mother's bosom to his own bed, *v.* 19. Probably he had taken a particular kindness to the child. He retired to his chamber, and, 1. He humbly reasons with God concerning the death of the child, *v.* 20. 2. He earnestly begs of God to restore the child to life again, *v.* 21. We do not read before this of any that were raised to life; yet Elijah, by a divine impulse, prays for the resurrection of this child, which yet will not warrant us to do the like. David expected not, by fasting and prayer, to bring his child back to life (2 Sam. xii. 23), but Elijah had a power to work miracles, which David had not. He *stretched himself upon the child*, to effect the restoration of the child—he would if he could put life into him by his own breath and warmth. He is very particular in his prayer: *I pray thee let this child's soul come into him again*, which plainly supposes the existence of the soul in a state of separation from the body, and consequently its immortality, which Grotius thinks God designed by this miracle to give intimation and evidence of, for the encouragement of his suffering people.

JAMIESON, FAUSSET, BROWN

The Spirit of God having prompted him to ask, and her to grant, some necessary succor, she received a prophet's reward (Matt. 10:41, 42), and for the one meal afforded to him, God, by a miraculous increase of the little stock, afforded many to her.

17-24. HE RAISES HER SON TO LIFE. 17. the son of the woman, the mistress of the house, fell sick—A severe domestic calamity seems to have led her to think that, as God had shut up heaven upon a sinful land in consequence of the prophet, she was suffering on a similar account.

Without answering her bitter upbraiding, the prophet takes the child, lays it on his bed, and after a very earnest prayer, had the happiness of seeing its restoration, and along with it, gladness to the widow's heart and home.

ADAM CLARKE

13. *But make me thereof a little cake first.* This was certainly putting the widow's faith to an extraordinary trial; to take and give to a stranger, of whom she knew nothing, the small pittance requisite to keep her child from perishing was too much to be expected.

16. *The barrel of meal wasted not.* She continued to take out of her jar and out of her bottle the quantity of meal and oil requisite for the consumption of her household.

17. *There was no breath left in him.* He ceased to breathe and died.

18. *To call my sin to remembrance.* She now seems to be conscious of some secret sin which she had either forgotten or too carelessly passed over, and to punish this she supposes the life of her son was taken away.

21. *Stretched himself upon the child three times.* It is supposed that he did this in order to communicate some natural warmth to the body of the child, in order to dispose it to receive the departed spirit. Elisha, his disciple, did the same in order to restore the dead child of the Shunammite, 2 Kings iv. 34. And Paul appears to have stretched himself on Eutychus in order to restore him to life, Acts xx. 10. *Let this child's soul come into him again.* Surely this means no more than the "breath." Though the word *nephesh* may sometimes signify the "life," yet does not this imply that the spirit must take possession of the body in order to produce and maintain the flame of animal life?

MATTHEW HENRY

IV. The resurrection of the child, and the great satisfaction it gave to the mother: the child revived, *v.* 22. See the power of prayer and the power of him that hears prayer, who *kills and makes alive*. Elijah brought him to his mother, who, we may suppose, could scarcely believe her own eyes. The good woman hereupon cries out, *Now I know that thou art a man of God*; though she knew it before, by the increase of her meal, yet the death of her child she took so unkindly that she began to question it; but now she was abundantly satisfied that he had both the power and goodness of a man of God. Thus the death of the child was for the glory of God and the honour of his prophet.

CHAPTER 18

Verses 1–16

I. The sad state of Israel at this time, upon two accounts:

1. *Jezebel cut off the prophets of the Lord* (*v.* 4), *slew them*, *v.* 13. Being an idolater, she was a persecutor, and made Ahab one. Even in those bad times there were some good people that feared God and served him, and some good prophets that assisted them in their devotions. The priests and the Levites had all gone to Judah and Jerusalem (2 Chron. xi. 13, 14), but, instead of them, God raised up these prophets, who read and expounded the law in private meetings, or in the families that retained their integrity; they had not the spirit of prophecy as Elijah, nor did they offer sacrifice, or burn incense, but taught people to live well, and keep close to the God of Israel. These Jezebel aimed to extirpate, and put many of them to death, which was as much a public calamity as a public iniquity, and threatened the utter ruin of religion's poor remains in Israel. Those few that escaped the sword were forced to abscond, and hide themselves in caves, where they were buried alive and cut off, though not from life, yet from usefulness, which is the end and comfort of life.

(1) There was one very good man, who was a great man at court, *Obadiah*, who answered his name—*a servant of the Lord*, one who feared God and was faithful to him, and yet was steward of the household to Ahab. He *feared the Lord greatly* (*v.* 3), and he *feared the Lord from his youth* (*v.* 12). [1] It was strange that so wicked a man as Ahab would prefer him; certainly it was because he was a man of celebrated honesty, industry, and ingenuity, and one in whom he could repose a confidence, whose eyes he could trust as much as his own, as appears here, *v.* 5. [2] It was strange that so good a man as Obadiah would accept of preferment in a court so addicted to idolatry and all manner of wickedness. Obadiah would not have accepted the place if he could not have had it without bowing the knee to Baal. Obadiah therefore could with a good conscience enjoy the place. Those that fear God need not go out of the world, bad as it is.

(2) This great good man used his power for the protection of God's prophets. He hid 100 of them in two caves, when the persecution was hot, and *fed them with bread and water*, *v.* 4. See how wonderfully God raises up friends for his ministers and people, for their shelter in difficult times, even where one would least expect them.

2. When Jezebel cut off God's prophets God cut off the necessary provisions by the extremity of the drought. Perhaps Jezebel persecuted God's prophets under pretence that they were the cause of the judgment, because Elijah had foretold it. But God made them know the contrary, for the famine continued till Baal's prophets were sacrificed, and so great a scarcity of water there was that the king himself and Obadiah went in person throughout the land to seek for grass for the cattle, *v.* 5, 6. Ahab's care was not to *lose all the beasts*, many being already lost; but he took no care about his soul, not to lose that; he took a deal of pains to seek grass, but none to seek the favour of God, fencing against the effect, but not enquiring how to remove the cause. The land of Judah lay close to the land of Israel, yet we find no complaint there of the want of rain; for *Judah yet ruled with God.*

II. The steps taken towards redressing the grievance, by Elijah's appearing again upon the stage, to act as a *Tishbite*, a *converter* or *reformer* of Israel, for so (some think) that title of his signifies. Turn them again to the Lord God of hosts, from whom they have revolted, and all will be well quickly; this must be Elijah's doing. See Luke i. 16, 17.

1. Ahab had made diligent search for him (*v.* 10), had offered rewards to any one that would discover him. It should seem, he made this diligent search

JAMIESON, FAUSSET, BROWN

The prophet was sent to this widow, not merely for his own security, but on account of her faith, to strengthen and promote which he was directed to go to her rather than to many widows in Israel, who would have eagerly received him on the same privileged terms of exception from the grinding famine. The relief of her bodily necessities became the preparatory means of supplying her spiritual wants, and bringing her and her son, through the teachings of the prophet, to a clear knowledge of God, and a firm faith in His word (Luke 4:25).

CHAPTER 18

3. Obadiah feared the Lord greatly—Although he did not follow the course taken by the Levites and the majority of pious Israelites at that time of emigration into Judah (II Chron. 11: 13-16), he was a secret and sincere worshipper. He probably considered the violent character of the government, and his power of doing some good to the persecuted people of God as a sufficient excuse for his not going to worship in Jerusalem.

4. an hundred prophets—not men endowed with the extraordinary gifts of the prophetic office, but who were devoted to the service of God, preaching, praying, praising, etc. (I Sam. 10:10-12). **fed them with bread and water**—These articles are often used to include sustenance of any kind. As this succor must have been given them at the hazard, not only of his place, but his life, it was a strong proof of his attachment to the true religion. **there was a sore famine in Samaria**—Elijah found that the famine was pressing with intense severity in the capital. Corn must have been obtained for the people from Egypt or the adjoining countries, else life could not have been sustained for three years; but Ahab, with the chamberlain of his royal household, is represented as giving a personal search for pasture to his cattle. On the banks of the rivulets, grass, tender shoots of grass, might naturally be expected; but the water being dried up, the verdure would disappear. In the pastoral districts of the East it would be reckoned a most suitable occupation still for a king or chief to go at the head of such an expedition. Ranging over a large tract of country, Ahab had gone through one district, Obadiah through another.

ADAM CLARKE

22. *And the soul* [*Nephesh*] *of the child came into him again; al kirbo,* into the midst of him; *and he revived,* "and he became alive."

24. *The word of the Lord in thy mouth is truth.* Three grand effects were produced by this temporary affliction: (1) The woman was led to examine her heart, and try her ways; (2) The power of God became highly manifest in the resurrection of the child; (3) She was convinced that the word of the Lord was truth, and that not one syllable of it could fall to the ground.

CHAPTER 18

13. *When Jezebel slew the prophets.* This persecution was probably during the dearth, for as this bad woman would attribute the public calamity to Elijah, not being able to find him, she would naturally wreak her vengeance on the prophets of Jehovah who were within her reach.

3. *Obadiah feared the Lord greatly.* He was a sincere and zealous worshipper of the true God, and his conduct towards the persecuted prophets was the full proof of both his piety and his humanity.

4. *Fed them with bread and water.* By these are signified the necessaries of life, of whatsoever kind.

5. *Unto all fountains of water.* All marshy or well-watered districts, where grass was most likely to be preserved.

10. *There is no nation or kingdom.* He had sent through all his own states and to the neighboring governments to find out the prophet, as he knew, from his own declaration, that both rain and drought were to be the effect of his prayers. *He took an oath.* Ahab must have had considerable power and authority among the neighboring nations to require and exact this, and Elijah must have kept himself very secret to have shunned such an extensive and minute search.

MATTHEW HENRY

for him, not so much that he might punish him for what he had done in denouncing the judgment as that he might oblige him to undo it again, by recalling the sentence.

2. God, at length, ordered Elijah to present himself to Ahab, because the time had now come when he would *send rain upon the earth* (*v.* 1), or rather *upon the land.* Above two years he had lain hid with the widow at Zarephath, after he had been concealed one year by the brook Cherith; so that the third year of his sojourning there, here spoken of (*v.* 1), was the fourth of the famine, which lasted in all three years and six months, as we find, Luke iv. 25; James v. 17.

3. Elijah first surrendered, or rather discovered, himself to Obadiah. He knew, by the Spirit, where to meet him.

(1) Obadiah saluted him with great respect, fell on his face, and humbly asked, *Art thou that my lord Elijah? v.* 7. As he had shown the tenderness of a father to the sons of the prophets, so he showed the reverence of a son to this father of the prophets; and by this made it appear that he did indeed *fear God greatly.*

(2) Elijah, in answer to him, [1] Transfers the title of honour he gave him to Ahab: "Call him thy lord, not me;" that is a fitter title for a prince than for a prophet, *who seeks not honour from men.* Prophets should be called *seers,* and *shepherds,* and *watchmen,* and *ministers,* rather than *lords,* as those that mind duty more than dominion. [2] He bids Obadiah go and tell the king that he is there to speak with him: *Tell thy lord, Behold, Elijah* is forth-coming, *v.* 8.

(3) Obadiah begs to be excused from carrying this message to Ahab, for it might prove as much as his life was worth. He thought Elijah was not in good earnest when he bade him tell Ahab where he was, but intended only to expose the impotency of his malice; for he knew Ahab was not worthy to receive any kindness from the prophet and it was not fit that the prophet should receive any mischief from him. He is sure Ahab would be so enraged that he would put him to death for making a fool of him, or for not laying hands on Elijah himself, when he had him in his reach, *v.* 12. He pleads that he did not deserve to be thus exposed, and put in peril of his life: *What have I said amiss? v.* 9. Nay (*v.* 13), *Was it not told my lord how I hid the prophets?* He mentions this to convince Elijah that though he was Ahab's servant he was not in his interest. He that had protected so many prophets, he hoped, should not have his own life hazarded by so great a prophet.

(4) Elijah satisfied him that he might with safety deliver this message to Ahab, by assuring him, with an oath, that he would, this very day, present himself to Ahab, *v.* 15.

(5) Notice is hereby soon brought to Ahab that Elijah had sent him a challenge to meet him immediately at such a place, and Ahab accepts the challenge: *He went to meet Elijah, v.* 16. We may suppose it was a great surprise to Ahab to hear that Elijah, whom he had so long sought and not found, was now found without seeking. He went in quest of grass, and found him from whose word, at God's mouth, he must expect rain. Yet his guilty conscience gave him little reason to hope for it, but, rather, to fear some other more dreadful judgment.

Verses 17–20

The meeting between Ahab and Elijah, as bad a king as ever the world was plagued with and as good a prophet as ever the church was blessed with. 1. Ahab, like himself, basely accused Elijah. He durst not strike him, remembering that Jeroboam's hand withered when it was stretched out against a prophet, but gave him bad language, which was no less an affront to him that sent him. *Art thou he that troubleth Israel? v.* 17. How unlike was this to that with which his servant Obadiah saluted him (*v.* 7): *Art thou that my lord Elijah?* Obadiah feared God greatly; Ahab had sold himself to work wickedness; and both discovered their character by the manner of their address to the prophet. It has been the lot of the best and most useful men to be called and counted *the troublers of the land,* and to be run down as public grievances. Even Christ and his apostles were thus misrepresented, Acts xvii. 6. 2. Elijah boldly returned the charge upon the king, and proved it upon him, that he was *the troubler of Israel, v.* 18. Those that procure God's judgments do the mischief, not he that merely foretells them and gives warning of them, that the nation may repent and prevent them. *I would have healed Israel, but they would not be healed.* Ahab is the troubler, who follows Baalim, those accursed things. 3. As one having authority immediately from the King of kings, he ordered a convention of the states to be forthwith summoned

JAMIESON, FAUSSET, BROWN

Vss. 1-16. Elijah Meets Obadiah. **1. the third year**—In the New Testament, it is said there was no rain "for the space of three years and six months." The early rain fell in our March, the latter rain in our October. Though Ahab might have at first ridiculed Elijah's announcement, yet when neither of these rains fell in their season, he was incensed against the prophet as the cause of the national judgment, and compelled him, with God's direction, to consult his safety in flight. This was six months after the king was told there would be neither dew nor rain, and from this period the three years in this passage are computed. **Go, show thyself unto Ahab**—The king had remained obdurate and impenitent. Another opportunity was to be given him of repentance, and Elijah was sent in order to declare to him the cause of the national judgment, and to promise him, on condition of his removing it, the immediate blessing of rain. **2. Elijah went**—a marvellous proof of the natural intrepidity of this prophet, of his moral courage, and his unfaltering confidence in the protecting care of God, that he ventured to approach the presence of the raging lion.

7-16. as Obadiah was in the way . . . Elijah met him—Deeming it imprudent to rush without previous intimation into Ahab's presence, the prophet solicited Obadiah to announce his return to Ahab. The commission, with a delicate allusion to the perils he had already encountered in securing others of God's servants, was, in very touching terms, declined, as unkind and peculiarly hazardous. But Elijah having dispelled all the apprehensions entertained about the Spirit's carrying him away, Obadiah undertook to convey the prophet's message to Ahab and solicit an interview.

But Ahab, bent on revenge, or impatient for the appearance of rain, went himself to meet Elijah.

17, 18. Art thou he that troubleth Israel—A violent altercation took place. Ahab thought to awe him into submission, but the prophet boldly and undisguisedly told the king that the national calamity was traceable chiefly to his own and his family's patronage and practice of idolatry. But, while rebuking the sins, Elijah paid all due respect to the high rank of the offender. He urged the king to convene, by virtue of his royal mandate, a public assembly, in whose presence it might be solemnly decided which was the troubler of Israel. The appeal could not well be resisted, and Ahab, from whatever motives, consented to the proposal. God directed and overruled the issue.

ADAM CLARKE

1. *After many days . . . in the third year.* We learn from our Lord, Luke iv. 25, that the drought which brought on the famine in Israel lasted three years and six months. Jas. v. 17 gives it the same duration. Probably Elijah spent six months at the brook Cherith, and three years with the widow at Sarepta. *I will send rain upon the earth.* The word *haadamah* should be translated "the ground" or "the land," as it is probable that this drought did not extend beyond the land of Judea.

F. B. MEYER:

"Behold, Elijah!" The word of the Lord came to Elijah on four successive occasions—17:2, 8; 18:1; 19:9. God has many things to say to us if we will only listen. His word may find us in very different places and direct us to varied duties; but to live by it is to execute the perfect plan of life.

Obadiah was a good man, but weak. He did his best to shield the prophets and to keep the true light from becoming extinguished (v. 13). But court favor had corrupted him. He stood before Ahab, while Elijah stood before God. Our Lord said that "soft raiment" and the king's court go together (Luke 7:25); and in the enervating atmosphere of a palace, it is granted to very few to retain the spirit and power of Elijah or of the Baptist. Who would not rather be Elijah than Obadiah! Elijah dared confront Ahab as the troubler of Israel, while Obadiah daily feared for his own life. Elijah rooted up idolatry, while Obadiah endeavored only to check its excesses. Obabiah sought grass for royal steeds, but Elijah's prayer brought the rain. Let us dare to stand for God though we stand alone!

—Bible Commentary

18. *I have not troubled Israel.* Here the cause of the dearth is placed on its true ground: the king and the people had forsaken the true God, and God shut up the heavens that there was no rain. Elijah was only the minister whom God used to dispense this judgment.

MATTHEW HENRY

to meet at Mount Carmel, where there had been an altar built to God, *v.* 30. Thither all Israel must come, to give Elijah the meeting; and the prophets of Baal who were dispersed all the country over, with those of the groves who were Jezebel's domestic chaplains, must there make their personal appearance. 4. Ahab issued out writs accordingly, for the convening of this great assembly (*v.* 20), either because he feared Elijah and durst not oppose him, or because he hoped Elijah would bless the land, and speak the word that they might have rain, and upon those terms they would be all at his beck.

Verses 21–40

Ahab and the people expected that Elijah would, in this solemn assembly, *bless the land*, and pray for rain; but he had other work to do first. The people must be brought to repent and reform, and then they may look for the removal of the judgment, but not till then. Deserters must not look for God's favour till they return to their allegiance. Elijah might have looked for rain seventy times seven times, and not have seen it, if he had not thus begun his work at the right end. God's cause is so incontestably just that it need not fear to have the evidences of its equity searched into and weighed.

I. Elijah reproved the people for mixing the worship of God and the worship of Baal together. Not only some Israelites worshipped God and others Baal, but the same Israelites sometimes worshipped one and sometimes the other. This he calls (*v.* 21) *halting between two opinions*, or *thoughts*. They worshipped God to please the prophets, but worshipped Baal to please Jezebel and curry favour at court. "There can be but one God, but one infinite and but one supreme: there needs but one God, one omnipotent, one all-sufficient. What occasion for addition to that which is perfect? Now if, upon trial, it appears that Baal is that one infinite omnipotent Being, that one supreme Lord and all-sufficient benefactor, you ought to renounce Jehovah and cleave to Baal only: but, if Jehovah be that one God, Baal is a cheat, and you must have no more to do with him." Those halt between, that are unresolved under their convictions, unstable and unsteady in their purposes, promise fair, but do not perform, begin well, but do not hold on, that are inconsistent with themselves, or indifferent and lukewarm in that which is good. *Their heart is divided* (Hos. x. 2), whereas God will have all or none. We are fairly put to our choice *whom we will serve*, Joshua xxiv. 15. To this fair proposal which Elijah here makes, the people knew not what to say: *They answered him not a word.*

II. He proposed to bring the matter to a fair trial; and Baal had all the external advantages on his side. The king and court were all for Baal; so was the body of the people. The managers of Baal's cause were 450 men (*v.* 22), besides 400 more, their supporters or seconds, *v.* 19. The manager of God's cause was but one man, lately a poor exile, hardly kept from starving; so that God's cause has nothing to support it but its own right. However, it is put to this experiment, "Let each side prepare a sacrifice, and pray to its God, and *the God that answereth by fire, let him be God*; if neither shall thus answer, let the people turn Atheists; if both, let them continue to *halt between two.*" It is an instance of the courage of Elijah that he durst stand alone in the cause of God against such powers and numbers; and the issue encourages all God's witnesses and advocates never to fear the face of man.

III. The people join issue with him: *It is well spoken*, *v.* 24. Ahab and the prophets of Baal durst not oppose for fear of the people. If, in this trial, they could but bring it to a drawn battle, their other advantages would give them the victory. Let it go on therefore to a trial.

IV. The prophets of Baal try first, but in vain, with their god. Elijah allows it to them (*v.* 25), gives them the lead for their greater confusion.

1. How importunate and noisy the prophets of Baal were in their applications to him. They got their sacrifices ready; and they cried as one man, and with all their might, *O Baal! hear us, O Baal! answer us.* How senseless, how brutish, were they in their addresses to Baal! (1) Like fools, *they leaped upon the altar*, as if they would themselves become sacrifices with their bullock. *They leaped up and down* to please their deity. (2) Like madmen they *cut themselves in pieces with knives and lancets* (*v.* 28) for vexation that they were not answered, or in a sort of prophetic fury, hoping to obtain the favour of their god by offering to him their own blood. God expressly forbade his worshippers to cut themselves, Deut. xiv. 1.

2. How sharp Elijah was upon them, *v.* 27. He stood by them, and patiently heard them for so

JAMIESON, FAUSSET, BROWN

19. gather . . . the prophets of Baal . . . the prophets of the groves—From the sequel it appears that the former only came. The latter, anticipating some evil, evaded the king's command. **which eat at Jezebel's table**—i.e., not at the royal table where she herself dined, but they were maintained from her kitchen establishment (see on I Sam. 20:24; ch. 4:22). They were the priests of Astarte, the Zidonian goddess. **20. mount Carmel**—is a bold, bluff promontory, which extends from the western coast of Palestine, at the bay of Acre, for many miles eastward, to the central hills of Samaria. It is a long range, presenting many summits, and intersected by a number of small ravines. The spot where the contest took place is situated at the eastern extremity, which is also the highest point of the whole ridge. It is called El-Mohhraka, "the Burning," or "the Burnt Place." No spot could have been better adapted for the thousands of Israel to have stood drawn up on those gentle slopes. The rock shoots up in an almost perpendicular wall of more than 200 feet in height, on the side of the vale of Esdraelon. This wall made it visible over the whole plain, and from all the surrounding heights, where gazing multitudes would be stationed. **21-40. Elijah said unto all the people, How long halt ye?**—They had long been attempting to conjoin the service of God with that of Baal. It was an impracticable union and the people were so struck with a sense of their own folly, or dread of the king's displeasure, that they "answered not a word."

Elijah proposed to decide for them the controversy between God and Baal by an appeal, not to the authority of the law, for that would have no weight, but by a visible token from Heaven. As fire was the element over which Baal was supposed to preside, Elijah proposed that two bullocks should be slain and placed on separate altars of wood, the one for Baal, and the other for God. On whichever the fire should descend to consume it, the event should determine the true God, whom it was their duty to serve.

The proposal, appearing every way reasonable, was received by the people with unanimous approval. The priests of Baal commenced the ceremony by calling on their god.

In vain did they continue invoking their senseless deity from morning till noon, and from noon till evening, uttering the most piercing cries, using the most frantic gesticulations, and mingling their blood with the sacrifice. No reponse was heard. No fire descended.

ADAM CLARKE

19. *Gather to me all Israel.* The heads of tribes and families, the rulers of the people. *The prophets of Baal four hundred and fifty . . . the prophets of the groves four hundred.* The king and queen had different religious establishments. The king and his servants worshipped Baal, the supreme lord and master of the world, the sun. For this establishment 450 priests were maintained. The queen and her women worshipped *Asherah*, Astarte or Venus; and for this establishment 400 priests were maintained. These latter were in high honor; they ate at Jezebel's table; they made a part of her household.

21. *How long halt ye between two opinions?* Literally, "How long hop ye about upon two boughs?" This is a metaphor taken from birds hopping about from bough to bough, not knowing on which to settle. Perhaps the idea of "limping" through lameness should not be overlooked. They were halt; they could not walk uprightly. They dreaded Jehovah, and therefore could not totally abandon Him; they feared the king and queen, and therefore thought they must embrace the religion of the state.

22. *I only, remain a prophet of the Lord.* That is, I am the only prophet of God present, and can have but the influence of an individual, while the prophets of Baal are 450 men! It appears that the queen's prophets, amounting to 400, were not at this great assembly; and these are they whom we meet in chap. xxii. 6, and whom the king consulted relative to the battle at Ramoth-gilead.

24. *The God that answereth by fire.* Elijah gave them every advantage when he granted that the God who answered by fire should be acknowledged as the true God; for as the Baal who was worshipped here was incontestably Apollo, or the sun, he was therefore the god of fire, and had only to work in his own element.

25. *For ye are many.* And therefore shall have the preference, and the advantage of being first in your application to the deity.

26. *From morning even until noon.* It seems that the priests of Baal employed the whole day in their desperate rites. The time is divided into two periods: (1) *From morning until noon;* this was employed in preparing and offering the sacrifice, and in earnest supplication for the celestial fire. Still there was no answer, and at noon Elijah began to mock and ridicule them, and this excited them to commence anew. And (2) They continued *from noon till the time of offering the evening sacrifice,* dancing up and down, cutting themselves with knives, mingling their own blood with their sacrifice, praying, supplicating, and acting in the most frantic manner. *And they leaped upon the altar.* Perhaps it will be more correct to read with the margin, "they leaped up and down at the altar"; they danced round it with strange and hideous cries and gesticulations, tossing their heads to and fro, with a great variety of bodily contortions.

27. *At noon . . . Elijah mocked them.* Had not Elijah been conscious of the divine protec-

MATTHEW HENRY

many hours praying to an idol, yet with secret indignation and disdain; and at noon bantered them: "*Cry aloud, for he is a god*, a goodly god that cannot be made to hear without all this clamour." Baal's prophets were so far from being convinced and put to shame by the just reproach Elijah cast upon them that it made them the more violent and led them to act more ridiculously.

3. How deaf Baal was to them. Elijah did not interrupt them, but let them go on till they were tired, and quite despaired of success, which was not *till the time of the evening sacrifice*, *v.* 29.

V. Elijah soon obtains from his God an answer by fire.

1. He fitted up an altar. He would not make use of theirs, which had been polluted with their prayers to Baal, but, finding the ruins of an altar there, which had formerly been used in the service of the Lord, he chose to repair that (*v.* 30), to intimate to them that he was not about to introduce any new religion, but to revive the faith and worship of their fathers' God. He repaired this altar with *twelve stones, according to the number of the twelve tribes*, *v.* 31. Though ten of the tribes had revolted to Baal, he would look upon them as belonging to God still, by virtue of the ancient covenant with their fathers.

2. Having built his altar *in the name of the Lord* (*v.* 32), he prepared his sacrifice, *v.* 33. *Behold the bullock and the wood; but where is the fire?* Gen. xxii. 7, 8. *God will provide himself fire.* If we, in sincerity, offer our hearts to God, he will, by his grace, kindle a holy fire in them. Elijah was no priest, nor were his attendants Levites. Carmel had neither tabernacle nor temple, yet never was any sacrifice more acceptable to God than this.

3. He ordered abundance of water to be poured upon his altar, for which he had prepared a trench for its reception (*v.* 32). Twelve barrels of water (probably sea-water, for the sea was near, and so much fresh water in this time of drought was too precious for him to be so prodigal of it) he poured upon this sacrifice, to prevent the suspicion of any fire under.

4. He then solemnly addressed himself to God by prayer before his altar, humbly beseeching him to *turn to ashes his burnt-offering* and to testify his acceptance of it. His prayer was not long, but it was very grave and composed, and showed his mind to be calm and sedate, and far from the heats and disorders that Baal's prophets were in, *v.* 36, 37. He addressed himself to God as "*the God of Abraham, Isaac, and Israel*," reminding people of their relation both to God and to the patriarchs. Two things he pleads here: (1) The glory of God: "Lord, hear me, and answer me, *that it may be known that thou art God in Israel*." (2) The edification of the people: "*That they may know that thou art the Lord, turning their heart back again to thee*, in order to thy return in a way of mercy to them."

5. God immediately answered him by fire, *v.* 38. While he was yet speaking, *the fire of the Lord fell, consumed the sacrifice and the wood, licked up all the water in the trench*. But this was not all; to complete the miracle, the fire consumed the *stones of the altar*, *and* the very *dust*. Moses's altar and Solomon's were consecrated by the fire from heaven; but this was destroyed, because no more to be used. We may well imagine what a terror the fire struck on guilty Ahab and all the worshippers of Baal.

VI. What was the result of this fair trial. The prophets of Baal had failed. Elijah had, by the most convincing and undeniable evidence, proved his claims on behalf of the God of Israel. And now, 1. The people, as the jury, gave in their verdict upon the trial, and they are all agreed in it: *They fell on their faces*, and all, as one man, said, "*Jehovah, he is the God*, and not Baal; *Jehovah, he is the God*" (*v.* 39), whence, one would think, they should have inferred, "If he be the God, he shall be our God, and we will serve him only." Some, we hope, had their hearts thus turned back, but the generality of them were convinced only, not converted, yielded to the truth of God, that he is the God, but consented not to his covenant, that he should be theirs. 2. The prophets of Baal, as criminals, are seized, condemned, and executed, according to law, *v.* 40. Elijah (acting still by an extraordinary commission, which is not to be drawn into a precedent) orders them all to be slain immediately as the troublers of the land. These were the 450 prophets of Baal; the 400 prophets of the groves (who, some think, were Sidonians), though summoned (*v.* 19), yet, as it should seem, did not attend, and so escaped this execution, but it proved they were reserved to be the instruments of Ahab's destruction, some time after, by encouraging him to go up to Ramoth-Gilead, *ch.* xxii. 6.

JAMIESON, FAUSSET, BROWN

Elijah exposed their folly and imposture with the severest irony and, as the day was far advanced, commenced his operations. Inviting the people to approach and see the entire proceeding, he first repaired an old altar of God, which Jezebel had demolished.

Then, having arranged the cut pieces of the bullock, he caused four barrels or jars of water to be dashed all over the altar and round in the trench.

Once, twice, a third time this precaution was taken, and then, when he had offered an earnest prayer, the miraculous fire descended (Lev. 9:24; Judg. 6:21; 13:20; I Chron. 21:26; II Chron. 7:1), and consumed not only the sacrifice, but the very stones of the altar. The impression on the minds of the people was that of admiration mingled with awe; and with one voice they acknowledged the supremacy of Jehovah as the true God. Taking advantage of their excited feelings, Elijah called on them to seize the priestly impostors, and by their blood fill the channel of the river (Kishon), which, in consequence of their idolatries, the drought had dried up—a direction, which, severe and relentless as it seems, it was his duty as God's minister to give (Deut. 15:5; 18:20). The natural features of the mount exactly correspond with the details of this narrative. The conspicuous summit, 1635 feet above the sea, on which the altars were placed, presents an esplanade spacious enough for the king and the priests of Baal to stand on the one side, and Elijah on the other. It is a rocky soil, on which there is abundance of loose stones, to furnish the twelve stones of which the altar was built—a bed of thick earth, in which a trench could be dug; and yet the earth not so loose that the water poured into it would be absorbed; 250 feet beneath the altar plateau, there is a perennial fountain, which, being close to the altar of the Lord, might not have been accessible to the people; and whence, therefore, even in that season of severe drought, Elijah could procure those copious supplies of water which he poured over the altar. The distance between this spring and the site of the altar is so short, as to make it perfectly possible to go thrice thither and back again, whereas it would have been impossible *once* in an afternoon to fetch water from the sea [VAN DE VELDE]. The summit is 1000 feet above the Kishon, which nowhere runs from the sea so close to the base of the mount as just beneath El-Mohhraka; so that the priests of Baal could, in a few minutes, be taken down to the brook (torrent), and slain there.

ADAM CLARKE

tion, he certainly would not have used such freedom of speech while encompassed by his enemies. *For he is a god. Ki Elohim hu*, "he is the supreme God," you worship him as such; he must needs be such, and no doubt jealous of his own honor and the credit of his votaries! A strong irony. *He is talking.* He may be giving audience to some others; let him know that he has other worshippers, and must not give too much of his attention to one. Perhaps the word *siach* should be interpreted as in the margin, "he meditateth." *He is pursuing.* He may be taking his pleasure in hunting.

28. *They cried aloud.* The poor fools acted as they were bidden. *And cut themselves after their manner.* This was done according to the rites of that barbarous religion; if the blood of the bullock would not move him, they thought their own blood might; and with it they smeared themselves and their sacrifice.

29. *They prophesied.* They made incessant prayer and supplication; a further proof that to pray or supplicate is the proper ideal meaning of the word *naba*, which we constantly translate "to prophesy," when even all the circumstances of the time and place are against such a meaning.

31. *Took twelve stones.* He did this to show that all the twelve tribes of Israel should be joined in the worship of Jehovah.

32. *He made a trench.* This was to detain the water that might fall down from the altar when the barrels should be poured upon it, v. 35.

33. *Fill four barrels.* This was done to prevent any kind of suspicion that there was fire concealed under the altar.

36. *Lord God of Abraham.* He thus addressed the Supreme Being, that they might know when the answer was given that it was the same God whom the patriarchs and their fathers worshipped, and thus have their hearts turned back again to the true religion of their ancestors.

38. *Then the fire of the Lord fell.* It did not burst out from the altar; this might still, notwithstanding the water, have afforded some ground for suspicion that fire had been concealed, after the manner of the heathens, under the altar. *Consumed the burnt sacrifice.* The process of this consumption is very remarkable, and all calculated to remove the possibility of a suspicion that there was any concealed fire.

39. *Fell on their faces.* Struck with awe and reverence at the sight of this incontestable miracle. *And they said.* We should translate the words thus: "Jehovah, He is the God! Jehovah, He is the God!" Baal is not the God; Jehovah alone is the God of Israel.

40. *Let not one of them escape.* They had committed the highest crime against the state and the people by introducing idolatry, and bringing down God's judgments upon the land; therefore their lives were forfeited to that law which had ordered every idolater to be slain. It seems also that Ahab, who was present, consented to this act of impartial justice.

MATTHEW HENRY

Verses 41–46

Israel being thus far reformed that they had acknowledged the Lord to be God, God thereupon opened the bottles of heaven, and poured out blessings upon his land, that very evening.

I. Elijah sent Ahab to *eat and drink.* Ahab had continued fasting all day, either religiously, it being a day of prayer, or for want of leisure, it being a day of great expectation; but now let him *eat and drink*, for, though others perceive no sign of it, Elijah, by faith, hears *the sound of abundance of rain, v.* 41.

II. He himself retired to pray and to give thanks for God's answer by fire, now hoping for an answer by water. 1. He withdrew to a strange place, to the *top of Carmel*, which was very high and very private. Hence we read of those that *hide themselves in the top of Carmel*, Amos ix. 3. There he would be alone. Those who are called to appear and act in public for God must yet find time to be private with him and keep up their converse with him in solitude. 2. He put himself into a strange posture. He cast himself down on his knees upon the earth, in token of humility, and *put his face between his knees.*

III. He ordered his servant to bring him notice as soon as he discerned a cloud arising out of the sea, the Mediterranean Sea, which he had a large prospect of from the top of Carmel. The sailors at this day call it *Cape Carmel.* Six times his servant goes to the point of the hill and sees nothing, brings no good news to his master; yet Elijah continues praying, but still sends his servant to see if he can discover any hopeful cloud, while he keeps his mind close and intent in prayer, and abides by it, as one that has taken up his father Jacob's resolution, *I will not let thee go except thou bless me.*

IV. A little cloud at length appeared, no bigger than a man's hand, which presently overspread the heaven's and watered the earth, *v.* 44, 45. Great blessings often arise from small beginnings, and showers of plenty from a cloud of a span long.

V. Elijah hereupon hastened Ahab home, and attended him himself. Ahab rode in his chariot, at ease and in state, *v.* 45. Elijah ran on foot before him. If Ahab had paid the respect to Elijah that he deserved he would have taken him into his chariot, as the eunuch did Philip, that he might honour him before the elders of Israel, and confer with him further about the reformation of the kingdom. But his corruptions got the better of his convictions, and he was glad to get clear of him, as Felix of Paul, when he dismissed him, and adjourned his conference with him to a more convenient season.

JAMIESON, FAUSSET, BROWN

41-46. ELIJAH, BY PRAYER, OBTAINS RAIN. **42. Ahab went up to eat and to drink**—Ahab, kept in painful excitement by the agonizing scene, had eaten nothing all the day. He was recommended to refresh himself without a moment's delay; and, while the king was thus occupied, the prophet, far from taking rest, was absorbed in prayer for the fulfilment of the promise (vs. 1). **put his face between his knees**—a posture of earnest supplication still used. **43. Go up now, look toward the sea**—From the place of worship there is a *small eminence*, which, on the west and northwest side, intercepts the view of the sea [STANLEY, VAN DE VELDE]. It can be ascended in a few minutes, and presents a wide prospect of the Mediterranean. Six times the servant went up, but the sky was clear—the sea tranquil. On the seventh he described the sign of approaching rain. **44. Behold, there ariseth a little cloud out of the sea, like a man's hand**—The clearness of the sky renders the smallest speck distinctly visible; and this is in Palestine the uniform precursor of rain. It rises higher and higher, and becomes larger and larger with astonishing celerity, till the whole heaven is black, and the cloud bursts in a deluge of rain. **Prepare thy chariot, and get thee down, that the rain stop thee not**—either by the river Kishon being suddenly so swollen as to be impassable, or from the deep layer of dust in the arid plain being turned into thick mud, so as to impede the wheels. **45. Ahab rode, and went to Jezreel**—now Zerin, a distance of about ten miles. This race was performed in the midst of a tempest of rain. But all rejoiced at it, as diffusing a sudden refreshment over all the land of Jezreel. **46. Elijah . . . girded up his loins, and ran before Ahab**—It was anciently, and still is in some countries of the East, customary for kings and nobles to have runners before their chariots, who are tightly girt for the purpose. The prophet, like the Bedouins of his native Gilead, had been trained to run; and, as the Lord was with him, he continued with unabated agility and strength. It was, in the circumstances, a most proper service for Elijah to render. It tended to strengthen the favorable impression made on the heart of Ahab and furnished an answer to the cavils of Jezebel for it showed that he who was so zealous in the service of God, was, at the same time, devotedly loyal to his king. The result of this solemn and decisive contest was a heavy blow and great discouragement to the cause of idolatry. But subsequent events seem to prove that the impressions, though deep, were but partial and temporary.

ADAM CLARKE

41. *Get thee up, eat and drink.* It appears most evidently that Ahab and the prophet were now on good terms, and this is a further evidence that the slaying of the false prophets was by the king's consent.

42. *Put his face between his knees.* He kneeled down, and then bowed his head to the earth, so that, while his face was between his knees, his forehead touched the ground.

43. *Look toward the sea.* From the top of Mount Carmel the Mediterranean Sea was in full view.

44. *There ariseth a little cloud out of the sea, like a man's hand.* "Like the hollow of a man's hand." In the form of the hand bent, the concave side downmost.

46. *Ran before Ahab.* Many think that Elijah ran before the king in order to do him honor. I believe all these entirely mistake the writer's meaning. Ahab yoked his chariot, and made all speed to Jezreel. The hand of the Lord, or, as the Targum says, the "spirit of strength," came upon Elijah, and he girded up his loins, that is, tucked up his long garments in his girdle, and ran; and notwithstanding the advantage the king had by means of his chariot, the prophet reached Jezreel before him. All this was intended to show that he was under the peculiar influence and inspiration of the Almighty, that the king might respect and fear him, and not do or permit to be done to him any kind of outrage.

MATTHEW HENRY

CHAPTER 19

Verses 1–8

One would have expected, after such a public and sensible manifestation of the glory of God that now they would all, as one man, return to the worship of the God of Israel and take Elijah for their guide and oracle. But he is neglected whom God honoured; no respect is paid to him, no care taken of him, nor any use made of him, but, on the contrary, the land of Israel is now made too hot for him. 1. Ahab incensed Jezebel against him. That queen-consort, it seems, was in effect queen-regent, as she was afterwards when she was queen-dowager, an imperious woman that managed king and kingdom and did what she would. Ahab's conscience would not let him persecute Elijah, but he told Jezebel all that Elijah had done (*v.* 1), not to convince, but to exasperate her. It is not said he told her what *God* had done, but what *Elijah* had done, as if he, by some spell or charm, had brought fire from heaven, and the hand of the Lord had not been in it. Especially he represented to her that he had slain the prophets. 2. Jezebel sent him a threatening message (*v.* 2), that she had vowed and sworn to be the death of him within twenty-four hours. But how came she to send him word of her design, and so to give him an opportunity of making his escape? I think that though she desired nothing more than his blood, yet, at this time, she durst not meddle with him *for fear of the people, all counting him a prophet*, a great prophet, and therefore sent this message to him merely to frighten him and get him out of the way. 3. Elijah, hereupon, fled for his life, it is likely by night, and came to Beer-sheba, *v.* 3. Where was the courage with which he had lately confronted Ahab and all the prophets of Baal? He could not but know that he might be very serviceable to Israel at this juncture, and had all the reason in the world to depend upon God's protection while he was doing God's work; yet he fled. In his former danger God had bidden him hide himself (*ch.* xvii. 3), therefore he supposed he might do so

JAMIESON, FAUSSET, BROWN

CHAPTER 19

Vss. 1-3. ELIJAH FLEES TO BEER-SHEBA. **3. he arose and went for his life**—He entered Jezreel full of hope. But a message from the incensed and hard-hearted queen, vowing speedy vengeance for her slaughtered priests, dispelled all his bright visions of the future. It is probable, however, that in the present temper of the people, even she would not have dared to lay violent hands on the Lord's servant, and purposely threatened him because she could do no more. The threat produced the intended effect, for his faith suddenly failed him. He fled out of the kingdom into the southernmost part of the territories in Judah; nor did he deem himself safe even there, but, dismissing his servant, he resolved to seek refuge among the mountain recesses of Sinai, and there longed for death (Jas. 5:17). This sudden and extraordinary depression of mind arose from too great confidence inspired by the miracles wrought at Carmel, and by the disposition the people evinced there. Had he remained steadfast and immovable, the impression on the mind of Ahab and

ADAM CLARKE

CHAPTER 19

1. *Ahab told Jezebel.* Probably with no evil design against Elijah.

2. *So let the gods do.* If I do not slay you, let the gods slay me with the most ignominious death.

3. *He arose, and went for his life.* He saw it was best to give place to this storm, and go to a place of safety. He probably thought that the miracle at Carmel would have been the means of effecting the conversion of the whole court and of the country, but, finding himself mistaken, he is greatly discouraged. *To Beer-sheba.* This being at the most southern extremity of the Promised Land, and under the jurisdiction of the king of Judah, he might suppose himself in a place of safety. *Left his servant there.* Being alone, he would be the more unlikely to be discovered; besides, he did not wish to risk the life of his servant.

MATTHEW HENRY

now. 4. From Beer-sheba he went forward into the wilderness, that vast howling wilderness in which the Israelites wandered. Beer-sheba was so far distant from Jezreel, and within the dominion of so good a king as Jehoshaphat, that he could not but be safe there; yet, as if his fears haunted him even when he was out of the reach of danger, he could not rest there, but went a day's journey into the desert. Yet perhaps he retired thither not so much for his safety as that he might be wholly retired from the world, in order to a more free and intimate communion with God. *He left his servant at Beer-sheba*, perhaps because he would not expose his servant, who was young and tender, to the hardships of the wilderness. 5. Being wearied with his journey, he grew cross (like children when they are sleepy) and *wished he might die, v.* 4. Those that are, in this manner, forward to die are not in the fittest frame for dying. Jezebel has sworn his death, and therefore he, in a fret, prays for it, runs from death to death, yet with this difference, he wishes to die by the hand of the Lord. He would rather die in the wilderness than as Baal's prophet died, according to Jezebel's threatening (*v.* 2), lest the worshippers of Baal should triumph and blaspheme the God of Israel. He pleads, "It is enough. I have done enough, and suffered enough. I am weary of living." He pleads, "*I am not better than my fathers.*" But is this *Elijah*? Can that great and gallant spirit shrink thus? God thus left him to himself, to show that when he was bold and strong it was *in the Lord and the power of his might*, but of himself he was *no better than his fathers* or brethren. 6. God, by an angel, fed him in that wilderness, into the wants and perils of which he had wilfully thrown himself. Elijah, in a pet, wished to die; God needed him not, yet he designed further to employ and honour him, and therefore sent an angel to *keep him alive*. Our case would be bad sometimes if God should take us at our word and grant us our foolish passionate requests. Having prayed that he might die, he *laid down and slept* (*v.* 5), wishing it may be to die in his sleep, but he is awakened and finds himself not only well provided for with bread and water (*v.* 6), but attended by an angel, who guarded him when he slept, and twice called him to his food when it was ready for him, *v.* 5, 7. Wherever God's children are, as they are still upon their Father's ground, so they are still under their Father's eye and care. They may lose themselves in a wilderness, but God has not lost them. 7. He was carried, in the strength of this meat, to Horeb, *the mount of God, v.* 8. Thither the Spirit of the Lord led him, probably beyond his own intention, that he might have communion with God in the same place where Moses had. The angel bade him eat the second time, because of the greatness *of the journey* that was *before him, v.* 7. Note God knows what he designs us for, that we be furnished with *grace sufficient*. He that appoints what the voyage shall be will victual the ship accordingly. See how many different ways God took to keep Elijah alive; he fed him by ravens, with multiplied meals—then by an angel—and now, to show that *man lives not by bread alone*, he kept him alive forty days without meat, continually traversing the mazes of the desert, a day for a year of Israel's wanderings; yet he neither needs food nor desires it.

Verses 9–18

Here is, I. Elijah housed in a cave at Mount Horeb, which is called *the mount of God*, because on it God had formerly manifested his glory. And perhaps this was the same cave, or cleft of a rock, in which Moses was hidden when the Lord *passed by before him and proclaimed his name*, Exod. xxxiii. 22.

II. The visit God paid to him there and the enquiry he made concerning him: *The word of the Lord came to him.* We cannot go anywhere to be out of the reach of God's eye, his arm, and his word. John saw visions of the Almighty when he was in banishment in the isle of Patmos, Rev. i. 9. The question God puts to the prophet is, *What dost* thou *here, Elijah? v.* 9, and again *v.* 13. This is a reproof, 1. For his fleeing hither. "What brings thee so far from home? Dost thou flee from Jezebel?" Lay the emphasis upon the pronoun *thou*. "What *thou*!" 2. For his fixing here. "What dost thou here, in this cave? Is this a place for a prophet of the Lord to lodge in? Is this a time for such men to retreat, when the public has such need of them?"

III. The account he gives of himself, in answer to the question put to him (*v.* 10), and repeated, in answer to the same question, *v.* 14.

1. He excuses his retreat. God knew, and his own conscience witnessed for him, that as long as there was any hope of doing good he had been *very jealous for the Lord God of Hosts*; but now that he had *laboured in vain*, and all his endeavours were to no

JAMIESON, FAUSSET, BROWN

the people generally might have been followed by good results. But he had been exalted above measure (II Cor. 12:7-9), and being left to himself, the great prophet, instead of showing the indomitable spirit of a martyr, fled from his post of duty.

4-18. HE IS COMFORTED BY AN ANGEL. **4. went a day's journey into the wilderness**—on the way from Beer-sheba to Horeb—a wide expanse of sand-hills, covered with the retem (not juniper, but broom shrubs), whose tall and spreading branches, with their white leaves, afford a very cheering and refreshing shade.

His gracious God did not lose sight of His fugitive servant, but watched over him, and, miraculously ministering to his wants, enabled him, in a better but not wholly right frame of mind, by virtue of that supernatural supply, to complete his contemplated journey.

In the solitude of Sinai, God appeared to instruct him. What dost thou here, Elijah? was a searching question addressed to one who had been called to so arduous and urgent a mission as his.

ADAM CLARKE

4. *A day's journey into the wilderness.* Probably on his way to Mount Horeb (see v. 8). *Juniper tree.* A tree that afforded him a shade from the scorching sun. *It is enough.* I have lived long enough! I can do no more good among this people; let me now end my days.

5. *As he lay and slept.* Excessive anguish of mind frequently induces sleep, as well as great fatigue of body. *An angel touched him.* He needed refreshment, and God sent an angel to bring him what was necessary.

6. *A cake baken on the coals.* All this seems to have been supernaturally provided.

7. *The journey is too great for thee.* From Beersheba to Horeb was about one hundred fifty miles.

8. *Forty days and forty nights.* So he fasted just the same time as Moses did at Horeb, and as Christ did in the wilderness.

9. *He came thither unto a cave.* Conjectured by some to be the same cave in which God put Moses that He might give him a glimpse of His glory (see Exod. xxxiii. 22). *What doest thou here, Elijah?* Is this a reproach for having fled from the face of Jezebel, through what some call unbelieving fears that God would abandon him to her rage?

MATTHEW HENRY

purpose, he thought it was time to give up the cause.

2. He complains of the people, their obstinacy in sin. "*The children of Israel have forsaken thy covenant*, and that is the reason I have forsaken them; who can stay among them, to see everything that is sacred ruined and run down?" He had often been, of choice, their advocate, but now he is necessitated to be their accuser, before God. He charges them (1) With having forsaken God's covenant; though they retained circumcision, the sign and seal of it, yet they had quitted his worship and service, which was the intention of it. (2) With having *thrown down his altars*, not only deserted them and suffered them to go to decay, but, in their zeal for the worship of Baal, wilfully demolished them. These separate altars, though breaking in upon the unity of the church, yet, being erected and attended by those that sincerely aimed at the glory of God, God owned them for his altars, as well as that at Jerusalem, and the putting of them down is charged upon Israel as a crying sin. (3) *They have slain thy prophets with the sword*, who, it is probable, ministered at those altars. Jezebel, a foreigner, slew them (*ch.* xviii. 4), but the crime is charged upon the body of the people because the generality of them were *consenting to their death*, and pleased with it.

3. He gives the reasons why he retired into this desert and took up his residence in this cave. (1) It was because he could not appear to any purpose: "*I only am left.* What can one do against thousands?" (2) It was because he could not appear with any safety: "*They seek my life to take it away*; and I had better spend my life in a useless solitude than lose my life in a fruitless endeavour to reform those that hate to be reformed."

IV. God's manifestation of himself to him. Did he come hither to meet with God? Moses was put into the cave when God's glory passed before him; but Elijah was called out of it: *Stand upon the mount before the Lord*, *v.* 11. He *saw no manner of similitude*, any more than Israel did when God *talked to them in Horeb*. But, 1. He heard a strong wind, and saw the terrible effects of it, for it rent the mountains and tore the rocks. 2. He felt the shock of an earthquake. 3. He saw an eruption of fire, *v.* 12. But, 4. At last he perceived a *still small voice*, in which *the Lord was*, that is, by which he spoke to him, and not out of the wind, or the earthquake, or the fire. Those struck an awe upon him, but God chose to make known his mind to him in whispers soft, not in those dreadful sounds. When he perceived this, (1) *He wrapped his face in his mantle*, as one afraid to look upon the glory of God. Elijah hid his face in token of shame for having been such a coward as to flee from his duty when he had such a God of power to stand by him in it. The wind, and earthquake, and fire, did not make him cover his face, but the still voice did. Gracious souls are more affected by the tender mercies of the Lord than by his terrors. (2) He stood at the entrance of the cave, ready to hear what God had to say to him. Elijah being now called to revive that law, especially the first two commandments of it, is here taught how to manage it; he must not only awaken and terrify the people with amazing signs, like the earthquake and fire, but he must endeavour, with a still small voice, to convince and persuade them. Faith comes by hearing the word of God; miracles do but make way for it.

V. The orders God gives him to execute. He repeats the question he had put to him before, "*What doest thou here?* This is not a place for thee now." Elijah gives the same answer (*v.* 14), complaining of Israel's apostasy from God and the ruin of religion among them. To this God gives him a reply. He sends him back with directions to appoint Hazael king of Syria (*v.* 15), Jehu king of Israel, and Elisha his successor in the eminency of the prophetical office (*v.* 16), which is intended as a prediction that by these God would chastise the degenerate Israelites, plead his own cause among them, and *avenge the quarrel of his covenant*, *v.* 17. Elisha, with the *sword of the Spirit*, shall terrify and wound the consciences of those who escape Hazael's sword of war and Jehu's sword of justice.

VI. The comfortable information God gives him of the number of Israelites who retained their integrity, though he thought he was left alone (*v.* 18): *I have left* 7,000 *in Israel* (besides Judea) *who have not bowed the knee to Baal.* In times of the greatest degeneracy and apostasy God has always had, and will have, a remnant faithful to him, some that keep their integrity and do not go down the stream. It is God's work to preserve that remnant, and distinguish them from the rest, for without his grace they could not have distinguished themselves. God's faithful ones are often his hidden ones (Ps. lxxxiii. 3), and the visible church is scarcely visible, the wheat lost in

JAMIESON, FAUSSET, BROWN

By an awful exhibition of divine power, he was made aware of the divine speaker who addressed him; his attention was arrested, his petulance was silenced, his heart was touched, and he was bid without delay return to the land of Israel, and prosecute the Lord's work there.

To convince him that an idolatrous nation will not be unpunished, He commissions him to anoint three persons who were destined in Providence to avenge God's controversy with the people of Israel. Anointing is used synonymously with appointment (Judg. 9:8), and is applied to all named, although Jehu alone had the consecrated oil poured over his head. They were all three destined to be eminent instruments in achieving the destruction of idolaters, though in different ways. But of the three commissions, Elijah personally executed only one; viz., the call of Elisha to be his assistant and successor, and by him the other two were accomplished (II Kings 8:7-13; 9:1-10). Having thus satisfied the fiery zeal of the erring but sincere and pious prophet, the Lord proceeded to correct the erroneous impression under which Elijah had been laboring, of his being the sole adherent of the true religion in the land; for God, who seeth in secret, and knew all that were His, knew that there were 7000 persons who had not done homage (lit., kissed the hand) to Baal. **16. Abel-meholah**—i.e., the meadow of dancing, in the valley of the Jordan.

ADAM CLARKE

10. *I have been very jealous for the Lord.* The picture which he draws here of apostate Israel is very affecting: (1) They *have forsaken thy covenant.* They have now cleaved to and worshipped other gods.

(2) *Thrown down thine altars.* Endeavored, as much as they possibly could, to abolish Thy worship, and destroy its remembrance from the land.

(3) *And slain thy prophets.* That there might be none to reprove their iniquity or teach the truth.

(4) *I only, am left.* They have succeeded in destroying all the rest of the prophets, and they are determined not to rest till they slay me.

11. *Stand upon the mount before the Lord.* God was now treating Elijah nearly in the same way that He treated Moses; and it is not unlikely that Elijah was now standing on the same place where Moses stood when God revealed himself to him in the giving of the law (see Exod. xix. 9, 16). *The Lord passed by.* It appears that the passing by of the Lord occasioned the strong wind, the earthquake, and the fire; but in none of these was God to make a discovery of himself unto the prophet. Yet these, in some sort, prepared His way, and prepared Elijah to hear the "still small voice."

13. *Wrapped his face in his mantle.* This he did to signify his respect; so Moses hid his face, for he dared not to look upon God, Exod. iii. 6. Covering the face was a token of respect among the Asiatics, as uncovering the head is among the Europeans.

15. *To the wilderness of Damascus.* He does not desire him to take a road by which he might be likely to meet Jezebel, or any other of his enemies. *Anoint Hazael.* For what reason the Lord was about to make all these revolutions, we are told in v. 17. God was about to bring His judgments upon the land, and especially on the house of Ahab. This He exterminated by means of Jehu, and Jehu himself was a scourge of the Lord to the people. Hazael also grievously afflicted Israel; see the accomplishment of these purposes, 2 Kings viii and ix.

17. *Shall Elisha slay.* The meaning of the prophecy may be this: Hazael, Jehu, and Elisha shall be the ministers of My vengeance against this disobedient and rebellious people. The order of time, here, is not to be regarded.

18. *Seven thousand in Israel.* That is, "many thousands"; for seven is a number of perfection, as we have often seen: so, "The barren has born seven"—has had a numerous offspring; "Gold seven times purified"—purified till all the dross is perfectly separated from it. The court and multitudes of the people had gone after Baal, but perhaps the majority of the common people still worshipped in secret the God of their fathers. *Every mouth which hath*

MATTHEW HENRY

the chaff and the gold in the dross, till the sifting, refining, separating day comes. *The Lord knows those that are his*, though we do not; he sees in secret. There are more good people in the world than some wise and holy men think there are. When we come to heaven, as we shall miss a great many whom we thought to meet there, so we shall meet a great many whom we little thought to find there. God's love often proves larger than man's charity and more extensive.

Verses 19–21

Elisha was named last in the orders God gave to Elijah, but he was first called, for by him the other two were to be called. He must come in Elijah's room; yet Elijah rejoices to think that he shall leave the work of God in such good hands. Concerning the call of Elisha observe, 1. That it was an unexpected surprising call. Elijah found him *in the field*, not reading, nor praying, nor sacrificing, but *ploughing*, *v.* 19. Though a great man (as appears by his feast, *v.* 21), master of the ground, and oxen, and servants, yet he did not think it any disparagement to lay his hand to the plough. An honest calling in the world does not at all put us out of the way of our heavenly calling, any more than it did Elisha, who was taken from following the plough to feed Israel and to sow the *seed of the word*, as the apostles were taken from fishing to catch men. 2. That it was a powerful call. Elijah did but *cast his mantle upon him* (*v.* 19), in token of friendship, that he would take him under his care and tuition as he did under his mantle, in token of his being clothed with the spirit of Elijah (now he put some of his honour upon him, as Moses on Joshua, Num. xxvii. 20); but, when Elijah went to heaven, he had the mantle entire, 2 Kings ii. 13. And immediately he *left the oxen* to go as they would, and *ran after Elijah*. An invisible hand touched his heart, and unaccountably inclined him by a secret power, without any external persuasions, to quit his husbandry and give himself to the ministry. Elisha came to a resolution presently, but begged a little time, not to *ask* leave, but only to *take* leave, of his parents. Elijah bade him go back and do it. He will not force him, nor take him against his will; let him sit down and count the cost, and make it his own act. The efficacy of God's grace preserves the native liberty of man's will, so that those who are good are good of choice and not by constraint, not pressed men, but volunteers. 3. That it was a pleasant and acceptable call to him, which appears by the farewell-feast he made for his family (*v.* 21). It was a discouraging time for prophets to set out in. A man that had consulted with flesh and blood would not be fond of Elijah's mantle, nor willing to wear his coat; yet Elisha cheerfully, and with a great deal of satisfaction, leaves all to accompany him. 4. That it was an effectual call. Elijah did not stay for him, lest he should seem to compel him, and he soon arose, went after him, and not only associated with him, but *ministered to him* as his servitor, *poured water on his hands*, 2 Kings iii. 11. Those that would be fit to teach must have time to learn; and those that hope hereafter to rise and rule must be willing at first to stoop and serve.

CHAPTER 20

Verses 1–11

I. The threatening descent which Ben-hadad made upon Ahab's kingdom, and the siege he laid to Samaria, his royal city, *v.* 1. David in his time had quite subdued the Syrians and made them tributaries to Israel, but Israel's apostasy from God makes them formidable again. Asa had tempted the Syrians to invade Israel once (*ch.* xv. 18–20), and now they did it of their own accord. It is dangerous bringing a foreign force into the country: posterity may pay dearly for it.

II. The treaty between these two kings.

1. Ben-hadad's proud spirit sends Ahab a very insolent demand, *v.* 2, 3. A parley is sounded to let Ahab know that he will raise the siege upon condition that Ahab becomes his vassal and not only pay him a tribute but make over his title to Ben-hadad, and hold all at his will, even his wives and children.

2. Ahab's poor spirit sends Ben-hadad a very disgraceful submission. *I am thine, and all that I have*, *v.* 4. See the effect of sin. (1) If he had not by sin provoked God to depart from him, Ben-hadad could not have made such a demand. If God may not rule us, our enemies shall. A rebel to God is a slave to all besides. (2) If he had not by sin wronged his own conscience, and set that against him, he could not have made such a mean surrender. Guilt dispirits men, and makes them cowards.

JAMIESON, FAUSSET, BROWN

19-21. ELISHA FOLLOWS ELIJAH. **19. Elisha the son of Shaphat**—Most probably he belonged to a family distinguished for piety, and for their opposition to the prevailing calf worship. **ploughing with twelve yoke of oxen**—indicating that he was a man of substance.

Elijah . . . cast his mantle upon him—This was an investiture with the prophetic office. It is in this way that the Brahmins, the Persian Sooffees, and other priestly or sacred characters in the East are appointed—a mantle being, by some eminent priest, thrown across their shoulders. Elisha had probably been educated in the schools of the prophets.

20. what have I done to thee?—i.e., Go, but keep in mind the solemn ceremony I have just performed on thee. It is not I, but God, who calls thee. Do not allow any earthly affection to detain you from obeying His call.

21. took a yoke of oxen—Having hastily prepared (II Sam. 24:22) a farewell entertainment to his family and friends, he left his native place and attached himself to Elijah as his minister.

CHAPTER 20

VSS. 1-12. BEN-HADAD BESIEGES SAMARIA. **1. Ben-hadad the king of Syria**—This monarch was the son of that Ben-hadad who, in the reign of Baasha, made a raid on the northern towns of Galilee (ch. 15:20). The thirty-two kings that were confederate with him were probably tributary princes. The ancient kings of Syria and Phœnicia ruled only over a single city, and were independent of each other, except when one great city, as Damascus, acquired the ascendency, and even then they were allied only in time of war. The Syrian army encamped at the gates and besieged the town of Samaria. **2-3. Thus saith Ben-hadad, Thy silver and thy gold is mine**—To this message sent him during the siege, Ahab returned a tame and submissive answer, probably thinking it meant no more than an exaction of tribute.

ADAM CLARKE

not kissed him. Idolaters often kissed their hands in honor of their idols; and hence the origin of "adoration"—bringing the hand to the mouth after touching the idol, if it were within reach; and if not, kissing the right hand in token of respect and subjection. The word is compounded of *ad*, "to," and *os*, *oris*, "the mouth."

19. *Twelve yoke of oxen.* Elisha must have had a considerable estate, when he kept twelve yoke of oxen to till the ground. If, therefore, he obeyed the prophetic call, he did it at considerable secular loss. *He with the twelfth.* Every owner of an inheritance among the Hebrews, and indeed among the ancients in general, was a principal agent in its cultivation.

Cast his mantle upon him. Either this was a ceremony used in a call to the prophetic office or it indicated that he was called to be the servant of the prophet. The *mantle* was the peculiar garb of the prophet, as we may learn from Zech. xiii. 4; and this was probably made of skin dressed with the hair on (see also 2 Kings i. 8). It is likely, therefore, that Elijah threw his mantle on Elisha to signify to him that he was called to the prophetic office.

20. *Let me . . . kiss my father and my mother.* Elisha fully understood that he was called by this ceremony to the prophetic office; and it is evident that he conferred not with flesh and blood, but resolved, immediately resolved, to obey; only he wished to bid farewell to his relatives. *What have I done to thee?* Your call is not from me, but from God; to Him, not to me, are you accountable for your use or abuse of it.

21. *He returned back.* He went home to his house; probably he yet lived with his parents, for it appears he was a single man. He slew a yoke of the oxen—he made a feast for his household, having boiled the flesh of the oxen with his agricultural implements, probably in token that he had abandoned secular life. Then, having bidden them an affectionate farewell, he arose, went after Elijah, who probably still awaited his coming in the field or its vicinity, and ministered unto him.

CHAPTER 20

1. *Ben-hadad.* Several MSS., and some early printed editions, have *Ben-hadar*, or "the son of Hadar," as the Septuagint. He is supposed to be the same whom Asa stirred up against the king of Israel, xv. 18; or, as others, his son or grandson. *Thirty and two kings.* Tributary chieftains of Syria and the adjacent countries. In former times every town and city had its independent chieftain. Both the Septuagint and Josephus place this war after the history of Naboth.

4. *I am thine, and all that I have.* He probably hoped by this humiliation to soften this barbarous king, and perhaps to get better conditions.

MATTHEW HENRY

3. Ben-hadad's proud spirit rises upon his submission, and becomes yet more insolent and imperious, *v.* 5, 6. (1) Ben-hadad is as covetous as he is proud, and cannot go away unless he have the possession as well as the dominion. (2) He is as spiteful as he is haughty. Had he come himself to select what he had a mind for, it would have shown some respect to a crowned head; but he will send his servants to insult the prince: *Whatsoever is pleasant in thy eyes they shall take away.* (3) He is as unreasonable as he is unjust, and will construe the surrender Ahab made for himself as made for all his subjects too.

4. Ahab's poor spirit begins to rise too, upon this growing insolence; and, if it becomes not bold, yet it becomes desperate, and he will rather hazard his life than give up all thus. (1) Now he takes advice of his privy-council, who encourage him to stand it out. (2) Yet he expresses himself very modestly in his denial, *v.* 9.

5. Ben-hadad proudly swears the ruin of Samaria.

6. Ahab sends him a decent rebuke to his assurance, dares not defy his menaces, only reminds him of the uncertain turns of war (*v.* 11).

Verses 12–21

The treaty between the besiegers and the besieged being broken off abruptly, we have here an account of the battle that ensued.

I. The Syrians, the besiegers, had their directions from a drunken king, who gave orders over his cups, as he was *drinking* (*v.* 12), *drinking himself drunk* (*v.* 16) *with the kings in the pavilions*, and this at noon. Had he not been very secure he would not have sat to drink; and, had he not been intoxicated, he would not have been so very secure. Security and sensuality went together in the old world, and Sodom, Luke xvii. 26, &c. Ben-hadad's drunkenness was the forerunner of his fall, as Belshazzar's was, Dan. v. In his drink, 1. He orders the town to be invested. 2. When the besieged made a sally he gave orders to take them alive (*v.* 18), not to kill them, which might have been done more easily and safely, but to seize them, which gave them an opportunity of killing the aggressors.

II. The Israelites, the besieged, had their directions from an inspired prophet, one of the prophets of the Lord, whom Ahab had hated and persecuted.

1. Behold, and wonder, that God should send a prophet with a kind and gracious message to so wicked a prince as Ahab was; but he did it, (1) For his people Israel's sake. (2) That he might magnify his mercy, in doing good to one so evil and unthankful, might either bring him to repentance or leave him the more inexcusable. (3) That he might mortify the pride of Ben-hadad and check his insolence. He enquired not for a prophet of the Lord, but God sent one to him unasked, for he waits to be gracious.

2. Two things the prophet does: (1) He animates Ahab with an assurance of victory, which was more than all the elders of Israel could give him (*v.* 8), though they promised to stand by him. He is informed what use he ought to make of this blessed turn of affairs: "*Thou shalt know that I am Jehovah*, the sovereign Lord of all." (2) He instructs him what to do for the gaining of this victory. [1] He must not stay till the enemy attacked him, but must sally out upon them and surprise them in their trenches. [2] The persons employed must be the *young men of the princes of the provinces*, the pages, the footmen, who were few in number, only 232, utterly unacquainted with war, and the unlikeliest men that could be thought of for such a bold attempt. [3] Ahab must himself so far testify his confidence in the word of God as to command in person, though, in the eye of reason, he exposed himself to the utmost danger by it. Yet, [4] He is allowed to make use of what other forces he has at hand, to follow the blow, when these young men have broken the ice. All he had in Samaria, or within call, were but 7,000 men, *v.* 15. It is observable that it is the same number with theirs that had not *bowed the knee to Baal* (*ch.* xix. 18), though, it is likely, not the same men.

III. The issue was accordingly. The proud Syrians were beaten, and the poor despised Israelites were more than conquerors. See how God *takes away the spirit of princes*, and makes himself *terrible to the kings of the earth.* Now where are the silver and gold he demanded of Ahab? Where are the handfuls of Samaria's dust?

Verses 22–30

An account of another successful campaign which Ahab, by divine aid, made against the Syrians, in which he gave them a greater defeat than in the former. Strange! Ahab idolatrous and yet victorious, a persecutor and yet a conqueror! God has wise

JAMIESON, FAUSSET, BROWN

But the demand was repeated with greater insolence; and yet, from the abject character of Ahab, there is reason to believe he would have yielded to this arrogant claim also, had not the voice of his subjects been raised against it. Ben-hadad's object in these and other boastful menaces was to intimidate Ahab.

But the weak sovereign began to show a little more spirit, as appears in his abandoning "my lord the king," for the single "tell him," and giving him a dry but sarcastic hint to glory no more till the victory is won. Kindling into a rage at the cool defiance, Ben-hadad gave orders for the immediate sack of the city.

12. as he was drinking, he and the kings in the pavilions—booths made of branches of trees and brushwood; which were reared for kings in the camp, as they still are for Turkish pashas or agas in their expeditions [KEIL]. **Set yourselves in array**—Invest the city.

13-20. THE SYRIANS ARE SLAIN. **13. behold, there came a prophet unto Ahab**—Though the king and people of Israel had highly offended Him, God had not utterly cast them off. He still cherished designs of mercy towards them, and here, though unasked, gave them a signal proof of His interest in them, by a prophet's animating announcement that the Lord would that day deliver the mighty hosts of the enemy into his hand by means of a small, feeble, inadequate band. Conformably to the prophet's instructions, 232 young men went boldly out towards the camp of the enemy, while 7000 more, apparently volunteers, followed at some little distance, or posted themselves at the gate, to be ready to reinforce those in front if occasion required it. Ben-hadad and his vassals and princes were already, at that early hour—scarcely midday—deep in their cups; and though informed of this advancing company, yet confiding in his numbers, or it may be, excited with wine, he ordered with indifference the proud intruders to be taken alive, whether they came with peaceful or hostile intentions. It was more easily said than done; the young men smote right and left, making terrible havoc among their intended captors; and their attack, together with the sight of the 7000, who soon rushed forward to mingle in the fray, created a panic in the Syrian army, who immediately took up flight. Ben-hadad himself escaped the pursuit of the victors on a fleet horse, surrounded by a squadron of horse-guards. This glorious victory, won so easily, and with such a paltry force opposed to overwhelming numbers, was granted that Ahab and his people might know (vs. 13) that God is the Lord. But we do not read of this acknowledgment being made, or of any sacrifices being offered in token of their national gratitude.

ADAM CLARKE

6. *Whatsoever is pleasant in thine eyes.* It is not easy to discern in what this second requisition differed from the first; for surely his silver, gold, wives, and children were among his most pleasant or desirable things. It is evident that Ben-hadad meant to sack the whole city, and after having taken the royal treasures, and the wives and children of the king, to deliver up the whole to be pillaged by his soldiers.

8. *Hearken not unto him.* The elders had everything at stake, and they chose rather to make a desperate defense than tamely to yield to such degrading and ruinous conditions.

10. *If the dust of Samaria shall suffice.* This is variously understood. Jonathan translates thus: "If the dust of Shomeron shall be sufficient for the soles of the feet of the people that shall accompany me"; i.e., I shall bring such an army that there will scarcely be room for them to stand in Samaria and its vicinity.

11. *Let not him that girdeth on.* This was no doubt a proverbial mode of expression. Jonathan translates, "Tell him, Let not him who girds himself and goes down to the battle, boast as he who has conquered and returned from it."

13. *There came a prophet.* Who this was we cannot tell.

14. *By the young men of the princes of the provinces.* These were probably some chosen persons out of the militia of different districts, raised by *the princes of the provinces.*

15. *Two hundred and thirty two.* These were probably the king's life or body guards; not all the militia, but 230 of them who constituted the royal guard in Samaria. They were therefore the king's own regiment, and he is commanded by the prophet to put himself at their head.

Seven thousand. How low must the state of Israel have been at this time!

18. *Take them alive.* He was confident of victory. Do not slay them; bring them to me, they may give us some useful information.

20. *The Syrians fled.* They were doubtless panic-struck.

MATTHEW HENRY

and holy ends in suffering wicked men to prosper.

I. Ahab is admonished by a prophet to prepare for another war, *v.* 22. The prophet told him they would renew their attempt at the return of the year, hoping to retrieve the honour they had lost and be avenged for the blow they had received. He therefore bade him strengthen himself. It concerns us always to expect assaults from our spiritual enemies, and therefore to mark and see what we do.

II. Ben-hadad is advised by those about him concerning the operations of the next campaign. 1. They advised him to *change his ground*, *v.* 23. They took it for granted that it was not Israel, but Israel's gods, that beat them, but they speak very ignorantly of Jehovah—that he was *many*, whereas he is one and his name one—that he was *their* God only, a local deity, peculiar to that nation, whereas he is the Creator and ruler of all the world. 2. They advised him to change his officers (*v.* 24, 25), not to employ the kings, who were commanders by birth, but captains rather, who were commanders by merit, who were inured to war.

III. Both armies take the field. Ben-hadad, with his Syrians, encamps near Aphek, in the tribe of Asher. Ahab, with his forces, posted himself at some distance over against them, *v.* 27. The disproportion of numbers was very remarkable. *The children of Israel*, who were cantoned in two battalions, looked like *two little flocks of kids*, their numbers small, their equipage mean, and the figure they made contemptible; *but the Syrians filled the country* with their numbers, their noise, their chariots, their carriages, and their baggage.

IV. Ahab is encouraged to fight the Syrians, notwithstanding their advantages and confidence. A man of God is sent to him, to tell him that this numerous army shall *all be delivered into his hand* (*v.* 28), but not for his sake; be it known to him, he is utterly unworthy for whom God will do this.

V. After the armies had faced one another seven days they engaged, and the Syrians were totally routed. Ben-hadad, who thought his city Aphek would hold out against the conquerers, finding it thus unwalled, and the remnant of his forces dispirited and dispersed, had nothing but secrecy to rely upon for safety, and therefore hid himself in *a chamber within a chamber*, lest the pursuers should seize him. See how the greatest confidence often ends in the greatest cowardice.

Verses 31–43

An account of what followed upon the victory which Israel obtained over the Syrians.

I. Ben-hadad's tame and mean submission. His servants, seeing him and themselves reduced to the last extremity, advised that they should surrender at discretion, and make themselves prisoners and petitioners to Ahab for their lives, *v.* 31. The servants will put their lives in their hands, and venture first. They had heard that the God of Israel proclaimed his name *gracious and merciful*, and they concluded their kings would make their God their pattern. This encouragement poor sinners have to repent and humble themselves before God. "Have we not heard that the God of Israel is a merciful God? Have we not found him so? Let us therefore rend our hearts and return to him." Joel ii. 13. That is evangelical repentance which flows from an apprehension of the mercy of God in Christ; *there is forgiveness with him.* Two things Ben-hadad's servants undertake to represent to Ahab: 1. Their master a penitent; for they *girded sackcloth on their loins*, as mourners, and *put ropes on their heads*, as condemned criminals going to execution. Many pretend to repent of their wrong-doing, when it does not succeed, who, if they had prospered in it, would have justified it and gloried in it. 2. Their master a beggar, a beggar for his life: *Thy servant Ben-hadad saith, "I pray thee, let me live," v.* 32. What a great change is here, (1) In his condition! How has he fallen from the height of power and prosperity to the depths of disgrace and distress. (2) In his temper—in the beginning of the chapter hectoring, swearing, and threatening, and none more high in his demands, but here crouching and whining and none more low in his requests!

II. Ahab's foolish acceptance of his submission, and the league he suddenly made with him upon it. He was proud to be thus courted by him whom he had feared. *Is he yet alive? Is he my brother*, brother-king, though not brother-Israelite; and Ahab valued himself more upon his royalty than on his religion. "*Is he thy brother, Ahab?* Did he use thee like a brother when he sent thee that barbarous message? *v.* 5, 6. Would he have called thee brother if he had been the conqueror? Would he now have called himself *thy servant* if he had not been reduced to the

JAMIESON, FAUSSET, BROWN

22. the prophet came to the king of Israel, and said—The same prophet who had predicted the victory shortly reappeared, admonishing the king to take every precaution against a renewal of hostilities in the following campaign. **at the return of the year**—i.e., in spring, when, on the cessation of the rainy season, military campaigns (II Sam. 11:1), were anciently begun. It happened as the prophet had forewarned. Brooding over their late disastrous defeat, the attendants of Ben-hadad ascribed the misfortune to two causes—the one arose from the principles of heathenism which led them to consider the gods of Israel as "gods of the hills"; whereas their power to aid the Israelites would be gone if the battle was maintained on the plains. The other cause to which the Syrian courtiers traced their defeat at Samaria, was the presence of the tributary kings, who had probably been the first to take flight; and they recommended "captains to be put in their rooms." Approving of these recommendations, Ben-hadad renewed his invasion of Israel the next spring by the siege of Aphek in the valley of Jezreel (I Sam. 29:1, with 28:4), not far from Endor. **27. like two little flocks of kids**—Goats are never seen in large flocks, or scattered, like sheep; and hence the two small but compact divisions of the Israelite force are compared to goats, not sheep. Humanly speaking, that little handful of men would have been overpowered by numbers. But a prophet was sent to the small Israelite army to announce the victory, in order to convince the Syrians that the God of Israel was omnipotent everywhere, in the valley as well as on the hills. And, accordingly, after the two armies had pitched opposite each other for seven days, they came to an open battle. 100,000 Syrians lay dead on the field, while the fugitives took refuge in Aphek, and there, crowding on the city walls, they endeavored to make a stand against their pursuers; but the old walls giving way under the incumbent weight, fell and buried 27,000 in the ruins. Ben-hadad succeeded in extricating himself, and, with his attendants, sought concealment in the city, fleeing from chamber to chamber; or, as some think it, an inner chamber, i.e., a harem but seeing no ultimate means of escape, he was advised to throw himself on the tender mercies of the Israelitish monarch.

32. put ropes on their heads—Captives were dragged by ropes round their necks in companies, as is depicted on the monuments of Egypt.

Their voluntary attitude and language of submission flattered the pride of Ahab, who, little concerned about the dishonor done to the God of Israel by the Syrian king, and thinking of nothing but victory, paraded his clemency, called the vanquished king "his brother," invited him to sit in the royal chariot, and dismissed him with a covenant of peace.

ADAM CLARKE

23. *Their gods are gods of the hills.* It is very likely that the small Israelitish army availed itself of the heights and uneven ground, that they might fight with greater advantage against the Syrian cavalry, for Ben-hadad came up against Samaria with horses and chariots, v. 1. These therefore must be soon thrown into confusion when charging in such circumstances; indeed, the chariots must be nearly useless. *Let us fight against them in the plain.* There our horses and chariots will all be able to bear on the enemy, and there their gods, whose influence is confined to the hills, will not be able to help them. It was a general belief in the heathen world that each district had its tutelary and protecting deity, who could do nothing out of his own sphere.

24. *Take the kings away.* These were not acquainted with military affairs, or they had not competent skill. Put experienced *captains* in their place, and fight not but on the plains, and you will be sure of victory.

26. *Ben-hadad numbered the Syrians, and went up to Aphek.* There were several towns of this name (see the notes on Josh. xii. 18). It is supposed that the town mentioned here was situated in Libanus, upon the river Adonis, between Heliopolis and Biblos.

28. *Because the Syrians have said.* God resents their blasphemy, and is determined to punish it. They shall now be discomfited in such a way as to show that God's power is everywhere, and that the multitude of a host is nothing against Him.

29. *Slew . . . an hundred thousand footmen in one day.* This number is enormous; but the MSS. and versions give no various reading.

30. *A wall fell upon twenty and seven thousand.* From the first view of this text it would appear that when the Syrians fled to Aphek, and shut themselves within the walls, the Israelites immediately brought all hands and sapped the walls, in consequence of which a large portion fell, and buried 27,000 men. But perhaps the hand of God was more immediately in this disaster; probably a burning wind is meant. *Came into the city, into an inner chamber.* However the passage above may be understood, the city was now, in effect, taken; and Ben-hadad either betook himself with his few followers to the citadel or to some secret hiding place, where he held the council with his servants immediately mentioned.

31. *Put sackcloth on our loins, and ropes upon our heads.* Let us show ourselves humbled in the deepest manner, and let us put ropes about our necks, and go submitting to his mercy, and deprecating his wrath.

32. *Thy servant Ben-hadad.* See the vicissitude of human affairs! A little before he was the haughtiest of all tyrants, and Ahab calls him his lord; now, so much is he humbled that he will be glad to be reputed Ahab's slave!

33. *Did hastily catch it.* They were watching to see if any kind word should be spoken by him, from which they might draw a favorable omen; and when they heard him use the word "brother," it gave them much encouragement.

MATTHEW HENRY

utmost strait? Canst thou suffer thyself to be thus imposed upon by a forced and counterfeit submission?" Ben-hadad, upon his submission, shall not only be honourably conveyed (he *took him up into the chariot*), but treated with as an ally (*v.* 34): he *made a covenant with him*, not consulting God's prophets, or the elders of the land. He might now have demanded some of Ben-hadad's cities, but was content with the restitution of his own. He might now have demanded the stores, and treasures, and magazines of Damascus, but was content with a poor liberty, at his own expense, to build streets there. With this covenant he sent him away, without so much as reproving him for his blasphemous reflections upon the God of Israel, for whose honour Ahab had no concern.

III. The reproof given to Ahab for his clemency to Ben-hadad and his covenant with him. It was given him by a prophet, in the name of the Lord, the Jews say by Micaiah, and not unlikely, for Ahab complains of him (*ch.* xxii. 8) that he used to *prophesy evil concerning him.* This prophet designed to reprove Ahab by a parable. To make his parable the more plausible, he finds it necessary to put himself into the posture of a wounded soldier. 1. With some difficulty he gets himself wounded, for he would not wound himself with his own hands. He commanded one of his brother prophets to smite him, and this in God's name (*v.* 35), but finds him not so willing to give the blow as he is to receive it. We cannot but think it was from a good principle he declined it. Good men can much more easily receive a wrongful blow than give one; yet because he disobeyed an express command of God (which was so much the worse if he was himself a prophet), like that other disobedient prophet (*ch.* xiii. 24), he was presently *slain by a lion*, *v.* 36. This was intended to intimate to Ahab that if a good prophet were thus punished for sparing his friend and God's, when God said, *Smite;* of much sorer punishment should a wicked king be thought worthy, who spared his enemy and God's, when God said, *Smite.* The next he met with made no difficulty of smiting him and did it so that he *wounded him*, *v.* 37. He fetched blood with the blow, probably in his face. 2. Wounded as he was, and disguised with ashes that he might not be known to be a prophet, he made his application to the king in a story wherein he charged himself with such a crime as the king was now guilty of in sparing Ben-hadad, and waited for the king's judgment upon it. The case in short is this—A prisoner taken in the battle was committed to his custody by a man with this charge, *If he be missing, thy life shall be for his life*, *v.* 39. The prisoner has made his escape through his carelessness. Can the chancery in the king's breast relieve him against his captain, who demands his life in lieu of the prisoner's? "By no means," says the king, "thou shouldst either not have undertaken the trust or been more careful and faithful to it; there is no remedy, thou hast forfeited thy bond, and execution must go out upon it: *So shall thy doom be, thou thyself hast decided it.*" Now the prophet has what he would have, puts off his disguise, and is known by Ahab himself to be a prophet (*v.* 41) and plainly tells him, *"Thou art the man.* Out of thy own mouth art thou judged. God delivered into thy hands one plainly marked for destruction both by his own pride and God's providence, and thou hast wittingly and willingly dismissed him, and so hast been false to thy trust." 3. We are told how Ahab resented this reproof. He *went to his house heavy and displeased* (*v.* 43), enraged at the prophet, exasperated against God, and yet vexed at himself.

JAMIESON, FAUSSET, BROWN

34. streets for thee in Damascus—implying that a quarter of that city was to be assigned to Jews, with the free exercise of their religion and laws, under a judge of their own.

This misplaced kindness to a proud and impious idolater, so unbecoming a theocratic monarch, exposed Ahab to the same censure and fate as Saul (I Sam. 15:9, etc.). It was in opposition to God's purpose in giving him the victory.

35-42. A PROPHET REPROVES HIM. **35. Smite me**—This prophet is supposed (vs. 8) to have been Micaiah. The refusal of his neighbor to smite the prophet was manifestly wrong, as it was a withholding of necessary aid to a prophet in the discharge of a duty to which he had been called by God, and it was severely punished, as a beacon to warn others (see on ch. 13:2-24).

The prophet found a willing assistant, and then, waiting for Ahab, leads the king unconsciously, in the parabolic manner of Nathan (II Samuel 12), to pronounce his own doom; and this consequent punishment was forthwith announced by a prophet (see on ch. 21). **39. a talent of silver**—about $ 2,000.00.

ADAM CLARKE

34. *Thou shalt make streets for thee in Damascus.* It appears that it was customary for foreigners to have a place assigned to them, particularly in maritime towns, where they might deposit and vend their merchandise.

35. *In the word of the Lord.* By the word or command of the Lord; that is, God has commanded thee to smite me. Refusing to do it, this man forfeited his life, as we are informed in the next verse. By this emblematical action he intended to inform Ahab that, as the man forfeited his life who refused to smite him when he had the Lord's command to do it, so he (Ahab) had forfeited his life, because he did not smite Ben-hadad when he had him in his power.

36. *A lion found him, and slew him.* This seems a hard measure, but there was ample reason for it. This person was also one of the sons of the prophets, and he knew that God frequently delivered His counsels in this way, and should have immediately obeyed. For the smiting could have had no evil in it when God commanded it, and it could be no outrage or injury to his fellow when he himself required him to do it.

38. *Disguised himself with ashes upon his face.* It does not immediately appear how putting *ashes* upon his face could disguise him. Instead of *apher*, "dust," Houbigant conjectures that it should be *aphad*, a "fillet" or "bandage." It is only the corner of the last letter which makes the difference, for the *daleth* and *resh* are nearly the same; only the shoulder of the former is square, the latter round. That "bandage," not "dust," was the original reading seems pretty evident from its remains in two of the oldest versions, the Septuagint and the Chaldee. The former has, "And he bound his eyes with a fillet." The latter has, "And he covered his eyes with a cloth."

39. *Keep this man.* The drift of this is at once seen; but Ahab, not knowing it, was led to pass sentence on himself.

41. *Took the ashes away.* He took the bandage from off his eyes (see on v. 38). It was no doubt of thin cloth, through which he could see, while it served for a sufficient disguise.

42. *Thy life shall go for his life.* This was fulfilled at the battle of Ramoth-gilead, where he was slain by the Syrians (see chap. xxii 34-35).

43. *Heavy and displeased.* Heavy or afflicted because of these dreadful tidings, and displeased with the prophet for having announced them. Had he been displeased with himself, and humbled his soul before God, even those judgments, so circumstantially foretold, might have been averted.

MATTHEW HENRY — CHAPTER 21

Verses 1–4

1. Ahab coveting his neighbour's vineyard, which unhappily lay near his palace and conveniently for a kitchen-garden. Ahab sets his eye and heart on this vineyard, *v.* 2. It will be a pretty addition to his demesne, and nothing will serve him but it must be his own. Yet he is not such a tyrant as to take it by force, but fairly proposes either to give Naboth the full value of it in money or a better vineyard in exchange. To desire a convenience to his estate was not evil, but to desire anything inordinately is a fruit of selfishness. 2. The repulse he met with in this desire. Naboth would by no means part with it (*v.* 3): *The Lord forbid it me.* Canaan was in a peculiar manner God's land; the Israelites were his tenants; and this was one of the conditions of their leases, that they should not alienate any part of that which fell to their lot, unless in case of extreme necessity, and then only till the year of jubilee, Lev. xxv. 28.

JAMIESON, FAUSSET, BROWN — CHAPTER 21

Vss. 1-4. NABOTH REFUSES AHAB HIS VINEYARD. **1. Naboth the Jezreelite had a vineyard, which was in Jezreel**—Ahab was desirous, from its contiguity to the palace, to possess it for a vegetable garden. He proposed to Naboth to give him a better in exchange, or to obtain it by purchase; but the owner declined to part with it.

In persisting in his refusal, Naboth was not actuated by any feelings of disloyalty or disrespect to the king, but solely from a conscientious regard to the divine law, which, for important reasons, had prohibited the sale of a paternal inheritance; or if, through extreme poverty or debt, an assignation of it to another was un-

ADAM CLARKE — CHAPTER 21

1. *After these things.* This and the twentieth chapter are transposed in the Septuagint, this preceding the account of the Syrian war with Ben-hadad. Josephus gives the history in the same order.

2-3. *Give me thy vineyard.* The request of Ahab seems at first view fair and honorable. Naboth's vineyard was nigh to the palace of Ahab, and he wished to add it to his own for a "kitchen garden," or perhaps a "grass-plat"; and he offers to give him either a better vineyard for it or to give him its worth in money. Naboth rejects the proposal with horror: *The Lord forbid it me, that I should give the inheritance of my fathers unto thee.* No man could finally alienate any part of the parental inheritance; it might be sold or mortgaged till

MATTHEW HENRY

Now Naboth foresaw that, if his vineyard were sold to the crown, it would never return to his heirs, no, not in the jubilee. He would gladly oblige the king, but he must obey God rather than men, and therefore in this matter desires to be excused. Some conceive that Naboth looked upon his earthly inheritance as an earnest of his lot in the heavenly Canaan, and therefore would not part with the former, lest it should amount to a forfeiture of the latter. 3. Ahab's great discontent and uneasiness hereupon. He was as before (*ch.* xx. 43) *heavy and displeased* (*v.* 4), grew melancholy upon it, threw himself upon his bed, would not eat nor admit company to come to him. He cursed the squeamishness of Naboth's conscience. Nor could he bear the disappointment; it cut him to the heart to be crossed in his desires, and he was perfectly sick for vexation. He had all the delights of Canaan, that pleasant land, at command, the wealth of a kingdom, the pleasures of a court, and the honours and powers of a throne; and yet *all this avails him nothing* without Naboth's vineyard.

Verses 5–16

Nothing but mischief is to be expected when Jezebel enters into the story—*that cursed woman,* 2 Kings ix. 34.

I. Under pretence of comforting her afflicted husband, she feeds his pride and passion, and blows the coals of his corruptions. He told her what troubled him (*v.* 6), yet invidiously concealed Naboth's reason for his refusal, representing it as peevish, when it was conscientious—*I will not give it thee,* whereas he said, *I may not.* What! says Jezebel (*v.* 7), *Dost thou govern Israel? Arise, and eat bread.* "*Dost thou govern Israel,* and shall any subject thou hast deny thee anything thou hast a mind to? If thou knowest not how to support the dignity of a king, let me alone to do it; give me but leave to make use of thy name, and I will soon *give thee the vineyard of Naboth*; right or wrong, it shall be thy own shortly, and cost thee nothing."

II. In order to gratify him, she projects and compasses the death of Naboth.

1. Had she aimed only at his land, her false witnesses might have sworn him out of that by a forged deed, but Naboth must die.

(1) Never were more wicked orders given by any prince than those which Jezebel sent to the magistrates of Jezreel, *v.* 8–10. She borrows the privy-seal, but the king shall not know what she will do with it. She makes use of the king's name; in short, she commands them, upon their allegiance, to put Naboth to death. She must have looked upon the elders of Jezreel as men perfectly lost to everything that is honest and honourable when she expected these orders should be obeyed. [1] It must be done under colour of religion: "*Proclaim a fast;* pretend to be afraid that there is some great offender among you undiscovered, for whose sake God is angry with your city; and at last let Naboth be fastened upon as the suspected person, probably because he does not join with his neighbours in their worship." [2] It must be done *under colour of justice* too, and with the formalities of a legal process. The crime they must lay to his charge was *blaspheming God and the king*—a complicated blasphemy.

(2) Never were wicked orders more wickedly obeyed than these were by the magistrates of Jezreel. They did *as it was written in the letters* (*v.* 11, 12), neither made any difficulty of it, nor met with any difficulty in it, but cleverly carried on the villainy. They stoned Naboth to death (*v.* 13), and, as it should seem, his sons with him, or after him.

2. Let us take occasion (1) To stand amazed at the wickedness of the wicked, and the power of Satan in the children of disobedience. (2) To lament the hard case of oppressed innocency. (3) To commit the keeping of our lives and comforts to God, for innocency itself will not always be our security. (4) To rejoice in the belief of a judgment to come, in which such wrong judgments as these will be called over.

III. Naboth being taken off, Ahab takes possession of his vineyard. 1. The elders of Jezreel sent notice to Jezebel very unconcernedly, sent it to her as a piece of agreeable news, *Naboth is stoned and is dead, v.* 14. 2. Jezebel, jocund enough that her plot succeeded so well, brings notice to Ahab that *Naboth is not alive, but dead*; therefore, says she, *Arise, take possession of his vineyard, v.* 15. He might have taken possession by one of his officers, but so pleased is he with this accession to his estate that he will make a journey to Jezreel himself to enter upon it; and it should seem he went in state too, as if he had obtained some mighty victory, for Jehu remembers long after that he and Bidkar attended him at this time, 2 Kings ix. 25.

JAMIESON, FAUSSET, BROWN

avoidable, the conveyance was made on the condition of its being redeemable at any time; at all events, of its reverting at the jubilee to the owner.

In short, it could not be alienated from the family, and it was on this ground that Naboth (vs. 3) refused to comply with the king's demand. It was not, therefore, any rudeness or disrespect that made Ahab heavy and displeased, but his sulky and pettish demeanor betrays a spirit of selfishness that could not brook to be disappointed of a favorite object, and that would have pushed him into lawless tyranny had he possessed any natural force of character. **4. turned away his face**—either to conceal from his attendants the vexation of spirit he felt, or, by the affectation of great sorrow, rouse them to devise some means of gratifying his wishes.

5-16. Jezebel Causes Naboth to Be Stoned. **7. Dost thou now govern the kingdom of Israel?**—This is not so much a question as an exclamation—a sarcastic taunt; "A pretty king thou art! Canst thou not use thy power and take what thy heart is set upon?" **arise, and eat bread, and let thine heart be merry: I will give thee the vineyard**—After upbraiding Ahab for his pusillanimity and bidding him act as a king, Jezebel tells him to trouble himself no more about such a trifle; she would guarantee the possession of the vineyard. **8. So she wrote letters in Ahab's name, and sealed them with his seal**—The seal-ring contained the name of the king and gave validity to the documents to which it was affixed (Esther 8:8; Dan. 6:17). By allowing her the use of his signet-ring, Ahab passively consented to Jezebel's proceeding. Being written in the king's name, it had the character of a royal mandate. **sent the letters unto the elders and nobles that were in his city**—They were the civic authorities of Jezreel, and would, in all likelihood, be the creatures and fit tools of Jezebel. It is evident that, though Ahab had recently been in Jezreel, when he made the offer to Naboth, both he and Jezebel were now in Samaria (ch. 20:43). **9. Proclaim a fast,** etc.—Those obsequious and unprincipled magistrates did according to orders. Pretending that a heavy guilt lay on one, or some unknown party, who was charged with blaspheming God and the king and that Ahab was threatening vengeance on the whole city unless the culprit were discovered and punished, they assembled the people to observe a solemn fast. Fasts were commanded on extraordinary occasions affecting the public interests of the state (II Chron. 20:3; Ezra 8:21; Joel 1:14; 2:15; Jonah 3:5). The wicked authorities of Jezreel, by proclaiming the fast, wished to give an external appearance of justice to their proceedings and convey an impression among the people that Naboth's crime amounted to treason against the king's life. **set Naboth on high**—During a trial the panel, or accused person, was placed on a high seat, in the presence of all the court; but as the guilty person was supposed to be unknown, the setting of Naboth on high among the people must have been owing to his being among the distinguished men of the place. **13. there came in two men**—worthless fellows who had been bribed to swear a falsehood. The law required two witnesses in capital offenses (Deut. 17:6; 19:15; Num. 35:30; Matt. 26:60). Cursing God and cursing the king are mentioned in the law (Exod. 22:28) as offenses closely connected, the king of Israel being the earthly representative of God in His kingdom. **they carried him forth out of the city, and stoned him**—The law, which forbade cursing the rulers of the people, does not specify the penalty for this offense but either usage had sanctioned or the authorities of Jezreel had originated stoning as the proper punishment. It was always inflicted out of the city (Acts 7:58). **14-16. Jezebel said to Ahab, Arise, take possession**—Naboth's execution having been announced, and his family being involved in the same fatal sentence (II Kings 9:26), his property became forfeited to the crown, not by law, but traditionary usage (see on II Sam. 16:4). **Ahab rose to go down**—from Samaria to Jezreel.

ADAM CLARKE

the jubilee, but at that time it must revert to its original owner, if not redeemed before; for this God had particularly enjoined, Lev. xxv. 14-17, 25-28. Ahab most evidently wished him to alienate it finally, and this is what God's law had expressly forbidden. Therefore he could not, consistently with his duty to God, indulge Ahab; and it was high iniquity in Ahab to tempt him to do it, and to covet it showed the depravity of Ahab's soul.

4. *He laid him down upon his bed.* Poor soul! He was lord over ten-twelfths of the land, and became miserable because he could not get a poor man's vineyard added to all that he possessed!

7. *Dost thou now govern the kingdom of Israel?* Naboth, not Ahab, is king. If he has authority to refuse, and you have no power to take, he is the greater man of the two. This is the vital language of despotism and tyranny.

8. *She wrote letters in Ahab's name.* She counterfeited his authority by his own consent, and he lent his signet to stamp that authority.

9. *Proclaim a fast.* Intimate that there is some great calamity coming upon the nation, because of some evil tolerated in it. *Set Naboth on high.* Bring him to a public trial.

10. *Set two men.* For life could not be attainted but on evidence of two witnesses at least. *Sons of Belial.* Men who will not scruple to tell lies and take a false oath. *Thou didst blaspheme God and the king.* The words literally are, "Naboth hath blessed God and the king"; or, as Parkhurst contends, "Thou hast blessed the false gods and Molech." And though Jezebel was herself an abominable idolatress, yet, as the law of Moses still continued in force, she seems to have been wicked enough to destroy Naboth, upon the false accusation of blessing the heathen Molech, which subjected him to death by Deut. xii. 6; xvii. 2-7. The first meaning appears the most simple.

13. *And stoned him with stones.* As they pretended to find him guilty of treason against God and the king, it is likely they destroyed the whole of his family; and then the king seized on his grounds as confiscated, without any heir at law. That his family was destroyed appears strongly intimated, 2 Kings ix. 26; "Surely I have seen yesterday the blood of Naboth, and the blood of his sons, saith the Lord."

MATTHEW HENRY

Verses 17–29

I. The very bad character that is given of Ahab (*v.* 25, 26), which comes in here to justify God in the heavy sentence passed upon him, and to show that though it was passed upon occasion of his sin in the matter of Naboth, yet God would not have punished him so severely if he had not been guilty of many other sins, especially idolatry. He was wholly given up to sin, and, upon condition he might have the pleasures of it, he would take the wages of it, which is death, Rom. vi. 23. It was no excuse of his crimes that *Jezebel his wife stirred him up* to do wickedly, and made him, in many respects, worse then otherwise he would have been.

II. The message with which Elijah was sent to him, when he went to take possession of Naboth's vineyard, *v.* 17–19.

1. Hitherto God kept silence, but now Ahab is reproved and his *sin set in order before his eyes.* (1) The person sent is Elijah. (2) The place is Naboth's vineyard and the time just when he is taking possession of it; then, and there, must his doom be read him. Now he is pleasing himself with his ill-gotten wealth, and giving direction for the turning of this vineyard into a flower-garden.

2. What passed between him and the prophet.

(1) Ahab vented his wrath against Elijah, fell into a passion at the sight of him, and, instead of humbling himself before the prophet, as he ought to have done (2 Chron. xxxvi. 12), was ready to fly in his face. *Hast thou found me, O my enemy? v.* 20. This shows, [1] That he hated him. The last time we found them together they parted very good friends, *ch.* xviii. 46. Then Ahab had countenanced the reformation, and therefore then all was well between him and the prophet; but now he had relapsed, and was worse than ever. His conscience told him he had made God his enemy, and therefore he could not expect Elijah should be his friend. [2] That he feared him: *Hast thou found me?* Never was poor debtor or criminal so confounded at the sight of the officer that came to arrest him.

(2) Elijah denounced God's wrath against Ahab: *I have found thee* (says he, *v.* 20), *because thou hast sold thyself to work evil.* [1] Elijah finds the indictment against him, and convicts him upon the notorious evidence of the fact (*v.* 19): *Hast thou killed, and also taken possession?* [2] He passes judgment upon him. He told him from God that his family should be ruined and rooted out (*v.* 21) and all his posterity cut off. "*Thy blood, even thine*, though it be royal blood, though it swell thy veins with pride and boil in thy heart with anger, shall ere long be an entertainment for the dogs," which was fulfilled, *ch.* xxii. 38.

III. Ahab's humiliation under the sentence passed upon him, and the favourable message sent him thereupon. 1. Ahab was a kind of penitent. The message Elijah delivered to him in God's name put him into a fright for the present, so that he *rent his clothes* and *put on sackcloth, v.* 27. Ahab put on the garb and guise of a penitent, and yet his heart was unhumbled and unchanged. 2. He obtained hereby a reprieve, which I may call a kind of pardon. Though it was but an outside repentance (lamenting the judgment only, and not the sin), though he did not leave his idols, nor restore the vineyard to Naboth's heirs, yet, because he did hereby give some glory to God, God took notice of it, and bade Elijah take notice of it: *Seest thou how Ahab humbles himself? v.* 29. This teaches us to take notice of that which is good even in those who are not so good as they should be: let it be commended as far as it goes. This gives a reason why wicked people sometimes prosper long; God is rewarding their external services with external mercies. This encourages all those that truly repent and unfeignedly believe the holy gospel. If a pretending partial penitent shall go to his house reprieved, doubtless a sincere penitent shall *go to his house justified.*

JAMIESON, FAUSSET, BROWN

17-29. Elijah Denounces Judgments against Ahab and Jezebel. **17-19. Hast thou killed, and also taken possession?**—While Ahab was in the act of surveying his ill-gotten possession, Elijah, by divine commission, stood before him. The appearance of the prophet, at such a time, was ominous of evil, but his language was much more so (cf. Ezek. 45:8; 46:16-18). Instead of shrinking with horror from the atrocious crime, Ahab eagerly hastened to his newly acquired property. **In the place where dogs licked,** etc.—a righteous retribution of Providence. The prediction was accomplished, not in Jezreel, but in Samaria; and not on Ahab personally, in consequence of his repentance (vs. 29), but on his son (II Kings 9:25). The words "in the place where" might be rendered "in like manner as."

20. thou hast sold thyself to work evil—i.e., allowed sin to acquire the unchecked and habitual mastery over thee (II Kings 17:17; Rom. 7:11).

21, 22. will make thine house, etc.—see on ch. 15:29; 16: 3-12). Jezebel, though included among the members of Ahab's house, has her ignominious fate expressly foretold (see on II Kings 9:30).

27-29. Ahab . . . rent his clothes, and put sackcloth upon his flesh, and fasted, and lay in sackcloth, and went softly—He was not obdurate, like Jezebel. This terrible announcement made a deep impression on the king's heart, and led, for a while, to sincere repentance. Going softly, i.e., barefoot, and with a pensive manner, within doors. He manifested all the external signs, conventional and natural, of the deepest sorrow. He was wretched, and so great is the mercy of God, that, in consequence of his humiliation, the threatened punishment was deferred.

ADAM CLARKE

25. *Did sell himself to work wickedness.* He hired himself to the devil for this very purpose, that he might work wickedness. *In the sight of the Lord, whom Jezebel his wife stirred up.* A good wife is from the Lord; a bad wife is from the devil. Jezebel was of this kind, and she has had many successors.

18. *Go down to meet Ahab.* This was the next day after the murder, as we learn from the above quotation, 2 Kings ix. 26.

19. *In the place where dogs licked.* Thus it would have been fulfilled, but the humiliation of Ahab induced the merciful God to say, "I will not bring the evil in his days, but in the days of his son" (see v. 29). Now dogs did lick the blood of Ahab; but it was at the pool of Samaria, where his chariot and his armor were washed, after he had received his death wound at Ramoth-gilead; but some think this was the place where Naboth was stoned (see chap. xxii. 38). And how literally the prediction concerning his son was fulfilled (see 2 Kings ix. 25), where we find that the body of Jehoram, his son, just then slain by an arrow that had passed through his heart, was thrown "into the portion of the field of Naboth the Jezreelite"; and there, doubtless, the dogs licked his blood, if they did not even devour his body!

20. *Thou hast sold thyself to work evil.* See a similar form of speech, Rom. vii. 14. You have totally abandoned yourself to the service of sin.

23. *The dogs shall eat Jezebel.* This was most literally fulfilled (see 2 Kings ix. 36).

27. *He rent his clothes.* He was penetrated with sorrow, and that evidently unfeigned. *Put sackcloth upon his flesh.* He humbled himself before God and man. *And fasted.* He afflicted his body for his soul's benefit. *Lay in sackcloth.* Gave the fullest proof that his repentance was real. *And went softly.* "Walked barefooted"; so the Chaldee, Syriac, and Arabic. The Vulgate has: "with his head hanging down." Houbigant translates "went groaning." Jarchi says that the word *at*, used here, signifies "to be unshod." This is its most likely sense. All these things prove that Ahab's repentance was genuine, and God's approbation of it puts it out of doubt.

29. *Seest thou how Ahab humbleth himself?* He did abase himself; he did truly repent him of his sins, and it was such a repentance as was genuine in the sight of God. *He humbleth himself before me.*

MATTHEW HENRY — CHAPTER 22

Verses 1–14

As a reward for his professions of repentance and humiliation, though the time drew near when he should descend into battle and perish, yet we have him blessed with a three years' peace (*v.* 1) and an honourable visit made him by Jehoshaphat king of Judah, *v.* 2. The Jews have a fabulous conceit, that when Ahab humbled himself for his sin, and lay in sackcloth, he sent for Jehoshaphat to come to him, to chastise him; and that he stayed with him for some time, and gave him so many stripes every day. This is a groundless tradition. He came now, it is probable,

JAMIESON, FAUSSET, BROWN — CHAPTER 22

Vss. 1-36. Ahab Slain at Ramoth-gilead. **1. continued three years without war between Syria and Israel**—The disastrous defeat of Ben-hadad had so destroyed his army and exhausted the resources of his country, that, however eager, he was unable to recommence active hostilities against Israel. But that his hereditary enmity remained unsubdued, was manifest by his breach of faith concerning the treaty by which he had engaged to restore all the cities which his father had seized (ch. 20:34). **2. Jehoshaphat the king of Judah came down to the king of Israel**—It was singular that a friendly league

ADAM CLARKE — CHAPTER 22

1. *Three years without war.* That is, from the time that Ahab made the covenant with Ben-hadad, mentioned in chap. xx. 34. And probably in that treaty it was stipulated that Ramoth-gilead should be restored to Israel; which not being done, Ahab formed a confederacy with Judah, and determined to take it by force.

MATTHEW HENRY

to consult him about the affairs of their kingdoms. The Syrians durst not give Ahab any disturbance. But,

I. Ahab here meditates a war against the Syrians, and advises concerning it with those about him, *v.* 3. The king of Syria gave him the provocation; when he lay at his mercy, he promised to restore him his cities (*ch.* xx. 34), and Ahab foolishly took his word. Ben-hadad is one of those princes that think themselves bound by their word no further and no longer than it is for their interest. Whether any other cities were restored we do not find, but Ramoth-Gilead was not, a considerable city in the tribe of Gad, on the other side Jordan, a Levites' city, and one of the cities of refuge. Ahab blames himself, and his people, that they did not bestir themselves to recover it out of the hands of the Syrians, and to chastise Ben-hadad's violation of his league.

II. He engages Jehoshaphat, and draws him in, to join with him in this expedition, for the recovery of Ramoth-Gilead, *v.* 4. But it is strange that Jehoshaphat will go so entirely into Ahab's interests as to say, *I am as thou art, and my people as thy people.* I hope not; Jehoshaphat and his people are not so wicked and corrupt as Ahab and his people. Too great a complaisance to evil-doers has brought many good people, through unwariness, into a dangerous fellowship with *the unfruitful works of darkness.* Jehoshaphat had like to have paid dearly for his compliment when, in battle, he was taken for Ahab. Yet some observe that in joining with Israel against Syria he atoned for his father's fault in joining with Syria against Israel, *ch.* xv. 19, 20.

III. At the special instance and request of Jehoshaphat, he asks counsel of the prophets concerning this expedition. Ahab thought it enough to consult with his statesmen, but Jehoshaphat moves that they should *enquire of the word of the Lord, v.* 5. Whithersoever a good man goes he ought to take his religion along with him, and not be ashamed to own it, no, not when he is with those who have no kindness for it.

IV. Ahab's 400 prophets (*prophets of the groves* they called them), agreed to encourage him in this expedition and to assure him of success, *v.* 6. He put the question to them: *Shall I go or shall I forbear?* But they knew which way his inclination was and designed only to humour the two kings. To please Jehoshaphat, they made use of the name *Jehovah*: He shall *deliver it into the hand of the king.* To please Ahab they said, *Go up.* "Thou shalt certainly recover Ramoth-Gilead." Zedekiah, a leading man among these prophets, illustrated his false prophecy with a sign, *v.* 11. He made himself a pair of iron horns, representing the two kings, and their honour and power (both of which were signified by horns, exaltation and force), and with these the Syrians must be pushed. All the prophets agreed, as one man, that Ahab should return from this expedition a conqueror, *v.* 12.

V. Jehoshaphat cannot relish this sort of preaching; it is not like what he was used to. The false prophets cannot so mimic the true but that he who had spiritual senses exercised could discern the fallacy, and therefore he enquired for a *prophet of the Lord besides, v.* 7.

VI. Ahab has another, but one he hates, Micaiah by name, a true prophet, and one that knew God's mind. And yet, 1. He hated him, and was not ashamed to own to the king of Judah that he did so, and to give this for a reason, He *doth not prophesy good concerning me, but evil.* And whose fault was that? If Ahab had done well, he would have heard nothing but good from heaven. Those are wretchedly hardened in sin, and are ripening apace for ruin, who hate God's ministers because they deal plainly with them. 2. He had imprisoned him. We may suppose that this was he that reproved him for his clemency to Ben-hadad (*ch.* xx. 38, &c.) and for so doing was cast into prison, where he had lain these three years. This was the reason why Ahab knew where to find him so readily, *v.* 9. He was bound, but *the word of the Lord was not.* Jehoshaphat gave too gentle a reproof to Ahab for expressing his indignation against a faithful prophet: *Let not the king say so, v.* 8. Such sinners as Ahab must be rebuked sharply. However he so far yielded to the reproof that, for fear of provoking Jehoshaphat to break off from his alliance with him, he orders Micaiah to be sent for with all speed, *v.* 9. The two kings sat each in their robes and chairs of state, in the gate of Samaria, ready to receive this poor prophet, and to hear what he had to say. They were attended with a crowd of flattering prophets, that could not think of prophesying anything but what was very sweet and very smooth to two such glorious princes now in confederacy.

VII. Micaiah is pressed by the officer that fetches him to follow the cry, *v.* 13. But Micaiah, who knows

JAMIESON, FAUSSET, BROWN

between the sovereigns of Israel and Judah should, for the first time, have been formed by princes of such opposite characters—the one pious, the other wicked. Neither this league nor the matrimonial alliance by which the union of the royal families was more closely cemented, met the Lord's approval (II Chron. 19:2). It led, however, to a visit by Jehoshaphat, whose reception in Samaria was distinguished by the most lavish hospitality (II Chron. 18:2). The opportunity of this visit was taken advantage of, to push an object on which Ahab's heart was much set. **3. Know ye that Ramoth in Gilead is ours**– a Levitical and free town on the north border of Gad (Deut. 4:43; Josh. 21:38), on the site of the present Salt Lake, in the province of Belka. It lay within the territories of the Israelitish monarch, and was unjustly alienated; but whether it was one of the cities usurped by the first Ben-hadad, which his son had promised to restore, or was retained for some other reasons, the sacred historian has not mentioned. In the expedition which Ahab meditated for the recovery of this town, the aid of Jehoshaphat was asked and promised (see on II Chron. 18:3).

Previous to declaring hostilities, it was customary to consult the prophets (see on I Sam. 28); and Jehoshaphat having expressed a strong desire to know the Lord's will concerning this war, Ahab assembled four hundred of his prophets. These could not be either the prophets of Baal or of Ashteroth (ch. 18:19), but seem (vs. 12) to have been false prophets, who conformed to the symbolic calf worship of Jehovah. Being the creatures of Ahab, they unanimously predicted a prosperous issue to the war.

But dissatisfied with them, Jehoshaphat inquired if there was any true prophet of the Lord.

Ahab agreed, with great reluctance, to allow Micaiah to be summoned. He was the only true prophet then to be found residing in Samaria, and he had to be brought out of prison (vs. 26), into which, according to Josephus, he had been cast on account of his rebuke to Ahab for sparing the king of Syria.

10. a void place—lit., a threshing-floor, formed at the gate of Samaria. **11. Zedekiah the son of Chenaanah made him horns of iron** —Small projections, of the size and form of our candle extinguishers (worn in many parts of the East as military ornaments), were worn by the Syrians of that time, and probably by the Israelite warriors also. Zedekiah, by assuming two horns, personated two heroes, and, pretending to be a prophet, wished in this manner to represent the kings of Israel and Judah in a military triumph. It was a symbolic action, to impart greater force to his language (see on Deut. 33:17); but it was little more than a flourish with a *spontoon* [CALMET'S FRAGMENT].

ADAM CLARKE

4. *Wilt thou go with me?* We find that there was a good understanding between Jehoshaphat and Ahab, which no doubt was the consequence of a matrimonial alliance between the son of the former, Jehoram, and the daughter of the latter, Athaliah (see 2 Chron. xviii. 1; 2 Kings viii. 18). This coalition did not please God, and Jehoshaphat is severely reproved for it by Jehu, the seer, 2 Chron. xix. 1-3.

6. *About four hundred men.* These were probably the prophets of Asherah maintained by Jezebel, who were not present at the contention on Mount Carmel (see chap. xviii. 19, etc.).

8. *Micaiah the son of Imlah.* The Jews suppose that it was this prophet who reproved Ahab for dismissing Ben-hadad, chap. xx. 35, etc. And that it was because of the judgments with which he had threatened him that Ahab hated him: *I hate him; for he doth not prophesy good concerning me, but evil.*

9. *The king of Israel called an officer. Saris,* literally "a eunuch"; probably a foreigner, for it was not lawful to disgrace an Israelite by reducing him to such a state.

11. *Zedekiah . . . made him horns of iron.* This was in imitation of that sort of prophecy which instructed by significative actions. This was frequent among the prophets of the Lord.

MATTHEW HENRY

better things, protests, and backs his protestation with an oath, that he will deliver his message from God with all faithfulness, whether it be pleasing or displeasing to his prince (*v.* 14): "*What the Lord saith to me, that will I speak.*"

Verses 15–28

I. We are told how faithfully he delivered his message. In three ways he delivers his message, and all displeasing to Ahab:

1. He spoke as the rest of the prophets had spoken, but ironically: *Go, and prosper*, *v.* 15. Ahab put the same question to him that he had put to his own prophets, seeming desirous to know God's mind, when, like Balaam, he was strongly bent to do his own, which Micaiah plainly took notice of when he bade him go, but he spoke by way of derision; as if he had said, go then, and take what follows. In answer to this Ahab adjured him to tell him the truth, and not to jest with him (*v.* 16).

2. Being thus pressed, he plainly foretold that the king would be cut off in this expedition, and his army scattered, *v.* 17. He saw them in a vision, dispersed upon the mountains, as sheep that had no one to guide them. This intimates, (1) That Israel should be deprived of their king, who was their shepherd. (2) That they would make a dishonourable retreat. *Let them return every man to his house in peace*, no great losers by the death of their king. Thus Micaiah, in his prophecy, testified what he had seen and heard. Now Ahab finds himself aggrieved, turns to Jehoshaphat and appeals to him whether Micaiah had not manifestly a spite against him, *v.* 18.

3. He informed the king how it was that all his prophets encouraged him to proceed, that God permitted Satan by them to deceive him into his ruin, and he by vision knew of it. God is a great king above all kings, and has a throne above all the thrones of earthly princes. The rise and fall of princes, the issues of war, and all the great affairs of state, which are the subject of the consultations of wise and great men, are no more above God's direction than the meanest concerns of the poorest cottages are below his notice. It is not without the divine permission that the devil deceives men, and even thereby God serves his own purposes. Thus Micaiah gave Ahab fair warning, not only of the danger of proceeding in this war, but of the danger of believing those that encouraged him to proceed.

II. We are told how he was abused for delivering his message thus faithfully. 1. Zedekiah, a wicked prophet, impudently insulted him in the face of the court, *smote him on the cheek*, to silence him and stop his mouth. To strike within the verge of the court, especially in the king's presence, is looked upon by our law as a high misdemeanour; yet this wicked prophet gives this abuse to a prophet of the Lord. Micaiah, though he returns not his blow leaves Ahab to be convinced of his error by the event: *Thou shalt know when thou hidest thyself in an inner chamber*, *v.* 25. It is likely Zedekiah went with Ahab to the battle, and took his horns of iron with him to encourage the soldiers, to see with pleasure the accomplishment of his prophecy, and return in triumph with the king; but, the army being routed, he fled among the rest from the sword of the enemy, sheltered himself as Ben-hadad had done in *a chamber within a chamber* (*ch.* xx. 30), lest he should perish. 2. Ahab, that wicked king, committed him to prison (*v.* 27), to be fed with bread and water, coarse bread and puddle-water, till he should return, not doubting but that he should return a conqueror, and then he would put him to death for a false prophet (*v.* 27)—hard usage for one that would have prevented his ruin! Micaiah put it upon the issue, and called all the people to be witnesses that he did so: "*If thou return in peace, the Lord has not spoken by me*, *v.* 28. Let me incur the reproach and punishment of a false prophet, if the king come home alive."

Verses 29–40

I. The two kings march with their forces to Ramoth-Gilead, *v.* 29. That Jehoshaphat, that pious prince, who had desired to enquire by a *prophet of the Lord*, discrediting Ahab's prophets, should yet proceed, after so fair a warning, is matter of astonishment. But by the easiness of his temper he was carried away with the delusion of his friends. He gave too much heed to Ahab's prophets, because it was 400 to one that they should succeed.

II. Ahab adopts a contrivance by which he hopes to secure himself and expose his friend (*v.* 30): "*I will disguise myself*, and go in the habit of a common soldier, but let *Jehoshaphat put on his robes*, to appear in the dress of a general." He pretended thereby to do honour to Jehoshaphat, but he intended, 1. To make a liar of a good prophet. Thus he hoped

JAMIESON, FAUSSET, BROWN

14. what the Lord saith unto me, that will I speak—On the way the messenger who conducted him to the royal presence informed him of the tenor of the prophecies already given and recommended him to agree with the rest, no doubt from the kindly motive of seeing him released from imprisonment. But Micaiah, inflexibly faithful to his divine mission as a prophet, announced his purpose to proclaim honestly whatever God should bid him. On being asked by the king, "Shall I go against Ramoth-gilead, or shall I forbear?" the prophet gave precisely the same answer as the previous oracles that had been consulted; but it must have been given in a sarcastic tone and in ironical mockery of their way of speaking. Being solemnly urged to give a serious and truthful answer, Micaiah then declared the visionary scene the Spirit had revealed to him;—"I saw all Israel scattered upon the hills as sheep that have not a shepherd." The purport of this was that the army of Israel would be defeated and dispersed; that Ahab would fall in the battle, and the people return without either being pursued or destroyed by the enemy.

18-23. Did I not tell thee that he would prophesy no good concerning me, but evil?—Since Ahab was disposed to trace this unwelcome truth to personal enmity, Micaiah proceeded fearlessly to tell the incensed monarch in full detail what had been revealed to him. The Hebrew prophets, borrowing their symbolic pictures from earthly scenes, described God in heaven as a king in His kingdom. And as earthly princes do nothing of importance without asking the advice of their counsellors, God is represented as consulting about the fate of Ahab. This prophetic language must not be interpreted literally, and the command must be viewed as only a permission to the lying spirit (Rom. 11:34) [CALMET].

24, 25. Zedekiah the son of Chenaanah went near, and smote Micaiah on the cheek—The insolence of this man, the leader of the false prophets, seems to have been provoked by jealousy at Micaiah's assumed monopoly of the spirit of inspiration. This mode of smiting, usually with a shoe, is both severe and ignominious. The calm reply of the Lord's prophet consisted in announcing the fate of the false prophets who suffered as the advisers of the disastrous expedition.

26-28. Take Micaiah, . . . Put this fellow in prison—Ahab, under the impulse of vehement resentment, remands the prophet until his return. **bread of affliction, water of affliction**—i.e., the poorest prison fare. Micaiah submitted, but reiterated aloud, in the presence of all, that the issue of the war would be fatal to Ahab.

29-38. went up to Ramoth-gilead—The king of Israel, bent on this expedition, marched, accompanied by his ally, with all his forces to the siege; but on approaching the scene of action, his courage failed, and, hoping to evade the force of Micaiah's prophecy by a secret stratagem, he assumed the uniform of a subaltern, while he advised Jehoshaphat to fight in his royal attire.

ADAM CLARKE

13. *The words of the prophets declare good.* What notion could these men have of prophecy, when they supposed it was in the power of the prophet to model the prediction as he pleased, and have the result accordingly?

15. *Go, and prosper.* This was a strong irony; as if he had said, All your prophets have predicted success; you wish me to speak as they speak. *Go, and prosper; for the Lord shall deliver it into the hand of the king.* These were the precise words of the false prophets (see vv. 6 and 12) and were spoken by Micaiah in such a tone and manner as at once showed to Ahab that he did not believe them. Hence the king adjures him, v. 16, that he would speak to him nothing but truth; and on this the prophet immediately relates to him the prophetic vision which pointed out the disasters which ensued.

17. *These have no master.* Here the prophet foretells the defeat of Israel, and the death of the king; they were as sheep that had not a shepherd, people that had no master. The political shepherd and master (Ahab) shall fall in battle.

22. *Go forth, and do so.* This is no more than, "God has permitted the spirit of lying to influence the whole of your prophets; and He now, by my mouth, apprizes you of this, that you may not go and fall at Ramoth-gilead." Never was a man more circumstantially and fairly warned; he had counsels from the God of truth, and counsels from the spirit of falsity. He obstinately forsook the former and followed the latter.

23. *The Lord hath put a lying spirit.* He has permitted or suffered a lying spirit to influence your prophets.

24. *Which way went the Spirit of the Lord from me?* This is an expression of as great insolence as the act was of brutal aggression. "Did the Spirit of the Lord, who rests solely upon me, condescend to inspire you? Was it at this ear [where he smote him] that it entered, in order to hold communion with you?"

25. *When thou shalt go into an inner chamber.* It is probable that this refers to some divine judgment which fell upon this deceiver. Hearing of the tragical result of the battle, he no doubt went into a secret place to hide himself from the resentment of Jezebel and the Israelitish courtiers, and there it is probable he perished; but how, when, or where is not mentioned.

27. *Feed him with bread of affliction.* Deprive him of all the conveniences and comforts of life; treat him severely; just keep him alive, that he may see my triumph.

30. *I will disguise myself.* Probably he had heard of the orders given by Ben-hadad to his thirty-two captains, to fight with the king of Israel only. *But put thou on thy robes.* What is meant by this? He could not mean, "Appear as the king of Judah, for they will not molest you, as the matter of contention lies between them and me." For if Jehoshaphat aided Ahab, is it to be supposed that the Syrians would spare him in battle? The Septuagint gives the clause a different and more intelligible turn: "I will cover (conceal) myself, and enter into the battle; but put thou on my robes." And does it not appear that he did put on Ahab's robes? And was it not this that caused the Syrians to mistake him for the king of Israel (v. 32)?

MATTHEW HENRY

to elude the danger. 2. To make a fool of a good king, whom he did not cordially love. How can it be expected that he should be true to his friend that has been false to his God?

III. Jehoshaphat, having more piety than policy, put himself into the post of honour, though it was the post of danger, and was thereby brought into peril of his life, but God graciously delivered him. The king of Syria charged his captains to level their force, not against the king of Judah, for with him he had no quarrel, but against the king of Israel only (*v.* 31). Some think that he designed only to have him taken prisoner. Whatever was the reason, the officers, seeing Jehoshaphat in his royal habit, took him for the king of Israel, and surrounded him. 1. By his danger God let him know that he was displeased with him for joining in confederacy with Ahab. 2. By his deliverance God let him know that, though he was displeased with him, yet he had not deserted him. Some of the captains that knew him perceived their mistake, and so retired from the pursuit of him.

IV. Ahab receives his mortal wound in the battle. Let no man think to hide himself from God's judgment. The Syrian that shot him *drew a bow at a venture*, not aiming particularly at any man, yet God so directed the arrow that, 1. He hit the right person. 2. He hit him in the right place, *between the joints of the harness*, the only place about him where this arrow of death could find entrance.

V. The army is dispersed by the enemy and sent home by the king. Ahab himself lived long enough to see that part of Micaiah's prophecy accomplished that all Israel should be scattered *upon the mountains of Gilead* (*v.* 17).

VI. The royal corpse is brought to Samaria and buried there (*v.* 37). Now Naboth's blood was avenged (*ch.* xxi. 19), and that word of David was fulfilled (Ps. lxviii. 23), *That thy foot may be dipped in the blood of thy enemies, and the tongue of thy dogs in the same*.

Lastly, The story of Ahab is here concluded in the usual form, *v.* 39, 40. Among his works mention is made of an ivory house, so called because many parts of it were inlaid with ivory; perhaps it was intended to vie with the stately palace of the kings of Judah, which Solomon built.

Verses 41–53

I. A short account of the reign of Jehoshaphat king of Judah, of which we have a much fuller narrative in the book of Chronicles, and of the greatness and goodness of that prince, neither of which was lessened or sullied by anything but his intimacy with the house of Ahab. His confederacy with Ahab in war we have already found dangerous to him, and his confederacy with Ahaziah his son in trade sped no better. He offered to go partner with him in a fleet of merchant-ships, that should fetch gold from Ophir. But, while they were preparing to set sail, they were disabled by a storm (*broken at Ezion-geber*). When Ahaziah desired a second time to be a partner with him, *Jehoshaphat would not*. The rod of God, expounded by the word of God, had effectually broken him off from his confederacy with that ungodly unhappy prince. Now Jehoshaphat's reign appears here to have been none of the longest, but one of the best. 1. It was none of the longest, for he reigned but twenty-five years (*v.* 42), but these twenty-five, added to his father's happy forty-one, give us a grateful idea of the flourishing condition of the kingdom of Judah, and of religion in it. 2. Yet it was one of the best, both in respect of piety and prosperity. (1) He did well: He *did that which was right in the eyes of the Lord* (*v.* 43). Yet the *high places were not taken away*, no, not out of Judah and Benjamin, though those tribes lay so near Jerusalem that they could not pretend, as some other of the tribes, the inconveniency of lying remote. (2) His affairs did well. He prevented the mischiefs which had attended their wars with the kingdom of Israel, establishing a lasting peace (*v.* 44); he put a deputy, or viceroy, in Edom, so that that kingdom was tributary to him (*v.* 47), and therein the prophecy concerning Esau and Jacob was fulfilled, that *the elder should serve the younger*. He pleased God, and God blessed him with strength and success.

II. The beginning of the story of Ahaziah the son of Ahab, *v.* 51–53. His reign was very short, not two years. Some sinners God makes quick work with. It is a very bad character that is here given him. He not only kept up Jeroboam's idolatry, but the worship of Baal likewise; though he had heard of the ruin of Jeroboam's family, and had seen his own father drawn into destruction by the prophets of Baal, who had often been proved false prophets, yet he followed the example of his wicked father and the counsel of his more wicked mother Jezebel, who was still living.

JAMIESON, FAUSSET, BROWN

The Syrian king, with a view either to put the speediest end to the war, or perhaps to wipe out the stain of his own humiliation (ch. 20:31), had given special instructions to his generals to single out Ahab, and to take or kill him, as the author of the war. The officers at first directed their assault on Jehoshaphat, but, becoming aware of their mistake, desisted.

Ahab was wounded by a random arrow, which, being probably poisoned, and the state of the weather increasing the virulence of the poison, he died at sunset.

The corpse was conveyed to Samaria; and, as the chariot which brought it was being washed, in a pool near the city, from the blood that had profusely oozed from the wound, the dogs, in conformity with Elijah's prophecy, came and licked it.

F. B. MEYER:

"Broken ships." Further details of Jehoshaphat's good reign are given in 2 Chron. 17—20. He made strenuous efforts to rid the land of the more obvious evils that disgraced it, though some of the abuses seemed too deeply rooted even for his strong hand (v. 43). The great defect of Jehoshaphat's character was the ease with which he associated himself with Ahab and his family; for this, subsequent generations paid a heavy penalty (2 Kings 11).

Jehoshaphat attempted to reopen sea commerce with Ophir, and entered into partnership with Ahaziah to build ships in Solomon's old port of Ezion-geber, to make the circuit of Africa en route for Spain. But as we learn from 2 Chron. 20:37, a prophet of Jehovah remonstrated with him for renewing the alliance with the king of Israel. The storm that shattered the ships on the rocks before they set sail gave evidence of the displeasure of the Almighty. Let us beware of these alliances and partnerships with the ungodly. Sooner or later they meet with disaster. God blocks our path and defeats our plans; and if only we are led to repentance, our broken ships may give us cause for thanksgiving in eternity.—*Bible Commentary*

Ahab was succeeded by his son Ahaziah.

ADAM CLARKE

34. *Drew a bow at a venture.* It is supposed that he shot, as the archers in general did, not aiming at any person in particular. The word *lethummo*, which we translate "in his simplicity," has been variously understood: "in his integrity, his uprightness; in his perfection"; i.e., to the utmost of his skill and strength. This is most probably the meaning.

35. *The king was stayed up.* He did not wish his misfortune should be known, lest his troops should be discouraged.

36. *Every man to his city.* It appears that the Israelites and Jews maintained the fight the whole of the day; but when at evening the king died, and this was known, there was a proclamation made, probably with the consent of both Syrians and Israelites, that the war was over. Ahab being dead, his subjects did not choose to contend for Ramoth-gilead; so the Israelites went to their own cities, and the Syrians to their own country.

38. *The dogs licked up his blood.* Some of the rabbins think that this was in the very place where Naboth was stoned (see on chap. xxi. 19).

39. *Ivory house.* A royal palace which he built in Samaria, decorated with ivory, and hence called the *ivory house*. Amos, the prophet, speaks against this luxury, chap. iii. 15.

43. *The high places were not taken away.* In 2 Chron. xvii. 6, it is expressly said that he did take away the high places. Allowing that the text is right in 2 Chronicles, the two places may be easily reconciled. There were two kinds of high places in the land: (1) those used for idolatrous purposes, (2) those that were consecrated *to God*, and were used before the Temple was built. The former he did take away; the latter he did not. But some think the parallel place in 2 Chron. xvii. 6 is corrupted, and that, instead of *veod*, "and moreover he took away," we should read, *velo hesir*, "and he did not take away."

46. *The remnant of the sodomites.* "Of the consecrated persons"; or it may rather apply here to the system of pollution, effeminacy, and debauch. He destroyed the thing itself—the abominations of Priapus, and the rites of Venus, Baal, and Ashtaroth. No more of that impure worship was to be found in Judea.

47. *There was then no king in Edom.* It is plain that the compiler of this book lived after the days of Jehoshaphat, in whose time the Edomites revolted (see 2 Kings viii. 22). David had conquered the Edomites, and they continued to be governed by deputies, appointed by the kings of Judah, till they recovered their liberty, as above. This note is introduced by the writer to account for Jehoshaphat's building ships at Ezion-geber, which was in the territory of the Edomites, and which showed them to be at that time under the Jewish yoke.

48. *Ships of Tharshish to go to Ophir for gold.* In the parallel place, 2 Chron. xx. 36, it is said that Jehoshaphat joined himself to Ahaziah "to make ships to go to Tharshish: and they made the ships in Ezion-gaber." Some translate, instead of ships of *Tharshish*, ships of "burden."

49. *But Jehoshaphat would not.* It appears from the above cited place in Chronicles that Jehoshaphat did join in making and sending ships to Tharshish, and it is possible that what is here said is spoken of a second expedition, in which Jehoshaphat *would not* join Ahaziah. But instead of *velo abah*, "he would not," perhaps we should read *velo abah*, "he consented to him"; two words pronounced exactly in the same way, and differing but in one letter, viz., an *aleph* for a *vau*. This reading, however, is not supported by any MS. or version. But the emendation seems just, for there are several places in these historical books in which there are mistakes of transcribers which nothing but criticism can restore, and to this it is dangerous to resort but in cases of the last necessity.

THE BOOK OF SECOND KINGS

I. Elisha (1:1-9:37)
- *A. Elijah (1:1-18)*
  1. The sin and sickness of Ahaziah (1:1-2)
  2. Elijah on behalf of God (1:3-8)
  3. The judgment of fire (1:9-18)
- *B. Elijah and Elisha (2:1-18)*
  1. The translation of Elijah (2:1-12)
  2. The succession of Elisha (2:13-18)
- *C. Elisha (2:19-9:37)*
  1. Healing of the waters of Jericho (2:19-22)
  2. Punishment of mocking children (2:23-25)
  3. The sign at the war with Moab (3:1-27)
  4. Wonders (4:1-7:20)
  5. The restoration of the Shunammite's land (8:1-6)
  6. Foretells Benhadad's death (8:7-15)
  7. Final events (8:16-9:37)

II. Corruption (10:1-17:41)
- *A. Israel (10:1-36)*
  1. The zeal of Jehu (10:1-28)
  2. The failure of Jehu (10:29-36)
- *B. Judah (11:1-12:21)*
  1. Athaliah and Jehoash (11:1-21)
  2. Jehoash (12:1-21)
- *C. Israel (13:1-25)*
  1. Jehoahaz, Jehoash (13:1-13)
  2. Death of Elisha (13:14-25)
- *D. Judah (14:1-22)*
  1. Amaziah (14:1-20)
  2. Azariah (14:21-22)
- *E. Israel (14:23-15:12)*
  1. Jeroboam II (14:23-28)
  2. Zachariah (14:29-15:12)
- *F. Israel and Judah (15:13-16:20)*
  1. Israel's throne (15:13-31)
  2. Judah's troubles (15:32-16:20)
- *G. Passing of Israel (17:1-41)*

III. Hezekiah and Josiah (18:1-23:30)
- *A. Hezekiah (18:1-20:21)*
  1. His accession and character (18:1-12)
  2. The coming of Sennacherib (18:13-37)
  3. Hezekiah and Isaiah's victory (19:1-37)
  4. The last things (20:1-21)
- *B. The reaction (21:1-26)*
  1. Manasseh (21:1-18)
  2. Amon (21:19-26)
- *C. Josiah (22:1-23:20)*
  1. The finding of the law (22:1-20)
  2. Reform and death (23:1-30)

IV. Captivity (23:31-25:30)
- *A. Tributary (23:31-24:7)*
- *B. Beginning of captivity (24:8-20)*
- *C. Carried away (25:1-30)*

This second book of the Kings (which the LXX, numbering from Samuel, called the *fourth*) is a continuation of the former book; and, some think, might better have been made to begin with the fifty-first verse of the preceding chapter, where the reign of Ahaziah begins. The former book had an illustrious beginning, in the glories of the kingdom of Israel, when it was entire; this has a melancholy conclusion, in the desolations of the kingdoms of Israel first, and then of Judah. But, as Elijah's mighty works were very much the glory of the former book (towards the latter end of it), so were Elisha's the glory of this (towards the beginning of it). These prophets outshone their princes; and therefore, as far as they go, the history shall be accounted for in them.

MATTHEW HENRY

CHAPTER 1

Verses 1–8

Ahaziah, the wicked king of Israel, under God's rebukes both by his providence and by his prophet, by his rod and by his word.

I. He is crossed in his affairs. How can those expect to prosper that *do evil in the sight of the Lord*, and *provoke him to anger*? When he rebelled against God, and revolted from his allegiance to him, Moab rebelled against Israel, and revolted from the subjection they had long paid to the kings of Israel, *v.* 1.

II. He is seized with sickness in body, not from any inward cause, but by a severe accident. *He fell down through a lattice.* Ahaziah would not attempt to reduce the Moabites, lest he should perish in the field of battle: but he is not safe, though he tarry at home. Royal palaces do not always yield firm footing.

III. In his distress he sends messengers to enquire of the god of Ekron whether he should recover or no, *v.* 2. 1. His enquiry was very foolish: *Shall I recover?* Even nature itself would rather have asked, "What means may I use that I may recover?" 2. His sending to Baal-zebub was very wicked. Baal-zebub, which signifies *the lord of a fly*, was one of their Baals that perhaps gave his answers, either by the power of the demons or the craft of the priests, with a humming noise, like that of a great fly, or that had (as they fancied) rid their country of the swarms of flies wherewith it was infested, or of some pestilential disease brought among them by flies. In the New Testament *the prince of the devils* is called *Beel-zebub* (Matt. xii. 24).

IV. Elijah, by direction from God, meets the messengers, and turns them back with an answer that shall save them the labour of going to Ekron.

1. He faithfully reproves his sin (*v.* 3): *Is it not because there is not* (that is, because you think there is not) a God in Israel *that you go to enquire of Baal-zebub, the god of Ekron*, a despicable town of the Philistines (Zech. ix. 7), long since vanquished by Israel? (1) The sin was bad enough, giving that honour to the devil which is due to God alone. (2) The construction which Elijah, in God's name, puts upon it, makes it much worse: "It is because you think not only that the God of Israel is not able to tell you, but that there is no God at all in Israel, else you would not send so far for a divine answer."

JAMIESON, FAUSSET, BROWN

CHAPTER 1

VS. 1. MOAB REBELS. **1. Then Moab rebelled**—Subdued by David (II Samuel 8:2), they had, in the partition of Israel and Judah, fallen to the share of the former kingdom. But they took advantage of the death of Ahab to shake off the yoke (see on ch. 3:6). The casualty that befell Ahaziah prevented his taking active measures for suppressing this revolt—which was accomplished as a providental judgment on the house of Ahab for all these crimes.

2-8. AHAZIAH'S JUDGMENT BY ELIJAH. **2-8. Ahaziah fell down through a lattice in his upper chamber**—This lattice was either a *part* of the wooden parapet, or fence, which surrounds the flat roofs of houses, and over which the king was carelessly leaning when it gave way; or it might be an opening like a skylight in the roof itself, done over with lattice-work, which, being slender or rotten, the king stepped on and slipped through. This latter supposition is most probably the true one, as Ahaziah did not fall either into the street or the court, but "in his upper chamber." **inquire of Baalzebub**—Anxious to learn whether he should recover from the effects of this severe fall, he sent to consult Baalzebub—i.e., the god of flies, who was considered the patron deity of medicine. A temple to that idol was erected at Ekron, which was resorted to far and wide, though it afterwards led to the destruction of the place (Zech. 9:5; Amos 1:8; Zeph. 2:4). "After visiting Ekron, 'the god of flies' is a name that gives me no surprise. The flies there swarmed, in fact so innumerably, that I could hardly get any food without these troublesome insects getting into it" [VAN DE VELDE]. **3. the angel of the Lord**—not *an* angel, but *the* angel, who carried on all communications between the invisible God and His chosen people [HENGSTENBERG]. This angel commissioned Elijah to meet the king's messengers, to stop them peremptorily on the idolatrous errand, and convey by them to the king information of his approaching death. This consultation of an idol, being a breach of the fundamental law of the kingdom (Exod. 20:3; Deut. 5:7), was a daring and deliberate rejection of the national relegion. The Lord, in making this announcement of his death, designed that he should see in that event a judgment for his idolatry.

ADAM CLARKE

CHAPTER 1

1. *Moab rebelled.* The Moabites had been subdued by David, and laid under tribute, chap. iii. 4 and 2 Sam. viii. 2. After the division of the two kingdoms, the Moabites fell partly under the dominion of Israel, and partly under that of Judah, until the death of Ahab, when they arose and shook off this yoke. Jehoram confederated with the king of Judah and the king of Edom, in order to reduce them. See this war, chap. iii. 5.

2. *Fell down through a lattice.* Perhaps either through the flat roof of his house or over or through the balustrades with which the roof was surrounded.

Go, enquire of Baal-zebub. Literally, the "fly-god," or "master of flies." The Septuagint has "Baal the fly." He was the tutelary god of Ekron, and probably was used at first to drive away flies. Afterwards he became a very respectable devil, and was supposed to have great power and influence. In the New Testament, Beelzebub is a common name for Satan himself, or the prince of devils.

MATTHEW HENRY

2. He plainly reads his doom: Go, tell him *he shall surely die*, *v.* 4.

V. The message being delivered to him by his servants, he enquires of them by whom it was sent to him, and concludes, by their description of him, that it must be Elijah, *v.* 7, 8. His dress was the same that he had seen him in, in his father's court. He was clad in a hairy garment, and had a leathern girdle about him, was plain and homely in his garb.

Verses 9–18

I. The king issues out a warrant for the apprehending of Elijah. If the God of Ekron had told him he should die, it is probable he would have taken it quietly; but now that a prophet of the Lord tells him so, reproving him for his sin and reminding him of the God of Israel, he cannot bear it.

II. The captain that was sent with his fifty soldiers found Elijah on the top of a hill (some think Carmel), and commanded him, in the king's name, to surrender himself, *v.* 9. Elijah was now so far from absconding, as formerly, into the close recesses of a cave, that he makes a bold appearance on the top of a hill; experience of God's protection makes him more bold. The captain calls him *a man of God*. Had he really looked upon him as a prophet, he would not have attempted to make him his prisoner; and, had he thought him entrusted with the word of God, he would not have pretended to command him with the word of a king.

III. Elijah calls for fire from heaven, to consume this haughty daring sinner, to prove his mission. It was not long since Elijah had fetched fire from heaven, to consume the sacrifice (1 Kings xviii. 38), but, they having slighted that, now the fire falls, not on the sacrifice, but on the sinners themselves, *v.* 10. 1. What an interest the prophets had in heaven; what the Spirit of God in them demanded the power of God effected. Elijah did but speak, and it was done. 2. What an interest heaven had in the prophets! God was always ready to plead their cause, and avenge the injuries done to them. Doubtless Elijah did this by a divine impulse, and yet our Saviour would not allow the disciples to draw it into a precedent, Luke ix. 54. "No," says Christ, "by no means, *you know not what manner of spirit you are of*," that is, (1) "You do not consider *what manner of spirit*, as disciples, you are called to, and how different from that of the Old Testament dispensation; it was agreeable enough to that dispensation of terror for Elias to call for fire, but the dispensation of the Spirit and of grace will by no means allow of it." (2) "You are not aware what manner of spirit you are, upon this occasion, actuated by, and how different from that of Elias: he did it in holy zeal, you in passion; he was concerned for God's glory, you for your own reputation only."

IV. Ahaziah sends, a second time, to apprehend Elijah (*v.* 11), as if he were resolved not to be baffled by omnipotence itself. Another captain is ready with his fifty. This is as impudent and imperious as the last, and more in haste. "*Come down quickly*, and do not trifle, the king's business requires haste." Elijah relents not, but calls for another flash of lightning, which instantly lays this captain and his fifty dead upon the spot.

V. The third captain humbled himself and cast himself upon the mercy of God and Elijah. He took warning by the fate of his predecessors, and, instead of summoning the prophet down, fell down before him, and begged for his life and the lives of his soldiers, acknowledging their own evil deserts and the prophet's power (*v.* 13, 14): *Let my life be precious in thy sight*.

VI. Elijah does more than grant the request of this third captain. God is as ready to show mercy to those that repent and submit to him; never any found it in vain to cast themselves upon the mercy of God. This captain, not only has his life spared, but is permitted to carry his point: Elijah, being so commanded by the angel, *goes down with him to the king*, *v.* 15. He comes boldly to the king, and tells him to his face what he had before sent to him (*v.* 16), that he shall surely and shortly die; he mitigates not the sentence, either for fear of the king's displeasure or in pity to his misery. The God of Israel has condemned him, let him send to see whether the god of Ekron can deliver him. So thunderstruck is Ahaziah with this message, when it comes from the prophet's own mouth, that neither he nor any of those about him durst offer him any violence, nor so much as give him an affront; but out of that den of lions he comes unhurt, like Daniel.

Lastly, The prediction is accomplished in a few days. Ahaziah died (*v.* 17), and, dying childless, left his kingdom to his brother Jehoram.

JAMIESON, FAUSSET, BROWN

Thou shall not come down from that bed—On being taken up, he had probably been laid on the divan—a raised frame, about three feet broad, extended along the sides of a room, covered with cushions and mattresses—serving, in short, as a sofa by day and a bed by night—and ascended by steps. **Elijah departed**—to his ordinary abode, which was then at Mount Carmel (ch. 2:25; I Kings 18:42). **5. the messengers turned back**—They did not know the stranger; but his authoritative tone, commanding attitude, and affecting message determined them at once to return. **8. an hairy man**—This was the description not of his person, as in the case of Esau, but of his dress, which consisted either of unwrought sheep or goatskins (Heb. 11:37), or of camel's haircloth—the coarser manufacture of this material—like our rough haircloth. The Dervishes and Bedouins are attired in this wild, uncouth manner, while their hair flows loose on the head, their shaggy cloak is thrown over their shoulders and tied in front on the breast, naked, except at the waist, round which is a skin girdle—a broad, rough leathern belt. Similar to this was the girdle of the prophets, as in keeping with their coarse garments and their stern, uncompromising office.

9-16. Elijah Brings Fire from Heaven on Ahaziah's Messengers. **9. Then the king sent unto him a captain of fifty**—Any appearance of cruelty that there is in the fate of the two captains and their men will be removed, on a full consideration of the circumstances. God being the King of Israel, Ahaziah was bound to govern the kingdom according to the divine law; to apprehend the Lord's prophet, for discharging a commanded duty, was that of an impious and notorious rebel. The captains abetted the king in his rebellion; and they exceeded their military duty by contemptuous insults. **man of God**—In using this term, they either spoke derisively, believing him to be no true prophet; or, if they regarded him as a true prophet, the summons to him to surrender himself bound to the king was a still more flagrant insult; the language of the second captain being worse than that of the first. **10. let fire come down**—rather, "fire shall come down." Not to avenge a personal insult of Elijah, but an insult upon God in the person of His prophet; and the punishment was inflicted, not by the prophet, but by the direct hand of God.

15. he arose, and went down with him—a marvellous instance of faith and obedience. Though he well knew how obnoxious his presence was to the king, yet, on receiving God's command, he goes unhesitatingly, and repeats, with his own lips, the unwelcome tidings conveyed by the messengers.

17, 18. Ahaziah Dies, and Is Succeeded by Jehoram. **17. Jehoram**—The brother of Ahaziah (see on ch. 3:1).

ADAM CLARKE

4. *But shalt surely die.* The true God tells you this, He in whose hands are both life and death, who can kill and make alive. Baal-zebub can do nothing; God has determined that your master shall die.

8. *He was an hairy man.* That is, he wore a rough garment, either made of camels' hair, as his successor John Baptist's was; or he wore a skin dressed with the hair on. Some think that the meaning is, he had very long hair and a long beard. The ancient prophets all wore rough garments, or upper coats made of the skins of beasts: "They wandered about in sheepskins and goatskins," says the apostle, Heb. xi. 37.

9. *A captain of fifty with his fifty.* It is impossible that such a man as Ahaziah, in such circumstances, could have had any friendly designs in sending a captain and fifty soldiers for the prophet; and the manner in which they are treated shows plainly that they went with a hostile intent. *And he spake unto him, Thou man of God.* You prophet of the Most High.

10. *And there came down fire.* Some have blamed the prophet for destroying these men, by bringing down fire from heaven upon them. But they do not consider that it was no more possible for Elijah to bring down fire from heaven than for them to do it. God alone could send the fire; and as He is just and good, He would not have destroyed these men had there not been a sufficient cause to justify the act. It was not to please Elijah, or to gratify any vindictive humor in him, that God thus acted; but to show His own power and justice. No entreaty of Elijah could have induced God to perform an act that was wrong in itself. God led him simply to announce on these occasions what He himself had determined to do. *If I be a man of God, fire [shall] come down from heaven, and [shall] consume thee and thy fifty.* This is the literal meaning of the original; and by it we see that Elijah's words were only declarative, and not imprecatory.

15. *And the angel of the Lord said . . . Go down with him.* This is an additional proof that Elijah was then acting under particular inspirations; he had neither will nor design of his own. *And he arose, and went down.* He did not even regard his personal safety or his life; he went to the king without the least hesitation, though he had reason to suppose he would be doubly irritated by his prediction and the death of 100 of his men.

17. *And Jehoram reigned in his stead.* The Vulgate, Septuagint, and Syriac say, "Jehoram his brother reigned in his stead, in the second year of Jehoram." There were two Jehorams who were contemporary: the first, the son of Ahab, brother to Ahaziah, and his successor in the kingdom of Israel; the second, the son of Jehoshaphat, king of Judah, who succeeded his father in Judah. But there is a difficulty here: "How is it that Jehoram the brother of Ahaziah began to reign in the second year of Jehoram son of Jehoshaphat, seeing that, according to chap. iii. 1, he began his reign in the eighteenth year of the reign of Jehoshaphat; and, according to chap. viii. 16, Jehoram son of Jehoshaphat began to reign in the fifth year of Jehoram king of Israel?" Calmet and others answer thus: "Jehoram king of Israel began to reign in the eighteenth year of Jehoshaphat king of Judah, which was the second year after this same Jehoshaphat had given the vice-royalty to his son Jehoram; and afterwards Jehoshaphat communicated the royalty to Jehoram his successor, two years before his death, and the fifth year of Jehoram, king of Israel."

MATTHEW HENRY

CHAPTER 2

Verses 1–8

Elijah's times, and the events concerning him, are as little dated as those of any great man in scripture; we are not told of his age, nor in what year of Ahab's reign he first appeared, nor in what year of Jehoram's he disappeared, and therefore cannot conjecture how long he flourished; it is supposed about twenty years in all.

I. God had determined to take him up into heaven by a whirlwind, *v.* 1. It is not for us to say why God would put such a peculiar honour upon Elijah above any other of the prophets; he was a man *subject to like passions as we are*, knew sin, and yet never tasted death. We may suppose that herein, 1. God looked back upon his past services, which were eminent and extraordinary, and intended a recompence for those and an encouragement to the sons of the prophets to tread in the steps of his zeal and faithfulness, and to witness against the corruptions of the age they lived in. 2. He looked down upon the present dark and degenerate state of the church, and would thus give a very sensible proof of another life after this, and draw the hearts of the faithful few upward towards himself, and that other life. 3. He looked forward to the evangelical dispensation, and, in the translation of Elijah, gave a type and figure of the ascension of Christ and the *opening of the kingdom of heaven to all believers*. Elijah had, by faith and prayer, conversed much with heaven, and now he is taken thither, to assure us that if we have our conversation in heaven, while we are here on earth, we shall be there shortly, the soul shall (and that is the man) be happy there, there for ever.

II. Elisha had determined, as long as he continued on earth to cleave to him, and not to leave him. Elijah seemed desirous to shake him off, would have had him stay behind at Gilgal, at Bethel, at Jericho, *v.* 2, 4, 6. Some think out of humility; he knew what glory God designed for him, but would not seem to glory in it. In vain does Elijah entreat him to tarry here and tarry there; he resolves to tarry nowhere behind his master, till he goes to heaven, and leaves him behind on this earth. "Whatever comes of it, *I will not leave thee*;" and why so? 1. Because he desired to be edified by his holy heavenly converse as long as he stayed on earth. 2. Because he desired to be satisfied concerning his departure, and to see him when he was taken up, that his faith might be confirmed and his acquaintance with the invisible world increased.

III. That Elijah, before his departure, visited the schools of the prophets and took leave of them. It seems that there were such schools in many of the cities of Israel, probably even in Samaria itself. Here we find *sons of the prophets*, and considerable numbers of them, even at Bethel, where one of the calves was set up, and at Jericho, which was lately built in defiance of a divine curse. At Jerusalem, and in the kingdom of Judah, they had priests and Levites, and the temple-service, the want of which, in the kingdom of Israel, God graciously made up by those colleges, where men were trained up and employed in the exercises of religion and devotion.

IV. That the sons of the prophets had intelligence that he was now shortly to be removed; and, 1. They told Elisha of it, both at Bethel (*v.* 3) and at Jericho (*v.* 5): *Knowest thou that the Lord will take away thy master from thy head today?* Elisha knew it too well and *sorrow had filled his heart* upon this account (as the disciples in a like case, John xvi. 6), and therefore he did not need to be told of it, did not care for hearing of it. *I know it; hold you your peace.* He speaks with an awful silence expecting the event: *I know it; be silent*, Zech. ii. 13. 2. They went themselves to be witnesses of it at a distance, though they might not closely attend (*v.* 7): *Fifty of them stood to view afar off*, intending to satisfy their curiosity, but God so ordered it that they might be eye-witnesses of the honour heaven did to that prophet, who was *despised and rejected of men.*

V. That the miraculous dividing of the river Jordan was the preface to Elijah's translation into the heavenly Canaan, as it had been to the entrance of Israel into the earthly Canaan, *v.* 8. He must go on to the other side Jordan to be translated, because it was his native country, and that he might be near the place where Moses died, and that thus honour might be put on that part of the country which was most despised. God would magnify Elijah in his exit, as he did Joshua in his entrance, by the dividing of this river, Joshua iii. 7. When God will take up his faithful ones to heaven death is the Jordan which, immediately before their translation, they must pass through, and they find a way through it, a safe and comfortable way;

JAMIESON, FAUSSET, BROWN

CHAPTER 2

Vss. 1-10. ELIJAH DIVIDES JORDAN. **1. when the Lord would take up Elijah**—A revelation of this event had been made to the prophet; but, unknown to him, it had also been revealed to his disciples, and to Elisha in particular, who kept constantly beside him.

Gilgal—This Gilgal (Jiljil) was near Ebal and Gerizim—a school of the prophets was established there. At Beth-el there was also a school of the prophets, which Elijah had founded, notwithstanding that place was the headquarters of the calf worship; and at Jericho there was another. In travelling to these places, which he had done through the impulse of the Spirit (vss. 2, 4-6), Elijah wished to pay a farewell visit to these several institutions, which lay on his way to the place of ascension and, at the same time, from a feeling of humility and modesty, to be in solitude. where there would be no eye-witnesses of his glorification. All his efforts, however, to prevail on his attendant to remain behind, were fruitless. Elisha knew that the time was at hand, and at every place the sons of the prophets spoke to him of the approaching removal of his master. Their last stage was at the Jordan. They were followed at a distance by fifty scholars of the prophets, from Jericho, who were desirous, in honor of the great occasion, to witness the miraculous translation of the prophet. The revelation of this striking event to so many was a necessary part of the dispensation; for it was designed to be under the law, like that of Enoch in the patriarchal age, a visible proof of another state, and a type of the resurrection of Christ.

3. take away thy master from they head—an allusion to the custom of scholars sitting at the feet of their master—the latter being over their heads (Acts 22:3).

8. Elijah took his mantle, and wrapped it together, and smote the waters—Like the rod of Moses, it had the divinely operating power of the Spirit.

ADAM CLARKE

CHAPTER 2

1. *When the Lord would take up Elijah.* It appears that God had revealed this intended translation, not only to Elijah himself, but also to Elisha, and to the schools of the prophets, at both Bethel and Jericho, so that they were all expecting this solemn event.

2. *Tarry here, I pray thee.* He either made these requests through humility, not wishing any person to be witness of the honor conferred on him by God, or with the desire to prove the fidelity of Elisha, whether he would continue to follow and serve him.

3. *Knowest thou that the Lord?* Thus we see that it was a matter well-known to all the sons of the prophets.

7. *Fifty men of the sons of the prophets.* They fully expected this extraordinary event, and they could have known it only from Elijah himself, or by a direct revelation from God.

8. *Took his mantle.* "His sheep-skin," says the Septuagint. *They were divided hither and thither.* This was a most astonishing miracle, and could be performed only by the almighty power of God.

MATTHEW HENRY

the death of Christ has divided those waters, that the ransomed of the Lord may pass over.

Verses 9–12

I. Elijah makes his will, and leaves Elisha his heir, now anointing him to be prophet in his room, more than when he *cast his mantle upon him*, 1 Kings xix. 19.

1. Elijah, being greatly pleased with the constancy of Elisha's affection and attendance, bade him ask what he should do for him, what blessing he should leave him at parting.

2. Elisha, having this fair opportunity to enrich himself with the best riches, prays for a *double portion of his spirit.* He asks not for wealth, nor honour, nor exemption from trouble, but to be qualified for the service of God and his generation; he asks, (1) For the Spirit, not that the gifts and graces of the Spirit were in Elijah's power to give, therefore, he says not, "Give me the Spirit" (he knew very well it was God's gift), but, "*Let it be upon me,* intercede with God for this for me." (2) For *his* spirit, because he was to be a prophet in his room, to carry on his work, to father the sons of the prophets and face their enemies, because he had the same difficulties to encounter. (3) For a *double portion of his spirit*; he does not mean double to what Elijah had, but double to what the rest of the prophets had, from whom so much would not be expected as from Elisha, who had been brought up under Elijah.

3. Elijah promised him that which he asked, but under two provisos, *v.* 10. (1) Provided he put a due value upon it and esteem it highly: this he teaches him to do by calling it *a hard thing,* not too hard for God to do, but too great for him to expect. (2) Provided he kept close to his master, even to the last, and was observant of him: *If thou see me when I am taken from thee, it shall be* so, otherwise not.

II. Elijah is carried up to heaven in a fiery chariot, *v.* 11. Like Enoch, he was translated, *that he should not see death*; and was (as Mr. Cowley expresses it) *the second man that leaped the ditch where all the rest of mankind fell, and went not downward to the sky.* Let it suffice that we are here told,

1. What his Lord, when he came, found him doing. He was talking with Elisha, instructing and encouraging him, directing him in his work, and quickening him to it, for the good of those whom he left behind. He was not meditating nor praying, as one wholly taken up with the world he was going to, but engaged in edifying discourse, as one concerned about the kingdom of God among men.

2. What convoy his Lord sent for him—*a chariot of fire and horses of fire,* that he may ride in state, may ride in triumph, like a prince, like a conqueror, yea, *more than a conqueror.* The angels are called in scripture *cherubim* and *seraphim,* and their appearance here, though it may seem below their dignity, answers to both those names; for (1) *Seraphim* signifies *fiery,* and God is said to make them *a flame of fire,* Ps. civ. 4. (2) *Cherubim* (as many think) signifies *chariots,* and they are called *the chariots of God* (Ps. lxviii. 17). The chariot and horses appeared like fire, not for burning, but brightness, not to torture or consume him, but to render his ascension conspicuous and illustrious in the eyes of those that stood afar off to view it. Elijah had burned with holy zeal for God and his honour, and now with a heavenly fire he was refined and translated.

3. How he was separated from Elisha. This chariot parted them both asunder.

4. Whither he was carried. He *went up by a whirlwind into heaven.* Elijah had once, in a passion, wished he might die; yet God was so gracious to him as to honour him with this singular privilege, that he should never see death; and by this instance, and that of Enoch, (1) God showed how men should have left the world if they had not sinned, not by death, but by a translation. (2) He gave a glimpse of that life and immortality which are brought to light by the gospel, and the *opening of the kingdom of heaven to all believers,* as then to Elijah. It was also a figure of Christ's ascension.

III. Elisha pathetically laments the loss of that great prophet. 1. He saw it; by which he was assured of the grant of his request for a double portion of Elijah's spirit. He looked steadfastly towards heaven, whence he was to expect that gift, as the disciples did, Acts i. 10. He saw it awhile, but the vision was presently out of his sight; and *he saw him no more.* 2. He rent his own clothes, in token of the sense he had of his own and the public loss. Though Elijah had gone triumphantly to heaven, yet this world could ill spare him. Surely their hearts are hard whose eyes are dry when God, by taking away faithful useful men, calls for weeping and mourning. Though Elijah's departure made way for Elisha's eminency,

JAMIESON, FAUSSET, BROWN

9. Elijah said unto Elisha, Ask what I shall do for thee—trusting either that it would be in his power to bequeath it, or that God, at his entreaty, would grant it. **let a double portion of thy spirit be upon me**—This request was not, as is commonly supposed, for the power of working miracles exceeding the magnitude and number of his master's, nor does it mean a higher endowment of the prophetic spirit; for Elisha was neither superior to, nor perhaps equally great with, his predecessor. But the phrase, "a double portion," was applied to the first-born, and therefore Elisha's request was, simply, to be heir to the prophetic office and gifts of his master.

10. Thou hast asked a hard thing—an extraordinary blessing which *I* cannot, and God only, can give. Nevertheless he, doubtless by the secret directions of the Spirit, proposed to Elisha a sign, the observation of which would keep him in the attitude of an anxious waiter, as well as suppliant for the favor.

11-18. HE IS TAKEN UP TO HEAVEN IN A CHARIOT OF FIRE. **11. behold, there appeared a chariot of fire, and horses of fire**—some bright effulgence, which, in the eyes of the spectators, resembled those objects.

went up by a whirlwind—a tempest or storm-wind accompanied with vivid flashes of fire, figuratively used for the divine judgments (Isa. 29:6).

ADAM CLARKE

9. *A double portion of thy spirit be upon me.* This in reference to the law, Deut. xxi. 17: "He shall acknowledge . . . the firstborn, by giving him a double portion of all that he hath . . . the right of the firstborn is his." Elisha considered himself the only child or firstborn of Elijah, as the disciples of eminent teachers were called their children; so here he claims a double portion of his spiritual influence, any other disciples coming in for a single share only. "Sons of the prophets" means no more than the disciples or scholars of the prophets. The original words *pi shenayim* mean rather "two parts" than double the quantity.

10. *A hard thing.* This is what is not in my power; God alone can give this. Yet *if thou see me . . . taken from thee, it shall be so.* Perhaps this means no more than, "If thou continue with me till I am translated, God will grant this to thee."

11. *A chariot of fire, and horses of fire.* That is, a chariot and horses of the most resplendent glory.

ALEXANDER MACLAREN:

Elijah's end is in keeping with his career. From his first abrupt appearance it had been fitly symbolized by the stormy wind and flaming fire which he heard and saw at Horeb, and now these were to be the vehicles which should sweep him into the heavens. He came like a whirlwind, he burned like a fire, and in fire and whirlwind he disappeared. The story is wonderful in emotion and simplicity. Surely never was such a miracle told so quietly. The actual ascension is narrated in a sentence. Its preliminaries take up the rest of this narrative.

—*Expositions of Holy Scripture*

MATTHEW HENRY

yet he lamented the loss of him, for he loved him, and could have served him for ever. 3. He gave him a very honourable character. He himself had lost the guide of his youth: *My father, my father.* The public had lost its best guard; he was *the chariot of Israel, and the horsemen thereof.* He would have brought them all to heaven, as in this chariot, if it had not been their own fault.

Verses 13–18

What followed immediately after the translation of Elijah.

I. The tokens of God's presence with Elisha, and the marks of his elevation into Elijah's room.

1. He was possessed of Elijah's mantle, the badge of his office, which, we may suppose, he put on and wore for his master's sake, *v.* 13. When Elijah went to heaven he left his mantle as a legacy to Elisha, and, as it was a token of the descent of the Spirit upon him, it was more than if he had bequeathed to him thousands of gold and silver. Elisha took it up as a significant garment to be worn. He that then so cheerfully obeyed the summons of it, and became Elijah's servant, is now dignified with it, and becomes his successor.

2. He was possessed of Elijah's power to divide Jordan, *v.* 14. Having parted with his father, he returns to his sons in the schools of the prophets. Jordan was between him and them; it had been divided to make way for Elijah to his glory; he will try whether it will divide to make way for him to his business. Elijah's last miracle shall be Elisha's first. In dividing the waters, (1) He made use of Elijah's mantle, as Elijah himself had done (*v.* 8), to signify that he designed to keep to his master's methods. (2) He applied to Elijah's God: *Where is the Lord God of Elijah?* He does not ask, "Where is Elijah?" "The God that owned, and protected, and provided for Elijah, and many ways honoured him, especially now at last, where is he? Lord, am not I promised Elijah's spirit? Make good that promise." The words which next follow in the original, *aph-his—even he,* which we join to the following clause, *when he also had smitten the waters,* some make an answer to this question, *Where is Elijah's God? "He is in being still,* and nigh at hand. We have lost Elijah, but we have not lost Elijah's God. He *has not forsaken the earth;* it is even he that is still with me." Those that walk in the spirit and steps of their godly faithful predecessors shall certainly experience the same grace that they experienced; Elijah's God will be Elisha's too. The Lord God of the holy prophets is the same yesterday, today, and for ever; and what will it avail us to have the mantles of those that are gone, their places, their books, if we have not their spirit, their God?

3. He was possessed of Elijah's interest in the sons of the prophets, *v.* 15. Some, who had placed themselves conveniently near Jordan, to see what passed, were surprised to see Jordan divided before Elisha in his return, and took that as a convincing evidence that *the spirit of Elijah did rest upon him.* Accordingly they went to meet him, to congratulate him on his safe passage through fire and water, and the honour God had put upon him; and they *bowed themselves to the ground before him.* They were trained up in the schools; Elisha was taken from the plough; yet when they perceived that God was with him, and that this was *the man whom he delighted to honour,* they readily submitted to him as their head and father, as the people to Joshua when Moses was dead, Joshua i. 17. Whomsoever God honours, we must.

II. The needless search which the sons of the prophets made for Elijah. 1. They suggested that possibly he was dropped, either alive or dead, upon some mountain, or in some valley, *v.* 16. Some of them perhaps started this as a demurrer to the choice of Elisha: "Let us first be sure that Elijah has quite gone." 2. Elisha consented not till they overcame him with importunity, *v.* 17. They urged him till he was ashamed to oppose it any further, lest he should be thought wanting in his respect to his old master or loth to resign the mantle again. 3. The issue made them ashamed of their proposal. Their messengers, after they had tired themselves with fruitless search, returned and gave Elisha an opportunity of upbraiding his friends with their folly: *Did I not say unto you, Go not? v.* 18. Traversing hills and valleys will never bring us to Elijah, but the imitation of his holy faith and zeal will, in due time.

Verses 19–25

Elisha wrought more miracles than Elijah. Some reckon them in number just double. Two are recorded in these verses—a miracle of mercy to Jericho and a miracle of judgment to Bethel, Ps. ci. 1.

I. Here is a blessing upon the waters of Jericho,

JAMIESON, FAUSSET, BROWN

12. Elisha saw it, and he cried, My father—i.e., spiritual father, as the pupils of the prophets are called their sons. **the chariot of Israel, and the horseman thereof**—i.e., that as earthly kingdoms are dependent for their defense and glory upon warlike preparations, there a single prophet had done more for the preservation and prosperity of Israel than all her chariots and horsemen. **took hold of his own clothes and rent them**—in token of his grief for his loss.

13. He took up also the mantle of Elijah—The transference of this prophetic cloak was, to himself, a pledge of his being appointed successor, and it was an outward token to others of the spirit of Elijah resting upon him.

14-18. smote the waters—The waving of the mantle on the river, and the miraculous division of the waters consequent upon it, was an evidence that the Lord God of Elijah was with him, and as this miracle was witnessed by the scholars of the prophets from Jericho, they forthwith recognized the pre-eminence of Elisha, as now the prophet of Israel.

16-18. fifty strong men, let them go, we pray thee, and seek thy master—Though the young prophets from Jericho had seen Elijah's miraculous passage of the Jordan, they had not witnessed the ascension. They imagined that he might have been cast by the whirlwind on some mountain or valley; or, if he had actually been admitted into heaven, they expected that his body would still be remaining somewhere on earth. In compliance with their importunity, he gave them permission, but told them what the result would be.

ADAM CLARKE

12. *The chariot of Israel and the horsemen thereof.* The Chaldee translates these words thus: "My master, my master! who, by thy intercession, wast of more use to Israel than horses and chariots." This is probably the sense. *And rent them in two pieces.* As a sign of sorrow for having lost so good and glorious a master.

13. *He took . . . the mantle.* The same with which he had been called by Elijah to the prophetic office, and the same by which Elijah divided Jordan. His having the mantle was a proof that he was invested with the authority and influence of his master.

15. *The spirit of Elijah doth rest on Elisha.* This was a natural conclusion, from seeing him with the mantle, and working the same miracle. This disposed them to yield the same obedience to him they had done to his master: and in token of this, they went out "to meet him, and bowed themselves to the ground before him."

16. *Fifty strong men.* Probably the same fifty who are mentioned in v. 7, and who saw Elijah taken up in the whirlwind. *Cast him upon some mountain.* Though they saw him taken up towards heaven, yet they thought it possible that the Spirit of the Lord might have descended with him, and left him on some remote mountain valley. *Ye shall not send.* He knew that he was translated to heaven, and that therefore it would be useless.

17. *Till he was ashamed.* He saw they would not be satisfied unless they made the proposed search; he felt therefore that he could not, with any good grace, resist their importunity any longer.

MATTHEW HENRY

which was effectual to heal them. Jericho was built in disobedience to a command, but even within those walls that were built by iniquity we find a nursery of piety. Hither Elisha came, to confirm the souls of the disciples with a more particular account of Elijah's translation than their spies, who saw at a distance, could give them. Here he stayed while the fifty men were searching for him. And, 1. The men of Jericho represented to him their grievance, *v.* 19. They had not applied to Elijah concerning the matter, perhaps because he was not so easy of access as Elisha was. The situation was pleasant and afforded a good prospect; but they had neither wholesome water to drink nor fruitful soil to yield them food. Some think that it was not all the ground about Jericho that was barren and had bad water, but some one part only. 2. He soon redressed their grievance. Prophets should endeavour to make every place they come to, some way or other, the better for them, endeavouring to sweeten bitter spirits, and to make barren souls fruitful, by the due application of the word of God. Elisha will heal their waters; but, (1) They must furnish him with salt in a new cruse, *v.* 20. If salt had been proper to season the water, yet what could so small a quantity do towards it and what the better for being in a new cruse? But thus those that would be helped must be employed and have their faith and obedience tried. God's works of grace are wrought, not by any operations of ours, but in observance of his institutions. (2) He cast the salt *into the spring of the waters,* and so healed the streams and the ground they watered. Thus the way to reform men's lives is to renew their hearts; let those be seasoned with the salt of grace, for *out of them are the issues of life.* Purify the heart and that will cleanse the hands. (3) He did not pretend to do this by his own power, but in God's name: *Thus saith the Lord, I have healed these waters.* By doing them this kindness with a *Thus saith the Lord,* they would be made the more willing, hereafter, to receive from him a reproof, admonition, or command, with the same preface. (4) The cure was lasting, and not for the present only: *The waters were healed unto this day, v.* 22.

II. A curse upon the children of Bethel. At Bethel there was another school of prophets. Thither Elisha went next, and the scholars welcomed him with all possible respect, but the townsmen were abusive to him. One of Jeroboam's calves was at Bethel; this they were proud of, and hated those that reproved them. We may suppose it was their usual practice to jeer the prophets as they went along the streets, to call them by some nickname or other, and, if possible, drive them out of their town. Had the abuse done to Elisha been the first offence of that kind, it is probable that it would not have been so severely punished. But *mocking the messengers of the Lord,* and *misusing the prophets,* was one of the *crying sins of Israel,* as we find, 2 Chron. xxxvi. 16. 1. An instance of that sin. The little *children of Bethel,* the boys and girls that were playing in the streets, went out to meet him, gathered about him and mocked him, as if he had been a fool. *Go up, thou bald head, go up, thou bald head.* It was his character as a prophet that they designed to abuse. The honour God had crowned him with should have been sufficient to cover his bald head and protect him from their scoffs. These children said as they were taught; they had learned of their idolatrous parents to call foul names and give bad language, especially to prophets. These young cocks, as we say, crowed after the old ones. 2. A specimen of that ruin which came upon Israel at last, for misusing God's prophets, and of which this was intended to give them fair warning. Elisha heard their taunts, a good while, with patience; but at length he *turned and looked upon them,* to try if a grave and severe look would put them out of countenance, but they *were not ashamed,* and therefore he *cursed them in the name of the Lord,* to punish the dishonour done to God. His summons was immediately obeyed; two she-bears came out of an adjacent wood, and presently killed forty-two children, *v.* 24. The prophet must be justified, for he did it by divine impulse. He intended hereby to punish the parents and to make them afraid of God's judgments. Let parents, that would have comfort in their children, train them up well. In vain do we look for good from those children whose education we have neglected; and in vain do we grieve for those miscarriages which our care might have prevented.

JAMIESON, FAUSSET, BROWN

19-25. ELISHA HEALS THE WATERS. **20. Bring me a new cruse, and put salt therein**—The noxious qualities of the water could not be corrected by the infusion of salt—for, supposing the salt was possessed of such a property, a whole spring could not be purified by a dishful for a day, much less in all future time. The pouring in of the salt was a symbolic act with which Elisha accompanied the word of the Lord, by which the spring was healed [KEIL].

23, 24. there came forth little children—i.e., the idolatrous, or infidel young men of the place, who affecting to disbelieve the report of his master's translation, sarcastically urged him to follow in the glorious career. **bald head**—an epithet of contempt in the East, applied to a person even with a bushy head of hair. The appalling judgment that befell them was God's interference to uphold his newly invested prophet.

ADAM CLARKE

19. *The water is naught, and the ground barren.* The barrenness of the ground was the effect of the badness of the water.

21. *And cast the salt in there.* He cast in the salt at the place where the waters sprang out of the earth. Jarchi well observes here, "Salt is a thing which corrupts water; therefore, it is evident that this was a true miracle."

23-24. *There came forth little children out of the city.* These were probably the school of some celebrated teacher; but under his instruction they had learned neither piety nor good manners. *Go up, thou bald head; go up, thou bald head.* Does not this imply the grossest insult? "Ascend, you empty skull, to heaven," as it is pretended your master did! This was blasphemy against God; and their punishment (for they were Bethelite idolaters) was only proportioned to their guilt. Elisha *cursed them,* i.e., pronounced a curse upon them, *in the name of the Lord, beshem Yehovah,* "by the name (or authority) of Jehovah." The spirit of their offense lies in their ridiculing a miracle of the Lord; the offense was against the Lord, and He punished it. It was no petulant humor of the prophet that caused him to pronounce this curse; it was God alone. Had it proceeded from a wrong disposition of the prophet, no miracle would have been wrought in order to gratify it.

"But was it not a cruel thing to destroy forty-two little children, who, in mere childishness, had simply called the prophet bare skull, or bald head?" I answer, Elisha did not destroy them; he had no power by which he could bring two she-bears out of the wood to destroy them. It was evidently either accidental or a divine judgment; and if a judgment, God must be the sole Author of it. Elisha's "curse" must be only declaratory of what God was about to do. "But then, as they were little children, they could scarcely be accountable for their conduct; and consequently, it was cruelty to destroy them." But were they *little children?* for here the strength of the objection lies. Now I suppose the objection means children from four to seven or eight years old, for so we use the word; but the original, *nearim ketannim,* may mean "young men," for *katon* signifies to be "young," in opposition to "old," and is so translated in various places in our Bible; and *naar* signifies not only a "child" but a "young man," a "servant," or even a "soldier," or one fit to go out to battle; and is so translated in a multitude of places in our common English version. Isaac was called *naar* when twenty-eight years old, Gen. xxi. 5-12; and Joseph was so called when he was thirty-nine, Gen. xli. 12. Add to these 1 Kings xx. 14: "And Ahab said, By whom [shall the Assyrians be delivered into my hand]? And he said, Thus saith the Lord, Even by the young men of the princes of the provinces." That these were soldiers, probably militia, or a selection from the militia, which served as a bodyguard to Ahab, the event sufficiently declares; and the persons that mocked Elisha were perfectly accountable for their conduct.

But is it not possible that these forty-two were a set of unlucky young men, who had been employed in the wood, destroying the whelps of these same *she-bears,* who now pursued them, and tore them to pieces, for the injury they had done? We have already heard of the ferocity of "a bear robbed of her whelps"; see at the end of 2 Samuel, chap. xvii. The mention of *she-bears* gives some color to the above conjecture; and, probably, at the time when these young fellows insulted the prophet, the bears might be tracing the footsteps of the murderers of their young, and thus came upon them in the midst of their insults, God's providence ordering these occurrences so as to make this natural effect appear as a divine cause.

MATTHEW HENRY

CHAPTER 3

Verses 1–5

Jehoram, the son of Ahab, and brother of Ahaziah, is here upon the throne of Israel; and, though he was a bad man, yet two commendable things are here recorded of him:

I. That he removed his father's idols. He did evil in many things, but not like his father Ahab or his mother Jezebel, *v.* 2. Perhaps Jehoshaphat, though by his alliance with the house of Ahab he made his own family worse, did something towards making Ahab's better. Jehoram *put away the image of Baal*, resolving to worship the God of Israel only, and consult none but his prophets. So far was well, yet it did not prevent the destruction of Ahab's family. 1. He only put away the image of Baal *which his father had made*. He did not destroy the worship of Baal among the people, for Jehu found it prevalent, *ch.* x. 19. It was well to reform his family, but he ought to have used his power for the reforming of his kingdom. 2. When he put away the image of Baal, he adhered to the worship of the calves, that politic sin of Jeroboam, *v.* 3. *He departed not therefrom*, by which the division between the two tribes was supported. Those do not truly reform, who only part with the sins that they lose by, but continue their affection to the sins that they get by. 3. He only *put away* the image of Baal, he did not break it in pieces, as he ought to have done.

II. That he did what he could to recover his brother's losses. As he had something more of the religion of an Israelite than his father, so he had something more of the spirit of a king than his brother. Moab rebelled against Israel immediately upon the death of Ahab, *ch.* i. 1. And we do not find that Ahaziah made any attempt to chastise or reduce them. The tribute which the king of Moab paid was a very considerable branch of the revenue of the crown of Israel: 100,000 *lambs, and* 100,000 *wethers, v.* 4. Taxes were then paid not so much in money as in the commodities of the country. The revolt of Moab was a great loss to Israel, yet Ahaziah sat still in sloth and ease. But an upper chamber in his house proved as fatal to him as the high places of the field could have been (*ch.* i. 2), and the breaking of his lattice let into his throne a man of a more active genius.

Verses 6–19

Jehoram has no sooner got the sceptre into his hand than he takes the sword to reduce Moab.

I. The concerting of this expedition between Jehoram king of Israel and Jehoshaphat king of Judah. Jehoram levied an army (*v.* 6), and such an opinion he had of the godly king of Judah that, 1. He courted him to be his confederate: *Wilt thou go with me against Moab?* And he gained him. Judah and Israel, though unhappily divided from each other, yet can unite against Moab a common enemy. Jehoshaphat treats with Israel as a sister-kingdom. Those are no friends to their own peace and strength who can never find in their hearts to forgive and forget an old injury. 2. He consulted him as his confidant, *v.* 8. He took advice of Jehoshaphat, who had more wisdom and experience than himself, which way they should make their descent upon the country of Moab; and he advised that they should not march against them the nearest way, over Jordan, but go round *through the wilderness of Edom*, that they might take the king of Edom (who was tributary to him) and his forces along with them.

II. The great straits that the army of the confederates was reduced to in this expedition. Before they saw the face of an enemy they were all in danger of perishing for want of water, *v.* 9. The king of Israel sadly lamented the present distress, and the imminent danger. It was he that had *called these kings together*; yet he charges it upon Providence, and reflects upon that as unkind.

III. Jehoshaphat's good motion to ask counsel of God in this exigency, *v.* 11. The place they were now in could not but remind them of the *wonders of which their fathers told them*, the waters fetched out of the rock. The thought of this, we may suppose, encouraged Jehoshaphat to ask, *Is there not here a prophet of the Lord*, like unto Moses? It was well that Jehoshaphat enquired of the Lord now, but it would have been much better if he had done it sooner, before he steered this course; so the distress might have been prevented.

IV. Elisha recommended as a proper person for them to consult with, *v.* 11. We may suppose it was by special direction from heaven that Elisha attended the war, as *the chariot of Israel and the horsemen thereof.* A servant of the king of Israel knew of his being there when the King himself did not. Probably

JAMIESON, FAUSSET, BROWN

CHAPTER 3

Vss. 1-3. JEHORAM'S EVIL REIGN OVER ISRAEL. **1. Jehoram the son of Ahab began to reign over Israel in Samaria the eighteenth year of Jehoshaphat**—(cf. I Kings 22:51). To reconcile the statements in the two passages, we must suppose that Ahaziah, having reigned during the seventeenth and the greater part of the eighteenth year of Jehoshaphat, was succeeded by his brother Joram or Jehoram, in the end of that eighteenth year, or else that Ahaziah, having reigned two years in conjunction with his father, died at the end of that period when Jehoram ascended the throne. His policy was as hostile as that of his predecessors to the true religion; but he made some changes. Whatever was his motive for this alteration—whether dread of the many alarming judgments the patronage of idolatry had brought upon his father; or whether it was made as a small concession to the feelings of Jehoshaphat, his ally, he abolished idolatry in its gross form and restored the symbolic worship of God, which the kings of Israel, from the time of Jeroboam, had set up as a partition wall between their subjects and those of Judah.

4, 5. MESHA, KING OF MOAB, REBELS. **4-6. Mesha king of Moab,** etc.—As his dominions embraced an extensive pasture country, he paid, as annual tribute, the wool of 100,000 lambs and 100,000 rams. It is still common in the East to pay custom and taxes in the fruits or natural produce of the land. **5. king of Moab rebelled**—This is a repetition of ch. 1:1, in order to introduce an account of the confederate expedition for crushing this revolt, which had been allowed to continue unchecked during the short reign of Ahaziah.

6-24. ELISHA PROMISES WATER AND VICTORY OVER MOAB. **6. King Jehoram . . . numbered Israel**—made a levy from his own subjects, and at the same time sought an alliance with Jehoshaphat, which, as on the former occasion with Ahab, was readily promised (I Kings 22:4).

8, 9. Which way shall we go? And he answered, The way through the wilderness of Edom—This was a long and circuitous route, by the southern bend of the Dead Sea. Jehoshaphat however preferred it, partly because the part of the Moabite territory at which they would arrive, was the most defenseless; and partly because he would thereby enlist, in the expedition, the forces of the king of Edom. But, in penetrating the deep, rocky valley of Ahsy, which forms the boundary between Edom and Moab, the confederate army was reduced, both man and beast, to the greatest extremities for want of water. They were disappointed by finding the wady of this valley, the brook Zered (Deut. 2:13-18) [ROBINSON], dry. Jehoram was in despair. But the pious mind of Jehoshaphat inquired for a prophet of the Lord; and, on being informed that Elisha was at hand, "the three kings went down to him"; i.e., to his tent, which was either in the camp, or close by it. He had been directed thither by the Spirit of God for this special purpose. They went to him, not only as a mark of respect, but to supplicate for his assistance.

11. which poured water on the hands of Elijah—i.e., was his servant—this being one of the common offices of a servant. The phrase is used here as synonymous with "a true and eminent prophet," who will reveal God's will to us.

ADAM CLARKE

CHAPTER 3

2. *He put away the image of Baal.* He abolished his worship; but he continued that of the calves at Dan and Bethel.

4. *Was a sheepmaster.* The original is *naked*, of which the Seputagint could make nothing, and therefore retained the Hebrew word; but the Chaldee has "a sheepmaster." The original signifies one who "marks" or "brands," probably from the marking of sheep. He fed many sheep and had them all marked in a particular way, in order to ascertain his property. *An hundred thousand lambs.* The Chaldee and Arabic have "a hundred thousand fat oxen."

7. *My people as thy people.* We find that Jehoshaphat maintained the same friendly intercourse with the son as he did with the father. See 1 Kings xxii. 4.

8. *Through the wilderness of Edom.* Because he expected the king of Edom to join them, as we find he did; for, being tributary to Judah, he was obliged to do it.

9. *A compass of seven days' journey.* By taking a circuitous route, to go round the southern part of the Dead Sea, they probably intended to surprise the Moabites; but it appears their journey was ill-planned, as they at last got into a country in which it was impossible to obtain water, and they were brought in consequence to the utmost extremity.

10. *The Lord hath called these three kings together.* That is, This is a divine judgment; God has judicially blinded us, and permitted us to take this journey to our destruction.

11. *Is there not here a prophet of the Lord.* The kings of Judah still acknowledged the true God, and Him only. *Poured water on the hands of Elijah.* That is, was his constant and confidential servant.

MATTHEW HENRY

it was such a servant as Obadiah was to his father Ahab, one that *feared the Lord*; to such a one Elisha made himself known, not to the kings.

V. The application which the kings made to Elisha. They went down to him to his quarters, *v.* 12. He that humbled himself was thus exalted, and looked great, when three kings came to knock at his door, and beg his assistance.

VI. The entertainment which Elisha gave them. 1. He was very plain with the wicked king of Israel (*v.* 13): "*What have I to do with thee? Get thee to the prophets of thy father and mother*, whom they hast countenanced and maintained in thy prosperity, and let them help thee now in thy distress. The world and the flesh have ruled you, let them help you; why should God be *enquired of by* you?" Ezek. xiv. 3. Elisha tells him to his face, in a holy indignation at his wickedness, that he can scarcely find in his heart to *look towards him* or to *see him*, *v.* 14. Jehoram is to be respected as a prince. Elisha, as a subject, will honour him, but as a prophet he will cause him to know his iniquity. Jehoram has so much self-command as to take this plain dealing patiently; he cares not now for hearing of the prophets of Baal, but is a humble suitor to the God of Israel and his prophet, representing the present case as very deplorable and humbly recommending it to the prophet's compassionate consideration. In effect, he owns himself unworthy, but let not the other kings be ruined for his sake. 2. Elisha showed a great respect to the godly king of Judah, *regarded his presence*, and, for his sake, would *enquire of the Lord* for them all. 3. He composed himself to receive instructions from God, yet his zeal for the present indisposed him for prayer and the operations of the Spirit, which required a mind very calm and sedate. He therefore called for a musician (*v.* 15), a devout musician, one accustomed to play upon his harp and sing psalms to it. Elisha being refreshed, and having the tumult of his spirits laid by this divine music, *the hand of the Lord came upon him*, and his visit did him more honour than that of three kings. 4. God, by him, gave them assurance that the issue of the present distress would be comfortable and glorious. (1) They should speedily be supplied with water, *v.* 16, 17. To try their faith and obedience, he bids them *make the valley full of ditches* to receive the water. Elijah, by prayer, obtained water out of the clouds, but Elisha fetches it nobody knows whence. **The spring of these waters shall be as secret as the head of the Nile. God is not tied to second causes.** Ordinarily it is by a plentiful rain that God *confirms his inheritance* (Ps. lxviii. 9), but here it is done without rain, at least without rain in that place. (2) That supply should be an earnest of victory (*v.* 18): "*This is but a light thing in the sight of the Lord;* you shall not only be saved from perishing, but shall return in triumph." It is promised that they shall be masters of the rebellious country.

Verses 20–27

I. We have here the divine gift of both those things which God had promised by Elisha—water and victory, and the former not only a pledge of the latter, but a means of it.

1. It relieved their armies, which were ready to perish, *v.* 20. And this relief came just at the time of the *offering of the morning sacrifice* upon the altar at Jerusalem. We now cannot pitch upon any hour more acceptable than another, because our high priest is always appearing for us, to present and plead his sacrifice. That time God chose for the hour of mercy to put an honour upon the daily sacrifice, which had been despised. God answered Daniel's prayer just at the *time of the evening sacrifice* (Dan. ix. 21).

2. It deceived their enemies, who were ready to triumph, promising themselves that it would be easy dealing with an army fatigued by so long a march through the wilderness of Edom.

(1) How easily they were drawn into their own delusions. [1] They saw the water in the valley where the army of Israel encamped, and conceited it was blood (*v.* 22), because they knew the valley to be dry, and could not imagine it should be water. The sun shone upon it, probably the sky was red and lowering, making the water look red, which made them willing to believe *This is blood.* [2] If their camp was thus full of blood, they conclude, "Certainly the kings have fallen out and they have *slain one another*" (*v.* 23). "*Now therefore, Moab, to the spoil.*"

(2) How fatally they thereby ran upon their own destruction. They rushed carelessly into the camp of Israel, to plunder it, but were undeceived when it was too late. The Israelites, animated by the assurances Elisha had given them of victory, fell upon

JAMIESON, FAUSSET, BROWN

13. What have I to do with thee, etc.—Wishing to produce a deep spirit of humility and contrition, Elisha gave a stern repulse to the king of Israel, accompanied by a sarcastic sneer, in bidding him go and consult Baal and his soothsayers.

But the distressed condition, especially the imploring language, of the royal suppliants, who acknowledged the hand of the Lord in this distress, drew from the prophet the solemn assurance, that solely out of respect to Jehoshaphat, the Lord's true servant, did he take any interest in Jehoram. **15. bring me a minstrel**—The effect of music in soothing the mind is much regarded in the East; and it appears that the ancient prophets, before entering their work, commonly resorted to it, as a preparative, by praise and prayer, to their receiving the prophetic afflatus. **the hand of the Lord**—a phrase significantly implying that the gift of prophecy was not a natural or inherent gift, but conferred by the power and grace of God. **16. Make this valley full of ditches**—capable of holding water. **17. Ye shall not see wind**—It is common in the East to speak of *seeing* wind, from the clouds of straw, dust, or sand, that are often whirled into the air, after a long drought.

20. when the meat offering was offered—i.e., at the time of the morning sacrifice, accompanied, doubtless, with solemn prayers; and these led, it may be, by Elisha on this occasion, as on a similar one by Elijah (I Kings 18:36).

behold, there came water by the way of Edom—Far from the Israelitish camp, in the eastern mountains of Edom, a great fall of rain—a kind of cloudburst took place, by which the wady was at once filled, but they saw neither the wind nor the rains. The divine interposition was shown by introducing the laws of nature to the determined end in the predetermined way [KEIL]. It brought not only aid to the Israelitish army in their distress, by a plentiful supply of water, but destruction on the Moabites, who, perceiving the water, under the refulgent rays of the morning sun, red like blood, concluded the confederate kings had quarrelled and deluged the field with their mutual slaughter; so that, rushing to their camp in full expectation of great spoil, they were met by the Israelites, who, prepared for battle, fought and pursued them.

ADAM CLARKE

12. *The word of the Lord is with him.* He has the gift of prophecy.

13. *Get thee to the prophets of thy father.* This was a just but cutting reproof.

14. *Were it not that I regard the presence of Jehoshaphat.* He worshipped the true God; Jehoram was an idolater.

15. *Bring me a minstrel.* A person who played on the harp. To be able to discern the voice of God, and the operation of His hand, it is necessary that the mind be calm, and the passions all in harmony, under the direction of reason, that reason may be under the influence of the Divine Spirit. *The hand of the Lord came upon him.* The playing of the harper had the desired effect; his mind was calmed, and the power of God descended upon him.

16. *Make this valley full of ditches.* The word *nachal* may be translated "brook," as it is by the Vulgate and Septuagint. There probably was a river here, but it was now dry; and the prophet desires that they would enlarge the channel, and cut out various canals from it, and reservoirs, where water might be collected for the refreshment of the army and of the cattle; and these were to be made so wide that the reflection of the sun's rays from this water might be the means of confounding and destroying the Moabites.

17. *Ye shall not see wind.* There shall be no wind to collect vapors, and there shall be no showers, and yet the whole bed of this river, and all the new-made canals, shall be filled with water.

19. *Shall fell every good tree.* Every tree by which your enemies may serve themselves for fortifications. But surely fruit trees are not intended here; for this was positively against the law of God, Deut. xx. 19-20. *Stop all wells of water.* In those hot countries this would lead sooner than anything else to reduce an enemy. *Mar every good piece of land with stones.* Such a multitude of men, each throwing a stone on a good field as they passed, would completely destroy it.

20. *When the meat offering was offered.* This was the first of all offerings, and was generally made at sunrising. *There came water.* This supply was altogether miraculous, for there was neither wind nor rain, nor any other natural means by which it could be supplied.

22. *Saw the water on the other side as red as blood.* This might have been an optical deception.

23. *Therefore, Moab, to the spoil.* Thus they came on in a disorderly manner, and fell an easy prey to their enemies.

MATTHEW HENRY

them with the utmost fury, routed them, and pursued them into their own country (*v.* 24), which they laid waste (*v.* 25), destroyed the cities, marred the ground, stopped up the wells, felled the timber, and left only the royal city standing, in the walls of which they made great breaches with their battering engines.

II. In the close of the chapter we are told what the king of Moab did when he found himself reduced to the last extremity. 1. He attempted that which was bold and brave. He got together 700 choice men, and with them sallied out upon the intrenchments of the king of Edom, who, being but a mercenary in this expedition, would not, he hoped, make any great resistance if vigorously attacked, and so he might make his escape that way. But it would not do; even the king of Edom proved too hard for him, and obliged him to retire, *v.* 26. 2. This failing, he did that which was brutish and barbarous; he took his own son, his eldest son, that was to succeed him, than whom nothing could be more dear to himself and his people, and *offered him for a burnt-offering upon the wall*, *v.* 27. He designed by this, (1) To obtain the favour of Chemosh his god, which, being a devil, delighted in blood and murder, and the destruction of mankind. (2) To terrify the besiegers, and oblige them to retire. Therefore he did it *upon the wall*, in their sight, that they might see what desperate courses he resolved to take rather than surrender, and how dearly he would sell his city and life.

JAMIESON, FAUSSET, BROWN

Their country was laid waste in the way, which has always been considered the greatest desolation in the East (vs. 24). **25. Kir-hareseth**—(now Kerak)—Castle of Moab—then, probably, the only fortress in the land.

27. took his eldest son that should have reigned in his stead, and offered him for a burnt offering, etc.—By this deed of horror, to which the allied army drove the king of Moab, a divine judgment came upon Israel; that is, the besiegers feared the anger of God, which they had incurred by giving occasion to the human sacrifice forbidden in the law (Lev. 18:21; 20:3), and hastily raised the siege.

ADAM CLARKE

25. *On every good piece of land.* On all cultivated ground, and especially fields that were sown. *Only in Kir-haraseth.* This was the royal city of the Moabites, and, as we learn from Scripture, exceedingly strong (see Isa. xvi. 7, 11), so that it is probable the confederate armies could not easily reduce it. The *slingers,* we are informed, went about the wall, and smote all the men that appeared on it, while no doubt the besieging army was employed in sapping the foundations.

26. *Seven hundred men.* These were no doubt the choice of all his troops, and being afraid of being hemmed up and perhaps taken by his enemies, whom he found on the eve of gaining possession of the city, he made a desperate sortie in order to regain the open country; and supposing that the quarter of the Edomites was weakest, or less carefully guarded, he endeavored to make his impression there; but they were so warmly received by the king of Edom that they failed in the attempt, and were driven back into the city. Hence he was led to that desperate act mentioned in the following verse.

MATTHEW HENRY

CHAPTER 4

Verses 1-7

Elisha's miracles were for use, not for show; this recorded here was an act of real charity. Such also were the miracles of Christ, not only great wonders, but great favours to those for whom they were wrought.

I. Elisha readily receives a poor widow's complaint. She was a prophet's widow. It seems, the prophets had wives as well as the priests. Marriage is honourable in all, and not inconsistent with the most sacred professions. Now, by the complaint of this poor woman (*v.* 1), we are given to understand, 1. That her husband, being *one of the sons of the prophets*, was well known to Elisha. 2. That he had the reputation of a godly man. He was one that kept his integrity in a time of general apostasy, one of the 7,000 that had not bowed the knee to Baal. 3. That he was dead. Those that were clothed with the spirit of prophecy were not thereby armed against the stroke of death. 4. That he died poor, and in debt more than he was worth. He did not contract his debts by prodigality, and luxury, and riotous living, for he was one that feared the Lord. Yet it may be the lot of those that fear God to be in debt, and insolvent, through afflictive providences, losses by sea, or bad debts, or their own imprudence, for the *children of light* are not always *wise for this world.* Perhaps this prophet was impoverished by persecution: when Jezebel ruled, prophets had much ado to live, and especially if they had families. 5. That the creditors were very severe with her. Two sons she had to be the support of her widowed state, and their labour is reckoned *assets* in her hand; that must go therefore, and they must be bondmen for seven years (Exod. xxi. 2) to work out this debt. In this distress the poor widow goes to Elisha, in dependence upon the promise that the seed of the righteous shall not be forsaken.

II. He effectually relieves this poor widow's distress, and puts her in a way both to pay her debt and to maintain herself and her family. He did not give her some small matter for her present provision, but set her up in the world to sell oil, and put a stock into her hand to begin with.

1. He directed her what to do, considered her case: *What shall I do for thee?* Elisha therefore enquired what she had to make money of, and found she had nothing to sell but one pot of oil, *v.* 2. If she had not had this pot of oil, the divine power could have supplied her; but, having this, it will work upon this, and so teach us to make the best of what we have. The prophet, knowing her to have credit among her neighbours, bids her borrow of them *empty vessels* (*v.* 3). He directs her to shut the door upon herself and her sons, while she filled all those vessels out of that one. The oil was to be multiplied in the pouring, as the other widow's meal in the spending. The way to increase what we have is to use it; to him that hath shall be given.

2. She did it firmly believing the divine power and goodness, and in obedience to the prophet. They were all amazed to find their pot, like a fountain of

JAMIESON, FAUSSET, BROWN

CHAPTER 4

Vss. 1-7. Elisha Augments the Widow's Oil. **1. there cried a certain woman of the wives of the sons of the prophets**—They were allowed to marry as well as the priests and Levites. Her husband, not enjoying the lucrative profits of business, had nothing but a professional income, which, in that irreligious age, would be precarious and very scanty, so that he was not in a condition to provide for his family.

the creditor is come to take unto him my two sons to be bondmen—By the enactment of the law, a creditor was entitled to claim the person and children of the insolvent debtor, and compel them to serve him as bondmen till the year of jubilee should set them free.

2. a pot—or cruet of oil. This comprising her whole stock of domestic utensils, he directs her to borrow empty vessels not a few; then, secluding herself with her children, she was to pour oil from her cruse into the borrowed vessels, and, selling the oil, discharge the debt, and then maintain herself and family with the remainder.

ADAM CLARKE

CHAPTER 4

1. *Sons of the prophets.* "Disciples of the prophets"; so the Targum here, and in all other places where the words occur, and properly too.

To take unto him my two sons to be bondmen. Children, according to the laws of the Hebrews, were considered the property of their parents, who had a right to dispose of them for the payment of their debts. And in cases of poverty, the law permitted them, expressly, to sell both themselves and their children; Exod. xxi. 7 and Lev. xxv. 39.

2. *Save a pot of oil.* Oil was used as aliment, for anointing the body after bathing, and to anoint the dead. Some think that this pot of oil was what this widow had kept for her burial (see Matt. xxvi. 12).

MATTHEW HENRY

living water, always flowing, and yet always full.

3. The oil continued flowing as long as she had any empty vessels to receive it. He gives above what we ask: were there more vessels, there is enough in God to fill them—enough for all, enough for each.

4. The prophet directed her what to do with the oil she had, *v.* 7. (1) She must sell the oil to those that were rich, and could afford to bestow it on themselves. (2) She must pay her debt with the money she received for her oil. It is one of the fundamental laws of our religion that we render to all their due, for conscience' sake. (3) The rest must not be laid up, but she and her children must live upon the money received, with which they must put themselves into a capacity of getting an honest livelihood. [1] Let those that are poor and in distress be encouraged to trust God. *Verily thou shalt be fed,* though not feasted. It is true we cannot now expect miracles, yet we may expect mercies, if we wait on God and seek to him. [2] Let those whom God has blessed with plenty use it for the glory of God and under the direction of his word.

Verses 8–17

The giving of a son to such as were old, and had been long childless, was an ancient instance of the divine power and favour; we find it here among the wonders wrought by Elisha.

I. The kindness of the Shunammite woman to Elisha. Shunem lay in the road between Samaria and Carmel, a road that Elisha often travelled, as we find *ch.* ii. 25. *There* lived *a great woman,* who was very hospitable. So famous a man as Elisha could not pass and repass unobserved. Probably this pious matron, having notice of his being there, constrained him to dine with her, *v.* 8. He was modest and loth to be troublesome, so that it was not without some difficulty that he was first drawn into an acquaintance there; but afterwards, whenever he went that way, he called. She suggests, 1. That the stranger she would invite was *a holy man of God,* who therefore would do good to their family. 2. That the kindness she intended him would be no great charge to them; she would build him only a little chamber. The furniture shall be very plain; a bed, and a table, a stool, and a candlestick, all that was needful for his convenience. Elisha seemed highly pleased with these accommodations.

II. Elisha's gratitude for this kindness. 1. He offered to use his interest for her in the king's court (*v.* 13): "*Wouldst thou be spoken for to the king, or the captain of the host,* for an office for thy husband, civil or military? Wherein can I serve thee?" But she needs not any good offices of this kind to be done for her: *I dwell* (says she) *among my own people,* that is, "We are well off as we are, and do not aim at preferment." Some years after this we find this Shunammite had occasion to be spoken for to the king, though now she needed it not, *ch.* viii. 3, 4. 2. He did use his interest for her in the court of heaven. Elisha consulted with his servant what kindness he should do for her. Gehazi reminded him that she was childless, had a great estate, but no son to leave it to, and was past hopes of having any, her husband being old. If Elisha could obtain this favour from God for her, it would be the removal of that which at present was her only grievance. He sent for her immediately. She very humbly and respectfully *stood in the door* (*v.* 15), according to her accustomed modesty, and then he assured her that within a year she should bring forth a son, *v.* 16. The event, within the time limited, confirmed the truth of the promise: *She bore a son* at the season that Elisha spoke of, *v.* 17.

Verses 18–37

We may well suppose that, after the birth of this son, the prophet was doubly welcome to the good Shunammite. He had thought himself indebted to her, but henceforth, as long as she lives, she will think herself in his debt, and that she can never do too much for him. We may also suppose that the child was very dear to the prophet, as the son of his prayers, and very dear to the parents, as the son of their old age.

I. The sudden death of the child. A child of promise, a child of prayer, and given in love, yet taken away. But how admirably does the prudent pious mother guard her lips under this surprising affliction! She had heard of the raising of the widow's son of Sarepta, and that the spirit of Elijah rested on Elisha; and such confidence had she of God's goodness that she was very ready to believe that he who so soon took away what he had given would restore what he had now taken away. In this faith she makes no preparation for the burial of her dead child, but for its resurrection; for she *lays him on the*

JAMIESON, FAUSSET, BROWN

6. the oil stayed—i.e., ceased to multiply; the benevolent object for which the miracle had been wrought having been accomplished.

8-17. PROMISES A SON TO THE SHUNAMMITE. **8. Elisha passed to Shunem**—now Sulam, in the plain of Esdraelon, at the southwestern base of Little Hermon. The prophet, in his journey, was often entertained here by one of its pions and opulent inhabitants.

10. Let us make a little chamber—not build, but prepare it. She meant a room in the *oleah,* the porch, or gateway (II Sam. 18:33; I Kings 17:19), attached to the front of the house, leading into the court and inner apartments. The front of the house, excepting the door, is a dead wall, and hence this room is called a chamber in the wall. It is usually appropriated to the use of strangers, or lodgers for a night, and, from its seclusion, convenient for study or retirement.

13. what is to be done for thee?—Wishing to testify his gratitude for the hospitable attentions of this family, he announced to her the birth of a son "about this time next year." The interest and importance of such an intelligence can only be estimated by considering that Oriental women, and Jewish in particular, connect ideas of disgrace with barrenness, and cherish a more ardent desire for children than women in any other part of the world (Gen. 18:10-15).

18-37. RAISES HER DEAD SON. **19. My head, my head!**—The cries of the boy, the part affected, and the season of the year, make it probable that he had been overtaken by a stroke of the sun. Pain, stupor, and inflammatory fever are the symptoms of the disease, which is often fatal.

ADAM CLARKE

6. *And the oil stayed.* While there was a vessel to fill, there was oil sufficient; and it ceased to flow only when there was no vessel to receive it. This is a good emblem of the grace of God. While there is an empty, longing heart, there is a continual overflowing fountain of salvation. If we find in any place or at any time that the oil ceases to flow, it is because there are no empty vessels there, no souls hungering and thirsting for righteousness. We find fault with the dispensations of God's mercy, and ask, Why were the former days better than these? Were we as much in earnest for our salvation as our forefathers were for theirs, we should have equal supplies, and as much reason to sing aloud of divine mercy.

8. *Elisha passed to Shunem.* This city was in the tribe of Issachar, to the south of the brook Kishon, and at the foot of Mount Tabor. *Where was a great woman.* Instead of *great woman,* the Chaldee has "a woman fearing sin"; the Arabic, "a woman eminent for piety before God." This made her truly great.

9. *This is an holy man of God.* That is, "a prophet," as the Chaldee interprets it. *Which passeth by us continually.* It probably lay in his way to some school of the prophets that he usually attended.

10. *Let us make a little chamber.* As the woman was convinced that Elisha was a prophet, she knew that he must have need of more privacy than the general state of her house could afford; and therefore she proposed what she knew would be a great acquisition to him, as he could live in this little chamber in as much privacy as if he were in his own house. The *bed,* the *table,* the *stool,* and the *candlestick* were really everything he could need by way of accommodation in such circumstances.

12. *Gehazi his servant.* This is the first time we hear of this very indifferent character.

13. *Wouldest thou be spoken for to the king?* Elisha must have had considerable influence with the king, from the part he took in the late war with the Moabites. *Or to the captain of the host?* As if he had said, Will you that I should procure you and your husband a place at court? *I dwell among mine own people.* I am perfectly satisfied and contented with my lot in life; I live on the best terms with my neighbors, and am here encompassed with my kindred, and feel no disposition to change my connections or place of abode. How few are there like this woman on the earth! How few are there that will not sacrifice everything—peace, domestic comfort, their friends, their conscience, and their God—for money, honors, grandeur, and parade?

14. *What then is to be done for her?* It seems that the woman retired as soon as she had delivered the answer mentioned in the preceding verse.

16. *Thou shalt embrace a son.* This promise, and the circumstances of the parties, are not very dissimilar to that relative to the birth of Isaac, and those of Abraham and Sarah.

18. *When the child was grown.* We know not of what age he was, very likely four or six, if not more years.

19. *My head, my head.* Probably affected by sunstroke, which might, in so young a subject, soon occasion death, especially in that hot country.

MATTHEW HENRY

prophet's bed (*v.* 21), expecting that he will stand her friend. *O woman! great is thy faith.*

II. The sorrowful mother's application to the prophet on this sad occasion; for it happened very opportunely that he was now at the college upon Mount Carmel, not far off.

1. She begged leave of her husband to go to the prophet, yet not acquainting him with her errand, lest he should not have faith enough to let her go, *v.* 22. See how this husband and wife vied with each other in showing mutual regard; she was so dutiful to him that she would not go till she had acquainted him with her journey, and he so kind to her that he would not oppose it, though she did not think fit to acquaint him with her business. 2. She made all the haste she could to the prophet (*v.* 24), and he, seeing her at a distance, sent his servant to enquire whether anything was amiss, *v.* 25, 26. The answer was general: *It is well.* Gehazi was not the man that she came to complain to, and therefore she put him off with this. Note, When God calls away our dearest relations by death it becomes us quietly to say, "It is well both with us and them;" it is well, for all is well that God does; all is well with those that are gone if they have gone to heaven, and all well with us that stay behind if by the affliction we are furthered in our way thither. 3. When she came to the prophet she humbly reasoned with him concerning her present affliction. Elisha waited to hear from her, since he might not know immediately from God, what was the cause of her trouble. What she said was very pathetic. She appealed to the prophet, (1) Concerning her indifference to this mercy which was now taken from her: "*Did I desire a son of my lord?* No, thou knowest I did not; it was thy own proposal, not mine; I did not fret for the want of a son, as Hannah, nor beg, as Rachel, *Give me children or else I die.*" (2) Concerning her entire dependence upon the prophet's word, pleading with the prophet for the raising of the child to life again: "*I said, Do not deceive me,* and I know thou wilt not."

III. The raising of the child to life again. We may suppose that the woman gave Elisha a more express account of the child's death, and he gave her a more express promise of his resurrection, than is here related, where we are briefly told,

1. That Elisha sent Gehazi to go in all haste to the dead child, gave him his staff, and bade him lay that on the face of the child, *v.* 29. Bishop Hall suggests that it was done out of human conceit, and not by divine instinct, and therefore it failed of the effect; God will not have such great favours made too cheap, nor shall they be too easily come by, lest they be undervalued.

2. The woman resolved not to go back without the prophet himself (*v.* 30): *I will not leave thee.* She had no great expectation from the staff, she would have the hand, and she was in the right of it.

3. The prophet, by earnest prayer, obtained from God the restoring of this dead child to life again. He found the child dead upon his own bed (*v.* 32), *and shut the door upon them twain, v.* 33.

(1) How closely the prophet applied himself to this great operation, perhaps being sensible that he had tempted God too much in thinking to effect it by the staff in Gehazi's hand. [1] He *prayed unto the Lord* (*v.* 33), probably as Elijah had done, *Let this child's soul come into him again.* Christ raised the dead to life as one having authority—*Damsel, arise—Young man, I say unto thee, Arise—Lazarus, come forth* (for he was powerful and faithful as a Son, the Lord of life), but Elijah and Elisha did it by petition, as servants. [2] He *lay upon the child* (*v.* 34), as if he would communicate to him some of his vital heat or spirits. He first *put his mouth to the child's mouth,* as if, in God's name, he would breathe into him the breath of life; then *his eyes to the child's eyes,* to open them again to the light of life; then *his hands to the child's hands,* to put strength into them. He then *returned, and walked in the house,* as one full of care and concern, and wholly intent upon what he was about. Then he went upstairs again, and, the second time, *stretched himself upon the child, v.* 35.

(2) How gradually the operation was performed. At the first application, *the flesh of the child waxed warm* (*v.* 34), which gave the prophet encouragement to continue instant in prayer. After a while, *the child sneezed seven times,* which was an indication, not only of life, but liveliness.

(3) How joyfully the child was restored alive to his mother (*v.* 36, 37), and all parties concerned *were not a little comforted,* Acts xx. 12.

Verses 38–44

Elisha in his place, in his element, among the sons of the prophets, teaching them, and, as a father,

JAMIESON, FAUSSET, BROWN

22. she called unto her husband—Her heroic concealment of the death from her husband is not the least interesting feature of the story.

24. Drive, and go forward—It is usual for women to ride on asses, accompanied by a servant, who walks behind and drives the beast with his stick, goading the animal at the speed required by his mistress. The Shunammite had to ride a journey of five or six hours to the top of Carmel. **26. And she answered, It is well**—Her answer was purposely brief and vague to Gehazi, for she reserved a full disclosure of her loss for the ear of the prophet himself. She had met Gehazi at the foot of the hill, and she stopped not in her ascent till she had disburdened her heavy-laden spirit at Elisha's feet. The violent paroxysm of grief into which she fell on approaching him, appeared to Gehazi an act of disrespect to his master; he was preparing to remove her when the prophet's observant eye perceived that she was overwhelmed with some unknown cause of distress. How great is a mother's love! how wondrous are the works of Providence! The Shunammite had not sought a son from the prophet—her child was, in every respect, the free gift of God. Was she then allowed to rejoice in the possession for a little, only to be pierced with sorrow by seeing the corpse of the cherished boy? Perish, doubt and unbelief! This event happened that "the works of God should be made manifest" in this prophet, "and for the glory of God."

29. take my staff . . . and lay . . . upon the face of the child—The staff was probably an official rod of a certain form and size. Necromancers used to send their staff with orders to the messengers to let it come in contact with nothing by the way that might dissipate or destroy the virtue imparted to it. Some have thought that Elisha himself entertained similar ideas, and was under an impression that the actual application of his staff would serve as well as the touch of his hand. But this is an imputation dishonorable to the character of the prophet. He wished to teach the Shunammite, who obviously placed too great dependence upon him, a memorable lesson to look to God. By sending his servant forward to lay his staff on the child, he raised her expectations, but, at the same time, taught her that his own help was unavailing—"there was neither voice, nor hearing." The command, to salute no man by the way, showed the urgency of the mission, not simply as requiring the avoidance of the tedious and unnecessary greetings so common in the East (Luke 10:1), but the exercise of faith and prayer. The act of Gehazi was allowed to fail, in order to free the Shunammite, and the people of Israel at large, of the superstitious notion of supposing a miraculous virtue resided in any *person,* or in any *rod,* and to prove that it was only through earnest prayer and faith in the power of God and for His glory that this and every miracle was to be performed. **34. lay upon the child,** etc.—(see on I Kings 17:21; Acts 20:10). Although this contact with a dead body would communicate ceremonial uncleanness, yet, in performing the great moral duties of piety and benevolence, positive laws were sometimes dispensed with, particularly by the prophets.

35. the child sneezed seven times, and the child opened his eyes—These were the first acts of restored respiration, and they are described as successive steps. Miracles were for the most part performed instantaneously; but sometimes, also, they were advanced progressively towards completion (I Kings 18:44, 45; Mark 8:24, 25).

ADAM CLARKE

21. *Laid him on the bed of the man of God.* She had no doubt heard that Elijah had raised the widow's son of Zarephath to life, and she believed that he who had obtained this gift from God for her could obtain his restoration to life.

23. *Wherefore wilt thou go?* She was a very prudent woman; she would not harass the feelings of her husband by informing him of the death of his son till she had tried the power of the prophet.

24. *Drive, and go forward.* It is customary in the East for a servant to walk alongside or drive the ass his master rides.

26. *It is well.* How strong was her faith in God and submission to His authority! Though the heaviest family affliction that could befall her and her husband had now taken place, yet, believing that it was a dispensation of Providence which was in itself neither unwise nor unkind, she said, "It is well with me, with my husband, and with my child."

27. *The Lord hath hid it from me, and hath not told me.* In reference to this point he had not now the discernment of spirits. This, and the gift of prophecy, were influences which God gave and suspended as His infinite wisdom saw good.

28. *Did I desire a son of my lord?* I expressed no such wish to you; I was contented and happy; and when you did promise me a son, *did I not say, Do not deceive me?*

29. *Salute him not.* Make all the haste you possibly can, and lay my staff on the face of the child. He probably thought that it might be a case of mere suspended animation or a swoon, and that laying the staff on the face of the child might act as a stimulus to excite the animal motions.

30. *I will not leave thee.* The prophet it seems had no design to accompany her; he intended to wait for Gehazi's return. But as the woman was well assured the child was dead, she was determined not to return till she brought the prophet with her.

33. *Prayed unto the Lord.* He had no power of his own by which he could restore the child.

34. *Lay upon the child.* Endeavored to convey a portion of his own natural warmth to the body of the child; and probably endeavored, by blowing into the child's mouth, to inflate the lungs and restore respiration. He uses every natural means in his power to restore life, while praying to the Author of it to exert a miraculous influence. Natural means are in our power; those that are supernatural belong to God. We should always do our own work, and beg of God to do His.

35. *Walked in the house to and fro.* In order, no doubt, that he might recover that natural warmth which was absorbed by the cold body of the child, that he might, by again taking it in his arms, communicate more warmth. *The child sneezed seven times.* That is, it sneezed "abundantly." When the nervous influence began to act on the muscular system, before the circulation could be in every part restored, particular muscles, if not the whole body, would be thrown into strong contractions and shiverings, and sneezing would be a natural consequence.

37. *She went in, and fell at his feet.* Few can enter into the feelings of this noble woman. What suspense must she have felt during the time that the prophet was employed in the slow process referred to above! for slow in its own nature it must have been, and exceedingly exhausting to the prophet himself.

MATTHEW HENRY

providing for them. There was a dearth in the land, for the wickedness of those that dwelt therein, the same that we read of, *ch.* viii. 1. It continued seven years, just as long again as that in Elijah's time.

I. He made hurtful food to become safe and wholesome. 1. The sons of the prophets being all to attend, he ordered his servant to provide food for their bodies, while he was breaking to them the bread of life for their souls. He orders only that pottage should be seethed for them of herbs, *v.* 38. The sons of the prophets should be examples of temperance and mortification. 2. One of the servitors, who was sent to gather herbs, by mistake brought in that which was noxious, and shred it into the pottage: *wild gourds* they are called, *v.* 39. Some think it was *coloquintida*, a herb strongly cathartic, and dangerous. 3. The guests complained to Elisha of the unwholesomeness of their food. They cried out, *There is death in the pot, v.* 40. 4. Elisha immediately cured the bad taste and prevented the bad consequences of this unwholesome pottage; as before he had healed the bitter waters with salt, so now the bitter broth with meal, *v.* 41. Now all was well, not only no death, but no harm in the pot.

II. He made a little food to go a great way. 1. Elisha had a present brought him of twenty barley-loaves and some ears of corn (*v.* 42), a present in a special manner valuable, when there was a dearth in the land. 2. Having freely received, he freely gave, ordering it all to be set before the sons of the prophets, reserving none for himself, none for hereafter. It well becomes the fathers of the prophets to be liberal to the sons of the prophets. 3. Though the loaves were little, yet with twenty of them he satisfied 100 men, *v.* 43, 44. His servant thought that to set so little meat before so many men was but to shame his master; but he, in God's name, pronounced it a full meal for them, and so it proved; they did eat, and left thereof, not because their stomachs failed them, but because the bread increased in the eating.

CHAPTER 5

Verses 1-8

Our Saviour's miracles were intended for the lost sheep of the house of Israel, yet one, like a crumb, fell from the table to a woman of Canaan; so this one miracle Elisha wrought for Naaman, a Syrian; for God does good to all, and will have all men to be saved.

I. The great affliction Naaman was under, in the midst of all his honours, *v.* 1. He was very acceptable to his prince, was his favourite, and prime-minister of state; a mighty man of valour, but he was a leper, a burden to himself. Every man has some *but* or other in his character, something that blemishes and diminishes him. Naaman was as great as the world could make him, and yet (as Bishop Hall expresses it) the basest slave in Syria would not change skins with him.

II. The notice that was given him of Elisha's power, by a little maid that waited on his lady, *v.* 2, 3. This maid was, by birth, an Israelite, providentially carried captive into Syria, into Naaman's family, where she published Elisha's fame to the honour of Israel and Israel's God. The unhappy dispersing of the people of God has sometimes proved the happy occasion of the diffusion of the knowledge of God, Acts viii. 4. This little maid, as became a true-born Israelite, consulted the honour of her country, and could give an account, though but a girl, of the famous prophet they had among them. As became a good servant, she desired the health and welfare of her master. *Elisha* had *not cleansed any leper in Israel* (Luke iv. 27), yet this little maid inferred that he *could* cure her master, and that he *would* do it, though he was a Syrian.

III. The application which the king of Syria hereupon made to the king of Israel on Naaman's behalf. See what Naaman did upon this little hint. 1. He would not send for the prophet to come to him, but such honour would he pay to one that had so much of a divine power with him as to be able to cure diseases that he would go to him himself. 2. He would not go *incognito—in disguise*, though his errand proclaimed his loathsome disease, but went in state, and with a great retinue, to do the more honour to the prophet. 3. He would not go empty-handed, but took with him gold, silver, and raiment, to present to his physician. 4. He would not go without a letter to the king of Israel from the king his master, who did himself earnestly desire his recovery.

IV. The alarm this gave to the king of Israel, *v.* 7. He apprehended there was in this letter, 1. A great affront upon God, and therefore he rent his clothes,

JAMIESON, FAUSSET, BROWN

38-41. PURIFIES DEADLY POTTAGE. **38. there was a dearth in the land**— (see on ch. 8:1). **the sons of the prophets were sitting before him**—When receiving instruction, the scholars sat under their masters. This refers to their being domiciled under the same roof (cf. ch. 6:1). **Set on the great pot**—As it is most likely that the Jewish would resemble the Egyptian "great pot," it is seen by the monumental paintings to have been a large goblet, with two long legs, which stood over the fire on the floor. The seethed pottage consisted of meat cut into small pieces, mixed with rice or meal and vegetables. **39. went out into the field to gather herbs**—Wild herbs are very extensively used by the people in the East, even by those who possess their own vegetable gardens. The fields are daily searched for mallow, asparagus, and other wild plants. **wild vine**—lit., "the vine of the field," supposed to be the *colocynth*, a cucumber, which, in its leaves, tendrils, and fruit, bears a strong resemblance to the wild vine. The "gourds," or fruit, are of the color and size of an orange bitter to the taste, causing colic, and exciting the nerves, eaten freely they would occasion such a derangement of the stomach and bowels as to be followed by death. The meal which Elisha poured into the pot was a symbolic sign that the noxious quality of the herbs was removed. **lap full**—The hyke, or large cloak, is thrown loosely over the left shoulder and fastened under the right arm, so as to form a lap or apron.

42-44. SATISFIES A HUNDRED MEN WITH TWENTY LOAVES. **43. They shall eat, and shall leave thereof**—This was not a miracle of Elisha, but only a prediction of one by the word of the Lord. Thus it differed widely from those of Christ (Matt. 15:37; Mark 8:8; Luke 9:17; John 6:12).

CHAPTER 5

VSS. 1-7. NAAMAN'S LEPROSY. **1. Naaman, captain of the host of the king of Syria, was a great man with his master**—highly esteemed for his military character and success. **and honourable**—rather, "very rich."

but he was a leper—This leprosy, which, in Israel, would have excluded him from society, did not affect his free intercourse in the court of Syria.

2. a little maid—who had been captured in one of the many predatory incursions which were then made by the Syrians on the northern border of Israel (see on I Sam. 30:8; ch. 13:21; 24:2). By this young Hebrew slave of his wife, Naaman's attention was directed to the prophet of Israel, as the person who would remove his leprosy.

Naaman, on communicating the matter to his royal master, was immediately furnished with a letter to the king of Israel, and set out for Samaria, carrying with him, as an indispensable preliminary in the East, very costly presents. **5. ten talents of silver**—$20,000 in silver, $60,000 in gold. **ten changes of raiment**—splendid dresses, for festive occasions—the honor being thought to consist not only in the beauty and fineness of the material, but on having a variety to put on one after another, in the same night. **7. when the king of Israel had read the letter, he rent his clothes**—According to an ancient practice among the Eastern people, the main

ADAM CLARKE

38. *Came again to Gilgal.* He had been there before with his master, a short time prior to his translation.

Set on the great pot, and seethe pottage for the sons of the prophets. It was in a time of dearth, and all might now stand in need of refreshment; and it appears that the prophet was led to put forth the power he had from God to make a plentiful provision for those who were present.

40. *There is death in the pot.* As if they had said, "We have here a deadly mixture; if we eat of it, we shall all die."

41. *Bring meal.* Though this might, in some measure, correct the strong acrid and purgative quality, yet it was only a miracle which could make a lapful of this fruit shred into pottage salutary.

42. *Bread of the firstfruits.* This was an offering to the prophet, as the firstfruits themselves were an offering to God. *Corn in the husk.* Probably parched corn or corn to be parched, a very frequent food in the East.

43. *Thus saith the Lord, They shall eat, and shall leave thereof.* It was God, not the prophet, who fed 100 men with these 20 loaves, etc. This is something like our Lord's feeding the multitude miraculously. Indeed, there are many things in this chapter similar to facts in our Lord's history.

CHAPTER 5

1. *Naaman, captain of the host.* Of Naaman we know nothing more than is related here. *King of Syria.* The Hebrew is *melech Aram,* "king of Aram," which is followed by the Chaldee and Arabic. The Septuagint and Vulgate have "Syria," and this is a common meaning of the term in Scripture. If the king of Syria be meant, it must be Ben-hadad; and the contemporary king of Israel was Jehoram. *A mighty man in valour.* "He was a giant, and very strong," according to the Arabic. He had, in a word, all the qualifications of an able general. *But he was a leper.* Here was a heavy tax upon his grandeur; he was afflicted with a disorder the most loathsome and the most humiliating that could possibly disgrace a human being.

2. *The Syrians had gone out by companies.* "Troops." *A little maid.* Who, it appears, had pious parents, who brought her up in the knowledge of the true God. Behold the goodness and the severity of the divine providence! Affectionate parents are deprived of their promising daughter by a set of lawless freebooters, without the smallest prospect that she should have any lot in life but that of misery, infamy, and woe. *Waited on Naaman's wife.* Her decent, orderly behavior, the consequence of her sober and pious education, entitled her to this place of distinction; in which her servitude was at least easy, and her person safe. If God permitted the parents to be deprived of their pious child by the hands of ruffians, He did not permit the child to be without a guardian.

3. *Would God my lord.* "I wish"; or, as the Chaldee, Syriac, or Arabic have, "Happy would it be for my master if he were with the prophet." Here the mystery of the divine providence begins to develop itself. By the captivity of this little maid one Syrian family at least, and that one of the most considerable in the Syrian empire, is brought to the knowledge of the true God.

5. *The king of Syria said.* He judged it the best mode of proceeding to send immediately to the king, under whose control he supposed the prophet must be, that he would order the prophet to cure his general.

according to the custom of the Jews when they heard or read that which they thought blasphemous; and what less could it be than to attribute to him a divine power? "*Am I a God, to kill* whom I will, and *make alive* whom I will? No, I pretend not to such an authority." 2. A bad design upon himself. He appeals to those about him for this: "*See how he seeketh a quarrel against me;* he requires me to recover the leper, and if I do not, though I cannot, he will make that a pretence to wage war with me," which he suspects the rather because Naaman is his general. If he had bethought himself of Elisha, and his power, he would easily have understood the letter, and have known what he had to do.

V. The proffer which Elisha made of his services. Hearing on what occasion the king had rent his clothes, he sent to him to let him know that if his patient would come to him he should not lose his labour (*v.* 8): *He shall know that there is a prophet in Israel* who can do that which the king of Israel dares not attempt, which the prophets of Syria cannot pretend to.

Verses 9-14

The cure of Naaman's leprosy.

I. The short and plain direction which the prophet gave him, with assurance of success. Naaman, with all his retinue, attended at Elisha's door as a beggar for an alms. Naaman expected to have his compliment returned, but Elisha gave him his answer without any formality, would not go to the door to him, lest he should seem too much pleased with the honour done him, but sent a messenger to him, saying, *Go wash in Jordan seven times*, and promising him that if he did so his disease should be cured. The promise was express: *Thou shalt be clean.* The method prescribed was plain: *Go wash in Jordan.* It was intended as a sign of the cure, and a trial of his obedience. Those that will be helped of God must do as they are bidden.

II. Naaman's disgust at the method prescribed, because it was not what he expected. Two things disgusted him:

1. That Elisha, as he thought, put a slight upon his person, in sending him orders by a servant, and not coming to him himself, *v.* 11. Being big with the expectation of a cure, he had been fancying how this cure would be wrought: "*He will surely come out to me*, that is the least he can do to me, a peer of Syria, to me that have so often been victorious over Israel. *He will stand*, and *call on the name of his God*, and name me in his prayer, and then he will *wave his hand over the place*, and so effect the cure." And, because the thing was not done just thus, he fell into a passion. He scorns to be healed, unless he be humoured.

2. That Elisha, as he thought, put a slight upon his country. He took it hard that he must be sent to wash in Jordan, a river of Israel, when he thought *Abana and Pharpar, rivers of Damascus, better than all the waters of Israel. May I not wash in them and be clean?* He might wash in them and be clean from dirt, but not wash in them and be clean from leprosy. Jordan was the river appointed, and, if he expected a cure from the divine power, he ought to acquiesce in the divine will, without asking why or wherefore. Naaman talked himself into such a heat (as passionate men usually do) that he turned away from the prophet's door in a rage, ready to swear he would never have anything more to say to Elisha; and who then would be the loser?

III. The modest advice which his servants gave him, to observe the prophet's prescriptions, with a tacit reproof of his resentments, *v.* 13. "*If the prophet had bidden thee do some great thing*, had ordered thee into a tedious course of physic, *Wouldst thou not have done it?* No doubt thou wouldst. And wilt thou not submit to so easy a method as this, *Wash and be clean?*" The reproof was very modest and respectful, very rational and considerate. If the servants had stirred up their master's angry resentment, and offered to avenge his quarrel upon the prophet, how mischievous would the consequences have been! They reasoned with him, (1) From his earnest desire of a cure: *Wouldst thou not do* anything? Note, When diseased sinners come to this, that they are content to do anything, to submit to anything, to part with anything, for a cure, then, and not till then, there begin to be some hopes of them. Then they will take Christ on his own terms when they are made willing to have Christ upon any terms. (2) From the easiness of the method prescribed: *Wash and be clean.* Note, The methods prescribed for the healing of the leprosy of sin are so plain that we are utterly inexcusable if we do not observe them. It is but, "Believe, and be saved"—"Repent, and be pardoned"—"Wash, and be clean."

object only was stated in the letter that was carried by the party concerned, while other circumstances were left to be explained at the interview. This explains Jehoram's burst of emotion—not horror at supposed blasphemy, but alarm and suspicion that this was merely made an occasion for a quarrel. Such a prince as he was would not readily think of Elisha, or, perhaps, have heard of his miraculous deeds.

8-15. ELISHA SENDS HIM TO JORDAN, AND HE IS HEALED. **8. when Elisha the man of God had heard that the king of Israel had rent his clothes, that he sent to the king, saying, . . . let him come to me**—This was the grand and ultimate object to which, in the providence of God, the journey of Naaman was subservient.

When the Syrian general, with his imposing retinue, arrived at the prophet's house, Elisha sent him a message to "go and wash in Jordan seven times."

This apparently rude reception to a foreigner of so high dignity incensed Naaman to such a degree that he resolved to depart, scornfully boasting that the rivers of Damascus were better than all the waters of Israel. **11. strike his hand over the place**—i.e., wave it over the diseased parts of his body. It was anciently, and still continues to be, a very prevalent superstition in the East that the hand of a king, or person of great reputed sanctity, touching, or waved over a sore, will heal it. **12. Abana and Pharpar**—the Barrady and one of its five tributaries—uncertain which. The waters of Damascus are still highly extolled by their inhabitants for their purity and coldness.

7. *Am I God, to kill and to make alive?* He spoke thus under the conviction that God alone could cure the leprosy; which, indeed, was universally acknowledged.

8. *Let him come now to me.* Do not be afflicted; the matter belongs to me, as the prophet of the Most High. Send him to me, and he shall know that I am such.

9. *Came with his horses and with his chariot.* In very great pomp and state. Closely inspected, this was preposterous enough; a leper sitting in state, and affecting it!

10. *Sent a messenger.* Did not come out to speak with him; he had got his orders from God, and he transmitted them to Naaman by his servant. *Wash in Jordan seven times.* The waters of Jordan had no tendency to remove this disorder, but God chose to make them the means by which He would convey His healing power.

11. *Naaman was wroth.* And why? Because the prophet treated him without ceremony, and because he appointed him an expenseless and simple mode of cure. *Behold, I thought.* God's ways are not as our ways; He appoints that mode of cure which He knows to be best. Naaman expected to be treated with great ceremony; and instead of humbling himself before the Lord's prophet, he expected the prophet of the Lord to humble himself before him! *Behold, I thought*—and what did he think? Hear his words, for they are all very emphatic: (1) *I thought, He will surely come out to me.* He will never make his servant the medium of communication between me and himself. (2) *And stand*—present himself before me, and stand as a servant to hear the orders of his God. (3) *And call on the name of the Lord his God,* so that both his God and himself shall appear to do me service and honor. (4) *And strike his hand over the place;* for can it be supposed that any healing virtue can be conveyed without contact?

13. *My father.* A title of the highest respect and affection. *Had bid thee do some great thing.* If the prophet had appointed you to do something very difficult in itself, and very expensive to you, would you not have done it? With much greater reason should you do what will occupy little time, be no expense, and is easy to be performed.

MATTHEW HENRY

IV. The cure effected, in the use of the means prescribed, *v.* 14. Naaman, upon second thoughts, yielded to make the experiment. *His flesh came again, like the flesh of a child,* to his great surprise and joy.

Verses 15–19

Of the ten lepers that our Saviour cleansed, the only one that *returned to give thanks* was a *Samaritan,* Luke xvii. 16. This Syrian did so, and here expresses himself.

I. Convinced of the power of the God of Israel, not only that he is God, but that he is God alone, and that indeed *there is no God in all the earth but in Israel* (*v.* 15). Had he seen other lepers cleansed, perhaps the sight would not have convinced him, but the mercy of the cure affected him more than the miracle of it. Those are best able to speak of the power of divine grace who have themselves experienced it.

II. Grateful to Elisha the prophet: "Therefore, for his sake whose servant thou art, I have a present for thee, silver, and gold, and raiment, whatever thou wilt please to accept." But Elisha generously refused the fee, not because he did not need it, for he was poor enough, but he would not be beholden to this Syrian. It would be much for the honour of God to show this new convert that the servants of the God of Israel were taught to look upon the wealth of this world with a holy contempt, which would confirm him in his belief that *there was no God but in Israel.* See 1 Cor. ix. 18; 2 Cor. xi. 9.

III. Proselyted to the worship of the God of Israel. He will not only offer a sacrifice to the Lord, in thanks for his present cure, but he resolves he will never offer sacrifice to any other gods, *v.* 17. It was a happy cure of his leprosy which cured him of his idolatry, a more dangerous disease. But, 1. In one instance he over-did it, that he would not only worship the God of Israel, but he would have clods of earth out of the prophet's garden to *make an altar of*, *v.* 17. He that awhile ago had spoken very slightly of the waters of Israel (*v.* 12) now is in another extreme, and over-values the earth of Israel, supposing that an altar of that earth would be most acceptable to him. 2. In another instance he under-did it, that he reserved to himself a liberty to bow in the house of Rimmon, in complaisance to the king his master, and according to the duty of his place at court (*v.* 18), *in this thing* he must be excused. If, in covenanting with God, we make a reservation for any known sin, which we will continue to indulge ourselves in, that reservation is a defeasance of his covenant. We must cast away all our transgressions and not except any house of Rimmon. If we ask for a dispensation to go on in any sin for the future, we mock God, and deceive ourselves.

Verses 20–27

Elisha, a holy prophet, a man of God, has but one servant, and he proves a base fellow. One would have expected that Elisha's servant should be a saint (even Ahab's servant, Obadiah, was), but even Christ himself had a Judas among his followers.

I. Gehazi's sin. 1. The love of money, that root of all evil, was at the bottom of it. His master contemned Naaman's treasures, but he coveted them, *v.* 20. His heart (says Bishop Hall) was packed up in Naaman's chests, and he must run after him to fetch it. 2. He blamed his master for refusing Naaman's present, envied and grudged his kindness and generosity to this stranger. 3. When Naaman alighted from his chariot to meet him (*v.* 21), he told him a deliberate lie, that his master sent him to him. 4. He abused his master, and basely misrepresented him to Naaman as one that had soon repented of his generosity. His story of the two sons of the prophets was as silly as it was false; if he would have begged a token for two young scholars, surely less than a talent of silver might serve them. 5. There was danger of his alienating Naaman from that holy religion which he had espoused, and lessening his good opinion of it. 6. His seeking to conceal what he had unjustly got added much to his sin. He hid it, till he should have an opportunity of laying it out, *v.* 24. He denied it: He *went in, and stood before his master,* ready to receive his orders. His master asked him where he had been. "Nowhere, sir" (said he), "out of the house."

II. The punishment of this sin. Elisha immediately called him to an account for it.

1. How he was convicted. He thought to impose upon the prophet, but was soon given to understand that the Spirit of prophecy could not be deceived, and that it was in vain to lie to the Holy Ghost. Elisha could tell him, (1) What he had done, though he had denied it. "Thou sayest thou wentest nowhere, but *went not my heart with thee?*" *v.* 26. (2) What he

JAMIESON, FAUSSET, BROWN

14. Then went he down, and dipped himself seven times in Jordan—Persuaded by his calmer and more reflecting attendants to try a method so simple and easy, he followed their instructions, and was cured. The cure was performed on the basis of God's covenant with Israel, by which the land, and all pertaining to it, was blessed. Seven was the symbol of the covenant [KEIL].

15-19. ELISHA REFUSES NAAMAN'S GIFTS. **15. he returned to the man of God**—After the miraculous cure, Naaman returned to Elisha, to whom he acknowledged his full belief in the sole supremacy of the God of Israel and offered him a liberal reward. But to show that he was not actuated by the mercenary motives of the heathen priests and prophets, Elisha, though he accepted presents on other occasions (ch. 4:42), respectfully but firmly declined them on this, being desirous that the Syrians should see the piety of God's servants, and their superiority to all worldly and selfish motives in promoting the honor of God and the interests of true religion.

17. two mules' burden of earth—with which to make an altar (Exod. 20:24) to the God of Israel. What his motive or his purpose was in this proposal—whether he thought that God could be acceptably worshipped only on his own *soil*; or whether he wished, when far away from the Jordan, to have the *earth* of Palestine to rub himself with, which the Orientals use as a substitute for water; or whether, by making such a request of Elisha, he thought the prophet's grant of it would impart some virtue; or whether, like the modern Jews and Mohammedans, he resolved to have a portion of this *holy earth* for his nightly pillow—it is not easy to say. It is not strange to find such notions in so newly a converted heathen. **18. goeth into the house of Rimmon**—a Syrian deity; probably the sun, or the planetary system, of which a pomegranate (*Heb., Rimmon*) was the symbol. **leaneth on my hand**—i.e., meaning the service which Naaman rendered as the attendant of his sovereign. Elisha's prophetic commission not extending to any but the conversion of Israel from idolatry, he makes no remark, either approving or disapproving, on the declared course of Naaman, but simply gives (vs. 19) the parting benediction.

20-27. GEHAZI, BY A LIE, OBTAINS A PRESENT, BUT IS SMITTEN WITH LEPROSY. **20. I will run after him, and take somewhat of him**—The respectful courtesy to Elisha, shown in the person of his servant, and the open-handed liberality of his gifts, attest the fulness of Naaman's gratitude; while the lie—the artful management is dismissing the bearers of the treasure, and the deceitful appearance before his master, as if he had not left the house—give a most unfavorable impression of Gehazi's character. **23. in two bags**—People in the East, when travelling, have their money, in certain sums, put up in bags.

ADAM CLARKE

14. *Then went he down.* He felt the force of this reasoning, and made a trial, probably expecting little success.

15. *He returned to the man of God.* He saw that the hand of the Lord was upon him; he felt gratitude for his cleansing; and came back to acknowledge, in the most public way, his obligation to God and His servant. *Stood before him.* He was now truly humbled, and left all his state behind him. *Take a blessing.* Accept a present.

16. *I will receive none.* It was very common to give presents to all great and official men; and among these, prophets were always included. But as it might have appeared to the Syrians that he had taken the offered presents as a remuneration for the cure performed, he refused; for as God alone did the work, He alone should have all the glory.

17. *Shall there not then, I pray thee?* This verse is understood two different ways. I will give them both in a paraphrase: (1) "Shall there not then be given unto thy servant [viz., Naaman] two mules' burden of this Israelitish earth, that I may build an altar with it, on which I may offer sacrifices to the God of Israel?" (2) "Shall there not be given to thy [Elisha's] servant [Gehazi] two mules' burden of this earth?" i.e., the gold and silver which he brought with him; and which he esteemed as earth, or dust, in comparison of the cure he received.

18. *In this thing the Lord pardon thy servant.* It is useless to enter into the controversy concerning this verse. By no rule of right reasoning, nor by any legitimate mode of interpretation, can it be stated that Naaman is asking pardon for offenses which he may commit, or that he could ask or the prophet grant indulgence to bow himself in the temple of Rimmon, thus performing a decided act of homage, the very essence of that worship which immediately before he solemnly assured the prophet he would never practice. The original may legitimately be read, and ought to be read, in the past, and not in the future tense. "For this thing the Lord pardon thy servant, for that when my master hath gone into the house of Rimmon to worship there, and he hath leaned upon mine hand, that I also have bowed myself in the house of Rimmon; for my worshipping in the house of Rimmon, the Lord pardon thy servant in this thing." This is the translation of Lightfoot, the most able Hebraist of his time in Christendom.

20. *My master hath spared . . . this Syrian.* He has neither taken anything from him for himself, nor permitted him to give anything to me.

21. *He lighted down from the chariot.* He treats even the prophet's servant with the profoundest respect, alights from his chariot, and goes to meet him. *Is all well? Hashalom;* "Is it peace (or prosperity)?"

22. *And he said. Shalom.* "It is peace"; all is right. This was a common mode of address and answer. *There be come to me from mount Ephraim.* There was probably a school of the prophets at this mount.

23. *He . . . bound two talents of silver.* It required two servants to carry these two talents, for, according to the computation above, each talent was about 120 pounds in weight.

24. *When he came to the tower.* The Chaldee, Septuagint, Syriac, and Arabic understand the word *ophel,* which we translate *tower,* as signifying a secret, dark, or hiding place.

26. *Went not mine heart with thee?* The Chaldee gives this a good turn: "By the prophetic spirit it was shown unto me, when the man returned from his chariot to meet thee." *Is it a time to receive money?* He gave him further

MATTHEW HENRY

designed, though he kept that in his own breast. He could tell him the very thoughts and intents of his heart, that he was projecting, now that he had got these two talents, to purchase ground and cattle, to leave Elisha's service, and to set up for himself. "*Is it a time to receive money?* Is this an opportunity of enriching thyself? Couldst thou find no better way of getting money than by belying thy master and laying a stumbling-block before a young convert?"

2. How he was punished for it: *The leprosy of Naaman shall cleave to thee, v.* 27. He *went out from his presence a leper as white as snow.* Thus he is stigmatised and made infamous, and carries the mark of his shame wherever he goes. What was Gehazi profited, though he gained his two talents, when thereby he lost his health, his honour, his peace, his service, and, if repentance prevented not, his soul for ever? See Job xx. 12, &c.

CHAPTER 6

Verses 1–7

I. Concerning the sons of the prophets, and their condition and character. The college here spoken of seems to be that at Gilgal, and it was near Jordan; and, probably, wherever Elisha resided as many as could of the sons of the prophets flocked to him for the advantage of his instructions, counsels, and prayers. Everyone would covet to dwell with him and be near him.

1. Their number increased so that they wanted room: *The place is too strait for us* (*v.* 1)—a good hearing, for it is a sign many are added to them. Elisha's miracles doubtless drew in many.

2. They were humble men. It becomes the sons of the prophets, who profess to look for great things in the other world, to be content with mean things in this.

3. They were poor men. Poverty is no bar to prophecy.

4. They were industrious men, and willing to take pains. Let no man think an honest employment either a burden or disparagement.

5. They were men that had a great value and veneration for Elisha. (1) They would not go about to build at all without his leave, *v.* 2. (2) They would not willingly go to fell timber without his company: "*Go with thy servants*" (*v.* 3). Good disciples desire to be always under good discipline.

6. They were honest men, and men that were in care to give all men their own. When one of them, accidentally fetching too fierce a stroke, threw off his axe-head into the water, he cries out with deep concern, *Alas, master! For it was borrowed, v.* 5. It is likely this prophet was poor, and had not wherewithal to pay for the axe, which made the loss of it so much the greater trouble.

II. Concerning the father of the prophets, Elisha. 1. That he was a man of great condescension and compassion; he went with the sons of the prophets to the woods, when they desired his company, *v.* 3. 2. That he was a man of great power; he could make iron to swim, contrary to its nature (*v.* 6). God's grace can thus raise the stony iron heart which has sunk into the mud of this world, and raise up affections naturally earthly, to things above.

Verses 8–12

Here we have Elisha, with his spirit of prophecy, serving the king, as before helping the sons of the prophets.

I. How the king of Israel was informed by Elisha of all the designs of his enemy, the king of Syria, *v.* 8–10. 1. The enemies of God's Israel are politic in their devices, and restless in their attempts, against him. 2. All those devices are known to God, even those that are deepest laid. He knows not only what men do, but what they design, and has many ways of countermining them. 3. It is a great advantage to us to be warned of our danger, that we may stand upon our guard against it. The work of God's prophets is to give us warning. The king of Israel would regard the warnings Elisha gave him of his danger by the Syrians, but not the warnings he gave him of his danger by his sins.

II. How the king of Syria resented this. He suspected treachery among his senators, and that his counsels were betrayed, *v.* 11. But one of his servants, that had heard, by Naaman and others, of Elisha's wondrous works, concludes it must needs be he that gave this intelligence to the king of Israel, *v.* 12.

Verses 13–23

I. The great force which the king of Syria sent to

JAMIESON, FAUSSET, BROWN

leper as white as snow—(See on Lev. 13:3). This heavy infliction was not too severe for the crime of Gehazi. For it was not the covetousness alone that was punished; but, at the same time, it was the ill use made of the prophet's name to gain an object prompted by a mean covetousness, and the attempt to conceal it by lying [KEIL].

CHAPTER 6

Vss. 1-7. ELISHA CAUSES IRON TO SWIM. **1. the place where we dwell with thee**—Marg., "sit before thee." The one points to a common residence—the other to a common place of meeting. The tenor of the narrative shows the humble condition of Elisha's pupils. The place was either Beth-el or Jericho, probably the latter. The ministry and miracles of Elisha brought great accessions to his schools.

2. Let us go, we pray thee, unto Jordan—whose wooded banks would furnish plenty of timber.

5. it was borrowed—lit., begged. The scholar's distress arose from the consideration that it had been presented to him; and that, owing to his poverty, he could not procure another.

6. cut down a stick, and cast it in thither—Although this means was used, it had no natural adaptation to make the iron swim. Besides, the Jordan is at Jericho so deep and rapid that there were 1000 chances to 1 against the stick falling into the hole of the axe-head. All attempts to account for the recovery of the lost implement on such a theory must be rejected. "The iron did swim"—only by the miraculous exertion of Elisha's power.

8-17. DISCLOSES THE KING OF SYRIA'S COUNSEL. **8. the king of Syria warred against Israel**—This seems to have been a sort of guerrilla warfare, carried on by predatory inroads on different parts of the country. Elisha apprised King Jehoram of the secret purpose of the enemy; so, by adopting precautionary measures, he was always enabled to anticipate and defeat their attacks. The frequency of his disappointments having led the Syrian king to suspect some of his servants of carrying on a treacherous correspondence with the enemy, he was informed about Elisha, whose apprehension he forthwith determined to effect. This resolution was, of course, grounded on the belief that however great the knowledge of Elisha might be, if seized and kept a prisoner, he could no longer give information to the king of Israel.

ADAM CLARKE

proof of this all-discerning prophetic spirit in telling him what he designed to do with the money; he intended to set up a splendid establishment, to have *menservants* and *maidservants*, to have *oliveyards* and *vineyards*, and *sheep* and *oxen*.

27. *The leprosy . . . of Naaman shall cleave unto thee.* You have received much money, and you shall have much to do with it. You have received Naaman's silver, and you shall have Naaman's leprosy. Gehazi is not the last who has received money in an unlawful way, and has received God's curse with it. *A leper as white as snow.* The moment the curse was pronounced, that moment the signs of the leprosy began to appear. The white shining spot was the sign that the infection had taken place (see Lev. xiii. 2).

CHAPTER 6

1. *The place . . . is too strait for us.* Notwithstanding the general profligacy of Israel, the schools of the prophets increased. This was no doubt owing to the influence of Elisha.

2. *Every man a beam.* They made a sort of log houses with their own hands.

5. *Alas, master! for it was borrowed.* "Ah! ah, my master; and it has been sought." It has fallen in, and I have sought it in vain. Or, "it was borrowed," and therefore I am the more afflicted for its loss.

6. *He cut down a stick.* This had no natural tendency to raise the iron; it was only a sign or ceremony which the prophet chose to use on the occasion. *The iron did swim.* This was a real miracle.

8. *The king of Syria warred against Israel.* This was probably the same Ben-hadad who is mentioned in v. 24. *In such and such a place.* The Syrian king had observed, from the disposition of the Israelitish army, in what direction it was about to make its movements; and therefore laid ambuscades where he might surprise it to the greatest advantage.

9. *Beware that thou pass not such a place.* Elisha must have had this information by immediate revelation from heaven.

10. *Sent to the place.* To see if it were so. But the Vulgate gives it quite a different turn: "The king of Israel sent previously to the place, and took possession of it"; and thus the Syrians were disappointed. This is very likely, though it is not expressed in the Hebrew text.

MATTHEW HENRY

seize Elisha. He found out where he was, at Dothan (*v.* 13), which was not far from Samaria; thither he sent a great host, who were to come upon him by night, and to bring him dead or alive, *v.* 14. Thus he hoped to make sure of him, especially coming upon him by surprise.

II. The grievous fright which the prophet's servant was in, when he perceived the city surrounded by the Syrians, and the effectual course which the prophet took to pacify him and free him from his fears. 1. What a consternation he was in. He ran straight to Elisha, to bring him an account of it: "*Alas, master!*" (said he), "*what shall we do?* We are undone: it is to no purpose to think either of fighting or flying, we must fall into their hands." Had he considered that he was embarked with his master, by whom God had done great things, and whom he would not now leave to *fall into the hands of the uncircumcised*, he would not have been thus at a loss. If he had only said, *What shall I do?* it would have been the more excusable. 2. How his master quieted him, (1) By word. What he said to him (*v.* 16) is spoken to all the faithful servants of God, when *without are fightings and within are fears:* "*Fear not* with that fear which has torment and amazement, *for those that are with us*, to protect us, *are more than those that are against us*, to destroy us—angels unspeakably more numerous—God infinitely more powerful." When we are magnifiying the causes of our fear we ought to possess ourselves with clear, and great, and high thoughts of God and the invisible world. *If God be for us*, we know what follows, Rom. viii. 31. (2) By vision, *v.* 17. [1] It seems Elisha was much concerned for the satisfaction of his servant, newly come into his service. [2] He saw himself safe, and wished no more than that his servant might see what he saw, a guard of angels round about him. [3] For the satisfaction of his servant there needed no more than the opening of his eyes; *that* therefore he prayed for, and obtained for him: *Lord, open his eyes that he may see.* The eyes of his body were open, and with them he saw the danger. "Lord, open the eyes of his faith, that with them he may see the protection we are under." The opening of our eyes will be the silencing of our fears. In the dark we are most apt to be frightened. The clearer sight we have of the sovereignty and power of heaven the less we shall fear the calamities of this earth.

III. The shameful defeat which Elisha gave to the host of Syrians who came to seize him. 1. He prayed to God to smite them with blindness, and they were all struck blind immediately, not stone-blind, but their sight was so altered that they could not know the persons and places they were before acquainted with, *v.* 18. They were so confounded that those among them whom they depended upon for information did not know this place to be Dothan nor this person to be Elisha, but *groped at noon day as in the night.*

2. When they were thus bewildered and confounded he led them to Samaria (*v.* 19), promising that he would show them the man whom they sought, and he did so. He did not lie to them when he told them, *This is not the way, nor is this the city* where Elisha is; for he had now come out of the city. 3. When he had brought them to Samaria he prayed to God so to open their eyes that they might see where they were (*v.* 20), *and behold*, to their great terror, *they were in the midst of Samaria*, where, it is probable, there was a standing force sufficient to cut them all off, or make them prisoners of war. 4. When he had them at his mercy he made it appear that he was influenced by a divine goodness as well as a divine power. (1) He took care to protect them from the danger into which he had brought them, and was content to show them what he could have done: *My father shall I smite them?* And, again, as if he longed for the assault, *Shall I smite them?* But the prophet would by no means suffer him to meddle with them; they were brought hither to be convinced and shamed, not to be killed, *v.* 22. They were not his prisoners; they were God's prisoners and the prophet's, and therefore he must do them no harm. (2) He took care to provide for them; he ordered the king to treat them handsomely and then dismiss them fairly, which he did, *v.* 23. [1] It was the king's praise that he was so obsequious to the prophet, contrary to his inclination, and, as it seemed, to his interest, 1 Sam. xxiv. 19. So willing was he to oblige Elisha that he *prepared great provision* for them, for the credit of his court and the country and of Elisha. [2] It was the prophet's praise that he was so generous to his enemies. The great duty of loving enemies, and doing good to those that hate us, was both commanded in the Old Testament (Prov. xxv. 21, 22, *If thy enemy hunger, feed him*, Exod. xxiii. 4, 5) and practised, as here by Elisha.

JAMIESON, FAUSSET, BROWN

13. Dothan—or Dothaim, a little north of Samaria (see on Gen. 37:17).

15. his servant said unto him, Alas, my master! how shall we do?—When the Syrian detachment surrounded the place by night, for the apprehension of the prophet, his servant was paralyzed with fear. This was a new servant, who had only been with him since Gehazi's dismissal and consequently had little or no experience of his master's powers. His faith was easily shaken by so unexpected an alarm.

17. Elisha prayed, and said, O Lord, I pray thee, open his eyes that he may see—The invisible guard of angels that encompass and defend us (Ps. 34:7). The opening of the eyes, which Elisha prayed for, were those of the Spirit, not of the body—the eye of faith sees the reality of the divine presence and protection where all is vacancy or darkness to the ordinary eye. The horses and chariots were symbols of the divine power (see on ch. 2:12); and their fiery nature denoted their supernatural origin; for fire, the most ethereal of earthly elements, is the most appropriate symbol of the Godhead [Keil].

18-23. His Army Smitten with Blindness. **18. Smite this people, I pray thee, with blindness**—not a total and material blindness, for then they could not have followed him—but a mental hallucination (see on Gen. 19:11) so that they did not perceive or recognize him to be the object of their search.

19. This is not the way, neither is this the city—This statement is so far true that, as he had now left the place of his residence, they would not have got him by that road. But the ambiguity of his language was purposely framed to deceive them; and yet the deception must be viewed in the light of a stratagem, which has always been deemed lawful in war. **he led them to Samaria**—When they were arrived in the midst of the capital, their eyes, at Elisha's request, were opened, and they then became aware of their defenseless condition, for Jehoram had received private premonition of their arrival.

The king, so far from being allowed to slay the enemies who were thus unconsciously put in his power, was recommended to entertain them with liberal hospitality and then dismiss them to their own country. This was humane advice; it was contrary to the usage of war to put war captives to death in cold blood, even when taken by the point of the sword, much more those whom the miraculous power and providence of God had unexpectedly placed at his disposal.

ADAM CLARKE

13. *Behold, he is in Dothan.* This is supposed to be the same place as that mentioned in Gen. xxxvii. 17. It lay about twelve miles from Samaria.

14. *He sent thither horses.* It is strange he did not think that he who could penetrate his secrets with respect to the Israelitish army could inform himself of all his machinations against his own life.

16. *For they that be with us are more.* What astonishing intercourse had this man with heaven! It seems the whole heavenly host had it in commission to help him.

18. *Smite this people . . . with blindness.* Confound their sight so that they may not know what they see, and so mistake one place for another.

19. *I will bring you to the man whom ye seek.* And he did so; he was their guide to Samaria, and showed himself to them fully in that city.

20. *Open the eyes of these men.* Take away their confusion of vision, that they may discern things as they are, and distinguish where they are.

21. *My father, shall I smite?* This was dastardly; the utmost he could have done with these men, when thus brought into his hand, was to make them prisoners of war.

22. *Whom thou hast taken captive.* Those who in open battle either lay down their arms, or are surrounded, and have their retreat cut off, are entitled to their lives, much more those who are thus providentially put into your hand, without having been in actual hostility against you. Give them meat and drink, and send them home to their master, and let them thus know that you fear him not, and are incapable of doing an ungenerous or unmanly action.

23. *He prepared great provision for them.* These, on the return to their master, could tell him strange things about the power of the God of Israel, and the magnanimity of its king.

MATTHEW HENRY

IV. The good effect this had, for the present, upon the Syrians. They *came no more into the land of Israel* (*v.* 23). The most glorious victory over an enemy is to turn him into a friend.

Verses 24–33

This last paragraph of this chapter begins a new story.

I. The siege which the king of Syria laid to Samaria. The Syrians had soon forgotten the kindnesses they had lately received in Samaria, and without any provocation, sought the destruction of it, *v.* 24. The country was plundered and laid waste when this capital city was brought to the last extremity, *v.* 25. The dearth which had of late been in the land was probably the occasion of the emptiness of their stores, so that, while the sword devoured without, the famine within was more grievous, for the Syrians designed not to storm the city, but to starve it. So great was the scarcity that an ass's head was sold for five pounds, and a small quantity of coarse corn, then called *dove's dung*, no more of it than the quantity of six eggs, for five pieces of silver. How contemptible money is, when, in time of famine, it is so freely parted with for anything that is eatable.

II. The sad complaint which a poor woman had to make to the king, in the extremity of the famine. He was *passing by upon the wall* to give orders for the mounting of the guard, when a woman of the city cried to him, *Help, my lord, O king! v.* 26. He returns but a melancholy answer (*v.* 27): *If the Lord do not help thee, whence shall I?* Some think it was a *quarrelling* word, but it rather seems to be a *quieting* word: "Let us be content, and make the best of our affliction, looking up to God, for, till he help us, I cannot help thee." 1. He laments the emptiness of the floor and the wine-press. 2. He acknowledges himself disabled to help, unless God would help them. However, though he cannot help her, he is willing to hear her (*v.* 28): "*What ails thee?* Is there anything singular in thy case, or dost thou fare worse than thy neighbours?" Truly yes; she and one of her neighbours had made a barbarous agreement, that, all provisions failing, they should boil and eat her son first and then her neighbour's; hers was eaten and now her neighbour hid hers, *v.* 28, 29.

III. The king's indignation against Elisha upon this occasion. He lamented the calamity, *rent his clothes, and had sackcloth upon his flesh* (*v.* 30), as one heartily concerned for the misery of his people, and that it was not in his power to help them; but he did not lament his own iniquity, nor the iniquity of his people. Instead of vowing to pull down the calves at Dan and Beth-el, he swears *the death of Elisha, v.* 31. Why? What has Elisha done? His head is the most innocent and valuable in all Israel. Thus in the days of the persecuting emperors, when the empire groaned under any extraordinary calamity, the fault was laid on the Christians, and they were doomed to destruction. *Christianos ad leones—Away with the Christians to the lions.*

IV. The foresight Elisha had of the king's design against him, *v.* 32. He sat in his house well composed, and the elders with him. He told the elders there was an officer coming from the king to cut off his head, and bade them stop him at the door, for the king his master was just following him, to revoke the order.

V. The king's passionate speech, when he came to prevent the execution of his edict for the beheading of Elisha. He seems to have been in a struggle between his convictions and his corruptions.

JAMIESON, FAUSSET, BROWN

In such circumstances, kind and hospitable treatment was every way more becoming in itself, and would be productive of the best effects. It would redound to the credit of the true religion, which inspired such an excellent spirit into its professors; and it would not only prevent the future opposition of the Syrians but make them stand in awe of a people who, they had seen, were so remarkably protected by a prophet of the Lord. The latter clause of verse 23 shows that these salutary effects were fully realized. A moral conquest had been gained over the Syrians.

24-33. BEN-HADAD BESIEGES SAMARIA. **Ben-hadad . . . besieged Samaria**—This was the predicted accomplishment of the result of Ahab's foolish and misplaced kindness (I Kings 20:42). **25. an ass's head was sold for fourscore pieces of silver**—Though the ass was deemed unclean food, necessity might warrant their violation of a positive law when mothers, in their extremity, were found violating the law of nature. The head was the worst part of the animal. Eighty pieces of silver, equal to $50.00. **the fourth part of a cab**—A cab was the smallest dry measure. The proportion here stated was nearly half a pint for $ 3.00. "Dove's dung" is thought by BOCHART to be a kind of pulse or pea, common in Judea, and still kept in the storehouses of Cairo and Damascus, and other places, for the use of it by pilgrim caravans; by LINNAEUS, and other botanists, it is said to be the root or white bulb of the plant *Ornithogalum umbellatum,* Star of Bethlehem. The sacred historian does not say that the articles here named were regularly sold at the rates described, but only that instances were known of such high prices being given. **26. as the king was passing**—to look at the defenses, or to give some necessary orders for manning the walls.

29. we boiled my son, and did eat him—(See on Deut. 28:53). **30. had sackcloth within upon his flesh**—The horrid recital of this domestic tragedy led the king soon after to rend his garment, in consequence of which it was discovered that he wore a penitential shirt of haircloth. It is more than doubtful, however, if he was truly humbled on account of his own and the nation's sins; otherwise he would not have vowed vengeance on the prophet's life. The true explanation seems to be, that Elisha having counselled him not to surrender, with the promise, on condition of deep humiliation, of being delivered, and he having assumed the signs of contrition without receiving the expected relief, regarded Elisha who had proved false and faithless as the cause of all the protracted distress. **32. But Elisha sat in his house, and the elders sat with him**—The latter clause of vs. 33, which contains the king's impatient exclamation, enables us to account for the impetuous order he issued for the beheading of Elisha. Though Jehoram was a wicked king and most of his courtiers would resemble their master, many had been won over, through the prophet's influence, to the true religion. A meeting, probably a prayer-meeting, of those was held in the house where he lodged, for he had none of his own (I Kings 19:20, 21); and them he not only apprised of the king's design against himself, but disclosed to them the proof of a premeditated deliverance.

ADAM CLARKE

So the bands of Syria came no more. Marauding parties were no more permitted by the Syrian king to make inroads upon Israel. And it is very likely that for some considerable time after this there was no war between these two nations. What is mentioned in the next verse was more than a year afterwards.

25. *And, behold, they besieged it.* They had closed it in on every side, and reduced it to the greatest necessity. *And the fourth part of a cab of dove's dung.* The *cab* was about a quart or three pints. *Dove's dung.* Whether this means pigeon's dung literally or a kind of pulse has been variously disputed by learned men. It is probable a sort of peas are meant, which the Arabs to this day call by this name.

27. *If the Lord do not help thee.* Some read this as an imprecation, "May God save thee not! how can I save thee?"

29. *So we boiled my son.* This very evil Moses had foretold should come upon them if they forsook God (see Deut. xxviii. 53, 57). The same evil came upon this wretched people when besieged by Nebuchadnezzar (see Ezek. v. 10). And also when Titus besieged Jerusalem (see Josephus, De Bell. Judaic., lib. vi, cap. 3).

30. *He had sackcloth within upon his flesh.* The king was in deep mourning for the distresses of the people.

31. *If the head of Elisha . . . shall stand on him.* Either he attributed these calamities to the prophet, or else he thought he could remove them and yet would not.

32. *This son of a murderer.* Jehoram, the son of Ahab and Jezebel. Ahab is called a *murderer* because of the murder of Naboth. *Shut the door.* He was obliged to make use of this method for his personal safety, as the king was highly incensed. *The sound of his master's feet behind him.* That is, King Jehoram is following his messenger, that he may see him take off my head.

33. *Behold, this evil is of the Lord.* It is difficult to know whether it be the prophet, the messenger, or the king that says these words. It might be the answer of the prophet from within to the messenger who was without, and who sought for admission, and gave his reason; to whom Elisha might have replied: "I am not the cause of these calamities; they are from the Lord; I have been praying for their removal; but why should I pray to the Lord any longer, for the time of your deliverance is at hand?" And *then Elisha said*—see the following chapter, where the removal of the calamity is foretold in the most explicit manner; and indeed the chapter is unhappily divided from this. The seventh chapter should have begun with v. 24 of this chapter, as by the present division the story is unnaturally interrupted.

MATTHEW HENRY — CHAPTER 7

Verses 1–2

I. Elisha foretells that within twenty-four hours they shall have plenty, *v.* 1. The king of Israel despaired of it and grew weary of waiting: then Elisha foretold it, when things were at the worst. Man's extremity is God's opportunity of magnifying his own power; his time to appear for his people is when *their strength is gone,* Deut. xxxii. 36. The king said, *Why shall I wait for the Lord any longer?* "Well," said Elisha, "*now hear you the word of the Lord,* hear what he says: tomorrow corn shall be sold at the usual rate in the gate of Samaria." 2. The consequence of that shall be great plenty. This would, in time, follow of course, but that corn should be thus cheap in so short a time was quite beyond what could be thought of.

II. A peer of Israel that happened to be present openly declared his disbelief of this prediction, *v.* 2. He was a courtier whom the king had an affection for, on whom he leaned, and in whom he reposed

JAMIESON, FAUSSET, BROWN — CHAPTER 7

Vss. 1-16. ELISHA PROPHESIES INCREDIBLE PLENTY IN SAMARIA. **1. Hear ye the word of the Lord**—This prediction, though uttered first to the assembled elders, was intimated to the king's messengers, who reported it to Jehoram (vs. 18). **Tomorrow, about this time, shall a measure of fine flour be sold for a shekel,** etc.—This may be estimated at a peck of fine flour for a dollar, and two pecks of barley at the same price. **in the gate of Samaria**—Vegetables, cattle, all sorts of country produce, are still sold every morning at the gates of towns in the East.

2. a lord on whose hand the king leaned—When an Eastern king walks or stands abroad in the open air, he always supports himself on the arm of the *highest* courtier present.

ADAM CLARKE — CHAPTER 7

1. *To morrow about this time.* This was in reply to the desponding language of the king, and to vindicate himself from the charge of being author of this calamity. See the end of the preceding chapter. *A measure of fine flour . . . for a shekel.* A *seah* of fine flour. The *seah* was about two gallons and a half; the *shekel,* two shillings and fourpence at the lowest computation. A wide difference between this and the price of the ass's head mentioned above!

2. *Then a lord. Shalish.* This word as a name of office occurs often, and seems to point out one of the highest offices in the state. So unlikely was this prediction to be fulfilled

MATTHEW HENRY

much confidence.

III. The just doom passed upon him for his infidelity, that he should see this great plenty for his conviction, and yet not eat of it to his comfort.

Verses 3–11

I. How the siege of Samaria was raised in the evening, at the edge of night (*v.* 6, 7), not by might or power, but by the Spirit of the Lord of hosts, striking terror upon the spirits of the besiegers. Here was not a sword drawn against them, but, 1. *The Lord made them to hear a noise of chariots and horses.* The Syrians that besieged Dothan had their *sight* imposed upon, *ch.* vi. 18. These had their *hearing* imposed upon. Whether the noise was really made in the air by the ministry of angels, or whether it was only a sound in their ears, is not certain; whichsoever it was, it was from God, who both *brings the wind out of his treasures*, and *forms the spirit of man within him.* Notices from the invisible world are either very comfortable or very dreadful, according as men are at peace with God or at war with him. 2. Hearing this noise, they concluded the king of Israel had certainly procured assistance from some foreign power: *He has hired against us the kings of the Hittites and the kings of the Egyptians.* 3. Hereupon they all fled with incredible precipitation, as for their lives, left their camp as it was: even their horses, that might have hastened their flight, they could not stay to take with them, *v.* 7. Those that will not fear God he can make to fear at the shaking of a leaf.

II. How the Syrians' flight was discovered by four leprous men. Samaria was delivered, and did not know it. The watchmen on the walls were not aware of the retreat of the enemy, so silently did they steal away. But Providence employed four lepers to be the intelligencers, who had their lodging without the gate, being excluded from the city, as ceremonially unclean: the Jews say they were Gehazi and his three sons. 1. How these lepers reasoned themselves into a resolution to make a visit in the night to the camp of the Syrians, *v.* 3, 4. They were ready to perish for hunger; none passed through the gate to relieve them. They therefore determine to go over to the enemy, and throw themselves upon their mercy: perhaps they would save them alive, as objects of compassion. According to this resolution, they went, in the beginning of the night, to the camp of the Syrians, and, to their great surprise, found it wholly deserted, not a man to be seen or heard in it, *v.* 5. 2. How they reasoned themselves into a resolution to bring tidings of this to the city. They feasted in the first tent they came to (*v.* 8) and then began to think of enriching themselves with the plunder; but they corrected themselves (*v.* 9): "*We do not well* to conceal these good tidings from the community we are members of, therefore let us bring them the news. Though it awake them from sleep, it will be *life from the dead* to them." According to this resolution, they returned to the gate, and acquainted the sentinel with what they had discovered (*v.* 10), who straightway brought the intelligence to court (*v.* 11), and it was not the less acceptable for being first brought by lepers.

Verses 12–20

I. The king's jealousy of a stratagem in the Syrian's retreat, *v.* 12. He feared that they had withdrawn into an ambush, to draw out the besieged, that they might fall on them with more advantage.

II. The course they took to prevent their falling into a snare. They sent out spies to see what had become of the Syrians, and found they had all fled indeed, commanders as well as common soldiers. They could track them by the garments, which they threw off, and left by the way, for their greater expedition, *v.* 15. He that gave this advice seems to have been very sensible of the deplorable condition the people were in (*v.* 13). He advised to send five horsemen, but. it should seem, there were only two horses fit to be sent, and those chariot-horses, *v.* 14.

III. The plenty that was in Samaria, from the plunder of the camp of the Syrians, *v.* 16. God determined that the besieging of Samaria, which was intended for its ruin, should turn to its advantage, and that Israel should now be enriched with the spoil of the Syrians as of old with that of the Egyptians. The word of Elisha fulfilled to a tittle: *A measure of fine flour was sold for a shekel;* those that spoiled the camp had not only enough to supply themselves with, but an overplus to sell at an easy rate for the benefit of others, and so even *those that tarried at home did divide the spoil*, Ps. lxviii. 12; Isa. xxxiii. 23.

IV. The death of the unbelieving courtier, that questioned the truth of Elisha's word. This lord, 1. Was preferred by the king to the *charge of the gate* (*v.* 17), to keep the peace, and to see that there was

JAMIESON, FAUSSET, BROWN

if the Lord would make windows in heaven—The scoffing infidelity of this remark, which was a sneer against not the prophet only, but the God he served, was justly and signally punished (see vs. 20).

6, 7. the Lord had made the host of the Syrians to hear a noise of chariots—This illusion of the sense of hearing, whereby the besiegers imagined the tramp of two armies from opposite quarters, was a great miracle which God wrought directly for the deliverance of His people.

3. there were four leprous men—The account of the sudden raising of the siege and the unexpected supply given to the famishing inhabitants of Samaria, is introduced by a narrative of the visit and discovery, by these poor creatures, of the extraordinary flight of the Syrians. **leprous men at the entering in of the gate**—living, perhaps, in some lazar-house there (Lev. 13:4-6; Num. 5:3).

5. they rose up in the twilight—i.e., the evening twilight (vs. 12). **the uttermost part of the camp of Syria**—i.e., the extremity nearest the city.

8-11. these lepers . . . did eat and drink—After they had appeased their hunger and secreted as many valuables as they could carry, their consciences smote them for concealing the discovery and they hastened to publish it in the city. **10. horses tied, and asses tied, and the tents as they were**—The uniform arrangement of encampments in the East is to place the tents in the center, while the cattle are picketed all around, as an outer wall of defense; and hence the lepers describe the cattle as the first objects they saw.

12-15. the king . . . said unto his servants, I will now show you what the Syrians have done—Similar stratagems have been so often resorted to in the ancient and modern wars of the East that there is no wonder Jehoram's suspicions were awakened. But the scouts, whom he despatched, soon found unmistakable signs of the panic that had struck the enemy and led to a most precipitate flight.

17-20. THE UNBELIEVING LORD TRODDEN TO DEATH. **17. the king appointed the lord on whose hand he leaned,** etc.—The news spread like lightning through the city, and was followed, as was natural,

ADAM CLARKE

that he thought God must pour out wheat and barley from heaven before it could have a literal accomplishment. *But shalt not eat thereof.* This was a mere prediction of his death, but not as a judgment for his unbelief; any person in his circumstances might have spoken as he did.

6. *The Lord had made the . . . Syrians to hear a noise.* This threw them into confusion; they imagined that they were about to be attacked by powerful auxiliaries, which the king of Israel had hired against them.

5. *The uttermost part of the camp.* Where the Syrian advanced guards should have been.

13. *And one of his servants answered.* This is a very difficult verse, and the great variety of explanations given of it cast but little light on the subject. I am inclined to believe, with Kennicott, that there is an interpolation here which puzzles, if not destroys, the sense. "Several instances," says he, "have been given of words improperly repeated by Jewish transcribers, who have been careless enough to make such mistakes, and yet cautious not to alter or erase, for fear of discovery. This verse furnishes another instance in a careless repetition of seven Hebrew words. The exact English of this verse is this: And the servant **said, Let** them take now five of the remaining horses, which remain in it; behold they are as all the multitude of Israel which remain in it; behold, they are as all the multitude of Israel which are consumed; and let us send and see. Whoever considers that the second set of these seven words is neither in the Septuagint nor Syriac versions, and that those translators who suppose these words to be genuine alter them to make them look like sense, will probably allow them to have been at first an improper repetition; consequently to be now an interpolation strangely continued in the Hebrew text."

That are consumed. The words should be translated, "which are perfect"; i.e., fit for service. The rest of the horses were either dead of the famine, killed for the subsistence of the besieged, or so weak as not to be able to perform such a journey.

14. *They took . . . two chariot horses.* They had at first intended to send five; probably they found on examination that only two were effective.

15. *All the way was full of garments and vessels.* A manifest proof of the hurry and precipitancy with which they fled.

MATTHEW HENRY

no tumult or disorder in dividing and disposing of the spoil. 2. Was trodden to death by the people in the gate, either by accident, the crowd being exceedingly great, or perhaps designedly, because he abused his power. However it was, God's justice was glorified, and the word of Elisha was fulfilled. He saw the plenty, corn cheap without *opening windows in heaven*, and therein saw his own folly in prescribing to God; but he did not eat of the plenty he saw. This event is compared with the prediction (*v.* 18–20), that we might take special notice of it, and might learn, (1) How deeply God resents our distrust of him, of his power, providence, and promise. (2) How uncertain life and the enjoyments of it are. Honour and power cannot secure men from sudden and inglorious deaths. He whom the king leaned upon the people trod upon.

JAMIESON, FAUSSET, BROWN

by a popular rush to the Syrian camp. To keep order at the gate, the king ordered his minister to keep guard; but the impetuosity of the famishing people could not be resisted. The lord was trodden to death, and Elisha's prophecy in all respects accomplished.

ADAM CLARKE

17. *And the people trode upon him.* This officer being appointed by the king to have the command of the *gate*, the people rushing out to get spoil, and to carry it to their houses, he was borne down by the multitude, and trodden to death.

MATTHEW HENRY

CHAPTER 8

Verses 1–6

I. The wickedness of Israel punished with a long famine, one of God's sore judgments often threatened in the law. The famine in Samaria was soon relieved by the raising of the siege, but neither that judgment nor that mercy had a due influence upon them. If less judgments do not prevail to bring men to repentance, he will send greater and longer. This famine continued seven years, as long again as that in Elijah's time; for, if men will walk contrary to him, he will heat the furnace yet hotter.

II. The kindness of the good Shunammite to the prophet rewarded by the care that was taken of her in that famine. 1. She had notice given her of this famine before it came, that she might provide accordingly, and was directed to remove to some other country; anywhere but in Israel she would find plenty. 2. Providence gave her a comfortable settlement in *the land of the Philistines*, who, though subdued by David, yet were not wholly rooted out. It seems the famine was peculiar to the land of Israel, and other countries that joined close to them had plenty at the same time, which plainly showed the immediate hand of God in it.

III. Her petition to the king at her return, favoured by the seasonableness of her application to him. 1. When the famine was over she *returned out of the land of the Philistines*. 2. At her return she found herself kept out of the possession of her own estate, it being either confiscated to the exchequer, or usurped in her absence by some of the neighbours. 3. She made her application to the king himself for redress. 4. She found the king talking with Gehazi about Elisha's miracles, *v.* 4. The law did not forbid all conversation with lepers, but only dwelling with them. There being then no priests in Israel, perhaps the king, or someone appointed by him, had the inspection of lepers, and passed the judgment upon them, which might bring him acquainted with Gehazi. 5. This happy coincidence befriended both Gehazi's narrative and her petition. (1) It made the king ready to believe Gehazi's narrative when it was thus confirmed by the persons most nearly concerned: "*This is the woman, and this her son;* let them speak for themselves," *v.* 5. (2) It made him ready to grant her request; for who would not be ready to favour one whom heaven had thus favoured, and to support a life which was given once and again by miracle? In consideration of this the king gave orders that her land should be restored to her and all the profits that were made of it in her absence. It is not enough for those in authority that they do no wrong themselves, but they must support the right of those that are wronged.

Verses 7–15

I. We may enquire what brought Elisha to Damascus, the chief city of Syria. Perhaps he went to pay a visit to Naaman his convert, and to confirm him in his choice of the true religion, which was the more needful now because he was now out of his place (for Hazael is supposed to be captain of the host); either he resigned it or was turned out of it, because he would not bow heartily, in the house of Rimmon. Some think he went to Damascus upon account of the famine, or rather he went thither in obedience to the orders God gave Elijah, 1 Kings xix. 15, "*Go to Damascus to anoint Hazael*, thou, or thy successor."

II. We may observe that Benhadad, a great king, rich and mighty, lay sick. No honour, wealth, or power, will secure men from the common diseases and disasters of human life; palaces and thrones lie as open to sickness and death as the meanest cottage.

III. We may wonder that the king of Syria, in his sickness, should make Elisha his oracle.

1. Notice was soon brought him that *the man of God* (for by that title he was well known in Syria

JAMIESON, FAUSSET, BROWN

CHAPTER 8

VSS. 1-6. THE SHUNAMMITE'S LAND RESTORED. **1. Then spake Elisha unto the woman**—rather "had spoken." The repetition of Elisha's direction to the Shunammite is merely given as an introduction to the following narrative; and it probably took place before the events recorded in chaps. 5 and 6. **6. The Lord hath called for a famine**—All such calamities are chastisements inflicted by the hand of God; and this famine was to be of double duration to that one which happened in the time of Elijah (Jas. 5:17)—a just increase of severity, since the Israelites still continued obdurate and incorrigible under the ministry and miracles of Elisha (Lev. 26: 21, 24, 28). **2. she . . . sojourned in the land of the Philistines seven years**—Their territory was recommended to her from its contiguity to her usual residence; and now that this state had been so greatly reduced, there was less risk than formerly from the seductions of idolatry; and many of the Jews and Israelites were residing there. Besides, an emigration thither was less offensive to the king of Israel than going to sojourn in Judah.

3. she went forth to cry unto the king for her house and for her land—In consequence of her long-continued absence from the country, her possessions were occupied by her kindred, or had been confiscated by the crown. No statute in the law of Moses ordained that alienation. But the innovation seems to have been adopted in Israel. **4. the king talked with Gehazi**—Ceremonial pollution being conveyed by contact alone, there was nothing to prevent a conference being held with this leper at a distance; and although he was excluded from the *town* of Samaria, this reported conversation may have taken place at the gate or in one of the royal gardens. The providence of God so ordained that King Jehoram had been led to inquire, with great interest, into the miraculous deeds of Elisha, and that the prophet's servant was in the act of relating the marvellous incident of the restoration of the Shunammite's son when she made her appearance to prefer her request. The king was pleased to grant it; and a state officer was charged to afford her every facility in the recovery of her family possession out of the hands of the occupier.

7-15. HAZAEL KILLS HIS MASTER, AND SUCCEEDS HIM. **7. Elisha came to Damascus**—He was directed thither by the Spirit of God, in pursuance of the mission formerly given to his master in Horeb (I Kings 19:15), to anoint Hazael king of Syria. On the arrival of the prophet being known, Ben-hadad, who was sick, sent to inquire the issue of his disease, and, according to the practice of the heathens in consulting their soothsayers, ordered a liberal present in remuneration for the service.

ADAM CLARKE

CHAPTER 8

1. *Then spake Elisha.* As this is the relation of an event far past, the words should be translated, "But Elisha *had spoken* unto the woman whose son he *had restored* unto life; and the woman *had arisen*, and acted according to the saying of the man of God, and *had gone* with her family, and *had sojourned* in the land of the Philistines seven years." What is mentioned in these two verses happened several years before the time specified in the third verse.

5. *This is the woman, and this is her son, whom Elisha restored to life.* This was a very providential occurrence in behalf of the Shunammite. The relation given by Gehazi was now corroborated by the woman herself; the king was duly affected, and gave immediate orders for the restoration of her land.

MATTHEW HENRY

since he cured Naaman) had come to Damascus, *v.* 7. "Never in better time," says Benhadad. "*Go, and enquire of the Lord by him.*" In his health he *bowed in the house of Rimmon*, but now that he is sick he distrusts his idol, and sends to enquire of the God of Israel. This is the more observable, (1) Because it was not long since a king of Israel had, in his sickness, sent to enquire of the god of Ekron (*ch.* i. 2), as if there had been no God in Israel. (2) Because it was not long since this Benhadad had sent a great force to treat Elisha as an enemy (*ch.* vi. 14), yet now he courts him as a prophet.

2. To put an honour upon the prophet, (1) He sends *to* him, and does not send *for* him, as if, with the centurion, he thought himself not worthy that the man of God should come under his roof. (2) He sends to him by Hazael, his prime-minister of state, and not by a common messenger. (3) He sends him a noble present, *of every good thing of Damascus*, as much as loaded forty camels (*v.* 9), bidding him welcome to Damascus. It is probable that Elisha accepted it, though he refused Naaman's. (4) He orders Hazael to call him *his son Ben-hadad*, conforming to the language of Israel, who called the prophets *fathers.* (5) He puts an honour upon him as one acquainted with the secrets of heaven, when he enquires of him, *Shall I recover?*

IV. What passed between Hazael and Elisha is especially remarkable.

1. Elisha answered his enquiry concerning the king, that he might recover, the disease was not mortal, but that he should die another way (*v.* 10), not a natural but a violent death.

2. He looked Hazael in the face with an unusual concern, till he made Hazael blush and himself weep, *v.* 11.

3. When Hazael asked him why he wept he told him what a great deal of mischief he foresaw he would do to the Israel of God (*v.* 12). Elisha wept to think that ever Israelites should be thus abused. See what havoc war makes, what havoc sin makes, and how the nature of man is changed by the fall, and stripped even of humanity itself.

4. Hazael was greatly surprised at this prediction (*v.* 13): *What*, says he, *Is thy servant a dog, that he should do this great thing?* This great thing he looks upon to be, (1) An act of great power, not to be done but by a crowned head. (2) An act of great barbarity, which could not be done but by one lost to all honour and virtue. It is possible for a wicked man, under the convictions and restraints of natural conscience, to express great abhorrence of a sin, and yet afterwards to be well reconciled to it.

5. In answer to this Elisha only told him *he should be king over Syria*; then he would have power to do it, and then he would find in his heart to do it.

V. What mischief Hazael did to his master hereupon. 1. He basely cheated his master, and belied the prophet (*v.* 14): *He told me thou shouldst certainly recover.* This was an injury to the king, who lost the benefit of this warning to prepare for death and an injury to Elisha, who would be counted a false prophet. 2. He barbarously murdered his master, and so made good the prophet's word, *v.* 15. He dipped a thick cloth in cold water, and stifled him. Hazael, who was Benhadad's confidant, was his murderer, and, some think, was not suspected, nor did the truth ever come out but by the pen of this inspired historian.

Verses 16–24

A brief account of the life and reign of Jehoram, one of the worst of the kings of Judah, but the son and successor of Jehoshaphat, one of the best. A nation is sometimes justly punished with the miseries of a bad reign for not improving the blessings and advantages of a good one.

Concerning Jehoram,

I. The general idea here given of his wickedness (*v.* 18): *He did as the house of Ahab*, and worse he could not do. Jehoram chose the house of Ahab for his pattern rather than his father's house, and this choice was his ruin.

II. The occasions of his wickedness. His father was a very good man, and no doubt took care to have him taught the good knowledge of the Lord, but, 1. It is certain he did ill to marry him to the daughter of Ahab. Those that are ill-matched are already half-ruined. 2. He did not do well to make him king in his own life-time. It is said here (*v.* 16) that he *began to reign, Jehoshaphat being then king*; hereby he gratified his pride. Jehoshaphat had made this wicked son of his viceroy once, when he went with Ahab to Ramoth-Gilead, from which Jehoshaphat's seventeenth year (1 Kings xxii. 51) is made Jehoram's second (2 Kings i. 17), but afterwards, in his twenty-second year, he made him partner in his

JAMIESON, FAUSSET, BROWN

9. forty camels' burden—The present, consisting of the rarest and most valuable produce of the land, would be liberal and magnificent. But it must not be supposed it was actually so large as to require forty camels to carry it. The Orientals are fond of display, and would, ostentatiously, lay upon forty beasts what might very easily have been borne by four. **Thy son Ben-hadad**—so called from the established usage of designating the prophet "father." This was the same Syrian monarch who had formerly persecuted him (see on ch. 6:13, 14). **10. Go, say . . ., Thou mayest certainly recover**—There was no contradiction in this message. This part was properly the answer to Ben-hadad's inquiry. The second part was intended for Hazael, who, like an artful and ambitious courtier, reported only as much of the prophet's statement as suited his own views (cf. vs. 14). **11. he settled his countenance steadfastly, until he was ashamed**—i.e., Hazael. The steadfast, penetrating look of the prophet seemed to have convinced Hazael that his secret designs were known. The deep emotions of Elisha were justified by the horrible atrocities which, too common in ancient warfare, that successful usurper committed in Israel (ch. 10:32; 13: 3, 4, 22).

15. took a thick cloth, etc.—a coverlet. In the East, this article of bedding is generally a thick quilt of wool or cotton, so that, with its great weight, when steeped in water, it would be a fit instrument for accomplishing the murderous purpose, without leaving any marks of violence. It has been supposed by many that Hazael purposely murdered the king. But it is common for Eastern people to sleep with their faces covered with a mosquito net; and, in some cases of fever, they dampen the bedclothes. Hazael, aware of those chilling remedies being usually resorted to, might have, with an honest intention, spread a refreshing cover over him. The rapid occurrence of the king's death and immediate burial were favorable to his instant elevation to the throne.

16-23. JEHORAM'S WICKED REIGN. **16. Jehoram the son of Jehoshaphat . . . began to reign**—(See on ch. 3:1). His father resigned the throne to him two years before his death.

18. daughter of Ahab—Athaliah, through whose influence Jehoram introduced the worship of Baal and many other evils into the kingdom of Judah (see II Chron. 21:2-20).

ADAM CLARKE

8. *Take a present in thine hand.* But what an immense present was this—forty camels' burden of every good thing of Damascus!

10. *Thou mayest certainly recover: howbeit the Lord hath shewed me that he shall surely die.* That is, God has not determined your death, nor will it be a necessary consequence of the disease by which you are now afflicted; but this wicked man will abuse the power and trust you have reposed in him, and take away your life.

11. *He settled his countenance stedfastly.* Of whom does the author speak? Of Hazael, or of Elisha? Several apply this action to the prophet. He had a murderer before him, and he saw the bloody acts he was about to commit, and was greatly distressed; but he endeavored to conceal his feelings. At last his face reddened with anguish, his feelings overcame him, and he burst out and wept. The Septuagint, as it stands in the Complutensian and Antwerp Polyglots, makes the text very plain: "And Hazael stood before his face, and he presented before him gifts till he was ashamed; and the man of God wept." The Codex Vaticanus and the Codex Alexandrinus are nearly as the Hebrew. All the versions follow the Hebrew.

12. *I know the evil that thou wilt do.* We may see something of the accomplishment of this prediction, chap. x. 32-33 and xiii. 3, 7.

13. *But what, is thy servant a dog, that he should do this great thing?* I believe this verse to be wrongly interpreted by the general run of commentators. It is generally understood that Hazael was struck with horror at the prediction; that these cruelties were most alien from his mind; that he then felt distressed and offended at the imputation of such evils to him; and yet so little did he know his own heart that when he got power, and had opportunity, he did the whole with a willing heart and a ready hand. On the contrary, I think he was delighted at the prospect; and his question rather implies a doubt whether a person so inconsiderable as he is shall ever have it in his power to do such great, not such evil things. The Hebrew text stands thus: "But, what! thy servant, this dog! that he should do this great work!" Or, "Can such a poor, worthless fellow, such a dead dog, perform such mighty actions? thou fillest me with surprise." And that this is the true sense, his immediate murder of his master on his return fully proves.

15. *A thick cloth.* The versions, in general, understand this of a hairy or woolen cloth. *So that he died.* He was smothered, or suffocated.

16. *In the fifth year of Joram.* The three Hebrew words, "and of Jehoshaphat king of Judah," greatly disturb the chronology in this place. It is certain that Jehoshaphat reigned twenty-five years, and that Jehoram, his son, reigned but eight; 1 Kings xxii. 42; 2 Kings viii. 17; 2 Chron. xx. 31 and xxi. 5. So that he could not have reigned during his father's life without being king twenty years, and eight years! These words are wanting in three of Kennicott's and De Rossi's MSS., in the Complutensian and Aldine editions of the Septuagint, in the Peshito Syriac, in the Arabic, and in many copies of the Vulgate.

17. *He reigned eight years in Jerusalem.* Beginning with the fifth year of Joram, king of Israel. He reigned three years with Jehoshaphat, his father, and five years alone.

18. *The daughter of Ahab was his wife.* This was the infamous Athaliah, and through this marriage Jehoshaphat and Ahab were confederates; and this friendship was continued after Ahab's death.

MATTHEW HENRY

government. It has been hurtful to many young men to come too soon to their estates. Samuel got nothing by *making his sons judges*.

III. The rebukes of Providence which he was under for his wickedness. 1. The Edomites revolted, who had been under the government of the kings of Judah ever since David's time, about 150 years, *v.* 20. He attempted to reduce them, and gave them a defeat (*v.* 21), but he could not recover his dominion over them: *Yet Edom revolted* (*v.* 22), and the Edomites were, after this, bitter enemies to the Jews, as appears by the prophecy of Obadiah and Ps. cxxxvii. 7. 2. Libnah revolted. This was a city in Judah, in the heart of his country, a priests' city; the inhabitants of this city shook off his government *because he had forsaken God*, and would have compelled them to do so too, 2 Chron. xxi. 10, 11. In order that they might preserve their religion they set up for a free state. 3. His reign was short. God cut him off in the midst of his days, when he was but forty years old, and had reigned but eight years.

IV. The gracious care of Providence for the keeping up of the kingdom of Judah, and the house of David, notwithstanding the apostasies and calamities of Jehoram's reign (*v.* 19): *Yet the Lord would not destroy Judah*.

V. The conclusion of this impious and inglorious reign, *v.* 23, 24. Nothing peculiar is here said of him; but we are told (2 Chron. xxi. 19, 20) that he *died of sore diseases* and *died without being desired*.

Verses 25–29

As among common persons there are some that we call *little men*, who make no figure, are little regarded, and less valued, so among kings there are some whom, in comparison with others, we may call *little kings*. This Ahaziah was one of these; he looks mean in the history, and in God's account vile, because wicked. Jehoshaphat and Ahab had the same names in their families at the same time, in which they designed to compliment one another. Ahab had two sons, Ahaziah and Jehoram, who reigned successively; Jehoshaphat had a son and grandson named Jehoram and Ahaziah, who, in like manner, reigned successively. Ahaziah king of Israel had reigned but two years, Ahaziah king of Judah reigned but one. We are here told that his relation to Ahab's family was the occasion, 1. Of his wickedness (*v.* 27): *He walked in the way of the house of Ahab*, that idolatrous bloody house: for his mother was Ahab's daughter (*v.* 26). When men choose wives for themselves they must remember they are choosing mothers for their children, and are concerned to choose accordingly. 2. Of his fall. Joram, his mother's brother, courted him to join with him for the recovery of Ramoth-Gilead, an attempt fatal to Ahab; so it was to Joram his son, for in that expedition he was wounded (*v.* 28), and returned to Jezreel to be cured, leaving his army there in possession of the place. Ahaziah likewise returned, but went to Jezreel to see how Jehoram did, *v.* 29.

JAMIESON, FAUSSET, BROWN

This apostasy would have led to the total extinction of the royal family in that kingdom, had it not been for the divine promise to David (II Sam. 7). A national chastisement, however, was inflicted on Judah by the revolt of Edom, which, being hitherto governed by a tributary ruler (ch. 3:9; I Kings 22:47), erected the standard of independence (see on II Chron. 21:9).

24. AHAZIAH SUCCEEDS HIM. **24. Ahaziah his son reigned in his stead**—(See on II Chron. 22: 1-6).

ADAM CLARKE

19. *To give him alway a light.* To give him a successor in his own family.

21. *Joram went over to Zair.* This is the same as Seir, a chief city of Idumea. So Isa. xxi. 11: "The burden of Dumah [Idumea]. He calleth to me out of Seir." *Smote the Edomites.* It appears that the Israelites were surrounded by the Idumeans; and that in the night Joram and his men cut their way through them, and so got every man to his tent, for they were not able to make any further head against these enemies; and therefore it is said, that "Edom revolted from under the hand of Judah unto this day."

23. *Are they not written in the book of the chronicles.* Several remarkable particulars relative to Joram may be found in 2 Chronicles xxi.

26. *Two and twenty years old was Ahaziah when he began to reign.* In 2 Chron. xxii. 2, it is said, "Forty and two years old was Ahaziah when he began to reign"; this is a heavy difficulty, to remove which several expedients have been used. It is most evident that, if we follow the reading in Chronicles, it makes the son two years older than his own father! for his father began to reign when he was thirty-two years old, and reigned eight years, and so died, being forty years old (see v. 17).

After all, here is a most manifest contradiction that cannot be removed but by having recourse to violent modes of solution. I am satisfied the reading in 2 Chron. xxii. 2 is a mistake; and that we should read there, as here, "twenty-two" instead of "forty-two" years. And may we not say with Calmet, Which is most dangerous, to acknowledge that transcribers have made some mistakes in copying the sacred books, or to acknowledge that there are contradictions in them, and then to have recourse to solutions that can yield no satisfaction to any unprejudiced mind?

28. *The Syrians wounded Joram.* Ahaziah went with Joram to endeavor to wrest Ramoth-gilead out of the hands of the Syrians, which belonged to Israel and Judah. Ahab had endeavored to do this before, and was slain there (see 1 Kings xxii. 3, etc.).

29. *Went back to be healed in Jezreel.* And there he continued till Jehu conspired against and slew him there. And thus the blood of the innocents, which had been shed by Ahab and his wife, Jezebel, was visited on them in the total extinction of their family. See the following chapters, where the bloody tale of Jehu's conspiracy is told at large.

MATTHEW HENRY — CHAPTER 9

Verses 1–10

The anointing of Jehu to be king. It does not appear that Jehu aimed at the government. Some think that he had been anointed before by Elijah, whom God ordered to do it, but privately, and with an intimation that he must not act till further orders, as Samuel anointed David long before he was to come to the throne: but that is not at all probable, for then we must suppose Elijah had anointed Hazael too.

I. The commission sent.

1. Elisha did not go himself to anoint Jehu, because he was old and unfit for such a journey and so well known that he could not do it privately, therefore he sends *one of the sons of the prophets* to do it, *v.* 1.

2. When he sent him, (1) He put the oil into his hand with which he must anoint Jehu: *Take this box of oil*. Solomon was anointed with *oil out of the tabernacle*, 1 Kings i. 39. That could not now be had, but oil from a prophet's hand was equivalent to oil out of God's house. (2) He put *the words into his mouth* which he must say (*v.* 3)—*I have anointed thee king*, *v.* 7–10. (3) He also ordered him, [1] To do it privately, to single out Jehu from the rest of the captains and anoint him *in an inner chamber* (*v.* 2). [2] To do it expeditiously. When he had done it he must *flee and not tarry*.

II. The commission delivered. The young prophet

JAMIESON, FAUSSET, BROWN — CHAPTER 9

VSS. 1-23. JEHU IS ANOINTED. **1. Ramoth-gilead**—a city of great importance to the Hebrew people, east of Jordan, as a fortress of defense against the Syrians. Jehoram had regained it (ch. 8:29). But the Israelitish army was still encamped there, under the command of Jehu.

Elisha . . . called one of the children of the prophets—This errand referred to the last commission given to Elijah in Horeb (I Kings 19:16).

box of oil—(See I Sam. 10:1). **2. carry him to an inner chamber**—both to ensure the safety of the messenger and to prevent all obstruction in the execution of the business. **3. I have anointed thee king over Israel**—This was only a part of the message; the full announcement of which is given (vss. 7-10). **flee, and tarry not**—for fear of being surprised and overtaken by the spies or servants of the court.

ADAM CLARKE — CHAPTER 9

1. *One of the children of the prophets.* The Jews say that this was Jonah, the prophet, the son of Amittai. *Gird up thy loins.* What you have to do requires the utmost dispatch.

MATTHEW HENRY

did his business with despatch, was at Ramoth-Gilead presently, *v.* 4. There he found the general officers in a council of war, *v.* 5. With the assurance that became a messenger from God, he called Jehu out from the rest as one having authority: *I have an errand to thee, O captain.* Perhaps Jehu had some intimation of his business; and therefore, that he might not seem too forward to catch at the honour, he asked, *To which of all us?* When the prophet had him alone he anointed him, *v.* 6.

1. He invests him with the royal dignity: *Thus saith the Lord God of Israel,* whose messenger I am, in his name *I have anointed thee king over the people of the Lord.* He reminds him that he was made king, (1) *By the God of Israel*; from him he must see his power derived, for him he must use it, and to him he must be accountable. (2) *Over the Israel of God.* Though the people of Israel had forfeited all the honour of relationship to God, yet they are here called the *people of the Lord,* for he had a right to them. Jehu must look upon the people he was made king of as the *people of the Lord,* God's freemen, not to be abused or tyrannised over, *God's people,* and therefore to be ruled for him, and according to his laws.

2. He instructs him in his present service, which was to destroy all the house of Ahab (*v.* 7), not that he might clear his own way to the throne, but that he might execute the judgments of God upon that guilty and obnoxious family. He calls Ahab his *master*: "But thou art under higher obligations to thy Master in heaven than to thy master Ahab. He has determined that *the whole house of Ahab shall perish,* and *by thy hand*; fear not danger; his command will secure and prosper thee." That he might intelligently do this execution on the house of Ahab, he tells him, (1) What was their crime. That they were idolaters was bad enough, but the controversy God has with them is for their being persecutors, not so much their *throwing down God's altars* as their *slaying his prophets with the sword.* This was the sin that brought on Jerusalem its first destruction (2 Chron. xxxvi. 16) and its final one, Matt. xxiii. 37, 38. Jezebel's whoredoms and witchcrafts were not so provoking as her persecuting the prophets, killing some and driving the rest into corners and caves, 1 Kings xviii. 4. (2) What was their doom. They were sentenced to utter destruction; and he is particularly directed to throw Jezebel to the dogs, *v.* 10.

Verses 11–15

Jehu, after some pause, returned to his place at the board, taking no notice of what had passed, but, as it should seem, designing, for the present, to keep it to himself.

I. With what contempt the captains speak of the young prophet (*v.* 11): "*Wherefore came this mad fellow to thee?* What business had he with thee?" They thought the prophets were fools and the *spiritual men were mad,* Hos. ix. 7. Those that have no religion commonly speak with disdain of those that are religious, and look upon them as mad. They said of our Saviour, *He is beside himself,* of John Baptist, *He has a devil,* of St. Paul, *Much learning has made him mad.* The highest wisdom is thus represented as folly, and those that best understand themselves are looked upon as beside themselves. Perhaps Jehu intended it for a rebuke to his friends when he said, "*You know the man* to be a prophet, why then do you call him a mad fellow?" Thus he thought to put them off, but they urged him to tell them. "It is false," say they, "we cannot conjecture what was his errand, and therefore tell us." Being thus pressed to it, he told them that the prophet had *anointed him king,* and it is probable showed them the oil upon his head, *v.* 12.

II. With what respect they compliment the new king upon the first notice of his advancement, *v.* 13. In token of their subjection and allegiance to him, they put their garments under him, that he might stand *on the top of the stairs,* in sight of the soldiers, who, upon the first intimation, came together to grace the solemnity.

III. With what caution Jehu proceeded. He had the army with him. Joram had left it, and had gone home badly wounded. Jehu's good conduct appears in two things:—1. That he complimented the captains, and would do nothing without their advice and consent. 2. That he contrived to surprise Joram; and, in order thereto, to come upon him with speed. The suddenness of an attack sometimes turns to as good an account as the force of it.

Verses 16–29

From Ramoth-Gilead to Jezreel was more than one day's march; about the mid-way between them the river Jordan must be crossed.

JAMIESON, FAUSSET, BROWN

4. So the young man . . . went to Ramoth-gilead—His ready undertaking of this delicate and hazardous mission was an eminent proof of his piety and obedience. The act of anointing being done through a commissioned prophet, was a divine intimation of his investiture with the sovereign power. But it was sometimes done long prior to the actual possession of the throne (I Sam. 16:13); and, in like manner, the commission had, in this instance, been given also a long time before to Elijah, who, for good reasons, left it in charge to Elisha; and he awaited God's time and command for executing it [POOLE].

10. in the portion of Jezreel—i.e., that had formerly been the vineyard of Naboth.

11. Is all well? etc.—Jehu's attendants knew that the stranger belonged to the order of the prophets by his garb, gestures, and form of address; and soldiers such as they very readily concluded such persons to be crackbrained, not only from the sordid negligence of their personal appearance and their open contempt of the world, but from the religious pursuits in which their whole lives were spent, and the grotesque actions which they frequently performed (cf. Jer. 29:26).

13. they hasted, and took every man his garment—the upper cloak which they spread on the ground, as a token of their homage to their distinguished commander (Matt. 21:7). **top of the stairs**—from the room where the prophet had privately anointed Jehu. That general returned to join his brother officers in the public apartment, who, immediately on learning his destined elevation, conducted him to the top of the stairs leading to the roof. This was the most conspicuous place of an Oriental structure that could be chosen, being at the very top of the gate-building, and fully in view of the people and military in the open ground in front of the building [KITTO]. The popularity of Jehu with the army thus favored the designs of Providence in procuring his immediate and enthusiastic proclamation as king, and the top of the stairs was taken as a most convenient substitute for a throne. **14, 15. Joram had kept Ramoth-gilead**—rather, was keeping, guarding, or besieging it, with the greater part of the military force of Israel. The king's wounds had compelled his retirement from the scene of action, and so the troops were left in command of Jehu. **16. So Jehu rode in a chariot, and went to Jezreel**—Full of ambitious designs, he immediately proceeded to cross the Jordan to execute his commission on the house of Ahab.

ADAM CLARKE

4. *The young man the prophet.* This should be translated, "The servant of the prophet"; that is, the servant which Elisha now had in place of Gehazi.

6. *King over the people of the Lord.* This pointed out to Jehu that he was to rule that people according to God's law; and consequently, that he was to restore the pure worship of the Most High in Israel.

7. *Thou shalt smite the house of Ahab.* For their most cruel murders they have forfeited their own lives, according to that immutable law, "He that sheddeth man's blood, by man shall his blood be shed." This and the following two verses contain the commission which Jehu received from the Lord against the bloody house of Ahab.

10. *The dogs shall eat Jezebel.* How most minutely was this prophecy fulfilled (see v. 33, etc.)!

11. *Wherefore came this mad fellow to thee?* Was it because he was a holy man of God that he was reputed by a club of irreligious officers to be a madman? *Ye know the man, and his communication.* You know that he is a madman, and that his message must be a message of folly. Jehu did not appear willing to tell them what had been done, lest it should promote jealousy and envy.

12. *They said, It is false.* Or, as the Chaldee has it, "Thou liest."

13. *Took every man his garment.* This was a ceremony by which they acknowledged him as king; and it was by such a ceremony that the multitudes acknowledged Jesus Christ for the Messiah and King of Israel, a little before His passion (see Matt. xxi. 7). The ceremony was expressive: "As we put our garments under his feet, so we place everything under his authority, and acknowledge ourselves his servants."

On the top of the stairs. The Chaldee, the rabbins, and several interpreters understand this of the public sundial; which, in those ancient times, was formed of steps like stairs, each step serving to indicate, by its shadow, one hour, or such division of time as was commonly used in that country. This dial was, no doubt, in the most public place; and upon the top of it, or on the platform on the top, would be a very proper place to set Jehu, while they blew their trumpets, and proclaimed him king. The Hebrew *maaloth* is the same word which is used in chap. xx. 9-11 to signify the "dial" of Ahaz, and this was probably the very same dial on which that miracle was afterwards wrought.

14. *Joram had kept Ramoth-gilead.* The confederate armies appear to have taken this city; but they were obliged to watch their conquests, as they perceived that Hazael was determined to retake it if possible.

16. *Jehu . . . went to Jezreel; for Joram lay there.* From the preceding verse we learn that Joram had been wounded in his attack on Ramoth-gilead, and had gone to Jezreel to be cured; and neither he nor Ahaziah knew anything of the conspiracy in Ramoth-gilead, because Jehu and his captains took care to prevent

MATTHEW HENRY

I. Joram's watchman discovers him first at a distance, him and his retinue, and gives notice to the king of the approach of a company, whether of friends or foes he cannot tell. But the king sent first one messenger, and then another, to bring him intelligence, *v.* 17–19. Each messenger asked the same question: "*Is it peace?* are you for us or for our adversaries?" Each had the same answer: *What hast thou to do with peace? Turn thee behind me*, *v.* 18, 19. The watchman gave notice that the messengers were taken prisoners, and at length observed that the leader of this troop drove like Jehu, who it seems was noted for driving furiously. A man of such a violent temper was fittest for the service to which Jehu was designated.

II. Joram himself goes out to meet him, and takes Ahaziah king of Judah along with him, neither of them equipped for war, as not expecting an enemy, but in haste to have their curiosity satisfied.

1. The place where Joram met Jehu was ominous: *In the portion of Naboth the Jezreelite*, *v.* 21. The very sight of that ground was enough to make Joram tremble and Jehu triumph; for Joram had the guilt of Naboth's blood fighting against him and Jehu had the force of Elijah's curse fighting for him.

2. Joram's demand was still the same: "*Is it peace, Jehu?* Is all well? Dost thou come home thus flying from the Syrians or more than a conqueror over them?"

3. Jehu's reply was very startling. He answered him with a question: *What peace* canst thou expect, *so long as the whoredoms of thy mother Jezebel and her witchcrafts are so many?* Observe, (1) He charges upon him his mother's wickedness. She stands impeached for whoredom, corporal and spiritual, for witchcraft likewise, enchantments and divinations, used in honour of her idols; and these multiplied, for those that abandon themselves to wicked courses know not where they will stop. (2) Upon that account he throws him off from all pretensions to peace: "What peace can come to that house in which there is so much wickedness unrepented of?" The way of sin can never be the way of peace, Isa. lvii. 21. No peace so long as sin is persisted in; but, as soon as it is repented of and forsaken there is peace.

4. The execution was done immediately. When Joram heard of his mother's crimes his heart failed him; he presently concluded the long-threatened day of reckoning had now come, and cried out, "*There is treachery, O Ahaziah!* Jehu is our enemy, and it is time for us to shift for our safety." Both fled, and, (1) Joram king of Israel was slain presently, *v.* 24. Jehu dispatched him with his own hands. He died a criminal, under the sentence of the law, which Jehu, the executioner, pursues in the disposal of the dead body. Naboth's vineyard was hard by, which put him in mind of that circumstance of the doom Elijah passed upon Ahab, "*I will requite thee in this plat, said the Lord* (*v.* 25, 26), *for the blood of Naboth* himself, and *for the blood of his sons.*" That very piece of ground which he, with so much pride and pleasure, had made himself master of at the expense of the guilt of innocent blood, now became the theatre on which his son's dead body lay exposed a spectacle to the world. (2) Ahaziah king of Judah was pursued, and slain in a little time, and not far off, *v.* 27, 28. Though he was now in Joram's company, he would not have been slain but that he was joined with the house of Ahab both in affinity and in iniquity.

Verses 30–37

The greatest delinquent in the house of Ahab was Jezebel: it was she that introduced Baal, slew the Lord's prophets, contrived the murder of Naboth, stirred up her husband first, and then her sons, to do wickedly; a *cursed woman* she is here called (*v.* 34). Three reigns her reign had lasted, but now, at length, her day had come to fall. So that Jezebel's destruction may be looked upon as typical of the destruction of idolaters and persecutors.

I. Jezebel daring the judgment. She heard that Jehu had slain her son, and slain him for her whoredoms and witchcrafts, and thrown his dead body into the portion of Naboth, and that he was now coming to Jezreel. She posted herself in a window at the entering of the gate, to affront Jehu and set him at defiance. 1. Instead of hiding herself, as one afraid of divine vengeance, she exposed herself to it and scorned to flee. 2. Instead of humbling herself, and putting herself into close mourning for her son, she *painted her face, and tired her head*, that she might appear like herself, that is (as she thought), great and majestic, hoping thereby to daunt Jehu. There is not a surer presage of ruin than an unhumbled heart under humbling providences. 3. Instead of trembling before Jehu, the instrument of God's vengeance, she thought to make him tremble with

JAMIESON, FAUSSET, BROWN

17. there stood a watchman on the tower of Jezreel—The Hebrew palaces, besides being situated on hills had usually towers attached to them, not only for the pleasure of a fine prospect, but as posts of useful observation. The ancient watchtower of Jezreel must have commanded a view of the whole region eastward, nearly down to the Jordan. Beth-shan stands on a rising ground about six or seven miles below it, in a narrow part of the plain; and when Jehu and his retinue reached that point between Gilboa and Beth-shan, they could be fully descried by the watchman on the tower. A report was made to Joram in his palace below. A messenger on horseback was quickly despatched down into the plain to meet the ambiguous host and to question the object of their approach. "Is it peace?" We may safely assume that this messenger would meet Jehu at the distance of three miles or more. On the report made of his being detained and turned into the rear of the still advancing troops, a second messenger was in like manner despatched, who would naturally meet Jehu at the distance of a mile or a mile and a half down on the plain. He also being turned into the rear, the watchman now distinctly perceived "the driving to be like the driving of Jehu, the son of Nimshi; for he driveth furiously."

The alarmed monarch, awakened to a sense of his impending danger, quickly summoned his forces to meet the crisis. Accompanied by Ahaziah, king of Judah, the two sovereigns ascended their chariots to make a feeble resistance to the impetuous onset of Jehu, who quickly from the plain ascended the steep northern sides of the site on which Jezreel stood, and the conflicting parties met in "the portion of Naboth the Jezreelite," where Joram was quickly despatched by an arrow from the strong arm of Jehu. We were impressed with the obvious accuracy of the sacred historian; the *localities* and *distances* being such as seem naturally to be required by the incidents related, affording just time for the transactions to have occurred in the order in which they are recorded [HOWE]. **25. cast him in the portion of the field of Naboth the Jezreelite,** etc.—according to the doom pronounced by divine authority on Ahab (I Kings 21:19), but which on his repentance was deferred to be executed on his son. **26. the blood of Naboth, and the blood of sons, saith the Lord**—Although their death is not expressly mentioned, it is plainly implied in the confiscation of his property (see on I Kings 21:16).

27-35. AHAZIAH IS SLAIN. **27. Ahaziah**—was grandnephew to King Joram, and great-grandson to King Ahab. **Ibleam**—near Megiddo, in the tribe of Issachar (Josh. 17:11; Judg. 1:27); and Gur was an adjoining hill.

30. Jezebel painted her face—lit., her eyes, according to a custom universal in the East among women, of staining the eyelids with a black powder made of pulverized antimony, or lead-ore mixed with oil, and applied with a small brush on the border, so that by this dark ligament on the edge, the largeness as well as the luster of the eye itself was thought to be increased. Her object was, by her royal attire, not to captivate, but to overawe Jehu.

ADAM CLARKE

any person from leaving the city.

17. *A watchman on the tower.* These watchmen, fixed on elevated places, and generally within hearing of each other, served as a kind of telegraphs, to communicate intelligence through the whole country. But, in some cases, it appears that the intelligence was conveyed by a horseman to the next stage, as in the case before us. At this time, when the armies were at Ramoth-gilead, they were, no doubt, doubly watchful to observe the state of the country and to notice every movement.

18. *What hast thou to do with peace?* "What is it to thee whether there be peace or war? Join my company, and fall into the rear."

20. *He driveth furiously.* Jehu was a bold, daring, prompt, and precipitate general. In his various military operations he had established his character, and now it was almost proverbial.

21. *Joram . . . and Ahaziah . . . went out.* They had no suspicion of what was done at Ramoth-gilead; else they would not have ventured their persons as they now did.

22. *What peace, so long as the whoredoms?* Though the words whoredom, adultery, and fornication are frequently used to express idolatry and false religion in general, yet here they may be safely taken in their common and most obvious sense, as there is much reason to believe that Jezebel was the patroness and supporter of a very impure system of religion.

23. *There is treachery, O Ahaziah.* This was the first intimation he had of it; he feels for the safety of his friend Ahaziah, and now they fly for their lives.

24. *Drew a bow with his full strength.* The marginal reading is correct: "He filled his hand with a bow." That is, "He immediately took up his bow, set his arrow, and let fly." *Between his arms.* That is, between his shoulders; for he was now turned, and was flying from Jehu.

25. *Cast him in the portion of the field.* This was predicted, 1 Kings xxi; and what now happened to the son of Ahab is foretold in v. 29 of that chapter.

26. *The blood of Naboth, and the blood of his sons.* We are not informed in 1 Kings xxi that any of Naboth's family was slain but himself. But as the object of both Ahab and Jezebel was to have Naboth's vineyard entirely, and forever, it is not likely that they would leave any of his posterity, who might at a future time reclaim it as their inheritance.

27. *Fled by the way of the garden.* The account of the death of Ahaziah, as given in 2 Chron. xxii. 8-9, is: "When Jehu was executing judgment upon the house of Ahab . . . he sought Ahaziah: and they caught him, (for he was hid in Samaria,) and brought him to Jehu: and when they had slain him, they buried him."

29. *In the eleventh year of Joram.* The note in our margin contains as good an account of this chronological difficulty as can be reasonably required: Then he began to reign "as viceroy to his father in his sickness, 2 Chron. xxi 18-19. But in Joram's twelfth year he began to reign alone, chap. viii. 25."

30. *She painted her face, and tired her head.* She endeavored to improve the appearance of her complexion by paint, and the general effect of her countenance by a tiara or turban headdress. Jonathan, the Chaldee Targumist, translates this, "She stained her eyes with *stibium* or *antimony.*"

MATTHEW HENRY

that threatening question, *Had Zimri peace, who slew his master?* (1) She took no notice of the hand of God gone out against her family, but flew in the face of him that was only the sword in his hand. (2) She pleased herself with the thought that what Jehu was now doing would certainly end in his own ruin, and that he would not have peace in it. (3) She quoted a precedent, to deter him from the prosecution of this enterprise: "*Had Zimri peace?* No, he had not; he came to the throne by blood and treachery, and within seven days was constrained to burn the palace over his head and himself in it: and canst thou expect to fare any better?" But Zimri had no warrant for what he did, but was incited to it merely by his own ambition and cruelty; whereas Jehu was anointed by one of the sons of the prophets, and did this by order from heaven, which would bear him out.

II. Jehu demanding aid against her. He looked up to the window, not daunted at the menaces of her impudent but impotent rage, and cried, *Who is on my side? Who? v.* 32. When reformation-work is set on foot, it is time to ask, "Who sides with it?"

III. Her own attendants delivering her up to his just revenge. Two or three chamberlains looked out to Jehu with such a countenance as encouraged him to believe they were on his side, and to them he called immediately to throw her down, which was one way of stoning malefactors, casting them headlong from some steep place. Thus was vengeance taken on her for the stoning of Naboth. They threw her down, *v.* 33. Thus she was most shamefully put to death, dashed against the wall and the pavement.

IV. The very dogs completing her shame and ruin, according to the prophecy. Jehu bethought himself of showing so much respect to Jezebel's sex and quality as to bury her. As bad as she was, she was a daughter, a king's daughter, a king's wife, a king's mother: *Go and bury her, v.* 34. While he was eating and drinking, the dogs had devoured her dead body. The hungry dogs had no respect to the dignity of her extraction; a king's daughter was no more to them than a common person. When notice was brought of this to Jehu, he remembered the threatening (**1 Kings xxi. 23**), *The dogs shall eat Jezebel by the wall of Jezreel.* Jezebel's name nowhere remained, but as stigmatised in sacred writ: they could not so much as say, "This is Jezebel's dust, This is Jezebel's grave."

JAMIESON, FAUSSET, BROWN

TODAY'S DICTIONARY OF THE BIBLE:

Jezebel—the daughter of Ethbaal, the king of the Zidonians, and the wife of Ahab, the king of Israel (1 Kings 16:31). This was the "first time that a king of Israel had allied himself by marriage with a heathen princess; and the alliance was in this case of a peculiarly disastrous kind. Jezebel has stamped her name on history as the representative of all that is designing, crafty, malicious, revengeful, and cruel. She is the first great instigator of persecution against the saints of God. Guided by no principle, restrained by no fear of either God or man, passionate in her attachment to her heathen worship, she spared no pains to maintain idolatry around her in all its splendor. Four hundred and fifty prophets ministered under her care to Baal, besides four hundred prophets of the groves—RSV, 'prophets of the Asherah,' who ate at her table (1 Kings 18:19). The idolatry, too, was of the most debased and sensual kind." Her conduct was in many respects very disastrous to the kingdom both of Israel and Judah (21:1–29). At length she came to an untimely end. As Jehu rode into the gates of Jezreel, she looked out at the window of the palace, and said, "Had Zimri peace, who slew his master?" He looked up and called to her chamberlains, who instantly threw her from the window, so that she was dashed in pieces on the street, and his horses trod her under their feet. She was immediately consumed by the dogs of the street (2 Kings 9:7–37), according to the word of Elijah the Tishbite (1 Kings 21:17, 19).

Her name afterward came to be used as the synonym for a wicked woman (Rev. 2:20).

35. found no more of her than the skull, and the palms of her hands, etc.—The dog has a rooted aversion to prey on the human hands and feet.

36, 37. JEZEBEL EATEN BY DOGS. **36. he said, This is the word of the Lord**—(see on I Kings 21:23). Jehu's statement, however, was not a literal but a paraphrased quotation of Elijah's prophecy.

ADAM CLARKE

33. *So they threw her down.* What a terrible death! She was already, by the fall, almost dashed to pieces; and the brutal Jehu trampled her already mangled body under his horses' feet!

34. *She is a king's daughter.* She was daughter of the king of Tyre; wife of Ahab, king of Israel; mother of Joram, king of Israel; mother-in-law of Joram, king of Judah; and grandmother of Ahaziah, king of Judah.

37. *And the carcase of Jezebel shall be as dung.* As it was not buried under the earth, but was eaten by the dogs, this saying was also literally fulfilled. *They shall not say, This is Jezebel.* There was not even a solitary stone to say, "Here lies Jezebel!"

MATTHEW HENRY

CHAPTER 10

Verses 1–14

Jehu knew the whole house of Ahab must be cut off.

I. He got the heads of all the sons of Ahab cut off by their own guardians at Samaria. These sons of Ahab were now at Samaria, a strong city, perhaps brought thither upon occasion of the war with Syria, as a place of safety, or upon notice of Jehu's insurrection; with them were the rulers of Jezreel, that is, the great officers of the court, who went to Samaria to secure themselves or to consult what was to be done. Jehu did not think fit to bring his forces to Samaria to destroy them, but, that the hand of God might appear the more remarkably in it, made their guardians their murderers. 1. He sent a challenge to their friends to stand by them, *v.* 2, 3. Not that he desired they should do this, or expected they would, but thus he upbraided them with their cowardice and utter inability to contest with the divine counsels. 2. Hereby he gained from them a submission. They prudently reasoned with themselves: "*Behold, two kings stood not before him*, but fell as sacrifices to his rage; *how then shall we stand?*" *v.* 4. Therefore they sent him a surrender of themselves: "*We are thy servants*, thy subjects, and *will do all that thou shalt bid us.*" 3. This was improved so far as to make them the executioners of those whom they had the tuition of (*v.* 6). These elders of Jezreel had been wickedly obsequious to Jezebel's order for the murder of Naboth, 1 Kings xxi. 11. She gloried, it is likely, in the power she had over them; and now the same base spirit makes them as pliable to Jehu and as ready to obey his orders for the murder of Ahab's sons. When the heads were presented to Jehu, he upbraided those that were the executioners, yet owned the hand of God in it. (1) He seems to blame those that had been the executioners of this vengeance. "I slew but one; they have slain all these. Let not the people of Samaria, nor any of the friends of the house of Ahab, ever reproach me for what I have done, when their own elders, and the very guardians of the orphans, have done this." But, (2) He resolves all into the righteous judgment of God (*v.* 10): *The Lord hath done that which he spoke by Elijah.*

II. He proceeded to destroy all that remained of

JAMIESON, FAUSSET, BROWN

CHAPTER 10

VSS. 1-17. JEHU CAUSES SEVENTY OF AHAB'S CHILDREN TO BE BEHEADED. **1. Ahab had seventy sons in Samaria**—As it appears (vs. 13) that grandsons are included, it is probable that this number comprehended the whole posterity of Ahab. Their being all assembled in that capital might arise from their being left there on the king's departure for Ramoth-gilead, or from their taking refuge in some of the strongholds of that city on the news of Jehu's conspiracy. It may be inferred from the tenor of Jehu's letters that their first intention was to select the fittest of the royal family and set him up as king. Perhaps this challenge of Jehu was designed as a stroke of policy on his part to elicit their views, and to find out whether they were inclined to be pacific or hostile. The bold character of the man, and the rapid success of his conspiracy, terrified the civic authorities of Samaria and Jezreel into submission. **5. he that was over the house**—the governor or chamberlain of the palace. **the bringers-up of the children**—Anciently, and still also in many Eastern countries, the principal grandees were charged with the support and education of the royal princes. This involved a heavy expense which they were forced to bear, but for which they endeavored to find some compensation in the advantages of their connection with the court. **6. take ye the heads of the men, your master's sons**—The barbarous practice of a successful usurper slaughtering all who may have claims to the throne, has been frequently exemplified in the ancient and modern histories of the East. **8. Lay ye them in two heaps at the entering in of the gate,** etc.—The exhibition of the heads of enemies is always considered a glorious trophy. Sometimes a pile of heads is erected at the gate of the palace; and a head of peculiarly striking appearance selected to grace the summit of the pyramid. **9. said to all the people, Ye be righteous,** etc. —A great concourse was assembled to gaze on this novel and ghastly spectacle. The speech which Jehu addressed to the spectators was artfully framed to impress their minds with the idea that so wholesale a massacre was the result of the divine judgments denounced on the house of Ahab; and the

ADAM CLARKE

CHAPTER 10

1. *Ahab had seventy sons.* As he had several wives, he might have many children. *Unto the rulers of Jezreel.* It certainly should be, "unto the rulers of Samaria"; for to them and to that city the whole context shows us the letters were sent (see v. 6). *To them that brought up Ahab's children.* It appears that the royal children of Israel and Judah were entrusted to the care of the nobles, and were brought up by them (see v. 6); and to these, therefore, Jehu's letters are directed. It is supposed Isaiah (xlix. 23) alludes to this custom: "Kings shall be thy nursing fathers, and queens thy nursing mothers."

2. *A fenced city also.* All here seems to refer to Samaria alone; in it were the magazines and implements of war. No reader need be told that these letters were all ironical. It was the same as if he had said, "Ye have no means of defense; Israel is with me. If you yield not up yourselves and the city, I will put you all to the sword."

4. *Two kings stood not before him.* That is, Joram and Ahaziah.

5. *He that was over the house.* Thus all the constituted authorities agreed to submit. *Will do all that thou shalt bid us.* They made no conditions, and stood pledged to commit the horrid murders which this most execrable man afterwards commanded.

6. *Come to me to Jezreel.* Therefore the letters were not written to Jezreel, but from Jezreel to Samaria.

7. *Put their heads in baskets.* What cold-blooded wretches were the whole of these people!

8. *Lay ye them in two heaps.* It appears that the heads of these princes had arrived at Jezreel in the nighttime. Jehu ordered them to be left at the gate of the city, a place of public resort, that all the people might see them, and be struck with terror, and conclude that all re-

MATTHEW HENRY

the house of Ahab, not only those that descended from him, but those that were in any relation to him. Having done this in Jezreel, he did the same in Samaria (*v.* 17), *slew all that remained to Ahab in Samaria.* This was bloody work, and is not now, in any case, to be drawn into a precedent. Let the guilty suffer, but not the guiltless for their sakes.

III. Providence bringing the brethren of Ahaziah in his way, as he was going on with this execution, he slew them likewise, *v.* 12–14. 1. They were branches of Ahab's house, being descended from Athaliah, and therefore fell within his commission. 2. They were tainted with the wickedness of the house of Ahab. 3. They were now going to make their court to the princes of the house of Ahab, to *salute the children of the king and the queen,* Joram and Jezebel, which showed that they were linked to them in affection as well as in affinity.

Verses 15–28

I. Courting the friendship of a good man, *Jehonadab the son of Rechab, v.* 15, 16. This Jehonadab, though mortified to the world and meddling little with the business of it (as appears by his charge to his posterity, which they religiously observed 300 years after, not to drink wine nor dwell in cities, Jer. xxxv. 6, &c.), yet, upon this occasion, went to meet Jehu, that he might encourage him in the work to which God had called him. Jehonadab, though no prophet, priest, or Levite, was generally respected for that life of self-denial and devotion which he lived: Jehu, though a soldier, knew him and honoured him. When he met him (though it is likely he drove now as furiously as ever) he stopped to speak to him. 1. Jehu saluted him; he *blessed him* (so the word is), paid him respect. 2. Jehu professed that *his heart was right with him,* that he had a true affection for his person and a veneration for the crown of his Nazariteship, and desired to know whether he had the same affection for him: *Is thy heart right?* Jehonadab gave him his word (*It is*), and gave him his hand as a pledge of his heart. 3. Jehu took him up into his chariot and took him along with him to Samaria. All sober people would think the better of Jehu when they saw Jehonadab in the chariot with him. This was not the only time in which the piety of some has been made to serve the policy of others, and designing men have strengthened themselves by drawing good men into their interests. Jehonadab is a stranger to the arts of fleshly wisdom, and therefore, if Jehu be a servant of God and an enemy to Baal, he will be his faithful friend. "Come then" (says Jehu), "come with me, *and see my zeal for the Lord.*" This is commonly taken as giving cause to suspect that the zeal he pretended for the Lord was really zeal for himself and his own advancement. For, (1) He boasted of it, and spoke as if God and man were mightily indebted to him for it. (2) He desired it might be seen and taken notice of, like the Pharisees, who did all to be seen of men. Jehonadab went with him, and, it is likely, animated and assisted him in the further execution of his commission (*v.* 17), destroying all Ahab's friends in Samaria. A man may hate cruelty and yet love justice.

II. Contriving the destruction of all the worshippers of Baal. Jehu's project is to cut them all off together. 1. By a wile he brought them together to the temple of Baal. He pretended he would worship Baal more than ever Ahab had done, *v.* 18. He issued a proclamation, requiring the attendance of all the worshippers of Baal to join with him in a sacrifice to Baal (*v.* 19, 20). 2. He took care that none of the servants of the Lord should be among them, *v.* 23. 3. He gave orders for the cutting of them all off, and Jehonadab joined with him therein, *v.* 23. Then the guards were sent in to put them all to the sword. 4. The idolators being thus destroyed, the idolatry itself was utterly abolished. The buildings about the house of Baal were destroyed; all the little images, statues, pictures, or shrines, which beautified Baal's temple, with the great image of Baal himself, were brought out and burnt (*v.* 26, 27), and the temple of Baal was broken down. Thus was the worship of Baal quite destroyed. Thus will God destroy all the gods of the heathen, and, sooner or later, triumph over them all.

Verses 29–36

The account of the reign of Jehu.

I. God's approbation of what Jehu had done. 1. God pronounced that to be right which he had done. The extirpating of idolaters and idolatry was a thing right in God's eyes. 2. God promised him a reward, that his children of the fourth generation from him should *sit upon the throne of Israel.*

II. Jehu's carelessness in what he was further to do. By this it appeared that his heart was not right with God, that he was partial in his reformation. 1. He

JAMIESON, FAUSSET, BROWN

effect of it was to prepare the public mind for hearing, without horror, of a similar revolting tragedy which was soon after perpetrated, viz., the extinction of all the influential friends and supporters of the dynasty of Ahab, including those of the royal house of Judah.

13. We are the brethren of Ahaziah—i.e., not full, but step-brothers, sons of Jehoram by various concubines. Ignorant of the revolution that had taken place, they were travelling to Samaria on a visit to their royal relatives of Israel, when they were seized and put to death, because of the apprehension that they might probably stimulate and strengthen the party that still remained faithful in their allegiance to Ahab's dynasty. **children of the queen**—i.e., of the queen mother, or regent, Jezebel.

15-18. Jehonadab the son of Rechab—(See on I Chron. 2:55). A person who, from his piety and simple primitive manner of life (Jer. 35), was highly esteemed, and possessed great influence in the country.

Jehu saw in a moment the advantage that his cause would gain from the friendship and countenance of this venerable man in the eyes of the people, and accordingly paid him the distinguished attention of inviting him to a seat in his chariot. **give me thine hand**—not simply to aid him in getting up, but for a far more significant and important purpose—the giving, or rather joining hands, being the recognized mode of striking a league or covenant, as well as of testifying fealty to a new sovereign; accordingly, it is said, "he [Jehonadab] gave him [Jehu] his hand."

18-29. HE DESTROYS THE WORSHIPPERS OF BAAL. **19. call unto me all the prophets of Baal**—The votaries of Baal are here classified under the several titles of prophets, priests, and servants, or worshippers generally. They might be easily convened into one spacious temple, as their number had been greatly diminished both by the influential ministrations of Elijah and Elisha, and also from the late King Joram's neglect and discontinuance of the worship. Jehu's appointment of a solemn sacrifice in honor of Baal, and a summons to all his worshippers to join in its celebration, was a deep-laid plot, which he had resolved upon for their extinction, a measure in perfect harmony with the Mosaic law, and worthy of a constitutional king of Israel. It was done, however, not from religious, but purely political motives, because be believed that the existence and interests of the Baalites were inseparably bound up with the dynasty of Ahab and because he hoped that by their extermination he would secure the attachment of the far larger and more influential party who worshipped God in Israel. Jehonadab's concurrence must have been given in the belief of his being actuated solely by the highest principles of piety and zeal. **22. Bring forth vestments for all the worshippers of Baal**—The priests of Baal were clad, probably, in robes of white byssus while they were engaged in the functions of their office, and these were kept under the care of an officer in a particular wardrobe of Baal's temple. This treacherous massacre, and the means taken to accomplish it, are paralleled by the slaughter of the Janissaries and other terrible tragedies in the modern history of the East.

ADAM CLARKE

sistance to such authority and power would be vain.

9. *Ye be righteous.* Another irony, intended partly to excuse himself, and to involve them in the odium of this massacre, and at the same time to justify the conduct of both, by showing that all was done according to the commandment of the Lord.

11. *Jehu slew all.* So it appears that the *great men* who had so obsequiously taken off the heads of Ahab's seventy sons fell also a sacrifice to the ambition of this incomparably bad man.

12. *The shearing house.* Probably the place where the shepherds met for the annual sheep shearing.

13. *The brethren of Ahaziah.* The relatives of his family; for it does not appear that he had any brethren, properly so called. But we know that the term brethren among the Jews signified the relatives of the same family, and especially brothers' and sisters' children; and that these were such (see 2 Chron. xxii. 8). *We go down to salute.* So promptly had Jehu executed all his measures that even the nearest relatives of the murdered kings had not heard of their death, and consequently had no time to escape. They were all taken as in a net.

14. *The pit of the shearing house.* Probably the place where they washed the sheep previously to shearing, or the fleeces after they were shorn off.

15. *Jehonadab the son of Rechab.* For particulars concerning this man, his ancestry, and posterity see the notes on Jeremiah xxxv. *Is thine heart right* with me, in the prosecution of a reform in Israel, *as my heart is with thy heart* in the true religion of Jehovah, and the destruction of Baal? *It is.* I wish a reform in the religion of the country; I am his friend who shall endeavor to promote it.

Give me thine hand. Jehonadab was doubtless a very honorable man in Israel; and by carrying him about with him in his chariot, Jehu endeavored to acquire the public esteem.

18. *Ahab served Baal a little.* Jehu had determined to have no worship in Israel but that of the golden calves at Dan and Bethel; therefore he purposes to destroy all the worshippers of Baal. And that he may do it without suspicion, he proclaims a great sacrifice; and that he may do it the more easily, he gathers them all together into one place.

19. *Whosoever shall be wanting, he shall not live.* Because, as he will thereby show himself without zeal for the service of his God, he will justly forfeit his life. All this was done in the very spirit of deceit.

22. *He said unto him that was over the vestry.* The word *vestry* comes from *vestiarium,* and that from *vestes,* "garments," from *vestio,* "I clothe"; and signifies properly the place where the sacerdotal robes are kept. The priests of Baal had their robes as well as the priests of the Lord, but the garments were such that one could be easily distinguished from the other.

25. *To the guard and to the captains.* To the couriers or runners, and the *shalashim,* the men of the third rank; those officers who were next to the nobles, the king and these being only their superiors. The runners were probably a sort of light infantry. *The city of the house of Baal.* Does not this mean a sort of holy of holies, where the most sacred images of Baal were kept?

27. *Made it a draught house.* A place for human excrement; so all the versions understand it. Nothing could be more degrading than this.

30. *Thy children of the fourth generation.* These four descendants of Jehu were Jehoahaz, Jehoash, Jeroboam II, and Zechariah (see chaps. xiv and xv). This was all the compensation Jehu had in either world, as a recompense of his zeal for the Lord.

MATTHEW HENRY

did not put away all the evil. He departed from the sins of Ahab, but not from the sins of Jeroboam—discarded Baal, but adhered to the calves. The worship of the calves was a politic idolatry, was begun and kept up for reasons of state, to prevent the return of the ten tribes to the house of David, and therefore Jehu clave to that. True conversion is not only from those sins that are destructive to the secular interest, but from those that support and befriend it, in forsaking which is the great trial whether we can deny ourselves and trust God. 2. He put away evil, but he did not mind that which was good (*v.* 31): *He took no heed to walk in the law of the Lord God of Israel.* He had shown great care and zeal for the rooting out of a false religion; but in the true religion, (1) He was not at all solicitious to please God. (2) He showed no zeal. It seems, he was a man that had little religion himself, and yet God made use of him as an instrument of reformation in Israel.

III. The judgment that came upon Israel in his reign. There was a general decay of piety and increase of profaneness; and therefore it is not strange that the next news we hear is, *In those days the Lord began to cut Israel short, v.* 32. Their neighbours encroached upon them on every side. Hazael king of Syria was, above any other, vexatious and mischievous to them, *smote them in all the coasts of Israel.*

Lastly, The conclusion of Jehu's reign, *v.* 34-36. Because he took no heed to serve God, the memorials of his mighty enterprises and achievements are justly buried in oblivion.

JAMIESON, FAUSSET, BROWN

29. Howbeit from the sins of Jeroboam . . . Jehu departed not from after them—Jehu had no intention of carrying his zeal for the Lord beyond a certain point, and as he considered it impolitic to encourage his subjects to travel to Jerusalem, he re-established the symbolic worship of the calves.

ADAM CLARKE

31. *Jehu took no heed.* He never made it his study; indeed, he never intended to walk in this way; it suited neither his disposition nor his politics.

32. *The Lord began to cut Israel short.* The marginal reading is best: "The Lord cut off the ends"; and this He did by permitting Hazael to seize on the *coasts,* to conquer and occupy the frontier towns. This was the commencement of those miserable ravages which Elisha predicted (see chap. viii. 12). And we find from the next verse that he seized on *all the land of Gilead,* and that of Reuben and Gad, and the half-tribe of Manasseh; in a word, whatever Israel possessed on the east side of Jordan.

34. *Are they not written in the book of the chronicles?* We have no chronicles in which there is anything further spoken of this bad man. His reign was long, twenty-eight years; and yet we know nothing of it but the commencement.

MATTHEW HENRY — CHAPTER 11

Verses 1–3

God had assured David of the continuance of his family, which is called his *ordaining a lamp for his anointed.* Now here we have David's promised lamp almost extinguished and yet wonderfully preserved.

I. It was almost extinguished by the barbarous malice of Athaliah, the queen-mother, who, when she heard that her son Ahaziah was slain by Jehu, *arose and destroyed all the seed-royal* (*v.* 1), all that she knew to be akin to the crown. She did it, 1. From a spirit of ambition. She thirsted after rule, and thought she could not get to it any other way. 2. From a spirit of revenge and rage against God. The house of Ahab being utterly destroyed, she resolved, as it were, by way of reprisal, to destroy the house of David. Well might she be called *Athaliah, that wicked woman* (2 Chron. xxiv. 7), Jezebel's own daughter.

II. It was wonderfully preserved by the pious care of one of Joram's daughters (who was wife to Jehoiada the priest), who stole away one of the king's sons, Joash by name, and hid him, *v.* 2, 3. The place of his safety was the house of the Lord, one of the chambers belonging to the temple, a place Athaliah seldom troubled. His aunt, by bringing him hither, put him under God's special protection, and so hid him by faith, as Moses was hidden. Now were David's words made good to one of his seed (Ps. xxvii. 5), *In the secret of his tabernacle shall he hide me.* With good reason did this Joash, when he grew up, set himself to repair the house of the Lord, for it had been a sanctuary to him. See the wisdom and care of Providence, and how it prepares for what it designs; and see what blessings those lay up in store for their families that marry their children to those that are wise and good.

Verses 4–12

Six years Athaliah tyrannised. While Jehu was extirpating the worship of Baal in Israel, she was establishing it in Judah, as appears, 2 Chron. xxiv. 7. All this while, Joash lay hid, entitled to a crown and intended for it, and yet buried alive in obscurity. Joash in his seventh year was ready to be shown, having served his first apprenticeship to life and arrived at his first climacterical year. By that time the people had grown weary of Athaliah's tyranny and ripe for a revolution. How that revolution was effected:

I. The manager of this great affair was Jehoiada the priest, probably the high priest. By his birth and office he was a man in authority. By marriage he was allied to the royal family, and, if all the seed-royal were destroyed, his wife, as daughter to Joram, had a better title to the crown than Athaliah had. By his eminent gifts and graces he was fitted to serve his country, and better service he could not do it than to free it from Athaliah's usurpation.

II. The management was very discreet as became so wise and good a man as Jehoiada.

1. He concerted the matter with the *rulers of hundreds and the captains,* the men in office, ecclesiastical, civil, and military; he got them to him to the temple, consulted with them, gave them an oath of

JAMIESON, FAUSSET, BROWN — CHAPTER 11

Vss. 1-3. Jehoash Saved from Athaliah's Massacre. **1. Athaliah**—(See on II Chron. 22:2). She had possessed great influence over her son, who, by her counsels, had ruled in the spirit of the house of Ahab. **destroyed all the seed royal**—all connected with the royal family who might have urged a claim to the throne, and who had escaped the murderous hands of Jehu (II Chron. 21:2-4; 22:1; ch. 10:13, 14). This massacre she was incited to perpetrate—partly from a determination not to let David's family outlive hers—partly as a measure of self-defense to secure herself against the violence of Jehu, who was bent on destroying the whole of Ahab's posterity to which she belonged (ch. 8:18-26); but chiefly from personal ambition to rule, and a desire to establish the worship of Baal. Such was the sad fruit of the unequal alliance between the son of the pious Jehoshaphat and a daughter of the idolatrous and wicked house of Ahab. **2. Jehosheba**—of Jehoshabeath (II Chron. 22:11). **daughter of King Joram**—not by Athaliah, but by a secondary wife. **stole him from among the king's sons which were slain**—either from among the corpses, he being considered dead, or out of the palace nursery. **hid him . . . in the bedchamber**—for the use of the priests, which was in some part of the temple (vs. 3), and of which Jehoiada and his wife had the sole charge. What is called, however, the bedchamber in the East is not the kind of apartment that we understand by the name, but a small closet, into which are flung during the day the mattresses and other bedding materials spread on the floors or divans of the sitting-rooms by day. Such a lumber-room was well suited to be a convenient place for the recovery of his wounds, and a hiding-place for the royal infant and his nurse.

4-12. He Is Made King. **4. the seventh year**—viz., of the reign of Athaliah, and the rescue of Jehoash.

Jehoiada sent and fetched the rulers, etc.—He could scarcely have obtained such a general convocation except at the time, or on pretext, of a public and solemn festival. Having revealed to

ADAM CLARKE — CHAPTER 11

1. *Athaliah.* This woman was the daughter of Ahab, and granddaughter of Omri, and wife of Joram, king of Judah, and mother of Ahaziah. *Destroyed all the seed royal.* All that she could lay her hands on whom Jehu had left, in order that she might get undisturbed possession of the kingdom.

2. *Daughter of . . . Joram, sister of Ahaziah.* It is not likely that Jehosheba was the daughter of Athaliah; she was sister, we find, to Ahaziah, the son of Athaliah, but probably by a different mother. The mother of Jehoash was Zibiah of Beersheba (see chap. xxii. 1).

3. *He was . . . hid in the house of the Lord.* This might be readily done, because none had access to the Temple but the priests; and the high priest himself was the chief manager of this business.

4. *And the seventh year Jehoiada sent.* He had certainly sounded them all, and brought them into the interests of the young king, before

MATTHEW HENRY

secrecy, and *showed them the king's son* (*v.* 4). What a pleasing surprise it was to them, who feared that the house and lineage of David were quite cut off, to find such a spark as this in the embers.

2. He posted the priests and Levites, who were more immediately under his direction, in the several avenues to the temple, to keep the guard. David had divided the priests into courses. Every sabbath-day morning a new company came into waiting, but the company of the foregoing week did not go out of waiting till the sabbath evening, so that on the sabbath day, when double service was to be done, there was a double number to do it. These Jehoiada employed to attend on this great occasion; he armed them out of the magazines of the temple with David's spears and shields. Two things they were ordered to do: (1) To protect the young king from being insulted. (2) To preserve the holy temple from being profaned by the concourse of people that would come together on this occasion (*v.* 6).

3. When the guards were fixed, then the king was brought forth, *v.* 12. Jehoiada, without delay, proceeded to the coronation of this young king. This was done with great solemnity, *v.* 12. (1) In token of his being invested with kingly power, he *put the crown upon him.* (2) In token of his obligation to govern by law, and to make the word of God his rule, he gave him the testimony, Deut. xvii. 18, 19. (3) In token of his receiving the Spirit, to qualify him for this great work to which he before was called, he anointed him. (4) In token of the people's acceptance of him and subjection to his government, they clapped their hands for joy, and expressed their hearty good wishes to him: *Let the king live;* and thus they made him their king and concurred with the divine appointment. They had reason to bid him welcome to the crown whose right it was, and to pray, *Let him live*, concerning him who came to them as life from the dead and in whom the house of David was to live. With such acclamations of joy and satisfaction must the kingdom of Christ be welcomed into our hearts when his throne is set up there and Satan the usurper is deposed.

Verses 13–16

It was designed when they had finished the solemnity of the king's inauguration, to pay a visit to Athaliah, and call her to an account for her murders, usurpation, and tyranny; but, like her mother Jezebel, she went out to meet them, and hastened her own destruction. 1. Hearing the noise, she came in a fright to see what was the matter, *v.* 13. Jehoiada and his friends proclaimed what they were doing. When she heard the noise it was strange that she was so ill advised as to come herself, and, for aught that appears, to come alone. 2. Seeing what was done she cried out for help. She saw the king's place by the pillar possessed by one to whom the princes and people did homage (*v.* 14). This made her rend her clothes and cry, "Treason! treason! Come and help against the traitors." 3. Jehoiada gave orders to put her to death as an idolater, a usurper, and an enemy to the public peace. Care was taken, (1) That she should not be killed in the temple. (2) That whoever appeared for her should die with her. She endeavouring to make her escape the back way to the palace, through the stalls, they pursued her, and there killed her, *v.* 16.

Verses 17–21

Jehoiada had now got over the hardest part of his work, when, by the death of Athaliah, the young prince had his way to the throne cleared of all opposition.

I. The good foundations he laid, by an original contract, *v.* 17. Now that prince and people were together in God's house, Jehoiada took care that they should jointly covenant with God, and mutually covenant with each other, that they might rightly understand their duty both to God and to one another. 1. He endeavoured to settle and secure the interests of religion among them, by a covenant between them and God. In this covenant, the king stands upon the same level with his subjects and is as much bound as any of them to serve the Lord. By this engagement they renounced Baal, whom many of them had worshipped, and resigned themselves to God's government. By our bonds to God the bonds of every relation are strengthened. They *first gave themselves to the Lord*, and then *to us*, 2 Cor. viii. 5. 2. He then settled both the coronation-oath and the oath of allegiance, the *pacta conventa—covenant*, between the king and the people, by which the king was obliged to govern according to law and to protect his subjects, and they were obliged, while he did so, to obey him and to bear faith and true allegiance to him.

JAMIESON, FAUSSET, BROWN

them the secret of the young king's preservation and entered into a covenant with them for the overthrow of the tyrant, he then arranged with them the plan and time of carrying their plot into execution (see on II Chron. 22:10-12; 23).

The conduct of Jehoiada, who acted the leading and chief part in this conspiracy, admits of an easy and full justification; for, while Athaliah was a usurper, and belonged to a race destined by divine denunciation to destruction, even his own wife had a better and stronger claim to the throne; the sovereignty of Judah had been divinely appropriated to the family of David, and therefore the young prince on whom it was proposed to confer the crown, possessed an inherent right to it, of which a usurper could not deprive him. Moreover, Jehoiada was most probably the high priest, whose official duty it was to watch over the due execution of God's laws, and who in his present movement, was encouraged and aided by the countenance and support of the chief authorities, both civil and ecclesiastical, in the country. In addition to all these considerations, he seems to have been directed by an impulse of the Divine Spirit, through the counsels and exhortations of the prophets of the time.

13-16. Athaliah Slain. **13. Athaliah heard the noise of the guard and of the people**—The profound secrecy with which the conspiracy had been conducted rendered the unusual acclamations of the vast assembled crowd the more startling and roused the suspicions of the tyrant. **she came . . . into the temple of the Lord**—i.e., the courts, which she was permitted to enter by Jehoiada's directions (vs. 8) in order that she might be secured. **14. the king stood by a pillar**—or on a platform, erected for that purpose (II Chron. 6:13). **15. without the ranges**—i.e., fences, that the sacred place might not be stained with human blood.

17. Jehoiada Restores God's Worship. **17. a covenant between the Lord and the king and the people**—The covenant with the Lord was a renewal of the national covenant with Israel (Exod. 19; 24; "to be unto him a people of inheritance," Deut. 4:6; 27:9). The covenant between the king and the people was the consequence of this, and by it the king bound himself to rule according to the divine law, while the people engaged to submit, to give him allegiance as the Lord's anointed.

ADAM CLARKE

this time. The plot having been laid, and now ripe for execution, he brings the chief officers of the army and those of the bodyguard into the Temple, and there binds them by an oath of secrecy, and shows them the king's son, in whose behalf they are to rise.

5. *That enter in on the sabbath.* It appears that Jehoiada chose the Sabbath day to proclaim the young king because, as that was a day of public concourse, the gathering together of the people who were in this secret would not be noticed; and it is likely that they all came unarmed, and were supplied by Jehoiada with the spears and shields which David had laid up in the Temple, v. 10.

12. *Put the crown upon him.* This was a diadem or golden band that went round the head. *And . . . the testimony.* Probably the book of the law, written on a roll of vellum. This was his sceptre. *They clapped their hands.* This I believe is the first instance on record of clapping the hands as a testimony of joy. *God save the king.* "May the king live!" So the words should be translated wherever they occur.

14. *The king stood by a pillar.* "Stood on a pillar or tribunal," the place or throne on which they were accustomed to put the kings when they proclaimed them. *Treason, Treason.* "A conspiracy, a conspiracy!" from *kashar,* "to bind, unite together."

15. *Have her forth.* She had pressed in among the guards into the Temple. *And him that followeth.* The person who takes her part, let him instantly be slain.

16. *By the way . . . which the horses came.* They probably brought her out near the king's stables.

17. *Jehoiada made a covenant.* A general covenant was first made between the *Lord*, the Supreme King, the *king*, His viceroy, and the *people*, that they should all be *the Lord's people*, each being equally bound to live according to the divine law. Then, secondly, a particular covenant was made between the *king* and the *people*, by which the king was bound to rule according to the laws and constitution of the kingdom, and to watch and live for the safety of the public. And the people were bound, on their part, to love, honor, succor, and obey the king.

MATTHEW HENRY

II. The good beginnings he raised on those foundations. 1. Pursuant to their covenant with God they immediately abolished idolatry. Every one, now that they were so well headed, would lend a hand to pull down Baal's temple, his altars, and his images. All his worshippers, it should seem, deserted him; only his priest Mattan stuck to his altar. Though all men forsook Baal, he would not, and there he was slain. Having destroyed Baal's temple, they appointed *officers over the house of God*, to see that the service of God was regularly performed by the proper persons, in due time, and according to the instituted manner. 2. Pursuant to their covenant with one another, (1) The king was brought in state to the royal palace, and sat there on the throne of judgment, *the thrones of the house of David* (*v.* 19), ready to receive petitions and appeals, which he would refer to Jehoiada to give answers to and to give judgment upon. (2) The people rejoiced, and Jerusalem was in quiet (*v.* 20).

CHAPTER 12

Verses 1–3

The general account given of Joash is, 1. That he reigned forty years. 2. That he did that which was right as long as Jehoiada lived to instruct him, *v.* 2. 3. That the *high places were not taken away*, *v.* 3. Up and down the country they had altars both for sacrifice and incense, to the honour of the God of Israel only. These private altars, perhaps, had been more used in the late bad reigns than formerly, because it was not safe to go up to Jerusalem, nor was the temple-service performed as it should have been; and, it may be, Jehoiada connived at them, because he hoped that the reforming of the temple, and putting things into a good posture there, would by degrees draw people from their high places and they would dwindle of themselves.

Verses 4–16

An account of the repairing of the temple in the reign of Joash.

I. Though Solomon built it of the best materials and in the best manner, yet in time it went to decay, and there were *breaches found in it* (*v.* 5). Even temples themselves are the worse for the wearing; but the heavenly temple will never wax old. Yet it was not only the teeth of time that made these breaches, the sons of Athaliah had *broken up the house of God* (2 Chron. xxiv. 7).

II. The king himself was the first and forwardest man that took care for the repair of it. 1. Because he was king, and God expects and requires from those who have power that they use it for the maintenance and support of religion, the redress of grievances, and reparation of decays. 2. Because the temple had been both his nursery and his sanctuary when he was a child, in a grateful remembrance of which he now appeared zealous for the honour of it. Those who have experienced the comfort and benefit of religious assemblies will make the support of them their care, and the prosperity of them their chief joy.

III. The priests were ordered to collect money for these repairs, and to take care that the work was done. 1. He gave them orders for the levying of the money. They must not stay till it was paid in, but they must call for it where they knew it was due, in their respective districts, as redemption-money (by virtue of the law, Exod. xxx. 12), or as estimation-money (by virtue of the law, Lev. xxvii. 2, 3), or as a free-will offering, *v.* 4.

IV. This method did not answer the intention, *v.* 6. Little money was raised. Either the priests were careless, and did not call on the people to pay in their dues, or the people had so little confidence in the priests' management that they were backward to pay money into their hands. But what money was raised was not applied to the proper use: *The breaches of the house were not repaired.*

V. Another method was therefore taken. The king had his heart much set upon having *the breaches of the house repaired*, *v.* 7. His apostasy, at last, gives us cause to question whether he had as good an affection for the service of the temple as he had for the structure. Many have been zealous for building and beautifying churches, and for other forms of godliness, who yet have been strangers to the power of it. However, we commend his zeal. Another course was taken,

1. For raising money, *v.* 9, 10. The money was put into a public chest, and then people brought it in readily and in great abundance. The money that was given, (1) Was dropped into the chest through a hole in the lid, past recall, to intimate

JAMIESON, FAUSSET, BROWN

The immediate fruit of this renewal of the covenant was the destruction of the temple and the slaughter of the priests of Baal (see on ch. 10:27); the restoration of the pure worship of God in all its ancient integrity; and the establishment of the young king on the hereditary throne of Judah.

CHAPTER 12

Vss. 1-18. JEHOASH REIGNS WELL WHILE JEHOIADA LIVED. **2. Jehoash did that which was right in the sight of the Lord**—so far as related to his outward actions and the policy of his government. But it is evident from the sequel of his history that the rectitude of his administration was owing more to the salutary influence of his preserver and tutor, Jehoiada, than to the honest and sincere dictates of his own mind. **3. But the high places were not taken away**—The popular fondness for the private and disorderly rites performed in the groves and recesses of hills was so inveterate that even the most powerful monarchs had been unable to accomplish their suppression; no wonder that in the early reign of a young king, and after the gross irregularities that had been allowed during the maladministration of Athaliah, the difficulty of putting an end to the superstitions associated with "the high places" was greatly increased.

4. Jehoash said to the priests, etc. There is here given an account of the measures which the young king took for repairing the temple by the levying of taxes: 1. "The money of every one that passeth the account," viz., half a shekel, as an offering to the Lord" (Exod. 30: 13). 2. "The money that every man is set at," i.e., the redemption-price of every one who had devoted himself or any thing belonging to him to the Lord, and the amount of which was estimated according to certain rules (Lev. 27:1-8). 3. Free-will or voluntary offerings made to the sanctuary. The first two were paid annually (see on II Chron. 24:5).

7-10. Why repair ye not the breaches of the house?—This mode of collection not proving so productive as was expected (the dilatoriness of the priests was the chief cause of the failure), a new arrangement was proposed.

A chest was placed by the high priest at the entrance into the temple, into which the money given by the people for the repairs of the temple was to be put by the Levites who kept the door. The object of this chest was to make a

ADAM CLARKE

18. *His altars and images brake they in pieces.* It is probable that Athaliah had set up the worship of Baal in Judah, as Jezebel had done in Israel; or probably it had never been removed since the days of Solomon. It was no wonder that Jehoiada began his reform with this act, when we learn from 2 Chron. xxiv. 7 that "the sons of Athaliah, that wicked woman, had broken up the house of God; and also all the dedicated things of the house of the Lord did they bestow upon Baalim."

20. *The people . . . rejoiced.* They were glad to get rid of the tyranny of Athaliah. *And the city was in quiet.* She had no partisans to rise up and disturb the king's reign.

21. *Seven years old was Jehoash.* The first instance on record of making a child seven years old the king of any nation, and especially of such a nation as the Jews, who were at all times very difficult to be governed.

CHAPTER 12

2. *Jehoash did . . . right in the sight of the Lord.* While Jehoiada, the priest, who was a pious, holy man, lived, Jehoash walked uprightly; but it appears from 2 Chron. xxiv. 17-18 that he departed from the worship of the true God after the death of this eminent high priest, lapsed into idolatry, and seems to have had a share in the murder of Zechariah, who testified against his transgressions and those of the princes of Judah.

3. *The high places were not taken away.* Without the total destruction of these there could be no radical reform. Jehoiada did not use his influence as he might have done; for as he had the king's heart and hand with him, he might have done what he pleased.

4. *All the money of the dedicated things.* From all this account we find that the Temple was in a very ruinous state; the walls were falling down, some had perhaps actually fallen, and there was no person so zealous for the pure worship of God as to exert himself to shore up the falling Temple! The king himself seems to have been the first who noticed these dilapidations, and took measures for the necessary repairs. The repairs were made from the following sources: (1) The *things* which pious persons had *dedicated* to the service of God. (2) The freewill offerings of strangers who had visited Jerusalem: *the money of every one that passeth.* (3) The half-shekel which the males were obliged to pay from the age of twenty years (Exod. xxx. 12) for the redemption of their souls, that is, their lives, which is here called *the money that every man is set at.*

6. *In the three and twentieth year.* In what year Jehoash gave the orders for these repairs, we cannot tell; but the account here plainly intimates that they had been long given, and that nothing was done, merely through the inactivity and negligence of the priests (see 2 Chron. xxiv. 5). It seems that the people had brought money in abundance, and the pious Jehoiada was over the priests, and yet nothing was done! Though Jehoiada was a good man, he does not appear to have had much of the spirit of an active zeal; and simple piety, without zeal and activity, is of little use when a reformation in religion and manners is necessary to be brought about.

9. *Jehoiada . . . took a chest.* This chest was at first set *beside the altar*, as is here mentioned; but afterwards, for the convenience of the people, it was set without the gate (see 2 Chron. xxiv. 8).

MATTHEW HENRY

that what has been once resigned to God must never be resumed. (2) The chest was put on the right hand as they went in, which, some think, is alluded to in that rule of charity which our Saviour gives, *Let not thy left hand know what thy right hand doeth.* But, while they were getting all they could for the repair of the temple, they did not break in upon that which was the stated maintenance of the priests, *v.* 16. Let not the servants of the temple be starved under colour of repairing the breaches of it.

2. For laying out the money that was raised.

(1) They did not put it into the hands of the priests, who were not versed in affairs of this nature, having other work to mind, but *into the hands of those that did the work,* or at least *had the oversight of it, v.* 11. [1] Carefully, purchasing materials and paying workmen, *v.* 12. [2] Faithfully, such a reputation they got for honesty that there was no occasion to examine their bills or audit their accounts. Those that think it is no sin to cheat the government, cheat the country, or cheat the church, will be of another mind when God shall set their sins in order before them.

(2) They did not lay it out in ornaments for the temple, in vessels of gold or silver, but in necessary repairs first (*v.* 13).

Verses 17–21

When Joash had revolted from God and become both an idolater and a persecutor the hand of the Lord went out against him, and his *last state was worse than his first.*

I. His wealth and honour became an easy prey to his neighbours. Hazael, when he had chastised Israel (*ch.* x. 32), threatened Judah and Jerusalem likewise, took Gath, a strong city (*v.* 17), and thence intended to march with his forces against Jerusalem. Joash had neither spirit nor strength to make head against him, but gave him all the hallowed things, and all the gold that was found both in his exchequer and in the treasures of the temple (*v.* 18), to bribe him to march another way. If he had not forsaken God, and forfeited his protection, his affairs would not have been brought to this extremity. He lost the honour of a prince and a soldier. He impoverished himself and his kingdom. He tempted Hazael to come again, when he could carry home so rich a booty without striking a stroke. And the next year the host of Syria came up against Jerusalem, destroyed the prince, and plundered the city, 2 Chron. xxiv. 23, 24.

II. His life became an easy prey to his own servants. They conspired against him and slew him (*v.* 20, 21), to be avenged on him for murdering the prophet, Jehoiada's son. Thus fell Joash, who began in the spirit and ended in the flesh.

JAMIESON, FAUSSET, BROWN

separation between the money to be raised for the building from the other moneys destined for the general use of the priests, in the hope that the people would be more liberal in their contributions when it was known that their offerings would be devoted to the special purpose of making the necessary repairs. The duty of attending to this work was no longer to devolve on the priests, but to be undertaken by the king.

11-13. they gave the money, being told, into the hands of them that did the work—The king sent his secretary along with an agent of the high priest (II Chron. 24:11) to count the money in the chest from time to time, and deliver the amount to the overseers of the building, who paid the workmen and purchased all necessary materials. The custom of putting sums of certain amount in bags, which are labelled and sealed by a proper officer, is a common way of using the currency in Turkey and other Eastern countries. **13-16. Howbeit there were not made . . . bowls,** etc.—When the repairs of the temple had been completed, the surplus was appropriated to the purchase of the temple furniture. The integrity of the overseers of the work being undoubted, no account was exacted of the way in which they applied the money given to them, while other moneys levied at the temple were left to the disposal of the priests as the law directed (Lev. 5:16; Num. 5:8). **17, 18. Then Hazael . . . fought against Gath**—(See on II Chron. 24:23, 24).

19-21. HE IS SLAIN. **20. his servants arose . . . and slew Joash in the house of Millo**—(See also II Chron. 24:25).

ADAM CLARKE

10. *The king's scribe and the high priest.* It was necessary to associate with the high priest some civil authority and activity, in order to get the neglected work performed.

13. *Howbeit there were not made . . . bowls.* That is, there were no vessels made for the service of the Temple till all the outward repairs were completed; but after this was done, "they brought the rest of the money before the king and Jehoiada, whereof were made . . . vessels of gold and silver," 2 Chron. xxiv. 14.

15. *They reckoned not with the men.* They placed great confidence in them, and were not disappointed, *for they dealt faithfully.*

17. *Hazael . . . fought against Gath, and took it.* This city, with its satrapy or lordship, had been taken from the Philistines by David (see 2 Sam. viii. 1 and 1 Chron. xviii. 1) and it had continued in the possession of the kings of Judah till this time.

18. *Took all the hallowed things.* He dearly bought a peace which was of short duration, for the next year Hazael returned, and Jehoash, having no more treasures, was obliged to hazard a battle, which he lost, with the principal part of his nobility, so that Judah was totally ruined, and Jehoash shortly after slain in his bed by his own servants, 2 Chron. xxiv. 23.

19. *The rest of the acts of Joash.* We have already seen that this man, so promising in the beginning of his reign, apostatized, became an idolater, encouraged idolatry among his subjects, and put the high priest Zechariah, the son of Jehoiada, his benefactor, to death; and now God visited that blood upon him by the hands of the tyrannous king of Syria, and by his own servants.

20. *The house of Millo.* Was a royal palace, built by David (see 2 Sam. v. 9), and *Silla* is supposed to be the name of the road or causeway that led to it. Millo was situated between the old city of Jerusalem and the city of David.

21. *For Jozachar.* This person is called Zabad in 2 Chron. xxiv. 26; and Shimeath, his mother, is said to be an Ammonitess, as Jehozabad is said to be the son, not of *Shomer,* but of Shimrith, a Moabitess. *They buried him with his fathers in the city of David.* But they did not bury him in the sepulchres of the kings; this is supposed to express the popular disapprobation of his conduct.

MATTHEW HENRY

CHAPTER 13

Verses 1–9

A general account of the reign of Jehoahaz, and of the state of Israel during his seventeen years.

I. The glory of Israel turned into shame. How is its crown profaned and its honour laid in the dust! 1. It was the honour of Israel that they worshipped the only living and true God, who is a Spirit, an eternal mind, and had rules by which to worship him of his own appointment; but by *changing the glory of their incorruptible God into the similitude of an ox, the truth of God into a lie,* they lost this honour, and levelled themselves with the nations that worshipped the work of their own hands. We find here that the king *followed the sins of Jeroboam* (*v.* 2), and the people departed *not from them, but walked therein, v.* 6. 2. It was the honour of Israel that they were taken under the special protection of heaven; God himself was their defence. But here, as often before, we find them stripped of this glory, and exposed to the insults of all their neighbours. They by their sins provoked God to anger, and then he *delivered them into the hands of Hazael and Benhadad, v.* 3. *Hazael oppressed Israel, v.* 22. Surely never was any nation so often plucked and pillaged by their neighbours as Israel was.

II. Some sparks of Israel's ancient honour appearing in these ashes. For, 1. It was the ancient honour of Israel that they were a praying people: and here we find somewhat of that honour revived; for Jehoahaz their king, in his distress, *besought the Lord* (*v.* 4), applied for help, not to the calves (what help could they give him?) but to the Lord. 2. It was the ancient honour of Israel that they had *God nigh unto them in all that which they called upon him for* (Deut. iv. 7), and so he was here. Though he might justly have rejected the prayer as an abomination to him, yet

JAMIESON, FAUSSET, BROWN

CHAPTER 13

Vss. 1-7. JEHOAHAZ'S WICKED REIGN OVER ISRAEL. **1. Jehoahaz . . . reigned seventeen years**—Under his government, which pursued the policy of his predecessors regarding the support of the calf-worship, Israel's apostasy from the true God became greater and more confirmed than in the time of his father Jehu.

The national chastisement, when it came, was consequently the more severe and the instruments employed by the Lord in scourging the revolted nation were Hazael and his son and general Ben-hadad, in resisting whose successive invasions the Israelitish army was sadly reduced and weakened. In the extremity of his distress, Jehoahaz besought the Lord, and was heard, not on his own account (Ps. 66:18; Prov. 1:28; 15:8), but that of the ancient covenant with the patriarchs (vs. 23). **4. he saw the oppression of Israel**—i.e., commiserated the fallen condition of His chosen people. The divine honor and the interests of true religion required that deliverance should be granted them to check the triumph of the idolatrous enemy and put an end to their blasphemous taunts that God had forsaken Israel (Deut. 32:27; Ps. 12:4).

ADAM CLARKE

CHAPTER 13

1. *In the three and twentieth year of Joash.* The chronology here is thus accounted for; Jehoahaz began his reign at the commencement of the twenty-third year of Joash, and reigned seventeen years—fourteen alone, and three years with his son Joash. The fourteenth year was but just begun.

MATTHEW HENRY

the Lord hearkened unto Jehoahaz, and to his prayer for himself and for his people (*v*. 4), and *he gave Israel a saviour* (*v*. 5), not Jehoahaz himself, for all his days Hazael oppressed Israel (*v*. 22), but his son, to whom, in answer to his father's prayers, God gave success against the Syrians, so that he recovered the cities which they had taken from his father, *v*. 25. This gracious answer God gave to the prayer of Jehoahaz in remembrance of his covenant with Abraham (*v*. 23). See how swift God is to show mercy, how willing to find out a reason to be gracious, else he would not look so far back as that ancient covenant.

Verses 10–19

Joash, the son of Jehoahaz and grandson of Jehu, upon the throne of Israel. Probably the house of Jehu intended some respect to the house of David when they gave this heir-apparent to the crown the same name with him that was then king of Judah.

I. He was none of the worst, and yet, because he kept up that ancient and politic idolatry of the house of Jeroboam, it is said, *He did that which was evil in the sight of the Lord*.

II. The particular account of what passed between him and Elisha:

1. Elisha fell sick, *v*. 14. (1) It was now about sixty years since he was first called to be a prophet. It was a great mercy to Israel, and especially to the sons of the prophets, that he was continued so long a burning and shining light. (2) All the latter part of his time, from the anointing of Jehu, which was forty-five years before Joash began his reign, we find no mention made of him, or of anything he did, till we find him here upon his death-bed.

2. King Joash visited him in his sickness, and *wept over him*, *v*. 14. This was an evidence of some good in him, that he had a value and affection for a faithful prophet. When the king heard of Elisha's sickness he came to visit him, and to receive his dying counsel and blessing. He lamented him in the same words with which Elisha had himself lamented the removal of Elijah: *My father, my father*.

3. Elisha gave the king great assurances of his success against the Syrians, Israel's present oppressors, and encouraged him to prosecute the war against them with vigour. *I die, but God will surely visit you*. He has the residue of the Spirit, and can raise up other prophets to pray for you. He gives him a sign, orders him to *take bow and arrow* (*v*. 15). God would be the agent, but he must be the instrument. And that he should be successful he gives him a token, by directing him,

(1) To shoot an arrow towards Syria, *v*. 16, 17. He received the words of command from the prophet: *Put thy hand upon the bow—Open the window—Shoot*. As if he had been a child that never drew a bow before, *Elisha put his hands upon the king's hands*, to signify that in all his expeditions against the Syrians he must look up to God for direction and strength. The trembling hands of a dying prophet, as they signified the concurrence and communication of the power of God, gave this arrow more force than the hands of the king in his full strength. The Syrians had made themselves masters of the country that lay eastward, *ch*. x. 33. Thitherward therefore the arrow was directed, and such an interpretation given by the prophet of the shooting of this arrow as made it, [1] A commission to the king to attack the Syrians. [2] A promise of success therein. It is the *arrow of the Lord's deliverance, even the arrow of deliverance from Syria*.

(2) To *strike with the arrows*, *v*. 18, 19. The prophet having in God's name assured him of victory over the Syrians, he will now try him and see what improvement he will make of his victories, whether he will push them on with more zeal than Ahab did when Benhadad lay at his mercy. For the trial of this he bids him *smite with the arrows on the ground*: Now show me what thou wilt do to them when thou hast them down. The king showed not that eagerness and flame which one might have expected upon this occasion, but smote thrice, and no more. But, by contemning the sign, he lost the thing signified, sorely to the grief of the dying prophet, who told him he should have smitten five or six times. Not being straitened in the power and promise of God, why should he be straitened in his own expectations and endeavours?

Verses 20–25

I. The sepulchre of Elisha: he died in a good old age, and they buried him. As soon as he was dead, the bands of the Moabites invaded the land—roving skulking bands, that murdered and plundered by surprise. The king was apprehensive of danger only from the Syrians, but, behold, the Moabites invade him. Elisha's dead body communicated life

JAMIESON, FAUSSET, BROWN

5. a saviour—This refers neither to some patriotic defender nor some signal victory, but to the deliverance obtained for Israel by the two successors of Jehoahaz, viz., Joash, who regained all the cities which the Syrians had taken from his father (vs. 25); and Jeroboam, who restored the former boundaries of Israel (ch. 14:25). **6. there remained the grove**—Asherah—the idol set up by Ahab (I Kings 16:33), which ought to have been demolished (Deut. 7:5). **7. made them like the dust in threshing**—Threshing in the East is performed in the open air upon a level plot of ground, daubed over with a covering to prevent, as much as possible, the earth, sand, or gravel from rising; a great quantity of them all, notwithstanding this precaution, must unavoidably be taken up with the grain; at the same time the straw is shattered to pieces. Hence it is a most significant figure, frequently employed by Orientals to describe a state of national suffering, little short of extermination (Isa. 21:10; Mic. 4:12; Jer. 51:33). The figure originated in a barbarous war custom, which Hazael literally followed (Amos 1:3, 4; cf. II Sam. 8:31; Judg. 8:7).

8-25. JOASH SUCCEEDS HIM. **8. his might**—This is particularly noticed in order to show that the grievous oppression from foreign enemies, by which the Israelites were ground down, was not owing to the cowardice or imbecility of their king, but solely to the righteous and terrible judgment of God for their foul apostasy. **12, 13. his might, wherewith he fought against Amaziah**—(See on ch. 14:8-14). The usual summary of his life and reign occurs rather early, and is again repeated in the account given of the reign of the king of Judah (ch. 14:15). **14-19. Elisha was fallen sick of his sickness whereof he died**—Every man's death is occasioned by some disease, and so was Elisha's. But in intimating it, there seems a contrast tacitly made between him and his prophetic predecessor, who did not die. **Joash the king of Israel came down unto him, and wept over his face**—He visited him where he was lying ill of this mortal sickness, and expressed deep sorrow, not from the personal respect he bore for the prophet, but for the incalculable loss his death would occasion to the kingdom. **my father, my father!** etc.—(See on ch. 2:12). These words seem to have been a complimentary phrase applied to one who was thought an eminent guardian and deliverer of his country. The particular application of them to Elisha, who, by his counsels and prayer, had obtained many glorious victories for Israel, shows that the king possessed some measure of faith and trust, which, though weak, was accepted, and called forth the prophet's dying benediction. **15. Take bow and arrows**—Hostilities were usually proclaimed by a herald, sometimes by a king or general making a public and formal discharge of an arrow into the enemy's country. Elisha directed Joash to do this, as a symbolical act, designed to intimate more fully and significantly the victories promised to the king of Israel over the Syrians. His laying his hands upon the king's hands was to represent the power imparted to the bow-shot as coming from the Lord through the medium of the prophet. His shooting the first arrow eastward—to that part of his kingdom which the Syrians had taken and which was east of Samaria—was a declaration of war against them for the invasion. His shooting the other arrows into the ground was in token of the number of victories he was taken to gain; but his stopping at the third betrayed the weakness of his faith; for, as the discharged arrow signified a victory over the Syrians, it is evident that the more arrows he shot the more victories he would gain. As he stopped so soon, his conquests would be incomplete.

20. Elisha died—He had enjoyed a happier life than Elijah, as he possessed a milder character, and bore a less hard commission. His rough garment was honored even at the court. **coming in of the year**—i.e., the spring, the usual season of beginning campaigns in ancient times. Predatory bands from Moab generally

ADAM CLARKE

5. *And the Lord gave Israel a saviour*. This was undoubtedly Joash, whose successful wars against the Syrians are mentioned at the conclusion of the chapter.

6. *The grove also in Samaria. Asherah*, or Astarte, remained in Samaria, and there she was worshipped, with all her abominable rites.

10. *In the thirty and seventh year*. Joash, the son of Jehoahaz, was associated with his father in the government two years before his death. It is this association that is spoken of here. He succeeded him two years after, a little before the death of Elisha. Joash reigned *sixteen years*, which include the years he governed conjointly with his father.

12. *Wherewith he fought against Amaziah*. This war with Amaziah may be seen in ample detail, 2 Chronicles xxv; it ended in the total defeat of Amaziah, who was taken prisoner by Joash, and afterwards slain in a conspiracy at Lachish. Joash took Jerusalem, broke down 400 cubits of the wall, and took all the royal treasures, and the treasures of the house of God (see 2 Chron. xxv. 20-27).

14. *Now Elisha was fallen sick*. This is supposed to have taken place in the tenth year of Joash; and if so, Elisha must have prophesied about sixty-five years. *O my father, my father*. "What shall I do now thou art dying? thou art the only defense of Israel." He accosts him with the same words which himself spoke to Elijah when he was translated (see chap. ii. 12).

15. *Take bow and arrows*. The bow, the arrows, and the smiting on the ground were all emblematical things, indicative of the deliverance of Israel from Syria.

17. *Open the window eastward*. This was towards the country beyond Jordan, which Hazael had taken from the Israelites. *The arrow of . . . deliverance from Syria*. That is, As surely as that arrow is shot towards the lands conquered from Israel by the Syrians, so surely shall those lands be reconquered and restored to Israel. It was an ancient custom to shoot an arrow or cast a spear into the country which an army intended to invade. *Thou shalt smite the Syrians in Aphek*. This was a city of Syria, and probably the place of the first battle; and there, it appears, they had a total overthrow. They were, in the language of the text, *consumed* or "exterminated."

MATTHEW HENRY

to another dead body, *v.* 21. This great miracle was a plain indication of another life after this. The neighbours were carrying the dead body of a man to the grave, and, fearing to fall into the hands of the Moabites, a party of whom they saw at a distance near the place where the body was to be interred, they laid the corpse in the next convenient place, which proved to be Elisha's sepulchre. The dead man, upon touching Elisha's bones, revived, and, it is likely, went home again with his friends. Elijah was honoured *in* his departure. Elisha was honoured *after* his departure. God thus dispenses honours as he pleases, but, one way or other, the rest of all the saints will be glorious, Isa. xi. 10.

II. The sword of Joash king of Israel successful against the Syrians. 1. The cause of his success was God's favour (*v.* 23): *The Lord was gracious to them, had compassion on them* in their miseries and *respect unto them.* It was of the Lord's mercies that they were not consumed, because he would give them space to repent. 2. The effect of his success. He recovered out of the hands of Benhadad the cities of Israel which the Syrians were possessed of, *v.* 25. Thrice Joash beat the Syrians, just as often as he had struck the ground with the arrows, and then a full stop was put to the course of his victories.

CHAPTER 14

Verses 1–7

Amaziah, the son and successor of Joash.

I. In the temple he acted, in some measure, well, like Joash, but not like David, *v.* 3. He began well, but did not persevere. It is not enough to do that which our pious predecessors did, merely to keep up the usage, but we must do it *as* they did it, from the same principle of faith and devotion and with the same sincerity and resolution. It is here taken notice of, as before, that *the high places were not taken away, v.* 4.

II. On the bench we have him doing justice on the traitors that murdered his father, not as soon as ever he came to the crown, lest it should occasion some disturbance, but he prudently deferred it till *the kingdom was confirmed in his hand, v.* 5. *The children of the murderers he slew not,* because the law of Moses had expressly provided that *the children should not be put to death for the fathers, v.* 6.

III. In the field we find him triumphing over the Edomites, *v.* 7. Edom had *revolted from under the hand of Judah* in Joram's time, *ch.* viii. 22. Now he makes war upon them to bring them back to their allegiance. We shall find a larger account of this expedition, 2 Chron. xxv. 5, &c.

Verses 8–14

For several successions after the division of the kingdoms that of Judah suffered much by the *enmity* of Israel. After Asa's time, for several successions, it suffered more by the *friendship* of Israel, and by the alliance and affinity made with them. But now we meet with hostility between them again.

I. Amaziah, upon no provocation, and without showing any cause of quarrel, challenged Joash into the field (*v.* 8): *Come, let us look one another in the face;* let us try our strength in battle. Hereby he showed himself proud, presumptuous, and prodigal of blood. Some think that he had the vanity to think of subduing the kingdom of Israel, and reuniting it to Judah.

II. Joash sent him a grave rebuke for his challenge, with advice to withdraw it, *v.* 9, 10. 1. He mortifies his pride, by comparing himself to a cedar, a stately tree, and Amaziah to a thistle, a sorry weed, telling him he was so far from fearing him that he despised him, and scorned as much to have anything to do with him, or make any alliance with him, as the cedar would to match his daughter to a thistle. The ancient house of David he thinks not worthy to be named the same day with the house of Jehu, though an upstart.

JAMIESON, FAUSSET, BROWN

made incursions at that time on the lands of Israel. The bearers of a corpse, alarmed by the appearance of one of these bands, hastily deposited, as they passed that way, their load in Elisha's sepulchre, which might be easily done by removing the stone at the mouth of the cave. According to the Jewish and Eastern custom, his body, as well as that of the man who was miraculously restored, was not laid in a coffin, but only swathed; so that the bodies could be brought into contact and the object of the miracle was to stimulate the king's and people of Israel's faith in the still unaccomplished predictions of Elisha respecting the war with the Syrians. Accordingly the historian forthwith records the historical fulfilment of the prediction (vss. 22-25), in the defeat of the enemy, in the recovery of the cities that had been taken, and their restoration to the kingdom of Israel.

CHAPTER 14

Vss. 1-6. Amaziah's Good Reign over Judah. **3-6. He did that which was right in the sight of the Lord, yet not like David his father**—The beginning of his reign was excellent, for he acted the part of a constitutional king, according to the law of God, yet not with perfect sincerity of heart (cf. II Chron. 25:2). As in the case of his father Joash, the early promise was belied by the devious course he personally followed in later life (see on II Chron. 20: 14), as well as by the public irregularities he tolerated in the kingdom. **5. as soon as the kingdom was confirmed in his hand**—It was an act of justice no less than of filial piety to avenge the murder of his father. But it is evident that the two assassins must have possessed considerable weight and influence, as the king was obliged to retain them in his service, and durst not, for fear of their friends and supporters, institute proceedings against them until his power had been fully consolidated. **6. But the children of the murderers he slew not**—This moderation, inspired by the Mosaic law (Deut. 24:16), displays the good character of this prince; for the course thus pursued toward the families of the regicides was directly contrary to the prevailing customs of antiquity, according to which all connected with the criminals were doomed to unsparing destruction.

7. He Smites Edom. **7. He slew of Edom in the valley of salt ten thousand**—In the reign of Joram the Edomites had revolted (see on ch. 8:20). But Amaziah, determined to reduce them to their former subjection, formed a hostile expedition against them, in which he routed their army and made himself master of their capital. **the valley of salt**—that part of the Ghor which comprises the salt and sandy plain to the south of the Dead Sea. **Selah**—lit., Selah—(rock) generally thought to be Petra. **Joktheel**—i.e., given or conquered by God. See the history of this conquest more fully detailed (II Chron. 25:6-16).

8-16. Joash Defeats Him. **8. Amaziah sent messengers to Jehoash, the son of Jehoahaz, son of Jehu, king of Israel**—This bold and haughty challenge, which was most probably stimulated by a desire of satisfaction for the outrages perpetrated by the discharged auxiliaries of Israel (II Chron. 25: 13) on the towns that lay in their way home, as well as by revenge for the massacre of his ancestors by Jehu (ch. 9) sprang, there is little doubt, from pride and self-confidence, inspired by his victory over the Edomites.

9. Jehoash the king of Israel sent to Amaziah—People in the East very often express their sentiments in a parabolic form, especially when they intend to convey unwelcome truths or a contemptuous sneer. This was the design of the ad-

ADAM CLARKE

23. *And the Lord was gracious unto them.* He had tender affection for them, as a husband has for his wife, or a father for his own children. *And had compassion on them.* "His bowels yearned over them"; He felt for them; He sympathized with them in all their distress. "Therefore my bowels are troubled for him; I will surely have mercy upon him, saith the Lord," Jer. xxxi. 20. *And had respect unto them.* "He turned face towards them"; He received them again into favor, and this because of His *covenant* with their fathers. They must not be totally destroyed; the Messiah must come from them.

25. *Three times did Joash beat him.* The particulars of these battles we have not, but these three victories were according to the prediction of Elisha, v. 19. That these victories were very decisive we learn from their fruits, for Joash took from the Syrians the cities which Hazael had taken from Israel: viz., Gilead, the possessions of Reuben, Gad, and the half-tribe of Manasseh, and the country of Bashan (see chap. x. 33).

CHAPTER 14

1. *In the second year of Joash.* This second year should be understood as referring to the time when his father, Jehoahaz, associated him with himself in the kingdom, for he reigned two years with his father; so this *second* year of Joash is the first of his absolute and independent government.

5. *As soon as the kingdom was confirmed in his hand.* No doubt those wicked men, Jozachar and Jehozabad, who murdered his father, had considerable power and influence; and therefore he found it dangerous to bring them to justice till he was assured of the loyalty of his other officers. When this was clear, he called them to account, and put them to death.

6. *But the children of the murderers he slew not.* Here he showed his conscientious regard for the law of Moses; for God had positively said, "The fathers shall not be put to death for the children, neither shall the children be put to death for the fathers: every man shall be put to death for his own sin," Deut. xxiv. 16.

7. *He slew of Edom in the valley of salt.* This war is more circumstantially related in 2 Chron. xxv. 5, etc. The Idumeans had arisen in the reign of Joram, king of Judah, and shaken off the yoke of the house of David. Amaziah determined to reduce them to obedience; he therefore levied an army of 300,000 men to his own kingdom, and hired 100,000 Israelites, at the price of 100 talents. When he was about to depart at the head of this numerous army, a prophet came to him and ordered him to dismiss the Israelitish army, for God was not with them; and on the king of Judah expressing regret for the loss of his 100 talents, he was answered that the Lord could give him much more than that. He obeyed, sent back the Israelities, and at the head of his own men attacked the Edomites in the valley of salt, slew 10,000 on the spot, and took 10,000 prisoners, all of whom he precipitated from the "rock," or *Selah,* a place or city supposed to be the same with Petra, where there must have been a great precipice, from which the place took its name of *Selah* or Petra.

8. *Come, let us look one another in the face.* This was a real declaration of war; and the ground of it is most evident from this circumstance: that the 100,000 men of Israel that had been dismissed, though they had the stipulated money, taking the advantage of Amaziah's absence, "fell upon the cities of Judah, from Samaria even unto Beth-horon, and smote three thousand of them, and took much spoil," 2 Chron. xxv. 10-13. Amaziah no doubt remonstrated with Jehoash, but to no purpose; and therefore he declared war against him.

9. *Jehoash . . . sent to Amaziah . . . saying.* The meaning of this parable is plain. The *thistle that was in Lebanon*—Amaziah, king of Judah, *sent to the cedar that was in Lebanon*—Jehoash, king of Israel, *saying, Give thy daugh-*

MATTHEW HENRY

2. He fortells his fall: *A wild beast trod down the thistle*, and so put an end to his treaty with the cedar; so easily does Joash think his forces can crush Amaziah. 3. He shows him the folly of his challenge. "Thou art proud of the blow thou hast given to Edom, as if that had made thee formidable to all mankind." 4. He counsels him to be content with the honour he has won, and not to hazard that, by grasping at more that was out of his reach.

III. Amaziah persisted in his resolution, and the issue was bad. 1. His army was routed and dispersed, *v.* 12. Josephus says, When they were to engage they were struck with such terror that they did not strike a stroke, but every one made the best of his way. 2. He himself was taken prisoner by the king of Israel, and then had enough of *looking him in the face*. 3. The conqueror entered Jerusalem, which tamely opened to him, and yet he broke down their wall (and, as Josephus says, drove his chariot in triumph through the breach), in reproach to them. 4. He plundered Jerusalem, took away all that was valuable, and returned to Samaria, laden with spoils, *v.* 14.

Verses 15–22

Here are three kings brought to their graves in these few verses:—1. Joash king of Israel, *v.* 15, 16. 2. Amaziah king of Judah. Fifteen years he survived his conqueror the king of Israel, *v.* 17. He was slain by his own subjects, who hated him for his maladministration (*v.* 19) and made Jerusalem too hot for him, the ignominious breach made in their walls being occasioned by his folly and presumption. He fled to Lachish. How long he continued concealed or sheltered there we are not told, but, at last, he was there murdered, *v.* 19. 3. Azariah succeeded Amaziah, but not till twelve years after his father's death, for he was but four years old at the death of his father, so that, for twelve years, till he came to be sixteen, the government was in the hands of protectors. He reigned very long (*ch.* xv. 2) and yet the account of his reign is here industriously huddled up, and broken off abruptly (*v.* 22): *He built Elath* which had belonged to the Edomites.

Verses 23–29

An account of the reign of Jeroboam the second.

I. His reign was long, the longest of all the reigns of the kings of Israel: *He reigned forty-one years;* yet his contemporary Azariah, the king of Judah, reigned longer, even fifty-two years. This Jeroboam reigned just as long as Asa had done (1 Kings xv. 10), yet one did that which was good and the other that which was evil. We cannot measure men's characters by the length of their lives or by their outward prosperity.

II. His character was the same with that of the rest of those kings: *He did that which was evil* (*v.* 24), for *he departed not from the sins of Jeroboam*; he kept up the worship of the calves. But a sin is never the less evil in God's sight for its being an ancient usage.

III. Yet he prospered more than most of them, for though, in that one thing, he did evil in the sight of the Lord, yet it is likely, in other respects, there was some good found in him and therefore God owned him, 1. By prophecy. He raised up Jonah the son of Amittai, a Galilean. It is a sign that God has not cast off his people if he continue faithful ministers among them; when Elisha, who strengthened the hands of Joash, was removed, Jonah was sent to encourage his son. It is probable that it was when he was a young man, that God sent him to Nineveh, and that he flew off and fretted as he did; and, if so, this is an undoubted evidence of the forgiveness of his faults and follies, that he was afterwards employed as a messenger of mercy to Israel. A commission amounts to a pardon. 2. By providence. The event was *according to the word of the Lord*: his arms were successful; he *restored the coast of Israel*, recovered those frontier-towns and countries that lay from Hamath in the north to the sea of the plain, *v.* 25. Two reasons why God blessed them with those victories:—(1) Because their distress was very great, which made them the objects of his compassion, *v.* 26. Those that lived in those countries which the enemies were masters of were miserably oppressed and enslaved, and the rest were much impoverished by the frequent incursions the enemy made upon them to plunder them. Let those whose case is pitiable take comfort from the divine pity: we read of God's bowels of mercy (Isa. lxiii. 15; Jer. xxxi. 20) and that he is full of compassion, Ps. lxxxvi. 15. (2) Because he had not as yet said *he would blot out the name of Israel* (*v.* 27). If this be understood of the dispersion of the ten tribes, he did say it and do it, not long after—if of the utter extirpation of the name of Israel, he never said it, nor will ever do it, for that

JAMIESON, FAUSSET, BROWN

monitory fable related by Joash in his reply. The thistle, a low shrub, might be chosen to represent Amaziah, a petty prince; the cedar, the powerful sovereign of Israel, and the wild beast that trampled down the thistle the overwhelming army with which Israel could desolate Judah. But, perhaps, without making so minute an application, the parable may be explained generally, as describing in a striking manner the effects of pride and ambition, towering far beyond their natural sphere, and sure to fall with a sudden and ruinous crash. The moral of the fable is contained in vs. 10.

11. But Amaziah would not hear—The sarcastic tenor of this reply incited the king of Judah the more; for, being in a state of judicial blindness and infatuation (II Chron. 25:20), he was immovably determined on war. But the superior energy of Joash surprised him ere he had completed his military preparations. Pouring a large army into the territory of Judah, he encountered Amaziah in a pitched battle, routed his army, and took him prisoner. Then having marched to Jerusalem, he not only demolished part of the city walls, but plundered the treasures of the palace and temple. Taking hostages to prevent any further molestation from Judah, he terminated the war. Without leaving a garrison in Jerusalem, he returned to his capital with all convenient speed, his presence and all his forces being required to repel the troublesome incursions of the Syrians.

17-20. HE IS SLAIN BY A CONSPIRACY. **19. they made a conspiracy against him in Jerusalem**—Amaziah's apostasy (II Chron. 25:27) was followed by a general maladministration, especially the disastrous issue of the war with Israel. The ruinous condition of Jerusalem, the plunder of the temple, and the loss of their children who were taken as hostages, lost him the respect and attachment not of the grandees only, but of his subjects generally, who were in rebellion. The king fled in terror to Lachish, a frontier town of the Philistines, where, however, he was traced and murdered. His friends had his corpse brought without any pomp or ceremony, in a chariot to Jerusalem, where he was interred among his royal ancestors.

21, 22. AZARIAH SUCCEEDS HIM. **21. all the people of Judah took Azariah**—or Uzziah (ch. 15:30; II Chron. 26:1). The popular opposition had been personally directed against Amaziah as the author of their calamities, but it was not extended to his family or heir. **22. He built Elath**—fortified that seaport. It had revolted with the rest of Edom, but was now recovered by Uzziah. His father, who did not complete the conquest of Edom, had left him that work to do.

23-29. JEROBOAM'S WICKED REIGN OVER ISRAEL. **23. Jeroboam, the son of Joash, the king of Israel**—This was Jeroboam II who, on regaining the lost territory, raised the kingdom to great political power (vs. 25), but adhered to the favorite religious policy of the Israelitish sovereigns (vs. 24). While God granted him so great a measure of national prosperity and eminence, the reason is expressly stated (vss. 26, 27) to be that the purposes of the divine covenant forbade as yet the overthrow of the kingdom of the ten tribes (see on ch. 13:23).

ADAM CLARKE

ter—a part of your kingdom, *to my son to wife*—to be united to, and possessed by the kings of Judah. *And there passed by a wild beast*—his troops, pillaged the Temple, and broke down *the thistle*—utterly discomfited Amaziah and his troops, pillaged the Temple, and broke down the walls of Jerusalem (see vv. 12-14). Probably Amaziah had required certain cities of Israel to be given up to Judah; if so, this accounts for that part of the parable, "Give thy daughter to my son to wife."

10. *Glory of this, and tarry at home.* There is a vast deal of insolent dignity in this remonstrance of Jehoash; but it has nothing conciliatory, no proposal of making amends for the injury his army had done to the unoffending inhabitants of Judah. The ravages committed by the army of Jehoash were totally unprovoked, and they were base and cowardly; they fell upon women, old men, and children, and butchered them in cold blood, for all the effective men were gone off with their king against the Edomites. The quarrel of Amaziah was certainly just, yet he was put to rout; he did meddle to his hurt; he fell, and Judah fell with him, as Jehoash had said. But why was this? Why, it came of God; for he had brought the gods "of Seir, and set them up to be his gods, and bowed down himself before them, and burned incense unto them." Therefore God delivered "them into the hand of their enemies, because they sought after the gods of Edom," 2 Chron. xxv. 14, 20. This was the reason why the Israelites triumphed.

13. *Took Amaziah king of Judah.* It is plain that afterwards Amaziah had his liberty; but how or on what terms he got it is not known. See on the following verse.

14. *And he took . . . hostages.* "Pledges"; from *arab*, "to pledge, give security," for the performance of some promise. It is likely that Amaziah gave some of the nobles or some of his own family as hostages, that he might regain his liberty; and they were to get their liberty when he had fulfilled his engagements; but of what kind these were we cannot tell, nor, indeed, how he got his liberty.

15. *How he fought with Amaziah.* The only fighting between them was the battle already mentioned, and this is minutely related in 2 Chronicles xxv.

19. *They made a conspiracy against him.* His defeat by Jehoash, and the consequent pillaging of the Temple, and emptying the royal exchequer, and the dismantling of Jerusalem, had made him exceedingly unpopular; so that probably the whole of the last fifteen years of his life were a series of troubles and distresses.

21. *Took Azariah.* He is also called Uzziah, 2 Chron. xxvi. 1. The former signifies, "The help of the Lord"; the latter, "The strength of the Lord."

22. *He built Elath.* This city belonged to the Edomites, and was situated on the eastern branch of the Red Sea. It had probably suffered much in the late war, and was now rebuilt by Uzziah, and brought entirely under the dominion of Judah.

25. *He restored the coast of Israel.* From the description that is here given it appears that Jeroboam reconquered all the territory that had been taken from the kings of Israel; so that Jeroboam II left the kingdom as ample as it was when the ten tribes separated under Jeroboam I.

26. *The Lord saw the affliction of Israel.* It appears that about this time Israel had been greatly reduced, and great calamities had fallen upon all indiscriminately; even the diseased and captives in the dungeon had the hand of God heavy upon them, and there was no helper. And then God sent Jonah to encourage them, and to assure them of better days. He was the first of the prophets, after Samuel, whose writings are preserved; yet the prophecy delivered on this occasion is not extant, for what is now in the prophecies of Jonah relates wholly to Nineveh.

28. *How he warred, and . . . recovered Damascus.* We learn from 1 Chron. xviii. 3-11 that David had conquered all Syria, and put garrisons in Damascus and other places, and laid all the Syrians under tribute; but this yoke

MATTHEW HENRY

name still remains under heaven in the *gospel Israel*, and will to the end of time.

IV. Here is the conclusion of Jeroboam's reign. We read (*v.* 28) of his might, and how he warred. Many prophets there had been in Israel, but none had left any of their prophecies in writing till those of this age began to do it, and their prophecies are part of the canon of scripture. It was in the reign of this Jeroboam that *Hosea* began to prophesy, and he was the first that wrote his prophecies; therefore the word of the Lord by him is called *the beginning of the word of the Lord*, Hos. i. 2. At the same time *Amos* prophesied, and wrote his prophecy, soon afterwards *Micah*, and then *Isaiah*, in the days of Ahaz and Hezekiah. Thus God never left himself without witness.

JAMIESON, FAUSSET, BROWN

ADAM CLARKE

they had not only shaken off, but they had conquered a considerable portion of the Israelitish territory and added it to Syria. These latter Jeroboam now recovered; and thus the places which anciently belonged to Judah by David's conquests, and were repossessed by Syria, he now conquered and added to Israel.

29. *Jeroboam slept with his fathers.* He died a natural death; and was regularly succeeded by his son Zachariah, who, reigning badly, was, after six months, slain by Shallum, who succeeded him, and reigned but one month, being slain by Menahem, who succeeded him, and reigned ten years over Israel. Amos, the prophet, lived in the reign of Jeroboam; and was accused by Amaziah, one of the idolatrous priests of Bethel, of having predicted the death of Jeroboam by the sword, but this was a slander. What he did predict, and which came afterwards to pass, may be seen in Amos vii. 10-17.

MATTHEW HENRY

CHAPTER 15

Verses 1–7

The reign of Azariah. 1. He began young and reigned long (*v.* 2), did, for the most part, that which was right, *v.* 3, only he had not zeal and courage to take away the high places, *v.* 4. 2. That which is peculiar, *v.* 5 (that God smote him with a leprosy) is more largely related, with the occasion of it, 2. Chron. xxvi. 16, &c., where we have also a fuller account of the glories of the former part of his reign, as well as of the disgraces of the latter part of it. Here we are told, (1) That he was a leper. (2) God smote him with this leprosy, to chastise him for his presumptuous invasion of the priests' office. (3) That he was a leper *to the day of his death.* Though we have reason to think he repented and the sin was pardoned, yet, for warning to others, he was continued under this mark of God's displeasure. (4) That he *dwelt in a separate house*, as being made ceremonially unclean by the law, to the discipline of which, though a king, he must submit. (5) That his son was his viceroy in the affairs both of his court (for *he was over the house*) and of his kingdom (for he was *judging the people of the land*); and it was both a comfort to him and a blessing to his kingdom that he had such a son to fill up his room.

Verses 8–31

The best days of the kingdom of Israel were while the government was in Jehu's family. In his reign, and the next three reigns, though there were many abominable corruptions and miserable grievances in Israel, yet the crown went in succession, the kings died in their beds, and some care was taken of public affairs; but, now that those days are at an end, the history which we have in these verses of about thirty-three years represents the affairs of that kingdom in the utmost confusion imaginable.

I. These unhappy revolutions—these bad times, as they may truly be called. 1. God had tried the people of Israel both with judgments and mercies, explained and enforced by his servants the prophets, and yet they continued impenitent and unreformed, and therefore God justly brought these miseries upon them. 2. God made good his promise to Jehu, that his sons to the fourth generation after him should sit upon the throne of Israel, which was a greater favour than was shown to any of the royal families either before or after his. Thus God rewarded Jehu for his zeal in destroying the worship of Baal and the house of Ahab; and yet, when the measure of the sins of the house of Jehu was full, God avenged upon it the blood then shed, called *the blood of Jezreel*, Hos. i. 4. 3. All these kings did that which was *evil in the sight of the Lord*, for *they walked in the sins of Jeroboam the son of Nebat.* Though at variance with one another, yet in this they agreed, to keep up idolatry, and the people loved to have it so. 4. Each of these (except one) conspired against his predecessor, and slew him—*Shallum, Menahem, Pekah*, and *Hoshea*, all traitors and murderers, and yet all kings awhile. One wicked man is often made a scourge to another, and every wicked man, at length, a ruin to himself. 5. The ambition of the great men made the nation miserable. Here is Tiphsah, a city of Israel, barbarously destroyed, with all the coasts thereof, by one of these pretenders (*v.* 16). 6. While the nation was thus shattered by divisions at home the kings of Assyria, first one (*v.* 19) and then another (*v.* 29), came against it and did what they pleased. 7. This was the condition of Israel just before they were quite ruined and carried away captive, for that was in the ninth year of Hoshea, the last of these

JAMIESON, FAUSSET, BROWN

CHAPTER 15

Vss. 1-4. Azariah's Reign over Judah. **1. In the twenty and seventh year of Jeroboam**—It is thought that the throne of Judah continued vacant eleven or twelve years, between the death of Amaziah and the inauguration of his son Azariah. Being a child only four years old when his father was murdered, a regency was appointed during Azariah's minority. **began Azariah . . . to reign**—The character of his reign is described by the brief formula employed by the inspired historian, in recording the religious policy of the later kings. But his reign was a very active as well as eventful one, and is fully related (II Chron. 26). Elated by the possession of great power, and presumptuously arrogating to himself, as did the heathen kings, the functions both of the real and sacerdotal offices, he was punished with leprosy, which, as the offense was capital (Num. 8:7), was equivalent to death, for this disease excluded him from all society. While Jotham, his son, as his viceroy, administered the affairs of the kingdom—being about fifteen years of age (cf. vs. 33)—he had to dwell in a place apart by himself (see on ch. 7:3). After a long reign he died, and was buried in the royal burying-field, though not in the royal cemetery of "the city of David" (II Chron. 26:33).

8-16. Zechariah's Reign over Israel. **8. In the thirty and eighth year of Azariah king of Judah did Zechariah the son of Jeroboam reign over Israel**—There was an interregnum from some unknown cause between the reign of Jeroboam and the accession of his son, which lasted, according to some, for ten or twelve years, according to others, for twenty-two years, or more. This prince pursued the religious policy of the calf-worship, and his reign was short, being abruptly terminated by the hand of violence. In his fate was fulfilled the prophecy addressed to Jehu (ch. 10:30; also Hos. 1:4), that his family would possess the throne of Israel for four generations; and accordingly Jehoahaz, Joash, Jehoram, and Zechariah were his successors—but there his dynasty terminated; and perhaps it was the public knowledge of this prediction that prompted the murderous design of Shallum.

ADAM CLARKE

CHAPTER 15

1. *In the twenty and seventh year of Jeroboam.* There are insuperable difficulties in the chronology of this place. The marginal note says, "This is the twenty-seventh year of Jeroboam's partnership in the kingdom with his father, who made him consort at his going to the Syrian wars. It is the sixteenth year of Jeroboam's monarchy." Lightfoot endeavors to reconcile this place with chap. xiv. 16-17 thus: "At the death of Amaziah, his son and heir Uzziah was but four years old, for he was about sixteen in Jeroboam's twenty-seventh year; therefore, the throne must have been empty eleven years, and the government administered by protectors while Uzziah was in his minority."

3. *He did that which was right.* It is said, 2 Chron. xxvi. 5, that he sought the Lord in the days of Zechariah the prophet, and "God made him to prosper."

10. *Smote him before the people.* In some public assembly: he probably became very unpopular.

12. *This was the word of the Lord . . . unto Jehu.* God had promised to Jehu that his sons **should sit on the throne of Israel to the fourth** generation; and so it came to pass, for Jehoahaz, Joash, Jeroboam, and Zachariah succeeded Jehu, to whom this promise was made. But because he executed the divine purpose with an uncommanded cruelty, therefore God cut his family short, according to his word by Hosea, "I will avenge the blood of Jezreel upon the house of Jehu, and will cause to cease the kingdom of the house of Israel," i. 4.

MATTHEW HENRY

usurpers. If they had, in these days of confusion and perplexity, humbled themselves before God and sought his face, that final destruction might have been prevented.

II. A short view of the particular reigns.

1. Zachariah, the son of Jeroboam, began to reign in the thirty-eighth year of Azariah, or Uzziah, king of Judah, *v.* 8. Some of the most critical chronologers reckon that between Jeroboam and his son Zachariah the throne was vacant twenty-two years through the disturbances and dissensions that were in the kingdom. Zachariah was deposed before he was well seated on the throne: he reigned but six months, and then Shallum *slew him before the people*, with the approbation of the people, to whom he had, some way or other, made himself odious; so ended the line of Jehu.

2. But had Shallum peace, who slew his master? No, he had not (*v.* 13), one month of days measured his reign and then he was cut off. Menaham, either provoked by his crime or animated by his example, soon served him as he had served his master—*slew him and reigned in his stead*, *v.* 14.

3. Menaham held the kingdom ten years, *v.* 17. He was so prodigiously cruel to those of his own nation who hesitated a little at submitting to him that he not only ruined a city, but *ripped up all the women with child*, *v.* 16. By these cruel methods he hoped to frighten all others into his interests; but when the king of Assyria came against him, (1) So little confidence had he in his people that he durst not meet him as an enemy, but was obliged, at a vast expense, to purchase a peace with him. (2) Such need had he of help *to confirm the kingdom in his hand* that he made it part of his bargain that he should assist him against his own subjects that were disaffected to him. Thus he got clear of the king of Assyria for this time; but his army now got so rich a booty with so little trouble that it encouraged them to come again, not long after, when they laid all waste.

4. Pekahiah, the son of Menahem, succeeded his father, but reigned only two years, and then was treacherously slain by Pekah.

5. Pekah, though he got the kingdom by treason, kept it twenty years (*v.* 27), so long it was before his violent dealing returned upon his own head, but it returned at last. This Pekah, son of Remaliah, (1) Made himself more considerable abroad than any of these usurpers, for he was a great terror to the kingdom of Judah, as we find, Isa. vii. 1, &c. (2) He lost a great part of his kingdom to the king of Assyria. By this judgment God punished him for his attempt upon Judah and Jerusalem. (3) Soon after this he forfeited his life to the resentments of his countrymen, who, it is probable, were disgusted at him for leaving them exposed to a foreign enemy, while he was invading Judah, of which Hoshea took advantage and, to gain his crown, seized his life, *slew him, and reigned in his stead*. Surely he was fond of a crown indeed who, at this time, would run such a hazard as a traitor did—a crown which a wise man would not have taken up in the street, yet Hoshea not only ventured *upon* it but ventured *for* it, and it cost him dear.

Verses 32–38

A short account of the reign of Jotham king of Judah, of whom we are told, 1. That he reigned very well, *did that which was right in the sight of the Lord*, *v.* 34. Josephus gives him a very high character, stating that he was pious towards God, just towards men, and laid out himself for the public good. Though the high places were not taken away, yet to draw people from them, and keep them close to God's holy place, he showed great respect to the temple, and built the higher gate to the temple. If magistrates cannot do all they would for the suppressing of vice and profaneness, let them do so much the more for the support and advancement of piety and virtue. If they cannot pull down the high places of sin, yet let them build and beautify the high gate of God's house. 2. That he died in the midst of his days, *v.* 33. By these accounts it appears that there was none of all the kings of Judah that reached David's age, seventy, the common age of man. Asa's age I do not find. Uzziah lived to be sixty-eight, Manasseh sixty-seven, and Jehoshaphat sixty; and these were the three oldest; many of those that were of note did not reach fifty. This Jotham died at forty-one. 3. That in his days the confederacy was formed against Judah by Rezin and Remaliah's son, the king of Syria and the king of Israel, which appeared so very formidable in the beginning of the reign of Ahaz that, upon notice of it, the heart of that prince was moved and *the heart of the people, as the trees of the wood are moved with the wind*, Isa. vii. 2.

JAMIESON, FAUSSET, BROWN

13-17. **Shallum . . . reigned a full month**—He was opposed and slain by Menahem, who, according to Josephus, was commander of the forces, which, on the report of the king's murder, were besieging Tirzah, a town twelve miles east of Samaria, and formerly a seat of the kings of Israel. Raising the siege, he marched directly against the usurper, slew him, and reigned in his stead. **16. Menahem . . . smote Tiphsah**—Thapsacus, on the Euphrates, the border city of Solomon's kingdom (I Kings 4:24). The inhabitants refusing to open their gates to him, Menahem took it by storm. Then having spoiled it, he committed the most barbarous excesses, without regard either to age or sex.

17-21. MENAHEM'S REIGN. **17. reigned ten years in Samaria**—His government was conducted on the religious policy of his predecessors. **19. Pul the king of Assyria**—This is the first Assyrian king after Nimrod who is mentioned in biblical history. His name has been recently identified with that of Phalluka on the monuments of Nineveh, and that of Menahem discovered also. **came against the land**—Elsewhere it is said "Ephraim [Israel] went to the Assyrian." The two statements may be reconciled thus: "Pul, of his own motion, induced, perhaps, by the expedition of Menahem against Thapsacus, advanced against the kingdom of Israel; then Menahem sent him 1000 talents in order not only to divert him from his plans of conquest, but at the same time to purchase his friendship and aid for the establishment of his own precarious sovereignty. So Menahem did not properly invite the Assyrian into the land, but only changed the enemy when marching against the country, by this tribute, into a confederate for the security of his usurped dominion. This the prophet Hosea, less concerned about the historical fact than the disposition betrayed therein, might very well censure as a going of Ephraim to the Assyrians (Hos. 5:13; 7:1; 8:9), and a covenant-making with Asshur (ch. 12:1) [KEIL]. **a thousand talents of silver**—equal to $ 2,000.00. This tribute, which Menahem raised by a tax on the grandees of Israel, bribed Pul to return to his own country (see on I Chron. 5:26).

22-24. PEKAHIAH'S REIGN. **23. Pekahiah . . . son of Menahem began to reign**—On comparing the date given with Azariah's reign, it seems that several months had intervened between the death of Menahem and the accession of Pekahiah, probably owing to a contest about the throne. **25. with Argob and Arieh**, etc.—Many commentators view these as the captain's accomplices. But it is more probable that they were influential friends of the king, who were murdered along with him.

27-30. PEKAH'S REIGN. **29. in the days of Pekah, king of Israel, came Tiglath-pileser**—This monarch, who succeeded Pul on the throne of Assyria, is the only one of all the kings who does not give his genealogy, and is therefore supposed to have been an usurper. His annals have been discovered in the Nimroud mound—describing this expedition into Syria. The places taken are here mentioned as they occurred and were conquered in the progress of an invasion. **30. Hoshea the son of Elah made a conspiracy . . . and slew him**—He did not, however, obtain possession of the kingdom till about nine or ten years after the perpetration of this crime [HALES].

30-38. JOTHAM'S REIGN OVER JUDAH. **30. in the twentieth year of Jotham**—Jotham's reign lasted only sixteen years, but the meaning is that the reign of Hoshea began in the twentieth after the beginning of Jotham's reign. The sacred historian, having not yet introduced the name of Ahaz, reckoned the date by Jotham, whom he had already mentioned (see on II Chron. 27:8). **33. Five and twenty years was he when he began to reign**—i.e., alone—for he had ruled as his father's viceroy. **35. the higher gate of the house of the Lord**—not the temple itself, but one of its courts—probably that which led into the palace (II Chron. 23:20). **37. the Lord began to send against Judah, Rezin the king of Syria**, etc. —This is the first intimation of the hostile feelings of the kings of Israel and Syria, to Judah, which led them to form an alliance and make joint preparations for war. However, war was not actually waged till the reign of Ahaz.

ADAM CLARKE

13. *He reigned a full month.* Menahem is supposed to have been one of Zachariah's generals. Hearing of the death of his master, when he was with the troops at Tirzah, he hastened to Samaria, and slew the murderer, and had himself proclaimed in his stead. But, as the people of Tiphsah did not open their gates to him, he took the place by assault; and as the text tells us, practiced the most cruel barbarities, even ripping up the women that were with child!

19. *Pul the king of Assyria.* This is the first time we hear of *Assyria* since the days of Nimrod, its founder, Gen. x. 11. *That his hand.* That is, "his power and influence," might be with him. In this sense is the word *hand* frequently used in Scripture.

20. *Each man fifty shekels of silver.* Upwards of five pounds sterling a man.

21. *Are they not written in . . . the chronicles?* There are no chronicles extant in which there is anything further relative to this king.

25. *Smote him in Samaria, in the palace of the king's house, with Argob and Arieh.* Who Argob and Arieh were we know not. Some make them men; some make them statues. Pekah had *fifty . . . Gileadites* in the conspiracy with him.

29. *Took Ijon.* These places belonged to Israel; and were taken by Ben-hadad, king of Syria, when he was in league with Asa, king of Judah (see 1 Kings xv. 20). They were regained by Jeroboam II, and now they are taken from Israel once more by Tiglath-pileser. From 1 Chron. v. 26 we learn that Pul and Tiglath-pileser, kings of Assyria, carried away into captivity the two tribes of Reuben, and Gad, and the half-tribe of Manasseh—all that belonged to Israel, on the other side of Jordan. These were never restored to Israel.

30. *Hoshea the son of Elah . . . in the twentieth year of Jotham.* There are many difficulties in the chronology of this place. To reconcile the whole Calmet says: "Hoshea conspired against Pekah, the twentieth year of the reign of this prince, which was the eighteenth after the beginning of the reign of Jotham, king of Judah. Two years after this, that is, the fourth year of Ahaz, and the twentieth of Jotham, Hoshea made himself master of a part of the kingdom, according to v. 30. Finally, the twelfth year of Ahaz, Hoshea had peaceable possession of the whole kingdom, according to chap. xvii. v. 1."

36. *Now the rest of the acts of Jotham.* These acts are distinctly stated in 2 Chronicles xxvii. He built the high gate of the house of the Lord, and he built much on the wall of Ophel. He built cities in the mountains of Judah, and in the forests he built castles and towers. He overthrew the Ammonites, and obliged them to give him 100 talents of silver, 10,000 measures of wheat, and 10,000 of barley, for three consecutive years. He was twenty-five years old when he began to reign, and he reigned sixteen years. These are the particulars which we learn from the place in Chronicles quoted above, few of which are mentioned in this place. As to the *higher gate* of the house of the Lord, commentators are not well agreed. Some think it was a gate which he then made, and which did not exist before, and is the same that is called the "new gate," Jer. xxvi. 10—which is very likely.

37. *In those days the Lord began to send.* It was about this time that the Assyrian wars so ruinous to the Jews began; but it was in the following reigns that they arrived at their highest pitch of disaster to those unfaithful and unfortunate people.

MATTHEW HENRY

CHAPTER 16

Verses 1–4

A general character of the reign of Ahaz. 1. He *did not that which was right like David* (*v.* 2). He had no love for the temple, made no conscience of his duty to God, nor had any regard to his law. He was a reproach to that honourable name and family, which therefore was really a reproach to him. 2. He walked *in the way of the kings of Israel* (*v.* 3), who all worshipped the calves. The kings of Israel pleaded policy and reasons of state for their idolatry, but Ahaz had no such pretence. They were his enemies, and had proved enemies to themselves too by their idolatry; yet he walked in their way. 3. He *made his sons to pass through the fire*, to the honour of his dunghill-deities. He burnt them (2 Chron. xxviii. 3), and made others pass between two fires, or to be drawn through a flame, in token of their dedication to the idol. 4. He did *according to the abominations of the heathen whom the Lord had cast out*. 5. *He sacrificed in the high places*, *v.* 4. If his father had but had zeal enough to take them away, the debauching of his sons might have been prevented; but those that connive at sin know not what dangerous snares they lay for those that come after them.

Verses 5–9

1. The attempt of his confederate neighbours, the kings of Syria and Israel, upon him. They thought to make themselves masters of Jerusalem, and to set a king of their own in it, Isa. vii. 6. In this they fell short, but the king of Syria recovered Elath, a considerable port upon the Red Sea, which Amaziah had taken from the Syrians, *ch.* xiv. 22. 2. His project to get clear of them. Having forsaken God, he had neither courage nor strength to make head against his enemies, nor could he, with any boldness, ask help of God; but he made his court to the king of Assyria, and got him to come in for his relief. The sin itself was its own punishment; for, though it is true that he gained his point the king of Assyria hearkened to him, and, to serve his own turn, made a descent upon Damascus, whereby he gave a powerful diversion to the king of Syria (*v.* 9), and obliged him to let fall his design against Ahaz, carrying the Syrians captive to Kir, yet, considering all, he made but a bad bargain; for, to compass this, (1) He enslaved himself (*v.* 7): *I am thy servant and thy son.* (2) He impoverished himself; for he took the silver and gold that were laid up in the treasury both of the temple and of the kingdom, and sent it to the king of Assyria, *v.* 8. I know not what authority he had thus to dispose of the public stock; but it is common for those that have brought themselves into straits by one sin to help themselves out by another.

Verses 10–16

Though Ahaz had himself sacrificed in high places (*v.* 4), yet God's altar had hitherto continued in its place and in use, but here we have it taken away by wicked Ahaz, and another altar, an idolatrous one, put in the room of it.

I. The model of this new altar, taken from one at Damascus, by the king himself, *v.* 10. The king of Assyria having taken Damascus, thither Ahaz went, to congratulate him and to receive his commands. At Damascus he saw an altar that pleased his fancy extremely. He must have an altar just like this: a pattern of it must be taken immediately.

II. The making of it by Urijah the priest, *v.* 11. Whatever pretence he had, it was a most base wicked thing for him that was a chief priest to make this altar, in compliance with an idolatrous prince, for hereby, 1. He prostituted his authority and profaned the crown of his priesthood, making himself a servant to the lusts of men. 2. He betrayed his trust.

III. The dedicating of it. Urijah set it near the brazen altar. The king was exceedingly pleased with it and offered thereon his burnt-offering, &c., *v.* 12, 13. His sacrifices were not offered to the God of Israel, but to the gods of Damascus.

IV. The removal of God's altar, to make room for it. Ahaz removed God's altar to an obscure corner in the north side of the court, and put his own before the sanctuary, in the place of it. His superstitious invention, at first, jostled *with* God's sacred institution, but at length jostled it *out*. Those will soon come to make nothing of God that will not be content to make him their all. Ahaz durst not quite demolish the brazen altar. He pretends to advance it above its institution. The altar was never designed for an oracle, yet Ahaz will have it for that use. The Jews say that, afterwards, of the brass of it he made that famous dial which was called *the dial of Ahaz*, *ch.* xx. 11.

JAMIESON, FAUSSET, BROWN

CHAPTER 16

Vss. 1-16. Ahaz' Wicked Reign over Judah. **1-4. Ahaz . . . did not that which was right in the sight of the Lord**—The character of this king's reign, the voluptuousness and religious degeneracy of all classes of the people, are graphically portrayed in the writings of Isaiah, who prophesied at that period. The great increase of worldly wealth and luxury in the reigns of Azariah and Jotham had introduced a host of corruptions, which, during his reign, and by the influence of Ahaz, bore fruit in the idolatrous practices of every kind which prevailed in all parts of the kingdom (see on II Chron. 28:24). **3. walked in the way of the kings of Israel**—This is descriptive of the early part of his reign, when, like the kings of Israel, he patronized the symbolic worship of God by images but he gradually went farther into gross idolatry (II Chron. 28:2). **made his son to pass through the fire**—(ch. 23:10). The hands of the idol Moloch being red-hot, the children were passed through between them, which was considered a form of lustration. There is reason to believe that, in certain circumstances, the children were burnt to death (Ps. 106:37). This was strongly prohibited in the law (Lev. 18:21; 20:2-5; Deut. 18:10), although there is no evidence that it was practised in Israel till the time of Ahaz. **5. Then Rezin king of Syria, and Pekah the son of Remaliah, king of Israel, came up to war against Jerusalem**—Notwithstanding their great efforts and military preparations, they failed to take it and, being disappointed, raised the siege and returned home (cf. Isa. 7:1). **6. Rezin . . . recovered Elath**—which Azariah had got into his possession (ch. 14:22). **the Syrians came to Elath, and dwelt there unto this day**—The Septuagint version has "the Edomites," which the most judicious commentators and travellers [Robinson] prefer. **7-9. So Ahaz sent messengers to Tiglath-pileser**—In spite of the assurance given him by Isaiah by two signs, the one immediate, the other remote (Isa. 7:14; 8:4), that the confederate kings would not prevail against him, Ahaz sought aid from the Assyrian monarch, to purchase which he sent the treasures of the palace and temple. Tiglath-pileser marched against Damascus, slew Rezin the king, and carried the people of Damascus into captivity to Kir, which is thought to have been the city Karine (now Kerend), in Media.

10-16. Ahaz went to Damascus to meet Tiglath-pileser—This was a visit of respect, and perhaps of gratitude. During his stay in that heathen city, Ahaz saw an altar with which he was greatly captivated. Forthwith a sketch of it was transmitted to Jerusalem, with orders to Urijah the priest to get one constructed according to the Damascus model, and let this new altar supersede the old one in the temple.

Urijah, with culpable complaisance, acted according to his instructions (vs. 16). The sin in this affair consisted in meddling with, and improving according to human taste and fancy, the altars of the temple, the patterns of which had been furnished by divine authority (Exod. 25:40; 26:30; 27:1; I Chron. 28:19). Urijah was one of the witnesses taken by Isaiah to bear his prediction against Syria and Israel (Isa. 8:2).

ADAM CLARKE

CHAPTER 16

2. *Twenty years old was Ahaz.* Here is another considerable difficulty in the chronology. Ahaz was but twenty years old when he began to reign, and he died after he had reigned sixteen years; consequently his whole age amounted only to thirty-six years. But Hezekiah, his son, was twenty-five years old when he began to reign; and if this were so, then Ahaz must have been the father of Hezekiah when he was but eleven years of age! Some think that the twenty years mentioned here respect the beginning of the reign of Jotham, father of Ahaz; so that the passage should be thus translated: "Ahaz was twenty years of age when his father began to reign"; and consequently he was fifty-two years old when he died, seeing Jotham reigned sixteen years; and therefore Hezekiah was born when his father was twenty-seven years of age. This however is a violent solution, and worthy of little credit. It is better to return to the text as it stands, and allow that Ahaz might be only eleven or twelve years old when he had Hezekiah. This is not at all impossible, as we know that the youth of both sexes in the Eastern countries are marriageable at ten or twelve years of age.

3. *Made his son to pass through the fire.* On this passage I beg leave to refer the reader to my notes on Lev. xviii. 21; xx. 2, 14, where the subject is considered at large.

5. *But could not overcome him.* It is likely that this was the time when Isaiah was sent to console Ahaz (see Isa. vii. 1); and predicted the death of both Rezin and Pekah, his enemies.

6. *Recovered Elath to Syria.* See the note on chap. xiv. 22.

7. *I am thy servant and thy son.* I will obey you in all, and become tributary to you; only help me against Syria and Israel.

9. *The king of Assyria hearkened unto him.* It is said, 2 Chron. xxviii. 20, that "Tilgath-pilneser . . . distressed him, but strengthened him not." Though he came against the Syrians, and took Damascus, and slew Rezin, yet he did not help Ahaz against the Philistines, nor did he lend him any forces to assist against Israel; and he distressed him by taking the royal treasures, and the treasures of the Temple, and did him little service for so great a sacrifice. He helped him a little, but distressed him on the whole. It appears that, about this time, Pekah, king of Israel, nearly ruined Judea: it is said, 2 Chron. xxviii. 6, that he slew 120,000 valiant men in one day; and that he carried away captive to Samaria 200,000 women and children, and much spoil; but, at the instance of the prophet Oded, these were all sent back, fed, and clothed, *ib.* 8-15.

10. *Ahaz went to Damascus.* He had received so much help on the defeat of Rezin that he went to Damascus to meet the king of Assyria and render him thanks. *Ahaz sent to Urijah the priest the fashion of the altar.* This was some idolatrous altar, the shape and workmanship of which pleased Ahaz so well that he determined to have one like it at Jerusalem. For this he had no divine authority, and the compliance of Urijah was both mean and sinful. That Ahaz did this for an idolatrous purpose is evident from 2 Chron. xxviii. 21-25.

14. *Put it on the north side.* He seems to have intended to conform everything in the Lord's house as much as possible to the idolatrous temples which he saw at Damascus, and to model the divine worship in the same way; in a word, to honor and worship the gods of Syria, and not the God of heaven. All the alterations specified here were in contempt of the true God. Thus "he provoked to anger the Lord God of his fathers," 2 Chron. xxviii. 25.

MATTHEW HENRY

Verses 17–20

Here is, I. Ahaz abusing the temple, not the building itself, but some of the furniture of it. 1. He defaced the bases on which the lavers were set (1 Kings vii. 28, 29) and took down the molten sea, *v.* 17. These the priests used for washing. 2. He removed *the covert for the sabbath*, erected either in honour of the sabbath or for the convenience of the priests, when, on the sabbath, they officiated in greater numbers than on other days. 3. The king's entry, which led to the house of the Lord, for the convenience of the royal family (perhaps that ascent which Solomon had made, and which the queen of Sheba admired, 1 Kings x. 5), he turned another way, to show that he did not intend to frequent the house of the Lord any more.

II. Ahaz resigning his life in the midst of his days, at thirty-six years of age (*v.* 19) and leaving his kingdom to a better man, Hezekiah his son (*v.* 20), who proved as much a friend to the temple as he had been an enemy to it.

CHAPTER 17

Verses 1–6

The reign and ruin of Hoshea, the last of the kings of Israel, concerning whom observe,

I. That though he forced his way to the crown by treason and murder (as we read *ch.* xv. 30), yet he gained not the possession of it till seven or eight years after.

II. That, though he was bad, yet not so bad as the kings of Israel had been before him (*v.* 2), not so devoted to the calves as they had been. And some say that this Hoshea took off the embargo which the former kings had put their subjects under, forbidding them to go up to Jerusalem to worship. But what shall we think of this dispensation of providence, that the destruction of the kingdom of Israel should come in the reign of one of the best of its kings? If Hoshea was not so bad as the former kings, yet the people were as bad as those that went before them. Their king gave them leave to do better, but they did as bad as ever, which laid the blame of their sin and ruin wholly upon themselves.

III. That the destruction came gradually.

IV. That they brought it upon themselves by the indirect course they took to shake off the yoke of the king of Assyria, *v.* 4. Had the king and the people of Israel applied to God, made their peace with him and their prayers to him, they might have recovered their liberty, ease, and honour; but they withheld their tribute, and trusted to the king of Egypt to assist them in their revolt, which, if it had taken effect, would have been but to change their oppressors. But Egypt became to them the staff of a broken reed.

V. That it was an utter destruction that came upon them. 1. The king of Israel was made a prisoner. 2. The land of Israel was made a prey. The army of the king of Assyria treated the people as traitors to be punished with the sword of justice rather than as fair enemies. 3. The royal city of Israel was besieged, and at length taken. Three years it held out after the country was conquered. 4. The people of Israel were carried captives into Assyria, *v.* 6. The generality of the people, those that were of any note, were forced away into the conqueror's country, to be slaves and beggars there. Those that forgot God were themselves forgotten. Many of the meaner sort of people were left behind, many of every tribe, who either went over to Judah or became subject to the Assyrian colonies, and their posterity were *Galileans* or *Samaritans.* But thus ended Israel as a nation; now they became *Lo-ammi—not a people*, and *Lo-ruhamah—unpitied.* James writes to the twelve tribes scattered abroad (James i. 1) and Paul speaks of the twelve tribes which *instantly served God day and night* (Acts xxvi. 7); so that though we never read of those that were carried captive, yet a remnant of them did escape, to keep up the name of Israel, till it came to be worn by the gospel church, the spiritual Israel, in which it will ever remain, Gal. vi. 16.

Verses 7–23

The destruction of the kingdom of the ten tribes and the reasons of it assigned. 1. It was *the Lord that removed Israel out of his sight*; whoever were the instruments, he was the author of this calamity. It was *destruction from the Almighty*; the Assyrian was but the *rod of his anger*, Isa. x. 5. But why would God ruin a people that were raised and incorporated, as Israel was, by miracles and oracles? Was it purely an act of sovereignty? No, it was an act of necessary justice. For, 2. They provoked him to do

JAMIESON, FAUSSET, BROWN

17-19. HE SPOILS THE TEMPLE. **17. cut off the borders of the bases,** etc.—It is thought that he did this to use the elaborate sculpture in adorning his palace. **18. the covert for the Sabbath**—the portico through which the priests entered the temple on the Sabbath. **the king's entry without**—a private external entrance for the king into the temple. The change made by Ahaz consisted in removing both of these into the temple from fear of the king of Assyria, that, in case of a siege, he might secure the entrance of the temple from him.

CHAPTER 17

VSS. 1-6. HOSHEA'S WICKED REIGN. **1. In the twelfth year of Ahaz king of Judah, began Hoshea . . . to reign**—The statement in ch. 15:30 may be reconciled with the present passage in the following manner: Hoshea conspired against Pekah in the twentieth year of the latter, which was the eighteenth of Jotham's reign. It was two years before Hoshea was acknowledged king of Israel, i.e., in the fourth of Ahaz, and twentieth of Jotham. In the twelfth year of Ahaz his reign began to be tranquil and prosperous [CALMET]. **2. he did evil . . . but not as the kings of Israel**—Unlike his predecessors from the time of Jeroboam, he neither established the rites of Baal, nor compelled the people to adhere to the symbolic worship of the calves. In these respects, Hoshea acted as became a constitutional king of Israel. Yet, through the influence of the nineteen princes who had swayed the scepter before him (all of whom had been zealous patrons of idolatry, and many of whom had been also infamous for personal crimes), the whole nation had become so completely demoralized that the righteous judgment of an angry Providence impended over it. **3. Against him came up Shalmaneser**—or Shalman (Hos. 10:14), the same as the Sargon of Isaiah. Very recently the name of this Assyrian king has been traced on the Ninevite monuments, as concerned in an expedition against a king of Samaria, whose name, though mutilated, Colonel Rawlinson reads as Hoshea. **4. found conspiracy in Hoshea**—After having paid tribute for several years, Hoshea, determined on throwing off the Assyrian yoke, withheld the stipulated tribute. Shalmaneser, incensed at this rebellion, proclaimed war against Israel. This was in the sixth year of Hoshea's reign. **he had sent messengers to So, king of Egypt**—the Sabaco of the classic historians, a famous Ethiopian who, for fifty years, occupied the Egyptian throne, and through whose aid Hoshea hoped to resist the threatened attack of the Assyrian conqueror. But Shalmaneser, marching against him, scoured the whole country of Israel, besieged the capital Samaria, and carried the principal inhabitants into captivity in his own land, having taken the king himself, and imprisoned him for life. This ancient policy of transplanting a conquered people into a foreign land, was founded on the idea that, among a mixed multitude, differing in language and religion, they would be kept in better subjection, and have less opportunity of combining together to recover their independence. **6. carried Israel away**—i.e., the remaining tribes (see on ch. 15:29). **and placed them,** etc.—This passage GESENIUS renders thus, omitting the particle *by*, which is printed in italics to show it is not in the original: "and placed them in Halah, and on the Chabor, a river of Gozan, and in the cities of the Medes." Halah, the same as Calah (Gen. 10:11, 12), in the region of the Laycus or Zab river, about a day's journey from the ruins of Nineveh. Chabor is a river, and it is remarkable that there is a river rising in the central highlands of Assyria which retains this name Khabour unchanged to the present day. Gozan (pasture) or Zozan, are the highlands of Assyria, which afford pasturage. The region in which the Chabor and the Zab rise, and through which they flow, is peculiarly of this character. The Nestorians repair to it with their numerous flocks, spending the summer on the banks or in the highlands of the Chabor or the Zab. Considering the high authority we possess for regarding Gozan and Zozan as one name, there

ADAM CLARKE

18. *And the covert for the sabbath.* There are a great number of conjectures concerning this *covert*, or, as it is in the Hebrew, the *musach*, of the Sabbath. As the word, and others derived from the same root, signify "covering" or "booths," it is very likely that this means either a sort of canopy which was erected on the Sabbath days for the accommodation of the people who came to worship, and which Ahaz took away to discourage them from that worship, or a canopy under which the king and his family reposed themselves, and which he transported to some other place to accommodate the king of Assyria when he visited him.

20. *Was buried with his fathers in the city of David.* But it is expressly declared, 2 Chron. xxviii. 27, that he was not buried in the sepulchres of the kings of Israel; and this was undoubtedly intended as a mark of degradation.

CHAPTER 17

3. *Shalmaneser.* This was the son and successor of Tiglath-pileser. He is called Shalman by Hosea, x. 14. *Gave him presents.* Became tributary to him.

4. *Found conspiracy in Hoshea.* He had endeavored to shake off the Assyrian yoke, by entering into a treaty with So, king of Egypt; and having done so, he ceased to send the annual tribute to Assyria.

5. *Besieged it three years.* It must have been well-fortified, well-provisioned, and well-defended to have held out so long.

6. *Took Samaria.* According to the prophets Hosea (xiii. 16) and Micah (i. 6), he exercised great cruelties on this miserable city, ripping up the women with child, dashing young children against the stones.

Thus ended the kingdom of Israel, after it had lasted 254 years, from the death of Solomon and the schism of Jeroboam till the taking of Samaria by Shalmaneser, in the ninth year of Hoshea, after which the remains of the ten tribes were carried away beyond the river Euphrates.

The rest of this chapter is spent in vindicating the divine providence and justice, showing the reason why God permitted such a desolation to fall on a people who had been so long His peculiar children.

MATTHEW HENRY

this by their wickedness. Was it God's doing? Nay, it was their own; by their *way and their doings* they *procured all this to themselves*, and it was their own wickedness that did correct them. This is here very movingly laid open as the cause of all the desolations of Israel.

I. What God had done for Israel, to engage them to serve him. 1. He gave them their liberty (*v.* 7). Thus they were bound in duty and gratitude to be his servants, for he had loosed their bonds; nor would he that rescued them out of the hand of the king of Egypt have contradicted himself so far as to deliver them into the hand of the king of Assyria, as he did, if they had not, by their iniquity, betrayed their liberty and sold themselves. 2. He gave them their law, and was himself their king. They could not plead ignorance of good and evil, sin and duty. 3. He gave them *their land*, for he *cast out the heathen from before them* (*v.* 8), to make room for them; and the casting out of them for their idolatries was as fair a warning as could be given to Israel not to do like them.

II. What they had done against God, notwithstanding these engagements which he had laid upon them. 1. They *sinned against the Lord their God* (*v.* 7), they *did those things that were not right* (*v.* 9), but *secretly*. They *sold themselves to do evil in the sight of the Lord*, that is, they wholly addicted themselves to sin, as slaves to the service of those to whom they are sold, and, by their obstinately persisting in sin, so hardened their own hearts that at length it had become morally impossible for them to recover themselves. Though they were guilty of many immoralities, and violated all the commands of the second table, yet nothing is here specified but their idolatry. *This* was the sin that did most easily beset them; this was, of all sins, most provoking to God: it was the spiritual adultery that broke the marriage-covenant, and was the inlet of all other wickedness. They feared other gods (*v.* 7), that is, worshipped them and paid their homage to them, as if they feared their displeasure. They *built themselves high places in all their cities*, *v.* 9. If in any place there was but the tower of the watchmen (a country town that had no walls, but only a tower to shelter the watch in time of danger), or but a lodge for shepherds, it must be honoured with a high place, and that with an altar. If there was a fenced city, it must be further fortified with a high place. They *set them up images and groves—Asherim* (even *wooden images*, so some think the term, which we translate *groves*, should be rendered) or *Ashtaroth* (so others)—directly contrary to the second commandment, *v.* 10. They served idols (*v.* 12), the works of their own hands. They *burnt incense in all the high places*, to the honour of strange gods, for it was to the dishonour of the true God, *v.* 11. Besides the molten images, even the two calves, they *worshipped all the host of heaven*—the sun, moon, and stars. They used divinations and enchantments, that they might receive directions from the gods.

III. What means God used with them, to bring them off from their idolatries, and to how little purpose. Though they had forsaken God's family of priests, he did not leave them without a succession of prophets, who made it their business to teach them the good knowledge of the Lord, but all in vain (*v.* 14).

IV. How God punished them for their sins. He *was very angry with them* (*v.* 18). He afflicted them (*v.* 20) and *delivered them into the hand of spoilers*, in the days of the judges and of Saul, and afterwards in the days of most of their kings, to see if they would be awakened by the judgments of God to consider and amend their ways; but, when all these corrections did not prevail to drive out the folly, God first *rent Israel from the house of David*, under which they might have been happy.

Lastly, Here is a complaint against Judah in the midst of all (*v.* 19): *Also Judah kept not the commandments of God:* though they were not as yet quite so bad as Israel, yet Israel communicated the infection to Judah.

Verses 24–41

When the children of Israel were dispossessed, and turned out of Canaan, the king of Assyria soon transplanted thither the supernumeraries of his own country, who should be servants to him and masters to the Israelites that remained; and here we have an account of these new inhabitants.

I. Concerning the Assyrians that were brought into the land of Israel we are here told, 1. That they possessed Samaria and *dwelt in the cities thereof*, *v.* 24. 2. That at their first coming God *sent lions among them*. They were probably insufficient to people the country, which occasioned *the beasts of the field*

JAMIESON, FAUSSET, BROWN

can be no doubt that this is the Gozan referred to in this passage. **cities of the Medes**—"villages," according to the Syriac and Vulgate versions, or "mountains," according to the Septuagint. The Medish inhabitants of Gozan, having revolted, had been destroyed by the kings of Assyria, and nothing was more natural than that they should wish to place in it an industrious people, like the captive Israelites, while it was well suited to their pastoral life [GRANT'S NESTORIANS].

7-41. SAMARIA TAKEN, AND ISRAEL FOR THEIR SINS CARRIED CAPTIVE. **7. For so it was, that the children of Israel had sinned**—There is here given a very full and impressive vindication of the divine procedure in punishing His highly privileged, but rebellious and apostate, people. No wonder that amid so gross a perversion of the worship of the true God, and the national propensity to do reverence to idols, the divine patience was exhausted; and that the God whom they had forsaken permitted them to go into captivity, that they might learn the difference between His service and that of their despotic conquerors.

24. the king of Assyria brought men from Babylon, etc.—This was not Shalmaneser, but Esar-haddon (Ezek. 4:2). The places vacated by the captive Israelites he ordered to be occupied by several colonies of his own subjects from Babylon and other provinces. **from Cuthah**—the Chaldee form of Cush or Susiana, now Khusistan. **Ava**—supposed to be Ahivaz, situated on the river Karuns, which empties into the head of the Persian Gulf. **Hamath**—on the Orontes. **Sepharvaim**—Siphara, a city on the Euphrates above Babylon. **placed them in the cities of Samaria,** etc.—It must not be supposed that the Israelites were universally removed to a man. A remnant was left, chiefly however of the poor and lower classes, with whom these foreign colonists mingled; so that the prevailing character of society about Samaria was heathen, not Israelite. For the Assyrian colonists became masters of the land; and, forming partial intermarriages with the remnant Jews, the inhabitants became a mongrel race, no longer a people of Ephraim (Isa. 7:6). These people, imperfectly instructed in the creed of

ADAM CLARKE

KEIL–DELITZSCH:

Verse 7. "And it came to pass when" (not because, or that): compare Gen. 6:1; 26:8; 27:1; 44:24; Ex. 1:21; Judg. 1:28; 6:7, etc. The apodosis does not follow till verse 18, as verses 7–17 simply contain a further explanation of Israel's sin. To show the magnitude of the sin, the writer recalls to mind the great benefit conferred in the redemption from Egypt, whereby the Lord had laid His people under strong obligation to adhere faithfully to Him. The words refer to the first commandment (Ex. 20:2, 3; Deut. 5:6, 7). It is from this that the "fearing of other gods" is taken.

Verse 8. The apostasy of Israel manifested itself in two directions: (1) in their walking in the statutes of the nations who were cut off from before them, instead of in the statutes of Jehovah, as God had commanded (cf. Lev. 18:4, 5, 26; 20:22, 23, etc.); and (2) in their walking the statutes which the kings of Israel had made, i.e., the worship of the calves.

—*Commentary on the Old Testament*

9. *From the tower of the watchmen to the fenced city.* That is, the idolatry was universal; every place was made a place for some idolatrous rite or act of worship; from the largest city to the smallest village, and from the public watchtower to the shepherd's cot.

10. *Images and groves.* Images of different idols, and places for the abominable rites of Ashtaroth.

13. *Yet the Lord testified against Israel.* What rendered their conduct the more inexcusable was that the Lord had preserved among them a succession of prophets, who testified against their conduct and preached repentance to them, and the readiness of God to forgive, provided they would return unto Him and give up their idolatries.

18. *None left but the tribe of Judah only.* Under this name all those of Benjamin and Levi and the Israelites who abandoned their idolatries and joined with Judah are comprised. It was the ten tribes that were carried away by the Assyrians.

24. *The king of Assyria brought men from Babylon.* He removed one people entirely, and substituted others in their place; and this he did to cut off all occasion for mutiny or insurrection. *From Cuthah.* This is supposed to be the same as *Cush*, the Chaldeans and Syrians changing *shin* into *tau*. *From Ava.* The Avim were an ancient people, expelled by the Caphtorim from Hazerim, Deut. ii. 23. *From Hamath.* This was Hemath or Emath of Syria, frequently mentioned in the sacred writings.

25. *The Lord sent lions among them.* The land being deprived of its inhabitants, wild beasts would necessarily increase, even without any supernatural intervention; and this the superstitious newcomers supposed to be a plague sent upon them, because they did not know how to worship Him who was the God of the land; for they thought, like other heathens, that every district had its own tutelary deity. Yet it is likely that God did send lions as a scourge on this bad people.

MATTHEW HENRY

to multiply against them (Exod. xxiii. 29); yet, besides the natural cause, there was a manifest hand of God in it. God ordered them this rough welcome to check their pride. 3. That they sent a remonstrance of this grievance to the king their master, setting forth, it is likely, the loss their infant colony had sustained by the lions and the continual fear they were in of them, and stating that they looked upon it to be a judgment upon them for not worshipping the God of the land, which they could not, because they knew not how, *v.* 26. Herein they shamed the Israelites, who were not so ready to hear the voice of God's judgments as they were. Assyrians begged to be taught that which Israelites hated to be taught. 4. That the king of Assyria took care to have them taught *the manner of the God of the land* (*v.* 27, 28), not out of any affection to that God, but to save his subjects from the lions. He sent back one of the priests of the calves, and he came and dwelt among them, to teach them how they should *fear the Lord.*

Being thus taught, they made a mongrel religion of it, worshipped the God of Israel for fear and their own idols for love (*v.* 33): *They feared the Lord*, but they *served their own gods.* If we may credit the traditions of the Jewish doctors, they tell us that Succoth-Benoth was worshipped in a hen and chickens, Nergal in a cock, Ashima in a smooth goat, Nibhaz in a dog, Tartak in an ass, Adrammelech in a peacock, Anammelech in a pheasant. Our own tell us, more probably, that Succoth-Benoth (signifying *the tents of the daughters*) was Venus. Nergal, being worshipped by the Cuthites, or Persians, was *the fire.* Adrammelech and Anammelech were only distinctions of Moloch. This medley superstition is here said to *continue unto this day* (*v.* 41), till the time when this book was written and long after, above 300 years in all, till the time of Alexander the Great, when Manasse drew over many of the Jews to him, and prevailed with the Samaritans to cast away all their idols and to worship the God of Israel only.

II. Concerning the Israelites that were carried into the land of Assyria. When the two tribes were afterwards carried into Babylon, they were cured by it of their idolatry, and therefore, after seventy years, they were brought back with joy; but the ten tribes were hardened in the furnace and therefore were justly lost in it and left to perish. When they were in the hand of their enemies, and stood in need of deliverance, they were so stupid that they did after the former manner (*v.* 40), they served both the true God and false gods, as if they knew no difference. *Ephraim is joined to idols, let him alone.* So they did, and so did the nations that succeeded them.

JAMIESON, FAUSSET, BROWN

the Jews, acquired also a mongrel doctrine. Being too few to replenish the land, lions, by which the land had been infested (Judg. 14:5; I Sam. 17:34; I Kings 13:24; 20:36; Song of Sol. 4:8), multiplied and committed frequent ravages upon them. Recognizing in these attacks a judgment from the God of the land, whom they had not worshipped, they petitioned the Assyrian court to send them some Jewish priests who might instruct them in the right way of serving Him. The king, in compliance with their request, sent them one of the exiled priests of Israel, who established his headquarters at Beth-el and taught them how they should fear the Lord. It is not said that he took a copy of the Pentateuch with him, out of which he might teach them. *Oral teaching* was much better fitted for the superstitious people than instruction out of a written book. He could teach them more effectually by word of mouth. Believing that he would adopt the best and simplest method for them, it is unlikely that he took the written law with him, and so gave origin to the Samaritan copy of the Pentateuch [DAVIDSON'S CRITICISM]. Besides, it is evident from his being one of the exiled priests, and from his settlement at Beth-el. that he was not a Levite, but one of the calf-worshipping priests. Consequently his instructions would be neither sound nor efficient. **29. Howbeit every nation made gods of their own**—These Assyrian colonists, however, though instructed in the worship, and acknowledging the being of the God of Israel, did not suppose Him to be the only God. Like other heathens, they combined His worship with that of their own gods; and as they formed a promiscuous society from different nations or provinces, a variety of idols was acknowledged among them. **30. Succoth-benoth**—i.e., the "tents or booths of the daughters," similar to those in which the Babylonian damsels celebrated impure rites (Amos 2:8). **Nergal**—The Jewish writers say this idol was in the form of a cock, and it is certain that a cock is often associated with a priest on the Assyrian monuments [LAYARD]. But modern critics, looking to the astrological character of Assyrian idolatry, generally consider Nergal as the planet Mars, the god of war. The name of this idol formed part of the appellation of two of the king of Babylon's princes (Jer. 39:3). **Ashima**—an idol under the form of an entirely bald he-goat. **31. Nibhaz**—under that of a dog—that Egyptian form of animal-worship having prevailed in ancient Syria, as is evident from the image of a large dog at the mouth of the Nahr-el-Kelb or Dog river. **Tartak**—According to the rabbis, it was in the form of an ass, but others understand it as a planet of ill-omen, probably Saturn. **Adrammelech**—supposed by some to be the same as Molech, and in Assyrian mythology to stand for the sun. It was worshipped in the form of a mule—others maintain in that of a peacock. **Anammelech**—worshipped in the form of a hare; others say in that of a goat. **34. Unto this day**—the time of the Babylonian exile, when this book was composed. Their religion was a strange medley or compound of the service of God and the service of idols. Such was the first settlement of the people, afterwards called Samaritans, who were sent from Assyria to colonize the land, when the kingdom of Israel, after having continued 356 years, was overthrown.

ADAM CLARKE

26. *The manner of the God of the land. Mishpat*, the "judgment," the way in which the God of the land is to be worshipped.

27. *Carry thither one of the priests.* Imperfect as this teaching was, it in the end overthrew the idolatry of these people, so that soon after the Babylonish captivity they were found to be as free from idolatry as the Jews themselves, and continue so to the present day. But they are now nearly annihilated; the small remains of them is found at Naplouse and Jaffa. They are about thirty families; and men, women, and children amount to about two hundred persons! They have a synagogue, which they regularly attend every Sabbath; and they go thither clothed in white robes.

29. *Every nation made gods of their own.* That is, they made gods after the fashion of those which they had worshipped in their own country.

30. *The men of Babylon made Succoth-benoth.* This, literally, signifies "the tabernacles of the daughters" or young women, and most evidently refers to those public prostitutions of young virgins at the temple of Venus among the Babylonians. *The men of Cuth made Nergal.* This is supposed to have been the solar orb or light. *The men of Hamath made Ashima.* Perhaps "the fire"; from *asham*, "to make atonement or to purify."

31. *The Avites made Nibhaz.* This was supposed to be the same as the Anubis of the Egyptians; and was in form partly of a dog, and partly of a man. *And Tartak.* This is supposed by some to be another name of the same idol. *Adrammelech.* From *adar*, "glorious," and *melech*, "king." Probably the sun. *Anammelech.* From *anah*, "to return," and *melech*, "king." Probably, the Moloch of the Ammonites.

32. *Of the lowest of them priests.* One priest was not enough for this motley population; and, as the priesthood was probably neither respectable nor lucrative, it was only the lowest of the people who would enter into the employment.

33. *They feared the Lord, and served their own gods.* They did not relinquish their own idolatry but incorporated the worship of the true God with that of their idols. They were afraid of Jehovah, who had sent lions among them, and therefore they offered Him a sort of worship that He might not thus afflict them; but they *served* other gods, devoted themselves affectionately to them, because their worship was such as gratified their grossest passions and most sinful propensities.

36. *But the Lord.* Jehovah, the supreme, self-existent, and eternal Being; Author of all being and life. This was to be the whole Object of their adoration. *Who brought you up.* This was a strong reason why they should adore Him only. He had saved them from the hands of their enemies, and He did it in such a way as to show His power to be irresistible; in such a Being they might safely confide. *Him shall ye fear.* Here is the manner in which He is to be worshipped. Him you shall "reverence" as your Lawgiver and Judge. *Him shall ye worship.* Before Him you shall bow the knee; living in the spirit of obedience, and performing every religious act in the deepest humility. *And to him shall ye do sacrifice.* You shall consider that, as you have sinned, so you deserve death; you shall therefore bring your living victims to the altar of the Lord, and let their life's blood be poured out there, as an atonement for your souls.

41. *So do they unto this day.* This must have been written before the Babylonish captivity, because after that time none of the Israelites ever lapsed into idolatry. But this may chiefly refer to the heathenish people who were sent to dwell among the remains of the ten tribes.

MATTHEW HENRY

CHAPTER 18

Verses 1–8

A general account of the reign of Hezekiah.

I. His great piety, which was the more wonderful because his father was one of the worst of the kings, yet he was one of the best. What good there is in any is not of nature, but of grace, which, contrary to nature, grafts into the good olive that which was

JAMIESON, FAUSSET, BROWN

CHAPTER 18

VSS. 1-3. HEZEKIAH'S GOOD REIGN. **Hezekiah . . . began to reign. Twenty and five years old**—According to this statement (cf. ch. 16:2), he must have been born when his father Ahaz was no more than eleven years old. Paternity at an age so early is not unprecedented in the warm climates of the

ADAM CLARKE

CHAPTER 18

MATTHEW HENRY

wild by nature (Rom. xi. 24), and also that grace gets over the greatest difficulties and disadvantages. Ahaz, it is likely, gave his son a bad education as well as a bad example; Urijah his priest perhaps had the tuition of him; his attendants and companions were such as were addicted to idolatry; and yet Hezekiah became eminently good. When God's grace will work what can hinder it?

1. He was a genuine son of David (*v.* 3): *He did that which was right, according to all that David his father did.* Hezekiah was a second David, had such a love for God's word, and God's house, as he had. Let us not be frightened with an apprehension of the continual decay of virtue, as if, when times and men are bad, they must needs, of course, grow worse and worse; that does not follow, for, after many bad kings, God raised up one that was like David himself.

2. He was a zealous reformer of his kingdom (2 Chron. xxix. 3). He found his kingdom very corrupt, the people in all things superstitious. They had always been so, but in the last reign worse than ever. Idolatry had overspread the land; his spirit was stirred against this idolatry and therefore, as soon as ever he had power in his hands, he set himself to abolish it (*v.* 4). (1) The images and the groves were idolatrous. These he broke and destroyed. (2) The high places, though they had sometimes been used by the prophets upon special occasions and had been hitherto connived at by the good kings, were nevertheless an affront to the temple and gave opportunity for the introducing of idolatrous usages. Hezekiah, therefore, who made God's word his rule, not the example of his predecessors, removed them, made a law for the removal of them, which law was put in execution with vigour. (3) The brazen serpent was originally of divine institution, and yet, because it had been abused to idolatry, he broke it to pieces. It seems, it had been carefully preserved, as a memorial of God's goodness to their fathers in the wilderness, Num. xxi. 9. But when they began to worship the creature more than the Creator, those that would not worship images borrowed from the heathen were drawn in by the tempter to burn incense to the brazen serpent, because that was made by order from God himself and had been an instrument of good to them. But Hezekiah, in his pious zeal for God's honour, not only forbade the people to worship it, but, that it might never be so abused any more, he showed the people that it was *Nehushtan*, nothing else but *a piece of brass*, and that therefore it was an idle wicked thing to burn incense to it; he then broke it to pieces. If any think that the just honour of the brazen serpent was hereby diminished they will find it abundantly made up again, John iii. 14, where our Saviour makes it a type of himself.

3. Two things he was eminent for in his reformation: (1) Courage and confidence in God. In abolishing idolatry, there was danger of disobliging his subjects, and provoking them to rebel; but *he trusted in the Lord God of Israel* to bear him out in what he did and save him from harm. (2) Constancy and perseverance in his duty.

II. His great prosperity, *v.* 7, 8. He was with God, and then God was with him. Finding himself successful, 1. He threw off the yoke of the king of Assyria, which his father had basely submitted to. When he had thrown out the idolatry of the nations he might well throw off the yoke of their oppression. 2. He made a vigorous attack upon the Philistines, and smote them even unto Gaza.

Verses 9–16

The kingdom of Assyria had now grown considerable.

I. Of the success of Shalmaneser, king of Assyria, against Israel, his besieging Samaria (*v.* 9), taking it (*v.* 10), and carrying the people into captivity (*v.* 11), with the reason why God brought this judgment upon them (*v.* 12): *Because they obeyed not the voice of the Lord their God.* This was related in the foregoing chapter, but it is here repeated, 1. As that which stirred up Hezekiah and his people to purge out idolatry, because they saw the ruin which it brought upon Israel. 2. As that which Hezekiah much lamented, but had not strength to prevent. Though the ten tribes had revolted from the house of David, yet being of the seed of Israel he could not be glad at their calamities. 3. As that which laid Hezekiah and his kingdom open to the king of Assyria, and made it much more easy for him to invade the land.

II. Of the attempt of Sennacherib, the succeeding king of Assyria, against Judah. The descent he made upon Judah was a great calamity to that kingdom, by which God would try the faith of Hezekiah and chastise the people, because they did not willingly part with their idols, but kept them up in their hearts.

JAMIESON, FAUSSET, BROWN

south, where the human frame is matured sooner than in our northern regions. But the case admits of solution in a different way. It was customary for the later kings of Israel to assume their son and heir into partnership in the government during their lives; and as Hezekiah began to reign in the third year of Hoshea (vs. 1), and Hoshea in the twelfth year of Ahaz (ch. 17:1), it is evident that Hezekiah began to reign in the fourteenth year of Ahaz his father, and so reigned two or three years before his father's death. So that, at the beginning of his reign in conjunction with his father, he might be only twenty-two or three, and Ahaz a few years older than the common calculation makes him. Or the case may be solved thus: As the ancient writers, in the computation of time, take notice of the year they mention, whether finished or newly begun, so Ahaz might be near twenty-one years old at the beginning of his reign, and near seventeen years older at his death; while, on the other hand, Hezekiah, when he began to reign, might be just entering into his twenty-fifth year, and so Ahaz would be near fourteen years old when his son Hezekiah was born —no uncommon age for a young man to become a father in southern latitudes [PATRICK].

4-37. HE DESTROYS IDOLATRY. **4. He removed the high places and brake the images,** etc.—The methods adopted by this good king for extirpating idolatry, and accomplishing a thorough reformation in religion, are fully detailed (II Chron. 20:3; 31:19). But they are indicated very briefly, and in a sort of passing allusion. **brake in pieces the brazen serpent**—The preservation of this remarkable relic of antiquity (Num. 21:5-10) might, like the pot of manna and Aaron's rod, have remained an interesting and instructive monument of the divine goodness and mercy to the Israelites in the wilderness: and it must have required the exercise of no small courage and resolution to destroy it. But in the progress of degeneracy it had become an object of idolatrous worship and as the interests of true religion rendered its demolition necessary, Hezekiah, by taking this bold step, consulted both the glory of God and the good of his country. **unto those days the children of Israel did burn incense to it**—It is not to be supposed that this superstitious reverence had been paid to it ever since the time of Moses, for such idolatry would not have been tolerated either by David or by Solomon in the early part of his reign, by Asa or Jehoshaphat had they been aware of such a folly. But the probability is, that the introduction of this superstition does not date earlier than the time when the family of Ahab, by their alliance with the throne of Judah, exercised a pernicious influence in paving the way for all kinds of idolatry. It is possible, however, as some think, that its origin may have arisen out of a misapprehension of Moses' language (Num. 21:8). Serpent-worship, how revolting soever it may appear, was an extensively diffused form of idolatry; and it would obtain an easier reception in Israel because many of the neighboring nations, such as the Egyptians and Phœnicians, adored idol gods in the form of serpents as the emblems of health and immortality. **5. He trusted in the Lord God of Israel**—without invoking the aid or purchasing the succor of foreign auxiliaries like Asa (I Kings 15:18, 19) and Ahaz (ch. 16:17; Isa. 7). **so that after him was none like him among all the kings of Judah**—Of course David and Solomon are excepted, they having had the sovereignty of the whole country. In the petty kingdom of Judah, Josiah alone had a similar testimony borne to him (ch. 23:25). But even he was surpassed by Hezekiah, who set about a national reformation at the beginning of his reign, which Josiah did not. The pious character and the excellent course of Hezekiah was prompted, among other secondary influences, by a sense of the calamities his father's wicked career had brought on the country, as well as by the counsels of Isaiah. **7. he rebelled against the king of Assyria**—i.e., the yearly tribute his father had stipulated to pay, he, with imprudent haste, withdrew. Pursuing the policy of a truly theocratic sovereign, he was, through the divine blessing which rested on his government, raised to a position of great public and national strength. Shalmaneser had withdrawn from Palestine, being engaged perhaps in a war with Tyre, or probably he was dead. Assuming, consequently, that full independent sovereignty which God had settled on the house of David, he both shook off the Assyrian yoke, and, by an energetic movement against the Philistines, recovered from that people the territory which they had taken from his father Ahaz (II Chron. 28:18).

ADAM CLARKE

4. *Brake in pieces the brasen serpent.* The history of this may be seen in Num. xxi. 8-9. We find that this brazen serpent had become an object of idolatry, and no doubt was supposed to possess extraordinary virtues, and that incense was burned before it which should have been burned before the true God. *And he called it Nehushtan.* Not one of the versions has attempted to translate this word. Jarchi says, "He called it Nechustan, through contempt, which is as much as to say, *a brazen serpent.*"

5-7. *He trusted in the Lord.* See the character of this good king: (1) *He trusted in the Lord God of Israel;* (2) He *clave to the Lord;* (3) He was steady in his religion; he *departed not from following* the Lord; (4) He *kept* God's *commandments.* And what were the consequences? (1) The *Lord was with him;* (2) *He prospered whithersoever he went.*

8. *From the tower of the watchmen.* See the same words, chap. xvii. 9. It seems a proverbial mode of expression. He reduced every kind of fortification; nothing was able to stand before him.

MATTHEW HENRY

Even times of reformation may prove troublesome times and then the blame is laid upon the reformers. This calamity will appear great upon Hezekiah if we consider, 1. How much he lost of his country, *v.* 13. The king of Assyria took all or most of the fenced cities of Judah, the frontier-towns and the garrisons. 2. How dearly he paid for his peace. He saw Jerusalem itself in danger of falling into the enemies' hand, and was willing to purchase its safety at the expense, (1) Of a mean submission (*v.* 14). Where was Hezekiah's courage? Where his confidence in God? (2) Of a vast sum of money—300 talents of silver and thirty of gold to be paid as a present ransom. To raise this sum, he was forced not only to empty the public treasures (*v.* 15), but to take the golden plates off from the doors of the temple, and from the pillars, *v.* 16. Though *the temple sanctified the gold* yet, the necessity being urgent, he thought he might make as bold with that as his father David did with the shew-bread. His father Ahaz had plundered the temple in contempt of it, 2 Chron. xxviii. 24. He had repaid with interest what his father took; and now, with all due reverence, he only begged leave to borrow it in an exigency and for a greater good.

Verses 17–37

I. Jerusalem besieged by Sennacherib's army, *v.* 17. He sent three of his great generals with a great host against Jerusalem. Is this the great king, the king of Assyria? Let him never be named with honour that could do such a dishonourable thing as this, to take Hezekiah's money, which he gave him upon condition he should withdraw his army, and then to advance against his capital city.

II. Hezekiah, and his princes and people, railed upon by Rabshakeh, the chief speaker of the three generals, and one that had the most satirical genius. He was instructed what to say by Sennacherib, who intended to pick a new quarrel with Hezekiah. He had promised, upon the receipt of Hezekiah's money, to withdraw his army, and therefore could not for shame make a forcible attack upon Jerusalem immediately; but he sent Rabshakeh to persuade Hezekiah to surrender it, and, if he should refuse, to besiege it, and to take it by storm. Rabshakeh had the impudence to desire audience of the king himself at the conduit of the upper pool, without the walls; but Hezekiah had the prudence to decline a personal treaty, and sent three commissioners to hear what he had to say. One interruption they gave him in his discourse, which was only to desire that he would speak to them now in the Syrian language, and they would consider what he said and report it to the king, and, if they did not give him a satisfactory answer, then he might appear to the people, by speaking *in the Jews' language*, *v.* 26. Hilkiah did not consider what an unreasonable man he had to deal with, else he would not have made this request, for it did but exasperate Rabshakeh, *v.* 27. Against all the rules of decency and honour he menaces the soldiery, persuades them to desert or mutiny, threatens if they hold out to reduce them to the last extremities of famine, and then goes on to persuade Hezekiah, and his princes and people, to surrender the city.

1. He magnifies his master the king of Assyria. Once and again he calls him, *That great king, the king of Assyria*, *v.* 19, 28. But to those who by faith see the King of Kings in his power and glory even the king of Assyria looks mean and little. Ps. lxxxii. 6, 7.

2. He endeavours to make them believe that it will be much for their advantage to surrender. If they would capitulate, seek his favour with a present and cast themselves upon his mercy, he would give them very good treatment, *v.* 31. If they would surrender upon discretion, though they must expect to be prisoners and captives, yet it would really be happy for them to be so. (1) Their imprisonment would be to their advantage, for they should *eat every man of his own vine* (*v.* 31); though the property of their estates would be vested in the conquerors, yet they should have the free use of them. (2) Their captivity would be much more to their advantage: *I will take you away to a land like your own land;* and what the better would they be for that, when they must have nothing in it to call their own?

3. That which he aims at especially is to convince them that it is to no purpose for them to stand out: *What confidence is this wherein thou trustest? v.* 19. To the people he says (*v.* 29), "*Let not Hezekiah deceive you* into your own ruin, for *he shall not be able to deliver you*; you must either bend or break." Three things he supposes Hezekiah might trust to, and he endeavours to make out the insufficiency of these:—(1) His own military preparations: *Thou sayest, I have counsel and strength for the war;* and we find that so he had, 2 Chron. xxxii. 3. But this

JAMIESON, FAUSSET, BROWN

13. Sennacherib—the son and successor of Shalmaneser. **all the fenced cities of Judah**—not absolutely all of them; for, besides the capital, some strong fortresses held out against the invader (vs. 17; ch. 19:8). The following account of Sennacherib's invasion of Judah and the remarkable destruction of his army, is repeated almost verbatim in II Chronicles 33; and Isaiah 36, 37. The expedition seems to have been directed against Egypt, the conquest of which was long a leading object of ambition with the Assyrian monarchs. But the invasion of Judah necessarily preceded, that country being the key to Egypt, the highway through which the conquerors from Upper Asia had to pass. Judah had also at this time formed a league of mutual defense with Egypt (vs. 24). Moreover, it was now laid completely open by the transplantation of Israel to Assyria. Overrunning Palestine, Sennacherib laid siege to the fortress of Lachish, which lay seven Roman miles from Eleutheropolis, and therefore southwest of Jerusalem on the way to Egypt [ROBINSON]. Among the interesting illustrations of sacred history furnished by the recent Assyrian excavations, is a series of bas-reliefs, representing the siege of a town, which the inscription on the sculpture shows to be Lachish, and the figure of a king, whose name is given, on the same inscription, as Sennacherib. The legend, sculptured over the head of the king, runs thus: "Sennacherib, the mighty king, king of the country of Assyria, sitting on the throne of judgment before the city of Lachish [Lakhisha], I give permission for its slaughter" [NINEVEH and BABYLON]. This minute confirmation of the truth of the Bible narrative is given not only by the name Lachish, which is contained in the inscription, but from the physiognomy of the captives brought before the king, which is unmistakably Jewish. **14. Hezekiah . . . sent to Lachish, saying, . . . that which thou puttest on me will I bear**—Disappointed in his expectations of aid from Egypt, and feeling himself unable to resist so mighty a conqueror who was menacing Jerusalem itself, Hezekiah made his submission. The payment of 300 talents of silver, and 30 talents of gold—$ 1,500,000.00—brought a temporary respite; but, in raising the imposed tribute, he was obliged not only to drain all the treasures of the palace and the temple, but even to strip the doors and pillars of the sacred edifice of the gold that adorned them.

SENNACHERIB BESIEGES JERUSALEM. **17. king of Assyria sent Tartan**—general (Isa. 20:1). **Rabsaris**—chief of the eunuchs. **Rab-shakeh**—chief cupbearer. These were the great officers employed in delivering Sennacherib's insulting message to Hezekiah. On the walls of the palace of Sennacherib, at Khorsabad, certain figures have been identified with the officers of that sovereign mentioned in Scripture. In particular, the figures, Rab-shakeh, Rabsaris, and Tartan, appear as full-length portraits of the persons holding those offices in the reign of Sennacherib. Probably they represent the very individuals sent on this embassy. **with a great host to Jerusalem**—Engaged in a campaign of three years in Egypt, Sennecharib was forced by the king of Ethiopia to retreat, and discharging his rage against Jerusalem, he sent an immense army to summon it to surrender. (See on II Chronicles 32: 30.) **the conduit of the upper pool, etc.**—the conduit which went from the reservoir of the Upper Gihon (Birket et Mamilla) to the lower pool, the Birket es Sultan. **the highway of the fuller's field**—the public road which passed by that district, which had been assigned them for carrying on their business without the city, on account of the unpleasant smell [KEIL]. **18. when they had called to the king**—Hezekiah did not make a personal appearance, but commissioned his three principal ministers to meet the Assyrian deputies at a conference outside the city walls. **Eliakim**—lately promoted to be master of the royal household (Isa. 22:20). **Shebna**—removed for his pride and presumption (Isa. 22:15) from that office, though still royal secretary. **Joah . . . the recorder**—i.e., the keeper of the chronicles, an important office in Eastern countries. **19. Rab-shakeh said**—The insolent tone he assumed appears surprising. But this boasting, both as to matter and manner, his highly colored picture of his master's powers and resources, and the impossibility of Hezekiah making any effective resistance, heightened by all the arguments and figures which an Oriental imagination could suggest, has been paralleled in all, except the blasphemy, by other messages of defiance sent on similar occasions in the history of the East.

ADAM CLARKE

TODAY'S DICTIONARY OF THE BIBLE:

Sennacherib—*Sin* (the god) *sends many brothers*—son of Sargon, whom he succeeded on the throne of Assyria (705 B.C.), in the 23rd year of Hezekiah. He first set himself to break up the powerful combination of princes who were in league against him. Among these was Hezekiah, who had entered into an alliance with Egypt against Assyria. He accordingly led a very powerful army of at least 200,000 men into Judea, and devastated the land on every side, taking and destroying many cities (2 Kings 18:13–16; comp. Isa. 22, 24, 29, and 2 Chron. 32:1–8).

Hezekiah was not disposed to become an Assyrian feudatory. He accordingly at once sought help from Egypt (2 Kings 18:20–24). Sennacherib, hearing this, marched a second time into Palestine (2 Kings 18:17–37; 19; 2 Chron. 32:9–23; Isa. 36:2–22). Isa. 37:25, "dried up all the rivers of the besieged places" (KJV), should be rendered, with the NIV, "all the streams of Egypt." The King James translators misread the Hebrew *Mazor*, a poetic form of *Mizraim*, i.e., Egypt. Sennacherib sent envoys to try to persuade Hezekiah to surrender, but in vain. He next sent a threatening letter (2 Kings 19:10–14), which Hezekiah carried into the temple and spread before the Lord. Isaiah again brought an encouraging message to the pious king (2 Kings 19:20–34).

26. *Talk not with us in the Jews' language.* The object of this blasphemous caitiff was to stir up the people to sedition, that the city and the king might be delivered into his hand.

17. *The king of Assyria sent Tartan.* Calmet has very justly remarked that these are not the names of persons but of offices. *Tartan* signifies him who presides over the gifts or tribute, chancellor of the exchequer. *Rabsaris.* "The chief of the eunuchs." *Rab-shakeh,* "Master or chief over the wine cellar," or he who had the care of the king's drink.

From Lachish. It seems as if the Assyrian troops had been worsted before Lachish, and were obliged to raise the siege, from which they went and sat down before Libnah. While Sennacherib was there with the Assyrian army, he heard that Tirhakah, king of Ethiopia, had invaded the Assyrian territories. Being obliged therefore to hasten, in order to succor his own dominions, he sent a considerable force under the aforementioned officers against Jerusalem, with a most fearful and bloody manifesto, commanding Hezekiah to pay him tribute, to deliver up his kingdom to him, and to submit, he and his people, to be carried away captives into Assyria! This manifesto was accompanied with the vilest insults and the highest blasphemies. God interposed and the evils threatened against others fell upon himself.

Conduit of the upper pool. The aqueduct that brought the water from the upper or eastern reservoir, near to the valley of Kidron, into the city. Probably they had seized on this in order to distress the city. *The fuller's field.* The place where the washermen stretched out their clothes to dry.

18. *Called to the king.* They wished him to come out that they might get possession of his person. *Eliakim . . . over the household.* What we would call lord chamberlain. *Shebna the scribe.* The king's secretary. *Joah . . . the recorder.* The writer of the public annals.

19. *What confidence is this?* The words are excessively insulting: "What little, foolish, or unavailing cause of confidence is it, in which thou trustest?"

MATTHEW HENRY

Rabshakeh turns off with a slight. With the greatest haughtiness he challenges him to produce 2,000 men that know how to manage a horse, and will venture to give him 2,000 horses if he can. He falsely insinuates that Hezekiah has no men fit to be soldiers, *v.* 23. (2) His alliance with Egypt. He supposes that Hezekiah trusts to Egypt for chariots and horsemen (*v.* 24), because the king of Israel had done so, and of this confidence he truly says, It is *a broken reed* (*v.* 21), it will not only fail a man when he leans on it, but *it will run into his hand and pierce it*, Ezek. xxix. 6, 7. So is the king of Egypt, says he. (3) His interest in God, *v.* 22. He supported himself by depending on the power and promise of God; with this he encouraged himself and his people (*v.* 30): *The Lord will surely deliver us*, and again, *v.* 32. This Rabshakeh was sensible was their great stay, and therefore his endeavours to shake this, as David's enemies, who used all the arts they had to drive him from his confidence in God (Ps. iii. 2; xi. 1), and thus did Christ's enemies, Matt. xxvii. 43. Three things Rabshakeh suggested to discourage their confidence in God, [1] That Hezekiah had forfeited God's protection, and thrown himself out of it, by *destroying the high places and the altars*, *v.* 22. Here he measures the God of Israel by the gods of the heathen, who delighted in the multitude of altars and temples, and concludes that Hezekiah has given a great offence to the God of Israel, in confining his people to one altar. [2] That God had given orders for the destruction of Jerusalem at this time (*v.* 25): *Have I now come up without the lord?* This is all banter and rhodomontade. He made this pretence to terrify the *people that were on the wall*. [3] That if Jehovah, the God of Israel, should undertake to protect them from the king of Assyria, yet he was not able to do it. With this blasphemy he concluded his speech (*v.* 33–35). See here, *First*, His pride. When he conquered a city he reckoned himself to have conquered its gods, and valued himself mightily upon it. *Secondly*, His profaneness. The God of Israel was not a local deity, but the God of the whole earth. The tradition of the Jews is that Rabshakeh was an apostate Jew, which made him so ready in the Jews' language; if so, his ignorance of the God of Israel was the less excusable and his enmity the less strange, for apostates are commonly the most bitter and spiteful enemies, witness Julian.

Lastly, We are told what the commissioners on Hezekiah's part did. 1. They held their peace, not for want of something to say both on God's behalf and Hezekiah's. But the king had commanded them not to answer him, and they observed their instructions. 2. They rent their clothes in detestation of his blasphemy and in grief for the despised afflicted condition of Jerusalem, the reproach of which was a burden to them. 3. They faithfully reported the matter to the king, their master, and *told him the words of Rabshakeh*.

CHAPTER 19

Verses 1–7

The contents of Rabshakeh's speech brought to Hezekiah.

I. Hezekiah discovered a deep concern at the dishonour done to God by Rabshakeh's blasphemy. When he heard it he *rent his clothes and covered himself with sackcloth*, *v.* 1. Royal robes are not too good to be rent, nor royal flesh too good to be clothed with sackcloth, in humiliation for indignities done to God and for the perils and terrors of his Jerusalem. The king was in sackcloth, but many of his subjects were in soft clothing.

II. He *went up to the house of the Lord*, to meditate and pray. He was not considering what answer to return to Rabshakeh, but refers the matter to God. "*Thou shalt answer, Lord, for me.*"

III. He sent to the prophet Isaiah, by honourable messengers, to desire his prayers, *v.* 2–4. Eliakim and Shebna were two of those that had heard the words of Rabshakeh and were able to acquaint Isaiah with the case. The messengers were to go in sackcloth, because they were to represent the king, who was so clothed.

1. Their errand to Isaiah was, "*Lift up thy prayer for the remnant that is left*, that is, for Judah, which is but a remnant now that the ten tribes are gone—for Jerusalem, which is but a remnant now that the defenced cities of Judah are taken." When we desire the prayers of others for us we must not think we are excused from praying for ourselves. When Hezekiah sent to Isaiah to pray for him he himself *went into the house of the Lord* to offer up his own prayers. When the interests of God's church are brought

JAMIESON, FAUSSET, BROWN

27. that they may eat, etc.—This was designed to show the dreadful extremities to which, in the threatened siege, the people of Jerusalem would be reduced.

CHAPTER 19

Vss. 1-5. Hezekiah in Deep Affliction. **1. when King Hezekiah heard it, he rent his clothes, etc.**—The rending of his clothes was a mode of expressing horror at the daring blasphemy—the assumption of sackcloth a sign of his mental distress—his entrance into the temple to pray, the refuge of a pious man in affliction—and the forwarding an account of the Assyrian's speech to Isaiah was to obtain the prophet's counsel and comfort. The expression in which the message was conveyed described, by a strong figure, the desperate condition of the kingdom, together with their own inability to help themselves; and it intimated also a hope, that the blasphemous defiance of Jehovah's power by the impious Assyrian might lead to some direct interposition for the vindication of His honor and supremacy to all heathen gods.

ADAM CLARKE

21. *The staff of this bruised reed.* Egypt had already been greatly bruised and broken, through the wars carried on against it by the Assyrians.

22. *Whose high places and whose altars Hezekiah hath taken away.* This was artfully malicious. Many of the people sacrificed to Jehovah on the high places; Hezekiah had removed them (v. 4) because they were incentives to idolatry. Rab-shakeh insinuates that by so doing he had offended Jehovah, deprived the people of their religious rights, and he could neither expect the blessing of God nor the cooperation of the people.

23. *I will deliver thee two thousand horses.* Another insult: Were I to give you 2,000 Assyrian horses, you could not find riders for them. How then can you think that you shall be able to stand against even the smallest division of my troops?

25. *Am I now come up without the Lord?* As Rab-shakeh saw that the Jews placed the utmost confidence in God, he wished to persuade them that by Hezekiah's conduct Jehovah had departed from them and was become Ally to the king of Assyria, and therefore they could not expect any help from that quarter.

34. *Where are the gods of Hamath?* Sennacherib is greater than any of the gods of the nations. The Assyrians have already overthrown the gods of *Hamath, Arpad, Hena,* and *Ivah;* therefore Jehovah shall be like one of them, and shall not be able to deliver Jerusalem out of the hand of my master. The impudent blasphemy of this speech is without parallel. Hezekiah treated it as he ought. It was not properly against him, but against the Lord; therefore he refers the matter to Jehovah himself, who punishes this blasphemy in the most signal manner.

36. *Answer him not.* The blasphemy is too barefaced. Jehovah is insulted, not you; let Him avenge His own quarrel. See the succeeding chapter.

37. ***Then came Eliakim . . . and Shebna . . . and Joah . . . to Hezekiah with their clothes rent.*** It was the custom of the Hebrews, when they heard any blasphemy, to rend their clothes, because this was the greatest of crimes, as it immediately affected the majesty of God; and it was right that a religious people should have in the utmost abhorrence every insult offered to the Object of their religious worship. These three ambassadors lay the matter before the king, as God's representative; he lays it before the prophet, as God's minister; and the prophet lays it before God, as the people's Mediator.

CHAPTER 19

2. *To Isaiah the prophet.* His fame and influence were at this time great in Israel; and it was well-known that the word of the Lord was with him.

MATTHEW HENRY

very low, so that there is but a remnant left, then it is time to *lift up our prayer for that remnant*.

2. Two things are urged to Isaiah, to engage his prayers for them:—(1) Their fears of the enemy (*v.* 3). "We are ready to perish; *if thou canst do anything, have compassion upon us and help us*." (2) Their hopes in God. To him they look, on him they depend, to appear for them. "He has heard and known the blasphemous words of Rabshakeh, and therefore, it may be, he will hear and rebuke them. We hope he will. Help us with thy prayers to bring the cause before him, and then we are content to leave it with him."

IV. God, by Isaiah, sent to Hezekiah, to assure him that he would glorify himself in the ruin of the Assyrians. Hezekiah sent to Isaiah, not to enquire concerning the event, but to desire his assistance in his duty. He encouraged Hezekiah, who was much dismayed: *Be not afraid of the words which thou hast heard;* they are but words (though swelling and fiery words), and words are but wind. He promised to frighten the king of Assyria worse than Rabshakeh had frightened him: "*I will send a blast upon him*" (that pestilential breath which killed his army).

Verses 8–19

Rabshakeh, having delivered his message and received no answer left his army before Jerusalem, under the command of the other generals, and went to the king for further orders. He found him besieging Libnah, a city that had revolted from Judah, *ch.* viii. 22. However, he was now alarmed with the rumour that the king of the Cushites, who bordered upon the Arabians, was coming out against him with a great army, *v.* 9. This made him very desirous to gain Jerusalem with all speed. To take it by force would cost him more time and men than he could well spare, and therefore he renewed his attack upon Hezekiah to persuade him tamely to surrender it.

I. Sennacherib sent a letter to Hezekiah, a railing letter, a blasphemous letter, to persuade him to surrender Jerusalem, "*Let not thy God deceive thee*," *v.* 10. To terrify Hezekiah, and drive him from his anchor, he magnifies himself and his own achievements. How proudly he boasts, 1. Of the lands he had conquered (*v.* 11): *All lands*, and destroyed utterly! So far was he from destroying all lands that at this time the land of Cush, and Tirhakah its king, were a terror to him. 2. Of the gods he had conquered, *v.* 12. 3. Of the kings he had conquered (*v.* 13), the *king of Hamath and the king of Arpad*. Whether he means the prince or the idol, he means to make himself appear greater than either.

II. Hezekiah was not so haughty as not to receive the letter. When he had read it he was not in such a passion as to write an answer to it in the same provoking language; but he immediately went up to the temple, presented himself, and then *spread the letter before the Lord* (*v.* 14); not as if God needed to have the letter shown to him, but hereby he signified that he acknowledged God in all his ways. In the prayer which Hezekiah prayed over this letter, 1. He adores the God whom Sennacherib had blasphemed (*v.* 15), calls him *the God of Israel*, because Israel was his peculiar people, and *the God that dwelt between the cherubim*, because there was the peculiar residence of his glory upon earth; but he gives glory to him as *the God of the whole earth*, and not, as Sennacherib fancied him to be, *the God of Israel only*, and confined to the temple. 2. He appeals to God concerning the insolence and profaneness of Sennacherib (*v.* 16). 3. He owns Sennacherib's triumphs over the gods of the heathen, but distinguishes between them and the God of Israel (*v.* 17, 18): He has indeed *cast their gods into the fire*; for *they were no gods*. 4. He prays that God will now glorify himself in the defeat of Sennacherib and the deliverance of Jerusalem out of his hands (*v.* 19): "*Now therefore save us;* and let all the world know, and be made to confess, that *thou art the Lord God*, the self-existent sovereign God, *even thou only*, and that all pretenders are vanity and a lie."

Verses 20–34

The gracious answer which God gave to Hezekiah's prayer. In general, God assured him that his prayer was heard, his prayer against Sennacherib, *v.* 20.

I. Confusion and shame to Sennacherib and his forces. It is here foretold that he should be humbled and broken. Sennacherib is here represented,

1. As the scorn of Jerusalem, *v.* 21. He thought himself the terror of the daughter of Zion, that chaste and beautiful virgin, and that by his threats he could force her to submit to him: "But, being a virgin in her Father's house and under his protection, she defies thee, despises thee, laughs thee to scorn. Thy impotent malice is ridiculous; he that sits in heaven

JAMIESON, FAUSSET, BROWN

4. the living God—is a most significant expression taken in connection with the senseless deities that Rabshakeh boasted were unable to resist his master's victorious arms.

6, 7. COMFORTED BY ISAIAH. **6. Isaiah said . . . Be not afraid**—The prophet's answer was most cheering, as it held out the prospect of a speedy deliverance from the invader. The blast, the rumor, the fall by the sword, contained a brief prediction that was soon fulfilled in all the three particulars—viz., the alarm that hastened his retreat, the destruction that overtook his army, and the violent death that suddenly ended his career.

8-13. SENNACHERIB SENDS A BLASPHEMOUS LETTER TO HEZEKIAH. **8. Rab-shakeh . . . found the king of Assyria warring against Libnah**—whether Lachish had fallen or not, is not said. But Sennacherib had transferred his battering-rams against the apparently neighboring fortress of Libnah (Josh. 10:29; cf. 31; 15:42), where the chief cup-bearer reported the execution of his mission. **9. when he heard say of Tirhakah . . ., Behold, he is come out to fight against thee,** etc. This was the "rumor" to which Isaiah referred. Tirhakah reigned in Upper Egypt, while So (or Sabaco) ruled in Lower Egypt. He was a powerful monarch, another Sesostris, and both he and Sabaco have left many monuments of their greatness. The name and figure of Tirhakah receiving war captives, are still seen in the Egyptian temple of Medinet Abou. This was the expected succor which was sneered at (ch. 16:21) by Rabshakeh as "a bruised reed." Rage against Hezekiah for allying himself with Egypt, or the hope of being better able to meet this attack from the south, induced him, after hearing the rumor of Tirhakah's advance, to send a menacing letter to Hezekiah, in order that he might force the king of Judah to an immediate surrender of his capital. This letter, couched in the same vaunting and imperious style as the speech of Rab-shakeh, exceeded it in blasphemy, and contained a larger enumeration of conquered places, with the view of terrifying Hezekiah and showing him the utter hopelessness of all attempts at resistance.

14-34. HEZEKIAH'S PRAYER. **14. Hezekiah received the letter . . . and went up into the house of the Lord**—Hezekiah, after reading it, hastened into the temple, spread it in the childlike confidence of faith before the Lord, as containing taunts deeply affecting the divine honor, and implored deliverance from this proud defier of God and man. The devout spirit of this prayer, the recognition of the Divine Being in the plenitude of His majesty—so strikingly contrasted with the fancy of the Assyrians as to His merely local power—his acknowledgment of the conquests obtained over other lands, and of the destruction of their wooden idols which, according to the Assyrian practice, were committed to the flames—because their tutelary deities were no gods; and the object for which he supplicated the divine interposition, that all the kingdoms of the earth might know that the Lord was the only God—this was an attitude worthy to be assumed by a pious theocratic king of the chosen people.

20. Then Isaiah . . . sent—A revelation having been made to Isaiah, the prophet announced to the king that his prayer was heard.

ADAM CLARKE

3. *The children are come to the birth.* The Jewish state is here represented under the emblem of a woman in travail, who has been so long in pangs that her strength is now entirely exhausted and her deliverance is hopeless, without a miracle. The image is very fine and highly appropriate.

4. *The remnant that are left.* That is, the Jews, the ten tribes having been already carried away captive by the kings of Assyria.

7. *Behold, I will send a blast . . . and he shall hear a rumour.* The *rumour* was that Tirhakah had invaded Assyria. The blast was that which slew 185,000 of them in one night (see v. 35). *Cause him to fall by the sword.* Alluding to his death by the hands of his two sons, at Nineveh (see vv. 35-37).

8. *Libnah . . . Lachish.* These two places were not very distant from each other; they were in the mountains of Judah, southward of Jerusalem.

10. *Let not thy God in whom thou trustest.* This letter is nearly the same with the speech delivered by Rab-shakeh (see chap. xviii. 29).

14. *Spread it before the Lord.* The Temple was considered to be God's dwelling place, and that whatever was there was peculiarly under His eye. Hezekiah spread the letter before the Lord, as he wished Him to read the blasphemies spoken against himself.

15. *Thou art the God.* Thou art not only God of Israel, but God also of Assyria, and of all the nations of the world.

MATTHEW HENRY

laughs at thee, and therefore so do those that abide under his shadow." By this word God intended to silence the fears of Hezekiah and his people.

2. As an enemy to God. Hezekiah pleaded this: "Lord, he has reproached thee," *v.* 16. "He has," saith God, "and I take it as against myself (*v.* 22): *Whom hast thou reproached?* Is it not the Holy One of Israel, whose honour is dear to him, and who has power to vindicate it, which the gods of the heathen have not?"

3. As a proud vainglorious fool, that spoke *great swelling words of vanity*, and *boasted of a false gift*, by his boasts, as well as by his threats, reproaching the Lord. For, (1) He magnified his own achievements out of measure (*v.* 23, 24): *Thou hast said* so and so. What a mighty figure does Sennacherib think he makes! Driving his chariots to the tops of the highest mountains, forcing his way through woods and rivers, breaking through all difficulties, making himself master of all he had a mind to. (2) He took to himself the glory of doing these great things, whereas they were all *the Lord's doing*, *v.* 25, 26. And as for the desolations thou hast made in the earth, and particularly in Judah, thou art but the instrument in God's hand, a mere tool: it is *I that have brought it to pass.* Sennacherib's boasts here are expounded in Isa. x. 13, 14, *By the strength of my hand I have done it, and by my wisdom*, &c.; and they are answered (*v.* 15), *Shall the axe boast itself against him that heweth therewith?*

4. As under the check and rebuke of that God whom he blasphemed. All his motions were, (1) Under the divine cognizance (*v.* 27): "*I know thy abode*, and what thou dost secretly devise and design, the noise and bluster thou makest: I know it all." (2) Under the divine control (*v.* 28): "*I will put my hook in thy nose*, thou great Leviathan (Job xli. 1, 2), *my bridle in thy jaws*, thou great Behemoth. I will restrain thee, manage thee, turn thee where I please, send thee home like a fool as thou camest."

II. Salvation and joy to Hezekiah and his people. This shall be a sign to them of God's favour, and that he is reconciled to them, and *his anger is turned away* (Isa. xii. 1), that a good issue shall be put to their present distress.

1. Provisions were scarce and dear; and what should they do for food? The fruits of the earth were devoured by the Assyrian army, Isa. xxxii. 9, 10, &c. Why, they shall not only dwell in the land, but *verily they shall be fed*. "*Eat you this year that which groweth of itself*, and you shall reap what you did not sow." But the next year was the sabbatical year, when the land was to rest, and they must neither sow nor reap. What must they do that year? Why, *Jehovah-jireh—The Lord will provide.* And then, the third year, their husbandry should return into its former channel, and they should sow and reap as they used to do. 2. The country was laid waste, families were broken up and scattered, and all was in confusion; how should it be otherwise when it was over-run by such an army? As to this, it is promised that *the remnant that has escaped of the house of Judah* shall yet again be planted in their own habitations, shall increase and grow rich, *v.* 30. See how their prosperity is described: it is *taking root downwards*, and *bearing fruit upwards*. Such is the prosperity of the soul: it is taking root downwards by faith in Christ, and then being fruitful in fruits of righteousness. 3. The city was shut up, none went out or came in; but now the remnant in Jerusalem and Zion shall go forth freely, and there shall be none to hinder them, or make them afraid, *v.* 31. Great destruction had been made both in city and country, but in both there was a remnant that escaped, which typified the saved remnant of Israelites indeed (as appears by comparing Isa. x. 22, 23, which speaks of this very event, with Rom. ix. 27, 28), and they shall go forth into the glorious liberty of the children of God. 4. The Assyrians were advancing towards Jerusalem, and would in a little time besiege it in form, and it was in great danger of falling into their hands. But it is here promised that, though the enemy had now encamped before the city, yet they should never *come into the city*, no, nor so much as *shoot an arrow* into it (*v.* 32, 33),—that he should be forced to retire with shame. 5. The honour and truth of God are engaged for the doing of all this. These are great things, but how will they be effected? Why, *the zeal of the Lord of hosts shall do this*, *v.* 31. His zeal, (1) For his own honour (*v.* 34): "I will do it for my own sake, to make myself an everlasting name." God's reasons of mercy are fetched from within himself. (2) For his own truth: "I will do it for my servant David's sake; not for the sake of his merit, but the promise made to him and the covenant made with him, those sure mercies of David."

JAMIESON, FAUSSET, BROWN

The prophetic message consisted of three different portions:—*First*, Sennacherib is apostrophized (vss. 21-28) in a highly poetical strain, admirably descriptive of the turgid vanity, haughty pretensions, and presumptuous impiety of the Assyrian despot.

Secondly, Hezekiah is addressed (vss. 29-31), and a sign is given him of the promised deliverance—viz., that for two years the presence of the enemy would interrupt the peaceful pursuits of husbandry, but in the third year the people would be in circumstances to till their fields and vineyards and reap the fruits as formerly.

Thirdly, the issue of Sennacherib's invasion is announced (vss. 32-34). **33. shall not come into this city**—nor approach near enough to shoot an arrow, not even from the most powerful engine which throws missiles to the greatest distance, nor shall he occupy any part of the ground before the city by a fence, a mantelet, or covering for men employed in a siege, nor cast (raise) a bank (mound) of earth, overtopping the city walls, whence he may see and command the interior of the city. None of these, which were the principal modes of attack followed in ancient military art, should Sennacherib be permitted to adopt. Though the army under Rabshakeh marched towards Jerusalem and encamped at a little distance with a view to blockade it, they delayed laying siege to it, probably waiting till the king, having taken Lachish and Libnah, should bring up his detachment, that with all the combined forces of Assyria they might invest the capital. So determined was this invader to conquer Judah and the neighboring countries (Isa. 10:7), that nothing but a divine interposition could have saved Jerusalem. It might be supposed that the powerful monarch who overran Palestine and carried away the tribes of Israel, would leave memorials of his deeds on sculptured slabs, or votive bulls. A long and minute account of this expedition is contained in the Annals of Sennacherib, a translation of which has recently been made into English, and, in his remarks upon it, Colonel Rawlinson says the Assyrian version confirms the most important features of the Scripture account. The Jewish and Assyrian narratives of the campaign are, indeed, on the whole, strikingly illustrative of each other [OUTLINES OF ASSYRIAN HISTORY].

ADAM CLARKE

23. *The tall cedar trees . . . the choice fir trees.* Probably meaning the princes and nobles of the country. *The forest of his Carmel.* Better in the margin: "the forest and his fruitful field."

24. *I have digged and drunk strange waters.* I have conquered strange countries, in which I have digged wells for my army; or, I have gained the wealth of strange countries. *With the sole of my feet.* My infantry have been so numerous that they alone have been sufficient to drink up the rivers of the places I have besieged.

25. *Hast thou not heard?* Here Jehovah speaks, and shows this boasting king that what he had done was done by the divine appointment, and that of his own counsel and might he could have done nothing. It was because God had appointed them to this civil destruction that he had overcome them, and it was not through his might; for God had made their inhabitants of small power, so that he got the victory only over men whom God had confounded, dismayed, and enervated, v. 26.

28. *I will put my hook in thy nose.* This seems to be an allusion to the method of guiding a buffalo. He has a sort of ring put into his nose, to which a cord or bridle is attached, by which he can be turned to the right, or to the left, or round about, according to the pleasure of his driver.

29. *This shall be a sign unto thee.* To Hezekiah; for to him this part of the address is made. *Ye shall eat this year.* Sennacherib had ravaged the country, and seedtime was now over, yet God shows them that He would so bless the land that what should grow of itself that year would be quite sufficient to supply the inhabitants and prevent all famine; and though the second year was the sabbatical rest or jubilee for the land, in which it was unlawful to plough or sow, yet even then the land, by an especial blessing of God, should bring forth a sufficiency for its inhabitants; and in the third year they should sow and plant and have abundance. Now this was to be a *sign* to Hezekiah that his deliverance had not been effected by natural or casual means; for as without a miracle the ravaged and uncultivated land could not yield food for its inhabitants, so not without miraculous interference could the Assyrian army be cut off and Israel saved.

30. *The remnant . . . shall yet again take root.* As your corn shall take root in the soil, and bring forth and abundantly multiply itself, so shall the Jewish people; the population shall be greatly increased, and the desolations occasioned by the sword soon be forgotten.

31. *Out of Jerusalem shall go forth a remnant.* The Jews shall be so multiplied as to fill not only Jerusalem, but all the adjacent country.

32. *He shall not.* Here follow the fullest proofs that Jerusalem shall not be taken by the Assyrians. (1) *He shall not come into this city;* (2) He shall not be able to get so near as to *shoot an arrow* into it; (3) He shall not be able to bring an army before it; (4) Nor shall he be able to raise any redoubt or mound against it.

33. *By the way that he came.* Though his army shall not return, yet he shall return to Assyria; for because of his blasphemy he is reserved for a more ignominious death.

MATTHEW HENRY

Verses 35–37

The word was no sooner spoken than the work was done.

I. The army of Assyria was entirely routed. Hezekiah had not force sufficient to sally out upon them and attack their camp, nor would God do it by sword or bow. It was *not by the sword of a mighty man or of a mean man*, that is, not of any man at all, but of an angel, that the Assyrian army was to fall (Isa. xxxi. 8). Josephus says it was done by a pestilential disease, which was instant death to them. The number slain was very great, 185,000 men, and Rabshakeh, it is likely, among the rest. When the besieged *arose, early in the morning, behold they were all dead corpses*, scarcely a living man among them. Some think the 76th Psalm was penned on this occasion, where we read that the *stout-hearted were spoiled and slept their sleep*, their last, their long sleep, *v.* 5.

II. The king of Assyria was hereby put into the utmost confusion. Ashamed to see himself, after all his proud boasts, thus defeated and disabled *He departed, and went, and returned*; the manner of the expression intimates the great disorder and distraction of mind he was in, *v.* 36. And it was not long before God cut him off too, by the hands of *two of his own sons, v.* 37. The God of Israel had done enough to convince him that he was the only true God, whom therefore he ought to worship; yet he persists in his idolatry, and seeks to his false god for protection against a God of irresistible power. His sons that murdered him were suffered to escape, and would be looked upon as the more excusable in what they had done if it be true (as Bishop Patrick suggested) that he was now vowing to sacrifice them to his god. His successor was another son, *Esarhaddon*, who did not aim, like his father, to enlarge his conquests, but rather to improve them; for he it was that first sent colonies of Assyrians to inhabit the country of Samaria, as appears, Ezra iv. 2, where the Samaritans say it was *Esarhaddon that brought them thither*.

CHAPTER 20

Verses 1–11

The historian, having shown us blaspheming Sennacherib destroyed in the midst of the prospects of life, here shows us praying Hezekiah delivered in the midst of the prospects of death.

I. Here is Hezekiah's sickness. *In those days*, that is, in the same year in which the king of Assyria besieged Jerusalem. Some think it was at the time that the Assyrian army was besieging the city or preparing for it. Others think it was soon after the defeat of Sennacherib. Hezekiah, in the midst of his triumphs, is seized with sickness. He was sick of the plague, for we read of the boil or plague-sore, *v.* 7. The same disease which was killing to the Assyrians was trying to him. Hezekiah, lately favoured of heaven above most men, yet is sick unto death.

II. Warning brought him to prepare for death. It is brought by Isaiah. The prophet tells him, 1. That his disease is mortal, and, if he be not recovered by a miracle of mercy, will certainly be fatal: *Thou shalt die, and not live*. 2. That therefore he must, with all speed, get ready for death: *Set thy house in order*. Set the heart in order by renewed acts of repentance, and faith, and resignation to God, with cheerful farewells to this world and welcomes to another; and set the house in order, make thy will, settle thy estate, put thy affairs in the best posture thou canst, for the ease of those that shall come after thee.

III. His prayer hereupon: *He prayed unto the Lord, v.* 2. Is any sick? Let him be prayed for, let him be prayed with, and let him pray. Hezekiah had found the prayers of faith bring in answers of peace. He had now received the sentence of death within himself, and, if it was reversible, it must be reversed by prayer. If the sentence was irreversible, yet prayer is one of the best preparations for death, because by

JAMIESON, FAUSSET, BROWN

35, 36. AN ANGEL DESTROYS THE ASSYRIANS. **35. in the morning . . . they were all dead corpses**—It was the miraculous interposition of the Almighty that defended Jerusalem. As to the secondary agent employed in the destruction of the Assyrian army, it is most probable that it was effected by a hot south wind—the simoon—such as to this day often envelops and destroys whole caravans. This conjecture is supported by verse 7, and Jeremiah 51:1. The destruction was during the night; the officers and soldiers, being in full security, were negligent; their discipline was relaxed; the camp-guards were not alert, or perhaps they themselves were the first taken off, and those who slept, *not wrapped up*, imbibed the poison plentifully. If this had been an evening of dissolute mirth (no uncommon thing in a camp), their joy (perhaps for a victory), or "the first night of their attacking the city," says Josephus, became, by its effects, one means of their destruction [CALMET'S FRAGMENT]. **36. So Sennacherib, king of Assyria . . . went and returned**—the same way as he came (vs. 33). The route is described (Isa. 10). The early chariot track near Beyrouth is on the rocky edge of Lebanon, which is skirted by the ancient Lycus (Nahr-el Kelb). On the perpendicular face of the limestone rock, at different heights, are seen slabs with Assyrian inscriptions, which having been deciphered, are found to contain the name of Sennacherib. Thus, by the preservation of these tablets, the wrath of the Assyrian invaders is made to praise the Lord. **dwelt at Nineveh**—This statement implies a considerable period of time, and his Annals carry on his history at least five years after his disastrous campaign at Jerusalem. No record of his catastrophe can be found, as the Assyrian practice was to record victories alone. The sculptures give only the sunny side of the picture.

37. SENNACHERIB SLAIN. **37. as he was worshipping in the house of Nisroeh**—Assarae, or Asshur, the head of the Assyrian Pantheon, represented not as a vulture-headed figure—that is now ascertained to be a priest—but as a winged figure in a circle, which was the guardian deity of Assyria. The king is represented on the monuments standing or kneeling beneath this figure, his hand raised in sign of prayer or adoration. **his sons smote him with the sword**—Sennacherib's temper, exasperated probably by his reverses, displayed itself in the most savage cruelty and intolerable tyranny over his subjects and slaves, till at length he was assassinated by his two sons, whom, it is said, he intended to sacrifice to pacify the gods and dispose them to grant him a return of prosperity. The parricides taking flight into Armenia, a third son, Esar-haddon, ascended the throne.

CHAPTER 20

VSS. 1-7. HEZEKIAH'S LIFE LENGTHENED. **1. In those days was Hezekiah sick**—As his reign lasted twenty-nine years (ch. 18:2), and his kingdom was invaded in the fourteenth (ch. 18:13), it is evident that this sudden and severe illness must have occurred in the very year of the Syrian invasion. Between the threatened attack and the actual appearance of the enemy, this incident in Hezekiah's history must have taken place. But according to the usage of the sacred historian, the story of Sennacherib is completed before entering on what was personal to the king of Judah (see also Isa. 38:39). **Set thine house in order**—Isaiah, being of the blood-royal, might have access to the king's private house. But since the prophet was commissioned to make this announcement, the message must be considered as referring to matters of higher importance than the settlement of the king's domestic and private affairs. It must have related chiefly to the state of his kingdom, he having not as yet any son (cf. vs. 6 with ch. 21:1). **for thou shalt die, and not live**—The disease was of a malignant character and would be mortal in its effects, unless the healing power of God should miraculously interpose.

ADAM CLARKE

35. *That night.* **The very night after the blasphemous message had been sent, and this prophecy delivered.** *The angel of the Lord went out.* **I believe this** *angel* **or "messenger of the Lord" was simply a suffocating or pestilential wind by which the Assyrian army was destroyed, as in a moment, without noise, confusion, or any warning. Thus was the threatening, v. 7, fulfilled, "I will send a blast upon him." For he had heard the rumor that his territories were invaded; and on his way to save his empire, in one night the whole of his army was destroyed, without anyone even seeing who had hurt them.** *When they arose early.* **That is, Sennacherib, and probably a few associates, who were preserved as witnesses and relaters of this most dire disaster. Rab-shakeh, no doubt, perished with the rest of the army.**

36. *Dwelt at Nineveh.* **This was the capital of the Assyrian empire.**

37. *Nisroch his god.* **We know nothing of this deity; he is nowhere else mentioned.**

CHAPTER 20

1. *Set thine house in order.* **It appears from the text that he was smitten with such a disorder as must terminate in death, without the miraculous interposition of God; and he is now commanded to set his house in order, or to give charge concerning his house. Hezekiah reigned only twenty-nine years, chap. xviii. 2. He had reigned fourteen years when the war with Sennacherib began, chap. xviii. 13, and he reigned fifteen years after this sickness, chap. xx. 6. That Hezekiah's sickness happened before the destruction of Sannacherib's army is asserted by the text itself (see v. 6).**

MATTHEW HENRY

it we fetch in strength and grace from God to enable us to finish well. Observe,

1. The circumstances of this prayer. (1) He *turned his face to the wall*, probably as he lay in his bed. This he did perhaps for privacy; he could not retire to his closet as he used to do, but he turned from the company that were about him, to converse with God. Or, as some think, he turned his face towards the temple, to show how willingly he would have gone up thither, to pray this prayer (as he did, *ch.* xix. 1, 14), if he had been able. (2) He *wept sorely*. Some gather from this that he was unwilling to die. It is in the nature of man to have some dread of the separation of soul and body. There was also something peculiar in Hezekiah's case: he was now in the midst of his usefulness, had begun a good work of reformation, which he feared would, through the corruption of the people, fall to the ground, if he should die. Let Hezekiah's prayer interpret his tears, and in *that* we find nothing that intimates him to have been under any of that fear of death which has either bondage or torment.

2. The prayer itself: "*Remember now, O Lord! how I have walked before thee in truth;* and either spare me to live, that I may continue thus to walk, or, if my work be done, receive me to that glory which thou hast prepared for those that have thus walked." Hezekiah does not pray, "Lord, spare me," or "Lord, take me; God's will be done;" but, *Lord, remember me; whether I live or die, let me be thine.*

IV. The answer which God immediately gave to this prayer of Hezekiah. The prophet had got but to the middle court when he was sent back with another message to Hezekiah (*v.* 4, 5), to tell him that he should recover. Upon Hezekiah's prayer God did that for him which otherwise he would not have done. God here calls Hezekiah *the captain of his people*, to intimate that he would reprieve him for his people's sake. He calls himself *the God of David*, to intimate that he would reprieve him out of a regard to the covenant made with David. In this answer, 1. God honours his prayers: *I have heard thy prayers, I have seen thy tears.* 2. God exceeds his prayers; he only begged that God would remember his integrity, but God here promises, (1) To restore him from his illness: *I will heal thee.* (2) To restore him to such a degree of health that *on the third day he should go up to the house of the Lord*, to return thanks. (3) To add fifteen years to his life. (4) To deliver Jerusalem from the king of Assyria, *v.* 6. This was the thing which Hezekiah's heart was upon as much as his own recovery, and therefore the promise of this is here repeated.

V. The means which were to be used for his recovery, *v.* 7. Isaiah was his physician. He ordered an outward application, a very cheap and common thing: "Lay a *lump of figs to the boil*, to ripen it and bring it to a head, that the matter of the disease may be discharged that way." It is our duty, when we are sick, to make use of such means as are proper to help nature, else we do not trust God, but tempt him. Plain and ordinary medicines must not be despised, for many such God has graciously made serviceable to man.

VI. The sign which was given for the encouragement of his faith. 1. He begged it, not in any distrust of the power or promise of God, but because he looked upon the things promised to be very great things and worthy to be so confirmed. Hezekiah asked, *What is the sign*, not that I shall go up to the thrones of judgment or up to the gate, but *up to the house of the Lord?* He desired to recover that he might glorify God *in the gates of the daughter of Zion.* It is not worth while to live for any other purpose than to serve God. 2. It was put to his choice whether the sun should go back or go forward. It is supposed that the degrees were half hours, and that it was just noon when the proposal was made, and the question is, "Shall the sun go back to its place at seven in the morning or forward to its place at five in the evening?" He humbly desired the sun might go back ten degrees, because, though either would be a great miracle, yet, it being the natural course of the sun to go forward, its going back would seem more strange, and would be more significant of Hezekiah's *returning to the days of his youth* (Job. xxxiii. 25) and the lengthening out of the day of his life. It was accordingly done, upon the prayer of Isaiah (*v.* 11): God brought the sun back ten degrees, which appeared to Hezekiah by the going back of the shadow upon the dial of Ahaz, which, it is likely, he could see through his chamber window; and the same was observed upon all other dials, even in Babylon, 2 Chron. xxxii. 31. Whether this retrograde motion of the sun was gradual—which would make the day ten hours longer than usual—or whether it

JAMIESON, FAUSSET, BROWN

2. he turned his face to the wall—not like Ahab (I Kings 21:4), in fretful discontent, but in order to secure a better opportunity for prayer.

3. remember now how I have walked before thee, etc.—The course of Hezekiah's thoughts was evidently directed to the promise made to David and his successors on the throne (I Kings 8:25). He had kept the conditions as faithfully as human infirmity admitted; and as he had been all along free from any of those great crimes by which, through the judgment of God, human life was often suddenly cut short, his great grief might arise partly from the love of life, partly from the obscurity of the Mosaic dispensation, where life and immortality had not been fully brought to light, and partly from his plans for the reformation of his kingdom being frustrated by his death. He pleaded the fulfilment of the promise. **4. afore Isaiah was gone out into the middle court**—of the royal castle. **5. Thus saith . . . the God of David thy father**—An immediate answer was given to his prayer, containing an assurance that the Lord was mindful of His promise to David and would accomplish it in Hezekiah's experience, both by the prolongation of his life, and his deliverance from the Assyrians.

on the third day—The perfect recovery from a dangerous sickness, within so short a time, shows the miraculous character of the cure (see his thanksgiving song, Isaiah 38:9).

The disease cannot be ascertained; but the text gives no hint that the plague was raging then in Jerusalem; and although Arab physicians apply a cataplasm of figs to plague-boils, they also do so in other cases, as figs are considered useful in ripening and soothing inflammatory ulcers.

8-20. THE SUN GOES TEN DEGREES BACKWARD. **8. Hezekiah said unto Isaiah, What will be the sign that the Lord shall heal me**—His recovery in the course of nature was so unlooked for, that the king asked for some token to justify his reliance on the truth of the prophet's communication; and the sign he specified was granted to him. The shadow of the sun went back upon the dial of Ahaz the ten degrees it had gone down. Various conjectures have been formed as to this dial. The word in the original is "degrees," or "steps," and hence many commentators have supposed that it was a stair, so artfully contrived, that the shadows on the steps indicated the hours and course of the sun. But it is more probable that it was a proper instrument, and, from the Hebrews having no term to designate it, that it was one of the foreign novelties imported from Babylon by Ahaz. It seems to have been of such magnitude, and so placed in the court, that Isaiah could point to it, and the king see it, from his chamber. The retrogression of the sun's shadow on the dial was miraculously accomplished by the omnipotent power of God; but the phenomenon was temporary, local, confined to the notice, and intended for the satisfaction, only of Hezekiah and his court.

ADAM CLARKE

3. *I beseech thee, O Lord.* Hezekiah knew that, although the words of Isaiah were delivered to him in an absolute form, yet they were to be conditionally understood; else he could not have prayed to God to reverse a purpose which he knew to be irrevocable. Even this passage is a key to many prophecies and divine declarations (see chap. xviii of Jeremiah).

7. *Take a lump of figs . . . and laid it on the boil.* We cannot exactly say in what Hezekiah's malady consisted. *Shechin* signifies any inflammatory tumor, boil, abscess.

8. *What shall be the sign?* He wishes to be fully convinced that his cure was to be entirely supernatural; and, in order to this, he seeks one miracle to prove the truth of the other, that nothing might remain equivocal.

11. *He brought the shadow ten degrees backward.* We cannot suppose that these *ten degrees* meant ten hours. There were ten divisions of time on this dial; and perhaps it would not be right to suppose that the sun went ten degrees back in the heavens, or that the earth turned back upon its axis from east to west, in a contrary direction to its natural course. But the miracle might be effected by means of refraction, for a ray of light we know can be refracted from a right line by passing through a dense medium. And we know also, by means of the refracting power of the atmosphere, the sun, when near rising and setting, seems to be higher above the horizon than he really is; and, by horizontal refraction, we find that the sun appears above the horizon when he is actually below it, and literally out of sight. Therefore, by using dense clouds or vapors, the rays of light in that place might be refracted from their direct course ten, or any other number, of degrees; so that the miracle might have been wrought by occasioning this extraordinary refraction, rather than by disturbing the course of the earth, or any other of the celestial bodies.

MATTHEW HENRY

darted back on a sudden, and, after continuing a little while, was restored again to its usual place, so that no change was made in the state of the heavenly bodies (as the learned Bishop Patrick thinks)—we are not told.

Verses 12–21

I. An embassy sent to Hezekiah by the king of Babylon, to congratulate him on his recovery, *v.* 12. The kings of Babylon had hitherto been tributaries to the kings of Assyria, and Nineveh was the royal city. We find Babylon subject to the king of Assyria, *ch.* xvii. 24. But by degrees things were so changed that Assyria became subject to the kings of Babylon. This king of Babylon sent to compliment Hezekiah upon a double account. 1. Upon the account of religion. The Babylonians worshipped the sun, and, perceiving what honour their god had done to Hezekiah, in going back for his sake, they thought themselves obliged to do honour to him likewise. 2. Upon the account of civil interest. If the king of Babylon was now meditating a revolt from the king of Assyria, it was policy to get Hezekiah into his interest. He found himself obliged to Hezekiah, and his God, for the weakening of the Assyrian forces, and had reason to think he could not have a more powerful and valuable ally than one that had so good an interest in the upper world.

II. The kind entertainment Hezekiah gave to these ambassadors, *v.* 13. 1. He was too fond of them. He *hearkened unto them.* Though they were idolaters, yet he was forward to come into a confederacy with the king their master. 2. He was too fond of showing them his palace, his treasures, and his magazines, that they might see, and might report to their master, what a great king he was.

III. The examination of Hezekiah concerning this matter, *v.* 14, 15. Isaiah, who had often been his comforter, is now his reprover. "Who are these? What is their business?" Hezekiah not only submitted to the examination but made an ingenuous confession: *There is nothing among my treasures that I have not shown them.* Why then did he not bring them to Isaiah, and show him to them who was the best treasure, and who by his prayers had been instrumental in all those wonders which these ambassadors came to enquire into?

IV. The sentence passed upon him for his pride and vanity. The sentence is (*v.* 17, 18), 1. That the treasures he was so proud of should hereafter become a prey. 2. That the king of Babylon, with whom he was so fond of an alliance, should be the enemy that should make a prey of them. The sins of Manasseh, his idolatries and murders, were the cause of that calamity; but it is now foretold to Hezekiah, to convince him of the folly of his pride. Hezekiah was fond of assisting the king of Babylon to rise, and to reduce the exorbitant power of the kings of Assyria; but he is told that his royal seed shall become the king of Babylon's slaves. Babylon will be the ruin of those that are fond of Babylon.

V. Hezekiah's humble and patient submission to this sentence, *v.* 19. It is not only just, but good; for he will bring good out of it, and do me good by the foresight of it.

Lastly, Here is the conclusion of Hezekiah's life and story, *v.* 20, 21. In 2 Chron. *ch.* xxix–xxxii much more is recorded of Hezekiah's work of reformation and it seems that in the civil chronicles there were many things recorded of his might and the good offices he did for Jerusalem, particularly his bringing water by pipes into the city. But this historian leaves him *asleep with his fathers,* and a son in his throne that proved very untoward. Wicked Ahaz was the son of a godly father and the father of a godly son; holy Hezekiah was the son of a wicked father and the father of a wicked son.

JAMIESON, FAUSSET, BROWN

12-19. Berodach-baladan—(Isa. 39), the first king of Babylon mentioned in sacred history; formerly its rulers were viceroys of the Assyrian monarchs. This individual threw off the yoke, and asserting his independence, made with varying success, a long and obstinate resistance [RAWLINSON'S OUTLINES]. The message of congratulation to Hezekiah, was, in all likelihood, accompanied with proposals for a defensive alliance against their common Assyrian enemy. The king of Judah, flattered with this honor, showed the ambassadors all his treasures, his armory and warlike stores; and his motive for this was evidently that the Babylonian deputies might be the more induced to prize his friendship.

13. the silver, and the gold—He paid so much tribute to Sennacherib as exhausted his treasury (cf. 18:16). But, after the destruction of Sennacherib, presents were brought him from various quarters, out of respect to a king who, by his faith and prayer, saved his country; and besides, it is by no means improbable that from the corpses in the Assyrian camp, all the gold and silver he had paid might be recovered. The vain display, however, was offensive to his divine liege lord, who sent Isaiah to reprove him. The answer he gave the prophet (vs. 14) shows how he was elated by the compliment of their visit; but it was wrong, as presenting a bait for the cupidity of these rapacious foreigners, who, at no distant period, would return and pillage his country, and transfer all the possessions he ostentatiously displayed to Babylon, as well as his posterity to be court attendants in that country—(see on II Chron. 32:31).

19. Good is the word of the Lord—indicating a humble and pious resignation to the divine will. The concluding part of his reply was uttered after a pause and was probably an ejaculation to himself, expressing his thankfulness, that, though great afflictions should befall his descendants, the execution of the divine judgment was to be suspended during his own lifetime. **20. pool and a conduit**—(See on II Chron. 32:30).

ADAM CLARKE

12. ***At that time Berodach-baladan.*** **He is called Merodach-Baladan, Isa. xxix. 1, and by the Septuagint, Syriac, and Arabic versions; and also by the Babylonian and Jerusalem Talmuds. The true reading seems to be Merodach.** ***Sent letters and a present.*** **It appears that there was friendship between the king of Babylon and Hezekiah, when the latter and the Assyrians were engaged in a destructive war. The king of Babylon had not only heard of his sickness, but he had heard of the miracle, as we learn from 2 Chron. xxxii. 31.**

13. ***Hezekiah hearkened unto them.*** **Instead of** ***vaiyishma,*** **"he hearkened,"** ***vaiyismach,*** **"he rejoiced" or "was glad," is the reading of twelve of Kennicott's and De Rossi's MSS., the parallel place, Isa. xxxix. 2, the Septuagint, Syriac, Vulgate, Arabic, some copies of the Targum, and the Babylonian Talmud.** ***All the house of his precious things.*** **Interpreters are not well-agreed about the meaning of the original** ***nechothoh,*** **which we here translate** ***precious things,*** **and in the margin "spicery" or "jewels." I suppose the last to be meant.** ***There was nothing in his house.*** **He showed them, through a spirit of folly and exultation, all his treasures, and no doubt those in the house of the Lord. And it is said, 2 Chron. xxxii. 31, that in this business "God left him, to try him, that he might know all that was in his heart"; and this trial proved that in his heart there was little else than pride and folly.**

17. ***Behold, the days come.*** **This was fulfilled in the days of the latter Jewish kings, when the Babylonians had led the people away into captivity, and stripped the land, the Temple, etc., of all their riches (see Dan. i. 1-3).**

18. ***They shall be eunuchs.*** **Perhaps this means no more than that they should become household servants to the kings of Babylon. See the fulfillment, chap. xxiv. 13-15 and Dan i. 1-3.**

CHAPTER 21

MATTHEW HENRY

Verses 1–9

The beauty of Jerusalem is stained, and all her glory, all her joy, sunk and gone. These verses give such an account of this reign as make it, in all respects, the reverse of the last, and, in a manner, the ruin of it.

I. Manasseh began young. He was but *twelve years old when he began to reign* (*v.* 1), born when his father was about forty-two years old, three years after his sickness. But being young, 1. He was puffed up with his honour, and thinking himself very wise, valued himself upon his undoing what his father had done. 2. He was easily wrought upon and drawn aside by seducers. Those that were enemies to Hezekiah's reformation, and retained an affection for

JAMIESON, FAUSSET, BROWN

VSS. 1-18. MANASSEH'S WICKED REIGN, AND GREAT IDOLATRY. **1. Manasseh was twelve years old when he began to reign**—He must have been born three years after his father's recovery; and his minority, spent under the influence of guardians who were hostile to the religious principles and reforming policy of his father, may account in part for the anti-theocratic principles of his reign. The work of religious reformation which Hezekiah had zealously carried on was but partially accomplished. There was little appearance of its influence on the heart and manners of the people at large. On the contrary, the true fear of God had vanished from the mass of the people; corruption and vice in-

ADAM CLARKE

1. ***Manasseh was twelve years old.*** **He was born about three years after his father's miraculous cure; he was carried captive to Babylon, repented, was restored to his kingdom, put down idolatry, and died at the age of sixty-seven years (see 2 Chron. xxxiii. 1-20).**

2. ***After the abominations of the heathen.*** **He exactly copied the conduct of those nations which God had cast out of that land.**

3. ***Made a grove.*** **"He made Asherah," the Babylonian Melitta or Roman Venus.** ***Worshipped all the host of heaven.*** **All the stars and planets, but particularly the sun and the**

MATTHEW HENRY

the old idolatries, flattered him, and used his power at their pleasure.

II. He reigned long, longest of any of the kings of Judah, fifty-five years. This was the only very bad reign that was a long one: in the beginning of his reign for some time affairs continued to move in the course that his father left them in, and in the latter end of his reign, after his repentance, religion got head again. Though he reigned long, yet some of this time he was a prisoner in Babylon.

III. He reigned very ill.

1. In general, (1) *He did that which was evil in the sight of the Lord.* (2) *He did after the abominations of the heathen* (*v.* 2) and as did Ahab (*v.* 3), nay (*v.* 9), he *did more evil than did the nations whom the Lord destroyed.*

2. More particularly, (1) He *rebuilt the high places which his father had destroyed, v.* 3. (2) He set up other gods, *Baal* and *Ashtaroth* (which we translate *a grove*), and all the host of heaven, the sun and moon, the other planets, and the constellations; these he worshipped and served (*v.* 3), gave their names to the images he made, and then did homage to them. To these he built altars (*v.* 5), and offered sacrifices, no doubt, on these altars. (3) He *made his son pass through the fire*, by which he dedicated him a votary to Moloch, in contempt of the seal of circumcision by which he had been dedicated to God. (4) He made the devil his oracle, and *used enchantments and dealt with familiar spirits* (*v.* 6) like Saul. Conjurers and fortune-tellers (who pretended, by the stars or the clouds, lucky and unlucky days, good and bad omens, the flight of birds, or the entrails of beasts, to foretell things to come) were his intimates. (5) We find afterwards (*v.* 16) that he shed innocent blood. The *blood of the prophets* is, in a particular manner, charged upon Jerusalem, and it is probable that he put to death many of them. The tradition of the Jews is that he caused the prophet Isaiah to be sawn asunder; and many think the apostle refers to this in Heb. xi. 37.

3. Three things are here mentioned as aggravations of Manasseh's idolatry:—(1) That he set up his images and altars *in the house of the Lord* (*v.* 4), in the two courts of the temple (*v.* 5), in the very house of which God had said to Solomon, *Here will I put my name, v.* 7. (2) That hereby he put a great slight upon the word of God, and his covenant with Israel.

Verses 10–18

Here is the doom of Judah and Jerusalem read. The prophets were sent, in the first place, to teach them the knowledge of God, to remind them of their duty. If they succeeded not in that, their next work was to reprove them for their sins, that they might repent. If in this they prevailed not, but sinners went on frowardly, their next work was to foretell the judgments of God, that the terror of them might awaken those to repentance who would not be made sensible of the obligations of his love.

I. A recital of the crime. The indictment is read upon which the judgment is grounded, *v.* 11.

II. A prediction of the judgment God would bring upon them for this: *They have done that which was evil*, and therefore *I am bringing evil upon them* (*v.* 12). It should make a great noise in the world and occasion many speculations. When God lays judgment to the plummet it shall be *the plummet of the house of Ahab*, marking out for the same ruin to which that wretched family was devoted. See Isa. xxviii. 17. *I will wipe it as a man wipes a dish.* The city should be emptied of its inhabitants, which had been the filth of it, as a dish is emptied when it is wiped: "They shall all be carried captive, the *land shall enjoy her sabbaths,* and be laid by as a dish when it is wiped." This should be in order to the purifying, not the destroying, of Jerusalem. The dish shall not be dropped, not broken to pieces, or melted down, but only wiped. Sin is spoken of here as the alpha and omega of their miseries.

This is all we have here of Manasseh; he stands convicted and condemned; but in the book of Chronicles we hear of his repentance, and acceptance with God. He was buried, it is likely by his own order, *in the garden of his own house* (*v.* 18); for, being truly

JAMIESON, FAUSSET, BROWN

creased, and were openly practised (Isa. 28:7, etc.) by the degenerate leaders, who, having got the young prince Manasseh into their power, directed his education, trained him up in their views, and seduced him into the open patronage of idolatry. Hence, when he became sovereign, he introduced the worship of idols, the restoration of high places, and the erection of altars or pillars to Baal, and the placing, in the temple of God itself, a graven image of Asherah, the sacred or symbolic tree, which represented "all the host of heaven." This was not idolatry, but pure star worship, of Chaldaic and Assyrian origin [KEIL]. The sun, as among the Persians, had chariots and horses consecrated to it (ch. 23:11); and incense was offered to the stars on the housetops (ch. 23:12; II Chron. 33:5; Jer. 19:13; Zeph. 1:5), and in the temple area with the face turned toward the sunrise (Ezek. 8:16). **5. the two courts of the house of the Lord**—the court of the priests and the large court of the people. **6. made his son pass through the fire**—(See on ch. 16:3). **observed times**—from an observation of the clouds. **used enchantments**—jugglery and spells. **dealt with familiar spirits**—*Sept.*, ventriloquists, who pretended to ask counsel of a familiar spirit and gave the response received from him to others. **and wizards**—wise or knowing ones, who pretended to reveal secrets, to recover things lost and hidden treasure, and to interpret dreams. A great influx of these impostors had, at various times, poured from Chaldea into the land of Israel to pursue their gainful occupations, especially during the reigns of the latter kings; and Manasseh was not only their liberal patron, but zealous to appear himself an adept in the arts. He raised them to be an influential class at his court, as they were in that of Assyria and Babylon, where nothing was done till they had ascertained the lucky hour and were promised a happy issue. **7. And he set a graven image**—The placing of the Asherah within the precincts of the temple, which was dedicated to the worship of the true God, is dwelt upon as the most aggravated outrage of the royal idolater. **8. Neither will I make the feet of Israel move . . . out of the land which I gave their fathers**—alluding to the promise (II Sam. 7:10). **only if they will observe,** etc.—This condition was expressed from the first plantation of Israel in Canaan. But that people not only did not keep it, but through the pernicious influence of Manasseh, were seduced into greater excesses of idolatrous corruption than even the original Canaanites. **10-17. the Lord spake by his servants the prophets**—These were Hosea, Joel, Nahum, Habakkuk, and Isaiah. Their counsels, admonitions, and prophetic warnings, were put on record in the national chronicles (II Chron. 33:18) and now form part of the sacred canon. **12. whosoever heareth of it, both his ears shall tingle**—a strong metaphorical form of announcing an extraordinary and appalling event (see I Sam. 3:11; Jer. 19:3; also Hab. 1:5). **13. the line of Samaria, and the plummet of the house of Ahab**—Captives doomed to destruction were sometimes grouped together and marked off by means of a measuring-line and plummet (II Sam. 8:2; Isa. 34:11; Amos 7:7); so that the line of Samaria means the line drawn for the destruction of Samaria; the plummet of the house of Ahab, for exterminating his apostate family; and the import of the threatening declaration here is that Judah would be utterly destroyed, as Samaria and the dynasty of Ahab had been. **I will wipe Jerusalem,** etc.—The same doom is denounced more strongly in a figure unmistakably significant. **14. I will forsake the remnant of mine inheritance**—The people of Judah, who of all the chosen people alone remained. The consequence of the Lord's forsaking them would be their fall into the power of their enemies. **16. Moreover, Manasseh shed innocent blood**—Not content with the patronage and the practice of idolatrous abomination, he was a cruel persecutor of all who did not conform. The land was deluged with the blood of good men; among whom it is traditionally said Isaiah suffered a horrid death, by being sawn asunder (see on Heb. 11:37).

ADAM CLARKE

moon.

4. *Built altars.* He placed idolatrous altars even in the Temple.

6. *Made his son pass through the fire.* Consecrated him to Moloch. *Observed times.* He practiced divination by the clouds; by observing their course at particular times, their different kinds, contrary directions. *Used enchantments.* He used incantations, spells, and charms. *Dealt with familiar spirits.* He was a necromancer; was a raiser of spirits, whom he endeavored to press into his service. *And wizards.* The "knowing ones."

7. *He set a graven image of the grove that he had made in the house.* Everyone may see that *Asherah* here must signify an idol, and not a grove.

8. *Neither will I make the feet of Israel.* Had they been faithful to God's testimonies, they never would have gone into captivity, and should even at this day have been in possession of the Promised Land.

9. *Seduced them to do more evil.* He did all he could to pervert the national character, and totally destroy the worship of the true God; and he succeeded.

10. *The Lord spake by . . . the prophets.* The prophets were Hosea, Joel, Nahum, Habakkuk, and Isaiah. These following five verses contain the sum of what these prophets spoke. It is said that Isaiah not only prophesied in those days, but also that he was put to death by Manasseh, being sawn asunder by a wooden saw.

12. *Both his ears shall tingle. Titstsalnah;* something expressive of the sound in what we call, from the same sensation, the "tingling" of the ears. This is the consequence of having the ears suddenly pierced with a loud and shrill noise; the ears seem to ring for some time after. The prophets spoke to them vehemently, so that the sound seemed to be continued even when they had left off speaking. This was a faithful and solemn testimony.

13. *The line of Samaria.* I will treat Jerusalem as I have treated Samaria. Samaria was taken, pillaged, ruined, and its inhabitants led into captivity; Jerusalem shall have the same measure. *I will wipe Jerusalem as a man wipeth a dish.* The Vulgate translates this clause as follows: "I will blot out Jerusalem as tablets are wont to be blotted out." This is a metaphor taken from the ancient method of writing. They traced their letters with a style on boards thinly spread over with wax; for this purpose one end of the style was sharp, the other end blunt and smooth, with which they could rub out what they had written, and so smooth the place and spread back the wax as to render it capable of receiving any other word. Thus the Lord had written down Jerusalem, never intending that its name or its memorial should be blotted out. But the idea of emptying out and wiping a dish expresses the same meaning equally well. Jerusalem shall be emptied of all its wealth, and of all its inhabitants, as truly as a dish turned up is emptied of all its contents; and it shall be turned upside down, never to be filled again.

14. *I will forsake the remnant of mine inheritance.* One part (the ten tribes) was already forsaken and carried into captivity; the *remnant* (the tribe of Judah) was now about to be forsaken.

16. *Shed innocent blood very much.* Like the deities he worshipped, he was fierce and cruel; an unprincipled, merciless tyrant. He slew innocent people and God's prophets.

17. *Now the rest of the acts.* In 2 Chron. xxxiii. 11, etc., we read that the Assyrians took Manasseh, bound him with fetters, and took him to Babylon; that there he repented, sought God, and was, we are not told how, restored to his kingdom; that he fortified the city of David, destroyed idolatry, restored the worship of the true God, and died in peace. *Are they not written?* There are several particulars referred to here, and in 2 Chronicles xxxiii, which are not found in any chronicles or books which now remain, and what the "books of the seers" were, mentioned in Chronicles, we cannot tell.

18. *In the garden of his own house.* It was

MATTHEW HENRY

humbled for his sins, he judged himself *no more worthy to be called a son*, a son of David, and therefore not worthy to have even his dead body buried *in the sepulchres of his fathers*. And better it is, and more honourable, for a sinner to die repenting, and be buried in a garden, than to die impenitent, and be buried in the abbey.

Verses 19–26

The short and inglorious reign of Amon, the son of Manasseh—a son not born till he was forty-five years old. 1. His reign was very wicked: *He forsook the God of his fathers* (*v.* 22), disobeyed the commands given to his fathers. He trod in the steps of his father's idolatry, and revived that which he, in the latter end of his days, had put down. 2. His end was very tragical. He having rebelled against God, his own servants *conspired against him and slew him*, when he had reigned but two years, *v.* 23. Two things the people of the land did, by their representatives, (1) They did justice on the traitors that had slain the king, and put them to death; for, though he was a *bad* king, he was *their* king, and it was a part of their allegiance to him to avenge his death. (2) They did a kindness to themselves in *making Josiah his son king in his stead*, encouraged, it may be, by the indications he gave, even in his early days, of a good disposition. Now they made a happy change from one of the worst to one of the best of all the kings of Judah.

JAMIESON, FAUSSET, BROWN

19-26. AMON'S WICKED REIGN. **18. Amon his son reigned in his stead**—This prince continued the idolatrous policy of his father; and, after an inglorious reign of two years, he was massacred by some of his own domestics. The people slew the regicide conspirators and placed his son Josiah on the throne.

ADAM CLARKE

probably a burying place made for his own family, for Amon, his son, is said to be buried in the same place, v. 26.

19. *He reigned two years in Jerusalem.* The remark of the rabbins is not wholly without foundation, that the sons of those kings who were idolaters and who succeeded their fathers seldom reigned more than two years. So Nadab, the son of Jeroboam, 1 Kings xv. 25; Elah, the son of Baasha, 1 Kings xvi. 8; Ahaziah, the son of Ahab, 1 Kings xxii. 51; and Amon, the son of Manasseh, as mentioned here, v. 19.

23. *The servants of Amon conspired.* What their reason was for slaying their king we cannot tell. It does not seem to have been a popular act, for the people of the land rose up and slew the regicides. We hear enough of this man when we hear that he was as bad as his father was in the beginning of his reign, but did not copy his father's repentance.

26. *The garden of Uzza.* The family sepulchre or burying place.

MATTHEW HENRY

CHAPTER 22

Verses 1–10

Concerning Josiah we are here told,

I. That he was very young when he began to reign (*v.* 1), only eight years old. Our English Israel had once a king that was such a child, Edward VI. Josiah, being young, had not received any bad impressions from the example of his father and grandfather, but soon saw their errors, and God gave him grace to take warning by them. See Ezek. xviii. 14, &c.

II. That he *did that which was right in the sight of the Lord*, *v.* 2. See the sovereignty of divine grace—the father passed by and left to perish in his sin, the son a chosen vessel. Nothing is too hard for that grace to do. There are errors on both hands, but God kept him in the right way; he fell neither into superstition nor profaneness.

III. That he took care for the repair of the temple. This he did in the eighteenth year of his reign, *v.* 3. Compare 2 Chron. xxxiv. 8. He began much sooner to *seek the Lord* (as appears, 2 Chron. xxxiv. 3), but it is to be feared the work of reformation went slowly on and met with much opposition. He sent Shaphan, the secretary of state, to Hilkiah the high priest, to take an account of the money that was collected for this use by the door-keepers (*v.* 4), for, it seems, they took much the same way of raising the money that Joash took, *ch.* xii. 9. This money, so collected, he ordered him to lay out for the repair of the temple, *v.* 5, 6. And now, it seems, the workmen (as in the days of Joash) acquitted themselves so well that *there was no reckoning made with them* (*v.* 7), which is certainly mentioned to the praise of the workmen.

IV. That, in repairing the temple, *the book of the law* was happily found and brought to the king, *v.* 8, 10. Some think this book was the autograph, or original manuscript, of the five books of Moses, under his own hand; others think it was only an ancient and authentic copy. 1. It seems, this book of the law was lost or missing. Perhaps it was carelessly mislaid and neglected, thrown by into a corner (as some throw their Bibles), by those that knew not the value of it, and forgotten there; or it was maliciously concealed by some of the idolatrous kings who buried it, in hopes it would never see the light again; or, as some think, it was carefully laid up by some of its friends, lest it should fall into the hands of its enemies. Whoever were the instruments of its preservation, we ought to acknowledge the hand of God in it. If this was the only authentic copy of the Pentateuch then in being, we now have reason to thank God, upon our knees, for that happy providence by which Hilkiah found this book at this time, found it when *he sought it not*, Isa. lxv. 1. God's care of the Bible is a plain indication of his interest in it. 2. Whether this was the only authentic copy in being or no, it seems the things contained in it were new both to the king himself and to the high priest; for the king, upon the reading of it, rent his clothes. If the book of the law was lost, it seems difficult to determine what rule *Josiah* went by in doing that which was *right in the sight of the Lord*, and how the priests and people kept up the rites of their religion.

JAMIESON, FAUSSET, BROWN

CHAPTER 22

VSS. 1, 2. JOSIAH'S GOOD REIGN. **1. Josiah was eight years old when he began to reign**—Happier than his grandfather Manasseh, he seems to have fallen during his minority under the care of better guardians, who trained him in the principles and practice of piety; and so strongly had his young affections been enlisted on the side of true and undefiled religion, that he continued to adhere all his life, with undeviating perseverance, to the cause of God and righteousness.

3-7. HE PROVIDES FOR THE REPAIR OF THE TEMPLE. **3. in the eighteenth year of King Josiah**—Previous to this period, he had commenced the work of national reformation. The preliminary steps had been already taken; not only the builders were employed, but money had been brought by all the people and received by the Levites at the door, and various other preparations had been made. But the course of this narrative turns on one interesting incident which happened in the eigthteenth year of Josiah's reign, and hence that date is specified. In fact the whole land was thoroughly purified from every object and all traces of idolatry. The king now addressed himself to the repair and embellishment of the temple and gave directions to Hilkiah the high priest to take a general survey, in order to ascertain what was necessary to be done (see on II Chron. 34:8-15).

8-15. HILKIAH FINDS THE BOOK OF THE LAW. **8. Hilkiah said . . . I have found the book of the law in the house of the Lord,** etc.—i.e., the law of Moses—the Pentateuch. It was the temple copy which, had been laid (Deut. 31:25, 26) beside the ark in the most holy place. During the ungodly reigns of Manasseh and Amon—or perhaps under Ahaz, when the temple itself had been profaned by idols, and the ark also (II Chron. 35:3) removed from its site—it was somehow lost, and was now found again during the repair of the temple [KEIL]. Delivered by Hilkiah the discoverer to Shaphan the scribe, it was by the latter shown and read to the king. It is thought, with great probability, that the passage read to the king, and by which the royal mind was so greatly excited, was a portion of Deuteronomy, the 28th, 29th, and 30th chapters, in which is recorded a renewal of the national covenant, and an enumeration of the terrible threats and curses denounced against all who violated the law, whether prince or people.

The impressions of grief and terror which the reading produced on the mind of Josiah have seemed to many unaccountable. But, as it is certain from the extensive and familiar knowl-

ADAM CLARKE

CHAPTER 22

1. *Josiah was eight years old.* He was one of the best, if not the best, of all the Jewish kings since the time of David. He began well, continued well, and ended well.

4. *That he may sum the silver.* As Josiah began to seek the Lord as soon as he began to reign, we may naturally conclude that the worship of God that was neglected and suppressed by his father was immediately restored, and the people began their accustomed offerings to the Temple. Ten years therefore had elapsed since these offerings began; no one had as yet taken account of them, nor were they applied to the use for which they were given, viz., the repairing the breaches of the Temple.

8. *I have found the book of the law.* Was this the autograph of Moses? It is very probable that it was, for in the parallel place, 2 Chron. xxxiv. 14, it is said to be the book of "the law of the Lord by Moses." It is supposed to be that part of Deuteronomy (xxviii; xxix; xxx; and xxxi) which contains the renewing of the covenant in the plains of Moab, and which contains the most terrible invectives against the corrupters of God's word and worship.

MATTHEW HENRY

I am apt to think that the people generally took up with abstracts of the law, like our abridgments of the statutes, a sort of ritual, directing them in the observances of their religion, but leaving out what they thought fit, and particularly the promises and threatenings (Lev. xxvi and Deut. xxviii &c.). These were the portions of the law which Josiah was so much affected with (*v.* 13), for these were new to him. No summaries, extracts, or collections, out of the Bible (though they may have their use) can be effectual to convey and preserve the knowledge of God and his will like the Bible itself. 3. It was a great instance of God's favour, and a token for good to Josiah and his people, that the book of the law was thus seasonably brought to light, to direct and quicken that blessed reformation which Josiah had begun. The translating of the scriptures into vulgar tongues was the glory, strength, and joy of the Reformation. It is observable that they were about a good work, repairing the temple, when they found the book of the law. Those that do their duty according to their knowledge shall have their knowledge increased. 4. Hilkiah the priest was exceedingly well pleased with the discovery. "O," says he to Shaphan, "rejoice with me, for *I have found the book of the law*, *ἕυρηκα, ἕυρηκα, I have found, I have found*, that jewel of inestimable value. Here, carry it to the king; it is the richest jewel of his crown. Read it before him. He walks in *the way of David his father*."

Verses 11–20

The book of the law is not laid up in the king's cabinet as a piece of antiquity, a rarity to be admired, but it is read before the king. Those put the truest honour upon their Bibles that study them and converse with them daily, feed on that bread and walk by that light.

I. The impressions which the reading of the law made upon Josiah. He had long thought the case of his kingdom bad, by reason of the idolatries and impieties that had been found among them, but he never thought it so bad as he perceived it to be by the book of the law now read to him. The rending of his clothes signified the rending of his heart.

II. The application he made to God hereupon: *Go, enquire of the Lord for me*, *v.* 13.

1. Two things we may suppose he desired to know:—"Enquire, (1) What we shall do; what course we shall take to turn away God's wrath and prevent the judgments which our sins have deserved." (2) "What we may expect and must provide for." He acknowledges, "*Our fathers have not hearkened to the words of this book*; if this be the rule of right, certainly our fathers have been much in the wrong. Certainly *great is the wrath that is kindled against us*; if this be the word of God, as no doubt it is, and he will be true to his word, as no doubt he will be, we are all undone."

2. This enquiry Josiah sent, (1) By some of his great men, who are named, *v.* 12, and again *v.* 14. (2) To Huldah the prophetess, *v.* 14. Miriam helped to lead Israel out of Egypt (Micah vi. 4), Deborah judged them, and now Huldah instructed them in the mind of God, and her being a wife was no prejudice at all to her being a prophetess; *marriage is honourable in all*. It was a mercy to Jerusalem that when Bibles were scarce they had prophets, as afterwards, when prophecy ceased, that they had more Bibles. The king's messengers made Huldah their oracle, probably because her husband had a place at court (for he was keeper of the wardrobe). They had, it is likely, consulted her upon other occasions, and had found that the word of God in her mouth was truth. She was near, for she dwelt at Jerusalem, in the second rank of buildings from the royal palace. The Jews say that she prophesied among the women, the court ladies, who it is probable had their apartments in that place.

III. The answer he received from God to his enquiry. Huldah returned it in the dialect of a prophetess, speaking from him before whom all stand upon the same level—*Tell the man that sent you to me*, *v.* 15.

1. She let him know what judgments God had in store for Judah and Jerusalem (*v.* 16, 17): *My wrath shall be kindled against this place.*

2. She let him know what mercy God had in store for him. (1) Notice is taken of his great tenderness and concern—*Thy heart was tender.* He received the impressions of God's word, trembled at it and yielded to it. This is tenderness of heart, and thus he *humbled himself before the Lord.* Those that most fear God's wrath are least likely to feel it. (2) A reprieve is granted till after his death (*v.* 20): *I will gather thee to thy fathers.* God promised him he should not live to see it, which would have been but a small reward for his eminent piety if there had

JAMIESON, FAUSSET, BROWN

edge displayed by the prophets, that there were numbers of other copies in popular circulation, the king must have known its sacred contents in some degree. But he might have been a stranger to the passage read him, or the reading of it might, in the peculiar circumstances, have found a way to his heart in a manner that he never felt before. His strong faith in the divine word, and his painful consciousness that the woeful and long-continued apostasies of the nation had exposed them to the infliction of the judgments denounced, must have come with overwhelming force on the heart of so pious a prince.

12-15. the king commanded . . . Go, inquire of the Lord for me, etc.—The agitated feelings of the king prompted him to ask immediate counsel how to avert those curses under which his kingdom lay; and forthwith a deputation of his principal officers was sent to one endowed with the prophetic spirit.

Ahikam—a friend of Jeremiah (Jer. 26:24). **14. Achbor**—or Abdon (II Chron. 34:20), a man of influence at court (Jer. 26:22). The occasion was urgent, and therefore they were sent—not to Zephaniah (Zeph. 1:1), who was perhaps young—nor to Jeremiah, who was probably absent at his house in Anathoth, but to one who was at hand and known for her prophetic gifts—to Huldah, who was probably at this time a widow. Her husband Shallum was grandson of one Harhas, "keeper of the wardrobe." If this means the priestly wardrobe, he must have been a Levite. But it probably refers to the royal wardrobe. **she dwelt . . . in the college**—rather in *the Misnah*, taking the original word as a proper name, not a school or college, but a particular suburb of Jerusalem. She was held in such veneration that Jewish writers say she and Jehoiada the priest were the only persons not of the house of David (II Chron. 24:16) who were ever buried in Jerusalem.

15. she said unto them, Thus saith the Lord God of Israel, Tell the man that sent you—On being consulted, she delivered an oracular response in which judgment was blended with mercy; for it announced the impending calamities that at no distant period were to overtake the city and its inhabitants. But at the same time the king was consoled with an assurance that this season of punishment and sorrow should not be during his lifetime, on account of the faith, penitence, and pious zeal for the divine glory and worship which, in his public capacity and with his royal influence, he had displayed.

ADAM CLARKE

ALEXANDER MACLAREN:

Nothing is more truthfullike than the statement that, in course of the repairs of the Temple, the book should be found—probably in the holiest place, to which the high priest would have exclusive access. How it came to have been lost is a more puzzling question; but if we recall that seventy-five years had passed since Hezekiah, and that these were almost entirely years of apostasy and of tumult, we shall not wonder that it was so. Unvalued things easily slip out of sight, and if the preservation of Scripture depended on the estimation which some of us have of it, it would have been lost long ago. But the fact of the loss suggests the wonder of the preservation. It would appear that this copy was the only one existing—at all events, the only one known. It alone transmitted the law to later days, like some slender thread of water that finds its way through the sand and brings the river down to broad plains beyond. Think of the millions of copies now, and the one dusty, forgotten roll tossing unregarded in the dilapidated Temple, and be thankful for the Providence that has watched over the transmission. Let us take care, too, that the whole Scripture is not as much lost to us, though we have half a dozen Bibles each, as the roll was to Josiah and his men.

Hilkiah's announcement to Shaphan has a ring of wonder and of awe in it. It sounds as if he had not known that such a book was anywhere in the Temple. And it is noteworthy that not he but Shaphan is said to have read it. Perhaps he could not—though, if he did not, how did he know what the book was? At all events he and Shaphan seem to have felt the importance of the find and to have consulted what was to be done. Observe how the latter goes cautiously to work, and at first only says that he has received "a book." He gives it no name, but leaves it to tell its own story—which it was then, and is still, well able to do. Scripture is its own best credentials and witnesses whence it comes.

—*Expositions of Holy Scripture*

14. *Went unto Huldah, the prophetess.* This is a most singular circumstance. At this time Jeremiah was certainly a prophet in Israel, but it is likely he now dwelt at Anathoth, and could not be readily consulted. Zephaniah also prophesied under this reign, but probably he had not yet begun. Hilkiah was high priest, and the priest's lips should retain knowledge. Shaphan was scribe, and must have been conversant in sacred affairs to have been at all fit for his office. And yet *Huldah*, a prophetess, of whom we know nothing but by this circumstance, is consulted on the meaning of the book of the law.

17. *My wrath shall be kindled.* The decree is gone forth. Jerusalem shall be delivered into the hands of its enemies; the people will revolt more and more; towards them long-suffering is useless. The wrath of God is kindled, *and shall not be quenched.* This was a dreadful message.

20. *Thou shalt be gathered into thy grave in peace.* During your life none of these calamities shall fall upon the people, and no adversary shall be permitted to disturb the peace of Judea, and you shall die in peace with God. But was Josiah gathered to the grave in peace? Is it not said, chap. xxiii. 29, that Pharaoh-nechoh slew him at Megiddo? On this we may remark that the Assyrians and the Jews were at peace; that Josiah might feel it his duty to oppose the Egyptian king going against his friend and ally, and endeavor to prevent him from passing through his territories; and that

MATTHEW HENRY

not been another world in which he should be abundantly recompensed, Heb. xi. 16. He died in the love and favour of God, which secure such a peace as no circumstances of dying, no, not dying in the field of war, could alter the nature of, or break in upon.

CHAPTER 23

Verses 1–3

Josiah had received a message from God that there was no preventing the ruin of Jerusalem, but he did not therefore sit down in despair. Here we have the preparations for reformation. 1. He summoned a general assembly of the states, the elders, the magistrates or representatives of Judah and Jerusalem, to meet him *in the house of the Lord*, with the priests and prophets, the ordinary and extraordinary ministers, that it might become a national act. 2. Instead of making a speech to this convention, he ordered the book of the law to be read to them; nay, it should seem, he read it himself (*v.* 2), as one much affected with it and desirous that they should be so too. Besides the convention of the great men, he had a congregation of the *men of Judah and the inhabitants of Jerusalem* to hear the law read. If the people be but as steadfastly resolved to obey by law as he is to govern by law, the kingdom will be happy. 3. Instead of proposing laws for the confirming of them in their duty, he proposed an association by which they should all jointly engage themselves to God, *v.* 3. The book of the law was the book of the covenant, that, if they would be to God a people, he would be to them a God; they here engage themselves to do their part, not doubting but that then God would do his. The covenanters were, in the first place, the king himself, who stood by his pillar (*ch.* xi. 14) and publicly declared his consent to this covenant. *All the people* likewise *stood to the covenant.*

Verses 4–24

An account of such a reformation as we have not met with in all the history of the kings of Judah, such thorough riddance made of all the abominable things and such foundations laid of a glorious good work. The generality of the people, after all, hated to be reformed.

I. What abundance of wickedness there was, and had been, in Judah and Jerusalem. 1. Even in the house of the Lord, that sacred temple which Solomon built, and dedicated to the honour and for the worship of the God of Israel, there were found vessels, all manner of utensils, for the worship of Baal, *and of the grove* (or *Ashtaroth*), and *of all the host of heaven*, *v.* 4. Though Josiah had suppressed the worship of idols, yet the utensils made for that worship were all carefully preserved, even in the temple itself. 2. Just *at the entering in of the house of the Lord* was a stable for horses kept for a religious use; they were holy horses, *given to the sun* (*v.* 11), as if he needed them who *rejoiceth as a strong man to run a race* (Ps. xix. 5), making their religion to conform to the poetical fictions of the chariot of the sun. Some say that those horses were to be led forth in pomp every morning to meet the rising sun, others that the worshippers of the sun rode out upon them to adore the rising sun; it should seem that they drew the chariots of the sun, which the people worshipped. 3. Hard *by the house of the Lord* there were *houses of the Sodomites*, where all manner of lewdness and filthiness, even that which was most unnatural, was practised, and under pretence of religion too, in honour of their impure deities. Those that dishonoured their God were justly left thus to dishonour themselves, Rom. i. 24, &c. There were women that *wove hangings for the grove* (*v.* 7), tents which encompassed the image of Venus, where the worshippers committed all manner of lewdness, and this *in the house of the Lord.* 4. There were many idolatrous altars found (*v.* 12), some in the palace, *on the top of the upper chamber of Ahaz*. The roofs of their houses being flat, they made them their high places, and set up altars upon them (Jer. xix. 13; Zeph. i. 5), domestic altars. 5. There was *Tophet, in the valley of the son of Hinnom*, very near Jerusalem, where the image of Moloch (that god of unnatural cruelty, as others were of unnatural uncleanness) was kept, to which some sacrificed their children, burning them in the fire, others dedicated them, making them to pass through the fire (*v.* 10), *labouring in the very fire*, Hab. ii. 13. It is supposed to have been called *Tophet* from *toph*, a drum, because they beat drums at the burning of the children, that their shrieks might not be heard. 6. There were *high places before Jerusalem*, which *Solomon had built*, *v.* 13. There were also high places all the kingdom over, from *Geba to Beer-sheba* (*v.* 8), and *high places of the gates, in the entering in of the*

JAMIESON, FAUSSET, BROWN

CHAPTER 23

VSS. 1-3. JOSIAH CAUSES THE LAW TO BE READ. **1. the king sent, and they gathered unto him all the elders**—This pious and patriotic king, not content with the promise of his own security, felt, after Huldah's response, an increased desire to avert the threatened calamities from his kingdom and people. Knowing the richness of the divine clemency and grace to the penitent, he convened the elders of the people, and placing himself at their head, accompanied by the collective body of the inhabitants, went in solemn procession to the temple, where he ordered the book of the law to be read to the assembled audience, and covenanted, with the unanimous concurrence of his subjects, to adhere steadfastly to all the commandments of the Lord. It was an occasion of solemn interest, closely connected with a great national crisis, and the beautiful example of piety in the highest quarter would exert a salutary influence over all classes of the people in animating their devotions and encouraging their return to the faith of their fathers. **2. he read in their ears**—i.e., caused to be read. **3. all the people stood to the covenant**—i.e., they agreed to the proposals made; they assented to what was required of them.

4-28. HE DESTROYS IDOLATRY. **4. the king commanded Hilkiah**, etc.—i.e., the high priest and other priests, for there was not a variety of official gradations in the temple. **all the vessels**, etc.—the whole apparatus of idol worship. **burned them without Jerusalem**—The law required them to be consigned to the flames (Deut. 7:25). **in the fields of Kidron**—most probably that part of the valley of Kidron, where lies Jerusalem and the Mount of Olives. It is a level, spacious basin, abounding at present with plantations [ROBINSON]. The brook winds along the east and south of the city, the channel of which is throughout a large portion of the year almost or wholly dry, except after heavy rains, when it suddenly swells and overflows. There were emptied all the impurities of the temple (II Chron. 29:15, 16) and the city. His reforming predecessors had ordered the mutilated relics of idolatry to be thrown into that receptacle of filth (I Kings 15:13; II Chron. 15:16; 30:14); but Josiah, while he imitated their piety, far outstripped them in zeal; for he caused the ashes of the burnt wood and the fragments of the broken metal to be collected and conveyed to Beth-el, in order thenceforth to associate ideas of horror and aversion with that place, as odious for the worst pollutions. **12. the altars that were on the top of the upper chamber of Ahaz**—Altars were reared on the flat roofs of houses, where the worshippers of "the host of heaven" burnt incense (Zeph. 1:5; Jer. 19:13). Ahaz had reared altars for this purpose on the *oleah,* or upper chamber of his palace, and Manasseh on some portion of the roof of the temple. Josiah demolished both of these structures.

10. Topheth—so called from Toph—a drum. It is the prevailing opinion among Jewish writers that the cries of the terrified children made to pass through the fire in that place of idolatrous horror were drowned by the sound of that instrument.

13. the high places . . . which Solomon . . . had builded—(See on I Kings 11:7). **the right hand of the mount of corruption**—The Mount of Olives is a hilly range on the east of Jerusalem. This range has three summits, of which the central one is the Mount of Corruption, so called from the idol temples built there, and of course the hill on the right hand denotes the southernmost peak. Josiah is said not to have destroyed, but only defiled, "the high places on the hill of corruption." It is most propable that Hezekiah had long before demolished the idolatrous temples erected there by Solomon but, as the superstitious people continued to regard the spot as consecrated ground, Josiah defiled it.

ADAM CLARKE

in his endeavors to oppose him he was mortally wounded at Megiddo, but certainly was not killed there. For his servants put him in his second chariot and brought him to Jerusalem, where he died in peace (see 2 Chron. xxxv. 24).

CHAPTER 23

2. *The king went up into the house of the Lord.* Here is another very singular circumstance. The high priest, scribes, priest, and prophets are gathered together, with all the elders of the people, and the king himself reads the book of the covenant which lately had been found! It is strange that either the high priest, Jeremiah, Zephaniah, or some other of the prophets, who were certainly present there, did not read the sacred book! It is likely that the king considered himself a mediator between God and them, and therefore read and made the covenant.

3. *Stood by a pillar.* He stood, *al haammud,* "upon the stairs or pulpit." This is what is called the brazen scaffold or pulpit which Solomon made, and on which the kings were accustomed to stand when they addressed the people (see 2 Chron. vi. 13 and the parallel places).

4. *The priests of the second order.* These were probably such as supplied the place of the high priest when he was prevented from fulfilling the functions of his office. But the words may refer to those of the second course or order established by David; though it does not appear that those orders were now in use, yet the distinction was continued even to the time of our Lord. We find the course of Abia, which was the eighth, mentioned in Luke i. 5. *All the vessels.* These had been used for idolatrous purposes; the king is now to destroy them; for although no longer used in this way, they might, if permitted to remain, be an incentive to idolatry at a future time.

12. *On the top of the upper chamber.* Altars built on the flat roof of the house. Such altars were erected to the sun, moon, and stars, etc.

10. *He defiled Topheth.* Jerome says that Topheth was a fine and pleasant place, well-watered with fountains, and adorned with gardens. The valley of the son of Hinnom, or *Gehenna,* was in one part; here it appears the sacred rites of Molech were performed, and to this all the filth of the city was carried, and perpetual fires were kept up in order to consume it. Hence it has been considered a type of hell, and in this sense it is used in the New Testament.

13. *Mount of corruption.* This, says Jarchi, following the Chaldee, was the mount of Olives, for this is the mount *hammishchah*, "of unction"; but because of the idolatrous purposes for which it was used, the Scripture changed the appellation to the mount *hammashchith,* "of corruption." *Ashtoreth the abomination* (see on 1 Kings xi. 7).

MATTHEW HENRY

gate of the governor. 7. There were idolatrous priests, that officiated at all those idolatrous altars (*v*. 5), chemarim, black men, or that wore black. See Zeph. i. 4. Those that sacrificed to Osiris, or that wept for Tammuz (Ezek. viii. 14), or that worshipped the infernal deities, put on black garments as mourners. 8. There were conjurers and wizards, and such as *dealt with familiar spirits*, *v*. 24.

II. What a full destruction good Josiah made of all those relics of idolatry. 1. He ordered Hilkiah, and the other priests, to clear the temple. Away with all the vessels that were made for Baal. They must all be burnt, and the ashes of them carried to Bethel. That place had been the common source of idolatry, for there was set up one of the calves. 2. The idolatrous priests were all put down. Those of them that were not of the house of Aaron, or had sacrificed to Baal or other false gods, he put to death, according to the law, *v*. 20. He *slew them upon their own altars*, the most acceptable sacrifice that ever had been offered upon them. Those that were descendants from Aaron, and yet had burnt incense in the high places, but to the true God only, he forbade ever to approach the altar of the Lord; but he allowed them to *eat of the unleavened bread among their brethren*, with whom they were to reside, that unleavened bread (heavy and unpleasant as it was), was better than they deserved, and that would serve to keep them alive. 3. All the images were broken to pieces and burnt. The image of the grove (*v*. 6), some goddess or other, was reduced to ashes, and the *ashes cast upon the graves of the common people* (*v*. 6), the common burying-place of the city. By the law a ceremonial uncleanness was contracted by the touch of a grave, so that in casting them here he declared them most impure. He *filled the places of the groves with the bones of men*; as he carried the ashes of the images to the graves, to mingle them with dead men's bones, so he carried dead men's bones to the places where the images had been, and put them in the room of them, that, both ways, idolatry might be rendered loathsome, and the people kept both from the dust of the images and from the ruins of the places where they had been worshipped. 4. All the wicked houses were suppressed, those nests of impiety that harboured idolaters, the houses of the Sodomites, *v*. 7. The high places were in like manner broken down and levelled with the ground (*v*. 8). Tophet, which, contrary to other places of idolatry, was in a valley, whereas they were on hills or high places, was likewise defiled (*v*. 10), was made the burying-place of the city. Concerning this we have a whole sermon, Jer. xix. 1, 2, &c., where it is said, *They shall bury in Tophet*, and the whole city is threatened to be made like Tophet. 5. The horses that had been given to the sun were taken away and put to common use, and the chariots of the sun he burnt with fire. 6. The workers with familiar spirits and the wizards were put away, *v*. 24.

III. How his zeal extended itself to the cities of Israel that were within his reach. The ten tribes were carried captive and the Assyrian colonies did not fully people the country, so that, it is likely, many cities had put themselves under the protection of the kings of Judah, 2 Chron. xxx. 1; xxxiv. 6. These he here visits, to carry on his reformation.

1. He defiled and demolished Jeroboam's altar at Bethel, with the high place and the grove that belonged to it, *v*. 15, 16. The golden calf, it should seem, was gone (*thy calf, O Samaria! has cast thee off*), but the altar was there. This was, (1) Defiled, *v*. 16. Josiah, in his pious zeal, was ransacking the old seats of idolatry, and spied the sepulchres in the mount, in which probably the idolatrous priests were buried. These he opened, took out the bones, and *burnt them upon the altar*, *v*. 20. Thus he polluted the altar, desecrated it, and made it odious. (2) It was demolished. He broke down the altar and all its appurtenances (*v*. 15), burnt what was combustible, and *stamped it small to powder* and made it *as dust before the wind*.

2. He destroyed all the houses of the high places, all those synagogues of Satan that were *in the cities of Samaria*, *v*. 19.

3. He carefully preserved the sepulchre of that man of God who came from Judah to foretell this. This was that good prophet who *proclaimed these things against the altar of Bethel*, and yet was himself slain by a lion, but to show that God's displeasure against him went no further than his death, God so ordered it that when all the graves about his were disturbed his was safe (*v*. 17, 18) and no man moved his bones.

IV. We are here told what a solemn passover Josiah and his people kept after all this. When they had cleared the country of the old leaven they then applied themselves to the keeping of the feast. We

JAMIESON, FAUSSET, BROWN

5. put down the idolatrous priests—*Hebrew, chemarim*, "scorched," i.e., Guebres, or fire-worshippers, distinguished by a girdle (Ezek. 23:14-17) or belt of wool and camel's hair, twisted round the body twice and tied with four knots, which had a symbolic meaning, and made it a supposed defense against evil. **them also that burned incense unto Baal, to the sun, and to the moon,** etc.—or Baal-shemesh—for Baal was sometimes considered the sun. This form of false worship was not by images, but pure star-worship, borrowed from the old Assyrians. **and**—rather, "even" to all the host of heaven. **6. brought out the grove**—i.e., Asherah, the mystic tree, placed by Manasseh in the temple, removed by him after his conversion, but replaced in the sanctuary by his wicked son Amon. Josiah had it taken to Kidron, burnt the wood, ground the metal about it to powder, and strewed the ashes "on the graves of the children of the people." The poor were buried in a common on part of the valley of Kidron. But reference is her made to the graves "of those that had sacrificed" (II Chron. 34:4). **7. brake down the houses of the sodomites**—not solid houses, but tents, called elsewhere Succoth-benoth, the booths of the young women who were devoted to the service of Asherah, for which they made embroidered hangings, and in which they gave themselves to unbridled revelry and lust. Or the hangings might be for Asherah itself, as it is a popular superstition in the East to hang pieces of cloth on trees. **8. he brought all the priests out of the cities of Judah, and defiled the high places,** etc.—Many of the Levitical order, finding in the reigns of Manasseh and Amon the temple worship abolished and the tithes and other offerings alienated, had been betrayed into the folly of officiating on high places, and presenting such sacrifices as were brought to them. These irregularities, even though the object of that worship was the true God, were prohibited in the law (Deut. 12: 11). Those who had been guilty of this sin, Josiah brought to Jerusalem. Regarding them as defiled, he debarred them from the service of the temple, but gave them an allowance out of the temple revenues, like the lame and disabled members of the priesthood (Lev. 21:21, 22). **from Geba to Beer-sheba**—the most northern and the most southern places in Judah—meaning all parts of the kingdom. **the high places . . . which were in the entering in of the gate of Joshua**—The governor's house and gate were on the left of the city gate, and close by the entrance of that civic mansion-house were public altars, dedicated, it might be, to the true God, but contrary to His own ordinance of worship (Isa. 57:8). **11. took away the horses which the kings of Judah had given to the sun**—Among the people who anciently worshipped the sun, horses were usually dedicated to that divinity, from the supposed idea that the sun himself was drawn in a chariot by horses. In some cases these horses were sacrificed; but more commonly they were employed either in the sacred processions to carry the images of the sun, or for the worshippers to ride in every morning to welcome his rise. It seems that the idolatrous kings, Ahaz, Manasseh, and Amon, or their great officers, proceeded on these horses early on each day from the east gate of the temple to salute and worship the sun at his appearing above the horizon.

14. filled their places with the bones of men—Every monument of idolatry in his dominion he in like manner destroyed, and the places where they stood he defiled by strewing them with dead men's bones. The presence of a dead carcass rendered both persons and places unclean in the eyes both of Jews and heathens. **15-20. Moreover, the altar that was at Beth-el,** etc.—Not satisfied with the removal of every vestige of idolatry from his own dominion, this zealous iconoclast made a tour of inspection through the cities of Samaria and all the territory formerly occupied by the ten tribes, destroying the altars and temples of the high places, consigning the Asherim to the flames, putting to death the priests of the high places, and showing his horror at idolatry by ransacking the sepulchers of idolatrous priests, and strewing the burnt ashes of their bones upon the altars before he demolished them. **16. according to the word of the Lord, which the man of God proclaimed,** etc.—In carrying on these proceedings, Josiah was prompted by his own intense hatred of idolatry. But it is remarkable that this act was predicted 326 years before his birth, and his name also was expressly mentioned, as well as the very place where it should be done (I Kings 13:2). This is one of the most remarkable prophecies contained in the Bible. **17. What title is that that I see?**—The king's attention,

ADAM CLARKE

6. *He brought out the grove.* He brought out the idol Asherah. *Upon the graves of the children of the people.* I believe this means the burial place of the common people.

7. *The houses of the sodomites.* We have already often met with these *kedeshim* or "consecrated persons." The word implies all kinds of prostitutes, as well as abusers of themselves with mankind. *Wove hangings for the grove.* For *Asherah;* curtains or tent coverings for the places where the rites of the impure goddess were performed.

8. *The gate of Joshua.* The place where he, as governor of the city, heard and decided causes. Near this we find there were public altars, where sometimes the true God, at other times false gods, were honored.

9. *The priests of the high places came not up.* As these priests had offered sacrifices on the high places, though it was to the true God, yet they were not thought proper to be employed immediately about the Temple; but as they were acknowledged to belong to the priesthood, they had a right to their support. Therefore a portion of the tithes, offerings, and unleavened bread, shewbread, was appointed to them for their support. Thus they were treated as priests who had some infirmity which rendered it improper for them to minister at the altar (see Lev. xxi. 17, etc., and particularly vv. 22 and 23).

11. *The horses that the kings of Judah had given to the sun.* Throughout the East the horse, because of his swiftness and utility, was dedicated to the sun; and the Greeks and Romans feigned that the chariot of the sun was drawn by four horses. Whether these were living or sculptured horses, we cannot tell; the latter is the more reasonable supposition.

14. *Filled their places with the bones of men.* This was allowed to be the utmost defilement to which anything could be exposed.

16. *And as Josiah turned himself.* See 1 Kings xiii. 2, where these things were predicted.

17. *What title is that?* There was either a stone, an image, or an inscription here; no doubt the old prophet took care to have the place made sufficiently remarkable.

MATTHEW HENRY

have not such a particular account of this passover as of that in Hezekiah's time, 2 Chron. xxx. But, in general, we are told that *there was not holden such a passover* in any of the foregoing reigns, no, not *from the days of the judges* (*v.* 22). This passover, it seems, was extraordinary for the number and devotion of the communicants, their sacrifices and offerings, and their exact observance of the laws of the feast. God was pleased to recompense their zeal in destroying idolatry with uncommon tokens of his presence and favour. All this concurred to make it a distinguished passover.

Verses 25–30

I. It is here owned that Josiah was one of the best kings that ever sat upon the throne of David, *v.* 25. As Hezekiah was a nonsuch for faith and dependence upon God in straits (*ch.* xviii. 5), so Josiah was a nonsuch for sincerity and zeal in carrying on a work of reformation. 1. He *turned to the Lord from whom his fathers had revolted.* He did what he could to turn his kingdom also to the Lord. 2. He did this *with his heart and soul.* 3. He did it with *all his heart*, and *all his soul*, and *all his might*—with vigour, and courage, and resolution. 4. He did this *according to all the law of Moses.* In all he did, he walked by rule.

II. Notwithstanding this he was cut off by a violent death in the midst of his days, and his kingdom was ruined within a few years after. Consequent upon such a reformation as this, one would have expected nothing but the prosperity and glory both of king and kingdom; but, quite contrary, we find both under a cloud. 1. Even the reformed kingdom continues marked for ruin. For all this (*v.* 26) *the Lord turned not from the fierceness of his great wrath.* That is certainly true, which God spoke by the prophet (Jer. xviii. 7, 8), that if a nation, doomed to destruction, *turn from the evil* of sin, God will *repent of the evil* of punishment; and therefore we must conclude that Josiah's people, though they submitted to Josiah's power, did not heartily imbibe Josiah's principles. They were turned by force, and did not voluntarily *turn from their evil way*, but still continued their affection for their idols; and therefore he that knows men's hearts would not recall the sentence, which was, That Judah should be removed, as Israel had been, and Jerusalem itself cast off, *v.* 27 Yet even this destruction was intended to be their effectual reformation; so that we must say that the disease had come to a crisis, and was ready for a cure. 2. As an evidence of this, even the reforming king is cut off in the midst of his usefulness—in mercy to him, that he might not see the evil which was coming upon his kingdom. The king of Egypt waged war with the king of Assyria: so the king of Babylon is now called. Josiah's kingdom lay between them. He therefore thought himself concerned to oppose the king of Egypt, and check the growing, threatening, greatness of his power. Therefore *Josiah went against him*, and was killed in the first engagement, *v.* 29, 30. We must adore God's righteousness in taking away such a jewel from an unthankful people that knew not how to value it. They greatly lamented his death (2 Chron. xxxv. 25), urged to it by Jeremiah, who told them the meaning of it, and what a threatening omen it was.

Verses 31–37

Jerusalem saw not a good day after Josiah was laid in his grave, but one trouble came after another, till within twenty-two years it was quite destroyed. Of the reign of two of his sons here is a short account; the former we find a prisoner and the latter a tributary to the king of Egypt. This king of Egypt having slain Josiah, bent all his force against his family and kingdom.

I. Jehoahaz, a younger son, was first made king by *the people of the land*, probably because he was of a more warlike genius than his elder brother, and likely to make head against the king of Egypt and to avenge his father's death. He did ill, *v.* 32. He did *according to all that his* wicked *fathers had done.* Though he had not time to do much, yet he had chosen his patterns. He was but three months a prince, and was then made a prisoner and lived and died so.

II. Eliakim, another son of Josiah, was made king by the king of Egypt. The crown of Judah had hitherto always descended from a father to a son, and never, till now, from one brother to another. The king of Egypt, having used his power in making him king, further showed it in changing his name; he called him *Jehoiakim*, a name that had reference to Jehovah, for he had no design to make him renounce or forget the religion of his country. Of this Jehoiakim we are here told the king of Egypt made him poor,

JAMIESON, FAUSSET, BROWN

probably, had been arrested by a tombstone more conspicuous than the rest around it, bearing on an inscription the name of him that lay beneath; and this prompted his curiosity to make the inquiry. **the men of the city**—not the Assyrian colonists—for they could know nothing about the ancient transactions of the place—but some of the old people who had been allowed to remain, and perhaps the tomb itself might not then have been discoverable, through the effects of time and neglect, had not some "Old Mortality" garnished the sepulcher of the righteous. **21-23. the king commanded all the people, saying, Keep the passover unto the Lord your God,** etc.—It was observed with great solemnity and was attended not only by his own subjects, but by the remnant people from Israel (see on II Chron. 35:1-19). Many of the Israelites who were at Jerusalem might have *heard of*, if they did *not hear*, the law read by Josiah. It is probable that they might even have procured a copy of the law, stimulated as they were to the better observance of Jehovah's worship by the unusual and solemn transactions at Jerusalem.

26. Notwithstanding, the Lord turned not from the fierceness of his wrath, etc. The national reformation which Josiah carried on was acquiesced in by the people from submission to the royal will; but they entertained a secret and strong hankering after the suppressed idolatries. Though outwardly purified, their hearts were not right towards God, as appears from many passages of the prophetic writings; their thorough reform was hopeless; and God, who saw no sign of genuine repentance, allowed His decree (ch. 21:12-15) for the subversion of the kingdom to take fatal effect.

29. In his days Pharaoh-nechoh—(See II Chron. 35: 20-27).

ADAM CLARKE

18. *The prophet that came out of Samaria.* See the note on 1 Kings xiii. 32.

19. *That were in the cities of Samaria.* Israel had now no king; and Josiah, of the blood royal of Judah, certainly had a direct right to the kingdom. He had, at this time, an especial commission from God to reform every abuse through the whole land—all that ground that was given by the Lord as an inheritance to the twelve sons of Jacob. Therefore he had every right to carry his plans of reformation into the Samaritan states.

20. *Slew all the priests.* The lives of these, as corrupters of the people, were forfeited to the law.

22. *Surely there was not holden such a passover.* Not one on purer principles, more heartily joined in by the people present, more literally consecrated, or more religiously observed. The words do not apply to the number present, but to the manner and spirit. See the particulars and mode of celebrating this Passover in 2 Chron. xxxv. 1-18.

24. *And the images.* The *teraphim.* See the note on Gen. xxxi. 19.

25. *Like unto him was there no king.* Perhaps not one from the time of David; and, morally considered, including David himself, none ever sat on the Jewish throne so truly exemplary in his own conduct, and so thoroughly zealous in the work of God. David was a greater but not a better man than Josiah.

26. *The Lord turned not.* It was of no use to try this fickle and radically depraved people any longer. They were respited merely during the life of Josiah.

30. *Dead from Megiddo.* The word *meth* should here be considered as a participle, "dying," for it is certain he was not *dead.* He was mortally wounded at Megiddo, was carried in a dying state to Jerusalem, and there he died and was buried (see 2 Chron. xxxv. 24).

31. *Jehoahaz was twenty and three years old.* This was not the eldest son of Josiah, which is evident from this, that he was twenty-three years old when he began to reign; that he reigned but three months; that, being dethroned, his brother Eliakim was put in his place, who was then twenty-five years of age. Eliakim, therefore, was the eldest brother; but Jehoahaz was probably raised to the throne by the people, as being of a more active and martial spirit.

33. *Nechoh put him in bands.* But what was the cause of his putting him in bands? It is conjectured, and not without reason, that Jehoahaz, otherwise called Shallum, raised an army, met Nechoh in his return from Carchemish, fought, was beaten, taken prisoner, put in chains, and taken into Egypt, where he died (v. 34 and Jer. xxii. 11-12). *Riblah* or Diblath, the place of this battle, was probably a town in Syria, *in the land* or district *of Hamath.*

34. *Turned his name to Jehoiakim.* These names are precisely the same in signification. Eliakim is "God shall arise"; Jehoiakim, "Jehovah shall arise." That is, God's rising again to show His power, justice. The change of the name was to show Nechoh's supremacy, and that Jehoiakim was only his vassal or viceroy. Proofs of this mode of changing the name, when a person of greater power put another in office under himself, may be seen in the case of Mattaniah, changed into Zedekiah; Daniel, Mishael, Hananiah, and Azariah into Belteshazzar, Shadrach, Meshach, and Abed-nego; and Joseph into Zaphnath-paaneah (see Dan. i. 6-7; Gen. xli. 45).

35. *Jehoiakim gave the silver and the gold.* Nechoh had placed him there as viceroy, simply to raise and collect his taxes. *Every one according to his taxation.* That is, each was assessed in proportion to his property. That was the principle avowed: but there is reason to fear that this bad king was not governed by it.

MATTHEW HENRY

exacted from him a vast tribute of 100 *talents of silver and a talent of gold* (*v.* 33), which, with much difficulty, he squeezed out of his subjects and gave to Pharaoh, *v.* 35. Notwithstanding the rebukes of Providence he was under, by which he should have been convinced, humbled, and reformed, he *did that which was evil in the sight of the Lord* (*v.* 37).

CHAPTER 24

Verses 1–7

We have here the first mention of *Nebuchadnezzar*, king of Babylon (*v.* 1), that head of gold. He was a potent prince, and one that was the terror of the mighty; and yet his name would not have been known in sacred writ if he had not been employed in the destruction of Jerusalem and the captivity of the Jews.

I. He made Jehoiakim his tributary and kept him in subjection three years, *v.* 1. Nebuchadnezzar began his reign in the fourth year of Jehoiakim. In his eighth year he made him his prisoner, but restored him upon his promise of faithfulness to him. That promise he kept about three years, but then rebelled, probably in hopes of assistance from the king of Egypt.

II. When he rebelled Nebuchadnezzar sent his forces against him to destroy his country, bands of Chaldeans, Syrians, Moabites, Ammonites, who were all now in the service and pay of the king of Babylon (*v.* 2), and withal retained, and now showed, their ancient enmity to the Israel of God. Two things God intended in suffering Judah to be thus harassed:— 1. The punishment of the sins of Manasseh, which God now visited upon *the third and fourth generation.* So long he waited before he visited them, to see if the nation would repent; but they continued impenitent. Though Manasseh repented, and we have reason to think even the persecutions and murders he was guilty of were pardoned, yet, as they were national sins, they lay still charged upon the land, crying for national judgments. Perhaps some were now living who were aiding and abetting. See what need nations have to lament the sins of their fathers, lest they smart for them.

III. The king of Egypt was likewise subdued by the king of Babylon, and a great part of his country taken from him, *v.* 7. He dares not *come any more out of his land.* Afterwards he attempted to give Zedekiah some relief, but was obliged to retire, Jer. xxxvii. 7.

IV. Jehoiakim, seeing his country laid waste and himself ready to fall into the enemy's hand, as it should seem, died of a broken heart, in the midst of his days (*v.* 6).

Verses 8–20

The history of king Jehoiachin's *captivity*, as it is called, Ezek. i. 2. He came to the crown, not to have the honour of wearing it, but the shame of losing it.

I. His reign was short and inconsiderable. He reigned but three months, and then was removed and carried captive to Babylon. Yet this young prince reigned long enough to show that he justly smarted for his fathers' sins, for he trod in their steps (*v.* 9).

II. The calamities that came upon him, and his family, and people, in the very beginning of his reign, 1. Jerusalem was besieged by the king of Babylon, *v.* 10, 11. 2. Jehoiachin immediately surrendered; wanting the faith and piety of an Israelite, he had not the resolution of a man, of a soldier, of a prince. He and his royal family delivered themselves up prisoners of war.

3. Nebuchadnezzar rifled the treasuries both of the church and of the state, and carried away the silver and gold of both, *v.* 13. Now the word of God by Isaiah was fulfilled (*ch.* xx. 17), *All that is in thy house shall be carried to Babylon.* 4. He carried away a great part of Jerusalem into captivity. There had been some carried away eight years before this, in the first year of Nebuchadnezzar and the third of Jehoiakim, among whom were Daniel and his fellows. See Dan. i. 1, 6. Now he carried off, (1) The young king himself and his family (*v.* 15), and we find (*ch.* xxv. 27–29) that for thirty-seven years he continued a close prisoner. (2) All the great men, the princes and officers. (3) All the military men, the *mighty men of valour* (*v.* 14), *the mighty of the land* (*v.* 15), *the men of might, even all that were strong and apt for war*, *v.* 16. (4) All the craftsmen and smiths who made weapons of war. In this captivity Ezekiel the prophet was carried away (Ezek. i. 1, 2).

JAMIESON, FAUSSET, BROWN

CHAPTER 24

Vss. 1-7. Jehoiakim Procures His Own Ruin. **1. Nebuchadnezzar**—the son of Nabopolassar, the founder of the Chaldee monarchy. This invasion took place in the fourth year of Jehoiakim's, and the first of Nebuchadnezzar's reign (Jer. 25:1; cf. 46:2). The young king of Assyria being probably detained at home on account of his father's demise, despatched, along with the Chaldean troops on his border, an army composed of the tributary nations that were contiguous to Judea, to chastise Jehoiakim's revolt from his yoke. But this hostile band was only an instrument in executing the divine judgment (vs. 2) denounced by the prophets against Judah for the sins of the people; and hence, though marching by the orders of the Assyrian monarch, they are described as sent by the Lord (vs. 3). **4. the Lord would not pardon**—(see on ch. 23:26; Jer. 15:1). **6. Jehoiakim slept with his fathers**—This phraseology can mean nothing more than that he died; for he was not buried with his royal ancestors; and whether he fell in battle, or his body was subjected to posthumous insults, he was, according to the prediction (Jer. 22:19), not honored with the rites of sepulture (Jer. 36:30). **Jehoiachin his son reigned in his stead**—The very brief reign of this prince, which lasted only three months, during which he was a humble vassal of the Assyrians, is scarcely deserving to be taken into account, and therefore is in no way contradictory to the prophetic menace denounced against his father (Jer. 36:30). **7. the king of Egypt**—i.e., Pharaoh-nechoh.

8, 9. Jehoiachin Succeeds Him. **8. Jehoiachin**—i.e., "God appointed," contracted into *Jeconiah* and *Coniah* (Jer. 22:24). **eighteen years old when he began to reign**—At the age of eight his father took him into partnership in the government (II Chron. 36:9). He began to reign alone at eighteen. **9. he did that which was evil in the sight of the Lord**—Untaught by experience, and deaf to the prophetic warnings, he pursued the evil courses which had brought so many disasters upon the royal family as well as the people of Judah. This bad character is figuratively but strongly depicted (Ezek. 19:5-7).

10-16. Jerusalem Taken. **10. At that time**—within three months after his accession to the throne. It was the spring of the year (II Chron. 36:10); so early did he indicate a feeling hostile to the interests of his Assyrian liege lord, by forming a league with Egypt. Nebuchadnezzar sent his generals to besiege Jerusalem, as Jeremiah had foretold (22:18; 24:30), and soon after he followed in person. Convinced of the hopelessness of making any effectual resistance, Jehoiachin, going to the camp of the besiegers, surrendered (vs. 12), in the expectation, probably, of being allowed to retain his throne as a vassal of the Assyrian empire. But Nebuchadnezzar's clemency towards the kings of Judah was now exhausted, so that Jehoiachin was sent as a captive to Babylon, according to Jeremiah's prediction (22: 24), accompanied by the queen mother (the same who had held that dignity under Jehoahaz) (ch. 23: 31), his generals, and officers. This happened in the eighth year of Nebuchadnezzar's reign, computing from the time when he was associated with his father in the government. Those that were left consisted chiefly of the poorer sort of people and the unskilled workmen. The palace and the temple were ransacked. The smaller golden vessels had been taken on the first capture of Jerusalem and placed by Nebuchadnezzar in the temple of his god as tokens of victory. They were used by Belshazzar at his impious feast, for the purpose of rewarding his army with these trophies, among which were probably the golden candlesticks, the ark, etc. (cf. II Chron. 36:7; Dan. 1:2). Now the gold plating was torn off all the larger temple furniture. **13. as the Lord had said**—(cf. ch. 20:17; Isa. 39:6; Jer. 15:13; 17:3). The elite of the nation for rank, usefulness, and moral worth, all who might be useful in Babylon or dangerous in Palestine, were carried off to Babylon, to the number of ten thousand (vs. 14). These are specified (vss. 15, 16), warriors, 7000; craftsmen and smiths, 1000; king's wives, officers, and princes, also priests and prophets (Jer. 29:1; Ezek. 1:1), 2000; equal to 10,000 captives in all.

ADAM CLARKE

37. *He did that which was evil in the sight of the Lord.* He was a most unprincipled and oppressive tyrant. Jeremiah gives us his character at large, chap. xxii. 13-19, to which the reader will do well to refer. Jeremiah was at that time in the land, and was an eyewitness of the abominations of this cruel king.

CHAPTER 24

1. *Nebuchadnezzar.* This man, so famous in the writings of the prophets, was son of Nabopolassar. He was sent by his father against the rulers of several provinces that had revolted; and he took Carchemish, and all that belonged to the Egyptians, from the Euphrates to the Nile. Jehoiakim, who was tributary to Nechoh, king of Egypt, he attacked and reduced, and obliged to become tributary to Babylon. At the end of three years he revolted; and then a mixed army, of Chaldeans, Syrians, Moabites, and Ammonites, was sent against him, who ravaged the country and took 3,023 prisoners, whom they brought to Babylon, Jer. lii. 28.

2. *According to the word of the Lord.* See what Huldah predicted, chap. xxii. 16; and see chaps. xiv; xv; and xvi of Jeremiah.

6. *Jehoiachin his son.* As this man reigned only three months, and was a mere vassal to the Babylonians, his reign is scarcely to be reckoned; and therefore Jeremiah says of Jehoiakim, "He shall have none to sit upon the throne of David," chap. xxxvi. 30, for at that time it belonged to the king of Babylon, and Jehoiachin was a mere viceroy or governor. Jehoiachin is called Jechonias in Matt. i. 11.

7. *The king of Egypt came not again.* He was so crushed by the Babylonians that he was obliged to confine himself within the limits of his own states, and could no more attempt any conquests. The text tells us how much he had lost by the Babylonians.

8. *Jehoiachin was eighteen years old.* He is called Jeconiah, 1 Chron. iii. 16; and Coniah, Jer. xxii. 24. In 2 Chron. xxxvi. 9, he is said to be only eight years of age, but this must be a mistake. For we find that, having reigned only three months, he was carried captive to Babylon, and there he had wives; and it is very improbable that a child between eight and nine years of age could have wives; and of such a tender age, it can scarcely be said that, as a king, "he did that which was evil in the sight of the Lord." The place in Chronicles must be corrupted.

12. *Jehoiachin . . . went out.* He saw that it was useless to attempt to defend himself any longer; and he therefore surrendered himself, hoping to obtain better terms.

13. *He carried out thence all the treasures.* It has been remarked that Nebuchadnezzar spoiled the Temple three times: (1) He took away the greater part of those treasures when he took Jerusalem under Jehoiakim, and the vessels that he took then he placed in the temple of his god, Dan. i. 2. And these were the vessels which Belshazzar profaned, Dan. v. 2; and which Cyrus restored to Ezra when he went up to Jerusalem, Ezra i. 2. It was at this time that he took Daniel and his companions. (2) He took the remaining part of those vessels, and broke them or cut them in pieces, when he came the second time against Jerusalem under Jeconiah; as is mentioned here, v. 13. (3) He pillaged the Temple, took away all the brass, the brazen pillars, brazen vessels, and vessels of gold and silver, which he found there when he besieged Jerusalem under Zedekiah, chap. xxv. 13-17.

14. *He carried away all Jerusalem.* That is, all the chief men, the nobles, and artificers. Among these there were of mighty men 7,000; of craftsmen and smiths, 1,000.

MATTHEW HENRY

III. The successor whom the king of Babylon appointed in the room of Jehoiachin. The king of Babylon made Mattaniah king, the son of Josiah; and to let all the world know, that he was his creature, he changed his name and called him *Zedekiah*, *v.* 17. This Zedekiah was the last of the kings of Judah. The name which the king of Babylon gave him signifies *The justice of the Lord.*

He rebelled against the king of Babylon (*v.* 20). This was the most foolish thing he could do, and hastened the ruin of his kingdom.

JAMIESON, FAUSSET, BROWN

17-20. ZEDEKIAH'S EVIL REIGN. **17. the king of Babylon made Mattaniah, his father's brother, king in his stead**—Adhering to his former policy of maintaining a show of monarchy, Nebuchadnezzar appointed the third and youngest son of Josiah (I Chron. 3:15), full brother of Jehoahaz, and uncle of the captive Jehoiachin. But, according to the custom of conquerors, who changed the names of the great men they took captives in war, in token of their supremacy, he gave him the new name of Zedekiah—i.e., "The righteous of God." This being a purely Hebrew name, it seems that he allowed the puppet king to choose his own name, which was confirmed. His heart towards God was the same as that of Jehoiakim, impenitent and heedless of God's word. **20. through the anger of the Lord . . . he cast them out from his presence**—i.e., in the course of God's righteous providence, his policy as king would prove ruinous to his country. **Zedekiah rebelled against the king of Babylon**—instigated by ambassadors from the neighboring states who came to congratulate him on his ascension to the throne (cf. Jer. 17:3, with 28:1), and at the same time get him to join them in a common league to throw off the Assyrian yoke. Though warned by Jeremiah against this step, the infatuated and perjured (Ezek. 17:13) Zedekiah persisted in his revolt.

ADAM CLARKE

17. *Made Mattaniah his father's brother king in his stead.* He was the son of Josiah, and brother to Jehoiakim. *Changed his name to Zedekiah.* See the note on chap. xxiii. 34.

19. *He did . . . evil.* How astonishing is this! not one of them takes warning by the judgments of God, which fell on their sinful predecessors.

20. *Zedekiah rebelled.* This was in the eighth year of his reign; and he is strongly reproved for having violated the oath he took to the king of Babylon (see 2 Chron. xxxvi. 13).

MATTHEW HENRY

CHAPTER 25

Verses 1–7

Zedekiah in rebellion against the king of Babylon (*ch.* xxiv. 20), contriving and endeavouring to shake off his yoke.

I. The king of Babylon's army laid siege to Jerusalem, *v.* 1. Two years this siege lasted; at first the army retired, for fear of the king of Egypt (Jer. xxxvii. 11), but, finding him not so powerful as they thought, they soon returned.

II. During this siege the famine prevailed (*v.* 3).

III. At length the city was taken by storm: it was *broken up*, *v.* 4. The besiegers made a breach in the wall, at which they forced their way into it.

IV. The king, his family, and all his great men, made their escape in the night, by some secret passages, *v.* 4. Intelligence was given to the Chaldeans of the king's flight, and they soon overtook him, *v.* 5.

1. He was brought to the king of Babylon, and tried by a council of war for rebelling against him to whom he had sworn fidelity. 2. His *sons were slain before his eyes.* 3. His eyes were put out, by which he was deprived of the light of the sun. Jeremiah prophesied that Zedekiah should be brought to Babylon, Jer. xxxii. 5; xxxiv. 3. Ezekiel prophesied that he should not see Babylon, Ezek. xii. 13. He was brought thither, but, his eyes being put out, he did not see it. Thus he ended his days, before he ended his life. 4. He was *bound in fetters of brass* and so *carried to Babylon.* For his greater disgrace, they led him bound.

Verses 8–21

About a month after (compare *v.* 8 with *v.* 3) Nebuzar-adan was sent with orders to complete the destruction of Jerusalem. This space God gave them to repent, after all the foregoing days of his patience,

JAMIESON, FAUSSET, BROWN

CHAPTER 25

VSS. 1-3. JERUSALEM AGAIN BESIEGED. **1. Nebuchadnezzar . . . came . . . against Jerusalem, and pitched against it**—Incensed by the revolt of Zedekiah, the Assyrian despot determined to put an end to the perfidious and inconstant monarchy of Judea. This chapter narrates his third and last invasion, which he conducted in person at the head of an immense army, levied out of all the tributary nations under his sway. Having overrun the northern parts of the country and taken almost all the fenced cities (Jer. 34:7), he marched direct to Jerusalem to invest it. The date of the beginning as well as the end of the siege is here carefully marked (cf. Ezek. 24:1; Jer. 39:1; 52:4-6); from which it appears, that, with a brief interruption caused by Nebuchadnezzar's marching to oppose the Egyptians who were coming to its relief but who retreated without fighting, the siege lasted a year and a half. So long a resistance was owing, not to the superior skill and valor of the Jewish soldiers, but to the strength of the city fortifications, on which the king too confidently relied (cf. Jer. 21; 37; 38). **pitched against it, and . . . built forts**—rather, perhaps, drew lines of circumvallation, with a ditch to prevent any going out of the city. On this rampart were erected his military engines for throwing missiles into the city. **3. on the ninth day of the fourth month the famine prevailed**—In consequence of the close and protracted blockade, the inhabitants were reduced to dreadful extremities; and under the maddening influence of hunger, the most inhuman atrocities were perpetrated (Lam. 2:20, 22; 4:9, 10; Ezek. 5:10). This was a fulfilment of the prophetic denunciations threatened on the apostasy of the chosen people (Lev. 26:29; Deut. 28:53-57; Jer. 15:2; 27:13; Ezek. 4:16).

4-30. ZEDEKIAH TAKEN. **4. the city was broken up**—i.e., a breach was effected, as we are elsewhere informed, in a part of the wall belonging to the lower city (II Chron. 32:5; 33:14). **the men of war fled by night by the way of the gate between two walls, which is by the king's garden**—The king's garden was (Neh. 3:15) at the pool of Siloam, i.e., at the mouth of the Tyropæon. A trace of the outermost of these walls appears to be still extant in the rude pathway which crosses the mouth of the Tyropæon, on a mound hard by the old mulberry tree, which marks the traditional spot of Isaiah's martyrdom [ROBINSON]. It is probable that the besiegers had overlooked this pass. **the king went . . . toward the plain**—i.e., the Ghor, or valley of Jordan, estimated at five hours' distance from Jerusalem. The plain near Jericho is about eleven or twelve miles broad. **6. they took the king, and brought him . . . to Riblah**—Nebuchadnezzar, having gone from the siege to oppose the auxiliary forces of Pharaoh-hophra, left his generals to carry on the blockade, he himself not returning to the scene of action, but taking up his station at Riblah in the land of Hamath (ch. 23:33). **they gave judgment upon him**—They, i.e., the counsel (Jer. 39:3, 13; Dan. 6:7, 8, 12), regarding him as a seditious and rebellious vassal, condemned him for violating his oath and neglecting the announcement of the divine will as made known to him by Jeremiah (cf. Jer. 32:5; 34:2; 38:17). His sons and the nobles who had

ADAM CLARKE

CHAPTER 25

1. *In the ninth year of his reign.* Zedekiah having revolted against the Chaldeans, Nebuchadnezzar, wearied with his treachery, and the bad faith of the Jews, determined the total subversion of the Jewish state. Having assembled a numerous army, he entered Judea on the tenth day of the tenth month of the ninth year of the reign of Zedekiah, which was a sabbatical year; whereon the men of Jerusalem, hearing that the Chaldean army was approaching, proclaimed liberty to their servants (see Jer. xxxiv. 8-10), according to the law, Exod. xxi. 2; Deut. xv. 1-2, 12. For Nebuchadnezzar, marching with his army against Zedekiah, having wasted all the country, and taken their strongholds, except Lachish, Azekah, and Jerusalem, came against the latter with all his forces (see Jer. xxxiv. 1-7). On the very day the siege and utter destruction of Jerusalem were revealed to Ezekiel, the prophet, then in Chaldea, under the type of a seething pot; and his wife died in the evening, and he was charged not to mourn for her, because of the extraordinary calamity that had fallen upon the land (see Ezek. xxiv. 1-2, etc.).

Jeremiah, having predicted the same calamities, Jer. xxxiv. 1-7, was by the command of Zedekiah shut up in prison, xxxii. 1-16. Pharaoh-hophra, hearing how Zedekiah was pressed, and fearing for the safety of his own dominions should the Chaldeans succeed against Jerusalem, determined to succor Zedekiah. Finding this, the Chaldeans raised the siege of Jerusalem, and went to meet the Egyptian army, which they defeated and put to flight, Joseph., *Antiq.*, lib. 10, cap. 10. In the interim the Jews, thinking their danger was passed, reclaimed their servants, and put them again under the yoke; Jer. xxxiv. 8, etc.

2-4. *And the city was besieged.* Nebuchadnezzar, having routed the Egyptian army, returned to Jerusalem, and besieged it so closely that, being reduced by famine, and a breach made in the wall, the Chaldeans entered it on the ninth day of the fourth month, Zedekiah and many others endeavoring to make their escape by night.

5. *The army of the Chaldeans pursued.* Zedekiah was taken, and brought captive to Riblah in Syria, where Nebuchadnezzar then lay, who ordered his sons to be slain before his face, and then put out his eyes; and having loaded him with chains, sent him to Babylon (see Jer. xxxix. 4, 7; lii. 7, 11), thus fulfilling the prophetic declarations that his eyes should see the eyes of the king of Babylon, Jer. xxxii. 4 and xxxiv. 3; but Babylon he should not see, though he was to die there, Ezek. xii. 13.

MATTHEW HENRY

but in vain. 1. The city and temple are burnt, *v.* 9. That house which David prepared for, and which Solomon built at such a vast expense—that house which had the eye and heart of God perpetually upon it (1 Kings ix. 3) must be turned into ashes. By the burning of the temple God would show how little he cares for the external pomp of his worship when the life and power of religion are neglected. The people trusted to the temple, as if that would protect them in their sins (Jer. vii. 4). It is observable that the second temple was burnt by the Romans the same month, and the same day of the month, that the first temple was burnt by the Chaldeans, which, Josephus says, was the tenth of August. 2. The walls of Jerusalem are demolished (*v.* 10), as if the victorious army would be revenged on them for having kept them out so long. These walls were never repaired till Nehemiah's time. 3. The residue of the people are carried away captive to Babylon, *v.* 11. Only the poor of the land were left behind (*v.* 12) to till the ground and dress the vineyards for the Chaldeans. Sometimes poverty is a protection; for those that have nothing have nothing to lose. 4. The brazen vessels, and other appurtenances of the temple, are carried away, those of silver and gold being most of them gone before. Those two famous columns of brass, *Jachin* and *Boaz*, which signified the strength and stability of the house of God, were broken to pieces and the brass of them was carried to Babylon, *v.* 13. 5. Several of the great men are slain in cold blood. This completed the calamity: *So Judah was carried away out of their land*, about 860 years after they were put in possession of it by Joshua. Sin kept their fathers forty years out of Canaan, and now turned *them* out.

Verses 22–30

I. The dispersion of the remaining people. The city of Jerusalem was quite laid waste. Some people there were in the land of Judah (*v.* 22) that had weathered the storm, and had *their lives given them for a prey*. The king of Babylon appointed Gedaliah, one of themselves, to be their governor and protector under him, a very good man, and one that would make the best of the bad, *v.* 22. His father Ahikam was one that countenanced and protected Jeremiah when the princes had vowed his death, Jer. xxvi. 24. It is probable that this Gedaliah, by the advice of Jeremiah, had gone over to the Chaldeans, and had conducted himself so well that the king of Babylon entrusted him with the government. He resided not at Jerusalem, but at Mizpah, in the land of Benjamin, a place famous in Samuel's time. Thither those came who had fled from Zedekiah (*v.* 4) and put themselves under his protection (*v.* 23). Gedaliah, though he had not the pomp and power of a sovereign prince, yet might have been a greater blessing to them than many of their kings had been. Yet this hopeful settlement is dashed to pieces, not by the Chaldeans, but by some of themselves. Ishmael, who was of the royal family, envying Gedaliah's advancement and the happy settlement of the people under him, basely slew him and all his friends, both Jews and Chaldeans. The Chaldeans had reason enough to be offended at the murder of Gedaliah; but if those that remained had humbly remonstrated, alleging that it was only the act of Ishmael and his party, those who were innocent of it would not have been punished for it: but contrary to the counsel of Jeremiah, they all went to Egypt, where, it is probable, they mixed with the Egyptians by degrees, and were never heard of more as Israelites. Thus was there a full end made of them by their own folly and disobedience, and Egypt had the last of them, that the last verse of that chapter of threatenings might be fulfilled, Deut. xxviii. 68, *The Lord shall bring thee into Egypt again*. These events are more largely related by the prophet Jeremiah, *ch.* xl. to *ch.* xlv.

II. The reviving of the captive prince. Of Jehoiachin, or Jeconiah, who surrendered himself (*ch.* xxiv. 12), we are here told that as soon as Evil-merodach came to the crown, upon the death of his father Nebuchadnezzar, he released him out of prison (where he had lain thirty-seven years, and was now fifty-five years old), *spoke kindly to him* (*v.* 28), gave him princely clothing instead of his prison-garments, maintained him in his own palace (*v.* 29), and allowed him a pension for himself and his family in some measure corresponding to his rank, *a daily rate for every day as long as he lived*. To have honour and liberty after he had been so long in confinement and disgrace was like the return of the morning after a very dark and tedious night. Let none say that they shall never see good again because they have long seen little but evil; the most miserable know not what blessed turn Providence may yet give to their affairs, Ps. xc. 15.

JAMIESON, FAUSSET, BROWN

joined in his flight were slain before his eyes (Jer. 39:6; 52:10). In conformity with Eastern ideas, which consider a blind man incapable of ruling, his eyes were put out, and being put in chains, he was carried to perpetual imprisonment in Babylon (Jer. 52:11), which, though he came to it, as Ezekiel had foretold, he did not see (Jer. 32:5; Ezek. 12:13; 17:16). **8-18. on the seventh day of the month . . . came Nebuzar-adan**—(cf. Jer. 52:12). In attempting to reconcile these two passages, it must be supposed either that, though he had set out on the 7th, he did not arrive in Jerusalem till the 10th, or that he did not put his orders in execution till that day. His office as captain of the guard (Gen. 37:36; 39:1) called him to execute the awards of justice on criminals; and hence, although not engaged in the siege of Jerusalem (Jer. 39:13), Nebuzar-adan was despatched to rase the city, to plunder the temple, to lay both in ruins, demolish the fortifications, and transport the inhabitants to Babylon. The most eminent of these were taken to the king at Riblah (vs. 27) and executed, as instigators and abettors of the rebellion, or otherwise obnoxious to the Assyrian government. In their number were Seraiah, the high priest, grandfather of Ezra (Ezra 7:1), his sagan or deputy, a priest of the second order (Jer. 21:2; 29:25, 29; 37:3). **the three keepers of the door**—not mere porters, but officers of high trust among the Levites (ch. 22:4; I Chron. 9:26). **19. five men of them that were in the king's presence**—i.e., who belonged to the royal retinue. It is probable that there were five at first, and that other two were found afterwards (Jer. 52:25).

22-26. Nebuchadnezzar . . . made Gedaliah . . . ruler—The people permitted to remain were, besides the king's daughters, a few court attendants and others (Jer. 40:7) too insignificant to be removed, only the peasantry who could till the land and dress the vineyards. Gedaliah was Jeremiah's friend (Jer. 26:24), and having, by the prophet's counsel, probably fled from the city as abandoned of God, he surrendered himself to the conqueror (Jer. 38:2, 17), and being promoted to the government of Judea, fixed his provincial court at Mizpeh. He was well qualified to surmount the difficulties of ruling at such a crisis. Many of the fugitive Jews, as well as the soldiers of Zedekiah who had accompanied the king in his flight to the plains of Jericho, left their retreats (Jer. 40:11, 12) and flocked around the governor; who having counselled them to submit, promised them on complying with this condition, security on oath that they would retain their possessions and enjoy the produce of their land (Jer. 40:9). **25. Ishmael . . . of the seed royal came, and ten men with him, and smote Gedaliah**—He had found refuge with Baalis, king of the Ammonites, and he returned with a bad design, being either instigated by envy of a governor not descended from the house of David, or bribed by Baalis to murder Gedaliah. The generous governor, though apprised of his intentions, refused to credit the report, much less to sanction the proposal made by an attached friend to cut off Ishmael. The consequence was, that he was murdered by this same Ishmael, when entertaining him in his own house (Jer. 41:1). **26. and all the people . . . came to Egypt**—In spite of Jeremiah's dissuasions (Jer. 43:7, 8) they settled in various cities of that country (Jer. 44:1).

27. seven and thirtieth year of the captivity of Jehoiachin—corresponding with the year of Nebuchadnezzar's death, and his son Evil-merodach's ascension to the throne. **Evil-merodach . . . did lift up the head of Jehoiachin . . . and spake kindly**—gave him liberty upon parole. This kindly feeling is said to have originated in a familiar acquaintance formed in prison, in which Evil-merodach had lain till his father's death, on account of some malversation while acting as regent during Nebuchadnezzar's seven years' illness (Dan. 4:32, 33). But doubtless the improvement in Zedekiah's condition is to be traced to the overruling providence and grace of Him who still cherished purposes of love to the house of David (II Sam. 7:14, 15). **29. Jeohiachin did eat . . . continually before him**—According to an ancient usage in Eastern courts, he had a seat at the royal table on great days, and had a stated provision granted him for the maintenance of his exiled court.

ADAM CLARKE

8. *In the fifth month*. On the seventh day of the fifth month Nebuzar-adan made his entry into the city; and having spent two days in making provision, on the tenth day of the same month he set fire to the Temple and the king's palace, and the houses of the nobility, and burned them to the ground (Jer. lii. 13, compared with xxxix. 8). Thus the Temple was destroyed in the eleventh year of Zedekiah, the nineteenth of Nebuchadnezzar.

10. *Brake down the walls*. In the same fifth month, Jer. i. 3, the walls of Jerusalem being razed to the ground, all that were left in the city, and all that had fled over formerly to Nebuchadnezzar, and all the common people of the city, with all the king's treasures, those of the nobles, and the whole furniture of the Temple, did Nebuzar-adan carry off to Babylon (see Jer. xxxix. 8-9; lii. 14, 23).

18. *Seraiah the chief priest . . . Zephaniah*. The person who is here called the *second priest* was what the Jews call *sagan*, a sort of deputy, who performed the functions of the high priest when he was prevented by any infirmity from attending the Temple service (see on chap. xxiii. 4).

19. *And five men of them that were in the king's presence*. These were principal counsellors and confidential officers. In Jer. lii. 25 it is said he took seven men who were near the king's person, and the same number is found in the Arabic in this place; and the Chaldee has no less than fifty men; but in Jeremiah this, as well as all the rest of the versions, reads "seven." Probably they were no more than five at first, or perhaps Jeremiah reckoned with the five the officer that was set over the men of war and the principal scribe of the host mentioned here, as two with the five; and thus made seven in the whole.

21. *The king of Babylon smote them*. He had, no doubt, found that these had counselled Zedekiah to revolt.

22. *Made Gedaliah . . . ruler*. This was no regal dignity; he was only a sort of overseer, appointed to regulate the husbandmen.

23. *To Mizpah*. This is said to have been situated on the east side of the river Jordan, and most contiguous to Babylon, and therefore the most proper for the residence of Gedaliah, because nearest to the place from which he was to receive his instructions.

24. *Gedaliah sware to them*. He pledged himself in the most solemn manner to encourage and protect them.

25. *Smote Gedaliah*. This was at an entertainment which Gedaliah had made for them (see Jer. xli. 1, etc.). He was not content with this murder, but slew fourscore more, who were coming with offerings to the Temple, and took several as prisoners, among whom were some of the king's daughters; and set off to go to the Ammonites. But Johanan, the son of Kareah, hearing of these outrages, raised a number of men, and pursued Ishmael; upon which Ishmael's prisoners immediately turned and joined Johanan; so that he, and eight of his accomplices, with difficulty escaped to the Ammonites (see Jer. xli. 1, etc.). Baalis, king of the Ammonites, had sent Ishmael to murder Gedaliah; and of this he was informed by Johanan, who offered to prevent it by taking away the life of this murderer. But Gedaliah could not believe that he harbored such foul designs, and therefore took no precaution to save his life (see Jer. xl. 13-16).

27. *And it came to pass*. Nebuchadnezzar was just now dead; and Evil-merodach, his son, succeeded to the kingdom in the thirty-seventh year of the captivity of Jehoiachin. And on the seven and twentieth day [Jeremiah says five and twentieth] of the twelfth month of that year, he brought the long captivated Jewish king out of prison, treated him kindly, and ever after, during his life, reckoned him among the king's friends. This is particularly related in the last four verses of the Book of Jeremiah.

30. *A continual allowance given him of the king*. He lived in a regal style, and had his court even in the city of Babylon, being supplied with every requisite by the munificence and friendship of the king.

THE BOOK OF FIRST CHRONICLES

I. Genealogies (1:1-10:14)
A. General—the nations (1:1-54)
1. Beginnings—Adam to Ishmael (1:1-28)
2. Related to Israel (1:29-54)

B. Particular—the chosen (2:1-10:14)
1. Sons of Israel (2:1, 2)
2. Judah (2:3-4:23)
3. Simeon, Reuben, Gad, and Manasseh (4:24-5:26)
4. Levi (6:1-81)
5. Issachar, Benjamin, Naphtali, Manasseh, Ephraim, and Asher (7:1-40)
6. Benjamin (8:1-40)
7. Conclusion (9:1-10:14)

II. David (11:1-29:30)
A. David made king (11:1-12:40)
1. The crowning at Hebron (11:1-3)
2. The taking of Jebus (11:4-9)
3. The mighty men (11:10-47)
4. The gathering of the people (12:1-40)

B. The Ark (13:1-17:27)
1. From Kiriath-jearim to House of Obed-edom—death of Uzza (13:1-14)
2. Parenthesis—David defeats the Philistines (14:1-17)
3. From Obed-edom to Jerusalem—Michal's contempt (15:1-16:6)
4. Parenthesis—the psalm (16:7-43)
5. Desire to build a home for the Ark—Nathan (17:1-27)

C. David's reign (18:1-21:30)
1. Victories and gathering of treasure for Temple (18:1-20:8)
2. The numbering of the people (21:1-30)

D. The Temple (22:1-29:30)
1. The site (22:1)
2. Preparation of material (22:2-5)
3. Charge to Solomon (22:6-16)
4. Charge to princes (22:17-19)
5. Arrangements of Levites (23:1-24:31)
6. Arrangements of song service (25:1-31)
7. Arrangements of porters (26:1-19)
8. Arrangements of keepers of treasure (26:20-32)
9. Parenthesis—internal order of the kingdom (27:1-34)
10. The final charge (28:1-21)
11. The ceremony of giving (29:1-25)
12. Death of David (29:26-30)

These books of Chronicles are in a great measure repetition; and yet there are no "vain repetitions." We could ill spare them; for there are many most excellent useful things in them, which we find not elsewhere. Abstracts, abridgments, and references, are of use in divinity as well as law. It is still of use, that "out of the mouth of two witnesses every word may be established."

These books are called in the Hebrew *words of days*—journals or annals, because, by divine direction, collected out of some public and authentic records. The collection was made after the captivity. The LXX call it a book of *things left*, or overlooked, by the preceding historians. It is the rereward, the gathering host, of this sacred camp, which gathers up what remained, that nothing might be lost.

MATTHEW HENRY

CHAPTER 1

Verses 1–27

This paragraph has *Adam* for its first word and *Abraham* for its last. Adam was the common father of our flesh, Abraham the common father of the faithful. By the breach which the former made of the covenant of innocency, we were all made miserable; by the covenant of grace made with the latter, we all are, or may be, made happy. We all are, by nature, the seed of Adam, branches of that wild olive. Let us see to it that, by faith, we become the seed of Abraham (Rom. iv. 11, 12), that we be grafted into the good olive and partake of its root and fatness.

I. The first four verses of this paragraph, and the last four, which are linked together by Shem (*v.* 4, 24), contain the sacred line of Christ from Adam to Abraham, and are inserted in his pedigree, Luke iii. 34–38, the order ascending as here it descends.

II. All the verses between repeat the account of the replenishing of the earth by the sons of Noah after the flood. The historian begins with those who were strangers to the church, the sons of Japhet, who were planted in the isles of the Gentiles, those western parts of the world, the countries of Europe. The sons of Ham moved southward towards Africa and those parts of Asia which lay that way. The posterity of Shem, *v.* 17–23, peopled Asia, and spread themselves eastward. The Assyrians, Syrians, Chaldeans, Persians, and Arabians, descended from these. At first the originals of the respective nations were known; but at this day the nations are so mingled with one another, by the enlargement of commerce and dominion, the transplanting of colonies, the carrying away of captives, and many other circumstances, that no one nation, no, nor the greatest part of any, is descended entire from any one of these fountains. Only this we are sure of, that God has *created of one blood all nations of men.* The great promise of the Messiah (says Bishop Patrick) was translated from Adam to Seth, from him to Shem, from him to Eber, and so to the Hebrew nation, who were entrusted, above all nations, with that sacred treasure, till the promise was performed and the Messiah had come.

Verses 28–54

All nations but the seed of Abraham are already shaken off from this genealogy: they have no part nor lot in this matter. *The Lord's portion is his people.* Not that we are to conclude that therefore

JAMIESON, FAUSSET, BROWN

CHAPTER 1

VSS. 1-23. ADAM'S LINE TO NOAH. **1. Adam, . . .**—"Begat" must be understood. Only that one member of the family is mentioned, who came in the direct order of succession.

4-23. Noah, Shem, Ham, and Japheth—The three sons of this patriarch are enumerated, partly because they were the founders of the new world, and partly because the fulfilment of Noah's prophecy (Gen. 9:25-27) could not otherwise appear to have been verified. **12. Casluhim (of whom came the Philistines), and Caphtorim**—a better rendering is, "and Casluhim, of whom came the Philistim and Caphtorim." They were brethren, the sons of Casluhim, and at first dwelt together, whence their names are used interchangeably. The Caphtorim are described as inhabiting Azzah, or Gaza, the seat of the Philistines. **14. the Jebusite,** etc.—From this verse to verse 17 the names are not those of individuals, but of people who all sprang from Canaan; and as several of them became extinct or were amalgamated with their brethren, their national appellations are given instead of the personal names of their ancestors. **17. Uz, and Hul, and Gether, and Meshech**—or Mash; these were the children of Aram, and *grandsons* of Shem (Gen. 10:23). **18. Arphaxad begat Shelah**—Cainan, the father's name, is omitted here. (See on Luke 3:36). **19. Peleg**—(See on Gen. 10:25). **22. Ebal**—or Obal (Gen. 10:28).

24-28. SHEM'S LINE TO ABRAHAM. **24. Shem,** etc.—This comprises a list of ten, inclusive of Abraham.

ADAM CLARKE

CHAPTER 1

1. *Adam, Sheth, Enosh.* That is, Adam was the father of Sheth or Seth, Seth was the father of Enosh, Enosh the father of Kenan, and so on. No notice is taken of Cain and Abel, or of any of the other sons of Adam. One line of patriarchs, from Adam to Noah, is what the historian intended to give.

MATTHEW HENRY

no particular persons of any other nation but the seed of Abraham found favour with God. There were many, very many, good people in the world, that lay out of the pale of God's covenant of peculiarity with Abraham, whose names were in the book of life, though not descended from any of the following families written in this book. *The Lord knows those that are his.* But Israel was a chosen nation, elect in type; and no other nation, in its national capacity, was so dignified and privileged as the Jewish nation was. That is the holy nation which is the subject of the sacred story; and therefore we are next to shake off all the seed of Abraham but the posterity of Jacob only.

I. We shall have little to say of the *Ishmaelites.* They were the sons of the bond-woman, that were to be cast out and not to be heirs with the child of the promise. Ishmael's twelve sons are just named here (*v.* 29–31), to show the performance of the promise God made to Abraham that he should become a great nation, and particularly that he should beget twelve princes, Gen. xvii. 20.

II. We shall have little to say of the *Midianites,* who descended from Abraham's children by Keturah. They were *children of the east* and were separated from Isaac, the heir of the promise (Gen. xxv. 6), and therefore they are only named here, *v.* 32.

III. We shall not have much to say of the *Edomites.* They had an inveterate enmity to God's Israel; yet because they descended from Esau, the son of Isaac, we have here an account of their families, and the names of some of their famous men, *v.* 35 to the end.

JAMIESON, FAUSSET, BROWN

29-31. SONS OF ISHMAEL. **29. These are their generations**—the heads of his twelve tribes. The great northern desert of Arabia, including the entire neck, was colonized by these tribes; and if we can recover, in the modern geography of this part of the country, Arab tribes bearing the names of those patriarchs, i.e., names corresponding with those preserved in the original catalogue of Scripture, we obtain at once so many evidences, not of mere similarity, but of absolute identification [FORSTER]. **Nebaioth**—gave rise to the Nabathæans of the classic, and the *Beni Nabat* of Oriental writers. **Kedar**—the Arab tribe, El Khedeyre, on the coast of Hedgar. **Abdeel**—Abdilla, the name of a tribe in Yemen. **30. Dumah**—Dumah and Tema, the great Arab tribes of Beni Teman. Thus this writer [HISTORICAL GEOGRAPHY OF ARABIA] traces the names of all the heads of the twelve tribes of Ishmael as perpetuated in the clans or tribes of the Arabs in the present day.

32, 33. SONS OF KETURAH. **32. sons of Keturah**—These became founders of nomadic tribes in the north of Arabia and Syria, as Midian of the Midianites (Gen. 36:35; Judg. 6:2). **and Shuah**—from whom Bildad sprang (Job 2:11).

34-42. POSTERITY OF ABRAHAM BY ESAU. **36. sons of Eliphaz**—the tribe Adites, in the center country of the Saracens, so called from his mother, Adah (Gen. 36:10). **Teman**—gave rise to the land of Teman, near the head of the Red Sea. **Omar**—the tribe Beni-Amma, settled at the northern point of Djebel Shera (Mount Seir). **Zephi**—the tribe Dzaf. **Gatam**—Katam, inhabited by the tribe Al Saruat, or "people of Sarah." **Kenaz**—the tribe Aenezes, a tribe whose settlement lies in the neighborhood of Syria. **Amalek**—the Beni Malak of Zohran, and the Beni Maledj of the Shat el Arab. **37. Reuel**—a powerful branch of the great Aeneze tribe, the *Rowalla* Arabs. **Shammah**—the great tribe Beni Shammar. In the same way, the names of the other kings and dukes are traced in the modern tribes of Arabia. But it is unnecessary to mention any more of these obscure nomads, except to notice that Jobab (vs. 44), one of the kings of Edom, is considered to be Job, and that his seat was in the royal city of Dinahab (Gen. 36:32), identified with O'Daeb, a well-known town in the center of Al Dahna, a great northern desert in the direction of Chaldea and the Euphrates [FORSTER].

ADAM CLARKE

C. J. BALL:

"The sons of Esau." Compare Gen. 36:9–13. In verse 36 the name of Timna occurs under the general heading, "Sons of Eliphaz." According to Gen. 36:12, Timna was a secondary wife of Eliphaz and mother of Amalek. Strange as this difference may at first sight appear, it is in fact absolutely unimportant. The writer's intention being simply to enumerate the principal branches of the sons of Eliphaz, the statement of the special relations between the different clans might be omitted here as fairly and naturally as the relations between Noah, Shem, Ham, and Japheth are left unnoticed in verse 4. Compare also verse 17, where Uz, Hul, etc., are apparently coordinated with Aram, although Gen. 10:23 expressly calls them "sons of Aram." The Vatican MS of the LXX has our text; the Alexandrine MS follows that of Gen. 36:12. It is at least curious that if Timna-Amalek be excluded from account, the sons of Esau are twelve in number. The fact is obscured in the compressed statement of the chronicler; but it becomes evident by reference to Gen. 36:11–14, where five sons are reckoned to Eliphaz (v. 11), four to Reuel (v. 13), and three to Esau's wife Aholibamah (v. 14), viz.: Jeush, Jaalam, and Korah.

—Ellicott's Commentary on the Whole Bible

43. *Before any king reigned over . . . Israel.* See Gen. xxxvi. 31, etc., where the same verses occur, as I have supposed borrowed from this place; and see the notes there.

For various particulars in this chapter see Genesis x and xxxvi and the parallel places.

MATTHEW HENRY

CHAPTER 2

Verses 1–17

I. The family of Jacob. His twelve sons are here named, that illustrious number so often celebrated almost throughout the whole Bible. At every turn we meet with the twelve tribes that descended from these twelve patriarchs. The personal character of several of them was none of the best (the first four were much blemished), and yet the covenant was entailed on their seed; for it was of grace, free grace, that it was said, *Jacob have I loved—not of works, lest any man should boast.*

II. The family of Judah. That tribe was most praised, most increased, of any of the tribes, and therefore the genealogy of it is the first and largest of them all. In the account of the first branches of that illustrious tree, of which Christ was to be the top branch, we meet, 1. With some that were very bad. Here is Er, Judah's eldest son, that was *evil in the sight of the Lord,* and was cut off, in the beginning of his days, *v.* 3. His next brother, Onan, fared no better. Here is Tamar, with whom Judah, her father-in-law, committed incest, *v.* 4. And here is Achan, called *Achar—a troubler,* that troubled Israel by taking of the accursed thing, *v.* 7. 2. With some that were very wise and good, as Heman and Ethan, Calcol and Dara, who were not perhaps the immediate sons of Zerah, but descendants from him, and are named because they were the glory of their father's house, 1 Kings iv. 31. 3. With some that were very great, as Nahshon, who was prince of Judah when the camp of Israel was formed in the wilderness, and so led the van in that glorious march, and Salman, or Salmon, who was in that post of honour when they entered into Canaan, *v.* 10, 11.

III. The family of Jesse, of which a particular account is kept for the sake of David, and the Son of David, who is *a rod out of the stem of Jesse,* Isa. xi. 1. Hence it appears that David was a seventh son, and that his three great commanders, Joab, Abishai, and Asahel, were the sons of one of his sisters, and Amasa of another.

JAMIESON, FAUSSET, BROWN

CHAPTER 2

Vss. 1, 2. SONS OF ISRAEL. Vss. 3-12. POSTERITY OF JUDAH. **3. The sons of Judah**—His descendants are enumerated first, because the right and privileges of the primogeniture had been transferred to him (Gen. 49:8), and because from his tribe the Messiah was to spring. **6. Zimri, and Ethan, and Heman, and Calcol, and Dara**—These five are here stated to be the sons of Zerah, i.e., of Ezra, whence they were called Ezrahites (I Kings 4:31). In that passage they are called "the sons of Mahol," which, however, is to be taken not as a proper name, but appellatively for "sons of music, dancing," etc. The traditional fame of their great sagacity and acquirements had descended to the time of Solomon and formed a standard of comparison for showing the superior wisdom of that monarch. Jewish writers say that they were looked up to as prophets by their countrymen during the abode in Egypt. **7. the sons of Carmi**—He was the son of Zimri, or Zabdi, as he is called (Josh. 7:1). **Achar**—or Achan (Josh. 7:1). This variety in the form of the name is with great propriety used here, since Achar means "troubler."

13-17. CHILDREN OF JESSE. **15. David the seventh**—As it appears (I Sam. 16:10; 17:12) that Jesse had eight sons, the presumption is from David being mentioned here as the seventh son of his father, that one of them had died at an early age, without leaving issue. **17. Jether the Ishmaelite**—(cf. II Sam. 17:25). In that passage he is called Ithra an Israelite; and there seems no reason why, in the early days of David, anyone should be specially distinguished as an Israelite. The presumption is in favor of the reading followed by the *Sept.,* which calls him "Jetra the Jezreelite." The circumstance of his settling in another tribe, or of a woman marrying out of her own tribe, was sufficiently rare and singular to call for the statement that Abigail was married to a man of Jezreel.

18-55. POSTERITY OF CALEB. **18. Caleb the son of Hezron**—The notices concerning this person appear confused in our version. In vs. 19 he is said to be the father of Hur, whereas in vs. 50 he is

ADAM CLARKE

CHAPTER 2

F. B. MEYER:

"These are the sons of Israel" (1 Chron. 2:1). It is noticeable how irrevocable the divine sentence is on a human life. Of Er, the grave, impartial voice of Scripture says he was "wicked in the sight of the Lord"; of Achan, he was the "troubler of Israel, and committed a trespass in the accursed thing." These sentences are recorded with such precision as to admit of no dispute, no appeal; and they sum up the life.

But was there not much else in each of these men? Were there not tender or chivalrous moments? Did they never shine for a moment in some transfiguring ray? Was all their life dyed with these sad and sombre hues? Ah, it may have been so—still the one thing that the Scripture tells of them is the sin in which all their life seemed to culminate and express itself. With unerring accuracy God can distinguish the one act or word by which the character is revealed. He may forgive it, but He holds it up as the epitome or summary of what that life was.

Let us see how we live, walking before God with reverent fear, watching and praying, because any moment may give birth to a word or act which may characterize our life in all coming time. *—Great Verses Through the Bible*

MATTHEW HENRY

Verses 18–55

Very few of those to whom this paragraph relates are mentioned anywhere else. 1. Here we find Bezaleel, who was head-workman in building the tabernacle, Exod. xxxi. 2. 2. Hezron was one of the seventy that went down with Jacob into Egypt, Gen. xlvi. 12.

The achievements of Jair, here mentioned (*v.* 22, 23), were long after the conquest of Canaan.

The pedigree of several of these terminates, not in a person, but in a place or country, as one is said to be *the father of Kirjath-jearim* (*v.* 50), another of Bethlehem (*v.* 51), which was afterwards David's city, because these places fell to their lot in the division of the land. Among all these great families we are glad to find some that were *families of scribes, v.* 55. *Would to God that all the Lord's people were prophets*—all the families of Israel families of scribes, well instructed to the kingdom of heaven.

JAMIESON, FAUSSET, BROWN

called "the son of Hur." The words in this latter passage have been transposed in the copying, and should be read thus, "Hur the son of Caleb." **begat children of Azubah his wife, and of Jerioth**—The former was his spouse, while Jerioth seems to have been a secondary wife, and the mother of the children whose names are here given. On the death of his principal wife, he married Ephrath, and by her had Hur. **21. Hezron . . . daughter of Machir the father of Gilead**—i.e., chief of that town, which with the lands adjacent was no doubt the property of Machir, who was so desirous of a male heir. He was grandson of Joseph. The wife of Machir was of the tribe of Manasseh (Num. 26:29). **22. Jair, who had three and twenty cities in the land of Gilead**—As the son of Segub and the grandson of Hezron, he was of the tribe of Judah; but from his maternal descent he is called (Num. 32:41; Deut. 3:14) "the son of Manasseh." This designation implies that his inheritance lay in that tribe in right of his grandmother; in other words, his *maternal* and *adopting* great-grandfather was Machir the son of Manasseh. Jair, inheriting his property, was his lineal representative; and accordingly this is expressly stated to be the case; for the village group of "Havoth-Jair" was awarded to him in that tribe, in consequence of his valiant and patriotic exploits. This arrangement, however, took place previous to the law (Num. 36), by which it was enacted that heiresses were to marry in their own tribe. But this instance of Jair shows that in the case of a man obtaining an inheritance in another tribe it required him to become thoroughly incorporated with it as a representative of the family through which the inheritance was received. He had been adopted into Manasseh, and it would never have been imagined that he was other than "a son of Manasseh" naturally, had not this passage given information supplementary to that of the passage in Numbers. **23. he took**—rather "he had taken." This statement is accounting for his acquisition of so large a territory; he got it by right of conquest from the former possessors. **Kenath**—This place, along with its group of surrounding villages, was gained by Nobah, one of Jair's officers sent by him to capture it (Num. 32:1, 2). **All these belonged to the sons of Machir**—In their number Jair is included as having completely identified himself by his marriage and residence in Gilead with the tribe of Manasseh. **24. Caleb-ephratah**—so called from uniting the names of husband and wife (vs. 19), and supposed to be the same as was afterwards called Bethlehem-ephratah. **Ashur, the father of Tekoa**—(II Sam. 14:2-4). He is called the father, either from his being the first founder, or perhaps the ruler, of the city. **34. Sheshan had no sons, but daughters**—either he had no sons alive at his death, or his family consisted wholly of daughters, of whom Ahlai (vs. 31) was one, she being specially mentioned on account of the domestic relations about to be noted. **35 Sheshan gave his daughter to Jarha his servant to wife**—The adoption and marriage of a foreign slave in the family where he is serving, is far from being a rare or extraordinary occurrence in Eastern countries. It is thought, however, by some to have been a connection not sanctioned by the law of Moses [MICHAELIS]. But this is not a well-founded objection, as the history of the Jews furnishes not a few examples of foreign proselytes in the same manner obtaining an inheritance in Israel; and doubtless Jarha had previously embraced the Jewish faith in place of the grovelling idolatries of his native Egypt. In such a case, therefore, there could be no legal difficulty. Being a foreign slave, he had no inheritance in a different tribe to injure by this connection; while his marriage with Sheshan's daughter led to his adoption into the tribe of Judah, as well as his becoming heir of the family property. **42. the sons of Caleb**—(cf. vss. 18, 25). The sons here noticed were the fruit of his union with a third wife. **55. the families of the scribes**—either civil or ecclesiastical officers of the Kenite origin, who are here classed with the tribe of Judah, not as being descended from it, but as dwelling within its territory, and in a measure incorporated with its people. **Jabez**—a place in Judah (ch. 4:9). **Kenites that came of Hemath**—who settled in Judah, and were thus distinguished from another division of the Kenite clan which dwelt in Manasseh (Judg. 4:11).

ADAM CLARKE

42. ***Now the sons of Caleb.*** **This was not Caleb the son of Jephunneh, but Caleb the son of Hezron, vv. 18, 50.**

KEIL–DELITZSCH:

The list of the twelve sons of Israel (2:1, 2) serves as foundation and starting point for the genealogies of the tribes of Israel which follow. The enumeration of the families of the tribe of Judah commences in verse 3 with the naming of Judah's sons, and extends to chapter 4:23. The tribe of Judah has issued from the posterity of only three of the five sons of Judah, viz. from Shelah, Pharez, and Zerah; but it was subdivided into five great families, as Hezron and Hamul, the two sons of Pharez, also founded families. The list of our three chapters give us: (1) from the family of Zerah only the names of some famous men (2:6–8); (2) the descendants of Hezron in the three branches corresponding to the three sons of Hezron, into which they divided themselves (2:9), viz. the descendants of Ram to David (2:10–17), of Caleb (2:18–24), and of Jerahmeel (2:25–41). Then there follow in chapter 2:42–55 four other lists of descendants of Caleb, who peopled a great number of the cities of Judah; and then in chapter 3 we have a list of the sons of David and the line of kings of the house of David, down to the grandsons of Zerubbabel; and finally, in chapter 4:1–23, other genealogical fragments as to the posterity of Pharez and Shelah. Of Hamul, consequently, no descendants are noticed, unless perhaps some of the groups ranged together in chapter 4:8–22, whose connection with the heads of the families of Judah is not given, are of his lineage. The lists collected in chapter 4:1–20 are clearly only supplements to the genealogies of the great families contained in chapters 2 and 3, which the author of the Chronicle found in the same fragmentary state in which they are communicated to us.

—Commentary on the Old Testament

CHAPTER 3 (MATTHEW HENRY)

Verses 1–9

We had an account of David's sons, 2 Sam. iii. 2, &c., and v. 14, &c. Some of them were a grief to him, as Amnon, Absalom, and Adonijah; and none

CHAPTER 3 (JAMIESON, FAUSSET, BROWN)

Vss. 1-9. SONS OF DAVID. **1-3. Now these were the sons of David which were born unto him in Hebron**—It is of consequence for the proper understanding of events in the domestic history of David,

CHAPTER 3 (ADAM CLARKE)

MATTHEW HENRY

imitated his piety or devotion except Solomon, and he came far short of it.

One of them, which Bath-sheba bore to him, he called Nathan, probably in honour of Nathan the prophet, who reproved him for his sin in that matter and was instrumental to bring him to repentance. It seems he loved him the better for it as long as he lived. It is wisdom to esteem those our best friends that deal faithfully with us. From this son of David our Lord Jesus descended, as appears Luke iii. 31. Here are two Elishamas, and two Eliphelets, *v.* 6, 8. Probably the two former were dead, and therefore David called two more by their names.

Verses 10–24

David having nineteen sons, we may suppose them to have raised many noble families in Israel whom we never hear of in the history. But the scripture gives us an account only of the descendants of Solomon here, and of Nathan, Luke iii. We have here, 1. The great and celebrated names by which the line of David is drawn down to the captivity, the kings of Judah in a lineal succession. Seldom has a crown gone in a direct line from father to son for seventeen descents together, as here. This was the recompence of David's piety. About the time of the captivity the lineal descent was interrupted, and the crown went from one brother to another and from a nephew to an uncle. 2. The less famous, and most of them very obscure names, in which the house of David subsisted after the captivity.

The only famous man of that house that we meet with at their return from captivity was Zerubbabel. Salathiel is said to be *the son of* Jeconiah because adopted by him, and because, as some think, he succeeded him in the dignity to which he was restored by Evil-merodach. Otherwise Jeconiah was written childless: he was *the signet God plucked from his right hand* (Jer. xxii. 24), and in his room Zerubbabel was placed, and therefore God saith to him (Hag. ii. 23), *I will make thee as a signet.* The posterity of Zerubbabel here bear not the same names that they do in the genealogies (Matt. i, or Luke iii), but those no doubt were taken from the public registers which the priests kept of all the families of Judah, especially that of David.

JAMIESON, FAUSSET, BROWN

to bear in mind the place and time of his sons' birth. The oldest son, born *after* his father's *accession* to the sovereign authority, is according to Eastern notions, the proper heir to the throne. And hence the natural aspirations of ambition in Ammon, who was long unaware of the alienation of the crown, and could not be easily reconciled to the claims of a younger brother being placed above his own (see on II Sam. 3:1-5). **3. Eglah his wife**—supposed to be another name of Michal, who, though she had no son after her mockery of David for dancing before the ark, might have had one previous to that time. She has the title of wife appended to her name because she was his proper wife; and the mention of her name last probably arose from the circumstance that, having been withdrawn from David and married to another husband but afterwards restored, she had in reality become the last of his wives. **5. four, of Bath-shua the daughter of Ammiel**—or Bath-sheba (II Sam. 11:3), and there her father is called Eliam. Of course Solomon was not her "only son," but he is called so (Prov. 4:3) from the distinguished affection of which he was the object; and though the oldest, he is named the last of Bath-sheba's children. **6. Elishama and Eliphelet**—Two sons of the same name are twice mentioned (vs. 8). They were the children of different mothers, and had probably some title or epithet appended by which the one was distinguished from the other. Or, it might be, that the former two were dead, and their names had been given to sons afterwards born to preserve their memories. **8. nine**—The number of David's sons born after his removal to Jerusalem, was eleven (II Sam. 5:14), but only nine are mentioned here: two of them being omitted, either in consequence of their early deaths or because they left no issue.

10-16. HIS LINE TO ZEDEKIAH. **10. Solomon's son was Rehoboam,** etc.—David's line is here drawn down to the captivity, through a succession of good and bad, but still influential and celebrated, monarchs. It has rarely happened that a crown has been transmitted from father to son, in lineal descent, for seventeen reigns. But this was the promised reward of David's piety. There is, indeed, observable some vacillation towards the close of this period—the crown passing from one brother to another, an even from uncle to nephew—a sure sign of disorderly times and a disjointed government. **15. Zedekiah**—called the son of Josiah (cf. Jer. 1:3; 37:1), but in II Chronicles 36:19 he is described as the brother of Jehoiachin, who was the son of Jehoiakim, and consequently the *grandson* of Josiah. Words expressive of affinity or relationship are used with great latitude in the Hebrew. **Shallum**—No king of this name is mentioned in the history of Josiah's sons (II Kings 23 and 14), but there is a notice of Shallum the son of Josiah (Jer. 22:11), who reigned in the stead of his father, and who is generally supposed to be Jehoahaz, a younger son, here called the fourth, of Josiah.

17-24. SUCCESSORS OF JECONIAH. **17. the sons of Jeconiah; Assir**—rather, "Jeconiah the prisoner, or captive." This record of his condition was added to show that Salathiel was born during the captivity in Babylon (cf. Matt. 1:12). Jeconiah was written childless (Jer. 22:30), a prediction which (as the words that follow explain) meant that this unfortunate monarch should have no son succeeding him on the throne. **18. Malchiram also**—As far as Jeconiah, everything is plain; but there is reason to suspect that the text in the subsequent verses has been dislocated and disarranged. The object of the sacred historian is to trace the royal line through Zerubbabel; yet, according to the present reading, the genealogical stem cannot be drawn from Jeconiah downwards. The following arrangement of the text is given as removing all difficulties [DAVIDSON'S HERM.] vs. 17. And the sons of Jeconiah the the captive, Salathiel (Shealtiel, Ezra 3:2; Neh. 12:1; Hag. 1:12, 14; 2:2) his son; vs. 18. And the sons of Salathiel; Zerubbabel and Shimei; and the sons of Zerubbabel; Meshullam, Hananiah, and Shelomith their sister. vs. 19. And Hashubah, and Ohel, and Berechiah, and Hasadiah, Jushab-hezed. vs. 20. And Malchiram, and Rephaiah, and Shenazar, Jecamiah, Hoshama, and Nedabiah. vs. 21. The sons of Hananiah; Pelatiah and Jesaiah; the sons of Rephaiah; his son Arnan, his son Obadiah, his son Shecaniah.

ADAM CLARKE

1. *The second, Daniel.* In 2 Sam. iii. 3, this person is called Chileab; he probably had two names. The Targum says, "The second, Daniel, who was also called Chileab, because he was in every respect like to his father." The Targumist refers here to the import of the word *ke-le-ab*, "like to the father."

5. *Shimea, and Shobab.* Solomon is mentioned last, though he was the eldest of these four sons, because the genealogy was to be continued from him. *Bath-shua* is the same as Bath-sheba.

6. *Elishama, and Eliphelet.* In this and the eighth verse these two names occur twice; some think this is a mistake, but others suppose that two persons of these names died young, and that the next born received the name of the deceased.

8. *Nine.* There are thirteen if we count the four sons of Bath-sheba, and nine without them; and in the Second Book of Samuel there are eleven, reckoning the above four, and without them only seven. In the Book of Samuel probably only those who were alive were reckoned, while the author of the Chronicles comprises those also who were dead in this enumeration. Jarchi supposes that the duplicate Elishama and Eliphelet are those which increase the regular number seven to nine.

9. *And Tamar their sister.* This is the only daughter of David whose name is on record; and yet he is said to have had both sons and daughters, 2 Sam. v. 13.

16. *Zedekiah his son.* If this be the same who was the last king of Judah, before the Captivity, the word *son* must be taken here to signify "successor"; for it is certain that Zedekiah was the successor of Jeconiah, and that Zedekiah was the son of Josiah, and not of Jehoiakim.

17. *The sons of Jeconiah.* Jeremiah has said, chap. xxii. 30, that Jeconiah, or as he calls him, Coniah, should be childless. But this must refer to his posterity being deprived of the throne, and indeed thus the prophet interprets it himself: "For no man of his seed shall prosper, sitting upon the throne of David, and ruling any more in Judah." *Assir.* Salathiel was not the son of Assir, but of Jeconiah, Matt. i. 12. Who then was Assir? Possibly nobody; for as the Hebrew *assir* signifies a "prisoner," it may be considered as an epithet of Jeconiah, who we know was a very long time prisoner in Babylon (see 2 Kings xxiv. 15).

19. *The sons of Pedaiah.* Houbigant thinks these words should be omitted. *Pedaiah* is wanting in the Arabic and Syriac. If this be omitted, Zerubbabel will appear to be the son of Salathiel, according to Matt. i. 12, and not the son of Pedaiah, as here stated.

22. *The sons of Shemaiah . . . six.* Five only are found in the text, and the versions give us no assistance; neither do the MSS. correct the place. If the father be not here included with his sons, some name must be lost out of the text.

MATTHEW HENRY — CHAPTER 4

Verses 1–10

One reason, no doubt, why Ezra is here most particular in the register of the tribe of Judah is

JAMIESON, FAUSSET, BROWN — CHAPTER 4

VSS. 1-8. POSTERITY OF JUDAH BY CALEB THE SON OF HUR. **1. the sons of Judah**—i.e., the descendants—for with the exception of Pharez, none of those

ADAM CLARKE — CHAPTER 4

1. *The sons of Judah.* A genealogy of this tribe has already been given in the second chapter. It is here introduced again, with some

MATTHEW HENRY

because it was that tribe which, with its appendages, Simeon, Benjamin, and Levi, made up the kingdom of Judah, which now when this was written, returned out of captivity, when the generality of the other tribes were lost in the kingdom of Assyria. The most remarkable person in this paragraph is Jabez, the founder of one of the families of Aharel, mentioned *v.* 8.

I. The reason of his name: his mother gave him the name with this reason, *Because I bore him with sorrow, v.* 9. Usually the sorrow in bearing is afterwards forgotten *for joy that the child is born*; but here it seems it was remembered when the child came to be circumcised, and care was taken to perpetuate the remembrance of it while he lived. 1. That it might be a continual memorandum to herself, to be thankful to God as long as she lived for bringing her through that sorrow. 2. That it might likewise be a memorandum to him what this world is into which she bore him, a vale of tears, in which he must expect *few days and full of trouble.* It might also remind him to love and honour his mother, and labour, in everything, to be a comfort to her who brought him into the world with so much sorrow.

II. The eminence of his character: *He was more honourable than his brethren.* We have most reason to think it was upon the account of his learning and piety. 1. In learning, because we find that *the families of the scribes dwelt at Jabez* (*ch.* ii. 55), a city which, it is likely, took its name from him. 2. In piety, because we find here that he was a praying man.

III. The prayer he made just when he was setting out in the world. He set himself to acknowledge God in all his ways, put himself under the divine blessing, and protection, and prospered accordingly. Observe,

1. To whom he prayed; he *called on the God of Israel*, a God in covenant with his people, the God with whom Jacob wrestled and prevailed and was thence called Israel.

2. What was the nature of his prayer. (1) As the *margin* reads it, it was a solemn vow—*If thou wilt bless me indeed, &c.*, and then the sense is imperfect, but may easily be filled up from Jacob's vow, or some such like—*then thou shalt be my God.* He does, as it were, give God a blank paper, let him write what he pleases: "Lord, if thou wilt bless me and keep me, do what thou wilt with me, I will be at thy command and disposal for ever." (2) As the *text* reads it, it was the language of a most ardent and affectionate desire: *O that thou wouldst bless me!*

3. What was the matter of his prayer. Four things he prayed for:—(1) That God would bless him indeed: "That, *blessing, thou wilt bless me*, bless me greatly with manifold and abundant blessings." (2) That he would enlarge his coast, that he would prosper his endeavours for the increase of what fell to his lot either by work or war. (3) That God's hand might be with him. God's hand with us, to lead us, protect us, strengthen us, and to work all our works in us and for us, is indeed a hand sufficient for us, all-sufficient. (4) That he would keep him from evil, the evil of sin, the evil of trouble, all the evil designs of his enemies, that they might not hurt him, or grieve him.

4. *God granted him that which he requested*, prospered him remarkably, and gave him success in his undertakings, in his studies, in his worldly business, in his conflicts with the Caananites.

Verses 11–23

1. Here is a whole family of craftsmen that applied themselves to all sorts of manufactures, in which they were ingenious and industrious above their neighbours, *v.* 14. There was a valley where they lived which was, from them, called *the valley of craftsmen.* 2. One of these married the daughter of Pharaoh (*v.* 18), which was the common name of the kings of Egypt. 3. Another is said to be the *father of the house of those that wrought fine linen, v.* 21. They were the best weavers in the kingdom, and they brought up their children, from one generation to another, to the same business. His posterity inhabited the city of Maseshah, the manufacture or staple commodity of which place was linen-cloth, with which their kings and priests were clothed. 4. Another family had had *dominion in Moab*, but were now in *servitude in Babylon, v.* 22, 23. (1) It was found among the *ancient things* that they had the *dominion in Moab.* Probably in David's time, when that country was conquered, they transplanted themselves thither. (2) Their posterity were now potters and gardeners in Babylon, where they *dwelt with the king for his work*, got a good livelihood and therefore cared not for returning to their own land, after the years of captivity had expired.

JAMIESON, FAUSSET, BROWN

here mentioned were his immediate sons. Indeed, the others are mentioned solely to introduce the name of Shobal, whose genealogy the historian intended to trace (ch. 2:52).

9-20. Of Jabez, and His Prayer. **9. Jabez**—was, as many think, the son of Coz, or Kenaz, and is here eulogized for his sincere and fervent piety, as well, perhaps, as for some public and patriotic works which he performed. The Jewish writers affirm that he was an eminent doctor in the law, whose reputation drew so many scribes around him that a town was called by his name (ch. 2:55); and to the piety of his character this passage bears ample testimony. The memory of the critical circumstances which marked his birth was perpetuated in his name (cf. Gen. 35:15); and yet, in the development of his high talents or distinguished worth in later life, his mother must have found a satisfaction and delight that amply compensated for all her early trials. His prayer which is here recorded, and which, like Jacob's, is in the form of a vow (Gen. 28:20), seems to have been uttered when he was entering on an important or critical service, for the successful execution of which he placed confidence neither on his own nor his people's prowess, but looked anxiously for the aid and blessing of God. The enterprise was in all probability the expulsion of the Canaanites from the territory he occupied; and as this was a war of extermination, which God Himself had commanded, His blessing could be the more reasonably asked and expected in preserving them from all the evils to which the undertaking might expose him. In the words, "that it may not grieve me," and which might be more literally rendered, "that I may have no more sorrow," there is an allusion to the meaning of his name—Jabez—signifying grief; and the import of this petition is, Let me not experience the grief which my name implies, and which my sins may well produce. **10. God granted him that which he requested**—Whatever was the kind of undertaking which roused his anxieties, Jabez enjoyed a remarkable degree of prosperity, and God, in this instance, proved that He was not only the hearer, but the answerer of prayer. **13. the sons of Kenaz**—the grandfather of Caleb, who from that relationship is called a Kenezite (Num. 32:12). **14. Joah, the father of the valley of Carashim**—lit., the father of the inhabitants of the valley—the valley of craftsmen, as the word denotes. They dwelt together, according to a custom which, independently of any law, extensively prevails in Eastern countries for persons of the same trade to inhabit the same street or the same quarter, and to follow the same occupation from father to son, through many generations. Their occupation was probably that of carpenters, and the valley where they lived seems to have been in the neighborhood of Jerusalem (Neh. 11:35). **17, 18. she bare Miriam**—It is difficult, as the verses stand at present, to see who is meant. The following readjustment of the text clears away the obscurity: "These are the sons of Bithiah the daughter of Pharaoh, which Mered took, and she bare Miriam, and his wife Jehudijah bare Jezreel," etc. **Jehudijah**—the Jewess, to distinguish her from his other wife, who was an Egyptian. This passage records a very interesting fact—the marriage of an Egyptian princess to a descendant of Caleb. The marriage must have taken place in the wilderness. The barriers of a different national language and national religion kept the Hebrews separate from the Egyptians; but they did not wholly prevent intimacies, and even occasional intermarriages between private individuals of the two nations. Before such unions, however, could be sanctioned, the Egyptian party must have renounced idolatry, and this daughter of Pharaoh, as appears from her name, had become a convert to the worship of the God of Israel.

21-23. Posterity of Shelah. **21. Laadah . . . the father . . . of the house of them that wrought fine linen**—Here, again, is another incidental evidence that in very early times certain trades were followed by particular families among the Hebrews, apparently in hereditary succession. Their knowledge of the art of linen manufacture had been, most probably, acquired in Egypt, where the duty of bringing up families to the occupations of their forefathers was a compulsory obligation, whereas in Israel, as in many parts of Asia to this day, it was optional, though common. **22, 23. had the dominion in Moab, and Jashubi-lehem**—"And these are ancient things" seems a strange rendering of a proper name; and, besides, it conveys a meaning that has no bearing on the record. The following improved translation has been suggested: "Sojourned in Moab, but returned to Bethlehem and Adaberim-athekim. These and the inhabitants of Netaim and Gedera

ADAM CLARKE

variations. Probably there were different copies in the public registers; and the writer of this book, finding that this second one contained some remarkable particulars, thought proper to insert it in this place.

7. *And Ethnan.* After this word we should, with the Targum, read Coz, whose posterity is mentioned in the next verse. Coz was probably the same as Kenaz.

8. *The son of Harum.* Jabez should be mentioned at the end of this verse, else he is as a consequent without an antecedent.

15. *Caleb the son of Jephunneh.* We have already met with this eminent person in Num. xiii. 6, 30; xiv. 24; and elsewhere, and seen his courageous piety and inflexible integrity.

23. *These were the potters.* They were probably brickmakers; perhaps potters also, who had their dwelling in low grounds, and fabricated the clay into pots and bricks that was digged up in forming fences in the king's domains.

MATTHEW HENRY

Verses 24–43

Some of the genealogies of the tribe of Simeon. Of this tribe it is said that they *increased greatly*, but *not like the children of Judah*, *v.* 27. 1. The cities allotted them (*v.* 28), of which see Joshua xix. 1, &c.

When it is said that they were theirs *unto the reign of David* (*v.* 31) intimation is given that when the ten tribes revolted from the house of David many of the Simeonites quitted these cities, because they lay within Judah, and seated themselves elsewhere. 2. The ground they got elsewhere. It was in the days of Hezekiah that a generation of Simeonites, whose tribe had long crouched and truckled, was animated to make these bold efforts. (1) Some of them attacked a place in Arabia called *the entrance of Gedor*, made themselves masters of it, and dwelt there. This adds to the glory of Hezekiah's pious reign, that, as his kingdom in general prospered, so did particular families. (2) Others of them, to the number of 500, under the command of four brethren, here named, made a descent upon Mount Seir, and smote the Amalekites, and took possession of their country, *v.* 42, 43.

JAMIESON, FAUSSET, BROWN

were potters employed by the king in his own work." Gedera or Gederoth, and Netaim, belonged to the tribe of Judah, and lay on the southeast border of the Philistines' territory (Josh. 15-36; II Chron. 28: 18).

24-43. OF SIMEON. **24. The sons of Simeon**—They are classed along with those of Judah, as their possession was partly taken out of the extensive territory of the latter (Josh. 19:1). The difference in several particulars of the genealogy given here from that given in other passages is occasioned by some of the persons mentioned having more than one name. **27. his brethren had not many children**—(see on Num. 1:22; 26:14).

31-43. These were their cities unto the reign of David—In consequence of the sloth or cowardice of the Simeonites, some of the cities within their allotted territory were only nominally theirs. They were never taken from the Philistines until David's time, when, the Simeonites having forfeited all claim to them, he assigned them to his own tribe of Judah (I Sam. 27:6). **38, 39. increased greatly, and they went to the entrance of Gedor**—Simeon having only a part of the land of Judah, they were forced to seek accommodation elsewhere; but their establishment in the new and fertile pastures of Gederah was soon broken up; for, being attacked by a band of nomad plunderers, they were driven from place to place till some of them effected by force a settlement on Mount Seir.

ADAM CLARKE

24. *The sons of Simeon.* This genealogy is very different from that given in Gen. xlvi. 10, and Num. xxvi. 12. This may be occasioned by the same person having several names, one list taking one name, another list some other, and so on. To reconcile is impossible; to attempt it, useless.

27. *Neither did all their family multiply.* In Num. i. 23 the number of all the families of Simeon was 59,300; and that of Judah was, v. 27, not less than 74,600. When the next census was made, Numbers xxvi, the tribe of Judah amounted to 76,500, an increase of 1,900; while the tribe of Simeon amounted only to 22,200, a decrease of 37,100. It was at that time the smallest tribe in Israel.

31. *These were their cities unto the reign of David.* It appears that David took some of the cities of the Simeonites, and added them to Judah; Ziklag, for instance, 1 Sam. xxvii. 6. As the tribe of Simeon had withdrawn their allegiance from the house of David, the kings of Judah extended their domination as far as possible into the territories of that tribe, so that they were obliged to seek pasture for their flocks at Gedor and in the mountains of Seir, as we find in vv. 39-42.

40. *They of Ham had dwelt there of old.* These were probably either Philistines or Egyptians, who dwelt at Gedor, which was situated in the environs of Joppa and Samnia. Those whom the 500 Simeonites expelled from Seir were Amalekites, v. 43.

43. *They smote the rest of the Amalekites.* Those who had escaped in the war which Saul made against them (see 1 Sam. xiv. 48) and from David, who had attacked them afterwards, 2 Sam. viii. 12.

MATTHEW HENRY

CHAPTER 5

Verses 1–17

An extract out of the genealogies,

I. Of the tribe of Reuben, where we have,

1. The reason why this tribe is thus postponed. Reuben the first born of Israel forfeited his birthright by defiling his father's concubine, Gen. xlix. 4. The advantages of the birthright were dominion and a double portion. Reuben having forfeited these, it was thought too much that both should be transferred to any one, and therefore they were divided. (1) Joseph had the double portion; for two tribes descended from him, Ephraim and Manasseh, each of whom had a child's part (for so Jacob by faith blessed them, Heb. xi. 21; Gen. xlviii. 15, 22), and each of those tribes was as considerable, and made as good a figure, as any one of the twelve, except Judah. But, (2) Judah had the dominion; on him the dying patriarch entailed the sceptre, Gen. xlix. 10. Of him came the chief ruler, David first, and, in the fulness of time, Messiah the Prince, Micah v. 2.

2. The genealogy of the princes of this tribe to Beerah, who was head of this clan when the king of Assyria carried them captive, *v.* 4–6.

3. The enlargement of the coasts of this tribe. They increasing, and their cattle being multiplied, they crowded out their neighbours the Hagarites, and extended their conquests, *v.* 9, 10.

II. Of the tribe of Gad. Some great families of that tribe are here named (*v.* 12), seven that were the children of Abihail, whose pedigree is carried upwards from the son to the father (*v.* 14, 15), as that *v.* 4, 5, is brought downwards from father to son.

JAMIESON, FAUSSET, BROWN

CHAPTER 5

VSS. 1-10. THE LINE OF REUBEN. **1. Now the sons of Reuben**—In proceeding to give this genealogy, the sacred historian states, in a parenthesis (vss. 1, 2), the reason why it was not placed first, as Reuben was the oldest son of Jacob. The birthright, which by a foul crime he had forfeited, implied not only dominion, but a double portion (Deut. 21:17); and both of these were transferred to Joseph, whose two sons having been adopted as the children of Jacob (Gen. 48:5), received each an allotted portion, as forming two distinct tribes in Israel. Joseph then was entitled to the precedency; and yet, as his posterity was not mentioned first, the sacred historian judged it necessary to explain that "the genealogy was not to be reckoned after the birthright," but with a reference to a superior honor and privilege that had been conferred on Judah—not the man, but the tribe, whereby it was invested with the pre-eminence over all the other tribes, and out of it was to spring David with his royal lineage, and especially the great Messiah (Heb. 7:14). These were the two reasons why, in the order of enumeration, the genealogy of Judah is introduced before that of Reuben. **9. Eastward he inhabited unto the entering in of the wilderness from the river Euphrates**—The settlement was on the east of Jordan, and the history of this tribe, which never took any part in the public affairs or movements of the nation, is comprised in "the multiplication of their cattle in the land of Gilead," in their wars with the Bedouin sons of Hagar, and in the simple labors of pastoral life. They had the right of pasture over an extensive mountain range—the great wilderness of Kedemoth (Deut. 2:26) and the Euphrates being a security against their enemies.

11-26. THE LINE OF GAD. **11-15. the children of Gad dwelt over against them**—The genealogy of the Gadites and the half-tribe of Manasseh (vs. 24) is given along with that of the Reubenites, as these three were associated in a separate colony. **16. Sharon**—The term Sharon was applied as descriptive of any place of extraordinary beauty and productiveness. There were three places in Palestine so called. This Sharon lay east of the Jordan. **upon their borders**—i.e., of Gilead and Bashan: Gilead proper, or at least the largest part, belonged to the Reubenites; and Bashan, the greatest portion of it, belonged to the Manassites. The Gadites occupied an intermediate settlement on the land which lay upon their borders. **17. All these were reckoned . . . in the days of Jotham**—His long reign and freedom from foreign wars as well as intestine troubles were favorable for taking a census of the people. **and in the days of Jeroboam**—the second of that name.

ADAM CLARKE

CHAPTER 5

1. *The sons of Reuben the firstborn.* As Reuben was the eldest son of Jacob, why was not his genealogy reviewed first? This verse answers the question; he lost the birthright because of the transgression mentioned in Gen. xxxv. 22 and xlix. 4, and the precedency was given to Judah; from him therefore came the chief ruler. This appears to be the meaning of the place.

2. *And of him came the chief ruler.* This is, by both the Syriac and Arabic, understood of Christ: "From Judah the King Messiah shall proceed."

6. *Beerah his son.* After their separation from the house of David the ten tribes continued to have princes of the tribes; and this continued till the time that Tiglath-pileser carried them captives into Assyria. At that time *Beerah* was their *prince* or "chief"; and with him this species of dominion or precedency terminated.

8. *Who dwelt in Aroer.* This town was situated on the river Arnon; and *Nebo* was both a city and a mountain in the same country. They both lay on the other side of Jordan.

10. *And they dwelt in their tents.* The *Hagarites* were tribes of nomad Arabs; people who lived in tents, without any fixed dwellings, and whose property consisted in cattle. The descendants of Reuben extirpated these Hagarites, seized on their property and their tents, and dwelt in their place.

16. *The suburbs of Sharon.* There were three places of this name: that mentioned here was a district in the country of Bashan beyond Jordan (see Josh. xii. 18); there was another that lay between Caesarea of Palestine and Joppa; and there was a third between Mount Tabor and the Sea of Tiberias.

MATTHEW HENRY

Verses 18–26

The heads of the half-tribe of Manasseh, that were seated on the other side Jordan, are named here, *v.* 23, 24. Their lot, at first, was Bashan only; but afterwards they increased so much in wealth and power that they spread far north, even unto Hermon. Two things only are here recorded concerning these tribes on the other side Jordan, in which they were all concerned. They all shared,

I. In a glorious victory over the Hagarites, so the Ishmaelites were now called, to remind them that they were *the sons of the bond-woman*, that was *cast out*.

1. What a brave army these frontier-tribes brought into the field against the Hagarites, 44,000 men and upwards, all strong, and brave, and skilful in war.

2. What course they took to engage God for them: They *cried to God*, and *put their trust in him*, *v.* 20. Though they had a powerful army, they relied not on that, but on the divine power. See the like done, 2 Chron. xiii. 14. In our spiritual conflicts, we must look up to heaven for strength; and it is the believing prayer that will be the prevailing prayer.

3. If the battle be the Lord's, there is reason to hope it will be successful.

II. They shared, at length, in an inglorious captivity. Had they kept close to God and their duty, they would have continued to enjoy both their ancient lot and their new conquests; but they *transgressed against the God of their fathers*, *v.* 25. They lay upon the borders and conversed most with the neighbouring nations, by which means they learned their idolatrous usages and transmitted the infection to the other tribes. These tribes were first placed, and they were first displaced. They would have the best land, not considering that it lay most exposed. But those who are governed more by sense than by reason or faith in their choices may expect to fare accordingly.

JAMIESON, FAUSSET, BROWN

18-22. Hagarites—or Hagarenes, originally synonymous with Ishmaelites, but afterwards applied to a particular tribe of the Arabs (cf. Ps. 83:6). **Jetur**—His descendants were called Itureans, and the country Auranitis, from Hauran, its chief city. These, who were skilled in archery, were invaded in the time of Joshua by a confederate army of the tribes of Reuben, Gad, and half Manasseh, who, probably incensed by the frequent raids of those marauding neighbors, took reprisals in men and cattle, dispossessed almost all of the original inhabitants, and colonized the district themselves. Divine Providence favored, in a remarkable manner, the Hebrew army in this just war. **26. the God of Israel stirred up the spirit of Pul**—the Phal-luka of the Ninevite monuments (see on II Kings 15:19). **and the spirit of Tilgath-pilneser**—the son of the former. By them the transjordanic tribes, including the other half of Manasseh, settled in Galilee, were removed to Upper Media. This was the *first* captivity (II Kings 15:29).

ADAM CLARKE

19. *They made war with the Hagarites.* This is probably the same war that is mentioned in v. 10.

21. *They took away their cattle.* This was a war of extermination as to the political state of the people, which nothing could justify but an especial direction of God; and this He could never give against any, unless the cup of their iniquity had been full. The Hagarites were full of idolatry (see v. 25).

22. *For there fell down many slain.* The hundred thousand men mentioned above were probably made slaves, and were not slain.

25. *The gods of the people of the land.* We see the reason why God delivered the Hagarites into the hands of these tribes; they were abominable idolaters, and therefore God destroyed them.

26. *Tilgath-pilneser.* Many MSS. have *Tiglath* instead of *Tilgath.* The Syriac, the Septuagint, and the Chaldee have the same reading as in 2 Kings xv. 29, etc.

MATTHEW HENRY — CHAPTER 6

Verses 1–30

The priests and Levites were more concerned than any other Israelites to preserve their pedigree clear and to be able to prove it, because all the honours and privileges of their office depended upon their descent. Very little is here recorded of the genealogies of this sacred tribe. 1. The first fathers of it are here named twice, *v.* 1, 16. Gershom, Kohath, and Merari, are three names which we were very conversant with in the book of Numbers. Aaron, and Moses, and Miriam, we have known much more of than their names, remembering that God honoured them in making them the instruments of Israel's deliverance and settlement and *figures of him that was to come*, Moses as a prophet and Aaron as a priest. And the mention of Nadab and Abihu cannot but remind us of the terrors of divine justice. 2. The line of Eleazar, the successor of Aaron, is here drawn down to the time of the captivity *v.* 4–15. It begins with Eleazar, who came out of the house of bondage in Egypt, and ends with Jehozadak, who went into the house of bondage in Babylon. All these here named were not high priests; for, in the time of the judges, that dignity was, upon some occasion or other, brought into the family of Ithamar, of which Eli was; but in Zadok it returned again to the right line. Of Azariah it is here said (*v.* 10), *He it is that executed the priest's office in the temple that Solomon built*. It is supposed that this was that Azariah who bravely opposed the presumption of king Uzziah when he invaded the priest's office (2 Chron. xxvi. 17, 18). This was done like a priest, like one that was truly zealous for his God. One of the families of Gershom (that of Libni) is here drawn down as far as Samuel, who had the honour of a prophet added to that of a Levite. One of the families of Merari (that of Mahli) is likewise drawn down for several descents, *v.* 29, 30.

Verses 31–53

When the Levites were first ordained in the wilderness much of the work then appointed them lay in carrying and taking care of the tabernacle and the utensils of it, while they were in their march through the wilderness. In David's time their number was increased; and, though the greater part of them were dispersed all the nation over, to teach the people the good knowledge of the Lord, yet those that attended the house of God were so numerous that there was not constant work for them all; and therefore David, by special commission and direction from God, new-modelled the Levites, as we shall find in the latter part of this book. Here we are told what the work was which he assigned them.

I. Singing-work, *v.* 31. David was raised up on

JAMIESON, FAUSSET, BROWN — CHAPTER 6

Vss. 1-48. Line of the Priests. **5. Uzzi**—It is supposed that, in his days, the high priesthood was, for unrecorded reasons, transferred from Eleazar's family to Ithamar's, in which it continued for several generations. **10. he it is that executed the priest's office in the temple that Solomon built in Jerusalem**—It is doubtful whether the person in favor of whom this testimony is borne be Johanan or Azariah. If the former, he is the same as Jehoiada, who rendered important public services (II Kings 11); if the latter, it refers to the worthy and independent part he acted in resisting the unwarrantable encroachments of Uzziah (II Chron. 26:17). **in the temple that Solomon built**—described in this particular manner to distinguish it from the second temple, which was in existence at the time when this history was written. **14. Azariah begat Seraiah**—He filled the supreme pontifical office at the destruction of Jerusalem, and, along with his deputy and others, he was executed by Nebuchadnezzar's orders at Riblah (II Kings 25:18, 21). The line of high priests, under the first temple, which from Zadok amounted to twelve, terminated with him. **16-48. The sons of Levi; Gershom,** etc.—This repetition (see vs. 1) is made, as the historian here begins to trace the genealogy of the Levitical families who were not priests. The list is a long one, comprising the chiefs or heads of their several families until David's reign, who made a new and different classification of them by courses. **20. Zimmah his son**—his grandson (vs. 42). **24. Uriel**—or Zephaniah (vs. 36). **27. Elkanah**—the father of the prophet Samuel (I Sam. 1:1). **28. the sons of Samuel**—are here named Vashni and Abiah. The first-born is called Joel (I Sam. 8:2); and this name is given to him in verse 33 of this chapter. It is now generally thought by the best critics that, through an error of the copyists, an omission has been made of the oldest son's name, and that Vashni, which is not the name of a person, merely signifies "and the second." This critical emendation of the text makes all clear, as well as consistent with other passages relating to the family of Samuel.

ADAM CLARKE — CHAPTER 6

1. *The sons of Levi.* It has been well remarked that the genealogy of *Levi* is given here more amply and correctly than that of any of the others. And this is perhaps an additional proof that the author was a priest, felt much for the priesthood, and took care to give the genealogy of the Levitical and sacerdotal families from the most correct tables; for with such tables we may presume he was intimately acquainted.

4. *Eleazar begat Phinehas.* As the high priesthood continued in this family for a long time, the sacred historian confines himself to this chiefly, omitting Nadab and Abihu, and even the family of Ithamar.

8. *Ahitub begat Zadok.* Through this person the high priesthood came again into the family of Eleazar.

10. *Johanan.* Supposed to be the same as Jehoiada. *Executed the priest's office.* Probably this refers to the dignified manner in which Azariah opposed King Uzziah, who wished to invade the priest's office, and offer incense in the Temple (see 2 Chron. xxvi. 17-18).

14. *Seraiah.* He was put to death by Nebuchadnezzar, 2 Kings xxv. 18, 21.

22. *Korah.* See the history of this man, and his rebellion, Numbers xvi.

28. *The firtsborn Vashni, and Abiah.* There is a great mistake in this verse: in 1 Sam. viii. 2 we read, "Now the name of his [Samuel's] firstborn was Joel; and the name of his second, Abiah." The word *Joel* is lost out of the text, in this place, and *vesheni*, which signifies "the second," and which refers to *Abiah*, is made here into a proper name. These, Joel and Abiah, were the two sons of Samuel, who administered justice so badly that the people, being oppressed, began to murmur, and demanded a king (see 1 Sam. viii. 1, etc).

MATTHEW HENRY

high to be the sweet psalmist of Israel (2 Sam. xxiii. 1), not only to pen psalms, but to appoint the singing of them in the house of the Lord, and this he did *after that the ark had rest.* While that was in captivity, obscure, and unsettled, the harps were hung upon the willow-trees: singing was then thought unseasonable, but the harps being resumed, and the songs revived, at the bringing up of the ark, they were continued afterwards. When the service of the ark was much superseded by its rest they had other work cut out for them (for Levites should never be idle) and were employed in the service of song. These singers kept up that service in the tabernacle till the temple was built, and then they *waited on their office* there, *v.* 32. We have here an account of the three great masters who were employed in the service of the sacred song, with their respective families; for they *waited with their children,* that is, such as descended from them or were allied to them, *v.* 33. Heman, Asaph, and Ethan, were the three that were appointed to this service, one of each of the three houses of the Levites. 1. Of the house of Kohath was Heman with his family (*v.* 33), a man of a sorrowful spirit, if it be the same Heman that penned the 88th psalm, and yet a singer. He was the grandson of Samuel the prophet, the son of Joel, of whom it is said that *he walked not in the ways of Samuel* (1 Sam. viii. 2, 3); but it seems, though the son did not, the grandson did. Perhaps David, in making Heman the chief, had some respect to his old friend Samuel. 2. Of the house of Gershom was Asaph, called *his brother,* because in the same office and of the same tribe, though of another family. He was posted on Heman's right hand in the choir, *v.* 39. Several of the psalms bear his name. It is plain that he was the penman of some psalms; for we read of those that praised the Lord in the words of David and of Asaph. He was a seer as well as a singer, 2 Chron. xxix. 30. His pedigree is traced up here, through names utterly unknown, as high as Levi, *v.* 39-43. 3. Of the house of Merari was Ethan (*v.* 44), who was appointed to Heman's left hand. His pedigree is also traced up to Levi, *v.* 47.

II. There was serving-work, abundance of service to be done *in the tabernacle of the house of God* (*v.* 48), to provide water and fuel,—to wash and sweep, and carry out ashes,—to kill, and flay, and boil the sacrifices; and to all such services there were Levites appointed, those of other families, or perhaps those that were not fit to be singers, that had either no good voice or no good ear. *As everyone has received the gift, so let him minister.*

III. There was sacrificing-work, and that was to be done by the priests only, *v.* 49. They only were to sprinkle the blood and burn the incense; as for *the work of the most holy place,* that was to be done by the high priest only. Each had his work, and they both needed one another and both helped one another in it. Concerning the work of the priests we are here told, they were to *make an atonement for Israel,* to mediate between the people and God; not to magnify and enrich themselves, but to serve the public. They presided in God's house, yet must do as they were bidden, according to all that God commanded.

Verses 54–81

An account of the Levites' cities. They and their possessions were, in a particular manner, the care of the divine providence: as God was their portion, so God was their protection; and a cottage will be a castle to those that abide under the shadow of the Almighty. It is common for cities to have several names. *Sarum* and *Salisbury, Salop* and *Shrewsbury,* are more unlike than *Hilen* (*v.* 58) and *Holon* (Joshua xxi. 15), *Ashan* (*v.* 59) and *Ain* (Joshua xxi. 16), *Alemeth* (*v.* 60) and *Almon* (Joshua xxi. 18); and time changes names. In this appointment of cities for the Levites God took care, 1. For Jacob's prediction concerning this tribe, that it should be *scattered in Israel,* Gen. xlix. 7. 2. For the diffusing of the knowledge of himself and his law to all parts of the land of Israel. Every tribe had Levites' cities in it. 3. For a comfortable maintenance for those that ministered in holy things. Some of the most considerable cities of Israel fell to the Levites' lot.

JAMIESON, FAUSSET, BROWN

32. before the dwelling place . . .—i.e., in the tent which David had erected for receiving the ark after it was removed from the house of Obed-edom. This was a considerable time before the temple was built. **they waited on their office according to their order**—which David, doubtless by the direction of the Holy Spirit, had instituted for the better regulation of divine worship.

33. Shemuel—i.e., Samuel. This is the exact representation of the Hebrew name.

39. his brother Asaph—They were brothers naturally, both being descended from Levi, as well as officially, both being of the Levitical order. **42. Ethan**—or Jeduthun (ch. 9:16; II Chron. 35:15).

48. Their brethren also, the Levites, were appointed unto all manner of service—Those of them who were endowed with musical tastes and talents were employed in various other departments of the temple service.

49-81. OFFICE OF AARON AND HIS SONS. **49. But Aaron and his sons offered,** etc.—The office and duties of the high priests having been already described, the names of those who successively filled that important office are recorded. **60. thirteen cities**—No more than eleven are named here; but two additional ones are mentioned (Josh. 21:16, 17), which makes up the thirteen. **61. unto the sons of Kohath which were left**—i.e., in addition to the priests belonging to the same family and tribe of Levi. **by lot, ten cities**—(Josh. 21:26). The sacred historian gives an explanation (vs. 66). Eight of these are mentioned, but only two of them are taken out of the half tribe of Manasseh (vs. 70). The names of the other two are given (Josh. 21:21), where full and detailed notices of these arrangements may be found. **62. to the sons of Gershom**—Supply "the children of Israel gave." **67. they gave unto them of the cities of refuge**—The names of the cities given here are considerably different from those applied to them (Josh. 21:14). In the lapse of centuries, and from the revolutions of society, changes might have been expected to take place in the form or dialectic pronunciation of the names of those cities; and this will sufficiently account for the variations that are found in the lists as enumerated here and in an earlier book. As to these cities themselves that were assigned to the Levites, they were widely remote and separated—partly in fulfilment of Jacob's prophecy (Gen. 49:7), and partly that the various districts of the country might obtain a competent supply of teachers who might instruct the people in the knowledge, and animate them to the observance, of a law which had so important a bearing on the promotion both of their private happiness and their national prosperity.

ADAM CLARKE

31. *After that the ark had rest.* That is, when it was brought from the house of Obed-edom.

32. *According to their order.* This order is specified below.

39. *Asaph.* This person, with Heman, the sons of Korah, Ethan, Jeduthun, etc., are celebrated in these books, and in the Psalms, for their skill in singing, and the part they performed in the public worship of God.

50. *These are the sons of Aaron.* We have already had a list of these (see vv. 3-16); this is a second, but less extensive, and is a proof that the writer of this book had several lists before him, from which he borrowed as he judged proper.

54. *Theirs was the lot.* All the tribes and families obtained their respective inheritances by lot, but to the sons of Aaron was the "first lot"; and so the Syriac and Arabic have understood this place. See an account of the possessions of the priests and Levites, Joshua xx; xxi.

60. *All their cities . . . were thirteen.* But there are only eleven reckoned here, Gibeon and Juttah being omitted, and the names of some of the others changed. None of the versions give the full number of names, although they all give the whole sum "thirteen."

65. *Which are called by their names.* Probably each family gave its own name to the city that fell to its lot.

69. *Aijalon with her suburbs.* There are two cities wanting here, Eltekeh and Gibethon (see Josh. xxi. 23).

71-77. We shall see from Josh. xxi. 28, etc., that several of these cities have different names.

MATTHEW HENRY

CHAPTER 7

Verses 1–19

A short view,

I. Of the tribe of Issachar, whom Jacob had compared to a *strong ass, couching between two burdens* (Gen. xlix. 14), an industrious tribe, that minded their country business very closely and *rejoiced in their tents,* Deut. xxxiii. 18. So fruitful their country was

JAMIESON, FAUSSET, BROWN

CHAPTER 7

Vss. 1-5. SONS OF ISSACHAR. **1. Jashub**—or Job (Gen. 46:13). **2. whose number was in the days of David two and twenty thousand and six hundred**—Although a census was taken in the reign of David by order of that monarch, it is not certain that the sacred historian had it in mind, since we find here the tribe of Benjamin enumerated, which was not

ADAM CLARKE

CHAPTER 7

2. *Whose number was in the days of David.* Whether this was the number returned by Joab and his assistants, when they made that census of the people with which God was so much displeased, we know not. It is worthy of remark that we read here the sum of three tribes, Ben-

MATTHEW HENRY

that they saw no danger of over-stocking the pasture, and so ingenious the people were that they could find work for all hands. Let no people complain of their numbers, provided they suffer none to be idle. The number of the respective families is here set down, amounting in the whole to above 145,000 men fit for war.

II. Of the tribe of Benjamin. Some account is here given of this tribe, but a much larger in the next chapter. The militia of this tribe scarcely reached to 60,000; but they are said to be *mighty men of valour, v.* 7, 9, 11. It was the honour of this tribe that it produced Saul the first king, and more its honour that it adhered to the rightful kings of the house of David when the other tribes revolted.

III. Of the tribe of Naphtali, *v.* 13. The first fathers only of that tribe are named, the very same that we find, Gen. xlvi. 24, only that *Shillem* there is *Shallum* here. None of their descendants are named, perhaps because their genealogies were lost.

IV. Of the tribe of Manasseh, that part of it which was seated within Jordan; for of the other part we had some account before, *ch.* v. 23, &c. One of them married an Aramitess, that is, a Syrian, *v.* 14. This was during their bondage in Egypt, so early did they begin to mingle with the nations. The father married a Syrian, Machir; the son of that marriage took to wife a daughter of Benjamin, *v.* 15.

Verses 20–40

An account,

I. Of the tribe of Ephraim. Great things we read of that tribe when it came to maturity. Here we have the disasters of its infancy, while it was in Egypt. 1. The great breach that was made upon the family of Ephraim. The men of Gath, Philistines, giants, slew many of the sons of that family, *because they came down to take away their cattle, v.* 21. It is uncertain who were the aggressors here. Some make the men of Gath the aggressors, supposing that they came down into the land of Goshen, to drive away the Ephraimites' cattle, and slew the owners, because they stood up in the defence of them. Others think that the Ephraimites made a descent upon the men of Gath to plunder them. I rather think that the men of Gath came down upon the Ephraimites, because the Israelites in Egypt were shepherds, not soldiers, abounded in cattle of their own, and therefore were not likely to venture their lives for their neighbours' cattle: and the words may be read, *The men of Gath slew them, for they came down to take away their cattle. Ephraim mourned many days.* Nothing brings the aged to the grave with more sorrow than their following the young that descend from them to the grave first, especially if in blood. It was a brotherly friendly office which his brethren did, when *they came to comfort him.* The repair of this breach, in some measure, by the addition of another son to his family in his old age (*v.* 23), like Seth, *another seed instead of that of Abel whom Cain slew*, Gen. iv. 25. When God thus restores comfort to his mourners, *makes glad according to the days wherein he afflicted*, setting the mercies over against the crosses, we ought therein to take notice of the kindness and tenderness of divine Providence; it is as if *it repented God concerning his servants*, Ps. xc. 13, 15. Yet joy that a man was born into his family could not make him forget his grief; for he gives a melancholy name to this son, *Beriah—in trouble*, for he was born when the family was in mourning, when *it went evil with his house.* It is added, as a further honour to the house of Ephraim, that a son of that tribe was employed in the conquest of Canaan, *Joshua the son of Nun, v.* 27.

JAMIESON, FAUSSET, BROWN

taken in David's time; and there are other points of dissimilarity. **3. five: all of them chief men**—Four only are mentioned; so that as they are stated to be five, in this number the father, Izrahiah, must be considered as included; otherwise one of the names must have dropped out of the text. They were each at the head of a numerous and influential division of their tribe. **5. fourscore and seven thousand**—exclusive of the 58,600 men which the Tola branch had produced (vs. 24), so that in the days of David the tribe would have contained a population of 45,600. This large increase was owing to the practice of polygamy, as well as the fruitfulness of the women. A plurality of wives, though tolerated among the Hebrews, was confined chiefly to the great and wealthy; but it seems to have been generally esteemed a privilege by the tribe of Issachar, "for they had many wives and sons."

6-12. OF BENJAMIN. **6. The sons of Benjamin**—Ten are named in Genesis 46:21, but only five later (ch. 8:1; Num. 26:38). Perhaps five of them were distinguished as chiefs of illustrious families, but two having fallen in the bloody wars waged against Benjamin (Judg. 20:46), there remained only three branches of this tribe, and these only are enumerated. **Jediael**—or Asbel (Gen. 46:21). **7. the sons of Bela**—Each of them was chief or leader of the family to which he belonged. In an earlier period seven great families of Benjamin are mentioned (Num. 26:38), five of them being headed by these five sons of Benjamin, and two descended from Bela. Here five families of Bela are specified, whence we are led to conclude that time or the ravages of war had greatly changed the condition of Benjamin, or that the five families of Bela were subordinate to the other great divisions that sprang directly from the five sons of the patriarch. **12. Shuppim also, and Huppim**—They are called Muppim and Huppim (Gen. 46:21) and Hupham and Shupham (Num. 26:39). They were the children of Ir, or Iri (vs. 7). **and Hushim, the sons** [son] **of Aher**—Aher signifies "another," and some eminent critics, taking Aher as a common noun, render the passage thus, "and Hushim, another son." Shuppim, Muppim, and Hushim are plural words, and therefore denote not individuals, but the heads of their respective families; and as they were not comprised in the above enumeration (vss. 7, 9) they are inserted here in the form of an appendix. Some render the passage, "Hushim, the son of another," i.e., tribe or family. The name occurs among the sons of Dan (Gen. 46:23), and it is a presumption in favor of this being the true rendering, that after having recorded the genealogy of Naphtali (vs. 13) the sacred historian adds, "the sons of Bilhah, the handmaid, who was the mother of Dan and Naphtali." We naturally expect, therefore, that these two will be noticed together, but Dan is not mentioned at all, if not in this passage.

13. OF NAPHTALI. **13. Shallum**—or Shillem (Gen. 46:24). **sons of Bilhah**—As Dan and Naphtali were her sons, Hushim, as well as these enumerated in vs. 13, were her grandsons.

14-40. OF MANASSEH. **14. The sons of Manasseh**—or descendants; for Ashriel was a grandson, and Zelophehad was a generation farther removed in descent (Num. 26:33). The text, as it stands, is so confused and complicated that it is exceedingly difficult to trace the genealogical thread, and a great variety of conjectures have been made with a view to clear away the obscurity. The passage should probably be rendered thus: "The sons of Manasseh were Ashriel, whom his Syrian concubine bare to him, and Machir, the father of Gilead (whom his wife bare to him). Machir took for a wife Maachah, sister to Huppim and Shuppim." **21. whom the men of Gath . . . slew,** etc.—This interesting little episode gives us a glimpse of the state of Hebrew society in Egypt; for the occurrence narrated seems to have taken place before the Israelites left that country. The patriarch Ephraim was then alive, though he must have arrived at a very advanced age; and the Hebrew people, at all events those of them who were his descendants, still retained their pastoral character. It was in perfect consistency with the ideas and habits of Oriental shepherds that they should have made a raid on the neighboring tribe of the Philistines for the purpose of plundering their flocks. For nothing is more common among them than hostile incursions on the inhabitants of towns, or on other nomad tribes with whom they have no league of amity. But a different view of the incident is brought out, if, instead of "because," we render the Hebrew particle "when" they came down to take their cattle, for the tenor of the context leads rather to the conclusion that "the men of Gath" were the aggressors, who, making a

ADAM CLARKE

jamin, Issachar, and Asher, under the reign of David, which is mentioned nowhere else; and yet we have no account here of the other tribes, probably because the author found no public registers in which such enumeration was recorded.

3. *The sons of Izrahiah . . . five.* There are, however, only four names in the text. Instead of *five*, the Syriac and Arabic read "four." If *five* be the true reading, then Izrahiah must be reckoned with his four sons.

6. *The sons of Benjamin; Bela, and Becher, and Jediael.* In Gen. xlvi. 21, ten sons of Benjamin are reckoned. In Num. xxvi. 38, etc., five sons only of Benjamin are mentioned. In the beginning of the following chapter, five sons of Benjamin are mentioned, viz., Bela, Ashbel, Aharah, Nohah, and Rapha; where also Addar, Gera, Abihud, Abishua, Naaman, Ahoah, a second Gera, Shephuphan, and Huram are all represented as grandsons, not sons, of Bejamin. Hence we see that in many cases grandsons are called sons, and both are often confounded in the genealogical tables. To attempt to reconcile such discrepancies would be a task as endless as it would be useless. The rabbins say that Ezra, who wrote this book, did not know whether some of these were sons or grandsons; and they intimate also that the tables from which he copied were often defective, and here we must leave all such matters.

21. *Whom the men of Gath . . . slew.* We know nothing of this circumstance but what is related here.

24. *His daughter was Sherah.* That is, "remnant"; "called so," says the Targum, "because she was the remnant that escaped from the slaughter mentioned above."

MATTHEW HENRY

II. Of the tribe of Asher. Some men of note of that tribe are here named. Their militia was not numerous in comparison with some other tribes, only 26,000 men in all; but their princes were *choice and mighty men of valour, chief of the princes* (*v.* 40), and perhaps it was their wisdom that they coveted not to make their trained bands numerous, but rather to have a few serviceable men.

CHAPTER 8

Verses 1–32

There is little or nothing of history in all these verses. In this and the foregoing genealogies some *a*scend, others *de*scend; some have *numbers* affixed, others *places*; some have historical remarks intermixed, others have not; some are shorter, others longer; some agree with other records, other differ; some, it is likely, were torn, erased, and blotted, others more legible. Those of Dan and Reuben were entirely lost. Many things in these genealogies which to us seem intricate, abrupt, and perplexed, were plain and easy to them then (who knew how to fill up the deficiencies). Many great and mighty nations there were now in being upon earth, and many illustrious men in them, whose names are buried in perpetual oblivion, while the names of multitudes of the Israel of God are here carefully preserved in everlasting remembrance. They are *Jasher, Jeshurun —just ones*, and *the memory of the just is blessed.* This tribe of Benjamin was once brought to a very low ebb, in the time of the judges, upon the occasion of the iniquity of Gibeah, when only 600 men escaped the sword of justice; and yet, in these genealogies, it makes as good a figure as almost any of the tribes. Here is mention of one Ehud (*v.* 6), in the preceding verse of one Gera (*v.* 5) and (*v.* 8) of one that descended from him, that *begat children in the country of Moab*, who was the second of the judges of Israel; for he is said to be *the son of Gera* and *a Benjamite* (Judges iii. 15), and he delivered Israel from the oppression of the Moabites by killing the king of Moab. Here is mention of some of the Benjamites that *drove away the inhabitants of Gath* (*v.* 13), perhaps those that had slain the Ephraimites (*ch.* vii. 21) and one of those that did this piece of justice was named *Beriah.*

Particular notice is taken of those that *dwelt in Jerusalem* (*v.* 28 and again *v.* 32), that those whose ancestors had had their residence there might thereby be induced, at their return from captivity, to settle there and therefore we find (Neh. xi. 2) *the people blessed those that willingly offered themselves to dwell at Jerusalem.*

Verses 33–40

Among all the genealogies of the tribes there is no mention of any of the kings of Israel after their defection from the house of David, much less of their families; not a word of Jeroboam's house or Baasha's, or Omri's or Jehu's; for they were all idolaters. But of the family of Saul, which was the royal family before the elevation of David, we have here a particular account. 1. Before Saul, Kish and Ner only are named, his father and grandfather, *v.* 33. He was in truth the son of Ner but the grandson of Abiel, as appears by 1 Sam. xiv. 51. 2. After Saul, divers of his sons are named, but the posterity of none of them, save Jonathan only, for the sake of his sincere kindness to David. This genealogy ends in Ulam, whose family became famous in the tribe of Benjamin for the number of its valiant men. Of that one man's posterity, there were at one time 150 archers.

CHAPTER 9

Verses 1–13

The first verse tells us of *the books of the kings of Israel and Judah.* Mentioning Israel and Judah, the historian takes notice of their being *carried away to Babylon for their transgression.* Then follows an account of the first inhabitants, after their return from captivity, that dwelt in their cities, especially in Jerusalem. 1. The Israelites. That general name is used (*v.* 2) because with those of Judah and Benjamin there were many of Ephraim and Manasseh, and the other ten tribes (*v.* 3), such as had escaped to Judah when the body of the ten tribes were carried captive or returned to Judah upon the revolutions in Assyria, and so went into captivity with them. It was foretold that the *children of Judah and of Israel* should be *gathered together and come up out*

JAMIESON, FAUSSET, BROWN

sudden foray on the Ephraimite flocks, killed the shepherds including several of the sons of Ephraim. The calamity spread a deep gloom around the tent of their aged father, and was the occasion of his receiving visits of condolence from his distant relatives, according to the custom of the East, which is remarkably exemplified in the history of Job (Job 2:11; cf. John 11:19).

CHAPTER 8

Vss. 1-32. SONS AND CHIEF MEN OF BENJAMIN. **1. Now Benjamin begat,** etc.—This chapter contains some supplementary particulars in addition to what has been already said regarding the tribe of Benjamin (ch. 7:6). The names of many of the persons mentioned are different from those given by Moses —a diversity which may be accounted for in part on grounds formerly stated, viz., either that the persons had more than one name, or that the word "sons" is used in a loose sense for grandsons or descendants. But there are other circumstances to be taken into account in considering the details of this chapter; viz., first, that the genealogies of the Benjamites were disordered or destroyed by the almost total extermination of this tribe (Judg. 20.); secondly, that a great number of Benjamites, born in Assyria, are mentioned here, who returned from the long captivity in Babylon, and established themselves—some in Jerusalem, others in different parts of Judea. There were more returned from Babylon of the families belonging to this tribe than to any other except Judah; and hence many strange names are here introduced; some of which will be found in the list of the restored exiles (cf. Ezra 2). **6. these are the sons of Ehud**—most probably the judge of Israel (Judg. 3:15). His descendants, who had at first been established in Geba in Benjamin, emigrated in a body under the direction of Gera (vs. 7) to Manahath, where their increased numbers would find more ample accommodation. Manahath was within the territory of Judah. **8. Shaharaim begat children in the country of Moab**—He had probably been driven to take refuge in that foreign land on the same calamitous occasion that forced Elimelech to emigrate thither (Ruth 1:1). But, destitute of natural affection, he forsook or divorced his two wives, and in the land of his sojourn married a third, by whom he had several sons. But there is another explanation given of the conduct of this Benjamite polygamist. His children by Hushim are mentioned (vs. 11), while his other wife is unnoticed. Hence it has been thought probable that it is Baara who is mentioned under the name of Hodesh, so called because her husband, after long desertion, returned and cohabited with her as before. **28. These dwelt in Jerusalem**—The ordinary and stated inhabitants of Jerusalem were Judahites, Benjamites, and Levites. But at the time referred to here, the chiefs or heads of the principal families who are enumerated (vss. 14-27) established themselves in the city after their return from the captivity.

33-40. STOCK OF SAUL AND JONATHAN. **33. Ner begat Kish**—The father of Ner, though not mentioned here, is stated (ch. 9:35) to have been Jehiel. Moreover, the father of Kish is said (I Sam. 9:1) to have been Abiel, the son of Zeror, whence it would seem that Abiel and Ner were names of the same person. **Abinadab**—the same as Ishui (I Sam. 14: 49). **Esh-baal**—that is, Ishbosheth. **34. Merib-baal**—that is, Mephibosheth. **36. Jehoada**—or Jara (ch. 9:42). **40. mighty men of valour, archers**—(see on Judg. 20-16). Great strength as well as skill was requisite in ancient archery, as the bow, which was of steel, was bent by treading with the feet, and pulling the string with both hands.

CHAPTER 9

Vss. 1-26. ORIGINAL REGISTERS OF ISRAEL AND JUDAH'S GENEALOGIES. **1. all Israel were reckoned by genealogies**—From the beginning of the Hebrew nation, public records were kept, containing a registration of the name of every individual, as well as the tribe and family to which he belonged. "The book of the kings of Israel and Judah" does not refer to the two canonical books that are known in Scripture by that name, but to authenticated copies of those registers, placed under the official care of the sovereigns; and as a great number of the Israelites (vs. 3) took refuge in Judah during the invasion of Shalmaneser, they carried the public records along with them. The genealogies given in the preceding chapters were drawn from the public records in the archives both of Israel and Judah; and those given

ADAM CLARKE

32. *And Shua their sister.* It is very rarely that women are found in the Jewish genealogies, and they are never inserted but for especial reasons.

CHAPTER 8

1. *Now Benjamin begat.* See what has been said on the preceding chapter, v. 6.

9. *He begat of Hodesh his wife.* In the preceding verse it is said that Hushim and Baara were his wives; and here it is said, *He begat of Hodesh his wife.* And then his children by Hushim are mentioned, but not a word of Baara! It is likely therefore that Hodesh was another name for Baara, and this is asserted by the Targum: "And he begot of Baara, that is Chodesh, his wife; so called because he espoused her anew." It is supposed that he had put her away before, and now remarried her.

29. *And at Gibeon.* This passage to the end of the thirty-eighth verse is found, with a little variety in the names, in chap. ix. 35-44. The rabbins say that Ezra, having found two books that had these passages with a variety in the names, as they agreed in general, he thought best to insert them both, not being able to discern which was the best.

34. *Merib-baal.* The same as Mephibosheth; for, as the Israelites detested *Baal,* which signifies "lord," they changed it into *bosheth,* which signifies "shame" or "reproach."

CHAPTER 9

1. *Were reckoned by genealogies.* Jarchi considers these as the words of Ezra, the compiler of the book; as if he had said: I have given the genealogies of the Israelites as I have found them in a book which was carried into Babylon, when the people were carried thither for their transgressions; and this book which I found is that which I have transcribed in the preceding chapters.

2. *Now the first inhabitants.* This is spoken of those who returned from the Babylonish captivity, and of the time in which they returned; for it is insinuated here that other persons afterwards settled at Jerusalem, though these mentioned here were the *first* on the

MATTHEW HENRY

of the land (Hosea i. 11), and that they should be one nation again, Ezek. xxxvii. 22. Pieces of metal that had been separated will run together again when melted in the same crucible. Many both of Judah and Israel stayed behind in captivity. 2. The priests, *v.* 10. It was their praise that they came with the first. (1) It is said of one of them that he was *the ruler of the house of God* (*v.* 11) not the chief ruler, for Joshua was then the high priest, but the sagan, the next under him. (2) It is said of many of them that they were *very able men for the service of the house of God*, *v.* 13. In the house of God there is service to be done, constant service; and it is well for the church when those are employed in that service who are qualified for it, *able ministers of the New Testament*, 2 Cor. iii. 6. The service of the temple required great courage and vigour of mind, as well as strength of body; and therefore they are praised as *mighty men of valour*.

Verses 14–34

The good posture which the affairs of religion were put into immediately upon the return of the people out of Babylon. The late want of ordinances made them very zealous in setting up the worship of God among them; and so they began their worship of God at the right end.

I. Before the house of the Lord was built they had the house of the tabernacle, a plain and movable tent. Those that cannot yet reach to have a temple must not be without a tabernacle, but be thankful for that and make the best of it. Never let God's work be left undone for want of a place to do it in.

II. In allotting to the priests and Levites their respective employments, they had the model that was drawn up by David, and Samuel the seer, *v.* 22. Samuel, in his time, had drawn the scheme of it, and laid the foundation, though the ark was then in obscurity, and David afterwards finished it, and both acted by immediate direction from God.

III. The most of them dwelt at Jerusalem (*v.* 34), yet there were some that dwelt in the villages (*v.* 16, 22), because, it may be, there was not yet room for them in Jerusalem. However they were employed in the service of the tabernacle (*v.* 25).

IV. Many of the Levites were employed as porters at the gates of the house of God, four chief porters (*v.* 26), and, under them, others, to the number of 212, *v.* 22. They had the oversight of the gates (*v.* 23), were keepers of the *thresholds*, as in the margin (*v.* 19), and keepers of the entry. This seemed a mean office; and yet David would rather have it than *dwell in the tents of wickedness*, Ps. lxxxiv. 10. Their office was, 1. To open the doors of God's house every morning (*v.* 27) and shut them at night. 2. To keep off the unclean, and hinder those from thrusting in that were forbidden by the law. 3. To direct and introduce into the courts of the Lord those that came thither to worship. Ministers have work to do of this kind.

V. Here is one Phinehas, a son of Eleazar, that is said to be a *ruler over them in time past* (*v.* 20), not the famous high priest of that name, but an eminent Levite, of whom it is here said that *the Lord was with him*, or (as the Chaldee reads it) *the Word of the Lord was his helper*.

VI. It is said of some of them that *they lodged roundabout the house of God*, *v.* 27. The Levites pitched about the tabernacle when they marched through the wilderness. Then they were porters in one sense, bearing the burdens of the sanctuary, now porters in another sense, attending the gates and the doors—in both instances keeping the charge of the sanctuary.

VII. Every one knew his charge. Some were entrusted with the ministering vessels, to bring them in and out, *v.* 28. Others were appointed to prepare the fine flour, wine, oil, &c., *v.* 29. Others, that were priests, made up the holy anointing oil, *v.* 30. Others took care of the meat-offerings, *v.* 31. Others of the shewbread, *v.* 32. God is the God of order: but that which is everybody's work will be nobody's work.

VIII. The singers *were employed in that work day and night*, *v.* 33. They were the *chief fathers of the Levites* that made a business of it, not mean singing-men that made a trade of it. They remained in the chambers of the temple, that they might closely and constantly attend it, and were therefore excused from all other services. It should seem, some companies were continually singing, at least at stated hours, both day and night. Thus was God continually praised.

Verses 35–44

These verses are the very same with *ch.* viii. 29–38, giving an account of the ancestors of Saul and the

JAMIESON, FAUSSET, BROWN

in this chapter relate to the period subsequent to the restoration; whence it appears (cf. ch. 3:17-24) that the genealogical registers were kept during the captivity in Babylon. These genealogical tables, then, are of the highest authority for truth and correctness, the earlier portion being extracted from the authenticated records of the nation; and as to those which belong to the time of the captivity, they were drawn up by a contemporary writer, who, besides enjoying the best sources of information, and being of the strictest integrity, was guided and preserved from all error by divine inspiration. **2. the first inhabitants that dwelt in their possessions**—This chapter relates wholly to the first returned exiles. Almost all the names recur in Nehemiah (chap. 11), although there are differences which will be explained there. The same division of the people into four classes was continued after as before the captivity; viz., the priests, Levites, natives, who now were called by the common name of Israelites, and the Nethinims (Josh. 9:27; Ezra 2:43; 8:20). When the historian speaks of "the first inhabitants that dwelt in their possessions," he implies that there were others who afterwards returned and settled in possessions not occupied by the first. Accordingly, we read of a great number returning successively under Ezra, Nehemiah, and at a later period. And some of those who returned to the ancient inheritance of their fathers, had lived before the time of the captivity (Ezra 3:12; Hag. 2:4, 10). **18. the king's gate**—The king had a gate from his palace into the temple (II Kings 16:18), which doubtless was kept constantly closed except for the monarch's use; and although there was no king in Israel on the return from the captivity, yet the old ceremonial was kept up, probably in the hope that the scepter would, ere long, be restored to the house of David. It is an honor by which Eastern kings are distinguished, to have a gate exclusively devoted to their own special use, and which is kept constantly closed, except when he goes out or returns (Ezek. 44:2). There being no king then in Israel, this gate would be always shut.

F. B. MEYER:

"Chosen to be porters . . . appointed over the furniture; . . . the singers" (1 Chron. 9:22, 29, 31, 33).

What a busy scene is suggested in these words! When the morning broke, it called to duty first the porters who opened the House of God; and then, after due ablution, each band of white-robed Levites began its special service. There was no running to and fro to disorder, no intrusion on one another's office, no clashing in duty, no jealousy of each other's ministry. It was enough to know that each had been appointed to his task, and was asked to be faithful to it. The right ordering of the whole depended on the punctuality, fidelity, and conscientiousness of each.

So it is in the Church of Christ, each is specially gifted for some post to which he has been set apart. One to see to the gates, admitting souls to the kingdom; one to the baking in pans, attending to the feeding of the household of God; some are appointed to the furnishing and maintaining of the House of Prayer; others to the psalmody, as the hymn writers of our praise and holy song. How beautiful it is when we dwell together in this unity, not envying one another, nor interfering in each other's ministry. "He gave some, apostles; and some, prophets; and some, evangelists; and some, pastors and teachers: for the perfecting of the saints, for the work of the ministry, for the edifying of the body of Christ."

—Great Verses Through the Bible

ADAM CLARKE

return from the Captivity. Properly speaking, the divisions mentioned in this verse constituted the whole of the Israelitish people, who were, ever since the days of Joshua, divided into the four following classes: (1) the *priests;* (2) the *Levites;* (3) the common people, or simple *Israelites;* (4) the *Nethinims*, or slaves of the Temple, the remains of the Gibeonites, who, having deceived Joshua, were condemned to this service, Josh. ix. 21, etc. In David's time it is probable that other conquered people were added, as the successors of the Gibeonites were not sufficient to perform all the drudgery of the Temple service.

3. *And in Jerusalem dwelt.* Several of the tribes of Judah, Benjamin, Ephraim, and Manasseh took advantage of the proclamation of Cyrus to return to Jerusalem, and so mingled with the Israelites, and those to whom Jerusalem had previously appertained; and this was necessary in order to provide a sufficient population for so large a city.

4. *Uthai the son of Ammihud.* The list here is nearly the same with those found in Ezra and Nehemiah, and contains those who returned to Jerusalem with Zerubbabel; but the list in Nehemiah is more ample, probably because it contains those who came afterwards. The object of the sacred writer here was to give the list of those who came *first.* "Now the first inhabitants."

11. *The ruler of the house of God.* The high priest at this time was Jeshua, the son of Jozadak (Ezra iii. 8); and Seraiah (Neh. xi. 11), called here *Azariah*, was the *ruler of the house;* the person next in authority to the high priest, and who probably had the guard of the Temple and command of the priests, Levites, etc. It is likely that the person here was the same as is called the "second priest," 2 Kings xxv. 18, who was the *sagan* or high priest's deputy.

13. *And their brethren.* What a prodigious number of ecclesiastics to perform the divine service of one temple! No less than 1,780 able-bodied men! And this number is reckoned independently of the 212 porters who served at the gates of the house of the Lord, v. 22.

18. *The king's gate.* That by which the kings of Judah went to the Temple (see 2 Kings xvi. 18).

19. *Keepers of the entry.* Whose business it was to suffer no person to come to the tabernacle but the priests, during the performance of the sacred service.

30. *The sons of the priests made the ointment.* Only the priests were permitted to make this ointment; all others were forbidden to do it on pain of death (see Exod. xxx. 34-38, and the notes there).

35. *Whose wife's name was Maachah.* Here our translators have departed from the original, for the word is *achotho*, "his sister"; but the Vulgate, Septuagint, Syriac, Arabic, and Chaldee have "wife"; to which may be added chap. viii. 29, the parallel place. Almost all the early editions, as well as the MS. editions, have the same reading. There is most certainly a fault somewhere, for Maachah could not be both the sister and the wife of Jehiel. Whether, therefore, chap. viii. 29 has been altered from this, or this altered from that, who can tell? A single letter makes the whole difference. If the word be written with *cheth*, it is "sister"; if with *shin*, it is "wife." The latter is most probably the true reading.

41. *And Ahaz.* This is added by our translators from chap. viii. 35, but such liberties should be taken only in a note; for although the words are now sufficiently distinguished from the text by being printed in italics, yet it is too much to expect that every editor of a Bible will attend to such distinctions, and in process of time the words will be found incorporated with the text.

35, and the following verses, are a repetition of what we find in chap. viii. 29-38.

MATTHEW HENRY

posterity of Jonathan. *There* it is the conclusion of the genealogy of Benjamin; *here* it is an introduction to the story of Saul.

CHAPTER 10

Verses 1–7

This account of Saul's death is the same which we had, 1 Sam. xxxi. 1, &c. Only let us observe, 1. Princes sin and the people suffer for it. 2. Parents sin and the children suffer for it. When the measure of Saul's iniquity was full, and his day came to fall (which David foresaw, 1 Sam. xxvi. 10), he not only descended into battle and perished himself, but his sons (all but Ishbosheth) perished with him, and Jonathan among the rest, that gracious, generous man; for *all things come alike to all.*

Verses 8–14

I. From the triumph of the Philistines over the body of Saul we may learn, 1. That the greater dignity men are advanced to the greater disgrace they are in danger of falling into. 2. That, if we give not to God the glory of our successes, even the Philistines will rise up in judgment against us and condemn us; for, when they had obtained a victory over Saul, they *sent tidings to their idols*—poor idols, that knew not what was done a few miles off till the tidings were brought them, nor then either! They also put Saul's armour *in the house of their gods, v.* 10.

II. From the triumph of the men of Jabesh-Gilead in the rescue of the bodies of Saul and his sons we learn that there is a respect due to the remains of the deceased. We must treat the dead body as those who remember it has been united to an immortal soul and must be so again.

III. From the divine Justice in the ruin of Saul we may learn, 1. That the sin of sinners will certainly find them out. 2. That no man's greatness can exempt him from the judgments of God.

CHAPTER 11

Verses 1–9

David is here brought to the possession,

I. Of the throne of Israel, after he had reigned seven years in Hebron, over Judah only. In consideration of his relation to them (*v.* 1), his former good services, and especially the divine designation (*v.* 2), they anointed him their king: he covenanted to protect them, and they to bear faith and true allegiance to him, *v.* 3.

II. Of the stronghold of Zion, which was held by the Jebusites till David's time. Whether David had a particular eye upon it as a place fit to make a royal city, or whether he had a promise of it from God, it seems that one of his first exploits was to make himself master of that fort; and, when he had it, he called it the *city of David, v.* 7. To this reference is had, Ps. ii. 6. *I have set my king upon my holy hill of Zion.*

Verses 10–47

An account of David's worthies, the great men of his time that served him and were preferred by him. The first edition of this catalogue we had, 2 Sam. xxiii. 8, &c. This is much the same, only that those named here from *v.* 41 to the end are added.

I. The connexion of this catalogue with that which is said concerning David, *v.* 9. *The Lord of hosts was with him, and these were the mighty men which he had.* God was with him and wrought for him, but by men and means and the use of second causes.

II. The title of this catalogue (*v.* 10): *These are the*

JAMIESON, FAUSSET, BROWN

CHAPTER 10

Vss. 1-7. Saul's Overthrow and Death. **1. Now the Philistines fought against Israel**—The details of this chapter have no relation to the preceding genealogies and seem to be inserted solely to introduce the narrative of David's elevation to the **throne of the whole kingdom.** The parallel between the books of Samuel and Chronicles commences with this chapter, which relates the issue of the fatal battle of Gilboa almost in the very same words as I Samuel 31. **3. the battle went sore against Saul; and the archers hit him, and he was wounded**—The *Heb.* words may be thus rendered: The archers found (attacked) him, and he feared the archers. He was not wounded, at least not dangerously, when he resolved on committing suicide. The deed was the effect of sudden terror and overwhelming depression of spirits [Calmet]. **4. his armour-bearer would not for he was sore afraid**—He was, of course, placed in the same perilous condition as Saul. But it is probable that the feelings that restrained him from complying with Saul's wish were a profound respect for royalty, mingled with apprehension of the shock which such a catastrophe would give to the national feelings and interests. **6. Saul died, and his three sons, and all his house**—his sons and courtiers who were there engaged in the battle. But it appears that Ish-bosheth and Mephibosheth were kept at Gibeah on account of their youth.

8-14. The Philistines Triumph over Him. **10. put his armour in the house of their gods**—It was common among the heathen to vow to a national or favorite deity, that, in the event of a victory, the armor of the enemy's king, or of some eminent leader, should be dedicated to him as an offering of gratitude. Such trophies were usually suspended on the pillars of the temple. **fastened his head in the temple of Dagon**—while the trunk or headless corpse was affixed to the wall of Beth-shan (I Sam. 31:10). **13. Saul died for his transgression which he committed against the Lord**—in having spared the king of the Amalekites and taken the flocks of the people as spoils, as well as in having consulted a pythoness. Both of these acts were great sins—the first as a violation of God's express and positive command, and the second as contrary to a well-known statute of the kingdom (Lev. 19:31). **14. And inquired not of the Lord**—He had done so in form (I Sam. 28:6), but not in the spirit of a humble penitent, nor with the believing confidence of a sincere worshipper. His inquiry was, in fact, a mere mockery, and his total want of all right religious impressions was manifested by his rushing from God to a wretched impostor in the service of the devil.

CHAPTER 11

Vss. 1-3. David Made King. **1. Then all Israel gathered themselves to David unto Hebron**—This event happened on the death of Ish-bosheth (see on II Sam. 5:1-3). The convention of the estates of the kingdom, the public and solemn homage of the representatives of the people, and the repeated anointing of the new king in their presence and by their direction, seem to have been necessary to the general acknowledgment of the sovereign on the part of the nation (cf. I Sam. 11:15).

4-9. He Wins the Castle of Zion from the Jebusites by Joab's Valor. **4. David and all Israel went to . . . Jebus**—(See on II Sam. 5:6-13). **8. Joab repaired the rest of the city**—David built a new town to the north of the old one on Mount Zion; but Joab was charged with a commission to restore the part that had been occupied by the ancient Jebus, to repair the breaches made during the siege, to rebuild the houses which had been demolished or burned in the sacking of the town, and to preserve all that had escaped the violence of the soldiery. This work of reconstruction is not noticed elsewhere [Calmet].

10-47. A Catalogue of His Worthies. **10. These . . . are the chief of the mighty men**—(See on II Sam. 23:8-39). They are here described as those who held strongly with him (Marg.) to make him king, etc. In these words the sacred historian assigns a reason for introducing the list of their names, immediately after his account of the election of David as king, and the conquest of Jerusalem; viz., that they assisted in making David king. In the

ADAM CLARKE

CHAPTER 10

1. *Now the Philistines fought against Israel.* The reader will find the same history in almost the same words, in 1 Sam. xxxi. 1-13.

6. *So Saul died . . . and all his house.* Every branch of his family that had followed him to the war was cut off; his three sons are mentioned as being the chief. No doubt all his officers were slain.

11. *When all Jabesh-gilead heard.* For a general account of the principles of heroism and gratitude from which this action of the men of Jabesh-gilead proceeded, see 1 Sam. xxxi. 11-12.

CHAPTER 11

1. *Then all Israel gathered themselves to David.* See 2 Sam. v. 1-10 for the history contained in the first nine verses of this chapter.

MATTHEW HENRY

men who strengthened themselves with him. In strengthening him they strengthened themselves and their own interest; for his advancement was theirs.

III. That which made all these men honourable was the good service that they did to their king and country; they helped to make David King (*v.* 10)—a good work. They slew the Philistines, and other public enemies, and were instrumental to save Israel. The honours of Christ's kingdom are prepared for those that *fight the good fight of faith,* that labour and suffer, and are willing to venture all, even life itself, for Christ and a good conscience.

IV. Among all the great exploits of David's mighty men, here is nothing great mentioned concerning David himself but his *pouring out water before the Lord* which he had *longed for, v.* 18, 19. Four very honourable dispositions of David appeared in that action. 1. Repentance for his own weakness. 2. Denial of his own appetite. He longed for the water of the well of Bethlehem; but, when he had it, he would not drink it, because he would not so far humour himself and gratify a foolish fancy. 3. Devotion towards God. That water which he thought too good, too precious, for his own drinking, he *poured out to the Lord* for a *drink-offering.* 4. Tenderness of his servants. It put him into the greatest confusion imaginable to think that three brave men should hazard their lives to fetch water for him.

V. In the wonderful achievements of these heroes the power of God must be acknowledged.

VI. One of these worthies is said to be *an Ammonite* (*v.* 39), another *a Moabite* (*v.* 46), and yet the law was that an *Ammonite* and *a Moabite should not enter into the congregation of the Lord,* Deut. xxiii. 3. These, it is likely, had approved themselves so hearty for the interest of Israel that in their case it was thought fit to dispense with that law, and the rather because it was an indication that the Son of David would have worthies among the Gentiles.

JAMIESON, FAUSSET, BROWN

original form of the list, and the connection in which it occurs in Samuel, there is no reference to the choice of a king; and even in this passage it is only in the clause introduced into the superscription that such a reference occurs [KEIL]. **11-13. Jashobeam, an Hachmonite**—or son of Hachmoni. He is called also son of Zabdiel (ch. 27:2), so that, strictly speaking, he was the grandson of Hachmoni (cf. ch. 27: 32). **lifted up his spear against three hundred, slain by him at one time**—The feat is said (II Sam. 23:8) to have been a slaughter of eight hundred in one day. Some endeavor to reconcile the statements in that passage and in this by supposing that he slew eight hundred on one occasion and three hundred on another; while others conjecture that he attacked a body of eight hundred, and, having slain three hundred of them, the rest fled [LIGHTFOOT]. **12. the three mighties**—Only two are mentioned; viz., Jashobeam and Eleazar—the third, Shammah (II Sam. 23:11), is not named in this passage. **13. He was with David at Pas-dammim**—It was at the time when he was a fugitive in the wilderness, and, parched with thirst under the burning heat of noonday, he wistfully thought of the cool fountain of his native village. This is a notice of the achievement to which Eleazar owed his fame, but the details are found only in II Sam. 23:9-11, where it is further said that he was aided by the valor of Shammah, a fact corroborated in the passage before us (vs. 14), where it is recorded of the heroes, that "they set themselves in the midst of that parcel." As the singular number is used in speaking of Shammah (II Sam. 23:12), the true view seems to be that when Eleazar had given up from exhaustion, Shammah succeeded, and by his fresh and extraordinary prowess preserved the field. **barley**—or lentils (II Sam. 23:11). Ephes-dammim was situated between Shocoh and Azekah, in the west of the Judahite territory. These feats were performed when David acted as Saul's general against the Philistines. **15-19. David longed and said, Oh that one would give me drink . . . of the well of Beth-lehem**—(See II Sam. 23:15). This chivalrous act evinces the enthusiastic devotion of David's men, that they were ready to gratify his smallest wish at the risk of their lives. It is probable that, when uttering the wish, David had no recollection of the military posted at Bethlehem. It is generally taken for granted that those who fought a way to the well of Bethlehem were the three champions just mentioned. But this is far from being clear. On the contrary, it would seem that three different heroes are referred to, for Abishai (vs. 20) was one of them. The camp of the Philistines was in the valley of Rephaim (vs. 15), which lay on the west of Jerusalem, but an outpost was stationed at Bethlehem (vs. 16), and through this garrison they had to force a passage. **21. howbeit he attained not to the first three**—(See on II Sam. 23:19). **22. Benaiah . . . of Kabzeel**—a town in the south of Judah (Josh. 15:21; Neh. 11:25). It is said that "he had done many acts"—though three only are mentioned as specimens of his daring energy and fearless courage. **slew two lionlike men of Moab**—lit., lions of God, i.e., great lions or champions. This gallant feat was probably achieved in David's hostile invasion of Moab (II Sam. 8:2). **also he went down and slew a lion in a pit in a snowy day**—probably a cave into which Benaiah had taken refuge from the snowstorm, and in which he encountered a savage lion which had its lair there. In a spacious cave the achievement would be far greater than if the monster had been previously snared or cabined in a pit. **23. he went down**—the ordinary phraseology for expressing an engagement in battle. The encounter of Benaiah with this gigantic Egyptian reminds us, in some respects, of David's combat with Goliath. At least, the height of this giant, which was about eight feet, and his armor, resembled his of Gath. **with a staff**—i.e., having no other weapon in his hand than his walking stick. **25. David set him over his guard**—the Cherethites and Pelethites that composed the small bodyguard in immediate attendance on the king. **26. Also the valiant men of the armies**—This was the third degree of military rank, and Asahel was their chief; the names of few of those mentioned are historically known. **27. Shammoth**—Between this name and Hebez, that of Elikah has evidently fallen out, as we may see (II Sam. 23:25) [BERTHEAU]. **30. Maharai**—chief of the detachment of the guards who attended on the king in the tenth month—January—(ch. 27:13; II Sam. 23:28). **39. Naharai**—armorbearer to Joab (II Sam. 23:37). The non-occurrence of Joab's name in any of the three catalogues is most probably to be accounted for by the circumstance that his office as commander-in-chief raised him to a position superior to all these orders

ADAM CLARKE

11. *The number of the mighty men.* See 2 Sam. xxiii. 8, etc.

JOSEPH PARKER:

When the men brought the water to David, "David would not drink of it, but poured it out to the Lord." Here again we come upon the line of instinct rather than upon the line of reason. David poured out the water as a libation or drink offering; he turned it indeed into a sacrifice before the Lord. There was no appointment in the law by which this should be done. There are times when we transcend the written law, the formal statute, the prescribed order of worship and ceremony, and under the impulse of unselfish thankfulness we become our greater selves. Whatever our form of worship may be, scope should always be left for free and spontaneous oblation and sacrifice.

While we have order we must also have liberty. Man was not intended to be enclosed in a cage: he is so constituted that he can worship under circumstances that have not been anticipated by mechanical laws and ordinances. Why should not men cry out aloud and praise God with a resounding voice, even at the risk of violating cold order? Can the heart always keep itself within statutory bounds? Is there to be no enthusiasm in the service of God? Is there not an instinctive worship, a psalmody of the heart, an outburst of love? Jesus Christ never restrained the enthusiasm of worship. Enthusiasm indeed is but a proof of earnestness. When the children cried out and sang before him he did not rebuke them; he said indeed that if these held their peace the very stones would cry out. We suffer immensely and continually for want of enthusiasm in our religious life. We are too orderly; our dignity is oppressive; our regulation schemes often threaten to devitalize our worship. There is no sadder condition in all human existence than to be "past feeling." Cold worship is worthless; cold worship is indeed a contradiction in terms. Not that men can be always equally passionate or enthusiastic; it would be impossible perhaps to live every day at the same altitude of religious excitement; at the same time it is possible for the heart to be in such a condition as to respond to the least appeal, to go out lovingly and consentingly after those who call to worship on the high mountains, and who would call to their aid trumpet, and harp, and organ many voiced and solemn.

Let us be careful that we do not wreck ourselves by prudence—miscalled, and perverted indeed. Who would talk of making love formal, orderly, and decorous? Who would set mechanical bounds to a child's enthusiasm on behalf of its parents? Who would bind down patriotism and forbid it to transgress certain limits of loyalty? If we do not so treat love, patriotism, friendship, neither should we so treat the religious instinct, the passion which surpasses and ennobles all other feeling.—*The People's Bible*

MATTHEW HENRY

JAMIESON, FAUSSET, BROWN

of military knighthood. **41. Uriah the Hittite**—The enrolment of this name in such a list, attesting, as it does, his distinguished merits as a brave and devoted officer, aggravates the criminality of David's outrage on his life and honor. The number of the names from verses 26 to 41 (exclusive of Asahel and Uriah, who were dead) is thirty, and from verses 41 to 47 is sixteen—making together forty-eight (see on ch. 27). Of those mentioned (vss. 26-41), the greater part belonged to the tribes of Judah and Benjamin; the sixteen names (vss. 41-47) are all associated with places unknown, or with cities and districts on the east of the Jordan. The northern tribes do not appear to have furnished any leaders [BERTHEAU].

ADAM CLARKE

MATTHEW HENRY

CHAPTER 12

Verses 1–22

An account of those that appeared and acted as David's friends, upon the death of Saul, to bring about the revolution. All the force he had, while he was persecuted, was but 600 men, but, when the time had come that he must begin to act offensively, Providence brought in more to his assistance. Even while he *kept himself close, because of Saul* (*v.* 1), while he did not appear, to invite or encourage his friends and well wishers to come in to him (not foreseeing that the death of Saul was so near), God was inclining and preparing them to come over to him. Those that trust God to do his work for them in his own way and time shall find his providence outdoing all their forecast and contrivance.

I. Some even of Saul's brethren, of the tribe of Benjamin, and a-kin to him, came over to David, *v.* 2. These Benjamites are described to be men of great dexterity, that were trained up in shooting and slinging, and used both hands alike—ingenious active men. See Judges xx. 16.

II. Some of the tribe of Gad, though seated on the other side Jordan, had such a conviction of David's title and fitness that they *separated themselves from their brethren* to go to David, though he was *in the hold in the wilderness* (*v.* 8). They were but few, eleven in all, here named, but they added much to David's strength. Those that had hitherto come were most of them men of broken fortunes, distressed, discontented, and soldiers of fortune, that came to him rather for protection than to do him any service, 1 Sam. xxii. 2. But these Gadites were brave men, *men of war, and fit for the battle*, *v.* 8. They were disciplined men in their own tribe (*v.* 14). What enemies those were that they met with in the valleys, when they had passed Jordan, does not appear; but they put them to flight with their lion-like faces, and pursued them with matchless fury, both *towards the east and towards the west.*

III. Some of Judah and Benjamin came to him, *v.* 16. Their leader was Amasai, whether the same with that Amasa that afterwards sided with Absalom (2 Sam. xvii. 25) does not appear.

1. David's prudent treaty with them, *v.* 17. He was surprised to see them, having been so often in danger by the treachery of the men of Ziph and the men of Keilah, who yet were all men of Judah. No marvel that he meets these men of Judah with caution.

(1) How fairly he deals with them. [1] If they be faithful and honourable, he will be their rewarder. But, [2] If they be false, and come to betray him into the hands of Saul, under colour of friendship, he leaves them to God to be their avenger. Never was man more violently run upon, and run down, than David was (except the Son of David himself), and yet he had the testimony of his conscience that there was no wrong in his hands.

(2) In this appeal observe, [1] He calls God the *God of our fathers*, both his fathers and theirs. Thus he reminded them not to deal ill with him; for they were both descendants from the same patriarchs, and both dependents on the same God. [2] He does not imprecate any fearful judgment upon them.

JAMIESON, FAUSSET, BROWN

CHAPTER 12

VSS. 1-22. THE COMPANIES THAT CAME TO DAVID AT ZIKLAG. **1-7. Now these are they that came to David to Ziklag**—There are three lists given in this chapter, arranged, apparently, according to the order of time when the parties joined the standard of David. **while he yet kept himself close because of Saul**—i.e., when the king's jealousy had driven him into exile from the court and the country. **Ziklag**—(See on I Sam. 27:6). It was during his retirement in that Philistine town that he was joined in rapid succession by the heroes who afterwards contributed so much to the glory of his reign. **2. of Saul's brethren of Benjamin**—i.e., of the tribe of Benjamin (cf. vs. 29), but some of them might be relatives of the king. This movement to which the parties were led, doubtless by the secret impulse of the Spirit, was of vast importance to the cause of David, as it must have been founded on their observation of the evident withdrawal of God's blessing from Saul, and His favoring presence with David, to whom it was universally known the Divine King of Israel had given the crown in reversion. The accession of the Benjamites who came first and their resolution to share his fortunes must have been particularly grateful to David. It was a public and emphatic testimony by those who had enjoyed the best means of information to the unblemished excellence of his character, as well as a decided protest against the grievous wrong inflicted by causelessly outlawing a man who had rendered such eminent services to his country. **4. Ismaiah the Gibeonite**—It appears that not only the Canaanites who were admitted into the congregation (Josh. 9), but people of the tribe of Benjamin, were among the inhabitants of Gibeon. The mention of "the Gederathite," probably from Gaderah (Josh. 15:36), in the lowlands of Judah; of the Korhites (vs. 6), from Korah (ch. 2:43), and of Gedor (vs. 7), a town in Judah, to the southwest of Bethlehem (cf. ch. 4: 4), shows that this first list contains men of Judah as well as Benjamin [BERTHEAU]. **8-13. of the Gadites there separated themselves unto David**—i.e., from the service of Saul and from the rest of the Gadites who remained steadfast adherents of his cause. **into the hold**—or fortress, i.e., of Ziklag, which was in the wilderness of Judah. **whose faces were like the faces of lions**, etc.—A fierce, lion-like countenance (II Sam. 1:23), and great agility in pursuit (II Sam. 2:18), were qualities of the highest estimation in ancient warfare. **14. one of the least was over an hundred, and the greatest over a thousand**—David, while at Ziklag, had not so large an amount of forces as to give to each of these the command of so many men. Another meaning, therefore, must obviously be sought, and excluding *was*, which is a supplement by our translators, the import of the passage is, that one of the least could discomfit a hundred, and the greatest was worth a thousand ordinary men; a strong hyperbole to express their uncommon valor. **15. These are they that went over Jordan in the first month**—i.e., in spring, when the swollen river generally fills up the banks of its channel (see on Josh. 3:15; 4:19; 5:10). **they put to flight all them of the valleys**—This was probably done at the time of their separating themselves and their purpose being discovered, they had to cut their passage through the opposing adherents of Saul, both on the eastern and western banks. The impossibility of taking the fords at such a time, and the violent rapidity of the current, make this crossing of the Jordan—in whatever way these Gadites accomplished it—a remarkable feat. **16. the children of Benjamin and Judah**—It is probable that the Benjamites invited the Judahites to accompany them, in order to prevent David being suspicious of them. Their anticipations, as the result showed, were well founded. He did suspect them, but the doubts of David as to their object in

ADAM CLARKE

CHAPTER 12

1. *Came to David to Ziklag.* Achish, king of Gath, had given Ziklag to David as a safe retreat from the wrath of Saul.

8. *And were as swift as the roes.* That swiftness was considered to be a grand accomplishment in a warrior appears from all ancient writings which treat of military affairs.

15. *In the first month.* Perhaps this was the month Nisan, which answers to a part of our March and April. This was probably before the snows on the mountains were melted, just as Jordan began to overflow its banks; or if we allow that it had already overflowed its banks, it made their attempt more hazardous, and afforded additional proof of their heroism.

MATTHEW HENRY

2. Their hearty closure with him, *v.* 18. Amasai was their spokesman, on whom the *Spirit of the Lord came.* Nothing could be said finer, more lively, or more pertinent to the occasion. *Thine are we, David, and on thy side, thou son of Jesse.* In calling him *son of Jesse* they reminded themselves that he was lineally descended from Nahshon and Salmon, who in their days were princes of the tribe of Judah. Saul called him so in disdain (1 Sam. xx. 27; xxii. 7), but they looked upon it as his honour. "*Peace, peace, be unto thee*, all the good thy heart desires, and *peace be to thy helpers*, among whom we desire to be reckoned, that peace may be on us." He assured him of help from heaven: "*For thy God helpeth thee.*" From these expressions of Amasai we may take instruction how to testify our affection and allegiance to the Lord Jesus.

3. David's cheerful acceptance of them into his interest and friendship. *David received them*, and preferred them to be *captains of the band.*

IV. Some of Manasseh likewise joined in with him, *v.* 19. Providence gave them a fair opportunity to do so when he and his men marched through their country upon this occasion. We have the story, 1 Sam. xxix. 4, &c. In his return some great men of Manasseh struck in with David to help him *against the band of Amalekites* who had plundered Ziklag.

Verses 23–40

An account of those who were active in perfecting the settlement of David upon the throne, after the death of Ishbosheth. The quota which every tribe brought in *ready armed to war*, in case there should be any opposition, *v.* 23.

I. Those tribes that lived nearest brought in the fewest—Judah but 6,800 (*v.* 24), Simeon but 7,100 (*v.* 25); whereas Zebulun, that lay remote, brought 50,000, Asher 40,000, and the two tribes and a half on the other side Jordan 120,000. Not as if the adjacent tribes were cold in the cause; but they showed prudence in bringing few, since all the rest lay within call.

II. The Levites themselves, and the priests (called here the Aaronites), appeared very hearty in this cause, and were ready, if there were occasion, to fight for David, as well as pray for him, because they knew he was called of God to the government, *v.* 26–28.

III. Even some of the kindred of Saul came over to David (*v.* 29).

IV. It is said of most of these that they were *mighty men of valour* (*v.* 25, 28, 30), of others that they were *expert in war* (*v.* 35, 36), and of them all that they *could keep rank*, *v.* 38.

V. Some were so considerate as to bring with them arms.

VI. The men of Issachar were the fewest of all, only 200, and yet as serviceable to David's interest as those that brought in the greatest numbers, these few being in effect the whole tribe. They were weather-wise. They understood public affairs, the temper of the nation, and the tendencies of the present events. We read of *the princes of Issachar*, Judges v. 15. They knew how to rule, and the rest knew how to obey.

VII. It is said of them all that they engaged in this enterprise *with a perfect heart* (*v.* 38).

VIII. The men of Judah, and others of the adjacent tribes, prepared for the victualling of their respective camps when they came to Hebron, *v.* 39, 40.

JAMIESON, FAUSSET, BROWN

repairing to him, were promptly dispelled by Amasai or Amasa, who, by the secret impulse of the Spirit, assured him of their strong attachment and their zealous service from a unanimous conviction that his cause was owned and blessed of God (I Sam. 18: 12-14). **19-22. there fell some of Manasseh**—The period of their accession is fixed as the time when David came with the Philistines against Saul to battle, "but they helped them not" (see on I Sam. 29:4). **20. As he went to Ziklag**—If those Manassites joined him on his return to Ziklag, after his dismissal from the Philistine army, then their arrival took place before the battle of Gilboa could have been fought (cf. I Sam. 29:11). Convinced of the desperate state of Saul's affairs, they abandoned him, and resolved to transfer their allegiance to David. But some learned men think that they came as fugitives from that disastrous field [CALMET and EWALD]. **captains of the thousands . . . of Manasseh**—Those seven were commanders of the large military divisions of their tribe. **21, 22. they helped David against the band**—i.e., the Amalekites who had pillaged Ziklag in David's absence. This military expedition was made by all his men (I Sam. 30: 9), who, as David's early helpers, are specially distinguished from those who are mentioned in the latter portion of the chapter. **the host of God**—i.e., a great and powerful army.

23-40. THE ARMIES THAT CAME TO HIM AT HEBRON. **23. these are the numbers of the bands . . . that came to David to Hebron**—after the death of Ish-bosheth (II Sam. 5:1). **to turn the kingdom of Saul to him according to the word of the Lord**—(ch. 10:14; 11:3, 10). The account commences with the southern tribes, Levi being associated with Judah and Simeon, as the great majority of the leading men in this tribe resided in Judah; and, after recounting the representatives of the northern tribes, it concludes with those on the east of Jordan. **27. Jehoiada, the leader of the Aaronites**—not the high priest, for that was Abiathar (I Sam. 23:9), but the leader of the Aaronite warriors, supposed to be the father of Benaiah (ch. 11:22). **29. Benjamin . . . 3000**—This small number shows the unpopularity of the movement in this tribe; and, indeed, it is expressly stated that the mass of the population had, even after Ish-bosheth's death, anxiously endeavored to secure the crown in the family of Saul. **32. children of Issachar, . . . that had understanding of the times,** etc.—Jewish writers say that the people of this tribe were eminent for their acquirements in astronomical and physical science; and the object of the remark was probably to show that the intelligent and learned classes were united with the military, and had declared for David. **33. Zebulun . . . could keep rank**—i.e., were more disciplined soldiers than the rest. **not of double heart**—Though their numbers were large, all were in a high degree well affected to David. **38. all the rest also of Israel were of one heart to make David king**—i.e., entertained a unanimous desire for his elevation. **39. 40. there they were with David three days, eating and drinking**—According to the statements made in the preceding verses, the number of armed warriors assembled in Hebron on this occasion amounted to 300,000. Supplies of provisions were abundantly furnished, not only by the people of the neighborhood, but from distant parts of the country, for all wished the festivities to be on a scale of liberality and magnificence suitable to the auspicious occasion.

ADAM CLARKE

23. *And came to David to Hebron.* That is, after the death of Ish-bosheth, Saul's son. See 2 Sam. iv. 5.

27. *Jehoiada was the leader of the Aaronites.* Abiathar was then high priest, and Jehoiada captain over the warriors of the house of Aaron.

32. *Children of Issachar.* According to the Targum they were all astronomers and astrologers. **It appears that in their wisdom, experience, and skill their brethren had the fullest confidence; and nothing was done but by their direction and advice.**

MATTHEW HENRY — CHAPTER 13

Verses 1–8

I. David's pious proposal to bring up the ark of God to Jerusalem, that the royal city might be the holy city, *v.* 1–3.

1. As soon as David was well seated on his throne he had thoughts concerning the ark of God: *Let us bring the ark to us*, *v.* 3. (1) To do honour to God, by showing respect to his ark, the token of his presence. (2) To have the comfort and benefit of that sacred

JAMIESON, FAUSSET, BROWN — CHAPTER 13

VSS. 1-8. DAVID FETCHES THE ARK FROM KIRJATH-JEARIM. **1-3. David consulted . . . And let us bring again the ark of our God**—Gratitude for the high and splendid dignity to which he had been elevated would naturally, at this period, impart a fresh animation and impulse to the habitually fervent piety of David; but, at the same time, he was animated by other motives. He fully understood his position as ruler under the theocracy, and, entering on his duties, he was resolved to fulfil his mission as a constitutional king of Israel. Accordingly, his first act as a sovereign related to the interests of religion. The ark being then the grand instrument and ornament of it, he takes the opportunity of the official representatives of the nation being with him, to consult them about the propriety of establishing it in a more public and accessible locality. The assembly at which he spoke of this consisted of the Sheloshim, princes of thousands (II Sam. 6:1). During the reign of the late king, the ark had been left in culpable neglect. Consequently

ADAM CLARKE — CHAPTER 13

1. *David consulted.* **Having taken the stronghold of Zion from the Jebusites, organized his army, got assurances of the friendly disposition of the Israelites towards him, he judged it right to do what he could for the establishment of religion in the land; and as a first step, consulted on the propriety of bringing the ark from an obscure village, where it had remained during the reign of Saul, to the royal city or seat of government.**

MATTHEW HENRY

oracle. "Let us bring it to us, not only that we may be a credit to it, but that it may be a blessing to us." It is the wisdom of those who are setting out in the world to take God's ark with them, to make his oracles their counsellors and his laws their rule.

2. He consulted with the leaders of the people about it, *v.* 1. (1) That he might show respect to the great men of the kingdom and put honour upon them. No prince that is wise will covet to be absolute. (2) That he might be advised by them in the manner of doing it.

3. He would have all the people summoned to attend on this occasion, both for the honour of the ark and for the people's satisfaction and edification, *v.* 2. (1) He calls the common people *brethren*, which bespeaks his humility and condescension. (2) He speaks of the people as a remnant that had escaped: *Our brethren that are left in all the land of Israel.* They had been under scattering providences. (3) He takes care that the priests and Levites especially should be summoned to attend the ark.

4. All this is upon supposition that it is *of the Lord their God.*

5. Thus it was requisite they should amend what had been amiss in the last reign: "For *we enquired not at it in the days of Saul*, and David makes no peevish reflections upon Saul, but, in general, *We enquired not at it*, making himself with others guilty of the neglect.

II. The people's ready agreement to this proposal (*v.* 4): *The thing* was *right in the eyes of all the people.*

III. The solemnity of bringing up the ark, *v.* 5, &c., which we read before, 2 Sam. vi. 1, &c.

Verses 9–14

This breach upon Uzza, which caused all the joy to cease, we had an account of, 2 Sam. vi. 6, &c. Let the sin of Uzza warn us all to take heed of presumption, rashness, and irreverence, in dealing about holy things (*v.* 9), and not to think that a good intention will justify a bad action.

JAMIESON, FAUSSET, BROWN

the people had, to a great extent, been careless about the ordinances of divine worship, or had contented themselves with offering sacrifices at Gibeon, without any thought of the ark, though it was the chief and most vital part of the tabernacle. The duty and advantages of this religious movement suggested by the king were apparent, and the proposal met with universal approval. **2. If it seem good unto you, and . . . it be of the Lord**—i.e., I shall conclude that this favorite measure of mine is agreeable to the mind of God, if it receive your hearty concurrence. **let us send abroad to our brethren everywhere**—He wished to make it known throughout the country, in order that there might be a general assembly of the nation, and that preparations might be made on a scale and of a kind suitable to the inauguration of the august ceremonial. **and with them also to the priests and Levites . . . in their cities and suburbs**—(See on Num. 35). The original terms, "Let us send," imply immediate execution; and, doubtless, the publication of the royal edict would have been followed by the appointment of an early day for the contemplated solemnity, had it not been retarded by a sudden invasion of the Philistines, who were twice repulsed with great loss (II Sam. 5:17), by the capture of Jerusalem, and the transference of the seat of government to that city. Finding, however, soon after, peace restored and his throne established, he resumed his preparations for removing the ark to the metropolis. **5. from Shihor of Egypt**—(Josh. 15:4, 47; Num. 34:5; I Kings 8:65; II Kings 24:7; II Chron. 7:8); a small brook flowing into the Mediterranean, near the modern El-arish, which forms the southern boundary of Palestine. **unto the entering of Hemath**—the defile between the mountain ranges of Syria and the extreme limit of Palestine on the north. **6-14. David went up, and all Israel, to Baalah**—(See on II Sam. 6:1-11). **6. whose name is called on it**—rather, "who is worshipped there" (II Sam. 6:2).

ADAM CLARKE

6. *Whose name is called on it.* "Where his name is invoked."—T. And so the Hebrew should be understood; his name was not *called on it*, but "invoked at it."

7. *In a new cart.* Lest it should be profaned by being placed on any carriage that had been employed about common uses. *Uzza and Ahio.* All the versions understand *achyo* as signifying "brother" or "brothers"; so does Jarchi, who observes, from 2 Sam. vi. 3, that these were the sons of Abinadab.

9. *Uzza put forth his hand.* See this transaction explained, 2 Sam. vi. 6, etc.

14. *The Lord blessed the house of Obed-edom.* That this man was only a sojourner at Gath, whence he was termed Gittite, and that he was originally a Levite, is evident from chap. xv. 17-18.

MATTHEW HENRY — CHAPTER 14

Verses 1–7

1. There is no man that has such a sufficiency in himself but he has need of his neighbours and has reason to be thankful for their help: David had a very large kingdom, Hiram a very little one; yet David could not build himself a house to his mind unless Hiram furnished him with both workmen and materials, *v.* 1. 2. It is a great satisfaction to a wise man to be settled, and to a good man to see the special providence of God in his settlement. The people had made David king; but he could not be easy till he perceived that *the Lord had confirmed him king over Israel*, *v.* 2. 3. We must look upon all our advancements as designed for our usefulness. We are blessed in order that we may be blessings. See Gen. xii. 2.

Verses 8–17

This narrative of David's triumph over the Philistines is much the same with that, 2 Sam. v. 17, &c. Let the attack which the Philistines made upon David forbid us to be secure in any settlement or advancement. When we are most easy something or other may come to be a terror or vexation to us. Christ's kingdom will thus be insulted by the serpent's seed, especially when it makes any advances. Let David's thankful acknowledgment of the hand of God in his successes direct us to bring all our sacrifices of praise to God's altar. ***Not unto us, O Lord! not unto us, but to thy name give glory.***

JAMIESON, FAUSSET, BROWN — CHAPTER 14

Vss. 1, 2. HIRAM'S KINDNESS TO DAVID; DAVID'S FELICITY. **1. Now Hiram king of Tyre**—The alliance with this neighboring king, and the important advantages derived from it, were among the most fortunate circumstances in David's reign. The providence of God appeared concurrent with His promise in smoothing the early course of his reign. Having conquered the Jebusites and made Zion the royal residence, he had now, along with internal prosperity, established an advantageous treaty with a neighboring prince; and hence, in immediate connection with the mention of this friendly league, it is said, "David perceived that the Lord had confirmed him king over Israel." **2. his kingdom was lifted up on high, because of his people Israel**—This is an important truth, that sovereigns are invested with royal honor and authority, not for their own sakes so much as for that of their people. But while it is true of all kings, it was especially applicable to the monarchs of Israel, and even David was made to know that all his glory and greatness were given only to fit him, as the minister of God, to execute the divine purposes towards the chosen people.

3-7. HIS WIVES. **3. David took more wives at Jerusalem**—(See on II Samuel 3:5). His concubines are mentioned (ch. 3:9), where also is given a list of his children (vss. 5-8), and those born in Jerusalem (II Sam. 5:14-16). In that, however, the names of Eliphalet and Nogah do not occur, and Beeliada appears to be the same as Eliada.

8-17. HIS VICTORIES OVER THE PHILISTINES. **8. all the Philistines went up to seek David**—in the hope of accomplishing his ruin (for so the phrase is used, I Sam. 23:15; 24:2, 3) before his throne was consolidated. Their hostility arose, both from a belief that his patriotism would lead him, erelong, to wipe out the national dishonor at Gilboa, and by fear, that in any invasion of their country, his thorough knowledge of their weak points would give him superior advantages. They resolved, therefore, to surprise and crush him before he was fairly seated on his throne. **11. they came to Baal-perazim; and David smote them there**—In an engagement fought at Mount Perazim (Isa. 28:21), in the valley of Rephaim, a few miles west of Jerusalem, the Philistines were defeated and put to flight. **12. when they had left their gods**—(See on II Sam. 5:21). **13. the Philistines yet again spread themselves**—They renewed the campaign the next season, taking the same route. David, according to divine directions, did not confront them. **14.**

ADAM CLARKE — CHAPTER 14

1. *Now Hiram king of Tyre.* See the transactions of this chapter related, 2 Sam. v. 11-25.

4. *These are the names of his children.* In 2 Sam. v. 14-16, eleven persons only are mentioned in the Hebrew text, but the Septuagint has twenty-four; here there are thirteen, and all the versions have the same number, with certain varieties in the names.

8. *The Philistines went up to seek David.* See 2 Sam. v. 17.

MATTHEW HENRY | JAMIESON, FAUSSET, BROWN | ADAM CLARKE

Go not up after them—The text in II Samuel 5:23, more correctly has, "Go not up." **turn away from them**—i.e., by stealing round a baca-grove, come upon their rear. **15. for God is gone forth before thee**—"a sound of going in the tops of the mulberry trees," i.e., the rustling of the leaves by a strong breeze suddenly rising, was the sign by which David was divinely apprised of the precise moment for the attack. The impetuosity of his onset was like the gush of a pent-up torrent, which sweeps away all in its course; and in allusion to this incident the place got its name. **16. from Gibeon . . . to Gazer**—Geba or Gibea (II Sam. 5:25), now Yefa, in the province of Judah. The line from this to Gazer was intersected by the roads which led from Judah to the cities of the Philistines. To recover possession of it, therefore, as was effected by this decisive battle, was equivalent to setting free the whole mountain region of Judah as far as their most westerly slope [BERTHEAU].

17. *Into all lands.* **That is, all the surrounding or neighboring lands and nations, for no others can possibly be intended.**

CHAPTER 15

Verses 1-24

Preparation is here made for the bringing of the ark home to the city of David from the house of Obed-edom. 1. David now prepared a place for the reception of the ark, before he brought it to him. He had not time to *build a house*, but he *pitched a tent* for it (*v.* 1), probably according to the pattern shown to Moses in the mount, or as near it as might be, of curtains and boards. Wherever we build for ourselves, we must be sure to make room for God's ark, for a church in the house.

2. David now ordered that the Levites or priests should carry the ark upon their shoulders. The Kohathites carried it in their ordinary marches, and therefore had no waggons allotted them, because their work was to *bear upon their shoulders*, Num. vii. 9. But upon extraordinary occasions, as when they passed Jordan and compassed Jericho, the priests carried it. This rule was express, and yet David himself forgot it, and put the ark upon a cart. David now took care not only to summon the Levites to the solemnity, as he did all Israel (*v.* 3) and had done before (*ch.* xiii. 2), but to see that they assembled (*v.* 4), especially the sons of Aaron, *v.* 11.

To them he gives that solemn charge (*v.* 12): *You are the chief of the fathers of the Levites*, therefore do you *bring up the ark of the Lord*. 3. The Levites and Priests sanctified themselves (*v.* 14) and were ready to carry the ark on their shoulders, according to the law, *v.* 15.

4. Officers were appointed to be ready to bid the ark welcome, with every possible expression of joy, *v.* 16. Heman, Asaph, and Ethan, were now first appointed, *v.* 17. They undertook to sound with symbols (*v.* 19), others with psalteries (*v.* 20), others with harps, on the *Sheminith*, or *eighth*, eight notes higher or lower than the rest, according to the rules of concert, *v.* 21.

CHAPTER 15

VSS. 1-24. DAVID BRINGS THE ARK FROM OBED-EDOM. **1. David made him houses in the city of David**—Through the liberality of his Tyrian ally (ch. 14:1), David was enabled to erect not only a palace for himself, but to furnish suitable accommodation for his numerous family. Where polygamy prevails, each wife has a separate house or suite of apartments for herself and children. **prepared a place for the ark of God, and pitched for it a tent**—i.e., made an entirely new one upon the model of the former. The old tabernacle, which Moses had constructed in the wilderness and which had hitherto served the purpose of a sacred covering, was to be left at Gibeon, either because of the unwillingness of the inhabitants to part with such a venerable relic, or because there was no use for it in Jerusalem, where a more solid and sumptuous edifice was contemplated. If it appear surprising that David "made him houses" before he prepared this new tabernacle, it should be remembered that he had received no divine intimation respecting such a work. **2. Then David said, None ought to carry the ark of God but the Levites**—After the lapse of three months (ch. 13:14) the purpose of transporting the ark to Jerusalem was resumed. Time and reflection had led to a discovery of the cause of the painful catastrophe that marred the first attempt. In preparing for the solemn procession that was now to usher the sacred symbol into its resting-place, David took special care that the carriage should be regulated in strict conformity to the law (Num. 4:5, 15; 7:9; 10:17). **3. David gathered all Israel together**—Some are of opinion that this was done on one of the three great festivals, but at whatever time the ceremonial took place, it was of great importance to summon a general convocation of the people, many of whom, from the long-continued disorders of the kingdom, might have had little or no opportunity of knowing anything of the ark, which had been allowed to remain so long in obscurity and neglect. **4. David assembled the children of Aaron, and the Levites**—The children of Aaron were the two priests (vs. 11), Zadok and Abiathar, heads of the two priestly houses of Eleazar and Ithamar, and colleagues in the high priesthood (II Sam. 20:25). The Levites were the chiefs of their father's house (vs. 12); four belonging to the Kohathite branch, on whose shoulders the ark was to be borne; viz., Uriel, Shemaiah—descended from Elizaphan or Elzaphan—(Exod. 6:22), Hebron (Exod. 6:18; ch. 6:2), and Amminadab from Uzziel (Exod. 6:22). **12. sanctify yourselves**—This special sanctification, which was required on all grave and important occasions, consisted in observing the strictest abstinence, as well as cleanliness, both in person and dress (see on Gen. 35:2; Exod. 19:10, 15); and in the neglect of these rules no step could have been taken (II Chron. 30:3). **16-24. David spake to the chief of the Levites to appoint . . . singers with instruments**—These eminent Levites were instructed to train the musicians and singers who were under them, for the solemn procession. The performers were ranged in three choirs or bands, and the names of the principal leaders are given (vss. 17, 18, 21), with the instruments respectively used by each. "Ben" (vs. 18) is omitted (vs. 20). Either it was used merely as a common noun, to intimate that Zechariah was the son of Jaaziel or Aziel, or Ben is the same as Azaziah. **22. Chenaniah, chief of the Levites**—He was not of the six heads of the Levitical families, but a chief in consequence of his office, which required learning, without regard to birth or family. **in-**

CHAPTER 15

1. *Made him houses.* One for himself, and one for the ark; in the latter was a tent, under which the ark was placed.

2. *None ought to carry the ark . . . but the Levites.* **It was their business; and he should have thought of this sooner, and then the unfortunate breach on Uzza would have been prevented; see v. 13.**

15. *Upon their shoulders.* **That is, the staves which went through the rings rested on their shoulders, but the ark itself rested on the staves like a sedan on its poles. *As Moses commanded.* See Num. iv. 5, 15.**

17. *Heman . . . Asaph . . . Ethan.* **These were the three chief musicians in the time of David; see chap. vi. 31.**

20. *With psalteries on Alamoth.* **Some suppose that the word signifies "virgins," or "women singers," the persons mentioned here being appointed to accompany them with psalteries, and preside over them.**

21. *On the Sheminith.* **According to the Targum, this signifies an instrument that sounded an octave, or, according to others, an instrument with eight strings.**

MATTHEW HENRY

Some that were priests blew with the trumpet (*v.* 24), as was usual at the removal of the ark (Num. x. 8) and at solemn feasts, Ps. lxxxi. 3. And one was appointed for song (*v.* 22), for he was skilful in it, could sing well himself and instruct others.

Verses 25–29

All things being got ready for the carrying of the ark to the city of David, and its reception there, we have here an account of the solemnity of this conveyance thither from the house of Obed-edom.

I. God helped the Levites that carried it. If God did not help us, we could not stir a step. The Levites, remembering the breach upon Uzza, were probably ready to tremble when they took up the ark; but God helped them, silenced their fears, and strengthened their faith. God's ministers that bear the vessels of the Lord have special need of divine help in their ministrations, that God in them may be glorified and his church edified.

II. When they experienced the tokens of God's presence with them they offered sacrifices of praise to him, *v.* 26.

III. There were great expressions of rejoicing used: the sacred music was played, David danced, the singers sang, and the common people shouted, *v.* 27, 28. This we had before, 2 Sam. vi. 14, 15.

JAMIESON, FAUSSET, BROWN

structed about the song—He directed all these bands as to the proper time when each was to strike in or change their notes; or, as some render the passage, "He led the burdens, for he was skilled," i.e., in the custom which it was necessary to observe in the carriage of the holy things [BERTHEAU]. **23. Berechiah and Elkanah were doorkeepers**—who marched immediately in front, while Obed-edom and Jeiel went in the rear, of the ark. **25. So David and the elders . . . and captains . . . went**—The pious design of David in ordering all his principal ministers and officers to take part in this solemn work and imparting so much pomp and imposing ceremony to the procession, was evidently to inspire the popular mind with a profound veneration for the ark and to give the young especially salutary impressions of religion, which would be renewed by the remembrance that they had been witnesses of the august solemnity in which the king and the highest aristocracy of the land participated, vying with all other classes to do honor to the God of Israel. **26. it came to pass,** etc.—(See on II Sam. 6:13-23). **they offered seven bullocks and seven rams**—The Levites seem to have entered on this duty with fear and trembling; and finding that they might advance without any such indications of divine wrath as Uzza had experienced (ch. 13:10), they offered an ox and a fatted sheep immediately after starting (II Sam. 6:13), and seven bullocks and seven rams—a perfect sacrifice— at the close of the procession (ch. 16:1). It is probable that preparations had been made for the offering of similar sacrifices at regular intervals along the way. **27. a robe of fine linen**—*Hebrew, Butz*—is rather supposed in the later books to denote cotton. **an ephod**—a shoulder garment, a cincture or cape over his dress. It was worn by the priests, but was not so peculiar to them as to be forbidden others (I Sam. 2:18; 22:18). **29. Michal . . . saw . . . David dancing and playing**—His movements would be slow and solemn, suitable to the grave and solemn character of the music. Though his royal robes were laid aside, he was attired like the other officials, showing a becoming humility in the immediate presence of God. The feelings manifested by Michal were only an ebullition of spleen from a proud and passionate woman.

ADAM CLARKE

22. *Chenaniah . . . instructed about the song.* This appears to have been the master singer; he gave the key and the time, for he presided *bemassa,* "in the elevation," probably meaning what is called pitching the tune, for *he was skilful* in music, and powerful in his voice, and well qualified to lead the band.

26. *God helped the Levites.* When they saw that God had made no breach among them, as he had in the case of Uzza, in gratitude for their preservation, and His acceptance of their labor, they sacrificed seven bullocks and seven rams.

27. *A robe of fine linen.* A robe made of *buts,* probably the tuft or beard of the Pinna Magna, a species of mussel found everywhere on the shores of the Mediterranean.

29. *Michal . . . saw . . . David dancing . . . and she despised him.* See this whole business explained, 2 Sam. vi. 20, etc.

MATTHEW HENRY

CHAPTER 16

Verses 1–6

It was a glorious day when the ark of God was safely lodged in the tent David had pitched for it.

I. The ark had been obscure in a country town, in the fields of the wood; now it was removed to a public place, to the royal city. It had been neglected, as a despised broken vessel; now it was attended with veneration, and God was enquired of by it. This was but a tent, a poor mean dwelling; yet this was the tabernacle, the temple, which David in his psalms often speaks of with so much affection. David, who pitched a tent for the ark and continued steadfast to it, did far better than Solomon, who built a temple for it and yet in his latter end turned his back upon it. The church's poorest times were its purest.

II. Now David was easy in his mind, the ark was fixed, and fixed near him. He takes care, 1. That God shall have the glory of it. (1) By sacrifices (*v.* 1), burnt-offerings in adoration of his perfections, peace-offerings in acknowledgment of his favours. (2) By songs; he appointed Levites to record this story in a song for the benefit of others. 2. That the people shall have the joy of it. They shall fare the better for this day's solemnity; for he gives them all not only a royal treat but also a *blessing in the name of the Lord,* as a father, as a prophet, *v.* 2.

Verses 7–36

The thanksgiving psalm which David, by the Spirit, composed, and delivered to the chief musician, to be sung upon occasion of the public entry the ark made into the tent prepared for it. It is gathered out of several psalms (from the beginning to *v.* 23 is taken from Ps. cv. 1, &c.; and then *v.* 23 to *v.* 34 is the whole 96th psalm, with little variation; *v.* 34 is taken from Ps. cxxxvi. 1 and divers others; and then the last two verses are taken from the close of Ps. cvi.), which some think warrants us to do likewise, and make up hymns out of David's psalms, a part of one and a part of another put together so as may be most proper to express and excite the devotion of Christians. In the midst of our praises we must not forget to pray for the succour and relief of those saints and

JAMIESON, FAUSSET, BROWN

CHAPTER 16

Vss. 1-6. DAVID'S FESTIVAL SACRIFICE AND LIBERALITY TO THE PEOPLE. **2. he blessed the people in the name of the Lord**—The king commended their zeal, supplicated the divine blessing upon them, and ordered the remains of the thank offerings which had been profusely sacrificed during the procession, to be distributed in certain proportions to every individual, that the ceremonial might terminate with appropriate festivities (Deut. 12:7). **3. flagon of wine**—The two latter words are a supplement by our translators, and the former is, in other versions, rendered not a "flagon," but a "cake," a confection, as the *Septuagint* renders it, made of flour and honey. **4-6. he appointed certain of the Levites to minister before the ark of the Lord**—No sooner was the ark deposited in its tent than the Levites, who were to officiate in the choirs before it, entered upon their duties. A select number of the musicians were chosen for the service from the list (ch. 15:19-21) of those who had taken a prominent part in the recent procession. The same arrangement was to be observed in their duties, now that the ark again was stationary; Asaph, with his associates, composing the first or principal company, played with cymbals; Zechariah and his colleagues, with whom were conjoined Jeiel and Obed-edom, forming the second company, used harps and similar instruments. **5. Jeiel**—is the same as Aziel (ch. 15:20). **6. Benaiah also and Jahaziel**—The name of the former is mentioned among the priests (ch. 15:24), but not the latter. The office assigned to them was that of blowing trumpets at regular intervals before the ark and in the tabernacle.

7-43. HIS PSALM OF THANKSGIVING. **7. Then on that day David delivered first this psalm**—Among the other preparations for this solemn inauguration, the royal bard had composed a special hymn for the occasion. Doubtless it had been previously in the hands of Asaph and his assistants, but it was now publicly committed to them as they entered for the first time on the performance of their sacred duties. It occupies the greater part of this chapter (vss. 8-36), and seems to have been compiled from other psalms of David, previously known to the Israelites, as the whole of it will be found, with very slight variations, in Psalms 96; 105:1-15; 106:47, 48. In the form, however, in which it is given by the sacred

ADAM CLARKE

CHAPTER 16

5. *Asaph.* See the preceding chapter, v. 17. etc.

7. *David delivered first this psalm.* I believe the meaning of this place to be this: David made the psalm on the occasion above specified; and delivered it to Asaph, who was the musician, and to his brethren, to be sung by them in honor of what God had done in behalf of His people.

12. *Remember his marvellous works.* The whole of the psalm refers to God's wondrous actions among the nations in behalf of Israel.

MATTHEW HENRY

servants of God that are in distress (*v.* 35): *Save us, gather us, deliver us from the heathen,* those of us that are scattered and oppressed. When we are rejoicing in God's favours to us we must remember our afflicted brethren, and pray for their salvation, and deliverance as our own. We are members one of another; and therefore when we mean, "Lord, save *them,*" it is not improper to say, "Lord, save *us.*" Let us make God the Alpha and Omega of our praises. David begins with (*v.* 8), *Give thanks to the Lord*; he concludes (*v.* 36), *Blessed be the Lord.* And whereas in the place whence this doxology is taken (Ps. cvi. 48) it is added, *Let all the people say, Amen, Hallelujah,* here we find they did according to that directory: *All the people said, Amen, and praised the Lord.*

Verses 37–43

The worship of God is not only to be the work of a solemn day now and then, brought in to grace a triumph; but it ought to be the work of every day. David therefore settles it here for a constancy. 1. At Jerusalem, where the ark was, Asaph and his brethren were appointed to attend, to *minister before the ark continually,* with songs of praise, *as every day's work required, v.* 37. No sacrifices were offered there, nor incense burnt, because the altars were not there, but David's prayers were *directed as incense, and the lifting up of his hands as the evening sacrifice* (Ps. cxli. 2), so early did spiritual worship take place of ceremonial. 2. Yet the ceremonial worship, being of divine institution, must by no means be omitted; and therefore at Gibeon were the altars where the priests attended, for their work was to sacrifice and burn incense, which they did *continually, morning and evening, according to the law of Moses, v.* 39, 40. These must be kept up, because, however in their own nature they were inferior to the moral services of prayer and praise, yet, as they were types of the mediation of Christ, they had a great deal of honour put upon them, and the observance of them was of great consequence. At Gibeon, where the altars were, David also appointed *singers to give thanks to the Lord,* and the burden of all their songs must be, *For his mercy endureth for ever, v.* 41. (1) The people were satisfied, and went home [pleased. (2) David returned to bless his house, resolving to keep up his family worship still, which public worship must not supersede.

JAMIESON, FAUSSET, BROWN

historian, it seems to have been the first psalm given for use in the tabernacle service. Abounding, as it does, with the liveliest ascriptions of praise to God for the revelation of His glorious character and the display of His marvellous works and containing, as it does, so many pointed allusions to the origin, privileges, and peculiar destiny of the chosen people, it was admirably calculated to animate the devotions and call forth the gratitude of the assembled multitude. **36. all the people said, Amen**—(Cf. Ps. 72:19, 20; 106:48). In the former, the author of the doxology utters the amen himself, while in the latter the people are exhorted to say amen. This may arise from the fact that the latter psalm originally concluded with the injunction to say amen. But in this historical account of the festival, it was necessary to relate that the people obeyed this injunction on the occasion referred to, and therefore the words "let them praise," were altered into "and they praised" [BERTHEAU]. **37-42. So he left there, before the covenant of the Lord, Asaph and his brethren,** etc.—The sequel of the chapter describes the appointment of the sacred musicians and their respective duties. **38. Obed-edom with their brethren**—Hosah, mentioned at the close of the verse, and a great number besides (see on ch. 26). **to be porters**—doorkeepers. **39, 40. And Zadok . . . before the tabernacle . . . at Gibeon**—While the above-mentioned officers under the superintendence of Abiathar, were appointed to officiate in Jerusalem, whither the ark had been brought, Zadok and the priests subordinate to him were stationed at Gibeon to perform the sacred service before the ancient tabernacle which still remained there. **continually morning and evening**—as the law enjoined (Exod. 29:38; Num. 28:3, 6). **and do according to all that is written in the law**—(See Num. 28). Thus, in the time of David, the worship was performed at two places, where the sacred things that had been transmitted from the age of Moses were preserved. Before the Ark in Jerusalem, Asaph and his brethren officiated as singers, Obed-edom and Hosah served as doorkeepers, and Benaiah and Jehaziel blew the trumpets. While at the tabernacle and burnt offering in Gibeon, Heman and Jeduthun presided over the sacred music, the sons of Jeduthun were doorkeepers, and Zadok, with his suite of attendant priests, offered the sacrifices.

ADAM CLARKE

22. *Touch not mine anointed.* By this title the patriarchs are generally understood; they had a regal and sacerdotal power in the order of God. In the behalf of the patriarchs God had often especially interfered: in behalf of Abraham, Gen. xii. 17 and xx. 3; and of Jacob, Gen. xxxi. 24; xxxiv. 26; and xxxv. 5. But the title may be applied to all the Jewish people, who were the anointed, as they were the elect and peculiar people of God. See Heb. xi. 26.

35. *Save us, O God of our salvation.* As He is the saving God, so we may pray to Him to save us.

39. *Zadok the priest.* Both Zadok and Abiathar were high priests at this time. The former David established at Gibeah, or Gibeon, where the ark had been all the days of Saul; and the latter he established at Jerusalem, where the ark now was. So there were two high priests, and two distinct services; but there was only one ark. How long the service at Gibeon was continued we cannot tell; the principal functions were no doubt performed at Jerusalem.

MATTHEW HENRY — CHAPTER 17

Verses 1–15

I. David could not be easy in a house of cedar while the ark was lodged within curtains, *v.* 1. Those that are contriving where to bestow their fruits and their goods would do well to enquire what condition the ark is in, and whether some may not be well bestowed upon it.

II. How ready God's prophets should be to encourage every good purpose (*v.* 2).

III. How little God affects external pomp and splendour in his service. His ark was content with a tabernacle (*v.* 5). He commanded the judges to *feed his people,* but never bade them *build him a house, v.* 6.

IV. How graciously God accepts his people's good purposes, yea, though he himself prevents the performance of them. David must not *build this house, v.* 4. He must prepare for it, but not do it; as Moses must bring Israel within sight of Canaan, but must then leave it to Joshua to put them in possession of it.

Yet David must not think that, because he was not permitted to build the temple, 1. His preferment was in vain; no, "*I took thee from the sheep-cote,* though not to be a builder of the temple, yet to be *ruler over my people Israel.*"

Nor, 2. Must he think that his good purpose was in vain, and that he should lose the reward of it; he shall be as fully recompensed as if he had done it: "*The Lord will build thee a house,* and annex the crown of Israel to it," *v.* 10. If there be a willing mind, it shall not only be accepted, but thus rewarded.

JAMIESON, FAUSSET, BROWN — CHAPTER 17

Vss. 1-10. DAVID FORBIDDEN TO BUILD GOD A HOUSE. **1. as David sat in his house**—The details of this chapter were given in nearly similar terms (II Sam. 7). The date was towards the latter end of David's reign, for it is expressly said in the former book to have been at the cessation of all his wars. But as to narrate the preparations for the removal of the ark and the erection of the temple was the principal object of the historian, the exact chronology is not followed. **5. I . . . have gone from tent to tent, and from one tabernacle to another**—The literal rendering is, "I was walking in a tent and in a dwelling." The evident intention (as we may see from vs. 6) was to lay stress upon the fact that God was a *Mithhallek* (a travelling God) and went from one place to another with His *tent* and His entire *dwelling* (the dwelling included not merely the tent, but the fore-courts with the altar of burnt offerings, etc.) [BERTHEAU]. **6 spake I a word to any of the judges**—In II Sam. 7:7 it is "any of the tribes" of Israel. Both are included. But the judges "who were commanded to feed the people," form the more suitable antithesis to David. **Why have ye not built me an house of cedars?**—i.e., a solid and magnificent temple. **7. Thus saith the Lord of hosts, I took thee from the sheepcote**—a round tower of rude construction, high walled, but open at the top, in which sheep are often enclosed at night to protect them from wild beasts. The meaning is, I elevated you to the throne from a humble condition solely by an act of divine grace, and not from any antecedent merits of your own (see on I Sam. 16:11), and I enabled you to acquire renown, equal or superior to any other monarch. Your reign will ever be afterwards regarded as the best and brightest era in the history of Israel, for it will secure to the nation a settled inheritance of prosperity and peace, without any of the oppressions or disorders that afflicted them in early times. **9, 10. at the beginning, and since the time I commanded judges**—i.e., including the whole period from Joshua to Saul. **I tell thee that the Lord will build thee an house**—This was the language of Nathan himself, who was specially directed to assure David, not only of personal blessing and prosperity, but of a continuous

ADAM CLARKE — CHAPTER 17

1. *Now it came to pass.* See everything recorded in this chapter amply detailed in the notes on 2 Sam. vii. 1, etc.

9. *Neither shall the children of wickedness.* They shall no more be brought into servitude as they were in the time they sojourned in Egypt. This is what is here referred to.

MATTHEW HENRY

Nor, 3. Must he think that because *he* might not do this good work therefore it would never be done, and that it was in vain to think of it; no, *I will raise up thy seed, and he shall build me a house*, *v.* 11, 12. Nor, 4. Must he confine his thoughts to the temporal prosperity of his family, but must entertain himself with the prospect of the kingdom of the Messiah, who should descend from his loins, and whose throne should be *established for evermore*, *v.* 14.

Verses 16–27

David's solemn address to God, in answer to the gracious message he had now received from him. By faith he receives the promises, embraces them, and is persuaded of them, as the patriarchs, Heb. xi. 13. What an example is this to us of humble, believing, fervent prayer! Observe only those few expressions in which the prayer, as we find it here, differs from the record of it in 2 Sam. vii.

I. That which is there expressed by way of question (*Is this the manner of men, O Lord God?*) is here an acknowledgment: "*Thou hast regarded me according to the estate of a man of high degree.*" God, by the covenant-relations into which he admits believers, regards them according to the estate of men of high degree, though they are mean and vile.

II. After the words *What can David say more unto thee*, it is here added, *for the honour of thy servant? v.* 18. The honour God puts upon his servants, by taking them into covenant and communion with himself, is so great that they need not, they cannot, desire to be more highly honoured.

III. It is very observable that what in Samuel is said to be *for thy word's sake* is here said to be *for thy servant's sake*, *v.* 19. Jesus Christ is both *the Word of God* (Rev. xix. 13) and *the servant of God* (Isa. xlii. 1), and it is for his sake, upon the score of his mediation, that the promises are both made and made good to all believers.

IV. In Samuel, the Lord of hosts is said to be the *God over Israel*; here he is said to be *the God of Israel, even a God to Israel*, *v.* 24. There were those that were called *gods* of such and such nations, gods of Assyria and Egypt, gods of Hamad and Arpad; but they were no gods to them, for they stood them in no stead at all, were mere ciphers, nothing but a name. But *the God of Israel* is a *God to Israel*; all his attributes and perfections redound to their real benefit and advantage.

V. The closing words in Samuel are, *With thy blessing let the house of thy servant be blessed for ever*. That is the language of a holy desire. But the closing words here are the language of a most holy faith: *For thou blessest, O Lord! and it shall be blessed for ever*, *v.* 27. David's prayer concludes as God's promise did (*v.* 14) with that which is *for ever*. God's word looks at things eternal, and so should our desires and hopes.

JAMIESON, FAUSSET, BROWN

line of royal descendants. **11. I will raise up thy seed**—(II Sam. 7:12). **13. I will not take my mercy away from him, as I took it from him that was before thee**—My procedure in dealing with him will be different from My disposal of Saul. Should his misconduct call for personal chastisement, I shall spare his family. If I see it necessary to withdraw My favor and help for a time, it will be a corrective discipline only to reform and restore, not to destroy. (On this passage some have founded an argument for Solomon's repentance and return to God.) **14. I will settle him in my house**—over My people Israel. **and in my kingdom**—God here asserts His right of supreme sovereignty in Israel. David and Solomon, with their successors, were only the vicegerents whom He nominated, or, in His providence, permitted. **his throne shall be established for evermore**—The posterity of David inherited the throne in a long succession—but not always. In such a connection as this, the phrase "for evermore" is employed in a restricted sense (see on Lam. 3:31). We naturally expect the prophet to revert to David before concluding, after having spoken (vs. 12) of the building of Solomon's temple. The promise that his house should be blessed was intended as a compensation for the disappointment of his wish to build the temple, and hence this assurance is appropriately repeated at the conclusion of the prophet's address [BERTHEAU]. **15. According to all ... this vision**—The revelation of the divine will was made to the prophet in a dream. **16. David the king ... sat before the Lord, and said**—(See on II Sam. 7:18-19).

ADAM CLARKE

12. *I will stablish his throne for ever.* David was a type of Christ, and concerning him the prophecy is literally true. See Isa. ix. 7, where there is evidently the same reference.

13. *I will not take my mercy away from him.* I will not cut off his family from the throne, as I did that of his predecessor, Saul.

16. *And what is mine house, that thou hast brought me hitherto?* I am not of any regal family, and have no natural right to the throne.

MATTHEW HENRY

CHAPTER 18

Verses 1–8

After this, it is said (*v.* 1), David did great exploits. After the sweet communion he had had with God by the word and prayer, he went on in his work with extraordinary vigour and courage, *conquering and to conquer*. The Philistines had, for several generations, been vexatious to Israel, but now *David subdued them*, *v.* 1.

Such is the uncertainty of this world that frequently men lose their wealth and power when they think to confirm it. Hadarezer was smitten *as he went to establish his dominion*, *v.* 3. The Syrians of Damascus were smitten when they came to help Hadarezer.

JAMIESON, FAUSSET, BROWN

CHAPTER 18

Vss. 1, 2. DAVID SUBDUES THE PHILISTINES AND MOABITES. **1. David ... took Gath and her towns**—The full extent of David's conquests in the Philistine territory is here distinctly stated, whereas in the parallel passage (II Sam. 8:1) it was only described in a general way. Gath was the "Metheg-ammah," or "arm-bridle," as it is there called—either from its supremacy as the capital over the other Philistine towns, or because, in the capture of that important place and its dependencies, he obtained the complete control of his restless neighbors. **2. he smote Moab**—The terrible severities by which David's conquest of that people was marked, and the probable reason of their being subjected to such a dreadful retribution, are narrated (II Sam. 8:2). **the Moabites ... brought gifts**—i.e., became tributary to Israel.

3-17. DAVID SMITES HADADEZER AND THE SYRIANS. **3. Hadarezer**—or Hadadezer (II Sam. 8:3), which was probably the original form of the name, was derived from Hadad, a Syrian deity. It seems to have become the official and hereditary title of the rulers of that kingdom. **Zobah**—Its situation is determined by the words "unto" or "towards Hamath," a little to the northeast of Damascus, and is supposed by some to be the same place as in earlier times was called Hobah (Gen. 14:15). Previous to the rise of Damascus, Zobah was the capital of the kingdom which held supremacy among the petty states of Syria. **as he went to establish his dominion by the river Euphrates**—Some refer this to David, who was seeking to extend his possessions in one direction towards a point bordering on the Euphrates, in accordance with the promise (Gen.

ADAM CLARKE

CHAPTER 18

1. *David . . . took Gath and her towns.* See 2 Sam. viii. 1, etc.

2. *Brought gifts.* Were laid under tribute.

MATTHEW HENRY

Verses 9–17

What God blesses us with we must honour him with. It was said before (*v.* 6) and here it is repeated (*v.* 13) that *the Lord preserved David whithersoever he went.* God gives men power, not that they may look great with it, but that they may do good with it.

CHAPTER 19

Verses 1–5

It becomes good people to be neighbourly, and especially to be grateful. David will pay respect to Hanun because he is his neighbour; and religion teaches us to be civil and to be ready to do all offices of kindness to those we live among; nor must difference in religion be any obstruction to this. But, besides this, David remembered the kindness which his father showed to him.

Those that are base, and design ill themselves, are apt to be jealous and to suspect ill of others without cause. Hanun's servants suggested that David's ambassadors came as spies, as if so great and mighty a man as David needed to do so mean a thing. Yet Hanun, against the law of nations, treated David's ambassadors villainously.

Verses 6–19

The hearts of sinners are hardened to their destruction. The children of Ammon saw that *they had made themselves odious to David* (*v.* 6); it would have been their wisdom to desire conditions of peace, to humble themselves and offer any satisfaction for the injury they had done him. But, instead of this, they prepared for war, and so brought upon themselves, by David's hand, those desolations which he never intended them.

The courage of brave men is heightened and invigorated by difficulties. When Joab saw that the battle was set against him before and behind (*v.* 10), instead of meditating a retreat, he doubled his resolution; and not only spoke, but acted, like a gallant man, that had great presence of mind when

JAMIESON, FAUSSET, BROWN

15:18; Num. 24:17). But others are of opinion that, as David's name is mentioned (vs. 4), this reference is most applicable to Hadadezer. **4-8. David took from him a thousand chariots**—(See on II Sam. 8:3-14). In that passage David is said to have taken 700 horsemen, whereas here it is said that he took 7000. This great discrepancy in the text of the two narratives seems to have originated with a transcriber in confounding the two Hebrew letters which indicate the numbers, and in neglecting to mark or obscure the points over one of them. We have no means of ascertaining whether 700 or 7000 be the more correct. Probably the former should be adopted [DAVIDSON'S HERM.]. **but reserved of them an hundred chariots**—probably to grace a triumphal procession on his return to Jerusalem, and after using them in that way, destroy them like the rest. **8. from Tibhath and from Chun**—These places are called Betah and Berothai (II Sam. 8:8). Perhaps the one might be the Jewish, the other the Syrian, name of these towns. Neither their situation nor the connection between them is known. The Arabic version makes them to be Emesa (now Hems) and Baal-bek, both of which agree very well with the relative position of Zobah. **9-13. Tou**—or Toi—whose dominions border on those of Hadadezer. (See on II Sam. 8:9-12; I Kings 11:15.) **17. the Cherethites and the Pelethites**—who formed the royal bodyguard. The Cherethites were, most probably, those brave men who all along accompanied David while among the Philistines, and from that people derived their name (I Sam. 30:14; Ezek. 25:16; Zeph. 12:5) as well as their skill in archery—while the Pelethites were those who joined him at Ziklag, took their name from Pelet, the chief man in the company (ch. 12:3), and, being Benjamites, were expert in the use of the sling.

CHAPTER 19

VSS. 1-5. DAVID'S MESSENGERS, SENT TO COMFORT HANUN, ARE DISGRACEFULLY TREATED. **1. after this**—This phrase seems to indicate that the incident now to be related took place immediately, or soon after the wars described in the preceding chapter. But the chronological order is loosely observed, and the only just inference that can be drawn from the use of this phrase is, that some farther account is to be given of the wars against the Syrians. **Nahash the king of the children of Ammon died**—There had subsisted a very friendly relation between David and him, begun during the exile of the former, and cemented, doubtless, by their common hostility to Saul. **3. are not his servants come unto thee for to search?**—i.e., thy capital, Rabbah (II Sam. 10:3). **4. shaved them**—not completely, but only the half of their face. This disrespect to the beard, and indecent exposure of their persons by their clothes being cut off from the girdle downwards, was the grossest indignity to which Jews, in common with all Orientals, could be subjected. No wonder that the men were ashamed to appear in public—that the king recommended them to remain in seclusion on the border till the mark of their disgrace had disappeared—and then they might, with propriety, return to the court.

6-15. JOAB AND ABISHAI OVERCOME THE AMMONITES. **6. when the children of Ammon saw that they had made themselves odious to David**—One universal feeling of indignation was roused throughout Israel, and all classes supported the king in his determination to avenge this unprovoked insult on the Hebrew nation. **Hanun . . . sent a thousand talents of silver**—a sum equal to about $2,000,000 to procure the services of **foreign mercenaries. chariots and horsemen out of Mesopotamia, . . . Syria-maachah, and . . . Zobah**—The Mesopotamian troops did not arrive during this campaign (vs. 16). Syria-maachah lay on the north of the possessions of the transjordanic Israelites, near Gilead. **Zobah**—(see on ch. 18:3). **7. they hired thirty and two thousand chariots**—*Heb.*, riders, or cavalry, accustomed to fight either on horseback or in chariots, and occasionally on foot. Accepting this as the true rendering, the number of hired auxiliaries mentioned in this passage agrees exactly with the statement in II Samuel 10:6. 20,000, 12,000 (from Tob), equal to 32,000, and 1000 with the king of Maachah. **8. David . . . sent Joab, and all the host of the mighty men**—All the forces of Israel, including the great military orders, were engaged in this war. **9. children of Ammon . . . put the battle in array before the gate of the city**—i.e., outside the walls of Medebah, a frontier town on the Arnon.

ADAM CLARKE

9. *Tou king of Hamath.* Called Toi in 2 Sam. viii. 9.

12. *Abishai . . . slew of the Edomites.* This victory is attributed to David, 2 Sam. viii. 13. He sent Abishai against them, and he defeated them; this is with great propriety attributed to David as commander in chief.

15. *Joab . . . was over the host.* General in chief. *Jehoshaphat . . . recorder.* The king's remembrancer, or historiographer royal.

16. *Zadok . . . and Abimelech . . . priests.* Both high priests; one at Gibeon, and the other at Jerusalem, as we have seen, chap. xvi. 39. *Shavsha was scribe.* Called Seraiah, 2 Sam. viii. 17.

CHAPTER 19

1. *Now it came to pass.* See the same history, 2 Sam. x. 1, etc.

6. *Chariots and horsemen out of Mesopotamia.* These are not mentioned in the parallel place in Samuel; probably they did not arrive till the Ammonites and their other allies were defeated by the Israelites in the first battle.

7. *Thirty and two thousand.* The whole number mentioned in Samuel is: Syrians, of Beth-rehob, and of Zoba, 20,000; of King Maacah, 1,000; of Ishtob, 12,000; in all, 33,000. Of chariots or cavalry there is no mention. These could not have been the whole army.

MATTHEW HENRY

he saw himself surrounded. He engaged with his brother for mutual assistance (*v.* 12), excited himself and the rest of the officers to act vigorously in their respective posts, and then left the issue to God: *Let the Lord do that which is right in his sight.* The Ammonites did their utmost to make the best of their position: they brought as good a force into the field, yet, having a bad cause, they were put to the worst. Right will prevail and triumph at last. The Syrians, though in no way concerned in the merits of the cause, but serving only as mercenaries to the Ammonites, when they were beaten, thought themselves concerned to retrieve their honour, and therefore called in the assistance of the Syrians on the other side Euphrates; but to no purpose, for still they *fled before Israel* (*v.* 18). The Syrians, finding that Israel was the conquering side, not only broke off their alliance with the Ammonites and would help them no more (*v.* 19), *but made peace with David and became his servants.*

CHAPTER 20

Verses 1–3

The destruction of Rabbah, the metropolis of their kingdom (*v.* 1), the putting of their king's crown upon David's head (*v.* 2), and the great severity that was used towards the people, *v.* 3. Of this we had a more full account in 2 Sam. xi, xii. While Joab was besieging Rabbah David fell into that greater sin in the matter of Uriah.

Verses 4–8

The Philistines were nearly subdued (*ch.* xviii. 1); but the giants of Gath were last brought down. In the conflicts between grace and corruption there are some sins which, like these giants, are not mastered without much difficulty and a long struggle. 1. We never read of giants among the Israelites, as we do of giants among the Philistines—giants of Gath, but not giants of Jerusalem. The growth of God's plants is in usefulness, not in bulk. 2. The servants of David, though men of ordinary stature, were too hard for the giants of Gath in every encounter, because they had God on their side. We need not fear great men against us while we have the great God for us. What will a finger more on each hand do, or a toe more on each foot, in contest with Omnipotence?

CHAPTER 21

Verses 1–6

Numbering the people, one would think, was no bad thing. Why should not the shepherd know the number of his flock? He did it in the pride of his heart; and there is no sin that has in it more of contradiction and therefore more of offence to God than pride. The sin was David's.

I. How active the tempter was in it (*v.* 1): *Satan stood up against Israel, and provoked David* to do it. It is said (2 Sam. xxiv. 1) that *the anger of the Lord was kindled against Israel, and he moved David* to do it. When it is said that he moved David to do it, it must be explained by what is intimated here, that, for wise and holy ends, he permitted the devil to do it. Now, when Satan meant to do Israel a mischief, what course did he take? He did not *move God against them to destroy them*, but he provoked David, the best friend they had, to number them, and so to offend God, and set him against them. The devil does us more mischief by tempting us to sin against our God than he does by accusing us before our God.

JAMIESON, FAUSSET, BROWN

the kings that were come were by themselves in the field—The Israelitish army being thus beset by the Ammonites in front, and by the Syrian auxiliaries behind, Joab resolved to attack the latter—the more numerous and formidable host—while he directed his brother Abishai, with a suitable detachment, to attack the Ammonites. Joab's address before the engagement displays the faith and piety that became a commander of the Hebrew people. The mercenaries being defeated, the courage of the Ammonites failed; so that, taking flight, they entrenched themselves within the fortified walls.

16-19. SHOPHACH SLAIN BY DAVID. **16. And when the Syrians saw that they were put to the worse**—(See on II Samuel 10:15-19). **18. David slew of the Syrians seven thousand men**—(Cf. II Samuel 10:18, which has seven hundred chariots). Either the text in one of the books is corrupt [KEIL, DAVIDSON], or the accounts must be combined, giving this result—7000 horsemen, 7000 chariots, and 40,000 footmen [KENNICOTT, HOUBIGANT, CALMET].

CHAPTER 20

Vss. 1-3. RABBAH BESIEGED BY JOAB, SPOILED BY DAVID, AND THE PEOPLE TORTURED. **1. at the time when kings go out to battle**—in spring, the usual season in ancient times for entering on a *campaign;* i.e., a year subsequent to the Syrian war. **Joab led forth the power of the army, and wasted the country . . . of Ammon**—The former campaign had been disastrous, owing chiefly to the hired auxiliaries of the Ammonites; and as it was necessary, as well as just, that they should be severely chastised for their wanton outrage on the Hebrew ambassadors, Joab ravaged their country and invested their capital, Rabbah. After a protracted siege, Joab took one part of it, the lower town or "city of waters," insulated by the winding course of the Jabbok. Knowing that the fort called "the royal city" would soon fall, he invited the king to come in person, and have the honor of storming it. The knowledge of this fact (mentioned in II Sam. 12:26) enables us to reconcile the two statements—"David tarried at Jerusalem" (vs. 1), and "David and all the people returned to Jerusalem" (vs. 3). **2. David took the crown of their king . . . , and found it to weigh a talent of gold**—equal to 125 lbs. Some think that *Malcom,* rendered in our version "their king," should be taken as a proper name, Milcom or Molech, the Ammonite idol, which, of course, might bear a heavy weight. But, like many other state crowns of Eastern kings, the crown got at Rabbah was not worn on the head, but suspended by chains of gold above the throne. **precious stones**—*Heb.*, a stone, or cluster of precious stones, which was set on David's head. **3. cut them with saws, etc.**—The Hebrew word, "cut them," is, with the difference of the final letter, the same as that rendered "put them," in the parallel passage of Samuel; and many consider that putting them to saws, axes, etc., means nothing more than that David condemned the inhabitants of Rabbah to hard and penal servitude.

4-8. THREE OVERTHROWS OF THE PHILISTINES AND THREE GIANTS SLAIN. **4. war at Gezer**—or Gob (see II Sam. 21:18-22).

CHAPTER 21

Vss. 1-13. DAVID SINS IN NUMBERING THE PEOPLE. **1. Satan stood up against Israel**—God, by withdrawing His grace at this time from David (see on II Sam. 24:1), permitted the tempter to prevail over him. As the result of this successful temptation was the entail of a heavy calamity as a punishment from God upon the people, it might be said that "Satan stood up against Israel." **number Israel**—In the act of taking the census of a people, there is not only no evil, but much utility. But numbering Israel—that people who were to become as the stars for multitude, implying a distrust of the divine promise, was a sin; and though it had been done with impunity in the time of Moses, at that enumeration each of the people had contributed "half a shekel towards the building of the tabernacle," that there might be no plague among them when he numbered them (Exod. 30:12). Hence the numbering of that people was in itself regarded as an undertaking by which the anger of God could be easily aroused; but when the arrangements were made by Moses for the taking of the census, God was not angry because the people were numbered for the express purpose of the tax for the sanctuary, and the money which was thus collected ("the atonement money," Exod. 30:16) appeased Him.

ADAM CLARKE

13. *Be of good courage.* See the note on 2 Sam. x. 12.

18. *Forty thousand footmen.* See this number accounted for in the note on 2 Sam. x. 18.

19. *They made peace with David, and became his servants.* See on 2 Sam. x. 19.

CHAPTER 20

1. *After the year was expired, at the time that kings go out to battle.* About the spring of the year; see the note on 2 Sam. xi. 1. After this verse the parallel place in Samuel relates the whole story of David and Bath-sheba, and the murder of Uriah, which the compiler of these books passes over as he designedly does almost everything prejudicial to the character of David. All he states is, *But David tarried at Jerusalem;* and while he thus tarried, and Joab conducted the war against the Ammonites, the awful transactions above referred to took place.

2. *David took the crown of their king . . . off his head.* See 2 Sam. xii. 30.

3. *He brought out the people.* See this transaction particularly explained in the notes on the parallel places, 2 Sam. xii. 30-31.

5. *Elhanan the son of Jair.* See 2 Sam. xxi. 19.

CHAPTER 21

1. *And Satan stood up against Israel.* See the notes on the parallel place, 2 Sam. xxiv. 1, etc.

MATTHEW HENRY

II. Joab, the person whom David employed, was an active man in public business; but to this he was perfectly forced, and did it with the greatest reluctance imaginable. No man more forward than he in anything that really tended to the honour of the king or the welfare of the kingdom; but in this matter he would gladly be excused. It was a needless thing. There was no occasion at all for it. It was a dangerous thing. In doing it he might be a cause of trespass to Israel, and might provoke God against them. There was a general disgust at these orders, which confirmed Joab in his dislike of them.

He left two tribes unnumbered (*v.* 5, 6), two considerable ones, Levi and Benjamin, and perhaps was not very exact in numbering the rest, because he did not do it with any pleasure, which might be one occasion of the difference between the sums here and 2 Sam. xxiv. 9.

Verses 7–17

David is here under the rod for numbering the people, that rod of correction which drives out the foolishness that is bound up in the heart, the foolishness of pride.

I. How he was corrected. God takes notice of, and is displeased with, the sins of his people; and no sin is more displeasing to him than pride of heart. David must have the people numbered: *Bring me the number of them,* says he, *that I may know it.* But now God numbers them after another manner, and David had another number of them brought, more to his confusion than to his satisfaction, namely, a black bill of mortality. He sees the destroying angel, with his sword drawn against Jerusalem, *v.* 16. Pestilences make the greatest devastations in the most populous places.

II. How he bore the correction. He owned that he had sinned, had done foolishly, and he entreated that, however he might be corrected for it, the iniquity of it might be done away. I submit to the rod, only let me be the sufferer, for I am the sinner. 1. He cast himself upon the mercy of God (though he knew he was angry with him) and did not entertain any hard thoughts of him. However it be, *Let us fall into the hands of the Lord, for his mercies are great, v.* 13. Good men, even when God frowns upon them, think well of him. *Though he slay me, yet will I trust in him.* 2. He expressed a very tender concern for the people, and it went to his heart to see them plagued for his transgression: *These sheep, what have they done?*

JAMIESON, FAUSSET, BROWN

Everything depended, therefore, upon the design of the census [BERTHEAU]. The sin of David numbering the people consisted in its being either to gratify his pride to ascertain the number of warriors he could muster for some meditated plan of conquest; or, perhaps, more likely still, to institute a regular and permanent system of taxation, which he deemed necessary to provide an adequate establishment for the monarchy, but which was regarded as a tyrannical and oppressive exaction—an innovation on the liberty of the people—a departure from ancient usage unbecoming a king of Israel. **3. why will he be a cause of trespass to Israel?**—or bring an occasion of punishment on Israel. In *Heb.*, the word sin is often used synonymously with the punishment of sin. In the course of Providence, the people frequently suffer for the misconduct of their rulers. **5. Joab gave the sum of the number of the children of Israel**—It amounted to one million one hundred thousand men in Israel, capable of bearing arms, inclusive of the 300,000 military (ch. 27), which, being already enlisted in the royal service, were not reckoned (II Sam. 24:9), and to 470,000 men in Judah, omitting 30,000 which formed an army of observation stationed on the Philistine frontier (II Sam. 6:1). So large a population at this early period, considering the limited extent of the country and comparing it with the earlier census (Num. 26), is a striking proof of the fulfilment of the promise (Gen. 15:5). **6. Levi and Benjamin counted he not**—If this census was ordered with a view to the imposition of taxes, this alone would account for Levi, who were not warriors (vs. 5), not being numbered (see on Num. 1:47-55). The population of Benjamin had been taken (see on ch. 7:6-11), and the register preserved in the archives of that tribe. This, however, was taken on another occasion, and by other agency than that of Joab. The non-numbering of these two tribes might have originated in the special and gracious providence of God, partly because Levi was devoted to His service, and Benjamin had become the least of all the tribes (Judg. 21); and partly because God foresaw that they would remain faithful to the house of David in the division of the tribes, and therefore He would not have them diminished [POOLE]. From the course followed in this survey (see on II Samuel 24: 4-8), it would appear that Judah and Benjamin were the last tribes that were to be visited; and that, after the census in Judah had been finished, Joab, before entering on that of Benjamin, had to return to Jerusalem, where the king, now sensible of his great error, gave orders to stop all further proceedings in the business. Not only the remonstrance of Joab at the first, but his slow progress in the survey (II Sam. 24:8) showed the strong repugnance and even horror of the old general at this unconstitutional measure. **9. the Lord spake unto Gad, David's seer**—Although David was himself endowed with a prophetic gift, yet, in matters relating to himself or his kingdom, he was in the habit of consulting the Lord through the medium of the priests; and when he failed to do so, a prophet was sent on extraordinary occasions to admonish or chastise him. Gad, a private friend, was occasionally employed as the bearer of these prophetic messages. **11, 12. Choose thee,** etc.—To the *three* evils these correspond in beautiful agreement: *three* years, *three* months, *three* days [BERTHEAU]. (See on II Samuel 24:13.) **13. let me fall now into the hand of the Lord . . . let me not fall into the hand of man**—Experience had taught him that human passion and vengeance had no bounds, whereas our wise and gracious Father in heaven knows the kind, and regulates the extent, of chastisement which every one needs. **14, 15. So the Lord . . . sent an angel unto Jerusalem to destroy it**—The infliction only of the pestilence is here noticed, without any account of its duration or its ravages, while a minute description is given of the visible appearance and menacing attitude of the destroying angel. **stood by the threshing-floor of Ornan the Jebusite**—Ornan was probably his Hebrew or Jewish, Araunah his Jebusite or Canaanitish, name. Whether he was the old king of Jebus, as that title is given to him (II Sam. 24:23), or not, he had been converted to the worship of the true God, and was possessed both of property and influence. **16. David and the elders . . . clothed in sackcloth, fell upon their faces**—They appeared in the garb and assumed the attitude of humble penitents, confessing their sins, and deprecating the wrath of God.

18-30. HE BUILDS AN ALTAR. **18. the angel of the Lord commanded Gad to say**—The order about the erection of an altar, as well as the indication of its site, is described (II Sam. 24:18) as brought directly by Gad. Here we are informed of the quarter

ADAM CLARKE

5. *All they of Israel were a thousand thousand . . . Judah was four hundred threescore and ten thousand.* In the parallel place, 2 Sam. xxiv. 9, the men of Israel are reckoned 800,000 and the men of Judah 500,000.

6. *Levi and Benjamin counted he not.* The rabbins give the following reason for this: Joab, seeing that this would bring down destruction upon the people, purposed to save two tribes. Should David ask, Why have you not numbered the Levites? Joab purposed to say, Because the Levites are not reckoned among the children of Israel. Should he ask, Why have you not numbered Benjamin? he would answer, Benjamin has been already sufficiently punished, on account of the treatment of the woman at Gibeah; if therefore this tribe were to be again punished, who would remain?

12. *Three days . . . the pestilence, in the land.* In 2 Sam. xxiv. 13, seven years of famine are mentioned.

MATTHEW HENRY

Verses 18–30

Upon David's repentance, his peace made with God. When David repented of the sin God repented of the judgment, and ordered the destroying angel to *stay his hand* and *sheath his sword*, *v.* 27. Direction was given to David to rear an altar in the threshing-floor of Ornan, *v.* 18. The commanding of David to build an altar was a blessed token of reconciliation.

David immediately made a bargain with Ornan for the threshing-floor. Ornan generously offered it to him gratis.

God testified his acceptance of David's offerings on this altar: He *answered him from heaven by fire*, *v.* 26. He continued to offer his sacrifices upon this altar. The brazen altar which Moses made was at Gibeon (*v.* 29), and there all the sacrifices of Israel were offered: but David was so terrified at the sight of the sword of the angel that he *could not go thither*, *v.* 30. The business required haste, when the plague was begun. And therefore God, in tenderness to him, bade him build an altar in that place. The symbols of unity were not so much insisted on as unity itself. When the present distress was over, David, as long as he lived, sacrificed there, though the altar at Gibeon was still kept up. "Here God has graciously met me, and therefore I will still expect to meet with him."

JAMIESON, FAUSSET, BROWN

whence the prophet got his commission. It is only in the later stages of Israel's history that we find angels employed in communicating the divine will to the prophets. **20, 21. Ornan was threshing wheat**—If the census was entered upon in autumn, the beginning of the civil year, the nine and a half months it occupied would end at wheat-harvest. The common way of threshing corn is by spreading it out on a high level area, and driving backwards and forwards upon it two oxen harnessed to a clumsy sledge with three rollers and some sharp spikes. The driver sits on his knees on the box, while another person is employed in drawing back the straw and separating it from the grain underneath. By this operation the chaff is very much chopped, and the grain threshed out. **23. I give thee . . . the threshing instruments for wood**—i.e., to burn the sacrifice of the oxen. Very little real import—the *haste* and the *value* of the present offered—can be understood in this country. The offering was made for *instant* use. Ornan, hereby hoping to terminate the pestilence without a moment's delay, "gave all," oxen, the large threshing machine, and the wheat. **25. David gave . . . for the place six hundred shekels of gold**—At first he bought only the cattle and the threshing instruments, for which he paid fifty shekels of silver (II Sam. 24:24); afterwards he purchased the whole property, Mount Moriah, on which the future temple stood. High in the center of the mountain platform rises a remarkable rock, now covered by the dome of "the Sakrah." It is irregular in its form, and measures about sixty feet in one direction and fifty feet in the other. It is the natural surface of Mount Moriah and is thought by many to be the rock of the threshing-floor of Araunah, selected by David, and continued by Solomon and Zerubbabel as "the unhewn stone" on which to build the altar [BARTLETT'S "WALKS ABOUT JERUSALEM," STANLEY]. **26. David built there an altar**—He went in procession with his leading men from the royal palace, down Mount Zion, and through the intervening city. Although he had plenty of space on his own property, he was commanded, under peremptory *direction,* to go a considerable distance from his home, up Mount Moriah, to erect an altar on premises which he had to buy. It was on or close to the spot where Abraham had offered up Isaac. **answered him by fire from heaven**—(See Lev. 9:24; I Kings 18:21-23; II Kings 1:12; II Chron. 7:1). **28. when David saw that the Lord had answered him . . . , he sacrificed there**—or, he continued to sacrifice there. Perceiving his sacrifice was acceptable, he proceeded to make additional offerings there, and seek favor by prayer and expiatory rites; for the dread of the menacing angel destroying Jerusalem while he was absent in the center of worship at Gibeon, especially reverence for the Divine Being, led him to continue his adorations in that place which God (II Chron. 3:1) had hallowed by the tokens of His presence and gracious acceptance.

ADAM CLARKE

20. *Ornan turned back, and saw the angel.* The Septuagint say, "And Orna turned and saw the king." The Syriac and Arabic say, "David saw the angel," and do not mention Ornan in this place.

24. *For the full price.* That is, 600 shekels full weight of pure gold.

26. *He answered him . . . by fire.* In answer to David's prayers, God, to show that He had accepted him, and was now pacified towards him and the people, sent fire from heaven and consumed the offerings.

30. *Because of the sword of the angel.* This is given as a reason why David built an altar in the threshing floor of Ornan. He was afraid to go to Gibeon, because of the sword of the destroying angel, or he was afraid of delaying the offerings so long as his going thither would require, lest the destroying angel should in the meanwhile exterminate the people. Therefore he hastily built an altar in that place, and on it made the requisite offerings; and by the fire from heaven God showed that He had accepted his act and his devotion. Such interventions as these must necessarily maintain in the minds of the people a full persuasion of the truth and divine origin of their religion.

MATTHEW HENRY

CHAPTER 22

Verses 1–5

I. The place fixed for the building of the temple (*v.* 1). The ground was a threshing-floor; for the church of the living God is his floor, his threshing, and *the corn of his floor*, Isa. xxi. 10. Christ's fan is in his hand, thoroughly to purge his floor. This is to be the house because this is the altar. The temple was built for the sake of the altar. There were altars long before there were temples.

II. Preparation made for that building. David must not build it, but he would do all he could towards it: He *prepared abundantly before his death*, *v.* 5.

1. What induced him to make such preparation. (1) Solomon was young and tender, and not likely to apply with any great vigour to this business at first; so that, unless he found the wheels set a-going, he would be in danger of losing a great deal of time at first. (2) The house must be very stately and sumptuous, strong and beautiful, everything about it the best in its kind, since it was intended for the honour of the Lord of the whole earth, and was to be a type of Christ, in whom all fulness dwells and in whom are hid all treasures. The grandeur of the house would help to affect the worshippers with a holy awe and reverence of God, and would invite strangers to come to see it, as the wonder of the world, who thereby would be brought acquainted with the true God.

2. What preparation he made. In general, he prepared abundantly cedar and stones, iron and brass, *v.* 2–4. Cedar he had from the Tyrians and the

JAMIESON, FAUSSET, BROWN

CHAPTER 22

Vss. 1-5. DAVID PREPARES FOR BUILDING THE TEMPLE. **1. David said, This is the home of the Lord God**—By the miraculous sign of fire from heaven, and perhaps other intimations, David understood it to be the will of God that the national place of worship should be fixed there, and he forthwith proceeded to make preparations for the erection of the temple on that spot.

ADAM CLARKE

CHAPTER 22

1. *David said, This is the house of the Lord.* Till a temple is built for His name, this place shall be considered the temple of God; and on this altar, and not on that at Gibeon, shall the burnt offerings of Israel be made. David probably thought that this was the place on which God designed that His house should be built.

3. *Iron . . . for the nails.* Iron for bolts, bars, hinges, etc.

MATTHEW HENRY

Zidonians. He also got workmen together, *the strangers that were in the land of Israel.*

Verses 6–16

Solomon was *to build a house for the Lord God of Israel, v.* 6.

I. David tells him why he did not do it himself. It was in his mind to do it (*v.* 7), but God forbade him, because *he had shed much blood, v.* 8. Some think this refers to the blood of Uriah, but that honour was forbidden him before he had shed that blood; therefore it must be meant of the blood he shed in his wars.

II. He gives him the reason why he imposed this task upon him. 1. Because God had nominated him as the man that should do it: *A son shall be born to thee*, that shall be called *Solomon*, and *he shall build a house for my name, v.* 9, 10. 2. Because he would have leisure and opportunity to do it. He should have rest from his enemies abroad and he should have peace and quietness at home; and therefore let him build the house.

III. He delivers him an account of the vast preparations he had made for this building (*v.* 14), as an encouragement to Solomon to engage cheerfully in the work, for which so solid a foundation was laid. The treasure here mentioned of 100,000 talents of gold, and 1,000,000 talents of silver, amounts to such an incredible sum that most interpreters either allow an error in the copy or think the talent here signifies no more than a plate or piece: *ingots* we call them.

IV. He charges him to keep God's commandments, *v.* 13. He must not think by building the temple to purchase a dispensation to sin.

V. He encourages him to go about this great work, and to go on in it (*v.* 13): It is God's work, and it shall come to perfection.

VI. He quickens him not to rest in the preparations he had made, *v.* 14. He prays for him: *The Lord give thee wisdom and understanding, and give thee charge concerning Israel, v.* 12. He concludes (*v.* 16), *Up and be going, and the Lord be with thee.*

Verses 17–19

David here engages the princes of Israel to assist Solomon in the great work he had to do. God had given them victory, and rest, and a good land for an inheritance, *v.* 18. He presses that upon them which should make them zealous in it (*v.* 19).

JAMIESON, FAUSSET, BROWN

2. David commanded to gather together the strangers—partly the descendants of the old Canaanites (II Chron. 8:7-10), from whom was exacted a tribute of bond-service, and partly war captives (II Chron. 2:7), reserved for the great work he contemplated.

6-19. He Instructs Solomon. **6. Then he called for Solomon . . . and charged him**—The earnestness and solemnity of this address creates an impression that it was given a little before the old king's decease. He unfolded his great and long cherished plan, enjoined the building of God's house as a sacred duty on him as his son and successor, and described the resources that were at command for carrying on the work.

The vast amount of personal property he had accumulated in the precious metals must have been spoil taken from the people he had conquered, and the cities he had sacked.

ADAM CLARKE

2. *The strangers that were in the land.* Those who had become proselytes to the Jewish religion, at least so far as to renounce idolatry, and keep what were called the seven Noahic precepts. These were to be employed in the more servile and difficult parts of the work; see on 1 Kings ix. 21. For the account of building the Temple, see 1 Kings v—ix.

9. *His name shall be Solomon. Shelomoh*, from *shalam*, "he was peaceable"; and therefore, says the Lord, alluding to the name, *I will give peace* [*shalom*] . . . *in his days.*

14. *In my trouble I have prepared.* Notwithstanding all the wars in which I have been engaged, all the treacheries with which I have been surrounded, all the domestic troubles with which I have been overwhelmed. I never lost sight of this great object, the building of a house for God, that His worship might be established in the land. *An hundred thousand talents of gold.* One hundred thousand talents would amount to 507,578,125 pounds sterling. *A thousand thousand talents of silver.* A thousand thousand, or a million, talents would amount to the immense sum of 353,591,666 pounds, 13 shillings, and 4 pence, sterling. *Thou mayest add thereto.* Save as I have saved, out of the revenues of the state, and thou mayest also add something for the erection and splendor of this house. This was a gentle though pointed hint, which was not lost on Solomon.

18. *Hath he not given you rest on every side?* David at this time was not only king of Judea, but had also subdued most of the surrounding nations.

CHAPTER 23 (Matthew Henry)

Verses 1–23

David made Solomon king, not to reign with him, or reign under him, but only to reign after him. He did it in a solemn assembly of all the princes of Israel, which made Adonijah's attempt to break in upon Solomon's title and set it aside, the more impudent and ridiculous.

II. The Levites numbered, according to the rule in Moses's time, from thirty years old to fifty, Num. iv. 2, 3. Their number in Moses's time, by this rule, was 8,580 (Num. iv. 47, 48), but the serviceable men of Levi's tribe were now 38,000.

III. The Levites distributed to their respective posts (*v.* 4, 5), that every hand might be employed (for, of all men, an idle Levite makes the worst figure). The work assigned the Levites was four-fold:—1. Some, and indeed far the greater number, were to set forward the work of the house of the Lord: 24,000, almost two-thirds, were appointed for this service, to attend the priests in killing the sacrifices, washing them, burning them, to have the meat-offerings and drink-offerings ready, to keep all the vessels of the temple clean, and everything in its place. These served 1,000 a week, and so went round in twenty-four courses. Perhaps while the temple was in building some of these were employed to set forward that work, to assist the builders. 2. Others were officers and judges, not in the affairs of the temple, but in the country. They were magistrates, to give the laws of God in charge, to resolve difficulties, and to determine controversies. Of these there were 6,000, in the several parts of the kingdom, that assisted the princes and elders of every tribe in the administration of justice. 3. Others were porters, to guard all the avenues of the house of God, to examine those that desired entrance, and to resist those that would force an entrance. 4. Others were singers and players on instruments, whose business it was to keep up that part of the service; this was a new-erected office.

IV. The Levites mustered into their respective families and kindreds, that an account of them might the better be kept by calling over the roll, which each family might do for itself. In this account of the

CHAPTER 23 (Jamieson, Fausset, Brown)

Vs. 1. David Makes Solomon King. **1. when David was old . . . he made Solomon . . . king**—This brief statement, which comprises the substance of I Kings 1:32-48, is made here solely to introduce an account of the preparations carried on by David during the latter years of his life for providing a national place of worship.

2-6. Number and Distribution of the Levites. **2. he gathered together all the princes of Israel**—All important measures relating to the public interest were submitted for consideration to a general assembly of the representatives of the tribes (ch. 13: 1; 15:25; 22:17; 26). **3. the Levites were numbered . . . thirty and eight thousand**—Four times their number at the early census taken by Moses (see on Num. 4 and 26). It was, in all likelihood, this vast increase that suggested and rendered expedient that classification, made in the last year of David's reign, which the present and three subsequent chapters describe. **by their polls, man by man**—Women and children were not included. **4. twenty and four thousand were to set forward the work of the house of the Lord**—They were not to preside over all the services of the temple. The Levites were subject to the priests, and they were superior to the Nethinim and other servants, who were not of the race of Levi. But they had certain departments of duty assigned, some of which are here specified. **5. praised the Lord with the instruments which I made**—David seems to have been an inventor of many of the musical instruments used in the temple (Amos 6:5). **6. David divided them into courses among the sons of Levi**—These are enumerated according to their fathers' houses, but no more of these are mentioned here than the twenty-four thousand who were engaged in the work connected with the Lord's house. The fathers' houses of those Levites corresponded with the classes into which they [Josephus' Antiquities] as well as the priests were divided (see on ch. 24: 20-31; 26:20-28).

7-11. Sons of Gershon. **7-11. the Gershonites**

CHAPTER 23 (Adam Clarke)

1. *David was old and full of days.* On the phrase *full of days*, see Gen. xxv. 8.

3. *Thirty years and upward.* The enumeration of the Levites made in the desert, Num. iv. 3, was from thirty years upwards to fifty years. In this place, the latter limit is not mentioned, probably because the service was not so laborious now; for the ark being fixed, they had no longer any heavy burdens to carry, and therefore even an old man might continue to serve the Tabernacle. David made another ordinance afterwards; see on vv. 24 and 27.

5. *Four thousand praised the Lord.* David made this distribution according to his own judgment, and from the dictates of his piety; but it does not appear that he had any positive divine authority for such arrangements. As to the instruments of music which he made, they are condemned elsewhere; see Amos vi. 5, to which this verse is allowed to be the parallel.

MATTHEW HENRY

families of the Levites the posterity of Moses stood upon the level with common Levites, whilst the posterity of Aaron were advanced to the priest's office, to *sanctify the most holy things, v.* 13. The levelling of Moses's family with the rest is an evidence of his self-denial. He was no self-seeking man, as appears from his leaving to his children no marks of distinction, which was a sign that he had the spirit of God and not the spirit of the world. The elevation of Aaron's family above the rest was a recompence for his self-denial. When Moses (his younger brother) was made a god to Pharaoh, and he only his prophet or spokesman, to observe his orders and do as he was bidden, Aaron never disputed it. Because he thus submitted himself, in his own person, to his junior, in compliance with the will of God, God highly exalted his family.

Verses 24–32

I. An alteration made in the computation of the effective men of the Levites—that whereas, in Moses's time, they were not enlisted, or taken into service, till they were thirty-years old, nor admitted as probationers till twenty-five (Num. viii. 24), David ordered, by direction from God, that they should be numbered *for the service of the house of the Lord,* from the age of twenty years and upwards, *v.* 24. Perhaps the young Levites, having no work appointed them till twenty-five years old, had many of them got a habit of idleness, to prevent which they are set to work, and brought under discipline, at twenty years old. There was no more occasion to carry the tabernacle and the vessels thereof, the service was much easier, and what would not over-work them nor over-load them if they entered upon it at twenty years old. Now it was requisite there should be more hands employed in the temple-service, that every Israelite who brought an offering might find a Levite ready to assist him.

II. The work of the priests was (*v.* 13): To *sanctify the most holy things, to burn incense before the Lord,* and to *bless in his name;* that work the Levites were not to meddle with, and yet they had work enough to which they were appointed, *v.* 4, 5. 1. Those that were to *set forward the work of the house of God* (*v.* 4) were therein to *wait on the sons of Aaron* (*v.* 28), were to do the drudgery-work of the house of God, to keep the courts and chambers clean, set things in their places. They were to prepare the shew-bread which the priests were to set on the table, to provide the flour and cakes for the meal-offerings, that the priests might have everything ready to their hands. 2. The standards of all weights and measures were kept in the sanctuary; and the Levites had the care of them, to see that they were exact, and to try other weights and measures by them when they were appealed to. 3. The work of the singers was to *thank* and *praise the Lord* (*v.* 30), at the offering of the morning and evening sacrifices, and other oblations on the sabbaths, new moons, &c., *v.* 31. Moses appointed that they should blow trumpets over their burnt offerings and other sacrifices, and on their solemn days, Num. x. 10. The sound of the trumpet was awful, and might be affecting to the worshippers, but was not articulate, nor such a reasonable service as this which David appointed, of singing psalms on those occasions. As the Jewish church grew up from its infancy, it grew more and more intelligent in its devotions. 4. The work of the porters (*v.* 5) was to keep *the charge of the tabernacle and of the holy place,* that none might come nigh but such as were allowed, *v.* 32.

CHAPTER 24

Verses 1–19

The particular account of these establishments, when Ezra published it, was of great use to direct their church affairs after their return from captivity. The title of this record we have *v.* 1—*These are the divisions of the sons of Aaron,* the distribution of them in order to the dividing of their work among themselves. 1. This distribution was made for the more regular discharge of the duties of their office. In the mystical body, every member has its use, for the good of the whole, Rom. xii. 4, 5; 1 Cor. xii. 12.

JAMIESON, FAUSSET, BROWN

–They had nine fathers' houses, six descended from Laadan, and three from Shimei.

12-20. OF KOHATH. **12. The sons of Kohath**–He was the founder of nine Levitical fathers' houses. **13. Aaron was separated**–as high priest (see on ch. 25:1-19). **14. concerning Moses**–His sons were ranked with the Levites generally, but not introduced into the distinctive portion of the descendants of Levi, who were appointed to the special functions of the priesthood.

21-23. OF MERARI. **21-23. The sons of Merari**–They comprised six fathers' houses. Summing them together, Gershon founded nine fathers' houses, Kohath nine, and Merari six: total, twenty-four.

24. OFFICE OF THE LEVITES. **24. These were the sons of Levi . . . that did the work . . . from the age of twenty years and upward**–The enumeration of the Levites was made by David (vs. 3) on the same rule as that followed by Moses (Num. 4:3), viz., from thirty years. But he saw afterwards that this rule might be beneficially relaxed, and that the enrolment of Levites for their proper duties might be made from twenty years of age. The ark and tabernacle being now stationary at Jerusalem, the labor of the Levites was greatly diminished, as they were no longer obliged to transport its heavy furniture from place to place. The number of 38,000 Levites, exclusive of priests, was doubtless more than sufficient for the ordinary service of the tabernacle. But this pious king thought that it would contribute to the glory of the Lord to employ as many officers in his divine service as possible. These first rules, however, which David instituted, were temporary, as very different arrangements were made after the ark had been deposited in the tabernacle of Zion.

CHAPTER 24

VSS. 1-19. DIVISION OF THE SONS OF AARON INTO FOUR AND TWENTY ORDERS. **1. Now these are the divisions of the sons of Aaron**–(See on ch. 23:6). **2. Nadab and Abihu died before their father**–i.e., not in his presence, but during his lifetime (see Marg. Ref). **therefore Eleazar and Ithamar executed the priest's office**–In consequence of the death of his two oldest sons without issue, the descendants of Aaron were comprised in the families of Eleazar and Ithamar. Both of these sons discharged the priestly functions as assistants to their father. Eleazar succeeded him, and in his line the high priesthood continued until it was transferred to the family of Ithamar, in the person of Eli. **3. Zadok . . . and Ahimelech of the sons of Ithamar**–This statement, taken in connection with verse 6, is not a little perplexing, since (II Sam. 15:24, 35; 20:25) Abiathar is mentioned as the person conjoined in David's time with Zadok, in the collegiate exercise of the high priesthood. Some think that the words have been.

ADAM CLARKE

11. *Therefore they were in one reckoning.* The family of Shimei, being small, was united with that of Laadan, that the two families might do that work which otherwise belonged to one, but which would have been too much for either of these separately.

13. *To bless in his name.* To bless the people by invoking the name of the Lord.

22. *Their brethren the sons of Kish took them.* This was according to the law made, Num. xxvii. 1, etc; and xxxvi. 5-9, in favor of the daughters of Zelophehad, that women who were heiresses should marry in the family of the tribe of their father, and that their estates should not be alienated from them.

24. *Twenty years and upward.* It appears that this was a different ordinance from that mentioned in v. 3. At first he appointed the Levites to serve from thirty years and upward; now from twenty years. These were David's last orders; see v. 27. They should begin at an earlier age, and continue later. This was not a very painful task; the ark being now fixed, and the Levites very numerous, there could be no drudgery.

28. *Purifying of all holy things.* Keeping all the vessels and utensils belonging to the sacred service clean and neat.

29. *Both for the shewbread.* It was the priests' office to place this bread before the Lord, and it was their privilege to feed on the old loaves when they were replaced by the new. *For all manner of measure and size.* The standards of all weights and measures were kept at the sanctuary, and by those there deposited all the weights and measures of the land were to be tried. See Exod. xxx. 13.

30. *To stand every morning.* At the offering of the morning and evening sacrifice they sounded their musical instruments and sang praises to God.

32. *The charge of the sons of Aaron.* It was the priests' business to kill, flay, and dress, as well as to offer, the victims; but being few, they were obliged to employ the Levites to flay those animals. The Levites were, properly speaking, servants to the priests, and were employed about the more servile part of divine worship.

CHAPTER 24

2. *Nadab and Abihu died before their father.* That is, during his lifetime. *Eleazar and Ithamar executed the priest's office.* These two served the office during the life of their father, Aaron; after his death Eleazar succeeded in the high priesthood. And under Eli, the high priest, the family of Ithamar reentered into that office.

3. *And Ahimelech.* Ahimelech is put here for Abiathar, who was high priest in the days of David. Abiathar had also the name of Ahimelech as well as his father.

MATTHEW HENRY

2. It was made by lot, that the disposal thereof might be of the Lord, and so all quarrels and contentions might be prevented. As God is the God of order, so he is the God of peace. 3. The lot was cast publicly, and with great solemnity, in the presence of the king, princes, and priests, that there might be no room for any fraudulent practices or the suspicion of them. 4. What those priests were chosen to was to preside in the affairs of the sanctuary (*v.* 5), in their several courses and turns. That which was to be determined by the lot was only the precedency, not who should serve but who should serve first, and who next. Of the twenty-four chief men of the priests sixteen were of the house of Eleazar and eight of Ithamar. The method of drawing the lots is intimated (*v.* 6), one chief household being taken for Eleazar, and one for Ithamar. The sixteen chief names of Eleazar were put in one urn, the eight for Ithamar in another, and they drew out of them alternately, as long as those for Ithamar lasted, and then out of those only for Eleazar, or two for Eleazar, and then one for Ithamar, throughout. 5. Among these twenty-four courses the eighth is that of Abijah or Abia (*v.* 10), which is mentioned (Luke i. 5) as the course which Zechariah was of, the father of John Baptist, by which it appears that these courses which David now settled, though interrupted perhaps in the bad reigns and long broken off by the captivity, yet continued in succession till the destruction of the second temple by the Romans.

Verses 20–31

Most of the Levites here named were mentioned before, *ch.* xxiii. 16, &c. But they are here mentioned as heads of the twenty-four courses of Levites who were to attend the twenty-four courses of the priests. The principal fathers cast lots over against their younger brethren; that is, those that were of the elder house came upon the level with those of the younger families, and took their place, not by seniority, but as God by the lot directed. The younger brethren, if they be faithful and sincere, shall be no less acceptable to Christ than the principal fathers.

JAMIESON, FAUSSET, BROWN

transposed, reading Abiathar, the son of Ahimelech. But there is no ground for regarding the text as faulty. The high priests of the line of Ithamar were the following: Ahiah or Ahimelech, his son Abiathar, his son Ahimelech. We frequently find the grandfather and grandson called by the same name (see list of high priests of the line of Eleazar, ch. 5:30-41). Hence the author of the Chronicles was acquainted with Ahimelech, son of Abiathar, who, for some reason, discharged the duties of high priest in David's reign, and during the lifetime of his father (for Abiathar was living in the time of Solomon, I Kings 2:27) [KEIL]. **4. there were more chief men found**—The *Heb.* may be translated, "There were more men as to heads of the sons of Eleazar." It is true, in point of fact, that by the census the number of individuals belonging to the family of Eleazar was found greater than in that of Ithamar. And this, of necessity, led to there being more fathers' houses, and consequently more chiefs or presidents in the former. **5. Thus were they divided by lot**—This method of allocation was adopted manifestly to remove all cause of jealousy as to precedence and the right of performing particular duties. **6. one principal household**—The marg. reading is preferable, "one house of the father." The lot was cast in a deliberate and solemn manner in presence of the king, the princes, the two high priests, and the chiefs of the priestly and Levitical families. The heads of families belonging to Eleazar and Ithamar were alternately brought forward to draw, and the name of each individual, as called, registered by an attendant secretary. To accommodate the casting of the lots to the inequality of the number, there being sixteen fathers' houses of Eleazar, and only eight of Ithamar, it was arranged that every house of Ithamar should be followed by two of Eleazar, or, what is the same thing, that every two houses of Eleazar should be followed by one of Ithamar. If, then, we suppose a commencement to have been made by Eleazar, the order would be as follows: one and two, Eleazar; three, Ithamar; four and five, Eleazar; six, Ithamar; seven and eight, Eleazar; nine, Ithamar; and so forth [BERTHEAU]. The lot determined also the order of the priests' service. That of the Levites was afterwards distributed by the same arrangement (vs. 31).

ADAM CLARKE

5. *They divided by lot.* This prevented jealousies; for, as all the families were equally noble, they had equal right to all ecclesiastical and civil distinctions.

6. *One principal household . . . for Eleazar.* The family of Eleazar was the most illustrious of the sacerdotal families, because Eleazar was the firstborn of Aaron; Ithamar's family was the second in order and dignity. Therefore one of the principal families of Eleazar was first taken, and then one of Ithamar's, and thus alternately till the whole was finished.

19. *Under Aaron their father.* That is, they followed the order and plans laid down by Aaron during his lifetime.

26. *The sons of Merari.* It is remarkable that not a word is here spoken of the family of Gershom.

31. *These likewise cast lots.* The Levites were divided into twenty-four orders; and these were appointed by lot to serve under the twenty-four orders of the priests: the first order of Levites under the first order of priests, and so on.

CHAPTER 25

MATTHEW HENRY

Verses 1–7

I. Singing the praises of God is here called *prophesying* (*v.* 1–3), not that all those who were employed in this service were honoured with visions of God. Heman indeed is said to be the *king's seer in the words of God* (*v.* 5); but the psalms they sang were composed by prophets, and many of them were prophetical. In Samuel's time singing the praises of God went by the name of *prophesying* (1 Sam. x. 5; xix. 20).

II. This is here called a *service*, and the persons employed in it *workmen*, *v.* 1. In our present state of corruption and infirmity, it will not be done as it should be done without labour and struggle.

III. Here were a great variety of musical instruments used, *harps, psalteries, cymbals* (*v.* 1, 6), and here was one that *lifted up the horn* (*v.* 5), that is, used wind-music.

IV. The glory and honour of God were principally intended in all this temple-music, whether vocal or instrumental. The intention of the perpetuating of psalmody in the gospel-church, is *to make melody with the heart*, in conjunction with the voice, *unto the Lord*, Eph. v. 19.

V. The order of the king is likewise taken notice of, *v.* 2 and again *v.* 6. His taking care for the due and regular observance of divine institutions, both ancient and modern, is an example to all in authority to use their power for the promoting of religion, and the enforcing of the laws of Christ.

VI. The fathers presided in this service, Asaph, Heman, and Jeduthun (*v.* 1), and the children were *under the hands of their father*, *v.* 2, 3, 6. It is probable that Heman, Asaph, and Jeduthun, were bred up under Samuel, and had their education in the schools of the prophets which he was the founder and president of; then they were pupils, now they came to be masters. Solomon perfects what David began, so David perfects what Samuel began.

VII. There were others also, besides the sons of these three great men, who are called their *brethren* who were *instructed in the songs of the Lord*, and were cunning or well skilled therein, *v.* 7. They were all Levites and were in number 288. Yet these were but a small number in comparison with the 4,000 whom

JAMIESON, FAUSSET, BROWN

Vss. 1-7. NUMBER AND OFFICE OF THE SINGERS. **1. David and the captains of the host**—i.e., the princes (ch. 23:2; 24:6). It is probable that the king was attended on the occasion of arranging the singers by the same parties that are mentioned as having assisted him in regulating the order of the priests and Levites. **2. according to the order of the king**—*Heb.*, "by the hands of the king," i.e., "according to the king's order," under the personal superintendence of Asaph and his colleagues. **which prophesied**—i.e., in this connection, played with instruments. This metaphorical application of the term "prophecy" most probably originated in the practice of the prophets, who endeavored to rouse their prophetic spirit by the animating influence of music (see on II Kings 3:15). It is said that Asaph did this "according to David's order," because by royal appointment he officiated in the tabernacle on Zion (ch. 16:37-41), while other leaders of the sacred music were stationed at Gibeon. **5. Heman the king's seer**—The title of seer or prophet of David is also given to Gad (ch. 21:9), and to Jeduthun (II Chron. 29:15), in the words (*marg. matters*) of God. **to lift up the horn**—i.e., to blow loudly in the worship of God; or perhaps it means nothing more than that he presided over the wind instruments, as Jeduthun over the harp. Heman had been appointed at first to serve at Gibeon (ch. 16:41). But his destination seems to have been changed at a subsequent period. **God gave to Heman fourteen sons and three daughters**—The daughters are mentioned, solely because from their musical taste and talents they formed part of the choir (Ps. 68:25). **6, 7. All these were under the hands of their father**—Asaph had four sons, Jeduthun six, and Heman fourteen, equal to twenty-four; making the musicians with their brethren the singers, an amount of 288. For, like the priests and Levites, they were divided into twenty-four courses of twelve men each, equal to 288, who served a week in rotation; and these, half of whom officiated every week with a proportionate number of assistants, were skilful and experienced musicians, capable of leading and instructing the general musical corps, which comprised no less than 4000

ADAM CLARKE

1. *David and the captains of the host.* The chiefs of those who formed the several orders, not military captains. *Should prophesy.* Should accompany their musical instruments with prayer and singing.

2. *Which prophesied.* Sung hymns and prayed.

3. *The sons of Jeduthun . . . six.* That is, six with their father; otherwise there are but five.

5. *Three daughters.* These also were employed among the singers.

MATTHEW HENRY

David appointed thus to *praise the Lord, ch.* xxiii. 5, and were disposed of, all the kingdom over, to preside in the country congregations, in this good work: for, though the sacrifices instituted by the hand of Moses might be offered but at one place, the psalms penned by David might be sung everywhere, 1 Tim. ii. 8.

Verses 8–31

Twenty-four persons are named in the beginning of this chapter as sons of those three great men, Asaph, Heman, and Jeduthun. Ethan was the third (*ch.* vi. 44), but probably he was dead before the establishment was perfected and Jeduthun came in his room. [Or perhaps Ethan and Jeduthun were two names for the same person]. All twenty-four (who were named, *v.* 2–4), were qualified for the service and called to it. In what order must they serve? This was determined by lot.

I. The lot was thrown impartially. They were placed in twenty-four companies, twelve in a company, in two rows, twelve companies in a row, and so they cast lots, *ward against ward*, putting them all upon a level, small and great, teacher and scholar.

II. God determined it as he pleased. The respective merits of the persons are of much more importance than seniority of age or priority of birth.

III. Probably twelve, some for the voice and others for the instrument, made up the concert. Let us learn with one mind and one mouth to glorify God, and that will be the best concern.

JAMIESON, FAUSSET, BROWN

(ch. 23:5).

8-31. Their Division by Lot into Four and Twenty Orders. **8. they cast lots, ward against ward**—"Ward" is an old English word for division or company. The lot was cast to determine the precedence of the classes or divisions over which the musical leaders presided; and, in order to secure an impartial arrangement of their order, the master and his assistants, the teacher and his scholars, in each class or company took part in this solemn casting of lots. In the first catalogue given in this chapter the courses are classed according to their employment as musicians. In the second, they are arranged in the order of their service.

ADAM CLARKE

9. *For Asaph to Joseph.* His firstborn. *The second to Gedaliah.* The firstborn of Jeduthun.

10. *The third to Saccur.* The firstborn of Asaph.

11. *The fourth to Izri.* The second son of Jeduthun.

12. *The fifth to Nethaniah.* The third son of Asaph. Thus we find the lot did not run in any particular kind of order.

14. *Jesharelah.* Supposed to be the same with Uzziel, son of Heman.

31. *Romamti-ezer.* Both these names belong to the same person. He is mentioned also in v. 4.

MATTHEW HENRY — CHAPTER 26

Verses 1–19

I. There were porters appointed to attend the temple, who guarded all the avenues that led to it, opened and shut all the outer doors to direct and instruct those who were going to worship in the courts of the sanctuary in the decorum they were to observe, to encourage those that were timorous, to send back the strangers and unclean, and to guard against enemies of the house of God. In allusion to this office, ministers are said to have *the keys of the kingdom of heaven* committed to them (Matt. xvi. 19), that they may admit, and exclude, according to the law of Christ.

II. Of several of those that were called to this service, it is taken notice of that they were *mighty men of valour* (*v.* 6), *strong men* (*v.* 7), *able men* (*v.* 8), and one of them that he was *a wise counsellor* (*v.* 14). Whatever service God calls men to he either finds them fit or makes them so.

III. The sons of Obed-edom were employed in this office, sixty-two of that family. This was he that entertained the ark with reverence and cheerfulness; and see how he was rewarded for it. 1. He had eight *sons* (*v.* 5), *for God blessed him*. 2. His sons were preferred to places of trust in the sanctuary. They had faithfully attended the ark in their own house, and now were called to attend it in God's house. He that keeps God's ordinances in his own tent is fit to have the custody of them in God's tabernacle, 1 Tim. iii. 4, 5.

IV. It is said of one here that *though he was not the first-born his father made him the chief* (*v.* 10), either because he was very excellent, or because the elder son was very weak.

V. The porters, as the singers, had their post assigned them by lot, so many at such a gate, and so many at such a one, that every one might know his post and make it good, *v.* 13.

JAMIESON, FAUSSET, BROWN — CHAPTER 26

Vss. 1-12. Divisions of the Porters. **1, 2. Concerning the divisions of the porters**—There were 4000 (ch. 23:6), all taken from the families of the Kohathites and Merarites (vs. 14), divided into twenty-four courses—as the priests and musicians. **Meshelemiah the son of Kore, of the sons of Asaph**—Seven sons of Meshelemiah are mentioned (vs. 2), whereas eighteen are given (vs. 9), but in this latter number his relatives are included. **5. God blessed him**—i.e., Obed-edom. The occasion of the blessing was his faithful custody of the ark (II Sam. 6:11, 12). The nature of the blessing (Ps. 127:5) consisted in the great increase of progeny by which his house was distinguished; seventy-two descendants are reckoned. **6. mighty men of valour**—The circumstance of physical strength is prominently noticed in this chapter, as the office of the porters required them not only to act as sentinels of the sacred edifice and its precious furniture against attacks of plunderers or popular insurrection— to be, in fact, a military guard—but, after the temple was built, to open and shut the gates, which were extraordinarily large and ponderous. **10. Simri the chief . . . though . . . not the first-born**—probably because the family entitled to the right of primogeniture had died out, or because there were none of the existing families which could claim that right. **12. Among these were the divisions of the porters, even among the chief men**—These were charged with the duty of superintending the watches, being heads of the twenty-four courses of porters.

13-19. The Gates Assigned by Lot. **13. they cast lots**—Their departments of duty, such as the gates they should attend to, were allotted in the same manner as those of the other Levitical bodies, and the names of the chiefs or captains are given, with the respective gates assigned them. **15. the house of Asuppim**—or collections, probably a storehouse, where were kept the grain, wine, and other offerings for the sustenance of the priests. **16. the gate Shallecheth**—probably the rubbish gate, through which all the accumulated filth and sweepings of the temple and its courts were poured out. **by the causeway of the going up**—probably the ascending road which was cast up or raised from the deep valley between Mount Zion and Moriah, for the royal egress to the place of worship (II Chron. 9:4). **ward against ward**— Some refer these words to Shuppim and Hosah, whose duty it was to watch both the western gate and the gate Shallecheth, which was opposite, while others take it as a general statement applicable to all the guards, and intended to intimate that they were posted at regular distances from each other, or that they all mounted and relieved guard at the same time in uniform order. **17-19. Eastward were six Levites**—because the gate there was the most frequented. There were four at the north gate; four at the south, at the storehouse which was adjoining the south, and which had two entrance gates, one leading in a southwesterly direction to the city, and the other direct west, two porters each. At the Parbar towards the west, there were six men posted—four at the causeway or ascent (vs.

ADAM CLARKE — CHAPTER 26

1. *The divisions of the porters.* There were four classes of these, each of which belonged to one of the four gates of the Temple, which opened to the four cardinal points of heaven. The eastern gate fell to Shelemiah; the northern, to Zechariah, v. 14; the southern, to Obed-edom, v. 15; the western, to Shuppim and Hosah, v. 16. These several persons were captains of these porter bands or doorkeepers at the different gates. There were probably a thousand men under each of these captains; as we find, from chap. xxiii. 5, that there were 4,000 in all.

6. *They were mighty men of valour.* They were not only porters or doorkeepers in the ordinary sense of the word, but they were a military guard for the gates; and perhaps in this sense alone we are to understand their office.

12. The rest of this chapter, with the whole of the twenty-eighth, is wanting in both the Syriac and Arabic.

13. *They cast lots . . . for every gate.* None of these captains or their companies were permitted to choose which gate they would guard, but each took his appointment by lot.

15. *The house of Asuppim.* The house of the "collections"; the place where either the supplies of the porters or the offerings made for the use of the priests and Levites were laid up.

16. *The gate Shallecheth.* The gate of the projections, probably that through which all the offal of the Temple was carried out.

17. *Eastward were six Levites.* It is supposed that there were more guards set at this eastern gate because it was more frequented than the others. At each of the other gates were only four; at this, six.

MATTHEW HENRY

Verses 20–28

1. There were *treasures of the house of God.* A great house cannot be well kept without stores of all manner of provisions. These treasures typified the plenty there is in our heavenly Father's house, enough and to spare. In Christ, the true temple, are hid *treasures of wisdom and knowledge*, and *unsearchable riches.* 2. There were *treasures of dedicated things* as a grateful acknowledgment of the divine protection. Abraham gave Melchisedec the *tenth of the spoils*, Heb. vii. 4. In Moses's time the officers of the army, when they returned victorious, brought of their spoils an *oblation to the Lord*, Num. xxxi. 50. Of late this pious custom had been revived; and not only Samuel and David, but Saul, and Abner, and Joab, had dedicated of their spoils to the honour and support of the house of God, *v.* 28.

Verses 29–32

The magistracy is an ordinance of God for the good of the church as truly as the ministry is. And here we are told, 1. That the Levites were employed in the administration of justice in concurrence with the princes and elders of the several tribes, who could not be supposed to understand the law so well as the Levites, who made it their business to study it. None of those Levites who were employed in the service of the sanctuary, none of the singers or porters, were concerned in this outward business; either one was enough to engage the whole man or it was presumption to undertake both. 2. Their charge was both *in all business of the Lord*, and *in the service of kings*, *v.* 30 and again *v.* 32. They managed the affairs of the country, as well ecclesiastical as civil, took care both of God's tithes and the king's taxes, punished offences committed immediately against God and his honour and those against the government and the public peace, guarded both against idolatry and against injustice, and took care to put the laws in execution against both. 3. There were more Levites employed as judges with the two tribes and a half on the other side Jordan than with all the rest of the tribes; there were 2,700; whereas on the west side of Jordan there were 1,700, *v.* 30, 32. Either those remote tribes were not so well furnished as the rest with judges of their own, or because they, lying furthest from Jerusalem and on the borders of the neighbouring nations, were most in danger of being infected with idolatry, and most needed the help of Levites to prevent it.

JAMIESON, FAUSSET, BROWN

16), and two at Parbar, amounting to twenty-four in all, who were kept daily on guard. **Parbar**—is, perhaps, the same as Parvar (suburbs, II Kings 23: 11), and if so, this gate might be so called as leading to the suburbs [CALMET].

20-28. LEVITES THAT HAD CHARGE OF THE TREASURES. **20. of the Levites, Ahijah**—The heading of this section is altogether strange as it stands, for it looks as if the sacred historian were going to commence a new subject different from the preceding. Besides, "Ahijah, whose name occurs after" the Levites, is not mentioned in the previous lists. It is totally unknown and is introduced abruptly without further information; and lastly, Ahijah must have united in his own person those very offices of which the occupants are named in the verses that follow. The reading is incorrect. The *Septuagint* has this very suitable heading, "And their Levitical brethren over the treasures," etc. [BERTHEAU]. The names of those who had charge of the treasure-chambers at their respective wards are given, with a general description of the precious things committed to their trust. Those treasures were immense, consisting of the accumulated spoils of Israelitish victories, as well as of voluntary contributions made by David and the representatives of the people.

29-32. OFFICERS AND JUDGES. **29. officers and judges**—The word rendered "officers" is the term which signifies scribes or secretaries, so that the Levitical class here described were magistrates, who, attended by their clerks, exercised judicial functions; there were 6000 of them (ch. 23:4), who probably acted like their brethren on the principle of rotation, and these were divided into three classes—one (vs. 29) for the outward business over Israel; one (vs. 30), consisting of 1700, for the west of Jordan "in all business of the Lord, and in the service of the king"; and the third (vss. 31, 32), consisting of 2700, "rulers for every matter pertaining to God, and affairs of the king."

ADAM CLARKE

20. *The treasures of the house of God.* Where the money was kept, which was to be expended in oblations for the Temple.

29. *Outward business.* Work done without the city: cutting the timber, hewing stones, ploughing the fields belonging to the sanctuary.

30. *In all the business of the Lord.* Everything that concerned ecclesiastical matters. *In the service of the king.* Everything that concerned civil affairs: see also v. 32.

MATTHEW HENRY

CHAPTER 27

Verses 1–15

An account of the regulation of the militia of the kingdom. David was himself a man of war. He contrived to keep up a constant force, and yet not a standing army. 1. He kept up 24,000 constantly in arms. This was a sufficient strength for the securing of the public peace and safety. 2. He changed them every month; so that the whole number of the militia amounted to 288,000, perhaps about a fifth part of the able men of the kingdom.

JAMIESON, FAUSSET, BROWN

CHAPTER 27

VSS. 1-15. TWELVE CAPTAINS FOR EVERY MONTH. **1. came in and went out month by month**—Here is an account of the standing military force of Israel. A militia formed, it would seem, at the beginning of David's reign (see on vs. 7) was raised in the following order: Twelve legions, corresponding to the number of tribes, were enlisted in the king's service. Each legion comprised a body of 24,000 men, whose term of service was a month in rotation, and who were stationed either at Jerusalem or in any other place where they might be required. There was thus always a force sufficient for the ordinary purposes of state, as well as for resisting sudden attacks or popular tumults; and when extraordinary emergencies demanded a larger force, the whole standing army could easily be called to arms, amounting to 288,000, or to 300,000, including the 12,000 officers that naturally attended on the twelve princes (vss. 16-24). Such a military establishment would be burdensome neither to the country nor to the royal treasury; for attendance on this duty being a mark of honor and distinction, the expense of maintenance would be borne probably by the militiaman himself, or furnished out of the common fund of his tribe. Nor would the brief period of actual service produce any derangement of the usual course of affairs; for, on the expiry of the term, every soldier returned to the pursuits and duties of private life during the other eleven months of the year. Whether the same individuals were always enrolled, cannot be determined. The probability is, that provided the requisite number was furnished, no stricter scrutiny would be made. A change of men might, to a certain degree, be encouraged, as it was a part of David's policy to train all his subjects to skill in arms; and to have made the enlistment fall always on the same individuals would have defeated that purpose. To have confined each month's levy rigidly within the limits of one tribe might have fallen hard upon those tribes which were weak and small. The rotation system being established, each division knew its own month, as well as the name of the commander under whom it was to serve. These

ADAM CLARKE

CHAPTER 27

1. *The chief fathers and captains of thousands.* The patriarchs, chief generals, or generals of brigade. This enumeration is widely different from the preceding. In that, we have the orders and courses of the priests and the Levites in their ecclesiastical ministrations; in this, we have the account of the order of the civil service, that which related simply to the political state of the king and the kingdom. Twenty-four persons, chosen out of David's worthies, each of whom had a second, were placed over 24,000 men, who all served a month in turn at a time; and this was the whole of their service during the year, after which they attended to their own affairs. Thus the king had always on foot a regular force of 24,000, who served without expense to him or the state, and were not oppressed by the service, which took up only a twelfth part of their time. And by this plan he could at any time, when the exigency of the state require it, bring into the field 12 times 24,000, or 288,000 fighting men, independently of the 12,000 officers, which made in the whole an effective force of 300,000 soldiers—and all these men were prepared, disciplined, and ready at a call, without the smallest expense to the state or the king. These were, properly speaking, the militia of the Israelitish kingdom.

MATTHEW HENRY

3. Every course had a commander-in-chief over it. All these twelve great commanders are mentioned among David's worthies and champions, 2 Sam. xxiii. and 1 Chron. xi. Benaiah is here called *a chief priest*, *v.* 5. But, *cohen* signifying both a *priest* and a *prince*, it might better be translated here *a chief ruler*, or (as in the margin) *a principal officer*. When his wars were over he revived this method, for the peaceable reign of his son Solomon.

Verses 16–34

An account,

I. Of the princes of the tribes. Something of the ancient order instituted by Moses in the wilderness was still kept up, that every tribe should have its prince or chief. Whether these princes were of the nature of lord-lieutenants that guided them in their military affairs, or chief-justices that presided in their courts of judgment, does not appear. Their power, we may suppose, was much less now that all the tribes were united under one king than it had been when, for the most part, they acted separately.

II. Of the numbering of the people, *v.* 23, 24. It is here said, 1. That when David ordered the people to be numbered he forbade the numbering of those under twenty years old.

2. That that account which David took of the people, in the pride of his heart, turned to no good account; for it was never perfected, nor done with exactness, nor was it ever recorded as an authentic account. Joab was disgusted with it, and did it by halves; David was ashamed of it, and willing it should be forgotten, because there fell wrath for it against Israel.

III. Of the officers of the court. 1. The *rulers of the* king's *substance* (as they are called, *v.* 31), such as had the oversight and charge of the king's tillage, his vineyards, his olive-yards, his herds, his camels, his asses, his flocks. Here are officers all for service, agreeable to the simplicity and plainness of those times. David was a great soldier, a great scholar, and a great prince, and yet a great husband of his estate. 2. The attendants on the king's person were such as were eminent for wisdom. His uncle, who was a wise man and a scribe, not only well skilled in politics, but well read in the scriptures, was his counsellor, *v.* 32. Hushai, an honest man, was his companion and confidant.

JAMIESON, FAUSSET, BROWN

commanders are styled, "the chief fathers," i.e., the hereditary heads of tribes who, like chieftains of clans, possessed great power and influence. **captains of thousands and hundreds**—The legions of 24,000 were divided into regiments of 1000, and these again into companies of 100 men, under the direction of their respective subalterns, there being, of course, twenty-four captains of thousands, and 240 centurions. **and their officers**—the Shoterim, who in the army performed the duty of the commissariat, keeping the muster roll, etc. **2, 3. Jashobeam the son of Zabdiel**—(See on ch. 11:11; II Sam. 23:8). Hachmoni was his father, Zabdiel probably one of his ancestors; or there might be different names of the same individual. In the rotation of the military courses, the dignity of precedence, not of authority, was given to the hero. **4. second month was Dodai**—or Dodo. Here the text seems to require the supplement of "Eleazar the son of Dodo" (II Sam. 23:9). **7. Asahel**—This officer having been slain at the very beginning of David's reign, his name was probably given to this division in honor of his memory, and his son was invested with the command.

16-24. PRINCES OF THE TWELVE TRIBES. **16. over the tribes of Israel: the ruler**—This is a list of the hereditary chiefs or rulers of tribes at the time of David's numbering the people. Gad and Asher are not included; for what reason is unknown. The tribe of Levi had a prince (vs. 17), as well as the other tribes; and although it was ecclesiastically subject to the high priest, yet in all civil matters it had a chief or head, possessed of the same authority and power as in the other tribes, only his jurisdiction did not extend to the priests. **18. Elihu**—probably the same as Eliab (I Sam. 16:16). **23. But David took not the number of them from twenty years old and under**—The census which David ordered did not extend to all the Israelites; for to contemplate such an enumeration would have been to attempt an impossibility (Gen. 28:14), and besides would have been a daring offense to God. The limitation to a certain age was what had probably quieted David's conscience as to the *lawfulness* of the measure, while its *expediency* was strongly pressed upon his mind by the army arrangements he had in view. **24. neither was the number put in the account of the chronicles of King David**—either because the undertaking was not completed, Levi and Benjamin not having been numbered (ch. 21:6), or the full details in the hands of the enumerating officers were not reported to David, and, consequently, not registered in the public archives. **the chronicles**—were the daily records or annals of the king's reign. No notice was taken of this census in the historical register, as from the public calamity with which it was associated it would have stood as a painful record of the divine judgment against the king and the nation. **25. over the king's treasures**—Those treasures consisted of gold, silver, precious stones, cedar-wood, etc.; those which he had *in* Jerusalem as distinguished from others *without* the city. **the storehouses in the fields**—Grain covered over with layers of straw is frequently preserved in the fields under little earthen mounds, like our potato pits. **27. the vineyards**—These seem to have been in the vine-growing districts of Judah, and were committed to two men of that quarter. **wine-cellars**—The wine is deposited in jars sunk in the court of the house. **28. olive trees and the sycamore trees . . . in the low plains**—i.e., the Shephela, the rich, low-lying ground between the Mediterranean and the mountains of Judah. **29. herds that fed in Sharon**—a fertile plain between Cæsarea and Joppa. **30. camels**—These were probably in the countries east of the Jordan, and hence an Ishmaelite and Nazarite were appointed to take charge of them. **31. rulers of the substance that was King David's**—How and when the king acquired these demesnes and this variety of property—whether it was partly by conquests, or partly by confiscation, or by his own active cultivation of waste lands—is not said. It was probably in all these ways. The management of the king's private possessions was divided into twelve parts, like his public affairs and the revenue derived from all these sources mentioned must have been very large.

ADAM CLARKE

5. *Benaiah the son of Jehoiada, a chief priest.* Why should not this clause be read as it is in the Hebrew? "Benaiah, the son of Jehoiada the priest, a captain; and in his course"? Or, as the Targum has it, "The third captain of the host for the month Sivan was Benaiah, the son of Jehoiada the priest, who was constituted a chief"?

7. *Asahel the brother of Joab.* This verse proves that the division and arrangement mentioned above were made before David was acknowledged king in Hebron; for Asahel, the brother of Joab, who was fourth captain, was slain by Abner, while Ish-bosheth reigned over Israel at Mahanaim, 2 Sam. ii. 19-23.

16. *Over the tribes of Israel.* In this enumeration there is no mention of the tribes of Asher and Gad. Probably the account of these has been lost from this register. These rulers appear to have been all honorary men, without pay, like the lords lieutenants of our counties.

24. *Neither was the number put in the account.* Joab did not return the whole number. Probably the plague began before he had finished; or he did not choose to give it in, as he had entered on this work with extreme reluctance, and he did not choose to tell the king how numerous they were.

25-31. *Over the king's treasures.* We see from these verses in what the personal property of David consisted: (1) *Treasures,* gold, silver. (2) Goods and grain in castles, *cities, villages,* and in the *fields.* (3) *Vineyards* and their produce. (4) *Olive trees* and their produce. (5) Meat cattle, in different districts. (6) *Camels* and *asses;* they had no horses. (7) *Flocks,* sheep, goats.

CHAPTER 28

MATTHEW HENRY

Verses 1–10

David had *served his generation according to the will of God,* Acts xiii. 36. But now the time draws nigh that he must die, and, as a type of the Son of David, the nearer he comes to his end the more busy he is.

JAMIESON, FAUSSET, BROWN

CHAPTER 28

ADAM CLARKE

CHAPTER 28

MATTHEW HENRY

I. He summoned all the great men to attend him, that he might take leave of them all together, *v.* 1. Thus Moses did (Deut. xxxi. 28), and Joshua, *ch.* xxiii. 2; xxiv. 1.

II. He addressed them with a great deal of respect and tenderness. He not only exerted himself to rise from his bed, but he rose out of his chair, and *stood up upon his feet* (*v.* 2), in reverence to God whose will he was to declare, and in reverence to this solemn assembly of the Israel of God, as if he looked upon himself, though *major singulis—greater than any individual among them*, yet *minor universis—less than the whole of them together*. It had been too much his pleasure that they were all his *servants* (*ch.* xxi. 3), but now he calls them his *brethren*, whom he loved, his people, whom he took care of, not his servants, whom he had the command of: *Hear me, my brethren, and my people.*

III. He declared the purpose he had formed to build a temple for God, and God's disallowing that purpose, *v.* 2, 3. He must serve the public with the sword; another must do it with the line and plummet. Times of rest are building times, Acts ix. 31.

IV. He produced his own title first, and then Solomon's, to the crown; both were undoubtedly *jure divino—divine*. 1. Judah was not the eldest son of Jacob, yet God chose that tribe to be the ruling tribe; Jacob entailed the sceptre upon it, Gen. xlix. 10. 2. It does not appear that the family of Jesse was the senior house of that tribe. 3. David was the youngest son of Jesse, yet God liked him to make him king; so it seemed good unto him. 4. Solomon was one of the youngest sons of David, and yet God chose him to sit upon the throne, because he was the likeliest of them all to build the temple, the wisest and best inclined.

V. He opened to them God's gracious purposes concerning Solomon (*v.* 6, 7): *I have chosen him to be my son.* Of him God said, as a figure of him that was to come, 1. *He shall build my house.* Christ is both the founder and the foundation of the gospel temple. 2. *I will establish his kingdom for ever.* This must have its accomplishment in the kingdom of the Messiah, which shall continue in his hands through all the ages of time (Isa. ix. 7; Luke i. 33) and shall then be delivered up to God, even the Father, yet perhaps to be delivered back to the Redeemer for ever. As to Solomon, this promise of the establishment of his kingdom is here made conditional: *If he be constant to do my commandments, as at this day.*

VI. He charged them to adhere steadfastly to God and their duty, *v.* 8. The matter of this charge: *Keep, and seek for all the commandments of the Lord your God.* The Lord was their God; his commandments must be their rule; they must be inquisitive concerning their duty, search the scriptures, take advice, seek the law at the mouth of those whose lips were to keep this knowledge, and pray to God to teach and direct them. God's commandments will not be kept without great care. 2. The solemnity of it. He charged them in the sight of all Israel, "God is witness, and this congregation is witness, that they have good counsel given them, and fair warning; if they do not take it, it is their fault, and God and man will be witnesses against them." See 1 Tim. v. 21; 2 Tim. iv. 1. 3. The motive to observe this charge. It was the way to be happy, to have the peaceable possession of this good land themselves and to preserve the entail of it upon their children.

VII. He concluded with a charge to Solomon himself, *v.* 9, 10. He was much concerned that Solomon should be religious.

1. The charge he gives him. He was born in God's house and therefore bound in duty to be his, brought up in his house and therefore bound in gratitude. *Thy own friend, and thy father's friend, forsake not.*

2. The arguments to enforce this charge.

(1) Two arguments of general inducement:—[1] That the secrets of our souls are open before God; he searches all hearts, even the hearts of kings, which to men are unsearchable, Prov. xxv. 3. [2] That we are happy or miserable here, and for ever, according as we do, or do not, serve God. *If we seek him diligently, he will be found of us,* and that is enough to make us happy, Heb. xi. 6. God never casts any off till they have first cast him off.

(2) One argument peculiar to Solomon (*v.* 10): "*Thou art to build a house for the sanctuary;* therefore seek and serve God, that that work may be done from a good principle, in a right manner, and may be accepted."

3. The means prescribed, and they are prescribed to us all. (1) Caution: *Take heed;* beware of everything that looks like, or leads to, that which is evil. (2) Courage: *Be strong, and do it.* We cannot do our work as we should unless we put on resolution, and

JAMIESON, FAUSSET, BROWN

Vss. 1-8. David Exhorts the People to Fear God. **1. David assembled all the princes of Israel**—i.e., the representatives of the people, the leading men of the kingdom, who are enumerated in this verse according to their respective rank or degree of authority. **princes of the tribes**—(ch. 27:16-22). Those patriarchal chiefs are mentioned first as being the highest in rank—a sort of hereditary noblesse. **the captains of the companies**—the twelve generals mentioned (ch. 27:1-15). **the stewards,** etc.—(ch. 27:25-31). **the officers**—*Hebrew,* eunuchs, or attendants on the court (I Sam. 8:15; I Kings 22:9; II Kings 22:18); and besides Joab, the commander-in-chief of the army, the heroes who had no particular office (ch. 11; II Sam. 23). This assembly, a very mixed and general one, as appears from the parties invited, was more numerous and entirely different from that mentioned (ch. 23:2). **2. Hear me, my brethren**—This was the style of address becoming a constitutional king of Israel (Deut. 17:20; I Sam. 30:23; II Sam. 5:1). **I had it in mine heart**—I proposed or designed. **to build an house of rest**—a solid and permanent temple. **for the footstool of our God**—God seated between the cherubim, at the two extremities of the ark, might be said to be enthroned in His glory, and the coverlet of the ark to be His footstool. **and had made ready for the building**—The immense treasures which David had amassed and the elaborate preparations he had made, would have been amply sufficient for the erection of the temple of which he presented the model to Solomon. **3. thou hast been a man of war, and hast shed much blood**—The church or spiritual state of the world, of which the temple at Jerusalem was to be a type, would be presided over by One who was to be pre-eminently the Prince of Peace, and therefore would be represented not so fitly by David, whose mission had been a preparatory one of battle and conquest, as by his son, who should reign in unbroken peace. **4, 5. he hath chosen Solomon**—The spirit of David's statement is this:—It was not my ambition, my valor, or my merit that led to the enthronement of myself and family; it was the grace of God which chose the tribe, the family, the person—myself in the first instance, and now Solomon, to whom, as the Lord's anointed, you are all bound to submit. Like that of Christ, of whom he was a type, the appointment of Solomon to the kingdom above all his brethren was frequently pre-intimated (ch. 17:12; 22:9; II Sam. 7:12-14; 12:24, 25; II Kings 1:13). **7. I will establish his kingdom for ever, if he be constant to do my commandments**—The same condition is set before Solomon by God (I Kings 3:14; 9:4). **8. Now . . . in the sight of all Israel, . . . keep, and seek for all the commandments of the Lord,** etc.—This solemn and earnest exhortation to those present, and to all Israel through their representatives, to continue faithful in observing the divine law as essential to their national prosperity and permanence, is similar to that of Moses (Deut. 39:15-20).

9-20. He Encourages Solomon to Build the Temple. **9, 10. And thou, Solomon my son**—The royal speaker now turns to Solomon, and in a most impressive manner presses upon him the importance of sincere and practical piety. **know thou**—He did not mean head knowledge, for Solomon possessed that already, but that experimental acquaintance with God which is only to be obtained by loving and serving Him.

ADAM CLARKE

1. *David assembled.* This refers to the persons whose names and offices we have seen in the preceding chapter.

2. *David . . . stood up upon his feet.* He was now very old, and chiefly confined to his bed (see 1 Kings i. 47); and while he was addressing his son Solomon he continued on the bed; but when all the principal nobles of his kingdom came before him, he received strength to arise and address them, standing on his feet.

3. *Thou shalt not build an house.* See 2 Sam. vii. 5, 13.

4. *Over Israel for ever.* The government should have no end, provided they continued to walk according to the commandments of God; see v. 7. The government, as referring to Christ, is, and will be, without end.

CHARLES H. SPURGEON:

"If thou seek him, he will be found of thee." The notion is that there are a great many very mysterious preliminaries, a great deal to do, and a great deal to be, and all quite beyond our power. It is not so, but seek Him. We will tell you what that means, and he that seeks Him finds Him. "If thou seek him, he will be found of thee." It has been supposed that we should want a good deal of help in seeking after salvation. Certain persons who step in to be absolutely necessary priests between us and God. A great delusion, but there are thousands who believe it and who fancy that God won't hear them if they pray unless they have some respect for these human mediators. Away with the whole, away with any pretense for anyone to stand between the soul and God, save Jesus Christ. "If thou seek him, he will be found of thee." Though thou bring no other man with thee, but come empty-handed as thou art to God here, without paraphernalia, or altar, or sacrifice, He will be found of thee. Take the text in its simplicity and sublimity. It is just this: that if any heart really seeks God in His way, it shall find Him; if any man really wants mercy from God and seeks it as God tells him to seek it, he shall have it. Any man of woman born, be he who he may, if he comes to God in the way laid down, and sincerely asks for salvation, that salvation he shall surely have. The matter is simple enough; our pride alone obscures it. The way to heaven is so plain that "a wayfaring man, though a fool, may not err therein." We do but muddle it because we dislike it; we do but add this and that and the other to it because, like Naaman, the Syrian, we want to do some great thing, and we are not content to take the prophetic word, "Wash and be clean."

—*The Treasury of the Old Testament*

MATTHEW HENRY

fetch in strength from divine grace.

Verses 11–21

As for the general charge that David gave his son to seek God and serve him, the book of the law was, in that, his only rule, and there needed no other; but, in building the temple, David was now to give him three things:—1. A model of the building, because it was to be such a building as neither he nor his architects ever saw. Moses had a pattern of the tabernacle shown him in the mount (Heb. viii. 5), so had David of the temple, by the immediate hand of God upon him, *v.* 19. It is said (*v.* 12), *He had this pattern by the Spirit.* The contrivance either of David's devotion or of Solomon's wisdom must not be trusted to in an affair of this nature. The temple must be a sacred thing and a type of Christ; it was a kind of sacrament, and therefore it must not be left to man's art or invention to contrive it, but must be framed by divine institution. This pattern David gave to Solomon, that he might know what to provide and might go by a certain rule. He gave him a table of the courses of the priests, patterns of the vessels of service (*v.* 13), and a pattern of the chariot of the cherubim, *v.* 18. Besides the two cherubim over the mercy-seat, there were two much larger, whose wings reached from wall to wall (1 Kings vi. 23, &c.), and of these David here gave Solomon the pattern, called a *chariot;* for the angels are the chariots of God, Ps. lxviii. 17. 2. Materials for the most costly of the utensils of the temple. That they might not be made any less than the patterns, he weighed out the exact quantity for each vessel both of gold and silver, *v.* 14. In the tabernacle there was but one golden candlestick; in the temple there were ten (1 Kings vii. 49), besides silver ones, which, it is supposed, were hand-candlesticks, *v.* 15. In the tabernacle there was but one table; but in the temple, besides that on which the shew-bread was set, there were ten others for other uses (2 Chron. iv. 8), besides silver tables; for, this house being much larger than that, it would look bare if it had not furniture proportionable. The gold for the altar of incense is particularly said to be *refined gold* (*v.* 18), purer than any of the rest; for that was typical of the intercession of Christ, than which nothing is more pure and perfect. 3. Directions which way to look for help in this great undertaking. God will help thee, and thou must look up to him in the first place (*v.* 20): *The Lord God, even my God,* whom I have chosen and served, who has all along been present with me and prospered me, and to whom, from my own experience of his power and goodness, I recommend thee, he will be with thee, to direct, strengthen, and prosper thee; he will not fail thee nor forsake thee. We may be sure that God, who owned our fathers and carried them through the services of their day, will, in like manner, if we be faithful to him, go along with us in our day, and will never leave us, while he has any work to do in us or by us. "Good men will help thee, *v.* 21. The priests and Levites will advise thee, and thou mayest consult them. Thou hast good workmen, who are both willing and skilful;" and these are two very good properties in a workman, especially in those that work at the temple. And, *lastly,* "The princes and the people will be so far from opposing or retarding the work that they will be wholly at thy command, every one in his place ready to further it."

JAMIESON, FAUSSET, BROWN

11. Then David gave to Solomon . . . the pattern—He now put into the hands of his son and successor the plan or model of the temple, with the elevations, measurements, apartments, and chief articles of furniture, all of which were designed according to the pattern given him by divine revelation (vs. 19).

12. the pattern of all that he had by the spirit—rather, with him in spirit; i.e., was floating in his mind.

15, 16. the candlesticks of silver—Solomon made them all of gold—in this and a few minor particulars departing from the letter of his father's instructions, where he had the means of executing them in a more splendid style. There was only one candlestick and one table in the tabernacle, but ten in the temple. **18. the chariot of the cherubim**—The expanded wings of the cherubim formed what was figuratively styled the throne of God, and as they were emblematical of rapid motion, the throne or seat was spoken of as a chariot (Ps. 18:10; 99:1). It is quite clear that in all these directions David was not guided by his own taste, or by a desire for taking any existing model of architecture, but solely by a regard to the express revelation of the divine will. In a vision, or trance, the whole edifice, with its appurtenances, had been placed before his eyes so vividly and permanently, that he had been able to take a sketch of them in the models delivered to Solomon. **20. Be strong and of good courage**—The address begun in verse 9 is resumed and concluded in the same strain.

21. behold, the courses of the priests and Levites—They were, most probably, represented in this assembly though they are not named. **also the princes and all the people**—i.e., as well the skilful, expert, and zealous artisan, as the workman who needs to be directed in all his labors.

ADAM CLARKE

11. *David gave to Solomon . . . the pattern.* He gave him an ichnography of the building, with elevations, sections, and specifications of every part; and all this he received by inspiration from God himself (see vv. 12 and 19), just as Moses had received the plan of the Tabernacle.

14. *Of gold by weight.* The quantity of gold which was to be put in each article.

15. *For the candlesticks.* There was but one chandelier in the Tabernacle; there were ten in the Temple. See 1 Kings vii. 49.

19. *Understand in writing.* In some vision of ecstasy he had seen a regularly sketched out plan, which had made so deep an impression on his mind that he could readily describe it to his son.

MATTHEW HENRY — CHAPTER 29

Verses 1–9

I. David spoke to the great men of Israel, to engage them to contribute towards the building of the temple. Though David would not impose on them, as a tax, what they should give towards it, he would recommend the present as a fair occasion for a free-will offering, because what is done in works of piety and charity should be done willingly and not by constraint; for God loves a cheerful giver. 1. He would have them consider that Solomon was young, and needed help; but that he was the person whom God had chosen to do this work. 2. That the work was great, and all hands should contribute to the carrying of it on. 3. He tells them what great preparations had been made for this work. He did not intend to throw all the burden upon them, but that they should show their goodwill, by adding to what was done (*v.* 2): *I have prepared with all my might.* 4. He sets them a good example. He had, out of his own share, offered largely for the beautifying and enriching of it, 2,000 talents of gold and 7,000 talents of silver (*v.* 4, 5), and this because he had set his affection on the house of his God. 5. He stirs them up to do as he had done (*v.* 5): *And who then is willing*

JAMIESON, FAUSSET, BROWN — CHAPTER 29

VSS. 1-9. DAVID CAUSES THE PRINCES AND PEOPLE TO OFFER FOR THE HOUSE OF GOD. **1. Solomon . . . is yet young and tender**—Though Solomon was very young when he was raised to the sovereign power, his kingdom escaped the woe pronounced (Eccles. 10:16). Mere childhood in a prince is not always a misfortune to a nation, as there are instances of the government being wisely administered during a minority. Solomon himself is a most illustrious proof that a young prince may prove a great blessing; for when he was but a mere child, with respect to his age, no nation was happier. His father, however, made this address before Solomon was endowed with the divine gift of wisdom, and David's reference to his son's extreme youth, in connection with the great national undertaking he had been divinely appointed to execute, was to apologize to this assembly of the estates—or, rather, to assign the reason of his elaborate preparations for the work. **3, 4. Moreover . . . I have of mine own proper good,** etc.—In addition to the immense amount of gold and silver treasure which David had already bequeathed for various uses in the service of the temple, he now made an additional

ADAM CLARKE — CHAPTER 29

2. *And marble stones. Abney shayish,* which the Vulgate translates, "Parian marble." Paros was one of the Cyclades islands, and produced the whitest and finest marble, that of which most of the finest works of antiquity have been made.

MATTHEW HENRY

to consecrate his service this day unto the Lord? We must make the service of God our business, must *fill our hands to the Lord*, so the Hebrew phrase is. The filling of our hands with the service of God intimates that we must serve him only, serve him liberally, and serve him in the strength of grace derived from him.

II. How handsomely they all contributed towards the building of the temple when they were thus stirred up to it. How generous they were appears by the sum total of the contributions, *v.* 7, 8. They gave like princes of Israel. *The people rejoiced*: they were glad of the opportunity of honouring God thus with their substance, and glad of the prospect of bringing this good work to perfection. *David rejoiced with great joy* that his son and successor would have those about him that were so well affected to the house of God, and that this work, upon which his heart was so much set, was likely to go on.

Verses 10–22

I. The solemn address which David made to God: *Wherefore David blessed the Lord before all the congregation.* David's psalms, towards the latter end of the book, are most of them psalms of praise. The nearer we come to the world of everlasting praise the more we should speak the language and do the work of that world. In this address,

1. He adores God, and ascribes glory to him as the God of Israel, *blessed for ever and ever.* Our Lord's prayer ends with a doxology much like this which David here begins with—*for thine is the kingdom, the power, and the glory.* This is properly praising God—with holy awe and reverence, acknowledging, (1) His infinite perfections. He is the fountain and centre of everything that is bright and blessed. His is the *greatness*; his greatness is immense and incomprehensible. His is the *power*, and it is almighty and irresistible. His is the *glory*; for his glory is his own end and the end of the whole creation. His is the *victory*; he transcends and surpasses all, and is able to conquer and subdue all things to himself. And his is the *majesty*, real and personal, inexpressible and inconceivable. (2) His sovereign dominion, as rightful owner and possessor of all: "*All that is in heaven, and in the earth, is thine: thine is the kingdom*, and all kings are thy subjects; for thou art head, and art to be exalted and worshipped as head above all." (3) His universal influence and agency. All that are rich and honourable among the children of men have their riches and honours from God. What they had returned to him was but a small part of what they had received from him.

2. He acknowledges with thankfulness the grace of God enabling him to contribute so cheerfully towards the building of the temple (*v.* 13, 14): *Now therefore, our God, we thank thee.* It is a great instance of the power of God's grace in us to be able to do the work of God willingly.

3. He speaks very humbly of himself, and his people, and the offerings they had now presented to God. (1) For himself, and those that joined with him, though they were princes, he wondered that God should take such notice of them and do so much for them (*v.* 14): *Who am I, O Lord?* for (*v.* 15) *we are strangers before thee, and sojourners*, poor despicable creatures. *Our days on the earth are as a shadow*, which intimates that our life is a vain life, a dark life, a transient life, and a life that will have its period either in perfect light or perfect darkness. The next words explain it: *There is no abiding*, Heb. vii. 3, *no expectation.* We cannot expect any great matters from it, nor can we expect any long continuance of it, which forbids us to boast of the service we do to God. Alas! it is confined to a scantling of time. (2) As to their offerings, *Lord*, says he, *of thy own have we given thee* (*v.* 14), and again (*v.* 16), *It cometh of thy hand, and is all thy own. Let him that glories* therefore *glory in the Lord.*

4. He appeals to God concerning his own sincerity in what he did, *v.* 17. It is a great satisfaction to a good man to think that God *tries the heart* and *has pleasure in uprightness.* It was David's comfort that God knew with what pleasure he both offered his own and saw the people's offering. He was neither proud of his own good work nor envious of the good works of others.

5. He prays to God both for the people and for Solomon, that both might hold on as they began. In this prayer he addresses God as *the God of Abraham, Isaac, and Jacob*, a God in covenant with them and with us for their sakes. (1) For the people he prays (*v.* 18) that what good God had put into their minds he would always keep there, that they might always have the same thoughts of things as they now seemed to have. Great consequences depend upon what is innermost, and what uppermost, in the imagination

JAMIESON, FAUSSET, BROWN

contribution destined to a specific purpose—that of overlaying the walls of the house. This voluntary gift was from the private fortune of the royal donor, and had been selected with the greatest care. The gold was "the gold of Ophir," then esteemed the purest and finest in the world (Job 22:24; 28:16; Isa. 13:12). The amount was 3000 talents of gold and 7000 talents of refined silver. **5. who then is willing to consecrate his service**—*Heb.*, fill his hand; i.e., make an offering (Exod. 32:29; Lev. 8:33; I Kings 13:33). The meaning is, that whoever would contribute voluntarily, as he had done, would be offering a freewill offering to the Lord. It was a sacrifice which every one of them could make, and in presenting which the offerer himself would be the priest. David, in asking freewill offerings for the temple, imitated the conduct of Moses in reference to the tabernacle (Exod. 25:1-8). **6-8. Then the chief of the fathers**—or heads of the fathers (ch. 24: 31; 27:1). **princes of the tribes**—(ch. 27:16-22). **the rulers of the king's work**—those who had charge of the royal demesnes and other possessions (ch. 27: 25-31). **offered willingly**—Influenced by the persuasive address and example of the king, they acted according to their several abilities, and their united contributions amounted to the gross sum—of gold worth about $125,000,000; and of silver, about $17,000,000, besides brass and iron. **7. drams**—rather, *darics*, a Persian coin, with which the Jews from the time of the captivity became familiar, and which was afterwards extensively circulated in the countries of Western Asia. It is estimated as equal in value to about $5.00 in American currency. **of brass eighteen thousand talents, and one hundred thousand talents of iron**—In Scripture, iron is always referred to as an article of comparatively low value, and of greater abundance and cheaper than bronze [NAPIER]. **8. and they with whom precious stones were found**—rather, "whatever was found along with it of precious stones they gave" [BERTHEAU]. These gifts were deposited in the hands of Jehiel, whose family was charged with the treasures of the house of the Lord (ch:26:21).

10-25. HIS THANKSGIVING. **10. Wherefore David blessed the Lord**—This beautiful thanksgiving prayer was the effusion overflowing with gratitude and delight at seeing the warm and widespread interest that was now taken in forwarding the favorite project of his life. Its piety is displayed in the fervor of devotional feeling—in the ascription of all worldly wealth and greatness to God as the giver, in tracing the general readiness in contributing to the influence of His grace, in praying for the continuance of this happy disposition among the people, and in solemnly and earnestly commending the young king and his kingdom to the care and blessing of God. **16. all this store that we have prepared**—It may be useful to exhibit a tabular view of the treasure laid up and contributions stated by the historian as already made towards the erection of the proposed temple. Omitting the brass and iron, and precious stones, which, though specified partly (vs. 7), are represented in other portions as "without weight" (ch. 22:3, 14), we shall give in this table only the amount of gold and silver. Taking the talent of gold as worth approximately $25,000 and the talent of silver as $1,700, we arrive at the following amounts of contributions:

Sum accumulated and in public treasury (22:14):	
Gold	$2,500,000,000
Silver	1,700,000,000
Contributed by David personally (29:4):	
Gold	82,000,000
Silver	12,000,000
Contributed by assembled rulers (29:7):	
Gold	125,000,000
Silver	17,000,000

A grand total of approximately $4,436,000,000. Though it has been the common practice of Eastern monarchs to hoard vast sums for the accomplishment of any contemplated project, this amount so far exceeds not only every Oriental collection on record, but even the bounds of probability, that it is very generally allowed that either there is a corruption of the text in ch. 22:14, or that the reckoning of the historian was by the Babylonian, which was only a half, or the Syrian, which was only a fifth part, of the Hebrew talent. This would bring the Scripture account more into accordance with the statements of Josephus, as well as within the range of credibility.

ADAM CLARKE

5. *To consecrate his service.* "To fill his hand"; to bring an offering to the Lord.

7. *Of gold five thousand talents.* These amount to 25,378,906 pounds, 5 shillings, sterling. *Ten thousand drams.* Probably golden *darics*, amounting to 10,000 pounds. *Of silver ten thousand talents.* These amount to 3,535,937 pounds. *Brass eighteen thousand talents.* Amount to 1,026 tons, 11 hundredweight, and one quarter. *One hundred thousand talents of iron.* Amount to 5,703 tons, 2 hundredweight, and a half.

15. *Our days on the earth are as a shadow.* They are continually declining, fading, and passing away. *There is none abiding.* However we may wish to settle and remain in this state of things, it is impossible, because every earthly form is passing swiftly away. All is in a state of revolution and decay, and there is no abiding, *mikveh*, no "expectation," that we shall be exempt from those changes and chances to which our fathers were subjected.

MATTHEW HENRY

of the thoughts of our heart, what we aim at and what we love to think of. If any good have got possession of our hearts, or the hearts of our friends, it is good by prayer to commit the custody of it to the grace of God: "Lord, keep it there, keep it for ever there. Confirm their resolutions. They are in a good mind; keep them so when I am gone, them and theirs for ever." (2) For Solomon he prays (*v.* 19), *Give him a perfect heart.* He does not pray, "Lord, make him a rich man, a great man, a learned man;" but, "Lord, make him an honest man;" for that is better than all. Yet his building the house would not prove him to have a perfect heart unless he made conscience of keeping God's commandments. It is not helping to build churches that will save us if we live in disobedience to God's law.

II. The cheerful concurrence of this great assembly in this great solemnity. 1. They joined with David in the adoration of God. (*Now bless the Lord your God, v.* 20), which accordingly they did, by *bowing down their heads*, a gesture of adoration. Whoever is the mouth of the congregation, those only have the benefit who join with him, not by *bowing down the head* so much as by *lifting up the soul.* 2. They paid their respects to the king, looking upon him as an instrument in God's hand of much good to them; and, in honouring him, they honoured God. 3. The next day they offered abundance of sacrifices to God (*v.* 21). 4. They feasted and rejoiced before God, *v.* 22. 5. They made Solomon king the second time. He having been before anointed in haste, upon occasion of Adonijah's rebellion, it was thought fit to repeat the ceremony, for the greater satisfaction of the people. They *anointed him to the Lord.*

Verses 23–30

These verses bring king Solomon to his throne and king David to his grave.

I. Here is Solomon rising (*v.* 23): *Solomon sat on the throne of the Lord.* The throne of Israel is called *the throne of the Lord* because not only is he King of all nations, and all kings rule under him, but he was in a peculiar manner King of Israel, 1 Sam. xii. 12. Solomon's kingdom typified the kingdom of the Messiah, and his is indeed *the throne of the Lord.* Solomon prospered; for, 1. His people paid honour to him, as one to whom honour is due: *All Israel obeyed him*, that is, were ready to swear allegiance to him (*v.* 23). God inclined their hearts to do so, that his reign might, from the first, be peaceable. His father was a better man that he, and yet came to the crown with much difficulty, after long delay, and by many and slow steps. David had more faith, and therefore had it more tried. *They submitted themselves* (Heb. *They gave the hand under Solomon*), that is, bound themselves by oath to be true to him (putting the hand under the thigh was a ceremony anciently used in swearing). 2. God put honour upon him; for those that honour him he will honour: *The Lord magnified Solomon exceedingly, v.* 25. None of all the judges or kings of Israel, his predecessors, made such a figure as he did nor lived in such splendour.

II. Here is David's setting, that great man going off the stage. The historian here brings him to the end of his day, leaves him asleep, and draws the curtains about him.

1. He gives a summary account of the years of his reign, *v.* 26, 27.

2. He gives a short account of his death (*v.* 28), that he died *full of days, riches, and honour.* Honoured both of God and man. He had been a man of war from his youth, but was preserved through all the dangers of a military life, lived to a good old age, and died in peace, died in his bed, and yet in the bed of honour. For a fuller account of David's life and reign he refers to the histories or records of those times, which were written by Samuel while he lived, and continued, after his death, by Nathan and Gad, *v.* 29.

JAMIESON, FAUSSET, BROWN

20. all the congregation . . . worshipped the Lord, and the king—Though the external attitude might be the same, the sentiments of which it was expressive were very different in the two cases—of divine worship in the one, of civil homage in the other.

21, 22. they sacrificed . . . And did eat and drink—After the business of the assembly was over, the people, under the exciting influence of the occasion, still remained, and next day engaged in the performance of solemn rites, and afterwards feasted on the remainder of the sacrifices. **before the Lord**—either in the immediate vicinity of the ark, or, perhaps, rather in a religious and devout spirit, as partaking of a sacrificial meal. **made Solomon . . . king the second time**—in reference to the first time, which was done precipitately on Adonijah's conspiracy (I Kings 1:35). **they . . . anointed . . . Zadok**—The statement implies that his appointment met the popular approval. His elevation as sole high priest was on the disgrace of Abiathar, one of Adonijah's accomplices. **23. Solomon sat on the throne of the Lord**—As king of Israel, he was the Lord's vicegerent.

24. submitted themselves—*Heb.*, put their hands under Solomon, according to the custom still practised in the East of putting a hand under the king's extended hand and kissing the back of it (II Kings 10:15).

26-30. HIS REIGN AND DEATH. **26. Thus David . . . reigned**—(See I Kings 2:11).

ADAM CLARKE

18. *Keep this for ever.* All the good dispositions which myself and my people have came from Thee; continue to support and strengthen them by the same grace by which they have been inspired!

19. *Give unto Solomon . . . a perfect heart.* This He did, but Solomon abused His mercies.

20. *Worshipped the Lord, and the king.* They did reverence to God as the supreme Ruler, and to the king as His deputy.

21. *With their drink offerings.* The Targum says a thousand drink offerings, making these libations equal in number to the other offerings. *And sacrifices.* These were peace offerings offered for the people, and on the flesh of which they feasted.

22. *They made Solomon . . . king the second time.* The first time of his being anointed and proclaimed king was when his brother Adonijah affected the throne; and Zadok, Nathan, and Benaiah anointed and proclaimed him in a hurry, and without pomp. See 1 Kings i. 39. Now that all is quiet, and David, his father, dead (for he was probably so at the time of the second anointing), they anointed and proclaimed him afresh, with due ceremonies, sacrifices, etc. *To be the chief governor.* To be the vicegerent or deputy of Jehovah; for God never gave up His right of king in Israel. Those called kings were only His lieutenants; hence it is said, v. 23, that "Solomon sat on the throne of the Lord as king instead of David his father."

24. *Submitted themselves.* "They gave the hand under Solomon"; they swore fealty to him.

28. *And he died.* David, at his death, had everything that his heart could wish. (1) *A good old age*; having lived as long as living could be desirable, and having in the main enjoyed good health. (2) *Full of days;* having lived till he saw everything that he lived for either accomplished or in a state of forwardness. (3) *Full of . . . riches;* witness the immense sums left for the Temple. (4) *Full of . . . honour;* having gained more renown than any crowned head ever did, either before his time or since.

29. *The acts of David . . . first and last.* Those which concerned him in private life, as well as those which grew out of his regal government. All these were written by three eminent men, personally acquainted with him through the principal part of his life. These were *Samuel* and *Gad*, the seers; and *Nathan*, the prophet. These writings are all lost, except the particulars interspersed in the books of Samuel, Kings, and Chronicles, none of which are the records mentioned here.

30. *The times that went over him.* The transactions of his reign, and the occurrences and vicissitudes in his own kingdom, as well as those which were over all the kingdoms of the countries, i.e., in the surrounding nations, in most of which David had a share during his forty years' reign.

THE BOOK OF SECOND CHRONICLES

I. Solomon (1:1-9:31)
A. First vision and things following (1:1-7:10)
1. The vision (1:1-13)
2. National prosperity (1:14-2:18)
3. The Temple (3:1-5:1)
4. Ceremonies of consecration (5:2-7:10)
B. Second vision and things following (7:11-9:31)
1. The second vision (7:11-22)
2. Various acts of the king (8:1-18)
3. The Queen of Sheba (9:1-28)
4. Epilogue (9:29-31)

II. The kings of Judah (10:1-36:23)
A. The revolt of the Ten Tribes (10:1-11:4)
B. Period of degeneracy (11:5-16:14)
1. Rehoboam (11:5-12:16)
2. Abijah (13:1-22)
3. Asa (14:1-16:14)
C. Reform under Jehoshaphat (17:1-20:37)
1. Reform (17:1-19)
2. Lapse and restoration (18:1-19:11)
3. Prevailing prayer (20:1-37)
D. Period of degeneracy (21:1-23:21)
1. Jehoram (21:1-20)
2. Ahaziah (22:1-9)
3. Athaliah (22:10-23:21)
E. Reform under Joash (24:1-27)
1. Influence of Jehoiada (24:1-16)
2. Failure of Joash (24:17-27)
F. Period of degeneracy (25:1-28:27)
1. Amaziah (25:1-28)
2. Uzziah (26:1-23)
3. Jotham (27:1-9)
4. Ahaz (28:1-27)
G. Reform under Hezekiah (29:1-32:33)
1. Consciousness of sin and consequent cleansing (29:1-36)
2. The Passover (30:1-27)
3. Practical reforms (31:1-21)
4. The trial of faith—Sennacherib (32:1-33)
H. Period of degeneracy (33:1-25)
1. Manasseh (33:1-20)
2. Amon (33:21-25)
I. Reform under Josiah (34:1-35:27)
1. Josiah's first reforms (34:1-13)
2. The finding of the book of the law (34:14-33)
3. The Passover (35:1-27)
J. Period of degeneracy (36:1-10)
1. Jehoahaz (36:1-4)
2. Jehoiakim (36:5-8)
3. Jehoiachin (36:9, 10)
K. Captivity (36:11-23)

This book begins with the reign of Solomon and the building of the temple and continues the history of the kings of Judah to the captivity and so concludes with the fall of that illustrious monarchy and the destruction of the temple. That monarchy of the house of David, as it was prior in time, so it was superior in worth and dignity to all those four celebrated ones of which Nebuchadnezzar dreamed. The succession was kept up in a lineal descent throughout the whole monarchy, which continued between 400 and 500 years, and, after a long eclipse, shone forth again in the kingdom of the Messiah, "of the increase of whose government and peace there shall be no end." We had the story of the house of David before (in the first and second books of Kings), intermixed with that of the kings of Israel, which there took more room than that of Judah; but here we have it entire. Much is repeated here which we had before, yet many of the passages of the story are enlarged upon and added to, especially relating to the affairs of religion; for it is a church history. All along the good kings prospered and the wicked kings suffered.

MATTHEW HENRY

CHAPTER 1

Verses 1–12

I. Solomon's great prosperity, *v.* 1. God being with him, he was *strengthened in his kingdom.*

II. His great piety and devotion.

1. All his great men must thus far be good men that they must join with him in worshipping God. He spoke to the captains and judges, the governors and chief of the fathers, to go with him to Gibeon, *v.* 2, 3. Solomon began his reign with this public pious visit to God's altar, and it was a very good omen. Magistrates are then likely to do well for themselves and their people when they thus take God along with them at their setting out.

2. He offered abundance of sacrifices to God there (*v.* 6). His father David had left him flocks and herds in abundance (1 Chron. xxvii. 29, 31), and thus he gave God his dues out of them. The ark was at Jerusalem (*v.* 4), but the altar was at Gibeon (*v.* 5), and thither he brought his sacrifices.

3. He prayed a good prayer to God: this, with the answer to it, we had before, 1 Kings iii. 5, &c. (1) God bade him ask what he would; not only that he might put him in the right way of obtaining the favours that were intended him, but that he might discover what was in his heart. Men's characters appear in their choices and desires. What wouldst thou *have*? tries a man as much as, What wouldst thou *do*? (2) Like a genuine son of David, he chose spiritual blessings rather than temporal. His petition here is, *Give me wisdom and knowledge.* God gave the faculty of understanding, and to him we must apply for the furniture of it. Two things are here pleaded which we had not in Kings. [1] *Thou hast made me reign in my father's stead, v.* 8. Must I reign in my father's stead? Lord, give me my father's spirit." [2] *Let thy promise to David my father be established, v.* 9. The promise was, *He shall build a house for my name, I will establish his throne, he shall be my son,* and *my mercy shall not depart from him.* "Now, Lord, unless thou give me wisdom, thy house will not be built, nor my throne established; therefore, *Lord, give me wisdom.*"

JAMIESON, FAUSSET, BROWN

CHAPTER 1

Vss. 1-6. Solemn Offering of Solomon at Gibeon. **2. Then Solomon spake unto all Israel**—The heads, or leading officers, who are afterwards specified, were summoned to attend their sovereign in a solemn religious procession. The date of this occurrence was the second year of Solomon's reign, and the high place at Gibeon was chosen for the performance of the sacred rites, because the tabernacle and all the ancient furniture connected with the national worship were deposited there. Zadok was the officiating high priest (I Chron. 16:39). It is true that the ark had been removed and placed in a new tent which David had made for it at Jerusalem. But the brazen altar, "before the tabernacle of the Lord," on which the burnt offerings were appointed by the law to be made, was at Gibeon; and although David had been led by extraordinary events and tokens of the divine presence to sacrifice on the threshing-floor of Araunah, Solomon considered it his duty to present his offerings on the legally appointed spot "before the tabernacle," and on the time-honored altar prepared by the skill of Bezaleel in the wilderness (Exod. 38:1). **6. offered a thousand burnt offerings**—This holocaust he offered, of course, by the hands of the priests. The magnitude of the oblation became the rank of the offerer on this occasion of national solemnity.

7-13. His Choice of Wisdom Is Blessed by God. **7. In that night did God appear unto Solomon**—(See on I Kings 3:5).

ADAM CLARKE

CHAPTER 1

1. *And Solomon the son of David.* The very beginning of this book shows that it is a continuation of the preceding, and should not be thus formally separated from it. See the preface to the first book.

2. *Then Solomon spake.* This is supposed to have taken place in the second year of his reign.

4. ***But the ark.*** **The Tabernacle and the brazen** altar remained still at Gibeon; but David had brought away the ark out of the Tabernacle, and placed it in a tent at Jerusalem; 2 Sam. vi. 2, 17.

5. *Sought unto it.* Went to seek the Lord there.

7. *In that night.* The night following the sacrifice. On Solomon's choice, see 1 Kings iii. 5-15.

9. *Let thy promise. Debarcha,* "thy word"; *pithgamach,* Targum. It is very remarkable that when either God or man is represented as having spoken a word then the noun *pithgam* is used by the Targumist; but when "word" is used personally, then he employs the noun *meymera,* which appears to answer to the *Logos* of St. John, ch. i. 1.

MATTHEW HENRY

4. He received a gracious answer to this prayer, *v.* 11, 12. (1) God gave him the wisdom that he asked for because he asked for it. God's grace shall never be wanting to those who sincerely desire to know and do their duty. (2) God gave him the wealth and honour which he did not ask for because he asked not for them. Those that make this world their end come short of the other and are disappointed in this too; but those that make the other world their end shall not only obtain that, and full satisfaction in it, but shall enjoy as much as is convenient of this world in their way.

Verses 13–17

Here is, 1. Solomon's entrance upon the government (*v.* 13): He came *from before the tabernacle, and reigned over Israel.* He would not do any acts of government till he had done his acts of devotion, would not take honour to himself till he had given honour to God—first the tabernacle, and then the throne. 2. The magnificence of his court (*v.* 14): *He gathered chariots and horsemen.* He made silver and gold very cheap and common, *v.* 15. The increase of gold lowers the value of it; but the increase of grace advances its price; the more men have of that the more they value it. *How much better* therefore *is it to get wisdom than gold*! He opened also a trade with Egypt, whence he imported horses and linen-yarn, which he exported again to the kings of Syria, with great advantage no doubt, *v.* 16, 17. This we had before, 1 Kings x. 28, 29.

JAMIESON, FAUSSET, BROWN

14-17. HIS STRENGTH AND WEALTH. **14. Solomon gathered chariots and horsemen**—His passion for horses was greater than that of any Israelitish monarch before or after him. His stud comprised 1400 chariots and 12,000 horses. This was a prohibited indulgence, whether as an instrument of luxury or power. But it was not merely for his own use that he imported the horses of Egypt. The immense equestrian establishment he erected was not for show merely, but also for profit. The Egyptian breed of horses was highly valued; and being as fine as the Arabian, but larger and more powerful, they were well fitted for being yoked in chariots.

These were light but compact and solid vehicles, without springs. From the price stated (vs. 17) as given for a chariot and a horse, it appears that the chariot cost four times the value of a horse. A horse brought 150 shekels, which amounts to about $100.00., while a chariot brought 600 shekels, equal to about $400. As an Egyptian chariot was usually drawn by two horses, a chariot and pair would cost about $600. As the Syrians, who were fond of the Egyptian breed of horses, could import them into their own country only through Judea, Solomon early perceived the commercial advantages to be derived from this trade, and established a monopoly.

His factors or agents purchased them in the markets or fairs of Egypt and brought them to the "chariot cities," the depots and stables he had erected on the frontiers of his kingdom, such as Beth-marcaboth, "the house of chariots," and Hazor-susah, "the village of horses" (Josh. 19:5; I Kings 10:28). **17. brought . . . for all the kings of the Hittites**—A branch of this powerful tribe, when expelled from Palestine, had settled north of Lebanon, where they acquired large possessions contiguous to the Syrians.

ADAM CLARKE

14. *He had a thousand and four hundred chariots.* For these numbers, see the notes on 1 Kings iv. 26.

17. *An horse for an hundred and fifty.* Suppose we take the shekel at the utmost value at which it has been rated, three shillings; then the price of a horse was about twenty-two pounds ten shillings.

MATTHEW HENRY — CHAPTER 2

Verses 1–10

Solomon's wisdom was given him, not merely for speculation, nor merely for conversation, to entertain his friends, but for action; and therefore to action he immediately applies himself.

I. His resolution concerning his business (*v.* 1): *He determined to build,* in the first place, a *house for the name of the Lord.* It is fit that he who is the first should be first served—first a temple and then a palace, a house not so much for his own convenience and magnitude, as for the kingdom, for the honour of it among its neighbours and for the decent reception of the people whenever they had occasion to apply to their prince; so that in both he aimed at the public good. We are not born for ourselves, but for God and our country.

II. His embassy to Huram, king of Tyre. The purport of his errand to him is much the same here as we had it 1 Kings v. 2, &c.

1. The reasons why he makes this application to Huram are here more fully represented, (1) He pleads his father's interest in Huram, and the kindness he had received from him (*v.* 3): *As thou didst deal with David, so deal with me.* (2) He represents his design in building the temple: he intended it for a place of religious worship (*v.* 4). The house was built that it might be dedicated to God and used in his service. He mentions various particular services that were there to be performed, for the instruction of Huram. (3) He endeavours to inspire Huram with very great and high thoughts of the God of Israel, by expressing the mighty veneration he had for his holy name: *Great is our God above all gods,* above all idols, above all princes. Therefore, [1] "The house must be great; not in proportion to the greatness of that God to whom it is to be dedicated (for between finite and infinite there can be no proportion), but in some proportion to the great value and esteem we have for this God." [2] "Yet, be it ever so great, it cannot be a habitation for the great God. Let not Huram think that the God of Israel, like the gods of the nations, *dwells in temples made with hands,* Acts xvii. 24. No, the *heaven of heavens cannot contain him.* It is intended only for the convenience of his priests and worshippers, that they may have a fit place wherein to burn sacrifice before him." [3] He looked upon himself, though a mighty prince, as unworthy the honour of being employed in this great work: *Who am I that I should build him a house?*

2. The requests he makes to him are more particularly set down here. (1) He desired Huram would furnish him with a good hand to work (*v.* 7): *Send me a man.* "There are ingenious men in Jerusalem, but not such engravers as are in Tyre; and therefore, since temple-work must be the best in its kind, let

JAMIESON, FAUSSET, BROWN — CHAPTER 2

VSS. 1, 2. SOLOMON'S LABORERS FOR BUILDING THE TEMPLE. **1. Solomon determined to build**—The temple is the grand subject of this narrative, while the palace—here and in other parts of this book—is only incidentally noticed. The duty of building the temple was reserved for Solomon before his birth. As soon as he became king, he addressed himself to the work, and the historian, in proceeding to give an account of the edifice, begins with relating the preliminary arrangements.

3-10. HIS MESSAGE TO HURAM FOR SKILFUL ARTIFICERS. **3. Solomon sent to Huram**—The correspondence was probably conducted on both sides in writing (vs. 11; see also on I Kings 5:8). **As thou didst deal with David my father**—This would seem decisive of the question whether the Huram then reigning in Tyre was David's friend (see on I Kings 5:1-6). In opening the business, Solomon grounded his request for Tyrian aid on two reasons: 1. The temple he proposed to build must be a solid and permanent building because the worship was to be continued in perpetuity; and therefore the building materials must be of the most durable quality. 2. It must be a magnificent structure because it was to be dedicated to the God who was greater than all gods; and, therefore, as it might seem a presumptuous idea to erect an edifice for a Being "whom the heaven and the heaven of heavens do not contain," it was explained that Solomon's object was not to build a house for Him to dwell in, but a temple in which His worshippers might offer sacrifices to His honor. No language could be more humble and appropriate than this. The pious strain of sentiment was such as became a king of Israel.

7. Send me now therefore a man cunning to work—Masons and carpenters were not asked for. Those whom David had obtained (I Chron. 14:1) were probably still remaining in Jerusalem, and had instructed

ADAM CLARKE — CHAPTER 2

1. *An house for the name of the Lord.* A temple for the worship of Jehovah. *An house for his kingdom.* A royal palace for his own use as king of Israel.

3. *Solomon sent to Huram.* This man's name is written *Chiram* in Kings; and in Chronicles, *Churam.* There is properly no difference, only a *yod* and a *vau* interchanged.

6. *Save only to burn sacrifice.* It is not under the hope that the house shall be able to contain Him, but merely for the purpose of burning incense to Him, and offering Him sacrifice, that I have erected it.

7. *Send me . . . a man cunning to work.* A person of great ingenuity, who is capable of planning and directing, and who may be over the other artists.

MATTHEW HENRY

me have the best workmen that can be got." (2) With good materials to work on (*v.* 8), cedar and other timber in abundance (*v.* 8, 9); for the house must be *wonderfully great*.

3. Here is Solomon's engagement to maintain the workmen (*v.* 10), to give them so much wheat and barley, so much wine and oil. He did not feed his workmen with bread and water, but with plenty, and everything of the best.

Verses 11–18

I. The return which Huram made to Solomon's embassy, in which he shows a great respect for Solomon and a readiness to serve him. 1. He congratulates Israel on having such a king as Solomon was (*v.* 11): *Because the Lord loved his people, he has made thee king*. 2. He blesses God for raising up such a successor to David, *v.* 12. Huram was not only very well affected to the Jewish nation, and well pleased with their prosperity, but worshipped Jehovah, *the God of Israel* (who was now known by that name to the neighbouring nations). Now that the people of Israel kept close to the law and worship of God, and so preserved their honour, the neighbouring nations were as willing to be instructed by them in the true religion as Israel had been, in the days of their apostasy, to be infected with the idolatries and superstitions of their neighbours. 3. He sent him a very ingenious curious workman, that would not fail to answer his expectations in everything, one that had both Jewish and Gentile blood meeting in him; for his mother was an Israelite, his father a Tyrian. 4. He engaged for the timber, as much as he would have occasion for, and undertook to deliver it at Joppa, and withal signified his dependence upon Solomon for the maintenance of the workmen as he had promised, *v.* 15, 16.

II. The orders which Solomon gave about the workmen. He would not employ the free-born Israelites in the drudgery work of the temple itself, not so much as to be overseers of it. In this he employed the strangers who were proselyted to the Jewish religion. There were, at this time, vast numbers of them in the land (*v.* 17), who fell under the law, of the Gibeonites, to be hewers of wood for the congregation. The distribution of them we have here (*v.* 2, and again *v.* 18), in all 150,000. Mr. Fuller suggests that the expedient peculiar to this structure, of framing all beforehand, must needs increase the work.

JAMIESON, FAUSSET, BROWN

others. But he required a master of works; a person capable, like Bezaleel (Exod. 35:31), of superintending and directing every department; for, as the division of labor was at that time little known or observed, an overseer had to be possessed of very versatile talents and experience. The things specified, in which he was to be skilled, relate not to the building, but the furniture of the temple. **Iron**, which could not be obtained in the wilderness when the tabernacle was built, was now, through intercourse with the coast, plentiful and much used. The cloths intended for curtains were, from the crimson or scarlet-red and hyacinth colors named, evidently those stuffs, for the manufacture and dyeing of which the Tyrians were so famous. "The graving," probably, included embroidery of figures like cherubim in needlework, as well as wood carving of pomegranates and other ornaments. **8. Send me . . . cedar trees,** etc.—The cedar and cypress were valued as being both rare and durable; the algum or almug trees (likewise a foreign wood), though not found on Lebanon, are mentioned as being procured through Huram (see on I Kings 10:11). **10. behold, I will give to thy servants . . . beaten wheat**—Wheat, stripped of the husk, boiled, and saturated with butter, forms a frequent meal with the laboring people in the East (cf. I Kings 5:11). There is no discrepancy between that passage and this. The yearly supplies of wine and oil, mentioned in the former, were intended for Huram's court in return for the cedars sent him; while the articles of meat and drink specified here were for the workmen on Lebanon.

11-18. HURAM'S KIND ANSWER. **11. Because the Lord hath loved his people,** etc.—This pious language creates a presumption that Huram might have attained some knowledge of the true religion from his long familiar intercourse with David. But the presumption, however pleasing, may be delusive (see on I Kings 5:7-12). **13, 14. I have sent a cunning man**—(See on I Kings 7:13-51). **17, 18. Solomon numbered all the strangers,** etc.—(See on I Kings 5:13, 18).

ADAM CLARKE

11. *Answered in writing.* Though correspondence among persons of distinction was in these early times carried on by confidential messengers, yet we find that epistolary correspondence did exist.

13. *I have sent a cunning man.* His name appears to have been *Hiram,* or *Hiram Abi;* see the notes on 1 Kings vii. 13-14.

16. *In floats by sea to Joppa.* See the note on 1 Kings v. 9, and on the parallel places, for other matters contained in this chapter.

MATTHEW HENRY — CHAPTER 3

Verses 1–9

I. The place where the temple was built. It was before determined (1 Chron. xxii. 1). 1. It must be at Jerusalem; for that was the place God had chosen. The royal city must be the holy city. 2. It must be on Mount Moriah, which, some think, was that very place in the land of Moriah where Abraham offered Isaac, Gen. xxii. 2. 3. It must be *where the Lord appeared to David*, and *answered him by fire*, 1 Chron. xxi. 18, 26. There atonement was made once; and therefore, in remembrance of that, there atonement must still be made. 4. It must be in the place which David had prepared, not only which he had purchased with his money, but which he had pitched upon by divine direction. 5. It must be in the threshing-floor of Ornan.

II. The time when it was begun; not till the fourth year of Solomon's reign, *v.* 2. The first three years were employed in the necessary preparations for it, wherein three years would be soon gone, considering how many hands were to be got together and set to work.

JAMIESON, FAUSSET, BROWN — CHAPTER 3

VSS. 1, 2. PLACE AND TIME OF BUILDING THE TEMPLE. **1. Mount Moriah, where the Lord appeared unto David**—These words seem to intimate that the region where the temple was built was *previously* known by the name of Moriah (Gen. 22:2), and do not afford sufficient evidence for affirming, as has been done [STANLEY], that the name was *first* given to the mount, in *consequence* of the vision seen by David. Mount Moriah was one summit of a range of hills which went under the general name of Zion. The platform of the temple is now, and has long been, occupied by the haram, or sacred enclosure, within which stand the three mosques of Omar (the smallest), of El Aksa, which in early times was a Christian church, and of Kubbet el Sakhara, "The dome of the rock," so called from a huge block of limestone rock in the center of the floor, which, it is supposed, formed the elevated threshing-floor of Araunah, and on which the great brazen altar stood. The site of the temple, then, is so far established for an almost universal belief is entertained in the authenticity of the tradition regarding the rock El Sakhara; and it has also been conclusively proved that the area of the temple was identical on its western, eastern, and southern sides with the present enclosure of the haram [ROBINSON]. "That the temple was situated *somewhere* within the oblong enclosure on Mount Moriah, all topographers are agreed, although there is not the slightest vestige of the sacred fane now remaining; and the greatest diversity of sentiment prevails as to its exact position within that large area, whether in the center of the haram, or in its southwest corner [BARCLAY]. Moreover, the full extent of the temple area is a problem that remains to be solved, for the platform of Mount Moriah being too narrow for the extensive buildings and courts attached to the sacred edifice, Solomon resorted to artificial means of enlarging and levelling it, by erecting vaults, which, as Josephus states, rested on immense earthen mounds raised from the slope of the hill. It should be borne in mind at the outset that the grandeur of the temple did not

ADAM CLARKE — CHAPTER 3

TODAY'S DICTIONARY OF THE BIBLE:

Moriah—according to the Samaritan tradition, Mount Gerizim is meant, but most probably we are to regard this as one of the hills of Jerusalem. Here Solomon's temple was built, on the spot that had been the threshing floor of Ornan the Jebusite (2 Sam. 24:24, 25; 2 Chron. 3:1). It is usually included in Zion, to the northeast of which it lay, and from which it was separated by the Tyropoean valley. This was "the land of Moriah" to which Abraham went to offer up his son Isaac (Gen. 22:2). It has been supposed that the highest point of the temple hill, which is now covered by the Mohammedan *Kubbet es-Sakhrah,* or "Dome of the Rock," is the actual site of Araunah's threshing floor. Here also 1,000 years after Abraham, David built an altar and offered sacrifices to God.

MATTHEW HENRY

III. The dimensions of it, in which Solomon was instructed (*v.* 3), as he was in other things, by his father. *This was the foundation* (so it may be read) *which Solomon laid for the building of the house.* This was the rule he went by, so many cubits the length and breadth, *after the first measure*, that is, according to the measure first fixed, for the dimensions were given by divine wisdom.

IV. The ornaments of the temple. The timber-work was very fine, and yet, within, it was *overlaid with pure gold* (*v.* 4), with *fine gold* (*v.* 5), and that embossed with *palm-trees* and chains. It was gold of *Parvain* (*v.* 6), the best gold. The *beams* and *posts*, the *walls* and *doors*, were *overlaid with gold*, *v.* 7. The most holy place, which was ten yards square, was all *overlaid with fine gold* (*v.* 8), even the *upper chambers*, or rather the *upper floor or roof*—top, bottom, and sides, were all overlaid with gold. Every nail, or screw, or pin, with which the golden plates were fastened to the walls that were overlaid with them, weighed fifty shekels, or was worth so much workmanship and all. A great many precious stones were dedicated to God (1 Chron. xxix. 2, 8), and these were set here and there, where they would show to the best advantage.

Verses 10–17

1. The two cherubim, which were set up in the holy of holies. There were two already over the ark, which covered the mercy-seat with their wings; these were small ones. Now that the most holy place was enlarged, though these were continued (being appurtenances to the ark, which was not to be made new, as all the other utensils of the tabernacle were), yet those two large ones were added. These cherubim are said to be of *image-work* (*v.* 10), to represent the angels who attend the divine Majesty. Each wing extended five cubits, so that the whole was twenty cubits (*v.* 12, 13), which was just the breadth of the most holy place, *v.* 8. They stood on their feet, as servants, their faces inward towards the ark (*v.* 13), that it might appear they were not set there to be adored (for then they would have been made sitting, as on a throne, and their faces towards their worshippers), but rather as themselves attendants on the invisible God. We must not worship angels, but we must worship *with* angels; for we have come into communication with them (Heb. xii. 22), and must do the will of God as the angels do it. Compare 1 Cor. xi. 10 with Isa. vi. 2. 2. The veil that parted between the temple and the most holy place, *v.* 14. This denoted the darkness of that dispensation, and the distance which the worshippers were kept at; but, at the death of Christ, this veil was rent; for through him we are made nigh, and have boldness not only to look, but to enter, into the holiest. On this he wrought cherubim. Heb. *he caused them to ascend*, that is, they were made in raised work, embossed. 3. The two pillars which were set up before the temple. Both together were somewhat above thirty-five cubits in length (*v.* 15), about eighteen cubits high a-piece. See 1 Kings vii. 15, &c., where we took a view of those pillars, *Jachin* and *Boaz*.

JAMIESON, FAUSSET, BROWN

consist in its colossal structure so much as in its internal splendor, and the vast courts and buildings attached to it. It was not intended for the reception of a worshipping assembly, for the people always stood in the outer courts of the sanctuary.

3-7. Measures and Ornaments of the House. **3. these are the things wherein Solomon was instructed for the building of the house of God**—by the written plan and specifications given him by his father. The measurements are reckoned by cubits, "after the first measure," i.e., the old Mosaic standard. But there is great difference of opinion about this, some making the cubit eighteen, others twenty-one inches. The temple, which embodied in more solid and durable materials the ground-form of the tabernacle (only being twice as large), was a rectangular building, seventy cubits long from east to west, and twenty cubits wide from north to south. **4. the porch**—The breadth of the house, whose length ran from east to west, is here given as the measure of the length of the piazza. The portico would thus be from thirty to thirty-five feet long, and from fifteen to seventeen and a half feet broad. **the height was an hundred and twenty cubits**—This, taking the cubit at eighteen inches, would be 180 feet; at twenty-one inches, 210 feet; so that the porch would rise in the form of a tower, or two pyramidal towers, whose united height was 120 cubits, and each of them about 90 or 105 feet high [Stieglitz]. This porch would thus be like the propylæum or gateway of the palace of Khorsabad [Layard], or at the temple of Edfou. **5. the greater house**—i.e., the holy places, the front or outer chamber (see on I Kings 6:17). **6. he garnished the house with precious stones for beauty**—better, he paved the house with precious and beautiful marble [Kitto]. It may be, after all, that these were stones with veins of different colors for decorating the walls. This was an ancient and thoroughly Oriental kind of embellishment. There was an under pavement of marble, which was covered with planks of fir. The whole interior was lined with boards, richly decorated with carved work, clusters of foliage and flowers, among which the pomegranate and lotus (or water-lily) were conspicuous; and overlaid, excepting the floor, with gold, either by gilding or in plates (I Kings 6).

8-13. Dimensions, etc., of the Most Holy House. **8. the most holy house**—It was a perfect cube (cf. I Kings 6:20). **overlaid it with . . . gold, amounting to six hundred talents**—equal to about $16,000,000. **10-13. two cherubim**—These figures in the tabernacle were of pure gold (Exod. 25) and overshadowed the mercy seat. The two placed in the temple were made of olive wood, overlaid with gold. They were of colossal size, like the Assyrian sculptures; for each, with expanded wings, covered a space of ten cubits in height and length—two wings touched each other, while the other two reached the opposite walls; their faces were inward, i.e., towards the most holy house, conformably to their use, which was to veil the ark.

14-17. Veil and Pillars (see on I Kings 6:21). The united height is here given; and though the exact dimensions would be thirty-six cubits. each column was only seventeen cubits and a half, a half cubit being taken up by the capital or the base. They were probably described as they were lying together in the mould before they were set up [Poole]. They would be from eighteen to twenty-one feet in circumference, and stand forty feet in height. These pillars, or obelisks, as some call them, were highly ornamented, and formed an entrance in keeping with the splendid interior of the temple.

ADAM CLARKE

4. *The height was an hundred and twenty.* Some think this should be twenty only; but if the same building is spoken of as in 1 Kings vi. 2, the height was only thirty cubits. "Twenty" is the reading of the Syriac, the Arabic, and the Septuagint in the Codex Alexandrinus. There is probably a mistake here, which, from the similarity of the letters, might easily occur.

6. The Vulgate translates the passage thus: "And he made the pavement of the temple of the most precious marble; and moreover the gold was of the best quality."

9. *The weight of the nails was fifty shekels.* "Bolts" must be here intended, as it would be preposterous to suppose nails of nearly two pounds' weight. *The upper chambers.* Probably the "ceiling" is meant.

MATTHEW HENRY — CHAPTER 4

Verses 1–10

David often speaks with much affection both of the *house of the Lord* and of the *courts of our God*.

I. Things in the open court, in the view of all the people, which were very significant.

1. There was the *brazen altar*, *v.* 1. On this all the sacrifices were offered, and it sanctified the gift. This altar was much larger than that which Moses made in the tabernacle; that was five cubits square, this was twenty cubits square. God had greatly enlarged their borders; it was therefore fit that they should enlarge his altars. Our returns should bear some proportion to our receivings. It was ten cubits high, so that the people who worshipped in the courts might see the sacrifices burnt, and their eye might affect their heart with sorrow for sin. And with the smoke of the sacrifices their hearts might ascend to heaven in holy desires towards God and

JAMIESON, FAUSSET, BROWN — CHAPTER 4

Vs. 1. Altar of Brass. **1. he made an altar of brass**—Steps must have been necessary for ascending so elevated an altar, but the use of these could be no longer forbidden (Exod. 20:26) after the introduction of an official costume for the priests (Exod. 28:42). It measured thirty-five feet by thirty-five, and in height seventeen and a half feet. The thickness of the metal used for this altar is nowhere given; but supposing it to have been three inches, the whole weight of the metal would not be under two hundred tons [Napier].

ADAM CLARKE — CHAPTER 4

MATTHEW HENRY

his favour. In all our devotions we must keep the eye of faith fixed upon Christ, the great propitiation.

2. There was the molten sea, a very large brass pan, in which they put water for the priests to wash in, *v.* 2, 6. (1) There is a fulness of merit in Jesus Christ for all those that by faith apply to him for the purifying of their consciences, that they may serve the *living God, Heb.* ix. 14. (2) Our great gospel duty, which is to cleanse ourselves by true repentance. Our hearts must be sanctified, or we cannot sanctify the name of God. Those that draw nigh to God must *cleanse their hands, and purify their hearts,* James iv. 8.

3. There were *ten lavers* of brass, in which *they washed such things as they offered for the burnt offerings, v.* 6. As the priests must be washed, so must the sacrifices. We must not only purify ourselves but carefully put away all those vain thoughts which cleave to our performances themselves and pollute them.

4. The doors of the court were overlaid with brass (*v.* 9), both for strength and beauty, and that they might not be rotted with the weather.

II. There were those things in *the house of the Lord* (into which the priests alone went to minister) that were very significant. All was of gold there. The nearer we come to God the purer we must be, the purer we shall be. 1. There were ten *golden candlesticks,* according to the form of that one which was in the tabernacle, *v.* 7. The written word is a lamp and a light, shining in a dark place. In Moses's time they had but one candlestick, the Pentateuch; but the additions which, in process of time, were to be made of other books of scripture might be signified by this increase of the number of the candlesticks. Light was growing. The candlesticks are the churches, Rev. i. 20. Moses set up but one, the church of the Jews; but, in the gospel temple, not only believers, but churches, are multiplied. 2. There were ten *golden tables* (*v.* 8), *tables whereon the shew-bread was set, v.* 19. To those tables belonged 100 golden basins, or dishes. 3. There was a *golden altar* (*v.* 19), on which they burnt incense.

Verses 11–22

A summary both of the brass-work and the goldwork of the temple. 1. Huram the workman was very punctual: *He finished all that he was to make* (*v.* 11). *Huram his father,* he is called, *v.* 16. Probably it was a sort of a nickname, for the king of Tyre called him *Huram Abi, my father,* he being a great artist and *father of the artificers* in brass and iron. 2. Solomon was very generous. He made *all the vessels in great abundance* (*v.* 18), that some might be laid up for use when others were worn out.

JAMIESON, FAUSSET, BROWN

2-5. MOLTEN SEA. **2. he made a molten sea**—(See on I Kings 7:23-26), as in that passage "knops" occur instead of "oxen." It is generally supposed that the rows of ornamental knops were in the form of ox heads. **3. Two rows of oxen were cast, when it was cast**—The meaning is, that the circular basin and the brazen oxen which supported it were all of one piece, being cast in one and the same mould. There is a difference in the accounts given of the capacity of this basin, for while in I Kings 7:26 it is said that two thousand baths of water could be contained in it, in this passage no less than three thousand are stated. It has been suggested that there is here a statement not merely of the quantity of water which the basin held, but that also which was necessary to work it, to keep it flowing as a fountain; that which was required to fill both it and its accompaniments. In support of this view, it may be remarked that different words are employed: the one in I Kings 7:26 rendered *contained;* the two here rendered, *received* and *held.* There was a difference between *receiving* and *holding.* When the basin played as a fountain, and all its parts were filled for that purpose, the latter, together with the sea itself, *received* 3000 baths; but the sea exclusively *held* only 2000 baths, when its contents were restricted to those of the circular basin. It received and held 3000 baths [CALMENT'S FRAGMENT].

6-18. THE TEN LAVERS, CANDLESTICKS, AND TABLES. **6. ten lavers**—(See on I Kings 7:27-39). The laver of the tabernacle had probably been destroyed. The ten new ones were placed between the porch and the altar, and while the molten sea was for the priests to cleanse their hands and feet, these were intended for washing the sacrifices. **7. ten candlesticks**—(See on I Kings 7:49). The increased number was not only in conformity with the characteristic splendor of the edifice, but also a standing emblem to the Hebrews, that the growing light of the word was necessary to counteract the growing darkness in the world [LIGHTFOOT]. **11. Huram made**—(See on I Kings 7:40-45).

ADAM CLARKE

3. *Under it was the similitude of oxen.* In 1 Kings vii. 24, instead of "oxen," *bekarim,* we have "knops," *pekaim;* and this last is supposed by able critics to be the reading which ought to be received here. What we call *knops* may signify grapes, mushrooms, apples, or some such ornaments placed round about under the turned-over lip or brim of this caldron. The reader will at once see that what are called the "oxen," v. 3, said to be round about the brim, are widely different from those in v. 4, by which this molten sea was supported.

5. *It . . . held three thousand baths.* In 1 Kings vii. 26, it is said to hold only 2,000 baths. As this book was written after the Babylonish captivity, it is very possible that reference is here made to the Babylonish bath, which might have been less than the Jewish.

6. *He made also ten lavers.* The lavers served to wash the different parts of the victims in, and the molten sea was for the use of the priests. In this they bathed, or drew water from it for their personal purification.

8. *An hundred basons of gold.* These were doubtless a sort of sacrificial spoons with which they made libations.

9. *He made the court of the priests.* This was the inner court. *And the great court.* This was the outer court, or place for the assembling of the people.

16. *Huram his father. Ab,* "father," is often used in Hebrew to signify a "master, inventor, chief operator," and is very probably used here in the former sense by the Chaldee: "All these Chiram his master made for King Solomon."

17. *In the clay ground.* See on 1 Kings vii. 46. Some suppose that he did not actually cast those instruments at those places, but that he brought the clay from that quarter, as being the most proper for making moulds to cast in.

21. *And the flowers, and the lamps.* Probably each branch of the chandelier was made like a plant in flower, and the opening of the flower was either the lamp or served to support it.

22. *The doors . . . were of gold.* That is, were overlaid with golden plates, the thickness of which we do not know.

MATTHEW HENRY

CHAPTER 5

Verses 1–10

This agrees with what we had 1 Kings viii. 2, &c., where an account was given of the solemn introduction of the ark into the new-erected temple. 1. There needed no great solemnity for the bringing in of the dedicated things, *v.* 1. They added to the wealth, and perhaps to the beauty of it; but they could not add to the holiness for it was the *temple that sanctified the gold,* Matt. xxiii. 17. See how just Solomon was both to God and to his father. Whatever David had dedicated to God he put it among the treasures of the temple. When Solomon had made all the vessels of the temple in abundance (*ch.* iv. 18), many of the materials were left, which he would not convert to any other use, but laid up in the treasury for a time of need. 2. But it was fit that the ark should be brought in with great solemnity; and so it was. All the other vessels were made new, and larger, in proportion to the house, than they had been in the tabernacle. But the ark, with the mercy-seat and the cherubim, was the same; for the presence and the grace of God are the same in little assemblies as they are in large ones. Wherever two or three are gathered together in Christ's name there is he as truly present with them as if there were 2,000 or 3,000. The ark was brought in attended by a very great assembly of the elders of Israel, who came to grace the solemnity, *v.* 2–4. It was carried by the priests (*v.* 7), brought into the most holy place, and put under the wings of the great cherubim which Solomon had set up there, *v.* 7, 8. *There they are unto this day* (*v.* 9), not the day when this book was written after the captivity, but when that was written out of which this story was transcribed. The ark was a type of Christ, and, as such, a token of the presence of God. The temple itself, if Christ leave it, is a desolate place, Matt. xxiii. 38. 3. With the ark they brought

JAMIESON, FAUSSET, BROWN

CHAPTER 5

VS. 1. THE DEDICATED TREASURES. **1. Solomon brought in all the things that David his father had dedicated**—the immense sums and the store of valuable articles which his father and other generals had reserved and appropriated for the temple (I Chron. 22:14; 26:26).

2-13. BRINGING UP OF THE ARK OF THE COVENANT. **2, 3. Then Solomon assembled . . . in the feast which was in the seventh month**—The feast of the dedication of the temple was on the eighth day of that month. This is related, word for word, the same as in I Kings 8:1-10. **9. there it is unto this day**—i.e., at the time when this history was composed; for after the Babylonish captivity there is no trace of either ark or staves.

ADAM CLARKE

CHAPTER 5

1. *Brought in all the things.* See the note on 1 Kings vii. 51.

3. *The feast.* "That is, the feast of tabernacles, which was held in the seventh month." —Targum. See 1 Kings viii. 2.

9. *They drew out the staves.* As the ark was no longer to be carried about, these were unnecessary.

MATTHEW HENRY

up the tabernacle and all the *holy vessels that were in the tabernacle*, v. 5. 4. This was done with great joy. They kept a holy feast upon the occasion (*v.* 3), and *sacrificed sheep and oxen without number*, v. 6. When Christ is formed in a soul, the law written in the heart, the ark of the covenant settled there, so that it becomes the temple of the Holy Ghost, there is true satisfaction in that soul.

Verses 11–14

Solomon, and the elders of Israel, had done what they could to grace the solemnity of the introduction of the ark; but God, by testifying his acceptance of what they did, put the greatest honour upon it. The cloud of glory that filled the house beautified it more than all the gold with which it was overlaid or the precious stones with which it was garnished; and yet that was no glory in comparison with the glory of the gospel dispensation, 2 Cor. iii. 8–10.

I. How God took possession of the temple: He *filled it with a cloud*, v. 13. 1. Thus he signified his acceptance of this temple to be the same to him that the tabernacle of Moses was, Exod. xl. 34. 2. Thus he considered the weakness and infirmity of those to whom he manifested himself, who could not bear the dazzling lustre of the divine light. Christ revealed things unto his disciples as they were able to bear them, and in parables, which wrapped up divine things as in a cloud.

II. When he took possession of it. 1. *When the priests had come out of the holy place*, v. 11. This is the way of giving possession. All must come out, that the rightful owner may come in. Would we have God dwell in our hearts? We must leave room for him; let everything else give way. 2. When the singers and musicians praised God, then the house was filled with a cloud. This is very observable; it was not when they *offered sacrifices*, but when they *sang the praises of God*, that God gave them this token of his favour; for the sacrifice of praise *pleaseth the Lord* better than that of *an ox or bullock*, Ps. lxix. 31. Where unity is the Lord commands the blessing. God's goodness is his glory, and he is pleased when we give him the glory of it.

III. What was the effect of it. The *priests themselves could not stand to minister, by reason of the cloud* (*v.* 14). The Word was made flesh; and when he comes to his temple, like a refiner's fire, *who may abide the day of his coming*? And *who shall stand when he appeareth*? Mal. iii. 1, 2.

JAMIESON, FAUSSET, BROWN

11. all the priests that were present . . . did not then wait by course—The rotation system of weekly service introduced by David was intended for the ordinary duties of the priesthood; on extraordinary occasions, or when more than wonted solemnity attached to them, the priests attended in a body. **12. the Levites which were the singers**—On great and solemn occasions, such as this, a full choir was required, and their station was taken with scrupulous regard to their official parts: the family of Heman occupied the central place, the family of Asaph stood on his right, and that of Jeduthun on his left; the place allotted to the vocal department was a space between the court of Israel and the altar in the east end of the priests' court. **with them an hundred and twenty priests sounding with trumpets**—The trumpet was always used by the priests, and in the divine service it was specially employed in calling the people together during the holy solemnities, and in drawing attention to new and successive parts of the ritual. The number of trumpets used in the divine service could not be less than two (Num. 10:2), and their greatest number never exceeded the precedent set at the dedication of the temple. The station where the priests were sounding with trumpets was apart from that of the other musicians; for while the Levite singers occupied an orchestra east of the altar, the priests stood at the marble table on the southwest of the altar. There both of them stood with their faces to the altar. The manner of blowing the trumpets was, first, by a long plain blast, then by one with breakings and quaverings, and then by a long plain blast again [BROWN'S JEWISH ANTIQUITIES]. **13. the house was filled with a cloud**—(See on I Kings 8:10, 11).

ADAM CLARKE

10. *There was nothing in the ark save.* The Chaldee paraphrases thus: "There was nothing put in the ark but the two tables which Moses placed there, after the first had been broken on account of the calf which they made in Horeb, and the two other tables had been confirmed which were written with writing expressed in the ten words."

11. *When the priests were come out.* After having carried the ark into the holy of holies, before the sacred service had commenced.

JOSEPH PARKER:

"The house was filled with a cloud . . . for the glory of the Lord had filled the house of God" (vv. 13, 14). Thus are all ministries reduced to insignificance and nothingness by the realized glory of the divine presence. Temples and altars, ritual and song, all come comparatively to nothing when God himself consciously, almost visibly, appears in his house. What would the temple have been without this "cloud"? Just what the sky would be on a starless night—a great gloom, a tremendous frown. So it is with our life-building. Unless the house of our life is owned by the living God, dwelt in by him, illumined and sanctified by his presence, it comes to nothing, it is an empty house—the emptier because of its very grandeur.

—*The People's Bible*

MATTHEW HENRY

CHAPTER 6

Verses 1–11

It is of great consequence, in all our religious actions, that we design well, and that our eye be single. If Solomon had built this temple in the pride of his heart it would not have turned at all to his account. 1. He did it for the glory and honour of God; this was his highest and ultimate end in it. It was *for the name of the Lord God of Israel* (*v.* 10), to be *a house of habitation for him*, v. 2. 2. He did it in compliance with the choice God had been pleased to make of Jerusalem, to be the city in which he would record his name (*v.* 6): *I have chosen Jerusalem.* 3. He did it in pursuance of his father's good intentions, which he never had an opportunity to put in execution: "*It was in the heart of David my father to build a house for God;*" the project was his, be it known, to his honour (*v.* 7), and God approved of it, though he permitted him not to put it in execution (*v.* 8), *Thou didst well that it was in thy heart.* Temple-work is often thus done; one sows and another reaps (John iv. 37, 38), one age begins that which the next brings to perfection. Every good piece is not an original. 4. He did it in performance of the word which God had spoken. God had said, *Thy son shall build the house for my name*; and now he had done it, *v.* 9, 10.

Verses 12–41

Solomon had, in the foregoing verses, signed and sealed, as it were, the deed of dedication, by which the temple was appropriated to the honour and service of God. Now here he prays the consecration-prayer, by which it was made a figure of Christ, the great Mediator, through whom we are to offer all our prayers.

I. Here are some doctrinal truths laid down. As, 1. That the God of Israel is a being of incomparable perfection. We cannot describe him; but this we know, there is *none like him in heaven or in earth*, v. 14. 2. That he is, and will be, true to every word that he has spoken; and all that serve him in sincerity shall certainly find him both faithful and kind. 3. That he is a being infinite and immense, whom the

JAMIESON, FAUSSET, BROWN

CHAPTER 6

VSS. 1-41. SOLOMON BLESSES THE PEOPLE AND PRAISES GOD. **1. The Lord hath said that he would dwell in the thick darkness**—This introduction to Solomon's address was evidently suggested by the remarkable incident recorded at the close of the last chapter: the phenomenon of a densely opaque and uniformly shaped cloud, descending in a slow and majestic manner and filling the whole area of the temple. He regarded it himself, and directed the people also to regard it, as an undoubted sign and welcome pledge of the divine presence and acceptance of the building reared to His honor and worship. He referred not to any particular declaration of God, but to the cloud having been all along in the national history of Israel the recognized symbol of the divine presence (Exod. 16:10; 24:16; 40:34; Num. 9:15; I Kings 8:10, 11). **13. Solomon had made a brazen scaffold**—a sort of platform. But the *Hebrew* term rendered scaffold, being the same as that used to designate the basin, suggests the idea that this throne might bear some resemblance, in form or structure, to those lavers in the temple, being a sort of round and elevated pulpit, placed in the middle of the court, and in front of the altar of burnt offering. **upon it he stood, and kneeled down upon his knees**—After ascending the brazen scaffold, he assumed those two attitudes in succession, and with different objects in view. He stood while he addressed and blessed the surrounding multitude (vss. 3-11). Afterwards he knelt down and stretched out his hands towards heaven, with his face probably turned towards the altar, while he gave utterance to the beautiful and impressive prayer which is recorded in the remainder of this chapter. It is deserving of notice that there was no seat in this pulpit—for the king either stood or knelt all the time he was in it. It is not improbable that it was surmounted by a canopy, or covered by a veil, to screen the royal speaker from the rays of the sun. **18-21. how much less this house which I have built! Have respect therefore to the prayer of thy servant**—No person who entertains just and exalted views

ADAM CLARKE

CHAPTER 6

1. *The Lord hath said that he would dwell.* Solomon, seeing the cloud descend and fill the house, immediately took for granted that the Lord had accepted the place, and was now present. What occurred now was precisely the same with what took place when Moses reared the Tabernacle in the wilderness; see Exod. xl. 34-35.

MATTHEW HENRY

heaven, and heaven of heavens, cannot contain, and to whose felicity nothing is added by the utmost we can do in his service, *v.* 18. He is infinitely beyond the bounds of the creation and infinitely above the praises of all intelligent creatures. 4. That he, and *he only, knows the hearts of the children of men*, *v.* 30. All men's thoughts, aims, and affections, are naked and open before him; and the imaginations and intents of our hearts cannot be hidden from God, who knows not only what is in the heart, but the heart itself and all the beatings of it. 5. That there is no such thing as a sinless perfection to be found in this life (*v.* 36).

II. Here are some suppositions. 1. He supposed that if doubts and controversies arose between man and man both sides would agree to appeal to God, and lay an oath upon the person whose testimony must decide the matter, *v.* 22. 2. He supposed that, though Israel enjoyed a profound peace and tranquillity, yet troublesome times would come. **3. He supposed that those who had not called upon God at other times, yet, in their affliction, would seek him early and earnestly. Trouble will drive those to God** who have said to him, Depart, *v.* 24, 26, 28. 4. He supposed that strangers would come from afar to worship the God of Israel and to pay homage to him.

III. Here are petitions. 1. That God would own this house, *v.* 20. 2. That God would hear and accept the prayers which should be made in or towards that place, *v.* 21. He prayed that God would hear from his dwelling-place, even from heaven. Heaven is his dwelling-place still, not this temple; and thence help must come. *When thou hearest forgive.* Note, The forgiveness of our sins is that which makes way for all the other answers to our prayers. 3. That God would give judgment according to equity upon all the appeals that should be made to him, *v.* 23, 30. 4. That God would return in mercy to his people when they repented, and reformed, and sought unto him, *v.* 25, 27, 38, 39. 5. That God would bid the strangers welcome to this house, and answer their prayers (*v.* 33). 6. That God would, upon all occasions, own and plead the cause of his people Israel, against all the opposers of it (*v.* 35): *Maintain their cause;* and again, *v.* 39. 7. He concludes this prayer with some expressions which he had learned of his good father, and borrowed from one of his psalms. We had them not in the Kings, but here we have them, *v.* 41, 42. He prayed (*v.* 41), (1) That God would take possession of the temple, and keep possession, that he would make it his resting-place: *Thou and the ark;* what will the ark do without the God of the ark—ordinances without the God of the ordinances?

(2) That he would make the ministers of the temple public blessings: *Clothe them with salvation*, that is, not only save them, but make them instrumental to save others, by offering the sacrifices of righteousness.

(3) That the service of the temple might turn abundantly to the joy and satisfaction of all the Lord's people.

JAMIESON, FAUSSET, BROWN

of the spiritual nature of the Divine Being will suppose that he can raise a temple for the habitation of Deity, as a man builds a house for himself. Nearly as improper and inadmissible is the idea that a temple can contribute to enhance the glory of God, as a monument may be raised in honor of a great man. Solomon described the true and proper use of the temple, when he entreated that the Lord "would hearken unto the supplications of His servant and His people Israel, which they should make towards this place." In short, the grand purpose for which the temple was erected was precisely the same as that contemplated by churches—to afford the opportunity and means of public and social worship, according to the ritual of the Mosaic dispensation—to supplicate the divine mercy and favor—to render thanks for past instances of goodness, and offer petitions for future blessings (see on I Kings 8:22-61). This religious design of the temple—the ONE temple in the world—is in fact its standpoint of absorbing interest. **22. If a man sin against his neighbour, and an oath be laid upon him to make him swear, and the oath come before thine altar in this house,** etc.—In cases where the testimony of witnesses could not be obtained and there was no way of settling a difference or dispute between two people but by accepting the oath of the accused, the practice had gradually crept in and had acquired the force of consuetudinary law, for the party to be brought before the altar, where his oath was taken with all due solemnity, together with the imprecation of a curse to fall upon himself if his disavowal should be found untrue. There is an allusion to such a practice in this passage. **38. If they return to thee . . . in the land of their captivity . . . and pray toward their land, which thou gavest unto their fathers**—These words gave rise to the favorite usage of the ancient as well as modern Jews, of turning in prayer toward Jerusalem, in whatever quarter of the world they might be, and of directing their faces toward the temple when in Jerusalem itself or in any part of the holy land (I Kings 8:44). **41. arise, O Lord God, into thy resting place**—These words are not found in the record of this prayer in the First Book of Kings; but they occur in Psalm 132, which is generally believed to have been composed by David, or rather by Solomon, in reference to this occasion. "Arise" is a very suitable expression to be used when the ark was to be removed from the tabernacle in Zion to the temple on Mount Moriah. **into thy resting place**—The temple so called (Isa. 66:1), because it was a fixed and permanent mansion (Ps. 132:14). **the ark of thy strength**—the abode by which Thy glorious presence is symbolized, and whence Thou dost issue Thine authoritative oracles, and manifest Thy power on behalf of Thy people when they desire and need it. It might well be designated the ark of God's strength, because it was through means of it the mighty miracles were wrought and the brilliant victories were won, that distinguish the early annals of the Hebrew nation. The sight of it inspired the greatest animation in the breasts of His people, while it diffused terror and dismay through the ranks of their enemies (cf. Ps. 78:61). **let thy priests . . . be clothed with salvation**—or with righteousness (Ps. 132:9), i.e., be equipped not only with the pure white linen garments Thou hast appointed for their robe of office, but also adorned with the moral beauties of true holiness, that their person and services may be accepted, both for themselves and all the people. Thus they would be "clothed with salvation," for that is the effect and consequence of a sanctified character. **42. turn not away the face of thine anointed**—i.e., of me, who by Thy promise and appointment have been installed as king and ruler of Israel. The words are equivalent in meaning to this: Do not reject my present petitions; do not send me from Thy throne of grace dejected in countenance and disappointed in heart. **remember the mercies of David thy servant**—i.e., the mercies promised to David, and in consideration of that promise, hear and answer my prayer (cf. Ps. 132:10).

ADAM CLARKE

22. *If a man sin against his neighbour.* For the seven cases put here by Solomon in his prayer, see the notes on 1 Kings viii. 31-46.

36. *For there is no man which sinneth not.* See this case considered in the note on 1 Kings viii. 46.

CHARLES H. SPURGEON:

The temple was intended to be the center of prayer for all the children of Israel. Those who could do so went up to it a certain number of times every year. Others, who were too far away to go, prayed with their window open towards Jerusalem; for there was the mercy seat, and beneath the wings of the overshadowing cherubim there dwelt that bright light of the Shekinah, which was the index of the presence of God in the midst of His people. It is not therefore to be wondered at that his great petition was that God would hear every prayer that should be offered in that place or toward that place. He wished the temple always to be to Israel the token that God's memorial is that He hears prayer. Solomon therefore presented a wonderfully comprehensive series of supplications, in which he appears to have included all the sorrowful conditions of the nation, and all the troubles that were likely to fall upon the chosen people.

MATTHEW HENRY — CHAPTER 7

Verses 1–11

I. The gracious answer which God immediately made to Solomon's prayer: The *fire came down from heaven and consumed the sacrifice*, *v.* 1. In this way God testified his acceptance of Moses (Lev. ix. 24), of Gideon (Judges vi. 21), of David (1 Chron. xxi. 26), of Elijah (1 Kings xviii. 38); and, in general, to accept the burnt-sacrifice is, in the Hebrew phrase, to turn it to ashes, Ps. xx. 3. Let us apply this, 1. To the sufferings of Christ. When it pleased the Lord

JAMIESON, FAUSSET, BROWN — CHAPTER 7

VSS. 1-3. GOD GIVES TESTIMONY TO SOLOMON'S PRAYER; THE PEOPLE WORSHIP. **1. the fire came down from heaven and consumed the burnt offering**—Every act of worship was accompanied by a sacrifice. The preternatural stream of fire kindled the mass of flesh, and was a token of the divine acceptance of Solomon's prayer (see on Lev. 9:24; I Kings 18:38). **the glory of the Lord filled the house**—The cloud, which was the symbol of God's presence and majesty, filled the interior of the

ADAM CLARKE — CHAPTER 7

1. *The fire came down.* The cloud had come down before; now the fire consumes the sacrifice, showing that both the house and the sacrifices were accepted by the Lord.

MATTHEW HENRY

to bruise him, and put him to grief, in that he showed his goodwill to men, having laid on him the iniquity of us all. His death was our life, and he was made sin and a curse that he might inherit righteousness and a blessing. 2. To the sanctification of the Spirit, who descends like fire, burning up our lusts and corruptions, those beasts that must be sacrificed or we are undone, and kindling in our souls a holy fire of pious and devout affections, always to be kept burning on the altar of the heart.

II. The grateful return made to God for this gracious token of his favour.

1. The people *worshipped and praised God*, *v.* 3. with reverence adoring the glory of God: *They bowed their faces to the ground and worshipped*, thus expressing their awful dread of the divine majesty, their cheerful submission to the divine authority, and the sense they had of their unworthiness to come into God's presence. Even when the fire of the Lord came down they praised him, saying, *He is good, for his mercy endureth for ever*. This is a song never out of season, and for which our hearts and tongues should be never out of tune.

2. The king and all the people offered sacrifices in abundance, *v.* 4, 5.

3. The priests did their part; they waited on their offices, and the singers and musicians on theirs (*v.* 6), with the instruments that David made, and the *hymn that David had put into their hand*, as some think it may be read (1 Chron. xvi. 7), or, as we read it, *when David praised by their ministry*.

4. The whole congregation expressed the greatest joy and satisfaction imaginable.

They kept the feast of the dedication of the altar seven days, from the second to the ninth; the tenth day was the day of atonement, when they were to afflict their souls for sin, and that was not unseasonable in the midst of their rejoicings; on the fifteenth day began the feast of tabernacles, which continued to the twenty-second, and they did not separate till the twenty-third.

Verses 12–22

God appeared to Solomon in the night, as he did once before (*ch.* i. 7), and after a day of sacrifice too, as then, and gave him a particular answer to his prayer. We had the substance of it before, 1 Kings ix. 2–9.

I. He promised to own this house for *a house of sacrifice to Israel* and a *house of prayer for all people* (Isa. lvi. 7): *My name shall be there for ever* (*v.* 12, 16).

II. He promised to answer the prayers of his people that should at any time be made in that place, *v.* 13–15. 1. National judgments are here supposed (*v.* 13), famine, and pestilence, and perhaps war, for by the locusts devouring the land may be meant enemies as greedy as locusts, and laying all waste. 2. National repentance, prayer, and reformation, are required, *v.* 14. 3. National mercy is then promised, that God will forgive their sin, which brought the judgment upon them, and then heal their land, redress all their grievances. Pardoning mercy makes way for healing mercy, Ps. ciii. 3; Matt. ix. 2.

III. He promised to perpetuate Solomon's kingdom, upon condition that he persevered in his duty, *v.* 17, 18. But he set before him death as well as life, the curse as well as the blessing. 1. He supposed it possible that though they had this temple built to the honour of God, yet they might be drawn aside to worship other gods, *v.* 19. 2. He threatened it as certain that, if they did so, it would certainly be the ruin of both church and state.

JAMIESON, FAUSSET, BROWN

temple (Exod. 40:35). **2. the priests could not enter**—Both from awe of the miraculous fire that was burning on the altar and from the dense cloud that enveloped the sanctuary, they were unable for some time to perform their usual functions (see on I Kings 8:10, 11). But afterwards, their courage and confidence being revived, they approached the altar and busied themselves in the offering of an immense number of sacrifices. **3. all the children of Israel . . . bowed themselves with their faces to the ground upon the pavement**—This form of prostration (that of lying on one's knees with the forehead touching the earth), is the manner in which the Hebrews, and Orientals in general, express the most profound sentiments of reverence and humility. The courts of the temple were densely crowded on the occasion, and the immense multitude threw themselves on the ground. What led the Israelites suddenly to assume that prostrate attitude on the occasion referred to, was the spectacle of the symbolical cloud slowly and majestically descending upon the temple, and then entering it.

4-11. Solomon's Sacrifices. **4. Then the king and all the people offered sacrifices**—Whether the individual worshippers slaughtered their own cattle, or a certain portion of the vast number of the Levitical order in attendance performed that work, as they sometimes did, in either case the offerings were made through the priests, who presented the blood and the fat upon the altar (see on I Kings 8:62-64). **5. so the king and all the people dedicated the house of God**—The ceremonial of dedication consisted principally in the introduction of the ark into the temple, and in the sacrificial offerings that were made on a scale of magnitude suitable to the extraordinary occasion. All present, the king, the people, and the priests, took part according to their respective stations in the performance of the solemn service. The duty, of course, devolved chiefly on the priests, and hence in proceeding to describe their several departments of work, the historian says, generally, "the priests waited on their offices." While great numbers would be occupied with the preparation and offering of the victims, others sounded with their trumpets, and the different bands of the Levites praised the Lord with vocal and instrumental music, by the 136th Psalm, the oft-recurring chorus of which is, "for His mercy endureth for ever." **7. Solomon hallowed the middle of the court**—On this extraordinary occasion, when a larger number of animals were offered than one altar and the usual place of rings to which the animals were bound would admit, the whole space was taken in that was between the place of rings and the west end of the court to be used as a temporary place for additional altars. On that part of the spacious court holocausts were burning all round. **8. Solomon kept the feast seven days**—The time chosen for the dedication of the temple was immediately previous to the feast of tabernacles (see on I Kings 8:1-12). That season, which came after the harvest, corresponding to our September and October, lasted seven days, and during so prolonged a festival there was time afforded for the offering of the immense sacrifices enumerated. A large proportion of these were peace offerings, which afforded to the people the means of festive enjoyment. **all Israel . . . from the entering in of Hamath**—i.e., the defile at Lebanon. **unto the river of Egypt**—i.e., Rhinocorura, now El-Arish, the south boundary of Palestine. **10. on the three and twentieth day of the seventh month**—This was the last day of the feast of tabernacles.

12-22. God Appears to Him. **12. the Lord appeared to Solomon by night**—(See on I Kings 9:1-9). The dedication of the temple must have been an occasion of intense national interest to Solomon and his subjects. Nor was the interest merely temporary or local. The record of it is read and thought of with an interest that is undiminished by the lapse of time. The fact that this was the only temple of all nations in which the *true God* was worshipped imparts a moral grandeur to the scene and prepares the mind for the sublime prayer that was offered at the dedication. The pure theism of that prayer—its acknowledgment of the unity of God as well as of His moral perfections in providence and grace, came from the same divine source as the miraculous fire. They indicated sentiments and feelings of exalted and spiritual devotion, which sprang not from the unaided mind of man, but from the fountain of revelation. The reality of the divine presence was attested by the miracle, and that miracle stamped the seal of truth upon the theology of the temple worship.

ADAM CLARKE

4. *The king and all the people offered sacrifices.* They presented the victims to the priests, and they and the Levites slew them, and sprinkled the blood. Or perhaps the people themselves slew them and, having caught the blood, collected the fat, etc., presented them to the priests to be offered as the law required.

5. *Twenty and two thousand oxen.* The amount of all the victims that had been offered during the seven days of the Feast of Tabernacles, and the seven days of the Feast of the Dedication.

10. *On the three and twentieth day.* This was the ninth day of the dedication of the Temple; but in 1 Kings viii. 66 it is called the eighth day. "The meaning is this," says Jarchi: "he gave them liberty to return on the eighth day, and many of them did then return: and he dismissed the remainder on the ninth, what is called here the twenty-third, reckoning the fourteen days for the duration of the two feasts; in all, twenty-three."

12. *The Lord appeared to Solomon.* This was a second manifestation; see 1 Kings ix. 2-9, and the notes there.

18. *There shall not fail thee a man.* This promise was not fulfilled, because the condition was not fulfilled; they forsook God, and He cut them off, and the throne also.

20. *Then will I pluck them up by the roots.* How completely has this been fulfilled! Not only all the branches of the Jewish political tree have been cut off, but the very *roots* have been plucked up; so that the day of the Lord's anger has left them neither root nor branch.

MATTHEW HENRY

CHAPTER 8

Verses 1–11

There is a similar account in 1 Kings ix. 10–24.

I. Though Solomon was a man of great learning and knowledge, yet he spent his days, not in contemplation, but in action, in building cities and fortifying them.

II. He employed a great many hands, kept abundance of people to work. A great many strangers there were in Israel, many that remained of the Canaanites; and they were welcome to live there, but not to live and do nothing.

III. When Solomon had begun with building the house of God, and made good work and quick work of that, he prospered in all his undertakings, so that *he built all that he desired to build*, *v.* 6. He knew how to set bounds to his desires. He finished all he desired, and then he desires no more.

IV. One reason why Solomon built a palace on purpose for the queen, and removed her and her court to it, was because he thought it by no means proper that she should *dwell in the house of David* (*v.* 11). She was proselyted, it is likely, to the Jewish religion; but it is a question whether all her servants were. Perhaps they had among them the idols of Egypt. Now, though Solomon had not zeal and courage enough to suppress and punish what was amiss there, yet he so far consulted the honour of his father's memory that he would not suffer that place to be thus profaned where the ark of God had been and where holy David had prayed many a good prayer and sung many a sweet psalm.

Verses 12–18

I. Solomon's devotion. The building of the temple was in order to the service of the temple. Whatever cost he was at in rearing the structure, if he had neglected the worship that was to be performed there, it would all have been to no purpose. When Solomon had built the temple, 1. He kept up the holy sacrifices there, according to the law of Moses, *v.* 12, 13. Those are spiritual sacrifices that are now required of us, which we are to bring daily and weekly; and it is good to be in a settled method of devotion. 2. He kept up the holy songs there, according to the *law of David*, who is here called *the man of God*, as Moses was, because he was both instructed and authorised of God to make these establishments; and Solomon took care to see them observed *as the duty of every day required*, *v.* 14. *None departed from the commandment of the king concerning any matter*, *v.* 15. When the service of the temple was put into this good order, *The house of the Lord was perfected*, *v.* 16.

II. Solomon's merchandise. He did himself in person visit the sea-port towns of Eloth and Ezion-geber. Canaan was a rich country, and yet must send to Ophir for gold; the Israelites were a wise and understanding people, and yet must be beholden to the king of Tyre for *men that had knowledge of the seas*, *v.* 18. Yet Canaan was God's peculiar land, and Israel God's peculiar people. This teaches us that grace, and not gold, is the best riches, and acquaintance with God and his law the best knowledge.

JAMIESON, FAUSSET, BROWN

CHAPTER 8

VSS. 1-6. SOLOMON'S BUILDINGS. **2. cities which Huram had restored . . . Solomon built them,** etc.—These cities lay in the northwest of Galilee. Though included within the limits of the promised land, they had never been conquered. The right of occupying them Solomon granted to Huram, who, after consideration, refused them as unsuitable to the commercial habits of his subjects (see on I Kings 9:11). Solomon, having wrested them from the possession of the Canaanite inhabitants, repaired them and filled them with a colony of Hebrews. **3-6. Solomon went to Hamath-zobah**—Hamath was on the Orontes, in Cæle-Syria. Its king, Toi, had been the ally of David; but from the combination, Hamath and Zobah, it would appear that some revolution had taken place which led to the union of these two petty kingdoms of Syria into one. For what cause the resentment of Solomon was provoked against it, we are not informed, but he sent an armed force which reduced it. He made himself master also of Tadmor, the famous Palmyra in the same regiion. Various other cities along the frontiers of his extended dominions he repaired and fitted up, either to serve as store-places for the furtherance of his commercial enterprises, or to secure his kingdom from foreign invasion (see on ch. 1:14; I Kings 9:15-24).

7-11. THE CANAANITES MADE TRIBUTARIES. **7. all the people that were left,** etc.—The descendants of the Canaanites who remained in the country were treated as war prisoners, being obliged to "pay tribute or to serve as galley slaves" (ch. 2:18), while the Israelites were employed in no works but such as were of an honorable character. **10. two hundred and fifty that bare rule**—(Cf. I Kings 9:23). It is generally agreed that the text of one of these passages is corrupt. **11. Solomon brought up the daughter of Pharaoh out of the city of David unto the house he had built for her**—On his marriage with the Egyptian princess at the beginning of his reign, he assigned her a temporary abode in the city of David, i.e., Jerusalem, until a suitable palace for his wife had been erected. While that palace was in progress, he himself lodged in the palace of David, but he did not allow her to occupy it, because he felt that she being a heathen proselyte, and having brought from her own country an establishment of heathen maidservants, there would have been an impropriety in her being domiciled in a mansion which was or had been hallowed by the reception of the ark. It seems she was received on her arrival into his mother's abode (Song of Sol. 3:4; 8:2).

15-18. SOLOMON'S FESTIVAL SACRIFICES. **15. they departed not from the commandment of the king**—i.e., David, in any of his ordinances, which by divine authority he established, either in regulating the courses of the priests and Levites, or in the destination of his accumulated treasures to the construction and adornment of the temple. **17. Then went Solomon to Ezion-geber, and to Eloth**—These two maritime ports were situated at the eastern gulf of the Red Sea, now called the Gulf of Akaba. Eloth is seen in the modern Akaba, Ezion-geber in El Gudyan [ROBINSON]. Solomon, determined to cultivate the arts of peace, was sagacious enough to perceive that his kingdom could become great and glorious only by encouraging a spirit of commercial enterprise among his subjects; and, accordingly, with that in mind he made a contract with Huram for ships and seamen to instruct his people in navigation. **18. Huram sent him . . . ships**—either sent him ship-*men,* able seamen, overland; or, taking the word "sent" in a looser sense, *supplied* him, i.e., *built* him ships—viz., in docks at Eloth (cf. I Kings 9:26, 27). This navy of Solomon was manned by Tyrians, for Solomon had no seamen capable of performing distant expeditions. The Hebrew fishermen, whose boats plied on the Sea of Tiberias or coasted the shores of the Mediterranean, were not equal to the conducting of large vessels laden with valuable cargoes on long voyages and through the wide and unfrequented ocean. **four hundred and fifty talents of gold**—(Cf. I Kings 9:28). The text in one of these passages is corrupt.

ADAM CLARKE

CHAPTER 8

1. *At the end of twenty years.* He employed seven years and a half in building the Temple, and twelve and a half, or thirteen, in building his own house. Compare this with 1 Kings vii. 1.

2. *The cities which Huram had restored.* See the note on 1 Kings ix. 11.

4. *Tadmor. Palmyra.* See the note on 1 Kings ix. 18 for an account of this superb city.

6. *All the store cities.* See 1 Kings ix. 19.

9. *But of the children of Israel.* See 1 Kings ix. 21.

11. *Because the places are holy.* Is not this a proof that he considered his wife to be a heathen, and not proper to dwell in a place which had been sanctified? Solomon had not yet departed from the true God.

13. *Three times in the year.* These were the three great annual feasts.

15. *The commandment of the king.* The institutions of David.

18. *Knowledge of the sea.* Skillful sailors. Solomon probably bore the expenses and his friend, the Tyrian king, furnished him with expert sailors; for the Jews, at no period of their history, had any skill in maritime affairs, their navigation being confined to the lakes of their own country, from which they could never acquire any nautical skill. The Tyrians, on the contrary, lived on and in the sea.

MATTHEW HENRY

CHAPTER 9

Verses 1–12

This passage of story has been largely considered in the Kings. Our Saviour has proposed it as an example to us in our enquiries after him (Matt. xii. 42). 1. *Those who honour God he will honour*, 1 Sam. ii. 30. Solomon had greatly honoured God, in building, beautifying, and dedicating the temple;

JAMIESON, FAUSSET, BROWN

CHAPTER 9

VSS. 1-12. THE QUEEN OF SHEBA VISITS SOLOMON; SHE ADMIRES HIS WISDOM AND MAGNIFICENCE. **1. when the queen of Sheba heard of the fame of Solomon**—(See on I Kings 10:1-13). It is said that among the things in Jerusalem which drew forth the admiration of Solomon's royal visitor was "his ascent by which he went up into the house of the

ADAM CLARKE

CHAPTER 9

1. *The queen of Sheba.* See all the particulars of this royal visit distinctly marked and explained in the notes on 1 Kings x. 1-10.

MATTHEW HENRY

all his wisdom and all his wealth were employed for the making of that a consummate piece: and now God made his wisdom and wealth to redound greatly to his reputation. 2. Those who know the worth of true wisdom will grudge no pains nor cost to obtain it. The queen of Sheba put herself to a great deal of trouble and expense to hear the wisdom of Solomon; and yet, learning from him to serve God and do her duty, she thought herself well paid for her pains. Heavenly wisdom is that *pearl of great price* which it is a good bargain to purchase by parting with all that we have. 3. As every man has received the gift so he ought to minister the same for the edification of others, as he has opportunity. Solomon was communicative of his wisdom and willing to teach others what he knew himself. The queen of Sheba was exceedingly affected to see the propriety with which Solomon's servants attended him and with which both he and they attended in the house of God. 5. Those are happy who have the opportunity of a constant converse with such as are knowing, wise, and good. The queen of Sheba thought Solomon's servants happy who continually *heard his wisdom*; it is observable that the posterity of those who had places in his court thought themselves sufficiently distinguished and dignified when they were called the *children of Solomon's servants* (Ezra ii. 55; Neh. vii. 57). It becomes those that are wise and good to be generous according to their place and power. The queen of Sheba was so to Solomon, Solomon was so to her, *v.* 9, 12. They both knew how to value wisdom, and therefore were neither of them covetous of their money, but cultivated the acquaintance and confirmed the friendship they had contracted by mutual presents.

Verses 13–30

I. Here is Solomon reigning in wealth and power, in ease and fulness, such as could never since be paralleled by any king whatsoever. The most illustrious of them were famed for their wars, whereas Solomon reigned forty years in profound peace. Some of those that might be thought to vie with Solomon affected retirement, kept people in awe by keeping them at a great distance; but Solomon went much abroad, and appeared in public business. The promise was fulfilled, that God would give him riches, and wealth, and honour, such as no kings *have had, or shall have, ch.* i. 12. 1. Never any prince appeared in public with greater splendour than Solomon did, which to those that judge by the sight of the eye, as most people do, would very much recommend him. He had 200 targets and 300 shields, all of beaten gold, carried before him (*v.* 15, 16), and sat upon a most stately throne, *v.* 17–19. *There was not the like in any kingdom.* 2. Never any prince had greater plenty of gold and silver, though there were no gold or silver mines in his own kingdom. 3. Never any prince had such presents brought him by all his neighbours as Solomon had: *All the kings of Arabia, and governors of the country, brought him gold and silver* (*v.* 14), not as tribute which he extorted from them, but as freewill offerings to procure his favour, or in a way of exchange for some of the productions of his husbandry, corn or cattle. Herein he was a type of Christ, to whom, as soon as he was born, the wise men of the east brought presents, *gold, frankincense, and myrrh* (Matt. ii. 11), and to whom all that are about him must bring presents, Ps. lxxvi. 11; Rom. xii. 1. 4. Never any prince was so renowned for wisdom, so courted, so consulted, so admired (*v.* 23).

II. Here is Solomon dying, stripped of his pomp, and leaving all his wealth and power, not to one concerning whom he knew not *whether he would be a wise man or a fool* (Eccles. ii. 19), but who he knew would be a fool. This was not only vanity but vexation of spirit, *v.* 29–31. Though he fell, yet he was not utterly cast down. His sin is not again recorded, because it was repented of, and pardoned, and so became as if it had never been. Scripture-silence sometimes speaks. I am willing to believe that its silence here concerning the sin of Solomon is an intimation that none of the sins he committed were mentioned against him, Ezek. xxxiii. 16. When God pardons sin he *casts it behind his back and remembers it no more.*

JAMIESON, FAUSSET, BROWN

Lord." This was the arched viaduct that crossed the valley from Mount Zion to the opposite hill. In the commentary on the passage quoted above, allusion was made to the recent discovery of its remains. Here we give a full account of what, for boldness of conceptions for structure and magnificence, was one of the greatest wonders in Jerusalem. "During our first visit to the southwest corner of the area of the mosque, we observed several of the large stones jutting out from the western wall, which at first seemed to be the effect of a bursting of the wall from some mighty shock or earthquake. We paid little regard to this at the moment; but on mentioning the fact not long after to a circle of our friends, the remark was incidentally dropped that the stones had the appearance of having once belonged to a large arch. At this remark, a train of thought flashed across my mind, which I hardly dared to follow out until I had again repaired to the spot, in order to satisfy myself with my own eyes as to the truth or falsehood of the suggestion. I found it even so. The courses of these immense stones occupy their original position; their external surface is hewn to a regular curve; and, being fitted one upon another, they form the commencement or foot of an immense arch which once sprung out from this western wall in a direction towards Mount Zion, across the Tyropœon valley. This arch could only have belonged to the bridge, which, according to Josephus, led from this part of the temple to the Xystus (covered colonnade) on Zion; and it proves incontestably the antiquity of that portion from which it springs" [ROBINSON]. The distance from this point to the steep rock of Zion Robinson calculates to be about three hundred and fifty feet, the probable length of this ancient viaduct. Another writer adds, that "the arch of this bridge, if its curve be calculated with an approximation to the truth, would measure *sixty* feet, and must have been one of five sustaining the viaduct (allowing for the abutments on either side), and that the piers supporting the center arch of this bridge must have been of great altitude–not less, perhaps, than one hundred and thirty feet. The whole structure, when seen from the southern extremity of the Tyropœon, must have had an aspect of grandeur, especially as connected with the lofty and sumptuous edifices of the temple, and of Zion to the right and to the left [ISAAC TAYLOR'S EDITION OF TRAILL'S JOSEPHUS].

13-28. HIS RICHES. **13. Now the weight of gold that came to Solomon in one year**–(See on I Kings 10:14-29). **six hundred and threescore and six talents of gold**–The sum named is equal to about $17,000,000; and if we take the proportion of silver (vs. 14), which is not taken into consideration, at 1 to 9, there would be about $2,000,000, making a yearly supply of nearly $19,000,000, being a vast amount for an infant effort in maritime commerce [NAPIER]. **21. the king's ships went to Tarshish**–rather, "the king's ships of Tarshish went" with the servants of Huram. **ships of Tarshish**–i.e., in burden and construction like the large vessels built for or used at Tarshish [CALMET'S FRAGMENTS]. **25. Solomon had four thousand stalls**–It has been conjectured [GESENIUS' HEBREW LEXICON] that the original term may signify not only stall or stable, but a number of horses occupying the same number of stalls. Supposing that ten were put together in one part, this would make 40,000. According to this theory of explanation, the historian in Kings refers to horses; while the historian in Chronicles speaks of the stalls in which they were kept. But more recent critics reject this mode of solving the difficulty, and, regarding the four thousand stalls as in keeping with the general magnificence of Solomon's establishments, are agreed in considering the text in Kings as corrupt, through the error of some copyist. **28. they brought unto Solomon horses out of Egypt**–(See on ch. 1:17). Solomon undoubtedly carried the Hebrew kingdom to its highest pitch of worldly glory. His completion of the grand work, the centralizing of the national worship at Jerusalem, whither the natives went up three times a year, has given his name a prominent place in the history of the ancient church. But his reign had a disastrous influence upon "the peculiar people," and the example of his deplorable idolatries, the connections he formed with foreign princes, the commercial speculations he entered into, and the luxuries introduced into the land, seem in a great measure to have altered and deteriorated the Jewish character.

ADAM CLARKE

12. *Beside that which she had brought unto the king.* In 1 Kings x. 13 it is stated that Solomon gave her all she asked, beside that which he "gave her of his royal bounty." It is not at all likely that he gave her back the presents which she brought to him, and which he had accepted. She had, no doubt, asked for several things which were peculiar to the land of Judea, and would be curiosities in her own kingdom; and besides these, he gave her other valuable presents.

25. *Four thousand stalls for horses.* See the note on 1 Kings iv. 26, where the different numbers in these two books are considered. The Targum, instead of *four thousand,* has *arba meah,* "four hundred."

29. *Nathan the prophet.* These books are all lost.

MATTHEW HENRY

CHAPTER 10

Verses 1–11

1. The wisest and best cannot give everybody content. Solomon enriched and advanced his kingdom, did all that could be done to make them happy and easy; and yet was indiscreet in burdening them with the imposition of taxes and services. No man is perfectly wise. It is probable that it was when Solomon had declined from God and his duty that his wisdom failed him, and God left him to himself to act in this impolitic manner. Even Solomon's treasures were exhausted by his love of women; and probably it was to maintain them, and their pride, luxury, and idolatry, that he burdened his subjects. 2. Turbulent and ungrateful spirits will find fault with the government, and complain of grievances. Had they not peace in Solomon's time? They were never plundered by invaders, as formerly, never put in fear by the alarms of war, nor obliged to hazard their lives in the high places of the field. Had they not plenty—meat enough, and money enough? And yet they complain that Solomon made their yoke grievous. 3. Many ruin themselves and their interests by trampling upon and provoking their inferiors. Rehoboam thought that because he was king he might assume as much authority as his father had done. But, though he wore his father's crown, he wanted his father's brains. Such a wise man as Solomon may do as he will, but such a fool as Rehoboam must do as he can. Rehoboam paid dearly for threatening, and talking big, and thinking to carry matters with a high hand. A tender consideration of those in subjection, and a forwardness to make them easy, will be the comfort and praise of all in authority, in the church, in the state, and in families. 4. Moderate counsels are generally wisest and best. Gentleness will do what violence will not do. Rehoboam's old experienced counsellors directed him to this method (*v.* 7): "*Be kind to this people, and please them, and speak good words to them,* and thou art sure of them for ever." Good words cost nothing but a little self-denial, and yet they purchase great things.

Verses 12–19

1. When public affairs are in a ferment violent proceedings do but make bad worse. Rough answers (such as Rehoboam here gave) do but stir up anger and bring oil to the flames. 2. Whatever the devices and designs of men are, God is, by all, doing his own work, and fulfilling the word which he has spoken, no iota or tittle of which shall fall to the ground. 3. Worldly wealth, honour, and dominion, are very uncertain things. *Solomon reigned over all Israel,* and, one would think, had done enough to secure the monarchy entire to his family for many ages; and yet he is scarcely cold in his grave before ten of the twelve tribes finally revolt from his son. All the good services he had done for Israel were now forgotten. 4. God often visits the iniquities of the fathers upon the children. Solomon forsakes God, and therefore his son after him, is forsaken by the greatest part of his people. Thus God, by making the penal consequences of sin to last long and visibly to continue after the sinner's death, would give an indication of its malignity, and perhaps some intimation of the perpetuity of its punishment. He that sins against God not only wrongs his soul, but perhaps wrongs his seed more than he thinks. 5. When God is fulfilling his threatenings, he will take care that, at the same time, promises do not fall to the ground. When Solomon's iniquity is remembered, and for it his son loses ten tribes, David's piety is not forgotten, nor the promise made to him; but for the sake of that his grandson had two tribes preserved to him.

CHAPTER 11

Verses 1–12

How the ten tribes deserted the house of David we read in the foregoing chapter. They had formerly sat loose to that family (2 Sam. xx. 1, 2), and now they quite threw it off, not considering how much it would weaken the common interest. But thus the *kingdom* must be corrected as well as the *house* of David. 1. Rehoboam at length, like a bold man, raises an army, with a design to reduce the revolters, *v.* 1. Judah and Benjamin were ready to give him the best assistance they could for the recovery of his right. Judah was his own tribe, that owned him some years before the rest did; Benjamin was the tribe in which Jerusalem, or the greatest part of it, stood. 2. Yet, like a conscientious man, when God

JAMIESON, FAUSSET, BROWN

CHAPTER 10

Vss. 1-15. Rehoboam Refusing the Old Men's Good Counsel. **1. Rehoboam went to Shechem**—(See on I Kings 12:1). This chapter is, with a few verbal alterations, the same as in I Kings. **3. And they sent**—rather, "for they had sent," etc. This is stated as the reason of Jeroboam's return from Egypt.

7. If thou be kind to this people, and please them, and speak good words to them—In the Book of Kings, the words are, "If thou wilt be a servant unto this people, and wilt serve them." The meaning in both is the same, viz., If thou wilt make some reasonable concessions, redress their grievances, and restore their abridged liberties, thou wilt secure their strong and lasting attachment to thy person and government.

15. the king hearkened not unto the people, for the cause was of God—Rehoboam, in following an evil counsel, and the Hebrew people, in making a revolutionary movement, each acted as free agents, obeying their own will and passions. But God, who permitted the revolt of the northern tribes, intended it as a punishment of the house of David for Solomon's apostasy. That event demonstrates the immediate superintendence of His providence over the revolutions of kingdoms; and thus it affords an instance, similar to many other striking instances that are found in Scripture, of divine predictions, uttered long before, being accomplished by the operation of human passions, and in the natural course of events.

CHAPTER 11

Vss. 1-17. Rehoboam, Raising an Army to Subdue Israel, Is Forbidden by Shemaiah. **1-4. Rehoboam . . . gathered of the house of Judah and Benjamin . . . to fight against Israel**—(See on I Kings 12:21-24). **5. built cities for defence in Judah**—This is evidently used as the name of the southern kingdom. Rehoboam, having now a bitter enemy in Israel, deemed it prudent to lose no time in fortifying several cities that lay along the frontier of his kingdom. Jeroboam, on his side, took a similar precaution (I Kings 12:25). Of the fifteen cities named Aijalon, now Yalo, and Zorah, now Surah, between Jerusalem and Jabneh [Robinson], lay within the province of Benjamin. Gath, though a Philistine city, had been subject to Solomon. And

ADAM CLARKE

CHAPTER 10

1. *Rehoboam went to Shechem.* This chapter is almost word for word the same as 1 Kings xii, to the notes on which the reader is referred.

10. *My little finger shall be thicker.* "My weakness shall be stronger than the might of my father."—Targum.

CHAPTER 11

1. *Gathered of the house of Judah.* See this account, 1 Kings xii. 21–24.

5. *And built cities for defence in Judah.* He was obliged to strengthen his frontiers against the encroachments of the men of Israel; and Jeroboam did the same thing on this part, to prevent the inroads of Judah. See 1 Kings xii. 25.

JOSEPH PARKER:

It might be supposed that the king had taken a most patriotic course in consulting the old and the young. He had done nothing of the kind: he had omitted to consult him who had called his house to the royalty. Rehoboam should have consulted the Kingmaker whose throne is on the circle of the earth, and whose sceptre toucheth the horizon, and whose will is the law of monarchy and commonwealth. All human consultation is a species of under-counsel, valuable within proper limits, and right as recognizing the education, the intelligence, and the political instinct of the times; but all consultation to result in profoundest wisdom must be intensely, almost exclusively, religious. Kings should talk to their King. The greater the man the nearer should he stand to God; yea, he should be within whisper-reach of the Lord of lords, asking him in every crisis of natural history what Israel ought to do, what the country ought to answer, what is the will of heaven.

—*The People's Bible*

MATTHEW HENRY

forbade him to prosecute this design, in obedience to him he let it fall, either because he reverenced the divine authority or because he knew that he should not prosper if he should go contrary to God's command. They *obeyed the words of the Lord*; and though it looked mean, and would turn to their reproach among their neighbours, yet, because God would have it so, they laid down their arms. 3. Like a discreet man, he fortified his own country. Now, his aged and experienced counsellors were hearkened to, and they advised him to submit to the will of God concerning what was lost, and to make it his business to keep what he had. It was probably by their advice that, (1) He fortified his frontiers, and many of the principal cities of his kingdom. (2) He furnished them with good store of victuals and arms, *v.* 11, 12. Because God forbade him to fight he prudently provided against an attack. Those that may not be conquerors, yet may be builders.

Verses 13–23

I. Rehoboam strengthened by the priests and Levites, and all the devout and pious Israelites.

1. Jeroboam set up such a way of worship as obliged them to withdraw from his altar, and he would not allow them to go up to Jerusalem to worship at the altar there; so that he totally *cast them off from executing the priest's office*, *v.* 14. And very willing he was that room might be made for those mean and scandalous persons whom he *ordained priests for the high places*, *v.* 15. Compare 1 Kings xii. 31.

2. They thereupon *left their suburbs and possessions*, *v.* 14. They were driven out of all their cities except those in Judah and Benjamin. But why did they leave their possessions? (1) Because they saw they could do no good among their neighbours, in whom (now that Jeroboam set up his calves), the old proneness to idolatry revived. (2) Because they themselves would be in continual temptation. (3) Because, they had reason to expect persecution from Jeroboam and his sons.

3. They *came to Judah and Jerusalem* (*v.* 14) and *presented themselves to Rehoboam*, *v.* 13, *margin.* (1) It was a mercy that when Jeroboam cast them off there were those so near that would bid them welcome. (2) It was an evidence that they loved their work better than their maintenance, in that they *left their suburbs* because they were restrained from serving God there, and cast themselves upon God's providence and the charity of their brethren. Better live upon alms, or die in a prison, with a good conscience, than roll in wealth and pleasure with a prostituted one. (3) Rehoboam and his people bade them welcome. Conscientious refugees will bring a blessing along with them to the countries that entertain them, as they leave a curse behind them with those that expel them.

4. When the priests and Levites came to Jerusalem all the devout pious Israelites of every tribe followed them.

5. They *strengthened the kingdom of Judah* (*v.* 17) by their piety and their prayers. See Zech. xii. 5. They made him and his people *strong three years*; for so long they *walked in the way of David and Solomon*, their *good* way. But when they forsook that, the best friends they had could no longer help to strengthen them.

II. Rehoboam was weakened by indulging himself in his pleasures. He *desired many wives*, as his father did (*v.* 23), yet, 1. In *this* he was more wise than his father, that he does not appear to have married strange wives. The wives mentioned here were daughters of Israel, of the family of David. 2. In *this* he was more happy than his father, that he had many sons and daughters; whereas we read not of more than one son that his father had. Several of Rehoboam's sons are here named (*v.* 19, 20) as men of note, and such active men that he thought it his wisdom to *disperse them throughout the countries of Judah and Benjamin* (*v.* 23). He could repose confidence in them for the preserving of the public peace and could trust them with fenced cities, that they might stand him in stead in case of an invasion.

JAMIESON, FAUSSET, BROWN

Etham, which was on the border of Simeon, now incorporated with the kingdom of Israel, was fortified to repel danger from that quarter. These fortresses Rehoboam placed under able commanders and stocked them with provisions and military stores, sufficient, if necessary, to stand a siege. In the crippled state of his kingdom, he seems to have been afraid lest it might be made the prey of some powerful neighbors. **13-17. the priests and the Levites . . . resorted to him out of all their coasts**—This was an accession of moral power, for the maintenance of the true religion is the best support and safeguard of any nation; and as it was peculiarly the grand source of the strength and prosperity of the Hebrew monarchy, the great numbers of good and pious people who sought an asylum within the territories of Judah contributed greatly to consolidate the throne of Rehoboam. The cause of so extensive an emigration from the kingdom of Israel was the deep and daring policy of Jeroboam, who set himself to break the national unity by entirely abolishing, within his dominions, the religious institutions of Judaism. He dreaded an eventual reunion of the tribes if the people continued to repair thrice a year to worship in Jerusalem as they were obliged by law to do. Accordingly, on pretense that the distance of that city was too great for multitudes of his subjects, he fixed upon two more convenient places, where he established a new mode of worshipping God under gross and prohibited symbols. The priests and Levites, refusing to take part in the idolatrous ceremonies, were ejected from their living. Along with them a large body of the people who faithfully adhered to the instituted worship of God, offended and shocked by the impious innovations, departed from the kingdom. **15. he ordained him priests**—The persons he appointed to the priesthood were low and worthless creatures (I Kings 12:31; 13:33); any were consecrated who brought a bullock and seven rams (Ch. 13:9; Exod. 29:37). **for the high places**—Those favorite places of religious worship were encouraged throughout the country. **for the devils**—a term sometimes used for idols in general (Lev. 17:7). But here it is applied distinctively to the goat deities, which were probably worshipped chiefly in the northern parts of his kingdom, where the heathen Canaanites still abounded. **and for the calves**—figures of the ox gods Apis and Mnevis, with which Jeroboam's residence in Egypt had familiarized him. (See on I Kings 12:26-33.) **17. they strengthened the kingdom of Judah**—The innovating measures of Jeroboam were not introduced all at once. But as they were developed, the secession of the most excellent of his subjects began, and continuing to increase for three years, lowered the tone of religion in his kingdom, while it proportionally quickened its life and extended its influence in that of Judah.

18-23. HIS WIVES AND CHILDREN. **18. Rehoboam took Mahalath**—The names of her father and mother are given. Jerimoth, the father, must have been the son of one of David's concubines (I Chron. 3:9.) Abihail was, of course, his cousin, previous to their marriage. **20. after her he took Maachah . . . daughter**—i.e., granddaughter (II Sam. 14:27) of Absalom, Tamar being, according to Josephus, her mother. (Cf. II Sam. 18:18.) **21. he took eighteen wives, and threescore concubines**—This royal harem, though far smaller than his father's, was equally in violation of the law, which forbade a king to "multiply wives unto himself." **22. made Abijah . . . chief . . . ruler among his brethren**—This preference seems to have been given to Abijah solely from the king's doting fondness for his mother and through her influence over him. It is plainly implied that Abijah was not the oldest of the family. In destining a younger son for the kingdom, without a divine warrant, as in Solomon's case, Rehoboam acted in violation of the law (Deut. 21:15). **23. he dealt wisely**—i.e., with deep and calculating policy (Exod. 1:10). **and dispersed of all his children . . . unto every fenced city**—The circumstance of twenty-eight sons of the king being made governors of fortresses would, in our quarter of the world, produce jealousy and dissatisfaction. But Eastern monarchs ensure peace and tranquillity to their kingdom by bestowing government offices on their sons and grandsons. They obtain an independent provision, and being kept apart, are not likely to cabal in their father's lifetime. Rehoboam acted thus, and his sagacity will appear still greater if the wives he desired for them belonged to the cities where each son was located. These connections would bind them more closely to their respective places.

ADAM CLARKE

11. *Store of victual.* In these places he laid up stores of provisions, not only to enable them to endure a siege, but also that they might be able, from their situation, to supply desolate places.

14. *The Levites left their suburbs.* They and the priests were expelled from their offices by Jeroboam, lest they should turn the hearts of the people to the true God, and then they would revolt to Judah, 1 Kings xii. 26; and therefore he established a new worship, and made new gods.

15. *And he ordained him priests . . . for the devils. Seirim*, "the hairy ones"; probably goats. For as the golden calves, or oxen, were in imitation of the Egyptian ox-god, Apis, so they no doubt paid divine honors to the goat, which we know was an object of religious veneration in Egypt.

16. *Such as set their hearts to seek the Lord.* All the truly pious joined him out of every tribe; and the whole tribe of Levi, being deprived of their functions, joined him also. Thus he had Judah, Benjamin, and Levi, and probably a part of Simeon; for he had Etam, which was in that tribe, and the truly religious out of all the other tribes, for they could not bear Jeroboam's idolatry.

17. *For three years they walked in the way of David.* During this time he prospered; but for fourteen years after this he and the people were unfaithful to the Lord, except at such intervals as the hand of God's judgments was upon them.

18. *Took him Mahalath.* By marrying thus in the family of David, he strengthened his right to the Jewish throne.

20. *Maachah the daughter of Absalom.* See the note on 1 Kings xv. 10. She is called Michaiah, the daughter of Uriel, chap. xiii. 2. For this the Targum gives the following reason: "Abijah reigned three years in Jerusalem; and his mother's name was Michaiah, daughter of Uriel of Gibeatha. She is the same as Michah, the daughter of Absalom; but because she was an upright woman, her name was changed into the more excellent name Michaiah, and her father's name into that of Uriel of Gibeatha, that the name of Absalom might not be remembered."

21. *Eighteen wives, and threescore concubines.* Bad enough, but not so abandoned as his father. Of these marriages and concubinage the issue was twenty-eight sons and sixty daughters; eighty-eight children in the whole, to the education of the whole of whom he could pay but little attention.

22. *Made Abijah . . . the chief.* Abijah certainly was not the firstborn of Rehoboam; but as he loved Maachah more than any of his wives, so he preferred her son, probably through his mother's influence.

23. *He dealt wisely.* It was true policy to disperse his own sons through the different provinces who were not likely to form any league with Jeroboam against their father.

MATTHEW HENRY

CHAPTER 12

Verses 1–12

Israel was disgraced and weakened by being divided into two kingdoms; yet the kingdom of Judah, having both the temple and the royal city, might have done very well if they had continued in the way of their duty.

I. Rehoboam and his people left God, *v.* 1. He walked in the way of David and Solomon (*ch.* xi. 17), but he grew remiss in the worship of God. As long as he thought his throne tottered he kept to his duty, that he might make God his friend; but, when he found it stood pretty firmly, he thought he had no more occasion for religion; he was safe enough without it.

II. God quickly brought troubles upon them, to recover them to repentance, before their hearts were hardened. It was in the fourth year of Rehoboam that they began to corrupt themselves, and in the fifth year the king of Egypt came up against them with a vast army, took *the fenced cities of Judah, and came against Jerusalem, v.* 2, 3, 4. This great calamity coming upon them so soon after they begun to desert the worship of God, by a hand they had little reason to suspect (having had a great deal of friendly correspondence with Egypt in the last reign), plainly showed that it was from the Lord, because they had transgressed against him.

III. Lest they should not rightly understand the meaning of this providence, God by the word explains the rod, *v.* 5. When the princes of Judah had all met at Jerusalem in a council of war, he sent a prophet to them, the same that had brought them an injunction from God not to fight against the ten tribes (*ch.* xi. 2), Shemaiah by name; he told them plainly that the reason why Shishak prevailed against them was because they had forsaken God.

IV. The rebukes both of the word and of the rod being thus joined, the king and princes humbled themselves before God for their iniquity, and patiently accepted the punishment, saying, *The Lord is righteous, v.* 6.

V. Upon the profession they made of repentance God saved them from ruin, and yet left them under some remaining fears of the judgment, to prevent their revolt again.

1. Such a vast and now victorious army as Shishak had what could be expected but that the whole country, and even Jerusalem itself, would in a little time be theirs? But when God saith, *Here shall the proud waves be stayed*, the most threatening force strangely dwindles and becomes impotent. The destroying angel, when he comes to Jerusalem, is forbidden to destroy it: "*My wrath shall not be poured out upon Jerusalem,*" *v.* 7, 12. So ready is the God of mercy to take the first occasion to show mercy.

2. He granted them some deliverance, not complete, but in part. They reformed but partially, and for a little while, soon relapsing again; and, as their reformation was, so was their deliverance. Yet it is said (*v.* 12), *in Judah things went well.* (1) In respect of piety. *There were good things in Judah* (so it is in the margin), good ministers, good people, good families. (2) In respect of prosperity. In Judah things went ill when all the fenced cities were taken (*v.* 4), but when they repented their affairs altered and things went well.

3. Yet he left them to smart sorely by the hand of Shishak, both in their liberty and in their wealth.

(1) In their liberty (*v.* 8): *They shall be his servants that they may know my service, and the service of the kingdoms of the countries.* They complained, it may be, of the strictness of their religion. Let them better themselves if they can; let the neighbouring princes rule them awhile. The more God's service is compared with other services the more reasonable and easy it will appear. Are the laws of temperance thought hard? The effects of intemperance will be much harder. The service of virtue is perfect liberty; the service of lust is perfect slavery.

(2) In their wealth. The king of Egypt plundered both the temple and the exchequer, the treasuries of both which Solomon left very full; but he *took them away*; yea, he *took all*, all he could lay his hands on, *v.* 9. This was what he came for.

Verses 13–16

The story of Rehoboam's reign concluded. Two things especially are observable. 1. That he was at length well *fixed in his kingdom, v.* 13. He *strengthened himself in Jerusalem*, and there he reigned seventeen years. He had his royal seat in the holy city, which yet was but an aggravation of his impiety—near the temple, but far from God. Frequent skirmishes there were between his subjects and Jeroboam's, such as

JAMIESON, FAUSSET, BROWN

CHAPTER 12

VSS. 1-12. REHOBOAM, FORSAKING GOD, IS PUNISHED BY SHISHAK. **1. when Rehoboam had established the kingdom, and had strengthened himself**—(See on ch. 11:17). During the first three years of his reign his royal influence was exerted in the encouragement of the true religion. Security and ease led to religious decline, which, in the fourth year, ended in open apostasy. The example of the court was speedily followed by his subjects, for "all Israel was with him," i.e., the people in his own kingdom. The very next year, the fifth of his reign, punishment was inflicted by the invasion of Shishak. **2. Shishak king of Egypt came up against Jerusalem**—He was the first king of the twenty-second or Bubastic Dynasty. What was the immediate cause of this invasion? Whether it was in resentment for some provocation from the king of Judah, or in pursuance of ambitious views of conquest, is not said. But the invading army was a vast horde, for Shishak brought along with his native Egyptians an immense number of foreign auxiliaries. **3. the Lubims**—the Libyans of northeastern Africa. **the Sukkiims**—Some think these were the Kenite Arabs, dwellers in tents, but others maintain more justly that these were Arab troglodytes, who inhabited the caverns of a mountain range on the western coast of the Red Sea. **the Ethiopians**—from the regions south of Egypt. By the overwhelming force of numbers, they took the fortresses of Judah which had been recently put in a state of defense, and marched to lay siege to the capital. While Shishak and his army was before Jerusalem, the prophet Shemaiah addressed Rehoboam and the princes, tracing this calamity to the national apostasy and threatening them with utter destruction in consequence of having forsaken God (vs. 6). **6. the princes of Israel**—(cf. vs. 5, "the princes of Judah"). **7, 8. when the Lord saw that they humbled themselves**—Their repentance and contrition was followed by the best effects; for Shemaiah was commissioned to announce that the phial of divine judgment would not be fully poured out on them—that the entire overthrow of the kingdom of Judah would not take place at that time, nor through the agency of Shishak; and yet, although it should enjoy a respite from total subversion, it should become a tributary province of Egypt in order that the people might learn how much lighter and better is the service of God than that of idolatrous foreign despots. **9. So Shishak . . . came up against Jerusalem**—After the parenthetical clause (vss. 5-8) describing the feelings and state of the beleaguered court, the historian resumes his narrative of the attack upon Jerusalem, and the consequent pillage both of the temple and the palace. **he took all**—i.e., everything valuable he found. The cost of the targets and shields has been estimated as about $1,200,000 [NAPIER'S METAL]. **the shields of gold**—(ch. 9:16) made by Solomon, were kept in the house of the forest of Lebanon (ch. 9:16). They seem to have been borne, like maces, by the guards of the palace, when they attended the king to the temple or on other public processions. Those splendid insignia having been plundered by the Egyptian conqueror, others were made of inferior metal and kept in the guardroom of the palace, to be ready for use; as, notwithstanding the tarnished glory of the court, the old state etiquette was kept up on public and solemn occasions. An account of this conquest of Judah, with the name of "king of Judah" in the cartouche of the principal captive, according to the interpreters, is carved and written in hieroglyphics on the walls of the great palace of Karnak, where it may be seen at the present day. This sculpture is about 2700 years old, and is of peculiar interest as a striking testimony from Egypt to the truth of Scripture history. **12. when he humbled himself, the wrath of the Lord turned from him**—The promise (vs. 7) was verified. Divine providence preserved the kingdom in existence, a reformation was made in the court, while true religion and piety were diffused throughout the land.

13-16. HIS REIGN AND DEATH. **13. Rehoboam strengthened himself . . . and reigned**—The Egyptian invasion had been a mere predatory expedition, not extending beyond the limits of Judah, and probably, erelong, repelled by the invaded. Rehoboam's government acquired new life and vigor by the general revival of true religion, and his reign continued many years after the departure of Shishak. But "he prepared not his heart to seek the Lord," i.e., he did not adhere firmly to the good course of reformation he had begun, "and he did evil," for through the unhappy influence of his

ADAM CLARKE

CHAPTER 12

1. ***He forsook the law of the Lord.*** **This was after the three years mentioned in chap. xi. 17.**

2. ***Shishak king of Egypt.*** **Concerning this man, and the motive which led him to attack the Jews, see the note on 1 Kings xiv. 31.**

3. ***The Lubims.*** **Supposed to be a people of Libya, adjoining to Egypt; sometimes called Phut in Scripture, as the people are called Lehabim and Ludim.** ***The Sukkiims.*** **The Troglodytes, a people of Egypt on the coast of the Red Sea. They were called** ***Troglodytes,*** **"because they dwelt in caves."** ***The Ethiopians. Cushim.*** **Various people were called by this name, particularly a people bordering on the northern coast of the Red Sea; but these are supposed to have come from a country of that name on the south of Egypt.**

6. ***Whereupon the princes of Israel and the king humbled themselves.*** **This is not mentioned in the parallel place, 1 Kings xiv. This was the sole reason why Jerusalem was not at this time totally destroyed, and the house of David entirely cut off; for they were totally incapable of defending themselves against this innumerable host.**

8. ***They shall be his servants.*** **They shall be preserved, and serve their enemies, that they may see the difference between the service of God and that of man. While they were pious, they found the service of the Lord to be perfect freedom; when they forsook the Lord, they found the fruit to be perfect bondage. A sinful life is both expensive and painful.**

9. ***Took away the treasures.*** **Such a booty as never had before, nor has since, come into the hand of man.** ***The shields of gold.*** **These shields were the mark of the king's bodyguard.**

13. ***Was one and forty years old.*** **Houbigant things he was but sixteen years old when he began to reign, and brings many and forcible arguments to prove that the number forty-one must be a mistake. That he was young when he came to the throne is evident from his consulting "the young men that were brought up with him," chap. x. 8, 10. Besides, Abijah, in his speech to Jeroboam, chap. xiii. 7, says that at the time Rehoboam came to the throne he was tenderhearted, and therefore could not withstand the children of Belial raised up against him**

amounted to *continual wars* (*v.* 15), but he held his own, and did not so grossly *forsake the law of God* as he had done (*v.* 1) in his fourth year. 2. That he was never rightly fixed in his religion, *v.* 14. He did not serve the Lord because he did not seek the Lord. He did not pray, as Solomon did, for wisdom and grace. If we prayed better, we should be every way better. He did evil because he was never determined for that which is good.

CHAPTER 13

Verses 1–12

Abijah's mother was called *Maachah*, the daughter of Absalom, *ch.* xi. 20; here she is called *Michaiah*, the daughter of Uriel. It is most probable that she was a granddaughter of Absalom, by his daughter Tamar (2 Sam. xiv. 27), and that her immediate father was this Uriel.

I. God gave Abijah leave to engage with Jeroboam; and owned him in the conflict. Jeroboam, it is probable, was now the aggressor, and what Abijah did was in his own necessary defence. Jeroboam claimed the crown of Judah. Against these impudent pretensions it was brave in Abijah to take up arms, and God stood by him. Abijah is allowed to chastise him.

II. Jeroboam's army was double in number to that of Abijah (*v.* 3), for he had ten tribes, while Abijah had but two. The inferior number however proved victorious.

III. Abijah, before he fought them, reasoned with them, to desist from fighting against the house of David. It is good to try reason before we use force. We must never fly to violent methods till all the arts of persuasion have been tried in vain. War must be the *ultima ratio regum—the last resort of kings.* Fair reasoning may do a great deal of good and prevent a great deal of mischief. Abijah had got with his army into the heart of their country; for he made this speech upon a hill in Mount Ephraim. Two things Abijah undertakes to make out,

1. That he had right on his side, a *jus divinum—a divine right*: "You know that *God gave the kingdom to David and his sons for ever*" (*v.* 5), by a covenant of salt, a lasting covenant, a covenant made by sacrifice, which was always salted; so Bishop Patrick. All Israel had owned that David was a king of God's making, and that God had entailed the crown upon his family; so that Jeroboam's taking the crown of Israel at first was not justifiable. Abijah shows, (1) That there was a great deal of dishonesty in Jeroboam's first setting himself up: He *rebelled against his lord* (*v.* 6) who had preferred him (1 Kings xi. 28), and basely took advantage of Rehoboam's weakness. Those that supported him are here called *vain men* (a character perhaps borrowed from Judges xi. 3). (2) That there was a great deal of impiety in his present attempt; for, in fighting against the house of David, he fought *against the kingdom of the Lord.*

2. That he had God on his side. This he insisted much upon, that the religion of Jeroboam and his army was false and idolatrous, but that he and his people, the men of Judah, had the pure worship of the true and living God among them. It appears from the character given of Abijah (1 Kings xv. 3) that he was not himself truly religious, and yet here he encouraged himself in this war chiefly from the religion of his kingdom. Whatever he was otherwise, it should seem that he was no idolater. Whatever corruptions there were in the kingdom of Judah, the state of religion among them was better than in the kingdom of Israel, with which they were now contending. It was the cause of his kingdom that he was pleading; and, though he was not himself so good as he should have been, yet he hoped that, for the sake of the good men and good things that were in Judah, God would now appear for them. "We *keep his charge, v.* 10, 11. We worship no images, have no priests but what he has ordained, no rites of worship but what he has prescribed. He is our captain, and we may therefore be sure that he is with us, because we are with him, *v.* 12. And in the day of battle we shall be *remembered before the Lord our God* and *saved from our enemies.*" He concludes with fair warning to his enemies. "*Fight not against the God of your fathers.*"

Verses 13–22

Jeroboam resolved not to heed, and therefore heard as though he heard not. He came to fight, not to dispute. The longest sword, he thought, would determine the matter, not the better cause.

I. Jeroboam, who trusted to his politics, was beaten. He was so far from fair reasoning that he was not for fair fighting. A parley, it is probable, was agreed on, yet Jeroboam basely takes advantage of it, and,

mother, a heathen foreigner, he had no doubt received in his youth a strong bias towards idolatry (see on I Kings 14:21-24).

CHAPTER 13

Vss. 1-20. Abijah, Succeeding, Makes War against Jeroboam, and Overcomes Him. **2. His mother's name also was Michaiah, the daughter of Uriel of Gibeah**—the same as Maachah (see on I Kings 15:2). She was "the daughter," i.e., granddaughter of Absalom (I Kings 15:2; cf. II Sam. 14), mother of Abijah, "mother," i.e., grandmother (I Kings 15:10, *marg.*) of Asa. **of Gibeah** probably implies that Uriel was connected with the house of Saul. **there was war between Abijah and Jeroboam**—The occasion of this war is not recorded (see I Kings 15:6, 7), but it may be inferred from the tenor of Abijah's address that it arose from his youthful ambition to recover the full hereditary dominion of his ancestors. No prophet now forbade a war with Israel (ch. 11:23) for Jeroboam had forfeited all claim to protection. **3. Abijah set the battle in array**—i.e., took the field and opened the campaign. **Abijah set the battle in array with . . . four hundred thousand chosen men . . . Jeroboam with eight hundred thousand**—These are, doubtless, large numbers, considering the smallness of the two kingdoms. It must be borne in mind, however, that Oriental armies are mere mobs—vast numbers accompanying the camp in hope of plunder, so that the gross numbers described as going upon an Asiatic expedition are often far from denoting the exact number of fighting men. But in accounting for the large number of soldiers enlisted in the respective armies of Abijah and Jeroboam, there is no need of resorting to this mode of explanation; for we know by the census of David the immense number of the population that was capable of bearing arms (I Chron. 21:5; cf. ch. 14:8; 17:14). **4-12. Abijah stood up upon Mount Zemaraim**—He had entered the enemy's territory and was encamped on an eminence near Beth-el (Josh. 18:22). Jeroboam's army lay at the foot of the hill, and as a pitched battle was expected, Abijah, according to the singular usage of ancient times, harangued the enemy. The speakers in such circumstances, while always extolling their own merits, poured out torrents of invective and virulent abuse upon the adversary. So did Abijah. He dwelt on the divine right of the house of David to the throne; and sinking all reference to the heaven-condemned offenses of Solomon and the divine appointment of Jeroboam, as well as the divine sanction of the separation, he upbraided Jeroboam as a usurper, and his subjects as rebels, who took advantage of the youth and inexperience of Rehoboam.

Then contrasting the religious state of the two kingdoms, he drew a black picture of the impious innovations and gross idolatry introduced by Jeroboam, with his expulsion and impoverishment (ch. 11:14) of the Levites. He dwelt with reasonable pride on the pure and regular observance of the ancient institutions of Moses in his own dominion and concluded with this emphatic appeal: "O children of Israel, fight ye not against Jehovah, the God of your fathers, for ye shall not prosper."

13-17. But Jeroboam caused an ambushment to come about behind them—The oration of Abijah, however animating an effect it might have produced on his own troops, was unheeded by the party to whom it was addressed; for while he was wasting time in useless words, Jeroboam had ordered a detachment of his men to move quietly round the base of the hill, so that when Abijah

by Jeroboam. But surely at that time no man could be reputed young and tenderhearted, quite devoid of experience, who was above forty years of age.

16. *Abijah his son.* Concerning the many varieties in this king's name, see the note on 1 Kings xiv. 31.

CHAPTER 13

2. *His mother's name . . . was Michaiah.* See on chap. xi. 20.

3. *Abijah set the battle in array.* The numbers in this verse and in the seventeenth seem almost incredible. Abijah's army consisted of 400,000 effective men; that of Jeroboam consisted of 800,000; and the slain of Jeroboam's army were 500,000. Now it is very possible that there is a cipher too much in all these numbers, and that they should stand thus: Abijah's army, 40,000; Jeroboam's, 80,000; the slain, 50,000.

9. *A young bullock and seven rams.* He who could provide these for his own consecration was received into the order of this spurious and wicked priesthood. Some think he who could give to Jeroboam a young bullock and seven rams was thereby received into the priesthood, this being the price for which the priesthood was conferred. The former is most likely.

10. *The Lord is our God.* We have not abandoned the Lord, and we still serve Him according to His own law.

12. *God himself is with us.* You have golden calves; we have the living and omnipotent Jehovah. *With . . . trumpets to cry alarm against you.* This was appalling. When the priests sound their trumpets, it will be a proof that the vengeance of the Lord shall speedily descend upon you.

13. *But Jeroboam caused an ambushment.* While Abijah was thus employed in reproving them, Jeroboam divided his army privately, and sent a part to take Abijah in the rear; and this must have proved fatal to the Jews had not the Lord interposed.

MATTHEW HENRY

while he was treating, *laid his ambushment behind Judah*, against all the laws of arms.

II. Abijah and his people, who trusted in their God, came off conquerors, notwithstanding the disproportion of their strength and numbers.

1. They were brought into a great strait, put into a great fright, for *the battle was before and behind*. A good cause may for a season be involved in embarrassment and distress.

2. In this distress, when danger was on every side, which way should they look but upwards for deliverance? It is an unspeakable comfort that no enemy, no stratagem or ambushment, can cut off our communication with heaven; our way thitherward is always open. (1) *They cried unto the Lord, v.* 14. (2) They *relied on the God of their fathers*, and committed themselves to him, *v.* 18. The prayer of faith is the prevailing prayer, and this is that by which we overcome the world, *even our faith*, 1 John v. 4. (3) The *priests sounded the trumpets* to put life into their faith. (4) They shouted in confidence of victory: "The day is our own, for God is with us." To the cry of prayer they added the shout of faith, and so became more than conquerors.

3. Thus they obtained a complete victory: *As the men of Judah shouted* for joy in God's salvation, *God smote Jeroboam* and his army with such terror that they fled with the greatest precipitation imaginable, and the conquerors gave no quarter, but the battle was the Lord's, who would thus chastise the idolatry of Israel and own the house of David.

4. The consequence of this was that the children of Israel, though they were not brought back to the house of David, yet, for that time, were *brought under, v.* 18. Many cities were taken, and remained in the possession of the kings of Judah; as Bethel particularly, *v.* 19.

Lastly, The death both of the conquered and of the conqueror, not long after. 1. Jeroboam never looked up after this defeat, though he survived it two or three years. He could not recover *strength again, v.* 20. 2. Abijah waxed mighty upon it. But soon after his triumphs, death conquered the conqueror.

JAMIESON, FAUSSET, BROWN

stopped speaking, he and his followers found themselves surprised in the rear, while the main body of the Israelitish forces remained in front.

A panic might have ensued, had not the leaders "cried unto the Lord," and the priests "sounded with the trumpets"—the pledge of victory (Num. 10:9; 31:6). Reassured by the well-known signal, the men of Judah responded with a war shout, which, echoed by the whole army, was followed by an impetuous rush against the foe. The shock was resistless. The ranks of the Israelites were broken, for "God smote Jeroboam and all Israel." They took to flight, and the merciless slaughter that ensued can be accounted for only by tracing it to the rancorous passions enkindled by a civil war. **19. Abijah pursued after Jeroboam**—This sanguinary action widened the breach between the people of the two kingdoms. Abijah abandoned his original design of attempting the subjugation of the ten tribes, contenting himself with the recovery of a few border towns, which, though lying within Judah or Benjamin, had been alienated to the new or northern kingdom. Among these was Beth-el, which, with its sacred associations, he might be strongly desirous to wrest from profanation. **20. Neither did Jeroboam recover strength again in the days of Abijah**—The disastrous action at Zemaraim, which caused the loss of the flower and chivalry of his army, broke his spirits and crippled his power. **the Lord struck him, and he died**—i.e., Jeroboam. He lived, indeed, two years after the death of Abijah (I Kings 14:20; 15:9). But he had been threatened with great calamities upon himself and his house, and it is apparently to the execution of these threatenings, which issued in his death, that an anticipatory reference is here made.

ADAM CLARKE

20. *The Lord struck him, and he died.* Who died? Abijah or Jeroboam? Some think it was Jeroboam; some, that it was Abijah. Both rabbins and Christians are divided on this point, nor is it yet settled. The prevailing opinion is that Jeroboam is meant, who was struck then with that disease of which he died about two years after, for he did not die till two years after Abijah; see 1 Kings xiv. 20; xv. 9.

21. *Married fourteen wives.* Probably he made alliances with the neighboring powers, by taking their daughters to him for wives.

22. *Written in the story. Bemidrash*, "in the commentary"; this, as far as I recollect, is the first place where a *midrash* or "commentary" is mentioned. *His ways, and his sayings.* The commentary *of the prophet Iddo* is lost. What his *sayings* were we cannot tell; but from the specimen in this chapter he appears to have been a very able speaker, and one who knew well how to make the best use of his argument.

MATTHEW HENRY — CHAPTER 14

Verses 1–8

I. Asa's general character (*v.* 2): He did *that which was good and right in the eyes of the Lord his God.* 1. He aimed at pleasing God, studied to approve himself to him. 2. He saw God's eye always upon him, and that helped much to keep him to what was good and right.

II. A blessed work of reformation which he set on foot immediately upon his accession to the crown. 1. He removed and abolished idolatry. Since Solomon admitted idolatry, in the latter end of his reign, nothing had been done to suppress it. Strange gods were worshipped and had their altars, images, and groves; and the temple service, though kept up by the priests (*ch.* xiii. 10), was neglected by many of the people. Asa, as soon as he had power in his hands, made it his business to destroy all those idolatrous altars and images (*v.* 3, 5). He hoped by destroying the idols to reform the idolaters, which he aimed at, rather than to ruin them. 2. He revived and established the pure worship of God; and, since the priests did their part in attending God's altars, he obliged the people to do theirs (*v.* 4): *He commanded Judah to seek the Lord God of their fathers*, and not the gods of the heathen, and *to do the law and the commandments*. In doing this, *the land was quiet before him, v.* 5.

III. The tranquillity of his kingdom, after constant alarms of war during the last two reigns: *In his days the land was quiet ten years* (*v.* 1), no war with the kingdom of Israel. Abijah's victory laid a foundation for Asa's peace, which was the reward of his piety and reformation. Though Abijah had little religion himself, he was instrumental to prepare the way for one that had much.

IV. The improvement he made of that tranquillity: *The land had rest, for the Lord had given him rest.* 1. Asa, takes notice of the rest they had as the gift of God, and as the reward of the reformation begun: *Because we have sought the Lord our God, he has given us rest.* We find by experience that it is good to *seek the Lord*; it *gives us rest.* 2. He consults with his people, by their representatives, how to make a good use of the peace they enjoyed, and concludes with them, (1) That they must not be idle, but busy. In the years when he had no war he said, "Let us build; still let us be doing." When the *churches had rest* they were *built up*, Acts ix. 31. When the sword is sheathed take up the trowel. (2) In times of peace we must be getting ready for trouble, expect it and lay

JAMIESON, FAUSSET, BROWN — CHAPTER 14

Vss. 1-5. ASA DESTROYS IDOLATRY. **2. Asa did that which was good and right**—(cf. I Kings 15:14). Still his character and life were not free from faults (ch. 16:7, 10, 12).

3. brake down the images—of Baal (see on ch. 34:4; Lev. 26:30). **cut down the groves**—rather, Asherim. **5. he took away . . . the high places**—i.e., those devoted to idolatrous rites. **took away out of all the cities of Judah the high places and the images**—All public objects and relics of idolatry in Jerusalem and other cities through his kingdom were destroyed; but those high places where God was worshipped under the figure of an ox, as at Beth-el, were allowed to remain (I Kings 15:14); so far the reformation was incomplete.

1. In his days the land was quiet ten years—This long interval of peace was the continued effect of the great battle of Zemaraim (cf. I Kings 15:11-14).

ADAM CLARKE — CHAPTER 14

2. *Did that which was good.* He attended to what the law required relative to the worship of God. He was no idolater, though, morally speaking, he was not exempt from faults, 1 Kings xv. 14.

He suppressed idolatry universally, and encouraged the people to worship the true God; see vv. 3-5.

1. *The land was quiet ten years.* Calmet thinks these years should be counted from the fifth to the fifteenth of Asa's reign.

MATTHEW HENRY

up in store for it. [1] He fortified his principal cities with *walls, towers, gates, and bars, v.* 7. He speaks as if he expected that trouble would arise, when it would be too late to fortify, and when they would wish they had done it. *So they built and prospered.* [2] He had a good army ready to bring into the field (*v.* 8). Judah and Benjamin were mustered severally; and Benjamin had almost as many soldiers as Judah. These two tribes were differently armed, both offensively and defensively. The men of Judah guarded themselves with targets, the men of Benjamin with shields, the former of which were much larger than the latter, 1 Kings x. 16, 17. The men of Judah fought with spears; the men of Benjamin drew bows, to reach the enemy at a distance.

Verses 9–15

I. Disturbance given to the peace of Asa's kingdom by a formidable army of Ethiopians that invaded them, *v.* 9, 10.

II. The application Asa made to God on occasion of the threatening cloud which now hung over his head, *v.* 11. He that sought God in the day of his prosperity could with holy boldness cry to God in the day of his trouble, and call him *his God.* His prayer is short. but has much in it. 1. He gives to God the glory of his infinite power and sovereignty: *It is nothing with thee to help* and save by many or few. God works in his own strength, not in the strength of instruments. "We do not say, Lord, take our part, for we have a good army for thee to work by; but, take our part, for without thee we have no power." 2. He takes hold of their covenant-relation to God as theirs. *O Lord our God!* 3. He pleads their dependence upon God. He was well prepared for it, yet trusted not to his preparations; but, "Lord, *we rest on thee, and in thy name we go against this multitude,* by warrant from thee, aiming at thy glory, and trusting to thy strength." 4. He interests God in their cause: "*Let not man*" (*mortal man,* so the word is) "*prevail against thee.*" The enemy is a mortal man; make it to appear what an unequal match he is for an immortal God.

III. The glorious victory God gave him over his enemies. 1. God defeated the enemy, and put their forces into disorder (*v.* 12): *The Lord smote the Ethiopians* with terror so that they fled, and knew neither why nor whither. 2. Asa and his soldiers took the advantage God gave them against the enemy. (1) They destroyed them. (2) They took the plunder of their camp. (3) They *smote the cities* that were in league with them, to which they fled for shelter (*v.* 14). (4) They fetched away the cattle out of the enemy's country, in vast numbers, *v.* 15.

JAMIESON, FAUSSET, BROWN

6-8. HAVING PEACE, HE STRENGTHENS HIS KINGDOM WITH FORTS AND ARMIES. **6. he built fenced cities in Judah**—(See on I Kings 15:22). **7. while the land is yet before us**—i.e., while we have free and undisputed progress everywhere; no foe is near; but, as this happy time of peace may not last always and the kingdom is but small and weak, let us prepare suitable defenses in case of need. He had also an army of 580,000 men. Judah furnished the heavily armed soldiers, and Benjamin the archers. This large number does not mean a body of professional soldiers but all capable of bearing arms and liable to be called into service.

9-15. HE OVERCOMES ZERAH, AND SPOILS THE ETHIOPIANS. **9. there came out against them Zerah the Ethiopian**—This could not have been from Ethiopia south of the cataracts of the Nile, for in the reign of Osorkon I., successor of Shishak, no foreign army would have been allowed a free passage through Egypt. Zerah must, therefore, have been chief of the Cushites, or Ethiopians of Arabia, as they were evidently a nomad horde who had a settlement of tents and cattle in the neighborhood of Gerar. **a thousand thousand, and three hundred chariots**—"Twenty camels employed to carry couriers upon them might have procured that number of men to meet in a short time. As Zerah was the aggressor, he had time to choose when he would summon these men and attack the enemy. Every one of these Cushite shepherds, carrying with them their own provisions of flour and water, as is their invariable custom, might have fought with Asa without eating a loaf of Zerah's bread or drinking a pint of his water" [BRUCE'S TRAVELS]. **10. Asa went out against him, and they set the battle in array . . . at Mareshah**—one of the towns which Rehoboam fortified (ch. 11:8), near a great southern pass in the low country of Judah (Josh. 15:44). The engagement between the armies took place in a plain near the town, called "the valley of Zephathah," supposed to be the broad way coming down Beit Jibrin towards Tell Es-Safren [ROBINSON]. **11-13. Asa cried unto the Lord his God**—Strong in the confidence that the power of God was able to give the victory equally with few as with many, the pious king marched with a comparatively small force to encounter the formidable host of marauders at his southern frontier. Committing his cause to God, **he engaged in the conflict**—completely routed the enemy, and succeeded in obtaining, as the reward of his victory, a rich booty in treasure and cattle from the tents of this pastoral horde.

ADAM CLARKE

6. *Fenced cities.* To preserve his territories from invasion, and strengthen the frontiers of his kingdom, see v. 7.

8. *Targets and spears.* Probably targets with the dagger in the center, and javelins for distant fight. *Bare shields and drew bows.* They were not only archers, but had shield and sword for close fight.

9. *Zerah the Ethiopian.* Probably of that Ethiopia which lay on the south of Egypt, near to Libya, and therefore the Libyans are joined with them, chap. xvi. 8. *A thousand thousand.* If this people had come from any great distance, they could not have had forage for such an immense army.

11. *Whether with many.* The same sentiment as that uttered by Jonathan, 1 Sam. xiv. 6, when he attacked the garrison of the Philistines.

14. *There was . . . much spoil in them.* These cities being on the rear of this vast army, they had laid up much forage in them, and to get this the Jews overthrew the whole.

MATTHEW HENRY — CHAPTER 15

Verses 1–7

Here was a prophet sent to Asa and his army, when they returned victorious from the war with the Ethiopians, not to congratulate them on their success, but to quicken them to their duty; this is the proper business of God's ministers. The *Spirit of God came* upon the prophet (*v.* 1), both to instruct him what he should say and to enable him to say it with clearness and boldness.

I. He told them plainly upon what terms they stood with God. Let them not think that, having obtained this victory, all was their own for ever. Let them do well, and it will be well with them, otherwise not. 1. *The Lord is with you while you are with him.* 2. *If you seek him, he will be found of you.* 3. If you forsake him and his ordinances, he is not tied to you, but will certainly forsake you.

II. He set before them the consequence of forsaking God and his ordinances, and that there was no way of having grievances redressed, but by repenting, and returning unto God. When Israel forsook their duty they were over-run with a deluge of atheism, impiety, irreligion, and all irregularity (*v.* 3), and were continually embarrassed with wars, foreign and domestic, *v.* 5, 6. But when their troubles drove them to God they found it not in vain to seek him, *v.* 4. But the question is, What time does this refer to? 1. Some think it looks as far back as the days of the Judges. These were sad times, when they were frequently oppressed by one enemy or other and grievously harassed by Moabites, Midianites, Ammonites, and other nations. When, in their perplexity, they turned to God by repentance, prayer, and reformation, he raised up deliverers for them. 2. Others think it describes the state of the ten tribes (who were now properly called *Israel*) in the days of Asa. In those times there was no peace, *v.* 5. Their war with Judah gave them frequent alarms; so did

JAMIESON, FAUSSET, BROWN — CHAPTER 15

VSS. 1-15. JUDAH MAKES A SOLEMN COVENANT WITH GOD. **1. Azariah the son of Oded**—This prophet, who is mentioned nowhere else, appears at this stage of the sacred story in the discharge of an interesting mission. He went to meet Asa, as he was returning from his victorious pursuit of the Ethiopians, and the congratulatory address here recorded was publicly made to the king in presence of his army. **2. The Lord is with you, while ye be with him**—You have had, in your recent signal success, a remarkable proof that God's blessing is upon you; your victory has been the reward of your faith and piety. If you steadfastly adhere to the cause of God, you may expect a continuance of His favor; but if you abandon it, you will soon reap the bitter fruits of apostasy. **3-6. Now for a long season Israel hath been without the true God,** etc.—Some think that Azariah was referring to the sad and disastrous condition to which superstition and idolatry had brought the neighboring kingdom of Israel. His words should rather be taken in a wider sense, for it seems manifest that the prophet had his eye upon many periods in the national history, when the people were in the state described—a state of spiritual destitution and ignorance—and exhibited its natural result as widespread anarchy, mutual dissension among the tribes, and general suffering (Judg. 9:23; 12:4; 20:21; II Chron. 13:17). These calamities God permitted to befall them as the punishment of their apostasy. Azariah's object in these remarks was to establish the truth of his counsel (vs. 2), threatening, in case of neglecting it by describing the uniform course of the divine procedure towards Israel, as shown in all periods of their history. Then after this appeal to national experience, he concluded with an earnest exhortation to the king to prosecute the work of reformation so

ADAM CLARKE — CHAPTER 15

1. *Azariah the son of Obed.* We know nothing of this prophet but what is related of him here.

2. *The Lord is with you, while ye be with him.* This the settled and eternal purpose of God; to them who seek Him, He will ever be found propitious, and them alone will He abandon who forsake Him.

5. *But great vexations.* Does not our Lord allude to this and the following verse in Matt. xxiv. 6-7, 9, 13?

MATTHEW HENRY

the late insurrection of Baasha. They provoked God with all iniquity, and then he *vexed them with all adversity*; yet, *when they turned to God*, he was entreated for them. 3. Others think the whole passage may be read in the future tense: Hereafter *Israel will be without the true God and a teaching priest*, and they will be destroyed by one judgment after another till they *return to God* and *seek him*. See Hos. iii. 4.

III. Upon this he grounded his exhortation to prosecute the work of reformation with vigour (*v.* 7): *Be strong, for your work shall be rewarded.*

Verses 8–19

The good effect the foregoing sermon had upon Asa.

I. He grew more bold for God than he had been. Now he took courage. He saw how necessary a further reformation was, and what assurance he had of God's presence with him in it. Now he ventured to destroy all the abominable idols. He also *renewed the altar of the Lord.*

II. He extended his influence further than before, *v.* 9. He summoned a solemn assembly, and brought the strangers to it, who had come over to him from the ten tribes. Their coming was a great encouragement to him; for the reason of their coming was because *they saw that the Lord his God was with him.* The invitation he gave them to the general assembly was a great encouragement to them. This meeting was held in the third month, probably at the feast of Pentecost, which was in that month.

III. He and his people offered sacrifices to God, as his share of the spoil they had got, *v.* 11. These sacrifices were intended by way of thanksgiving for the favours they had received, and supplication for further favours. Prayers and praises are now our spiritual sacrifices. *He brought into the house of God all the dedicated things*, *v.* 18. It is honesty to render to God the things that are his.

IV. *They entered into covenant with God*, repenting that they had violated their engagements to him and resolving to do better for the future. It is proper for penitents, for converts, to renew their covenants. 1. What was this covenant. It would help to increase their sense of the obligation, to arm them against temptations, and would be a testimony. And, by joining all together in this covenant, they strengthened the hands one of another. Two things they engaged themselves to:—(1) That they would diligently seek God themselves, seek his precepts, seek his favour. What is religion but seeking God, enquiring after him, applying to him, upon all occasions? (2) That they would, to the utmost of their power, oblige others to seek him, *v.* 13. They agreed that *whosoever would not seek the Lord God of Israel* (that is, an obstinate idolater or an obstinate atheist) he should be put to death.

2. In what manner they made this covenant. (1) With great cheerfulness, and all possible expressions of joy: *They swore unto the Lord* with a loud voice, and they all rejoiced at the oath, *v.* 14, 15. Every honest Israelite was pleased with his own engagements to God, and they were all pleased with one another's. They rejoiced in it as a hopeful expedient to prevent their apostasy from God and a happy indication of God's presence with them. It is an honour and happiness to be in bonds to God. (2) They did it with great sincerity, zeal, and resolution: *They swore to God with all their hearts*, and *sought him with their whole desire*. If God has the heart, we have the joy.

V. The effect of this their solemn covenanting with God. 1. God did well for them: *He* was *found of them, and gave them rest round about* (*v.* 15), so that there was no war for a long time after (*v.* 19), though there were constant bickerings between Judah and Israel upon the frontiers, 1 Kings xv. 16. 2. They did, on the whole, well for him. They carried on the reformation so far that Maachah the queen-mother was deposed for idolatry and her idol destroyed, *v.* 16. Asa knows he must honour God more than his grandmother, and dares not leave an idol in an apartment of his palace while he is destroying idols in the cities of his kingdom. We may suppose Maachah was convinced of her sin and therefore was not put to death. But because she had been an idolater Asa thought fit to divest her of the dignity and authority she had. But the reformation was not complete; the high places were not all taken away, though many of them were, *ch.* xiv. 3, 5. There may be defects in some particular duties where yet the heart, in the main, is upright with God. Sincerity is something less than sinless perfection.

JAMIESON, FAUSSET, BROWN

well begun. **7. Be ye strong**—Great resolution and indomitable energy would be required to persevere in the face of the opposition your reforming measures will encounter. **your work shall be rewarded**—What you do in the cause and for the glory of God will assuredly be followed by the happiest results both to yourself and your subjects. **8. when Asa heard . . . the prophecy of Oded the prophet**—The insertion of these words, "of Oded the prophet," is generally regarded as a corruption of the text. "The sole remedy is to erase them. They are, probably, the remains of a note, which crept in from the margin into the text" [BERTHEAU]. **he took courage**—Animated by the seasonable and pious address of Azariah, Asa became a more zealous reformer than ever, employing all his royal authority and influence to extirpate every vestige of idolatry from the land. **and out of the cities which he had taken from Mount Ephraim**—He may have acquired cities of Ephraim, the conquest of which is not recorded (ch. 17:2); but it has been commonly supposed that the reference is to cities which his father Abijah had taken in that quarter (ch. 13:19). **renewed the altar of the Lord . . . before the porch**—i.e., the altar of burnt offering. As this was done on or about the fifteenth year of the reign of this pious king, the renewal must have consisted in some splendid repairs or embellishments, which made it look like a new dedication, or in a reconstruction of a temporary altar, like that of Solomon (ch. 7:7), for extraordinary sacrifices to be offered on an approaching occasion. **9-15. he gathered all Judah and Benjamin**—Not satisfied with these minor measures of purification and improvement, Asa meditated a grand scheme which was to pledge his whole kingdom to complete the work of reformation, and with this in view he waited for a general assembly of the people. **and the strangers with them out of Ephraim and Manasseh**—The population of Asa's kingdom had been vastly increased by the continued influx of strangers, who, prompted by motives either of interest or of piety, sought in his dominions that security and freedom which they could not enjoy amid the complicated troubles which distracted Israel. **and out of Simeon**—Although a portion of that tribe, located within the territory of Judah, were already subjects of the southern kingdom, the general body of the Simeonites had joined in forming the northern kingdom of Israel. But many of them now returned of their own accord. **10. the third month**—when was held the feast of pentecost. On this occasion, it was celebrated at Jerusalem by an extraordinary sacrifice of 700 oxen and 7000 sheep, the spoil of the Ethiopians being offered.

The assembled worshippers entered with great and holy enthusiasm into a national covenant "to seek the Lord God . . . with all their heart and with all their soul"; and, at the same time, to execute with rigor the laws which made idolatry punishable with death (Deut. 17:2-5; Heb. 10:28). The people testified unbounded satisfaction with this important religious movement, and its moral influence was seen in the promotion of piety, order, and tranquillity throughout the land. **18. the things which his father had dedicated**—probably part of the booty obtained by his signal victory over Jeroboam, but which, though dedicated, had hitherto been unrepresented. **and that he himself had dedicated**—of the booty taken from the Ethiopians. Both of these were now deposited in the temple as votive offerings to Him whose right hand and holy arm had given them the victory.

ADAM CLARKE

8. *Renewed the altar.* Dedicated it afresh, or perhaps enlarged it, that more sacrifices might be offered on it than ever before; for it cannot be supposed that this altar had no victims offered on it till the fifteenth year of the reign of Asa, who had previously been so zealous in restoring the divine worship.

9. *And the strangers.* Many out of the different tribes, particularly out of Simeon, Ephraim, and Manasseh, having reflected that the divine blessing was promised to the house of David, and finding the government of Jeroboam founded in idolatry, would naturally, through a spirit of piety, leave their own country and go where they might enjoy the worship of the true God.

10. *The third month.* At the Feast of Pentecost, which was held on the third month.

11. *The spoil which they had brought.* The spoil which they had taken from Zerah and his auxiliaries, chap. xiv. 14-15.

12. *They entered into a covenant.* The covenant consisted of two parts: (1) We will seek the God of our fathers with all our hearts, and with all our souls. (2) Whosoever, great or small, man or woman, will not worship the true God, and serve Him alone, shall be put to death. Thus no toleration was given to idolatry, so that it must be rooted out; and that this covenant might be properly binding, they confirmed it with an oath; and God accepted them and their services.

16. *Concerning Maachah.* See the matter fully explained in the note on 1 Kings xv. 13.

17. *The high places were not taken away.* He had totally suppressed or destroyed the idolatry; but some of the places, buildings, or altars, he permitted to remain.

18. *The things that his father had dedicated.* As it was a custom to dedicate a part of the spoils taken from an enemy to the service and honor of God, it is natural to suppose that Abijah, having so signally overthrown Jeroboam (chap. xiii. 15-19), had dedicated a part of the spoils to the Lord; but they had not been brought into the Temple till this time. *Silver, and gold, and vessels.* The word *kelim,* which we translate *vessels,* signifies "instruments, utensils, ornaments."

19. *The five and thirtieth year of the reign of Asa.* Archbishop Ussher thinks that this should be counted from the separation of the kingdom, and that this fell on the fifteenth year of Asa's reign. Probably we should read here "the five and twentieth year." See the margin, and the note on 1 Kings xv. 16.

MATTHEW HENRY

CHAPTER 16

Verses 1–6

This passage we had before (1 Kings xv. 17, &c.) and Asa was in several ways faulty in it. 1. He did not do well to make a league with Benhadad, a heathen king, *v.* 3. Had he relied more upon his covenant, and his father's, with God, he would not have boasted so much of his league, and his fathers, with the royal family of Syria. 2. If he had had a due regard to the honour of Israel in general, he would have found some other expedient to give Baasha a diversion than by calling in a foreign force, and inviting into the country a common enemy, who, in process of time, might be a plague to Judah too. 3. It was doubtless a sin in Benhadad to break his league with Baasha upon no provocation, but merely through the influence of a bribe; and, if so, certainly it was a sin in Asa to move him to it, especially to hire him to do it. 4. To take silver and gold out of the house of the Lord for this purpose was a great aggravation of the sin. 5. Perhaps Asa intended not that they should carry the matter so far. However the project succeeded. Benhadad gave Baasha a powerful diversion, obliged him to leave off building Ramah and betake himself to the defence of his own country northward, which gave Asa an opportunity, not only to demolish his fortifications, but to sieze the materials and convert them to his own use.

Verses 7–14

I. A plain and faithful reproof given to Asa by a prophet of the Lord, for making this league with Baasha. The reprover was Hanani the seer, the father of Jehu, another prophet, whom we read of 1 Kings xvi. 1; 2 Chron. xix. 2. That which the prophet here charges upon him as the greatest fault is his *relying on the king of Syria and not on the Lord his God*, *v.* 7. He plainly tells the king that herein he had done foolishly, *v.* 9. It is a foolish thing to lean on a broken reed, when we have the rock of ages to rely upon. To convince him of his folly he shows him,

1. That he acted against his experience, *v.* 8. He, of all men, had no reason to distrust God, who had found him such a present powerful helper. "*What!*" said the prophet, "*Were not the Ethiopians and the Lubim a huge host*, enough to swallow up a kingdom? And yet, *because thou didst rely on the Lord, he delivered them into thy hand*; and was not he sufficient to help thee against Baasha?" But see how deceitful our hearts are! We trust in God when we have nothing else to trust to, but, when we have other things to stay on, we are apt to stay too much on them.

2. That he acted against his knowledge of God and his providence, *v.* 9. Asa could not trust God and therefore made court to Benhadad.

3. That he acted against his interest. (1) He had lost an opportunity of checking the growing greatness of the king of Syria (v. 7): His *host has escaped out of thy hand*, which otherwise would have joined with Baasha's and fallen with it. (2) He had incurred God's displeasure and henceforth must expect no peace, but the constant alarms of war, *v.* 9.

II. Asa's displeasure at this reproof. Though it came from God by one that was known to be his messenger, yet he was wroth with the seer for telling him of his folly; *he was in a rage with him*, *v.* 10. 1. In his rage he committed the prophet to the jail, *put him in a prison-house*, as a malefactor, *in the stocks* (so some read it), or into *little-ease*. 2. Having proceeded thus far, *he oppressed some of the people*, probably such as owned the prophet in his sufferings, or were known to be his particular friends.

III. His sickness. Two years before he died *he was diseased in his feet* (*v.* 12), afflicted with the gout in a high degree. He had put the prophet in the stocks, and now God put him in the stocks; so his punishment answered his sin. His making use of physicians was his duty; but trusting to them, and expecting that from them which was to be had from God only, were his sin and folly.

IV. His death and burial. His funeral had something of extraordinary solemnity in it, *v.* 14. They made a very magnificent *burying for him*. This funeral pomp was an expression of the great respect his people retained for him, notwithstanding the failings and infirmities of his latter days. The eminent piety and usefulness of good men ought to be remembered to their praise, though they have had their blemishes. Let their faults be buried in their graves, while their services are remembered over their graves.

JAMIESON, FAUSSET, BROWN

CHAPTER 16

Vss. 1-14. Asa, by a League with the Syrians, Diverts Baasha from Building Ramah. **1-6. In the six and thirtieth year of the reign of Asa, Baasha . . . came up**—Baasha had died several years before this date (I Kings 15:33), and the best biblical critics are agreed in considering this date to be calculated from the separation of the kingdoms, and coincident with the sixteenth year of Asa's reign. This mode of reckoning was, in all likelihood, generally followed in the book of the kings of Judah and Israel, the public annals of the time (vs. 11), the source from which the inspired historian drew his account. **Baasha . . . built Ramah**—i.e., fortified it. The blessing of God which manifestly rested at this time on the kingdom of Judah, the signal victory of Asa, the freedom and purity of religious worship, and the fame of the late national covenant, were regarded with great interest throughout Israel, and attracted a constantly increasing number of emigrants to Judah. Baasha, alarmed at this movement, determined to stem the tide; and as the high road to and from Jerusalem passed by Ramah, he made that frontier town, about six miles north of Asa's capital, a military station, where the vigilance of his sentinels would effectually prevent all passage across the boundary of the kingdom (see on I Kings 15:16-22; also Jer. 41:9). **4. Ben-hadad . . . sent the captains of his armies . . . and they smote . . . Abel-maim**—"The meadow of waters," supposed to have been situated on the marshy plain near the uppermost lake of the Jordan. The other two towns were also in the northern district of Palestine. These unexpected hostilities of his Syrian ally interrupted Baasha's fortifications at Ramah, and his death, happening soon after, prevented his resuming them. **7-10. Hanani the seer came to Asa . . . and said**—His object was to show the king his error in forming his recent league with Ben-hadad. The prophet represented the appropriation of the temple treasures to purchase the services of the Syrian mercenaries, as indicating a distrust in God most blameable with the king's experience. He added, that in consequence of this want of faith, Asa had lost the opportunity of gaining a victory over the united forces of Baasha and Benhadad, more splendid than that obtained over the Ethiopians. Such a victory, by destroying their armies, would have deprived them of all power to molest him in the future; whereas by his foolish and worldly policy, so unworthy of God's vicegerent, to misapply the temple treasures and corrupt the fidelity of an ally of the king of Israel, he had tempted the cupidity of the one, and increased the hostility of the other, and rendered himself liable to renewed troubles (I Kings 15:32). This rebuke was pungent and, from its truth and justness, ought to have penetrated and afflicted the heart of such a man as Asa. But his pride was offended at the freedom taken by the honest reprover of royalty, and in a burst of passionate resentment, he ordered Hanani to be thrown into prison. **10. Asa oppressed some of the people the same time**—The form or degree of this oppression is not recorded. The cause of his oppressing them was probably due to the same offense as that of Hanani—a strong expression of their dissatisfaction with his conduct in leaguing with Ben-hadad, or it may have been his maltreatment of the Lord's servant. **12. Asa . . . was diseased in his feet**—probably the gout. **his disease was exceeding great**—better, "moved upwards" in his body, which proves the violent and dangerous type of the malady. **yet in his disease he sought not to the Lord, but to the physicians**—most probably Egyptian physicians, who were anciently in high repute at foreign courts, and who pretended to expel diseases by charms, incantations, and mystic arts. Asa's fault consisted in his trusting to such physicians, while he neglected to supplicate the aid and blessing of God. The best and holiest men have been betrayed for a time into sins, but through repentance have risen again; and as Asa is pronounced a good man (ch. 15:17), it may be presumed that he also was restored to a better state of mind. **14. they buried him in his own sepulchre**—The tombs in the neighborhood of Jerusalem were excavated in the side of a rock. One cave contained several tombs or sepulchers. **laid him in the bed . . . filled with sweet odours and divers kinds of spices**—It is evident that a sumptuous public funeral was given him as a tribute of respect and gratitude for his pious character and patriotic government. But whether "the bed" means a state couch on which he lay exposed to public view, the odoriferous perfumes being designed to neutralize the offensive smell of the corpse, or whether it refers to an embalmment, in which aromatic spices were

ADAM CLARKE

CHAPTER 16

1. *The six and thirtieth year.* After the division of the kingdoms of Israel and Judah, according to Ussher. This opinion is followed in our margin; see the note on 1 Kings xv. 16, where this subject is further considered. Concerning Baasha's building of Ramah, see the note on 1 Kings xv. 17.

3. *There is a league.* Let there be a treaty, offensive and defensive, between me and thee: see on 1 Kings xv. 22.

6. *Took all Judah.* See on 1 Kings xv. 22.

7. *Escaped out of thine hand.* It is difficult to know what is here intended. Perhaps the divine providence had intended to give Asa a grand victory over the Syrians, who had always been the inveterate enemies of the Jews; but by this unnecessary and very improper alliance between Asa and Ben-hadad, this purpose of the divine providence was prevented, and thus the Syrians escaped out of his hands.

9. *Therefore . . . thou shalt have wars.* And so he had with Israel during the rest of his reign, 1 Kings xv. 32.

10. *Asa was wroth with the seer.* Instead of humbling himself, and deprecating the displeasure of the Lord, he persecuted His messenger; and having thus laid his impious hands upon the prophet, he appears to have got his heart hardened through the deceitfulness of sin. Then he began to oppress the people, either by unjust imprisonments or by excessive taxations.

12. *Diseased in his feet.* He had a strong and long fit of the gout; this is most likely.

14. *And laid him in the bed.* It is very likely that the body of Asa was burnt; that the *bed* spoken of here was a funeral pyre, on which much spices and odoriferous woods had been placed; and then they set fire to the whole and consumed the body with the aromatics. Some think the body was not burned, but the aromatics only, in honor of the king.

MATTHEW HENRY | JAMIESON, FAUSSET, BROWN | ADAM CLARKE

always used in great profusion, it is impossible to say. **they made a very great burning for him**—according to some, for consuming the spices. According to others, it was a magnificent pile for the cremation of the corpse—a usage which was at that time, and long after, prevalent among the Hebrews, and the omission of which in the case of royal personages was reckoned a great indignity (ch. 21: 19; I Sam. 31:12; Jer. 34:5; Amos 6:10).

MATTHEW HENRY

CHAPTER 17

Verses 1–9

Concerning Jehoshaphat,

I. What a wise man he was. As soon as he came to the crown he *strengthened himself against Israel, v.* 1. Ahab, an active warlike prince, had been three years upon the throne of Israel. The first thing Jehoshaphat had to do was to check the growing greatness of the king of Israel, which he did so effectually, and without bloodshed, that Ahab soon courted his alliance. Jehoshaphat strengthened himself not to act offensively against Israel or invade them, but only to maintain his own, which he did by fortifying the cities that were on his frontiers, and putting garrisons, stronger than had been, in the cities of Ephraim.

II. What a good man he was. 1. He *walked in the ways of his father David.* In the characters of the kings, David's ways are often made the standard, as 1 Kings xv. 3, 11; 2 Kings xiv. 3; xvi. 2; xviii. 3. Jehoshaphat followed David as far as he followed God and no further. The words here will admit another reading; they run thus: *He walked in the ways of David his father* (*Hareshonim*), *those first ways*, or those *ancient ways.* He proposed to himself, for his example, the primitive times of the royal family, those purest times, before the corruptions of the late reigns came in. It is good to be cautious in following the best men, lest we step aside after them. 2. He *sought not to Baalim, but sought to the Lord God of his father, v.* 3, 4. 3. He *walked in God's commandments*, not only worshipped the true God, but worshipped him according to his own institution, *and not after the doings of Israel, v.* 4. 4. *His heart was lifted up in the ways of the Lord* (*v.* 6), or *he lifted up his heart.* He was lively and affectionate in his religion, *fervent in spirit, serving the Lord*, cheerful and pleasant in it; he went on in his work with alacrity, as Jacob, who, after his vision of God at Bethel, *lifted up his feet*, Gen. xxix. 1, *margin.*

III. What a useful man he was, not only a good man, but a good king. He not only was good himself, but did good. 1. He took away the teachers of lies, so images are called (Hab. ii. 18), the *high places* and *the groves, v.* 6. It is meant of those in which idols were worshipped. 2. He sent forth teachers of truth. When he enquired into the state of religion in his kingdom he found his people generally very ignorant: they *knew not that they did evil.* Jehoshaphat resolves to begin his work at the right end, will not lead them blindfold, no, not into a reformation, but endeavours to have them well taught, knowing that that was the way to have them well cured. In this good work he employed, (1) His princes. He ordered them, in the administration of justice, not only to correct the people when they did ill, but to teach them how to do better, and to give a reason for what they did. (2) The *Levites* and *priests* went *with the princes*, and *taught in Judah, having the book of the law with them, v.* 8, 9. They were teachers by office, Deut. xxxiii. 10.

What an abundance of good may be done when Moses and Aaron thus go hand in hand in the doing of it, when princes with their power, and priests and Levites with their scripture learning, agree to teach the people the good knowledge of God and their duty! These itinerant judges and itinerant preachers together were instrumental to diffuse a blessed light throughout the cities of Judah. *They had the book of the law of the Lord with them* for the conviction of the people, that they might see that they had a divine warrant for what they said and delivered to them that only which they received from the Lord.

IV. What a happy man he was. *The Lord was with him* (*v.* 3); *the word of the Lord was his helper* (so the Chaldee paraphrase); *the Lord established the kingdom in his hand, v.* 5. *All Judah brought him presents*, in acknowledgment of his kindness in sending preachers among them. The more there is of true religion among a people the more there will be of conscientious loyalty. Riches and honour in abundance prove to many a hindrance, an occasion of pride, but they had a quite contrary effect upon Jehoshaphat; his abundance was oil to the wheels of his obedience, and the more he had of the wealth of this world the more was his heart *lifted up in the ways of the Lord.*

JAMIESON, FAUSSET, BROWN

CHAPTER 17

Vss. 1-6. Jehoshaphat Reigns Well and Prospers. **1. Jehoshaphat . . . strengthened himself against Israel**—The temper and proceedings of the kings of Israel rendered it necessary for him to prepare vigorous measures of defense on the northern frontier of his kingdom. These consisted in filling all the fortresses with their full complement of troops and establishing military stations in various parts of the country, as well as in the cities of Mount Ephraim, which belonged to Jehoshaphat (ch. 15:8).

3-5. he walked in the first ways of his father David—He imitated the piety of his great ancestor in the early part of his reign before he made those unhappy lapses which dishonored his character.

and sought not unto Baalim—a term used for idols generally in contradistinction to the Lord God of his father. **and not after the doings of Israel**—He observed with scrupulous fidelity, and employed his royal influence to support the divine institutions as enacted by Moses, abhorring that spurious and unlawful calf-worship that now formed the established religion in Israel. Being thus far removed, alike from gross idolatry and Israelitish apostasy, and adhering zealously to the requirements of the divine law, the blessing of God rested on his government. Ruling in the fear of God, and for the good of his subjects, "the Lord established the kingdom in his hand." **6. his heart was lifted up in the ways of the Lord**—Full of faith and piety, he possessed zeal and courage to undertake the reformation of manners, to suppress all the works and objects of idolatry (see on ch. 20:33), and he held out public encouragement to the pure worship of God.

7-11. He Sends Levites to Teach in Judah. **7-11. Also in the third year of his reign he sent to his princes, . . . to teach in the cities of Judah**—The ordinary work of teaching devolved on the priests. But extraordinary commissioners were appointed, probably to ascertain whether the work had been done or neglected. This deputation of five princes, assisted by two priests and nine Levites, was to make a circuit of the towns in Judah. It is the first practical measure we read of as being adopted by any of the kings for the religious instruction of the people. Time and unbroken opportunities were afforded for carrying out fully this excellent plan of home education, for the kingdom enjoyed internal tranquillity as well as freedom for foreign wars. It is conformable to the pious style of the sacred historian to trace this profound peace to the "fear of the Lord having fallen on all kingdoms of the lands that were round about Judah." **the book of the law**—i.e., either the whole Pentateuch or only the book of Deuteronomy, which contains an abridgment of it.

all Judah brought . . . presents—This was customary with the people generally at the beginning of a reign (I Sam. 10:27), and with the nobles and high functionaries yearly afterwards. They were given in the form of voluntary offerings, to avoid the odious idea of a tax or tribute.

ADAM CLARKE

CHAPTER 17

1. *Jehoshaphat . . . and strengthened himself against Israel.* The kingdoms of Israel and Judah were rivals from the beginning; sometimes one, sometimes the other, prevailed. Asa and Baasha were nearly matched; but after Baasha's death Israel was greatly weakened by civil contentions, and Jehoshaphat got the ascendancy. See 1 Kings xvi. 16-23.

2. *The cities of Ephraim.* This conquest from the kingdom of Israel is referred to in chap. xv. 8, but when it was made we do not know.

7-9. *To teach in the cities of Judah.* "To teach the fear of the Lord in the cities of Judah."—Targum.

In these verses we find a remarkable account of an itinerant ministry established by Jehoshaphat; and in this work he employed three classes of men: (1) the *princes,* (2) the *Levites,* (3) the *priests.* We may presume that the princes instructed the people in the nature of the civil law and constitution of the kingdom; the Levites instructed them in everything that appertained to the Temple service and ritual law; and the priests instructed them in the nature and design of the religion they professed. Thus the nation became thoroughly instructed in their duty to God, to the king, and to each other.

9. *Had the book of the law of the Lord with them.* This was their textbook; it was the book of God; they taught it as such, and as such the people received it. By these means the nation enjoyed peace and prosperity; and all insurrections, seditions, and popular commotions were prevented. The surrounding nations, perceiving this, saw that there was no hope of subduing such a people, so "they made no war against Jehoshaphat," v. 10. And they took care not to provoke such a people to fall on them; therefore it is said, "The fear of the Lord fell upon all the kingdoms of the lands that were round about Judah."

MATTHEW HENRY

Verses 10–19

A further account of Jehoshaphat's great prosperity and the flourishing state of his kingdom.

I. He had good interest in the neighbouring princes and nations. Though he was not perhaps so great a soldier as David, nor so great a scholar as Solomon, yet *the fear of the Lord fell so upon them* that they had all a reverence for him, *v.* 10. And, 1. *None of them made war against him.* 2. Many of them brought presents to him (*v.* 11), to secure his friendship.

II. He had very considerable stores laid up in the cities of Judah.

III. He had the militia in good order. Five *lord-lieutenants* are here named, with the numbers of those under their command. It is said of one of these great commanders, *Amasiah*, that *he willingly offered himself unto the Lord* (*v.* 16), not only to the king, to serve him in this post, but to the Lord, to glorify him in it. It was usual for great generals then to offer of their spoils to the Lord, 1 Chron. xxvi. 26. But this good man offered himself first to the Lord, and then his dedicated things. The armies, we may suppose, were dispersed all the country over, and each man resided for the most part on his own estate; but they appeared often, to be mustered and trained, and were ready at call whenever there was occasion.

But, *lastly*, observe, It was not this formidable army that struck a terror upon the neighbouring nations, but the fear of God which fell upon them when Jehoshaphat reformed his country and set up a preaching ministry in it, *v.* 10.

JAMIESON, FAUSSET, BROWN

11. Also some of the Philistines brought Jehoshaphat presents, and tribute silver—either they had been his tributaries, or they were desirous of securing his valuable friendship, and now made a voluntary offer of tribute. Perhaps they were the Philistines who had submitted to the yoke of David (II Sam. 8:1; Ps. 60:8). **the Arabians**—the nomad tribes on the south of the Dead Sea, who, seeking the protection of Jehoshaphat after his conquest of Edom, paid their tribute in the way most suitable to their pastoral habits—the present of so many head of cattle.

12-19. His Greatness, Captains, and Armies. **14. these are the numbers**—The warriors were arranged in the army according to their fathers' houses. The army of Jehoshaphat, commanded by five great generals and consisting of five unequal divisions, comprised one million one hundred and sixty thousand men, without including those who garrisoned the fortresses. No monarch, since the time of Solomon, equalled Jehoshaphat in the extent of his revenue, in the strength of his fortifications, and in the number of his troops.

ADAM CLARKE

11. *The Philistines brought . . . presents.* They and the *Arabians* purchased peace with the king of Judah by paying an annual *tribute.* The Philistines brought *silver,* and no doubt different kinds of merchandise. The Arabs, whose riches consisted in cattle, *brought him flocks* in great abundance, principally *rams* and *he goats.*

13. *He had much business in the cities.* He kept the people constantly employed; they had wages for their work, and by their labors the empire was both enriched and strengthened.

14. *Adnah the chief.* He was generalissimo of all his host.

19. *These waited on the king.* They were disposable forces, always at the king's command, and were independent of those by which the cities of Judah were garrisoned.

MATTHEW HENRY

CHAPTER 18

Verses 1–3

I. Jehoshaphat growing greater.

II. Not growing wiser, else he would not have joined with Ahab, that degenerate Israelite, who had sold himself to work wickedness. With him he joined in affinity, that is, married his son Jehoram to Ahab's daughter Athaliah.

1. This was the worst match that ever was made by any of the house of David. (1) Perhaps pride made the match. His religion forbade him to marry his son to a daughter of any of the heathen princes that were about him, and, having riches and honour in abundance, he thought it a disparagement to marry him to a subject. A king's daughter it must be, and therefore Ahab's, little considering that Jezebel was her mother. (2) Some think he did it in policy, hoping by this expedient to unite the kingdoms in his son.

2. This match drew Jehoshaphat, (1) Into an intimate familiarity with Ahab. He paid him a visit at Samaria, and Ahab, proud of the honour which Jehoshaphat did him, gave him entertainment, according to the splendour of those times. (2) Into a league with Ahab against the Syrians. Ahab persuaded him to join forces with him in an expedition for the recovery of Ramoth-Gilead, a city in the tribe of Gad, on the other side Jordan. Did not Ahab know that that, and all the other cities of Israel, did of right belong to Jehoshaphat, as heir of the house of David? The feast Ahab made for Jehoshaphat was designed only to wheedle him into this expedition.

Verses 4–27

This is almost word for word the same with 1 Kings xxii. 1. Of the great duty of acknowledging God in all our ways *and enquiring at his word,* whatever we undertake. Jehoshaphat was not willing to proceed till he had done this, *v.* 4. 2. Of the great danger of bad company even to good men. Jehoshaphat here, in complaisance to Ahab, sits in his robes, and dares not rebuke that false prophet who basely abused the faithful seer nor oppose Ahab who committed him to prison. 3. Of the unhappiness of those who are surrounded with flatterers, especially flattering prophets, who cry peace to them and prophesy nothing but smooth things. Thus was Ahab cheated into his ruin, and justly; for he hearkened to such, and preferred those that humoured him before a good prophet that gave him fair warning of his danger. 4. Of the power of Satan, by the divine permission, *in the children of disobedience.* One lying spirit can make 400 lying prophets and make use of them to deceive Ahab, *v.* 21. 5. Of the justice of God in giving those up to strong delusions, to believe a lie, who will not receive the love of the truth, but rebel against it, *v.* 21. 6. Of the hard case of faithful ministers, whose lot it has often been to be hated, and persecuted, and ill-treated, for being true to their God and just and kind to the souls of men. Micaiah, for discharging a good conscience, was buffeted, imprisoned, and

JAMIESON, FAUSSET, BROWN

CHAPTER 18

Vss. 1-34. Jehoshaphat and Ahab Go against Ramoth-Gilead.

2. after certain years he went down to Ahab to Samaria—This is word for word, the same as I Kings 22. (See commentary on that chapter.)

ADAM CLARKE

CHAPTER 18

1. *Jehoshaphat had riches and honour.* The preceding chapter gives ample proof of this. *Joined affinity with Ahab.* **Took his daughter Athaliah to be wife to his son Joram.**

3. *To Ramoth-gilead.* **This place belonged to the Israelites, and was now held by the king of Syria. The whole of this chapter is circumstantially explained in the note on 1 Kings xxii.**

F. B. MEYER:

"I hate him; for he never prophesied good unto me, but always evil" (2 Chron. 18:7). This was a very naïve confession. Of course, Micaiah could not speak good of Ahab, whose life was diametrically opposed to all that was Godlike and holy. Micaiah had no animosity toward the king of Israel; it was not a personal matter with him. He simply read from the page of the future as God opened it to his eyes, and in which the outworking of the king's evil life was disclosed in gloomy characters. It was as absurd to hate him because he read such dark lessons from the inevitable future as for a householder to shoot his dog, that bays all night to warn his master against the burglar engaged in rifling his home.

The Bible, the pastor, the whole Church of God are hated by worldlings for the same reason, because they cannot speak hopefully of their future. It is as though a card-playing crew were to hate the watchman who told them that the course of their vessel was straight for the surf and rocks of the shore. If men will persist in violating God's law, in breaking through the hedge of thorns, and in pursuing their own wild ways, they cannot possibly expect the blessedness of the Beatitudes. However, their hatred against those who warn them is really directed towards God. They are indignant that they cannot have their way; their proud spirit would like to overturn the very order of the universe rather than that it should be thwarted. They cannot endure the contrast between God's children and themselves. Do not be surprised if the world hate you. It shows that you are no more of the world than your Master was. Jesus said: "If they have persecuted me, they will also persecute you; if they have kept my saying, they will keep yours also."—*Great Verses Through the Bible*

MATTHEW HENRY

condemned to the bread and water of affliction. But he could with assurance appeal to the issue, as all those may do who are persecuted for their faithfulness, *v.* 27.

Verses 28–34

1. Good Jehoshaphat exposing himself in his robes, thereby endangered, and yet delivered. We have reason to think that Ahab, while he pretended friendship, really aimed at Jehoshaphat's life, else he would never have advised him to enter into the battle with his robes on, which was but to make himself an easy mark to the enemy. The enemy had soon an eye upon the robes, and vigorously attacked the unwary prince who now, when it was too late, wished himself in the habit of the poorest soldier, rather than in his princely raiment. *The Lord helped him out* of his distress, by *moving the captains to depart from him*, *v.* 31. God has all men's hearts in his hand, and turns them as he pleases, contrary to their own first intentions, to serve his purposes. Many are moved unaccountably both to themselves and others, but an invisible power moves them. 2. Wicked Ahab disguising himself, thereby as he thought securing himself, and yet slain, *v.* 33. Jehoshaphat is safe in his robes, Ahab killed in his armour.

CHAPTER 19

Verses 1–4

I. The great favour God showed to Jehoshaphat,

1. In bringing him back in safety from his dangerous expedition with Ahab, which had like to have cost him dearly (*v.* 1): *He returned to his house in peace.* Whenever we return in peace to our houses we ought to acknowledge God's providence in preserving our going out and our coming in. He fared better than he deserved.

2. In sending him a reproof for his affinity with Ahab. It is a great mercy to be told in time wherein we have erred, that we may repent and amend the error before it be too late. The prophet by whom the reproof is sent is Jehu the son of Hanani. The father was an eminent prophet in the last reign, as appeared by Asa's putting him in the stocks for his plain dealing; yet the son was not afraid to reprove another king. The prophet told him plainly that he had done very ill in joining with Ahab: *Shouldst thou love those that hate the Lord?* God was displeased with him for doing this: "*There is wrath upon thee from before the Lord*, and thou must, by repentance, make thy peace with him, or it will be the worse for thee." He did so, and God's anger was turned away. Yet he took notice of that which was praiseworthy, as it is proper for us to do when we give a reproof (*v.* 3): "*There are good things found in thee;* and therefore, though God be displeased with thee, he does not, he will not, cast thee off."

II. Jehoshaphat took the reproof well, was not wroth with the seer as his father was, but submitted. He *dwelt at Jerusalem* (*v.* 4), minded his own business at home, and would not expose himself by paying any more such visits to Ahab. To atone for the visit he had paid to Ahab, he made a pious profitable visitation of his own kingdom: He *went out through the people* in his own person from Beersheba in the south to Mount Ephraim in the north, and *brought them back to the Lord God of their fathers*, that is, did all he could towards recovering them. His late affinity with the idolatrous house of Ahab had had a bad influence upon his own kingdom. Many were emboldened to revolt to idolatry when they saw even their reforming king so intimate with idolaters; and therefore he thought himself doubly obliged to do all he could to restore them.

Verses 5–11

Jehoshaphat, having done what he could to make his people good, is here providing, if possible, to keep them so by the influence of a settled magistracy. He had sent preachers among them, to instruct them (*ch.* xvii. 7–9), but now he saw it further requisite to send judges among them, to see the laws put in execution, and to be a terror to evil-doers.

I. He erected inferior courts of justice in the several cities of the kingdom, *v.* 5. The judges of these courts were to keep the people in the worship of God, to punish the violations of the law, and to decide controversies between man and man. Here is the charge he gave them (*v.* 6): *Take heed what you do*, *v.* 6. And again, "*Take heed and do it* (*v.* 7). Mind your business; take heed of making any mistakes." Judges of all men, have need to be cautious, because so much depends upon the correctness of their judgment. "*Let the fear of God be upon you,* and that will be a restraint upon you to keep you from doing wrong

JAMIESON, FAUSSET, BROWN

CHAPTER 19

Vss. 1-4. JEHOSHAPHAT VISITS HIS KINGDOM. **1. Jehoshaphat . . . returned to his house in peace**—(See on ch. 18:16). Not long after he had resumed the ordinary functions of royalty in Jerusalem, he was one day disturbed by an unexpected and ominous visit from a prophet of the Lord. This was Jehu, of whose father we read in ch. 16:7. He himself had been called to discharge the prophetic office in Israel. But probably for his bold rebuke to Baasha (I Kings 16:1), he had been driven by that arbitrary monarch within the territory of Judah, where we now find him with the privileged license of his order, taking the same religious supervision of Jehoshaphat's proceedings as he had formerly done of Baasha's. At the interview here described, he condemned, in the strongest terms, the king of Judah's imprudent and incongruous league with Ahab—God's open enemy (I Kings 22:2)—as an unholy alliance that would be conducive neither to the honor and comfort of his house nor to the best interests of his kingdom. He apprised Jehoshaphat that, on account of that grave offense, "wrath was upon him from before the Lord," a judgment that was inflicted soon after (see on ch. 20). The prophet's rebuke, however, was administered in a mingled strain of severity and mildness; for he interposed "a nevertheless" (vs. 3), which implied that the threatened storm would be averted, in token of the divine approval of his public efforts for the promotion of the true religion, as well as of the sincere piety of his personal character and life.

4. he went out again through the people—This means his reappointing the commissioners of public instruction (ch. 17:7-9), perhaps with new powers and a larger staff of assistants to overtake every part of the land. The complement of teachers required for that purpose would be easily obtained because the whole tribe of Levites was now concentrated within the kingdom of Judah.

5-7. HIS INSTRUCTIONS TO THE JUDGES. **5-7. he set judges in the land**—There had been judicial courts established at an early period. But Jehoshaphat was the first king who modified these institutions according to the circumstances of the now fragmentary kingdom of Judah. He fixed local courts in each of the fortified cities, these being the provincial capitals of every district (see on Deut. 16: 18-20).

ADAM CLARKE

29. *I will disguise myself.* See the note on 1 Kings xxii. 30.

34. *Stayed himself up . . . against the Syrians.* There was a great deal of true personal courage and patriotism in this last act of the king of Israel. He well knew that if his troops found that he was mortally wounded they would immediately give way, and the battle would not only be lost, but the slaughter would be great in the pursuit. Therefore he stayed himself up till the evening, when the termination of the day must necessarily bring the battle to a close, and when this was done, the Israelites found that their king was slain, and so they left the field of battle to their foes. Thus Israel had a great loss, and the Syrians had got a great deliverance. Had it not been for this accident, the Syrians had probably been defeated. See on 1 Kings xxii. 36.

CHAPTER 19

1. *Returned to his house in peace.* That is, in safety, notwithstanding he had been exposed to a danger so imminent, from which only the especial mercy of God could have saved him.

2. *Jehu the son of Hanani.* We have met with this prophet before; see the note on 1 Kings xvi. 7.

Therefore is wrath upon thee. That is, Thou deservest to be punished. And who can doubt this, who knows that he did help the ungodly, and did love them that hated Jehovah?

4. *From Beer-sheba to Mount Ephraim.* Before the separation of the ten tribes, in speaking of the extent of the land it was said, "From Dan to Beer-sheba"; but since that event, the kingdom of Judah was bounded on the south by Beer-sheba, and on the north by the mountains of Ephraim. This shows that Jehoshaphat had gone through all his territories to examine everything himself, to see that judgment and justice were properly administered among the people.

6. *Take heed what ye do.* A very solemn and very necessary caution; judges should feel themselves in the place of God, and judge as those who know they shall be judged for their judgments.

MATTHEW HENRY

and an engagement to you to be active in doing the duty of your place." The powers that be are ordained by God and for him: "*You judge not for man, but for the Lord*; your business is to glorify him, and serve the interests of his kingdom among men." "He is *with you in the judgment*, to take notice what you do and call you to an account if you do amiss."

II. He erected a supreme court at Jerusalem, which was appealed to, in all the difficult causes that occurred in the inferior courts. This court sat in Jerusalem; for *there were set the thrones of judgment*; there they would be under the inspection of the king himself.

1. The causes cognizable in this court were of two kinds, (1) Pleas of the crown, called here *the judgment of the Lord*, because the law of God was the law of the realm. All criminals were charged with the breach of some part of his law and were said to offend against his peace, his crown and dignity. (2) Common pleas, between party and party, called here *controversies* (*v.* 8) and *causes of their brethren* (*v.* 10), differences *between blood and blood* (this refers to Deut. xvii. 8). Since the revolt of the ten tribes all the cities of refuge, except Hebron, belonged to the kingdom of Israel; and therefore, we may suppose, the courts of the temple, or the horns of the altar, were chiefly used as sanctuaries in that case, and hence the trial of homicides was reserved for the court at Jerusalem.

2. The judges of this court were some of *the Levites and priests* that were most learned in the law, eminent for wisdom, and of approved integrity, and some of *the chief of the fathers of Israel*, or persons of age and experience.

3. The two chiefs, or presidents, of this court. Amariah, the high priest, was to preside in ecclesiastical causes. Zebadiah, the prime-minister of that state, was to preside in all civil causes, *v.* 11.

4, The inferior officers of the court. "Some of *the Levites shall be officers before you*," *v.* 11.

5. They must see to it that they acted from a good principle; they must do all in the *fear of the Lord*, and *with a perfect upright heart*, *v.* 9. They must act with resolution. "Deal courageously, and fear not the face of man; be bold and daring in the discharge of your duty, and, whoever is against you, God will protect you."

JAMIESON, FAUSSET, BROWN

8-11. TO THE PRIESTS AND LEVITES. **8. set of the Levites . . . priests, and of the chief of the fathers of Israel**—A certain number of these three classes constituted a supreme court, which sat in Jerusalem to review appellate cases from the inferior courts. It consisted of two divisions: the first of which had jurisdiction in ecclesiastical matters; the second, in civil, fiscal, and criminal cases. According to others, the two divisions of the supreme court adjudicated: the one according to the law contained in the sacred books; the other according to the law of custom and equity. As in Eastern countries at the present day, the written and unwritten law are objects of separate jurisdiction.

ADAM CLARKE

8. *And for controversies, when they returned to Jerusalem.* Who were they that returned to Jerusalem? Some suppose that it means Jehoshaphat and his courtiers, who returned to Jerusalem after the expedition mentioned in v. 4. But if this were so, or if the text spoke of any person returning to Jerusalem, would not "to Jerusalem," and not the simple word *Yerushalem*, without the preposition, be used? Learned men have supposed, with great plausibility, that the word *vaiyashubu*, "and they returned," should be written *yoshebey*, "the inhabitants," and that the words should be read, "And for the controversies of the inhabitants of Jerusalem." That this was the original reading is very probable from its vestiges in the Vulgate, "its inhabitants"; and in the Septuagint it is, "And to judge the inhabitants of Jerusalem."

10. *Between blood and blood.* Cases of manslaughter or accidental murder, or cases of consanguinity, the settlement of inheritance, family claims, etc. *Between law and commandment.* Whatsoever concerns the moral precepts, rites, and ceremonies of the law, or whatsoever belongs to civil affairs.

11. *Behold, Amariah.* Here was a twofold jurisdiction, ecclesiastical and civil. In the ecclesiastical court, Amariah, the high priest, was supreme judge; in the civil court, Zebadiah was supreme. To assist both, the Levites were a sort of counsellors.

CHAPTER 20

MATTHEW HENRY

Verses 1–13

Jehoshaphat in distress, which was followed by such a glorious deliverance as was an abundant recompence for his piety.

I. A formidable invasion of Jehoshaphat's kingdom by the Moabites and Ammonites, *v.* 1. Jehoshaphat was surprised when the enemy entered his country, *v.* 2. What pretence they had to quarrel with Jehoshaphat does not appear; they are said to come *from beyond the sea*, meaning *the Dead Sea*, where Sodom had stood. The neighbouring nations had feared Jehoshaphat (*ch.* xvii. 10), but perhaps his affinity with Ahab had lessened him in their esteem.

II. The preparation Jehoshaphat made against the invaders. No mention is made of his mustering his forces, which yet it is most probable he did. But his great care was to obtain the favour of God. But he is of the mind of his father David. If we must be corrected, yet *let us not fall into the hands of man.* Consciousness of guilt made him fear. *He set himself to seek the Lord*, and, in the first place, to make him his friend. He *proclaimed a fast throughout all Judah*, appointed a day of humiliation and prayer, that they might join together in confessing their sins and *asking help of the Lord*. The people readily assembled out of all the cities of Judah in the court of the temple to join in prayer (*v.* 4). Jehoshaphat himself was the mouth of the congregation to God. The prayer Jehoshaphat prayed is here recorded.

CHAPTER 20

JAMIESON, FAUSSET, BROWN

VSS. 1-21. JEHOSHAPHAT, INVADED BY THE MOABITES, PROCLAIMS A FAST. **1. the children of Moab . . . Ammon, and with them other beside the Ammonites**—supposed to be rather the name of a certain people called Mohammonim or Mehunim (ch. 26:7), who dwelt in Mount Seir—either a branch of the old Edomite race or a separate tribe who were settled there. **2. from beyond the sea, on this side Syria**—Instead of Syria, some versions read "Edom," and many able critics prefer this reading, both because the nomad tribes here mentioned were far from Syria, and because express mention is made of Mount Seir, i.e., Edom. The meaning then is: this confederate horde was composed of the different tribes that inhabited the far distant regions bordering on the northern and eastern coasts of the Red Sea. Their progress was apparently by the southern point of the Dead Sea, as far as En-gedi, which, more anciently, was called Hazezon-tamar (Gen. 14:7). This is the uniform route taken by the Arabs in their marauding expeditions at the present day; and in coming round the southern end of the Dead Sea, they can penetrate along the low-lying Ghor far north, without letting their movements be known to the tribes and villages west of the mountain chain [ROBINSON]. Thus, anciently, the invading horde in Jehoshaphat's time had marched as far north as En-gedi, before intelligence of their advance was conveyed to the court. En-gedi is recognized in the modern Ainjidy and is situated at a point of the western shore, nearly equidistant from both extremities of the lake [ROBINSON]. **3, 4. Jehoshaphat . . . proclaimed a fast throughout all Judah**—Alarmed by the intelligence and conscious of his total inability to repel this host of invaders, Jehoshaphat felt his only refuge was at the horns of the altar. He resolved to employ the aid of his God, and, in conformity with this resolution, he summoned all his subjects to observe a solemn fast at the sanctuary. It was customary with the Hebrew kings to proclaim fasts in perilous circumstances, either in a city, a district, or throughout the entire kingdom, according to the greatness of the emergency. On this occasion, it was a universal fast, which extended to infants (vs. 13; see also Joel 2:15, 16; Jonah 3:7). **5-13. Jehoshaphat stood . . . in the house of the Lord, before the new court**—i.e.,

CHAPTER 20

ADAM CLARKE

1. *Children of Ammon, and with them other beside the Ammonites.* Here there must be a mistake; surely the *Ammonites* are the same as the *children of Ammon.* Our translators have falsified the text by inserting the words "other beside," which have nothing properly to represent them in the Hebrew. Literally translated, the words are: "And it happened after this, the children of Moab, and the children of Ammon, and with them of the Ammonites"; and thus the Vulgate. "And with them some of the Edomites." This is very likely to be the true reading, as we find from vv. 10, 22-23 that they procured men from Mount Seir; and these were the Idumeans or Edomites. We should, in my opinion, read the text thus: "The children of Moab, and the children of Ammon, and with them some of the Edomites."

2. *On this side Syria.* Instead of *mearam*, "from Syria," I would read with one of Kennicott's MSS. *meedom*, "from Edom," which alteration brings it to truth, and does not require the change of half a letter, as it consists in the almost imperceptible difference between *resh* and *daleth.* We do not read of any Syrians in the invasion, but we know there were Edomites, or inhabitants of Mount Seir. *Hazazon-tamar.* "In the wood of palm trees, that is, in Engedi."—Targum. This is the meaning of the word, and it is probable that they lay hid there.

3. *Jehoshaphat feared.* He found that he could not possibly stand against such a numerous army, and therefore could not expect to be delivered except by the strong arm of God. To get this assistance, it was necessary to seek it; and to get such extraordinary help, they should seek it in an extraordinary way; hence he proclaimed a universal fast, and all the people came up to Jerusalem to seek the Lord.

5. *Jehoshaphat stood.* What an instructive sight was this! The king who proclaimed the

MATTHEW HENRY

He acknowledges the sovereign dominion of the divine Providence, gives to God the glory of it and takes to himself the comfort of it (*v.* 6): "*Art not thou God in heaven?* Control these heathen then; set bounds to their daring threatening insults." He lays hold on their covenant-relation to God. "Thou that art *God in heaven* art the *God of our fathers* (*v.* 6) and *our God*, *v.* 7. Whom should we seek to, whom should we trust to, for relief, but to the God we have chosen and served?" "We hold this land by grant from thee. Suffer us not to be *cast out of thy possession*." *v.* 11. He makes mention of the temple they had built for God's name (*v.* 8), not as if that merited anything at God's hand, for *of his own they gave him*, but it was a token of God's favourable presence with them, *v.* 8, 9. "Lord, when it was built it was intended for the encouragement of our faith at such a time as this. Here thy name is; here we are. Lord, help us, for the glory of thy name." He professes his entire dependence upon God for deliverance. Though he had a great army on foot, and well disciplined, yet he said, "*We have no might against this great company*, but *our eyes are upon thee. In thee, O God! do we put our trust; our souls wait on thee.*"

Verses 14–19

God's gracious answer to Jehoshaphat's prayer. *While he was yet speaking God heard:* before the congregation was dismissed they had assurance given them that they should be victorious; for it is never in vain to seek God. 1. The spirit of prophecy came upon a Levite *in the midst of the congregation*, *v.* 14. He was of the sons of Asaph, and therefore one of the singers; on that office God would put an honour. There needed no sign, the thing itself was to be performed the very next day, and that would be confirmation enough to his prophecy. 2. He encouraged them to trust in God, though the danger was very threatening (*v.* 15): "*Be not afraid. The battle is not yours;* the *battle is God's*." 3. He gives them intelligence of the motions of the enemy, and orders them to march towards them, with particular directions where they should find them. *To-morrow* (the day after the fast) *go you down against them*, *v.* 16, 17. 4. He assures them that they should be, not the glorious instruments, but the joyful spectators, of the total defeat of the enemy: "You shall not need to strike a stroke; the work shall be done to your hands; only stand still and see it," *v.* 17. Let but the Christian soldier go out against his spiritual enemies, and the God of peace will *tread them under his feet* and make *him more than a conqueror*. 5. Jehoshaphat and his people received these assurances with faith, reverence, and thankfulness. They *bowed their heads*, Jehoshaphat first, and then all the people *fell before the Lord, and worshipped*. They lifted up their voices in praise to God, *v.* 19.

Verses 20–30

The foregoing prayer answered and the foregoing promise performed, in the total overthrow of the enemies' forces and the triumph of Jehoshaphat's forces over them.

I. Never was army drawn out to the field of battle as Jehoshaphat's army was. He had soldiers *ready prepared for war* (*ch.* xvii. 18), but here is no notice taken of their military equipment, their swords or spears, their shields or bows. But Jehoshaphat took care, 1. That faith should be their armour. As they went forth, instead of calling them to handle their arms, he bade them *believe in the Lord God* and give credit to his word in the mouth of his prophets, and assured them that then they should *prosper* and *be established*, *v.* 20. 2. That praise and thanksgiving should be their vanguard, *v.* 21. Jehoshaphat called a council of war, and it was resolved to appoint *singers to go out before the army* to praise God, with that ancient and good doxology which eternity itself will not wear thread-bare, *Praise the Lord; for his mercy endureth for ever*. By this strange advance towards the field of battle, Jehoshaphat intended to express his firm reliance upon the word of God.

II. Never was army so unaccountably destroyed as that of the enemy; not by thunder, or hail, or the sword of an angel, not by dint of sword, but the Lord set ambushments against them, as Bishop Patrick thinks, their own ambushments, whom God struck with such confusion that they fell upon their own friends as if they had been enemies, and *everyone helped to destroy another*, so that *none escaped*. This God did *when his people began to sing and to praise* (*v.* 22). When they did but begin the work of praise God perfected the work of their deliverance.

III. Never was spoil so cheerfully divided, for Jehoshaphat's army had nothing to do besides; the rest was done for them. The spoil *was more than they could carry away* at once, and they were *three days*

JAMIESON, FAUSSET, BROWN

the great or outer court (ch. 4:9) called the new court, probably from having been at that time enlarged or beautified. **6. And said, O Lord God of our fathers**—This earnest and impressive prayer embraces every topic and argument which, as king and representative of the chosen people, he could urge.

Then it concludes with an earnest appeal to the justice of God to protect those who, without provocation, were attacked and who were unable to defend themselves against overwhelming numbers.

14-18. Then upon Jahaziel . . . came the Spirit of the Lord—This prophet is not elsewhere mentioned, but his claim to the inspiration of a prophetic spirit was verified by the calm and distinct announcement he gave, both of the manner and the completeness of the deliverance he predicted.

16. they come up by the cliff of Ziz—This seems to have been nothing else than the present pass which leads northwards, by an ascent from En-gedi to Jerusalem, issuing a little below Tekoa. The wilderness of Jeruel was probably the large flat district adjoining the desert of Tekoa, called el-Husasah, from a wady on its northern side [ROBINSON]. **18. Jehoshaphat bowed his head . . . and all Judah, . . .**—This attitude was expressive of reverence to God and His Word, of confidence in His promise, and thankfulness for so extraordinary a favor. **19. the Levites . . . stood up to praise the Lord**—doubtless by the king's command. Their anthem was sung with such a joyful acclaim as showed that they universally regarded the victory as already obtained. **20, 21. as they went forth, Jehoshaphat stood . . . Hear me, O Judah, and ye inhabitants of Jerusalem**—probably in the gate of Jerusalem, the place of general rendezvous; and as the people were on the eve of setting out, he exhorted them to repose implicit trust in the Lord and His prophet, not to be timid or desponding at sight of the enemy, but to remain firm in the confident assurance of a miraculous deliverance, without their striking a single stroke. **he appointed singers . . . that they should praise . . . as they went out before the army**—Having arranged the line of procession, he gave the signal to move forwards. The Levites led the van with their musical instruments; and singing the 136th Psalm, the people went on, not as an army marching against an enemy, but returning in joyful triumph after a victory.

22-30. THE OVERTHROW OF HIS ENEMIES. **22. when they began to sing and to praise, the Lord set ambushments against the children of Ammon, Moab, and Mount Seir**—Some think that this was done by angels in human form, whose sudden appearance diffused an uncontrollable panic. Others entertain the more probable opinion that, in the camp of this vast horde, composed of different tribes, jealousies and animosities had sprung up, which led to widespread dissensions and fierce feuds, in which they drew the sword against each other. The consequence was, that as the mutual strife commenced when the Hebrew procession set out from Jerusalem, the work of destruction was completed before Jehoshaphat and his people arrived at the battlefield. Thus easy is it for God to make the wrath of man to praise Him, to confound the counsels of His enemies and employ their own passions in defeating the machinations they have devised for the overthrow of His Church and people. **24. when Judah came to the watchtower in the wilderness**—Most probably the conical hill, Jebel Fereidis, or Frank Mountain, from the summit of which they obtained the first view of the scene of

ADAM CLARKE

fast was foremost to observe it, and was on this occasion the priest of the people; offering in the congregation, without form or any premeditation, one of the most sensible, pious, correct, and as to its composition one of the most elegant prayers ever offered under the Old Testament dispensation.

12. *Wilt thou not judge them?* That is, Thou wilt inflict deserved punishment upon them.

15. *For the battle is not yours, but God's.* God will not employ you in the discomfiture of this great host; He himself will take the matter in hand, deliver you, and destroy them.

22. *The Lord set ambushments.* Houbigant translates the place thus: "The Lord set against the children of Ammon and Moab ambushments of those who came from Mount Seir against Judah; and the children of Ammon and Moab were smitten: but they afterwards rose up against the inhabitants of Mount Seir, and utterly destroyed each other." This is probably the meaning of these verses.

MATTHEW HENRY

in gathering it, v. 25.

IV. Never was victory celebrated with more solemn and enlarged thanksgivings. They kept a day of praise in the camp, before they drew their forces out of the field. On the fourth day they assembled in a valley, where they blessed God with so much zeal and fervency that that day's work gave a name to the place, the valley of *Berechah*, that is, *of blessing, v.* 26. Yet they did not think this enough, but came in solemn procession, and Jehoshaphat at the head of them, to Jerusalem, that the country, as they passed along, might join with them in their praises, and that they might give thanks for the mercy where they had by prayer obtained it, *in the house of the Lord, v.* 27, 28. Public mercies call for public acknowledgments *in the courts of the Lord's house*, Ps. cxvi. 19.

V. Never did victory turn to a better account than this; for, 1. Jehoshaphat's kingdom was hereby made to look very great and considerable abroad, *v.* 29. It begat in the neighbours a reverence of God and a cautious fear of doing any injury to his people. 2. It was made very easy and quiet at home, *v.* 30. They were quiet from the fear of insults from their neighbours, God having given them rest round about. And, if he give rest, who can give disturbance?

Verses 31–37

The close of the history of Jehoshaphat's reign. This was the general character of his reign, that he did that which was right in the sight of the Lord, kept close to the worship of God himself and did what he could to keep his people close to it. But two things are to be lamented:—1. The people still retained a partiality for the high places, *v.* 33. Those that were erected to the honour of strange gods were taken away (*ch.* xvii. 6); but those where the true God was worshipped, being less culpable, were thought allowable. 2. Jehoshaphat himself still retained a partiality for the house of Ahab, because he had married his son to a daughter of that family, though he had been plainly reproved for it and had like to have smarted for it. He joined himself with him, not in war, as with his father, but in trade, became his partner in a fleet bound for Tarshish, *v.* 35, 36. God sends to him, to show him his error and bring him to repentance, (1) By a prophet, who foretold the blasting of his project, *v.* 37. And, (2) By a storm, which broke the ships in the port before they set sail, by which he was warned to break off his alliance with Ahaziah; and it seems he took the warning, for, when Ahaziah afterwards pressed him to join with him, he *would not*, 1 Kings xxii. 49.

JAMIESON, FAUSSET, BROWN

slaughter. Jehoshaphat and his people found the field strewed with dead bodies, so that they had not to fight at all, but rather to take possession of an immense booty, the collection of which occupied three days. On the fourth they set out on their return to Jerusalem in the same order and joyful mood as they came. The place where they mustered previous to departure was, from their public thanksgiving service, called, "The Valley of Berachah" (benediction), now Wady Bereikut.

31-37. HIS REIGN. **31. Jehoshaphat reigned over Judah**—(See ch. 24:1). **32. he walked in the way of Asa his father, and departed not from it**—He was more steadfast and consistently religious (cf. ch. 15:18). **33. the high places were not taken away**—Those on which idolatry was practised were entirely destroyed (ch. 17:6); but those where the people, notwithstanding the erection of the temple, continued to worship the true God, prudence required to be slowly and gradually abolished, in deference to popular prejudice. **35-37. after this did Jehoshaphat . . . join himself with Ahaziah . . . to make ships**—A combined fleet was built at Ezion-geber, the destination of which was to voyage to Tartessus, but it was wrecked. Jehoshaphat's motive for entering into this partnership was to secure a free passage through Israel, for the vessels were to be conveyed across the Isthmus of Suez, and to sail to the west of Europe from one of the ports of Palestine on the Mediterranean. Eliezar, a prophet, denounced this unholy alliance, and foretold, as divine judgment, the total wreck of the whole fleet. The consequence was, that although Jehoshaphat broke off—in obedience to the divine will—his league with Ahaziah, he formed a new scheme of a merchant fleet, and Ahaziah wished to be admitted a partner. The proposal of the Israelitish king was respectfully declined. The destination of this new fleet was to Ophir, because the Israelitish seaports were not accessible to him for the Tartessus trade; but the ships, when just off the docks, were wrecked in the rocky creek of Ezion-geber.

ADAM CLARKE

25. *Both riches with the dead bodies.* For *pegarim,* "dead bodies," *begadim,* "garments," is the reading of eight MSS. in the collections of Kennicott and De Rossi, and in several ancient editions. None of the versions have *dead bodies* except the Chaldee. The words might be easily mistaken for each other, as the *pe,* if a little faint in the under dot, might easily pass for a *beth;* and we know that the *resh* and *daleth* are frequently interchanged and mistaken for each other, in both Hebrew and Syriac. I believe "garments" to be the true reading.

26. *Assembled themselves in the valley of Berachah.* "The valley of Benediction"; and so in the latter clause.—Targum.

27. *Jehoshaphat in the forefront of them.* He was their leader in all these spiritual, holy, fatiguing, and self-denying exercises. What a noble and persuasive pattern!

33. *The high places were not taken away.* The idolatry, as we have seen, was universally suppressed; but some of the places where that worship had been performed were not destroyed. Some of them still remained; and these, to such a fickle people, became the means of idolatry in reigns less propitious to truth and religion.

34. *In the book of Jehu.* This is totally lost, though it is evident that it was in being when the Books of Chronicles were written.

36. *To go to Tarshish.* "In the great sea."—Targum. By which expression they always meant the Mediterranean Sea.

MATTHEW HENRY

CHAPTER 21

Verses 1–11

I. Jehoshaphat was a very careful indulgent father to Jehoram. He had many sons, who are here named (*v.* 2), and it is said (*v.* 13) that they were better than Jehoram, and any of them more fit for the crown than he; and yet, because he was the firstborn (*v.* 3), his father secured the kingdom to him. His birthright entitled him to a double portion of his father's estate, Deut. xxi. 17. But if he appeared utterly unfit for government (the end of which is the good of the people), and likely to undo all that his father had done, it would have been better perhaps to have set him aside, and taken the next that was hopeful, and not inclined as he was to idolatry.

II. Jehoram was a most barbarous brother to his father's sons. As soon as he had settled himself in the throne he slew all his brethren with the sword, either by false accusation, under colour of law, or by assassination. With them he slew divers of the princes of Israel, who adhered to them, or were likely to avenge their death.

III. Jehoram was a most wicked king, who corrupted and debauched his kingdom, and ruined the reformation that his good father and grandfather had carried on: He *walked in the way of the house of Ahab* (*v.* 6), made high places, and did his utmost to set up idolatry again, *v.* 11. 1. As for the inhabitants of Jerusalem, where he kept his court, he easily drew them into his spiritual whoredom. 2. The country people seem to have been brought to it with more difficulty; but those that would not be corrupted by flatteries were driven by force to partake in his abominable idolatries.

IV. When he forsook God and his worship his subjects withdrew from their allegiance to him. 1. Some of the provinces abroad that were tributaries to him did so. The Edomites revolted (*v.* 8), and, though he chastised them (*v.* 9), yet he could not reduce them, *v.* 10. 2. One of the cities of his own kingdom did so. Libnah revolted (*v.* 10) and set up for a free state, as of old it had a king of its own,

JAMIESON, FAUSSET, BROWN

CHAPTER 21

Vss. 1-4. JEHORAM SUCCEEDS JEHOSHAPHAT. **1. Jehoshaphat slept with his fathers . . . Jehoram . . . reigned**—The late king left seven sons; two of them are in our version named Azariah; but in the Hebrew they appear considerably different, the one being spelt Azariah, and the other Azariahu. Though Jehoshaphat had made his family arrangements with prudent precaution, and while he divided the functions of royalty in his lifetime (cf. II Kings 8:16), as well as fixed the succession to the throne in his oldest son, he appointed each of the others to the government of a fenced city, thus providing them with an honorable independence. But this good intentions were frustrated; for no sooner did Jehoram find himself in the sole possession of sovereign power than, from jealousy, or on account of their connections, he murdered all his brothers, together with some leading influential persons who, he suspected, were attached to their interest, or would avenge their deaths. Similar tragedies have been sadly frequent in Eastern courts, where the heir of the crown looks upon his brothers as his most formidable enemies, and is therefore tempted to secure his power by their death.

5-7. HIS WICKED REIGN. **6. he walked . . . as did the house of Ahab, for he had the daughter of Ahab to wife**—The precepts and examples of his excellent father were soon obliterated by his matrimonial alliance with a daughter of the royal house of Israel. Through the influence of Athaliah he abolished the worship of the Lord, and encouraged an introduction of all the corruptions prevalent in the sister kingdom. The divine vengeance was denounced against him, and would have utterly destroyed him and his house, had it not been for a tender regard to the promise made to David (II Sam. 7; II Kings 8:19).

8-17. EDOM AND LIBNAH REVOLT. **8. the Edomites revolted**—That nation had been made dependent

ADAM CLARKE

CHAPTER 21

2. *And he had brethren . . . the sons of Jehoshaphat king of Israel.* Jehoshaphat certainly was not king of Israel, but king of Judah. *Yisrael* must be a corruption in the text, for *Yehudah,* which is the reading of the Syriac, Arabic, Septuagint, and Vulgate; the Chaldee only agrees with the Hebrew text. And the reading of the versions is supported by thirty-eight of Kennicott's and De Rossi's MSS. The word "Judah" should therefore be restored to the text.

3. *The kingdom gave he to Jehoram.* He made him copartner with himself in the kingdom about three years before his death, so that he reigned only five years after the death of his father, Jehoshaphat. See the notes on 2 Kings viii. 16, etc.; and on the same, chap. i. 17, where an attempt is made to settle this disturbed chronology.

6. *He had the daughter of Ahab to wife.* This was Athaliah, daughter of Ahab and Jezebel, who was famous for her impieties and cruelty, as was her most profligate mother. It is likely that she was the principal cause of Jehoram's cruelty and profaneness.

7. *To give a light to him.* To give him a descendant.

8. *In his days the Edomites revolted.* See on 2 Kings viii. 21.

MATTHEW HENRY

Joshua xii. 15.

V. God was tender of his covenant with the house of David, and therefore would not destroy the royal family, though it was so wretchedly corrupted and degenerated, *v.* 7.

Verses 12–20

I. A warning from God sent to Jehoram by a writing from Elijah the prophet. By this it appears that Jehoram came to the throne, and showed himself what he was, before Elijah's translation. We will suppose that the time of his departure was at hand, so that he could not go in person to Jehoram; but that, hearing of his great wickedness in murdering his brethren, he left this writing with Elisha, to be sent him by the first opportunity, that it might either be a means to reclaim him or a witness against him.

1. His crimes are plainly charged upon him—his departure from the good ways of God, in which he had been educated (*v.* 12)—his conformity to the ways of the house of Ahab, his setting up and enforcing idolatry in his kingdom—and his murdering his brethren, *v.* 13. 2. Judgment is given against him for these crimes; he is plainly told that his sin should certainly be the ruin, (1) Of his kingdom and family (*v.* 14). His people justly suffer because they had complied with his idolatry, and his wives because they had drawn him to it. (2) Of his health and life. And now, if he had learned to humble himself upon the receipt of his threatening message from Elijah, who knows but he might have obtained at least a reprieve? But it does not appear that he took any notice of it; Elijah seemed to him *as one that mocked.*

II. The threatened judgments brought upon him because he slighted the warning.

1. Jehoram stripped of all his comforts. God *stirred up the spirit of his neighbours* against him. Some occasion or other they took to quarrel with him, invaded his country, but fought against the king's house only; they made directly to that, and *carried away all the substance that was found in it.* They *carried away* his sons; but we find (*ch.* xxii. 1) that they *slew all the eldest.* Now all his sons are slain but one. If he had not been of the house of David, that one would not have escaped.

2. His disease was very grievous. Two years he continued ill, and could get no relief. These sore diseases seized him just after his house was plundered and his wives and children were carried away. Perhaps his grief and anguish of mind for that calamity might occasion his sickness. To be sick and poor, sick and solitary, but especially to be sick and in sin, sick and destitute of grace to bear the affliction, and of comfort to counter-balance it—is a most deplorable case.

3. He reigned but eight years, and then *departed without being desired, v.* 20. To show what little affection or respect they had for him, they would not *bury him in the sepulchres of the kings*, as thinking him unworthy. This further disgrace they put upon him, that they *made no burning for him, like the burning of his fathers, v.* 19. They did not honour him with any sweet odours or precious spices.

JAMIESON, FAUSSET, BROWN

by David, and down to the time of Jehoshaphat was governed by a tributary ruler (I Kings 22:47; II Kings 3:9). But that king having been slain in an insurrection at home, his successor thought to ingratiate himself with his new subjects by raising the flag of independence [JOSEPHUS]. The attempt was defeated in the first instance by Jehoram, who possessed all the military establishments of his father; but being renewed unexpectedly, the Edomites succeeded in completely emancipating their country from the yoke of Judah (Gen. 27:40). Libnah, which lay on the southern frontier and towards Edom, followed the example of that country. **12-15. there came a writing to him from Elijah**—That prophet's translation having taken place in the reign of Jehoshaphat, we must conclude that the name of Elijah has, by the error of a transcriber, been put for that of Elisha. **13. hast made Judah and the inhabitants of Jerusalem . . . like to the whoredoms of the house of Ahab**—i.e., introduced the superstitions and vices of Phœnician idolatry (see on Deut. 13:6-14). On this account, as well as for his unnatural cruelties, divine vengeance was denounced against him, which was soon after executed exactly as the prophet had foretold.

A series of overwhelming calamities befell this wicked king; for in addition to the revolts already mentioned, two neighboring tribes (see ch. 17:11) made hostile incursions on the southern and western portions of his kingdom. His country was ravaged, his capital taken, his palace plundered, his wives carried off, and all his children slain except the youngest.

He himself was seized with an incurable dysentery, which, after subjecting him to the most painful suffering for the unusual period of two years, carried him off, a monument of the divine judgment.

To complete his degradation, his death was unlamented, his burial unhonored by his subjects. This custom, similar to what obtained in Egypt, seems to have crept in among the Hebrews, of giving funeral honors to their kings, or withholding them, according to the good or bad characters of their reign.

ADAM CLARKE

11. *To commit fornication.* That is, to serve idols. The Israelites were considered as joined to Jehovah as a woman is joined to her husband. When she associates with other men, this is adultery; when they served other gods, this was called by the same name—it was adultery against Jehovah. This is frequently the only meaning of the terms adultery and fornication in the Scriptures.

12. *There came a writing to him from Elijah the prophet.* From 2 Kings ii. 11, it is evident that Elijah had been translated in the reign of Jehoshaphat, the father of Jehoram. How then could he send a letter to the son? It is certainly a possible case that this writing might have been a prediction of Jehoram's impiety and miserable death, delivered in the time of the prophet, and which was now laid before this wicked king for the first time; and by it the prophet, though not among mortals, still continued to speak. I can see no solid reason against this opinion.

16. *The Philistines, and . . . the Arabians.* We have no other account of this war. Though it was a predatory war, yet it appears to have been completely ruinous and destructive.

17. *Save Jehoahaz the youngest.* This person had at least three names, Jehoahaz, Ahaziah (chap. xxii. 1), and Azariah (v. 6.)

20. *Departed without being desired.* He was hated while he lived, and neglected when he died; visibly cursed of God, and necessarily execrated by the people whom he had lived only to corrupt and oppress. No annalist is mentioned as having taken the pains to write any account of his vile life.

MATTHEW HENRY

CHAPTER 22

Verses 1–9

An account of the reign of Ahaziah, a short reign (of one year only). He was called *Jeho-ahaz* (*ch.* xxi. 17); here he is called *Ahaz-iah*, the same name transposed. He is here said to be forty-two years old when he began to reign (*v.* 2), but it is said (2 Kings viii. 26) that he was twenty-two years old. Some make this forty-two to be the age of his mother Athaliah, for in the original it is, *he was the son of forty-two years.*

The history of Ahaziah's reign is briefly summed up in two clauses, *v.* 3, 4.

I. He did wickedly, *walked in the way of the house of Ahab, did evil in the sight of the Lord* like them (*v.* 3, 4), that is, he worshipped the same false gods that they worshipped, Baalim and Ashtaroth. These Baalim encouraged in their worshippers all manner of lewdness and sensuality, which the God of Israel strictly forbade.

II. He was counselled by his mother and her relations to do so. *She was his counsellor* (*v.* 3) and so

JAMIESON, FAUSSET, BROWN

CHAPTER 22

VSS. 1-9. AHAZIAH SUCCEEDING JEHORAM, REIGNS WICKEDLY. **1. the inhabitants of Jerusalem made Ahaziah . . . king**—or Jehoahaz (ch. 21:17). All his older brothers having been slaughtered by the Arab marauders, the throne of Judah rightfully belonged to him as the only legitimate heir. **2. Forty and two years old was Ahaziah when he began to reign**—(Cf. II Kings 8:26). According to that passage, the commencement of his reign is dated in the twenty-second year of his age, and, according to this, in the forty-second year of the kingdom of his mother's family [LIGHTFOOT]. "If Ahaziah ascended the throne in the twenty-second year of his life, he must have been born in his father's nineteenth year. Hence, it may seem strange that he had older brothers; but in the East they marry early, and royal princes had, besides the wife of the first rank, usually concubines, as Jehoram had (ch. 21:17); he might, therefore, in the nineteenth year of his age, very well have several sons" [KEIL] (cf. ch. 21:20; II Kings 8:17). **Athaliah, the daughter of Omri**—more properly, granddaughter. The expression is used loosely, as the statement was made simply for the purpose of intimating that she belonged to that idolatrous race. **3, 4. his mother was his counsellor . . . they were his counsellors**—The facile king surrendered himself wholly to the influence of his mother and her relatives. Athaliah and her son

ADAM CLARKE

CHAPTER 22

1. *Made Ahaziah his youngest son king.* All the others had been slain by the Arabians, etc.; see the preceding chapter, v. 17.

2. *Forty and two years old was Ahaziah.* See the note on 2 Kings viii. 26. Ahaziah might have been twenty-two years old, according to 2 Kings viii. 26, but he could not have been forty-two, as stated here, without being two years older than his own father! The Syriac and Arabic have "twenty-two," and the Septuagint, in some copies, "twenty." And it is very probable that the Hebrew text read so originally; for when numbers were expressed by single letters it was easy to mistake *mem*, "forty," for *caph*, "twenty." And if this book was written by a scribe who used the ancient Hebrew letters, now called the Samaritan, the mistake was still more easy and probable, as the difference between *caph* and *mem* is very small, and can in many instances be discerned only by an accustomed eye. The reading in 2 Kings is right, and any attempt to reconcile this in Chronicles with that is equally futile and absurd. Both readings cannot be true; is that therefore likely to be genuine that makes the son two years older than the *father* who begat him?

3. *His mother was his counsellor.* Athaliah,

MATTHEW HENRY

were *they*, after the death of his father, *v.* 4. The counsel of the ungodly is the ruin of many young persons when they are setting out in the world. This young prince might have had better advice from the princes and the judges, the priests and the Levites, that had been famous in his good grandfather's time for teaching the knowledge of God; but the house of Ahab humoured him, and *he walked after their counsel.*

III. He was counselled by them to his destruction. It was bad enough that they exposed him to the sword of the Syrians, drawing him in to join with Joram king of Israel in an expedition to Ramoth-Gilead, where Joram was wounded, an expedition that was not for his honour. But that was not all: by engaging him in an intimacy with Joram king of Israel, they involved him in the common ruin of the house of Ahab. He came on a visit to Joram (*v.* 6) just at the time that Jehu was executing the judgment of God upon that idolatrous family, and so was cut off with them, *v.* 7–9.

Verses 10–12

1. A wicked woman endeavouring to destroy the house of David, that she might set up a throne for herself upon the ruins of it. Athaliah barbarously cut off all the seed-royal (*v.* 10), perhaps intending to transmit the crown of Judah after herself to some of her own relations.

2. A good woman effectually preserving it from being wholly extirpated. One of the late king's sons, a child of a year old, was rescued from among the dead, and saved alive by the care of Jehoiada's wife (*v.* 11, 12).

JAMIESON, FAUSSET, BROWN

introduced a universal corruption of morals and made idolatry the religion of the court and the nation. By them he was induced not only to conform to the religion of the northern kingdom, but to join a new expedition against Ramoth-gilead (see on II Kings 9:10). **5. went . . . to war against Hazael, king of Syria**—It may be mentioned as a very minute and therefore important confirmation of this part of the sacred history that the names of Jehu and Hazael, his contemporary, have both been found on Assyrian sculptures; and there is also a notice of Ithbaal, king of Sidon, who was the father of Jezebel. **6. Azariah . . . went down**—i.e., from Ramoth-gilead, to visit the king of Israel, who was lying ill of his wounds at Jezreel, and who had fled there on the alarm of Jehu's rebellion. **9. he sought Ahaziah, and they caught him (for he was hid in Samaria)**—(cf. II Kings 9:27-29). The two accounts are easily reconciled. "Ahaziah fled first to the garden-house and escaped to Samaria; but was here, where he had hid himself, taken by Jehu's men who pursued him, brought to Jehu, who was still near or in Jezreel, and at his command slain at the hill Gur, beside Ibleam, in his chariot; that is, mortally wounded with an arrow, so that he, again fleeing, expired at Megiddo" [KEIL]. Jehu left the corpse at the disposal of the king of Judah's attendants, who conveyed it to Jerusalem, and out of respect to his grandfather Jehoshaphat's memory, gave him an honorable interment in the tombs of the kings. **So the house of Ahaziah had no power to keep still the kingdom**—His children were too young to assume the reins of government, and all the other royal princes had been massacred by Jehu (vs. 8).

10-12. ATHALIAH, DESTROYING THE SEED ROYAL SAVE JOASH, USURPS THE KINGDOM. **10. Athaliah . . . arose and destroyed all the seed royal**—(See on II Kings 11:1-3.) Maddened by the massacre of the royal family of Ahab, she resolved that the royal house of David should have the same fate. Knowing the commission which Jehu had received to extirpate the whole of Ahab's posterity, she expected that he would extend his sword to her. Anticipating his movements, she resolved, as her only defense and security, to usurp the throne and destroy "the seed royal," both because they were hostile to the Phœnician worship of Baal, which she was determined to uphold, and because, if one of the young princes became king, his mother would supersede Athaliah in the dignity of queen mother. **12. he was with them hid in the house of God**—Certain persons connected with the priesthood had a right to occupy the buildings in the outer wall, and all within the outer wall was often called the temple. Jehoiada and his family resided in one of these apartments.

ADAM CLARKE

the wicked daughter of a wicked parent, and the wicked spouse of an unprincipled king.

5. *Went with Jehoram.* See on 2 Kings viii. 28.

9. *He sought Ahaziah.* See a different account, 2 Kings ix. 27, and the note there, where the accounts are reconciled.

10. *All the seed royal of the house of Judah.* Nothing but the miraculous intervention of the divine providence could have saved the line of David at this time, and preserved the prophecy relative to the Messiah. The whole truth of that prophecy, and the salvation of the world, appeared to be now suspended on the brittle thread of the life of an infant of a year old (see chap. xxiv. 1), to destroy whom was the interest of the reigning power! But God can save by few as well as by many.

MATTHEW HENRY

CHAPTER 23

Verses 1–11

Imagine the bad position of affairs in Jerusalem during Athaliah's six years' usurpation. After such a dark and tedious night the returning day in this revolution was the brighter and the more welcome. The continuance of David's seed and throne was what God had sworn by his holiness (Ps. lxxxix. 35), and the stream of government here runs again in the right channel. The instrument and chief manager of the restoration is Jehoiada. 1. A man of great prudence, who reserved the young prince for so many years till he was fit to appear in public, who prepared his work beforehand, and then effected it with admirable secrecy and expedition. 2. A man of great interest. The captains joined with him, *v.* 1. The Levites and the chief of the fathers of Israel came at his call to Jerusalem (*v.* 2). *The Levites and all Judah did as Jehoiada commanded* (*v.* 8). 3. A man of great faith. *The king's son shall reign*, must reign, *as the Lord hath said.* 4. A man of great religion. He gave special order that none of the people should come into the house of the Lord, but the priests and Levites only, who were holy, upon pain of death, *v.* 6, 7. Never let sacred things be profaned, no, not for the support of civil rights.

5. A man of great resolution. When he had undertaken this business he went through with it, *brought out the king, crowned him, and gave him the testimony*, *v.* 11.

JAMIESON, FAUSSET, BROWN

CHAPTER 23

VSS. 1-11. JEHOIADA MAKES JOASH KING. **1. in the seventh year Jehoiada . . . took the captains of hundreds, etc.**—(See on II Kings 11:4, 17). The five officers mentioned here had been probably of the royal guard, and were known to be strongly disaffected to the government of Athaliah. **2. chief of all the fathers of Israel**—This name is frequently used in Chronicles for Judah and Benjamin, now all that remained of Israel. Having cautiously entrusted the secret of the young prince's preservation to all the leading men in the kingdom, he enlisted their interest in the royal cause and got their pledge to support it by a secret oath of fidelity. **they came to Jerusalem**—The time chosen for the grand discovery was, probably, one of the annual festivals, when there was a general concourse of the nation at the capital. **4. This is the thing that ye shall do**—The arrangements made for defense are here described. The people were divided into three bodies; one attended as guards to the king, while the other two were posted at all the doors and gates, and the captains and military officers who entered the temple unarmed to lull suspicion, were furnished with weapons out of the sacred armory, where David had deposited his trophies of victory and which was reopened on this occasion. **8. Jehoiada . . . dismissed not the courses**—As it was necessary to have as large a disposable force as he could command on such a crisis, the high priest detained those who, in other circumstances, would have returned home on the expiry of their week of service. **11. Then they brought out the king's son, and put upon him the crown, and gave to him the testimony**—Some think that the original word rendered "testimony," as its derivation warrants, may signify here the regalia, especially the bracelet (II Sam. 1:10); and this view they support on the ground that "gave him" being

ADAM CLARKE

CHAPTER 23

1. *And in the seventh year.* See on 2 Kings xi. 4, etc.

9. *Spears, and bucklers.* See on 2 Kings xi. 10.

MATTHEW HENRY

Verses 12–21

I. The people pleased, *v.* 12, 13. When the king stood at his pillar, whose right it was to stand there, *all the people of the land rejoiced to see a rod sprung out of the stem of Jesse*, Isa. xi. 1.

II. Athaliah slain. She ventured *into the house of the Lord* at that time, and cried, *Treason, treason!* But nobody seconded her, or sided with her. Jehoiada, as protector in the king's minority, ordered her to be slain (*v.* 14), which was done immediately (*v.* 15).

III. The original contract agreed to, *v.* 16. In the *Kings* it is said that Jehoiada made a covenant between the *Lord*, the people, and the king, 2 Kings xi. 17. Here it is said to be between *himself*, the people, and the king; for he, as God's priest, was his representative in this transaction, or a sort of mediator, as Moses was. Let us look upon ourselves and one another as *the Lord's people*, and this will have a powerful influence upon us in the discharge of all our duty both to God and man.

IV. Baal destroyed, *v.* 17. They would not have done half their work if they had only destroyed the usurper of the *king's* right, and not the usurper of *God's* right—if they had asserted the honour of the throne, and not that of the altar. Down with Baal's house, his altars, his images; down with them all, Deut. xiii. 5, 6.

V. The temple service revived, *v.* 18, 19. Jehoiada restored *the offices of the house of the Lord*. 1. He appointed the priests to their courses, for the due offering of sacrifices. 2. The singers to theirs, according to the appointment of David. 3. The porters were put in their respective posts as David ordered (*v.* 19), to take care that none who were ceremonially unclean should be admitted into the courts of the temple.

VI. The civil government re-established, *v.* 20. They brought the king in state to his own palace, and set him *upon the throne of the kingdom*, to give law, and give judgment, either in his own person or by Jehoiada his tutor. Thus was this happy revolution perfected.

CHAPTER 24

Verses 1–14

An account of Joash's good beginnings. 1. It is a happy thing for young people, when they are setting out in the world, to be under the direction of those that are wise and good and faithful to them, as Joash was under the influence of Jehoiada, during whose time he *did that which was right*. Let those that are young reckon it a blessing to have those that will caution them against that which is evil and quicken them to that which is good; and let them reckon it not a mark of weakness to hearken to such. He that will not be counselled cannot be helped. It is especially prudent for young people to take advice in their marriages. 2. Men may go far in the external performances of religion, merely by the power of their education and the influence of their friends, who are not actuated by a living principle of grace in their hearts. 3. In the outward expressions of devotion it is possible that those who have only the form of godliness may out-strip those who have the power of it. Joash is more solicitous and more zealous about the repair of the temple than Jehoiada himself, whom he reproves for his remissness in that matter, *v.* 6. It is easier to build temples than to be temples to God. 4. The repairing of churches is a good work. When Joash found that money did not come in as he expected in one way he tried another. The throwing of money into a chest, through a hole in the lid of it, was a way that had not been used before, and perhaps the very novelty of the thing made it a successful expedient for the raising of money; a great deal was thrown in and with a great deal of cheerfulness: they all rejoiced, *v.* 10.

JAMIESON, FAUSSET, BROWN

supplemented, the text properly runs thus, "put upon him the crown and testimony." At the same time, it seems equally pertinent to take "the testimony" in the usual acceptation of that term; and, accordingly, many are of opinion that a roll containing a copy of the law (Deut. 17:18) was placed in the king's hands, which he held as a scepter or truncheon. Others, referring to a custom of Oriental people, who when receiving a letter or document from a highly respected quarter, lift it up to their heads before opening it, consider that Joash, besides the crown, had the book of the law laid upon his head (see Job 31:35, 36). **God save the king**—lit., Long live the king.

12-15. ATHALIAH SLAIN. **12. Athaliah heard the noise of the people**—The unusual commotion, indicated by the blast of the trumpets and the vehement acclamations of the people, drew her attention, or excited her fears. She might have flattered herself that, having slain all the royal family, she was in perfect security; but it is just as likely that, finding on reflection, one had escaped her murderous hands, she might not deem it expedient to institute any inquiries; but the very idea would keep her constantly in a state of jealous suspicion and irritation. In that state of mind, the wicked usurper, hearing across the Tyropœon the outburst of popular joy, rushed across the bridge to the temple grounds, and, penetrating from a single glance the meaning of the whole scene, raised a shriek of "Treason!" **13. behold, the king stood at the pillar at the entering in**—The king's pillar was in the people's court, opposite that of the priests'. The young king, arrayed in the royal insignia, had been brought out of the inner, to stand forth in the outer court, to the public view. Some think that he stood on the brazen scaffold of Solomon, erected beside the pillar. **14, 15. Slay her not in the house of the Lord . . . and when she was come to the entering of the horse gate by the king's house, they slew her there**—The high priest ordered her immediately to be taken out of the temple grounds and put to death. "And they laid hands on her; and she went by the way by the which horses came into the king's house: and there was she slain" (II Kings 11:16). "Now, we are not to suppose that horses came into" the king's house "of residence, but into the king's (horses') house or hippodrome (the gate of the king's mules) [JOSEPHUS], he had built for them on the southeast of the temple, in the immediate vicinity of the horse gate in the valley of Kedron—a valley which was at that time a kind of desecrated place by the destruction of idols and their appurtenances" (II Kings 23:2, 6, 12), [BARCLAY'S CITY OF THE GREAT KING].

16. JEHOIADA RESTORES THE WORSHIP OF GOD, AND SETTLES THE KING. **16. Jehoiada made a covenant**—(See on II Kings 11:17).

CHAPTER 24

Vss. 1-14. JOASH REIGNS WELL ALL THE DAYS OF JEHOIADA. **1-3. Joash . . . began to reign**—(See on II Kings 12:1-3).

Jehoiada took for him two wives—As Jehoiada was now too old to contract such new alliances, the generality of interpreters apply this statement to the young king.

4-14. Joash was minded to repair the house of the Lord—(See on II Kings 12:4-16).

ADAM CLARKE

11. *God save the king.* "May the king live!" See on 2 Kings xi. 12.

14. *And whoso followeth her, let him be slain with the sword.* He who takes her part, or endeavors to prevent the present revolution, let him be immediately slain.

15. *Of the horse gate.* See on 2 Kings xi. 16.

16. *Made a covenant between him.* The high priest was, on this occasion, the representative of God, whom both the people and the king must have had in view, through the medium of His priest.

21. *The city was quiet.* There was no attempt at a counterrevolution.

CHAPTER 24

1. *Joash was seven years old.* As he was hidden six years in the Temple, and was but seven when he came to the throne, he could have been but one year old when he was secreted by his aunt; see on chap. xxii. 10.

4. *To repair the house of the Lord.* During the reigns of Joram and Athaliah, the temple of God had been pillaged to enrich that of Baal, and the whole structure permitted to fall into decay; see v. 7.

5. *Gather of all Israel money.* As the Temple was the property of the whole nation, and the services performed in it were for the salvation of the people at large, it was right that each should come forward on an occasion of this kind and lend a helping hand. This is the first instance of such a general collection for building or repairing a house of God. *From year to year.* It must have been in a state of great dilapidation when it required such annual exertions to bring it into a thorough state of repair.

6. *The collection . . . of Moses.* This was the poll tax, fixed by Moses, of half a shekel, which was levied on every man from twenty years old and upward, and which was considered as a ransom for their souls, that there might be no plague among them. See Exod. xxx. 12-14.

8. *They made a chest.* See the notes on the parallel places, 2 Kings xii. 4, etc.

MATTHEW HENRY

Verses 15–26

A sad account of the degeneracy and apostasy of Joash. God had done great things for him; he had done something for God; but now he proved ungrateful to his God.

I. The occasions of his apostasy. He never was sincere, never acted from principle, but in compliance to Jehoiada, who had helped him to the crown, and because he had been protected in the temple and rose upon the ruins of idolatry; and therefore, when the wind turned, he turned with it. 1. His good counsellor left him, and was by death removed from him. *They buried him among the kings*, with this honourable encomium, that *he had done good in Israel*. Judah is called *Israel* because, the other tribes having revolted from God, they only were Israelites indeed. Jehoiada finished his course with honour; but the little religion that Joash had was all buried in his grave, and, after his death, both king and kingdom miserably degenerated. See how necessary it is that, as our Saviour speaks, we *have salt in ourselves*, that we act in religion from an inward principle, which will carry us on through all changes. Then the loss of a parent, a minister, a friend, will not involve the loss of our religion. 2. Bad counsellors got about him, insinuated themselves into his affections, and, instead of condoling, congratulated him upon the death of his old tutor, as his release from discipline. They tell him he must be priest-ridden no longer, he may do as he pleases: and the princes of Judah were industrious to debauch him, *v.* 17. His father and grandfather were corrupted by the house of *Ahab*, from whom no better could be expected. But that the princes of Judah should be seducers to their king was very sad. And he hearkened to them: their discourse pleased him, and was more agreeable than Jehoiada's dictates used to be.

II. The apostasy itself: *They left the house of God, and served groves and idols*, *v.* 18. The princes had a request to the king that they may set up the groves and idols again which were thrown down in the beginning of his reign, for they hate to be always confined to the dull old-fashioned service of the temple. And he not only gave them leave to do it themselves, but he joined with them.

III. The aggravations of this apostasy. God *sent prophets to them* (*v.* 19) to reprove them. It is the work of ministers to bring people, not to themselves, but to God—to bring those again to him who have gone a-whoring from him. They slighted all the prophets and slew one of the most eminent, *Zechariah the son of Jehoiada*. The people were assembled in the court of the temple when this Zechariah, being filled with the spirit of prophecy, stood up and plainly told the people of their sin and what would be the consequences of it. He did not impeach any particular persons, but reminded them of what was written in the law. "*You transgress the commandments of the Lord*, you know you do so, in serving groves and idols: and why will you so offend God and wrong yourselves?" By the conspiracy of the princes, or some of their party, and *by the commandment of the king*, they stoned him to death immediately, not under colour of law, accusing him as a blasphemer, a traitor, or a false prophet, but in a popular tumult, *in the court of the house of the Lord*. The *person* was sacred—a priest, the *place* sacred—the court of the temple (the inner court, *between the porch and the altar*), the *message* yet more sacred. The reproof was just, the warning fair, both backed with scripture, and the delivery very gentle and tender. The Jews say there were seven transgressions in this; for they killed a priest, a prophet, a judge, they shed innocent blood, and polluted the court of the temple, the sabbath, and the day of expiation: for on that day, their tradition says, this happened. This Zechariah, who suffered martyrdom for his faithfulness to God and his country, was the son of Jehoiada, who had done so much good in Israel, and particularly had been as a father to Joash, *v.* 22. The dying martyr's prophetic imprecation upon his murderers: *The Lord look upon it, and require it!* This came not from a spirit of revenge, but a spirit of prophecy: *He will require it.* This precious blood was quickly reckoned for in the judgments that came upon this apostate prince; it came into the account afterwards in the destruction of Jerusalem by the Chaldeans (*ch.* xxxvi. 16); nay, our Saviour makes the persecutors of him and his gospel answerable for the blood of this Zechariah; so loud, so long, does the blood of the martyrs cry. See Matt. xxiii. 35.

JAMIESON, FAUSSET, BROWN

15, 16. JEHOIADA BEING DEAD. **15, 16. Jehoiada waxed old . . . and died**—His life, protracted to unusual longevity and spent in the service of his country, deserved some tribute of public gratitude, and this was rendered in the posthumous honors that were bestowed on him. Among the Hebrews, intramural interment was prohibited in every city but Jerusalem, and there the exception was made only to the royal family and persons of eminent merit, on whom the distinction was conferred of being buried in the city of David, among the kings, as in the case of Jehoiada.

17-22. JOASH FALLS INTO IDOLATRY. **17-22. Now came the princes of Judah, and made obeisance to the king**—Hitherto, while Joash occupied the throne, his uncle had held the reins of sovereign power, and by his excellent counsels had directed the young king to such measures as were calculated to promote both the civil and religious interests of the country. The fervent piety, practical wisdom, and inflexible firmness of that sage counsellor exerted immense influence over all classes. But now that the helm of the state-ship was no longer steered by the sound head and firm hand of the venerable high priest, the real merits of Joash's administration appear; and for want of good and enlightened principle, as well as, perhaps, of natural energy of character, he allowed himself to be borne onward in a course which soon wrecked the vessel upon hidden rocks. **the king hearkened unto them,** etc.—They were secretly attached to idolatry, and their elevated rank affords sad proof how extensively and deeply the nation had become corrupted during the reigns of Jehoram, Ahaziah, and Athaliah. With strong professions of allegiance they humbly requested that they might not be subjected to the continued necessity of frequent and expensive journeys to Jerusalem, but allowed the privilege their fathers had enjoyed of worshipping God in high places at home. They framed their petition in this plausible and least offensive manner, well knowing that, if excused attendance at the temple, they might —without risk of discovery or disturbance—indulge their tastes in the observance of any private rites they pleased. The weak-minded king granted their petition; and the consequence was, that when they left the house of the Lord God of their fathers, they soon "served groves and idols." **18. wrath came upon Judah and Jerusalem**—The particular mention of Jerusalem as involved in the sin implies that the neglect of the temple and the consequent idolatry received not only the king's toleration, but his sanction; and it naturally occurs to ask how, at his mature age, such a total abandonment of a place with which all his early recollections were associated can be accounted for. It has been suggested that what he had witnessed of the conduct of many of the priests in the careless performance of the worship, and especially their unwillingness to collect the money, as well as apply a portion of their revenues for the repairs of the temple, had alienated and disgusted him [LECLERC]. **19. Yet he sent prophets** —Elisha, Micah, Jehu son of Hanani, Jahaziel son of Zechariah (ch. 20:14), Eliezar son of Dodavah (ch. 20:37), lived and taught at that time. But all their prophetic warnings and denunciations were unheeded. **20. the Spirit of God came upon Zechariah, the son of Jehoiada**—probably a younger son, for his name does not occur in the list of Aaron's successors (I Chron. 6). **stood above the people**— Being of the priestly order, he spoke from the inner court, which was considerably higher than that of the people. **and said unto them, Thus saith God, Why transgress ye the commandments of the Lord, that ye cannot prosper,** etc.—His near relationship to the king might have created a feeling of delicacy and reluctance to interfere; but at length he, too, was prompted by an irresistible impulse to protest against the prevailing impiety. The bold freedom and energy of his remonstrance, as well as his denunciation of the national calamities that would certainly follow, were most unpalatable to the king; while they so roused the fierce passions of the multitude that a band of miscreants, at the secret instigation of Joash, stoned him to death. This deed of violence involved complicated criminality on the part of the king. It was a horrid outrage on a prophet of the Lord—base ingratitude to a family who had preserved his life—atrocious treatment of a true Hebrew patriot—an illegal and unrighteous exercise of his power and authority as a king. **22. when he died, he said, The Lord look upon it and require it**—These dying words, if they implied a vindictive imprecation, exhibit a striking contrast to the spirit of the first Christian martyr (Acts 7:60). But, instead of being the expression of a personal wish, they might be the utterance of a prophetic

ADAM CLARKE

16. *They buried him . . . among the kings.* He had, in fact, been king in Judah; for Joash, who appears to have been a weak man, was always under his tutelage. Jehoiada governed the state in the name of the king, and his being buried among the kings is a proof of the high estimation in which he was held among the people.

17. *The princes of Judah . . . made obeisance to the king.* I believe the Targum has given the true sense of this verse: "After the death of Jehoiada, the great men of Judah came and adored King Joash, and seduced him; and then the king received from them their idols."

CHARLES H. SPURGEON:

There is a book called *The Museum of Natural History*, and the most singular animal in that museum is man. It would be far more easy to understand any other creature than to understand a human being. He is worthy of very great study; and the more he is studied, the more he will surprise you. There are certain characters that are great curiosities. Alas, there are also other characters that are great monstrosities! You can never tell, from what a man is, what he will be. The case before us is a very extraordinary one, because here is a man with every possible advantage, who through a number of years exhibited the brightest form of character; and yet in the end he was not thought worthy to be laid in the sepulchres of his fathers with others of the kings of Judah; neither was he worthy of any royal interment, for the latter part of his life blackened and defiled the whole of his career, and he who began his reign like the dawning of the day ended it like the middle of the night.

—The Treasury of the Old Testament

20. *And the Spirit of God came upon Zechariah.* "When he saw the transgression of the king and of the people, burning incense to an idol in the house of the sanctuary of the Lord, on the day of expiation; and preventing the priests of the Lord from offering the burnt-offerings, sacrifices, daily oblations, and services, as written in the book of the law of Moses; he stood above the people, and said."—Targum.

21. *Stoned him . . . at the commandment of the king.* What a most wretched and contemptible man was this, who could imbrue his hands in the blood of a prophet of God, and the son of the man who had saved him from being murdered, and raised him to the throne!

22. *The Lord look upon it, and require it.* And so he did; for at the end of that year the Syrians came against Judah, destroyed all the princes of the people, sent their spoils to Damascus; and Joash, the murderer of the prophet, the son of his benefactor, was himself murdered by his own servants. Here was a most signal display of the divine retribution.

MATTHEW HENRY

IV. The judgments of God which came upon Joash for this aggravated wickedness of his. 1. A small army of Syrians made themselves masters of Jerusalem, destroyed the princes, plundered the city, and sent the spoil of it to Damascus, *v.* 23, 24. 2. God smote him with great diseases, of body, or mind, or both. 3. His own servants conspired against him. They slew him in his bed *for the blood of the sons of Jehoiada*, by which it should seem that he did not only slay Zechariah, but others of the sons of Jehoiada for his sake. 4. His people would not bury him in the sepulchres of the kings because he had stained his honour by his mal-administration.

JAMIESON, FAUSSET, BROWN

doom.

23-27. HE IS SLAIN BY HIS SERVANTS. **23. at the end of the year the host of Syria came up**—This invasion took place under the personal conduct of Hazael, whom Joash, to save the miseries of a siege, prevailed on to withdraw his forces by a large present of gold (II Kings 12:18). Most probably, also, he promised the payment of an annual tribute, on the neglect or refusal of which the Syrians returned the following year, and with a mere handful of men inflicted a total and humiliating defeat on the collected force of the Hebrews. **25. they left him in great diseases**—The close of his life was embittered by a painful malady, which long confined him to bed. **his own servants conspired against him**—These two conspirators (whose fathers were Jews, but their mothers aliens) were probably courtiers, who, having constant access to the bed-chamber, could the more easily execute their design. **for the blood of the sons**—read "the son" of Jehoiada. Public opinion seems to have ascribed the disasters of his life and reign to that foul crime, and as the king had long lost the esteem and respect of his subjects, neither horror nor sorrow was expressed for his miserable end!

ADAM CLARKE

26. *These are they that conspired against him.* The two persons here mentioned were certainly not Jews; the mother of one was an Ammonitess, and the mother of the other was a Moabitess. Who their fathers were we know not; they were probably foreigners and aliens. Some suppose that these persons were of the king's chamber, and therefore could have the easiest access to him.

27. *The greatness of the burdens laid upon him.* Meaning, probably, the heavy tribute laid upon him by the Syrians, though some think the vast sums amassed for the repairs of the Temple are here intended. *Written in the story, Midrash*, the "commentary," *of the book of the kings.* We have met with this before; but these works are all lost, except the extracts found in Kings, Chronicles, and Ezra. These abridgments were the cause of the neglect, and finally of the destruction, of the originals.

MATTHEW HENRY

CHAPTER 25

Verses 1–13

I. The general character of Amaziah: *He did that which was right in the eyes of the Lord*, worshipped the true God, kept the temple service going, and countenanced religion in his kingdom; but he did not do it *with a perfect heart* (*v.* 2), that is, he was not a man of serious piety or devotion himself. He was no enemy to it, but a cool and indifferent friend. Such is the character of too many in this Laodicean age: they do that which is good, but not with a perfect heart.

II. A necessary piece of justice which he did upon the traitors that murdered his father: he put them to death, *v.* 3. Though they intended to avenge on their king the death of the prophet, *they* presumptuously took God's work out of his hands: and therefore Amaziah did what became him in calling them to an account for it, *v.* 4.

III. An expedition of his against the Edomites. 1. The great preparation he made for this expedition. (1) He mustered his own forces (*v.* 5), and found Judah and Benjamin in all but 300,000 men fit for war, whereas, in Jehoshaphat's time they were four times as many. Sin weakens a people, diminishes them, dispirits them, and lessens their number. (2) He hired auxiliary troops out of the kingdom of Israel, *v.* 6.

2. The command which God sent him by a prophet to dismiss the forces of Israel, *v.* 7, 8. If he made sure of God's presence, the army he had of his own was sufficient. But particularly he must not take in *their* assistance: *For the Lord is not with the children of Ephraim, because they are not with him*, but worship the calves.

3. The objection which Amaziah made against this command, and the satisfactory answer which the prophet gave to that objection, *v.* 9. The king had remitted 100 talents to the men of Israel for advance-money. "Now," says he, "if I send them back, I shall lose that: *But what shall we do for the* 100 *talents?*" This is an objection men often make against their duty: they are afraid of losing by it. "Regard not that," says the prophet: "*The Lord is able to give thee much more than this;* and, thou mayest depend upon it, he will not see thee lose by him." What is it to trust in God, but to be willing to venture the loss of anything for him, in confidence of the goodness of the security he gives us that we shall not lose by him, but that whatever we part with for his sake shall be made up to us in kind or kindness. He is just, and he is good, and he is solvent. The king lost 100 talents by his obedience; and we find just that sum given to his grandson Jotham as a present (*ch.* xxvii. 5); then the principal was repaid, and, for interest, 10,000 measures of wheat and as many of barley.

4. His obedience to the command of God, which is upon record to his honour. *He separated the army of Ephraim, to go home again, v.* 10. And they went home in great anger.

5. His triumphs over the Edomites, *v.* 11, 12. He left dead upon the spot, in the field of battle, 10,000 men; 10,000 more he took prisoners, and barbarously killed them all by throwing them down some steep and craggy precipice. What provocation he had to exercise this cruelty towards them we are not told.

6. The mischief which the disbanded soldiers of Israel did to the cities of Judah, either in their return

JAMIESON, FAUSSET, BROWN

CHAPTER 25

VSS. 1-4. AMAZIAH BEGINS TO REIGN WELL. **1. Amaziah was twenty and five years old,** etc.—(See on II Kings 4:1-6).

5-10. HAVING HIRED AN ARMY OF ISRAELITES AGAINST THE EDOMITES, AT THE WORD OF A PROPHET HE LOSES A HUNDRED TALENTS AND DISMISSES THEM. **5. Amaziah . . . made captains,** etc.—As all who were capable of bearing arms were liable to serve, it was quite natural in making up the muster roll to class them according to their respective families and to appoint the officers of each corps from the same quarter; so that all the soldiers who formed a regiment were brothers, relatives, friends. Thus the Hebrew troops were closely linked together, and had strong inducements to keep steady in their ranks. **found them three hundred thousand choice men**—This was only a fourth part of Jehoshaphat's army (ch. 17:14-19), showing how sadly the kingdom of Judah had, in the space of eighty-two years, been reduced in population by foreign wars, no less than by internal corruptions. But the full amount of Amaziah's troops may not be here stated. **6. He hired also an hundred thousand mighty men of valour . . . for an hundred talents of silver**—This sum was paid into the treasury of Jehoahaz—not given as bounty to the mercenaries who were obliged to serve at the sovereign's call; their remuneration consisting only in the booty they might obtain. It was about $170,000 in our currency, or $17 per man, including officers—a very paltry pay, compared with the bounty given for a soldier in this country. But it must be remembered that in ancient times campaigns were short and the hazards of the service comparatively small. **7, 8. there came a man of God**—sent to dissuade Amaziah from the course he was following, on the ground that "the Lord is not with Israel." This statement was perfectly intelligible to the king. But the historian, writing long after, thought it might require explanation, and therefore added the comment, "with all the children of Ephraim." Idolatry had long been the prevailing religion in that kingdom, and Ephraim its headquarters. As to the other part of the prophet's advice (vs. 8), considerable obscurity hangs over it, as the text stands; and hence some able critics have suggested the insertion of "not" in the middle clause, so that the verse will be thus: "But if thou wilt go [alone], do, be strong for the battle; God shall *not* make thee fall before the enemy." **10. separated them . . . the army . . . out of Ephraim . . . their anger was greatly kindled against Judah**—Amaziah, who knew his position as the Lord's viceroy, complied with the prophet's counsel, and, consenting to forfeit the purchase-money of the Israelitish soldiers, discharged them. Exasperated at this treatment, they resolved to indemnify themselves for the loss of their expected booty, and so on their return home they plundered all the towns in their way, committing great havoc both of life and property without any stoppage, as the king of Judah and his army had set out on their expedition (II Kings 14:7). **11. valley of salt**—This ravine lies to the south of the Dead Sea. The arms of Amaziah, in reward for his obedience to the divine will, were crowned with victory—ten thousand of the Edomites were slain on the field, and as many taken prisoners, who were put to death by precipitation "from the top of the rock." This rock might be situated in the neighbor-

ADAM CLARKE

CHAPTER 25

2. *He did that which was right.* He began his reign well, but soon became an idolater, vv. 14-15.

5. *Gathered Judah together.* He purposed to avenge himself of the Syrians, but wished to know his military strength before he came to a rupture.

9. *The Lord is able to give thee much more than this.* Better lose the money than keep the men, for they will be a curse unto thee.

10. *They returned home in great anger.* They thought they were insulted, and began to meditate revenge. See the notes on 2 Kings xiv. 1-20, where almost every circumstance in this chapter is examined and explained.

MATTHEW HENRY

or soon after, *v.* 13. They were so enraged at being sent home that, if they might not go to share with Judah in the spoil of Edom, they would make a prey of Judah. Several cities that lay upon the borders they plundered, killing 3,000 men that made resistance. But why should God suffer this to be done? Doubtless God intended hereby to chastise those cities of Judah for their idolatries, which were found most in those parts that lay next to Israel.

Verses 14–16

I. The revolt of Amaziah from the God of Israel to the gods of the Edomites. Egregious folly! Ahaz worshipped the gods of those that had conquered him, for which he had some little colour, *ch.* xxviii. 23. But to worship the gods of those whom he had conquered, who could not protect their own worshippers, was the greatest absurdity that could be. If he had cast the idols down from the rock and broken them to pieces, instead of the prisoners, he would have manifested more of the piety as well as more of the pity of an Israelite; but perhaps for that barbarous inhumanity he was given up to this ridiculous idolatry.

II. The reproof which God sent to him, by a prophet, for this sin. The prophet reasoned with him very fairly and very mildly: *Why hast thou sought* the favour of those gods *which could not deliver their own people? v.* 15.

III. The check he gave to the reprover, *v.* 16. He could say nothing in excuse of his own folly; but he fell into a passion. 1. He taunted him as meddling with that which did not belong to him: *Art thou made of the king's counsel?* 2. He silenced him, bade him say not a word more to him. He *said to the seer, See not,* Isa. xxx. 10. 3. He threatened him. He seems to remind him of Zechariah's fate in the last reign, who was put to death for making bold with the king; and bids him take warning by him.

IV. The doom which the prophet passed upon him for this. He had made to say to him by way of instruction and advice; but, finding him obstinate in his iniquity, he forbore. Miserable is the condition of that man with whom the blessed Spirit, by ministers and conscience, *forbears to strive,* Gen. vi. 3. And both the reprovers in the gate and that in the bosom, if long brow-beaten and baffled, will at length forbear. So I *gave them up to their own heart's lusts.*

Verses 17–28

This degenerate prince mortified by his neighbour and murdered by his own subjects.

I. Never was proud prince more thoroughly mortified than Amaziah was by Joash king of Israel.

1. This part of the story (which was as fully related 2 Kings xiv. 8, &c., as it is here)—embracing the foolish challenge which Amaziah sent to Joash (*v.* 17), his haughty scornful answer to it (*v.* 18), with the friendly advice he gave him to sit still and know when he was well off (*v.* 19),—his wilfully persisting in his challenge (*v.* 20, 21) the defeat that was given him (*v.* 22), and the calamity he brought upon himself and his city thereby (*v.* 23, 24),—verifies two of Solomon's proverbs:—(1) That *a man's pride will bring him low,* Prov. xxix. 23. (2) That he that *goes forth hastily to strive* will probably not know what to do in the end thereof, *when his neighbour has put him to shame,* Prov. xxv. 8.

2. But there are two passages in this story not in the *Kings.* (1) That *Amaziah took advice* before he challenged the king of Israel, *v.* 17. But of whom? Not of the prophet but of his statesmen that would flatter him and bid him go up and prosper. (2) Amaziah's imprudence is here made the punishment of his impiety (*v.* 20).

II. Never was poor prince more violently pursued by his own subjects. *From the time* that he departed from the Lord (so it may be read, *v.* 27) the hearts of his subjects departed from him, and they began to form a design against him in Jerusalem. At length the ferment grew so high, and he perceived the plot to be laid so deeply, that he thought fit to quit his royal city and flee to Lachish, but they sent after him thither, and slew him there.

JAMIESON, FAUSSET, BROWN

hood of the battlefield, but more probably it formed one of the high craggy cliffs of Selah (Petra), the capital of the Edomites, whither Amaziah marched directly from the Valley of Salt, and which he captured (II Kings 14:7). The savage cruelty dealt out to them was either in retaliation for similar barbarities inflicted on the Hebrews, or to strike terror into so rebellious a people for the future. The mode of execution, by dashing against stones (Ps. 137:9), was common among many ancient nations. **14-16. Amaziah . . . brought the gods of the children of Seir**—The Edomites worshipped the sun under different forms and with various rites. But burning incense upon altars was a principal act of worship, and this was the very thing Amaziah is described as having with strange infatuation performed. Whether he had been captivated with the beauty of the images, or hoped by honoring the gods to disarm their spite at him for his conquest and harsh treatment of their votaries, his conduct in establishing these objects of religious homage in Jerusalem was foolish, ignorant, and highly offensive to God, who commissioned a prophet to rebuke him for his apostasy, and threaten him with the calamity that soon after befell him.

16. as he talked with him, etc.—Those who were invested with the prophetic character were entitled to counsel kings. Amaziah, had he not been offended by unwelcome truths, would have admitted the claim of this prophet, who was probably the same that had given him counsel previous to the war with Edom. But victory had elated and blinded him.

17. HE PROVOKES JOASH TO HIS OVERTHROW. **17. Then Amaziah . . . sent to Joash . . . Come, let us see one another in the face**—(See on II Kings 14: 8-20).

ADAM CLARKE

16. *Art thou made of the king's counsel?* How darest *thou* give advice to, or reprove, a king?

18. *The thistle that was in Lebanon.* See the explanation of this 2 Kings xiv. 9.

24. *In the house of God with Obed-edom.* From 1 Chron. xxvi. 15 we learn that to Obed-edom and his descendants was allotted the keeping of the house of *Asuppim* or "collections" for the divine treasury. *And . . . the hostages.* See on 2 Kings xiv. 14.

CHAPTER 26

Verses 1–15

An account of two things concerning Uzziah:—

I. His piety. In this he was not very eminent or zealous; yet *he did that which was right in the sight of the Lord.* He kept up the pure worship of the true God *as his father* did, and was better than his father, inasmuch as he never worshipped idols as his father did. It is said (*v.* 5), He *sought God in the days of Zechariah,* who, some think, was the son of that

CHAPTER 26

VSS. 1-8. UZZIAH SUCCEEDS AMAZIAH AND REIGNS WELL IN THE DAYS OF ZECHARIAH. **1. Then all the people of Judah took Uzziah**—(See on II Kings 14: 21, 22; 15:1-3). **2. He built Eloth**—or, "He it was who built Eloth." The account of the fortifications of this port on the Red Sea, which Uzziah restored to the kingdom of Judah (ch. 33:13), is placed before the chronological notices (vs. 3), either

CHAPTER 26

1. *The people of Judah took Uzziah.* They all agreed to place this son on his father's throne.

2. *He built Eloth.* See the notes on 2 Kings xiv. 21. This king is called by several different names; see the note on 2 Kings xv. 1.

MATTHEW HENRY

Zechariah whom his grandfather Joash slew. This Zechariah was one that *had understanding in the visions of God*, and had great influence with Uzziah.

II. His prosperity.

1. In general, *as long as he sought the Lord*, and minded religion, *God made him to prosper.*

2. Here are several particular instances of his prosperity:—(1) His success in his wars: *God helped him* (*v.* 7), and then he triumphed over the Philistines, demolished the fortifications of their cities, and put garrisons of his own among them, *v.* 6. He obliged the Ammonites to pay him tribute, *v.* 8. (2) The greatness of his fame and reputation. His name was celebrated throughout all the neighbouring countries (*v.* 8) and it was a good name, a name for good things with God and good people. (3) His buildings. While he acted offensively abroad, he did not neglect the defence of his kingdom at home, but *built towers in Jerusalem* and fortified them, *v.* 9. Much of the wall of Jerusalem was in his father's time broken down (*ch.* xxv. 23); and he *built a tower at the corner gate*. But his best fortification of Jerusalem was his close adherence to the worship of God. While he fortified the city, he did not forget the country, but *built towers in the desert* too (*v.* 10), to protect the country people from the inroads of the plunderers, *ch.* xxi. 16. (4) His husbandry. He dealt much in cattle and corn for he *loved husbandry* (*v.* 10). (5) His standing armies. He had, as it should seem, two military establishments. [1] A *host of fighting men* that were to make excursions abroad. These *went out to war by bands*, *v.* 11. They fetched in spoil from the neighbouring countries by way of reprisal for the depredations they had so often made upon Judah, [2] Another army for *guards and garrisons*, that were ready to defend the country in case it should be invaded, *v.* 12, 13. Uzziah furnished himself with a great armoury (*v.* 14), spears, bows, and slings, shields, helmets, and habergeons: swords are not mentioned, because it is probable that every man had a sword of his own. Engines were invented, in his time, for annoying besiegers with darts and stones shot from the towers and bulwarks, *v.* 15. What a pity it is that the wars and fightings which come from men's lusts have made it necessary for cunning men to employ their skill in inventing instruments of death.

Verses 16–23

The only blot we find on the name of king Uzziah.

I. His sin was invading the priest's office. The transgression of his predecessors was forsaking the temple of the Lord (*ch.* xxiv. 18), and burning incense upon idolatrous altars, *ch.* xxv. 14. *His* was intruding *into the temple of the Lord* further than was allowed him, and attempting himself to *burn incense upon the altar* of God.

1. That which was at the bottom of his sin was pride of heart (*v.* 16): *When he was strong* (and he was marvellously helped by the good providence of God *till he was so*, *v.* 15), when he had grown very great and considerable in wealth and power, instead of lifting up the name of God in gratitude his *heart was lifted up to his destruction.*

2. His sin was *going into the temple of the Lord to burn incense*, probably when he himself had some special occasion for supplicating the divine favour. (1) Perhaps he fancied the priests did not do their office so devoutly, as they ought, and he could do it better. Or, (2) He observed that the idolatrous kings did themselves burn incense at the altars of their gods; his father did so, and Jeroboam (1 Kings xiii. 1), and he, being resolved to cleave to God's altar, would try to come as near it as the idolatrous kings did to their altars. But it is called a *transgression against the Lord his God.*

3. He was opposed in this attempt by the chief priest and other priests that attended and assisted him, *v.* 17, 18. They were ready to burn incense for the king, according to the duty of their place; but, when he offered to do it himself, they plainly let him know that he meddled with that which did not belong to him, and that it was at his peril. "*It appertaineth not to thee, O Uzziah*! but *to the priests*, whose birthright it is, as sons of Aaron, and who are consecrated to the service." Aaron and his sons were appointed by the law to burn incense, Exod. xxx. 7. See Deut. xxxiii. 10; 1 Chron. xxiii. 13. David had blessed the people and Solomon and Jehoshaphat had prayed with them and preached to them. Uzziah might have done this, and it would have been to his praise; but, as for burning incense, that service was to be performed by the priests only. Korah and his accomplices, though Levites, paid dearly for offering to burn incense, which was the work of the priests only, Num. xvi. 35. The incense of our prayers must be by faith put into the hands of our Lord Jesus, the great high priest of our profession, else we cannot

JAMIESON, FAUSSET, BROWN

on account of the importance attached to the conquest of Eloth, or from the desire of the historian to introduce Uzziah as the king, who was known as the conqueror of Eloth. Besides, it indicates that the conquest occurred in the early part of his reign, that it was important as a port, and that Hebrew merchants maintained the old trade between it and the countries of the East [BERTHEAU]. **5. he sought God in the days of Zechariah**—a wise and pious counsellor, who was skilled in understanding the meaning and lessons of the ancient prophecies, and who wielded a salutary influence over Uzziah. **6, 7. he went forth and warred against the Philistines**—He overcame them in many engagements—dismantled their towns, and erected fortified cities in various parts of the country, to keep them in subjection. **Jabneh**—the same as Jabneel (Josh. 15:11). **Gur-baal**—thought by some to be Gerar, and by others Gebal. **8. the Ammonites gave gifts**—The countries east of the Jordan became tributary to him, and by the rapid succession and extent of his victories, his kingdom was extended to the Egyptian frontier.

9, 10. HIS BUILDINGS. **9. Uzziah built towers in Jerusalem,** etc.—whence resistance could be made, or missiles discharged against assailants. The sites of the principal of these towers were: at the corner gate (ch. 25:23), the northwest corner of the city; at the valley gate on the west, where the Joppa gate now is; at the "turning"—a curve in the city wall on the eastern side of Zion. The town, at this point, commanded the horse gate which defended Zion and the temple hill on the southeast [BERTHEAU]. **10. Also he built towers in the desert**—for the threefold purpose of defense, of observation, and of shelter to his cattle. He dug also a great many wells, for he loved and encouraged all branches of agriculture. Some of these "were in the desert," i.e., in the district to the southeast of Jerusalem, on the west of the Dead Sea, an extensive grazing district "in the low country" lying between the mountains of Judah and the Mediterranean; "and in the plains," east of the Jordan, within the territory of Reuben (Deut. 4:43; Josh. 20:8). **in Carmel**—This mountain, being within the boundary of Israel, did not belong to Uzziah; and as it is here placed in opposition to the vine-bearing mountains, it is probably used, not as a proper name, but to signify, as the word denotes, "fruitful fields" (*Margin*).

11-15. HIS HOST, AND ENGINES OF WAR. **11-15. an host of fighting men, who went out to war by bands**—He raised a strong body of militia, divided into companies or regiments of uniform size, which served in rotation. The enumeration was performed by two functionaries expert in the drawing up of military muster rolls, under the superintendence of Hananiah, one of the high officers of the crown. The army consisted of 307,500 picked men, under the command of two thousand gallant officers, chiefs or heads of fathers' houses, so that each fathers' house formed a distinct band. They were fully equipped with every kind of military accoutrements, from brazen helmets, a habergeon or coat of mail, to a sling for stones. **15. he made . . . engines, invented by cunning men . . . to shoot arrows and great stones**—This is the first notice that occurs in history of the use of machines for throwing projectiles. The invention is apparently ascribed to the reign of Uzziah, and PLINY expressly says they originated in Syria. **he was marvellously helped till he was strong**—He conducted himself as became the viceroy of the Divine King, and prospered.

16-21. HE INVADES THE PRIEST'S OFFICE, AND IS SMITTEN WITH LEPROSY. **16-21. he transgressed against the Lord,** etc.—(See on II Kings 15:5). This daring and wicked act is in both records traced to the intoxicating influence of overweening pride and vanity. But here the additional circumstances are stated, that his entrance was opposed, and strong remonstrances made (I Chron. 6:10) by the high priest, who was accompanied by eighty inferior priests.

ADAM CLARKE

5. *In the days of Zechariah.* Who this was we know not, but by the character that is given of him here. He was wise in the visions of God—in giving the true interpretation of divine prophecies. He was probably the tutor of Uzziah.

8. *The Ammonites gave gifts.* Paid an annual tribute.

10. *Built towers in the desert.* For the defense of his flocks, and his shepherds and husbandmen.

14. *Shields, and spears.* He prepared a vast number of military weapons, that he might have them in readiness to put into the hands of his subjects on any exigency.

15. *Engines . . . to shoot arrows and great stones.* This is the very first intimation on record of any warlike engines for the attack or defense of besieged places, and this account is long prior to anything of the kind among either the Greeks or Romans. Previously to such inventions the besieged could only be starved out, and hence sieges were very long and tedious. Shalmaneser consumed three years before such an inconsiderable place as Samaria, 2 Kings xvii. 5-6. The Jews alone were the inventors of such engines; and the invention took place in the reign of Uzziah, about eight hundred years before the Christian era. It is no wonder that, in consequence of this, *his name spread far abroad* and struck terror into his enemies.

16. *Went into the temple . . . to burn incense.* Thus assuming to himself the priest's office. See this whole transaction explained in the notes on 2 Kings xv. 5.

MATTHEW HENRY

expect it should be accepted by God, Rev. viii. 3.

4. He fell into a passion with the priests that reproved him (*v.* 19): *Uzziah was wroth*, and would not part with the censer out of his hand.

II. His punishment was an incurable leprosy, which rose up in his forehead while he was contending with the priests. When the leprosy appeared, they were emboldened to thrust him out of the temple; nay, he himself *hasted to go out, because the Lord had smitten him* with a disease which was in a particular manner a token of his displeasure, and which he knew secluded him from common converse with men, much more from the altar of God. 2. It remained a lasting punishment of his transgression; for he continued a *leper to the day of his death*, *v.* 21. 3. It was a punishment that answered the sin as face does face in a glass. (1) Pride was at the bottom of his transgression, and thus God humbled him and put dishonour upon him. (2) He invaded the office of the priests in contempt of them, and God struck him with a disease which in a particular manner made him subject to the inspection and sentence of the priests; for to them pertained the *judgment of the leprosy*, Deut. xxiv. 8. (3) He thrust himself into the temple of God, whither the priests only had admission, and for that was thrust out of the very courts of the temple, into which the meanest of his subjects that was ceremonially clean had free access.

CHAPTER 27

Verses 1-9

Concerning Jotham.

I. He reigned well. He *did that which was right in the sight of the Lord*; he *prepared his ways before the Lord his God* (*v.* 6). He walked steadily and constantly in the way of his duty, not like some of those that went before him, who, though they had some good in them, lost their credit by their inconstancy and inconsistency with themselves. Two things are observed here in his character:—1. What was amiss in his father he amended in himself (*v.* 2). 2. What was amiss in his people he could not prevail to amend: *The people did yet corruptly*,

II. He prospered. 1. He built. He began with *the gate of the house of the Lord*, which he repaired, beautifully, and raised. He then *fortified the wall of Ophel, and built cities in the mountains of Judah* (*v.* 3, 4).

2. He conquered. He prevailed against the Ammonites, who had invaded Judah in Jehoshaphat's time, *ch.* xx. 1. 3. He *became mighty* (*v.* 6) in wealth and power, and influence upon the neighbouring nations, who courted his friendship and feared his displeasure; and this he got by *preparing his ways before the Lord his God*.

III. He finished his course too soon, but finished it with honour. He died when he was but forty-one years of age (*v.* 8); but *his wars and his ways*, his wars abroad and his ways at home, were so glorious that they were recorded in the book of the kings of Israel, as well as of the kings of Judah, *v.* 7.

CHAPTER 28

Verses 1-5

Never surely had a man greater opportunity of doing well than Ahaz had, and yet here we have him in these few verses, 1. Wretchedly corrupted and debauched. He had had a good education given him, but *He did not that which was right in the sight of the Lord* (*v.* 1), nay, he did a great deal that was wrong, a wrong to God, to his own soul, and to his people; he walked in the way of the revolted Israelites and the Canaanites, made molten images and worshipped them. He forsook the temple of the Lord and sacrificed and burnt incense on the hills, as if they would place him nearer heaven, and under every green tree, as if they would signify the protection and influence of heaven by their shade and dropping. To complete his wickedness, as one perfectly divested of all natural affection as well as religion, he *burnt his children in the fire to Moloch* (*v.* 3). 2. Wretchedly spoiled. (1) The Syrians insulted him and triumphed over him, beat him in the field and carried away a

JAMIESON, FAUSSET, BROWN

Rage and threats were the only answers he deigned to return, but God took care to vindicate the sacredness of the priestly office. At the moment the king lifted the censer, He struck him with leprosy. The earthquake mentioned (Amos 1:1) is said to have been felt at the moment [JOSEPHUS].

21. dwelt in a several house—in an infirmary [BERTHEAU]. **23. they buried him . . . in the field of the burial which belonged to the kings**—He was interred not in, but near, the sepulcher of the kings, as the corpse of a leper would have polluted it.

CHAPTER 27

VSS. 1-4. JOTHAM, REIGNING WELL, PROSPERS. **1. Jotham was twenty and five years old**—(See on II Kings 15:32-35). **His mother's name . . . was Jerushah, the daughter of Zadok**—or descendant of the famous priest of that name. **2. he did that which was right**—The general rectitude of his government is described by representing it as conducted on the excellent principles which had guided the early part of his father's reign. **the people did yet corruptly**—(See II Kings 15:35); but the description here is more emphatic, that though Jotham did much to promote the good of his kingdom and aimed at a thorough reformation in religion, the widespread and inveterate wickedness of the people frustrated all his laudable efforts. **3. He built the high gate of the house of the Lord**—situated on the north—that portion of the temple hill which was high compared with the southern part—hence "the higher," or upper gate (II Kings 15:35). He built, i.e., repaired or embellished. **and on the wall of Ophel**—*Hebrew*, the Ophel, i.e., the mound, or eminence on the southeastern slope of the temple mount, a ridge lying between the valleys Kedron and Tyropœon, called "the lower city" [JOSEPHUS]. He "built much," having the same desire as his father to secure the defense of Jerusalem in every direction. **4. in the mountains of Judah, and in the forests he built castles and towers**—i.e., in the elevated and wooded spots where fortified cities could not be placed, he erected castles and towers.

5-9 HE SUBDUES THE AMMONITES. **5. He fought also with the king of the Ammonites**—This invasion he not only repelled, but, pursuing the Ammonites into their own territory, he imposed on them a yearly tribute, which, for two years, they paid. But when Rezin, king of Syria, and Pekah, king of Israel, combined to attack the kingdom of Judah, they took the opportunity of revolting, and Jotham was too distracted by other matters to attempt the reconquest (see on II Kings 15:37).

CHAPTER 28

VSS. 1-21. AHAZ, REIGNING WICKEDLY, IS AFFLICTED BY THE SYRIANS. **1-4. Ahaz was twenty years old**—(See on II Kings 16:1-4). This prince, discarding the principles and example of his excellent father, early betrayed a strong bias to idolatry. He ruled with an arbitrary and absolute authority, and not as a theocratic sovereign: he not only forsook the temple of God, but embraced first the symbolic worship established in the sister kingdom, and afterwards the gross idolatry practised by the Canaanites.

5, 6. the Lord . . . delivered him into the hand of the king of Syria . . . he was also delivered into the hand of the king of Israel—These

ADAM CLARKE

21. *And dwelt in a several house.* He was separated, because of the infectious nature of his disorder, from all society, domestic, civil, and religious.

Jotham . . . was over the king's house. He became regent of the land, his father being no longer able to perform the functions of the regal office.

22. *The rest of the acts of Uzziah, first and last, did Isaiah the prophet . . . write.* This work, however, is totally lost; for we have not any history of this king in the writings of Isaiah. He is barely mentioned, Isa. i. 1 and vi. 1.

23. *They buried him . . . in the field of the burial.* As he was a leper, he was not permitted to be buried in the common burial place of the kings, as it was supposed that even a place of sepulture must be defiled by the body of one who had died of this most afflictive and dangerous malady.

CHAPTER 27

2. *He entered not into the temple.* He copied his father's conduct as far as it was constitutional, and avoided his transgression. See the preceding chapter.

3. *On the wall of Ophel.* The wall, says the Targum, of the interior palace. Ophel was some part of the wall of Jerusalem that was most pregnable, and therefore Jotham fortified it in a particular manner.

4. *Castles and towers.* These he built for the protection of the country people against marauders.

5. *He fought also with . . . the Ammonites.* We find here that he brought them under a heavy tribute for three years, but whether this was the effect of his prevailing against them is not so evident. Some think that they paid this tribute for three years and then revolted; that, in consequence, he attacked them, and their utter subjection was the result.

7. *The rest of the acts of Jotham, and all his wars, and his ways.* It was in his days, according to 2 Kings xv. 37, that Rezin, king of Syria, and Pekah, king of Israel, began to cut Judah short. See the notes on 2 Kings xv. 36-37. *Written in the book of the kings.* There is not so much found in the Books of Kings which we have now as in this place of the Chronicles. In both places we have abridged accounts only; the larger histories have long been lost. The reign of Jotham was properly the last politically prosperous reign among the Jews. Hezekiah and Josiah did much to preserve the divine worship, but Judah continued to be cut short, till at last it was wholly ruined.

CHAPTER 28

1. *Ahaz was twenty years old.* For the difficulties in this chronology, see the notes on 2 Kings xvi. 1.

5. *Delivered him into the hand of the king of Syria.* For the better understanding of these passages the reader is requested to refer to

MATTHEW HENRY

great many of his people into captivity. (2) The king of Israel, though an idolater, too was made a scourge to him, and *smote him with a great slaughter*.

Verses 6–15

I. Treacherous Judah under the rebukes of God's providence. Never was such bloody work made among them since they were a kingdom, and by Israelites too. It is just with God to make those our plagues whom we make our patterns or make ourselves partners with in sin. A war broke out between Judah and Israel, in which Judah was worsted. 1. There was a great slaughter of men in the field of battle. Vast numbers were slain (*v.* 6) and some of the first rank, the king's son for one. The kingdom of Israel was not strong at this time, and yet strong enough to bring this great destruction upon Judah. 2. There was a great captivity of *women and children*, *v.* 8.

II. Even victorious Israel under the rebuke of God's word.

1. The message which God sent them by a prophet, who went out to meet them, not to applaud their valour, but in God's name to tell them of their faults.

(1) He told them how they came by this victory of which they were so proud. *Not for your righteousness*, be it known to you, but *for their wickedness* (Deut. ix. 5) *they are broken off*; therefore *be not you high-minded but fear, lest God also spare not you*, Rom. xi. 20, 21.

(2) He charged them with the abuse of the power God had given them over their brethren. The conquerors are here reproved, [1] For the cruelty of the slaughter they had made in the field. They had indeed *shed the blood of war in war*; they did it from a bad principle of enmity to their brethren and after a bad manner, with a barbarous fury. *The wrath of man worketh not the righteousness of God.* [2] For the imperious treatment they gave their prisoners. "*You now purpose to keep them under*, to use them or sell them as slaves, though they are your brethren and free-born Israelites."

(3) He reminded them of their own sins, by which they also were obnoxious to the wrath of God: *Are there not with you, even with you, sins against the Lord your God? v.* 10. This is intended as a check, [1] To their triumph in their success. "You are sinners, and it ill becomes sinners to be proud; for, if judgment begin thus with those that have *the house of God* among them, what shall be the end of such as worship the calves?" [2] To their severity towards their brethren. It ill becomes sinners to be cruel. You have transgressions enough to answer for already, and need not add this to the rest.

(4) He commanded them to release the prisoners, and to send them home again carefully (*v.* 11); "for you having sinned, *the fierce wrath of God is upon you*, and there is no other way of escaping it than by showing mercy."

2. The resolution of the princes thereupon not to detain the prisoners. They *stood up against those that came from the war*, though flushed with victory, and told them plainly that they should not bring their captives into Samaria, *v.* 12, 13.

3. The armed men acquiesced, and left their captives and the spoil to the disposal of *the princes* (*v.* 14), and herein they showed more truly heroic bravery than they did in taking them. It is a great honour for any man to yield to the authority of reason and religion against his interest. The princes generously sent home the poor captives well accommodated, *v.* 15.

Verses 16–27

I. The great distress which the kingdom of Ahaz was reduced to for his sin. In general, 1. *The Lord brought Judah low*, *v.* 19. They had lately been very high in wealth and power; but God found means to bring them down, and make them as despicable as they had been formidable. 2. Ahaz made Judah naked. As his sin debased them, so it exposed them. It made them naked to their shame; for it exposed them to contempt, as a man unclothed. It made them naked to their danger; for it exposed them to assaults, as a man unarmed, Exod. xxxii. 25. Sin strips men. In particular, the Edomites, to be revenged for Amaziah's cruel treatment of them (*ch.* xxv. 12), smote Judah, and carried off many captives, *v.* 17. The Philistines also insulted them, took and kept possession of several cities and villages that lay near them (*v.* 18), and so they were revenged for the incursions which Uzziah had made upon them, *ch.* xxvi. 6.

II. The addition which Ahaz made both to the national distress and the national guilt.

1. He added to the distress, by making court to strange kings, in hopes they would relieve him. When the Edomites and Philistines were vexatious to him, *he sent to the kings of Assyria to help him* (*v.* 16).

JAMIESON, FAUSSET, BROWN

verses, without alluding to the formation of a confederacy between the Syrian and Israelitish kings to invade the kingdom of Judah, or relating the commencement of the war in the close of Jotham's reign (II Kings 15:37), give the issue only of some battles that were fought in the early part of the campaign. **delivered him . . . smote him . . . he was also delivered**—i.e., his army, for Ahaz was not personally included in the number either of the slain or the captives. The slaughter of 120,000 in one day was a terrible calamity, which, it is expressly said (vs. 6), was inflicted as a judgment on Judah, "because they had forsaken the Lord God of their fathers." Among the slain were some persons of distinction: "Maaseiah the king's son" (the sons of Ahaz being too young to take part in a battle, this individual must have been a younger son of the late King Jotham); "Azrikam, the governor of the house," i.e., the palace; and "Elkanah that was next to the king," i.e., the vizier or prime minister (Gen. 41:40; Esther 10:3). These were all cut down on the field by Zichri, an Israelitish warrior, or as some think, ordered to be put to death after the battle. A vast number of captives also fell into the power of the conquerors; and an equal division of war prisoners being made between the allies, they were sent off under a military escort to the respective capitals of Syria and Israel. **8. the children of Israel carried away captive of their brethren two hundred thousand**—These captives included a great number of women, boys, and girls, a circumstance which creates a presumption that the Hebrews, like other Orientals, were accompanied in the war by multitudes of non-combatants (see on Judg. 4:8). The report of these "brethren," being brought as captives to Samaria, excited general indignation among the better-disposed inhabitants; and Oded, a prophet, accompanied by the princes (vs. 12, compared with vs. 14), went out, as the escort was approaching, to prevent the disgraceful outrage of introducing such prisoners into the city. The officers of the squadron were, of course, not to blame; they were simply doing their military duty in conducting those prisoners of war to their destination. But Oded clearly showed that the Israelitish army had gained the victory—not by the superiority of their arms, but in consequence of the divine judgment against Judah. He forcibly exposed the enormity of the offense of keeping "their brethren" as slaves got in war. He protested earnestly against adding this great offense of unnatural and sinful cruelty (Lev. 25:43, 44; Mic. 2:8, 9) to the already overwhelming amount of their own national sins.

Such was the effect of his spirited remonstrance and the opposing tide of popular feeling, that the armed men left the captives and the spoil before the princes and all the congregation." **15. the men which were expressed by name rose up**—These were either the "heads of the children of Ephraim" (mentioned vs. 12), or some other leading individuals chosen for the benevolent office. Under their kindly superintendence, the prisoners were not only released, but out of the spoils were comfortably relieved with food and clothing, and conveyed as far as Jericho on their way back to their own homes. This is a beautiful incident, and full of interest, as showing that even at this period of national decline, there were not a few who steadfastly adhered to the law of God. **16. At that time did King Ahaz send unto the kings of Assyria**—"kings," the plural for the singular, which is found in many ancient versions. "At that time," refers to the period of Ahaz' great distress, when, after a succession of defeats, he retreated within the walls of Jerusalem. Either in the same or a subsequent campaign, the Syrian and Israelitish allies marched there to besiege him (see on II Kings 16: 7-9). Though delivered from this danger, other enemies infested his dominions both on the south and the west. **17. again the Edomites had come and smitten Judah**—This invasion must have been after Rezin (at the beginning of the recent Syro-Israelitish war), had released that people from the yoke of Judah (ch. 15:11; cf. II Kings 16:6). **18. Gederoth**—on the Philistine frontier (Josh. 15:41). **Shocho**—or Socah (Josh. 15:35), now Shuweikeh, a town in the Valley of Judah (see on I Sam. 17:1). **Gimzo**—now Jimza, a little east of Ludd (Lydda) [ROBINSON]. All these disasters, by which the "Lord brought Judah low," were because of Ahaz, king of Israel (Judah), see ch. 21:2; 24:16; 28:27, who made Judah naked, and transgressed sore against the Lord.

ADAM CLARKE

what has been advanced in the notes on the sixteenth chapter of 2 Kings, vv. 5, etc.

6. *An hundred and twenty thousand.* It is very probable that there is a mistake in this number. It is hardly possible that 120,000 men could have been slain in one day, yet all the versions and MSS. agree in this number. The whole people seem to have been given up into the hands of their enemies.

9. *But a prophet of the Lord . . . whose name was Oded.* To this beautiful speech nothing can be added by the best comment; it is simple, humane, pious, and overwhelmingly convincing —no wonder it produced the effect mentioned here.

16. *The kings of Assyria to help him.* Instead of *malchey*, "kings," the Vulgate, Syriac, Arabic, and Chaldee, and the parallel place, 2 Kings xvi. 7, have *melek*, "king," in the singular number. This king was Tiglath-pileser, as we learn from the Second Book of Kings.

MATTHEW HENRY

He pillaged the house of God, and the king's house, and squeezed the princes for money to hire these foreign forces into his service, *v.* 21. But what did Ahaz get by the king of Assyria? Why, he *came to him*, but he *distressed him*, and *strengthened him not* (*v.* 20), *helped him not*, *v.* 21. The forces of the Assyrian quartered upon his country, and so impoverished and weakened it.

2. He added to the guilt, by making court to strange gods, in hopes they would relieve him. (1) He abused the house of God; for he *cut in pieces the vessels* of it, that the priests might not perform the service of the temple for want of vessels; and, at length, he *shut up the doors*, that the people might not attend it, *v.* 24. (2) He confronted the altar of God, for he *made himself altars in every corner of Jerusalem*; so that, as the prophet speaks, they were like *heaps in the furrows of the fields*, Hos. xii. 11. And in the cities of Judah he erected high places for the people to burn incense to what idols they pleased, as if on purpose to *provoke the God of his fathers*, *v.* 25. (3) He cast off God himself; for he *sacrificed to the gods of Damascus* (*v.* 23), because he feared them, thinking that they helped his enemies, and that, if he could bring them into his interest, they would help him. And what comes of it? The gods of Syria befriend Ahaz no more than the kings of Assyria did; they were *the ruin of him and of all Israel*. This sin debauched the people so that the reformation of the next reign could not prevail to cure them of their inclination to idolatry, but they retained that root of bitterness till the captivity in Babylon plucked it up.

For aught that appears, he died impenitent, and therefore died inglorious, for he was not buried *in the sepulchres of the kings*.

JAMIESON, FAUSSET, BROWN

20. Tilgath-pilneser . . . distressed him, but strengthened him not—i.e., Notwithstanding the temporary relief which Tilgath-pilneser afforded him by the conquest of Damascus and the slaughter of Rezin (II Kings 16:9), little advantage resulted from it, for Tilgath-pilneser spent the winter in voluptuous revelry at Damascus; and the connection formed with the Assyrian king was eventually a source of new and greater calamities and humiliation to the kingdom of Judah (vss. 2, 3).

22-27. HIS IDOLATRY IN HIS DISTRESS. **22. in the time of his distress did he trespass yet more against the Lord**—This infatuated king surrendered himself to the influence of idolatry and exerted his royal authority to extend it, with the intensity of a passion—with the ignorance and servile fear of a heathen (vs. 23) and a ruthless defiance of God (see on II Kings 16:10-20).

ADAM CLARKE

21. *But he helped him not.* He did him no ultimate service. See the note on 2 Kings xvi. 9.

23. *He sacrificed unto the gods of Damascus, which smote him.* "This passage," says Mr. Hallet, "greatly surprised me; for the sacred historian himself is here represented as saying, *The gods of Damascus had smitten Ahaz.* But it is impossible to suppose that an inspired author could say this; for the Scripture everywhere represents the heathen idols as nothing and vanity, and as incapable of doing either good or hurt. All difficulty is avoided if we follow the old Hebrew copies, from which the Greek translation was made, *And King Ahaz said, I will seek to the gods of Damascus which have smitten me;* and then it follows, both in Hebrew and Greek, *He said moreover, Because the gods of the king of Syria help them; therefore will I sacrifice to them, that they may help me.* Both the Syriac and Arabic give it a similar turn; and say that *Ahaz sacrificed to the gods of Damascus, and said, Ye are my gods and my lords; you will I worship, and to you will I sacrifice.*"

24. *Shut up the doors.* He caused the divine worship to be totally suspended; and they continued shut till the beginning of the reign of Hezekiah, one of whose first acts was to reopen them, and thus to restore the divine worship, chap. xxix. 3.

27. *The kings of Israel.* It is a common thing for the writer of this book to put *Israel* for "Judah." He still considers them as one people, because proceeding from one stock. The versions and MSS. have the same reading with the Hebrew; the matter is of little importance, and with this interpretation none can mistake.

MATTHEW HENRY — CHAPTER 29

Verses 1–11

I. Hezekiah was *twenty-five years old*. Joash, who came to the crown after two bad reigns, was but seven years old; Josiah, who came after two bad reigns, was but eight, which occasioned the delay of the reformation; but Hezekiah had come to years, and so applied himself immediately to it.

II. His general character. He *did that which was right like David*, *v.* 2. Of several of his predecessors it had been said that they did that which was right, *but not like David*, not with David's integrity and zeal. But here was one that had as hearty an affection for the ark and law of God as ever David had.

III. His speedy application to the great work of restoring religion. The first thing he did was to *open the doors of the house of the Lord*, *v.* 3. He found Judah low and naked, yet did not make it his first business to revive the civil interests of his kingdom, but to restore religion. Those that begin with God begin at the right end of their work.

IV. His speech to the priests and Levites. Hezekiah's exhortation to the Levites is very pathetic.

1. He laid before them the desolations of religion and the deplorable state to which it was brought among them (*v.* 6, 7): *Our fathers have trespassed.* He complained, (1) That the house of God had been deserted: *They have forsaken God, and turned their backs upon his habitation.* (2) That the instituted worship of God there had been let fall. The lamps were not lighted, and incense was not burnt. There are still such neglects as these, and they are no less culpable, when the word is not duly read and opened (for that was signified by the *lighting of the lamps*) and when prayers and praises are not duly offered up, for that was signified by *the burning of incense*.

2. He showed the sad consequences of the neglect and decay of religion among them, *v.* 8, 9.

3. He declared his own full purpose and resolution to revive religion and make it his business to promote it (*v.* 10): "*It is in my heart to make a covenant with the Lord God of Israel* (that is, to worship him only, and in that way which he has appointed)." This covenant he would not only make himself, but bring his people into the bond of.

4. He engaged and excited the Levites and priests to do their duty on this occasion. This he begins with (*v.* 5); this he ends with, *v.* 11. He called them *Levites* to remind them of their obligation to God, called them his *sons* to remind them of their relation to himself, that he expected that, *as a son with the father, they should serve with him* in the reformation of the land. (1) He told them what was their duty, to sanctify *themselves* first by repenting of their neglects, and renewing their covenants with God, and then to *sanctify the house of God*, as his servants, to make it

JAMIESON, FAUSSET, BROWN — CHAPTER 29

VSS. 1, 2. HEZEKIAH'S GOOD REIGN. **1. Hezekiah began to reign,** etc.—(see on II Kings 18:1-3). His mother's name, which, in the passage referred to, appears in an abridged form, is here given in full.

3-11. HE RESTORES RELIGION. **3. in the first year of his reign, in the first month**—not the first month after his accession to the throne, but in Nisan, the first month of the sacred year, the season appointed for the celebration of the passover. **he opened the doors of the house of the Lord**—which had been closed up by his father (ch. 28:24). **and repaired them**—or embellished them (cf. II Kings 18:16). **4. the east street**—the court of the priests, which fronted the eastern gate of the temple. Assembling the priests and Levites there, he enjoined them to set about the immediate purification of the temple. It does not appear that the order referred to the removal of idols, for objects of idolatrous homage could scarcely have been put there, seeing the doors had been shut up; but in its forsaken and desolate state the temple and its courts had been polluted by every kind of impurity. **6. our fathers have trespassed**—Ahaz and the generation contemporary with him were specially meant, for they "turned away their faces from the habitation of the Lord," and whether or not they turned east to the rising sun, they abandoned the worship of God. They "shut up the doors of the porch," so that the sacred ritual was entirely discontinued. **8. Wherefore the wrath of the Lord was upon Judah and Jerusalem**—This pious king had the discernment to ascribe all the national calamities that had befallen the kingdom to the true cause, viz., apostasy from God. The country had been laid waste by successive wars of invasion, and its resources drained. Many families mourned members of their household still suffering the miseries of foreign captivity; all their former prosperity and glory had fled; and to what was this painful and humiliating state of affairs to be traced, but to the manifest judgment of God upon the kingdom for its sins? **10, 11. Now it is in mine heart to make a covenant with the Lord God**—Convinced of the sin and bitter fruits of idolatry, Hezekiah intended to reverse the policy of his father, and to restore, in all its ancient purity and glory, the worship of the true God. His commence-

ADAM CLARKE — CHAPTER 29

2. *He did that which was right.* See the note on 2 Kings xviii. 3.

10. *To make a covenant.* To renew the covenant under which the whole people were constantly considered, and of which circumcision was the sign; and the spirit of which was, "I will be your God; ye shall be My people."

MATTHEW HENRY

clean and to set it up for the purposes for which it was made. (2) He stirred them up to do it (*v.* 11): *Be not deceived*, so the *margin*. Those that by their negligence in the service of God think to mock God, do but deceive themselves. God expected work from them. They were not chosen to be idle, to enjoy the dignity and leave the duty to be done by others, but to serve him and to minister to him.

Verses 12–19

Busy work, good work, and needful work, the cleansing of the house of the Lord.

I. The persons employed in this work were the priests and Levites, who should have kept the temple clean. Several of the Levites are here named, two of each of the three principal houses, Kohath, Gershon, and Merari (*v.* 12), and two of each of the three families of singers, Asaph, Heman, and Jeduthun, *v.* 13, 14, because they were more zealous and active than the rest. When God has work to do he will raise up leading men to preside in it. And it is not always that the first in place and rank are most fit for service or most forward to it.

II. The work was *cleansing the house of God*, 1. From the common dirt it had contracted while it was shut up—dust, and cobwebs, and the rust of the vessels. 2. From the idols and idolatrous altars that were set up in it, which, though kept ever so neat, were a greater pollution to it than if it had been made the common sewer of the city. The priests were none of them mentioned as leading men in this work, yet none but they durst go *into the inner part of the house, no, not to cleanse it*, which they did, and perhaps the high priest into the holy of holies, to cleanse that. What filth the priests brought into the court the Levites carried to the brook Kidron.

III. The expedition with which they did this work was remarkable. They began on the first day of the first month, a happy beginning of the new-year, and one that promised a good year. Thus should every year begin with the reformation of what is amiss, and the purging away, by true repentance, of all the defilements contracted the foregoing year. In eight days they cleared and cleansed the temple, and in eight days more the *courts* of the temple, *v.* 17.

IV. The report they made of it to Hezekiah was very agreeable, *v.* 18, 19. They knew the good king had set his heart upon God's altar, and longed to be attending that, and therefore they insisted most upon the readiness they had put that into—that the vessels of the altar were scoured and brightened. Those vessels which Ahaz, in his *transgression, had cast away* as vessels in which there was no pleasure, they gathered them together, sanctified them, and laid them in their place *before the altar*.

Verses 20–36

A solemn assembly was called to meet the king at the temple, the very next day (*v.* 20); and very glad, no doubt, all the good people in Jerusalem were, when it was said, *Let us go up to the house of the Lord*, Ps. cxxii. 1. As soon as Hezekiah heard that the temple was ready for him he lost no time, but was ready for it. He rose early to go up to the house of the Lord, earlier on that day than on other days, to show that his heart was upon his work there.

I. Atonement must be made for the sins of the last reign. They thought it not enough to lament and forsake those sins, but they brought a sin-offering. Even our repentance and reformation will not obtain pardon but in and through Christ, who was made *sin* (that is, a sin-offering) for us. No peace but through his blood, no, not for penitents. 1. The sin-offering was *for the kingdom, for the sanctuary*, and *for Judah* (*v.* 21), that is, to make atonement for the sins of princes, priests, and people, for they had all corrupted their way. The law of Moses appointed sacrifices to make atonement for the sins of the whole congregation (Lev. iv. 13, 14; Num. xv. 24, 25), that the national judgments which their national sins deserved might be turned away. For this purpose we must now have an eye to Christ the great propitiation, as well as for the remission and salvation of particular persons. 2. The law appointed only one goat for a sin-offering, as on the day of atonement (Lev. xvi. 15) and on such extraordinary occasions as this, Num. xv. 24. But they here offered seven (*v.* 21), because the sins of the congregation had been very great and long continued in. Seven is a number of perfection. Our great sin-offering is but one, yet that one *perfects* for ever *those that are sanctified*. 3. The king and the *congregation* (that is, the representatives of the congregation) *laid their hands on the heads of the goats* that were for the *sin-offering* (*v.* 23), thereby owning themselves guilty before God and expressing their desire that the guilt of the sinner might be transferred to the sacrifice. By faith we lay

JAMIESON, FAUSSET, BROWN

ment of this resolution at the beginning of his reign attests his sincere piety. It also proves the strength of his conviction that righteousness exalteth a nation; for, instead of waiting till his throne was consolidated, he devised measures of national reformation at the beginning of his reign and vigorously faced all the difficulties which, in such a course, he had to encounter, after the people's habits had so long been moulded to idolatry. His intentions were first disclosed to this meeting of the priests and Levites—for the agency of these officials was to be employed in carrying them into effect.

12-36. THE HOUSE OF GOD CLEANSED. **12. Then the Levites arose**—Fourteen chiefs undertook the duty of collecting and preparing their brethren for the important work of cleansing the Lord's house.

Beginning with the outer courts—that of the priests and that of the people—the cleansing of these occupied eight days, after which they set themselves to purify the interior; but as the Levites were not allowed to enter within the walls of the temple, the priest brought all the sweepings out to the porch, where they were received by the Levites and thrown into the brook Kedron. This took eight days more.

At the end of this period they repaired to the palace and announced that not only had the whole of the sacred edifice, within and without, undergone a thorough purification, but all the vessels which the late king had taken away and applied to a common use in his palace, had been restored, "and sanctified."

20. Then Hezekiah the king rose early, and gathered the rulers of the city—His anxiety to enter upon the expiatory service with all possible despatch, now that the temple had been properly prepared for it, prevented his summoning all the representatives of Israel.

The requisite number of victims having been provided, and the officers of the temple having sanctified themselves according to the directions of the law, the priests were appointed to offer sacrifices of atonement successively for "the kingdom," i.e., for the sins of the king and his predecessors; "for the sanctuary," i.e., for the sins of the priests themselves and for the desecration of the temple; "and for Judah," i.e., for the people who, by their voluntary consent, were involved in the guilt of the national apostasy.

ADAM CLARKE

16. *And the priests went.* The priests and Levites cleansed first the courts both of the priests and of the people. On this labor they spent eight days. Then they cleansed the interior of the Temple; but as the Levites had no right to enter the Temple, the priests carried all the dirt and rubbish to the porch, whence they were collected by the Levites, carried away, and cast into the brook Kidron. In this work eight days more were occupied, and thus the Temple was purified in sixteen days.

ALEXANDER MACLAREN:

The first thing to be noted is that the whole movement back to Jehovah was a one-man movement. It was Hezekiah's doing and his only. No priest is named as prominent in it, and the slowness of the whole order is especially branded in verse 34. No prophet is named; was there any one prompting the king? Perhaps Isaiah did, though his chapter 1, with its scathing repudiation of the "burnt offerings of rams and the fat of fed beasts," suggests that he did not think the restoration of sacrifice so important as that the nation should "cease to do evil and learn to do well." The people acquiesced in the king's worship of Jehovah, as they had acquiesced in other kings' worship of Baal or Moloch or Hadad. When kings take to being religious reformers, they make swift converts, but their work is as slight as it is speedy, and as short-lived as it is rapid. Manasseh was Hezekiah's successor, and swept away all his work after twenty-nine years, and apparently the mass of his people followed him just as they had followed Hezekiah. Religion must be a matter of personal conviction and individual choice. Imposed from without, or adopted because other people adopt it, it is worthless.—*Expositions of Holy Scripture*

23. *They laid their hands upon them.* That is, they confessed their sin; and as they had by their transgression forfeited their lives, they now offer these animals to die as vicarious offerings, their life being taken for the life of their owners.

MATTHEW HENRY

our hands on the Lord Jesus, and so *receive the atonement*, Rom. v. 11. 4. Burnt-offerings were offered with the sin-offerings, *seven bullocks, seven rams*, and *seven lambs*. The intention of the burnt-offerings was to give glory to the God of Israel, whom they owned as the only true God, which it was proper to do at the same time that they were by the sin-offering making atonement for their offences. The blood of those, as well as of the sin-offering, was *sprinkled upon the altar* (*v.* 22), to make reconciliation *for all Israel* (*v.* 24), and not for Judah only. Christ is a propitiation, not for the sins of Israel only, but *of the whole world*, 1 John ii. 1, 2. 5. While the offerings were burning upon the altar the *Levites* sang *the song of the Lord* (*v.* 27), the Psalms composed by David and Asaph (*v.* 30), accompanied by the musical instruments which God by his prophets had commanded the use of (*v.* 25), and which had been long neglected. Even sorrow for sin must not put us out of tune for praising God. 6. The king and all the congregation testified their consent to and concurrence in all that was done, by *bowing their heads* and *worshipping*. This is taken notice of, *v.* 28-40.

II. The solemnities of this day did likewise look forward. The temple service was to be set up again that it might be continually kept up; and this Hezekiah calls them to, *v.* 31. "Now that you have *consecrated yourselves to the Lord*—have both made an atonement and made a covenant by sacrifice, are solemnly reconciled and engaged to him—now *come near, and bring sacrifices*." Having consecrated ourselves, in the first place, to the Lord, we must bring the sacrifices of prayer, and praise, and alms, to his house. Now, in this work, it was found,

1. That the people were free. Being called to it by the king, they brought in their offerings, though not in such abundance as in the glorious days of Solomon, but according to what they had, considering their poverty and the great decay of piety among them. (1) Some were so generous as to bring burnt-offerings, which were wholly consumed to the honour of God, and of which the offerer had no part. (2) Others brought peace-offerings and thank-offerings, the fat of which was burnt upon the altar, and the flesh divided between the priests and the offerers, *v.* 35.

2. That *the priests were few*, too few for the service, *v.* 34.

3. That the Levites were forward. They had been *more upright in heart to sanctify themselves than the priests* (*v.* 34), were better affected to the work and better prepared and qualified for it. This was their praise, and, in recompence for it, they had the honour to be employed in that which was the priests' work: they *helped them to flay the offerings*. This was not according to the law (Lev. i. 5, 6), but the irregularity was dispensed with in cases of necessity, and thus encouragement was given to the faithful zealous Levites and a just disgrace put upon the careless priests.

4. That all were pleased. The king and all the people rejoiced in this blessed turn of affairs and the new face of religion which the kingdom had put on, *v.* 36. Two things in this matter pleased them:—(1) That it was soon brought about: *The thing was done suddenly*, in a little time, with a great deal of ease, and without any opposition. (2) That the hand of God was plainly in it: *God had prepared the people* by the secret influences of his grace, so that many of those who had in the last reign doted on the idolatrous altars were now as much in love with God's altar.

JAMIESON, FAUSSET, BROWN

Animals of the kinds used in sacrifice were offered by sevens—that number indicating completeness.

The Levites were ordered to praise God with musical instruments, which, although not originally used in the tabernacle, had been enlisted in the service of divine worship by David on the advice of the prophets Gad and Nathan, as well calculated to animate the devotions of the people. At the close of the special services of the occasion, viz., the offering of atonement sacrifices, the king and all civic rulers who were present joined in the worship. A grand anthem was sung (vs. 30) by the choir, consisting of some of the psalms of David and Asaph, and a great number of thank offerings, praise offerings, and freewill burnt offerings were presented at the invitation of the king. **31. Hezekiah . . . said, Now ye have consecrated yourselves unto the Lord, come near**—This address was made to the priests as being now, by the sacrifice of the expiation offerings, anew consecrated to the service of God and qualified to resume the functions of their sacred office (Exod. 28:41; 29:32). **the congregation brought in**—i.e., the body of civic rulers present.

34. the priests were too few, . . . wherefore their brethren the Levites did help them—The skins of beasts intended as peace offerings might be taken off by the officers, because, in such cases, the carcass was not wholly laid upon the altar; but animals meant for burnt offerings which were wholly consumed by fire could be flayed by the priests alone, not even the Levites being allowed to touch them, except in cases of unavoidable necessity (ch. 35:11). The duty being assigned by the law to the priests (Lev. 1:6), was construed by consuetudinary practice as an exclusion of all others not connected with the Aaronic family. **for the Levites were more upright in heart to sanctify themselves than the priests**—i.e., displayed greater alacrity than the priests. This service was hastened by the irrepressible solicitude of the king. Whether it was that many of the priests, being absent in the country, had not arrived in time—whether from the long interruption of the public duties, some of them had relaxed in their wonted attentions to personal cleanliness, and had many preparations to make—or whether from some having participated in the idolatrous services introduced by Ahaz, they were backward in repairing to the temple—a reflection does seem to be cast upon their order as dilatory and not universally ready for duty (cf. ch. 30:15). Thus was the newly consecrated temple reopened to the no small joy of the pious king and all the people.

ADAM CLARKE

21. *They brought seven bullocks.* This was more than the law required; see Lev. iv. 13, etc. It ordered one calf or ox for the sins of the people, and one he-goat for the sins of the prince; but Hezekiah here offers many more. And the reason appears sufficiently evident: the law speaks only of sins of ignorance; but here were sins of every kind and every die—idolatry, apostasy from the divine worship, profanation of the Temple, etc., etc. The sin offerings, we are informed, were offered, first for the kingdom—for the transgressions of the king and his family; secondly, for the sanctuary, which had been defiled and polluted, and for the priests who had been profane, negligent, and unholy; and, finally, for Judah—for the whole mass of the people, who had been led away into every kind of abomination by the above examples.

34. *They could not flay all the burnt offerings.* Peace offerings, and suchlike, the Levites might flay and dress; but the whole burnt offerings, that is, those which were entirely consumed on the altar, could be touched only by the priests, unless in a case of necessity, such as is mentioned here.

The Levites were more upright in heart. The priests seem to have been very backward in this good work; the Levites were more ready to help forward this glorious reformation. Why the former should have been so backward is not easy to tell, but it appears to have been the fact. Indeed it often happens that the higher orders of the priesthood are less concerned for the prosperity of true religion than the lower.

36. *And Hezekiah rejoiced.* Both he and the people rejoiced that God had prepared their hearts to bring about so great a reformation in so short a time; *for*, it is added, *the thing was done suddenly.*

MATTHEW HENRY — CHAPTER 30

Verses 1–12

I. A passover resolved upon. Shall we revive it? The time has elapsed for this year; the priests are not prepared, *v.* 3. Many, it is likely, were for deferring it; but Hezekiah finding a proviso in the law of Moses that particular persons who were unclean in the first month might keep the passover the fourteenth day of the second month (Num. ix. 11), doubted not but what it might be extended to the congregation. Whereupon they resolved to keep the passover *in the second month.*

II. A proclamation to give notice of this passover and to summon the people to it.

1. An invitation was sent to the ten revolted tribes to stir them up to come and attend this solemnity. Letters were written to Ephraim and Manasseh to invite them to Jerusalem to keep this passover (*v.* 1), with a pious design to bring them back to the Lord God of Israel. "Let them take whom they will for their king," says Hezekiah, "so they will but take him for their God."

(1) The contents of the letters that were despatched

JAMIESON, FAUSSET, BROWN — CHAPTER 30

Vss. 1-12. Hezekiah Proclaims a Passover. **1. Hezekiah sent to all . . . Judah . . . to come to . . . Jerusalem, to keep the passover**—This great religious festival had not been regularly observed by the Hebrews in their national capacity for a long time because of the division of the kingdom and the many disorders that had followed that unhappy event. Hezekiah longed extremely to see its observance revived; and the expression of his wishes having received a hearty response from the princes and chief men of his own kingdom, the preparatory steps were taken for a renewed celebration of the national solemnity. **letters also to Ephraim and Manasseh**—The names of these leading tribes are used for the whole kingdom of Israel. It was judged impossible, however, that the temple, the priests, and people could be all duly sanctified at the usual time appointed for the anniversary, viz., the fourteenth day of the first month (Nisan). Therefore it was resolved, instead of postponing the feast till another year, to observe it on the fourteenth

ADAM CLARKE — CHAPTER 30

1. *Hezekiah sent to all Israel.* It is not easy to find out how this was permitted by the king of Israel; but it is generally allowed that Hoshea, who then reigned over Israel, was one of their best kings. And as the Jews allow that at this time both the golden calves had been carried away by the Assyrians—that at Dan by Tiglath-pileser, and that at Bethel by Shalmaneser—the people who chose to worship Jehovah at Jerusalem were freely permitted to do it, and Hezekiah had encouragement to make the proclamation in question.

2. *In the second month.* In Ijar, as they could not celebrate it in Nisan, the fourteenth of which month was the proper time. But as they could not complete the purgation of the Temple till the sixteenth of that month, therefore they were obliged to hold it now, or else adjourn it till the next year, which would have been fatal to that spirit of reformation which had now

MATTHEW HENRY

upon this occasion, in which Hezekiah discovers a great concern both for the honour of God and for the welfare of the neighbouring kingdom. "*Yield yourselves unto the Lord.* Before you can come into communion with him you must come into covenant with him," *Give the hand to the Lord* (so the word is), that is, "Consent to take him for your God." "The doors of the sanctuary are now opened, and you have liberty to enter; the temple service is now revived, and you are welcome to join in it. You are children of Israel. The God you are called to return to is the God of Abraham, Isaac, and Jacob, a God in covenant with your first fathers. Your late fathers that forsook him and trespassed against him have been given up to desolation; their apostasy and idolatry have been their ruin, as you see (*v.* 7). You yourselves are but a *remnant* narrowly *escaped out of the hands of the kings of Assyria* (*v.* 6). If you return to God in a way of duty, he will return to you in a way of mercy." This he begins with (*v.* 6) and concludes with, *v.* 9. Could anything be expressed more pathetically, more movingly? Could there be a better cause, or could it be better pleaded?

(2) The entertainment which Hezekiah's messengers and message met with. It does not appear that Hoshea, who was now king of Israel, forbade his subjects to accept the invitation. They might go to Jerusalem to worship if they pleased; for, though he did evil, yet *not like the kings of Israel that were before him*, 2 Kings xvii. 2. The generality of them slighted the call and turned a deaf ear to it. The messengers went from city to city, but they *laughed them to scorn, and mocked them* (*v.* 10). The destruction of the kingdom of the ten tribes was now at hand. It was but two or three years after this that the king of Assyria laid siege to Samaria, which ended in the captivity of those tribes. Yet there were some few that accepted the invitation. In the worst of times God has had a remnant; so he had here, many of Asher, Manasseh, and Zebulun (here is no mention of any out of Ephraim, though some of that tribe are mentioned, *v.* 18), *humbled themselves, and came to Jerusalem.*

2. A command was given to the men of Judah to attend this solemnity; and they universally obeyed it, *v.* 12. They did it with one heart, were all of a mind in it, and *the hand of God gave* them that *one heart.*

Verses 13–20

The time appointed for the passover having arrived, a very great congregation came together upon the occasion, *v.* 13.

I. The preparation they made for the passover, and good preparation it was: *They took away* all *the* idolatrous *altars* that were found, not only in the temple, but *in Jerusalem*, *v.* 14. The best preparation we can make for the gospel passover is to cast away our iniquities, our spiritual idolatries.

II. The celebration of the passover. In this the people were so forward and zealous that the priests and Levites blushed to see them more ready to bring sacrifices than they were to offer them. This put them upon sanctifying themselves (*v.* 15).

III. The irregularities they were guilty of in this solemnity. 1. The *Levites killed the passover*, which should have been done by the priests only, *v.* 17. 2. Many were permitted to eat the passover who were not purified according to the strictness of the law, *v.* 18. Grotius observes from this that ritual institutions must give way, not only to a public necessity, but to a public benefit and advantage.

IV. Hezekiah's prayer to God for the forgiveness of this irregularity.

1. A short prayer, but to the purpose: *The good Lord pardon every one* in the congregation that has *prepared his heart* to those services, though the ceremonial preparation be wanting. For *this* is the *one thing needful*, that we *seek God*, his favour, his honour, and that we set our hearts to do it. Where this sincerity and fixedness of heart are there may still be many defects and infirmities. These defects need pardoning healing grace; for omissions in duty are sins as well as omissions of duty. The way to obtain pardon for our deficiencies in duty is to seek it of God by prayer.

2. A successful prayer: *The Lord hearkened to Hezekiah* and, in answer to his prayer, *healed the people* (*v.* 20), not only did not lay their sin to their charge, but graciously accepted their services, for healing denotes not only forgiveness (Isa. vi. 10; Ps. ciii. 3), but comfort and peace, Isa. lvii. 18; Mal. iv. 2.

Verses 21–27

After the passover followed the feast of unleavened bread, which continued seven days. 1. Abundance

JAMIESON, FAUSSET, BROWN

day of the second month; a liberty which, being in certain circumstances (Num. 9:6-13) granted to individuals, might, it was believed, be allowed to all the people. Hezekiah's proclamation was, of course, authoritative in his own kingdom, but it could not have been made and circulated in all the towns and villages of the neighboring kingdom without the concurrence, or at least the permission, of the Israelitish sovereign. Hoshea, the reigning king, is described as, though evil in some respects, yet more favorably disposed to religious liberty than any of his predecessors since the separation of the kingdom. This is thought to be the meaning of the mitigating clause in his character (II Kings 17:2). **6. the posts**–i.e., runners, or royal messengers, who were taken from the king's bodyguard (ch. 23:1, 2). Each, well mounted, had a certain number of miles to traverse. Having performed his course, he was relieved by another, who had to scour an equal extent of ground; so that, as the government messengers were despatched in all directions, public edicts were speedily diffused throughout the country. The proclamation of Hezekiah was followed by a verbal address from himself, piously urging the duty, and setting forth the advantages, of a return to the pure faith and institutions which God had delivered to their ancestors through Moses. **the remnant of you that are escaped out of the hand of the kings of Assyria**–This implies that several expeditions against Israel had already been made by Assyrian invaders–by Pul (II Kings 15:19), but none of the people were then removed; at a later period by Tiglath-pileser, when it appears that numbers among the tribes east of Jordan (I Chron. 5:26), and afterwards in the northern parts of Israel (II Kings 15:20), were carried into foreign exile. The invasion of Shalmaneser cannot be alluded to, as it did not take place till the sixth year of Hezekiah's reign (II Kings 17:6; 18:9-12). **10 the posts passed from city to city**–It is not surprising that after so long a discontinuance of the sacred festival, this attempt to revive it should, in some quarters, have excited ridicule and opposition. Accordingly, among the tribes of Ephraim, Manasseh, and Zebulun, Hezekiah's messengers met with open insults and ill usage. Many, however, in these very districts, as well as throughout the kingdom of the ten tribes, generally complied with the invitation; while, in the kingdom of Judah, there was one unanimous feeling of high expectation and pious delight. The concourse that repaired to Jerusalem on the occasion was very great, and the occasion was ever after regarded as one of the greatest passovers that had ever been celebrated.

13-27. THE ASSEMBLY DESTROYS THE ALTARS OF IDOLATRY. **14. they arose and took away the altars that were in Jerusalem**–As a necessary preparation for the right observance of the approaching solemnity, the removal of the altars, which Ahaz had erected in the city, was resolved upon (ch. 28:24); for, as the people of God, the Hebrews were bound to extirpate all traces of idolatry; and it was a happy sign and pledge of the influence of the Spirit pervading the minds of the people when they voluntarily undertook this important preliminary work. **15. the priests and Levites were ashamed**–Though the Levites are associated in this statement, the priests were principally referred to; those of them who had been dilatory or negligent in sanctifying themselves (ch. 29:34) were put to the blush and stimulated to their duty by the greater alacrity and zeal of the people. **16-18. the priests sprinkled the blood, which they received of the hand of the Levites**–This was a deviation from the established rules and practices in presenting the offerings of the temple. The reason was, that many present on the occasion having not sanctified themselves, the Levites slaughtered the paschal victims (see on ch. 35:5) for everyone that was unclean. At other times the heads of families killed the lambs themselves, the priests receiving the blood from their hands and presenting it on the altar. Multitudes of the Israelites, especially from certain tribes (vs. 18), were in this unsanctified state, and yet they ate the passover–an exceptional feature and one opposed to the law (Num. 9:6); but this exception was allowed in answer to Hezekiah's prayer (vss. 18-20). **20. the Lord . . . healed the people**–We imagine the whole affair to have been the following: In consequence of their transgressions they had cause to fear disease and even death (Lev. 15:31). Hezekiah prayed for the nation, which was on the point of being diseased, and might therefore be regarded as sick already [BERTHEAU]. **21. the children of Israel . . . kept the feast**–The time appointed by the law for the continuance of the feast was seven days; but in consequence of its having been allowed to fall so long into

ADAM CLARKE

taken place. The law itself had given permission to those who were at a distance and could not attend to the fourteenth of the first month, and to those who were accidentally defiled and ought not to attend, to celebrate the Passover on the fourteenth of the second month; see Num. ix. 10-11.

6. *So the posts went.* "The runners or couriers"; persons who were usually employed to carry messages; men who were light of foot, and confidential.

F. B. MEYER:

"The good Lord pardon every one that prepareth his heart to seek God" (2 Chron. 30:18, 19). A very touching prayer that opens up deep thoughts as to the progress of the true knowledge of God in Israel and of the comparative value of heart preparation and ceremonial cleansing. Here were crowds of well-meaning people who had come from all parts of the land in answer to Hezekiah's invitation. Unaccustomed to temple usage, strangers to the temple rites, they had participated in the festivities of this great Passover without submitting first to the necessary ablutions. Their heart was prepared to seek God, they were proud of the great past, they desired to stand right with the Lord God of their fathers; but they were sadly ignorant and careless. The only thing to be done was to pray that their ignorances and negligences might be forgiven.

It is thus that Jesus pleads in heaven; and there are many that obtain mercy on the ground of his merit, because when they sin they do so ignorantly, and from want of knowledge rather than from want of heart. The devout ritualist who lays an excessive stress on outward forms; the man who has sensuous and distorted views of Christ, but sincerely desires to be accepted through Him; the soul that touches the hem of the garment as though the healing power were independent of the willpower of the Redeemer; the dying malefactor, who, in his last hours, catches at some distorted representation of Christ which is filtered through to him from the chance word of an uninstructed preacher—these are included in the fruitful pleading of the Great High Priest, who has compassion on the ignorant and on those who are out of the way. You may not understand doctrine, creed, or rite; but be sure to seek God. No splendid ceremonial nor rigorous etiquette can intercept the seeking soul.—*Great Verses Through the Bible*

18. *A multitude of the people . . . had not cleansed themselves.* As there were men from Ephraim, Manasseh, Issachar, and Zebulun, they were excusable, because they came from countries that had been wholly devoted to idolatry.

MATTHEW HENRY

of sacrifices were offered to God in peace-offerings, by which they both acknowledged and implored the favour of God. 2. Many good prayers were put up to God with the peace-offerings, *v.* 22. They *made confession to the Lord God of their fathers*, in which the intent and meaning of the peace-offerings were directed and explained. 3. There was a great deal of good preaching. The Levites (whose office it was, Deut. xxxiii. 10) *taught the people the good knowledge of the Lord.* Hezekiah did not himself preach, but he *spoke comfortably to the Levites* that did, attended their preaching, commended their diligence, and assured them of his protection and countenance. 4. They sang psalms every day (*v.* 21): *The Levites and priests praised the Lord day by day.* 5. Having kept the seven days of the feast in this religious manner they had so much comfort in the service that they *kept other seven days, v.* 23. The case was extraordinary: they had been long without the ordinance; guilt had been contracted by the neglect of it; they had now got a very great congregation together, and were in a devout serious frame; they knew not when they might have such another opportunity, and therefore could not now find in their hearts to separate till they had doubled the time. How unlike those who snuffed at God's service, and said, *What a weariness is it!* Or those who asked, *When will the sabbath be gone?* 6. All this they did *with gladness* (*v.* 23); they all rejoiced, and particularly *the strangers, v.* 25. *So there was great joy in Jerusalem, v.* 26. Never was the like since the dedication of the temple in Solomon's time. 7. The congregation was at length dismissed with a solemn blessing, *v.* 27. (1) The priests pronounced it; for it was part of their office to *bless the people* (Num. vi. 22, 23), in which they were both the people's mouth to God by way of prayer and God's mouth to the people by way of promise; for their blessing included both. What a comfort is it to a congregation to be sent home thus crowned! (2) God said *Amen* to it. The prayer that comes up to heaven will come down again to this earth in showers of blessings.

CHAPTER 31

Verses 1–10

An account of what was done after the passover. What was wanting in the solemnities of preparation for it before was made up in that which is better, a due improvement of it after

I. They applied themselves with vigour to destroy all the monuments of idolatry, *v.* 1. 1. This was done immediately after the passover. If our hearts have been made to burn within us at an ordinance, that spirit of burning will consume the dross of corruption. Hoshea king of Israel not forbidding it, their zeal carried them out to the destruction of idolatry even in many parts of his kingdom. At least those that came out of Ephraim and Manasseh to keep the passover (as many did, *ch.* xxx. 18) destroyed all their own images and groves, and did the like for many more. 2. They destroyed all: though ever so ancient, ever so costly, ever so beautiful, and ever so well patronised, yet they must all be destroyed.

II. Hezekiah revived and restored the courses of the priests and Levites, which David had appointed and which had of late been put out of course, *v.* 2. And all this in the *gates* or *courts* of *the tents of the Lord.* The temple is here called a tent because the temple privileges are movable things and this temple was shortly to be removed.

III. He appropriated a branch of the revenue of his crown to the maintenance and support of the altar. It was a generous act of piety, wherein he consulted both God's honour and his people's ease, as a faithful servant to him and a tender father to them.

IV. He issued out an order to the inhabitants of Jerusalem first, *v.* 4, but afterwards extended to the *cities of Judah*, that they should carefully pay in their dues, according to the law, to the priests and Levites.

JAMIESON, FAUSSET, BROWN

desuetude, they doubled the period of celebration and kept it fourteen days with unabated satisfaction and joy. Materials for the additional sacrificial meals were supplied by the munificence of the king and the princes.

24. and a great number of priests sanctified themselves—so that there would be a sufficient number of hands for the additional services.

CHAPTER 31

VSS. 1-10. THE PEOPLE FORWARD IN DESTROYING IDOLATRY. **1. all Israel . . . present went out to the cities of Judah**—The solemnities of this paschal season left a deep and salutary impression on the minds of the assembled worshippers; attachment to the ancient institutions of their country was extensively revived; ardor in the service of God animated every bosom; and under the impulse of the devout feelings inspired by the occasion, they took measures at the close of the passover for extirpating idolatrous statues and altars out of every city, as at the beginning of the festival they had done in Jerusalem. **Judah and Benjamin**—denote the southern kingdom. **Ephraim also and Manasseh**—refer to the northern kingdom. This unsparing demolition of the monuments of idolatry would receive all encouragement from the king and public authorities of the former; and the force of the popular movement was sufficient to effect the same results among the tribes of Israel, whatever opposition the power of Hoshea or the invectives of some profane brethren might have made. Thus the reign of idolatry being completely overthrown and the pure worship of God re-established throughout the land, the people returned every one to his own home, in the confident expectation that, through the divine blessing, they would enjoy a happy future of national peace and prosperity. **2. Hezekiah appointed the course of the priests,** etc.—The king now turned his attention to provide for the orderly performance of the temple-worship—arranging the priests and Levites in their courses, assigning to every one his proper place and functions—and issuing edicts for the regular payment of those dues from which the revenues of the sanctuary were derived. To set a proper example to his subjects, his own proportion was announced in the first instance, for to the king it belonged, out of his privy purse, to defray the expenses of the altar, both stated and occasional (Num. 28:3, 4, 9, 11, 19); and in making this contribution from his own means, Hezekiah followed the course which David and Solomon had taken before him (see on ch. 8:14; I Kings 9:25). Afterwards he reappointed the people's dues to the temple; and from its being necessary to issue a royal mandate in reference to this matter, it appears that the sacred tribute had been either totally neglected, or (as the idolatrous princes were known to appropriate it to their own purposes) the people had in many cases refused or evaded the duty. But with the improved state of public feeling, Hezekiah's

ADAM CLARKE

22. *Spake comfortably unto all the Levites.* On such occasions the priests and Levites had great fatigue and suffered many privations, and therefore had need of that encouragement which this prudent and pious king gave. It is a fine and expressive character given of these men, "They taught the good knowledge of God to the people."

25. *The strangers that came out of the land of Israel.* That is, the proselytes of the covenant who had embraced Judaism and had submitted to the rite of circumcision, for none others could be permitted to eat of the Passover.

26. *Since the time of Solomon . . . there was not the like in Jerusalem.* For from that time the ten tribes had been separated from the true worship of God, and now many of them for the first time, especially from Asher, Issachar, Ephraim, Manasseh, and Zebulun, joined to celebrate the Passover.

27. *And their voice was heard.* God accepted the fruits of that pious disposition which himself had infused. *And their prayer came up.* As the smoke of their sacrifices ascended to the clouds, so did their prayers, supplications, and thanksgivings ascend to the heavens.

CHAPTER 31

1. *Brake the images in pieces.* This species of reformation was not only carried on through Judah, but they carried it into Israel; whether through a transport of religious zeal or whether with the consent of Hoshea the Israelitish king, we cannot tell.

2. *In the gates of the tents of the Lord.* That is in the Temple; for this was the house, tabernacle, tent, and camp of the Most High.

3. *The king's portion of his substance for the burnt offerings.* It is conjectured that the Jewish kings, at least from the time of David, furnished the morning and evening sacrifice daily at their own expense, and several others also.

MATTHEW HENRY

V. The people thereupon brought in their tithes very readily. What the priests had occasion for, for themselves and their families, they made use of, and the overplus was *laid in heaps, v.* 6. All harvest-time they were increasing these heaps, as the fruits of the earth were gathered in; for God was to have his dues out of them all. When harvest ended they finished their heaps, *v.* 7. Hezekiah *questioned the priests and Levites* concerning them, why they did not use what was paid in, but hoarded it up thus (*v.* 9), to which it was answered that they had made use of all they had occasion for, for the maintenance of themselves and their families and for their winter store, and that this was that which was left over and above, *v.* 10. They did not hoard these heaps for covetousness, but to show what plentiful provision God had made for them. See the acknowledgment which the king and princes made of it, *v.* 8. They gave thanks to God for his good providence, which gave them something to bring, and his good grace, which gave them hearts to bring it.

Verses 11–21

I. Two particular instances of the care of Hezekiah concerning church matters. The tithes and other holy things being brought in, he provided, 1. That they should be carefully laid up, and not left exposed in loose heaps, liable to be wasted and embezzled. He ordered chambers to be made ready in some of the courts of the temple for store-chambers (*v.* 11), and into them the offerings were brought. 2. That they should be faithfully laid out, according to the uses they were intended for. Church treasures are not to be hoarded any longer than till there is occasion for them. Out of the offerings of the Lord distribution was made, (1) To the priests in the cities (*v.* 15), who stayed at home while their brethren went to Jerusalem, and did good there in *teaching the good knowledge of the Lord.* (2) To those that *entered into the house of the Lord,* all the *males from three years old and upwards*; for the male children even at that tender age, were allowed to come into the temple with their parents, and shared with them in this distribution, *v.* 16. (3) Even the Levites from twenty years old and upwards had their share, *v.* 17. (4) The wives and children of the priests and Levites had a comfortable maintenance out of those offerings, *v.* 18. In maintaining ministers, regard must be had to their families.

II. A general character of Hezekiah's services for the support of religion, *v.* 20, 21. 1. His pious zeal reached to all the parts of his kingdom: *Thus he did throughout all Judah.* 2. He sincerely designed to please God, and approved himself to him in all he did: He *wrought that which was good before the Lord his God.*

JAMIESON, FAUSSET, BROWN

commandment was readily obeyed, and contributions of first fruits and tithes were poured in with great liberality from all parts of Judah, as well as from Israel. The first fruits, even of some articles of produce that were unfit for sacrifice (Lev. 2:11), such as honey (*Marg.* dates), were appropriated to the priests (Num. 18:12, 13; Deut. 18:4). The tithes (Lev. 27:31) were intended for the support of the whole Levitical tribe (Num. 18:8, 20, 24). **6. and laid them by heaps**—The contributions began to be sent in shortly after the celebration of the passover, which had taken place in the middle of the second month. Some time would elapse before the king's order reached all parts of the kingdom. The wheat harvest occurred in the third month, so that the sheaves of that grain, being presented before any other, formed "the foundation," an under-layer in the corn stores of the temple. The first fruits of their land produce which were successively sent in all the summer till the close of the fruit and vintage season, i.e., the seventh month, continued to raise heap upon heap. **9. Hezekiah questioned with the priests and the Levites concerning the heaps**—The object of his inquiries was to ascertain whether the supplies afforded the prospect of a sufficient maintenance for the members of the sacred order. **10. Azariah . . . answered . . . we have had enough**—This is probably the person mentioned (ch. 26:17), and his reply was to the following purport: There has been an abundant harvest, and a corresponding plenty in the incoming of first fruits and tithes; the people have testified their gratitude to Him who has crowned the year with His goodness by their liberality towards His servants.

11-19. Hezekiah Appoints Officers to Dispose of the Tithes. **11. Hezekiah commanded to prepare chambers in the house of the Lord**—storehouses, granaries, or cellars; either the old ones, which had been allowed through neglect to fall into decay, were to be repaired, or additional ones built. Private individuals brought their own first fruits to the temple; but the tithes were levied by the Levites, who kept a faithful account of them in their several places of abode and transmitted the allotted proportion to the priests. Officers were appointed to distribute equal rations to all in the cities of the priests who, from age or other reasons, could not repair to the temple. With the exception of children under three years of age—an exception made probably from their being considered too young to receive solid food—lists were kept of the number and age of every male; of priests according to their fathers' house, and Levites from twenty years (see Num. 4:3; 28:24; I Chron. 23:24). But, besides, provision was also made for their wives, daughters, and servants. **18. for in their set office they sanctified themselves**—This is the reason assigned for providing for the wives and children out of the revenues of the sanctuary, that priests, withdrawing from those secular pursuits by which they might have maintained their households, devoted themselves entirely to the functions of the ministry.

20, 21. His Sincerity of Heart. **20. Hezekiah . . . wrought that which was good and right**—He displayed the qualities of a constitutional king, in restoring and upholding the ancient institutions of the kingdom; while his zealous and persevering efforts to promote the cause of true religion and the best interests of his subjects entitled him to be ranked with the most illustrious of his predecessors (II Kings 18:15).

ADAM CLARKE

5. *Brought . . . the firstfruits.* These were principally for the maintenance of the priests and Levites. They brought tithes of all the produce of the field, whether commanded or not, as we see in the instance of *honey,* which was not to be offered to the Lord, Lev. ii. 11, yet it appears it might be offered to the priests as firstfruits, or in the way of tithes.

7. *In the third month.* "The month *Sivan;* the seventh, *Tisri.*"—Targum. *The heaps.* The vast collections of grain which they had from the tithes over and above their own consumption; see v. 10.

11. *To prepare chambers.* To make granaries to lay up this superabundance.

12. *Shimei . . . was the next.* He was assistant to Cononiah.

15. *And Miniamin.* Instead of *Miniamin, Benjamin* is the reading of three of Kennicott's and De Rossi's MSS.; and this is the reading of the Vulgate, Syriac, Septuagint, and Arabic.

17. *From twenty years old.* Moses had ordered that the Levites should not begin their labor till they were thirty years of age; but David changed this order, and obliged them to begin at twenty.

CHAPTER 32

MATTHEW HENRY

Verses 1–8

1. The formidable design of Sennacherib against Hezekiah's kingdom. Sennacherib was now, as Nebuchadnezzar was afterwards, the terror and scourge of that part of the world. He aimed to raise a boundless monarchy for himself upon the ruins of all his neighbours. His predecessor Shalmaneser had lately made himself master of the kingdom of Israel, and carried the ten tribes captives. Sennacherib thought, in like manner, to win Judah for himself. It is observable that, just about this time, Rome, a city which afterwards came to reign more than any other had done *over the kings of the earth,* was built by Romulus. Sennacherib invaded Judah immediately after the re-establishment of religion in it: *After these things he entered into Judah, v.* 1. Perhaps he intended to chastise Hezekiah for destroying that idolatry to which he himself was devoted. One would have expected to hear of nothing but perfect peace, and that none durst meddle with a people thus qualified for the divine favour; yet the next news we hear is that a threatening destroying army enters the

JAMIESON, FAUSSET, BROWN

Vss. 1-20. Sennacherib Invades Judah. **1. After these things, and the establishment thereof**—i.e., the restoration of the temple-worship. The precise date is given, II Kings 18:13. Determined to recover the independence of his country, Hezekiah had decided to refuse to pay the tribute which his father had bound himself to pay to Assyria. **Sennacherib . . . entered into Judah, and encamped against the fenced cities**—The whole land was ravaged; the strong fortresses of Ashdod (Isa. 20:1) and Lachish had fallen; the siege of Libnah had commenced, when the king of Judah, doubting his ability to resist, sent to acknowledge his fault, and offer terms of submission by paying the tribute. The commencement of this Assyrian war was disastrous to Hezekiah (II Kings 18:13). But the misfortunes of the early period of the war are here passed over, as the historian hastens to relate the remarkable deliverance which God wrought for His kingdom of Judah.

ADAM CLARKE

1. *After these things.* God did not permit this pious prince to be disturbed till he had completed the reformation which he had begun.

MATTHEW HENRY

country, and is ready to lay all waste. The little opposition which Sennacherib met with in entering Judah induced him to imagine that all was his own. He thought to *win all the fenced cities* (*v.* 1), and purposed to *fight against Jerusalem*, *v.* 2. See 2 Kings xviii. 7, 13.

II. The preparation which Hezekiah made against this storm that threatened him: *He took counsel with his princes*, *v.* 3. With their advice he provided, 1. That the country should give him a cold reception, for he took care that he should find no water in it. All hands were set immediately to work to *stop up the fountains*, and *the brook that ran through the midst of the land.* Such as this is the policy commonly practised now-a-days of destroying the forage before an invading army. 2. That the city should give him a warm reception. In order to do this he repaired the wall, raised towers, and made darts and shields in abundance (*v.* 5), and appointed captains, *v.* 6.

III. The encouragement which he gave to his people to depend upon God in this distress. He gathered them together in a broad open street, and *spoke comfortably to them*, *v.* 6. With what he said he put life into his people, his captains especially, and *spoke to their heart*, as the word is. 1. He endeavoured to keep down their fears: "*Be strong and courageous*"; do not think of surrendering the city or capitulating, but resolve to hold it out to the last man. The prophet had thus encouraged them from God (Isa. x. 24): *Be not afraid of the Assyrians;* and here the king from him. 2. He endeavoured to keep up their faith, in order to the silencing and suppressing of their fears. "Sennacherib has a *multitude with him*, and yet there are *more with us than with him*; for we have God with us, and how many do you reckon him for? With our enemy is an arm of flesh, which he trusts to; but *with us is the Lord*, whose power is irresistible, our God, whose promise, is inviolable, a God in covenant with us, *to help us, and to fight our battles.*" God will raise us above the prevailing fear of man. He that *feareth the fury of the oppressor forgetteth the Lord his Maker*, Isa. li. 12, 13. It is probable that Hezekiah said more concerning the presence of God with them and his power to relieve them. Let the good subjects and soldiers of Jesus Christ rest thus upon his word, and boldly say, *Since God is for us, who can be against us?*

Verses 9–23

This story of the rage and blasphemy of Sennacherib, Hezekiah's prayer, and the deliverance of Jerusalem by the destruction of the Assyrian army, we had more at large in the book of Kings, 2 Kings xviii and xix.

I. Sennacherib has his hands full in besieging Lachish (*v.* 9), but hears that Hezekiah is fortifying Jerusalem and encouraging his people to stand it out; and therefore, before he come in person to besiege it, he sends messengers, and writes letters to frighten Hezekiah and his people into a surrender of the city. He did not treat with Hezekiah as a man of honour, nor propose fair terms to him, but used mean and base artifices, to terrify the common people and persuade them to desert him. He represented Hezekiah as one who designed to betray them *to famine and thirst* (*v.* 11), as one who had exposed them already to the divine displeasure by taking away the high places and altars (*v.* 12). This proud blasphemer compared the great Jehovah, the Maker of heaven and earth, with the dunghill gods of the nations, the work of men's hands, and thought him no more able to deliver his worshippers than they were to deliver theirs (*v.* 19), as if an infinite and eternal Spirit had no more wisdom and power than a stone or the stock of a tree. He boasted of his triumphs over the gods of the nations, that they could none of them protect their people (*v.* 13–15), and thence inferred as if he were inferior to them all, *How much less shall your God deliver you?* All this was intended to frighten the people from their hope in God. Thus they hoped to take the city by weakening the hands of those that should defend it. Satan, in his temptations, aims to destroy our faith in God's all-sufficiency, knowing that he shall gain his point if he can do that; as we keep our ground if our *faith fail not*, Luke xxii. 32.

II. The duty is in the day of distress to pray and cry to Heaven. So Hezekiah did, and the prophet Isaiah, *v.* 20. It was a happy time when the king and the prophet joined thus in prayer.

III. The power and goodness of God. He is able both to control his enemies, be they ever so high, and to relieve his friends, be they ever so low.

1. As the blasphemies of his enemies engage him against them (Deut. xxxii. 27), so the prayers of his people engage him for them. The army of the Assyrians was cut off by the sword of an angel, which triumphed particularly in the slaughter of the mighty men of valour. The king of the Assyrians, having

JAMIESON, FAUSSET, BROWN

2-8. when Hezekiah saw that Sennacherib . . . was purposed to fight against Jerusalem—An account of the means taken to fortify Jerusalem against the threatened siege is given only in this passage. The polluting or filling up of wells, and the altering of the course of rivers, is an old practice that still obtains in the wars of the East. Hezekiah's plan was to cover the fountain-heads, so that they might not be discovered by the enemy, and to carry the water by subterranean channels or pipes into the city—a plan which, while it would secure a constant supply to the inhabitants, would distress the besiegers, as the country all around Jerusalem was very destitute of water. **4. So there was gathered much people . . . who stopped all the fountains, and the brook that ran through the midst of the land**—"Where these various fountains were, we have now no positive means of ascertaining; though Enrogel, and the spring now called the Virgin's Fount, may well be numbered among them. *Josephus* mentions the existence of various fountains without the city, but does not mention any of them in this connection but Siloam. 'The brook,' however, is located with sufficient precision to enable us to trace it very definitely. We are told that 'it ran through the midst of the land.' Now a stream running through either the Kedron or Hinnom Valley, could, in no proper sense, be said to run 'through the midst of the land,' but one flowing through the true Gihon valley, and separating Akra and Zion from Bezetha, Moriah, and Ophel, as a stream once, doubtless, did, could, with peculiar propriety, be said to run *through the midst of the land* on which the [Holy] City was built. And that this is the correct meaning of the phrase is not only apparent from the force of circumstances, but is positively so declared in the Septuagint, where, moreover, it is called a 'river,' which, at least, implies a much larger stream than the Kedron, and comports well with the marginal reading, where it is said to 'overflow through the midst of the land.' Previous to the interference of man, there was, no doubt, a very copious stream that gushed forth in the upper portion of that shallow, basin-like concavity north of Damascus Gate, which is unquestionably the upper extremity of the Gihon valley, and pursuing its meandering course through this valley, entered the Tyropœon at its great southern curve, down which it flowed into the valley of the Kedron" [BARCLAY'S CITY OF THE GREAT KING]. **5, 6. he strengthened himself**—He made a careful inspection of the city defenses for the purpose of repairing breaches in the wall here, renewing the masonry there, raising projecting machines to the towers, and especially fortifying the lower portion of Zion, i.e., Millo, "(in) the original city of David." "In" is a supplement of our translators, and the text reads better without it, for it was not the whole city that was repaired, but only the lower portion of Zion, or the original "city of David." **he . . . gathered them together . . . in the street**—i.e., the large open space at the gate of Eastern cities. Having equipped his soldiers with a full suit of military accoutrements, he addressed them in an animated strain, dwelling on the motives they had to inspire courage and confidence of success, especially on their consciousness of the favor and helping power of God. **9-20.** (See on II Kings 18:17-35; also 19: 8-34.) **18. they cried with a loud voice . . . unto the people of Jerusalem . . . on the wall**—It appears that the wall on the west side of the city reached as far to the side of the uppermost pool of Gihon at that time as it does now, if not farther; and the wall was so close to that pool that those sent to negotiate with the Assyrian general answered him in their own tongue (see on II Kings 18:27).

21-23. AN ANGEL DESTROYS THE ASSYRIANS. **21. an angel . . . cut off all the mighty men**—(see on II Kings 19:35-37).

ADAM CLARKE

2. *When Hezekiah saw.* This was in the fourteenth year of the reign of Hezekiah; and at first the Jewish king bought him off at the great price of 300 talents of silver and 30 talents of gold; and even emptied his own treasures, and spoiled the house of the Lord, to gratify the oppressive avarice of the Assyrian king. See the whole account, 2 Kings xviii. 13, etc.

4. *Stopped all the fountains.* This was prudently done, for without water how could an immense army subsist in an arid country?

5. *Raised it up to the towers.* He built the wall up to the height of the towers, or, having built the wall, he raised towers on it.

6. *Set captains of war over the people . . . in the street of the gate of the city.* That is, the open places at the gate of the city, whither the people came for judgment.

7. *There be more with us than with him.* We have more power than they have. (These words he quotes from the prophet Elisha, 2 Kings vi. 16). This was soon proved to be true by the slaughter made by the angel of the Lord in the Assyrian camp.

9. *After this did Sennacherib.* Having received the silver and gold mentioned above, he withdrew his army, but shortly after he sent Rabshakeh with a blasphemous message. This is the fact mentioned here.

10. *Thus saith Sennacherib.* See all these circumstances largely explained, 2 Kings xviii. 17-36.

17. *Wrote also letters.* See 2 Kings xix. 9, 14.

21. *The Lord sent an angel.* See 2 Kings xix. 35 and the note there. *House of his god.* Nisroch. *They that came forth of his own bowels.* His sons Adrammelech and Sharezer.

MATTHEW HENRY

received this disgrace, was cut off by the sword of his own sons.

2. By this work of wonder God was glorified, as the protector of his people. Thus he saved Jerusalem, not only from the hand of Sennacherib, but from the hand *of all others*, *v.* 22; for such a deliverance as this was an earnest of much mercy in store; and he *guided them*, that is, he guarded them, on every side.

Verses 24–33

The story of Hezekiah concluded:

I. His sickness and his recovery from it, *v.* 24. The account of his sickness is but briefly mentioned here; we had a large narrative of it, 2 Kings xx. His disease seemed likely to be mortal. In the extremity of it he prayed. God answered him, and gave him a sign that he should recover, the going back of the sun ten degrees.

II. His sin and his repentance for it, which were also more largely related, 2 Kings xx. 12, &c. The occasion of it was the king of Babylon's sending an honourable embassy to him to congratulate him on his recovery. But here it is added that they came to enquire of *the wonder that was done in the land* (*v.* 31), either the destruction of the Assyrian army or the going back of the sun. The Assyrians were their enemies; they came to enquire concerning their fall, that they might triumph in it. The sun was their god; they came to enquire concerning the favour he had shown to Hezekiah, that they might honour him whom their god honoured, *v.* 31. His sin was that *his heart was lifted up*, *v.* 25. He was proud of the honour God had put upon him in so many instances, the honour his neighbours did him in bringing him presents, and now that the king of Babylon should send an embassy to him to caress and court him: this exalted him above measure. When Hezekiah had destroyed other idolatries he began to idolize himself. Though we cannot render an equivalent, or the payment of a debt, we must render the acknowledgment of a favour. His repentance for this sin: *He humbled himself for the pride of his heart*.

III. Here is the honour done to Hezekiah, while he lived. He had *exceeding much riches and honour* (*v.* 27). Among his great performances, his turning the water-course of Gihon is mentioned (*v.* 30), which was done upon occasion of Sennacherib's invasion, *v.* 3, 4. The water had come into that which is called the *old pool* (Isa. xxii. 11) and the *upper pool* (Isa. vii. 3); but he gathered the waters into a new place, for the greater convenience of the city, called the *lower pool*, Isa. xxii. 9. And, in general, he *prospered in all his works*, for they were good works. The prophet Isaiah wrote his life and reign (*v.* 132), his acts and his goodness or piety.

The people *did him honour at his death* (*v.* 33), buried him in the chief of the sepulchres, made as great a burning for him as for Asa, or, which is a much greater honour, made great lamentation for him, as for Josiah.

JAMIESON, FAUSSET, BROWN

24-26. HEZEKIAH'S SICKNESS AND RECOVERY. **24. In those days Hezekiah was sick to the death**—(See on II Kings 20:1-11).

27-33. HIS RICHES AND WORKS. **he had exceeding much riches and honour**—(cf. II Kings 20:13; Isa. 39:2). A great portion of his personal wealth, like that of David and Uzziah, consisted in immense possessions of agricultural and pastoral produce. Besides, he had accumulated large treasures in gold, silver, and precious things, which he had taken as spoils from the Philistines, and which he had received as presents from neighboring states, among which he was held in great honor as a king under the special protection of Heaven. Much of his great wealth he expended in improving his capital, erecting forts, and promoting the internal benefit of his kingdom. **30. stopped the . . . watercourse of Gihon, and brought it . . . to the west side of the city,** etc.—(cf. II Kings 20:20). Particular notice is here taken of the aqueduct, as among the greatest of Hezekiah's works. "In exploring the subterranean channel conveying the water from Virgin's Fount to Siloam, I discovered a similar channel entering from the north, a few yards from its commencement; and on tracing it up near the Mugrabin gate, where it became so choked with rubbish that it could be traversed no farther, I there found it turn to the *west* in the direction of the south end of the cleft, or saddle, of Zion, and if this channel was not constructed for the purpose of conveying the waters of Hezekiah's aqueduct, I am unable to suggest any purpose to which it could have been applied. Perhaps the reason why it was not brought down on the Zion side, was that Zion was already well watered in its lower portion by the Great Pool, 'the lower pool of Gihon.' And accordingly *Williams* (HOLY CITY) renders this passage, 'He stopped the upper outflow of the waters of Gihon, and led them down westward to the city'" [BARCLAY'S CITY OF THE GREAT KING]. The construction of this aqueduct required not only masonic but engineering skill; for the passage was bored through a continuous mass of rock. Hezekiah's pool or reservoir made to receive the water within the northwest part of the city still remains. It is an oblong quadrangular tank, 240 feet in length, from 144 to 150 in breadth, but, from recent excavations, appears to have extended somewhat farther towards the north. **31. in the business of the ambassadors who sent . . . to inquire of the wonder that was done in the land,** etc.—They brought a present (vs. 23, see on II Kings 20:12, 13), and a letter of congratulation on his recovery, in which particular inquiries were made about the miracle of the sun's retrocession—a natural phenomenon that could not fail to excite great interest and curiosity at Babylon, where astronomy was so much studied. At the same time, there is reason to believe that they proposed a defensive league against the Assyrians. **God left him, to try him,** etc.—Hezekiah's offense was not so much in the display of his military stores and treasures, as in not giving to God the glory both of the miracle and of his recovery, and thus leading those heathen ambassadors to know Him.

ADAM CLARKE

23. *Many brought gifts unto the Lord*. They plainly saw that Jehovah was the Protector of the land. *And presents to Hezekiah*. They saw that God was his Friend and would undertake for him, and they did not wish to have such a man for their enemy.

24. *Hezekiah was sick*. See 2 Kings xx. 1, etc., and the notes there.

25. *Hezekiah rendered not again*. He got into a vain confidence, took pleasure in his riches, and vainly showed them to the messengers of the king of Babylon. See on 2 Kings xx. 12, etc.

26. *Humbled himself*. Awoke from his sleep, was sorry for his sin, deprecated the wrath of God, and the divine displeasure was turned away from him.

27. *Pleasant jewels*. Desirable "vessels" or "utensils."

30. *The upper watercourse*. He made canals to bring the waters of Gihon from the west side of Jerusalem to the west side of the city of David.

31. *Of the ambassadors*. See 2 Kings xx. 13.

32. *The vision of Isaiah*. See this prophet, cc. xxxvi—xxxix.

33. *Chiefest of the sepulchres*. This respect they paid to him who, since David, had been the best of all their kings.

MATTHEW HENRY — CHAPTER 33

Verses 1–10

An account of the great wickedness of Manasseh. It is the same almost word for word with that which we had, 2 Kings xxi. 1–9. This foolish young prince, in contradiction to the good example and good education his father gave him, abandoned himself to all impiety, transcribed the abominations of the heathen (*v.* 2), ruined the established religion, unravelled his father's glorious reformation (*v.* 3), profaned the house of God with his idolatry (*v.* 4, 5), dedicated his children to Moloch, and made the devil's lying oracles his guides and his counsellors, *v.* 6. We may here admire the grace of God in speaking to them, and their obstinacy in turning a deaf ear to him, that either their badness did not quite turn away his goodness, but still he waited to be gracious, or that his goodness did not turn them from their badness, but still they hated to be reformed. Corruptions in worship are such diseases of the church as it is very apt to relapse into again even when they seem to be cured. The god of this world has strangely blinded men's minds, and has a wonderful power over those that are led captive by him; else he could not draw them from God, their best friend, to depend upon their sworn enemy.

Verses 11–20

Manasseh by his wickedness undid the good that his father had done; by repentance undid the evil

JAMIESON, FAUSSET, BROWN — CHAPTER 33

VSS. 1-10. MANASSEH'S WICKED REIGN. **1, 2. Manasseh . . . did that which was evil in the sight of the Lord**—(See on II Kings 21:1-16).

11-19. HE IS CARRIED UNTO BABYLON, WHERE HE HUMBLES HIMSELF BEFORE GOD, AND IS RESTORED TO HIS KINGDOM. **11. the captains of the host of the king of Assyria**—This king was Esarhaddon. After having devoted the first years of his reign to the consolidation of his government at home, he turned his attention to repair the loss of the tributary provinces west of the Euphrates, which, on the disaster and death of Sennacherib, had taken the opportunity of shaking off the Assyrian yoke.

ADAM CLARKE — CHAPTER 33

1. *Manasseh was twelve years old*. We do not find that he had any godly director; his youth was therefore the more easily seduced. But surely he had a pious education; how then could the principles of it be so soon eradicated?

3. *Altars for Baalim*. The sun and moon. *And made groves, Asheroth*, "Astarte"; *the host of heaven*, all the planets and stars. These were the general objects of his devotion.

5. *He built altars*. See the principal facts in this chapter explained in the notes on 2 Kings xxi. 1-17.

MATTHEW HENRY

that he himself had done. A memorable instance it is of the riches of God's pardoning mercy and the power of his renewing grace.

I. The occasion of Manasseh's repentance was his affliction. God brought a foreign enemy upon him; the king of Babylon, that courted his father who faithfully served God, invaded him now that he had treacherously departed from God. He is here called *king of Assyria*, because he had made himself master of Assyria, which he would the more easily do for the defeat of Sennacherib's army, and its destruction before Jerusalem. The captain took *Manasseh among the thorns*, in some bush or other, perhaps in his garden, where he had hid himself. Or it is spoken figuratively: he was perplexed in his counsels and embarrassed in his affairs. He was, as we say, in the briers, and knew not which way to extricate himself, and so became an easy prey to the Assyrian captains, who no doubt plundered his house and took away what they pleased, as Isaiah had foretold, 2 Kings xx. 17, 18. What was Hezekiah's pride was their prey. They bound Manasseh, who had been held before with the cords of his own iniquity, and carried him prisoner to Babylon.

II. The expressions of his repentance (*v.* 12, 13): *When he was in affliction* he had time to bethink himself and reason enough too. 1. He was convinced that Jehovah is the only living and true God. Had he been a prince in the palace of Babylon, it is probable he would have been confirmed in his idolatry; but, being a captive in the prisons of Babylon, he was convinced of it and reclaimed from it. 2. He applied to him as *his* God now, renouncing all others, and resolving to cleave to him only, the God of his fathers, and a God in covenant with him. 3. He humbled himself greatly before him. 4. He prayed to him for the pardon of sin and the return of his favour. That is a good prayer, and very pertinent in this case, which we find among the apocryphal books, entitled, *The prayer of Manasses, king of Judah, when he was holden captive in Babylon.*

III. God's gracious acceptance of his repentance: *God was entreated of him, and heard his supplication.* Though affliction drive us to God, he will not therefore reject us if in sincerity we seek him, for afflictions are sent on purpose to bring us to him. Let not great sinners despair, when Manasseh himself, upon his repentance, found favour with God; in whom God *showed forth a pattern of longsuffering*, as 1 Tim. i. 16; Isa. i. 18.

IV. The *fruits meet for repentance* which he brought forth after his return to his own land, *v.* 15, 16. He *took away the strange gods*, the images of them, and that idol (whatever it was) which he had set up with so much solemnity *in the house of the Lord*. He returned to his duty; for he *repaired the altar of the Lord*. He sacrificed thereon peace-offerings to implore God's favour, and thank-offerings to praise him for his deliverance.

V. His prosperity, in some measure, after his repentance. When he returned to God in a way of duty, God returned to him in a way of mercy. Josephus says that all the rest of his time he was so changed for the better that he was looked upon as a very happy man.

Verses 21–25

Concerning Amon,

I. His great wickedness. He did as *Manasseh had done* in the days of his apostasy, *v.* 22. Manasseh, when he *cast out the images*, did not utterly deface and destroy them, according to the law which required Israel to *burn the images with fire*, Deut. vii. 5. How necessary that law was this instance shows; for the *carved images* being only thrown by, and not burnt, Amon knew where to find them, soon set them up, and sacrificed to them It is added, *He trespassed more and more*, *v.* 23. He *humbled not himself before the Lord, as his father had humbled himself.* He fell like him, but did not get up again like him. It is not so much sin as impenitence in sin that ruins men.

II. His speedy destruction. He reigned but two years and then his servants *conspired against him* and *slew him*, *v.* 24.

JAMIESON, FAUSSET, BROWN

Having overrun Palestine and removed the remnant that were left in the kingdom of Israel, he despatched his generals, the chief of whom was Tartan (Isa. 20:1), with a portion of his army for the reduction of Judah also. In a successful attack upon Jerusalem, they took multitudes of captives, and got a great prize, including the king himself, among the prisoners. **took Manasseh among the thorns**—This may mean, as is commonly supposed, that he had hid himself among a thicket of briers and brambles. We know that the Hebrews sometimes took refuge from their enemies in thickets (I Sam. 13:6). But, instead of the *Hebrew, Bacochim*, "among the thorns," some versions read *Bechayim*, "among the living," and so the passage would be "took him alive." **bound him with fetters, and carried him to Babylon**—The *Hebrew* word rendered "fetters" denotes properly two chains of brass. The humiliating state in which Manasseh appeared before the Assyrian monarch may be judged of by a picture on a tablet in the Khorsabad palace, representing prisoners led bound into the king's presence. "The captives represented appear to be inhabitants of Palestine. Behind the prisoners stand four persons with inscriptions on the lower part of their tunics; the first two are bearded, and seem to be accusers; the remaining two are nearly defaced; but behind the last appears the eunuch, whose office it seems to be to usher into the presence of the king those who are permitted to appear before him. He is followed by another person of the same race as those under punishment; his hands are manacled, and on his ankles are strong rings fastened together by a heavy bar" [NINEVEH AND ITS PALACES]. No name is given, and, therefore, no conclusion can be drawn that the figure represents Manasseh. But the people appear to be Hebrews, and this pictorial scene will enable us to imagine the manner in which the royal captive from Judah was received in the court of Babylon. Esar-haddon had established his residence there; for though from the many revolts that followed the death of his father, he succeeded at first only to the throne of Assyria, yet having some time previous to his conquest of Judah, recovered possession of Babylon, this enterprising king had united under his sway the two empires of Babylon and Chaldea and transferred the seat of his government to Babylon. **12, 13. when he was in affliction, he besought the Lord his God**—In the solitude of exile or imprisonment, Manasseh had leisure for reflection. The calamities forced upon him a review of his past life, under a conviction that the miseries of his dethronement and captive condition were owing to his awful and unprecedented apostasy (vs. 7) from the God of his fathers. He humbled himself, repented, and prayed for an opportunity of bringing forth the fruits of repentance. His prayer was heard; for his conqueror not only released him, but, after two years' exile, restored him, with honor and the full exercise of royal power, to a tributary and dependent kingdom. Some political motive, doubtless, prompted the Assyrian king to restore Manasseh, and that was most probably to have the kingdom of Judah as a barrier between Egypt and his Assyrian dominions. But God overruled this measure for higher purposes. Manasseh now showed himself, by the influence of sanctified affliction, a new and better man. He made a complete reversal of his former policy, by not only destroying all the idolatrous statues and altars he had formerly erected in Jerusalem, but displaying the most ardent zeal in restoring and encouraging the worship of God. **14. he built a wall without the city . . . on the west side of Gihon . . . even to the entering in at the fish gate**—"The well-ascertained position of the fish-gate, shows that the valley of Gihon could be no other than that leading northwest of Damascus gate, and gently descending southward, uniting with the Tyropœon at the northeast corner of Mount Zion, where the latter turns at right angles and runs towards Siloam. The wall thus built by Manasseh on the west side of the valley of Gihon, would extend from the vicinity of the northeast corner of the wall of Zion in a northerly direction, until it crossed over the valley to form a junction with the outer wall at the trench of Antonia, precisely in the quarter where the temple would be most easily assailed" [BARCLAY]. **17. the people did sacrifice still in the high places, yet unto the Lord their God only**—Here it appears that the worship on high places, though it originated in a great measure from the practice of heathenism, and too often led to it, did not necessarily imply idolatry.

20-25. HE DIES AND AMON SUCCEEDS HIM. **20, 21. Manasseh slept with his fathers . . . Amon . . . began to reign**—(See on II Kings 21:17-26).

ADAM CLARKE

ALEXANDER MACLAREN:

Here we see that merciful chastisement was meant to secure a hearing for God's voice. 2 Kings tells the threat, but not the fulfillment; Chronicles tells the fulfillment but not the threat. We note how emphatically God's hand is recognized behind the political complications which brought the Assyrians to Jerusalem, and how particularly it is stated that the invasion was not headed by Esarhaddon but by his generals. The place of Manasseh's captivity also is specified, not as Nineveh, as might have been expected, but as Babylon. These details, especially the last, look like genuine history. It is history which carries a lesson. Here is one conspicuous instance of the divine method, which is working today as it did then. God's hand is behind the secondary causes of events. Our sorrows and "misfortunes" are sent to us by Him, not hurled at us by human hands only, or occurring by the working of impersonal laws. They are meant to make us bethink ourselves, and drop evil things from our hands and hearts. It is best to be guided by His eye and not need "bit and bridle"; but if we make ourselves stubborn, it is second best that we should taste the whip that it may bring us to run in harness on the road which He wills. If we habitually looked at calamities as His loving chastisement, intended to draw us to himself, we should not have to stand perplexed so often at what we call the mysteries of His providence.

The next step in the story is the yielding of the sinful heart when smitten. The worst affliction is an affliction wasted, which does us no good. And God has often to lament, "In vain have I smitten your children; they received no correction." Sorrow has in itself no power to effect the purpose for which it is sent; but all depends on how we take it. It sometimes makes us hard, bitter, obstinate in clinging to evil. A heart that has been disciplined by it, and still is undisciplined, is like iron hammered on an anvil, and made the more close-grained thereby.

—*Expositions of Holy Scripture*

14. *He built a wall.* This was probably a weak place that he fortified; or a part of the wall which the Assyrians had broken down, which he now rebuilt.

15. *He took away the strange gods.* He appears to have done everything in his power to destroy the idolatry which he had set up and to restore the pure worship of the true God. His repentance brought forth fruits meet for repentance. How long he was in captivity, and when or by whom he was delivered, we know not. The fact of his restoration is asserted, and we believe it on divine testimony.

21. *Amon . . . reigned two years.* See on 2 Kings xxi. 19.

22. *Sacrificed unto all the carved images.* How astonishing is this! with his father's example before his eyes, he copies his father's vices, but not his repentance.

23. *Trespassed more and more.* He appears to have exceeded his father, and would take no warning.

25. *The people of the land slew all them.* His murder was not a popular act, for the people slew the regicides. They were as prone to idolatry as their king was. We may rest satisfied that idolatry was accompanied with great licentiousness and sensual gratifications, else it never, as a mere religious system, could have had any sway in the world.

MATTHEW HENRY

CHAPTER 34

Verses 1–7

Josiah came to the crown when he was very young, only eight years old and he reigned *thirty-one years* (*v.* 1). In the beginning of his reign things went much as they had done in his father's time, because, being a child, he must have left the management of them to others; so that it was not till his twelfth year that the reformation began, *v.* 3. He reigned very well (*v.* 2), approved himself to God, trod in the steps of David, and did not decline either *to the right hand or to the left*. While he was young, about sixteen years old, he *began to seek after God*, *v.* 3. In the twelfth year of his reign, when it is probable he took the administration of the government entirely into his own hands, he *began to purge his kingdom from the remains of idolatry*; he destroyed the high places, groves, images, altars, all the utensils of idolatry, *v.* 3, 4. He not only cast them out as Manasseh did, but broke them to pieces, and made dust of them. This destruction of idolatry is here said to be in his twelfth year, but it was said (2 Kings xxiii. 23) to be in his eighteenth year. Something was probably done towards it in his twelfth year; then he began to purge out idolatry, but that good work met with opposition, so that it was not thoroughly done till they had found the book of the law six years afterwards.

Verses 8–13

Orders are given by the king for the repair of the temple, *v.* 8. When he had purged the house of the corruptions of it he began to fit it up for the services that were to be performed in it. Those that truly love God will *love the habitation of his house*. The Levites went about the country and gathered money towards it, which was returned to the three trustees mentioned, *v.* 8. They brought it to Hilkiah the high priest (*v.* 9), and he and they put it into the hands of workmen, both overseers and labourers, *v.* 10, 11. It is observed that the workmen were industrious and honest: They *did the work faithfully* (*v.* 12). It is also intimated that the overseers were ingenious; for it is said that all those were employed to inspect this work who were skilful in *instruments of music*; not that their skill in music could be of any use in architecture, but it was an evidence that they were men of sense and ingenuity. They had need of one another, and the work needed both. Let not the overseers of the work despise the bearers of burdens, nor let those that work in the service grudge at those whose office it is to direct; but let each esteem and serve the other in love, and let God have the glory and the church the benefit of the different gifts and dispositions of both.

Verses 14–28

This whole paragraph we had, just as it is here related, 2 Kings xxii. 8–20, and have nothing to add here to what was there observed. We take occasion to bless God that we have plenty of Bibles, and that they are, or may be, in all hands,—that the book of the law and gospel is not lost, is not scarce. Bibles are jewels, but, thanks be to God, they are not rarities. Were the things contained in the scripture new to us, as they were here to Josiah, surely they would make deeper impressions upon us than commonly they do; but they are not the less weighty, and therefore should not be the less considered by us, for their being well known. We are here directed when we are under convictions of sin, and apprehensions of divine wrath, to enquire of the Lord; so Josiah did, *v.* 21. It concerns us to ask (as they did, Acts ii. 37), *Men and brethren, what shall we do?* and more particularly (as the jailor), *What must I do to be saved?* Acts xvi. 30. Blessed be God, we have the lively oracles to which to apply with these enquiries. We are here encouraged to humble ourselves before God and seek unto him, as Josiah did.

Verses 29–33

An account of the further advances which Josiah made towards the reformation of his kingdom upon the hearing of the law read and the receipt of the message God sent him by the prophetess. Happy the people that had such a king. They were well taught. He did not go about to force them to do their duty, till he had first instructed them in it. He called all the people together, great and small, young and old, rich and poor, high and low. *He that hath ears to hear, let him hear* the words of *the book of the covenant*. The king himself read the book to the people (*v.* 30). The articles of agreement between God and Israel being read, that they might intelligently covenant with God, both king and people with great solemnity did as it were subscribe the articles. He caused *all that were present to stand to it* (*v.* 32), and made them all

JAMIESON, FAUSSET, BROWN

CHAPTER 34

Vss. 1, 2. Josiah's Good Reign. **1. Josiah was eight years old**—(See on II Kings 22:1, 2). The testimony borne to the undeviating steadfastness of his adherence to the cause of true religion places his character and reign in honorable contrast with those of many of his royal predecessors.

3-7. He Destroys Idolatry. **3. in the eighth year of his reign**—This was the sixteenth year of his age, and, as the kings of Judah were considered minors till they had completed their thirteenth year, it was three years after he had attained majority. He had very early manifested the piety and excellent dispositions of his character. In the twelfth year of his reign, but the twentieth of his age, he began to take a lively interest in the purgation of his kingdom from all the monuments of idolatry which, in his father's short reign, had been erected. At a later period, his increasing zeal for securing the purity of divine worship led him to superintend the work of demolition in various parts of his dominion. The course of the narrative in this passage is somewhat different from that followed in the Book of Kings. For the historian, having made allusion to the early manifestation of Josiah's zeal, goes on with a full detail of all the measures this good king adopted for the extirpation of idolatry; whereas the author of the Book of Kings sets out with the cleansing of the temple, immediately previous to the celebration of the passover, and embraces that occasion to give a general description of Josiah's policy for freeing the land from idolatrous pollution. The exact chronological order is not followed either in Kings or Chronicles. But it is clearly recorded in both that the abolition of idolatry began in the twelfth and was completed in the eighteenth year of Josiah's reign. Notwithstanding Josiah's undoubted sincerity and zeal and the people's apparent compliance with the king's orders, he could not extinguish a strongly rooted attachment to idolatries introduced in the early part of Manasseh's reign. This latent predilection appears unmistakably developed in the subsequent reigns, and the divine decree for the removal of Judah, as well as Israel, into captivity was irrevocably passed. **4. the graves of them that had sacrificed unto them.** He treated the graves themselves as guilty of the crimes of those who were lying in them [Bertheau]. **5. he burnt the bones of the priests upon their altars**—A greater brand of infamy could not have been put on idolatrous priests than the disinterment of their bones, and a greater defilement could not have been done to the altars of idolatry than the burning upon them the bones of those who had there officiated in their lifetime. **6. with their mattocks**—or "in their deserts"—so that the verse will stand thus: "And so did [viz., break the altars and burn the bones of priests] he in the cities of Manasseh, and Ephraim, and Simeon, even unto Naphtali, in their deserted suburbs." The reader is apt to be surprised on finding that Josiah, whose hereditary possessions were confined to the kingdom of Judah, exercised as much authority among the tribes of Ephraim, Manasseh, Simeon, and others as far as Naphtali, as he did within his own dominion. Therefore, it is necessary to observe that, after the destruction of Samaria by Shalmaneser, the remnant that continued on the mountains of Israel maintained a close intercourse with Judah, and looked to the sovereigns of that kingdom as their natural protectors. Those kings acquired great influence over them, which Josiah exercised in removing every vestige of idolatry from the land. He could not have done this without the acquiescence of the people in the propriety of this proceeding, conscious that this was conformable to their ancient laws and institutions. The Assyrian kings, who were now masters of the country, might have been displeased at the liberties Josiah took beyond his own territories. But either they were not informed of his doings, or they did not trouble themselves about his religious proceedings, relating, as they would think, to the god of the land, especially as he did not attempt to seize upon any place or to disturb the allegiance of the people [Calmet].

8-18. He Repairs the Temple. **in the eighteenth year of his reign . . . he sent Shaphan**—(See on II Kings 22:3-9).

19-33. And, Causing the Law to Be Read, Renews the Covenant between God and the People. **19. when the king had heard the words of the law**, etc.—(See on II Kings 22:11-20; 23:1-3).

ADAM CLARKE

CHAPTER 34

2. *He . . . declined neither to the right hand, nor to the left.* He never swerved from God and truth; he never omitted what he knew to be his duty to God and his kingdom; he carried on his reformation with a steady hand; timidity did not prevent him from going far enough; and zeal did not lead him beyond due bounds.

4. *The altars of Baalim.* How often have these been broken down, and how soon set up again! We see that the religion of a land is as the religion of its king. If the king were idolatrous, up went the altars; on the other hand, when the king was truly religious, down went the idolatrous altars.

6. *The cities of Manasseh.* Even those who were under the government of the Israelitish king permitted their idols and places of idolatry to be hewn down and destroyed; after the truth was declared and acknowledged, the spade and the axe were employed to complete the reformation.

9. *And they returned to Jerusalem.* Instead of *vaiyashubu*, "they returned," we should read *yoshebey*, "the inhabitants"—a reading which is supported by many MSS., printed editions, and all the versions, as well as by necessity and common sense. See the note on chap. xix. 8, where a similar mistake is rectified.

14. *Found a book of the law.* See on 2 Kings xxii. 8.

22. *Huldah the prophetess.* See on 2 Kings xxii. 14.

28. *Gathered to thy grave in peace.* See particularly the note on 2 Kings xxii. 20.

30. *The king went.* See on 2 Kings xxiii. 1.

31. *Made a covenant.* See on 2 Kings xxiii. 3.

32. *To stand to it.* It is likely that he caused

MATTHEW HENRY

to serve, even to serve the Lord their God (*v.* 33). *All his days they departed not from following the Lord;* he kept them, with much ado, from running into idolatry again. *All his days* were days of restraint upon them; but this intimated that there was in them a *bent to backslide*, a strong inclination to idolatry. Josiah was sincere in what he did, but the generality of the people were averse to it and hankered after their idols still. This God saw, and therefore from that time, when one would have thought the foundations had been laid for a perpetual security and peace, from that very time did the decree go forth for their destruction.

CHAPTER 35

Verses 1–19

The destruction which Josiah made of idols and idolatry was more largely related in the *Kings*, and but just mentioned here in the foregoing chapter (*v.* 33); but his solemnizing the passover, which was touched upon there (2 Kings xxiii. 21), is very particularly related here. Many were the feasts of the Lord, appointed by the ceremonial law, but the passover was the chief. In the celebration of it Hezekiah and Josiah, those two great reformers, revived religion in their day. The ordinance of the Lord's supper resembles the passover; and the due observance of that ordinance is an instance and means both of the growing purity and beauty of churches and of the growing piety and devotion of particular Christians.

In the account we had of Hezekiah's passover the great zeal of the people was observable, and the transport of devout affection that they were in; but little of the same spirit appears here. It was more in compliance with the king that they all kept the passover (*v.* 17, 18) than from any great inclination they had to it themselves. Some pride they took in this form of godliness, but little pleasure in the power of it.

I. The king exhorted and directed, quickened and encouraged, the priests and Levites to do their office in this solemnity. Let us see how this good king managed his clergy upon this occasion. 1. He reduced them to the office they were appointed to by the law of Moses (*v.* 6) and the order they were put into by David and Solomon, *v.* 4. 2. He ordered the ark to be put in its place. 3. He charged them to *serve God and his people Israel*, *v.* 3. 4. He charged them to *sanctify themselves*, and *prepare their brethren*, *v.* 6. Ministers' work must begin at home. But it must not end there; they must do what they can to *prepare their brethren* by admonishing, instructing, exhorting, quickening, and comforting them. 5. He *encouraged them to the service*, *v.* 2. He spoke comfortably to them, as Hezekiah did, *ch.* xxx. 22.

II. The king and the princes, influenced by his example, gave liberally for the bearing of the charges of this passover. Josiah, at his own proper cost, furnished the congregation with paschal lambs, and other sacrifices, to be offered during the seven days of the feast. The chief of the priests contributed towards the priests' charges, as Josiah did towards the people's.

III. The priests and Levites performed their office very readily, *v.* 10. The priests and Levites took care to honour God by *eating of the passover* themselves, *v.* 14.

JAMIESON, FAUSSET, BROWN

CHAPTER 35

VSS. 1-19. JOSIAH KEEPS A SOLEMN PASSOVER. **1. Moreover Josiah kept a passover**—(See on II Kings 23:21-23). The first nine verses give an account of the preparations made for the celebration of the solemn feast. The day appointed by the law was kept on this occasion (cf. ch. 30:2, 13). The priests were ranged in their courses and exhorted to be ready for their duties in the manner that legal purity required (cf. ch. 29:5). The Levites, the ministers or instructors of the people in all matters pertaining to the divine worship, were commanded (vs. 3) to "put the holy ark in the house which Solomon did build." Their duty was to transport the ark from place to place according to circumstances. Some think that it had been ignominiously put away from the sanctuary by order of some idolatrous king, probably Manasseh, who set a carved image in the house of God (ch. 33:7), or Amon; while others are of opinion that it had been temporarily removed by Josiah himself into some adjoining chamber, during the repairs on the temple. In replacing it, the Levites had evidently carried it upon their shoulders, deeming that still to be the duty which the law imposed on them. But Josiah reminded them of the change of circumstances. As the service of God was now performed in a fixed and permanent temple, they were not required to be bearers of the ark any longer; and, being released from the service, they should address themselves with the greater alacrity to the discharge of other functions. **4. prepare yourselves by the houses of your fathers, after your courses**—Each course or division was to be composed of those who belonged to the same fathers' house. **according to the writing of David and . . . Solomon.** Their injunctions are recorded (ch. 8:14; I Chron. 23; 24; 25; 26). **5. stand in the holy place**—in the court of the priests, the place where the victims were killed. The people were admitted according to their families in groups or companies of several households at a time. When the first company entered the court (which consisted commonly of as many as it could well hold), the gates were shut and the offering was made. The Levites stood in rows from the slaughtering-places to the altar, and handed the blood and fat from one to another of the officiating priests (ch. 30:16-18). **6. So kill the passover,** etc.—The design of the minute directions given here was to facilitate the distribution of the paschal lambs. These were to be eaten by the respective families according to their numbers (Exod. 12:3). But multitudes of the people, especially those from Israel, having been reduced to poverty through the Assyrian devastations, were to be provided with the means of commemorating the passover. Therefore, the king enjoined the Levites that when the paschal lambs were brought to them to be killed (7-9) they should take care to have everything put in so orderly a train, that the lambs, after due presentation, might be easily delivered to the various families to be roasted and eaten by themselves apart. **7. Josiah gave to the people . . . lambs and kids**—These were in all probability destined for the poor; a lamb or a kid might be used at convenience (Exod. 12:5). **and . . . bullocks**—which were offered after the lambs on each of the successive days of the feast. **8. his princes**—They gave to the priests and Levites; as those of Hezekiah's princes (ch. 30:24). They were ecclesiastical princes; viz., Hilkiah the high priest (ch. 34:9), Zechariah, probably the second priest of the Eleazar (II Kings 16:18), and Jehiel of the Ithamar, line. And as the Levitical tribes were not yet sufficiently provided (vs. 9), some of their eminent brethren who had been distinguished in Hezekiah's time (ch. 31:12-15), gave a large additional contribution for the use of the Levites exclusively. **10. So the service was prepared,** etc.—All the necessary preparations having been completed, and the appointed time having arrived for the passover, the solemnity was celebrated.

ADAM CLARKE

them all to arise when he read the terms of the covenant, and thus testify their approbation of the covenant itself, and their resolution to observe it faithfully and perseveringly.

CHAPTER 35

3. *Put the holy ark in the house.* It is likely that the priests had secured this when they found that the idolatrous kings were determined to destroy everything that might lead the people to the worship of the true God. And now, as all appears to be well-established, the ark is ordered to be put into its own place. For an ample account of this Passover and the reformation that was then made, see on 2 Kings xxiiii. 1, etc.

KEIL–DELITZSCH:

Josiah said to them, "Set the ark in the house which Solomon did build; not is to you to bear upon the shoulder"; i.e., ye have not any longer to bear it on your shoulders, as formerly on the journey through the wilderness, and indeed till the building of the temple, when the ark and the tabernacle had not yet any fixed resting place (1 Chron. 17:5). The summons is variously interpreted. Several Rabbins regard it as a command to remove the ark from its place in the most holy place into some subterranean chamber of the temple, so as to secure its safety in the event of the threatened destruction of the temple taking place. But his hypothesis needs no refutation since it in no way corresponds to the words used. Most ancient and modern commentators, on the other hand, suppose that the holy ark had, during the reigns of the godless Manasseh and Amon, either been removed by them from its place or taken away from the most holy place, from a desire to protect it from profanation, and hidden somewhere; and that Josiah calls upon the Levites to bring it back again to its place. Certainly this idea is favored by the circumstance that, just as the book of the law, which should have been preserved in the ark of the covenant, had been lost, and was only recovered when the temple was being repaired, so the ark also may have been removed from its place. But even in that case the sacred ark would have been brought back to its place, according to the law, at the completion of the purification of the temple, before the king and people made the covenant with Jahve, after the law had been read to them in the temple, and could not have remained in its hiding place until the passover.

—*Commentary on the Old Testament*

MATTHEW HENRY

F. B. MEYER:

"Prepare" (2 Chron. 35:4, 6, 10, 14, 15, 16). No great court function can be carried through successfully, without careful preparation. And Josiah's passover was so vast and rare a success because of the large amount of previous preparation, as is described in this chapter. The priests and Levites were prepared by careful washings and ceremonial rites. The course of the sacrifices was ordered according to the law of Moses. The routine of sacred song and praise was also provided for. Nothing was left to haphazard or chance.

We are taught to rely on the promptings and inspirations of the Holy Spirit; and it is certain that He would use us more on special errands, if we were to trust and obey Him better. But these extraordinary ministries should not lead us to a life of haphazard. We should prepare ourselves for service so far as we may, laying our plans, anticipating the calls and exigencies of coming days, and preparing for the demands which almost certainly will be made on us. We may have to give our special words and addresses and arrangements to the winds; but we shall always need that preparedness of heart which is necessary for those who are to be used of God.

Remember what is said of the vessels that were purged from uncleanness, sanctified, meet for the Master's use, and prepared unto every good work. Be always in your own place, clean so far as you can be, filled with the Holy Ghost, with the handle of your life turned towards the Master's hand, that at any moment He may take hold of you and use you for his holy service. By the diligent study of his Word, as well as by earnest prayer and waiting upon God, you will be prepared to do his will.

—*Great Verses Through the Bible*

IV. The singers expressed the joy of the congregation, and the porters at the gates took care that there should be no breaking in of anything to defile or disquiet the assembly, nor going out of any from it, that none should steal away till the service was done.

V. The whole solemnity was performed according to the law (*v.* 16, 17), there was none like it since Samuel's time (*v.* 18).

JAMIESON, FAUSSET, BROWN

One remarkable feature in the account is the prominent part that was taken by the Levites in the preparation of the sacrifices; viz., the killing and stripping of the skins, which were properly the peculiar duties of the priests; but as those functionaries were not able to overtake the extraordinary amount of work and the Levites had been duly sanctified for the service, they were enlisted for the time in this priestly employment. At the passover in Hezekiah's time, the Levites officiated in the same departments of duty, the reason assigned for that deviation from the established rule being the unprepared state of many of the people (ch. 30:17). But on this occasion the whole people had been duly sanctified, and therefore the exceptional enlistment of the Levites' services must have been rendered unavoidably necessary from the multitudes engaged in celebrating the passover. **12. they removed the burnt offerings**—Some of the small cattle being designed for burnt offerings were put apart by themselves, that they might not be intermingled with the paschal lambs, which were carefully selected according to certain rules, and intended to be sacramentally eaten; and the manner in which those burnt offerings were presented seems to have been the following: "All the subdivisions of the different fathers' houses came one after another to the altar in solemn procession to bring to the priests the portions which had been cut off, and the priests laid these pieces upon the fire of the altar of burnt offering." **13. they roasted the passover with fire according to the ordinance**—(See Exod. 12:7-9). This mode of preparation was prescribed by the law exclusively for the paschal lamb; the other offerings and thank offerings were cooked in pots, kettles, and pans (I Sam. 2:14). **divided them speedily among the people**—The haste was either owing to the multiplicity of the priests' business, or because the heat and flavor of the viands would have been otherwise diminished. Hence it appears that the meal consisted not of the paschal lambs alone, but of the meat of the thank offerings—for part of the flesh fell to the portion of the offerer, who, being in this instance, the king and the princes, were by them made over to the people, who were recommended to eat them the day they were offered, though not absolutely forbidden to do so on the next (Lev. 7:15-18). **14. afterwards they made ready for themselves, and for the priests**—The Levites rendered this aid to the priests solely because they were so engrossed the entire day that they had no leisure to provide any refreshments for themselves. **15. And the singers . . . , were in their place**—While the priests and people were so much engaged, the choir was not idle. They had to sing certain psalms, viz., 113 to 118 inclusive, once, twice, and even a third time, during the continuance of each company of offerers. As they could not leave their posts, for the singing was resumed as every fresh company entered, the Levites prepared for them also; for the various bands relieved each other in turn, and while the general choir was doing duty, a portion of the tuneful brethren, relieved for a time, partook of the viands that were brought them. **18. there was no passover like to that kept in Israel from the days of Samuel**—One feature by which this passover was distinguished was the liberality of Josiah. But what distinguished it above all preceding solemnities was, not the imposing grandeur of the ceremonies, nor the immensity of the assembled concourse of worshippers; for these, with the exception of a few from the kingdom of Israel, were confined to two tribes; but it was the ardent devotion of the king and people, the disregard of purely traditional customs, and the unusually strict adherence, even in the smallest minutiæ, to the forms of observance prescribed in the book of the law, the discovery of an original copy of which had produced so great a sensation. Instead of "from the days of Samuel," the author of the Book of Kings says, "from the days of the judges who judged Israel." The meaning is the same in both passages, for Samuel concluded the era of the judges. **all Judah and Israel were present**—The great majority of the people of the northern kingdom were in exile, but some of the remaining inhabitants performed the journey to Jerusalem on this occasion. 37,600 paschal lambs and kids were used, which, at ten to a company, would make 376,000 persons attending the feast. **19. In the eighteenth year of the reign of Josiah was this passover kept**—"It is said (II Kings 22:3) that Josiah sent Shaphan to Hilkiah in the eighth month of that year." If this statement rests upon an historical basis, all the events narrated here (from ch. 34:8 to ch. 35:19) must have happened in about the space of five months and a half. We should then have a proof that the eighteenth year of Josiah's reign was

ADAM CLARKE

11. *They killed the passover.* The people themselves might slay their own paschal lambs, and then present the blood to the priests, that they might sprinkle it before the altar; and the Levites flayed them, and made them ready for dressing.

JOSEPH PARKER:

"There was no passover like to that" (v. 18). Herein is a law of nature, an operation of the soul familiar to us in the higher education, and in the higher excitements of commercial, political, and literary life. But the occasional passover, how memorable, how tender, how good to recall! What an inspiration to revive in the soul. Pity the man whose calendar is all written alike, who has no red-letter days of the heart, no memory of prayer that thrills him with unutterable joy. You remember the early struggle with sin and the devil, and how by the grace of God you were enabled to fling the monster to the ground and stand upon him in sign of victory? Never let that writing in the record fade out. You remember the first glimpse of God in prayer? You prayed on with difficulty, words seemed to come hesitantly to your use, as if they were partly afraid of you: but you persevered, and from sentence you passed to sentence, until the whole soul glowed with a new delight; and for the moment heaven was opened, and you by the cross of Christ had right of entry. Never forget that day. When temptation thickens upon you, and the devil's hand is on your throat, remember that blessed passover, and the memory of it shall be a protection, a benediction, and an inspiration. Comfort one another with these words.—*The People's Bible*

18. *There was no passover like to that.* "That which distinguished this passover from all the former was," says Calmet, "the great liberality of Josiah, who distributed to his people a greater number of victims than either David or Solomon had done."

MATTHEW HENRY

Verses 20–27

It was thirteen years from Josiah's famous passover to his death. During this time things went well in his kingdom, and religion flourished. The next news we hear of Josiah is that he is cut off in the midst of his days and usefulness, before he is full forty years old. We had this sad story, 2 Kings xxiii. 29, 30.

I. Josiah was a very good prince, yet he was to be blamed for his rashness in going out to war against the king of Egypt without cause. It was bad enough, as it appeared in the *Kings*, that he meddled with strife which belonged not to him.

But here it looks worse; for the king of Egypt sent ambassadors to him, to warn him against this enterprise, *v.* 21.

1. The king of Egypt argued with Josiah, (1) From principles of justice. If even a *righteous man* engage in an *unrighteous cause*, let him not expect to prosper. (2) From principles of religion: "*God is with me;* nay, *He commanded me to make haste*, and therefore, it thou retard my motions, thou meddlest with God." It cannot be that the king of Egypt only pretended this, hoping thereby to make Josiah desist, for it is said here (*v.* 22) that the words of Necho were from the mouth of God. Either by a dream, or by a strong impulse which he had reason to think was from God, or by Jeremiah or some other prophet, he had ordered him to make war upon the king of Assyria. (3) From principles of policy: "*That he destroy thee not;* it is at thy peril if thou engage against one that has not only a better army and a better cause, but God on his side."

2. Josiah, whose heart was upright with the Lord his God, in wrath to a hypocritical nation, was so far infatuated as not to hearken to these fair reasonings and desist from his enterprise. He *would not turn his face from him*, but went in person and fought the Egyptian army in the *valley of Megiddo*, *v.* 22. In this matter he walked not in the ways of David his father; for, had it been his case, he would have enquired of the Lord, *Shall I go up? Wilt thou deliver them into my hands?*

II. The people were a wicked people, yet they were to be commended for lamenting the death of Josiah as they did. All Judah and Jerusalem, that stupid senseless people, *mourned for him* (*v.* 24). Elegies were inserted in the collections of state poems; they are written in the Lamentations. It appeared, 1. That they had some respect to their good prince, and that, though they did not cordially comply with him in all his good designs, they could not but greatly honour him. 2. That they had some sense of their own danger now that he was

JAMIESON, FAUSSET, BROWN

reckoned from the autumn (cf. ch. 29:3). "The eighth month" of the sacred year in the eighteenth year of his reign would be the second month of his eighteenth year, and the first month of the new year would be the seventh month [BERTHEAU].

20-27. HIS DEATH. **20. After all this, when Josiah had prepared the temple**—He most probably calculated that the restoration of the divine worship, with the revival of vital religion in the land, would lead, according to God's promise and the uniform experience of the Hebrew people, to a period of settled peace and increased prosperity. His hopes were disappointed. The bright interval of tranquillity that followed his re-establishment of the true religion was brief. But it must be observed that this interruption did not proceed from any unfaithfulness in the divine promise, but from the state into which the kingdom of Judah had brought itself by the national apostasy, which was drawing down upon it the long threatened but long deferred judgments of God. **Necho king of Egypt came ap to fight against Carchemish by Euphrates**—Necho, son of Psammetichus, succeeded to the throne of Egypt in the twentieth year of Josiah. He was a bold and enterprising king, who entered with all his heart into the struggle which the two great powers of Egypt and Assyria had long carried on for the political ascendency. Each, jealous of the agressive movements of its rival, was desirous to maintain Palestine as a frontier barrier. After the overthrow of Israel, the kingdom of Judah became in that respect doubly important. Although the king and people had a strong bias for alliance with Egypt, yet from the time of Manasseh it had become a vassal of Assyria. Josiah, true to his political no less than his religious engagements, thought himself bound to support the interests of his Assyrian liege lord. Hence, when "Necho king of Egypt came up to fight Carchemish, Josiah went out against him." Carchemish, on the eastern side of the Euphrates, was the key of Assyria on the west, and in going thither the king of Egypt would transport his troops by sea along the coast of Palestine, northwards. Josiah, as a faithful vassal, resolved to oppose Necho's march across the northern parts of that country. They met in the "valley of Megiddo," i.e., the valley or plain of Esdraelon. The Egyptian king had come either by water or through the plains of Philistia, keeping constantly along the coast, round the northwest corner of Carmel, and so to the great plain of Megiddo. This was not only his direct way to the Euphrates, but the only route fit for his chariots, while thereby also he left Judah and Jerusalem quite to his right. In this valley, however, the Egyptian army had necessarily to strike across the country, and it was on that occasion that Josiah could most conveniently intercept his passage. To avoid the difficulty of passing the river Kishon, Necho kept to the south of it, and must, therefore, have come past Megiddo. Josiah, in following with his chariots and horsemen from Jerusalem, had to march northwards along the highway through Samaria by Kefr-Kud (the ancient Caper-Cotia) to Megiddo [VAN DE VELDE]. **21. But he sent ambassadors . . . What have I to do with thee, thou king of Judah?**—Not wishing to spend time or strength in vain, Necho informed the king of Judah that he had no intention of molesting the Jews; that his expedition was directed solely against his old Assyrian enemy; and that he had undertaken it by an express commission from God. Commentators are not agreed whether it was really a divine commission given him through Jeremiah, or whether he merely used the name of God as an authority that Josiah would not refuse to obey. As he could not know the truth of Necho's declaration, Josiah did not sin in opposing him; or, if he sinned at all, it was a sin of ignorance. The engagement took place. Josiah was mortally wounded. **24. took him out of that chariot, and put him in the second chariot**—the carriage he had for ordinary use, and which would be more comfortable for the royal sufferer than the war chariot. The death of this good king was the subject of universal and lasting regret. **25. Jeremiah lamented for Josiah,** etc.—The elegy of the prophet has not reached us; but it seems to have been long preserved among his countrymen and chanted on certain public occasions by the professional singers, who probably got the dirges they sang from a collection of funeral odes composed on the death of good and great men of the nation. The spot in the valley of Megiddo where the battle was fought was near the town of Hadadrimmon; hence the lamentation for the death of Josiah was called "the lamentation of Hadadrimmon in the valley of Megiddo," which was so great and so long continued, that the lamentation of

ADAM CLARKE

20. *Necho king of Egypt.* "Pharaoh the lame," says the Targum.

TODAY'S DICTIONARY OF THE BIBLE:

Necho II, an Egyptian king, the son and successor of Psammetichus (610–594 B.C.), the contemporary of Josiah, king of Judah. After the defeat of Assyria, Necho saw the opportunity to establish a weak Assyria as a buffer state between Egypt and his own territory, so he marched northward to confront the forces of Nebuchadnezzar which were attempting to dispose of the remnants of the Assyrian army at Haran. He was at least partially successful, as the westward advance of Babylon was checked in 609 B.C. Josiah of Judah, opposing Necho's imperial plans, attempted to stop him in his northward advance, but his army was routed and he himself was killed at Megiddo (2 Chron. 35:20–24).

On his return march he deposed Jehoahaz, who had succeeded his father Josiah, and made Eliakim, Josiah's eldest son, whose name he changed into Jehoiakim, king. Jehoahaz he carried down into Egypt, where he died (2 Kings 23:31, 34; 2 Chron. 36:1–4). Four years after this conquest Necho again marched to the Euphrates; but here he was met and his army routed by the Chaldeans (605 B.C.) under Nebuchadnezzar, who drove the Egyptians back, and took from them all the territory they had conquered, from the Euphrates unto the "river of Egypt" (Jer. 46:2; 2 Kings 24:7, 8). In 601 B.C. Nebuchadnezzar pressed the attack to the borders of Egypt itself but was held off by Necho. Soon after this Necho died, and was succeeded by his son, Psammetichus II.

24. *The second chariot.* Perhaps this means no more than that they took Josiah out of his own chariot and put him into another, either for secrecy or because his own had been disabled. The chariot into which he was put might have been that of the officer who attended his master to the war. See the note on 2 Kings xxii. 20.

MATTHEW HENRY

gone. They lamented the death of him that was their defence. Many will shed tears for their troubles, but will not be prevailed upon to part with their sins.

CHAPTER 36

Verses 1–10

The destruction of Judah and Jerusalem by degrees. God gives them both time and inducement to repent and waits to be gracious. The history of these reigns was more largely recorded in the last three chapters of the second of *Kings*.

1. Jehoahaz was set up by the people (*v.* 1), but was deposed by Pharaoh-necho, and carried a prisoner to Egypt, *v.* 2-4. Of this young prince we hear no more.

2. Jehoiakim was set up by the king of Egypt, and reigned eleven years. How low was Judah brought when the king of Egypt, an old enemy to their land, gave what king he pleased to the kingdom and what name he pleased to the king! *v.* 4. He made Eliakim king, and called him *Jehoiakim*, in token of his authority over him. *Jehoiakim did that which was evil* (*v.* 5), we read of the *abominations which he did* (*v.* 8). We hear no more of the king of Egypt, but the king of Babylon came up against him (*v.* 6), seized him, and bound him with a design to carry him to Babylon; but, it seems, he either suffered him to reign as his vassal, or death released the prisoner before he was carried away. However, the best and most valuable vessels of the temple were now carried away and made use of in Nebuchadnezzar's temple in Babylon (*v.* 7). As the carrying away of these vessels to Babylon began the calamity of Jerusalem, so Belshazzar's daring profanation of them there filled the measure of the iniquity of Babylon; for, when he drank wine in them to the honour of his gods, the handwriting on the wall presented him with his doom, Dan. v. 3, &c. In the reference to the book of the *Kings* concerning this Jehoiakim mention is made of *that which was found in him* (*v.* 8), which seems to be meant of the treachery that was found in him towards the king of Babylon; but some of the Jewish writers understand it of certain private marks or signatures found in his dead body, in honour of his idol, such cuttings as God had forbidden, Lev. xix. 28. 3. Jehoiachin, or Jeconiah, the son of Jehoiakim, attempted to reign in his stead, and reigned long enough to show his evil inclination; but, after three months and ten days, the king of Babylon sent and fetched him away captive, with more of the goodly vessels of the temple.

Verses 11–21

An account of the destruction of the kingdom of Judah and the city of Jerusalem by the Chaldeans. Abraham, God's friend, was called out of that country, from Ur of the Chaldees, when God took him into covenant and communion with himself; and now his degenerate seed were carried into that country again, to signify that they had forfeited all that kindness wherewith they had been regarded for the father's sake.

I. The sins that brought this desolation.

1. Zedekiah, the king in whose days it came, brought it upon himself by his own folly. (1) If he had but made God his friend, that would have prevented the ruin. Jeremiah brought him messages from God, but it is here charged upon him that he *humbled not himself before Jeremiah*, *v.* 12. Because he would not thus make himself a servant to God, he

JAMIESON, FAUSSET, BROWN

Hadad passed afterwards into a proverbial phrase to express any great and extraordinary sorrow (Zech. 12:11).

CHAPTER 36

VSS. 1-4. JEHOAHAZ, SUCCEEDING, IS DEPOSED BY PHARAOH. **1. the people of the land took Jehoahaz**—Immediately after Josiah's overthrow and death, the people raised to the throne Shallum (I Chron. 3:15), afterwards called Jehoahaz, in preference to his older brother Eliakim, from whom they expected little good. Jehoahaz is said (II Kings 23: 30) to have received at Jerusalem the royal anointing—a ceremony not usually deemed necessary in circumstances of regular and undisputed succession. But, in the case of Jehoahaz, it seems to have been resorted to in order to impart greater validity to the act of popular election; and, it may be, to render it less likely to be disturbed by Necho, who, like all Egyptians, would associate the idea of sanctity with the regal anointing. He was the youngest son of Josiah, but the popular favorite, probably on account of his martial spirit (Ezek. 19:3) and determined opposition to the aggressive views of Egypt. At his accession the land was free from idolatry; but this prince, instead of following the footsteps of his excellent father, adopted the criminal policy of his apostatizing predecessors. Through his influence, directly or indirectly used, idolatry rapidly increased (see on II Kings 23:32). **2. he reigned three months in Jerusalem**—His possession of sovereign power was of but very brief duration; for Necho determined to follow up the advantage he had gained in Judah; and, deeming it expedient to have a king of his own nomination on the throne of that country, he deposed the popularly elected monarch and placed his brother Eliakim or Jehoiakim on the throne, whom he anticipated to be a mere obsequious vassal. The course of events seems to have been this: on receiving intelligence after the battle of the accession of Jehoahaz to the throne, and perhaps also in consequence of the complaint which Eliakim brought before him in regard to this matter, Necho set out with a part of his forces to Jerusalem, while the remainder of his troops pursued their way at leisure towards Riblah, laid a tribute on the country, raised Eliakim (Jehoiakim) as his vassal to the throne, and on his departure brought Jehoahaz captive with him to Riblah. The old expositors mostly assumed that Necho, after the battle of Megiddo, marched directly against Carchemish, and then on his return came to Jerusalem. The improbability, indeed the impossibility, of his doing so appears from this: Carchemish was from four hundred to five hundred miles from Megiddo, so that within "three months" an army could not possibly make its way thither, conquer the fenced city of Carchemish, and then march back a still greater distance to Jerusalem, and take that city [KEIL]. **3. an hundred talents of silver**—about $170,000. **and a talent of gold**—about $25,000; total amount of tribute, about $195,000. **4. carried him** [Jehoahaz] **to Egypt**—There he died (Jer. 22:10-12).

5-8. JEHOIAKIM, REIGNING ILL, IS CARRIED INTO BABYLON. **5. Jehoiakim . . . did that which was evil in the sight of the Lord**—He followed the course of his idolatrous predecessors; and the people, to a great extent, disinclined to the reforming policy of his father, eagerly availed themselves of the vicious license which his lax administration restored. His character is portrayed with a masterly hand in the prophecy of Jeremiah (ch. 22:13-19). As the deputy of the king of Egypt, he departed further than his predecessor from the principles of Josiah's government; and, in trying to meet the insatiable cupidity of his master by grinding exactions from his subjects, he recklessly plunged into all evil. **6. Against him came up Nebuchadnezzar king of Babylon**—This refers to the first expedition of Nebuchadnezzar against Palestine, in the lifetime of his father Nabopolassar, who, being old and infirm, adopted his son as joint sovereign and despatched him, with the command of his army, against the Egyptian invaders of his empire. Nebuchadnezzar defeated them at Carchemish, drove them out of Asia, and reduced all the provinces west of the Euphrates to obedience—among the rest the kingdom of Jehoiakim, who became a vassal of the Assyrian empire (II Kings 24:1). Jehoiakim at the end of three years threw off the yoke, being probably instigated to revolt by the solicitations of the king of Egypt, who planned a new expedition against Carchemish. But he was completely vanquished by the Babylonian king, who stripped him of all his

ADAM CLARKE

27. *And his deeds, first and last.* These general histories are lost, but in the Books of Kings and Chronicles we have the leading facts.

CHAPTER 36

1. *Took Jehoahaz.* It seems that after Necho had discomfited Josiah he proceeded immediately against Charchemish, and in the interim, Josiah dying of his wounds, the people made his son king.

3. *The king of Egypt put him down.* He now considered Judah to be conquered and tributary to him, and because the people had set up Jehoahaz without his consent, he dethroned him, and put his brother in his place, perhaps for no other reason but to show his supremacy. For other particulars see the notes on 2 Kings xxiii. 31-35.

6. *Came up Nebuchadnezzar.* See the notes on 2 Kings xxiv. 1.

F. B. MEYER:

At the mercy of the foe. The narrative here runs parallel with 2 Kings, but the events are described with a certain gravity of warning which enforces the lesson of history. Here was the final catastrophe. Long predicted, at last it fell. The Jewish kings named here were mere puppets, and instead of turning to Jehovah, followed each other in persistent idolatry. Jehoahaz was deposed by Necho, who hoped for a more obsequious tool in his brother Jehoiakim; and the latter in his turn was deposed by Nebuchadnezzar because he was Necho's nominee. Jehoiachin was carried into captivity because he was the choice of the people, and Zedekiah became he rebelled. These are the superficial reasons for the changes that followed each other with such terrible rapidity. But the pages of Jeremiah and Ezekiel reveal other and deeper reasons, alluded to subsequently in this chapter.

It was a long process of pruning through which Israel had to pass before this stock could bear that one pure flower, the mother of our Lord, who was to give the human side of his holy nature to the world.—*Bible Commentary*

MATTHEW HENRY

was made a slave to his enemies. (2) If he had but been true to his covenant with the king of Babylon, that would have prevented his ruin; but he *rebelled against him*, though he had sworn to be his faithful tributary, *v.* 13. It was this that provoked the king of Babylon to deal so severely with him as he did. The thing that ruined Zedekiah was not only that he *turned not to the Lord God of Israel*, but that he *stiffened his neck and hardened his heart from turning to him*, and so, in effect, he *would not be healed*, he *would not live*.

2. The great sin that brought this destruction was idolatry. The priests, the chief of the priests, who should have opposed idolatry, were ring-leaders in it.

3. The great aggravation of their sin was the abuse they gave to God's prophets, who were sent to call them to repentance, *v.* 15, 16. (1) God's tender compassion towards them in sending prophets to them. The reason given why God by his prophets did thus strive with them is because *he had compassion on his people and on his dwelling-place*, and would by these means have prevented their ruin. The methods God takes to reclaim sinners by his word, by ministers, by conscience, by providences, are all instances of his compassion towards them and his unwillingness *that any should perish.* (2) *They mocked the messengers of God, despised his word* in their mouths, and *misused the prophets*, treating them as their enemies. The ill usage they gave Jeremiah who lived at this time, and which we read much of in the book of his prophecy, is an instance of this. This brought wrath upon them without remedy, for it was sinning against the remedy. Nothing is more provoking to God than abuses given to his faithful ministers; for what is done against them he takes as done against himself. *Saul, Saul, why persecutest thou me?* Persecution was the sin that brought upon Jerusalem its final destruction by the Romans. See Matt. xxiii. 34–37.

II. The desolation itself, and some few of the particulars of it, which we had more largely, 2 Kings xxv. 1. Multitudes were put to the sword, even *in the house of their sanctuary* (*v.* 17), whither they fled for refuge, hoping that the holiness ofthe place would be their protection. The Chaldeans not only paid no reverence to the sanctuary, but showed no natural pity either to the tender sex or to venerable age. 2. All the remaining vessels of the temple, great and small, and all the treasures, sacred and secular, the treasures of God's house and of the king and his princes, were seized, and brought to Babylon, *v.* 18. 3. The temple was burnt, the walls of Jerusalem were demolished, the houses (called here the *palaces*, as Ps. xlviii. 3, so stately, rich, and sumptuous were they) laid in ashes, and all the furniture, called here *the goodly vessels thereof*, destroyed, *v.* 19. 4. The remainder of the people that escaped the sword were carried captives to Babylon (*v.* 20), impoverished, enslaved, insulted, and exposed to all the miseries of a strange and barbarous land. Now they sat down by the rivers of Babylon, with the streams of which they mingled their tears, Ps. cxxxvii. 1. And though there, it should seem, they were cured of idolatry, yet, as appears by the prophet Ezekiel, they were not cured of mocking the prophets. 5. The land lay desolate while they were captives in Babylon, *v.* 21. Now this may be considered, (1) As the just punishment of their former abuse of it. They had served Baal with its fruits; *cursed* therefore *is the ground for their sakes.* Now the land *enjoyed her sabbaths* (*v.* 21); as God had threatened by Moses, Lev. xxvi. 34. (2) Yet we may consider it as giving some encouragement to their hopes that they should, in due time, return to it again. Had others come and taken possession of it, they might have despaired of ever recovering it; but, while it lay desolate, it did, as it were, lie waiting for them again.

Verses 22–23

These last two verses of this book have a double aspect. 1. They look back to the prophecy of Jeremiah, and show how that was accomplished, *v.* 22. God had, by him, promised the restoring of the captives and the rebuilding of Jerusalem, at the end of seventy years; and that time to favour Sion, that set time, came at last. After a long and dark night the day-spring from on high visited them. 2. They look forward to the history of Ezra, which begins with the repetition of these last two verses. They are there the introduction to a pleasant story; here they are the conclusion of a very melancholy one; and so we learn from them that, though God's church be cast down, it is not cast off, though his people be corrected, they are not abandoned, though thrown into the furnace, yet not lost there, nor left there any longer than till the dross be separated. It may be long, but the vision is for an appointed time, and at the end it shall speak and not lie; therefore, though it tarry, wait for it.

JAMIESON, FAUSSET, BROWN

possessions between the Euphrates and the Nile (II Kings 24:7). Then marching against the Egyptian's ally in Judah, he took Jerusalem, carried away a portion of the sacred vessels of the temple, perhaps in lieu of the unpaid tribute, and deposited them in the temple of his god, Belus, at Babylon (Dan. 1:2; 5:2). Though Jehoiakim had been taken prisoner (and it was designed at first to transport him in chains to Babylon), he was allowed to remain in his tributary kingdom. But having given not long after some new offense, Jerusalem was besieged by a host of Assyrian dependents. In a sally against them Jehoiakim was killed (see on Kings 24:2-7; also Jer. 22:18, 19; 36:30). **9. Jehoiachin was eight years old**—called also Jeconiah or Coniah (Jer. 22:23)—"eight" should have been "eighteen," as appears from II Kings 24:8, and also from the full development of his ungodly principles and habits (see Ezek. 19:5-7). His reign being of so short duration cannot be considered at variance with the prophetic denunciation against his father (Jer. 36:30). But his appointment by the people gave umbrage to Nebuchadnezzar, who, "when the year was expired" (vs. 10)—i.e., in the spring when campaigns usually began—came in person against Jerusalem, captured the city, and sent Jehoiachin in chains to Babylon, removing at the same time all the nobles and most skilful artisans, and pillaging all the remaining treasures both of the temple and palace (see on II Kings 24:8-17).

11-21. ZEDEKIAH'S REIGN. **11. Zedekiah**—Nebuchadnezzar appointed him. His name, originally Mattaniah, was, according to the custom of Oriental conquerors, changed into Zedekiah. Though the son of Josiah (I Chron. 3:15; Jer. 1:2, 3; 37:1), he is called (vs. 10) the brother of Jehoiachin, i.e., according to the latitude of Hebrew style in words expressing affinity, his relative or kinsman (see on II Kings 24:18; 26:1-21). **13. who had made him swear**—Zedekiah received his crown on the express condition of taking a solemn oath of fealty to the king of Babylon (Ezek. 17:13); so that his revolt by joining in a league with Pharaoh-hophra, king of Egypt, involved the crime of perjury. His own pride and obdurate impiety, the incurable idolatry of the nation, and their reckless disregard of prophetic warnings, brought down on his already sadly reduced kingdom the long threatened judgments of God. Nebuchadnezzar, the executioner of the divine vengeance, commenced a third siege of Jerusalem, which, after holding out for a year and a half, was taken in the eleventh year of the reign of Zedekiah. It resulted in the burning of the temple, with, most probably, the ark, and in the overthrow of the kingdom of Judah (see on II Kings 25; Ezek. 12:13; 17:16).

21. until the land had enjoyed her sabbaths—The return of every seventh was to be held as a sabbatic year, a season of rest to all classes, even to the land itself, which was to be fallow. This divine institution, however, was neglected—how soon and how long, appears from the prophecy of Moses (Lev. 26:34), and of Jeremiah in this passage (see also *Marginal Reference*), which told that for divine retribution it was now to remain desolate seventy years. As the Assyrian conquerors usually colonized their conquered provinces, so remarkable a deviation in Palestine from their customary policy must be ascribed to the overruling providence of God.

22, 23. CYRUS' PROCLAMATION. **22. the Lord stirred up the spirit of Cyrus**—(See on Ezra 1:1-3).

ADAM CLARKE

9. *Jechoiachin was eight.* See on 2 Kings xxiv.

10. *Made Zedekiah . . . king.* His name was at first Mattaniah, but the king of Babylon changed it to Zedekiah. See 2 Kings xxiv. 17, and the notes there.

12. *Did that which was evil.* Was there ever such a set of weak, infatuated men as the Jewish kings in general? They had the fullest evidence that they were only deputies to God Almighty, and that they could not expect to retain the throne any longer than they were faithful to their Lord; and yet with all this conviction they lived wickedly, and endeavored to establish idolatry in the place of the worship of their Maker! After bearing with them long, the divine mercy gave them up, as their case was utterly hopeless.

19. *They burnt the house of God.* Here was an end to the Temple, the most superb and costly edifice ever erected by man. *Brake down the wall of Jerusalem.* So it ceased to be a fortified city. *Burnt all the palaces.* So it was no longer a dwelling place for kings or great men. *Destroyed all the goodly vessels.* Beat up all the silver and gold into masses, keeping only a few of the finest in their own shape. See v. 18.

21. *To fulfil the word of the Lord.* See Jer. xxv. 9, 12; xxvi. 6-7; xxix. 12. For the miserable death of Zedekiah, see 2 Kings xxv. 4, etc.

22. *Now in the first year of Cyrus.* This and the following verse are supposed to have been written by mistake from the Book of Ezra, which begins in the same way. The Book of the Chronicles, properly speaking, does close with the twenty-first verse, as then the Babylonish captivity commences; and these two verses speak of the transactions of a period seventy years after.

THE BOOK OF EZRA

I. Zerubbabel (1:1-6:22)

A. Return (1:1-2:70)

1. The edict of Cyrus (1:1-11)
2. The returning exiles (2:1-70)

B. Reorganization (3:1-6:22)

1. Resumption of worship (3:1-13)
2. Opposition (4:1-24)
   a. General statement (4:1-6)
   b. Particular account (4:7-24)
3. Resumption of building (5:1-17)
4. Darius (6:1-22)

II. Ezra (7:1-10:44)

A. Return—interval of sixty years (7:1-8:36)

1. The coming of Ezra (7:1-28)
2. The returning exiles (8:1-14)
3. The preliminary convention (8:15-30)
4. The return (8:31-36)

B. Reformation (9:1-10:44)

1. The conditions in Jerusalem (9:1, 2)
2. Ezra's intercession (9:3-15)
3. The reformation (10:1-44)

The history of this book is the accomplishment of Jeremiah's prophecy concerning the return of the Jews out of Babylon at the end of seventy years. Ezra preserved the records of that great revolution and transmitted them to the church in this book. His name signifies a helper; and so he was to that people. A particular account concerning him we shall meet with (ch. 7), where he himself enters upon the stage of action.

MATTHEW HENRY

CHAPTER 1

Verses 1–4

1. What was the state of the captive Jews in Babylon. They were under the power of those that hated them, had nothing they could call their own; no temple, no altar; if they sang psalms, their enemies ridiculed them; and yet they had prophets among them. Some of them were preferred at court, others had comfortable settlements in the country, and they were all borne up with hope that, in due time, they should return to their own land again, in expectation of which they preserved among them the distinction of their families, the knowledge of their religion, and an aversion to idolatry. 2. What was the state of the government under which they were. Nebuchadnezzar carried many of them into captivity in the first year of his reign, which was the fourth of Jehoiakim; he reigned forty-five years, his son Evil-merodach twenty-three, and his grandson Belshazzar three years, which make up the seventy years. It is charged upon Nebuchadnezzar that he *opened not the house of his prisoners*, Isa. xiv. 17. And, if he had shown mercy to the poor Jews, Daniel told him it would have been the *lengthening of his tranquillity*, Dan. iv. 27. But the measure of the sins of Babylon was at length full, and then destruction was brought upon them by Darius the Mede and Cyrus the Persian, which we read of, Dan. v. Darius, being old, left the government to Cyrus, and he was employed as the instrument of the Jews' deliverance, as soon as ever he was master of the kingdom of Babylon, perhaps in a pious regard to the prophecy of Isaiah, where he was expressly named as the man that should do this for God, and for whom God would do great things (Isa. xliv. 28; xlv. 1, &c.). His name (some say) in the Persian language signifies the *sun*, for he brought light and healing to the church of God, and was an eminent type of Christ the *Sun of righteousness*.

I. *The Lord stirred up the spirit of Cyrus.* It is said of Cyrus that he knew not God, nor how to serve him; but God knew him, and how to serve himself by him, Isa. xlv. 4. God governs the world by his influence on the spirits of men, and whatever good is done at any time, it is God that stirs up the spirit to do it, puts thoughts into the mind, gives to the understanding to form a right judgment, and directs the will which way he pleases.

II. The reference it had to the prophecy of Jeremiah, by whom God had not only promised that they should return, but had fixed the time. What Cyrus now did was long since said to be the *confirming of the word of God's servants*, Isa. xliv. 26. Jeremiah, while he lived, was hated and despised; yet thus did Providence honour him long after, that a mighty monarch was influenced to act in pursuance of the word of the Lord by his mouth.

III. The date of this proclamation. It was in his first year, not the first of his reign over Persia, the kingdom he was born to, but the first of his reign over Babylon, the kingdom he had conquered.

IV. The publication of it, both by word of mouth and also in black and white: he put it in writing, that it might be the more satisfactory, and might be sent to those distant provinces where the ten tribes were scattered in Assyria and Media, 2 Kings xvii. 6.

V. The purport of this proclamation of liberty.

1. The preamble shows the causes and considerations by which he was influenced, *v.* 2. His mind was enlightened with the knowledge of *Jehovah*, the God of Israel, as the only *living and true God*, the *God of heaven*, who is the sovereign Lord and disposer of all *the kingdoms of the earth*; of him he says (*v.* 3), *He is the God*, God alone, God above all. He professes that he does it, (1) In gratitude to God for

JAMIESON, FAUSSET, BROWN

CHAPTER 1

VSS. 1-6. PROCLAMATION OF CYRUS FOR BUILDING THE TEMPLE.

1. in the first year of Cyrus king of Persia—The Persian empire, including Persia, Media, Babylonia, and Chaldea, with many smaller dependencies, was founded by Cyrus, 536 B.C. [HALES].

that the word of the Lord by the mouth of Jeremiah might be fulfilled—(See Jer. 25:12; 29:10). This reference is a parenthetic statement of the historian, and did not form part of the proclamation.

2. The Lord God of heaven hath given me all the kingdoms of the earth—Though this is in the Oriental style of hyperbole (see also Dan. 4:1), it was literally true that the Persian empire was the greatest ruling power in the world at that time.

ADAM CLARKE

CHAPTER 1

1. *Now in the first year.* This is word for word with the two last verses of the preceding book, which stand here in their proper place and connection, but there are entirely destitute of chronological connection and reference. *Cyrus.* This prince, so eminent in antiquity, is said to have been the son of Cambyses, king of Persia, and Mandane, daughter of Astyages, king of the Medes, and was born about six hundred years before Christ. Josephus accounts for his partiality to the Jews from this circumstance, that he was shown the places in Isaiah the prophet where he is mentioned by name, and his exploits and conquests foretold: see Isa. xliv. 28 and xlv. 1. Finding himself thus distinguished by the God of the Jews, he was anxious to give Him proofs of his gratitude in return; and so made the decree in favor of the Jews, restored their sacred vessels, gave them liberty to return to their own land, and encouraged them to rebuild the temple of Jehovah. It is very probable that when Cyrus took Babylon he found Daniel there, who had been long famed as one of the wisest ministers of state in all the East; and it is most likely that it was this person who pointed out to him the prophecy of Isaiah, and gave him those further intimations relative to the divine will which were revealed to himself.

By . . . Jeremiah. This prophet, chap. xxv. 12 and xxix. 11, had foretold that the Babylonish captivity should last only seventy years; these were now ended. Cyrus had given the Jews permission and encouragement to return to Judea and rebuild the temple of the Lord, and thus the prediction of Jeremiah was fulfilled.

2. *The Lord God of heaven.* It is not unworthy of remark that, in all the books written prior to the Captivity, Jehovah is called "The Lord of Hosts"; but in all the books written after the Captivity, as 2 Chronicles, Ezra, Nehemiah, and Daniel, He is styled "The God of Heaven." The words however have the same

MATTHEW HENRY

the favours he had bestowed upon him: *The God of heaven has given me all the kingdoms of the earth.* He means that God had given him all that was given to Nebuchadnezzar, whose dominion, Daniel says, was *to the end of the earth,* Dan. iv. 22; v. 19.

2. He gives free leave to all the Jews that were in his dominions to go up to Jerusalem, and to *build the temple of the Lord* there, *v.* 3.

3. He subjoins a brief for a collection to bear the charges of such as were poor and not able to bear their own, *v.* 4. "Whosoever remaineth, because he has not the means to bear his charges to Jerusalem, *let the men of his place help him.*" Cyrus not only gave his good wishes with those that went (*Their God be with them, v.* 3), but took care also to furnish them with such things as they needed.

Verses 5–11

I. How Cyrus's proclamation succeeded with others. 1. He having given leave to the Jews to go up to Jerusalem, many of them went up accordingly, *v.* 5. The same God that had raised up the spirit of Cyrus to proclaim this liberty raised up their spirits to take the benefit of it; for it was done, *not by might, nor by power, but by the Spirit of the Lord of hosts,* Zech. iv. 6. The temptation perhaps was strong to some of them to stay in Babylon. The discouragements of their return were many and great, the journey long, their wives and children unfit for travelling, their own land was to them a strange land, the road to it an unknown road. Go up to Jerusalem! And what should they do there? It was all in ruins, and in the midst of enemies to whom they would be an easy prey. Many were wrought upon by these considerations to stay in Babylon, at least not to go with the first. But there were some that got over these difficulties, and they were those whose spirits God raised. He, by his Spirit and grace, filled them with a generous ambition of liberty, a gracious affection to their own land, and a desire of the free and public exercise of their religion. The call and offer of the gospel are like Cyrus's proclamation. *Deliverance is preached to the captives,* Luke iv. 18. Those that are bound under the unrighteous dominion of sin, and bound over to the righteous judgment of God, may be made free by Jesus Christ. Whoever will, by repentance and faith, return to God, Jesus Christ has opened the way for him, and let him go up out of the slavery of sin into the *glorious liberty of the children of God.* The offer is general to all. Christ makes it, in pursuance of the grant which the Father has made him of *all power both in heaven and in earth* and of the charge given him to *build God a house,* to set him up a church in the world, a kingdom among men, Many that hear this joyful sound choose to sit still in Babylon, are in love with their sins and will not venture upon the difficulties of a holy life; but some there are that break through the discouragements, and resolve to *build the house of God,* to make heaven of their religion, whatever it cost them. Thus will the heavenly Canaan be replenished, though many perish in Babylon; and the gospel-offer will not be made in vain. 2. Cyrus having given order that their neighbours should help them, they did so, *v.* 6. All those that were about them furnished them with plate and goods to bear the charges of their journey, and to help them in building and furnishing both their own houses and God's temple. As the tabernacle was made of the spoils of Egypt, and the first temple built by the labours of the strangers, so the second by the contributions of the Chaldeans, all intimating the admission of the Gentiles into the church in due time.

II. How this proclamation was seconded by Cyrus himself. To give proof of the sincerity of his affection to the house of God, he not only released the people of God, but restored the vessels of the temple, *v.* 7, 8. Judah had a prince, even in captivity. Sheshbazzar, supposed to be the same with Zerubbabel, is here called *prince of Judah*; the Chaldeans called him *Sheshbazzar,* which signifies *joy in tribulation*; but among his own people he went by the name of *Zerubbabel—a stranger in Babylon*; so he looked upon himself, and considered Jerusalem his home, though, as Josephus says, he was captain of the life-guard to the king of Babylon. He took care of the affairs of the Jews. To him the sacred vessels were numbered out (*v.* 8), and he took care for their safe conveyance to Jerusalem, *v.* 11.

JAMIESON, FAUSSET, BROWN

he hath charged me to build him an house at Jerusalem—The phraseology of this proclamation, independently of the express testimony of Josephus, affords indisputable evidence that Cyrus had seen (probably through means of Daniel, his venerable prime minister and favorite) those prophecies in which, 200 years before he was born, his name, his victorious career, and the important services he should render to the Jews were distinctly foretold (Isa. 44:28; 46:1-4). The existence of predictions so remarkable led him to acknowledge that all his kingdoms were gifts bestowed on him by "the Lord God of heaven," and prompted him to fulfil the duty which had been laid upon him long before his birth. This was the source and origin of the great favor he showed to the Jews. The proclamation, though issued "in the first year of Cyrus," did not take effect till the year following. **3. Who is there among you of all his people**—The purport of the edict was to grant full permission to those Jewish exiles, in every part of his kingdom, who chose, to return to their own country, as well as to recommend those of their countrymen who remained to aid the poor and feeble on their way, and contribute liberally towards the rebuilding of the temple. **5, 6. Then rose up the chief of the fathers,** etc.—The paternal and ecclesiastical chiefs of the later captivity, those of the tribes of Judah and Benjamin, with some also from other tribes (I Chron. 9:3), who retained their attachment to the pure worship of God, naturally took the lead in this movement. Their example was followed by all whose piety and patriotism were strong enough to brave the various discouragements attending the enterprise. They were liberally assisted by multitudes of their captive countrymen, who, born in Babylonia or comfortably established in it by family connections or the possession of property, chose to remain.

It seems that their Assyrian friends and neighbors, too, either from a favorable disposition toward the Jewish faith, or from imitation of the court policy, displayed hearty good will and great liberality in aiding and promoting the views of the emigrants.

7-11. CYRUS RESTORES THE VESSELS. **7. Cyrus . . . brought forth the vessels of the house of the Lord**—Though it is said (II Kings 24:13) that these were *cut in pieces,* that would not be done to the large and magnificent vases; and, if they had been divided, the parts could be reunited. But it may be doubted whether the *Hebrew* word rendered *cut in pieces,* does not signify merely *cut off,* i.e., from further use in the temple. **8. Sheshbazzar, the prince of Judah**—i.e., Zerubbabel, son of Salathiel (cf. ch. 3:8; 5:16). He was born in Babylon, and called by his family Zerubbabel, i.e., stranger or exile in Babylon. Sheshbazzar, signifying "fire-worshipper," was the name given him at court, as other names were given to Daniel and his friends. He was recognized among the exiles as hereditary prince of Judah. **11. All the vessels of gold and of silver were five thousand and four hundred**—The vessels here specified amount only to the number of 2499. Hence it is probable that the larger vases only are mentioned, while the inventory of the whole, including great and small, came to the gross sum stated in the text. **them of the captivity that were brought up from Babylon unto Jerusalem**—All the Jewish exiles did not embrace the privilege which the Persian king granted them. The great proportion, born in Babylon, preferred continuing in their comfortable homes to undertaking a distant, expensive, and hazardous journey to a desolate land. Nor did the returning exiles all go at once. The first band went with Zerubbabel, others afterwards with Ezra, and a large number with Nehemiah at a still later period.

ADAM CLARKE

meaning. *All the kingdoms of the earth.* At this time the empire of the Medo-Persians was very extensive; according to ancient writers, Cyrus, at this time, reigned over the Medes, Persians, Hyrcanians, Armenians, Syrians, Assyrians, Arabians, Cappadocians, Phrygians, Lydians, Phoenicians, Babylonians, Bactrians, Indians, Saci, Cilicians, Paphlagonians, Moriandrians, and many others. His empire extended on the east to the Red Sea; on the north, to the Euxine Sea; on the west, to the island of Cyprus and Egypt; and on the south, to Ethiopia.

4. *Whosoever remaineth in any place.* Everyone was at liberty to go, but none was obliged to go. Thus their attachment to God was tried. He whose heart was right with God went; he who was comfortably settled in Babylon might go if he chose. Those who did not go were commanded to assist their brethren who went.

6. *Vessels of silver.* Articles of silver, gold, etc.

7. *The king brought forth the vessels.* See on vv. 9-11.

8. *Sheshbazzar, the prince of Judah.* This was probably the Chaldean name of him who was originally called Zerubbabel. The former signifies "joy in affliction"; the latter, "a stranger in Babylon." The latter may be designed to refer to his captive state; the former, to the prospect of release. Some think this was quite a different person; a Persian or Chaldean, sent by Cyrus to superintend whatever officers or men Cyrus might have sent to assist the Jews on their return and to procure them help in the Chaldean provinces, through which they might be obliged to travel.

11. *All the vessels . . . were five thousand and four hundred.* This place is without doubt corrupted; here it is said the sum of all the vessels, of every quality and kind, was 5,400; but the enumeration of the articles, as given in vv. 9 and 10, gives the sum of 2,499 only. But we can correct this account from 1 Esdras ii. 13-14.

MATTHEW HENRY — CHAPTER 2

Verses 1–35

1. An account was kept in writing of the families that came up out of captivity, and the numbers of each family. This was done for their honour, as

JAMIESON, FAUSSET, BROWN — CHAPTER 2

Vss. 1-70. NUMBER OF THE PEOPLE THAT RETURNED. **1. children of the province**—i.e., Judea (ch. 5:8), so called as being now reduced from an illustrious, independent, and powerful kingdom to

ADAM CLARKE — CHAPTER 2

1. *These are the children of the province.* That is, of Judea—once a kingdom and a flourishing nation; now a province, subdued, tributary, and ruined! Some think Babylon is meant

MATTHEW HENRY

part of their recompence for their faith and courage, and their affection to their own land, and to stir up others to follow their good example. The names of all those Israelites indeed that accept the offer of deliverance by Christ shall be found, to their honour, in a more sacred record than this, even in *the Lamb's book of life*. The account that was kept of the families that came up from the captivity was intended also for the benefit of posterity, that they might know from whom they descended and to whom they were allied. 2. They are called *children of the province*. Judah, which had been an illustrious kingdom, to which other kingdoms had been made provinces, subject to it and dependent on it, was now itself made a province, to receive laws and commissions from the king of Persia and to be accountable to him. 3. They are said to come *every one to his city*, that is, the city appointed them, in which appointment an eye, no doubt, was had to their former settlement by Joshua; and to that, as near as might be, they returned. 4. That the leaders are first mentioned, *v.* 2. Zerubbabel and Jeshua were their Moses and Aaron, the former their chief prince, the latter their chief priest. 5. Some of these several families are named from the persons that were their ancestors, others from the places in which they had formerly resided. Here are two families that are called *the children of Elam* (one *v.* 7, another *v.* 31), and, which is strange, the number of both is the same, 1,254. The children of Bethlehem (*v.* 21) were but 123, though it was David's city; for Bethlehem was *little among the thousands of Judah*, yet there must the Messiah arise, Micah v. 2. Anathoth had been a famous place in the tribe of Benjamin and yet here it numbered but 128 (*v.* 23), which is to be imputed to the divine curse which the men of Anathoth brought upon themselves by persecuting Jeremiah, who was of their city. Jer. xi. 21, 23.

Verses 36–63

An account, I. Of the priests that returned, and they were a considerable number, about a tenth part of the whole company: for the whole were above 42,000 (*v.* 64), and four families of priests made up above 4,200 (*v.* 36–39).

II. Of the Levites. The small number of them, for, taking in both the singers and the porters (*v.* 40–42), they did not make 350.

III. Of the Nethinim, the Gibeonites, *given* (so their name signifies) by Joshua first (Joshua ix. 27), and again by David (Ezra viii. 20), when Saul had expelled them, to be employed by the Levites in the work of God's house as hewers of wood and drawers of water.

IV. Of some that were looked upon as Israelites by birth, and others as priests, and yet could not make out a clear title to the honour. 1. There were some that could not prove themselves Israelites (*v.* 59, 60), a considerable number, who presumed they were of the seed of Jacob, but could not produce their pedigrees, and yet would go up to Jerusalem, having an affection to the house and people of God. 2. There were others that could not prove themselves priests, and yet were supposed to be of the seed of Aaron.

Verses 64–70

I. The sum total of the company that returned out of Babylon. The before mentioned amount not quite to 30,000 (29,818), so that there were above 12,000 who, it is probable, were of the rest of the tribes of Israel, besides Judah and Benjamin. This was more than double the number that were carried captive into Babylon by Nebuchadnezzar, so that, as in Egypt, the time of their affliction was the time of their increase.

II. Their retinue. Their servants were comparatively few (*v.* 65) and their beasts of burden about as many, *v.* 66, 67. But notice is taken of 200 *singing-men and women* whom they had among them, who were intended (as those 2 Chron. xxxv. 25) to excite *their mourning*.

III. Their oblations. It is said (*v.* 68, 69), 1. That they *came to the house of the Lord at Jerusalem*; and yet that house, that holy and beautiful house, was now in ruins. 2. That they offered freely towards the *setting of it up in its place*. That, it seems, was the first house they talked of setting up. Their offering was nothing in comparison with the offerings of the princes in David's time; then they offered by talents

JAMIESON, FAUSSET, BROWN

an obscure, servile, tributary province of the Persian empire. This name is applied by the sacred historian to intimate that the Jewish exiles, though now released from captivity and allowed to return into their own land, were still the subjects of Cyrus, inhabiting a province dependent upon Persia. **came again unto Jerusalem and Judah, every one unto his city**—either the city that had been occupied by his ancestors, or, as most parts of Judea were then either desolate or possessed by others, the city that was rebuilt and allotted to him now. **2. Which came with Zerubbabel**—He was the chief or leader of the first band of returning exiles. The names of other influential persons who were associated in the conducting of the caravans are also mentioned, being extracted probably from the Persian archives, in which the register was preserved: conspicuous in the number are Jeshua, the high priest, and Nehemiah. **3. The children**—This word, as used throughout this catalogue, means posterity or descendants. **5. children of Arah, seven hundred seventy and five**—The number is stated in Nehemiah 7 to have been only 652. It is probable that all mentioned as belonging to this family repaired to the general place of rendezvous, or had enrolled their names at first as intending to go; but in the interval of preparation, some died, others were prevented by sickness or insurmountable obstacles, so that ultimately no more than 652 came to Jerusalem. **23. The men of Anathoth**—It is pleasant to see so many of this Jewish town returning. It was a city of the Levites; but the people spurned Jeremiah's warning and called forth against themselves one of his severest predictions (Jer. 32:27-35). This prophecy was fulfilled in the Assyrian conquest. Anathoth was laid waste and continued a heap of ruins. But the people, having been brought during the captivity to a better state of mind, returned, and their city was rebuilt. **36-39. The priests**—Each of their families was ranged under its prince or head, like those of the other tribes. It will be remembered that the whole body was divided into twenty-four courses, one of which, in rotation, discharged the sacerdotal duties every week, and each division was called after the name of its first prince or chief. It appears from this passage that only four of the courses of the priests returned from the Babylonish captivity; but these four courses were afterwards, as the families increased, divided into twenty-four, which were distinguished by the names of the original courses appointed by David. Hence we find the course of Abijah or Abia (I Chron. 24:10) subsisting at the commencement of the Christian era (Luke 1: 5). **55. The children of Solomon's servants**—either the strangers that monarch enlisted in the building of the temple, or those who lived in his palace, which was deemed a high honor. **61, 62. the children of Barzillai**—He preferred that name to that of his own family, deeming it a greater distinction to be connected with so noble a family, than to be of the house of Levi. But by this worldly ambition he forfeited the dignity and advantages of the priesthood. **63. Tirshatha**—a title borne by the Persian governors of Judea (see also Neh. 7:65-70; 8:9; 10: 1). It is derived from the Persian *torsh*, severe, and is equivalent to "your severity," "your awfulness." **64. The whole congregation together was forty-two thousand three hundred and threescore**—This gross amount is 12,000 more than the particular numbers given in the catalogue, when added together, come to. Reckoning up the smaller numbers, we shall find that they amount to 29,818 in this chapter, and to 31,089 in the parallel chapter of Nehemiah. Ezra also mentions 494 persons omitted by Nehemiah, and Nehemiah mentions 1765 not noticed by Ezra. If, therefore, Ezra's surplus be added to the sum in Nehemiah, and Nehemiah's surplus to the number in Ezra, they will both become 31,583. Subtracting this from 42,360, there will be a deficiency of 10,777. These are omitted because they did not belong to Judah and Benjamin, or to the priests, but to the other tribes. The servants and singers, male and female, are reckoned separately (vs. 65), so that putting all these items together, the number of all who went with Zerubbabel amounted to 50,000, with 8000 beasts of burden (ALTING, quoted DAVIDSON'S HERMENEUTICS). **68. some of the chief of the fathers, when they came to the house of the Lord, offered freely for the house of God,** etc.—The sight of a place hallowed by the most endearing and sacred associations, but now lying in desolation and ruins, made the well-springs of their piety and patriotism gush out afresh. Before taking any active measures for providing accommodation to themselves and their families, the chief among them raised a large sum by voluntary contributions towards the restoration

ADAM CLARKE

by *the province;* and that *the children of the province* means those Jews who were born in Babylon. But the first is most likely to be the meaning, for thus we find Judea styled, chap. v. Besides, the *province* is contradistinguished from *Babylon* even in this first verse. *The children of the province*—"that had been carried away unto Babylon."

2. *Which came with Zerubbabel.* There are many difficulties in this table of names; but as we have no less than three copies of it, that contained here from vv. 1-67, a second in Neh. vii. 6-69, and a third in 1 Esdras v. 7-43, on a careful examination they will be found to correct each other. Though the sum total at the end of each of these enumerations is equal, namely, 42,360, yet the particulars reckoned up make in Ezra only 29,818, and in Nehemiah 31,089. We find that Nehemiah mentions 1,765 persons which are not in Ezra, and Ezra has 494 not mentioned by Nehemiah. Mr. Alting thinks that this circumstance, which appears to render all hope of reconciling them impossible, is precisely the very point by which they can be reconciled; for if we add Ezra's surplus to the sum in Nehemiah, and the surplus of Nehemiah to the number in Ezra, the numbers will be equal.

3. *The children of Parosh.* Where the word *children* is found in this table, prefixed to the name of a man, it signifies the descendants of that person, as from this verse to v. 21. Where it is found prefixed to a place, it signifies the inhabitants of that place, as from v. 21 to v. 35.

33. *The children of Lod, Hadid, and Ono.* There were cities in the tribe of Benjamin; see on 1 Chron. viii. 12.

36. *The priests.* The preceding list takes in the census of Judah and Benjamin.

55. *The children of Solomon's servants.* The Nethinim, and others appointed to do the meaner services of the holy house.

63. *The Tirshatha.* This is generally supposed to be Nehemiah, or the person who was the commandant; see Neh. viii. 9 and x. 1, for the word appears to be the name of an office. *Should not eat of the most holy things.* There was a high priest then, but no Urim and Thummim, these having been lost in the Captivity.

66. *Their horses . . . seven hundred.* They went into captivity, stripped of everything; they now return from it, abounding in the most substantial riches, viz., horses 736, or, according to Esdras, 7,036; mules, 245; camels, 435; asses, 6,720; besides gold, and silver, and rich stuffs.

69. *Threescore and one thousand drams of gold. Drakmons* or darics; a Persian coin, always of gold, and worth about 1*£.* 5*s.*; not less than £76,250 sterling in gold. *Five thousand pound of silver.* Manehs or minas. As a weight, the

MATTHEW HENRY

(1 Chron. xxix. 7), now by drams, yet these drams, being after their ability, were as acceptable to God as those talents, like the widow's two mites. 3. That they *dwelt in their cities, v.* 70. Though their cities were out of repair, yet, because they were their cities, such as God had assigned them, they were content to dwell in them. Their poverty was a bad cause, but their unity and unanimity were a good effect of it.

CHAPTER 3

Verses 1–7

I. A general assembly of the returned Israelites at Jerusalem, in the *seventh month, v.* 1. We may suppose that they came from Babylon in the spring. The seventh month therefore soon came, in which many of the feasts of the Lord were to be solemnized. Such was their zeal for religion that they left all their business in the country, to attend God's altar; and they came *as one man.* Let worldly business be postponed to the business of religion and it will prosper the better.

II. The care which their leading men took to have an altar ready for them to attend upon.

1. Joshua and his brethren the priests, Zerubbabel and his brethren the princes, built *the altar of the God of Israel* (*v.* 2), in the same place where it had stood, *v.* 3. They could not immediately have a temple, but they would not be without an altar. Abraham, wherever he came, *built an altar*; and wherever we come, though we may perhaps want the benefit of the candlestick of preaching, and the showbread of the eucharist, yet, if we bring not the sacrifices of prayer and praise, we are wanting in our duty, for we have an altar that sanctifies the gift ever ready.

2. The reason here given why they hastened to set up the altar: *Fear was upon them, because of the people of the land.* They were in the midst of enemies that bore ill will to them and their religion. *Because* they were so, therefore they set up the altar. Apprehension of danger should stir us up to our duty. This good use we should make of our fears, we should be driven by them to our knees.

III. The sacrifices they offered upon the altar. Let not those that have an altar starve it.

1. They began *on the first day of the seventh month, v.* 6.

2. Having begun, they kept up the *continual burnt-offering* (*v.* 5), *morning and evening, v.* 3. They had known by sad experience what it was to want the comfort of the daily sacrifice to plead in their daily prayers.

3. They observed all the *set feasts of the Lord*, and offered the sacrifices appointed for each, and particularly *the feast of tabernacles, v.* 4, 5. Now that they were beginning to settle in their cities it might serve well to remind them of their fathers dwelling in tents in the wilderness.

4. They offered *every man's free-will offering, v.* 5. The law required much, but they brought more; for, though they had little wealth to support the expense of their sacrifices, they had much zeal, and, we may suppose, spared at their own tables that they might plentifully supply God's altar.

IV. The preparation they made for the building of the temple, *v.* 7. Tyre and Sidon must now, as of old, furnish them with workmen, and Lebanon with timber, orders for both which they had from Cyrus.

Verses 8–13

There was no dispute among the returned Jews whether they should build the temple or no. An account of the beginning of that good work.

I. When it was begun—as soon as ever the season of the year would permit (*v.* 8), and when they had ended the solemnities of the passover. They took little more than half a year for making preparation of the ground and materials.

II. Who began it—Zerubbabel, and Jeshua, and their brethren. Then the work of God is likely to go on well when magistrates, ministers, and people, are hearty for it.

III. They appointed the *Levites to set forward the work* (*v.* 8), and they did it by *setting forward the workmen* (*v.* 9), and strengthening their hands with good and comfortable words.

IV. How God was praised at the laying of the foundation of the temple (*v.* 10, 11); the priests with the trumpets appointed by Moses, and the Levites with the cymbals appointed by David to assist the singing of that everlasting hymn which will never be out of date, and to which our tongues should never be out

JAMIESON, FAUSSET, BROWN

of the temple. **69. drams of gold**—rather darics, a Persian coin (see on I Chron. 29:7). **priests' garments** (cf. Neh. 7:70). This—in the circumstances—was a very appropriate gift. In general, it may be remarked that presents of garments, or of any other usable commodities, however singular it may seem to us, is in harmony with the established notions and customs of the East.

CHAPTER 3

Vss. 1-13. The Altar Set Up. **1. when the seventh month was come**—The departure of the returning exiles from Babylon took place in the spring. For some time after their arrival they were occupied in the necessary work of rearing habitations to themselves amid the ruins of Jerusalem and its neighborhood. This preliminary work being completed, they addressed themselves to rebuild the altar of burnt offering. As the seventh month of the sacred year was at hand—corresponding to the latter end of our September—when the feast of tabernacles (Lev. 23) fell to be observed, they resolved to celebrate that religious festival, just as if the temple had been fully restored. **2. Jeshua**—the grandson of Seraiah, the high priest, put to death by Nebuchadnezzar at Riblah (II Kings 25:18-21). His father, Josedech, had been carried captive to Babylon, and died there, some time before this. **Zerubbabel**—was, according to the order of nature, son of Pedaiah (I Chron. 3:17-19); but having been brought up by Salathiel, he was called his son. **builded the altar of the God of Israel, to offer burnt offerings thereon**—This was of urgent and immediate necessity, in order, first, to make atonement for their sins; secondly, to obtain the divine blessing on their preparations for the temple, as well as animate their feelings of piety and patriotism for the prosecution of that national work. **3. they set the altar upon his bases**—They reared it upon its old foundation, so that it occupied as nearly as possible the site on which it had formerly stood.

they offered burnt offerings . . . morning and evening—Deeming it their duty to perform the public rites of religion, they did not wait till the temple should be rebuilt and dedicated; but, at the outset, they resumed the daily service prescribed by the law (Exod. 29:38, 39; Lev. 6:9, 11), as well as observed the annual seasons of solemn observance.

4-7. Offerings Renewed. **4, 6. They kept also the feast of tabernacles . . . From the first day of the seventh month**—They revived at that time the daily oblation, and it was on the fifteenth day of that month the feast of tabernacles was held.

7. They gave . . . meat . . . drink, and oil, unto them of Zidon—They opened negotiations with the Tyrians for workmen, as well as for timber, on the same terms and with the same views as Solomon had done (I Kings 5:11; II Chron. 2:15, 16).

8-13. The Foundation of the Temple Laid. **8. appointed the Levites . . . to set forward the work**—i.e., to act as overseers of the workmen, and to direct and animate the laborers in the various departments. **9. Jeshua with his sons**—not the high priest, but a Levite (ch. 2:40). To these, as probably distinguished for their mechanical skill and taste, the duty of acting as overseers was particularly committed.

ADAM CLARKE

maneh was 100 shekels; as a coin, 60 shekels in value, or about 9£; 5,000 of these manehs therefore will amount to £45,000, making in the whole a sum of about £120,000; and in this are not included the 100 garments for priests.

70. *Dwelt in their cities.* They all went to those cities which belonged originally to their respective families.

CHAPTER 3

1. *When the seventh month was come.* The month Tisri, which answers to the latter part of our September and beginning of October. It seems that the Israelites had left Babylon about the spring of the year; that on their arrival at Jerusalem they constructed themselves huts and sheds to lodge in among the ruins, in which they must have spent some months. After this they rebuilt the altar of burnt offerings and kept the Feast of Tabernacles, which happened about this time, and continued to offer sacrifices regularly, as if the Temple were standing.

2. *Jeshua the son of Jozadak.* He was grandson of Seraiah, the high priest, who was put to death by Nebuchadnezzar, 2 Kings xxv. 18, 21. This Jeshua or Joshua was the first high priest after the Captivity.

3. *They set the altar upon his bases.* Rebuilt it on the same spot on which it had formerly stood. As it was necessary to keep up the divine worship during the time they should be employed in reedifying the Temple, they first reared this altar of burnt offerings; and all this they did, though *fear was upon them*, because of the unfriendly disposition of their surrounding neighbors.

4. *They kept also the feast of tabernacles, as it is written.* This began on the fifteenth day of the seventh month; but they had begun the regular offerings from the first day of this month, v. 6. And these were religiously continued all the time they were building the Temple.

7. *They gave money also.* They copied the conduct of Solomon while he was building his temple; see 1 Kings v. 11. He employed the Tyrians, gave them meat and drink; and this permission they now had from Cyrus.

8. *In the second year.* The previous time had been employed in clearing the ground, felling timber, hewing stones, and transporting them to the place, and making other necessary preparations for the commencement of the building.

10. *After the ordinance of David.* With psalms which he composed, acting in the manner which he directed.

MATTHEW HENRY

of tune, *God is good, and his mercy endureth for ever*. Let all the streams of mercy be traced up to the fountain. However it be, yet *God is good to Israel* (Ps. lxxiii. 1), good to us. Let the reviving of the church's interests, when they seemed dead, be ascribed to the continuance of God's mercy for ever, for therefore the church continues.

V. How the people were affected. Different sentiments there were among the people of God, and each expressed himself according to his sentiments, and yet there was no disagreement among them. 1. Those that only knew the misery of having no temple at all praised the Lord with shouts of joy when they saw but the foundation of one laid, *v.* 11. To them even this foundation seemed great, and was as life from the dead. They shouted, so that *the noise was heard afar off.* 2. Those that remembered the glory of the first temple which Solomon built, and considered how far this was likely to be inferior to that, perhaps in dimensions, certainly in magnificence and sumptuousness, *wept with a loud voice, v.* 12. If we date the destruction of the first temple 586 B.C., and the return from Babylon 537 B.C., the foundation of the new temple was laid in 536 B.C., fifty years after the temple was burnt. So that many now alive might remember it standing. These lamented the disproportion between this temple and the former. And, (1) There was some reason for it; and if they turned their tears into the right channel, and bewailed the sin that was the cause of this melancholy change, they did well. (2) Yet it was their infirmity to mingle those tears with the common joys and so to cast a damp upon them. In the harmony of public joys, let not us be jarring strings. They were priests and Levites, who should have known and taught others how to be duly affected under various providences, and not to let the remembrance of former afflictions drown the sense of present mercies. This mixture of sorrow and joy here is a representation of this world. We can scarcely ***discern the shouts of joy from the noise of the weeping.***

JAMIESON, FAUSSET, BROWN

12. But many of the priests and Levites and chief of the fathers . . . wept with a loud voice—Those painful emotions were excited by the sad contrast between the prosperous circumstances in which the foundations of the first temple had been laid and the desolate, reduced state of the country and city when the second was begun; between the inferior size and less costliness of the stones used in the foundations of the second (I Kings 7:9, 10), and the much smaller extent of the foundation itself, including all the appurtenances of the building (Hag. 2:3); between the comparative smallness of their present means and the immense resources of David and Solomon. Perhaps, however, the chief cause of grief was that the second temple would be destitute of those things which formed the great and distinguishing glory of the first; viz., the ark, the shekinah, the Urim and Thummim, etc. Not that this second temple was not a very grand and beautiful structure. But no matter how great its material splendor was, it was inferior in this respect to that of Solomon. Yet the glory of the second far outshone that of the first temple in another and more important point of view, viz., the receiving within its walls the incarnate Saviour (Hag. 2:9). **13. the people could not discern the shout of joy from the noise of the weeping**—Among Eastern people, expressions of sorrow are always very loud and vehement. It is indicated by wailing, the howl of which is sometimes not easily distinguishable from joyful acclamations.

ADAM CLARKE

12. *Wept with a loud voice.* They saw that the glory had departed from Israel; in their circumstances it was impossible to build such a house as the first Temple was; and had this been even possible, still it would have been greatly inferior, because it wanted the ark of the covenant, the heavenly fire, the mercy seat, the heavenly manna, Aaron's rod that budded, the divine Shekinah, the spirit of prophecy, and most probably the Urim and Thummim. *Many shouted . . . for joy.* Finding they were now restored to their own land, and to the worship of their God in His own peculiar city. These, in general, had not seen the original Temple, and therefore could not feel affected in that way which the elderly people did.

MATTHEW HENRY — CHAPTER 4

Verses 1–5

An instance of the old enmity that was put between the seed of the woman and the seed of the serpent. God's temple cannot be built, but Satan will rage, and the *gates of hell* will *fight against it.* The gospel kingdom was, in like manner, to be set up with much struggling and contention.

I. The *children of the captivity* (*v.* 1) had newly come out of captivity, were born in captivity, had still the marks of their captivity upon them; though they were not now captives, they were under the control of those whose captives they had lately been. Israel was God's son, his first-born; but by their iniquity the people sold and enslaved themselves, and so became children of the captivity.

II. The opposers of the undertaking are here said to be *the adversaries of Judah and Benjamin*, not the Chaldeans or Persians, but the relics of the ten tribes, and the foreigners that had joined themselves to them, and patched up that mongrel religion we had an account of, 2 Kings xvii. 33. *They feared the Lord, and served their own gods too.* They are called *the people of the land, v.* 4.

III. The opposition they gave had in it much of the subtlety of the old serpent. When they heard that the temple was in building they were immediately aware that it would be a fatal blow to their superstition, and set themselves to oppose it.

1. They offered their service to build with the Israelites only that thereby they might get an opportunity to retard the work, while they pretended to further it. Their offer was plausible enough, and looked kind: "*We will build with you*, will help you to contribute, and will contribute towards the expense; *for we seek your God as you do*," *v.* 2. This was false, for, though they sought the same God, they did not seek him only, nor seek him in the way he appointed. *The chief of the fathers of Israel* were soon aware that they meant them no kindness, whatever they pretended, but really designed to do them a mischief, and therefore told them plainly, "*You have nothing to do with us*, have no part nor lot in this matter, are not true-born Israelites nor faithful worshippers of God; *you worship you know not what*, John iv. 22. You are none of those with whom we dare hold communion, and therefore we ourselves will build it."

2. When this plot failed they did what they could to divert them from the work and discourage them in it. Those that were cool and indifferent were by these artifices drawn off from the work, which wanted their help, *v.* 4. Wonder not at the restlessness of

JAMIESON, FAUSSET, BROWN — CHAPTER 4

Vss. 1-6. THE BUILDING HINDERED.

1. the adversaries of Judah and Benjamin—i.e., strangers settled in the land of Israel. **2. we seek your God, as ye do; and we do sacrifice unto him since the days of Esarhaddon . . . which brought us up hither**—A very interesting explanation of this passage has been recently obtained from the Assyrian sculptures. On a large cylinder, deposited in the British Museum, there is inscribed a long and perfect copy of the annals of Esarhaddon, in which the details are given of a large deportation of Israelites from Palestine, and a consequent settlement of Babylonian colonists in their place. It is a striking confirmation of the statement made in this passage. Those Assyrian settlers intermarried with the remnant of Israelite women, and their descendants, a mongrel race, went under the name of Samaritans. Though originally idolaters, they were instructed in the knowledge of God, so that they could say, "We seek your God"; but they served Him in a superstitious way of their own (see on II Kings 17:26-34, 41). **3. But Zerubbabel and Jeshua . . . said . . . Ye have nothing to do with us to build an house unto our God**—This refusal to co-operate with the Samaritans, from whatever motives it sprang, was overruled by Providence for ultimate good; for, had the two peoples worked together, familiar acquaintanceship and intermarriage would have ensued, and the result might have been a relapse of the Jews into idolatry. Most certainly, confusion and obscurity in the genealogical evidence that proved the descent of the Messiah would have followed; whereas, in their hostile and separate condition, they were jealous observers of each other's proceedings, watching with mutual care over the preservation and integrity of the sacred books, guarding the purity and honor of the Mosaic worship, and thus contributing to the maintenance of religious knowledge and truth. **4. Then the people of the land weakened the hands of the people of Judah,** etc.—Exasperated

ADAM CLARKE — CHAPTER 4

1. *Now when the adversaries.* These were the Samaritans, and the different nations with which the kings of Assyria had peopled Israel, when they had carried the original inhabitants away into captivity, see v. 9.

2. *Let us build with you.* We acknowledge the same God, are solicitous for His glory, and will gladly assist you in this work. But that they came with no friendly intention, the context proves.

3. *Ye have nothing to do with us.* We cannot acknowledge you as worshippers of the true God, and cannot participate with you in anything that relates to His worship.

4. *Weakened the hands.* Discouraged and opposed them by every possible means.

MATTHEW HENRY

the church's enemies in their attempts against the building of God's temple. He whom they serve, and whose work they are doing, is *unwearied* in *walking to and fro through the earth* to do mischief.

Verses 6–16

Cyrus steadfastly adhered to the Jews' interest. His successor was Ahasuerus (*v.* 6), called also *Artaxerxes* (*v.* 7), supposed to be the same that in heathen authors is called *Cambyses,* who had never taken such cognizance of the despised Jews as to concern himself for them. To him these Samaritans applied for an order to stop the building of the temple; and they did it in the beginning of his reign, being resolved to lose no time when they thought they had a king for their purpose. See how watchful the church's enemies are to take the first opportunity of doing it a mischief; let not its friends be less careful to do it a kindness.

I. The general purport of the letter which they sent to the king, to inform him of this matter. It is called (*v.* 6) *an accusation against the inhabitants of Judah and Jerusalem.*

II. The persons concerned in writing this letter. The contrivers are named (*v.* 7) that plotted the thing, the writers (*v.* 8) that put it into form, and the subscribers (*v.* 9) that concurred in it and joined with them. The *rulers take counsel together against the Lord* and his temple. The building of the temple would do them no harm, yet they appear against it with the utmost concern and virulence, perhaps because the prophets of the God of Israel had foretold the *famishing* and *perishing* of all the *gods of the heathen,* Zeph. ii. 11; Jer. x. 11. The people concurred with them in imagining this vain thing. All the several colonies from the cities or countries of Assyria, Chaldea, Persia, &c., whence they came, set their hands, by their representatives, to this letter.

III. A copy of the letter itself, which Ezra inserts here out of the records of the kingdom of Persia.

1. They represent themselves as very loyal to the government, and greatly concerned for the honour and interest of it. *Because we are salted with the salt of the palace* (so it is in the *margin*), we have our salary from the court, and could no more live without it than flesh could be preserved without salt. Now, in consideration of this, "*it is not meet for us to see the king's dishonour;*" and therefore they urge him to stop the building of the temple.

2. They represent the Jews as disloyal, and dangerous to the government, that Jerusalem was *the rebellious and bad city* (*v.* 12), *hurtful to kings and provinces, v.* 15.

(1) Their history of what was past was invidious, that *within this city sedition had been moved of old time,* and, for *that cause, it was destroyed, v.* 15. There was some colour given for this suggestion by the attempts of Jehoiakim and Zedekiah to shake off the yoke of the king of Babylon. But their efforts to recover their rights would have been justifiable had they taken the right method and made their peace with God first. Though these Jews, and their princes, had been guilty of rebellion, yet it was unjust therefore to fasten this as an indelible brand upon this city. The Jews, in their captivity, had given such specimens of good behaviour as were sufficient, with any reasonable men, to roll away that one reproach.

(2) Their information concerning what was now doing was grossly false in matter of fact. Very careful they were to inform the king that the Jews had *set up the walls of this city.* They had only begun to build the temple, which Cyrus commanded them to do, but, as for the walls, there was nothing done nor designed towards the repair of them, as appears by the condition they were in many years after (Neh. i. 3), all in ruins.

(3) Their prognostics of the consequences were altogether groundless and absurd. They were very confident that if this city should be built, not only the Jews would *pay no toll, tribute, or custom* (*v.* 13), but that all the countries on this side Euphrates would instantly revolt, drawn in to do so by their example; and, if the prince in possession should connive at this, he would wrong, not only himself, but his successors: *Thou shalt endamage the revenue of the kings.* See how every line in this letter breathes both the subtlety and malice of the old serpent.

Verses 17–24

I. The orders which the king of Persia gave, in answer to the information sent him by the Samaritans against the Jews. He suffered himself to be imposed upon by their falsehood, but was very willing to gratify them with an order to stay proceedings. He

JAMIESON, FAUSSET, BROWN

by this repulse, the Samaritans endeavored by every means to molest the workmen as well as obstruct the progress of the building; and, though they could not alter the decree which Cyrus had issued regarding it, yet by bribes and clandestine arts indefatigably plied at court, they labored to frustrate the effects of the edict. Their success in those underhand dealings was great; for Cyrus, being frequently absent and much absorbed in his warlike expeditions, left the government in the hands of his son Cambyses, a wicked prince, and extremely hostile to the Jews and their religion. The same arts were assiduously practised during the reign of his successor, Smerdis, down to the time of Darius Hystaspes. In consequence of the difficulties and obstacles thus interposed, for a period of twenty years, the progress of the work was very slow. **6. in the reign of Ahasuerus, in the beginning of his reign, wrote they . . . an accusation**—Ahasuerus was a regal title, and the king referred to was successor of Darius, the famous Xerxes.

7-24. LETTER TO ARTAXERXES. **7. in the day of Artaxerxes wrote Bishlam,** etc.—The three officers named are supposed to have been deputy-governors appointed by the king of Persia over all the provinces subject to his empire west of the Euphrates. **the Syrian tongue**—or Aramæan language, called sometimes in our version, Chaldee. This was made use of by the Persians in their decrees and communications relative to the Jews (cf. II Kings 18:26; Isa. 36:11). The object of their letter was to press upon the royal notice the inexpediency and danger of rebuilding the walls of Jerusalem. They labored hard to prejudice the king's mind against that measure.

9. the Dinaites—The people named were the colonists sent by the Babylonian monarch to occupy the territory of the ten tribes. "The great and noble Asnapper" was Esar-haddon. Immediately after the murder of Sennacherib, the Babylonians, Medes, Armenians, and other tributary people seized the opportunity of throwing off the Assyrian yoke. But Esar-haddon having, in the thirtieth year of his reign, recovered Babylon and subdued the other rebellious dependents, transported numbers of them into the waste cities of Samaria, most probably as a punishment of their revolt [HALES]. **14. we have maintenance from the king's palace**—lit., we are salted with the king's salt. "Eating a prince's salt" is an Oriental phrase, equivalent to "receiving maintenance from him."

12. the Jews which came up from thee to us—The name "Jews" was generally used after the return from the captivity, because the returning exiles belonged chiefly to the tribes of Judah and Benjamin. Although the edict of Cyrus permitted all who chose to return, a permission of which some of the Israelites availed themselves, the great body who went to settle in Judea were the men of Judah.

13. toll, tribute, and custom—The first was a poll tax; the second was a property tax; the third the excise dues on articles of trade and merchandise. Their letter, and the edict that followed, commanding an immediate cessation of the work at the city walls, form the exclusive subject of narrative from vs. 7 to vs. 23. And now from this digression he returns at vs. 24 to resume the thread of his narrative concerning the building of the temple.

ADAM CLARKE

5. *Hired counsellors.* They found means to corrupt some of the principal officers of the Persian court, so that the orders of Cyrus were not executed—or at least so slowly as to make them nearly ineffectual. *Until the reign of Darius.* This was probably Darius the son of Hystaspes.

6. *In the reign of Ahasuerus.* This is the person who is called Cambyses by the Greeks. He reigned seven years and five months, and during the whole of that time the building of the Temple was interrupted.

7. *In the days of Artaxerxes.* It is generally believed that, from the time of Cyrus the great, Xerxes and Artaxerxes were names assumed by the Persian sovereigns, whatever their names had been before. *Written in the Syrian tongue.* That is, the Syrian or Chaldean character was used—not the Hebrew. *Interpreted in the Syrian tongue.* That is, the language, as well as the character, was the Syriac or Chaldaic.

8. *Rehum the chancellor.* With this verse the Chaldee part of the chapter begins, and the same language continues to the end of v. 18 of chap. vi. These men wrote to Darius in their own language; and the king in the same dialect returns an answer, chap. v. This circumstance adds authenticity to what is written; so scrupulous was the inspired penman that he not only gave the words which each spoke and wrote, but he gave them also in the very language in which they were conceived, and in the character peculiar to that language.

10. *The great and noble Asnapper.* Whether this was Shalmaneser, or Esar-haddon, or some other person, learned men and chronologists are not agreed.

11. *And at such a time.* The word *ucheeneth* has greatly perplexed all commentators and critics. The versions give us no light; and the Vulgate translates it "and they wish prosperity." Some translate it "and so forth"; and our translators supposed that it referred to the date, which however is not specified, and might have been as easily entered as the words *and at such a time.*

14. *Now because we have maintenance from the king's palace.* More literally: "Now because at all times we are salted with the salt of the palace"; i.e., We live on the king's bounty, and must be faithful to our benefactor. Salt was used as the emblem of an incorruptible covenant, and those who ate bread and salt together were considered as having entered into a very solemn covenant. These hypocrites intimated that they felt their conscience bound by the league between them and the king, and therefore could not conscientiously see the thing going on that was likely to turn to the king's damage. They were probably also persons in the pay of the Persian king.

15. *The book of the records of thy fathers.* That is, the records of the Chaldeans, to whom the Persians succeeded.

13. *Toll, tribute, and custom.* The first term is supposed to imply the capitation tax; the second, an excise on commodities and merchandise; the third, a sort of land tax. Others suppose the first means a property tax; the second, a poll tax; and the third, what was paid on imports and exports. In a word, if you permit these people to rebuild and fortify their city, they will soon set you at naught, and pay you no kind of tribute.

17. *Peace, and at such a time.* The word *ucheeth* is like that which we have already considered on v. 10, and probably has the same meaning.

MATTHEW HENRY

consulted the records concerning Jerusalem, and found that it had indeed rebelled against the king of Babylon, and therefore that it was, as they called it, a *bad city* (*v.* 19), and that in times past kings had reigned there, to whom all the countries on that side the river had been tributaries (*v.* 20). He appointed these Samaritans to stop the building of the city immediately, *v.* 21, 22. Neither they, in their letter, nor he, in his order, make any mention of the temple, and the building of that, because both they and he knew that they had a command from Cyrus to rebuild that. They spoke only of the *city*: "Let not *that* be built," that is, as a city with walls and gates.

II. The use which the enemies of the Jews made of these orders, so fraudulently obtained. The order was only to prevent the walling of the *city*, but, having force and power on their side, they construed it as relating to the *temple*, for it was that to which they had an ill will. The consequence was that *the work of the house of God ceased* for a time, through the power and insolence of its enemies.

JAMIESON, FAUSSET, BROWN

24. Then ceased the work of the house of God—It was this occurrence that first gave rise to the strong religious antipathy between the Jews and the Samaritans, which was afterwards greatly aggravated by the erection of a rival temple on Mount Gerizim.

ADAM CLARKE

19. *Hath made insurrection against kings.* The struggles of the Israelites to preserve or regain their independency, which they had from God, are termed insurrection, rebellion, and sedition, because at last they fell under the power of their oppressors.

20. *Beyond the river.* That is, the Euphrates. Both David and Solomon carried their conquests beyond this river. See 2 Sam. viii. 3, etc., and 1 Kings iv. 21, where it is said, "Solomon reigned over all kingdoms from the river [Euphrates] unto the land of the Philistines, and unto the border of Egypt."

21. *Until another commandment shall be given from me.* The rebuilding was only provisionally suspended. The decree was, Let it cease for the present; nor let it proceed at any time without an order express from me.

MATTHEW HENRY — CHAPTER 5

Verses 1–2

During this time they had an altar and a tabernacle. But the counsellors that were hired to hinder the work (*ch.* iv. 5) told them that the time had not come for the building of the temple (Hag. i. 2), urging that it was long ere the time came for the building of Solomon's temple; and thus the people were made easy in their own *ceiled houses,* while *God's house lay waste.*

I. They had two good ministers, who, in God's name, earnestly persuaded them to put the wheel of business in motion again. Haggai and Zechariah both began to prophesy in the second year of Darius, as appears, Hag. i. 1; Zech. i. 1. The temple of God among men is to be built not by secular force but by *the word of God.* As the *weapons of our warfare,* so the instruments of our building *are not carnal,* but *spiritual.* It is the business of God's prophets to stir up God's people to that which is good, and to help them in it, to strengthen their hands, and, by suitable considerations fetched from the word of God, to quicken them to their duty and encourage them in it. They prophesied in the name, or (as some read it) *in the cause,* or for the sake, *of the God of Israel*; they spoke by commission from him, and argued from his authority.

II. They had two good magistrates, who were forward and active in this work. Zerubbabel their chief prince, and Jeshua their chief priest, *v.* 2. These great men thought it no disparagement to them, but a happiness, to be taught and prescribed to by the prophets of the Lord, and were glad of their help in reviving this good work. Read the first chapter of the prophecy of Haggai here (for that is the best comment on these two verses) and see what great things God does by his word, which he magnifies above all his name, and by his Spirit working with it.

Verses 3–17

I. The cognizance which their neighbours soon took of the reviving of this good work. No sooner did the Spirit of God stir up the friends of the temple to appear for it than the evil spirit stirred up its enemies to appear against it. While the people built and ceiled their own houses their enemies gave them no molestation (Hag. i. 4), but when they fell to work again at the temple then the alarm was taken, and all heads were at work to hinder them, *v.* 3, 4. The adversaries are here named: *Tatnai* and *Shethar-boznai.* These, though real enemies to the building of the temple, made some conscience of telling truth. If *all men have not faith* (2 Thess. iii. 2), it is well some have, and a sense of honour. The church's enemies are not all equally wicked and unreasonable.

II. The care which the divine Providence took of this good work (*v.* 5): *The eye of their God was upon the elders of the Jews,* who were active in the work, so that their enemies could not cause them to cease, as they would have done, till the matter came to Darius. They desired they would only cease till they had instructions from the king about it. But they would not so much as yield them that, for *the eye of God was upon them,* even their God. The elders of the Jews saw *the eye of God upon them,* to observe what they did and own them in what they did well, and then they had courage enough to face their enemies and to go on vigorously with their work, notwithstanding all the opposition they met with.

III. The account they sent to the king of this matter.

JAMIESON, FAUSSET, BROWN — CHAPTER 5

Vss. 1-17. Zerubbabel and Jeshua Set Forward the Building of the Temple in the Reign of Darius. **1. Then the prophets . . . prophesied . . . in the name of the God of Israel**—From the recorded writings of Haggai and Zechariah, it appears that the difficulties experienced and the many obstacles thrown in the way had first cooled the zeal of the Jews in the building of the temple, and then led to an abandonment of the work, under a pretended belief that the time for rebuilding it had not yet come (Hag. 1:2-11). For fifteen years the work was completely suspended. These two prophets upbraided them with severe reproaches for their sloth, negligence, and worldly selfishness (Hag. 1:4), threatened them with severe judgments if they continued backward, and promised that they would be blessed with great national prosperity if they resumed and prosecuted the work with alacrity and vigor. **Zechariah the son of Iddo**—i.e., grandson (Zech. 1:1). **2. Then rose up Zerubbabel . . . and Jeshua . . . and began to build the house of God**—The strong appeals and animating exhortations of these prophets gave a new impulse to the building of the temple. It was in the second year of the reign of Darius Hystaspes that the work, after a long interruption, was resumed. **3, 4. At the same time came to them Tatnai, governor on this side the river**—The Persian empire west of the Euphrates included at this time Syria, Arabia, Egypt, Phœnicia, and other provinces subject to Darius. The empire was divided into twenty provinces, called satrapies. Syria formed one satrapy, inclusive of Palestine, Phœnicia, and Cyprus, and furnished an annual revenue of 350 talents. It was presided over by a satrap or viceroy, who at this time resided at Damascus. Though superior to the native governors of the Jews appointed by the Persian king, he never interfered with their internal government except when there was a threatened disturbance of order and tranquillity. Tatnai, the governor (whether this was a personal name or an official title is unknown), had probably been incited by the complaints and turbulent outrages of the Samaritans against the Jews; but he suspended his judgment, and he prudently resolved to repair to Jerusalem, that he might ascertain the real state of matters by personal inspection and inquiry, in company with another dignified officer and his provincial council. **5. But the eye of their God was upon the elders of the Jews,** etc.—The unusual presence, the imposing suite, the authoritative inquiries of the satrap appeared formidable, and might have produced a paralyzing influence or led to disastrous consequences, if he had been a partial and corrupt judge or actuated by unfriendly feelings towards the Jewish cause. The historian, therefore, with characteristic piety, throws in this parenthetical verse to intimate that God averted the threatening cloud and procured favor for the elders or leaders of the Jews, that they were not interrupted in their proceedings till communications with the court should be made and received. Not a word was uttered to dispirit the Jews or afford cause of triumph to their opponents. Matters were to go on till contrary orders arrived from Babylon. After surveying the work in progress, he inquired: first, by what authority this national temple was undertaken; and, secondly, the names of the principal promoters and directors of the undertaking. To these two heads of inquiry the Jews returned ready and distinct replies. Then having learned that it originated in

ADAM CLARKE — CHAPTER 5

1. *Haggai . . . and Zechariah.* These are the same whose writings we have among the twelve minor prophets. *The son of Iddo.* That is, the grandson of Iddo; for Zechariah was the son of Berechiah, the son of Iddo. See his prophecy, chap. i. 1.

2. *Then rose up Zerubbabel.* Here we find three classes of men joining in the sacred work: Zerubbabel, the civil governor; Jeshua, the high priest or ecclesiastical governor; and Haggai and Zechariah, the prophets.

3. *Tatnai, governor.* He was governor of the provinces which belonged to the Persian Empire on their side of the Euphrates, comprehending Syria, Arabia Deserta, Phoenicia, and Samaria. He seems to have been a mild and judicious man, and to have acted with great prudence and caution, and without any kind of prejudice. The manner in which he represented this to the king is a full proof of this disposition.

4. *What are the names?* It is most evident that this is the answer of the Jews to the inquiry of Tatnai, v. 3, and the verse should be read thus: "Then said we unto them after this manner: These are the names of the men who make this building."

MATTHEW HENRY

1. How fully the elders of the Jews gave the Samaritans an account of their proceedings. They put these questions to them:—"By what authority do you do these things, and who gave you that authority?" To this they answered: "*We are the servants of the God of heaven and earth.* The God we worship is not a local deity, and therefore we cannot be charged with making a faction, or setting up a sect, in building this temple, to his honour: but we pay our homage to a God on whom the whole creation depends, and therefore ought to be protected and assisted by all and hindered by none. . . . It was to punish us for our sins that we were, for a time, put out of the possession of this house; not because the gods of the nations had prevailed against our God, but because we had provoked him (*v.* 12), for which he delivered us and our temple into the hands of the king of Babylon. We have the royal decree of Cyrus to justify us."

This is the account they give of their proceedings, not asking what authority they had to examine them, nor upbraiding them with their idolatry, and superstitions, and medley religion. Let us learn hence with meekness and fear to *give a reason of the hope that is in us* (1 Peter iii. 15), rightly to understand, and then readily to declare, what we do in God's service and why we do it.

2. How fairly the Samaritans represented this to the king. They called the temple at Jerusalem the *house of the great God* (*v.* 8); for though the Samaritans had yet gods many and lords many, they owned the God of Israel to be the *great God*, who is above all gods. They told him truly what was done, not stating, as their predecessors did, that they were fortifying the city as if they intended war, but only that they were rearing the temple as those that intended worship, *v.* 8. God's people could not be persecuted if they were not belied, could not be baited if they were not dressed up in bears' skins. Let but the cause of God and truth be fairly stated, and fairly heard, and it will keep its ground.

JAMIESON, FAUSSET, BROWN

a decree of Cyrus, who had not only released the Jewish exiles from captivity and permitted them to return to their own land for the express purpose of rebuilding the house of God, but, by an act of royal grace, had restored to them the sacred vessels which Nebuchadnezzar had carried off as trophies from the former temple, Tatnai transmitted all this information in an official report to his imperial master, accompanying it with a recommendatory suggestion that search should be made among the national archives at Babylon for the original decree of Cyrus, that the truth of the Jews' statement might be verified. The whole conduct of Tatnai, as well as the general tone of his despatch, is marked by a sound discretion and prudent moderation, free from any party bias, and evincing a desire only to do his duty. In all respects he appears in favorable contrast with his predecessor, Rehum (ch. 4:9). **8. the house of the great God, which is builded with great stones**—lit., "stones of rolling"—i.e., stones of such extraordinary size that they could not be carried—they had to be rolled or dragged along the ground. **13. Cyrus the king . . . made a decree**—The Jews were perfectly warranted according to the principles of the Persian government to proceed with the building in virtue of Cyrus' edict. For everywhere a public decree is considered as remaining in force until it is revoked but the "laws of the Medes and Persians changed not." **16. Then came . . . Sheshbazzar . . . since that time even until now hath it been in building**—This was not a part of the Jews' answer—they could not have said this, knowing the building had long ceased. But Tatnai used these expressions in his report, either looking on the stoppage as a temporary interruption, or supposing that the Jews were always working a little, as they had means and opportunities.

ADAM CLARKE

8. *With great stones.* They are making a very strong and a very costly building.

16. *Sheshbazzar.* Probably the military officer that conducted the people from Babylon, and had the oversight of the work; but some think that Ezra is meant.

17. *The . . . treasure house.* This is a Persian word, "a treasury."

MATTHEW HENRY

CHAPTER 6

Verses 1–12

I. The decree of Cyrus for the building of the temple repeated. Search was ordered to be made for it among the records. It was looked for in Babylon (*v.* 1). But it was not found there. At length it was found at Achmetha, in the province of the Medes, *v.* 2. It is here inserted, *v.* 3–5. 1. Here is a warrant for the building of the temple: *Let the house of God at Jerusalem*, yea, *let that house be built* within such and such dimensions, and with such and such materials. 2. A warrant for the taking of the expenses of the building out of the king's revenue, *v.* 4. We do not find that they had received what was here ordered them, the face of things at court being changed. 3. A warrant for the restoring of the vessels and utensils of the temple, which Nebuchadnezzar had taken away (*v.* 5), with an order that the priests, the Lord's ministers, should return them all to their places in the house of God.

II. The confirmation of it by a decree of Darius, grounded upon it and in pursuance of it.

1. The decree of Darius is very explicit and satisfactory.

(1) He forbids his officers to do anything in opposition to the building of the temple. The manner of expression intimates that he knew they had a mind to hinder it: *Be you far hence* (*v.* 6); *let the work of this house of God alone*, *v.* 7.

(2) He orders them out of his own revenue to assist the builders with money. I. For carrying on the building, *v.* 8. Herein he pursues the example of Cyrus, *v.* 4. II. For maintaining the sacrifices there when it was built, *v.* 9. See here how he gives honour, *First*, To Israel's God, whom he calls once and again the *God of heaven*. *Secondly*, To his ministers, in ordering his commissioners to give out supplies for the temple service at the appointment of the priests. *Thirdly*, To prayer: *That they may pray for the life of the king*.

(3) He enforces his decree with a penalty (*v.* 11).

(4) He entails a divine curse upon all those kings and people that should ever have any hand in the destruction of this house, *v.* 12.

2. The heart of kings is in the hand of God, and he turns it which way soever he pleases; what they are he makes them to be, for he is *King of kings*. When God's time has come for the accomplishing of his gracious purposes concerning his church he will raise up instruments to promote them from whom such good service was not expected. *The earth sometimes helps the woman* (Rev. xii. 16), and those are made use of for the defence of religion, who have little religion themselves. The enemies of the Jews, in appealing to Darius, hoped to get an order to sup-

JAMIESON, FAUSSET, BROWN

CHAPTER 6

Vss. 1-12. Darius' Decree for Advancing the Building. **1. Darius the king**—This was Darius **Hystaspes.** Great and interesting light has been thrown on the history of this monarch and the transaction of his reign, by the decipherment of the cuneatic inscriptions on the rocks at Behistun. **in the house of the rolls, where the treasures were laid up in Babylon**—An idea of the form of this Babylonian register house, as well as the manner of preserving public records within its repositories, can be obtained from the discoveries at Nineveh. Two small chambers were discovered in the palace of Koyunjik, which, from the fragments found in them, Mr. Layard considers "as a house of the rolls." After reminding his readers that the historical records and public documents of the Assyrians were kept on tablets and cylinders of baked clay, many specimens of which have been found, he goes on to say, "The chambers I am describing appear to have been a depository in the palace of Nineveh for such documents. To the height of a foot or more from the floor they were entirely filled with them; some entire, but the greater part broken into many fragments, probably by the falling in of the upper part of the building. They were of different sizes; the largest tablets were flat, and measured about 9 inches by 6½ inches; the smaller were slightly convex, and some were not more than an inch long, with but one or two lines of writing. The cuneiform characters on most of them were singularly sharp and well defined, but so minute in some instances as to be almost illegible without a magnifying glass. These documents appear to be of various kinds. The documents that have thus been discovered 'in the house of rolls' at Nineveh probably exceed all that have yet been afforded by the monuments of Egypt, and when the innumerable fragments are put together and transcribed, the publication of these records will be of the greatest importance to the history of the ancient world" [Nineveh and Babylon]. **2. Achmetha**—long supposed to be the capital of Greater Media—the Ecbatana of classical, the Hamadan of modern times, at the foot of the Elwund range of hills, where, for its coolness and salubrity, Cyrus and his successors on the Persian throne established their summer residence. There was another city, however, of this name, the Ecbatana of Atropatene, and the most ancient capital of northern Media, and recently identified by Colonel Rawlinson in the remarkable ruins of *Takht-i-Soleiman*. Yet as everything tends to show the attachment of Cyrus to his native city, the Atropatenian Ecbatana, rather than to the stronger

ADAM CLARKE

CHAPTER 6

1. *In the house of the rolls.* The "house of the books," the king's library. This is the first time we hear of a library.

2. *At Achmetha.* Ecbatana in India, whither it is probable all the records of Cyrus had been carried. This was a sort of summer residence for the kings of Persia.

3. *The height thereof threescore cubits.* This was much larger than the temple of Solomon. This was sixty cubits high and sixty cubits broad, whereas Solomon's was only twenty cubits broad and thirty cubits high.

4. *Three rows of great stones, and a row of new timber.* We have noticed this kind of building before, three courses of stones, and then a course of strong balk; and this continued to the square of the building. *And let the expenses be given.* Cyrus had ordered wood to be cut at Libanus, and conveyed to Joppa at his expense; but it does not appear that he furnished the other expenses of the building, for we have already seen that the Jews contributed for the defraying of all others. But it appears that he provided at his own expense the sacrifices and offerings for the Temple. See v. 9.

6. *Be ye far from thence.* Do not interrupt the Jews in their building but, on the contrary, further them all in your power.

MATTHEW HENRY

press them, but, instead of that, they got an order to supply them.

Verses 13–22

I. The Jews' enemies made their friends. When they received this order from the king they came with as much haste to encourage and assist the work as their predecessors had done to put a stop to it, *ch.* iv. 23.

II. The building of the temple carried on, and finished in a little time, *v.* 14, 15. Now the *elders of the Jews built* with cheerfulness. They found themselves bound to it *by the commandment of the God of Israel.* They found themselves shamed into it by the commandment of the heathen kings, Cyrus formerly, Darius now, and Artaxerxes some time after. They found themselves encouraged in it by the prophesying of Haggai and Zechariah. And now the work went on so prosperously that, in four years' time, it was brought to perfection. The gospel church, that spiritual temple, is long in the building, but it will be finished at last, when the mystical body is completed. Every believer is a *living temple, building up himself in his most holy faith.* Much opposition is given to this work by Satan and our own corruptions. We trifle, and proceed in it with many stops and pauses; but he that has *begun the good work* will see it performed, and will *bring forth judgment unto victory.*

III. The dedication of the temple. When it was built, being designed only for sacred uses, *they showed by an example how it should be used,* which (says Bishop Patrick) is the proper sense of the word *dedicate.* They entered upon it with solemnity and probably with a public declaration of the separating of it from common uses and the surrender of it to the honour of God, to be employed in his worship. 1. The persons employed in this service were not only *the priests and Levites* who officiated, but *the children of Israel,* some of each of the *twelve tribes,* though Judah and Benjamin were the chief, and *the rest of the children of the captivity.* 2. The sacrifices that were offered upon this occasion were *bullocks, rams, and lambs* (*v.* 17), for burnt-offerings and peace-offerings; not to be compared, in number, with what had been offered at the dedication of Solomon's temple, but, being according to their present ability, they were accepted. These hundreds were more to them than Solomon's thousands were to him. 3. This service was performed with joy. 4. When they dedicated the house they settled the household. Though the temple service could not now be performed with so much pomp and plenty as formerly, because of their poverty, yet perhaps it was performed with as much purity and close adherence to the divine institution as ever, which was the true glory of it. No beauty like the beauty of holiness.

IV. The celebration of the passover in the newly-erected temple. Now that they were newly delivered out of their bondage in Babylon it was seasonable to commemorate their deliverance out of their bondage in Egypt. Fresh mercies should put us in mind of former mercies. Now they made a joyful festival of it, it falling out in the next month after the temple was finished and dedicated, *v.* 19. Notice is here taken, 1. Of the purity of the priests and Levites that *killed the passover, v.* 20. They joined together in their preparations, that they might help one another, so that all of them were pure, to a man. The purity of ministers adds much to the beauty of their ministrations; so does their unity. 2. Of the proselytes that communicated with them in this ordinance: *All such as had separated themselves unto them,* had left their country and the superstitions of it and cast in their lot with the Israel of God, and had *turned from the filthiness of the heathen of the land,* both their idolatries and immoralities, *to seek the Lord God of Israel* as their God, did eat the passover. 3. Of the great pleasure and satisfaction wherewith they *kept the feast of unleavened bread, v.* 22. *The Lord had made them joyful,* had given them both cause to rejoice and hearts to rejoice.

JAMIESON, FAUSSET, BROWN

capital of Greater Media, Colonel Rawlinson is inclined to think that he deposited there, in his fortress, the famous decree relating to the Jews, along with the other records and treasures of his empire [NINEVEH and PERSEPOLIS]. **8-10. of the king's goods, even of the tribute beyond the river . . . expenses be given unto these men**—The decree granted them the privilege of drawing from his provincial treasury of Syria, to the amount of whatever they required for the furthering of the work and providing sacrifice for the service of the temple, that the priests might daily pray for the health of the king and the prosperity of the empire. **11. whosoever shall alter this word**—The warning was specially directed against the turbulent and fanatical Samaritans. The extremely favorable purport of this edict was no doubt owing in some measure to the influence of Cyrus, of whom Darius entertained a high admiration, and whose two daughters he had married. But it proceeded still more from the deep impressions made even on the idolatrous people of that country and that age, as to the being and providence of the God of Israel.

13-15. THE TEMPLE FINISHED. **13. Then Tatnai . . . did speedily**—A concurrence of favorable events is mentioned as accelerating the restoration of the temple and infusing a new spirit and energy into the workmen, who now labored with unabating assiduity till it was brought to a completion. Its foundation was laid in April, 536 B.C. (ch. 3:8-10), and it was completed on February 21, 515 B.C., being 21 years after it was begun [LIGHTFOOT].

16-18. FEASTS OF THE DEDICATION. **16. the the children of Israel . . . kept the dedication . . . with joy**—The ceremonial was gone through with demonstrations of the liveliest joy. The aged who had wept at the laying of the foundation were most, if not all of them, now dead; and all rejoiced at the completion of this national undertaking.

17. twelve he-goats—as at the dedication of the tabernacle (Num. 8:17). **18. they set the priests in their divisions, and the Levites in their courses . . . as it is written in the book of Moses**—Although David arranged the priests and Levites in courses according to their families, it was Moses who assigned to the priests and Levites their rights and privileges, their stations and several duties.

19-22. AND OF THE PASSOVER. **21. all such as had separated themselves . . . from the filthiness of the heathen**—i.e., who had given satisfactory evidence of being true proselytes by not only renouncing the impure worship of idolatry, but by undergoing the rite of circumcision, a condition indispensable to a participation of the passover. **22. kept the feast . . . with joy: for the Lord . . . turned the heart of the king of Assyria unto them**—i.e., king of the Persian empire, which now included the possessions, and had surpassed the glory, of Assyria. The favorable disposition which Darius had evinced towards the Jews secured them peace and prosperity and the privileges of their own religion during the rest of his reign. The religious joy that so remarkably characterized the celebration of this feast, was testified by expressions of lively gratitude to God, whose overruling power and converting grace had produced so marvellous a change in the hearts of the mighty potentates, and disposed them, pagans though they were, to aid the cause and provide for the worship of the true God.

ADAM CLARKE

10. *And pray for the life of the king, and of his sons.* Even heathens believed that offerings made in their behalf to the God of the Jews would be available.

11. *Let timber be pulled down.* Whether this refers to the punishment of hanging and gibbeting, or whipping at a post, or of impaling, is not quite clear. *Let his house be made a dunghill.* Let it be reduced to ruins, and never more used, except for the most sordid and unclean purposes.

14. *According to the commandment of the God of Israel.* He first gave the order, and stirred up the hearts of the following Persian kings to second that order.

17. *Twelve he goats.* This was a sin offering for every tribe.

18. *And they set the priests.* With this verse the Chaldee or Aramitic part of this chapter ends.

20. *The Levites were purified together.* They were all ready at one time to observe the proper rites and ceremonies, and had no need of having a second Passover, which was appointed by the law for those who had been accidentally defiled or were at a distance from the Tabernacle. See 2 Chron. xxx. 3.

21. *And all such as had separated themselves.* These were the proselytes who had embraced the Jewish religion by having mingled with the Jews in their captivity. This proves that there the poor captives had so acted according to the principles of their religion that the heathen saw it and walked in the light of the Lord with them.

22. *Turned the heart of the king of Assyria.* I am of Calmet's mind, that *king of Assyria* is here put for "king of Persia." Cyrus and his successors possessed all the rights and estates of the ancient kings of Assyria and therefore the same monarch may be styled king of Assyria as well as king of Persia.

MATTHEW HENRY — CHAPTER 7

Verses 1–10

I. Ezra's pedigree. He was one of the sons of Aaron, a priest. Him God chose to be an instrument of good to Israel, that he might put honour upon the priesthood, the glory of which had been much eclipsed by the captivity. He is said to be *the son of Seraiah,* that Seraiah, as is supposed, whom the king of Babylon put to death when he sacked Jerusalem, 2 Kings xxv. 18, 21. If we take the shortest computation, it was seventy-five years since Seraiah died; many

JAMIESON, FAUSSET, BROWN — CHAPTER 7

Vss. 1-10. EZRA GOES UP TO JERUSALEM. **1. in the reign of Artaxerxes**—the Ahasuerus of Esther. **Ezra the son of Seraiah**—i.e., grandson or great-grandson. Seraiah was the high priest put to death by Nebuchadnezzar at Riblah (II Kings 25:18). A period of 130 years had elapsed between that catastrophe and the journey of Ezra to Jerusalem. As a grandson of Seraiah, viz., Jeshua, who held the office of high priest, had accompanied Zerubbabel in the first caravan of returning exiles, Ezra must have

ADAM CLARKE — CHAPTER 7

1. *In the reign of Artaxerxes.* This was Artaxerxes Longimanus. *Son of Seraiah.* Either this could not have been Seraiah, the high priest, who had been put to death by Nebuchadnezzar 121 years before this time, or the term *son* here must signify only one of his descendants. In this place there are only 16 generations reckoned between Ezra and Aaron, but in 1 Chron. vi. 3-4, etc., there are not less than 22. We must therefore supply the deficient generations from the

MATTHEW HENRY

reckon it much longer, and, because they suppose Ezra called out in the prime of his time to public service, therefore think that Seraiah was not his immediate parent, but his grandfather or great-grandfather, 1 Chron. vi. 4, &c.

II. His character. Though of the younger house, his personal qualifications made him very eminent. 1. He was a man of great learning, a scribe, a *ready scribe, in the law of Moses, v.* 6. He was very much conversant with the scriptures, especially the writings of Moses, had the words ready and was well acquainted with the sense and meaning of them. It is to be feared that learning ran low among the Jews in Babylon; but Ezra was instrumental to revive it. The Jews say that he collected and collated all the copies of the law he could find out, and published an accurate edition of it, with all the prophetical books, historical and poetical, that were given by divine inspiration, and so made up the canon of the Old Testament, with the addition of the prophecies and histories of his own time. Now that prophecy was about to cease it was time to promote scripture-knowledge, Mal. iv. 4. 2. He was a man of great piety and holy zeal (*v.* 10): *He had prepared his heart to seek the law of the Lord,* &c. The Chaldeans, among whom he was born and bred, were famed for literature, especially the study of the stars, to which, being a studious man, we may suppose that Ezra was tempted to apply himself. But he got over the temptation; the law of his God was more to him than all the writings of their magicians and astrologers. He *sought the law of the Lord,* that is, he searched the scriptures, and sought the knowledge of God, of his mind and will. He set it before him as his rule. He set himself *to teach Israel the statutes and judgments* of that law. He first learned and then taught. He also first did and then taught. He *prepared his heart* to do all this, or he fixed his heart.

III. His expedition to Jerusalem for the good of his country: *He went up from Babylon* (*v.* 6), and, in four months' time, came to Jerusalem, *v.* 8. 1. How kind the king was to him. He *granted him all his request,* whatever he desired to put him into a capacity to serve his country. 2. How kind his people were to him. When he went many more went with him, because they would venture to dwell in Jerusalem when he had gone thither. 3. How kind his God was to him. He obtained this favour from his king and country by *the good hand of the Lord that was upon him, v.* 6, 9.

Verses 11–26

The commission which the Persian emperor granted to Ezra, giving him authority to act for the good of the Jews. The commission runs *Artaxerxes, King of kings.* This however is too high a title for any mortal man to assume; he was indeed king of some kings, but to speak as if he were king of all kings was to usurp *his* prerogative who hath *all power both in heaven and in earth.* He sends greeting to his trusty and well-beloved Ezra, whom he calls a *scribe of the law of the God of heaven* (*v.* 12). He reckoned it more his honour to be a *scribe of God's law* than to be a peer or prince of the empire.

I. He gives Ezra leave to go up to Jerusalem, and as many of his countrymen as pleased to go up with him, *v.* 13.

II. He gives him authority to enquire into the affairs of Judah and Jerusalem, *v.* 14. The rule of his enquiry was to be *the law of his God, which was in his hand.* He must enquire whether the Jews, in their religion, had and did according to that law—whether the temple was built, the priesthood was settled, and the sacrifices were offered conformably to the divine appointment. If he found anything amiss, he must get it amended, and, like Titus in Crete, must *set in order the things that were wanting,* Titus i. 5. Thus are the Jews restored to their ancient privilege of governing themselves by that law.

III. He entrusts him with the money that was freely given by the king himself and his counsellors, and collected among his subjects, for the service of the house of God, *v.* 15, 16. Ezra was entrusted, (1) To receive this money and to carry it to Jerusalem. (2) To lay out this money in the best manner, in sacrifices to be offered upon the altar of God (*v.* 17), and in whatever else he or his brethren thought fit (*v.* 18), with this limitation only that it should be *after the will of their God.*

IV. He draws him a bill, or warrant rather, upon the *treasurers on that side the river,* requiring them to furnish him with what he had occasion for out of the king's revenues, and to place it to the king's account, *v.* 20, 22. This was considerately done; for Ezra, having yet to enquire into the state of things, knew not what he should have occasion for and was modest in his demand.

JAMIESON, FAUSSET, BROWN

been in all probability a grandson, descended, too, from a younger son, the older branch being in possession of the pontificate. **6. This Ezra . . . was a ready scribe in the law of Moses**—The term "scribe" does not mean merely a penman, nor even an attorney well versed in forms of law and skilled in the method of preparing public or private deeds. He was a rabbi, or doctor, learned in the Mosaic law, and in all that related to the civil and ecclesiastical polity and customs of the Hebrew people. Scribes of this description possessed great authority and influence (cf. Matt. 23:25; Mark 12:28). **the king granted him all his request**—He left Babylon entrusted with an important commission to be executed in Jerusalem. The manner in which he obtained this office is minutely related in a subsequent passage. Here it is noticed, but with a pious acknowledgment of the divine grace and goodness which disposed the royal mind in favor of Ezra's patriotic objects. The Levites, etc., did not go at that time, but are mentioned here by anticipation. **8. he came to Jerusalem in the fifth month**—i.e., corresponding to the end of our July or beginning of our August. As he left Babylon on the Jewish New Year's Day (vs. 9), the journey must have occupied not less than four months—a long period—but it was necessary to move at a slow pace and by short, easy stages, as he had to conduct a large caravan of poor people, including women, children, and all their household gear (see on ch. 8). **10. Ezra had prepared his heart to seek the law of the Lord,** etc.—His reigning desire had been to study the divine law—its principles, institutions, privileges, and requirements; and now from love and zeal, he devoted himself, as the business of his life, to the work of instructing, reforming, and edifying others.

11-26. Gracious Commission of Artaxerxes. **11. this is the copy of the letter that the king Artaxerxes gave**—The measure which this document authorized, and the remarkable interest in the Jews displayed in it, were most probably owing to the influence of Esther, who is thought to have been raised to the high position of queen a few months previous to the departure of Ezra [Hales]. According to others, who adopt a different chronology, it was more probably pressed upon the attention of the Persian court by Ezra, who, like Daniel, showed the prophecies to the king; or by some leading Jews on his accession, who, seeing the unsettled and disordered state of the colony after the deaths of Zerubbabel, Jeshua, Haggai, and Zechariah, recommended the appointment of a commission to reform abuses, suppress disorder, and enforce the observance of the law. **12. Artaxerxes, king of kings**—That title might have been assumed as, with literal truth, applicable to him, since many of the tributary princes of his empire still retained the name and authority of kings. But it was a probably a mere Orientalism, denoting a great and powerful prince, as the heaven of heavens signified the highest heaven, and vanity of vanities, the greatest vanity. This vainglorious title was assumed by the kings of Assyria, from whom it passed to the sovereigns of Persia. **unto Ezra the priest, a scribe of the law of the God of heaven**—The appointment of Ezra to this influential mission was of the highest importance to the Hebrew people, as a large proportion of them were become, in a great measure, strangers both to the language and the institutions of their forefathers. **14. sent of the king, and of his seven counsellors**—This was the fixed number of the privy council of the kings of Persia (Esther 1:10, 14). The document describes, with great clearness and precision, the nature of Ezra's commission and the extent of power and prerogatives with which he was invested. It gave him authority, in the first place, to organize the colony in Judea and institute a regular government, according to the laws of the Hebrew people, and by magistrates and rulers of their own nation (vss. 25, 26), with power to punish offenders by fines, imprisonment, exile, or death, according to the degree of their criminality. Secondly, he was empowered to carry a large donation in money, partly from the royal treasury and partly raised by voluntary contributions among his countrymen, to create a fund out of which to make suitable provision for maintaining the regular worship of God in Jerusalem (vss. 16, 17). Thirdly, the Persian officers in Syria were commanded to afford him every assistance by gifts of money within a certain specified limit, in carrying out the objects of his patriotic mission (vs. 21). **22. and hundred talents of silver**—about $110,000, according to the rate of the silver talent of Babylon. Fourthly, Artaxerxes gave his royal sanction in the establishment of the divine law, which exempted priests and Levites from taxation or tribute and confirmed to them the ex-

ADAM CLARKE

above place, between Amariah son of Meraioth, 1 Chron. vi. 7, and Azariah the son of Johanan, v. 10.

6. *A ready scribe. Sopher machir* does not merely signify a speedy writer or an excellent penman, but one who was eminently skillful in expounding the law. In this sense the word *scribe* is repeatedly used in the New Testament, and we find that in both the Old and New Testament it had the same signification.

8. *He came to Jerusalem in the fifth month.* From the following verse we learn that Ezra and his company set off from Babylon on the first day of the first month, and thus we find they were upwards of four months on their journey. They could not travel fast, as they were a great company, composed in part of the aged and infirm, besides multitudes of women and children. They appear also to have taken a circuitous route. See on chap. viii.

10. *Ezra had prepared his heart.* Here is a fine character of a minister of God: He prepares, he fixes, purposes, and determines; with his heart, with all his powers and affections; *to seek the law of the Lord, and to do it* himself, that he may be properly qualified to *teach* its *statutes* and *judgments* to Israel.

12. *Artaxerxes, king of kings.* This letter, from the beginning of this verse to the end of v. 26, is in the Aramitic or Chaldee language.

13. *Their own freewill.* None shall be forced either to go or to stay. He who loves his God will avail himself of this favorable opportunity.

14. *His seven counsellors.* It is very likely that the privy counsel of the king consisted of seven persons simply. The names of these seven counsellors or chamberlains may be found in the Book of Esther, chap. i. 10.

16. *And all the silver and gold.* The king and his counsellors had already made a present to the house of the God of Israel, and Ezra is now empowered to receive any contribution which any of the inhabitants of the province of Babylon may think proper to give.

18. *After the will of your God.* He gave them the fullest liberty to order everything according to their own institutions, binding them to no form or mode of worsnip.

22. *An hundred talents of silver.* The talent of silver was 450 *l. An hundred measures of wheat.* A hundred cors; each cor was a little more than seventy-five gallons, one quart, and a pint, wine measure. *An hundred baths of wine.* Each bath was seven gallons and five pints.

MATTHEW HENRY

V. He charges him to let nothing be wanting that was requisite to be done in or about the temple for the honour of the God of Israel. In this charge (*v.* 23), 1. How honourably he speaks of God. He had called him before *the God of Jerusalem*; but here, lest it should be thought that he looked upon him as a local deity, he calls him twice, with great veneration, the *God of heaven*. 2. How strictly he eyes the word and law of God, which, it is likely, he had read and admired: "Whatsoever is *commanded by your God* let it be done, let it be diligently done, with care and speed."

VI. He exempts all the ministers of the temple from paying taxes to the government. From the greatest of the priests to the least of the Nethinim, *it shall not be lawful* for the king's officers *to impose* that *toll, tribute, or custom upon them*, which the rest of the king's subjects paid, *v.* 24.

VII. He empowers Ezra to nominate and appoint judges and magistrates for all the Jews on that side the river, *v.* 25, 26. It was a great favour to the Jews to have such nobles of themselves, and especially to have them of Ezra's nomination. 1. All that *knew the laws of Ezra's God* (that is, all that professed the Jewish religion) were to be under the jurisdiction of these judges, which intimates that they were exempted from the jurisdiction of the heathen magistrates. 2. These judges were allowed and encouraged to make proselytes: Let them *teach the laws of God* to *those that do not know them*. They were not allowed to make new laws, but must see the laws of God duly executed; and they were entrusted with the sword in order that they might be *a terror to evil doers.*

Verses 27–28

Two things Ezra blessed God for:—1. For his commission. *Blessed be God* (says he) *that put such a thing as this into the king's heart.* God can put things into men's hearts which would not arise there of themselves, and into their heads too, both by his providence and by his grace, in things *pertaining both to life and godliness.* If any good appear to be in our own hearts, or in the hearts of others, we must own it was God that put it there, and bless him for it. When princes and magistrates act for the suppression of vice, and the encouragement of religion, we must thank God that *put it into their hearts* to do so. 2. For the encouragement he had in pursuance of his commission (*v.* 28): *He has extended mercy to me.* Ezra himself was a man of courage, yet he attributed his encouragement not to his own heart, but to God's hand: "I was strengthened to undertake the services, *as the hand of the Lord my God was upon me*, to direct and support me."

JAMIESON, FAUSSET, BROWN

clusive right to officiate in the sacred services of the sanctuary. And, finally, in the expression of the king's desire for the divine blessing upon the king and his government (vs. 23), we see the strong persuasion which pervaded the Persian court, and had been produced by the captivity of the Hebrew people, as to the being and directing providence of the God they worshipped. It will be observed, however, that the commission related exclusively to the rebuilding of the temple—not of the walls. The Samaritans (ch. 4:20-22) had succeeded in alarming the Persian court by their representations of the danger to the empire of fortifying a city notorious for the turbulent character of its inhabitants and the prowess of its kings.

27, 28. EZRA BLESSES GOD FOR THIS FAVOR. **27. Blessed be the Lord God of our fathers**—This devout thanksgiving is in unison with the whole character of Ezra, who discerns the hand of God in every event, and is always ready to express a pious acknowledgment for the divine goodness.

ADAM CLARKE

23. *Why should there be wrath?* As he believed he was appointed by the Almighty to do this work, he therefore wished to do it heartily, knowing that if he did not, God would be displeased, and that the kingdom would be cut off from him or his posterity.

24. *It shall not be lawful to impose toll.* As these persons had no private revenues, it would have been unreasonable to have laid them under taxation.

26. *Whether it be unto death.* These include almost every species of punishment which should be inflicted on culprits in any civilized state. With this verse the Chaldee part of this chapter ends.

MATTHEW HENRY — CHAPTER 8

Verses 1–20

Ezra, having received his commission from the king, beats up for volunteers, as it were, sets up an ensign to assemble the outcasts of Israel and the dispersed of Judah, Isa. xi. 12. "Whoever of the sons of Sion, that *dwell with the daughters of Babylon*, is disposed to go to Jerusalem, now that the temple there is finished and the temple-service set a-going, now is their time."

I. Some offered themselves willingly to go with Ezra. The heads of the several families are here named, for their honour, and the numbers of the males that each brought in, amounting in all to 1,496. Several of their families, or clans, here named, we had before, *ch.* ii.

II. The Levites who went in this company were in a manner pressed into the service. Ezra appointed a general rendezvous of all his company at a certain place upon new-year's day, the first day of the first month, *ch.* vii. 9. There he mustered them, and *found there none of the sons of Levi*, *v.* 15. Some priests there were, but no others that were Levites. Where was the spirit of that sacred tribe? Ezra had money enough for the service of the temple, but wanted men. Eleven men of understanding, he chooses out of his company, to be employed for the filling up of this lamentable vacancy. Ezra sent them to a proper place, where there was a college of Levites, *the place Casiphia*, probably a street or square in Babylon allowed for that purpose—*Silver Street* one may call it, for *ceseph* signifies *silver*. He sent them to a proper person, to Iddo, the chief president of the college, to urge him to send some of the juniors, *ministers for the house of our God*, *v.* 17. Though the warning was short, they brought about forty Levites to attend Ezra. Of the Nethinim, the servitors of the sacred college, more appeared forward to go. Of them 220, upon this hasty summons, enlisted themselves, and had the honour to be expressed by name

JAMIESON, FAUSSET, BROWN — CHAPTER 8

VSS. 1-14. EZRA'S COMPANIONS FROM BABYLON. **1. this is the genealogy of them that went up with me from Babylon**—The number given here amounts to 1754. But this is the register of adult males only, and as there were women and children also (vs. 21), the whole caravan may be considered as comprising between 6000 and 7000.

15-20. HE SENDS TO IDDO FOR MINISTERS FOR THE TEMPLE SERVICE. **15. I gathered them together to the river that runneth to Ahava**—This river has not been ascertained. It is probable that the Ahava was one of the streams or numerous canals of Mesopotamia communicating with the Euphrates [CYCLOPÆDIA OF BIBLICAL LITERATURE]. But it was certainly in Babylonia on the banks of that stream; and perhaps the place appointed for general rendezvous was in the neighborhood of a town of the same name. The emigrants encamped there for three days, according to Oriental custom, while the preparations for the departure were being completed and Ezra was arranging the order of the caravan. **I . . . found there none of the sons of Levi**—i.e., the ordinary Levites. Notwithstanding the privilege of exemption from all taxes granted to persons engaged in the temple service, none of the Levitical tribes were induced to join the settlement in Jerusalem; and it was even not without difficulty Ezra persuaded some of the priestly families to accompany him. **16, 17. then sent I for Eliezer . . . with commandment unto Iddo the chief**—Ezra sent this deputation, either by virtue of authority which by his priestly character he had over the Levites, or of the royal commission with which he was invested. The deputation was despatched to Iddo, who was a prince or chief of the Nethinims—for the Persian government allowed the Hebrews during their exile to retain their ecclesiastical government by their own chiefs, as well as to enjoy the privilege of free worship. Iddo's

ADAM CLARKE — CHAPTER 8

2. *Gershom.* One of the descendants of Phinehas, son of Eleazar.

3. *Of the sons of Shechaniah.* There were three of this name; the second is mentioned in v. 5, and the third in chap. x. 2. They were all different persons, as may be seen from their fathers' houses.

15. *The river that runneth to Ahava.* Ahava was a river itself.

None of the sons of Levi. None that were simply Levites.

MATTHEW HENRY

in Ezra's muster-roll, *v.* 20.

Verses 21–23

Ezra has procured Levites, but what will that avail, unless he have God with him?

I. The steadfast confidence he had in God and in his gracious protection. God's servants have his power engaged for them; his enemies have it engaged against them. This Ezra believed with his heart, and with his mouth made confession of it before the king; and therefore he was ashamed to ask of the king a convoy, lest the king, and those about him, suspected either God's power to help his people or Ezra's confidence in that power. Not but that those who depend upon God must use proper means for their preservation, and they need not be ashamed to do so.

II. The solemn application he made to God in that confidence: He *proclaimed a fast, v.* 21. For public mercies public prayers must be made. Their fasting was, 1. To express their humiliation. This he declares to be the meaning of it, "*that we might afflict ourselves before our God* for our sins, and so be qualified for the pardon of them." 2. To excite their supplications. Prayer was always joined with religious fasting. Their errand to the throne of grace was *to seek of God the right way*, that is, to commit themselves to the guidance of the divine Providence, to put themselves under the divine protection, and to beg of God to guide and keep them in their journey and bring them safely to their journey's end.

III. The good success of their doing so (*v.* 23): *We besought our God* by joint-prayer, *and he was entreated of us.*

Verses 24–30

An account of the particular care which Ezra took of the treasure he had with him, that belonged to God's sanctuary, 1. Having committed the keeping of it to God, he committed the keeping of it to proper men, whose business it was to watch it, though without God they would have waked in vain. 2. Having prayed to God to preserve all the substance they had with them, he shows himself especially solicitous for that part of it which belonged to the house of God and was an offering to him. Twelve chief priests, and as many Levites, he appointed to this trust (*v.* 24, 30). Ezra tells them why he put those things into their hands (*v.* 28): *You are holy unto the Lord, the vessels are holy also;* and who so fit to take care of holy things as holy persons? He *weighed to them the silver, the gold, and the vessels* (*v.* 25), because he expected to have it from them again by weight. The charge he gave them with these treasures (*v.* 29): "*Watch you, and keep them*, that they be not lost, nor embezzled, nor mingled with the other articles. Keep them together; keep them by themselves; keep them safely, till you weigh them in the temple, before the great men there."

Verses 31–36

Ezra goes to Jerusalem, but his multitude made his marches slow and his stages short. His God was good, and he acknowledged his goodness: *The hand of our God was upon us.* Even the common perils of journeys oblige us to sanctify our going out with prayer and our returns in peace with praise and thanksgiving; much more in such a dangerous expedition as this was. They were brought in safety to their journey's end, *v.* 32. His companions were devout. As soon as they came to be near the altar they thought themselves obliged to offer sacrifice, whatever they had done in Babylon, *v.* 35. Among their sacrifices they had a sin-offering; for it is the atonement that sweetens and secures every mercy to us. The number of their offerings related to the number of the tribes, twelve bullocks, twelve he-goats, and ninety-six rams, intimating the union of the two kingdoms, according to what was foretold, Ezek. xxxvii. 22. They did not any longer go two tribes one way and ten another, but all the twelve met by their representatives at the same altar. Even the enemies of the Jews became their friends, bowed to Ezra's commission, and, instead of hindering the people of God, furthered them (*v.* 36).

CHAPTER 9

Verses 1–4

Ezra saw nothing amiss, but information is brought him that many of the people, and some of the rulers, had married wives out of heathen families, and joined themselves in affinity with strangers.

I. The sin was *mingling with the people of those lands* (*v.* 2), associating with them both in trade and in conversation, and taking *their daughters in marriages* to their sons. They disobeyed the express command of

JAMIESON, FAUSSET, BROWN

influence procured and brought to the camp at Ahava thirty-eight Levites, and 220 Nethinims, the descendants of the Gibeonites, who performed the servile duties of the temple.

21-36. A FAST PROCLAIMED. **21. Then I proclaimed a fast there**—The dangers to travelling caravans from the Bedouin Arabs that prowl through the desert were in ancient times as great as they still are; and it seems that travellers usually sought the protection of a military escort. But Ezra had spoken so much to the king of the sufficiency of the divine care of His people that he would have blushed to apply for a guard of soldiers. Therefore he resolved that his followers should, by a solemn act of fasting and prayer, commit themselves to the Keeper of Israel. Their faith, considering the many and constant perils of a journey across the Bedouin regions, must have been great, and it was rewarded by the enjoyment of perfect safety during the whole way.

24-32. Then I separated twelve of the chief of the priests . . . and weighed unto them the silver, etc.—The custody of the contributions and of the sacred vessels was, during the journey, committed to twelve of the chief priests, who, with the assistance of ten of their brethren, were to watch closely over them by the way, and deliver them into the house of the Lord in Jerusalem. The treasures in silver and gold, according to the value of the Babylonian talent, amounted to over $3,000,000. **27. two vessels of fine copper, precious as gold**—Almost all commentators agree in maintaining that the vessels referred to were not made of copper, but of an alloy capable of taking on a bright polish, which we think highly probable, as copper was then in common use among the Babylonians, and would not be as precious as gold. This alloy, much esteemed among the Jews, was composed of gold and other metals, which took on a high polish and was not subject to tarnish [NOYES]. **31. we departed from the river of Ahava on the twelfth day of the first month**—Computing from the time of their setting out to the period of their arrival, they occupied about four months on the way. Their health and security were marvellous during so long a journey. The pilgrim-caravans of the present day perform long journeys through the wildest deserts of the East under the protection of a firman from the Porte, and an escort of soldiers. But for a large body, composed as that of Ezra—of some thousands of men, women, and children, unaccustomed to travel, undisciplined to order, and without military strength, and with so large an amount of treasure tempting the cupidity of the marauding, plundering tribes of the desert—to accomplish a journey so long and so arduous in perfect safety, is one of the most astonishing events recorded in history. Nothing but the vigilant care of a superintending Providence could have brought them securely to their destination. **33. Now on the fourth day was the silver . . . weighed in the house of our God**—The first three days after their arrival in Jerusalem were undoubtedly given to repose; on the next, the treasures were weighed and handed over to the custody of the officiating priests of the temple. The returned exiles offered burnt offerings, and Ezra delivered the royal commission to the satraps and inferior magistrates; while the Levitical portion of them lent all the assistance they could in performing the additional work which the arrival of so many new worshippers occasioned.

CHAPTER 9

Vss. 1-4. EZRA MOURNS FOR THE AFFINITY OF THE PEOPLE WITH STRANGERS. **1. Now when these things were done**—The first days after Ezra's arrival in Jerusalem were occupied in executing the different trusts committed to him. The nature and design of the office with which the royal authority had invested him was publicly made known to his own people by the formal delivery of the contribu-

ADAM CLARKE

22. *I was ashamed to require . . . a band.* **He had represented God, the object of his worship, as supremely powerful, and as having the strongest affection for His true followers. He could not therefore, consistently with his declarations, ask a band of soldiers from the king to protect them on the way, when they were going expressly to rebuild the temple of Jehovah and restore His worship. He therefore found it necessary to seek the Lord by fasting and prayer, that they might have from Him those succors without which they might become a prey to their enemies; and then the religion which they professed would be considered by the heathen as false and vain. Thus we see that this good man had more anxiety for the glory of God than for his own personal safety.**

26. *Silver vessels an hundred talents.* **That is, The weight of all the silver vessels amounted to 100 talents; not that there were 100 vessels of silver, each a talent in weight.**

35. *Twelve bullocks for all Israel.* **Though of tribes there were only Judah and Benjamin, yet they offered a bullock for every tribe, as if present. There can be little doubt that there were individuals there from all the twelve tribes, possibly some families of each, but no complete tribe but those mentioned above.**

CHAPTER 9

1. *The people of Israel.* **These were they who had returned at first with Zerubbabel, and were settled in the land of Judea, and whom Ezra found on his arrival to be little better than the Canaanitish nations from whom God had commanded them ever to keep separate.**

MATTHEW HENRY

God, which forbade all intimacy with the heathen, and particularly in matrimonial contracts, Deut. vii. 3. They exposed themselves, and much more their children, to the peril of idolatry, the very sin that had once been the ruin of their nation.

II. The persons that were guilty of this sin, not only some of the unthinking people of Israel, that knew no better, but *many of the priests and Levites*, whose office it was to teach the law, and in whom it was a greater crime. Miserable is the case of that people whose leaders debauch them and cause them to err.

III. The information was given to Ezra. It was given by the princes, those of them that had kept their integrity and with it their dignity. They applied to Ezra, hoping that his wisdom, authority, and interest would prevail.

IV. The impression this made upon Ezra (*v.* 3): *He rent his clothes, plucked off his hair*, and *sat down astonished*. It grieved him to the heart to think that a people called by God's name should so grossly violate his law. Sorrow for sin must be great sorrow; such Ezra's was, *as for an only son or a first-born*.

V. The influence which Ezra's grief for this had upon others. Public notice was soon taken of it, and all the devout serious people that were at hand assembled themselves to him. All good people ought to own those that appear and act in the cause of God against vice and profaneness, to stand by them, and do what they can to strengthen their hands.

Verses 5–15

A most pathetic address Ezra makes to Heaven upon this occasion.

I. He made this address—*at the evening sacrifice*, *v.* 5. Then devout people used to come into the courts of the temple to offer up their own prayers. In their hearing Ezra chose to make this confession, that they might be made duly sensible of the sins of their people. The sacrifice, and especially the evening sacrifice, was a type of the great propitiation. Ezra had faith in this penitential address to God; he makes confession with his hand, as it were, upon the head of that great sacrifice, through which *we receive the atonement*.

II. His preparation for this address. 1. He *rose up from his heaviness*, and so far shook off the burden of his grief as was necessary to the lifting up of his heart to God. 2. He *fell upon his knees*, put himself into the posture of a penitent, representing the people for whom he was now an intercessor. 3. He *spread out his hands*, as one affected with what he was going to say, offering it up unto God.

III. The address itself. If we give prayer its full latitude, it is the offering up of pious and devout affections to God. His address is a penitent confession of sin, not his own, but the sin of his people. Though he himself was wholly clear from this guilt, yet he puts himself into the number of the sinners, because he was a member of the same community—*our sins and our trespass*. He owns their sins to have been very great: "*Our iniquities are increased over our heads* (*v.* 6); we are ready to perish in them as in deep waters." But let this be the comfort of true penitents that though their sins reach to the heavens God's mercy is *in the heavens*, Ps. xxxvi. 5. They were *not forsaken in their bondage*, but even in Babylon had the tokens of God's presence,—they were a remnant of Israelites left, a few out of many, and those narrowly escaped out of the hands of their enemies, by the favour of the kings of Persia. They had *a nail in his holy place*, that is (as it is explained, *v.* 9), that they had set up the *house of God*. They had their religion settled and the service of the temple in a constant method. This enlightened their eyes and revived their hearts; it was life from the dead to them. "Now," says Ezra, "how ungrateful are we to offend a God that has been so kind to us!" The sin was against an express command: *We have forsaken thy commandments*, *v.* 10. Gen. xxxiv. 14. But, besides that, God had strictly forbidden it. He recites the command, *v.* 11, 12. Nothing could be more express: *Give not your daughters to their sons, nor take their daughters to your sons*. The reason given is because, if they mingled with those nations, they would pollute themselves. It was an unclean land, and they were a holy people. Ezra, in a penitential sense of the great malignity that was in their sin, acknowledged that, though the punishment was very great, it was less than they deserved. He speaks as one much ashamed. With this he begins (*v.* 6), *O my God! I am ashamed and blush, O my God! to lift up my face unto thee*. Sin is a shameful thing. Holy shame is as necessary an ingredient in true and ingenuous repentance as holy sorrow. The sins of others should be our shame, and we should blush for those who do not

JAMIESON, FAUSSET, BROWN

tion and the sacred vessels brought from Babylon to the priests to be deposited in the temple. Then his credentials were privately presented to the provincial governors; and by this prudent, orderly proceeding he put himself in the best position to avail himself of all the advantages guaranteed him by the king. On a superficial view everything contributed to gratify his patriotic feelings in the apparently flourishing state of the church and country. But a further acquaintance discovered the existence of great corruptions, which demanded immediate correction. One was particularly brought under his notice as being the source and origin of all others; viz., a serious abuse that was practised respecting the law of marriage. **the princes came to me, saying**—The information they lodged with him was to the effect that numbers of the people, in violation of the divine law (Deut. 7:2, 3), had contracted marriages with Gentile women, and that the guilt of the disorderly practice, far from being confined to the lower classes, was shared in by several of the priests and Levites, as well as of the leading men in the country. This great irregularity would inevitably bring many evils in its train; it would encourage and increase idolatry, as well as break down the barriers of distinction which, for important purposes, God had raised between the Israelites and all other people. Ezra foresaw these dangerous consequences, but was overwhelmed with a sense of the difficulty of correcting the evil, when matrimonial alliances had been formed, families had been reared, affections engaged, and important interests established. **3. when I heard this thing I rent my garment and my mantle**, etc.—the outer and inner garment, which was a token not only of great grief, but of dread at the same time of the divine wrath; "plucked off the hair of my head and my beard," which was a still more significant sign of overpowering grief. **4. Then were assembled unto me every one that trembled at the words of the God of Israel**, etc.—All the pious people who reverenced God's word and dreaded its threatenings and judgments joined with Ezra in bewailing the public sin, and devising the means of redressing it. **I sat astonied until the evening sacrifice**—The intelligence of so gross a violation of God's law by those who had been carried into captivity on account of their sins, and who, though restored, were yet unreformed, produced such a stunning effect on the mind of Ezra that he remained for a while incapable either of speech or of action. The hour of the evening sacrifice was the usual time of the people assembling; and at that season, having again rent his hair and garments, he made public prayer and confession of sin.

5-15. PRAYS TO GOD. **5. I fell upon my knees, and spread out my hands unto the Lord my God**—The burden of his prayer, which was dictated by a deep sense of the emergency, was that he was overwhelmed at the flagrant enormity of this sin, and the bold impiety of continuing in it after having, as a people, so recently experienced the heavy marks of the divine displeasure. God had begun to show returning favor to Israel by the restoration of some. But this only aggravated their sin, that, so soon after their re-establishment in their native land, they openly violated the express and repeated precepts which commanded them to extirpate the Canaanites.

ADAM CLARKE

3. *I rent my garment and my mantle*. The outer and inner garment, in sign of great grief. This significant act is frequently mentioned in the sacred writings, and was common among all ancient nations. *Plucked off the hair*. Shaving the head and beard were signs of excessive grief; much more so the plucking off the hair, which must produce exquisite pain. All this testified his abhorrence, not merely of the act of having taken strange wives, but their having also joined them in their idolatrous abominations.

4. *Those that had been carried away*. Those that had returned long before with Zerubbabel; see v. 1. *Until the evening sacrifice*. The morning sacrifice was the first of all the offerings of the day, the evening sacrifice the last. As the latter was offered between the two evenings, i.e., between sunset and the end of twilight, so the former was offered between break of day and sunrise. Ezra *sat astonied*—confounded in his mind, distressed in his soul, and scarcely knowing what to do. He probably had withdrawn himself into some sequestered place, or into some secret part of the Temple, spending the time in meditation and reflection.

5. *Fell upon my knees*. In token of the deepest humility. *Spread out my hands*, as if to lay hold on the mercy of God.

8. *And now for a little space*. This interval in which they were returning from servitude to their own land. *Grace hath been shewed*. God has disposed the hearts of the Persian kings to publish edicts in our favor. *To leave us a remnant to escape*. The ten tribes are gone irrecoverably into captivity; a great part even of Judah and Benjamin had continued beyond the Euphrates; so that Ezra might well say there was but a *remnant* which had escaped. *A nail in his holy place*. Even so much ground as to fix our tent poles in. *May lighten our eyes*. To give us a thorough knowledge of ourselves and of our highest interest, and to enable us to re-establish His worship, is the reason why God has brought us back to this place. *A little reviving*. We were perishing, and our hopes were almost dead; and, because of our sins, we were sentenced to death. But God in His great mercy has given us a new trial; and He begins with little, to see if we will make a wise and faithful use of it.

6. *I am ashamed and blush*. God had been so often provoked, and had so often pardoned them, and they had continued to transgress, that he was ashamed to go back again to the throne of grace to ask for mercy in their behalf.

MATTHEW HENRY

blush for themselves. The publican, when he went to the temple to pray, hung down his head more than ever, as one ashamed, Luke xviii. 13. True penitents are at a loss what to say. Shall we say, We have *not sinned*, or, *God will not require it?* If we do, *we deceive ourselves, and the truth is not in us.* Shall we say, Have patience with us and we will pay thee all, with *thousands of rams, or our first-born for our transgression?* God will not thus be mocked: he knows we are insolvent. Shall we say, *There is no hope*, and *let come on us what will?* That is but to make bad worse. True penitents should, as Ezra, beg of God to teach them. What shall we say? Say, "I have sinned; I have done foolishly; God be merciful to me a sinner;" and the like. See Hos. xiv. 2. He speaks as one much assured of the righteousness of God. "*Thou art righteous*, wise, just, and good; thou wilt neither do us wrong nor be hard upon us; and therefore behold *we are before thee*, we lie at thy feet, waiting our doom; *we cannot stand before thee*, insisting upon any righteousness of our own, having no plea to support us and therefore we fall down before thee, in our trespass, and cast ourselves on thy mercy. *Do unto us whatsoever seemeth good unto thee*, Judges x. 15. We have nothing to say, nothing to do, but to *make supplication to our Judge*," Job ix. 15. Thus does this good man lay his grief before God and then leave it with him.

JAMIESON, FAUSSET, BROWN

Such conduct, he exclaimed, could issue only in drawing down some great punishment from offended Heaven and ensuring the destruction of the small remnant of us that is left, unless, by the help of divine grace, we repent and bring forth the fruits of repentance in an immediate and thorough reformation.

ADAM CLARKE

10. *What shall we say after this?* Even in the midst of these beginnings of respite and mercy we have begun to provoke Thee anew!

11. *Have filled it from one end to another.* The abominations have been like a sweeping, mighty torrent that has increased till it filled the whole land and carried everything before it.

13. *Hast punished us less than our iniquities.* Great, numerous, and oppressive as our calamities have been, yet merely as temporal punishments, they have been much less than our provocations have deserved.

15. *Thou art righteous.* Thou art "merciful." This is one of the many meanings of the word *tsedek;* and to this meaning St. Paul refers when he says, God declares "his righteousness for the remission of sins that are past," Rom. iii. 25. *We remain yet escaped.* Because of this righteousness or mercy. *In our trespasses.* We have no righteousness; we are clothed and covered with our trespasses. *We cannot stand before thee because of this.* The parallel place is Ps. cxxx. 3: "If thou, Lord, shouldest mark iniquities, O Lord, who shall stand?" Every man must stand before the judgment seat of Christ; but who shall stand there with joy? No man against whom the Lord marks iniquities.

MATTHEW HENRY — CHAPTER 10

Verses 1–5

I. What good impressions were made upon the people by Ezra's humiliation and confession of sin. No sooner was it noised in the city that their new governor, in whom they rejoiced, was himself in grief, for them and their sin, than presently there *assembled to him a very great congregation*, to mingle their tears with him, *v.* 1. See what a happy influence the good examples of great ones may have upon their inferiors. When Ezra, a scribe, a scholar, a man in authority under the king, so deeply lamented the public corruptions, they concluded that they were indeed very grievous.

II. What a good motion Shechaniah made upon this occasion. The place was *Bochim*—a place of *weepers*; but, for aught that appears, there was a profound silence among them till Shechaniah (one of Ezra's companions from Babylon, *ch.* viii. 3, 5) stood up, and made a speech addressed to Ezra, in which he owns the national guilt, sums up all Ezra's confession in one word, and sets to his seal that it is true: "*We have trespassed against God, and have taken strange wives*," *v.* 2. It does not appear that Shechaniah was himself culpable in this matter, but his father was guilty, and several of his father's house (as appears *v.* 26), and therefore he reckons himself among the trespassers. *Now there is hope;* now that the disease is discovered it is half-cured. The sin that truly troubles us shall not ruin us. The case is plain; what has been done amiss must be undone again as far as possible. *Let us put away all the wives, and such as are born of them, v.* 3. Ezra despaired of ever bringing the people to it, but Shechaniah, who conversed more with the people than he did, assured him the thing was practicable if they went wisely to work. As to the case of being *unequally yoked with unbelievers*, Shechaniah's counsel will not hold now; such marriages, it is certain, are sinful, and ought not to be made, but they are not null. *Quod fieri non debuit, factum valet—That which ought not to have been done must, when done, abide.* Our rule, under the gospel is, *If a brother has a wife that believeth not*, and *she be pleased to dwell with him, let him not put her away*, 1 Cor. vii. 12, 13. Shechaniah said to Ezra and the people: Let us covenant, not only that, if we have strange wives ourselves, we will put them away, but that, if we have not, we will do what we can in our places to oblige others to put away theirs.

Verses 6–14

An account of the proceedings concerning the strange wives. Ezra sent orders to all the children of the captivity to attend him at Jerusalem *within three days* (*v.* 7, 8). Within the time limited the generality of the people met at Jerusalem and made their appearance *in the street of the house of God, v.* 9. Ezra gave the charge at this great assize. He found that since their return out of captivity they had *increased the trespass of Israel* by *marrying strange wives*, which would certainly be a means of again introducing idolatry. He called them together that they might *confess their sin to God*, and that they might separate themselves from all idolaters, especi-

JAMIESON, FAUSSET, BROWN — CHAPTER 10

Vss. 1-17. Ezra Reforms the Strange Marriages. **1. Now when Ezra had prayed**—As this prayer was uttered in public, while there was a general concourse of the people at the time of the evening sacrifice and as it was accompanied with all the demonstrations of poignant sorrow and anguish, it is not surprising that the spectacle of a man so respected, a priest so holy, a governor so dignified as Ezra, appearing distressed and filled with fear at the sad state of things, should produce a deep sensation; and the report of his passionate grief and expressions in the court of the temple having rapidly spread through the city, a great multitude flocked to the spot.

2-4. Shechaniah . . . answered and said unto Ezra, We have trespassed—This was one of the leading men, who was not himself a delinquent in the matter, for his name does not occur in the following. He spoke in the general name of the people, and his conduct evinced a tender conscience, as well as no small fortitude in making such a proposal; for as his father and five paternal uncles (vs. 26) were involved in the guilt of unlawful marriages, he showed, by the measure he recommended, that he deemed it better to obey God than to please his nearest relatives. **yet now there is hope in Israel concerning this thing**—This hope, however, depended on timely measures of reformation, and therefore, instead of surrendering themselves to despair or despondency, he counselled them to amend their error without delay, relying on God's mercy for the past. Though the proposal may seem harsh and cruel, yet in the peculiar circumstances of the Jews it was just as well as necessary; and he urged the duty of seeing it executed on Ezra, as the only person competent to carry it into effect, being possessed of skill and address for so delicate and difficult a work, and invested by God, and under Him by the Persian king (ch. 7:23-28), with the requisite authority to enforce it. **5-8. Then Ezra . . . went into the chamber of Johanan**—At a private council of the princes and elders held there, under the presidency of Ezra, it was resolved to enter into a general covenant to put away their foreign wives and children; that a proclamation should be made for all who had returned from Babylon to repair within three days to Jerusalem, under pain of excommunication and confiscation of their property. **9-11. Then all the men of Judah and Benjamin**—The returned captives belonged chiefly to these tribes; but other Israelites are also included under these names, as they all were then occupying the territory formerly assigned to those two tribes. **It was the ninth month**—i.e., between the end of December and the beginning of January, which is the coldest and most rainy season of the year in Palestine. **all the people sat in the street**—i.e., the court. **10. Ezra the priest stood up, and said**—Having fully

ADAM CLARKE — CHAPTER 10

1. *The people wept very sore.* They were deeply affected at the thought of God's displeasure, which they justly feared was about to light upon them because of their transgressions.

2. *Shechaniah the son of Jehiel.* He speaks here in the name of the people, not acknowledging himself culpable, for he is not in the following list.

Yet now there is hope in Israel. Mikveh, "expectation," of pardon; for the people were convinced of the evil, and were deeply penitent. Hence it is said, v. 1, that they wept sore.

3. *Let us make a covenant. Nichrath berith,* "Let us cut or divide the covenant sacrifice." See the notes on Gen. xv. 10.

4. *Arise; for this matter belongeth unto thee.* By the decree of Artaxerxes, he was authorized to do everything that the law of God required; see chap. vii. 23-28. And all officers were commanded to be aiding and assisting; hence Shechaniah says, "We are with you."

5. *And they sware.* The thing was evidently contrary to the law of God, and now he bound them by an oath to rectify the abuse.

6. *Johanan the son of Eliashib.* Eliashib was high priest, and was succeeded in that office by his son Joiada, Neh. xii. 10. Probably Johanan here is the same as Jonathan in Nehemiah, who was the son of Joiada, and grandson of Eliashib. Some suppose that Johanan and Joiada were two names for the same person.

8. *All his substance should be forfeited.* To the use of the Temple. So the Septuagint understood the place: "All his substance shall be devoted to a holy use." *Himself separated.* Excommunicated from the church of God, and exiled from Israel.

9. *Ninth month.* Answering to a part of our December. *Trembling because of . . . the great rain.* "Because of the winter," Septuagint; it was now December, the coldest and most rainy part of the year in Palestine.

MATTHEW HENRY

ally idolatrous wives, *v.* 10, 11. The people submitted not only to Ezra's jurisdiction in general, but to his inquisition and determination in this matter: "*As thou hast said, so must we do,*" *v.* 12.

Verses 15–44

The congregation dismissed, that each in his respective place might gain and give intelligence to facilitate the matter. The commissioners that sat upon this matter. Ezra was president, and with him *certain chief* men *of the fathers* who were qualified with wisdom and zeal above others for this service, *v.* 16. They began *the first day of the tenth month to examine the matter* (*v.* 16), which was but ten days after this method was proposed (*v.* 9), and they finished in three months, *v.* 17.

About 113 in all are here named who had married strange wives, and some of them, it is said (*v.* 44), had children by them, which implies that not many of them had, God not crowning those marriages with the blessing of increase. Whether the children were turned off with the mothers, as Shechaniah proposed, does not appear; it should seem not: however, it is probable that the wives which were put away were well provided for, according to their rank.

JAMIESON, FAUSSET, BROWN

represented the enormity of their sin and urged them to dissolve their unlawful connections, he was gratified by receiving a prompt acknowledgment of the justice of his reproof and a promise of compliance with his recommendation. But as the weather was ungenial and the defaulters were too numerous to be passed in review at one time, it was resolved that a commission should be appointed to examine into the whole matter. These commissioners, assisted by the judges and elders of the respective cities, made a minute investigation into every case, and after three months' labor completely removed all traces of the abuse. Doubtless, an adequate provision was made for the repudiated wives and children, according to the means and circumstances of the husbands.

18-44. THOSE THAT HAD TAKEN STRANGE WIVES. **18. among the sons of the priests**—From the names of so many men of rank appearing in the following list, some idea may be formed of the great and complicated difficulties attending the reformatory work. **19. they gave their hands**—i.e., came under a solemn engagement, which was usually ratified by pledging the right hand (Prov. 6:1; Ezek. 17:18). The delinquents of the priestly order bound themselves to do like the common Israelites (vs. 25), and sought to expiate their sin by sacrificing a ram as a trespass offering.

ADAM CLARKE

11. *Make confession.* Acknowledge your sins before God, with deep compunction of heart, and the fullest resolution to forsake them.

12. *As thou hast said, so must we do.* They all resolved to do what Ezra then commanded. They did put away their wives, even those by whom they had children, v. 44; this was a great hardship on the women and children. Though by the Jewish laws such marriages were null and void, yet as the women they had taken did not know these laws, their case was deplorable. However, we may take it for granted that each of them received a portion according to the circumstances of their husbands, and that they and their children were not turned away desolate, but had such a provision as their necessities required.

17. *The first day of the first month.* So they were three whole months in examining into this affair, and making those separations which the law required.

19. *They gave their hands.* They bound themselves in the most solemn manner to do as the rest of the delinquents had done, and they made an acknowledgment of their iniquity to God by offering each a ram for a trespass offering.

25. *Moreover of Israel.* That is, as Calmet observes, "simple Israelites," to distinguish them from the priests, Levites, and singers, mentioned in vv. 18, 23-24.

44. *Some of them had wives by whom they had children.* This observation was probably intended to show that only a few of them had children; but it shows also how rigorously the law was put in execution.

THE BOOK OF NEHEMIAH

I. Building of the wall (1:1-7:73a)
- *A. Initiation (1:1-2:20)*
  1. Nehemiah's grief concerning Jerusalem (1:1-11)
  2. Nehemiah's coming to Jerusalem (2:1-20)
- *B. Process (3:1-5:19)*
  1. The building of the wall (3:1-32)
  2. The opposition and persistence (4:1-23)
  3. Internal difficulties (5:1-19)
- *C. Completion (6:1-7:73a)*
  1. Opposition and victory (6:1-19)
  2. The people (7:1-73a)

II. The reading of the law (7:73b-10:39)
- *A. The reading of the law and Feast of Tabernacles (7:73b-8:18)*
  1. The reading of the law (7:73b-8:12)
  2. The Feast of Tabernacles (8:13-18)
- *B. The great prayer of the Levites (9:1-38)*
  1. The day of humiliation (9:1-4)
  2. The offering of praise (9:5-29)
  3. Prayer (9:30-38)
- *C. The reestablishment of a covenant (10:1-39)*
  1. The sealing (10:1-28)
  2. The covenant (10:29-39)

III. The settlement of the cities (11:1-13:31)
- *A. The people in Jerusalem (11:1-12:26)*
  1. The repeopling of Jerusalem (11:1, 2)
  2. Lists (11:3-12:26)
- *B. The dedication of the wall (12:27-13:3)*
  1. Two processions of singers (12:27-47)
  2. The reading of the law (13:1, 2)
  3. Separation (13:3)
- *C. Nehemiah's final reformation (13:4-31)*
  1. Twelve years later (13:4-9)
  2. Correction of four abuses (13:10-24)
  3. His method of correction (13:25-31)

This book continues the history of the "children of the captivity," the poor Jews, that had lately returned out of Babylon to their own land. At this time not only the Persian monarchy flourished in great pomp and power, but Greece and Rome began to make a figure. Of the affairs of those high and mighty states we have authentic accounts extant; but the sacred and inspired history takes observation only of the state of the Jews. Ezra the scribe and Nehemiah the governor, though neither of them ever wore a crown, commanded an army, conquered any country, or was famed for philosophy or oratory, yet both of them, being pious praying men and very serviceable in their day to the interests of religion, were really greater men and more honorable, not only than any of the Roman consuls or dictators, but than Xenophon, or Demosthenes, or Plato himself, who lived at the same time, the bright ornaments of Greece.

Nehemiah's agency for the advancing of the settlement of Israel we have a full account of in this book, wherein he records not only the works of his hands, but the workings of his heart, in the management of public affairs. Twelve years, from his twentieth year (ch. 1:1) to his thirty-second year (ch. 8:6), he was governor of Judea, under Artaxerxes king of Persia.

MATTHEW HENRY

CHAPTER 1

Verses 1–4

I. Nehemiah's station at the court of Persia. He was *in Shushan the palace*, or royal city, of the king of Persia, where the court was ordinarily kept (*v.* 1), and (*v.* 11) he was *the king's cup-bearer*. By this place at court he would be the bettter qualified for the service of his country in that post for which God had designed him, as Moses was the fitter to govern for being bred up in Pharaoh's court, and David in Saul's. He would also have the fairer opportunity of serving his country by his interest in the king and those about him. God has his remnant in all places; we read of Obadiah in the house of Ahab, saints in Cæsar's household, and a devout Nehemiah in Shushan the palace. God can make the courts of princes sometimes nurseries and sometimes sanctuaries to the friends and patrons of the church's cause.

II. Nehemiah's tender and compassionate enquiry concerning the state of the Jews in their own land, *v.* 2. It happened that a friend and relation of his came to the court, with some other company, by whom he had an opportunity of informing himself fully how it went with the children of the captivity and what posture Jerusalem, the beloved city, was in. Nehemiah lived at ease, in honour and fulness, himself, but could not forget that he was an Israelite, nor shake off the thoughts of his brethren in distress, but in spirit (like Moses, Acts vii. 23) he *visited them and looked upon their burdens*. Though he was a great man yet he did not think it below him to take cognizance of his brethren that were low and despised, nor was he ashamed to own his relation to them and concern for them. Though he did not go to settle at Jerusalem himself he did not therefore judge nor despise those that had returned.

III. The melancholy account which is here given him of the present state of the Jews and Jerusalem, *v.* 3. Hanani, the person he enquired of, has this character given of him (*ch.* vii. 2), that he *feared God above many*, and therefore would not only speak truly, but, when he spoke of the desolations of Jerusalem, would speak tenderly. It is probable that his errand to court at this time was to solicit some favour, some relief or other, that they stood in need of. Now the account he gives is, 1. That the holy seed was miserably trampled on and abused, *in great affliction and reproach*, insulted upon all occasions by their neighbours, and *filled with the scorning of those that were at ease*. 2. That the holy city was exposed and in ruins. *The wall of Jerusalem was* still *broken*

JAMIESON, FAUSSET, BROWN

CHAPTER 1

Vss. 1-3. Nehemiah, Understanding by Hanani the Afflicted State of Jerusalem, Mourns, Fasts, and Prays. **1. Nehemiah the son of Hachaliah**—This eminently pious and patriotic Jew is to be carefully distinguished from two other persons of the same name—one of whom is mentioned as helping to rebuild the walls of Jerusalem (ch. 3:16), and the other is noticed in the list of those who accompanied Zerubbabel in the first detachment of returning exiles (Ezra 2:2; ch. 7:7). Though little is known of his genealogy, it is highly probable that he was a descendant of the tribe of Judah and the royal family of David. **in the month Chisleu**—answering to the close of November and the larger part of December. **Shushan the palace**—the capital of ancient Susiana, east of the Tigris, a province of Persia. From the time of Cyrus it was the favorite winter residence of the Persian kings.

2. Hanani, one of my brethren, came, he and certain men of Judah—Hanani is called his brother (ch. 7:2). But as that term was used loosely by Jews as well as other Orientals, it is probable that no more is meant than that he was of the same family. According to Josephus, Nehemiah, while walking around the palace walls, overheard some persons conversing in the Hebrew language. Having ascertained that they had lately returned from Judea, he was informed by them, in answer to his eager inquiries, of the unfinished and desolate condition of Jerusalem, as well as the defenseless state of the returned exiles. The commissions previously given to Zerubbabel and Ezra extending only to the repair of the temple and private dwellings, the walls and gates of the city had been allowed to remain a mass of shattered ruins, as they had been laid by the Chaldean siege.

ADAM CLARKE

CHAPTER 1

1. *The words of Nehemiah.* That this book was compiled out of the journal or memoranda made by Nehemiah himself, there can be no doubt; but that he was not the compiler is evident from several passages in the work itself. As it is written consecutively as one book with Ezra, many have supposed that this latter was the author. But whoever compares the style of each, in the Hebrew, will soon be convinced that this is not correct; the style is so very different that they could not possibly be the work of the same person. *The month Chisleu.* Answering to a part of our November and December. *Twentieth year.* That is, of Artaxerxes. *Shushan the palace.* The ancient city of Susa, the winter residence of the Persian kings.

3. *The wall of Jerusalem also is broken down.* This must refer to the walls which had been rebuilt after the people returned from their captivity, for it could not refer to the walls which were broken down and levelled with the dust by Nebuchadnezzar; to hear of this could be no news to Nehemiah.

MATTHEW HENRY

down, and the gates were, as the Chaldeans left them, in ruins. This made the condition of the inhabitants both very despicable under the abiding marks of poverty and slavery, and very dangerous, for their enemies might when they pleased make an easy prey of them. The temple was built, the government settled, and a work of reformation brought to some head, but here was one good work yet undone; this was still wanting.

IV. The great affliction this gave to Nehemiah and the deep concern it put him into, *v.* 4. 1. He *wept and mourned.* 2. He *fasted and prayed.*

Verses 5–11

Nehemiah's prayer, a prayer that has reference to all the prayers which he had for some time before been putting up to God day and night, while he continued his sorrows for the desolations of Jerusalem, and withal to the petition he was now intending to present to the king his master for his favour to Jerusalem.

I. His humble and reverent address to God. It teaches us to draw near to God, 1. With a holy awe of his majesty and glory, remembering that he is the God of heaven, infinitely above us, infinitely excelling all the principalities and powers both of the upper and of the lower world, angels and kings. 2. With a holy confidence in his grace and truth, for he *keepeth covenant and mercy for those that love him,* not only the mercy that is promised, but even more than he promised.

II. His general request for the audience and acceptance of all the prayers and confessions he now made to God (*v.* 6): "*Let thy ear be attentive to the prayer,* which I *pray before thee.*"

III. His penitent confession of sin; not only Israel has sinned but *I and my father's house have sinned, v.* 6.

IV. The pleas he urges for mercy for his people Israel.

1. He pleads what God had of old said to them. He had said indeed that, if they broke covenant with him, he would *scatter them among the nations,* and that threatening was fulfilled in their captivity: never was people so widely dispersed as Israel was at this time, though at first so closely incorporated; but he had said withal that if they *turned to him* (as now they began to do, having renounced idolatry and kept to the temple service) he would *gather them again.* This he quotes from Deut. xxx. 1–5, and begs leave to put God in mind of it (though the Eternal Mind needs no remembrancer) as that which he guided his desires by, and grounded his faith and hope upon, in praying this prayer. If God were not more mindful of his promises than we are of his precepts we should be undone. Our best pleas therefore in prayer are those that are taken from the promise of God, the *word on which he has caused us to hope,* Ps. cxix. 49.

2. He pleads the relation wherein of old they stood to God: "These are *thy servants and thy people* (*v.* 10), whom thou hast set apart for thyself, and taken into covenant with thee. Wilt thou suffer thy sworn enemies to trample upon and oppress thy sworn servants? If thou wilt not appear for thy people, whom wilt thou appear for?" See Isa. lxiii. 19. As an evidence of their being God's servants he gives them this character (*v.* 11): "*They desire to fear thy name;* they are not only called by thy name, but really have a reverence for thy name; they now worship thee, and thee only, according to thy will, and have an awe of all the discoveries thou art pleased to make of thyself; this they have a desire to do."

3. He pleads the great things God had formerly done for them (*v.* 10).

Lastly, He concludes with a particular petition, that God would prosper him in his undertaking, and give him favour with the king. *Mercy in the sight of this man* is what he prays for, meaning not the king's mercy, but mercy from God in his address to the king. Favour with men is then comfortable when we can see it springing from the mercy of God.

JAMIESON, FAUSSET, BROWN

4-11. HIS PRAYER. **4. when I heard these words that I sat down . . . and mourned, . . . and fasted, and prayed**—The recital deeply affected the patriotic feelings of this good man, and no comfort could he find but in earnest and protracted prayer, that God would favor the purpose, which he seems to have secretly formed, of asking the royal permission to go to Jerusalem.

ALEXANDER MACLAREN:

Ninety years had passed since the returning exiles had arrived at Jerusalem. They had encountered many difficulties which had marred their progress and cooled their enthusiasm. The Temple, indeed, was rebuilt, but Jerusalem lay in ruins and its walls remained as they had been left by Nebuchadnezzar's siege some century and a half before. A little party of pious pilgrims had gone from Persia to the city, and had come back to Shushan with a sad story of weakness and despondency, affliction and hostility. One of the travellers had a brother, a youth named Nehemiah, who was a cupbearer in the court of the Persian king. Living in a palace and surrounded with luxury, his heart was with his brethren; and the ruins of Jerusalem were dearer to him than the pomp of Shushan.

My text tells how the young cupbearer was affected by the tidings, and how he wept and prayed before God. The accurate dates given in this book show that this period of brooding contemplation of the miseries of his brethren lasted for four months. Then he took a great resolution, flung up brilliant prospects, identified himself with the afflicted colony, and asked for leave to go and share, and, if it might be, to redress the sorrows which had made so deep a dint upon his heart.—*Expositions of Holy Scripture*

11. I was the king's cupbearer—This officer, in the ancient Oriental courts, was always a person of rank and importance; and, from the confidential nature of his duties and his frequent access to the royal presence, he possessed great influence.

ADAM CLARKE

4. *And mourned certain days.* From the month Chisleu to the month Nisan—about four months from the time he received the above information till the time that Artaxerxes noticed his grief, chap. ii. 1. All this time he probably spent in supplication to God, waiting for a favorable opening in the divine providence.

5. *Lord God of heaven.* What was, before the Captivity, "Jehovah, God of hosts." *Great*—able to do mighty things. *Terrible*—able to inflict the heaviest judgments.

6. *Let thine ear.* Hear what we say and confess. *Thine eyes open*—see what we suffer.

7. *Have not kept thy commandments.* The moral precepts by which our lives should be regulated. *Statutes.* What refers to the rites and ceremonies of Thy religion. *Judgments.* The precepts of justice relative to our conduct to each other.

8. *Thy servant Moses.* Though in an enemy's country, and far from the ordinances of God, Nehemiah did not forget the law; he read his Bible well, and quotes correctly.

11. *Mercy in the sight of this man.* Favor before the king, Ahasuerus. He seems then to have been giving him the cup. *For I was the king's cupbearer.* The king's "butler," which gave him the opportunity of being frequently with the king; and to be in such a place of trust, he must be in the king's confidence.

MATTHEW HENRY — CHAPTER 2

Verses 1–8

Nehemiah had prayed for the relief of his countrymen. Nearly four months passed, from Chisleu to Nisan (from November to March), before Nehemiah made his application to the king for leave to go to Jerusalem, either because the winter was not a proper time for such a journey, or because it was so long before his month of waiting came, and there was no coming into the king's presence uncalled, Esther iv. 11. Now that he attended the king's table he hoped to have his ear.

I. The occasion which he gave the king to enquire

JAMIESON, FAUSSET, BROWN — CHAPTER 2

VSS. 1-20. ARTAXERXES, UNDERSTANDING THE CAUSE OF NEHEMIAH'S SADNESS, SENDS HIM WITH LETTERS AND A COMMISSION TO BUILD AGAIN THE WALLS OF JERUSALEM. **1. it came to pass in the month Nisan**—This was nearly four months after he had learned the desolate and ruinous state of Jerusalem (ch. 1:1). The reasons for so long a delay cannot be ascertained.

ADAM CLARKE — CHAPTER 2

1. *Month Nisan.* Answering to a part of our March and April.

MATTHEW HENRY

into his cares and griefs, by appearing sad in his presence. He took up the wine and gave it to the king when he called for it, expecting that then he would look him in the face. He had not used to be sad in the king's presence, but conformed to the rules of the court (as courtiers must do), which would admit no sorrows, Esther iv. 2. Good men should do what they can by their cheerfulness to convince the world of the pleasantness of religious ways and to roll away the reproach cast upon them as melancholy; but there is a time for all things, Eccles. iii. 4. Nehemiah now saw cause both to be sad and to appear. so. The miseries of Jerusalem gave him cause to be sad, and his showing his grief would give occasion to the king to enquire into the cause.

II. The kind notice which the king took of his sadness and the enquiry he made into the cause of it (*v.* 2): *Why is thy countenance sad, seeing thou art not sick?*

III. The account which Nehemiah gave the king of the cause of his sadness, which he gave with meekness and fear. He modestly asked, "*Why should not my countenance be sad* as it is *when the city, the place of my fathers' sepulchres, lieth waste?*" He assigns the ruins of Jerusalem as the true cause of his grief.

IV. The encouragement which the king gave him to tell his mind, and the application he thereupon made in his heart to God, *v.* 4. The king had an affection for him, and was not pleased to see him melancholy. It is also probable that he had a kindness for the Jews' religion; he had discovered it before in the commission he gave to Ezra, who was a churchman, and now again in the power he put Nehemiah into, who was a statesman. Wanting therefore only to know how he might be serviceable to Jerusalem, he asks this its anxious friend, "*For what dost thou make request?* Something thou wouldst have; what is it?" Nehemiah immediately *prayed to the God of heaven* that he would give him wisdom to ask properly and incline the king's heart to grant him his request. It was a secret sudden ejaculation; he lifted up his heart to that God who understands the language of his heart: *Lord, give me a mouth and wisdom; Lord, give me favour in the sight of this man.*

V. His humble petition to the king. He asked for a commission to go as governor to Judah, to build the wall of Jerusalem. He also asked for a convoy (*v.* 7), and an order upon the governors, not only to permit and suffer him to pass through their respective provinces, but to supply him with what he had occasion for, with another order upon the keeper of the forest of Lebanon to give him timber for the work that he designed.

VI. The king's great favour to him in asking him *when he would return*, *v.* 6. He intimated that he was unwilling to lose him. He would spare him awhile, and let him have what clauses he pleased inserted in his commission, *v.* 8. Here was an immediate answer to his prayer. In the account he gives of the success of his petition he takes notice, 1. Of the presence of the queen; she sat by (*v.* 6), which (they say) was not usual in the Persian court, Esther i. 11. 2. Of the power and grace of God. He gained his point *according to the good hand of his God upon him.*

Verses 9–20

I. How Nehemiah was dismissed by the court he was sent from. The king appointed *captains of the army* and *horsemen* to go *with him* (*v.* 9), both for his guard and to show that he was a man whom *the king did delight to honour*, that all the king's servants might respect him accordingly.

II. How he was received by the country he was sent to.

1. By the Jews and their friends at Jerusalem.

(1) While he concealed his errand they took little notice of him. He was at *Jerusalem three days* (*v.* 11), and it does not appear that any of the great men of the city waited on him to congratulate him on his arrival, but he remained unknown.

(2) Though they took little notice of him he took great notice of them and their state. He arose in the night, and viewed the ruins of the walls, probably by moonlight (*v.* 13), that he might see what was to be done and in what method they must go about it, whether the old foundation would serve, and what there was of the old materials that would be of use. Those that would build up the church's walls must first take notice of the ruins of those walls. Those that would know how to amend must enquire what is amiss, what needs reformation, and what may serve as it is.

(3) When he disclosed his design to the rulers and people they cheerfully concurred with him in it. He did not tell them, at first, what he came about (*v.* 16), because he would not seem to do it for ostentation, and because, if he found it impracticable, he might retreat the more honourably. But when he had viewed and considered the thing, and probably

JAMIESON, FAUSSET, BROWN

I took up the wine, and gave it unto the king—Xenophon has particularly remarked about the polished and graceful manner in which the cupbearers of the Median, and consequently the Persian, monarchs performed their duty of presenting the wine to their royal master. Having washed the cup in the king's presence and poured into their left hand a little of the wine, which they drank in his presence, they then handed the cup to him, not grasped, but lightly held with the tips of their thumb and fingers. This description has received some curious illustrations from the monuments of Assyria and Persia, on which the cupbearers are frequently represented in the act of handing wine to the king. **2. the king said unto me, Why is thy countenance sad?**—It was deemed highly unbecoming to appear in the royal presence with any weeds or signs of sorrow (Esther 4:2); and hence it was no wonder that the king was struck with the dejected air of his cupbearer, while that attendant, on his part, felt his agitation increased by his deep anxiety about the issue of the conversation so abruptly begun. But the piety and intense earnestness of the man immediately restored him to calm self-possession and enabled him to communicate, first, the cause of his sadness, and next, the patriotic wish of his heart to be the honored instrument of reviving the ancient glory of the city of his fathers. **6-9. the queen also sitting by him**—As the Persian monarchs did not admit their wives to be present at their state festivals, this must have been a private occasion. The queen referred to was probably Esther, whose presence would tend greatly to embolden Nehemiah in stating his request; and through her influence, powerfully exerted it may be supposed, also by her sympathy with the patriotic design, his petition was granted, to go as deputy-governor of Judea, accompanied by a military guard, and invested with full powers to obtain materials for the building in Jerusalem, as well as to get all requisite aid in promoting his enterprise. **6. I set him a time**—Considering the great despatch made in raising the walls, it is probable that this leave of absence was limited at first to a year or six months, after which he returned to his duties in Shushan. The circumstance of fixing a set time for his return, as well as entrusting so important a work as the refortification of Jerusalem to his care, proves the high favor and confidence Nehemiah enjoyed at the Persian court, and the great estimation in which his services were held. At a later period he received a new commission for the better settlement of the affairs of Judea and remained governor of that province for twelve years (ch. 5:14). **7. letters be given me to the governors beyond the river**—The Persian empire at this time was of vast extent, reaching from the Indus to the Mediterranean. The Euphrates was considered as naturally dividing it into two parts, eastern and western (see Ezra 5:3, 4). **8. according to the good hand of my God upon me**—The piety of Nehemiah appears in every circumstance. The conception of his patriotic design—the favorable disposition of the king, and the success of the undertaking are all ascribed to God. **9, 10. Sanballat the Horonite**—Horonaim being a town in Moab, this person, it is probable, was a Moabite. **Tobiah the servant, the Ammonite**—The term used indicates him to have been a freed slave, elevated to some official dignity. These were district magistrates under the government of the satrap of Syria; and they seem to have been leaders of the Samaritan faction. **11, 12. So I came to Jerusalem, and was there three days**—Deeply affected with the desolations of Jerusalem, and uncertain what course to follow, he remained three days before informing any one of the object of his mission. At the end of the third day, accompanied with a few attendants, he made, under covert of night, a secret survey of the walls and gates. **13-15. I went out by night by the gate of the valley**—i.e., the Jaffa gate, near the tower of Hippicus. **even before the dragon well**—i.e., fountain on the opposite side of the valley. **and to the dung port**—the gate on the east of the city, through which there ran a common sewer to the brook Kedron and the valley of Hinnom. **14. Then**—i.e., after having passed through the gate of the Essenes. **I went on to the gate of the fountain**—i.e., Siloah, from which turning round the fount of Ophel. **to the king's pool; but there was no place for the beast that was under me to pass**—i.e., by the sides of this pool (Solomon's) there being water in the pool, and too much rubbish about it to permit the passage of the beast. **15. Then I went up . . . by the brook**—i.e., Kedron. **and entered by the gate of the valley, and so returned**—the gate leading to the valley of Jehoshaphat, east of the city. He went out by this gate, and having made the circuit

ADAM CLARKE

4. *So I prayed to the God of heaven.* Before he dared to prefer his request to the king, he made his prayer to God, that his suit might be acceptable; and this he does by mental prayer. To the spirit of prayer every place is a praying place.

5. *The city of my fathers' sepulchres.* The tombs of the dead were sacred among the ancients, and nothing could appear to them more detestable than disturbing the ashes or remains of the dead. Nehemiah knew that in mentioning this circumstance he should strongly interest the feelings of the Persian king.

6. *The queen also sitting by him.* Who probably forwarded his suit. This was not Esther, as Dean Prideaux supposes, nor perhaps the same Artaxerxes who had taken her to be queen; nor does *shegal* signify "queen," but rather harlot or concubine, she who was chief favorite. The Septuagint translate it "harlot"; and properly too. *I set him a time.* How long this time was we are not told; it is by no means likely that it was long, probably no more than six months or a year; after which he either returned, or had his leave of absence lengthened. For in the same year we find he was made governor of the Jews, in which office he continued twelve years, viz., from the twentieth to the thirty-second year of Artaxerxes, chap. v. 14. He then returned to Susa; and after staying a short time, had leave to return to rectify some abuses that Tobiah the Ammonite had introduced into the Temple, chap. xiii. 6-7, and several others of which the people themselves were guilty. After having performed this service, it is likely he returned to the Persian king, and died in his office of cupbearer; but of this latter circumstance we have no mention in the text.

8. *Asaph the keeper of the king's forest.* The "paradise" of the king. This I believe is originally a Persian word; it frequently occurs in Arabic and in Greek, and in both signifies a "pleasant garden, vineyard, pleasure garden," and what we call a "paradise." *And the king granted me.* This noble-spirited man attributes everything to God. He might have said, I had been long a faithful servant to the king; and he was disposed, in reward of my fidelity, to grant my request; but he would not say so. "He granted my request, because the good hand of my God was upon me."

10. *Sanballat the Horonite.* Probably a native of Horonaim, a Moabite by birth, and at this time governor of the Samaritans under the king of Persia. *Tobiah the servant.* He was an Ammonite; and here, under the Persian king, joint governor with Sanballat. Some suppose that the Sanballat here mentioned was the same who persuaded Alexander to build a temple on Mount Gerizim in favor of the Samaritans. Pelagius thinks there were two governors of this name.

13. *The dragon well.* Perhaps so called because of the representation of a dragon, out of whose mouth the stream issued that proceeded from the well. *Dung port.* This was the gate on the eastern side of the city, through which the filth of the city was carried into the valley of Hinnom.

14. *The gate of the fountain.* Of Siloah. *The king's pool.* Probably the aqueduct made by Hezekiah, to bring the waters of Gihon to the city of David. See 2 Chron. xxxii. 30.

15. *By the brook.* Kidron. *By the gate of the valley.* The valley through which the brook Kidron flowed. It was by this gate he went out; so he went all round the city, and entered by the same gate from which he had gone out.

MATTHEW HENRY

felt the pulse of the rulers and people, he told them *what God had put into his heart* (*v.* 12), even to *build up the wall of Jerusalem*, *v.* 17. "*Come, therefore, and let us build up the wall.*" He did not undertake to do the work without them (it could not be the work of one man), nor did he charge or command imperiously, though he had the king's commission; but in a friendly brotherly way he exhorted and excited them to join with him in this work. To encourage them hereto, he speaks of the design, *First*, As that which owed its origin to the special grace of God. He takes not the praise of it to himself, as a good thought of his own, but acknowledges that God *put it into his heart*. *Secondly*, As that which owed its progress hitherto to the special providence of God. He produced the king's commission, told them how readily it was granted and how forward the king was to favour his design, in which he saw the hand of his God *good upon him*. They presently came to a resolution, one and all, to concur with him: *Let us rise up and build*. *So they strengthened their hands*, their own and one another's, *for this good work*. Many a good work would find hands enough to be laid to it if there were but one good head to lead in it.

2. By those that wished ill to the Jews. Sanballat and Tobiah, two of the Samaritans, but by birth the former a Moabite, the latter an Ammonite, when they saw one come armed with a commission from the king to do service to Israel, *were exceedingly grieved* that all their little paltry arts to weaken Israel were thus baffled and frustrated by a fair, and noble, and generous project to strengthen them. When they saw a man come in that manner, who professedly *sought the welfare of the children of Israel*, it vexed them to the heart. When he began to act they set themselves to hinder him, but in vain, *v.* 19, 20. With what good reason the Jews slighted these discouragements. They bore up themselves with this that they were the *servants of the God of heaven*, the only true and living God, that they were acting for him in what they did, and that therefore he would bear them out and prosper them, though the heathen raged, Ps. ii. 1.

JAMIESON, FAUSSET, BROWN

of the city, went in by it again [BARCLAY'S CITY OF THE GREAT KING]. **16-18. the rulers knew not**—The following day, having assembled the elders, Nehemiah produced his commission and exhorted them to assist in the work. The sight of his credentials, and the animating strain of his address and example, so revived their drooping spirits that they resolved immediately to commence the building, which they did, despite the bitter taunts and scoffing ridicule of some influential men.

ADAM CLARKE

16. *The rulers knew not whither I went.* He made no person privy to his design, that he might hide everything as much as possible from their enemies till he had all things in readiness, lest they should take measures to defeat the work.

18. *Then I told them.* He opened to them his design and his commission.

19. *Geshem the Arabian.* Some chief of the Arabs contiguous to Samaria, who had joined with Sanballat and Tobiah to distress the Jews and hinder their work. *Will ye rebel against the king?* This they said in order to raise jealousies in the king's mind, and induce him to recall his ordinance.

20. *Ye have no portion, nor right.* To be a citizen of Jerusalem was a high honor, and they would not permit those who did not belong to the tribes of Israel to dwell there. Zerubbabel gave the same answer to the Samaritans, Ezra iv. 3.

MATTHEW HENRY — CHAPTER 3

Verses 1–32

Several things are observable in the account here given of the buildings of the wall about Jerusalem:—

I. That Eliashib the high priest, with his brethren the priests, led the van in this troop of builders, *v.* 1. If there be labour in it, who so fit as they to work? if danger, who so fit as they to venture? The priests repaired the *sheep-gate*, so called because through it were brought the sheep that were to be sacrificed in the temple; and therefore the priests undertook the repair of it because *the offerings of the Lord made by fire were* their inheritance. And of this gate only it is said that *they sanctified it* with the word and prayer.

II. That the undertakers were very many, who each took his share, some more and some less, in this work, according as their ability was.

III. That many were active in this work who were not themselves inhabitants of Jerusalem, and therefore consulted purely the public welfare and not any private interest or advantage of their own. Here are the men of Jericho with the first (*v.* 2), the men of Gibeon and Mizpah (*v.* 7), and Zanoah, *v.* 13. Every Israelite should lend a hand towards the building up of Jerusalem.

IV. That several rulers, both of Jerusalem and of other cities, were active in this work, thinking themselves bound in honour to do the utmost that their wealth and power enabled them to do for the furtherance of this good work.

V. Here is a just reproach fastened upon the nobles of Tekoa, that they *put not their necks to the work of their Lord* (*v.* 5), that is, they would not come under the yoke of an obligation to this service; as if the dignity and liberty of their peerage were their discharge from serving God and doing good.

VI. Two persons joined in repairing *the old gate* (*v.* 6), and so were co-founders, and shared the honour of it between them. The good work which we cannot compass ourselves we must be thankful to those that will go partners with us in. Some think that this is called the *old gate* because it belonged to the ancient Salem, which was said to be first built by Melchizedek.

VII. Several good honest tradesmen, as well as priests and rulers, were active in this work—*goldsmiths, apothecaries, merchants*, *v.* 8, 32. They did not think their callings excused them, nor plead that they could not leave their shops to attend the public business, knowing that what they lost would certainly be made up to them by the blessing of God upon their callings.

JAMIESON, FAUSSET, BROWN — CHAPTER 3

VSS. 1-32. THE NAMES AND ORDER OF THEM THAT BUILDED THE WALL OF JERUSALEM. **1. Then Eliashib the high priest**—the grandson of Jeshua, and the first high priest after the return from Babylon. **rose up, with his brethren the priests**—i.e., set an example by commencing the work—their labors being confined to the sacred localities. **they builded the sheep gate**—close to the temple. Its name arose either from the sheep-market, or from the pool of Bethesda, which was there (John 5:2). There the sheep were washed and then taken to the temple for sacrifice. **they sanctified it, and set up the doors**—Being the common entrance into the temple, and the first part of the building repaired, it is probable that some religious ceremonies were observed in gratitude for its completion. "It was the first-fruits, and therefore, in the sanctification of it, the whole lump and building was sanctified" [POOLE]. **the tower of Meah**—This word is improperly considered, in our version, as the name of a tower; it is the *Hebrew* word for "a hundred," so that the meaning is: they not only rebuilt the sheep gate, but also a hundred cubits of the wall, which extended as far as the tower of Hananeel. **2. next unto him builded the men of Jericho,** etc.—The wall was divided into portions, one of which was assigned respectively to each of the great families which had returned from the captivity. This distribution, by which the building was carried on in all parts simultaneously with great energy, was eminently favorable to despatch. "The villages where the restorers resided being mostly mentioned, it will be seen that this circumstance affords a general indication of the part of the wall upon which they labored, such places being on that side of the city nearest their place of abode; the only apparent exception being, perhaps, where they repaired more than their piece. Having completed their first undertaking (if they worked any more), there being no more work to be done on the side next their residence, or having arrived after the repairs on that part of the city nearest them under operation were completed, they would go wherever their services would be required" [BARCLAY'S CITY OF THE GREAT KING]. **8. they fortified Jerusalem unto the broad wall**—or double wall, extending from the gate of Ephraim to the corner gate, 400 cubits in length, formerly broken down by Joash, king of Israel, but afterwards rebuilt by Uzziah, who made it so strong that the Chaldeans, finding it difficult to demolish, had left it standing.

ADAM CLARKE — CHAPTER 3

1. *Eliashib the high priest.* It was right that the priests should be first in this holy work, and perhaps *the sheep gate* which is mentioned here is that by which the offerings or sacrifices were brought into the Temple.

They sanctified it. As they began with the sacred offering as soon as they got an altar built, it was proper that the gate by which these sacrifices entered should be consecrated for this purpose, i.e., set apart, so that it should be for this use only.

3. *The fish gate.* We really know scarcely anything about these gates—what they were, why called by these names, or in what part of the wall situated.

7. *The throne of the governor.* His house, and the place where he dispensed justice and judgment. Previously to the days of Nehemiah, Jerusalem was governed by a deputy from the Persian king (see chap. v. 15); but after this time they were governed by governors and judges chosen from among themselves.

8. *Goldsmiths.* From the remotest period of the history of the Jews they had artists in all elegant and ornamental trades; and it is also evident that goldsmiths, apothecaries, and merchants were formed into companies in the time of Nehemiah. *Apothecaries.* Rather such as dealt in drugs, aromatics, spices, for embalming or for furnishing the Temple with the incense consumed there.

MATTHEW HENRY

VIII. Some ladies are spoken of as helping forward this work—*Shallum and his daughters* (*v.* 12), who, though not capable of personal service, yet having their portions in their own hands, or being rich widows, contributed money for buying materials and paying workmen. St. Paul speaks of some good women that *laboured with him in the gospel*, Phil. iv. 3.

IX. Of some it is said that they repaired *over against their houses* (*v.* 10, 23, 28, 29), and of one (who, it is likely, was only a lodger) that he repaired *over against his chamber*, *v.* 30. When a general good work is to be done each should apply himself to that part of it that falls nearest to him and is within his reach. If every one will sweep before his own door, the street will be clean; if everyone will mend one, we shall be all mended. If he that has but a chamber will repair before that, he does his part.

X. Of one it is said that he *earnestly* repaired that which fell to his share (*v.* 20). It is good to be thus *zealously affected in a good thing*; and it is probable that this good man's zeal provoked very many to take the more pains and make the more haste.

XI. Of one of these builders it is observed that he was *the sixth son* of his father, *v.* 30. His five elder brethren, it seems, laid not their hands to this work, but he did. In doing that which is good we need not stay to see our elders go before us; if they decline it, it does not therefore follow that we must. Thus the younger brother, if he be the better man, and does God and his generation better service, is indeed the better gentleman; those are most honourable that are most useful.

XII. Some of those that had *first done helped their fellows*, and undertook another share where they saw there was most need. Meremoth repaired, *v.* 4 and again, *v.* 21. And the Tekoites, besides the piece they repaired (*v.* 5), undertook another piece (*v.* 27), which is the more remarkable because their nobles set them a bad example by withdrawing from the service, which, instead of serving them for an excuse to sit still, perhaps made them the more forward to do double work, that by their zeal they might either shame or atone for the covetousness and carelessness of their nobles.

Lastly, Here is no mention of any particular share that Nehemiah himself had in this work. A namesake of his is mentioned, *v.* 16. But did he do nothing? Yes, though he undertook not any particular piece of the wall, yet he did more than any of them, for he had the oversight of them all; half of his servants worked where there was most need, and the other half stood sentinel, as we find afterwards (*ch.* iv. 16), while he himself in his own person walked the rounds, directed and encouraged the builders, set his hand to the work where he saw occasion, and kept a watchful eye upon the motions of the enemy, as we shall find in the next chapter. The pilot need not haul at a rope; it is enough for him to steer.

JAMIESON, FAUSSET, BROWN

12. Shallum . . . he and his daughters—who were either heiresses or rich widows. They undertook to defray the expenses of a part of the wall next them.

13. the inhabitants of Zanoah—There were two towns so called in the territory of Judah (Josh. 15:34, 56). **14. Beth-haccerem**—a city of Judah, supposed to be now occupied by Bethulia, on a hill of the same name, which is sometimes called also the mountain of the Franks, between Jerusalem and Tekoa.

16. the sepulchres of David, and to the pool that was made, and unto the house of the mighty—i.e., along the precipitous cliffs of Zion [BARCLAY].

19. at the turning of the wall—i.e., the wall across the Tyropœon, being a continuation of the first wall, connecting Mount Zion with the temple wall [BARCLAY].

25. the tower which lieth out from the king's high house—i.e., watchtower by the royal palace [BARCLAY]. **26. the Nethinims**—Not only the priests and the Levites, but the common persons that belonged to the house of God, contributed to the work. The names of those who repaired the walls of Jerusalem are commemorated because it was a work of piety and patriotism to repair the holy city. It was an instance of religion and courage to defend the true worshippers of God, that they might serve Him in quietness and safety, and, in the midst of so many enemies, go on with this work, piously confiding in the power of God to support them [BISHOP PATRICK].

ADAM CLARKE

9. *Ruler of the half part of Jerusalem.* Probably the city was divided into two parts: one for Judah, and the other for Benjamin, each having its proper governor. *Rephaiah* mentioned here was one of these governors, and Shallum, mentioned in v. 12, was the other.

11. *Repaired the other piece.* That which was left by Jedaiah after he had repaired the wall opposite to his own house. Probably some of the principal people were obliged to repair those parts of the wall opposite to their own dwellings. Perhaps this was the case generally.

12. *The son of Halohesh.* Or the son of the "Enchanter," conjectured to be thus named from having the art to charm serpents. *The ruler of the half part.* See on v. 9.

13. *The inhabitants of Zanoah.* This was a town in the tribe of Judah, Josh. xv. 34.

14. *Beth-haccerem.* A village or town in the tribe of Benjamin. See Jer. vi. 1.

15. *The pool of Siloah.* This is probably the same as that mentioned by the Evangelists. *The stairs that go down from the city of David.* Jerusalem being built on very uneven ground, and some hills being taken within the walls, there was a necessity that there should be in different places steps by which they could ascend and descend.

16. *The pool that was made.* Calmet supposes that this was the reservoir made by Hezekiah, when besieged by Sennacherib, 2 Chron. xxxii. 4. *The house of the mighty.* Probably a place where a band of soldiers was kept, or the city guard.

19. *The going up to the armoury.* This was either a tower that defended the angle where the two walls met or the city arsenal, where shields, spears, etc., were kept to arm the people in time of danger.

20. *Earnestly repaired.* He distinguished himself by his zeal and activity.

22. *The priests, the men of the plain.* Some of the officers of the Temple, particularly the singers, dwelt in the plain country round about Jerusalem, chap. xii. 28; and it is likely that several of the *priests* dwelt in the same place.

28. *The horse gate.* The place through which the horses passed in order to be watered; it was near the Temple.

MATTHEW HENRY — CHAPTER 4

Verses 1–6

Here is, I. The spiteful scornful reflection which Sanballat and Tobiah cast upon the Jews for their attempt to build the wall about Jerusalem. The intelligence was brought to Samaria, that nest of enemies to the Jews, and here we are told how they received the tidings. 1. In heart. They were very angry at the undertaking, and had *great indignation*, *v.* 1. It vexed them that Nehemiah came to seek the welfare of the children of Israel (*ch.* ii. 10); but, when they heard of this great undertaking for their good, they were out of all patience. 2. In word. They despised it, and made it the subject of their ridicule. "*These feeble Jews*" (*v.* 2), "what will they do for materials? *Will they revive the stones out of the rubbish?* And what mean they by being so hasty? Do they think to make the walling of a city but one day's work, and to keep the feast of dedication with sacrifice the next day? Poor silly people! See how ridiculous they made themselves!" "*If a fox go up*, not with his subtlety, but with his weight, he *will break down their stone wall.*"

II. Nehemiah's humble and devout address to God when he heard of these reflections. He did not answer these fools according to their folly; he did not upbraid them with their weakness, but looked up to God by prayer.

1. He begs of God to take notice of the indignities that were done them (*v.* 4), and in this we are to imitate him: *Hear, O our God! for we are despised.*

2. He begs of God to avenge their cause and turn the reproach upon the enemies themselves (*v.* 4, 5); and this was spoken rather by a spirit of prophecy than by a spirit of prayer, and is not to be imitated

JAMIESON, FAUSSET, BROWN — CHAPTER 4

Vss. 1-6. WHILE THE ENEMIES SCOFF, NEHEMIAH PRAYS TO GOD, AND CONTINUES THE WORK. **1. when Sanballat heard that we builded the wall, he was wroth**—The Samaritan faction showed their bitter animosity to the Jews on discovering the systematic design of refortifying Jerusalem. Their opposition was confined at first to scoffs and insults, in heaping which the governors made themselves conspicuous, and circulated all sorts of disparaging reflections that might increase the feelings of hatred and contempt for them in their own party. The weakness of the Jews in respect of wealth and numbers, the absurdity of their purpose apparently to reconstruct the walls and celebrate the feast of dedication in one day, the idea of raising the walls on their old foundations, as well as using the charred and mouldering debris of the ruins as the materials for the restored buildings, and the hope of such a parapet as they could raise being capable of serving as a fortress of defense—these all afforded fertile subjects of hostile ridicule. **3. if a fox go up**—The foxes were mentioned because they were known to infest in great numbers the ruined and desolate places in the mount and city of Zion (Lam. 5:18).

4, 5. Hear, O our God; for we are despised—The imprecations invoked here may seem harsh, cruel, and vindictive; but it must be remembered that Nehemiah and his friends regarded those Samaritan leaders as enemies to the cause of God and His

ADAM CLARKE — CHAPTER 4

2. *The army of Samaria.* As he was governor, he had the command of the army, and he wished to excite the soldiers to second his views against Nehemiah and his men. *What do these feeble Jews?* We may remark here, in general, that the enemies of God's work endeavor by all means to discredit and destroy it, and those who are employed in it.

4. *Turn their reproach upon their own head.* A prayer of this kind, understood literally, is not lawful for any Christian. Jesus, our great Master, has said, "Love your enemies . . . do good to them that hate you, and pray for them

MATTHEW HENRY

by us who are taught of Christ to *pray for* those that *despitefully use and persecute us*. Christ himself prayed for those that reproached him: *Father, forgive them.*

III. The vigour of the builders, notwithstanding these reflections, *v.* 6. They made such good speed that in a little time they had run up the wall to half its height, for *the people had a mind to work*; their hearts were upon it, and they would have it forwarded.

Verses 7–15

I. The conspiracy which the Jews' enemies formed against them, to stay the building by slaying the builders. The conspirators were not only Sanballat and Tobiah, but other neighbouring people whom they had drawn into the plot. *They were very wroth. Cursed be their anger, for it was fierce, and their wrath, for it was cruel.* Nothing would serve but they would *fight against Jerusalem*, *v.* 8. Why, what quarrel had they with the Jews? They hated the Jews' piety, and were therefore vexed at their prosperity and sought their ruin. The hindering of good work is that which bad men aim at and promise themselves; but good work is God's work, and it shall prosper.

II. The discouragements which the builders themselves laboured under. At the very time when the adversaries said, Let us *cause the work to cease*, Judah said, "Let us even let it fall, for we are not able to go forward with it," *v.* 10. They represent the labourers as tired, and the remaining difficulties, even of that first part of their work, the removing of the rubbish, as insuperable, and therefore they think it advisable to desist for the present. Active leading men have many times as much ado to grapple with the fears of their friends as with the terrors of their enemies.

III. The information that was brought to Nehemiah of the enemies' designs, *v.* 12. There were *Jews that dwelt by them*, in the country, who, though they had not zeal enough to bring them to Jerusalem to help their brethren in building the wall, yet, having by their situation opportunity to discover the enemies' motions, had so much honesty and affection to the cause as to give intelligence of them; nay, that their intelligence might be the more credited, they came themselves to give it, and they said it ten times, repeating it as men in earnest, and under a concern, and the report was confirmed by many witnesses. "*Whatever place you turn to, they are against us*, so that you have need to be upon your guard on all sides."

IV. The pious and prudent methods which Nehemiah, hereupon, took to baffle the design, and to secure his work and workmen.

1. It is said (*v.* 14) he *looked.* (1) He looked up, engaged God for him, and put himself and his cause under the divine protection (*v.* 9): *We made our prayer unto our God.* That was the way of this good man, and should be our way; all his cares, all his griefs, all his fears, he spread before God, and thereby made himself easy. This was the first thing he did; before he used any means, he made his prayer to God, for with him we must always begin. (2) He looked about him. Having prayed, he *set a watch against them.* The instructions Christ has given us in our spiritual warfare agree with this example, Matt. xxvi. 41. *Watch and pray.* If we think to secure ourselves by prayer only, without watchfulness, we are slothful and tempt God; if by watchfulness, without prayer, we are proud and slight God; and, either way, we forfeit his protection.

2. Observe, (1) How he posted the guards, *v.* 13. *In the lower places* he set them *behind the wall*, that they might annoy the enemy over it, as a breast-work; but *in the higher places*, where the wall was raised to its full height, he set them upon it, that from the top of it they might throw down stones or darts upon the heads of the assailants: he set them *after their families*, that mutual relation might engage them to mutual assistance. (2) How he animated and encouraged the people, *v.* 14. "Come," says he, "*be not afraid of them*, but behave yourselves valiantly, considering, [1] Whom you fight under. You cannot have a better captain: *Remember the Lord, who is great and terrible;* you think your enemies *great and terrible*, but what are they in comparison with God, especially in opposition to him? He is great above them to control them, and will be terrible to them when he comes to reckon with them." The reigning fear of God is the best antidote against the ensnaring fear of man.

V. The disappointment which this gave to the enemies, *v.* 15. When they found that their design was discovered, and that the Jews were upon their guard, they concluded that it was to no purpose to attempt anything, but that *God had brought their counsel to nought.* They knew they could not gain

JAMIESON, FAUSSET, BROWN

people, and therefore as deserving to be visited with heavy judgments. The prayer, therefore, is to be considered as emanating from hearts in which neither hatred, revenge, nor any inferior passion, but a pious and patriotic zeal for the glory of God and the success of His cause, held the ascendant sway.

6. all the wall was joined together unto the half thereof—The whole circuit of the wall had been distributed in sections to various companies of the people, and was completed to the half of the intended height.

7-23. HE SETS A WATCH. **7. But . . . when Sanballat . . . heard that the walls . . . were made up, and . . . the breaches . . . stopped**—The rapid progress of the fortifications, despite all their predictions to the contrary, goaded the Samaritans to frenzy. So they, dreading danger from the growing greatness of the Jews, formed a conspiracy to surprise them, demolish their works, and disperse or intimidate the builders. The plot being discovered, Nehemiah adopted the most energetic measures for ensuring the common safety, as well as the uninterrupted building of the walls.

By these vigilant precautions, the counsels of the enemy were defeated, and the work was carried on apace.

ADAM CLARKE

which despitefully use you." Such sayings as the above are excusable in the mouth of a Jew, under severe irritation. See the next verse.

5. *Let not their sin be blotted out.* These are the most terrible imprecations; but probably we should understand them as declaratory, for the same form of the verb, in the Hebrew, is used as precative and imperative. *Turn their reproach*—Their reproach "shall be turned." *Give them for a prey*—"They shall be given for a prey." *Cover not their iniquity*—"Their iniquity shall not be covered." *Let not their sin be blotted out*—"Their sin shall not be blotted out." All who know the genius of the Hebrew language know that the future tense is used to express all these senses. Besides, we may rest assured that Neheimah's curses, or declaration of God's judgments, had respect only to their bodies, and to their life—not to their souls and the world to come. And then they amount to no more than this: What a man soweth, that shall he reap.

6. *For the people had a mind to work.* The original is very emphatic: *vayehi leb leam laasoth*, "For the people had a *heart* to work." Their hearts were engaged in it; and where the heart is engaged, the work of God goes on well. The whole of this sixth verse is omitted by the Septuagint.

7. *The walls of Jerusalem were made up.* That is, they were made up to the half height of the wall; for the preceding verse seems to intimate that the whole wall was thus far built—not half of the wall completed, but the whole wall built to half its height.

10. *The strength of the bearers of burdens is decayed.* They worked both day and night, scarcely ever putting off their clothes, except for the purpose of being washed, vv. 21, 23. *Much rubbish.* The ruins they were obliged to clear away before they could dig the foundation for a new wall; and in this labor they were nearly exhausted; see chap. v. 15.

12. *From all places whence ye shall return unto us.* This verse is extremely difficult. Our translators have supplied the words, "they will be upon you," which have nothing correspondent in the Hebrew. The Septuagint have given a good sense. "They come up from all places against us." The sense appears to be this: The Jews which dwelt among the Samaritans came often to Nehemiah from all quarters where they sojourned, and told him the designs of his enemies against him. Therefore he set people with their swords, spears, and bows, to defend the walls. It is probable that instead of *tashubu*, "ye shall return," we should read *chashebu*, "they designed or meditated." This word is very similar to the other, and makes the sense very clear. "The Jews who dwelt among them told us frequently, from all places, what they designed against us."

9. *We made our prayer unto our God, and set a watch.* The strongest confidence in the protection and favor of God does not preclude the use of all or any of the means of self-preservation and defense which His providence has put in our power.

14. *Be not ye afraid of them.* Are they more terrible or stronger than God? *Fight for your brethren.* Your own countrymen, who worship the same God, and are come from the same stock; *your sons*, whom they wish to slay or lead into captivity; *your daughters* and *wives*, whom they wish to deflower and defile; and *your houses*, which they wish to seize and occupy as their own. They had everything at stake; and therefore they must fight for their religion, their lives, and their property.

15. *Their counsel to nought.* The word *counsel* used here countenances the emendation in the twelfth verse.

MATTHEW HENRY

their point but by surprise, and, if their plot was known, it was quashed. The Jews hereupon *returned everyone to his work,* with so much the more cheerfulness because they saw plainly that God owned it and owned them in the doing of it.

Verses 16–23

When the builders had so far reason to think the design of the enemies broken *as to return to their work,* yet they were not so secure as to lay down their arms. 1. While one half were at work, the other half were under their arms, holding *spears, and shields, and bows,* not only for themselves but for the labourers too, who would immediately quit their work, and betake themselves to their weapons, upon the first alarm, *v.* 16. Thus dividing their time between the trowels and the spears they are said to *work with one hand* and hold their weapons *with the other* (*v.* 17), which cannot be understood literally, for the work would require both hands; but it intimates that they were equally employed in both. 2. Every builder had a sword by his side (*v.* 18). which he could carry without hindering his labour. The word of God is the sword of the Spirit, which we ought to have always at hand and never to seek, both in our labours and in our conflicts as Christians. 3. Care was taken both to get and give early notice of the approach of the enemy, in case they should endeavour to surprise them. Nehemiah kept a trumpeter always by him to sound an alarm upon the first intimation of danger. The work was large, and the builders were dispersed; for in all parts of the wall they were labouring at the same time. Nehemiah continually walked round to oversee the work and encourage the workmen. When they acted as workmen, it was requisite they should be dispersed wherever there was work to do; but when as soldiers it was requisite they should come into close order, and be found in a body. Thus should the labourers in Christ's building be ready to unite against a common foe. 4. The inhabitants of the villages were ordered to lodge within Jerusalem, with their servants, not only that they might be the nearer to their work in the morning, but that they might be ready to help in case of an attack in the night, *v.* 22. 5. Nehemiah himself, and all his men, kept closely to their business. The spears were held up, with the sight of them to terrify the enemy, not only from sun to sun, but from twilight to twilight every day, *v.* 21.

JAMIESON, FAUSSET, BROWN

Hitherto the governor, for the sake of despatch, had set all his attendants and guards on the work—now half of them were withdrawn to be constantly in arms. The workmen labored with a trowel in one hand and a sword in the other; and as, in so large a circuit, they were far removed from each other, Nehemiah (who was night and day on the spot, and, by his pious exhortations and example, animated the minds of his people) kept a trumpeter by his side, so that, on any intelligence of a surprise being brought to him, an alarm might be immediately sounded, and assistance rendered to the most distant detachment of their brethren.

God, when He has important public work to do, never fails to raise up instruments for accomplishing it, and in the person of Nehemiah, who, to great natural acuteness and energy added fervent piety and heroic devotion, He provided a leader, whose high qualities fitted him for the demands of the crisis. Nehemiah's vigilance anticipated every difficulty, his prudent measures defeated every obstruction, and with astonishing rapidity this Jerusalem was made again "a city fortified."

ADAM CLARKE

16. *Half . . . wrought in the work.* This is no unusual thing, even in the present day, in Palestine. People sowing their seed are often attended by an armed man, to prevent the Arabs from robbing them of their seed, which they will not fail to do if not protected. *Habergeons.* Breastplates, or armor for the breast.

17. *With one of his hands wrought in the work, and with the other hand held a weapon.* That is, he had his arms at hand, and was as fully prepared to fight as to work.

20. *Ye hear the sound of the trumpet.* As the walls were very extensive, and the workmen consequently much scattered, their enemies might easily attack and destroy them successively. He therefore ordered them all to work as near to each other as they could; and himself, who was everywhere surveying the work, kept a trumpeter always with him, who was to sound when the enemy approached; and all were instantly to run to the place where they heard the sound.

22. *Let every one with his servant lodge within Jerusalem.* The country people were accustomed, after their day's labor, to return to their families; now being so formidably threatened, he obliged them all to sleep in Jerusalem, that they might be ready, in case of attack, to help their brethren. All this man's arrangements were wise and judicious.

MATTHEW HENRY — CHAPTER 5

Verses 1–5

Hard times and hard hearts made the poor miserable.

I. The times they lived in were hard. There was a dearth of corn (*v.* 3), probably for want of rain. When the markets are high, and provisions scarce and dear, the poor soon feel from it, and are pinched by it. That which made the scarcity here complained of the more grievous was that their *sons and their daughters were many, v.* 2. The families that were most necessitous were most numerous. As corn was dear, so the taxes were high; the king's tribute must be paid, *v.* 4. This mark of their captivity still remained upon them. Now, it seems, they had not wherewithal of their own to buy corn and pay taxes, but were necessitated to borrow. Their families came poor out of Babylon; they had been at great expense in building them houses, and had not yet got up their strength, when these new burdens came upon them.

II. The persons they dealt with were hard. Money must be had, but it must be borrowed; and those that lent them money, taking advantage of their necessity, were very hard upon them. 1. They exacted interest from them at twelve per cent, the hundredth part every month, *v.* 11. But if the poor borrow to maintain their families, and we be able to help them, it is certain we ought either to lend freely what they have occasion for, or (if they be not likely to repay it) to give freely something towards it. 2. They forced them to mortgage to them their lands and houses for the securing of the money (*v.* 3), and not only so, but took the profits of them for interest (*v.* 5, compare *v.* 11), that by degrees they might make themselves masters of all they had. Yet this was not the worst. 3. They took their children for bond-servants, to be enslaved or sold at pleasure, *v.* 5. "Our heirs must be their slaves, and *it is not in our power to redeem them.*" This they made a humble remonstrance of to Nehemiah, not only because they saw he was a great man that could relieve them, but a good man that would. Let us lament the hardships which many in the world are

JAMIESON, FAUSSET, BROWN — CHAPTER 5

Vss. 1-5. The People Complain of Their Debt, Mortgage, and Bondage. **1. there was a great cry of the people . . . against their brethren**—Such a crisis in the condition of the Jews in Jerusalem—fatigued with hard labor and harassed by the machinations of restless enemies, the majority of them poor, and the bright visions which hope had painted of pure happiness on their return to the land of their fathers being unrealized—must have been very trying to their faith and patience. But, in addition to these vexatious oppressions, many began to sink under a new and more grievous evil. The poor made loud complaints against the rich for taking advantage of their necessities, and grinding them by usurious exactions. Many of them had, in consequence of these oppressions, been driven to such extremities that they had to mortgage their lands and houses to enable them to pay the taxes to the Persian government, and ultimately even to sell their children for slaves to procure the means of subsistence. The condition of the poorer inhabitants was indeed deplorable; for, besides the deficient harvests caused by the great rains (Ezra 10: 9; also Hag. 1:6-11), a dearth was now threatened by the enemy keeping such a multitude pent up in the city, and preventing the country people bringing in provisions.

ADAM CLARKE — CHAPTER 5

2. *We, our sons, and our daughters, are many.* Our families are larger than we can provide for; we are obliged to go in debt; and our richer brethren take advantage of our necessitous situation, and oppress us. The details which are given in the next verse are sufficiently plain.

3. *Because of the dearth.* About the time of Zerubbabel, God had sent a judicial dearth upon the land, as we learn from Haggai, chap. i. 9, etc.; for the people, it seems, were more intent on building houses for themselves than on rebuilding the house of the Lord. This dearth might have been continued, or its effects still felt; but it is more likely that there was a new dearth owing to the great number of people, for whose support the land that had been brought into cultivation was not sufficient.

4. *We have borrowed money.* This should be read, "We have borrowed money for the king's tribute on our lands and vineyards." They had a tax to pay to the Persian king in token of their subjection to him, and though it is not likely it was heavy, yet they were not able to pay it.

5. *We bring into bondage our sons.* The law permitted parents to sell their children in times of extreme necessity, Exod. xxi. 7.

MATTHEW HENRY

groaning under; putting our souls into their souls' stead, and remembering in our prayers and succours those that are burdened, as burdened with them. But let those who show no mercy expect *judgment without mercy*. It was an aggravation of the sin of these oppressing Jews that they were themselves so lately delivered out of the house of bondage, which obliged them in gratitude to *undo the heavy burdens*, Isa. lviii. 6.

Verses 6–13

The foregoing complaint was made to Nehemiah at the time when he had his head and hands as full as possible of the public business about building the wall; yet, perceiving it to be just, he did not reject it. The case called for speedy interposition, and therefore he applied himself immediately to the consideration of it, knowing that, let him build Jerusalem's walls ever so high, so thick, so strong, the city could not be safe while such abuses as these were tolerated.

I. He *was very angry* (*v.* 6).

II. He *consulted with himself*, *v.* 7. By this it appears that he did not say or do anything unadvisedly. Before he rebuked the nobles, he consulted with himself what to say, and when, and how.

III. He *rebuked the nobles and rulers*, who were the monied men, and whose power perhaps made them the more bold to oppress. Let no man imagine that his dignity sets him above reproof.

IV. He set a great assembly against them. He called the people together to bear their testimony (which the people will generally be forward to do) against the oppressions and extortions, *v.* 12. Ezra and Nehemiah were both of them very wise, good, useful men, yet, in cases not unlike, there was a great deal of difference between their management: when Ezra was told of the sin of the rulers in marrying strange wives he rent his clothes, and wept, and prayed, and was hardly persuaded to attempt a reformation, fearing it to be impracticable, for he was a man of a mild tender spirit; when Nehemiah was told of as bad a thing he kindled immediately, reproached the delinquents, incensed the people against them, and never rested till, by all the rough methods he could use, he forced them to reform; for he was a man of a hot and eager spirit. Very holy men may differ much from each other in their natural temper. 2. God's work may be well done and yet different methods taken in the doing of it, which is a good reason why we should neither arraign the management of others nor make our own a standard.

V. He fairly reasoned the case with them, and showed them the evil of what they did. The regular way of reforming men's lives is to endeavour, in the first place, to convince their consciences. He lays it before them, 1. That those whom they oppressed were their brethren. 2. That they were but lately redeemed *out of the hand of the heathen*. The body of the people were so by the wonderful providence of God. "Now," says he, "have we taken all this pains to get their liberty out of the hands of the heathen, and shall their own rulers enslave them?" 3. That it was a great sin thus to oppress the poor (*v.* 9). 4. That it was a reproach to their profession. "Consider *the reproach of the heathen our enemies;* they will say, These Jews, that profess so much devotion to God, see how barbarous they are one to another." Nothing exposes religion more to the reproach of its enemies than the worldliness and hard-heartedness of the professors of it.

VI. He earnestly pressed them not only not to make their poor neighbours any more such hard bargains, but to restore that which they had got into their hands, *v.* 11. See how familiarly he speaks to them: *Let us leave off this usury*, putting himself in, as becomes reprovers, though far from being any way guilty of the crime. Though he had authority to command, yet, *for love's sake, he rather beseeches.*

VII. He got a promise from them (*v.* 12): *We will restore them.* He sent for the priests to give them their oath that they would perform this promise. *So let God shake out every man that performeth not this promise*, *v.* 13. This was a threatening to which the people said *Amen*. With this *Amen* the people *praised the Lord*. This cheerfulness in promising was well, but that which follows was better: *They did according to this promise*, and adhered to what they had done.

Verses 14–19

Nehemiah relates more particularly what his practice was, not in pride or vainglory, but as an inducement both to his successors and to the inferior magistrates to be as tender as might be of the people's ease.

I. He intimates what had been the way of his predecessors, *v.* 15. He does not name them, because

JAMIESON, FAUSSET, BROWN

JOSEPH PARKER:

How difficult it is to permeate a whole nation with the spirit of high patriotism. Nehemiah will be faithful—a man here and a man there may be equal to the occasion, but how difficult to inspire a nation with the common sentiment of distrust of the enemy, with the common sentiment of mutual confidence. If an enemy were assaulting England, there are men who would sacrifice all they had to defend their paternal shores, and there are also Englishmen who would be within the lines turning the occasion to selfish profit, building up their personal fortunes out of the catastrophes of the empire. This is exactly what the wealthier and better-to-do Jews did in the days of Nehemiah: they oppressed the hireling, they added toil to the labor of the weary man; their one purpose was to increase themselves, to aggrandize their possessions, no matter what became of the name of the Jews or the fortunes of Israel. How is it with us?—*The People's Bible*

6-19. THE USURERS REBUKED. **6. I was very angry when I heard their cry and these words**—When such disorders came to the knowledge of the governor, his honest indignation was roused against the perpetrators of the evil.

Having summoned a public assembly, he denounced their conduct in terms of just severity. He contrasted it with his own in redeeming with his money some of the Jewish exiles who, through debt or otherwise, had lost their personal liberty in Babylon.

He urged the rich creditors not only to abandon their illegal and oppressive system of usury, but to restore the fields and vineyards of the poor, so that a remedy might be put to an evil the introduction of which had led to much actual disorder, and the continuance of which would inevitably prove ruinous to the newly restored colony, by violating the fundamental principles of the Hebrew constitution. The remonstrance was effectual. The conscience of the usurious oppressors could not resist the touching and powerful appeal. With mingled emotions of shame, contrition, and fear, they with one voice expressed their readiness to comply with the governor's recommendation. The proceedings were closed by the parties binding themselves by a solemn oath, administered by the priests, that they would redeem their pledge, as well as by the governor invoking, by the solemn and significant gesture of shaking a corner of his garment, a malediction on those who should violate it. The historian has taken care to record that the people did according to this promise. **14. Moreover from the time that I was appointed . . . I and my brethren have not eaten the bread of the governor**—We have a remarkable proof both of the opulence and the disinterestedness of Nehemiah. As he declined, on conscientious grounds, to accept the lawful emoluments attached to his government, and yet main-

ADAM CLARKE

7. *Ye exact usury.* This was expressly contrary to the law of God; and was doubly cruel at this time, when they were just returning out of the land of their captivity, and were suffering from the effects of a dearth. *I set a great assembly against them.* Brought all these delinquents before the rulers of the people.

9. *Ought ye not to walk in the fear of our God?* If ye wish to accredit that religion ye profess which comes from the God of justice and mercy, should you not, in the sight of the heathen, abstain from injustice and cruelty?

11. *Also the hundredth part of the money.* Houbigant contends, (1) That the word *meath,* which we and the Vulgate translate one *hundredth* part, never means so anywhere; and (2) That it would have answered no end to remit to people so distressed merely the one-hundredth part of the money which had been taken from them by usury. He understands *meath* as signifying the same as *min eth,* contracted into *meeth*, a preposition and demonstrative particle joined together, "also a part from the money." Neither the Syriac, Septuagint, nor Arabic acknowledges this *hundredth part.*

13. *Also I shook my lap.* This was a significant action frequent among the Hebrews, and something of the same nature was practiced among other nations.

14. *I and my brethren have not eaten the bread of the governor.* From what is related here, and in the following verse, we find that the table of the governor was always supplied by the people with bread and wine; and, besides, they had forty shekels per diem for their other expenses. The people were also greatly op-

MATTHEW HENRY

what he had to say of them was not to their honour, and in such a case it is good to spare names. The government allowed them *forty shekels of silver* (so much a day, it is probable); but, besides that, they obliged the people to furnish them with *bread and wine*, and they suffered their servants to squeeze the people, and to get all they could out of them.

II. He tells us what had been his own way.

1. In general, he had not done as the former governors did. The fear of God restrained him from oppressing the people. He was thus generous purely for conscience' sake. Nehemiah, for his part, got nothing, except the satisfaction of doing good: *Neither bought we any land*, v. 16.

2. More particularly, observe (1) How little Nehemiah received of what he might have required. So far was he from extorting more than his due that he never demanded that, but lived upon what he had got in the king of Persia's court and his own estate in Judæa: the reason he gives for this piece of self-denial is, *Because the bondage was heavy upon the people*. In our demands we must consider not only the justice of them, but the ability of those on whom we make them. (2) How much he gave which he might have withheld. [1] His servants' work, *v.* 16. [2] His own meat, *v.* 17, 18.

III. He concludes with a prayer (*v.* 19): *Think upon me, my God, for good*. 1. Nehemiah here mentions what he had *done for this people* to shame the rulers out of their oppressions. 2. He mentions it to God in prayer, not as if he thought he had hereby merited any favour from God, as a debt. "If God do but *think upon me for good*, I have enough."

JAMIESON, FAUSSET, BROWN

tained a style of princely hospitality for twelve years out of his own resources, it is evident that his office of cupbearer at the court of Shushan must have been very lucrative. **15. the former governors . . . had taken . . . bread and wine, besides forty shekels of silver**—The income of Eastern governors is paid partly in produce, partly in money. "Bread" means all sorts of provision. The forty shekels of silver per day would amount to a yearly salary of about $9,000.

17. Moreover there were at my table an hundred and fifty of the Jews—In the East it has been always customary to calculate the expense of a king's or grandee's establishment, not by the amount of money disbursed, but by the quantity of provisions consumed (see I Kings 4:22; 18:19; Eccles. 5:11).

ADAM CLARKE

pressed by the servants and officers of the governor; but during the twelve years that Nehemiah had been with them, he took not this salary, and ate none of their bread. Nor were his servants permitted to take or exact anything from them. Having such an example, it was scandalous for their chiefs, priests, and nobles thus to oppress an afflicted and distressed people.

16. *Neither bought we any land.* Neither he nor his officers took any advantage of the necessities of the people to buy their lands. He even made his own servants to work at the wall.

17. *An hundred and fifty of the Jews.* He kept open house, entertained all comers, besides having 150 Jews who had their food constantly at his table and at his expense. To be able to bear all these expenses, no doubt Nehemiah had saved money while he was cupbearer to the Persian king in Susa.

18. *One ox and six choice sheep.* This was food sufficient for more than two hundred men. *Once in ten days store of all sorts of wine.* It is supposed that every tenth day they drank wine; at all other times they drank water—unless we suppose the meaning of the phrase to be that his servants laid in a stock of wine every ten days.

19. *Think upon me, my God, for good.* Nehemiah wishes for no reward from man; and he only asks mercy at the hand of his God for what His providence enabled him to do; and which, according to the good hand of his God upon him, he had done faithfully.

MATTHEW HENRY — CHAPTER 6

Verses 1–9

Two plots upon Nehemiah.

I. A plot to trepan him into a snare. The enemies had an account that all the breaches of the wall were made up, so that they considered it as good as done, though at that time the *doors of the gates* were off the hinges (*v.* 1); they must therefore now or never, by one bold stroke, take off Nehemiah. 1. With subtlety they courted him to meet them in a village in the lot of Benjamin: "*Come, let us meet together* to consult about the common interests of our provinces." *But they thought to do him a mischief.* 2. He declined the motion. His care was that the work might not cease; he knew it would if he left it ever so little; and *why should it cease while I come down to you?* Four times *I answered them* (says he) *after the same manner*, *v.* 4.

II. A plot to terrify him from his work. This therefore Sanballat attempts, but in vain. 1. He endeavours to possess Nehemiah with an apprehension that his undertaking to build the walls of Jerusalem was generally represented as factious and seditious, *v.* 5–7. This is written to him in *an open letter*, as a thing generally known and talked of, and Gashmu will aver it for truth, that Nehemiah was aiming to make himself king and to shake off the Persian yoke. Now Sanballat pretends to inform Nehemiah of this as a friend—"*Let us take counsel together* how to quell the report." He hoped, like Judas, to kiss and kill. Nehemiah not only denied that such things were true, but that they were reported; he was better known than to be thus suspected. 2. Thus he escaped the snare and kept his ground. While we keep a good conscience, let us trust God with our good name.

He lifts up his heart to Heaven in this short prayer: *Now therefore, O God! strengthen my hands.* When, in our Christian work and warfare, we are entering upon any particular services or conflicts, this is a good prayer—"*Now therefore, O God! strengthen my hands.*"

Verses 10–14

The Jews' enemies leave no stone unturned, to take Nehemiah off from building the wall about Jerusalem. Now they try to drive him into the temple for his own safety; let him be anywhere but at his work.

I. How basely the enemies managed this temptation.

1. That which they designed was to bring Nehemiah to do a foolish thing, that they might laugh at him (*v.* 13): *That I should be afraid*, and so they might have *matter for an evil report*, and *might reproach me.*

2. The tools they made use of were a pretended prophet and prophetess, whom they hired to persuade Nehemiah to quit his work and retire for his own safety. The pretended prophet was Shemaiah, of whom it is said that he was *shut up* in his own house, under pretence of retirement for meditation. Nehe-

JAMIESON, FAUSSET, BROWN — CHAPTER 6

Vss. 1-19. Sanballat Practises against Nehemiah by Insidious Attempts. **2. Sanballat and Geshem sent unto me**—The Samaritan leaders, convinced that they could not overcome Nehemiah by open arms, resolved to gain advantage over him by deceit and stratagem. With this in view, under pretext of terminating their differences in an amicable manner, they invited him to a conference. The place of rendezvous was fixed "in *some one* of the villages in the plain of Ono." "In the villages" is, *Heb.*, "in Cephirim," or Cephirah, the name of a town in the territory of Benjamin (Josh. 9:17; 18: 26). Nehemiah, however, apprehensive of some intended hischief, prudently declined the invitation. Though it was repeated four times, his uniform answer was that his presence could not be dispensed with from the important work in which he was engaged. This was one, though not the only, reason. The principal ground of his refusal was that his seizure or death at their hands would certainly put a stop to the further progress of the fortifications. **5-9. Then sent Sanballat his servant . . . the fifth time with an open letter in his hand**—In Western Asia, letters, after being rolled up like a map, are flattened to the breadth of an inch; and instead of being sealed, they are pasted at the ends. In Eastern Asia, the Persians make up their letters in the form of a roll about six inches long, and a bit of paper is fastened round it with gum, and sealed with an impression of ink, which resembles our printers' ink, but it is not so thick. Letters were, and are still, sent to persons of distinction in a bag or purse, and even to equals they are enclosed—the tie being made with a colored ribbon. But to inferiors, or persons who are to be treated contemptuously, the letters were sent open—i.e., not enclosed in a bag. Nehemiah, accustomed to the punctillious ceremonial of the Persian court, would at once notice the want of the usual formality and know that it was from designed disrespect. The strain of the letter was equally insolent. It was to this effect: The fortifications with which he was so busy were intended to strengthen his position in the view of a meditated revolt: he had engaged prophets to incite the people to enter into his design and support his claim to be their native king; and, to stop the circulation of such reports, which would soon reach the court, he was earnestly besought to come to the wished-for conference. Nehemiah, strong in the consciousness of his own integrity, and penetrating the purpose of this shallow artifice, replied that there were no rumors of the kind described, that the idea of a revolt and the stimulating addresses of hired demagogues were stories of the writer's own invention, and that he declined now, as formerly, to leave his work. **10-14. Afterward I came unto the house of Shemaiah,** etc.—This man was the son of a priest, who was an intimate and

ADAM CLARKE — CHAPTER 6

2. *Come, let us meet together in . . . the plain of Ono.* They wished to get him out of Jerusalem from among his friends, that they might either carry him off or murder him. Ono is supposed to have been in the tribe of Benjamin, near Jordan.

3. *I am doing a great work.* Though he knew their design, he did not think it prudent to mention it. Had he done so, they would probably have gone to extremities, finding that they were discovered; and perhaps in a formidable body attacked Jerusalem, when ill provided to sustain such a shock. They wished to effect their purpose rather by treachery than by open violence.

5. *With an open letter in his hand.* This was an insult to a person of Nehemiah's quality, as letters sent to chiefs and governors in the East are always carefully folded up, and put in costly silken bags, and these carefully sealed. The circumstance is thus marked to show the contempt he (Sanballat) had for him.

6. *And Gashmu saith it.* You are accused of crimes against the state, and Geshem, the Arabian, is your accuser.

7. *Thou hast also appointed prophets.* Persons who pretend to be commissioned to preach to the people, and say, "Nehemiah reigneth!" *Come now therefore, and let us take counsel.* Come and justify yourself before me. This was a trick to get Nehemiah into his power.

8. *There are no such things done.* You well know that what you say is false. I shall not, therefore, trouble myself about a false charge.

10. *Who was shut up.* Lived in a sequestered, solitary state, pretending to sanctity and to close intercourse with God.

MATTHEW HENRY

miah went to his house to consult him, *v.* 10. Other prophets there were, and one prophetess, Noadiah (*v.* 14), that were in the interest of the Jews' enemies.

3. The pretence was plausible. These prophets suggested to Nehemiah that the enemies would come and slay him, *in the night*. They pretended to be much concerned for his safety. They very gravely advised him to hide himself in the temple till the danger was over. If Nehemiah had been prevailed upon to do this, immediately the people would both have left off their work and thrown down their arms and everyone would have shifted for his own safety and then the enemies might easily, and without opposition, have broken down the wall again.

II. Nehemiah vanquished this temptation, and came off conqueror.

1. He immediately resolved not to yield to it, *v.* 11. "*Should such a man as I flee?* I will not go in. I will rather die at my work than live in an inglorious retreat from it."

2. He was immediately aware of what was the rise of it (*v.* 12): "*I perceived that God had not sent him*, that he gave this advice, not by any divine direction, but with a design against me." Two things Nehemiah says he dreaded (1) Offending God: *That I should be afraid, and do so, and sin*. Sin is that which above anything we should dread; and a good preservative it is against sin to be afraid of nothing but sin. (2) Shaming himself: *That they might reproach me*.

3. He humbly begs of God to reckon with them for their base designs upon him (*v.* 14): *My God, think thou upon Tobiah*, and the rest of them, *according to their works*.

Verses 15–19

Nehemiah is here finishing the wall of Jerusalem, and yet still has trouble created by his enemies.

I. Tobiah, and the other adversaries of the Jews, had the mortification to see the wall built up, notwithstanding all their attempts to hinder it. The wall was finished *in fifty-two days*, and we have reason to believe they rested on the sabbaths, *v.* 15. Many were employed, and what they did they did cheerfully, because they loved it. When the enemies heard that the wall was finished before they thought it was well begun, they were *much cast down in their own eyes*, *v.* 16. They envied the prosperity and success of the Jews, grieved to see the walls of Jerusalem built. If it were of God, it was to no purpose to think of opposing it; it would certainly prevail and be victorious.

II. Nehemiah had the vexation notwithstanding this, to see some of his own people treacherously corresponding with Tobiah. Many in Judah were in a strict but secret confederacy with him to advance the interest of his country, though it would certainly be the ruin of their own. They were *sworn unto him*, not as their prince, but as their friend and ally, because both he and his son had married daughters of Israel, *v.* 18. See the mischief of marrying with strangers; for one heathen that was converted by it ten Jews were perverted. They had the impudence to court Nehemiah himself into a friendship with him. They were so false as to betray Nehemiah's counsels to him. Thus were all their thoughts against him for evil, yet God thought upon him for good.

JAMIESON, FAUSSET, BROWN

confidential friend of Nehemiah. The young man claimed to be endowed with the gift of prophecy. Having been secretly bribed by Sanballat, he, in his pretended capacity of prophet, told Nehemiah that his enemies were that night to make an attempt upon his life. He advised him, at the same time, to consult his safety by concealing himself in the sanctuary, a crypt which, from its sanctity, was strong and secure.

But the noble-minded governor determined at all hazards to remain at his post, and not bring discredit on the cause of God and religion by his unworthy cowardice in leaving the temple and city unprotected.

This plot, together with a secret collusion between the enemy and the nobles of Judah who were favorably disposed towards the bad Samaritan in consequence of his Jewish connections (vs. 18), the undaunted courage and vigilance of Nehemiah were enabled, with the blessing of God, to defeat, and the erection of the walls thus built in troublous times (Dan. 9:25) was happily completed (vs. 15) in the brief space of fifty-two days. So rapid execution, even supposing some parts of the old wall standing, cannot be sufficiently accounted for, except by the consideration that the builders labored with the ardor of religious zeal, as men employed in the work of God.

ADAM CLARKE

14. *And on the prophetess Noadiah*. Whether this was a prophet or prophetess, we cannot tell. Only the Hebrew text makes her a *prophetess;* all the versions have "Noadiah the prophet," except the Arabic, which has "Younadaa the prophet." I think we should read, "Noadiah the prophet."

15. *The twenty and fifth . . . of . . . Elul*. This Jewish month answers to a part of our August and September. *Fifty and two days*. I see no difficulty in supposing that several thousand workmen, each of whom was working as for God, should be able to complete this wall in fifty-two days. There is little doubt that several parts of the old wall were entire; in many places the foundations still remained; there were all the materials of the old wall still at hand; and though they had to clear and carry away much rubbish, yet they do not appear to have had any stones to quarry.

16. *This work was wrought of our God*. This is an additional reason why we should not wonder at the shortness of the time in which so great a work was done, for God helped them by an especial providence; and this was so very observable that their *carnal* enemies could discover it.

17. *The nobles of Judah sent many letters*. The circumstances marked in this and the following verses show still more clearly the difficulties which Nehemiah had to encounter; he had enemies without and false friends within. A treacherous correspondence was carried on between the nobles of Judah and the Ammonites; and had almost any other man been at the head of the Jewish affairs, Jerusalem had never been reestablished.

18. *He was the son in law of Shechaniah*. Previously to the coming of Nehemiah, the Jews seemed to be fast intermixing with the heathen, by intermarriages with Ashdodites, Ammonites, and Moabites; see chap. xiii. 23. Ezra had many evils of this kind to redress (Ezra ix. 3, etc.), chiefly among the common people, though there were both chiefs and priests in that trespass. But here we find the heathen and Jewish nobles interlinked; and the latter were so far imbued with the spirit of idolatry that they forgot God, His service, their brethren, and their own souls.

MATTHEW HENRY

CHAPTER 7

Verses 1–4

God saith concerning his church (Isa. lxii. 6), *I have set watchmen upon thy walls, O Jerusalem!* This is Nehemiah's care here; for dead walls, without living watchmen, are but a poor defence to a city.

I. He appointed *the porters, singers, and Levites*, in their places to their work. God's worship is the defence of a place, and his ministers, when they mind their duty, are watchmen on the walls.

II. He appointed two governors or consuls, to whom he committed the care of the city, and gave them in charge to provide for the public peace and safety. Hanani, his brother, who came to him with the tidings of the desolations of Jerusalem, was one, a man of approved integrity and affection to his country; the other was Hananiah, who had been ruler of the palace. Of this Hananiah it is said that he was a *faithful man and one that feared God above many*, *v.* 2.

JAMIESON, FAUSSET, BROWN

CHAPTER 7

Vss. 1-4. NEHEMIAH COMMITS THE CHARGE OF JERUSALEM TO HANANI AND HANANIAH. **2. I gave my brother Hanani . . . charge over Jerusalem**—If, as is commonly supposed, Nehemiah was now contemplating a return to Shushan according to his promise, it was natural that he should wish to entrust the custody of Jerusalem and the management of its civic affairs to men on whose ability, experience, and fidelity, he could confide. Hanani, a near relative (ch. 1:2), was one, and with him was associated, as colleague, Hananiah, "the ruler of the palace"—i.e., the marshal or chamberlain of the viceregal court, which Nehemiah had maintained in Jerusalem. The high religious principle, as well as the patriotic spirit of those two men, recommended them as pre-eminently qualified for being invested with an official trust of such peculiar importance. **he . . . feared God above many**—The piety of Hananiah is especially mentioned as the ground of his eminent fidelity in the discharge of all his duties and, consequently, the reason of the confidence which Nehemiah reposed in him; for he was fully persuaded that Hananiah's fear of God would preserve him from those temptations to treachery and unfaithfulness which he was likely to encounter on the governor's departure from Jerusalem. **3. Let not**

ADAM CLARKE

CHAPTER 7

2. *My brother Hanani*. This was the person who gave Nehemiah the account of the desolate state of the Jews, chap. i. 2. He is now made ruler of Jerusalem, probably because Nehemiah was about to return to the Persian court.

MATTHEW HENRY

III. He gave orders about the shutting of the gates and the guarding of the walls, *v.* 3, 4. The city, in compass, was large. The walls enclosed the same ground as formerly; but much of it lay waste, for the houses were not built; so that Nehemiah walled the city in faith, and with an eye to that promise of the replenishing of it which God had lately made by the prophet, Zech. viii. 3, &c. Though the people were now few, he believed they would be multiplied and therefore built the walls so as to make room for them. The care of Nehemiah for it. He ordered the rulers of the city themselves, 1. To stand by, and see the city-gates shut up and barred every night. 2. To take care that they should not be opened in the morning till they could see that all was clear and quiet. 3. To set sentinels who should, in case of the approach of the enemy, give timely notice to the city of the danger; and, as it came to their turn to watch, they must post themselves *over against their own houses,* because of them, they would be in a particular manner careful. The public safety depends upon everyone's particular care to guard himself and his own family against sin, that common enemy. They were made sensible that *except the Lord kept the city the watchman waked but in vain,* Ps. cxxvii. 1.

Verses 5–73

Another good project of Nehemiah's. He knew very well that the safety of a city, under God, depends more upon the number and valour of the inhabitants than upon the height or strength of its walls; and therefore he thought fit to take an account of the people, that he might find what families had formerly had their settlement in Jerusalem, that he might bring them back, and what families could be influenced by their religion, or by their business, to come and rebuild the houses in Jerusalem and dwell in them. It is the wisdom of the governors of a nation to keep the balance even between the city and country, that the metropolis be not so extravagantly large as to drain and impoverish the country, nor yet so weak as not to be able to protect it.

I. Whence this good design of Nehemiah's came. He owns, *My God put it into my heart, v.* 5.

II. What method he took in prosecution of it.

1. He called the rulers together, and the people, that he might have an account of the present state of their families—their number and strength, and where they were settled.

2. He reviewed the old *register of the genealogy of those who came up at the first,* and compared the present accounts with that; and here we have the repetition of that out of Ezra ii. There are many differences in the numbers between this catalogue and that in Ezra. What differences there are we may suppose to arise either from the mistakes of transcribers, or from the diversity of the copies from which they were taken. Or perhaps one was the account of them when they set out from Babylon with Zerubbabel, the other when they came to Jerusalem. The sum totals are all just the same there and here, except of the singing-men and singing-women, which there are 200, here 245. An account of the offerings which were given towards the work of God, *v.* 70, &c. differs much from that in Ezra ii. 68, 69, and it must be questioned whether it refers to the same contribution; here the tirshatha, or chief governor, who there was not mentioned, begins the offering; and the single sum mentioned there exceeds all those here put together; yet it is probable that it was the same, but that followed one copy of the lists, this another; for the last verse is the same here that it was Ezra ii. 70, and Ezra iii. 1. Blessed be God that our faith and hope are not built upon the niceties of names and numbers, genealogy, and chronology, but on the great things of the law and gospel.

JAMIESON, FAUSSET, BROWN

the gates of Jerusalem be opened until the sun be hot, etc.—In the East it is customary to open the gates of a city at sunrise, and to bar them at sunset—a rule which is very rarely, and not except to persons of authority, infringed upon. Nehemiah recommended that the gates of Jerusalem should not be opened so early; a precaution necessary at a time when the enemy was practising all sorts of dangerous stratagems, to ensure that the inhabitants were all astir and enjoyed the benefit of clear broad daylight for observing the suspicious movements of any enemy. The propriety of regularly barring the gates at sunset was, in this instance, accompanied with the appointment of a number of the people to act as sentinels, each mounting guard in front of his own house. **4. Now the city was large and great**—The walls being evidently built on the old foundations, the city covered a large extent of surface, as all Oriental towns do, the houses standing apart with gardens and orchards intervening. This extent, in the then state of Jerusalem, was the more observable as the population was comparatively small, and the habitations of the most rude and simple construction—mere wooden sheds or coverings of loose, unmortared stones.

5-38. Genealogy of Those Who Came at the First out of Babylon. **5. my God put into mine heart to gather together the nobles,** etc.—The arrangement about to be described, though dictated by mere common prudence, is, in accordance with the pious feelings of Nehemiah, ascribed not to his own prudence or reflection, but to the grace of God prompting and directing him. He resolved to prepare a register of the returned exiles, containing an exact record of the family and ancestral abode of every individual. While thus directing his attention, he discovered a register of the first detachment who had come under the care of Zerubbabel. It is transcribed in the following verses, and differs in some few particulars from that given in Ezra 2. But the discrepancy is sufficiently accounted for from the different circumstances in which the two registers were taken; that of Ezra having been made up at Babylon, while that of Nehemiah was drawn out in Judea, after the walls of Jerusalem had been rebuilt. The lapse of so many years might well be expected to make a difference appear in the catalogue, through death or other causes; in particular, one person being, according to Jewish custom, called by different names. Thus Hariph (vs. 24) is the same as Jorah (Ezra 2:18), Sia (vs. 47) the same as Siaha (Ezra 2:44), etc. Besides other purposes to which this genealogy of the nobles, rulers, and people was subservient, one leading object contemplated by it was to ascertain with accuracy the parties to whom the duty legally belonged of ministering at the altar and conducting the various services of the temple. For guiding to exact information in this important point of inquiry, the possession of the old register of Zerubbabel was invaluable.

39-73. Of the Priests. **39. The priests**—It appears that only four of the courses of the priests returned from the captivity; and that the course of Abia (Luke 1:5) is not in the list. But it must be noticed that these four courses were afterwards divided into twenty-four, which retained the names of the original courses which David appointed. **70. some of the chief of the fathers,** etc.—With verse 69 the register ends, and the thread of Nehemiah's history is resumed. He was the *tirshatha* or governor, and the liberality displayed by him and some of the leading men for the suitable equipment of the ministers of religion, forms the subject of the remaining portion of the chapter. Their donations consisted principally in garments. This would appear a singular description of gifts to be made by any one among us; but, in the East, a present of garments, or of any article of use, is conformable to the prevailing sentiments and customs of society. **drams of gold**—i.e., darics. A daric was a gold coin of ancient Persia. **71. pound of silver**—i.e., *mina* (sixty shekels, or about $45). **73. So . . . all Israel, dwelt in their cities**—The utility of these genealogical registers was thus found in guiding to a knowledge of the cities and localities in each tribe to which every family anciently belonged.

ADAM CLARKE

3. *Until the sun be hot.* The meaning of this is, the gates were not to be opened before sunrise, and always shut at sunset. *Every one . . . over against his house.* Each was obliged to guard that part of the wall that was opposite to his own dwelling.

4. *The houses were not builded.* The city was not yet rebuilt, only a row of houses in the inside of the wall all round.

5. *God put into mine heart.* With this good man every good thing was of God. If he purposed any good, it was because God put in into his heart; if he did any good, it was because the good hand of his God was upon him; if he expected any good, it was because he earnestly prayed God to remember him for good.

7. *Who came with Zerubbabel.* The register which he found was that of the persons only who came long before Zerubbabel, Ezra, and Joshua, the son of Josedek, which register could not answer in every respect to the state of the people then. Several persons and families were no doubt dead, and others had arrived since. Nehemiah probably altered it only in such parts, leaving the body of it as it was before; and this will account for the difference between it and the register that is found in Ezra, chap. ii.

8. *The children of Parosh.* As this chapter is almost entirely the same with the second chapter of the Book of Ezra, it is not necessary to add anything to what is said there.

19. *The children of Bigvai, two thousand threescore and seven.* Some MSS. read 2,066, as in Ezra ii.

33. *The men of the other Nebo.* The word *other* is not in the parallel place, Ezra ii. 29, and is wanting in many of Kennicott's and De Rossi's MSS. This *Nebo* is supposed to be the same as Nob or Nobah, in the tribe of Benjamin.

34. *The other Elam.* To distinguish him from the Elam mentioned in v. 12.

73. *All Israel, dwelt in their cities.* It was in reference to this particularly that the public registers were examined; for by them they found the different families, and consequently the cities, villages, etc., which belonged to them, according to the ancient division of the lands. It seems that the examination of the registers occupied about a month; for as soon as the walls were finished, which was in the sixth month, chap. vi. 15, Nehemiah instituted the examination mentioned in this chapter, v. 5; and by the concluding verse we find that the different families had got into their paternal cities in the seventh month, answering to a part of our September and October. Thus the register determined everything; there was not room for complaint, and none to accuse the governor of partiality.

MATTHEW HENRY — CHAPTER 8

Verses 1–8

An account of a solemn religious assembly, and the good work that was done in that assembly.

I. The time of it was the *first day of the seventh month, v.* 2. That was the day of the *feast of trumpets,* which is called a *sabbath,* and on which they were to

JAMIESON, FAUSSET, BROWN — CHAPTER 8

Vss. 1-8. Religious Manner of Reading and Hearing the Law. **1. all the people gathered themselves together as one man**—The occasion was the celebration of the feast of the seventh month (ch. 7:73). The beginning of every month was ushered in as a sacred festival; but this, the com-

ADAM CLARKE — CHAPTER 8

MATTHEW HENRY

have a *holy convocation*, Lev. xxiii. 24; Num. xxix. 1. But that was not all: it was on that day that the altar was set up, and they began to offer their burnt-offerings after their return out of captivity, a recent mercy in the memory of many then living.

II. The place was in the *street that was before the water-gate* (*v.* 1), a spacious broad street, able to contain so great a multitude, which the court of the temple was not; for probably it was not now built nearly so large as it had been in Solomon's time. Sacrifices were to be offered only at the door of the temple, but praying, and praising, and preaching, were, and are, services of religion as acceptably performed in one place as in another. When this congregation thus met in the street of the city no doubt God was with them.

III. The persons that met were all the people, who were not compelled to come, but voluntarily gathered themselves together by common agreement, as one man: not only men came, but women and children. Little ones, as they come to the exercise of reason, must be trained up in the exercises of religion.

IV. The master of this assembly was Ezra the priest. 1. His call to the service was very clear; for being in office as a priest, and qualified as a scribe, the *people spoke to him to bring the book of the law* and read it to them, *v.* 1. 2. His post was very convenient. He stood in a pulpit or tower of wood, *which they made for the word, for the preaching of the word*, that what he said might be the more gracefully delivered and the better heard, and that the eyes of the hearers might be upon him, Luke iv. 20. 3. He had several assistants. Some of these stood with him (*v.* 4), six on his right hand and seven on his left. Others who are mentioned (*v.* 7) seem to have been employed at the same time in other places near at hand, to read and expound to those who could not come within hearing of Ezra.

V. The religious exercises performed in this assembly were not ceremonial, but moral, praying and preaching. Ezra, as president of the assembly, was, 1. The people's mouth to God, and they affectionately joined with him, *v.* 6. He blessed the Lord as the great God, and the people said *Amen, Amen, lifted up up their hands* and *bowed their heads* in reverence. 2. God's mouth to the people, and they attentively hearkened to him. *Ezra brought the law before the congregation*, *v.* 2. Ministers, when they go to the pulpit, should take their Bibles with them; Ezra did so; thence they must fetch their knowledge. See 2 Chron. xvii. 9. He opened the book with great reverence and solemnity, *in the sight of all the people v.* 5. He and others read in the book of the law, *from morning till noon* (*v.* 3), and they read *distinctly*, *v.* 8. Let those that read and preach the word learn also to deliver themselves distinctly, as those who understand what they say and are affected with it themselves, and who desire that those they speak to may understand it, retain it, and be affected with it likewise. *It is a snare for a man to devour that which is holy.* What they read they expounded. It is requisite that those who hear the word should understand it. It is therefore required of those who are teachers by office that they explain the word and give the sense of it. When Ezra opened the book *all the people stood up* (*v.* 5), thereby showing respect both to Ezra and to the word he was about to read.

Verses 9–12

I. The people were wounded with the words of the law that were read to them. The law shows men their sins, and their misery and danger because of sin. Therefore when they heard it they *all wept* (*v.* 9): it was a good sign that their hearts were tender, like Josiah's when he heard the words of the law. They wept to think how they had offended God.

II. They were healed and comforted with the words of peace that were spoken to them. It was one of the solemn feasts, on which it was their duty to rejoice; and even sorrow for sin must not hinder our joy in God, but rather lead us to it. Ezra was pleased to see them so affected with the word, but Nehemiah observed to him, and Ezra concurred in the thought, that it was now unseasonable. This day was holy and therefore was to be celebrated with joy and praise, not as if it were *a day to afflict their souls.* They forbade the people to *mourn and weep* (*v.* 9): *Be not sorry* (*v.* 10); *hold your peace, neither be you grieved*, *v.* 11. They commanded them to testify their joy, to put *on the garments of praise instead of the spirit of heaviness.* They allowed them, in token of their joy, to feast themselves. But then it must be, 1. With charity to the poor: "*Send portions to those for whom nothing is prepared* that your abundance may supply their want, that they may rejoice with you." 2. It must be with piety and devotion: *The joy of the Lord is your strength.* Holy joy will be oil to the

JAMIESON, FAUSSET, BROWN

mencement of the seventh month, was kept with distinguished honor as "the feast of trumpets," which extended over two days. It was the first day of the seventh ecclesiastical year, and the new year's day of the Jewish civil year, on which account it was held as "a great day." The place where the general concourse of people was held was "at the water gate," on the south rampart. Through that gate the Nethinims or Gibeonites brought water into the temple, and there was a spacious area in front of it.

they spake unto Ezra the scribe to bring the book of the law of Moses—He had come to Jerusalem twelve or thirteen years previous to Nehemiah. He either remained there or had returned to Babylon in obedience to the royal order, and for the discharge of important duties. He had returned along with Nehemiah, but in a subordinate capacity. From the time of Nehemiah's appointment to the dignity of *tirshatha*, Ezra had retired into private life. Although cordially and zealously co-operating with the former patriot in his important measures of reform, the pious priest had devoted his time and attention principally toward producing a complete edition of the canonical Scriptures. The public reading of the Scriptures was required by the law to be made every seventh year; but during the long period of the captivity this excellent practice, with many others, had fallen into neglect, till revived on this occasion. That there was a strong and general desire among the returned exiles in Jerusalem to hear the word of God read to them indicates a greatly improved tone of religious feeling. **4. Ezra . . . . stood upon a pulpit of wood**—Not made in the form known to us, but only a raised scaffold or platform, broad enough to allow fourteen persons to stand with ease upon it. Ezra's duty was very laborious, as he continued reading aloud from morning until midday, but his labor was lightened by the aid of the other priests present. Their presence was of importance, partly to show their cordial agreement with Ezra's declaration of divine truth; and partly to take their share with him in the important duty of publicly reading and expounding the Scripture. **5. when he opened it, all the people stood up**—This attitude they assumed either from respect to God's word, or, rather, because the reading was prefaced by a solemn prayer, which was concluded by a general expression of amen, amen. **7, 8. caused the people to understand the law . . . gave the sense**—Commentators are divided in opinion as to the import of this statement. Some think that Ezra read the law in pure Hebrew, while the Levites, who assisted him, translated it sentence by sentence into Chaldee, the vernacular dialect which the exiles spoke in Babylon. Others maintain that the duty of these Levites consisted in explaining to the people, many of whom had become very ignorant, what Ezra had read.

9-15. THE PEOPLE COMFORTED. **9. This day is holy unto the Lord . . . mourn not, nor weep**—A deep sense of their national sins, impressively brought to their remembrance by the reading of the law and its denunciations, affected the hearts of the people with penitential sorrow.

ADAM CLARKE

1. *The street that was before the water gate.* The gate which led from the Temple to the brook Kidron.

2. *Upon the first day of the seventh month.* This was the first day of what was called the civil year; and on it was the Feast of Trumpets, the year being ushered in by the sound of these instruments.

4. *Stood upon a pulpit of wood. Migdal*, a "tower," a "platform," raised up for the purpose, to elevate him sufficiently for the people both to see and hear him; for it is said, v. 5, that "he was above all the people."

5. *All the people stood up.* This was out of respect to the sacred word; in imitation of this, when the Gospel for the day is read in our churches, all the people stand up.

8. *So they read in the book.* For an explanation of this verse, see the observations at the end of the chapter.

9. *Nehemiah, which is the Tirshatha.* This puts it out of doubt that, when the Tirshatha is mentioned, Nehemiah himself is intended, Tirshatha being the name of his office. *Mourn not, nor weep.* This is a holy day to God; a day appointed for general rejoicing in Him who has turned our captivity, restored to us His law, and again established among us His ordinances.

10. *Eat the fat, and drink the sweet.* Eat and drink the best that you have; and while ye are feeding yourselves in the fear of the Lord, remember those who cannot feast, and send portions to them, that the joy and the thanksgiving may be general. Let the poor have reason to rejoice as well as you. *For the joy of the Lord*

MATTHEW HENRY

wheels of our obedience.

III. The assembly complied with the directions that were given them. Their weeping was *stilled* (*v.* 11) and they *made great mirth*, *v.* 12. Those that *sow in tears shall reap in joy*; those that tremble at the convictions of the word may triumph in the consolations of it. They made mirth, not because they had the fat to eat and the sweet to drink, and a great deal of good company, but because they had *understood the words that were declared to them.* The darkness of trouble arises from the darkness of ignorance and mistake. When the words were first declared to them they wept; but, when they understood them, they rejoiced, finding at length precious promises made to those who repented and reformed and that therefore there was hope in Israel.

Verses 13–18

I. The people's renewed attendance upon the word. The next day after, though it was no festival, the chief of them came together again to hear Ezra expound (*v.* 13). Now the priests and the Levites themselves came with *the chief of the people to Ezra*, as it is in the margin, *that they might instruct in the words of the law*; they came to be taught themselves, that they might be qualified to teach others. Now, they being by trial made more sensible than ever of their own deficiencies and his excellencies, on the second day their humility set them at Ezra's feet, as learners of him.

II. The people's ready obedience to the word as soon as they were made sensible of their duty therein. It is probable that Ezra, *after the wisdom of his God that was in his hand* (Ezra vii. 25), when they applied to him for instruction out of the law on the second day of the seventh month, read to them those laws which concerned the feasts of that month, and, among the rest, that of the feast of tabernacles, Lev. xxiii. 34; Deut. xvi. 13. 1. The divine appointment of the feast of tabernacles reviewed, *v.* 14, 15. *They found written in the law* a commandment concerning it. This feast of tabernacles was a memorial of their dwelling in tents in the wilderness, a representation of our tabernacle state in this world. The conversion of the nations to the faith of Christ is foretold under the figure of this feast (Zech. xiv. 16); they shall come to *keep the feast of tabernacles*, as having here no continuing city. The people were themselves to fetch boughs of trees (they of Jerusalem fetched them from the mount of Olives) and to make booths, or arbours, of them, in which they were to lodge. 2. This appointment religiously observed, *v.* 16, 17. (1) They observed the ceremony: *They sat in booths*, which the priests and Levites set up in the courts of the temple; those that had houses of their own set up booths on the roofs of them, or in their courts; and those that had not, set them up in the streets. All their holy feasts, but this especially, were to be celebrated with joy. (2) They attended the reading and expounding of the word of God during all the days of the feast, *v.* 18.

JAMIESON, FAUSSET, BROWN

But notwithstanding the painful remembrances of their national sins which the reading of the law awakened, the people were exhorted to cherish the feelings of joy and thankfulness associated with a sacred festival (see on Lev. 23:23-25).

By sending portions of it to their poorer brethren (Deut. 16:11, 14; Esther 9:19), they would also enable them to participate in the public rejoicings.

16-18. THEY KEEP THE FEAST OF TABERNACLES. **16. the people went forth, and brought . . . and made themselves booths,** etc.—(See on Lev. 23:34-44; Deut. 16:13-17). **17. since the days of Jeshua . . . had not the children of Israel done so**—This national feast had not been neglected for so protracted a period. Besides that it is impossible that such a flagrant disregard of the law could have been tolerated by Samuel, David, and other pious rulers, its observance is sufficiently indicated (I Kings 8:2, 65; II Chron. 7:9) and expressly recorded (Ezra 3:4). But the meaning is, that the popular feelings had never been raised to such a height of enthusiastic joy since the time of their entrance into Canaan, as now on their return after a long and painful captivity. **18. Also day by day . . . he read in the book of the law of God**—This was more than was enjoined (Deut. 31:10-12), and arose from the exuberant zeal of the time. **on the eighth day was a solemn assembly**—This was the last and great day of the feast (Num. 30:35). In later times, other ceremonies which increased the rejoicing were added (John 7: 37).

ADAM CLARKE

is your strength. This is no gluttonous and drunken festival that enervates the body and enfeebles the mind. From your religious feast your bodies will acquire strength and your minds power and fervor, so that you shall be able to do His will, and to do it cheerfully.

14. *In the feast of the seventh month.* That is, the Feast of Tabernacles, which was held in commemoration of the sojourning of their fathers in the wilderness after they had been delivered from the Egyptian bondage. Now, having been delivered from the Babylonish captivity, and the proper time of the year occurring, it was their especial duty to keep the same feast.

15. *Fetch olive branches.* For everything concerning this Feast of Tabernacles, see the notes on Leviticus xxiii.

16. *Upon the roof of his house.* It need scarcely be repeated that the houses in the East are generally built with flat roofs. On these they reposed; on these they took the air in the heats of summer; and on these they oftentimes slept.

17. *Since the days of Jeshua.* No Feast of Tabernacles since Joshua's time had been so heartily and so piously celebrated.

On the subject in v. 8, I beg leave to make observation: "So they read in the book in the law of God distinctly, and gave the sense, and caused them to undertsand the reading." The Israelites, having been lately brought out of the Babylonish captivity, in which they had continued seventy years, according to the prediction of Jeremiah, chap. xxv. 11, were not only extremely corrupt, but it appears that they had in general lost the knowledge of the ancient Hebrew to such a degree that, when the book of the law was read, they did not understand it; but certain Levites stood by and "gave the sense," i.e., translated into the Chaldee dialect.

MATTHEW HENRY

CHAPTER 9

Verses 1–3

A general account of a public fast which the children of Israel kept, probably by order from Nehemiah. It was a fast that men appointed, but such *a fast as God had chosen*; for, 1. It was a day *to afflict the soul*, Isa. lviii. 5. Probably they assembled in the courts of the temple, and they there appeared in sackcloth and in the posture of mourners, with earth on their heads, *v.* 1. They were restrained from *weeping*, *ch*, viii. 9, but now they were directed to weep. 2. It was a day *to loose the bands of wickedness*, and that is the fast that God has chosen, Isa. lviii. 6. Without this, spreading sackcloth and ashes under us is but a jest. 3. It was a day of communion with God. *They fasted to him, even to him* (Zech. vii. 5); for, (1) They spoke to him in prayer. Fasting without prayer is a body without a soul, a worthless carcase. (2) They heard him speaking to them by his word; for they read in the book of the law that, in the glass of the law, we may see our deformities and defilements, and know what to acknowledge and what to amend. The time was equally divided between these two. Three hours they spent in reading, expounding, and applying the scriptures, and three hours in confessing sin and praying; so that they stayed together six hours, and spent all the time in the solemn acts of religion, without saying, *Behold, what a weariness is it!*

Verses 4–38

An account how the work of this fast-day was carried on. 1. The names of the ministers that were

JAMIESON, FAUSSET, BROWN

CHAPTER 9

Vss. 1-3. A SOLEMN FAST AND REPENTANCE OF THE PEOPLE. **1. Now in the twenty and fourth day of this month**—i.e., on the second day after the close of the feast of tabernacles, which commenced on the fourteenth and terminated on the twenty-second (Lev. 23). The day immediately after that feast, the twenty-third, had been occupied in separating the delinquents from their unlawful wives, as well, perhaps, as in taking steps for keeping aloof in future from unnecessary intercourse with the heathen around them. For although this necessary measure of reformation had been begun formerly by Ezra (Ezra 10), and satisfactorily accomplished at that time (in so far as he had information of the existing abuses, or possessed the power of correcting them) yet it appears that this reformatory work of Ezra had been only partial and imperfect. Many cases of delinquency had escaped, or new defaulters had appeared who had contracted those forbidden alliances; and there was an urgent necessity for Nehemiah again to take vigorous measures for the removal of a social evil which threatened the most disastrous consequences to the character and prosperity of the chosen people. A solemn fast was now observed for the expression of those penitential and sorrowful feelings which the reading of the law had produced, but which had been suppressed during the celebration of the feast; and the sincerity of their repentance was evinced by the decisive steps taken for the correction of existing abuses in the matter of marriage. **2. confessed their sins, and the iniquities of their fathers**—Not only did they read in

ADAM CLARKE

CHAPTER 9

1. *Now in the twenty and fourth day.* The Feast of Trumpets was on the first day of this month; on the fourteenth began the Feast of Tabernacles, which, lasting seven days, finished on the twenty-second; on the twenty-third they separated themselves from their illegitimate wives and children; and on the twenty-fourth they held a solemn day of fasting and confession of sin, and reading the law, which they closed by renewing their covenants.

2. *The seed of Israel separated themselves.* A reformation of this kind was begun by Ezra, x. 3; but it appears that either more were found out who had taken strange wives, or else those who had separated from them had taken them again. *And stood and confessed their sins, and the iniquities of their fathers.* They acknowl-

MATTHEW HENRY

employed. They are twice named (*v.* 4, 5). Either they prayed successively, or, as some think, there were eight several congregations at some distance from each other, and each had a Levite to preside in it. 2. The work itself in which they employed themselves. (1) They prayed to God for the pardon of the sins of Israel and God's favour to them. (2) They praised God; for the work of praise is not unseasonable on a fast-day; in all acts of devotion we must aim at this, *to give unto God the glory due to his name.* The summary of their prayers we have here upon record.

I. An awful adoration of God, as a perfect and glorious Being, and the fountain of all beings, *v.* 5, 6. The congregation is called upon to signify their concurrence herewith by standing up; and so the minister directs himself to God, *blessed be thy glorious name.* God is here adored, 1. As the only living and true God: *Thou art Jehovah alone.* 2. As the Creator of all things: *Thou hast made heaven, earth, and seas,* and all that is in them. 3. As the great Protector of the whole creation: "Thou preservest in being all the creatures thou hast given being to." 4. As the object of the creatures' praises: "*The host of heaven,* the world of holy angels, *worshippeth thee, v.* 6. But thy *name is exalted above all blessing and praise.*"

II. A thankful acknowledgment of God's favours to Israel.

1. Many of these are here reckoned up in order before him.

2. The particular instances of God's goodness to Israel here recounted. (1) The call of Abraham, *v.* 7. (2) The covenant God made with him to give the land of Canaan to him and his seed, a type of the better country, *v.* 8. (3) The deliverance of Israel out of Egypt, *v.* 9–11. It was seasonable to remember this now that they were interceding for the perfecting of their deliverance out of Babylon. (4) The conducting of them through the wilderness, by the pillar of cloud and fire, which showed them which way they should go, when they should remove, and when and where they should rest, directed all their stages and all their steps, *v.* 12. It was also a visible token of God's presence with them, to guide and guard them. (5) The plentiful provision made for them in the wilderness, that they might not perish for hunger: Thou *gavest them bread from heaven,* and *water out of the rock* (*v.* 15), and, to hold up their hearts, a promise that they should go in and possess the land of Canaan. They had meat and drink, food convenient in the way, and the good land at their journey's end; what would they more? This also is repeated (*v.* 20, 21) as that which was continued, notwithstanding their provocations: *Forty years didst thou sustain them.* (6) The giving of the law upon Mount Sinai. The Lawgiver was very glorious, *v.* 13. "Thou didst not only send, but camest down thyself, and *didst speak with them,*" Deut. iv. 33. No nation under the sun had such *right judgments, true laws,* and *good statutes,* Deut. iv. 8. And with *the law* and *the sabbath,* he *gave his good Spirit to instruct them, v.* 20. Besides the law given on Mount Sinai, the five books of Moses, which he wrote *as he was moved by the Holy Ghost,* were constant instructions to them. (7) The putting of them in possession of Canaan, that good land, *kingdoms and nations, v.* 22. They were made so numerous as to replenish it (*v.* 23) and so victorious as to be masters of it (*v.* 24). (8) God's great readiness to pardon their sins, and work deliverance for them, when they had by their provocations brought his judgments upon themselves. Afterwards, when they were settled in Canaan and sold themselves by their sins into the hands of their enemies, upon their submission and humble request he *gave them saviours* (*v.* 27), the judges, by whom God wrought many a great deliverance for them when they were on the brink of ruin. (9) The admonitions and fair warnings he gave them by his servants the prophets. When he delivered them from their troubles he *testified against their sins* (*v.* 28, 29), that they might not misconstrue their deliverances as connivances at their wickedness. The testimony of the prophets was the testimony of the Spirit in the prophets, and it was the Spirit of Christ in them, 1 Peter i. 10, 11. They *spoke as they were moved by the Holy Ghost,* and what they said is to be received accordingly. (10) The lengthening out of his patience and the moderating of his rebukes: *Many years did he forbear them* (*v.* 30), as loth to punish them, and waiting to see if they would repent; and when he did punish them, he did not *utterly consume them nor forsake them, v.* 31.

III. A penitent confession of sin, their own sins, and the sins of their fathers.

1. They begin with the sins of Israel in the wilderness: *They, even our fathers dealt proudly and hardened their necks, v.* 16. Pride is at the bottom of men's

JAMIESON, FAUSSET, BROWN

their recent sufferings a punishment of the national apostasy and guilt, but they had made themselves partakers of their fathers' sins by following the same evil ways. **3. they . . . read in the book of the law**—Their extraordinary zeal led them to continue this as before. **one fourth part of the day**—i.e., for three hours, twelve hours being the acknowledged length of the Jewish day (John 11:9). This solemn diet of worship, which probably commenced at the morning sacrifice, was continued for six hours, i.e., till the time of the evening sacrifice. The worship which they gave to the Lord their God, at this season of solemn national humiliation, consisted in acknowledging and adoring His great mercy in the forgiveness of their great and multiplied offenses, in delivering them from the merited judgments which they had already experienced or which they had reason to apprehend, in continuing amongst them the light and blessings of His word and worship, and in supplicating the extension of His grace and protection.

4-38. THE LEVITES CONFESS GOD'S MANIFOLD GOODNESS, AND THEIR OWN WICKEDNESS. **4. Then stood up upon the stairs**—the scaffolds or pulpits, whence the Levites usually addressed the people. There were probably several placed at convenient distances, to prevent confusion and the voice of one drowning those of the others. **cried with a loud voice unto the Lord**—Such an exertion, of course, was indispensably necessary, in order that the speakers might be heard by the vast multitude congregated in the open air. But these speakers were then engaged in expressing their deep sense of sin, as well as fervently imploring the forgiving mercy of God; and "crying with a loud voice" was a natural accompaniment of this extraordinary prayer meeting, as violent gestures and vehement tones are always the way in which the Jews, and other people in the East, have been accustomed to give utterance to deep and earnest feelings. **5. Then the Levites . . . said, Stand up and bless the Lord your God**—If this prayer was uttered by all these Levites in common, it must have been prepared and adopted beforehand, perhaps, by Ezra; but it may only embody the substance of the confession and thanksgiving. **6. Thou, even thou, art Lord alone,** etc.—In this solemn and impressive prayer, in which they make public confession of their sins, and deprecate the judgments due to the transgressions of their fathers, they begin with a profound adoration of God, whose supreme majesty and omnipotence is acknowledged in the creation, preservation, and government of all. Then they proceed to enumerate His mercies and distinguished favors to them as a nation, from the period of the call of their great ancestor and the gracious promise intimated to him in the divinely bestowed name of Abraham, a promise which implied that he was to be the Father of the faithful, the ancestor of the Messiah, and the honored individual in whose seed all the families of the earth should be blessed. Tracing in full and minute detail the signal instances of divine interposition for their deliverance and their interest—in their deliverance from Egyptian bondage—their miraculous passage through the Red Sea—the promulgation of His law—the forbearance and long-suffering shown them amid their frequent rebellions—the signal triumphs given them over their enemies—their happy settlement in the promised land—and all the extraordinary blessings, both in the form of temporal prosperity and of religious privilege, with which His paternal goodness had favored them above all other people, they charge themselves with making a miserable requital. They confess their numerous and determined acts of disobedience. They read, in the loss of their national independence and their long captivity, the severe punishment of their sins. They acknowledge that, in all heavy and continued judgments upon their nation, God had done right, but they had done wickedly. And in throwing themselves on His mercy, they express their purpose of entering into a national covenant, by which they pledge themselves to dutiful obedience in future. **22. Moreover, thou gavest them kingdoms and nations**—i.e., put them in possession of a rich country, of an extensive territory, which had been once occupied by a variety of princes and people. **and didst divide them into corners**—i.e., into tribes. The propriety of the expression arose from the various districts touching at points or angles on each other. **the land of Sihon, and the land of the king of Heshbon**—Heshbon being the capital city, the passage should run thus: the land of Sihon or the land of the king of Heshbon.

ADAM CLARKE

edged that they had been sinners against God throughout all their generations; that their fathers had sinned and were punished; and that they, with this example before their eyes, had copied their fathers' offenses.

3. *One fourth part of the day.* As they did no manner of work on this day of fasting and humiliation, so they spent the whole of it in religious duties.

5. *Stand up and bless the Lord your God.* It is the shameless custom of many congregations of people to sit still while they profess to bless and praise God by singing the psalms of David or hymns made on the plan of the gospel! I ask such persons, Did they ever feel the spirit of devotion while thus employed?

6. *Thou preservest them all.* "And Thou givest life to them all; and the host of the heavens prostrate themselves unto Thee."

14. *Madest known unto them thy holy sabbath.* They appear to have forgotten this first of all the commandments of God, during their sojourning in Egypt.

17. *And in their rebellion appointed a captain.* This clause, read according to its order in the Hebrew text, is thus: "And appointed a captain to return to their bondage in their rebellion." But it is probable that *bemiryam,* "in their rebellion," is a mistake for *bemitsrayim,* "in Egypt." This is the reading in Num. xiv. 4. The clause should undoubtedly be read, "They appointed a captain to return to their bondage in Egypt."

19. *The pillar of the cloud departed not from them.* "From over them."

21. *Their clothes waxed not old.* See Deut. viii. 4.

22. *The land of Og king of Bashan.* It is most evident that Sihon was king of Heshbon. How then can it be said that they possessed *the land of Sihon, and the land of the king of Heshbon?* The words *the land of the king of Heshbon* are wanting in two of De Rossi's MSS. In another MS. the words *and the land of* are wanting; so that the clause is read, "They possessed the land of Sihon, king of Heshbon." The Septuagint has the same reading; the Arabic nearly the same, viz., "the land of Sihon, the land of the king of Heshbon." The Syriac has, "They possessed the land of Sihon, the land of the kings of Heshbon." The reading of the text is undoubtedly wrong; that supported by the MSS. and by the Septuagint is most likely to be the true one. Those of the Arabic and Syriac contain at least no contradictory sense. The *and* in the Hebrew and our version distinguishes two lands and two kings, when it is most certain that only one land and one king can be meant; but the *vau* may be translated here as it often is, *even:* "even the land of the king of Heshbon."

25. *Became fat, and delighted themselves.* They became effeminate, fell under the power of luxury, got totally corrupted in their manners, sinned against all the mercies of God, and then were destroyed by His judgments.

27. *Thou gavest them saviours.* The whole Book of Judges is a history of God's mercies and their rebellions.

30. *Many years didst thou forbear.* It is supposed that Nehemiah refers here principally to

MATTHEW HENRY

obstinacy and disobedience. When men make no right use either of God's ordinances or of his providences, what can be expected from them? Two great sins are here specified, which they were guilty of in the wilderness—meditating a return, (1) To Egyptian slavery, which, for the sake of the garlick and onions, they preferred before the glorious liberty of the Israel of God attended with some difficulty and inconvenience. (2) To Egyptian idolatry: *They made a molten calf*, and were so sottish as to say, *This is thy God.*

2. They next bewail the provocations of their fathers after they were put in possession of Canaan.

3. They at length come nearer to their own day, and lament the sins which had brought those judgments upon them which they had long been groaning under and were now but in part delivered from. Two things they charge upon themselves and their fathers, as the cause of their troubles:—(1) A contempt of the good law God had given them: They *sinned against thy judgments*, the dictates of divine wisdom, and the demands of divine sovereignty. (2) A contempt of the good land God had given them (*v.* 35). Those that would not serve God in their own land were made to serve their enemies in a strange land, as was threatened, Deut. xxviii. 47, 48.

IV. A humble representation of the judgments of God, which they had been and were now under.

1. Former judgments are remembered. They had not taken warning. In the days of the judges their *enemies vexed them* (*v.* 27); and, when they did evil again, God did again *leave them in the hand of their enemies.*

2. Their present calamitous state is laid before the Lord (*v.* 36, 37): *We are servants this day.* Free-born Israelites are enslaved, and the land which they had long held by a much more honourable tenure, they now held by, from, and under, the kings of Persia, whose vassals they were. This, they honestly own, was for their sins. Poverty and slavery are the fruits of sin; it is sin that brings us into all our distresses.

V. Their address to God under these calamities. 1. By way of request, that their trouble might not *seem little*, *v.* 32. It is the only petition in all this prayer. The trouble was universal; it had come on their *kings, princes, priests, prophets, fathers, and all their people*; they had all shared in the sin (*v.* 34), and now all shared in the judgment. It was of long continuance: *From the time of the kings of Assyria*, who carried the ten tribes captive, *unto this day.* "Lord, let it not all seem little and not worthy to be regarded, or not needing to be relieved." They do not prescribe to God what he shall do for them, but leave it to him. 2. By way of acknowledgment, notwithstanding, that really it was less than they deserved, *v.* 33. They own the justice of God in all their troubles.

VI. The result and conclusion of this whole matter. After this long remonstrance of their case was made they came at last to this resolution. "Because of all this, we make a sure covenant with God; in consideration of our frequent departures from God, we will now more firmly than ever bind ourselves to him. Because we have smarted so much for sin, we will now steadfastly resolve against it, that we may not any more withdraw the shoulder." A certain number of the princes, priests, and Levites, were chosen as the representatives of the congregation, to subscribe and seal it for and in the name of the rest.

JAMIESON, FAUSSET, BROWN

36. Behold, we are servants this day—Notwithstanding their happy restoration to their native land, they were still tributaries of a foreign prince whose officers ruled them. They were not, like their fathers, free tenants of the land which God gave them. **37. it yieldeth much increase unto the kings whom thou hast set over us because of our sins**—Our agricultural labors have been resumed in the land—we plough, and sow, and till, and Thou blessest the work of our hands with a plentifull return; but this increase is not for ourselves, as once it was, but for our foreign masters, to whom we have to pay large and oppressive tribute. **they have dominion over our bodies**—Their persons were liable to be pressed, at the mandate of their Assyrian conqueror, into the service of his empire, either in war or in public works. And our beasts are taken to do their pleasure.

32. Now therefore our God . . . who keepest covenant and mercy—God's fidelity to His covenant is prominently acknowledged, and well it might; for their whole national history bore testimony to it. But as this could afford them little ground of comfort or of hope while they were so painfully conscious of having violated it, they were driven to seek refuge in the riches of divine grace; and hence the peculiar style of invocation here adopted: "Now therefore, our God, the great, the mighty, and the terrible God, who *keepest covenant and mercy*."

38. we make a sure covenant, and write—i.e., subscribe or sign it. This written document would exercise a wholesome influence in restraining their backslidings or in animating them to duty, by being a witness against them if in the future they were unfaithful to their engagements.

ADAM CLARKE

the ten tribes. And many years did God bear with them, not less than 254 years from their separation from the house of David, till their captivity and utter dispersion under Shalmaneser, during the whole of which time God invariably warned them by His prophets; or, as it is here said, *by thy spirit in thy prophets,* which gives us the true notion of divine inspiration. God's Spirit was given to the prophets; and they testified to the people, according as they were taught and influenced by this Spirit.

35. *For they have not served thee in their kingdom.* Instead of *in their kingdom,* "in thy kingdom" is the reading of two of Kennicott's MSS., as also of the Septuagint, Syriac, and Arabic. This is most likely to be the true reading.

36. *Behold, we are servants.* They had no king of their own, and were under the government of the kings of Persia, to whom they paid a regular tribute.

37. *It yieldeth much increase unto the kings.* Good and fruitful as the land is, yet it profits us little, as the chief profits on all things go to the kings of Persia.

32. *On our kings, on our princes.* I believe Nehemiah in this place mentions the whole of civil society in its officers as they stand related to each other in dignity: (1) *kings,* as supreme; (2) *princes;* (3) *priests;* (4) *prophets;* (5) the *fathers,* heads or chiefs of tribes and families; (6) the common *people.*

MATTHEW HENRY — CHAPTER 10

Verses 1–31

When Israel was first brought into covenant with God it was done by sacrifice and the sprinkling of blood, Exod. xxiv. But here it was done by the more natural and common way of sealing and subscribing the written articles of the covenant.

I. The names of those public persons who, as the representatives and heads of the congregation, set their hands and seals to this covenant. Nehemiah, who was the governor, signed first. Next to him subscribed twenty-two priests. Next to the priests, seventeen Levites subscribed this covenant, among whom we find all or most of those who were the mouth of the congregation in prayer, *ch.* ix. 4, 5. Those that lead in prayer should lead in every other good work. Next to the Levites, forty-four of the chief of the people gave it under their hands for themselves and all the rest.

II. The concurrence of the rest of the people with them, and the rest of the priests and Levites, who signified their consent to what their chiefs did. With them joined, 1. Their wives and children; for they had transgressed, and they must reform. 2. The

JAMIESON, FAUSSET, BROWN — CHAPTER 10

VSS. 1-27. THE NAMES OF THOSE WHO SEALED THE COVENANT. **1. Nehemiah, the Tirshatha**—His name was placed first in the roll on account of his high official rank, as deputy of the Persian monarch. All classes were included in the subscription; but the people were represented by their elders (vs. 14), as it would have been impossible for every one in the country to have been admitted to the sealing.

28. THE REST OF THE PEOPLE BOUND THEMSELVES TO OBSERVE IT. Those who were not present at the sealing ratified the covenant by giving their assent, either in words or by lifting up their hands, and bound themselves, by a solemn oath, to walk in

ADAM CLARKE — CHAPTER 10

1. *Now those that sealed.* Four classes here seal. Nehemiah first, as their governor. And after him, secondly, the priests, vv. 2-8. Thirdly, the Levites, vv. 9-13. Fourthly, the chiefs of the people, vv. 14-27.

28. *And the rest of the people.* All had, in one or other of the classes which sealed, their representatives; and by their sealing they considered themselves bound.

MATTHEW HENRY

proselytes of other nations, *all that had separated themselves from the people of the lands*, their gods and their worship, *unto the law of God*, and the observance of that law. See what conversion is; it is separating ourselves from the course and custom of this world, and devoting ourselves to the conduct of the word of God. And, as there is one law, so there is one covenant, one baptism, for the stranger and for him that is born in the land. The concurrence of the people is expressed, *v.* 29. *They clave to their brethren* one and all.

III. The general purport of this covenant. They laid upon themselves no other burden than this necessary thing, which they were already obliged to by all other engagements of duty, interest, and gratitude—*to walk in God's law, and to do all his commandments, v.* 29.

IV. Some of the particular articles of this covenant, such as were adopted to their present temptations. 1. That they would not intermarry with the heathen, *v.* 30. 2. That they would keep no markets on the sabbath day, or any other day of which the law has said, *You shall do no work therein*. The sabbath is a market day for our souls, but not for our bodies. 3. That they would not be severe in exacting their debts, but would observe the seventh year as a year of release, according to the law, *v.* 31.

Verses 32–39

I. It was resolved, in general, that the temple service should be carefully kept up, that the work of the house of their God should be done in its season, according to the law, *v.* 33. It is likely to go well with our houses when care is taken that the work of God's house may go well. It was likewise resolved that they would never *forsake the house of their God* (*v.* 39), for the house of any other god, or for the high places, as idolaters did, nor forsake it for their farms and merchandises, as those did that were atheistical and profane. Those that forsake the worship of God forsake God.

II. It was resolved, in pursuance of this, that they would liberally maintain the temple service, and not starve it if the people would do theirs, which was to find them materials to work upon. Now here it was agreed and concluded, 1. That a stock should be raised for the furnishing of God's table and altar plentifully. The people therefore agreed to contribute yearly, every one of them, the third part of a shekel, about ten pence a-piece for the bearing of this expense. When everyone will act, and everyone will give, though but little, towards a good work, the whole amount will be considerable. The tirshatha did not impose this tax, but the people made it an ordinance for themselves, and charged themselves with it, *v.* 32, 33. 2. That particular care should be taken to provide wood for the altar, to keep the fire always burning upon it. 3. That all those things which the divine law had appointed for the maintenance of the priests and Levites should be duly paid in, that they might not be under any temptation to neglect it for the making of necessary provision for their families. First-fruits and tenths were then the principal branches of the minister's revenues; and they here resolve to bring in the first fruits justly and to bring in their tenths likewise. This was the law (Num. xviii. 21–28); but these dues had been withheld, in consequence of which God, by the prophet, charges them with *robbing him* (Mal. iii. 8, 9), at the same time encouraging them to be more just to him and his receivers, with a promise that, if they brought the *tithes into the store-house*, he would *pour out blessings upon them, v.* 10. This therefore they resolved to do, that there might be meat in God's house. "We will do it (say they) *in all the cities of our tillage*," *v.* 37. *In all the cities of our servitude*, so the LXX, for they were servants in their own land, *ch.* ix. 36. Though they paid great taxes to the kings of Persia, and had much hardship put upon them, they would not make that an excuse for not paying their tithes, but would render to God the things that were his, as well as to Cæsar the things that were his.

JAMIESON, FAUSSET, BROWN

God's law, imprecating a curse upon themselves in the event of their violating it.

29-39. Points of the Covenant. **29. to observe and do all the commandments,** etc.—This national covenant, besides containing a solemn pledge of obedience to the divine law generally, specified their engagement to some particular duties, which the character and exigency of the times stamped with great urgency and importance, and which may be summed up under the following heads: that they abstain from contracting matrimonial alliances with the heathen; that they would rigidly observe the sabbath; that they would let the land enjoy rest and remit debts every seventh year; that they would contribute to the maintenance of the temple service, the necessary expenses of which had formerly been defrayed out of the treasury of the temple (I Chron. 26:20), and when it was drained, given out from the king's privy purse (II Chron. 31:3); and that they would make an orderly payment of the priests' dues. A minute and particular enumeration of the first fruits was made, that all might be made fully aware of their obligations, and that none might excuse themselves on pretext of ignorance from withholding taxes which the poverty of many, and the irreligion of others, had made them exceedingly prone to evade.

39. we will not forsake the house of our God—This solemn pledge was repeated at the close of the covenant as an expression of the intense zeal by which the people at this time were animated for the glory and the worship of God. Under the pungent feelings of sorrow and repentance for their national sins, of which apostasy from the service of the true God was the chief, and under the yet fresh and painful remembrance of their protracted captivity, they vowed, and (feeling the impulse of ardent devotion as well as of gratitude for their restoration) flattered themselves they would never forget their vow, to be the Lord's.

32. the third part of a shekel for the service of the house of our God—The law required every individual above twenty years of age to pay half a shekel to the sanctuary. But in consequence of the general poverty of the people, occasioned by war and captivity, this tribute was reduced to a third part of a shekel. **34. we cast the lots ... for the wood offering**—The carrying of the wood had formerly been the work of the Nethinims. But few of them having returned, the duty was assigned as stated in the text. The practice afterwards rose into great importance, and Josephus speaks [Wars, 2. 17, sect. 6] of the Xylophoria, or certain stated and solemn times at which the people brought up wood to the temple. **38. the priest the son of Aaron shall be with the Levites, when the Levites take tithes**—This was a prudential arrangement. The presence of a dignified priest would ensure the peaceful delivery of the tithes; at least his superintendence and influence would tend to prevent the commission of any wrong in the transaction, by the people deceiving the Levites, or the Levites defrauding the priests. **the tithe of the tithes**—The Levites, having received a tenth of all land produce, were required to give a tenth of this to the priests. The Levites were charged with the additional obligation to carry the tithes when received, and deposit them in the temple stores, for the use of the priests.

ADAM CLARKE

29. *They clave to their brethren.* Though they did not sign this instrument, yet they found themselves under a solemn oath that they would fulfil the conditions of the covenant, and walk according to the law of Moses.

30. *Not give our daughters.* Make no affinity with the people of the land.

31. *Bring ware.* We will most solemnly keep the Sabbath. *Leave the seventh year.* We will let the land have its Sabbath, and rest every seventh year. See on Exod. xxiii. 10-11.

39. *We will not forsake the house of our God.* Here was a glorious resolution; and had they been faithful to it, they had been a great and good people to the present day.

32. *Charge ourselves yearly with the third part of a shekel.* According to the law, everyone above twenty years of age was to give half a shekel to the sanctuary, which was called a ransom for their souls. See Exod. xxx. 11-16. But why is one *third* of a shekel now promised instead of the half-shekel, which the law required? To this question no better answer can be given than this: The general poverty of the people occasioned by their wars, overthrows, heavy tributes, etc., in the land of their captivity; and now on their return, having little property, it was impossible for them to give more. Though only a third part of a shekel was given at this time, and probably for the reason above assigned, yet when the people got into a state of greater prosperity the half-shekel was resumed, for it is clear that this sum was paid in the time of our Lord.

34. *Cast the lots . . . for the wood offering.* There does not appear to have been any wood offering under the law. It was the business of the Nethinim to procure this; and hence they were called "hewers of wood and drawers of water" to the congregation. But it is very likely that after the Captivity few Nethinim were found; for as such, who were the descendants of the Gibeonites, were considered only as slaves among the Israelites, they would doubtless find it as much, if not more, to their interest to abide in the land of their captivity than to return with their former masters.

36. *Also the firstborn.* See this law, and the reasons of it, Exod. xiii. 1-13. As by this law the Lord had a right to all the firstborn, instead of these He was pleased to take the tribe of Levi for the whole; and thus the Levites served at the Tabernacle and Temple, instead of the firstborn of all the tribes.

38. *Tithe of the tithes.* The tithes of all the produce of the fields were brought to the Levites; out of these a tenth part was given to the priests. This is what is called the "tithe of the tithes." The law for this is found in Num. xviii. 26.

MATTHEW HENRY — CHAPTER 11

Verses 1–19

Jerusalem is called here *the holy city* (*v.* 1), because there the temple was, and God had chosen to put his name there; the holy seed should all have chosen to dwell there, but, on the contrary, they declined. 1. Because a greater strictness was expected from the inhabitants of Jerusalem than from others. Those who care not for being holy themselves are shy of dwelling in a holy city. Or, 2. Because Jeru-

JAMIESON, FAUSSET, BROWN — CHAPTER 11

Vss. 1, 2. The Rulers, Voluntary Men, and Every Tenth Man Chosen by Lot, Dwell at Jerusalem. **1. the rulers ... dwelt at Jerusalem**—That city being the metropolis of the country, it was right and proper that the seat of government should be there. But the exigency of the times required that special measures should be taken to insure the residence of an adequate population for the custody of the buildings and the defense of the city.

ADAM CLARKE — CHAPTER 11

MATTHEW HENRY

salem, of all places, was most hated by the heathen their neighbours, which made that the post of danger (as the post of honour usually is) and therefore they were not willing to expose themselves there. Fear of persecution and reproach, keeps many out of the holy city, and makes them backward to appear for God and religion, not considering that, as Jerusalem is threatened and insulted by its enemies, so it is with a special care protected by its God and made a *quiet habitation*, Isa. xxxiii. 20; Ps. xlvi. 4, 5. Or, 3. Because it was more for their worldly advantage to dwell in the country. Jerusalem was no trading city, and therefore there was no money to be got there by merchandise, as there was in the country by corn and cattle.

I. By what means it was replenished. 1. The rulers dwelt there, *v.* 1. That was the proper place for them to reside in, because *there were set the thrones of judgment* (Ps. cxxii. 5). Their dwelling there would invite and encourage others too. *Magnates magnetes—the mighty are magnetic.* 2. There were some that willingly offered themselves to dwell at Jerusalem, nobly foregoing their own secular interest for the public welfare, *v.* 2. They *sought the good of Jerusalem, because of the house of the Lord their God.* 3. They, finding that *yet there was room,* concluded upon a review of their whole body to bring one in ten to dwell in Jerusalem; who they should be was determined by lot, the disposal whereof, all knew, was of the Lord.

II. By what persons it was replenished. 1. Many of the children of Judah and Benjamin dwelt there; for, originally, part of the city lay in the lot of one of those tribes and part in that of the other; but the greater part was in the lot of Benjamin, and therefore here we find of the children of Judah only 468 families in Jerusalem (*v.* 6), but of Benjamin 928, *v.* 7, 8. Though the Benjamites were more in number, yet of the men of Judah it is said (*v.* 6) that they were valiant men, fit for service, and able to defend the city in case of an attack. Judah has not lost its ancient character of a lion's whelp, bold and daring. Of the Benjamites that dwelt in Jerusalem we are here told who was *overseer*, and who was second, *v.* 9. 2. The priests and Levites did many of them settle at Jerusalem. Of those that did the work of the house in their courses here were 822 of one family, 242 of another, and 128 of another, *v.* 12–14. It is said of some of them that they were *mighty men of valour* (*v.* 14). Some of the Levites also came and dwelt at Jerusalem, yet but few in comparison, 284 in all (*v.* 18), with 172 porters (*v.* 19), for much of their work was to *teach the good knowledge of God* up and down the country, for which purpose they were to be scattered in Israel. (1) It is said of one of the Levites that he had *the oversight of the outward business of the house of God*, *v.* 16. The priests were chief managers of the business within the temple gates; but this Levite was entrusted with the secular concerns of God's house, the collecting of the contributions, the providing of materials for the temple service, and the like. Those who take care of the *outward concerns* of the church, the serving of its tables, are as necessary in their place as those who take care of *its inward concerns*, who give themselves to the word and prayer. (2) It is said of another that he was *the principal to begin the thanksgiving in prayer.* Probably he had a good ear and a good voice, and was a scientific singer, and therefore was chosen to lead the psalm. He was precentor in the temple.

Verses 20–36

Some account of the other cities, in which dwelt *the residue of Israel*, *v.* 20. It was requisite that Jerusalem should be replenished, yet not so as to drain the country. 1. The Nethinims, the posterity of the Gibeonites, dwelt in Ophel, which was upon the wall of Jerusalem (*ch.* iii. 26). 2. Though the Levites were dispersed through the cities of Judah, yet they had an overseer who resided in Jerusalem, superior of their order and their provincial. 3. Some of the singers were appointed to look after the necessary repairs of the temple, they were *over the business of the house of God*, *v.* 22. The king of Persia allotted a particular maintenance for them, besides what belonged to them as Levites, *v.* 23.

JAMIESON, FAUSSET, BROWN

From the annoyances of restless and malignant enemies, who tried every means to demolish the rising fortifications, there was some danger attending a settlement in Jerusalem. Hence the greater part of the returned exiles, in order to earn as well as secure the rewards of their duty, preferred to remain in the country or the provincial towns. To remedy this state of things, it was resolved to select every tenth man of the tribes of Judah and Benjamin by lot, to become a permanent inhabitant of the capital. The necessity of such an expedient commended it to the general approval. It was the more readily submitted to because the lot was resorted to on all the most critical conjunctures of the Jewish history, and regarded by the people as a divine decision (Prov. 18:18). This awakened strongly the national spirit; and patriotic volunteers came forward readily to meet the wishes of the authorities, a service which, implying great self-denial as well as courage, was reckoned in the circumstances of so much importance as entitled them to the public gratitude. No wonder that the conduct of these volunteers drew forth the tribute of public admiration; for they sacrificed their personal safety and comfort for the interests of the community because Jerusalem was at that time a place against which the enemies of the Jews were directing a thousand plots. Therefore, residence in it at such a juncture was attended with expense and various annoyances from which a country life was entirely free.

3-36. THEIR NAMES. **3. the chief of the province**—i.e., Judea. Nehemiah speaks of it, as it then was, a small appendix of the Persian empire. **in the cities of Judah dwelt every one in his possession in their cities**—The returned exiles, who had come from Babylon, repaired generally, and by a natural impulse, to the lands and cities throughout the country which had been anciently assigned them. **Israel**—This general name, which designated the descendants of Jacob before the unhappy division of the two kingdoms under Rehoboam, was restored after the captivity, the Israelites being then united with the Jews, and all traces of their former separation being obliterated. Although the majority of the returned exiles belonged to the tribes of Judah and Benjamin, they are here called Israel because a large number out of all the tribes were now intermingled, and these were principally the occupiers of the rural villages, while none but those of Judah and Benjamin resided in Jerusalem. **the Levites**—These took possession of the cities allotted to them, according as they had opportunity. **the Nethinims**—A certain order of men, either Gibeonites or persons joined with them, who were devoted to the service of God. **4. at Jerusalem dwelt certain of the children of Judah**—The discrepancy that is apparent between this and the list formerly given in I Chron. 9:1-9, arose not only from the Jewish and Oriental practice of changing or modifying the names of persons from a change of circumstances, but from the alterations that must have been produced in the course of time. The catalogue in Chronicles contains those who came with the first detachment of returned exiles, while the list in this passage probably included also those who returned with Ezra and Nehemiah; or it was most probably made out afterwards, when several had died, or some, who had been inserted as going on the journey, remained, and others came in their stead. **9. overseer** i.e., captain or chief. **11. the ruler of the house of God**—assistant of the high priest (Num. 3:32; 1 Chron. 9:11; II Chron. 19:11). **16. the oversight of the outward business of the house of God**—i.e., those things which were done outside, or in the country, such as the collecting of the provisions (I Chron. 26:29). **17. the principal to begin the thanksgiving in prayer**—i.e., the leader of the choir which chanted the public praise at the time of the morning and evening sacrifice. That service was always accompanied by some appropriate psalm, the sacred music being selected and guided by the person named. **22. the sons of Asaph, the singers were over the business of the house of God**—They were selected to take charge of providing those things which were required for the interior of the temple and its service, while to others was committed the care of the "outward business of the house of God" (vs. 16). This duty was very properly assigned to the sons of Asaph; for, though they were Levites, they did not repair in rotation to Jerusalem, as the other ministers of religion. Being permanent residents, and employed in duties which were comparatively light and easy, they were very competent to undertake this charge. **23. it was the king's commandment**—It was the will of the Persian monarch in issuing his edict that the temple service should be revived in all its religious fulness

ADAM CLARKE

1. *To bring one of ten.* Jerusalem certainly had many inhabitants at this time; but not sufficient to preserve the city, which was now encompassed with a wall, and the rebuilding of which was going on fast. Nehemiah therefore obliged one-tenth of the country people to come and dwell in it, that the population might be sufficient for the preservation and defense of the city. Ten were set apart, and the lot cast among them to see which one of the ten should take up his residence in the city.

2. *All the men, that willingly offered.* Some volunteered their services, which was considered a sacrifice to patriotism at that time, as Jerusalem afforded very few advantages and was a place of considerable danger; hence the people "spoke well of them," and no doubt prayed for God's blessing upon them.

3. *Now these are the chief.* A good deal of difference will be found between the enumeration here and that in 1 Chron. ix. 2, etc. There, those only who came with Zerubbabel appear to be numbered; here, those, and the persons who came with Ezra and Nehemiah, enter into the account.

9. *And Joel . . . was their overseer.* Joel was chief or magistrate over those, and Judah was his *second* or "deputy." Perhaps each had a different office, but that of Joel was the chief.

11. *Ruler of the house of God.* He had the command over all secular matters, as the high priest had over those which were spiritual.

14. *Mighty men of valour.* Noted for strength of body and military courage.

16. *And Shabbethai.* This verse, with vv. 20-21, 28-29, 32-35, are all wanting in the Septuagint and the whole chapter is wanting in the Arabic, the translator not being concerned in Jewish genealogies. *The outward business.* Calmet supposes that he provided the victuals for the priests, victims for the sacrifices, the sacerdotal vestments, the sacred vessels, and other necessaries for the service of the Temple.

17. *The principal to begin the thanksgiving.* The pitcher of the tune.

22. *The overseer also of the Levites.* The "visitant," the "inspector."

23. *It was the king's commandment.* By the *king* some understand David, and others Artaxerxes. It is most probable that it was the latter, who wished that a provision should be made for these, a part of whose office was to offer up

MATTHEW HENRY

4. Here is one that was the king's commissioner at Jerusalem. He is said to be *at the king's hand*, or *on the king's part*, in *all matters concerning the people*, to determine controversies that arose between the king's officers and his subjects, to see that what was due to the king from the people was duly paid in and what was allowed by the king for the temple service was duly paid out, and happy it was for the Jews that one of themselves was in this post. 5. An account of the villages, or country towns, which were inhabited by the residue of Israel—the towns in which the children of Judah dwelt (*v.* 25–30), those that were inhabited by the children of Benjamin (*v.* 31–35), and divisions for the Levites among both, *v.* 36.

CHAPTER 12

Verses 1–26

The names, of a great many priests and Levites, that were eminent in their day among the returned Jews. Perhaps it is intended to stir up their posterity, who succeeded them in the priest's office and inherited their dignities and preferments, to imitate their courage and fidelity.

The succession of high priests during the Persian monarchy, from Jeshua, who was high priest at the time of the restoration, to Jaddua (or Jaddus), who was high priest when Alexander the Great, after the conquest of Tyre, came to Jerusalem, and paid great respect to this Jaddus, who met him in his pontifical habit, and showed him the prophecy of Daniel, which foretold his conquests. The next generation of priests, who were chief men, and active in the days of Joiakim, sons of the first set. All those who are mentioned *v.* 1, &c., as eminent in their generation, are again mentioned, though with some variation in several of the names, *v.* 12, &c., except two, as having sons that were likewise eminent in their generation—a rare instance, that twenty good fathers should leave behind them twenty good sons. The next generation of Levites, or rather a latter generation; for those priests who are mentioned flourished in the days of Joiakim the high priest, these Levites in the days of Eliashib, *v.* 22. Then a generation of Levites was *raised up*, who were *recorded chief of the fathers* (*v.* 22), and were eminently serviceable to the interests of the church, and their service not the less acceptable for their being Levites only. Eliashib the high priest being allied to Tobiah (*ch.* xiii. 4), the other priests grew remiss; but then the Levites appeared the more zealous. Those who were now employed in expounding (*ch.* viii. 7) and in praying (*ch.* ix. 4, 5) were all Levites, not priests, regard being had to their personal qualifications more than to their order.

Verses 27–43

The dedication of the wall of Jerusalem.

I. The meaning of this dedication of the wall. It was not done till the city was pretty well replenished, *ch.* xi. It was a solemn thanksgiving to God for his great mercy. They devoted the city in a peculiar manner to God and to his honour, and took possession of it for him and in his name. This city was (as never any other was) a *holy city*, the *city of the great king* (Ps. xlviii. 2 and Matt. v. 35). They put the city and its walls under the divine protection, owning that *unless the Lord kept the city* the walls were *built in vain.*

JAMIESON, FAUSSET, BROWN

and solemnity. As this special provision for the singers is said to have been by the king's commandment, the order was probably given at the request or suggestion of Ezra or Nehemiah. **24. Pethahiah . . . was at the king's hand in all matters concerning the people**—This person was entrusted with judicial power, either for the interest, or by the appointment, of the Persian monarch, and his duty consisted either in adjusting cases of civil dispute, or in regulating fiscal concerns. **25. some of the children of Judah dwelt at Kirjath-arba**—The whole region in which the villages here mentioned were situated had been completely devastated by the Chaldean invasion; and, therefore, it must be assumed, that these villages had been rebuilt before "the children dwelt in them." **36. And of the Levites were divisions in Judah, and in Benjamin**—Rather, there were divisions for the Levites; i.e., those who were not resident in Jerusalem were distributed in settlements throughout the provinces of Judah and Benjamin.

CHAPTER 12

Vss. 1-9. Priests and Levites Who Came Up with Zerubbabel. **1. these are the priests**—according to verse 7 "the chief of the priests," the heads of the twenty-four courses into which the priesthood was divided (I Chron. 24:1-20). Only four of the courses returned from the captivity (ch. 7:39-42; Ezra 2:36-39). But these were divided by Zerubbabel, or Jeshua, into the original number of twenty-four. Twenty-two only are enumerated here, and no more than twenty in verses 12-21. The discrepancy is due to the extremely probable circumstance that two of the twenty-four courses had become extinct in Babylon; for none belonging to them are reported as having returned (vss. 2-5). Hattush and Maadiah may be omitted in the account of those persons' families (vs. 12), for these had no sons. **Shealtiel**—or Salathiel. **Ezra**—This was most likely a different person from the pious and patriotic leader. If he were the same person, he would now have reached a very patriarchal age—and this longevity would doubtless be due to his eminent piety and temperance, which are greatly conducive to the prolongation of life, but, above all, to the special blessing of God, who had preserved and strengthened him for the accomplishment of the important work he was called upon to undertake in that critical period of the Church's history. **4. Abijah**—one of the ancestors of John the Baptist (Luke 1:5). **9. their brethren were over against them in the watches**—i.e., according to some, their stations—the places where they stood when officiating—"ward over against ward" (vs. 24); or, according to others, in alternate watches, in course of rotation.

10-47. Succession of the High Priests. **10. Jeshua begat Joiakim,** etc. This enumeration was of great importance, not only as establishing their individual purity of descent, but because the chronology of the Jews was henceforth to be reckoned, not as formerly by the reigns of their kings, but by the successions of their high priests. **11. Jaddua**—It is an opinion entertained by many commentators that this person was the high priest whose dignified appearance, solemn manner, and splendid costume overawed and interested so strongly the proud mind of Alexander the Great; and if he were not this person (as some object that this Jaddua was not in office till a considerable period after the death of Nehemiah), it might probably be his father, called by the same name. **12. in the days of Joiakim were priests, the chief of the fathers**—As there had been priests in the days of Jeshua, so in the time of Joiakim, the son and successor of Jeshua, the sons of those persons filled the priestly office in the place of their fathers, some of whom were still alive, though many were dead. **23. The sons of Levi . . . were written in the book of the chronicles**—i.e., the public registers in which the genealogies were kept with great regularity and exactness. **27-43. at the dedication of the wall of Jerusalem**—This ceremony of consecrating the wall and gates of the city was an act of piety on the part of Nehemiah, not merely to thank God in a general way for having been enabled to bring the building to a happy completion, but especially because that city was the place which He had chosen. It also contained the temple which was hallowed by the manifestation of His presence, and anew set apart to His service. It was on these accounts that Jerusalem was called "the holy city," and by this public and solemn act of religious observance, after a long period of neglect and desecration, it was, as it were, restored to its rightful proprietor. The dedication consisted in a solemn

ADAM CLARKE

prayers also, as well as praises. For we know that Darius made an ample provision for the priests, "that they may offer sacrifices of sweet savours unto the God of heaven, and pray for the life of the king, and of his sons," Ezra vi. 10. Some have thought that they had been Jewish singers employed in the service of the Persian king, to whom he had given a salary, and to whom he wished still to continue the same.

24. *Pethahiah . . . was at the king's hand.* He was the governor appointed by the Persian king over the Jewish nation in those matters in which the civil government interfered with Jewish concerns. He no doubt fixed, levied, and received the tribute.

36. *And of the Levites were divisions.* The Levites had their dwellings in the divisions of Judah and Benjamin. This is probably the meaning.

CHAPTER 12

1. *Now these are the priests.* Not the whole, but the chief of them, as we are informed, vv. 7, 22-24.

7. *The chief of the priests.* They were twenty-four orders or courses in number, all subordinate to each other; as established by David, 1 Chron. xxiv. 18. And these orders or courses were continued till the destruction of Jerusalem by the Romans.

8. *Over the thanksgiving.* The principal singers: see on chap. xi. 17.

23. *The book of the chronicles.* This is not the Book of Chronicles which we have now, no such list being found in it; but some other book or register, which is lost.

27. *At the dedication of the wall.* They sent for the Levites from all quarters, that this dedication might be as solemn and majestic as possible; and it is likely that this was done as soon as convenient after the walls were finished. The dedication seems to have consisted in processions of the most eminent persons around the walls, and thanksgivings to God, who had enabled them to bring the work to so happy a conclusion.

29. *From the house of Gilgal, and out of the fields of Geba and Azmaveth.* Or from Beth-Gilgal; a village erected in the place where the Israelites encamped after they had, under the direction of Joshua, passed over Jordan.

MATTHEW HENRY

II. With what solemnity it was performed, under the direction of Nehemiah. The Levites from all parts of the country were summoned to attend. There was a general rendezvous, *v.* 28. 29. They *purified themselves*, *v.* 30, then the people. Then they purified *the gates and the wall.* This purification was performed by sprinkling the *water of purifying* (or of *separation*, as it is called, Num. xix. 9) on *themselves* and the *people*, the walls and the gates—a type of the blood of Christ, with which our consciences being *purged from dead works*, we become fit to *serve the living God* (Heb. ix. 14). The princes, priests, and Levites, walked round upon the wall in two companies, with musical instruments, to signify the dedication of it all to God (*v.* 36). They had a rendezvous where they divided themselves into two companies. Half of the princes, with several priests and Levites, went on the right hand, Ezra leading their van, *v.* 36. The other half of the princes and priests, who gave thanks likewise, went to the left hand, Nehemiah bringing up the rear, *v.* 38.

At length both companies met in the temple, where they joined their thanksgivings, *v.* 40. The crowd of people, it is likely, walked some within the wall and others without. The people *greatly rejoiced*, *v.* 43. Their shouts, coming from a sincere and hearty joy, are here taken notice of; for God graciously accepts honest zealous services, though there is in them little of part. *The women and children rejoiced;* and their hosannas were not despised.

Verses 44–47

When the solemnities of a thanksgiving day leave such impressions on ministers and people as that both are more careful and cheerful in doing their duty afterwards, then they are indeed acceptable to God. So it was here. 1. The ministers were more careful than they had been of their work, *v.* 45. *The singers kept the ward of their God*, attending in due time to the duty of their office; the *porters*, too, *kept the ward of the purification*, that is, they took care to preserve the purity of the temple. 2. The people were more careful than they had been of the maintenance of their ministers, *v.* 44. Now, (1) Care is here taken for the collecting of their dues. They were modest, and would rather lose their right than call for it themselves. The people were many of them careless and would not bring their dues unless they were called upon; and therefore *some were appointed* whose office it should be to gather into the treasuries, *out of the fields of the cities, the portions of the law for the priests and Levites* (*v.* 44). (2) Care is taken that, being *gathered in*, they might be duly *paid out*, *v.* 47. They gave the singers and porters their daily portion, over and above what was due to them as Levites; for we may suppose that when David and Solomon appointed them their work (*v.* 45, 46), above what was required from them as Levites, they settled a fund for their further encouragement. For the other Levites, the tithes, here called *the holy things*, were duly set apart for them, out of which they paid the priests their tithe according to the law.

JAMIESON, FAUSSET, BROWN

ceremonial, in which the leading authorities, accompanied by the Levitical singers, summoned from all parts of the country, and by a vast concourse of people, marched in imposing procession round the city walls, and, pausing at intervals to engage in united praises, prayer, and sacrifices, supplicated the continued presence, favor, and blessing on "the holy city." "*The assembly convened near Jaffa Gate, where the procession commences.* Then (vs. 31) I brought up the princes of Judah upon the wall (*near the Valley Gate*), and appointed two great companies of them that gave thanks, whereof one went on the right hand upon the wall towards the dung-gate (*through Bethzo*). And after them went Hoshaiah, and half of the princes of Judah. And (vs. 37) at the fountain-gate, which was over against them, they (*descending by the Tower of Siloam on the interior, and then reascending*) went up by the stairs of the city of David, at the going up of the wall, above the house of David, even unto the water-gate eastward (*by the staircase of the rampart, having descended to dedicate the fountain structures*). And the other company of them that gave thanks went over against them (*both parties having started from the junction of the first and second walls*), and I after them, and the half of the people upon the wall, from beyond the tower of the furnaces even unto the broad wall (*beyond the corner-gate*). And from above the gate of Ephraim, and above the old gate (*and the gate of Benjamin*), and above the fish-gate, and the tower of Hananeel, and the tower of Meah, even unto the sheep-gate; and they stood still in the prison-gate (*or high gate, at the east end of the bridge*). So stood the two companies of them that gave thanks in the house of God, and I, and half of the rulers with me (*having thus performed the circuit of the investing walls*), and arrived in the courts of the temple" [BARCLAY'S CITY OF THE GREAT KING]. **43. the joy of Jerusalem was heard even afar off**—The events of the day, viewed in connection with the now repaired and beautified state of the city, raised the popular feeling to the highest pitch of enthusiasm, and the fame of their rejoicings was spread far and near. **44. portions of the law**—i.e., prescribed by the law. **for Judah rejoiced for the priests and . . . Levites that waited**—The cause of this general satisfaction was either the full restoration of the temple service and the reorganized provision for the permanent support of the ministry, or it was the pious character and eminent gifts of the guardians of religion. **45. the singers and the porters kept . . . the ward of the purification**—i.e., took care that no unclean person was allowed to enter within the precincts of the sacred building. This was the official duty of the porters (II Chron. 23:19), with whom, owing to the pressure of circumstances, it was deemed expedient that the singers should be associated as assistants. **47. all Israel . . . sanctified holy things unto the Levites,** etc.—The people, selecting the tithes and first fruits, devoted them to the use of the Levites, to whom they belonged by appointment of the law. The Levites acted in the same way with the tithes due from them to the priests. Thus all classes of the people displayed a conscientious fidelity in paying the dues to the temple and the servants of God who were appointed to minister in it.

ADAM CLARKE

30. *The priests and the Levites purified themselves.* This consisted in washings, abstinence from wine, and other matters, which, on all other occasions, were lawful. And as to the purifying of the gates and the walls, nothing was requisite but to remove all filth from the former, and all rubbish that might have been laid against the latter.

31. *Then I brought up the princes.* Perhaps this verse should be read thus: "Then I caused the princes of Judah to go up on the wall, and appointed two great choirs [to sing praises], and two processions, one on the right hand," etc.

F. B. MEYER:

"David, the man of God" (Neh. 12:24, 36, 37, 45, 46). How long the influence of David has lingered over the world, like the afterglow of a sunset! Mark the characteristic in him which laid the foundation of his supremacy over the hearts of his countrymen. He was preeminently "a man of God." Notwithstanding his terrible fall, his people recognized that his salient characteristic was Godward. Would you be one of God's men?

(1) Give all to God. Too many live lives of piecemeal consecration, giving a bit here and a bit there, but never all. David surrendered himself to do God's will utterly, and in all, and so became a man after God's own heart. With what joy God's voice seems to quiver, as He says, "I have found David, the son of Jesse, a man after mine own heart, who shall fulfil all my will" (Acts 13:22). Without reserve, holding nothing back, yield yourself to God, to be, and do, and suffer his will, whatever it may be.

(2) Take all from God. "It is not what we give to Jesus, but what we take from Him, that makes us strong, helpful, and victorious day by day." Accept this as a fact, that in Jesus God has made all his fulness dwell. There is nothing we require, for life or godliness, that is not stored in Him; but the terrible loss of our lives is that we take so little.

(3) Use all for God. It sometimes appears as though Christian people were urged to yield themselves to God only that their lives might be more comfortable. But the supreme and final end in all surrender must be that his will be done, his glory promoted, and himself magnified whether in life or death.

—*Great Verses Through the Bible*

MATTHEW HENRY — CHAPTER 13

Verses 1–9

Israel was not to mingle with the nations, nor suffer any of them to incorporate with them.

I. The law to this purport happened to be read *on that day, in the audience of the people* (*v.* 1), on the day of the dedication of the wall. They found a law, that the Ammonites and Moabites should not be naturalised, should not settle among them, nor unite with them, *v.* 1. The reason given is because they had been injurious and ill-natured to the Israel of God (*v.* 2), had not shown them common civility, but sought their ruin. This law we have, with this reason, Deut. xxiii. 3–5.

II. The people's ready compliance with this law, *v.* 3. See the benefit of the public reading of the word of God; it discovers to us sin and duty, good and evil, and shows us wherein we have erred. They *separated from Israel all the mixed multitude*, which had of old been a snare to them, for the *mixed multitude fell a-lusting*, Num. xi. 4. These they expelled.

III. The particular case of Tobiah, who was an Ammonite. He had the same enmity to Israel that his ancestors had, the spirit of an Ammonite, witness his indignation at Nehemiah (*ch.* ii. 10).

1. How basely Eliashib the chief priest took this Tobiah in to be a lodger even in the courts of the

JAMIESON, FAUSSET, BROWN — CHAPTER 13

VSS. 1-9. UPON THE READING OF THE LAW SEPARATION IS MADE FROM THE MIXED MULTITUDE. **1. On that day**—This was not immediately consequent on the dedication of the city wall and gates, but after Nehemiah's return from the Persian court to Jerusalem, his absence having extended over a considerable period. The transaction here described probably took place on one of the periodical occasions for the public readings of the law, when the people's attention was particularly directed to some violations of it which called for immediate correction. There is another instance afforded, in addition to those which have already fallen under our notice, of the great advantages resulting from the public and periodical reading of the divine law. It was an established provision for the religious instruction of the people, for diffusing a knowledge and a reverence for the sacred volume, as well as for removing those errors and corruptions which might, in the course of time, have crept in. **the Ammonite and the Moabite should not come into the congregation of God for ever**—i.e., not be incorporated into the Israelitish kingdom, nor united in marriage relations with that people (Deut. 23:3, 4). This appeal to the authority of the divine law led to a dis-

ADAM CLARKE — CHAPTER 13

1. *Should not come into the congregation.* That is, You shall not form any kind of matrimonial alliance with them. This, and this alone, is the meaning of the law.

3. *They separated from Israel all the mixed multitude.* They excluded all strange women, and all persons, young and old, who had been born of these illegal connections.

MATTHEW HENRY

temple. He was allied to Tobiah (*v.* 4), by marriage first and then by friendship. His grandson had married Sanballat's daughter, *v.* 28. Probably some other of his family had married Tobiah's. It was expressly provided by the law that the high priest should marry *one of his own people*, else he *profanes his seed among his people*, Lev. xxi. 14, 15. In the courts of the temple, out of several little chambers used for store-chambers, he contrived to make a state-room for Tobiah, *v.* 5. That Tobiah the Ammonite should be entertained with respect in Israel, in the courts of God's house, as if to confront God himself; this was next to setting up an idol there. An Ammonite must not *come into the congregation*; and shall one of the worst and vilest of the Ammonites be courted into the temple itself?

Well might Nehemiah add (*v.* 6), *But all this time was not I at Jerusalem.* If he had been there, the high priest durst not have done such a thing.

2. How bravely Nehemiah, the chief governor, threw him out, and all that belonged to him, and restored the chambers to their proper use. When he came to Jerusalem, and was informed by the good people who were troubled at it what an intimacy had grown between their chief priest and their chief enemy, it *grieved him sorely* (*v.* 7, 8). Nehemiah has power and he will use it for God. Tobiah shall be expelled. He fears not his resentments, or Eliashib's, but expels the intruder, by casting forth all his household stuff. Our Saviour thus *cleansed the temple*, that the *house of prayer* might not be a *den of thieves*. And thus those that would expel sin out of their hearts, those living temples, must throw out all those things that are the food and fuel of lust. The temple stores shall be brought in again, and the *vessels of the house of God put in their places*; but the chambers must first be sprinkled with the water of purification, and so cleansed. Thus, when sin is cast out of the heart by repentance, let the blood of Christ be applied to it by faith, and then let it be furnished with the graces of God's Spirit for every good work.

Verses 10–14

Another grievance redressed by Nehemiah.

I. The Levites had been wronged. Their *portions had not been given them*, *v.* 10. The Levites were so modest as not to sue for them; *for the Levites and singers fled every one to his field.* This comes in as a reason either, 1. Why their payments were withheld. The Levites were non-residents: when they should have been doing their work about the temple, they were at their farms in the country; and therefore the people were little inclined to give them their maintenance. Or rather, 2. It is the reason why Nehemiah soon perceived that their dues had been denied them, because he missed them from their posts. "They have gone to get a livelihood for themselves and their families out of their grounds; for their profession would not maintain them." A scandalous maintenance makes a scandalous ministry.

II. Nehemiah laid the fault upon the rulers. Nehemiah began with the rulers, and called them to an account: "*Why is the house of God forsaken? v.* 11. Why are the Levites starved out of it?"

III. He delayed not to bring the dispersed Levites to *their places* again, and set them in *their stations* (as the word is), *v.* 11.

IV. He obliged the people to bring in their tithes, *v.* 12.

V. He provided that just and prompt payment should be made of the Levites' stipends. Commissioners were appointed to see to this (*v.* 13).

VI. Having no recompence from those for whom he did these good services, he looks up to God as his paymaster (*v.* 14): *Remember me, O my God! concerning this.* Nehemiah was a man much in pious ejaculations. He only prays, *Remember me*, not *Reward me.*

JAMIESON, FAUSSET, BROWN

solution of all heathen alliances (ch. 9:2; Ezra 10:3). **4. before this**—The practice of these mixed marriages, in open neglect or violation of the law, had become so common, that even the pontifical house, which ought to have set a better example, was polluted by such an impure mixture. **Eliashib the priest . . . was allied unto Tobiah**—This person was the high priest (vs. 28; also ch. 3:1), who, by virtue of his dignified office, had the superintendence and control of the apartments attached to the temple. The laxity of his principles, as well as of his practice, is sufficiently apparent from his contracting a family connection with so notorious an enemy of Israel as Tobiah. But his obsequious attentions had carried him much farther; for to accommodate so important a person as Tobiah on his occasional visits to Jerusalem, Eliashib had provided him a splendid apartment in the temple. The introduction of so gross an impropriety can be accounted for in no other way than by supposing that in the absence of the priests and the cessation of the services, the temple was regarded as a common public building, which might, in the circumstances, be appropriated as a palatial residence. **6. But in all this was not I at Jerusalem**—Eliashib—concluding that, as Nehemiah had departed from Jerusalem, and, on the expiry of his allotted term of absence, had resigned his government, he had gone not to return—began to use great liberties, and, there being none left whose authority or frown he dreaded, allowed himself to do things most unworthy of his sacred office, and which, though in unison with his own irreligious character, he would not have dared to attempt during the residence of the pious governor. Nehemiah resided twelve years as governor of Jerusalem, and having succeeded in repairing and refortifying the city, he at the end of that period returned to his duties in Shushan. How long he remained there is not expressly said, but "after certain days," which is a Scripture phraseology for a year or a number of years, he obtained leave to resume the government of Jerusalem; to his deep mortification and regret, he found matters in the neglected and disorderly state here described. Such gross irregularities as were practised, such extraordinary corruptions as had crept in, evidently imply the lapse of a considerable time. Besides, they exhibit the character of Eliashib, the high priest, in a most unfavorable light; for while he ought, by his office, to have preserved the inviolable sanctity of the temple and its furniture, his influence had been directly exercised for evil; especially he had given permission and countenance to a most indecent outrage—the appropriation of the best apartments in the sacred building to a heathen governor, one of the worst and most determined enemies of the people and the worship of God. The very first reform Nehemiah on his second visit resolved upon, was the stopping of this gross profanation. The chamber which had been polluted by the residence of the idolatrous Ammonite was, after undergoing the process of ritual purification (Num. 15:9), restored to its proper use—a storehouse for the sacred vessels.

10-14. NEHEMIAH REFORMS THE OFFICERS IN THE HOUSE OF GOD. **10. And I perceived that the portions of the Levites had not been given them**—The people, disgusted with the malversations of Eliashib, or the lax and irregular performance of the sacred rites, withheld the tithes, so that the ministers of religion were compelled for their livelihood to withdraw to their patrimonial possessions in the country. The temple services had ceased; all religious duties had fallen into neglect. The money put into the sacred treasury had been squandered in the entertainment of an Ammonite heathen, an open and contemptuous enemy of God and His people. The return of the governor put an end to these disgraceful and profane proceedings. He administered a sharp rebuke to those priests to whom the management of the temple and its services was committed, for the total neglect of their duties, and the violation of the solemn promises which they had made to him at his departure. He upbraided them with the serious charge of having not only withheld from men their dues, but of having robbed God, by neglecting the care of His house and service. And thus having roused them to a sense of duty and incited them to testify their godly sorrow for their criminal negligence by renewed devotedness to their sacred work, Nehemiah restored the temple services. He recalled the dispersed Levites to the regular discharge of their duties; while the people at large, perceiving that their contributions would be no longer perverted to improper uses, willingly brought in their tithes as formerly. Men of integrity and good report were appointed to act as trustees of the sacred treasures, and thus order, regularity, and active serv-

ADAM CLARKE

4. *Eliashib the priest.* Perhaps this was a different person from Eliashib, the high priest; but there is no indubitable evidence that he was not the same. If he was high priest, he was very unfaithful to the high charge which he had received, and a reproach to the priesthood. He had married his grandson to Sanballat's daughter; this produced a connection with Tobiah, the fast friend of Sanballat, in whose favor he polluted the house of God, giving him one of the chambers for his ordinary residence, which were appointed for the reception of the tithes, oblations, etc., that came to the house of God.

6. *Was not I at Jerusalem.* Nehemiah came to Jerusalem in the twentieth year of Artaxerxes, and remained there till the thirty-second year, twelve years; then returned to Babylon, and staid one year; got leave to revisit his brethren; and found matters as stated in this chapter.

8. *I cast forth all the household stuff of Tobiah.* He acted as Jesus Christ did when He found the courts of the Lord's house profaned: "He overthrew the tables of the money-changers, and the seats of them that sold doves."

10. *The portions of the Levites had not been given.* Hence we find they were obliged to abandon the sacred service and betake themselves to cultivate the land for their support. This was the fault of the rulers, who permitted all these abuses.

11. *Why is the house of God forsaken?* They had all solemnly promised, chap. x. 39, that they would never forsake the house of their God; but, alas, how soon is this forgotten! Nehemiah used their own words here by way of reproof.

13. *They were counted faithful.* They were reported to me as persons in whom I could confide; they had been steady in God's ways and work, while others had been careless and relaxed.

MATTHEW HENRY

Verses 15–22

Another instance of that blessed reformation in which Nehemiah was so active. He revived sabbath-sanctification, and maintained the authority of the fourth commandment.

I. The law of the sabbath was very strict and much insisted on, and with good reason, for religion is never in the throne while sabbaths are trodden under foot. But Nehemiah discovered even in Judah this law was wretchedly violated. 1. The husbandmen trod their winepresses and brought home their corn on that day (*v.* 15), though there was an express command that *in earing-time, and in harvest-time, they should rest* on the sabbaths (Exod. xxxiv. 21). 2. The carriers *loaded their asses with all manner of burdens*, and made no scruple of it, though there was a particular proviso in the law for the cattle resting (Deut. v. 14) and that they should *bear no burden on the sabbath day*, Jer. xvii. 21. 3. The hawkers, and pedlars, and petty chapmen, that were men of Tyre, that famous trading city, *sold all manner of wares* on the sabbath day (*v.* 16).

II. The reformation of it.

1. *He testified against those* who profaned it, *v.* 15, and again *v.* 21.

2. He reasoned with the rulers concerning it, took the nobles of Judah to task, *v.* 17. He charges them with it: *You do it.* They did not carry corn, nor sell fish, but, they connived at those that did, and did not use their power to restrain them, and so made themselves guilty, as those magistrates do who bear the sword in vain. They set a bad example in other things. If the nobles allowed themselves in sports and recreations, in idle visits and idle talk, on the sabbath day, the men of business, both in city and country, would profane it by their worldly employments, as more justifiable. He reasons the case with them (*v.* 18). If they did not take warning, but returned to the same sins again, they had reason to expect further judgments: *You bring more wrath upon Israel by profaning the sabbath.*

3. He took care to prevent the profanation of the sabbath, as one that aimed only at reformation. If he could reform them, he would not punish them, and, if he should punish them, it was but that he might reform them. This is an example to magistrates to be heirs of restraint, and prudently to use the bit and bridle, that there may be no occasion for the lash. He ordered the gates of Jerusalem to be kept shut from the evening before the sabbath to the morning after, and set his own servants to watch them, that no burdens should be brought in on the sabbath day, nor late the night before, nor early in the morning after, lest sabbath time should be encroached upon, *v.* 19. He threatened those who came with goods to the gates, telling them that, if they came again, he would certainly lay hands on them (*v.* 21). He charged the Levites to take care about the due sanctifying of the sabbath, that they should cleanse themselves in the first place, and so give a good example to the people, and *that they should* some of them *come and keep the gates*, *v.* 22. Then there is likely to be a reformation, in this and other respects, when magistrates and ministers join their forces. The cure he wrought was lasting. In our Saviour's time, we find the Jews in the other extreme, over-scrupulous in the ceremonial part of Sabbath-sanctification.

4. He concludes this passage with a prayer (*v.* 22).

Verses 23-31

One instance more of Nehemiah's pious zeal for the purifying of his countrymen as a peculiar people to God.

I. They had corrupted themselves by marrying strange wives. This was complained of in Ezra's time, and much done towards a reformation, Ezra ix and x. Nehemiah, like a good governor, enquired into the state of the families of those that were under his charge, that he might reform what was amiss in them, and so heal the streams by healing the springs. He found that many of the Jews had *married wives of Ashdod, of Ammon, and of Moab* (*v.* 23). He talked with the children, and found they were *children of strangers*, for their *speech betrayed them.* The children were bred up with their mothers, and learned of them and their nurses and servants to speak, so that they could not speak the Jews' language, or not purely, but *half in the speech of Ashdod*, or Ammon, or Moab, according as the country was which the mother was a native of.

II. What course Nehemiah took to purge out this corruption.

1. He showed them the evil of it, and the obligation he lay under to witness against it. He quotes a precept, to prove that it was in itself a great sin; and makes

JAMIESON, FAUSSET, BROWN

ice were re-established in the temple.

15-31. The Violation of the Sabbath. **15. In those days saw I in Judah some treading wine presses on the sabbath**—The cessation of the temple services had been necessarily followed by a public profanation of the Sabbath, and this had gone so far that labor was carried on in the fields, and fish brought to the markets on the sacred day.

Nehemiah took the decisive step of ordering the city gates to be shut, and not to be opened, till the Sabbath was past; and in order to ensure the faithful execution of this order, he stationed some of his own servants as guards, to prevent the introduction of any commodities on that day. On the merchants and various dealers finding admission denied them, they set up booths outside the walls, in hopes of still driving a traffic with the peasantry; but the governor threatened, if they continued, to adopt violent measures for their removal. For this purpose a body of Levites was stationed as sentinels at the gate, with discretionary powers to protect the sanctification of the Sabbath.

24. could not speak in the Jews' language, but according to the language of each people—a mongrel dialect imbibed from their mothers, together with foreign principles and habits.

ADAM CLARKE

15. *Treading wine presses.* The Sabbath appears to have been totally disregarded.

17. *I contended with the nobles.* These evils took place through their negligence, and this I proved before them.

19. *When the gates . . . began to be dark.* After sunset on Friday evening he caused the gates to be shut, and kept them shut all the Sabbath; and, as he could not trust the ordinary officers, he set some of his own servants to watch the gates, that no person might enter for the purpose of traffic.

20. *So the merchants . . . lodged without Jerusalem.* They exposed their wares for sale on the outside of the walls.

21. *I will lay hands on you.* I will imprison every man of you. This had the desired effect; they *came . . . no more.*

24. *Half in the speech of Ashdod.* There were children in the same family by Jewish and Philistine mothers. As the Jewish mother would always speak to her children in Hebrew or Chaldee, so they learned to speak these languages; and as the Ashdod mother would always speak to her children in the Ashdod language, so they learned that tongue.

MATTHEW HENRY

them swear to that precept: *You shall not give your daughters unto their sons*, &c., which is taken from Deut. vii. 3. He quotes a precedent, to show the pernicious consequences of it, which made it necessary to be animadverted upon by the government (*v.* 26): *Did not Solomon king of Israel sin by these things?*

2. He showed himself highly displeased at it, that he might awaken them to a due sense of the evil of it: *He contended with them*, *v.* 25. He showed them how frivolous their excuses were, and argued it warmly with them. When he had silenced them he *cursed them*, that is, he denounced the judgments of God against them, and showed them what their sin deserved. Ezra, in this case, had plucked off his own hair, in holy sorrow for the sin; Nehemiah plucked off their hair, in a holy indignation at the sinners.

3. He obliged them not to take any more such wives, and separated those whom they had taken: *He cleansed them from all strangers*, both men and women (*v.* 30), and made them promise with an oath that they would never do so again, *v.* 25.

4. He took particular care of the priests' families, that they might not lie under this stain, this guilt. He found, upon enquiry, that a branch of the high priest's own family, one of his grandsons, had married a daughter of Sanballat, that notorious enemy of the Jews (*ch.* ii. 10; iv. 1), and so had, in effect, twisted interests with the Samaritans, *v.* 28. It seems this young priest would not put away his wife, and therefore Nehemiah *chased him from him*, deprived him, degraded him, and made him for ever incapable of the priesthood. Josephus says that this expelled priest was Manasseh, and that when Nehemiah drove him away he went to his father-in-law Sanballat, who built him a temple upon Mount Gerizim, like that at Jerusalem, and promised him he should be high priest in it, and that then was laid the foundation of the Samaritans' pretensions, which continued warm to our Saviour's time. Here are Nehemiah's prayers on this occasion. (1) He prays, *Remember them, O my God! v.* 29. "Lord, convince and convert them; put them in mind of what they should be and do, that they may come to themselves." (2) He prays, *Remember me, O my God! v.* 31.

JAMIESON, FAUSSET, BROWN

25. cursed them—i.e., pronounced on them an anathema which entailed excommunication. **smote . . . and plucked off their hair**—To cut off the hair of offenders seems to be a punishment rather disgraceful than severe; yet it is supposed that pain was added to disgrace, and that they tore off the hair with violence as if they were plucking a bird alive.

ADAM CLARKE

25. *I contended with them.* Proved the fact against these iniquitous fathers, in a legal assembly. *And cursed them.* Denounced the judgments of God and the sentence of the law upon them. *Smote certain of them.* Had them punished by whipping. *And plucked off their hair.* Had them shaven, as a mark of the greatest ignominy. *And made them swear by God, saying, Ye shall not give.* Caused them to bind themselves by an oath that they would make no intermarriages with those who were not of the seed of Israel.

26. *Did not Solomon?* Have you not had an awful example before you? What a heavy curse did Solomon's conduct bring upon himself and upon the people, for a conduct such as yours?

27. *Shall we then hearken unto you?* If God spared not Solomon, who was so much beloved of Him, shall we spare you, who by your conduct are bringing down God's judgments upon Israel?

28. *One of the sons of Joiada.* This was Manasseh, brother of Jaddua, son of Joiada, and grandson of Eliashib, the high priest. *I chased him from me.* Struck him off the list of the priests, and deemed him utterly unworthy of all connection and intercourse with truly religious people.

29. *Because they have defiled the priesthood.* God, therefore, will remember their iniquities against them, and punish them for their transgressions. These words of Nehemiah are to be understood declaratively.

31. *For the word offering.* This was a most necessary regulation; without it the Temple service could not have gone forward; and therefore Nehemiah mentions this as one of the most important services he had rendered to his nation. See chap. x. 34, *Remember me, O my God, for good.* This has precisely the same meaning with, "O my God, have mercy upon me!" and thus alone it should be understood.

THE BOOK OF ESTHER

I. The king's court (1:1-3:15)
A. The feast at Shushan (1:1-22)
B. The new queen (2:1-23)
C. Haman (3:1-15)

II. The country (4:1-3)
A. Mordecai (4:1, 2)
B. The Jews (4:3)

III. The king's court (4:4-8:17)
A. Esther and Mordecai (4:4-17)
B. Esther and the king (5:1-8)
C. Haman (5:9-14)
D. The sleepless king (6:1-14)
E. The queens's banquet (7:1-10)
F. Mordecai (8:1-17)

IV. The country (9:1-32)
A. Poetic retribution (9:1-19)
B. The Feast of Purim (9:20-32)

V. Conclusion (10:1-3)
A. Ahasuerus (10:1, 2)
B. Mordecai (10:3)

God deals not with us according to our folly and weakness. Those Jews who were scattered in the provinces of the heathen were taken care of as well as those who were gathered in the land of Judaea, and were wonderfully preserved when doomed to destruction and appointed as sheep for the slaughter. Who drew up this story is uncertain. Mordecai was as able as any man to relate, on his own knowledge, the several passages of it. That he wrote such an account of them as was necessary to inform his people of the grounds of their observing the feast of Purim we are told (ch. 9:20, "Mordecai wrote these things," and sent them enclosed in letters to all the Jews). It is the narrative of a plot laid against the Jews to cut them all off. The name of God is not found in this book; but the apocryphal addition to it (which is not in the Hebrew, nor was ever received by the Jews into the canon), containing six chapters, begins thus, "Then Mordecai said, God has done these things." But, though the name of God be not in it, the finger of God is, directing many minute events for the bringing about of his people's deliverance. In such ways as God here took to defeat Haman's plot he will still protect his people.

MATTHEW HENRY

CHAPTER 1

Verses 1–9

Which of the kings of Persia this Ahasuerus was the learned are not agreed. Mordecai is said to have been one of those that were *carried* captive from *Jerusalem* (*ch.* ii. 5, 6), whence it should seem that this Ahasuerus was one of the first kings of that empire. Dr. Lightfoot thinks that he was that Artaxerxes who hindered the building of the temple, who is called also *Ahasuerus* (Ezra iv. 6, 7), after his great-grandfather of the Medes, Dan. ix. 1.

I. Of the vast extent of his dominion. In the time of Darius and Cyrus there were but 120 provinces (Dan. vi. 1); now there were 127, *from India to Ethiopia*, *v.* 1. It had become an over-grown kingdom, which in time would sink with its own weight.

II. Of the great pomp and magnificence of his court. He made a most extravagant feast *to show the riches of his glorious kingdom and the honour of his excellent majesty*, *v.* 4. This was vain glory, to no purpose at all. If he had shown the riches of his kingdom as some of his successors did, in contributing towards the building of the temple (Ezra vi. 8; vii. 22), it would have turned to a much better account. Two feasts Ahasuerus made:—1. One for his nobles and princes, which lasted *a hundred and eighty days*, *v.* 3, 4. 2. Another was made for *all the people, both great and small*, which lasted *seven days in the court of the garden*, *v.* 5. The tents which were there pitched for the company, were very fine and rich; so were the beds and the pavement under their feet, *v.* 6.

III. Of the good order which in some respects was kept there notwithstanding. Yet the Chaldee paraphrase says that the vessels of the sanctuary were used in this feast, to the great grief of the pious Jews. Two things which are laudable from the account here given:—1. *The drinking was according to the law*, probably some law lately made; *none did compel*, no, not by a continual proposing of it (as Josephus explains it). This caution of a heathen prince, even when he would show his generosity, may shame many who are called Christians, who think they do not bid their friends welcome, unless they make them drunk, and, under pretence of sending the health round, send the sin round, and death with it. 2. There was no mixed dancing, Vashti feasted the women in her own apartment, *in the royal house*, *v.* 9. Thus, while the king showed the honour of his majesty, she and her ladies showed the honour of their modesty, which is truly the majesty of the fair sex.

Verses 10–22

Ahasuerus's feast; it ended in heaviness by his own folly. An unhappy falling out between the king and queen, broke off the feast abruptly, and sent the guests away silent and ashamed.

I. It was certainly the king's weakness to send for Vashti into his presence when he was drunk, and in company with gentlemen in the same condition. *When his heart was merry with wine* Vashti must come, well dressed as she was, with *the crown on*

JAMIESON, FAUSSET, BROWN

CHAPTER 1

Vss. 1-22. Ahasuerus Makes Royal Feasts. **1. Ahasuerus**—It is now generally agreed among learned men that the Ahasuerus mentioned in this episode is the Xerxes who figures in Grecian history. **3. made a feast unto all his princes and his servants**—Banquets on so grand a scale, and extending over so great a period, have been frequently provided by the luxurious monarchs of Eastern countries, both in ancient and modern times. The early portion of this festive season, however, seems to have been dedicated to amusement, particularly an exhibition of the magnificence and treasures of the court, and it was closed by a special feast of seven days' continuance, given within the gardens of the royal palace. The ancient palace of Susa has been recently disinterred from an incumbent mass of earth and ruins; and in that palace, which is, beyond all doubt, the actual edifice referred to in this passage, there is a great hall of marble pillars. "The position of the great colonnade corresponds with the account here given. It stands on an elevation in the center of the mound, the remainder of which we may well imagine to have been occupied, after the Persian fashion, with a garden and fountains. Thus the colonnade would represent the 'court of the garden of the king's palace' with its 'pillars of marble.' I am even inclined to believe the expression, 'Shushan the palace,' applies especially to this portion of the existing ruins, in contradistinction to the citadel and the city of Shushan" [Loftus' Chaldæa and Susiana]. **6. Where were white, green, and blue hangings,** etc.—The fashion, in the houses of the great, on festive occasions, was to decorate the chambers from the middle of the wall downward with damask or velvet hangings of variegated colors suspended on hooks, or taken down at pleasure. **the beds were of gold and silver**—i.e., the couches on which, according to Oriental fashion, the guests reclined, and which were either formed entirely of gold and silver or inlaid with ornaments of those costly metals, stood on an elevated floor of parti-colored marble. **7. they gave them drink in vessels of gold**—There is reason to believe from this account, as well as from ch. 5:6, 7:2, 7, 8, where the drinking of wine occupies by far the most prominent place in the description, that this was a banquet rather than a feast. **9. Also Vashti the queen made a feast for the women**—The celebration was double; for, as according to the Oriental fashion, the sexes do not intermingle in society, the court ladies were entertained in a separate apartment by the queen.

10-12. On the seventh day, when the heart of the king was merry with wine—As the feast-days advanced, the drinking was more freely indulged in, so that the close was usually marked by great excesses of revelry. **he commanded**

ADAM CLARKE

CHAPTER 1

1. *Now it came to pass.* The Ahasuerus of the Romans, the Artaxerxes of the Greeks, and Ardsheer of the Persians are the same. *Reigned, from India even unto Ethopia.* This is nearly the same account that is given by Xenophon.

2. *Sat on the throne of his kingdom.* Having subdued all his enemies, and brought universal peace to his empire. *Shushan the palace.* The ancient city of Susa. This, with Ecbatana and Babylon, was a residence of the Persian kings. The word which we render *the palace* should be rendered "the city," as in the Septuagint.

4. *The riches of his glorious kingdom.* Luxury was the characteristic of the Eastern monarchs, and particularly of the Persians. In their feasts, which were superb and of long continuance, they made a general exhibition of their wealth, grandeur, etc., and received the highest encomiums from their poets and flatterers.

5. *A feast unto all the people.* The first was a feast for the nobles in general; this, for the people of the city at large. *In the court of the garden.* As the company was very numerous that was to be received, no apartments in the palace could be capable of containing them; therefore the *court of the garden* was chosen.

6. *White, green, and blue hangings.* It was customary, on such occasions, not only to hang the place about with elegant curtains of the above colors, but also to have a canopy of rich stuffs suspended on cords from side to side of the place in which they feasted. The *beds . . . of gold and silver* mentioned here were the couches covered with gold and silver cloth, on which the guests reclined.

7. *Vessels being diverse.* They had different services of plate.

8. *None did compel: for so the king had appointed.* Every person drank what he pleased; he was not obliged to take more than he had reason to think would do him good.

9. *Also Vashti the queen. Vashti* is a mere Persian word, and signifies a "beautiful or excellent woman." *Made a feast for the women.* The king, having subdued all his enemies, left no competitor for the kingdom; and being thus quietly and firmly seated on the throne, made this a time of general festivity. As the women of the East never mingle with the men in public, Vashti made a feast for the Persian ladies by themselves; and while the men were in the court of the garden, the women were in the royal house.

MATTHEW HENRY

her head, that the princes and people might see what a handsome woman she was, *v.* 10, 11. Hereby, 1. He dishonoured himself as a husband, who ought to be to her *a covering of the eyes* (Gen. xx. 16), not to uncover them. 2. It was against the custom of the Persians for the women to appear in public, and he put a great hardship upon her when he did not court, but command her to do so uncouth a thing, and make her a show.

II. *She refused to come* (*v.* 12); though he sent his command by seven honourable messengers, yet she persisted in her denial. Had she come, while it was evident that she did it in pure obedience, it would have been no reflection upon her modesty. Perhaps she refused in a haughty manner, and then it was certainly evil; she *scorned to come at the king's commandment*. What a mortification was this to him!

III. The king thereupon grew outrageous. He that had rule over 127 provinces had no rule over his own spirit, but his *anger burned in him*, *v.* 12.

IV. Though he was very angry, he would not do anything till he advised with his privy-counsellors. Of these counsellors it is said that they were learned men, for they *knew law* and *judgment*,—that they were wise men, for they *knew the times*,—and that the king put great confidence in them and honour upon them, for they *saw the king's face and sat first in the kingdom*, *v.* 13, 14.

1. The question proposed to this cabinet-council (*v.* 15): *What shall we do to the queen Vashti according to the law?*

2. The proposal which Memucan made, that Vashti should be divorced for her disobedience. (1) He shows what would be the bad consequences of the queen's disobedience to her husband, if it were passed by. (2) He shows what would be the good consequence of a decree against Vashti that she should be divorced. Therefore they gave this judgment against her, that she *come no more before the king*, and this judgment so ratified as never to be reversed, *v.* 19.

3. The edict that passed according to this proposal, signifying that the queen was divorced for contumacy, according to the law, and that, if other wives were in like manner undutiful to their husbands, they must expect to be in like manner disgraced (*v.* 21, 22): were they better than the queen?

JAMIESON, FAUSSET, BROWN

. . . the seven chamberlains—These were the eunuchs who had charge of the royal harem.

The refusal of Vashti to obey an order which required her to make an indecent exposure of herself before a company of drunken revellers, was becoming both the modesty of her sex and her rank as queen; for, according to Persian customs, the queen, even more than the wives of other men, was secluded from the public gaze. Had not the king's blood been heated with wine, or his reason overpowered by force of offended pride, he would have perceived that his own honor, as well as hers, was consulted by her dignified conduct. **13. Then the king said to the wise men**—These were probably the magi, without whose advice as to the proper time of doing a thing the Persian kings never did take any step whatever; and the persons named in the following verse were the "seven counsellors" (cf. Ezra 7:14) who formed the state ministry. The combined wisdom of all, it seems, was enlisted to consult with the king what course should be taken after so unprecedented an occurrence as Vashti's disobedience of the royal summons. It is scarcely possible for us to imagine the astonishment produced by such a refusal in a country and a court where the will of the sovereign was absolute. The assembled grandees were petrified with horror at the daring affront. Alarm for the consequences that might ensue to each of them in his own household next seized on their minds; and the sounds of bacchanalian revelry were hushed into deep and anxious consultation what punishment to inflict on the refractory queen. But a purpose was to be served by the flattery of the king and the enslavement of all women. The counsellors were too intoxicated or obsequious to oppose the courtly advice of Memucan. It was unanimously resolved, with a wise regard to the public interests of the nation, that the punishment of Vashti could be nothing short of degradation from her royal dignity. The doom was accordingly pronounced and made known in all parts of the empire.

ADAM CLARKE

10. *He commanded Mehuman.* All these are doubtless Persian names, but so disguised by passing through a Hebrew medium that some of them can scarcely be known. *Mehuman* signifies a "stranger or guest."

12. *Vashti refused to come.* And much should she be commended for it. What woman, possessing even a common share of prudence and modesty, could consent to expose herself to the view of such a group of drunken Bacchanalians? Her courage was equal to her modesty: she would resist the royal mandate rather than violate the rules of chaste decorum.

14. *And the next unto him . . . the seven princes.* Probably the privy counsellors of the king. *Which saw the king's face*—were at all times admitted to the royal presence.

18. *The ladies of Persia.* The "princesses."

19. *That it be not altered.* Let it be inserted among the permanent laws.

MATTHEW HENRY — CHAPTER 2

Verses 1–20

Vashti being humbled for her height, Esther is advanced for her humility. Observe,

I. The extravagant course that was taken to please the king with another wife instead of Vashti. Josephus says that when his anger was over he would have been reconciled to Vashti but that, by the constitution of the government, the judgment was irrevocable. Therefore, to make him forget her, they contrived how to entertain him first with a great variety of concubines. All the provinces of his kingdom must be searched for fair young virgins, and officers appointed to choose them, *v.* 3. After the king had once taken them to his bed they were looked upon as secondary wives, were maintained by the king accordingly, and might not marry. We may see, by this instance, to what absurd practices those came who were destitute of divine revelation, and who, as a punishment for their idolatry, were given up to vile affections. Having broken through that law of creation which resulted from God's making man, they broke through another law, which was founded upon his making one man and one woman. See what need there was of the gospel of Christ to purify men from the lusts of the flesh and to reduce them to the original institution.

II. The overruling providence of God bringing Esther to be queen. She came in her turn, after several others, and it was found that Esther excelled them all. Concerning Esther,

1. Her origin and character. (1) She was one of the *children of the captivity*, a Jewess and a sharer with her people in their bondage. (2) She was an orphan; her father and mother were both dead (*v.* 7), but, when they had forsaken her, then the Lord took her up, Ps. xxvii. 10. (3) She was a beauty, *fair of form, good of countenance*; so it is in the margin, *v.* 7. Her wisdom and virtue were her greatest beauty, but it is an advantage to a diamond to be well set. (4) Mordecai, her cousin-german, was her guardian, *brought her up, and took her for his own daughter*. Let God be acknowledged in raising up friends for the fatherless and motherless; let it be an encouragement to that pious instance of charity that many who have taken care of the education of orphans have lived to see the good fruit of their care and pains, abund-

JAMIESON, FAUSSET, BROWN — CHAPTER 2

Vss. 1-20. Esther Chosen to Be Queen. **1. After these things, when the wrath of King Ahasuerus was appeased**—On recovering from the violent excitement of his revelry and rage, the king was pierced with poignant regret for the unmerited treatment he had given to his beautiful and dignified queen. But, according to the law, which made the word of a Persian king irrevocable, she could not be restored. His counsellors, for their own sake, were solicitous to remove his disquietude, and hastened to recommend the adoption of all suitable means for gratifying their royal master with another consort of equal or superior attractions to those of his divorced queen. In the despotic countries of the East the custom obtains that when an order is sent to a family for a young damsel to repair to the royal palace, the parents, however unwilling, dare not refuse the honor for their daughter; and although they know that when she is once in the royal harem, they will never see her again, they are obliged to yield a silent and passive compliance. On the occasion referred to, a general search was commanded to be made for the greatest beauties throughout the empire, in the hope that, from their ranks, the disconsolate monarch might select one for the honor of succeeding to the royal honors of Vashti. The damsels, on arrival at the palace, were placed under the custody of "Hege, the king's chamberlain, keeper of the women," i.e., the chief eunuch, usually a repulsive old man, on whom the court ladies are very dependent, and whose favor they are always desirous to secure. **5. Now in Shushan the palace there was a certain Jew**—Mordecai held some office about the court. But his "sitting at the king's gate" (vs. 21) does not necessarily imply that he was in the humble condition of a porter; for, according to an institute of Cyrus, all state officers were required to wait in the outer courts till they were summoned into the presence-chamber. He might, therefore, have been a person of some official dignity. This man had an orphan cousin, born during the exile, under his care, who being distinguished by great personal beauty, was one of the young damsels taken into the royal harem on this occasion. She had the good fortune at once to gain the good-will of the chief

ADAM CLARKE — CHAPTER 2

2. *Let there be fair young virgins sought for the king.* This was the usual way in which the harem was furnished; the finest women in the land, whether of high or low birth, were sought out, and brought to the harem. They all became the king's concubines; but one was raised, as chief wife, to the throne, and her issue was specially entitled to inherit.

3. *Hege the king's chamberlain.* "Hege, the king's *eunuch*"; so the Septuagint, Vulgate, Targum, and Syriac. In the Eastern countries the women are intrusted to the care of the eunuchs only. *Let their things for purification be given them.* "Their cosmetics." What these were we are told in v. 12; "oil of myrrh" and "sweet odours." The myrrh was employed for six months, and the "odours" for six months more, after which the person was brought to the king. This space was sufficient to show whether the young woman had been chaste, whether she were with child or not, that the king might not be imposed on, and be obliged to father a spurious offspring, which might have been the case had not this precaution been used.

7. *He brought up Hadassah. Hadassah* signifies a "myrtle" in Chaldee; this was probably her first or Babylonish name. When she came to the Persian court, she was called Esther, which signifies a "star" in Persian. Esther was the daughter of Abihail, the uncle of Mordecai, and therefore must have been Mordecai's cousin.

9. *The maiden pleased him.* He conceived a partiality for her above the rest, probably because of the propriety of her deportment, and her engaging though unassuming manners. *Seven maidens.* These were to attend her to the bath, to anoint and adorn her, and be her servants in general.

MATTHEW HENRY

antly to their comfort. Mordecai being Esther's guardian we are told, [1] How tender he was of her, as if she had been his own child (*v.* 11). [2] How respectful she was to him. Though in relation she was his equal, yet, being in age and dependance his inferior, she honoured him as her father—*did his commandment, v.* 20. She did not *show her people or her kindred,* because Mordecai had charged her that she should not, *v.* 10. He did not bid her tell a lie to conceal her parentage; he only told her not to proclaim her country. She being born in Shushan, and her parents being dead, all took her to be of Persian extraction.

2. Her preferment. Who would have thought that a Jewess, a captive, an orphan, was born to be a queen, an empress! The king's chamberlain honoured her (*v.* 9), and was ready to serve her. The king himself fell in love with her. The more natural beauty is the more agreeable. *The king loved Esther above all the women, v.* 17. Now he needed not to take time to deliberate; he is soon determined to *set the royal crown upon her head, and make her queen, v.* 17. This was done in his seventh year (*v.* 16). He graced the solemnity of her coronation with a *royal feast* (*v.* 18). He also granted a *release to the provinces,* either a remittance of the taxes in arrear or an act of grace for criminals. Esther still *did the commandment of Mordecai, as when she was brought up with him, v.* 20. Mordecai sat *in the king's gate*; that was the height of his preferment: he was one of the porters or doorkeepers of the court.

Verses 21–23

This good service which Mordecai did to the government, in discovering a plot against the life of the king, is here recorded, because the mention of it will again occur to his advantage. No step is yet taken towards Haman's design of the Jews' destruction, but several steps are taken towards God's design of their deliverance. God now gives Mordecai an opportunity of doing the king a good turn, that he might have the fairer opportunity afterwards of doing the Jews a good turn. 1. A design was laid against the king by two of his own servants, who sought *to lay hands on him,* not only to make him a prisoner, but to take away his life, *v.* 21. 2. Mordecai got notice of their treason, and, by Esther's means, discovered it to the king, hereby confirming her in and recommending himself to the king's favour. 3. The traitors were hanged, as they deserved, but not till their treason was, upon search, fully proved against them (*v.* 23), and the whole matter was recorded in the king's journals, with a particular remark that Mordecai was the man who discovered the treason.

JAMIESON, FAUSSET, BROWN

eunuch. Her sweet and amiable appearance made her a favorite with all who looked upon her (vs. 15, last clause). Her Hebrew name (vs. 7) was Hadassah, i.e., myrtle, which, on her introduction into the royal harem, was changed to Esther, i.e., the star Venus, indicating beauty and good fortune [GENESIUS]. **11. Mordecai walked every day before the court of the women's house**—The harem is an inviolable sanctuary, and what is transacted within its walls is as much a secret to those without as if they were thousands of miles away. But hints were given him through the eunuchs. **12. Now when every maid's turn was come to go in to King Ahasuerus**—A whole year was spent in preparation for the intended honor. Considering that this took place in a palace, the long period prescribed, together with the profusion of costly and fragrant cosmetics employed, was probably required by state etiquette. **17. the king loved Esther above all the women**—The choice fell on Esther, who found favor in the eyes of Ahasuerus. He elevated her to the dignity of chief wife, or queen. The other competitors had apartments assigned them in the royal harem, and were retained in the rank of secondary wives, of whom Oriental princes have a great number. **he set the royal crown upon her head**—This consisted only of a purple ribbon, streaked with white, bound round the forehead. The nuptials were celebrated by a magnificent entertainment, and, in honor of the auspicious occasion, "he made a release to the provinces, and gave gifts, according to the state of the king." The dotation of Persian queens consisted in consigning to them the revenue of certain cities, in various parts of the kingdom, for defraying their personal and domestic expenditure. Some of these imposts the king remitted or lessened at this time.

21-23. MORDECAI, DISCOVERING A TREASON, IS RECORDED IN THE CHRONICLES. **21. In those days . . . two of the king's chamberlains . . . were wroth and sought to lay hand on the king,** etc.—This secret conspiracy against the king's life probably arose out of revenge for the divorce of Vashti, in whose interest, and at whose instigation, these eunuchs may have acted. Through the vigilance of Mordecai, whose fidelity, however, passed unnoticed, the design was frustrated, while the conspirators were condemned to be executed and as the matter was recorded in the court annals, it became the occasion afterwards of Mordecai's preferment to the place of power and influence for which, in furtherance of the national interests of the Jews, divine providence intended him.

ADAM CLARKE

10. *Esther had not shewed her people.* This might have prejudiced her with the king, for it was certainly no credit at the Persian court to be a Jew; and we shall find from the sequel that those who were in the Persian dominions were far from being reputable, or in a safe state. Besides, had her lineage been known, envy might have prevented her from ever having access to the king.

13. *Whatsoever she desired.* When any of the young women were called to go to the king, it appears that it was an ordinance that whatever kind of dress stuff, color, jewels, etc., they thought best to set off their persons, and render them more engaging, should be given them.

14. *She returned into the second house.* This was the place where the king's concubines were kept. They went out no more, and were never given in marriage to any man, and saw the king's face no more unless specially called. *Custody of Shaashgaz.* This is probably another Persian name; "beardless," a proper epithet of a eunuch.

15. *She required nothing.* She left this entirely to her friend Hege, who seems to have been intent on her success. She therefore left her decorations to his judgment alone, and went in that dress and in those ornaments which he deemed most suitable.

16. *The tenth month . . . Tebeth.* Answering to part of our December and January.

18. *Made a release to the provinces.* Remitted some kind of tribute or impost in honor of Esther at her coronation.

21. *Mordecai sat in the king's gate.* Mordecai might have been one of the officers of the king, as the gate was the place where such usually attended to await the king's call. It has been observed that the name of God does not once occur in this book. This is true of the Hebrew text, and all translations from it; but in the Septuagint we find the following words, in v. 20, after, "Esther had not yet shewed her kindred": "For so Mordecai had charged her to fear God, and to keep his commandments, as she did when with him."

MATTHEW HENRY — CHAPTER 3

Verses 1–6

I. Haman advanced by the prince, and adored thereupon by the people. Haman was an Agagite (an Amalekite, says Josephus), probably of the descendants of Agag, a common name of the princes of Amalek, as appears, Num. xxiv. 7. The king took a fancy to him (princes are not bound to give reasons for their favours), made him his favourite, his confidant, his prime-minister of state. It is plain that he was not a man of honour or justice, of any true courage or steady conduct, but proud, and passionate, and revengeful; yet was he promoted, and caressed, and there was none so great as he.

II. Mordecai adhering to his principles with a bold and daring resolution, and therefore refusing to reverence Haman as the rest of the king's servants did, *v.* 2. He was urged to it by his friends. They *spoke daily to him* (*v.* 4), to persuade him to conform, but all in vain: he hearkened not to them, but told them plainly that he was a Jew, and could not in conscience do it. It does not appear that anyone scrupled at conforming to it except Mordecai; and yet his refusal was pious, conscientious, and pleasing to God, for the religion of a Jew forbade him, 1. To give such extravagant honours as were required to any mortal man, especially so wicked a man as Haman was. In the apocryphal chapters of this book (*ch.* xiii. 12–14) Mordecai is brought in thus appealing to God in this matter: *Thou knowest, Lord, that it was neither in contempt nor pride, nor for any desire of glory, that I did not bow down to proud Haman, for I could have been content with goodwill, for the salvation of Israel, to kiss the soles of his feet; but I did this that I might not prefer the glory of man above the glory of God, neither will I worship any but thee.* 2. He especially thought it a piece of injustice to his nation to give such honour to an Amalekite, one of that

JAMIESON, FAUSSET, BROWN — CHAPTER 3

VSS. 1-15. HAMAN, ADVANCED BY THE KING, AND DESPISED BY MORDECAI, SEEKS REVENGE ON ALL THE JEWS. **1. After these things did Ahasuerus promote Haman . . . and set his seat above all the princes**—i.e., raised him to the rank of vizier, or prime confidential minister, whose pre-eminence in office and power appeared in the elevated state chair appropriated to that supreme functionary. Such a distinction in seats was counted of vast importance in the formal court of Persia.

2. all the king's servants, that were in the king's gate, bowed, and reverenced Haman—Large mansions in the East are entered by a spacious vestibule, or gateway, along the sides of which visitors sit, and are received by the master of the house; for none, except the nearest relatives or special friends, are admitted farther. There the officers of the ancient king of Persia waited till they were called, and did obeisance to the all-powerful minister of the day. **But Mordecai bowed not, nor did him reverence**—The obsequious homage of prostration not entirely foreign to the manners of the East, had not been claimed by former viziers; but this minion required that all subordinate officers of the court should bow before him with their faces to the earth. But to Mordecai, it seemed that such an attitude of profound reverence was due only to God. Haman being an Amalekite, one of a doomed and accursed race, was, doubtless, another element in the refusal; and on learning that the recusant was a Jew, whose nonconformity was grounded on religious scruples, the magnitude of the affront appeared so much the greater, as the example of Mordecai would be imitated by all his compatriots. Had the homage

ADAM CLARKE — CHAPTER 3

1. *Haman . . . the Agagite.* Perhaps he was some descendant of that Agag, king of the Amalekites, spared by Saul, but destroyed by Samuel; and on this ground might have an antipathy to the Jews. *Set his seat above all the princes.* Made him his prime minister, and put all the officers of state under his direction.

2. *The king's servants, that were in the king's gate.* By *servants* here, certainly a higher class of officers are intended than porters; and Mordecai was one of those officers, and came to the gate with the others who were usually there in attendance to receive the commands of the king.

Mordecai bowed not. "He did not bow down"; *nor did him reverence, velo yishtachaveh,* "nor did he prostrate himself." I think it most evident, from these two words, that it was not civil reverence merely that Haman expected and Mordecai refused; this sort of respect is found in the word *cara,* to "bow." This sort of reverence Mordecai could not refuse without being guilty of the most inexcusable obstinacy, nor did any part of the Jewish law forbid it. But Haman expected, what the Persian kings frequently received, a species of divine adoration; and this is implied in the word *shachah,* which signifies that kind of prostration which implies the highest

MATTHEW HENRY

nation with which God had sworn that he would have perpetual war (Exod. xvii. 16) and concerning which he had given that solemn charge (Deut. xxv. 17), *Remember what Amalek did.*

III. Haman meditating revenge. Some that hoped thereby to curry favour with Haman took notice to him of Mordecai's rudeness, waiting to see whether he would bend or break, *v.* 4. Haman then observed it himself, and was *full of wrath, v.* 5. It is soon resolved that Mordecai must die. Haman thinks his life nothing towards a satisfaction for the affront: thousands of innocent and valuable lives must be sacrificed to his indignation; and therefore he vows the destruction of all the people of Mordecai, for his sake, because his being a Jew was the reason he gave why he did not reverence Haman.

Verses 7–15

Haman doubts not but to find desperate and bloody hands enough to cut all their throats if the king will but give him leave. He obtained leave, and commission to do it.

I. He makes a false and malicious representation of the Jews, and their character, to the king, *v.* 8. He would have the king believe, 1. That the Jews were a despicable people, and that it was not for his credit to harbour them: "*A certain people there is, scattered abroad and dispersed in all the provinces* as fugitives and vagabonds on the earth, and inmates in all countries, the burden and scandal of the places where they live." 2. That they were a dangerous people. "They have laws of their own, and conform not to the statutes of the kingdom, and may be looked upon as disaffected to the government, which may end in a rebellion."

II. He bids leave to destroy them all, *v.* 9. He knew there were many that hated the Jews. *Let it be written* therefore *that they may be destroyed.* Give but orders for a general massacre of all the Jews. If the king will gratify him in this matter, he will make him a present of *ten thousand talents*, which shall be *paid into the king's treasuries.* This, he thought, would obviate the strongest objection that the government must needs sustain loss in its revenues by the destruction of so many of its subjects. No doubt Haman knew how to re-imburse himself out of the spoil of the Jews, which his janizaries were to seize for him (*v.* 13), and so to make them bear the charges of their own ruin.

III. He obtains what he desired, a full commission to do what he would with the Jews, *v.* 10, 11. The king was so bewitched with Haman, that he was willing to believe the worst concerning the Jews, and therefore he gave them up into his hands, as lambs to the lion: *The people are thine, do with them as it seemeth good unto thee.* So little did he consider how much Haman would gain in the spoil, that he gave him withal the ten thousand talents: *The silver is thine.*

IV. He then consults with his soothsayers to find out a lucky day for the designed massacre, *v.* 7. The resolve was taken up in the first month, in the twelfth year of the king, when Esther had been his wife about five years. The lot fell upon the twelfth month, so that Mordecai and Esther had eleven months for the defeating of the design. Haman, though eager to have the Jews cut off, yet will submit to the laws of his superstition. God's wisdom serves its own purposes by men's folly. Haman has appealed to the lot, and to the lot he shall go, which, by adjourning the execution, gives judgment against him and breaks the neck of the plot.

V. The bloody edict is drawn up, signed, and published, giving orders to the militia of every province to be ready against *the thirteenth day of the twelfth month*, and, on that day, to murder all the Jews, men, women, and children, and seize their effects, *v.* 12–14. No crime is laid to their charge; but die they must, without mercy.

VI. The different temper of the court and city hereupon. The court was very merry upon it: *The king and Haman sat down to drink.* Haman was afraid lest the king's conscience should smite him for what he had done, to prevent which he kept him drinking. This cursed method many take to drown their convictions, and harden their own hearts and the hearts of others in sin. The city was very sad upon it: *The city of Shushan was perplexed*, not only the Jews themselves, but all their neighbours that had any principles of justice and compassion. It grieved them to see men that lived peaceably treated so barbarously. But the king and Haman cared for none of these things.

JAMIESON, FAUSSET, BROWN

been a simple token of civil respect, Mordecai would not have refused it; but the Persian kings demanded a sort of adoration, which, it is well known, even the Greeks reckoned it degradation to express. As Xerxes, in the height of his favoritism, had commanded the same honors to be given to the minister as to himself, this was the ground of Mordecai's refusal.

Vowing revenge but scorning to lay hands on a single victim, he meditated the extirpation of the whole Jewish race, who, he knew, were sworn enemies of his countrymen; and by artfully representing them as a people who were aliens in manners and habits, and enemies to the rest of his subjects, he procured the king's sanction of the intended massacre. One motive which he used in urging his point was addressed to the king's cupidity. Fearing lest his master might object that the extermination of a numerous body of his subjects would seriously depress the public revenue, Haman promised to make up the loss.

9. I will pay ten thousand talents of silver . . . into the king's treasuries—This sum, reckoning by the Babylonish talent, will be about $10,000,000 in our money; but estimated according to the Jewish talent, it will considerably exceed $15,000,000 an immense contribution to be made out of a private fortune. But classic history makes mention of several persons whose resources seem almost incredible.

10. the king took his ring from his hand, and gave it unto Haman—There was a seal or signet in the ring. The bestowment of the ring, with the king's name and that of his kingdom engraven on it, was given with much ceremony, and it was equivalent to putting the sign manual to a royal edict.

7. In the first month . . . they cast Pur, that is, the lot—In resorting to this method of ascertaining the most auspicious day for putting his atrocious scheme into execution, Haman acted as the kings and nobles of Persia have always done, never engaging in any enterprise without consulting the astrologers, and being satisfied as to the lucky hour.

12-15. Then were the king's scribes called . . . and there was written—The government secretaries were employed in making out the proclamation authorizing a universal massacre of the Jews on one day. It was translated into the dialects of all the people throughout the vast empire, and swift messengers were sent to carry it into all the provinces. On the day appointed, all Jews were to be put to death and their property confiscated; doubtless, the means by which Haman hoped to pay his stipulated tribute into the royal treasury. To us it appears unaccountable how any sane monarch could have given his consent to the extirpation of a numerous class of his subjects. But such acts of frenzied barbarity have, alas! been not rarely authorized by careless and voluptuous despots, who have allowed their ears to be engrossed and their policy directed by haughty and selfish minions, who had their own passions to gratify, their own ends to serve. **15. the king and Haman sat down to drink; but the city Shushan was perplexed**—The completeness of the word-painting in this verse is exquisite. The historian, by a simple stroke, has drawn a graphic picture of an Oriental despot, wallowing with his favorite in sensual enjoyments, while his tyrannical cruelties were rending the hearts and homes of thousands of his subjects.

ADAM CLARKE

degree of reverence that can be paid to God or man, lying down flat on the earth, with the hands and feet extended, and the mouth in the dust.

8. *Their laws are diverse from all people.* Such they certainly were, for they worshipped the true God according to His own laws; and this was not done by any other people then on the face of the earth.

9. *Let it be written that they may be destroyed.* Let it be enacted that they may all be put to death. By this he would throw all the odium off himself, and put it on the king and his counsellors; for he wished the thing to pass into a law, in which he could have but a small share of the blame. *I will pay ten thousand talents of silver.* He had said before that it was not for the king's profit to suffer them; but here he is obliged to acknowledge that there will be a loss to the revenue, but that loss he is willing to make up out of his own property. Ten thousand talents of silver is an immense sum indeed, which, counted by the Babylonish talent, amounts to 2,119,000 pounds sterling; but, reckoned by the Jewish talent, it makes more than double that sum.

10. *The king took his ring.* In this ring was no doubt included his privy seal, and he gave this to Haman, that when he had formed such a decree as he thought fit, he might seal it with this ring, which would give it its due force and influence among the rulers of the provinces.

7. *The first month.* That is, of the civil year of the Jews. *The month Nisan.* Answering to a part of our March and April. *The twelfth year of King Ahasuerus.* According to the chronology in our Bibles, about five hundred and ten years before Christ. *They cast Pur, that is, the lot.* This appears to be the Hebrew corruption of the pure Persian word *pari*, which signifies anything that "happens fortuitously." We see plainly intimated by the Hebrew text that they cast lots, or used a species of divination, to find which of the twelve months would be the most favorable for the execution of Haman's design; and, having found the desired month, then they cast lots, or used divination, to find out which day of the said month would be the lucky day for the accomplishment of the enterprise. The Hebrew text does not tell us the result of this divination; we are left to guess it out. But the Greek supplies this deficiency, and makes all clear. From it we find that, when they cast for the month, the month Adar was taken; and when they cast for the day, the fourteenth (Heb., thirteenth) of that month was taken.

12. *Unto the king's lieutenants. Achashdarpeney.* This is in all probability another Persian word, for there is nothing like it in the Hebrew language, nor can it be fairly deduced from any roots in that tongue. The Vulgate translates "to all the *satraps* of the king." It is very likely that this is the true sense of the word.

13. *To destroy, to kill, and to cause to perish.* To put the whole of them to death in any manner, or by every way and means. *Take the spoil of them for a prey.* Thus, whoever killed a Jew had his property for his trouble! And thus the hand of every man was armed against this miserable people.

15. *The posts.* Literally, the "couriers," those who carried the public dispatches. *The decree was given in Shushan.* It was dated from the royal Susa, where the king then was. *The city Shushan was perplexed.* They saw that in a short time, by this wicked measure, the whole city would be thrown into confusion; for, although the Jews were the only objects of this decree, yet, as it armed the populace against them, even the Persians could not hope to escape without being spoiled, when a desperate mob had begun to taste of human blood, and enrich themselves with the property of the murdered.

MATTHEW HENRY

CHAPTER 4

Verses 1–4

An account of the general sorrow that there was among the Jews upon the publishing of Haman's bloody edict against them. 1. Mordecai cried bitterly, *rent his clothes, and put on sackcloth, v.* 1, 2. He not only thus vented his grief, but proclaimed it, that all might take notice of it that he was not ashamed to own himself a friend to the Jews, and a fellow-sufferer with them. It was nobly done thus publicly to espouse what he knew to be a righteous cause, and the cause of God, even when it seemed a desperate and a sinking cause. Mordecai knew that Haman's spite was against him primarily, and that it was for his sake that the rest of the Jews were struck at; and therefore it troubled him greatly that his people should suffer for his scruples. But, being able to appeal to God that what he did he did from a principle of conscience, he could with comfort commit his own cause and that of his people to him. Notice is here taken of a law that *none might enter into the king's gate clothed with sackcloth.* None must come near the king in a mourning dress, because he was not willing to hear the complaints of such. Nothing but what was gay and pleasant must appear at court. This obliged Mordecai to keep his distance and only to come before the gate, not to take his place in the gate. 2. All the Jews in every province laid it much to heart, *v.* 2. They denied themselves the comfort of their tables (for they fasted and mingled tears with their meat and drink), and *they lay in sackcloth and ashes.* 3. Esther the queen, upon a general intimation of the trouble Mordecai was in, *was exceedingly grieved, v.* 4. Mordecai's grief was hers, and the Jews' danger was her distress. Esther sent change of raiment to Mordecai, but because he would make her sensible of the greatness of his grief, and consequently of the cause of it, *he received it not,* but was as one that refused to be comforted.

Verses 5–17

So strictly did the laws of Persia confine the wives, especially the king's wives, that it was not possible for Mordecai to have a conference with Esther, but divers messages are here carried between them by Hatach, whom the king had appointed to attend her.

I. She sent to Mordecai to know more fully what the trouble was which he was now lamenting (*v.* 5) and why it was that he would not put off his sackcloth.

II. Mordecai sent her an authentic account of the whole matter, with a charge to her to intercede with the king: *Mordecai told him all that had happened unto him* (*v.* 7), what a pique Haman had against him for not bowing to him, and by what arts he had procured this edict. He sent her also a true copy of the edict, that she might see what imminent danger she and her people were in, and charged her, if she had any respect for him or any kindness for the Jewish nation, that she should rectify the misinformations with which the king was imposed upon.

III. She sent her case to Mordecai, that she could not, without peril of her life, address the king.

1. The law was express, and all knew it, that whosoever came to the king uncalled should be put to death, unless he was pleased to *hold out the golden sceptre to them.* This made the royal palace little better than a royal prison, and the kings themselves could not but become morose. It was bad for their subjects; for what good had they of a king that they might never have liberty to apply to for the redress of grievances. It is not thus in the court of the King of kings; to the footstool of his throne of grace we may at any time *come boldly,* and may be sure of an answer of peace to the prayer of faith. It was particularly very uncomfortable for their wives (for there was not a proviso in the law to except them).

2. Her case was at present very discouraging. Providence so ordered it that, just at this juncture, she was under a cloud, and the king's affections cooled towards her, for she had been *kept from his presence thirty days.*

IV. Mordecai still insisted upon it that, whatever hazard she might run, she must apply to the king in this great affair, *v.* 13, 14. He suggested to her, 1. That it was her own cause, for that the decree to *destroy all the Jews* did not except her: "*Think not* therefore that *thou shalt escape in the king's house,* that the palace will be thy protection, and the crown save thy head: no, thou art a Jewess, and, if the rest be cut off, thou wilt be cut off too." 2. That it was a cause which, one way or other, would certainly be carried, and which therefore she might safely venture in. "If thou shouldst decline the service, *enlargement and deliverance will arise to the Jews from another place.*" This was the language of a strong faith, which *staggered not at the promise* when the danger was most

JAMIESON, FAUSSET, BROWN

CHAPTER 4

Vss. 1-14. Mordecai and the Jews Mourn. **1. When Mordecai perceived all that was done**—Relying on the irrevocable nature of a Persian monarch's decree (Dan. 6:15), Haman made it known as soon as the royal sanction had been obtained; and Mordecai was, doubtless, among the first to hear of it. On his own account, as well as on that of his countrymen, this astounding decree must have been indescribably distressing.

The acts described in this passage are, according to the Oriental fashion, expressive of the most poignant sorrow; and his approach to the gate of the palace, under the impulse of irrepressible emotions, was to make an earnest though vain appeal to the royal mercy. Access, however, to the king's presence was, to a person in his disfigured state, impossible: "for none might enter into the king's gate clothed with sackcloth." But he found means of conveying intelligence of the horrid plot to Queen Esther.

4. Then was the queen . . . grieved; and . . . sent raiment to . . . Mordecai—Her object in doing so was either to qualify him for resuming his former office, or else, perhaps, of fitting him to come near enough to the palace to inform her of the cause of such sudden and extreme distress.

5. Then called Esther for Hatach, one of the king's chamberlains, whom he had appointed to attend upon her—Communication with the women in the harem is very difficult to be obtained, and only through the medium of the keepers. The chief eunuch receives the message from the lips of the queen, conveys it to some inferior office of the seraglio. When the commission is executed, the subaltern communicates it to the superintendent, by whom it is delivered to the queen. This chief eunuch, usually an old man who has recommended himself by a long course of faithful service, is always appointed by the king; but it is his interest, as well as his duty, to ingratiate himself with the queen also. Accordingly, we find Hatach rendering himself very serviceable in carrying on those private communications with Mordecai who was thereby enabled to enlist Esther's powerful influence. **8. charge her that she should go in unto the king**—This language is exceedingly strong. As it can scarcely be supposed that Mordecai was still using authority over Esther as his adopted daughter, he must be considered as imploring rather than commanding her, in the name of her brethren and in the name of her God, to make a direct appeal to the feelings of her royal husband. **11. whosoever, whether man or woman, shall come unto the king into the inner court, who is not called**—The Persian kings surrounded themselves with an almost impassable circle of forms. The law alluded to was first enacted by Deioces, king of Media, and afterwards, when the empires were united, adopted by the Persians, that all business should be transacted and petitions transmitted to the king through his ministers. Although the restriction was not intended, of course, to apply to the queen, yet from the strict and inflexible character of the Persian laws and the extreme desire to exalt the majesty of the sovereign, even his favorite wife had not the privilege of *entree,* except by special favor and indulgence. Esther was suffering from the severity of this law; and as, from not being admitted for a whole month to the king's presence, she had reason to fear that the royal affections had become alienated from her, she had little hope of serving her country's cause in this awful emergency. **13, 14. Then Mordecai commanded to answer Esther**—His answer was to this effect, that Esther need not indulge the vain hope she would, from her royal connection, escape the general doom of her race—that he (Mordecai) confidently believed God would interpose, and, if not through her, by some other deliverer, save His people;

ADAM CLARKE

CHAPTER 4

1. *Mordecai rent his clothes.* He gave every demonstration of the most poignant and oppressive grief. Nor did he hide this from the city; and the Greek says that he uttered these words aloud: "A people are going to be destroyed, who have done no evil!"

2. *Before the king's gate.* He could not enter into the gate of the place where the officers waited, because he was in the habit of a mourner, for this would have been contrary to law.

3. *Fasting, and weeping, and wailing.* How astonishing that in all this there is not the slightest intimation given of praying to God!

4. *Sent raiment.* She supposed that he must have been spoiled of his raiment by some means, and therefore sent him clothing.

5. *Then called Esther for Hatach.* This eunuch the king had appointed to wait upon her, partly, as is still the case in the East, to serve her, and partly to observe her conduct; for no despot is ever exempt from a twofold torture, jealousy and suspicion.

11. *Into the inner court.* The Persian sovereigns affected the highest degree of majesty, even to the assuming of divine honors. No man nor woman dared to appear unveiled before them without hazarding their lives; into the inner chamber of the harem no person ever entered but the king, and the woman he had chosen to call thither.

13. *Think not . . . that thou shalt escape.* This confirms the suspicion that Haman knew something of the relationship between Mordecai and Esther; and therefore he gives her to understand that, although in the king's palace, she should no more escape than the Jews.

14. *Then shall there enlargment and deliverance arise.* He had a confidence that deliverance would come by some means, and he thought that

MATTHEW HENRY

threatening, but *against hope believed in hope*. 3. That if she deserted her friends now, through cowardice and unbelief, she would have reason to fear that some judgment from heaven would be the ruin of her and her family: "*Thou and thy father's house shall be destroyed*, when the rest of the families of the Jews shall be preserved." 4. That divine Providence had an eye to this in bringing her to be queen: "*Who knows whether thou hast come to the kingdom for such a time as this?*" We should every one of us consider for what end God has put us in the place where we are, and, when any particular opportunity of serving God and our generation offers itself, we must take care that we do not let it slip. These things Mordecai urges to Esther; and some of the Jewish writers, who are fruitful in invention, add another thing which had *happened to him* (*v.* 7) which he desired she might be told, "that going home, the night before, in great heaviness, upon the notice of Haman's plot, he met three Jewish children coming from school, of whom he enquired what they had learned that day; one of them told him his lesson was, Prov. iii. 25, 26, *Be not afraid of sudden fear*; the second told him his was, Isa. viii. 10, *Take counsel together, and it shall come to nought*; the third told him his was Isa. xlvi. 4, *I have made, and I will bear, even I will carry and will deliver you*.

V. Esther hereupon resolved, whatever it might cost her, to apply to the king, but not till she and her friends had first applied to God. Let them first by fasting and prayer obtain God's favour, and then she should hope to find favour with the king, *v.* 15, 16. She spoke,

1. With the piety and devotion that became an Israelite, for she believed that God's favour was obtained by prayer. She knew it was the practice of good people, in extraordinary cases, to join fasting with prayer. She therefore, (1) Desired that Mordecai would direct the Jews that were in Shushan to *sanctify a fast* and *call a solemn assembly*, to meet in the respective synagogues to which they belonged, and to pray for her, and to keep a solemn fast. (2) She promised that she and her family would sanctify this fast in her apartment of the palace, for she might not come to their assemblies. Those who are confined to privacy may join their prayers with those of the solemn assemblies of God's people; those that are absent in body may be present in spirit.

2. With the courage and resolution that became a queen. "When we have sought God in this matter, *I will go in unto the king* to intercede for my people. *I know it is not according to the king's law*, but it is according to God's law; and therefore I will venture, and, *if I perish, I perish*. I cannot lose my life in a better cause. Better do my duty and die with them." She said not this in despair or passion, but in a holy resolution to do her duty and trust God with the issue.

JAMIESON, FAUSSET, BROWN

but that the duty evidently devolved on her, as there was great reason to believe that this was the design of Providence in her elevation to the dignity of queen, and therefore that she should go with a courageous heart, not doubting of success.

16. so will I go in unto the king, which is not according to the law—The appeal of Mordecai was irresistible. Having appointed a solemn fast of three days, she expressed her firm resolution to make an appeal to the king, though she should perish in the attempt. **I . . . and my maidens**—It is probable that she had surrounded herself with Jewish maidens, or women who were proselytes to that religion.

ADAM CLARKE

Esther would be the most likely; and that, if she did not use the influence which her providential station gave her, she would be highly culpable.

16. *Fast ye for me, and neither eat nor drink three days*. What a strange thing that still we hear nothing of prayer, nor of God! What is the ground on which we can account for this total silence? I know it not. She could not suppose there was any charm in fasting, sackcloth garments, and lying on the ground. If these were not done to turn away the displeasure of God, which seemed now to have unchained their enemies against them, what were they done for?

MATTHEW HENRY

CHAPTER 5

Verses 1–8

I. Esther's bold approach to the king, *v.* 1. When the time appointed for their fast was finished she lost no time, but on the third day, when the impressions of her devotions were fresh upon her spirit, she addressed the king. Now she *put on her royal apparel*, that she might the better recommend herself to the king, and laid aside her fast-day clothes. In the Apocrypha (Esther xiv. 16), she thus appeals to God: *Thou knowest, Lord, I abhor the sign of my high estate which is upon my head, in the days wherein I show myself*, &c. She stood *in the inner court over against the king*, expecting her doom, between hope and fear.

II. The favourable reception which the king gave her. When he *saw her* she *obtained favour in his sight*. The apocryphal author and Josephus say that she took two maids with her, on one of whom she leaned, while the other bore up her train,—that her countenance was cheerful and very amiable, but her heart was in anguish,—that the king, lifting up his countenance that shone with majesty, at first looked very fiercely upon her, whereupon she grew pale, and fainted, and bowed herself on the head of the maid that went by her; but then God changed the spirit of the king, and, in a fear, he leaped from his throne, took her in his arms till she came to herself, and comforted her with loving words. Here we are only told,

1. That he protected her from the law, and assured her of safety, by *holding out to her the golden sceptre* (*v.* 2), which she thankfully *touched the top of*, thereby presenting herself to him as a humble petitioner.

2. That he encouraged her address (*v.* 3): *What wilt thou, queen Esther, and what is thy request?* Esther

JAMIESON, FAUSSET, BROWN

CHAPTER 5

VSS. 1-14. ESTHER INVITES THE KING AND HAMAN TO A BANQUET. **1. Esther put on her royal apparel**—It was not only natural, but, on such occasions, highly proper and expedient, that the queen should decorate herself in a style becoming her exalted station. On ordinary occasions she might reasonably set off her charms to as much advantage as possible; but, on the present occasion, as she was desirous to secure the favor of one who sustained the twofold character of her husband and her sovereign, public as well as private considerations—a regard to her personal safety, no less than the preservation of her doomed countrymen—urged upon her the propriety of using every legitimate means of recommending herself to the favorable notice of Ahasuerus. **the king sat upon his royal throne in the royal house, over against the gate of the house**—The palace of this Persian king seems to have been built, like many more of the same quality and description, with an advanced cloister, over against the gate, made in the fashion of a large penthouse, supported only by one or two contiguous pillars in the front, or else in the center. In such open structures as these, in the midst of their guards and counsellors, are the *bashaws*, kadis, and other great officers, accustomed to distribute justice, and transact the public affairs of the provinces [SHAW'S TRAVELS]. In such a situation the Persian king was seated. The seat he occupied was not a *throne*, according to our ideas of one, but simply a chair, and so high that it required a footstool. It was made of gold, or, at least, inlaid with that metal, and covered with splendid tapestry, and no one save the king might sit down on it under pain of death. It is often found pictured on the Persepolitan monuments, and al-

ADAM CLARKE

CHAPTER 5

1. *On the third day*. Most probably the third day of the fast which she has prescribed to Mordecai and the Jews.

MATTHEW HENRY

feared that she should perish, but was promised that she should have what she might ask for, though it were *the half of the kingdom*. Let us from this story infer, as our Saviour does from the parable of the unjust judge, an encouragement to *pray always* to our God, *and not faint*, Luke xviii. 6–8. Esther came to a proud imperious man; we come to the God of love and grace. She was not called; we are: the Spirit says, *Come*, and the bride says, *Come*. She had a law against her; we have a promise, many a promise, in favour of us: *Ask, and it shall be given you*. She had no friend to introduce her, or intercede for her, while on the contrary he that was then the king's favourite was her enemy; but we have an advocate with the Father, in whom he is well pleased. *Let us therefore come boldly to the throne of grace*.

3. That all the request she had to make to him, at this time, was that he would please to come to a banquet which she had prepared for him, and bring Haman along with him, *v.* 4, 5. She would endeavour to bring him into a pleasant humour, and soften his spirit, that he might with the more tenderness receive the complaint she had to make to him. She would please him, by making court to Haman his favourite, and inviting him to come whose company she knew he loved and whom she desired to have present when she made her complaint.

4. That he readily came, and ordered Haman to come along with him (*v.* 5). There he renewed his kind enquiry (*What is thy petition?*) and his generous promise, that it should be granted, *even to the half of the kingdom* (*v.* 6), a proverbial expression, by which he assured her that he would deny her nothing in reason.

5. That then Esther thought fit to ask no more than a promise that he would please to accept of another treat, the next day, in her apartment, and Haman with him (*v.* 7, 8), intimating to him that then she would let him know what her business was. The putting of it off thus she knew would be well taken as an expression of the great reverence she had for the king, and her unwillingness to be too pressing upon him.

Verses 9–14

Haman, in whom pride and wrath had so much the ascendant.

I. Puffed up with the honour of being invited to Esther's feast. He was *joyful and glad of heart* at it, *v.* 9. He thought it was because she was exceedingly charmed with his conversation that the next day she had invited him also to come with the king.

II. Mordecai was as determined as ever: *He stood not up, nor moved for him*, *v.* 9. Haman can as ill bear it as ever; nay, the higher he is lifted up, the more impatient is he of contempt and the more enraged at it. Gladly would he have drawn his sword and run Mordecai through for affronting him thus; but he hoped shortly to see him fall with all the Jews, and therefore with much ado prevailed with himself to forbear stabbing him.

III. Meditating revenge, Haman was assisted by his wife and his friends, *v.* 14. For the pleasing of his fancy they advise him to get *a gallows ready*, and have it set up before his own door, that, as soon as ever he could get the warrant signed, there might be no delay of the execution. This is very agreeable to Haman, who has the gallows made and fixed immediately; it must be fifty cubits high, for the greater disgrace of Mordecai and to make him a spectacle to everyone that passed by. They advised him to go early in the morning to the king, and get an order from him for the hanging of Mordecai.

JAMIESON, FAUSSET, BROWN

ways of the same fashion. **2. the king held out to Esther the golden sceptre that was in his hand**—This golden scepter receives an interesting illustration from the sculptured monuments of Persia and Assyria. In the bas-reliefs of Persepolis, copied by Sir Robert Ker Porter, we see King Darius enthroned in the midst of his court, and walking abroad in equal state; in either case he carries in his right hand a slender rod or wand, about equal in length to his own height, ornamented with a small knob at the summit. In the Assyrian alabasters, those found at Nimroud as well as those from Khorsabad, "the great king" is furnished with the same appendage of royalty, a slender rod, but destitute of any knob or ornament. On the Khorsabad reliefs the rod is painted red, *doubtless* to *represent gold;* proving that "the golden sceptre" was a simple wand of that precious metal, commonly held in the right hand, with one end resting on the ground, and that whether the king was sitting or walking. "The gold sceptre" has received little alteration or modification since ancient times [Goss]. It was extended to Esther as a token not only that her intrusion was pardoned, but that her visit was welcome, and a favorable reception given to the suit she had come to prefer. **touched the top of the sceptre**—This was the usual way of acknowledging the royal condescension, and at the same time expressing reverence and submission to the august majesty of the king. **3. it shall be even given thee to the half of the kingdom**—This mode of speaking originated in the Persian custom of appropriating for the maintenance of great men, or royal favorites, one city for his bread, another for his wine, a third for his clothes, etc., so that the phrase denoted great liberality. **4. let the king and Haman come this day unto the banquet that I have prepared for him**—There was great address in this procedure of Esther's; for, by showing such high respect to the king's favorite, she would the better insinuate herself into the royal affections; and gain a more suitable opportunity of making known her request. **8. let the king and Haman come to the banquet that I shall prepare**—The king ate alone, and his guests in an adjoining hall; but they were admitted to sit with him at wine. Haman being the only invited guest with the king and queen, it was natural that he should have been elated with the honor.

ADAM CLARKE

F. B. MEYER:

Hatred breeds crime. Thus the soul clad in the royal garments of Christ's righteousness stands in the throne room with its request. It has already obtained favor, for has it not been accepted in the beloved? The Lord waits that he may be gracious. Delay is not denial, and in the meanwhile there are things to be seen and heard which fill the soul with rapture. Have you touched the top of the sceptre? Have you claimed unto the half of the kingdom? Have you invited the King himself to your banqueting table? For the King himself is willing to be your guest. We feast at his table, but he also comes and sups with us at ours. In all earthly joy there is alloy, something which detracts from full gratification; a Mordecai for Haman, because of whom all else availed nothing. The joy that this world gives is at the mercy of unfavorable circumstances, but "he that drinketh of the water that I shall give him shall never thirst."

—*Bible Commentary*

4. *Let the king and Haman come this day unto the banquet.* It was necessary to invite Haman to prevent his suspicion, and that he might not take any hasty step which might have prevented the execution of the great design.

6. *The banquet of wine.* At that part of the banquet when *wine* was introduced.

8. *I will do tomorrow.* She saw she was gaining on the king's affections; but she was not yet sufficiently confident, and therefore wished another interview, that she might ingratiate herself more fully in the king's favor, and thus secure the success of her design. But Providence disposed of things thus, to give time for the important event mentioned in the succeeding chapter.

9. *That he stood not up, nor moved for him.* This was certainly carrying his integrity or inflexibility to the highest pitch. But still we are left to conjecture that some reverence was required which Mordecai could not conscientiously pay.

11. *The multitude of his children.* The Asiatic sovereigns delight in the number of their children, and this is one cause why they take so many wives and concubines.

13. *Yet all this availeth me nothing.* Pride will ever render its possessor unhappy. He has such a high opinion of his own worth that he conceives himself defrauded by everyone who does not pay him all the respect and homage which he conceives to be his due.

14. *Let a gallows be made of fifty cubits high.* The word *ets*, which we translate *gallows*, signifies simply "wood, a tree, or pole"; and this was to be seventy-five feet high, that he might suffer the greater ignominy, and be a more public spectacle.

CHAPTER 6

Verses 1–3

When Satan put it into the heart of Haman to contrive Mordecai's death, God put it into the heart of the king to contrive Mordecai's honour. The steps which Providence took towards the advancement of Mordecai.

I. *On that night could not the king sleep.* His *sleep fled away* (so the word is); and perhaps, like a shadow, the more carefully he pursued it the further it went from him.

II. When he could not sleep he called to have the book of records, the Journals of his reign, read to him, *v.* 1. But God put it into his heart to call for it, rather than for music or songs, which would have been more likely to compose him to rest.

III. The servant that read to him lighted on that article which concerned Mordecai. Among other things it was found written that Mordecai had discovered a plot against the life of the king which prevented the execution of it, *v.* 2. How Mordecai's

CHAPTER 6

VSS. 1-14. AHASUERUS REWARDS MORDECAI FOR FORMER SERVICE. **1. the king . . . commanded to bring the book of records of the chronicles**—In Eastern courts, there are scribes or officers whose duty it is to keep a journal of every occurrence worthy of notice. A book of this kind, abounding with anecdotes, is full of interest. It has been a custom with Eastern kings, in all ages, frequently to cause the annals of the kingdom to be read to them. It is resorted to, not merely as a pastime to while away the tedium of an hour, but as a source of instruction to the monarch, by reviewing the important incidents of his own life, as well as those of his ancestors. There was, therefore, nothing uncommon in this Persian monarch calling for the court journal. But, in his being unable to sleep at that particular juncture, in his ordering the book then to be read to him, and in his attention having been specially directed to the important and as yet unrewarded serv-

CHAPTER 6

MATTHEW HENRY

good service was recorded we read *ch.* ii. 23, and here it is found upon record.

IV. The king enquired *what honour and dignity had been done to Mordecai* for this, suspecting that this good service had gone unrewarded.

V. The servants informed him that nothing had been done to Mordecai for that eminent service; in the king's gate he sat before, and there he still sat. Humility, modesty, and self-denial, though in God's account of great price, yet commonly hinder men's preferment in the world. Mordecai rises no higher than the king's gate, while proud ambitious Haman gets the king's ear and heart; but, though the aspiring rise fast, the humble stand fast. Mordecai is at this time, by the king's edict, doomed to destruction, with all the Jews, though it is owned that he deserved dignity.

Verses 4–11

It is now morning, and people begin to stir.

I. Haman is so impatient to get Mordecai hanged that he comes early to court, before any other business is brought to get a warrant for his execution (*v.* 4), which he makes sure that he shall have at the first word. He could tell the king that he was so confident of the justice of his request, and the king's favour to him in it, that he had got the gallows ready: one word from the king would complete his satisfaction.

II. The king is so impatient to have Mordecai honoured that he sends to know who is in the court that is fit to be employed in it. Word is brought him that Haman is in the court, *v.* 5. *Let him come in*, says the king, the fittest man to be made use of both in directing and in dispensing the king's favour; and the king knew nothing of any quarrel he had with Mordecai. Haman is brought in immediately, proud of the honour done him in being admitted into the king's bed-chamber *before he was up*. Now Haman thinks he has the fairest opportunity he can wish for to solicit against Mordecai; but the king's heart is as full as his, and it is fit he should speak first.

III. The king asks Haman how he should express his favour to one whom he had marked for a favourite: *What shall be done to the man whom the king delights to honour? v.* 6.

IV. Haman concludes that he himself is the favourite intended, and therefore prescribes the highest expressions of honour that could be bestowed upon a subject. Now Haman thinks he is carving out honour for himself, and therefore does it very liberally, *v.* 8, 9.

V. The king confounds him with a positive order that he should immediately go himself and put all this honour upon Mordecai the Jew, *v.* 10. If the king had but said, as Haman expected, *Thou art the man!* But how is he thunderstruck when the king bids him not to order all this to be done, but to do it himself to Mordecai the Jew, the very man he hated above all men and whose ruin he was now designing!

VI. Haman dares not dispute nor so much as seem to dislike the king's order, but, with the greatest reluctance brings it to Mordecai, who did no more cringe to Haman now than he had done, valuing his counterfeit respect no more than he had valued his concealed malice. The apparel is brought, Mordecai is dressed up, and rides in state through the city, recognized as the king's favourite, *v.* 11.

Verses 12–14

I. How little Mordecai was puffed up with his advancement. He *came again to the king's gate* (*v.* 12); he returned to his place and the duty of it immediately, and minded his business as closely as he had done before.

II. How much Haman was cast down with his disappointment. To wait upon any man, especially Mordecai, and at this time, when he hoped to have seen him hanged, was enough to break such a proud heart.

III. How his doom was read to him by his wife and his friends: "If Mordecai be, as they say he is, *of the seed of the Jews, before whom thou hast begun to fall*, never expect to *prevail against him*; for thou *shalt surely fall before him*," *v.* 13. This Mordecai was *of the seed of the Jews*; *feeble Jews* their enemies sometimes called them, but formidable Jews they sometimes found them. They are a holy seed, a praying seed, in covenant with God, and a seed that the Lord hath all along blessed, and therefore let not their enemies expect to triumph over them.

IV. He was now sent for to the banquet that Esther had prepared, *v.* 14. He thought it seasonable in hopes it would revive his drooping spirits and save his sinking honour.

JAMIESON, FAUSSET, BROWN

ices of Mordecai, the immediate interposition of Providence is distinctly visible.

4. Now Haman was come into the outward court—This was early in the morning. It is the invariable custom for kings in Eastern countries to transact business before the sun is hot, often in the open air, and so Haman was in all probability come officially to attend on his master.

6. What shall be done unto the man whom the king delighteth to honour?—In bestowing tokens of their favor, the kings of Persia do not at once, and as it were by their own will, determine the kind of honor that shall be awarded; but they turn to the courtier standing next in rank to themselves, and ask him what shall be done to the individual who has rendered the service specified; and according to the answer received, the royal mandate is issued. **8. the royal apparel . . . which the king useth to wear**—A coat which has been on the back of a king or prince is reckoned a most honorable gift, and is given with great ceremony. **the horse that the king rideth upon**—Persia was a country of horses, and the high-bred charger that the king rode upon acquired, in the eyes of his venal subjects, a sort of sacredness from that circumstance. **and the crown royal which is set upon his head**—either the royal turban, or it may be a tiara, with which, on state processions, the horse's head was adorned. **9. delivered to the hand of one of the king's most noble princes . . . array the man**—On grand and public occasions, the royal steed is led by the highest subject through the principal streets of the city, a ceremony which may occupy several hours. **11. Then Haman took,** etc.—This sudden reverse, however painful to Haman as an individual, is particularly characteristic of the Persian manners.

14. came the king's chamberlains, and hasted to bring Haman unto the banquet—Besides the invitation given to an entertainment, a message is always sent to the guests, immediately at the day and hour appointed, to announce that all things are ready.

ADAM CLARKE

3. *What honour and dignity hath been done to Mordecai?* It is certain he found nothing in the record; and had anything been done, that was the most likely place to find it.

6. *The king said unto him.* He did not give him time to make his request; and put a question to him which, at the first view, promised him all that his heart could wish.

8. *Let the royal apparel be brought.* Pride and folly ever go hand in hand. What he asked would have been in any ordinary case against his own life; but he wished to reach the pinnacle of honor, never reflecting that the higher he rose, the more terrible would be his fall. The *royal apparel* was never worn but by the king; even when the king had lain them aside, it was death to put them on. *And the horse . . . and the crown royal.* Interpreters are greatly divided whether what is called here the *crown royal* be not rather an ornament worn on the head of the horse than what may be called the royal crown. The original may be understood both ways, and our version seems to favor the former opinion; but I think it more likely that the royal crown is meant, for why mention the ordinary trappings of the royal steed?

9. *One of the king's most noble princes.* Alas, poor Haman! Never was the fable of the dog and shadow more literally fulfilled. Thou didst gape at the shadow, and didst lose the substance.

12. *Mordecai came again to the king's gate.* He resumed his former humble state; while Haman, ashamed to look up, covered his face, and ran home to hide himself in his own house. Covering the head and face was a sign of shame and confusion, as well as of grief, among most people of the earth.

14. *Hasted to bring Haman.* There was a dreadful banquet before him, of which he knew nothing, and he could have little appetite to enjoy that which he knew was prepared at the palace of Esther.

MATTHEW HENRY

CHAPTER 7

Verses 1–6

The king in humour, and Haman out of humour, meet at Esther's table.

I. The king urged Esther, a third time, to tell him what her request was, for he longed to know, and repeated his promise that it should be granted, *v.* 2.

II. Esther, at length, surprises the king with a petition for the preservation of herself and her countrymen from death and destruction, *v.* 3, 4. That a friend, a wife, should have occasion to present such a petition was very affecting: *Let my life be given me at my petition, and my people at my request.* To move the king the more she suggests she and her people were bought and sold. They had not sold themselves by any offence against the government, but were sold to gratify the pride and revenge of one man. That it was not their liberty only, but their lives that were sold. "Had we been sold" (says she) "into slavery, I would not have complained; for in time we might have recovered our liberty, though the king would have made but a bad bargain of it. Whatever had been paid for us, the loss of so many industrious hands out of his kingdom would have been more damage to the treasury than the price would countervail." *We are sold* (says she) *to be destroyed, to be slain, and to perish.* She refers to the words of the decree (*ch.* iii. 13), which aimed at nothing short of their destruction.

III. The king stands amazed at the remonstrance, and asks (*v.* 5). "*Who is he, and where is he, that durst presume in his heart to do so?* We sometimes startle at the mention of that evil which yet we ourselves are chargeable with. Ahasuerus is amazed at that wickedness which he himself was guilty of; for he consented to that bloody edict against the Jews. *Thou art the man,* might Esther too truly have said.

IV. Esther plainly charges Haman with it before his face: "Here he is, let him speak for himself, for therefore he is invited: *The adversary and enemy is this wicked Haman* (*v.* 6); it is he that has designed our murder."

V. Haman is apprehensive of his danger: *He was afraid before the king and queen;* and it was time for him to fear when the queen was his prosecutor, the king his judge, and his own conscience a witness against him.

Verses 7–10

I. The king retires in anger. He rose from table in a great passion, and *went into the palace garden* to cool himself and to consider what was to be done, *v.* 7. He blames himself, that he should be such a fool as to doom a guiltless nation to destruction, and his own queen among the rest, upon the base suggestions of a self-seeking man, without examining the truth of his allegations. He condemned Haman whom he had laid in his bosom, that he should be such a villain as to draw him to consent to so wicked a measure.

II. Haman becomes a humble petitioner to the queen for his life. He might easily perceive by the king's hastily flying out of the room that *there was evil determined against him.* How mean Haman looks, when he stands up first and then falls down at Esther's feet, to beg she would save his life and take all he had. How great Esther looks, who of late had been neglected and doomed! Now her sworn enemy owns that he lies at her mercy, and begs his life at her hand. The day is coming when those that hate and persecute God's chosen ones would gladly be beholden to them.

III. The king returns yet more exasperated against Haman.

IV. Those about him were ready to be the instruments of his wrath. The courtiers that adored Haman when he was the rising sun set themselves as much against him now that he is a falling star. As soon as the king spoke an angry word *they covered Haman's face,* as a condemned man; they marked him for execution. Those that are hanged commonly have their faces covered. One of those that had been lately sent to Haman's house, to fetch him to the banquet, informed the king of the gallows which Haman had prepared for Mordecai, *v.* 9.

V. The king gave orders that he should be hanged upon his own gallows, which was done accordingly.

CHAPTER 8

Verses 1–2

1. Esther enriched. Haman was hanged as a traitor, therefore his estate was forfeited to the crown, and the king gave it all to Esther. 2. Mordecai advanced. His procession, this morning, through the streets of

JAMIESON, FAUSSET, BROWN

CHAPTER 7

VSS. 1-6. ESTHER PLEADS FOR HER OWN LIFE AND THE LIFE OF HER PEOPLE.

4. we are sold, I and my people, to be destroyed—i.e., by the cruel and perfidious scheme of that man, who offered an immense sum of money to purchase our extermination. Esther dwelt on his contemplated atrocity, in a variety of expressions, which both evinced the depth of her own emotions, and were intended to awaken similar feelings in the king's breast. **But if we had been sold for bondmen and bondwomen, I had held my tongue**—Though a great calamity to the Jews, the enslavement of that people might have enriched the national treasury; and, at all events, the policy, if found from experience to be bad, could be altered. But the destruction of such a body of people would be an irreparable evil, and all the talents Haman might pour into the treasury could not compensate for the loss of their services.

7-10. THE KING CAUSES HAMAN TO BE HANGED ON HIS OWN GALLOWS. **7. he saw that there was evil determined against him by the king**—When the king of Persia orders an offender to be executed, and then rises and goes into the women's apartment, it is a sign that no mercy is to be hoped for. Even the sudden rising of the king in anger was the same as if he had pronounced sentence. **8. Haman was fallen upon the bed whereon Esther was**—We do not know the precise form of the couches on which the Persians reclined at table. But it is probable that they were not very different from those used by the Greeks and Romans. Haman, perhaps, at first stood up to beg pardon of Esther; but driven in his extremity to resort to an attitude of the most earnest supplication, he fell prostrate on the couch where the queen was recumbent. The king returning that instant was fired at what seemed an outrage on female modesty. **they covered Haman's face**—The import of this striking action is, that a criminal is unworthy any longer to look on the face of the king, and hence, when malefactors are consigned to their doom in Persia, the first thing is to cover the face with a veil or napkin. **9. Harbonah, one of the chamberlains, said before the king, Behold also, the gallows**—This eunuch had probably been the messenger sent with the invitation to Haman, and on that occasion had seen the gallows. The information he now volunteered, as well it may be from abhorrence of Haman's cold-blooded conspiracy as from sympathy with his amiable mistress, involved with her people in imminent peril. **10. So they hanged Haman on the gallows that he had prepared**—He has not been the only plotter of mischief whose feet have been taken in the net which they hid (Ps. 9:15). But never was condemnation more just, and retribution more merited, than the execution of that gigantic criminal.

CHAPTER 8

VSS. 1-6. MORDECAI ADVANCED. **1. On that day did . . . Ahasuerus give the house of Haman . . . unto Esther**—His property was confiscated, and everything belonging to him, as some compensation for

ADAM CLARKE

CHAPTER 7

3. *Let my life be given me.* This was very artfully, as well as very honestly, managed, and was highly calculated to work on the feelings of the king. What! is the life of the queen, whom I most tenderly love, in any kind of danger?

4. *To be destroyed, to be slain.* She here repeats the words which Haman put into the decree. See chap. iii. 13. *Could not countervail the king's damage.* Even the 10,000 talents of silver could not be considered as a compensation to the state for the loss of a whole nation of people throughout all their generations.

5. *Who is he, and where is he?* There is a wonderful abruptness and confusion in the original words, highly expressive of the state of mind in which the king then was: *mi hu zeh veey zeh hu asher melao libbo laasoth ken.* "Who? He? This one? And where? This one? He? Who hath filled his heart to do thus?" He was at once struck with the horrible nature of a conspiracy so cruel and diabolic.

7. *Haman stood up.* He rose from the table to make request for his life, as soon as the king had gone out; and then he fell on his knees before the queen, she still sitting upon her couch.

8. *Will he force the queen?* On the king's return he found him at the queen's knees; and, professing to think that he intended to do violence to her honor, used the above expressions; though he must have known that, in such circumstances, the thought of perpetrating an act of this kind could not possibly exist.

They covered Haman's face. This was a sign of his being devoted to death, for the attendants saw that the king was determined on his destruction.

9. *Behold also, the gallows.* As if he had said, Besides all he has determined to do to the Jews, he has erected a very high gallows, on which he had determined, this very day, to hang Mordecai, who has saved the king's life. *Hang him thereon.* Let him be instantly impaled on the same post.

CHAPTER 8

1. *The king . . . give the house of Haman.* As Haman was found guilty of treasonable practices against the peace and prosperity of the king and his empire, his life was forfeited, and his

MATTHEW HENRY

the city, was but a sudden blaze of honour; but here we have the more durable preferments to which he was raised. He is owned as the queen's cousin, which till now, though Esther had been four years queen, the king did not know. So humble, so modest, a man was Mordecai, and so far from being ambitious of a place at court, that he concealed his relation to the queen, and her obligations to him as her guardian. Now, at length, *Esther had told what he was to her*, near akin, who took care of her when she was an orphan, and one whom she still respected as a father. All the trust he had reposed in Haman, and all the power he had given him, are here transferred to Mordecai; for the ring which he had taken from Haman he gave to Mordecai, and made this trusty humble man his confidant. The queen makes him her steward, for the management of Haman's estate, *She set Mordecai over the house of Haman.*

Verses 3–14

Haman, the chief enemy of the Jews, was hanged, Mordecai and Esther, their chief friends, were sufficiently protected; but many others there were in the king's dominions that hated the Jews and desired their ruin, and to their rage and malice all the rest of that people lay exposed for the edict against them was still in force.

I. The queen here makes intercession with much affection and importunity. She came, a second time, uncalled into the king's presence (*v.* 3), and was as before encouraged to present her petition, by the king's holding out the golden sceptre to her, *v.* 4. Her petition is that the king, having put away Haman, would put away the mischief of Haman and his device against the Jews. This petition Esther presents with much affection: She *fell down at the king's feet and besought him with tears* (*v.* 3), every tear as precious as any of the pearls with which she was adorned. *If it please the king and if I have found favour in his sight*—and again, "If the thing itself seem right and reasonable before the king, and if I that ask it *be pleasing in his eyes*, let the decree be reversed." She enforces her petition with a pathetic plea: "*For how can I endure to see the evil that shall come upon my people?*"

II. The king here takes a course for the preventing of the mischief that Haman had designed. The king knew, and informed the queen, that, according to the constitution of the Persian government, the former edict could not be revoked (*v.* 8): What is *written in the king's name, and sealed with the king's ring*, may not, under any pretence whatsoever, be reversed. Yet he found an expedient to undo the devices of Haman, and defeat his design, by singing and publishing another decree to authorize the Jews to stand upon their defence, *vim vi repellere, et invasorem occidere—to oppose force to force, and destroy the assailant.* This would be their effectual security. "*Write for the Jews as it liketh you* (*v.* 8), saving only the honour of our constitution. Let the mischief be put away as effectually as may be without reversing the letters." This edict was to be drawn up and published in the respective languages of all the provinces. The purport of this decree was to commission the Jews, upon the day which was appointed for their destruction, to draw together in a body for their own defence. And, 1. To stand for their life, that, whoever assaulted them, it might be at their peril. 2. They might not only act defensively, but might *destroy, and slay, and cause to perish, all the power of the people that would assault them.* Now, (1) This showed his kindness to the Jews, and sufficiently provided for their safety; for the latter decree would be looked upon as a tacit revocation of the former. But, (2) It shows the absurdity of their constitution that none of the king's edicts might be repealed; for it laid the king here under a necessity of enacting a civil war in his own dominions, between the Jews and their enemies, so that both sides took up arms *by* his authority, and yet *against* his authority.

Verses 15–17

Here is a blessed change, Mordecai in purple and all the Jews in joy. 1. Mordecai in purple, *v.* 15. Having obtained an order for the relief of all the Jews, he was easy, he put on the *royal apparel.* His robes were rich, *blue and white, of fine linen and purple*; so was his coronet: it was *of gold.* These things were marks of the king's favour, and the fruit of God's favour to his church. The *city Shushan* was sensible of its advantage in the preferment of Mordecai, and therefore *rejoiced and was glad.* 2. The Jews in joy, *v.* 16, 17. The Jews, who awhile ago were under a dark cloud, dejected and disgraced, now had *light and gladness, joy and honour, a feast and a good lay.* One good effect of this deliverance was that *many of the people of the land*, that were

JAMIESON, FAUSSET, BROWN

the peril to which she had been exposed. **Mordecai came before the king**—i.e., was introduced at court and appointed one of the seven counsellors. Esther displayed great prudence and address in acknowledging Mordecai's relation to her at the moment most fitted to be of eminent service to him. **2. the king took off his ring . . . and gave it unto Mordecai**—By that act transferring to him all the power and authority which the ring symbolized, and promoting him to the high dignity which Haman had formerly filled. **Esther set Mordecai over the house of Haman**—as her steward or factor, to manage that large and opulent estate which had been assigned to her. **3. Esther spake yet again before the king, and fell down at his feet**—The king was then not reclining at table, but sitting on a divan, most probably in the Persian attitude, leaning back against the cushions, and one foot under him. **besought him with tears to put away the mischief of Haman**—i.e., to repeal the sanguinary edict which, at the secret instigation of Haman, had been recently passed (ch. 3:12). **4. Then the king held out the golden sceptre toward Esther**—in token that her request was accepted, and that she needed no longer to maintain the humble attitude of a suppliant. **5, 6. reverse the letters devised by Haman . . . to destroy the Jews**—The whole conduct of Esther in this matter is characterized by great tact, and the variety of expressions by which she describes her willing submission to her royal husband, the address with which she rolls the whole infamy of the meditated massacre on Haman, and the argument she draws from the king's sanction being surreptitiously obtained, that the decree should be immediately reversed—all indicate the queen's wisdom and skill, and she succeeded in this point also.

7-14. Ahasuerus Grants to the Jews to Defend Themselves. **8. Write . . . in the king's name, and seal it with the king's ring**—Hence it is evident that the royal ring had a seal in it, which, being affixed to any document, authenticated it with the stamp of royal authority. **which . . . may no man reverse**—This is added as the reason why he could not comply with the queen's request for a direct reversal of recall of Haman's letters; viz., that the laws of the Medes and Persians, once passed, were irrevocable. **10. sent . . . by posts . . . and riders on . . . camels, and young dromedaries**—The business being very urgent, the swiftest kind of camel would be employed, and so the word in the original denotes—the *wind-camel.* Young dromedaries also are used to carry expresses, being remarkable for the nimbleness and ease of their movements. Animals of this description could convey the new rescript of Ahasuerus over the length and breadth of the Persian empire in time to relieve the unhappy Jews from the ban under which they lay. **11-13. the king granted the Jews . . . to stand for their life . . . to slay . . . all . . . that would assault them**—The fixed and unalterable character claimed for Persian edicts often placed the king in a very awkward dilemma; for, however bitterly he might regret things done in a moment of haste and thoughtlessness, it was beyond even his power to prevent the consequences. This was the reason on account of which the king was laid under a necessity not to reverse, but to issue a contradictory edict; according to which it was enacted that if, pursuant to the first decree, the Jews were assaulted, they might, by virtue of the second, defend themselves and even slay their enemies. However strange and even ridiculous this mode of procedure may appear, it was the only one which, from the peculiarities of court etiquette in Persia, could be adopted. Instances occur in sacred (Dan. 6:14), no less than profane, history. Many passages of the Bible attest the truth of this, particularly the well-known incident of Daniel's being cast into the den of lions, in conformity with the rash decree of Darius, though, as it afterwards appeared, contrary to the personal desire of that monarch. That the law of Persia has undergone no change in this respect, and the power of the monarch not less immutable, appear from many anecdotes related in the books of modern travellers through that country.

15-17. Mordecai's Honors, and the Jews' Joy. **15. Mordecai went out . . . in royal apparel**—He was invested with the khelaat of official honor. A dress of blue and white was held in great estimation among the Persians; so that Mordecai, whom the king delighted to honor, was in fact arrayed in the royal dress and insignia. The variety and the kind of insignia worn by a favorite at once makes known to the people the particular dignity to which he has been raised.

ADAM CLARKE

goods confiscated. And as Mordecai had been the means of preserving the king's life, and was the principal object of Haman's malice, it was but just to confer his property upon him, as well as his dignity and office, as Mordecai was found deserving of the former, and fit to discharge the duties of the latter.

2. *The king took off his ring.* In the ring was the seal of the king. Giving the ring to Mordecai was tantamount to giving him the seal of the kingdom, and constituting him the same as lord chancellor among us.

6. *To see the destruction of my kindred?* She had now informed the king that she was cousin to Mordecai, and consequently a Jewess; and though her own life and that of Mordecai were no longer in danger, Haman being dead, yet the decree that had gone forth was in full force against the Jews; and if not repealed, their destruction would be inevitable.

8. *May no man reverse.* Whatever had passed the royal signet could never be revoked; no succeeding edict could destroy or repeal a preceding one. But one of a similar nature to the Jews against the Persians, as that to the Persians was against the Jews, might be enacted, and thus the Jews be enabled legitimately to defend themselves and, consequently, placed on an equal footing with their enemies.

9. *The month Sivan.* This answers to a part of our May and June.

10. *On mules, camels, and young dromedaries.* What these beasts were is difficult to say. The word which we translate *mules* signifies a "swift chariot horse."

11. *To destroy, to slay, and to cause to perish.* The same words as in Haman's decree; therefore the Jews had as much authority to slay their enemies as their enemies had to slay them. *Little ones and women.* This was the ordinary custom, to destroy the whole family of those convicted of great crimes; and whether this was right or wrong, it was the custom of the people, and according to the laws. Besides, as this edict was to give the Jews the same power against their enemies as they had by the former decree against them, and the women and children were there included, consequently they must be included here.

14. *The decree was given at Shushan.* The contrary effect which it was to produce considered, this decree was in every respect like the former. See chap. iii.

15. *Blue and white.* Probably stripe interchanged with stripe, or blue faced and bordered with white fur. *A great crown of gold.* A large turban, ornamented with gold, jewels, etc. *Shushan . . . was glad.* Haman was too proud to be popular; few lamented his fall.

MATTHEW HENRY

considerate, sober, and well inclined, became Jews, were proselyted to the Jewish religion, renounced idolatry, and worshipped the true God only. *We will go with you, for we have heard,* we have seen, *that God is with you, the shield of your help, and the sword of your excellency,* Deut. xxxiii. 29.

CHAPTER 9

Verses 1–19

A decisive battle fought between the Jews and their enemies, in which the Jews were victorious. Neither side could call the other *rebels*, for they were both supported by the royal authority.

I. The enemies of the Jews were the aggressors.

II. But the Jews were the conquerors. That very day when the king's decree for their destruction was to be put in execution, and which the enemies thought would have been *their* day, proved *God's day*, Ps. xxxvii. 13. *They gathered themselves together in their cities*, embodied, and stood upon their defence, offering violence to none, but bidding defiance to all. If they had not had an edict to warrant them, they durst not have done it, but, being so supported, they strove lawfully. Had they acted separately, each family apart, they would have been an easy prey to their enemies; but acting in concert, and gathering together in their cities, they strengthened one another, and durst face their enemies. All the officers of the king, who, by the bloody edict, were ordered to help forward their destruction (*ch.* iii. 12, 13), conformed to the latter edict and *helped the Jews*, which turned the scale on their side, *v.* 3. The provinces would generally do as the rulers of the provinces inclined, and therefore their favouring the Jews would greatly further them. But why did they help them? Not because they had any kindness for them, but because *the fear of Mordecai fell upon them*, he having manifestly the countenance both of God and the king. *No man could withstand them* (*v.* 2), but *they did what they would to those that hated them*, *v.* 5. So strangely were the Jews strengthened and animated, and their enemies weakened and dispirited, that none of those who had marked themselves for their destruction escaped. On the thirteenth day of the month Adar they slew in the city Shushan 500 men (*v.* 6) and the ten sons of *Haman*, *v.* 10. On the fourteenth day they slew in Shushan 300 more, who had escaped the sword on the former day of execution, *v.* 15. This Esther obtained leave of the king for them to do, for the greater terror of their enemies, and the utter crushing of that malignant party of men. That which justifies them in the execution of so many is that they did it in their own just and necessary defence; they *stood for their lives*, authorized to do so by the law of self-preservation, as well as by the king's decree. The king's commission had warranted them to *take the spoil* of their enemies *for a prey* (*ch.* viii. 11), and a fair opportunity they had of enriching themselves with it. But the Jews would not do so by them, 1. That they might, to the honour of their religion, evidence a holy and generous contempt of worldly wealth, in imitation of their father Abraham, who scorned to enrich himself with the spoils of Sodom. 2. That they might make it to appear that they aimed at nothing but their own preservation, and used their interest at court for the saving of their lives, not for the raising of their estates. 3. Their commission empowered them to destroy the families of their enemies, even the *little ones* and *the women*, *ch.* viii. 11. But their humanity forbade them to do that. They slew none but those they found in arms; and therefore they did not take the spoil, but left it to the women and little ones. Herein they acted with a consideration and compassion well worthy of imitation.

Verses 20–32

To perpetuate the remembrance of it to posterity,

I. The history was written, and copies of it were dispersed among all the Jews in all the provinces of the empire, *both nigh and far*, *v.* 20. Mordecai *wrote all these things.* And if this book be the same that he wrote, as many think it is, what a difference there is between Mordecai's style and Nehemiah's. Nehemiah, at every turn, takes notice of divine Providence and the *good hand of his God* upon him, which is very proper to stir up devout affections in the minds of his readers; but Mordecai never so much as mentions the name of God in the whole story. Nehemiah wrote his book at Jerusalem, where religion was in fashion. Mordecai wrote his at Shushan the palace, where policy reigned more than piety, and he wrote according to the genius of the place. Because there is so little of the language of Canaan in this book, many think it was not written by Mordecai, but was an extract out of the journals

JAMIESON, FAUSSET, BROWN

CHAPTER 9

Vss. 1-19. THE JEWS SLAY THEIR ENEMIES WITH THE TEN SONS OF HAMAN. **1. in the twelfth month, . . . on the thirteenth day of the same**—This was the day which Haman's superstitious advisers had led him to select as the most fortunate for the execution of his exterminating scheme against the Jews. **2. The Jews gathered themselves . . . no man could withstand them**—The tables were now turned in their favor; and though their enemies made their long meditated attack, the Jews were not only at liberty to act on the defensive, but through the powerful influence enlisted on their side at court together with the blessing of God, they were everywhere victorious. **the fear of them fell upon all people**—This impression arose not alone from the consciousness of the all-powerful vizier being their countryman, but from the hand of God appearing so visibly interposed to effect their strange and unexpected deliverance. **5-16. Thus the Jews smote all their enemies**—The effect of the two antagonistic decrees was, in the meantime, to raise a fierce and bloody war between the Jews and their enemies throughout the Persian empire; but through the dread of Esther and Mordecai, the provincial governors universally favored their cause, so that their enemies fell in great numbers. **13. let it be granted to the Jews which are in Shushan to do to-morrow also according unto this day's decree**—Their enemies adroitly concealing themselves for the first day might have returned on the next, when they imagined that the privilege of the Jews was expired; so that that people would have been surprised and slain. The extension of the decree to another day at the queen's special desire has exposed her to the charge of being actuated by a cruel and vindictive disposition. But her conduct in making this request is capable of full vindication, on the ground (1) that Haman's sons having taken a prominent part in avenging their father's fall, and having been previously slain in the *melee,* the order for the exposure of their dead bodies on the gallows was only intended to brand them with public infamy for their malice and hatred to the Jews; and (2) the anti-Jewish party having, in all probability, been instigated through the arts or influence of Haman to acts of spiteful and wanton oppression, the existing state of feeling among the natives required some vigorous and decisive measure to prevent the outbreak of future aggressions. To order an extension, therefore, of the permissive edict to the Jews to defend themselves, was perhaps no more than affording an opportunity for their enemies to be publicly known. Though it led to so awful a slaughter of 75,000 of their enemies, there is reason to believe that these were chiefly Amalekites, in the fall of whom on this occasion, the prophecies (Exod. 17:14, 16; Deut. 25:19) against that doomed race were accomplished. **19. a day of . . . feasting . . . and of sending portions one to another**—The princes and people of the East not only invite their friends to feasts, but it is their custom to send a portion of the banquet to those who cannot well come to it, especially their relations, and those who are detained at home in a state of sorrow or distress.

20-32. THE TWO DAYS OF PURIM MADE FESTIVAL. **20. Mordecai wrote these things**—Commentators are not agreed what is particularly meant by "these things"; whether the letters following, or an account of these marvellous events to be preserved in the families of the Jewish people, and transmitted from one generation to another.

ADAM CLARKE

CHAPTER 9

1. *Now in the twelfth month.* What a number of providences, and none of them apparently of an extraordinary nature, concurred to preserve a people so signally, and to all human appearance so inevitably, doomed to destruction!

3. *And all the rulers of the provinces.* Mordecai being raised to the highest confidence of the king, and to have authority over the whole realm, these officers assisted the Jews, no doubt, with the troops under their command, to overthrow those who availed themselves of the former decree to molest the Jews. For it does not appear that the Jews slew any person who did not rise up to destroy them. See v. 5.

6. *And in Shushan.* It is strange that in this city, where the king's mind must have been so well known, there should be found 500 persons to rise up in hostility against those whom they knew the king befriended!

10. *The ten sons of Haman.* Their names are given above. And it is remarked here, and in v. 16, where the account is given of the number slain in the provinces, that the Jews laid no hands on the spoil. They stood for their lives, and gave full proof that they sought their own personal safety, and not the property of their enemies, though the decree in their favor gave them authority to take the property of all those who were their adversaries, chap. viii. 11.

13. *Let Haman's ten sons be hanged.* They had been slain the preceding day, and now she requests that they may be exposed on posts or gibbets, as a terror to those who sought the destruction of the Jews.

15. *And slew three hundred men.* Esther had probably been informed by Mordecai that there were still many enemies of the Jews who sought their destruction, who had escaped the preceding day, and therefore begs that this second day be added to the former permission. This being accordingly granted, they found 300 more, in all 800. And thus Susa was purged of all their enemies.

18. *The Jews . . . assembled . . . on the thirteenth . . . and on the fourteenth.* These two days they were employed in slaying their enemies, and they rested on the fifteenth.

19. *The Jews of the villages.* They joined that to the preceding day, and made it a day of festivity, and of sending portions to each other; that is, the rich sent portions of the sacrifices slain on this occasion to the poor, that they also might be enabled to make the day a day of festivity; that as the sorrow was general, so also might the joy be.

20. *Mordecai wrote these things.* It has been supposed that thus far that part of the Book of Esther which was written by Mordecai extends. What follows, to the end, was probably added either by Ezra or the men of the Great Synagogue—though what is said here may refer only to the letters sent by Mordecai to the Jews of the provinces. From this to the end of the chapter is nothing else than a recapitulation of the chief heads of the preceding history, and an account of the appointment of an annual feast, called the Feast of Purim, in commemoration of their providential deliverance from the malice of Haman.

MATTHEW HENRY

of the kings of Persia.

II. A festival was instituted, to be observed yearly from generation to generation by the Jews. in remembrance of this wonderful work which God wrought for them, that *the children who should be born* might know it, and *declare it to their children, that they might set their hope in God*, Ps. lxxviii. 6, 7. Posterity would reap the benefit of this deliverance, and therefore ought to celebrate the memorial of it. Concerning this festival

1. It was observed—every year on *the fourteenth and fifteenth days of the twelfth month*, just a month before the passover, *v.* 21. They kept two days together as thanksgiving days, and did not think them too much to spend in praising God. On the fourteenth day country-Jews rested, and on the fifteenth those in Shushan, and both those days they kept.

2. It was called—*The feast of Purim* (*v.* 26), from *Pur*, a Persian word which signifies *a lot*, because Haman had by lot determined this to be the time of the Jews' destruction, but the Lord, at whose disposal the lot is, had determined it to be the time of their triumph.

3. It was not a divine institution, and therefore it is not called a *holy day*, but a human appointment, by which it was made a *good day*, *v.* 19, 22. (1) The Jews ordained it, and took it upon themselves (*v.* 27), voluntarily *undertook to do as they had begun*, *v.* 23. (2) Mordecai and Esther confirmed their resolve, that it might be the more binding on posterity, and might come well recommended by those great names. They *wrote*, [1] *With all authority* (*v.* 29), Esther being queen and Mordecai prime-minister of state. [2] *With words of peace and truth.* Though they wrote with authority, they wrote with tenderness,

4. It was to be observed—by *all the Jews*, and by *their seed*, and by all such as *joined themselves to them*, *v.* 27. A concurrence in joys and praises is one branch of the communion of saints.

5. It was to be observed—that the memorial of the great things God had done for his church might never *perish from their seed*, *v.* 28. When Esther, in peril of her life, *came before the king*, he repealed the edict, *v.* 25. This also must be remembered. Good deeds done for the Israel of God ought to be remembered, for the encouragement of others to do the like. The more cries we have offered up in our trouble, and the more prayers for deliverance, the more we are obliged to be thankful to God for deliverance.

6. How it was to be observed. They should make it, (1) A day of cheerfulness, *a day of feasting and joy* (*v.* 22). (2) A day of generosity, *sending portions one to another*, in token of mutual respect, and being knit by this and other public common dangers and deliverances so much the closer to each other in love. (3) A day of charity, sending *gifts to the poor*. Those that have received mercy must, in token of their gratitude, show mercy. Thanksgiving and almsgiving should go together, that, when we are rejoicing and blessing God, the heart of the poor may rejoice with us. They always, at the feast, read the whole story over in the synagogue each day, and put up three prayers to God, in the first of which they praise God for counting them worthy to attend this divine service; in the second they thank him for the miraculous preservation of their ancestors; in the third they praise him that they have lived to observe another festival in memory of it.

JAMIESON, FAUSSET, BROWN

26. they called these days Purim, after the name of Pur—Pur, in the Persian language, signifies lot; and the feast of Purim, or lots, has a reference to the time having been pitched upon by Haman through the decision of the lot. In consequence of the signal national deliverance which divine providence gave them from the infamous machinations of Haman, Mordecai ordered the Jews to commemorate that event by an anniversary festival, which was to last for two days, in accordance with the two days' war of defense they had to maintain. There was a slight difference in the time of this festival; for the Jews in the provinces, having defended themselves against their enemies on the thirteenth, devoted the fourteenth to festivity; whereas their brethren in Shushan, having extended that work over two days, did not observe their thanksgiving feast till the fifteenth. But this was remedied by authority, which fixed the fourteenth and fifteenth of Adar. It became a season of sunny memories to the universal body of the Jews; and, by the letters of Mordecai, dispersed through all parts of the Persian empire, it was established as an annual feast, the celebration of which is kept up still. On both days of the feast, the modern Jews read over the *Megillah* or Book of Esther in their synagogues. The copy read must not be printed, but written on vellum in the form of a roll; and the names of the ten sons of Haman are written on it a peculiar manner, being ranged, they say, like so many bodies on a gibbet. The reader must pronounce all these names in one breath. Whenever Haman's name is pronounced, they make a terrible noise in the synagogue. Some drum with their feet on the floor, and the boys have mallets with which they knock and make a noise. They prepare themselves for their carnival by a previous fast, which should continue three days, in imitation of Esther's; but they have mostly reduced it to one day [JENNING'S JEWISH ANTIQUITIES].

ADAM CLARKE

23. *The Jews undertook to do as they had begun.* They had already kept the fifteenth day, and some of them in the country the fourteenth also, as a day of rejoicing. Mordecai wrote to them to bind themselves and their successors, and all their proselytes, to celebrate this as an annual feast throughout all their generations; and this they undertook to do. And it has been observed among them, in all places of their dispersion, from that day to the present time, without any interruption.

26. *They called these days Purim.* That is from *pari*, "the lot"; because, as we have seen, Haman cast lots to find what month, and what day of the month, would be the most favorable for the accomplishment of his bloody designs against the Jews. See on chap. iii. 7. *And of that which they had seen.* The first letter to which this second refers must be that sent by Mordecai himself. See v. 20.

29. *Esther . . . wrote with all authority.* Esther and Mordecai had the king's license so to do, and their own authority was great and extensive.

31. *As they had decreed for themselves and for their seed.* There is no mention of their receiving the approbation of any high priest, nor of any authority beyond that of Mordecai and Esther. The king could not join in such a business, as he had nothing to do with the Jewish religion, that not being the religion of the country.

32. *The decree of Esther confirmed these matters.* It was received by the Jews universally with all respect, and they bound themselves to abide by it.

MATTHEW HENRY

CHAPTER 10

Verses 1–3

I. How great and powerful king Ahasuerus was. He had a vast dominion, both in the continent and among the islands, from which he raised a vast revenue. Besides the usual customs which the kings of Persia exacted (Ezra iv. 13), he laid an additional tribute upon his subjects (*v.* 1): *The king laid a tribute.* Besides this instance of the grandeur of Ahasuerus, many more might be given, that were *acts of his power and of his might*. These however are not recorded here in the sacred story, which is confined to the Jews, and relates the affairs of other nations only as they fell in with their affairs.

II. How great and good Mordecai was. Long had Mordecai sat contentedly in the king's gate, and now at length he is advanced. The declaration of the greatness to which the king advanced Mordecai was *written in the chronicles of the kingdom*, as very memorable, and contributing to the great achievements of the king. He was *great among the Jews* (*v.* 3), not only great above them, but great with them, dear to them, and much respected by them. He was good, for he did good. He did not disown his people the Jews, though they were strangers and captives, dispersed and

JAMIESON, FAUSSET, BROWN

CHAPTER 10

VSS. 1-3. AHASUERUS' GREATNESS. MORDECAI'S ADVANCEMENT. **1. Ahasuerus laid a tribute**—This passage being an appendix to the history, and improperly separated from the preceding chapter, it might be that the occasion of levying this new impost arose out of the commotions raised by Haman's conspiracy. Neither the nature nor the amount of the tax has been recorded; only it was not a local tribute, but one exacted from all parts of his vast empire. **2. the declaration of the greatness of Mordecai**—The experience of this pious and excellent Jew verified the statement, "he that humbleth himself shall be exalted." From sitting contentedly at the king's gate, he was raised to the dignity of highest subject, the powerful ruler of the kingdom. Acting uniformly on the great principles of truth and righteousness, his greatness rested on a firm foundation. His faith was openly avowed, and his influence as a professor of the true religion was of the greatest usefulness for promoting the welfare of the Jewish people, as well as for advancing the glory of God. **3. Mordecai . . . was next unto King Ahasuerus . . . great among the Jews,** etc.—The elevation of this pious and patriotic Jew to the possession of

ADAM CLARKE

CHAPTER 10

1. *Laid a tribute upon the land.* On the 127 provinces of which we have already heard. *The isles of the sea.* Probably the isles of the Aegean Sea, which were conquered by Darius Hystaspes.

2. *The book of the chronicles . . . of Media and Persia?* The Persians have ever been remarkable for keeping exact chronicles of all public events.

3. *Was next unto king Ahasuerus.* He was his prime minister; and, under him, was the governor of the whole empire.

MATTHEW HENRY

despised. Still he wrote himself *Mordecai the Jew.* He did not seek his own wealth, or the raising of an estate for himself and his family.

His power, his wealth, and all his interest in the king and queen, he improved for the public good. He did not side with any one party of his people against another, but, whatever differences there were among them, he was a common father to them all.

JAMIESON, FAUSSET, BROWN

the highest official power was of very great importance to the suffering church at that period; for it enabled him, who all along possessed the disposition, now to direct the royal influence and authority in promoting the interests and extending the privileges of his exiled countrymen. Viewed in this light, the providence of God is plainly traceable in all the steps that led to his unexpected advancement. This providential interposition is all the more remarkable, that, as in the analogous case of Joseph, it was displayed in making the ordinary and natural course of things lead to the most marvellous results. To use the pious words of an eminent prelate, "though in the whole of this episode there was no extraordinary manifestation of God's power, no particular cause or agent that was in its working advanced above the ordinary pitch of nature, yet the contrivance, and suiting these ordinary agents appointed by God, is in itself more admirable than if the same end had been effected by means that were truly miraculous." The sudden advancement of individuals from obscurity and neglect to the highest stations of power and influence is, in Eastern courts, no extraordinary nor infrequent occurrence. The caprice, the weak partiality of the reigning sovereign, or, it may be, his penetrating discernment in discovering latent energy and talent, has often "raised the beggar from the dunghill, and set him among princes." Some of the all-powerful viziers in modern Persia, and not a few of the beys in Egypt, have been elevated to their respective dignities in this manner. And, therefore, the advancement of "Mordecai, who was next unto Ahasuerus, and great among the Jews," was in perfect accordance with the rapid revolution of "the wheel of fortune" in that part of the world. But, considering all the circumstances of Mordecai's advancement, not only his gaining the favor of the king, but his being "accepted of the multitude of his brethren, it was beyond all controversy the doing of the Lord, and was truly marvellous in his people's eyes." **accepted of the multitude of his brethren**—Far from being envious of his grandeur, they blessed God for the elevation to official power of so good a man. **speaking peace to all his seed**—While his administration was conducted with a mild and impartial hand, he showed a peculiarly warm and friendly feeling to all his countrymen when asked his counsel or his aid.

ADAM CLARKE

JOSEPH PARKER:

"Mordecai the Jew was next unto king Ahasuerus, and great among the Jews, and accepted of the multitude of his brethren, seeking the wealth of his people, and speaking peace to all his seed" (10:3).

What narrow escapes we have in life! How near being hanged was even Mordecai one night! Who can tell what will happen tomorrow? Blessed is that servant who when his Lord cometh shall be found waiting. The faithful servant shall be called up into friendship and honor and coronation. You are in great straits today—tomorrow you may have great riches. "Hope springs eternal in the human breast." There is a sentimental hope which is never to be trusted; there is a hope which is the blossom of righteousness or the music of reason. Every Christian has the spirit of hope given to him as part of his divine estate: quench not the Spirit. We are not delivered in order that we may crush our enemies; we are not Christians in order that we may slay the heathen; we have not been adopted into God's family that we may go out with a naked sword to cut down every infidel, sceptic, atheist, and unbeliever: we are saved that we may save, we have this honor given to us that we may call others to the same great joy. Let us, if we are delivered men—let us, if we are saved from peril, strait, and sore extremity—let us show our gratitude by our benevolence.
—*The People's Bible*

THE BOOK OF JOB

I. Prologue—the man before the process (1:1-5)

II. A controversy between heaven and hell (1:6-2:10)

A. The first cycle (1:6-22)

1. Council in heaven (1:6-12)
2. Conflict on earth (1:13-22)

B. The second cycle (2:1-10)

1. Council in heaven (2:1-6)
2. Conflict on earth (2:7-10)

III. Controversy between Job and his friends (2:11-37:24)

A. Their coming (2:11-3:26)

1. Their sympathy (2:11-13)
2. Job's lament (3:1-26)

B. The controversy (4:1-31:40)

1. First cycle (4:1-14:22)
   a. The argument: God is righteous. He punishes the wicked. He blesses the good. (4:1-5:27; 8:1-22; 11:1-20)
   b. The answer of Job: He is not wicked but just and yet he is afflicted. (6:1-7:21; 9:1-10:22; 12:1-14:22)
2. Second cycle (15:1-21:34)
   a. The argument: It is the wicked who are afflicted. (15:1-35; 18:1-21; 20:1-29)
   b. The answer of Job: The righteous also are afflicted. The wicked are not always afflicted. (16:1-17:16; 19:1-29; 21:1-34)
3. Third cycle (22:1-31:40)
   a. The argument: Job has sinned; therefore he suffers. (22:1-30; 25:1-6)
   b. The answer of Job: Solemn protestation of innocence. (23:1-24:25; 26:1-31:40)

C. The last voice—suffering is educational (32:1-37:24)

IV. Controversy between Jehovah and Job (38:1-42:6)

A. Jehovah, the first unveiling—the creation and sustenance of the universe (38:1-39:30)

B. Interlude (40:1-5)

C. Jehovah, the second unveiling—the government of the material universe (40:6-41:34)

D. Job's answer (42:1-6)

V. Epilogue—the man beyond the process (42:7-17)

The book of Job stands by itself, is not connected with any other, and is therefore to be considered alone. Many copies of the Hebrew Bible place it after the book of Psalms, and some after the Proverbs, which perhaps has given occasion to some learned men to imagine it to have been written by Isaiah or some of the later prophets. It is most properly placed first in this collection of divine morals: also, being doctrinal, it is proper to precede and introduce the book of Psalms, which is devotional, and the book of Proverbs, which is practical; for how shall we worship or obey a God whom we know not? As to this book:

I. We are sure that it is given by inspiration of God, though we are not certain who was the penman of it. The Jews, though no friends to Job because he was a stranger to the commonwealth of Israel, yet, as faithful conservators of the "oracles of God" committed to them, always retained this book in their sacred canon. The history is referred to by one apostle (James 5:11) and one passage (5:13) is quoted by another apostle with the usual form of quoting scripture, "It is written" (1 Cor. 3:19).

II. It is, for the substance of it, a true history, and not a romance, though the dialogues are poetical. No doubt there was such a man as Job; the prophet Ezekiel names him with Noah and Daniel (Ezek. 14:14).

III. It is very ancient, though we cannot fix the precise time either when Job lived or when the book was written. So many, so evident, are its hoary hairs, the marks of its antiquity, that we have reason to think that holy Job was contemporary with Isaac and Jacob; though not co-heir with them of the promise of the earthly Canaan, yet a joint-expectant with them of the "better country," that is "the heavenly." Probably he was of the posterity of Nahor, Abraham's brother, whose first-born was Uz (Gen. 31:21), and in whose family religion was for some ages kept up, as appears (Gen. 53) where God is called not only "the God of Abraham," but "the God of Nahor." He lived before the age of man was shortened to seventy or eighty, as it was in Moses' time; before sacrifices were confined to one altar; before the general apostasy of the nations from the knowledge and worship of the true God; and while yet there was no other idolatry known than the worship of the sun and moon, and that punished by the judges (31:26–28). He lived while God was known by the name of "God Almighty" more than by the name of "Jehovah"; for he is called "Shaddai—the Almighty" above thirty times in this book. He lived while divine knowledge was conveyed, not by writing, but by tradition; for to that appeals are here made (8:8; 21:29; 15:18; 5:1). And we have therefore reason to think that he lived before Moses, because here is no mention at all of the deliverance of Israel out of Egypt or the giving of the law. We conclude therefore that we are here got back to the patriarchal age, and, besides its authority, we receive this book with veneration for its antiquity.

IV. We are sure that it is of great use to the church and to every Christian, though there are many passages in it dark and hard to be understood.

A. This noble poem presents to us, in very clear and lively characters, these five things among others:

1. *A monument of primitive theology.* The first and great principles of the light of nature, on which natural religion is founded, are here, in a warm and long and learned dispute, not only taken for granted, but by common consent plainly laid down as eternal truths. Were ever the being of God, his glorious attributes and perfections, his unsearchable wisdom, his irresistible power, his inconceivable glory, his inflexible justice, and his incontestable sovereignty, discoursed of with more clearness, fullness, reverence, and divine eloquence, than in this book?
2. *A specimen of Gentile piety.* This great saint was out of the pale of the covenant, no Israelite, no proselyte, and yet none like him for religion, nor such a favorite of heaven upon this earth.
3. *An exposition of the book of Providence.* The prosperity of the wicked and the afflictions of the righteous have always been reckoned two as hard chapters as any in that book; but they are here expounded and reconciled with the divine wisdom, purity, and goodness.
4. *A great example of patience and close adherence to God in the midst of the sorest calamities.* Sir Richard Blackmore's most ingenious pen, in his excellent preface to his paraphrase on this book, makes Job a hero proper for an epic poem; for, says he, "He appears brave in distress and valiant in affliction, maintains his virtue, and with that his character, under the most exasperating provocations that the malice of hell could invent, and thereby gives a most noble example of passive fortitude, a character no way inferior to that of the active hero."
5. *An illustrious type of Christ,* the particulars of which we shall endeavor to take notice of as we go along.

B. In this book we have:

1. The history of Job's sufferings, and his patience under them (chs. 1, 2), not without a mixture of human frailty (ch. 3).
2. A dispute between him and his friends upon them, in which:
   a. The opponents were Eliphaz, Bildad, and Zophar.
   b. The respondent was Job.
   c. The moderators were, first, Elihu (chs. 32–37); secondly, God himself (chs. 39–41).
3. The issue of all in Job's honor and prosperity (ch. 42).

MATTHEW HENRY

CHAPTER 1

Verses 1–3

Concerning Job,

I. He was a man; therefore subject to like passions as we are. He was *Ish*, a man in authority. The country he lived in was the land of Uz, in the eastern part of Arabia, near Euphrates. God has his remnant in all places. It was the privilege of the land of Uz to have so good a man as Job in it; the worse others were round about him the better he was. His name *Job*, or *Jjob*, some say, signifies *one hated* and counted as an enemy. Others make it to signify one that grieves or groans.

II. He was a very good man, eminently pious, and better than his neighbours: *He was perfect and upright*. It is the judgment of God concerning him, and we are sure that is according to truth. 1. Job was a religious man, *one that feared God*, that is, worshipped him. 2. He was sincere in his religion: He was *perfect*; not sinless, as he himself owns (*ch.* ix. 20): *If I say I am perfect, I shall be proved perverse*. But, having a respect to all God's commandments, aiming at perfection, he was really as good as he seemed to be, his heart was sound and his eye single. 3. He was upright in his dealings both with God and man, was faithful to his promises, steady in his counsels, true to every trust. 4. The fear of God reigning in his heart was the principle that governed his whole conversation. 5. He dreaded the thought of doing what was wrong; with the utmost abhorrence and detestation he *eschewed evil. The fear of the Lord is to hate evil* (Prov. viii. 13) and then *by the fear of the Lord men depart from evil*, Prov. xvi. 6.

III. He was prosperous and yet pious. Though it is hard and rare, it is not impossible, for *a rich man to enter into the kingdom of heaven*. He was prosperous, and his prosperity put a lustre upon his piety, and gave him who was so good so much greater opportunity of doing good. 1. He had a numerous family. He was eminent for religion, and yet not a hermit, not a recluse, but the father and master of a family. 2. He had a good estate for the support of his family; his *substance* was considerable, *v.* 3. Riches are called *substance*. Job's substance is described, not by the acres of land he was lord of, but, (1) By his cattle—*sheep and camels, oxen and asses*. As soon as God had made man, and provided for his maintenance by the herbs and fruits, he made him rich and great by giving him *dominion over the crea.ures*, Gen. i. 28. (2) By his servants. He had a very good household or husbandry, and thus he both had honour and did good. Job's wealth, with his wisdom, entitled him to the honour and power he had in his country, which he describes (*ch.* xxix). Job was upright and *therefore* grew rich; for honesty is the best policy, and piety and charity are ordinarily the surest ways of thriving. The account of Job's piety and prosperity comes before the history of his great afflictions, to show that neither will secure us from the calamities of human life. Piety will not secure us, as Job's mistaken friends thought, for *all things come alike to all*; prosperity will not, as a careless world thinks, Isa. xlvii. 8.

Verses 4–5

A further account of Job's prosperity and his piety.

I. His great comfort in his children is taken notice of as an instance of his prosperity; for our temporary comforts are borrowed, depend upon others, and are as those about us are. It was a comfort to this good man, 1. To see his children grown up and settled in the world. All his sons were in houses of their own, probably married. 2. To see them thrive in their affairs, and able to feast one another, as well as to feed themselves. 3. To see them in health. 4. Especially to see them live in love, and unity, and mutual good affection, no jars or quarrels among them. 5. It added to his comfort to see the brothers so kind to their sisters, that they sent for them to feast with them. 6. They feasted in their own houses.

II. His great care about his children is taken notice of as an instance of his piety. Observe (*v.* 5) Job's pious concern for the spiritual welfare of his children.

1. He was jealous over them with a godly jealousy; and so we ought to be over ourselves and those that are dearest to us, as far as is necessary to our care and endeavour for their good.

2. As soon as the days of their feasting were over he called them to the solemn exercises of religion.

3. He sent to them to prepare for solemn ordinances, *sent and sanctified them*, ordered them to examine their own consciences and repent of what they had done amiss in their feasting. Thus he kept his authority over them for their good, and they submitted to it, though they had got into houses of their own.

JAMIESON, FAUSSET, BROWN

CHAPTER 1

PART I—PROLOGUE OR HISTORICAL INTRODUCTION IN PROSE—CHAPTERS I, II

Vss. 1-5. THE HOLINESS OF JOB, HIS WEALTH, etc. **1. Uz**—north of Arabia Deserta, lying towards the Euphrates. It was in this neighborhood, and not in that of Idumea, that the Chaldeans and Sabeans who plundered him dwelt. The Arabs divide their country into the north, called Sham, or "the left"; and the south, called Yemen, or "the right"; for they faced east; and so the west was on their left, and the south on their right. Arabia Deserta was on the east, Arabia Petræa on the west, and Arabia Felix on the south. **Job**—The name comes from an *Arabic* word meaning "to return," viz., to God, "to repent," referring to his end [EICHORN]; or rather from a *Hebrew* word signifying one to whom enmity was shown, "greatly tried" [GESENIUS]. Significant names were often given among the Hebrews, from some event of later life (cf. Gen. 4:2, Abel—a "feeder" of sheep). So the emir of Uz was by general consent called Job, on account of his "trials." The only other person so called was a son of Issachar (Gen. 46:13). **perfect**—not absolute or faultless perfection (cf. 9:20); Eccles. 7:20), but *integrity, sincerity, and consistency* on the whole, in all relations of life (Gen. 6:9; 17:1; Prov. 10:9; Matt. 5:48). It was the fear of God that kept Job from evil (Prov. 8:13).

3. she-asses—prized on account of their milk, and for riding (Judg. 5:10). Houses and lands are not mentioned among the emir's wealth, as nomadic tribes dwell in movable tents and live chiefly by pasture, the right to the soil not being appropriated by individuals. The "five hundred yoke of oxen" imply, however, that Job tilled the soil. He seems also to have had a dwelling in a town, in which respect he differed from the patriarchs. Camels are well called "ships of the desert," especially valuable for caravans, as being able to lay in a store of water that suffices them for days, and to sustain life on a very few thistles or thorns. **household**—(Gen. 26:14). The other rendering which the *Hebrew* admits, "husbandry," is not so probable. **men of the east**—denoting in Scripture those living east of Palestine; as the people of North Arabia Deserta (Judg. 6:3; Ezek. 25:4).

4. every one his day—viz., the birthday (ch. 3:1). Implying the love and harmony of the members of the family, as contrasted with the ruin which soon broke up such a scene of happiness. The *sisters* are specified, as these feasts were not for revelry, which would be inconsistent with the presence of sisters. These latter were invited by the brothers, though they gave no invitations in return.

5. when the days of feasting were gone about—i.e., at the end of all the birthdays collectively, when the banquets had gone round through all the families. **Job . . . sanctified them**—by offering up as many expiatory burnt offerings as he had sons (Lev. 1:4). This was done "in the morning" (Gen. 22:3; Lev. 6:12). Jesus also began devotions early (Mark 1:35). The holocaust, or burnt offer-

ADAM CLARKE

CHAPTER 1

1. *In the land of Uz.* This country was situated in Idumea, or the land of Edom, in Arabia Petraea, of which it comprised a very large district.

Whose name was Job. The original is *Aiyob*. From the Vulgate we borrow *Job*, not very dissimilar from the *Iob* of the Septuagint. The name signifies "sorrowful," or "he that weeps."

Perfect and upright. "Complete" as to his mind and heart, and "straight" or "correct" as to his moral deportment. *Feared God.* Had Him in continual reverence. *Eschewed evil.* Departing from or avoiding evil. We have the word "eschew" from the old French *eschever*, which signifies "to avoid."

3. *His substance also was seven thousand sheep.* A thousand, says the Chaldee, for each of his sons. *Three thousand camels*, a thousand for each of his daughters. *Five hundred yoke of oxen* for himself. And *five hundred she asses* for his wife. Thus the Targum divides the substance of this eminent man. *A very great household.* "A very great estate." The word *abuddah* refers chiefly to husbandry, including all manner of labor in the field, with cattle, and every description of servants.

The greatest of all the men of the east. He was more eminent than any other person in that region in wisdom, wealth, and piety.

4. *Feasted in their houses, every one his day.* It is likely that a birthday festival is here intended. When the birthday of one arrived, he invited his brothers and sisters to feast with him; and each observed the same custom.

5. *When the days of their feasting were gone about.* At the conclusion of the year, when the birthday of each had been celebrated, the pious father appears to have gathered them all together, that the whole family might hold a feast to the Lord, offering burnt offerings in order to make an atonement for sins of all kinds, whether presumptuous or committed through ignorance.

MATTHEW HENRY

Still he was the priest of the family, and at his altar they all attended, valuing their share in his prayers more than their share in his estate. Parents cannot give grace to their children (it is God that sanctifies) but they ought by seasonable admonitions and counsels to further their sanctification.

4. He offered sacrifice for them. Job, like Abraham, had an altar for his family. On this extraordinary occasion, he offered more sacrifices than usual, *according to the number of them all*, one for each child. "For this child I prayed, according to its particular temper, genius, and condition," to which the prayers, as well as the endeavours, must be accommodated. He rose early as one whose heart was upon his work. He required his children to attend the sacrifice.

5. Thus he did *continually*. The acts of repentance and faith must be often renewed, because we often repeat our transgressions. He that serves God uprightly will serve him continually.

Verses 6–12

Job was not only so rich and great, but withal so wise and good, that one would think the mountain of his prosperity stood so strong that it could not be moved; but here we have a thick cloud gathering over his head. The devil, having a great enmity to Job for his eminent piety, begged and obtained leave to torment him. It does not at all derogate from the credibility of Job's story in general to allow that this discourse between God and Satan, in these verses, is parabolical, like that of Micaiah (1 Kings xxii. 19, &c.), and an allegory designed to represent the malice of the devil against good men and the divine check and restraint which that malice is under.

I. Satan among the sons of God (*v.* 6), an *adversary* (*so Satan* signifies) to God, to men, to all good: he thrust himself into an assembly of the *sons of God* that came to *present themselves before the Lord*. This means either, 1. A meeting of the saints on earth. Professors of religion, in the patriarchal age, were called *sons of God* (Gen. vi. 2); they had then religious assemblies and stated times for them. But there was a Satan among the sons of God; when they came together he is among them, to distract and disturb them. Or, 2. A meeting of the angels in heaven. They are *the sons of God, ch.* xxxviii. 7. Satan was one of them originally.

II. His examination, how he came thither (*v.* 7): *The Lord said unto Satan, Whence comest thou?* He knew very well whence he came, and with what design he came thither, that as the good angels came to do good he came for a permission to do hurt; but he would, by calling him to an account, show him that he was under check and control.

III. The account he gives of himself and of the tour he had made. I come (says he) *from going to and fro on the earth*. 1. He could not pretend he had been doing any good. 2. He would not own he had been doing any hurt. While we are on this earth we are within his reach, and with so much subtlety, swiftness, and industry, does he penetrate into all the corners of it, that we cannot be in any place secure from his temptations. 3. He yet seems to give some representation of his own character. Perhaps it is spoken proudly. Perhaps it is spoken fretfully, and with discontent. He had been walking to and fro, and could find no rest, but was as much a fugitive and a vagabond as Cain in the land of Nod. Perhaps it is spoken carefully: "I have been hard at work, going to and fro," in quest of an opportunity to do mischief.

IV. The question God puts to him concerning Job (*v.* 8): *Hast thou considered my servant Job?* How honourably God speaks of Job: "Yonder is *my servant Job*; there is *none like him*." How closely he gives to Satan this good character of Job: *Hast thou set thy heart to my servant Job?* designing hereby to answer the devil's seeming boast of the interest he had in this earth. Saith God, "Job is my faithful servant." Satan may boast, but he shall not triumph. As if he had said, "Satan, I know thy errand; thou hast come to inform against Job; but *hast thou considered him?*"

V. The devil's base insinuation against Job, in answer to God's encomium of him. He could not deny but that Job feared God, but suggested that he was mercenary in his religion, and therefore a hypocrite (*v.* 9): *Doth Job fear God for nought?* How impatient the devil was of hearing Job praised, though it was God himself that praised him. Those are like the devil who cannot endure that anybody should be praised but themselves. How slily he censured him as a hypocrite, not asserting that he was so, but only asking, "Is he not so?" This is the common way of slanderers, whisperers, backbiters, to suggest that by way of query which yet they have no reason

JAMIESON, FAUSSET, BROWN

ing, in patriarchal times, was offered (lit., "caused to ascend," referring to the smoke ascending to heaven) by each father of a family officiating as priest in behalf of his household. **cursed God**—The same *Hebrew* word means to "curse," and to "bless"; GESENIUS says, the original sense is to "kneel," and thus it came to mean bending the knee in order to invoke either a blessing or a curse. Cursing is a perversion of blessing, as all sin is of goodness. Sin is a degeneracy, not a generation. It is not, however, likely that Job should fear the possibility of his sons *cursing* God. The sense "bid farewell to," derived from the *blessing* customary at parting, seems sufficient (Gen. 47:10). Thus UMBREIT translates "may have dismissed God from their hearts"; viz., amid the intoxication of pleasure (Prov. 20:1). This act illustrates Job's "fear of God" (vs. 1).

6-12. SATAN, APPEARING BEFORE GOD, FALSELY ACCUSES JOB. **6. sons of God**—angels (ch. 38:7; I Kings 22:19). They present themselves to render account of their "ministry" in other parts of the universe (Heb. 1:14). **the Lord**—*Heb.*, JEHOVAH—the self-existing God, faithful to His promises. God says (Exod. 6:3) that He was not known to the patriarchs by this name. But, as the name occurs previously in Genesis 2:7-9, etc., what must be meant is, not until the time of delivering Israel by Moses was He known peculiarly and publicly in the *character* which the name means; viz., "making things to be," fulfilling the promises made to their forefathers. This name, therefore, here, is no objection against the antiquity of the Book of Job. **Satan**—The tradition was widely spread that *he* had been the agent in Adam's temptation. Hence his name is given without comment. The feeling with which he looks on Job is similar to that with which he looked on Adam in Paradise: emboldened by his success in the case of one not yet fallen, he is confident that the piety of Job, one of a fallen race, will not stand the test. He had fallen himself (ch. 4:19; 15:15; Jude 6). In the Book of Job, Satan is first designated by *name:* "Satan," *Heb.*, "one who lies in wait"; an "adversary" in a court of justice (I Chron. 21:1; Ps. 109:6; Zech. 3:1); "accuser" (Rev. 12:10). He has the law of God on his side by man's sin, and against man. But Jesus Christ has fulfilled the law for us; justice is once more on man's side against Satan (Isa. 42:21); and so Jesus Christ can plead as our Advocate against the adversary. "Devil" is the *Greek* name—the "slanderer," or "accuser." He is subject to God, who uses his ministry for chastising man. In *Arabic,* Satan is often applied to a serpent (Gen. 3:1). He is called prince of this world (John 12:31); the god of this world (II Cor. 4:4); prince of the power of the air (Eph. 2:2). God here questions him, in order to vindicate His own ways before angels. **7. going to and fro**—rather, "hurrying rapidly to and fro." The original idea in *Arabic* is the heat of haste (Matt. 12:43; I Pet. 5:8). Satan seems to have had some peculiar connection with this earth. Perhaps he was formerly its ruler under God. Man succeeded to the vice royalty (Gen. 1: 26; Ps. 8:6). Man then lost it and Satan became prince of this world. The Son of man (Ps. 8:4)—the representative man, regains the forfeited inheritance (Rev. 11:15). Satan's replies are characteristically curt and short. When the angels appear before God, Satan is among them, even as there was a Judas among the apostles. **8. considered**—*Marg.* "set thine heart on"; i.e., considered attentively. No true servant of God escapes the eye of the adversary of God. **9. fear God for naught**—It is a mark of the children of Satan to sneer and not give credit to any for disinterested piety. Not so much God's gifts, as God Himself is "the reward" of His people (Gen. 15:1).

ADAM CLARKE

This we may consider as a general custom among the godly in those ancient times. *And cursed God in their hearts.* In this book, according to most interpreters, the verb *barach* signifies both to "bless" and to "curse"; and the noun *Elohim* signifies the true God, false gods, and great or mighty. The reason why Job offered the burnt offerings appears to have been this: In a country where idolatry flourished, he thought it possible that his children might, in their festivity, have given way to idolatrous thoughts, or done something prescribed by idolatrous rites; and therefore the words may be rendered thus: "It may be that my children have blessed the gods in their hearts."

Job appears to have thought that his children might have sinned through ignorance, or sinned privately; and it was consequently necessary to make the due sacrifices to God in order to prevent His wrath and their punishment; he therefore offered the burnt offering, which was prescribed by the law in cases of sins committed through ignorance. See the ordinances, Lev. iv. 1-35; v. 15-19, and particularly Num. xv. 24-29.

6. *There was a day when the sons of God.* All the versions, and indeed all the critics, are puzzled with the phrase *sons of God; beney haelohim*, literally, "sons of the God," or "sons of the gods." The Vulgate has simply "sons of God." The Septuagint, "the angels of God." But what are we to make of this whole account? Expositions are endless. That of Mr. Peters appears to me to be at once the most simple and the most judicious: The Scripture speaks of God after the manner of men. As kings, therefore, transact their most important affairs in a solemn council or assembly, so God is pleased to represent himself as having His council likewise, and as passing the decrees of His providence in an assembly of His holy angels. We have here, in the case of Job, the same grand assembly held as was before in that of Ahab, I Kings xxii. *And Satan came also.* This word *also* is emphatic in the original, *hassatan,* "the Satan," or "the adversary." St. Peter, 1st Epist., chap. v, v. 8, plainly refers to this place; and fully proves that *hassatan,* which he literally translates "the adversary," is no other than "the devil," or chief of bad demons, which he adds to others by way of explanation. There are many demons mentioned in Scripture; but the word "Satan" or "devil" is never found in the originals of the Old and New Testaments in the plural number. Hence we reasonably infer that all evil spirits are under the government of one chief, the devil, who is more powerful and more wicked than the rest.

7. *From going to and fro in the earth.* The translation of the Septuagint is curious: "Having gone round the earth, and walked over all that is under heaven, I am come hither." St. Peter, as has been already stated, v. 8, refers to this: "Be sober, be vigilant; for your adversary the devil, as a roaring lion, walketh about, seeking whom he may devour."

8. *Hast thou considered my servant Job?* Literally, "Hast thou placed thy heart on My servant Job?" Hast thou viewed his conduct with attention, whilst thou wert roaming about, seeking whom thou mightest devour?

9. *Doth Job fear God for nought?* Thou hast made it his interest to be exemplary in his conduct. For this assertion Satan gives his reasons in what immediately follows.

MATTHEW HENRY

to think is true. How unjustly he accused him as mercenary, to prove him a hypocrite. It was a great truth that Job did not fear God for nought; he got much by it, for godliness is great gain: but it was a falsehood that he would not have feared God if he had not got this by it, as the event proved. Job's friends charged him with hypocrisy because he was greatly afflicted, Satan because he greatly prospered.

VI. The complaint Satan made of Job's prosperity, *v.* 10. God's peculiar people are taken under his special protection, they and all that belong to them; divine grace makes a hedge about their spiritual life, and divine providence about their natural life. He had prospered him, not in idleness or injustice but in the way of honest diligence: *Thou hast blessed the work of his hands.* The devil speaks of it with vexation. "I see thou hast *made a hedge about him, round about.*" *The wicked* one *saw it and was grieved*, and argued against Job that the only reason why he served God was because God prospered him so well.

VII. The proof Satan undertakes to give of the hypocrisy and mercenariness of God's religion, if he might but have leave to strip him of his wealth. "Let it be put to this issue," says he (*v.* 11); "make him poor, frown upon him, turn thy hand against him, and then see where his religion will be; touch what he has and it will appear what he is. How spitefully he speaks of the impression it would make upon Job: "He will not only let fall his devotion, but *even curse thee to thy face.*" God declared Job the best man then living: now, if Satan can prove him a hypocrite, it will follow that God had not one faithful servant among men and that there was no such thing as true and sincere piety in the world, but religion was all a sham, and Satan was king *de facto—in fact*, over all mankind.

VIII. The permission God gave to Satan to afflict Job for the trial of his sincerity. 1. It is matter of wonder that God should give Satan such a permission as this, but he did it for his own glory, the honour of Job, the explanation of Providence, and the encouragement of his afflicted people in all ages. He suffered Job to be tried, as he suffered Peter to be sifted, but took care that *his faith should not fail* (Luke xxii. 32). 2. It is matter of comfort that God has the devil *in a chain.* He could not afflict Job without leave from God first asked and obtained, and then no further than he had leave: "*Only upon himself put not forth thy hand;* meddle not with his body, but only with his estate." It is a limited power that the devil has.

IX. Satan's departure from this meeting of the sons of God. He went forth now, not to go to and fro, rambling through the earth, but with a direct course, to fall upon poor Job, who is carefully going on in the way of his duty, and knows nothing of the matter.

Verses 13–19

A particular account of Job's troubles.

I. Satan brought them upon him on the very day that his children began their course of feasting, at their *elder brother's house* (*v.* 13).

II. They all come upon him at once; while one messenger of evil tidings was speaking another came, and, before he had told his story, a third, and a fourth, followed immediately. 1. That there might appear a more than ordinary displeasure of God against him in his troubles. 2. That he might not have leisure to consider, and reason himself into a gracious submission, but might be overwhelmed by a complication of calamities.

III. They took from him all that he had, and made a full end of his enjoyments.

1. He had 500 *yoke of oxen*, and 500 *she-asses*, and a competent number of servants to attend them; and all these he lost at once, *v.* 14, 15. His neighbours the Sabeans, carried off the oxen and asses, and slew the servants that faithfully and bravely did their best to defend them, and *one only escaped.* When Satan has God's permission to do mischief he will not want mischievous men to be his instruments in doing it.

2. He had 7,000 *sheep*, and shepherds that kept them; and all those he lost at the same time by lightning, *v.* 16. Job was ready to reproach the Sabeans, and fly out against them for their injustice and cruelty, when the next news immediately directs him to look upwards. *The fire of God has fallen from heaven.* All his sheep and shepherds were not only killed, but consumed by it at once, and one shepherd only was left alive to carry the news to poor Job. This would tempt Job to say, *It is in vain to serve God.* The messenger called the lightning the *fire of God.* How terrible then were the tidings of this destruction, which came immediately from the hand of God!

JAMIESON, FAUSSET, BROWN

10. his substance is increased—Lit., "spread out like a flood"; Job's herds covered the face of the country.

11. curse thee to thy face—in antithesis to God's praise of him (vs. 8), "one that feareth God." Satan's words are too true of many. Take away their prosperity and you take away their religion (Mal. 3:14).

12. in thy power—Satan has no power against man till God gives it. God would not touch Job with His own hand, though Satan asks this (vs. 11, "thine"), but He allows the enemy to do so.

13-22. JOB, IN AFFLICTION, BLESSES GOD, etc. **13. wine**—not specified in verse 4. The mirth inspired by the "wine" here contrasts the more sadly with the alarm which interrupted it.

14. the asses feeding beside them—*Heb.*, "she-asses." A graphic picture of rural repose and peace; the more dreadful, therefore, by contrast is the sudden attack of the plundering Arabs. **15. Sabeans**—not those of Arabia Felix, but those of Arabia Deserta, descending from Sheba, grandson of Abraham and Keturah (Gen. 25:3). The Bedouin Arabs of the present day resemble, in marauding habits, these Sabeans (cf. Gen. 16:12). **I alone am escaped**—cunningly contrived by Satan. One in each case escapes (vss. 16, 17, 19), and brings the same kind of message. This was to overwhelm Job, and leave him no time to recover from the rapid succession of calamities—"misfortunes seldom come single." **16. fire of God**—Hebraism for "a mighty fire"; as "cedars of God"—"lofty cedars." Not lightning, which would not consume *all* the sheep and servants. UMBREIT understands it of *the burning wind* of Arabia, called by the Turks "wind of poison." "The prince of the power of the air" is permitted to have control over such destructive agents.

ADAM CLARKE

10. *Hast not thou made an hedge about him?* Thou hast fortified him with spikes and spears. Thou hast defended him as by an unapproachable hedge. He is an object of Thy peculiar care, and is not exposed to the common trials of life.

11. *But put forth thine hand.* Shoot the dart of poverty and affliction against him. *And he will curse thee to thy face.* "If he will not bless Thee to Thy appearances." He will bless Thee only in proportion to the temporal good Thou bestowest upon him, to the providential and gracious appearances or displays of Thy power in his behalf. The exact maxim of a great statesman Sir Robert Walpole: "Every man has his price."

13. *There was a day.* It no doubt refers to one of those birthday festivals mentioned before.

14. *The asses feeding beside them.* The she-asses, which appear to have been more domesticated, as of more worth and use than the others, for both their milk and their work.

15. *And the Sabeans fell.* The Vulgate alone understands this of a people. The Septuagint, Syriac, and Arabic understand it as implying a marauding party.

16. *The fire of God is fallen.* Though *the fire of God* may mean a great, a tremendous fire, yet it is most natural to suppose lightning is meant; for as thunder was considered to be the voice of God, so lightning was the fire of God.

MATTHEW HENRY

3. He had 3,000 *camels*, and servants tending them; and he lost them all at the same time by the Chaldeans, who came in three bands, and drove them away, and slew the servants, *v.* 17. When the way of the wicked prospers, and they carry off their booty, while just and good men are suddenly cut off, God's righteousness is like the great deep, the bottom of which we cannot find, Ps. xxxvi. 6.

4. His dearest and most valuable possessions were his ten children; and, to conclude the tragedy, news is brought him, at the same time, that they were killed and buried in the ruins of the house in which they were feasting, and all the servants that waited on them, except one that came express with the tidings, of it *v.* 18, 19. This was the greatest of Job's losses, and therefore the devil reserved it for the last, that, if the other provocations failed, this might make him curse God. Our children are pieces of ourselves; it is very hard to part with them, and touches a good man in as tender a part as any. But to part with them all at once, and for them to be all cut off in a moment, who had been so many years his cares and hopes, went to the quick indeed. They all died together. They died suddenly. They died when they were feasting and making merry. Had they died suddenly when they were praying, he might the better have borne it. They were taken away when he had most need of them to comfort him under all his other losses.

Verses 20–22

The devil had done all he desired leave to do against Job, to provoke him to curse God. He whom the rising sun saw the richest of all the men in the east was before night poor to a proverb. If his riches had been, as Satan insinuated, the only principle of his religion, now that he had lost his riches he would certainly have lost his religion; but the account we have, in these verses, of his pious deportment under his affliction, sufficiently proved the devil a liar and Job an honest man.

I. He conducted himself like a man under his afflictions (*v.* 20), he *arose, and rent his mantle, and shaved his head*, which were the usual expressions of great sorrow, to show that he was sensible of the hand of the Lord that had gone out against him; yet he did not break out into any extravagant passion. He kept his temper, and bravely maintained the possession and repose of his own soul, in the midst of all these provocations. The time when he began to show his feelings was not till he heard of the death of his children, and then he rent his mantle. A worldly unbelieving heart would have said, "Now that the meat is gone it is well that the mouths are gone too." But Job knew better, and would have been thankful if Providence had spared his children, though he had had little or nothing for them, for *Jehovah-jireh—the Lord will provide.*

II. He conducted himself like a wise and good man under his affliction, like *one that feared God* and *eschewed* the *evil* of sin more than that of outward trouble.

1. He humbled himself under the hand of God, and accommodated himself to the providences he was under, as one that knew how to want as well as how to abound.

2. He composed himself with quieting considerations, that he might not be disturbed and put out of the possession of his own soul by these events. He reasons from the common state of human life, which he describes with application to himself: *Naked came I* (as others do) *out of my mother's womb, and naked shall I return thither.* St. Paul refers to this of Job, 1 Tim. vi. 7. *We brought nothing* of this world's goods *into the world*, but have them from others; and *it is certain that we can carry nothing out*, but must leave them to others. This consideration silenced Job under all his losses. He is but where he was at first. He looks upon himself only as naked, not maimed, not wounded; he was himself still his own man, when nothing else was his own, and therefore but reduced to his first condition. He is but where he must have been at last, and is only unclothed, or unloaded rather, a little sooner than he expected. If we put off our clothes, before we go to bed, it is some inconvenience, but it may be the better borne when it is near bed-time.

3. We may well rejoice to find Job in this good frame, because this was the very thing upon which the trial of his integrity was put. The devil said that he would, under his affliction, curse God; but he blessed him, and so proved himself an honest man.

(1) He acknowledged the hand of God both in the mercies he had formerly enjoyed and in the afflictions he was now exercised with: *The Lord gave, and the Lord has taken away.* The same that gave hath

JAMIESON, FAUSSET, BROWN

17. Chaldeans—not merely robbers as the Sabeans; but experienced in war, as is implied by "they *set in array* three bands" (Hab. 1:6-8). RAWLINSON distinguishes three periods: 1. When their seat of empire was in the south, towards the confluence of the Tigris and Euphrates. The Chaldean period, from 2300 B.C. to 1500 B.C. In this period was Chedorlaomer (Gen. 14), the Kudur of Hur or Ur of the Chaldees, in the Assyrian inscriptions, and the conqueror of Syria. 2. From 1500 to 625 B.C., the Assyrian period. 3. From 625 to 538 B.C. (when Cyrus the Persian took Babylon), the Babylonian period. "Chaldees" in *Hebrew—Chasaim*. They were akin, perhaps, to the Hebrews, as Abraham's sojourn in Ur, and the name "Chesed," a nephew of Abraham, imply. The *three* bands were probably in order to attack the three separate thousands of Job's camels (vs. 3). **19. wind from the wilderness**—south of Job's house. The tornado came the more violently over the desert, being uninterrupted (Isa. 21:1; Hos. 13:15). **the young men**—rather, "the young people"; including the daughters (so in Ruth 2:21).

20. Job arose—not necessarily from sitting. Inward excitement is implied, and the beginning to do anything. He had heard the other messages calmly, but on hearing of the death of his children, *then* he arose; or, as EICHORN translates, he *started up* (II Sam. 13:31). The rending of the mantle was the conventional mark of deep grief (Gen. 37:34). Orientals wear a tunic or shirt, and loose pantaloons; and over these a flowing mantle (especially great persons and women). Shaving the head was also usual in grief (Jer. 41:5; Mic. 1:16).

21. Naked—(I Tim. 6:7). "Mother's womb" is poetically the earth, the universal mother (Eccles. 5:15; 12:7; Ps. 139:15).

Job herein realizes God's assertion (vs. 8) against Satan's (vs. 11). Instead of cursing, he blesses the name of JEHOVAH (*Hebrew*). The *name* of Jehovah, is Jehovah *Himself*, as manifested to us in His attributes (Isa. 9:6).

ADAM CLARKE

17. *The Chaldeans made out three bands.* The *Chaldeans* inhabited each side of the Euphrates near to Babylon, which was their capital. They were also mixed with the wandering Arabs, and lived like them on rapine. They divided themselves into *three bands*, in order the more speedily and effectually to encompass, collect, and drive off the 3,000 camels; probably they mounted the camels and rode off.

19. *A great wind from the wilderness.* Here was another proof of the influence of "the prince of the power of the air." What mischief might he not do with this tremendous agent, were he not constantly under the control of the Almighty! He seems to have directed four different currents, which, blowing against the four corners or sides of the house, crushed it together, and involved all within in one common ruin.

20. *Rent his mantle.* Tearing the garments, shaving or pulling off the hair of the head, throwing dust or ashes on the head, and sitting on the ground were acts by which immoderate grief was expressed. Job must have felt the bitterness of anguish when he was told that, in addition to the loss of all his property, he was deprived of his ten children by a violent death. *Worshipped.* Prostrated himself; lay all along upon the ground, with his face in the dust.

21. *Naked came I out of my mother's womb.* I had no earthly possessions when I came into the world; I cannot have less going out of it. *Naked shall I return thither.* As I came out of my mother's womb destitute of the earthly possessions, so shall I return there; i.e., to the earth on which he was now falling.

MATTHEW HENRY

taken away; and may he not do what he will with his own? See how Job looks above instruments, and keeps his eye upon the first Cause.

(2) He adored God in both. When all was gone he fell down and worshipped. Afflictions must not divert us from, but quicken us to, the exercises of religion. Weeping must not hinder sowing, nor hinder worshipping. He gives God thanks for good designed him by his afflictions, for gracious supports under his afflictions, and the believing hopes he had of a happy issue at last.

Lastly, Here is the honourable testimony which the Holy Ghost gives to Job's constancy and good conduct under his afflictions. He passed his trials with applause, *v.* 22.

JAMIESON, FAUSSET, BROWN

22. nor charged God foolishly—rather, "allowed himself to commit no folly against God" [UMBREIT]. Chapter 2:10 proves that this is the meaning. Not as *marg.* "attributed no folly to God." Hasty words against God, though natural in the bitterness of grief, are *folly;* lit., an "insipid, unsavory" thing (ch. 6:6; Jer. 23:13, margin). Folly in Scripture is continually equivalent to wickedness. For when man sins, it is himself, not God, whom he injures (Prov. 8:36). We are to submit to trials, not because we see the reasons for them, nor yet as though they were matters of chance, but because *God wills* them, and has a right to send them, and has His own good reasons in sending them.

ADAM CLARKE

22. *In all this Job sinned not.* He did not give way to any action, passion, or expression offensive to his Maker. That Job lived after the giving of the law seems to me clear from many references to the rites and ceremonies instituted by Moses. In chap. i. 5, we are informed that he sanctified his children, and offered burnt offerings daily in the morning for each of them. This was a general ordinance of the law, as we may see, Lev. ix. 7.

MATTHEW HENRY

CHAPTER 2

Verses 1–6

Satan will have Job's cause called over again.

I. The court set, and the prosecutor making his appearance (*v.* 1, 2), as before, *ch.* i, 6, 7. The angels attended God's throne and Satan among them. He is asked the same question as before, *Whence comest thou?* and answers as before, *From going to and fro in the earth*; as if he had been doing no harm.

II. The judge himself pleading for him (*v.* 3): "*Hast thou considered my servant Job* better than thou didst, *a perfect and an upright man*; for thou seest he *still holds fast his integrity*?" Satan is condemned for his allegations against Job: "*Thou movedst me against him,* as an accuser, *to destroy him without cause.*" How well it is for us that neither men nor devils are to be our judges, for perhaps they would destroy us, right or wrong; but our judgment proceeds from the Lord, whose judgment never errs nor is biassed. Job is commended for his constancy notwithstanding the attacks made upon him. *Still he holds fast his integrity.* Constancy crowns integrity.

III. The accusation further prosecuted, *v.* 4. *Skin for skin, and all that a man has, will he give for his life.* Men will not only venture, but give, their estates to save their lives. Satan grounds upon this an accusation of Job, slyly representing him, 1. As unnatural to those about him, and one that laid not to heart the death of his children and servants. 2. As wholly selfish, and minding nothing but his own ease and safety.

IV. A challenge given to make a further trial of Job's integrity (*v.* 5): "*Put forth thy hand now and touch his bone and his flesh*, and then *he will curse thee to thy face*, and let go his integrity." Nothing is more likely to ruffle the thoughts and put the mind into disorder than acute pain and distemper of body. St. Paul himself had much ado to bear a thorn in the flesh, nor could he have borne it without special grace from Christ, 2 Cor. xii. 8, 9.

V. A permission granted to Satan to make this trial, *v.* 6. "*He is in thy hand*, do thy worst with him; *only save his life*, or his soul. Afflict him, but not to death." "Save his soul," that is, "his reason" (or some), "preserve to him the use of that, for otherwise it will be no fair trial; if in his delirium, he should curse God, that will be no disproof of his integrity. It would be the language not of his heart, but of his distemper."

Verses 7–10

The devil, having got leave to tear and worry poor Job, presently fell to work with him, as a tormentor first and then as a tempter. Artfully is the temptation managed with all the subtlety of the old serpent, who is here playing the same game against Job that he played against our first parents (Gen. iii).

I. He provokes him to curse God by smiting him with sore boils, and so making him a burden to himself, *v.* 7, 8.

1. The disease with which Job was seized was very grievous: Satan *smote him with boils, sore boils*, all over him, from head to foot, an erysipelas, perhaps, in a higher degree.

2. Instead of healing salves, *he took a potsherd*, a piece of a broken pitcher, *to scrape himself withal.* A very sad pass this poor man had come to. Even Lazarus had some ease from the tongues of the dogs that came and *licked his sores*; but poor Job has no help afforded him. None of those he had formerly been kind to had so much gratitude as to minister to him in his distress, either because the disease was loathsome and noisome or because they apprehended it to be infectious. Instead of reposing in a soft and warm bed, he *sat down among the ashes.* Thus did he humble himself under the mighty hand of God, and bring his mind to the meanness and poverty of his condition. The Septuagint reads it, He sat *down upon a dunghill without the city*, but the

JAMIESON, FAUSSET, BROWN

CHAPTER 2

Vss. 1-8. SATAN FURTHER TEMPTS JOB. **1. a day**—appointed for the angels giving an account of their ministry to God. The words "to present himself before the Lord" occur here, though not in 1:6, as Satan has now a special report to make as to Job.

3. integrity—lit., "completeness"; so "perfect," another form of the same Hebrew word, ch. 11. **movedst . . . against**—So I Samuel 26:19; cf. I Chron. 21:1 with II Sam. 24:1.

4. Skin for skin—a proverb. Supply, "He will give." The "skin" is figurative for any outward good. Nothing outward is so dear that a man will not exchange it for some other outward good; "but" (not "yea") "life," the inward good, cannot be replaced; a man will sacrifice everything else for its sake. Satan sneers bitterly at man's egotism and says that Job bears the loss of property and children because these are mere *outward and exchangeable goods,* but he will give up all things, even his religion, in order to save his life, if you touch his bones and flesh. "Skin" and "life" are in antithesis [UMBREIT]. The martyrs prove Satan's sneer false. ROSENMULLER explains it not so well. A man willingly gives up *another's* skin (life) for *his own* skin (life). So Job might bear the loss of his children, etc., with equanimity, so long as he remained unhurt himself; but when touched in his own person, he would renounce God. Thus the first "skin" means the *other's* skin, i.e., body; the second "skin," *one's own,* as in Exodus 21:28. **6. but save**—rather, "only spare." Satan shows his ingenuity in inflicting pain, and also his knowledge of what man's body can bear without vital injury.

7. sore boils—malignant boils; rather, as it is singular in the Hebrew, a "burning sore." Job was covered with one universal inflammation. The use of the potsherd agrees with this view. It was that form of leprosy called *black* (to distinguish it from the *white*), or *elephantiasis*, because the feet swell like those of the elephant. The *Arabic judham* (Deut. 28:35), where "sore botch" is rather the black burning boil (Isa. 1:6). **8. a potsherd**—not a piece of a broken earthen vessel, but an instrument made for scratching (the root of the *Hebrew* word is "scratch"); the sore was too disgusting to touch. "To sit in the ashes" marks the deepest mourning (Jonah 3:6); also humility, as if the mourner were nothing but dust and ashes; so Abraham (Gen. 18: 27).

ADAM CLARKE

CHAPTER 2

3. *To destroy him without cause.* Thou wishedst Me to permit thee to destroy a man whose sins have not called for so heavy a judgment. The original word signifies to "swallow down" or "devour"; and this word Peter had no doubt in view in the place quoted on v. 7 of the preceding chapter: "Your adversary the devil, as a roaring lion, walketh about, seeking whom he may devour"—seeking whom he may swallow or gulp down.

4. *Skin for skin.* That is, A man will part with all he has in the world to save his life.

5. *He will curse thee to thy face.* Literally, "If he will not bless Thee to Thy face." See the note on chap. i. 11.

6. *But save his life.* His body thou shalt have permission to afflict, but against his life thou shalt have no power.

7. *Sore boils.* "With an evil inflammation." What this diabolical disorder was interpreters are not agreed. Some think it was the leprosy; and this is the reason why he dwelt by himself, and had his habitation in an unclean place, without the city, or in the open air; and the reason why his friends beheld him "afar off," v. 12, was because they knew that the disorder was infectious. His scraping himself with a potsherd indicates a disease accompanied with intolerable itching, one of the characteristics of smallpox.

MATTHEW HENRY

original says no more than that he sat *in the midst of the ashes*.

II. Satan urges him, by the persuasions of his own wife, to curse God, *v.* 9. She was spared to him, when the rest of his comforts were taken away, for this purpose, to be a troubler and tempter to him. If Satan leaves anything that he has permission to take away, it is with a design of mischief. She banters Job for his constancy in his religion: "*Dost thou still retain thy integrity?* Art thou so tame and sheepish as thus to truckle to a God who is so far from rewarding thy services with marks of his favour that he strips thee, and scourges thee, without any provocation given? Is this a God to be still loved, and blessed, and served?" She urges him to renounce his religion, to blaspheme God, and dare him to do his worst: *Curse God and die*; be thy own deliverer by being thy own executioner; end thy troubles by ending thy life. These are two of the blackest and most horrid of all Satan's temptations. Nothing is more contrary to natural conscience than blaspheming God, nor to natural sense than self-murder.

III. He bravely resists and overcomes the temptation, *v.* 10.

1. He was very indignant at having such a thing mentioned to him: "What! Curse God? I abhor the thought of it. *Get thee behind me, Satan.*" In other cases Job reasoned with his wife with a great deal of mildness, even when she was unkind to him (*ch.* xix. 17): *I entreated her for the children's sake of my own body*. But, when she persuaded him to curse God, he was much displeased, and showed her the evil of what she said. In such a pious household as Job had his wife was one that had been well affected to religion, but now, when all their estate and comfort were gone, she could not bear the loss with that temper of mind that Job had. When Peter was a Satan to Christ he told him plainly, *Thou art an offence to me*. If those whom we think wise and good at any time speak that which is foolish and bad, we ought to reprove them faithfully.

2. He reasoned against the temptation: *Shall we receive good at the hand of God, and shall we not receive evil also?* Those whom we reprove we must endeavour to convince. He argues for, not only the bearing, but the receiving of evil: *Shall we not receive evil*, that is, "Shall we not expect to receive it? If God give us so many good things, shall we be surprised, or think it strange, if he sometimes afflict us, when he has told us that prosperity and adversity are set the one over against the other?" 1 Peter iv. 12. "Shall we not set ourselves to receive it aright?" The word signifies to receive as a gift, and denotes a pious affection and disposition of soul under our afflictions, accounting them gifts (Phil. i. 29), accepting them as punishments of our iniquity (Lev. xxvi. 41), acquiescing in the will of God in them ("Let him do with me as seemeth him good"). "Shall we receive so much good as has come to us from the hand of God during all those years of peace and prosperity, and shall we not now receive evil, when God thinks fit to lay it on us?" If we receive so much good for the body, shall we not receive some good for the soul; something which, by saddening the countenance, makes the heart better?

IV. Thus Job still held fast his integrity, and Satan's design against him was defeated: *In all this did not Job sin with his lips*. Grace got the upper hand and he took care that the root of bitterness might not spring up to trouble him, Heb. xii. 15.

Verses 11–13

An account of the kind visit which Job's three friends paid him in his affliction. Some, who were his enemies, triumphed in his calamities, *ch.* xvi. 10; xix. 18; xxx. 1, &c. But his friends concerned themselves for him, and endeavoured to comfort him. Three of them are here named (*v.* 11), Eliphaz, Bildad, and Zophar. These three were eminently wise and good men, as appears by their discourses. They were old men, had a great reputation for knowledge, and much deference was paid to their judgment, *ch.* xxxii. 6.

I. Job, in his prosperity, had contracted a friendship with them. Much of the comfort of this life lies in acquaintance and friendship with those that are prudent and virtuous; and he that has a few such friends ought to value them highly. Job's three friends are supposed to have been all of them of the posterity of Abraham. Eliphaz descended from Teman, the grandson of Esau (Gen. xxxvi. 11), Bildad (it is probable) from Shuah, Abraham's son by Keturah, Gen. xxv. 2. Zophar is thought by some to be the same with Zepho, a descendant from Esau, Gen. xxxvi. 11. The preserving of so much wisdom and piety among those that were strangers to the covenants of promise was a happy presage of God's grace

JAMIESON, FAUSSET, BROWN

9-13. Job Reproves His Wife. **9. curse God**—rather "renounce" God. (*Note,* 1:5.) [Umbreit]. However, it was usual among the heathens, when disappointed in their prayers accompanied with offerings to their gods, to reproach and *curse* them. **and die**—i.e., take thy farewell of God and so die For no good is to be got out of religion, either here or hereafter; or, at least, not in this life [Gill]. Nothing makes the ungodly so angry as to see the godly under trial not angry.

10. the foolish women—Sin and folly are allied in Scripture (I Sam. 25:25; II Sam. 13:13; Ps. 14:1). **receive evil**—bear willingly (Lam. 3:39).

11. Eliphaz—The view of Rawlinson that "the names of Job's three friends represent the Chaldean times, about 700 B.C.," cannot be accepted. Eliphaz is an Idumean name, Esau's oldest son (Gen. 36:4); and Teman, son of Eliphaz (15), called "duke." Eusebius places Teman in Arabia Petræa (but see *Note,* 6:19). Teman means "at the right hand"; and then the south, viz., part of Idumea; capital of Edom (Amos 1:12). Hebrew geographers faced the east, not the north as we do; hence with them "the right hand" was the south. Temanites were famed for wisdom (Jer. 49:7). Baruch mentions them as "authors of fables (viz., proverbs embodying the results of observation), and searchers out of understanding." **Bildad the Shuhite**—Shuah (a pit), son of Abraham and Keturah (Gen. 25:2). Ptolemy mentions the region Syccea, in Arabia Deserta, east of Batanea. **Zophar the Naamathite**—not of the Naamans in Judah (Josh. 15:41), which was too distant; but some region in Arabia Deserta. Fretelius says there was a Naamath in Uz.

ADAM CLARKE

9. *Then said his wife.* We translate *barech Elohim vamuth,* "Curse God, and die." The verb *barach* is supposed to include in it the ideas of cursing and blessing; but it is not clear that it has the former meaning in any part of the sacred writings, though we sometimes translate it so. Here it seems to be a strong irony. Job was exceedingly afflicted, and apparently dying through sore disease, yet his soul was filled with gratitude to God. His wife, destitute of the salvation which her husband possessed, gave him this ironical reproof. "Bless God, and die"—What! bless Him for His goodness while He is destroying all that thou hast! bless Him for His support while He is casting thee down and destroying thee! Bless on, and die.

10. *Thou speakest as one of the foolish.* Thou speakest like an infidel; like one who has no knowledge of God, of religion, or of a future state.

11. *Job's three friends.* The first was *Eliphaz the Temanite.* Eliphaz was one of the sons of Esau; and Teman, of Eliphaz, Gen. xxxvi. 10-11. Teman was a city of Edom, Jer. xlix. 7-20; Ezek. xxv. 13; Amos i. 11-12. *Bildad the Shuhite.* Shuah was the son of Abraham by Keturah, and his posterity is reckoned among the Easterns. *Zophar the Naamathite.* He most probably came from that Naamah which was bordering upon the Edomites to the south and fell by lot to the tribe of Judah, Josh. xv. 21-41. These circumstances prove that Job must have dwelt in the land of Edom, and that all his friends dwelt in Arabia Petraea, or in the countries immediately adjacent. That some of those Eastern people were highly cultivated, we have at least indirect proof in the case of the Temanites, Jer. xlix. 7: "Concerning Edom, thus saith the Lord of hosts; Is wisdom no more in Teman? is counsel perished from the prudent? is their wisdom vanished?" It is evident that the inhabitants of those districts were celebrated for their knowledge, and the sayings of Job's three friends are proofs that their reputation for wisdom stood on a very solid foundation.

MATTHEW HENRY

to the Gentiles, when the partition-wall should in the latter days be taken down. Esau was rejected; yet many that came from him inherited some of the best blessings.

II. They continued their friendship with Job in his adversity, when most of his friends had forsaken him, *ch.* xix. 14. They come to share with him in his griefs, as formerly they had come to share with him in his comforts. Many a good lesson is to be learned from the troubles of others; we may look upon them and receive instruction, and be made wise and serious. Some good word may be spoken to them which may help to make them easy. Job's friends came to mourn with him, to mingle their tears with his, and so to comfort him. It is much more pleasant to visit those in affliction to whom comfort belongs than those to whom we must first speak conviction. They were not sent for, but came of their own accord (*ch.* vi. 22). They came with a design to comfort him, and yet proved miserable comforters, through their unskilful management of his case. When they saw him at some distance he was so disfigured and deformed with his sores that *they knew him not, v.* 12. What a change will a sore disease, or oppressing care and grief, make in the countenance, in a little item! *Is this Job?* Observing him thus miserably altered, they did not leave him, in a fright or loathing, but expressed so much the more tenderness towards him. The sight of them revived Job's grief, and set him a weeping afresh, which fetched floods of tears from their eyes. *They rent their clothes, and sprinkled dust upon their heads*, as men that would strip themselves, and abase themselves, with their friend that was stripped and abased. They had many a time, it is likely, sat with him on his couches and at his table, in his prosperity, and were therefore willing to share with him in his grief and poverty because they had shared with him in his joy and plenty. They resolved to stay with him till they saw him mend or end, and therefore took lodgings near him, though he was not now able to entertain them. Every day, for seven days together, they came and sat with him, as his companions in tribulation. They sat with him, but *none spoke a word* to him, only they all attended to the particular narratives he gave of his troubles. By their silence so long they would intimate that what they afterwards said was well considered and digested and the results of many thoughts. We should think twice before we speak once, especially in such a case as this, think long, and we shall be the better able to speak short and to the purpose.

JAMIESON, FAUSSET, BROWN

12. toward heaven—They threw ashes violently upwards, that they might fall on their heads and cover them—the deepest mourning (Josh. 7:6; Acts 22:23).

13. seven days . . . nights—They did not remain in the same posture and without food, etc., all this time, but for most of this period daily and nightly. Sitting on the earth marked mourning (Lam. 2:10). Seven days was the usual length of it (Gen. 50:10; I Sam. 31:13). This silence may have been due to a rising suspicion of evil in Job; but chiefly because it is only ordinary griefs that find vent in language; extraordinary griefs are too great for utterance.

ADAM CLARKE

12. *They rent every one his mantle.* I have already had frequent occasions to point out and illustrate, by quotations from the ancients, the actions that were used in order to express profound grief; such as wrapping themselves in sackcloth, covering the face, strewing dust or ashes upon the head, sitting upon the bare ground, etc., etc.—significant actions which were in use among all nations.

13. *They sat down with him upon the ground seven days.* They were astonished at the unprecedented change which had taken place in the circumstances of this most eminent man; they could not reconcile his present situation with anything they had met with in the history of divine providence. The *seven days* mentioned here were the period appointed for mourning. The Israelites mourned for Jacob seven days, Gen. l. 10. The men of Jabesh mourned so long for the death of Saul, 1 Sam. xxxi. 13; 1 Chron. x. 12. And Ezekiel sat on the ground with the captives at Chebar, and mourned with and for them seven days, Ezek. iii. 15. The wise son of Sirach says, "Seven days do men mourn for him that is dead," Ecclus. xxii. 12. So calamitous was the state of Job that they considered him as a dead man, and went through the prescribed period of mourning for him. *They saw that his grief was very great.* This is the reason why they did not speak to him. They believed him to be suffering for heavy crimes and, seeing him suffer so much, they were not willing to add to his distresses by invectives or reproach. Job himself first broke silence.

MATTHEW HENRY — CHAPTER 3

Verses 1–10

Long was Job's heart hot within him; and, while he was musing the fire burned, and the more for being stifled and suppressed. So long Job and his friends sat thinking, but said nothing; *they* were afraid of speaking what they thought, lest they should grieve him, and *he* durst not give vent to his thoughts, lest he should offend them. Job first gives vent to his thoughts. In short, he cursed the day of his birth, wished he had never been born.

I. The extremity of his troubles and the discomposure of his spirits may excuse it in part, but he can by no means be justified in it. Now he has forgotten the good he was born to, the lean kine have eaten up the fat ones, and he is filled with thoughts of the evil only, and wishes he had never been born. The prophet Jeremiah himself expressed his painful sense of his calamities in language, not much unlike this: *Woe is me, my mother, that thou hast borne me!* Jer. xv. 10. *Cursed be the day wherein I was born*, Jer. xx. 14, &c. There is no condition of life a man can be in in this world but he may in it (if it be not his own fault) so honour God, and work out his own salvation, and make sure a happiness for himself in a better world, that he will have no reason at all to wish he had never been born, but a great deal of reason to say that he had his being to good purpose. Yet it must be owned, if there were not another life after this, so many are the sorrows and troubles of this that we might sometimes be tempted to say that we were *made in vain* (Ps. lxxxix. 47), and to wish we had never been. Let us observe it, to the honour of the spiritual life above the natural, that though many have cursed the day of their first birth, never any cursed the day of their new-birth, nor wished they never had had grace, and the Spirit of grace, given them.

II. Job cursed his day, but he did not curse his God—was weary of his life, and would gladly have parted with that, but not weary of his religion; he resolutely cleaves to that, and will never let it go. The

JAMIESON, FAUSSET, BROWN — CHAPTER 3

THE POEM OR DEBATE ITSELF, 2-42:6; FIRST SERIES IN IT, 3-14; JOB FIRST 3

VSS. 1-19. JOB CURSES THE DAY OF HIS BIRTH AND WISHES FOR DEATH. **1. opened his mouth**—The Orientals speak seldom, and then sententiously; hence this formula expressing deliberation and gravity (Ps. 78:2). He formally began. **cursed his day**—the strict *Hebrew* word for "cursing": not the same as in ch. 1:5. Job cursed his birthday, but not his God. **2. spake**—*Hebrew,* "answered," i.e., not to any actual question that preceded, but to the question virtually involved in the case. His outburst is singularly wild and bold (Jer. 20:14). To desire to die so as to be free from sin is a mark of grace; to desire to die so as to escape troubles is a mark of corruption. He was ill-fitted to die who was so unwilling to live. But his trials were greater, and his light less, than ours. **3. the night** *in which*—rather "the night which said." The words in italics are not in the *Hebrew*. Night is personified and poetically made to speak. So in verse 7, and in Psalm 19:2. The birth of a male in the East is a matter of joy; often not so of a female.

ADAM CLARKE — CHAPTER 3

1. *After this opened Job his mouth.* After the seven days' mourning was over, there being no prospect of relief, Job is represented as thus cursing the day of his birth. Here the poetic part of the book begins. *Cursed his day.* That is, the day of his birth. We find a similar execration to this in Jeremiah, chap. xx. 14-18, and in other places; which, by the way, are no proofs that the one borrowed from the other, but that this was the common mode of Asiatic thinking, speaking, and feeling on such occasions.

3. *There is a man child conceived.* The word *harah* signifies to "conceive"; yet here, it seems, it should be taken in the sense of being born, as it is perfectly unlikely that the night of conception should be either distinctly known or published.

MATTHEW HENRY

dispute between God and Satan concerning Job was not whether Job had his infirmities, and whether he was subject to like passions as we are (that was granted), but whether he was a hypocrite, who secretly hated God, and, if he were provoked, would show his hatred; and, upon trial, it proved that he was no such man. The particular expressions which Job used in cursing his day are full of poetical fancy, flame, and rapture. We need not be particular in our observations upon them. When he would express his passionate wish that he had never been, he falls foul upon the day, and wishes,

(1) That earth might forget it.

(2) That Heaven might frown upon it: *Let not God regard it from above, v.* 4. Let the gloominess of the day represent Job's condition, whose sun went down at noon.

(3) That all joy might forsake it: *Let no joyful voice come therein* (*v.* 7); let it be a long night, and not *see the eye-lids of the morning* (*v.* 9), which bring joy with them.

(4) That all curses might follow it (*v.* 8): "Let none ever desire to see it, but, on the contrary, *let those curse it that curse the day.* Whatever day any are tempted to curse, let them at the same time bestow one curse upon my birth-day." What a foolish thing it was to wish that his eyes had never seen the light, that so they might not have seen sorrow, which yet he might hope to see through, and beyond which he might see joy!

Verses 11–19

Job, perhaps reflecting upon himself for his folly in wishing he had never been born, follows it, and thinks to mend it, with another, little better, that he had died as soon as he was born. Job here complains of life as a curse, and covets death and the grave as the greatest and most desirable bliss. Surely Satan was deceived in Job when he applied that maxim to him, *All that a man hath will he give for his life;* for never any man valued life at a lower rate than he did.

I. He ungratefully quarrels with life, and is angry that it was not taken from him as soon as it was given him (*v.* 11, 12): *Why died not I from the womb?* What a weak and helpless creature man is when he comes into the world, and how slender the thread of life is when it is first drawn. What a merciful and tender care divine Providence took of us at our entrance into the world. What a great deal of vanity and vexation of spirit attends human life. If we had not a God to serve in this world, and better things to hope for in another world, considering the faculties we are endued with and the troubles we are surrounded with, we should be strongly tempted to wish that we had *died from the womb.* How much soever life is embittered, we must say, "It was of the Lord's mercies that we died not from the womb, that we were not consumed." Hatred of life is a contradiction to the common sense and sentiments of mankind, and to our own at any other time. When the old man in the fable, being tired with his burden, threw it down with discontent and called for Death, and Death came to him and asked him what he would have with him, he then answered, "Nothing, but to help me up with my burden."

II. He passionately applauds death and the grave, and seems quite in love with them. To desire to die that we may be with Christ, that we may be free from sin, and that we may be *clothed upon with our house which is from heaven,* is the effect and evidence of grace; but to desire to die only that we may be quiet in the grave, and delivered from the troubles of this life, savours of corruption. Job here frets himself with thinking that if he had but died as soon as he was born: I should have been (says he, *v.* 14) *with kings and counsellors of the earth,* whose pomp, power, and policy, cannot set them out of the reach of death, nor secure them from the grave, nor distinguish theirs from common dust in the grave. Though they filled their houses with silver, yet they were forced to leave it all behind them, no more to return to it. Some, by the *desolate places* which the kings and counsellors are here said *to build for themselves,* understand the sepulchres or monuments they prepared for themselves in their life-time; and by the gold which the princes had, and the silver with which they filled their houses, they understand the treasures which, they say, it was usual to deposit in the graves of great men. Such arts have been used to preserve their dignity, if possible, on the other side death, and to keep themselves from lying with those of inferior rank; but it will not do: death is, and will be, an irresistible leveller. *Death mingles sceptres with spades.* There a *hidden untimely birth* (*v.* 16), a child that either never saw light or but just opened its eyes and peeped

JAMIESON, FAUSSET, BROWN

4. let not God regard it—rather, more poetically, "seek it out." "Let not God stoop from His bright throne to raise it up from its dark hiding-place." The curse on the *day* in vs. 3, is amplified in vss. 4, 5; that on the *night,* in vss. 6-10. **5. Let . . . the shadow of death**—(deepest darkness, Isaiah 9:2). **stain it**—This is a later sense of the verb [GESENIUS]; better the old and more poetic idea, "Let darkness (the ancient night of chaotic gloom) resume its rights over light (Gen. 1:2), and claim that day as its own." **a cloud**—collectively, a gathered mass of dark clouds. **the blackness of the day terrify it**—lit., the obscurations; whatever darkens the day [GESENIUS]. The verb in *Hebrew* expresses sudden terrifying. May it be suddenly affrighted at its own darkness. UMBREIT explains it as "magical incantations that darken the day," forming the climax to the previous clauses; vs. 8 speaks of "cursers of the day" similarly. But the former view is simpler. Others refer it to the poisonous simoom wind. **6. seize upon it**—as its prey, i.e., utterly dissolve it. **joined unto the days of the year**—rather, by poetic personification, "Let it not *rejoice* in the circle of days and nights and months, which form the circle of years." **7. solitary**—rather, unfruitful. "Would that it had not *given birth* to me." **8. them . . . that curse the day**—If "mourning" be the right rendering in the latter clause of this verse, these words refer to the hired mourners of the dead (Jer. 9:17). But the *Hebrew* for "mourning" elsewhere always denotes an animal, whether it be the crocodile or some huge serpent (Isa. 27:1), such as is meant by leviathan. Therefore, the expression, "cursers of day," refers to magicians, who were believed to be able by charms to make a day one of evil omen. (So Balaam, Num. 22:5.) This accords with UMBREIT's view (vs. 7); or to the Ethiopians and Atlantes, who "used to curse the sun at his rising for burning up them and their country" [HERODOTUS]. Necromancers claimed power to control or rouse wild beasts at will, as do the Indian serpent-charmers of our day (Ps. 58:5). Job does not say they had the power they claimed; but, supposing they had, may they curse the day. SCHUTTENS renders it by supplying words (?). Let those that are ready *for anything, call it* (the day) the raiser up of leviathan, i.e., of a host of evils. **9. dawning of the day**—lit., "eyelashes of morning." The Arab poets call the sun the eye of day. His early rays, therefore, breaking forth before sunrise, are the opening eyelids or eyelashes of morning. **12. Why did the knees prevent me?**—Old English for "anticipate my wants." The reference is to the solemn recognition of a newborn child by the father, who used to place it on his knees as his own, whom he was bound to rear (Gen. 30:3; 50:23; Isa. 66:12). **13. lain . . . quiet . . . slept**—a gradation. I should not only have *lain,* but been *quiet,* and not only *been quiet,* but *slept.* Death in Scripture is called sleep (Ps. 13:3); especially in the New Testament, where the resurrection-awakening is more clearly set forth (I Cor. 15:51; I Thess. 4:14; 5:10).

14. With kings . . . which built desolate places for themselves—who built up for themselves what proved to be (not palaces, but) ruins! The wounded spirit of Job, once a great emir himself, sick of the vain struggles of mortal great men, after grandeur, contemplates the palaces of kings, now desolate heaps of ruins. His regarding the repose of death the most desirable end of the great ones of earth, wearied with heaping up perishable treasures, marks the irony that breaks out from the black clouds of melancholy [UMBREIT]. The "for themselves" marks their selfishness. MICHAELIS explains it weakly of mausoleums, such as are found still, of stupendous proportions, in the ruins of Petra of Idumea. **15. filled their houses with silver**—Some take this to refer to the treasures which the ancients used to bury with their dead. But see last verse. **16. untimely birth**—(Ps. 58:8); preferable to the life of the restless miser (Eccles. 6: 3-5).

ADAM CLARKE

4. *Let that day be darkness.* The meaning is exactly the same with our expression, "Let it be blotted out of the calendar." *Let not God regard it from above.* "Let Him not require it"—let Him not consider it essential to the completion of the days of the year; and therefore he adds, *neither let the light shine upon it.* If it must be a part of duration, let it not be distinguished by the light of the sun.

5. *Let darkness and the shadow of death stain it.* "Pollute or avenge it," from *gaal,* to "vindicate, avenge"; hence *goel,* the nearest of kin, whose right it was to redeem an inheritance, and avenge the death of his relative by slaying the murderer. Let this day be pursued, overtaken, and destroyed. *Let a cloud dwell upon it.* "Let the thickest clouds have there their dwelling-place." *Let the blackness of the day terrify it.* Leaving out the semicolon, we had better translate the whole clause thus: "Let the thickest cloud have its dwelling-place upon it, and let the bitterness of a day fill it with terror."

6. *As for that night, let darkness seize upon it.* I think the Targum has hit the sense of this whole berse: "Let darkness seize upon that night; let it not be reckoned among the annual festivals; in the number of the months of the calendar let it not be computed."

7. *Lo, let that night be solitary.* "Let that night be grievous, oppressive, as destitute of good as a bare rock is of verdure." *Let no joyful voice come therein.* The word *renanah* signifies any brisk movement, such as the vibration of the rays of light, or the brisk modulation of the voice in a cheerful ditty.

8. *Let them curse it that curse the day.* "Let them curse it who detest the day; them who are ready to raise up the leviathan." That is, Let them curse my birthday who hate daylight, such as adulterers, murderers, thieves, and banditti, for whose practices the night is more convenient; and let them curse it who. being like me weary of life, are desperate enough to provoke the leviathan, the crocodile, to tear them to pieces.

9. *Let the stars of the twilight thereof.* The stars of the twilight may here refer to the planets Venus, Jupiter, Mars, and Mercury, as well as to the brighter fixed stars. *Let it look for light.* The darkness is represented as waiting for the lustre of the evening star, but is disappointed; and then for the dawn, but equally in vain.

12. *Why did the knees prevent me?* Why was I dandled on the knees? Why was I nourished by *the breasts?*

13. *For now should I have lain still.* In that case I had been insensible; *quiet*—without these overwhelming agitations; *slept*—unconscious of evil; *been at rest*—been out of the reach of calamity and sorrow.

14. *With kings and counsellors of the earth.* These mighty agitators of the world are at rest in their graves, after the lives of commotion which they have led among men, most of whom indeed have been the troublers of the peace of the globe. *Which built desolate places.* Who erect mausoleums, funeral monuments, sepulchral pyramids to keep their names from perishing, while their bodies are turned to corruption.

15. *Or with princes that had gold.* Chief or mighty men who got gold in abundance, filled their houses with silver, left all behind, and had nothing reserved for themselves but the empty places which they had made for their last dwelling, and where their dust now sleeps, devoid of care, painful journeys, and anxious expectations.

16. *Or as a hidden untimely birth.* An early miscarriage, which was scarcely perceptible by the parent herself; and in this case he *had not been*—he had never had the distinguishable form of a human being.

MATTHEW HENRY	JAMIESON, FAUSSET, BROWN	ADAM CLARKE

MATTHEW HENRY

into the world, and, not liking it, closed them again and hastened out of it, lies as soft and easy, lies as high and safe, as kings, and counsellors, and princes, that had gold. "And therefore," says Job, "would I have lain there in the dust, rather than live to lie here in the ashes! *Then should I have lain still, and been quiet*, which now I cannot do, I cannot be, but am still tossing and unquiet; then *I should have slept*, where as now sleep departeth from my eyes; *then had I been at rest*, whereas now I am restless." Now that life and immortality are brought to a much clearer light by the gospel than before good Christians can give a better account than this of the gain of death. But all that poor Job dreamed of was rest and quietness in the grave out of the fear of evil tidings and out of the feeling of sore boils. *Then should I have been quiet.* How finely he describes the repose of the grave. Those that now are troubled will there be out of the reach of trouble (*v.* 17): *There the wicked cease from troubling.* Those that are now toiled will there see the period of their toils. *There the weary are at rest.* Those that were here enslaved are there at liberty. Death is the prisoner's discharge, the relief of the oppressed, and the servant's manumission (*v.* 18).

Verses 20–26

Job here complains that his life was now continued and not cut off.

I. He thinks it hard, in general, that miserable lives should be prolonged (*v.* 20–22): *Wherefore is light in life given to those that are bitter in soul?* Life is called *light*, because pleasant and serviceable for walking and working. It is candle-light; the longer it burns the shorter it is, and the nearer to the socket. This light is said to be given us. Job reckons that to those who are in misery it is δῶρον ἄδωρον—*gift and no gift*, while the light only serves them to see their own misery. He here speaks of those who long for death, when they have outlived their comforts and usefulness, are burdened with age and infirmities, with pain or sickness, poverty or disgrace, and yet it comes not; while, at the same time, it comes to many who dread it and would put it far from them. The continuance and period of life must be according to God's will, not according to ours. It is not fit that we should be consulted how long we would live and when we would die; our times are in a better hand than our own. *Some dig for it as for hidden treasures*, that is, would give anything for a fair dismission out of this world. It may be a sin to long for death, but I am sure it is no sin to long for heaven.

II. He thinks himself, in particular, hardly dealt with, that he might not be eased of his pain and misery by death. To be thus impatient of life for the sake of the troubles we meet with is not only unnatural in itself, but ungrateful to the giver of life. Grace teaches us, in the midst of life's greatest comforts, to be willing to die, and, in the midst of its greatest crosses, to be willing to live. He had no comfort of his life: *My sighing comes before I eat*, *v.* 24. His griefs returned as duly as his meals, and affliction was his daily bread. He had no prospect of bettering his condition: *His way was hidden*, and God had *hedged him in*, *v.* 23. That which made his grief now the more grievous was that he was not conscious either of negligence or security in the day of his prosperity, which might provoke God thus to chastise him. He had kept up such a fear of trouble as was necessary to the maintaining of his guard. He was afraid for his children when they were feasting, lest they should offend God (*ch.* i. 5), afraid for his servants lest they should offend his neighbours; he took all the care he could of his own health, yet all would not do. He had not been secure, nor indulged himself in ease and softness, yet trouble came. Thus his way was hidden, for he knew not wherefore God contended with him.

CHAPTER 4

Verses 1–6

I. Eliphaz excuses the trouble he is now about to give to Job by his discourse (*v.* 2): "*If we assay a word with thee*, offer a word of reproof and counsel, wilt thou be grieved and take it ill? We have reason to fear thou wilt; but there is no remedy: *Who can refrain from words?*" With what tenderness he speaks of Job, and his present afflicted condition: "If we tell thee our mind, *wilt thou be grieved?*" We should show ourselves backward to say that which we foresee will be grievous, though ever so necessary. With what assurance he speaks of the truth of what he was about to say: *Who can withhold himself from speaking?* It is foolish pity not to reprove our friends, even our

JAMIESON, FAUSSET, BROWN

17. the wicked—the original meaning, "those ever restless," "full of desires" (Isa. 57:20, 21). **weary**—lit., "those whose strength is wearied out" (Rev. 14:13). **18. There the prisoners rest**—from their chains. **19. servant**—The slave is there manumitted from slavery.

20-26. He Complains of Life because of His Anguish. **20. Wherefore giveth he light**—viz., God; often omitted reverentially (ch. 24:23; Eccles. 9:9). Light, i.e., life. The joyful light ill suits the mourners. The grave is most in unison with their feelings.

23. whose way is hid—The picture of Job is drawn from a wanderer who has lost his way, and who is hedged in, so as to have no exit of escape (Hos. 2:6; Lam. 3:7, 9). **24. my sighing cometh before I eat**—i.e., prevents my eating [Umbreit]; or, conscious that the effort to eat brought on the disease, Job must sigh before eating [Rosenmuller]; or, sighing takes the place of good (Ps. 42:3) [Good]. But the first explanation accords best with the text. **my roarings are poured out like the waters**—an image from the rushing sound of water streaming. **25. the thing which I . . . feared is come upon me**—In the beginning of his trials, when he heard of the loss of one blessing, he feared the loss of another; and when he heard of the loss of that, he feared the loss of a third. **that which I was afraid of is come unto me**—viz., the ill opinion of his friends, as though he were a hypocrite on account of his trials. **26. I was not in safety . . . yet trouble came**—referring, not to his former state, but to the *beginning* of his troubles. From that time I had no rest, there was no intermission of sorrows. "And" (not, "yet") a fresh trouble is coming, viz., my friends' suspicion of my being a hypocrite. This gives the starting-point to the whole ensuing controversy.

CHAPTER 4

Vss. 1-21. First Speech of Eliphaz. **Eliphaz**—the mildest of Job's three accusers. The greatness of Job's calamities, his complaints against God, and the opinion that calamities are proofs of guilt, led the three to doubt Job's integrity. **2. If we assay to commune**—Rather, two questions, "May we attempt a word with thee? Wilt thou be grieved at it?" Even pious friends often count that only a touch which we feel as a wound.

ADAM CLARKE

17. *There the wicked cease.* In the grave the oppressors of men cease from irritating, harassing, and distressing their fellow creatures and dependents. *And there the weary be at rest.* Those who were worn out with the cruelties and tyrannies of the above.

18. *The prisoners rest together.* Those who were slaves, feeling all the troubles, and scarcely tasting any of the pleasures of life, are quiet in the grave together; and the voice of the oppressor, the hard, unrelenting taskmaster, which was more terrible than death, is heard no more.

19. *The small and great are there.* All sorts and conditions of men are equally blended in the grave, and ultimately reduced to one common dust; and between the bond and free there is no difference.

20. *Wherefore is light given?* Why is life granted to him who is incapable of enjoying it, or of performing its functions?

21. *Which long for death.* They look to it as the end of all their miseries, and long more for a separation from life than those who love gold do for a rich mine.

22. *Which rejoice exceedingly.* Literally, "They rejoice with joy, and exult when they find the grave."

23. *To a man whose way is hid.* Who knows not what is before him in either world, but is full of fears and trembling concerning both. *God hath hedged in.* Leaving him no way to escape, and not permitting him to see one step before him. There is an exact parallel to this passage in Lam. iii. 7, 9: "He hath hedged me about, that I cannot get out . . . He hath inclosed my ways with hewn stone."

24. *For my sighing cometh.* Some think that this refers to the ulcerated state of Job's body, mouth, hands, etc. He longed for food, but was not able to lift it to his mouth with his hands, nor masticate it when brought thither. But perhaps it is most natural to suppose that he means his sighing took away all appetite, and served him in place of meat. There is the same thought in Ps. xlii. 3: "My tears have been my meat day and night." *My roarings are poured out.* My lamentations are like the noise of the murmuring stream, or the dashings of the overswollen torrent.

25. *For the thing which I greatly feared.* Literally, "the fear that I feared"; or, "I feared a fear," as in the margin. While I was in prosperity I thought adversity might come, and I had a dread of it. I feared the loss of my family and my property, and both have occurred.

26. *I was not in safety.* If this verse be read interrogatively, it will give a good and easy sense: "Was I not in safety? Had I not rest? Was I not in comfort? Yet trouble came."

CHAPTER 4

1. *Then Eliphaz the Temanite answered.* For seven days this person and his two friends had observed a profound silence, being awed and confounded at the sight of Job's unprecedented affliction. Having now sufficiently contemplated his afflicted state, and heard his bitter complaint, forgetting that he came as a comforter, and not as a reprover, he loses the feeling of the friend in the haughtiness of the censor, endeavoring to strip him of his only consolation by insinuating that, if his ways had been upright, he would not have been abandoned to such distress and affliction, and if his heart possessed

MATTHEW HENRY

friends in affliction, for what they say or do amiss, only for fear of offending them.

II. He exhibits a twofold charge against Job.

1. As to his particular conduct under this affliction. He charges him with weakness and faint-heartedness.

(1) He takes notice of Job's former serviceableness to the comfort of others. He owns that Job had instructed many, not only his own children and servants. With suitable counsels and comforts he *strengthened the weak hands* for work and service and the spiritual warfare. Those who have abundance of spiritual riches should abound in spiritual charity. But why does Eliphaz mention this here? Perhaps he praises him thus for the good he had done that he might make the intended reproof the more passable with him. He remembers how Job had comforted others as a reason why he might justly expect to be himself comforted. He speaks in pity, lamenting that through the extremity of his affliction he could not apply those comforts to himself which he had formerly administered to others. He mentions it, upbraiding him with his knowledge, and the good offices he had done for others, as if he had said, "Thou that hast taught others, why dost thou not teach thyself?"

(2) He upbraids him with his present low-spiritedness, *v.* 5. "*Now* that *it has come upon thee*, now that *it touches thee, thou faintest, thou art troubled.*" He makes too light of Job's afflictions: "It *touches* thee." The very word that Satan himself had used, *ch.* i. 11; ii. 5. Had Eliphaz felt but the one-half of Job's affliction, he would have said, "It smites me, it wounds me;" but, speaking of Job's afflictions, he makes a mere trifle of it. He makes too much of Job's resentments. Men in deep distress must have grains of allowance, and a favourable construction put upon what they say.

2. As to his general character before this affliction. He charges him with wickedness and false-heartedness, and this article of his charge was utterly groundless and unjust. How unkindly does he upbraid him with the great profession of religion he had made, as if it had all now come to nothing and proved a sham (*v.* 6): "*Is not this thy fear, thy confidence, thy hope, and the uprightness of thy ways?* Does it not all appear now to be a mere pretence? For, hadst thou been sincere in it, God would not thus have afflicted thee, nor wouldst thou have behaved thus under the affliction." This was the very thing Satan aimed at, to prove Job a hypocrite. When he could not himself do this to God, he endeavoured, by his friends, to do it to Job himself, and to persuade him to confess himself a hypocrite. But, by the grace of God, Job was enabled to hold fast his integrity, and would not bear false witness against himself. Those that pass rash and uncharitable censures upon their brethren, and condemn them as hypocrites, do Satan's work. This verse is differently read in several editions of our common English Bibles. One of the first, in 1612, has it, "*Is not this thy fear, thy confidence, the uprightness of thy ways, and thy hope?* Does it not appear now that all the religion both of thy devotion and of thy conversation was only in hope and confidence that thou shouldst grow rich by it? If it had been sincere, would it not have kept thee from this despair? It is true, *if thou faint in the day of adversity, thy strength,* thy grace, *is small* (Prov. xxiv. 10); but it does not therefore follow that thou hast no grace, no strength at all." A man's character is not to be taken from a single act.

Verses 7–11

Eliphaz here advances another argument to prove Job a hypocrite, and will have not only his impatience under his afflictions to be evidence against him, but even his afflictions themselves.

I. Good men were never thus ruined. For the proof of this he appeals to Job's own observation (*v.* 7): "*Remember, I pray thee;* and give me an instance of any one that was righteous, and yet was cut off as thou art." If we understand it of a final destruction, his principle is true. None that are righteous perish for ever, 2 Thess. ii. 3. But, if we understand it of any temporal calamity, his principle is not true.

II. Wicked men were often thus ruined. For the proof of this he vouches his own observation (*v.* 8): "*Even as I have seen,* many a time, *those that plough iniquity, and sow wickedness, reap accordingly; by the blast of God they perish, v.* 9." We have reason to think that, whatever profession of religion thou hast made, thou hast but ploughed iniquity and sown wickedness. Some, by iniquity and wickedness, understand wrong and injury done to others. They shall be paid in their own coin. Those who are troublesome shall be troubled. He further describes their destruction (*v.* 9): *By the blast of God they perish.* Some think that in attributing the destruction

JAMIESON, FAUSSET, BROWN

3. weak hands—Isaiah 35:3; II Samuel 4:1.

5. thou art troubled—rather, "unhinged," hast lost thy self-command (I Thess. 3: 3).

6. Is not this thy fear, thy confidence, etc.—Does thy fear, thy confidence, come to nothing? Does it come only to this, that thou faintest now? Rather, by transposition, ""Is not thy fear (of God) thy hope? and the uprightness of thy ways thy confidence? If so, bethink thee, who ever perished being innocent?" [UMBREIT]. But Luke 13:2, 3 shows that, though there *is* a retributive divine government even in this life, yet *we* cannot judge by the mere outward *appearance*. "One event is outwardly to the righteous and to the wicked" (Eccles. 9:2); but yet we must take it on trust, that God deals righteously even now (Ps. 37:25; Isa. 33: 16). Judge not by a part, but by the whole of a godly man's life, and by his end, even here (James 5:11). The one and the same outward event is altogether a different thing in its inward bearings on the godly and on the ungodly even here. Even prosperity, much more calamity, is a punishment to the wicked (Prov. 1:32). Trials are chastisements for their good (to the righteous) (Ps. 119:67, 71, 75).

8. they that plough iniquity . . . reap the same—(Prov. 22:8; Hos. 8:7; 10:13; Gal. 6:7, 8).

ADAM CLARKE

that righteousness of which he boasted, he would not have been so suddenly cast down by adversity.

2. *If we assay to commune with thee.* As if he had said, Should I and my friends endeavor to reason with you ever so mildly, because we shall have many things to say by way of reprehension, you will be grieved and faint; and this we may reasonably infer from the manner in which you bear your present afflictions. Yet as you have uttered words which are injurious to your Maker, who can forbear speaking? It is our duty to rise up on the part of God, though thereby we shall grieve him who is our friend. This was a plausible beginning, and certainly was far from being insincere.

5. *But now it is come upon thee.* Now it is your turn to suffer, and give an example of the efficacy of your own principles; but instead of this, behold, you faint. Either, therefore, you pretended to what you had not or you are not making a proper use of the principles which you recommended to others.

6. *Is not this thy fear?* I think Coverdale hits the true meaning: "Where is now thy feare of God, thy stedfastnesse, they pacience, and the perfectnesse of thy life?" If these be genuine, surely there is no cause for all this complaint, vexation, and despair.

7. *Remember, I pray thee.* Recollect, if you can, a single instance where God abandoned an innocent man, or suffered him to perish. Did you ever hear of a case in which God abandoned a righteous man to destruction? Were you a righteous man, and innocent of all hidden crimes, would God abandon you thus to the malice of Satan? or let loose the plagues of affliction and adversity against you?

8. *They that plow iniquity.* A proverbial form of speech drawn from nature. Whatever seed a man sows in the ground, he reaps the same kind, for every seed produces its like. Thus Prov. xxii. 8: "He that soweth iniquity shall reap vanity." And Gal. vi. 7-8: "Be not deceived, God is not mocked: for whatsoever a man soweth, that shall he also reap. For he that soweth to his flesh shall of the flesh reap corruption; but he that soweth to the Spirit shall of the Spirit reap life everlasting." The same figure is employed by the prophet Hosea, viii. 7: "They have sown the wind, and they shall reap the whirlwind"; and chap. x. 12-13: "Sow to yourselves in righteousness, reap in mercy . . . Ye have plowed wickedness, ye have reaped iniquity." The last sentence contains not only the same image but almost the same words as those used by Eliphaz.

9. *By the blast of God they perish.* As the noxious and parching east wind blasts and destroys vegetation, so the wicked perish under the indignation of the Almighty.

MATTHEW HENRY

of sinners to the blast of God, and *the breath of his nostrils*, he refers to the wind which blew the house down upon Job's children. He speaks particularly of tyrants and cruel oppressors, under the similitude of lions, *v.* 10, 11. The Hebrew tongue has five several names for lions, and they are all here used to set forth the terrible tearing power, fierceness, and cruelty, of proud oppressors. The voice of their roaring shall be stopped. God will take away their power to do hurt: *The teeth of the young lions are broken.* They shall not enrich themselves with the spoil of their neighbours. Even *the old lion* is famished, and *perishes for lack of prey*. They shall not leave a succession: *The stout lion's whelps are scattered abroad*, to seek for food themselves, which the old ones used to bring in for them, Nah. ii. 12. Perhaps Eliphaz intended, in this, to reflect upon Job, as if he, being the *greatest of all the men of the east*, had got his estate by spoil, but now his power and estate were gone, and his family was scattered: if so, it was a pity that a man whom God praised should be thus abused.

Verses 12–21

Eliphaz, having undertaken to convince Job of the sin and folly of his discontent and impatience, here vouches a vision which he relates to Job. It would have been well if he had kept to the purport of this vision, which would serve for a ground on which to reprove Job for his murmuring, but not to condemn him as a hypocrite. The people of God had not then any written word to quote, and therefore God sometimes notified to them even common truths by the extraordinary ways of revelation. We that have Bibles have there (thanks be to God) a more sure word to depend upon than even visions and voices, 2 Peter i. 19.

I. This message was sent to Eliphaz *secretly*. Some of the sweetest communion gracious souls have with God is in secret, where no eye sees but that of him who is all eye. God has ways of bringing conviction, counsel, and comfort, to his people, unobserved by the world, by private whispers, as powerfully and effectually as by the public ministry. *He received a little thereof*, *v.* 12. We know little in comparison with what is to be known, and with what we shall know when we come to heaven. It was brought to him in the *visions of the night* (*v.* 13), when he had retired from the world and the hurry of it, and all about him was composed and quiet. It was prefaced with terrors: *Fears came upon him, and trembling*, *v.* 14. A holy awe and reverence of God and his majesty being struck upon his spirit, he was thereby prepared for a divine visit.

II. Concerning this apparition which Eliphaz saw we are here told (*v.* 15, 16) it was real, and not a dream. If some have been so knavish as to impose false visions on others, and some so foolish as to be themselves imposed upon, it does not therefore follow but that there may have been apparitions of spirits, both good and bad. He *could not discern the form thereof*, so as to frame any exact idea of it in his own mind, much less to give a description of it. His conscience was to be awakened and informed, not his curiosity gratified.

III. The message was delivered in a still small voice, and this was it (*v.* 17): "*Shall mortal man be more just than God*, the immortal God? *Shall a man be* thought to be, or pretend to be, *more pure than his Maker?*" It is a reproof of Job's murmuring and discontent: "Shall a man pretend to be more just and pure than God? more truly to understand, and more strictly to observe, the rules and laws of equity than God?"

IV. Eliphaz shows how little the angels themselves are in comparison with God, *v.* 18. Angels are God's servants, waiting servants, working servants. If the world were left to the government of the angels, and they were trusted with the sole management of affairs, they would take false steps, and everything would not be done for the best, as now it is. Angels are intelligences, but finite ones. Thence he infers how much less man is, how much less to be trusted in or gloried in. If there is such a distance between God and angels, what is there between God and man! Look upon man in his life, and he is very mean, *v.* 19. Take man in his best estate, and he is a very despicable creature in comparison with the holy angels, though honourable if compared with the brutes. Angels are pure spirits; the souls of men *dwell in houses of clay*: such the bodies of men are. Angels are free; human souls are houses, and the body is a cloud, a clog, to it; it is its cage; it is its prison. Angels are fixed, but the very *foundation* of that house of clay in which man dwells *is in the dust*. We stand but upon the dust; some have a higher heap of dust to stand upon than others, but still it is the

JAMIESON, FAUSSET, BROWN

9. breath of his nostrils—God's anger; a figure from the fiery winds of the East (ch. 1:16; Isa. 5:25; Ps. 18:8, 15). **10. lion**—i.e., wicked men, upon whom Eliphaz wished to show that calamities come in spite of their various resources, just as destruction comes on the lion in spite of his strength (Ps. 58:6; II Tim. 4:17). Five different *Hebrew* terms here occur for "lion." The raging of the lion (*the tearer*), and the roaring of the *bellowing lion* and the teeth of the *young lions*, not *whelps*, but grown up enough to hunt for prey. The *strong* lion, the whelps of the *lioness* (not the *stout lion*, as in *English Version*) [BARNES and UMBREIT]. The various phases of wickedness are expressed by this variety of terms: obliquely, Job, his wife, and children, may be hinted at by the lion, lioness, and whelps. The one verb, "are broken," does not suit both subjects; therefore, supply "the roaring of the bellowing lion *is silenced*." The strong lion dies of want at last, and the whelps, torn from the mother, are scattered, and the race becomes extinct.

12. a thing—*Hebrew*, a "word." Eliphaz confirms his view by a divine declaration which was secretly and unexpectedly imparted to him.

a little—lit., a whisper; implying the still silence around, and that more was conveyed than articulate words could utter (ch. 26:14; II Cor. 12:4). **13. In thoughts from the visions**—[So WINER]. While revolving night visions previously made to him (Dan. 2:29). Rather, "In my manifold (*Hebrew*, divided) thoughts, *before* the visions of the night commenced"; therefore not a delusive dream (Ps. 4:4) [UMBREIT]. **deep sleep**—(Gen. 2:21; 15:12).

16. It stood still—At first the apparition glides before Eliphaz, then stands still, but with that shadowy indistinctness of form which creates such an impression of awe; a gentle murmur: not (*English Version*): *there was silence*; for in I Kings 19:12, the voice, as opposed to the previous storm, denotes a gentle, still murmur.

17. mortal man . . . a man—Two *Hebrew* words for "man" are used; the first implying his feebleness; the second his strength. Whether feeble or strong, man is not righteous before God. **more just than God . . . more pure than his maker**—But this would be self-evident without an oracle.

18. folly—Imperfection is to be attributed to the angels, in comparison with Him. The holiness of some of them had given way (II Pet. 2:4), and at best is but the holiness of a creature. Folly is the want of *moral* consideration [UMBREIT].

19. houses of clay—(II Cor. 5:1). Houses made of sun-dried clay bricks are common in the East; they are easily washed away (Matt. 7:27). Man's foundation is this dust (Gen. 3:19). **before the moth**—rather, "as before the moth," which devours a garment (ch. 13: 28; Ps. 39:11; Isa. 50:9). Man, who cannot, in a physical point of view, stand before the very moth, surely cannot, in a moral, stand before God. **20. from morning to evening**—unceasingly; or, better, between the morning and evening of one short day (so Exod. 18:14; Isa. 38:12). "They are destroyed"; better, "they *would be* destroyed," if God withdrew His loving protection. Therefore man must not

ADAM CLARKE

10. *The roaring of the lion.* By the roaring lion, fierce lion, old lion, stout lion, and lion's whelps, tyrannous rulers of all kinds are intended. The design of Eliphaz in using these figures is to show that even those who are possessed of the greatest authority and power—the kings, rulers, and princes of the earth—when they become wicked and oppressive to their subjects are cast down, broken to pieces, and destroyed by the incensed justice of the Lord; and their *whelps*, their children and intended successors, scattered without possessions over the face of the earth.

11. *The old lion perisheth.* In this and the preceding verse the word *lion* occurs five times; and in the original the words are all different.

12. *Now a thing was secretly brought to me.* To give himself the more authority, he professes to have received a vision from God, by which he was taught the secret of the divine dispensations in providence, and a confirmation of the doctrine which he was now stating to Job, and which he applied in a different way to what was designed in the divine communication. *Mine ear received a little thereof.* Mr. Good translates, "And mine ear received a whisper along with it."

18. *Behold, he put no trust in his servants.* This verse is generally understood to refer to the fall of angels; for there were some of those heavenly beings who "kept not their first estate" and are "reserved in . . . chains under darkness unto the judgment of the great day," Jude 6. *And his angels he charged with folly.* Not "chargeth," as many quote the passage. He *charged* those with folly who kept not their first estate. It does not appear that He is charging the others in the same way, who continue steadfast.

19. *How much less?* Rather, with the Vulgate, "How much more?" If angels may be unstable, how can man arrogate stability to himself, who dwells in an earthly tabernacle, and who must shortly return to dust? *Crushed before the moth.* The slightest accident oftentimes destroys. "A fly, a grapestone, or a hair can kill."

20. *They are destroyed from morning to evening.* In almost every moment of time some human being comes into the world, and someone departs from it. Thus are they *destroyed from morning to evening. They perish for ever.* They "pass by"; they "go out of sight"; they moulder

MATTHEW HENRY

earth that stays us up and will shortly swallow us up. Angels are immortal, but man is soon *crushed like a moth* between one's fingers. A little thing will destroy his life. He is *crushed before the face of the moth*, so the word is. Is such a creature as this to be trusted in, or can any service be expected from him by that God who puts no trust in angels themselves? In his death he appears yet more despicable, and unfit to be trusted. Men are mortal and dying, *v.* 20, 21. They are dying daily, and continually wasting: *Destroyed from morning to evening*. In death all their excellency passes away; beauty, strength, learning, not only cannot secure them from death, but must die with them, nor shall their pomp, their wealth, or power, descend after them. Their wisdom cannot save them from death. Shall such a mean, weak, foolish, sinful, dying creature as this pretend to be *more just than God and more pure than his Maker?* No, instead of quarrelling with his afflictions, let him wonder that he is out of hell.

CHAPTER 5

Verses 1–5

So well assured is Eliphaz of the goodness of his own cause that he moves Job himself to choose the arbitrators (*v.* 1): *Call now, if there be any that will answer thee.* "Canst thou produce an instance of anyone that was really a saint that was reduced to such an extremity as thou art now reduced to? God never dealt with any that love his name as he deals with thee, and therefore surely thou art none of them. Did ever any good man curse his day as thou dost?" *To which of the saints wilt thou turn?* Good people are called *saints* even in the Old Testament; and therefore I know not why we should appropriate the title to those of the New Testament, and not say St. Abraham, St. Moses, and St. Isaiah, as well as St. Matthew and St. Mark; and St. David the psalmist, as well as St. David the British bishop. There are two things which Eliphaz here maintains, and in which he doubts not but all the saints concur with him:—

I. That the sin of sinners directly tends to their own ruin (*v.* 2): *Wrath kills the foolish man*, his own wrath, and therefore he is foolish for indulging it. *Envy* is the rottenness of the bones, and so *slays the silly one* that frets himself with it. "So it is with thee," says Eliphaz, "while thou quarrellest with God thou doest thyself the greatest mischief." Job had told his wife she spoke as the foolish women; now Eliphaz tells him he acted as the foolish men, the silly ones.

II. That their prosperity is short and their destruction certain, *v.* 3–5. He seems here to parallel Job's case with that which is commonly the case of wicked people. Job's prosperity was now at an end, and so has the prosperity of other wicked people quickly been. Eliphaz foresaw their ruin. Those who looked only at present things blessed their habitation, and thought them happy. He saw, at length, what he had foreseen. His family was undone, and his estate ruined. In these particulars he plainly and very invidiously reflects on Job's calamities. His children were crushed, *v.* 4. This is commonly understood of the destruction of the families of wicked men, to oblige them to restore what they have ill-gotten. They leave it to their children; but the rightful owners will crush their children, and cast them by due course of law. His estate was plundered, *v.* 5. Job's was so. The hungry robbers, the Sabeans and Chaldeans, ran away with it, and swallowed it; and this, says he, I have often observed in others. What has been got by spoil and rapine has been lost in the same way. The careful owner hedged it about with thorns, and then thought it safe; but the fence proved insignificant against the greediness of the spoilers, which will go through the thorns and briers, and *burn them together*, Isa. xxvii. 4.

Verses 6–16

Eliphaz, having touched Job, in mentioning the loss of his estate and the death of his children as the just punishment of his sin, that he might not drive him to despair, here begins to encourage him. Now he speaks in the accents of kindness, as if he would atone for the hard words he had given him.

I. He reminds him that no affliction comes by chance, nor is to be attributed to second causes: It *doth not come forth of the dust*, nor *spring out of the ground*, as the grass doth, *v.* 6. If men be bad, they must not lay the blame upon the soil, the climate, or the stars, but on themselves.

II. He reminds him that trouble and affliction are what we have all reason to expect in this world: *Man is brought to trouble* (*v.* 7), not as man, but as sinful man. Such is the frailty of our bodies, and the vanity

JAMIESON, FAUSSET, BROWN

think to be *holy before God*, but to draw holiness and all things else *from God* (vs. 17). **21. their excellency**—(Ps. 39:11; 146:4; I Cor. 13:8). But UMBREIT, by an Oriental image from a bow, useless because unstrung. "*Their nerve* or *string* would be torn away." MICHAELIS, better in accordance with vs. 19, makes the allusion be to the *cords* of a tabernacle taken down (Isa. 33:20). **they die, even without wisdom**—rather, "They would perish, yet not according to wisdom," but according to arbitrary choice, if God were not infinitely wise and holy. The design of the spirit is to show that the continued existence of weak man proves the inconceivable wisdom and holiness of God, which alone save man from ruin [UMBREIT]. BENGEL shows from Scripture that God's holiness (*Hebrew, kadosh*) comprehends all His excellencies and attributes. DE WETTE loses the scope, in explaining it, of the shortness of man's life, contrasted with the angels "before they have attained to wisdom."

CHAPTER 5

VSS. 1-27. ELIPHAZ' CONCLUSION FROM THE VISION. **1. if there be any**, etc.—Rather, will He (God) reply to thee? Job, after the revelation just given, cannot be so presumptuous as to think God or any of the holy ones (Dan. 4:17; angels) round His throne, will vouchsafe a *reply* (a judicial expression) to his rebellious complaint.

2. wrath . . . envy—fretful and passionate complaints, such as Eliphaz charged Job with (ch. 4:5; so Prov. 14:30). Not, the wrath *of God* killeth the foolish, and *His* envy, etc.

3. the foolish—the wicked. I have seen the sinner spread his "root" wide in prosperity, yet circumstances "suddenly" occurred which gave occasion for his once prosperous dwelling being "cursed" as desolate (Ps. 37:35, 36; Jer. 17:8).

4. His children . . . crushed in the gate—A judicial formula. The gate was the place of judgment and of other public proceedings (Ps. 127:5; Prov. 22:22; Gen. 23:10; Deut. 21:19). Such propylæa have been found in the Assyrian remains. Eliphaz obliquely alludes to the calamity which cut off Job's children. **5. even out of the thorns**—Even when part of the grain remains hanging on the thorn bushes (or, "is growing among thorns," Matthew 13:7), the hungry gleaner does not grudge the trouble of even taking it away, so clean swept away is the harvest of the wicked. **the robber**—as the Sabeans, who robbed Job. rather, translate "the thirsty," as the antithesis in the parallelism, "the hungry," proves.

6. Although—rather, "for truly" [UMBREIT]. **affliction cometh not forth of the dust**—like a weed, of its own accord. Eliphaz hints that the cause of it lay with Job himself.

7. Yet—rather, "Truly," or, *But* affliction does not come from chance, but is the appointment of God for sin; i.e., the original birth-sin of man. Eliphaz passes from

ADAM CLARKE

with the dust, and are soon forgotten.

21. *Doth not their excellency . . . go away?* Personal beauty, corporeal strength, powerful eloquence, and various mental endowments pass away, or are "plucked up by the roots"; they are no more seen or heard among men, and their memory soon perisheth. *They die, even without wisdom.* If wisdom means "the pursuit of the best end, by the most legitimate and appropriate means," the great mass of mankind appear to perish without it. But, if we consider the subject more closely, we shall find that all men die in a state of comparative ignorance. With all our boasted science and arts, how little do we know!

CHAPTER 5

1. *Call now, if there be any.* This appears to be a strong irony. From whom among those whose foundations are in the dust, and who are crushed before the moth, canst thou expect succor? *To which of the saints wilt thou turn?* To whom among the *holy ones (kedoshim)* or among those who are equally dependent on divine support with thyself, and can do no good but as influenced and directed by God, canst thou turn for help?

2. *For wrath killeth the foolish man.* "Foolish," "silly," and "simple," are epithets given by Solomon to sinners and transgressors of all kinds. Such parallelisms have afforded a presumptive argument that Solomon was the author of this book. The words of Eliphaz may be considered as a sort of maxim, which the wisdom and experience of ages had served to establish; viz., The wrath of God is manifested only against the wicked and impious; and if you were not such, God would not thus contend with you.

3. *I have seen the foolish taking root.* I have seen wicked men for a time in prosperity, and becoming established in the earth; but I well knew, from God's manner of dealing with men, that they must soon be blasted. I even ventured to pronounce their doom; for I knew that, in the order of God's providence, that was inevitable.

4. *His children are far from safety.* His posterity shall not continue in prosperity. "Ill gotten, ill spent"; whatever is got by wrong must have God's curse on it. *They are crushed in the gate.* There is reference here to a custom which I have often had occasion to notice: viz., that in the Eastern countries the courthouse, or tribunal of justice, was at the gate of the city; here the magistrates attended, and hither the plaintiff and defendant came for justice.

5. *Whose harvest.* Their possessions, because acquired by unjust means, shall not be under the protection of God's providence; He shall abandon them to be pillaged and destroyed by the wandering, half-starved hordes of the desert banditti. *The robber swalloweth up.* Or, more properly, the *thirsty*, as is plain from their "swallowing up" or "gulping down"; opposed to the "hungry" or half-starved, mentioned in the preceding clause. The hungry shall eat up their grain, and the thirsty shall drink down their wine and oil, here termed their "strength" or "power," for the most obvious reasons.

6. *Affliction cometh not forth of the dust.* If there were not an adequate cause, you could not be so grievously afflicted. *Spring out of the ground.* It is not from mere natural causes that affliction and trouble come; God's justice inflicts them upon offending man.

7. *Yet man is born unto trouble.* "To labour." He must toil and be careful; and if in the course of his labor he meet with trials and difficulties,

MATTHEW HENRY

of our enjoyments, that our troubles arise as naturally *as the sparks fly upwards*. Why then should we be surprised at our afflictions as strange, or quarrel with them as hard.

III. He directs him how to behave himself under his affliction (*v.* 8): *I would seek unto God; surely I would:* so it is in the original. It is easy to say what we would do if we were in such a one's case; but, when it comes to the trial, perhaps it will be found not so easy to do as we say. Good and seasonable advice Eliphaz transfers to himself in a figure: "For my part, the best way I should think I could take, if I were in thy condition, would be to apply to God." We must by prayer fetch in mercy and grace from God, though he contend with us. His favour we must seek when we have lost all we have in the world. *Is any afflicted? let him pray*. It is heart's ease, a salve for every sore. *To God would I commit my cause*, having laid it at his feet, I would lodge it in his hand.

IV. He encourages him thus to seek to God, and commit his cause to him. In general, he *doeth great things* (*v.* 9), great indeed, for he can do anything, he doth do everything, and all according to the counsel of his own will. The works of nature are mysterious; and the wisest philosophers have owned themselves at a loss. The designs of Providence are much more deep and unaccountable, Rom. xi. 33. He doeth great *things without number*; his power is never exhausted, nor will all his purposes ever be fulfilled till the end of time. Now, by the consideration of this, Eliphaz intends to convince Job of his fault and folly in quarrelling with God. He gives some instances of God's dominion and power. God doeth great things in the kingdom of nature: *He gives rain upon the earth* (*v.* 10), put here for all the gifts of common providence, all the *fruitful seasons* by which he *filleth our hearts with food and gladness*, Acts xiv. 17. He doeth great things in the affairs of the children of men, not only enriches the poor and comforts the needy, by the rain he sends (*v.* 10), but, in order to the advancing of those that are low, he *disappoints the devices of the crafty*; for *v.* 11 is to be joined to *v.* 12. God can defeat all the designs of his and his people's enemies. How were the plots of Ahithophel, Sanballat, and Haman baffled! How were the confederacies of Syria and Ephraim against Judah, of Gebal, and Ammon, and Amalek, against God's Israel, the kings of the earth and the princes against the Lord and against his anointed, broken! The learned men of the heathen were befooled by their own vain philosophy. When God infatuates men they are perplexed, and at a loss, even in those things that seem most plain and easy (*v.* 14): *They meet with darkness* even *in the daytime*: nay (as in the margin), *They run themselves into darkness* by the violence and precipitation of their own counsels. See *ch.* xii. 20, 24, 25. He exalts the humble, *v.* 11. The lowly in heart, and those that mourn, he advances, comforts, and makes to *dwell on high*, in the *munitions of rocks*, Isa. xxxiii. 16. *So the poor*, who began to despair, *has hope*. The experiences of some are encouragements to others to hope the best in the worst of times; for it is the glory of God to send help to the helpless and hope to the hopeless.

Verses 17–27

Eliphaz gives Job a comfortable prospect of the issue of his afflictions, if he did but recover his temper and accommodate himself to them.

I. The seasonable word of caution and exhortation that he gives him (*v.* 17): "*Despise not thou the chastening of the Almighty*. Call it a chastening, which comes from the father's love and is designed for the child's good. Let grace conquer the antipathy which nature has to suffering, and reconcile thyself to the will of God in it." We must never think it a thing below us to come under his discipline, but reckon, on the contrary, that God really magnifies man when he thus *visits and tries him, ch.* vii. 17, 18. Do not overlook and disregard it, as if it were only a chance, and the production of second causes, but take great notice of it as the voice of God and a messenger from heaven.

II. The comfortable words of encouragement which he gives him.

1. *Happy is the man whom God correcteth* if he make but a due improvement of the correction. Correction is an evidence of his sonship and a means of his sanctification; it mortifies his corruptions, weans his heart from the world, draws him nearer to God, brings him to his Bible, brings him to his knees, and so is working for him, a far more exceeding and eternal weight of glory. The issue and consequence of it would be very good, *v.* 18. When God makes sores by the rebukes of his providence he binds up by the consolations of his Spirit.

2. In the following verses Eliphaz addresses him-

JAMIESON, FAUSSET, BROWN

the particular sin and consequent suffering of Job to the universal sin and suffering of mankind. Troubles spring from man's common sin by as necessary a law of natural consequences as sparks (*Hebrew*, sons of coal) fly upward. Troubles are many and fiery, as sparks (I Pet. 4:12; Isa. 43:2). UMBREIT for "sparks" has "birds of prey." **8.** Therefore (as affliction is ordered by God, on account of sin), "I would" have you to "seek unto God" (Isa. 8:19; Amos 5:8; Jer. 5:24).

12. enterprise–lit., "realization." The *Hebrew* combines in the one word the two ideas, wisdom and happiness, "enduring existence" being the etymological and philosophical root of the combined notion [UMBREIT].

14. Judicial blindness often is sent upon keen men of the world (Deut. 28:29; Isa. 59:10; John 9: 39). **15.** "From the sword" which proceedeth "from their mouth" (Ps. 59:7; 57:4). **11.** Connected with vs. 9. His "unsearchable" dealings are with a view to raise the humble and abase the proud (Luke 1:52). Therefore Job ought to turn humbly to Him. **16. the poor hath hope**–of the interposition of God. **iniquity stoppeth her mouth**–(Ps. 107:42; Mic. 7:9, 10; Isa. 52:15). Especially at the last day, through shame (Jude 15; Matt. 22:12). The "mouth" was the offender (vs. 15), and the mouth shall then be stopped (Isa. 25:8) at the end.

17. happy–not that the actual suffering is joyous; but the consideration of the *righteousness* of Him who sends it, and the *end* for which it is sent, make it a cause for thankfulness, not for complaints, such as Job had uttered (Heb. 12: 11). Eliphaz implies that the end in this case is to call back Job from the particular sin of which he takes for granted that Job is guilty. Paul seems to allude to this passage in Hebrews 12:5; so James 1: 12; Proverbs 3:12. Eliphaz does not give due prominence to this truth, but rather to *Job's sin*. It is Elihu alone (chs. 32-37) who fully dwells upon the truth, that affliction is mercy and justice in disguise, for the good of the sufferer. **18. he maketh sore, and bindeth up**–(Deut. 32:39; Hos. 6:1; I Sam. 2: 6). An image from binding up a wound. The healing art consisted much at that time in external applications.

ADAM CLARKE

he should rise superior to them, and not sink as you do. *As the sparks fly upward*. "And the sons of the coal lift up their flight," or "dart upwards." And who are the sons of the coal? Are they not bold, intrepid, ardent, fearless men, who rise superior to all their trials; combat what are termed chance and occurrence; succumb under no difficulties; and rise superior to time, tide, fate, and fortune?

8. *I would seek unto God*. Were I in your place, instead of wasting my time, and irritating my soul with useless complaints, I would apply to my Maker, and, if conscious of my innocence, would confidently commit my cause to Him.

9. *Which doeth great things*. No work, however complicated, is too deep for His counsel to plan; none, however stupendous, is too great for His power to execute. He who is upright is always safe in referring his cause to God, and trusting in Him.

14. *They meet with darkness in the daytime*. They act in noonday as if the sun were extinct, and their eyes put out.

11. *To set up on high those that be low*. He so distributes His providential blessings without partiality that the land of the poor man is as well sunned and watered as that of the rich, so that he is thus set upon a level with the lords of the soil.

16. *So the poor*. He who is made "thin," who is wasted, extenuated; *hath hope*—he sees what God is accustomed to do, and he expects a repetition of gracious dealings in his own behalf; and because God deals thus with those who trust in Him, therefore the mouth of impiety is stopped.

17. *Behold, happy is the man*. See Heb. xii. 5; Jas. i. 12; and Prov. iii. 12.

18. *For he maketh sore, and bindeth up*. Thus nervously rendered by Coverdale, "For though he make a wounde, he giveth a medicyne agayne; though he smyte, his hande maketh whole agayne."

MATTHEW HENRY

self directly to Job, and gives him many precious promises of great and kind things which God would do for him if he did but humble himself under his hand. And, though Job's friends spoke both of God and Job some things that were not right, yet the general doctrines they laid down expressed the pious sense of the patriarchal age, and as St. Paul quoted *v.* 13 for canonical scripture, and as the command *v.* 17 is no doubt binding on us, so these promises must be, received and applied as divine promises, and we may *through patience and comfort of this* part of *scripture have hope.*

(1) It is here promised that as afflictions and troubles recur deliverances shall be graciously repeated, be it ever so often: *In six troubles he shall* be ready to *deliver thee*; *yea, and in seven, v.* 19.

(2) Whatever troubles good men may be in, *there shall no evil touch them*; they shall do them no real harm; they may hiss, but they cannot hurt, Ps. xci. 10.

(3) When desolating judgments are abroad, they shall be taken under special protection, *v.* 20.

(4) Whatever is maliciously said against them, it shall not affect them to do them any hurt, *v.* 21. The best men, and the most inoffensive, cannot secure themselves from calumny, reproach, and false accusation. From these a man cannot hide himself, but God can hide him, so that the most malicious slanders shall not disturb his peace nor blemish his reputation.

(5) They shall have a holy security and serenity of mind, arising from their hope and confidence in God. When dangers are most threatening they *shall not be afraid of destruction,* no, not when they see it coming (*v.* 21), nor *of the beasts of the field* when they set upon them, nor of men as cruel as beasts; *at destruction and famine thou shalt laugh* (*v.* 22). Blessed Paul laughed at destruction when he said, *O death! where is thy sting?* when, in the name of all the saints, he defied all the calamities of this present time to *separate us from the love of God,* concluding that *in all these things we are more than conquerors*, Rom. viii. 35, &c.

(6) Being at peace with God, there shall be a covenant of friendship between them and the whole creation, *v.* 23. "When thou walkest over thy grounds thou shalt not need to fear stumbling, for *thou shalt be at league with the stones of the field*, not to dash thy foot against any of them, nor shalt thou be in danger from *the beasts of the field*, for they shall all be at peace with thee."

(7) Their houses and families shall be comfortable to them, *v.* 24. *That peace is thy tabernacle* (so the word is); peace is the house in which those dwell who dwell in God, and are at home in him. "*Thou shalt visit*" (that is, enquire into the affairs of) "*thy habitation*, and take a review of them, *and shalt not sin.*" God will provide a settlement for his people, mean perhaps and movable, a cottage, a tabernacle, but a fixed and quiet habitation. "Thou shalt not sin," or *wander*; that is, as some understand it, "thou shalt not be a fugitive and a vagabond." They shall have wisdom to govern their families aright, to order their affairs with discretion, which is here called *visiting their habitation.* Family piety crowns family peace and prosperity.

(8) Their posterity shall be numerous and prosperous. Job had lost all his children; "but," says Eliphaz, "if thou return to God, he will again build up thy family." It is a comfort to parents to see the prosperity, especially the spiritual prosperity, of their children; if they are truly good, they are truly great, how small a figure soever they may make in the world.

(9) Their death shall be seasonable, and they shall finish their course, at length, with joy and honour, *v.* 26. If the providence of God do not give us long life, yet if the grace of God give us to be satisfied with the time allotted us, we may be said to come to a full age. Our times are in God's hand; it is well they are so, for he will take care that those who are his shall die in the best time: however their death may seem to us untimely, it will be found not unseasonable.

3. In the last verse he recommends these promises to Job, as faithful sayings, which he might be confident of the truth of: "*Lo, this we have searched, and so it is.* We have indeed received these things by tradition from our fathers, but we have diligently studied them, and been confirmed in our belief of them from our own observation and experience; and we are all of a mind that so it is." *Hear it, and know thou it for thy good.* It is not enough to hear and know the truth, but we must improve it, and be made wiser and better by it. *Know it for thyself* (so the word is) not only "This is true," but "this is true concerning me." That is indeed a good sermon to us which does us good.

JAMIESON, FAUSSET, BROWN

13. Paul (I Cor. 3: 19) quoted this clause with the formula establishing its inspiration, "it is written." He cites the exact *Hebrew* words, not as he usually does the LXX, *Greek* version (Ps. 9:15). Haman was hanged on the gallows he prepared for Mordecai (Esther 5:14; 7:10). The wise—i.e., the cunning. **is carried headlong**—Their scheme is precipitated before it is ripe. **19. in six . . . yea, in seven**—(Prov. 6: 16; Amos 1:3). The *Hebrew* idiom fixes on a certain number (here "six"), in order to call attention as to a thing of importance; then increases the force by adding, with a "yea, nay seven," the next higher number; here "seven," the sacred and perfect number. In *all* possible troubles; not merely in the precise number "seven." **20. power**—(Jer. 5:12). *Hebrew,* hands. **of the sword**—(Ezek. 35:5, *Margin*). Hands are given to the sword personified as a living agent. **21.** (Ps. 31:20; Jer. 18:18.)

22. famine thou shalt laugh—Not, in spite of destruction and famine, which is true (Hab. 3:17, 18), though not *the* truth meant by Eliphaz, but because those calamities shall not come upon thee. A different *Hebrew* word from that in vs. 20; there, famine *in general;* here, *the languid state* of those wanting proper nutriment [BARNES]. **23. in league with the stones of the field**—They shall not hurt the fertility of thy soil; nor the wild beasts thy fruits; spoken in Arabia Deserta, where stones abounded. *Arabia,* derived from *Arabah*—a desert plain. The first clause of this verse answers to the first clause of verse 22; and the last of this verse to the last of that verse. The full realization of this is yet future (Isa. 65:23, 25; Hos. 2:18). **24. know**—"Thou shalt rest in the assurance, that thine habitation is the abode of peace; and (if) thou numberest thine herd, thine expectations prove not fallacious" [UMBREIT]. "Sin" does not agree with the context. The *Hebrew* word—"to miss" a mark, said of archers (Judg. 20:16). The *Hebrew* for "habitation" primarily means "the fold for cattle"; and for "visit," often to "take an account of, to number." "Peace" is the common Eastern salutation; including inward and outward prosperity. **25. as the grass**—(Ps. 72:16). Properly, herb-bearing seed (Gen. 1:11, 12).

26. in a full age—So "full of days" (42:17; Gen. 35:29). Not mere length of years, but ripeness for death, one's inward and outward full development not being prematurely cut short, is denoted (Isa. 65:22). "Thou shalt come," not lit., but expressing willingness to die. Eliphaz speaks from the Old Testament point of view, which made full years a reward of the righteous (Ps. 91:16; Exod. 20:12), and premature death the lot of the wicked (Ps. 55:23). The righteous are immortal till their work is done. To keep them longer would be to render them less fit to die. God takes them at their best (Isa. 57:1). The good are compared to wheat (Matt. 13:30). **cometh in**—lit., "ascends." The corn is lifted up off the earth and carried home; so the good man "is raised into the heap of sheaves" [UMBREIT]. **27. searched it . . . for thy good**—lit., for thyself (Ps. 111:2; Prov. 2:4; 9:12).

ADAM CLARKE

13. *He taketh the wise in their own craftiness.* So counterworks them as to cause their feet to be taken in their own snares, and their evil dealings to fall on their own pate.

19. *He shall deliver thee in six troubles.* The numbers *six* and *seven* are put here for "many."

21. *Thou shalt be hid from the scourge of the tongue.* Perhaps no evil is more dreadful than the *scourge of the tongue*: evil speaking, detraction, backbiting, calumny, slander, talebearing, whispering, and scandalizing are some of the terms which we use when endeavoring to express the baleful influence and effects of that member, which is a "world of fire," kindled from the nethermost hell. The Scripture abounds with invectives and execrations against it. See Ps. xxxi. 20; lii. 2-4; Prov. xii. 18; xiv. 3; Jas. iii. 5-8.

23. *Thou shalt be in league with the stones of the field.* Coverdale translates the verse thus: "But the castels in the londe shall be confederate with the, And the beastes of the felde shall give the peace."

24. *Thou shalt know.* You shall be so fully satisfied of the friendly disposition of all your neighbors that you shall rest secure in your bed, and not be afraid of any danger, though sleeping in your "tent" in the field; and when you return from your country excursions, you shall find that your habitation has been preserved in peace and prosperity, and that you have "made no mistake" in your trust, in your confidence, or in your confederates.

The word *thy tabernacle* means simply a tent, or movable dwelling, composed of poles, pins, and cloth, or skin, to be pitched anywhere in a few moments, and struck again with the same ease. The word which we properly translate *thy habitation* signifies solid, permanent dwelling place. As to *techeta,* which we translate *thou . . . shalt not sin,* it comes from *chata,* to "err," to "mistake," to "miss the mark," hence to sin. And it is very likely, from the connection above, that to "mistake" or "err" is its meaning in this place. I need not add that the Arab chiefs, who had their castles or strongholds, frequently in their country excursions lodged in tents in the open fields; and that on such occasions a hostile neighbor sometimes took advantage of their absence, attacked and pillaged their houses, and carried off their families and household.

26. *Thou shalt come to thy grave.* You shall not die before your time; you shall depart from life like a full-fed guest, happy in what you have known, and in what you have enjoyed. *Like as a shock of corn.* You shall completely run through the round of the spring, summer, autumn, and winter of life; and you shall be buried like a wholesome seed in the earth; from which you shall again rise up into an eternal spring!

27. *Lo this, we have searched it.* What I have told you is the sum of our wisdom and experience on these important points. These are established maxims, which universal experience supports. *Know*—understand, and reduce them to practice *for thy good.* Thus ends Eliphaz, the Temanite, "full of wise saws and ancient instances"; but he miserably perverted them in his application of them to Job's case and character. They contain, however, many wholesome truths, of which the wise in heart may make a very advantageous, practical use.

MATTHEW HENRY

CHAPTER 6

Verses 1–7

Eliphaz, in the beginning of his discourse, had been very sharp upon Job, and yet it does not appear that Job gave him any interruption, but when he had concluded, he makes his reply, in which he speaks very feelingly.

I. He represents his calamity, in general, as much heavier than either he had expressed it or they had apprehended it, *v.* 2, 3. He would gladly appeal to a third person, who had just weights and just balances with which to weigh his grief and calamity. He wished that they would set his grief and all the expressions of it in one scale, his calamity and all the particulars of it in the other, and they would find (as he says, *ch.* xxiii. 2) that *his stroke was heavier than his groaning*; for, whatever his grief was, his calamity was *heavier than the sand of the sea.* "Therefore (says he) *my words are swallowed up*;" that is, "Therefore you must excuse both the brokenness and the bitterness of my expressions." He complains that his friends undertook to administer spiritual physic to him before they thoroughly understood his case. He excuses the passionate expressions he had used when he cursed his day. Though he could not himself justify all he had said, yet he thought his friends should not thus violently condemn it. He bespeaks the charitable and compassionate sympathy of his friends with him.

II. He complains of the trouble and terror of mind he was in as the sorest part of his calamity, *v.* 4. Herein he was a type of Christ, who, in his sufferings, complained most of the sufferings of his soul. *Now is my soul troubled,* John xii. 27. *My soul is exceedingly sorrowful,* Matt. xxvi. 38. *My God, my God, why hast thou forsaken me?* Matt. xxvii. 46. Poor Job sadly complains *The arrows of the Almighty are within me.* That which cut him to the heart was to think that the God he loved and served had laid him under these marks of his displeasure. Note, Trouble of mind is the sorest trouble. *A wounded spirit who can bear!* The poison or heat of these arrows is said to drink up his spirit, because it disturbed his reason, shook his resolution, exhausted his vigour, and threatened his life. He saw himself charged by *the terrors of God,* as by an army set in battle-array, and surrounded by them.

III. He reflects upon his friends for their severe censures of his complaints. Their reproofs were causeless. He complained, it is true, now that he was in this affliction, but he never used to complain. He did not *bray when he had grass,* nor *low over his fodder, v.* 5. But, now that he was utterly deprived of all his comforts, he must be a stock or a stone, and not have the sense of an ox or a wild ass, if he did not give some vent to his grief. He was forced to eat unsavoury meats, and was so poor that he had not a grain of salt wherewith to season them, nor to give a little taste to the white of an egg, which was now the choicest dish he had at his table, *v.* 6. Food which once he would have scorned to touch was his *sorrowful meat, v.* 7.

Verses 8–13

The troubled sea rages most when it dashes against a rock. Job, instead of unsaying what he had said, says it here again with more vehemence than before.

I. He is still most passionately desirous to die. He could see no end of his trouble but death, and had not patience to wait the time appointed for that. He has a request to make; there is a thing he longs for (*v.* 8): *That it would please God to destroy me, v.* 9. Though Job was extremely desirous of death, and very angry at its delays, yet he did not offer to destroy himself, nor to take away his own life, only he begged *that it would please God to destroy him.*

II. He puts this desire into a prayer, that God would grant him this request.

III. He promises himself effectual relief, and the redress of all his grievances, by the stroke of death (*v.* 10): *Then should I yet have comfort.* If Job had not had a good conscience, he could not have spoken with this assurance of comfort on the other side death.

IV. He challenges death to do its worst. If he could not die without bitter pains yet, in prospect of dying at last, he would make nothing of dying pangs: "*I would harden myself in sorrow. Let him not spare;* I desire no mitigation of that pain which will put a happy period to all my pains."

V. He grounds his comfort upon the testimony of his conscience for him that he had been faithful and firm to his profession of religion: *I have not concealed the words of the Holy One.*

VI. He justifies himself, in this extreme desire of

JAMIESON, FAUSSET, BROWN

CHAPTER 6

Vss. 1-30. Reply of Job to Eliphaz. **2. thoroughly weighed**—Oh, that instead of censuring my complaints when thou oughtest rather to have sympathized with me, thou wouldst accurately compare my sorrow, and my misfortunes; these latter "outweigh in the balance" the former.

3. the sand—(Prov. 27:3). **are swallowed up**—See *Margin.* So Psalm 77:4. But Job plainly is apologizing, not for not having had words *enough,* but for having spoken *too much* and *too boldly;* and the *Hebrew* is, "to speak rashly" [Umbreit, Gesenius, Rosenmuller]. "Therefore were my words *so rash.*"

4. arrows . . . within me—have pierced me. A poetic image representing the avenging Almighty armed with bow and arrows (Ps. 38:2, 3). Here the arrows are poisoned. Peculiarly appropriate, in reference to *the burning pains* which penetrated, like poison, into *the inmost parts*—("spirit"; as contrasted with mere *surface flesh wounds*) of Job's body. **set themselves in array**—a military image (Judg. 20: 33). All the terrors which the divine wrath can muster are set in array against me (Isa. 42:13). **5.** Neither wild animals, as the wild ass, nor tame, as the ox, are dissatisfied when well supplied with food. The braying of the one and the lowing of the other prove distress and want of palatable food. So, Job argues, if he complains, it is not without cause; viz., his pains, which are, as it were, disgusting food, which God feeds him with (end of verse 7). But he should have remembered a rational being should evince a better spirit than the brute. **6. unsavoury**—tasteless, insipid. Salt is a chief necessary of life to an Easterner, whose food is mostly vegetable. **the white**—lit., "spittle" (I Sam. 21:13), which the white of an egg resembles. **7.** To "touch" is contrasted with "meat." "My *taste* refused *even to touch* it, and yet am I *fed* with such *meat* of sickness." The second clause literally, is, "Such is like the sickness of my food." The natural taste abhors even to touch insipid food, and such forms my nourishment. For my sickness is like such nauseous food [Umbreit]. (Ps. 42:3; 80:5; 102:9). No wonder, then, I complain. **8.** To desire death is no necessary proof of fitness for death. The ungodly sometimes desire it, so as to escape troubles, without thought of the hereafter. The godly desire it, in order to be with the Lord; but they patiently wait God's will. **9. destroy**—lit., grind or crush (Isa. 3:15). **let loose his hand**—God had put forth His hand only so far as to wound the *surface* of Job's flesh (ch. 1:12; 2:6); he wishes that hand to be *let loose,* so as to wound *deeply and vitally.* **cut me off**—metaphor from a weaver cutting off the web, when finished, from the thrum fastening it to the loom (Isa. 38:12).

10. I would harden myself—rather, "I would *exult* in the pain," if I knew that that pain would hasten my death [Gesenius]. Umbreit translates the *Hebrew* of "Let Him not spare," as "unsparing"; and joins it with "pain." **concealed**—I have not disowned, in word or deed, the commands of the Holy One (Ps. 119:46; Acts 20:20). He says this in answer to Eliphaz' insinuation that he is a hypocrite. God is here called "the Holy One," to imply man's reciprocal obligation to be holy, as He is holy (Lev. 19:2).

ADAM CLARKE

CHAPTER 6

2. ***Oh that my grief were thoroughly weighed!*** **Job wished to be dealt with according to justice, as he was willing that his sins, if they could be proved, should be weighed against his sufferings; and if this could not be done, he wished that his sufferings and his complainings might be weighed together; and it would then be seen that, bitter as his complaint had been, it was little when compared with the distress which occasioned it.**

3. ***Heavier than the sand of the sea.*** **This includes two ideas: their number was too great to be counted; their weight was too great to be estimated.**

4. *The arrows of the Almighty.* There is an evident reference here to wounds inflicted by poisoned arrows; and to the burning fever occasioned by such wounds, producing such an intense, parching thirst as to dry up all the moisture in the system, stop all the salivary ducts, thicken and inflame the blood, induce putrescency, and terminate in raging mania, producing the most terrifying images, from which the patient is relieved only by death.

5. *Doth the wild ass?* This meaning of Job appears to be this: You condemn me for complaining; do I complain without a cause? The wild ass will not bray, and the ox will not low, unless in want.

8. *Oh that I might have!* As Job had no hope that he should ever be redeemed from his present helpless state, he earnestly begs God to shorten it by taking away his life.

9. *Let loose his hand.* A metaphor taken from an archer drawing his arrow to the head, and then loosing his hold, that the arrow may fly to the mark.

10. *Then should I yet have comfort.* The expectation that He will speedily make an end of me would cause me to rejoice with great joy. *I would harden myself in sorrow.* To know that I should shortly have an end put to my miseries would cause me to endure the present with determinate resolution. *Let him not spare*—let Him use whatever means he chooses, for I will not resist His decree; He is *holy,* and His decrees must be just.

MATTHEW HENRY

death, from the deplorable condition he was now in, *v.* 10, 12, and very ingeniously, yet perversely, argues against the encouragements that were given him. "*What is my strength, that I should hope?* You see how I am weakened and brought low, and therefore what reason have I to hope that I should see better days? *Is my strength the strength of stones?* Are my muscles brass and my sinews steel? No, they are not, and therefore I cannot hold out always in this pain and misery, but must needs sink under the load." *What is our strength?* It is depending strength. We have no more strength than God gives us; for in him we live and move. "*What is my end, that I should desire to prolong my life?* What comfort can I promise myself in life, comparable to the comfort I promise myself in death?"

VII. He obviates the suspicion of his being delirious (*v.* 13): *Is not my help in me?* "Do you think wisdom is driven quite from me, and that I am gone distracted? No, I am not mad, most noble Eliphaz, but *speak the words of truth and soberness.*"

Verses 14–21

Eliphaz had been very severe in his censures of Job; and his companions had intimated their concurrence with him. Their unkindness poor Job complains of, as an aggravation of his calamity and a further excuse of his desire to die; for what satisfaction could he expect in this world when those that should have been his comforters thus proved his tormentors?

I. He shows what reason he had to expect kindness from them. His expectation was grounded upon the common principles of humanity (*v.* 14): "*To him that is afflicted pity should be shown from his friend;* and he that does not show that pity *forsakes the fear of the Almighty.*" Inhumanity is impiety and irreligion. *He that withholds compassion from his friend forsakes the fear of the Almighty.* So the Chaldee. When a man is afflicted he will see who are his friends indeed and who are but pretenders.

II. He shows how wretchedly he was disappointed in his expectations from them (*v.* 15): "*My brethren,* who should have helped me, *have dealt deceitfully as a brook.*" None questioned but that the drift of their discourses would be to comfort Job with the remembrance of his former piety, the assurance of God's favour to him, and the prospect of a glorious issue; but, instead of this, they fall upon him with their reproaches and censures, condemn him as a hypocrite, and pour vinegar instead of oil, into his wounds. We cannot expect too little from the creature nor too much from the Creator. God will out-do our hopes as much as men come short of them. This disappointment which Job met with he here illustrates by the failing of brooks in summer.

His expectations from them, which their coming so solemnly to comfort him had raised, he compares to the expectation which the weary thirsty travellers have of finding water in the summer where they have often seen it in great abundance in the winter, *v.* 19. *The troops of Tema and Sheba,* the caravans of the merchants of those countries, whose road lay through the deserts of Arabia, looked and waited for supply of water from those brooks. "Hard by here," says one, "A little further," says another, "when I last travelled this way, there was water enough; we shall have that to refresh us." The disappointment of his expectation is here compared to the confusion which seizes the poor travellers when they find heaps of sand where they expected floods of water. In the winter, when they were not thirsty, there was water enough. Everyone will applaud and admire those that are full and in prosperity. But in the heat of summer, when they needed water, then it failed them; it was consumed (*v.* 17); it was turned aside, *v.* 18.

JAMIESON, FAUSSET, BROWN

11. What strength have I, so as to warrant the hope of restoration to health? a hope which Eliphaz had suggested. "And what" but a miserable "end" of life is before me, "that I should" desire to "prolong life"? [UMBREIT]. UMBREIT and ROSENMULLER not so well translate the last words "to be patient." **12.** Disease had so attacked him that his strength would need to be hard as a stone, and his flesh like brass, not to sink under it. But he has only flesh, like other men. It must, therefore, give way; so that the hope of restoration suggested by Eliphaz is vain (see *Note,* 5:11). **13. Is not my help in me?**—The interrogation is better omitted. "There is no help in me!" For "wisdom," "deliverance" is a better rendering. "And deliverance is driven quite from me." **14. pity**—a proverb. Charity is the love which judges indulgently of our fellow men: it is put on a par with truth in Proverbs 3:3, for they together form the essence of moral perfection [UMBREIT]. It is the spirit of Christianity (I Pet. 4:8; I Cor. 13;7; Prov. 10:12; 17:17). If it ought to be used towards all men, much more towards friends. But he who does not use it forsaketh (renounceth) the fear of the Almighty (Jas. 2:13). **15.** Those whom I regarded as "my brethren," from whom I looked for faithfulness in my adversity, have disappointed me, as the streams failing from drought—wadies of Arabia, filled in the winter, but dry in the summer, which disappoint the caravans expecting to find water there. The fulness and noise of these temporary streams answer to the past large and loud professions of my friends; their dryness in summer, to the failure of the friendship when needed. The Arab proverb says of a treacherous friend, "I trust not in thy torrent" (Isa. 58:11, *Margin*). **streams of brooks**—rather, "the brook in the ravines which passes away." It has no perpetual spring of water to renew it (unlike "the fountain of living waters," Jer. 2:13; Isa. 33:16, at the end); and thus it passes away as rapidly as it arose. **16. blackish**—lit., Go as a mourner in black clothing (Ps. 34:14). A vivid and poetic image to picture the stream turbid and black with melted ice and snow, descending from the mountains into the valley. In the next clause, the snow dissolved is, in the poet's view, "hid" in the flood [UMBREIT]. **17. wax warm**—rather, at the time when. ("But they soon") [UMBREIT]. "they become narrower (flow in a narrower bed), they are silent (cease to flow noisily); in the heat (of the sun) they are consumed or vanish out of their place. First the stream flows more narrowly—then it becomes silent and still; at length every trace of water disappears by evaporation under the hot sun" [UMBREIT]. **18. turned aside**—rather, caravans (Hebrew travellers) turn aside from their way, by circuitous routes, to obtain water. They had seen the brook in spring full of water: and now in the summer heat, on their weary journey, they turn off their road by a devious route to reach the living waters, which they remembered with such pleasure. But, when "they go," it is "into a desert" [NOYES and UMBREIT]. Not as *English Version,* "They go *to nothing,*" which would be a tame repetition of the drying up of the waters in verse 17; instead of waters, they find an "empty wilderness"; and, not having strength to regain their road, bitterly disappointed, they "perish." The terse brevity is most expressive. **19. the troops**—i.e., caravans. **Tema**—north of Arabia Deserta, near the Syrian desert; called from Tema son of Ishmael (Gen. 25:15; Isa. 21:14; Jer. 25:23), still so called by the Arabs. Verses 19, 20 give another picture of the mortification of disappointed hopes, viz., those of the caravans on the direct road, anxiously awaiting the return of their companions from the distant valley. The mention of the locality whence the caravans came gives living reality to the picture. "Sheba" refers here not to the marauders in North Arabia Deserta (ch. 1:15), but to the merchants (Ezek. 27:22) in the south, in Arabia Felix or Yemen, "afar off" (Jer. 6:20; Matt. 12:42; Gen. 10:28). Caravans are first mentioned in Genesis 37:25; men needed to travel thus in companies across the desert, for defense against the roving robbers and for mutual accommodation. "The companies waited for them," cannot refer to the caravans who had gone in quest of the waters; for verse 18 describes their utter destruction. **20.** lit., each had hoped; viz., that their companions would find water. The greater had been their hopes the more bitter now their disappointment; "they came thither," to the place, "and were ashamed"; lit., their countenances burn, an Oriental phrase for the shame and consternation of deceived expectation; so "ashamed" as to disappointment (Rom. 5:5). **21.** As the dried-up brook is to the

ADAM CLARKE

11. *What is my strength?* I can never suppose that my strength will be restored; and, were that possible, have I any comfortable prospect of a happy termination of my life? Had I any prospect of future happiness, I might well bear my present ills; but the state of my body and the state of my circumstances preclude all hope.

12. *Is my strength the strength of stones?* I am neither a rock, nor is my flesh brass, that I can endure all these calamities. This is a proverbial saying, and exists in all countries.

13. *Is not my help in me?* My help is all in myself; and, alas! that is perfect weakness: "and my subsistence," all that is real, stable, and permanent, is *driven quite from me.* My friends have forsaken me, and I am abandoned to myself; my property is all taken away, and I have no resources left. I believe Job neither said, nor intended to say, as some interpreters have it, "Reason is utterly driven from me." Surely there is no mark in this chapter of his being deranged, or at all impaired in his intellect.

14. *To him that is afflicted pity should be shewed from his friend; but he forsaketh the fear of the Almighty.* The Vulgate gives a better sense, "He who takes away mercy from his friend, hath cast off the fear of the Lord."

15. *Have dealt deceitfully as a brook.* There is probably an allusion here to those land torrents which make a sudden appearance, and as suddenly vanish, being produced by the rains that fall upon the mountains during the rainy season, and are soon absorbed by the thirsty sands over which they run. At first they seem to promise a permanent stream, and are noticed with delight by the people, who fill their tanks or reservoirs from their waters; but sometimes they are so large and rapid as to carry everything before them—and then suddenly fail, so that there is no time to fill the tanks. The approach of Job's friends promised much of sympathy and compassion; his expectations were raised, but their conduct soon convinced him that they were physicians of no value.

16. *Blackish by reason of the ice.* He represents the waters as being sometimes suddenly frozen, their foam being turned into the semblance of snow. When the heat comes, they are speedily liquefied; and the evaporation is so strong from the heat, and the absorption so powerful from the sand, that they soon disappear.

18. *The paths of their way.* They sometimes forsake their ancient channels; and, growing smaller and smaller from being divided into numerous streams, *they go to nothing, and perish*—are at last utterly lost in the sands.

19-20. *The troops of Tema looked.* The caravans coming from Tema are represented as arriving at those places where it was well known torrents did descend from the mountains, and they were full of expectation that here they could not only slake their thirst, but fill their waterskins; but when they arrive, they find the waters totally dissipated and lost. In vain did the caravans of Sheba wait for them; they did not reappear; and they *were confounded because they had hoped* to find here refreshment and rest.

MATTHEW HENRY

When Job was in prosperity his friends were something to him, but "*Now you are nothing*, now I can find no comfort but in God." You are not what you have been, what you should be, what you pretend to be, what I thought you would have been; *for you see my casting down and are afraid*. You are afraid lest, if you own me, you should be obliged to keep me.

Verses 22–30

Poor Job goes on here to upbraid his friends with their unkindness. If they would but think impartially, and speak as they thought, they could not but own,

I. That though he was necessitous, yet he was not craving, nor burdensome to his friends. Job would be glad to see his friends, but he did not say, *Bring unto me* (*v.* 22), or, *Deliver me*, *v.* 23. He did not desire to put them to any expense. "Did I send for you to *deliver me out of the hand of the mighty*? No, I never expected you should either expose yourselves to any danger or put yourselves to any charge upon my account." Job's not asking their help did not excuse them from offering it when he needed it and it was in the power of their hands to give it. It often happens that from man, even when we expect little, we have less, but from God, even when we expect much, we have more, Eph. iii. 20.

II. That, though he differed in opinion from them, yet he was not obstinate, but ready to yield to conviction (*v.* 24, 25): *Teach me, and I will hold my tongue;* for I have often found, with pleasure and wonder, *how forcible right words are*. But the method you take will never make proselytes: *What doth your arguing prove?* Your hypothesis is false, your surmises are groundless, your management is weak, and your application peevish and uncharitable.

III. That, though he had been indeed in a fault, yet they ought not to have given him such hard usage (*v.* 26, 27): "*Do you imagine*, or contrive with a great deal of art" (for so the word signifies), "*to reprove words*, some passionate expressions of mine in this desperate condition, as if they were certain indications of reigning impiety and atheism? A little charity would have served to excuse them, and to put a better construction upon them. Shall a man's spiritual state be judged of by some rash and hasty words, which a surprising trouble extorts from him? Is it kind, is it just, to criticise in such a case?" They took advantage of his weakness and the helpless condition he was in: *You overwhelm the fatherless*, a proverbial expression, denoting that which is most barbarous and inhuman. They made pretence of kindness: "*You dig a pit for your friend;* not only you are unkind to me, who am your friend, but, under colour of friendship, you ensnare me." When they came to see and sit with him he thought he might speak his mind freely to them. But this freedom of speech, which their professions of concern for him made him use, had exposed him to their censures, and so they might be said to dig a pit for him.

IV. That, though he had let fall some passionate expressions, yet in the main he was in the right, and that his afflictions, though very extraordinary, did not prove him to be a hypocrite or a wicked man. "*Be content*, and *look upon me*; what do you see in me that bespeaks me either a madman or a wicked man? Let the show of my countenance witness for me that, though I have cursed my day, I do not curse my God. You hear what I have to say: *Is there iniquity in my tongue?* that iniquity that you charge me with? Have I blasphemed God or renounced him? *Return, I pray you*, consider the thing over again without prejudice and you will find *my righteousness is in it*," that is, "I am in the right in this matter; and, though I cannot keep my temper as I should, I keep my integrity."

CHAPTER 7

Verses 1–6

Job is here excusing what he could not justify, even his inordinate desire of death. I. Every man must die shortly. "Pray mistake not my desires of death, as if I thought the time appointed of God could be anticipated: no, I know very well that that is fixed; only in such language as this I take the liberty to express my present uneasiness: *Is there not an appointed time* (*a warfare*, so the word is) to *man upon earth?* and *are not his days* here *like the days of a hireling*?" Certainly there is, and it is easy to say by whom the appointment is made, even by him that made us and set us here. We are not to think that we are governed by the blind fate of the Stoics, nor by the blind fortune of the Epicureans, but by the wise, holy, and sovereign counsel of God. Man's life is

JAMIESON, FAUSSET, BROWN

caravan, so are ye to me, viz., a nothing; ye might as well not be in existence [UMBREIT]. *The* Margin "like to them" or "it" (viz., the waters of the brook), is not so good a reading. **ye see, and are afraid**—Ye are struck aghast at the sight of my misery, and ye lose presence of mind. Job puts this mild construction on their failing to relieve him with affectionate consolation.

22. And yet I did not ask you to "bring me" a gift; or to "pay for me out of your substance a reward" (to the Judge, to redeem me from my punishment); all I asked from you was affectionate treatment. **23. the mighty**—the oppressor, or creditor, in whose power the debtor was [UMBREIT].

24, 25. Irony—If you can "teach me" the right view, I am willing to be set right, and "hold my tongue"; and to be made to see my error. But then if your words be really the right words. how is it that they are so feeble? "Yet how feeble are the words of what you call the right view." So the *Hebrew* is used (in Mic. 2:10; 1:9). The *English Version*, "How powerful," etc., does not agree so well with the last clause of the verse. "And what will your arguings reprove?" lit., "the reproofs which proceed from you"; the emphasis is on *you; you* may find fault, who are not in *my* situation [UMBREIT]. **26. Do you imagine** [mean] **to reprove words and** [to reprove] **the speeches of one desperate, (which are) as wind**—mere nothings, not to be so narrowly taken to task? UMBREIT not so well takes the *Hebrew* for "as wind," as "sentiments"; making formal "sentiments" antithetical to mere "speeches," and supplying, not the word "reprove," but "would you regard," from the first clause. **27.** Ye overwhelm—lit., ye cause (supply, "your anger") [UMBREIT], a net, viz., of sophistry [NOYES and SCHUTTENS], to fall upon the desolate (one bereft of help, like the fatherless orphan); **and ye dig (a pit) for your friend,** i.e., try to ensnare him, to catch him in the use of unguarded language [NOYES]. (Ps. 57:6); metaphor from hunters catching wild beasts in a pit covered with brushwood to conceal it. UMBREIT from the *Syriac*, and answering to his interpretation of the first clause, has, "Would you be *indignant* against your friend?" The *Hebrew* in ch. 41:6, means to "feast upon." As the first clause asks, "Would you *catch him in a net*?" so this follows up the image, "And would you next *feast upon him*, and his miseries?" So LXX. **28. be content**—rather, be pleased to—look. Since you have so falsely judged my words, look upon me, i.e., upon my countenance: for (it is evident before your faces) if I lie; my countenance will betray me, if I be the hypocrite that you suppose. **29. Return**—rather, "retract" your charges: "Let it not be iniquity"; i.e., (retract) that injustice may not be done me. Yea retract, "my righteousness is in it"; i.e., my right is involved in this matter. **30.** Will you say that my guilt lies in the organ of speech, and will you call it to account? or, Is it that my taste (palate) or discernment is not capable to form a judgment of perverse things? Is it thus you will explain the fact of my having no consciousness of guilt? [UMBREIT].

CHAPTER 7

Vss. 1-21. JOB EXCUSES HIS DESIRE FOR DEATH. **1. appointed time**—better, "warfare," hard conflict with evil (so in Isa. 40:2; Dan. 10:1). Translate it "appointed time" (ch. 14:14). Job reverts to the sad picture of man, however great, which he had drawn (ch. 3:14), and details in this chapter the miseries which his friends will see, if, according to his request (ch. 6:28), they will look on him. Even the Christian soldier, "warring a good warfare," rejoices when it is completed (I Tim. 1:18; II Tim. 2: 3; 4:7, 8).

ADAM CLARKE

21. *For now ye are nothing.* Ye are just to me as those deceitful torrents to the caravans of Tema and Sheba. *Ye see my casting down.* Ye see that I have been hurried from my eminence into want and misery, as the flood from the top of the mountains, which is divided, evaporated, and lost in the desert. *And are afraid.* Ye are terrified at the calamity that has come upon me; and instead of drawing near to comfort me, ye start back at my appearance.

22. *Did I say, Bring unto me?* Why do you stand aloof? Have I asked you to bring me any presents? or to supply my wants out of your stores?

23. *Or, Deliver me?* Did I send to you to come and avenge me of the destroyers of my property, or to rescue my substance out of the hands of my enemies?

24. *Teach me.* Show me where I am mistaken. Bring proper arguments to convince me of my errors, and you will soon find that I shall gladly receive your counsels, and abandon the errors of which I may be convicted.

25. *How forcible are right words!* A well-constructed argument, that has truth for its basis, is irresistible. *But what doth your arguing reprove?* Your reasoning is defective, because your premises are false; and your conclusions prove nothing, because of the falsity of the premises whence they are drawn. The last clause, literally rendered, is, "What reproof, in a reproof from you?"

26. *Do ye imagine to reprove words?* Is it some expressions which in my hurry, and under the pressure of unprecedented affliction, I have uttered, that ye catch at? You can find no flaw in my conduct; would ye make me an offender for a word? Why endeavor to take such advantage of a man who complains in the bitterness of his heart, through despair of life and happiness?

27. *Ye overwhelm the fatherless.* Ye see that I am as destitute as the most miserable ophan; would ye overwhelm such a one? And would you *dig a pit for your friend*—do ye lay wait for me, and endeavor to entangle me in my talk?

28. *Look upon me.* View me; consider my circumstances; compare my words; and you must be convinced that I have spoken nothing but truth.

29. *Return, I pray you.* Reconsider the whole subject. Do not be offended. *My righteousness is in it*—my argumentation is a sufficient proof of my innocence.

30. *Is there iniquity in my tongue?* Am I not an honest man? And if in my haste my tongue had uttered falsity, would not my conscience discern it? And do you think that such a man as your friend is would defend what he knew to be wrong?

CHAPTER 7

1. *Is there not an appointed time to man?* The Hebrew literal rendering is as follows: "Is there not a warfare to miserable man upon the earth?" Coverdale: "Is not the life off man upon earth a very batayle?"

MATTHEW HENRY

a warfare, and *as the days of a hireling*. We are to look upon ourselves in this world, 1. As soldiers, exposed to hardship and in the midst of enemies; we must serve under command; and, when our warfare is accomplished, we must be disbanded. 2. As day-labourers, that have the work of the day to do in its day and must make up their account at night.

II. He had as much reason, he thought, to wish for death, as a poor servant or hireling that is tired with his work has to wish for the shadows of the evening, when he shall receive his penny and go to rest, *v.* 2. The comparison is plain, the application is somewhat obscure. Exactness of language is not to be expected from one in Job's condition. "*As a servant earnestly desires the shadow, so* and for the same reason I earnestly desire death; for *I am made to possess*, &c." Hear his complaint.

1. His days were useless, and had been so a great while. Every day was a burden to him, because he was in no capacity of doing good, or of spending it to any purpose. But when we are disabled to work for God, if we will but sit still quietly for him, it is all one; we shall be accepted.

2. His nights were restless, *v.* 3, 4. The night relieves the toil and fatigue of the day, not only to the labourers, but to the sufferers. But poor Job could not gain this relief. This made him dread the night as much as the servant desires it.

3. His body was noisome, *v.* 5.

4. His life was hastening apace towards a period, *v.* 6. He thought he had no reason to expect a long life, for he found himself declining fast (*v.* 6): *My days are swifter than a weaver's shuttle*, and he was therefore without hope of being restored to his former prosperity.

Verses 7–16

Job is here begging of God either to ease him or to end him. He represents himself to God,

I. As a dying man, surely and speedily dying (*v.* 7): *O remember that my life is wind.* He recommends himself to God as an object of his pity and compassion, with this consideration, that he was a frail creature and his abode in this world uncertain. *The eye of him that hath* here *seen me shall see me no more* there. Dying is work that is to be done but once. This is illustrated by the plotting out and scattering of a cloud. It is consumed and vanisheth away, is resolved into air and never knits again. Other clouds arise, but the same cloud never returns: so a new generation of the children of men is raised up (*v.* 10): *He shall return no more to his house.* From these premises he might have drawn a better conclusion than this (*v.* 11): *Therefore I will not refrain my mouth; I will speak; I will complain.* Better die praying and praising than die complaining and quarrelling.

II. As a distempered man, sorely and grievously distempered both in body and mind. In this part of his representation he is very peevish: "*Am I a sea, or a whale* (*v.* 12), a raging sea, that must be kept within bounds, or an unruly whale, that must be restrained by force from devouring all the fishes of the sea?" With poor Job, his bed, instead of comforting him, terrified him; and his couch, instead of easing his complaint, added to it. In Job's dreams, though they might partly arise from his distemper, we have reason to think Satan had a hand, for he delights to terrify those whom it is out of his reach to destroy; but Job looked up to God and mistook Satan's representations for the *terrors of God setting themselves in array against him.* We have reason to pray to God that our dreams may neither defile nor disquiet us. He covets to rest in his grave, that bed where there are no tossings to and fro, nor any frightful dreams, *v.* 15, 16. Doubtless this was Job's infirmity; for though a good man would not wish to live always in this world, and would choose strangling and death rather than sin, as the martyrs did, yet he will not choose death rather than life, because life is our opportunity of glorifying God and getting ready for heaven.

Verses 17–21

Job here reasons with God,

I. Concerning his dealings with man in general (*v.* 17, 18): *What is man, that thou shouldst magnify him?* We mistake God, and the nature of his providence, if we think it any lessening to him to take notice of the meanest of his creatures. Job owns God's favour to man in general, even when he complains of his own particular troubles. "*What is man*, a poor, mean, weak creature, *that thou*, the great and glorious God, shouldst deal with him as thou dost? What is man, 1. That thou shouldst put such honour upon him, *shouldst magnify him*, by taking him into covenant and communion with thyself?

JAMIESON, FAUSSET, BROWN

2. earnestly desireth—*Hebrew*, "pants for the [evening] shadow." Easterners measure time by the length of their shadow. If the servant longs for the evening when his wages are paid, why may not Job long for the close of his hard service, when he shall enter on his "reward"? This proves that Job did not, as many maintain, regard the grave as a mere sleep. **3.** Months of comfortless misfortune. "I am made *to possess*," lit., "to be heir to." Irony. "To be heir to," is usually a matter of joy; but here it is the entail of an involuntary and dismal inheritance. "Months," for days, to express its long duration. **Appointed**—lit., "they have numbered to me"; marking well the unavoidable doom assigned to him. **4.** Lit., "When shall be the flight of the night?" [GESENIUS]. UMBREIT, not so well, "The night is long extended"; lit., measured out (so Margin). **5.** In elephantiasis maggots are bred in the sores (Acts 12:23; Isa. 14:11). **clods of dust**—rather, a crust of dried filth and accumulated corruption (ch. 2:7, 8). **my skin is broken and . . . loathsome**—rather, comes together so as to heal up, and again breaks out with running matter [GESENIUS]. More simply the *Hebrew* is, "My skin rests (for a time) and (again) melts away" (Ps. 58:7). **6.** (Isa. 38:12.) Every day like the weaver's shuttle leaves a thread behind; and each shall wear, as he weaves. But Job's thought is that his days must swiftly be cut off as a web; **without hope,**—viz., of a recovery and renewal of life (ch. 14:19; I Chron. 29:15). **7.** Address to God. **Wind**—a picture of evanescence (Ps. 78:39). **shall no more see**—rather, "shall no more return to see good." This change from the different wish in ch. 3:17, etc., is most true to nature. He is now in a softer mood; a beam from former days of prosperity falling upon memory and the thought of the unseen world, where one is seen no more (vs. 8), drew from him an expression of regret at leaving this world of light (Eccles. 11:7); so Hezekiah (Isa. 38:11). Grace rises above nature (II Cor. 5:8). **8.** The eye of him who beholds me (present, not past), i.e., in the very act of beholding me, seeth me no more. **Thine eyes [are] upon me, and I [am] not.** He disappears, even while God is looking upon him. Job cannot survive the gaze of Jehovah (Ps. 104:32; Rev. 20:11). Not, "Thine eyes seek me and I am not to be found"; for God's eye penetrates even to the unseen world (Ps. 139:8). UMBREIT unnaturally takes "thine" to refer to one of the three friends. **9.** (II Sam. 12:23.) **the grave**—the Sheol, or place of departed spirits, not disproving Job's belief in the resurrection. It merely means, "He shall come up no more" in the present order of things. **10.** (Ps. 103:16.) The Oriental keenly loves his dwelling. In Arabian elegies the desertion of abodes by their occupants is often a theme of sorrow. Grace overcomes this also (Luke 18:29; Acts 4:34). **11.** Therefore, as such is my hard lot, I will at least have the melancholy satisfaction of venting my sorrow in words. The *Hebrew* opening words, "Therefore I, at all events," express self-elevation [UMBREIT]. **12-14.** Why dost thou deny me the comfort of care-assuaging sleep? Why scarest thou me with frightful dreams? **Am I a sea**—regarded in Old Testament poetry as a violent rebel against God, the Lord of nature, who therefore curbs his violence (Jer. 5:22). **or a whale**—or some other sea monster (Isa. 27:1), that Thou needest thus to watch and curb me? The Egyptians watched the crocodile most carefully to prevent its doing mischief. **14.** The frightful dreams resulting from elephantiasis he attributes to God; the common belief assigned all night visions to God. **15.** UMBREIT translates, "So that I could wish to strangle myself—dead by my own hands." He softens this idea of Job's harboring the thought of suicide, by representing it as entertained only in agonizing dreams, and immediately repudiated with horror in next verse, "Yet that (self-strangling) I loathe." This is forcible and graphic. Perhaps the meaning is simply, "My soul chooses (even) strangling (or any violent death) rather than my life," lit., "my bones" (Ps. 35:10); i.e., rather than the wasted and diseased skeleton, left to him. In this view, "I loathe it" (vs. 16) refers to his life. **16. Let me alone**—i.e., cease to afflict me for the few and vain days still left to me. **17.** (Ps. 8:4; 144:3.) Job means, "What is man that thou shouldst make him (of so much importance, and that thou shouldst expend such attention (heart-thought) upon him" as to make him the subject of so severe trials? Job ought rather to have reasoned from God's condescending so far to notice man as to try him, that there must be a wise and loving purpose in trial. David uses the same words, in their right application, to express wonder that God should do so much as He does for insignificant man. Christians who know God mani-

ADAM CLARKE

2. *Earnestly desireth the shadow.* As a man who labors hard in the heat of the day earnestly desires to get under a shade, or wishes for the long evening shadows, that he may rest from his labor, get his day's wages, retire to his food, and then go to rest.

3. *So am I made to possess.* But night is no relief to me; it is only a continuance of my anxiety and labor. I am like the hireling; I have my appointed labor for the day. I am like the soldier harassed by the enemy; I am obliged to be continually on the watch, always on the lookout, with scarcely any rest.

4. *When I lie down.* I have so little rest that when I do lie down I long for the return of the light, that I may rise. Nothing can better depict the state of a man under continual afflictions, which afford him no respite, his days and his nights being spent in constant anguish, utterly unable to be in any one posture, so that he is continually changing his position in his bed, finding ease nowhere; thus, as himself expresses it, he is *full of tossings.*

5. *My flesh is clothed with worms.* This is perhaps no figure, but is literally true. *Clods of dust.* I suppose Job to allude to those incrustations of dried pus which are formed on the tops of pustules in a state of decay, such as the scales which fall from the pustules of the smallpox, when the patient becomes convalescent.

9. *As the cloud is consumed.* As the cloud is dissipated, so is the breath of those that go down to the grave. As that cloud shall never return, so shall it be with the dead; they return no more to sojourn with the living.

10. *He shall return no more to his house, neither shall his place know him any more.* He does not mean that he shall be annihilated, but that he shall nevermore become an inhabitant of the earth.

11. *Therefore I will not refrain.* All is hopeless; I will therefore indulge myself in complaining.

12. *Am I a sea, or a whale?* Job was hedged about and shut in with insuperable difficulties of various kinds. He was entangled as a wild beast in a net; the more he struggled, the more he lost his strength, and the less probability there was of his being extricated from his present situation. The *sea* is shut in with barriers, over which it cannot pass; Jer. v. 22; Ps. civ. 9; chap. xxxviii. 8.

14. *Thou scarest me with dreams.* There is no doubt that Satan was permitted to haunt his imagination with dreadful dreams and terrific appearances, so that, as soon as he fell asleep, he was suddenly roused and alarmed by those appalling images. He needed rest by sleep, but was afraid to close his eyes because of the horrid images which were presented to his imagination. Could there be a state more deplorable than this?

16. *I loathe it: I would not live alway.* Life, in such instances, is hateful to me; and though I wished for long life, yet if length of days were offered to me with the sufferings which I now undergo, I would despise the offer and spurn the boon.

17. *What is man, that thou shouldest magnify him? and that thou shouldest set thine heart upon him?* Two different ideas have been drawn from these words:

(*a*) Man is not worth Thy notice; why therefore dost Thou contend with him?

(*b*) How astonishing is Thy kindness that Thou shouldest fix Thy heart—Thy strongest affections—on such a poor, base, vile, impotent creature as man (*enosh*), that Thou shouldest so highly exalt him beyond all other creatures, and mark him with the most particular notice of Thy providence and grace!

The paraphrase of Calmet is as follows: "Does man, such as he at present is, merit thy attention! What is man that God should make it his business to examine, try, prove, and afflict him? Is it not doing him too much honour to think thus seriously about him? O Lord! I am not worthy that thou shouldest concern thyself about me!"

MATTHEW HENRY

2. That thou *shouldst set thy heart upon him*, as dear to thee. 3. *That thou shouldst visit him* with thy compassions *every morning*."

II. Concerning his dealings with him in particular. 1. That he was the butt to God's arrows: "*Thou hast set me as a mark against thee*," *v.* 20. "My case is singular, and none is shot at as I am." 2. That he was a *burden to himself*, ready to sink under the load of his own life. 3. That he had no intermission of his griefs (*v.* 19): "*How long* will it be ere thou cause thy rod to *depart from me*, or abate the rigour of the correction, at least for so long as that I may *swallow down my spittle*?" It should seem, Job's distemper lay much in his throat, and almost choked him, so that he could not swallow his spittle. He complains (*ch.* xxx. 18) that it *bound him about like the collar of his coat*. "Lord," says he, "wilt not thou give me some respite, some breathing time?" *ch.* ix. 18. He ingenuously owns himself guilty before God: *I have sinned.* God had said of him that he was a *perfect and an upright man*; yet he says of himself, *I have sinned.* Those may be upright who yet are not sinless; and those who are sincerely penitent are accepted, through a Mediator, as evangelically perfect. Job maintained, against his friends, that he was not a hypocrite, not a wicked man; and yet he owned to his God that he had sinned. Penitent confessions would drown and silence passionate complaints. He seriously enquires how he may make his peace with God: "*What shall I do unto thee*, having done so much against thee?" In our repentance we must keep up good thoughts of God, as one that delights not in the ruin of his creatures, but would rather they should return and live. "Thou art the Saviour of men; be my Saviour, for I cast myself upon thy mercy." He earnestly begs for the forgiveness of his sins, *v.* 21. The heat of his spirit, as, on the one hand, it made his complaints the more bitter, so, on the other hand, it made his prayers the more lively and importunate; as here: "*Why dost thou not pardon my transgression?*" When the mercy of God pardons the transgression that is committed by us the grace of God takes away the iniquity that reigns in us. Wherever God removes the guilt of sin he breaks the power of sin.

JAMIESON, FAUSSET, BROWN

fest in the man Christ Jesus may use them still more. **18.** With each new day (Ps. 73:14). It is rather God's mercies, not our trials, that are new every morning (Lam. 3:23). The idea is that of a shepherd taking count of his flock every morning, to see if all are there [COCCEIUS]. **19.** How long (like a jealous keeper) wilt thou never take thine eyes off (so the *Heb.* for "depart from") me? Nor let me alone for a brief respite (lit., "so long as I take to swallow my spittle"), an Arabic proverb, like our, "till I draw my breath." **20. I have sinned**—Yet what sin can I do against (to: ch. 35:6) thee (of such a nature that thou shouldst jealously watch and deprive me of all strength, as if thou didst fear me)? Yet thou art one who hast men ever in view, ever watchest them—O thou *Watcher* (vs. 12; Dan. 9:14) of men. Job had borne with patience his trials, as sent by God (ch. 1:21; ch. 2:10); only his reason cannot reconcile the ceaseless continuance of his mental and bodily pains with his ideas of the divine nature. **set me as a mark**—Wherefore dost thou make me thy point of attack? i.e., ever assail me with new pains? [UMBREIT]. (Lam. 3:12.)

21. for now—very soon. **in the morning**—not the resurrection; for then Job will be found. It is a figure, from one seeking a sick man in the morning, and finding he has died in the night. So Job implies that, if God does not help him at once, it will be too late, for he will be gone. The reason why God does not give an immediate sense of pardon to awakened sinners is that they think they have a claim on God for it.

ADAM CLARKE

19. *Till I swallow down my spittle?* This is a proverbial expression, and exists among the Arabs to the present day, the very language being nearly the same. It signifies the same as, *Let me draw my breath; give me a moment's space; let me have even the twinkling of an eye.* I am urged by my sufferings to continue my complaint; but my strength is exhausted, my *mouth dry* with speaking. Suspend my sufferings even for so short a space as is necessary to swallow my spittle, that my parched tongue may be moistened, so that I may renew my complaint.

20. *I have sinned; what shall I do?* Dr. Kennicott contends that these words are spoken to Eliphaz, and not to God, and would paraphrase them thus: "You say I must have been a sinner. What then? I have not sinned against thee, O thou spy upon mankind! Why hast thou set up me as a butt or mark to shoot at? Why am I become a burden unto thee? Why not rather overlook my transgression, and pass by mine iniquity? I am now sinking to the dust! Tomorrow, perhaps, I shall be sought in vain!" Others consider the address as made to God. Taken in this light, the sense is plain enough. Those who suppose that the address is made to God translate the twentieth verse thus: "Be it that I have sinned, what injury can I do unto thee, O thou Observer of man? Why hast thou set me up as a mark for thee, and why am I made a burden to thee?"

21. *And why dost thou not pardon?* These words are spoken after the manner of men. If Thou have any design to save me, if I have sinned, why dost Thou not pardon my transgression, as Thou seest that I am a dying man; and tomorrow morning Thou mayest seek me to do me good, but in all probability I shall then be no more, and all Thy kind thoughts towards me shall be unavailing? If I have sinned, then why should not I have a part in that mercy that flows so freely to all mankind?

MATTHEW HENRY

CHAPTER 8

Verses 1–7

I. Bildad reproves Job for what he had said (*v.* 2), checks his passion, but (as is too common) with greater passion. Job spoke a great deal of good sense, but Bildad turns it all off with this, *How long wilt thou speak these things?* Bildad compares Job's discourse to a *strong wind.*

II. He justifies God in what he had done. This he had no occasion to do at this time (for Job did not condemn God, as he would have it thought he did), or he might at least have done it without reflecting upon Job's children, as he does here. 1. He is right in general, that *God doth not pervert judgment*, nor ever go contrary to any settled rule of justice, *v.* 3. 2. Yet he takes it for granted that Job's children (the death of whom was one of the greatest of his afflictions) had been guilty of some notorious wickedness, *v.* 4. Job readily owned that God did not pervert judgment; and yet it did not therefore follow either that his children died for some great transgression. It is true that we and our children have sinned against God, but extraordinary afflictions are not always the punishment of extraordinary sins, but sometimes the trial of extraordinary graces; and, in our judgment of another's case we ought to take the more favourable side, as our Saviour directs, Luke xiii. 2–4.

III. He put Job in hope that, if he were indeed upright, as he said he was, he should yet see a good issue of his present troubles: "*Although thy children have sinned against him, and are cast away in their transgression*, yet if thou be pure and upright thyself, and as an evidence of that wilt now seek unto God and submit to him, all shall be well yet," *v.* 5–7. This may be taken two ways, either, 1. As designed to prove Job a hypocrite and a wicked man by the continuance of his afflictions. Herein Bildad was not in the right; for a good man may be afflicted for his trial, not only very sorely, but very long, and yet, if for life, it is in comparison with eternity but for a moment. Or, 2. As designed to direct and encourage Job, that he might not thus run himself into despair, there might yet be hope if he would take the right course. He gives him good hopes that he shall yet again see good days, secretly suspecting, however, that he was not qualified to see them. Let not Job object that he had so little left to begin the world with again that it was impossible he should ever prosper as he had done; no, "Though thy beginning

JAMIESON, FAUSSET, BROWN

CHAPTER 8

FIRST SERIES—FIRST SPEECH OF BILDAD, MORE SEVERE AND COARSE THAN THAT OF ELIPHAZ

Vss. 1-22. THE ADDRESS OF BILDAD. **2. like a . . . wind**—disregarding restraints, and daring against God. **3.** The repetition of "pervert" gives an emphasis galling to Job (ch. 34:12). "Wouldst thou have God (as thy words imply) pervert judgment," by letting thy sins go unpunished? He assumes Job's guilt from his sufferings. **4. If**—Rather, "*Since* thy children have sinned against Him, and (*since*) He has cast them away for (*Hebrew, by the* **hand** of) their transgressions, (yet) if thou wouldst seek unto God, etc., if thou wert pure, etc., surely (even) now He would awake for thee." UMBREIT makes the apodosis to, "since thy children," etc., begin at "He has cast them away." Also, instead of "*for*," "He gave them up to (lit., *into* the hand of) their own guilt." Bildad expresses the justice of God, which Job had arraigned. Thy children have sinned; God leaves them to the consequence of their sin; most cutting to the heart of the bereaved father.

5. seek unto God betimes—early. Make it the first and chief anxiety (Ps. 78:34; Hos. 5:15; Isa. 26:9; Prov. 8:17; 13:24).

6. He would awake for thee—i.e., arise to thy help. God seemed to be asleep toward the sufferer (Ps. 35:23; 7:6; Isa. 51:9). **make . . . prosperous**—restore to prosperity thy (their) righteous habitation. Bildad assumes it to have been heretofore the habitation of guilt. **7. thy beginning**—the beginning of thy new happiness after restoration. **latter end**—(ch. 42:12; Prov. 23:18).

ADAM CLARKE

CHAPTER 8

1. *Bildad the Shuhite.* Supposed to be a descendant of Shuah, one of the sons of Abraham, by Keturah, who dwelt in Arabia Deserta, called in Scripture the "east country." See Gen. xxv. 1-2, 6.

2. *How long wilt thou speak these things?* Will you still go on to charge God foolishly? Your heavy affliction proves that you are under His wrath; and His wrath, thus manifested, proves that it is for your sins that He punishes you. *Be like a strong wind?* Will you continue to "breathe forth a tempest of words?"

3. *Doth God pervert judgment?* God afflicts you; can He afflict you for naught? As He is just, His judgment is just; and He could not inflict punishment unless there be a cause.

4. *If thy children have sinned.* I know your children have been cut off by a terrible judgment; but was it not because by transgression they had filled up the measure of their iniquity?

5. *If thou wouldest seek unto God.* Though God has so severely afflicted you, and removed your children by a terrible judgment, yet if you will now humble yourself before Him, and implore His mercy, you shall be saved. He cut them off in their sins, but He spares you; and this is a proof that He waits to be gracious to you.

6. *If thou wert pure and upright.* Concerning your guilt there can be no doubt; for if you had been a holy man, and these calamities had occurred through accident, or merely by the malice of your enemies, would not God, long ere this, have manifested His power and justice in your behalf, punished your enemies, and restored you to affluence? *The habitation of thy righteousness.* Strongly ironical. If your house had been as a temple of God, in which His worship had been performed, and His commandments obeyed, would it now be in a state of ruin and desolation?

MATTHEW HENRY

should be ever so small, a little meal in the barrel and a little oil in the cruse, God's blessing shall multiply that to a great increase." This is God's way of enriching the souls of his people with graces and comforts, not *per saltum*—as by a bound, but *per gradum—step by step.*

Verses 8–19

Bildad will not be so bold as to say with Eliphaz that none that were righteous were ever cut off thus (*ch.* iv. 7); yet he takes it for granted that God does ordinarily bring wicked men to shame and ruin in this world, and that, by making their prosperity short, he discovers their piety to be counterfeit. Whether this will certainly prove that all who are thus ruined must be concluded to have been hypocrites he will not say.

I. He proves the certain destruction of all the hopes and joys of hypocrites, by an appeal to antiquity. He insists not on his own judgment and that of his companions: *We are but of yesterday, and know nothing, v.* 9. He refers to the testimony of the ancients, *v.* 8. *They will teach thee,* and inform thee (*v.* 10), that all along, in their time, the judgments of God followed wicked men. The learned Bishop Patrick suggests that Bildad being a Shuhite, descended from Shuah one of Abraham's sons by Keturah (Gen. xxv. 2), in this appeal which he makes to history has a particular respect to the rewards which the blessing of God secured to the posterity of faithful Abraham.

II. He illustrates this truth by some similitudes.

1. The hopes and joys of the hypocrite are compared to a rush or flag, *v.* 11–13. It grows up out of the mire and water. The hypocrite cannot gain his hope without some false rotten ground or other out of which to raise it, and with which to support it and keep it alive, any more than the rush can grow without mire. He grounds it on his worldly prosperity, the plausible profession he makes of religion, the good opinion of his neighbours, and his own good conceit of himself, which are no solid foundation on which to build his confidence. It may look green and gay for a while (the rush outgrows the grass), but it is light, and hollow and empty. It withers presently, *before any other herb, v.* 12. Even *while it is in its greenness* it is dried away and gone in a little time. *So are the paths of all that forget God* (*v.* 13); they take the same way that the rush does, *for the hypocrite's hope shall perish.*

2. They are compared to *a spider's web,* or *a spider's house* (as it is in the margin), a cobweb, *v.* 14, 15. The hope of the hypocrite is the creature of his own fancy, and arises merely from a conceit of his own merit and sufficiency. There is a great deal of difference between the work of the bee and that of the spider. A diligent Christian, like the laborious bee, fetches in all his comfort from the heavenly dews of God's word; but the hypocrite, like the subtle spider, weaves his out of a false hypothesis of his own concerning God, as if he were altogether such an one as himself. He is very fond of it, as the spider of her web; wraps himself in it, calls it his house, *leans upon it, and holds it fast.* It is said of the spider that *she takes hold with her hands, and is in kings' palaces,* Prov. xxx. 28. So does a carnal worldling hug himself in the fulness and firmness of his outward prosperity; he prides himself in that house as his palace. It will be swept away, as the cobweb with the besom, when God shall come to purge his house.

3. The hypocrite is here compared to a flourishing and well-rooted tree, which, though it do not wither of itself, yet will easily be cut down and its place know it no more. See this tree fair and flourishing (*v.* 16) under the protection of his garden-wall and with the benefit of his garden-soil, taking deep root, never likely to be overthrown by stormy winds, *for his roots are interwoven with the stones* (*v.* 17); it grows in firm ground, not, as the rush, in mire and water.

JAMIESON, FAUSSET, BROWN

8, 9. The sages of the olden time reached an age beyond those of Job's time (*Note,* 42:16), and therefore could give the testimony of a fuller experience. **of yesterday**—i.e., a recent race. We know nothing as compared with them because of the brevity of our lives; so even Jacob (Gen. 47:9). Knowledge consisted then in the results of observation, embodied in poetical proverbs, and handed down by tradition. Longevity gave the opportunity of wider observation. **a shadow**—(Ps. 144:4; I Chron. 29:15). **10. teach thee**—Chapter 6:24 had said, "Teach me." Bildad, therefore, says, "Since you want *teaching,* inquire of the fathers. They will teach thee." **utter words**—more than mere speaking; "put forth well-considered words." **out of their heart**—from observation and reflection; not merely, from their mouth: such, as Bildad insinuates, were Job's words. Verses 11, 12, 13 embody in poetic and sententious form (probably the fragment of an old poem) the observation of the elders. The double point of comparison between the ungodly and the paper-reed is: 1. the luxuriant prosperity at first; and, 2. the sudden destruction. **11. rush**—rather, paper-reed: the papyrus of Egypt, which was used to make garments, shoes, baskets, boats. and paper (a word derived from it) It and the flag or bulrush grow only in marshy places (such as are along the Nile). So the godless thrives only in external prosperity; there is in the hypocrite no inward stability; his prosperity is like the rapid growth of water plants. **12. not cut down**—Before it has ripened for the scythe, it withers more suddenly than any herb, having no self-sustaining power, once that the moisture is gone, which other herbs do not need in the same degree. So ruin seizes on the godless in the zenith of prosperity, more suddenly than on others who appear less firmly seated in their possessions [UMBREIT]. (Ps. 112:10.)

13. paths—so "ways" (Prov. 1:19). **all that forget God**—the distinguishing trait of the godless (Ps. 9: 17; 50:22).

14. cut off—so GESENIUS; or, to accord with the metaphor of the spider's "house," "The confidence (on which he builds) shall be laid in ruins" (Isa. 59:5, 6).

15. he shall hold it fast—implying his eager grasp, when the storm of trial comes: as the spider "holds fast" by its web; but with this difference: the light spider is sustained by that on which it rests; the godless is not by the thin web on which he rests. The expression, "Hold fast," properly applies to the spider holding his web, but is transferred to the man. Hypocrisy, like the spider's web, is fine-spun, flimsy, and woven out of its own inventions, as the spider's web out of its own bowels. An Arab proverb says, "Time destroys the well-built house, as well as the spider's web." **16. before the sun**—i.e., he (the godless) is green only before the sun rises; but he cannot bear its heat, and withers. So succulent plants like the gourd (Jonah 4:7, 8). But the widespreading in the garden does not quite accord with this. Better, "in sunshine"; the sun representing the smiling fortune of the hypocrite, during which he wondrously progresses [UMBREIT]. The image is that of weeds growing in rank luxuriance and spreading over even heaps of stones and walls, and then being speedily torn away.

ADAM CLARKE

8. *Enquire . . . of the former age.* "Of the first age"; of the patriarchs.

9. *For we are but of yesterday, and know nothing.* The writer of this book probably had before his eyes these words of David, in his last prayer, 1 Chron. xxix. 15: "For we are strangers before thee, and sojourners, as were all our fathers: our days on the earth are as a shadow, and there is no expectation" (marg.)

10. *Shall not they teach thee?* Will you not treat their maxims with the utmost deference and respect? They *utter words out of their heart*—what they say is the fruit of long and careful experience.

11. *Can the rush grow?* The word *gome,* which we translate *rush,* is, without doubt, the Egyptian papyrus, on which the ancients wrote, and from which our paper derives its name. The Septuagint render *gome* by "papyrus," thus: "Can the papyrus flourish without water?" Their translation leaves no doubt concerning the meaning of the original. They were probably writing on the very substance in question, while making their translation. *Can the flag grow without water?* Parkhurst supposes that the word *achu,* which we render *flag,* is the same with that species of reed which Mr. Hasselquist found growing near the river Nile.

12. *Whilst it is yet in his greenness.* We do not know enough of the natural history of this plant to be able to discern the strength of this allusion; but we learn from it that, although this plant be very succulent, and grow to a great size, yet it is short-lived, and speedily withers; and this we may suppose to be in the dry season, or on the retreat of the waters of the Nile. However, "Soon ripe, soon rotten," is a maxim in horticulture.

13. *So are the paths.* The papyrus and the rush flourish while they have a plentiful supply of ooze and water; but take these away, and their prosperity is speedily at an end. So it is with the wicked and profane; their prosperity is of short duration, however great it may appear to be in the beginning. *The hypocrite's hope shall perish.* A *hypocrite,* or rather "profligate," has no inward religion, for his heart is not right with God; he has only hope, and that perishes when he gives up the ghost. This is the first place in which the word *hypocrite* occurs, or the noun *chaneph,* which rather conveys the idea of pollution and defilement than of hypocrisy. A hypocrite is one who only carries the mask of godliness, to serve secular purposes; who wishes to be taken for a religionist, though he is conscious he has no religion. Such a person cannot have hope of any good, because he knows he is insincere. But the person in the text has hope; therefore *hypocrite* cannot be the meaning of the original word. But all the vile, the polluted, and the profligate have hope; they hope to end their iniquities before they end life, and they hope to get at last to the kingdom of Heaven. *Hypocrite* is a very improper translation of the Hebrew.

14. *Whose hope shall be cut off.* Such persons, subdued by the strong habits of sin, hope on fruitlessly, till the last thread of the web of life is cut off from the beam; and then they find no more strength in their hope than is in the threads of the spider's web.

15. *He shall lean upon his house.* This is an allusion to the spider. When he suspects his web, here called his *house,* to be frail or unsure, he leans upon it in different parts, propping himself on his hinder legs, and pulling with his fore claws, to see if all be safe. If he find any part of it injured, he immediately adds new cordage to that part, and attaches it strongly to the wall. When he finds all safe and strong, he retires into his hole at one corner, supposing himself to be in a state of complete security, when in a moment the *brush* sweeps away both himself, his house, and his confidence. The wicked, whose hope is in his temporal possessions, strengthens and keeps his house in repair, and thus leans on his earthly supports. In a moment, as in the case of the spider, his house is overwhelmed by the blast of God's judgments, and himself probably buried in its ruins.

16. *He is green before the sun.* This is another metaphor. The wicked is represented as a luxuriant plant, in a good soil, with all the advantages of a good situation; well exposed to the

MATTHEW HENRY

Thus does a wicked man, when he prospers in the world, think himself secure. See this tree felled and forgotten notwithstanding, *destroyed from his place* (*v.* 18).

Verses 20–22

Bildad sums up what he has to say in a few words, 1. On the one hand, if Job were a perfect upright man, God would not *cast him away*, *v.* 20. Though now he seemed forsaken of God, he would yet return to him, and his *mouth* should be *filled with laughing*, *v.* 21. Those that loved him would rejoice with him; but those that hated him, and had triumphed in his fall, would be ashamed of their insolence. Now it is true that *God will not cast away an upright man*; he may be cast down for a time, but he shall not be cast away for ever. 2. On the other hand, if he were a wicked man and an evil-doer, God would not help him, but leave him to perish in his present distresses (*v.* 20), and his *dwelling-place* should *come to nought*, *v.* 22. It is true that *the dwelling-place of the wicked*, sooner or later, *will come to nought*. Those only *who make God their dwelling-place* are safe for ever, Ps. xc. 1; xci. 1. Sin brings ruin on persons and families. Yet to argue (as Bildad slyly does) that because Job's family was sunk, and he himself at present seemed helpless, therefore he certainly was an ungodly wicked man, was neither just nor charitable.

JAMIESON, FAUSSET, BROWN

17. seeth the place of stones—*Hebrew*, "the house of stones"; i.e., the wall surrounding the garden. The parasite plant, in creeping towards and over the wall—the utmost bound of the garden—is said figuratively to "see" or regard it. **18.** If He (God) tear him away (properly, "to tear away rapidly and violently") from his place, "then it (the place personified) shall deny him" (Ps. 103:16). The very soil is ashamed of the weeds lying withered on its surface, as though it never had been connected with them. So, when the godless falls from prosperity, his nearest friends disown him. **19.** Bitter irony. The hypocrite boasts of joy. This then is his "joy" at the last. **and out of the earth**—others immediately, who take the place of the man thus punished; not *godly men* (Matt. 3:9). For the place of the weeds is among stones, where the gardener wishes no plants. But, *ungodly;* a fresh crop of weeds always springs up in the place of those torn up: there is no end of hypocrites on earth [UMBREIT]. **20.** Bildad regards Job as a righteous man, who has fallen into sin. **God will not cast away a perfect man**—(or godly man, such as Job was), if he will only repent. Those alone who persevere in sin God will not help (*Hebrew*, "take by the hand," Ps. 73:23; Isa. 41:13; 42:6) when fallen. **21. Till**—lit., "to the point that"; God's blessing on thee, when repentant, will go on increasing to the point that, or until, etc. **22.** The haters of Job are the wicked. They shall be clothed with shame (Jer. 3:25; Ps. 35:26; 109:29), at the failure of their hope that Job would utterly perish, and because they, instead of him, come to naught.

ADAM CLARKE

sun; the roots intervolving themselves with stones, so as to render the tree more stable. But suddenly a blast comes, and the tree begins to die.

18. *If he destroy him from his place.* Is not this a plain reference to the alienation of his inheritance? God destroys him from it; it becomes the property of another; and on his revisiting it, the place says, "I know thee not; I have never seen thee."

19. *Behold, this is the joy of his way.* A strong irony. Here is the issue of all his mirth, of his sports, games, and pastimes! *Out of the earth shall others grow.* As in the preceding case, when one plant or tree is blasted or cut down, another may be planted in the same place; so, when a spendthrift has run through his property, another possesses his inheritance.

20. *Behold, God will not cast away a perfect man.* This is another of the maxims of the ancients, which Bildad produces: "As sure as he will punish and root out the wicked, so surely will he defend and save the righteous."

21. *Till he fill thy mouth with laughing.* Perhaps it may be well to translate after Mr. Good, "Even yet may he fill thy mouth with laughter!" The two verses may be read as a prayer; and probably they were thus expressed by Bildad, who speaks with less virulence than his predecessor, though with equal positiveness in respect to the grand charge, viz., If you were not a sinner of no mean magnitude, God would not have inflicted such unprecedented calamities upon you.

MATTHEW HENRY

CHAPTER 9

Verses 1–13

Bildad began with a rebuke to Job for talking so much, *ch.* viii. 2. Job makes no answer to that, but in what he next lays down as his principle, that God never perverts judgment, Job agrees with him: *I know it is so of a truth*, *v.* 2. *How should man be just with God?* Some understand this as a passionate complaint of God's strictness and severity, and it cannot be denied that there are, in this chapter, some peevish expressions. But I take this rather as a pious confession of man's sinfulness, and his own in particular, that, if God should deal with any of us according to the desert of our iniquities, we should certainly be undone.

I. He lays this down for a truth, that man is an unequal match for his Maker.

1. In dispute (*v.* 3): *If he will contend with him*, either at law or at any argument, *he cannot answer him one of a thousand.* When God spoke to Job out of the whirlwind he asked him a great many questions (*Dost thou know* this? *Canst thou do* that?) to none of which Job could give an answer, *ch.* xxxviii, xxxix. God can lay to our charge a thousand offences, and we cannot answer him so as to acquit ourselves from any of them.

2. In combat (*v.* 4): "*Who hath hardened himself against him and hath prospered?*" You cannot produce any instance of any daring sinner who has *hardened himself against God*, who did not find God too hard for him and pay dearly for his folly.

II. He proves it by showing what a God he is with whom we have to do: *He is wise in heart*, and therefore we cannot answer him at law; he is *mighty in strength*, and therefore we cannot fight it out with him. The devil promised himself that Job, in the day of his affliction, would curse God and speak ill of him, but, instead of that, he sets himself to honour God and to speak highly of him. The God of nature acts with an uncontrollable power and does what he pleases; for all the orders and all the powers of nature are derived from him and depend upon him. When he pleases he alters the course of nature, and turned back its streams, *v.* 4–5. Nothing more firm than the mountains. When we speak of removing mountains we mean that which is impossible; yet the divine power can make them change their seat. He can level them, and overturn them. Men have much ado to pass over them, but God, when he pleases, can make them pass away. Nothing more fixed than the earth on its axletree; yet God can, when he pleases, *shake the earth out of its place*, heave it off its centre, and make even *its pillars to tremble.* God has power enough to shake the earth from under that guilty race of mankind which makes it groan under the burden of sin, and so to *shake the wicked out of it* (Chap. xxxviii. 13); yet he continues the earth, and man upon it, and does not make it, as once, to

JAMIESON, FAUSSET, BROWN

CHAPTER 9

Vss. 1-35. REPLY OF JOB TO BILDAD. **2. I know that it is so**—that God does not "pervert justice" (8:3). But (even though I be sure of being in the right) how can a mere man assert his right—(be just) with God. The Gospel answers (Rom. 3:26).

If he [God] **will contend with him**—lit., "*deign* to enter into judgment." **he cannot answer . . .**—He (man) would not dare, even if he had a thousand answers in readiness to one question of God's, to utter one of them, from awe of His Majesty.

4. wise in heart—in understanding!—and mighty in power! God confounds the ablest arguer by His wisdom, and the mightiest by His power. **hardened himself**—or his neck (Prov. 29:1); i.e., defied God. To prosper, one must fall in with God's arrangements of providence and grace. **5. and they know not**—*Hebrew* for "suddenly, unexpectedly, before they are aware of it" (Ps. 35:8); "at unawares"; *Hebrew*, which "he knoweth not of" (Joel 2:14; Prov. 5:6).

6. The earth is regarded, poetically, as resting on pillars, which tremble in an earthquake (Ps. 75:3; Isa. 24:20). The literal truth as to the earth is given (26:7).

ADAM CLARKE

CHAPTER 9

2. *I know it is so of a truth.* I acknowledge the general truth of the maxims you have advanced. God will not ultimately punish a righteous person, nor shall the wicked finally triumph; and though righteous before man, and truly sincere in my piety, yet I know, when compared with the immaculate holiness of God, all my righteousness is nothing.

3. *If he will contend with him.* God is so holy, and His law so strict, that if He will enter into judgment with His creatures, the most upright of them cannot be justified in His sight. *One of a thousand.* Of a thousand offenses of which he may be accused, he cannot vindicate himself in even one. How little that any man does, even in the way of righteousness, truth, and mercy, can stand the penetrating eye of a just and holy God, when all motives, feelings, and objects come to be scrutinized! In His sight, on this ground, no man living can be justified. Oh, how necessary to fallen, weak, miserable, imperfect, and sinful man is the doctrine of justification by faith, and sanctification through the Divine Spirit, by the sacrificial death and mediation of the Lord Jesus Christ!

4. *He is wise in heart, and mighty in strength.* By His infinite knowledge He searches out and sees all things, and by His almighty power He can punish all delinquencies. He that rebels against Him must be destroyed.

5. *Removeth the mountains, and they know not.* This seems to refer to earthquakes. By those strong convulsions, mountains, valleys, hills, even whole islands, are removed in an instant; and to this latter circumstance the words *they know not* most probably refer.

6. *The pillars thereof tremble.* This also refers to an earthquake, and to that tremulous motion which sometimes gives warning of the approaching catastrophe, and from which this violent convulsion of nature has received its name.

MATTHEW HENRY

swallow up the rebels. Nothing more constant than the rising sun, it never misses its appointed time; yet God, when he pleases, can suspend it. Thus great is God's power; and how great then is his goodness, which causes his sun to shine even upon the evil and unthankful, though he could withhold it! Job here speaks of what God can do; but, if we must understand it of what he has done in fact, all these verses may perhaps be applied to Noah's flood. As long as he pleases he preserves the settled course and order of nature; and this is a continued creation. He himself alone, by his own power, and without the assistance of any other, *Spreads out the heaven* (*v.* 8), not only did spread them out at first, but still spreads them out. *He treads upon the waves of the sea;* that is, he suppresses them and keeps them under, that they return not to deluge the earth (Ps. civ. 9), which is given as a reason why we should all fear God and stand in awe of him, Jer. v. 22. God makes the constellations; three are named for all the rest (*v.* 9), *Arcturus, Orion,* and *Pleiades,* and in general *the chambers of the south.* The stars he makes to be what they are to man, and inclines the hearts of men to observe them, which the beasts are not capable of doing. Not only those stars which we see and give names to, but those also in the other hemisphere, about the antarctic pole, which never come in our sight, called here *the chambers of the south,* are under the divine direction and dominion. Consider what God does in the government of the world, and you will say, He is *wise in heart* and *mighty in strength.* He does many things and great, many and great to admiration, *v.* 10. God is a great God, and *doeth great things,* a wonder-working God; his works of wonder are so many that we cannot number them and so mysterious that we cannot find them out. He acts invisibly and undiscerned, *v.* 11. "*He goes by me* in his operations, *and I see him not, I perceive him not.* His *way is in the sea,*" Ps. lxxvii. 19. Our finite understandings cannot fathom his counsels, apprehend his motions, or comprehend the measures he takes; we are therefore incompetent judges of God's proceedings, because we know not what he does nor what he designs. The *arcania imperii—secrets of government,* are things above us, which therefore we must not pretend to expound. He acts with an incontestable sovereignty, *v.* 12. What action can be brought against him? Or *who will say unto him, What dost thou?* God is not obliged to give us a reason of what he does. The meaning of his proceedings we know not now; it will be time enough to know hereafter, when it will appear that what seemed now to be done by prerogative was done in infinite wisdom and for the best. He acts with an irresistible power, which no creature can resist, *v.* 13. *If God will not withdraw his anger the proud helpers do stoop under him;* that is, He certainly breaks and crushes those that proudly help one another against him.

Verses 14–21

What Job had said of man's utter inability to contend with God he here applies to himself, and in effect despairs of gaining his favour. It arises from the dark and cloudy apprehensions which at present he had of God's displeasure against him.

I. He durst not dispute with God (*v.* 14): "*If the proud helpers do stoop under him, how much less shall I* (a poor weak creature, so far from being a helper that I am very helpless) *answer him?* What can I say against that which God does?"

II. He durst not insist upon his own justification before God. Though he vindicated his own integrity to his friends, and would not yield that he was a hypocrite and a wicked man, as they suggested, yet he would never plead it as his righteousness before God.

1. He knew so much of God that he durst not stand a trial with him, *v.* 15–19. God knew him better than he knew himself and therefore (*v.* 15), "*Though I were righteous* in my own apprehension, and my own heart did not condemn me, *yet God is greater than my heart,* and knows those secret faults and errors of mine which I do not and cannot understand, and is able to charge me with them, and therefore *I would not answer.*" Job will therefore cast himself upon God's mercy, and not think to come off by his own merit. God answers before we call and not because we call, and gives gracious answers to our prayers, but not for our prayers (*v.* 16): "*If I had called, and he had answered,* had given the thing I called to him for, yet, so weak and defective are my best prayers, that *I would not believe he had* therein *hearkened to my voice*; I could not say that he had *saved with his right hand and answered me*" (Ps. lx. 5), "but that he did it purely for his own name's sake." Job was not conscious to himself of any extraordinary

JAMIESON, FAUSSET, BROWN

7. The sun, at His command, does not rise; viz., in an eclipse, or the darkness that accompanies earthquakes (vs. 6). **sealeth up**—i.e., totally covers as one would seal up a room, that its contents may not be seen.

8. **spreadeth out**—(Isa. 40:22; Ps. 104:2). But throughout it is not so much God's creating, as His governing, power over nature that is set forth. A storm seems a struggle between Nature and her Lord! Better, therefore, "Who *boweth* the heavens alone," without help of any other. God descends from the bowed-down heaven to the earth (Ps. 18:9). The storm, wherein the clouds descend, suggests this image. In the descent of the vault of heaven, God has come down from His high throne and walks majestically over the mountain waves (*Hebrew,* "heights"), as a conqueror taming their violence. So "tread upon" (Deut. 33:29; Amos 4:13; Matt. 14:26). The Egyptian hieroglyphic for impossibility is a man walking on waves. **9. maketh**—rather, from the Arabic, "covereth up." This accords better with the context, which describes His boundless power as controller rather than as creator [UMBREIT]. **Arcturus**—the great bear, which always revolves about the pole, and never sets. The Chaldeans and Arabs, early named the stars and grouped them in constellations; often travelling and tending flocks by night, they would naturally do so, especially as the rise and setting of some stars mark the distinction of seasons. BRINKLEY, presuming the stars here mentioned to be those of Taurus and Scorpio, and that these were the cardinal constellations of spring and autumn in Job's time, calculates, by the precession of equinoxes, the time of Job to be 818 years after the deluge, and 184 before Abraham. **Orion**—*Hebrew,* "the fool"; in ch. 38:31 he appears fettered with "bands." The old legend represented this star as a hero, who presumptuously rebelled against God, and was therefore a fool, and was chained in the sky as a punishment; for its rising is at the stormy period of the year. He is Nimrod (the exceedingly impious rebel) among the Assyrians; Orion among the Greeks. Sabaism (worship of the heavenly hosts) and hero-worship were blended in his person. He first subverted the patriarchal order of society by substituting a chieftainship based on conquest (Gen. 10:9, 10). **Pleiades**—lit., "the heap of stars"; *Arabic,* "knot of stars." The various names of this constellation in the East express the close union of the stars in it (Amos 5:8). **chambers of the south**—the unseen regions of the southern hemisphere, with its own set of stars, as distinguished from those just mentioned of the northern. The true structure of the earth is here implied. **10.** Repeated from Eliphaz (ch. 5:9). **11. I see him not: he passeth on**—The image is that of a howling wind (Isa. 21:1). Like it when it bursts invisibly upon man, so God is felt in the awful *effects* of His wrath, but is not *seen* (John 3:8). Therefore, reasons Job, it is impossible to contend with Him. **12.** If "He taketh away," as in my case all that was dear to me, still a mortal cannot call Him to account. He only takes His own. He is an absolute King (Eccles. 8:4; Dan. 4:35). **13. If God**—rather, "God will not withdraw His anger," i.e., so long as a mortal obstinately resists [UMBREIT]. **the proud helpers**—The arrogant, who would help one contending with the Almighty, are of no avail against Him. **14. How much less shall I . . . ?**—who am weak—seeing that the mighty have to stoop before Him. Choose words (use a well-chosen speech, in order to reason) with Him. **15.** (Ch. 10:15). Though I were conscious of no sin, yet I would not dare to say so, but leave it to His judgment and mercy to justify me (I Cor. 4:4).

16, 17. would I not believe that he had hearkened unto my voice—who breaketh me (as a tree stript of its leaves) with a tempest.

ADAM CLARKE

7. *Which commandeth the sun.* Obscures it either with clouds, with thick darkness, or with an eclipse. *Sealeth up the stars.* Like the contents of a letter, wrapped up and sealed, so that it cannot be read. Sometimes the heavens become as black as ebony, and no star, figure, or character in this great book of God can be read.

8. *And treadeth upon the waves.* This is a very majestic image. God not only walks upon the waters, but, when the sea runs mountains high, He steps from billow to billow in His almighty and essential majesty. There is a similar sentiment in David, Ps. xxix. 10: "The Lord sitteth upon the flood; yea, the Lord sitteth King for ever." But both are far outdone by the Psalmist, Ps. xviii. 9-15, and especially in these words, v. 10, "He did fly upon the wings of the wind."

9. *Which maketh Arcturus, Orion, and Pleiades, and the chambers of the south.* The original words are thus rendered by the Septuagint: "Who makes the Pleiades, and Hesperus, and Arcturus, and Orion, and the chambers of the south."

11. *Lo, he goeth by me, and I see him not.* He is incomprehensible in all His ways, and in all His works; and He must be so if He be God, and work as God; for His own nature and His operations are past finding out.

12. *He taketh away.* He never gives, but He is ever lending, and while the gift is useful or is improved, He permits it to remain; but when it becomes useless or is misused, He recalls it. *Who can hinder him?* Literally, "Who can cause Him to restore it?"

13. *If God will not withdraw his anger.* It is of no use to contend with God; He cannot be successfully resisted; all His opposers must perish.

14. *How much less shall I answer?* I cannot contend with my Maker. He is the Lawgiver and the Judge. How shall I stand in judgment before Him?

15. *Though I were righteous.* Though clear of all the crimes, public and secret, of which you accuse me, yet I would not dare to stand before His immaculate holiness.

16. *If I had called, and he had answered.* These sentiments sufficiently confuted that slander of his friends, who said he was presumptuous, had not becoming notions of the majesty of God, and used blasphemous expressions against His sovereign authority.

MATTHEW HENRY

guilt, and yet fell under extraordinary afflictions, *v.* 17, 18. Job was *broken with a tempest.* Job's troubles came so thickly upon him that he had no breathing time, and he was filled with bitterness. And he presumes to say that all this was *without cause,* without any great provocation given. Here, no doubt, *he spoke unadvisedly with his lips*; he reflected on God's goodness in saying that he was not suffered *to take his breath* (while yet he had such good use of his reason and speech as to be able to talk thus) and on his justice in saying that it was without cause. There is no disputing (said one once to Cæsar) with him that commands legions. Much less is there any with him that has legions of angels at command.

2. He knew so much of himself that he durst not stand a trial, *v.* 21, 20. "*If I go* about *to justify myself,* and to plead a righteousness of my own, my defence will be my offence, and *my own mouth shall condemn me* even when it goes about to acquit me." A good man, who knows the deceitfulness of his own heart, is suspicious of more evil in himself than he is really conscious of, and therefore will by no means think of justifying himself before God. "Though I were free from gross sin, though my conscience should not charge me with any enormous crime, yet would I not believe my own heart so far as to insist upon my innocency nor think my life worth striving for with God."

Verses 22–24

Here Job touches briefly upon the main point now in dispute between him and his friends. They maintained that those who are righteous and good always prosper in this world, and none but the wicked are in misery and distress; he asserted, on the contrary, that it is a common thing for the wicked to prosper and the righteous to be greatly afflicted. "I said it, and say it again, that all things come alike to all." Now, 1. It must be owned that there is very much truth in what Job here means, that temporal judgments, when they are sent abroad, fall both upon good and bad. Let this reconcile God's children to their troubles; they are but trials, designed for their honour and benefit, and, if God be pleased with them, let not them be displeased. On the other hand, the wicked are so far from being made the marks of God's judgments that *the earth is given into their hand, v.* 24, *into the hand of the wicked one* (in the original, the word is singular). The wicked have the earth given them, but the righteous have heaven given them, and which is better—heaven without earth or earth without heaven? Job ought not to have said, *He laughs at it,* for God doth not afflict willingly. When the spirit is heated, either with dispute or with discontent, we need to set a watch before the door of our lips.

Verses 25–35

Job grows more querulous. When we are in trouble we are allowed to complain to God, as the Psalmist often, but must by no means complain of God, as Job here.

I. His complaint here of the passing away of the days of his prosperity is proper enough (*v.* 25, 26): "*My days* (that is, all my good days) are gone, never to return, gone of a sudden, gone ere I was aware."

II. His complaint of his present uneasiness is excusable, *v.* 27, 28. He did his endeavour to compose himself as his friends advised him. He would fain *forget his complaints* and praise God. He found he could not do it: "*I am afraid of all my sorrows.*"

III. His complaint of God as implacable and inexorable was by no means to be excused. He knew better, and, at another time, would have been far from harbouring any such hard thoughts of God. Good men do not always speak like themselves; but God, who considers their frame and the strength of their temptations, gives them leave afterwards to unsay what was amiss by repentance and will not lay it to their charge.

1. Job seems to speak here, (1) As if he despaired of obtaining from God any relief or redress of his grievances: "*I know that thou wilt not hold me innocent.* My afflictions have continued so long upon me. *Why then do I labour in vain* to clear myself and maintain my own integrity?" *v.* 29. With men it is often labour in vain for the most innocent to go about to clear themselves. But it is not so in our dealings with God, to whom it was never in vain to commit a righteous cause (*v.* 30, 31): "*If I wash myself with snow-water,* and make my integrity ever so evident, it will be all to no purpose; judgment must go against me. *Thou shalt plunge me in the ditch* (the pit of destruction, so some, or rather the filthy kennel, or sewer), which will make me so offensive in the nostrils of all about

JAMIESON, FAUSSET, BROWN

19. UMBREIT takes these as the words of God, translating, "What availeth the might of the strong?" "Here (saith he) behold! what availeth justice? Who will appoint me a time to plead?" (So Jer. 49:19). The last words certainly apply better to God than to Job. The sense is substantially the same if we make "me" apply to Job. The "lo!" expresses God's swift readiness for battle when challenged. **20. it**—(ch. 15:6; Luke 19:22); or "He," God. **21.** Lit., here (and in vs. 20), "I perfect! I should not know my soul! I would despise (disown) my life"; i.e., Though conscious of innocence, I should be compelled, in contending with the infinite God, to ignore my own soul and despise my past life as if it were guilty [ROSENMULLER].

22. one thing—"It is all one; whether perfect or wicked—He destroyeth." This was the point Job maintained against his friends, that the righteous and wicked alike are afflicted, and that great sufferings *here* do not prove great guilt (Luke 13:1-5; Eccles. 9:2). **23. If**—Rather, "While (His) scourge slays suddenly (the wicked, vs. 22), He laughs at (disregards; not derides) the pining away of the innocent." The only difference, says Job, between the innocent and guilty is, the latter are slain by a *sudden* stroke, the former pine away *gradually.* The translation, "trial," does not express the antithesis to "slay suddenly," as "pining away" does [UMBREIT]. **24.** Referring to righteous "judges," in antithesis to "the wicked" in the parallel first clause, whereas the wicked oppressor often has the earth given into his hand, the righteous judges are led to execution—culprits had their faces covered preparatory to execution (Esther 7:8). Thus the contrast of the wicked and righteous here answers to that in vs. 23. **if not, where and who?**—If God be *not* the cause of these anomalies, *where* is the cause to be found, and *who* is *he*?

25. a post—a courier. In the wide Persian empire such couriers, on dromedaries or on foot, were employed to carry the royal commands to the distant provinces (Esther 3:13, 15; 8:14). "My days" are not like the slow caravan, but the fleet post. The "days" are themselves poetically said to "see no good," instead of Job in them (I Pet. 3:10). **26. swift ships**—rather, canoes of reeds or papyrus skiffs, used on the Nile, swift from their lightness (Isa. 18:2). **28.** The apodosis to 27—"If I say," etc. "I still am afraid of all my sorrows (returning), for I know that thou wilt (dost) not (by removing my sufferings) hold or declare me innocent. How then can "I leave off my heaviness"?

29. The "if" is better omitted; I (am treated by God as) wicked; why then labor I in vain (to disprove His charge)? Job submits, not so much because he is *convinced* that God is *right,* as because God is *powerful* and he *weak* [BARNES].

30. snow water—thought to be more cleansing than common water, owing to the whiteness of snow (Ps. 51:7; Isa. 1:18). **never so clean**—Better, to answer to the parallelism of the first clause which expresses the cleansing material, "lye": the Arabs used alkali mixed with oil, as soap (Ps. 73:13; Jer. 2:22).

ADAM CLARKE

17. *He breaketh me with a tempest.* The Targum, Syriac, and Arabic have this sense: "He powerfully smites even every hair of my head, and multiplies my wounds without cause." That is, There is no reason known to myself, or to any other man, why I should be thus most oppressively afflicted. It is, therefore, cruel and inconsequent to assert that I suffer for my crimes.

18. *He will not suffer me to take my breath.* I have no respite in my afflictions; I suffer continually in my body, and my mind is incessantly harassed.

19. *If I speak of strength, lo, he is strong.* Human wisdom, power, and influence avail nothing before Him. *Who shall set me a time?* "Who would be a witness for me?" or, Who would dare to appear in my behalf? Almost all the terms in this part of the speech of Job, from v. 11 to v. 24, are forensic or juridical, and are taken from legal processes and pleadings in their gates or courts of justice.

20. *If I justify myself.* God must have some reason for His conduct towards me. I therefore do not pretend to justify myself; the attempt to do it would be an insult to His majesty and justice. Though I am conscious of none of the crimes of which you accuse me, and know not why He contends with me, yet He must have some reason, and that reason He does not choose to explain.

24. *The earth is given into the hand of the wicked.* Is it not most evident that the worst men possess most of this world's goods, and that the righteous are scarcely ever in power or affluence? This was the case in Job's time; it is the case still. Therefore prosperity and adversity in this life are no marks of either God's approbation or His disapprobation. *He covereth the faces of the judges thereof.* Or, "The faces of its decisions he shall cover." God is often stated in Scripture as doing a thing which He only permits to be done. So He permits the eyes of judgment to be blinded, and hence false decisions. *Where, and who is he?* If God does not permit these things, who is it that orders them?

25. *Swifter than a post.* "Than a runner." The light-footed messenger or courier who carries messages from place to place. *They flee away.* The Chaldee says, "My days are swifter than the shadow of a flying bird."

26. *As the swift ships.* "Ships of desire," or "ships of Ebeh," says our margin; perhaps more correctly, "inflated ships," the sails bellying out with a fair brisk wind, tide favorable, and the vessels themselves lightly freighted.

27. *I will forget my complaint.* I will "forsake" or "forego" my complaining. *I will leave off my heaviness.* Vulgate, "I will change my countenance"—force myself to smile, and endeavor to assume the appearance of comfort.

29. *If I be wicked.* If I am the sinner you suppose me to be, in vain should I labor to counterfeit joy, and cease to complain of my sufferings.

30. *If I wash myself with snow water.* Supposed to have a more detergent quality than common water, and it was certainly preferred to common water by the ancients.

MATTHEW HENRY

me that *my own clothes shall abhor me* and I shall even loathe to touch myself." He saw his afflictions coming from God. Yet these words are capable of a good construction. If we keep our hands ever so clean from the pollutions of gross sin, which fall under the eye of the world,—yet God, who knows our hearts, can charge us with so much secret sin as will for ever take off all our pretensions to purity and innocency, and make us see ourselves odious in the sight of the holy God. Paul, while a Pharisee, made his hands very clean; but when the commandment came and discovered to him his heart-sins, made him know lust, that *plunged him in the ditch.* (2) As if he despaired to have a fair hearing with God. He complains that he was not upon even terms with God (*v.* 32): "*He is not a man, as I am.* I could venture to dispute with a man like myself." *Neither is there any daysman between us.* This complaint that there was not is in effect a wish that there were, and so the LXX read it: *O that there were a mediator between us!* Job would gladly refer the matter, but no creature was capable of being a referee, and therefore he must even refer it still to God himself and resolve to acquiesce in his judgment. Our Lord Jesus is the blessed days-man, who has mediated between heaven and earth. The gospel leaves no room for such a complaint as this. Job knew not how to address God with the confidence with which he was formerly wont to approach him, *v.* 34, 35. "*Let him take his rod away from me.*" He means not so much his outward afflictions as *his fear* which *terrified him.*

2. From all this let us pity those that are wounded in spirit, and keep up good thoughts of God in our minds, for hard thoughts of him are the inlets of much mischief.

JAMIESON, FAUSSET, BROWN

32. (Eccles. 6:10; Isa. 45:9.) **33. daysman**—mediator or umpire; the imposition of whose hand expresses power to adjudicate between the persons. There might be one on a level with Job, the one party; but Job knew of none on a level with the Almighty, the other party (I Sam. 2:25). We Christians know of such a Mediator (not, however, in the sense of umpire on a level with both—the God-man, Christ Jesus (I Tim. 2:5).

34. rod—not here the symbol of punishment, but of *power.* Job cannot meet God on fair terms so long as God deals with him on the footing of His almighty power. **35. it is not so with me**—As it now is, God not taking His rod away, I am not on such a footing of equality as to be able to vindicate myself.

ADAM CLARKE

32. *For he is not a man, as I am.* I cannot contend with Him as with one of my fellows in a court of justice.

33. *Neither is there any daysman.* A "reprover," "arguer," or "umpire" between us. Daysman, in our law, means an arbitrator or umpire between party and party; instead of *lo yesh,* "there is not," fifteen of Kennicott's and De Rossi's MSS., with the Septuagint, Syriac, and Arabic, read *lu yesh,* "I wish there were"; or, "Oh, that there were!"

34. *Let him take his rod away.* As *shebet* signifies, not only *rod,* but also "sceptre" or the ensign of royalty, Job might here refer to God sitting in His majesty upon the judgment seat; and this sight so appalled Him that, filled with terror, he was unable to speak.

35. *But it is not so with me.* I am not in such circumstances as to plead with my Judge.

MATTHEW HENRY

CHAPTER 10

Verses 1–7

I. A passionate resolution to persist in his complaint, *v.* 1. He resolves to give himself some ease by giving vent to his resentments. "*My soul is weary of my life.*" He will give vent to the bitterness of his soul by violent words. Job's corruption speaks here, yet grace puts in a word. 1. He will complain, but he will *leave his complaint upon himself.* 2. He will speak, but it shall be the *bitterness of his soul* that he will express, not his settled judgment. If I speak amiss, it is *not I, but sin that dwells in me,* not my soul, but its bitterness.

II. A humble petition to God. He will speak, but the first word shall be a prayer, *v.* 2. 1. That he might be delivered from the sting of his afflictions, which is sin. "Thou dost correct me; I will bear that as well as I can; but O do not condemn me!" It is the comfort of those who are in Christ Jesus, that though they are in affliction, there is *no condemnation to them,* Rom. viii. 1. "Lord, do not condemn me; my friends condemn me, but do not thou." 2. That he might be made acquainted with the true cause of his afflictions, and that is sin too: Lord, *show me wherefore thou contendest with me.* When God afflicts us he contends with us, and when he contends with us there is always a reason.

III. A peevish expostulation with God concerning his dealings with him.

1. He thinks it unbecoming the goodness of God, and the mercifulness of his nature, to deal so hardly with his creature as to lay upon him more than he can bear (*v.* 3): *Is it good unto thee that thou shouldst oppress? What profit is there in my blood?* Far be it from Job to think that God did him wrong, but he is quite at a loss how to reconcile his providences with his justice, as good men have often been, and must wait until the day shall declare it.

2. He thinks it unbecoming the infinite knowledge of God to put his prisoner thus upon the rack, as it were, by torture, to extort a confession from him, *v.* 4–6. Many things are hidden from eyes of flesh, the most curious and piercing; *there is a path which* even *the vulture's eye has not seen*: but nothing is, or can be, hidden from the eye of God, to which all things are naked and open. Eyes of flesh see the outward appearance only, but God sees everything truly. Eyes of flesh discover things gradually, but God sees everything at one view. Eyes of flesh are soon tired, but the keeper of Israel neither slumbers nor sleeps, nor does his sight every decay. *God sees not as man sees,* that is, he does not judge as man judges, *but we are sure that the judgment of God is according to truth.* God is not short-sighted, like man, so he is not short-lived (*v.* 5): "*Are thy days as the days of man,* few and evil?" Men grow wiser by experience and must take time for their searches. But it is not so with God; to him nothing is past, nothing future, but everything present.

JAMIESON, FAUSSET, BROWN

CHAPTER 10

Vss. 1-22. Job's Reply to Bildad Continued.

1. leave my complaint upon myself—rather, "I will *give loose* to my complaint" (ch. 7:11).

2. show me ...—Do not, by virtue of Thy mere sovereignty, treat me as guilty without showing me the reasons.

3. Job is unwilling to think God can have pleasure in using His power to "oppress" the weak, and to treat man, the work of His own hands, as of no value (vs. 8; Ps. 138:8). **shine upon**—favor with prosperity (Ps. 50:2).

4-6. Dost Thou see as feebly as man? i.e., with the same uncharitable eye, as, for instance, Job's friends? Is Thy time as short? Impossible! Yet one might think, from the rapid succession of Thy strokes, that Thou hadst no time to spare in overwhelming me.

ADAM CLARKE

CHAPTER 10

2. *Do not condemn me.* Let me not be afflicted in Thy wrath.

Shew me wherefore thou contendest. If I am afflicted because of my sins, show me what that sin is. God never afflicts but for past sin, or to try His followers, or for the greater manifestation of His grace in their support and deliverance.

3. *Is it good unto thee?* Surely it can be no gratification to Thee to distress the children of men, as if Thou didst despise the work of Thy own hands. *And shine upon the counsel.* For by my afflictions the harsh judgments of the wicked will appear to be confirmed, viz., that God regards not His most fervent worshippers, and it is no benefit to lead a religious life.

4. *Hast thou eyes of flesh?* Dost Thou judge as *man* judges? Illustrated by the next clause, *Seest thou as man seeth?*

5. *Are thy days as the days of man? Enosh,* "wretched, miserable man." *Thy years as man's days? Gaber,* "the strong man." Thou art not short-lived, like man in his present imperfect state; nor can the years of the long-lived patriarchs be compared with Thine.

6. *That thou enquirest.* Is it becoming Thy infinite dignity to concern thyself so much with the affairs or transgresions of a despicable mortal? A word spoken in the heart of most sinners.

MATTHEW HENRY

3. He thinks it looked like an abuse of his omnipotence to keep a poor prisoner in custody, whom he knew to be innocent, only because there was none that could deliver him out of his hand (*v.* 7): *Thou knowest that I am not wicked.* He had already owned himself a sinner, but he here stands to it that he was not devoted to sin, not an enemy to God. I cannot say that I am not wanting, or I am not weak; but through grace, I can say, *I am not wicked*: thou knowest I am not, for *thou knowest I love thee.*

Verses 8–13

I. Job eyes God as his Creator and preserver, and describes his dependence upon him as the author and upholder of his being.

1. God made us, he, and not our parents, who were only the instruments of his power and providence in our production. *He made us, and not we ourselves.* The soul also, which animates the body, is his gift. Job takes notice of both here. (1) The body is *made as the clay* (*v.* 9), cast into shape as the clay is formed into a vessel, according to the skill and will of the potter. The formation of human bodies in the womb is described by an elegant similitude (*v.* 10, *Thou hast poured me out like milk, which is coagulated into cheese*), and by an induction of some particulars, *v.* 11. Though we come into the world naked, yet the body is itself both clothed and armed. The skin and flesh are its clothing; the bones and sinews are its armour, not offensive, but defensive. The vital parts, the heart and lungs, are thus clothed, not to be seen—thus fenced, not to be hurt. The admirable structure of human bodies is an illustrious instance of the wisdom, power, and goodness of the Creator. What a pity it is that these bodies should be instruments of unrighteousness which are capable of being temples of the Holy Ghost! (2) The soul is the life, the soul is the man, and this is the gift of God: *Thou hast granted me life*, breathed into me the breath of life, without which the body would be but a worthless carcase. God is the Father of spirits: he made us living souls, and endued us with the powers of reason; he gave us *life and favour*, and life is a favour. Now Job was in a better mind than he was when he quarrelled with life as a burden, and asked, *Why died I not from the womb?*

2. God maintains us. Having lighted the lamp of life, he does not leave it to burn upon its own stock, but continually supplies it with fresh oil: "*Thy visitation has preserved my spirit*, kept me alive, protected me from the adversaries of life, and blessed me with the daily supplies it needs and craves."

II. He pleads this with God (*v.* 9): *Remember, I beseech thee, that thou hast made me.* 1. "Thou hast made me, and needest not to examine me by scourging, not to put me upon the rack for the discovery of what is within me." 2. "Thou hast made me, as the clay, by an act of sovereignty; and wilt thou by a like act of sovereignty unmake me again?" 3. "Wilt thou destroy the work of thy own hands? Wilt thou not spare and help me, and stand by *the work of thy own hands*?" Ps. cxxxviii. 8. Job knew not how to reconcile God's former favours and his present frowns, but concludes (*v.* 13), "*These things hast thou hidden in thy heart.*"

Verses 14–22

I. Job's passionate complaints. On this harsh and unpleasant string he harps much, in which, though he cannot be justified, he may be excused. If we think it looks ill in him, let it be a warning to us to keep our temper better.

1. He complains of the strictness of God's judgment and the rigour of his proceedings against him, and is ready to call it *summum jus—justice bordering on severity.* (1) That he took all advantages against him: "*If I sin, then thou markest me,*" *v.* 14. (2) That he prosecuted those advantages to the utmost: *Thou wilt not acquit me from my iniquity.* While his troubles continued he could not take the comfort of his pardon, nor hear that voice of joy and gladness; so hard is it to see love in God's heart when we see frowns in his face and a rod in his hand. (3) That, whatever was his character, his case at present was very uncomfortable, *v.* 15. [1] If he be wicked, he is certainly undone in the other world: *If I be wicked, woe to me.* [2] If he be *righteous*, yet he dares not *lift up his head*, dares not answer as before, *ch.* ix. 15. He is so oppressed and overwhelmed with his troubles that he cannot look up with any comfort or confidence.

2. He complains of the severity of the execution. God (he thought) did not only punish him for every failure, but punish him in a high degree, *v.* 16, 17. God *hunted him* as a lion. God was not only strange to him, but *showed himself marvellous upon him*, by bringing him into uncommon troubles and so making him a prodigy, a wonder unto many. That which

JAMIESON, FAUSSET, BROWN

7. "Although Thou (the Omniscient) knowest," etc. (connected with vs. 6), "Thou searchest after my sin." **and . . . [that] none can deliver out of thine hand**—Therefore Thou hast no need to deal with me with the rapid violence which man would use (*Note,* vs. 6).

8. Made—with pains; implying a work of difficulty and art; applying to God language applicable only to man. **together round about**—implying that the human body is a *complete unity,* the parts of which *on all sides* will bear the closest scrutiny. **9. clay**—Next verse proves that the reference here is, not so much to the *perishable* nature of the materials, as to their *wonderful fashioning* by the divine potter. **10.** In the organization of the body from its rude commencements, the original liquid gradually assumes a more solid consistency, like milk curdling into cheese (Ps. 139: 15, 16). Science reveals that the chyle circulated by the lacteal vessels is the supply to every organ. **11. fenced**—or "inlaid" (Ps. 139:15); curiously wrought" [UMBREIT]. In the fœtus the skin appears first, then the flesh, then the harder parts.

12. visitation—Thy watchful Providence, **spirit**—breath.

13. is with thee—was Thy purpose. All God's dealings with Job in his creation, preservation, and present afflictions were part of His secret counsel (Ps. 139: 16; Acts 15:18; Eccles. 3:11).

14, 15. Job is perplexed because God "marks" every sin of his with such ceaseless rigor. Whether "wicked" (godless and a hypocrite) or "righteous" (comparatively sincere), God condemns and punishes alike.

lift up my head—in conscious innocence (Ps. 3:3). **see thou**—rather, "and seeing I see (I too well see) mine affliction," (which seems to prove me guilty) [UMBREIT].

16. increaseth—rather, "(if) I *lift* up (my head) Thou wouldest hunt me, etc. [UMBREIT]. **and again**—as if a lion should not kill his prey at once, but come back and torture it again.

ADAM CLARKE

8. *Thine hands have made me.* Thou art well acquainted with human nature, for Thou art its Author. *And fashioned me together round about.* It is Thou who hast refined the materials out of which I have been formed, and modified them into that excellent symmetry and order in which they are now found, so that the union and harmony of the different parts (*yachad*) and their arrangement and completion (*sabib*) proclaim equally Thy wisdom, skill, power, and goodness. *Yet thou dost destroy me.* "And thou wilt swallow me up." Men generally care for and prize those works on which they have spent most time, skill, and pains: but, although Thou hast formed me with such incredible skill and labor, yet Thou art about to destroy me!

KEIL–DELITZSCH:

The development of the embryo was regarded by the Israelitish Chokma as one of the greatest mysteries (Eccles. 11:5; 2 Macc. 7:22 sq.). There are two poetical passages which treat explicitly of this mysterious existence: this strophe of the book of Job, and the Psalm by David, 139:13–16. The assertion of Scheuchzer, Hoffmann, and Oetinger, that these passages of Scripture "include, and indeed go beyond, all recent *systemata generationis,*" attributes to Scripture a design of imparting instruction—a purpose which is foreign to it. Scripture nowhere attempts an analysis of the workings of nature, but only traces them back to their final cause. According to the view of Scripture, a creative act similar to the creation of Adam is repeated at the origin of each individual; and the continuation of development according to natural laws is not less the working of God than the creative planting of the very beginning. Thy hands, says Job, had formed (to cut, carve, fashion; cognate are without the accompanying notion of toil, which makes this word specially appropriate, as describing the fashioning of the complicated nature of man) and perfected me.

—*Commentary on the Old Testament*

MATTHEW HENRY

made his afflictions most grievous was that he felt God's *indignation* in them. It was growing, still growing worse and worse. This he insists much upon; when he hoped the tide would turn, and begin to ebb, still it flowed higher and higher.

3. He complains of his life, and that ever he was born to all this trouble and misery (*v.* 18, 19): "If this was designed for my lot, *why was I brought out of the womb,* and not smothered there, or stifled in the birth?" Mr. Caryl gives this a good turn in favour of Job. "We may charitably suppose," says he, "that that which troubled Job was that he was in a condition of life which (as he conceived) hindered the main end of his life, which was the glorifying of God. He feared lest his troubles should reflect dishonour upon God and give occasion to his enemies to blaspheme; and therefore he wishes, *O that I had given up the ghost!* A godly man reckons that he lives to no purpose if he do not live to the praise and glory of God." If that was his meaning, it was grounded on a mistake; for we may *glorify the Lord in the fires.*

II. Job's humble requests. He prays, 1. That God would *see his affliction* (*v.* 15). 2. That God would grant him some ease.

JAMIESON, FAUSSET, BROWN

17. witnesses—His accumulated trials were like a succession of witnesses brought up in proof of his guilt, to wear out the accused. **changes and war**—rather, ("thou settest in array) against me host after host" (lit., "changes and a host," i.e,, a succession of hosts); viz., his afflictions, and then reproach upon reproach from his friends. **20.** But, since I was destined from my birth to these ills, at least give me a little breathing time during the few days left me (ch. 9:34; 13:21; Ps. 39:13). **22.** The ideas of order and light, disorder and darkness, harmonize (Gen. 1:2). Three *Hebrew* words are used for darkness; in vs. 21 (1) the common word "darkness"; here (2) "a land of *gloom"* (from a *Hebrew* root, "to cover up"); (3) as "thick darkness" or blackness (from a root, expressing sunset). "Where the light thereof is like blackness." Its only sunshine is thick darkness. A bold figure of poetry. Job in a better frame has brighter thoughts of the unseen world. But his views at best wanted the definite clearness of the Christian's. Compare with his words here Revelation 21:23; 22:5; II Timothy 1:10.

ADAM CLARKE

17. *Thou renewest thy witnesses.* In this speech of Job he is ever referring to trials in courts of judicature, and almost all his terms are forensic. Thou bringest witnesses in continual succession to confound and convict me. *Changes and war.* I am as if attacked by successive troops; one company being wearied, another succeeds to the attack, so that I am harassed by continual warfare.

MATTHEW HENRY

CHAPTER 11

Verses 1–6

It is sad to see what intemperate passions even wise and good men are sometimes betrayed into by the heat of disputation, of which Zophar here is an instance. Eliphaz began with a very modest preface, *ch.* iv. 2. Bildad was a little more rough upon Job, *ch.* viii. 2. But Zophar falls upon him without mercy. *Should a man full of talk be justified? And should thy lies make men hold their peace?* Is this the way to comfort Job? Does this become one that appears as an advocate for God and his justice?

I. He represents Job otherwise than what he was, *v.* 2, 3. He would have him thought one that loved to hear himself talk; and all this that it might be looked upon as a piece of justice to chastise him. We have read and considered Job's discourses in the foregoing chapters, and have found them full of good sense, that his principles are right, his reasonings strong, and that what there is in them of heat and passion a little charity will excuse and overlook; and yet Zophar here invidiously represents him, 1. As a man that never considered what he said. *Should not the multitude of words be answered?* Truly, sometimes it is no great matter whether it be or no. *Should a man full of talk* (margin, *a man of lips,* that is all tongue, *a mere voice*) *be justified?* Should he be justified in his loquacity, as in effect he is if he be not reproved for it? No, for *in the multitude of words there wanteth not sin.* 2. As a man that made no conscience of what he said—a liar, and one that hoped by the impudence of lies to silence his adversaries (*should thy lies make men hold their peace?*)—one that bantered all mankind. Job was not mad, but spoke the words of truth and soberness, and yet was thus misrepresented.

II. He charges Job with saying that which he had not said (*v.* 4): *Thou hast said, My doctrine is pure.* Job spoke better of God than his friends did. If he had expressed himself unwarily, yet it did not therefore follow but that his doctrine was true. But he charges him with saying, *I am clean in thy eyes.* Job had not said so: he had indeed said, *Thou knowest that I am not wicked* (*ch.* x. 7); but he had also said, *I have sinned.* He had indeed maintained that he was not a hypocrite as they charged him; but to infer thence that he would not own himself a sinner was an unfair insinuation.

III. He appeals to God, and wishes him to appear against Job. Nothing will serve him but that God must immediately appear to silence and condemn him. We are commonly ready with too much assurance to interest God in our quarrels, and to conclude that, if he would but speak, he would take our part and speak for us, as Zophar here: *O that God would speak!* for he would certainly *open his lips against thee*; whereas, when God did speak, he opened his lips for Job against his three friends. Zophar despairs to convince Job himself, and therefore desires God would convince him of two things:—

1. The unsearchable depth of God's counsels. Zophar desires that God himself would show Job so much of the secrets of the divine wisdom as might convince him *that they are* at least *double to that which is, v.* 6. What we know of God is nothing to what we cannot know. What is hidden is more than double to what appears, Eph. iii. 9. God knows a great deal more evil of us than we do of ourselves; so some understand it.

JAMIESON, FAUSSET, BROWN

CHAPTER 11

VSS. 1-20. FIRST SPEECH OF ZOPHAR.

2. Zophar assails Job for his empty words, and indirectly, the two friends, for their weak reply. Taciturnity is highly prized among Orientals (Prov. 10:8, 19). **3. lies**—rather, "vain boasting" (Isa. 16:6; Jer. 48:30). The "men" is emphatic; men of sense; in antithesis to "vain boasting." **mockest**—upbraidest God by complaints.

4. doctrine—purposely used of Job's speeches, which sounded like lessons of doctrine (Deut. 32:2; Prov. 4:2). **thine**—addressed to God. Job had maintained his *sincerity* against his friends' suspicions, not *faultlessness.*

6. to that which is!—Rather, "they are double to [man's] *wisdom*" [MICHAELIS]. So the *Hebrew* is rendered (Prov. 2:7). God's ways, which you arraign, if you were shown their secret wisdom, would be seen vastly to exceed that of men, including yours (I Cor. 1:25).

ADAM CLARKE

CHAPTER 11

1. *Zophar the Naamathite.* Of this man and his friends, see chap. ii. 11. He is the most inveterate of Job's accusers, and generally speaks without feeling or pity. In sour godliness he excelled all the rest. This chapter and the twentieth comprehend all that he said. He was too crooked to speak much in measured verse.

2. *Should not the multitude of words be answered?* Some translate, "To multiply words profiteth nothing." *And should a man full of talk be justified?* "A man of lips," a proper appellation for a great talker.

4. *My doctrine is pure.* "My assumptions."

MATTHEW HENRY

2. The unexceptionable justice of his proceedings. "*God exacteth of thee less than thy iniquity deserves*," or (as some read it), "he *remits thee part of thy iniquity*."

Verses 7–12

Zophar here speaks concerning God and his greatness and glory, concerning man and his vanity and folly.

I. God is an incomprehensible Being. We that are so little acquainted with the divine nature are incompetent judges of the divine providence; and, when we censure the dispensations of it, we talk of things that we do not understand. Zophar here shows, that God's nature infinitely exceeds the capacities of our understandings: "*Canst thou find out God, find him out to perfection?*" *v.* 7, 8. We may, by searching find God (Acts xvii. 27); we may apprehend him, but we cannot comprehend him; we may know that he is, but cannot know what he is. This is a good reason why we should always speak of God with humility and caution and never quarrel with him, why we should be thankful for what he has revealed of himself and long to be where we shall see him as he is, 1 Cor. xiii. 9, 10. We cannot fathom God's designs, nor find out the reasons of his proceedings. His judgments are a great deep. Paul attributes such immeasurable dimensions to the divine love as Zophar here attributes to the divine wisdom, and yet recommends it to our acquaintance. Eph. iii. 18, 19, *That you may know the breadth, and length, and depth, and height, of the love of Christ*. God is a sovereign Lord (*v.* 10): *If he cut off* by death (margin, *If he make a change*, for death is a change; if he make a change in nations, in families, in the posture of our affairs), or *if he gather to himself man's spirit, then who can hinder him?* God is a strict and just observer of the children of men (*v.* 11): *He knows vain men.* He takes knowledge of the vanity of men (that is, their little sins; so some) their vain thoughts and vain words, and unsteadiness in that which is good. He observes bad men: *He sees* gross *wickedness also. Will he not then consider it?*

II. See here what man is, and let him be humbled, *v.* 12. God sees vain man that he *would be wise*, would be thought so, *though he is born like a wild ass's colt*, so sottish and foolish, unteachable and untameable. He is a vain creature—*empty*; so the word is. God made him full, but he emptied himself, and now he is *raca*, a creature that has nothing in him. He has become *like the beasts that perish* (Ps. xlix. 20; lxxiii. 22), an idiot, born like an ass, the most stupid animal, an ass's colt, not yet brought to any service. If ever he come to be good for any thing, it is owing to the grace of Christ, who once, in the day of his triumph, served himself by an ass's colt. He is a wilful ungovernable creature. An ass's colt may be made good for something, but the wild ass's colt will never be reclaimed, nor regards the crying of the driver. See Chap. xxxix. 5–7. Yet he is a proud creature and self-conceited. Now is such a creature as this fit to contend with God or call him to an account?

Verses 13–20

Zophar, as the other two, here encourages Job to hope for better times if he would but come to a better temper.

I. He gives him good counsel (*v.* 13, 14), as Eliphaz did (*ch.* v. 8), and Bildad, (*ch.* viii. 5). He must look within, and get his mind changed and the tree made good. He must *prepare his heart*; there the work of conversion and reformation must begin. He must look up, and *stretch out his hands towards God*, that is, must pray to him with earnestness and importunity. To *give the hand to the Lord* signifies to yield ourselves to him and to covenant with him, 2 Chron. xxx. 8. Job had prayed, but Zophar would have him to pray in a better manner, not as an appellant, but as a petitioner and humble suppliant. He must amend what was amiss (*v.* 14): "*If iniquity be in thy hand* (that is, if there be any sin which thou dost yet live in the practice of) *put it far away*." The guilt of sin is not removed if the gain of sin be not restored. He must do his utmost to reform his family too: "*Let not wickedness dwell in thy tabernacles;* let not thy house harbour or shelter any wicked persons, any wicked practices, or any wealth gotten by wickedness."

II. He assures him of comfort if he took this counsel, *v.* 15, &c. "*Then shalt thou lift up thy face towards heaven* without spot; thou mayest come boldly to the throne of grace, and not with that terror and amazement expressed," *ch.* ix. 34. *Thou shalt be steadfast, and shalt not fear*. Job was full of confusion (*ch.* x. 15), while he looked upon God as his enemy and quarrelled with him; but Zophar assures him that, if he would submit and humble himself, his mind

JAMIESON, FAUSSET, BROWN

exacteth—Rather, "God *consigns to oblivion* in thy favor much of thy guilt."

7. Rather, "Penetrate to the perfections of the Almighty" (ch. 9:10; Ps. 139:6). **8. It**—the "wisdom" of God (vs. 6). The abruptness of the *Hebrew* is forcible: "The heights of heaven! What canst thou do" (as to attaining to them with thy gaze, Ps. 139:8)? **know**—viz., of His perfections.

10. cut off—Rather, as in ch. 9:11, "pass over," as a storm; viz., rush upon in anger, **shut up**—in prison, with a view to trial. **gather together**—the parties for judgment: hold a judicial assembly; to pass sentence on the prisoners. **11.** (Ps. 94:11.) **consider**—so as to punish it. Rather, from the connection, vs. 6, "He seeth wickedness also, which man does not *perceive*"; lit., "But no (other, save He) perceiveth it" [UMBREIT]. God's "wisdom" (vs. 6), detects sin where Job's human eye cannot reach (vs. 8), so as to see any.

12. vain—hollow. **would be**—"wants to consider himself wise"; opposed to God's "wisdom" (*Note*, vs. 11); refuses to see sin, where God sees it (Rom. 1:22). **wild ass's colt**—a proverb for untamed wildness (ch. 39:5, 8; Jer. 2:24; Gen. 16:12; *Hebrew*, "a wild-ass man"). Man wishes to appear wisely obedient to his Lord, whereas he is, from his birth, unsubdued in spirit.

13. The apodosis to the "If" is at vs. 15. The preparation of the heart is to be obtained (Prov. 16:1) by stretching out the hands in prayer for it (Ps. 10:17; I Chron. 29:18).

14. Rather, "if thou wilt put far away the iniquity in thine hand" (as Zaccheus did, Luke 19:8). The apodosis or conclusion is at vs. 15, "*then* shalt thou," etc.

15. Zophar refers to Job's own words (ch. 10:15), "yet will I not lift up my head," even though righteous. Zophar declares, if Job will follow his advice, he may "lift up his face." **spot**—(Deut. 32:5). **steadfast**—lit., "run fast together," like metals which become firm and hard by fusion. The sinner on the contrary is wavering.

ADAM CLARKE

F. B. MEYER:

"Canst thou by searching find out God?" Zophar waxes vehement as he censures Job's self-justification and his refusal to acknowledge the guilt which his friends attribute to him. There is some truth in his allegations, though it was cruel to goad Job with them, notwithstanding his repeated protestations.

It is quite true that many of us are filled with self-complacency, because we judge our best by others' worst. It may be also that we have a very poor conception of what God is and asks. It is best for us to strike our breasts with the publican and to confess ourselves the chief of sinners.

What a magnificent challenge is that of verses 7–12! Canst thou reach God's depths, or his perfections, or his heights? But, oh my soul, remember that through all his unsearchable depths God is love. Job had said he could not lift up his face (10:15), but when sin is put away, we may exchange glances with our Father (cf. v. 15).—*Bible Commentary*

10. *If he cut off.* Perhaps Zophar may refer to Job's former state, his losses and afflictions. *If he cut off*, as He has done, your children; *if he . . . shut up*, as He has done, yourself by this sore disease; or *gather together* hostile bands to invade your territories and carry away your property; *who can hinder him?*

11. *He knoweth vain men.* "Men of falsehood."

12. *For vain man would be wise.* The original is difficult and uncertain. *Though man be born like a wild ass's colt.* Man is full of self-conceit; and imagines himself born to act as he pleases, to roam at large, to be under no control, and to be accountable to none for his actions.

MATTHEW HENRY

would be composed. *"Thou shalt forget thy misery;* thou shalt be perfectly freed from the impressions it makes upon thee, and *thou shalt remember it as waters that pass away,* or are poured out of a vessel, which leave no taste or tincture behind them as other liquors do." Job had endeavoured to forget his complaint (*ch.* ix. 27), but found he could not. Zophar here thinks to please Job. Though now his light was eclipsed it should shine out again, and more brightly than ever (*v.* 17). Though now he was in a continual fear and terror, he should live in a holy rest and security, and find himself continually safe and easy (*v.* 18): *Thou shalt be secure, because there is hope. "Thou shalt dig about thee,"* that is, "Thou shalt be as safe as an army in its intrenchments." Those that submit to God's government are safe both day and night. *"Thou shalt dig in safety,* thou and thy servants for thee, and not be again set upon by the plunderers, who fell upon thy servants at plough," *ch.* i. 14, 15. It is no part of the promised prosperity that he should live in idleness, but that he should have a calling and follow it, and, when he was about the business of it, should be under the divine protection. *"Thou shalt lie down* (*v.* 19), not forced to wander where there is no place to lay thy head on, but thou shalt go to bed at bedtime, and not only shall none hurt thee, but none shall make thee afraid nor so much as give thee an alarm." Though now he was slighted, yet he should be courted: *"Many shall make suit to thee,* and think it their interest to secure thy friendship."

III. Zophar concludes with a brief account of the doom of wicked people (*v.* 20): *But the eyes of the wicked shall fail.* He suspected that Job would not take his counsel, and here tells him what would then come of it, setting death as well as life before him. *When a wicked man dies his expectation perishes,* Prov. xi. 7. *Their hope shall be as a puff of breath* (margin), vanished and gone past recall. Those that will not fly to God will find it in vain to think of flying from him.

CHAPTER 12

Verses 1–5

The reproofs Job gives to his friends.

I. He upbraids them with their conceit of themselves, and the good opinion they seemed to have of their own wisdom. 1. He represents them as claiming the monopoly of wisdom, *v.* 2. He speaks ironically: *"No doubt you are the people;* you think yourselves fit to dictate and give law to all mankind, and therefore every top-sail must lower to you, and, right or wrong, we must all say as you say, and you three must be the people, the majority, to have the casting vote. You not only think there are none, but that there will be none, as wise as you, and therefore that *wisdom must die with you,* that all the world must be fools when you are gone, and in the dark when your sun has set." It is folly for us to think that there will be any great irreparable loss of us when we are gone, since God can raise up others, more fit than we are, to do his work. 2. He does himself the justice to put in his claim as a sharer in the gifts of wisdom (*v.* 3). *"But I have understanding* (*a heart*) *as well as you;* nay, *I fall not lower than you;"* as it is in the margin. "I am as well able to judge of the methods and meanings of the divine providence, and to construe the hard chapters of it, as you are." He says not this to magnify himself. *"Yea, who knows not such things as these?* What things you have said that are true are plain truths, which many can talk as excellently of as either you or I." But he says it to humble them, and check the value they had for themselves as doctors of the chair.

II. He complains of the great contempt with which they had treated him (*v.* 4): *I am as one mocked.* We are apt to call reproofs reproaches, and to think ourselves mocked when we are but advised and admonished. Yet there was colour for this charge; they came to comfort him, but they vexed him, and therefore he thought they mocked him. They were his *neighbours,* his friends, his companions (so the word signifies), and they were professors of religion, such as *called upon God,* and said that he *answered them.* Job had a God to go to, with whom he could lodge his appeal. The mockers were themselves rich and at ease, and therefore they despised him who had fallen into poverty. It is the way of the world. Those that prosper are praised, but of those that are going down it is said, "Down with them."

Verses 6–11

Job's friends went upon this principle, that wicked people cannot prosper long in this world; *the eyes of the wicked shall fail, ch.* xi. 20. This principle

JAMIESON, FAUSSET, BROWN

16. Just as when the stream runs dry (ch. 6:17), the danger threatened by its wild waves is forgotten (Isa. 65:16) [UMBREIT].

17. age—days of life. **the noon-day**—viz., of thy former prosperity; which, in the poet's image, had gone on increasing, until it reached its height, as the sun rises higher and higher until it reaches the meridian (Prov. 4:18). **shine forth**—rather, "though now in darkness, thou shalt be as the morning"; or, "thy darkness (if any dark shade should arise on thee, it) shall be as the morning" (only the dullness of morning twilight, not nocturnal darkness) [UMBREIT]. **18.** The experience of thy life will teach thee there is hope for man in every trial. **dig**—viz., wells; the chief necessity in the East. Better, "though now *ashamed* (Rom. 5:5, opposed to the previous 'hope'), thou shalt then rest safely" [GESENIUS]. **19.** (Ps. 4:8; Prov. 3:24; Isa. 14:30); oriental images of prosperity.

19. make suit—lit., stroke thy face, caress thee (Prov. 19:6).

20. A warning to Job, if he would not turn to God. **The wicked**—i.e., obdurate sinners. **eyes . . . fail**—i.e., in vain look for relief (Deut. 28:65). Zophar implies Job's only hope of relief is in a change of heart. **they shall not escape**—lit., "every refuge shall vanish from them." **giving up the ghost**—Their hope shall leave them as the breath does the body (Prov. 11:7).

CHAPTER 12

Vss. 1-25. JOB'S REPLY TO ZOPHAR, chs. 12-14.

2. wisdom shall die with you—Ironical, as if all the wisdom in the world was concentrated in them and would expire when they expired. Wisdom makes "a people": a foolish nation is "not a people" (Rom. 10:19).

3. not inferior—not vanquished in argument and "wisdom" (ch. 13:2). **such things as these**—such commonplace maxims as you so pompously adduce.

4. The unfounded accusations of Job's friends were a "mockery" of him. He alludes to Zophar's word, "mockest" (ch. 11:3). **his neighbour, who calleth . . .**—rather, "I who *call* upon God *that he may answer* me favorably [UMBREIT]. **5.** Rather, "a torch" (lamp) is an object of contempt in the thoughts of him who rests securely (is at ease), though it was prepared for the falterings of the feet [UMBREIT]. (Prov. 25:19.) "Thoughts" and "feet" are in contrast; also rests "securely," and "falterings." The wanderer, arrived at his night-quarters, contemptuously throws aside the torch which had guided his uncertain steps through the darkness. As the torch is to the wanderer, so Job to his friends. Once they gladly used his aid in their need; now they in prosperity mock him in his need.

ADAM CLARKE

17. *Thine age shall be clearer than the noon-day.* The rest of your life shall be unclouded prosperity.

18. *Yea, thou shalt dig.* I believe this neither refers to digging his grave nor to curiously investigating surrounding circumstances, but to the custom of digging for water in the places where they pitched their tents.

CHAPTER 12

2. *No doubt but ye are the people.* Doubtless ye are the wisest men in the world; all wisdom is concentrated in you; and when ye die, there will no more be found on the face of the earth! This is a strong irony.

3. *I am not inferior to you.* I do not fall short of any of you in understanding, wisdom, learning, and experiece. *Who knoweth not such things as these?* All your boasted wisdom consists only in strings of proverbs which are in every person's mouth, and are no proof of wisdom and experience in them that use them.

MATTHEW HENRY

Job here opposes, and maintains that God, in disposing men's outward affairs, acts as a sovereign, reserving the exact distribution of rewards and punishments for the future state.

I. He asserts it as an undoubted truth that wicked people may, and often do, prosper long in this world, *v.* 6. They are *robbers*, and such as provoke God, the worst kind of sinners, blasphemers and persecutors. (Perhaps he refers to the Sabeans and Chaldeans, who had robbed him, and had always lived by spoil and rapine, and yet prospered.) Even *their tabernacles prosper*, those that live with them and those that come after them and descend from them. It seems as if a blessing were entailed upon their families; and that is sometimes preserved to succeeding generations which was got by fraud. We cannot therefore judge of men's piety by their plenty, nor of what they have in their heart by what they have in their hand.

II. He appeals even to the inferior creatures for the proof of this—the beasts, and fowls, and trees, and even the earth itself; consult these, and they shall tell thee, *v.* 7, 8. Even among the brute creatures the greater devour the less and the stronger prey upon the weaker, and men are as the fishes of the sea, Hab. i. 14. If sin had not entered, we may suppose there would have been no such disorder among the creatures, but the wolf and the lamb would have lain down together. Zophar had made a vast mystery of it, *ch.* xi. 7. "So far from that," says Job, "what we are concerned to know we may learn even from the inferior creatures; for *who knows not from all these? v.* 9. Anyone may easily gather from the book of the creatures that *the hand of the Lord has wrought this*." A wise Providence guides and governs all these things by rules. From God's sovereign dominion over the inferior creatures we should learn to acquiesce in all his disposals of the affairs of the children of men.

III. He resolves all into the absolute propriety which God has in all the creatures (*v.* 10): *In whose hand is the soul of every living thing*. All the creatures, and mankind particularly, derive their being from him. All souls are his; and may he not do what he will with his own? The name *Jehovah* is used here (*v.* 9), and it is the only time that we meet with it in all the discourses between Job and his friends; for God was, in that age, more known by the name of *Shaddai—the Almighty*.

IV. Those words—(*v.* 11), *Doth not the ear try words, as the mouth tastes meat?*—may be taken either as the conclusion to the foregoing discourse or the preface to what follows. The mind of man has as good a faculty of discerning between truth and error, when duly stated, as the palate has of discerning between what is sweet and what is bitter. Job seems to appeal to any man's impartial judgment in this controversy.

Verses 12–25

This is a noble discourse of Job's concerning the wisdom, power, and sovereignty of God. It were well if wise and good men, that differ about minor things, would dwell most upon those great things in which they are agreed. On this subject Job speaks like himself. Here are no passionate complaints, no peevish reflections, but everything masculine and great.

I. He asserts the unsearchable wisdom and irresistible power of God. It is allowed that among men there is *wisdom and understanding, v.* 12. But it is to be found only *with the ancient*, who get it by long experience and constant experience; and, when they have got the wisdom, they have lost their strength. But now *with God there are* both *wisdom and strength*, wisdom to design the best and strength to accomplish what is designed. He does not get counsel or understanding, as we do, by observation, but he has it essentially and eternally in himself, *v.* 13. Happy are those who have this God for their God, for they have infinite wisdom and strength engaged for them. Foolish and fruitless are all the attempts of men against him (*v.* 14): *He breaketh down, and it cannot be built again*.

II. He gives an instance, for the proof of this doctrine in nature, *v.* 15. God has the command of *the waters, binds them as in a garment* (Prov. xxx. 4), holds them *in the hollow of his hand* (Isa. xl. 12). 1. Great droughts are sometimes great judgments: *He withholds the waters, and they dry up;* if the heaven be as brass, the earth is as iron. 2. Great wet is sometimes a great judgment. He raises the waters, and *overturns the earth*, the productions of it, the buildings upon it.

III. He gives many instances of it in God's powerful management of the children of men.

1. In general (*v.* 16): *With him are strength and reason* (so some translate it), strength and consistency with himself: it is an elegant word in the original.

JAMIESON, FAUSSET, BROWN

6. Job shows that the matter of *fact* opposes Zophar's *theory* (ch. 11:14, 19, 20) that wickedness causes insecurity in men's "tabernacles." On the contrary, they who rob the "tabernacles" (dwellings) of others "prosper securely" in their own. **Into whose hand . . .** —rather, "who make a god of their own hand," i.e,, who regard their might as their only ruling principle [UMBREIT].

7, 8. Beasts, birds, fishes, and plants, reasons Job, teach that the violent live the most securely (vs. 6). The vulture lives more securely than the dove, the lion than the ox, the shark than the dolphin, the rose than the thorn which tears it. **speak to the earth**—rather, "the *shrubs* of the earth" [UMBREIT].

9. In all these cases, says Job, the agency must be referred to Jehovah, though they may seem to man to imply imperfection (vs. 6; ch. 9:24). This is the only undisputed passage of the poetical part in which the name "Jehovah" occurs; in the historical parts it occurs frequently.

10. The soul, i.e., the animal life. Man, reasons Job, is subjected to the same laws as the lower animals.

11. As the mouth by tasting meats selects what pleases it, so the ear tries the words of others and retains what is convincing. Each chooses according to his taste. The connection with verse 12 is in reference to Bildad's appeal to the "ancients" (ch:8. 8). You are right in appealing to them, since "with them was wisdom," etc. But you select such proverbs of theirs as suit your views; so I may borrow from the same such as suit mine.

12. ancient—aged (ch. 15:10).

13. In contrast to, "with the ancient is wisdom" (vs. 12), Job quotes a saying of the ancients which suits his argument, "with Him (God) is (the true) wisdom" (Prov. 8:14); and by that "wisdom and strength" "He breaketh down," etc., as an absolute Sovereign, not allowing man to penetrate His mysteries; man's part is to bow to His unchangeable decrees (ch. 1: 21). The Mohammedan saying is, "if God will, and how God will." **14. shutteth up**—(Isa. 22:22). Job refers to Zophar's "shut up" (ch. 11:10). **15.** Probably alluding to the flood.

16. (Ezek. 14:9).

ADAM CLARKE

CHARLES H. SPURGEON:

These verses occur in Job's answer to Zophar the Naamathite. Job had his failings, but certainly he appears less faulty in this dialogue than those three men who sought to reprove him and convict him of error. Zophar the Naamathite had the very highest opinion of his own personal wisdom. He addressed Job as though he had been an inferior and in the eleventh chapter he used language which though extremely beautiful, must have been very grating upon the ear of such a sufferer as Job; for it is a lecture full of high-flown language, abounding in poetry and noble images, but containing little solid sense and less sympathy. Job being exceedingly irritated both with the style and with the matter of Zophar's speech begins at once to pluck off his plumes and to pull to pieces his fine language. In biting irony Job cries from his dunghill: "No doubt but ye are the people, and wisdom shall die with you. But I have understanding as well as you; I am not inferior to you; yea, who knoweth not such things as these?" You have put into flowery language things which an ordinary observer might discover. You have pointed to the heaven above, and to the depth beneath, to prove a truth which the creeping insect of the earth could tell you, and which the fishes of the sea might proclaim. "Ask now the beasts, and they shall teach thee; and the fowls of the air, and they shall tell thee: or speak to the earth, and it shall teach thee: and the fishes of the sea shall declare unto thee. Who knoweth not in all these that the hand of the Lord hath wrought this?"

There is much temper here, but there is very much also of good common sense. I would we had another Job to chastise the high-sounding language of modern theologians. There are starting up in our midst men who if they are not heretics in doctrine are aliens in speech. They are men described by the old preachers who say, "Mark!" and there is nothing to mark, and who shout, "Observe!" and there is nothing to observe, except the want of everything that is worth observing. I pray God the time may come when some man may unmask them, when all these wind-bags may be rent, when if teachers have anything to tell us they will deliver themselves so that all can understand. If they cannot use plain language let their tongues go to school till they have learned it. A man with an education that may be complete in every department except that in which he should excel, stands up and would teach Christians that all they have learned at the feet of Paul has been a mistake; that a new theology has been discovered. Well, what shall we do to this wiseacre and his fellow sages? Serve them, wherever you meet them or their disciples, as Job did Zophar: laugh at them, dash their language to pieces, and remind them that the best thing they tell us are only what the fishes of the sea, or the fowls of the air, knew before them.

—*The Treasury of the Old Testament*

16. *With him is strength and wisdom.* "Strength and sufficiency." Strength or power, springing from an exhaustless and infinite source of potency.

MATTHEW HENRY

With him are the very quintessence and extract of wisdom. *With him are power and all that is;* so some read it. *He* is what he is of himself, and by him and in him all things subsist. Having this strength and wisdom, he knows how to make use, not only of those who are wise and good, but even of those who are foolish and bad, who, one would think, could be made no way serviceable to the designs of his providence: *The deceived and the deceiver are his;* the simplest men that are deceived are not below his notice; the subtlest men that deceive cannot with all their subtlety escape his cognizance.

2. He next descends to the particular instances of the wisdom and power of God in the revolutions of states and kingdoms. Some think that Job here refers to the extirpation of those powerful nations, the Rephaim, the Zuzim, the Emim, and the Horites (mentioned Gen. xiv. 5, 6; Deut. ii. 10, 20), in which perhaps it was particularly noticed how strangely they were infatuated and enfeebled: if so, it is designed to show it is God that does it, and we must therein observe his sovereign dominion, even over those that think themselves most powerful, politic, and absolute. Compare this with that of Eliphaz, *ch.* v. 12, &c. Those that were wise are sometimes strangely infatuated, and in this the hand of God must be acknowledged (*v.* 17): *He leadeth counsellors away spoiled.* His counsel stands, while all their devices are brought to nought. *He maketh the judges fools.* By a work on their minds he deprives them of their qualifications for business, and so they become really fools. Let not the wise man therefore glory in his wisdom, nor the ablest counsellors and judges be proud of their station, but humbly depend upon God for the continuance of their abilities. Even the aged, who seem to hold their wisdom, by prescription, may yet be deprived of it by the infirmities of age, which make them twice children: He *taketh away the understanding of the aged, v.* 20. Those that were high and in authority are strangely brought down, impoverished, and enslaved, and it is God that humbles them (*v.* 18): *He looseth the bond of kings,* and taketh from them the power wherewith they ruled their subjects, unbuckles their belts, so that the sword drops from their side, and then no marvel if the crown quickly drops from their head, on which immediately follows the *girding of their loins with a girdle,* a badge of servitude. Those that were strong are strangely weakened, and it is God that weakens them (*v.* 21) and *overthrows the mighty, v.* 19. Those that were famed for eloquence, and entrusted with public business, are strangely silenced, and have nothing to say (*v.* 20): *He removeth away the speech of the trusty,* so that they cannot speak as they intended and as they used to do, with freedom and clearness, but blunder, and falter, and make nothing of it. Those that were honoured and admired strangely fall into disgrace (*v.* 21): He *poureth contempt upon princes.* That which was secret, and lay hidden, is strangely brought to light and laid open (*v.* 22): *He discovers deep things out of darkness.* Plots closely laid are discovered and defeated; wickedness closely committed and artfully concealed is discovered. Kingdoms have their ebbings and flowings, their waxings and wanings; and both are from God (*v.* 23). *He taketh away the heart of the chief of the people,* their leaders most famed for their martial fire. They are heartless, and ready to flee at the shaking of a leaf. Those that were driving on their projects with full speed are strangely bewildered and at a loss, wandering like men in a desert (*v.* 24), groping like men in the dark, and staggering like men in drink, *v.* 25. Heaven and earth are shaken, but the Lord sits King for ever, and with him we look for *a kingdom that cannot be shaken.*

JAMIESON, FAUSSET, BROWN

JOSEPH PARKER:

In the latter part of the twelfth chapter Job shows that he has a fuller and grander conception of God than any of his three comforters have. He is not behind them in the instinct or in the enjoyment of divine worship. When he speaks of God he lifts up our thought to a new and sublime level: "With him is wisdom and strength, he hath counsel and understanding" (12:13). Regarded metaphysically or spiritually, God is the great mystery of all things; he covers all the range appropriate to counsel, wisdom, and understanding: he is spiritually incomprehensible. Then actively—"Behold, he breaketh down, and it cannot be built again: he shutteth up a man, and there can be no opening. Behold, he withholdeth the waters, and they dry up: also he sendeth them out, and they overturn the earth" (12:14, 15).

What can man do? He cannot bring a single rain cloud into the dry sky with promise of refreshment and fertility for the barren and languishing earth; he cannot make the sun rise one moment sooner than he is appointed by law astronomical to rise. Poor man! He can but stand in presence of natural phenomena with notebook in hand, putting down what he calls memoranda, looking these very carefully and critically over, and turning them into classical utterances which the vulgar cannot understand. But he is kept outside; he is not allowed to go to the other side of the door on which is marked the word Private. And as for God's actions among the great and mighty of the earth, they are as grasshoppers before him: "He leadeth counsellers away spoiled, and maketh the judges fools. He looseth the bonds of kings, and girdeth their loins with a girdle" (12:17, 18).
—*The People's Bible*

18. He looseth the authority of kings—the "bond" with which they bind their subjects (Isa. 45:1; Gen. 14:4; Dan. 2:21). **a girdle**—the *cord,* with which they are bound as captives, instead of the royal "girdle" they once wore (Isa. 22:21), and the bond they once bound others with. So "gird"—put on one the bonds of a prisoner instead of the ordinary girdle (John 21:18). **19. princes**—rather, "priests," as the *Hebrew* is rendered (Ps. 99:6). Even the sacred ministers of religion are not exempt from reverses and captivity. **the mighty**—rather, "the firm-rooted in power"; the *Arabic* root expresses ever-flowing *water* [UMBREIT]. **20. the trusty**—rather, "those secure in their eloquence"; e.g., the speakers in the gate (Isa. 3:3) [BEZA]. **understanding**—lit., "taste," i.e., insight or spiritual discernment, which experience gives the aged. The same *Hebrew* word is applied to Daniel's wisdom in interpretation (Dan. 2:14). **21.** Psalm 107:40 quotes, in its first clause, this verse and, in its second, the 24th verse of the chapter. **weakeneth the strength**—lit., "looseth the girdle"; Orientals wear flowing garments; when active strength is to be put forth, they gird up their garments with a girdle. Hence here—"He destroyeth their power" in the eyes of the people. **22.** (Dan. 2:22.) **23.** Isaiah 9:3; Psalm 107:38, 39, which Psalm quotes this chapter elsewhere. (See *Note,* vs. 21.) **straiteneth**—lit., "leadeth in," i.e., reduces.

24. heart—intelligence. **wander in a wilderness**—figurative; not referring to any actual fact. This cannot be quoted to prove Job lived after Israel's wanderings in the desert. Psalm 107:4, 40 quotes this passage. **25.** Deuteronomy 28: 29; Psalm 107: 27 again quote Job, but in a different connection.

ADAM CLARKE

25. *They grope in the dark.* The writer seems to have had his eye on those words of Moses, Deut. xxviii. 28-29: "The Lord shall smite thee with madness, and blindness, and astonishment of heart: and thou shalt grope at noonday, as the blind gropeth in darkness."

MATTHEW HENRY

CHAPTER 13

Verses 1–12

Job warmly expresses his resentment of the unkindness of his friends.

I. He comes up with them as one that did not need to be taught by them, *v.* 1, 2. They compelled him, as the Corinthians did Paul, to commend himself and his own knowledge, yet not in a way of self-applause, but of self-justification. Happy are those who not only see and hear, but understand, the greatness, glory, and sovereignty of God. This, he thought, would justify what he had said before (*ch.* xii. 3), which he repeats here (*v.* 2): "*What you know, the same do I know also,* so that I need not come to you to be taught; *I am not inferior unto you* in wisdom."

II. He turns from them to God (*v.* 3): *Surely I would speak to the Almighty.* Job would rather argue with God himself than with his friends.

III. He condemns them for their unjust and un-

JAMIESON, FAUSSET, BROWN

CHAPTER 13

Vss. 1-28. JOB'S REPLY TO ZOPHAR CONTINUED. **1. all this**—as to the dealings of Providence (ch. 12: 3).

3. Job wishes to plead his cause before God (ch. 9:34, 35), as he is more and more convinced of the valueless character of his would-be "physicians" (ch. 16:2).

ADAM CLARKE

CHAPTER 13

3. *Surely I would speak to the Almighty.* "Oh, that—I wish I could speak to the Almighty!" *I desire to reason with God.* He speaks here in reference to the proceedings in a court of justice.

MATTHEW HENRY

charitable treatment of him, *v.* 4. They falsely accused him, and that was unjust: *You are forgers of lies.* They framed a wrong hypothesis concerning the divine Providence, as if it did never remarkably afflict any but wicked men in this world, and thence they drew a false judgment concerning Job, that he was certainly a hypocrite. They undertook his cure, and pretended to be his physicians; but they were all *physicians of no value*, "idol-physicians, who can do me no more good than an idol can."

IV. He begs they would be silent and give him a patient hearing, *v.* 5, 6. "*Hold your peace, and it shall be your wisdom*, for thereby you will conceal your ignorance and ill-nature." *Hear now my reasoning.* Perhaps, though they did not interrupt him in his discourse, yet they seemed careless, and did not much heed what he said. He therefore begged that they would not only hear, but hearken.

V. He endeavours to convince them of the wrong they did to God's honour, while they pretended to plead for him, *v.* 7, 8. God and his cause did not need such advocates: "*Will you* think to *contend for God*, as if his justice were clouded and wanted to be cleared up, or as if he were at a loss what to say and wanted you to speak for him? If you were for ever silent, the heavens would declare his righteousness." Under pretence of justifying God in afflicting Job they magisterially condemned him as a hypocrite and a bad man. "This" (says he) "is *speaking wickedly*" (for uncharitableness and censoriousness are wickedness, great wickedness). God's truth needs not our lie, nor God's cause either our sinful policies or our sinful passions.

VI. He endeavours to possess them with a fear of God's judgment, and so to bring them to a better temper. Let them consider whether they could give him a good account of what they did (*v.* 9): "*Is it good that he should search you out?*" It is good to an upright man who means honestly that God should search him. But it is bad to him who looks one way and rows another that God should search him out. The severity of his rebukes and displeasure against them (*v.* 10): "*If you do accept persons*, though but secretly and in heart, *he will surely reprove you.* You that have great knowledge of God, and profess a fear of him, how dare you talk at this rate and give yourselves so great a liberty of speech?" There is in God a dreadful excellency. His excellencies in themselves are amiable, but considering man's distance from God by nature, and his defection and degeneracy by sin, his excellencies are dreadful. Let them consider themselves, and what an unequal match they were for this great God (*v.* 12): "*Your remembrances* (all that in you for which you hope to be remembered when you are gone) *are like unto ashes*, worthless and weak, and easily trampled on and blown away. *Your bodies are like bodies of clay.* Your remonstrances on God's behalf are no better than dust, and the arguments you accumulate but like so many heaps of dirt."

Verses 13–22

Job here takes fresh hold, fast hold, of his integrity, as one that was resolved not to let it go, nor suffer it to be wrested from him.

I. He entreats his friends and all the company to let him alone, and not interrupt him in what he was about to say (*v.* 13), but diligently to hearken to it, *v.* 17. He would have his own protestation to be decisive, for none but God and himself knew his heart. "Be silent therefore, and let me hear no more of you, but hearken diligently to what I say, and let my own oath for confirmation be an end of the strife."

II. He resolves to adhere to the testimony his own conscience gave of his integrity: "I will speak in my own defence, and *let come on me what will*, *v.* 13. I hope God will not make my necessary defence to be my offence, as you do. He will justify me (*v.* 18) and then nothing can come amiss to me." He resolves (*v.* 15) that he will *maintain his own ways.* "*If I hold my tongue*, and do not speak for myself, my silence now will for ever silence me, for *I shall* certainly *give up the ghost*," *v.* 19.

III. He complains of the extremity of pain and misery he was in (*v.* 14): *Wherefore do I take my flesh in my teeth?* That is, "Why do I suffer such agonies? I cannot but wonder that God should lay so much upon me when he knows I am not a wicked man." It would vex the most patient man, when he had lost everything else, to be denied the comfort (if he deserves it) of a good conscience and a good name.

IV. He still depends upon God for—justification and salvation, the two great things we hope for through Christ (*v.* 18): *I have ordered my cause, and*, upon the whole matter, *I know that I shall be justified.* Those whose hearts are upright with God, in walking

JAMIESON, FAUSSET, BROWN

4. forgers of lies—lit., "artful twisters of vain speeches" [UMBREIT].

5. (Prov. 17:28). The Arabs say, "The wise are dumb; silence is wisdom."

7. deceitfully—use fallacies to vindicate God in His dealings; as if the end justified the means. Their "deceitfulness" for God, against Job, was that they asserted he was a sinner, because he was a sufferer. **8. accept his person**—God's; i.e., be partial for Him, as when a judge favors one party in a trial, because of personal considerations. **contend for God**—viz., with fallacies and prepossessions against Job before judgment (Judg. 6:31). Partiality can never please the impartial God, nor the goodness of the cause excuse the unfairness of the arguments.

9. Will the issue to you be good, when He searches out you and your arguments? Will you be regarded by Him as pure and disinterested? **mock**—(Gal. 6:7.) Rather, "Can you deceive Him as one man?" etc. **10. If** ye do, though secretly, act partially. (*Note*, vs. 8; Ps. 82:1, 2.) God can successfully vindicate His acts, and needs no fallacious argument of man.

11. make you afraid?—viz., of employing sophisms in His name (Jer. 10:7, 10). **12. remembrances**—"proverbial maxims," so called because well remembered. **like unto ashes**—or, "parables of ashes"; the image of lightness and nothingness (Isa. 44:20). **bodies**—rather, "entrenchments"; those of clay, as opposed to those of stone, are easy to be destroyed; so the proverbs, behind which they entrench themselves, will not shelter them when God shall appear to reprove them for their injustice to Job.

13. Job would wish to be spared their speeches, so as to speak out all his mind as to his wretchedness (vs. 14), happen what will.

19. if . . .—Rather, *Then* would I hold my tongue and give up the ghost; i.e., if any one can contend with me and prove me false, I have no more to say. "I will be silent and die." Like our "I would stake my life on it" [UMBREIT].

14. A proverb for, "Why should I anxiously desire to save my life?" [EICHORN]. The image in the first clause is that of a wild beast, which in order to preserve his prey, carries it in his teeth. That in the second refers to men who hold in the hand what they want to keep secure.

18. ordered—implying a constant preparation for defense in his confidence of innocence.

ADAM CLARKE

Ye pretend to be advocates for God, but ye are forgers of lies. Oh, that God himself would appear! Before Him I could soon prove my innocence of the evils with which ye charge me.

4. *Ye are forgers of lies.* Ye frame deceitful arguments; ye reason sophistically, and pervert truth and justice, in order to support your cause.

6. *Hear now my reasoning.* The speeches in this book are conceived as if delivered in a court of justice, different counsellors pleading against each other. Hence most of the terms are forensic.

12. *Your remembrances are like unto ashes.* Your memorable sayings are proverbs of dust.

14. *Wherefore do I take my flesh in my teeth?* A proverbial expression. I risk everything on the justice of my cause. "I put my life in my hand," 1 Sam. xxviii. 21.

MATTHEW HENRY

not after the flesh but after the Spirit, may be sure that through Christ there shall be no condemnation to them, but that, whoever lays anything to their charge, they shall be justified (*v.* 16): *He also shall be my salvation.* He means it not of temporal salvation (he had little expectation of that); but concerning his eternal salvation he was very confident. He knew himself not to be a hypocrite, and therefore concluded he should not be rejected. Sincerity is our evangelical perfection; nothing will ruin us but the want of that. *Though he slay me, yet will I trust in him, v.* 15. This is a high expression of faith. We must rejoice in God when we have nothing else to rejoice in, and cleave to him, yea, though we cannot for the present find comfort in him.

V. He wishes to argue the case even with God himself, if he might but have leave to settle the preliminaries of the treaty, *v.* 20–22. "*Withdraw thy hand far from me;* for, while I am in this extremity, I am fit for nothing." "*Let not thy dread make me afraid*"; "Lord," says Job, "let me not be put into such a consternation of spirit, together with this bodily affliction; for then I must certainly drop the cause, and shall make nothing of it." How can even a good man, much less a bad man, reason with God, so as to be justified before him, when he is upon the rack of pain.

Verses 23–28

I. Job enquires after his sins, and begs to have them discovered to him. *Make me to know my transgressions, v.* 23. His friends were ready enough to tell him how numerous and how heinous they were, *ch.* xxii. 5. "But Lord," says he, "let me know them from thee; *for thy judgment is according to truth,* theirs is not." *That which I see not, teach thou me.* A true penitent is willing to know the worst of himself; and we should all desire to know what our transgressions are, that we may be particular in the confession of them and on our guard against them for the future.

II. He bitterly complains of God's withdrawings from him (*v.* 24): *Wherefore hidest thou thy face?* This must be meant of something more than his outward afflictions; *his soul was also sorely vexed.* God hid his face as one strange to him, displeased with him. Note, The Holy Ghost sometimes denies his favours to the best and dearest of his saints and servants in this world. Evidences for heaven are eclipsed, communications interrupted, and the returns of comfort, for the present, despaired of, Ps. lxxvii. 7–9; lxxxviii. 7, 15, 16. These are grievous burdens to a gracious soul, that values God's loving-kindness as better than life, Prov. xviii. 14. *A wounded spirit who can bear?* Job, by asking here, *Why hidest thou thy face?* teaches us that, when at any time we are under the sense of God's withdrawings, we are to enquire into the reason of them—what is the sin for which he corrects us and what the good he designs us. Job's sufferings were typical of the sufferings of Christ, from whom not only men hid their faces (Isa. liii. 3), but God hid his, witness the darkness which surrounded him on the cross when he cried out, *My God, my God, why hast thou forsaken me?*

III. He humbly pleads with God his own utter inability to stand before him (*v.* 25): "*Wilt thou break a leaf, pursue the dry stubble?*" We ought to have such an apprehension of the goodness and compassion of God as to believe that he will not *break the bruised reed,* Matt. xii. 20.

IV. He sadly complains of God's severe dealings with him. He owns it was for his sins that God thus contended with him, but thinks it hard (*v.* 26): *Thou writest bitter things against me.* Afflictions are bitter things. "Herein *thou makest me to possess the iniquities of my youth,*" that is, "thou punishest me for them, and thereby puttest me in mind of them, and obligest me to renew my repentance for them." Time does not wear out the guilt of sin. God writes bitter things against us to bring forgotten sins to mind, and so to bring us to remorse for them as to break us off from them. "*Thou puttest my feet also in the stocks* to correct me for every false step. Thou *settest a print upon the heels of my feet* no sooner have I trodden wrong, though ever so little, than immediately I smart for it; the punishment treads upon the very heels of the sin." Now, (1) It was not true that God did thus seek advantages against him. But he is so far from this that he deals not with us according to the desert. This therefore was the language of Job's melancholy; his sober thoughts never represented God thus as a hard Master. (2) But we should keep such a strict and jealous eye as this upon ourselves and our own steps, both for the discovery of sin past and the prevention of it for the future.

JAMIESON, FAUSSET, BROWN

15. in him—So the *margin* or *keri* reads. But the textual reading or *chetib* is "not," which agrees best with the context, and other passages wherein he says he has no hope (ch. 6:11; 7:21; 10:20; 19:10). "Though He slay me, and I dare no more hope, yet I will maintain," etc., i.e., **"I desire to vindicate myself before Him,"** as not a hypocrite [UMBREIT and NOYES]. **16. He**—rather, "*This* also already speaks in my behalf (lit., "for my saving acquittal"), for an hypocrite would not wish to come before Him" (as I do) [UMBREIT]. (See last clause of vs. 15.) **17. my declaration**—viz., that I wish to be permitted to justify myself immediately before God. **with your ears**—i.e., attentively.

20. Address to God. **not hide**—stand forth boldly to maintain my cause. **21.** (*Note,* 9:34; Ps. 39:10.) **22. call**—a challenge to the defendant to answer to the charges. **answer**—the defense begun. **speak**—as plaintiff. **answer**—to the plea of the plaintiff. Expressions from a trial.

23. The catalogue of my sins ought to be great, to judge from the severity with which God ever anew crushes one already bowed down. Would that He would reckon them up! He then would see how much my calamities outnumber them. **sin?**—singular, "I am unconscious of a *single* particular sin, much less many" [UMBREIT].

hidest . . . face—a figure from the gloomy impression caused by the sudden clouding over of the sun. **enemy**—God treated Job as an enemy who must be robbed of power by ceaseless sufferings (ch. 7:17, 21).

25. (Lev. 26:36; Ps. 1:4.) Job compares himself to a leaf already fallen, which the storm still chases hither and thither. **break**—lit., "shake with (Thy) terrors." Jesus Christ does not "break the bruised reed" (Isa. 42:3, 27:8).

26. writest—a judicial phrase, to note down the determined punishment. The sentence of the condemned used to be *wrtten down* (Isa. 10:1; Jer. 22:30; Ps. 149:9) [UMBREIT]. **bitter things**—bitter punishments. **makest me to posses**—or "inherit." In old age he receives possession of the inheritance of sin thoughtlessly acquired in youth. "To inherit *sins*" is to inherit the *punishments* inseparably connected with them in *Hebrew* ideas (Ps. 25:7). **27. stocks**—in which the prisoner's feet were made fast until the time of execution (Jer. 20:2). **lookest narrowly**—as an overseer would watch a prisoner. **print**—Either the stocks, or his disease, *marked* his *soles* (*Hebrew,*"roots") as the bastinado would. Better, thou drawest (or diggest) [GESENIUS] a line (or trench) [GESENIUS] round my soles, beyond which I must not move [UMBREIT].

ADAM CLARKE

15. *Though he slay me.* I have no dependence but God; I trust in Him alone. Should He even destroy my life by this affliction, yet will I hope that when He has tried me, I shall come forth as gold. In the common printed Hebrew text we have *lo ayachel,* "I will not hope"; but the Vulgate, Syriac, Arabic, and Chaldee have read "him," instead of "not." Our translators have followed the best reading.

22. *Then call thou.* Begin thou first to plead, and I will answer for myself; or I will first state and defend my own case, and then answer *thou* me.

23. *How many are mine iniquities?* What are the specific charges in this indictment? To say I must be a sinner to be thus afflicted is saying nothing; tell me what are the sins, and show me the proofs.

24. *Wherefore hidest thou thy face?* Why is it that I no longer enjoy thy approbation? *Holdest me for thine enemy?* treatest me as if I were the vilest of sinners?

27. *Thou puttest my feet also in the stocks.* "In a clog," such as was tied to the feet of slaves, to prevent them from running away.

MATTHEW HENRY

V. He finds himself wasting away apace under the heavy hand of God, *v.* 28. *He* (that is, man) *as a rotten thing*, the principle of whose putrefaction is in itself, *consumes even like a moth-eaten garment*, which becomes continually worse and worse. While there is so little soundness in the soul, no marvel there is so little soundness in the flesh, Ps. xxxviii. 3.

CHAPTER 14

Verses 1–6

We are here led to think,

I. Of the original of human life. God is indeed its great original, for he *breathed into man the breath of life* and in him we live; but we date it from our birth, and thence we must date both its frailty and its pollution. 1. Its frailty: *Man, that is born of a woman, is* therefore *of few days*, *v.* 1. This may refer to the first woman, who was called *Eve*, or it may refer to every man's immediate mother. 2. Its pollution (*v.* 4): *Who can bring a clean thing out of an unclean?* Our blood is not only attainted by a legal conviction, but tainted with an hereditary disease. Our Lord Jesus, being made sin for us, is said to be *made of a woman*, Gal. iv.,4.

II. Of the nature of human life: it is *a flower*, it is a *shadow*, *v.* 2. The flower is fading, and all its beauty soon withers and is gone. The shadow is fleeting, and its very being will soon be lost and drowned in the shadows of the night.

III. Of the shortness and uncertainty of human life: Man is *of few days*. Life is here computed, not by months or years, but by days, for we cannot be sure of any day. Man sometimes no sooner comes forth than he *is cut down*—comes forth into the world and enters into the business of it than he is hurried away as soon as he has laid his hand to the plough. If not cut down immediately, yet *he flees as a shadow*, and never continues in one stay.

IV. Of the calamitous state of human life. Man, as he is short-lived, so he is sad-lived. During these few days he is *full of trouble*, not only troubled, but full of trouble, either toiling or fretting, grieving or fearing. When we come to heaven our days will be many, and perfectly free from trouble, and in the mean time faith, hope, and love, balance the present grievances.

V. Of the sinfulness of human life, arising from the sinfulness of the human nature. So some understand that question (*v.* 4), *Who can bring a clean thing out of an unclean?* He intends it as a plea with God for compassion: "Lord, be not extreme to mark my sins of human frailty and infirmity, for thou knowest my weakness. *O remember that I am flesh!*" The Chaldee paraphrase has an observable reading of this verse: *Who can make a man clean that is polluted with sin? Cannot one? that is, God.*

VI. Of the settled period of human life, *v.* 5. Nothing comes to pass by chance, so, not the execution done by a bow drawn at a venture. We are no more governed by the Stoic's blind fate than by the Epicurean's blind fortune. The consideration of our own inability to contend with God, of our own sinfulness and weakness, should engage us to pray, *Lord, enter not into judgment with thy servant.* Thus may we find some relief under great troubles by recommending ourselves to the compassion of that God who knows our frame and will consider it, and our being out of frame too.

Verses 7–15

Job here shows,

I. That death is a removal for ever out of this world. A man cut down by death will not revive again, as a tree cut down will. What hope there is of a tree he shows very elegantly, *v.* 7–9. If the body of the tree be cut down, and only the stem or stump left in the ground, though it seem dead and dry, yet it will shoot out young boughs again, as if it were but newly planted. But man has no such prospect of a return to life. The vegetable life is a cheap and easy thing: the scent of water will recover it. The animal life, in some insects and fowls, is so: the heat of the sun retrieves it. But the rational soul, when once retired, is too great, too noble, a thing to be recalled by any of the powers of nature; it is out of the reach of sun or rain, and cannot be restored but by the immediate operations of Omnipotence itself; for (*v.* 10) *man dieth and wasteth away, yea, man giveth up the ghost, and where is he?* Two words are here used for man:—*Geber, a mighty man*, though mighty, dies; *Adam, a man of the earth*, because earthy, gives up the ghost. After death: *Where is he?* He is not where he was; his place knows him no more; but *is he nowhere?* So some read it. Yes, he is some-

JAMIESON, FAUSSET, BROWN

28. Job speaks of himself in the third person, thus forming the transition to the *general* lot of man (ch. 14:1; Ps. 39:11; Hos. 5:12).

CHAPTER 14

Vss. 1-22. Job Passes from His Own to the Common Misery of Mankind.

1. woman—feeble, and in the East looked down upon (Gen. 2:21). Man being born of one so frail must be frail himself (Matt. 11:11). **few days**—(Gen. 47:9; Ps. 90:10). Lit., "short of days." Man is the reverse of full of days and short of trouble. **2.** (Ps. 90:6; *Note,* ch. 8:9.)

3. open . . . eyes upon—Not in graciousness; but, "Dost Thou sharply fix Thine eyes upon?" (*Note,* 7:20; also 1:7). Is one so frail as man worthy of such constant watching on the part of God? Zech. 12:4). **me**—so frail. **thee**—so almighty.

4. A plea in mitigation. The doctrine of original sin was held from the first. "Man is unclean from his birth, how then can God expect perfect cleanness from such a one and deal so severely with me?"

5. determined—(ch. 7:1; Isa. 10:23; Dan. 9:27; 11:36). **6. Turn**—viz., Thine eyes from watching him so jealously (vs. 3). **hireling**—(ch. 7:1). **accomplish**—rather, "enjoy." That he may at least enjoy the measure of rest of the hireling who though hard worked reconciles himself to his lot by the hope of his rest and reward [Umbreit].

7. Man may the more claim a peaceful life, since, when separated from it by death, he never returns to it. This does not deny a future life, but a return to the *present condition* of life. Job plainly hopes for a future state (vs. 13; ch. 7:2). Still, it is but vague and trembling *hope,* not *assurance;* excepting the one bright glimpse in ch. 19:25. The Gospel revelation was needed to change fears, hopes, and glimpses into clear and definite certainties. **9. scent**—exhalation, which, rather than the humidity of water, causes the tree to germinate. In the antithesis to *man* the *tree* is personified, and volition is poetically ascribed to it. **like a plant**—"as if newly planted" [Umbreit]; not as if trees and plants were a different species. **10. man . . . man**—Two distinct *Hebrew* words are here used; *Geber,* a *mighty* man: though mighty, he dies. *Adam,* a man of earth: because earthly, he gives up the ghost. **wasteth**—is reduced to nothing: he cannot revive in the present state, as the tree does. The cypress and pine, which when cut down do not revive, were the symbols of death among the Romans. **11. sea**—i.e., a lake, or pool formed from the outspreading of a river. Job lived near the Euphrates: and "sea" is applied to it (Jer. 51:36; Isa. 27:1). So of the Nile (Isa. 19:5). **fail**—utterly disappeared by drying up. The rugged channel of the once flowing water answers to the outstretched corpse ("lieth down," vs. 12) of the once living man.

ADAM CLARKE

CHAPTER 14

1. *Man . . . born of a woman.* There is a delicacy in the original not often observed: *Adam yelud ishah.* "Adam born of a woman, few of days, and full of tremor."

3. *Dost thou open thine eyes upon such an one?* The whole of this chapter is directed to God alone; in no part of it does he take any notice of his friends.

4. *Who can bring a clean thing?* The text refers to man's original and corrupt nature.

5. *Seeing his days are determined.* The general term of human life is fixed by God himself; in vain are all attempts to prolong it beyond this term. Several attempts have been made in all nations to find an elixir that would expel all the seeds of disease and keep men in continual health, but all these attempts have failed.

MATTHEW HENRY

where; and it is a very awful consideration to think where those are that have given up the ghost, and where we shall be when we give it up. It has gone to the world of spirits, gone into eternity, gone to return no more to this world.

II. That yet there will be a return of man to life again in another world, at the end of time, when *the heavens* are *no more*. Then *they shall awake and be raised out of their sleep*. The resurrection of the dead was doubtless an article of Job's creed, as appears, *ch.* xix. 26.

1. A humble petition for a hiding-place in the grave, *v.* 13. It was not only in a passionate weariness of this life that he wished to die, but in a pious assurance of a better life, to which at length he should arise.

2. A holy resolution patiently to attend the will of God both in his death, and in his resurrection (*v.* 14): *If a man die, shall he live again? All the days of my appointed time will I wait until my change come.* Job's friends proving miserable comforters, he set himself to be the more his own comforter. His case was now bad, but he pleases himself with the expectation of a change.

3. A joyful expectation of bliss and satisfaction in this (*v.* 15): Then *thou shalt call, and I will answer thee.* Now, he was under such a cloud that he could not, he durst not, answer (*ch.* ix. 15, 35; xiii. 22); but he comforted himself with this, that there would come a time when God would call and he should answer. "Thou *wilt have a desire to the work of thy hands.* Thou hast mercy in store for me, not only as made by thy providence, but new-made by thy grace; otherwise *he that made them will not save them.*" Grace in the soul is the work of God's own hands, and therefore he will not forsake it in this world (Ps. cxxxviii. 8), but will have a desire to it, to perfect it in the other, and to crown it with endless glory.

Verses 16—22

Job returns to his complaints; and, though he is not without hope of future bliss, he finds it very hard to get over his present grievances.

I. He complains of the particular hardships he apprehended himself under from the strictness of God's justice, *v.* 16, 17. *Therefore* he longed to go hence to that world where God's wrath will be past, because now he was under the continual tokens of it, as a child, under the severe discipline of the rod, longs to be of age. "When shall my change come? *For now thou* seemest to me to *number my steps*, and *watch over my sin*, and *seal it up in a bag*, as bills of indictment are kept safely, to be produced against the prisoner." See Deut. xxxii. 34. 1. Job does right to the divine justice in owning that he smarted for his sins and transgressions, that he had done enough to deserve all that was laid upon him. But, 2. He does wrong to the divine goodness in suggesting that God was extreme to mark what he did amiss, and made the worst of everything. He spoke to this purport, *ch.* xiii. 27, but we are punished less than our iniquities deserve. God does indeed seal and sew up, against the day of wrath, the transgression of the impenitent, but the sins of his people he blots out as a cloud.

II. He complains of the wasting condition of mankind in general. We live in a dying world.

1. We see the decays of the earth itself. (1) Of the strongest parts of it, *v.* 18. Nothing will last always, for we see even mountains moulder and come to nought; they wither and fall as a leaf; rocks wax old and pass away by the continual beating of the sea against them. *The waters wear the stones* with constant dropping, *non vi, sed sæpe cadendo—not by the violence, but by the constancy with which they fall.* On this earth everything is the worse for the wearing. *Tempus edax rerum—Time devours all things.* (2) Of the natural products of it. The things which grow out of the earth, and seem to be firmly rooted in it, are sometimes by an excess of rain washed away, *v.* 19.

2. No marvel then if we see the decays of man upon the earth, for he is of the earth, earthy. Job begins to think his case is not singular, and therefore he ought to reconcile himself to the common lot. How vain it is to expect much from the enjoyments of life: "*Thou destroyest the hope of man*," that is, "puttest an end to all the projects he had framed and all the prospects of satisfaction he had flattered himself with." Death will be the destruction of all those hopes which are built upon worldly confidences and confined to worldly comforts. Hope in Christ, and hope in heaven, death will consummate and not destroy. The consideration of this should moderate our cares concerning our children and families. God will know what comes of them when we are gone. To him therefore let us commit them, with him let

JAMIESON, FAUSSET, BROWN

12. heavens be no more—This only implies that Job had no hope of living again in the *present* order of the world, not that he had no hope of life again in a new order of things. Psalm 102:26 proves that early under the Old Testament the dissolution of the present earth and heavens was expected (cf. Gen. 8:22). Enoch *before Job* had implied that the "saints shall live again" (Jude 14; Heb. 11:13-16). Even if, by this phrase, *Job* meant "never" (Ps. 89:29) in his gloomier state of feelings, yet the *Holy Ghost* has made him unconsciously (I Pet. 1: 11, 12) use language expressing the truth, that the resurrection is to be preceded by the dissolution of the heavens. In vss. 13-15 he plainly passes to brighter hopes of a world to come. **13.** Job wishes to be kept hidden in the grave until God's wrath against him shall have passed away. So while God's wrath is visiting the earth for the abounding apostasy which is to precede the second coming, God's people shall be hidden against the resurrection-glory (Isa. 26:19-21). **set time**—a decreed time (Acts 1:7). **14. shall he live?**—The answer implied is, *There is a hope that he shall, though not in the present order of life,* as is shown by the words following. Job had denied (vss. 10-12) that man shall live again in this present world. But hoping for a "set time," when God shall remember and raise him out of the hiding-place of the grave (vs. 13), he declares himself willing to "wait all the days of his appointed time" of continuance in the grave, however long and hard that may be. "Appointed time," lit., "warfare, hard service"; implying the *hardship* of being shut out from the realms of life, light, and God for the time he shall be in the grave (ch. 7:1). **change**—my release, as a soldier at his post released from duty by the relieving guard (*Note,* 10:17) [UMBREIT and GESENIUS], but elsewhere GESENIUS explains it, "renovation," as of plants in spring (vs. 7), but this does not accord so well with the metaphor in "appointed time" or "warfare." **15.** viz., at the resurrection (John 5:28; Ps. 17:15). **have a desire to**—lit., "become pale with anxious desire": the same word is translated "sore longedst after" (Gen. 31:30; Ps. 84:2), implying the utter unlikelihood that God would leave in oblivion the "creature of His own hands so fearfully and wonderfully made." It is objected that if Job knew of a future retribution, he would make it the *leading* topic in solving the problem of the permitted afflictions of the righteous. But, (1) "He did not intend to exceed the limits of what was *clearly revealed;* the doctrine was then in a vague form only; (2) The doctrine of God's moral government in *this* life, even *independently of the future,* needed vindication. **16.** Rather, "Yea, thou wilt number my steps, and wilt not (as now) jealously watch over my sin." Thenceforward, instead of severe watching for every sin of Job, God will guard him against every sin. "Number . . . steps," i.e., minutely attend to them, that they may not wander" [UMBREIT] (I Sam. 2:9, Ps. 37: 23). **17. scaled up**—(ch. 9:7). Is shut up in eternal oblivion, i.e., God thenceforth will think no more of my former sins. *To cover* sins is to *completely forgive* them (Ps. 32:1; 85:2). Purses of money in the East are usually sealed. **sewest up**—rather, "coverest"; akin to an *Arabic* word, "to color over," to forget wholly. **18. cometh to naught**—lit., "fadeth"; a poetical image from a leaf (Isa. 34:4). Here Job falls back into his gloomy bodings as to the grave. Instead of "and surely," translate "yet"; marking the transition from his brighter hopes. Even the solid mountain falls and crumbles away; man therefore cannot "hope" to escape decay or to live again in the present world (vs. 19). **out of his place**—so man (Ps. 103:16). **19.** The *Hebrew* order is more forcible: "Stones themselves are worn away by water." **things which grow out of**—rather, "*floods* wash away the dust of the earth." There is a gradation from "mountains" to "rocks" (vs. 18), then "stones," then last "dust of the earth"; thus the solid mountain at last disappears utterly. **20. prevailest**—dost overpower by superior strength. **passeth**—dieth. **changest countenance**—the change in the visage at death. Differently (Dan. 5:9). **21.** One striking trait is selected from the sad picture of the severance of the dead from all that passes in the world (Eccles. 9:5), viz., the utter separation of parents and children. **22.** "Flesh" and "soul" describe the whole man. Scripture rests the hope of a future life, not on the inherent immortality of the soul, but on the restoration of the *body* with the soul. In the unseen world, Job in a gloomy frame anticipates, man shall be limited to the thought of his own misery. "Pain is by personification, from *our* feelings while *alive,* attributed to the flesh and soul, as if the man could feel in his body when dead. It is the dead in

ADAM CLARKE

13. *O that thou wouldest hide me in the grave!* Dreadful as death is to others, I shall esteem it a high privilege; it will be to me a covert from the wind and from the tempest of this affliction and distress. *Keep me secret.* Hide my soul with thyself, where my enemies cannot invade my repose.

14. *If a man die, shall he live again?* The Septuagint: "If a man die, shall he live, having accomplished the days of his life? I will endure till I live again." Here is no doubt, but a strong persuasion, of the certainty of the general resurrection. *All the days of my appointed time.* "Of my warfare." *Will I wait, till* "my renovation come." This word is used to denote the springing again of grass, Ps. xc. 5-6, after it had once withered, which is in itself a very expressive emblem of the resurrection.

15. *Thou wilt have a desire.* "Thou wilt pant with desire"; or, "Thou wilt yearn over the work of thy hands."

16. *For now thou numberest my steps.* "Although thou."

17. *My transgression is sealed up in a bag.* An allusion to the custom of collecting evidence of state transgressions, sealing them up in a bag, and presenting them to the judges.

20. *Thou changest his countenance.* Probably an allusion to the custom of covering the face when the person was condemned, and sending him away to execution. See the case of Haman, Esther vii. 8.

MATTHEW HENRY

us leave them, and not burden ourselves with needless fruitless cares concerning them. It is true wisdom, by making our peace with God in Christ and keeping a good conscience, to treasure up comforts which will support and relieve us against the pains and sorrows of a dying hour.

CHAPTER 15

Verses 1–16

Eliphaz here falls very foul upon Job, because he contradicted what he and his colleagues had said. Several great crimes Eliphaz here charges Job with, only because he would not own himself a hypocrite.

I. He charges him with folly and absurdity (*v.* 2, 3), that, whereas he had been reputed a wise man, he had now quite forfeited his reputation. It is common for angry disputants thus to represent one another's reasonings as impertinent and ridiculous. There is a great deal of vain knowledge, science falsely so called, that is useless, and therefore worthless. This is the knowledge that puffs up, with which men swell in a fond conceit of their own accomplishments. Vain knowledge or unprofitable talk ought to be reproved and checked, especially in a wise man, whom it worst becomes.

II. He charges him with impiety and irreligion (*v.* 4): "*Thou castest off fear,*" that is, "the fear of God, and that regard to him which thou shouldst have; and then *thou restrainest prayer.*" See what religion is summed up in, fearing God and praying to him, the former the most needful principle, the latter the most needful practice. Those who are prayerless are fearless and graceless. Those who either omit prayer or straiten and abridge themselves in it, quenching the spirit of adoption and denying themselves the liberty they might take in the duty, restrain prayer. This is bad enough, but it is worse to restrain others from prayer, to prohibit and discourage prayer, as Darius, Dan. vi. 7. Eliphaz charges this upon Job. He thought that Job talked of God with such liberty as if he had been his equal, that he had quite thrown off all religious regard to him. This charge was utterly false, and yet wanted not some colour. We ought not only to take care that we keep up prayer and the fear of God, but that we never drop any unwary expressions which may give occasion to those who seek occasion to question our sincerity and constancy in religion. "If this be true" (thinks Eliphaz) "which Job says, that a man may be thus surely afflicted and yet be a good man, then farewell all religion, farewell prayer and the fear of God. *Thy mouth utters thy iniquity—teaches it,*" so the word is. "Thou teachest others to have the same hard thoughts of God and religion that thou thyself hast." But *thou choosest the tongue of the crafty,* that is, "Thou utterest thy iniquity with some show and pretence of piety, mixing some good words with the bad, as tradesmen do with their wares to help them off." Eliphaz, in his first discourse, had proceeded against Job upon mere surmise (*ch.* iv. 6, 7), but now he has got proof against him from his own discourses (*v.* 6): *Thy own mouth condemns thee, and not I.* But he should have considered that he and his fellows had provoked him to say that which now they took advantage of; and that was not fair.

III. He charges him with intolerable arrogancy and self-conceitedness. It was a just, and reasonable, and modest demand that Job had made (*ch.* xii. 3), Allow that *I have understanding as well as you*; but see how they seek occasion against him: that is misconstrued, as if he pretended to be wiser than any man. "*Art thou the first man that was born? Wast thou made before the hills,* as Wisdom herself was? (Prov. viii. 23, &c.) Dost thou know more of the world than any of us do? No, thou art but of yesterday even as we are," *ch.* viii. 9. In intimacy of acquaintance with God (*v.* 8): "*Hast thou heard the secret of God?*" He also represents him, (1) As assuming to himself such knowledge as none else had: "*Dost thou restrain wisdom to thyself,* as if none were wise besides?" Job had said (*ch.* xiii. 2), *What you know, the same do I know also.* (2) As opposing the stream of antiquity, a venerable name, under the shade of which all contending parties strive to shelter themselves: "*With us are the grey-headed and very aged men* (*v.* 10). We have the fathers on our side."

IV. He charges him with a contempt of the counsels and comforts that were given him by his friends (*v.* 11): *Are the consolations of God small with thee?* Eliphaz takes it ill that Job did not value the comforts which he and his friends administered to him more than it seems he did. He represents this as a slight put upon divine consolations in general, as if they were of small account with him, whereas really they were

JAMIESON, FAUSSET, BROWN

general, not the wicked, who are meant here."

CHAPTER 15

Vss. 1-35. SECOND SPEECH OF ELIPHAZ. **2. a wise man**—which Job claims to be. **vain knowledge**—*Hebrew,* "windy knowledge," lit., "of wind" (ch. 8:2). In Ecclesiastes 1:14, Hebrew "to catch wind," expresses to strive for what is vain. **east wind**—stronger than the previous "wind," for in that region the east wind is the most destructive of winds (Isa. 27:8). Thus here,—empty violence. **belly**—the inward parts, the breast (Prov. 18:8).

4. fear—reverence for God (ch. 4:6; Ps. 2:11). **prayer**—meditation, in Psalm 104:34; so *devotion.* If thy views were right, reasons Eliphaz, that God disregards the afflictions of the righteous and makes the wicked to prosper, all devotion would be at an end.

5. The sophistry of thine own speeches proves thy guilt. **6.** No *pious* man would utter such sentiments.

7—I.e., Art thou wisdom personified? Wisdom existed before the hills; i.e., the eternal Son of God (Prov. 8:25; Ps. 90:2). Wast thou in existence before Adam? The farther back one existed, the nearer he was to the Eternal Wisdom. **8. secret,**—rather, "Wast thou a listener *in the secret council* of God?" The *Hebrew* means properly the *cushions* of a divan on which counsellors in the East usually sit. God's servants are admitted to God's secrets (Ps. 25:14; Gen. 18:17; John 15:15). **restrain**—Rather, didst thou take away, *or borrow,* thence (viz., from the divine secret council) thy wisdom? Eliphaz in this (vss. 8, 9) retorts Job's words upon himself (ch. 12:2, 3; 13:2). **9. in us**—or, "with us," Hebraism for "we are aware of." **10.** On our side, thinking with us are the aged. Job had admitted that wisdom is with them (ch. 12:12). Eliphaz seems to have been himself older than Job; perhaps the other two were also (ch. 32:6). Job, in ch. 30:1, does not refer to his three friends; it therefore forms no objection. The Arabs are proud of fulness of years. **11. consolations**—viz., the revelation which Eliphaz had stated as a consolatory reproof to Job, and which he repeats in vs. 14. **secret**—Hast thou some *secret* wisdom and source of consolation, which makes thee disregard those suggested by me? (vs. 8). Rather, from a different *Hebrew* root, Is the word of *kindness* or *gentleness* addressed by me treated by thee as valueless? [UMBREIT].

ADAM CLARKE

CHAPTER 15

2. *Should a wise man utter vain knowledge?* Or rather, "Should a wise man utter the science of wind?" A science without solidity or certainty. *And fill his belly with the east wind? Beten,* which we translate *belly,* is used to signify any part of the body; here it evidently refers to the lungs, and may include the cheeks. The *east wind* is a very stormy wind in the Levant, or the eastern part of the Mediterranean Sea. Eliphaz, by these words, seems to intimate that Job's speech was a perfect storm or tempest of words.

4. *Thou castest off fear.* Thou hast no reverence for God. *And restrainest prayer.* Instead of humbling yourself, and making supplication to your Judge, you spend your time in arraigning His providence and justifying yourself.

7. *Art thou the first man that was born?* Literally, "Wert thou born before Adam?" Art thou in the pristine state of purity and innocence?

8. *Hast thou heard the secret of God?* "Hast thou hearkened in God's council?"

MATTHEW HENRY

not. If he had not highly valued them, he could not have borne up as he did under his sufferings.

V. He charges him with opposition to God himself and to religion (*v.* 12, 13): "*Why doth thy heart carry thee away* into such indecent irreligious expressions?" He thought Job's spirit was soured against God, and so turned from what it had been, and exasperated at his dealings with him. Eliphaz wanted candour and charity, else he would not have put such a harsh construction upon the speeches of one that had such a settled reputation for piety and was now in temptation.

VI. He charges him with justifying himself to such a degree as even to deny his share in the common corruption and pollution of the human nature (*v.* 14): *What is man, that he should be clean?* that is, that he should pretend to be so, or that any should expect to find him so. What is *he that is born of a woman, a sinful woman, that he should be righteous?* With these plain truths Eliphaz thinks to convince Job, whereas he had just now said the same (*ch.* xiv. 4): *Who can bring a clean thing out of an unclean?* But does it therefore follow that Job is a hypocrite and a wicked man, which is all that he denied? By no means. Though man, as born of a woman, is not clean, yet, as born again of the Spirit, he is clean. Further to evince this he here shows, (1) That the brightest creatures are imperfect and impure before God, *v.* 15. He takes no complacency in the heavens themselves. How pure soever they seem to us, in his eye they had many a speck and many a flaw: *The heavens are not clean in his sight.* If the stars have no light in the sight of the sun, what light has the sun in the sight of God! See Isa. xxiv. 23. (2) That man is much more so (*v.* 16): *How much more abominable and filthy is man!* If saints are not to be trusted, much less sinners. If the heavens are not pure, which are as God made them, much less man, who is degenerated. Nay, he is abominable and filthy in the sight of God, and if ever he repent he is so in his own sight, and therefore he abhors himself.

Verses 17–35

Eliphaz comes to maintain his own thesis, upon which he built his censure of Job. Those who are wicked are certainly miserable, those who are miserable are certainly wicked, therefore Job was so.

I. His solemn preface (*v.* 17): "*I will show thee* that which is worth hearing, and not reason, as thou dost, with unprofitable talk." He promises to teach him, 1. From his own experience and observation: "*That which I have* myself *seen*, in divers instances, *I will declare.*" 2. From the wisdom of the ancients (*v.* 18): *Which wise men have told from their fathers.* The wisdom and learning of the moderns are very much derived from those of the ancients. Good children will learn a good deal from their good parents; and what we have learned from our ancestors we must transmit to our posterity.

II. The discourse itself.

1. Those who are wise and good do ordinarily prosper in this world. This he only hints at (*v.* 19), that those were such as had the earth given to them, and to them only; they enjoyed it entirely and peaceably. Job had said, *The earth is given into the hand of the wicked, ch.* ix. 24. "No," says Eliphaz, "it is given into the hands of the saints, and they are not robbed and plundered by strangers making inroads upon them, as thou art by the Sabeans and Chaldeans."

2. Wicked people, and particularly tyrannizing rulers, are subject to continual terrors, and perish very miserably. Even those who impiously dare God's judgments will feel them at last. He speaks in the singular number—*the wicked man.* He meant Job himself, whom he expressly charges both with the tyranny and with the timorousness here described, *ch.* xxii. 9, 10. Here he thinks Job might, in this description, see his own face.

(1) He describes the sinner who lives thus miserably, *v.* 25–28. It is no ordinary sinner, that bids defiance to God, *v.* 25. Tell him of the divine law, and its obligations; he breaks those bonds asunder. Tell him of the divine wrath, and he bids the Almighty do his worst, and will not be controlled by law, or conscience. *He stretches out his hand against God* to show that, if it were in his power, he would ungod him. *He strengthens himself* (*he would be valiant*, so some read it) *against the Almighty.* It is the prodigious madness of presumptuous sinners that they enter the lists with Omnipotence. *He runs upon him*, upon God himself, *even upon his neck*, as a desperate combatant, when he finds himself an unequal match for his adversary, flies in his face, though, at the same time, he falls on his sword's point, or the sharp spike of his buckler. He wraps himself up in security and sensuality (*v.* 27): *He covers his face with his fatness.* This signifies both the pampering of his flesh with daily

JAMIESON, FAUSSET, BROWN

12. wink—i.e., why do thy eyes *evince pride*? (Prov. 6:13, Ps. 35:19). **13**—i.e., frettest against God and lettest fall rash words.

14. Eliphaz repeats the revelation (ch. 4:17) in substance, but using Job's own words (ch. 14:1, *Note* on "born of a woman") to strike him with his own weapons.

15. Repeated from ch. 4: 18; "servants" there are "saints"; here, viz., holy angels. **heavens**—lit., or else answering to "angels" (ch. 4:18; see *Note* there, and ch. 25:5).

16. filthy—in *Arabic* "sour" (Ps. 14:3; 53:3), corrupted from his original purity. **drinketh**—(Prov. 19:28).

17. In direct contradiction of Job's position (ch. 12:6, etc.), that the lot of the wicked was the most prosperous here, Eliphaz appeals (1) to his own experience, (2) to the wisdom of the ancients. **18.** Rather, "and which as handed down from their fathers, they have not concealed."

19. Eliphaz speaks like a genuine Arab when he boasts that his ancestors had ever possessed the land unmixed with foreigners [UMBREIT]. His words are intended to oppose Job's (ch. 9:24); "the earth" in their case was *not* "given into the hand of the wicked." He refers to the division of the earth by divine appointment (Gen. 10:5; 25:32). Also he may insinuate that Job's sentiments had been corrupted from original purity by his vicinity to the Sabeans and Chaldeans [ROSENMULLER].

25. stretcheth . . . hand—wielding the spear, as a bold rebel against God (ch .9:4; Isa. 27:4). **26. on his neck**—rather, "with outstretched neck," viz., that of the rebel [UMBREIT] (Ps. 75:5). **upon . . . bucklers**—rather, "*with*—his (the rebel's, not God's) bucklers." The rebel and his fellows are depicted as joining shields together, to form a compact covering over their heads against the weapons hurled on them from a fortress [UMBREIT and GESENIUS]. **27.** The well-nourished body of the rebel is the sign of his prosperity. **collops**—masses of fat. He pampers and fattens himself with sensual indulgences; hence his rebellion against God (Deut. 32:15; I Sam. 2:29).

ADAM CLARKE

16. *How much more abominable and filthy is man?* As in the preceding verse it is said, "He putteth no trust in his saints," it has appeared both to translators and commentators that the original words should be rendered "how much less," not "how much more": How much less would He put confidence in man, who is filthy and abominable in his nature, and profligate in his practice, as he drinks down *iniquity like water?* A man who is under the power of sinful propensities commits sin as greedily as the thirsty man or camel drinks down water. He thinks he can never have enough.

17. *I will shew thee, hear me; and that which I have seen I will declare.* Eliphaz is now about to quote a whole collection of wise sayings from the ancients; all good enough in themselves, but sinfully misapplied to the case of Job.

19. *Unto whom alone the earth was given.* He very likely refers to the Israelites, who got possession of the Promised Land from God himself, *no stranger* being permitted to dwell in it, as the old inhabitants were to be exterminated.

26. *He runneth upon him.* Calmet has properly observed that this refers to God, who, like a mighty conquering hero, marches against the ungodly, rushes upon him, seizes him.

27. *Maketh collops of fat on his flanks. A* proverbial expression for "His ambition is boundless."

MATTHEW HENRY

delicious fare and the hardening of his heart hereby against the judgments of God. The fat that covers his face makes him look bold and haughty, and that which covers his flanks makes him lie easy and soft, and feel little; but this will prove poor shelter against the darts of God's wrath. He enriches himself with the spoils of all about him, *v.* 28. *They conceive mischief,* and then they effect it by *preparing deceit,* pretending to protect those whom they design to subdue, and making leagues of peace the more effectually to carry on the operations of war.

(2) The miserable condition of this wicked man, both in spiritual and temporal judgments. His inward peace is continually disturbed. His own conscience accuses him, and with the pangs of that *he travaileth in pain all his days, v.* 20. His sins stare him in the face at every turn. He is vexed at the uncertainty of the continuance of his wealth and power: *The number of years is hidden to the oppressor.* He is under a *certain fearful expectation of judgment. A dreadful sound is in his ears, v.* 21. He knows that God is angry with him and that all the world hates him; he has done nothing to make his peace with either. Again (*v.* 23): *He knows that the day of darkness* (or the *night* of darkness rather) *is ready at his hand,* that it is appointed to him and cannot be put by. 'No marvel that it follows (*v.* 24), *Trouble and anguish shall make him afraid* of worse to come. If at any time he be in trouble, he despairs of getting out (*v.* 22). Such a dread he has of poverty, and such a waste does he discern upon his estate, that he is already, in his own imagination, *wandering abroad for bread.* How can he prosper when God runs upon him? so some understand that, *v.* 26. Whom God runs *upon* he will certainly run *down.* Many that get much by fraud and injustice, yet do not grow rich: it goes as it comes; it is got by one sin and spent upon another. He is in care to leave what he has got and kept to his children after him. But the branches of his family shall perish. *They shall not be green, v.* 32. *The flame shall dry them up, v.* 30. He shall shake them off as blossoms that never knit, or as the *unripe grape, v.* 33. Many a man's family is ruined by his iniquity. He is in care, when he is in trouble, how to get out of it (not how to get good by it); but in this also he is crossed (*v.* 30): *He shall not depart out of darkness.* He is in care to secure his partners, but that is in vain too, *v.* 34, 35. *The congregation* of them, the whole confederacy they and all their tabernacles, *shall be desolate.*

(3) Will the prosperity of presumptuous sinners end thus miserably? Then (*v.* 31) *let not him that is deceived trust in vanity.* Those who trust to their sinful ways of getting wealth *trust in vanity,* and *vanity will be their recompence.* Those who trust to their wealth when they have gotten it, especially to the wealth they have gotten dishonestly, trust in vanity; for it will yield them no satisfaction. They will own at length, with the utmost confusion, that *a deceived heart turned them aside,* and that they cheated themselves with *a lie in their right hand.*

CHAPTER 16

Verses 1–5

Both Job and his friends undervalue one another's sense, and wisdom, and management. The longer the saw of contention is drawn the hotter it grows. Eliphaz had represented Job's discourses as idle, and unprofitable, and Job here gives his the same character. Job here reproves Eliphaz, 1. For needless repetitions (*v.* 2): "*I have heard many such things.*" 2. For unskilful applications. "*Miserable comforters are you all,* who, instead of offering anything to alleviate the affliction add affliction to it, and make it yet more grievous." The patient's case is sad indeed when his medicines are poisons and his physicians his worst disease. 3. For endless impertinence. Job wishes that *vain words might have an end, v.* 3. 4. For obstinacy. *What emboldeneth thee, that thou answerest?* It is a great piece of confidence, to pass a judgment on men's spiritual state upon the view of their outward condition. 5. For the violation of the sacred laws of friendship. This is a cutting reproof, *v.* 4, 5. He desires his friends, in imagination, to suppose themselves in misery like him and him at ease like them. He represents the unkindness of their conduct towards him, by showing what he could do to them if they were in his condition: *I could speak as you do.* He shows them what they should do, by telling them what in that case he would do (*v.* 5): "*I would strengthen you,* and say all I could to assuage your grief, but nothing to aggravate it." What is the duty we owe to our brethren in their affliction? We should say and do all we can to strengthen them, to encourage their confidence in God, to support their sinking spirits, to

JAMIESON, FAUSSET, BROWN

28. The class of wicked here described is that of robbers who plunder "cities," and seize on the houses of the banished citizens (Isa. 13:20). Eliphaz chooses this class because Job had chosen the same (ch. 12:6). **heaps**—of ruins. **29.** Rather, he shall not *increase* his riches; he has reached his highest point; his prosperity shall not continue. **perfection**—rather, "His *acquired* wealth—what he possesses—shall not *be extended,*" etc.

20. travaileth—rather, "trembleth of himself," though there is no real danger [UMBREIT]. **and the number of [his] years . . .**—This gives the reason why the wicked man trembles continually; viz., because he knows not the moment when his life must end. **21.** An evil conscience conceives alarm at every sudden sound, though it be in a time of peace ("prosperity"), when there is no real danger (Lev. 26:36; Prov. 28:1; II Kings 7:6). **22. darkness**—viz., danger or calamity. Glancing at Job, who despaired of restoration: in contrast to good men when in darkness (Mic. 7:8, 9). **waited for of**—i.e., He is destined for the sword [GESENIUS]. Rather (in the night of danger), "he *looks anxiously towards* the sword," as if every sword was drawn against him [UMBREIT]. **23.** Wandereth *in anxious search* for bread. Famine in Old Testament depicts sore need (Isa. 5:13). Contrast the pious man's lot (ch. 5:20-22). **knoweth**—has the firm conviction. Contrast the same word applied to the pious (ch. 5: 24, 25). **ready at his hand**—an *Arabic* phrase to denote a thing's *complete readiness* and *full presence,* as if in the hand. **24. prevail**—break upon him suddenly and terribly, as a king, etc. (Prov. 6: 11). **30. depart**—i.e., escape (vss. 22, 23). **branches**—viz., his offspring (ch. 1:18, 19; Ps. 37:35). **dry up**—The "flame" is the sultry wind in the East by which plants most full of sap are suddenly shrivelled. **his mouth**—i.e., God's wrath (Isa. 11:4). **31.** Rather, let him not trust in vanity or he will be deceived, etc. **vanity**—that which is unsubstantial. Sin is its own punishment (Prov. 1:31; Jer. 2:19). **32.** lit., "it (*the tree* to which he is compared, vs. 30, or else *his life*) shall not be filled up in its time"; i.e., "he shall be ended before his time." **shall not be green**—image from a withered tree; the childless extinction of the wicked. **33.** Images of incompleteness. The loss of the unripe grapes is poetically made the vine tree's own act, in order to express more pointedly that the sinner's ruin is the fruit of his own conduct (Isa. 3: 11; Jer. 6:19). **34.** Rather, The binding together of the hypocrites (wicked) shall be *fruitless* [UMBREIT]. Tabernacles of bribery, viz., dwellings of unjust judges, often reprobated in the Old Testament (Isa. 1:23). The "fire of God" that consumed Job's possessions (ch. 1:16) Eliphaz insinuates may have been on account of Job's bribery as an Arab sheik or emir. **35.** Bitter irony, illustrating the "unfruitfulness" (vs. 34) of the wicked. Their conceptions and birth-givings consist solely in mischief, etc. (Isa. 33:11). **prepareth**—hatcheth.

CHAPTER 16

Vss. 1-22. JOB'S REPLY. **2.** (Ch. 13:4.)

3. "Words of wind," *Hebrew.* He retorts upon Eliphaz his reproach (ch. 15:2). **emboldeneth**—lit., "What wearies you so that ye contradict"? i.e., What have I said to *provoke* you? etc. [SCHUTTENS]. Or, as better accords with the first clause, "Wherefore do ye weary yourselves contradicting?" [UMBREIT]. **4. heap up**—rather, marshal together (an army of) words. **shake . . . head**—in mockery; it means *nodding,* rather than *shaking;* nodding is not with us, as in the East, a gesture of scorn (Isa. 37:22; Jer. 18: 16; Matt. 27:39).

5. strengthen . . . with . . . mouth—bitter irony. In allusion to Eliphaz' boasted "consolations" (ch. 15:11). Opposed to strengthening with the *heart,* i.e., with real consolation. Translate, "I also (like you) could strengthen with the *mouth,*" i.e., with *heartless* talk: "And the moving

ADAM CLARKE

29. *He shall not be rich.* The whole of what follows, to the end of the chapter, seems to be directed against Job himself, whom Eliphaz indirectly accuses of having been a tyrant and oppressor.

20. *The wicked man travaileth with pain.* This is a most forcible truth: a life of sin is a life of misery, and he that will sin must suffer. The sense of the original is, "He torments himself." He is a true self-tormentor, and he alone is author of his own sufferings and of his own ruin.

22. *That he shall return out of darkness.* If he take but a few steps in the dark, he expects the dagger of the assassin.

32. *It shall be accomplished before his time.* I believe the Vulgate gives the true sense: "He shall perish before his time; before his days are completed."

34. *The congregation of hypocrites.* Job is here classed with *hypocrites,* or rather the impious of all kinds. The *congregation,* or "society," of such shall be *desolate,* or a "barren rock." See the Arabic word explained in the note on chap. iii. 7. *Fire shall consume the tabernacles of bribery.* Another insinuation against Job, that he had perverted justice and judgment, and had taken bribes.

CHAPTER 16

3. *Vain words.* Literally, "words of air."

MATTHEW HENRY

assuage their grief—the causes of their grief, if possible, or at least their resentment of those causes. Good words cost nothing; but they may be of good service to those that are in sorrow, not only as it is some comfort to them to see their friends concerned for them, but as they may be so reminded of that which, through the prevalency of grief, was forgotten. Though hard words break no bones, yet kind words may help to make broken bones rejoice.

Verses 6–16

Job's complaint is here as bitter as anywhere in all his discourses. Sometimes giving vent to grief gives ease; but, "*Though I speak*" (says Job), "*my grief is not assuaged*, what I speak is so misconstrued as to be turned to the aggravation of my grief." At other times keeping silence makes the trouble the easier and the sooner forgotten; but (says Job) *though I forbear what am I eased?* If he complained he was censured as passionate; if not, as sullen. If he maintained his integrity, that was his crime; if he made no answer to their accusations, his silence was taken for a confession of his guilt.

I. His family was scattered (*v.* 7). He had company indeed, but such as he would rather have been without, for they seemed to triumph in his desolation.

II. His body was worn away with diseases and pains, *v.* 8. His face was furrowed, not with age, but sickness: *Thou hast filled me with wrinkles.* "They are witnesses *for* me, that my complaint is not causeless."

III. His enemy threatened him (*v.* 9): *He tears me in his wrath.* But who is this enemy? 1. Eliphaz, who showed himself very much exasperated against him, and what he said tore Job's good name and thundered nothing but terror to him. Or, 2. Satan. He was his enemy that hated him, and aimed to make him curse God. It is not improbable that this is the enemy he means. Or, 3. God himself. If we understand it of him, the expressions are indeed as rash as any he used. God hates none of his creatures; but Job's melancholy did thus represent to him the terrors of the Almighty.

IV. All about him were abusive to him, *v.* 10. Herein Job was a type of Christ, as many of the ancients make him: these very expressions are used in the predictions of his sufferings, Ps. xxii. 13, *They gaped upon me with their mouths;* and (Mic. v. 1), *They shall smite the Judge of Israel with a rod upon the cheek*, which was literally fulfilled, Matt. xxvi. 67.

V. God, instead of delivering him out of their hands, as he hoped, delivered him into their hands (*v.* 11): *He hath turned me over into the hands of the wicked.* Herein also Job was a type of Christ, who was delivered into wicked hands, to be crucified and slain, by the *determinate counsel and foreknowledge of God*, Acts ii. 23.

VI. God not only delivered him into the hands of the wicked, but took him into his own hands too (*v.* 12): "*I was at ease* in the comfortable enjoyment of the gifts of God's bounty, yet *he has broken me asunder*, put me upon the rack of pain, and torn me limb from limb." "*He has set me up for his mark*, the butt at which he is pleased to let fly all his arrows." When God set him up for a mark *his archers* presently *compassed him round.* Whoever are our enemies, we must look upon them as God's archers, and see him directing the arrow. *It is the Lord; let him do what seemeth him good.* As if he had no mercy in reserve for him, he does not spare nor abate anything of the extremity. "*He breaketh me with breach upon breach*, follows me with one wound after another." Thus he thought that God ran upon him *like a giant*, whom he could not possibly stand before or confront. Even good men, when they are in great and extraordinary troubles, have much ado not to entertain hard thoughts of God.

VII. He had divested himself of all his honour, and all his comfort. Job, as one truly penitent and truly patient, humbled himself under the mighty hand of God, *v.* 15, 16. He consulted not either his ease or finery in his dress, but sewed sackcloth upon his skin; that clothing he thought good enough for such a defiled distempered body as he had. He insisted not upon any points of honour, but humbled himself under humbling providences: *He defiled his horn in the dust*, and refused the respect that used to be paid to his dignity. "*My face is foul with weeping* so constantly for my sins, for God's displeasure against me, and for my friends' unkindness: this has brought a *shadow of death upon my eyelids.*"

Verses 17–22

Job's condition was very deplorable; but,

I. He had the testimony of his conscience that he had walked uprightly, and had never allowed himself in any gross sin. None was ever more ready than he

JAMIESON, FAUSSET, BROWN

of my lips (mere lip comfort) could console" (in the same fashion as you do) [UMBREIT]. "*Hearty* counsel" (Prov. 27:9) is the opposite.

6. eased—lit., "What (portion of my sufferings) goes from me?" **7. But now**—rather, "ah!" **he**—God. **company**—rather, "band of *witnesses*," viz., those who could attest his innocence (his children, servants, etc.). So the same *Hebrew* is translated next verse. UMBREIT makes his "band of witnesses" *himself*, for, alas! he had no other witness for him. But this is too recondite. **8. filled . . . with wrinkles**—Rather (as also the same *Hebrew* word in ch. 22:16; *English Version*, "cut down"), "thou hast *fettered* me, thy witness" (*besides* cutting off my "band of witnesses," vs. 7), i.e., hast disabled me by pains from properly attesting my innocence. But another "witness" arises against him, viz., his "leanness" or wretched state of body, construed by his friends into a proof of his guilt. The radical meaning of the *Hebrew* is "to draw together," whence flow the double meaning "to bind" or "fetter," and in *Syriac*, "to wrinkle." **leanness**—meaning also "lie"; implying it was a *false* "witness." **9.** Image from a wild beast. So God is represented (ch. 10:16). **who hateth me**—rather, "and pursues me hard." Job would not ascribe "hatred" to God (Ps. 50:22). **mine enemy**—rather, "he sharpens, etc., *as an enemy*" (Ps. 7:12). Darts wrathful glances at me, like a foe (ch. 13:24). **10. gaped**—not in order to devour, but to mock him. To fill his cup of misery, the mockery of his friends (vs. 10) is added to the hostile treatment from God (vs. 9). **smitten . . . cheek**—figurative for contemptuous abuse (Lam. 3:30; Matt. 5:39). **gathered themselves**—"conspired unanimously" [SCHUTTENS]. **11. the ungodly**—viz., his professed friends, who persecuted him with unkind speeches. **turned me over**—lit., cast me headlong into, etc.

12. I was at ease—in past times (ch. 1). **by my neck**—as an animal does its prey (so ch. 10:16). **shaken**—violently; in contrast to his former "ease" (Ps. 102:10). **Set me up** (*again*). **mark**—(ch. 7:20; Lam. 3:12). God lets me always recover strength, so as to torment me ceaselessly. **13. his archers**—The image of previous verse is continued. God, in making me His "mark," is accompanied by the three friends, whose words wound like sharp arrows. **gall**—put for a vital part; so the liver (Lam. 2:11). **14.** The image is from storming a fortress by making breaches in the walls (II Kings 14:13). **a giant**—a mighty warrior.

15. sewed—denoting the tight fit of the mourning garment; it was a sack with armholes closely sewed to the body. **horn**—image from horned cattle, which when excited tear the earth with their horns. The horn was the emblem of power (I Kings 22:11). Here, it is "in the *dust*," which as applied to Job denotes *his humiliation* from former greatness. To throw one's self in the dust was a sign of mourning; this idea is here joined with that of excited despair, depicted by the fury of a horned beast. The Druses of Lebanon still wear horns as an ornament. **16. foul**—rather, "is red," i.e., flushed and heated [UMBREIT and NOYES]. **shadow of death**—i.e., darkening through many tears (Lam. 5:17). Job here refers to Zophar's implied charge (ch. 11:14). Nearly the same words occur as to Jesus Christ (Isa. 53:9). So vs. 10 above answers to the description of Jesus Christ (Ps. 12:13; Isa. 50:6, and vs. 4 to Ps. 22:7). He alone realized what Job aspired after, viz., outward *righteousness* of acts and inward *purity* of devotion. Jesus Christ as the representative man is typified in some degree in every servant of God in the Old Testament.

ADAM CLARKE

7. ***But now he hath made me weary.*** **The Vulgate translates thus: "But now my grief oppresses me, and all my joints are reduced to nothing."**

9. ***He teareth me in his wrath. He*** **(Satan)** ***gnasheth upon me with his teeth; mine enemy sharpeneth his eyes upon me.***

10. ***They*** **(demons)** ***have gaped on me with their mouth; they have gathered themselves together against me.***

11. ***God hath delivered me to the ungodly*** **(to the evil one),** ***and turned me over into the hands of the wicked.***

15. ***Defiled my horn in the dust.*** **The** ***horn*** **was an emblem of power.**

MATTHEW HENRY

to acknowledge his sins of infirmity; but he could not charge himself with any enormous crime, for which he should be made more miserable than other men, *v.* 17. Eliphaz had represented him as a tyrant and an oppressor. "No," says he, "I never did any wrong to any man, but always despised the gain of oppression." Eliphaz had charged him with hypocrisy in religion, but he specifies prayer, the great act of religion, and professes that in that he was pure, though not from all infirmity. It was not like the prayers of the Pharisees, who looked no further than to be seen of men, and to serve a turn.

1. This assertion of his own integrity he backs with a solemn imprecation of shame and confusion to himself if it were not true, *v.* 18. If there were any injustice in his hands, he wished it might not be concealed: *O earth! cover thou not my blood,* that is, "the innocent blood of others, which I am suspected to have shed." If there were any impurity in his prayers, he wished they might not be accepted: *Let my cry have no place.*

II. He could appeal to God's omniscience concerning his integrity, *v.* 19. The witness in our own bosoms for us will stand us in little stead if we have not a witness in heaven for us too; for *God is greater than our hearts,* and we are not to be our own judges. This therefore is Job's triumph, *My witness is in heaven.* It is an unspeakable comfort to a good man, when he lies under the censure of his brethren, that there is a God in heaven who knows his integrity and will clear it up sooner or later.

III. He had a God to go to before whom he might unbosom himself, *v.* 20, 21. "My friends (so they call themselves) scorn me; they set themselves not only to resist me, but to use all their art and eloquence" (so the word signifies) "to run me down." He doubted not but that God did now take cognizance of his sorrows: *My eye pours out tears to God.* Even tears, when sanctified to God, give ease to troubled spirits; and, if men slight our grief, this may comfort us, that God regards them. If he could but now have the same freedom at God's bar that men commonly have at the bar of the civil magistrate, he doubted not but to carry his cause, for the Judge himself was a witness to his integrity. The language of this wish is like that in Isa. l. 7, 8, *I know that I shall not be ashamed, for he is near that justifies me.*

IV. He had a prospect of death which would put a period to all his troubles. Such confidence had he towards God that he could take pleasure in thinking of the approach of death, when he should be determined to his everlasting state, as one that doubted not but it would be well with him then: *When a few years have come* (*the years of number* which are determined and appointed to me) *then I shall go the way whence I shall not return.* To die is to *go the way whence we shall not return.* It is to go a journey from the world of sense to the world of spirits. It is a journey to our long home. We must all of us very certainly go this journey; and it is comfortable to those who keep a good conscience to think of it, for it is the crown of their integrity.

JAMIESON, FAUSSET, BROWN

18. my blood—i.e., my undeserved suffering. He compares himself to one murdered, whose blood the earth refuses to drink up until he is avenged (Gen. 4:10, 11; Ezek. 24:1, 8; Isa. 26:21). The Arabs say that the dew of heaven will not descend on a spot watered with innocent blood (cf. II Sam. 1:21). **no place**—no resting-place. "May my cry never stop!" May it go abroad! "Earth" in this verse in antithesis to "heaven" (vs. 19). May my innocence be as well known to *man* as it is even now to God! **19. Also now**—Even now, when I am so greatly misunderstood on earth, God in *heaven* is sensible of my innocence. **record**—*Hebrew,* "my witness." Amidst all his impatience, Job still trusts in God. **20.** *Hebrew,* more forcibly, "my mockers—my friends!" A heart-cutting paradox [UMBREIT]. God alone remains to whom he can look for attestation of his innocence; plaintively with tearful eye, he supplicates for this. **21. one**—rather, He (God). "Oh, that He would plead for a man (viz., me) against God." Job quaintly says," God must support me against God; for He makes me to suffer, and He alone knows me to be innocent" [UMBREIT]. So God helped Jacob in wrestling against Himself (cf. 23:6; Gen. 32:25). *God* in Jesus Christ does plead with *God* for man (Rom. 8:26, 27). **as a man**—lit,. the Son of man. A prefiguring of the advocacy of Jesus Christ—a boon longed for by Job (ch. 9:33), though the spiritual pregnancy of his own words, designed for all ages, was but little understood by him (Ps. 80:17). **for his neighbour**—*Hebrew,* "friend." Job himself (ch. 42:8) pleaded as intercessor for his "friends," though "his scorners" (vs. 20); so Jesus Christ the Son of man (Luke 23:34); "for *friends*" (John 15:13-15). **22. few**—lit., "years *of number,*" i.e., few, opposed to *numberless* (Gen. 34:30).

ADAM CLARKE

18. *O earth, cover not thou my blood.* This is evidently an allusion to the murder of Abel. Job here calls for justice against his destroyers.

CHARLES H. SPURGEON:

"When a few years are come, then I shall go the way whence I shall not return." To the occupations of life—to sow and reap, and mow; to the abodes of life—to the store and to the country house; to the pleasures of life—the festival and the family—we shall not return. To the engagements of the sanctuary, the communion table, the pulpit, or the pew, we shall not return. To the chamber of love, to the hearth of affection, to the walk of friendship we shall not return. To hopes and fears, and joys, and pains we shall not return. To summer's flowers and winter's snows we shall not return. To our brothers, children, husband, or wife we shall not return. To nothing that is done under the sun shall we return. Soul, unsaved soul, to the land of the gospel and the mercy seat thou shalt not return. If you die unsaved, you will not be able to come back to the house of God to hear again the ministry of reconciliation; you will hear no more invitations and expostulations, neither will Jesus be set before you as your hope. You will not be able to come back to the prayer meeting and to the earnest entreaties of a godly mother and other loving friends, nor even back to your Bible and to the opportunity of searching it that you may find eternal life. You will not return to find space for repentance, nor a second opportunity for prayer, nor another season for believing in Jesus. It shall be said concerning you, "He which is filthy, let him be filthy still." Where the tree falleth there must it lie. Once pass the barriers of life unsaved, and ye cannot return to a new probation. The die is cast.

—*The Treasury of the Old Testament*

MATTHEW HENRY

CHAPTER 17

Verses 1–9

Job's discourse is broken and he passes suddenly from one thing to another, as is usual with men in trouble.

I. The deplorable condition which he describes to justify his own complaints.

1. He was a dying man, *v.* 1. He had said (*ch.* xvi. 22), "*When a few years have come,* I shall go that long journey." But here he corrects himself. "Why do I talk of years to come? *My breath is* already *corrupt,* I am a gone man." It concerns us therefore carefully to redeem the days of time, and to spend them in getting ready for the days of eternity. We are expected in our long home: *The graves are ready for me.* He speaks of the *sepulchres of his fathers,* to which he must be gathered.

2. He was a despised man (*v.* 6): "*He*" (that is, Eliphaz, so some, or God) "*has made me a byword of the people,* a laughing-stock to many, and *aforetime I was as a tabret,* that whoever chose might play upon." They made ballads of him; his name became a proverb; it is so still, *As poor as Job.* "*He has* now *made me a by-word,*" a reproach of men, whereas, aforetime, in my prosperity, I was as a tabret, *deliciæ humani generis—the darling of the human race.*

3. He was a man of sorrows, *v.* 7. He wept so much that he had almost lost his sight: *My eye is dim by reason of sorrow, ch.* xvi. 16. He had become a perfect skeleton. "*All my members are as a shadow.* I am not to be called a man, but the *shadow of a man.*"

II. The ill use which his friends made of his miseries. They condemned him as a hypocrite, because he was

JAMIESON, FAUSSET, BROWN

CHAPTER 17

Vss. 1-16. JOB'S ANSWER CONTINUED. **1. breath . . . corrupt**—result of elephantiasis. But UMBREIT, "my strength (spirit) is spent." **extinct**—Life is compared to an expiring light. "The light of my day is extinguished." **graves**—plural, to heighten the force.

6. He—God. The poet reverentially suppresses the name of God when speaking of calamities inflicted. **by-word**—(Deut. 28:37; Ps. 69:11). My awful punishment makes my name execrated everywhere, as if I must have been superlatively bad to have earned it. **aforetime . . . tabret**—as David was honored (I Sam. 18:6). Rather from a different *Hebrew* root, "I am treated to my face as an object of disgust," lit., an object to be spit upon in the face (Num. 12:14). So *Raca* means (Matt. 5:22), [UMBREIT]. **7.** (Ps. 6:7; 31:9; Deut. 34:7.) **members**—lit., "figures"; all the individual members being peculiar *forms* of the body; opposed to "shadow," which looks like a figure without solidity.

ADAM CLARKE

CHAPTER 17

1. *My breath is corrupt.* Rather, "My spirit is oppressed."

6. *He hath made me also a byword.* My afflictions and calamities have become a subject of general conversation, so that my poverty and affliction are proverbial. "As poor as Job," "As afflicted as Job," are proverbs that have reached even our times and are still in use. *Aforetime I was as a tabret.* "I shall be as a furnace, or consuming fire (Topheth) before them." They shall have little reason to mock when they see the end of the Lord's dealings with me; my example will be a consuming fire to them, and my false friends will be confounded.

7. *Mine eye also is dim.* Continual weeping impairs the sight; and indeed any affliction that debilitates the frame generally, weakens the *sight* in the same proportion. *All my members are as a shadow.* Nothing is left but skin and bone. I am but the shadow of my former self.

MATTHEW HENRY

thus grievously afflicted.

1. Job looks upon himself as basely abused by them. "They are *mockers*, who deride my calamities, because I am thus brought low." They had all promised him that he would be happy if he would take their advice. Now all this he looked upon as flattery, and as designed to vex him so much the more. All this he calls their *provocation*, *v.* 2.

2. He condemns it. It was a sign that *God had hidden their heart from understanding* (*v.* 4). Those that are void of compassion are so far void of understanding. Where there is not the tenderness of a man one may question whether there be the understanding of a man. *Therefore shalt thou not exalt them.* Those are certainly kept back from honour whose hearts are hidden from understanding. He that thus violates the sacred laws of friendship forfeits the benefit of it, not only for himself, but for his posterity: "*Even the eyes of his children shall fail*, and, when they look for succour and comfort from their own and their father's friends, they shall look in vain as I have done, and be as much disappointed as I am in you." Those that wrong their neighbours may thereby, in the end, wrong their own children.

3. He appeals from them to God (*v.* 3): *Lay down now, put me in a surety with thee.* Those whose hearts condemn them not have confidence towards God, and can with humble and believing boldness beg of him to search and try them. Our English annotations give this reading of the verse: "*Appoint, I pray thee, my surety with thee*, namely, Christ who is with thee in heaven." "Who dares then contend with me? Who shall lay anything to my charge if Christ be an advocate for me?" Rom. viii. 32, 33.

III. The good use which the righteous should make of Job's afflictions from God, from his enemies, and from his friends, *v.* 8, 9. They are *upright men*, honest and sincere, and that act from a steady principle, with a single eye. This was Job's own character (*ch.* i. 1), and probably he speaks of such upright men especially as had been his intimates and associates. They are *the innocent*, not perfectly so, but innocence is what they aim at and press towards. Sincerity is evangelical innocency. They have *clean hands*, kept clean from the gross pollutions of sin, and, when spotted with infirmities, *washed with innocency*, Ps. xxvi. 6. Job's troubles will amaze them: *Upright men shall be astonished at this;* they will wonder to hear that so good a man as Job should be so grievously afflicted in body, name, and estate, that God should lay his hand so heavily upon him, and that his friends, who ought to have comforted him, should add to his grief. They would hereby be animated to confront the corrupt and pernicious inferences which evil men would draw from Job's sufferings, as that God has forsaken the earth, that it is in vain to serve him, and the like. The boldness of the attacks which profane people make upon religion should sharpen the courage and resolution of its friends and advocates. When vice is daring it is no time for virtue, through fear, to hide itself. *The righteous*, instead of drawing back at this frightful spectacle, *shall* with so much the more constancy and resolution *hold on his way* and press forward. Those who keep their eye upon heaven as their end will keep their feet in the paths of religion as their way, whatever difficulties and discouragements they meet with in it. By the sight of other good men's trials, and the experience of his own, he will be made more vigorous and lively in his duty, more warm and affectionate, more resolute and undaunted. The blustering wind makes the traveller gather his cloak the closer about him and gird it the faster.

Verses 10–16

Job's friends had pretended to comfort him with the hopes of his return to a prosperous estate.

I. It was their folly to talk so (*v.* 10): "*Return, and come now*, be convinced that you are in an error, and let me persuade you to be of my mind; *for I cannot find one wise man among you*, that knows how to explain the difficulties of God's providence or how to apply the consolations of his promises." It is our wisdom to comfort ourselves, and others, in distress, with that which will not fail, the promise of God, his love and grace, and a well-grounded hope of eternal life.

II. It would be his folly to heed them.

1. All his measures were already broken and he was full of confusion, *v.* 11, 12. He had had thoughts about enlarging his border, increasing his stock, and settling his children, and many pious thoughts, it is likely, of promoting religion in his country, but he concluded that all these thoughts of his heart were now at an end, and that he should never have the satisfaction of seeing his designs effected. But, if with full purpose of heart we cleave to the Lord, death

JAMIESON, FAUSSET, BROWN

2. [UMBREIT], more emphatically, "had I only not to endure *mockery*, in the midst of their *contentions* I (mine eye) would remain quiet." "Eye continue," or *tarry all night* (*Hebrew*), is a figure taken from sleep at night, to express undisturbed *rest;* opposed to (ch. 16:20), when the eye of Job is represented as pouring out tears to God *without rest*. **3. Lay down**—viz., a pledge or security, i.e., be my surety; do Thou attest my innocence, since my friends only mock me (vs. 2). Both litigating parties had to lay down a sum as security before the trial. **put me in a surety**—Provide a surety for me (in the trial) with Thee. A presage of the "surety" (Heb. 7:22), or "one Mediator between God and man" (see *Note*, 16:21). **strike hands**—"who else (save God Himself) could strike hands with me?" i.e,, be my securtiy (Ps. 119:122). The Hebrew strikes the hand of him for whom he goes security (Prov. 6:1). **4. their heart**—The *intellect* of his friends. **shalt . . . exalt**—Rather imperative, exalt them not; allow them not to conquer [UMBREIT], (Isa. 6:9, 10). **5.** The *Hebrew* for "flattery" is "smoothness"; then it came to mean a *prey* divided by *lot*, because a smooth stone was used in casting the lots (Deut. 18:8), "a portion" (Gen. 14:24). Therefore translate, "He that delivers up his friend as a prey (which the conduct of my friends implies that they would do), even the eyes," etc. [NOYES] (Ch. 11:20). Job says this as to the sinner's *children*, retorting upon their reproach as to the cutting off of his (ch. 5:4; 15:30). This accords with the Old Testament dispensation of legal retribution (Exod. 20:5).

8. astonied—at my unmerited sufferings. **against the hypocrite**—The upright shall feel their sense of justice wounded ("will be indignant") because of the prosperity of the wicked. By "hypocrite" or "ungodly," he perhaps glances at his false friends.

9. The strength of religious principle is heightened by misfortune. The pious shall take fresh courage to persevere from the example of suffering Job. The image is from a warrior acquiring new courage in action (Isa. 40:30, 31; Phil. 1:14).

10. "Return." If you have anything to advance really wise, though I doubt it, recommence your speech. For as yet I cannot find one wise man among you all.

11. Only do not vainly speak of the restoration of health to me; for "my days are past." **broken off**—as the threads of the web cut off from the loom (Isa. 38:12). **thoughts**—lit., "possessions," i.e., all the feelings and fair hopes which my heart once nourished. These belong to the *heart*, as "purposes" to the *understanding;* the two together here describe the entire inner man.

ADAM CLARKE

3. *Lay down now.* Deposit a pledge; stake your conduct against mine, and your life and soul on the issue. Let the cause come before God; let Him try it, and see whether any of you shall be justified by Him, while I am condemned.

4. *For thou hast hid their heart.* This address is to God; and here He is represented as doing that which in the course of His providence He only permits to be done. *Shalt thou not exalt them.* This was exactly fulfilled; not one of Job's friends was exalted. On the contrary, God condemned the whole, and they were not received into the divine favor till Job sacrificed and made intercession for them.

5. *He that speaketh flattery.* The man who expects much from his friends will be disappointed; while depending on them, his children's eyes may fail in looking for bread.

9. *The righteous also shall hold on his way.* There shall be no doubt concerning the dispensations of the divine providence. My case shall illustrate all seemingly intricate displays of God's government. *Shall be stronger and stronger.* He shall take encouragement from my case, stay himself on the Lord, and thus gain strength by every blast of adversity. This is one grand use of the Book of Job. It casts much light on seemingly partial displays of divine providence, and has ever been the great textbook of godly men in a state of persecution and affliction.

MATTHEW HENRY

will not break off that purpose. Job was under a constant uneasiness (*v.* 12): *The thoughts of his heart* being broken, they *changed the night into day and shortened the light.*

2. All his expectations from this world would very shortly be buried in the grave with him; so that it was a jest for him to think of such mighty things as they had flattered him with the hopes of, *ch.* v. 19, viii. 21; xi. 17. "Alas! you do but make a fool of me." He endeavours not only to reconcile himself to the grave, but to recommend it to himself: "It is my house." The grave is a house; to the wicked it is a prison-house (*ch.* xxiv. 19, 20); to the godly it is *Bethabara, a passage-house* in their way home. "There," says he, "*I have made my bed.*" The grave is a bed, for we shall rest in it in the evening of our day on earth, and rise from it in the morning of our everlasting day, Isa. lvii. 2. Let this make good people willing to die; it is but going to bed; they are weary and sleepy, and it is time that they were in their beds. Why should they not go willingly, when their father calls? He saw all his hopes from this world dropping into the grave with him (*v.* 15, 16): "Seeing I must shortly leave the world, *where is now my hope*? How can I expect to prosper who do not expect to live?" He is not hopeless, but his hope is not where they would have it be. "No, that hope which I comfort myself with is something out of sight, not things that are seen, that are temporal, but things not seen, that are eternal."

CHAPTER 18

Verses 1–4

Bildad shoots his arrows, even bitter words, against poor Job, little thinking that, though he was a wise and good man, in this instance he was serving Satan's design in adding to Job's affliction.

I. He charges him with idle endless talk, as Eliphaz had done (*ch.* xv. 2, 3): *How long will it be ere you make an end of words? v.* 2. Bildad was weary of hearing others speak, and impatient till it came to his turn. How unbecoming this conduct is in others everyone can see; but few that are guilty of it can see it in themselves. Time was when Job had the last word in all debates (*ch.* xxix. 22): *After my words they spoke not again.* Then he was in power and prosperity; but now that he was impoverished and brought low he could scarcely be allowed to speak at all.

II. With a regardlessness of what was said to him, intimated in that, *Mark, and afterwards we will speak.*

III. With a haughty contempt and disdain of his friends and of that which they offered (*v.* 3): *Wherefore are we counted as beasts?* Job had indeed called them *mockers*, had represented them both as unwise and as unkind, but he did not count them beasts; yet Bildad so represents the matter. His hot spirit was willing to find a pretence to be hard upon Job. Those that incline to be severe upon others will have it thought that others have first been so upon them.

IV. With outrageous passion: *He teareth himself in his anger, v.* 4. Herein he seems to reflect upon what Job had said (*ch.* xiii. 14): *Wherefore do I take my flesh in my teeth?*

V. With a proud and arrogant expectation to give law even to Providence itself: "*Shall the earth be forsaken for thee?* There is no reason that the course of nature should be changed and the settled rules of government violated to gratify the humour of one man. Job, dost thou think the world cannot stand without thee; but that, if thou art ruined, all the world is ruined and forsaken with thee?" To expect that God's counsels should change, his method alter, and his word fail, to please us, is as absurd and unreasonable as to think that *the earth should be forsaken for us and the rock removed out of its place.*

Verses 5–10

The rest of Bildad's discourse is entirely taken up in an elegant description of the miserable condition of a wicked man, in which there is a great deal of truth. But it is not true that all wicked people are made miserable in this world; nor is it true that all who are brought into great distress are *therefore* to be deemed wicked men. Therefore, though Bildad thought the application of it to Job was easy, yet it was not safe nor just.

I. The destruction of the wicked foreseen and foretold, under the similitude of darkness (*v.* 5, 6): *Yea, the light of the wicked shall be put out.* "Yea," says Bildad, "so it is; thou art clouded, and straitened, and made miserable, and no better could be expected; for *the light of the wicked shall be put out*, and therefore thine shall."

JAMIESON, FAUSSET, BROWN

12. They—viz., *my friends* would change the night into day, i.e., would try to persuade me of the change of my misery into joy, which is impossible [UMBREIT] (ch. 11:17); (but) the light of prosperity (could it be enjoyed) would be short because of the darkness of adversity. Or better for "short," the *Hebrew* "near"; and the light of new prosperity should be near in the face of (before) the darkness of death;" i.e., they would persuade me that light is near, even though darkness approaches. **13.** Rather, "if I wait for this grave (Sheol, or the unseen world) as my house, and make my bed in the darkness (vs. 14), and say to corruption," rather, to the pit or grave, etc. (vs. 15.) Where then is my hope? [UMBREIT]. The apodosis is at vs. 15. **14. Thou art my father . . .**—expressing most intimate connection (Prov. 7:4). His diseased state made him closely akin to the grave and worm.

15. Who shall see it fulfilled? viz., the "hope" (ch. 11:18) which they held out to him of restoration. **16. They**—viz., my hopes shall be buried with me. **bars**—(Isa. 38:10). Rather, the *wastes* or *solitudes* of the pit (sheol, the unseen world). **rest together**—the rest of me and my hope is in, etc. Both expire together. The word "rest" implies that man's ceaseless hopes only rob him of rest.

CHAPTER 18

Vss. 1-21. REPLY OF BILDAD. **2. ye**—the other two friends of Job, whom Bildad charges with having spoken mere "words," i.e., empty speeches; opposed to "mark," i.e., come to *reason,* consider the question *intelligently;* and then let us speak.

3. beasts—alluding to what Job said (ch. 12:7; so Isa. 1:3). **vile**—rather from a *Hebrew* root, "to stop up." "Stubborn," answering to the stupidity implied in the parallel first clause [UMBREIT]. Why should we give occasion by your empty speeches for our being mutually reputed, in the sight of Job and one another, as unintelligent? (ch. 17:4, 10). **4.** Rather, turning to Job, thou that tearest thyself in anger (ch. 5:2).

be forsaken—become desolate. He alludes here to Job's words as to the "rock," crumbling away (ch. 14:18, 19); but in a different application. He says bitterly "for thee." Wert thou not punished as thou art, and as thou art unwilling to bear, the eternal order of the universe would be disturbed and the earth become desolate through unavenged wickedness [UMBREIT]. Bildad takes it for granted Job is a great sinner (ch. 8:3-6; Isa. 24:5, 6). "Shall that which stands fast as a rock be removed for your special accommodation?"

5. That (vs. 4) cannot be. The decree of God is unalterable, the light (prosperity) of the wicked shall at length be put out. **his fire**—alluding to Arabian hospitality, which prided itself on welcoming the stranger to the fire in the tent, and even lit fires to direct him to it. The ungodly shall be deprived of the means to show hospitality. His dwelling shall be dark and desolate! **6. candle**—the lamp which in the East is usually fastened to the ceiling. Oil abounds in those regions, and the lamp was kept burning all night, as now in Egypt, where the poorest would rather dispense with food than the night-lamp (Ps. 18:28). To put out the lamp was an image of utter desolation.

ADAM CLARKE

12. *They change the night into day.* These purposes and thoughts are so very gloomy that they change day into night. *The light is short because of darkness.* "The light is near from the face of darkness."

CHAPTER 18

2. *How long will it be ere ye make an end?* It is difficult to say to whom this address is made; being in the plural number, it can hardly be supposed to mean Job only. It probably means all present; as if he had said, It is vain to talk with this man, and follow him through all his quibbles; take notice of this, and then let us all deliver our sentiments fully to him, without paying any regard to his self-vindications. It must be owned that this is the plan which Bildad followed, and he amply unburdens a mind that was laboring under the spirit of rancor and abuse.

3. *Counted as beasts.* You treat us as if we had neither reason nor understanding.

5. *The light of the wicked shall be put out.* Some think it would be better to translate the original, "Let the light of the wicked be extinguished!" You are a bad man, and you have perverted the understanding which God has given you. Let that understanding, that abused gift, be taken away. From this verse to the end of the chapter is a continual invective against Job.

6. *The light shall be dark in his tabernacle.* His property shall be destroyed, his house pillaged, and himself and his family come to an untimely end. *His candle shall be put out.* He shall have no posterity.

MATTHEW HENRY

II. The destruction represented under the similitude of a beast or bird caught in a snare, or a malefactor arrested and taken into custody in order to his punishment, *v.* 7-10. 1. Satan is preparing for his destruction. He is *the robber that shall prevail against him* (*v.* 9). He *hunts for the precious life.* 2. He is himself preparing for his own destruction by going on in sin, and *so treasuring up wrath against the day of wrath. His own counsels cast him down*, *v.* 7. He is *cast into a net by his own feet* (*v.* 8). 3. God is preparing for his destruction. The sinner is infatuated to run himself into the snare. *The steps of his strength*, his mighty designs and efforts, *shall be straitened*, so that he shall not compass what he intended; and the more he strives to extricate himself the more will he be entangled. *The gin shall take him by the heel.* He can no more escape the divine wrath that is in pursuit of him than a man, so held, can flee from the pursuer.

Verses 11-21

Bildad describes the destruction itself.

I. The dread of God's wrath (*v.* 11, 12): *Terror shall make him afraid on every side.* The terrors of the sinner's conscience shall haunt him, so that he shall never be easy. His feet will do him no service; they are fast in the snare, *v.* 9. He sees his ruin approaching. He feels himself utterly unable to grapple with it, either to escape it or to bear up under it.

II. Miserable indeed a wicked man's death is, how secure and jovial soever his life was. 1. See him dying, arrested by *the first-born of death*—some disease, or some stroke that has in it a more than ordinary resemblance of death itself. The harbingers of death *devour the strength of his skin*, bring rottenness into his bones and consume them. *His confidence shall then be rooted out of his tabernacle* (*v.* 14), that is, all that he trusted to for his support shall be taken from him. 2. See him dead. (1) He is then brought to *the king of terrors.* Death is terrible to nature; our Saviour himself prayed, *Father, save me from this hour.* But to the wicked it is in a special manner *the king of terrors.* How happy then are the saints, and how much indebted to the Lord Jesus, by whom death is so far abolished, and the property of it altered, that this king of terrors becomes a friend and servant! (2) He is then *driven from light into darkness* (*v.* 18), from the light of this world, and his prosperous condition in it, into darkness. (3) He is then *chased out of the world*, hurried and dragged away by the messengers of death, sorely against his will, chased as Adam out of paradise, for the world is his paradise. All the world is weary of him, and glad to get rid of him. This is death to a wicked man.

III. His family sunk and cut off, *v.* 15. Even the dwelling shall be ruined for the sake of his owner: *Brimstone shall be scattered upon his habitation*, rained upon it as upon Sodom, to the destruction of which this seems to have reference. Some think he here upbraids Job with the burning of his sheep and servants with fire from heaven. The reason is here given: *Because it is none of his*; that is, it was unjustly got. His children shall perish, either with him or after him, *v.* 16. Those who consult the true honour of their family, and the welfare of its branches, will be afraid of withering it by sin. The extirpation of the sinner's family is mentioned again (*v.* 19): *He shall neither have son nor nephew.* Sin entails a curse upon posterity. It is probable that Bildad reflects upon the death of Job's children and servants, as a further proof of his being a wicked man.

IV. His memory buried with him, or made odious; he shall either be forgotten or spoken of with dishonour (*v.* 17): *His remembrance shall perish from the earth.* All his honour shall be lost in the dust, so that *he shall have no name in the street*, departing without being desired.

V. Amazement at his fall, *v.* 20. Those that see it are affrighted. Horrible sins bring strange punishments. Ignorance of God is a wilful ignorance, for there is that to be known of him which is sufficient to leave them for ever inexcusable. They know not God, and then they commit all iniquity.

JAMIESON, FAUSSET, BROWN

7. "Steps of strength," *Hebrew*, for "His strong steps." A firm step marks health. To be straitened in steps is to be no longer able to move about at will (Prov. 4:12). **his own counsel**—Plans shall be the means of his fall (ch. 5:13). **8. he walketh upon**—rather, "he *lets himself go into* the net" [UMBREIT]. If the *English Version* be retained, then understand "snare" to be the pitfall, covered over with branches and earth, which when walked upon give way (Ps. 9:15, 35:8). **9. robber**—rather answering to "gin" in the parallel clause, "the *noose* shall hold him fast" [UMBREIT].

11. Terrors—often mentioned in this book (vs. 14; ch. 24:17; etc.). The terrors excited through an evil conscience are here personified. "Magor-missabib" (Jer. 20:3). **drive . . . to his feet**—rather, shall pursue (lit., "scatter," Hab. 3:14) him close at his heels (lit., "immediately after his feet," Hab. 3:5; I Sam. 25:42; *Hebrew*). The image is that of a pursuing conqueror who scatters the enemy [UMBREIT]. **12.** The *Hebrew* is brief and bold, "his strength is hungry." **destruction**—i.e., a great calamity (Prov. 1:27). **ready at his side**—close at hand to destroy him (Prov. 19:29). **13.** UMBREIT has "he" for "it," i.e., "in the rage of hunger he shall devour his own body"; or, "his own children" (Lam. 4:10). Rather, "destruction" from the last verse is nominative to "devour." **strength**—rather, "members" (lit., the "branches" of a tree). **the first-born of death**—a personification full of poetical horror. The first-born son held the chief place (Gen. 49:3); so here *the chiefest* (*most deadly*) *disease* that death has ever engendered (Isa. 14:30; "first-born of the poor"—the poorest). The Arabs call fever, "daughter of death." **14. confidence**—all that the father trusted in for domestic happiness, children, fortune, etc., referring to Job's losses. **rooted out**—suddenly torn away, it shall bring—i.e., he shall be brought; or, as UMBREIT better has, "*Thou* (God) shalt bring him *slowly*." The *Hebrew* expresses, "to stride slowly and solemnly." The godless has a fearful death for long before his eyes, and is at last taken by it. Alluding to Job's case. The King of terrors, not like the heathen Pluto, the fabled ruler of the dead, but Death, with all its terrors to the ungodly, personified. **15. It**—"Terror" shall haunt, etc., and not as UMBREIT "another," which the last clause of the verse disproves. **none of his**—It is his no longer. **brimstone**—probably comparing the calamity of Job by the "fire of God" (ch. 1:16) to the destruction of guilty Sodom by fire and brimstone (Gen. 19:24). **16. Roots**—himself. **branch**—his children (ch. 8:12; 15:30; Mal. 4:1).

17. street—Men shall not speak of him in meeting in the highways; rather, in the field or meadow; the shepherds shall no more mention his name—a picture from nomadic life [UMBREIT]. **18. light . . . darkness**—existence—nonexistence. **19. nephew**—(so Isa. 14:22). But it is translated "grandson" (Gen. 21:23); translate "kinsman." **20. after . . . before**—rather, "those in the West—those in the East"; i.e., all people; lit., those behind—those before"; for Orientals in geography turn with their faces to the east (not to the north as we), and back to the west; so that *before*—east; *behind*—north (so Zech. 14:8). **day**—of ruin (Obad. 12). **affrighted**—seized with terror (ch. 21:6; Isa. 13:8). **21.** (Ch. 8:22, *Marg.*)

ADAM CLARKE

F. B. MEYER:

"The king of terrors" (v. 14). So the ancients spoke of death. They were constantly pursued by the dread of the unknown. Every unpeopled or distant spot was the haunt and dwelling-place of evil and dreadful objects. But the grave, and the world beyond, were above all terrible, and death the King of Terrors. It is difficult for us, who inherit centuries of Christian teaching, to realize how dark and fearsome was all the realm that lay under the dominion of death and the grave. What a shiver in those words, King of Terrors!

But for us how vast the contrast! Jesus has abolished death, and brought life and immortality to light. He has gone through the grave, and come again to assure us that it is the back door into our Father's house, with its many mansions. At his girdle hang the keys of death and Hades; none can shut the door when He opens it, and none open when He keeps it shut. He was Himself dead; but He lives for evermore, and comes to the side of each dying saint to escort him through the valley to his own bright abode.

There is something better. In the case of immense numbers, who shall be alive and remain when He comes again, death will be entirely evaded. "He that liveth and believeth in him shall never die." They shall be caught away to meet the Lord in the air. Suddenly, in the twinkling of an eye, this mortal shall put on immortality, this corruptible incorruption. At his coming the grave shall be despoiled of its treasures, and death shall miss its expected prey.

"O death, where is thy sting! O grave, where is thy victory! Thanks be to God which giveth us the victory through our Lord Jesus Christ."

—*Great Verses Through the Bible*

18. ***He shall be driven from light.*** **He shall be taken off by a violent death.** ***And chased out of the world.*** **The wicked is driven away in his iniquity. This shows his reluctance to depart from life.**

MATTHEW HENRY

CHAPTER 19

Verses 1-7

Bildad had twice begun with a *How long* (*ch.* viii. 2; xviii. 2), and therefore Job begins with a *How long* too, *v.* 2. Job had more reason to think those long who assaulted him than they had to think him long who only vindicated himself.

I. They *vexed his soul.* They were his friends; they came to comfort him, but with a great deal of gravity, and affectation of wisdom and piety, they set themselves to rob him of the only comfort he had now left

JAMIESON, FAUSSET, BROWN

CHAPTER 19

Vss. 1-29. JOB'S REPLY TO BILDAD. **2. How long,** etc.—retorting Bildad's words (ch. 18:2). Admitting the punishment to be deserved, is it kind thus ever to be harping on this to the sufferer? And yet even this they have not yet proved.

ADAM CLARKE

CHAPTER 19

MATTHEW HENRY

him in a good God, a good conscience, and a good name; and this vexed him to the heart. They *broke him in pieces with words.* They *reproached him* (*v.* 3), gave him a bad character and *made themselves strange to him*, were shy of him now that he was in his troubles, and seemed as if they did not know him. They *magnified themselves against him* (*v.* 5), not only looked shy of him, but insulted him, magnifying themselves to depress him. *They pleaded against him his reproach*, that is, they made use of his affliction as an argument to prove him a wicked man.

II. They had thus abused him often (*v.* 3): *These ten times you have reproached me*, that is, very often. They were not ashamed of what they did, *v.* 3. They had reason to be ashamed of their hard-heartedness, of their uncharitableness, and of their deceitfulness, so ill becoming friends.

III. He answers their harsh censures, by showing them that what they condemned was capable of excuse, which they ought to have considered. The errors of his judgment were excusable (*v.* 4): "*Be it indeed that I have erred*, that I am in the wrong through ignorance or mistake." "But be it so," said Job, "*my error remaineth with myself*," that is, "I speak according to the best of my judgment, with all sincerity, and not from a spirit of contradiction." *Hast thou faith? Have it to thyself.* Some give this sense of these words: "If I be in an error, it is I that must smart for it; and therefore you need not concern yourselves." The breakings out of his passion, though not justifiable, yet were excusable, considering the vastness of his grief and the extremity of his misery. *Know then that God has overthrown me, v.* 6. Three things he would have them consider:—(1) He was overthrown, and could not help himself, enclosed as in a net, and could not get out. (2) God was the author of it, and that, in it, he fought against him. "I have enough to do to grapple with God's displeasure; let me not have yours also." (3) He could not obtain any hope of the redress of his grievances, *v.* 7. *I cry out of wrong, but I am not heard.*

Verses 8–22

Bildad had perverted Job's complaints by making them the description of the miserable condition of a wicked man; and yet he repeats them here, to move their pity, if they had any left in them.

I. He complains of the tokens of God's displeasure. "*He hath kindled his wrath against me*, which burns and pains me," *v.* 11. Enlightened consciences fear it now, but shall not feel it hereafter. Job's present apprehension was that *God counted him as one of his enemies*; and yet, at the same time, God loved him as his faithful friend. It is a gross mistake, but a very common one, to think that whom God afflicts he treats as his enemies; whereas, on the contrary, *as many as he loves he rebukes and chastens*; it is the discipline of his sons. "*He has stripped me of my glory*, my wealth, honour, power, and all the opportunity I had of doing good. My children were my glory, but I have lost them; and whatever was a crown to my head he has taken it from me, and has laid all my honour in the dust." Did he look down upon his present troubles? He saw God giving them their commission, and their orders to attack him. They are *his troops*, that act by his direction, which *encamp against me, v.* 12. It did not so much trouble him that his miseries came upon him in troops as that they were *God's* troops in whom it seemed as if God fought against him and intended his destruction. Time was when God's hosts encamped round him for safety. Now they surrounded him and *destroyed him on every side, v.* 10. He saw the hand of God cutting off all hope (*v.* 8): "*He hath fenced up my way, that I cannot pass.* I have now no way left to help myself." Hope in this life is a perishing thing, but the hope of good men, when it is cut off from this world, is but removed like a tree, transplanted from this nursery to the garden of the Lord. We shall have no reason to complain if God thus remove our hopes from the sand to the rock, from things temporal to things eternal.

II. He complains of the unkindness of his relations and of all his old acquaintance. In this also he owns the hand of God (*v.* 13): *He has put my brethren far from me*, that is, "He has laid those afflictions upon me which frighten them from me, and make them stand aloof from my sores." Yet this does not excuse Job's relations and friends from the guilt of horrid ingratitude and injustice to him. His kindred and acquaintance, his neighbours, and such as he had formerly been familiar with, who were bound by all the laws of friendship and civility, were *estranged from him, v.* 13. Poor Job was misused by his own family, and some of his worst foes were those of his own house. His own servants slighted him. His maids did not attend him in his illness, but *counted him for*

JAMIESON, FAUSSET, BROWN

3. These—prefixed emphatically to numbers (Gen. 27:36). **ten**—i.e., often (Gen. 31:7). **make yourselves strange**—rather, *stun* me [GESENIUS]. (See *Marg.* for a different meaning.)

4. erred—The *Hebrew* expresses *unconscious error.* Job was unconscious of wilful sin. **remaineth**—lit., passeth the night." An image from harboring an unpleasant guest for the night. I bear the consequences. **5. magnify**, etc.—Speak proudly (Obad. 12; Ezek. 35:13). **against me**—emphatically repeated (Ps. 38:16). **plead . . . reproach**—*English Version* makes this part of the protasis, "if" being understood, and the apodosis beginning at vs. 6. Better with UMBREIT, If ye would become great heroes against me in truth, ye must *prove* (evince) against me my *guilt*, or *shame*, which you assert. In the *English Version* "reproach" will mean Job's *calamities,* which they "pleaded" against him as a "reproach," or proof of guilt. **6. compassed . . . net**—alluding to Bildad's words (ch. 18:8). Know, that it is not that I as a wicked man have been caught in my "*own* net"; *it is God* who has compassed me in His—why, I know not. **7. wrong**—violence: brought on him by God. **no judgment**—God will not remove my calamities, and so vindicate my just cause; and my friends will not do *justice* to my past character. **8.** Image from a benighted traveller.

11. enemies—(ch. 13:24; Lam. 2:5).

9. stripped . . . crown—image from a deposed king, deprived of his robes and crown; appropriate to Job, once an emir with all but royal dignity (Lam. 5:16; Ps. 89:39).

12. troops—Calamities advance together like hostile troops (ch. 10:17). **raise up . . . way**—An army must *cast up a way* of access before it, in marching against a city (Isa. 40:3).

10. destroyed . . . on every side—"Shaken all round, so that I fall in the dust"; image from a tree uprooted by violent shaking from every side [UMBREIT]. The last clause accords with this (Jer. 1:10). **mine hope**—as to this life (in opposition to Zophar, ch. 11:18); not as to the world to come (vs. 25; ch. 14:15). **removed**—uprooted.

13. brethren—nearest kinsmen, as distinguished from "acquaintance." So "kinsfolk" and "familiar friends" (vs. 14) correspond in parallelism. The Arabic proverb is, "The brother, i.e., the true friend, is only known in time of need."

estranged—lit., "turn away with disgust." Job again unconsciously uses language prefiguring the desertion of Jesus Christ (ch. 16:10; Luke 23:49; Ps. 38:11).

ADAM CLARKE

3. *These ten times.* The exact arithmetical number is not to be regarded, *ten times* being put for many times, as we have already seen. See particularly Gen. xxxi. 7. *Ye make yourselves strange to me.* When I was in affluence and prosperity, ye were my intimates, and appeared to rejoice in my happiness; but now ye scarcely know me, or ye profess to consider me a wicked man because I am in adversity.

11. *And he counteth me unto him as one of his enemies.* From the seventh to the thirteenth verse there seems to be an allusion to a hostile invasion, battles, sieges, etc.

14. *My kinsfolk have failed.* Literally, "departed"; they have all left my house, now that there is no more hope of gain.

MATTHEW HENRY

a stranger and an alien, v. 15. Though he was now sickly, yet he was not cross and imperious, but entreated his servants with his mouth, when he had authority to command; and yet they would not be civil to him, neither kind nor just. But, one would think, when all forsook him, the wife of his bosom should have been tender of him: no, because he would not curse God and die, as she persuaded him, she did not care for coming near him, nor took any notice of what he said, *v.* 17. Even the little children who were born in his house, the children of his own servants, despised him (*v.* 18); they let him know that they neither feared him nor loved him.

III. He complains of the decay of his body; all the beauty and strength of that were gone (*v.* 20): *My bone cleaves now to my skin.*

IV. Upon all these accounts he recommends himself to the compassion of his friends. *"Have pity upon me, have pity upon me, O you my friends! Have pity upon me, for the hand of God hath touched me."* If they would not ease his affliction by their pity, yet they must not be so barbarous as to add to it by their censures and reproaches (*v.* 22): *"Why do you persecute me as God?"* If they did delight in his calamity, let them be satisfied with his flesh, which was wasted and gone, but let them not wound his spirit. Great tenderness is due to those that are in affliction, especially to those that are troubled in mind.

Verses 23–29

Here is much both of Christ and heaven in these verses: and he that said such things as these *declared plainly that he sought the better country, that is, the heavenly*; as the patriarchs of that age did, Heb. xi. 14. We have here Job's creed, or confession of faith. His belief in God the Father Almighty, the Maker of heaven and earth, and the principles of natural religion, he had often professed: but here we find him no stranger to revealed religion; though the revelation of the promised Seed, and the promised inheritance, was then discerned only like the dawning of the day, yet Job was taught of God to believe in a living Redeemer, and to *look for the resurrection of the dead and the life of the world to come*, for of these, doubtless, he must be understood to speak. These were the things he comforted himself with the expectation of, and not a deliverance from his trouble or a revival of his happiness in this world, as some would understand him. The expressions he here uses, of the Redeemer's *standing at the latter day upon the earth*, of his seeing God, and *seeing him for himself*, are wretchedly forced if they be understood of any temporal deliverance. Job was now under an extraordinary impulse of the blessed Spirit, which raised him above himself, gave him light, and gave him utterance. And some observe that, after this, we do not find in Job's discourses such passionate complaints of God and his providence as before. This hope quieted his spirit, stilled the storm, and, having here cast anchor within the veil, his mind was kept steady from this time forward.

I. Job makes this confession of his faith here. Never did anything come in more pertinently, or to better purpose. His friends reproached him as a hypocrite, but he appeals to his creed, to his faith, to his hope, and to his own conscience, which comforted him with the expectation of a blessed resurrection. *These are not the words of him that has a devil.* He appeals to the coming of the Redeemer, from this wrangle at the bar to the judgment of the bench. Job was now afflicted, and this was his cordial; when he was pressed above measure this kept him from fainting—he believed that he should *see the goodness of the Lord in the land of the living*; not in this world, for that is the land of the dying.

II. With what a solemn preface he introduces it, *v.* 23, 24. He breaks off his complaints abruptly, to triumph in his comforts. That which Job here somewhat passionately wished for God graciously granted him. His words are written; they are printed in God's book; so that, wherever that book is read, there shall this be told for a memorial concerning Job.

III. His confession itself is written, *v.* 25–27.

1. He believes the glory of the Redeemer (*v.* 25): *I know that my Redeemer liveth*, that he is in being and is my life, *and that he shall stand at last upon the earth*. There is a Redeemer provided for fallen man, and Jesus Christ is that Redeemer. The word is *Goël* which is used for the next of kin, to whom, by the law of Moses, the right of redeeming a mortgaged estate did belong, Lev. xxv. 25. Our heavenly inheritance was mortgaged by sin; we are ourselves utterly unable to redeem it; Christ is near of kin to us, the next kinsman that is able to redeem; he has paid our debt, satisfied God's justice for sin, and so has taken off the mortgage and made a new settlement of the inheritance. Our persons also want a Redeemer;

JAMIESON, FAUSSET, BROWN

15. They that dwell, etc.—rather, sojourn: male servants, sojourning in his house. Mark the contrast. The stranger admitted to sojourn as a dependent treats the master as a stranger in his own house. **16. servant**—born in my house (as distinguished from those sojourning in it), and so altogether belonging to the family. Yet even he disobeys my call **mouth**—i.e., calling aloud; formerly a *nod* was enough. Now I no longer look for *obedience*, I try *entreaty*. **17. strange**—His breath by elephantiasis had become so strongly altered and offensive, that his wife turned away as estranged from him (vs. 13; ch. 17:1). **children . . . of mine own body**—lit., "belly." But "loins" is what we should expect, not "belly" (womb), which applies to the woman. The "mine" forbids it being taken of his wife. Besides their children were dead. In ch. 3:10 the same words "my womb" mean, *my mother's womb:* therefore translate, "and I must entreat (as a suppliant) the children of my mother's womb"; i.e., my own brothers—a heightening of force, as compared with last clause of vs. 16 [UMBREIT]. Not only must I entreat suppliantly my *servant*, but my own *brothers* (Ps. 69:8). Here too, he unconsciously foreshadows Jesus Christ (John 7: 5). **18. young children**—So the *Hebrew* means (ch. 21:11). Reverence for age is a chief duty in the East. The word means "wicked" (ch. 16:11). So UMBREIT has it here, not so well. **I arose**—Rather, supply "if," as Job was no more in a state to stand up. "If I stood up (arose), they would speak against (abuse) me" [UMBREIT]. **19. inward**—confidential: lit., "men of my secret"—to whom I entrusted my most intimate confidence. **20.** Extreme meagerness. The bone seemed to stick in the skin, being seen through it, owing to the flesh drying up and falling away from the bone. The *Margin,* "as to my flesh," makes this sense clearer. The *English Version*, however, expresses the same: "*And* to my flesh," viz., which has fallen away from the bone, instead of firmly covering it. **skin of my teeth**—proverbial. I have *escaped with* bare life; I am whole *only with the skin of my teeth;* i.e., my gums alone are whole, the rest of the skin of my body is broken with sores (ch. 7:5; Ps. 102:5). Satan left Job his speech, in hope that he might therewith curse God. **21.** When God had made him such a piteous spectacle, his friends should spare him the additional persecution of their cruel speeches. **22. as God**—has persecuted me. Prefiguring Jesus Christ (Ps. 69:26). That God afflicts is no reason that man is to add to a sufferer's affliction (Zech. 1: 15). **satisfied with my flesh**—It is not enough that God afflicts my flesh literally (vs. 20), but you must "eat my flesh" metaphorically (Ps. 27:2); i.e., utter the worst calumnies, as the phrase often means in *Arabic*. **23.** Despairing of justice from his friends in his lifetime, he wishes his words could be preserved imperishably to posterity, attesting his hope of vindication at the resurrection. **printed**—not our modern printing, but engraven. **24. pen**—graver. **lead**—poured into the engraven characters, to make them better seen [UMBREIT]. Not on leaden plates; for it was "in the rock" that they were engraved. Perhaps it was the hammer that was of "lead," as sculptors find more delicate incisions are made by it, than by a harder hammer. FOSTER (*One Primev. Lang.*) has shown that the inscriptions on the rocks in Wady-Mokatta, along Israel's route through the desert, record the journeys of that people, as Cosmas Indicopleustes asserted, A.D. 535. **for ever**—as long as the rock lasts. **25. redeemer**—UMBREIT and others understand this and vs. 26, of God appearing as Job's avenger *before his death,* when his body would be wasted to a skeleton. But Job uniformly despairs of restoration and vindication of his cause in this life (ch. 17:15, 16). One hope alone was left, which the Spirit revealed—a vindication in a future life: it would be no full vindication if his soul alone were to be happy *without the body,* as some explain (vs. 26) *out of* the flesh." It was his body that had chiefly suffered: the resurrection of his body, therefore, alone could vindicate his cause: to see God with *his own eyes,* and in a renovated body (vs. 27), would disprove the imputation of guilt cast on him because of the sufferings of his present body. That this truth is not further dwelt on by Job, or noticed by his friends, only shows that it was *with him* a bright passing glimpse of *Old Testament* hope, rather than the steady light of *Gospel assurance; with us* this passage has a definite clearness, which it had not in *his* mind (see *Note,* 21:30). The idea in "redeemer" with Job is Vindicator (ch. 16:19; Num. 35:27), redressing his wrongs; also including at least with *us,* and probably with *him,* the idea of the predicted Bruiser of the serpent's head. Tradition would inform him of the prediction. FOSTER

ADAM CLARKE

19. *My inward friends.* Those who were my greatest intimates.

20. *My bone cleaveth to my skin.* My flesh is entirely wasted away, and nothing but skin and bone left.

I am escaped with the skin of my teeth. To *escape with the skin of the teeth* seems to have been a proverbial expression, signifying great difficulty. I had as narrow an escape from death as the thickness of the enamel on the teeth. I was within a hair's breadth of destruction.

21. *Have pity upon me.* The iteration here strongly indicates the depth of his distress, and that his spirit was worn down with the length and severity of his suffering.

23. *Oh that my words were now written!* Our translators have made a strange mistake by rendering the verb *yuchaku, printed,* when they should have used "described, traced out." Oh, that my words were fairly traced out in a book! Three kinds of writing Job alludes to, as being practiced in his time: (1) writing in a book, (2) cutting with an iron style on plates of lead, (3) engraving on large stones or rocks, many of which are still found in different parts of Arabia.

25. *For I know that my redeemer liveth.* I shall therefore lay down one principle, without which no mode of interpretation hitherto offered can have any weight. The principle is this: Job was now under the especial inspiration of the Holy Spirit, and spoke prophetically. I arrive at the conclusion that the prophecy in question was not designed to point out the future prosperity of Job, but rather the future redemption of mankind by Jesus Christ, and the general resurrection of the human race.

I know, yadati, I have a firm and full persuasion, *that my redeemer, goali,* my **"kinsman,"** he whose right it was among the ancient Hebrews to redeem the forfeited heritages belonging to the family (Lev. xxv. 25; Num. xxv. 12; Ruth iii. 13); but here it must refer to Christ, who has truly the right of redemption, being of the same kindred, who was born of woman, flesh of our flesh and bone of our bone. *Liveth, chai,* is the living One, who has the keys of hell and death; the Creator and Lord of the spirits of all flesh, and the principle and support of all *life.*

MATTHEW HENRY

we are sold for sin, and sold under sin; our Lord Jesus has wrought out a redemption for us, and proclaims redemption to us, and so he is truly the Redeemer. *Because he lives we shall live also*, John xiv. 19. When Job had lost all his wealth and all his friends, yet he was not separated from Christ, nor cut off from his relation to him: "Still he is my Redeemer." That next kinsman adhered to him when all his other kindred forsook him, and he had the comfort of it. *I know* (observe with what an air of assurance he speaks it, as one confident of this very thing), *I know that my Redeemer lives.*

2. He believes the happiness of the redeemed, and his own title to that happiness. He counts upon the corrupting of his body in the grave, and speaks of it with a holy carelessness and unconcernedness: *Though, after my skin they destroy this body.* Job mentions this, that the glory of the resurrection he believed and hoped for might shine the more brightly. The same power that made man's body at first, out of common dust, can raise it out of its own dust. He comforts himself with the hopes of happiness on the other side death and the grave: *After I shall awake* (so the margin reads it), *though this body be destroyed, yet out of my flesh shall I see God.* Soul and body shall come together again. That body which must be destroyed in the grave shall be raised again, a glorious body, *Yet in my flesh I shall see God.* Job speaks of seeing him with eyes of flesh, *in my flesh, with my eyes*; the same body that died shall rise again, a glorified body, a *spiritual body*, 1 Cor. xv. 44. Job and God shall come together again: *In my flesh shall I see God. My eyes shall behold him, and not another.*

IV. His creed spoke comfort to himself, but warning and terror to those that set themselves against him. It was a word of caution to them not to proceed and persist in their unkind usage of him, *v.* 28. A living, quickening, commanding, principle of grace in the heart, is the root of the matter, as necessary to our religion as the root to the tree. Love to God and our brethren, faith in Christ, hatred of sin—these are the root of the matter; other things are but leaves in comparison with these. Serious godliness is the one thing needful. We are to believe that many have the root of the matter in them who are not in everything of our mind—who have their follies, and weaknesses, and mistakes—and to conclude that it is at our peril if we persecute any such. Job and his friends differed in some notions concerning the methods of Providence, but they agreed in the root of the matter, the belief of another world. Good men need to be frightened from sin by the terrors of the Almighty, particularly from the sin of rashly judging their brethren, Matt. vii. 1; James iii. 1.

JAMIESON, FAUSSET, BROWN

shows that the fall by the serpent is represented perfectly on the temple of Osiris at Philæ; and the resurrection on the tomb of the Egyptian Mycerinus, dating 4000 years back. Job's sacrifices imply sense of sin and need of atonement. Satan was the injurer of Job's body; Jesus Christ his Vindicator, the Living One who giveth life (John 5:21,26). **at the latter day**—Rather, "the Last," the peculiar title of Jesus Christ, though Job may not have known the pregnancy of his own inspired words, and may have understood merely *one that comes after* (I Cor. 15: 45; Rev. 1:17). Jesus Christ is *the last.* The day of Jesus Christ *the last day* (John 6:39). **stand**—rather, arise: as God is said to "raise up" the Messiah (Jer. 23:5; Deut. 18:15). **earth**—rather, dust: often associated with the body crumbling away in it (ch. 7:21; 17:16); therefore appropriately here. Above that very *dust* wherewith was mingled man's decaying body shall man's Vindicator arise. "Arise above the dust," strikingly expresses that fact that Jesus Christ *arose* first Himself *above the dust,* and then is to *raise* His people *above* it (I Cor. 15:20, 23). The Spirit intended in Job's words more than Job fully understood (I Pet. 1:12). Though He *seems,* in forsaking me, to be as one *dead,* He now truly "liveth" in heaven; hereafter He shall appear also above the *dust* of earth. The Goel or vindicator of blood was the nearest kinsman of the slain. So Jesus Christ took our flesh, to be our kinsman. Man lost life by Satan the "murderer" (John 8:44), here Job's persecutor (Heb. 2:14). Compare also as to *redemption of the inheritance* by the kinsman of the dead (Ruth 4:3-5; Eph. 1:14). **26.** Rather, though after my skin (is no more) this (body) is destroyed ("body" being omitted, because it was so wasted as not to deserve the name), yet *from* my flesh (*from my renewed body,* as the starting-point of vision, Song of Sol. 2:9; "looking out *from* the windows") "shall I see God." Next clause proves *bodily* vision is meant, for it specifies "mine eyes" [ROSENMULLER, 2d ed.]. The *Hebrew* opposes "*in* my flesh." The "skin" was the first destroyed by elephantiasis, then the "body." **27. for myself**—for my advantage, as my friend. **not another**—Mine eyes shall behold Him, but *no longer* as one *estranged* from me, as now [BENGEL]. **though**—better omitted: my reins (inward recesses of the heart) are consumed within me; i.e., pine with longing desire for that day (Ps. 84:2; 119:81). The Gentiles had but few revealed promises: how gracious that the few should have been so explicit (cf. Num. 24:17; Matt. 2:2). **28.** Rather ye will then (when the Vindicator cometh) say, Why, etc. **root . . . in me**—The root of pious integrity, which was the *matter* at issue, whether it could be in one so afflicted, is found in me. UMBREIT, with many MSS. and versions, reads "in him." "Or how found we in him *ground of contention.*" **29.** "Wrath (the passionate violence with which the friends persecuted Job) bringeth," etc., lit., "is sin of the sword." **that ye may know**—Supply, "I say this." **judgment**—inseparably connected with the coming of the Vindicator. The "wrath" of God at His appearing for the temporal vindication of Job against the friends (ch. 42:7) is a pledge of the eternal wrath at the final coming to glorify the saints and judge their enemies (II Thess. 1:6-10; Isa. 25:8).

ADAM CLARKE

And that he shall stand at the latter day upon the earth. The latter day, or time, when God comes to judgment.

He shall stand, "he shall arise, or stand up," i.e., to give sentence in judgment; or He himself shall arise from the dust, as the passage has been understood by some to refer to the resurrection of Christ from the dead. *Upon the earth, al aphar,* "over the dead," or from the dead. *Upon the earth, al aphar,* "over the dead," or those who are reduced to dust. This is the meaning of *aphar* in Ps. xxx. 9: "What profit is there in my blood, when I go down to the pit? Shall the dust [i.e., the dead] praise thee?"

26. *And though after my skin worms destroy this body. My skin,* which is now almost all that remains of my former self, except the bones; see v. 20. *They destroy this*—not body. *They*—diseases and affliction, destroy this wretched composition of misery and corruption. *Yet in my flesh shall I see God.* Either, I shall arise from the dead, have a renewed body, and see Him with eyes of flesh and blood, though what I have now shall shortly molder into dust; or, I shall see Him in the flesh, my Kinsman, who shall partake of my flesh and blood, in order that He may ransom the lost inheritance.

27. *Whom I shall see for myself.* Have a personal interest in the resurrection, as I shall have in the Redeemer. *And mine eyes shall behold.* That very Person who shall be the Resurrection, as He is the Life. *And not another.* And not a "stranger," one who has no relation to human nature; but *goali,* my redeeming Kinsman. *Though my reins be consumed within me.* Though I am now apparently on the brink of death, the thread of life being spun out to extreme tenuity.

28. *But ye should say.* Or, "Then ye shall say." *Why persecute we him?* Or, as Mr. Good, How did we persecute him! Alas! we are not convinced that we did wrong. *Seeing the root of the matter.* Instead of *bi,* "in me," *bo,* "in him," is the reading of more than one hundred of Kennicott's and De Rossi's MSS., and in several of the versions: "Seeing the root of the matter is found in him."

MATTHEW HENRY

CHAPTER 20

Verses 1-9

Here, I. Zophar begins very passionately (*v.* 2): *Therefore do my thoughts cause me to answer.* He takes no notice of what Job had said to move their pity. He excuses his haste with two things:—1. That Job had given him a strong provocation (*v.* 3): "*I have heard the check of my reproach.*" Job's friends, I doubt, had spirits too high to deal with a man in his low condition; and high spirits are impatient of contradiction. They cannot bear a check but they call it *the check of their reproach.* 2. That his own heart caused him to answer (*v.* 2), for *out of the abundance of the heart the mouth speaks*; but he fathers the instigation (*v.* 3) upon *the spirit of his understanding.*

II. Zophar proceeds to show the ruin and destruction of wicked people, insinuating that because Job was destroyed and ruined he was certainly a wicked man.

1. He appeals, (1) To Job's own knowledge and conviction: "*Knowest thou not this?*" (2) To the experience of all ages. It was known of old that the sin of sinners will be their ruin.

2. It is laid down (*v.* 5): *The triumphing of the wicked is short, and the joy of the hypocrite but for a moment.* Job's friends were loth to own, at first, that wicked

JAMIESON, FAUSSET, BROWN

CHAPTER 20

Vss. 1-29. REPLY OF ZOPHAR. **2. Therefore**—Rather, the more excited I feel by Job's speech, the more *for that very reason* shall my reply be supplied by my calm consideration. Lit., "Notwithstanding; my calm thoughts (as in ch. 4:13) shall furnish my answer, because of the excitement (haste) within me" [UMBREIT]. **3. check of my reproach**—i.e., the castigation intended as a reproach (lit., shame) to me. **spirit of . . . understanding**—my rational spirit; answering to "calm thoughts" (vs. 2). In spite of thy reproach urging me to "hastiness." I will answer in calm reason.

5. hypocrite—lit., "the ungodly" (Ps. 37:36, 36).

ADAM CLARKE

CHAPTER 20

2. *Therefore do my thoughts.* It has already been observed that Zophar was the most inveterate of all Job's *enemies,* for we really must cease to call them *friends.* He sets no bounds to his invective, and outrages every rule of charity. A man of such a bitter spirit must have been, in general, very unhappy. With him Job is, by insinuation, everything that is base, vile, and hypocritical. *For this I make haste.* "There is sensibility in me, and my feelings provoke me to reply."

3. *I have heard the check of my reproach.* Zophar assumes his old ground, and retracts nothing of what he had said. Like many of his own complexion in the present day, he was determined to believe that his judgment was infallible and that he could not err.

4. *Knowest thou not this of old?* This is a maxim as ancient as the world; it began with the first man: A wicked man shall triumph but a short time; God will destroy the proud doer.

MATTHEW HENRY

people might prosper at all (*ch.* iv. 9), until Job proved it plainly (*ch.* ix. 24; xii. 6), and now Zophar yields it; but lays it down that they will not prosper long.

3. It is illustrated, *v.* 6-9. (1) He supposes his prosperity to be very high, as high as you can imagine, *v.* 6. (2) He is confident that his ruin will accordingly be very great, and his fall the more dreadful for his having risen so high: *He shall perish for ever*, *v.* 7.

Verses 10–22

The instances of the miserable condition of the wicked man in this world are expressed with great fulness.

I. What his wickedness is for which he is punished.

1. The lusts of the flesh, here called *the sins of his youth* (*v.* 11). The forbidden pleasures of sense are said to be *sweet in his mouth* (*v.* 12); he indulges himself in all the gratifications of the carnal appetite, as yielding the satisfaction which *he hides under his tongue*, as the most dainty delicate thing that can be. *He keeps it still within his mouth* (*v.* 13); let him have that, and he desires no more. Or his hiding it and keeping it under his tongue denotes his industrious concealment of his beloved lust.

2. The love of the world and the wealth of it. *He has swallowed down riches* as eagerly as ever a hungry man swallowed down meat. It is that which he desired (*v.* 20). It is *that which he laboured for* (*v.* 18), all ways and methods, *per fas, per nefas—right or wrong*, to be rich. We must *labour*, not *to be rich* (Prov. xxiii. 4), but to be charitable, *that we may have to give* (Eph. iv. 28), not to spend. He expected rivers of sensual delights.

3. Violence and oppression, and injustice in his poor neighbours, *v.* 19. It is charged upon this wicked man, that *he has forsaken the poor*. He has *oppressed* them. He has *violently taken away their houses*.

II. His punishment for this wickedness. *He shall never see the rivers, the floods, the brooks of honey and butter*, with which he hoped to glut himself. The enjoyment sinks far below the raised expectation. He shall be diseased and distempered in his body; and how little comfort a man has in riches if he has not health! The sins of his youth shall *lie down with him in the dust*. He shall be disquieted and troubled in his mind: *Surely he shall not feel quietness in his belly*, *v.* 20. Let none expect to enjoy that comfortably which they have gotten unjustly. Even that wickedness which was sweet in the commission, and was rolled under the tongue as a delicate morsel, becomes bitter in the reflection, and, when it is reviewed, fills him with horror and vexation. It is turned into *the gall of asps*, than which nothing is more bitter, *the poison of asps* (*v.* 16), than which nothing more fatal, and so it will be to him. *In the fulness of his sufficiency*, when he thinks himself most sure of the continuance of his happiness, *he shall be in straits*, through the anxieties and perplexities of his own mind. He shall be dispossessed of his estate; that shall sink and dwindle away to nothing, so that *he shall not rejoice therein*, *v.* 18. *His children shall seek to please the poor*, while his own hands shall restore them their goods with shame (*v.* 18). Thus, *he shall not save of that which he desired* (*v.* 20), not only he shall not save it all, but he shall save nothing of it. In all this Zophar reflects upon Job, who had lost all and was reduced to the last extremity.

Verses 23–29

Zophar here comes to show their utter ruin at last.

I. Their ruin will take its rise from God's wrath and vengeance, *v.* 23. *God shall cast the fury of his wrath upon him and rain it upon him*. Every word here speaks terror. There is no fence against this, but in Christ, who is the only covert from the storm and tempest, Isa. xxxii. 2. Perhaps Zophar here reflects on the death of Job's children when they were eating and drinking.

II. Their ruin will be inevitable (*v.* 24). *He shall flee from the iron weapon*. If he escape the sword, yet *the bow of steel shall strike him through*.

III. It will be a total terrible ruin. O what *terrors are upon him*!

IV. Sometimes it is a ruin that comes upon him insensibly, *v.* 26. 1. The darkness he is wrapped up in is a hidden darkness, and it is *hid in his secret place*, whither he has retreated and where he hopes to shelter himself; he never retires into his own conscience but he finds himself in the dark and utterly at a loss. He is wasted by a soft gentle fire—the fire needs no blowing, and that is his case; he is ripe for ruin.

V. It is a ruin, not only to himself, but to his family: *It shall go ill with him that is left in his tabernacle*, for the curse shall reach him, and he shall be cut off. *His goods shall flow away* from his family as fast as ever they flowed into it.

JAMIESON, FAUSSET, BROWN

6. (Isa. 14:13; Obad. 3:4.) **7.** dung—in contrast to the haughtiness of the sinner (vs. 6); this strong term expresses disgust and the lowest degradation (Ps. 83:10; I Kings 14:10). **8.** (Ps. 73:20.) **9.** Rather "the eye followeth him, but can *discern* him no more." A *sharp-looking* is meant (ch. 28:7; ch. 7:10). **10. seek to please**—"Atone to the poor" (by restoring the property of which they had been robbed by the father) [DE WETTE]. Better than *English Version*, "The children" are reduced to the humiliating condition of "seeking the favor of those very poor," whom the father had oppressed. But UMBREIT translates as *Margin*. **his hands**—rather, *their* (the children's) hands. **their goods**—the goods of the poor. Righteous retribution! (Exod. 20:5.) **11.** (Ps. 25:7), so *Vulgate*. GESENIUS has "full of youth"; viz., *in the fulness of his youthful strength* he shall be laid in the dust. But "bones" plainly alludes to Job's disease, probably to Job's own words (ch. 19:20). UMBREIT translates, "full of his *secret* sins," as in Psalm 90:8; his secret guilt in his time of seeming righteousness, like secret poison, at last lays him in the dust. The *English Version* is best. Zophar alludes to Job's own words (ch. 17:16). **with him**—His sin had so pervaded his nature that it accompanies him to the grave: for eternity the sinner cannot get rid of it (Rev. 22:11). **12. be**—"*taste sweet.*" Sin's fascination is like poison sweet to the taste, but at last deadly to the vital organs (Prov. 20:17; ch. 9:17, 18). **hide . . . tongue**—seek to prolong the enjoyment by keeping the sweet morsel long in the mouth (so vs. 13). **14. turned**—*Hebrew* denotes a total change into a disagreeable contrary (Jer. 2:21; cf. Rev. 10:9, 10). **14. gall**—in which the poison of the asp was thought to lie. It rather is contained in a sack in the mouth. Scripture uses popular language, where no moral truth is thereby endangered. **15.** He is forced to disgorge his ill-gotten wealth. **16. shall suck**—It shall turn out that he has sucked the poison, etc. **17. floods**—lit., "stream of floods," plentiful streams flowing with milk, etc. (ch. 29:6; Exod. 3:17). Honey and butter are more fluid in the East than with us and are poured out from jars. These "rivers" or waterbrooks are in the sultry East emblems of prosperity. **18.** Image from food which is taken away from one before he can swallow it. **restitution**—(So Prov. 6: 31). The parallelism favors the *Eng. Version* rather than the translation of GESENIUS, "As a possession to be restored in which he rejoices not." **he shall not rejoice**—His enjoyment of his ill-gotten gains shall then be at an end (vs. 5). **19. oppressed**—whereas he ought to have espoused their cause (II Chron. 16:10). **forsaken**—left helpless. **house**—thus leaving the poor without shelter (Isa. 5:8; Mic. 2:2). **20.** UMBREIT translates, "His inward parts know no rest" from desires. **his belly**—i.e., peace *inwardly*. **not save**—lit., "not *escape* with that which," etc., alluding to Job's having been stripped of his all. **21. look for**—rather, *because* his goods, i.e., prosperity *shall have* no *endurance*. **22. shall be**—rather, "he is (feeleth) straitened." The next clause explains in what respect. **wicked**—Rather, "the whole hand of the *miserable* (whom he had oppressed) cometh upon him"; viz., the sense of his having oppressed the poor, now in turn comes with all its power (hand) on him. This caused his "straitened" feeling even in prosperity. **23.** Rather, "God shall cast (may God send) [UMBREIT] upon him the fury of His wrath *to fill his belly!*" **while . . . eating**—rather, "shall rain it upon him *for his food*! Fiery rain, i.e., lightning (Ps. 11:6; alluding to Job's misfortune, ch. 1:16). The force of the image is felt by picturing to one's self the opposite nature of a refreshing rain in the desert (Exod. 16:4; Ps. 68:9). **24. steel**—rather, "brass." While the wicked flees from one danger, he falls into a greater one from an opposite quarter [UMBREIT]. **25. It is drawn**—Rather, "He (God) draweth (the sword, Josh. 5:13) and (no sooner has He done so, than) it cometh out of (i.e., passes right through) the (sinner's) body" (Deut. 32:41, 42; Ezek. 21:9, 10). The *glittering* sword is a happy image for lightning. **gall**—i.e., his life (ch. 16:13). "Inflicts a deadly wound." **terrors**—Zophar repeats Bildad's words (ch. 17:11; Ps. 88:16; 55:4). **26.** "All darkness," i.e., every calamity that befalls the wicked shall be *hid* (in store for him) *in His* (God's) *secret places*, or treasures (Jude 13; Deut. 32:34). **not blown**—not kindled by man's hands, but by God's (Isa. 30:33; LXX in ALEXANDRIAN MS. reads "unquenchable fire," Matt. 3:12). Tact is shown by the friends in not expressly mentioning, but alluding under color of general cases, to Job's calamities; here (ch. 1:16) UMBREIT explains it, *wickedness*, is a "self-igniting fire"; in it lie the principles of destruction. **ill . . . tabernacle**—Every trace of the sinner must be obliterated (ch. 18:15).

ADAM CLARKE

6. *Though his excellency mount up to the heavens.* Probably referring to the original state of Adam, of whose fall he appears to have spoken, v. 4. He was created in the image of God; but by his sin against his Maker he fell into wretchedness, misery, death, and destruction.

10. *His children shall seek to please the poor.* They shall be reduced to the lowest degree of poverty and want, so as to be obliged to become servants to the poor.

15. *He shall vomit them up again.* This is also an allusion to an effect of most ordinary poisons; they occasion a nausea, and often excruciating vomiting—nature striving to eject what it knows, if retained, will be its bane.

16. *He shall suck the poison of asps.* That delicious morsel, that secret, easily besetting sin, of his soul as the poison of asps would do on the life of his body.

19. *He hath oppressed and hath forsaken the poor.* Literally, *He hath broken in pieces the forsaken of the poor.*

20. *Surely he shall not feel quietness in his belly.* The meaning seems to be, "He shall never be satisfied; he shall have an endless desire after secular good, and shall never be able to obtain what he covets."

22. *In the fulness of his sufficiency he shall be in straits.* This is a fine saying. It is literally true of every great, rich, wicked man.

23. *When he is about to fill his belly.* Here seems a plain allusion to the lustings of the children of Israel in the desert. God showered down quails upon them, and showered down His wrath while the flesh was in their mouths.

24. *He shall flee from the iron weapon.* Or, "Though he should flee from the iron armour, the brazen bow should strike him through."

26. *A fire not blown shall consume him.* As Zophar is here showing that the wicked cannot escape from the divine judgments, so he points out the different instruments which God employs for their destruction. The "wrath" of God—any secret or supernatural curse. The "iron weapon"—the spear or suchlike. The "bow," and its swift-flying arrow. "Darkness"—deep horror and perplexity. "A fire not blown"—a supernatural fire, lightning—such as fell on Korah and his company, to whose destruction there is probably here an allusion; hence the words, *It shall go ill with him that is left in his tabernacle.*

MATTHEW HENRY

VI. It is a ruin which will manifestly appear to be just and righteous, and what he has brought upon himself by his own wickedness; for (*v.* 27) *the heaven shall reveal his iniquity.*

VII. Zophar concludes like an orator (*v.* 29): *This is the portion of a wicked man from God.* Never was any doctrine better explained, or worse applied, than this by Zophar, who intended by all this to prove Job a hypocrite. Let us receive the good explication, and make a better application.

JAMIESON, FAUSSET, BROWN

27. All creation is at enmity with him, and proclaims his guilt, which he would fain conceal.

28. increase—prosperity. Ill got—ill gone. **flow away**—like waters that run dry in summer; using Job's own metaphor against himself (ch. 6:15-17; II Sam. 14:14; Mic. 1:4). **his wrath**—God's **29. appointed**—not as a matter of chance, but by the divine "decree" (*Margin*) and settled principle.

ADAM CLARKE

27. *The heaven shall reveal his iniquity; and the earth shall rise up against him.* Another allusion, if I mistake not, to the destruction of Korah and his company. "And the glory of the Lord appeared unto all the congregation," Num. xvi. 19, etc. And then "the earth rose up against them." "The ground clave asunder that was under them: and the earth opened her mouth, and swallowed them up, and . . . they . . . went down alive into the pit, and the earth closed upon them," Num. xvi. 31-33.

28. *The increase of his house shall depart, and his goods shall flow aawy in the day of his wrath.* A further allusion to the punishment of the rebellious company of Korah, who not only perished themselves, but their houses also, and their goods, Num. xvi. 32.

MATTHEW HENRY

CHAPTER 21

Verses 1–6

Job here recommends himself to the compassionate consideration of his friends. That which he entreats of them is very fair, that they would suffer him to speak (*v.* 3) and not break in upon him. They came to comfort him. "Now," says he, "*let this be to your consolations* (*v.* 2); if you have no other comforts to administer to me, be so just, as to give me a patient hearing. After I have spoken you may go on with what you have to say, and I will not hinder you, no, though you go on to mock me. If you will but give me a fair hearing, I believe I shall say that which will change your note and make you pity me rather than mock me. *Is my complaint to man?* No, if it were I see it would be to little purpose to complain. But my complaint is to God, and to him do I appeal. Let him be Judge between you and me." It was not a common case, but a very extraordinary one. He himself was amazed at it. "*When I remember* that terrible day in which I was on a sudden stripped of all my comforts, that day in which I was stricken with sore boils,—when I remember all the hard speeches with which you have grieved me,—I confess *I am afraid, and trembling takes hold of my flesh,* especially when I compare this with the prosperous condition of many wicked people, and the applauses of their neighbours, with which they pass through the world."

Verses 7–16

All Job's three friends, in their last discourses, had been very copious in describing the miserable condition of a wicked man in this world. "It is true," says Job, "remarkable judgments are sometimes brought upon notorious sinners, but not always; for we have many instances of the great and long prosperity of those that are openly and avowedly wicked; though they are hardened in their wickedness by their prosperity, yet they are still suffered to prosper."

I. He here describes their prosperity in the height, and breadth, and length of it. They live, and are not suddenly cut off by the strokes of divine vengeance. Not only do they live but they *live in prosperity*, 1 Sam. xxv. 6. They are *mighty in power*, are preferred to places of authority and trust. This is the day of God's patience, and, in some way or other, he makes use of their prosperity to serve his own counsels, while it ripens them for ruin. *Their seed is established in their sight.* They are easy and quiet, *v.* 9. Whereas Zophar had spoken of their continual frights and terrors, Job says, *Their houses are safe* both from danger and from the fear of it (*v.* 9). They are rich and thrive in their estates. Of this he gives only one instance, *v.* 10. They are merry and live a jovial life (*v.* 11, 12).

II. He shows how they abuse their prosperity and are confirmed and hardened by it in their impiety, *v.* 14, 15. God suffers them to prosper; but let us not wonder at it, for *the prosperity of fools destroy them*, by hardening them in sin, Prov. i. 32; Ps. lxxiii. 7–9. How light these prospering sinners make of God and religion, as if because they have so much of this world they had no need to look after another. How ill affected they are to God and religion; they abandon them, and cast off the thoughts of them. The world is the portion they have chosen, and take up with, and think themselves happy in; while they have that they can live without God. *We desire not the knowledge of thy ways.* The two great bonds by which we are drawn and held to religion are those of duty and interest. They will not believe it is their duty to be religious: *What is the Almighty, that we should serve him?* How slightly they speak of God: *What is the Almighty?* As if he were a mere name. How hardly they speak of religion. They call it a *service* which they look upon as a task and drudgery.

JAMIESON, FAUSSET, BROWN

CHAPTER 21

Vss. 1-34. Job's Answer. **2. consolations**—If you will listen calmly to me, this will be regarded as "consolations"; alluding to Eliphaz' boasted "consolations" ch. 15:11), which Job felt more as aggravations ("mockings," vs. 3) than consolations (ch. 16:2). **3.** Lit., "*Begin* your mockings" (ch. 17:2). **4.** Job's difficulty was not as to *man,* but as to *God,* why He so afflicted him, as if he were the guilty hypocrite which the friends alleged him to be. Vulgate translates it, "my disputation." **if it were**—rather, since this is the case. **5. lay . . . hand upon . . . mouth**—(Prov. 30:32; Judg. 18:19). So the heathen god of silence was pictured with his hand on his mouth. There was enough in Job's case to awe them into silence (ch. 17:8). **6. remember**—Think on it. Can you wonder that I broke out into complaints, when the struggle was not with men, but with the Almighty? Reconcile, if you can, the ceaseless woes of the innocent with the divine justice! Is it not enough to make one tremble? [Umbreit].

7. The answer is Romans 2:4; I Timothy 1:16; Psalm 73:18; Ecclesiastes 8:11-13; Luke 2:35-end; Proverbs 16:4; Romans 9:22. **old**—in opposition to the friends who asserted that sinners are "cut off" early (ch. 8:12, 14). **8.** In opposition to ch. 18:19, 5:4. **9.** Lit., "Peace from fear": with poetic force. Their house is *peace itself,* far removed from fear. Opposed to the friends' assertion, as to the bad (ch. 15:21-24; 20:26-28), and conversely, the good (ch. 5:23, 24). **10.** Rather, their cattle conceive. The first clause of the verse describes an *easy conception,* the second, a happy *birth* [Umbreit]. **11.** "Send forth," viz., out of doors, to their happy sports under the skies, like a joyful flock sent to the pastures. **little ones**—like lambkins. **children**—somewhat older than the former. **dance**—not formal dances; but skip, like lambs, in joyous and healthful play. **12. take**—rather, *lift up the voice* (sing) to the note of [Umbreit]. **timbrel**—rather, tambourine. **organ**—not the modern "organ," but the "pipe" (Gen. 4:21). The first clause refers to stringed, the latter, to wind instruments; thus, with "the voice" all kinds of music are enumerated. **13. wealth**—Old *English Version* for *prosperity.* **in a moment**—not by a lingering disease. Great blessings! Lengthened life with prosperity, and a sudden painless death (Ps. 73:4). **14. Therefore**—rather, *And yet* they are such as say, etc., i.e., say, not in so many words, but virtually, by their conduct (so the Gergesenes, Matt. 8:34). How differently the godly (Isa. 2:3). **ways**—The course of action, which God points out; as in Psalm 50:23; *Margin.*

ADAM CLARKE

CHAPTER 21

2. *Let this be your consolations.* "And let this be your retractations." Let what I am about to say induce you to retract what you have said, and to recall your false judgments. *Nacham* signifies, not only to "comfort," but to "change one's mind, to repent."

4. *As for me.* "Alas for me!"

7. *Wherefore do the wicked live?* You have frequently asserted that the wicked are invariably punished in this life, and that the righteous are ever distinguished by the strongest marks of God's providential kindness. How then does it come that many wicked men live long and prosperously, and at last die in peace, without any evidence whatever of God's displeasure? This is a fact that is occurring daily; how then will you reconcile it with your maxims?

12. *They take the timbrel and harp.* They "rise up" or "lift themselves up," probably alluding to the rural exercise of dancing. *Toph,* which we translate *timbrel,* means a sort of "drum," such as the tom-tom of the Asiatics. *Kinnor* may mean something of the *harp* kind. *Ugab, organ,* means nothing like the instrument now called the organ. It probably means the syrinx, composed of several unequal pipes, closed at the bottom, which, when blown into at the top, gives a very shrill and lively sound.

13. *They spend their days in wealth.* "They grow old," or wear out as with old age.

MATTHEW HENRY

How highly they speak of themselves: "*That we should serve him;* we who are rich and mighty in power, shall we be subject and accountable to him? No, we are lords," Jer. ii. 31. They will not believe it is their interest to be religious: *What profit shall we have if we pray unto him?* Is nothing to be called gain but the wealth and honour of this world? If we obtain the favour of God, and spiritual and eternal blessings, we have no reason to complain of losing by our religion.

III. He shows their folly herein, and utterly disclaims all concurrence with them (*v.* 19): *Lo, their good is not in their hand*, that is, they did not get it without God, and therefore they are very ungrateful to slight him thus. It was *not their might, nor the power of their hand*, that got them this wealth, and therefore they ought to remember God who gave it them. Nor can they keep it without God, and therefore they are very unwise to lose their interest in him and bid him to depart from them. Some give this sense of it: "Their good is in their barns and their bags, hoarded up there; it is not in their hand, to do good to others with it; and then what good does it do them? Therefore," says Job, "*the counsel of the wicked is far from me*. Far be it from me that I should be of their mind, say as they say, do as they do, and take my measures from them. Their *posterity approve their sayings*, though *their way* be *their folly* (Ps. xlix. 13); but I know better things than to walk in their counsel."

Verses 17–26

Job had described the prosperity of wicked people; now,

I. He opposes this to what his friends had maintained concerning their certain ruin in this life. "Tell me *how often* do you see *the candle of the wicked put out?* Do you not as often see it burnt down to the socket, until it goes out of itself? *v.* 17. How often do you see *their destruction come upon them*, or *God distributing sorrows in his anger* among them? Do you not as often see their mirth and prosperity continuing to the last?"

II. He reconciles this to the holiness and justice of God. Though wicked people prosper thus all their days, they are *as stubble and chaff before the stormy wind*, *v.* 18. They are light and worthless, and of no account either with God or with wise and good men. They are fitted to destruction, and continually lie exposed to it, and in the height of their pomp and power there is but a step between them and ruin. Though they prosper in this world, yet they shall be reckoned with in another world. He shall know it (*v.* 20): *His eyes shall see his destruction* which he would not be persuaded to believe. They *will not see, but they shall see*, Isa. xxvi. 11. The eyes that have been wilfully shut against the grace of God shall be opened to see his destruction. *What pleasure has he in his house after him? v.* 21. Little will the gain of the world profit him that has lost his soul.

III. He resolves this difference which Providence makes between one wicked man and another into the wisdom and sovereignty of God (*v.* 22): *Shall any pretend to teach God knowledge?* Shall we take upon us to tell God how he should govern the world, what sinner he should spare and whom he should punish? So vast is the disproportion between time and eternity that, if hell be the lot of every sinner at last, it makes little difference if one goes singing thither and another sighing. One dies suddenly, *in his full strength*, not weakened by age or sickness (*v.* 23), *being wholly at ease and quiet*, under no apprehension at all of the approach of death, nor in any fear of it; but, on the contrary, because *his breasts are full of milk and his bones moistened with marrow* (*v.* 24), that is, he is healthful and vigorous, and of a good constitution, he counts upon nothing but to live many years in mirth and pleasure. Yet he is cut off in a moment by the stroke of death. Another dies slowly, and with a great deal of previous pain and misery (*v.* 23), *in the bitterness of his soul*, such as poor Job was himself now in, *and never eats with pleasure*, through sickness, or age, or sorrow of mind.

Verses 27–34

I. Job opposes the opinion of his friends, that the wicked are sure to fall into such visible ruin as Job had now fallen into, upon which principle they condemned Job as a wicked man. "*I know your thoughts*," says Job (*v.* 27), "*and the devices which you wrongfully imagine against* my comfort and honour: and how can such men be convinced?" Job's friends were ready to say, "*Where is the house of the prince?* (*v.* 28). Where is Job's house, or the house of his eldest son, in which his children were feasting? Enquire into the circumstances of Job's house and family, and then ask, *Where are the dwelling-places of the wicked?* and you will soon see that Job's house is in the same predicament with the houses of tyrants and oppressors."

JAMIESON, FAUSSET, BROWN

15. (Cf. Jer. 2:20; *Margin;* Prov. 30:9; Exod. 5:2). **what profit**—(ch. 35:3; Mal. 3:14; Ps. 73:13). Sinners ask, not what is *right*, but what is for the *profit of self*. They forget, "If religion cost self something, the want of it will cost self infinitely more."

16. not in their hand—but in the hand of God. This is Job's difficulty, that God who has sinners' prosperity (good) in His hand should allow them to have it.

is—rather, "may the counsel of the wicked be far from me!" [UMBREIT]. This naturally follows the sentiment of the first clause: Let me not hereby be thought to regard with aught but horror the ways of the wicked, however prosperous.

17. Job in this whole passage down to verse 21 quotes the assertion of the friends, as to the short continuance of the sinner's prosperity, not his own sentiments. In verse 22 he proceeds to refute them. "How oft is the candle" (lamp) etc., quoting Bildad's sentiment (ch. 18:5, 6), in order to question its truth (cf. Matt. 25:8). **how oft**—"God distributeth," etc. (alluding to ch. 20:23, 29). **sorrows**—UMBREIT translates "snares," lit., "cords," which lightning in its twining motion resembles (Ps. 11:6).

18. Job alludes to a like sentiment of Bildad (ch. 18:18), using his own previous words (ch. 13:25). **19.** Equally questionable is the friends' assertion that if the godless himself is not punished, the children are (ch. 18:19; 20:10); and that *God rewardeth him* here for his iniquity, and that *he shall know* it to his cost. So "know" (Hos. 9:7). **20.** Another questionable assertion of the friends, that the sinner sees his own and his children's destruction in his lifetime. **drink**—(Ps. 11:6; Isa. 51:17; Lam. 4:21.) **21.** The argument of the friends, in proof of vs. 20, What pleasure can he have from his house (children) when he is dead—("after him"; Eccles. 3:22). **when the number . . .**—(ch. 14:21). Or, rather, What hath he to do with his children, etc.? (so the *Hebrew* in Eccles. 3:1; 8:6). It is therefore necessary that "*his eyes* should *see* his and their destruction." **cut off**—rather, when the number of his *allotted* months is *fulfilled* (ch. 14:5). From an Arabic word, "arrow," which was used to draw lots with. Hence "arrow"—inevitable destiny [UMBREIT]. **22.** Reply of Job, "In all these assertions you try to teach God how He *ought* to deal with men, rather than prove that He does *in fact* so deal with them. Experience is against you. God gives prosperity and adversity as it pleases Him, not as man's wisdom would have it, on principles inscrutable to us" (Isa. 40:13; Rom. 11:34). **those . . . high**—the high ones, not only angels, but men (Isa. 2:12-17). **23.** Lit., in the bone of his perfection," i.e., the full strength of unimpaired prosperity [UMBREIT]. **24. breasts**—rather, skins, or vessels for fluids [LEE]. But [UMBREIT] "stations or resting-places of his herds near water"; in opposition to Zophar (ch. 20:17); the first clause refers to his abundant substance, the second to his vigorous health. **moistened**—comparing man's body to a well-watered field (Prov. 3:8; Isa. 58:11). **26.** (Eccles. 9:2.) **27.** Their wrongful thoughts against Job are stated by him in vs. 28. They do not honestly *name* Job, but *insinuate* his *guilt*. **28. ye say**—referring to Zophar (ch. 20:7). **the house**—referring to the fall of the *house* of Job's oldest son (ch. 1:19) and the destruction of his *family*. **prince**—The parallel "wicked" in the second clause requires this to be taken in a bad sense, *tyrant, oppressor* (Isa. 13:2), the same *Hebrew*, "nobles"—oppressors. **dwelling-places**—rather, pavilions, a tent containing many dwellings, such as a great emir, like Job, with many dependents, would have.

ADAM CLARKE

JOSEPH PARKER:

We could take you to many scenes that would show the infinite profitableness of faith in God. We should not withdraw the flowered curtain behind which sinful life drinks its poisoned cups. We should take you to houses that have been desolated by misfortune, and show you the profitableness of religion in the sweet patience which it has wrought in sad hearts; we should take you to the house of affliction, where youth has been turned into old age by long-continued pain, and show how the fire has left the gold and only consumed the dross; we should take you to men who once were the curse and terror of society, and show you the light of Christian intelligence in their countenances and the love of Christian charity in their actions; we should take you to the chamber "where the good man meets his fate," and as he smiles at the last enemy, and passes upward to the quiet and holy place, calm, fearless, exultant, we should say, Behold the profit which comes of knowing and loving the Savior of the world!—*The People's Bible*

18. *They are as stubble before the wind.* The original signifies that they shall be "carried away by a furious storm."

19. *God layeth up his iniquity for his children.* This is according to the declaration of God, Exod. xx. 5: "Visiting the iniquity of the fathers upon the children unto the third and fourth generation of them that hate me." This always supposes that the children, who are thus visited, have copied their parents' example.

23. *One dieth in his full strength.* In this and the three following verses Job shows that the inequality of fortune, goods, health, strength, etc., decides nothing either for or against persons in reference to the approbation or disapprobation of God, as these various lots are no indications of their wickedness or innocence.

MATTHEW HENRY

II. He lays down his own judgment to the contrary. He is willing to refer the cause to the next man that comes by (*v.* 29): "*Have you not asked those that go by the way.* Turn to which you will, and you will find them all of my mind, that the punishment of sinners is designed more for the other world than for this. *Do you not know the tokens* of this truth?"

1. What is it that Job here asserts? Two things:—(1) That impenitent sinners will certainly be punished in the other world.

(2) That therefore we are not to think it strange if they prosper greatly in this world. *Therefore* they are spared now, because they are to be punished then. The sinner is here supposed to be the terror of the wise and good, whom he keeps in such awe that none dares *declare his way to his face, v.* 31. None will take the liberty to reprove him. And, if none dares declare his way to his face, much less dare any repay him what he has done and make him refund what he has obtained by injustice. But there is a day coming when those shall be told of their faults. and those who would not repay the wrongs they had done shall have them repaid to them. He must die; but everything you can think of shall be done to take off the reproach of death. He shall have a splendid funeral—a poor thing for any man to be proud of the prospect of; yet with some it passes for a mighty thing. Well, *he shall be brought to the grave* in state. He shall have a stately monument erected over him. *He shall remain in the tomb* with a *Hic jacet—Here lies*, over him, and a large encomium. *The clods of the valley shall be sweet to him;* there shall be as much done as can be to take off the noisomeness of the grave. But it is all a jest; what is the light, or what the perfume, to a man that is dead? It shall be alleged, for the lessening of the disgrace of death, that it is the common lot: He has only yielded to fate, *and every man shall draw after him, as there are innumerable before him.*

2. From all this Job infers the impertinency of their discourses, *v.* 34. They went upon a wrong hypothesis: "*In your answers there remains falsehood.*" "*You comfort me in vain.*" Where there is not truth there is little comfort to be expected.

JAMIESON, FAUSSET, BROWN

29. Job, seeing that the friends will not admit him as an impartial judge, as they consider his calamities prove his guilt, begs them to ask the opinion of travellers (Lam. 1:12), who have the experience drawn from observation, and who are no way connected with him. Job opposes this to Bildad (ch. 8:8) and Zophar (ch. 20:4). **tokens**—rather, intimations (e.g., inscriptions, proverbs, signifying the results of their observation), testimony. Lit., "signs" or proofs in confirmation of the word spoken (Isa. 7:11). **30.** Their testimony (referring perhaps to those who had visited the region where Abraham who enjoyed a revelation then lived) is that "the wicked is (now) spared (reserved) against the day of destruction" (hereafter). The *Hebrew* does not so well agree with [UMBREIT] "in the day of destruction." Job does not deny sinners' *future* punishment, but their punishment *in this life.* They have their "good things" *now.* Hereafter, their lot, and that of the godly, shall be reversed (Luke 16:25). Job, by the Spirit, often utters truths which solve the difficulty under which he labored. His afflictions mostly clouded his faith, else he would have seen the solution furnished by his own words. This answers the objection, that if he knew of the resurrection in ch. 19:25, and future retribution (ch. 21:30), why did he not draw his reasonings elsewhere from them, which he did not? God's righteous government, however, needs to be vindicated as to *this* life also, and therefore the Holy Ghost has caused the argument mainly to turn on it at the same time giving glimpses of a future fuller vindication of God's ways. **brought forth**—not "carried away safe" or "escape" (referring to *this life*), as UMBREIT has it. **wrath**—lit., "wraths," i.e., multiplied and fierce wrath. **31.** I.e., who dares to charge him openly with his bad ways? viz., in this present life. He shall, I grant (vs. 30), be "repaid" hereafter. **32. Yet**—rather, "and." **brought**—with solemn pomp (Ps. 45:15). **grave**—lit., "graves"; i.e., the place where the graves are. **remain in**—rather, *watch on* the tomb, or sepulchral mound. Even after death he seems still to live and watch (i.e., have his "remembrance" preserved) by means of the monument over the grave. In opposition to Bildad (ch. 18:17). **33.** As the classis saying has it, "The earth is light upon him." His repose shall be "sweet." **draw**—follow. He shall share the common lot of mortals; no worse off than they (Heb. 9:27). UMBREIT not so well (for it is not true of "*every* man"). "*Most* men follow in his bad steps, as countless such preceded him." **34. falsehood**—lit., "wickedness." **Your** boasted "consolations" (ch. 15:11) are contradicted by facts ("vain"); they therefore only betray your *evil intent* ("wickedness") against me.

ADAM CLARKE

29. *Have ye not asked them that go by the way?* This appears to be Job's answer. Consult travellers who have gone through different countries, and they will tell you that they have seen both examples—the wicked in great prosperity in some instances, while suddenly destroyed in others.

33. *The clods of the valley shall be sweet unto him.* Perhaps there is an allusion here to the Asiatic mode of interment for princes, saints, and nobles; a well-watered valley was chosen for the tomb, where a perpetual spring might be secured. This was intended to be the emblem of a resurrection, or of a future life; and to conceal as much as possible the disgrace of the rotting carcass.

CHAPTER 22

Verses 1–4

What Eliphaz says here is unjustly applied to Job, but in itself it is very true and good,

I. That when God does us good it is not because he is indebted to us. Eliphaz here shows that the righteousness and perfection of the best man in the world are no real benefit or advantage to God, and therefore cannot be thought to merit anything from him. The gains of religion are infinitely greater than the losses of it, and so it will appear when they are balanced. But can a man be thus profitable to God? No, for such is the perfection of God that he cannot receive any benefit or advantage by men; what can be added to that which is infinite? *Is it any gain to him*, any real addition to his glory or wealth, *if we make our way perfect?* God has indeed expressed himself in his word well pleased with the righteous; his countenance beholds them and his delight is in them and their prayers; but all that adds nothing to the infinite satisfaction which the Eternal Mind has in itself.

II. That when God restrains or rebukes us it is not because he is in danger from us, or jealous of us (*v.* 4): "*Will he reprove thee for fear of thee.*" Satan indeed suggested to our first parents that God forbade them the tree of knowledge, for fear of them, lest they should be as gods, and so become rivals with him; but it was a base insinuation. God rebukes the good because he loves them, but he never rebukes the great because he fears them.

Verses 5–14

Eliphaz and his companions had condemned Job, in general, as a wicked man and a hypocrite. Eliphaz here positively and expressly charges him with many high crimes and misdemeanours. "Come," says Eliphaz, "we have been too long beating about the

CHAPTER 22

Vss. 1-30. AS BEFORE, ELIPHAZ BEGINS. **1.** Eliphaz shows that man's goodness does not add to, or man's badness take from, the happiness of God; therefore it cannot be that God sends prosperity to some and calamities on others for His own advantage; the cause of the goods and ills sent must lie in the men themselves (Ps. 16:2; Luke 17:10; Acts 17:25; I Chron. 29:14). So Job's calamities must arise from guilt. Eliphaz, instead of meeting the *facts*, tries to show that it *could not* be so. **2. as he that is wise**—rather, *yea* the *pious* man profiteth himself. So "understanding" or "wise"—*pious* (Dan. 12:3, 10; Ps. 14:2) [MICHAELIS]. **3. pleasure**—accession of happiness; God has pleasure in man's righteousness (Ps. 45:7), but He is not dependent on man's character for His happiness.

4. Is the punishment inflicted on thee from fear of thee, in order to disarm thee? as Job had implied (*Notes*, 7:12, 20; 10:17). **will he enter . . . into judgment?**—Job had desired this (ch. 13:3, 21). He ought rather to have spoken as in Psalm 143:2.

CHAPTER 22

2. *Can a man be profitable unto God?* God does not afflict you because you have deprived Him of any excellency.

MATTHEW HENRY

bush, too tender of Job. It is high time to deal plainly with him. We must plainly tell him, *Thou art the man*, the tyrant, the oppressor, the atheist, we have been speaking of all this while. *Is not thy wickedness great?* Certainly it is, or else thy troubles would not be so great." For aught I know, Eliphaz, in accusing Job falsely, as he does here, was guilty of as great a sin and as great a wrong to Job as the Sabeans and Chaldeans that robbed him; for a man's good name is more precious and valuable than his wealth. Eliphaz could produce no instances of Job's guilt in any of the particulars that follow here, but seems resolved to calumniate boldly, and throw all the reproach he could on Job, not doubting but that some would cleave to him. Job, whom God himself praised as the best man in the world, is here represented by one of his friends, and he a wise and good man too, as one of the greatest villains in nature.

I. He charges him with oppression and injustice, that, when he was in prosperity, he not only did no good with his wealth and power, but did a great deal of hurt with them. This was utterly false, as appears by the account Job gives of himself (*ch.* xxix. 12, &c.) and the character God gave of him, *ch.* i. He tells him he had been cruel and unmerciful to the poor. *Thou hast taken a pledge from thy brother for nought*, or, as the LXX. read it, *Thou hast taken thy brethren for pledges*, and that for nought, imprisoned them, enslaved them, because they had nothing to pay,—that he had taken the very clothes of his insolvent tenants and debtors, so that he had *stripped them naked.* He had not been charitable to the poor: "*Thou hast not given* so much as a cup of cold *water to the weary to drink*, nay, *thou hast withholden bread from the hungry* in their extremity. Poor widows thou hast sent away empty from thy doors with a sad heart, *v.* 9. Those who came to thee for justice, thou didst send away unheard, unhelped; and, worst of all, *the arms of the fatherless have been broken*; those that could help themselves but little thou hast quite disabled to help themselves." This, which is the blackest part of the charge, is but insinuated: *The arms of the fatherless have been broken.* "They have been broken by those under thee, and thou hast connived at it, which brings thee under the guilt." He had been partial to the rich and great (*v.* 8): "The poor were not fed at thy door, while the rich were feasted at thy table." He attributes all his present troubles to these supposed sins (*v.* 10, 11). "*Snares are round about thee*, and others are as hard upon thee as thou hast been upon the poor. No sin makes a louder cry there than unmercifulness; and, accordingly, *sudden fear troubles thee.*" Those that have not shown mercy may justly be denied the comfortable hope that they shall find mercy; and then what can they expect but snares, and darkness, and continual fear?

II. He charges him with atheism, infidelity, and gross impiety; he that did not fear God did not regard men. He would have it thought that Job was an Epicurean, who did indeed own the being of God, but denied his providence.

1. Eliphaz referred to an important truth, which he thought, if Job had duly considered it, would have prevented him from being so passionate in his complaints and bold in justifying himself (*v.* 12): *Is not God in the height of heaven?* There he is pleased to manifest himself in a way peculiar to the upper world, and thence he is pleased to manifest himself in a way suited to this lower world. When we *behold the height of the stars, how high they are*, we should, at the same time, also consider the transcendant majesty of God, who is above the stars, and how high he is.

2. He charged it upon Job that he made a bad use of this doctrine, which he might have made so good a use of, *v.* 13. "This is *holding the truth in unrighteousness*; thou art willing to own that *God is in the height of heaven* but thence thou inferrest, *How doth God know?*" Eliphaz suspected that Job had such a notion of God as this, that, because he is in the height of heaven, it is therefore impossible for him to see and hear what is done at so great a distance as this earth, especially since there is a *dark cloud* (*v.* 13), many *thick clouds* (*v.* 14), that come between him and us, and *are a covering to him*; so as if God had *eyes of flesh*, *ch.* x. 4. Distance of place creates no difficulty to him who fills immensity, any more than distance of time to him who is eternal. Or, *He walks in the circuit of heaven*, and has enough to do to enjoy himself and his own perfections and glory in that bright and quiet world; why should he trouble himself about us? This is gross absurdity, as well as gross impiety, which Eliphaz here fathers upon Job; for it supposes that the administration of government is a burden and disparagement to the supreme governor and that the acts of justice and mercy are a toil to a mind infinitely wise, holy, and good. If the sun, a creature, and inanimate, can with the light

JAMIESON, FAUSSET, BROWN

5. Heretofore Eliphaz had only insinuated, now he plainly asserts Job's guilt, merely on the ground of his sufferings.

6. The crimes alleged, on a harsh inference, by Eliphaz against Job are such as he would think likely to be committed by a rich man. The Mosaic law (Exod. 22:26; Deut. 24:10) subsequently embodied the feeling that existed among the godly in Job's time against oppression of debtors as to their pledges. Here the case is not quite the same; Job is charged with taking a pledge where he had *no just claim to it;* and in the second clause, that pledge (the outer garment which served the poor as a covering by day and a bed by night) is represented as taken from one who had not "changes of raiment" (a common constituent of wealth in the East), but was poorly clad—"naked" (Matt. 25:36; Jas. 2:15); a sin the more heinous in a rich man like Job. **7.** Hospitality to the weary traveller is regarded in the East as a primary duty (Isa. 21:14). **8. mighty**—*Hebrew*, "man of *arm*" (Ps. 10:15; viz., Job). **honourable**—*Hebrew*, "accepted of countenance" (Isa. 3:3; II Kings 5:1); i.e., possessing authority. Eliphaz repeats his charge (ch. 15:28; so Zophar, ch. 20:19), that it was by violence Job wrung houses and lands from the poor, to whom now he refused relief (vss. 7, 9) [MICHAELIS]. **9. empty**—without their wants being relieved (Gen. 31:42). The Mosaic law especially protected the widow and fatherless (Exod. 22:22); the violation of it in their case by the great is a complaint of the prophets (Isa. 1:17). **arms**—supports, helps, on which one leans (Hos. 7:15). Thou hast robbed them of their only stay. Job replies in ch. 29:11-16. **10. snares**—alluding to Job's admission (ch. 19:6; cf. ch. 18:10; Prov. 22:5). **11. that**—so that thou. **abundance**—floods. Danger by floods is a less frequent image in this book than in the rest of the Old Testament (ch. 11:16; 27:20).

12. Eliphaz says this to prove that God can from His height behold all things; gratuitously *inferring* that Job denied it, because he denied that the wicked are punished here. **height**—*Hebrew*, "head" i.e., elevation (ch. 11:8).

13. Rather, *And yet* thou sayest, God does not *concern Himself with* ("know") human affairs (Ps. 73:11).

14. "In the circuit of heaven" only, not taking any part in earthly affairs. Job is alleged as holding this Epicurean sentiment (Lam. 3:44; Isa. 29:15; 40:27; Jer. 23:24; Ezek. 8:12; Ps. 139:12).

ADAM CLARKE

6. *Thou hast taken a pledge.* You have exacted where nothing was due, so that through you the poor have been unable to procure their necessary clothing.

7. *Thou hast not given water.* It was esteemed a great virtue in the East to furnish thirsty travellers with water; especially in the deserts, where scarcely a *stream* was to be found, and where *wells* were very rare. Some of the Indian devotees are accustomed to stand with a *girbah* or skin full of water, on the public roads, to give drink to weary travellers who are parched with thirst.

8. *But as for the mighty man, he had the earth.* "The man of arm." Finger, hand, and arm are all emblems of strength and power. *The honourable man.* Literally, the man whose "face is accepted," the respectable man, the man of wealth. You were an enemy to the poor and needy, but you favored and flattered the rich and great.

12. *Is not God in the height of heaven?* It appears, from this and the following verses, that Eliphaz was attributing infidel and blasphemous speeches or sentiments to Job.

MATTHEW HENRY

and influence reach this earth, and every part of it (Ps. xix. 6), even from that vast height of the visible heavens in which he is, and in the circuit of which he walks, and that through many a thick and dark cloud, shall we question it concerning the Creator?

Verses 15–20

Eliphaz, having endeavoured to convict Job, here endeavours to awaken him to a sense of his danger by reason of sin; and this he does by comparing his case with that of the sinners of the old world, *who were overflown with a flood* (v. 16), and the *remnant of whom the fire consumed* (*v.* 20), namely, the Sodomites, who, in comparison of the old world, were but a remnant. Eliphaz would have Job to *mark the old way which wicked men have trodden* (*v.* 15). They said to God, *Depart from us;* and then *what could the Almighty do with them but cut them off?* Those who will not submit to God's golden sceptre must expect to be broken to pieces with his iron rod. Others make it to denote: "What has he done to oblige us? What can he do in a way of wrath to make us miserable, or in a way of favour to make us happy?" *The Lord will not do good, neither will he do evil.* Eliphaz shows the absurdity of this in one word, and that is, calling God *the Almighty*; for, if he be so, what cannot he do? *Yet he had filled their houses with good things, v.* 18. Many have their houses full of goods but their hearts empty of grace, and thereby are marked for ruin. *But the counsel of the wicked is far from me.* Job had said so (*ch.* xxi. 16) and Eliphaz will not be behind with him. If they cannot agree in their own principles concerning God, yet they agree in renouncing the principles of those that live without God in the world. They take occasion thence to expose the folly of sinners and show how ridiculous their principles are. "*Our substance is not cut down*, as theirs was, and as thine is; we continue to prosper, which is a sign that we are the favourites of Heaven, and in the right." The same rule that served him to condemn Job by served him to magnify himself and his companions by. *His* substance is cut down; therefore he is a wicked man; *ours* is not; therefore we are righteous.

Verses 21–30

Eliphaz had laid before Job the miserable condition of a wicked man, that he might frighten him into repentance. Here, on the other hand, he shows him the happiness which those may be sure of that do repent, that he might allure and encourage him to it. Ministers must try both ways in dealing with people, must speak to them from Mount Sinai by the terrors of the law, and from Mount Sion by the comforts of the gospel, must set before them both life and death, good and evil, the blessing and the curse.

I. The good counsel which Eliphaz gives to Job; it was built upon a false supposition that he was a wicked man. 1. *Acquaint now thyself with God:* be not such a stranger to him as thou hast made thyself by casting off the fear of him and restraining prayer before him. It is our honour that we are made capable of this acquaintance, our misery that by sin we have lost it, our privilege that through Christ we are invited to return to it. 2. "*Be at peace*, at peace with thyself. Be at peace with thy God; be reconciled to him." 3. *Receive the law from his mouth, v.* 22. "Having made thy peace with God, submit to his government, and resolve to be ruled by him, that thou mayest keep thyself in his love." 4. *Lay up his word in thy heart.* It is not enough to receive it, but we must retain it, Prov. iii. 18. 5. *Return to the Almighty, v.* 23. "Do not only turn from sin, but turn to God and thy duty. Do not only turn towards the Almighty in some good inclinations and good beginnings, but *return to him*; return home to him, quite to him." 6. *Put away iniquity far from thy tabernacle.* This was the advice Zophar gave him, *ch.* xi. 14. "*Let not wickedness dwell in thy tabernacle.* Put iniquity far off, the further the better, not only from thy heart and hand, but from thy house."

II. The encouragement which Eliphaz gives Job, that he shall be very happy, if he will but take this good counsel. In general, "*Thereby good shall come unto thee* (*v.* 21). Thou art now ruined and brought down, but, if thou return to God, *thou shalt be built up* again, and thy present ruins shall be repaired. Thy family shall be built up in children, thy estate in wealth, and thy soul in holiness and comfort."

1. Temporal blessings should be bestowed abundantly on him. It is promised, He shall be very rich (*v.* 23): "*Thou shalt lay up gold as dust*, in such great abundance, and *shalt have plenty of silver* (*v.* 25), whereas now thou art poor and stripped of all." *Thou shalt have silver of strength* (for so the word is), which, being honestly got, will wear well—silver like steel. Wealth is a blessing indeed when we are not

JAMIESON, FAUSSET, BROWN

15. marked—Rather, Dost thou *keep to*? i.e., wish to follow (so *Hebrew*, II Sam. 22:22). If so, beware of sharing their end. **the old way**—the degenerate ways of the world before the flood (Gen. 6:5). **16. cut down**—rather, "fettered," as in ch. 16:8; i.e., arrested by death. **out of time**—prematurely, suddenly (ch. 15:32; Eccles. 7:17); lit., whose foundation was poured out (so as to become) a stream or flood. The solid earth passed from beneath their feet into a flood Gen. 7:11). **17.** Eliphaz designedly uses Job's own words (ch. 21:14,15). **do for them**—They think they can do everything for themselves. **18.** "Yet you say (ch. 21:16, see *Note*) that it is "*He* who filled their houses with good"—"their" "good is not in *their* hand," but comes from *God*. **but the counsel . . . is . . .**—rather, may the counsel be, etc. Eliphaz sarcastically quotes in continuation Job's words (ch. 21:16). Yet, after uttering this godless sentiment, thou dost hypocritically add, "May the counsel," etc. **19.** Triumph of the pious at the fall of the recent followers of the antediluvian sinners. While in the act of denying that God can do them any good or harm, they are cut off by Him. Eliphaz hereby justifies himself and the friends for their conduct to Job: not derision of the wretched, but joy at the vindication of God's ways (Ps. 107:42; Rev. 15:3; 16:7; 19:1, 2). **20.** The triumphant speech of the pious. If "substance" be retained, translate, rather as LXX, "Has not their substance been taken away, and . . . ? But the *Hebrew* is rather, "Truly our *adversary* is cut down" [GESENIUS]. The same opposition exists between the godly and ungodly seed as between the unfallen and restored Adam and Satan (*adversary*); this forms the groundwork of the book (chs. 1 and 2; Gen. 3: 15). **remnant**—all that "is left" of the sinner; repeated from 20:26, which makes UMBREIT's rendering "glory" (*margin*), "excellency," less probable. **fire**—alluding to Job (ch. 1:16; 15:34; 18:15). First is mentioned destruction by *water* (vs. 16); here, by *fire* (II Pet. 3:5-7).

21. Eliphaz takes it for granted, Job is not yet "acquainted" with God; lit., become a *companion* of God. **Turn with familiar** confidence to God. **and be**—*So* thou *shalt* be: the 2d *imperatively* expresses the consequence of obeying the 1st (Ps. 37:27). **peace**—prosperity and restoration to *Job*; true spiritually also to *us* (Rom. 5:1; Col. 1:20).

good—(I Tim. 4:8). **22. lay up**—(Ps. 119:11). **23.** "Built up" anew, as a *restored* house. **thou shalt put away**—rather, If thou put away [MICHAELIS]. **24.** Rather, containing the protasis from the last clause of vs. 23, If thou regard the glittering metal *as dust;* lit., "lay it on the dust"; to regard it of as little value as the dust on which it lies. The apodosis is at vs. 25, *Then* shall the Almighty be, etc. God will take the place of the wealth, in which thou didst formerly trust. **gold**—rather, "precious" or "glittering metal," parallel to "(gold) of Ophir," in the second clause [UMBREIT and MAURER]. **Ophir**—derived from a *Hebrew* word "dust," viz., gold dust. HEEREN thinks it a general name for the rich countries of the South, on the African, Indian, and especially the Arabian coast

ADAM CLARKE

16. *Whose foundation was overflown with a flood.* The unrighteous in the days of Noah, who appear to have had an abundance of all temporal good (v. 18) and who surpassed the deeds of all the former wicked, said in effect to God, "Depart from us."

18. *But the counsel of the wicked is far from me.* Sarcastically quoting Job's words, chap. xxi. 14, 16.

19. *The righteous see it, and are glad.* They see God's judgments on the incorrigibly wicked, and know that the Judge of all the earth does right; hence they rejoice in all the dispensations of His providence.

ALEXANDER MACLAREN:

"Acquaint now thyself with Him, and be at peace: thereby good shall come unto thee" (22:21). In the sense in which the speaker meant them, these words are not true. They mean little more than "It pays to be religious." What kind of notion of acquaintance with God Eliphaz may have had, one scarcely knows, but at any rate, the whole meaning of the text on his lips is poor and selfish.

The peace promised is evidently only outward tranquillity and freedom from trouble, and the good that is to come to Job is plainly mere worldly prosperity. This strain of thought is expressed even more clearly in that extraordinary bit of bathos, which with solemn irony the great dramatist who wrote this book makes this Eliphaz utter immediately after the text, "The Almighty shall be thy defence and—thou shalt have plenty of silver!" It has not been left for commercial Englishmen to recommend religion on the ground that it produces successful merchants and makes the best of both worlds.

These friends of Job's all err in believing that suffering is always and only the measure of sin, and that you can tell a man's great guilt by observing his great sorrows. And so they have two main subjects on which they preach at their poor friend, pouring vitriol into his wounds: first, how wicked he must be to be so haunted by sorrows; second, how surely he will be delivered if he will only be religious after their pattern, that is, speak platitudes of conventional devotion and say, I submit.—*Expositions of Holy Scripture*

MATTHEW HENRY

ensnared with the love of it. Thou shalt *lay up gold as dust*, and *as the stones of the brooks*. So little shalt thou value it or expect from it that thou shalt lay it at thy feet (Acts iv. 35), not in thy bosom. Yet he shall be very safe; for *the Almighty shall be thy defender*; nay, he shall be *thy defence*, *v.* 25. He *shall be thy gold*; so it is in the margin, and it is the same word that is used (*v.* 24) for gold, but it signifies also a strong-hold, because *money is a defence*, Eccles. vii. 12. Worldlings make gold their god, saints make God their gold; and those that are enriched with his favour and grace may truly be said *to have abundance of the best gold*, and best laid up.

2. He should be enriched with spiritual blessings: "*For then shalt thou have thy delight in the Almighty;* and *thus* the Almighty comes to be thy gold by thy delighting in him, as worldly people delight in their money." Then *shalt* thou *lift up thy face to God* with boldness, and not be afraid, as thou now art, to draw near to him. "Thou shalt by prayer send letters to God: *Thou shalt make thy prayer*" (the word is, *Thou shalt multiply* thy prayers) "unto him, and he will not think thy letters troublesome, though many and long. *He shall hear thee*, and make it to appear he does so by what he does for thee and in thee." He should have inward satisfaction in the management of all his outward affairs (*v.* 28): "*Thou shalt decree a thing and it shall be established unto thee,*" that is, "Thou shalt frame all thy projects and purposes with so much wisdom, and grace, and resignation to the will of God, that the issue of them shall be to thy heart's content. Thou shalt *commit thy works unto the Lord* by faith and prayer, and then *thy thoughts shall be established*; thou shalt be easy and pleased, whatever occurs, Prov. xvi. 3. "Whereas now thou complainest of darkness round about thee, then *the light shall shine on thy ways;*" that is, "God shall guide and direct thee." Even in times of common calamity and danger he should have abundance of joy and hope (*v.* 29): "*When men are cast down* round about thee, desponding, *then shalt thou say, There is lifting up.*"

3. He should be a blessing to his country and an instrument of good to many (*v.* 30): *God shall*, in answer to thy prayers, *deliver the island of the innocent*, and have a regard therein to *the pureness of thy hands. He shall deliver those that are not innocent, and they are delivered by the pureness of thy hands;* so it may be read, and most probably. Note, A good man is a public good. Sinners fare the better for saints, whether they are aware of it or no. Eliphaz and his three friends were delivered by the *pureness of Job's hands, ch.* xlii. 8.

CHAPTER 23

Verses 1-7

Job, ill as he is, will not give up the cause.

I. He justifies his own resentments and representations of his trouble (*v.* 2): "*Even today*, I own, *my complaint is bitter. Even today is my complaint* counted *rebellion.* But," says he, "I do not complain more than there is cause; *for my stroke is heavier than my groaning.* The pains of my body and the wounds of my spirit are such that I have reason enough for my complaints."

II. He appeals from the censures of his friends to the just judgment of God; and this he thought was an evidence for him that he was not a hypocrite, for then he durst not have made such an appeal as this.

1. He is so sure of the equity of God's tribunal that he longs to appear before it (*v.* 3): *O that I knew where I might find him!* This may properly express the pious breathings of a soul convinced that it has by sin lost God and is undone for ever if it recover not its interest in his favour.

2. He is so sure of the goodness of his own cause that he longs to be opening it at God's bar (*v.* 4): "*I would order my cause before him*, and set it in a true light." We may apply this to the duty of prayer, in which we have *boldness to enter into the holiest* and to come even to the footstool of the throne of grace. We have not only liberty of access, but liberty of speech. We have leave *to order our cause before God.* We durst not be so free with earthly princes as a humble holy soul may be with God. We are allowed, not only to pray, but to plead, not only to ask, but to argue; nay, to *fill our mouths with arguments*, not to move God (he is perfectly apprized of the merits of the cause without our showing), but to move ourselves, to excite our fervency and encourage our faith in prayer.

3. He is so sure of a sentence in favour of him that he even longed to hear it (*v.* 5): "*I would know the words which he would answer me.*" This becomes us, in all controversies; let the word of God determine

JAMIESON, FAUSSET, BROWN

(where was the port Aphar. El Ophir, too, a city of Oman, was formerly the center of Arabian commerce). It is curious that the natives of Malacca still call their mines *Ophirs*. **stones of the brooks**—If thou dost let the gold of Ophir remain in its native valley among the stones of the brooks; i.e., regard it as of little worth as the stones, etc. The gold was washed down by mountain torrents and lodged among the stones and sand of the valley. **25.** Apodosis. **Yea**—rather, *Then* shall the Almighty be, etc. **defence**—rather, as the same *Hebrew* means in vs. 24 (see *Note*)—Thy *precious metals;* God will be to thee in the place of riches. **plenty of silver**—rather, "And shall be to thee in the place of *laboriously-obtained treasures* of silver" [GESENIUS]. Elegantly implying, it is less labor to find God than the hidden metals; at least to the humble seeker (ch. 28:12-28). But [MAURER] "the shining silver." **26. lift up . . . face,** etc.—repeated from Zophar (ch. 11:15). **27.** (Isa. 58:9, 14.) **pay thy vows**—which thou hast promised to God in the event of thy prayers being heard: God will give thee occasion to pay the former, by hearing the latter. **28. light**—success. **29.** Rather, When (thy ways; from vs. 28) are cast down (for a time), thou shalt (soon again have joyful cause to) say, There is lifting up (prosperity returns back to me) [MAURER]. **he**—God. **humble**—*Hebrew*, him that is of low eyes. Eliphaz implies that Job is not so now in his affliction; therefore it continues: with this he contrasts the blessed effect of being humble under it (Jas. 4:6, and I Pet. 5:5, probably quote this passage). Therefore it is better, I think, to take the first clause as referred to by "God resisteth the *proud*." When (men) are cast down, thou shalt say (behold the effects of) *pride*. Eliphaz hereby justifies himself for attributing Job's calamities to his *pride*. "Giveth grace to the humble," answers to the second clause. **30. island**—i.e., dwelling. But the *Hebrew* expresses the *negative* (I Sam. 4:21); translate "Thus He (God) shall deliver him who was *not* guiltless," viz., one, who like Job himself on conversion shall be saved, but not because he was, as Job so constantly affirms of himself, guiltless, but because he *humbles* himself (vs. 29); an oblique attack on Job, even to the last. **and it**—Rather, "*he* (the *one* not heretofore guiltless) shall be delivered through the purity (acquired since conversion) of thy hands"; by thy intercession (as Gen. 18:26, etc.) [MAURER]. The irony is strikingly exhibited in Eliphaz unconsciously uttering words which exactly answer to what happened at last: he and the other two were "delivered" by God accepting the intercession of Job for them (ch. 42:7, 8).

CHAPTER 23

Vss. 1-17. JOB'S ANSWER. **2. to-day**—implying, perhaps, that the debate was carried on through more days than one (see Introduction). **bitter**—(ch. 7:11; 10:1).—**my stroke**—the *hand* of God *on me* (*margin;* ch. 19:21; Ps. 32:4). **heavier than**—is so heavy that I cannot relieve myself adequately by groaning.

3. The same wish as in ch. 13:3 (cf. Heb. 10:19-22). **Seat**—The idea in the *Hebrew* is *a well-prepared throne* (Ps. 9:7).

4. order—state methodically (ch. 13:18; Isa. 43:26). **fill . . .**—I would have abundance of arguments to adduce.

5. he—emphatic: it little matters what *man* may say of me, if only I know what *God* judges of me.

ADAM CLARKE

29. *When men are cast down.* The following is nearly a literal version: "When they shall humble themselves, thou shalt say, Be exalted [or, There is exaltation]: for the downcast of eye he will save." The same sentiment as that of our Lord, "Every one that exalteth himself shall be abased; and he that humbleth himself shall be exalted."

30. *He shall deliver the island of the innocent.* The text may be translated, "He shall deliver every innocent person: He [the innocent person] shall be delivered by the pureness of thy hands"; i.e., as you love justice, so you will do justice.

CHAPTER 23

3. *Oh that I knew where I might find him!* This and the following verse may be read thus: "Who will give me the knowledge of God, that I may find Him out? I would come to His establishment (the place or way in which He has promised to communicate himself); I would exhibit, in detail, my judgment (the cause I wish to be tried) before His face; and my mouth would I fill with convincing or decisive arguments."

MATTHEW HENRY

them; let us know what he answers, and understand what he says.

III. He comforts himself with the hope that God would deal favourably with him in this matter, *v.* 6, 7. The same power that is engaged against proud sinners is engaged for humble saints, who prevail with God by strength derived from him, as Jacob did, Hos. xii. 3. See Ps. lxviii. 35. There in the court of heaven, when the final sentence is to be given, *the righteous might dispute with him* and come off in his righteousness. Now, even the upright are often *chastened of the Lord*, and they cannot dispute against it; integrity itself is no fence either against calamity or calumny. *Then you shall discern between the righteous and the wicked*, whereas now we can scarcely distinguish them, so little is the difference between them as to their outward condition. Then "*I shall be delivered for ever from my Judge.*" Those that are delivered up to God as their owner and ruler shall be for ever delivered from him as their judge and avenger; and there is no flying from his justice but by flying to his mercy.

Verses 8–12

I. Job complains that he cannot understand the meaning of God's providence concerning him (*v.* 8, 9): *I go forward, but he is not there*, &c. He had a great desire to appear before God, and get a hearing of his case, but the Judge was not to be found. Job, no doubt, believed that God is everywhere present, but by reason of the disorder and tumult his spirit was in, he could not fasten upon that which he knew to be in God. He could not perceive wherein he had sinned more than others, nor could he discern what other end God should aim at in afflicting him thus. He was quite at a loss to know what God designed to do with him.

II. He satisfies himself with this, that God himself was a witness to his integrity, and therefore did not doubt but the issue would be good.

1. After Job had almost lost himself in the labyrinth, how contentedly does he sit down with this thought: "Though *I* know not the way that he takes yet *he knows the way that I take*," *v.* 10. It is a great comfort to those who mean honestly that God understands their meaning, though men do not, cannot, or will not. "He knows that, however I may sometimes have *taken a false step*, yet I have still *taken a good way*, have *chosen the way of truth*," that is, he accepts it, and is well pleased with it, as he is said to *know the way of the righteous*, Ps. i. 6. Job infers, *When he hath tried me I shall come forth as gold.* The trial will have an end. *God will not contend for ever.* They shall come forth as gold approved and improved, found to be good and made to be better.

2. Now that which encouraged Job to hope that his present troubles would thus end well was the testimony of his conscience. God's way was the way he walked in (*v.* 11): "*My foot hath held his steps*," that is, "held to them, adhered closely to them; the steps he takes." God's word was the rule he walked by, *v.* 12. He governed himself by *the commandment of God's lips*. Job kept closely to the law of God. *I have esteemed the words of his mouth more than my necessary food;* that is, he could as well have lived without his daily bread as without the word of God. *I have laid it up* (so the word is), as those that lay up provision for a siege, or as Joseph laid up corn before the famine. The word of God is to our souls what our necessary food is to our bodies; it sustains the spiritual life and strengthens us for the actions of life.

Verses 13–17

Job reasons himself into a sort of *patience per force*, which he cannot do without reflecting upon God as dealing hardly with him; the worst he says is that God deals unaccountably with him.

I. He lays down good truths, *v.* 13, 14. 1. That God's counsels are immutable: *He is in one mind, and who can turn him? He is one* (so some read it) or *in one*; he has no counsellors by whose interest he might be prevailed with to alter his purpose. Prayer has prevailed to change God's way and his providence, but never was his will or purpose changed; for *known unto God are all his works*. 2. That his power is irresistible: *What his soul desires* or designs *even that he does. None can stay his hand. Whatever the Lord pleased that did he* (Ps. cxxxv. 6), and always will, for it is always best. *He performs the thing that is appointed for me. Many such things are with him*, that is, He does many things in the course of his providence which we can give no account of, but must resolve into his absolute sovereignty.

II. He makes but a bad use of these good truths. He said, *Therefore am I troubled at his presence*, *v.* 15. What confusion poor Job was now in, for he contradicted himself: just now he was troubled for God's

JAMIESON, FAUSSET, BROWN

6. An objection suggests itself, while he utters the wish (vs. 5). Do I hereby wish that He should plead against me with His omnipotence? Far from it! (ch. 9:19, 34; 13:21; 30:18). **strength**—so as to prevail with Him: as in Jacob's case (Hos. 12:3, 4). UMBREIT and MAURER better translate as in ch. 4:20 (I only wish that He) "would *attend* to me," i.e., give me a patient hearing as an ordinary judge, not using His omnipotence, but only His divine knowledge of my innocence. **7. There**—rather, Then: if God would "attend" to me (vs. 6). **righteous**—i.e., the result of my *dispute* would be, He would acknowledge me as *righteous.* **delivered**—from suspicion of guilt on the part of *my Judge.*

8. But I wish in vain. For "behold," etc. **forward . . . backward**—rather, "to *the east*—to the *west.*" The Hebrew geographers faced the east, i.e., sunrise: not the north, as we do. So "before" means east: "behind," west (so the Hindoos). *Para,* "before"—east: *Apara,* "behind" —west: *Daschina,* "the right hand"—south: *Bama,* "left"—north. A similar reference to sunrise appears in the name Asia, "sunrise," Europe, "sunset"; pure Babylonian names, as RAWLINSON shows. **9.** Rather, "To the north." **work**—God's glorious *works* are especially seen towards the north region of the sky by one in the northern hemisphere. The antithesis is between God *working* and yet *not* being *beheld:* as in ch. 9:11, between "He *goeth by,*" and "I *see* Him *not.*" If the *Hebrew* bears it, the parallelism to the second clause is better suited by translating, as UMBREIT, "doth hide himself"; but then the antithesis to "behold" would be lost. **right hand** —"in the south." **hideth**—appropriately, of the unexplored south, then regarded as uninhabitable because of its heat (see ch. 34:29). **10. But**—correcting himself for the wish that his cause should be known before God. The omniscient One already *knoweth the way in me* (my *inward* principles: His *outward* way or course of acts is mentioned in vs. 11. So *in me,* ch. 4:21); though for some inscrutable cause He as yet hides Himself (vss. 8, 9). **when**—let Him only but try my cause, I shall, etc.

11. held—fast by *His steps.* The law is in Old Testament poetry regarded as *a way,* God going before us as our guide, in whose footsteps we must tread (Ps. 17:5). **declined**—(Ps. 125:5). **12. esteemed**—rather, laid up, viz., as a treasure found (Matt. 13:44; Ps. 119:11); alluding to the words of Eliphaz (ch. 22:22). There was no need to tell me so; I have done so already (Jer. 15:16). **necessary** —"Appointed portion" (of food; as in Prov. 30:8). UMBREIT and MAURER translate, "More than my *law,*" my own will, in antithesis to "the words of His mouth" (John 6:38). Probably under the general term, "what is *appointed* to me" (the same *Hebrew* is in vs. 14), all that ministers to the appetites of the body and carnal will is included.

13. in one mind—notwithstanding my innocence, He is *unaltered* in His purpose of proving me guilty (ch. 9:12). **soul**—His *will* (Ps. 115:3). God's sovereignty. He has one great purpose; nothing is haphazard; everything has its proper place with a view to His purpose.

14. many such—He has yet many more such ills in store for me, though hidden in His breast (ch. 10:13). **15.** God's decrees, impossible to be resisted, and leaving us in the dark as to what may come next, are calculated to fill the mind with holy awe [BARNES]. **16. soft**—faint; hath melted my courage. Here again Job's language is that of Jesus Christ (Ps. 22:14). **17.** Because I was not taken away by death from the evil to come (lit., "from before the face of the darkness," Isa. 57:1). Alluding to the words of Eliphaz (ch. 22:11), "dark-

ADAM CLARKE

7. *There the righteous might dispute with him.* Might "argue" or "plead." To dispute with God sounds very harsh.

8. *Behold, I go forward.* These two verses paint in vivid colors the distress and anxiety oi a soul in search of the favor of God.

JOSEPH PARKER:

Hear the patriarch—had he lived now he could not have been wiser—"He knoweth the way that I take"—the dark, sinuous way; not one straight mile in it; sometimes uphill, so that my very strength gives way, and I would almost return to the starting point, and then suddenly down a deep and threatening declivity, the end of which no eye can see; and then off into stony places, and across broad wildernesses; and then up to the very lips in cold, cold rivers: but he watches all the way; the light and the darkness are both alike unto him; he knoweth my downsitting and mine uprising, my going out and my coming in; he watches me as if I were an only child: blessed be his name forever: when he hath tried me, tested me, pierced me through and through, thrown me into the fire, watched the burning in all its effect upon me—when he has got out the last speck of dross, he will put me into his crown; I shall be for the King's use through eternal day. Who says that Job has fallen, taken the wrong view, lapsed into infidelity? He is now hiding himself in rocks; he is now standing in the very sanctuary of God: see how he pulls himself together! God is forbearing, because he is not issuing against me all his strength: God knows the way that I take, and he is trying me: he knows there is some gold in me: who would try dross, knowing it to be dross only? The very fact of the trial means that there is something to be tried, and something worth saving, and something that God can turn to high uses.

—*The People's Bible*

14. *For he performeth the thing that is appointed for me.* "For he hath appointed me my lot; and like these there are multitudes with him." He diversifies human affairs; scarcely any two men have the same lot, nor has the same person the same portion at all times. He has multitudes of resources, expedients, means, etc., which he employs in governing human affairs.

16. *For God maketh my heart soft.* Prostrates my strength, deprives me of courage.

17. *Because I was not cut off.* This verse should be read in connection with the preceding, and then we shall have the following sense. Verse 16: "The Lord hath beaten down my

MATTHEW HENRY

absence (*v.* 8, 9); now he is troubled at his presence. *When I consider, I am afraid of him. The Almighty troubled him*, and so *made his heart soft*, a grievous softness, which apprehends everything that is present to be pressing and everything future to be threatening. He quarrels with God. *Because I was not cut off before the darkness, v.* 17.

CHAPTER 24

Verses 1–12

Job's friends had been very positive in it that they should soon see the fall of wicked people, how much soever they might prosper for a while. By no means, says Job; *though times are not hidden from the Almighty*, yet *those that know him do not presently see his day, v.* 1. God governs the world. Bad times are not hidden from him, though the bad men that make the times bad say one to another, He has *forsaken the earth*, Ps. xciv. 6, 7. Before Job will enquire into the reasons of the prosperity of wicked men he asserts God's omniscience. He yet asserts that those who know him (that is, wise and good people who are acquainted with him, and with whom his secret is) *do not see his day*,—the day of his judging for them. We shall shortly know why the judgment is deferred; even the wisest, and those who know God best, do not yet see it. God will exercise their faith and patience, and excite their prayers for the coming of his kingdom, for which they are to *cry day and night to him*, Luke xviii. 7. Job specifies two sorts of unrighteous ones, whom all the world saw thriving in their iniquity:—

I. Tyrants, and those that do wrong under pretence of law and authority. They *remove the land-marks*, under pretence that they were misplaced (*v.* 2), and so they think they effectually secure that to their posterity which they have got wrongfully. This was forbidden by the law of Moses (Deut. xix. 14), under a curse, Deut. xxvii. 17. *They violently take away flocks*, pretending they are forfeited, *and feed thereof*. If a poor fatherless child has but an ass of his own to get a little money with, they find some colour or other to take it away. It is all one if a widow has but an ox for what little husbandry she has; under pretence of distraining for some small debt, or arrears of rent, this ox shall be taken for a pledge, though perhaps it is the widow's all. God has taken it among the titles of his honour to be a *Father of the fatherless and a judge of the widows*; and therefore those will not be reckoned his friends that do not to their utmost protect them; but those he will certainly reckon with as his enemies that vex and oppress them. They love in their hearts to triumph over poor people, whom they turn out of the way of getting relief, threaten to punish them as vagabonds, and so force them to abscond. *They pluck the fatherless from the breast;* that is, having made poor infants fatherless, they make them motherless too; having taken away the father's life, they break the mother's heart, and so starve the children and leave them to perish. Those who show no mercy to such as lie at their mercy shall themselves have judgment without mercy. They squeeze them so with their extortion that they *cause them to go naked without clothing* (*v.* 10). They are very oppressive to the labourers they employ in their service. *Those that carry their sheaves are hungry;* so some read it (*v.* 10), and it agrees with *v.* 11, that those who *make oil within their walls*, and with a great deal of toil labour at the wine-presses, yet suffer thirst. In the cities also, we see the tears of the oppressed (*v.* 12): *Men groan from out of the city*, where the rich merchants and traders are as cruel with their poor debtors as the landlords in the country are with their poor tenants.

II. He speaks of robbers, and those that do wrong by downright force, as the bands of the Sabeans and Chaldeans, which had lately plundered him. Their character is that they are *as wild asses in the desert*, untamed, untractable, unreasonable. They choose the deserts for their dwelling. The desert is indeed the fittest place for such wild people, *ch.* xxxix. 6. But no desert can set men out of the reach of God's eye and hand. Their trade is to steal, and to make a prey of all about them. They are diligent and take pains at it: They *rise betimes for a prey*. They not only rob travellers, but they make incursions upon their neighbours, and *reap every one his corn in the field* (*v.* 6), that is, they enter upon other people's ground, cut their corn, and carry it away as freely as if it were their own. *They cause the naked*, whom they have stripped, not leaving them the clothes to their backs, *to lodge*, in the cold nights, *without clothing*, so that *they are wet with the showers of the mountains, and, for want of* a better *shelter, embrace the rock*, and are glad of a cave or den in it to preserve them

JAMIESON, FAUSSET, BROWN

ness," i.e., calamity. "Cut off"; rather, in the *Arabic* sense, *brought to* the land of *silence;* my sad complaint hushed in death [UMBREIT]. "Darkness" in the second clause, not the same *Hebrew* word as in the first, "cloud," "obscurity." Instead of "covering the cloud (of evil) from my face," He "covers" me with it (ch. 22:11).

CHAPTER 24

Vss. 1-25. **1.** Why is it that, seeing that the times of punishment (Ezek. 30:3; "time" in the same sense) are not hidden from the Almighty, they who know Him (His true worshippers, ch. 18:21) do not see His days (of vengeance; Joel 1:15; II Pet. 3:10)? Or, with UMBREIT less simply, making the parallel clauses more nicely balanced, Why are not times of punishment hoarded up ("laid up"; ch. 21:19; *appointed*) by the Almighty? i.e., Why are they not so appointed as that man may now see them? as the second clause shows. Job does not doubt that they are appointed: nay, he asserts it (ch. 21:30); what he wishes is that God would let all now *see* that it is so. **2-24.** Instances of the wicked doing the worst deeds with seeming impunity. **Some**—the wicked. **landmarks**—boundaries between different pastures (Deut. 19:14; Prov. 22:28). **3. pledge**—alluding to ch. 22:6. Others really do, and with impunity, that which Eliphaz falsely charges the afflicted Job with. **4.** Lit., they push the poor out of their road in meeting them. Fig., they take advantage of them by force and injustice (alluding to the charge of Eliphaz (ch. 22:8; I Sam. 8:3). **poor**—in spirit and in circumstances (Matt. 5:3). **hide**—from the injustice of their oppressors, who have robbed them of their all and driven them into unfrequented places (ch. 20:19; 30:3-6; Prov. 28:28). **5. wild asses**—(ch. 11:12.) So Ishmael is called a wild ass-man; *Hebrew* (Gen. 16:12). These Bedouin robbers, with the unbridled wildness of the ass of the desert, go forth thither. Robbery is their lawless "work." The desert, which yields no food to other men, yields food for the robber and his children by the plunder of caravans. **rising betimes**—In the East travelling is begun very early, before the heat comes on. **6.** Like the wild asses (vs. 5), they (these Bedouin robbers) reap (metaphorically) their various grain (so the *Hebrew* for "corn" means). The wild ass does not let man pile his mixed provender up in a stable (Isa. 30:24); so these robbers find their food in the open air, at one time in the desert (vs. 5), at another in the fields. **the vintage of the wicked**—the vintage of robbery, not of honest industry. If we translate "belonging to the wicked," then it will imply that the wicked alone have vineyards, the "pious poor" (vs. 4) have none. "Gather" in *Hebrew*, is "gather late." As the first clause refers to the *early* harvest of corn, so the second to the vintage *late* in autumn. **7.** UMBREIT understands it of the Bedouin robbers, who are quite regardless of the comforts of life, "They pass the night naked, and uncovered," etc. But the allusion to ch. 22:6, makes the *English Version* preferable (see *Note* below, vs. 10). Frost is not uncommon at night in those regions (Gen. 31: 40). **8. They**—the plundered travellers. **embrace the rock**—take refuge under it (Lam. 4:5). **9. from the breast**—of the widowed mother. Kidnapping children for slaves. Here Job passes from wrongs in the desert to those done among the habitations of men. **pledge**—viz., the garment of the poor debtor, as next verse shows. **10.** (*Note*, ch. 22:6.) In vs. 7 a like sin is alluded to: but *there* he implies open robbery of garments in the desert; *here*, the more refined robbery in civilized life, under the name of a "pledge." Having stripped the poor, they make them besides labor in their harvest-fields and do not allow them to satisfy their hunger with any of the very corn which they carry to the heap. Worse treatment than that of the ox, according to Deut. 25:4. Translate: "they (the poor laborers) hungering carry the sheaves" [UMBREIT]. **11. Which**—"They," the poor, "press the oil within their wall"; viz., not only in the open fields (vs. 10), but also in the wall-enclosed vineyards and olive gardens of the oppressor (Isa. 5:5). Yet they are not allowed to quench their "thirst" with the grapes and olives. Here, *thirsty;* vs. 10, *hungry*. **12. Men**—rather, "mortals" (not the common *Hebrew* for "men"); so the Masoretic vowel points read as *English Version*. But the vowel points are modern. The true reading is, "The dying," answering to "the wounded" in the next clause, so *Syriac*. Not merely in the country (vs. 11), but also in the city there are oppressed sufferers, who cry for help in vain. *"From out of* the city;" i.e., they long to get forth and be free outside

ADAM CLARKE

strength, and my soul has been terrified by His fear." Verse 17: "For it is not this deep night in which I am enveloped, nor the evils which I suffer, that have overwhelmed me; I sink only through the fear which the presence of His majesty inspires."

CHAPTER 24

1. *Why, seeing times are not hidden from the Almighty?* The wish is that God would appoint such times that the falsely accused might look forward to them with comfort; knowing that, on their arrival, they should have a fair hearing, and their innocence be publicly declared.

2. *Some remove the landmarks.* Stones or posts were originally set up to ascertain the bounds of particular estates, and this was necessary in open countries, before hedges and fences were formed. Wicked and covetous men often removed the landmarks and set them in on their neighbors' ground, that, by contracting their boundaries, they might enlarge their own. The law of Moses denounces curses on those who remove their neighbors' landmarks.

4. *They turn the needy out of the way.* They will not permit them to go by the accustome paths; they oblige them to take circuitous routes.

9. *They pluck the fatherless from the breast.* They forcibly take young children in order that they may bring them up in a state of slavery. *Take a pledge of the poor.* Oppressive landlords who let out their grounds at an exorbitant rent, which the poor laborers, though using the utmost diligence, are unable at all times to pay; and then the unfeeling wretch "sells them up," as the phrase here is, or takes their cow or their bed in pledge that the money shall be paid in such a time.

10. *They cause him to go naked.* These cruel, hardhearted oppressors seize the cloth made for the family wear, or the wool and flax out of which such clothes should be made. *And they take away the sheaf.* Seize the grain as soon as it is reaped, that they may pay themselves the exorbitant rent at which they have leased out their land.

11. *Make oil within their walls.* Thus stripped of all that on which they depended for clothing and food, they are obliged to become vassals to their lord, labor in the fields on scanty fare, or tread their winepresses, from the produce of which they are not permitted to quench their thirst.

12. *Men groan from out of the city.* After having shown the oppressions carried on in the country, he takes a view of those carried on in the town. Here the miseries are too numerous to be detailed.

MATTHEW HENRY

from the injuries of the weather. The impunity of these oppressors and spoilers is expressed in one word (*v.* 12): *Yet God layeth not folly to them,* that is, he does not prosecute them with his judgments until he saith, *Thou fool, this night thy soul shall be required of thee,* Luke xii. 20.

Verses 13–17

Another sort of sinners who go unpunished, because they go undiscovered. *They rebel against the light, v.* 13. Some understand it figuratively. Of their own consciences they profess to know God, but they rebel against the knowledge they have of him. Others understand it literally: they have the daylight, and choose the night as the most advantageous season for their wickedness. In this paragraph Job specifies three sorts of sinners that shun the light:—1. Murderers, *v.* 14. 2. Adulterers. 3. Housebreakers, *v.* 16.

And, *lastly,* Job observes that they are in a continual terror for fear of being discovered (*v.* 17): *The morning is to them even as the shadow of death.* The light of the day, which is welcome to honest people, is a terror to bad people. They curse the sun because it discovers them.

Verses 18–25

Job in the conclusion of his discourse,

I. Gives some further instances of the wickedness of these cruel bloody men. 1. Some are pirates and robbers at sea. To this many interpreters apply those difficult expressions (*v.* 18), *He is swift upon the waters.* Their *portion is cursed in the earth,* and they *behold not the way of the vineyards,* that is, they despise the employment of those who till the ground and plant vineyards as poor and unprofitable. But others make this a further description of the conduct of those sinners that are afraid of the light: if they be discovered, they get away as fast as they can, and choose to lurk, not in the vineyards, for fear of being discovered, but in some cursed portion, a lonely and desolate place, which nobody looks after. 2. Some are abusive to those that are in trouble, and add affliction to the afflicted. Barrenness was looked upon as a great reproach, and those that fall under that affliction they upbraid with it. This is *evil entreating the barren that beareth not* (*v.* 21), or those that are childless. 3. There are those who, by inuring themselves to cruelty, come at last to be *the terror of the mighty in the land of the living* (*v.* 22): *He draws the mighty* into a snare with his power; *he rises up* in his passion, and lays about him with so much fury that *no man is sure of his life.*

II. Shows that these daring sinners prosper, and are at ease for a while, nay, and often end their days in peace. It is *given them to be in safety, v.* 23. *They are exalted for a while.* At length, they are carried out of the world very silently and gently. "They go down to the grave as easily as snow-water sinks into the dry ground when it is melted by the sun;" so Bishop Patrick explains *v.* 19. He paraphrases, *v.* 20, *The womb shall forget him,* &c. "God sets no such mark of his displeasure upon him but that his mother may soon forget him. Neither he nor his wickedness is any more remembered than a tree which is broken to shivers." And *v.* 24, *They are taken out of the way as all others,* that is, "they are shut up in their graves like all other men; nay, they die as easily as an ear of corn is cropped with your hand."

III. Foresees their fall however. God's *eyes are upon their ways, v.* 23. Though he keep silence yet he will make it to appear shortly that their most secret sins, which they thought *no eye should see* (*v.* 15), were under his eye and will be called over again. The *grave shall consume those that have sinned*; that land of darkness will be the lot of those that *love darkness rather than light.* Their pride shall be brought down and laid in the dust (*v.* 24). Job owns that wicked people will be miserable on the other side death, but utterly denies what his friends asserted, that ordinarily they are miserable in this life.

IV. Concludes with a bold challenge to all that were present to disprove what he had said (*v.* 25): "*If it be not so now,* as I have declared, and if it do not thence follow that I am unjustly condemned and censured, let those that can undertake to prove me a liar."

JAMIESON, FAUSSET, BROWN

of it (Exod. 1:11; 2:23). **wounded**—by the oppressor (Ezek. 30:24). **layeth not folly**—takes no account of (by punishing) their *sin* ("folly" in Scripture; ch. 1:22). This is the gist of the whole previous list of sins (Acts 17:30). UMBREIT with *Syriac* reads by changing a vowel point, "Regards not their supplication." **13.** So far as to openly committed sins; now, those done in the dark. Translate: "There are those among them (the wicked) who rebel," etc. **light**—both literal and figurative (John 3:19, 20; Prov. 2:13). **paths thereof**—places where the light shines. **14. with the light**—at early dawn, while still dark, when the traveller in the East usually sets out, and the poor laborer to his work; the murderous robber lies in wait then (Ps. 10:8). **is as a thief**—*Thieves* in the East steal while men sleep at night; *robbers* murder at early dawn. The same man who steals at night, when light dawns not only robs, but murders to escape detection. **15.** (Prov. 7:9; Ps. 10:11.) **disguiseth**—puts a veil on. **16. dig through**—Houses in the East are generally built of sun-dried mud bricks (so Matt. 6:19). "Thieves break through," lit., "dig through" (Ezek. 12:7). **had marked**—Rather, as in ch. 9:7, "They shut themselves up (in their houses); lit., "they seal up." **for themselves**—for their own ends, viz., to escape detection. **know not**—shun. **17.** They shrink from the "morning" light, as much as other men do from *the blackest darkness* ("the shadow of *death*"). **if one know**—i.e., recognize them. Rather, "They know well (are familiar with) the terrors of," etc. [UMBREIT]. Or, as MAURER, "They know the terrors of (this) darkness," viz., of morning, the light, which is as terrible to them as darkness ("the shadow of death") is to other men. **18-21.** In these verses Job quotes the opinions of his adversaries ironically; he quoted them so before. In vss. 22-24 he states his own observation as the opposite. You say, "The sinner is swift, i.e., swiftly passes away (as a thing floating) on the surface of the waters" (Eccles. 11:1; Hos. 10:7). **is cursed**—by those who witness their "swift" destruction. **beholdeth not**—"turneth not to"; figuratively, for He cannot enjoy his pleasant possessions (ch. 20:17; 15:33). **the way of the vineyards**—including his fields, fertile as vineyards; opposite to "the way of the desert." **19.** Arabian image; melted snow, as contrasted with the living fountain, quickly dries up in the sunburnt sand, not leaving a trace behind (ch. 6:16-18). The Hebrew is terse and elliptical to express the swift and utter destruction of the godless; (so) "the grave—they have sinned!" **20. The womb**—The very mother that bare him, and who is the last to "forget" the child that *sucked* her (Isa. 49:15), shall dismiss him from her memory (ch. 18:17; Prov. 10:7). The worm shall *suck,* i.e., "feed sweetly" on him as a delicate morsel (ch. 21:33). **wickedness**—i.e., the wicked; abstract for concrete (as ch. 5:16). **as a tree**—utterly (ch. 19:10); UMBREIT better, "as a staff." A broken staff is the emblem of irreparable ruin (Isa. 14:5; Hos. 4:12). **21.** The reason given by the friends why the sinner deserves such a fate. **barren**—without sons, who might have protected her. **widow**—without a husband to support **her. 22-25.** Reply of Job to the opinion of the friends. Experience proves the contrary. Translate: "But He (God) prolongeth the life of (lit., draweth out at length; *Margin,* Ps. 36:10) the mighty with His (God's) power. He (the wicked) riseth up (from his sick bed) although he had given up hope of (lit., when he no longer believed in) life" (Deut. 28:66). **23.** Lit., "He (God omitted, as often; ch. 3:20; Eccles. 9:9; reverentially) giveth to him (the wicked, to be) in safety, or security." **yet**—Job means, How strange that God should so favor them, and yet have His eyes all the time open to their wicked ways (Prov. 15:3; Ps. 73:4)! **24.** Job repeats what he said (ch. 21:13), that sinners die in exalted positions, not the painful and lingering death we might expect, but a *quick and easy death.* Join "for a while" with "are gone," not as *English Version.* Translate: "A moment—and they are no more! They are brought low, as all (others) gather up their feet to die" (so the *Hebrew* of "are taken out of the way"). A natural death (Gen. 49:33). **ears of corn**—in a ripe and full age, not prematurely (ch. 5:26). **25.** (So ch. 9:24.)

ADAM CLARKE

Yet God layeth not folly to them. He does not impute their calamities to their own folly. But the Hebrew may be translated, "And God doth not attend to their prayers." Job's object was to show, in opposition to the mistaken doctrine of his friends, that God did not hastily punish every evil work, nor reward every good one.

13. *They . . . rebel against the light.* Speaking of wicked men. They rebel against the light of God in their consciences, and His light in His Word.

F. B. MEYER:

"Yet a little while, and they are gone" (24:24). Job here describes the insecurity of the wicked. He may have raged against the poor and innocent; but in a moment he comes down to Sheol, is hurried to stand before his Maker to receive his sentence. As he had treated the poor, so he is treated. As he had devoured the houses of the innocent, so he is devoured. "How are they become a desolation in a moment! They are utterly consumed with terrors. As a dream when one awaketh; so, O Lord, when Thou awakest, Thou shalt despise their image."

For those who fear God there is a greatly contrasted lot. They receive a kingdom that cannot be moved. Zion may be a desolation, and Jerusalem a wilderness; the holy and beautiful institutions in which their early religious impressions were made may crumble; but they are come to the heavenly Jerusalem. The removing of those things that are capable of being shaken only makes more apparent those which cannot be shaken.

Where do you build your nest? In the trees of this world, that sway in the tempest, or may be hewn down by the woodman's axe; or have you learnt to build in the clefts of the Rock of Ages? Is your treasure in human friendships, which may change or be cut in twain by the sharp shears of death; or is it in the love of God, the unchangeable and everlasting Lover of souls? Let us look off from ourselves; from that diseased introspection that so confuses and dims our life; from the old fears that made us tremble and the old matters of which we must speak no more. And let us look upward and forward to that near future, which is so much larger and better than the past has been, and where we shall attain more than the heights of our dreams.

—*Great Verses Through the Bible*

CHAPTER 25 (Matthew Henry)

Verses 1–6

Bildad is to be commended, 1. For speaking no more on the subject about which Job and he differed. 2. For speaking so well on the matter about which Job and he were agreed.

CHAPTER 25 (Jamieson, Fausset, Brown)

Vss. 1-6. BILDAD'S REPLY. He tries to show Job's rashness (ch. 23:3), by arguments borrowed from Eliphaz (ch. 15:15), with which cf. ch. 11:17.

CHAPTER 25 (Adam Clarke)

1. *Bildad the Shuhite.* This is the last attack on Job; the others felt themselves foiled, though they had not humility enough to acknowledge it, but would not again return to the attack. Bildad

MATTHEW HENRY

Two ways Bildad takes here to exalt God and abase man:

I. He shows how glorious God is, and thence infers how guilty and impure man is before him, *v.* 2–4. God is the sovereign Lord of all, and *with him is terrible majesty. Dominion and fear are with him, v.* 2. He that gave being has an incontestable authority to give laws, and can enforce the laws he gives. His having dominion (or being *Dominus—Lord*) bespeaks him both owner and ruler of all the creatures. They are all his, and they are all under his direction and at his disposal. *He maketh peace in his high places.* The holy angels never quarrel with him, nor with one another, but acquiesce in his will, and execute it without murmuring or disquieting. The high places are *his* high places; for *the heaven, even the heavens, are the Lord's* (Ps. cxv. 16). Peace is God's work; where it is made it is he that makes it, Isa. lvii. 19. In heaven there is perfect peace; for there is perfect holiness, and there is God, who is love. He is a God of irresistible power: *Is there any number of his armies? v.* 3. His providence extends itself to all: *Upon whom does not his light arise? How then can man be justified with God? Or how can he be clean?* Man is not only mean, but vile, not only earthy, but filthy; he cannot be justified, he cannot be clean, (1) In comparison with God. (2) In debate with God. (3) In the sight of God. If God is so great and glorious, how can man, who is guilty and impure, appear before him?

II. He shows how dark and defective even the heavenly bodies are in the sight of God, and in comparison with him, and thence infers how little, and mean, and worthless, man is. The lights of heaven have no glory by reason of the glory which excelleth, as a candle, though it burn, yet does not shine when it is set in the clear light of the sun. *The moon shall be confounded, and the sun ashamed, when the Lord of hosts shall reign in Mount Sion.* How durst Job then so confidently appeal to God, who would discover that amiss in him which he was not aware of in himself? The children of men, though noble creatures, are before God but as worms of the earth (*v.* 6): *How much less* does *man* shine in honour, how much less is he pure in righteousness *that is a worm.* What little reason has man to be proud, and what great reason to be humble! Shall man be such a fool as to contend with his Maker?

JAMIESON, FAUSSET, BROWN

2. Power and terror, i.e., terror-inspiring power. **peace in his high places**—implying that His power is such on high as to quell all opposition, not merely there, but on earth also. The Holy Ghost here shadowed forth Gospel truths (Col. 1:20; Eph. 1:10).

3. armies—angels and stars (Isa. 40:26; Jer. 33:22; Gen. 15:5; countless, Dan. 7:10). **his light**—(Jas. 1:17). **4.** (ch. 4:17, 18; 14:4, 15:14.)

5. "Look up even unto the moon" (ch. 15:15). "Stars" here answer to "saints" (angels) there; "the moon" here to "the heavens" there. Even the "stars," the most dazzling object to man's eye, and the angels, of which the stars are emblems (ch. 4:18; Rev. 9:1), are imperfect in His sight. Theirs is the light and purity but of creatures; His of the Creator. **6.** (ch. 4:19-21; 15:16). **worm ... worm**—two distinct *Hebrew* words. The first, a worm bred in putridity; alluding to man's *corruption.* The second a crawling worm; implying that man is *weak and grovelling.*

ADAM CLARKE

has little to say, and that little is very little to the point. He makes a few assertions, particularly in reference to what Job had said in the commencement of the preceding chapter, of his desire to appear before God, and have his case tried by Him, as he had the utmost confidence that his innocence should be fully proved. For this Bildad reprehends Job with arguments which had been brought forth often in this controversy, and as repeatedly confuted, chap. iv. 18 and xv. 14-16.

This speech of Bildad is both confused and inconclusive. His reasoning is absurd, and he draws false conclusions from his premises. In the third verse, he says, "Is there any number of his armies? and upon whom doth not his light arise?" But how absurd is the conclusion which he draws from his questions! "How then can a man be justified with God? or how can he be clean that is born of a woman?" This has no relation to the premises; still, to us the question is not difficult. A man can be "justified with God," through the blood of Christ; and he can "be clean that is born of a woman," through the sanctification of the Spirit.

6. *How much less man, that is a worm?* Or as the Targum: "How much more man, who in his life is a reptile; and the son of man, who in his death is a worm?"

Thus endeth Bildad the Shuhite, who endeavored to speak on a subject which he did not understand; and, having got on bad ground, was soon confounded in his own mind, spoke incoherently, argued inconclusively, and came abruptly and suddenly to an end. Thus, his three friends being confounded, Job was left to pursue his own way. They trouble him no more, and he proceeds in triumph to the end of the thirty-first chapter.

MATTHEW HENRY — CHAPTER 26

Verses 1–4

Bildad thought that he had made a fine speech, but Job peevishly enough shows that his performance was not so valuable as he thought it.

I. There was no great matter to be found in it (*v.* 3): *How hast thou plentifully declared the thing as it is?* This is spoken ironically, upbraiding Bildad. 1. He thought he had spoken very clearly, had *declared the thing as it is.* 2. He thought he had spoken very fully. It was but poorly and scantily that he declared it, in comparison with the vast compass of the subject.

II. There was no great use to be made of it. *Cui bono—What good hast thou done* by all that thou hast said? *How hast thou,* with all this mighty flourish, *helped him that is without power? v.* 2. Job would convince him, 1. That he had done God no service by it. 2. That he had done his cause no service by it. 3. That he had done him no service by it. He pretended to convince, instruct, and comfort, Job; but, alas! what he had said was little to the purpose. *"To whom hast thou uttered words? v.* 4. Was it to me that thou didst direct thy discourse? And dost thou take me for such a child as to need these instructions?" Everything that is true and good is not suitable and seasonable. To one that was humbled, and broken, as Job was, he ought to have preached of the grace and mercy of God, rather than of his greatness and majesty. Job asks him, *Whose spirit came from thee?* that is, "What troubled soul would ever been revived, and relieved, and brought to itself, by such discourses as these?"

Verses 5–14

Now they are upon a subject in which they were all agreed, the infinite glory and power of God.

I. Many instances are here given of the wisdom and power of God in the creation and preservation of the world.

JAMIESON, FAUSSET, BROWN — CHAPTER 26

VSS. 1-14. JOB'S REPLY. **2, 3. without power ... no strength ... no wisdom**—The negatives are used instead of the positives, *powerlessness,* etc., designedly (so Isa. 31:8; Deut. 32:21). Granting I am, as you say (ch. 18:17; 15:2), *powerlessness* itself, etc. *How hast thou helped* such a one? **savest**—supportest. **plentifully ... the thing as it is**—rather, "abundantly—wisdom." Bildad had made great pretensions to abundant wisdom. How has he shown it? **4.** For whose instruction were thy words meant? If for me I know the subject (God's omnipotence) better than my instructor; vss. 5-14 is a sample of Job's knowledge of it. **whose spirit**—not that of God (ch. 32:8); nay, rather, the borrowed sentiment of Eliphaz (ch. 4:17-19; 15:14-16). **5-14.** As before in chs. 9 and 12, Job had shown himself not inferior to the friends' inability to describe God's greatness, so now he describes it as manifested in hell (the world of the dead), 5, 6; on earth, 7; in the sky, 8-11; the sea, 12; the heavens, 13. **Dead things are formed**—Rather, "The souls of the dead (Rephaim) tremble." Not only does God's power exist, as Bildad says (ch. 25:2), "in high places" (heaven), but reaches to the region of the dead. *Rephaim* here, and in Proverbs 21:16 and Isaiah 14:9, is from a *Hebrew* root, meaning "to be weak," hence "deceased"; in Genesis 14:5 it is applied to the Canaanite giants; perhaps in derision, to express their *weakness,* in spite of their gigantic size, as compared with Jehovah [UMBREIT]; or, as the imagination of the living magnifies apparitions, the term originally was applied to *ghosts,* and then to *giants* in general [MAGEE]. **from under**—UMBREIT joins this with the previous word tremble *from beneath* (so Isa. 14:9). But the Masoretic text joins it to "under the waters." Thus the place of the dead will be represented as "under the waters" (Ps. 18:4, 5); and the waters as under the earth (Ps. 24:2). MAGEE well translates thus: "The souls of the dead tremble; (the places) under the waters, and their inhabitants." Thus the Masoretic connection is retained; and at the same time the parallel clauses are evenly balanced. "The inhabitants of the places

ADAM CLARKE — CHAPTER 26

2. *How hast thou helped him?* This seems a species of irony.

4. *Whose spirit came from thee?* Mr. Good renders the verse thus: "From whom hast thou pillaged speeches? And whose spirit hath issued forth from thee?" The retort is peculiarly severe, and refers immediately to the proverbial sayings which in several of the preceding answers have been adduced against the irritated sufferer, for which see chap. viii. 11-19; xv. 20-35. I concur most fully therefore with Dr. Stock in regarding the remainder of this chapter as a sample, ironically exhibited by Job, of the harangues on the power and greatness of God which he supposes his friends to have taken out of the mouths of other men, to deck their speeches with borrowed lustre. Only, in descanting on the same subject, he shows how much he himself can go beyond them in eloquence and sublimity.

5. *Dead things are formed from under the waters.* This verse, as it stands in our version, seems to convey no meaning, and the Hebrew is obscure; *harephaim,* "the Rephaim," certainly does not mean *dead things.* There is probably here an allusion to the destruction of the earth by the general deluge. Moses, speaking concerning the state of the earth before the Flood, says, Gen. vi. 4, "There were giants [*nephilim*] in the earth in those days." Now it is likely that Job means the same by *rephaim* as Moses does by the *nephilim;* and that both refer to the antediluvians, who were all, for their exceeding great iniquities, overwhelmed by the waters of the Deluge. Can those mighty men and their neighbors, all the sinners who have been gathered to them since, be rejected from under the waters, by which they were judicially overwhelmed?

MATTHEW HENRY

1. If we look about us, to the earth and waters here below, we shall see striking instances of omnipotence, which we may gather out of these verses. (1) *He hangs the earth upon nothing*, *v.* 7. The art of man could not hang a feather upon nothing, yet the divine wisdom hangs the whole earth so. (2) He *sets bounds to the waters of the sea*, and compasses them in (*v.* 10), that they may not *return to cover the earth.* (3) He *forms dead things under the waters. Rephaim—giants, are formed under the waters*, that is, vast creatures, of prodigious bulk, as whales. (4) By mighty storms and tempests he shakes the mountains, which are here called *the pillars of heaven* (*v.* 11), and even *divides the sea, and smites through its proud waves*, *v.* 12.

2. By *hell and destruction* (*v.* 6) we may understand the grave, and those who are buried in it, that they are under the eye of God, though laid out of our sight, which may strengthen our belief of the resurrection of the dead. We may also consider them as referring to the place of the damned.

3. If we look up to heaven above, we shall see instances of God's sovereignty and power. *He stretches out the north over the empty place*, *v.* 7. So he did at first, when *he stretched out the heavens like a curtain* (Ps. civ. 2). *He binds up the waters in his thick clouds*, as if they were tied closely in a bag, and, notwithstanding the vast weight of water so raised and laid up, yet *the cloud is not rent under them*, but they distil through the cloud, and so come drop by drop, in mercy to the earth, in small rain, or great rain, as he pleases. *He holds back the face of his throne*, that light in which he dwells, *and spreads a cloud upon it*, through which *he judges*, *ch.* xxii. 13. *By his Spirit*, the eternal Spirit that moved upon the face of the waters, *he has garnished the heavens*, not only made them, but beautified them, has curiously bespangled them with stars by night and painted them with the light of the sun by day. "If the pavement be so richly inlaid, what must the palace be! If the visible heavens be so glorious, what are those that are out of sight!" What is meant here by *the crooked serpent* which his hands have formed is not certain. Some make it part of the garnishing of the heavens, the milky-way, say some; some particular constellation, so called, say others. It is the same word that is used for leviathan (Isa. xxvii. 1), and probably may be meant of the whale or crocodile, in which appears much of the power of the Creator; and why may not Job conclude with that inference, when God himself does so? *ch.* xli.

II. He concludes (*v.* 14): *Lo, these are parts of his ways*, by which he makes himself known to the children of men. Here he acknowledges, with adoration, the discoveries that were made of God. These things which he himself had said, and which Bildad had said, are his ways, and this is something of God. He admires the depth of that which is undiscovered. What we know of God is nothing in comparison with what is in God and what God is. He is infinite and incomprehensible; our understandings and capacities are weak and shallow, and the full discoveries of the divine glory are reserved for the future state.

JAMIESON, FAUSSET, BROWN

under the waters" are those in Gehenna, the lower of the two parts into which Sheol, according to the Jews, is divided; they answer to "destruction," i.e., the place of the wicked in vs. 6, as "Rephaim" (vs. 5) to "Hell" (Sheol) (vs. 6). Sheol comes from a *Hebrew* root—"ask," because it is insatiable (Prov. 27:20); or "ask as a loan to be returned," implying Sheol is but a *temporary* abode, previous to the resurrection; so for *English Version* "formed," LXX and *Chaldee* translate; *shall be born*, or *born again*, implying the dead are to be *given back* from Sheol and *born again into a new state* [MAGEE]. **6.**—(ch. 38:17; Ps. 139:8; Prov. 5:11). **destruction**—the abode of destruction, i.e., of lost souls. *Hebrew, Abaddon* (Rev. 9:11). **no covering**—from God's eyes. **7.** Hint of the true theory of the earth. Its suspension in empty space is stated in the second clause. The north in particular is specified in the first, being believed to be the highest part of the earth (Isa. 14:13). The northern hemisphere or vault of *heaven* is included; often compared to a stretched-out canopy (Ps. 104:2). The chambers of the south are mentioned (ch. 9:9), i.e., the southern hemisphere, consistently with the earth's globular form. **8. in . . . clouds**—as if in airy vessels, which, though light, do not burst with the weight of water in them (Prov. 30:4). **9.** Rather, He *encompasseth* or *closeth*. God makes the clouds a veil to screen the glory not only of His person, but even of the exterior of His throne from profane eyes. His agency is everywhere, yet He Himself is invisible (Ps. 18:11; 104:3). **10.** Rather, "He hath drawn a circular bound round the waters" (Prov. 8:27; Ps. 104:9). The horizon seems a circle. Indication is given of the globular form of the earth. **until the day . . .**—to the confines of light and darkness. When the light falls on our horizon, the other hemisphere is dark. UMBREIT and MAURER translate "He has *most perfectly* (lit., "to perfection") drawn the bound (taken from the first clause) between light and darkness" (cf. Gen. 1:4, 6, 9): where the bounding of the light from darkness is similarly brought into proximity with the bounding of the waters. **11. pillars**—poetically for the mountains which seem to bear up the sky (Ps. 104:32). **astonished**—viz., from terror. Personification. **his reproof**—(Ps. 104:7). The thunder, reverberating from cliff to cliff (Hab. 3:10; Nahum 1:5). **12. divideth**—(Psalm 74:13). Perhaps at creation (Gen. 1:9, 10). The parallel clause favors UMBREIT, "He stilleth." But the *Hebrew* means "He moves." Probably such a "moving" is meant as that at the assuaging of the flood by the wind which "God made to pass over" it (Gen. 8:1; Ps. 104:7). **the proud**—rather, its pride, viz., of the sea (ch. 9:13). **13.** UMBREIT less simply, "By His breath He maketh the heavens to revive": viz., His wind dissipates the clouds, which obscured the shining stars. And so the next clause in contrast, "His hand doth strangle," i.e., obscures the north constellation, the dragon. Pagan astronomy typified the flood trying to destroy the ark by the dragon constellation, about to devour the moon in its eclipsed crescent-shape like a boat (ch. 3:8, *Margin*). But better as *English Version* (Ps. 33:6). **crooked**—implying the oblique course, of the stars, or the ecliptic. "Fleeing" or "swift" [UMBREIT] (Isa. 27:1). This particular constellation is made to represent the splendor of all the stars. **14. parts**—Rather, "only the extreme boundaries of, etc., and how faint is the whisper that we hear of Him!" **thunder**—the entire fulness. In antithesis to "whisper" (I Cor. 13:9, 10, 12).

ADAM CLARKE

6. *Hell is naked before him. Sheol*, the place of the dead, or of separate spirits, is always in his view. "And there is no covering to Abaddon"—the place of the "destroyer," where destruction reigns, and where those dwell who are eternally separated from God. The ancients thought that hell or Tartarus was a vast space in the center or at the very bottom of the earth.

7. *He stretcheth out the north over the empty place. Al tohu*, "to the hollow waste." The same word as is used, Gen. i. 2, "The earth was without form," *tohu.*

8. *He bindeth up the waters.* Drives the aqueous particles together, which were raised by evaporation, so that, being condensed, they form clouds which float in the atmosphere, till, meeting with strong currents of wind, or by the agency of the electric fluid, they are further condensed; and then, becoming too heavy to be sustained in the air, fall down in the form of rain, when, in this poetic language, *the cloud is . . . rent under them.*

9. *He holdeth back the face of his throne.* The great Agent is not personally discoverable. The words, however, may refer to those obscurations of the face of heaven, and the hiding of the body of the sun, when the atmosphere is laden with dense vapors, and the rain begins to be poured down on the earth.

10. *He hath compassed the waters with bounds.* Perhaps this refers merely to the circle of the horizon, the line that terminates light and commences darkness, called here "until the completion of light with darkness."

11. *The pillars of heaven tremble.* This is probably a poetical description either of thunder or of an earthquake.

12. *He divideth the sea with his power.* Here is a manifest allusion to the passage of the Red Sea by the Israelites, and the overthrow of Pharaoh and his host. *He smiteth through the proud. Rahab*, the very name by which Egypt is called Isa. li. 9 and elsewhere. Let Job live when he might, I am satisfied the Book of Job was written long after the death of Moses, and not earlier than the days of Solomon, if not later. The farther I go in the work, the more this conviction is deepened.

14. *Lo, these are parts of his ways. Ketsoth*, "the ends" or "extremities," the outlines, an indistinct sketch, of his eternal power and Godhead. *How little a portion is heard? Shemets*, "a mere whisper"; admirably opposed to *raam, the thunder*, mentioned in the next clause.

MATTHEW HENRY — CHAPTER 27

Verses 1-6

Job's discourse here is called a *parable* (*mashal*), the title of Solomon's proverbs, because it was very instructive, and he spoke as one having authority. It comes from a word that signifies *to rule*, or *have dominion*; and some think it intimates that Job now triumphed over his opponents. We say of an excellent preacher that he knows how *to command his hearers.* Job here backs all he had said in maintainance of his own integrity with a solemn oath, to silence contradiction, and take the blame entirely upon himself if he prevaricated.

I. The form of his oath (*v.* 2): *As God liveth, who hath taken away my judgment.* He speaks highly of God, in calling him *the living God* (which means *ever-living*, the eternal God, that has life in himself). Yet he speaks hardly of him, and unbecomingly, in saying that he had taken away his judgment (that is, refused to do him justice in this controversy and to appear in defence of him), and that by continuing his troubles, on which his friends grounded their censures of him,

JAMIESON, FAUSSET, BROWN — CHAPTER 27

Vss. 1-23. It was now Zophar's turn to speak. But as he and the other two were silent, virtually admitting defeat, after a pause Job proceeds. **1. parable**—applied in the East to a figurative sententious embodiment of wisdom in poetic form, a gnome (Ps. 49:4). **continued**—proceeded to put forth: implying elevation of discourse.

2. (I Sam. 20:3.) **taken away . . . judgment**—words unconsciously foreshadowing Jesus Christ (Isa. 53:8; Acts 8:33). God will not give Job his right, by declaring his innocence.

ADAM CLARKE — CHAPTER 27

1. *Continued his parable.* After having delivered the preceding discourse, Job appears to have paused to see if any of his friends chose to make any reply; but finding them all silent, he resumed his discourse, which is here called *meshalo, his parable*, his "authoritative weighty discourse"; from *mashal*, "to exercise rule, authority, dominion, or power." And it must be granted that in this speech he assumes great boldness, exhibits his own unsullied character, and treats his friends with little ceremony.

2. *Who hath taken away my judgment.* Who has turned aside my cause, and has not permitted it to come to a hearing, where I might have justice done to me, but has abandoned me to the harsh and uncharitable judgment of my enemies. There appears to be a great want of reverence in these words of Job; he speaks with a degree of irritation, if not bitterness, which

MATTHEW HENRY

he had taken from him the opportunity he hoped ere now to have of clearing himself. He also charges it upon God that he had *vexed his soul* by laying such grievous afflictions upon him. Yet see Job's confidence in the goodness both of his cause and of his God, that though God seemed to be angry with him, and to act against him for the present, yet he could cheerfully commit his cause to him.

II. The matter of his oath, *v.* 3, 4. 1. That he would not *speak wickedness, nor utter deceit*—that, as in this debate he had all along spoken as he thought so he would never wrong his conscience by speaking otherwise; he would never maintain any doctrine, nor assert any matter of fact, but what he believed to be true; nor would he deny the truth, how much soever it might make against him. He would not be brought by their unjust censures, falsely to accuse himself. 2. That he would adhere to this resolution as long as he lived (*v.* 3): *All the while my breath is in me.* In things doubtful and indifferent, it is not safe to be thus peremptory. We know not what reason we may see to change our mind. But in so plain a thing as this we cannot be too positive that we will never speak wickedness.

III. The explication of his oath (*v.* 5, 6): "*God forbid that I should justify you* in your uncharitable censures of me, by owning myself a hypocrite: no, *until I die I will not remove my integrity from me; my righteousness I hold fast, and I will not let it go.*" Job complained much of the reproaches of his friends; but (says he) *my heart shall not reproach me*, that is, "I will never give my heart cause to reproach me, but will keep a conscience void of offence; and, while I do so, I will not give my heart leave to reproach me."

Verses 7–10

Job here expresses the dread he had of being found a hypocrite.

I. He looked upon the condition of a hypocrite to be certainly the most miserable condition that any man could be in (*v.* 7): *Let my enemy be as the wicked*, a proverbial expression. If he might wish the greatest evil to the worst enemy he had, he would wish him the portion of a wicked man, knowing that worse he could not wish him.

II. The reasons of it.

1. Because the hypocrite's hopes will not be crowned (*v.* 8): *For what is the hope of the hypocrite?* Job's friends would persuade him that all his hope was but the hope of the hypocrite, *ch.* iv. 6. "Nay," says he, "I would not, for all the world, be so foolish as to build upon such a rotten foundation; for *what is the hope of the hypocrite?*" It is certain that a formal hypocrite, with all his gains and all his hopes, will be miserable in a dying hour.

2. Because the hypocrite's prayer will not be heard (*v.* 9): *Will God hear his cry when trouble comes upon him?* If true repentance come upon him, God will hear his cry and accept him (Isa. i. 18); but if he continue impenitent and unchanged, let him not think to find favour with God.

3. Because the hypocrite's religion is neither comfortable nor constant (*v.* 10): *Will he delight himself in the Almighty? Will he always call upon God?* No, in prosperity he will not call upon God, but slight him; in adversity he will not call upon God but curse him. The reason why hypocrites do not persevere in religion is because they have no pleasure in it.

Verses 11–23

Now that the heat of the battle was nearly over Job was willing to own how far he agreed with his friends, and where the difference between his opinion and theirs lay. 1. He agreed with them that wicked people are miserable people, that God will surely reckon with cruel oppressors, make reprisals upon them for all the affronts they have put upon God and all the wrongs they have done to their neighbours. This truth is abundantly confirmed by the entire concurrence even of these angry disputants in it. But, 2. In *this* they differed—they held that these deserved judgments are presently and visibly brought upon wicked oppressors. Now Job held that, in many cases, judgments do not fall upon them quickly, but are deferred for some time.

I. Job here undertakes to set this matter in a true light (*v.* 11, 12): *I will teach you.* 1. What he would teach them: "*That which is with the Almighty*," that is, "the counsels and purposes of God concerning wicked people." This, says Job, *will I not conceal. Things revealed belong to us and our children.* 2. How he would teach them: *By the hand of God.* Those whom God teaches with a strong hand are best able to teach others, Isa. viii. 11. 3. What reason they had to learn those things which he was about to teach them (*v.* 12), "*You yourselves have seen it. Why then*

JAMIESON, FAUSSET, BROWN

vexed—*Hebrew*, "made bitter" (Ruth 1:20).

3. Implying Job's knowledge of the fact that the living soul was breathed into man by God (Gen. 2:7). "All the while." But MAURER, "As yet all my breath is in me" (notwithstanding my trials): the reason why I can speak so boldly. **4.** (Ch. 6:28, 30). The "deceit" would be if he were to admit guilt against the witness of his conscience. **5. justify you**—approve of your views. **mine integrity**—which you deny, on account of my misfortunes. **6.** Rather, my "heart" (conscience) reproaches "not one of my days," i.e., I do not repent of any of my days since I came into existence [MAURER].

7. Let . . . be—Let mine enemy be accounted as wicked, i.e., He who opposes my asseveration of innocence must be regarded as actuated by criminal hostility. Not a curse on his enemies.

8. "What hope hath the hypocrite, notwithstanding all his gains, when?" etc. "Gained" is antithetic to "taketh away." UMBREIT's translation is an unmeaning tautology. "When God cuts off, when He *taketh away* his life." **taketh away**—lit., "draws out" the soul from the body, which is, as it were, its scabbard (ch. 4:21; Ps. 104:29; Dan. 7:15). Job says that he admits what Bildad said (ch. 8:13) and Zophar (ch. 20:5). But he says the very fact of his still calling upon God (vs. 10) amid all his trials, which a hypocrite would not dare to do, shows he is no "hypocrite." **9.** (Ps. 66:18.)

10. Alluding to ch. 22:26. **always call**—He may do so in times of prosperity in order to be thought religious. But he will not, as I do, call on God in calamities verging on death. Therefore I cannot be a "hypocrite" (ch. 19:25; 20:5; Ps. 62:8). **11-23.** These words are contrary to Job's previous sentiments (*Notes*, ch. 21:22-33; 24:22-25). They therefore seem to be Job's statement, not so much of his own sentiments, as of what Zophar would have said had he spoken when his turn came (end of ch. 26). So Job stated the friends' opinion (ch. 21:17-21; 24:18-21). The objection is, why, if so, does not Job answer Zophar's opinion, as stated by himself? The fact is, it is probable that Job tacitly, by giving, in ch. 28, only a general answer, implies, that in spite of the wicked *often* dying, as he said, in prosperity, he does not mean to deny that the wicked are *in the main* dealt with according to right, and that God herein vindicates His moral government *even here.* Job therefore states Zophar's argument more strongly than Zophar would have done. But by comparing vs. 13 with ch. 20:29 ("portion," "heritage"), it will be seen, it is Zophar's argument, rather than his own, that Job states. Granting it to be true, implies Job, you ought not to use it as an argument to criminate *me.* For (ch. 28) the ways of divine wisdom in afflicting the godly are inscrutable: all that is sure to man is, the fear of the Lord is wisdom (vs. 28). **by the hand**—rather, *concerning* the hand of God, viz., what God does in governing men. **with the Almighty**—the counsel or principle which regulates God's dealings. **12.** "Ye yourselves see" that the wicked *often* are afflicted (though often the reverse, ch. 21:33). But do you "vainly"

ADAM CLARKE

cannot be justified. No man should speak thus of his Maker.

3. *All the while my breath is in me.* "As long as I live and have my understanding."

5. *God forbid.* Far be it from me, *that I should justify you.*

8. *What is the hope of the hypocrite?* The word *chaneph,* which we translate, most improperly, *hypocrite,* means a "wicked fellow, a defiled, polluted wretch, a rascal, a knave."

11. *I will teach you by the hand of God.* Job felt that the good hand of his God was upon him, and that therefore he should make no mistake in his doctrines.

12. *Ye yourselves have seen it.* Your own experience and observation have shown you that the righteous are frequently in affliction, and the wicked in affluence. *Why then are ye thus altogether vain?* "Why then should ye thus *babble babblings?*" If our language would allow it, we might say "vanitize vanity."

13. *This is the portion of a wicked man.* Job now commences his promised teaching; and what follows is a description of the lot or portion of the wicked man and of tyrants, in general, though the hand of man be not laid upon them. Though God does not at all times show His displeasure against the wicked, by reducing them to a state of poverty and affliction, yet He often does it so that men may see it; and at other times He seems to pass them by, reserving their

MATTHEW HENRY

are you thus altogether vain, to condemn me for a wicked man because I am afflicted?" He offers now to lay before them *the portion of a wicked man with God,* particularly of *oppressors, v.* 13. Compare *ch.* xx. 29. Their portion in the world may be wealth and preferment, but their portion with God is ruin and misery.

II. He does it, by showing that wicked people may, in some instances, prosper, but that ruin follows them and that is their portion.

1. They may prosper in their children, but ruin attends them. *His children* perhaps *are multiplied* (*v.* 14) or *magnified* (so some); they are very numerous and are raised to honour and great estates. (1) Some of them shall die by the sword, the sword of war, by the sword of justice for their crimes, or the sword of the murderer for their estates. (2) Others of them shall die by famine (*v.* 14): *His offspring shall not be satisfied with bread.* (3) Those that *remain shall be buried in death,* that is, shall die of the plague, which is called *death* (Rev. vi. 8), and be buried privately and in haste, without any solemnity, *buried with the burial of an ass*; and even their *widows shall not weep.*

2. They may prosper in their estates, but ruin attends *them* too, *v.* 16–18. *They heap up silver* in abundance *as the dust,* and *prepare raiment as the clay*; they have heaps of clothes about them, as plentiful as heaps of clay. But what comes of it? God will so order it that *the just shall wear his raiment and the innocent shall divide his silver.* Good men shall come honestly by that wealth which the wicked man came dishonestly by. They shall do good with it. The innocent shall not hoard the silver, but shall divide it to the poor. Money is like manure, good for nothing if it be not spread. Suppose them to have built themselves strong and stately houses; but they are like the house which the moth makes for herself in an old garment, out of which she will soon be shaken, *v.* 18. He is very secure in it, as a moth, and has no apprehension of danger; but it will prove of as short continuance as *a booth which the keeper makes,* which will quickly be taken down.

3. Destruction attends their persons, though they lived long in health and at ease (*v.* 19): *The rich man shall lie down* to sleep, *but he shall not be gathered,* that is, he shall not have his mind composed, and gathered in, to enjoy his wealth. He does not sleep so contentedly as people think he does. *His abundance will not suffer him to sleep* so sweetly as the *labouring man,* Eccles. v. 12. His cares increase his fears, and both together make him uneasy. He is miserable in death. It is to him the king of terrors, *v.* 20, 21. *Terrors take hold of him as waters,* as if he were surrounded by the flowing tides. He trembles to think of leaving this world, and much more of removing to another. The tempest of death, may be said *to steal him away in the night.* He is said *to be carried away,* and hurled out of his place as with a storm, and with an east wind, violent, and noisy, and very dreadful. Death, to a godly man, is like a fair gale of wind to convey him to the heavenly country. But the wicked man is miserable after death. His soul falls under the just indignation of God. *For God shall cast upon him and not spare.* Those who will not be persuaded now to fly to the arms of divine grace, which are stretched out to receive them, will not be able to flee from the arms of divine wrath. *Men shall clap their hands at him,* that is, they shall be well pleased in his fall.

JAMIESON, FAUSSET, BROWN

make this an argument to prove from my afflictions that I am wicked? **13.** (*Note,* vs. 11.)

14. His family only increases to perish by sword or famine (Jer. 18:21; ch. 5:20, the converse). **15.** Those that escape war and famine (vs. 14) shall be buried by *the deadly plague*—"death" (ch. 18:13; Jer. 15:2; Rev. 6:8). The plague of the Middle Ages was called "the black death." *Buried by* it implies that they would have none else but the death plague itself (poetically personified) to perform their funeral rites, i.e., would have no one. **his**—rather, their **widows.** Transitions from *singular* to *plural* are frequent. Polygamy is not implied. **16. dust . . . clay**—images of multitudes (Zech. 9:3). Many changes of raiment are a chief constituent of wealth in the East. **17.** Introverted parallelism. (See my introduction). Of the four clauses in the two verses, 1 answers to 4, 2 to 3 (so Matt. 7:6). **18.** (Ch. 8:14; 4:19.) The transition is natural from "raiment" (vs. 16) to the "house" of the "moth" in it, and of it, when in its larva state. The *moth worm's house* is broken whenever the "raiment" is shaken out, so frail is it.

booth—a bough-formed hut which the guard of a vineyard raises for temporary shelter (Isa. 1:8). **19. gathered**—buried honorably (Gen. 25:8; II Kings 22:20). But UMBREIT, agreeably to vs. 18, which describes *the short continuance of the sinner's prosperity,* "He layeth himself rich in his bed, *and nothing is robbed from him,* he openeth his eyes, and *nothing more is there.*" If *English Version* be retained, the first clause probably means, rich though he be in *dying,* he shall not be honored with a *funeral;* the second, When he opens his eyes *in the unseen world,* it is only to see *his destruction:* LXX reads for "not gathered," *He does not proceed,* i.e., goes to his bed no more. So MAURER. **20.** (Ch. 18:11; 22:11, 21.) Like a sudden violent flood (Isa. 8:7, 8; Jer. 47:2): conversely (Ps. 32:6). **21.** (Ch. 21:18; 15:2; Ps. 58:9.)

22. cast—viz., thunderbolts (ch. 6:4; 7:20; 16:13; Ps. 7:12, 13). **23. clap . . . hands**—for joy at his downfall (Lam. 2:15; Nah. 3:19). **hiss**—deride (Jer. 25:9). Job alludes to Bildad's words (ch. 18:18).

ADAM CLARKE

judgment for *another world,* that men may not forget that there is a day of judgment and perdition for ungodly men, and a future recompense for the righteous.

14. *If his children be multiplied.* As numerous families were supposed to be a proof of the benediction of the Almighty, Job shows that this is not always the case; for the offspring of the wicked shall be partly cut off by *violent deaths,* and partly reduced to great *poverty.*

15. *Those that remain of him.* "His remains," whether meaning himself personally, or his family.

16. *Though he heap up silver.* Though he amass riches in the greatest abundance, he shall not enjoy them. Unsanctified wealth is a curse to its possessor.

17. *The just shall put it on.* Money is God's property. "The silver is mine, and the gold is mine, saith the Lord"; and though it may be abused for a time by unrighteous hands, God, in the course of His providence, brings it back to its proper use; and often the righteous possess the inheritance of the wicked.

18. *He buildeth his house as a moth.* With great skill, great pains, and great industry; but the structure, however skilful, shall be dissolved. To its owner it shall be only a temporary habitation, like that which the moth makes in its caterpillar state. *As a booth that the keeper maketh.* A shed which the watchman or keeper of a vineyard erects to cover him from the scorching sun, while watching the ripening grapes, that they may be preserved from depredation. Travellers in the East have observed that such booths or sheds are made of the lightest and most worthless materials; and after the harvest or vintage is in, they are quite neglected, and by the winter rains are soon dissolved and destroyed.

19. *The rich man shall lie down.* In the grave. *But he shall not be gathered.* Neither have a respectable burial among men nor be gathered with the righteous in the kingdom of God. *He openeth his eyes.* In the morning of the resurrection. *And he is not.* He is utterly lost and undone forever.

22. *God shall cast upon him.* Or, rather, the storm mentioned above shall incessantly pelt him, and give him no respite; nor can he by any means escape from its fury.

23. *Men shall clap their hands at him.* These two verses refer to the storm which is to sweep away the ungodly; therefore the word *God,* in v. 22, and *men* in this verse, should be omitted. Verse 22: "For it shall fall upon him, and not spare: flying from its power, he shall continue to fly. Verse 23: "It shall clap its hands against him, and *hiss,* 'shriek,' him out of his place." Here the storm is personified, and the wicked actor is hissed and driven by it from off the stage. It seems it was an ancient method to clap the hands against and hiss a man from any public office who had acted improperly in it.

MATTHEW HENRY

CHAPTER 28

Verses 1–11

Here Job shows, 1. What a great way the wit of man may go in diving into the depths of nature and seizing the riches of it. But does it therefore follow that men may, by their wit, comprehend the reasons why some wicked people prosper and others are punished. By no means. The caverns of the earth may be discovered, but not the counsels of heaven. 2. What a great deal of pains worldly men take to get riches. He shows whence that silver came and how it was obtained, to show what little reason wicked rich men have to be proud of their wealth and pomp.

I. The wealth of this world is hidden in the earth. Thence the silver and the gold, which afterwards they refine, are fetched, *v.* 1. Iron and less costly but more serviceable metals. are *taken out of the earth* (*v.* 2), and are there found in great abundance, which abates their price indeed, but is a great kindness to man, who could much better be without gold than without iron. Nay, *out of the earth comes bread,* that is, bread-corn, the necessary support of life, *v.* 5. Thence man's maintenance is fetched, to remind him of his own original; he is of the earth. *Under it is turned up as it were fire,* precious stones, that sparkle as fire—coal, that is proper to feed fire.

JAMIESON, FAUSSET, BROWN

CHAPTER 28

Vss. 1-28. JOB'S SPEECH CONTINUED. In ch. 27 Job had tacitly admitted that the statement of the friends was often true, that God vindicated His justice by punishing the wicked here; but still the affliction of the godly remained unexplained. Man has, by skill, brought the precious metals from their concealment. But the Divine Wisdom, which governs human affairs, he cannot similarly discover (vs. 12, etc.). However, the image from the same metals (ch. 23:10) implies Job has made some way towards solving the riddle of his life; viz., that affliction is to him as the refining fire is to gold. **1. vein**—a mine, from which it *goes forth, Hebrew,* is dug. **place for gold**—a place where gold may be found, *which* men refine. Not as English Version, "A place—*where,*" (Mal. 3:3). Contrasted with gold found in the bed and sand of rivers, which does not need refining; as the gold *dug from a mine does.* Golden ornaments have been found in Egypt, of the times of Joseph. **2. brass**—i.e., copper; for brass is a mixed metal of copper and zinc, of modern invention. Iron is less easily discovered, and wrought, than copper; therefore copper was in common use long before iron. Copper-stone is called

ADAM CLARKE

CHAPTER 28

1. *Surely there is a vein for the silver.* This chapter is the oldest and finest piece of natural history in the world, and gives us very important information on several curious subjects; and could we ascertain the precise meaning of all the original words we might, most probably, find out allusions to several useful arts which we are apt to think are of modern, or comparatively modern, invention. *A place for gold where they fine it.* This should rather be translated, "A place for gold which they refine."

MATTHEW HENRY

The wisdom of the Creator has placed these things, 1. Out of our sight, to teach us not to set our eyes upon them, Prov. xxiii. 5. 2. Under our feet, to teach us to trample upon them with a holy contempt.

II. The wealth that is hidden in the earth cannot be obtained but with a great deal of difficulty. 1. It is hard to be found out: there is but here and there *a vein for the silver*, v. 1. 2. When found out it is hard to be fetched out. If one method fail, they must try another, till they have *searched out all perfection*, and turned every stone to effect it, v. 3. They must grapple with subterraneous waters (v. 4, 10, 11), and force their way through rocks which are, as it were, the roots of the mountains, v. 9. Now God has made the getting of gold, and silver, and precious stones, so difficult, (1) For the engaging of industry. If valuable things were too easily obtained men would never learn to take pains. (2) For the checking and restraining of pomp and luxury. What is for necessity is had with a little labour from the surface of the earth; but what is for ornament must be dug with a great deal of pains out of the bowels of it. To be fed is cheap, but to be fine is chargeable.

III. Though the subterraneous wealth is thus hard to obtain, yet men will have it. They *search out all perfection*, v. 3. They have arts and engines to dry up the waters, and carry them off, when they break in upon them in their mines and threaten to drown the work, v. 4. They have pumps and pipes, and canals, to clear their way, and, obstacles being removed, they tread *the path which no fowl knoweth* (v. 7, 8), unseen by the vulture's eye, which is piercing and quick-sighted, and untrodden by the lion's whelps, which traverse all the paths of the wilderness. They work their way through the rocks and undermine the mountrains, v. 10. Those that dig in the mines have their lives in their hands; for they are obliged to *bind the floods from overflowing* (v. 11), and are continually in danger of being suffocated by damps or crushed or buried alive by the fall of the earth upon them. *Their eye sees every precious thing*, v. 10. In the prospect of laying hold of them, they make nothing of all these difficulties. Go to the miner's then, thou sluggard in religion; consider their ways, and be wise. Let their courage, diligence, and constancy in seeking the wealth that perisheth shame us out of slothfulness and faint-heartedness in labouring for the true riches.

Verses 14–19

Job here comes to speak of another more valuable jewel, and that is, *wisdom and understanding*, the knowing and enjoying of God and ourselves. There is more true knowledge, satisfaction, and happiness, in sound divinity, which shows us the way to the joys of heaven, than in natural philosophy or mathematics, which help us to find a way into the bowels of the earth. Two things cannot be found out concerning this wisdom:—

I. The price of it, for that is inestimable; its worth is infinitely more than all the riches in this world: *Man knows not the price thereof* (v. 13). Few put a due value upon it. The cock in the fable knew not the value of the precious stone he found in the dunghill, and therefore would rather have lighted on a barley-corn. Men know not the worth of grace, and therefore will take no pains to get it. None can possibly give valuable consideration for it. This Job enlarges upon v. 15, &c., where he makes an inventory of the *bona notabilia—the most valuable treasures* of this world. There is no purchasing wisdom with these. It is a gift of *the Holy Ghost*, which *cannot be bought with money*, Acts viii. 20. Spiritual gifts are conferred without money and without price, because no money can be a price for them. It is *better to get wisdom than gold*. Gold is another's, wisdom our own; gold is for the body and time, wisdom for the soul and eternity.

II. The place of it, for that is undiscoverable. *Where shall wisdom be found?* v. 12. This is a question we should all put. While the most of men are asking, "Where shall money be found?" we should ask, *Where may wisdom be found?* not vain philosophy, or carnal policy, but true religion; for that is the only true wisdom, *It is not found in* this *land of the living*, v. 13. We cannot attain to a right understanding of God and his will, of ourselves and our duty and interest, by reading any books or men, but by reading God's book and the men of God. Such is the degeneracy of human nature that there is no true wisdom to be found with any but those who are born again, and who, through grace, partake of the divine nature. Ask the miners, and by them *the depth will say, It is not in me*, v. 14. Ask the mariners, and by them *the sea will say, It is not in me*. It can never be got either by trading on the waters or diving into them, can never be *sucked from the abundance of the seas or the treasures hidden in the sand.*

JAMIESON, FAUSSET, BROWN

"cadmium" by PLINY [NATURAL HISTORY 34:1; 36: 21]. Iron is fitly said to be taken out of the "earth" (dust), for ore looks like mere earth. **3.** "Man makes an end of darkness," by exploring the darkest depths (with torches). **all perfection**—rather, carries out his search to the utmost perfection; most thoroughly searches the stones of darkness and of the shadow of death (thickest gloom); i.e., the stones, whatever they be, embedded in the darkest bowels of the earth [UMBREIT] (ch. 26:10). **4.** Three hardships in mining: 1. "A stream (flood) breaks out at the side of the stranger"; viz., *the miner, a strange newcomer* into places heretofore unexplored; his surprise at the sudden stream breaking out *beside* him is expressed (*English Version*, "from the inhabitant"); 2. "Forgotten (unsupported) by the foot they *hang*," viz., by ropes, in descending. In the *Hebrew*, "Lo there" precedes this clause, graphically placing it as if before the eyes. "The waters" is inserted by *English Version*. "Are dried up," ought to be, "hang," "are suspended." *English Version* perhaps understood, waters of whose existence man was previously *unconscious*, and near which he *never trod;* and yet man's energy is such, that by pumps, etc., he soon causes them to "dry up and go away" [So HERDER]. 3. "Far away from men, they move with uncertain step"; they stagger; not "they are gone" [UMBREIT]. **5.** Its fertile surface yields food; and yet "beneath it is turned up as it were with fire." So PLINY [NATURAL HISTORY, 33] observes on the ingratitude of man who repays the debt he owes the earth for food, by digging out its bowels. "Fire" was used in mining [UMBREIT]. *English Version* is simpler, which means precious stones which glow *like fire;* and so vs. 6 follows naturally (Ezek. 28:14). **6.** Sapphires are found in alluvial soil near rocks and embedded in gneiss. The ancients distinguished two kinds: 1. The real, of transparent blue: 2. That improperly so called, opaque, with gold spots; i.e., lapis lazuli. To the latter, looking like gold dust, UMBREIT refers "dust of gold." *English Version* better, "The *stones* of the earth are, etc., and the *clods* of it (*Vulgate*) are gold"; the parallel clauses are thus neater. **7. fowl** —rather, "ravenous bird," or "eagle," which is the most sharp-sighted of birds (Isa. 46:11). A vulture will spy a carcass at an amazing distance. The miner penetrates the earth by a way unseen by birds of keenest sight. **8. lion's whelps**—lit., "the sons of pride," i.e., the fiercest beasts. **passed**—The *Hebrew* implies *the proud gait* of the lion. The miner ventures where not even the fierce lion dares to go in pursuit of his prey. **9. rock**—flint. He puts forth his hand to cleave the *hardest rock*. **by the roots**—from their foundations, by undermining them. **10.** *He cuts* channels to drain off the waters, which hinder his mining; and when the waters are gone, he he is able to *see the precious things* in the earth. **11. floods**—"He restrains *the streams* from *weeping*"; a poetical expression for the *trickling* subterranean *rills*, which impede him; answering to the first clause of vs. 10; so also the two latter clauses in each verse correspond. **12.** Can man discover the Divine Wisdom by which the world is governed, as he can the treasures hidden in the earth? Certainly not. Divine Wisdom is conceived as a person (vss. 12-27) distinct from God (vs. 23; also in Prov. 8:23, 27). The Almighty Word, Jesus Christ, *we* know now, is that Wisdom. The order of the world was originated and is maintained by the breathing forth (Spirit) of Wisdom, unfathomable and unpurchasable by man. In verse 28, the only aspect of it, which relates to, and may be understood by, *man*, is stated. **understanding**—insight into the plan of the divine government. **13.** Man can fix no price upon it, as it is nowhere to be found in man's abode (Isa. 38:11). Job implies both its valuable worth, and the impossibility of buying it at any price. **15.** Not the usual word for "gold"; from *a Hebrew* root, "to shut up" with care; i.e., purest gold (I Kings 6:20, *Margin*). **weighed**—The precious metals were *weighed* out before coining was known (Gen. 23:16). **16. gold of Ophir**—the most precious (*Note*, 22:24; Ps. 45:9). **onyx**—(Gen. 2:12.) More valued formerly than now. The term is Greek, meaning "thumb nail," from some resemblance in color. The *Arabic* denotes, of two colors, white preponderating. **17. crystal**—Or else glass, if then known, very costly. From a root, "to be transparent." **jewels**—rather, vessels. **18.** Red coral (Ezek. 27: 16). **18. pearls**—lit., "what is frozen." Probably *crystal;* and vs. 17 will then be *glass*. **rubies**—UMBREIT translates "pearls" (see Lam. 4:1; Prov. 3: 15). The Urim and Thummim, the means of consulting God by the twelve stones on the high priest's breastplate, "the stones of the sanctuary" (Lam. 4:1), have their counterpart in this chapter; the precious

ADAM CLARKE

2. *Iron is taken out of the earth.* This most useful metal is hidden under the earth, and men have found out the method of separating it from its ore.

3. *He setteth an end to darkness.* As it is likely Job still refers to mining, the words above may be understood as pointing out the persevering industry of man in penetrating into the bowels of the earth, in order to seek for metals and precious stones.

4. *The flood breaketh out from the inhabitant.* This passage is very difficult. Some think it refers to mining; others, to navigation. *Forgotten of the foot.* No man treads there anymore.

5. *The earth, out of it cometh bread.* Or the earth, *mimmennah*, "from itself," by its own vegetative power, "it sends out bread," or the corn of which bread is made.

9. *He putteth forth his hand upon the rock.* Still there appears to be a reference to mining. Man puts his hand upon the rock, he breaks that to pieces, in order to extract the metals which it contains. *He overturneth the mountains.* He excavates, undermines, or digs them away, when in search of the metals contained in them.

10. *He cutteth out rivers among the rocks.* He cuts canals in the rocks, and drives levels under ground, in order to discover *veins* of ore. *His eye seeth every precious thing.* He sinks those shafts, and drives those levels, in order to discover where the precious minerals lie.

11. *He bindeth the floods.* Prevents the risings of springs from drowning the mines; and conducts rivers and streams from their wonted course, in order to bring forth to light what was hidden under their beds.

12. *But where shall wisdom be found?* Now as these terms *chochmah*, "wisdom," and *binah*, "understanding" or "discernment," are often applied in the sacred writings in their common acceptations, we must have recourse to what Job says of them, to know their meaning in this place. In v. 28, he says, "The fear of the Lord . . . is wisdom; and to depart from evil is understanding." We know that the "fear of the Lord" is often taken for the whole of that religious reverence and holy obedience which God prescribes to man in His Word, and which man owes to his Maker. Hence the Septuagint render *chochmah*, "wisdom," by "Divine worship"; wisdom—all true religion—must come by divine revelation.

14. *The depth saith, It is not in me.* Men may dig into the bowels of the earth, and there find gold, silver, and precious stones; but these will not give them true happiness. *The sea saith, It is not with me.* Men may explore foreign countries, and by navigation connect as it were the most distant parts of the earth; but every voyage and every enjoyment proclaim, True happiness is not here.

15. *It cannot be gotten for gold.* Genuine religion and true happiness are not to be acquired by earthly property.

16. *The gold of Ophir.* Gold is five times mentioned in this and vv. 17 and 19, and four of the times in different words. I shall consider them all at once. (1) *Segor*, from *sagar*, to "shut up": gold in the mine, or shut up in the ore. (2) *Kethem*, from *catham*, to "sign" or "stamp": gold made current by being coined, or stamped with its weight or value.

17. (3) *Zahab*, from *zahab*, to be "clear, bright, or resplendent": the untarnishing metal; the only metal that always keeps its lustre. But probably here it means burnished gold. (4) *Paz*, from *paz*, to *consolidate*, joined here with *keley*, "vessels, ornaments, instruments": hammered or wrought gold; gold in the finest forms, and most elegant utensils. In these verses there are also seven kinds of precious stones mentioned: onyx, sapphire, crystal, coral, pearls, rubies, and topaz.

MATTHEW HENRY

Verses 20–28

There is a twofold wisdom, one *hidden in God*, which is secret and *belongs not to us*, the other made known by him and revealed to man, which *belongs to us and to our children*.

I. The knowledge of God's secret will, the will of his providence, is out of our reach. It *belongs to the Lord our God*. To know what God will do hereafter, and the reasons of what he is doing now, is the knowledge Job first speaks of.

1. This knowledge is hidden from us. It is high, we cannot attain unto it (*v.* 21, 22): *It is hid from the eyes of all living*, even of philosophers, politicians, and saints; it is *kept close from the fowls of the air*; though their eyes behold afar off (*ch.* 29). Even those who, in their speculations, soar highest above the heads of other people, cannot pretend to this knowledge. "What fools are we" (says Job) "to fight in the dark thus, to dispute about that which we do not understand!" The line and plummet of human reason can never fathom the abyss of the divine counsels. Yet there is a world on the other side death and the grave, and there we shall see clearly what we are now in the dark about. When *the mystery of God shall be finished* it will be laid open, and we shall know as we are known: when the veil of flesh is rent, and the interposing clouds are scattered, we shall know what God does, though we know not now, John xiii. 7.

2. This knowledge is hidden in God, as the apostle speaks, Eph. iii. 9. Men sometimes do that which they cannot give a good reason for, but in every will of God there is a counsel: he knows both what he does and why he does it. Two reasons why God must needs understand his own way, and he only:—

(1) Because all events are now directed by an all-seeing and almighty Providence, *v.* 24, 25. He that governs the world is Omniscient. One day's events, and one man's affairs, have such a reference to, and such a dependence upon, another's, that he only to whom all events and all affairs are naked and open, and who sees the whole at one entire and certain view, is a competent Judge of every part. He is omnipotent. For proof of this Job mentions the winds and waters, *v.* 25. What is lighter than the wind? Yet God hath ways of poising it. The waters of the sea, and the rainwaters, he both weighs and measures, allotting the proportion of every tide and every shower. A great and constant communication there is between clouds and seas, the waters above the firmament and those under it. Vapours go up, rains come down, air is condensed into water, water rarefied into air; but the great God keeps an exact account of all the stock with which this trade is carried on for the public benefit. Now, if in these things, Providence be so exact, much more in dispensing frowns and favours, rewards and punishments, to the children of men, according to the rules of equity.

(2) Because all events were from eternity designed and determined by an infallible prescience and immutable decree, *v.* 26, 27. He settled the course of nature. Job mentions particularly *a decree for the rain* and *a way for the thunder and lightning*. The general method, and the particular uses of these strange performances, both their causes and their effects, were appointed by the divine purpose. Some make Job to speak of wisdom here as a person, and translate it, *Then he saw her and showed her*, &c.

II. The knowledge of God's revealed will is within our reach; it is level to our capacity, and will do us good (*v.* 28): *Unto man he said, Behold, the fear of the Lord that is wisdom*. Let it not be said that when God concealed his counsels from man, it was because he grudged him anything that would contribute to his real bliss and satisfaction. He let him know as much as is needful and fit for a subject, but he must not think himself fit to be a privy-counsellor. No less wisdom (says Archbishop Tillotson) than that which made the world can thoroughly understand the philosophy of it. But let him look upon this as his wisdom, to fear the Lord and to depart from evil. When God forbade man the tree of knowledge he allowed him the tree of life. We cannot attain true wisdom but by divine revelation. *The fear of the Lord, that is the wisdom*. Pure religion, and undefiled, is to *fear the Lord and depart from evil*, which agrees with God's character of Job, *ch.* i. 1. The *fear of the Lord* is the spring and summary of all religion. There is a slavish fear of God, springing from hard thoughts of him, which is contrary to religion, Matt. xxv. 24. There is a selfish fear of God springing from dreadful thoughts of him, which may be a good step towards religion, Acts ix. 5. But there is a filial fear of God, springing from great and high thoughts of him, which is the life and soul of all religion. And, wherever this reigns in the heart, it will appear by a constant care to *depart from evil*, Prov. xvi. 6.

JAMIESON, FAUSSET, BROWN

stones symbolizing the "light" and "perfection" of the divine wisdom. **19. Ethiopia**—*Cush* in the *Hebrew*. Either Ethiopia, or the south of Arabia, near the Tigris. **20.** Verse 12 repeated with great force.

21. None can tell *whence* or *where, seeing* it, etc. **fowls**—The gift of divination was assigned by the heathen especially to birds. Their rapid flight heavenwards and keen sight originated the superstition. Job may allude to it. Not even the boasted divination of birds has an insight into it (Eccles. 10:20). But it may merely mean, as in vs. 7, It escapes the eye of the most keen-sighted bird. **22.**—I.e., the abodes of *destruction* and of the *dead*. "Death" put for Sheol (ch. 30:23; 26:6, *Note*; Ps. 9: 13). **We have** [only] **heard**—the report of her. We have not *seen* her. In the land of the living (vs. 13) the workings of Wisdom are seen, though not herself. In the regions of the dead she is only *heard of*, her actings on nature not being seen (Eccles. 9:10). **23.** God hath, and is Himself, wisdom.

24. "Seeth (all that is) under," etc. **25.** God has adjusted the weight of the winds, so seemingly imponderable, lest, if too weighty, or too light, injury should be caused. He measureth out the waters, fixing their bounds, with wisdom as His counsellor (Prov. 8:27-31; Isa. 40:12).

26. The decree regulating at what time and place, and in what quantity, the rain should fall. **a way**—through the parted clouds (ch. 38:25; Zech. 10:1). **27. declare**—manifest her, viz., in His works (Ps. 19:1, 2). So the approval bestowed by the Creator on His works (Gen. 1:10, 31); cf. the "rejoicing" of wisdom at the same (Prov. 8:30; which UMBREIT translates; "I was the skilful artificer by His side"). **prepared**—not *created*, for wisdom is from everlasting (Prov. 8); but "established" her as Governor of the world. **searched . . . out**—examined her works to see whether she was adequate to the task of governing the world [MAURER]. **28.** Rather, *But* unto man, etc., *My* wisdom is that whereby all things are governed; *Thy* wisdom is *in fearing God and shunning evil*, and in feeling assured that My wisdom always acts aright, though thou dost not understand the principle which regulates it; e.g., in afflicting the godly (John 7:17). The friends, therefore, as not comprehending the Divine Wisdom, should not infer Job's guilt from his sufferings. Here alone in Job the name of God, *Adonai*, occurs; "Lord" or "master," often applied to Messiah in Old Testament. Appropriately here, in speaking of the Word or Wisdom, by whom the world was made (Prov. 8; John 1; Eccles. 24).

ADAM CLARKE

22. *Destruction and death say, We have heard the fame thereof. Abaddon*, the destroyer, and his offspring, death. This is the very name that is given to the devil in Greek letters, Rev. ix. 11, and is rendered by the Greek word *Apollyon*, a word exactly of the same meaning.

23. *God understandeth the way thereof*. It can be taught only by a revelation from himself.

25. *And he weigheth the waters by measure*. He has exactly proportioned the aqueous surface of the earth to the terrene parts, so that there shall be an adequate surface to produce, by evaporation, moisture sufficient to be treasured up in the atmosphere for the irrigation of the earth.

26. *When he made a decree for the rain*. When he determined how that should be generated. *A way for the lightning of the thunder*. *Kol* signifies "voice" of any kind; and *koloth* is the plural, and is taken for the frequent claps or rattlings of thunder. *Chaz* signifies to "notch, indentate," as in the edges of the leaves of trees; *chaziz* must refer to the zigzag form which lightning assumes in passing from one cloud into another.

27. *Then did he see it, and declare it*. When He had finished all His creative operations, and tried and proved His work, investigated and found it to be very good, then He gave the needful revelation to man.

28. *Unto man he said. Laadam*, "unto man," He said. This probably refers to the revelation of His will which God gave to Adam after his fall.

MATTHEW HENRY

CHAPTER 29

Verses 1–6

Job begins here with a wish (*v.* 2): *O that I were as in months past!* so he brings in this account of his prosperity. "O that I might be restored to my prosperity, and then the censures and reproaches of my friends would be effectually silenced, even upon their own principles, and for ever rolled away!" He wishes he now had his spirit as much encouraged in the service of God as he had then, and that he had as much freedom and fellowship with him. This was *in the days of his youth* (*v.* 4), when he was in the prime. Two things made the months past pleasant to Job:—

I. That he had comfort in his God. This was the chief thing he rejoiced in, in his prosperity, as the spring of it and the sweetness of it, that he had the favour of God and the tokens of that favour. They were *the days when God preserved me*, *v.* 2. *God's candle shone upon his head*, that is, God lifted up the light of his countenance upon him. That guided him in his doubts, comforted him in his griefs, bore him up under his burdens, and helped him through all his difficulties. *The secret of God was upon my tabernacle*, that is, God conversed freely with him, as one bosom-friend with another. He knew God's mind, and was not in the dark about it, as, of late, he had been. *The Almighty was yet with me.* Now he thought God had departed from him, but in those days he was *with him*, and that was all in all to him. God's presence with a man in his house, though it be but a cottage, makes it both a castle and a palace.

II. That he had comfort in his family. Everything was agreeable there: he had both mouths for his meat and meat for his mouths; the want of either is a great affliction. Job speaks very feelingly of this comfort now that he was deprived of it. Yet we reckon amiss if, when we have lost our children, we cannot comfort ourselves with this, that we have not lost our God. He had a plentiful estate for the support of this numerous family, *v.* 6. His dairy abounded to such a degree that he might, if he pleased, *wash his steps with butter*; and his olive-yards were so fruitful that it seemed as if the *rock poured him out rivers of oil.* He reckons his wealth, not by his silver and gold, which were for hoarding, but by his butter and oil, which were for use; for what is an estate good for unless we take the good of it ourselves and do good with it to others?

Verses 7–17

Job in a post of honour and power. Judgment was administered in the gate, in the street, in the places of concourse, to which every man might have a free access, that every one who would might be a witness to all that was said and done. Job being a magistrate, we are here told,

I. What a profound respect was paid to him, not only for the dignity of his place, but for his personal merit. The people honoured him and stood in awe of him, *v.* 8. *The young men*, who, it may be, were conscious of something amiss, *hid themselves*, and got out of his way; *and the aged*, though they kept their ground, yet would not keep their seats: they *arose and stood up* to do homage to him. The princes and nobles paid great deference to him, *v.* 9, 10. When he came into court *the princes refrained talking, the nobles held their peace*, that they might the more diligently hearken to what he said.

II. What a great deal of good he did in his place. Job valued himself, not by the honour of his family, the great estate he had, and the court that was made to him, but by his usefulness. All that heard what he said, and saw how he laid out himself for the public good with all the authority and tender affection of a father to his country, blessed him, and gave witness to him, *v.* 11. Such was the blessing of him who was ready to perish (*v.* 13) and who by Job's means was rescued from perishing. If the poor were injured or oppressed, they might cry to Job, and, if he found the allegations of their petitions true he *delivered the poor that cried* (*v.* 12) and would not suffer them to be trampled upon. He was *a father to the poor*, not only a judge to protect them and to see that they were not wronged, but a father to provide for them and to see that they did not want, to counsel and direct them. Those that were ready to perish he saved from perishing, taking care of those that were sick, that were outcasts, that were falsely accused, or in danger of being turned out of their estates. The widows that were sighing for grief, and trembling for fear, he made to sing for joy. Those that were upon any account at a loss Job gave suitable and seasonable relief to (*v.* 15): *I was eyes to the blind*, and *feet to the lame.* He devoted himself to the administration of justice (*v.* 14): *I put on righteousness and it clothed me*, that is, he had an habitual disposition to execute justice. He always appeared in it, as in his clothing,

JAMIESON, FAUSSET, BROWN

CHAPTER 29

Vss. 1-25. **1.** Job pauses for a reply. None being made, he proceeds to illustrate the mysteriousness of God's dealings, as set forth (ch. 28) by his own case.

4. youth—lit., "autumn"; the time of the ripe fruits of my prosperity. Applied to *youth*, as the Orientalists *began* their year with autumn, the most temperate season in the East. **secret**—when the intimate friendship of God rested on my tent (Prov. 3:32; Ps. 31:20; Gen. 18:17; John 15:15). The *Hebrew* often means a *divan for deliberation*. **2. preserved me**—from calamity. **3. candle**—when His favor shone on me (*Note,* 18:6; Ps. 18:28). **darkness**—By His safeguard I passed secure through *dangers.* Perhaps alluding to the lights carried before caravans in nightly travels through deserts [Noyes].

6. butter—rather, "cream," lit., "thick milk." Wherever I turned my steps, the richest milk and oil flowed in to me abundantly. Image from pastoral life. Literal *washing of the feet in milk* is not meant, as the second clause shows; *Margin,* "with me," i.e., "near" my path, wherever I walked (Deut. 32:13). Olives amidst *rocks* yield the best oil. Oil in the East is used for food, light, anointing, and medicine. **7-10.** The great influence Job had over young and old, and noblemen. **through . . . street**—rather, When I went out of my house, in the country (see ch. 1, prologue) to the gate (ascending), *up* to the city (which was on elevated ground), and when I prepared my (judicial) seat in *the market place.* The market place was the place of judgment, at the gate or propylæa of the city, such as is found in the remains of Nineveh and Persepolis (Isa. 59:14; Ps. 55:11; 127:5). **8. hid**—not lit.; rather, *stepped backwards,* reverentially. *The aged,* who were already seated, *arose and remained standing* (*Hebrew*) until Job seated himself. Oriental manners. **9.** (Ch. 4:2; *Note,* 21:5.) **Refrained**—stopped in the middle of their speech. **10.** *Margin,* "voice–hid," i.e., "hushed" (Ezek. 3:26). **Tongue cleaved . . .** i.e., awed by my presence, the emirs or sheiks were silent.

11. blessed—extolled my virtues (Prov. 31:28). Omit "me" after "heard"; whoever *heard of* me (in general, not in the market place, 7-10) praised me. **gave witness**—to my honorable character. Image from a court of justice (Luke 4:22). "The eye"—i.e., "face to face"; antithesis to "ear"—i.e., report of me. **12-17.** The grounds on which Job was praised (vs. 11), his helping the afflicted (Ps. 72:12) who cried to him for help, as a judge, or as one possessed of means of charity. Translate; The fatherless who had none to help him. **13.** So far was I from sending "widows" away empty (ch. 22:9). **ready to perish**—(Prov. 31:6.)

15. Lit., "the blind" (Deut. 27:18); "lame" (II Sam. 9:13); fig., also the spiritual support which the more enlightened gives to those less so (ch. 4:3; Heb. 12:13; Num. 10:31).

ADAM CLARKE

CHAPTER 29

2. *Oh that I were as in months past.* Job seems here to make an apology for his former prosperity, which was very great, but was now entirely at an end. He shows that it was not removed because of any bad use he had made of it; and describes how he behaved himself before God and man, and how much, for justice, benevolence, and mercy, he was esteemed and honored by the wise and good.

7. *When I went out to the gate.* Courts of justice were held at the gates or entrances of the cities of the East, and Job was "supreme magistrate."

8. *The young men saw me, and hid themselves.* From all classes of persons I had the most marked respect.

11. *When the ear heard me.* This and the six following verses present us with a fine exhibition of a man full of benevolence and charity, acting up to the highest dictates of those principles, and rendering the miserable of all descriptions happy, by the constant exercise of his unconfined philanthropy.

12. *Because I delivered the poor that cried.* This appears to be intended as a refutation of the charges produced by Eliphaz, chap. xxii. 5-10, to confute which Job appeals to facts, and to public testimony.

MATTHEW HENRY

and never without it. *My judgment was as a robe and a diadem.* If a magistrate do the duty of his place, that is an honour to him far beyond his gold or purple. If he do not make conscience of his duty, his robe and diadem, his gown and cap, are but a reproach. As clothes on a dead man will never make him warm, so robes on a base man will never make him honourable. *The cause which I knew not I searched out.* He diligently enquired into the matters of fact, patiently and impartially heard both sides. He valued himself by the check he gave to the violence of proud and evil men (*v.* 17): *I broke the jaws of the wicked.* He does not say that he broke their necks. He did not take away their lives, but he broke their jaws, he took away their power of doing mischief. Good magistrates must thus be a terror and restraint to evil-doers and a protection to the innocent. A judge upon the bench has as much need to be bold and brave as a commander in the field.

Verses 18–25

I. Job's thoughts in his prosperity (*v.* 18): *Then I said, I shall die in my nest.* He saw no storm arising to shake down his nest; and therefore concluded, *Tomorrow shall be as this day.* In the midst of his prosperity he thought of dying. Yet he flattered himself he should *multiply his days as the sand.* He means as the sand on the sea-shore; whereas we should rather reckon our days by the sand in the hour-glass, which will have run out in a little time.

II. The ground of these thoughts. He found no bodily distemper growing upon him; his estate did not lie under any incumbrance; nor was he sensible of any worm at the root of it.

He was like a tree whose root is not only spread out, which fixes it and keep it firm, so that it is in no danger of being overturned, but *spread out by the waters,* which feed it. Blessed with the fatness of the earth, so also with the kind influences of heaven too; for the *dew lay all night upon his branch.* His *bow* also *was renewed in his hand,* that is, his power to protect himself, so that he had little reason to fear the insults of the Sabeans and Chaldeans. Neither had he any reason to distrust the fidelity of his friends. Nothing surely could be done against him when really nothing was done without him. He was consulted as an oracle, *v.* 21. When others could not be heard all men *gave ear* to him, *and kept silence at his counsel,* knowing that, as nothing could be said against it, so nothing needed to be added to it. And therefore, *after his words, they spoke not again, v.* 22. He had the hearts and affections of all his neighbours. Those were thought happy to whom he spoke. His speech dropped upon them, and they waited for it as for the rain (*v.* 22, 23). "*If I laughed on them,* designing thereby to show myself pleased in them, or pleasant with them, it was such a favour that *they believed it not* for joy," or because it was so rare a thing to see this grave man smile.

He *chose out their way,* sat at the helm, and steered for them. He *dwelt as a king in the army,* giving orders which were not to be disputed. Everyone that has the spirit of wisdom has not the spirit of government, but Job had both. Yet he had the tenderness of a comforter. Our Lord Jesus is such a King as Job was, the poor man's King.

JAMIESON, FAUSSET, BROWN

14. (Isa. 61:10; I Chron. 12:18.) **judgment**—justice. **diadem**—tiara. Rather, turban, head-dress. It and the full flowing outer mantle or "robe," are the prominent characteristics of an Oriental grandee's or high priest's dress (Zech. 3:5). So Job's righteousness especially characterized him. **16.** So far was I from "breaking the arms of the *fatherless,*" as Eliphaz asserts (ch. 22:9), I was a "father" to such. **the cause which I knew not**—rather—"of him whom I knew not," the stranger (Prov. 29:7 [UMBREIT]; contrast Luke 18:1, etc.). Applicable to almsgiving (Ps. 41:1); but here primarily, judicial conscientiousness (ch. 31:13). **17.** Image from combating with wild beasts (ch. 4:11; Ps. 3:7). So compassionate was Job to the oppressed, so terrible to the oppressor! **jaws**—Job broke *his power,* so that he could do no more hurt, and tore from him the spoil, which he had torn from others. **18. I said**—in my heart (Ps. 30:6). **in**—rather, "*with* my nest"; as the second clause refers to long life. Instead of my family dying before me, as now, I shall live so long as to die with them: proverbial for long life. Job did realize his hope (ch. 42:16). However, *in* the bosom of my family, gives a good sense (Num. 24:21; Obad. 4). Use "nest" for a *secure dwelling.* **sand**—(Gen. 22:17; Hab. 1:9). But LXX and Vulgate, and Jewish interpreters, favor the translation, "the phœnix bird." "Nest" in the parallel clause supports the reference to a bird. "Sand" for *multitude,* applies to men, rather than to *years.* The myth was, that the phœnix sprang from a nest of myrrh, made by his father before death, and that he then came from Arabia (Job's country) to Heliopolis (the city of the Sun) in Egypt, once in every 500 years, and there burnt his father [HERODOTUS, 2:73]. Modern research has shown that this was the Egyptian mode of representing hieroglyphically a particular chronological era or cycle. The death and revival every 500 years, and the reference to *the sun,* implies such a grand cycle commencing afresh from the same point in relation to the sun from which the previous one started. Job probably refers to this. **19.** Lit., "opened to the waters." Opposed to ch. 18:16. Vigorous health. **20.** My renown, like my bodily health, was continually fresh. **bow**—Metaphor from war, for, *my strength,* which gains me "renown," was ever renewed (Jer. 49:35). **21.** Job reverts with peculiar pleasure to his former dignity in assemblies (vss. 7-10). **22. not again**—did not contradict me. **dropped**—affected their minds, as the genial rain does the soil on which it gently drops (Amos 7:16; Deut. 32:2; Song of Sol. 4:11). **23.** Image of vs. 22 continued. They waited for my salutary counsel, as the dry soil does for the refreshing rain. **opened . . . mouth**—*panted for;* Oriental image (Ps. 119:131). The "early rain" is in autumn and onwards, while the seed is being sown. The "latter rain" is in March, and brings forward the harvest, which ripens in May or June. Between the early and latter rains, some rain falls, but not in such quantities as those rains. Between March and October no rain falls (Deut. 11:14; Jas. 5:7). **24.** When I relaxed from my wonted gravity (a virtue much esteemed in the East) and smiled, they could hardly credit it; and yet, notwithstanding my condescension, *they did not cast aside reverence* for *my gravity.* But the parallelism is better in UMBREIT's translation, "I smiled kindly on those who trusted not," i.e., in times of danger I cheered those in despondency. And they could not cast down (by their despondency) my *serenity of countenance* (flowing from trust in God) (Prov. 16:15; Ps. 104: 15). The opposite phrase (Gen. 4:5, 6). "Gravity" cannot well be meant by "light of countenance." **25. I chose out their way**—i.e., I willingly went up to their assembly (from my country residence, vs. 7). **in the army**—as a king supreme in the midst of his army. **comforteth the mourners**—Here again Job unconsciously foreshadows Jesus Christ (Isa. 61:2, 3). Job's afflictions, as those of Jesus Christ, were fitting him for the office hereafter (Isa. 50:4; Heb. 2:18).

ADAM CLARKE

JOSEPH PARKER:

Job brought to their remembrance that he was the friend of the poor, and that whenever he met oppression on the high road he rent it in twain, and left the two sundered pieces to come together again if they could. Now what Job says he was personally, religion, as represented by Christ, ought to be influentially. We cannot indeed be all these to the letter, for every man is not a Job in mental capacity or in material possessions; but the Church can be what Job was in its unity. The Church must play the Job of this twenty-ninth chapter of his book. Religion should be the greatest figure in society: it should be the great voice in council; it should represent what we find Job was in the twenty-fifth verse—"I . . . dwelt as a king in the army, as one that comforteth the mourners." The Church that is not all this is not Christ's Church, or if it be Christ's Church it is ungrown, undeveloped, unaware of its privileges and responsibilities. Do not let us lose the golden thought of the occasion by imagining that there was but one Job, and that when he died all the actualities and possibilities of this chapter died along with him. What the one man was the one Church may be. —*The People's Bible*

19. *My root was spread out by the waters.* A metaphor taken from a healthy tree growing beside a rivulet where there is plenty of water, which in consequence flourishes in all seasons; its leaf does not wither, nor its fruit fall off. See Ps. i. 3; Jer. xvii. 8.

24. *I laughed on them, they believed it not.* We have a similar phrase: "The news was too good to be true."

MATTHEW HENRY — CHAPTER 30

Verses 1–14

Here Job makes complaint of the great disgrace he had fallen into, from the height of honour and reputation. Two things he insists upon as greatly aggravating his affliction:

I. The meanness of the persons that affronted him. He was spurned by the meanest and most contemptible of mankind. They were young, younger than he (*v.* 1), *the youth* (*v.* 12), who ought to have behaved

JAMIESON, FAUSSET, BROWN — CHAPTER 30

Vss. 1-31. **1. younger**—not the three friends (ch. 15:10; 32:4, 6, 7). A general description: 1-8, the lowness of the persons who derided him; 9-15, the derision itself. Formerly old men rose to me (ch. 29:8). Now not only my *juniors,* who are bound to reverence me (Lev. 19:32), but even the mean and *base-born* actually *deride* me; opposed to, "smiled upon" (ch. 29:24). This goes farther than even the "mockery" of Job by *relations* and *friends* (ch. 12:4;

ADAM CLARKE — CHAPTER 30

1. *But now they that are younger than I have me in derision.* Compare this with chap. xxix. 8, where he speaks of the respect he had from the youth while in the days of his prosperity. Now he is no longer affluent, and they are no longer respectful.

MATTHEW HENRY

themselves respectfully towards him for his age and gravity. Their fathers were so very despicable that such a man as Job would have disdained to take them into the lowest service about his house, as that of tending the sheep and attending the shepherds with the dogs of his flock, *v.* 1.

Job himself, with all his prudence and patience, could make nothing of them, *v.* 2. The young were not fit for labour, they were so lazy. *Whereto might the strength of their hands profit me?* The old were not to be advised with in the smallest matters, for their *old age was perished,* they were twice children. **Being brought into straits by their own slothfulness and wastefulness,** nobody was forward to relieve them.

Hence **they were forced to flee into the deserts both** for shelter and sustenance, and were put to sorry shifts indeed, when they *cut up mallows by the bushes,* and were glad to eat them, for want of food that was fit for them, *v.* 4. This beggarly world is full of the devil's poor. *They were driven forth from among men, v.* 5. An idle fellow is a public nuisance; but it is better to drive such into a workhouse than, as here, into a wilderness, which will punish them indeed, but never reform them. They were forced to dwell in *caves of the earth,* and *they brayed* like asses *among the bushes, v.* 6, 7. *They groan among the trees* (so Broughton) *and smart among the nettles;* they are stung and scratched there, where they hoped to be sheltered and protected. But such as these were abusive to Job because when he was in prosperity and power, like a good magistrate, he put in execution the laws which were in force against vagabonds, and rogues, and sturdy beggars, which these base people now remembered against him. They thought he had now become like one of them.

II. The greatness of the affronts that were given him. *I am their song and their byword.* They shunned him as a loathsome spectacle, abhorred him, fled far from him (*v.* 10), as an ugly monster or as one infected. They tripped up his heels, pushed away his feet (*v.* 12), kicked him, either in wrath or in sport. *They raise up against me the ways of their destruction;* or (as some read it), *They cast upon me the cause of their woe;* that is, "They lay the blame of their being driven out upon me;" and it is common for criminals to hate the judges and laws by which they are punished. They misrepresented his former conversation, which is here called *marring his path.* They reflected upon him as a tyrant because he had done justice upon them; and perhaps Job's friends grounded their uncharitable censures of him (*ch.* xxii. 6, &c.) upon the clamours of these sorry people. They are fools in other things, but wise enough to do mischief, and need no help in inventing that. Some read it thus, *They hold my heaviness a profit, though they be never the better. They came upon me as a wide breaking in of waters,* when the dam is broken; or, "They came as soldiers into a broad breach which they have made in the wall of a besieged city, pouring in upon me with the utmost fury." *They rolled themselves in the desolation* with all the weight of their malice.

III. All this contempt put upon him was caused by the troubles he was in (*v.* 11): "*Because he has loosed my cord,* has taken away the honour and power with which I was girded (*ch.* xii. 18), because he has afflicted me, therefore *they have let loose the bridle before me,*" that is, "have given themselves a liberty to say and do what they please against me." "Because he hath loosed *his* cord," that is, "because he has taken off his bridle of restraint from off their malice, they cast away the bridle from me," that is, "they make no account of my authority, nor stand in any awe of me." Those that today cry *Hosannah* may tomorrow cry *Crucify.* But there is an honour which comes from God, which if we secure, we shall find it not thus changeable and losable.

JAMIESON, FAUSSET, BROWN

16:10, 20; 17:2, 6; 19:22). Orientals feel keenly any indignity shown by the young. Job speaks as a rich Arabian emir, proud of his descent. **dogs**—regarded with disgust in the East as unclean (I Sam. 17:43; Prov. 26:11). They are not allowed to enter a house, but run about wild in the open air, living on offal and chance morsels (Ps. 59:14, 15). Here again we are reminded of Jesus Christ (Ps. 22:16). "Their fathers, my coevals, were so mean and famished that I would not have associated them *with* (not to say, set them over) my dogs in guarding my flock." **2.** If their fathers could be of no profit to me, much less the sons, who are feebler than their sires; and in whose case the hope of attaining old age is utterly gone, so puny are they (ch. 5:26). [MAURER]. Even if they had "strength of hands," that could be now of no use to me, as all I want in my present affliction is sympathy. **3. solitary**—lit., *hard* as a rock; so translate, rather, "dried up," emaciated with hunger. Job describes the rudest race of Bedouins of the desert [UMBREIT]. **fleeing**—So LXX. Better, as *Syriac, Arabic,* and *Vulgate,* "*gnawers* of the wilderness." What they gnaw follows in vs. 4. **in former time**—lit., the "*yesternight* of desolation and waste" (the most utter desolation; Ezek. 6:14); i.e., those deserts frightful as night to man, and even there from time immemorial. I think both ideas are in the words *darkness* [GESENIUS] and *antiquity* [UMBREIT]. (Isa. 30:33, *Margin.*) **4. mallows**—rather, "salt-wort," which grows in deserts and is eaten as a salad by the poor [MAURER]. **by the bushes**—among the bushes. **juniper**—rather, a kind of broom, *Spartium junceum* [LINNÆUS], still called in Arabia, as in the *Hebrew* of Job, *retem,* of which the bitter roots are eaten by the poor. **5. they cried**—i.e., a cry is raised. Expressing the contempt felt for this race by civilized and well-born Arabs. When these wild vagabonds make an incursion on villages, they are driven away, as thieves would be. **6.** They are forced "to dwell." **cliffs of the valleys**—rather, "in the gloomy (lit., gloom of) valleys," or wadies. To dwell in valleys is, in the East, a mark of wretchedness. The troglodytes, in parts of Arabia, lived in such dwellings as caves. **7. brayed**—like the wild ass (ch. 6:5 for food). The inarticulate tones of this uncivilized rabble are but little above those of the beast of the field. **gathered together**—rather, sprinkled here and there. Lit., "poured out," graphically picturing their disorderly mode of encampment, lying up and down behind the thorn-bushes. **nettles**—or brambles [UMBREIT]. **8. fools**—i.e., the impious and abandoned (I Sam. 25:25). **base**—nameless, low-born rabble. **viler than . . .**—rather, they were *driven* or *beaten out of the land.* The Horites in Mount Seir (Gen. 14:6, with which cf. Gen. 36:20, 21; Deut. 2:12, 22) were probably the aborigines, driven out by the tribe to which Job's ancestors belonged; their name means troglodytæ, or "dwellers in caves." To these Job alludes here (vss. 1-8, and Gen. 24:4-8, which cf. together). **9.** (Ch. 17:6.) Strikingly similar to the derision Jesus Christ underwent (Lam. 3:14; Ps. 69:12). Here Job returns to the sentiment in vs. 1. It is to such I am become a song of "derision." **10. in my face**—rather, refrain not to spit in deliberate contempt *before* my face. To spit at all in presence of another is thought in the East insulting, much more so when done to mark "abhorrence." Cf. the further insult to Jesus Christ (Isa. 50:6; Matt. 26:67). **11. He**—i.e., God; antithetical to *they; English Version* here follows the marginal reading (KERI). **my cord,**—image from a bow unstrung; opposed to ch. 29:20. The text (CHETIB), "*His* cord" or "reins" is better; "yea, each lets loose his reins" [UMBREIT]. **12. youth**—rather, a (low) *brood.* To rise on the right hand is to accuse, as that was the position of the accuser in court (Zech. 3:1; Ps. 109:6). **push . . . feet**—jostle me out of the way (ch. 24:4). **ways of**—i.e., their ways of (i.e., with a view to my) destruction. Image, as in ch. 19:12, from a besieging army throwing up a way of approach for itself to a city. **13.** Image of an assailed fortress continued. They tear up the path by which succor might reach me. **set forward**—(Zech. 1:15). **they have no helper**—Arabic proverb for *contemptible* persons. Yet even such afflict Job. **14. waters**—(So II Sam. 5:20). But it is better to retain the image of vss. 12, 13. "They came (upon me) as through a wide *breach,*" viz., made by the besiegers in the wall of a fortress (Isa. 30:13) [MAURER]. **in the desolation**—"Amidst the crash" of falling masonry, or "with a shout like the crash" of, etc. **15. they**—terrors. **soul**—rather, my dignity [UMBREIT]. **welfare**—prosperity. **cloud**—(Ch. 7:9; Isa. 44:22). **16-23.** Job's outward calamities affect his mind. **poured out**—in irrepressible complaints (Ps. 42:4; Josh. 7:5). **17.** In the

ADAM CLARKE

2. *The strength of their hands profit me.* He is speaking here of the fathers of these young men. What was the strength of their hands to me? Their old age also has perished.

7. *Among the bushes they brayed.* They cried out among the bushes, seeking for food, as the wild ass when he is in want of provender. *Under the nettles.* The "briers" or "brambles," under the brushwood in the thickest parts of the underwood; they huddled together like wild beasts.

8. *Children of fools.* Children of *nabal. Viler than the earth.* Rather, "driven out of the land"; persons not fit for civil society.

11. *Because he hath loosed my cord.* Instead of *yithri,* "my cord," which is the marginal reading, *yithro,* "his cord," is the reading of the text in many copies; and this reading directs us to a metaphor taken from an archer, who, observing his butt, sets his arrow on the string, draws it to a proper degree of tension, levels, and then loosing his hold, the arrow flies at the mark. He hath let loose his arrow against me; it has hit me, and I am wounded. *They have also let loose the bridle.* When they perceived that God had afflicted me, they then threw off all restraints, like headstrong horses.

12. *Upon my right hand rise the youth. "Younglings." They push away my feet.* They trip up my heels, or they in effect trample me under their feet.

13. *They mar my path.* They destroy the waymarks, so that there is no safety in travelling through the deserts, the guideposts and waymarks being gone.

MATTHEW HENRY

Verses 15–31

This second part of Job's complaint is very bitter.

I. Affliction seized him, and surprised him. *The days of affliction have taken hold upon me, have caught me* (so some); *they have arrested me,* as the bailiff arrests the debtor. It surprised him (*v.* 27): "*The days of affliction prevented me,*" that is, "they came upon me without giving me any previous warning. I did not make any provision for such an evil day." He was in great sorrow by reason of it. His *bowels boiled* with grief, *and rested not, v.* 27. The sense of his calamities was continually preying upon his spirits without any intermission. He *went mourning* from day to day, and such a cloud was constantly upon his mind that he went, in effect, *without the sun, v.* 28. Thus he was *a brother to dragons and owls* (*v.* 29), both in choosing solitude and retirement, as they do (Isa. xxxiv. 13), and in making a fearful hideous noise as they do. The terror and trouble that seized his soul were the sorest part of his calamity, *v.* 15, 16. He complained, at first, of the *terrors of God setting themselves in array against him, ch.* vi. 4. And still, which way soever he looked, they turned upon him; which way soever he fled, they pursued him. The soul is the principal part of the man and therefore that which pursues the soul, and threatens, should be most dreaded. *My welfare* and prosperity *pass away,* as suddenly, swiftly, and irrecoverably, *as a cloud.* If he looked within, he found his spirit not only wounded, but *poured out upon him, v.* 16. His bodily diseases went to the bone, *v.* 17. It was a *sword in his bones,* which *pierced him in the night season.* His *sinews took no rest.* By reason of his pain, sleep departed from his eyes. *His bones were burnt with heat, v.* 30. He was in a constant fever. He was full of sores. His *skin was black upon him, v.* 30. Some think that Job was ill of a quinsy and that it was this which bound him like a collar. Thus was he *cast into the mire* (*v.* 19), *compared to mire* (so some); his body looked more like a heap of dirt than anything else. That which afflicted him most of all was that God seemed to be his enemy and to fight against him. "*I cry unto thee,* as one in earnest, *I stand up* and cry, as one waiting for an answer, but thou hearest not, *thou regardest not,* for anything I can perceive." That which he here says of God is one of the worst words that ever Job spoke (*v.* 21): *Thou hast become cruel to me.* Job was unjust and ungrateful when he said so of him. He thought God fought against him and stirred up his whole strength to ruin him: *With thy strong hand thou opposest thyself,* or art an adversary against me. He thought he insulted over him (*v.* 22): *Thou liftest me up to the wind,* as a feather or the chaff which the wind plays with. He expected now that God would shortly make an end of him: "*I know that thou wilt bring me,* with so much the more terror, *to death,* though I might have been brought thither without all this ado, for it is *the house appointed for all living,*" *v.* 23. "*When I looked for good,* for more good, or at least for the continuance of what I had, *then evil came*"—such uncertain things are all our worldly enjoyments. "*My harp is turned to mourning, and my organ into the voice of those that weep.*" Job, in his prosperity, had taken *the timbrel and harp,* and *rejoiced at the sound of the organ, ch.* xxi. 12.

II. Something in the midst of all with which he comforts himself. He foresees that death will be the period of all his calamities (*v.* 24): Though God now opposed himself against him, "yet," says he, "*he will not stretch out his hand to the grave.*" He reflects with comfort upon the concern he always had for the calamities of others when he was himself at ease (*v.* 25): *Did not I weep for him that was in trouble?* His conscience witnessed for him that he had always sympathised with persons in misery and done what he could to help them, and therefore he had reason to expect that, at length, both God and his friends would pity him. *Did not my soul burn for the poor?* so some read it, comparing it with that of St. Paul, 2 Cor. xi. 29, *Who is offended, and I burn not?*

JAMIESON, FAUSSET, BROWN

Hebrew, night is poetically personified, as in ch. 3:3: "night pierceth my bones (so that they fall) *from* me" (not as *English Version,* "*in* me"; see vs. 30). **sinews**—so the *Arabic,* "veins," akin to the *Hebrew;* rather, gnawers, as in vs. 3 (*Note*), viz., my gnawing pains never cease. Effects of elephantiasis. **18. of my disease**—rather, "of God" (ch. 23:6). **garment changed**—from a robe of honor to one of mourning, literally (ch. 2:8; John 3:6) and metaphorically [UMBREIT]. Or rather, as SCHUTTENS, following up vs 17, My *outer* garment is changed into affliction; i.e., affliction has become my outer garment; it also bindeth me fast round (my throat) as the collar of the *inner* coat; i.e., it is both my inner and outer garment. Observe the distinction between the inner and outer garments. The latter refers to his afflictions *from without* (vss. 1-13); the former his personal afflictions (vss. 14-23). UMBREIT makes "God" subject to "bindeth," as in vs. 19. **19.** God is poetically said to do that which the mourner had done to himself (ch. 2:8). With lying in the ashes he had become, like them, in dirty color. **20. stand up**—the reverential attitude of a suppliant before a king (I Kings 8:14; Luke 18:11-13). **not**—supplied from the first clause. But the intervening affirmative "stand" makes this ellipsis unlikely. Rather, as in ch. 16:9 (not only dost thou refuse aid to me "standing" as a suppliant, but), *thou dost regard me with a frown:* eye me sternly. **22. liftest . . . to wind**—as a "leaf" or "stubble" (ch. 13:25). The moving pillars of sand, raised by the wind to the clouds, as described by travellers, would happily depict Job's agitated spirit, if it be to them that he alludes. **dissolvest . . . substance**—The *marginal Hebrew* reading (KERI), "my wealth," or else "wisdom," i.e., sense and spirit, or "my hope of *deliverance.*" But the text (CHETIB) is better: Thou dissolvest me (with fear, Exod. 15:15) *in the crash* (of the whirlwind; as vs. 14, *Note*) [MAURER]. UMBREIT translates as a verb, "Thou *terrifiest* me." **23.** This shows ch. 19:25 cannot be restricted to Job's hope of a *temporal* deliverance. **death**—as in ch. 28:22, the realm of the dead (Heb. 9:27; Gen. 3:19). **24.** Expressing Job's faith as to the state after death. Though one must go to the grave, yet He will no more afflict *in the ruin* of the body (so *Hebrew* for *grave*) there, if one has cried to Him when being destroyed. The "stretching of His hand" to punish after death answers antithetically to the raising "the cry" of prayer in the second clause. MAURER gives another translation which accords with the scope of vss. 24-31; if it be natural for one in affliction to ask aid, why should it be considered (by the friends) wrong in my case? "Nevertheless does not a man in ruin stretch out his hand" (imploring help, vs. 20; Lam. 1:17)? If one be in his calamity (destruction) is there not therefore a "cry" (for aid)? Thus in the parallelism "cry" answers to "stretch—hand"; "in his calamity," to "in ruin." The negative of the first clause is to be supplied in the second, as in vs. 25 (ch. 28:17). **25.** May I not be allowed to complain of my calamity, and beg relief, seeing that I myself sympathized with those "in trouble" (lit., "hard of day"; those who had a hard time of it). **26.** I may be allowed to crave help, seeing that, "when I looked for food (on account of my piety and charity), yet evil," etc. **light**—(ch. 22:28). **27. bowels**—regarded as the seat of deep feeling (Isa. 16:11). **boiled**—violently heated and agitated. **prevented**—Old English for unexpectedly came upon me, surprised me. **28. mourning**—rather, I move about *blackened,* though not by the sun; i.e., whereas many are blackened by the sun, I am, by the heat of God's wrath (so "boiled," vs. 27); the elephantiasis covering me with blackness of skin (vs. 30), as with the garb of mourning (Jer. 14:2). This striking enigmatic form of *Hebrew* expression occurs, Isaiah 29:9. **stood up**—as an innocent man crying for justice in an assembled court (vs. 20). **29. dragons . . . owls**—rather, "jackals," "ostriches," both of which utter dismal screams (Mic. 1:8); in which respect, as also in their living amidst solitudes (the emblem of desolation), Job is their brother and companion; i.e., resembles them. "Dragon," *Hebrew, tannim,* usually means the crocodile; so perhaps here, its open jaws lifted towards heaven, and its noise making it seem as if it mourned over its fate [BOCHART]. **30. upon me**—rather, as in vs. 17 (*Note*), my skin is black (and falls away) *from* me. **my bones**—(ch. 19:20; Ps. 102:5). **31. organ**—rather, *pipe* (ch. 21:12); "My joy is turned into the voice of weeping" (Lam. 5:15). These instruments are properly appropriated to joy (Isa. 30:29, 32), which makes their use now in sorrow the sadder by contrast.

ADAM CLARKE

CHARLES H. SPURGEON:

Job suffered from a terrible sickness which filled him with pain both day and night. It is supposed that, in addition to his grievous eruptions upon the skin, he endured great difficulty in breathing. He says in the eighteenth verse, "By the great force of my disease is my garment changed: it bindeth me about as the collar of my coat." His clothes were sodden, and clung to him: his skin was blackened, and seemed to be tightened. He was like a man whose tunic strangles him; the collar of his garment seemed to be fast bound about his throat. Those who have suffered from it know what distress is occasioned by this complaint, especially when they are also compelled to cry, "My bones are pierced in me in the night season: and my sinews take no rest." At such a time Job thought of death, and surely if at any period in our lives we should consider our latter end, it is when the frail tent of our body begins to tremble, because the cords are loosened and the curtain is rent. It is the general custom with sick people to talk about "getting well"; and those who visit them, even when they are gracious people, will see the tokens of death upon them and yet will speak as if they were hopeful of their recovery. I remember a father asking me when I prayed with a consumptive girl to be sure not to mention death. In such cases it would be far more sensible for the sick man to turn his thoughts towards eternity, and stand prepared for the great change. When our God by our affliction calls upon us to number our days, let us not refuse to do so. I admire the wisdom of Job, that he does not shirk the subject of death but dwells upon it as an appropriate topic, saying, "I know that thou wilt bring me to death, and to the house appointed for all living."

—*The Treasury of the Old Testament*

24. *He will not stretch out his hand to the grave.* As if he said, Though I suffer here, I shall not suffer hereafter. Though He add stroke to stroke, so as to destroy my life, yet His displeasure shall not proceed beyond the grave.

25. *Did not I weep for him that was in trouble?* "Should I not then weep for the ruthless day?"

28. *I went mourning without the sun. Chammah,* which we here translate *the sun,* comes from a root of the same letters, which signifies to hide, protect, and may be translated, "I went mourning without a protector or guardian."

29. *I am a brother to dragons.* By my mournful and continual cry I resemble *tannim,* the jackals or hyenas. *And a companion to owls.* "To the daughters of howling," generally understood to be the ostrich; for both the jackal and the female ostrich are remarkable for their mournful cry, and for their attachment to desolate places.

MATTHEW HENRY

CHAPTER 31

Verses 1–8

The lusts of the flesh, and the love of the world, are the two fatal rocks on which multitudes split; against these Job protests he was always careful to stand upon his guard.

I. Against the lusts of the flesh. He not only kept himself clear from adultery, from defiling his neighbours' wives (*v.* 9), but from all lewdness with any woman whatsoever. *I made a covenant with my eyes*, that is, "I watched against the occasions of the sin; *why then should I think upon a maid?*" that is, "by that means, through the grace of God, I kept myself from the very first step towards it." He would not so much as admit a wanton look. Those that would keep their hearts pure must guard their eyes, which are both the outlets and inlets of uncleanness. He would not so much as allow a wanton thought. It was not for fear of reproach among men, though that is to be considered (Prov. vi. 33), but for fear of the wrath and curse of God. Uncleanness is a sin that forfeits all good, and shuts us out from the hope of it (*v.* 2): *What portion of God is there from above? Is not destruction*, a swift and sure destruction, *to* those *wicked* people, *and a strange punishment to the workers of* this *iniquity*? *Is there not alienation* (so some read it) *to the workers of iniquity?* This is the sinfulness of the sin that it alienates the mind from God (Eph. iv. 18, 19). *Doth not he see my ways? O God! thou hast searched me and known me.* God sees what rule we walk by, what company we walk with, what end we walk towards, and therefore what ways we walk in. He *counts all my steps*, all my false steps in the way of duty, all my by-steps into the way of sin. God takes a more exact notice of us than we do of ourselves; for who ever counted his own steps? yet God counts them.

II. He stood upon his guard against the love of the world, and carefully avoided all sinful means of getting wealth. He dreaded all forbidden profit as much as all forbidden pleasure. He never *walked with vanity* (*v.* 5), that is, he never durst tell a lie to get a good bargain. He never *hasted to deceit*. He never made haste to be rich by deceit, but always acted cautiously, lest, through inconsideration, he should do an unjust thing. His *steps never turned out of the way*, the way of justice and fair dealing; from that he never deviated, *v.* 7. His heart did not *walk after his eyes*, that is, he did not covet what he saw that was another's nor wish it his own. Covetousness is called the *lust of the eye*, 1 John ii. 16. *No blot had cleaved to his hands*, that is, he was not chargeable with getting anything dishonestly, or keeping that which was another's. Injustice is a blot, a blot to the estate, a blot to the owner; it spoils the beauty of both. Job ratifies his protestation. He is willing to have his goods searched (*v.* 6): *Let me be weighed in an even balance*, that is, "Let what I have got be enquired into and it will be found to weigh well." He is willing to forfeit the whole cargo if there be found any prohibited or contraband goods, anything but what he came honestly by (*v.* 8): *"Let me sow, and let another eat,"* which was already agreed to be the doom of oppressors (*ch.* v. 5), "and *let my offspring*, all the trees that I have planted, *be rooted out*." He knew himself innocent and would venture all the poor remains of his estate upon the issue of the trial.

Verses 9–15

Two more instances of Job's integrity:

I. He had a very great abhorrence of the sin of adultery. He was careful not to offer any injury to his neighbour's marriage bed. He did not so much as covet his neighbour's wife; for even *his heart was not deceived by a woman*. He never *laid wait at his neighbour's door*, to get an opportunity to debauch his wife in his absence. He owns that, if he were guilty: *Let my wife grind to another*. Let her be a *slave* (so some), a *harlot*, so others. God often punishes the sins of one with the sin of another, the adultery of the husband with the adultery of the wife. Those who are not just and faithful to their relations must not think it strange if their relations be unjust and unfaithful to them. *For it is an iniquity to be punished by the judges.* Adultery is a crime which the civil magistrate ought to take cognizance of and punish. *It is a fire*. Lust is a fire in the soul: those that indulge it are said to burn.

II. He had a very great tenderness for his servants and ruled them with a gentle hand. He did not *despise the cause of his man-servant*, no, nor of his *maid-servant, when they contended with him*. If they had offended him, or were accused to him, if they complained of any hardship he put upon them, he gave them leave to tell their story, and redressed their grievances as far as it appeared they had right on their side. He considered, "If I should be im-

JAMIESON, FAUSSET, BROWN

CHAPTER 31

Vss. 1-40. **1.** Job proceeds to prove that he deserved a better lot. As in ch. 29, he showed his uprightness as an emir, or magistrate in *public* life, so in this chapter he vindicates his character in *private* life. **1-4.** He asserts his guarding against being allured to sin by his senses. **1. think**—rather, *cast* a (lustful) *look*. He not merely did not so, but put it out of the question by covenanting with his eyes against leading him into temptation (Prov. 6: 25; Matt. 5:28).

2. Had I let my senses tempt me to sin, "what portion (would there have been to me, i.e., must I have expected) from (lit. "of") God above, and what inheritance from (lit. "of") the Almighty," etc. [MAURER] (ch. 20:29; 27:13). **3.** Answer to the question in vs. 2. **strange**—extraordinary. **4.** Doth not he see . . . ? Knowing this, I could only have expected "destruction" (vs. 3), had I committed this sin (Prov. 5:21).

5. Job's abstinence from evil deeds. **vanity**—i.e., falsehood (Ps. 12:2).

7. Connected with vs. 6. **the way**—of God (ch. 23:11; Jer. 5:5). A godly life. **heart . . . after . . . eyes**—if my heart coveted, what my eyes beheld (Eccles. 11: 9; Josh. 7:21). **hands**—(Ps. 24:4).

6. Parenthetical. Translate: "Oh, that God would weigh me . . . *then* would He know . . ."

8. Apodosis to vss. 5 and 7; the curses which he imprecates on himself, if he had done these things (Lev. 26:16; Amos 9:14; Ps. 128:2). **offspring**—rather, *what I plant*, my harvests.

9-12. Job asserts his innocence of adultery. **deceived**—hath let itself be seduced (Prov. 7:8; Gen. 39:7-12). **laid wait**—until the husband went out. **10. grind**—turn the handmill. Be the most abject slave and concubine (Isa. 47:2; II Sam. 12-11). **11.** In the earliest times punished with death (Gen. 38:24). So in later times (Deut. 22:22). Heretofore he had spoken only of sins against conscience; now, one against the community, needing the cognizance of the judge. **12.** (Prov. 6:27-35; 8:6-23, 26, 27.) No crime more provokes God to send *destruction as a consuming fire;* none so desolates the soul.

13-23. Job affirms his freedom from unfairness towards his servants, from harshness and oppression towards the needy. **despise the cause**—refused to do them justice. **14, 15.** Parenthetical; the reason why Job did not despise the cause of his servants. Translate: What then (had I done so) could I have done, when God arose

ADAM CLARKE

CHAPTER 31

1. *I made a covenant with mine eyes.* "I have cut" or divided "the covenant sacrifice with my eyes." My conscience and my eyes are the contracting parties; God is the Judge; and I am therefore bound not to look upon anything with a delighted or covetous eye by which my conscience may be defiled or my God dishonored. *Why then should I think upon a maid?* "And why should I set myself to contemplate, or think upon, Bethulah?" That Bethulah may here signify an idol is very likely.

5. *If I have walked with vanity.* If I have been guilty of idolatry, or the worshipping of a false god; for thus *shav*, which we here translate "vanity," is used Jer. xviii. 15 (compare with Ps. xxxi. 6; Hos. xii. 11; and Jonah ii. 9) and it seems evident that the whole of Job's discourse here is a vindication of himself from all idolatrous dispositions and practices.

7. *If my step hath turned out of the way.* I am willing to be sifted to the uttermost—for every step of my foot, for every thought of my heart, for every look of mine eye, and for every act of my hands.

6. *Mine integrity. Tummathi*, my perfection; the totality of my unblamable life.

9. *If mine heart have been deceived by a woman.* The Septuagint add, "another man's wife."

10. *Let my wife grind unto another.* Let her work at the handmill, grinding corn, which was the severe work of the meanest slave.

MATTHEW HENRY

perious and severe with my servants, *what then shall I do when God riseth up*?" When he was tempted to be harsh with his servants this thought came very seasonably into his mind, "*Did not he that made me in the womb make him?* I am a creature as well as he, and my being is derived and depending as well as his. He partakes of the same nature that I do and is the work of the same hand.

Verses 16–23

Eliphaz had particularly charged Job with unmercifulness to the poor (*ch.* xxii. 6, &c.). It appears, by Job's protestation, that it was utterly false and groundless.

I. He was always compassionate to the poor, and careful of them, especially the widows and fatherless, always ready to grant their desires and answer their expectations, *v.* 16. If he could but perceive by the widow's look that she expected an alms from him, he had compassion enough to give it, and *never caused the eyes of the widow to fail.* He was a father to the fatherless, took care of orphans. He provided food convenient for them; they ate of the same morsels that he did (*v.* 17), did not eat after him, of the crumbs that fell from his table, but with him, of the best dish upon his table. He took particular care to clothe those that were without covering, which would be more expensive to him than feeding them, *v.* 19. If Job knew of any that were in this distress he had good warm strong clothes made on purpose for them of *the fleece of his sheep* (*v.* 20). He never so much as *lifted up his hand against the fatherless* (*v.* 21). He never used his power to crush those that stood in his way, though he *saw his help in the gate*, that is, though he had interest enough, both in the people and in the judges, both to enable him to do it and to bear him out when he had done it.

II. The imprecation with which he confirms this protestation (*v.* 22): "If I have been oppressive to the poor, *let my arm fall from my shoulder-blade and my arm be broken from the bone*," that is, "let the flesh rot off from the bone and one bone be disjoined and broken off from another."

III. The principles by which Job was restrained from all uncharitableness and unmercifulness. "*Destruction from God was a terror to me*, whenever I was tempted to this sin, and *by reason of his highness I could not endure* the thought of making him my enemy." He thought of the infinite distance between him and God. Those who oppress the poor, and pervert judgment and justice, forget that *he who is higher than the highest regards*, and *there is a higher than they*, who is able to deal with them (Eccles. v. 8); but Job considered this.

Verses 24–32

Four articles more of Job's protestation not only assure us what he was and did, but teach us what we should be and do:

I. He protests that he never set his heart upon the wealth of this world. His *wealth was great*, and he *had gotten much.* Job put no great confidence in it: he did not *make gold his hope*, *v.* 24. It is hard to have riches and not to trust in riches; and it is this which makes it so difficult for *a rich man to enter into the kingdom of God*, Matt. xix. 23; Mark x. 24.

II. He protests that he never gave the worship and glory to the creature which are due to God only; he was never guilty of idolatry, *v.* 26–28. He not only never bowed the knee to Baal (which, some think, was designed to represent the sun), never fell down and worshipped the sun, but he kept his eye, his heart, and his lips, clean from this sin. This was his covenant, that, whenever he looked at the lights of heaven, he should by faith look through them, and beyond them, to the Father of lights. He did not perform the least and lowest act of adoration: *His mouth did not kiss his hand*, which, it is likely, was a ceremony then commonly used even by some that yet would not be thought idolaters. In giving divine honours to the sun and moon, they could not reach to kiss them, but to show their goodwill, they kissed their hand, reverencing those as their masters which God has made servants to this lower world, to hold the candle for us. He looked upon it as an affront to the civil magistrate: It *were an iniquity to be punished by the judge*, as a public nuisance. He looked upon it as a much greater affront to the God of heaven, and no less than high treason against his crown and dignity. Idolatry is in effect atheism.

III. He protests that he was so far from doing or designing mischief to any that he neither desired nor delighted in the hurt of the worst enemy he had. He did not so much as rejoice when any mischief befell them, *v.* 29. He did not so much as wish in his own mind that evil might befall them, *v.* 30. He was violently urged to revenge, and yet he kept himself

JAMIESON, FAUSSET, BROWN

(to call me to account); and when He visited (came to inquire), what could I have answered Him? **15.** Slaveholders try to defend themselves by maintaining the *original* inferiority of the slave. But Malachi 2:10; Acts 17:26; Ephesians 6:9, make the common origin of masters and servants the argument for brotherly love being shown by the former to the latter.

16. fail–in the vain expectation of relief (ch. 11:20). **17.** Arabian rules of hospitality require the stranger to be helped first, and to the best. **18.** Parenthetical: asserting that he did the contrary to the things in vss. 16, 17. **he**–the orphan. **guided her**–viz., the widow, by advice and protection. On this and "a father," see ch. 29:16. **19. perish**–i.e., ready to perish (ch. 29:13). **20. loins**–The parts of the body benefited by Job are poetically described as thanking him; the loins before naked, when clad by me, wished me every blessing. **21.** "When (i.e., because) I saw" that I might calculate on the "help" of a powerful party in the court of justice–("gate"), if I should be summoned by the injured fatherless. **22.** Apodosis to vss. 13, 16, 17, 19, 20, 21. If I had done those crimes, **I** should have made a bad use of my influence (my arm, figuratively, vs. 21): therefore, if I have done them let my arm (literally) suffer. Job alludes to Eliphaz' charge (ch. 22:9). The first "arm" is rather the *shoulder*. The second "arm" is the *forearm*. **from the bone**–lit., "a reed"; hence the upper arm, above the elbow. **23. For**–i.e., the reason why Job guarded against such sins. *Fear of God,* though he could escape man's judgment (Gen. 39:9). UMBREIT more spiritedly translates, Yea, destruction and terror from God might have befallen me (had I done so): mere *fear* not being the motive. **highness**–majestic might. **endure**–I could have availed nothing against it.

24, 25. Job asserts his freedom from trust in money (I Tim. 6:17). Here he turns to his duty towards God, as before he had spoken of his duty towards *himself* and his *neighbor*. Covetousness is covert idolatry, as it transfers the heart from the Creator to the creature (Col. 3:5). In vss. 26, 27 he passes to overt idolatry. **26. If I** looked unto the sun (as an object of worship) *because* he shined; or to the moon *because* she walked, etc. Sabaism (from *tsaba*, the heavenly hosts) was the earliest form of false worship. God is hence called in contradistinction, "Lord of Sabaoth." The sun, moon, and stars, the brightest objects in nature, and seen everywhere, were supposed to be visible representatives of the invisible God. They had no temples, but were worshipped on high places and roofs of houses (Ezek. 8:16; Deut. 4:19; II Kings 23:5, 11). The *Hebrew* here for "sun" is *light.* Probably light was worshipped as the emanation from God, before its embodiments, the sun, etc. This worship prevailed in Chaldea; wherefore Job's exemption from the idolatry of his neighbors was the more exemplary. Our "Sun-day," "Mon-day," or Moon-day, bear traces of Sabaism. **27. enticed**–away from God to idolatry. **kissed . . . hand**–"adoration," literally means this. In worshipping they used to kiss the hand, and then throw the kiss, as it were, towards the object of worship (I Kings 19:18; Hos. 13:2). **28.** The Mosaic law embodied subsequently the feeling of the godly from the earliest times against idolatry, as deserving judicial penalties: being treason against the Supreme King (Deut. 13:9; 17:2-7; Ezek. 8:14-18). This passage therefore does not prove Job to have been subsequent to Moses. **29. lifted up himself**–in malicious triumph (Prov. 17:5; 24:17; Ps. 7:4). **30. mouth**–lit., "palate" (ch. 6:30, *Note*). **wishing**–lit., "so as to demand his (my enemy's) soul, i.e., life by a curse." This verse parenthetically confirms vs. 30. Job in the patriarchal age of the promise, anterior to the law, realizes the Gospel spirit, which was the end of the law (cf. Lev. 19:18; Deut. 23:6, with Matt. 5:43, 44).

ADAM CLARKE

17. *Or have eaten my morsel myself alone.* Hospitality was a very prominent virtue among the ancients in almost all nations.

24. *Gold my hope, Zahab,* polished gold, and *kethem,* stamped gold (see on chap. xxviii. 15-17).

26. *If I beheld the sun when it shined.* In this verse Job clears himself of that idolatrous worship which was the most ancient and most consistent with reason of any species of idolatry: the worship of the heavenly bodies.

"Adoration," or the religious act of "kissing the hand," comes to us from the Latin; *ad*, to, and *oris*, the mouth.

MATTHEW HENRY

thus clear from it (*v.* 31): *The men of his tabernacle,* his domestics, his servants, and those about him, were enraged at Job's enemy who hated him. "*O that we had of his flesh!* Our master is satisfied to forgive him, but *we cannot be so satisfied.*"

IV. He protests that he had never been unkind or inhospitable to strangers (*v.* 32). *The stranger lodged not in the street. He opened his door to the road* (so it may be read); he kept the street-door open, that he might see who passed by and invite them in, as Abraham, Gen. xviii. 1.

Verses 33–40

Job's protestation against three more sins.

I. Of dissimulation and hypocrisy. The general crime of which his friends accused him was that really he was as bad as other people, but had the art of concealing it. Zophar insinuated (*ch.* xx. 12) that he *hid his iniquity under his tongue.* "No," says Job, "I never did (*v.* 33), *I never covered my transgression as Adam,* never palliated a sin with frivolous excuses, nor ever *hid my iniquity in my bosom.*"

II. His courage in that which is good he produces as an evidence of his sincerity in it (*v.* 34): *Did I fear a great multitude, that I kept silence?* No, all that knew Job knew him to be a man of undaunted resolution in a good cause, and did not fear the face of man, but set his face as a flint. He did not, he durst not, keep silence when he had a call to speak in an honest cause, or keep within doors when he had a call to go abroad to do good. He valued not the clamours of the mob, feared not a great multitude, nor did he value the menaces of the mighty: *The contempt of families never terrified him.*

III. The charge of oppression and violence, and doing wrong to his poor neighbours. The estate he had he both got and used honestly, so that his *land* could not *cry out against him nor the furrows thereof complain* (*v.* 38), as they do against those who get the possession of them by fraud and extortion, Hab. ii. 9–11. Two things he could say safely concerning his estate:—1. That he *never ate the fruits of it without money, v.* 39. What he purchased he paid for. The labourers that he employed had their wages duly paid them. 2. That he never caused the owners thereof to lose their life, never got an estate, as Ahab got Naboth's vineyard, by killing the heir and seizing the inheritance, never starved those that held lands of him nor killed them with hard bargains and hard usage. "If I have got my estate unjustly, *let thistles grow instead of wheat,* the worst of weeds instead of the best of grains." Job, towards the close of his protestation, appeals to the judgment-seat of God concerning the truth of it (*v.* 35–37): *O that he would hear me,* even *that the Almighty would answer me!* An upright heart does not dread a scrutiny. He that means honestly wishes he had a window in his breast, that all men might see the intents of his heart. But an upright heart does particularly desire to be determined in everything by the judgment of God which we are sure is according to truth. "*O that my adversary had written a book*—that my friends, who charge me with hypocrisy, would draw up their charge in writing, that it might be reduced to a certainty, and that we might the better join issue upon it." If it discovered to him any sin he had been guilty of, which he did not yet see, he should be glad to know it, that he might repent of it and get it pardoned. If it charged him with what was false, he doubted not but to disprove the allegations. The defendant is ready to make his appearance and to give his accusers all the fair play they can desire. He will *declare unto them the number of his steps, v.* 37. He will let them into the history of his own life. So confident he is of his integrity that as a prince to be crowned, rather than as a prisoner to be tried, he would *go near to him,* both to his accuser to hear his charge and to his judge to hear his doom. He has now said all he would say in answer to his friends: he afterwards said something in a way of self-reproach and condemnation (*ch.* xl. 4, 5; xlii. 2, &c.), but here ends what he had to say in a way of self-defence and vindication.

JAMIESON, FAUSSET, BROWN

31. i.e., Job's household said, Oh, that we had Job's enemy to devour, we cannot rest satisfied till we have! But Job refrained from even wishing revenge (I Sam. 26:8; II Sam. 16:9, 10). So Jesus Christ (Luke 9:54, 55). But, better (see vs. 32), translated, "Who can show (lit., give) the man who was not satisfied with the flesh (meat) provided by Job?" He never let a poor man leave his gate without giving him enough to eat. **32. traveller**—lit., "way," i.e., wayfarers; so expressed to include all of every kind (II Sam. 12:4). **33. Adam**—translated by UMBREIT, "as men do" (Hos. 6, 7, where see *Margin*). But *English Version* is more natural. The very same word for "hiding" is used in Genesis 3:8, 10, of Adam *hiding* himself from God. Job elsewhere alludes to the flood. So he might easily know of the fall, through the two links which connect Adam and Abraham (about Job's time), viz., Methuselah and Shem. Adam is representative of fallen man's propensity to concealment (Prov. 28: 13). It was *from God* that Job did not "hide his iniquity in his bosom," as on the contrary it was from God that "Adam" hid in his lurking-place. This disproves the translation, "as men"; for it is *from their fellow men* that "men" are chiefly anxious to hide their real character as guilty. MAGEE, to make the comparison with Adam more exact, for my "bosom" translates, "lurking-place." **34.** Rather, the apodosis to vs. 33, "Then let me be fear-stricken before a great multitude, let the contempt, etc., let me keep silence (the greatest disgrace to a patriot, heretofore so prominent in assemblies), and not go out," etc. A just retribution that he who hides his sin from God, should have it exposed before man (II Sam. 12:12). But Job had not been so exposed, but on the contrary was esteemed in the assemblies of the "tribes"—("families"); a proof, he implies, that God does not hold him guilty of hiding sin (ch. 24:16, contrast with ch. 29:21-25). **35.** Job returns to his wish (ch. 13:22; 19:23). Omit "is"; "Behold my *sign,*" i.e., my mark of subscription to the statements just given in my defense: the *mark* of signature was originally a *cross;* and hence the letter Tau or T. Translate, also "Oh, *that* the Almighty," etc. He marks "God" as the "One" meant in the first *clause.* Adversary, i.e., he who contends with me, refers also to God. The vagueness is designed to express "whoever it be that judicially opposes me"—the Almighty if it be He. **had written a book**—rather, "would write down his charge." **36.** So far from hiding the adversary's "answer" or "charge" through fear, "I would take it on my shoulders" as a public honor (Isa. 9:6). **a crown**—not a mark of shame, but of distinction (Isa. 62:3). **37.** A good conscience imparts a princely dignity before man and free assurance in approaching God. This can be realized, not in Job's way (42:5, 6); but only through Jesus Christ (Heb. 10:22). **38.** Personification. The complaints of the unjustly ousted proprietors are transferred to the lands themselves (vs. 20; Gen. 4:10; Hab. 2:11). If I have unjustly acquired lands (ch. 24:2; Isa. 5:8). **furrows**—The specification of these makes it likely, he implies in this, "If I paid not the laborer for *tillage*"; as next verse, "If I paid him not for gathering in the fruits." Thus of the four clauses in vss. 38, 39, the 1st refers to the same subject as the 4th, the 2d is connected with the 3d by introverted parallelism. Cf. James 5:4, which plainly alludes to this passage: cf. "Lord of Sabaoth" with vs. 26 here. **39. lose . . . life**—not literally, but "harassed to death;" until he gave me up his land gratis [MAURER]; as in Judges 16:16; "suffered him to languish" by taking away his means of living [UMBREIT] (I Kings 21:19). **40. thistles**—or brambles, thorns. **cockle**—lit., "noxious weeds." **The words . . . ended**—i.e., in the controversy with the friends. He spoke in the book afterwards, but not to *them.* At vs. 37 would be the regular conclusion in strict art. But vss. 38-40 are naturally added by one whose mind in agitation recurs to its sense of innocence, even after it has come to the usual stopping point; this takes away the appearance of rhetorical artifice. Hence the transposition by EICHORN of vss. 38-40 to follow vs. 25 is quite unwarranted.

ADAM CLARKE

31. *If the men of my tabernacle said.* I believe the Targum gives the best sense here: "If the men of my tabernacle have not said, Who hath commanded that we should not be satisfied with his flesh?" My domestics have had all kindness shown them; they have lived like my own children, and have been served with the same viands as my family.

33. *If I covered my transgressions as Adam.* Here is a most evident allusion to the Fall. Adam transgressed the commandment of his Maker, and he endeavored to conceal it.

34. *Did I fear a great multitude?* Was I ever prevented by the voice of the many from decreeing and executing what was right?

35. *Oh that one would hear me!* I wish to have a fair and full hearing. *Behold, my desire is.* "There is my pledge." I bind myself, on a great penalty, to come into court, and abide the issue. *That the Almighty would answer me.* That He would call this case immediately before himself, and oblige my adversary to come into court, to put His accusations into a legal form, that I might have the opportunity of vindicating myself in the presence of a Judge who would hear dispassionately my pleadings, and bring the cause to a righteous issue. *And that mine adversary had written a book.* That he would not indulge himself in vague accusations, but would draw up a proper "bill of indictment," that I might know to what I had to plead, and find the accusation in a tangible form.

36. *Surely I would take it upon my shoulder.* I would be contented to stand before the bar as a criminal, bearing upon my shoulder the board to which the accusation is affixed.

37. *I would declare unto him the number of my steps.* I would show this adversary the different stations I had been in, and the offices which I had filled in life, that he might trace me through the whole of my civil, military, and domestic life, in order to get evidence against me. *As a prince would I go near.* Though carrying my own accusation, I would go into the presence of my Judge as the *nagid,* "chief," or sovereign commander and judge, of the people and country, and would not shrink from having my conduct investigated by even the meanest of my subjects.

38. *If my land cry.* Job seems here to refer to that law, Lev. xxv. 1-7, by which the Israelites were obliged to give the land rest every seventh year. He, conscious that he had acted according to this law, states that his land could not cry out against him, nor its *furrows . . . complain.*

39. *If I have eaten the fruits thereof without money.* If I have eaten the fruits of it, I have cultivated it well to produce those fruits; and this has not been without money, for I have gone to expenses on the soil, and remunerated the laborers.

40. *The words of Job are ended.* That is, his defense of himself against the accusations of his friends, as they are called. He spoke afterwards, but never to them; he addresses only God, who came to determine the whole controversy.

MATTHEW HENRY — CHAPTER 32

Verses 1–5

When old men were the disputants, as a rebuke to them for their unbecoming heat, a young man is raised up to be the moderator.

I. The reason why Job's three friends were now silent. They *ceased to answer him,* and let him have

JAMIESON, FAUSSET, BROWN — CHAPTER 32

Vss. 1-22. SPEECH OF ELIHU (ch. 32-37). 1-6. Prose (poetry begins with "I am young").

ADAM CLARKE — CHAPTER 32

1. *These three men ceased to answer Job.* They supposed that it was of no use to attempt to reason any longer with a man who justified himself before God. The truth is, they failed to convince Job of any point because they argued

MATTHEW HENRY

his saying, *because he was righteous in his own eyes.* It was to no purpose to argue with a man that was so opinionative, *v.* 1. But they did not judge fairly concerning Job: he was really righteous before God, and not righteous in his own eyes only.

II. The reasons why Elihu, the fourth, now spoke. His name *Elihu* signifies *My God is he.* He is said to be a *Buzite*, from Buz, Nahor's second son (Gen. xxii. 21), and *of the kindred of Ram*, that is, *Aram* (so some), whence the Syrians or Aramites descended and were denominated, Gen. xxii. 21. *Of the kindred of Abram;* so the Chaldee-paraphrase, supposing him to be first called *Ram—high*, then *Abram—a high father*, and lastly *Abraham—the high father of a multitude.*

1. Elihu spoke because he was angry and thought he had good cause to be so. He was angry at Job, because he thought he did not speak so reverently of God as he ought to have done; and that was too true (*v.* 2): *He justified himself more than God*, that is, took more care and pains to clear himself from the imputation of unrighteousness in being thus afflicted than to clear God from the imputation of unrighteousness in afflicting him. Elihu owned Job to be a good man. He was angry at his friends because he thought they had not conducted themselves so charitably towards Job as they ought to have done (*v.* 3): *They had found no answer, and yet had condemned Job.* Seldom is a quarrel carried on to the length that this was, in which there is not a fault on both sides. Elihu, as became a moderator, took part with neither.

2. Elihu had waited on Job's speeches, had patiently heard him out, until the words of Job were ended.

Verses 6–14

Elihu appears to have been,

I. A man of great modesty and humility. "*I am young, and therefore I was afraid, and durst not show you my opinion*, for fear I should either prove mistaken or do that which was unbecoming me." It becomes us to be swift to hear the sentiments of others and slow to speak our own, especially when we go contrary to the judgment of those for whom, upon the score of their learning and piety, we justly have a veneration. *I said, Days should speak.* Age and experience give a man great advantage in judging of things, both as they furnish a man with so much the more matter for his thoughts to work upon and as they ripen and improve the faculties. It is good *lodging with an old disciple*, Acts xxi. 16; Titus ii. 4. Elihu's modesty appeared in the patient attention he gave to what his seniors said, *v.* 11, 12. He attended to them with diligence and care. Though they had often to seek for matter and words, paused and hesitated, yet he *gave ear to their reasons.* We must often be willing to hear what we do not like, else we cannot prove all things. Those that have heard may speak, and those that have learned may teach.

II. A man of great sense and courage, and one that knew as well when and how to speak as when and how to keep silence. Though he had so much respect to his friends as not to interrupt them with his speaking, yet he had so much regard to truth and justice (his better friends) as not to betray them by his silence.

1. Man is a rational creature, and therefore has for himself a judgment of discretion and ought to be allowed a liberty of speech in his turn. He means the same that Job did (*ch.* xii. 3, *But I have understanding as well as you*) when he says (*v.* 8), *But there is a spirit in man;* only he expresses it a little more modestly, that one man has understanding as well as another, and no man can pretend to have the monopoly of reason. *Therefore hearken to me.* The soul is a spirit, neither material itself nor dependent upon matter. It is an understanding spirit. It is able to discover and receive truth, to discourse and reason upon it, and to direct and rule accordingly. This understanding spirit is in every man; it is the light *that lighteth every man*, John i. 9. It is the inspiration of the Almighty that gives us this understanding spirit.

2. Those who are advanced above others in grandeur and gravity do not always proportionably go beyond them in knowledge and wisdom (*v.* 9): *Great men are not always wise;* it is a pity but they were, for then they would never do hurt with their greatness and would do so much the more good with their wisdom. The aged do not always understand judgment; even *they* may be mistaken, and they must not take it as an affront to be contradicted, but rather take it as a kindness to be instructed, by their juniors: *Therefore I said, hearken to me*, *v.* 10. He that has a good eye can see further upon level ground than he that is purblind can from the top of the highest mountain. *Better is a poor and wise child than an old and foolish king*, Eccles. iv. 13.

JAMIESON, FAUSSET, BROWN

1. because . . .—and because they could not prove to him that he was unrighteous. **2. Elihu**—meaning "God is Jehovah." In his name and character as messenger between God and Job, he foreshadows Jesus Christ (ch. 33:23-26). **Barachel**—meaning "God blesses." Both names indicate the piety of the family and their separation from idolaters. **Buzite**—Buz was son of Nahor, brother of Abraham. Hence was named a region in Arabia Deserta (Jer. 25:23). **Ram**—Aram, nephew of Buz. Job was probably of an older generation than Elihu. However, the identity of names does not necessarily prove the identity of persons. The particularity with which Elihu's descent is given, as contrasted with the others, led LIGHTFOOT to infer Elihu was the author of the book. But the reason for particularity was, probably, that Elihu was *less known* than the three called "friends" of Job; and that it was right for the poet to mark especially him who was mainly to solve the problem of the book. **rather than God**—i.e., was more eager *to vindicate himself than God.* In ch. 4:17, Job denies *that man can be more just than God.* UMBREIT translates, "Before (in the presence of) God." **3.** Though silenced in argument, they held their opinion still.

4. had spoken—*Hebrew*, "in words" referring rather to *his own* "words" of reply, which he had long ago ready, but kept back in deference to the seniority of the friends *who spoke.* **6. was afraid**—The root meaning in *Hebrew is* "to crawl" (Deut. 32:24).

7. Days—i.e., the aged (ch. 15:10).

11. Therefore Elihu was present from the first. **reasons**—lit., "understandings," i.e., the meaning intended by words. **whilst**—I waited *until* you should discover a suitable reply to Job.

8. Elihu claims inspiration, as a divinely commissioned messenger to Job (ch. 33: 6, 23); and that claim is not contradicted in ch. 42. Translate: "But the spirit (which God puts) in man, and the inspiration . . ., is that which giveth . . ."; it is not mere "years" which give understanding (Prov. 2:6; John 20:22).

9. Great—rather, old (vs. 6). So *Hebrew*, in Gen. 25:23. "Greater, less" for *the older, the younger.* **judgment**—what is right. **10.** Rather, I say. **opinion**—rather, knowledge.

ADAM CLARKE

from false principles; and, as we have seen, Job had the continual advantage of them. There were points on which he might have been successfully assailed, but they did not know them. Elihu, better acquainted with both human nature and the nature of the divine law, and of God's moral government of the world, steps in, and makes the proper discriminations; acquits Job on the ground of their accusations, but condemns him for his too great self-confidence, and his trusting too much in his external righteousness; and, without duly considering his frailty and imperfections, his incautiously arraigning the providence of God of unkindness in its dealings with him. This was the point on which Job was particularly vulnerable, and which Elihu very properly clears up. *Because he was righteous in his own eyes.* The Septuagint, Syriac, Arabic, and Chaldee, all read, "Because he was righteous in their eyes," intimating that they were now convinced that he was a holy man, and that they had charged him foolishly.

2. *Then was kindled the wrath.* This means no more than that Elihu was greatly excited, and felt a strong and zealous desire to vindicate the justice and providence of God against the aspersions of Job and his friends. *Elihu the son of Barachel the Buzite.* Buz was the second son of Nahor, the brother of Abram, Gen. xxii. 21. *Of the kindred of Ram.* Kemuel was the third son of Nahor; and is called in Genesis (see above) "the father of Aram," which is the same as Ram. A city of the name of *Buz* is found in Jer. xxv. 23, which probably had its name from this family; and, as it is mentioned with Dedan and Tema, we know it must have been a city in Idumea, as the others were in that district. *Because he justified himself rather than God.* Literally, "he justified his soul," *naphhso*, "before God." He defended, not only the whole of his conduct, but also his motives, thoughts.

6. *I am young.* Among the Asiatics the youth never spoke in the presence of the elders, especially on any subject of controversy.

7. *Days should speak.* That is, men are to be reputed wise and experienced in proportion to the time they have lived. The Easterners were remarkable for treasuring up wise sayings; indeed, the principal part of their boasted wisdom consisted in proverbs and maxims on different subjects.

11. *Whilst ye searched out what to say.* "Whilst ye were searching up and down for words." A fine irony, which they must have felt.

8. *But there is a spirit in man.* "The spirit itself is in miserable man, and the breath of the Almighty causeth them to understand." The spirit itself is in man as the spring or fountain of his animal existence; and by the afflatus of this spirit he becomes capable of understanding and reason, and consequently of discerning divine truth. The animal and intellectual lives are here stated to be from God, and this appears to be an allusion to man's creation, Gen. ii. 7. In this one saying Elihu spoke more sense and sound doctrine than all Job's friends did in the whole of the controversy.

MATTHEW HENRY

3. It was requisite for something to be said, for the setting of this controversy in a true light. "I must speak, *lest you should say, We have found out wisdom*, lest you should think your argument against Job conclusive and that he cannot be convinced and humbled by any other argument than this of yours, *that God casteth him down and not man*, that it appears by his extraordinary afflictions that God is his enemy, and therefore he is certainly a wicked man. I must show you that this is a false hypothesis and that Job may be convinced without maintaining it."

4. He had something new to offer. He will not reply to Job's protestations of his integrity, but allows the truth of them, and therefore does not interpose as his enemy: "*He hath not directed his words against me.*" He will not repeat their arguments, nor go upon their principles: "*Neither will I answer him with your speeches*—not with the same matter, for should I only say what has been said I might justly be silenced as impertinent,—nor in the same manner; I will not be guilty of that peevishness towards him myself which I dislike in you."

Verses 15–22

Three things here apologize for Elihu's interposing as he does in this controversy which had already been canvassed by such learned disputants:—

1. The stage was clear, and he did not break in upon any of the managers on either side: *They were amazed* (*v.* 15); *they stood still, and answered no more, v.* 16. The judgment is the Lord's, and by him it must be determined who is in the right and who is in the wrong; but, since you have each of you shown your opinion, I also will show mine, and let it take its fate with the rest.

2. He was uneasy, and even in pain, to be delivered of his thoughts upon this matter. "*I am full of matter*, having carefully attended to all that has hitherto been said, and made my own reflections upon it. *The spirit within me* not only instructs me what to say, but puts me on to say it; so that if I have not vent I shall *burst like bottles of new wine* when it is working," *v.* 19. *I will speak, that I may be refreshed*, not only that I may be eased of the pain of stifling my thoughts, but that I may have the pleasure of endeavouring, according to my place and capacity, to do good.

3. That he was resolved to speak, with sincerity, what he thought was true, not what he thought would please (*v.* 21, 22): "*Let me not accept any man's person*, as partial judges do, that aim to enrich themselves, not to do justice. I am resolved to flatter no man." He that made us hates all dissimulation and flattery, and will soon *put lying lips to silence* and *cut off flattering lips*, Ps. xii. 3.

JAMIESON, FAUSSET, BROWN

13. This has been so ordered, "lest you should" pride yourselves on having overcome him by your "wisdom" (Jer. 9:23, the great aim of the Book of Job); and that you may see, "God alone can thrust him down," i.e., confute him, "not man." So Elihu grounds his confutation, not on the maxims of sages, as the friends did, but on his special commission from God (vs. 8; ch. 33:4, 6).

14. I am altogether unprejudiced. For it is not I, whom he addressed. "Your speeches" have been influenced by irritation.

15. Here Elihu turns from the friends to Job: and so passes from the second person to the third; a transition frequent in a rebuke (ch. 18:3, 4). **they left off**—Words were taken from them.

17. my part—for my part. **opinion**—knowledge. **18.** "I am full of words," whereas the friends have not a word more to say. **the spirit**—(vs. 8; ch. 33:4; Jer. 20:9; Acts 18:5). **19. belly**—bosom: from which the words of Orientalists in speaking seem to come more than with us; they speak gutturally. "Like (new) wine (in fermentation) without a vent," to work itself off. *New* wine is kept in new goatskin bottles. This fittingly applies to the *young* Elihu, as contrasted with the *old* friends (Matt. 9:7). **20. refreshed**—lit., "that there may be air to me" (I Sam. 16:23). **21.** "May I never accept. . . ." Elihu alludes to Job's words (ch. 13:8, 10), wherein he complains that the friends plead for God partially, "accepting His person." Elihu says he will not do so, but will act impartially between God and Job. "And I will not give flattery . . . ." (Prov. 24:23). **22. take me away**—as a punishment (Ps. 102:24).

ADAM CLARKE

12. *Behold, there was none of you that convinced Job.* "Confuted Job." They spoke multitudes of words, but were unable to overthrow his arguments.

14. *He hath not directed.* He has not spoken a word against me; therefore I have no cause of irritation. I shall speak for truth, not for conquest or revenge. *Neither will I answer him with your speeches;* your passions have been inflamed by contradiction, and you have spoken foolishly with your lips.

16. *When I had waited.* I waited to hear if they had anything to reply to Job; and when I found them in effect speechless, then I ventured to come forward.

17. *I will answer also my part.* "I will recite my portion." We have already seen that the Book of Job is a sort of drama, in which several persons have their different parts to recite. Probably the book was used in this way, in ancient times, for the sake of public instruction. Eliphaz, Zophar, and Bildad had recited their parts, and Job had responded to each; nothing was brought to issue. Elihu, a bystander, perceiving this, comes forward and takes a part, when all the rest had expended their materials. Yet Elihu, though he spoke well, was incapable of closing the controversy; and God himself appears, and decides the case.

18. *I am full of matter.* "I am full of words," or sayings; i.e., wise sentences, and ancient opinions.

19. *My belly is as wine which hath no vent.* New wine in a state of effervescence. *Like new bottles.* Rather "bags," made of goatskins. When the wine is in a state of fermentation, and the skin has no vent, these bags are ready to *burst;* and if they be old, the new wine destroys them, breaks the old stitching, or rends the old skin. Our Lord makes use of the same figure, Matt. ix. 17.

21. *Let me not . . . accept any man's person.* I will speak the truth without fear or favor. *Neither let me give flattering titles.* I will not give epithets to any man that are not descriptive of his true state.

MATTHEW HENRY

CHAPTER 33

Verses 1–7

Elihu does not join with his three friends against him. He has, in the foregoing chapter, declared his dislike of their proceedings, disclaimed their hypothesis, and quite set aside the method they took of healing Job. "*Wherefore, Job, I pray thee, hear my speech, v.* 1. I am trying a new way, *therefore hearken to all my words.*" He *opened his mouth* (*v.* 2), with deliberation and design. "*My words shall be of the uprightness of my heart*, the genuine product of my convictions and sentiments." What he said should be easy, and not dark and hard to be understood: *My lips shall utter knowledge clearly.* He owns himself unfit to enter into the lists with his seniors, yet he desires they will not despise his youth. He would be very willing to hear what Job could object against what he had to say (*v.* 5): "*If thou canst, answer me.*" He had often wished for one that would appear for God, with whom he might freely expostulate, and to whom, as arbitrator, he might refer the matter, and such a one Elihu would be (*v.* 6): *I am, according to thy wish, in God's stead.* "*I also am formed out of the clay.* I also as well as thou." Job had urged this with God as a reason why he should not bear hard upon him (*ch.* x. 9), *Remember that thou hast made me as the clay.* "I," says Elihu, "am *formed out of the clay* as well as thou," *formed of the same clay*, so some read it. "*My terror shall not make thee afraid.*" If we would rightly convince men, it must be by reason, not by terror, by fair arguing, not by a heavy hand.

Verses 8–13

I. Elihu particularly charges Job with some expressions that had dropped from him, reflecting upon the justice and goodness of God in his dealings with him. "*Thou hast spoken it in my hearing*, and in the hearing of all this company." When we hear any-

JAMIESON, FAUSSET, BROWN

CHAPTER 33

Vss. 1-33. ADDRESS TO JOB, AS (ch. 32) TO THE FRIENDS. **2. mouth**—rather, "palate," whereby the taste *discerns*. Every man speaks with his mouth, but few, as Elihu, *try* their words *with discrimination* first, and only say what is really good (ch. 6:30; 12:11). **hath spoken**—rather, "proceeds to speak." **3.** I will speak according to my inward conviction. **clearly**—rather, "purely"; sincerely, not distorting the truth through passion, as the friends did. **4.** "The Spirit of God hath made me," as He did thee: latter clause of vs. 6 (Gen. 2:7). Therefore thou needest not fear me, as thou wouldest God (vs. 7; ch. 9:34). On the other hand, "the breath of the Almighty hath *inspired* me" (as ch. 32:8); not as *English Version,* "given me life"; therefore "I am according to thy wish (ch. 9:32, 33) in God's stead" to thee; a "daysman," umpire, or mediator, between God and thee. So Elihu was designed by the Holy Ghost to be a type of Jesus Christ (vss. 23-26). **5.** Images from a court of justice. **stand up**—alluding to Job's words (ch. 30:20). **6.** Note (vs. 4; ch. 31:35; 13:3, 20, 21). **formed**—Though acting as God's representative, I am but a creature, like thyself. *Arabic,* "pressed together," as a mass of clay by the potter, in forming a vessel [UMBREIT]. *Hebrew* "cut off," as the portion taken from the clay to form it [MAURER]. **7. hand**—alluding to Job's words (ch. 13:21).

8. thy words—(ch. 10:7; 16:17; 23:11, 12; 27:5, 6; 29:14). In ch. 9:30; 13:23, Job had acknowledged sin; but the general *spirit* of his words was to maintain himself to be "clean," and to charge God with injustice. He went too far on the

ADAM CLARKE

CHAPTER 33

6. *I am according to thy wish in God's stead: I also am formed out of the clay.* Mr. Good, and before him none other that I have seen, has most probably hit the true meaning: "Behold, I am thy fellow. I too was formed by God out of the clay."

7. *My terror shall not make thee afraid.* This is an allusion to what Job had said, chap. ix. 34: "Let him take his rod away from me, and let not his fear terrify me." Being thy equal, no fear can impose upon thee so far as to overawe thee, so that thou shouldst not be able to conduct thy own defense.

8. *Surely thou hast spoken.* What Elihu speaks here, and in the three following verses, contains, in general, simple quotations from Job's own words, or the obvious sense of them.

MATTHEW HENRY

thing said that tends to God's dishonour we ought publicly to bear our testimony against it. What is said amiss in our hearing we are concerned to reprove; for *you are my witnesses, saith the Lord,* to confront the accuser. Job had represented himself as innocent (*v.* 9): *I am clean without transgression.* Job had not said this *in so many words*; he had owned himself to have sinned and to be impure before God; but he had indeed said, *Thou knowest that I am not wicked, my righteousness I hold fast.* Elihu did not deal fairly in charging Job with saying that he was clean and innocent from all transgression, when he only pleaded that he was upright and innocent from the great transgression. He had represented God as severe in marking what he did amiss (*v.* 10, 11), as if he sought opportunity to pick quarrels with him. *He findeth occasions against me.*

II. He endeavours to convince him that he had spoken amiss in speaking thus, and that he ought to humble himself before God for it, and by repentance to unsay it (*v.* 12): *Behold, in this thou art not just.* See the difference between the charge which Elihu exhibited against Job and that which was preferred against him by his other friends; they would not own that he was just at all, but Elihu only says, "In this, in saying this, thou art not just." Job himself said a great deal, and admirably well, concerning the greatness of God, his irresistible power and incontestable sovereignty, his terrible majesty and unsearchable immensity. "Now," said Elihu, "do but consider what thou thyself hast said concerning the greatness of God, and apply it to thyself; if he is greater than man, he is greater than thou, and thou wilt see reason enough to repent of these ill-natured reflections upon him, and tremble to think of thy own presumption." There is enough in this one plain truth, *That God is greater than man,* to put to silence all our complaints of his providence and our exceptions against his dealings with us. He is not only more wise and powerful than we are, but more holy, just, and good, for these are the transcendent glories and excellencies of the divine nature; in these God is greater than man, and therefore it is absurd and unreasonable to find fault with him. God is not accountable to us (*v.* 13): *Why dost thou strive against him?* It is an unreasonable thing for us, weak, foolish, sinful, creatures, to strive with a God of infinite wisdom, power, and goodness. *He gives not account of all his matters* (so some read it); he reveals as much as it is fit for us to know, as follows here (*v.* 14).

Verses 14–18

Job had complained that God kept him wholly in the dark concerning the meaning of his dealings with him, and therefore concluded he dealt with him as his enemy. "No," says Elihu, "he speaks to you, but you do not perceive him; so that the fault is yours, not his; and he is designing your real good even in those dispensations which you put this harsh construction upon." 1. What a friend God is to our welfare: *He speaketh to us once, yea, twice, v.* 14. When one warning is neglected he gives another. 2. What enemies we are to our own welfare: *Man perceives it not,* is not aware that it is the voice of God. He stops his ear, stands in his own light, rejects the counsel of God against himself. God teaches and admonishes the children of men by their own consciences.

I. The proper season and opportunity for these admonitions (*v.* 15): *In a dream, in slumberings upon the bed,* when men are retired from the world and the business and conversation of it. Thus he made his mind known to the prophets by visions and dreams (Num. xii. 6). When he stirred up conscience, that ordinary deputy of his, in the soul, to do its office, he took that opportunity, either when deep sleep fell on men (for, though dreams mostly come from fancy, some may come from conscience) or in slumberings, when men are between sleeping and waking, reflecting at night upon the business of the foregoing day or projecting in the morning the business of the ensuing day; then is a proper time for their hearts to reproach them for what they have done ill and to admonish them what they should do.

II. The power and force with which those admonitions come, *v.* 16. *Then he opens the ears of men,* which were before shut. He opens the heart, as he opened Lydia's, and so opens the ears. *He sealeth their instruction,* that is, the instruction that is designed for them and is suited to them; this he makes their souls to receive the deep and lasting impression of, as the wax of the seal.

III. The end and design of these admonitions that are sent. 1. To keep men from sin, and particularly the sin of pride (*v.* 17). *That he may withdraw man from his purpose,* that is, from his evil purposes. Many a man has been stopped in the full career of a

JAMIESON, FAUSSET, BROWN

opposite side in opposing the friends' false charge of hypocrisy. Even the godly, though willing to confess themselves sinners in *general,* often dislike sin in particular to be brought as a charge against them. Affliction is therefore needed to bring them to feel that sin *in them* deserves even worse than they suffer and that God does them no injustice. Then at last humbled under God they find, *affliction is for their real good,* and so at last it is taken away either here, or at least at death. To teach this is Elihu's mission. **9. clean**—spotless. **10. occasions**—for hostility: lit., "enmities" (ch. 13:24; 16:9; 19:11; 30:21). **11.** (Ch. 13:27.) **marketh**—narrowly watches (ch. 14:16; 7: 12; 31:4).

12. in this—view of God and His government. It cannot be that God should jealously "watch" man, though "spotless," as an "enemy," or as one afraid of him as an equal. For "God is greater than man!" There must be sin in man, even though he be no hypocrite, which needs correction by suffering for the sufferer's good.

13. (Isa. 45: 9.) **his matters**—ways. Our part is, not to "strive" with God, but to *submit.* To believe it is right because He does it, not because *we see all the reasons* for His doing it.

14. Translate, "Yet, man *regardeth* it not"; or rather, as UMBREIT, "Yea, twice (He repeats the warning)—if man gives no heed" to the first warning. Elihu implies that God's reason for sending affliction is because, when God has communicated His will in various ways, man in prosperity has not heeded it; God therefore must try what affliction will effect (John 15:2; Ps. 62:11; Isa. 28:10, 13).

15. slumberings—light is opposed to "deep sleep." Elihu has in view Eliphaz (ch. 4:13), and also Job himself (ch. 7:14). "Dreams" in sleep, and "visions" of actual apparitions, were among the ways whereby God then spake to man (Gen. 20:3).

16. Lit., "sealeth (their ears) to Himself by warnings," i.e., with the sureness and secrecy of a seal He reveals His warnings [UMBREIT]. To seal up securely (ch. 37:7). On the "openeth," see ch. 36: 10.

17. purpose—Margin, "work." So ch. 36:9. So "business" in a bad sense (I Sam. 20:19). Elihu alludes to Job's words (ch. 17:11).

ADAM CLARKE

12. *In this thou art not just.* Thou hast laid charges against God's dealings, but thou hast not been able to justify those charges; and were there nothing else against thee, these irreverent speeches are so many proofs that thou art not clear in the sight of God.

13. *Why dost thou strive against him?* Is it not useless to contend with God? Can He do anything that is not right? As to His giving thee any account of the reasons why He deals thus and thus with thee, or anyone else, thou needest not expect it; He is sovereign, and is not to be called to the bar of His creatures.

14. *For God speaketh once.* Elihu, having made the general statement that God would not come to the bar of His creatures to give account of His conduct, shows the general means which He uses to bring men to an acquaintance with themselves and with Him. He states these in the six following particulars, which may be collected from vv. 15-24.

15. (1) *In a dream . . . when deep sleep falleth upon men.* Many, by such means, have had the most salutary warnings. (2) *In a vision of the night . . . in slumberings upon the bed.* Visions or images presented in the imagination during slumber, when men are betwixt sleeping and waking, or when, awake and in bed, they are wrapt up in deep contemplation, the darkness of the night having shut out all objects from their sight, so that the mind is not diverted by images of earthly things impressed on the senses.

16. *Then he openeth the ears of men.* (3) By secret inspirations. A dream or a vision simply considered is likely to do no good; it is the opening of the understanding, and the pouring in of the light, that make men wise to salvation.

MATTHEW HENRY

sinful pursuit by the seasonable checks of his own conscience, saying, *Do not this abominable thing which the Lord hates.* Particularly, God does, by this means, *hide pride from man.* That he may *take away pride from man* (so some read it), that he may pluck up that root of bitterness which is the cause of so much sin. 2. To keep men from ruin, *v.* 18. God, by the admonitions of conscience, withdraws them from sin, he thereby *keeps back* their souls *from the pit.* What a mercy it is to be under the restraints of an awakened conscience. Faithful are the wounds, and kind are the bonds, of that friend.

Verses 19–28

God speaks a second time, and tries another way to convince and reclaim sinners, and that is by providences, afflictive and merciful (in which he speaks twice). Job complained much of his diseases and judged by them that God was angry with him; but Elihu shows that God often afflicts the body in love, and with gracious designs of good to the soul. This part of Elihu's discourse will be of great use to us for the due improvement of sickness, by which God speaks to men.

I. See what work sickness makes (*v.* 19, &c.) when God sends it with commission. 1. The sick man is full of pain all over him (*v.* 19): *He is chastened with pain upon his bed.* Pain and sickness will turn a bed of down into a bed of thorns. Frequently the stronger the patient the stronger the pain. It is not the smarting of the flesh that is complained of, but the aching of the bones. It is an inward rooted pain; and not only the bones of one limb, but *the multitude of the bones,* are thus chastened. By the grace of God, the pain of the body is often made a means of good to the soul. 2. He has quite lost his appetite, the common effect of sickness (*v.* 20): *His life abhorreth bread,* the most necessary food. 3. He has become a perfect skeleton, nothing but skin and bones, *v.* 21. 4. *His soul draws near to the grave,* and in the apprehension of all about him, as well as in his own, he is a dying man. The pangs of death, here called *the destroyers,* are ready to seize him.

II. The provision made for his instruction, that, when God in that way speaks to man, he may be heard and understood, *v.* 23. He is happy *if there be a messenger with him an interpreter* to expound the providence and give him to understand the meaning of it, *a man of wisdom* that knows the voice of the rod and its interpretation. The advice and help of a good minister are as needful and seasonable, and should be as acceptable, in sickness, as of a good physician, especially if he be well skilled in the art of explaining and improving providences. His business at such a time is *to show his uprightness,* that is, God's uprightness, that in faithfulness he afflicts him. If it appear that the sick person is truly pious, the interpreter will not do as Job's friends had done, make it his business to prove him a hypocrite because he is afflicted, but will show him his uprightness, notwithstanding his afflictions, that he may be easy.

III. God's gracious acceptance of him, upon his repentance, *v.* 24. Wherever God finds a gracious heart he will be found a gracious God; and, 1. He will give a gracious order for his discharge. He says, *Deliver him* (that is, let him be delivered) *from going down to the pit,* from that death which is the wages of sin. 2. He will give a gracious reason for this order: *I have found a ransom,* or propitiation; Jesus Christ is that ransom, so Elihu calls him, as Job had called him his Redeemer, for he is both the purchaser and the price, the priest and the sacrifice. God glories in the invention here, ἑυρηκα, ἑυρηκα—*"I have found, I have found, the ransom;* I, even I, am he that has done it."

IV. The recovery of the sick man hereupon. When the patient becomes a penitent see what a blessed change follows. 1. His body recovers its health, *v.* 25. This is not always the consequence of a sick man's repentance and return to God, but sometimes it is; and recovery from sickness is a mercy indeed when it arises from the remission of sin. Interest him in the ransom, and then *his flesh shall be fresher than a child's* and there shall be no remains of his distemper, but *he shall return to the days of his youth,* to the beauty and strength which he had then. 2. His soul recovers its peace, *v.* 26. (1) The patient, being a penitent, is a supplicant, and has learned to pray. (2) His prayers are accepted. All true penitents rejoice more in the returns of God's favour than in any instance whatsoever of prosperity or pleasure, Ps. iv. 6, 7.

V. The general rule which God will go by in dealing with the children of men inferred from this instance, *v.* 27, 28. As sick people, upon their submission, are restored so all others that truly repent of their sins shall find mercy with God. Would we know the nature of sin and the malignity of it? It is the

JAMIESON, FAUSSET, BROWN

"Pride" is an open "pit" (vs. 18) which God hides or covers up, lest man should fall into it. Even the godly need to learn the lesson which trials teach, to *"humble* themselves under the mighty hand of God." **18. his soul**—his life. **the pit**—the grave; a symbol of hell. **perishing by the sword**—i.e., a violent death; in the Old Testament a symbol of the future punishment of the ungodly. **19.** When man does not heed warnings of the night, he is chastened, etc. The new thought suggested by Elihu is that affliction is *disciplinary* (ch. 36:10); *for the good* of the godly. **multitude**—so the *Margin, Hebrew* (KERI). Better with the text (CHETIB), "And with the perpetual (strong) *contest* of his bones"; the never-resting fever in his bones (Ps. 38:3) [UMBREIT]. 20. life—i.e., the appetite, which ordinarily sustains "life" (ch. 38:39; Ps. 107:18; Eccles. 12:5). The taking away of desire for food by sickness symbolizes the removal by affliction of lust, for things which foster the spiritual fever of pride. **soul**—desire. **21.** His flesh once prominent "can no more be seen." His bones once not seen now appear prominent. **stick out**—lit., "are bare." The *Margin, Hebrew* (KERI) reading. The text (CHETIB) reads it a noun (are become) "bareness." The KERI was no doubt an explanatory reading of transcribers. **22. destroyers**—angels of death commissioned by God to end man's life (II Sam. 24:16; Ps. 78:49). The *death pains* personified may, however, be meant; so "gnawers" (*Note,* ch. 30:17). **23.** Elihu refers to himself as the divinely-sent (ch. 32:8; 33:6) "messenger," the "interpreter" to explain to Job and vindicate God's righteousness; such a one Eliphaz had denied that Job could look for (ch. 5:1), and Job (ch. 9:33) had wished for such a "daysman" or umpire between him and God. The "messenger" of good is antithetical to the "destroyers" (vs. 23). **with him**—if there be vouchsafed *to the sufferer.* The office of the interpreter is stated "to show unto man *God's* uprightness" in His dealings; or, as UMBREIT, "man's upright course towards God" (Prov. 14:2). The former is better; Job maintained his own "uprightness" (ch. 16:17; 27:5, 6); Elihu on the contrary maintains God's, and that man's true uprightness lies in submission to God. "One among a thousand" is a man rarely to be found. So Jesus Christ (Song of Sol. 5:10). Elihu, the God-sent mediator of a *temporal* deliverance, is a type of the God-man Jesus Christ the Mediator of *eternal* deliverance: "the *messenger* of the covenant" (Mal. 3:1). This is the wonderful work of the Holy Ghost, that persons and events move in their own sphere in such a way as unconsciously to shadow forth Him, whose "testimony is the Spirit of prophecy"; as the same point may be center of a small and of a vastly larger concentric circle. **24.** Apodosis to vs. 23. **he**—God. **Deliver**—lit., "redeem"; in it and "ransom" there is reference to the *consideration,* on account of which God pardons and relieves the sufferers; here it is primarily the intercession of Elihu. But the language is too strong for its full meaning to be *exhausted* by this. The Holy Ghost has suggested language which receives its *full* realization only in the "eternal redemption found" by God in the price paid by Jesus Christ for it; i.e., His blood and meritorious intercession (Heb. 9:12). "Obtained," lit., "found"; implying the earnest zeal, wisdom, and faithfulness of the *finder,* and the newness and joyousness of the *finding.* Jesus Christ could not but have *found* it, but still His *seeking* it was needed [BENGEL], (Luke 15:8.) God the Father, is the Finder (Ps. 89:19). Jesus Christ the Redeemer, to whom He saith, *Redeem* (so *Hebrew*) him from going, etc. (II Cor. 5:19). **ransom**—used in a general sense by Elihu, but meant by the Holy Ghost in its strict sense as applied to Jesus Christ, of a *price* paid for deliverance (Exod. 21:30), an *atonement* (i.e., means of selling *at once,* i.e., reconciling *two* who are estranged), *a covering,* as of the ark with pitch, typical of what covers us sinners from wrath (Gen. 6:14; Ps. 32:1). The pit is primarily here the *grave* (Isa. 38:17), but the spiritual pit is mainly shadowed forth (Zech. 9:11). **25-28.** Effects of restoration to God's favor; lit., to Job a temporal revival; spiritually, an eternal *regeneration.* The striking words cannot be restricted to their temporal meaning, as used by Elihu (I Pet. 1:11, 12). **his flesh shall be fresher than a child's**—so Naaman, II Kings 5:14 spiritually, John 3:3-7. **26.** Job shall no longer pray to God, as he complains, in vain (ch. 23:3, 8, 9). True especially to the redeemed in Jesus Christ (John 16:23-27). **he [Job] shall see his face**—or, God shall make him to see His face [MAURER]. God shall no longer "hide His face" (ch. 13:24). True to the believer now (John 14:21, 22); eternally (Ps. 17:15; John 17:24). **his**

ADAM CLARKE

19. *He is chastened also with pain upon his bed.* (4) Afflictions are a fourth means which God makes use of to awaken and convert sinners. In the hand of God these were the cause of the salvation of David, as himself testifies: "Before I was afflicted I went astray," Ps. cxix. 67, 71, 75.

23. *If there be a messenger with him, an interpreter.* (5) The messengers of righteousness this is a fifth method, "If there be over him an interpreting or mediatorial angel or messenger." *One among a thousand,* "One from the chief, head, or teacher."

24. *Then he is gracious unto him.* He exercises mercy towards fallen man, and gives command for His respite and pardon.

(6) *I have found a ransom. Copher,* "an atonement." It is this that gives efficacy to all the preceding means, without which they would be useless, and the salvation of man impossible. I must think that the redemption of a lost world, by Jesus Christ, is not obscurely signified in vv. 23-24.

25. *His flesh shall be fresher than a child's.* He shall be born a new creature. *He shall return to the days of his youth.* He shall be born again, and become a child of God, through faith in Christ Jesus.

MATTHEW HENRY

perverting of that which is right; it is a most unjust unreasonable thing; it is the rebellion of the creature against the Creator, the usurped dominion of the flesh over the spirit. Would we know what is to be got by sin? *It profiteth us not.* What reason we have to repent. We must confess the fault of sin, the iniquity, the dishonesty of it (*I have perverted that which was right*); we must confess the folly of sin—"so foolish have I been and ignorant, for *it profited me not.*" God looked upon sinners with an eye of compassion, desiring to hear this from them; for he has no pleasure in their ruin. He shall be happy in everlasting life and joy: *His life shall see the light,* that is, all good, in the vision and fruition of God.

Verses 29–33

Elihu briefly sums up what he had said, showing that God's great and gracious design, in all the dispensations of his providence towards the children of men, is to save them from being for ever miserable and bring them to be for ever happy, *v.* 29, 30. He deals with them by conscience, by providences, by ministers, by mercies, by afflictions. He makes them sick, and makes them well again. All providences are to be looked upon as God's workings with man, his strivings with him. Why does he take all this pains with man? It is *to bring back his soul from the pit, v.* 30. Job is welcome to make what objections he can (*v.* 32): *If thou hast anything to say* for thyself, in thy own vindication, *answer me. Speak, for I desire to justify thee.* Elihu lets him know that he has something more to say, which he desires him patiently to attend to (*v.* 33): *Hold thy peace, and I will teach thee wisdom.*

CHAPTER 34

Verses 1–9

I. Elihu addresses himself to the auditors, and endeavours to gain their goodwill and attention. 1. He calls them *wise men*, and men that *had knowledge, v.* 2. It is comfortable dealing with such as understand sense. Elihu differed in opinion from them, and yet he calls them wise and knowing men. 2. He appeals to their judgment, and therefore submits to their trial, *v.* 3. *The ear* of the judicious *tries words,* whether what is said to be true or false, right or wrong, and he that speaks must stand the test of the intelligent. 3. He takes them into partnership with him in the examination and discussion of this matter, *v.* 4. He does not pretend to be sole dictator. "Let us agree to lay aside all animosities and prejudices and *let us choose to ourselves judgment*; and *let us know among ourselves*, by comparing notes and communicating our reasons, *what is good* and what is otherwise."

II. He warmly accuses Job for some passionate words which he had spoken, that reflected on the divine government.

1. He recites the words which Job had spoken, as nearly as he can remember. Job hath said, *I am righteous* (*v.* 5), and, when urged to confess his guilt, had stiffly maintained his plea of, *Not guilty: Should I lie against my right? v.* 6. *My wound is incurable*, and likely to be mortal, and yet *without transgression*; *not for any injustice in my hand, ch.* xvi. 16, 17. He had, in effect, said that there is nothing to be got in the service of God and that no man will be the better at last for his religion (*v.* 9). This Elihu gathers as Job's opinion, by an innuendo from what he said (*ch.* ix. 22), *He destroys the perfect and the wicked*, which has a truth in it (for all things come alike to all), but it was ill expressed. Job sat down silently under it and attempted not his own vindication, whence Mr. Caryl well observes that good men sometimes speak worse than they mean, and that a good man will rather bear more blame than he deserves than stand to excuse himself when he has deserved any blame.

2. He charges Job: *What man is like Job? v.* 7. Did you ever know such a man as Job, or ever hear a man talk at such an extravagant rate? "He *drinketh up scorning like water.*" By these foolish expressions of his he makes himself the object of scorn, lays himself very open to reproach, and gives occasion to others to laugh at him. He *goes in company with the workers of iniquity* (*v.* 8), not that in his conversation he did associate with them, but in his opinion he did favour and countenance them, and strengthen their hands.

Verses 10–15

The scope of Elihu's discourse is to reconcile Job to his afflictions. God meant him no hurt in afflicting him, but intended it for his spiritual benefit. In these verses he directs his discourse to all the company:

JAMIESON, FAUSSET, BROWN

[God's] **righteousness**—God will again make the restored Job no longer ("I perverted . . . right," vs. 27) doubt God's justice, but to justify Him in His dealings. The penitent justifies God (Ps. 51:4). So the believer is made to see God's righteousness in Jesus Christ (Isa. 45:24; 46:13). **27. he looketh**—God. Rather, with UMBREIT, "Now he (*the restored penitent*) *singeth joyfully* (answering to 'joy,' vs. 26; Ps. 51:12) before men, and saith," etc. (Prov. 25:20; Ps. 66:16; 116:14). **perverted**—made the straight crooked: as Job had misrepresented God's character. **profited**—lit., "was made even" to me; rather, "My punishment was not commensurate with my sin" (so Zophar, ch. 11:6); the reverse of what Job heretofore said (ch. 16:17; Ps. 103:10; Ezra 9:13). **28.** *Note,* vs. 24; rather, as *Hebrew* text (*English Version* reads as *Margin, Hebrew,* KERI, "his soul, his life"), "He hath delivered *my* soul . . . *my* life." Continuation of the penitent's testimony to the people. **light**—(vs. 30; ch. 3:16, 20; Ps. 56:13; Eccles. 11:7). **29.** Margin, "twice and thrice," alluding to vs. 14; once, by visions, vss. 15-17; secondly, by afflictions, vss. 19-22; now, by the "messenger," thirdly, vs. 23.

30. Referring to vs. 28 (Ps. 50:13). **32. justify**—to do thee justice; and, if I can, consistently with it, to declare thee innocent. At vs. 33 Elihu pauses for a reply; then proceeds in ch. 34.

CHAPTER 34

Vss. 1-37. **1. answered**—proceeded. **2.** This chapter is addressed also to the "friends" as ch. 33, to Job alone.

3. palate (*Note*, ch. 12:11; ch. 33:2).

4. judgment—Let us select among the conflicting sentiments advanced, what will stand the test of examination.

5. judgment—my right. Job's own words (ch. 13:18; 27:2). **6.** Were I to renounce my right (i.e., confess myself guilty), I should die. Job virtually had said so (ch. 27:4, 5; 6:28). MAURER, not so well, "Notwithstanding my right (innocence) I am treated as a liar," by God, by His afflicting me. **my wound**—lit., "mine arrow," viz., by which I am pierced. So "*my* stroke" (hand, *Margin,* ch. 23:2). My sickness (ch. 6:4; 16:13). **without transgression**—without fault of mine to deserve it (ch. 16:17).

7. (Ch. 15:16.) Image from the camel. **scorning**—against God (ch. 15:4). **8.** Job virtually goes in company (makes common cause) with the wicked, by taking up their sentiments (ch. 9:22, 23, 30; 21: 7-15), or at least by saying, that those who act on such sentiments are unpunished (Mal. 3:14). To deny God's righteous government because we do not see the reasons of His acts, is virtually to take part with the ungodly. **9. with God**—in intimacy (Ps. 50: 18).

ADAM CLARKE

27. *He looketh upon men. Anashim,* wretched, fallen men. He "shines into them," to convince them of sin; and if any, under this convincing light of God, say, *"I have sinned, and perverted* the *right"*—abused the powers, faculties, mercies, and advantages, which Thou didst give me, by seeking rest and happiness in the creature—*and it profited me not,* "and it was not equal to me," did not come up to my expectation, nor supply my wants;

28. *He will deliver his soul.* He will do that to every individual penitent sinner which He has promised in His Word to do for a lost world—He will deliver his soul from going down to the *pit* of hell.

29. *Lo, all these things worketh God.* God frequently uses one, or another, or all of these means to bring men, *gaber,* stouthearted men, who are far from righteousness, to holiness and heaven.

CHAPTER 34

5. *Job hath said, I am righteous.* Job had certainly said the words attributed to him by Elihu, particularly in chap. xxvii. 2, etc.; but it was in vindication of his aspersed character that he had asserted is own righteousness, and in a different sense to that in which Elihu appears to take it up. He asserted that he was righteous as to the charges his friends had brought against him. And he never intimated that he had at all times a pure heart, and had never transgressed the laws of his Maker. It is true also that he said, *God hath taken away my judgment;* but he most obviously does not mean to charge God with injustice, but to show that He had dealt with him in a way wholly mysterious; and that He did not interpose in his behalf, while his friends were overwhelming him with obloquy and reproach.

8. *Which goeth in company with the workers of iniquity.* Job makes a "track to join fellowship" with the workers of iniquity; i.e., Job's present mode of reasoning, when he says, "I am righteous, yet God hath taken away my judgment," is according to the assertion of sinners, who say, "There is no profit in serving God."

MATTHEW HENRY

"*Hearken to me, you men of understanding*" (*v.* 10). The righteous God never did, nor ever will do, any wrong to any of his creatures, but his ways are equal, ours are unequal.

I. This truth is laid down, both negatively and positively. *God cannot do wickedness*, nor *the Almighty commit iniquity*, *v.* 10. It is inconsistent with the perfection of his nature, and so it is also with the purity of his will (*v.* 12): *God will not do wickedly, neither will the Almighty pervert judgment.* He will never either do any man wrong or deny any man right, but *the heavens will shortly declare his righteousness.* Though he be Almighty, yet he never uses his power for the support of injustice. He is *Shaddai*—God *all-sufficient*, and therefore he cannot be *tempted with evil* (James i. 13). He ministers justice to all (*v.* 11): *The work of a man shall he render unto him.*

II. How warmly it is asserted, 1. With an assurance of the truth of it: *Yea, surely*, *v.* 12. 2. With an abhorrence of the very thought of the contrary (*v.* 10): *Far be it from God that he should do wickedness*, and from us that we should imagine such a thing.

III. How evidently it is proved by two arguments: 1. His independent absolute sovereignty and dominion (*v.* 13): *Who has given him a charge over the earth?* He has the sole administration of the kingdoms of men, and has it of himself.

2. His irresistible power (*v.* 14): *If he set his heart upon man*, to contend with him, much more *if* (as some read it) *he set his heart against man*, to ruin him, if he should deal with man either by *summa potestas—mere sovereignty*, or by *summum jus—strict justice*, there were no standing before him; man's spirit and breath would soon be gone and *all flesh would perish together*, *v.* 15.

Verses 16–30

Elihu here addresses himself more directly to Job.

I. God is not to be quarrelled with for anything that he does. *Shall even he that hates right govern? v.* 17. The righteous Lord so loves righteousness that, in comparison with him, even Job himself, though a perfect and upright man, might be said to hate right; and shall he govern? Shall he pretend to direct God or correct what he does? *Wilt thou condemn him that is righteous in all his ways*, and cannot but he so? *He regardeth not the rich more than the poor*, and therefore it is fit he should rule, and it is not fit we should find fault with him, *v.* 19. A great man shall fare never the better, nor find any favour, for his wealth and greatness; nor shall a poor man fare ever the worse for his poverty, nor an honest cause be starved.

II. God is to be acknowledged and submitted to in all that he does. Divers considerations Elihu here suggests to Job, to beget in him great and high thoughts of God, and so to persuade him to submit and proceed no further in his quarrel with him.

1. God is almighty, and able to deal with the strongest of men when he enters into judgment with them (*v.* 20); even *the people*, the body of a nation, though ever so numerous, *shall be troubled*, unhinged, and put into disorder, when God pleases; even *the mighty* man, the prince, *shall*, if God speak the word, *be taken away* out of his throne. Nor is it one single mighty man only that he can thus overpower, but even hosts of them (*v.* 24).

2. God is omniscient, and can discover that which is most secret. As the strongest cannot oppose his arm, so the most subtle cannot escape his eye; and therefore, if some are punished either more or less than we think they should be, instead of quarrelling with God, it becomes us to ascribe it to some secret cause known to God only. Everything is open before him (*v.* 21): *His eyes are upon the ways of man. There is no darkness nor shadow of death* so close, so remote from light or sight as that in it *the workers of iniquity may hide themselves* from the discovering eye of the righteous God. The workers of iniquity may find ways and means to hide themselves from men, but not from God: *He knows their works* (*v.* 25), both what they do and what they design.

3. God is righteous. *He will not lay upon man more than right*, *v.* 23. As he will not punish the innocent, so he will not exact of those that are guilty more than their iniquities deserve; and of the proportion between the sin and the punishment Infinite Wisdom shall be the judge. Therefore Job was to be blamed for his complaints of God. These unjust judges were rebels to God: They *turned back from him*, cast off the fear of him, and abandoned the very thoughts of him; for *they would not consider any of his ways*, took no heed either to his precepts or to his providences, but lived without God in the world. They were tyrants to all mankind, *v.* 28.

4. God has an uncontrollable dominion in all the affairs of the children of men, and so guides and

JAMIESON, FAUSSET, BROWN

10. The true answer to Job, which God follows up (ch. 38). Man is to *believe* God's ways are right, because they are His, not because we fully *see* they are so (Rom. 9:14; Deut. 32:4; Gen. 18:25). **11.** Partly here; fully, hereafter (Jer. 32:19; Rom. 2:6; I Pet. 1:17; Rev. 22:12).

12. (Ch. 8:3.) In opposition to Job, vs. 5, will not—cannot. **13.** If the world were not God's property, as having been made by Him, but committed to His charge by some superior, it might be possible for Him to act unjustly, as He would not thereby be injuring Himself; but as it is, for God to act unjustly would undermine the whole order of the world, and so would injure God's own property (ch. 36:23). **disposed**—hath founded (Isa. 44:7), established the circle of the globe. **14, 15.** "If He were to set His heart on man," either to injure him, or to take strict account of his sins. The connection supports rather [UMBREIT], "If He had regard to himself (only), and were to gather unto Himself (Ps. 104:29) man's spirit, etc. (which he sends forth, Ps. 104:30; Eccles. 12:7), all flesh must perish together," etc. (Gen. 3:19). God's loving preservation of His creatures proves He cannot be selfish, and therefore cannot be unjust. **16.** In vs. 2, Elihu had spoken *to all* in general, now he calls Job's special attention. **17.** "Can even He who (in thy view) hateth right (justice) govern?" The government of the world would be impossible if injustice were sanctioned. God must be just, because He governs (II Sam. 23:3). **govern**—lit., "bind," viz., by authority (so "reign," *Margin,* I Sam. 9:17). UMBREIT translates for "govern," *repress wrath,* viz., against Job for his accusations. **most just**—rather, "Him who is at once mighty and just" (in His government of the world). **18.** Lit., (Is it fit) *to be said* to a king? It would be a gross outrage to reproach thus an earthly monarch, much more the King of kings (Exod. 22:28). But MAURER with LXX and *Vulgate* reads, (It is not fit to accuse of injustice Him) *who says* to a king, Thou art wicked; to princes, Ye are ungodly; i.e., who punishes impartially the great, as the small. This accords with vs. 19. **19.** Acts 10:34; II Chron. 19:7; Prov. 22:2; ch. 31:15.

20. they—"the rich" and "princes" who offend God. **the people**—viz., of the guilty princes: guilty also themselves. **at midnight**—image from a night attack of an enemy on a camp, which becomes an easy prey (Exod. 12:29, 30). **without hand**—without *visible* agency, by the mere word of God (so ch. 20:26; Zech. 4:6; Dan. 2:34). **21.** God's omniscience and omnipotence enable Him to execute immediate justice. He needs not to be long on the "watch," as Job thought (ch. 7:12; II Chron. 16:9; Jer. 32:19). **22. shadow of death**—thick darkness (Amos 9:2, 3; Ps. 139:12). **23.** (I Cor. 10:13; Lam. 3:32; Isa. 27:8.) Better, as UMBREIT, "He does not (needs not to) *regard* (as in vs. 14; Isa. 41:20) man *long* (so *Hebrew,* Gen. 46:29) in order that he may go (be brought by God) into judgment." Lit., "*lest* his (attention) upon men" (ch. 11:10, 11). So vs. 24, "without number" ought to be translated, "without (needing any) searching out," such as has to be made in human judgments. **24. break in pieces**—(Ps. 2:9; ch. 12:18; Dan. 2:21). **25. Therefore**—because He knows all things (vs. 21). He knows their works, without a formal investigation (vs. 24). **in the night**—suddenly, unexpectedly (vs. 20). Fitly *in the night,* as it was in it that the godless hid themselves (vs. 22). UMBREIT, *less* simply, for "overturneth," translates, "walketh"; i.e., God is ever on the alert, discovering all wickedness. **26. striketh**—chasteneth. **as**—i.e., because they are wicked. **sight of others**—Sinners hid themselves in darkness; therefore they are punished before all, in open day. Image from the place of public execution (ch. 40:12; Exod. 14:30; II Sam. 12:12). **27, 28.** The grounds of their punishment in vs. 26; vs. 28 states in what respect they "considered not God's ways," viz., by *oppression,* whereby "they caused the cry," etc.

ADAM CLARKE

10. *Far be it from God.* Rather, "Wickedness, far be that from God; and from iniquity, the Almighty." The sense is sufficiently evident without the paraphrase in our version.

13. *Who hath given him a charge?* Who is it that governs the world? Is it not God? Who disposes of all things in it? Is it not the Almighty, by His just and merciful providence? The government of the world shows the care, the justice, and the mercy of God.

14. *If he set his heart upon man.* I think this and the following verse should be read thus: "If He set His heart upon man, He will gather his soul and breath to himself; for all flesh shall perish together, and man shall turn again unto dust."

17. *Shall . . . he that hateth right govern?* Or, "Shall he who hateth judgment lie under obligation?" It is preposterous to suppose that he who lives by no rule should impose rules upon others.

18. *Is it fit to say to a king, Thou art wicked?* Literally, "Who calls a king Belial? Who calls princes wicked?" Civil governors should be treated with respect; no man should speak evil of the ruler of the people.

19. *That accepteth not.* If it be utterly improper to speak against a king or civil governor, how much more so to speak disrespectfully of God, who is not influenced by human caprices or considerations, and who regards the rich and the poor alike!

23. *For he will not lay upon man.* The meaning appears to be this: He will not call man a second time into judgment.

25. *He knoweth their works.* He knows what they have done, and what they are plotting to do. *He overturneth them in the night.* In the revolution of a single night the plenitude of power on which the day closed is annihilated. See the cases of Belshazzar and Babylon.

26. *He striketh them as wicked men.* At other times He executes His judgments more openly, and they are suddenly destroyed in the sight of the people.

MATTHEW HENRY

governs whatever concerns both communities and particular persons, that, as what he designs cannot be defeated, so what he does cannot be changed, *v.* 29. The frowns of all the world cannot trouble those whom God quiets with his smiles. *When he gives quietness* who then *can make trouble? v.* 29. If God give outward peace to a nation, he can secure what he gives. If God give inward peace to a man only, neither the accusations of Satan nor the afflictions of this present time, no, nor the arrests of death itself, can give trouble. See Phil. iv. 7. If God in displeasure, *hide his face*, and withhold the comfort of his favour, *who then can behold him?*

5. God is wise, and careful of the public welfare, and therefore provides *that the hypocrite reign not, lest the people be ensnared, v.* 30. The pride of hypocrites. They aim to reign; the praise of men, and power in the world, are their reward. The policy of tyrants. When they aim to set up themselves they sometimes make use of religion as a cloak and cover for their ambition. The danger the people are in when hypocrites reign. They are likely to be ensnared in sin, or trouble, or both.

Verses 31–37

I. Elihu instructs Job what he should say under his affliction, *v.* 31, 32. In general, he would have him repent of his expressions, under his affliction. Job's other friends would have had him own himself a wicked man, and by overdoing they undid. Elihu will oblige him only to own that he had, in the management of this controversy, *spoken unadvisedly with his lips.* He directs Job, 1. To humble himself before God for his sins, and to accept the punishment of them: "*I have borne chastisement.*" Many are chastised that do not bear chastisement, do not bear it well, and so, in effect, do not bear it at all. Penitents, if sincere, will take all well that God does, and will bear chastisement as a medicinal operation intended for good. 2. To pray to God to discover his sins to him (*v.* 32). 3. To promise reformation (*v.* 31): *I will not offend any more.* "*If I have done iniquity* (or *seeing I have*), *I will do so no more;* whatever thou shalt discover to me to have been amiss, by thy grace I will amend it for the future."

II. He reasons with him concerning his discontent and uneasiness under his affliction, *v.* 33. We are ready to think every thing that concerns us should be just as we would have it; but Elihu here shows it is absurd and unreasonable to expect this: "*Should it be according to thy mind?* No, what reason for that?"

III. He appeals to all intelligent indifferent persons whether there was not sin and folly in that which Job said. "*My desire is that Job may be tried unto the end.* Let the trial be continued till the end be obtained." He appeals both to God and man, and desires the judgment of both upon it. Some read *v.* 36 as an appeal to God: *O my Father! let Job be tried.* So the margin of our Bibles, for the same word signifies *my desire* and *my father*; and some suppose that he lifted up his eyes when he said this, meaning, "*O my Father who art in heaven!* let Job be tried till he be subdued."

JAMIESON, FAUSSET, BROWN

(Prov. 16:7; Isa. 26:3.) **make trouble**–rather, condemn (Rom. 8:33, 34). MAURER, from the reference being only to *the godless,* in the next clause, and vs. 20 translates, "When God keeps quiet" (leaves men to *perish*) Ps. 83:1; [UMBREIT] from the *Arabic* (*strikes to the earth*), "who shall *condemn* Him as unjust?" vs. 17. **hideth . . . face**–(ch. 23:8, 9; Ps. 13:1). **it be done**–Whether it be against a guilty nation (II Kings 18:9-12) or an individual, that God acts so. **30.** "Ensnared" into sin (I Kings 12:28, 30). Or rather, "enthralled by further oppression," vss. 26-28.

31. Job accordingly says so (ch. 40:3-5; Micah 7:9; Lev. 26:41). It was to lead him to this that Elihu was sent. Though no hypocrite, Job, like all, had sin; therefore through affliction he was to be brought to humble himself under God. All sorrow is a proof of the common heritage of sin, in which the godly shares; and therefore he ought to regard it as a merciful correction. UMBREIT and MAURER lose this by translating, as the *Hebrew* will bear, "Has any a right to say to God, I have borne chastisement and yet have not sinned?" (so vs. 6). **borne**–viz., the penalty of sin, as in Leviticus 5:1, 17. **offend**–lit., "to deal destructively or corruptly" (Neh. 1:7). **32.** ch. 10:2; Ps. 32:8; 19:12; 139:23, 24. **no more**–Prov. 28:13; Eph. 4:22.

33. Rather, "should God recompense (sinners) according to thy mind? Then it is for thee to reject and to choose, and not me," UMBREIT; or as MAURER, "*For thou hast rejected* God's way of recompensing; state therefore thy way, *for thou must choose, not I,*" i.e., it is thy part, not mine, to show a better way than God's. **34, 35.** Rather, men . . . will say to me, and the wise man (vs. 2, 10) who hearkens to me (will say), "Job hath spoken . . . ." **36.** Margin, not so well, "My father," Elihu addressing God. This title does not elsewhere occur in Job. **tried**–by calamities. **answers for wicked men**–(See *Note,* vs. 8.) Trials of the godly are not removed until they produce the effect designed. **37. clappeth . . . hands**–in scorn (ch. 27:23; Ezek. 21:17). **multiplieth . . . words**–(ch. 11:2; 35:16). To his original "sin" to correct which trials have been sent, "he adds *rebellion,*" i.e., words arraigning God's justice.

ADAM CLARKE

31. *Surely it is meet to be said unto God.* This is Elihu's exhortation to Job: Humble thyself before God, and say, "I have suffered—I will not offend."

37. *He addeth rebellion unto his sin.* An ill-natured, cruel, and unfounded assertion, borne out by nothing which Job had ever said or intended; and indeed, more severe than the most inveterate of his friends (so called) had ever spoken.

MATTHEW HENRY

CHAPTER 35

Verses 1–8

I. The bad words which Elihu charges upon Job, *v.* 2, 3. It intimates his good opinion of Job, that he thought better than he spoke, and that, when he perceived his mistake, he would not stand to it. "Thou hast, in effect, said, *My righteousness is more than God's.*" Job did in effect say, *My righteousness is more than God's* (*v.* 2); for if he got nothing by his religion, God was more beholden to him than he was to God. But, though there might be some colour for it, yet it was not fair to charge these words upon Job, when he himself had made them the wicked words of prospering sinners (*ch.* xxi. 15, *What profit shall we have if we pray to him?*).

II. The good answer which Elihu gives to this (*v.* 4): "*I will* undertake to *answer thee, and thy companions with thee,*" that is, all those that approve thy sayings. To do this he has recourse to his old maxim (*ch.* xxxiii. 12), *that God is greater than man.* Elihu needs not prove that God is above man; it is agreed by all; but he endeavours to affect Job and us with it, by an ocular demonstration of the height of the heavens and the clouds, *v.* 5. They are far above us, and God is far above them; how much then is he set out of the reach either of our sins or of our services! *Look unto the heavens, and behold the clouds.* He utterly denies that God can be either prejudiced or advantaged by what any, even the greatest men of the earth, do, or can do. Sin is said to *be against God* because so the sinner intends it

JAMIESON, FAUSSET, BROWN

CHAPTER 35

Vss. 1-16. **2. more than**–rather as in ch. 9:2; 25:4: "I am righteous (lit., my righteousness is) before God." *English Version,* however, agrees with ch. 9:17; 16:12-17; 27:2-6. Ch. 4:17 is susceptible of either rendering. Elihu means Job said so, not in so many words, but *virtually.* **3.** Rather, explanatory of "this" in vs. 2, "That thou sayest (to thyself, as if a distinct person) What advantage is it (thy integrity) to thee? What profit have I (by integrity) more than (I should have) by my sin?" i.e., more than if I had sinned (ch. 34:9). Job had said that the wicked, who use *these very words,* do not suffer for it (ch. 21:13-15); whereby he virtually sanctioned their sentiments. The same change of persons from oblique to direct address occurs (ch. 19:28; 22:17). **4. companions**–those entertaining like sentiments with thee (ch. 34:8, 36). **5-8.** Elihu like Eliphaz (ch. 22:2, 3, 12) shows that God is too exalted in nature to be susceptible of benefit or hurt from the righteousness or sin of men respectively; it is themselves that they benefit by righteousness, or hurt by sin. **behold the clouds, which are higher than thou**–spoken with irony. Not only are they higher than thou, but thou canst not even reach them clearly with

ADAM CLARKE

CHAPTER 35

2. *My righteousness is more than God's.* This would indeed be a blasphemous saying; but Job never said so, neither directly nor constructively. It would be much better to translate the words, "I am righteous before God." And Job's meaning most certainly was, "Whatever I am in your sight, I know that in the sight of God I am a righteous man"; and he had a right to assume this character, because God himself had given it to him.

3. *What advantage will it be unto thee?* As if he had said to God, "My righteousness cannot profit Thee, nor do I find that it is of any benefit to myself. Or perhaps Elihu makes here a general assertion, which he afterwards endeavors to exemplify: Thou hast been reasoning how it may profit thee, and thou hast said, "What profit shall I have in righteousness more than in sin?"

MATTHEW HENRY

and so God takes it, and it is an injury to his honour; yet it cannot *do anything against him.* Job therefore spoke amiss in saying *What profit is it that I am cleansed from my sin?* God was no gainer by his reformation; and who then would gain if he himself did not? The services of the best saints are no profit to him (*v.* 7): *If thou be righteous, what givest thou to him?*

Verses 9–13

Elihu returns an answer to another word that Job had said, which, he thought, reflected upon the justice and goodness of God.

I. Job complained that God did not regard the cries of the oppressed against their oppressors (*v.* 9): "*By reason of the multitude of oppressions they make the oppressed to cry;* but it is to no purpose: God does not appear to right them." This seems to refer to those words of Job (*ch.* xxiv. 12), *Men groan from out of the city, and the soul of the wounded cries out* against the oppressors, *yet God lays not folly to them. Is there a righteous God, and can it be that he should so slowly hear, so slowly see?*

II. How Elihu solves the difficulty. If the cries of the oppressed be not heard, the fault is in themselves; they *ask and have not,* but it is *because they ask amiss,* James iv. 3. *They cry out by reason of the arm of the mighty,* but it is not a penitent praying cry, the cry of nature and passion, not of grace.

1. They do not enquire after God, nor seek to acquaint themselves with him, under their affliction (*v.* 10): *But none saith, Where is God my Maker?* God is our Maker, the author of our being. It is our duty therefore to enquire after him. Where is he, that we may pay our homage to him? All are asking, Where is mirth? Where is wealth? Where is a good bargain? But none ask, *Where is God my Maker?*

2. They do not take notice of the mercies they enjoy in their afflictions. He provides for our inward comfort and joy under our outward troubles. He *gives songs in the night,* that is, when our condition is ever so dark, and sad, and melancholy, there is that in God, in his providence and promise. He preserves to us the use of our reason and understanding (*v.* 11): *Who teaches us more than the beasts of the earth,* that is, who has endued us with more noble powers and faculties than they are endued with and has made us capable of more excellent pleasures and employments here and for ever. Now this furnishes us with matter for thanksgiving, even under the heaviest burden of affliction. Whatever we are deprived of, we have our immortal souls continued to us; even those that kill the body cannot hurt *them.* This is the greatest excellency of reason, that it makes us capable of religion, and it is in that especially that we are *taught more than the beasts and the fowls.* They have wonderful instincts and sagacities in seeking out their food, their physic, their shelter; but none of them are capable of enquiring, *Where is God my Maker?* Something like logic, and philosophy, and politics, has been observed among the brute-creatures, but never anything of divinity or religion; these are peculiar to man. If therefore the oppressed only *cry by reason of the arm of the mighty,* and do not look up to God, they do no more than the brutes (who complain when they are hurt). God relieves the brute-creatures because they cry to him according to the best of their capacity, *ch.* xxxviii. 41; Ps. civ. 21. But what reason have men to expect relief, who are capable of enquiring after God as their Maker and yet cry to him no otherwise than as brutes do? *There they cry but none gives answer.* God does not work deliverance for them, *because of the pride of evil men;* they *regard iniquity in their hearts,* and therefore God will not hear their prayers, Ps. lxvi. 18; Isa. i. 15. The case is plain then, If we cry to God for the removal of the oppression and affliction we are under, and it is not removed, the reason is not because the Lord's hand is shortened or his ear heavy, but because the affliction has not done its work; we are not sufficiently humbled, and therefore must thank ourselves that it is continued.

Verses 14–16

I. Another improper word for which Elihu reproves Job (*v.* 14): ***Thou sayest thou shalt not see him;*** that is, 1. "Thou complainest that thou dost not understand the meaning of his severe dealings with thee." As, when we are in prosperity, we are ready to think our mountain will never be brought low, so when we are in adversity we are ready to think our valley will never be filled, but, in both, to conclude that *to-morrow must be as this day,* which is as absurd as to think, when the weather is either fair or foul, that it will be always so, that the flowing tide will always flow, or the ebbing tide will always ebb.

II. The answer which Elihu gives is this, 1. That,

JAMIESON, FAUSSET, BROWN

the eye. Yet these are not as high as God's seat. God is therefore too exalted to be dependent on man. Therefore He has no inducement to injustice in His dealings with man. When He afflicts, it must be from a different motive; viz., the good of the sufferer. **6. what dost**—how canst thou affect Him? **unto him**—that can hurt Him? (Jer. 7:19; Prov. 8: 36). **7.** (Ps. 16:2; Prov. 9:12; Luke 17:10.)

9. (Eccles. 4:1.) Elihu states in Job's words (ch. 24: 12; 30:20) the difficulty; the "cries" of "the oppressed" not being heard might lead man to think that wrongs are not punished by Him.

10-13. But the reason is that the innocent sufferers often do not humbly seek God for succor; so to their "pride" is to be laid the blame of their ruin; also because (13-16) they, as Job, instead of waiting God's time in pious trust, are prone to despair of His justice, when it is not immediately visible (ch. 33:19-26). If the sufferer would apply to God with a humbled, penitent spirit, He would hear. **Where . . .**—(Jer. 2:6, 8; Isa. 51:13).

songs—of joy at deliverance (Ps. 42:8; 149:5; Acts 16:25). **in the night**—unexpectedly (ch. 34:20, 25). Rather, in calamity. **11.** Man's spirit, which distinguishes him from the brute, is the strongest proof of God's beneficence; by the use of it we may understand that God is the Almighty helper of all sufferers who humbly seek Him; and that they err who do not so seek Him. **fowls**—(ch. 28:21, *Note*).

12. There—rather, *Then* (when none humbly casts himself on God, vs. 10). They cry proudly *against* God, rather than humbly *to* God. So, as the design of affliction is to humble the sufferer, there can be no answer until "pride" gives place to humble, penitent prayer (Ps. 10:4; Jer. 13: 17). **13.** Vanity, i.e., cries uttered in an unhumbled spirit, vs. 12, which applies in some degree to Job's cries; still more to those of the wicked (ch. 27:9; Prov. 15:29).

14. Although thou sayest, thou shalt not see Him (as a *temporal* deliverer; for he did look for a Redeemer *after death,* ch. 19:25-27; which passage cannot consistently with Elihu's assertion here be interpreted of "seeing" a *temporal* "redeemer"), ch. 7:7; 9:11; 23:3, 8, 9; yet, judgment . . .; therefore trust . . . But the *Hebrew* favors MAURER, "*How much less* (will God . . . regard, vs. 13), since thou sayest, that He does not regard thee." So in ch. 4:19. Thus Elihu alludes to Job's words (ch. 19:7; 30:20).

ADAM CLARKE

9. *By reason of the multitude.* Or rather, "From among the multitude" the oppressed clamor, "They shout because of the mighty." The wicked rich oppress the wicked poor; these cry aloud because of their oppressors; but they have no relief, because they call not upon God.

JOSEPH PARKER:

Whatever may be the exact definition of the phrase, who can fail to receive it as throwing an explanatory lustre upon many a human experience? Consider the words in their relation to one another. First look at them separately—"songs"; then look at the next word, "night"; now connect them, "songs in the night"—apparently songs out of place, songs out of season, songs that have gone astray, angels that have lost their foothold in heaven and have fallen down into wildernesses and valleys of darkness. Such is not the case. "Song" and "night" are words which seem to have no reciprocal relation: but human experience is larger than human definitions, and it is true to the experience of mankind that while there has been a night the night has been made alive with music. Who will deny this? No man who has had experience of life; only he will deny it who has seen life in one aspect, and who has seen so little of life as really to have seen none of it. Life is not a flash, a transient phase, a cloud that comes and goes without leaving any impression behind it: life is a long, complicated, changeful experience—now joyous to ecstasy, now sad to despair; now a great harvest field rich with the gold of wheat, and now a great sandy desert in which no flower can be found. Taking life through and through, in all its relations and interrelations, how many men can testify that in the night they have heard sweeter music than they ever heard in the day! Do not the surroundings sometimes help the music? Some music is out of place at midday; we must wait for the quiet wood, for the heart of the deep plantation, for the top of the silent hill: some music must come to the heart in solitude—a weird, mystic, tender thing, frightful sometimes as a ghost, yet familiar oftentimes as a friend. Who has not seen more of God at the graveside than he ever saw elsewhere? Who has not had Scripture interpreted to him in the house of death which was never interpreted to him by eloquent Apollos or by reasoning Paul? and who has not had occasion to go back upon his life, and say, It was good for me that I was afflicted: now that I have had time to reflect, I see that all the while God was working for me, secretly, beneficently, and the result is morning, beauty, promise, early summer, almost heaven!

—The People's Bible

MATTHEW HENRY

when he looked up to God, he had no just reason to speak thus despairingly: *Judgment is before him*, that is, "He knows what he has to do, and will do all in infinite wisdom and justice; he has the entire plan and model of providence before him. *Therefore trust in him*, depend upon him, wait for him, and believe that the issue will be good at last." He is a God of judgment (Isa. xxx. 18), we shall see no reason to despair of relief from him, but all the reason in the world to hope in him. "*Because it is not so*, because thou dost not thus trust in him, therefore the affliction which came at first from love has now displeasure mixed with it. Now God *has visited* thee *in his anger*." Elihu concludes therefore that *Job opens his mouth in vain* (*v*. 16), because he does not trust in God and wait for him. Let not that man who distrusts God *think that he shall receive anything from him*, James i. 7. He did not, as his other friends, condemn him for a hypocrite, but charged him only with Moses's sin, *speaking unadvisedly with his lips* when his spirit was provoked.

CHAPTER 36

Verses 1–4

Once more Elihu begs the patience of the auditory, and Job's particularly. To gain this he pleads, 1. That he had a good cause, and a noble and very fruitful subject: *I have yet to speak on God's behalf*. 2. That he had something to offer: *I will fetch my knowledge from afar* (*v*. 3), that is, we will have recourse to our first principles. It is worth while to go far for this knowledge of God, to dig for it, to travel for it; it will recompense our pains, and, though far-fetched, is not dear-bought. "*My words shall not be false*. He who is perfect or upright in knowledge is now reasoning with thee; and therefore let him not only have a fair hearing, but let what he says be taken in good part, as meant well."

Verses 5–14

Elihu, being to speak on God's behalf, shows that the disposals of divine Providence are all according to the eternal rules of equity. God acts as a righteous governor, for,

I. He does not think it below him to take notice of the meanest of his subjects, but *God is mighty*, infinitely so, and yet he *despises not any*, *v*. 5. Job thought himself and his cause slighted because God did not immediately appear for him. "No," says Elihu, *God despises not any*, which is a good reason why we should honour all men.

II. He gives no countenance to the greatest, if they be bad (*v*. 6): *He preserves not the life of the wicked*. Though their life may be prolonged, yet not under any special care of the divine Providence, but only its common protection.

III. He is always ready to right those that are any way injured, and to plead, their cause (*v*. 6). If men will not right the injured poor, God will.

IV. He takes a particular care for the protection of his good subjects, *v*. 7. He not only looks on them, but he never looks off them: *He withdraws not his eyes from the righteous*. Though they may seem sometimes neglected and forgotten, yet the tender careful eye of their heavenly Father never withdraws from them.

1. Sometimes he prefers good people to places of trust and honour (*v*. 7): *With kings are* they *on the throne*, and every sheaf is made to bow to theirs. When righteous persons are advanced to places of honour and power, it is in mercy to them. It is also in mercy to those over whom they are set: *When the righteous bear rule the city rejoices*.

2. If at any time he bring them into affliction, it is for the good of their souls, *v*. 8–10. *If they be bound in fetters*, laid in prison as Joseph was, or *holden in the cords of* any other *affliction*, confined by pain and sickness, hampered by poverty, it is for the benefit of their souls, the consideration of which should reconcile us to affliction. Three things God intends when he afflicts us:—(1) To discover past sins to us. *He shows them their work*. Sin is our own work. (2) To dispose our hearts to receive present instructions: Then *he opens their ear to discipline*, *v*. 10. Whom God chastens *he teaches* (Ps. xciv. 12), and the affliction makes people willing to learn, softens the wax, that it may receive the impression of the seal; yet it does not do this of itself, but the grace of God working with and by it. (3) To deter and draw us off from iniquity for the future.

3. If the affliction do its work, and accomplish that for which it is sent, he will comfort them again, according to the time that he has afflicted them (*v*. 11). If we faithfully serve God, (1) We have the

JAMIESON, FAUSSET, BROWN

judgment—i.e., thy cause, thy right; as in Ps. 9:16; Prov. 31:5, 8. **trust**—rather, *wait thou* on Him, patiently, until He take up thy cause (Ps. 37:7). **15.** *As it is, because* Job waited *not* trustingly and patiently (vs. 14; Num. 20:12; Zeph. 3:2; Mic. 7:9), *God hath visited . . . ; yet still he has not taken* (severe) *cognizance of the great multitude* (*English Version* wrongly, "extremity") of sins; therefore Job should not complain of being punished with undue severity (ch. 7:20; 11: 6). MAURER translates: "Because His anger hath not visited (hath not immediately punished Job for his impious complaints), nor has He taken *strict* (great) cognizance of his *folly* (sinful speeches); therefore . . ." For "folly," UMBREIT translates with the Rabbins, "multitude." GESENIUS reads with LXX and *Vulgate* needlessly, "transgression." **16.** Apodosis to vs. 15. **in vain**—rashly.

CHAPTER 36

Vss. 1-33. **1, 2.** Elihu maintains that afflictions are to the godly disciplinary, in order to lead them to attain a higher moral worth, and that the reason for their continuance is not, as the friends asserted, on account of the sufferer's extraordinary guilt, but because the discipline has not yet attained its object, viz., to lend him to humble himself penitently before God (Isa. 9:13; Jer. 5:3). This is Elihu's *fourth* speech. He thus exceeds the ternary number of the others. Hence his formula of politeness (vs. 2). Lit., Wait yet but a little for me." Bear with me a little farther. *I have yet* (much, ch. 32:18-20). There are Chaldeisms in this verse, agreeably to the view that the scene of the book is near the Euphrates and the Chaldees. **3. from afar**—not trite commonplaces, but drawn from God's mighty works. **ascribe righteousness**—whereas Job ascribed unrighteousness (ch. 34:10, 12). A man, in inquiring into God's ways, should at the outset *presume* they are all just, be *willing* to find them so, and *expect* that the result of investigation will prove them to be so; such a one will never be disappointed [BARNES]. **4.** I will not "speak wickedly for God," as the friends (ch. 13:4, 7, 8)—i.e., vindicate God by unsound arguments. **he that is perfect . . . .**—Rather, as the parallelism requires, "a man of *integrity in sentiments* is with thee" (is he with whom thou hast to do). Elihu means himself, as opposed to the dishonest reasonings of the friends (ch. 21:34). **5.** Rather, *strength of understanding* (heart) the force of the repetition of "mighty"; as "mighty" as God is, none is too low to be "despised" by Him; for His "might" lies especially in "His strength of understanding," whereby He searches out the most minute things, so as to give to each his right. Elihu confirms his exhortation (ch. 35:14). **6. right . . . poor**—He espouses the cause of the afflicted. **7.** (I Pet. 3:12.) God does not forsake the godly, as Job implied, but "establishes," or *makes* them *sit* on the throne as kings (I Sam. 2:8; Ps. 113:7, 8). True of believers in the highest sense, already in part (I Pet. 2:9; Rev. 1:6); hereafter fully (Rev. 5:10; ch. 22:5). **and they are**—*that they may be*.

8-10. If they be afflicted, it is no proof that they are hypocrites, as the friends maintain, or that God disregards them, and is indifferent whether men are good or bad, as Job asserts: God is thereby "disciplining them," and "showing them their sins," and if they bow in a right spirit under God's visiting hand, the greatest blessings ensue. **9. work**—transgression. **that . . . exceeded**—"In that they behaved themselves mightily (lit., "great"); i.e., presumptuously, or, at least, self-confidently. **10.** (Ch. 33:16-18, 23.)

11. serve—i.e., worship; as in Isaiah 19:23. *God* is to be supplied (cf. Isa. 1:19, 20).

ADAM CLARKE

15. *But . . . because it is not so*. Rather, "But now, because He visiteth not in His anger." The sense of the place appears to be this: Because vengeance is not speedily executed on an evil work, therefore are the hearts of the children of men set in them to do iniquity. This is, in effect, the charge which Elihu brings against Job.

16. *Therefore doth Job open his mouth in vain*. God will execute vengeance when it may best serve the ends of His justice, providence, and mercy. *He multiplieth words without knowledge*. However this may apply to Job, it most certainly applies very strongly and generally to the words, not only of Job's three friends, but to those also of Elihu himself. The contest is frequently a strife of words.

CHAPTER 36

3. *I will fetch my knowledge from afar*. "From the distant place," meaning probably both remote antiquity and heaven. I will show thee that all antiquity and experience are on my side.

4. *He that is perfect in knowledge is with thee*. "The perfection of knowledge is with thee."

5. *God is mighty, and despiseth not any*. He reproaches no man for his want of knowledge. *He is mighty*. Literally, "He is mighty in strength of heart"; He can never be terrified nor alarmed.

6. *He preserveth not the life*. He will not give life to the wicked; all such forfeit life by their transgressions. *But giveth right*. Justice will He give to the afflicted or "humble."

MATTHEW HENRY

promise of outward prosperity, the promise of the life that now is, and the comforts of it, as far as is for God's glory and our good; and who would desire them any further? (2) We have the possession of inward pleasures, the comfort of communion with God and a good conscience, and that great peace which those have that love God's law.

4. If the affliction do not do its work, let them expect the consuming fire will prevail if the refining fire do not; for when God judges he will overcome.

V. He brings ruin upon hypocrites, the secret enemies of his kingdom (such as Elihu described, *v.* 12). *They cry not when he binds them,* that is, when they are in affliction, bound with the cords of trouble, their hearts are hardened, they are stubborn and unhumbled, and will not cry to God nor make their application to him. *They die in youth, and their life is among the unclean, v.* 14.

Verses 15–23

Elihu here comes more closely to Job; and,

I. He tells him what God would have done for him before this if he had been duly humbled under his affliction (*v.* 15). "The poor in spirit, those that are of a broken and contrite heart, he looks upon with tenderness, and, when they are in affliction, is ready to help them. He *opens their ears,* and makes them to hear joy and gladness, even *in* their *oppressions.* If thou hadst accommodated thyself to the will of God, thy liberty and plenty would have been restored to thee with advantage." 1. "Thou wouldst have been enlarged, and not confined thus by thy sickness and disgrace: *He would have removed thee into a broad place where is no straitness,* and thou wouldst no longer have been cramped thus and have had all thy measures broken." 2. "Thou wouldst have been enriched, and wouldst not have been left in this poor condition; thou wouldst have had thy table richly spread, not only with food convenient, but with the finest of the wheat."

II. He charges him with standing in his own light, and makes him the cause of the continuance of his own trouble (*v.* 17): "*But thou hast fulfilled the judgment of the wicked,*" that is, "Whatever thou art really, in this thing thou hast conducted thyself like a wicked man, and *therefore* judgment and justice take hold on thee as a wicked man."

III. He cautions him not to persist in his frowardness. "*Because there is wrath*" (that is, "because God is a righteous governor, because thou hast reason to fear that thou art under God's displeasure) therefore *beware lest he take thee away* suddenly *with his stroke,* and be so wise as to make thy peace with him quickly and get his anger turned away from thee." This was a friendly caution to Job, and necessary. There is no escaping by money, no purchasing a pardon with silver, or gold, and such corruptible things: "Even *a great ransom cannot deliver thee* when God enters into judgment with thee. If *all the forces of strength* were at thy command, if thou couldst muster ever so many servants and vassals to appear for thee it were all in vain. There is *none that can deliver out of his hand.*" There is no escaping by absconding (*v.* 20): "*Desire not the night,* which often favours the retreat of a conquered army and covers it; think not that thou canst so escape the righteous judgment of God, for the *darkness hideth not from him,*" Ps. cxxxix. 11, 12. "*Take heed,* look well to thy own spirit, and *regard not iniquity,* return not to it (so some), for it is at thy peril if thou do." Let him not dare to prescribe to God, nor give him his measures (*v.* 22, 23): "*Behold, God exalteth by his power,*" that is, "He does, may, and can set up and pull down whom he pleases, and therefore it is not for thee nor me to contend with him." He is an incomparable teacher: *Who teaches like him?* It is absurd for us to teach him who is himself the fountain of light, truth, knowledge, and instruction. *He that teaches man knowledge,* and so as none else can, *shall not he know?* Shall we light a candle to the sun? When Elihu would give glory to God as a ruler he praises him as a teacher, for rulers must teach. He teaches by the Bible, and that is the best book, teaches by his Son, and he is the best Master.

Verses 24–33

Elihu is here endeavouring to give Job great and high thoughts of God, and so to persuade him into a cheerful submission to his providence.

I. He represents the work of God, in general, *v.* 24. God does nothing mean. His visible works, those of nature, are such as we admire and commend, and in which we observe the Creator's wisdom, power, and goodness; shall we then find fault with his dispensations concerning us. Look which way we will, we see: "This is *the work of God,*" the finger of God; it is the Lord's doing. Every man may see, afar off,

JAMIESON, FAUSSET, BROWN

12. (Ch. 33:18.) **without knowledge**—i.e., on account of their foolishness (ch. 4:20, 21). **13-15.** Same sentiment as vss. 11, 12, expanded. **13. hypocrites**—or, the ungodly [MAURER]; but "hypocrites" is perhaps a distinct class from the openly wicked (vs. 12). **heap up wrath**—of God against themselves (Rom. 2:5). UMBREIT translates, "nourish *their* wrath *against God,*" instead of "crying" unto Him. This suits well the parallelism and the *Hebrew.* But *English Version* gives a good parallelism, "hypocrites" answering to "cry not" (ch. 27:8, 10); "heap up wrath" against themselves, to "He bindeth them" with fetters of affliction (vs. 8). **14.** Rather (Deut. 23:17), *Their life* is (ended) as that of (lit., "among") *the unclean,* prematurely and dishonorably. So the second clause answers to the first. A warning that Job make not common cause with the wicked (ch. 34:36). **15. poor**—*the afflicted* pious. **openeth . . . ears**—(vs. 10); so as to be *admonished* in their straits ("oppression") to seek God penitently, and so be "delivered" (ch. 33:16, 17, 23-27). **16.** Rather, "He *will* lead forth thee also out of *the jaws of* a strait" (Ps. 18:19; 118:5). The "broad place" expresses the *liberty,* and the well-supplied "table" the *abundance* of the prosperous (Ps. 23:5; Isa. 25:6). **17.** Rather, "But *if* thou art fulfilled (i.e., entirely filled) with the judgment of the wicked" (i.e., the *guilt* incurring judgment [MAURER]; or rather, as UMBREIT, referring to ch. 34:5, 6, 7, 36, the *judgment pronounced on God by the guilty* in misfortunes), judgment (*God's judgment on the wicked;* Jer. 51:9, playing on the double meaning of "judgment") and justice shall closely follow each other [UMBREIT]. **18.** (Num. 16:45; Ps. 49:6, 7; Matt. 16:26.) Even the "ransom" by Jesus Christ (ch. 33:24) will be of no avail to wilful despisers (Heb. 10:26-29). **with his stroke**—(ch. 34: 26). UMBREIT translates, "Beware lest the wrath of God (thy severe calamity) *lead thee to scorn*" (ch. 34:7; 27:23). This accords better with the verb in the parallel clause, which ought to be translated, "Let not the great ransom (of money, which thou canst give) *seduce* thee (*Margin, Turn thee aside,* as if thou couldst deliver thyself from "wrath" by it). As the "scorn" in the first clause answers to the "judgment of the wicked" (vs. 17), so "ransom, seduce" to "will he esteem riches" (vs. 19). Thus, vs. 18 is the transition between vs. 17 and vs. 19. **19. forces of strength**—i.e., resources of wealth (Ps. 49:7; Prov. 11:4). **20. Desire**—rant for. Job had *wished for death* (ch. 3:3-9, etc.). **night**—(John 9:4). **when**—rather, "whereby." **cut off**—lit., "ascend," as the corn cut and lifted upon the wagon or stack (vs. 26); so "cut off," "disappear." **in their place**—lit., "under themselves"; so, without moving from their place, on the spot, suddenly (ch. 40:12) [MAURER]. UMBREIT's translation: "To *ascend* (which is really, as thou wilt find to thy cost, *to descend*) to the people *below*" (lit., "under themselves"), answers better to the parallelism and the *Hebrew.* Thou pantest for death as desirable, but it is a "night" or *region of darkness;* thy fancied *ascent* (amelioration) will prove a *descent* (deterioration) (ch. 10:22); therefore desire it not. **21. regard**—lit., "turn thyself to." **iniquity**—viz., presumptuous speaking against God (ch. 34:5, and above, vss. 17, 18, *Note*). **rather than**—to bear "affliction" with pious patience. Men think it an alleviation to complain against God, but this is adding sin to sorrow; it is sin, not sorrow, which can really hurt us (contrast Heb. 11:25). **22-25.** God is not to be impiously arraigned, but to be praised for His might, shown in His works. **exalteth**—rather, doeth lofty things, shows His exalted power [UMBREIT] (Ps. 21:13). **teacheth**—(Ps. 94:12, etc.). The connection is, returning to vs. 5, God's "might" is shown in His "wisdom"; He alone can *teach;* yet, because He, as a sovereign, explains not all His dealings, forsooth Job must presume to *teach Him* (Isa. 40:13, 14; Rom. 11:34; I Cor. 2:16). So the transition to vs. 23 is natural. UMBREIT with LXX translates, "Who is *Lord,*" wrongly, as this meaning belongs to later *Hebrew.* **23.** Job dared to *prescribe* to God what He should do (ch. 34:10, 13). **24.** Instead of arraigning, let it be thy fixed principle to *magnify* God in His works (Ps. 111:2-8; Rev. 15:3); these, which all may "see," may convince us that what we do not see is altogether wise and good (Rom. 1:20). **behold**—As "see," (vs. 25), shows; not, as MAURER, "sing," laud (*Note,* 33:27). **25.** "See," viz., with wondering admiration [MAURER]. **man may behold**— rather, (yet) *mortals* (a different *Hebrew* word from "man") behold it (only) from afar off," see but a small "part" (ch. 26:14).

ADAM CLARKE

13. *But the hypocrites in heart.* "The profligates, the impious." *They cry not.* "Though he binds them, yet they cry not." They are too obstinate to humble themselves even under the mighty hand of God.

14. *They die in youth.* Exactly what the Psalmist says, "Bloody and deceitful men shall not live out half their days," Ps. lv. 23. Literally, the words of Elihu are, "They shall die in the youth of their soul."

20. *Desire not the night.* Thou hast wished for death (here called *night*).

21. *Regard not iniquity.* It is sinful to entertain such wishes; it is an insult to the providence of God. He sends affliction; He knows this to be best for thee. But thou hast preferred death to affliction, thereby setting thy wisdom against the wisdom of God.

MATTHEW HENRY

the heaven and all its lights, the earth and all its fruits, to be the work of Omnipotence. Look at the minutest works of nature through a microscope; do they not appear curious? The eternal power and godhead of the Creator are *clearly seen and understood* by the *things that are made*, Rom. i. 20. It ought to be marvellous in our eyes. The beauty and excellency of the work of God, and the agreement of all the parts of it, are what we must remember to magnify and highly to extol.

II. He represents God, the author of them, as infinite and unsearchable, *v.* 26. The streams of being, power, and perfection should lead us to the fountain. *God is great*, infinitely so, and therefore greatly to be praised,—great, and therefore *we know him not.* We know that he is, but not what he is. We know what he is not, but not what he is. We know in part, but not in perfection. *The number of his years cannot* possibly *be searched out*, for he is eternal; there is no number of them. He is a Being without beginning, succession, or period, who ever was, and ever will be, and ever the same, the great *I AM.* This is a good reason why we should not prescribe to him, nor quarrel with him.

III. He gives some instances of God's wisdom, power, and sovereign dominion, beginning in this chapter with the clouds and the rain that descends from them. We need not be critical in examining either the phrase or the philosophy of this noble discourse. The general scope of it is to show that God is infinitely great, and the Lord of all, the first cause and supreme director of all the creatures, and *has all power in heaven and earth* (whom therefore we ought, with all humility and reverence, to adore, to speak well of, and to give honour to), and that it is presumption for us to prescribe to him the rules and methods of his special providence towards the children of men. Elihu, to affect Job with God's sublimity and sovereignty, had directed him (*ch.* xxxv. 5) to look unto the clouds. Consider the clouds,

1. As springs to this lower world, the source and treasure of its moisture. The clouds above distil upon the earth below. If the heavens become brass, the earth becomes iron; therefore thus the promise of plenty runs, *I will hear the heavens and they shall hear the earth.* Every good gift is from above, from him who is both Father of lights and Father of the rain. They are here said to *distil upon man* (*v.* 28); for, though indeed God *causes it to rain in the wilderness where no man is* (*ch.* xxxviii. 26; Ps. civ. 11), yet special respect is had to man herein, to whom the inferior creatures are all made serviceable. Among men, he *causes his rain to fall upon the just and upon the unjust*, Matt. v. 45. They are said to distil the water in *small drops*, not in spouts, as when the *windows of heaven were opened*, Gen. vii. 11. God waters the earth with that with which he once drowned it. Though it comes down in drops, yet it distils upon man *abundantly* (*v.* 28), and therefore is called *the river of God which is full of water*, Ps. lxv. 9. The clouds *pour down according to the vapour* that they draw up, *v.* 27. So just the heavens are to the earth, but the earth is not so in the return it makes.

2. As shadows to the upper world (*v.* 29): *Can any understand the spreading of the clouds?* Shall we then pretend to understand the reasons and methods of God's judicial proceedings with the children of men whose characters and cases are so various. By the interposition of the clouds between us and the sun, we are favoured; for they serve as an umbrella to shelter us from the violent heat of the sun. A *cloud of dew in the heat of harvest* is spoken of as a very great refreshment, Isa. xviii. 4. Sometimes we are by them frowned upon; for they darken the earth at noon-day and eclipse the light of the sun. Sin is compared to a cloud (Isa. xliv. 22), because it comes between us and the light of God's countenance and obstructs the shining of it. But though the clouds darken the sun for a time, and pour down rain, yet after he has wearied the cloud, *he spreads his light upon it, v.* 30. There is a *clear shining after rain*, 2 Sam. xxiii. 4.

JAMIESON, FAUSSET, BROWN

(Ch. 37:13.) God's greatness in heaven and earth: a reason why Job should bow under His afflicting hand. **26. know him not**—only in part (vs. 25; I Cor. 13:12). **his years**—(Ps. 90:2; 102:24, 27); applied to Jesus Christ (Heb. 1:12).

27, 28. The marvellous formation of rain (so ch. 5:9, 10). **maketh small**—Rather, "He *draweth* (up) *to* Him, He *attracts* (from the earth below) the drops of water; they (the drops of water) pour down rain, (*which is*) *His* vapor." "Vapor" is in apposition with "rain," marking the way in which rain is formed; viz., from the vapor drawn up by God into the air and then condensed into drops, which fall (Ps. 147:8). The suspension of such a mass of water, and its descent not in a deluge, but in *drops of vapory rain*, are the marvel. The selection of this particular illustration of God's greatness forms a fit prelude to the storm in which God appears (ch. 40:1). **28. abundantly**—lit., "upon many men." **29.** (ch. 37:5). God's marvels in thunder and lightnings. **29. spreadings . . .**—the canopy of thick clouds, which covers the heavens in a storm (Ps. 105:39). **the noise** [crashing] **of his tabernacle**—viz., thunder; God being poetically said to have *His pavilion* amid dark clouds (Ps. 18:11; Isa. 40:22). **30. light**—lightning. **it**—His tabernacle. The light, in an instant spread over the vast mass of dark clouds, forms a striking picture. "Spread" is repeated from vs. 29 to form an antithesis. "He spreads not only *clouds*, but *light*." **coveteth the bottom** [*roots*] **of the sea**—viz., with the light. In the storm the depths of ocean are laid bare; and the light "covers" them, at the same moment that it "spreads" across the dark sky. So in Psalm 18:14, 15, the discovering of "the channels of waters" follows the "lightnings." UMBREIT translates: "He spreadeth His light *upon Himself*, and *covereth Himself with* the roots of the sea" (Ps. 104:2). God's garment is woven of celestial light and of the watery depths, raised to the sky to form His cloudy canopy. The phrase, "cover Himself with the roots of the sea," is harsh; but the image is grand. **31.** These (rain and lightnings) are marvellous and *not* to be *understood* (vs. 29), yet necessary. "*For* by them He judgeth (chastiseth on the one hand), etc. (and on the other, by them) He giveth meat" (food), etc. (ch. 37:13; 38:23, 27; Acts 14:17). **32.** Rather, "He covereth (both) *His hands* with light (*lightning*, ch. 37:3, *Margin*), and giveth it a command *against his adversary*" (lit., the one "assailing" Him; Ps. 8:2; 139:20; 21:19). Thus, as in vs. 31, the twofold effects of His *waters* are set forth, so here, of His *light*; in the one hand, *destructive lightning* against the wicked; in the other, *the genial light* for good to His friends, etc. (vs. 33) [UMBREIT]. **33. noise**—rather, He revealeth it (lit., "announceth concerning it") to *His friend* (antithesis to *adversary*, vs. 32, so the *Hebrew* is translated, ch. 2:11); also to cattle and plants (lit., "that which shooteth up"; Gen. 40:10; 41:22). As the genial effect of "water" in the growth of food, is mentioned, vs. 31, so here that of "light" in cherishing *cattle* and *plants* [UMBREIT]. If *English Version*, "noise" be retained, translate, "His noise (thunder) announces concerning Him (His coming in the tempest), the cattle (to announce) concerning Him when He is in the act of *rising up*" (in the storm). Some animals give various intimations that they are sensible of the approach of a storm [*Virg. Georg.* I. 373, etc.].

ADAM CLARKE

26. *God is great.* He is omnipotent. *We know him not.* He is unsearchable. *Neither can the number of his years be searched out.* He is eternal.

27. *He maketh small the drops of water.* This appears simply to refer to evaporation.

29. *The noise of his tabernacle?* By the *tabernacle* we may understand the whole firmament, whence He sends forth the rain of His strength, and the thunder of His power.

32. *With clouds he covereth the light.* "By the hollow of his hands he concealeth the light," the fountain of light, i.e., the sun. *And commandeth it not to shine by the cloud that cometh betwixt.* I am afraid this is no translation of the original. Old Coverdale is better: "And at his commandement it cometh agayne."

33. *The noise thereof sheweth concerning it, the cattle also concerning the vapour. I* think this may be translated without any violence to any word in the text: Its loud noise (or His thunder) shall proclaim concerning Him; a magazine of wrath against iniquity.

MATTHEW HENRY — CHAPTER 37

Verses 1–5

Thunder and lightning are sensible indications of the glory and majesty of Almighty God. In these God leaves not himself without witness of his greatness, as, in the rain from heaven and fruitful seasons, he leaves not himself without witness of his goodness (Acts xiv. 17). It is very probable that at this time, when Elihu was speaking, it thundered and lightened, for he speaks of the phenomena as present; and, God being about to speak (*ch.* xxxviii. 1), these were, as on Mount Sinai, the proper prefaces to command

JAMIESON, FAUSSET, BROWN — CHAPTER 37

Vss. 1-24. **1. At this**—when I hear the thundering of the Divine Majesty. Perhaps the storm already had begun, out of which God was to address Job (ch. 38:1).

ADAM CLARKE — CHAPTER 37

MATTHEW HENRY

attention and awe. Elihu was himself affected, and desired to affect Job, with the appearance of God's glory in the thunder and lightning (*v.* 1, 2): "For my part," says Elihu, "*my heart trembles* at it; it is still terrible to me, and makes my heart beat as if it would move *out of its place.*" He also calls upon Job to attend to it (*v.* 2): *Hear attentively the noise of his voice.* To apprehend and understand the instructions God thereby gives us, we have need to hear with great attention and application of mind. God directs the thunder, and the lightning is his, *v.* 3. Their production and motion are not from chance, though to us they seem accidental and ungovernable. The claps of thunder roll *under the whole heaven,* and are heard far and near; so are the lightnings darted to *the ends of the earth.* The lightning is first directed, and *after it a voice roars, v.* 4. The thunder is here called *the voice of God's excellency,* because by it he proclaims his transcendent power and greatness. He will not stay the rains and showers that usually follow upon the thunder, but will pour them out upon the earth *when his voice is heard.* Does God thunder thus marvellously with his voice? From this one instance we may argue to all, that, in the dispensations of his providence, there is that which is too great, too strong, for us to oppose or strive against.

Verses 6–13

The changes and extremities of the weather, wet or dry, hot or cold, are the subject of a great deal of our common talk, but how seldom do we think and speak of these things, as Elihu does here, with regard to God. We must take notice of the glory of God, not only in the thunder and lightning, but in the more common revolutions of the weather.

I. In the snow and rain, *v.* 6. Then *he saith to the snow, Be thou on the earth.* He speaks, and it is done: as in the creation of the world, *Let there be light,* so in the words of common providence, *Snow, be thou on the earth.* Saying and doing are not two things with God, though they are with us. When he speaks the word *the small rain* distils and *the great rain pours down* as he pleases—*the winter-rain.* The providence of God is to be acknowledged, both by husbandmen in the fields and travellers upon the road, in every shower of rain, whether it does them a kindness or a diskindness. It is sin and folly to contend with God's providence in the weather. The effect of the extremity of the winter-weather obliges both men and beasts to retire. *He seals up the hand of every man.* In frost and snow, husbandmen cannot follow their business, nor some tradesmen, nor travellers. The plough is laid by, the shipping laid up. Men, being taken off from their own work, *may know his work,* and contemplate that, and give him the glory. When we are confined to our houses we should thereby be driven to our Bibles and ours knees. *The beasts* also *retire to* their *dens and remain in their* close *places, v.* 8. The wild beasts must seek a shelter for themselves, to which by instinct they are directed, while the tame beasts, which are serviceable to man, are housed and protected by his care.

II. In the winds, which blow from different quarters and produce different effects (*v.* 9): *Out of the hidden place* (so it may be read) *comes the whirlwind;* it turns round, and so it is hard to say from which point it comes but it comes from *the secret chamber,* as the word signifies, which I am not so willing to understand of the *south,* because he says here (*v.* 17) that the wind out of the south is so far from being a whirlwind that it is a warming, quieting, wind.

III. In the frost, *v.* 10. See the cause of it: It *is given by the breath of God,* that is, by the word of his power and the command of his will; or, as some understand it, by the wind, which is the breath of God, as the thunder is his voice; it is caused by the cold freezing wind out of the north. See the effect of it: *The breadth of the waters is straightened,* that is, the waters are congealed, benumbed, arrested, bound up in crystal fetters. This is such an instance of the power of God as, if it were not common, would be next to a miracle.

IV. In the clouds. Three sorts of clouds he here speaks of: 1. Close, black, thick clouds, pregnant with showers; and these with watering *he wearies* (*v.* 11), that is, they spend themselves, and are exhausted by the rain into which they melt and are dissolved, pouring out water till they are weary and can pour out no more. The clouds water the earth till they are weary; they spend and are spent for our benefit. 2. Bright thin clouds, clouds without water; and these *he scattereth;* they are dispersed of themselves. 3. Flying clouds, which do not dissolve, as the thick cloud, into a close rain, but are carried upon the wings of the wind from place to place, dropping showers as they go; and these are said to be *turned round about* by his counsels, *v.* 12.

JAMIESON, FAUSSET, BROWN

2. Hear attentively—the thunder (noise), etc., and then you will feel that there is good reason to tremble. **sound**—*muttering* of the thunder. **3. directeth it**—however zigzag the lightning's course; or, rather, it applies to the pealing roll of the thunder. God's *all-embracing* power. **ends**—lit., "wings," "skirts," the habitable earth being often compared to an extended garment (ch. 38:13; Isa. 11:12). **4.** The thunderclap follows at an interval after the flash. **stay them**—He will not hold back the lightnings (vs. 3), when the thunder is heard [MAURER]. Rather, take "them" as the usual concomitants of thunder, viz., *rain and hail* [UMBREIT] (ch. 40:9). **5.** (Ch. 36:26; Ps. 65:6; 139:14). The sublimity of the description lies in this, that God is everywhere in the storm, directing it whither He will [BARNES]. See Psalm 29, where, as here, the "voice" of God is repeated with grand effect. The thunder in Arabia is sublimely terrible.

6. Be—more forcible than "fall," as UMBREIT translates Genesis 1:3. **to the small rain . . .**—He saith, Be on the earth. The shower increasing from "small" to "great," is expressed by the *plural showers* (*Margin*), following the *singular shower.* Winter rain (Song of Sol. 2:11).

7. In winter God stops man's out-of-doors activity. **sealeth**—closeth up (ch. 9:7). Man's "hands" are then tied up. **his work**—in antithesis to *man's own work* ("hand") which at other times engages men so as to make them liable to forget their dependence on God. UMBREIT more literally translates, That all men *whom He has made* (lit., "of His making") may be brought to acknowledgment. **8. remain**—rest in their lairs. It is beautifully ordered that during the cold, when they could not obtain food, many lie torpid, a state wherein they need no food. The desolation of the fields, at God's bidding, is poetically graphic. **9. south**—lit., "chambers"; connected with the south (ch. 9:9). The whirlwinds are poetically regarded as pent up by God in His southern chambers, whence He sends them forth (so ch. 38:22; Ps. 135:7). As to the southern whirlwinds (see Isa. 21:1; Zech. 9:14), they drive before them burning sands; chiefly from February to May. **the north**—lit., "scattering"; the north wind *scatters* the clouds. **10. the breath of God**—poetically, for the ice-producing north wind. **frost**—rather, *ice.* **straitened**—physically accurate; frost *compresses* or *contracts* the expanded liquid into a congealed mass (ch. 38:29, 30; Ps. 147:17, 18). **11-13.** How the thunderclouds are dispersed, or else employed by God, either for correction or mercy. **by watering**—by loading it with water. **wearieth**—*burdeneth* it, so that it falls in rain; thus "wearieth" answers to the parallel "scattereth" (cf. *Note,* vs. 9); a clear sky resulting alike from both. **bright cloud**—lit., "cloud of His light," i.e., of His lightning. UMBREIT for "watering," etc., translates; "*Brightness* drives away the clouds, His *light* scattereth the thick clouds"; the parallelism is thus good, but the *Hebrew* hardly sanctions it. **12. it**—the cloud of lightning. **counsels**—guidance (Ps. 148:8); lit., "steering"; the clouds obey God's guidance, as the ship does the helmsman. So the lightning (*Note,* 36:31, 32); neither is haphazard in its movements. **they**—*the clouds,* implied in the collective *singular* "it." **face of the world . . .**—in the face of the earth's circle. **13.** Lit., "He maketh it (the rain-cloud) find place," whether for correction, if (it be destined) for His land (i.e., for the part *inhabited by man,* with whom *God* deals, as opposed to the parts *uninhabited,* on which rain is at other times appointed to fall, ch. 38:26, 27) or for mercy. "If it be destined for His land" is a parenthetical supposition [MAURER]. In *English Version,* this clause spoils the even balance of the antithesis between the "rod" (*Margin*) and "mercy" (Ps. 68:9; Gen. 7).

ADAM CLARKE

1. *My heart trembleth.* A proper consideration of God's majesty in the thunder and lightning is enough to appall the stoutest heart.

2. *Hear attentively.* "Hear with hearing." The words seem to intimate that there was actually at that time a violent storm of thunder and lightning, and that the successive peals were now breaking over the house, and the lightning flashing before their eyes. The storm continued till Elihu had finished, and out of that storm the Almighty spoke. See the beginning of the succeeding chapter. *The noise of his voice.* The sudden clap. *And the sound that goeth out.* The peal or continued rattling, pounding, and thumping, to the end of the peal.

3. *He directeth it under the whole heaven.* He directs it (the lightning) under the whole heaven, in the twinkling of an eye from east to west; and its light—the reflection of the flash, not the lightning—*unto the ends of the earth,* so that a whole hemisphere seems to see it at the same instant.

4. *After it a voice roareth.* After the flash has been seen, the peal is heard. *He thundereth with the voice of his excellency.* "Of his majesty"; nor is there a sound in nature more descriptive of, or more becoming, the majesty of God than that of thunder. *And he will not stay them.* "And he hath not limited or circumscribed them."

5. *God thundereth marvellously with his voice.* This is the conclusion of Elihu's description of the lightning and thunder; and here only should chap. xxxvi. have ended. He began, chap. xxxvi. 29, with the noise of God's tabernacle; and he ends here with the marvellous thundering of Jehovah. *Great things doeth he.* This is the beginning of a new paragraph, and relates particularly to the phenomena which are afterwards mentioned.

7. *He sealeth up the hand of every man.* I think that the act of freezing is probably intended; that when the earth is bound up by intense frost, *the hand,* "labour," *of every man* is sealed up; he can do no more labor in the field till the south wind blow, by which a thaw takes place. While the earth is in this state of rigidity, *the beasts go into their* [*dens,*] *and remain in their places,* v. 8, some of them sleeping out the winter in a state of torpor, and others of them feeding on the stores which they had collected in autumn.

11. *By watering he wearieth the thick cloud.* Perhaps it would be better to say, "The brightness dissipates the cloud"; or, if we follow our version, *By watering the earth he wearieth,* weareth out or emptieth, *the thick cloud*—causes it to pour down all its contents upon the earth, that they may cause it to bring forth and bud.

MATTHEW HENRY

Verses 14–20

Elihu here addresses himself closely to Job, desiring him to apply what he had hitherto said to himself. He begs that he would hearken to this discourse (*v.* 14), that he would pause awhile: *Stand still, and consider the wondrous works of God.* Elihu, for the humbling of Job, shows him,

I. That he had no insight into natural causes, could neither see the springs of them nor foresee the effects of them (*v.* 15–17): *Dost thou know* this and know that which are *the wondrous works of him who is perfect in knowledge?* We are here taught, 1. The perfection of God's knowledge. It is one of the most glorious perfections of God that he is perfect in knowledge; he is omniscient. His knowledge is intuitive: he *sees.* It is intimate and entire. To his knowledge there is nothing distant, but all near—nothing future, but all present—nothing hid, but all open. 2. The imperfection of our knowledge. The greatest philosophers are much in the dark concerning the powers and works of nature. We are a paradox to ourselves, and about us is a mystery. It is good for us to be made sensible of our own ignorance. Some have confessed their ignorance, and those that would not do this have betrayed it. But what incompetent judges we are of the divine politics, when we understand so little even of the divine mechanics. If we foresee the change of weather a few hours before, by vulgar observation, or when second causes have begun to work by the weather-glass, yet how little do these show us of the purposes of God by these changes! We know not how the clouds are poised in the air, the *balancing* of them, which is one of the wondrous works of God, so balanced that they do not fall at once, nor burst into cataracts or water-spouts. *He quiets the earth by the south wind,* when the spring comes. As he has a blustering freezing north wind, so he has a thawing, composing, south wind; the Spirit is compared to both, because he both convinces and comforts, Cant. iv. 16.

II. That he had no share at all in the first making of the world (*v.* 18): *Hast thou with him spread out the sky?* It *is strong,* and has its name from its stability. It still is what it was, and suffers no decay, nor shall the ordinances of heaven be altered till the lease expires with time. It is a *molten looking-glass,* smooth and polished, and without the least flaw or crack. In this, as in a looking-glass, we may *behold the glory of God* and the wisdom of *his handiwork,* Ps. xix. 1.

III. That neither he nor they were able to speak of the glory of God in any proportion to the merit of the subject, *v.* 19, 20. He challenges Job ironically: "*Teach us,* if thou canst, *what we shall say unto him, v.* 19. Thou hast a mind to reason with God, and wouldst have us to contend with him on thy behalf; teach us then what we shall say." He owns his own insufficiency: *We cannot order our speech by reason of darkness.* Those that through grace know much of God, yet know little in comparison with what is to be known, and what will be known, when that which is perfect shall come and the veil shall be rent. He is even ashamed of what he has said, not of the cause, but of his own management of it: "*Shall it be told him that I speak? v.* 20. By no means; let it never be spoken of," for he fears that the subject has suffered by his undertaking it, as a fine face is wronged by a bad painter.

Verses 21–24

Elihu here concludes his discourse with some short but great sayings concerning the glory of God, who has said that he will *dwell in the thick darkness* and *make that his pavilion* (2 Chron. vi. 1; Ps. xviii. 11). He saw the cloud, with a whirlwind in the bosom of it, coming out of the south; but now it hung so thick, so black, over their heads, that they could none of them *see the bright light which* just before *was in the clouds.* Yet he looks to the north, and sees it clear that way, which gives him hope that the clouds are not gathering for a deluge; they are covered, but not surrounded, with them. He expects that *the wind will pass* (so it may be read) *and cleanse them,* and then *fair weather will come out of the north* (*v.* 22) and all will be well. God will not always frown, nor contend for ever. He hastens to conclude, now that God is about to speak. He observes, (1) That *with God is terrible majesty.* He is a God of glory and transcendent perfection. (2) That when we speak *touching the Almighty* we must own that *we cannot find him out*; our finite understandings cannot comprehend his infinite perfections, *v.* 23. Can we put the sea into an egg-shell? (3) That *he is excellent in power.* (4) That he is no less excellent in wisdom and righteousness, *in judgment and plenty of justice,* else there would be little excellency in his power. (5) That *he will not afflict,* that is, that he will not afflict willingly; it is no pleasure to him to grieve the children of men,

JAMIESON, FAUSSET, BROWN

14. (Ps. 111:2.) **15. when**—rather, "how." **disposed them**—*lays His charge on these* "wonders" (vs. 14) to arise. **light**—lightning. **shine**—flash. How is it that *light* arises from the *dark* thundercloud? **16.** *Hebrew,* "*Hast thou understanding of* the balancings," etc., how the clouds are poised in the air, so that their watery gravity does not bring them to the earth? The condensed moisture, descending by gravity, meets a warmer temperature, which dissipates it into vapor (the tendency of which is to ascend) and so counteracts the descending force. **perfect in knowledge**—God; not here in the sense that Elihu uses it of himself (ch. 36:4).

17. Dost thou know—**how, thy garments . . .**—i.e., how thy body grows warm, so as to affect thy garments with heat? **south wind**—lit., "region of the south." "When He *maketh still* (and sultry) the earth (i.e., the atmosphere) by (during) the south wind (Song of Sol. 4:16).

18. with him—like as He does (ch. 40:15). **spread out**—given expanse to. **strong**—firm; whence the term "firmament" (Gen. 1:6; *Margin, expansion,* Isa. 44:24). **molten looking glass**—image of the bright smiling sky. Mirrors were then formed of molten polished metal, not glass.

19. Men cannot explain God's wonders; we ought, therefore, to be dumb and not contend with God. If Job thinks we ought, "let him teach us, what we shall say." **order**—frame. **darkness**—of mind; ignorance. "The eyes are bewilderingly blinded, when turned in bold controversy with God towards the sunny heavens" (vs. 18) [UMBREIT]. **20.** What **I** a mortal say against God's dealings is not worthy of being told HIM. In opposition to Job's wish to "speak" before God (ch. 13:3, 18-22). **if . . . surely he shall be swallowed up**—The parallelism more favors UMBREIT, "Durst a man speak (before Him, complaining) *that he is* (without cause) *being destroyed?*" **21. cleanseth** i.e., *cleareth* the air of clouds. When the "bright light" of the sun, previously not seen through "clouds," suddenly shines out from behind them, owing to the wind clearing them away, the effect is dazzling to the eye; so if God's majesty, now hidden, were suddenly revealed in all its brightness, it would spread darkness over Job's eyes, anxious as he is for it (cf. *Note,* vs. 19) [UMBREIT]. It is because now man sees not the bright sunlight (God's dazzling majesty), owing to the intervening "clouds" (ch. 26:9), that they dare to wish to "speak" before God (vs. 20). Prelude to God's appearance (ch. 38:1). The words also hold true in a sense not intended by Elihu, but perhaps included by the Holy Ghost. Job and other sufferers cannot see the *light* of God's countenance through the *clouds* of trial: but the wind will soon clear them off, and God shall appear again: let them but wait patiently, for He still shines, though for a time they see Him not (see *Note,* 23:9). **22.** rather, golden splendor. MAURER translates "gold." *It* is found in northern regions. But *God* cannot be "found out," because of His "Majesty" (vs. 23). Thus ch. 28 corresponds; *English Version* is simpler. **the north**—*Brightness* is chiefly associated with it (*Note,* 23:9). Here, perhaps, because the north wind clears the air (Prov. 25:23). Thus this clause answers to the last of vs. 21; as the second of this verse to the first of vs. 21. Inverted parallelism. (See Isa. 14:13; Ps. 48:2). **with God**—rather, *upon God,* as a garment (Ps. 104:1, 2). **majesty**—splendor.

ADAM CLARKE

15. *And caused the light of his cloud to shine?* Almost every critic of note understands this of the rainbow.

F. B. MEYER:

"Men see not the bright light which is in the clouds" (37:21). The world owes much of its beauty to cloudland. The unchanging blue of the Italian sky hardly compensates for the changefulness and glory of the clouds. Clouds also are the cisterns of the rain. Earth would become a wilderness apart from their ministry. There are clouds in human life, shadowing, refreshing, and sometimes draping it in blackness of night; but there is never a cloud without its bright light. "I do set my bow in the cloud!"

If only we could see the clouds from the other side where they lie in billowy glory, bathed in the light they intercept, like heaped ranges of Alps, we should be amazed at their splendid magnificence. We look at their under side; but who shall describe the bright light that bathes their summits, and searches their valleys, and is reflected from every pinnacle of their expanse? Is not every drop drinking in health-giving qualities, which it will carry to the earth?

O child of God! If you could see your sorrows and troubles from the other side; if instead of looking up at them from earth, you would look down on them from the heavenly places where you sit with Christ; if you knew how they are reflecting in prismatic beauty before the gaze of heaven, the bright light of Christ's face—you would be content that they should cast their deep shadows over the mountain slopes of existence. Only remember that clouds are always moving, and passing before God's cleansing wind.—*Great Verses Through the Bible*

21. *And now men see not the bright light.* Elihu seems to refer to the insufferable brightness of the sun. Can any man look at the sun shining in his strength, when a clear and strong wind has purged the sky from clouds and vapors? Much less can any gaze on the majesty of God.

22. *Fair weather cometh out of the north.* Is this any version of the original, which is rendered by almost every version, ancient and modern, thus, or to this effect: "From the north cometh gold"?

23. *Touching the Almighty, we cannot find him out.* This is a very abrupt exclamation, and highly descriptive of the state of mind in which Elihu was at this time; full of solemnity, wonder, and astonishment at his own contemplation of this "great First Cause, least understood." The Almighty! we cannot find Him out.

MATTHEW HENRY

much less his own children. Some read it thus: "*The Almighty, whom we cannot find out, is great in power, but he will not afflict in judgment, and with him is plenty of justice*, nor is he extreme to mark what we do amiss." (6) He values not the censures of those who are wise in their own conceit: *He respecteth them not*, *v.* 24.

CHAPTER 38

Verses 1–3

1. Who speaks—*The Lord*, Jehovah, not a created angel, but the eternal Word himself, the second person in the blessed Trinity, for it is he by whom the worlds were made, and that was no other than the Son of God. He begins with the creation of the world. Elihu had said, *God speaks to men and they do not perceive it* (*ch.* xxxiii. 14); but this they could not but perceive. 2. When he spoke—*Then.* When they had all had their saying, then it was time for God to interpose, whose judgment is according to truth. Job had silenced his three friends, and yet could not convince them of his integrity in the main. Elihu had silenced Job, and yet could not bring him to acknowledge his mismanagement of this dispute. But now God comes, and does both, convinces Job first of his unadvised speaking and makes him cry, *Peccavi—I have done wrong;* and, having humbled him, he puts honour upon him, by convincing his three friends that they had done him wrong. 3. How he spoke—*Out of the whirlwind*, the rolling and involving cloud. A whirlwind prefaced Ezekiel's vision (Ezek. i. 4), and Elijah's, 1 Kings xix. 11. God is said to have *his way in the whirlwind* (Nah. i. 3), and, to show that even the stormy wind fulfils his word, here it was made the vehicle of it. 4. To whom he spoke: He *answered Job*, directed his speech to him, to convince him of what was amiss, before he cleared him from the unjust aspersions cast upon him. 5. What he said. The preface is very searching. (1) God charges him with ignorance and presumption in what he had said (*v.* 2): "*Who is this* that talks at this rate? Is it Job? What! my servant Job, a perfect and an upright man? Can he so far forget himself, and act unlike himself? Who, where is he *that darkens counsel thus by words without knowledge?* Let him show his face if he dare and stand to what he has said." A humble faith and sincere obedience shall see further and better into the secret of the Lord than all the philosophy of the schools, and the searches of science. This first word which God spoke is the more observable because Job, in his repentance, fastens upon it as that which silenced and humbled him, *ch.* xlii. 3. This he repeated and echoed as the arrow that stuck fast in him: "I am the fool that has darkened counsel." (2) He challenges him to give such proofs of his knowledge as would serve to justify his enquiries into the divine counsels (*v.* 3): "*Gird up now thy loins like a* stout *man; I will demand of thee*, will put some questions to thee, *and answer me* if thou canst, before I answer thine."

Verses 4–11

For the humbling of Job, God here shows him his ignorance even concerning the earth and the sea.

I. Concerning the founding of the earth.

1. Let him tell where he was when this lower world was made (*v.* 4): "*Where wast thou when I laid the foundations of the earth?* Wast thou present when the world was made?" See here, (1) The greatness and glory of God: *I laid the foundations of the earth.* (2) The meanness of man: *Where wast thou* then? So far were we from having any hand in the creation of the world, which might entitle us to a dominion in it, or so much as being witnesses of it, by which we might have gained an insight into it, that we were not then in being. The first man was not, much less were we. It is the honour of Christ that he was present when this was done (Prov. viii. 22, &c.; John i. 1, 2); but *we are of yesterday and know nothing.* Let us not therefore find fault with the works of God.

2. Let him describe how this world was made, "*Declare, if thou hast* so much *understanding*, what were the advances of that work. Stand forth, and *tell who laid the measures thereof* and *stretched out the line upon it.* Wast thou the architect that formed the model and then drew the dimensions by rule according to it?" The vast bulk of the earth is moulded as regularly as if it had been done by line and measure; but who can describe how it was cast into this figure? How it came to be so firmly fixed. Though it is hung upon nothing, yet it is established, but who can tell *upon what the foundations of it are fastened*, that it may not sink with its own weight, or *who laid the corner-stone thereof*, that the parts

JAMIESON, FAUSSET, BROWN

23. afflict—oppressively, so as to "pervert *judgment*" as Job implied (*Note*, 8:3); but see end of *Note*, vs. 21, above. The reading, "He answereth not," i.e., gives no account of His dealings, is like a transcriber's correction, from ch. 33:13; *Margin.* **24. do**—rather, "*ought.*" **wise**—in their own conceits.

CHAPTER 38

Vss. 1-41. **1.** Jehovah appears unexpectedly in a whirlwind (already gathering ch. 37:1, 2), the symbol of "judgment" (Ps. 50:3, 4, etc.), to which Job had challenged Him. He asks him now to get himself ready for the contest. Can he explain the phenomena of God's *natural* government? How can he, then, hope to understand the principles of His *moral* government? God thus confirms Elihu's sentiment, that *submission to,* not *reasonings on,* God's ways is man's part. This and the *disciplinary* design of trial to the godly is the great lesson of this book. He does not solve the difficulty by reference to future retribution: for this was not the immediate question; *glimpses* of that truth were already given in chs. 14 and 19, the *full revelation* of it being reserved for Gospel times. Yet even *now* we need to learn the lesson taught by Elihu and God in Job.

2. this—Job. **counsel**—impugning My divine wisdom in the providential arrangements of the universe. Such "words" (including those of the friends) rather obscure, than throw light on My ways. God is about to be Job's Vindicator, but must first bring him to a *right state of mind* for receiving relief.

3. a man—*hero*, ready for battle (I Cor. 16:13), as he had wished (ch. 9:35; 13:22; 31:37). The robe, usually worn flowing, was girt up by a girdle when men ran, labored, or fought (I Pet. 1:13).

4. To understand the cause of things, man should have been present at their origin. The finite creature cannot fathom the infinite wisdom of the Creator (ch. 28:12; 15:7, 8).

hast [knowest] **understanding**—(Prov. 4:1). **5. measures**—of its proportions. Image from an architect's plans of a building. **line**—of measurement (Isa. 28:17). The earth is formed on an all-wise *plan.*

6. foundations—not *sockets,* as *Margin.* **fastened**—lit., "made to sink," as a foundation stone let down till it settles firmly in the clay (ch. 26:7). Gravitation makes and keeps the earth a sphere.

ADAM CLARKE

He will not afflict. "He will not answer." "He will give account of none of His matters to us. We cannot comprehend His motives, nor the ends He has in view.

CHAPTER 38

1. *The Lord answered Job out of the whirlwind.* It is not *suphah,* as in the preceding chapter, v. 9; but *searah,* which signifies something turbulent, tumultuous, or violently agitated; and here may signify what we call a "tempest," and was intended to fill Job's mind with solemnity, and an awful sense of the majesty of God.

5. *Who hath laid the measures thereof?* Who hath adjusted its polar and equatorial distances from the center? *Who hath stretched the line?* Who hath formed its zones and its great circles, and adjusted the whole of its magnitude and gravity to the orbit in which it was to move, as well as its distance from that great center about which it was to revolve?

F. B. MEYER:

Divine power and human ignorance. When the storm had ceased and the thunder was hushed, a voice spoke out of the golden splendor of the sky (Job 37:21, 22). Job had challenged God to answer him and now he is taken at his word. We recall Horeb's ancient cave, where, after wind and earthquake, there came a sound of gentle stillness. "Gird up now thy loins," said the Eternal to Job. In later years, under similar circumstances, the Spirit entered Ezekiel to strengthen him. Surely some such strengthening was forthwith given the patriarch!

A sublime series of questions is now addressed to him, not by a God of judgment and wrath, but by a Father arguing and pleading with his child and pointing out two things: first, the inability of mortal man to understand the ways of God; and second, the minuteness and tenderness of God's providence. Job had thought of him as remote, but he is near and is ordering all things wisely and lovingly. Can he forget his child?—*Bible Commentary*

MATTHEW HENRY

of it may not fall asunder? *v.* 6.

3. Let him repeat if he can, the songs of praise which were sung at that solemnity (*v.* 7), *when the morning-stars sang together*, the blessed angels, who, in the morning of time, shone as brightly as the morning star, going immediately before the light which God commanded to shine out of darkness upon the earth, which was without form and void. They were *the sons of God*, who *shouted for joy* when they saw the foundations of the earth laid. The angels are called *the sons of God* because they bear much of his image, are with him in his house above, and serve him as a son does his father.

II. Concerning the limiting of the sea to the place appointed for it, *v.* 8, &c. This refers to the third day's work, when God said (Gen. i. 9), *Let the waters under the heaven be gathered together unto one place, and it was so.* 1. Out of the great deep or chaos, in which earth and water were intermixed, in obedience to the divine command the waters *broke forth like a child out of the* teeming *womb*, *v.* 8. 2. This new-born babe is clothed and swaddled, *v.* 9. *The cloud* is made *the garment thereof*, with which it is covered, and *thick darkness* (that is, shores vastly remote and distant from one another and quite in the dark one to another) *is a swaddling-band for it*. It is not said, He made *rocks and mountains* its swaddling bands, but *clouds and darkness*, something that we are not aware of and should think least likely for such a purpose. 3. There is a cradle too provided for this babe: *I broke up for it my decreed place*, *v.* 10. Valleys were sunk for it in the earth, capacious enough to receive it, and there it is laid to sleep; and, if it be sometimes tossed with winds, that (as Bishop Patrick observes) is but the rocking of the cradle, which makes it sleep the faster. As for the sea, so for every one of us, there is a decreed place; for he that determined the times before appointed determined also the bounds of our habitation. 4. This babe being made unruly and dangerous by the sin of man, which was the original of all unquietness and danger in this lower world, there is also a prison provided for it; *bars and doors are set*, *v.* 10. And it is said to it, by way of check to its insolence, *Hitherto shalt thou come, but no further.* The sea is God's, for he made it, he restrains it; he says to it, *Here shall thy proud waves be stayed*, *v.* 11. This may be considered as an act of God's power over the sea. Though it is so vast a body, and though its motion is sometimes extremely violent, yet God has it under check. Its waves rise no higher, its tides roll no further, than God permits; and this is mentioned as a reason why we should stand in awe of God (Jer. v. 22), and yet why we should encourage ourselves in him, for he that stops the noise of the sea, even the noise of her waves, can, when he pleases, still the tumult of the people, Ps. lxv. 7.

Verses 12–24

The Lord here proceeds to ask Job many puzzling questions, to convince him of his ignorance, and so to shame him for his folly in prescribing to God. Job is here challenged to give an account of six things:—

I. Of the springs of the morning, the dayspring from on high, *v.* 12–15. It was not we, it was not any man, that commanded the morning-light at first, or appointed the place of its springing up and shining forth, or the time of it. The constant and regular succession of day and night was no contrivance of ours; it is the glory of God that it shows, and his handy work, not ours, Ps. xix. 1, 2. It is quite out of our power to alter this course: "*Hast thou countermanded the morning since thy days?* No, never. Why then wilt thou pretend to direct the divine counsels, or expect to have the methods of Providence altered in favour of thee?" It is God that has appointed the day-spring to visit the earth, and diffuses the morning light through the air, which receives it as readily as the clay does the seal (*v.* 14), immediately admitting the impressions of it, so as of a sudden to be all over enlightened by it, as the seal stamps its image on the wax; *and they stand as a garment*, or as if they were clothed with a garment. The earth puts on a new face every morning, and dresses itself as we do, puts on light as a garment, and is then to be seen. This is made a terror to evil-doers. God makes the light a minister of his justice as well as of his mercy. It is designed *to shake the wicked out of the earth*, and for that purpose *it takes hold of the ends of it*, as we take hold of the ends of a garment to shake the dust and moths out of it. Job had observed what a terror the morning light is to criminals, because it discovers them (*ch.* xxiv. 13, &c.), and God here asks him whether the world was indebted to him for that kindness? No, the great Judge of the world sends forth the beams of the morning light as his messengers to detect criminals (*v.* 15), that their light may be *with-*

JAMIESON, FAUSSET, BROWN

7. So at the founding of Zerubbabel's temple (Ezra 3:10-13). So hereafter at the completion of the Church, the temple of the Holy Ghost (Zech. 4:7); as at its foundation (Luke 2:13, 14). **7. morning stars**—especially beautiful. The creation *morn* is appropriately associated with these, it being the *commencement* of this world's *day*. The stars are figuratively said to sing God's praises, as in Psalm 19:1; 148:3. They are symbols of the angels, bearing the same relation to our earth, as angels do to us. Therefore they answer to "sons of God," or angels, in the parallel. See *Note,* 25:5.

8. doors—floodgates; these when opened caused the flood (Gen. 8:2); or else, *the shores.* **womb**—of chaos. The bowels of the earth. Image from childbirth (vss. 8, 9; Ezek. 32:2; Mic. 4:10). Ocean at its birth was wrapped in clouds as its swaddling bands.

10. brake up for—i.e., appointed it. Shores are generally broken and abrupt cliffs. The *Greek* for *shore* means a *broken place.* I *broke off* or measured off for it *my limit,* i.e., the limit which I thought fit (ch. 26:10).

11. stayed—*Hebrew*, "a limit shall be set to."

12-15. Passing from creation to phenomena in the existing inanimate world. **12. Hast thou**—as God daily does. **commanded the morning**—to rise. **since thy days**—since thou hast come into being. **his place**—It varies in its place of rising from day to day, and yet it has its place each day according to fixed laws. **13. take hold of the ends . . .**—spread itself over the earth to its utmost bounds in a moment. **wicked**—who hate the light, and do their evil works in the dark (ch. 24:13). **shaken out of it**—The corners (*Hebrew*, "wings" or "skirts") of it, as of a garment, are taken hold of by the dayspring, so as to shake off the wicked. **14.** Explaining the first clause of vs. 13, as vs. 15 does the second clause. As the plastic clay presents the various figures impressed on it by a seal, so the earth, which in the dark was void of all form, when illuminated by the dayspring, presents a variety of forms, hills, valleys, etc. **Turned** ("turns itself," *Hebrew*) alludes to the rolling cylinder seal, such as is found in Babylon, which leaves its impressions on the clay, as it is turned about; so the morning light rolling on over the earth. **they stand**—The forms of beauty, unfolded by the dawn, stand forth as a garment, in which the earth is clad.

ADAM CLARKE

7. *When the morning stars sang together.* This must refer to some intelligent beings who existed before the creation of the visible heavens and earth, and it is supposed that this and the following clause refer to the same beings; that by the *sons of God* and the *morning stars,* the angelic host is meant, as they are supposed to be first, though perhaps not chief, in the order of creation.

10. *And brake up for it my decreed place.* This refers to the decree, Gen. i. 9: "Let the waters under the heaven be gathered together unto one place."

13. *That the wicked might be shaken out of it.* The meaning appears to be this: As soon as the light begins to dawn upon the earth, thieves, assassins, murderers, and adulterers, who all hate and shun the light, fly like ferocious beasts to their several dens and hiding places.

14. *And they stand as a garment.* The earth receiving these impressions from the solar light and heat, plants and flowers spring up, and decorate its surface as the most beautiful stamped garment does the person of the most sumptuously dressed female.

MATTHEW HENRY

holden from them (that is, that they may lose their comfort, their confidence, their liberties, their lives) and that their *high arm*, which they have listed up against God and man, may be *broken*, and they deprived of their power to do mischief. Here we are reminded of the *Benedictus* (Luke i. 78, By the *tender mercy of our God the day-spring from on high has visited us, to give light to those that sit in darkness*, 2 Cor. iv. 6), and the *Magnificat* (Luke i. 51), showing that God, in his gospel, has *shown strength with his arm, scattered the proud, and put down the mighty*, by that light by which he designed to shake the wicked, to shake wickedness itself out of the earth, and break its high arm.

II. Of the springs of the sea (*v.* 16): "*Hast thou entered into* them, or *hast thou walked in the search of the depth?* God's way in the government of the world is said to be *in the sea*, and *in the great waters* (Ps. lxxvii. 19), intimating that it is hidden from us and not to be pried into by us.

III. Of the gates of death: *Have* these *been open to thee? v.* 16. Death is a grand secret. *Man knows not his time*. We cannot describe what death is. Let us make sure that the gates of heaven shall be opened to us on the other side death, and then we need not fear the opening of the gates of death, though it is a way we are to go but once. While we are here, in a world of sense, we speak of the world of spirits as blind men do of colours.

IV. Of the breadth of the earth (*v.* 18): *Hast thou perceived* that? The knowledge of this might seem most level to him and within his reach; yet he is challenged to declare this if he can. It is but a point to the universe yet, small as it is, we cannot be exact in declaring the dimensions of it. Job had never sailed round the world, nor any before him; so little did men know the breadth of the earth that it was but a few ages ago that the vast continent of America was discovered, which had, time out of mind, lain hidden. It is presumption for us, who perceive not the breadth of the earth, to dive into the depth of God's counsels.

V. Of the place and way of light and darkness. Of the day-spring he had spoken before (*v.* 12) and he returns to speak of it again (*v.* 19): *Where is the way where light dwells?* And again (*v.* 24): *By what way is the light parted?* When God, in the beginning, first spread darkness upon the face of the deep, and afterwards commanded the light to shine out of darkness, by that mighty word, *Let there be light*, was Job a witness to the order, to the operation? Though we long ever so much either for the shining forth of the morning or the shadows of the evening, we know not whither to send, or go, to fetch them, nor can tell *the paths to the house thereof*, *v.* 20. We were not then born, nor is the number of our days so great that we can describe the birth of that first-born of the visible creation, *v.* 21. Shall we then undertake to discourse of God's counsels, which were from eternity, or to find out the paths to the house thereof, to solicit for the alteration of them? It is no order of ours, that is executed by the outgoings of the morning light and the darkness of the night. We cannot so much as tell whence they come nor whither they go (*v.* 24): *By what way is the light parted* in the morning, when, in an instant, it shoots itself into all the parts of the air above the horizon. It is a marvellous change that passes over us every morning by the return of the light and every evening by the return of the darkness; but we expect them, and so they are no surprise nor uneasiness to us. If we would, in like manner, reckon upon changes in our outward condition, we should neither in the brightest noon expect perpetual day nor in the darkest midnight despair of the return of the morning. God has set the one over against the other, like the day and night; and so must we, Eccles. vii. 14.

VI. Of the *treasures of the snow and hail* (*v.* 22, 23): "*Hast thou entered* into these and taken a view of them?" In the clouds the snow and hail are generated, and thence they come in such abundance that one would think there were treasures of them laid up in store there, whereas indeed they are produced *for the occasion*. What folly it is to strive against God, who is thus prepared for battle and war, and how much it is our interest to make our peace with him and to keep ourselves in his love.

Verses 25–41

Hitherto God had put questions to Job to convince him of his ignorance. Now he comes, in the same manner, to show his weakness. It is but little that he knows, and therefore he ought not to arraign the divine counsels. It is but little that he can do, and therefore he ought not to oppose the proceedings of Providence. Let him consider what great things God does, and try whether he can do the like.

JAMIESON, FAUSSET, BROWN

15. their light—by which they work; viz., darkness, which is *their day* (ch. 24:17), is extinguished by daylight.

high—Rather, *The arm uplifted* for murder or other crime is broken; it falls down suddenly, powerless, through their fear of light.

16. springs—fountains beneath the sea (Ps. 95:4, 5). **Search**—Rather, the inmost recesses; lit., "that which is only found by searching," the deep caverns of ocean.

17. seen—The second clause heightens the thought in the first. Man during life does not even "see" the gates of the realm of the dead ("death," ch. 10:21); much less are they "opened" to him. But those are "naked before God" (ch. 26:6).

18. Hast thou—as God doth (ch. 28:24).

19-38. The marvels in heaven. **19.** "What is the way (to the place wherein) light dwelleth?" The origin of light and darkness. In Genesis 1, "light" is created distinct from, and previous to, light-emitting bodies, the luminaries of heaven.

20. Dost thou know its place so well as to be able to *guide*, ("take" as in Isa. 36:17) it to (but UMBREIT, "*reach* it in") its own boundary, i.e., the limit between light and darkness (ch. 26:10)? **21.** Or without the interrogation, in an ironical sense [UMBREIT]. then—when I created light and darkness (ch. 15:7).

24. is . . . parted—parts, so as to diffuse itself over the whole earth, though seeming to come from one point. Light travels from the sun to the earth, ninety millions of miles, in eight minutes. **which scattereth**—rather, "And by what way the east wind (personified) spreads (scattereth) itself." The light and east wind are associated together, as both come from one quarter, and often arise together (Jonah 4:8).

22. treasures—storehouses, from which God draws forth snow and hail. Snow is vapor congealed in the air before it is collected in drops large enough to form hail. Its shape is that of a crystal in endless variety of beautiful figures. Hail is formed by rain falling through dry cold air. **23. against the time of trouble**—the time when I design to chastise men (Exod. 9:18; Josh. 10:11; Rev. 16:21; Isa. 28:17; Ps. 18:12, 13; Hag. 2:17).

ADAM CLARKE

CHARLES H. SPURGEON:

The question is, "Hast thou seen the doors of the shadow of death?" and the answer implied is—"No." In this chapter God is questioning Job in order to show him his inability and his ignorance; to each question which the Lord puts to the patriarch a negative answer is expected. "Hast thou entered into the springs of the sea?" "Hast thou walked in the search of the depth?" "Have the gates of death been opened to thee?" "Hast thou perceived the breadth of the earth?" Job had done none of these things.

Well, then, Job, "Hast thou seen the doors of the shadow of death?" The only answer the patriarch could haven given or that we can give is "No." We can get as far as the gates of death, but we cannot pry within. Apart from revelation we have no information about the dreary land beyond, that land which lies enshrouded, as far as we are concerned, in perpetual gloom. We cannot tell when or how we ourselves shall die, so little do we know of the dread mystery. The message will some day come to us that the pitcher is to be broken at the cistern, but when it shall come we little dream. It may be much nearer than we think, and, on the other hand, it may be farther off than we have feared.

Neither do we know what it is to die. We know, in a certain sense, what the act of death is; but what is the strange feeling with which the soul finds itself houseless, forsaken of the body which falls about it like a crumbling tenement—what it is to have the link severed which keeps the mortal bound to the immortal, the spiritual caged within the material—what that is, we do not know; neither hath any told it to us. We have watched others passing; we have stood by the bedside of the dying; we have witnessed the last gasp; and still it remains a secret what it is to die. We only know that these gates of the shadow of death are so shut upon us that we cannot hold any intercourse whatever with the world beyond, save only as there is an everlasting fellowship in the person of Christ between all that are in Him; so that

"The saints on earth, and all the dead,
But one communion make."

—*The Treasury of the Old Testament*

23. *Reserved against the time of trouble.* "To the season of strictness," i.e., the season when the earth is bound by the frost. *Against the day of battle and war.* Hailstones being often employed as instruments of God's displeasure against His enemies, and the enemies of His people. There is probably an allusion here to the plague of hail sent on the Egyptians. See Exod. ix. 23.

MATTHEW HENRY

I. God has thunder, and lightning, and rain, and frost, at command, but Job has not, and therefore let him not dare to compare himself with God, or to contend with him. He has a sovereign dominion over the waters, even when they seem to overflow and to be from under his check, *v.* 25. He has *divided a water-course.* Thus the hearts of kings are said to be *in God's hand*; and as the rains, those rivers of God, he turns them whithersoever he will. The lightning or the thunder, are not blind bullets, but go the way that God himself, who means no hurt to them, directs.

In directing the course of the rain he does not neglect the wilderness, the desert land (*v.* 26, 27), *where no man is.* God's providence reaches further than man's industry. If he had not more kindness for many of the inferior creatures than man has, it would go ill with them. When *there was not a man to till the ground*, yet there went up a mist and watered it. But we cannot make it fruitful without God; it is he that gives the increase. God has enough for all, and wonderfully provides even for those creatures that man neither has service from nor makes provision for. He is, in a sense, *the Father of the rain*, *v.* 28. Even the small drops of the dew he distils upon the earth, as the God of nature; and, as the God of grace, he rains righteousness upon us and is himself as the dew unto Israel. See Hos. xiv. 5, 6; Micah v. 7. The ice and the frost, by which the waters are congealed are produced by his providence, *v.* 29, 30. These are very common things, which lessens the strangeness of them. But, considering what a vast change is made by them in a very little time, we may well ask, "*Out of whose womb came the ice?* What created power could produce such a wonderful work?" No power but that of the Creator himself. Job cannot command one shower of rain: "*Canst thou lift up thy voice to the clouds*, those bottles of heaven, *that abundance of waters may cover thee*, to water thy fields when they are dry and parched? *Canst thou send lightnings, that they may go* on thy errand. Will they come at thy call, and say unto thee, *Here we are?*" No, the ministers of God's wrath will not be ministers of ours.

II. God has the stars of heaven under his command and cognizance. God mentions particularly the fixed stars. It is supposed that they have an influence upon this earth, notwithstanding their vast distance, not upon the minds of men or the events of providence (men's fate is not determined by their stars), but upon the ordinary course of nature. And if the stars have such a dominion over this earth (*v.* 33), though they are but mere matter, much more has he who is their Maker and ours, and who is an Eternal Mind. *Canst thou bind the sweet influences of Pleiades? Canst thou loose the bands of Orion?* Both summer and winter will have their course. God can change them when he pleases, can make the spring cold, and so bind the sweet influences of Pleiades, and the winter warm, and so loose the bands of Orion; but we cannot. God, who *calls the stars by their names* (Ps. cxlvii. 4), calls them forth in their respective seasons, appointing them the time of their rising and setting. But this is not our province; we cannot *bring forth Mazzaroth*—the stars in the southern signs, nor *guide Arcturus*—those in the northern, *v.* 32. We *know not the ordinances of heaven*, *v.* 33. So far are we from being able to change them that we can give no account of them; they are a secret to us. Shall we then pretend to know God's counsels. Shall we then teach God how to govern the world?

III. God is the author and giver, the father and fountain of all wisdom and understanding, *v.* 36. The souls of men are nobler and more excellent beings than the stars of heaven and shine more brightly. The powers and faculties of reason with which man is endued bring him into some alliance to the blessed angels; and whence comes this light, but from the Father of lights? *Who* else *has put wisdom into the inner parts* of man, and *given understanding to the heart?* The rational soul itself, and its capacities, come from him as the God of nature; for he forms the spirit of man within him. We did not make our own souls, nor can we describe how they act, nor how they are united to our bodies. He only that made them knows them. Shall we pretend to be wiser than God, when we have all our wisdom from him?

IV. God has the clouds under his cognizance and government, *v.* 37. Can any man, with all his wisdom, undertake to *number the clouds.* And when the clouds have poured down rain in abundance, so that *the dust grows into* solid mire and *the clods cleave fast together* (*v.* 38), *who can stay the bottles of heaven?* As we cannot command a shower of rain, so we cannot command a fair day, without God.

V. God provides food for the inferior creatures. The following chapter is wholly taken up with the instances of God's power and goodness about animals,

JAMIESON, FAUSSET, BROWN

25. waters—Rain falls, not in a mass on one spot, but in countless separate canals in the air marked out for them. **way for the lightning**—(ch. 28:26.)

26. Since rain falls also on places uninhabited by man, it cannot be that *man* guides its course. Such rain, though man cannot explain the reason for it, is not lost. *God* has some wise design in it. **27.** As though the desolate ground thirsted for God's showers. Personification. The beauty imparted to the uninhabited desert pleases God, for whom primarily all things exist, and He has ulterior designs in it.

28. Can any visible origin of rain and dew be assigned by man? Dew is moisture, which was suspended in the air, but becomes condensed on reaching the—in the night—lower temperature of objects on the earth. **29.** Ch. 37:10. **30.** The unfrozen *waters are hid* under the frozen, as *with* a covering of *stone.* **frozen**—lit., "is taken"; the particles take hold of one another so as to cohere.

31. sweet influences—the joy diffused by spring, the time when the Pleiades appear. The Eastern poets, Hafiz, Sadi, etc., describe them as "brilliant rosettes." GENESIUS translates: "bands" or "knot," which answers better the parallelism. But *English Version* agrees better with the *Hebrew.* The seven stars are closely "bound" together (*Note,* 9:9). "Canst thou bind or loose the tie?" "Canst thou loose the bonds by which the constellation Orion (represented in the East as an impious giant chained to the sky) is held fast?" (*Note,* 9:9). **32.** *Canst thou bring forth* from their places or *houses* (*Mazzaloth, Margin,* II Kings 23:5; to which *Mazzaroth* here is equivalent) into the sky the signs of the Zodiac at their respective seasons—the twelve lodgings in which the sun successively stays, or appears, in the sky? **Arcturus**—Ursa Major. **his sons**—the three stars in his tail. Canst thou make them appear in the sky? (ch. 9:9). The great and less Bear are called by the Arabs "Daughters of the Bier," the quadrangle being the bier, the three others the mourners. **33. ordinances**—which regulate the alternations of seasons, etc. (Gen. 8:22). **dominion**—*controlling influence* of the heavenly bodies, the sun, moon, etc., on the earth (on the tides, weather) (Gen. 1:16; Ps. 136:7-9). **34.** Jeremiah 14:22; above ch. 22:11, metaphorically. **35. Here we are**—at thy disposal (Isa. 6:8).

36. inward parts . . . heart—But [UMBREIT] "dark clouds ("shining phenomena") [MAURER]—"meteor," referring to the consultation of these as signs of weather by the husbandman (Eccles. 11:4). But *Hebrew* supports *English Version.* The connection is, "Who hath given thee the intelligence to comprehend in any degree the phenomena just specified?" **heart**—not the usual *Hebrew* word, but one from a root "to view"; perception. **37.** Who appoints by his wisdom the due measure of the clouds? **stay**—rather, "empty"; lit., "lay down" or "incline" so as to pour out. **bottles of heaven**—rain-filled clouds. **38. groweth . . .**—rather, pour itself into a mass by the rain, like molten metal; then translate vs. 38, "Who is it that *empties,* etc., "when," etc.? *English Version,* however, is tenable: "*Is caked into a mass*" by heat, like molten metal, *before* the rain falls; "Who is it that *can empty* the rain vessels, and bring down rain *at such a time?*" (vs. 38).

ADAM CLARKE

25. *Divided a watercourse.* The original may signify rather a "cloud," or clouds in general, where the waters are stored up.

26. *To cause it to rain on the earth.* It is well-known that rain falls copiously in thunder-storms. The flash is first seen, the clap is next heard, and last the rain descends.

31. *Canst thou bind the sweet influences of Pleiades?* The Pleiades are a constellation in the sign Taurus. They consist of six stars visible to the naked eye; to a good eye, in a clear night, seven are discernible; but with a telescope ten times the number may be readily counted.

32. *Mazzaroth in his season?* This is generally understood to mean the signs of the zodiac.

37. *Who can number the clouds?* Perhaps the word *saphar,* which is commonly rendered to *number,* may here mean, as in Arabic, to "irridiate," and may refer to those celestial and inimitable tinges which we sometimes behold in the sky. *Bottles of heaven.* The clouds; it is an allusion to the *girbahs,* or bottles made of skin, in which they are accustomed to carry their water from swells.

MATTHEW HENRY

and therefore some transfer to it the last three verses of this chapter, which speak of the provision made, *v.* 39, 40. "Let us try that then: *Wilt thou hunt the prey for the lion?* Thou valuest thyself upon thy possessions of cattle which thou wast once owner of, the oxen, and asses, and camels, that were fed at thy crib; but wilt thou undertake the maintenance of the lions, and *the young lions, when they couch in their dens,* waiting for a prey? No, they can shift for themselves without thee: But I do it." The all-sufficiency of the divine providence has wherewithal to satisfy the desire of every living thing. See the bounty of the divine Providence, that, wherever it has given life, it will give livelihood. The young ravens, *v.* 41, ravenous birds, are fed by the divine Providence. *Who* but God *provides for the raven his food?* They *cry* and this is interpreted a crying to God. It being the cry of nature, it is looked upon as directed to the God of nature. Some way or other he provides for them, so that they grow up, and come to maturity. And he that takes this care of the young ravens certainly will not be wanting to his people.

JAMIESON, FAUSSET, BROWN

39. From this verse to ch. 39:30, the instincts of animals. Is it thou that givest it the instinct to hunt its prey? (Ps. 104:21.) **appetite**—lit., "life"; which depends on the *appetite* (ch. 33:20). **40. lie in wait**—for their prey (Ps. 10:9).

41. Luke 12:24. Transition from the noble lioness to the croaking raven. Though man dislikes it, as of ill-omen, God cares for it, as for all His creatures.

ADAM CLARKE

39. *Wilt thou hunt the prey for the lion?* Rather the lioness, or strong lion. In the best Hebrew Bibles, the thirty-ninth chapter begins with this verse, and begins properly, as a new subject now commences, relating to the natural history of the earth, or the animal kingdom, as the preceding chapter does to astronomy and meteorology.

40. *When they couch in their dens.* Before they are capable of trusting themselves abroad. *Abide in the covert.* Before they are able to hunt down the prey by running. It is a fact that the young lions, before they have acquired sufficient strength and swiftness, lie under cover, in order to surprise those animals which they have not fleetness enough to overtake in the forest; and from this circumstance the *kephirim,* "young lions, or lions' whelps," have their name. The root is *caphar,* to "cover" or "hide."

41. *Who provideth for the raven?* This bird is chosen, perhaps, for his voracious appetite, and general hunger for prey, beyond most other fowls.

MATTHEW HENRY — CHAPTER 39

Verses 1–12

God here shows Job what little acquaintance he had with the untamed creatures that run wild in the deserts, but are the care of the divine Providence.

I. The *wild goats* and the *hinds.* Though they bring forth their young with a great deal of difficulty and sorrow, and have no assistance from man, yet, by the good providence of God, their young ones are safely produced, *v.* 3. Concerning the growth of their young (*v.* 4): *They are in good liking;* after their dams have suckled them awhile they shift for themselves in the cornfields, and are no more burdensome to them, which is an example to children, when they have grown up, not to be always hanging upon their parents.

II. The *wild ass,* a creature we frequently read of in Scripture, some say untameable. *Who* but God *has sent out the wild ass free?* He has given a disposition to it, and therefore a dispensation for it. Freedom from service, and liberty to range at pleasure, are but the privileges of a wild ass. It is a pity that any of the children of men should covet such a liberty. It is better to labour and be good for something than ramble and be good for nothing (v. 6). *Whose house I have made the wilderness,* where he has room enough to traverse his ways. The tame ass, that labours, and is serviceable to man, has his master's crib to go to both for shelter and food, and lives in a fruitful land: but the wild ass, that will have his liberty, must have it in a barren land. He has no owner, nor will he be in subjection: *He scorns the multitude of the city,* and *the crying of the driver* is nothing to him. *The range of the mountains is his pasture,* and a bare pasture it is; there he *searches after here and there a green thing,* as he can find it and pick it up; whereas the labouring asses have green things in plenty, without their searching for them. From the untamableness of this and other creatures we may infer how unfit we are to give law to Providence, who cannot give law even to a wild ass's colt.

III. The unicorn—*rhem,* a strong creature (Num. xxiii. 22), a stately proud creature, Ps. xcii. 10. He is able to serve, but not willing; and God here challenges Job to force him to it. "Since thou dost pretend" (says God) "to bring everything beneath thy sway, begin with the unicorn, and try thy skill upon him. Now that thy oxen and asses are all gone, try whether he will be willing to serve thee in their stead (*v.* 9) and whether he will be content with the provision thou usedst to make for them: *Will he abide by thy crib?* No; Thou canst not tame him, nor *bind him with his band,* nor set him to *draw the harrow,*" *v.* 10. Though the wild bull (which some think is meant here by the unicorn) will not serve him, nor submit to his band in the furrows, yet there are tame bullocks that will. "Thou darest not trust him; though *his strength is great,* yet thou wilt not *leave thy labour to him,* as thou dost with thy asses or oxen. Thou wilt never depend upon the wild bull, as likely to come to thy harvest-work, much less to go through it, to *bring home thy seed and gather it into thy barn,*" *v.* 11, 12.

Verses 13–18

The ostrich is a very large bird, but it never flies. Some have called it *a winged camel.*

I. Something that it has in common with the peacock, that is, beautiful feathers (*v.* 13): *Gavest thou proud wings unto the peacocks?* Fine feathers make proud birds. The peacock is an emblem of pride;

JAMIESON, FAUSSET, BROWN — CHAPTER 39

Vss. 1-30. **1.** Even wild beasts, cut off from all care of *man,* are cared for by *God* at their seasons of greatest need. Their instinct comes direct from God and guides them to help themselves in parturition; the very time when the herdsman is most anxious for his herds. **wild goats**—ibex (Ps. 104:18; I Sam. 24:2). **hinds**—fawns; most timid and defenseless animals, yet cared for by God. **2.** They bring forth with ease and do not need to reckon the months of pregnancy, as the shepherd does in the case of his flocks. **3.** "Bow themselves" in parturition; bend on their knees (I Sam. 4:19). **bring forth**—lit., "cause their young to cleave the womb and break forth." **sorrows**—their young ones, the cause of their momentary pains. **4. are in good liking**—in good condition, grow up strong. **with corn**—rather, "in the field," without man's care. **return not**—being able to provide for themselves. **5. wild ass**—Two different *Hebrew* words are here used for the same animal, "the ass of the woods" and "the wild ass." (*Note,* 6:5; ch. 11:12, 24:5; Jer. 2:24.) **loosed the bands**—given its liberty to. Man can rob animals of freedom, but not, as God, give freedom, combined with subordination to fixed laws.

6. barren—lit., "salt," i.e., unfruitful. (So *Margin,* Ps. 107:34.) **7. multitude**—rather, "din"; he sets it at defiance, being far away from it in the freedom of the wilderness. **driver**—who urges on the tame ass to work. The wild ass is the symbol of uncontrolled freedom in the East; even kings have, therefore, added its name to them. **8. The range**—lit., "searching," "that which it finds by searching is," etc.

9. unicorn—Pliny (*Natural History* 8. 21), mentions such an animal; its figure is found depicted in the ruins of Persepolis. The *Hebrew reem* conveys the idea of *loftiness* and *power* (cf. *Ramah,* Indian *Ram,* Latin *Roma*). The rhinoceros was perhaps the original type of the unicorn. The Arab *rim* is a two-horned animal. Sometimes "unicorn" or *reem* is a mere poetical symbol or abstraction; but the buffalo is the animal referred to here, from the contrast to the tame ox, used in ploughing (vss. 10, 12). **abide**—lit., "pass the night." **crib**—(Isa. 1:3). **10. his band**—fastened to the horns, as its chief strength lies in the head and shoulders. **after thee**—obedient to thee; willing to follow, instead of being goaded on *before* thee. **11. thy labour**—rustic work. **12. believe**—trust **seed**—produce (I Sam. 8:15). **into thy barn**—rather, *gather* (the contents of) *thy threshing-floor* [MAURER]; the corn threshed on it.

13. Rather, "the wing of the ostrich hen—lit., "the crying bird"; as the Arab name for it means "song"; referring to its night cries (ch. 30:29; Mic. 1:8) vibrating joyously. Is it

ADAM CLARKE — CHAPTER 39

F. B. MEYER:

"Knowest thou?" "Canst thou?" The series of questions is continued, and God asks more especially with respect to animated and organic nature: the wild goats (vv. 1–4), the wild ass (vv. 5–8), the wild ox (vv. 9–12), the peacocks and ostriches (vv. 13–18), the war horse (vv. 19–25), the hawk (vv. 26–30). In each case some special point is asked, hidden from the observation of ordinary men. If Job were unable to know more than they on such matters as these, how could he expect to know more than they of the reasons that dictate God's dealings with his people?

There is mystery in every part of the universe of God. He hides himself so that we cannot discover him. His thoughts are deeper, his ways profounder than our mind can fathom. There is not a single pathway leading out of the garden of life along which a man, traversing it, will not come to a point when the track dies away in the grass and there is no further progress. In nature and in Scripture alike we have to deal with the inscrutability of God's ways. Nor can we wonder, if the God of the Bible and of nature be the God of providence, that we find mystery also there.
—*Bible Commentary*

9. *Will the unicorn be willing to serve thee?* The animal in question, called *reim,* is undoubtedly the rhinoceros, which has the latter name from the horn that grows on his nose.

12. *That he will bring home thy seed.* Thou canst make no domestic nor agricultural use of him.

13. *The goodly wings unto the peacocks?* I believe *peacocks* are not intended here; and the Hebrew word should be translated "ostriches"; and the term which we translate *ostrich* should

MATTHEW HENRY

the ostrich too has goodly feathers, and yet is a foolish bird. God gives his gifts variously, and those gifts are not always the most valuable that make the finest show. Who would not rather have the voice of the nightingale than the tail of the peacock, the eye of the eagle and her soaring wing, and the natural affection of the stork, than the beautiful wings and feathers of the ostrich, which can never rise above the earth, and is without natural affection?

II. Something that is peculiar to itself. Most birds, as well as other animals, are strangely guided by natural instinct in providing for the preservation of their young. But the ostrich is a monster, for she drops her eggs anywhere upon the ground and takes no care to hatch them. If the sand and the sun will hatch them, well and good; for she will not warm them, *v.* 14. *The foot* of the traveller *may crush them,* and *the wild beast break them, v.* 15. *She is hardened against her young ones.* Her labour in laying her eggs is in vain, because she has not that tender concern for them that she should have. *God has deprived her of wisdom.* This intimates that the art which other animals have to nourish and preserve their young is God's gift, and that, where it exists not, God denies it, that by the folly of the ostrich, as well as by the wisdom of the ant, we may learn to be wise. So careless are many parents of their children; some of their bodies, not providing for their own house, and therefore as bad as the ostrich; but many more are thus careless of their children's souls, take no care of their education, send them abroad into the world untaught, unarmed, forgetting what corruption there is in the world through lust. She leaves her eggs in danger, but, if she herself be in danger, she lifts up her wings, and, with the help of them, runs so fast that a horseman at full speed cannot overtake her: *She scorneth the horse and his rider.* Those that are least under the law of natural affection often contend most for the law of self-preservation.

Verses 19–25

God, having displayed his power in those creatures that despise man, here shows it in one serviceable to man, and that is the horse, especially *the horse that is prepared against the day of battle.* It seems, there was, in Job's country, a noble breed of horses. The great horse has a great deal of strength and spirit (*v.* 19): *Hast thou given the horse strength?* He uses his strength for man, but God gave it to him, who is the fountain of all the powers of nature. It is a mercy to man to have such a servant, which, though very strong, submits to the management of a child, and rebels not against his owner. His neck is *clothed with thunder,* with a large and flowing mane. *The glory of his nostrils,* when he snorts, flings up his head, and throws foam about, *is terrbile, v.* 20. How frolicsome he is (*v.* 21): *He paws in the valley. He goes on to meet the armed men,* animated only by *the sound of the trumpet, the thunder of the captains, and the shouting* of the soldiers, *v.* 25. How fearless he is (*v.* 22): *He mocks at fear,* and makes a jest of it. High mettle is the praise of a horse rather than of a man, whom fierceness and rage ill become. This description of the war-horse will help to explain that character which is given of presumptous sinners, Jer. viii. 6.

Verses 26–30

The birds of the air are proofs of the wonderful power and providence of God. 1. The *hawk,* a noble bird of great strength and sagacity, and yet a bird of prey, *v.* 26. This bird is here taken notice of for her flight, which is swift and strong, and especially for the course she steers *towards the south,* whither she follows the sun in winter. This is her wisdom, and it was God that gave her this wisdom, not man. 2. The *eagle,* a royal bird is here taken notice of. (1) For the height of her flight. No bird soars so high, has so strong a wing, nor can so well bear the light of the sun. Now, "*Doth she mount at thy command? v.* 27. No; it is by the natural power and instinct God has given her." (2) For the strength of her nest. Her house is her castle and stronghold; she makes it *on high* and *on the rock, the crag of the rock* (*v.* 28), which sets her and her young out of the reach of danger. (3) For her quicksightedness (*v.* 29): *Her eyes behold afar off,* not upwards, but downwards, in quest of her prey. In this she is an emblem of a hypocrite, who, while, in the profession of religion, he seems to rise towards heaven, keeps his eye and heart upon the prey on earth, some temporal advantage, some widow's house or other that he hopes to devour, under pretence of devotion. (4) For the way she has of maintaining herself and her young. She preys upon living animals, which she seizes and tears to pieces, and then carries to her young ones, which are taught to *suck up blood;* they do it by instinct, and know no better. Our Saviour refers to this instinct of the eagle, Matt. xxiv. 28.

JAMIESON, FAUSSET, BROWN

not like the quill and feathers of *the pious bird*" (the stork)? [UMBREIT]. The *vibrating, quivering wing,* serving for sail and oar at once, is characteristic of the ostrich in full course. Its white and black feathers in the wing and tail are like the stork's. But, unlike that bird, the symbol of parental love in the East, it with seeming want of natural (pious) affection deserts its young. Both birds are poetically called by descriptive, instead of their usual appellative, names. **14.** Yet (unlike the stork) she "leaveth . . ." Hence called by the Arabs "the impious bird." However, the fact is, she lays her eggs with great care and hatches them, as other birds do; but in hot countries the eggs do not need so constant incubation; she therefore often leaves them and sometimes forgets the place on her return. Moreover, the outer eggs, intended for food, she feeds to her young; these eggs, lying separate in the sand, exposed to the sun, gave rise to the idea of her altogether leaving them. God describes her as she *seems to man;* implying, though she may seem foolishly to neglect her young, yet really she is guided by a sure instinct from God, as much as animals of instincts widely different. **16.** On a slight noise she often forsakes her eggs, and returns not, *as if* she were "hardened towards her young." **her labour**—in producing eggs, *is in vain,* (yet) *she has not disquietude* (about her young), unlike other birds, who, if one egg and another are taken away, will go on laying till their full number is made up. **17. wisdom**—such as God gives to other animals, and to man (ch. 35:11). The Arab proverb is, "foolish as an ostrich." Yet her very seeming want of wisdom is not without wise design of God, though man cannot see it; just as in the trials of the godly, which seem so unreasonable to Job, there lies hid a wise design. **18.** Notwithstanding her deficiencies, she has distinguishing excellences. **lifteth . . . herself**—for running; she cannot mount in the air. GESENIUS translates: "lashes herself" up to her course by flapping her wings. The old versions favor *English Version,* and the parallel "scorneth" answers to her *proudly* "lifting up herself." **19.** The allusion to "the horse" (vs. 18), suggests the description of him. Arab poets delight in praising the horse; yet it is not mentioned in the possessions of Job (chs. 1 and 42). It seems to have been at the time chiefly used for war, rather than "domestic purposes." **thunder**—poetically for, "he with arched neck inspires fear as thunder does." Translate, "majesty" [UMBREIT]. Rather "the trembling, quivering mane," answering to the "vibrating wing" of the ostrich (*Note,* vs. 13) [MAURER]. "Mane" in Greek also is from a root meaning "fear." *English Version* is more sublime. **20. make . . . afraid**—rather, "canst thou (as I do) make him *spring* as the *locust?"* So in Joel 2:4 the comparison is between *locusts* and *war-horses.* The heads of the two are so similar that the Italians call the locusts *cavaletta,* "little horse." **nostrils**—snorting furiously. **21. valley**—where the battle is joined. **goeth on**—goeth forth (Num. 1:3; 21:23). **23. quiver**—for the arrows, which they contain, and which are directed "against him." **glittering spear**—lit., "glittering of the spear," like "lightning of the spear" (Hab. 3:11). **shield**—rather, "lance." **24. swalloweth**—Fretting with impatience, he *draws the ground towards him* with his hoof, as if he would *swallow* it. The parallelism shows this to be the sense; not as MAURER, "scours over it." **neither believeth**—for joy. Rather, "he will not *stand still,* when the note of the trumpet" (soundeth). **25. saith**—poetically applied to his mettlesome neighing, whereby he shows his love of the battle. **smelleth**—snuffeth; discerneth (*Margin,* Isa. 11:3). **thunder**—thundering voice. **26.** The instinct by which some birds migrate to warmer climes before winter. Rapid flying peculiarly characterizes the whole hawk genus. **27. eagle**—It flies highest of all birds: thence called "the bird of heaven." **28. abideth**—securely (Ps. 91:1); it occupies the same abode mostly for life. **crag**—lit., "tooth" (*Margin,* I Sam. 14:5). **strong place**—citadel, fastness. **29. seeketh**—is on the lookout for. **behold**—The eagle descries its prey at an astonishing distance, by sight, rather than smell. **30.** Quoted partly by Jesus Christ (Matt. 24:28). The food of young eagles is the blood of victims brought by the parent, when they are still too feeble to devour flesh. **slain**—As the vulture chiefly feeds on carcasses, *it* is included probably in the eagle genus.

ADAM CLARKE

be, as it is elsewhere translated, "stork"; and perhaps the word rendered here *feathers* should be translated "hawk," or "pelican." Mr. Good has come nearest both to the original and to the meaning by translating thus: "The wing of the ostrich tribe is for flapping; but of the stork and falcon for flight."

17. *God hath deprived her of wisdom.* Of this foolishness we have an account from the ancients: "It covers its head in the reeds, and thinks itself all out of sight because itself cannot see."

18. *She lifteth up herself.* "When she raiseth up herself to run away." It neither flies nor runs distinctly, but has a motion composed of both; and, using its wings as sails, makes great speed.

21. *He paweth in the valley.* "They dig in the valley," i.e., in his violent galloping, in every pitch of his body, he scoops up sods out of the earth.

25. *He saith among the trumpets, Ha, ha.* The original is peculiarly emphatical: *Heach!* a strong, partly nasal, partly guttural sound, exactly resembling the first note which the horse emits in neighing.

26. *Doth the hawk fly by thy wisdom?* It may very probably mean the falcon. It was owing to its swiftness that the Egyptians in their hieroglyphics made it the emblem of the wind. *Stretch her wings toward the south?* Most of the falcon tribe pass their way toward warmer regions on the approach of winter.

29. *Her eyes behold afar off.* The eagle was proverbial for her strong and clear sight.

30. *Her young ones also suck up blood.* The eagle does not feed her young with carrion, but with prey newly slain, so that they may *suck up blood.* Where the slain are, there is she. These words are quoted by our Lord. "Wheresoever the carcase is, there will the eagles be gathered together," Matt. xxiv. 28. It is likely, however, that this was a proverbial mode of expression; and our Lord adapts it to the circumstances of the Jewish people, who were about to fall a prey to the Romans.

MATTHEW HENRY

CHAPTER 40

Verses 1–5

I. A humbling challenge which God gave to Job. Job remained silent, and therefore God put him upon replying, *v.* 1, 2. Some think God said it in a still small voice, which wrought more upon Job than the whirlwind did, as upon Elijah, 1 Kings xix. 12, 13. 1. God puts a convincing question to him: "*Shall he that contendeth with the Almighty instruct him?*" Those who quarrel with God do, in effect, go about to teach him how to mend his work. Some read it, *Is it any wisdom to contend with the Almighty?* 2. He demands a speedy reply to it: "*He that reproaches God let him answer* this question to his own conscience, and answer it thus, *Far be it from me to contend with the Almighty* or to *instruct him.*"

II. Job's humble submission. Now Job came to himself, and began to melt into godly sorrow. When his friends reasoned with him he did not yield. They had condemned him for a wicked man; Elihu himself had been very sharp upon him (*ch.* xxxiv. 7, 8, 37); but God had not given him such hard words. We may expect better treatment from God than we meet with from our friends. This the good man is here overcome by, and yields himself a conquered captive to the grace of God. 1. He owns himself an offender (*v.* 4): "*Behold, I am vile*, and abominable in my own eyes." Repentance changes men's opinion of themselves. When God talked with him, he had nothing to say. *What shall I answer thee?* Here he gives the reason of his silence; it was not because he was sullen, but because he was convinced he had been in the wrong. 2. He promises not to offend any more. He enjoins himself silence (*v.* 4): "*I will lay my hand upon my mouth*, will keep that as with a bridle, to suppress all passionate thoughts which may arise in my mind, and keep them from breaking out in intemperate speeches." Job had suffered his evil thoughts to vent themselves: "*Once have I spoken* amiss, *yea, twice*," that is, "divers times, in one discourse and in another; but I have done: *I will not answer*; I will not stand to what I have said, nor say it again; *I will proceed no further.*"

Verses 6–14

Job was greatly humbled for what God had already said, but not sufficiently; God here proceeds to reason with him as before, *v.* 6. God begins with a challenge (*v.* 7): "*Gird up thy loins now like a man;* if thou hast the courage and confidence thou hast pretended to, show them now."

I. We cannot vie with God for justice, the Lord is righteous and holy in his dealings with us, but we are unrighteous and unholy in our conduct towards him; we have a great deal to blame ourselves for, but nothing to blame him for (*v.* 8): "*Wilt thou disannul my judgment?*" "*Wilt thou*," says God, "*condemn me, that thou mayest be righteous?* Must my honour suffer for the support of thy reputation?"

II. We cannot vie with God for power; and therefore, as it is great impiety, so it is great impudence to contest with him: "*Hast thou an arm like God*, equal to his in length and strength? *Or canst thou thunder with a voice like him*, as he did (*ch.* xxxvii. 1, 2), or does now out of the whirlwind?" Man cannot speak so convincingly, so powerfully, nor with such a commanding conquering force as God can, who *speaks, and it is done.* His creating voice is called his *thunder* (Ps. civ. 7), so is that voice of his with which he terrifies and discomfits his enemies, 1 Sam. ii. 10. *Out of heaven shall he thunder upon them.*

III. We cannot vie with God for beauty and majesty, *v.* 10. "If thou wilt enter into a comparison with him, and appear more amiable, put on thy best attire: *Deck thyself now with majesty and excellency.* Appear in all the martial pomp, in all the royal pageantry that thou hast; make the best of everything that will set thee off: *Array thyself with glory and beauty*, such as may awe thy enemies and charm thy friends; but what is it all to the divine majesty and beauty? No more than the light of a glow-worm to that of the sun when he goes forth in his strength."

IV. We cannot vie with God for dominion over the proud, *v.* 11–14. If Job can humble and abase proud tyrants and oppressors as easily and effectually as God can, it shall be acknowledged that he has some colour to compete with God.

1. The justice Job is here challenged to do is to bring the proud low with a look.

(1) It is here supposed that God can do it and will do it himself, else he would not have put it thus upon Job. By this God proves himself to be God, that he resists the proud, sits Judge upon them, and is able to bring them to ruin. Proud people are wicked people, and pride is at the bottom of a great deal of the wickedness that is in this world. Proud people will certainly be abased and brought low; for *pride*

JAMIESON, FAUSSET, BROWN

CHAPTER 40

Vss. 1-24. GOD'S SECOND ADDRESS. He had paused for a reply, but Job was silent. **1. the Lord**—*Hebrew*, JEHOVAH.

2. he that contendeth—as Job had so often expressed a wish to do. Or, *rebuketh.* Does Job now still (after seeing and hearing of God's majesty and wisdom) wish to set God right? **answer it**—viz., the questions I have asked. **3. Lord**—JEHOVAH.

4. I am (too) vile (to reply). It is a very different thing to vindicate ourselves before God, from what it is before men. Job could do the latter, not the former.

lay . . . hand upon . . . mouth—I have no plea to offer (ch. 21:5; Judg. 18: 19).

5. Once . . . twice—oftentimes, more than once (ch. 33:14, cf. with 29; Ps. 62:11): "I have spoken," viz., against God. **not answer**—not plead against Thee.

6. the Lord—JEHOVAH. **7.** (*Note*, 38:3.) Since Job has not only spoken against God, but accused Him of injustice, God challenges him to try, could *he* govern the world, as *God* by His power doth, and punish the proud and wicked (vss. 7-14).

8. Wilt thou not only contend with, but *set aside My judgment* or justice in the government of the world? **condemn**—declare Me unrighteous, in order *that thou mayest be* accounted *righteous* (innocent; undeservingly afflicted). **9. arm**—God's omnipotence (Isa. 53:1).

thunder—God's voice (ch. 37:4). **10.** See, hast thou power and majesty like God's, to enable thee to judge and govern the world?

ADAM CLARKE

CHAPTER 40

1. *Moreover the Lord answered.* That is, the Lord continued His discourse with Job. *Answered* does not refer to any thing said by Job, or any question asked.

2. *He that reproveth God, let him answer it.* Let the man who has made so free with God and His government answer to what he has now heard.

F. B. MEYER:

"I am of small account; what shall I answer Thee? I lay mine hand upon my mouth" (40:4). What a different tone is here! This is he who so vehemently protested his innocence and defended himself against the attacks of his accusers. The Master is come, and the servant who had contended with his fellows takes a lowly place of humility and silence.

The first step in the noblest life, possible to any of us, is to learn and say that we are of small account. We may learn it by successive and perpetual failures which abash and confound us. It is better to learn it by seeing the light of God rise in majesty above the loftiest of earth's mountains. "When I was young," said Gounod to a friend, "I used to talk of 'I and Mozart.' Later I said, 'Mozart and I.' But now I only say 'Mozart.' " Substitute God, and you have the true story of many a soul.

The next step is to choke back words and lay the hand on the mouth. Silence and meditation! Not arguing or contending! Not complaining or murmuring! Not cavilling or criticizing! But just being still—still, that you may feel God near; still, that you may hear Him speak. "Take heed of many words," said George Fox, "keep down, keep low, that nothing may reign in you but life itself."

The greatest saints avoided, when they could, the society of men, and did rather choose to live to God in secret. A certain one said, "As oft as I have been among men I returned home less a man than I was before. Shut thy door upon thee, and call unto Jesus, thy Beloved. Stay with Him in thy closet, for thou shalt not find elsewhere so great peace." How good it would be to lay our hands on our mouths rather oftener, whether in silence with our fellows, or in the hour of secret prayer!

—*Great Verses Through the Bible*

9. *Hast thou an arm like God?* Every word from this to the end of v. 14, has a wonderful tendency to humble the soul; and it is no wonder that at the conclusion of these sayings Job fell in the dust confounded, and ascribed righteousness to his Maker.

MATTHEW HENRY

goes before destruction. The wrath of God, scattered among the proud, will humble them, and break them, and bring them down. *Who knows the power of his anger?* God can and does easily abase proud tyrants; he can *look upon them, and bring them low,* by one angry look, as he can, by a gracious look, revive the hearts of the contrite ones. He can not only bring them to the dust, from which they might hope to arise, but *hide them in the dust,* like the proud Egyptian whom Moses slew and *hid in the sand* (Exod. ii. 12). They were proud of the figure they made, but they shall be buried in oblivion and be no more remembered than those that are hidden in the dust. They were linked in leagues and confederacies to do mischief, and are now bound in bundles. They are hidden *together, ch.* xvii. 16. He *binds their faces in secret* or as dead men. Thus complete will be the victory that God will gain, at last, over proud sinners that set themselves in opposition to him.

(2) It is here proposed to Job to do it. He had been passionately quarrelling with God and his providence. "Come," says God, "try thy hand first upon proud men, and thou wilt soon see how little they value the rage of thy wrath; and shall I then regard it, or be moved by it?" If God, and he only, has power enough to humble and bring down proud men, no doubt he has wisdom enough to know when and how to do it, and it is not for us to prescribe to him or to teach him how to govern the world.

2. The justice which is here promised to be done him if he can perform such mighty works as these (*v.* 14): "*Then I will also confess unto thee that thy right hand* is sufficient to save thee, though, after all, it would be too weak to contend with me."

Verses 15–24

God, for the further proving of his own power, concludes his discourse with the description of two mighty animals, far exceeding man in bulk and strength, one he calls *behemoth,* the other *leviathan.* In these verses we have the former described. "*Behold now behemoth,* and consider whether thou art able to contend with him who made that beast and gave him all the power he has, and whether it is not thy wisdom rather to submit to him and make thy peace with him." *Behemoth* signifies *beasts* in general, but must here be meant of some one particular species. Some understand it of the *bull;* others of an amphibious animal called the *river-horse* (*hippopotamus*), living in the river Nile.

I. The description here given of the behemoth.

1. His body is very strong and well built. *His strength is in his loins, v.* 16. *His bones,* compared with those of other creatures, *are like bars of iron, v.* 18. His back-bone is so strong that, though his tail be not large, yet he moves it like a cedar, with a commanding force, *v.* 17.

2. He feeds on the productions of the earth and does not prey upon other animals: He *eats grass as an ox* (*v.* 15), the *mountains bring him forth food* (*v.* 20), and the beasts of the field do not tremble before him nor flee from him, as from a lion, but they play about him, knowing they are in no danger from him.

3. He *lodges under the shady trees* (*v.* 21), which *cover him with their shadow* (*v.* 22), where he has a free and open air to breathe in, while lions, which live by prey, when they would repose themselves, are obliged to retire into a close and dark den, to live therein, and to abide in the covert of that, *ch.* xxxviii. 40. Those who are a terror to others cannot but be sometimes a terror to themselves too; but those will be easy who will let others be easy about them; and the reed and fens, and the willows of the brook, though a very weak and slender fortification, yet are sufficient for the defence and security of those who *therefore* dread no harm, because they design none.

4. He is a very great and greedy drinker. His size is prodigious, and therefore he must have supply accordingly, *v.* 23. His eye anticipates more than he can take; for, when he is very thirsty *he trusts that he can drink up Jordan in his mouth,* and even *takes it with his eyes, v.* 24. His nose has in it strength for, when he goes greedily to drink with it, he *pierces through snares* or nets.

II. This description of this mountain of a beast is an argument with us to humble ourselves before the great God. He made this vast animal; it is *behemoth which I made, v.* 15. This beast is here called the *chief,* in its kind, *of the ways of God* (*v.* 19), an eminent instance of the Creator's power and wisdom. "It is *behemoth, which I made with thee*; I made that beast as well as thee, and he does not quarrel with me; why then dost thou? *He that made him can make his sword to approach to him* (*v.* 19), that is, the same hand that made him, notwithstanding his great bulk and strength can unmake him again at pleasure and kill an elephant as easily as a worm or a fly, without any difficulty.

JAMIESON, FAUSSET, BROWN

11. rage—rather, pour out *the redundant floods of* . . . . **behold**—Try, canst thou, as God, by a mere *glance* abase the proud (Isa. 2:12, etc.)? **12. proud**—high (Dan. 4:37). **in their place**—on the spot; suddenly, before they can move from their place (*Note,* 34:26; 36:20). **13.** (Isa. 2:10.) *abase* and remove them out of the sight of men.

bind . . . faces—i.e., shut up their persons [MAURER]. But it refers rather to the custom of binding a cloth over the faces of persons about to be executed (ch. 9:24; Esther 7:8). **in secret**—consign them to *darkness.*

14. confess—rather, extol; "I also," who now *censure* thee. But since thou canst not do these works, thou must, instead of censuring, extol *My* government. **thine own . . . hand . . . save**—(Ps. 44:3). So as to eternal salvation by Jesus Christ (Isa. 59:16; 63:5). **15-24.** God shows that if Job cannot bring under control the lower animals (of which he selects the two most striking, behemoth on land, leviathan in the water), much less is he capable of governing the world. **15. behemoth**—The description in part agrees with the hippopotamus, in part with the elephant, but exactly in all details with neither. It is rather a poetical personification of the great *Pachydermata,* or *Herbivora* (so "he eateth grass"), the idea of the hippopotamus being predominant. In vs. 17, "the tail like a cedar," hardly applies to the latter (so also vss. 20, 23, "Jordan," a river which elephants alone could reach, but see *Note,* vs. 23). On the other hand, vss. 21, 22 are characteristic of the *amphibious* river horse. So leviathan (the twisting animal), ch. 41:1, is a generalized term for cetacea, pythons, saurians of the neighboring seas and rivers, including the crocodile, which is the most prominent, and is often associated with the river horse by old writers. "Behemoth" seems to be the Egyptian *Pehemout,* "water-ox," Hebraized, so-called as being like an ox, whence the Italian *bombarino.* **with thee**—as I made thyself. Yet how great the difference! The *manifold* wisdom **and** power of God! **he eateth grass**—marvellous in an animal living so much in the water; also strange, that such a monster should not be carnivorous. **16. navel**—rather, *muscles* of his belly; the weakest point of the elephant, therefore *it* is not meant. **17. like a cedar**—As the tempest *bends* the cedar, so it can move its smooth thick tail [UMBREIT]. But the cedar implies straightness and length, such as do not apply to the river horse's short tail, but perhaps to an extinct species of animal (see *Note,* vs. 15). **stones**—rather, thighs. **wrapped**—firmly *twisted together,* like a thick rope. **18. strong pieces**—rather, *tubes* of copper [UMBREIT]. **19.** Chief of the *works* of God; so "ways" (ch. 26:14; Prov. 8:22). **can make his sword to approach**—rather, has furnished him with his sword (*harpe*), viz., the *sickle-like* teeth with which he cuts down grain. *English Version,* however, is literally right. **20.** The mountain is not his *usual* haunt. BOCHART says it is *sometimes* found there(?). **beasts . . . play**—a graphic trait: though armed with such teeth, he lets the beasts play near him unhurt, for his food is grass. **21. lieth**—He leads an inactive life. **shady trees**—rather, lotus bushes; as vs. 22 requires. **22.** Translate: "lotus bushes." **23.** Rather, "(Though) a river be violent (overflow), he trembleth not"; (for though living on land, he can live in the water, too); he is secure, though a Jordan swell up to his mouth. "Jordan" is used for *any great river* (consonant with the "behemoth"), being a poetical generalization (*Note,* vs. 5). The author cannot have been a Hebrew as UMBREIT asserts, or he would not adduce the Jordan, where there were no river horses. He alludes to it as a name for *any* river, but not as one known to him, except by hearsay. **24.** Rather, "Will any take him by open force" (lit., "before his eyes"), "or pierce his nose with cords?" No; he can only be taken by guile, and in a pitfall (ch. 41:1, 2).

ADAM CLARKE

13. *Hide them in the dust together.* Blend the high and the low, the rich and the poor, in one common ruin.

Bind their faces in secret. This seems to refer to the custom of preserving mummies.

15. *Behold now behemoth.* I am of the opinion that the animal here described is now extinct. The mammoth, for size, will answer the description in this place, especially v. 19: "He is the chief of the ways of God."

JOSEPH PARKER:

The argument would seem to be, Until you can understand these comparatively inferior matters, let other subjects alone: if you cannot explain the ground you tread upon, the probability is that you will not be able to explain the sky you gaze upon: if you know not yourself, how can you know God? And yet let us not be discouraged. If man has any superiority, it must be in other directions. How great, then, must those directions be, how sublime in their scope and energy? Is man altogether overwhelmed by these inquiries? In a certain limited way he is; but does he not recover his breath, and return and say, After all, I am crowned above all these things? He does, but we must wait until he has had time to recover his breath or regain his composure. The questions come upon him like a cataract! they roar upon him from all points of the compass in great overwhelming voices, so that he is deafened and stunned and thrown down, and asks for time. Presently we shall see that man is greater than all the stars put together, and that although he cannot search the past to exhaustion, he will live when the sun himself grows dim and nature fades away; he will abide in the secret of the Almighty, long as eternal ages roll.—*The People's Bible*

MATTHEW HENRY

God that gave to all the creatures their being may take away the being he gave; for may he not do what he will with his own? The *behemoth* perhaps is here intended (as well as the *leviathan* afterwards) to represent those proud tyrants and oppressors whom God had just now challenged Job to abase and bring down. He that framed the engine, and put the parts of it together, knows how to take it in pieces.

CHAPTER 41

Verses 1–10

Whether this leviathan be a whale or a crocodile is a great dispute among the learned. The whale is much larger and a nobler animal and the creation of whales was generally looked upon as a most illustrious proof of the eternal power of the Creator.

I. How unable Job was to master the leviathan. 1. He could not catch him with angling, *v.* 1, 2. He had no bait wherewith to deceive him, no hook wherewith to catch him, no fish-line wherewith to draw him out of the water, nor a thorn to run through his gills, on which to carry him home. 2. He could not force him to cry for quarter, *v.* 3, 4. "He knows his own strength too well to *make many supplications to thee*, and to *make a covenant with thee* to be thy servant on condition thou wilt save his life." 3. He could not entice him into a cage, and keep him there as a bird for the children to play with, *v.* 5. 4. He could not have him served up to his table; he and his companions could not make a banquet of him. 5. They could not enrich themselves with the spoil of him: *Shall they part him among the merchants*, the bones to one, the oil to another? If they can catch him, they will; but the art of fishing for whales was not brought to perfection then, as it has been since. 6. They could not destroy him, could not *fill his head with fish-spears*, *v.* 7. 7. It was to no purpose to attempt it: *The hope of* taking *him is in vain*, *v.* 9. *Shall not one be cast down even at the sight of him?* "Touch him if thou dare; *remember the battle*, how unable thou art to encounter such a force." Job is hereby admonished not to proceed in his controversy with God, but to make his peace with him.

II. Thence he infers how unable he was to contend with the Almighty. *None is so fierce*, none so foolhardy, *that he dares to stir up* the leviathan (*v.* 10), and *who then is able to stand before God.*

Verses 11–34

I. God's sovereign dominion and independency laid down, *v.* 11. 1. That he is indebted to none of his creatures. "*Who has prevented me?*" that is, "who has laid any obligations upon me by any services he has done me?" 2. That he is the rightful Lord and owner of all the creatures: "*Whatsoever is under the whole heaven*, animate or inanimate, is *mine*."

II. The proof and illustration of it, from the wonderful structure of the leviathan, *v.* 12.

1. The parts of his body, the power he exerts, are what God will not conceal. Though he is a creature of monstrous bulk, yet there is in him a *comely proportion.* (1) The leviathan, *at first sight*, appears formidable and inaccessible, *v.* 13, 14. Who dares come so near him while he is alive as to take a distinct view of *the face of the garment*, the skin with which he is clothed, so near him as to bridle him, or to be within reach of his jaws, which are like *a double bridle*? Who will venture to look into his mouth, as we do into a horse's mouth? He that *opens the doors of his face* will see *his teeth terrible round about.* (2) *His scales are* his beauty and strength, and therefore *his pride*, *v.* 15–17. The crocodile is indeed remarkable for his scales; if we understand it of the whale, we must understand by these *shields* (for so the word is) the several coats of his skin. (3) He scatters terror with his very breath; if he spout up water, it is like a light shining, either with the froth or the light of the sun shining through it. *v.* 18. The eyes of the whale are reported to shine in the night-time *like the eye-lids of the morning*; the same they say of the crocodile.

Probably these hyperbolical expressions (*v.* 19–21) are used concerning the leviathan to intimate the terror of the wrath of God. (4) He is of invincible strength so that he frightens all that come in his way, but is not himself frightened by any. Take a view of his neck, and there remains strength, *v.* 22.

JAMIESON, FAUSSET, BROWN

CHAPTER 41

Vss. 1-34. **1. leviathan**—lit., "the twisted animal," gathering itself in folds: a synonym to the Thannin (ch. 3:8, *Margin;* see Ps. 74:14; type of the Egyptian tyrant; Ps. 104:26; Isa. 27:1; the Babylon tyrant). A poetical generalization for all cetacean, serpentine, and saurian monsters (*Note,* 40:15, hence *all* the description applies to no *one* animal); especially the crocodile; which is naturally described after the *river horse,* as both are found in the Nile. **tongue . . . lettest down**—The crocodile has no tongue, or a very small one cleaving to the lower jaw. But as in fishing the tongue of the fish draws the baited hook to it, God asks, Canst thou in like manner take leviathan? **2. hook**—rather, a rope of rushes. **thorn**—rather, a ring or hook. So wild beasts were led about when caught (Isa. 37:29; Ezek. 29:4); fishes also were secured thus and thrown into the water to keep them alive. **3. soft words**—that thou mayest spare his life. No: he is untamable. **4.** Can he be tamed for domestic use (so ch. 39:10-12)? **5. a bird**—that is tamed. **6.** Rather, partners (viz., in fishing). **make a banquet**—The parallelism rather supports UMBREIT, "Do partners (in trade) *desire to purchase* him?" So the *Hebrew* (Deut. 2: 6). **merchants**—lit., "Canaanites," who were great merchants (Hos. 12:7, *Margin*). His hide is not penetrable, as that of fishes. **8.** If thou *lay . . .*, thou wilt have reason ever to *remember . . .*, and thou wilt never try it again. **9. the hope**—of taking *him.* **cast down**—with fear "at the (mere) sight of him." **10. fierce**—courageous. If a man *dare* attack one of My creatures (Gen. 49:9; Num. 24:9), who will dare (as Job has wished) oppose himself (Ps. 2:2) to Me, the Creator? This is the main drift of the description of leviathan. **11. prevented**—done Me a favor first: anticipated Me with service (Ps. 21:3). None can call Me to account ("stand before Me," vs. 10) as unjust, because I have withdrawn favors from him (as in Job's case): for none has laid Me under a prior obligation by conferring on Me something which was not already My own. What can man give to Him who possesses all, including man himself? Man cannot constrain the creature to be his "servant" (vs. 4), much less the Creator. **12. I will not conceal**—a resumption of the description broken off by the digression, which formed an agreeable change. **his power**—lit., "the way," i.e., true proportion or expression *of his strength* (so *Hebrew,* Deut. 19:4). **comely proportion**—lit., "the comeliness of his structure" (his *apparatus:* so "suit of apparel" Judg. 17:10) [MAURER]. UMBREIT translates, "his armor." But that follows after. **13. discover**—rather, *uncover the surface* of his garment (*skin,* ch. 10:11): strip off the hard *outer coat* with which the inner skin is covered. **with**—rather, within his double jaws; lit., "bridle"; hence that into which the bridle is put, the double row of teeth; but "bridle" is used to imply that none dare put his hand in to insert a bridle where in other animals it is placed (vs. 4; ch. 39:10). **14. doors of . . . face**—his mouth. His teeth are sixty in number, larger in proportion than his body, some standing out, some serrated, fitting into each other like a comb [BOCHART]. **15.** Rather, his *furrows of shields* (as "tubes," "*channels,*" *Note,* 40:18), are, etc., i.e., the *rows of scales,* like *shields* covering him: he has seventeen such rows. **shut up**—firmly closed together. A musket ball cannot penetrate him, save in the eye, throat, and belly. **18.** Transate: "his sneezing, causeth a light to shine." Amphibious animals, emerging after having long held their breath under water, respire by violently expelling the breath like one sneezing: in the effort the *eyes* which are usually directed towards the sun, seem to flash fire; or it is the expelled *breath* that, in the sun, seems to emit light. **eyelids of morning**—The Egyptian hieroglyphics paint the *eyes of the crocodile* as the symbol for *morning,* because the eyes appear the first thing, before the whole body emerges from the deep [*Hor. Hierog.,* 1. 65. BOCHART]. **19. burning lamps**—"torches"; viz., in respiring (vs. 18), *seem* to go out. **20. seething**—boiling: lit., "blown under," under which a fire is blown. **21. kindleth coals**—poetical imagery (Ps. 18:8). **22. remaineth**—abideth permanently. His chief strength

ADAM CLARKE

CHAPTER 41

1. ***Canst thou draw out leviathan?*** **A species of whale has been supposed to be the creature in question, but the description suits no animal but the crocodile or alligator. The crocodile is a natural inhabitant of the Nile, and other Asiatic and African rivers. It is a creature of enormous voracity and strength, as well as fleetness in swimming. He will attack the largest animals, and even men, with the most daring impetuosity. In proportion to his size he has the largest mouth of all monsters. The upper jaw is armed with forty sharp, strong teeth, and the under jaw with thirty-eight.** ***With an hook.*** **That crocodiles were caught with a baited hook, at least one species of crocodile, we have the testimony of Herodotus, lib. ii., c. 70.**

8. ***Lay thine hand upon him.*** **Mr. Heath translates, "Be sure thou strike home. Mind thy blow: rely not upon a second stroke."**

MATTHEW HENRY

Sorrow rejoices (or *rides in triumph*) *before him*, for he makes terrible work wherever he comes. *His flesh is of brass*, which Job had complained his was not, *ch.* vi. 12.

His heart is as firm as a stone, *v.* 24. He has spirit equal to his bodily strength. *When he raises up himself* like a moving mountain in the great waters even *the mighty are afraid* lest he should overturn their ships.

(5) All the instruments of slaughter that are used against him do him no hurt and therefore are no terror to him, *v.* 26-29.

(6) His very motion in the water troubles it and puts it into a ferment, *v.* 31, 32.

2. He concludes with four things in general concerning this animal:—(1) *Upon earth there is not his like*, *v.* 33. No creature in this world is comparable to him for strength. It is well for man that he is confined to the waters and there has *a watch set upon him* (*ch.* vii. 12). (2) He *is made without fear.* (3) He is himself very proud; though lodged in the deep, yet *he beholds all high things*, *v.* 34. (4) *He is a king over all the children of pride.* Whatever bodily accomplishments men are proud of, and puffed up with, the leviathan excels them and is a *king over them.* Some read it so as to understand it of God: *He that beholds all high things, even he, is King over all the children of pride;* he can tame the behemoth (*ch.* xl. 15) and the leviathan. This discourse concerning those two animals was brought in to prove that it is God only who can *look upon proud men and abase them* (*ch.* xl. 11-13). He is *King over all the children of pride*, whether brutal or rational, and can make them all either bend or break before him, Isa. ii. 11.

JAMIESON, FAUSSET, BROWN

is in the neck. **sorrow**—anxiety or dismay personified. **is turned into joy**—rather, danceth, exulteth; wherever he goes, he spreads terror "before him." **23. flakes**—rather, dewlaps; that which *falls* down (*Margin*). They are "joined" *fast and firm,* together, not *hanging loose,* as in the ox. **are firm**—UMBREIT and MAURER, "are spread." **in themselves**—rather, upon him. **24. heart**—"In large beasts which are less acute in feeling, there is great firmness of the *heart,* and slower motion" [BOCHART]. The nether millstone, on which the upper turns, is especially hard. **25. he**—the crocodile: a type of the awe which the Creator inspires when He rises in wrath. **breakings**—viz., of the mind, i.e., terror. **purify themselves**—rather, they wander from the way, i.e., flee away bewildered [MAURER and UMBREIT]. **26. cannot hold**—on his hard skin. **habergeon**—coat of mail; *avail* must be taken by zeugma out of "hold," as the verb in the second clause: "hold" cannot apply to the "coat of mail." **27. iron . . . brass**—viz., weapons. **28. arrow**—lit., "son of the bow"; Oriental imagery (Lam. 3:13; *Margin*). **stubble**—Arrows produce no more effect than it would to throw stubble at him. **29. Darts**—rather, *clubs;* darts have been already mentioned. **30. stones**—rather, potsherds, i.e., the sharp and pointed scales on the belly, like broken pieces of pottery, **sharp-pointed things**—rather, *a threshing instrument,* but not on the *fruits* of the earth, but "on the *mire*"; irony. When he lies on the mire, he leaves the marks of his scales so imprinted on it, that one might fancy a threshing instrument with its sharp teeth had been drawn over it (Isa. 28:27). **31.** Whenever he moves. **sea**—the Nile (Isa. 19:5; Nah. 3:8). **pot of ointment**—the vessel in which it is mixed. Appropriate to the crocodile, which emits a musky smell. **32. path**—the foam on his track. **hoary**—as hair of the aged. **33. who**—being one who. . . . **34. beholdeth**—as their superior. **children of pride**—the proud and fierce beasts. So ch. 28:8; *Hebrew,* sons of pride. To humble the *pride* of man and to teach implicit submission, is the aim of Jehovah's speech and of the book; therefore with this as to leviathan, the type of God in His lordship over creation, He closes.

ADAM CLARKE

25. *By reason of breakings they purify themselves.* No version, either ancient or modern, appears to have understood this verse; nor is its true sense known.

29. *Darts are counted as stubble.* All these verses state that he cannot be wounded by any kind of weapon, and that he cannot be resisted by any human strength.

CHAPTER 42 (MATTHEW HENRY)

Verses 1-6

The words of Job justifying himself were ended, *ch.* xxxi. 40. The words of Job judging and condemning himself began, *ch.* xl. 4, 5. Here he goes on with words to the same purport. Though his patience had not its perfect work, his repentance for his impatience had. He is here thoroughly humbled for his folly and unadvised speaking, and it was forgiven him. When God had said all that to him concerning his own greatness and power appearing in the creatures *then Job answered the Lord* (*v.* 1), by way of submission.

I. He subscribes to the truth of God's unlimited power, knowledge, and dominion, to prove which was the scope of God's discourse out of the whirlwind, *v.* 2. 1. He owns that God can do everything. What can be too hard for him that made behemoth and leviathan, and manages both as he pleases? He knew this before, and had himself discoursed very well upon the subject, but now he knew it with application. "*Thou canst do everything*, and therefore canst raise me out of this low condition, which I have so often foolishly despaired of as impossible: I now believe thou art able to do this." 2. *No thought can be withholden from him.* Not a fretful, discontented, unbelieving thought is in our minds at any time but God is a witness to it. *Whatever the Lord pleased, that did he.* Job had said this passionately, complaining of it (*ch.* xxiii. 13), *What his soul desireth even that he doeth;* now he says, with pleasure and satisfaction, that *God's counsels shall stand.* If God's thoughts concerning us be *thoughts of good, to give us an unexpected end*, he cannot be withheld from accomplishing his gracious purposes.

II. He owns himself to be guilty of that which God had charged him with in the beginning of his discourse, *v.* 3. "Lord, the first word thou saidst was, *Who is this that darkens counsel by words without knowledge?* That word convinced me. I own *I am the man* that has been so foolish. That word reached my conscience, and set my sin in order before me. I have ignorantly overlooked the counsels and designs of God in afflicting me, and therefore have quarrelled with God, and insisted too much upon my own justification: *Therefore I uttered that which I understood not*," that is, "I have passed a judgment upon the dispensations of Providence, though I was utterly a stranger to the reasons of them." He owns himself

CHAPTER 42 (JAMIESON, FAUSSET, BROWN)

VSS. 1-6. JOB'S PENITENT REPLY.

2. In the first clause he owns God to be omnipotent over nature, as contrasted with his own feebleness, which God had proved (ch. 40:15; 41:34); in the second, that God is supremely just (which, in order to be governor of the world, He must needs be) in all His dealings, as contrasted with his own vileness (vs. 6), and incompetence to deal with the wicked as a just judge (ch. 40:8-14). **thought**—*purpose,* as in ch. 17:11; but it is usually applied to *evil devices* (ch. 21:27; Ps. 10:2): the ambiguous word is designedly chosen to express that, while to Job's finite view, God's plans seem bad, to the All-wise One they continue unhindered in their development, and will at last be seen to be as good as they are infinitely wise. No evil can emanate from the Parent of good (Jas. 1;13, 17); but it is His prerogative to overrule evil to good. **3.** I am the man! Job *in God's own words* (ch. 38: 2) expresses his deep and humble penitence. God's word concerning our guilt should be engraven on our hearts and form the groundwork of our confession. Most men in confessing sin palliate rather than confess. Job in omitting "by words" (ch. 38: 2), goes even further than God's accusation. Not merely my *words,* but my whole thoughts and ways were "without knowledge." **3. too wonderful**—I rashly denied that Thou hast any fixed plan in governing human affairs, merely because Thy plan was "too wonderful" for my comprehension.

CHAPTER 42 (ADAM CLARKE)

2. *I know that thou canst do every thing.* Thy power is unlimited, Thy wisdom infinite.

3. *Who is he that hideth counsel?* These are the words of Job, and they are a repetition of what Jehovah said, chap. xxxviii. 2: "Who is this that darkeneth counsel by words without knowledge?" Job now, having heard the Almighty's speech, and having received His reproof, echoes back His words: "Who is he that hideth counsel without knowledge?" Alas, I am the man.

MATTHEW HENRY

ignorant of the divine counsels; and so we are all. We see what God does, but we neither know why he does it nor what he will bring it to. The reason why we quarrel with Providence is because we do not understand it. He owns himself presumptuous in undertaking to discourse of that which he did not understand and to arraign that which he could not judge of. *He that answereth a matter before he heareth it, it is folly and shame to him.*

III. He will not answer, but he will *make supplication to his Judge*, as he had said, *ch.* ix. 15. "*Hear, I beseech thee, and I will speak* (*v.* 4), not speak either as plaintiff or defendant (*ch.* xiii. 22), but as a humble petitioner."

IV. He puts himself into the posture of a penitent. In true repentance there must be not only conviction of sin, but contrition and godly sorrow for it, sorrow *according to God*, 2 Cor. vii. 9.

1. "*I have heard of thee by the hearing of the ear.* I have known something of thy greatness, and power, and sovereign dominion. *But now* thou hast by immediate revelation discovered thyself to me in thy glorious majesty; *now my eyes see thee*; and therefore now I repent, and unsay what I have foolishly said." It is a great mercy to have a good education, and to know the things of God by the instructions of his word and ministers. When the understanding is enlightened by the Spirit of grace our knowledge of divine things as far exceeds what we had before as that by ocular demonstration exceeds that by report and common fame. By the teachings of men God reveals his Son to us; but by the teachings of his Spirit he reveals his Son in us (Gal. i. 16), and so *changes us into the same image*, 2 Cor. iii. 18. God is pleased sometimes to manifest himself most fully to his people by the rebukes of his word and providence. *Blessed is the man whom thou chastenest and teachest.*

2. Job thought hardly of himself (*v.* 6): *Wherefore I abhor myself, and repent in dust and ashes.* Even good people, that have no gross enormities to repent of, must be greatly afflicted in soul for the workings and breakings out of pride, passion, peevishness, and discontent, and all their hasty unadvised speeches. The more we see of the glory and majesty of God, and the more we see of the vileness and odiousness of sin and of ourselves because of sin, the more we shall abase and abhor ourselves for it. Let us leave it to God to govern the world, and make it our care, in the strength of his grace, to govern ourselves and our own hearts well.

Verses 7-9

While God was catechising Job out of the whirlwind one would have thought that he only was in the wrong, and that the cause would certainly go against him; but here we find the sentence given in Job's favour. Wherefore judge nothing before the time. Those who are truly righteous before God may have their righteousness clouded and eclipsed by great and uncommon affections, by the severe censures of men, by the sharp reproofs of conscience, and yet, in due time, these clouds shall all blow over, and God will *bring forth their righteousness as the light and their judgment as the noon-day*, Ps. xxxvii. 6.

I. Judgment given against Job's three friends, upon the controversy between them and Job. Elihu is not censured here, for he acted, not as a party, but as a moderator. Job is magnified and his three friends are mortified. Something of truth we thought they both had on their side, but it is well that the judgment is the Lord's and by it we will abide.

1. Job is greatly magnified and comes off with honour. When God appeared for him he had brought him to repentance for what he had said amiss, then he owned him in what he had said well. True penitents shall find favour with God, and what they have said and done amiss shall no more be mentioned against them. God calls him again and again *his servant Job*, four times in two verses, and he seems to take a pleasure in calling him so, as before his troubles (*ch.* i. 8), "*Hast thou considered my servant Job?* Though he is poor and despised, he is my servant notwithstanding, and as dear to me as when he was in prosperity. Though he has his faults, and has appeared to be a man subject to like passions as others, though he has contended with me, has gone about to disannul my judgment, and has darkened counsel by words without knowledge, yet he sees his error and retracts it, and therefore he is my servant Job still." If God says, *Well done, good and faithful servant*, it is of little consequence who says otherwise. He owns that he had *spoken of him the thing that was right*, beyond what his antagonists had done. Job had given a much better and truer account of the divine Providence than they had done. They had wronged God by making prosperity a mark of the

JAMIESON, FAUSSET, BROWN

4. When I said, "Hear," etc., Job's *demand* (ch. 13:22) convicted him of being "without knowledge." God alone could speak thus to Job, not Job to God: therefore he quotes again God's words as the groundwork of retracting his own foolish words. **5. hearing of the ear**—(Ps. 18:44, *Margin*). *Hearing* and *seeing* are often in antithesis (ch. 29:11; Ps. 18:8). **seeth**—not God's *face* (Exod. 33:20), but His presence in the veil of a dark cloud (ch. 38:1). Job implies also that, besides this literal *seeing*, he now saw spiritually what he had indistinctly taken on hearsay before God's infinite wisdom. He "now" proves this; he had seen in a *literal* sense before, at the beginning of God's speech, but he had not seen *spiritually* till "now" at its close.

6. myself—rather "I abhor," and retract *the rash speeches* I made against thee (vss. 3, 4) [UMBREIT].

7-17. EPILOGUE, in prose. **7. to Eliphaz**—because he was the foremost of the three friends; their speeches were but the echo of his. **right**—lit., "well-grounded," sure and true. Their spirit towards Job was unkindly, and to justify themselves in their unkindliness they used false arguments (ch. 13:7); (viz., that calamities always prove *peculiar* guilt); therefore, though it was "for God" they spake thus falsely, God "reproves" them, as Job said He would (ch. 13:10). **as . . . Job hath**—Job had spoken rightly in relation to *them* and their argument, denying their *theory*, and the *fact* which they alleged, that he was peculiarly guilty and a hypocrite; but wrongly in relation to *God*, when he fell into the opposite extreme of almost denying *all* guilt. This extreme *he* has now repented of, and therefore God speaks of him as now altogether "right."

ADAM CLARKE

CHARLES H. SPURGEON:

In the confession which now lies before us, *Job acknowledges God's boundless power*; for he exclaims, "I know that thou canst do everything, and that no thought can be withholden from thee." He felt that whatever the Lord chose to think or desire, He could at once accomplish. Job had a glimpse of that omnipotence of which the height and depth no mind can ever measure.

Job sees his own folly. He speaks like a man in a maze or a muse, and he says, "Who is he that hideth counsel without knowledge?" Look at the second verse of chapter thirty-eight, and you will see that he is quoting what God had said to him. The Lord's words are ringing in his ears, and in his anguish he repeats them, accepting them as justly applicable to himself. It is not far from being right with us when the words of God can fitly become our words. "The Lord answered Job out of the whirlwind, and said, Who is this that darkeneth counsel by words without knowledge?" And now Job replies, "I am that foolish one: I uttered that I understood not; things too wonderful for me, which I knew not." Job felt that what he had spoken concerning the Lord was in the main true; and the Lord himself said to Job's three friends. "Ye have not spoken of me the thing that is right, as my servant Job hath"; but under a sense of the divine presence Job felt that even when he had spoken aright, he had spoken beyond his own proper knowledge, uttering speech whose depths of meaning he could not himself fathom. Many a holy prophet has done this, for inspired men are described as those who "enquired and searched diligently; searching what, or what manner of time the Spirit which was in them did signify, when it testified beforehand the sufferings of Christ, and the glory that should follow." It is not the thoughts of the prophets which have been inspired of God so much as their words; for frequently they were moved to speak prophecies which were quite beyond their own understanding; in fact, my brethren, are not all the great mysteries of the faith above human thought? and may we not fearlessly assert that no inspired man has ever known all the depth of God's meaning treasured up in the words which he himself has been led by the Spirit of God to write? Hence I assert that there is a verbal inspiration, or no inspiration at all worthy of the name. Job, as he comes before us in the text, is impressed with his own folly. He had to a large degree spoken what he felt sure was true, but he now feels that he did not understand what he said; and he at the same time tacitly confesses that he may have said in his bitterness many an unwise and unseemly thing, and therefore he bows his head before the Lord his God, and confesses that he has darkened counsel by words without knowledge, and uttered things that he understood not.

—*The Treasury of the Old Testament*

MATTHEW HENRY	JAMIESON, FAUSSET, BROWN	ADAM CLARKE

true church and affliction a certain indication of God's wrath. Job had referred things to the future judgment, and the future state, more than his friends had done, and therefore he spoke of God that which was right, better than his friends had done. Though he had spoken some things amiss, even concerning God, yet he is commended for what he spoke that was right. Job was in the right, and his friends were in the wrong, and yet he was in pain and they were at ease—a plain evidence that we cannot judge of men by looking in their faces or purses. He only can do it infallibly who sees men's hearts. Notwithstanding all the wrong his friends had done him, he is so good a man, and of such a humble, tender, forgiving spirit, that he will very readily pray for them. *My servant Job will pray for you.* True penitents shall not only find favour as petitioners for themselves, but be accepted as intercessors for others also. And, as Job prayed and offered sacrifice for those that had grieved and wounded his spirit, so Christ prayed and died for his persecutors, and ever lives *making intercession for the transgressors.*

2. Job's friends are greatly mortified, and come off with disgrace. They were good men and belonged to God, and therefore he would not let them lie still in their mistake any more than Job, but, having humbled them by a discourse out of the whirlwind, he takes another course to humble them. In most disputes and controversies there is something amiss on both sides, either in the merits of the cause or in the management, if not in both; and it is fit that both sides should be told of it, and made to see their errors. God tells them plainly that they had *not spoken of him the thing that was right, like Job,* that is, they had censured and condemned Job upon a false hypothesis, had represented God fighting against Job as an enemy when really he was only trying him as a friend. Those do not say well of God who represent his fatherly chastisements of his own children as judicial punishments. It is a dangerous thing to judge uncharitably of the spiritual and eternal state of others, for in so doing we may perhaps condemn those whom God has accepted. *My wrath is kindled against thee and thy two friends.* He requires from them a sacrifice, to make atonement for what they had said amiss. They must bring each of them *seven bullocks,* and each of them *seven rams,* to be offered up to God for a *burnt-offering.* He orders them to go to Job, and beg of him to offer their sacrifices, and pray for them, otherwise they should not be accepted. They thought that they only were the favourites of Heaven, and that Job had no interest there; but God gives them to understand that he had a better interest there than they had. Job and his friends had differed in their opinion about many things, but now they were to be made friends. They must agree in a sacrifice and a prayer, and that must reconcile them. Those who differ in judgment about minor things are yet one in Christ the great sacrifice, and meet at the same throne of grace, and therefore ought to love and bear with one another. Our quarrels with God always begin on our part, but the reconciliation begins on his.

II. The acquiescence of Job's friends in this judgment given, *v.* 9. They were good men, and, as soon as they understood what the mind of the Lord was, they did as he commanded them. Peace with God is to be had only in his own way and upon his own terms, and they will never seem hard to those who know how to value the privilege. Job's friends had all joined in accusing Job, and now they join in begging his pardon. Those that have sinned together should repent together.

Verses 10–17

You have heard of the patience of Job (says the apostle, James v. 11) *and have seen the end of the Lord,* that is, what end the Lord, at length, put to his troubles. In the beginning of this book we had Job's patience under his troubles, for an example; here, in the close, for our encouragement to follow that example, we have the happy issue of his troubles and the prosperous condition to which he was restored. Perhaps, too, the extraordinary prosperity which Job was crowned with after his afflictions was intended to be to us Christians a type and figure of the glory and happiness of heaven, which the afflictions of this present time are working for us. He that rightly endures temptation, when he is tried, shall receive a *crown of life* (James i. 12).

I. God returned in ways of mercy to him. This put a new face upon his affairs immediately, and everything now looked as pleasing and promising as before it had looked gloomy and frightful. God *turned his captivity,* that is, he redressed his grievances and took away all the causes of his complaints; he loosed him from the bond with which Satan had now, for a great while, bound him. What was more, he felt a very

ALEXANDER MACLAREN:

The close of the Book of Job must be taken in connection with its prologue in order to get the full view of its solution of the mystery of pain and suffering. Indeed the prologue is more completely the solution than the ending is; for it shows the purpose of Job's trials as being, not his punishment, but his testing. The whole theory that individual sorrows were the result of individual sins, in the support of which Job's friends poured out so many eloquent and heartless commonplaces, is discredited from the beginning. The magnificent prologue shows the source and purpose of sorrow. The epilogue in this last chapter shows the effect of it in a good man's character, and afterwards in his life.

So we have the grim thing lighted up, as it were, at the two ends. Suffering comes with the mission of trying what stuff a man is made of, and it leads to closer knowledge of God, which is blessed; to lowlier self-estimation, which is also blessed; and to renewed outward blessings, which hide the old scars and gladden the tortured heart.

Job's final word to God is in beautiful contrast with much of his former unmeasured utterances. It breathes lowliness, submission, and contented acquiescence in a providence partially understood. It does not put into Job's mouth a solution of the problem, but shows how its pressure is lightened by getting closer to God. Each verse presents a distinct element of thought and feeling.

—Expositions of Holy Scripture

him—rather, "His *person* [face] only" (*Note,* 22:30). The "person" must be first accepted, before God can accept his offering and work (Gen. 4:4); *that* can be only through Jesus Christ. **folly**—impiety (ch. 1:22; 2:10).

8. seven—(See Introduction). The number offered by the Gentile prophet (Num. 23:1). Job plainly lived before the legal priesthood, etc. The patriarchs acted as priests for their families; and sometimes as praying mediators (Gen. 20:17), thus foreshadowing the true Mediator (I Tim. 2:5), but sacrifice accompanies and is the groundwork on which the mediation rests.

9. The forgiving spirit of Job foreshadows the love of Jesus Christ and of Christians to enemies (Matt. 5:44; Luke 23:34; Acts 7:60; 16:24, 28, 30, 31).

10. turned . . . captivity—proverbial for *restored,* or *amply indemnified him for all he had lost* (Ezek. 16:53; Ps. 14:7; Hos. 6:11). Thus the future vindication of man, body and soul, against Satan (ch. 1:

8. *Take . . . seven bullocks and seven rams.* From this it appears that Job was considered a priest, not only in his own family, but also for others. For his children he offered burnt offerings, chap. i. 5; and now he is to make the same kind of offerings, accompanied with intercession, in behalf of his three friends. This is a full proof of the innocence and integrity of Job. A more decided one could not be given that the accusations of his friends, and their bitter speeches, were as untrue as they were malevolent.

MATTHEW HENRY

great alteration in his mind; the tumult was all over, and the consolations of God were now as much the delight of his soul as his terrors had been its burden. The tide thus turned, his troubles began to ebb as fast as they had flowed, just then *when he was praying for his friends.* We are really doing our business when we are praying for our friends, if we pray in a right manner, for in those prayers there is not only faith, but love. Christ has taught us to pray with and for others in teaching us to say, *Our Father*; and, in seeking mercy for others, we may find mercy ourselves. God doubled his possessions: *Also the Lord gave Job twice as much as he had before.* He suffered for the glory of God, and therefore God made it up to him with advantage, and allowed him more than interest upon interest. God will take care that none shall lose by him. Job's friends had often said, *If thou wert pure and upright, surely now he would awake for thee, ch.* viii. 6. But he does not awake for thee; therefore thou art not upright. "Well," says God, "though your argument be not conclusive, I will even by that demonstrate the integrity of my servant Job; his latter end shall greatly increase."

II. His old acquaintance, neighbours, and relations, were very kind to him, *v.* 11. They wept for his griefs, and rejoiced in his joys, and proved not such miserable comforters as his three friends, that, at first, were so forward and officious to attend him. These were not such great men nor such learned and eloquent men as those, but they proved much more skilful and kind in comforting Job. They made a collection among them for the repair of his losses and the setting of him up again. *Every one gave him a piece of money and everyone an ear-ring of gold,* which would be as good as money to him. When God was friendly to him they were all willing to be friendly too, Ps. cxix. 74, 79. Others of them, it may be, withdrew because he was poor, and sore, and a rueful spectacle, but now that he began to recover they were willing to renew their acquaintance with him. Swallow-friends, that are gone in winter, will return in the spring, though their friendship is of little value. Job *prayed for his friends,* and then they flocked about him, overcome by his kindness, and everyone desiring an interest in his prayers.

III. His estate strangely increased, by the blessing of God upon the little that his friends gave him. He thankfully received their courtesy, and did not think it below him to have his estate repaired by contributions. God gave him that which was far better than their money and ear-rings, and that was his blessing, *v.* 12. The Lord comforted him now according to the days wherein he had afflicted him, and *blessed his latter end more than his beginning.* The last days of a good man sometimes prove his best days, his last works his best works, his last comforts his best comforts; for his path, like that of the morning light, shines more and more to the perfect day. We know not what good times we may yet be reserved for in our latter end.

IV. His family was built up again, and he had great comfort in his children, *v.* 13–15. The number of his children was the same as before, *seven sons and three daughters.* Some give this reason why they were not doubled as his cattle were, because his children that were dead were not lost, but gone before to a better world; and therefore he has two fleeces of children (as I may say) *mahanaim—two hosts,* one in heaven, the other on earth. The names of his daughters are here registered (*v.* 14), because, in the significations of them, they seemed designed to perpetuate the remembrance of God's great goodness to him in the surprising change of his condition. He called the first *Jemima—The day,* because of the shining forth of his prosperity after a dark night of affliction. The next *Kezia,* a spice of a very fragrant smell. The third *Keren-happuch* (that is, *Plenty restored,* or *A horn of paint*), because (says he) God had wiped away the tears which fouled his face, *ch.* xvi. 16. Concerning these daughters, God adorned them with great beauty, *no women so fair as the daughters of Job, v.* 15. He made them co-heirs with their brethren.

V. His life was long. He lived to have much of the comfort of this life, for he saw his posterity to the fourth generation, *v.* 16. Though his children were not doubled to him, yet in his children's children (and those are the crown of old men) they were more than doubled. God has ways to repair the losses and balance the griefs of those who are written childless, as Job was when he had buried all his children. He died full of days, satisfied with living in this world, and willing to leave it; not peevishly so, as in the days of his affliction, but piously so, and thus, as Eliphaz had encouraged him to hope, he *came to his grave like a shock of corn in his season.*

JAMIESON, FAUSSET, BROWN

9-12), at the resurrection (ch. 19:25-27), has its earnest and adumbration in the temporal vindication of Job at last by Jehovah in person.

twice—so to the afflicted literal and spiritual Jerusalem (Isa. 40:2, 60:7; 61:7; Zech. 9:12). As in Job's case, so in that of Jesus Christ, the glorious recompense follows the "intercession" for enemies (Isa. 53:12).

11. It was Job's complaint in his misery that his "brethren," were "estranged" from him (ch. 19:13); these now return with the return of his prosperity (Prov. 14:20; 19:6, 7); the true friend loveth at all times (Prov. 17: 17; 18:24). "Swallow friends leave in the winter and return with the spring" [HENRY]. **eat bread**—in token of friendship (Ps. 41:9). **piece of money**—Presents are usual in visiting a man of rank in the East, especially after a calamity (II Chron. 32:23). *Hebrew, kesita.* MAGEE translates *"a lamb"* (the medium of exchange then before money was used), as it is in *Margin* of Genesis 33:19; Joshua 24:32. But it is from the *Arabic kasat,* "weighed out" [UMBREIT], not coined; so Genesis 42:35; 33:19; cf. with Genesis 23:15, makes it likely it was equal to four shekels; *Hebrew kashat,* "pure," viz., metal. The term, instead of the usual "shekel," etc., is a mark of antiquity. **earring**—whether for the nose or ear (Gen. 35:4; Isa. 3:21). Much of the gold in the East, in the absence of banks, is in the shape of ornaments.

12. Probably by degrees, not all at once.

13. The same number as before; perhaps by a second wife; in ch. 19:17 his wife is last mentioned.

14. Names significant of his restored prosperity (Gen. 4:25; 5:29). Jemima, "daylight," after his "night" of calamity; but MAURER, "a dove." Kezia, "cassia," an aromatic herb (Ps. 45:8), instead of his offensive breath and ulcers. Keren-happuch, "horn of stibium," a paint with which females dyed their eyelids; in contrast to his "horn defiled in the dust" (ch. 16:15). The names also imply the beauty of his daughters. **15. inheritance among . . . brethren**—An unusual favor in the East to daughters, who, in the Jewish law, only inherited, if there were no sons (Num. 27:8), a proof of wealth and unanimity. **16.** LXX makes Job live 170 years after his calamity, and 240 in all. This would make him seventy at the time of his calamity, which added to 140 in *Hebrew* text makes up 210; a little more than the age (205) of Terah, father of Abraham, perhaps his contemporary. Man's length of life gradually shortened, till it reached threescore and ten in Moses' time (Ps. 90:10). **16. sons' sons**—a proof of divine favor (Gen. 50:23; Ps. 128:6; Prov. 17:6). **17. full of days**—*fully sated and contented* with all the happiness that life could give him; realizing what Eliphaz had painted as the lot of the godly (ch. 5:26; Ps. 91:16; Gen. 25:8; 35:29). LXX adds, "It is written, that he will rise again with those whom the Lord will raise up." Cf. Matthew 27:52, 53, from which it perhaps was derived spuriously.

ADAM CLARKE

10. *The Lord turned the captivity of Job.* It is said that *the Lord turned the captivity of Job, when he prayed for his friends.* He had suffered much through the unkindness of these friends. They had criticized his conduct without feeling or mercy, and he had just cause to be irritated against them; and that he had such a feeling toward them several parts of his discourses sufficiently prove. God was now about to show Job His mercy; but mercy can be shown only to the merciful. Job must forgive his unfeeling friends if he would be forgiven by the Lord.

11. *A piece of money. Kesitah* signifies a "lamb"; and it is supposed that this piece of money had a lamb stamped on it, as that quantity of gold was generally the current value for a lamb. The Vulgate, Chaldee, Septuagint, Arabic, and Syriac have "one lamb or sheep"; so it appears that they did not understand the *kesitah* as implying a piece of money of any kind, but a sheep or a lamb. *Earring of gold.* Literally, a "nose-jewel."

12. *The Lord blessed the latter end of Job.* Was it not in consequence of his friends bringing him a lamb, sheep, or other kind of cattle, and the quantity of gold mentioned, that his stock of sheep was increased so speedily to 14,000, his camels to 6,000, his oxen to 2,000, and his she-asses to 1,000? *He had fourteen thousand sheep.* The reader, by referring to chap. i. 3, will perceive that the whole of Job's property was exactly *doubled.*

13. *Seven sons and three daughters.* This was the same number as before.

14. *The name of the first, Jemima.* "Days upon days." *Kezia.* "Cassia," a well-known aromatic plant. *Keren-happuch.* The "horn of plenty."

15. *Gave them inheritance among their brethren.* This seems to refer to the history of the daughters of Zelophehad, given in Num. xxviii. 1-8, who appear to have been the first who were allowed an inheritance among their brethren.

16. *After this lived Job an hundred and forty years.* How long he had lived before his afflictions we cannot tell.

17. *Job died, being old and full of days.* He died when he was "satisfied with this life"; this the word *seba* implies.

THE BOOK OF PSALMS

I. Book I (1-41)
- *A. Dominant notes of worship*
  - 1. Jehovah
    - a. The Becoming One
    - b. The Helper
  - 2. Adoring worship
- *B. Occurrences of divine names*
  - 1. Jehovah—275
  - 2. Elohim—68
  - 3. Adonai—14
- *C. Doxology (41:13)*

II. Book II (42-72)
- *A. Dominant notes of worship*
  - 1. Elohim—the wonder-working God
  - 2. Wondering worship
- *B. Occurrences of divine names*
  - 1. Jehovah—32
  - 2. Elohim—214
  - 3. Adonai—19
  - 4. Jah—1
- *C. Doxology (72:18, 19)*

III. Book III (73-89)
- *A. Dominant notes of worship*
  - 1. Elohim-Jehovah: the mighty helper
  - 2. Ceaseless worship
- *B. Occurrences of divine names*
  - 1. Jehovah—44
  - 2. Elohim—80
  - 3. Adonai—15
- *C. Doxology (89:52)*

IV. Book IV (90-106)
- *A. Dominant notes of worship*
  - 1. Elohim-Jehovah: the governing king
  - 2. Submissive worship
- *B. Occurrences of divine names*
  - 1. Jehovah—103
  - 2. Elohim—72
  - 3. Adonai—2
  - 4. Jah—7
- *C. Doxology (106:48)*

V. Book V (107-150)
- *A. Dominant notes of worship*
  - 1. Jehovah: the redeemer
  - 2. Perfected worship
- *B. Occurrences of divine names*
  - 1. Jehovah—236
  - 2. Elohim—40
  - 3. Adonai—12
  - 4. Jah—32
- *C. Doxology (150)*

The History of Israel led us to camps and council boards, and there instructed us in the knowledge of God. The book of Job brought us into the schools and treated us with disputations concerning God and his providence. But this book brings us into the sanctuary, draws us off from converse with the politicians, philosophers, or disputers of this world, and directs us into communion with God, lifting up and letting out our hearts toward him. Thus may we be in the mount with God.

I. The title of this book. It is called:

A. The *Psalms*; under that title is it referred to (Luke 24:44). The Hebrew calls it *Tehillim*, which properly signifies *Psalms of praise*, because many of them are such; but *Psalms* is a more general word, meaning all metrical compositions fitted to be sung, which may as well be historical, doctrinal, or supplicatory, as laudatory. Though singing be properly the voice of joy, yet the intention of songs is to assist the memory, and to express and excite all the other affections as well as this of joy. The priests had a mournful muse as well as joyful ones; and the divine institution of singing psalms is thus largely intended; for we are directed not only to praise God, but to teach and admonish ourselves and one another "in psalms, and hymns and spiritual songs" (Col. 3:16).

B. It is called the *Book of Psalms*: so it is quoted by Peter (Acts 1:20). It is a collection of psalms, of all the psalms that were divinely inspired.

II. The author of this book. It is, no doubt, derived originally from the blessed Spirit. They are spiritual songs, words which the Holy Ghost taught. The penman of most of them was David the son of Jesse, who is therefore called the "sweet psalmist of Israel" (2 Sam. 23:1). Some that have not his name in their titles yet are expressly ascribed to him elsewhere, as Psalm 2 (Acts 4:25) and Psalms 96 and 105 (1 Chron. 16). One psalm is expressly said to be "the prayer of Moses" (Ps. 90); and that some of the psalms were penned by Asaph is intimated (2 Chron. 29:30), where they are said to "praise the Lord in the words of David and Asaph," who is there called a "seer" or "prophet." Some of the psalms seem to have been penned long after, as Psalm 137, at the time of the captivity in Babylon; but the far greater part of them were certainly penned by David himself.

III. The scope of it. It is manifestly intended:

A. To assist the exercises of natural religion, and to kindle in the souls of men those devout affections which we owe to God as our Creator, owner, ruler, and benefactor. The book of Job helps to prove our first principles of the divine perfections and providence; but this helps to improve them in prayers and praises, and professions of dependence on him. Other parts of scripture show that God is infinitely above man, and is his sovereign Lord; but this shows us that there are ways in which we may keep up communion with him in all the various conditions of human life.

B. To advance the excellencies of revealed religion, and in the most pleasing powerful manner to recommend it to the world. There is indeed little or nothing of the ceremonial law in the book of Psalms. Though sacrifice and offering were yet to continue many ages, yet they are here represented as things which God did not desire (Ps. 40:6; 51:16), as things comparatively little, and which in time were to vanish away. But the word and law of God, those parts of it which are moral and of perpetual obligation, are here magnified and made honorable. And Christ, the crown and center of revealed religion, the foundation, corner, and top-stone, of that blessed building, is here clearly spoken of in type and prophecy, his sufferings and the glory that should follow, and the kingdom that he should set up in the world.

IV. The use of it. All scripture is profitable to convey divine light into our understandings; but this book is of singular use to convey divine life and power, and a holy warmth, into our affections.

A. It is of use to be sung. What the rules of the Hebrew metre were even the learned are not certain. But these psalms ought to be rendered according to the metre of every language, at least so that they may be sung for the edification of the church. So rich, so well made, are these divine poems, that they can never be exhausted, can never be worn thread-bare.

B. It is of use to be read by the ministers of Christ, as containing excellent truths and rules concerning good and evil.

C. It is of use to be read and meditated upon by all good people. The Psalmist's experiences are of great use for our direction, caution, and encouragement. In telling us, as he often does, what passed between God and his soul, he lets us know what we may expect from God, and what He will expect, and require, and graciously accept from us. Even the Psalmist's expressions too are of great use; and by them the Spirit helps our praying infirmities. If we make David's psalms familiar to us, whatever errand we have at the throne of grace, we may there find apt words wherewith to clothe it, sound speech which cannot be condemned. We may take sometimes one choice psalm and sometimes another, and pray it over, that is, enlarge upon each verse in our own thoughts, and offer up our own meditations to God as they arise from the expressions we find there.

MATTHEW HENRY

PSALM 1

Verses 1–3

The psalmist begins with the character and condition of a godly man.

I. The Lord knows those that are his by name, but we must know them by their character. The character of a good man is here given by the rules he chooses to walk by.

1. A godly man (*v.* 1) *walks not in the council of the ungodly*, &c. This part of his character is put first, because departing from evil is that in which wisdom begins. (1) He sees evil-doers round about him; the the world is full of them. They are here described by three characters, *ungoldly*, *sinners*, and *scornful*. They are *ungodly* first, casting off the fear of God. When the services of religion are laid aside, they come to be *sinners*, that is, they break out into open rebellion against God. Omissions make way for commissions, and by these the heart is so hardened that at length they come to be *scorners*, that is, they openly defy all that is sacred, scoff at religion, and make a jest of sin. The word which we translate *ungodly* signifies such as are unsettled, aim at no certain end and walk by no certain rule, but are at the command of every lust and at the beck of every temptation. These the good man sees with a sad heart. He does not do as they do. He does *not walk in the counsel of the ungodly*. He does not take his measures from their principles, nor act according to the advice which they give and take. He *stands not in the way of sinners*; he avoids doing as they do; their way shall not be his way. He *sits not in the seat of the scornful*. He does not associate with those that sit in close cabal to find out ways and means for the support and advancement of the devil's kingdom.

2. A godly man, that he may do that which is good and cleave to it, submits to the guidance of the word of God and makes that familiar to him, *v.* 2. All who are well pleased that there is a God must be well pleased that there is a Bible, a revelation of God, of his will, and of the only way to happiness in him. *In that law doth he meditate day and night.* To meditate in God's word is to discourse with ourselves concerning the great things contained in it, with a close application of mind, a fixedness of thought, till we be suitably affected with those things and experience the savour and power of them in our hearts.

II. An assurance given of the godly man's happiness. God blesses him, and that blessing will make him happy. Goodness and holiness are not only the way to happiness (Rev. xxii. 14) but happiness itself; supposing there were not another life after this, yet that man is a happy man that keeps in the way of his duty. *He shall be like a tree*, fruitful and flourishing. The divine blessing produces real effects. A good man is planted by the grace of God. These trees were by nature wild olives, and will continue so till they are grafted anew, and so planted by a power from above. Never any good tree grew of itself; it is *the planting of the Lord*, and therefore he must in it be glorified. Isa. lxi. 3. He is placed by the means of grace, here called *the rivers of water*; from these a good man receives supplies of strength and vigour, but in secret undiscerned ways. It is expected from those who enjoy the mercies of grace that, both in the temper of their minds and in the tenor of their lives, they comply with the intentions of that grace, and bring forth fruit. *His leaf also shall not wither.* As to those who bring forth only the leaves of profession, without any good fruit, even their leaf will wither; but, if the word of God rule in the heart, that will keep the profession green; the laurels thus won shall never wither.

Verses 4–6

I. The description of the ungodly given, *v.* 5. 1. In general, they are the reverse of the righteous, both in character and condition: they bring forth no fruit but grapes of Sodom; they cumber the ground. In particular, whereas the righteous are like valuable, useful, fruitful trees, *they are like the chaff which the wind drives away*, the very lightest of the chaff, the dust which the owner of the floor desires to have driven away, as not capable of being put to any use.

II. The doom of the ungodly read, *v.* 5. *They shall not stand in the judgment*, that is, they shall be found guilty. They shall not stand *in the congregation of the righteous*. The wicked shall not have a place in that congregation. Into the new Jerusalem none unclean nor unsanctified shall enter. Hypocrites in this world, under the disguise of a plausible profession, may thrust themselves into the congregation of the righteous and remain undisturbed and undiscovered there; but Christ cannot be imposed upon, though his ministers may.

III. The reason rendered of this different state of the

JAMIESON, FAUSSET, BROWN

PSALM 1

Vss. 1-6. The character and condition, and the present and future destiny, of the pious and the wicked are described and contrasted, teaching that true piety is the source of ultimate happiness, and sin of misery. As this is a summary of the teachings of the whole book, this Psalm, whether designedly so placed or not, forms a suitable preface.

1. Blessed—lit., "oh, the happiness"—an exclamation of strong emotion, as if resulting from reflecting on the subject. The use of the plural may denote fulness and variety (II Chron. 9:7). **counsel . . . way . . . seat**—With their corresponding verbs, mark gradations of evil, as acting on the principles, cultivating the society, and permanently conforming to the conduct of the wicked, who are described by three terms, of which the last is indicative of the boldest impiety (cf. Ps. 26:4, 5; Jer. 15:17).

2. law—all of God's word then written, especially the books of Moses (cf. Ps. 119:1, 55, 97, etc.).

3. like a tree—(Jer. 17:7, 8). **planted**—settled, fast. **by**—or, over. **the rivers**—canals for irrigation. **shall prosper**—lit., "make prosper," brings to perfection. The basis of this condition and character is given (Ps. 32:1).

4. not so—either as to conduct or happiness. **like the chaff**—which, by Eastern modes of winnowing against the wind, was utterly blown away.

–5. stand in the judgment—be acquitted. They shall be driven from among the good (Matt. 25:45, 46).

ADAM CLARKE

PSALM 1

1. *Blessed is the man.* This psalm has no title, and has been generally considered, but without especial reason, as a preface or introduction to the whole book.

The Word which we translate *blessed* is properly in the plural form, "blessednesses"; or may be considered as an exclamation produced by contemplating the state of the man who has taken God for his Portion; "Oh, the blessedness of the man!" And the word *haish* is emphatic: "that man"; that one among a thousand who lives for the accomplishment of the end for which God created him. *That walketh not in the counsel of the ungodly.* There is a double climax in this verse: First, there are here three characters, each exceeding the other in sinfulness. (1) The ungodly, *reshaim*, from *rasha*, to be "unjust"; rendering to none his due. (2) Sinners, *chattaim*, from *chata*, "to miss the mark," "to pass over the prohibited limits," "to transgress." This man not only does no good, but he does evil. (3) Scornful, *letsim*, from *latsah*, "to mock, deride." The second climax is found in the words, (1) Walk; (2) Stand; (3) Sit, which mark three different degrees of evil in the conduct of those persons. The ungodly man walks, the sinner stands, and the scornful man sits down in the way of iniquity.

2. *But his delight is in the law of the Lord.* His will, desire, affection, every motive in his heart, and every moving principle in his soul are on the side of God and His truth.

3. *Like a tree planted.* Not like one growing wild, but one that has been carefully cultivated.

His leaf also shall not wither. His profession of true religion shall always be regular and unsullied, and his faith be ever shown by his works.

MATTHEW HENRY

godly and wicked, *v.* 6. The Lord approves and is well pleased with the way of the righteous, and therefore, under the influence of his gracious smiles, it shall prosper and end well; but he is angry at the way of the wicked, all they do is offensive to him and therefore it shall perish, and they in it.

In singing these verses, and praying over them, let us possess ourselves with a holy dread of the wicked man's portion, and with a holy care to approve ourselves to God in everything, entreating his favour with our whole hearts.

PSALM 2

Verses 1–6

We have here a very great struggle about the kingdom of Christ, hell and heaven contesting it; the seat of the war is this earth.

I. The mighty opposition that would be given to the Messiah and his kingdom, *v.* 1–3. One would have expected that so great a blessing to this world would be universally welcomed and embraced. Never were the notions of any sect of philosophers, nor the powers of any prince, opposed with so much violence as the doctrine and government of Christ. Princes and people, court and country, have sometimes separate interests, but here they are united against Christ. Though his kingdom is not of this world, nor in the least calculated to weaken their interests, yet the kings of the earth and rulers are up in arms immediately. As the Philistines and their lords, Saul and his courtiers, the disaffected party and their ringleaders, opposed David's coming to the crown, so Herod and Pilate, the Gentiles and the Jews, did their utmost against Christ and his interest in men, Acts iv. 27. They quarrel *against the Lord and against his anointed*, that is, against all religion in general and the Christian religion in particular. The great author of our holy religion is here called *the Lord's anointed*, or *Messiah*, or *Christ*, in allusion to the anointing of David to be king. It is a most spiteful and malicious opposition. They *rage* and fret; they gnash their teeth for vexation at the setting up of Christ's kingdom. It is a deliberate and politic opposition. They *imagine*, that is, they contrive means to suppress the rising interests of Christ's kingdom. It is a resolute and obstinate opposition. They *set themselves* in defiance of reason. It is a combined and confederate opposition. They *take counsel together*, to assist and animate one another. They will be content to entertain such notions of the kingdom of God and the Messiah as will serve to support their own dominion. If the Lord and his anointed will make them rich and great in the world, they will bid them welcome; but if they will restrain their corrupt appetites and passions, *they will not have this man to reign over them*, Luke xix. 14. Christ has *bands and cords* for us; but they are *cords of a man*, agreeable to right reason, and *bands of love*, conductive to our true interest. Why do men oppose religion but because they are impatient of its restraints and obligations? They would break asunder the bands of conscience they are under and the cords of God's commandments. They are here reasoned with concerning it, *v.* 1. Why do they do this? They can show no good cause for opposing so just, holy, and gracious a government. They can hope for no good success in opposing so powerful a kingdom. It is *a vain thing*; when they have done their worst Christ will have a church in the world glorious and triumphant. It is *built upon a rock, and the gates of hell shall not prevail against it.*

II. The mighty conquest gained over all this threatening opposition. The perfect repose of the Eternal Mind may be our comfort under all the disquietments of our mind. We are tossed on earth, and in the sea, but he sits in the heavens, where he has prepared his throne for judgment.

1. The attempts of Christ's enemies are easily ridiculed. God *laughs at* them as a company of fools.

2. They are justly punished, *v.* 5. Though God despises them as impotent, yet he is justly displeased with them. The enemies rage, but cannot vex God. His setting up this kingdom of his Son, in spite of them, is the greatest vexation to them that can be.

3. They are certainly defeated, and all their counsels turned headlong (*v.* 6): *Yet have I set my king upon my holy hill of Zion.* Jesus Christ is a King, and God is pleased to call him *his* King, because he is appointed by him, and entrusted by him with the sole administration of government and judgment. He is his King, for he is dear to the Father, and one in whom he is well pleased. Christ took not this honour to himself, but was called to it. Being called to this honour, he was confirmed in it: "*I have set him*, I have settled him."

We are to sing these verses with a holy exultation,

JAMIESON, FAUSSET, BROWN

6. knoweth the way—attends to and provides for them (Ps. 101:6; Prov. 12:10; Hos. 13:5). **way of the wicked**—All their plans will end in disappointment and ruin (Ps. 37: 13; 146:8; Prov. 4:19).

PSALM 2

Vss. 1-12. The number and authorship of this Psalm are stated (Acts 4:25; 13:33). Though the warlike events of David's reign may have suggested its imagery, the scenes depicted and the subjects presented can only find a fulfilment in the history and character of Jesus Christ, to which, as above cited and in Hebrews 1:5; 5:5, the New Testament writers most distinctly testify. In a most animated and highly poetical style, the writer, in "four stanzas of three verses each," sets forth the inveterate and furious, though futile, hostility of men to God and His anointed, God's determination to carry out His purpose, that purpose as stated more fully by His Son, the establishment of the Mediatorial kingdom, and the imminent danger of all who resist, as well as the blessing of all who welcome this mighty and triumphant king.

1. Why do the heathen . . .—Beholding, in prophetic vision, the peoples and nations, as if in a tumultuous assembly, raging with a fury like the raging of the sea, designing to resist God's government, the writer breaks forth into an exclamation in which are mingled surprise at their folly, and indignation at their rebellion. **heathen**—nations generally, not as opposed to Jews. **people**—or, lit., "peoples," or races of men. **2.** The kings and rulers lead on their subjects. **set themselves**—take a stand. **take counsel**—lit., "sit together," denoting their deliberation. **anointed**—*Hebrew*, Messiah; *Greek*, Christ (John 1:41). Anointing, as an emblem of the gifts of the Holy Spirit, was conferred on prophets (Isa. 6:1); priests (Exod. 30: 30); and kings (I Sam. 10:1; 16:13; I Kings 1:39). Hence this title well suited Him who holds all these offices, and was generally used by the Jews before His coming, to denote Him (Dan. 9:26). While the prophet has in view men's opposition generally, he here depicts it in its culminating aspect as seen in the events of Christ's great trial. Pilate and Herod, and the rulers of the Jews (Matt. 27:1; Luke 23:1-25), with the furious mob, are vividly portrayed. **3.** The rebellious purposes of men are more distinctly announced by this representation of their avowal in words, as well as actions. **bands . . . and . . . cords**—denote the restraints of government.

4. By a figure whose boldness is only allowable to an inspired writer, God's conduct and language in view of this opposition are now related. **He that sitteth in the heavens**—enthroned in quiet dignities (cf. Ps. 29:10; Isa. 40: 22). **shall laugh**—in supreme contempt; their vain rage excites His derision. He is still *the Lord*, lit., "Sovereign," though they rebel. **5. Then shall he speak**—His righteous indignation as well as contempt is roused. For God to speak is for Him to act, for what He resolves He will do (Gen. 1:3; Ps. 33:9). **vex them**—agitate or terrify them (Ps. 83:15). **6.** The purpose here declared, in its execution, involves their overthrow. **Yet**—lit., "and," in an adversative sense. **I have set**—anointed, or firmly placed, with allusion in the *Hebrew* to "casting an image in a mould." The sense is not materially varied in either case. **my king**—appointed by Me and for Me (Num. 27:18). **upon my holy hill of Zion**—Zion, selected by David as the abode of the ark and the seat of God's visible residence (I King 8:1); as also David, the head of the Church and nation, and type of Christ, was called holy, and the Church itself came to be thus named (Ps. 9:11; 51:18; 99:2; Isa. 8:18; 18:7, etc.).

ADAM CLARKE

6. *The Lord knoweth.* "Approveth" the way, of the righteous, *tsaddikim*, from *tsadak*, to "give even weight"—the men who give to all their due; opposed to *reshaim*, v. 1, they who withhold right from all.

PSALM 2

1. *Why do the heathen rage?* It has been supposed that David composed this psalm after he had taken Jerusalem from the Jebusites, and made it the head of the kingdom; 2 Sam. vv. 7-9. The Philistines, hearing this, encamped in the valley of Rephaim, nigh to Jerusalem, and Josephus, *Antiq.* lib. vii. c. 4, says that all Syria, Phoenicia, and the other circumjacent warlike people, united their armies to those of the Philistines, in order to destroy David before he had strengthened himself in the kingdom. David, having consulted the Lord, 2 Sam. vv. 17-19, gave them battle, and totally overthrew the whole of his enemies. In the first place, therefore, we may suppose that this psalm was written to celebrate the taking of Jerusalem, and the overthrow of all the kings and chiefs of the neighboring nations. In the second place we find, from the use made of this psalm by the apostles, Acts iv. 27, that David typified Jesus Christ, and that the psalm celebrates the victories of the gospel. *The heathen, goyim,* the nations; those who are commonly called "the Gentiles." *Rage, rageshu;* the gnashing of teeth, and tumultuously rushing together, of those indignant and cruel people are well expressed by the sound as well as the meaning of the original word.

2. *Against his anointed.* "Against his Messiah." But as this signifies "the anointed" person, it may refer first to David, as it does secondly to Christ.

4. *He that sitteth in the heavens shall laugh.* Words spoken after the manner of men; shall utterly contemn their puny efforts.

MATTHEW HENRY

triumphing in Jesus Christ as the great trustee of power; and we are to pray, in firm belief of the assurance here given, "Father in heaven, *Thy kingdom come*; let thy Son's kingdom come."

Verses 7–9

Let us now hear what the Messiah himself has to say for his kingdom.

I. The kingdom of the Messiah is founded upon a decree, an eternal decree, of God the Father. It was not a sudden resolve, it was not the trial of an experiment, but the result of the counsels of the divine wisdom.

II. There is a declaration of that decree, as far as is necessary for the satisfaction of all those who are called and commanded to yield themselves subjects to this king, and to leave those inexcusable who will not have him to reign over them. Christ here makes a twofold title to his kingdom:—1. A title by inheritance (*v.* 7): *Thou art my Son, this day have I begotten thee.* This scripture the apostle quotes (Heb. i. 5) to prove that Christ has a more excellent name than the angels, but that he *obtained it by inheritance*, *v.* 4. He is the Son of God, and therefore of the same nature with the Father, has in him all the fulness of the godhead, infinite wisdom, power, and holiness. Upon this account we are to receive him as a King; for because *the Father loveth the Son he hath given all things into his hand*, John iii. 35 v. 20. Being a Son, he is heir of all things, and, the Father having made the worlds by him, it is easy to infer thence that by him also he governs them; for he is the eternal Wisdom and the eternal Word. Immediately after his resurrection he entered upon the administration of his mediatorial kingdom; it was then that he said, *All power is given unto me.* 2. A title by agreement, *v.* 8, 9. The agreement is, in short, this: the Son must undertake the office of an intercessor, and, upon that condition, he shall have the honour and power of a universal monarch. The Father will grant more than the half of the kingdom, even the kingdom itself. It is here promised him, he shall have *the heathen* for his inheritance, not the Jews only, but the Gentiles also. A great part of the Gentile world received the gospel when it was first preached, and it is to be yet further accomplished when *the kingdoms of this world shall become the kingdoms of the Lord and of his Christ*, Rev. xi. 15. It shall be victorious: *Thou shalt break them* (those of them that oppose thy kingdom) *with a rod of iron*, *v.* 9. This was in part fulfilled when the nation of the Jews, those that persisted in unbelief and enmity to Christ's gospel, were destroyed by the Roman power. It had a further accomplishment in the destruction of the pagan powers, when the Christian religion came to be established; but it will not be completely fulfilled till all opposing rule, principality, and power, shall be finally put down, 1 Cor. xv. 24. See cx. 5, 6.

In singing this, and praying it over, we must give glory to Christ as the eternal Son of God and our rightful Lord, and must take comfort from this promise, and plead it with God, that the kingdom of Christ shall be enlarged and established and shall triumph over all opposition.

Verses 10–12

The practical application of this gospel doctrine concerning the kingdom of the Messiah, by way of exhortation to the kings and judges of the earth. They hear that it is in vain to oppose Christ's government; let them therefore be so wise for themselves as to submit to it. He that has power to destroy them shows that he has no pleasure in their destruction, for he puts them into a way to make themselves happy, *v.* 10. What is said to them is said to all. We are exhorted,

I. To reverence God and to stand in awe of him, *v.* 11. This is the great duty of natural religion. We must serve God in all ordinances of worship, with a holy fear. We must rejoice in God, but still with a holy trembling. Our salvation must be wrought out *with fear and trembling*, Phil. ii. 12.

II. To welcome Jesus Christ and to submit to him, *v.* 12. This is the great duty of the Christian religion. 1. The command given to this purport: *Kiss the Son.* Christ is called the *Son* because so he was declared (*v.* 7), *Thou art my Son.* He is the Son of God by eternal generation, and, upon that account, he is to be adored by us. Our duty to Christ is here expressed figuratively: *Kiss the Son*, not with a betraying kiss, as Judas kissed him, but with a believing kiss. With a kiss of affection and sincere love: "*Kiss the Son;* enter into a covenant of friendship with him, and let him be very dear and precious to you; love him above all, love him in sincerity, love him much, as she did to whom much was forgiven, and, in token of it, kissed his feet," Luke vii. 38. With a kiss of

JAMIESON, FAUSSET, BROWN

7. The king thus constituted declares the fundamental law of His kingdom, in the avowal of His Sonship, a relation involving His universal dominion. **this day have I begotten thee**—as II Samuel 7:14, "he shall be My son," is a solemn recognition of this relation. The interpretation of this passage to describe the inauguration of Christ as Mediatorial King, by no means impugns the Eternal Sonship of His divine nature. In Acts 13:33, Paul's quotation does not imply an application of this passage to the resurrection; for "raised up" in verse 32 is used as in Acts 2:30; 3:22, etc., to denote bringing Him into being as a man; and not that of resurrection, which it has only when, as in verse 34, allusion is made to His death (Rom. 1:4). That passage says He was declared as to His divine nature to be the Son of God, by the resurrection, and only teaches that that event manifested a truth already existing. A similar recognition of His Sonship is introduced in Hebrews 5:5, by these ends, and by others in Matthew 3:17; 17:5. **8.** The hopes of the rebels are thus overthrown, and not only so; the kingdom they opposed is destined to be coextensive with the earth. **heathen**—or, nations (vs. 1). **and the uttermost parts of the earth**—(Ps. 22:27); denotes universality.

9. His enemies shall be subject to His terrible power (Job 4:9; II Thess. 2:8), as His people to His grace (Ps. 110:2, 3). **rod of iron**—denotes severity (Rev. 2:27). **a potter's vessel**—when shivered cannot be mended, which will describe utter destruction.

10-12. kings . . . judges—For rulers generally (Ps. 148:11), who have been leaders in rebellion, should be examples of penitent submission, and with fear for His terrible judgments, mingled with trust in His mercy, acknowledge—**Kiss**—the authority of the Son.

ADAM CLARKE

7. *This day have I begotten thee.* We have St. Paul's authority for applying to the resurrection of our Lord these words, "Thou art my Son; this day have I begotten thee"—see Acts xiii. 3; see also Heb. v. 5. "I have begotten" is here taken in the sense of "manifesting, exhibiting, or declaring"; and to this sense of it St. Paul (Rom. i. 3-4) evidently alludes when speaking of "Jesus Christ . . . which was made of the seed of David according to the flesh; and declare [exhibited or determined] to be the Son of God with power, according to the spirit of holiness."

8. *Ask of me, and I shall give thee.* Here a second branch of Christ's office as Saviour of the world is referred to; viz., His mediatorial office. Having died as an atoning Sacrifice, and risen again from the dead, He was now to make intercession for mankind.

9. *Thou shalt break them with a rod of iron.* This may refer to the Jewish nation, whose final rejection of the gospel was foreseen, and in whose place the Gentiles or heathen were brought into the Church of Christ.

10. *Be instructed, ye judges.* Rather, "Be ye reformed"; and receive the gospel as the law, or the basis of the law, of the land.

11. *Serve the Lord with fear.* A general direction to all men. Fear God with that reverence which is due to His supreme majesty, and as servants should their Master. *Rejoice with trembling.* If ye serve God aright, ye cannot but be happy; but let a continual filial fear moderate all your joys. Ye must all stand at last before the judgment seat of God; watch, pray, believe, work, and keep humble.

12. *Kiss the Son, lest he be angry.* It is remarkable that the word *son* (*bar*, a Chaldee word) is not found in any of the versions except

MATTHEW HENRY

allegiance and loyalty, submit to his government, take his yoke upon you.

2. The reasons to enforce this command;

(1) The certain ruin we run upon if we refuse and reject Christ: "*Kiss the Son;* for it is at your peril if you do not." Do it, *lest he be angry.*

(2) The happiness we are sure of if we yield ourselves to Christ. Blessed will those be in the day of wrath, who, by trusting in Christ, have made him their refuge and patron; when the hearts of others fail them for fear they shall lift up their heads with joy.

In singing this, and praying it over, we should have our hearts filled with a holy awe of God, but at the same time borne up with a cheerful confidence in Christ, in whose mediation we may comfort and encourage ourselves and one another.

JAMIESON, FAUSSET, BROWN

perish from the way—i.e., suddenly and hopelessly. **kindled but a little**—or, in a little time. **put their trust in him**—or take refuge in Him (Ps. 5:11). Men still cherish opposition to Christ in their hearts and evince it in their lives. Their ruin, without such trust, is inevitable (Heb. 10:29), while their happiness in His favor is equally sure.

ADAM CLARKE

the Syriac, nor indeed anything equivalent to it. The Chaldee, Vulgate, Septuagint, Arabic, and Aethiopic, have a term which signifies "doctrine" or "discipline": "Embrace discipline, lest the Lord be angry with you."

This psalm is remarkable, not only for its subject, the future kingdom of the Messiah, but also for the change of person. In the first verse the prophet speaks; in the third, the adversaries; in the fourth and fifth, the prophet answers; in the sixth, Jehovah speaks; in the seventh, the Messiah; in the eighth and ninth, Jehovah answers; and in the tenth to the twelfth, the prophet exhorts the opponents to submission and obedience.

PSALM 3 (Matthew Henry)

A psalm of David, when he fled from Absalom his son.

Verses 1–3

The title of this psalm and many others is as a key hung ready at the door, to open it. When we know upon what occasion a psalm was penned we know the better how to expound it. 1. David was in great grief; when, in his flight, he went up the Mount of Olives, he wept greatly, with his head covered, and marching bare-foot; yet *then* he composed this comfortable psalm. He wept and prayed, wept and sung, wept and believed. Is any afflicted with undutiful disobedient children? David was; and yet that did not hinder his joy in God, nor put him out of tune for holy songs. 2. He was in great danger; the plot against him was laid deep, the party that sought his ruin was very formidable, and his own son at the head of them, so that his affairs seemed to be at the last extremity; yet *then* he kept hold of his interest in God and improved that. Perils and frights should drive us to God, not drive us from him. 3. He had now a great deal of provocation given him by those from whom he had reason to expect better things, from his son, whom he had been indulgent of, from his subjects, whom he had been so great a blessing to. 4. He was suffering for his sin in the matter of Uriah; this was the evil which, for that sin, God threatened to *raise up against him out of his own house* (2 Sam. xii. 11). Yet he did not *therefore* cast away his confidence in the divine power and goodness, nor despair of succour. Even our sorrow for sin must not hinder either our joy in God or our hope in God. 5. He seemed cowardly in fleeing from Absalom, and quitting his royal city, before he had had one struggle for it; and yet, by this psalm, it appears he was full of true courage arising from his faith in God.

In these three verses he applies to God. Whither else should we go but to him when anything grieves us or frightens us?

I. With a representation of his distress, *v.* 1, 2. He looks round, and as it were takes a view of his enemies' camp. David had had the hearts of his subjects as much as ever any king had, and yet now, of a sudden, he had lost them. They rose up against him; they aimed to trouble him; but that was not all: they said of his soul, *There is no help for him in God.* They put a spiteful and invidious construction upon his troubles, as Job's friends did upon his, concluding that, because his servants and subjects forsook him thus and did not help him, God had deserted him and abandoned his cause, and he was therefore to be looked *on*, or rather to be looked *off*, as a hypocrite and a wicked man. They endeavoured to shake his confidence in God and drive him to despair of relief from him: "They have said it *to* my soul"; so it may be read; compare xi. 1; xlii. 10. David comes to God, and tells him what his enemies said of him. "They say, *There is no help for me in thee*; but, Lord, if it be so, I am undone. They say to my soul, *There is no salvation*" (for so the word is) *"for him in God*; but, Lord, do thou say unto my soul, *I am thy salvation* (xxxv. 3) and that shall satisfy me, and in due time silence them." To this complaint he adds *Selah.* Some refer it to the music with which, in David's time, the psalms were sung; others to the sense, and that it is a note commanding a solemn pause. *Selah—Mark that*, or, "*Stop there*, and consider a little." As here, they say, *There is no help for him in God, Selah.*

II. With a profession of his dependence upon God, *v.* 3. David here, when his enemies said, *There is no help for him in God*, cries out with so much the more assurance, "*But thou, O Lord! art a shield for me. Thou art a shield for me*, a shield *about* me" (so some), "to secure me on all sides, since my enemies surrounded me." *Thou art my glory Thou*

PSALM 3 (Jamieson, Fausset, Brown)

Vss. 1-8. For the historical occasion mentioned, cf. II Samuel, chaps. 15-17. David, in the midst of great distress, with filial confidence, implores God's aid, and, anticipating relief, offers praise.

PSALM 3 (Adam Clarke)

This is said to be *A Psalm of David, when he fled from Absalom his son.* See the account, 2 Sam. xv. 1, etc. And David is supposed to have composed it when obliged to leave Jerusalem, passing by the mount of Olives, weeping, with his clothes rent, and with dust upon his head. This psalm is suitable enough to these circumstances, and they mutually cast light on each other. If the inscription be correct, this psalm is a proof that the psalms are not placed in any chronological order.

CHARLES H. SPURGEON:

The poor brokenhearted father complains of the multitude of his enemies, and if you turn to 2 Sam. 15:12, you will find it written that "the conspiracy was strong; for the people increased continually with Absalom," while the troops of David constantly diminished! *"Lord; how are they increased that trouble me!"* Here is a note of exclamation to express the wonder of woe which amazed and perplexed the fugitive father. Alas! I see no limit to my misery, for my troubles are enlarged! There was enough at first to sink me very low; but lo! my enemies multiply. When Absalom, my darling, is in rebellion against me, it is enough to break my heart; but lo! Ahithophel hath forsaken me, my faithful counsellors have turned their backs on me; lo! my generals and soldiers have deserted my standard. "How are they increased that trouble me!" Troubles always come in flocks. Sorrow hath a numerous family.—*The Treasury of David*

Jamieson, Fausset, Brown

1. Lord . . . increased—The extent of the rebellion (II Sam. 15:13) surprises and grieves him.

2. say of my soul—i.e., of me (cf. Ps. 25:3). This use of "soul" is common; perhaps it arose from regarding the soul as man's chief part. **no help . . . in God**—rejected by Him. This is the bitterest reproach for a pious man, and denotes a spirit of malignant triumph.

Selah—This word is of very obscure meaning. It probably denotes *rest* or *pause,* both as to the music and singing, intimating something emphatic in the sentiment (cf. Ps. 9:16).

3. But—lit., "and" (Ps. 2:6). He repels the reproach by avowing his continued trust. **shield**—a favorite and often-used figure for protection. **my glory**—its

Adam Clarke

1. *Lord, how are they increased that trouble me!* We are told that the hearts of all Israel went after Absalom, 2 Sam. xv. 13.

2. *No help for him in God.* These were some of the reproaches of his enemies, Shimei and others. These reproaches deeply affected his heart; and he mentions them with that note which so frequently occurs in the Psalms, and which occurs here for the first time, *Selah.* Much has been said on the meaning of this word, and we have nothing but conjecture to guide us. The Septuagint always translate it by *diapsalma,* "a pause in the Psalm." The Chaldee sometimes translates it by *lealmin,* "for ever." The rest of the versions leave it unnoticed. It either comes from *sal,* to "raise or elevate," and may denote a particular elevation in the voices of the performers, which is very observable in the Jewish singing to the present day; or it may come from *salah,* to "strew or spread out," intimating that the subject to which the word is attached should be spread out, meditated on, and attentively considered by the reader.

3. *Thou, O Lord, art a shield.* As a shield covers and defends the body from the strokes of an adversary, so wilt Thou cover and defend me from them that rise up against me.

MATTHEW HENRY

art the lifter up of my head. If, in the worst of times, God's people can lift up their heads with joy, knowing that all shall work for good to them, they will own it is God that is the lifter up of their head, that gives them both cause to rejoice and hearts to rejoice.

Verse 4–8

David, having stirred up himself by the irritations of his enemies to take hold on God as his God, and so gained comfort in looking upward when, if he looked round about him, nothing appeared but what was discouraging, here looks back with pleasing reflections and looks forward with pleasing expectations of a happy issue to which the dark dispensation he was now under would shortly be brought.

I. David had been exercised with many difficulties, often oppressed and brought very low; but still he had found God all-sufficient.

1. His troubles had always brought him to his knees, and, in all his difficulties and dangers, he had been enabled to acknowledge God and to lift up his heart to him, and his voice too: *I cried unto God with my voice.*

2. He had always found God ready to answer his prayers: *He heard me out of his holy hill*, from heaven, the high and holy place, from the ark on Mount Sion, whence he used to give answers to those that sought to him. Christ was *set King upon the holy hill of Zion* (ii. 6), and it is through him, whom the Father hears always, that our prayers are heard.

3. He had always been very safe and very easy under the divine protection (*v.* 5): "*I laid myself down and slept*, composed and quiet; *and awaked* refreshed, *for the Lord sustained me.*" (1) This is applicable to the common mercies of every night, which we ought to give thanks for alone, and with our families, every morning. (2) It seems here to be meant of the wonderful quietness and calmness of David's spirit, in the midst of his dangers. Having by prayer committed himself and his cause to God, and being sure of his protection, his heart was fixed, and he was easy.

4. God had often broken the power and restrained the malice of his enemies, had *smitten them upon the cheek-bone* (*v.* 7), had silenced them and spoiled their speaking.

II. See with what confidence he looks forward to the dangers he had yet in prospect. 1. His *fears were all stilled and silenced, v.* 6. "*I will not be afraid of ten thousands of people*, that either in a foreign invasion or an intestine rebellion *set themselves*, or encamp, *against me round about.*" When David, in his flight from Absalom, bade Zadok carry back the ark, he spoke doubtfully of the issue of his present troubles, and concluded, like a humble penitent, *Here I am; let him do to me what seemeth to him good*, 2 Sam. xv. 26. But now, like a strong believer, he speaks confidently, and has no fear concerning the event. 2. His prayers were quickened and encouraged, *v.* 7. He believed God was his Saviour, and yet prays: nay, he *therefore* prays, *Arise, O Lord! save me, O my God!* 3. His faith became triumphant. He began the psalm with complaints of the strength and malice of his enemies, but concludes it with exultation in the power and grace of his God, and now sees more with him than against him, *v.* 8. Two great truths he here builds his confidence upon. (1) That *salvation belongeth unto the Lord*; he has power to save, be the danger ever so great. (2) That his blessing is upon his people; he not only has power to save them, but he has assured them of his gracious intentions. He has, in his word, pronounced a blessing upon his people; and we are bound to believe that that blessing does accordingly rest upon them, though there be not the visible effects of it.

JAMIESON, FAUSSET, BROWN

source. **lifter up of mine head**—one who raises me from despondency.

4. cried . . . heard—Such has been my experience. The latter verb denotes a gracious hearing or answering. **out of** [or, from] **his holy hill**—Zion (Ps. 2:6). His visible earthly residence.

5. the Lord sustained me—lit., "will sustain me," the reason of his composure.

6. ten thousands of people—or, myriads, any very great number (cf. II Sam. 16:18).

7. Arise, O Lord—God is figuratively represented as asleep to denote His apparent indifference (Ps. 7:6). The use of "*cheekbone*" and "*teeth*" represents his enemies as fierce, like wild beasts ready to devour (Ps. 27:2), and smiting their cheekbone (I Kings 22:24) denotes violence and insult. **thou hast broken**—God took his part, utterly depriving the enemy of power to injure. **8.** an ascription of praise to a delivering God, whose favor is an efficient benefit.

ADAM CLARKE

The lifter up of mine head. Thou wilt restore me to the state from which my enemies have cast me down. This is the meaning of the phrase, and this he speaks prophetically.

5. *I laid me down and slept.* He who knows that he has God for his Protector may go quietly and confidently to his bed.

7. *Thou hast smitten.* "Thou wilt smite. Breaking the jaws and *the teeth* are expressions which imply confounding and destroying an adversary.

PSALM 4

MATTHEW HENRY

To the chief musician on Neginoth. A psalm of David.

Verses 1–5

The title of the psalm acquaints us that David, having penned it by divine inspiration for the use of the church, delivered it to the chief musician. We have a particular account of the constitution, the modelling of the several classes of singers, each with a chief, and the share each bore in the work, 1 Chron. xxv.

I. David addresses himself to God, *v.* 1. All the notice God is pleased to take of our prayers, and all the returns he is pleased to make to them, must be ascribed, not to our merit, but purely to his mercy. "Hear me for thy mercy-sake" is our best plea. Two things David here pleads further:—1. "Thou art *the God of my righteousness*; not only a righteous God

JAMIESON, FAUSSET, BROWN

Vss. 1-8. *On Neginoth,* i.e., stringed instruments, as the kind of musical accompaniment. On other parts of title, see Introduction. The historical occasion was probably the same as that of the foregoing. The writer, praying for further relief, admonishes his enemies of the vanity of attacking God's servant, exhorts them to repentance, and avows his confidence and peace in God's favor.

1. Hear—as in Psalm 3:4. **God of my righteousness**—or, my righteousGod, as my holy hill (Ps. 2:6), who will act towards me on righteous principles.

ADAM CLARKE

This psalm seems to have been composed on the same occasion with the preceding, viz., Absalom's rebellion. It appears to have been an evening hymn, sung by David and his company previously to their going to rest. It is inscribed "to the chief Musician on Neginoth." *Neginoth* seems to come from *nagan*, "to strike"; and probably may signify some such instruments as the cymbal, drum, and stringed instruments in general.

MATTHEW HENRY

thyself, but the author of my righteous dispositions, who hast by thy grace wrought that good that is in me, hast made me a righteous man; therefore *hear me.*" 2. "*Thou hast* formerly *enlarged me when I was in distress,* enlarged my heart in holy joy and comfort under my distresses, enlarged my condition by bringing me out of my distresses; therefore *now, Lord,* have mercy upon me, and hear me." "*Thou hast; wilt thou not?* For thou art God, and changest not; thy work is perfect."

II. He addresses himself to the children of men, for the conviction and conversion of those that are yet strangers to God, and that will not have the Messiah, the Son of David, to reign over them.

1. He endeavours to convince them of the folly of their impiety (*v.* 2). "You debase yourselves, for you are *sons of men*" (the word signifies man as a noble creature); "consider the dignity of your nature, and do not act thus irrationally and unbecoming yourselves." "You dishonour your Maker, and *turn his glory into shame.*" Those that profane God's holy name, that ridicule his word and ordinances, and, while they profess to know him, in works deny him, do what in them lies to *turn his glory into shame.* "You set your hearts upon that which will prove, at last, but vanity and a lie." Those that love the world, and seek the things that are beneath, love vanity, and seek lies.

2. He shows them the peculiar favour which God has for good people, the special protection they are under, and the singular privileges to which they are entitled, *v.* 3. It is at their peril if they *offend one of these little ones,* whom God has *set apart for himself,* Matt. xviii. 6. God reckons that those who touch them touch the apple of his eye; and he will make their persecutors to know it, sooner or later. *They shall be mine, saith the Lord, in that day when I make up my jewels. Know this;* let godly people know it, and let wicked people know it, and take heed how they hurt those whom God protects.

3. He warns them against sin, and exhorts them both to frighten and to reason themselves out of it (*v.* 4): "*Stand in awe and sin not*" (*be angry and sin not,* so the LXX). One good means of preventing sin, and preserving a holy awe, is to be frequent and serious in *communing with our own hearts*: "*Talk with your hearts;* you have a great deal to say to them; they may be spoken with at any time; let it not be unsaid." A thinking man is in a fair way to be a wise and a good man. "Choose a solitary time; do it when you lie awake *upon your beds.* Before you turn yourself to go to sleep at night" (as some of the heathen moralists have directed) "examine your consciences with respect to what you have done that day, particularly what you have done amiss, that you may repent of it. When you awake in the night meditate upon God, and the things that belong to your peace."

4. He counsels them to make conscience of their duty (*v.* 5): *Offer to God the sacrifice of righteousness.* We must not only cease to do evil, but learn to do well. "*Offer sacrifices to him,* your own selves first, and your best sacrifices." "Let all your devotions come from an upright heart; let all your alms be sacrifices of righteousness." Honour him, by trusting in him only, and not in your wealth nor in an arm of flesh; trust in his providence, and lean not to your own understanding; trust in his grace, and go not about to establish your own righteousness or sufficiency.

Verses 6–8

I. The foolish wish of worldly people: *There be many that say, Who will show us any good? Who will make us to see good?* What good they meant is intimated, *v.* 7. It was the increase of their corn and wine; all they desired was plenty of the wealth of this world, that they might enjoy abundance of the delights of sense. They enquire for good that may be seen, and they show no concern for the good things that are out of sight and are the objects of faith only. As we must be taught to worship an unseen God, so to seek an unseen good, 2 Cor. iv. 18. We look with an eye of faith further than we can see with an eye of sense. All they want is outward good, present good, partial good, good meat, good drink, a good trade, and a good estate; and what are all these worth without a good God and a good heart? Any good will serve the turn of most men, but a gracious soul will not be put off so.

II. The wise choice which godly people make. David, and the pious few that adhered to him, joined in this prayer, *Lord lift thou up the light of thy countenance upon us.* He and his friends agree in their choice of God's favour as their felicity; it is this which in their account is better than life and all the comforts of life. Though David speaks of himself only in the

JAMIESON, FAUSSET, BROWN

thou hast enlarged—expresses relief afforded in opposition to "distress," which is expressed by a word denoting straits or pressure. Past favor is a ground of hope for the future.

2. sons of men—men of note or prominence (cf. II Chron. 21:9). **turn my glory**—or, royal dignity. **into shame**—or reproach.

vanity—a foolish and hopeless enterprise (Ps. 2:1). **leasing**—a lie.

3. godly—an object as well as subject of divine favor (cf. Ps. 105:14, 15).

4. Stand in awe—(Eph. 4:26), from *Septuagint*—be angry. Both clauses are qualified by "not."

5. Not only repent, but manifest penitence by sacrifices or righteousness or righteous sacrifices, etc.

corn and wine—lit., "new corn and wine." **increased**—an abundant harvest giving great joy (Isa. 9:3).

6, 7. Contrast true with vain confidence. **light of thy countenance**—figure for favor (Num. 6:26; Ps. 44:3; 81:16).

ADAM CLARKE

1. *Thou hast enlarged me.* I was in prison, and Thou hast brought me forth abroad. *Have mercy upon me*—continue to act in the same way.

2. *Love vanity.* The poor, empty, shallow-brained, pretty-faced Absalom, whose prospects are all vain, and whose promises are all empty! *Seek after leasing?* "Falsehood."

3. *The Lord hath set apart him that is godly. Chasid,* the pious, benevolent man. He has marked such, and put them aside as His own property.

4. *Stand in awe, and sin not.* The Septuagint, which is copied by St. Paul, Eph. iv. 26, translate this clause, "Be ye angry, and sin not." The Vulgate, Syriac, Aethiopic, and Arabic, give the same reading; and thus the original *rigzu* might be translated: If ye be angry, and if ye think ye have cause to be angry, do not let your disaffection carry you to acts of rebellion against both God and your king. *And be still.* "And be dumb." Hold your peace; fear lest ye be found fighting against God.

6. *Who will shew us any good?* This is not a fair translation. The word *any* is not in the text, nor anything equivalent to it. The place is sufficiently emphatic without this. There are multitudes who say, Who will show us good?

Lift thou up the light of thy countenance. This alone, *the light of thy countenance*—Thy peace and approbation—constitute the supreme good.

MATTHEW HENRY

7th and 8th verses, he speaks, in this prayer, for others also,—"*upon us*," as Christ taught us to pray, "*Our Father.*" All the saints come to the throne of grace on the same errand, and in this they are one, they all desire God's favour as their chief good. We should beg it for others as well as for ourselves, for in God's favour there is enough for us all and we shall have never the less for others sharing in what we have. This is what, above anything, they rejoice in (*v.* 7): "*Thou hast* hereby often *put gladness into my heart.*" When God puts grace in the heart he *puts gladness in the heart*; inward, solid, substantial joy. "*I will lay myself down* (having the assurance of thy favour) *in peace, for thou only makest me to dwell in safety.*" When he comes to sleep the sleep of death, he will then, with good old Simeon, *depart in peace* (Luke ii. 29), being assured that God will receive his soul. He commits all his affairs to God, and contentedly leaves the issue of them with him.

JAMIESON, FAUSSET, BROWN

8. both lay me down, . . .—or, will lie down at once, and sleep in sure confidence and quiet repose (Ps. 3:5).

ADAM CLARKE

7. *Thou hast put gladness in my heart.* Thou hast given my soul what it wanted and wished for. I find now a happiness which earthly things could not produce. I have peace of conscience, and joy in the Holy Ghost; such inward happiness as they cannot boast who have got the highest increase of *corn* and *wine,* those two things in the abundance of which many suppose happiness to be found.

8. *I will both lay me down in peace, and sleep.* Most men lie down, and most sleep, daily, for without rest and sleep life could not be preserved; but alas! how few lie down in peace! peace with their own consciences, and peace with God!

MATTHEW HENRY

PSALM 5

To the chief musician upon Nehiloth. A psalm of David.

Verses 1–6

In these verses David prays to God,

I. As a prayer-hearing God; such he has always been ever since men began to call upon the name of the Lord, and yet is still as ready to hear prayer as ever. David here styles him: *O Lord* (*v.* 1, 3), *Jehovah,* a self-existent, self-sufficient, Being, whom we are bound to adore, and, "*my King and my God* (*v.* 2), to whom I have sworn allegiance, and under whose protection I have put myself as my King." We believe that the God we pray to is a King and a God. The most powerful plea in prayer, is to look upon him as *our* King and *our* God.

1. What David here prays for, which may encourage our faith and hopes in all our addresses to God. *Give ear to my words, O Lord!* Men perhaps will not or cannot hear us; our enemies are so haughty that they will not, our friends at such a distance that they cannot; but God, though high, though in heaven, can, and will. *Consider my meditation.* David's prayers were not his words only, but his meditations. Meditation and prayer should go together, xix. 14.

2. Four things David here promises, and so must we:—(1) That he will pray, that he will make conscience of praying. The assurances God has given us of his readiness to hear prayer should confirm our resolution to live and die praying. (2) That he will pray *in the morning.* Morning prayer is our duty; we are the fittest for prayer when we are in the most fresh, and lively, and composed frame, got clear of the slumbers of the night, revived by them, and not yet filled with the business of the day. We have then most need of prayer. (3) That he will have his eye single: *I will direct my prayer,* as a marksman directs his arrow to the white; with such a fixedness and steadiness of mind should we address ourselves to God. Let our first petition be, *Hallowed,* glorified, *be thy name,* and then we may be sure of the same gracious answer to it that was given to Christ himself: *I have glorified it, and I will glorify it yet again.* (4) That he will patiently wait for an answer of peace: "I *will look up,* will look after my prayers, and *hear what God the Lord will speak* (lxxxv. 8; Hab. ii. 1), that, if he grant what I asked, I may be thankful—if he deny, I may be patient—if he defer, I may continue to pray and wait and may not faint."

II. As a sin-hating God, *v.* 4–6. David takes notice of this. As the God with whom we have to do is gracious and merciful, so he is pure and holy; though he is ready to hear prayer, yet, if we regard iniquity in our heart, he will not hear our prayers, lxvi. 18. God has no pleasure in wickedness, though covered with a cloak of religion. Let those therefore who delight in sin know that God has no delight in them. Those whom thou hatest thou shalt destroy; particularly two sorts of sinners, who are here marked for destruction: Those that are fools, that speak leasing or lying, and that are deceitful. Those that are cruel: *Thou wilt abhor the bloody man;* for inhumanity is no less contrary, no less hateful, to the God of mercy, whom mercy pleases.

Verses 7–12

In these verses David gives three characters—of himself, of his enemies, and of all the people of God, and subjoins a prayer to each of them.

I. He gives an account of himself and prays for himself, *v.* 7, 8.

1. He is steadfastly resolved to keep closely to God and to his worship. (1) To worship God, to

JAMIESON, FAUSSET, BROWN

PSALM 5

Vss. 1-12. *Upon Nehiloth*—flutes or wind instruments. The writer begs to be heard, on the ground of God's regard for His covenant people and true worshippers as contrasted with His holy hatred to the wicked. He prays for divine guidance, on account of his watchful, malignant, and deceitful enemies; and for their destruction as being also God's enemies. At the same time he expresses his confidence that God will extend aid to His people.

1. meditation—moanings of that half-uttered form to which deep feeling gives rise—groanings, as in Romans 8:26, 27. **2. Hearken**—incline the ear (Ps. 10:17; cf. Ps. 61:2)—give close attention. **my cry**—i.e., for help (Ps. 61:2; Jer. 8:19). **my King**—thus by covenant relation interested in my cause.

3. direct—lit., "set in order," as the shewbread was placed or set in order (Exod. 40:23).

4. For, etc.—God only regards sincere worshippers. **evil**—or, the evil man. **dwell**—lodge, remain under protection. **5. foolish**—vainglorious and insolent. **iniquity**—especially such as denotes a negation, or defect, i.e., of moral principle.

6. leasing—a lie, **the bloody . . . man**—lit., "man of blood"—murderer.

ADAM CLARKE

PSALM 5

This psalm is inscribed "to the chief Musician upon Nehiloth, A Psalm of David." As *neginoth* may signify all kinds of instruments struck with a plectrum, stringed instruments, those like the drum, cymbals, etc.; so *nechiloth,* from *chal,* to be "hollow," to "bore through," may signify any kind of wind instruments, such as the horn, trumpet, flute.

1. *Give ear to my words.* This is properly a morning hymn, as the preceding was an evening hymn. We have seen from the conclusion of the last psalm that David was very happy, and lay down and slept in the peace and love of his God. When he opens his eyes on the following morning, he not only remembers but feels the happiness of which he spoke; and with his first recollections he meditates on the goodness and mercy of God, and the glorious state of salvation into which he has been brought.

3. *My voice shalt thou hear in the morning.* He finds it good to begin the day with God, to let divine things occupy the first place in his waking thoughts, as that which first occupies the mind on awaking is most likely to keep possession of the heart all the day through.

4. *Neither shall evil dwell with thee.* As Thou art holy, so Thou hast pleasure only in holiness; and as to *evil men,* they shall never enter into Thy glory; *lo yegurecha ra,* "the evil man shall not even *sojourn* with thee."

5. *The foolish shall not stand.* He is a fool and a madman who is running himself out of breath for no prize, who is fighting against the Almighty. This every wicked man does; therefore is every *wicked* man a *fool* and a *madman. Thou hatest all workers of iniquity.* Some sin *now* and *then,* others *generally;* some *constantly,* and some *labor* in it with all their might. These are the *workers of iniquity.* Such even the God of infinite love and mercy *hates.* Alas! what a portion have *the workers of iniquity!* the hatred of God Almighty!

6. *That speak leasing.* See on Ps. iv. 2. *The Lord will abhor the bloody and deceitful man.* "The man of bloods"; for he who has the spirit of a murderer will rarely end with one blood-shedding.

7. *In the multitude of thy mercy.* David considered it an inexpressible privilege to be permitted to attend public worship; and he knew that it was only through the multitude of God's

MATTHEW HENRY

pay his homage to him, and give unto God the glory due unto his name. (2) To worship him publicly: "*I will come into thy house*, the courts of thy house, to worship there with other faithful worshippers." David was much in secret worship, prayed often alone (*v.* 2, 3), and yet was very constant and devout in his attendance on the sanctuary. (3) To worship him reverently and with a due sense of the infinite distance there is between God and man. (4) To take his encouragement in worship, from God himself only. The mercy of God should ever be both the foundation of our hopes and the fountain of our joy in everything wherein we have to do with him.

2. He earnestly prays that God by his grace, would guide and preserve him always in the way of his duty (*v.* 8): *Lead me in thy righteousness, because of my enemies*—Heb. "*Because of those who observe me*, who watch for my halting and seek occasion against me."

II. He gives an account of his enemies, and prays against them, *v.* 9, 10. He had spoken (*v.* 6) of God's hating the bloody and deceitful man. "Now, Lord," says he, "that is the character of my enemies: they are deceitful; there is no trusting them, for there is no faithfulness in their mouth." "They have by their sins deserved destruction; there is enough to justify God in their utter rejection: *Cast them out in the multitude of their transgressions*, by which they have filled up the measure of their iniquity and have become ripe for ruin." He pleads, "*They have rebelled against thee.* Had they been only my enemies, I could safely have forgiven them; but they are rebels against God, his crown and dignity; they oppose his government, and will not repent, to give him glory, and therefore I plainly foresee their ruin." His prayer for their destruction comes not from a spirit of revenge, but from a spirit of prophecy, by which he foretold that all who rebel against God will certainly be destroyed by their own counsels.

III. He gives an account of the people of God, and prays for them, concluding with an assurance of their bliss. They are the righteous (*v.* 12); for they *put their trust in God*, are well assured of his power and all-sufficiency, venture their all upon his promise, and are confident of his protection. *Let them rejoice;* let them have cause to rejoice and hearts to rejoice; fill them with joy, with great joy and unspeakable. Let all that are entitled to God's promises have a share in our prayers; grace be with all that love Christ in sincerity. "They are safe under the protection of thy favour; with that thou wilt *crown* him." A shield, in war, guards only one side, but the favour of God is to the saints a defence on every side; like the hedge about Job, round about, so that, while they keep themselves under the divine protection, they are entirely safe and ought to be entirely satisfied.

JAMIESON, FAUSSET, BROWN

7. But—as in Psalm 2:6, lit., "and." **house**—(I Chron. 9:23), the tabernacle. **temple**—lit., "palace," applied to God's residence, the Holy of Holies (I Sam. 3:3; II Sam. 22:7); the inner part of the tabernacle. **toward**—not in; the high priest alone was allowed to enter.

8. enemies—lit., "watchers," (Ps. 27:11), hence special need of guidance. **in thy righteousness**—an attribute implying faithfulness in promises as well as threatenings. **make thy way straight**—i.e., make the way of providence plain.

9. The wicked are not reliable because by nature they are full of wickedness, or lit., "wickednesses," of every kind (Rom. 8:7). **sepulchre**—a dwelling-place of corruption, emitting moral putridness. **flatter**—or, make smooth. **their tongue**—speaks deceitfully. 10. **Destroy**—or, condemn them to destruction as guilty.

11. defendest—(cf. *Margin*). **love thy name**—Thy manifested perfections (Ps. 9:10). **12. with favour**—or, acceptance, alluding to the favor shown to an acceptable offering and worshipper (Lev. 7:18, 19:7). **shield**—(cf. Ps. 3:3).

ADAM CLARKE

mercy that he, or any man else, could enjoy such a privilege. He who takes David's views of this subject will never, willingly, be absent from the means of grace. *In thy fear.* Duly considering the infinite holiness of Thy majesty *will I worship*, "will I bow and prostrate myself" in the deepest self-abasement and humility. *Toward thy holy temple.* If David was the author of this psalm, as is generally agreed, the Temple was not built at this time; only the Tabernacle then existed; and in the preceding clause he speaks of coming into the house, by which he must mean the Tabernacle. But *temple* here may signify the holy of holies, before which David might prostrate himself while in the house, i.e., the court of the Tabernacle.

10. *Destroy thou them, O God.* All these apparently imprecatory declarations should be translated in the future tense, to which they belong, and which shows them to be prophetic. "Thou wilt *destroy* them; Thou wilt *cast them out.*"

11. *Let all those that put their trust in thee rejoice.* Such expressions as these should be translated in the same way, declaratively and prophetically: "All those who put their trust in Thee shall *rejoice*—shall *ever shout for joy.*"

12. *With favour.* Literally, "Like a shield Thy favor will crown him."

MATTHEW HENRY

PSALM 6

To the chief musician on Neginoth upon Sheminith. A psalm of David.

Verses 1-7

These verses speak the language of a heart truly humbled under humbling providences, of a broken and contrite spirit under great afflictions.

I. The representation he makes to God of his grievances. He pours out his complaint before him. Whither else should a child go with his complaints, but to his father? He complains of bodily pain and sickness (*v.* 2): *My bones are vexed.* His bones and his flesh, like Job's, were touched. He complains of inward trouble: *My soul is also sorely vexed;* and that is much more grievous than the vexation of the bones. It is a sad thing for a man to have his bones and his soul vexed at the same time. *Thou, O Lord! how long?* To the living God we must, at such a time, address ourselves, who is the only physician both of body and mind, and not to the Assyrians, not to the god of Ekron.

II. The impression which his troubles made upon him. They lay very heavily; he *groaned till he was weary.* David had more courage and consideration than to mourn thus for any outward affliction; but, when sin sat heavily upon his conscience then he thus grieved and mourned in secret, and even his soul refused to be comforted. True penitents weep in their retirements. David mourned in the night upon the bed where he lay communing with his own heart, and no eye was a witness to his grief, but the eye of him who is all eye. Peter went out, covered his face, and wept. David's eye waxed old because of his enemies, who rejoiced in his afflictions and put bad constructions upon his tears.

III. The petitions which he offers up to God in this sorrowful and distressed state. That which he dreads as the greatest evil is the anger of God.

JAMIESON, FAUSSET, BROWN

PSALM 6

Vss. 1-10. *On Neginoth* (cf. Psalm 4) *upon Sheminith*—the eighth—an instrument for the eighth key—or, more probably, the bass, as it is contrasted with Alamoth (the treble, Ps. 46) in I Chronicles 15:20, 21. In deep affliction the Psalmist appeals to God's mercy for relief from chastisement, which otherwise must destroy him, and thus disable him for God's service. Sure of a gracious answer, he triumphantly rebukes his foes.

1. He owns his ill desert in begging a relief from chastisement. **2. I am weak**—as a culled plant (Isa. 24:4). **my bones**—the very frame. **are vexed**—(Ps. 2:5)—shaken with fear.

3. how long?—shall this be so (cf. Ps. 79:5). **but**—or, and. **thou**—The sentence is incomplete as expressive of strong emotion.

ADAM CLARKE

PSALM 6

This psalm has the following inscription: "To the chief Musician on Neginoth, upon Sheminith, A Psalm of David," which the Chaldee translates, "To be sung on neginoth, a harp of eight strings." We have already seen that *neginoth* probably signifies all instruments which emitted sounds by strokes, or stringed instruments in general. This psalm was to be accompanied with such instruments; but one of a particular kind is specified, viz., *sheminith*, so called from its having eight strings. The "chief musician" is directed to accompany the recital of this psalm with the above instrument.

2. *Have mercy.* I have no merit. I deserve all I feel and all I fear. *O Lord, heal me.* No earthly physician can cure my malady. Body and soul are both diseased, and only God can help me. *I am weak. Umlal.* "I am exceedingly weak"; I cannot take nourishment, and my strength is exhausted.

MATTHEW HENRY

Therefore he prays (*v.* 1), *O Lord! rebuke me not in thy anger*, though I have deserved it, *neither chasten me in thy hot displeasure.* He can bear the rebuke and chastening well enough if God, at the same time, lift up the light of his countenance upon him and by his Spirit make him to hear the joy and gladness of his loving-kindness; the affliction of his body will be tolerable if he have but comfort in his soul. That which he desires as the greatest good, and which would be to him the restoration of all good, is the favour and friendship of God. He prays, That God would pity him and look upon him with compassion. That God would pardon his sins. That God would put forth his power for his relief: *Lord, heal me* (*v.* 2), *save me* (*v.* 4). That he would be at peace with him: *Return, O Lord!* receive me into thy favour again, and be reconciled to me. That he would especially preserve the inward man and the interests of that, whatever might become of the body: "*O Lord! deliver my soul.*"

IV. The pleas with which he enforces his petitions, not to move God but to move himself. He pleads his own misery. He pleads God's mercy. He pleads God's glory (*v.* 5): "*For in death there is no remembrance of thee.*"

Verses 8–10

What a sudden change is here for the better! He that was groaning, and weeping, and giving up all for gone (*v.* 6, 7), here looks and speaks very pleasantly.

I. He distinguishes himself from the wicked and ungodly, and fortifies himself against their insults (*v.* 8): *Depart from me, all you workers of iniquity.* The workers of iniquity had teased him, and taunted him, and asked him, "Where is thy God?" triumphing in his despondency and despair; but now he had wherewith to answer those that reproached him, for God had now comforted his spirit and would shortly complete his deliverance. But now, "*depart from me:* I will never lend an ear to your counsel; you would have had me to curse God and die, but I will bless him and live." When God has done great things for us, this would put us upon studying what we shall do for him.

II. He assures himself that God was, and would be, propitious to him, notwithstanding the present intimations of wrath which he was under. He is confident of a gracious answer to this prayer which he is now making. While he is yet speaking, he is aware that God hears and therefore speaks of it with an air of triumph, "*The Lord hath heard.*" (*v.* 8), and again (*v.* 9), "*The Lord hath heard.*" Thence he infers the like favourable audience of all his other prayers: "He *has heard the voice of my supplication*, and therefore he *will receive my prayer.*"

III. He either prays for the conversion or predicts the destruction of his enemies and persecutors, *v.* 10. 1. It may very well be taken as a prayer for their conversion: "Let them all be ashamed of the censures they have passed upon me. Let them be (as all true penitents are) vexed at themselves for their own folly; let them return to a better temper and disposition of mind." 2. If they be not converted, it is a prediction of their confusion and ruin. *They shall be ashamed and sorely vexed* (so it may be read), and that justly. They rejoiced that David was vexed (*v.* 2, 3), and therefore, as usually happens, the evil returns upon themselves; they also shall be sorely vexed.

PSALM 7

Shiggaion of David, which he sang unto the Lord concerning the words of Cush the Benjamite.

Verses 1–9

Shiggaion is a *song* or *psalm* (the word is used so only here and Hab. iii. 1)—a *wandering* song (so some), the matter and composition of the several parts being different, but artificially put together—a *charming* song (so others), very delightful. David not only penned it, but sang it himself in a devout religious manner unto the Lord, *concerning the words* or affairs *of Cush the Benjamite*, that is, of some kinsman of Saul named *Cush*, who was an inveterate enemy to David, and made mischief between him and Saul. David, thus basely abused, has recourse to the Lord. His spirit was not ruffled by it, and it did not occasion one jarring string in his harp. Thus let the injuries we receive from men, instead of provoking our passions, kindle and excite our devotions.

I. He puts himself under God's protection (*v.* 1): "*Lord, save me, and deliver me* from the power and malice of *all those that persecute me*, that they may not have their will against me." He pleads, 1. His relation to God. "Thou art *my God*, and therefore whither else should I go but to thee?" 2. His con-

JAMIESON, FAUSSET, BROWN

4. Return—i.e., to my relief—or, "turn," as now having His face averted. **for thy mercies' sake**—to illustrate Thy mercy.

5. (Cf. Ps. 115:17, 18; Isa. 38:18.) There is no incredulity as to a future state. The contrast is between this scene of life, and the grave or *Sheol*, the unseen world of the dead. **give . . . thanks**—or, praise for mercies.

6. By a strong figure the abundance as well as intensity of grief is depicted. **7. consumed**— or, has failed, denoting general debility (Ps. 13:3; 38:10). **waxeth old**—or, dim. **grief**—mingled with indignation. **8, 9.** Assured of God's hearing, he suddenly defies his enemies by an address indicating that he no longer fears them;

10. and knows they will be disappointed and in their turn (cf. vs. 3) be terror-stricken or confounded.

PSALM 7

Vss. 1-17. *Shiggaion*—a plantive song or elegy. Though obscure in details, this title seems to intimate that the occasion of this Psalm was some event in David's persecution by Saul. He prays for relief because he is innocent, and God will be glorified in his vindication. He thus passes to the celebration of God's righteous government, in defending the upright and punishing the wicked, whose malignant devices will result in their own ruin; and, confident of God's aid, he closes with rejoicing.

ADAM CLARKE

1. *O Lord, rebuke me not.* This psalm, which is one of the seven "Penitential Psalms," is supposed to have been written during some grievous disease with which David was afflicted after his transgression with Bath-sheba. It argues a deep consciousness of sin, and apprehension of the just displeasure of God.

7. *Mine eye is consumed.* Is blasted, withered, sunk in my head.

10. *Ashamed and sore vexed.* May they as deeply deplore their transgressions as I have done mine! May they return; may they be suddenly converted! The original will bear this meaning, and it is the most congenial to Christian principles.

PSALM 7

This psalm is entitled, "Shiggaion of David, which he sang unto the Lord, concerning the words of Cush the Benjamite." The word *shiggayon* comes from *shagah*, "to wander," a wandering song; i.e., a psalm composed by David in his wanderings, when he was obliged to hide himself from the fury of Saul.

As to "Cush the Benjamite," he is a person unknown in the Jewish history. The name is probably a name of disguise, and by it he may covertly mean Saul himself, the son of Kish, who was of the tribe of Benjamin. The subject of the psalm will better answer to Saul's unjust persecution and David's innocence than to any other subject in the history of David.

1. *O Lord my God. Yehovah Elohai*, words expressive of the strongest confidence the soul can have in the Supreme Being.

MATTHEW HENRY

fidence in God: "Lord, save me, for I depend upon thee: *In thee do I put my trust*, and not in any arm of flesh." 3. The rage and malice of his enemies, and the imminent danger he was in of being swallowed up by them: "Lord, save me, or I am gone; he will *tear my soul like a lion* tearing his prey." 4. The failure of all other helpers: "*Lord*, be thou pleased to deliver me, for otherwise *there is none to deliver*," *v.* 2.

II. He makes a solemn protestation of his innocency as to those things whereof he was accused, and by a dreadful imprecation appeals to God, the searcher of hearts, concerning it, *v.* 3–5. David had no court on earth to appeal to. But he had the court of heaven, and a righteous Judge there, whom he could call *his God.* He was charged with a traitorous design against Saul's crown and life. This he utterly denies. *I have delivered him that without cause is my enemy*, *v.* 4. David had no design against Saul's life—Providence so ordered it that Saul lay at his mercy, and there were those about him that would soon have dispatched him, but David prevented it, when he cut off his skirt (1 Sam. xxiv. 4) and afterwards when he took away his spear (1 Sam. xxvi. 12), to attest for him what he could have done. If he were guilty (*v.* 5): *Let the enemy persecute my soul* to the death, and my good name when I am gone: let him *lay my honour in the dust.* With such an oath, or imprecation, David here ratifies the protestation of his innocency.

III. Having this testimony of his conscience concerning his innocency, he humbly prays to God to appear for him against his persecutors, and backs every petition with a proper plea.

1. He prays that God would manifest his wrath against his enemies. "Lord, they are unjustly angry at me, be thou justly angry with them and let them know that thou art so, *v.* 6. *In thy anger lift up thyself* to the seat of judgment, *because of the rage of my enemies.*"

2. He prays that God would plead his cause. *Awake for me to judgment* (that is, let my cause have a hearing), to *the judgment which thou hast commanded;* He prays (*v.* 7), "*Return thou on high* that it may be universally acknowledged that heaven itself owns and pleads David's cause." He prays again (*v.* 8), "*Judge me*, judge for me, give sentence on my side" *The Lord shall judge the people*, *v.* 8. It is his place; it is his promise. *God is the judge;* "Therefore, Lord, judge me." It would be much for the glory of God and the edification and comfort of his people if God would appear for him: "*So shall the congregation of the people compass thee about;* therefore do it for their sakes, that they may attend thee with their praises and services in the courts of thy house."

3. He prays, in general, for the conversion of sinners and the establishment of saints (*v.* 9): "*O let the wickedness*, not only of my wicked enemies, but *of all the wicked, come to an end! but establish the just.*" Here are two things which every one of us must desire and may hope for:— (1) The destruction of sin, that it may be brought to an end in ourselves and others. And this is that which all that love God, and for his sake hate evil, desire and pray for. (2) The perpetuity of righteousness: *But establish the just.* As we pray that the bad may be made good, so we pray that the good may be made better.

Verses 10–17

David having lodged his appeal with God by prayer and a solemn profession of his integrity, does, as it were, take out judgment upon the appeal, by faith in the word of God, and the assurance it gives of the happiness and safety of the righteous and the certain destruction of wicked people that continue impenitent.

I. David is confident that he shall find God his powerful protector and Saviour, and the patron of his oppressed innocency (*v.* 10): "*My defence is of God. My shield is upon God* (so some read it); there is that in God which gives an assurance of protection to all that are his. Two things David builds this confidence upon:—1. The particular favour God has for all that are sincere: *He saves the upright in heart*, and therefore will *preserve them to his heavenly kingdom*; he saves them out of their present troubles, as far as is good for them. 2. The general respect he has for justice and equity: *God judgeth the righteous;* he owns every righteous cause, and will maintain it in every righteous man, and will protect him. *God is a righteous Judge* (so some read it), who not only doeth righteousness himself, but will take care that righteousness be done by the children of men and will avenge and punish all unrighteousness.

II. He is no less confident of the destruction of all his persecutors, even as many of them as would not *repent, to give glory to God.* He reads their doom here, for their good, if possible, that they might

JAMIESON, FAUSSET, BROWN

1, 2. Though many enemies set upon him, one is singled out as prominent, and compared to a wild beast tearing his prey to pieces (cf. I Sam. 20:1; 23:23; 26:19).

3. if I have done this—i.e., the crime charged in the "words of Cush" (cf. I Sam. 24:9). **4. If I have injured my friend. yea, I have delivered . . .**—This makes a good sense, but interrupts the course of thought, and hence it is proposed to render—"if I have spoiled my enemy"—in either case (cf. I Sam. 24:4-17; 31:8, 11.

5. This is the consequence, if such has been his conduct. **mine honour**—(cf. Ps. 3:3; 4:2)—my personal and official dignity.

6. God is involved as if hitherto careless of him (Ps. 3:7; 9:18). **rage**—the most violent, like a flood rising over a river's banks.

the judgment . . . commanded—or, ordained; a just decision. **7. compass thee**—as those seeking justice. **return thou on high**—assume the judgment seat, to be honored as a just Ruler by them. **8.** Though not claiming innocence in general, he can confidently do so in this case, and in demanding from the Judge of all the earth a judgment, he virtually asks acquittal.

9. the hearts and reins—the affections and motives of men, or the seat of them (cf. Ps. 16:7; 26:2); as we use heart and bosom or breast.

10. defence—lit., "shield" (Ps. 5:12).

11. judgeth—as in verse 8. **the wicked**—Though not expressed, they are implied, for they alone are left as objects of anger.

ADAM CLARKE

2. *Lest he tear my soul like a lion.* These words seem to answer well to Saul. As the lion is king in the forest, so was Saul king over the land. As the lion in his fierceness seizes at once, and tears his prey in pieces, so David expected to be seized and suddenly destroyed by Saul.

3. *If I have done this.* David was accused by Saul of affecting the kingdom and of waiting for an opportunity to take away the life of his king, his patron, and his friend. In his application to God he refers to these charges, meets them with indignation, and clears himself of them by a strong appeal to his Judge.

4. *Yea, I have delivered him.* When, in the course of Thy providence, Thou didst put his life in my hand in the cave, I contented myself with cutting off his skirt, merely to show him the danger he had been in, and the spirit of the man whom he accused of designs against his life; and yet even for this my heart smote me, because it appeared to be an indignity offered to him who was the Lord's anointed.

7. *For their sakes therefore return thou on high.* Ascend the judgment seat; and let them see, by the dispensations of Thy providence, who is innocent and who is guilty.

11. *God is angry with the wicked every day.* The Hebrew for this sentence according to the *points* is, "And God is angry every day." Our translation seems to have been borrowed from the Chaldee, where the whole verse is as follows: "God is a righteous Judge; and in strength he is angry against the wicked every day." The Vulgate: "God is a Judge righteous, strong, and patient;—will he be angry every day?" The Septuagint: "God is a righteous Judge, strong and long-suffering; not bringing forth his anger every day." Syriac: "God is the Judge of righteousness; he is not angry every day." The Arabic is the same as the Septuagint. The Aethiopic: "God is a just Judge, and strong and long-suffering; he will not bring forth tribulation daily." I have judged it of consequence to trace this verse through all the ancient versions in order to be able to ascertain what is the true reading, where the evidence on one side amounts to a positive affirmation, "God is angry every day"; and, on the other side, to as positive a negation, "He is not angry every day." The

MATTHEW HENRY

cease from their enmity, or, however, for his own comfort, that he might not be afraid of them nor aggrieved at their prosperity and success for a time. God is angry with the wicked even in the merriest and most prosperous of their days. The destruction of sinners may be prevented by their conversion, for it is threatened with that proviso: *If he turn not* from his evil way, if he do not let fall his enmity against the people of God, then let him expect it will be his ruin; but, if he turn, it is implied that his sin shall be pardoned and all shall be well. Thus even the threatenings of wrath are introduced with a gracious implication of mercy. While God is preparing his instruments of death, he gives the sinners timely warning of their danger, and space to repent and prevent it. He is slow to punish, and *longsuffering to us-ward, not willing that any should perish.* Of all sinners persecutors are set up as the fairest marks of divine wrath; against them, more than any other, God has ordained his arrows. They set God at defiance, but cannot set themselves out of the reach of his judgments. They will destroy themselves, *v.* 14–16. The sinner is here described as taking a great deal of pains to ruin himself. The sinner's head with its politics *conceives mischief,* contrives it with a great deal of art, lays the plot deep, and keeps it close; the sinner's heart with its passions *travails with iniquity,* and is in pain to be delivered of the malicious projects it is hatching against the people of God. But what does it come to when it comes to the birth? It is falsehood; it is a cheat upon himself; it is a lie in his right hand. A labouring man works hard to dig a pit, and then falls into it and perishes in it. This is true, in a sense, of all sinners. They prepare destruction for themselves by preparing themselves for destruction.

PSALM 8

To the chief musician upon Gittith, A psalm of David.

Verses 1–2

The psalmist here sets himself to give to God the glory due to his name. Two things David here admires:—

I. How plainly God displays his glory himself, *v.* 1. He addresses himself to God with all humility and reverence, as the Lord and his people's Lord: *O Lord our Lord!* If we believe that God is the Lord, we must avouch and acknowledge him to be ours. 1. How brightly God's glory shines even in this lower world: *How excellent is thy name in all the earth!* The works of creation and Providence evince and proclaim to all the world that there is an infinite Being. There is no speech or language but the voice of God's name either is heard in it or may be. 2. How much more brightly it shines in the upper world: *Who hast set thy glory above the heavens.* (1) God is infinitely more glorious and excellent than the noblest of creatures and those that shine most brightly. (2) Whereas we, on this earth, only hear God's excellent name, and praise that, the angels and blessed spirits above see his glory, and praise that, and yet he is exalted far above even their blessing and praise. (3) In the exaltation of the Lord Jesus to the right hand of God, who is the brightness of his Father's glory and the express image of his person, God set his glory above the heavens, far above all principalities and powers.

II. How powerfully he proclaims it by the weakest of his creatures (*v.* 2): *Out of the mouth of babes and sucklings hast thou ordained strength,* or perfected praise, the praise of thy strength, Matt. xxi. 16. This intimates the glory of God, 1. In the kingdom of nature. The care God takes of little children (when they first come into the world the most helpless of all animals), the special protection they are under, and the provision nature has made for them, ought to be acknowledged by every one of us, to the glory of God, as a great instance of his power and goodness, and the more because we have all had the benefit of it. 2. In the kingdom of Providence. In the government of this lower world he makes use of the children of men. 3. In the kingdom of grace, the kingdom of the Messiah. It is here foretold that by the apostles, who were looked upon but as babes, *unlearned and ignorant men* (Acts iv. 13), mean and despicable, and *by the foolishness of their preaching,* the devil's kingdom should be thrown down, as Jericho's walls were by the sound of rams' horns. The gospel is called *the arm of the Lord* and *the rod of his strength*; this was ordained to work wonders, not out of the mouth of philosophers or orators, politicians or statesmen, but of a company of poor fishermen. We hear children crying, *Hosanna to the Son of David,* when the chief priests and Pharisees owned him not.

JAMIESON, FAUSSET, BROWN

12, 13. They are here distinctly pointed out, though by changing the person, a very common mode of speech, one is selected as a representative of wicked men generally. The military figures are of obvious meaning. **against the persecutors**—Some render "for burning," but the former is the best sense. Arrows for burning would be appropriate in besieging a town, not in warring against one man or a company in open fight. **14.** The first clause expresses the general idea that wicked men labor to do evil, the others carry out the figure fully. **15, 16.** I Samuel 18:17; 31:2 illustrate the statement whether alluded to or not. These verses are expository of verse 14, showing how the devices of the wicked end in disappointment, falsifying their expectations. **17. his righteousness**—(Ps. 5:8). Thus illustrated in the defense of His servant and punishment of the wicked.

PSALM 8

Vss. 1-19. *Upon* [or according to the] *Gittith,* probably means that the musical performance was directed to be according to a tune of that name; which, derived from *Gath,* a wine press, denotes a tune (used in connection with gathering the vintage) of a joyous character. All the Psalms to which this term is prefixed are of such a character. The Psalmist gives vent to his admiration of God's manifested perfections, by celebrating His condescending and beneficent providence to man as evinced by the position of the race, as originally created and assigned a dominion over the works of His hands.

1. thy name—perfections (Ps. 5:11; 7:17). **who hast set**—lit., "which set Thou Thy glory," etc., or "which glory of Thine set Thou," etc., i.e., make it more conspicuous as if earth were too small a theater for its display. A similar exposition suits the usual rendering.

2. So manifest are God's perfections, that by very weak instruments He conclusively sets forth His praise. Infants are not only wonderful illustrations of God's power and skill, in their physical constitution, instincts, and early developed intelligence, but also in their spontaneous admiration of God's works, by which they put to shame—**still**—or, silence men who rail and cavil against God. A special illustration of the passage is afforded in Matthew 21:16, when our Saviour *stilled* the cavillers by quoting these words; for the glories with which God invested His incarnate Son, even in His humiliation, constitute a most wonderful display of the perfections of His wisdom, love, and power. In view of the scope of verses 4-8 (see below), this quotation by our Saviour may be regarded as an exposition of the prophetical character of the words. **sucklings**—among the Hebrews were probably of an **age to speak** (cf. I Sam. 1:22-24; Mark 7:27). **ordained**—founded, or prepared, and perfected, which occurs in Matthew 21:16; taken from the *Septuagint,* has the same meaning. **strength**—In the quotation in the New Testament, *praise* occurs as the consequence or effect put for the cause (cf. Ps. 118:14). **avenger**—as in Psalm 44:16; one desirous of revenge, disposed to be quarrelsome, and so apt to cavil against God's government.

ADAM CLARKE

mass of evidence supports the latter reading. The Chaldee first corrupted the text by making the addition, "with the wicked," which our translators have followed, though they have put the words into italics, as not being in the Hebrew text. The true sense may be restored thus: *el,* with the vowel point *tsere,* signifies "God"; *al,* the same letters, with the point *pathach,* signifies "not." Several of the versions have read it in this way: "God judgeth the righteous, and is not angry every day."

12. *If he turn not.* Most of the versions read, "If ye return not."

13. *He hath also prepared for him the instruments of death.* This appears to be all a prophecy of the tragic death of Saul. He was wounded by the arrows of the Philistines; and his own keen sword, on which he fell, terminated his woeful days!

14. *He travaileth with iniquity.* All these terms show the pitch of envy, wrath, and malevolence to which Saul had carried his opposition against David.

15. *He made a pit.* The metaphor is taken from pits dug in the earth, and slightly covered over with reeds, so as not to be discerned from the solid ground; but the animal steps on them, the surface breaks, and he falls into the pit and is taken. "All the world agrees to acknowledge the equity of that sentence, which inflicts upon the *guilty* the punishment intended by them for the *innocent.*"—Horne.

16. *Shall come down upon his own pate.* Upon his *scalp,* the top of the head.

PSALM 8

The inscription of this psalm is the following: "To the chief Musician upon Gittith, A Psalm of David." This has been metaphrased, "To the conqueror, concerning the winepresses," and has been supposed to be a psalm intended for the time of vintage. That the psalm has respect to our Lord and the time of the gospel is evident from the reference made to v. 2, in Matt. xi. 25, the express quotation of it in Matt. xxi. 16, and another reference to it in 1 Cor. i. 27. The *fourth* and *sixth* verses are quoted Heb. ii. 6-9. See also 1 Cor. xv. 27 and Eph. i. 22. The first and second Adam are both referred to, and the first and second creation also; and the glory which God has received, and is to receive, through both. It relates to Christ and redemption.

1. *O Lord our Lord. Yehovah Adoneynu;* "O Jehovah our Prop, our Stay, or Support."

2. *Out of the mouth of babes and sucklings.* We have seen how our Lord applied this passage to the Jewish children, who, seeing His miracles, cried out in the Temple, "Hosanna to the Son of David" Matt. xxi. 16. And we have seen how the *enemy* and the *avenger*—the *chief priests* and the *scribes*—were offended because of these things; and as the psalm wholly concerns Jesus Christ, it is most probable that in this act of the Jewish children the prophecy had its primary fulfilment, and was left to the Jews as a witness and a sign of the Messiah, which they should have acknowledged when our Lord directed their attention to it.

MATTHEW HENRY

Sometimes the grace of God appears wonderfully in young children, and he *teaches* those *knowledge and makes* those *to understand doctrine, who are* but *newly weaned from the milk and drawn from the breasts*, Isa. xxviii. 9. Sometimes the power of God brings to pass great things in his church by very weak and unlikely instruments.

Verses 3–9

David here goes on to magnify the honour of God by recounting the honours he has put upon man, especially the man Christ Jesus. The condescensions of the divine grace call for our praises as much as the elevations of the divine glory. See here,

I. What it is that leads him to admire the condescending favour of God to man; it is his consideration of the lustre and influence of the heavenly bodies, which are within the view of sense (*v.* 3): *I consider thy heavens*, and there, particularly, *the moon and the stars.* It is our duty to consider the heavens. We see them, we cannot but see them. By this, among other things, man is distinguished from the beasts, that, while *they* are so framed as to look downwards to the earth, man is made erect to look upwards towards heaven. *The heavens, even the heavens, are the Lord's* (cxv. 16), because they are the work of his fingers. He made them; he made them easily. The stretching out of the heavens needed not any outstretched arm; it was done with a word; it was but *the work of his fingers.* Even the inferior lights, the moon and stars, show the glory and power of the Father of lights, and furnish us with matter for praise. God not only made them, but *ordained* them, and the ordinances of heaven can never be altered. When we consider how the glory of God shines in the upper world we may well wonder that he should take cognizance of such a mean creature as man. When we consider of what great use the heavens are to men on earth, we may well say, "*Lord, what is man* that thou shouldst settle the ordinances of heaven with an eye to him and to his benefit, and that his comfort and convenience should be so consulted in the making of the lights of heaven and directing their motions!"

II. How he expresses this admiration (*v.* 4): "*Lord, what is man* (*enosh*, sinful, weak, miserable man, a creature so forgetful of thee and his duty to thee) *that thou art* thus *mindful of him*, that thou takest cognizance of him and of his actions and affairs, that in the making of the world thou hadst a respect to him! What is the *son of man, that thou visitest him* as one friend visits another, art pleased to converse with him and concern thyself for him!"

1. To mankind in general. Though man is a worm (Job xxv. 6), yet God puts a respect upon him, and shows him abundance of kindness; man is, above all the creatures in this lower world, the favourite and darling of Providence. We may be sure he takes precedence of all the inhabitants of this lower world, for he is made but a *little lower than the angels* (*v.* 5), lower indeed, because by his body he is allied to the earth and to the beasts that perish, and yet by his soul, which is spiritual and immortal, he is so near akin to the holy angels that he may be truly said to be but *a little lower than they*, and is, in order, next to them. He is but for a little while lower than the angels, while his great soul is cooped up in a house of clay, but the children of the resurrection shall be *ἰσάγγελοι—angels' peers* (Luke xx. 36) and no longer lower than they. He is endued with noble faculties and capacities: *Thou hast crowned him with glory and honour.* Man's reason is his crown of glory; let him not profane that crown by disturbing the use of it nor forfeit that crown by acting contrary to its dictates. God has put all things under man's feet, that he might serve himself, not only of the labour, but of the productions and lives of the inferior creatures; they are all delivered into his hand, nay, they are all *put under his feet.* He specifies some of the inferior animals (*v.* 7, 8), not only *sheep and oxen*, which man takes care of and provides for, but *the beasts of the field*, as well as those of the flood, yea, and those creatures which are most at a distance from man, as *the fowl of the air*, yea, *and the fish of the sea*, which live in another element and pass unseen through the paths of the seas. Man has arts to take these; though many of them are much stronger and many of them much swifter than he.

2. But this refers, in a particular manner, to Jesus Christ. Of him we are taught to expound it, Heb. ii. 6–8, where the apostle, to prove the sovereign dominion of Christ both in heaven and in earth, shows that he is that man, that son of man, here spoken of, whom God *has crowned with glory and honour* and made to *have dominion over the works of his hands.* We have reason humbly to value ourselves by it and thankfully to admire the grace of God in it, (1) That

JAMIESON, FAUSSET, BROWN

3, 4. The allusion to the magnificence of the visible heavens is introduced for the purpose of illustrating God's condescension, who, though the mighty Creator of these glorious worlds of light, makes man the object of regard and recipient of favor.

man—lit., "frail man," an allusion to his essential infirmity.

son of man—only varies the form of speech. **visitest**—in favor (Ps. 65:10). This favor is now more fully illustrated.

5-8. God has placed man next in dignity to angels, and but a little lower, and has crowned him with the empire of the world.

glory and honour—are the attributes of royal dignity (Ps. 21:5; 45:3). The position assigned man is that described (Gen. 1:26-28) as belonging to Adam, in his original condition, the terms employed in detailing the subjects of man's dominion corresponding with those there used. In a modified sense, in his present fallen state, man is still invested with some remains of this original dominion. It is very evident, however, by the apostle's inspired expositions (Heb. 2:6-8: I Cor. 15:27, 28) that the language here employed finds its fulfilment only in the final exaltation of Christ's human nature. There is no limit to the "all things" mentioned, God only excepted, who "puts all things under." Man, in the person and glorious destiny of Jesus of Nazareth, the second Adam, the head and representative of the race, will not only be restored to his original position, but exalted far beyond it. "The last enemy, death," through fear of which, man, in his present estate, is "all his lifetime in bondage," "shall be destroyed." Then *all things* will have been put under his feet, "principalities and powers being made subject to him." This view, so far from being alien from the scope of the passage, is more consistent than any other; for man as a race cannot well be conceived to have a higher honor put upon him than to be thus exalted in the person and destiny of Jesus of Nazareth. And at the same time, by no

ADAM CLARKE

JOSEPH PARKER:

It does us good to go to nature. The Psalmist considered the "heavens," "the moon, and the stars." Good nature! sweet mother! What medicine is like her smile, or her breath, or her benediction! What a sanctuary is on the top of her mountains; what altars are in the sighs of her winds; what immortality, as it were, breathes across her seas! "Lift up thine eyes," said God to a dejected one, "and behold." It does us good to look upward: there is a healing influence in space—its vastness, its purity, its solemnity. What can they be who have never seen the sky? There are millions of men who have never seen it because they have never looked at it; it seems to be no business of theirs; they seem to have no relation to it; they forget that if there were no sky, there could be no earth; if there were no sun, there could be no food to eat. But men do not connect things; they are not logical; they do not perceive sequences, and trace results to origins. And many are so shut up that they cannot see the sky, only little blue strips of it, with space enough for a star or two; but the great city of stars—the infinite metropolis of light, they have never seen. If they could see—really see it—they would lose all their care and fear, and their tears would be but part of the common rain that makes the earth glad. But men will not look up; they live with inclined heads; and who ever saw anything in the earth but a grave? The earth is not worth thinking about, except as a part of something else.—*The People's Bible*

4. *What is man? Mah enosh*, what is wretched, miserable man; man in his fallen state, full of infirmity, ignorance, and sin? *That thou art mindful of him?* That thou settest Thy heart upon him, keepest him continually in Thy merciful view. *And the son of man. Uben Adam*, and the son of Adam, **the first** great rebel, the fallen child of a fallen **parent**.

5. *Thou hast made him a little lower than the angels.* The original is certainly very emphatic: "Thou hast made him less than God for a little time." See these passages explained at large in the notes on Heb. ii. 6.

6. *Thou madest him to have dominion.* See the notes referred to above, and those on Phil. ii. 6-9. *Thou hast put all things under his feet.* Though the whole of the brute creation was made subject to Adam in his state of innocence, yet it could never be literally said of him that God had put all things under his feet, or that he had dominion over the work of God's hands; but all this is most literally true of our Lord Jesus, and to Him the apostle, Heb. ii. 6, etc., applies all these passages.

7. *All sheep and oxen.* All domestic animals. *Beasts of the field.* All wild beasts.

8. *The fowl of the air.* All these were given to man in the beginning, and he has still a general dominion over them; for thus saith the Lord:

MATTHEW HENRY

Jesus Christ assumed the nature of man, and, in that nature, humbled himself. He was, *for a little while* (so the apostle interprets it), made lower than the angels, when he took upon him the form of a servant and made himself of no reputation. (2) That, in that nature, he is exalted to be Lord of all. God the Father exalted him, because he had humbled himself, *crowned him with glory and honour*, the glory which he had with him before the worlds were. All the creatures are put under his feet; and, even in the days of his flesh, he gave some specimens of his power over them, as when he commanded the winds and the seas.

PSALM 9

To the chief musician upon Muth-labben. A psalm of David.

Verses 1–10

The title of this psalm gives a very uncertain sound concerning the occasion of penning it. It is upon *Muth-labben*, which some make to refer to the death of Goliath, others of Nabel, others of Absolom; but I incline to think it signifies only some tune, or some musical instrument, to which this psalm was intended to be sung; and that the enemies are the Philistines, and other neighbouring nations, 2 Sam. v. 8.

I. David praises God for his mercies and the great things he had of late done for him and his government, *v.* 1, 2. Holy joy is the life of thankful praise, as thankful praise is the language of holy joy: *I will be glad and rejoice in thee.* The triumphs of the Redeemer ought to be the triumphs of the redeemed; see Rev. xii. 10; xix. 5; xv. 3, 4.

II. He acknowledges the almighty power of God as that which the strongest and stoutest of his enemies were no way able to contest with or stand before, *v.* 3. They are forced to turn back. When once they turn back, they fall and perish; even their retreat will be their ruin, and they will save themselves no more by flying than by fighting. The presence of the Lord and the glory of his power, are sufficient for the destruction of his and his people's enemies. This was fulfilled when our Lord Jesus, with one word, *I am he*, made his enemies to *fall back at his presence* (John xviii. 6).

III. He gives to God the glory of his righteousness, in his appearing on his behalf (*v.* 4): *"Thou hast maintained my right and my cause*, that is, my righteous cause; when that came on, *thou satest in the throne judging right*."

IV. He records, with joy, the triumphs of the God of heaven over all the powers of hell and attends those triumphs with his praises, *v.* 5. *"Thou hast rebuked the heathen*, hast given them real proofs of thy displeasure against them." *Thou hast destroyed the wicked.* He had buried them in oblivion.

V. He exults over the enemy whom God thus appears against (*v.* 6): *Thou hast destroyed cities.* Either, "Thou, O enemy! hast destroyed our cities, at least in intention and imagination," or "Thou, O God! hast destroyed their cities by the desolation brought upon their country." It may be taken either way.

VI. He comforts himself and others in God, and pleases himself with the thoughts of him. 1. With the thoughts of his eternity. On this earth we see nothing durable, even strong cities are buried in rubbish and forgotten; *but the Lord shall endure for ever, v.* 7. 2. With the thoughts of his sovereignty both in government and judgment: *He has prepared his throne*, has fixed it by his infinite wisdom, has fixed it by his immutable counsel. 3. With the thoughts of his justice and righteousness in all the administrations of his government. *He shall judge the world*, all persons and all controversies, *shall minister judgment* to the people (shall determine their lot both in this and in the future state) in righteousness and *in uprightness*, so that there shall not be the least colour of exception against it. 4. With the thoughts of that peculiar favour which God bears to his own people and the special protection which he takes them under. *He will be a refuge for the oppressed*, a high place, a strong place, for the oppressed, *in times of trouble*. 5. With the thoughts of that sweet satisfaction and repose of mind which those have that make God their refuge (*v.* 10): *"Those that know thy name will put their trust in thee*, as I have done, and then they will find, as I have found, that thou dost not forsake those that seek thee." The better God is known the more he is trusted. Those who know him to be a God of infinite wisdom will trust him *further than they can see him* (Job xxxv. 14); those who know him to be a God of almighty power will trust him when creature-confidences fail and they have nothing else to trust to (2 Chron. xx. 12); and those who know him to be a God of infinite grace and goodness will

JAMIESON, FAUSSET, BROWN

other of His glorious manifestations has God more illustriously declared those attributes which distinguish His name than in the scheme of redemption, of which this economy forms such an important and essential feature. In the generic import of the language, as describing man's present relation to the works of God's hands, it may be regarded as typical, thus allowing not only the usual application, but also this higher sense which the inspired writers of the New Testament have assigned it. **9.** Appropriately, the writer closes this brief but pregnant and sublime song of praise with the terms of admiration with which it was opened.

PSALM 9

Vss. 1-20. *Upon Muth-labben*, or, *after the manner according to "death to the Son,"* by which some song was known, to whose air or melody the musician is directed to perform this Psalm. This mode of denoting a song by some prominent word or words is still common (cf. Ps. 22). The Psalmist praises God for deliverance from his enemies and celebrates the divine government, for providing security to God's people and punishment to the wicked. Thus encouraging himself, he prays for new occasions to recount God's mercies, and confident of His continued judgment on the wicked and vindication of the oppressed, he implores a prompt and efficient manifestation of the divine sovereignty.

1. Heartfelt gratitude will find utterance.

3-5. When . . . are turned back—It is the result of God's power alone.

He, as a righteous Judge (Ps. 7:11), vindicates His people.

He rebukes by acts as well as words (Ps. 6:1; 18:15), and so effectually as to destroy the names of nations as well as persons.

6. Lit., "As to the enemy finished are his ruins for ever. Thou [God] hast destroyed," etc. (I Sam. 15:3, 7; 27: 8, 9). The wicked are utterly undone. Their ruins shall never be repaired.

7, 8. God's eternal possession of a throne of justice is contrasted with the ruin of the wicked.

9, 10. The oppressed, and all who know Him (Ps. 5:3, 7:1), find Him a sure refuge.

ADAM CLARKE

"The fear of you and the dread of you shall be upon every beast of the earth, and upon every fowl of the air, upon all that moveth upon the earth, and upon all the fishes of the sea; into your hand are they delivered," Gen. ix. 2.

9. *O Lord our Lord.* The Psalmist concludes as he began. Jehovah, our Prop and Support! His name is excellent in all the earth. The name of Jesus is celebrated in almost every part of the habitable globe; for His gospel has been preached, or is in the progress of being preached, through the whole world.

PSALM 9

The inscription to this psalm in the Hebrew text is, "To the chief Musician upon Muth-labben, A Psalm of David." The title and the psalm have been so variously understood that it would be as painful as it would be useless to follow the different commentators, both ancient and modern, through all their conjectures.

1. *I will praise thee, O Lord, with my whole heart.* And it is only when the *whole heart* is employed in the work that God can look upon it with acceptance. *I will shew forth.* "I will number out, or reckon up," a very difficult task, "thy miracles," supernatural interventions of Thy power and goodness.

5. *Thou hast rebuked the heathen.* We know not what this particularly refers to, but it is most probably to the Canaanitish nations, which God destroyed from off the face of the earth; hence it is said, *Thou hast put out their name for ever and ever.*

6. *Destructions are come to a perpetual end.* Rather, "The enemy is desolated for ever; for thou hast destroyed their cities, and their memory is perished with them." Multitudes of the cities of the Canaanites have perished so utterly that neither name nor vestige remains of them.

9. *A refuge.* "A high place," where their enemies can neither reach nor see them.

MATTHEW HENRY

trust him *though he slay them*, Job xiii. 15. Those who know him to be a God of inviolable truth and faithfulness will rejoice in his word of promise, and rest upon that. Those who know him to be the Father of spirits, and an everlasting Father, will trust him with their souls even to the end.

Verses 11–20

I. David, having praised God himself, calls upon and invites others to praise him likewise, *v.* 11. *Sing praises to the Lord who dwelleth in Zion.* As the special residence of his glory is in heaven, so the special residence of his grace is in his church, of which Zion was a type. Let them particularly take notice of the justice of God in avenging the blood of his people Israel on the Philistines and their other wicked neighbours, who had, in making war upon them, used them barbarously and given them no quarter, *v.* 12.

II. David, having praised God for former mercies and deliverances, earnestly prays that God would still appear for him; for he sees not yet all things put under him. "*Have mercy upon me*, who, having misery only, and no merit, to speak for me, must depend upon mere mercy for relief. *Lord, consider my trouble*, and do for me as thou thinkest fit." The experience he had had of divine succours and the expectation he now had of the continuance of them: "*O thou that liftest me up*, that canst do it, that hast done it, that wilt do it, whose prerogative it is to **lift up thy people** *from the gates of death!*" We are never brought so low, so near to death, but God can raise us up. If he has saved us from spiritual and eternal death, we may thence take encouragement to hope that in all our distresses he will be a very present help to us. His sincere purpose to praise God when his victories should be completed (*v.* 14).

III. David by faith foresees and foretells the certain ruin of all wicked people, both in this world and in that to come. God executes judgment upon them when the measure of their iniquities is full, for they sink into the pit which they themselves digged (vii. 15). Drunkards kill themselves; prodigals beggar themselves, the contentious bring mischief upon themselves. In these judgments the wrath of God is revealed from heaven against all ungodliness and unrighteousness of men. *The wicked shall be turned into hell*, as captives into the prison-house, even *all the nations that forget God.* Forgetfulness of God is the cause of all the wickedness of the wicked.

IV. David encourages the people of God to wait for his salvation, though it should be long deferred, *v.* 18. The needy may think themselves, and others may think them, forgotten for a while, and their expectation of help from God may seem to have perished. But he that believes does not make haste; the vision is for an appointed time, and at the end it shall speak. We may build upon it as undoubtedly true that God's people shall not always be forgotten, nor shall they be disappointed of their hopes from the promise.

V. He concludes with prayer that God would humble the pride, break the power, and blast the projects, of all the wicked enemies of his church: "*Arise, O Lord!* (*v.* 19), stir up thyself, exert thy power, take thy seat, and deal with all these proud and daring enemies of thy name, and cause, and people. *Let not man prevail;* consult thy own honour, and let not weak and mortal men prevail against the kingdom and interest of the almighty and immortal God. *Shall mortal man be too hard for God, too strong for his Maker?*" It is a very desirable thing, much for the glory of God and the peace and welfare of the universe, that men should know and consider themselves to be but men, depending creatures, mutable, mortal, and accountable.

JAMIESON, FAUSSET, BROWN

11. (Cf. Ps. 2:6; 3:4.) **12. for blood**—i.e., murders (Ps. 5:6), including all the oppressions of His people. **maketh inquisition**—(cf. Gen. 9:5). He will avenge their cause.

13. gates—or, regions—**of death**—Gates being the entrance is put for the bounds. **14. gates . . . Zion**—The enclosure of the city (cf. Ps. 48:12; Isa. 23:12), or, church, as denoted by this phrase contrasted with that of death, carries out the idea of exaltation as well as deliverance. Signal favors should lead us to render signal and public thanks. **15, 16.** The undesigned results of the devices of the wicked prove them to be of God's overruling or ordering, especially when those results are destructive to the wicked themselves. **Higgaion**—means "meditation," and, combined with **Selah**, seems to denote a pause of unusual solemnity and emphasis (cf. Ps. 3:2). Though Selah occurs seventy-three times, this is the only case in which Higgaion is found. In the view which is given here of the retribution on the wicked as an instance of God's wise and holy ordering, we may well pause in adoring wonder and faith. **17. shall be turned**—or, shall turn, retreating under God's vengeance, and driven by Him to the extreme of destruction, even hell itself. Those who forget God are classed with the depraved and openly profane. **18.** (Cf. Ps. 13.) **the needy**—lit., "poor," as deprived of anything; hence miserable. **expectation of the poor**—or, meek, humble, made so by affliction.

19. Arise—(cf. Ps. 4:7). **let not man**—(Ps. 8:4). **let . . . be judged**—and of course condemned. **20.** By their effectual subjection, make them to realize their frail nature Ps. 8:4), and deter them from all conceit and future rebellion.

ADAM CLARKE

CHARLES H. SPURGEON:

The heavenly spirit of praise is gloriously contagious, and he that hath it is never content unless he can excite all who surround him to unite in his sweet employ. Singing and preaching, as means of glorifying God, are here joined together, and it is remarkable that, connected with all revivals of gospel ministry, there has been a sudden outburst of the spirit of song. Luther's Psalms and Hymns were in all men's mouths, and in the modern revival under Wesley and Whitefield, the strains of Charles Wesley, Cennick, Berridge, Toplady, Hart, Newton, and many others, were the outgrowth of restored piety. The singing of the birds of praise fitly accompanies the return of the gracious spring of divine visitation through the proclamation of the truth. Sing on, brethren, and preach on, and these shall both be a token that the Lord still dwelleth in Zion. It will be well for us, when coming up to Zion to remember that the Lord dwells among his saints, and is to be had in peculiar reverence of all those that are about him.

—The Treasury of David

15. *The heathen are sunk down in the pit.* See on Ps. vii. 15.

17. *The wicked shall be turned into hell.* "Headlong into hell, down into hell." The original is very emphatic.

20. *Put them in fear.* "O Lord, place a teacher among them," that they may know they also are accountable creatures, grow wise unto salvation, and be prepared for a state of blessedness. *That the nations may know themselves to be but men. Enosh;* Let the Gentiles be taught by the preaching of Thy gospel that they are weak and helpless and stand in need of the salvation which Christ has provided for them.

MATTHEW HENRY

PSALM 10

Verses 1–11

David, in these verses, discovers,

I. A very great affection to God and his favour; for, in the time of trouble, that which he complains of most feelingly is God's withdrawing his gracious presence (*v.* 1): "*Why standest thou afar off*, as one unconcerned in the indignities done to thy name and the injuries done to the people?" It is because we judge by outward appearance; we stand afar off from God by our unbelief, and then we complain that God stands afar off from us.

II. A very great indignation against sin. He beholds the transgressors and is grieved, is amazed, and brings to his heavenly Father their evil report. Passionate and satirical invectives against bad men do more hurt than good; if we will speak of their badness, let it be to God in prayer, for he alone can make

JAMIESON, FAUSSET, BROWN

PSALM 10

Vss. 1-18. The Psalmist mourns God's apparent indifference to his troubles, which are aggravated by the successful malice, blasphemy, pride, deceit, and profanity of the wicked. On the just and discriminating providence of God he relies for the destruction of their false security, and the defense of the needy.

1. These are, of course, figurative terms (cf. Ps. 7:6; 13:1; etc.). **hidest**—Supply "thine eyes" or "face."

ADAM CLARKE

PSALM 10

1. *Why standest thou afar off, O Lord?* This psalm makes a part of the preceding in the Vulgate and Septuagint, and in four of Kennicott's and De Rossi's MSS. It seems to belong to the time of the Captivity, or the return of the captives. It was probably made in reference to Sanballat, and the other enemies of the Jews. There is a great similarity between this and Psalms xiii; xiv; xxxv; and liii. In these we find the same complaints, the same sentiments, and almost the same expressions. God is represented here as standing at some distance, beholding the oppression of His people, and yet apparently disregarding it.

MATTHEW HENRY

them better. This long representation of the wickedness of the wicked is here summed up in the first words of it (*v.* 2), *The wicked in his pride doth persecute the poor*, where two things are laid to their charge, pride and persecution, the former the cause of the latter. Tyranny, both in state and church, owes its origin to pride. The psalmist, having begun this description, presently inserts a short prayer, a prayer in a parenthesis. *Let them be taken*, as proud people often are, *in the devices that they have imagined*, *v.* 2. The sinner proudly glories in his power and success. He *boasts of his heart's desire*, boasts that he can do what he pleases. He proudly contradicts the judgment of God, which, we are sure, is according to truth; for he *blesses the covetous, whom the Lord abhors*. See how God and men differ in their sentiments of persons: God abhors covetous worldlings who make money their God and idolise it; he looks upon them as his enemies, and will have no communion with them. *The friendship of the world is enmity to God.* But proud persecutors bless them, and approve their sayings, xlix. 13. He proudly casts off the thoughts of God (*v.* 4). *God is not in all his thoughts*, not in any of them. *All his thoughts are that there is no God.* The cause of this impiety and irreligion is pride. Men will not seek after God because they think they have no need of him, their own hands are sufficient for them. He proudly makes light of God's commandments and judgments (*v.* 5): *His ways are always grievous.* Tell him of God's judgments which will be executed upon those that go on still in their trespasses, and he will not be convinced that there is any reality in them; they are *far above out of his sight*, and therefore he thinks they are mere bugbears. He proudly sets trouble at defiance and is confident of the continuance of his own prosperity (*v.* 6): *He hath said in his heart*, and pleased himself with the thought, *I shall not be moved*, my goods are laid up for many years, and *I shall never be in adversity*: like Babylon, that said, *I shall be a lady for ever*, Isa. xlvii. 7; Rev. xviii. 7. Those are nearest ruin who thus set it furthest from them. For the gratifying of their pride and covetousness, and in opposition to God and religion, they are very oppressive to all within their reach. They are very bitter and malicious (*v.* 7): *His mouth is full of cursing.* They are very false and treacherous. Like Esau, that cunning hunter, *he sits in the lurking places, in the secret places*, and *his eyes are privily set* to do mischief (*v.* 8), not because he is ashamed of what he does (if he blushed, there were some hopes he would repent), nor because he is afraid of the wrath of God, for he imagines God will never call him to an account (*v.* 11), but because he is afraid lest the discovery of his designs should be the breaking of them. Those that have power ought to protect the innocent and provide for the poor; yet these will be the destroyers of those whose guardians they ought to be. And what do they aim at? It is to *catch the poor*, and *draw them into their net*, that is, get them into their power, not to strip them only, but to *murder them.* They hunt for the precious life. It is God's poor people that they are persecuting, against whom they bear a mortal hatred for his sake whose they are and whose image they bear. *He lies in wait as a lion* that thirsts after blood, and feeds with pleasure upon the prey. *He crouches and humbles himself*, as beasts of prey do, that they may get their prey within their reach. This intimates that the sordid spirits of persecutors and oppressors will stoop to anything, though ever so mean, for the compassing of their wicked designs. They could not thus break through all the laws of justice and goodness towards man if they had not first shaken off all sense of religion, and risen up in rebellion against the light of its most sacred and self-evident principles: *He hath said in his heart, God has forgotten.*

Verses 12–18

David, upon the foregoing representation of the inhumanity and impiety of the oppressors, ground an address to God.

I. What he prays for. 1. That God would himself appear (*v.* 12): "*Arise, O Lord! O God! lift up thy hand*, manifest thy presence and providence in the affairs of this lower world. *Arise, O Lord!* to the confusion of those who say that thou hidest thy face." 2. That he could appear for his people: "*Forget not the humble, the afflicted*, that are poor, that are made poorer, and are poor in spirit. Their oppressors, in their presumption, say that thou hast forgotten them; and they, in their despair, are ready to say the same. Lord, make it to appear that they are both mistaken." 3. That he would appear against their persecutors, *v.* 15. *Break thou the arm of the wicked*, take away his power, *that the hypocrite reign not, lest the people be ensnared*, Job xxxiv. 30.

II. What he pleads for the encouraging of his own

JAMIESON, FAUSSET, BROWN

2. Lit., "In pride of the wicked they (the poor or humble, vs. 17; Ps. 12:5) shall be taken in the devices they (the proud) have imagined.

3. his heart's [or "soul's"] **desire**–i.e., his success in evil. **and blesseth . . .**–he (the wicked) blesseth the covetous, he despiseth the Lord.

4. The face expresses the self-conceit, whose fruit is practical atheism (Ps. 14:1).

5, 6. Such is his confidence in the permanence of his way or course of life, that he disregards God's providential government (*out of sight*, because he will not look, Isa. 26:11), sneers at his enemies, and boasts perpetual freedom from evil.

7-10. The malignity and deceit (Ps. 140:3) of such are followed by acts combining cunning, fraud, and violence (cf. Prov. 1:11, 18), aptly illustrated by the habits of the lion, and of hunters taking their prey. "Poor," in verses 8, 10, 14, represents a word peculiar to this Psalm, meaning the sad or sorrowful; in verse 9, as usual, it means the pious or meek sufferer. **8. eyes . . . privily set**–He watches with half-closed eyes, appearing not to see. **10. croucheth**–as a lion gathers himself into as small compass as possible to make the greater spring. **fall by his strong ones**–The figure of the lion is dropped, and this phrase means the accomplices of the chief or leading wicked man. **11.** As before, such conduct implies disbelief or disregard of God's government.

12. (Cf. Ps. 9:19; 3:7.) **humble**–(Cf. vs. 17, and *Margin.*) **lift up thine hand**–exert thy power.

ADAM CLARKE

3. *Blesseth the covetous, whom the Lord abhorreth.* Or, "He blesseth the covetous, he abhorreth the Lord."

8-9. *He sitteth in the lurking places.* In this and the following verse there appears to be an allusion to espionage, or setting of spies on a man's conduct; or to the conduct of an assassin or private murderer. *He sitteth in the lurking places . . . in the secret places . . . his eyes*—spies—*are privily set. He lieth in wait secretly . . . he doth catch the poor, when he draweth him into his net.* He is like a hunter that lays his traps and gins, digs his pits, sets his nets; and when the prey falls into them, he destroys its life.

10. *He croucheth.* The lion squats down and gathers himself together, that he may make the greater spring.

MATTHEW HENRY

faith in these petitions.

1. He pleads the great affronts which these proud oppressors put upon God himself (*v.* 13): "*Wherefore do the wicked contemn God?*" He does so; for he says, "*Thou wilt not require it;* thou wilt never call us to an account for what we do," than which they could not put a greater indignity upon the righteous God. *Wherefore do the wicked thus contemn God?* It is because they do not know him. Why are they suffered thus to contemn God? It is because the day of reckoning is yet to come.

2. He pleads the notice God took of the impiety and iniquity of these oppressors (*v.* 14).

3. He pleads the dependence which the oppressed had upon him: "*The poor commits himself unto thee,* each of them does so, I among the rest. *They leave themselves with thee*" (so some read it), "not prescribing, but subscribing, to thy wisdom and will. They are thy willing subjects, and put themselves under thy protection; therefore protect them."

4. He pleads the relation in which God is pleased to stand to us, (1) As a great God. He *is King for ever and ever, v.* 16. "Lord, let all that pay homage and tribute to thee as their King have the benefit of thy government and find thee their refuge." (2) As a good God. He is the helper of the fatherless (*v.* 14), of those who have no one else to help them and have many to injure them.

5. He pleads the experience which God's church and people had had of God's readiness to appear for them. "*The heathen have perished out of this land;* the remainders of the Canaanites, the seven devoted nations, which have long been as thorns in the eyes and goads in the sides of Israel, are now, at length, utterly rooted out; and this is an encouragement to us to hope that God will, in like manner, break the arm of the oppressive Israelites, who were, in some respects, worse than heathens." He had heard and answered their prayers (*v.* 17): "*Lord, thou hast* many a time *heard the desire of the humble,* and never saidst to a distressed suppliant, *Seek in vain.* Why may not we hope for the continuance and repetition of the wonders, the favours, which our father told us of?" Thou art the same, and thy power, and promise, and relation to thy people are the same, and the work and workings of grace are the same in them; why therefore may we not hope that he who has been will still be, will ever be, a God hearing prayer? He prepares the heart for prayer by kindling holy desires, and strengthening our most holy faith, fixing the thoughts and raising the affections and then he graciously accepts the prayer. He will plead the cause of the persecuted, will judge the fatherless and oppressed, clear up their innocency, restore their comforts, and recompense them for all the loss and damage. He will put an end to the fury of the persecutors. See how light the psalmist now makes of the power of that proud persecutor whom he had been describing in this psalm. He is but *a man of the earth,* a man *out of* the earth (so the word is), sprung out of the earth, and therefore mean, and weak. He is but *man that shall die, a son of man that shall be as grass?* Isa. li. 12. He that protects us is the Lord of heaven; he that persecutes us is but a man of the earth.

JAMIESON, FAUSSET, BROWN

13, 14. It is in vain to suppose God will overlook sin, however forbearing; for He carefully examines or beholds all wickedness, and will mark it by His providential (Thine hand) punishment.

14. mischief and spit—provocation and trouble of the sufferer (cf. Ps. 6:7; 7:14). **committeth**—or, leaves (his burden) on Thee. **15. arm**—power. **till thou find none**—So far from not requiting (vss. 11, 13), God will utterly destroy the wicked and his deeds (Ps. 9:5, 6; 34:16; 37:36).

16-18. God reigns. The wicked, if for a time successful, shall be cut off. He hears and confirms the hearts of His suffering people (Ps. 112:7), executes justice for the feeble, and represses the pride and violence of conceited, though frail, men (cf. Ps. 9:16).

ADAM CLARKE

16. *The Lord is King for ever.* He has, and ever will have, the supreme power.

18. *That the man of the earth may no more oppress.* I believe the Hebrew will be better translated thus: "That he may not add any more to drive away the wretched man from the land." Destroy the influence of the tyrant, and let him not have it again in his power to add even one additional act of oppression to those which he has already committed.

MATTHEW HENRY

PSALM 11

To the chief musician. A psalm of David.

Verses 1–3

I. David's fixed resolution to make God his confidence: *In the Lord put I my trust, v.* 1. The psalmist before he gives an account of the temptation he was in to distrust God, records his resolution to trust in him, as that which he was resolved to live and die by.

II. His resentment of a temptation to the contrary: "*How say you to my soul, Flee as a bird to your mountain,* to be safe there out of the reach of the fowler?" This may be taken either,

1. As the serious advice of his timorous friends: some that were hearty wellwishers to David, when they saw how Saul maliciously sought his life, pressed him by all means to flee. (1) Because he could not be safe where he was, *v.* 2. "Observe," say they, "how *the wicked bend their bow;* Saul and his instruments aim at thy life, and the uprightness of thy heart will not be thy security." (2) Because he could be no longer useful where he was. "For," say they, "*if the foundations be destroyed*" (as they were by Saul's mal-administration), "if the civil state and government be unhinged and all out of course" (lxxv. 3; lxxxii. 5), "what canst thou do with thy righteousness to redress the grievances?"

2. It may be taken as a taunt wherewith his er[illegible] bantered him, upbraiding him with the prof[illegible]

JAMIESON, FAUSSET, BROWN

PSALM 11

Vss. 1-7. Alluding to some event in his history, as in I Samuel 23:13, the Psalmist avows his confidence in God, when admonished to flee from his raging persecutors, whose destruction of the usual foundations of safety rendered all his efforts useless. The grounds of his confidence are God's supreme dominion, His watchful care of His people, His hatred to the wicked and judgments on them, and His love for righteousness and the righteous.

1. my soul—me (Ps. 3:2). **Flee**—lit., "flee ye"; i.e., he and his companion. **as a bird to your mountain**—having as such no safety but in flight (cf. I Sam. 26:20; Lam. 3:52).

ADAM CLARKE

PSALM 11

The inscription is, "To the chief Musician, A Psalm of David." By the "chief musician" we may understand the master singer, the leader of the band, the person who directed the choir; but we know that the word has been translated, "To the Conqueror."

1. *In the Lord put I my trust: how say ye?* Some of David's friends seem to have given him this advice when they saw Saul bent on his destruction: *Flee as a bird to your mountain.*

MATTHEW HENRY

he used to make of confidence in God, and scornfully bidding him try what stead that would stand him in now. "You say, God is your mountain; flee to him now, and see what the better you will be." Taking it thus, the two following verses are David's answer to this sarcasm, in which, (1) He complains of the malice of those who did thus abuse him (*v.* 2): *They bend their bow and make ready their arrows;* and we are told (lxiv. 3) what their arrows are, even bitter words, by which they endeavour to discourage hope in God. (2) He resists the temptation with a gracious abhorrence, *v.* 3. The principles of religion are the foundations on which the faith and hope of the righteous are built.

Verses 4–7

The shaking of a tree (they say) makes it take the deeper and faster root. The attempt of David's enemies to discourage his confidence in God engages him to cleave so much the more closely to his first principles. That which was shocking to his faith, and has been so to the faith of many, was the prosperity of wicked people in their wicked ways, and the straits and distresses which the best men are sometimes reduced to: hence an evil thought was apt to arise, *Surely it is vain to serve God.* But, in order to stifle and shame all such thoughts, consider,

I. That there is a God in heaven: *The Lord is in his holy Temple* above, where, though he is out of our sight, we are not out of his. Or, He is in his holy temple, that is, in his church; he is a God in covenant and communion with his people.

II. That this God governs the world. The Lord has not only his residence, but his throne, in heaven, and he has *set the dominion thereof in the earth* (Job xxxviii. 33). Let us by faith see God on his throne, on his throne of glory—on his throne of government, giving law, giving motion, and giving aim, to all the creatures—on his throne of judgment—and on his throne of grace, to which his people may come boldly for mercy and grace; we shall then see no reason to be discouraged by the pride and power of oppressors, or any of the afflictions that attend the righteous.

III. That this God perfectly knows every man's true character: *His eyes behold, his eyelids try, the children of men;* he not only sees them, but he sees through them, not only knows all they say and do, but knows what they think, what they design, whatever they pretend.

IV. That, if he afflict good people, it is for their trial and therefore for their good, *v.* 5. The Lord tries all the children of men that he may *do them good in their latter end,* Deut. viii. 16.

V. That, however persecutors and oppressors may prosper and prevail awhile, they now lie under, and will for ever perish under, the wrath of God. *The wicked and him that loveth violence, his soul hateth.* Their prosperity is so far from being an evidence of God's love that their abuse of it does certainly make them the objects of his hatred. He that hates nothing that he has made, yet hates those who have thus ill-made themselves. *Upon the wicked he shall rain snares.* Here is a double metaphor, to denote the unavoidableness of the punishment of wicked men. It shall surprise them as a sudden shower sometimes surprises the traveller in a summer's day. It shall be as snares upon them, to hold them fast, and keep them prisoners, till the day of reckoning comes. It is *fire, and brimstone, and a horrible tempest,* which plainly alludes to the destruction of Sodom and Gomorrah.

VI. That, though honest good people may be run down, yet God does and will own them, and favour them, and that is the reason why God will severely reckon with persecutors and oppressors, because those whom they oppress and persecute are dear to him; so that *whosoever toucheth them toucheth the apple of his eye, v.* 7. He looks graciously upon them: *His countenance doth behold the upright.* He, like a tender father, looks upon them with pleasure, and they, like dutiful children, are pleased and abundantly satisfied with his smiles. They walk in the light of the Lord.

JAMIESON, FAUSSET, BROWN

2. privily—lit., "in darkness," treacherously. **3.** Lit., The foundations (i.e., of good order and law) will be destroyed, what has the righteous done (to sustain them)? All his efforts have failed.

4. temple . . . heaven—The connection seems to denote God's heavenly residence; the term used is taken from the place of His visible earthly abode (Ps. 2:6; 3:4; 5:7). Thence He inspects men with close scrutiny.

5. The trial of the righteous results in their approval, as it is contrasted with God's hatred to the wicked.

6. Their punishment is described by vivid figures denoting abundant, sudden, furious, and utter destruction (cf. Gen. 19: 24; Job 18:15; Ps. 7:15; 9:15). **cup**—is a frequent figure for God's favor or wrath (Ps. 16:5; 23:5; Matt. 20:22, 23).

7. his countenance—lit., "their faces"—a use of the plural applied to God, as in Genesis 1:26; 3:22; 11:7; Isaiah 6:8, etc., denoting the fulness of His perfections, or more probably originating in a reference to the trinity of persons. "Faces" is used as "eyes" (vs. 4), expressing here God's complacency towards the upright (cf. Ps. 34:15, 16).

ADAM CLARKE

3. *If the foundations be destroyed.* If Saul, who is the vicegerent of God, has cast aside his fear, and now regards neither truth nor justice, a righteous man has no security for his life. Kimchi supposes this refers to the priests who were murdered by Doeg, at the command of Saul.

4. *The Lord is in his holy temple.* He is still to be sought and found in the place where He has registered His name. Though the priests be destroyed, the God in whose worship they were employed still lives, and is to be found in His temple by His upright worshippers.

5. *The Lord trieth the righteous.* He does not abandon them; He tries them to show their faithfulness, and He afflicts them for their good. *His soul hateth.* The wicked man must ever be abhorred of the Lord; and the violent man—the destroyer and murderer—*his soul hateth.* An expression of uncommon strength and energy—all the perfections of the divine nature have such in abomination.

6. *Upon the wicked he shall rain.* This is a manifest allusion to the destruction of Sodom and Gomorrah. *An horrible tempest.* "The spirit of terrors."

PSALM 12

MATTHEW HENRY

To the chief musician upon Sheminith. A psalm of David.

Verses 1–8

This psalm furnishes us with good thoughts for bad times.

I. Let us see here what it is that makes the times bad, and when they may be said to be so. Scarcity of money, decay of trade, and the desolations of war, make the times bad. But the scripture lays the badness of the times upon causes of another nature. 2 Tim. iii. 1, *Perilous times shall come,* for iniquity

JAMIESON, FAUSSET, BROWN

Vss. 1-8.

The Psalmist laments the decrease of good men. The pride and deceit of the wicked provokes God's wrath, whose promise to avenge the cause of pious sufferers will be verified even amidst prevailing iniquity.

ADAM CLARKE

The inscription to this psalm is: "To the chief Musician upon Sheminith, A Psalm of David." See on the title of Psalm vi. Some think that this psalm was made when Doeg and the Ziphites betrayed David to Saul, see 1 Samuel xxii and xxiii; but it is most likely that was written during the Babylonish captivity.

MATTHEW HENRY

shall abound; and that is the thing David here complains of. The times are bad:—

1. When there is a general decay of piety and honesty among men the times are then truly bad (*v.* 1): *When the godly man ceases and the faithful fail.* Observe how these two characters are here put together, the godly and the faithful. As there is no true policy, so there is no true piety, without honesty. Godly men are faithful men, *fast* men, so they have sometimes been called; they make conscience of being true both to God and man. They are here said to cease and fail. Those that were godly and faithful were taken away, and those that were left had sadly degenerated and were not what they had been.

2. When men are so spiteful as to design against their neighbours the worst of mischiefs, and yet so base as to cover the design with plausible professions of friendship. Thus *they speak vanity* (that is, falsehood and a lie) *everyone to his neighbour, with flattering lips and a double heart.* They will kiss and kill. This is the devil's image complete, a complication of malice and falsehood. The times are bad indeed when there is no such thing as sincerity to be met with.

3. The times are very bad, when proud sinners have arrived at such a pitch of impiety as to say, "*With our tongue will we prevail* against the cause of virtue; *our lips are our own* and we may say what we will; *who is lord over us,* either to restrain us or to call us to an account?" *v.* 4. *Our lips are our own* (an unjust pretension, for who made man's mouth, in whose hand is his breath, and whose is the air he breathes in?) and as if he had no authority either to command them or to judge them: *Who is Lord over us?* Like Pharaoh, Exod. v. 2.

4. When the poor and needy are oppressed, and abused, and puffed at, then the times are very bad. This is implied (*v.* 5) where God himself takes notice of *the oppression of the poor* and *the sighing of the needy.*

5. When wickedness abounds, and goes barefaced under the protection and countenance of those in authority, then the times are very bad, *v.* 8. *When the vilest men are exalted* to places of trust and power then *the wicked walk on every side. When the wicked bear rule the people mourn.*

II. When times are thus bad it is comfortable to think,

1. That we have a God to go to, from whom we may ask and expect the redress of all our grievances. This he begins with (*v.* 1): "*Help, Lord, for the godly man ceaseth. It is time for thee, Lord, to work.*"

2. That God will certainly reckon with false and proud men, and will punish and restrain their insolence. Men cannot discover the falsehood of flatterers, nor humble the haughtiness of those that speak proud things; but the righteous God will *cut off all flattering lips* (*v.* 3). Some translate it as a prayer, "May God cut off those false and spiteful lips."

3. That God will, in due time, work deliverance for his oppressed people, and shelter them from the malicious designs of their persecutors (*v.* 5): *Now, will I arise, saith the Lord.* When the oppressors are in the height of their pride and insolence—when they say, *Who is lord over us?*—then is God's time to let them know, to their cost, that he is above them. When the oppressed are in the depth of their distress and despondency, then is God's time to appear for them, as for Israel when they were most dejected and Pharaoh was most elevated. *Now will I arise. I will set him in safety*, or in salvation, not only protect him, but restore him to his former prosperity, will *bring him out into a wealthy place* (lxvi. 12), so that, upon the whole, he shall lose nothing by his sufferings.

4. That, though men are false, God is faithful; *the words of the Lord are pure words* (*v.* 6), not only all true, but all pure, like silver tried in a furnace of earth or a crucible.

5. That God will secure his chosen remnant to himself, how bad soever the times are (*v.* 7): *Thou shalt preserve them from this generation for ever.* In times of general apostasy the Lord knows those those that are his, and they shall be enabled to keep their integrity.

JAMIESON, FAUSSET, BROWN

1. the faithful—or lit., "faithfulness" (Ps. 31:23).

2. The want of it is illustrated by the prevalence of deceit and instability.

3, 4. Boasting (Dan. 7:25) is, like flattery, a species of lying. **lips and . . . tongue**—for persons.

8. The wicked roam undisturbed doing evil, when vileness and vile men are exalted.

5. The writer intimates his confidence by depicting God's actions (cf. Ps. 9:19; 10:12) as coming to save the poor at whom the wicked sneer (Ps. 10:5).

6. The words—lit., "saying of" (vs. 5). **seven times**—thoroughly (Dan. 3:19). **7. them**—(*Margin.*)

ADAM CLARKE

2. *They speak vanity every one with his neighbour.* They are false and hollow; they say one thing while they mean another; there is no trusting to what they say. *With flattering lips and with a double heart do they speak.* "With a heart and a heart." They seem to have two hearts: one to speak fair words, and the other to invent mischief.

3. *Proud things. Gedoloth,* "Great things."

8. *The wicked walk on every side.* The land is full of them. *When the vilest men are exalted;* rather, "As villainy gains ground among the sons of Adam."

5. *For the oppression of the poor.* This seems to refer best to the tribulations which the poor Israelites suffered while captives in Babylon. The Lord represents himself as looking on and seeing their affliction; and, hearing their cry, He determines to come forward to their help.

MATTHEW HENRY

PSALM 13

To the chief musician. A psalm of David.

Verses 1-6

David, in affliction, is here pouring out his soul before God.

I. It is some ease to a troubled spirit to give vent to its griefs, especially to give vent to them at the throne of grace, where we are sure to find one who is afflicted in the afflictions of his people. Thither

JAMIESON, FAUSSET, BROWN

PSALM 13

Vss. 1-6. The Psalmist, mourning God's absence and the triumph of his enemies, prays for relief before he is totally destroyed, and is encouraged to hope his trust will not be in vain.

ADAM CLARKE

PSALM 13

There is nothing particular in the inscription. The psalm is supposed to have been written during the Captivity, and to contain the prayers and supplications of the distressed Israelites, worn out with their long and oppressive bondage.

MATTHEW HENRY

we have boldness of access by faith, and there we have παῤῥησία—*freedom of speech.* David thought God had forgotten him. Not that any good man can doubt the omniscience, goodness, and faithfulness of God; but it is a peevish expression of prevailing fear, which yet, when it arises from a high esteem and earnest desire of God's favour, though it be indecent and culpable, shall be passed by and pardoned, for the second thought will retract it and repent of it. He was racked with care, which filled his head: *I take counsel in my soul;* "I am at a loss, and am *without a friend* that I can put any confidence in. *I have sorrow in my heart daily.*" The bread of sorrow is sometimes the saint's daily bread. Our Master himself was a man of sorrows. His enemies' insolence added to his grief. He expostulates with God "*How long* shall it be thus?" And, "Shall it be thus *for ever*?" It is a common temptation, when trouble lasts long, to think it will last always; despondency then turns into despair, and those that have long been without joy begin, at last, to be without hope.

II. His complaints stir up his prayers, *v.* 3, 4. We should never allow ourselves to make any complaints but what are fit to be offered up to God and what drive us to our knees. "*Consider* my case, *hear* my complaints and *enlighten my eyes.* Strengthen my faith"; for faith is the eye of the soul, with which it sees above, and sees through, the things of sense. "Lord, enable me to look beyond my present troubles and to foresee a happy issue of them." If his eyes were not enlightened quickly he must perish: "I shall *sleep the sleep of death*; I cannot live under the weight of all this care and grief." It would gratify the pride of his enemy: He will say, "*I have prevailed,* I have gotten the day, and been too hard for him and his God."

III. His prayers are soon turned into praises (*v.* 5, 6): But *my heart shall rejoice and I will sing to the Lord.* What a surprising change is here in a few lines! In the beginning of the psalm we have him drooping, trembling, and ready to sink into melancholy and despair; but, in the close of it, rejoicing in God, and elevated and enlarged in his praises. See the power of faith, the power of prayer, and how good it is to draw near to God. "In former distresses *I have trusted in the mercy of God,* and I never found that it failed me. Even in the depth of this distress, when God hid his face from me, when without were fightings and within were fears, yet *I trusted in the mercy of God* and that was as an anchor in a storm, by the help of which, though I was tossed, I was not overset." And still *I do trust in thy mercy*; so some read it. His faith in God's mercy filled his heart with *joy in his salvation*; for joy and peace come *by believing*, Rom. xv. 13. *Believing, you rejoice*, 1 Pet. i. 8. "*I will sing unto the Lord,* sing in remembrance of what he has done formerly; though I should never recover the peace I have had, I will die blessing God that ever I had it. He has dealt bountifully with me formerly, and he shall have the glory of that, however he is pleased to deal with me now. I will sing in hope of what he will do for me at last, being confident that all will end well, will end everlastingly well."

JAMIESON, FAUSSET, BROWN

1. The forms of expression and figure here used are frequent (cf. Ps. 9:12, 18; 10:11, 12). **How long . . . for ever**—Shall it be for ever?

2. The counsels or devices of his heart afford no relief.

3. lighten mine eyes—dim with weakness, denoting approaching death (cf. I Sam. 14:27-29; Ps. 6:7; 38:10). **4. rejoice**—lit., "shout as in triumph." **I am moved**—cast down from a firm position (Ps. 10:6).

5, 6. Trust is followed by rejoicing in the deliverance which God effects, and, instead of his enemy, he can lift the song of triumph.

ADAM CLARKE

1. *How long wilt thou forget me?* The words *ad anah,* "to what length, to what time," translated here *how long?* are four times repeated in the two first verses, and point out at once great dejection and extreme earnestness of soul. *Hide thy face from me?* How long shall I be destitute of a clear sense of Thy approbation?

3. *Consider and hear me.* Rather, "Answer me."

4. *Lest mine enemy say.* Satan's ordinary method in temptation is to excite strongly to sin, to blind the understanding, inflame the passions; and when he succeeds, he triumphs by insults and reproaches.

6. *I will sing unto the Lord.* That heart is turned to God's praise which has a clear sense of God's favor. *Because he hath dealt bountifully with me.* "Because he hath recompensed me."

MATTHEW HENRY

PSALM 14

To the chief musician. A psalm of David.

Verses 1–3

Sin is the disease of mankind, and it appears here to be malignant and epidemic.

1. See how malignant it is (*v.* 1) in two things:—

(1) The contempt it puts upon the honour of God: for there is something of practical atheism at the bottom of all sin. *The fool hath said in his heart, There is no God.* We are sometimes tempted to think, "Surely there never was so much atheism and profaneness as there is in our days"; but we see the former days were no better. The sinner is one that *saith in his heart, There is no God*; he is an atheist. He cannot be sure there is one, and therefore he is willing to think there is none. He is a fool; he is simple and unwise, and this is an evidence of it; he is wicked and profane, and this is the cause of it.

(2) The disgrace and debasement it puts upon the nature of man. Sinners are corrupt, quite degenerated from what man was in his innocent estate: *They have become filthy* (*v.* 3), putrid. *They are corrupt* indeed; for they do God no service, bring him no honour, nor do themselves any real kindness. They do a great deal of hurt. *They have done abominable works*, for such all sinful works are. This follows upon their saying, *There is no God;* for those that *profess they know God, but in works deny him, are abominable, and to every good work reprobate,*

JAMIESON, FAUSSET, BROWN

PSALM 14

Vss. 1-7. The practical atheism and total and universal depravity of the wicked, with their hatred to the good, are set forth. Yet, as they dread God's judgments when He vindicates His people, the Psalmist prays for His delivering power.

1. Sinners are termed "fools," because they think and act contrary to right reason (Gen. 34:7; Josh. 7:15; Ps. 39:8; 74:18, 22). **in his heart**—to himself (Gen. 6:12).

3. filthy—lit., "spoiled," or, "soured," "corrupted" (Job. 15:16; Rom. 3:12).

ADAM CLARKE

PSALM 14

There is nothing particular in the title; only it is probable that the word *ledavid,* "of David," is improperly prefixed, as it is sufficiently evident, from the construction of the psalm, that it speaks of the Babylonish captivity.

1. *The fool hath said in his heart, There is no God. Nabal,* which we render *fool,* signifies "an empty fellow, a contemptible person, a villain." One who has a muddy head and an unclean heart; and, in his darkness and folly, says in his heart, "There is no God." "And none," says one, "but a *fool* would say so." The word is not to be taken in the strict sense in which we use the term "atheist," that is, one who denies the being of a God, or confounds Him with matter. (1) There have been some, not many, who have denied the existence of God. (2) There are others who, without absolutely denying the divine existence, deny His providence. (3) There are others, and they are very numerous, who, while they profess to acknowledge both, deny them in their heart, and live as if they were persuaded there was no God to either punish or reward.

3. *They are all gone aside.* They will not

MATTHEW HENRY

Titus. i. 16.

2. See how epidemic this disease is; it has infected the whole race of mankind. God himself is here brought in for a witness, *v.* 2, 3. *The Lord looked down from heaven*, he took a view of all *the children of men*, and the question was, *Whether there were any* among them *that did understand* themselves aright, their duty and interests, and did seek God and set him before them. The result of this enquiry, *v.* 3. Upon his search, it appeared, *They have all gone aside*, the apostasy is universal, *there is none that doeth good, no, not one*, till the free and mighty grace of God has wrought a change. When God had made the world he looked upon his own work, and *all was very good* (Gen. i. 31); but, some time after, he looked upon man's work, and, behold, all was very bad (Gen. vi. 5).

Verses 4–7

In these verses the psalmist endeavours,

I. To convince sinners of the evil and danger of the way they are in, how secure soever they are in that way. Three things he shows them, which, it may be, they are not very willing to see—their wickedness, their folly, and their danger.

1. Their wickedness. This is described in four instances:—(1) They are themselves *workers of iniquity*; and take as much pleasure in it as ever any man did in his business. (2) They *eat up God's people* with as much greediness *as they eat bread* because they really hate God, whose people they are. It is meat and drink to persecutors to be doing mischief. (3) They *call not upon the Lord*. What good can be expected from those that live without prayer? (4) They *shame the counsel of the poor*, and upbraid them with making God their refuge, as David's enemies upbraided him, *xi.* 1.

2. Their folly: *They have no knowledge*.

3. Their danger (*v.* 5): *There were they in great fear*. Many instances there have been of proud and cruel persecutors who have been made *terrors to themselves* and all about them.

II. He endeavours to comfort the people of God. They have God's presence (*v.* 5): He *is in the generation of the righteous*. They have his protection (*v.* 6): *The Lord is their refuge*. When David was driven out by Absalom and his rebellious accomplices, he comforted himself with an assurance that God would in due time *turn again his captivity*. But surely this pleasing prospect looks further. He had, in the beginning of the psalm, lamented the general corruption of mankind; and, in the melancholy view of that, wishes for the salvation which in the fulness of time was to come out of Zion—salvation from sin, that great salvation which should be wrought out by the Redeemer, who was expected *to come to Zion*, to *turn away ungodliness from Jacob*, Rom. xi. 26.

PSALM 15

A psalm of David.

Verses 1–5

I. A very serious and weighty question concerning the character of a citizen of Zion (*v.* 1): "*Lord, who shall abide in thy tabernacle?* Let me know who shall go to heaven." Not, who by name (in this way the *Lord* only knows those that are his), but who by description: "What kind of people are those whom thou wilt own and crown with distinguishing and everlasting favours?" It concerns us all to put this question to ourselves, *Lord, what shall I be, and do, that I may abide in thy tabernacle?* Luke xviii. 18; Acts xvi. 30. 1. Observe to whom this enquiry is addressed—to God himself. 2. How it is expressed in Old Testament language. (1) By the *tabernacle* we may understand the church militant, typified by Moses's tabernacle, fitted to a wilderness-state, mean and movable. There God manifests himself, and there he meets his people, as of old in the tabernacle of the testimony, the tabernacle of meeting. (2) By the *holy hill* we may understand the church triumphant, alluding to Mount Zion, on which the temple was to be built by Solomon. It concerns us to know who shall dwell there, that we may make it sure to ourselves that we shall have a place among them.

II. A very plain and particular answer to this question of the particular character of a citizen of Zion.

1. He is one that is sincere and entire in his religion: He *walketh uprightly*, according to the condition of the covenant (Gen. xvii. 1), "*Walk before me, and be thou perfect*" (it is the same word that is here used) "and then thou shalt find me a God all-sufficient." He is really what he professes to be, is sound at heart, and can approve himself to God, in his integrity, in all he does. His eye perhaps is weak, but it is single; he has his spots indeed, but he does

JAMIESON, FAUSSET, BROWN

2. looked—in earnest inquiry. **understand**—as opposed to fool.

4-6. Their conduct evinces indifference rather than ignorance of God; for when He appears in judgment, they are stricken with great fear. **who eat up my people**—to express their beastly fury—(Prov. 30:14; Hab. 3:14). To "call on the Lord" is to worship Him.

7. captivity—denotes any great evil. **Zion**—God's abode, from which He revealed His purposes of mercy, as He now does by the Church (cf. 3:4; 20:2), and which He rules and in which He does all other things for the good of His people (Eph. 1:22).

PSALM 15

Vss. 1-5. Those who are fit for communion with God may be known by a conformity to His law, which is illustrated in various important particulars.

1. abide—or, sojourn (cf. Ps. 5:4), where it means under God's protection here, as (Ps. 23:6, 27:4, 6) communion.

tabernacle—seat of the ark (II Samuel 6:17), the symbol of God's presence.

holy hill—(Cf. Ps. 2:6).

2. walketh—(Cf. Ps. 1:1). **uprightly**—in a complete manner, as to all parts of conduct (Gen. 17:1), not as to degree.

ADAM CLARKE

walk in the straight path. *They are all together become filthy.* They are become "sour" and "rancid"; a metaphor taken from milk that has fermented, and turned sour, rancid, and worthless. *There is none that doeth good, no, not one.* This is not only the state of heathen Babylon, but the state of the whole inhabitants of the earth, till the grace of God changes their heart. By nature, and from nature, by practice, every man is sinful and corrupt.

5. *There were they in great fear.* This is a manifest allusion to the history of the Canaanitish nations; they were struck with terror at the sight of the Israelites, and by this allusion the Psalmist shows that a destruction similar to that which fell upon them should fall on the Babylonians.

7. *Oh that the salvation!* Or, more literally, "Who will give from Zion salvation to Israel?" From Zion the deliverance must come, for God alone can deliver them; but whom will He make His instruments?

PSALM 15

1. *Lord, who shall abide in thy tabernacle?* The literal translation of this verse is, "Lord, who shall sojourn in Thy tabernacle? who shall dwell in the mountain of Thy holiness?"

2. *He that walketh uprightly.* (1) He walks perfectly. *And worketh righteousness.* (2) He is not satisfied with a contemplative life; he has duties to perform. *And speaketh the truth in his heart.* (3) He is a true man; in him there is no false way.

MATTHEW HENRY

not paint; he is an *Israelite indeed in whom is no guile*, John i. 47; 2 Cor. i. 12. I know no religion but sincerity.

2. He is one that is conscientiously honest and just in all his dealings, faithful and fair to all with whom he has to do: He *worketh righteousness*. He reckons that that cannot be a good bargain, nor a saving one, which is made with a lie, and that he who wrongs his neighbour, though ever so plausibly, will prove, in the end, to have done the greatest injury to himself.

3. He is one that contrives to do all the good he can to his neighbours, but is very careful to do hurt to no man, and is, in a particular manner, tender of his neighbour's reputation, *v.* 3. He makes the best of everybody, and the worst of nobody. If an ill-natured character of his neighbour be given him, or an ill-natured story be told him, he will disprove it if he can; if not, it shall die with him and go no further. His *charity will cover a multitude of sins*.

4. He is one that values men by their virtue and piety, and not by the figure they make in the world, *v.* 5. He thinks the worse of no man's piety for his poverty and meanness, *but he knows those that fear the Lord*. He reckons that serious piety, wherever it is found, puts an honour upon a man, and makes his face to shine, more than wealth, or wit, or a great name among men, does or can. He honours such.

5. He is one that always prefers a good conscience before any secular interest or advantage whatsoever; for, if he has promised upon oath to do anything, though afterwards it appear much to his damage and prejudice in his worldly estate, yet he adheres to it and *changes not*, *v.* 4.

6. He is one that will not increase his estate by any unjust practices, *v.* 5. *He putteth not out his money to usury*, that he may live at ease upon the labours of others. Not that it is any breach of the law of justice or charity for the lender to share in the profit which the borrower makes of his money, any more than for the owner of the land to demand rent from the occupant, money being, by art and labour, as improvable as land. But a citizen of Zion will freely lend to the poor, according to his ability, and not be rigorous and severe in recovering his right from those that are reduced by Providence. He will not *take a reward against the innocent*; if he be any way employed in the administration of public justice, he will not, for any gain, or hope of it, to himself, do anything to the prejudice of a righteous cause.

III. The psalm concludes with a ratification of this character of the citizen of Zion. He is like Zion-hill itself, which cannot be moved. Every true living member of the church, like the church itself, is built upon a rock, which the gates of hell cannot prevail against: *He that doeth these things shall never be moved*.

JAMIESON, FAUSSET, BROWN

worketh—or, does. **righteousness**—what is right. **in his heart**—sincerely (Prov. 23:7).

3. He neither slanders nor spreads slander.

4. Love and hate are regulated by a regard to God. **sweareth . . . hurt**—or what so results (cf. Lev. 5:4). **5.** (Cf. Lev. 25:37; Deut. 23:19, 20.) **usury**—is derived from a verb meaning "to bite." All gains made by the wrongful loss of others are forbidden.

taketh reward . . .—The innocent would not otherwise be condemned (cf. Exod. 23:8; Deut. 16:19). Bribery of all sorts is denounced.

doeth these . . .—Such persons admitted to God's presence and favor shall never be moved (Ps. 10:6; 13:5).

ADAM CLARKE

3. *He that backbiteth not with his tongue.* "He foots not upon his tongue." (4) He is one who treats his neighbor with respect. He says nothing that might injure him in his character, person, or property. *Nor doeth evil to his neighbour.* (5) He not only avoids evil speaking, but he avoids also evil acting towards his neighbor. *Nor taketh up a reproach against his neighbour.* (6) The word *cherpah,* which we here translate *a reproach,* comes from *charaph,* "to strip, or make bare, to deprive one of his garments." The application is easy: A man, for instance, of a good character is reported to have done something wrong; the tale is spread, and the slanderers and backbiters carry it about; and thus the man is stripped of his fair character, of his clothing of righteousness, truth, and honesty. The good man *taketh* it not *up.* He cannot prevent the detractor from laying it down; but it is in his power not to take it up, and thus the progress of the slander may be arrested.

4. *In whose eyes a vile person is contemned.* (7) This man judges of others by their conduct; he tries no man's heart. *A vile person,* the "reprobate," one abandoned to sin; is despised, is "loathsome," as if he were covered with leprosy, for so the word implies. *He honoureth them that fear the Lord.* (8) The truly pious man, while he has in contempt the "honourable" profligate, yet *honoureth them that fear the Lord,* though found in the most abject poverty. *Sweareth to his own hurt, and changeth not.* (9) If at any time he have bound himself by a solemn engagement to do so and so, and he finds afterwards that to keep his oath will be greatly to his damage, yet such reverence has he for God and for truth that he will not change, be the consequences what they may. The Hebrew might be thus translated: "He sweareth to afflict himself, and does not change"; and thus the Chaldee has rendered this clause. He has promised to the Lord to keep his body under, and bring it into subjection; to deny himself that he may not pamper the flesh, and have the more to give to the poor.

5. *Putteth not out his money to usury.* (10) As *usury* signifies unlawful interest, or that which is got by taking advantage of the necessity of a distressed neighbor, no man that fears God can be guilty of it. The word *neshech,* which we translate *usury,* comes from *nashach,* "to bite as a serpent"; and here must signify that biting or devouring usury which ruins the man who has it to pay. *Nor taketh reward against the innocent.* (11) He neither gives nor receives a bribe in order to pervert justice or injure an innocent man in his cause.

MATTHEW HENRY — PSALM 16

Michtam of David.

Verses 1–7

This psalm is entitled *Michtam,* which some translate *a golden* psalm, more to be valued than much fine gold, because it speaks so plainly of Christ and his resurrection, who is the true treasure hidden in the field of the Old Testament.

JAMIESON, FAUSSET, BROWN — PSALM 16

Vss. 1-11. *Michtam,* or, by the change of one letter, *Michtab*—a "writing," such as a poem or song (cf. Isa. 38:9). Such a change of the letter *m* for *b* was not unusual. The position of this word in connection with the author's name, being that usually occupied by some term, such as Psalm or song, denoting the style or matter of the composition, favors this view of its meaning, though we know not why this and Psalms 56-60 should be specially called "a writing." "A golden" (Psalm), or a "memorial" are explanations proposed by some—neither of which, however applicable here, appears adapted to the other Psalms where the term occurs. According to Peter (Acts 2:25) and Paul (Acts 13:35), this Psalm relates to Christ and expresses the feelings of His human nature, in view of His sufferings and victory over death and the grave, including His subsequent exaltation at the right hand of God. Such was the exposition of the best earlier Christian interpreters. Some moderns have held that the Psalm relates exclusively to David; but this view is expressly contradicted by the apostles; others hold that the language of the Psalm is applicable to David as a type of Christ, capable of the higher sense assigned it in the New Testament. But then the language of vs. 10 cannot be used of David in any sense, for "he saw corruption." Others again propose to refer the first part to David, and the last to Christ; but it is evident that no change in the subject of the Psalm is indicated. Indeed, the person who appeals to God for help is evidently the same who rejoices in having found it. In referring the whole Psalm to Christ, it is, however, by no means denied that much of its language is expressive of the

ADAM CLARKE — PSALM 16

The title of this psalm in the Hebrew is *michtam ledavid,* which the Chaldee translates, "A straight sculpture of David." That David was the author there can be no doubt. It is most pointedly attributed to him by St. Peter, Acts ii. 25-31. That its principal parts might have some relation to his circumstances is also probable; but that Jesus Christ is its main scope not only appears from quotations made by the apostle as above, but from the circumstance that some parts of it never did and never could apply to David. From the most serious and attentive consideration of the whole psalm, I am convinced that every verse of it belongs to Jesus Christ, and none other.

MATTHEW HENRY

I. David here flies to God's protection: "*Preserve me, O God!* from the deaths, and especially from the sins, to which I am continually exposed: *for in thee*, and in thee only, *do I put my trust*." This is applicable to Christ, who prayed, *Father, save me from this hour*, and trusted in God that he would deliver him.

II. He recognises his solemn dedication of himself to God as his God (*v.* 2): "*O my soul! thou hast said unto the Lord, Thou art my Lord*, and therefore thou mayest venture to trust him." *Adonai* signifies *My stayer*, the strength of my heart.

III. He devotes himself to the honour of God in the service of the saints (*v.* 2, 3): *My goodness extends not to thee, but to the saints*. If God be ours, we must, for his sake, extend our goodness to those that are his, to the saints in the earth; for what is done to them he is pleased to take as done to himself, having constituted them his receivers. Those that are renewed by the grace of God, and devoted to the glory of God, are saints on earth. Christ delights even in the saints on earth, notwithstanding their weaknesses and manifold infirmities, which is a good reason why we should (John xvii. 19).

IV. He disclaims the worship of all false gods and all communion with their worshippers, *v.* 4. He reads the doom of idolaters. *Their sorrows shall be multiplied*, both by the judgments they bring upon themselves from the true God whom they forsake and by the disappointment they will meet with in the false gods they embrace. "*Their drink-offerings of blood will I not offer*, not only because the gods they are offered to are a lie, but because the offerings themselves are barbarous." At God's altar, because the blood made atonement, the drinking of it was most strictly prohibited, and the drink-offerings were of wine; but the devil prescribed to his worshippers to drink of the blood of the sacrifices, to teach them cruelty. Some make this also applicable to Christ and his undertaking, showing the nature of the sacrifice he offered (it was not the blood of bulls and goats, which was offered according to the law; that was never named, nor did he ever make any mention of it, but his own blood).

V. He repeats the solemn choice he had made of God for his portion and happiness (*v.* 5), takes to himself the comfort of the choice (*v.* 6), and gives God the glory of it, *v.* 7. Heaven is an inheritance. We must take that for our home, our rest, our everlasting good, and look upon this world to be no more ours than the country through which our road lies when we are on a journey. Confiding in him for the securing of this portion: "*Thou maintainest my lot*. Thou that hast by promise made over thyself to me, wilt graciously make good what thou hast promised. *The lines have fallen to me in pleasant places*. Those have reason to say so that have God for their portion. What can they desire more? *Return unto thy rest, O my soul!* and look no further. Those whose lot is cast, as David's was, in a land of light, in a valley of vision, where God is known and worshipped, have, upon that account, reason to say, *The lines have fallen to me in pleasant places;* much more those who have not only Immanuel's land, but Immanuel's love.

"*I will bless the Lord who has given me counsel*, this counsel, to take him for my portion and happiness." If we have the pleasure of it, let God have the praise of it. God having given him counsel by his word and Spirit, his own *reins* also (his own thoughts) instructed him in the night-season; when he was silent and solitary, and retired from the world, then his own conscience (which is called the reins, Jer. xvii. 10) not only reflected with comfort upon the choice he had made, but instructed or admonished him concerning the duties arising out of this choice.

All this may be applied to Christ, who made the Lord his portion and was pleased with that portion, made his Father's glory his highest end. We may also apply it to ourselves, in singing it, renewing our choice of God as ours, with a holy complacency and satisfaction.

Verses 8–11

All these verses are quoted by St. Peter in his first sermon, after the pouring out of the Spirit on the day of Pentecost (Acts ii. 25–28); and he tells us expressly that David in them speaks concerning Christ and particularly of his resurrection. Something we may allow here of the workings of David's own pious and devout affections towards God, but in these holy elevations towards God and heaven he was carried by the spirit of prophecy quite beyond the consideration of himself and his own case, to foretell the glory of the Messiah. The New Testament furnishes us with a key to let us into the mystery of these lines.

I. These verses must certainly be applied to Christ; of him speaks the prophet this, as did many of the

JAMIESON, FAUSSET, BROWN

feelings of His people, so far as in their humble measure they have the feelings of trust in God expressed by Him, their head and representative. Such use of His language, as recorded in His last prayer (John 17), and even that which He used in Gethsemane, under similar modifications, is equally proper. The propriety of this reference of the Psalm to Christ will appear in the scope and interpretation. In view of the sufferings before Him, the Saviour, with that instinctive dread of death manifested in Gethsemane, calls on God to "preserve" Him; He avows His delight in holiness and abhorrence of the wicked and their wickedness; and for "the joy that was set before Him, despising the shame," encourages Himself; contemplating the glories of the heritage appointed Him. Thus even death and the grave lose their terrors in the assurance of the victory to be attained and "the glory that should follow."

1. Preserve me—keep or watch over my interests. **in thee . . . I . . . trust**—as one seeking shelter from pressing danger. **2. my soul**—must be supplied; expressed in similar cases (Ps. 42:5, 11). **my goodness . . . thee**—This obscure passage is variously expounded. Either one of two expositions falls in with the context. "My goodness" or merit is not on account of Thee—i.e., is not for Thy benefit. Then follows the contrast of vs. 3 (but is), in respect, or for the saints, etc.—i.e., it enures to them. Or, *my goodness*—or happiness is not *besides Thee*—i.e., without Thee I have no other source of happiness. Then, "*to the saints*," etc., means that the same privilege of deriving happiness from God only is theirs. The first is the most consonant with the Messianic character of the Psalm, though the latter is not inconsistent with it. **3. saints**—or, persons consecrated to God, set apart from others to His service. **in the earth**—i.e., land of Palestine—the residence of God's chosen people—figuratively for the Church. **excellent**—or, nobles, distinguished for moral excellence. **4.** He expresses his abhorrence of those who seek other sources of happiness or objects of worship, and, by characterizing their rites by drink offerings of blood, clearly denotes idolaters. The word for "sorrows" is by some rendered idols; but, though a similar word to that for idols, it is not the same. In selecting such a term, there may be an allusion, by the author, to the sorrows produced by idolatrous practices. **5-7.** God is the chief good, and supplies all need (Deut. 10:9). **portion of mine inheritance and of my cup**—may contain an allusion to the daily supply of food, and also to the inheritance of Levi (Deut. 18:1, 2). **maintainest**—or, *drawest out* my lot—enlargest it. The next verse carries out this idea more fully.

7. given me counsel—cared for me. **my reins**—the supposed seat of emotion and thought (Ps. 7:9, 26:2). **instruct me**—or, excite to acts of praise (Isa. 53:11, 12; Heb. 12:2).

8. With God's presence and aid he is sure of safety (Ps. 10:6; 15:5; John 12:27, 28; Heb. 5:7, 8). **9. glory**—as heart (Ps. 7:5), for self. In Acts 2:26, after the Septuagint, *my tongue* as "the glory of the frame"—the instrument for praising God. **flesh**—If taken as opposed to soul (vs. 10), it may mean the body; otherwise, the whole person (cf. Ps. 63:1; 84:2). **rest in hope**—(cf. *Margin*). **10. soul**—or, self. This use of soul for the person is frequent (Gen. 12:5; 46:26; Ps. 3:2; 7:2; 11:1), even when the body may be the part chiefly affected, as in Psalm 35:13; 105:18. Some cases are cited, as Leviticus 22:4; Numbers 6:6; 9:6, 10; 19:13; Haggai 2:13, etc., which seem to justify assigning the meaning of *body*,

ADAM CLARKE

1. *Preserve me, O God: for in thee do I put my trust.* I consider this a prayer of the *man* Christ Jesus on His entering on His great atoning work, particularly His passion in the Garden of Gethsemane. In that passion, Jesus Christ most evidently speaks as man; and with the strictest propriety, as it was the manhood, not the Godhead, that was engaged in the suffering. *Shomreni,* "keep me"—preserve, sustain this feeble humanity, now about to bear the load of that punishment due to the whole of the human race. "For in thee have I hoped." No human fortitude, or animal courage, can avail in My circumstances. It is worthy of remark that our Lord here uses the term, *El,* which signifies the "strong God," an expression remarkably suited to the frailty of that human nature which was now entering upon its vicarious sufferings. It will be seen with what admirable propriety the Messiah varies the appellations of the Divine Being in this address, a circumstance which no translation without paraphrase can express.

2-3. *Thou hast said unto the Lord, Thou art my Lord.* Thou hast said to Jehovah, the supreme, self-existing, and eternal Being; *Thou art my Lord, adonai attah,* "Thou art my *Prop, Stay,* or *Support.*" As the Messiah, or Son of God, Jesus derived His being and support from Jehovah; and the man Christ was supported by the eternal divinity that dwelt within Him, without which He could not have sustained the sufferings which He passed through, nor have made an atonement for the sin of the world. It is the suffering Messiah, or the Messiah in prospect of His sufferings, who here speaks. *My goodness extendeth not to thee.* There are almost endless explanations of this clause. I think the words should be understood of what the Messiah was doing for men. My goodness, "my bounty," is not to Thee. What I am doing can add nothing to Thy divinity. Thou art not providing this astonishing sacrifice because Thou canst derive any excellence from it; but this bounty extends *to the saints*—to all the spirits of just men made perfect, whose bodies are still in the earth; *and to the excellent,* "the noble or supereminent ones," those who through faith and patience inherit the promises.

4. *Their sorrows shall be multiplied that hasten after another god.* In the Hebrew text there is no word for *God,* and therefore *Messiah* or *Saviour* might be as well substituted, and then the whole will refer to the unbelieving Jews. They would not have the true Christ; they have sought, and are seeking, another Messiah; and how amply fulfilled has the prophetic declaration been in them! *Their drink offerings of blood will I not offer. Nesech* is a "libation," whether of wine or of water, poured out on the sacrifice. A drink offering of blood is not a correct form of expression; it is rather the libation on the blood of the sacrifice already made.

5. *The Lord is the portion of mine inheritance.* The Messiah speaks. Jehovah is the Portion of mine inheritance. I seek no earthly good; I desire to do the will of God, and that only.

6. *The lines are fallen unto me in pleasant places.* Here is an allusion to the ancient division of the land by lot among the Israelites, the breadth and length being ascertained by lines which were used in measuring. I have got a rich inheritance of immortal spirits. *I have a goodly heritage.* A Church, an innumerable multitude of saints, partakers of the divine nature, and filled with all the fullness of God.

7. *Who hath given me counsel.* Jesus, as man, received all His knowledge and wisdom from God, Luke ii. 40-52. And in Him were hidden all the treasures of wisdom and knowledge. *My reins also instruct me. Reins* or "kidneys," which from their retired situation in the body, says Parkhurst, and being hidden in fat, are often used in Scripture for the most secret workings and affections of the heart. The kidneys and their fat were always to be burnt in sacrifice, to indicate that the most secret purposes and affections of the soul are to be devoted to God. *In the night seasons.* That is, in the time of My passion, My secret purposes and determinations concerning the redemption of man support Me. "For the joy that was set before him [he] endured the cross, despising the shame," Heb. xii. 2.

MATTHEW HENRY

Old Testament prophets, who *testified beforehand the sufferings of Christ and the glory that should follow* (1 Pet. i. 11), and that is the subject of this prophecy here.

1. That he should suffer and die. When he says, "*My flesh shall rest*," it is implied that he must put off the body, that he should not only die, but be buried, and abide for some time under the power of death.

2. That he should be wonderfully borne up by the divine power in suffering and dying. That he should not be moved till he could say, *It is finished*. That his heart should rejoice and his glory be glad, that he should go on with his undertaking, not only resolutely, but cheerfully. By his glory is meant his *tongue*, as appears, Acts ii. 26. Now there were three things which carried him on thus cheerfully:—(1) The respect he had to his Father's will and glory in what he did: *I have set the Lord always before me*. (2) The assurance he had of his Father's presence with him in his sufferings: *He is at my right hand*, a present help to me, nigh at hand in the time of need. (3) The prospect he had of a glorious issue of his sufferings. It was *for the joy set before him* that *he endured the cross*, Heb. xii. 2. He rested in hope, and that made his rest glorious, Isa. xi. 10. See John xiii. 31, 32.

3. That he should be brought through his sufferings, and brought from under the power of death by a glorious resurrection.

4. That he should be abundantly recompensed for his sufferings, with the joy set before him, *v.* 11. "*Thou wilt show me the path of life*, and lead me to that life through this darksome valley." In confidence of this, when he gave up the ghost, he said, *Father, into thy hands I commit my spirit;* and, a little before, *Father, glorify me with thy own self*.

II. Christ being the Head of the body, the church, these verses may, for the most part, be applied to all good Christians, who are guided and animated by the Spirit of Christ; and, in singing them, when we have first given glory to Christ, we may then encourage and edify ourselves and one another with them. Dying Christians, as well as a dying Christ, may cheerfully put off the body, in a believing expectation of a joyful resurrection: *My flesh also shall rest in hope*.

JAMIESON, FAUSSET, BROWN

or dead body; but it will be found that the latter sense is given by some adjunct expressed or implied. In those cases *person* is the proper sense. **wilt not leave . . . hell**—abandon to the power of (Job 39:14; Ps. 49:10). Hell as (Gen. 42:38; Ps. 6:5; Jonah 2:2) the state or region of death, and so frequently —or the *grave itself* (Job 14:13, 17:13; Eccles. 9:10, etc.). So the *Greek Hades* (cf. Acts 2:27, 31). The context alone can settle whether the state mentioned is one of suffering and place of the damned (cf. Ps. 9:17; Prov. 5:5; 7:27). **wilt . . . suffer**—lit., "give" or "appoint." **Holy One**—(Ps. 4:3), one who is the object of God's favor, and so a recipient of divine grace which he exhibits—*pious.* **to see**—or, experience—undergo (Luke 2:26). **corruption**—Some render the word, *the pit*, which is possible, but for the obvious sense which the apostle's exposition (Acts 2:27; 13:36, 37) gives. The sense of the whole passage is clearly this: by the use of *flesh* and *soul*, the disembodied state produced by death is indicated; but, on the other hand, no more than the *state of death* is intended; for the last clause of vs. 10 is strictly parallel with the first, and *Holy One* corresponds to *soul*, and *corruption* to *hell*. As *Holy One*, or David (Acts 13:36, 37), which denotes the *person*, including soul and body, is used for *body*, of which only corruption can be predicated (cf. Acts 2:31); so, on the contrary, *soul*, which literally means the immaterial part, is used for the person. The language may be thus paraphrased, "In death I shall hope for resurrection; for I shall not be left under its dominion and within its bounds, or be subject to the corruption which ordinarily ensues." **11.** Raised from the dead, he shall die no more; death hath no more dominion over him. **Thou wilt show me**—guide me to attain. **the path of life**—or, "lives"—the plural denoting variety and abundance—immortal blessedness of every sort—as life often denotes. **in thy presence**—or, "before Thy faces." The frequent use of this plural form for faces may contain an allusion to the Trinity (Num. 6:25, 26; Ps. 17:15; 31:16). **at thy right hand**—to which Christ was exalted (Ps. 110:1; Acts 2:33; Col. 3:1; Heb. 1:3). In the glories of this state, He shall see of the travail (Isa. 53:10, 11; Phil. 2:9) of His soul, and be satisfied.

ADAM CLARKE

8. *I have set the Lord always before me.* This verse and all to the end of v. 11 are applied by St. Peter to the death and resurrection of Christ, Acts ii. 25, etc. *He is at my right hand.* That is, I have His constant presence, approbation, and support. All this is spoken by Christ as *man. I shall not be moved.* Nothing can swerve Me from My purpose; nothing can prevent Me from fulfilling the divine counsel, in reference to the salvation of men.

9. *Therefore my heart is glad.* Unutterably happy in God, always full of the divine presence, because whatsoever I do pleaseth Him. *My glory rejoiceth.* My "tongue," so called by the Hebrews (see Ps. lvii. 8; xxx. 12) because it was bestowed on us to glorify God, and because it is our *glory*, being the instrument of expressing our thoughts by words. *My flesh also shall rest in hope.* There is no sense in which these and the following words can be spoken of David. Jesus, even on the Cross, and breathing out His soul with His life, saw that His rest in the grave would be very short—just a sufficiency of time to prove the reality of His death, but not long enough to produce corruption; and this is well argued by St. Peter, Acts ii. 31.

11. *Thou wilt shew me the path of life.* I first shall find the way out of the regions of death, to die no more. Thus Christ was the Firstfruits of them that slept. Several had before risen from the dead, but they died again. Jesus Christ's resurrection from the dead was the first entrance out of the grave to eternal life or lives, *chaiyim*, for the word is in the plural, and with great propriety too, as this resurrection implies the life of the body, and the life of the rational soul also. *In thy presence.* "Thy faces." Every holy soul has, throughout eternity, the beatific vision, i.e., it sees God as He is, because it is like Him, 1 John iii. 2. *Thy right hand.* The place of honor and dignity; repeatedly used in this sense in the Scriptures. *Pleasures for evermore.* "Onwardly; perpetually, continually," well expressed by our translation, *ever* and *more*—an eternal progression.

MATTHEW HENRY

PSALM 17

A prayer of David.

Verses 1–7

This psalm is a prayer. A time for praise and a time for prayer. David was now persecuted, probably by Saul. He addresses himself to God in these verses both by way of appeal (*Hear the right, O Lord!* let my righteous cause have a hearing before thy tribunal, and give judgment upon it) and by way of petition (*Give ear unto my prayer, v.* 1, and again (*v.* 6), *Incline thy ear unto me and hear my speech*). He was sincere, and did not dissemble with God in his prayer: *It goeth not out of feigned lips.* Feigned prayers are fruitless. "*I have called upon thee* formerly (*v.* 6); therefore, Lord, hear me now." It will be a great comfort to us if trouble, when it comes, find the wheels of prayer a-going, for then we may come with the more boldness to the throne of grace. He was encouraged by his faith to expect God would take notice of his prayers: "*I know thou wilt hear me*, and therefore, O God, *incline thy ear to me*."

I. He makes his appeal to the court of heaven. "Lord, do thou hear the right, for Saul is so passionate, so prejudiced, that he will not hear it. Lord, *let my sentence come forth from thy presence, v.* 2. Men sentence me to be pursued and cut off as an evil-doer. Lord, I appeal from them to thee." Sincerity dreads no scrutiny, no, not that of God himself, according to the tenor of the covenant of grace: *Let thy eyes behold the things that are equal. Thou hast proved my heart.* He knew God had tried him, by his own conscience, which is God's deputy in the soul. *The spirit of a man is the candle of the Lord*, with this God had searched him, and *visited him in the night*, when he *communed with his own heart upon his bed.* God had tried him by the fair opportunity he had, once and again, to kill Saul. He had a fixed resolution against all sins of the tongue: "*I have purposed* and fully determined, in the strength of God's grace, *that my mouth shall not transgress*." He had been as careful to refrain from sinful actions as from sinful words (*v.* 4): "*Concerning the* common *works of men*, the actions and affairs of human life, *I have*, by the direction of thy word, *kept myself from the paths of the destroyer*." Some understand it particularly, that he had not been himself a destroyer of Saul, when it lay in his power. But it may be taken more generally; he kept himself from all evil works, and

JAMIESON, FAUSSET, BROWN

PSALM 17

Vss. 1-15. This Psalm is termed a prayer because the language of petition is predominant. With a just cause, sincerely presented, the writer prays for a just decision and help and protection. Pleading former mercies as a ground of hope, he urges his prayer in view of the malice, pride, rapacity, and selfishness of his foes, whose character is contrasted with his pious devotion and delight in God's favor.

2. sentence—acquitting judgment. **from thy presence**—Thy tribunal.

things that are equal—just and right, do Thou regard. **3. proved . . . visited . . . tried**—His character was most rigidly tested, at all times, and by all methods, affliction and others (Ps. 7:10).

purposed that . . .—or, my mouth does not exceed my purpose—I am sincere.

4. works of men—sinful practices. **by the word of thy lips**—as a guide (Ps. 119:9, 11, 95). **destroyer**—violent man.

ADAM CLARKE

PSALM 17

David was most probably the author of this psalm; and it appears to have been written about the time in which Saul had carried his persecution against him to the highest pitch. See 1 Samuel xxvii.

1. *Hear the right.* Attend to the justice of my cause. "O righteous Jehovah, attend unto my cry."

3. *Thou hast tried me.* "Thou hast put me to the test," as they do metals, in order to detect their alloy, and to purify them; well expressed by the Vulgate, "Thou hast tried me by fire."

4. *The paths of the destroyer.* Some render, "hard or difficult paths."

MATTHEW HENRY

endeavoured, according to the duty of his place, to keep others from them too.

II. His petition is that he might experience the good work of God in him, as an evidence of and qualification for the goodwill of God towards him: this is grace and peace from God the Father. 1. He prays for the work of God's grace in him (*v.* 5): "*Hold up my goings in thy paths.* Lord, I have, by thy grace, kept myself from the paths of the destroyer; by the same grace let me be kept in thy paths. 2. He prays for the tokens of God's favour to him, *v.* 7. *O thou that savest by thy right hand* (by thy own power, and needest not the agency of any other) *those who put their trust in thee from those that rise up against them.* Those that trust in God have many enemies, but they have one friend that is able to deal with them all. The margin reads it, *O thou that savest those who trust in thee from those that rise up against thy right hand.* Those that are enemies to the saints are rebels against God and his right hand. *Show thy marvellous loving-kindness.* "Set apart thy loving-kindnesses for me; put me not off with common mercies, but be gracious to me, *as thou usest to do to those who love thy name.*"

Verses 8–15

I. What David prays for. This prayer is both a prediction of the preservation of Christ through all the hardships and difficulties of his humiliation, and a pattern to Christians to commit the keeping of their souls to God, trusting him to *preserve them to his heavenly kingdom.* He prays,

1. That he himself might be protected (*v.* 8): "Keep me safe, hide me close, where I may not be found, where I may not be come at. Deliver my soul, not only my mortal life from death, but my immortal spirit from sin." He prays that God would keep him as a man keeps the apple of his eye, which nature has wonderfully fenced and teaches us to guard. If we keep God's law as the *apple of our eye* (Prov. vii. 2), we may expect that God will so keep us; for it is said concerning his people that whoso *touches them touches the apple of his eye,* Zech. ii. 8. He prays that God would keep him with as much tenderness as the hen gathers her young ones under her wings. Christ uses the similitude, Matt. xxiii. 37. "*Hide me under the shadow of thy wings,* where I may be both safe and warm." Or, perhaps, it rather alludes to the wings of the cherubim shadowing the mercy-seat: "Let me be taken under the protection of that glorious grace which is peculiar to God's Israel." David further prays, "Lord, keep me from the wicked, from men of the world."

2. That all the designs of his enemies to bring him either into sin or into trouble might be defeated (*v.* 13): "*Arise, O Lord!* appear for me, disappoint him, and cast him down in his own eyes by the disappointment." While Saul persecuted David, how often did he miss his prey, when he thought he had him sure! And how were Christ's enemies disappointed by his resurrection, who thought they had gained their point when they had put him to death!

II. For the encouraging of his own faith in these petitions, he pleads,

1. The malice and wickedness of his enemies: They are *my deadly enemies, enemies against the soul,* so the word is. They are sensual, insolent and haughty (*v.* 10): *They are enclosed in their own fat,* wrap themselves, hug themselves, in their own honour, and power, and plenty, and then make light of God, and set his judgments at defiance, lxxiii. 7; Job xv. 27. They *compass me about, v.* 9. "They are watchful and intent upon it, to do us a mischief; they are down-looked, and never let slip any opportunity of compassing their design." "The ringleader of them (that was Saul) is in a special manner bloody and barbarous (*v.* 12), *like a lion* that lives by prey and is therefore greedy of it." This is fitly applied to Saul, who sought David *on the rocks of the wild goats* (1 Sam. xxiv. 2) and in *the wilderness of Ziph* (*ch.* xxvi. 2), where lions used to lurk for their prey.

2. The power God had over them, to control and restrain them. Lord, they are *thy sword*—God's sword, which he can manage as he pleases, which cannot move without him, and which he will sheathe when he has done his work with it. "They are *thy hand,* by which thou dost chastise thy people and make them feel thy displeasure."

3. Their outward prosperity (*v.* 14). They are *men of the world,* actuated by the spirit of the world, in love with the wealth and pleasure of this world. They *have their portion in this life.* They have abundance of the world. *Their bellies thou fillest with thy hidden treasures.* The things of this world are called *treasures,* because they are so accounted; otherwise, to a soul, and in comparison with eternal blessings, they are but trash. Those that fare deliciously every

JAMIESON, FAUSSET, BROWN

5. May be read as an assertion "my steps or goings have held on to Thy paths." **6. wilt hear me**—i.e., graciously (Ps. 3:4). **7. Show**—set apart as special and eminent (Exod. 8:18; Ps. 4:3). **thy right hand**—for Thy power.

8. Similar figures, denoting the preciousness of God's people in His sight, in Deuteronomy 32:10, 11; Matthew 23:37.

13-15. disappoint—lit., "come before," or, "encounter him."

9. compass me—(cf. Ps. 118:10-12). **10. enclosed . . . fat**—are become proud in prosperity, and insolent to God (Deut. 32:15; Ps. 73:7). **11.** They pursue us as beasts tracking their prey. **12.** The figure made more special by that of a lion lurking.

Supply "with" before "sword" (vs. 13), and "hand" (vs. 14). These denote God's power. **men . . . world**—all men of this present time.

ADAM CLARKE

8. *Keep me as the apple of the eye.* Or, "as the black of the daughter of eye." *Hide me under the shadow of thy wings.* This is a metaphor taken from the hen and her chickens. See Matt. xxiii. 37. The Lord says of His followers, Zech. ii. 8: "He that toucheth you toucheth the apple of mine eye." How dear are our eyes to us! how dear must His followers be to God!

13. *Arise, O Lord, disappoint him.* When *he* arises to spring upon and tear me to pieces, arise Thou, O Lord; disappoint him of his prey; seize him, and cast him down. *Deliver my soul.* Save my life. *From the wicked, which is thy sword.* Saul is still meant.

9. *From my deadly enemies, who compass me about.* This is a metaphor taken from huntsmen who spread themselves around a large track of forest, driving in the deer from every part of the circumference, till they are forced into the nets or traps which they have set for them in some particular narrow passage. The metaphor is carried on in the following verses.

10. *They are inclosed in their own fat.* Dr. Kennicott, Bishop Horsley, Houbigant, and others read the passage thus: "They have closed their net upon me." This continues the metaphor which was introduced in the preceeding verse, and which is continued in the two following.

11. *They have set their eyes bowing down to the earth.* It is the attitude of the huntsmen looking for the track of the hart's, hind's, or antelope's foot on the ground.

12. *Like as a lion that is greedy of his prey.* I believe the word *lion* is here used to express Saul in his strength, kingly power, and fierce rapacity.

14. *From men of the world, which have.* "From mortal men of time"; temporizers; men who shift with the times; who have no fixed principle but one, that of securing their own secular interest. And this agrees with what follows—*which have their portion in this life;* who never seek after anything spiritual; who have bartered heaven for earth, and have got the portion they desired.

MATTHEW HENRY

day have their *bellies filled with these hidden treasures*; and they will but *fill the belly* (1 Cor. vi. 13); they will not fill the soul. They have numerous families, and a great deal to leave to them: *They are full of children*, and they have enough for them all, and *leave the rest of their substance to their babes*, to their grand-children.

4. He pleads his own dependence upon God as his portion and happiness. "They have their portion in this life, but as for me (*v.* 15) I am none of them, I have but little of the world." When the soul awakes, at death, out of its slumber in the body, and when the body awakes, at the resurrection, out of its slumber in the grave blessedness will consist in three things:—(1) The immediate vision of God and his glory: *I shall behold thy face*, not, as in this world, through a glass darkly. (2) The participation of his likeness. *When he shall appear we shall be like him, for we shall see him as he is.* (3) A complete and full satisfaction resulting from all this: *I shall be satisfied*, abundantly satisfied with it.

PSALM 18

To the chief musician, *A psalm* of David, the servant of the Lord, who spoke unto the Lord the words of this song, in the day *that* the Lord delivered him from the hand of all his enemies, and from the hand of Saul.

Verses 1–19

This psalm we had before (2 Sam. xxii. 1), only here we are told that the psalm was delivered *to the chief musician*, or precentor, in the temple-songs. David is here called *the servant of the Lord*, as Moses was. It was more his honour that he was a servant of the Lord than that he was king of a great kingdom; and so he himself accounted it (cxvi. 16): *O Lord! truly I am thy servant*.

I. He triumphs in God and his relation to him. The first words of the psalm, *I will love thee, O Lord! my strength*, are here prefixed as the scope and contents of the whole. An interest in the person loved is the lover's delight; this string therefore he touches, and on this he harps with much pleasure (*v.* 2): "*The Lord* Jehovah *is my* God; and then he is my *rock, my fortress*, all that I need and can desire in my present distress."

II. He sets himself to magnify the deliverances God had wrought for him, that he might be the more affected in his returns of praise.

JAMIESON, FAUSSET, BROWN

They appear, by fulness of bread and large families, to be prosperous; but (vs. 15) he implies this will be transient, contrasting his better portion in a joyful union with God hereafter.

PSALM 18

Vss. 1-50. "The servant of the LORD," which in the *Hebrew* precedes "David," is a significant part of the title (and not a mere epithet of David), denoting the inspired character of the song, as the production of one entrusted with the execution of God's will. He was not favored by God because he served Him, but served Him because selected and appointed by God in His sovereign mercy. After a general expression of praise and confidence in God for the future, David gives a sublimely poetical description of God's deliverance, which he characterizes as an illustration of God's justice to the innocent and His righteous government. His own prowess and success are celebrated as the results of divine aid, and, confident of its continuance, he closes in terms of triumphant praise. II Samuel 22 is a copy of this Psalm, with a few unimportant variations recorded there as a part of the history, and repeated here as part of a collection designed for permanent use.

1. I will love thee—with most tender affection. **2, 3.** The various terms used describe God as an object of the most implicit and reliable trust. **rock**—lit., "a cleft rock," for concealment.

strength—a firm, immovable rock.

horn of my salvation—The horn, as the means of attack or defense of some of the strongest animals, is a frequent emblem of power or strength efficiently exercised (cf. Deut. 33:17; Luke 1:69). **tower**—lit., "high place," beyond reach of danger. **to be praised**—for past favors, and worthy of confidence.

ADAM CLARKE

For Thou *fillest* their *belly . . . with thy hid treasure*. Their *belly*—their sensual appetites—is their god; and, when their animal desires are satisfied, they take their rest without consideration, like the beasts that perish.

PSALM 18

The title: "To the chief Musician, A Psalm of David, the servant of the Lord, who spake unto the Lord the words of this song in the day that the Lord delivered him from the hand of all his enemies, and from the hand of Saul." Except the first clause, this title is taken from 2 Sam. xxii. 1.

1. *I will love thee*. Love always subsists on motive and reason. The verb *racham* signifies to "love with all the tender feelings of nature." Why should he love Jehovah? Not merely because He was infinitely great and good, possessed of all possible perfections, but because He was good to him; and he here enumerates some of the many blessings he received from Him. *My strength*. (1) Thou who hast given me power over my adversaries, and hast enabled me to avoid evil and do good.

2. *The Lord is my rock*. (2) I stand on Him as my Foundation, and derive every good from Him who is the Source of good. The word *sela* signifies those craggy precipices which afford shelter to men and wild animals. (3) He was his *fortress*; a place of strength and safety, where he could be safe from his enemies. He refers to those inaccessible heights in the rocky, mountainous country of Judea where he had often found refuge from the pursuit of Saul. What these have been to my body, such has the Lord been to my soul. *Deliverer*. (4) He who causes me to escape. He was often almost surrounded and taken, but still the Lord made a way for his escape—made a way out as his enemies got in. These escapes were so narrow and so unlikely that he plainly saw the hand of the Lord was in them. (5) *My God, Eli*, "my strong God," not only the Object of my adoration, but He who puts strength in my soul. (6) *My strength, tsuri*. This is a different word from that in the first verse. Rabbi Maimon has observed that *tsur*, when applied to God, signifies "fountain, source, origin." God is not only the Source whence my being was derived, but He is the Fountain whence I derive all my good; *in whom*, says David, *I will trust*. And why? Because he knew Him to be an eternal and inexhaustible Fountain of goodness. This fine idea is lost in our translation; for we render two Hebrew words of widely different meaning by the same term in English, "strength." (7) *My buckler*, my Shield, my Defender, He who covers my head and my heart, so that I am neither slain nor wounded by the darts of my adversaries. (8) *Horn of my salvation. Horn* was the emblem of power, and power in exercise. This has been already explained; see on 1 Sam. ii. 1. The *horn of salvation* means a powerful, an efficient salvation. (9) *My high tower;* not only a place of defense, but one from which I can discern the country round about, and always be able to discover danger before it approaches me.

3. *I will call upon the Lord*. When he was conscious that the Object of his worship was such as he has pointed out in the above nine particulars, it is no wonder that he resolves to call upon Him; and no wonder that he expects, in consequence, to be saved from his enemies. For who can destroy him whom such a God undertakes to save?

MATTHEW HENRY

1. The more imminent and threatening the danger was out of which we were delivered the greater is the mercy of the deliverance. David now remembered how the forces of his enemies poured in upon him, which he calls *the floods of Belial.*

2. The more earnest we have been with God for deliverance, and the more direct answer it is to our prayers, the more we are obliged to be thankful. David's deliverances were so, *v.* 6. David was found a praying man, and God was found a prayer-hearing God.

3. The more wonderful God's appearances are in any deliverance the greater it is: such were the deliverances wrought for David, in which God's manifestation of his presence and glorious attributes is most magnificently described, *v.* 7, &c. Little appeared of man, but much of God, in these deliverances. He moved even the *foundations of the hills* (*v.* 7), as of old at Mount Sinai. He showed his anger and displeasure against the enemies and persecutors of his people: *He was wroth, v.* 7. His wrath smoked (*v.* 8), and *coals were kindled by it.* He showed his readiness to plead his people's cause and work deliverance for them; for he rode upon a cherub and did fly, for the maintaining of right and the relieving of his distressed servants, *v.* 10. No opposition, no obstruction, can be given to him *who rides upon the wings of the wind, who rides on the heavens, for the help of his people, and, in his excellency, on the skies.* He showed his condescension, in taking cognizance of David's case: *He bowed the heavens and came down* (*v.* 9), did not send an angel, but came himself, as one afflicted in the afflictions of his people. He wrapped himself in darkness, and yet commanded light to shine out of darkness for his people, Isa. xlv. 15. He *made darkness his pavilion, v.* 11. His glory is invisible; we know not the way that he takes, even when he is coming towards us in ways of mercy; but, when his designs are secret, they are kind; for, though he hide himself, he is the God of Israel, the Saviour. And, *at his brightness, the thick clouds pass* (*v.* 12).

4. The greater the difficulties are that lie in the way of deliverance the more glorious the deliverance is. For the rescuing of David, the waters were to be divided till the very channels were seen; the earth was to be cloven till the very foundations of it were discovered, *v.* 15. There were waters deep and many, waters out of which he was to be drawn (*v.* 16), as Moses, who had his name from being drawn out of the water literally, as David was figuratively.

JAMIESON, FAUSSET, BROWN

4. sorrows—lit., "bands as of a net" (Ps. 116:3). **floods**—denotes multitude.

5. death—and *hell* (cf. Ps. 16:10) are personified as man's great enemies (cf. Rev. 20:13, 14). **prevented**—encountered me, crossed my path, and endangered my safety. He does not mean he was in their power. **6.** He relates his methods to procure relief when distressed, and his success. **temple**—(Cf. Ps. 11:4). **7, 8.** God's coming described in figures drawn from His appearance on Sinai (cf. Deut. 32:22). **smoke out . . . his nostrils**—bitter in His wrath (cf. Ps. 74:1). **by it**—i.e., the fire (Exod. 19:18). **9. darkness**—or, a dense cloud (Exod. 19:16; Deut. 5:22). **10. cherub**—angelic agents (cf. Gen. 3:24), the figures of which were placed over the ark (I Sam. 4:4), representing God's dwelling; used here to enhance the majesty of the divine advent. *Angels* and *winds* may represent all rational and irrational agencies of God's providence (cf. Ps. 104:3, 4). **did fly**—Rapidity of motion adds to the grandeur of the scene.

11. dark waters—or, clouds heavy with vapor.

12. Out of this obscurity, which impresses the beholder with awe and dread, He reveals Himself by sudden light and the means of His terrible wrath (Josh. 10:11; Ps. 78:47).

13. The storm breaks forth—thunder follows lightning, and hail with repeated lightning, as often seen, like balls or coals of fire, succeed (Exod. 9:23).

14. The fiery brightness of lightning, in shape like burning arrows rapidly shot through the air, well represents the most terrible part of an awful storm. Before the terrors of such a scene the enemies are confounded and overthrown in dismay. **15.** The tempest of the air is attended by appropriate results on earth. The language, though not expressive of any special physical changes, represents the utter subversion of the order of nature. Before such a God none can stand. **16-19. from above**—As seated on a throne, directing these terrible scenes, God—**sent**—His hand (Ps. 144: 7), reached down to His humble worshipper, and delivered him. **many waters**—calamities (Job 30: 14; Ps. 124:4, 5).

ADAM CLARKE

4. *The sorrows of death compassed me.* "The cables or cords of death." He was almost taken in those nets or stratagems, by which, if he had been entangled, he would have lost his life. *The floods of ungodly men.* Troops of wicked men were rushing upon him like an irresistible torrent; or like the waves of the sea, one impelling another forward in successive ranks; so that, thinking he must be overwhelmed by them, he was for the moment affrighted. But God turned the torrent aside, and he escaped.

5. *The sorrows of hell.* "The cables or cords of the grave." Is not this a reference to the cords or ropes with which they lowered the corpse into the grave? or the bandages by which the dead were swathed? He was as good as dead. *The snares of death prevented me.* I was just on the point of dropping into the pit which they had digged for me. In short, I was all but a dead man; and nothing less than the immediate interference of God could have saved my life.

10. *He rode upon a cherub, and did fly.* I.e., the cherub supported and led on the tempest, in which the Almighty rode as in His chariot. This is agreeable to the office elsewhere ascribed to the cherubim. Thus they supported the mercy seat, which was peculiarly the throne of God under the Jewish economy. God is expressly said to make "the clouds his chariot," Ps. civ. 3; and to ride "upon a swift cloud," Isa. xix. 1: so that riding upon a cherub, and riding upon a swift cloud, are riding in the cloud as His chariot, supported and guided by the ministry of the cherubim.

11. *He made darkness his secret place.* God is represented as dwelling in the thick darkness, Deut. iv. 11; Ps. xcvii. 2. This representation in the place before us is peculiarly proper; as thick, heavy clouds deeply charged, and with lowering aspects, are always the forerunners and attendants of a tempest, and greatly heighten the horrors of the appearance; and the representation of them, spread about the Almighty as a tent, is truly grand and poetic. *Dark waters.* The vapors strongly condensed into clouds, which, by the stroke of the lightning, are about to be precipitated in torrents of rain.

12. *At the brightness that was before him his thick clouds passed.* The word *nogah signifies* the "lightning." This goes before Him; the flash is seen before the thunder is heard, and before the rain descends; and then the thick cloud passes. Its contents are precipitated on the earth, and the cloud is entirely dissipated. *Hail stones and coals of fire.* This was the storm that followed the flash and the peal, for it is immediately added—

13. *The Lord also thundered in the heavens, and the Highest gave his voice.* And then followed the hail and coals of fire. The former verse mentioned the lightning, with its effects; this gives us the report of the thunder, and the increasing storm of hail and fire that attended it.

14. *He sent out his arrows . . . he shot out lightnings.* I believe the latter clause to be an illustration of the former. *He sent out his arrows*—that is, He shot out *lightnings.*

15. *The channels of water were seen.* This must refer to an earthquake; for in such cases, the ground being rent, water frequently gushes out at the fissures, and often rises to a tremendous height.

16. *He drew me out of many waters.* Here the allusion is still carried on. The waters thus poured out were sweeping the people away; but God, by a miraculous interference, sent and drew David out. Sometimes *waters* are used to denote multitudes of people, and here the word may have that reference; multitudes were gathered together against David, but God delivered him from them all. This seems to be countenanced by the following verse.

17. *He delivered me from my strong enemy.* Does not this refer to his conflict with Ishbi-benob? "And Ishbi-benob, which was of the sons of the giant . . . thought to have slain David. But Abishai the son of Zeruiah succoured him, and smote the Philistine, and killed him. Then the men of David sware unto him, saying, Thou shalt go no more out with us to battle, that thou quench not the light of Israel," 2 Sam. xxi. 16-17. It appears that at this time he was in the most imminent danger of his life, and that he

MATTHEW HENRY

His enemies were too quick for him; for they *prevented him* in the day of his calamity, *v.* 18. But, in the midst of his troubles, the Lord was his stay, so that he did not sink. Note, God will not only deliver his people out of their troubles in due time, but he will sustain them and bear them up under their troubles in the mean time.

5. That which especially magnified the deliverance was that his comfort was the fruit of it. "He brought me forth also out of my straits into a large place, where I had room, not only to turn, but to thrive in." "*He delivered me because he delighted in me*, not for my merit, but for his own grace and goodwill."

In singing this we may apply it to Christ the Son of David. The sorrows of death surrounded him; in his distress he prayed (Heb. v. 7); God made the earth to shake and tremble, and the rocks to cleave, and brought him out, in his resurrection, into a large place, because he delighted in him and in his undertaking.

Verses 20–28

I. David reflects with comfort upon his own integrity, and rejoices in the testimony of his conscience that he had had his conversation in godly sincerity and not with fleshly wisdom, 2 Cor. i. 12. His deliverances were an evidence of this, and this was the great comfort of his deliverances. His deliverances cleared his innocency before men, and acquitted him from those crimes which he was falsely accused of. This he calls *rewarding him according to his righteousness* (*v.* 20, 24). They confirmed the testimony of his own conscience for him, which he here reviews with a great deal of pleasure, *v.* 21–23. Though we are conscious of many a stumble, and many a false step taken, yet if we recover ourselves by repentance, and go on in the way of our duty, it shall not be construed into a departure, for it is not a wicked departure, from our God. He had kept his eye upon the rule of God's commands (*v.* 22): *All his judgments were before me.*

II. He takes occasion thence to lay down the rules of God's government and judgment, that we may know not only what God expects from us, but what we may expect from him, *v.* 25, 26. Those that show mercy to others shall find mercy with God, Matt. v. 7. Wherever God finds an upright man, he will be found an upright God.

III. Hence he speaks comfort to the humble "*Thou wilt save the afflicted people*, that are wronged and bear it patiently", terror to the proud "Thou *wilt bring down high looks*, that aim high, and expect great things for themselves, and look with scorn and disdain upon the poor and pious", and encouragement to himself—"*Thou wilt light my candle*, that is, thou wilt revive and comfort my sorrowful spirit, and not leave me melancholy. Thou wilt light my candle to work by, and give me an opportunity of serving thee and the interests of thy kingdom among men."

Verses 29–50

I. David looks back, with thankfulness, upon the great things which God had done for him. When we set ourselves to praise God for one mercy we must be led by that to observe the many more with which we have been compassed about, and followed, all our days. Many things had contributed to David's advancement, and he owns the hand of God in them all, to teach us to do likewise. 1. God had given him all his skill and understanding in military affairs, which he was not bred up to nor designed for, his genius leading him more to music, and poetry, and a contemplative life: *He teaches my hands to war*, *v.* 34. 2. God had given him bodily strength to go through the business and fatigue of war: God *girded him with strength* (*v.* 32, 39) to such a degree that he could break even a bow of steel, *v.* 34. What service God designs men for he will be sure to fit them for. 3. God had likewise given him great swiftness, not to flee from the enemies but to fly upon them (*v.* 33): *He makes my feet like hinds' feet*, *v.* 36. "*Thou hast enlarged my steps under me;* but" (whereas those that take large steps are apt to tread awry) "my feet did not slip." 4. God had made him very bold. If a troop stood in his way, he made nothing of running through them; if a wall, he made nothing of leaping over it (*v.* 29); if ramparts and bulwarks, he soon mounted them, and by divine assistance set his feet upon the high places of the enemy, *v.* 33. 5. God had protected him, and kept him safe, in the midst of the greatest perils. "*Thou hast given me the shield of thy salvation* (*v.* 35), and that has compassed me on every side. By that I have been delivered from the strivings of the people who aimed at my destruction (*v.* 43), particularly from the violent man"

JAMIESON, FAUSSET, BROWN

prevented—(vs. 3).

a large place—denotes safety or relief, as contrasted with the straits of distress (Ps. 4:1). All his deliverance is ascribed to God, and this sublime poetical representation is given to inspire the pious with confidence and the wicked with dread. **20-24.** The statements of innocence, righteousness, etc., refer, doubtless, to his personal and official conduct and his purposes, during all the trials to which he was subjected in Saul's persecutions and Absalom's rebellions, as well as the various wars in which he had been engaged as the head and defender of God's Church and people. **upright before him**—In my relation to God I have been perfect as to all parts of His law. The perfection does not relate to degree. **mine iniquity**—perhaps the thought of his heart to kill Saul (I Sam. 24:6). That David does not allude to all his conduct, in all relations, is evident from Psalm 51:1, etc. **25-27.** God renders to men according to their deeds in a penal, not vindictive, sense (Lev. 26:23, 24). **merciful**—or, kind (Ps. 4:3). **froward**—contrary to. **the afflicted people**—i.e., the humbly pious. **high looks**—pide (Ps. 101:5; 131:1). **28.** *To give one light* is to make prosperous (Job. 18:5, 6; 21:17). **thou**—is emphatic, as if to say, I can fully confide in *Thee* for help. **29.** And this on past experience in his military life, set forth by these figures. **30-32.** God's perfection is the source of his own, which has resulted from his trust on the one hand, and God's promised help on the other. **tried**—"as metals are tried by fire and proved genuine" (Ps. 12:6). *Shield* (Ps. 3:3).

Girding was essential to free motion on account of the looseness of Oriental dresses; hence it is an expressive figure for describing the gift of strength.

33-36. God's help farther described—He gives swiftness to pursue or elude his enemies (Hab. 3:19), strength, protection, and a firm footing.

thy gentleness— as applied to God—condescension—or, that which He gives, in the sense of *humility* (cf. Prov. 22:4). **enlarged my steps**—made ample room (cf. Prov. 4:12). **37-41.** In actual conflict, with God's aid, the defeat of his enemies is certain. A present and continued success is expressed. **that rose up against me**—lit., "insurgents" (Ps. 3:1; 44:5). **given me the necks**—lit., "backs of the necks"—made them retreat (Exod. 23:27; Josh. 7:8).

42. This conquest was complete. **43-45.** Not only does He conquer civil foes, but foreigners, who are driven from their places of refuge.

ADAM CLARKE

must have fallen by the hands of the giant if God had not sent Abishai to his assistance. *They were too strong for me.* He was nearly overpowered by the Philistines, and his escape was such as evidently to show it to be supernatural.

18. *They prevented me in the day of my calamity.* They took advantage of the time in which I was least able to make head against them, and their attack was sudden and powerful. I should have been overthrown, *but the Lord was my stay.* He had been nearly exhausted by the fatigue of the day, when the giant availed himself of this advantage.

19. *He brought me forth also into a large place.* He enabled me to clear the country of my foes, who had before cooped me up in holes and corners.

20. *The Lord rewarded me.* David proceeds to give the reasons why God had so marvellously interposed in his behalf. *According to my righteousness.* Instead of being an enemy to Saul, I was his friend. I dealt righteously with him while he dealt unrighteously with me.

26. *With the froward.* "The perverse man"; he that is crooked in his tempers and ways. *Thou wilt shew thyself froward.* "Thou wilt set thyself to twist, twine, and wrestle." If he contend, Thou wilt contend with him.

28. *For thou wilt light my candle.* Thou wilt restore me to prosperity, and give me a happy issue out of all my afflictions. By the lamp of David the Messiah may be meant; Thou wilt not suffer my family to become extinct, nor the kingdom which Thou hast promised me utterly to fail.

29. *I have run through a troop.* This may relate to some remarkable victory, and the taking of some fortified place, possibly Zion, from the Jebusites. See the account 2 Sam. v. 6-8.

30. *God, his way is perfect.* His conduct is like His nature, absolutely pure. *The word of the Lord is tried.* Literally "tried in the fire."

31. *For who is God save the Lord?* "For who is Eloah, except Jehovah?" None is worthy of adoration but the self-existent, eternal, infinitely perfect, and all-merciful Being.

32. *God . . . girdeth me with strength.* The girdle was a necessary part of the Eastern dress; it strengthened and supported the loins, served to confine the garments close to the body; and in it they tucked them up when journeying. The strength of God was to his soul what the girdle was to the body.

33. *My feet like hinds' feet.* Swiftness, or speed of foot, was a necessary qualification of an ancient hero.

34. *He teacheth my hands to war.* The success which I have had in my military exercises I owe to the divine help. *A bow of steel is broken by mine arms.* All the versions render this: "Thou hast made my arm like a brazen bow." A bow of steel is out of the question.

35. *The shield of thy salvation.* In all battles and dangers God defended him. *Thy gentleness,* thy "meekness" or "humility."

40. *The necks of mine enemies.* Thou hast made me a complete conqueror. Treading on the neck of an enemy was the triumph of the conqueror, and the utmost disgrace of the vanquished.

41. *They cried.* The Philistines called upon their gods, but there was none to save them. *Even unto the Lord.* Such as Saul, Ish-bosheth, Absalom, who, professing to worship the true God, called on Him while in their opposition to David.

42. *Then did I beat them.* God was with him, and they had only an arm of flesh.

43. *The strivings of the people.* Disaffections and insurrections among my own subjects, as in the revolt of Absalom, the civil war of Abner in favor of Ish-bosheth. *The head of the heathen. Rosh goyim*, "the chief," or "governor, of the nations," all the circumjacent heathen people; all these were subdued by David, and brought under tribute. *A people whom I have not known.* The people whom he knew were those of the twelve tribes; those whom he did not know were the Syrians, Philistines, Idumeans, etc. All these served him, that is, paid him tribute.

MATTHEW HENRY

(*v.* 48), that is, Saul, who more than once threw a javelin at him. 6. God had prospered him in his designs; he it was that made his way perfect (*v.* 32) and it was his right hand that held him up, *v.* 35. 7. Those whom God has abandoned are easily vanquished: *Then did I beat them small as the dust*, *v.* 42. But those whose cause is just he avenges (*v.* 47), and those whom he favours will certainly be *lifted up above those that rise up against them*, *v.* 48. 8. God had raised him to the throne, and not only delivered him and kept him alive but dignified him and made him great (*v.* 35): *Thy gentleness has increased me*—thy *discipline* and *instruction*; so some. The good lessons David learned in his affliction prepared him for the dignity and power that were intended him; and the lessening of him helped very much to increase his greatness.

II. David looks up with humble and reverent adorations of the divine glory and perfection. He endeavours, with his praises, to magnify God, to bless him and exalt him, *v.* 46. He gives honour to him, 1. As a living God: *The Lord liveth*, *v.* 46. The gods of the heathen were dead gods. But God lives, lives for ever, and will not fail those that trust in him, but, because he lives, they shall live also; for he is their life. 2. As a finishing God: *As for God*, he is not only perfect himself, but *his way is perfect*, *v.* 30. What God begins to build he is able to finish. 3. As a faithful God: *The word of the Lord is tried.* "I have tried it" (says David), "and it has not failed me." David, in God's providences concerning him, takes notice of the performance of his promises to him, which, as it puts sweetness into the providence, so it puts honour upon the promise. 4. As the protector and defender of his people. David had found him so to him: "*He is the God of my salvation* (*v.* 46), by whose power and grace I am and hope to be saved; but not of mine only: he is *a buckler to all those that trust in him* (*v.* 30); he shelters and protects them all, is both able and ready to do so."

III. David looks forward, with a believing hope that God would still do him good. He promises himself his enemies should be completely subdued, and that his government should be extensive, so that even a people whom he had not known should serve him (*v.* 43). *As soon as they hear of me they shall obey me*, *v.* 44. His seed should be for ever continued in the Messiah, who, he foresaw, should come from his loins, *v.* 50. He *shows mercy to his anointed*, his Messiah, *to David* himself, the anointed of the God of Jacob in the type, *and to his seed for evermore.*

JAMIESON, FAUSSET, BROWN

submit . . .—(cf. *Margin*)—i.e., show a forced subjection.

46. The Lord liveth—contrasts Him with idols (I Cor. 8:4). **47, 48. avengeth me**—His cause is espoused by God as His own. **liftest me up**—to safety and honors.

49, 50. Paul (Rom. 15:9) quotes from this doxology to show that under the Old Testament economy, others than the Jews were regarded as subjects of that spiritual government of which David was head, and in which character his deliverances and victories were typical of the more illustrious triumphs of David's greater Son. The language of vs. 50 justifies this view in its distinct allusion to the great promise (cf. II Sam. 7). In all David's successes he saw the pledges of a fulfilment of that promise, and he mourned in all his adversities, not only in view of his personal suffering, but because he saw in them evidences of danger to the great interests which were committed to his keeping. It is in these aspects of his character that we are led properly to appreciate the importance attached to his sorrows and sufferings, his joys and successes.

ADAM CLARKE

44. *As soon as they hear of me.* His victories were so rapid and splendid over powerful enemies that they struck a general terror among the people, and several submitted without a contest.

45. *The strangers shall fade away.* "They shall fall as the leaves fall off the trees in winter." *And be afraid out of their close places.* Those who have formed themselves into banditti, and have taken possession of rocks and fortified places, shall be so afraid when they hear of my successes that they shall surrender at discretion, without standing a siege. Perhaps all these verbs should be understood in the perfect tense, for David is here evidently speaking of a kingdom at rest, all enemies having been subdued; or, as the title is, when the Lord had "delivered him from the hand of all his enemies."

48. *He delivereth me.* That is, He hath delivered me, and continues to deliver me, from all that rise up against me. *The violent man.* Saul; this applies particularly to him.

49. *Will I give thanks unto thee . . . among the heathen.* Quoted by Paul, Rom. xv. 9, to prove that the calling of the Gentiles was predicted, and that what then took place was the fulfillment of that prediction.

50. *Great deliverance giveth he to his king.* David was a king of God's appointment, and was peculiarly favored by Him. Literally, "He is magnifying the salvations of His king." *To his seed.* His "posterity." So the words in the Old and New Testament should be universally translated. The common translation is totally improper. *For evermore. Ad olam,* "forever"; through all duration of created worlds. And *more*—the eternity that is beyond time. This shows that another David is meant, with another kind of posterity, and another sort of kingdom. From the family of David came the man Christ Jesus; His posterity are the genuine Christians; His kingdom, in which they are subjects, is spiritual. This government shall last through all time.

MATTHEW HENRY

PSALM 19

To the chief musician. A psalm of David.

Verses 1-6

From the things that are seen every day by all the world the psalmist, in these verses, leads us to the consideration of the invisible things of God, whose glory shines transcendently bright in the visible heavens, the structure and beauty of them, and the order and influence of the heavenly bodies. This instance of the divine power serves not only to show the folly of atheists, who see there is a heaven and yet say, "There is no God," who see the effect and yet say, "There is no cause," but to show the folly of idolaters also, and the vanity of their imagination, who, though the heavens declare the glory of God, yet gave that glory to the lights of heaven which those very lights directed them to give to God only, the Father of lights.

I. What that is which the creatures notify to us. They are in many ways useful and serviceable to us, but in nothing so much as in this, that they declare the glory of God, by showing his handiworks, *v.* 1. They plainly speak themselves to be God's handiworks; all succession and motion must have had a beginning; they could not make themselves, that is a contradiction; they could not be produced by a casual hit of atoms, that is an absurdity, fit rather to be bantered than reasoned with: therefore they must have a Creator, who can be no other than an eternal mind, infinitely wise, powerful, and good. From the excellency of the work we may easily infer the infinite perfection of its great author. From the brightness of the heavens we may collect that the Creator is light; their vastness of extent bespeaks his immensity, their height his transcendency and sovereignty, their influence upon this earth his dominion, and providence, and universal beneficence: and all declare his almighty power.

II. What are some of those things which notify this? 1. The heavens and the firmament—the vast expanse of air and ether, and the spheres of the planets and fixed stars. Man has this advantage

JAMIESON, FAUSSET, BROWN

PSALM 19

Vss. 1-14. After exhibiting the harmonious revelation of God's perfections made by His works and His word, the Psalmist prays for conformity to the divine teaching.

1. the glory of God—is the sum of His perfections (Ps. 24:7-10; Rom. 1:20). **firmament**—another word for "heavens" (Gen. 1:8). **handywork**—old English for "work of His hands."

ADAM CLARKE

PSALM 19

1. *The heavens declare the glory of God.* Literally, "The heavens number out the glory of the strong God." *The firmament.* The whole visible expanse; not only containing the celestial bodies above referred to, but also the air, light rains, dews.

MATTHEW HENRY

above the beasts, in the structure of his body, that whereas they are made to look downwards, as their spirits must go, he is made erect, to look upwards, because upwards his spirit must shortly go and his thoughts should now rise. 2. The constant and regular succession of day and night (*v.* 2): *Day unto day, and night unto night,* speak the glory of that God who first divided between the light and the darkness. He not only glorifies himself, but gratifies us, by this constant revolution; for, as the light of the morning befriends the business of the day, so the shadows of the evening befriend the repose of the night; every day and every night speak the goodness of God, and, when they have finished their testimony, leave it to the next day, to the next night, to say the same. 3. The light and influence of the sun do, in a special manner, declare the glory of God; for of all the heavenly bodies that is the most conspicuous in itself and most useful to this lower world, which would be all dungeon, and all desert, without it. In the heavens God has *set a tabernacle for the sun.* The heavenly bodies are called *hosts of heaven,* and therefore are fitly said to *dwell in tents,* as soldiers in their encampments. That glorious creature was not made to be idle, but *his going forth* (at least as it appears to our eye) *is from one point of the heavens, and his circuit* thence to the opposite point, and thence (to complete his diurnal revolution) to the same point again; and this with such steadiness and constancy that we can certainly foretell the hour and the minute at which the sun will rise at such a place, any day to come. The brightness wherein he appears. He is *as a bridegroom coming out of his chamber,* richly dressed and adorned, as fine as hands can make him, looking pleasantly himself and making all about him pleasant. The cheerfulness wherewith he makes his tour. For the service of man he *rejoices as a strong man to run a race.*

III. To whom this declaration is made of the glory of God. It is made to all parts of the world (*v.* 3, 4): *There is no speech nor language where their voice is not heard. Their line has gone through all the earth* (the equinoctial line suppose) *and* with it *their words to the end of the world,* proclaiming the eternal power of the God of nature, *v.* 4. *They have no speech or language* (so some read it) *and yet their voice is heard.* All people may hear these natural immortal preachers speak to them in their own tongue the wonderful works of God.

Verses 7–14

God's glory (that is, his goodness to man) appears much in the works of creation, but much more in and by divine revelation. The holy scripture, as it is a rule both of our duty to God and of our expectation from him, is of much greater use and benefit to us than day or night, than the air we breathe in, or the light of the sun.

1. The psalmist gives an account of the excellent properties and uses of the word of God, in six sentences (*v.* 7–9), in each of which the name *Jehovah* is repeated. Here are six several titles of the word of God, to take in the whole of divine revelation, precepts, and promises, and especially the gospel. 1. *The law of the Lord is perfect.* It is perfectly free from all corruption, perfectly filled with all good, and perfectly fitted for the end for which it is designed, 2 Tim. iii. 17. Nothing is to be added to it nor taken from it. It is of use to *convert the soul,* to bring us back to ourselves, to our God, to our duty. 2. *The testimony of the Lord is sure.* It is a sure fountain of living comforts and a sure foundation of lasting hopes. It will make even *the simple* wise for their souls and eternity. Those that are humbly simple, sensible of their own folly and willing to be taught, shall be made wise by the word of God, xxv. 9. 3. *The statutes of the Lord are right,* exactly agreeing with the eternal rules and principles of good and evil. Because they are right, they *rejoice the heart.* The law, as we see it in the hands of Christ, gives cause for joy; and, when it is written in our hearts, it lays a foundation for lasting joy, by restoring us to our right mind. 4. *The commandment of the Lord is pure.* It is the ordinary means which the Spirit uses in *enlightening the eyes*; it brings us to a sight and sense of our sin and misery, and directs us in the way of duty. 5. *The fear of the Lord* will cleanse our way, cxix. 9. And it *endureth for ever.* The ceremonial law is long since done away, but the law concerning the fear of God is ever the same. Time will not alter the nature of moral good and evil. 6. *The judgments of the Lord* (all his precepts, which are framed in infinite wisdom) *are true altogether.* They are all of a piece.

II. He expresses the great value he had for the word of God, and the great advantage he had, and hoped to have, from it, *v.* 10, 11. He prized the com-

JAMIESON, FAUSSET, BROWN

2. uttereth—pours forth—as a stream—a perpetual testimony.

5, 6. The sun, as the most glorious heavenly body, is specially used to illustrate the sentiment; and his vigorous, cheerful, daily, and extensive course, and his reviving heat (including light), well display the wondrous wisdom of his Maker.

3. Though there is no articulate speech or words, yet without these their voice is heard (cf. *Margin*). **4. Their line**—or instruction—the influence exerted by their tacit display of God's perfections. Paul (Rom.10:18), quoting from the *Septuagint,* uses *sound,* which gives the same sense.

7-9. The law is described by six names, epithets, and effects. It is a rule, God's testimony for the truth, His special and general prescription of duty, fear (as its cause) and judicial decision. It is distinct and certain, reliable, right, pure, holy, and true. Hence it revives those depressed by doubts, makes wise the unskilled (II Tim. 3:15), rejoices the lover of truth, strengthens the desponding (Ps. 13:4; 34:6), provides permanent principles of conduct, and by God's grace brings a rich reward.

ADAM CLARKE

5. *Which is as a bridegroom.* The sun is compared to a bridegrrom in his ornaments, because of the glory and splendor of his rays; and to a giant or strong man running a race, because of the power of his light and heat.

3. *There is no speech nor language, where their voice is not heard.* Leave out the expletives here, which pervert the sense; and what remains is a tolerable translation of the original: "No speech, and no words; their voice without hearing. Into all the earth hath gone out their sound; and to the extremity of the habitable world, their eloquence." St. Paul applies this as a prophecy relative to the universal spread of the gospel of Christ, Rom. x. 18; for God designed that the light of the gospel should be diffused wheresoever the light of the celestial luminaries shone.

7. *The law of the Lord.* And here are two books of divine revelation: (1) the visible heavens, and the works of creation in general; (2) the Bible, or divinely inspired writings contained in the Old and New Testaments. These may all be called *the law of the Lord; torah,* from *yarah,* to "instruct, direct, put straight, guide." *Is perfect. Temimah,* it is perfection; it is perfect in itself as a law, and requires perfection in the hearts and lives of men. *Converting the soul.* Turning it back to God. *The testimony of the Lord. Eduth,* from *ad,* "beyond, forward." The various types and appointments of the law, which refer to something beyond themselves, and point forward to the Lamb of God, who takes away the sin of the world. *Is sure. Neemanah,* are "faithful"; they point out the things beyond them fairly, truly, and fully. They all bear testimony to the great atonement. *Making wise the simple.* The simple is he who has but one end in view, who is concerned about his soul.

8. *The statutes of the Lord. Pikkudim,* from *pakad,* "He visited, cared, took notice of, appointed to a charge." The appointments or charge delivered by God to man for his regard and observance. *Are right. Yesharim,* from *yashar,* "to make straight, smooth, right, upright." *Rejoicing the heart.* As they show a man what he is to observe and keep in charge, and how he is to please God, and the divine help he is to receive from the visitations of God, they contribute greatly to the happiness of the upright—they rejoice the heart. *The commandment. Mitsvah,* from *tsavah,* "to command, give orders, ordain." *Is pure.* From *barah,* "to clear, cleanse, purify." *Enlightening the eyes.* Showing men what they should *do,* and what they should avoid. It is by God's commandments that we see the exceeding sinfulness of sin, and the necessity of redemption.

9. *The fear of the Lord. Yirah,* from *yara,* "to fear, to venerate"; often put for the whole of divine worship. The reverence we owe to the Supreme Being. *Is clean. Tehorah,* from *tahar,* "to be pure, clean"; not differing much from *barah* (see above), to be clean and bright as the heavens. Its object is to purge away all defilement, to make a spotless character. *The judgments of the Lord. Mishpatim,* from *shaphat,* "He judged, regulated, disposed." All God's regulations, all His decisions; what He has pronounced to be right and proper. *Are true. Emeth, truth,* from *am,* "to support, confirm, make stable, and certain." *And righteous altogether.* They are not only according to truth, but they are righteous, *tsadeku;* they give to "all their due." They show what belongs to *God,* to *man,* and to *ourselves.* And hence the word *altogether, yachdav, equally,* is added; or *truth and righteousness united.*

MATTHEW HENRY

mandments of God before all the wealth of the world. Gold is of the earth, earthly; but grace is the image of the heavenly. Gold is only for the body and the concerns of time; but grace is for the soul and the concerns of eternity. The word of God, received by faith, is sweet to the soul, *sweeter than honey and the honeycomb.* The pleasures of sense are deceitful, will soon surfeit, and yet never satisfiy; but those of religion are substantial and satisfying, and there is no danger of exceeding in them. The word of God is a word of warning to the children of men; it warns us of the duty we are to do, the dangers we are to avoid. There is a reward, not only after keeping, but in keeping, God's commandments, a present great reward of obedience in obedience.

III. The excellency of the word of God.

1. He takes occasion to make a penitent reflection upon his sins; for *by the law is the knowledge of sin.* "Is the commandment thus holy, just, and good? Then *who can understand his errors*? I cannot, whoever can." From the rectitude of the divine law he learns to call his sins his *errors.* Every transgression of the commandment is an error, a deviation from the rule we are to work by. God knows a great deal more evil of us than we do of ourselves.

2. He takes occasion hence to pray against sin. Finding himself unable to specify all the particulars of his transgressions, he cries out, *Lord, cleanse me from my secret faults*; not secret to God, so none are, nor only such as were secret to the world, but such as were hidden from his own observation of himself. Having prayed that his sins of infirmity might be pardoned, he prays that presumptuous sins might be prevented, *v.* 13. His plea: "*So shall I be upright;* and I *shall be innocent from the great transgression*"; so he calls a presumptuous sin, because no sacrifice was accepted for it, Num. xv. 28–30.

3. He takes occasion humbly to beg the divine acceptance of his thoughts and affections, *v.* 14, and then begs he would accept his performances. His services were—the *words of his mouth and the meditations of his heart,* his holy affections offered up to God. His care that they might be acceptable with God; for, if our services be not acceptable to God, what do they avail us?

JAMIESON, FAUSSET, BROWN

12-14. The clearer our view of the law, the more manifest are our sins. Still for its full effect we need divine grace to show us our faults, acquit us, restrain us from the practice, and free us from the power, of sin. Thus only can our conduct be blameless, and our words and thoughts acceptable to God.

ADAM CLARKE

10. *Honeycomb.* Honey is sweet; but honey just out of the comb has a sweetness, richness, and flavor far beyond what it has after it becomes exposed to the air.

11. *By them is thy servant warned. Nizhar,* from *zahar,* "to be clear." By these laws, testimonies, etc., Thy servant is fully instructed; he sees all clearly, and he discerns that in keeping of them there is great reward.

14. *Let the words of my mouth.* He has prayed against practical sin, the sins of the body; now, against the sins of the mouth and of the heart. *My redeemer. Goali,* my "kinsman," he whose right it is to redeem the forfeited inheritance.

MATTHEW HENRY — PSALM 20

To the chief musician. A psalm of David.

Verses 1–5

This prayer for David is entitled *a psalm of David.* It is very proper for those who desire the prayers of their friends to tell them particularly what they would have to be asked of God for them. Paul often begged of his friends to pray for him.

I. What it is that they are taught to ask of God for the king. *The Lord hear thee in the day of trouble* (*v.* 1), and *the Lord fulfil all thy petitions, v.* 5. It was often a day of trouble with David himself, of disappointment and distress, of treading down and of perplexity. Neither the crown on his head nor the grace in his heart would exempt him from trouble. The prayers of others for us must be desired, not to supersede, but to second, our own for ourselves. "*The name of the God of Jacob defend thee,* and set thee out of the reach of thy enemies." Mercies out of the sanctuary are the sweetest mercies, *v.* 2. *The Lord remember all thy offerings and accept thy burnt-sacrifices* (*v.* 3) or *turn them to ashes*; that is, "The Lord give thee the victory and success which thou didst by prayer with sacrifices ask of him, and thereby give as full proof of his acceptance of the sacrifice as ever he did by kindling it with fire from heaven." By this we may now know that God accepts our spiritual sacrifices, if by his Spirit he kindles in our souls a holy fire of pious and divine affection and with that makes our hearts burn within us. *The Lord grant thee according to thy own heart.* This they might in faith pray for, because they knew David was a man after God's own heart, and would design nothing but what was pleasing to him.

II. What confidence they had of an answer of peace to these petitions for themselves and their good king (*v.* 5): "*We will rejoice in thy salvation.* We that are subjects will rejoice in the preservation and prosperity of our prince." *In the name of our God will we set up our banners.* These prayers for David are prophecies concerning Christ the Son of David, and in him they were abundantly answered; he undertook the work of our redemption, and made war upon the powers of darkness. In the day of trouble, when his soul was exceedingly sorrowful, the Lord heard him, heard him in that he feared (Heb. v. 7), *sent him help out of the sanctuary.*

JAMIESON, FAUSSET, BROWN — PSALM 20

Vss. 1-9. David probably composed this Psalm to express the prayers of the pious for his success as at once the head of the Church and nation. Like other compositions of which David in such relations is the subject, its sentiments have a permanent value —the prosperity of Christ's kingdom being involved, as well as typified, in that of Israel and its king.

1. hear thee—graciously (Ps. 4:1). **name of**—or manifested perfections, as power, wisdom, etc. **defend thee**—set thee on high from danger (Ps. 9:9; 18: 3). **2. strengthen thee**—*sustain* in conflict; even physical benefits may be included, as courage for war, etc., as such may proceed from a sense of divine favor, secured in the use of spiritual privileges. **3. all thy offerings**—or gifts, vegetable offerings. **accept**—lit., "turn to ashes" (cf. I Kings 18:38). **Selah**—(Ps. 3:2). **4. thy counsel** —or plan.

5. salvation—that wrought and experienced by him. **set up our banners**—(Num. 2:3, 10). In usual sense, or, as some render, *may we be made great.*

ADAM CLARKE — PSALM 20

It is most likely that this psalm was penned on the occasion of David's going to war; and most probably with the Ammonites and Syrians, who came with great numbers of horses and chariots to fight with him. See 2 Sam. x. 6-8; 1 Chron. xix. 7. It is one of the Dialogue Psalms, and appears to be thus divided: Previously to his undertaking the war, David comes to the Tabernacle to offer sacrifice. This being done, the people, in the king's behalf, offer up their prayers; these are included in the three first verses. The fourth was probably spoken by the high priest; the fifth, by David and his attendants; the last clause, by the high priest; the sixth, by the high priest, after the victim was consumed; the seventh and eighth, by David and his men; and the ninth, as a chorus by all the congregation.

1. *The Lord hear thee.* David had already offered the sacrifice and prayed. The people implore God to succor him in the day of trouble. *The name of the God of Jacob.* This refers to Jacob's wrestling with the Angel, Gen. xxxii. 24, etc. And who was this Angel? Evidently none other than the *Angel of the Covenant,* the Lord Jesus.

2. *Send thee help from the sanctuary.* This was the place where God recorded His name, the place where He was to be sought, and the place where He manifested himself. He is now in Christ, reconciling the world to himself. This is the true sanctuary where God must be sought.

3. *Remember all thy offerings.* The *minchah,* which is here mentioned, was a gratitude offering. *Burnt sacrifice.* The *olah* here mentioned was a bloody sacrifice.

4. *Grant thee according to thine own heart.* This was probably the prayer of the high priest.

5. *We will rejoice in thy salvation.* The words of this verse were spoken by David and his officers; immediately after which I suppose the high priest to have added, *The Lord fulfil all thy petitions.*

MATTHEW HENRY

Verses 6–9

I. Holy David himself triumphs in the interest he had in the prayers of good people (*v.* 6): "*Now know I that the Lord saveth his anointed*, because he hath stirred up the hearts of the seed of Jacob to pray for him." *He will hear him from his holy heaven*, of which the sanctuary was a type (Heb. ix. 23), from the throne he hath prepared in heaven, of which the mercy-seat was a type. He will hear him *with the saving strength of his right hand*; not by letter, nor by word of mouth, but by his right hand, by the saving strength of his right hand. He will make it to appear that he hears him by what he does for him.

II. His people triumph in God and their relation to him, and his revelation of himself to them. The children of this world trust in second causes, and think all is well if those do but smile upon them; they trust *in chariots and in horses*, and the more of them they can bring into the field the more sure they are of success in their wars. "But," say the Israelites, "we neither have chariots and horses to trust to nor do we want them, nor, if we had them, would we build our hopes of success upon that; *but we will remember*, and rely upon, *the name of the Lord our God.* Those that trusted in their chariots and horses are brought down and fallen, and their chariots and horses were so far from saving them that they helped to sink them, and made them the easier and the richer prey to the conqueror, 2 Sam. viii. 4. But we that trust in the name of the Lord our God not only stand upright, and keep our ground, but have risen, and have got ground against the enemy, and have triumphed over them.

III. They conclude their prayer for the king with a *Hosanna*, "*Save now, we beseech thee*, O Lord!" *v.* 9. As we read this verse, it may be taken as a prayer that God would not only bless the king, "Save, Lord, give him success," but that he would make him a blessing to them, "*Let the king hear us* when we call to him for justice and mercy." Those that would have good of their magistrates must thus pray for them, for they, as all other creatures, are that to us (and no more) which God makes them to be.

JAMIESON, FAUSSET, BROWN

6. He speaks as if suddenly assured of a hearing. **his anointed**—not only David personally, but as the specially appointed head of His Church. **his holy heaven**—or, lit., "the heavens of His holiness," where He resides (Ps. 2: 6; 11:4). **saving . . . hand**—His power which brings salvation.

7. remember—or cause to remember, mention thankfully (I Sam. 17:45; Ps. 33:16).

8. They—i.e., who trust in horses, etc. **stand upright**—lit., "we have straightened ourselves up from our distress and fears."

9. let the king hear—as God's representative, delivered to deliver. Perhaps a better sense is, "LORD, save the king; hear us when we call," or pray.

ADAM CLARKE

6. *Now know I that the Lord saveth his anointed.* These are probably the words of the priest after the victim had been consumed.

7. *Some trust in chariots.* The words of the original are short and emphatic: "These in chariots; and these in horses; but we will record in the name of Jehovah our God." This and the following verse I suppose to be the words of David and his officers.

9. *Save, Lord.* This verse was spoken by all the congregation, and was the chorus and conclusion of the piece.

MATTHEW HENRY — PSALM 21

To the chief musician. A psalm of David.

Verses 1–6

David here speaks professing that his joy was in God's strength and in his salvation, and not in the strength or success of his armies. He also directs his subjects herein to rejoice with him, and to give God all the glory of the victories he had obtained. They congratulate the king on his joys: "*The king rejoices*, and so do we." They give God all the praise of those things which were the matter of their king's rejoicing. *Thou hast given him his heart's desire. Thou preventest him with the blessings of goodness.* The psalmist here reckons that these blessings were given in a preventing way. When God's blessings come sooner and prove richer than we imagine, when they are given before we prayed for them, before we were ready for them, nay, when we feared the contrary, then it may be truly said that he prevented us with them. "*Thou hast set a crown of pure gold upon his head* and kept it there, when his enemies attempted to throw it off." When he went forth upon a perilous expedition *he asked* his *life of thee, and thou* not only *gavest him that*, but withal gavest him *length of days for ever and ever*, didst not only prolong his life far beyond his expectation, but didst assure him of a blessed immortality in a future state and of the continuance of his kingdom in the Messiah that should come of his loins. "*His glory is great*, far transcending that of all the neighbouring princes, in the salvation thou hast wrought for him and by him." The glory which every good man is ambitious of is to see the salvation of the Lord. God had given him the satisfaction of being the channel of all bliss to mankind (*v.* 6): "*Thou hast set him to be blessings for ever*" (so the margin reads it), "thou has made him to be a universal everlasting blessing to the world, in whom the families of the earth are, and shall be, blessed." See how the spirit of prophecy gradually rises here to that which is peculiar to Christ, for none besides is blessed for ever, much less a blessing for ever.

Verses 7–13

The psalmist, having taught his people to look back with joy and praise on what God had done for him and them, here teaches them to look forward with faith, and hope, and prayer, upon what God would further do for them: *The king rejoices in God* (*v.* 1), and therefore we will be thankful; *the king trusteth*

JAMIESON, FAUSSET, BROWN — PSALM 21

Vss. 1-13. The pious are led by the Psalmist to celebrate God's favor to the king in the bounties already conferred and in prospective victories. The doxology added may relate to both Psalms; the preceding of petition, chiefly this of thanksgiving, ascribing honor to God for His display of grace and power to His Church in all ages, not only under David, but also under his last greatest successor, "the King of the Jews."

1. thy strength . . . thy salvation—as supplied by Thee. **2.** The sentiment affirmed in the first clause is reaffirmed by the negation of its opposite in the second. **3. preventest**—lit., "to meet here in good sense," or "friendship" (Ps. 59:10; cf. opposite, Ps. 17:13). **blessings of goodness**—which confer happiness. **crown of pure gold**—a figure for the highest royal prosperity.

4-6. (Cf. II Sam. 7:13-16.) The glory and blessedness of the king as head of his line, including Christ, as well as in being God's specially selected servant, exceeded that of all others. **made him most blessed**—or set him "to be blessings," as Abraham (Gen. 12:2). **with thy countenance**—by sight of thee (Ps. 16:11), or by Thy favor expressed by the light of Thy countenance (Num. 6: 25), or both.

ADAM CLARKE — PSALM 21

1. *The king shall joy. Melech Meshicha,* "the King Messiah."

3. *Thou preventest him.* To "prevent," from *praevenio,* literally signifies "to go before." "For thou shalt go before him with the blessings of goodness."

6. *Thou hast made him most blessed for ever.* Literally, "Thou hast set him for blessings for ever." Thou hast made the Messiah the Source whence all blessings for time and for eternity shall be derived.

MATTHEW HENRY

in God (*v.* 7), therefore will we be encouraged. The joy and confidence of Christ our King is the ground of all our joy and confidence.

I. They are confident of the stability of David's kingdom. *Through the mercy of the Most High*, and not through his own merit or strength, *he shall not be moved.*

II. They are confident of the destruction of all the impenitent implacable enemies of David's kingdom. The success with which God had blessed David's arms hitherto was an earnest of the rest which God would give him from all his enemies round about. They hated David because God had set him apart for himself, hated Christ because they hated the light; but both were hated without any just cause, and in both God was hated, John xv. 23, 25. *They intended evil against thee, and imagined a mischievous device;* they pretended to fight against David only, but their enmity was against God himself. Those that aimed to un-king David aimed, in effect, to un-God Jehovah. "They devise what they are *not able to perform,*" *v.* 11. Their malice is impotent, and they *imagine a vain thing*, ii. 1. The discovery of them (*v.* 8): "*Thy hand shall find them out.* Though ever so artfully disguised by the pretences and professions of friendship, though mingled with the faithful subjects of this kingdom and hardly to be distinguished from them, though flying from justice and absconding in their close places, yet thy hand shall find them out wherever they are." *Their fruit and their seed shall be destroyed*, *v.* 10.

III. In this confidence they beg of God that he would still appear for his anointed (*v.* 13), that he would act for him in his own strength, by the immediate operations of his power as Lord of hosts and Father of spirits.

JAMIESON, FAUSSET, BROWN

7. The mediate cause is the king's faith, the efficient, God's mercy.

8. The address is now made to the king. **hand**—denotes power, and —**right hand**—a more active and efficient degree of its exercise. **find out**—reach, lay hold of, indicating success in pursuit of his enemies. **9.** The king is only God's agent. **anger**—lit., "face," as appearing against them. **as a fiery oven**—as in it. **10. fruit**—children (Ps. 37:25; Hos. 9:16). **11.** This terrible overthrow, reaching to posterity, is due to their crimes (Exod. 20:5, 6). **12. turn their back**—lit., "place them [as to the] shoulder." **against the face of them**—The shooting against their faces would cause them to turn their backs in flight. **13.** The glory of all is ascribable to God alone.

ADAM CLARKE

CHARLES H. SPURGEON:

"Thine hand shall find out all thine enemies: thy right hand shall find out those that hate thee" (21:8). Saul killed himself for fear of falling into the hands of his enemies, and thought death less terrible than the shame that he would have endured in seeing himself in their power. What will it be then "to fall into the hands of the living God" (Heb. 10:31), of an offended God? of God unchangeably determined to be avenged? "Who can stand before his indignation?" says the prophet Nahum (1:6). Who will dare look on him? Who will dare show himself? "Who may abide the day of his coming" (Mal. 3:2) without shuddering and fainting for fear?

—The Treasury of David

13. *Be thou exalted.* "Exalt thyself, O Lord" —Thy creatures cannot exalt Thee.

MATTHEW HENRY

PSALM 22

To the chief musician upon Aijeleth Shahar. A psalm of David.

Verses 1–10

I. A sad complaint of God's withdrawings, *v.* 1, 2.

1. This may be applied to David, or any other child of God, apprehending himself forsaken of God, unhelped, unheard, yet calling him, again and again, "*My God,*" and continuing to **cry day and night** earnestly desiring his gracious return. Spiritual desertions are the saints' sorest afflictions. To cry out, "My God, why am I sick? Why am I poor?" would give cause to suspect discontent and worldliness. But, *Why hast thou forsaken me?* is the language of a heart binding up its happiness in God's favour. When we want the faith of assurance we must live by a faith of adherence. "However it be, yet God is good, and he is mine; *though he slay me, yet will I trust in him.*"

2. But it must be applied to Christ; for, in the first words of this complaint, he poured out his soul before God when he was upon the cross (Matt. xxvii. 46); and, some think, repeated the whole psalm, if not aloud yet to himself. Christ, in his sufferings, cried earnestly to his Father *in the daytime*, upon the cross, *and in the night season*, when he was in his agony in the garden. But, Christ having made himself sin for us, in conformity thereunto the Father laid him under the present impressions of his wrath and displeasure against sin. *It pleased the Lord to bruise him and put him to grief*, Isa. liii. 10.

II. Encouragement taken, in reference hereunto, *v.* 3-5. "*But thou art holy*, not unjust, untrue, nor unkind, in any of thy dispensations. Though thou dost not immediately come in to the relief of thy afflicted people, yet thou lovest them, art true to thy covenant with them, and dost not countenance the iniquity of their persecutors, Hab. i. 13. *Thou inhabitest the praises of Israel;* thou art pleased to manifest thy glory, and grace, and special presence with thy people, in the sanctuary, where they attend thee with their praises. There thou art always ready to receive their homage, and of the tabernacle of meeting thou hast said, *This is my rest for ever.*" Though God seem, for a while, to turn a deaf ear yet he is so well pleased with his people's praises that he will, in due time, give them cause to change their note: *Hope in God, for I shall yet praise him.* He will take comfort from the experiences which the saints in former ages had of the benefit of faith and prayer (*v.* 4, 5): "*Our fathers trusted in thee, cried unto thee, and thou didst deliver them*; therefore thou wilt, in due time, deliver me, for never any that hoped in thee were made ashamed of their hope, never any that sought thee sought thee in vain. And thou art still the same in thyself."

III. The complaint renewed of another grievance,

JAMIESON, FAUSSET, BROWN

PSALM 22

Vss. 1-31. The obscure words *Aijeleth Shahar* in this title have various explanations. Most interpreters agree in translating them by "hind of the morning." But great difference exists as to the meaning of these words. By some they are supposed (cf. Ps. 9) to be the name of the tune to which the words of the Psalm were set; by others, the name of a musical instrument. Perhaps the best view is to regard the phrase as enigmatically expressive of the subject—the sufferer being likened to a hind pursued by hunters in the early morning (lit., "the dawn of day")—or that, while *hind* suggests the idea of a meek, innocent sufferer, the addition of morning denotes relief obtained. The feelings of a pious sufferer in sorrow and deliverance are vividly portrayed. He earnestly pleads for divine aid on the ground of his relation to God, whose past goodness to His people encourages hope, and then on account of the imminent danger by which he is threatened. The language of complaint is turned to that of rejoicing in the assured prospect of relief from suffering and triumph over his enemies. The use of the words of the first clause of vs. 1 by our Saviour on the cross, and the quotation of vs. 18 by John (19: 24), and of vs. 22 by Paul (Heb. 2:12), as fulfilled in His history, clearly intimate the prophetical and Messianic purport of the Psalm. The intensity of the grief, and the completeness and glory of the deliverance and triumph, alike appear to be unsuitable representations of the fortunes of any less personage. In a general and modified sense (cf. on Ps. 16), the experience here detailed may be adapted to the case of all Christians suffering from spiritual foes, and delivered by divine aid, inasmuch as Christ in His human nature was their head and representative.

1. A summary of the complaint. Desertion by God, when overwhelmed by distress, is the climax of the sufferer's misery. **words of my roaring**—shows that the complaint is expressed intelligently, though the term "roaring" is figurative, taken from the conduct of irrational creatures in pain. **2.** The long distress is evinced by—**am not silent**—lit., "not silence to me," either meaning, I continually cry; or, corresponding with "thou hearest not," or answerest not, it may mean, there is no rest or quiet to me. **3.** Still he not only refrains from charging God foolishly, but evinces his confidence in God by appealing to Him. **thou art holy**—or possessed of all the attributes which encourage trust, and the right object of the praises of the Church: hence the sufferer need not despair. **4, 5.** Past experience of God's people is a ground of trust. The mention of "our fathers" does not destroy the applicability of the words as the language of our Saviour's human nature.

ADAM CLARKE

PSALM 22

F. B. MEYER:

The cry of the forsaken. The Hebrew inscription of this exquisite ode is, "The hind of the morning." The hind is the emblem of loveliness (Song of Songs 2:7, 9). The cruel persecutors are designated as bulls, lions, and dogs. Perhaps the allusion to the morning refers to the daybreak of resurrection hope.

Of course our blessed Lord is in every syllable. Indeed, the psalm reads more as history than as prophecy. The divine Sufferer seems to have recited it to himself when on the cross; for it begins with "My God, my God, why hast thou forsaken me?" and ends, according to some, with a word in the Hebrew meaning, "It is finished." The psalm is indeed a photograph of Calvary, a memorial of the heartbreak of Jesus.

Sometimes to the soul in agony God seems not to hear; but through those hours of darkness the Easter day is hastening to break in resplendent glory. He will not suffer his holy one to see corruption (Ps. 16:10).

—Bible Commentary

1. *My God, my God, why hast thou forsaken me?* I beg the reader to refer to my note on Matt. xxvii. 46. *The words of my roaring. Shaagathi*, The Vulgate, Septuagint, Syriac, Aethiopic, and Arabic, with the Anglo-Saxon, make use of terms which may be thus translated: "My sins (or foolishness) are the cause why deliverance is so far from me." It appears that these versions have read *shegagathi*, "my sin of ignorance," instead of *shaagathi*, "my roaring"; but no MS. extant supports this reading.

MATTHEW HENRY

and that is the contempt and reproach of men. This complaint is by no means so bitter as that before of God's withdrawings; but, as that touches a gracious soul, so this a generous soul, in a very tender part, *v.* 6–8. Man, at the best, is a worm; but he became *a worm, and no man.* If he had not made himself a worm, he could not have been trampled upon as he was. He was reproached as a bad man, as a blasphemer, a sabbath-breaker, a wine-bibber, a false prophet, an enemy to Caesar, a confederate with the prince of the devils. He was despised of the people as a mean contemptible man, not worth taking notice of, his country in no repute, his relations poor mechanics, his followers none of the rulers, or the Pharisees, but the mob. He was ridiculed as a foolish man, and one that not only deceived others, but himself too. David was sometimes taunted for his confidence in God; but in the sufferings of Christ this was literally and exactly fulfilled. *He trusted in God; let him deliver him.*

IV. Encouragement taken as to this also (*v.* 9, 10): Men despise me, *but thou art he that took me out of the womb.* David and other good men have often, for direction to us, encouraged themselves with this, that God was not only the *God of their fathers,* as before (*v.* 4) but the God of their infancy who began betimes to take care of them, as soon as they had a being, and therefore, they hope, will never cast them off. He that did so well for us in that helpless useless state will not leave us when he has reared us and nursed us up into some capacity of serving him. See the early instances of God's providential care for us: *He took us also out of the womb,* else we had died there, or been stifled in the birth. *"Then didst thou make me hope"*; that is, "thou didst that for me, in providing sustenance for me and protecting me from the dangers to which I was exposed, which encourages me to hope in thee all my days." The blessings of the breasts, as they crown the blessings of the womb, so they are earnests of the blessings of our whole lives; surely he that fed us then will never starve us, Job iii. 12. *I was cast upon thee from the womb,* which perhaps refers to his circumcision on the eighth day; he was then by his parents committed and given up to God as his God in covenant; for circumcision was a seal of the covenant; and this encouraged him to trust in God. In the experience we have had of God's goodness to us all along ever since, drawn out in a constant uninterrupted series of preservations and supplies: *Thou art my God,* providing for me and watching over me for good, *from my mother's belly,* that is, from my coming into the world unto this day. This is applicable to our Lord Jesus, over whose incarnation and birth the divine Providence watched with a peculiar care, when he was born in a stable, laid in a manger, and immediately exposed to the malice of Herod, and forced to flee into Egypt.

Verses 11–21

I. Here is Christ suffering. David indeed was often in trouble, and beset with enemies; but many of the particulars here specified are such as were never true of David, and therefore must be appropriated to Christ in the depth of his humiliation.

1. He is here deserted by his friends: *Trouble* and distress are *near,* and *there is none to help,* none to uphold, *v.* 11. He trod the wine-press alone; for all his disciples forsook him and fled.

2. He is here insulted and surrounded by his enemies, who, for their strength and fury, are compared to bulls, *strong bulls of Bashan* (*v.* 12), such were the chief priests and elders that persecuted Christ; and others who are compared to dogs (*v.* 16), filthy and greedy, and unwearied in running him down. There was an assembly of the wicked plotting against him (*v.* 16); for the chief priests sat in council, to consult of ways and means to take Christ. They have enclosed me, *v.* 16. They are formidable and threatening (*v.* 13): *They gaped upon me with their mouths,* to show me that they would swallow me up.

3. He is here crucified. The very manner of his death is described, though never in use among the Jews: *They pierced my hands and my feet* (*v.* 16), which were nailed to the accursed tree.

4. He is here dying (*v.* 14, 15), dying in pain and anguish, because he was to satisfy for sin. *I am poured out like water. My heart is like wax. My strength is dried up. My tongue cleaveth to my jaws. "Thou hast brought me to the dust of death;* I am just ready to drop into the grave"; for nothing less would satisfy divine justice. The life of the sinner was forfeited, and therefore the life of the sacrifice must be the ransom for it. The sentence of death passed upon Adam was thus expressed: *Unto dust thou shalt return.* And therefore Christ, in his obedience to death, here uses a similar expression: *Thou hast*

JAMIESON, FAUSSET, BROWN

6. He who was despised and rejected of His own people, as a disgrace to the nation, might well use these words of deep abasement, which express not His real, but esteemed, value. **7, 8.** For the Jews used one of the gestures (Matt. 27:39) here mentioned, when taunting Him on the cross, and (vs. 43) reproached Him almost in the very language of this passage.

trusted on the Lord—lit., "rolled"—i.e., his burden (Ps. 37:5; Prov. 16:3) on the Lord. This is the language of enemies sporting with his faith in the hour of his desertion. **shoot out** [or, open] **the lip**—(Cf. Ps. 35:21). **9, 10.** Though ironically spoken, the exhortation to trust was well founded on his previous experience of divine aid, the special illustration of which is drawn from the period of helpless infancy.

didst make me hope—or lit., "made me secure."

11. From this statement of reasons for the appeal, he renews it, pleading his double extremity, the nearness of trouble, and the absence of a helper. **12, 13.** His enemies, with the vigor of bulls and rapacity of lions, surround him, eagerly seeking his ruin. The force of both figures is greater without the use of any particle denoting comparison. **14, 15.** Utter exhaustion and hopeless weakness, in these circumstances of pressing danger, are set forth by the most expressive figures; the solidity of the body is destroyed, and it becomes like water; the bones are parted; the heart, the very seat of vitality, melts like wax; all the juices of the system are dried up; the tongue can no longer perform its office, but lies parched and stiffened (cf. Gen. 49:4; II Sam. 14:14; Ps. 58:8). In this, God is regarded as the ultimate source, and men as the instruments. **15. the dust of death**—of course, denotes the grave. We need not try to find the exact counterpart of each item of the description in the particulars of our Saviour's sufferings. Figurative language resembles pictures of historical scenes, presenting substantial truth, under illustrations, which, though not essential to the facts, are not inconsistent with them. Were any portion of Christ's terrible sufferings specially designed, it was doubtless that of the garden of Gethsemane. **16.** Evildoers are well described as dogs, which, in the East, herding together, wild and rapacious, are justly objects of great abhorrence. The last clause has been a subject of much discussion (involving questions as to the genuineness of the *Hebrew* word translated "pierce)" which cannot be made intelligible to the English reader. Thought not quoted in the New Testament, the remarkable aptness of the description to the facts of the Saviour's history, together with difficulties attending any other mode of explaining the clause in the *Hebrew,* justify an adherence to the terms of our version and their obvious meaning.

ADAM CLARKE

6. *But I am a worm, and no man.* I can see no sense in which our Lord could use these terms. David might well use them to express his vileness and worthlessness.

7. *Laugh me to scorn.* They utterly despised me, set me at naught, treated me with the utmost contempt.

They shoot out the lip, they shake the head. This is applied by Matthew, chap. xxvii. 39, to the conduct of the Jews toward our Lord when He hung upon the Cross; as is also the following verse.

12. *Many bulls have compassed me.* The bull is the emblem of brutal strength, that gores and tramples down all before it. Such were Absalom, Ahithophel, and others who rose up in rebellion against David; and such were the Jewish rulers who conspired against Christ. *Strong bulls of Bashan.* Bashan was a district beyond Jordan, very fertile, where they were accustomed to fatten cattle, which became, in consequence of the excellent pasture, the largest, as well as the fattest, in the country.

16. *For dogs have compassed me.* This may refer to the Gentiles, the Roman soldiers, and others by whom our Lord was surrounded in His trial, and at His cross. *They pierced my hands and my feet.* The other sufferings David, as a type of our Lord, might pass through, but the piercing of the hands and feet was peculiar to our Lord; therefore this verse may pass for a direct revelation.

MATTHEW HENRY

brought me to the dust of death.

5. He was stripped. The shame of nakedness was the immediate consequence of sin; and therefore our Lord Jesus was stripped of his clothes, when he was crucified, that he might clothe us with the robe of his righteousness, and that the shame of our nakedness might not appear. Now here we are told, (1) How his body looked when it was thus stripped: *I may tell all my bones, v.* 17. *They look and stare upon me,* "the standers by, the passers by, are amazed to see my bones start out thus; and, instead of pitying me, are pleased even with such a rueful spectacle." (2) What they did with his clothes, which they took from him (*v.* 18): *They part my garments among them,* to every soldier a part, and *upon my vesture,* the seamless coat, *do they cast lots.* This very circumstance was exactly fulfilled, John xix. 23, 24. And, though it was no great instance of Christ's suffering, yet it is a great instance of the fulfilling of the scripture in him. *Thus it was written,* and therefore *thus it behoved Christ to suffer.*

II. Christ, in his agony, prayed that the cup might pass from him. And of that David's praying here was a type. He calls God his *strength, v.* 19. He prays, *Be thou not far from me* (*v.* 11), and again, *v.* 19. "Whoever stands aloof from my sore, Lord, do not thou." And the Father *heard him in that he feared* (Heb. v. 7) and enabled him to go through with his work. The psalmist here calls his soul his *darling,* his *only one* (so the word is): "*My soul* is *my only one.* I have but one soul to take care of, and therefore the greater is my shame if I neglect it." He prays to be delivered, *from the sword,* the flaming sword of divine wrath, which turns every way. "O deliver my soul from that. Lord, though I lose my life, let me not lose thy love. Save me from *the power of the dog,* and *from the lion's mouth.*" This seems to be meant of Satan, that old enemy. "Lord, save me from being overpowered by his terrors." He pleads, "Thou hast formerly *heard me from the horns of the unicorn,*" that is, "saved me from him in answer to my prayer." Has God delivered us *from the horns of the unicorn,* that we be not tossed? Let that encourage us to hope that we shall be delivered from the lion's mouth, that we be not torn. This prayer of Christ was answered, for the Father suffered him not to see corruption, but, the third day, raised him out of the dust of death, which was a greater instance of God's favour to him than if he had helped him down from the cross; for that would have hindered his undertaking, whereas his resurrection crowned it.

Verses 22–30

As the first words of the complaint were used by Christ himself upon the cross, so the first words of the triumph are expressly applied to him (Heb. ii. 12) and are made his own words: *I will declare thy name unto my brethren, in the midst of the church will I sing praise unto thee.*

Five things are here spoken of the satisfaction and triumph of Christ in his sufferings:—

I. That he should have a church in the world. This is implied here; that he should *see his seed,* Isa. liii. 10. By the declaring of God's name, by the preaching of the everlasting gospel in its plainness and purity, many should be effectually called to him and to God by him. Those who are thus called in should be brought into a very near and dear relation to him as his brethren; not the believing Jews only, but those of the Gentiles also who became fellow-heirs and of the same body, Heb. ii. 11. These his brethren should be incorporated into a great congregation; such is the universal church, the whole family that is named from him, into which all the *children of God that were scattered abroad are collected,* and in which they are united (John xi. 52, Eph. i. 10), and that they should also be incorporated into smaller societies, members of that great body. These should be accounted the seed of Jacob and Israel (*v.* 23), that on them, though Gentiles, the blessing of Abraham might come (Gal. iii. 14). The gospel church is called *the Israel of God,* Gal. vi. 16.

II. That God should be greatly honoured and glorified in him by that church. He foresees with pleasure, 1. That God would be glorified by the church that should be gathered to him. All that fear the Lord will praise him (*v.* 23), even every Israelite indeed. See cxviii. 2–4; cxxxv. 19, 20. 2. That God would be glorified in the Redeemer and in his undertaking. *Therefore* Christ is said to *praise God in the church.* All our praises must centre in the work of redemption.

III. That all humble gracious souls should have a full satisfaction and happiness in him, *v.* 26. Those that are much in praying shall be much in thanksgiving: *Those shall praise the Lord that seek him,* because through Christ they are sure of finding him,

JAMIESON, FAUSSET, BROWN

17. His emaciated frame, itself an item of his misery, is rendered more so as the object of delighted contemplation to his enemies. The verbs, *look* and *stare,* often occur as suggestive of feelings of satisfaction (cf. Ps. 27:13; 54:7; 118:7). **18.** This literally fulfilled prediction closes the sad picture of the exposed and deserted sufferer.

19, 20. He now turns with unabated desire and trust to God, who, in His strength and faithfulness, is contrasted with the urgent dangers described. **my soul**—or self (cf. Ps. 3:2; 16:10). **my darling**—lit., "my only one," or, "solitary one," as desolate and afflicted (Ps. 25:16; 35:17). **21.** Deliverance pleaded in view of former help, when in the most imminent danger, from the most powerful enemy, represented by the unicorn or wild buffalo. **the lion's mouth**—(Cf. vs. 13.) The lion often used as a figure representing violent enemies; the connecting of the *mouth* intimates their rapacity.

22-24. He declares his purpose to celebrate God's gracious dealings and publish His manifested perfections (name, Ps. 5:11), etc., and forthwith invites the pious (those who have a reverential fear of God) to unite in special praise for a deliverance, illustrating God's kind regard for the lowly, whom men neglect. *To hide the face* (or eyes) expresses a studied neglect of one's cause, and refusal of aid or sympathy (cf. Ps. 30:7; Isa. 1:15).

25, 26. My praise shall be of thee—or, perhaps better, "from thee'—i.e., God gives grace to praise Him. With offering praise, he farther evinces his gratitude by promising the payment of his vows, in celebrating the usual festival, as pro-

ADAM CLARKE

17. *I may tell all my bones.* This may refer to the violent extension of His body when the whole of its weight hung upon the nails which attached His hands to the transverse beam of the Cross. The body being thus extended, the principal bones became prominent, and easily discernible.

18. *They part my garments.* This could be true in no sense of David. The fact took place at the crucifixion of our Lord. The soldiers divided His upper garment into four parts, each soldier taking a part; but His tunic or inward vestment being without seam, woven in one entire piece, they agreed not to divide, but to cast lost whose the whole should be.

20. *Deliver my soul from the sword.* Deliver *naphshi,* "my life"; save Me alive, or raise Me again. *My darling.* "My only one." The only human being that was ever produced since the creation, even by the power of God himself, without the agency of man.

21. *Save me from the lion's mouth.* Probably our Lord here includes His Church with himself. The *lion* may then mean the Jews; the *unicorns,* the Gentiles. For the *unicorn,* see the note on Num. xxiii. 22.

24. *For he hath not despised.* Perhaps it may mean, Though ye have despised Me in My humiliation, yet God has graciously received Me in the character of a sufferer on account of sin, as by that humiliation unto death the great atonement was made for the sin of the world.

26. *The meek shall eat.* "The poor shall eat." In the true only Sacrifice there shall be such a provision for all believers that they shall have a fullness of joy. Those who offered the sacrifice fed on what they offered. Jesus, the true Sacri-

MATTHEW HENRY

in the hopes of which they have reason to praise him even while they are seeking him. The souls that are devoted to him shall be for ever happy with him: "*Your heart shall live for ever.*"

IV. That the church of Christ, and with it the kingdom of God among men, should extend itself to all corners of the earth (*v.* 27, 28). Whereas the Jews had long been the only professing people of God, now all the ends of the world should come into the church, and, the partition-wall being taken down, the Gentiles should be taken in. It is here prophesied, they should be converted: They *shall remember, and turn to the Lord.* Serious reflection is the first step, and a good step it is, towards true conversion. We must consider and turn. The prodigal came first to himself, and then to his father. Then they should be admitted into communion with God and with the assemblies that serve him: *They shall worship before thee,* for *in every place incense shall be offered to God,* Mal. i. 11; Isa. lxvi. 23. For (*v.* 28) *the kingdom is the Lord's.* 1. The kingdom of nature is the Lord Jehovah's, and his providence rules among the nations. 2. The kingdom of grace is the Lord Christ's, and he, as Mediator, is appointed governor among the nations, head over all things to his church. High and low, rich and poor, bond and free, meet in Christ. Christ shall have the homage of many of the great ones. *Those that are fat upon the earth,* that *shall eat and worship.* The poor also shall receive his gospel: *Those that go down to the dust,* that sit in the dust (cxiii. 7), that can scarcely keep life and soul together, *shall bow before him,* before the Lord Jesus, who reckons it his honour to be the poor man's King (lxxii. 12). Seeing we cannot keep alive our own souls, it is our wisdom, by an obedient faith, to commit our souls to Jesus Christ, who is able to save them and keep them alive for ever.

V. That the church of Christ, and with it the kingdom of God among men, should continue through all the ages of time. *A seed shall serve him;* there shall be a remnant, enough to preserve the entail. *They shall be accounted to him for a generation;* he will be the same to them that he was to those who went before them. *They shall come,* shall rise up in their day, not only to keep up the virtue of the generation that is past, but to serve the welfare of souls in the generations to come; they shall transmit to them the gospel of Christ.

In singing this we must triumph in the name of Christ, rejoice in the honours others do him, and in the assurance we have that there shall be a people praising him on earth when we are praising him in heaven.

JAMIESON, FAUSSET, BROWN

vided in the law (Deut. 12:18; 16:11), of which the pious or humble, and they that seek the Lord (His true worshippers) shall partake abundantly, and join him in praise. In the enthusiasm produced by his lively feelings, he addresses such in words, assuring them of God's perpetual favor. *The dying of the heart* denotes death (I Sam. 25:37); so its living denotes life. **27-31.** His case illustrates God's righteous government.

Beyond the existing time and people, others shall be brought to acknowledge and worship God; the *fat ones,* or the rich as well as the poor, the helpless who cannot keep themselves alive, shall together unite in celebrating God's delivering power, and transmit to unborn people the records of His grace.

it shall be accounted to the Lord for . . .—or, it shall be told of the Lord to a generation. God's wonderful works shall be told from generation to generation. **that he hath done**—supply *it,* or *this*—i.e., what the Psalm has unfolded.

ADAM CLARKE

fice, is the Bread that came down from heaven; they who eat of this Bread shall never die.

27. *All the ends of the world.* The gospel shall be preached to every nation under heaven; and *all the kindreds of the nations, mishpechoth,* the "families" of the nations.

28. *The kingdom is the Lord's.* That universal sway of the gospel which in the New Testament is called the kingdom of God.

29. *All they that be fat upon earth.* The rich, the great, the mighty, even princes, governors, and kings, shall embrace the gospel. *That go down to the dust.* Every dying man shall put his trust is Christ, and shall expect glory only through the great Saviour of mankind. *None can keep alive his own soul.* The Vulgate has: "And my soul shall live to him, and my seed shall serve him." And with this agree the Syriac, Septuagint, Aethiopic, Arabic, and Anglo-Saxon.

30. *Shall be accounted to the Lord for a generation.* They shall be called Christians after the name of Christ.

MATTHEW HENRY

PSALM 23

A psalm of David.

Verses 1–6

I. From God's being his shepherd he infers that he shall not want anything that is good for him, *v.* 1. Time was when David was himself a shepherd; he was taken from following the ewes great with young (lxxviii. 70, 71), and so he knew by experience the cares and tender affections of a good shepherd towards his flock. He remembered what need they had of a shepherd, and he once ventured his life to rescue a lamb. By this therefore he illustrates God's care of his people; and to this our Saviour seems to refer when he says, *I am the shepherd of the sheep; the good shepherd,* John x. 11. He takes them into his fold, and provides for them. We must know the shepherd's voice, and follow him. When David considers that God is his shepherd, he can boldly say, *I shall not want.* More is implied than is expressed, not only, *I shall not want,* but, "I shall be supplied with whatever I need; and, if I have not everything I desire, I may conclude it is either not fit for me or not good for me, or I shall have it in due time."

II. From his performing the office of a good shepherd to him he infers that he needs not fear any evil in the greatest dangers and difficulties he could be in, *v.* 2–4. See the happiness of the saints as the sheep of God's pasture. (1) They are well placed, well laid: *He maketh me to lie down in green pastures.* We have the comforts of this life from God's good hand, our daily bread from him as our Father. The greatest abundance is but a dry pasture to a wicked man, who relishes that only in it which pleases the senses; but to a godly man, who tastes the goodness of God in all his enjoyments, though he has but little of the world, it is a green pasture, xxxvii. 16; Prov. xv. 16, 17. God makes his saints to lie down; he gives them quiet and contentment in their own minds, whatever their lot is; their souls dwell at ease in him, and that makes every pasture green. (2) They are well

JAMIESON, FAUSSET, BROWN

PSALM 23

Vss. 1-6. Under a metaphor borrowed from scenes of pastoral life, with which David was familiar, he describes God's providential care in providing refreshment, guidance, protection, and abundance, and so affording grounds of confidence in His perpetual favor.

1. Christ's relation to His people is often represented by the figure of a shepherd (John 10:14; Heb. 13:20; I Pet. 2:25; 5:4), and therefore the opinion that He is *the Lord* here so described, and in Genesis 48:15; Psalm 80:1; Isaiah 40:11, is not without some good reason.

2. green pastures—or, pastures of tender grass, are mentioned, not in respect to food, but as places of cool and refreshing rest.

ADAM CLARKE

PSALM 23

1. *The Lord is my shepherd.* There are two allegories in this psalm which are admirably well adapted to the purpose for which they are produced. The first is that of a shepherd; the second, that of a great feast, set out by a host the most kind and the most liberal.

2. *He maketh me to lie down in green pastures.* Not *green pastures,* but "cottages of turf or sods," such as the shepherds had in open champaign countries; places in which themselves could repose safely; and pens thus constructed where the flock might be safe all the night.

MATTHEW HENRY

guided, well led. *He leadeth me beside the still waters.* Those that feed on God's goodness must follow his direction; he directs their eye, their way, and their heart, into his love. God provides for his people not only food and rest, but refreshment also and pleasure. God leads his people, not to the standing waters which corrupt and gather filth, nor to the troubled sea, nor to the rapid rolling floods, but to the silent purling waters; for the still but running waters agree best with those spirits that flow out towards God and yet do it silently. *He leadeth me in the paths of righteousness,* in the way of my duty; in that he instructs me by his word and directs me by conscience and providence. The way of duty is the truly pleasant way. In these paths we cannot walk unless God both lead us into them and lead us in them. (3) They are well helped when anything ails them: *He restoreth my soul.* When, after one sin, David's heart smote him, and, after another, Nathan was sent to tell him, *Thou art the man,* God restored his soul. Though God may suffer his people to fall into sin, he will not suffer them to lie still in it. "Having had such experience of God's goodness to me all my days, in six troubles and in seven, I will never distrust him, no, not in the last extremity." "*Though I walk through the valley of the shadow of death,* that is, though I am in peril of death, though in the midst of dangers, deep as a valley, yet I am easy." But, even in the supposition of the distress, there are four words which lessen the terror. It is but the *shadow* of death; there is no substantial evil in it; the shadow of a serpent will not sting nor the shadow of a sword kill. It is the *valley* of the shadow, deep indeed, and dark, and dirty; but the valleys are fruitful, and so is death itself fruitful of comforts to God's people. It is but a *walk* in this valley, a gentle pleasant walk. It is a walk *through* it; they shall not be lost in this valley, but get safely to the mountain of spices on the other side of it. There is no evil in it to a child of God; death cannot separate us from the love of God; it kills the body, but cannot touch the soul. The good shepherd will not only conduct, but convoy, his sheep through this valley. His presence shall comfort them: *Thou art with me.* His word and Spirit shall comfort them—*his rod and staff,* alluding to the shepherd's crook, or the rod under which the sheep passed when they were counted (Lev. xxvii. 32), or the staff with which the shepherds drove away the dogs that would worry the sheep.

III. From the good gifts of God's bounty to him now he infers the constancy and perpetuity of his mercy, *v.* 5, 6. "*Thou preparest a table before me;* thou hast provided for me all things requisite both for body and soul, for time and eternity": food convenient, a table spread, a cup filled, meat for his hunger, drink for his thirst. "*My cup runs over,* enough for myself and my friends too." *Thou anointest my head with oil.* He had said (*v.* 1), *I shall not want;* but now he speaks more positively, *Surely goodness and mercy shall follow me all the days of my life.* His hope rises, and his faith is strengthened, by being exercised. It shall *follow* me, as the water out of the rock followed the camp of Israel through the wilderness. It shall follow me *all my life long,* even to the last; for whom God loves he loves to the end. *Surely* it shall. "Goodness and mercy having followed me all the days of my life on this earth, when that is ended I shall remove to a better world, to *dwell in the house of the Lord for ever,* in our Father's house above, where there are many mansions."

JAMIESON, FAUSSET, BROWN

the still waters—are, lit., "waters of stillness," whose quiet flow invites to repose. They are contrasted with boisterous streams on the one hand, and stagnant, offensive pools on the other.

3. To restore the soul is to revive or quicken it (Ps. 19:7), or relieve it (Lam. 1:11, 19). **paths of righteousness**—those of safety, as directed by God, and pleasing to Him. **for his name's sake**—or, regard for His perfections, pledged for His people's welfare.

4. In the darkest and most trying hour God is near. **the valley of the shadow of death**—is a ravine overhung by high precipitous cliffs, filled with dense forests, and well calculated to inspire dread to the timid, and afford a covert to beasts of prey. While expressive of any great danger or cause of terror, it does not exclude the greatest of all, to which it is most popularly applied, and which its terms suggest.

thy rod and thy staff—are symbols of a shepherd's office. By them he guides his sheep.

5, 6. Another figure expresses God's provided care. **a table**—or, food, anointing **oil**—the symbol of gladness, and the overflowing **cup** (which represents abundance)—are prepared for the child of God, who may feast in spite of his enemies, confident that this favor will ever attend him. This beautiful Psalm most admirably sets before us, in its chief figure, that of a shepherd, the gentle, kind, and sure care extended to God's people, who, as a shepherd, both *rules and feeds them.* The closing verse shows that the blessings mentioned are spiritual.

ADAM CLARKE

Beside the still waters. "Deep waters," that the strongest heat could not exhale; not by a rippling current, which argues a shallow stream.

4. *Yea, though I walk through the valley of the shadow of death.* The reference is still to the shepherd. Though I, as one of the flock, should walk through the most dismal valley, in the dead of the night, exposed to pitfalls, precipices, devouring beasts, I should fear no evil under the guidance and protection of such a Shepherd. He knows all the passes, dangerous defiles, hidden pits, and abrupt precipices in the way; and He will guide me around, about, and through them.

Thy rod and thy staff. "Thy sceptre, rod, ensign" of a tribe, staff of office; for so *shebet* signifies in Scripture. *And thy staff,* "Thy prop or support." The former may signify the shepherd's crook; the latter, some sort of rest or support.

5. *Thou preparest a table before me.* Here the second allegory begins. A magnificent banquet is provided by a most liberal and benevolent host, who has not only the bounty to feed me, but power to protect me; and, though surrounded by enemies, I sit down to this table with confidence, knowing that I shall feast in perfect security. *Thou anointest my head with oil.* Perfumed oil was poured on the heads of distinguished guests when at the feasts of great personages. The woman in the Gospel who poured the box of ointment of spikenard on the head of our Lord (see Matt. xxvi. 6-7; Mark xiv. 8; Luke vii. 46) only acted according to the custom of her own country, which the host, who invited our Lord, had shamefully neglected.

6. *Goodness and mercy shall follow me.* As I pass on through the vale of life, Thy goodness and mercy shall follow my every step; as I proceed, so shall they. *I will dwell in the house,* "and I shall return to the house of the Lord," *for ever,* "for length of days."

PSALM 24 (Matthew Henry)

A psalm of David.

Verses 1–2

I. We are not to think that the heavens, even the heavens only, are the Lord's, and that this earth, being so small and inconsiderable a part of the creation, is neglected, and that he claims no interest in it. No, even the earth is his. 1. When God gave the earth to the children of men he still reserved to himself the property, and only let it out to them as tenants: *The earth is the Lord's and the fulness thereof.* The mines, the fruits it produces, all the beasts of the forest and the cattle upon a thousand hills, our lands and houses, and all the improvements that are made of this earth by the skill and industry of man, are all his. These indeed, in the kingdom of grace, are justly looked upon as emptiness; for they are vanity of vanities, nothing to a soul; but, in the kingdom of providence, they are fulness. *The earth is full of God's riches, so is the great and wide sea also.* 2. The habitable part of this earth (Prov. viii. 31) is his in a special manner—*the world and those that dwell therein.* We ourselves are not our own, our bodies, our souls, are not.

PSALM 24 (Jamieson, Fausset, Brown)

Vss. 1-10. God's supreme sovereignty requires a befitting holiness of life and heart in His worshippers; a sentiment sublimely illustrated by describing His entrance into the sanctuary, by the symbol of His worship—the ark, as requiring the most profound homage to the glory of His Majesty.

1. fulness—everything.

world—the habitable globe, with **they that dwell**—forming a parallel expression to the first clause.

PSALM 24 (Adam Clarke)

It is probable that this psalm was composed on occasion of bringing the ark from the house of Obed-edom to Mount Zion, and the questions may respect the fitness of the persons who were to minister before this ark. The last verses may refer to the opening of the city gates in order to admit it. Many of the expressions here are nearly the same with those in Psalm xv.

1. *The earth is the Lord's.* He is the Creator and Governor of it; it is His own property. *The fulness thereof.* "All its creatures."—*Targum.*

They that dwell therein. All human beings.

MATTHEW HENRY

II. The earth is his by an indisputable title, *for he hath founded it upon the seas* and *established it upon the floods, v.* 2. He made it and fitted it for the use of man. The matter is his, for he made it out of nothing; the form is his, for he made it according to the eternal counsels and ideas of his own mind. He continues it, he has *established* it, fixed it, so that, though one generation passes and another comes, the earth abides, Eccles. i. 4. And his providence is a continued creation, cxix. 90.

Verses 3–6

From this world, and the fulness thereof, the psalmist's meditations rise, of a sudden, to the great things of another world, the foundation of which is not on the seas, nor on the floods.

I. This earth is God's footstool; we must be here but a while, must shortly go hence, and *Who then shall ascend into the hill of the Lord?* Who shall go to heaven hereafter, and, as an earnest of that, have communion with God in holy ordinances now? A soul that knows and considers its own nature, origin, and immortality, when it has viewed the earth and the fulness thereof, will sit down unsatisfied; "What shall I do to rise to that high place, that hill, where the Lord dwells, that I may abide in that happy holy place where he meets his people?"

II. An answer to this enquiry. The properties of God's peculiar people, who shall have communion with him in grace and glory. They are such as keep themselves from all the gross acts of sin. They have *clean hands.* The hands lifted up in prayer must be pure hands, no blot of unjust gain cleaving to them, nor anything else that defiles the man and is offensive to the holy God. They are such as make conscience of being inwardly good as they seem to be outwardly. They have *pure hearts.* That is a pure heart which is sincere, purified by faith, and conformed to the image and will of God; see Matt. v. 8. They are such as do not set their affections upon the things of this world, do not *lift up their souls unto vanity.* They are such as deal honestly both with God and man. They are a praying people (*v.* 6): *This is the generation of those that seek him.* In every age there is a remnant of such as these, men of this character, who are *accounted to the Lord for a generation,* xxii. 30. It is to the hill of the Lord that we must ascend, and, the way being up-hill, we have need to put forth ourselves to the utmost, as those that seek diligently. They join themselves to the people of God, to seek God with them. They seek God's face, as Jacob, who was *therefore* surnamed *Israel,* because he wrestled with God and prevailed, sought him and found him. As soon as ever Paul was converted he *joined himself to the disciples,* Acts ix. 26. *Thy face, O God of Jacob!* so our margin supplies it, and makes it easy. They shall be made truly and for ever happy. They shall be justified and sanctified. These are the spiritual blessings in heavenly things which they shall receive, even righteousness, the very thing they hunger and thirst after, Matt. v. 6. They shall be saved; for God himself will be the God of their salvation.

Verses 7–10

What is spoken once is spoken a second time; such repetitions are usual in songs. Entrance once and again demanded for the King of glory; the doors and gates are to be thrown open. *Who is this King of glory? It is the Lord, strong and mighty, the Lord, mighty in battle, the Lord of hosts, v.* 8, 10.

I. This splendid entry here described probably refers to the solemn bringing in of the ark into the tent David pitched for it or the temple Solomon built for it; for, when David prepared materials for the building of it, it was proper for him to prepare a psalm for the dedication of it. The doors are called *everlasting doors,* because much more durable than the door of the tabernacle, which was but a curtain. God, in his word and ordinances, is thus to be welcomed by us. The doors and gates must be thrown open to him.

II. Doubtless it points at Christ, of whom the ark, with the mercy-seat, was a type. We may apply it to the ascension of Christ into heaven and the welcome given to him there. The gates of heaven must then be opened to him, those doors that may be truly called *everlasting.* Our Redeemer found them shut, but, having by his blood made atonement for sin and gained a title to *enter into the holy place* (Heb. ix. 12), as one having authority, he demanded entrance, not for himself only, but for us; for, as the forerunner, he has for us entered and *opened the kingdom of heaven to all believers.* We may apply it to Christ's entrance into the souls of men by his word and Spirit, that they may be his temples. Christ's presence in them is like that of the ark in the temple; it sancti-

JAMIESON, FAUSSET, BROWN

2. poetically represents the facts of Genesis 1:9.

hill of the Lord—(cf. Ps. 2:6, etc.). His Church—the true or invisible, as typified by the earthly sanctuary.

3, 4. The form of a question gives vivacity. *Hands, tongue,* and *heart* are organs of action, speech, and feeling, which compose character. **lifted up his soul**—is to set the affections (Ps. 25:1) on an object; here, **vanity**—or, any false thing, of which swearing falsely, or *to falsehood,* is a specification.

6. Jacob—By "Jacob," we may understand God's people (cf. Isa. 43:22; 44:2, etc.), corresponding to "the generation," as if he had said, "those who seek Thy face are Thy chosen people."

5. righteousness—the rewards which God bestows on His people, or the grace to secure those rewards as well as the result.

7-10. The entrance of the ark, with the attending procession, into the holy sanctuary is pictured to us. The repetition of the terms gives emphasis. **Lord of hosts**—or fully, *Lord God of hosts* (Hos. 12:5; Amos 4:13), describes God by a title indicative of supremacy over all creatures, and especially the heavenly armies (Josh. 5:14; I Kings 22:19). Whether, as some think, the actual enlargement of the ancient gates of Jerusalem be the basis of the figure, the effect of the whole is to impress us with a conception of the matchless majesty of God.

ADAM CLARKE

3. *Who shall ascend?* Who is sufficiently holy to wait in His temple? Who is fit to minister in the holy place?

4. *He that hath clean hands.* He whose conscience is irreproachable.

6. *This is the generation.* This is the description of people who are such as God can approve of, and delight in.

That seek thy face, O Jacob. It is most certain that *Elohey,* "O God," has been lost out of the Hebrew text in most MSS., but it is preserved in two of Kennicott's MSS., and also in the Syriac, Vulgate, Septuagint, Aethiopic, Arabic, and Anglo-Saxon. "Who seek thy face, O God of Jacob."

5. *He shall receive the blessing.* Perhaps alluding to Obed-edom, at whose house the ark had been lodged, and on whom God had poured out especial blessings. *And righteousness.* Mercy; every kind of necessary good.

7. *Lift up your heads, O ye gates.* The address of those who preceded the ark, the gates being addressed instead of the keepers of the gates.

8. *Who is this King of glory?* This is the answer of those who are within. Who is this glorious King, for whom ye demand entrance? To which they reply: *The Lord strong and mighty, the Lord mighty in battle.* It is Jehovah, who is come to set up His abode in His imperial city—He who has conquered His enemies and brought salvation to Israel. To make the matter still more solemn, and give those without an opportunity of describing more particularly this glorious Personage, those within hesitate to obey the first summons; and then it is repeated, v. 9—*Lift up your heads, O ye gates; even lift them up, ye everlasting doors; and the King of glory shall come in.* To which a more particular question is proposed: *Who is [He], this King of glory?* To which an answer is given that admits of no reply. *The Lord of hosts*—He who is coming with innumerable armies.

MATTHEW HENRY

fies them. *Behold, he stands at the door and knocks,* Rev. iii. 20. It is required that the gates and doors of the heart be opened to him, not only as admission is given to a guest, but as possession is delivered to the rightful owner. This is the gospel call and demand, that we let Jesus Christ, the King of glory, come into our souls, and welcome him with hosannas, *Blessed is he that cometh.*

PSALM 25

A psalm of David.

Verses 1–7

David's professions of desire towards God and dependence on him. He often begins his psalms with such professions, not to move God, but to move himself.

I. He professes his desire towards God: *Unto thee, O Lord! do I lift up my soul, v.* 1. In worshipping God we must lift up our souls to him. Prayer is the ascent of the soul to God. *Sursum corda—Up with your hearts,* was anciently used as a call to devotion.

II. He professes his dependence upon God (*v.* 2): *O my God! I trust in thee.* His conscience witnessed for him that he had no confidence in himself nor in any creature. He pleases himself with this profession of faith in God. "*Let me not be ashamed* of my confidence in thee; let me not be shaken from it by any prevailing fears, and let me not be, in the issue, disappointed of what I depend upon thee for; but, Lord, *keep what I have committed unto thee.*" *Let those be ashamed that transgress without cause,* or *vainly,* as the word is. The weaker the temptation is by which men are drawn to sin the stronger the corruption is by which they are driven to it. Those are the worst transgressors that sin for sinning-sake.

III. He begs direction from God in the way of his duty, *v.* 4, 5. Once and again he here prays to God to teach him. "*Teach me,* not fine words or fine notions, but *thy ways, thy paths, thy truth,* the ways in which thou walkest towards me, which are *all mercy and truth* (*v.* 10), and the ways in which thou wouldst have me to walk towards thee. *Show me thy way,* and so *teach me.*" In doubtful cases we should pray earnestly that God would make it plain to us what he would have us to do. "*Lead me,* and so teach me." *Thou art the God of my salvation.* If God save us, he will teach us and lead us. He that gives salvation will give instruction. *On thee do I wait all the day.* Whence should a servant expect direction but from his own master, on whom he waits all the day?

IV. He appeals to God's infinite mercy, not pretending to any merit of his own (*v.* 6): "*Remember, O Lord! thy tender mercies,* and, for the sake of those mercies, lead me, and teach me; for they *have been ever of old.*"

V. He is earnest for the pardon of his sins (*v.* 7): "*O remember not the sins of my youth.* Lord, remember thy mercies (*v.* 6), which speak for me, and not my sins, which speak against me." When God pardons sin he is said to *remember it no more,* which denotes a plenary remission; he forgives and forgets.

Verses 8–14

God's promises are here mixed with David's prayers. Many petitions there were in the former part of the psalm, and many we shall find in the latter; and here, in the middle of the psalm, he meditates upon the promises. The promises of God are not only the best foundation of prayer, telling us what to pray for, but they are a present answer to prayer. Let the prayer be made according to the promise, and then the promise may be read as a return to the prayer; and we are to believe the prayer is heard because the promise will be performed. But, in the midst of the promises, we find one petition which seems to come in somewhat abruptly, and should have followed upon *v.* 7. It is (*v.* 11), *Pardon my iniquity.* He enforces this petition with a double plea. "*For thy name's sake pardon my iniquity. Pardon my iniquity, for it is great,* and therefore I am undone, if infinite mercy do not interpose for the pardon of it."

Let us now view the great and precious promises which we have in these verses,

I. These promises are sure to those who, though they have been sinners, yet now keep God's word. Though, through the infirmity of the flesh, they sometimes break the command, yet by a sincere repentance when at any time they do amiss, and a constant adherence by faith to God as their God, they keep the covenant and do not break that. Such as fear him (*v.* 12 and again *v.* 14), such as stand in awe of his majesty and worship him with reverence, submit to his authority and obey him

JAMIESON, FAUSSET, BROWN

PSALM 25

Vss. 1-22. The general tone of this Psalm is that of prayer for help from enemies. Distress, however, exciting a sense of sin, humble confession, supplication for pardon, preservation from sin, and divine guidance, are prominent topics.

1. lift up my soul—(Ps. 24:4; 86:4), set my affections (cf. Col. 3:2).

2. not be ashamed—by disappointment of hopes of relief. **3.** The prayer generalized as to all who *wait on God*—i.e., who expect His favor. On the other hand, the disappointment of the perfidious, who, unprovoked, have done evil, is invoked (cf. II Sam. 22:9).

4, 5. On the ground of former favor, he invokes divine guidance, according to God's gracious ways of dealing and faithfulness.

6, 7. Confessing past and present sins, he pleads for mercy, not on palliations of sin, but on God's well-known benevolence.

11. God's perfections of love, mercy, goodness, and truth are manifested (*his name,* cf. Ps. 9:10) in pardoning sin, and the greatness of sin renders pardon more needed.

ADAM CLARKE

Several, both among ancients and moderns, have thought this psalm speaks of the resurrection of our Lord, and is thus to be understood. It is easy to apply it in this way: Jesus has conquered sin, Satan, and death, by dying. He now rises from the dead; and, as a mighty Conqueror, claims an entrance into the realms of glory.

PSALM 25

This psalm seems to refer to the case of the captives in Babylon, who complain of oppression from their enemies, and earnestly beg the help and mercy of God. It is the first of those called acrostic psalms, i.e., psalms each line of which begins with a several letter of the Hebrew alphabet in their common order. Of acrostic psalms there are seven, viz., xxv, xxxiv, xxxvii, cxi, cxii, cxix, and cxlv. The letter *vau* is wanting in the fifth verse, and *koph* in the eighteenth; the letter *resh* being twice inserted, once instead of *koph;* and a whole line added at the end, entirely out of the alphabetical series.

1. *Do I lift up my soul.* His soul was cast down, and by prayer and faith he endeavors to lift it up to God.

2. *I trust in thee.* I depend upon Thy infinite goodness and mercy for my support and salvation, *Let me not be ashamed.* Hide my iniquity, and forgive my guilt.

3. *Let none that wait on thee be ashamed.* Though he had burden enough of his own, he felt for others in similar circumstances, and became an intercessor in their behalf.

4. *Shew me thy ways.* That he may get this *showing, teaching,* and *leading,* he comes to God, as the God of his salvation; and that he may not lose his labor, he waits on Him all the day. Many lose the benefit of their earnest prayers because they do not persevere in them.

ALEXANDER MACLAREN:

This consciousness of sin and cry for pardon lie at the foundation of vigorous practical religion. It seems to me that the differences between different types of Christianity, insipid elegance and fiery earnestness, between coldness and fervor, the difference between a sapless and a living ministry and between a formal and a real Christianity are very largely due to the differences in realizing the fact and the gravity of transgression. The prominence which we give to that in our thoughts will largely determine our notions of ourselves, and of Christ's work, and to a great extent settle what we think Christianity is for and what in itself it is. If a man has no deep consciousness of sin, he will be satisfied with a very superficial kind of religion. "Every man his own redeemer" will be his motto. And not knowing the necessity for a Savior, he will not recognize that Christianity is fundamentally and before anything else, a system of redemption.—*Expositions of Holy Scripture*

MATTHEW HENRY

with cheerfulness.

II. Two things which ratify and confirm all the promises:—1. The perfections of God's nature. We value the promise by the character of him that makes it. We may therefore depend upon God's promises; for *good and upright is the Lord*, and therefore he will be as good as his word. 2. The agreeableness of all he says and does with the perfections of his nature (*v.* 10): *All the paths of the Lord* (that is, all his promises and all his providences) *are mercy and truth*; they are, like himself, good and upright.

III. What these promises are.

1. That God will instruct and direct them in the way of their duty. This is most insisted upon, because it is an answer to David's prayers (*v.* 4, 5), *Show me thy ways and lead me*. We should fix our thoughts on those promises which suit our present case. (1) He will *teach sinners in the way*, because they are sinners, and therefore need teaching. When they desire teaching, then he will teach them the way of reconciliation to God, the way to a well-grounded peace of conscience, and the way to eternal life. (2) *The meek will he guide*, that is, those that are humble, distrustful of themselves, desirous to be taught, and honestly resolved to follow the divine guidance. These he will guide *in judgment*, that is, by the rule of the written word. (3) *Him that feareth the Lord he will teach in the way that he shall choose*, either in the way that God shall choose or that the good man shall choose. It comes all to one, for he that fears the Lord chooses the things that please him.

2. That God will make them easy (*v.* 13): *His soul shall dwell at ease, shall lodge in goodness*, marg. Those that devote themselves to the fear of God, and give up themselves to be taught of God, will be easy.

3. That he will give to them and theirs as much of this world as is good for them: *His seed shall inherit the earth*. Their children shall fare the better for their prayers when they are gone.

4. That God will admit them into the secret of communion with himself (*v.* 14): *The secret of the Lord is with those that fear him*. They understand his word; for, *if any man do his will, he shall know of the doctrine whether it be of God*, John vii. 17.

Verses 15–22

David, encouraged by the promises he had been meditating upon, concludes the psalm, as he began, with professions of dependence upon God and desires towards him.

I. He lays open before God the calamitous condition he was in. His feet were in the net, held fast and entangled, so that he could not extricate himself out of his difficulties, *v.* 15. He was *desolate and afflicted*, *v.* 16. David calls himself *desolate and solitary* because he depended not upon his servants and soldiers, but relied as entirely upon God as if he had no prospect at all of help and succour from any creature. *The troubles of his heart were enlarged* (*v.* 17), he grew more and more melancholy and troubled in mind.

II. He expresses the dependence he had upon God in these distresses (*v.* 15): *My eyes are ever towards the Lord*. Those that have their eye ever towards God shall not have their feet long in the net. He repeats his profession of dependence upon God (*v.* 20)—*Let me not be ashamed, for I put my trust in thee;* and of expectation from him—*I wait on thee*, *v.* 21.

III. He prays earnestly to God for relief and succour, *Forgive all my sins*, Lord, *forgive all, take away all iniquity*. It is observable that, as to his affliction, he asks for no more than God's regard to it: "*Look upon my affliction and my pain*, and do with it as thou pleasest." But, as to his sin, he asks for no less than a full pardon: *Forgive all my sins. Turn thou unto me*. His condition was troubled, and, in reference to that, he prays, "*O bring thou me out of my distresses*. I see no way of deliverance open; but thou canst either find one or make one." He pleads God's mercy: *Have mercy upon me*. Men of the greatest merits would be undone if they had not to do with a God of infinite mercies. He pleads his own misery, which made him the proper object of divine mercy. He pleads the iniquity of his enemies: "Lord, consider them, how cruel they are, and deliver me out of their hands." He pleads his own integrity, *v.* 21. Though he had owned himself guilty before God, yet, as to his enemies, he had the testimony of his conscience that he had done them no wrong. Sincerity will be our best security in the worst of times. *Redeem Israel, O God! out of all his troubles*. David's troubles were enlarged, and very earnest he was with God to deliver him, yet he forgets not the distresses of God's church.

JAMIESON, FAUSSET, BROWN

8, 9. upright—acting according to His promise. **sinners**—the general term, limited by the **meek**—who are *penitent*. **in judgment**—rightly. **the way**—and **his way**—God's way of providence. **10. paths**—similar sense—His modes of dealing (cf. vs. 4). **mercy and truth**—(Job 14), God's grace in promising and faithfulness in performing.

12, 13. What he asks for himself is the common lot of all the pious. The phrase—**inherit the earth**—(cf. Matt. 5:5), alluding to the promise of Canaan, expresses all the blessings included in that promise, temporal as well as spiritual. **14.** The reason of the blessing explained—the pious enjoy communion with God (cf. Prov. 3:21, 22), and, of course, learn His gracious terms of pardon.

15. His trust in God is fixed. **net**—is frequently used as a figure for dangers by enemies (Ps. 9:15; 10:9). **16-19.** A series of earnest appeals for aid because God had seemed to desert him (cf. Ps. 13:1; 17:13, etc.), his sins oppressed him, his enemies had enlarged his troubles and were multiplied, increasing in hate and violence (Ps. 9:8; 18:48).

20. keep my soul—(Ps. 16:1). **put my trust**—flee for refuge (Ps. 2:12).

21. In conscious innocence of the faults charged by his enemies, he confidently commits his cause to God. Some refer—**integrity . . .**—to God, meaning His covenant faithfulness. This sense, though good, is an unusual application of the terms. **22.** Extend these blessings to all Thy people in all their distresses.

ADAM CLARKE

9. *The meek will he guide. Anavim,* the "poor," the "distressed."

10. *All the paths of the Lord. Orchoth* signifies the "tracks" or "ruts" made by the wheels of wagons by often passing over the same ground. Mercy and truth are the paths in which God constantly walks in reference to the children of men.

13. *His soul shall dwell at ease.* "Shall lodge in goodness"; this is the marginal reading in our version, and is preferable to that in the text. *His seed shall inherit.* His posterity shall be sent up to God by their pious fathers, and God has registered these prayers in their behalf.

16. *Turn thee unto me.* Probably the prayer of the poor captives in Babylon, which is continued through this and the remaining verses.

17. *The troubles of my heart are enlarged.* The evils of our captive state, instead of lessening, seem to multiply, and each to be extended.

21. *Let integrity and uprightness.* I wish to have a perfect heart and an upright life.

MATTHEW HENRY

PSALM 26

A psalm of David.

Verses 1–5

It is probable that David penned this psalm when he was persecuted by Saul, who represented him as a very bad man, and falsely accused him of many crimes. Herein he was a type of Christ, who was made a reproach of men. Now see what David does in this case.

I. He appeals to God's righteous sentence (*v.* 1): "*Judge me, O God!* be thou Judge between me and my accusers." He cannot justify himself against the charge of sin; he owns his iniquity is great and he is undone if God, in his infinite mercy, do not forgive him; but he can justify himself against the charge of hypocrisy. It is a comfort to all who are sincere in religion that God himself is a witness to their sincerity.

II. He submits to his unerring search (*v.* 2): *Examine me, O Lord! and prove me*, as gold is proved, whether it be standard. So sincere was he in his devotion to his God that he wished he had a window in his bosom, that whoever would might look into his heart.

III. He solemnly protests his sincerity (*v.* 1): "*I have walked in my integrity;* my conversation has agreed with my profession, and one part of it has been of a piece with another." Proofs of his integrity encouraged him to trust in the Lord as his righteous Judge, *therefore I shall not slide.* Those that are sincere in religion may trust in God that they shall not slide, that is, that they shall not apostatize from their religion.

1. He had a constant regard to God and to his grace, *v.* 3. *Thy loving-kindness is before my eyes.* He governed himself by the word of God as his rule: "*I have walked in thy truth*, that is, according to thy law, for thy law is truth."

2. He had no fellowship with the unfruitful works of darkness, nor with the workers of those works, *v.* 4, 5. Great care to avoid bad company is both a good evidence of our integrity and a good means to preserve us in it. "*I have not sat with them*, and I *will not go in with them.*" The company of dissemblers is as dangerous company as any, and as much to be shunned. Evil-doers pretend friendship to those whom they would decoy into their snares, but they dissemble. *When they speak fair, believe them not.* Though sometimes he could not avoid being in the company of bad people, yet he would not *go in with them*, he would not choose such for his companions. I have hated *ecclesiam malignantium —the church of the malignant;* so the Latin reads it. As good men, in concert, make one another better, and are enabled to do so much the more good, so bad men, in combination, make one another worse, and do so much the more mischief.

Verses 6–12

I. David mentions, as a further evidence of his integrity, the sincere affection he had to the ordinances of God.

1. He was very careful and conscientious in his preparation for holy ordinances: *I will wash my hands in innocency.* In our preparations for solemn ordinances we must not only be able to clear ourselves from the charge of hypocrisy, and to protest our innocency of that (which was signified by *washing the hands*, Deut. xxi. 6), but we must take pains to cleanse ourselves by renewing our repentance.

2. He was very diligent and serious in his attendance upon them: *I will compass thy altar*, alluding to the custom of the priests, who, while the sacrifice was in offering, walked round the altar, and probably the offerers likewise did so at some distance, denoting a diligent regard to what was done and a dutiful attendance in the service.

3. In all his attendance on God's ordinances he aimed at the glory of God.

4. He did this with delight. "*Lord*, thou knowest how dearly *I have loved the habitation of thy house* (*v.* 8), the tabernacle where thou art pleased to manifest thy residence among thy people and receive their homage, *the place where thy honour dwells.*"

II. David, having given proofs of his integrity, earnestly prays that he might not fall under the doom of the wicked (*v.* 9, 10). *Gather not my soul with sinners.* "They are *bloody men*, that thirst after blood and lie under a great deal of the guilt of blood. They do mischief, and mischief is always in their hands. Though they get by their wickedness (for *their right hand is full of bribes* which they have taken to pervert justice), yet that will make their case never the better; for *what is a man profited if he gain the world and lose his soul?*" He dreads having his lot with them.

III. David, with a holy humble confidence, commits

JAMIESON, FAUSSET, BROWN

PSALM 26

Vss. 1-12. After appealing to God's judgment on his avowed integrity and innocence of the charges laid by his enemies, the Psalmist professes delight in God's worship, and prays for exemption from the fate of the wicked, expressing assurance of God's favor.

1. Judge—decide on my case—the appeal of innocence.

2. He asks the most careful scrutiny of his affections and thoughts (Ps. 7:9), or motives.

in mine integrity—freedom from blemish (cf. Ps. 25:21). His confidence of perseverance results from trust in God's sustaining grace.

3. As often, the ground of prayer for present help is former favor.

4-8. As exemplified by the fruits of divine grace, presented in his life, especially in his avoiding the wicked and his purposes of cleaving to God's worship.

wash mine hands—expressive symbol of freedom from sinful acts (cf. Matt. 27:24).

the habitation of thy house—where Thy house rests—as the tabernacle was not yet permanently fixed. **honour dwelleth**—conveys an allusion to the Holy of Holies.

9. Gather not . . .—Bring me not to death. **bloody men**—(cf. Ps. 5:6). **10.** Their whole conduct is that of violence and fraud.

ADAM CLARKE

PSALM 26

This psalm, and the two following, are supposed by Calmet to be all parts of one ode, and to relate to the time of the Captivity, containing the prayers, supplications, complaints, and resolutions of the Israelites in Babylon.

1. *Judge me, O Lord.* There are so many strong assertions in this psalm concerning the innocence and uprightness of its author that many suppose he wrote it to vindicate himself from some severe reflections on his conduct or accusations relative to plots, conspiracies, etc. This seems to render the opinion probable that attributes it to David during his exile, when all manner of false accusations were brought against him at the court of Saul.

4. *I have not sat with vain persons.* "Men of lies," dissemblers, backbiters. *Neither will I go in with dissemblers.* The "hidden ones," the dark designers, the secret plotters and conspirators in the state.

9. *Gather not my soul with sinners.* Let not my eternal lot be cast with them!

10. *Their right hand is full of bribes.* He speaks of persons in office who took bribes to pervert judgment and justice.

MATTHEW HENRY

himself to the grace of God, *v.* 11, 12. "*As for me*, whatever others do, *I will walk in my integrity*." He prays for the divine grace both to enable him to do so and to give him the comfort of it: "*Redeem me* out of the hands of my enemies, *and be merciful to me*, living and dying." He pleases himself with his steadiness: "*My foot stands in an even place*, where I shall not stumble and whence I shall not fall." He promises himself that though he was now perhaps banished from public ordinances, yet he should again have an opportunity of blessing God in the congregation of his people.

PSALM 27

Verses 1–6

I. With what a lively faith David triumphs in God, glories in his holy name. 1. *The Lord is my light*. David's subjects called him *the light of Israel*, 2 Sam. xxi. 17. And he was indeed a burning and a shining light: but he owns that he shone, as the moon does, with a borrowed light; what light God darted upon him reflected upon them: *The Lord is my light*. 2. "He is *my salvation*, in whom I am safe and by whom I shall be saved." 3. "He is *the strength of my life*, not only the protector of my exposed life, but the strength of my frail weak life."

II. With what an undaunted courage he triumphs over his enemies; no fortitude like that of faith. If God be for him, who can be against him? *Whom shall I fear? Of whom shall I be afraid?* His enemies came upon him, *to eat up his flesh*, aiming at no less and assured of that, but they fell; not, "He smote them and they fell," but, "They *stumbled and fell*"; they were so confounded and weakened that they could not go on with their enterprise. "Though they be numerous, *a host* of them, though they *encamp against me*, an army against one man, yet *my heart shall not fear*." Hosts cannot hurt us if the Lord of hosts protect us. Nay, in this assurance that God is for me *I will be confident*. "*He shall hide me*, not in the strongholds of En-gedi (1 Sam. xxiii. 29), but *in the secret of his tabernacle. Now shall my head be lifted up above my enemies*, not only so as that they cannot reach it with their darts, but so as that I shall be exalted to bear rule over them."

III. With what a gracious earnestness he prays for a constant communion with God in holy ordinances, *v.* 4.

1. What it is he desires—*to dwell in the house of the Lord*. In the courts of God's house the priests had their lodgings, and David wished he had been one of them. All God's children desire to dwell in God's house; where should they dwell else? Do we hope that praising God will be the blessedness of our eternity? Surely then we ought to make it the business of our time.

2. How earnestly he covets this: "This is the *one thing I have desired of the Lord* and which I will seek after." If he were to ask but one thing of God, this should be it; for this he had at heart more than anything. He would dwell in God's house *to behold the beauty of the Lord and to enquire in his temple*. He knew something of the beauty of the Lord; his holiness is his beauty (cx. 3); his goodness is his beauty, Zech. ix. 17. The harmony of all his attributes is the beauty of his nature. In God's house troubles would not find him. Joash, one of David's seed, was hidden in the house of the Lord six years, and there not only preserved from the sword, but reserved to the crown, 2 Kings xi. 3. The temple was thought a safe place for Nehemiah to abscond in, Neh. vi. 10. The safety of believers however is not in the walls of the temple, but in the God of the temple and their comfort in communion with him.

Verses 7–14

David in these verses expresses,

I. His desire towards God, in many petitions. If he cannot now go up to the house of the Lord, yet, wherever he is, he can find a way to the throne of grace by prayer. "*Hear, O Lord, when I cry*, not only with my heart, but, as one in earnest, *with my voice* too." If we pray and believe, God will graciously hear and answer. David fastens, in his thoughts, upon the call God had given him to the throne of his grace. *My heart said unto thee* (so it begins in the original) or *of* thee, *Seek you my face*; he first revolved that, and preached that over again to himself (and that is the best preaching; it is hearing twice what God speaks once)—*Thou saidst Seek you my face;* and then he returns what he had so meditated upon, in this pious resolution, *Thy face, Lord, will I seek*. The opening of his hand will satisfy the desire of living things (cxlv. 16), but it is only the

JAMIESON, FAUSSET, BROWN

11, 12. But . . .—He contrasts his character and destiny with that of the wicked (cf. vss. 1, 2).

even place—free from occasions of stumbling—safety in his course is denoted. Hence he will render to God his praise publicly.

PSALM 27

Vss. 1-14. With a general strain of confidence, hope, and joy, especially in God's worship, in the midst of dangers, the Psalmist introduces prayer for divine help and guidance.

1. light—is a common figure for comfort.

strength—or, stronghold—affording security against all violence. The interrogations give greater vividness to the negation implied.

2. eat . . . my flesh—(Job 19:22; Ps. 14:4). The allusion to wild beasts illustrates their rapacity. **they stumbled**—"they" is emphatic; *not I*, but *they* were destroyed. **3.** In the greatest dangers. **in this**—i.e., then, in such extremity.

4, 5. The secret of his confidence is his delight in communion with God (Ps. 16:11; 23:6), beholding the harmony of His perfections, and seeking His favor in His temple or palace; a term applicable to the tabernacle (cf. Ps. 5:7). There he is safe (Ps. 31:21; 61:5). The figure is changed in the last clause, but the sentiment is the same. **6. head be lifted up**—I shall be placed beyond the reach of my enemies. Hence he avows his purpose of rendering joyful thank offerings.

7. Still pressing need extorts prayer for help. **cry with my voice**—denotes earnestness. Other things equal, Christians in earnest pray audibly, even in secret. **8.** The meaning is clear, though the construction in a literal translation is obscure. The *English Version* supplies the implied clause. To *seek God's face* is to seek His favor (Ps. 105:4).

ADAM CLARKE

PSALM 27

In the Hebrew and Chaldee this psalm has no other title than simply *ledavid*. "To or for David."

5. *He shall hide me in his pavilion*. "In his tabernacle." I would make His temple my residence. *He shall set me up upon a rock*. He shall so *strengthen* and *establish* me that my enemies shall not be able to prevail against me.

6. *Now shall mine head be lifted up*. We shall most assuredly be redeemed from this captivity, and restored to our own land, and to the worship of our God in His own temple. There shall we offer *sacrifices of joy;* we *will sing praises unto the Lord*, and acknowledge that it is by His might and mercy alone that we have been delivered.

7. *Hear, O Lord, when I cry*. This is the utmost that any man of common sense can expect—to be heard when he cries. But there are multitudes who suppose God will bless them whether they cry or not; and there are others, and not a few, who, although they listlessly pray and *cry* not, yet imagine God must and will hear them! God will answer them that pray and cry; those who do not are most likely to be without the blessings which they so much need.

8. *When thou saidst, Seek ye my face*. I believe the true rendering to be as follows: "Unto thee, my heart, He hath said, Seek ye My face. Thy face, O Jehovah, I will seek. O my heart, God hath commanded thee to seek His face." Then, "His face I will seek."

MATTHEW HENRY

shining of his face that will satisfy the desire of a living soul, iv. 6, 7. He owns he had deserved God's displeasure, but begs that, however God might correct him, he would not cast him away from his presence. "*O leave me not, neither forsake me;* withdraw not the operations of thy power from me, for then I am helpless; withdraw not the tokens of thy goodwill to me, for then I am comfortless." "*Teach me thy way, O Lord!* give me to understand the meaning of thy providences towards me that I may not mistake it, but may walk rightly, and that I may not do it with hesitation, but may walk surely." He begs to be guided *in a plain path, because of his enemies,* or (as the margin reads it) his *observers.* "*Deliver me not over to the will of my enemies.* Lord, let them not gain their point, for it aims at my life, and I have no fence against them, but thy power over their consciences; for *false witnesses have risen up against me,* that aim further than to take away my reputation, for they *breathe out cruelty*; it is the blood they thirst after."

II. He expresses his dependence upon God: "*When my father and my mother forsake me,* the nearest and dearest friends I have in the world, from whom I may expect most relief and with most reason, when they die, or are at a distance from me, or are disabled to help me in the time of need, or are unkind to me or unmindful of me, and will not help me, when I am as helpless as ever poor orphan was that was left fatherless and motherless, then I know *the Lord will take me up.*" He believed he should *see the goodness of the Lord in the land of the living*; and, if he had not done so, he would *have fainted* under his afflictions. Those that walk by faith in the goodness of the Lord shall in due time walk in the sight of that goodness. It is his comfort, not so much that he shall see the land of the living as that he shall see the goodness of God in it; for that is the comfort of all creature-comforts to a gracious soul. In heaven is that land that may truly be called *the land of the living.* This earth is the land of the dying. There is nothing like the believing hope of eternal life to keep us from fainting under all the calamities of this present time. In the meantime he says to himself, or to his friends, *He shall strengthen thy heart,* shall sustain the spirit. In that strength, *Wait on the Lord* by faith, and prayer, and a humble resignation to his will; *wait, I say, on the Lord*; whatever you do, grow not remiss in your attendance upon God. Those that wait upon the Lord have reason to be of good courage.

JAMIESON, FAUSSET, BROWN

9. Hide not . . .—(Ps. 4:6; 22:24). Against rejection he pleads former mercy and love. **10.** In the extremity of earthly destitution (Ps. 31:11; 38:11), God provides (cf. Matt. 25:35). **11. thy way**—of providence.

a plain path—(Ps. 26:12). **enemies**—lit., "watchers for my fall" (Ps. 5:8). **12. will**—lit., "soul," "desire" (Ps. 35:25). **enemies**—lit., "oppressors." Falsehood aids cruelty against him.

breathe out—as being filled with it (Acts 9:1).

13. The strong emotion is indicated by the incomplete sentence, for which the *English Version* supplies a proper clause; or, omitting that, and rendering, *yet I believed . . .*, the contrast of his faith and his danger is expressed. **to see**—is to experience (Ps. 22:17).

14. Wait . . .—in confident expectation. The last clause is, lit., "and wait . . . ," as if expecting new measures of help.

ADAM CLARKE

10. *When my father and my mother forsake me.* Or, more literally, "For my father and my mother have forsaken me; but the Lord hath gathered me up."

13. "*I had fainted,* unless I had believed." The words in italics are supplied by our translators; but, far from being necessary, they injure the sense. Throw out the words "I had fainted," and leave a break after the verse, and the elegant figure of the Psalmist will be preserved: "Unless I had believed to see the goodness of the Lord in the land of the living"—what! what, alas! should have become of me!

MATTHEW HENRY

PSALM 28

A psalm of David.

Verses 1–5

David is very earnest in prayer.

I. He prays that God would graciously hear and answer him, now that, in his distress, he called upon him, *v.* 1, 2. "*O Lord, my rock* (denoting his belief of God's power), *to thee will I cry,* as one in earnest, being ready to sink, unless thou come in with seasonable succour. *If thou be silent to me,* and I have not the tokens of thy favour, I am *like those that go down into the pit* (that is, I am a dead man, lost and undone); if God be not my friend my hope and my help will have perished." *I lift up my hands towards thy holy oracle,* thence to receive an answer of peace. The most holy place within the veil is here, as elsewhere, called the *oracle*; there the ark and the mercy-seat were, there God was said to *dwell between the cherubim,* and thence he spoke to his people, Num. vii. 89. That was a type of Christ, and it is to him that we must lift up our eyes and hands, for through him all good comes from God to us.

II. He deprecates the doom of wicked people. "Lord, I attend thy holy oracle, *draw me not away* from that *with the wicked, and with the workers of iniquity,*" *v.* 3. "Lord, never leave me to myself, to use such arts of deceit and treachery for my safety as they use for my ruin."

III. He imprecates the just judgments of God upon the workers of iniquity (*v.* 4): *Give them according to their deeds.* This is not the language of passion or revenge, nor is it inconsistent with the duty of praying for our enemies. But he would show how far he was from complying with the workers of iniquity. If what has been done amiss be not undone by repentance, there will certainly come a reckoning day, when God will render to every man who persists in his evil deeds according to them. It is a prophecy particularly of the destruction of destroyers: "*They speak peace to their neighbours, but mischief is in their hearts;* Lord, *give them according to their deeds.*"

IV. He foretells their destruction for their contempt of God and his hand (*v.* 5): "*Because they regard*

JAMIESON, FAUSSET, BROWN

PSALM 28

Vss. 1-9. An earnest cry for divine aid against his enemies, as being also those of God, is followed by the Psalmist's praise in assurance of a favorable answer, and a prayer for all God's people.

1. my rock—(Ps. 18:2, 31). **be not silent to me**—lit., "from me," deaf or inattentive. **become like them . . .**—share their fate. **go down into the pit**—or, grave (Ps. 30:3).

2. lift up my hands—a gesture of prayer (Ps. 63:4; 141:2). **oracle**—place of *speaking* (Exod. 25:22; Num. 7:89), where God answered His people (cf. Ps. 5:7).

3. Draw me not . . .—implies punishment as well as death (cf. Ps. 26:9). Hypocrisy is the special *wickedness* mentioned.

4. The imprecation is justified in vs. 5. The force of the passage is greatly enhanced by the accumulation of terms describing their sin. **endeavours**—points out their deliberate sinfulness.

ADAM CLARKE

PSALM 28

This psalm is of the same complexion with the two preceding, and belongs most probably to the times of the Captivity, though some have preferred it to David in his persecutions. In the first five verses the author prays for support against his enemies, who appear to have acted treacherously against him. In the sixth and seventh he is supposed to have gained the victory, and returns with songs of triumph. The eighth is a chorus of the people sung to their conquering king. The ninth is the prayer of the king for his people.

1. *O Lord my rock. Tsuri* not only means *my rock,* but "my fountain," and the origin of all the good I possess.

4. *Give them.* Is the same as "Thou wilt give them," a prophetic declaration of what their lot will be.

MATTHEW HENRY

not the works of the Lord and the operations of his hands, by which he manifests himself and speaks to the children of men, *he will destroy them* in this world and in the other, *and not build them up."* Why do men question the being or attributes of God, but because they do not duly regard his handiworks, which declare his glory, and in which the invisible things of him are clearly seen?

Verses 6-9

I. David gives God thanks. It was in faith that David prayed (*v.* 2), *Hear the voice of my supplications;* and by the same faith he gives thanks (*v.* 6) that *God has heard the voice of his supplications.* Those that pray in faith may rejoice in hope. What we win by prayer we must wear with praise.

II. He encourages himself to hope in God for the perfecting of everything that concerned him. This is the method of attaining peace: let us begin with praise that it is attainable. His experience of the benefit of that dependence: "*My heart trusted in him,* and in his power and promise; and it has not been in vain to do so, for *I am helped,* I have been often helped; not only God has given to me, in his due time, the help I trusted to him for, but my very trusting in him has helped me, in the mean time, and kept me from fainting," xxvii. 13. *Therefore my heart greatly rejoices.*

III. He pleases himself with the interest which all good people, through Christ, have in God (*v.* 8): "*The Lord is their strength;* not mine only, but the strength of every believer." This is our communion with all saints, that God is their strength and ours, Christ their Lord and ours, 1 Cor. i. 2.

IV. He concludes with a short but comprehensive prayer for the church of God, *v.* 9. He prays for Israel, not as his people ("save my people, and bless my inheritance"), though they were so, but, "*thine.*" *The Lord's portion is his people.* That which he begs of God for them is, 1. That he would save them from their enemies. 2. That he would bless them with all good. 3. That he would *feed them.* "Direct their counsels and actions aright, and overrule their affairs for good. Feed them, and rule them; set pastors, set rulers, over them, that shall do their office with wisdom and understanding." 4. That he would *lift them up for ever,* lift them up out of their troubles and distresses, and do this, not only for those of that age, but for his people in every age to come, even to the end.

JAMIESON, FAUSSET, BROWN

5. Disregard of God's judgments brings a righteous punishment. **destroy . . . build . . . up**—The positive strengthened by the negative form.

6. supplications—or, cries for mercy.

7. The repetition of heart denotes his sincerity.

8. The distinction made between the people. **their strength**—and the **anointed**—may indicate Absalom's rebellion as the occasion.

9. The special prayer for the people sustains this view. **feed them**—as a shepherd (Ps. 23:1, etc.).

ADAM CLARKE

8. *The Lord is their strength.* Instead of *lamo,* "to them," eight MSS. of Kennicott and De Rossi have *leammo,* "to His people"; and this reading is confirmed by the Septuagint, Syriac, Vulgate, Aethiopic, Arabic, and Anglo-Saxon. This makes the passage more precise and intelligible; and of the truth of the reading there can be no reasonable doubt. *The Lord is* the *strength* of His people, and *the saving strength of his anointed.* Both king and people are protected, upheld, and saved by Him.

9. *Save thy people.* Continue to preserve them from all their enemies, from idolatry, and from sin of every kind. *Feed them. Raah* signifies both to "feed" and to "govern." Feed them, as a shepherd does his flock; rule them, as a father does his children.

MATTHEW HENRY

PSALM 29

A psalm of David.

Verses 1-11

I. A demand of the homage of the great men of the earth to be paid to the great God. Every clap of thunder David interpreted as a call to himself and other princes to give glory to the great God. "*O you mighty* (*v.* 1), you sons of the mighty, who have power, *give unto the Lord,* and again, and a third time, *Give unto the Lord* the recognition of his glory, and of his dominion over us. *Give unto the Lord* your ownselves, in the first place, and then your services. *Give unto the Lord glory and strength;* acknowledge his glory and strength, and whatever glory or strength he has entrusted you with offer it to him, to be used for his honour, in his service. Give him your crowns; let them be laid at his feet; give him your sceptres, your swords, your keys; put all into his hand, that you, in the use of them, may be to him for a name and a praise." What is here said to the mighty is said to all: *Worship God;* it is the sum and substance of the everlasting gospel, Rev. xiv. 6, 7. Religious worship is *giving to the Lord the glory due to his name, v.* 2. *Worship the Lord in the beauty of holiness.* Adore him, not only as infinitely awful and therefore to be feared above all, but as infinitely amiable and therefore to be loved and delighted in above all; especially we must have an eye to the beauty of his holiness. There is a beauty in holiness, and it is that which puts an acceptable beauty upon all the acts of worship.

II. Good reason given for this demand.

1. His sufficiency in himself, intimated in his name *Jehovah—I am that I am,* which is repeated here no fewer than eighteen times in this short psalm, twice in every verse but three, and once in two of those three.

2. His sovereignty over all things. The psalmist here sets forth God's dominion,

(1) In the kingdom of nature. In the wonderful effects of natural causes, and the operations of the powers of nature. It is the God of glory that thunders, *v.* 3. Every one that hears the thunder will own that *the voice of the Lord is full of majesty* (xxix. 4). For if his voice be so terrible, what is

JAMIESON, FAUSSET, BROWN

PSALM 29

Vss. 1-11. Trust in God is encouraged by the celebration of His mighty power as illustrated in His dominion over the natural world, in some of its most terrible and wonderful exhibitions.

1. Give—or, ascribe (Deut. 32:3). **mighty**—or, sons of the mighty (Ps. 89:6). Heavenly beings, as angels.

2. name—as (Ps. 5:11; 8:1). **beauty of holiness**—the loveliness of a spiritual worship, of which the perceptible beauty of the sanctuary worship was but a type.

3. The voice of the Lord—audible exhibition of His power in the tempest, of which thunder is a specimen, but not the uniform or sole example. **the waters**—the clouds or vapors (Ps. 18:11; Jer. 10:13). **4. powerful . . . majesty**—lit., "in power, in majesty."

ADAM CLARKE

PSALM 29

In the Hebrew, this is called "A Psalms for David." The psalm was probably written to commemorate the abundant rain which fell in the days of David, after the heavens had been shut up for three years, 2 Sam. xxi. 1-10. The whole psalm is employed in describing the effects produced by a thunderstorm which had lately taken place.

2. *In the beauty of holiness.* "The beautiful garments of holiness."

3. *The voice of the Lord.* Thunder, so called, Exod. ix. 23, 28-29; Job xxxvii. 4; Ps. xviii. 13; Isa. xxx. 30. *Upon many waters.* The clouds, which Moses calls the waters which are above the firmament.

4. *Is powerful.* There is no agent in universal nature so powerful as the electric fluid. *Full of majesty.* No sound in nature is so tremendous and majestic as that of thunder; it is the most fit to represent the voice of God.

MATTHEW HENRY

his arm? *The voice of the Lord*, in the thunder, often *broke the cedars*, even those of Lebanon, the strongest, the stateliest. Some understand it of the violent winds which shook the cedars, and tore off their tops. Earthquakes also shook the ground itself on which the trees grew, and made *Lebanon and Sirion* to dance; *the wilderness of Kadesh* also was in like manner shaken (*v.* 8), the trees by winds, the ground by earthquakes. Dr. Hammond understands it of the conquest of the neighbouring kingdoms that warred with Israel and opposed David, as the Syrians, whose country lay near the forest of Lebanon, the Amorites that bordered on Mount Hermon, and the Moabites and Ammonites that lay about the wilderness of Kadesh. Fires have been kindled by lightnings, accordingly the voice of the Lord, in the thunder, is here said to *divide the flames of fire* (*v.* 7). The terror of thunder makes the hinds to calve sooner, and some think more easily, than otherwise they would. The thunder is said here to *discover the forest*, that is, it so terrifies the wild beasts of the forest that they quit the dens and thickets in which they hid themselves and so are discovered.

(2) In the kingdom of providence, *v.* 10. God is to be praised as the governor of the world of mankind. He *sits upon the flood; he sits King for ever*. The ebbings and flowings of this lower world, and the agitations and revolutions of the affairs in it, give not the least shake to the repose nor to the counsels of the Eternal Mind. *He sits King for ever;* no period can, or shall, be put to his government. The administration of his kingdom is consonant to his counsels from eternity and pursuant to his designs for eternity.

(3) In the kingdom of grace. Here his glory shines most brightly. *In his temples*, where his people attend his discoveries of himself and his mind and attend him with their praises *everyone speaks of his glory. All his works do praise him*, but his saints only do bless him, and speak of his glory in his works, cxlv. 10. *He will give strength to his people*, to fortify them against every evil work and to furnish them for every good work. *He will bless his people with peace* Peace is a blessing of inestimable value, which Goc designs for all his people.

JAMIESON, FAUSSET, BROWN

5, 6. The tall and large cedars, especially of Lebanon, are shivered, utterly broken. The waving of the mountain forests before the wind is expressed by the figure of skipping or leaping.

8. the wilderness—especially Kadesh, south of Judea, is selected as another scene of this display of divine power, as a vast and desolate region impresses the mind, like mountains, with images of grandeur.

7. divideth—lit., "hews off." The lightning, like flakes and splinters hewed from stone or wood, flies through the air.

9. Terror-stricken animals and denuded forests close the illustration. In view of this scene of awful sublimity, God's worshippers respond to the call of vs. 2, and speak or cry, "Glory!" By temple, or palace (God's residence, Ps. 5:7), may here be meant heaven, or the whole frame of nature, as the angels are called on for praise. **10, 11.** Over this terrible raging of the elements God is enthroned, directing and restraining by sovereign power; and hence the comfort of His people. "This awful God is ours, our Father and our Love."

ADAM CLARKE

5. *Breaketh the cedars*. Very tall trees attract the lightning from the clouds, by which they are often torn to pieces.

8. *The wilderness of Kadesh*. This was on the frontiers of Idumea and Paran. There may be a reference to some terrible thunderstorm and earthquake which had occurred in that place.

7. *Divideth the flames of fire*. The forked, zigzag lightning is the cause of thunder; and in a thunderstorm these lightnings are variously dispersed.

9. *Maketh the hinds to calve*. Strikes terror through all the tribes of animals, which sometimes occasions those which are pregnant to cast their young. *Discovereth the forests*. Makes them sometimes evident in the darkest night, by the sudden flash, and often by setting them on fire.

10. *The Lord sitteth upon the flood*. "Jehovah sat upon the deluge." *Sitteth King for ever*. He governs universal nature.

MATTHEW HENRY — PSALM 30

A psalm *and* song *at* the dedication of the house of David.

Verses 1–5

It was the laudable practice of the pious Jews, and, though not expressly appointed, yet allowed and accepted, when they had built a new house, to *dedicate it to God*, Deut. xx. 5. David did so when his house was built, and he took possession of it (2 Sam. v. 11). The houses we dwell in should, at our first entrance upon them, be dedicated to God, as little sanctuaries. We must solemnly commit ourselves, our families, and all our family affairs, to God's guidance and pray for his presence and blessing.

I. David does himself give God thanks for the great deliverances he had wrought for him (*v.* 1): "*I will extol thee, O Lord!* I will exalt thy name, will praise thee as one high and lifted up. *I cried to thee, and thou hast* not only heard me, but *healed me*, healed the distempered body, healed the disturbed and disquieted mind, healed the disordered distracted affairs of the kingdom." He was brought to the last extremity, dropping into the grave, and ready *to go down into the pit*, and yet rescued and kept alive, *v.* 3. A life from the dead ought to be spent in extolling the God of our life.

II. He calls upon others to join with him in praise. *Sing unto the Lord, O you saints of his!* "Let them *give thanks at the remembrance of his holiness*; let them praise his holy name, for holiness is his memorial throughout all generations." It is a good sign that we are in some measure partakers of his holiness if we can heartily rejoice and give thanks at the remembrance of it. We have found his frowns very short. Though we have deserved that they should be everlasting, and that he should be angry with us till he had consumed us, and should never be reconciled, yet *his anger endureth but for a moment*, *v.* 5. If *weeping endureth for a night*, yet, as sure as the light of the morning returns, so sure will joy and comfort return in a short time to the people of God; for the covenant of grace is as firm as the covenant of the day. *In his favour is life*, that is, all good. It is the life of the soul, it is spiritual life, the earnest of life eternal.

Verses 6–12

An account of three several states that David was in successively, and of the workings of his heart towards God in each of those states.

I. "*In my prosperity*, when I was in health of body

JAMIESON, FAUSSET, BROWN — PSALM 30

Vss. 1-12. Lit., "A Psalm-Song"—a composition to be sung with musical instruments, or without them—or, "*Song of the dedication . . . ,*" specifying the particular character of the Psalm. Some suppose that "*of David*" should be connected with the name of the composition, and not with "house"; and refer for the occasion to the selection of a site for the temple (I Chron. 21:26-30; 22:1). But "house" is never used absolutely for the temple, and "dedication" does not well apply to such an occasion. Though the phrase in the *Hebrew*, "dedication of the house of David," is an unusual form, yet it is equally unusual to disconnect the name of the author and the composition. As a "dedication of David's house" (as provided, Deut. 20:25), the scope of the Psalm well corresponds with the state of repose and meditation on his past trials suited to such an occasion (II Sam. 5:11; 7:2). For beginning with a celebration of God's delivering favor, in which he invites others to join, he relates his prayer in distress, and God's gracious and prompt answer.

1. lifted me up—as one is drawn from a well (Ps. 40:2). **2. healed me**—Affliction is often described as disease (Ps. 6:2; 41:4; 107:20), and so relief by healing. **3.** The terms describe extreme danger. **soul**—or, myself. **grave**—lit., "hell," as in Psalm 16:10. **hast kept me . . . pit**—quickened or revived me from the state of dying (cf. Ps. 28:1). **4. remembrance**—the thing remembered or memorial. **holiness**—as the sum of God's perfections (cf. Ps. 22:3), used as *name* (Exod. 3:15; Ps. 135:13).

5. Relatively, the longest experience of divine anger by the pious is momentary. These precious words have consoled millions.

ADAM CLARKE — PSALM 30

This psalm or song is said to have been made or used at the dedication of the house of David, or rather the dedication of a house or temple; for the word *David* refers not to the house, but to *mizmor*, a psalm. But what temple or house could this be? Calmet supposes it to have been made by David on the dedication of the place which he built on the threshing floor of Araunah, after the grievous plague which had so nearly desolated the kingdom, 2 Sam. xxiv. 25; 1 Chron. xxi. 26. All the parts of the psalm agree to this; and they agree to this so well, and to no other hypothesis, that I feel myself justified in modelling the comment on this principle alone.

2. *Thou hast healed me*. Thou hast removed the plague from my people by which they were perishing in thousands before my eyes.

3. *Thou hast brought up my soul from the grave*. I and my people were both about to be cut off, and Thou hast spared us in mercy, and given us a most glorious respite.

4. *Sing unto the Lord, O ye saints of his*. Ye priests, who wait upon Him in His sanctuary, and whose business it is to offer prayers and sacrifices for the people, magnify Him for the mercy He has now showed in staying this most destructive plague. *Give thanks at the remembrance of his holiness*. "Be ye holy," saith the Lord, "for I am holy." He who can give thanks at the remembrance of His holiness is one who loves holiness.

5. *For his anger endureth but a moment*. There is an elegant abruptness in these words in the Hebrew text. This is the literal translation: "For a moment in His anger. Lives in His favor. In the evening weeping may lodge: but in the morning exultation."

MATTHEW HENRY

and God had *given me rest from all my enemies, I said I shall never be moved;* I never had any apprehensions of danger upon any account." He thought his prosperity fixed like a mountain; *Thou, through thy favour, hast made my mountain to stand strong, v.* 7. He does not look upon it as his *heaven* (as worldly people do, who make their prosperity their felicity), only his *mountain;* it is earth still, only raised a little higher than the common level.

II. On a sudden he fell into trouble, and then he prayed to God, and pleaded earnestly for relief and succour. His mountain was shaken and he with it; it proved, when he grew secure, that he was least safe: "*Thou didst hide thy face and I was troubled,* in mind, body, or estate." If God hide his face, a good man is certainly troubled, though no other calamity befall him; when the sun sets night certainly follows, and the moon and all the stars cannot make day. When his mountain was shaken he lifted up his eyes above the hills. Is any troubled? *Let him pray. I cried to thee, O Lord!* It seems God's withdrawings made his prayers the more vehement. *What profit is there in my blood?* implying that he would willingly die if he could thereby do any real service to God or his country (Phil. ii. 17), but he saw not what good could be done by his dying in the bed of sickness, as might be if he had died in the bed of honour. *Shall the dust praise thee?* The sanctified spirit, which returns to God shall be still praising him; but the dust, which returns to the earth, shall not praise him, nor declare his truth.

III. In due time God delivered him out of his troubles and restored him to his former prosperity. His prayers were answered and his *mourning was turned into dancing, v.* 11. But what temper of mind was he in upon this happy change of the face of his affairs? What does he say now? He tells us, *v.* 12. His complaints were turned into praises. *I will give thanks unto thee for ever.* Thus must we learn to accommodate ourselves to the various providences of God.

JAMIESON, FAUSSET, BROWN

6, 7. What particular prosperity is meant we do not know; perhaps his accession to the throne. In his self-complacent elation he was checked by God's *hiding His face* (cf. Ps. 22:24; 27:9).

troubled—confounded with fear (Ps. 2:5). **8-11.** As in Psalm 6:5; 88:10; Isaiah 38:18, the appeal for mercy is based on the destruction of his agency in praising God here, which death would produce.

The terms expressing relief are poetical, and not to be pressed, though "dancing" is the translation of a word which means a *lute,* whose cheerful notes are contrasted with mourning, or (Amos 5:16) wailing. **sackcloth**—was used, even by kings, in distress (I Chron. 21:16; Isa. 37:1) but "gladness," used for a garment, shows the language to be figurative. **12. Though—my—**is supplied before—**glory**—it is better as in Psalm 16:10, to receive it as used for *tongue,* the organ of praise. The ultimate end of God's mercies to us is our praise to Him.

ADAM CLARKE

6. *In my prosperity I said, I shall never be moved.* Peace and prosperity had seduced the heart of David, and led him to suppose that his "mountain"—his dominion—stood so strong that adversity could never affect him. He wished to know the physical and political strength of his kingdom; and, forgetting to depend upon God, he desired Joab to make a census of the people, which God punished in the manner related in 2 Samuel xxiv.

8. *I cried to thee, O Lord.* See his confession and prayer, 2 Sam. xxiv. 17.

11. *Thou hast turned . . . my mourning into dancing.* Rather "into piping." I have not prayed in vain. Though I deserved to be cut off from the land of the living, yet Thou hast spared me, and the remnant of my people. Thou hast taken away *my sackcloth,* the emblem of my distress and misery, *and girded me with gladness,* when Thou didst say to the destroying angel, when he stood over Jerusalem ready to destroy it: "It is enough: stay now thy hand," 2 Sam. xxiv. 16.

MATTHEW HENRY

PSALM 31

To the chief musician. A psalm of David.

Verses 1–8

Faith and prayer must go together.

I. David, in distress, is very earnest with God in prayer for succour and relief. He prays that God, not only in mercy, but in righteousness, would deliver him, as a righteous Judge betwixt him and his unrighteous persecutors. The psalmist prays also that he would deliver him speedily, lest, if the deliverance were long deferred, his faith should fail. "*Be thou my strong rock,* immovable, impregnable, as a fastness framed by nature, and my *house of defence,* a fortress framed by art, and all *to save me. Lord, lead me and guide me*" (*v.* 3). Those that resolve to follow God's direction may in faith pray for it.

II. In this prayer he gives glory to God by a repeated profession of his confidence in him and dependence on him. "*In thee, O Lord! do I put my trust,* and not in myself, or any sufficiency of my own, or in any creature; *let me never be ashamed,* let me not be disappointed of any of that good which thou hast promised me. *Thou art my rock and my fortress,* by thy covenant with me and my believing consent to that covenant; therefore *be my strong rock,*" *v.* 2. If God be our strength, we may hope that he will both put his strength in us and put forth his strength for us. *Into thy hands I commit my spirit* (*v.* 5). David is here to be looked upon as a man in distress and trouble. His great care is about his soul, his spirit, his better part. Our outward afflictions should increase our concern for our souls. Many think that while they are perplexed about their worldly affairs, they may be excused if they neglect their souls; whereas the greater hazard our lives and secular interests lie at the more we are concerned to look to our souls, that we may keep possession of our souls when we can keep possession of nothing else, Luke xxi. 19. He thinks the best he can do for his soul is to commit it into the hand of God. He had prayed (*v.* 4) to be plucked out of the net of outward trouble, but, as not insisting upon that (God's will be done), he immediately lets fall that petition, and commits the spirit, the inward man, into God's hand. "Lord, however it goes with me, as to my body, let it go well with my soul."

III. He disclaimed all confederacy with those that made an arm of flesh their confidence (*v.* 6): *I have hated those that regard lying vanities*—idolaters (so some), who expect aid from false gods, which are vanity and a lie—astrologers, and those that give heed to them, so others.

JAMIESON, FAUSSET, BROWN

PSALM 31

Vss. 1-24. The prayer of a believer in time of deep distress. In the first part, cries for help are mingled with expressions of confidence. Then the detail of griefs engrosses his attention, till, in the assurance of strong but submissive faith, he rises to the language of unmingled joyful trust and exhorts others to like love and confidence towards God.

1. Expresses the general tone of feeling of the Psalm.

2-4. He seeks help in God's righteous government (Ps. 5:8), and begs for an attentive hearing, and speedy and effectual aid. With no other help and no claim of merit, he relies solely on God's regard to His own perfections for a safe guidance and release from the snares of his enemies. On the terms "rock," etc., (cf. Ps. 17:2 18:2, 50; 20:6; 23:3; 25:21).

5, 6. commit my spirit—my life, or myself. Our Saviour used the words on the Cross, not as prophetical, but, as many pious men have done, **as** expressive of His unshaken confidence in God.

The Psalmist rests on God's faithfulness to His promises to His people, and hence avows himself one of them, detesting all who revere objects of idolatry (cf. Deut. 32:21; I Cor. 8:4).

ADAM CLARKE

PSALM 31

2. *Strong rock.* Rocks, rocky places, or caves in the rocks were often strong places in the land of Judea.

4. *Pull me out of the net.* They have hemmed me in on every side, and I cannot escape but by miracle.

5. *Into thine hand I commit my spirit.* "And when Jesus had cried with a loud voice, he said, Father, into thy hands I commend my spirit," Luke xxiii. 46. The rest of the verse was not suitable to the Saviour of the world, and therefore he omits it; but it is suitable to us who have been redeemed by that sacrificial death. Stephen uses nearly the same words, and they were the last that he uttered, Acts vii. 59.

6. *I have hated them.* That is, I have abominated their ways. *I trust in the Lord.* While they trust in vanities, vain things (for an idol is nothing in the world) and in *lying vanities* (for much is promised and nothing given), I trust in Jehovah, who is God all-sufficient, and is my Shepherd, and therefore I shall lack no good thing.

MATTHEW HENRY

IV. He comforted himself with his hope in God, and made himself, not only easy, but cheerful, with it, *v.* 7.

V. He encouraged himself in this hope with the experiences he had had of late. "*Thou hast considered my trouble*, with wisdom to suit relief to it, with condescension and compassion regarding the low estate of thy servant. *Thou hast known my soul in adversities*, with a tender concern and care for it. *Thou hast not shut me up into the hand of the enemy*, but set me at liberty, in *a large room*, where I may shift for my own safety," *v.* 8.

Verses 9–18

In the foregoing verses David had appealed to God's righteousness; here he appeals to his mercy, and pleads the greatness of his own misery, which made his case the proper object of that mercy.

I. The complaint he makes of his trouble and distress (*v.* 9): "*Have mercy upon me, O Lord! for I am in trouble*, and need thy mercy." His troubles had made him a man of sorrows. We may guess by David's complexion, which was ruddy and sanguine, by his genius for music, and by his daring enterprises in his early days, that his natural disposition was both cheerful and firm, that he was apt to be cheerful, and not to lay trouble to his heart; yet here we see he has almost wept out his eyes, and sighed away his breath. His body was affected with the sorrows of his mind (*v.* 10): *My strength fails, my bones are consumed*, and all *because of my iniquity*. His friends were unkind and became shy of him. He was *a fear to his acquaintance*, when they saw him they *fled from him*, *v.* 11. He was forgotten by them, *as a dead man out of mind* (*v.* 12), and looked upon with contempt *as a broken vessel*. Such swallow-friends the world is full of, that are gone in winter. His enemies were unjust in their censures of him. He was a *reproach among all his enemies, but especially among his neighbours*, *v.* 11. Thus he *heard the slander of many*; everyone had a stone to throw at him, because *fear was on every side*.

II. His confidence in God in the midst of these troubles. Everything looked black and dismal round about him, and threatened to drive him to despair: "*But I trusted in thee, O Lord!* (*v.* 14) and was thereby kept from sinking." His enemies robbed him of his reputation among men, but they could not rob him of his comfort in God, because they could not drive him from his confidence in God. "*Thou art my God;* I have chosen thee for mine, and thou hast promised to be mine." *My times are in thy hand.* Join this with the former and it makes the comfort complete. If God have our times in his hand, he can help us; and, if he be our God, he will help us; and then what can discourage us?

III. His petitions to God, in this faith and confidence. Our opportunities are in God's hand (so some read it), and therefore he knows how to choose the best and fittest time for our deliverance, and we must be willing to wait that time. When David had Saul at his mercy in the cave those about him said, "*This is the time* in which God will deliver thee," 1 Sam. xxiv. 4. "No," says David, "the time has not come for my deliverance till it can be wrought without sin; and I will wait for that time; for it is God's time, and that is the best time." Particularly, he prays for the silencing of those that reproach and calumniate the people of God (*v.* 18): *Let lying lips be put to silence, that speak grievous things proudly and contemptuously against the righteous.* One would think they thought it no sin to tell a deliberate lie if it might but serve to expose a good man either to hatred or contempt. *Hear, O our God! for we are despised.*

Verses 19–24

I. The acknowledgment which David makes of God's goodness to his people in general, *v.* 19, 20. God is good to all, but he is, in a special manner, good to Israel. Those who are interested in this goodness are described to be such as fear God and trust in him, as stand in awe of his greatness and rely on his grace. This goodness is said to be *laid up for them* and *wrought for them.* There is enough in bank and enough in hand. This goodness is wrought, in the actual performance of the promise, for those that trust in him. If what is laid up for us in the treasures of the everlasting covenant be not wrought for us, it is our own fault, because we do not believe. God is, in a special manner, the protector of his own people (*v.* 20): *Thou shalt hide them.* The saints are God's hidden ones. See the defence they are under: *Thou shalt hide them in the secret of thy presence, in a pavilion.* God's providence shall keep them safe from the malice of their enemies. He has many ways of sheltering them. When Baruch and Jeremiah were sought for *the Lord hid them*, Jer. xxxvi. 26.

II. The thankful returns which David makes for

JAMIESON, FAUSSET, BROWN

7. hast known my soul . . .—had regard to me in trouble.

8. shut me up . . . enemy—abandon to (I Sam. 23:11). **large room**—place of safety (cf. Ps. 18:19).

9. 10. mine eye . . . denotes extreme weakness (cf. Ps. 6:7). **grief**—mingled sorrow and indignation (Ps. 6:7). **soul and . . . belly**—the whole person. Though the effects ascribed to grief are not mere figures of speech—**spent . . . consumed**—must be taken in the modified sense of *wasted* and *decayed.* **iniquity**—or, suffering by it (cf. on Ps. 40:12). **11. among**—or, lit., "from," or, "by" my enemies. The latter clauses describe the progress of his disgrace to the lowest degree, till, **12.** he is forgotten as one dead, and contemned as a useless broken vessel. **13. For**—introduces further reasons for his prayer, the unjust, deliberate, and murderous purposes of his foes.

14-18. In his profession of trust he includes the terms of the prayer expressing it. **times**—course of life. **deliver . . . hand**—opposed to "shut me up . . ." of vs. 8. **Make . . . shine**—(Cf. Num. 6:25; Ps. 4:6). Deprecating from himself, he imprecates on the wicked God's displeasure, and prays that their virulent persecution of him may be stopped.

19-21. God displays openly His purposed goodness to His people. **the secret of thy presence**—or, *covering* of Thy countenance; the protection He thus affords; cf. Ps. 27:5 for a similar figure; "dwelling" used there for "presence" here. The idea of security further presented by the figure of a tent and a fortified city.

ADAM CLARKE

10. *My life is spent with grief.* My life is a life of suffering and distress, and by grief my days are shortened. *My years with sighing. Anachah.* This is a mere natural expression of grief, the very sounds which proceed from a distressed mind; *an-ach-ah!* common, with little variation, to all nations, and nearly the same in all languages.

13. *I have heard the slander of many.* To this and the two foregoing verses the reader may find several parallels: Jer. xviii. 18 to the end of chap. xix, and first ten verses of chap. xx. This has caused several to suppose that Jeremiah was the author of this psalm.

16. *Make thy face to shine upon thy servant.* Only let me know that Thou art reconciled to and pleased with me, and then, come what will, all must be well. *Save me for thy mercies' sake.* Literally, "Save me in Thy mercy."

20. *Thou shalt hide them in the secret of thy presence.* "With the covering of thy countenance."

21. *In a strong city.* If this psalm was written by David, this must refer to his taking refuge with Achish, king of Gath, who gave him

F. B. MEYER:

"Jehovah preserveth the faithful." What a change ensues in the spirit of our life when we look from men and things to God. Do not look at God through circumstances but at circumstances through God's environing presence, as through a golden haze. Our Lord's times were in the hands of the Father, and he would not move an inch until the clock had struck in heaven (John 2:4; 7:6, 8, 30; 8:20).

As God has laid up coal and ore in the earth, and as explorers in Arctic regions deposit provisions in cairns that those who follow in their steps, or they themselves returning, may be supplied on their march, so unsearchable riches are stored in Christ awaiting our appropriation (2 Pet. 1:3).

What a hiding place is the secret of his presence! Have you ever been inside that royal withdrawing room? God's pavilion is soundproof; the strife of tongues cannot penetrate.—*Bible Commentary*

MATTHEW HENRY

God's goodness to him in particular, *v.* 21, 22. "*He has shown me his marvellous loving-kindness*, beyond what I could have expected." Special preservations call for particular thanksgiving. Within were fears; but God was better to him than his fears, *v.* 22. Though his faith failed, God's promise did not: *Thou heardest the voice of my supplication*, for all this. He mentions his own unbelief as a foil to God's fidelity, serving to make his loving-kindness the more marvellous, the more illustrious.

III. The exhortation and encouragement which he hereupon gives to all the saints, *v.* 23, 24. *O love the Lord! all you his saints.* It is the character of the saints that they do love God; and yet they must be still called upon to love him, to love him more and love him better, and give proofs of their love. He would have them set their hope in God (*v.* 24): "*Be of good courage;* have a good heart on it; whatever difficulties or dangers you may meet with, the God you trust in shall by that trust strengthen your heart."

JAMIESON, FAUSSET, BROWN

22. For I said—lit., "And I said," in an adversative sense. I, thus favored, was despondent. **in my haste**—in my terror. **cut off . . . eyes**—from all the protection of Thy presence.

23, 24. the Lord . . . proud doer—lit., "the Lord is keeping faith"—i.e., with His people, and is repaying, etc. Then let none despair, but take courage; their hopes shall not be in vain.

ADAM CLARKE

Ziklag, a fortified city, to secure himself and followers in. See 1 Sam. xxvii. 6. Perhaps the passage may mean that, under the protection of God, he was as safe as if he had been in a fortified city.

MATTHEW HENRY

PSALM 32

A psalm of David, Maschil.

Verses 1–6

This psalm is entitled *Maschil*, which some take to be only the name of the tune to which it was set and was to be sung. But others think it is significant; our margin reads it, *A psalm of David giving instruction*, and there is nothing in which we have more need of instruction than in the nature of true blessedness—what we must do that we may be happy. In general our happiness consists in the favour of God, and not in the wealth of this world—in spiritual blessings. When it is here said, *Blessed is the man whose iniquity is forgiven*, the meaning is, "This is the ground of his blessedness: this is that fundamental privilege from which all the other ingredients of his blessedness flow."

I. Concerning the nature of the pardon of sin. 1. It is the forgiving of transgression. *Sin is the transgression of the law.* Upon our repentance, the transgression is forgiven; that is, the obligation to punishment which we lay under is cancelled: it is *lifted off* (so some read it), that by the pardon of it we may be eased of a burden, a heavy burden. 2. It is the covering of sin, as nakedness is covered, that it may not appear to our shame, Rev. iii. 18. When sin is pardoned, it is covered with the robe of Christ's righteousness. 3. It is the not imputing of iniquity, not laying it to the sinner's charge. The righteousness of Christ being imputed to us, and we being made *the righteousness of God in him*, our iniquity is not imputed, God having *laid upon him the iniquity of us all* and made him *sin for us.*

II. Concerning the character of those whose sins are pardoned: *in whose spirit there is no guile.* He does not say, "There is no *guilt*" (for who is there that lives and sins not?), but no *guile*; the pardoned sinner is one that does not dissemble with God in his professions of repentance and faith. *While I kept silence my bones waxed old.* Those may be said to keep silence who stifle their convictions, who, when they cannot but see the evil of sin and their danger by reason of it, ease themselves by not thinking of it and diverting their minds to something else, who will not unburden their consciences by a penitent confession, and who choose rather to pine away in their iniquities than to take the method which God has appointed of finding rest for their souls.

III. Concerning the true and only way to peace of conscience. We are here taught to confess our sins, that they may be forgiven, to declare them, that we may be justified. This course David took: *I acknowledged my sin unto thee*, and no longer *hid my iniquity*, *v.* 5.

IV. Concerning God's readiness to pardon sin to those who truly repent of it: "*I said, I will confess and* immediately *thou forgavest the iniquity of my sin*, and gavest me the comfort of the pardon in my own conscience; immediately I found rest to my soul." Thus the father of the prodigal saw his returning son *when he was yet afar off*, and ran to meet him with the kiss that sealed his pardon. *For this shall every one that is godly pray unto thee.* All godly people are praying people. As soon as ever Paul was converted, *Behold, he prays*, Acts ix. 11. Those that are sincere and abundant in prayer will find the benefit of it when they are in trouble: *Surely in the floods of great waters*, which are very threatening, *they shall not come nigh them.*

Verses 7–11

I. David speaks to God, and professes his confidence in him and expectation from him, *v.* 7. "*Thou*

JAMIESON, FAUSSET, BROWN

PSALM 32

Vss. 1-11. *Maschil*—lit., "giving instruction." The Psalmist describes the blessings of His forgiveness, succeeding the pains of conviction, and deduces from his own experience instruction and exhortation to others.

1, 2. (Cf. Rom. 4:6.) **forgiven**—lit., "taken away," opposed to *retain* (John 20:23). **covered**—so that God no longer regards the sin (Ps. 85:3). **imputeth**—charge to him, and treat him accordingly.

no guile—or, *deceit*, no false estimate of himself, nor insincerity before God (cf. Rom. 8:1). **3, 4.** A vivid description of felt, but unacknowledged, sin. **When**—lit., "for," as in vs. 4. **thy hand**—of God, or, power in distressing him (Ps. 38:2). **moisture**—vital juices of the body, the parching heat of which expresses the anguish of the soul. On the other figures, cf. Psalm 6:2, 7; 31:9-11. If composed on the occasion of the fifty-first Psalm, this distress may have been protracted for several months.

5. A prompt fulfilment of the purposed confession is followed by a prompt forgiveness.

6. For this—i.e., my happy experience. **godly**—pious in the sense of Psalm 4:3. **a time**—(Isa. 55:6); when God's Spirit inclines us to seek pardon, He is ready to forgive. **floods . . .**—denotes great danger (Ps. 18:17; 66:12).

ADAM CLARKE

PSALM 32

The title of this psalm is significant, *ledavid maskil*, "A Psalm of David, giving instruction," an instructive psalm; so called by way of eminence, because it is calculated to give the highest instruction relative to the guilt of sin, and the blessedness of pardon and holiness, or justification and sanctification. It is supposed to have been composed after David's transgression with Bath-sheba, and subsequently to his obtaining pardon.

1. *Blessed is he whose transgression is forgiven.* In this and the following verse four evils are mentioned: *Transgression, sin, iniquity, guile.* The first signifies the passing over a boundary, doing what is prohibited. The second signifies the missing of a mark, not doing what was commanded; but is often taken to express sinfulness, or sin in the future, producing transgression in the life. The third signifies what is turned out of its proper course or situation, anything morally distorted or perverted. The fourth signifies fraud, deceit, guile. To remove these evils, three acts are mentioned: forgiving, covering, and not imputing. St. Paul quotes this passage, Rom. iv. 6-7, to illustrate the doctrine of justification by faith.

3. *When I kept silence.* Before I humbled myself, and confessed my sin, my soul was under the deepest horror.

5. *I acknowledged my sin.* When this confession was made thoroughly and sincerely, and I ceased to cover my offense, then Thou didst forgive *the iniquity of my sin.*

6. *Surely in the floods.* In violent trials, afflictions, and temptations.

MATTHEW HENRY

art my hiding-place; when by faith I have recourse to thee I shall see all the reason in the world to be easy, and to think myself out of the reach of any real evil. *Thou shalt preserve me from trouble,* from the sting of it, and from the strokes of it as far as is good for me. *Thou shalt preserve me from* such trouble as I was in *while I kept silence,*" *v.* 3. When God has pardoned our sins, if he leaves us to ourselves, we shall soon run as far in debt again as ever, and therefore, when we have received the comfort of our remission, we must fly to the grace of God to be preserved from returning to folly again. "Thou shalt not only deliver me, but *compass me about with songs of deliverance.* As *everyone that is godly shall pray with me,* so they shall give thanks with me."

II. He turns his speech to the children of men. Being himself converted, he does what he can to *strengthen his brethren* (Luke xxii. 32): *I will instruct thee,* whoever thou art that desirest instruction, *and teach thee in the way which thou shalt go, v.* 8. When Solomon became a penitent he immediately became a preacher, Eccles. i. 1. *I will guide thee with my eye.* Some apply this to God's conduct and direction. But it is rather to be taken as David's promise to those who sat under his instruction, his own children and family especially: "*I will counsel thee; my eye shall be upon thee*" (so the margin reads it); "I will give thee the best counsel I can and then observe whether thou takest it or no." Spiritual guides must be overseers. Here is a word of caution to sinners, not to be unruly and ungovernable: *Be you not as the horse and the mule, which have no understanding, v.* 9. It is our honour and happiness that we have understanding, that we are capable of being governed by reason and of reasoning with ourselves. Where there is renewing grace there is no need of the bit and bridle of restraining grace. The reason for this caution is because the way of sin will certainly end in sorrow (*v.* 10). Here is a word of comfort to saints. They are assured that if they will but trust in the Lord, and keep closely to him, *mercy shall compass them about* on every side (*v.* 10).

JAMIESON, FAUSSET, BROWN

7. His experience illustrates the statement of vs. 6.

8. Whether, as most likely, the language of David (cf. Ps. 51:13), or that of God, this is a promise of divine guidance. **I will . . . mine eye**—or, My eye shall be on thee, watching and directing thy way.

9. The latter clause, more literally, *"in that they come not near thee"*—i.e., *because* they will not come, etc., unless forced by bit and bridle.

10. The sorrows of the impenitent contrasted with the peace and safety secured by God's mercy. **11.** The righteous and upright, or those conforming to the divine teaching for securing the divine blessing, may well rejoice with shouting.

ADAM CLARKE

7. *Thou art my hiding place.* An allusion, probably, to the city of refuge. *Thou shalt preserve me from trouble.* The avenger of blood shall not be able to overtake me.

8. *I will instruct thee.* These are probably the Lord's words to David.

MATTHEW HENRY

PSALM 33

Verses 1–11

I. The great desire that God might be praised. Holy joy is the heart and soul of praise (*v.* 1): *Rejoice in the Lord, you righteous;* so the foregoing psalm concluded and so this begins. Thankful praise is holy joy (*v.* 2): "*Praise the Lord;* speak well of him, and give him the glory due to his name." Religious songs are the proper expressions of thankful praise (*v.* 3): "*Sing unto him a new song,* the best you have." Music was then used with the temple-songs (*v.* 2): *Sing unto him with the psaltery.* A good rule for this duty: "Do it *skilfully,* and *with a loud noise;* let it have the best both of head and heart; let it be done intelligently and with a clear head, affectionately and with a warm heart." A good reason for this duty: *For praise is comely for the upright.*

II. The high thoughts he had of God, and of his infinite perfections, *v.* 4, 5. God makes himself known to us, 1. In his *word,* here put for all divine revelation, all that which God at sundry times and in divers manners spoke to the children of men. 2. In his *works,* and those are all *done in truth.* The copy in all God's works agrees exactly with the great original, the plan laid in the Eternal Mind, and varies not in the least jot. God has made it to appear in his works that he is a God of inflexible justice: *He loveth righteousness and judgment.* He is a God of inexhaustible bounty: *The earth is full of his goodness,* that is, of the proofs and instances of it. The benign influences which the earth receives from above, and the fruits it is thereby enabled to produce, the provision that is made both for man and beast, and the common blessings with which all the nations of the earth are blessed, plainly declare that *the earth is full of his goodness*—the darkest, the coldest, the hottest, and the most dry and desert part of it not excepted. What a pity it is that this earth, which is so full of God's goodness, should be so empty of his praises, and that of the multitudes that live upon his bounty there are so few that live to his glory!

III. The conviction he was under of the almighty power of God, evidenced in the creation of the world. We "believe in God," and therefore we praise him as "the Father Almighty, maker of heaven and earth", so we are here taught to praise him.

1. God made the world, and brought all things into being. (1) How easily: All things were made *by the word of the Lord and by the breath of his mouth.* Christ is the Word, the Spirit is the breath, so that God the Father made the world, as he rules it and redeems it, by his Son and Spirit. *He spoke,*

JAMIESON, FAUSSET, BROWN

PSALM 33

Vss. 1-22. A call to lively and joyous praise to God for His glorious attributes and works, as displayed in creation, and His general and special providence, in view of which, the Psalmist, for all the pious, professes trust and joy and invokes God's mercy.

1-3. The sentiment falls in with Psalm 32:11 (cf. I Cor. 14:15). The instruments (Ps. 92:3; 144:9) do not exclude the voice. **a new song**—fresh, adapted to the occasion (Ps. 40:3; 96:1). **play skilfully**—(Cf. Ps. 15, 16, 21).

4-9. Reasons for praise—first, God's truth, faithfulness, and mercy, generally; then, His creative power which all must honor.

In word and breath—or, spirit, there may be an allusion to the Son (John 1:1) and Holy Spirit.

ADAM CLARKE

PSALM 33

This psalm has no title in the Hebrew and it was probably written on no particular occasion, but was intended as a hymn of praise in order to celebrate the power, wisdom, and mercy of God. Creation and providence are its principal subjects, and these lead the Psalmist to glance at different parts of the ancient Jewish history.

1. *Rejoice in the Lord.* It is very likely that the last verse of the preceding psalm was formerly the first verse of this. As this psalm has no title, the verse was the more easily separated. In the preceding psalm we have an account of the happiness of the justified man; in this such are taught how to glorify God, and to praise Him for the great things He had done for them.

2. *The psaltery.* Our translation seems to make a third instrument in this place, by rendering *an instrument of ten strings,* whereas they should both be joined together.

MATTHEW HENRY

and he commanded (*v.* 9), and that was enough; there needed no more. With men saying and doing are two things, but it is not so with God. (2) How effectually it was done: *And it stood fast.* What God does he does to purpose; he does it and it stands fast.

2. What he made. He made all things, but notice is here taken, (1) Of *the heavens, and the host of them, v.* 6. The visible heavens, and the sun, moon, and stars, their hosts—the highest heavens, and the angels, their hosts. (2) Of the waters, and the treasures of them, *v.* 7. The earth was at first covered with the water, and *he gathered the waters together on a heap,* that the dry land might appear, yet left them not to continue on a heap, but *laid up the depth in storehouses.*

3. What use is to be made of this (*v.* 8): *Let all the earth fear the Lord,* and *stand in awe of him;* that is, let all the children of men worship him and give glory to him, xcv. 5, 6.

IV. The satisfaction he had of God's sovereignty and dominion, *v.* 10, 11. Come and see with an eye of faith God in the throne, 1. Frustrating the devices of his enemies: *He bringeth the counsel of the heathen to nought.* 2. Fulfilling his own decrees: *The counsel of the Lord standeth for ever.* Through all the revolutions of time God never changed his measures, but in every event, even that which to us is most surprising, the eternal counsel of God is fulfilled.

Verses 12–22

Give to God the glory,

I. Of his common providence towards all the children of men. 1. The children of men are all under his eye, even their hearts are so; and all the motions and operations of their souls, which none know but they themselves, he knows better than they themselves, *v.* 13, 14. He not only beholds them, but he *looks upon them;* he looks narrowly upon them (so the word here used is sometimes rendered). 2. *He fashions their hearts.* He formed the spirit of each man within him. Hence he is called *the Father of spirits.* The artist that made the clock, can account for the motions of every wheel. David uses this argument with application to himself, cxxxix. 1, 14. *He fashions them together* (so some read it); as the wheels of a watch, though of different shapes, sizes, and motions, are yet all put together, to serve one and the same purpose, so the hearts of men and their dispositions, however varying from each other and seeming to contradict one another, are yet all overruled to serve the divine purpose, which is one. All the powers of the creature have a dependence upon him, and are of no account, of no avail at all, without him, *v.* 16, 17. The strength of an army is nothing without God. *The multitude of a host* cannot secure those under whose command they act, unless God make them a security to them. The strength of a giant is nothing without God. *A mighty man,* such as Goliath was, *is not delivered by* his *much strength,* when his day comes to fall. *Let not the strong man* then *glory in his strength,* but let us all strengthen ourselves in the Lord our God. The strength of a horse is nothing without God (*v.* 17): *A horse is a vain thing for safety.* In war horses were then so highly accounted of, and so much depended on, that God forbade the kings of Israel to *multiply horses* (Deut. xvii. 16), lest they should be tempted to trust to them and their confidence should thereby be taken off from God. David houghed the horses of the Syrians (2 Sam. viii. 4); here he houghs all the horses in the world, by pronouncing a horse a vain thing for safety in the day of battle.

II. We are to give God the glory of his special grace. *Blessed is the nation whose God is the Lord.* It is their wisdom that they take the Lord for their God. It is their happiness that they are the people whom God has chosen for his own inheritance, whom he protects and cultivates and improves as a man does his inheritance, Deut. xxxii. 9. God beholds all the sons of men with an eye of observation, but his eye of favour and complacency is upon those that fear him. While those that depend on arms and armies, on chariots and horses, perish in the disappointment of their expectations, God's people, under his protection, are safe, for he shall deliver their soul from death when there seems to be but a step between them and it. If he do not deliver the body from temporal death, yet he will deliver the soul from spiritual and eternal death. Their souls, whatever happens, shall live and praise him, either in this world or in a better. He shall *keep them alive in famine.* When visible means fail, God will find out some way or other to supply them. We must attend the motions of his providence, and accommodate ourselves to them. Our souls must wait for him, *v.* 20. We must rely on God, *hope in his mercy.* This is *trusting in his holy name* (*v.* 21). We must rejoice in God, *v.* 21. Our expectations from God are not to supersede,

JAMIESON, FAUSSET, BROWN

he spake—lit., "said." **it was**—The addition of "done" weakens the sense (cf. Gen. 1:3-10).

10, 11. In God's providence He thwarts men's purposes and executes His own. **heathen**—lit., "nations."

12-19. The inference from the foregoing in vs. 12 is illustrated by God's special providence, underlying which is His minute knowledge of all men. **looketh**—intently (Isa. 14:16). **fashioneth**—or, forms, and hence knows and controls (Prov. 21:1). **alike**—without exception. **considereth**—or, understands; God knows men's motives.

16, 17. Men's usual reliances in their greatest exigencies are, in themselves, useless. *On the war horse* (cf. Job 39:19-25). **a vain thing**—a lie, which deceives us.

18, 19. Contrasted is God's guidance and power to save from the greatest earthly evil and its most painful precursor, and hence from all.

20-22. waiteth—in earnest expectation. **holy name**—(Cf. Ps. 5:12; 22:(22; 30:4).

ADAM CLARKE

10. *The counsel of the heathen to nought.* This appears to be similar to what is mentioned in the second psalm, the useless attempts of the Gentiles to prevent the extension of the kingdom of Christ in the earth, and it may refer to similar attempts of ungodly nations or men to prevent the promulgation of the gospel and the universal dissemination of truth in the world.

11. *The counsel of the Lord.* What He has determined shall be done. He determined to make a world, and He made it; to create man, and He created him. He determined that at a certain period God should be manifested in the flesh, and it was so; that He should taste death for every man, and He did so; that His gospel should be preached in all the world, and, behold, it has already nearly overrun the whole earth.

13. *The Lord looketh from heaven.* This and the following verse seem to refer to God's providence. He sees all that is done in the earth, and His eye is on all the children of men.

CHARLES H. SPURGEON:

"There is no king saved by the multitude of an host" (33:16). At the battle of Arbela, the Persian hosts numbered between five hundred thousand and a million men, but they were utterly put to the rout by Alexander's band of fifty thousand; and the once mighty Darius was soon vanquished. Napoleon led more than half a million men into Russia—

"Not such the numbers, or the host so dread,
By northern Bren, or Scythian Timour led."

But the terrible winter left the army a mere wreck, and their leader was soon a prisoner on the lone rock of St. Helena. All along the line of history this verse has been verified. The strongest battalions melt like snowflakes when God is against them.—*The Treasury of David*

20. *Our soul waiteth.* Our whole life is employed in this blessed work; we trust in nothing but Him—neither in multitudes of armed men, nor in natural strength, nor in the fleetest animals, nor in anything human. We trust in Him alone who is *our help and our shield.*

MATTHEW HENRY

but to quicken and encourage, our applications to him; and therefore the psalm concludes with a short but comprehensive prayer, "*Let thy mercy, O Lord! be upon us;* let us always have the comfort and benefit of it, not according as we merit from thee, but *according as we hope in thee*, that is, according to the promise which thou hast in thy word given to us and according to the faith which thou hast by thy Spirit and grace wrought in us."

PSALM 34

A psalm of David when he changed his behaviour before Abimelech, who drove him away, and he departed.

Verses 1–10

David, being forced to flee from his country, which was made too hot for him by the rage of Saul, sought shelter as near it as he could, in the land of the Philistines. There it was soon discovered who he was, and he was brought before the king, here *Abimelech* (his title); and lest he should be treated as a spy, he feigned himself to be a madman that Achish might dismiss him as a contemptible man, rather than take cognizance of him as a dangerous man. And by this stratagem he escaped the hand that otherwise would have handled him roughly. Even when he was in danger his heart was so fixed, trusting in God, that he penned this excellent psalm, which has as much in it of the marks of a calm sedate spirit as any psalm in all the book; and there is something curious too in the composition, for it is what is called an alphabetical psalm, that is, a psalm in which every verse begins with each letter in its order as it stands in the Hebrew alphabet.

I. David engages and excites himself to praise God. "*I will bless the Lord at all times*, upon all occasions. *His praise shall continually be in my mouth.*" He will praise him heartily: "*My soul shall make her boast in the Lord*, in my relation to him, my interest in him, and expectations from him."

II. He calls upon others to join with him herein. He expects they will (*v.* 2): "*The humble shall hear thereof*, both of my deliverance and of my thankfulness, *and be glad.*" We cannot make God greater or higher than he is; but if we adore him as infinitely great, and higher than the highest, he is pleased to reckon this magnifying and exalting him. This we must do together. God's praises sound best in concert. David has found him a prayer-hearing God (*v.* 4): "*I sought the Lord*, in my distress, entreated his favour, begged his help, *and he heard me*, answered my request immediately, *and delivered me from all my fears*, both from the death I feared and from the disquietude and disturbance produced by my fear of it." The former he does by his providence working for us, the latter by his grace working in us, to silence our fears and still the tumult of the spirits. Many besides him have *looked unto God* by faith and prayer, *and have been lightened by it*, *v.* 5. It has wonderfully revived and comforted them; witness Hannah, who, when she had prayed, *went her way, and did eat and her countenance was no more sad.* These here spoken of had their expectations raised. *Their faces were not ashamed* of their confidence. *This poor man cried*, a single person, mean and inconsiderable, whom no man looked upon with any respect or looked after with any concern; yet he was as welcome to the throne of grace as David or any of his worthies: *The Lord heard him*, took cognizance of his case and of his prayers, *and saved him out of all his troubles*, *v.* 6. *The angel of the Lord*, a guard of angels (so some), *encamps round about those that fear God*, as the life-guard about the prince, *and delivers them.* David would have us to join with him in kind and good thoughts of God (*v.* 8): *O taste and see that the Lord is good!* The goodness of God includes both the beauty and amiableness of his being and the bounty and beneficence of his providence and grace. He would have us join with him in a resolution to seek God and serve him, and continue in his fear (*v.* 9): *O fear the Lord! you his saints. Fear the Lord;* that is, worship him, and make conscience of your duty to him in everything, not fear him and shun him, but fear him and seek him (*v.* 10). To encourage us to fear God and seek him, it is here promised that those that do so, even in this wanting world, *shall want no good thing.* They shall have grace sufficient for the support of the spiritual life (2 Cor. xii. 9; Ps. lxxxiv. 11); and, as to this life, they shall have what is necessary to the support of it from the hand of God: as a Father, he will feed them with food convenient. What further comforts they desire they shall have, as far as Infinite Wisdom sees good, and what they want in one thing shall be made up in another. What God denies them he will give them grace to be content

JAMIESON, FAUSSET, BROWN

Our faith measures mercy (Matt. 9:29); and if of grace, it is no more of debt (Rom. 11:6).

PSALM 34

Vss. 1-22. On the title cf. I Samuel 21:13. Abimelech was the general name of the sovereign (Gen. 20:2). After celebrating God's gracious dealings with him, the Psalmist exhorts others to make trial of His providential care, instructing them how to secure it. He then contrasts God's care of His people and His punitive providence towards the wicked.

1-4. Even in distress, which excites supplication, there is always matter for praising and thanking God (cf. Eph. 5:20); Phil. 4:6). **make her boast**—glory (Ps. 105:3; cf. Gal. 6:14).

humble—the pious, as in Psalm 9:12; 25:9.

magnify the Lord—ascribe greatness to Him, an act of praise. **together**—alike (Ps. 33:15), or, equally, without exception. **delivered . . . fears**—as well as actual evil (Ps. 64:1).

5-7. God's favor to the pious generally, and to himself specially, is celebrated. **looked**—with desire for help. **lightened**—or, brightened, expressing joy, opposed to the downcast features of those who are ashamed or disappointed (Ps. 25:2, 3).

This poor man—lit., "humble," himself as a specimen of such.

angel—of the covenant (Isa. 63:9), of whom as a leader of God's host (Josh. 5:14; I Kings 22:19), the phrase—**encampeth . . .**—is appropriate; or, "angel" used collectively for angels (Heb. 1:14). **8. taste and see**—try and experience.

9. that fear him—who are pious—fear and love (Prov. 1:7; 9:10). **saints**—consecrated to His service (Isa. 40:31). **10. not want any good**—"good" is emphatic; they may be afflicted (cf. vs. 10); but this may be a *good* (II Cor. 4:17, 18; Heb. 12:10, 11).

ADAM CLARKE

PSALM 34

The title states that this is "A Psalm of David, when he changed his behaviour before Abimelech, who drove him away, and he departed." The history of this transaction may be found in 1 Samuel xxi. But Abimelech is not the person there mentioned; it was Achish, king of Gath, called here Abimelech, because that was a common name of the Philistine kings. This is the second of the acrostic or alphabetical psalms, each verse beginning with a consecutive letter of the Hebrew alphabet. But in this psalm some derangement has taken place. The verse which begins with *vau*, and which should come in between the fifth and sixth, is totally wanting; and the twenty-second verse is entirely out of the series. It is, however, my opinion that this verse (the twenty-second), which now begins with *phe, podeh*, "redeemeth," was originally written *vepodeh* or with *padah*, as more than a hundred of Dr. Kennicott's MSS. read it, thus making *vepodah*, "and will redeem," and this reads admirably in the above connection.

2. *My soul shall make her boast.* Shall "set itself to praise" the Lord—shall consider this its chief work. *The humble.* The afflicted, such as David had been.

6. *This poor man cried.* "This afflicted man," David.

7. *The angel of the Lord encampeth round.* I should rather consider this angel in the light of a watchman going round his circuit, and having for the objects of his especial care such as fear the Lord.

MATTHEW HENRY

without and then they do not want it, Deut. iii. 26. Paul had all and abounded, because he was content, Phil. iv. 11, 18.

Verses 11–22

David, in this latter part of the psalm, undertakes to teach children. It does not appear that he had now any children of his own, he instructs the children of his people, and therefore calls together a congregation of them (*v.* 11): "*Come, you children, hearken unto me,* leave your play, lay by your toys, and hear what I have to say to you; not only give me the hearing, but observe and obey me." He undertakes to teach them—*the fear of the Lord,* inclusive of all the duties of religion.

I. He supposes that we all aim to be happy (*v.* 12): *What man is he that desireth life?*

II. He prescribes the true and only way to happiness both in this world and that to come, *v.* 13, 14. 1. We must learn to bridle our tongues, and be careful what we say, that we never speak amiss, to God's dishonour or our neighbour's prejudice: *Keep thy tongue from evil speaking, lying, and slandering.* 2. We must be upright and sincere in everything we say, and not double-tongued. 3. We must *depart from evil,* from evil works and evil workers. 4. It is not enough not to do hurt in the world, but we must study to be useful, and live to some purpose. 5. We must *seek peace and pursue it; follow peace with all men,* willing to deny ourselves a great deal, both in honour and interest, for peace' sake.

III. Here are life and death, good and evil, the blessing and the curse, plainly stated before us, that we may choose life and live. See Isa. iii. 10, 11.

1. *Woe to the wicked, it shall be ill with them,* however they may bless themselves in their own way. *The face of the Lord is against those that do evil, v.* 16. *Evil shall slay the wicked, v.* 21. Their death shall be miserable; and so it will certainly be, though they die on a bed of down or on the bed of honour. The *evil* here, which slays the wicked, is the same word, in the singular number, that is used (*v.* 19) for the afflictions of the righteous, to intimate that godly people have many troubles, and yet they do them no hurt, for God will deliver them out of them all; whereas wicked people have fewer troubles, perhaps but one, and yet that one may prove their utter ruin. One trouble with a curse in it kills, but many, with a blessing in them, are harmless, nay, gainful.

2. Yet *say to the righteous, It shall be well with them.* All good people are under God's special favour and protection. *The eyes of the Lord are upon the righteous* (*v.* 15), to direct and guide them, to protect and keep them. Parents that are very fond of a child will not let it be out of their sight; none of God's children are ever from under his eye. They *cry, and the Lord hears them,* and hears them as the tender mother the cry of her sucking child, which another would take no notice of. He not only takes notice of what we say, but is ready to us for our relief (*v.* 18): *He is nigh to those that are of a broken heart, and saves them.* He is near them to good purpose. *He keepeth all his bones;* not only his soul, but his body; not only his body in general, but every bone in it: *Not one of them is broken.* He that has a broken heart shall not have a broken bone; for David himself had found that, when he had a contrite heart, the *broken bones* were *made to rejoice,* li. 8, 17. *Many are the afflictions of the righteous,* witness David and his afflictions, cxxxii. 1. God has engaged for their deliverance and salvation: *He delivers them out of all their troubles* (*v.* 17, 19); he saves them (*v.* 18), so that, though they may fall into trouble, it shall not be their ruin.

JAMIESON, FAUSSET, BROWN

11. children—subjects of instruction (Prov. 1:8, 10).

12. What man—Whoever desires the blessings of piety, let him attend. **13, 14.** Sins of thought included in those of speech (Luke 6:45), avoiding evil and doing good in our relations to men are based on a right relation to God.

16. face . . . against—opposed to them (Lev. 17:10; 20:3). **cut off the remembrance**—utterly destroy (Ps. 109:13).

15. eyes of the Lord are upon—(Ps. 32:8; 33:18).

17, 18. Humble penitents are objects of God's special tender regard (Ps. 51:19; Isa. 57:15).

20. bones—framework of the body.

21, 22. Contrast in the destiny of righteous and wicked; the former shall be delivered and never come into condemnation (John 5:24; Rom. 8:1); the latter are left under condemnation and desolate.

ADAM CLARKE

11. ***Come, ye children.*** **All ye that are of a humble, teachable spirit.**

CHARLES H. SPURGEON:

"The eyes of the Lord are upon the righteous" (34:15). He observes them with approval and tender considerations; they are so dear to him that he cannot take his eyes off them; he watches each one of them as carefully and intently as if there were only that one creature in the universe.

"His ears are open unto their cry." His eyes and ears are thus both turned by the Lord towards his saints; his whole mind is occupied about them: if slighted by all others, they are not neglected by him. Their cry he hears at once, even as a mother is sure to hear her sick babe; the cry may be broken, plaintive, unhappy, feeble, unbelieving, yet the Father's quick ear catches each note of lament or appeal, and he is not slow to answer his children's voice.

—*The Treasury of David*

18. ***A broken heart.*** **The heart "broken to shivers."** ***A contrite spirit.*** **"The beaten-out spirit." In both words the hammer is necessarily implied. This will call to the reader's remembrance Jer. xxiii. 29: "Is not my word like as a fire? saith the Lord; and like a hammer that breaketh the rock in pieces?" The** ***broken heart*** **and the** ***contrite spirit*** **are two essential characteristics of true repentance.**

22. ***The Lord redeemeth.*** **Both the life and soul of God's followers are ever in danger, but God is continually redeeming both.** ***Shall be desolate.*** **Literally, "shall be guilty." They shall be preserved from sin, and forfeit neither life nor soul.**

MATTHEW HENRY

PSALM 35

A psalm of David.

Verses 1–10

I. David's representation of his case to God, setting forth the restless rage and malice of his persecutors. They persecuted him with an unwearied enmity, *sought after his soul* (*v.* 4), that is, his life, no less would satisfy their bloody minds.

II. His appeal to God concerning his integrity and the justice of his cause. If a fellow-subject had wronged him, he might have appealed to his prince, as St. Paul did to Caesar; but, when his prince wronged him, he appealed to his God, who is prince and Judge of the kings of the earth: *Plead my cause, O Lord! v.* 1.

III. His prayer to God to manifest himself both for him and to him, in this trial. He prays that God would *fight against* his enemies, so as to disable them to hurt him, and defeat their designs against him. If God be our friend, no matter who is our

JAMIESON, FAUSSET, BROWN

PSALM 35

Vss. 1-28. The Psalmist invokes God's aid, contrasting the hypocrisy, cunning, and malice of his enemies with his integrity and generosity. The imprecations of the first part including a brief notice of their conduct, the fuller exposition of their hypocrisy and malice in the second, and the earnest prayer for deliverance from their scornful triumph in the last, are each closed (vss. 9, 10, 18, 27, 28) with promises of praise for the desired relief, in which his friends will unite. The historical occasion is probably I Samuel 24.

1-3. God is invoked in the character of a warrior (Exod. 15:3; Deut. 32:41). **fight against**—lit., "devour my devourers." **stop the way against**—lit., "shut up" (the way), to meet or oppose, etc. **I . . . thy salvation**—who saves thee. **4.** (Cf. Psalm 9:17.) **devise my hurt**—purpose for evil to me. **5, 6.**—(Cf.

ADAM CLARKE

PSALM 35

1. ***Plead my cause, O Lord.*** **Literally, "Contend, Lord, with them that contend with me." The word is often used in a forensic or law sense. The imprecations in these verses against enemies are all legitimate. They are not against the souls or eternal welfare of those sinners, but**

MATTHEW HENRY

enemy.

IV. His prospect of the destruction of his enemies, which he prays for, not in malice or revenge. In *v.* 4–6 Dr. Hammond reads, *They shall be confounded, they shall be turned back*. This may be taken as a prayer for their repentance, for all penitents are put to shame for their sins and turned back from them. *They shall be as chaff before the wind*, so unable will wicked men be to stand before the judgments of God. Their way shall be *dark and slippery, darkness and slipperiness* (so the margin reads it).

V. His prospect of his own deliverance, which, having committed his cause to God, he did not doubt of, *v.* 9, 10. 1. He hoped that he should have the comfort of it: "*My soul shall be joyful*, not in my own ease and safety, but *in the Lord* and in his favour, in his promise and *in his salvation* according to the promise." He promised that then God should have the glory of it (*v.* 10): *All my bones shall say, Lord, who is like unto thee?*

Verses 11–16

Two very wicked things David here lays to the charge of his enemies—perjury and ingratitude.

I. Perjury, *v.* 11. When Saul would have David attainted of treason, in order to his being outlawed, *False witnesses did rise up*, who would swear anything; *they laid to my charge things that I knew not*. This instance of the wrong done to David was typical, and had its accomplishment in the Son of David, against whom false witnesses did arise, Matt. xxvi. 60.

II. Ingratitude. Call a man ungrateful and you can call him no worse. This was the character of David's enemies (*v.* 12): *They rewarded me evil for good*. He had deserved well not only of the public in general, but of those particular persons that were now most bitter against him. Probably it was then well known whom he meant; it may be Saul himself.

1. How tenderly, and with what a cordial affection, he had behaved towards them in their afflictions (*v.* 13, 14). He prayed for them. With his prayers he joined humiliation and self-affliction, both in his diet (he fasted, at least from pleasant bread) and in his dress; he clothed himself with sackcloth, thus expressing his grief, not only for their affliction, but for their sin; for this was the guise and practice of a penitent. His fasting also put an edge upon his praying. He was so intent in his devotions that he had no appetite to meat, nor would allow himself time for eating: *My prayer returned into my own bosom*.

2. How basely and insolently and with what a brutish enmity, and worse than brutish, they had behaved towards him (*v.* 15, 16): *In my adversity they rejoiced. They gnashed upon him with their teeth.* David was the fool in the play, and his disappointment all the table-talk of the hypocritical mockers at feasts; it was the song of the drunkards. Such has often been the hard fate of the best of men. The apostles were made a spectacle to the world.

Verses 17–28

I. David describes the great injustice, malice, and insolence, of his persecutors, pleading this with God as a reason why he should protect him from them. *They hated him without a cause*; nay, for that for which they ought rather to have loved and honoured him. This is quoted, with application to Christ, and is said to be fulfilled in him. John xv. 25, *They hated me without cause. They speak not peace;* if they met him, they had not the good manners to give him the time of the day; like Joseph's brethren, that could not *speak peaceably to him*, Gen. xxxvii. 4. *They opened their mouth wide against me.* They set themselves against all the sober good people that adhered to David (*v.* 20): *They devised deceitful matters*, to trepan and ruin *those that were quiet in the land*. He appeals to God against them, the *God to whom vengeance belongs*, appeals to his knowledge (*v.* 22): *This thou hast seen.* He appeals to God's justice: *Awake to my judgment, even to my cause*, and let it have a hearing at thy bar, *v.* 23. "*Judge me, O Lord my God!* pass sentence upon this appeal, *according to the righteousness* of thy nature and government," *v.* 24.

II. He prays earnestly to God to appear graciously for him and his friends, that God would act for him, and not stand by as a spectator (*v.* 17): "*Lord, how long wilt thou look on? Rescue my soul from the destructions* they are plotting against it; rescue *my darling*, my only one, *from the lions*. My soul is my only one, and therefore the greater is the shame if I neglect it and the greater the loss if I lose it: it is my only one, and therefore ought to be my darling, ought to be carefully protected and provided for. It is my soul that is in danger; Lord, rescue it. He desires that his innocency might be so cleared that

JAMIESON, FAUSSET, BROWN

Ps. 1:4)—a terrible fate; driven by wind on a slippery path in darkness, and hotly pursued by supernatural violence (II Sam. 24:16; Acts 12:23). **7, 8. net in a pit**—or, pit of their net—or, net-pit—as holy hill for hill of holiness—(Ps. 2:6)—a figure from hunting (Ps. 7:15). Their imprecations on impenitent rebels against God need no vindication; His justice and wrath are for such; His mercy for penitents. Cf. Psalms 7:16; 11:5, on the peculiar fate of the wicked here noticed.

9, 10. All my bones—every part. **him that spoileth him**—(Cf. Ps. 10:2).

11. False witnesses—lit., "Witnesses of injustice and cruelty" (cf. Ps. 11:5; 25:19).

12-14. Though they rendered evil for good, he showed a tender sympathy in their affliction.

spoiling—lit., "bereavement." The usual modes of showing grief are made, as figures, to express his sorrow. **prayer . . . bosom**—may denote either the posture—the head bowed—(cf. I Kings 18: 42)—or, that the prayer was in secret. Some think there is a reference to the result—the prayer would benefit him if not them. **behaved**—lit., "went on" —denoting his habit. **heavily**—or, squalidly, his sorrowing occasioning neglect of his person. Altogether, his grief was that of one for a dearly loved relative. **15, 16.** On the contrary, they rejoiced in his affliction. *Halting*, or lameness, as in Psalm 38: 17 for any distress. **abjects**—either as cripples (cf. II Sam. 4:4), contemptible; or, degraded persons, such as had been beaten (cf. Job 30:1-8). **I knew it not**—either the persons, or, reasons of such conduct. **tear me, and ceased not**—lit., "were not silent"—showing that the *tearing* meant slandering. **mockers**—who were hired to make sport at feasts (Prov. 28:21).

19. enemies wrongfully—by false and slanderous imputations. **wink with the eye**—an insulting gesture (Prov. 6:13). **without a cause** —manifests more malice than having a wrong cause.

20. deceitful matters—or, words of deceit. **quiet in the land**—the pious lovers of peace. **21.** On the gesture cf. Psalm 22:7, and on the expressions of malicious triumph, cf. Psalms 10:13; 28:3. **23, 24.** (Cf. Ps. 7:6; 26:1; II Thess. 1:6.) God's righteous government is the hope of the pious and terror of the wicked.

17. darling—(Cf. Ps. 22:20, 21.)

ADAM CLARKE

against their schemes and plans for destroying the life of an innocent man; and the holiest Christian may offer up such prayers against his adversaries.

7. *For without cause have they hid for me their net in a pit.* The word *pit* belongs to the second member of this verse, and the whole should be read thus: For without a cause they have hidden for me their net; without a cause they have digged a pit for my life.

14. *Mourneth for his mother.* As a mourning mother. How expressive is this word!

15. *But in mine adversity they rejoiced.* How David was mocked and insulted in the case of Absalom's rebellion by Shimei and others is well-know. *The abjects.* "The smiters," probably hired assassins. They were everywhere lying in wait, to take away my life.

16. *With hypocritical mockers in feasts.* These verses seem to be prophetic of the treatment of Christ.

21. *They opened their mouth wide.* Gaped upon me to express their contempt. *And said, Aha, aha, our eye hath seen it.* They said, *Heach, heach*, the last syllable in each word being a protracted, strongly guttural sound, marking insult and triumph at the same time. It is the word which we translate, "Ah," v. 25.

17. *My darling.* "My only one," Ps. xxii. 20.

MATTHEW HENRY

they might be ashamed of the calumnies with which they had loaded him, that his interest might be so confirmed that they might be ashamed of their designs against him and their expectations of his ruin, that they might either be brought to that shame which would be a step towards their reformation or that that might be their portion which would be their everlasting misery. Notwithstanding the arts that were used to blacken David, and make him odious, and to frighten people from owning him, there were some that favoured his righteous cause, and he prays for them. *Let them say continually, The Lord be magnified*, by us and others, *who hath pleasure in the prosperity of his servant*.

III. The mercy he hoped to win by prayer he promises to wear with praise: "*I will give thee thanks*, as the author of my deliverance (*v.* 18), *and my tongue shall speak of thy righteousness*, the justice of thy judgments and the equity of all thy dispensations."

PSALM 36

To the chief musician. A psalm of David the servant of the Lord.

Verses 1–4

David, in the title of this psalm, is styled *the servant of the Lord*; why in this, and not in any other, except in xviii (*title*), no reason can be given; but so he was, not only as every good man is God's servant, but as a king, as a prophet.

David, in these verses, describes the wickedness of the wicked, sin in its causes and sin in its colours, in its root and in its branches.

I. Here is the root of bitterness, from which all the wickedness of the wicked comes. "*The transgression of the wicked* (as it is described afterwards, *v.* 3, 4) *saith within my heart* (makes me to conclude within myself) *that there is no fear of God before his eyes:* for, if there were, he would not break the laws of God, and violate his covenants with him, if he had any awe of his majesty or dread of his wrath." *He flattereth himself in his own eyes;* that is, while he goes on in sin he thinks he does wisely and well for himself, and either does not see or will not own the evil and danger of his wicked practices; he calls evil good and good evil; his licentiousness he pretends to be but his just liberty, his fraud passes for his prudence and policy, and his persecuting the people of God, he suggests to himself, is a piece of necessary justice. But the day is coming when the sinner will be undeceived, when *his iniquity shall be found to be hateful*.

II. Here are the cursed branches which spring from this root of bitterness. The sinner defies God. *The words of his mouth are iniquity and deceit*, contrived to do wrong, and yet to cover it with specious and plausible pretences. The sparks of virtue are extinguished, their convictions baffled, their good beginnings come to nothing: They have *left off to be wise and to do good. He devises mischief upon his bed.* Those that leave off to do good begin to do evil. Doing evil themselves, they have no dislike at all of it in others: *He abhors not evil*, but, on the contrary, takes pleasure in it, and is glad to see others as bad as himself.

Verses 5–12

David, having looked round with grief upon the wickedness of the wicked, here looks up with comfort upon the goodness of God.

I. His meditations upon the grace of God.

1. The transcendent perfections of the divine nature. *Thy mercy, O Lord! is in the heavens.* How bad soever the world is, let us never think the worse of God nor of his government; but, let us take occasion, instead of reflecting upon God's purity, as if he countenanced sin, to admire his patience, that he bears so much with those that so impudently provoke him, nay, and causes his sun to shine and his rain to fall upon them. He is a God of inviolable truth: *Thy faithfulness reaches unto the clouds.* God's faithfulness reaches so high that it does not change with the weather, as men's does, for it reaches to the *skies* (so it should be read, as some think), above the clouds, and all the changes of the lower region. He is a God of incontestable justice and equity: *Thy righteousness is like the great mountains*, immovable and inflexible. He is a God of unsearchable wisdom and design: "*Thy judgments are a great deep*, not to be fathomed with the line and plummet of any finite understanding."

2. The extensive care and beneficence of the divine Providence: "*Thou preservest man and beast*, not only protectest them from mischief, but suppliest them with that which is needful for the support of life."

3. The peculiar favour of God to the saints.

JAMIESON, FAUSSET, BROWN

25. swallowed him up—utterly destroyed him (Ps. 21:9; Lam. 2:16). **26. clothed**—covered wholly (Job 8:22). **27. favour . . . cause**—delight in it, as vindicated by Thee. **Let the Lord . . .** Let Him be greatly praised for His care of the just. **28.** In this praise of God's equitable government (Ps. 5:8) the writer promises ever to engage.

18. (Cf. Ps. 22:22.)

PSALM 36

Vss. 1-12. On *servant of the Lord*, cf. title of Psalm 18. The wickedness of man contrasted with the excellency of God's perfections and dispensations; and the benefit of the latter sought, and the evils of the former deprecated.

1. The general sense of this difficult verse is, "that the wicked have no fear of God." The first clause may be rendered, "Saith transgression in my heart, in respect to the wicked, there is no fear," etc., i.e., such is my reflection on men's transgressions. **2-4.** This reflection detailed.

until his iniquity . . .—lit., "for finding his iniquity for hating"; i.e., he persuades himself God will not so find it—"for hating" involving the idea of punishing. Hence his words of **iniquity** and **deceit,** and his bold rejection of all right principles of conduct. The climax is that he deliberately adopts and patronizes evil. The negative forms affirm more emphatically their contraries.

5, 6. mercy . . . and . . . faithfulness—as mercy and truth (Ps. 25:10).

righteousness [and] **judgments**—qualities of a good government (Ps. 5:8; 31:1). These all are set forth, by the figures used, as unbounded.

ADAM CLARKE

25. *Swallowed him up.* "We have gulped him down."

PSALM 36

The title in the Hebrew is, "To the conqueror, to the servant of Jehovah, to David." It is one of the finest psalms in the whole collection.

1. *The transgression of the wicked saith within my heart.* It is difficult to make any sense of this line as it now stands. How can the transgression of the wicked speak within my heart? But instead of *libbi*, "my heart," four of Kennicott's and De Rossi's MSS. have *libbo*, "his heart." "The speech of transgression to the wicked is in the midst of his heart. There is no fear of God before his eyes." The principle of transgression, sin in the heart, says, or suggests to every sinner, There is no cause for fear; go on, do not fear, for there is no danger. He obeys this suggestion, goes on, and acts wickedly, as God is not *before his eyes*.

5. *Thy mercy, O Lord, is in the heavens.* That is, Thou art abundant, infinite in Thy mercy, else such transgressors must be immediately cut off; but Thy long-suffering is intended to lead them to repentance.

Thy faithfulness reacheth unto the clouds. To the eternal regions, above all visible space.

6. *Thy righteousness is like the great mountains.* "Like the mountains of God"; exceeding high mountains. *Thy judgments are a great deep.* "The great abyss"; as incomprehensible as the great chaos.

MATTHEW HENRY

(1) Their character, *v.* 7. They are such as are allured by the *excellency of God's loving-kindness to put their trust under the shadow of his wings.*

(2) Their privilege. *They shall be abundantly satisfied with the fatness of thy house,* their wants supplied, their cravings gratified, and their capacities filled. In God all-sufficient they shall have enough, all that which an enlightened enlarged soul can desire or receive. A gracious soul, though still desiring more of God, never desires more than God. *I have all, and abound,* Phil. iv. 18. Their joys shall be constant: *Thou shalt make them drink of the river of thy pleasures.* There are pleasures that are truly divine. "They are *thy pleasures,* not only which come from thee as the giver of them, but which terminate in thee as the matter and centre of them." There is a river of these pleasures, always full, always fresh, always flowing. The pleasures of sense are putrid puddle-water; those of faith are pure and pleasant, *clear as crystal,* Rev. xxii. 1. Having God himself for their felicity they have a fountain of life, from which those rivers of pleasure flow, *v.* 8. In him they have light in perfection, wisdom, knowledge, and joy, all included in this light: *In thy light we shall see light.* "In the knowledge of thee in grace, and the vision of thee in glory, we shall have that which will abundantly suit and satisfy our understandings." That divine light which shines in the scripture, and especially in the face of Christ, the light of the world, has all truth in it. "In communion with thee now; by the communications of thy grace to us and the return of our devout affections to thee, we have all the good we can desire."

II. We have here David's prayers, intercessions, and holy triumphs, grounded upon these meditations.

1. He intercedes for all saints, *v.* 10. (1) The persons he prays for are those that know God—the upright in heart, that are sincere in their profession of religion, and faithful both to God and man. (2) The blessing he begs for them is God's loving-kindness (that is, the tokens of his favour towards them) and his righteousness (that is, the workings of his grace in them).

2. He prays for himself, that he might be preserved in his integrity and comfort (*v.* 11): "*Let not the foot of pride come against me,* to trip up my heels, or trample upon me; *and let not the hand of the wicked,* which is stretched out against me, prevail to *remove me,* either from my purity and integrity, by any temptation, or from my peace and comfort, by any trouble."

JAMIESON, FAUSSET, BROWN

7. shadow of thy wings—(Cf. Deut. 32: 11; Ps. 91:1). **8. fatness**—richness. **thy house**—residence—for the privileges and blessings of communion with God (Ps. 23:6; 27:4). **river of thy pleasures**—plenteous supply—may allude to Eden.

9. Light is an emblem of all blessings—given of God as a means to gain more.

10. that know thee—right knowledge of God is the source of right affections and conduct.

11. foot of . . . hand . . . wicked—all kinds of violent dealing. **12. There**—in the acting of violence, they are overthrown. A signal defeat.

ADAM CLARKE

8. *They shall be abundantly satisfied.* "They shall be saturated," as a thirsty field is by showers from heaven.

10. *O continue thy lovingkindness.* Literally, "Draw out Thy mercy." *To the upright in heart.* "To the straight of heart"; to those who have but one end in view, and one aim to that end.

11. *Let not the foot of pride come against me.* Let me not be trampled underfoot by proud and haughty men. *Let not the hand of the wicked remove me.* "Shake me" or "cause me to wander."

MATTHEW HENRY

PSALM 37

A psalm of David.

Verses 1–6

I. We are here cautioned against discontent at the prosperity and success of evildoers (*v.* 1, 2): *Fret not thyself, neither be thou envious.* We may suppose that David speaks this to himself first. That is preached best, and with most probability of success, to others, which is first preached to ourselves. When we look abroad we see the world full of evildoers and workers of iniquity, that flourish and prosper. When we look within we find ourselves tempted to fret at this, and to be envious. We are apt to fret at God, as if he were unkind to the world and unkind to his church in permitting such men to live, and prosper, and prevail, as they do. We are apt to envy them the liberty they take in getting wealth, and perhaps by unlawful means, and in the indulgence of their lusts, and to wish that we should shake off the restraints of conscience and do so too. When we look forward with an eye of faith we shall see no reason to envy wicked people their prosperity, for their ruin is at the door and they are ripening apace for it, *v.* 2. They flourish, but as the grass, and as the green herb, which nobody envies nor frets at. They will soon wither of themselves. Outward prosperity is a fading thing, and so is the life itself to which it is confined.

II. We are here counselled to live a life of confidence in God, and that will keep us from fretting at the prosperity of evil-doers; if we do well for our own souls, we shall see little reason to envy those that do so ill for theirs. Here are three excellent precepts, and three precious promises,

1. We must make God our hope in the way of duty and then we shall have a comfortable subsistence in this world, *v.* 3. It is required that we *trust in the Lord and do good.* We must not think to trust in God and then live as we list. It is promised that we shall be well provided for in this world: *So shalt thou dwell in the land, and verily thou shalt be fed.* "Thou shalt have a settlement, a quiet settlement, and a maintenance, a comfortable maintenance:

JAMIESON, FAUSSET, BROWN

PSALM 37

Vss. 1-40. A composed and uniform trust in God and a constant course of integrity are urged in view of the blessedness of the truly pious, contrasted in various aspects with the final ruin of the wicked. Thus the wisdom and justice of God's providence are vindicated, and its seeming inequalities, which excite the cavils of the wicked and the distrust of the pious, are explained. David's personal history abundantly illustrates the Psalm.

1, 2. The general sentiment of the whole Psalm is expressed. The righteous need not be vexed by the prosperity of the wicked; for it is transient, and their destiny undesirable.

3. Trust—sure of safety. **shalt thou dwell**—or, dwell thou—repose quietly. **verily . . . , fed**—or, feed on truth—God's promise (Ps. 36:5; cf. Hos. 12:1).

ADAM CLARKE

PSALM 37

This psalm is one of the acrostic or alphabetical kind; but it differs from those we have already seen in having two verses under each letter, the first only exhibiting the alphabetical letter consecutively.

MATTHEW HENRY

Verily thou shalt be fed." Some read it, *Thou shalt be fed by faith,* as the just are said to live by faith, and it is good living, good feeding, upon the promises.

2. We must make God our heart's delight and then we shall have our heart's desire, *v.* 4. We were commanded (*v.* 3) to do good, and then follows this command to delight in God, which is as much a privilege as a duty. And this pleasant duty has a promise annexed to it, *He shall give thee the desires of thy heart.* He has not promised to gratify all the appetites of the body, but to grant all the desires of the heart, all the cravings of the soul. What is the desire of the heart of a good man? It is this, to know, and love, and live to God, to please him and to be pleased in him.

3. We must make God our guide, and submit in everything to his guidance, and then all our affairs, even those that seem most intricate and perplexed, shall be made to issue well, *v.* 5, 6. The duty is very easy; and, if we do it aright, it will make us easy: *Commit thy way unto the Lord; roll thy way upon the Lord* (so the margin reads it), Prov. xvi. 3; Ps. lv. 22. *Cast thy burden upon the Lord,* the burden of thy care, 1 Pet. v. 7. *Reveal thy way unto the Lord* (so the LXX), that is, "By prayer spread thy case, and all thy cares about it, before the Lord, and then trust in him to bring it to a good issue, with a full satisfaction that all is well that God does." We must follow Providence, and not force it, subscribe to Infinite Wisdom and not prescribe. The promise is very sweet. "*He shall bring that to pass,* whatever it is, which thou hast committed to him, if not to thy contrivance, yet to thy content. He will find means to extricate thee out of thy straits, to prevent thy fears, and bring about thy purposes, to thy satisfaction." *He shall bring forth thy righteousness as the light and thy judgment as the noon-day*" (*v.* 6), that is, "he shall make it to appear that thou art an honest man, and that is honour enough." If we take care to keep a good conscience, we may leave it to God to take care of our good name.

Verses 7–20

I. The foregoing precepts inculcated. 1. Let us compose ourselves by believing in God: "*Rest in the Lord, and wait patiently for him*" (*v.* 7), that is, be well reconciled to all he does and acquiesce in it, and be well satisfied that he will still make all to work for good to us, though we know not how or which way. *Be silent to the Lord* (so the word is), not with a sullen, but a submissive silence. 2. Let us not discompose ourselves at what we see in this world: "*Fret not thyself, because of him who prospers in his wicked way,* who, though he is a bad man, yet thrives and grows rich and great in the world. If thy heart begins to rise at it, stroke down thy folly, and *cease from anger* (*v.* 8). *Fret not thyself in any wise to do evil;* do not envy them their prosperity, lest thou be tempted to fall in with them and to take the same evil course that they take to enrich and advance themselves or some desperate course to avoid them and their power."

II. The foregoing reasons repeated.

1. Good people have no reason to envy the worldly prosperity of wicked people. *Evil-doers shall be cut off* by some sudden stroke of divine justice in the midst of their prosperity. The condition of the righteous, even in this life, is every way better and more desirable than that of the wicked, *v.* 16. A godly man's little is really better than a wicked man's much, see Prov. xv. 16, 17; xiv 8; xxviii. 6. **It comes from** a better hand, from a hand of special love and not merely from a hand of common providence. *Those that wait upon the Lord,* as dependents on him, expectants from him, and suppliants to him, *shall inherit the earth,* as a token of his present favour to them and an earnest of better things intended for them in the other world. *The meek shall inherit the earth.* Our Saviour has made this a gospel promise, and a confirmation of the blessing he pronounced on the meek, Matt. v. 5. They *shall delight themselves in the abundance of peace, v.* 11. That peace which the world cannot give (John xiv. 27), they shall delight themselves in. God *knows their days, v.* 18. He takes particular notice of them, of all they do and of all that happens to them. He keeps account of the days of their service, and not one day's work shall go unrewarded. *Their inheritance shall be for ever.* Their time on earth is reckoned by days, which will soon be numbered. God takes cognizance of them, and gives them the blessings of every day in its day; but it was never intended that their inheritance should be confined within the limits of those days. No, that must be the portion of an immortal soul, and therefore must last as long as that lasts, and will run parallel with the longest line of eternity itself: *Their inheritance shall be for ever;* not their

JAMIESON, FAUSSET, BROWN

4. desires–(Ps. 20:5; 21:2), what is lawful and right, really good (Ps. 84:11).

5. Commit thy way–(Prov. 16:3). *Works*–what you have to do and cannot–set forth as a burden. **trust . . . in him**–lit., "on Him."

He will do what you cannot (cf. Ps. 22:8; 31:6). He will not suffer your character to remain under suspicion.

7, 8. Rest in–lit., "Be silent to the Lord." **and wait**–Be submissive–avoid petulance and murmurings, anger and rash doing.

9. Two reasons: The prosperity of the wicked is short; and the pious, by humble trust, will secure all covenant blessing, denoted here by "inherit the earth" (cf. Ps. 25:13).

16. riches–lit., "noise and tumult," as incidental to much wealth (cf. Ps. 39:6). Thus the contrast with the "little" of one man is more vivid.

10, 11. shall not be–lit., "is not"–is not to be found. **peace**–includes prosperity.

18, 19. God, who knows His people's changes, provides against evil and supplies all their need. **20.** While the wicked, however mighty, are destroyed, and that utterly, as smoke which vanishes and leaves no trace.

ADAM CLARKE

4. *Delight thyself also in the Lord.* Expect all thy happiness from Him, and seek it in Him. *The desires of thine heart.* The "petitions." The godly man never indulges a desire which he cannot form into a prayer to God.

5. *Commit thy way unto the Lord.* "Roll thy way upon the Lord."

He shall bring it to pass. "He will work." Trust God, and He will work for thee.

7. *Rest in the Lord.* "Be silent, be dumb." Do not find fault with thy Maker. He does all things well for others; He will do all things well for thee. *And wait patiently for him.* And "set thyself" to expect Him; and be determined to expect or wait for Him.

9. *They shall inherit the earth.* The word *arets* throughout this psalm should be translated "land," not *earth;* for it is most probable that it refers to the land of Judea, and in this verse there is a promise of their return thither.

10. *For yet a little while, and the wicked shall not be.* A prediction of the destruction of Babylon. This empire was now in its splendor; and the captives lived to see it totally overturned by Cyrus, so that even the shadow of its power did not remain. *Thou shalt diligently consider his place.* "And he is not." The ruler is killed, the city is taken, and the whole empire is overthrown, in one night!

11. *But the meek. Anavim,* the "afflicted," the poor Jewish captives. *Shall inherit the earth. Arets,* the "land" of Judea, given by God himself as an inheritance to their fathers, and to their posterity forever. See v. 9.

20. *The enemies of the Lord shall be as the fat of lambs.* This verse has given the critics some trouble. Several of the versions read thus: "But the enemies of the Lord, as soon as they are exalted to honour, shall vanish; like smoke they vanish." If we follow the Hebrew, it intimates that "they shall consume as the fat of lambs." That is, as the fat is wholly consumed in sacrifices by the fire on the altar, so shall they consume away in the fire of God's wrath.

MATTHEW HENRY

inheritance in the earth, but that incorruptible indefeasible one which is laid up for them in heaven.

2. Good people have no reason to fret at the occasional success of the designs of the wicked against the just.

(1) Their plots will be their shame, *v.* 12, 13. It is true *the wicked plotteth against the just.* They are proud and insolent, but God despises all their attempts as vain and ineffectual. Men have their day now. God's day will give a decisive judgment.

(2) Their attempts will be their destruction, *v.* 14, 15. They *have drawn the sword, and bent the bow*; and all these military preparations are made against the helpless, *the poor and needy* and against the guiltless, *such as are of upright conversation.* How justly their malice recoils upon themselves: *Their sword shall turn into their own heart.*

(3) Those that are not suddenly cut off shall yet be so disabled for doing any further mischief: *Their bows shall be broken* (*v.* 15); the instruments of their cruelty shall fail them and *their arms shall be broken*, so that they shall not be able to go on with their enterprises, *v.* 17.

Verses 21–33

I. What is required of us as the way to our happiness. If we would be blessed of God, 1. We must make conscience of giving everybody his own; for *the wicked borrows and pays not again, v.* 21. It is the first thing which the Lord our God requires of us, that we do justly, and render to all their due. 2. We must be ready to all acts of charity and beneficence; for, as it is an instance of God's goodness to the righteous that he puts it into the power of his hand to be kind and to do good, so it is an instance of the goodness of the righteous man that he has a heart proportionable to his estate: *He shows mercy, and gives, v.* 21. *He is ever merciful and lends*, and sometimes there is as true charity in lending as in giving. 3. We must leave our sins, and engage in the practice of serious godliness (*v.* 27): *Depart from evil and do good.* 4. We must abound in good discourse, and with our tongues must glorify God and edify others. It is part of the character of a righteous man (*v.* 30) that his *mouth speaketh wisdom.* Out of the abundance of a good heart will the mouth speak that which is good and to the use of edifying. 5. We must have our wills brought into an entire subjection to the will and word of God (*v.* 31): *The law of God*, of his God, *is in his heart*; and in vain do we pretend that God is our God if we do not receive his law into our hearts and resign ourselves to the government of it.

II. What is assured to us, as instances of our happiness and comfort, upon these conditions.

1. That we shall have the blessing of God, and that blessing shall be the spring, and sweetness, and security of all our temporal comforts and enjoyments (*v.* 22): *Such as are blessed of God*, as all the righteous are, with a Father's blessing, by virtue of that *shall inherit the earth*, or *the land* (for so the same word is translated, *v.* 29), the land of Canaan, that glory of all lands.

2. That God will direct and dispose of our actions and affairs so as may be most for his glory (*v.* 23): *The steps of a good man are ordered by the Lord.* God orders the steps of a good man; not only his way in general, by his written word, but his particular steps, by the whispers of conscience, saying, *This is the way, walk in it.* He does not always show him his way at a distance, but leads him step by step, as children are led, and so keeps him in a continual dependence upon his guidance.

3. That God will keep us from being ruined by our falls either into sin or into trouble (*v.* 24): *Though he fall, he shall not be utterly cast down.* A good man may be overtaken in a fault, but the grace of God shall recover him to repentance, so that he shall not be utterly cast down. Though he may, for a time, lose the joys of God's salvation, yet they shall be restored to him; for God shall uphold him with his hand, uphold him with his free Spirit. The root shall be kept alive, though the leaf wither; and there will come a spring after the winter.

4. That we shall not want the necessary supports of this life (*v.* 25): "*I have been young and now am old*, and, among all the changes I have seen in men's outward condition and the observations I have made upon them, *I never saw the righteous forsaken* of God and man." There are very few instances of good men, or their families, that are reduced to such extreme poverty as many wicked people bring themselves to by their wickedness. Some make this promise relate especially to those that are charitable and liberal to the poor, and to intimate that David never observed any that brought themselves to poverty by their charity.

5. That God will not desert us, but graciously

JAMIESON, FAUSSET, BROWN

12. gnasheth . . . teeth—in beastly rage. **13.** (Cf. Ps. 2:4.) **seeth**—knows certainly. **his day**—of punishment, long delayed, shall yet come (Heb. 10:37).

14, 15. sword, and . . . bow—for any instruments of violence. **slay**—lit., "slaughter" (I Sam. 25:11). **poor and needy**—God's people (Ps. 10:17; 12:5). The punishment of the wicked as drawn on themselves—often mentioned (cf. Ps. 7:15, 16; 35:8).

17. Even the members of the body needed to hold weapons are destroyed.

21, 22. payeth not—not able; having grown poor (cf. Deut. 15:7). Ability of the one and inability of the other do not exclude moral dispositions. God's blessing or cursing makes the difference. **cut off**—opposed to "inherit the earth" (cf. Lev. 7:20, 21).

30, 31. The righteous described as to the elements of character, thought, word, and action. **steps**—or, goings—for conduct which is unwavering (Ps. 18:36).

23, 24. steps—way, or, course of life; as ordered by God, failures will not be permanent.

25, 26. his seed is blessed—lit., "for a blessing" (Gen. 12:2; Ps. 21:6). This position is still true as the rule of God's economy (I Tim. 4:8; 6:6).

ADAM CLARKE

21. *The wicked borroweth.* Is often reduced to penury, and is obliged to become debtor to those whom he before despised. *And payeth not again.* May refuse to do it, and because he is a wicked man; or be unable to do it, because he is reduced to beggary. *But the righteous sheweth mercy.* Because he has received mercy from God, therefore he shows mercy to men.

22. *Shall inherit the earth. Arets*, the "land," as before. See v. 11.

31. *None of his steps shall slide.* His holy heart always dictates to his *eyes*, his *mouth*, his *hands*, and his *feet.* The precepts which direct his conduct are not only *written in his Bible*, but also *in his heart.*

23. *The steps of a good man are ordered by the Lord.* There is nothing for *good* in the text. *Geber* is the original word, and it properly signifies a "strong man," a "conqueror" or "hero"; and it appears to be used here to show that even the most powerful must be supported by the Lord, otherwise their strength and courage will be of little avail.

24. *Though he fall, he shall not be utterly cast down.* The original is short and emphatic *ki yippol, lo yutal*, which the Chaldee translates, "Though he should fall into sickness, he shall not die." Neither the text nor any of the versions intimate that a falling into sin is meant; but a falling into trouble, difficulty.

25. *I have been young, and now am old.* I believe this to be literally true in all cases. I am now grey-headed myself; I have travelled in different countries, and have had many opportunities of seeing and conversing with religious people in all situations in life; and I have not, to my knowledge, seen one instance to the contrary.

26. *He is ever merciful, and lendeth.* "All the day he is compassionate."

MATTHEW HENRY

protect us in our difficulties and straits (*v.* 28): *The Lord loves judgment;* he delights in doing justice himself and he delights in those that do justice.

6. That we shall have a comfortable settlement in this world, and in a better when we leave this. That we shall *dwell for evermore* (*v.* 27), and not be *cut off* as the *seed of the wicked*, *v.* 28. That we *shall inherit the land* which the Lord our God gives us *and dwell therein for ever*, *v.* 29. But on this earth there is no dwelling for ever, no continuing city; it is in heaven only, that city which has foundations, that the righteous shall dwell for ever; that will be their everlasting habitation.

7. That we shall not become a prey to our adversaries who seek our ruin, *v.* 32, 33.

Verses 34-40

The psalmist's conclusion of this sermon.

I. The duty here pressed upon us is still the same (*v.* 34): *Wait on the Lord and keep his way.* If we make conscience of *keeping God's way*, we may with cheerfulness wait on him and commit to him our way; and we shall find him a good Master both to his working servants and to his waiting servants.

II. The reasons to enforce this duty are much the same too, taken from the certain destruction of the wicked and the certain salvation of the righteous.

1. The misery of the wicked at last, however they may prosper awhile: *The end of the wicked shall be cut off* (*v.* 38); and that cannot be well that will undoubtedly end so ill. *The transgressors shall be destroyed together*, *v.* 38. In this world God singles out here one sinner and there another, out of many, to be made an example *in terrorem*—as a warning; but in the day of judgment there will be a general destruction of all the transgressors, and not one shall escape.

2. The blessedness of the righteous, at last. Those that keep God's way may be assured that in due time he will *exalt them to inherit the land* (*v.* 34); he will advance them to a place in the heavenly mansions, to dignity, and honour, and true wealth, in the New Jerusalem, to inherit that good land, that land of promise, of which Canaan was a type; he will exalt them above all contempt and danger. Let all people *mark the perfect man, and behold the upright*; take notice of him to observe what comes of him, and you will find that *the end of that man is peace. The salvation of the righteous is of the Lord*; it will be the Lord's doing. He shall *save them*, not only keep them safe, but make them happy, *because they trust in him.*

JAMIESON, FAUSSET, BROWN

27-29. The exhortation is sustained by the assurance of God's essential rectitude in that providential government which provides perpetual blessings for the good, and perpetual misery for the wicked.

32, 33. The devices of the wicked against the good fail because God acquits them.

37. By **the end** is meant reward (Prov. 23:18; 24:14), or expectation of success, as in vs. 38, which describes the *end of the wicked* in contrast, and that is *cut off* (cf. Ps. 73:17). **38. together**—at once—entirely (Ps. 4:8).

34. On the contrary, the good are not only blessed, but made to see the ruin of their foes. **35, 36.** of which a picture is given, under the figure of a flourishing tree (cf. *Margin*), which soon withers. **he was not**—(Cf. vs. 10).

39, 40. strength—(Ps. 27:1; 28:8). **trouble**—straits Ps. 9:9; 10:1). In trust and quietness is the salvation of the pious from all foes and all their devices.

ADAM CLARKE

28. *Forsaketh not his saints.* "His merciful or compassionate ones"; those who, through love to Him and all mankind, are ever ready to give of their substance to the poor.

29. *The righteous shall inherit the land.* If this be not another promise of return to their own land, from that of their captivity, it must be spiritually understood and refer to their eternal dwelling with God in glory.

32. *The wicked watcheth the righteous, and seeketh to slay him.* Similar to what is said in v. 12: "The wicked plotteth against the just [righteous]." But it is added, v. 33: "The Lord will not leave him in his hands"; He will confound his devices, and save His own servants.

34. *Wait on the Lord, and keep his way.* This is the true mode of waiting on God which the Scripture recommends: keeping God's way—using all His ordinances, and living in the spirit of obedience. *When the wicked are cut off, thou shalt see it.* They did see the destruction of the Babylonish king, Belshazzar, and his empire; and it was in consequence of that destruction that they were enlarged.

35. *I have seen the wicked in great power, and spreading himself like a green bay tree.* Does not this refer to Nebuchadnezzar, king of Babylon, and to the vision he had of the great tree which was in the midst of the earth, the head of which reached up to heaven? See Dan. iv. 10, etc.

36. *Yet he passed away.* Both Nebuchadnezzar and his wicked successor, Belshazzar.

37. *Mark the perfect man.* Him who is described above. Take notice of him. He is perfect in his soul, God having saved him from all sin, and filled him with His own love and image. And he is upright in his conduct; and his end, die when he may or where he may, is peace, quietness, and assurance forever.

PSALM 38 (MATTHEW HENRY)

A psalm of David to bring to remembrance.

Verses 1-11

The title of this psalm is a psalm *to bring to remembrance*; the 70th psalm, which was likewise penned in a day of affliction, is so entitled.

I. He deprecates the wrath of God and his displeasure in his affliction (*v.* 1): *O Lord! rebuke me not in thy wrath.* However God rebukes and chastens us, it may not be in wrath and displeasure, for that will be wormwood and gall in the affliction and misery. Those that would escape the wrath of God must pray against that more than any outward affliction, and be content to bear any outward affliction while it comes from, and consists with, the love of God.

II. He bitterly laments the impressions of God's displeasure upon his soul (*v.* 2): *Thy arrows stick fast in me.* He complains of God's wrath as that which inflicted the bodily distemper he was under (*v.* 3): *There is no soundness in my flesh because of thy anger.* The bitterness of it, infused in his mind, affected his body; but that was not the worst: it caused the disquietude of his heart, by reason of which he forgot the courage of a soldier, the dignity of a prince, and all the cheerfulness of the sweet psalmist of Israel, and roared terribly, *v.* 8.

III. He acknowledges his sin to be the cause of all his troubles, and groans more under the load of guilt than any other load, *v.* 3. He complains that his flesh had no soundness. "It is *because of thy anger*; that kindles the fire which burns so fiercely"; but, in the next words, he justifies God herein, and takes all the blame upon himself: "It is *because of my sin.* I have deserved it, and so have brought it upon myself. My own iniquities do correct me." It is sin therefore that this good man complains most of, a burden, a heavy burden (*v.* 4): "*My iniquities have gone over my head*, as proud waters over a man that is sinking and drowning, or as a heavy burden upon my head, pressing me down more than I am able to bear or to bear up under." It keeps men from soaring upward and pressing forward. "*My*

PSALM 38 (JAMIESON, FAUSSET, BROWN)

Vss. 1-22. *To bring to remembrance,* or, remind God of His mercy and himself of his sin. Appealing to God for relief from His heavy chastisement, the Psalmist avows his integrity before men, complains of the defection of friends and persecution of enemies, and in a submissive spirit, casting himself on God, with penitent confession he pleads God's covenant relation and his innocence of the charges of his enemies, and prays for divine comfort and help.

1-4. He deprecates deserved punishment, which is described (Ps. 6:1), under the figure of bodily disease.

arrows . . . and thy hand—the sharp and heavy afflictions he suffered (Deut. 32:23).

iniquities—afflictions in punishment of sin (II Sam. 16:12; Ps. 31:10; 40:12). **gone over mine head**—as a flood.

PSALM 38 (ADAM CLARKE)

CHARLES H. SPURGEON:

"O Lord, rebuke me not in thy wrath" (38:1). Rebuked I must be, for I am an erring child and thou a careful Father, but throw not too much anger into the tones of thy voice; deal gently although I have sinned grievously. The anger of others I can bear, but not thine. As thy love is most sweet to my heart, so thy displeasure is most cutting to my conscience.

"Neither chasten me in thy hot displeasure." Chasten me if thou wilt; it is a Father's prerogative, and to endure it obediently is a child's duty; but oh, turn not the rod into a sword, smite not so as to kill. True, my sins might well inflame thee, but let thy mercy and longsuffering quench the glowing coals of thy wrath. Oh, let me not be treated as an enemy or dealt with as a rebel. Bring to remembrance thy covenant, thy fatherhood, and my feebleness, and spare thy servant.—*The Treasury of David*

MATTHEW HENRY

wounds stink and are corrupt (as wounds in the body rankle, and fester, and grow foul, for want of being dressed and looked after), and it is through my own *foolishness.*" Sins are wounds (Gen. iv. 23), painful mortal wounds. A slight sore, neglected, may prove of fatal consequence, and so may a slight sin slighted and left unrepented of.

IV. He bemoans himself because of his afflictions, and gives ease to his grief by giving vent to it and pouring out his complaint before the Lord.

1. He was troubled in mind, his conscience was pained, and he had no rest in his own spirit; and a wounded spirit who can bear? He was *troubled,* or distorted, *bowed down greatly,* and went *mourning all the day long, v.* 6.

2. He was sick and weak in body; his loins were filled with a loathsome disease, some swelling, or ulcer, or inflammation (some think a plague-sore, such as Hezekiah's boil), and there was *no soundness in his flesh,* but, like Job, he was all over distempered. Sickness will tame the strongest body and the stoutest spirit. David was famed for his courage and great exploits; and yet, when God contended with him by bodily sickness and the impressions of his wrath upon his mind, his heart fails him, and he becomes weak as water.

3. His friends were unkind to him (*v.* 11): *My lovers* (such as had been merry with him in the day of his mirth) now *stand aloof from my sore.* Even *his kinsmen,* that were bound to him by blood and alliance, *stood afar off.*

V. In the midst of his complaints, he comforts himself with the cognizance God graciously took both of his griefs and of his prayers (*v.* 9): "*Lord, all my desire is before thee.* Thou knowest what I want and what I would have: *My groaning is not hidden from thee.* Thou knowest the burdens I groan under and the blessings I groan after."

Verses 12–22

I. David complains of the power and malice of his enemies, who, it should seem, not only took occasion from the weakness of his body and the trouble of his mind to insult over him, but took advantage thence to do him a mischief. He has a great deal to say against them, which he humbly offers as a reason why God should appear for him, as xxv. 19, *Consider my enemies.* "They are very subtle and politic. They *lay snares,* they *imagine deceits,* and herein they are restless and unwearied: they do it *all the day long.* They are very insolent and abusive: *When my foot slips,* when I make any mistake, or take a false step, they magnify themselves against me; they are pleased with it. They are not only unjust, but very ungrateful: They *hate me wrongfully, v.* 19. I never did them any ill turn; *they render evil for good, v.* 20. Many a kindness I have done them, for which I might have expected a return of kindness; but *for my love they are my adversaries,* cix. 4. "*They are my adversaries* merely *because I follow the thing that*" good is. They hated him, not only for his kindness to them, but for his devotion and obedience to God; they hated him because they hated God and all that bear his image.

II. He reflects, with comfort, upon his own peaceable and pious behaviour under all the injuries and indignities that were done him. If still we hold fast our integrity and our peace, who can hurt us? This David did here. He kept his temper, and was not ruffled nor discomposed by any of the mischievous things that were said or done against him (*v.* 13, 14): *I, as a deaf man, heard not.* Herein David was a type of Christ, who was as a sheep dumb before the shearer, and, when he was reviled, reviled not again; and both are examples to us not to render railing for railing. He kept close to his God by faith and prayer. His friends, that should have owned him, and stood by him, and appeared as witnesses for him, withdrew from him, *v.* 10. But God is a friend that will never fail us if we hope in him. *Thou shalt answer, Lord, for me.*

III. He here bewails his own follies and infirmities. *I am ready to halt, v.* 17. This will best be explained by a reflection like this which the psalmist made upon himself in a similar case (lxxiii. 2): *My feet were almost gone, when I saw the prosperity of the wicked.* So here: *I was ready to halt,* ready to say, *I have cleansed my hands in vain.* Good men, by setting their sorrow continually before them, have been ready to halt, who, by setting God always before them, have kept their standing. Though before men he could justify himself, before God he will judge and condemn himself (*v.* 18): "*I will declare my iniquity,* and not cover it; *I will be sorry for my sin,* and not make a light matter of it"; and this helped to make him silent under the rebukes of Providence and the reproaches of men.

JAMIESON, FAUSSET, BROWN

5-8. The loathsomeness, corruption, and wasting torture of severe physical disease set forth his mental anguish. It is possible some bodily disease was connected. The **loins** are the seat of strength. His exhaustion left him only the power to groan.

9. That God can hear (Rom. 8:26). **10. My heart panteth**—as if barely surviving. **light . . . from me**—utter exhaustion (Ps. 6: 7; 13:3).

11, 12. Friends desert, but foes increase in malignity. **seek after my life**—(I Sam. 20:1; 22:23).

19, 20. Still, while humbled before God, he is the victim of deadly enemies, full of malice and treachery. **enemies are lively**—lit., "of life," who would take my life, i.e., deadly.

13, 14. He patiently submits, uttering no reproaches or replies (John 19:9) to their insulting speeches;

15-17. for he is confident the **Lord**—lit., "Sovereign" (to whom he was a servant), would answer his prayer (Ps. 3:4; 4:1), and not permit their triumph in his partial halting, of which he was in danger.

18. Consciousness of sin makes suffering pungent, and suffering, rightly received, leads to confession.

ADAM CLARKE

6. *I am troubled.* In mind. *I am bowed down*—in body. I am altogether afflicted, and full of distress.

7. *For my loins are filled with a loathsome disease.* Or rather, a "burning," strongly feverish disease.

11. *My lovers.* Those who professed much affection for me; *my friends,* my "companions," who never before left my company, *stand aloof. My kinsmen.* My "neighbors," stand afar off. I am deserted by all, and they stand off because of my "plague."

10. *My heart panteth.* "Flutters, palpitates," through fear and alarm. *My strength faileth.* Not being able to take nourishment. *The light of mine eyes . . . is gone.* I can scarcely discern anything through the general decay of my health and vigor, particularly affecting my sight.

19. *But mine enemies are lively.* Instead of *chaiyim,* "lively," I would read *chinam,* "without cause."

20. *Because I follow the thing that good is.* The translation is as bad as the sentence is awkward. "Because I follow goodness."

13. *But I, as a deaf man.* I was conscious of my guilt; I could not vindicate myself; and I was obliged in silence to bear their insults.

14. *No reproofs.* "Arguments" or "vindications"; a forensic term. I was as a man accused in open court, and I could make no defense.

17. *For I am ready to halt.* Literally, "I am prepared to halt." So completely infirm is my soul that it is impossible for me to take one right step in the way of righteousness, unless strengthened by Thee.

18. *I will declare mine iniquity.* I will confess it with the deepest humiliation and self-abasement.

MATTHEW HENRY

IV. He concludes with very earnest prayers to God for his gracious presence (*v.* 21, 22): "*Forsake me not, O Lord!* though my friends forsake me, and though I deserve to be forsaken by thee. Be not far from me, as my unbelieving heart is ready to fear thou art."

PSALM 39

To the chief musician, *even* to Jeduthun. A psalm of David.

Verses 1–6

David here recollects, and leaves upon record, the workings of his heart under his afflictions.

I. He remembered the covenants he had made with God. When at any time we are tempted to sin we must call to mind the solemn vows we have made against the particular sin we are upon the brink of.

1. He remembers that he had resolved to be circumspect in his walking (*v.* 1): *I said, I will take heed to my ways.* Having resolved to take heed to our ways, we must, upon all occasions, remind ourselves of that resolution.

2. He remembers that he had in particular covenanted against tongue-sins. It is not so easy as we could wish not to sin in thought; but, if an evil thought should arise in his mind, he would lay his hand upon his mouth, and suppress it, that it should go no further. "*I will keep a bridle*, or muzzle, *upon my mouth.*" Watchfulness in the habit is the bridle upon the head; watchfulness in the act and exercise is the hand upon the bridle. He would keep a muzzle upon it, as upon an unruly dog that is fierce and does mischief; by particular steadfast resolution corruption is restrained from breaking out at the lips, and so is muzzled. When he was in company with the wicked he would take heed of saying any thing that might harden them or give occasion to them to blaspheme.

II. Pursuant to these covenants he made a shift with much ado to bridle his tongue (*v.* 2): *I was dumb with silence; I held my peace even from good.* But what shall we say of his keeping silence *even from good*? I rather think it was his weakness; because he might not say anything, he would say nothing, but ran into an extreme.

III. The less he spoke the more he thought and the more warmly. Binding the distempered part did but draw the humour to it: *My sorrow was stirred, my heart was hot within me*, *v.* 3. He could bridle his tongue but he could not keep his passion under. Note, Those that are of a fretful discontented spirit ought not to pore much, for, while they suffer their thoughts to dwell upon the causes of the calamity, the fire of their discontent is fed with fuel and burns the more furiously. If therefore we would prevent the mischief of ungoverned passions, we must redress the grievance of ungoverned thoughts.

IV. When he did speak, at last, it was to the purpose: *At the last I spoke with my tongue.* I rather take it to be, not the breach of his good purpose, but the reformation of his mistake in carrying it too far; he had kept silence from good, but now he would so keep silence no longer.

1. He prays to God to make him sensible of the shortness and uncertainty of life and the near approach of death (*v.* 4): *Lord, make me to know my end and the measure of my days.* He does not mean, "Lord, let me know how long I shall live and when I shall die." But, *Lord, make me to know my end*, means, "Lord, give me wisdom and grace to consider it (Deut. xxxii. 29) and to improve what I know concerning it. Lord, make me to consider the end of my life." It is a final period to our state of probation. To the wicked man it is the end of all joys; to a godly man it is the end of all griefs. When we look upon death as a thing at a distance we are tempted to adjourn the necessary preparations for it; but, when we consider how short life is, we shall see ourselves concerned to do what our hand finds to do, not only with all our might, but with all possible expedition.

2. He meditates upon the brevity and vanity of life, pleading them with God for relief under the burdens of life and pleading them with himself for his quickening to the business of life. *Behold, thou hast made my days as a hand-breadth*, the breadth of four fingers, a certain dimension, a small one, and the measure whereof we have always about us, always before our eyes. We need no skill in arithmetic wherewith to compute the number of them. No; we have the standard of them at our fingers' end, and it is but one hand-breadth in all. Our time is short, and God has made it so; for *the number of our months is with him.* It is short, and he knows it to be so: It *is as nothing before thee.* All time is nothing to God's eternity, much less our share of time. Men's life on

JAMIESON, FAUSSET, BROWN

22. (Cf. Ps. 22:19; 35:3.) All terms of frequent use. In this Psalm the language is generally susceptible of application to Christ as a sufferer, David, as such, typifying Him. This does not require us to apply the confessions of sin, but only the pains or penalties which He bore for us.

PSALM 39

Vss. 1-13. *To Jeduthun* (I Chron. 16:41, 42), one of the chief singers. His name mentioned, perhaps, as a special honor. Under depressing views of his frailty and the prosperity of the wicked, the Psalmist, tempted to murmur, checks the expression of his feelings, till, led to regard his case aright, he prays for a proper view of his condition and for the divine compassion.

1. I said—or, resolved. **will take heed**—watch. **ways**—conduct, of which the use of the tongue is a part (Jas. 1:26).

bridle—lit., "muzzle" (cf. Deut. 25:4). **while . . . before me**—in beholding their prosperity (Ps. 37:10, 36).

2. even from good—(Gen. 31:24), everything.

3. His emotions, as a smothered flame, burst forth.

4-7. Some take these words as those of fretting, but they are not essentially such. The tinge of discontent arises from the character of his suppressed emotions. But, addressing God, they are softened and subdued. **4. make me to know**—experimentally appreciate. **how frail I am**—lit., "when I shall cease."

ADAM CLARKE

PSALM 39

The title says, "To the chief Musician, Jeduthun himself, A Psalm of David." It is supposed that this Jeduthun is the same with *Ethan*, 1 Chron. vi. 44, compared with 1 Chron. xvi. 41; and is there numbered among the sons of Merari. And he is supposed to have been one of the four masters of music, or leaders of bands, belonging to the Temple. And it is thought that David, having composed this psalm, gave it to Jeduthun and his company to sing. But several have supposed that Jeduthun himself was the author. It is very likely that this psalm was written on the same occasion with the preceding. It relates to a grievous malady by which David was afflicted after his transgression with Bath-sheba.

1. *I said, I will take heed to my ways.* I must be cautious because of my enemies; I must be patient because of my afflictions; I must be watchful over my tongue, lest I offend my God, or give my adversaries any cause to speak evil of me.

CHARLES H. SPURGEON:

"My heart was hot within me" (39:3). The friction of inward thoughts produced an intense mental heat. The door of his heart was shut, and with the fire of sorrow burning within, the chamber of his soul soon grew unbearable with heat. Silence is an awful thing for a sufferer, it is the surest method to produce madness. Mourner, tell your sorrow; do it first and most fully to God, but even to pour it out before some wise and godly friend is far from being wasted breath.

"While I was musing the fire burned." As he thought upon the ease of the wicked and his own daily affliction, he could not unravel the mystery of providence, and therefore he became greatly agitated. While his heart was musing it was fusing, for the subject was confusing. It became harder every moment to be quiet; his volcanic soul was tossed with an inward ocean of fire, and heaved to and fro with a mental earthquake; an eruption was imminent, the burning lava must pour forth in a fiery stream. "Then spake I with my tongue." The original is grandly laconic. "I spake." The muzzled tongue burst all its bonds. The gag was hurled away. Misery, like murder, will out. You can silence praise, but anguish is clamorous. Resolve or no resolve, heed or no heed, sin or no sin, the impetuous torrent forced for itself a channel and swept away every restraint.

—*The Treasury of David*

5. *My days as a handbreadth.* My life is but a "span." *And mine age is as nothing.* "As if it were not before thee." All time is swallowed up in Thy eternity.

MATTHEW HENRY

earth is vain and therefore it is wisdom to make sure of a better life. *All man is all vanity* (so it may be read); everything about him is uncertain; nothing is substantial and durable but what relates to the new man. *Selah* is annexed, as a note commanding observation. "Stop here, and pause awhile, that you may take time to consider and apply this truth, that every man is vanity." For the proof of the vanity of man, as mortal, he here mentions three things, *v.* 6, *First*, The vanity of our joys and honours: *Surely every man walks* (even when he walks in state, when he walks in pleasure) in a shadow, in an image, *in a vain show*. *Secondly*, The vanity of our griefs and fears. *Surely they are disquieted in vain.* The occasions of our trouble are often the creatures of our own fancy and they are always fruitless. *Thirdly*, The vanity of our cares and toils. Man takes a great deal of pains to *heap up riches*, and they are but like heaps of manure in the furrows of the field, good for nothing unless they be spread.

Verses 7–13

The psalmist, in these verses, turns his eyes and heart heaven-ward. When there is no solid satisfaction to be had in the creature it is to be found in God, and in communion with him; and to him we should be driven by our disappointments in the world.

I. His dependence on God, *v.* 7. He despairs of a happiness in the things of the world, and disclaims all expectations from it: "*Now, Lord, what wait I for?* Even nothing from the things of sense and time; I have nothing to wish for, nothing to hope for, from this earth." We cannot reckon upon constant health and prosperity, nor upon comfort in any relation; for it is all as uncertain as our continuance here. He takes hold of happiness and satisfaction in God: *My hope is in thee.*

II. His submission to God, and his cheerful acquiescence in his holy will, *v.* 9. "*Because thou didst it;* it did not come to pass by chance, but according to thy appointment." Of every event we may say, "This is the finger of God; it is the Lord's doing," whoever were the instruments.

III. His desire towards God, and the prayers he puts up to him.

1. For the pardoning of his sin and the preventing of his shame, *v.* 8. Before he prays (*v.* 10), *Remove thy stroke from me*, he prays (*v.* 8), "*Deliver me from all my offences*, from the guilt I have contracted, the punishment I have deserved." He pleads, *Make me not a reproach to the foolish.* Wicked people are foolish people; and they then show their folly most when they think to show their wit, by scoffing at God's people.

2. For the removal of his affliction, that he might speedily be eased of his present burdens (*v.* 10): *Remove thy stroke away from me. I am consumed by the blow of thy hand.* His sickness prevailed to such a degree that his spirits failed, his strength was wasted, and his body emaciated. Our ways and our doings procure the trouble to ourselves, and we are beaten with a rod of our own making. It is the yoke of our transgressions, though it be *bound with his hand*, Lam. i. 14. God's rebukes make man's *beauty to consume away like a moth.* Some make the moth to represent man, who is as easily crushed as a moth with the touch of a finger, Job iv. 19. Others make it to represent the divine rebukes, which silently and insensibly waste and consume us, as the moth does the garment. He pleads the good impressions made upon him by his affliction. He hoped that the end was accomplished for which it was sent, and that therefore it would be removed in mercy. It had set him a-weeping, and he hoped God would take notice of that. *Lord, hold not thy peace at my tears*, *v.* 12. He that does not willingly afflict and grieve the children of men, much less his own children, will not hold his peace at their tears, but will either speak deliverance for them or in the meantime speak comfort to them. It had set him a-praying; and afflictions are sent to stir up prayer. It had helped to wean him from the world and to take his affections off from it. Now he began, more than ever, to look upon himself as *a stranger and sojourner* here, like all his fathers, not at home in this world, but travelling through it to another, to a better, and would never reckon himself at home till he came to heaven.

3. He prays for a reprieve yet a little longer (*v.* 13): "*O spare me*, ease me, raise me up from this illness, that I may recover strength both in body and mind, that I may get into a more calm and composed frame of spirit, and may be better prepared for another world, *before I go hence* by death, *and* shall *be no more* in this world." *Let my soul live, and it shall praise thee.*

JAMIESON, FAUSSET, BROWN

5-6. His prayer is answered in his obtaining an impressive view of the vanity of the life of all men, and their transient state. Their pomp is a mere image, and their wealth is gathered they know not for whom.

7. The interrogation makes the implied negative stronger. Though this world offers nothing to our expectation, God is worthy of all confidence.

8-10. Patiently submissive, he prays for the removal of his chastisement, and that he may not be a reproach.

11. From his own case, he argues to that of all, that the destruction of man's enjoyments is ascribable to sin.

12, 13. Consonant with the tenor of the Psalm, he prays for God's compassionate regard to him as a stranger here; and that, as such was the condition of his fathers, so, like them, he may be cheered instead of being bound under wrath and chastened in displeasure.

ADAM CLARKE

Verily every man at his best state. "Every man that exists is vanity."

6. *Walketh in a vain shew.* In a "shadow." He is but the semblance of being; he appears for a while, and then vanisheth away. *He heapeth up riches, and knoweth not who shall gather them.* He "raketh together." This is a metaphor taken from agriculture. The husbandman rakes the corn, etc., together in the field, and yet, so uncertain is life, that he knows not who shall gather them into the granary!

CHARLES H. SPURGEON:

"My hope is in thee" (39:7). The Lord is self-existent and true, and therefore worthy of the confidence of men; he will live when all the creatures die, and his fullness will abide when all second causes are exhausted; to him, therefore, let us direct our expectation, and on him let us rest our confidence. Away from sand to rock let all wise builders turn themselves, for if not today, yet surely ere long, a storm will rise before which nothing will be able to stand but that which has the lasting element of faith in God to cement it. David had but one hope, and that hope entered within the veil; hence he brought his vessel to safe anchorage, and after a little drifting all was peace.—*The Treasury of David*

11. *When thou with rebukes dost correct man. Tochachoth* signifies a "vindication of proceedings in a court of law," a "legal defense." When God comes to maintain the credit and authority of His law against a sinner, He causes *his beauty to consume away*—a metaphor taken from the case of a culprit who, by the arguments of counsel and the unimpeachable evidence of witnesses, has the facts all proved against him, grows pale, looks terrified; his fortitude forsakes him, and he faints in court.

13. *O spare me.* Take me not from this state of probation till I have a thorough preparation for a state of blessedness. This he terms recovering his strength—being restored to the favor and image of God, from which he had fallen. This should be the daily cry of every human spirit: Restore me to Thine image, guide me by Thy counsel, and then receive me to Thy glory!

MATTHEW HENRY

PSALM 40

To the chief musician. A psalm of David.

Verses 1–5

I. The great distress and trouble that the psalmist had been in.

II. His humble attendance upon God and his believing expectations from him in those depths: *I waited patiently for the Lord, v.* 1. *Waiting, I waited.* He expected relief from no other than from God; the same hand that tears must heal, that smites must bind up (Hos. vi. 1), or it will never be done. But he waited patiently, which intimates that the relief did not come quickly; yet he doubted not but it would come, and resolved to continue believing, and hoping, and praying, till it did come. Now this is very applicable to Christ. His agony, both in the garden and on the cross, was the same continued, and it was a horrible pit and miry clay. Then was his soul troubled and exceedingly sorrowful; but then he prayed, *Father, glorify thy name; Father, save me;* then he kept hold of his relation to his Father, "My God, my God," and thus waited patiently for him.

III. His comfortable experience of God's goodness to him in his distress, which he records for the honour of God and his own and others' encouragement. *He inclined unto me and heard my cry.* Those that have been under the prevalency of a religious melancholy, and by the grace of God have been relieved, may apply this very feelingly to themselves; they are brought up out of a horrible pit. The mercy is completed by the setting of their feet upon a rock, where they find firm footing, are as much elevated with the hopes of heaven as they were before cast down with the fears of hell. "*He has put a new song in my mouth;* he has given me cause to rejoice and a heart to rejoice." He was brought, as it were, into a new world, and that filled his mouth with a new song, *even praise to our God.*

IV. David's experience would be an encouragement to many to hope in God, and, for that end, he leaves it here upon record: *Many shall see, and fear, and trust in the Lord.* There is a holy reverent fear of God, which is not only consistent with, but the foundation of our hope in him. They shall not fear him and shun him, but fear him and trust in him in their greatest straits, not doubting but to find him as able and ready to help as David did in his distress. The psalmist invites others to make God their hope, as he did, by pronouncing those happy that do so (*v.* 4): "*Blessed is the man that makes the Lord his trust, and respects not the proud,* does not do as those do that trust in themselves, nor depends upon those who proudly encourage others to trust in them; for both the one and the other turn aside to lies, as indeed all those do that turn aside from God." This is applicable, particularly, to our faith in Christ. Blessed are those that trust in him, and in his righteousness alone. The joyful sense he had of this mercy led him to observe, with thankfulness, the many other favours he had received from God, *v.* 5. "*Many, O Lord my God, are thy wonderful works which thou hast done,* both for me and others; this is but one of many." All his wonderful works are the product of his thoughts to us-ward. They are the projects of infinite wisdom, the designs of everlasting love (1 Cor. ii. 7, Jer. xxxi. 3), *thoughts of good and not of evil,* Jer. xxix. 11. How the links of the golden chain are joined, is a mystery to us, and what we shall not be able to account for till the veil be rent and the mystery of God finished. When we have said the most we can of the wonders of divine love to us we must conclude with an *et cetera*—and such like, and adore the depth, despairing to find the bottom.

Verses 6–10

The psalmist, being struck with amazement at the wonderful works that God had done for his people, is strangely carried out here to foretell that work of wonder which excels all the rest and is the foundation and fountain of all, that of our redemption by our Lord Jesus Christ. This paragraph is quoted by the apostle (Heb. x. 5, &c.) and applied to Christ and his undertaking for us.

I. The utter insufficiency of the legal sacrifices to atone for sin in order to our peace with God and our happiness in him: *Sacrifice and offering thou didst not desire;* thou wouldst not have the Redeemer to offer them. Something he must have to offer, but not these (Heb. viii. 3). Even while the law concerning them was in full force it might be said, God did not desire them, nor accept them, for their own sake. They could not take away the guilt of sin by satisfying God's justice. The life of a sheep, which is so much inferior in value to that of a man (Matt. xii. 12), could not pretend to be an equivalent, much less an expedient to preserve the honour of God's government and

JAMIESON, FAUSSET, BROWN

PSALM 40

Vss. 1-17. In this Psalm a celebration of God's deliverance is followed by a profession of devotion to His service. Then follows a prayer for relief from imminent dangers, involving the overthrow of enemies and the rejoicing of sympathizing friends. In Hebrews 10:5, etc., Paul quotes vss. 6-8 as the words of Christ, offering Himself as a better sacrifice. Some suppose Paul thus accommodated David's words to express Christ's sentiments. But the value of his quotation would be thus destroyed, as it would have no force in his argument, unless regarded by his readers as the original sense of the passage in the Old Testament. Others suppose the Psalm describes David's feelings in suffering and joy; but the language quoted by Paul, in the sense given by him, could not apply to David in any of his relations, for as a type the language is not adapted to describe any event or condition of David's career, and as an individual representing the pious generally, neither he nor they could properly use it (cf. on vs. 7 below). The Psalm must be taken then, as the sixteenth, to express the feelings of Christ's human nature. The difficulties pertinent to this view will be considered as they occur.

1-3. The figures for deep distress are illustrated in Jeremiah's history (Jer. 38:6-12). Patience and trust manifested in distress, deliverance in answer to prayer, and the blessed effect of it in eliciting praise from God's true worshippers, teach us that Christ's suffering is our example, and His deliverance our encouragement (Heb. 5:7, 8; 12:3; I Pet. 4:12-16). **inclined**—(the ear, Ps. 17:6), as if to catch the faintest sigh. **a new song**—(Ps. 33:3).

fear, and . . . trust— revere with love and faith.

4. Blessed—(Ps. 1:1; 2: 12). **respecteth**—lit., "turns towards," as an object of confidence. **turn aside**—from true God and His law to falsehood in worship and conduct.

5. be reckoned up in order—(cf. Ps. 5:3; 33:14; Isa. 44:7), too many to be set forth regularly. This is but one instance of many. The use of the plural accords with the union of Christ and His people. In suffering and triumph, they are one with Him.

6-8. In Paul's view this passage has more meaning than the mere expression of grateful devotion to God's service. He represents Christ as declaring that the sacrifices, whether vegetable or animal, general or special expiatory offerings, would not avail to meet the demands of God's law, and that He had come to render the required satisfaction, which he states was effected by "the offering of the body of Christ," for that is the "will of God" which Christ came to fulfil or do, in order to effect man's redemption. We thus see that the contrast to the unsatisfactory character assigned the Old Testament offerings in vs.

ADAM CLARKE

PSALM 40

I am satisfied the psalm was composed by David, and about the same time and on the same occasion as the two preceding; with this difference, that here he magnifies God for having bestowed the mercy which he sought there. It is, therefore, a thanksgiving for his recovery from the sore disease by which he was afflicted in his body, and for his restoration to the divine favor. The sixth, seventh, and eighth verses contain a remarkable prophecy of the incarnation and sacrificial offering of Jesus Christ. From the eleventh to the end contains a new subject, and appears to have belonged to another psalm. It is the same as the seventieth psalm; only it wants the first two verses.

1. *I waited patiently for the Lord.* The two preceding psalms are proofs of the patience and resignation with which David waited for the mercy of God. *And heard my cry.* The two preceding psalms show how he prayed and waited; this shows how he succeeded.

2. *An horrible pit.* Literally, the "sounding pit," where nothing was heard except the howlings of wild beasts, or the hollow sounds of winds reverberated and broken from the craggy sides and roof. *The miry clay.* Where the longer I stayed, the deeper I sank, and was utterly unable to save myself.

5. *Many . . . are thy wonderful works.* The Psalmist seems here astonished and confounded at the counsels, loving-kindnesses, and marvellous works of the Lord, not in nature, but in grace; for it was the mercy of God towards himself that he had now particularly in view.

6. *Sacrifice and offering.* The apostle, Heb. x. 5, etc., quoting this and the two following verses, says, "When he [the Messiah] cometh into the world"—was about to be incarnated, "he saith"—to God the Father, "Sacrifice and offering thou wouldest not"—it was never Thy will and design that the sacrifices under Thy own law should be considered as making atonement for sin; they were designed only to point out My incarnation and consequent sacrificial death; and therefore "a body hast thou prepared me," by a miraculous conception in the womb of a virgin.

MATTHEW HENRY

laws and repair the injury done to that honour by the sin of man. They could not take away the terror of sin by pacifying the conscience, nor the power of sin by sanctifying the nature; it was impossible, Heb. ix. 9; x. 1-4. What there was in them that was valuable resulted from their reference to Jesus Christ, of whom they were types—shadows indeed, but shadows of good things to come, and trials of the faith and obedience of God's people, of their obedience to the law and their faith in the gospel. But the substance must come, which is Christ, who must bring that glory to God and that grace to man which it was impossible those sacrifices should ever do.

II. The designation of our Lord Jesus to the work and office of Mediator: *My ears hast thou opened.* God the Father disposed him to the undertaking (Isa. l. 5, 6) and then obliged him to go through with it. *My ear hast thou digged.* It is supposed to allude to the law and custom of binding servants to serve for ever by boring their ear to the doorpost; see Exod. xxi. 6.

III. His own voluntary consent to this undertaking: "*Then said I, Lo, I come;* then, when sacrifice and offering would not do, rather than the work should be undone, I said, Lo, I come, to enter the lists with the powers of darkness, and to advance the interests of God's glory and kingdom." He freely offered himself to this service. He firmly obliged himself to it: "I come; I promise to come in the fulness of time." He frankly owned himself engaged: He said, *Lo, I come,* said it all along to the Old Testament saints, who therefore knew him by the title of ὁ ἐρχόμενος—*He that should come.*

IV. The reason why he came, in pursuance of his undertaking—because *in the volume of the book it was written of him,* 1. In the close rolls of the divine decree and counsel; there it was written that his ear was opened, and he said, *Lo, I come*; there the covenant of redemption was recorded.

V. The pleasure he took in his undertaking. Having freely offered himself to it, he did not fail, nor was discouraged, but proceeded with all possible satisfaction to himself (*v.* 8, 9): *I delight to do thy will, O my God!*

VI. The publication of the gospel to the children of men, even *in the great congregation, v.* 9, 10. The same that as a priest wrought out redemption for us, as a prophet, by his own preaching first, then by his apostles, and still by his word and Spirit, makes it known to us. The *great salvation began to be spoken by the Lord,* Heb. ii. 3. What is preached is *righteousness* (*v.* 9), God's righteousness (*v.* 10), God's *faithfulness* to his promise, God's *loving-kindness* and his *truth,* his mercy according to his word. It is preached—*to the congregation, v.* 9, and again *v.* 10. The gospel was preached both to Jews and Gentiles, to great congregations of both. It is preached—freely and openly: *I have not refrained my lips; I have not hid it; I have not concealed it.*

Verses 11-17

The psalmist, having meditated upon the work of redemption, and spoken of it in the person of the Messiah, now speaks in his own person.

I. This may encourage us to pray for the mercy of God, and to put ourselves under the protection of that mercy, *v.* 11. "Lord, thou hast not spared thy Son, nor withheld him; *withhold not thou thy tender mercies* then, which thou hast laid up for us in him; for wilt thou not *with him also freely give us all things?* Rom. viii. 32. *Let thy lovingkindness and thy truth continually preserve me.*"

II. This may encourage us in reference to the guilt of sin, that Jesus Christ has done that towards our discharge from it which sacrifice and offering could not do. The psalmist saw his iniquities to be evils, the worst of evils; he saw that they *compassed him about more than the hairs of his head.* The sight of sin so oppressed him that he could not hold up his head—*I am not able to look up;* much less could he keep up his heart—*therefore my heart fails me.* With what a holy passion does he cry out, "*Be pleased, O Lord! to deliver me* (*v.* 13). In a case of this nature, where the bliss of an immortal soul is concerned, delays are dangerous; therefore, *O Lord! make haste to help me.*"

III. This may encourage us to hope for victory over our spiritual enemies that seek after our souls to destroy them (*v.* 14). If Christ has triumphed over them, we, through him, shall be more than conquerors. In the belief of this we may pray, with humble boldness, *Let them be ashamed and confounded together,* and *driven backward, v.* 14. *Let them be desolate, v.* 15. When a child of God is brought into that horrible pit, and the miry clay, Satan cries *Aha! aha!* thinking he has gained his point; but he shall rage when he sees the brand plucked out of the fire, and

JAMIESON, FAUSSET, BROWN

6 is found in the compliance with God's law (cf. vss. 7, 8). Of course, as Paul and other New Testament writers explain Christ's work, it consisted in more than being made under the law or obeying its precepts. It required an "obedience unto death," and that is the compliance here chiefly intended, and which makes the contrast with vs. 6 clear.

mine ears hast thou opened—Whether allusion is made to the custom of boring a servant's ear, in token of voluntary and perpetual enslavement (Exod. 21:6), or that *the opening of the ear,* as in Isa. 48:8; 50:5 (though by a different word in *Hebrew*) denotes obedience by the common figure of hearing for obeying, it is evident that the clause is designed to express a devotion to God's will as avowed more fully in vs. 8, and already explained. Paul, however, uses the words, "a body hast thou prepared me," which are found in the *Septuagint* in the place of the words, "*mine* ears hast thou opened." He does not lay any stress on this clause, and his argument is complete without it. It is, perhaps, to be regarded rather as an interpretation or free translation by the *Septuagint,* than either an addition or attempt at verbal translation. The *Septuagint* translators may have had reference to Christ's vicarious sufferings as taught in other Scriptures, as in Isaiah 53; at all events, the sense is substantially the same, as a body was essential to the required obedience (cf. Rom. 7:4; I Pet. 2:24). **7. Then**—in such case, without necessarily referring to order of time. **Lo, I come**—I am prepared to do, etc. **in the volume of the book**—*roll of the book.* Such rolls, resembling maps, are still used in the synagogues. **written of me**—or on me, prescribed to me (II Kings 22:13). The first is the sense adopted by Paul. In either case, the Pentateuch, or law of Moses, is meant, and while it contains much respecting Christ directly, as Genesis 3:15; 49:10; Deuteronomy 18:15, and, indirectly, in the Levitical ritual, there is nowhere any allusion to David. **9, 10.** Christ's prophetical office is taught. He "preached" the great truths of God's government of sinners. **I have preached**—lit., "announced good tidings."

11. may be rendered as an assertion, that God *will not withhold* . . . (Ps. 16: 1). **12. evils**—inflicted by others. **iniquities**—or penal *afflictions,* and sometimes calamities in the wide sense. This meaning of the word is very common. (Ps. 31:11; 38:4; cf. Gen. 4:13, Cain's punishment; Gen. 19:15, that of Sodom; I Sam. 28:10, of the witch of Endor; also II Sam. 16:12; Job 19:29; Isa. 5:18; 53:11). This meaning of the word is also favored by the clause, "taken hold of me," which follows, which can be said appropriately of *sufferings,* but not of *sins* (cf. Job. 27:20; Ps. 69:24). Thus, the difficulties in referring this Psalm to Christ, arising from the usual reading of this verse, are removed. Of the terrible *afflictions,* or sufferings, alluded to and endured for us, cf. Luke 22:39-44, and the narrative of the scenes of Calvary. **my heart faileth me**—(Matt. 26:38), "My soul is exceeding sorrowful, even unto death." **cannot look up**—lit., "I cannot see," not denoting the depression of conscious guilt, as Luke 18:13, but exhaustion from suffering, as *dimness* of eyes (cf. Ps. 6:7; 13:3; 38: 10). The whole context thus sustains the sense assigned to *iniquities.* **13.** (Cf. Ps. 22:19.) **14, 15.** The language is not necessarily imprecatory, but rather a confident expectation (Ps. 5:11), though the former sense is not inconsistent with Christ's prayer for the forgiveness of His murderers, inasmuch as their confusion and shame might be the very means to prepare them for humbly seeking forgiveness (cf. Acts. 2:37). **for a reward**—lit., "in consequence of." **Aha**—(Cf. Ps. 35:21, 25).

ADAM CLARKE

A body hast thou prepared me. The quotation of this and the two following verses by the apostle, Heb. x. 5, etc., is taken from the Septuagint, with scarcely any variety of reading: but, although the general meaning is the same, they are widely different in verbal expression in the Hebrew. David's words we translate, *Mine ears hast thou opened;* but they might be more properly rendered, "My ears hast Thou bored;" that is, Thou hast made me Thy servant forever, to dwell in Thine own house. For the allusion is evidently to the custom mentioned Exod. xxi. 2, etc.: "If thou buy an Hebrew servant, six years he shall serve: and in the seventh he shall go out free . . . and if the servant shall plainly say, I love my master, etc., I will not go out free: then his master shall bring him to . . . the door post; and . . . shall bore his ear through with an aul; and he shall serve him for ever."

But how is it possible that the Septuagint and the apostle should take a meaning so totally different from the sense of the Hebrew? Dr. Kennicott has a very ingenious conjecture here. He supposes that the Septuagint and the apostle express the meaning of the words as they stood in the copy from which the Greek translation was made; and that the present Hebrew text is corrupted in the word *oznayim,* "ears," which has been written through carelessness for *az gevah,* "then, a body."

It is remarkable that all the offerings and sacrifices which were considered to be of an atoning or cleansing nature, offered under the law, are here enumerated by the Psalmist and the apostle, to show that none of them, nor all of them, could take away sin; and that the grand sacrifice of Christ was that alone which could do it.

Four kinds are here specified, by both the Psalmist and the apostle; viz., sacrifice, offering, burnt offering, sin offering. Of all these we may say, with the apostle, it was impossible that the blood of bulls and goats should take away sin.

7. *In the volume of the book.* "In the roll of the book." Anciently, books were written on skins and rolled up. Among the Romans these were called *volumina,* from *volvo,* "I roll"; and the Pentateuch in the Jewish synagogues is still written in this way. There are two wooden rollers; on one they roll on, on the other they roll off, as they proceed in reading. One now lying before me, written on vellum, is 2 feet 2 inches in breadth, and 102 feet long. To roll and unroll such a MS. was no easy task; and to be managed, must lie flat on a table. This contains the Pentateuch only, and is without points, or any other Masoretic distinction. The *book* mentioned here must be the Pentateuch, or five books of Moses; for in David's time no other part of divine revelation had been committed to writing. This whole book speaks about Christ, and His accomplishing the will of God, not only in "The Seed of the woman shall bruise the head of the serpent" and "In thy seed shall all the nations of the earth be blessed," but in all the sacrifices and sacrificial rites mentioned in the law.

9. *I have preached righteousness.* I think it best to refer these words to Christ and His apostles. In consequence of His having become a Sacrifice for sin, the Jewish sacrificial system being ended, the middle wall of partition was broken down, and the door of faith, the doctrine of justification by faith, opened to the Gentiles. Hence the gospel was preached in all the world, and the mercy of God made known to the Gentiles; and thus *righteousness,* justification by faith, was preached *in the great congregation*—to Jews and Gentiles, throughout the Roman Empire. *The great congregation,* in both this and the following verse, I think, means the Gentiles, contradistinguished from the Jews.

10. *Thy faithfulness.* This means the exact fulfilment of the promises made by the prophets relative to the incarnation of Christ, and the opening of the door of faith to the Gentiles. *Lovingkindness.* Shows the gift itself of Jesus Christ, the highest proof that God could give to a lost world of His loving-kindness.

12. *Innumerable evils have compassed me about.* This part does not comport with the preceding, and either argues a former experience or must be considered a part of another psalm, written at a different time and on another occasion; and were we to prefix the first two verses of the seventieth psalm to it we

MATTHEW HENRY

shall be *desolate, for a reward of his shame.*

IV. This may encourage all that seek God, and love his salvation, to rejoice in him and to praise him, *v.* 16.

V. This may encourage the saints, in distress and affliction, to trust in God and comfort themselves in him, *v.* 17. David himself was one of these: *I am poor and needy, yet the Lord thinketh upon me* in and through the Mediator, by whom we are made accepted.

JAMIESON, FAUSSET, BROWN

16. (Cf. Psalm 35:27.) **love thy salvation**—delight in its bestowal on others as well as themselves. **17.** A summary of his condition and hopes. **thinketh upon**—or provides for me. "He was heard," "when he had offered up prayers and supplications with strong crying and tears, unto Him that was able to save him from death."

ADAM CLARKE

should find it to be a psalm as complete in itself as that is.

15. *That say unto me, Aha, aha. Heach, heach.* See on Ps. xxxv. 21.

17. *But I am poor.* "Afflicted," greatly depressed. *And needy.* "A beggar." One utterly destitute, and seeking help. *The Lord thinketh upon me.* The words are very emphatic; *Adonai,* my Prop, my Support, *thinketh,* "meditateth," *upon me.*

MATTHEW HENRY — PSALM 41

To the chief musician. A psalm of David.

Verses 1–4

I. God's promises of succour and comfort to those that consider the poor;

1. David makes mention of these with application either, (1) To his friends, who were kind to him, *Blessed is he that considers* poor David. The provocations which his enemies gave him did but endear his friends so much the more to him. Or, (2) To himself. He had considered the poor and had provided for their relief, and therefore was sure God would, according to his promise, strengthen and comfort him in his sickness.

2. We must regard them more generally with application to ourselves. *Blessed are the merciful, for they shall obtain mercy.* The mercy which is required of us is to consider the poor or afflicted, whether in mind, body, or estate. We must take notice of their affliction and enquire into their state, must sympathise with them and judge charitably concerning them. He that considers the poor *shall be blessed upon the earth.* This branch of godliness, as much as any, has the promise of the life that now is and is usually recompensed with temporal blessings. Those who thus distinguish themselves from those that have hard hearts God will distinguish from those that have hard usage. *"They shall be preserved and kept alive,* when the arrows of death fly thickly round about them." The goodwill of a God that loves us is sufficient to secure us from the ill-will of all that hate us, men and devils; and that goodwill we may promise ourselves if we have considered the poor and helped to relieve and rescue them. In sickness (*v.* 3): *The Lord will strengthen him,* both in body and mind, *upon the bed of languishing,* on which he had lain sick, and *he will make all his bed*—a very condescending expression, alluding to the care of those that nurse and tend sick people, especially of mothers for their children when they are sick, which is to make their beds easy for them. He will make all his bed from head to foot, so that no part shall be uneasy; he will *turn* his bed (so the word is), to shake it up and make it very easy; or he will turn it into a bed of health. He has not promised that they shall never be sick, nor that their sickness shall not be unto death; but he has promised to enable them to bear their affliction with patience, and cheerfully to wait the issue. The soul shall by his grace be made to dwell at ease when the body lies in pain.

II. David's prayer, directed and encouraged by these promises (*v.* 4): *I said, Heal my soul.* Sin is the sickness of the soul; pardoning mercy heals it; renewing grace heals it; and this spiritual healing we should be more earnest for than for bodily health.

Verses 5–13

David often complains of the insolent conduct of his enemies towards him when he was sick. *My enemies speak evil of me,* designing thereby to grieve his spirit, to ruin his reputation.

I. His enemies longed for his death: *When shall he die, and his name perish* with him? They envied him his name, and the honour he had won, and doubted not but, if he were dead, that would be laid in the dust with him; but his name lives and flourishes to this day in the sacred writings, and will to the end of time; for *the memory of the just is,* and shall be, *blessed.* They picked up everything they could to reproach him with (*v.* 6): *"If he come to see me"* (as it has always been reckoned a piece of neighbourly kindness to visit the sick) *"he speaks vanity;* that is, he pretends friendship, but it is all flattery and falsehood." We complain, and justly, of the want of sincerity in our days, and that there is scarcely any true friendship to be found among men; but it seems, by this, that the former days were no better than these. They make invidious remarks upon everything he said or did: *His heart gathereth iniquity to itself,* puts ill constructions upon everything. If he prayed, or gave them good counsel, they would banter it, and call it *canting;* if he kept silence from good, when the wicked were before him, they would say that he

JAMIESON, FAUSSET, BROWN — PSALM 41

Vss. 1-13. The Psalmist celebrates the blessedness of those who compassionate the poor, conduct strongly contrasted with the spite of his enemies and neglect of his friends in his calamity. He prays for God's mercy in view of his ill desert, and, in confidence of relief, and that God will vindicate his cause, he closes with a doxology.

1-3. God rewards kindness to the poor (Prov. 19:17). From vss. 2 and 11 it may be inferred that the Psalmist describes his own conduct, **poor**—in person, position, and possessions.

shall be blessed—lit., "led aright," or "safely," prospered (Ps. 23:3). **upon the earth**—or land of promise (Ps. 25:13; 27:3-9, etc.).

The figures of vs. 3 are drawn from the acts of a kind nurse.

4. I said—I asked the mercy I show. **heal my soul**—(Cf. Ps. 30:2). "Sin and suffering are united," is one of the great teachings of the Psalms.

5, 6. A graphic picture of the conduct of a malignant enemy.

to see me—as if to spy out my case. **he speaketh . . . itself**—or, "he speaketh vanity as to his heart"—i.e., does not speak candidly, "he gathereth iniquity to him," collects elements for mischief, and then divulges the gains of his hypocrisy.

ADAM CLARKE — PSALM 41

F. B. MEYER:

"Blessed is he that considereth the poor" (41:1). The realm of blessedness is all around. It may be entered at any minute, and we may dwell in it all the days of our life. Our enjoyment of blessedness is totally undetermined by outward circumstances. If you stand in some great retail emporium and watch the faces of the women, you will be greatly instructed. Yonder sits a richly-dressed lady with society and fashion, dress and money at her command, but her manner and tone are utterly weary and dissatisfied; across the counter a girl waits on her, whose thin face and simple attire tell their own story, but her expression and bearing betoken the possession of an inner calm and strength, an inexhaustible fund of patience and sweetness. Such contrasts meet us everywhere. The realm of blessedness dips down into humble and lowly lives on every side of us. Have we entered it?

Christ's beatitudes give us eight gates, any one of which will immediately conduct us within its confines. But here is another: "Blessed is he that considereth the poor." Even if you cannot help or relieve them to any appreciable extent, consider them; let them feel that you are thinking of and for them; do not hurry them when they recite their long, sad story; put them at their ease; treat them with Christian courtesy and consideration. Begin at once. There are plenty around you, who, if not poor in the things of this world, are poor in love and hope and the knowledge of God. Tell them of "the blessing of the Lord," which "maketh rich, and he addeth no sorrow with it." Silver and gold you may have none; but such as you have be sure and give. Learn to consider people. Try and look on things from their standpoint.

—*Great Verses Through the Bible*

3. *Thou wilt make all his bed.* Thou hast "turned up, tossed, and shaken" it; and Thou wilt do so to all his bed—Thou wilt not leave one uneasy place in it—not one lump, or any unevenness, to prevent him from sleeping.

MATTHEW HENRY

had forgotten his religion now that he was sick. They *whispered together against him* (*v.* 7), speaking that secretly in one another's ears which they could not for shame speak out, and which, if they did, they knew would be confuted. Whisperers and backbiters are put together among the worst of sinners, Rom. i. 29, 30. "The disease he is now under will certainly make an end of him; for it is the punishment of some great enormous crime, which he will not be brought to repent of, and proves him, however he has appeared, a son of Belial." There was one particularly in whom he had reposed a great deal of confidence, that took part with his enemies (*v.* 9): *My own familiar friend;* probably he means Ahithophel, who had been his bosom-friend and prime-minister of state, in whom he trusted, and who *did eat of his bread*, that is, with whom he had been very intimate. Yet this base and treacherous confidant of David's forgot all the eaten bread, and *lifted up his heel against him* that had lifted up his head. Let us not think it strange if we receive abuses from such: David did, and the Son of David; our Saviour himself so expounds this, and *therefore* gave Judas the sop, that the scripture might be fulfilled, *He that eats bread with me has lifted up his heel against me*, John xiii. 18, 26. Nay, have not we ourselves behaved thus perfidiously and disingenuously towards God? We *eat of his bread* daily, and yet *lift up the heel against him.*

II. How did David bear this insolent ill-natured conduct of his enemies towards him. He said nothing to them, but turned himself to God: "*O Lord! be thou merciful to me*, for they are unmerciful, *v.* 10. Raise me up *that I may requite them*, that I may render them good for evil" (so some), for that was David's practice, vii. 4; xxxv. 13. They hoped for his death, but he found himself, through mercy, recovering, and this would add to the comfort of his recovery. "Because thou dost, by thy grace, uphold me in my integrity, I know that thou wilt, in thy glory, set me for ever before thy face." The best man in the world holds his integrity no longer than God upholds him in it; for by his grace we are what we are; if we be left to ourselves, we shall not only fall, but fall away. The psalm concludes with a solemn doxology, or adoration of God as *the Lord God of Israel*, *v.* 13. It is not certain whether this verse pertains to this particular psalm or whether it was added as the conclusion of the first book of *Psalms*, which is reckoned to end here (the like being subjoined to lxxii, lxxxix, cvi), and then it teaches us to make God the Omega who is the Alpha, to make him the end who is the beginning of every good work.

JAMIESON, FAUSSET, BROWN

7, 8. So of others, *all* act alike. **An evil disease**—lit., "a word of Belial," some slander. **cleaveth**—lit., "poured on him." **that he lieth**—*who has* now laid down, "he is utterly undone and our victory is sure."

9. mine . . . friend—lit., "man of my peace." **eat . . . bread**—who depended on me or was well treated by me. **lifted up his heel**—in scornful violence. As David and his fortunes typified Christ and His (cf. *Introduction*), so these words expressed the treatment he received, and also that of his Son and Lord; hence, though not distinctly prophetical, our Saviour (John 13:18) applies them to Judas, "that the Scripture may be fulfilled." This last phrase has a wide use in the New Testament, and is not restricted to denote special prophecies.

10. A lawful punishment of criminals is not revenge, nor inconsistent with their final good (cf. Ps. 40:14, 15).

11-13. favourest—or tenderly lovest me (Gen. 34:19), evinced by relief from his enemies; and, farther, God recognizes his innocence by upholding him. **settest . . .before thy face**—under thy watch and care, as God *before man's face* (Ps. 16:8) is an object of trust and love.

Blessed—praised, usually applied to God. The word usually applied to men denotes *happiness* (Ps. 1:1; 32:1). With this doxology the first book closes.

ADAM CLARKE

8. *An evil disease, say they, cleaveth fast unto him.* A "thing, word, or pestilence of Belial, is poured out upon him." His disease is of no common sort; it is a diabolical malady.

9. *Mine own familiar friend.* This is either a direct prophecy of the treachery of Judas or it is a fact in David's distresses which our Lord found so similar to the falsity of His treacherous disciple that He applies it to him, John xiii. 18. What we translate *mine own familiar friend* is "the man of my peace." The man who, with the "Peace be to thee!" kissed me, and thus gave the agreed-on signal to my murderers that I was the person whom they should seize, hold fast, and carry away. *Did eat of my bread.* Applied by our Lord to Judas, when eating with Him out of the same dish. See John xiii. 18, 26. Possibly it may refer to Ahithophel, his counsellor, the man of his peace, his prime minister, who, we know, was the strength of Absalom's conspiracy.

10. *Raise me up.* Restore me from this sickness, *that I may requite them.* This has also been applied to our Lord, who, knowing that He must die, prays that He may rise again, and thus disappoint the malice of His enemies.

13. *Blessed be the Lord God of Israel.* By all these circumstances and events glory shall redound to the name of God forever; for the record of these things shall never perish, but be published from one generation to another; and it has been so. *From everlasting, and to everlasting.* "From the hidden time to the hidden time"; from that which had no beginning to that which has no end.

Thus ends what the Hebrews call the First Book of Psalms; for the reader will recollect that this book is divided by the Jews into five books, the first of which ends with this psalm.

PSALM 42 (MATTHEW HENRY)

To the chief musician, Maschil, for the sons of Korah.

Verses 1–5

Holy love to God is the very life and soul of religion. Here we have some of the expressions of that love.

I. Holy love thirsting, love upon the wing, soaring upwards in holy desires towards the Lord and towards the remembrance of his name (*v.* 1, 2): "*My soul panteth, thirsteth, for God*, for nothing more than God, but still for more and more of him."

1. David thus expressed his vehement desire towards God, when he was debarred from his outward opportunities of waiting on God, when he was banished to the land of Jordan, a great way off from the courts of God's house. Note, Sometimes God teaches us effectually to know the worth of mercies by the want of them, and whets our appetite for the means of grace by cutting us short in those means. He now went mourning, but he went on panting.

2. What is the object of his desire and what it is he thus thirsts after. He pants after God, he thirsts for God, not the ordinances themselves, but the God of the ordinances. Living souls can never take up their rest anywhere short of a living God. He longs to *come and appear before God,*—to make himself known to him, as being conscious to himself of his own sincerity,—to attend on him, as a servant appears before his master. To appear before God is as much the desire of the upright as it is the dread of the hypocrite.

3. What is the degree of this desire. His longing for the water of the well of Bethlehem was nothing to this. He compares it to the *panting of a hart*, or deer, which is naturally hot and dry, especially of a hunted buck, *after the water-brooks.* Thus earnestly does a gracious soul desire communion with God.

II. Holy love mourning for God's present with-

PSALM 42 (JAMIESON, FAUSSET, BROWN)

Vss. 1-11. *Maschil*—(Cf. Ps. 32, title). *For*, or *of* (cf. *Introduction*) the sons of Korah. The writer, perhaps one of this Levitical family of singers accompanying David in exile, mourns his absence from the sanctuary, a cause of grief aggravated by the taunts of enemies, and is comforted in hopes of relief. This course of thought is repeated with some variety of detail, but closing with the same refrain.

1, 2.—Cf. (Ps. 63:1.) **panteth**—desires in a state of exhaustion.

appear before God—in acts of worship, the terms used in the command for the stated personal appearance of the Jews at the sanctuary.

PSALM 42 (ADAM CLARKE)

The title, "to the chief Musician, giving instruction to the sons of Korah." This is the first of the psalms that has this title prefixed, and it is probable that such psalms were composed by the descendants of Korah during the Babylonish captivity, or by some eminent person among those descendants, and that they were used by the Israelites during their long captivity, as a means of consolation. Indeed, most of the psalms which bear this inscription are of the consoling kind and the sentiments appear to belong to that period of the Jewish history, and to none other. The word *maskil*, from *sakal*, signifies to "make wise," to "direct wisely," to "give instruction."

1. *As the hart panteth after the water brooks.* The hart feels himself almost entirely spent; he is nearly hunted down; the dogs are in full pursuit; he is parched with thirst; and in a burning heat pants after the water, and when he comes to the river, plunges in as his last refuge.

MATTHEW HENRY

drawings (*v.* 3): "*My tears have been my meat day and night* during this forced absence from God's house." Even the royal prophet was a weeping prophet when he wanted the comforts of God's house. His tears were mingled with his meat; nay, they were *his meat day and night*; he fed, he feasted, upon his own tears. His enemies teased him: *They continually say unto me, Where is thy God?* Because he was absent from the ark, the token of God's presence, they concluded he had lost his God. Those are mistaken who think that when they have robbed us of our Bibles, and our ministers, and our solemn assemblies, they have robbed us of our God; for, though God has tied us to them when they are to be had, he has not tied himself to them. We know where our God is, and where to find him, when we know not where his ark is, nor where to find that. Wherever we are there is a way open heaven-ward. Because God did not immediately appear for his deliverance they concluded that he had abandoned him; but herein also they were deceived: it does not follow that the saints have lost their God because they have lost all their other friends. However, by this base reflection on God and his people, they added affliction to the afflicted, and that was what they aimed at. Nothing is more grievous to a gracious soul than that which is intended to shake its hope and confidence in God. David remembered the *days of old*, and then *his soul was poured out in him*; he melted away, and the thought almost broke his heart. He poured out his soul within him in sorrow, and then poured out his soul before God in prayer. It was not the remembrance of the pleasures at court, or the entertainments of his own house, from which he was now banished, that afflicted him, but the remembrance of the free access he had formerly had to God's house. He *went to the house of God*, though in his time it was but a tent; at the time of his being persecuted by Saul, the ark was in a private house, 2 Sam. vi. 3. But the meanness of the place did not lessen his esteem of that sacred symbol of the divine presence. He *went with the multitude*, and thought it no disparagement to his dignity to be at the head of a crowd in attending upon God. Nay, this added to the pleasure of it, that he was accompanied with a multitude, and therefore it is twice mentioned, as that which he greatly lamented the want of now. He went *with the voice of joy and praise*, not only with joy and praise in his heart, but with the outward expressions of it. He went to keep holy-days, not to keep them in vain mirth and recreation, but in religious exercises.

III. Holy love hoping (*v.* 5): *Why art thou cast down, O my soul?* His sorrow was upon a very good account, and yet it must not exceed its due limits, nor prevail to depress his spirits; he therefore communes with his own heart, for his relief. "Thou art disquieted, in confusion and disorder; now why art thou so?" Our disquietudes would in many cases vanish before a strict scrutiny into the grounds and reasons of them. "*Why am I cast down?* Is there a cause, a real cause? Have not others more cause, that do not make so much ado? Have not we, at the same time, cause to be encouraged?" A believing confidence in God is a sovereign antidote against prevailing despondency and disquietude of spirit. And therefore, when we chide ourselves for our dejections, we must charge ourselves to hope in God; when the soul embraces itself it sinks; if it catch hold on the power and promise of God, it keeps the head above water. *Hope thou in God for I shall yet praise him;* I shall experience such a change in my spirit that I shall not want a heart for praise. We shall praise him *for the help of his countenance*, for his favour, the support we have by it and the satisfaction we have in it.

Verses 6–11

Complaints and comforts here take their turn, like day and night in the course of nature.

I. He complains of the dejections of his spirit, but comforts himself with the thoughts of God, *v.* 6. His soul was dejected, and he goes to God and tells him so: *O my God! my soul is cast down within me.* He had often remembered God and was comforted, and therefore had recourse to that expedient now. He was now driven to the utmost borders of the land of Canaan, to shelter himself there from the rage of his persecutors—sometimes to *the country about Jordan*, and, when discovered there, to *the land of the Hermonites*, or to a hill called *Mizar*, or *the little hill.* Wherever he went he took his religion along with him. In all these places, he remembered God, and lifted up his heart to him, and kept his secret communion with him. Distance and time could not make him forget that which his heart was so much upon and which lay so near it.

JAMIESON, FAUSSET, BROWN

3. Where is thy God?—implying that He had forsaken him (cf. II Sam. 16:7; Ps. 3:2; 22:8).

4. The verbs are properly rendered as futures, "I will remember," etc.,—i.e., the recollection of this season of distress will give greater zest to the privileges of God's worship, when obtained.

5. Hence he chides his despondent soul, assuring himself of a time of joy.

help of his countenance—or, face (cf. Num. 6:25; Ps. 4:6; 16:11).

6. Dejection again described. **therefore**—i.e., finding no comfort in myself, I turn to Thee, even in this distant "*land of Jordan and the* (mountains) *Hermons*," the country east of Jordan. **hill Mizar**—as a name of a small hill contrasted with the mountains round about Jerusalem, perhaps denoted the contempt with which the place of exile was regarded.

ADAM CLARKE

3. *My tears have been my meat day and night.* My longing has been so intense after spiritual blessings that I have forgotten to take my necessary food, and my sorrow has been so great that I have had no appetite for any.

4. *When I remember these things.* Or "these things I shall remember." My soul is dissolved, becomes weak as water, when I reflect on what I have had, and on what I have lost. Or, "I pour out my soul to myself" in deep regrets and complaints, when reflecting on these things. There was a *multitude* to worship God in public; with these I often went. But, alas, this is no more; now there are found only a few solitary individuals who sigh for the desolations of Zion. There we had our holy days, our appointed feasts, to commemorate the wonderful works of the Lord; now there are no processions, no festivals, no joyous assemblies. All is desolation in Zion, and all is mourning in our captivity.

5. *Why art thou cast down, O my soul?* Bad as the times are, desolate as Jerusalem is, insulting as are our enemies, hopeless as in the sight of man our condition may be, yet there is no room for despair. All things are possible to God. We have a promise of restoration. He is as good as He is powerful; hope therefore in Him. I *shall yet praise him.* For my restoration from this captivity.

6. *Therefore will I remember thee from the land of Jordan.* That is, from Judea, this being the chief river of that country. *And of the Hermonites.* The "Hermons," used in the plural because Hermon has a double ridge joining in an angle, and rising in many summits. The river Jordan, and the mountains of Hermon, were the most striking features of the Holy Land. *From the hill Mizar.* "From the little hill." The little hill probably means Sion, which was little in comparison of the Hermons.

MATTHEW HENRY

II. He complains of the tokens of God's displeasure against him, but comforts himself with the hopes of the return of his favour in due time.

1. He saw his troubles coming from God's wrath, and that discouraged him (*v.* 7): "*Deep calls unto deep,* one affliction comes upon the neck of another, as if it were called to hasten after it; and thy water-spouts give the signal and sound the alarm of war." The waves and billows are under a divine check. Let not good men think it strange if they be exercised with many and various trials, and if they come thickly upon them; God knows what he does, and so shall they shortly.

2. He expected his deliverance to come from God's favour (*v.* 8): *Yet the Lord will command his loving-kindness.* After the storm there will come a calm, and the prospect of this supported him when deep called unto deep. He eyes the favour of God as the fountain of all the good he looked for. God's conferring his favour is called his *commanding* it. This intimates the freeness of it; we cannot pretend to merit it, but it is bestowed in a way of sovereignty, he gives like a king. By commanding his loving-kindness, he commands down the waves and the billows, and they shall obey him. This he will do *in the daytime,* for God's lovingkindness will make day in the soul at any time. If God command his lovingkindness for him, he will meet it, and bid it welcome, with his best affections and devotions. He will rejoice in God: *In the night his song shall be with me. My prayer shall be to the God of my life.* God is the God of our life, in whom we live and move, the author and giver of all our comforts; and therefore to whom should we apply by prayer, but to him?

III. He complains of the insolence of his enemies, and yet comforts himself in God as his friend, *v.* 9–11. He did not break out into indecent passions, but silently wept out his grief and for this we cannot blame him: it must needs grieve a man that truly loves his country, to see himself persecuted, as if he were an enemy to it. Yet David ought not hence to have concluded that God had forgotten him and cast him off. *Why go I mourning?* and *why hast thou forgotten me?* We may complain to God, but we are not allowed thus to complain of him. *They say daily unto me, Where is thy God?*—a reproach which was intended to discourage his hope in God. His comfort is that God is his rock (*v.* 9)—a rock to build upon, a rock to take shelter in. To God his rock he might say what he had to say, and be sure of a gracious audience. He therefore repeats what he had before said (*v.* 5), and concludes with it (*v.* 11): *Why art thou cast down, O my soul?* But here, at length, his faith came off a conqueror and forced the enemies to quit the field. And he gains this victory, (1) By repeating what he had before said, chiding himself, as before, for his dejections and disquietudes, and encouraging himself to trust in the name of the Lord and to stay himself upon his God. It may be of great use to us to think our good thoughts over again, and, if we do not gain our point with them at first, perhaps we may the second time.

JAMIESON, FAUSSET, BROWN

7. The roar of successive billows, responding to that of floods of rain, represented the heavy waves of sorrow which overwhelmed him.

8. Still he relies on as constant a flow of divine mercy which will elicit his praise and encourage his prayer to God;

9, 10, in view of which he dictates to himself a prayer based on his distress, aggravated as it was by the cruel taunts and infidel suggestions of his foes.

11. This brings on a renewed self-chiding, and excites hopes of relief. **health** [or, help] **of my countenance**—(cf. vs. 5) who cheers me, driving away clouds of sorrow from my face. **my God**—It is He of whose existence and favor my foes would have me doubt.

ADAM CLARKE

7. *Deep calleth unto deep.* One wave of sorrow rolls on me, impelled by another. There is something dismal in the sound of the original, *tehom el tehom kore;* something like, "And hollow howlings hung in air."

9. *I will say unto God my rock.* God, my Fortress and Support. *Why hast thou forgotten me?* This and the following verse are badly pointed in our Bibles: "Why go I mourning as with a sword in my bones because of the oppression of the enemy? Mine enemies reproach me daily, while they say unto me, Where is thy God?" Their reproaches are to my soul as cutting and severe as a sword thrust into my body.

11. *Why art thou cast down?* There is no reason why you should despair. God will appear and release you and your brother captives, and soon your sighing and sorrowing shall flee away. *Who is the health of my countenance.* As a healthy state of the constitution shows itself in the appearance of the face, God will so rejoice your heart, heal all your spiritual maladies, that your face shall testify the happiness that is within you.

MATTHEW HENRY

PSALM 43

Verses 1–5

David here makes application to God, by faith and prayer, as his judge, his strength, his guide, his joy, his hope.

I. As his Judge (*v.* 1): *Judge me, O God! and plead my cause.* There were those that impeached him; against them he is defendant. Here was a sinful body of men, whom he calls an *ungodly* or *unmerciful nation.* And here was one bad man the head of them, a deceitful and unjust man, most probably Saul, who not only showed no kindness to David, but dealt most perfidiously and dishonestly with him. If Absalom was the man he meant, his character was no better. As to the quarrel God had with him for sin, he prays, "*Enter not into judgment with me,* for then I shall be condemned"; but, as to the quarrel his enemies had with him he prays, "Lord, *judge me,* for I know that I shall be justified; *plead my cause against them,* take my part, and in thy providence appear on my behalf."

II. As his strength, his all-sufficient strength; so he eyes God (*v.* 2): "*Thou art the God of my strength, my God, my strength,* from whom all my strength is derived, in whom I strengthen myself, who hast often strengthened me, and without whom I am weak as water and utterly unable either to do or suffer anything for thee." David now went mourning, destitute of spiritual joys, yet he found God to be the God of his strength. If we cannot comfort ourselves in God, we may stay ourselves upon him, and may have spiritual supports when we want spiritual de-

JAMIESON, FAUSSET, BROWN

PSALM 43

Vss. 1-5. Excepting the recurrence of the refrain, there is no good reason to suppose this a part of the preceding, though the scope is the same. It has always been placed separate.

1. Judge—or, vindicate (Ps. 10:18). **plead . . .**—(Ps. 35:1). **ungodly**—neither in character or condition objects of God's favor (cf. Ps. 4:3).

2. God of my strength—by covenant relation my stronghold (Ps. 18:1).

ADAM CLARKE

PSALM 43

There is no title to this psalm in the Hebrew. It is most evidently on the same subject with the forty-second psalm, had the same author or authors, and contains the remaining part of the complaint of the captive Jews in Babylon. It is written as a part of the forty-second psalm in forty-six of Kennicott's and De Rossi's MSS.

1. *Judge me, O God, and plead my cause. Ribah ribi,* a forensic term, properly enough translated, "plead my cause," be my Counsellor and Advocate. *Ungodly nation.* The Babylonians. *The deceitful and unjust man.* Nebuchadnezzar.

2. *For thou art the God of my strength.* The Psalmist speaks here, as in other places, in the person of the whole Israelitish people then captive in Babylon. We still acknowledge Thee for our God.

MATTHEW HENRY

lights. "Thou art the God on whom I depend as my strength; why then dost thou cast me off?" This was a mistake; for God never cast off any that trusted in him, whatever melancholy apprehensions they may have had of their own state.

III. As his guide, his faithful guide (*v.* 3): *Lead me, bring me to thy holy hill.* His heart is upon *the holy hill and the tabernacles*, not upon his family-comforts, his court-preferments, or his diversions; but he is impatient to see God's tabernacles again. In order to this he prays, "*Send out thy light and thy truth;* let me have this as a fruit of thy favour, which is light, and the performance of thy promise, which is truth." We are still to pray for God's light and truth, the Spirit of light and truth, who supplies the want of Christ's bodily presence, to lead us into the mystery of godliness and to guide us in the way to heaven.

IV. As his joy, his exceeding joy. If God guide him to his tabernacles, if he restore him to his former liberties, he knows very well what he has to do: *Then will I go unto the altar of God, v.* 4. He will get as near as he can unto God, his exceeding joy. Those that come unto God must come to him as their exceeding joy, not only as their future bliss, but as their present joy, and that not a common, but an exceeding joy, far exceeding all the joys of sense and time. The phrase, in the original, is very emphatic—*unto God the gladness of my joy*, or of my triumph.

V. As his hope, his never-failing hope, *v.* 5. Here, as before, David quarrels with himself for his dejections and despondencies: *Why art thou cast down O my soul?* He then quiets himself in the believing expectation he had of giving glory to God (*Hope in God, for I shall yet praise him*) and of enjoying glory with God; (*He is the health of my countenance and my God.*)

JAMIESON, FAUSSET, BROWN

cast me off—in scorn. **because**—or, in, i.e, in such circumstances of oppression.

3. light—as in Psalm 27:1. **truth**—or, faithfulness (Ps. 25:5), manifest it by fulfilling promises. *Light* and *truth* are personified as messengers who will bring him to the privileged place of worship. **tabernacles**—plural, in allusion to the various courts.

4. the altar—as the chief place of worship. The mention of the harp suggests the prominence of praise in his offering.

ADAM CLARKE

3. *O send out thy light and thy truth.* We are in darkness and distress; oh, send light and prosperity. We look for the fulfillment of Thy promises; oh, send forth Thy truth. Let Thy light guide me to Thy holy hill, to the country of my fathers; let Thy truth lead me to Thy tabernacles, there to worship Thee in spirit and in truth.

4. *Then will I go unto the altar.* When Thy light, a favorable turn in our affairs, leads us to the land of our fathers, and Thy truth, the fulfillment of Thy gracious promises, has placed us again at the door of Thy tabernacles, then will we go to Thy altar, and joyfully offer those sacrifices and offerings which Thy law requires, and rejoice in Thee with exceeding great joy.

MATTHEW HENRY

PSALM 44

To the chief musician for the sons of Korah, Maschil.

Verses 1–8

In these verses the church, though now trampled upon, calls to remembrance the days of her triumph. This is mentioned here, 1. As an aggravation of the present distress. The yoke of servitude cannot but lie very heavily on the necks of those that used to wear the crown of victory; and the tokens of God's displeasure must needs be most grievous to those that have been long accustomed to the tokens of his favour. 2. As an encouragement to hope that God would yet turn again their captivity; accordingly he mixes prayers and comfortable expectations with his record of former mercies.

I. Their commemoration of the great things God had formerly done for them. *Our fathers have told us what work thou didst in their days.* "They have told us the *work* which thou didst"; for there is a wonderful harmony and uniformity in all that God does, and the many wheels make but one wheel (Ezek. x. 13), many works make but one work. It is a debt which every age owes to posterity to keep an account of God's works of wonder, and to transmit the knowledge of them to the next generation. Children must attend to what their parents tell them of the wonderful works of God. How wonderfully God planted Israel in Canaan at first, *v.* 2, 3. This was not owing to their own merit, but to God's favour and free grace: It was *through the light of thy countenance, because thou hadst a favour to them.* It was not by their own sword that they got the land in possession, though they had great numbers of mighty men; nor did their own arm save them from being driven back by the Canaanites and put to shame. It was God that planted Israel in that good land, as the careful husbandman plants a tree, from which he promises himself fruit. This is applicable to the planting of the Christian church in the world, by the preaching of the gospel. Paganism was driven out, as the Canaanites, not all at once, but by little and little, not by any human policy or power (for God chose to do it by the weak and foolish things of the world), but by the wisdom and power of God—Christ by his Spirit went forth conquering and to conquer; and the remembrance of that is a great support and comfort to those that groan under the yoke of antichristian tyranny. *Thou hast*, many a time, *saved us from our enemies*, and hast put to flight, and so put to shame, *those that hated us*, witness the successes of the judges against the nations that oppressed Israel. Many a time have the persecutors of the Christian church, and those that hate it, been put to shame by the power of truth, Acts vi. 10.

JAMIESON, FAUSSET, BROWN

PSALM 44

Vss. 1-26. In a time of great national distress, probably in David's reign, the Psalmist recounts God's gracious dealings in former times, and the confidence they had learned to repose in Him. After a vivid picture of their calamities, he humbly expostulates against God's apparent forgetfulness, reminding Him of their faithfulness and mourning their heavy sorrows.

1-3. This period is that of the settlement of Canaan (Josh. 24:12; Judg. 6:3). **have told**—or, related (cf. Exod. 10:2).

plantedst them—i.e., our fathers, who are also, from the parallel construction of the last clause, to be regarded as the object of "*cast* them out," which means—lit., "send" them out, or, "extend them." *Heathen* and *people* denote the nations who were driven out to make room for the Israelites.

ADAM CLARKE

PSALM 44

The title here is the same as that in Psalms xlii, which see. Like the preceding, it appears to belong to the time of the Captivity.

1. *We have heard with our ears.* The Psalmist begins with recounting the marvellous interpositions of God in behalf of the Jewish people, that he might the better strengthen his confidence, and form a ground on which to build his expectation of additional help.

2. *Thou didst drive out the heathen.* The Canaanites were as a bad tree planted in a good soil, and bringing forth bad fruit with great luxuriance. God plucked up this bad tree from the roots, and in its place planted the Hebrews as a good tree, a good vine, and caused them to take root, and fill the land.

MATTHEW HENRY

II. The good use they make of this record of the great things God had done for their fathers of old. They had taken God for their sovereign Lord (*v.* 4): *Thou art my King, O God!* The psalmist speaks for himself here: "Lord, *Thou art my King*; whither shall I go with my petitions, but to thee? The favour I ask is not for myself, but for thy church." They had always applied to him by prayer for deliverance when at any time they were in distress: *Command deliverances for Jacob.* "Command it, as one having authority, whose command will be obeyed." As they owned it was not their own sword and bow that had saved them (*v.* 3), so neither did they trust to their own sword or bow to save them for the future (*v.* 6): "*I will not trust in my bow*, nor in any of my military preparations, as if those would stand me in stead without God. *Through thy name* (by virtue of thy wisdom directing us, thy power strengthening us and working for us, and thy promise securing success to us) we shall, we *will, tread those under that rise up against us. In God we have boasted;* in him we do and will boast, every day, and all the day long."

Verses 9–15

The people of God here complain to him of the low and afflicted condition that they were now in, under the prevailing power of their enemies and oppressors.

I. They wanted the usual tokens of God's favour to them and presence with them (*v.* 9): "*Thou hast cast off;* thou seemest to have cast us off and our cause, and so hast put us to shame." God's people, when they are cast down, are tempted to think themselves cast off and forsaken of God; but it is a mistake.

II. They were put to the worst before their enemies in the field of battle (*v.* 10): *Thou makest us to turn back from the enemy*, as Joshua complained when they met with a repulse at Ai (Joshua vii. 8): "We are dispirited. Attempts to shake off the Babylonish yoke have been ineffectual, and we have rather lost ground by them."

III. They were doomed to the sword and to captivity (*v.* 11): "*Thou hast given us like sheep appointed for meat.* They make no more scruple of killing an Israelite than of killing a sheep." They looked upon themselves as bought and sold, and charged it upon God, *Thou sellest thy people*, when they should have charged it upon their own sin. *Thou dost not increase thy wealth by their price*, intimating that they could have suffered this contentedly if they had been sure that it would redound to the glory of God.

IV. They were loaded with contempt, and all possible ignominy was put upon them. In this also they acknowledge God: "*Thou makest us a reproach.*" The heathen, the people that were strangers to the commonwealth of Israel and aliens to the covenants of promise, made them a by-word. The reproach was constant and incessant (*v.* 15): *My confusion is continually before me. The shame of my face has covered me.* It reflected upon God himself; the reproach which the enemy and the avenger cast upon them was downright blasphemy against God, *v.* 16, and 2 Kings xix. 3.

Verses 17–26

The people of God, being greatly afflicted and oppressed, here apply to him.

I. By way of appeal, concerning their integrity, though they suffered these hard things, yet they kept close to God and to their duty (*v.* 17): "*All this has come upon us*, and it is as bad perhaps as bad can be, *yet have we not forgotten thee*, neither cast off the thoughts of thee nor deserted the worship of thee; for, though we cannot deny but that we have dealt foolishly, yet we have not *dealt falsely in thy covenant*, so as to cast thee off and take to other gods. Though idolaters were our conquerors, yet we have not therefore forsaken thee." The trouble they had been long in was very great: "We have been *sorely broken in the place of dragons*, among men as fierce, and furious, and cruel, as dragons. We have been *covered with the shadow of death*, that is, we have been under deep melancholy and apprehensive of nothing short of death. Though thou hast slain us, we have continued to trust in thee: *Our heart has not turned back;* we have not secretly withdrawn our affections from thee, neither have our steps *declined from thy way* (*v.* 18), the way which thou hast appointed us to walk in." While our troubles do not drive us from our duty to God we should not suffer them to drive us from our comfort in God; for he will not leave us if we do not leave him. "*If we have forgotten the name of our God*, under pretence that he had forgotten us, or in our distress have *stretched out our hands to a strange god*, as more likely to help us,

JAMIESON, FAUSSET, BROWN

4. Thou art my King—lit., "he who is my King," sustaining the same covenant relation as to the "fathers."

5. The figure drawn from the habits of the ox. **6-8.** God is not only our sole help, but only worthy of praise. **thy name**—as in Psalm 5:11. **put . . . to shame**—(cf. Ps. 6:10), disgraced.

9. But—contrasting, *cast off* as abhorrent (Ps. 43:2). **goest not forth**—lit., "will not go" (II Sam. 5:23). In several consecutive verses the leading verb is *future*, and the following one *past* (in *Hebrew*), thus denoting the causes and effects. Thus (vss. 10, 11, 12), when defeated, spoiling follows; when delivered as sheep, dispersion follows, etc.

11. The Babylonian captivity not necessarily meant. There were others (cf. I Kings 8:46).

13, 14. (Cf. Deut. 28:37; Ps. 79:4). **15. shame of . . . face**—blushes in disgrace. **16.** Its cause, the taunts and presence of malignant enemies (Ps. 8:2).

17-19. They had not apostatized totally—were still God's people.

sore broken—crushed. **place of dragons**—desolate, barren, rocky wilderness (Ps. 63:10; Isa. 13:22), **shadow of death**—(Cf. Ps. 23:4).

declined—turned aside from God's law.

20, 21. A solemn appeal to God to witness their constancy. **stretched out . . . hands**—gesture of worship (Exod. 9:29; Ps. 88:9).

ADAM CLARKE

4. *Thou art my King.* What Thou wert to *them*, be to *us*. We believe in Thee as they did; we have sinned and are in captivity, but we repent and turn unto Thee; *command*, therefore, *deliverances for Jacob*, for we are the descendants of him in whose behalf Thou hast wrought such wonders.

5. *Through thee will we push down.* "Through Thy words." Literally, "We will toss them in the air with our horn," a metaphor taken from an ox or bull tossing into the air the dogs which attack him. *Through thy name.* Jehovah; the infinite, the omnipotent, the eternal Being, whose power none is able to resist.

6. *I will not trust in my bow.* As he is speaking of what God had already done for his forefathers, these words should be read in the past tense: "We have not trusted."

8. *In God we boast.* We have told the heathen how great and powerful our God is. If Thou do not deliver us by Thy mighty power, they will not believe our report, but consider that we are held in bondage by the superior strength of their gods.

11. *And hast scattered us among the heathen.* This most evidently alludes to the Captivity. From the successful wars of the kings of Assyria and Chaldea against the kings of Israel and Judah, and the dispersion of the tribes under Tiglath-pileser, Shalmaneser, and Nebuchadnezzar, Jews have been found in every province of the East; there they settled, and there their successors may be found to the present day.

12. *Thou sellest thy people for nought.* An allusion to the mode of disposing of slaves by their proprietors or sovereigns. Instead of seeking profit, Thou hast made us a present to our enemies.

14. *Thou makest us a byword.* We are evidently abandoned by Thee, and are become so very miserable in consequence that we are a proverb among the people.

17. *Yet have we not forgotten thee.* These are bold words, but they must be understood in a qualified sense. We have not apostatized from Thee; we have not fallen into idolatry. And this was strictly true; the charge of idolatry could never be brought against the Jewish nation from the time of the Captivity.

19. *Thou hast sore broken us in the place of dragons.* Thou hast delivered us into the hands of a fierce, cruel, and murderous people. We, as a people, are in a similar state to one who has strayed into a wilderness where there are no human inhabitants.

20. *If we have forgotten the name of our God.* That name, Yehovah, by which the true God was particularly distinguished, and which implied the exclusion of all other objects of adoration.

MATTHEW HENRY

shall not God search this out? Shall he not judge it, and call us to an account for it?" They suffered these hard things because they kept close to God and to their duty (*v.* 22): "It is *for thy sake that we are killed all the day long,* because we stand related to thee, are called by thy name, call upon thy name, and will not worship other gods."

II. By way of petition, with reference to their present distress, that God would work deliverance for them. *Awake, arise, v.* 23. *Arise for our help; redeem us* (*v.* 26). They had complained (*v.* 12) that God had sold them; here they pray (*v.* 26) that God would redeem them; for there is no appealing from God, but by appealing to him. They had complained (*v.* 9), *Thou hast cast us off;* but here they pray (*v.* 23), "*Cast us not off for ever;* let us not be finally forsaken of God." The expostulations are very moving: *Why sleepest thou? v.* 23. The expression is figurative (as lxxviii. 65, *Then the Lord awaked as one out of sleep*); but it was applicable to Christ in the letter (Matt. viii. 24); he was asleep when his disciples were in a storm, and they awoke him, saying, *Lord, save us, we perish.* They plead the poor sinner's pleas. "*Our soul is bowed down to the dust* under prevailing grief and fear. We have become as creeping things, the most despicable animals: *Our belly cleaves unto the earth;* we cannot lift up ourselves, neither revive our own drooping spirits nor recover ourselves out of our low and sad condition, and we lie exposed to be trodden on by every insulting foe. *O redeem us for thy mercies' sake.*"

JAMIESON, FAUSSET, BROWN

22. Their protracted sufferings as God's people attests the constancy. Paul (Rom. 8:36) uses this to describe Christian steadfastness in persecution.

23-26. This style of addressing God, as indifferent, is frequent (Ps. 3:7; 9:19; 13:1, etc.). However low their condition, God is appealed to, on the ground, and for the honor, of His mercy.

ADAM CLARKE

22. *For thy sake are we killed all the day long.* Because of our attachment to Thee and to Thy religion we are exposed to continual death; and some of us fall a daily sacrifice to the persecuting spirit of our enemies, and we all carry our lives continually in our hands. In the same state were the primitive Christians, and St. Paul applies these words to their case, Rom. viii. 36.

23. *Awake, why sleepest thou, O Lord?* That is, Why dost Thou appear as one asleep, who is regardless of the safety of his friends?

MATTHEW HENRY

PSALM 45

To the chief musician upon Shoshannim, for the sons of Korah, Maschil. A song of loves.

Verses 1–5

Some make *Shoshannim,* in the title, to signify an instrument of six strings; others take it in its primitive signification for lilies or roses, which probably were strewed, with other flowers, at nuptial solemnities. It is *a song of loves,* concerning the holy love that is between Christ and his church. It is a *song of the well-beloved,* the virgins, the companions of the bride (*v.* 14), prepared to be sung by them.

I. The preface (*v.* 1) speaks, 1. The dignity of the subject. It is *a good matter.* It is *touching the King,* King Jesus, and his kingdom and government. 2. The excellency of the management. This song was a confession with the mouth of faith in the heart concerning Christ and his church. *My heart is inditing it.* We speak best of Christ and divine things when we speak from the heart that which has warmed and affected us. It was well expressed: *I will speak of the things which I have made.* Not, "I will speak the things I have heard from others," that is speaking by rote; but, "the things which I have myself studied. *My tongue is* as *the pen of a ready writer,* guided by my heart in every word as the pen is by the hand." We call the prophets the *penmen* of scripture, whereas really they were but the pen. The tongue of the most subtle disputant, and the most eloquent orator, is but the pen with which God writes what he pleases.

II. In these verses the Lord Jesus is represented,

1. As most beautiful and amiable in himself. It is a marriage-song; and therefore the transcendent excellencies of Christ are represented by the beauty of the royal bridegroom (*v.* 2): *Thou art fairer than the children of men,* than any of them. He proposed (*v.* 1) to speak of the King, but immediately directs his speech to him. Those that have an admiration and affection for Christ love to go to him and tell him so. *Thou art fair,* thou art *fairer than the children of men.*

2. As the great favourite of heaven. He is *fairer than the children of men.* He has grace, and he has it for us: *Grace is poured into thy lips.* By his word, his promise, his gospel, the goodwill of God is made known to us and the good work of God is begun and carried on in us. The gospel of grace is poured into his lips; for it *began to be spoken by the Lord,* and from him we receive it. He has the words of eternal life. *The spirit of prophecy is put into thy lips;* so the Chaldee. "Therefore, because thou art the great trustee of divine grace for the use and benefit of the children of men, *therefore God has blessed thee for ever,* has made thee an everlasting blessing, so that in thee all the nations of the earth shall be blessed."

3. As victorious over all his enemies. The royal bridegroom is to rescue his spouse by dint of sword out of her captivity, to conquer her, and to conquer for her, and then to marry her.

(1) His preparations for war (*v.* 3): *Gird thy sword upon thy thigh, O Most Mighty!* The word of God is the sword of the Spirit. By the promises of that word,

JAMIESON, FAUSSET, BROWN

PSALM 45

Vss. 1-17. *Shoshannim*—lit., "Lilies," either descriptive of an instrument so shaped, or denoting some tune or air so called, after which the Psalm was to be sung (cf. Ps. 8, title). A *song of loves,* or, *of beloved ones* (plural and feminine)—a conjugal song. *Maschil* (cf. Ps. 32 and 42) denotes the didactic character of the Psalm; that it gives *instruction,* the song being of allegorical, and not literal, import. *The union and glories of Christ and his Church are described.* He is addressed as a king possessed of all essential graces, as a conqueror exalted on the throne of a righteous and eternal government, and as a bridegroom arrayed in nuptial splendor. The Church is portrayed in the purity and loveliness of a royally adorned and attended bride, invited to forsake her home and share the honors of her affianced lord. The picture of an Oriental wedding thus opened is filled up by representing the complimentary gifts of the wealthy with which the occasion is honored, the procession of the bride clothed in splendid raiment, attended by her virgin companions, and the entrance of the joyous throng into the palace of the king. A prediction of a numerous and distinguished progeny, instead of the complimentary wish for it usually expressed (cf. Gen. 24:60; Ruth 4:11, 12), and an assurance of a perpetual fame, closes the Psalm. All ancient Jewish and Christian interpreters regarded this Psalm as an allegory of the purport above named. In the Song of Songs the allegory is carried out more fully. Hosea (chs. 1-3) treats the relation of God and His people under the same figure, and its use to set forth the relation of Christ and His Church runs through both parts of the Bible (cf. Isa. 54:5; 62:4, 5; Matt. 22:3; 25:1; John 3:29; Eph. 5:25-32, etc.). Other methods of exposition have been suggested. Several Jewish monarchs, from Solomon to the wicked Ahab, and various foreign princes, have been named as the hero of the song. But to none of them can the terms here used be shown to apply, and it is hardly probable that any mere nuptial song, especially of a heathen king, would be permitted a place in the sacred songs of the Jews. The advocates for any other than the Messianic interpretation have generally silenced each other in succession, while the application of the most rigorous rules of a fair system of interpretation has but strengthened the evidences in its favor. The scope of the Psalm above given is easy and sustained by the explication of its details. The quotation of vss. 6, 7 by Paul (Heb. 1:8, 9), as applicable to Christ, *ought to be conclusive,* and their special exposition shows the propriety of such an application.

1. An animated preface indicative of strong emotion. *Lit., "My heart overflows: a good matter I speak; the things which I have made,"* etc. **inditing**—lit., "boiling up," as a fountain overflows. **my tongue is the pen**—a mere instrument of God's use. **of a ready writer**—i.e., it is fluent. The theme is inspiring and language flows fast. **2.** To rich personal attractions is added grace of the lips, captivating powers of speech. This is given, and be-

ADAM CLARKE

PSALM 45

The title is nearly the same with that of Psalms lxix and lxxx. "To the chief musician, or master of the band of those who played on the six-stringed instruments, giving instruction, for the sons of Korah; a song of loves, or a song of the beloved maids." I believe it to be a nuptial song, which primarily respected Solomon's marriage with the daughter of Pharaoh, and that it probably has a prophetic reference to the conversion of the Gentiles.

1. *My heart is inditing a good matter.* Boileth or bubbleth up. It is a metaphor taken from a fountain that sends up its waters from the earth in this way.

I speak of the things which I have made touching the king. Literally, "I dedicate my work unto the king." *My tongue is the pen of a ready writer.* I shall compose and speak as fluently the divine matter which is now in my heart as the most expert scribe can write from my recitation.

2. *Thou art fairer than the children of men.* By whom are these words spoken? It seems that the whole psalm, except the first verse, was spoken by those who are called in the title the "beloved maids," or female companions, who begin with his perfections and then describe hers. And afterwards there is a prophetical declaration concerning his issue. We may, therefore, consider that what is spoken here is spoken by companions of the bride. *Grace is poured into thy lips.* This probably refers to his speech, or the gracious words which he spoke. Solomon was renowned for wisdom, and especially the wisdom of his conversation.

God hath blessed thee for ever. This, I am afraid, could in no sense be ever spoken of Solomon; but of the man Christ Jesus it is strictly true.

3. *Gird thy sword upon thy thigh, O most mighty.* This clause should be translated, "O hero, gird thy sword upon thy thigh!" This,

MATTHEW HENRY

and the grace contained in those promises, souls are made willing to submit to Jesus Christ and become his loyal subjects. By the gospel of Christ many Jews and Gentiles were converted.

(2) His expedition to this holy war: He goes forth *with his glory and his majesty*, as a great king takes the field with abundance of pomp and magnificence—his sword, his glory, and majesty. In his gospel he appears transcendently great and excellent, bright and blessed, in the honour and majesty which the Father has laid upon him. Christ, both in his person and in his gospel, had nothing of external glory or majesty, nothing to charm men (for he had no form nor comeliness), nothing to awe men, for he *took upon him the form of a servant*; it was all spiritual glory, spiritual majesty. *In thy majesty ride prosperously, v.* 4. "*Thy kingdom come;* Go on and prosper."

(3) The glorious cause in which he is engaged—*because of truth, and meekness, and righteousness*, which were, in a manner, sunk and lost among men, and which Christ came to retrieve and rescue. The gospel itself is *truth, meekness, and righteousness*; it commands by the power of truth and righteousness; for Christianity has these, incontestably, on its side, and yet it is to be promoted by meekness and gentleness, 1 Cor. iv. 12, 13; 2 Tim. ii. 25. Christ appears in it in his *truth, meekness,* and *righteousness*, and these are his glory and majesty, and because of these he shall prosper. Men are brought to believe on him because he is true, to learn of him because he is meek, Matt. xi. 29 (the gentleness of Christ is of mighty force, 2 Cor. x. 1), and to submit to him because he is righteous and rules with equity.

(4) The success of his expedition: "*Thy right hand shall teach thee terrible things.*" In order to the conversion and reduction of souls to him, there are terrible things to be done; the heart must be pricked, conscience must be startled, and the terrors of the Lord must make way for his consolations. The next verse describes these terrible things (*v.* 5): *Thy arrows are sharp in the heart of the king's enemies.* Those that were by nature enemies are thus wounded, in order to their being subdued and reconciled. Convictions are like the arrows of the bow, which are sharp in the heart on which they fasten, and bring people to fall under Christ, in subjection to his laws and government.

Verses 6–9

We have here the royal bridegroom filling his throne with judgment and keeping his court with splendour.

I. He here fills his throne with judgment. It is God the Father that says to the Son here, *Thy throne, O God! is for ever and ever*, as appears Heb. i. 8, 9, where this is quoted to prove that he is God and has a *more excellent name than the angels.* Concerning his government observe, 1. The eternity of it; it is *for ever and ever.* It shall continue on earth throughout all the ages of time. Even when the kingdom shall be *delivered up to God even the Father* (1 Cor. xv. 24) the throne of the Redeemer will continue. 2. The equity of it: *The sceptre of thy kingdom*, the administration of thy government, *is right*, exactly according to the eternal counsel and will of God, which is the eternal rule and reason of good and evil. 3. The establishment and elevation of it: *Therefore God, even thy God* (Christ, as Mediator, called God *his God*, John xx. 17, as commissioned by him, and the head of those that are taken into covenant with him), *has anointed thee with the oil of gladness.* "In recompence of what thou hast done and suffered for the advancement of righteousness and the destruction of sin God has anointed thee with the oil of gladness, has brought thee to all the honours and all the joys of thy exalted state." *Because he humbled himself, God has highly exalted him*, Phil. ii. 8, 9. His anointing him denotes the power and glory to which he is exalted; he is invested in all the dignities and authorities of the Messiah.

II. He keeps his court with splendour and magnificence. 1. His robes of state, wherein he appears, are taken notice of, not for their pomp, which might strike an awe upon the spectator, but their pleasantness and the gratefulness of the odours with which they were perfumed (*v.* 8): *They smell of myrrh, aloes, and cassia* (the *oil of gladness* with which he and his garments were anointed); these were some of the ingredients of the holy anointing oil which God appointed, the like to which was not to be made up for any common use (Exod. xxx. 23, 24), which was typical of the unction of the Spirit which Christ, the great high priest of our profession, received, and to which therefore there seems here to be a reference. 2. His royal palaces are said to be *ivory* ones, such as were then reckoned most magnificent. The man-

JAMIESON, FAUSSET, BROWN

comes a source of power and proves a blessing. Christ is a prophet (Luke 4:22). **3, 4.** The king is addressed as ready to go forth to battle. **sword**—(Cf. Rev. 1:16; 19:15.) **mighty**—(Cf. Isa. 9:6.) **glory and . . . majesty**—generally used as divine attributes Ps. 96:6; 104:1; 111:3), or as specially conferred on mortals (Ps. 21:5), perhaps these typically.

ride prosperously—or conduct a successful war.

because of—for the interests of truth, etc. **meekness . . . righteousness**—without any connection—i.e., a righteousness or equity of government, distinguished by meekness or condescension (Ps. 18:35).

right hand—or power, as its organ. **shall teach thee**—point the way to terrible things i.e., in conquest of enemies.

5. The result. **people**—Whole nations are subdued.

6. No lawful construction can be devised to change the sense here given and sustained by the ancient versions, and above all by Paul (Heb. 1:8). Of the perpetuity of this government, cf. II Samuel 7:13; Psalm 10:16; 72:5; 89:4; 110:4; Isaiah 9:7.

7. As in vs. 6 the divine nature is made prominent, here the moral qualities of the human are alleged as the reason or ground of the mediatorial exultation. Some render "O God, thy God," instead of **God thy God**—but the latter is sustained by the same form (Ps. 50:7), and it was only of His human nature that the anointing could be predicated (cf. Isa. 61:3). **oil of gladness**—or token of gladness, as used in feasts and other times of solemn joy (cf. I Kings 1:39, 40). **fellows**—other kings.

8. The king thus inaugurated is now presented as a bridegroom, who appears in garments richly perfumed, brought out from *ivory palaces,* His royal residence; by which, as indications of the happy bridal occasion, He has been gladdened.

ADAM CLARKE

I think, cannot be spoken of Solomon. The words more properly apply to Christ, who is King of Kings, and Lord of Lords. *With thy glory and thy majesty.* Be as warlike as thou art glorious and majestic. Solomon's court was splendid, and his person was majestic. But the majesty and glory of Christ are above all.

4. *In thy majesty ride prosperously.* These words cannot be spoken of Solomon; they are true only of Christ. His riding is the prosperous progress of His gospel over the earth. He uses no sword but the Sword of the Spirit.

And thy right hand shall teach thee terrible things. The Chaldee is different; "And the Lord will teach thee to perform terrible things by thy right hand." The meaning is, Nothing shall be able to resist thee, and the judgments which thou shalt inflict on thine enemies shall be terrible.

5. *Thine arrows are sharp.* The arrows here may mean the convictions produced in the hearts of man by the preaching of the gospel.

6. *Thy throne, O God, is for ever.* "O God, thy throne is for ever, and eternal!" The word *Elohim* here is the very *first* term or *name* by which the Supreme God has made himself known to the children of men. See Gen. i. 1; and this very verse the apostle, Heb. i. 8, has applied to Jesus Christ.

7. *Oil of gladness.* As an evidence that all causes of *mourning, sorrow,* and *death* were at an end, as in the state of mourning the ancients did not anoint themselves.

8. *All thy garments smell of myrrh.* The Asiatics are very partial to perfumes; everything with them is perfumed, and especially their garments. *Myrrh* and *aloes* are well-known; *cassia* is probably the bark or wood of the cinnamon tree. *Whereby they have made thee glad.* Referring to the effect of strong perfumes refreshing and exhilarating the spirits.

MATTHEW HENRY

sions of light above are the *ivory palaces*, whence all the joys both of Christ and believers come, and where they will be for ever in perfection. *Kings' daughters are among thy honourable women.* All true believers are born from above; they are the children of the King of kings. The church is here compared to the queen herself—the queen-consort, whom, by an everlasting covenant, he hath betrothed to himself. She stands *at his right hand in gold of Ophir.* This is *the bride, the Lamb's wife*, whose graces, which are her ornaments, are compared to *fine linen, clean and white* (Rev. xix. 8), for their purity, here to *gold of Ophir*, for their costliness; for, as we owe our redemption, so we owe our adorning, not to corruptible things, but to *the precious blood of the Son of God.*

Verses 10–17

This latter part of the psalm is addressed to the royal bride, standing on the right hand of the royal bridegroom. God, who said to the Son, *Thy throne is for ever and ever*, says this to the church.

I. He tells her of the duties expected from her, which ought to be considered by all those that come into relation to the Lord Jesus: "*Hearken*, therefore, *and consider* this, *and incline thy ear*, that is, submit to those conditions of thy espousals, and bring thy will to comply with them."

1. She must renounce all others. "*Forget thy own people and thy father's house*, according to the law of marriage." This shows, (1) How necessary it was for those who were converted from Judaism or paganism to the faith of Christ wholly to cast out the old leaven, and not to bring into their Christian profession either the Jewish ceremonies or the heathen idolatries, for these would make such a mongrel religion in Christianity as the Samaritans had. (2) How necessary it is for us all, when we give up our names to Jesus Christ, to hate father and mother, and all that is dear to us in this world, in comparison, that is, to love them less than Christ. *So shall the king greatly desire thy beauty*, which intimates that the mixing of her old rites and customs, whether Jewish or Gentile, with her religion, would blemish her beauty. The beauty of holiness, both on the church and on particular believers, is in the sight of Christ of great price.

2. She must reverence him, must love, honour, and obey him: *He is thy Lord, and worship thou him.* We must worship him as God, and our Lord; for this is the will of God, that *all men should honour the Son even as they honour the Father.*

II. He tells her of the honours designed for her.

1. Great court should be made to her, and rich presents brought her (*v.* 12): "*The daughter of Tyre*," a rich and splendid city, "the *daughter of the King of Tyre* shall be *there with a gift*; every royal family round about shall send a branch, as a representative of the whole, to seek thy favour and to make an interest in thee; *even the rich among the people* shall entreat thy favour, for his sake to whom thou art espoused, that by thee they may make him their friend."

2. She shall be very splendid, and highly esteemed in the eyes of all (*v.* 13): *The king's daughter is all glorious within.* The glory of the church is spiritual glory, and that is indeed all glory; it is the glory of the soul, and that is the man; it is glory in God's sight, and it is an earnest of eternal glory. Though all her glory is within yet *her clothing* also *is of wrought gold*; the conversation of Christians, in which they appear in the world, must be enriched with good works, like wrought gold, which is worked with a great deal of care and caution.

3. Her nuptials shall be celebrated with a great deal of honour and joy (*v.* 14, 15): *She shall be brought to the king.* None are brought to Christ but whom the Father brings, and he has undertaken to do it; none besides are so brought *to the king* (*v.* 14) as to *enter into the king's palace*, *v.* 15.

4. The progeny of this marriage shall be illustrious (*v.* 16): *Instead of thy fathers shall be thy children.* Instead of the Old Testament church, the economy of which had waxed old, and ready to *vanish away* (Heb. viii. 13), as the fathers that are going off, there shall be a New Testament church, drafted into the same olive.

5. The praise of this marriage shall be perpetual in the praises of the royal bridegroom (*v.* 17): *I will make thy name to be remembered.* His Father has given him *a name above every name*, and here promises to make it perpetual, by keeping up a succession of ministers and Christians in every age, that shall bear up his name, which shall thus *endure for ever* (lxxii. 17).

JAMIESON, FAUSSET, BROWN

9. In completion of this picture of a marriage festival, female attendants or bridesmaids of the highest rank attend Him, while the queen, in rich apparel (vs. 13), stands ready for the nuptial procession. **10, 11.** She is invited to the union, for forming which she must leave her father's people. She representing, by the form of the allegory, the Church, this address is illustrated by all those scriptures, from Genesis 12:1 on, which speak of the people of God as a chosen, separate, and peculiar people. The relation of subjection to her spouse at once accords with the law of marriage, as given in Genesis 3:16; 18:12; Ephesians 5:22; I Peter 3:5, 6, and the relation of the Church to Christ (Eph. 5:24). The love of the husband is intimately connected with the entire devotion to which the bride is exhorted. **12. daughter of Tyre**—(Ps. 9:14)—denotes the people. Tyre, celebrated for its great wealth, is selected to represent the richest nations, an idea confirmed by the next clause. These gifts are brought as means to conciliate the royal parties, representing the admitted subjection of the offerers. This well sets forth the exalted position of the Church and her head, whose moral qualities receive the homage of the world. The contribution of material wealth to sustain the institutions of the Church may be included (cf. "riches of the Gentiles," Ps. 72:10; Isa. 60:5-10). **13. the king's daughter**—a term of dignity. It may also intimate, with some allusion to the teaching of the allegory, that the bride of Christ, the Church, is the daughter of the great king, God. **within**—Not only is her outward raiment costly, but all her apparel is of the richest texture. **wrought gold**—gold embroidery, or cloth in which gold is woven. **14, 15.** The progress of the procession is described; according to the usual custom the bride and attendants are conducted to the palace. Some for the words—**in raiment of needlework**—propose another rendering, "on variegated (or embroidered) cloths"—i.e., in the manner of the East, richly wrought tapestry was spread on the ground, on which the bride walked. As the dress had been already mentioned, this seems to be a probable translation. **shall be brought**—in solemn form (cf. Job 10:19; 21:22). The entrance into the palace with great joy closes the scene. So shall the Church be finally brought to her Lord, and united amid the festivities of the holy beings in heaven. **16.** As earthly monarchs govern widely extended empires by viceroys, this glorious king is represented as supplying all the principalities of earth with princes of his own numerous progeny. **17.** The glories of this empire shall be as wide as the world and lasting as eternity. **therefore**—Because thus glorious, the praise shall be universal and perpetual. Some writers have taxed their ingenuity to find in the history and fortunes of Christ and His Church exact parallels for every part of this splendid allegory, not excepting its gorgeous Oriental imagery. Thus, by the dresses of the king and queen, are thought to be meant the eminent endowments and graces of Christ and His people. The attendant women, supposed (though inconsistently it might seem with the inspired character of the work) to be concubines, are thought to represent the Gentile churches, and the bride the Jewish, etc. But it is evident that we cannot pursue such a mode of interpretation. For, following the allegory, we must suspend to the distant future the results of a union whose consummation as a marriage is still distant (cf. Rev. 21:9). In fact, the imagery here and elsewhere sets before us the Church in two aspects. As a body, it is yet incomplete, the whole is yet ungathered. As a moral institution, it is yet imperfect. In the final catastrophe it will be complete and perfect. Thus, as a bride adorned, etc., it will be united with its Lord. Thus the union of Christ and the Church triumphant is set forth. On the other hand, in regard to its component parts, the relation of Christ as head, as husband, etc., already exists, and as these parts form an institution in this world, it is by His union with it, and the gifts and graces with which He endows it, that a spiritual seed arises and spreads in the world. Hence we must fix our minds only on the *one simple but grand truth, that Christ loves the Church, is head over all things for it, raises it in His exaltation to the highest moral dignity—a dignity of which every, even the meanest, sincere disciple will partake.* As to the *time*, then, in which this allegorical prophecy is to fulfilled, it may be said that no periods of time are specially designated.

ADAM CLARKE

9. *Kings' daughters were among.* Applied to Solomon, these words have no difficulty. We know he had 700 wives, princesses.

10-11. *Hearken, O daughter, and consider.* This is the beginning of the address by the companions of the bride to their mistress; after having, in the preceding verses, addressed the bridegroom; or, rather, given a description of his person, qualities, and magnificence. Supposing the daughter of Pharaoh to be intended, the words import: Thou art now become the spouse of the most magnificent monarch in the universe. To thee he must be all in all. *Forget* therefore *thine own people*—the Egyptians—and take the Israelites in their place. *Forget* also *thy father's house;* thou art now united to a new family. *So shall the king*, Solomon, *greatly desire thy beauty*—thou wilt be, in all respects, pleasing to him. And it is right thou shouldst act so, for he is now become *thy Lord*—thy supreme governor. *And worship thou him*—submit thyself reverently and affectionately to all his commands.

Taken in reference to Christ and the gospel, this is an address to the Gentiles to forsake their idolatrous customs and connections, to embrace Christ and His gospel in the spirit of reverence and obedience, with the promise that, if beautified with the graces of His Spirit, Christ will delight in them, and take them for His peculiar people—which has been done.

12. *The daughter of Tyre shall be there with a gift.* The Tyrians shall pay tribute to thy spouse, and assist him in all his grand and magnificent operations.

13. *The king's daughter is all glorious within.* This, in some sense, may be spoken of Solomon's bride, the daughter of the king of Egypt; and then the expression may refer either to the cultivation of her mind or the ornaments and splendor of her palace. Spiritually, the *king's daughter* may mean the Christian Church filled with the mind that was in Christ, and adorned with the graces of the Holy Spirit.

16. *Instead of thy fathers shall be thy children.* This is the third part, or prophetic declaration relative to the numerous and powerful issue of this marriage. This cannot refer either to Solomon or to the daughter of Pharaoh, for there is no evidence that he ever had a child by Pharaoh's daughter. The *children* mentioned here are generally supposed to mean the apostles and their successors in the Christian ministry, founding churches all over the world, by whom the Christian name becomes a memorial through all the earth.

17. *Therefore shall the people praise thee.* They shall magnify the heavenly Bridegroom, and sing the wonderful displays of His love to the Church, His spouse. And the constant use of this psalm in the Christian Church is a literal fulfillment of the prophecy.

MATTHEW HENRY

PSALM 46

To the chief musician for the sons of Korah.
A song upon Alamoth.

Verses 1–5

The psalmist teaches us by his own example.

I. To triumph in God, and his presence with us, especially when we have had some fresh experiences of his appearing in our behalf (*v.* 1): *God is our refuge and strength.* Are we in distress? He is a help, *a present help, a help found* (so the word is), one whom we have found to be so, a help on which we may write *Probatum est—It is tried,* as Christ is called a *tried stone,* Isa. xxviii. 16.

II. To triumph over the greatest dangers: *God is our strength and our help,* a God all-sufficient to us; *therefore will not we fear.* It is our duty, it is our privilege, to be thus fearless; it is an evidence of a clear conscience, of an honest heart, and of a lively faith in God and his providence and promise. We will suppose the earth to be removed, and thrown into the sea, even the mountains, the strongest and firmest parts of the earth, to lie buried in the unfathomed ocean; we will suppose the sea to roar and rage, even to *shake the mountains, v.* 3. Though kingdoms and states be in confusion, embroiled in wars, tossed with tumults—though their powers combine against the church and people of God—yet will not we fear, knowing that all these troubles will end well for the church. It is not any private particular concern of our own that we are in pain about; it is the city of God, *the holy place of the tabernacles of the Most High*; it is the ark of God for which our hearts tremble. But, when we consider what God has provided for the comfort and safety of his church, we shall see reason to have our hearts fixed, and set above the fear of evil tidings. *There is a river the streams whereof shall make* it *glad,* even then when the waters of the sea roar and threaten it. The covenant of grace is the river, the promises of which are the streams; or the Spirit of grace is the river (John vii. 38, 39), the comforts of which are *the streams, that make glad the city of our God.* Though heaven and earth are shaken, yet *God is in the midst of her, she shall not be moved, v.* 5. The church shall survive the world, and be in bliss when that is in ruins. God shall help her out of her troubles, *and that right early*—when the morning appears; that is, very speedily, for he is *a present help* (*v.* 1), and very seasonably, when things are brought to the last extremity and when the relief will be most welcome.

Verses 6–11

These verses give glory to God both as King of nations and as King of saints.

I. As King of nations. He checks the rage and breaks the power of the nations that oppose him and his interests in the world (*v.* 6): *The heathen raged* at David's coming to the throne, and at the setting up of the kingdom of the Son of David; compare ii. 1, 2. *The kingdoms were moved* with indignation, and rose in a tumultuous furious manner to oppose it; but God *uttered his voice, spoke to them in his wrath,* and they were moved in another sense, they were struck into confusion and consternation. Such a melting of the spirits of the enemies is described, Judges v. 4, 5; and see Luke xxi. 25, 26. When he pleases he can make great havoc among the nations and lay all waste (*v.* 8): *Come, behold the works of the Lord*; they are to be observed (lxvi. 5), and to be sought out, cxi. 2. War is a tragedy which commonly destroys the stage it is acted on; David carried the war into the enemies' country; and O what desolations did it make there! Stand in awe of God; say, *How terrible art thou in thy works!* lxvi. 3. When he pleases to sheathe his sword, he puts an end to the wars of the nations and crowns them with peace, *v.* 9. *He makes wars to cease unto the end of the earth,* sometimes in pity to the nations, that they may have a breathing-time, when, by long wars with each other, they have run themselves out of breath. The total destruction of Gog and Magog is prophetically described by the burning of their weapons of war (Ezek. xxxix. 9, 10), which intimates likewise the church's perfect security and assurance of lasting peace, which made it needless to lay up those weapons of war for their own service. The bringing of a long war to a good issue is a work of the Lord, which we ought to behold with wonder and thankfulness.

II. As King of saints, and as such we must own that *great and marvellous are his works,* Rev. xv. 3. He does and will do great things. Let his enemies be still, and threaten no more, but know that he is God, one infinitely above them; let them rage no more, for it is all in vain: *he that sits in heaven, laughs at them*; and, in spite of all their impotent malice, he will be exalted in the earth and not merely

JAMIESON, FAUSSET, BROWN

PSALM 46

Vss. 1-11. *Upon Alamoth*—most probably denotes the *treble,* or part sung by female voices, the word meaning "virgins"; and which was sung with some appropriately keyed instrument (cf. I Chron. 15:19-21; Ps. 6, title). The theme may be stated in Luther's well-known words, "A mighty fortress is our God." The great deliverance (II Kings 19:35; Isa. 37:36) may have occasioned its composition.

1. refuge—lit., "a place of trust" (Ps. 2:12). **strength**—(Ps. 18:2). **present help**—lit., "a help He has been found exceedingly." **trouble**—as in Psalm 18:7.

2, 3. The most violent civil commotions are illustrated by the greatest physical commotions. **swelling**—well represents the *pride* and haughtiness of insolent foes.

4. God's favor is denoted by a **river** (cf. Ps. 36:8; Zech. 14:8; Rev. 22:1). **city of God, the holy place**—His earthly residence, Jerusalem and the temple (cf. Ps. 2:6, 3:4; 20:2; 48:2, etc.). God's favor, like a river whose waters are conducted in channels, is distributed to all parts of His Church. **most High**—denoting His supremacy (Ps. 17:2).

5. right early—lit., "at the turn of morning, or change from night to day, a critical time (Ps. 30:5; cf. Isa. 37:36).

6. (Cf. vs. 4.) **earth melted**—all powers dissolved by His mere word (Ps. 75:3; Hos. 2:22). **7. with us**—on our side; His presence is terror to our enemies, safety to us. **refuge**—high place (Ps. 9:9; cf. also Ps. 24:6, 10).

8. what desolations—lit., "who hath put desolations," destroying our enemies.

9. *The usual weapons of war* (Ps. 7:12), as well as those using them, are brought to an end.

ADAM CLARKE

PSALM 46

The title in the Hebrew is, "To the chief musician for the sons of Korah; an ode upon *Alamoth,* or concerning the virgins," possibly meaning a choir of singing girls.

1. *God is our refuge.* It begins abruptly, but nobly; you may trust in whom and in what you please, but *God* (Elohim) *is our refuge and strength. A very present help.* The words are very emphatic: "He is found an exceeding, or superlative, Help in difficulties."

3. *Though the waters thereof roar. Waters,* in prophetic language, signify people; and, generally, people in a state of political commotion, here signified by the term *roar.* And by these strong agitations of the people, the *mountains*—the secular rulers—*shake with the swelling thereof*—tremble, for fear that these popular tumults should terminate in the subversion of the state.

4. *There is a river, the streams whereof.* The Chaldee understands the *river,* and its *streams* or divisions, as pointing out various peoples who should be converted to the faith, and thus *make glad the city of God,* Jerusalem, by their flowing together to the worship of the true God.

7. *The Lord of hosts is with us.* We, feeble Jews, were but a handful of men; but the *Lord of hosts*—the God of armies—was on our side. *The God of Jacob.* The God who appeared to Jacob in his distress, and saved him out of all his troubles, appeared also for us His descendants, and has amply proved to us that He has not forgotten His covenant.

8. *Come, behold the works of the Lord.* See empires destroyed and regenerated, and in such a way as to show that a supernatural agency has been at work. By the hand of God alone could these great changes be effected.

9. *He maketh wars to cease.* By the death of Cambyses, and setting Darius, son of Hystaspes, upon the Persian throne, he has tranquillized the whole empire. That same God who for our unfaithfulness has delivered us into the hand of our enemies, and subjected us to a long and grievous captivity and affliction, has now turned our captivity, and raised us up the most powerful friends and protectors in the very place in which we have been enduring so great a fight of afflictions.

MATTHEW HENRY

in the church. Men will set up themselves, but let them know that God will be exalted, will glorify his own name, and *wherein they deal proudly he will be above them*, and make them know that he is so. Let his own people be still and tremble no more, but know, to their comfort, that the Lord is God. When we pray, *Father, glorify thy name*, we ought to exercise faith upon the answer given to that prayer when Christ himself prayed it, *I have both glorified it and I will glorify it yet again*. Amen. Lord, so be it. Let all believers triumph in this. 1. They have the presence of a God of power, of all power: *The Lord of hosts is with is*. This sovereign Lord is with us, sides with us, acts with us, and has promised he will never leave us. Hosts may be against us, but we need not fear them if the Lord of hosts be with us. 2. They are under the protection of a God in covenant, who not only is able to help them, but is engaged in honour and faithfulness to help them. He is the God of Jacob, not only Jacob the person, but Jacob the people.

PSALM 47

To the chief musician. A psalm for the sons of Korah.

Verses 1–4

The psalmist, his own heart filled with great and good thoughts of God, endeavours to engage all about him in the blessed work of praise.

I. Who are called upon to praise God: "*All you people*, all you people of Israel"; so it may be taken as a prophecy of the conversion of the Gentiles and the bringing of them into the church; see Rom. xv. 11.

II. What they are called upon to do: "*Clap your hands*, as men that cannot contain themselves; *shout unto God*, not to make him hear, but to make all about you hear. Shout *with the voice of triumph* in him, and in his power and goodness, that others may join with you in the triumph."

III. What is suggested to us as matter for our praise. *The Lord most high is terrible, a King over all the earth;* and he takes a particular care of his people and their concerns, has done so and ever will. This God had done for them, witness the planting of them in Canaan, and their continuance there unto this day. The kingdom of the Messiah was to be set over all the earth, and not confined to the Jewish nation. Jesus Christ shall subdue the Gentiles; he shall bring *them in as sheep into the fold* (so the word signifies), not for slaughter, but for preservation. *He shall choose our inheritance for us.* He had chosen the land of Canaan to be an inheritance for Israel; it was the land which the Lord their God spied out for them; see Deut. xxxii. 8. And the setting up of God's sanctuary in it made it *the excellency*, the honour, *of Jacob* (Amos vi. 8). Apply this spiritually, 1. The happiness of the saints, that God himself has chosen their inheritance for them, and has laid up for them in the other world an inheritance incorruptible, 1 Pet. i. 4. 2. The faith and submission of the saints to God. This is the language of every gracious soul, "God shall choose my inheritance for me. He knows what is good for me better than I do for myself, and therefore I will have no will of my own but what is resolved into his."

Verses 5–9

Should not subjects praise their king? God is our God, our King, and therefore we must praise him. But here is a needful rule subjoined (*v.* 7): *Sing you praises with understanding*, with *Maschil*. 1. "Intelligently; as those that do yourselves understand why and for what reasons you praise God and what is the meaning of the service." This is the gospel-rule (1 Cor. xiv. 15). 2. "Instructively, as those that desire to make others understand God's glorious perfections, and to teach them to praise him."

I. We must praise God going up (*v.* 5): *God has gone up with a shout*, which may refer, 1. To the carrying up of the ark to the hill of Zion. The ark being the instituted token of God's special presence with them, when that was brought up by warrant from him he might be said to *go up*. 2. To the ascension of our Lord Jesus into heaven, when he had finished his work on earth, Acts i. 9. Then *God went up with a shout*, the shout of a King, of a conqueror.

II. We must praise God reigning, *v.* 7, 8. *He sits upon the throne of his holiness*, which he has prepared in the heavens, and there he rules over all. See here the extent of God's government; all are born within his allegiance; even the heathen that serve other gods are ruled by the true God, our God, whether they will or no. See the equity of his government; it is a throne of holiness, on which he sits, whence he gives warrants, orders, and judgment, in which we are

JAMIESON, FAUSSET, BROWN

10. Be still . . .—lit., "Leave off to oppose Me and vex My people. I am over all for their safety". (cf. Isa. 2:11; Eph. 1:22).

PSALM 47

Vss. 1-9 Praise is given to God for victory, perhaps that recorded (II Chron. 20); and His dominions over all people, Jews and Gentiles, is asserted.

1. clap . . . hands . . . people—lit., "peoples," or "nations" (cf. Deut. 32:43; Ps. 18:49; 98:9).

2, 3. His universal sovereignty now exists, and will be made known. **under us**—i.e., His saints; Israel's temporal victories were types of the spiritual conquests of the true Church.

4. He shall . . . inheritance—the heathen to be possessed by His Church (Ps. 2:8), as Canaan by the Jews.

excellency of Jacob—lit., "pride," or, that in which he glories (not necessarily, though often, in a bad sense), the privileges of the chosen people—**whom he loved**—His love being the sole cause of granting them.

5-7. God, victorious over His enemies, reascends to heaven, amid the triumphant praises of His people, who celebrate His sovereign dominion. This sovereignty is what the Psalm teaches; hence he adds—**sing . . . praises with understanding**—lit., "sing and play an instructive (Psalm)." The whole typifies Christ's ascension (cf. Ps. 68:18).

8, 9. The instruction continued. **throne of . . . holiness**—or, holy throne (cf. on Ps. 2:6; 23:3).

ADAM CLARKE

10. *Be still, and know that I am God.* "Cease" from your provocations of the divine justice; cease from murmuring against the dispensations of His providence.

11. *The Lord of hosts is with us.* Having heard these declarations of God, the people cry out with joy and exultation, *The Lord of hosts*, the God of armies, *is with us;* we will not fear what man can do unto us. *The God of Jacob is our refuge.* He who saved our fathers will save us, and will never abandon His people in distress.

PSALM 47

The title, "A Psalm for the sons of Korah," has nothing remarkable in it. The psalm was probably written about the same time with the preceding, and relates to the happy state of the Jews when returned to their own land. They renew their praises and promises of obedience, and celebrate Him for the deliverance they had received. In a spiritual sense, it appears to relate to the calling of the Gentiles to be made partakers of the blessings of the gospel with the converted Jews.

1. *O clap your hands, all ye people.* Let both Jews and Gentiles magnify the Lord: the Jews, for being delivered from the Babylonish captivity; the Gentiles, for being called to enter into the glorious liberty of the children of God.

6. *Sing praises. Zammeru.* This word is four times repeated in this short verse, and shows at once the earnestness and happiness of the people. They are the words of exultation and triumph.

7. *For God is the King of all the earth.* He is not your King only, but the King of the universe. *Sing ye praises with understanding. Zammeru maskil*, "sing an instructive song." Let sense and sound go together. Let your hearts and heads go with your voices. Understand what you sing, and feel what you understand; and let the song be what will give instruction in righteousness to them that hear it.

8. *God reigneth over the heathen.* Though this is literally true in God's universal dominion, yet more is here meant. God reigns over the heathen when, by the preaching of the gospel, they are brought into the Church of Christ.

MATTHEW HENRY

sure there is no iniquity. Jesus Christ, who is God, and whose *throne is for ever and ever, reigns over the heathen*; not only is he entrusted with the administration of the providential kingdom, but he shall set up the kingdom of his grace in the Gentile world, and rule in the hearts of multitudes that were bred up in heathenism, Eph. ii. 12, 13.

III. We must praise God as attended and honoured by *the princes of the people, v.* 9. It was the honour of Israel that they were *the people of the God of Abraham.* 1. It was their happiness that they had a settled government, *princes of their people*, who were the *shields of their land.* Magistracy is the shield of a nation, it is likewise the honour of God that, in another sense, the *shields of the earth do belong to him*; magistracy is his institution, and he serves his own purposes by it in the government of the world. The unanimous agreement of the great ones of a nation in the things that belong to its peace is a very happy omen, which promises abundance of blessings. 2. It may be applied to the calling of the Gentiles into the church of Christ, and taken as a prophecy that in the days of the Messiah the kings of the earth and their people should join themselves to the church. When the *shields of the earth*, the ensigns of royal dignity (1 Kings xiv. 27, 28), are surrendered to the Lord Jesus, as the keys of a city are presented to the conqueror or sovereign, when princes use their power for the advancement of the interests of religion, then Christ is greatly exalted.

JAMIESON, FAUSSET, BROWN

princes—who represent *peoples.* For—**even**—supply, "as," or, "to"—i.e., they all become united under covenant with Abraham's God.

shields—as in Hosea 4:18, rulers.

ADAM CLARKE

9. *The princes of the people are gathered together.* The princely, noble, or free-willed people; those who gladly receive the word of life; those who, like the Bereans, were of a noble or liberal disposition, and when they heard the gospel, searched the Scriptures to see whether these things were so. It is a similar word which is used Ps. cx. 3; and I believe both texts speak of the same people—the Gentiles who gladly come unto His light, and present themselves a freewill offering to the Lord. *The people of the God of Abraham.* The people of the God of Abraham are the Gentiles, who, receiving the gospel, are made partakers of the faith of Abraham, and are his spiritual children. *The shields of the earth belong unto God.* The Septuagint translates this "the strong ones of the earth."

MATTHEW HENRY

PSALM 48

A song *and* psalm for the sons of Korah.

Verses 1–7

What is here said to the honour of Jerusalem is,

I. Of Zion he said kinder things than ever he said of any place upon earth. *This is my rest for ever; here will I dwell, for I have desired it,* cxxxii. 13, 14. It is *the city of the great King* (*v.* 2), the King of all the earth, who is pleased to declare himself in a special manner present there. *In Judah God is known, and his name is great.* In Jerusalem *God is great* (*v.* 1). It is therefore called *the mountain of his holiness*, for *holiness to the Lord* is written upon it and all the furniture of it, Zech. xiv. 20, 21. God was known, not only in the streets, but even in the palaces of Jerusalem, for a refuge. Upon all these accounts, Jerusalem, and especially Mount Zion, on which the temple was built, were universally beloved and admired—*beautiful for situation,* and *the joy of the whole earth, v.* 2. The situation must needs be every way agreeable, when Infinite Wisdom chose it for the place of the sanctuary; and that which made it beautiful was that it was the mountain of holiness, for there is a beauty in holiness. Mount Zion was on the north side of Jerusalem and so was a shelter to the city from the cold and bleak winds that blew from that quarter.

II. That the kings of the earth were afraid of it. They had had but too much occasion to fear their enemies; for *the kings were assembled, v.* 4. They passed, advanced, and marched on together, not doubting but they should soon make themselves masters of that city which should have been the joy, but was the envy of the whole earth. The very sight of Jerusalem struck them into a consternation and gave check to their fury, as the sight of the tents of Jacob frightened Balaam from his purpose to curse Israel (Num. xxiv. 2): *They saw it and marvelled, and hasted away, v.* 5. Not that there was anything to be seen in Jerusalem that was so very formidable; but the sight of it brought to mind what they had heard concerning the special presence of God in that city and the divine protection it was under. They knew themselves an unequal match for Omnipotence, and therefore *fear came upon them, and pain, v.* 6. The fright they were in upon the sight of Jerusalem is here compared to the throes of a woman in travail. The defeat hereby given to their designs upon Jerusalem is compared to the dreadful work made with a fleet of ships by a violent storm, when some are split, others shattered, all dispersed (*v.* 7).

Verses 8–14

I. Let our faith in the word of God be hereby confirmed. "As we have heard done in former providences, in the days of old, so have we seen done in our own days. We have heard that God is the Lord of hosts, and that Jerusalem is the city of our God, is dear to him, in his particular care; and now we have seen it; we have seen the power of our God; we have seen his goodness; we have seen his care and concern for us, that he is a *wall of fire round about Jerusalem and the glory in the midst of her.*"

JAMIESON, FAUSSET, BROWN

PSALM 48

Vss. 1-14. This is a spirited Psalm and song (cf. Ps. 30), having probably been suggested by the same occasion as the foregoing. It sets forth the privileges and blessings of God's spiritual dominion as the terror of the wicked and joy of the righteous.

1. to be praised—always: it is an epithet, as in Psalm 18:3. **mountain of his holiness**—His Church (cf. Isa. 2:2, 3; 25:6, 7, 10); the sanctuary was erected first on Mount Zion, then (as the temple) on Moriah; hence the figure.

2, 3. situation—lit., "elevation." **joy of . . .**—source of joy. **sides of the north**—poetically for eminent, lofty, distinguished, as the ancients believed the *north* to be the highest part of the earth (cf. Isa. 14:13). **palaces**—lit., "citadels." **refuge**—(Ps. 9:10; 18:3). He was so known in them because they enjoyed His presence.

4-6. **For**—The reason is given. Though the kings (perhaps of Moab and Ammon, cf. Ps. 83:3-5) combined, a conviction of God's presence with His people, evinced by the unusual courage with which the prophets (cf. II Chron. 20:12-20) had inspired them, seized on their minds, and smitten with sudden and intense alarm, they fled astonished.

7. **ships of Tarshish**—as engaged in a distant and lucrative trade, the most valuable. The phrase may illustrate God's control over all material agencies, whether their literal destruction be meant or not.

ADAM CLARKE

PSALM 48

The title: "A Song and Psalm for the sons of Korah." It is evidently of the same complexion with the two preceding, and refers to the Jews returned from captivity; and perhaps was sung at the dedication of the second Temple, in order to return thanks to the Lord for the restoration of their political state and the reestablishment of their worship.

1. *Great is the Lord.* This verse should be joined to the last verse of the preceding psalm, as it is a continuation of the same subject. *The mountain of his holiness.* Mount Moriah, on which the Temple was built. The ancient city of Jerusalem, which David took from the Jebusites, was on the south of Mount Zion, on which the Temple was built, though it might be said to be more properly on Mount Moriah, which is one of the hills of which Mount Zion is composed. The Temple therefore was to the north of the city, as the Psalmist here states, v. 2: "Beautiful for situation, the joy of the whole earth, is Mount Zion, on the sides of the north, the city of the great King."

2. *The joy of the whole earth.* Commentators have been greatly puzzled to show in what sense Zion, or the Temple, could be said to be the joy of the whole earth. If we take the earth here for the habitable globe, there is no sense in which it ever was the joy of the whole earth; but if we take *col haarets* as signifying the "whole of this land" (and it has no other meaning), the assertion is plain and easy to be understood, for the Temple was considered the ornament and glory of the whole land of Judea.

3. *God is known in her palaces for a refuge.* All those who worship there in spirit and truth find God for their Refuge. But the words may be understood: God is known for the defense of her palaces; and with this view of the subject agree the three following verses.

4-6. *For, lo, the kings were assembled.* Many of the neighboring potentates, at different times, envied the prosperity of the Jewish nation and coveted the riches of the Temple, but they had no power against it till the cup of Jewish transgression was full. In vain did they assemble —confederate, and invade the land. *Saw it*— reconnoitered the place; *marvelled* at its excellence and strength, for *they were troubled* —struck with fear; *hasted away* for fear of destruction, for *fear took hold upon them* as pains seize on *a woman in travail.* Those who came to destroy were glad to make their own escape.

MATTHEW HENRY

II. Let our hope of the stability and perpetuity of the church be hereby encouraged. "From what we have seen, compared with what we have heard, in the city of our God, we may conclude that God will establish it for ever." This was not fulfilled in Jerusalem (that city was long since destroyed, and all its glory laid in the dust), but has its accomplishment in the gospel church.

III. Let our minds be hereby filled with good thoughts of God. "From what we have heard, and seen, and hope for, we may take occasion to think much of God's lovingkindness, whenever we meet *in the midst of his temple*," *v*. 9.

IV. Let us give to God the glory of the great things which he has done for us, and mention them to his honour (*v*. 10): "*According to thy name, O God! so is thy praise*, not only in Jerusalem, but to the ends of the earth." As far as his name goes his praise will go, at least it should go, and, at length, it shall go, when all the ends of the world shall praise him, xxii. 27; Rev. xi. 15. Some, by his *name*, understand especially that glorious name of his, *the Lord of hosts*; according to that name, so is his praise; for all the creatures, even to the ends of the earth, are under his command.

V. Let all the members of the church in particular take to themselves the comfort of what God does for his church in general (*v*. 11): "*Let Mount Zion rejoice*, the priests and Levites that attend the sanctuary, and then *let* all *the daughters of Judah*, the country towns, and the inhabitants of them, be glad: let the women in their songs and dances, as usual on occasion of public joys, celebrate with thankfulness the great salvation which God has wrought for us."

VI. Let us diligently observe the instances and evidences of the church's beauty, strength, and safety, and faithfully transmit our observations to those that shall come after us (*v*. 12, 13): *Walk about Zion*. Some think this refers to the ceremony of the triumph; let those who are employed in that solemnity walk round the walls (as they did, Neh. xii. 31), singing and praising God. In doing this let *them tell the towers and mark well the bulwarks*, magnify the late wonderful deliverance God had wrought for them. Let them observe, with wonder, that the towers and bulwarks are all in their full strength and none of them damaged by the kings that were assembled. *Tell this to the generation following*, as a wonderful instance of God's care of his holy city. *Set your heart to her bulwarks*. This intimates that the principal bulwarks of Zion were not the objects of sense, which they might set their eye upon, but the objects of faith, which they must set their hearts upon. Calvin observes here that when they are directed to transmit to posterity a particular account of the towers, and bulwarks, and palaces of Jerusalem, it is intimated that in process of time they would all be destroyed and remain no longer to be seen; for, otherwise, what need was there to preserve the description and history of them? When the disciples were admiring the buildings of the temple their Master told them that in a little time one stone of it should not be *left upon another*, Matt. xxiv. 1, 2. This must certainly be applied to the gospel church. See it founded on Christ, the rock fortified by the divine power, guarded by him that neither slumbers nor sleeps.

VII. Let us triumph in God, and in the assurances we have of his everlasting loving-kindness, *v*. 14. Tell this to the generation following: That *this God*, who has now done such great things for us, *is our God for ever and ever*. If he be our God, *he will be our guide*, our faithful constant guide. He will be our guide *above* death (so some); he will so guide us as to set us above the reach of death. He will be our guide *beyond* death (so others); he will conduct us safely to a happiness on the other side death, to a life in which there shall be no more death.

PSALM 49

To the chief musician. A psalm for the sons of Korah.

Verses 1–5

This is the psalmist's preface to his discourse concerning the vanity of the world and its insufficiency to make us happy.

I. He demands attention (*v*. 1, 2): *Hear, all you people, and give ear, all you inhabitants of the world;* for this doctrine is not peculiar to those that are blessed with divine revelation, but even the light of nature witnesses to it. All men may know, and therefore let all men consider, that their riches will not profit them in the day of death. Poor people are as much in danger from an inordinate desire towards the wealth of the world as rich people from an inordinate delight in it. *My mouth shall speak*

JAMIESON, FAUSSET, BROWN

8. This present experience assures of that perpetual care which God extends to His Church.

9. thought of—lit., "compared," or considered, in respect of former dealings. **in the . . . temple**—in acts of solemn worship (cf. II Chron. 20:28).

10. According . . . praise—i.e., As Thy perfections manifested (cf. Ps. 8:1; 20:1-7), demand praise, it shall be given, everywhere. **thy right hand . . .**—Thy righteous government is displayed by Thy power.

11. the daughters . . .—*the small towns*, or the people, with the chief city, or rulers of the Church. **judgments**—decisions and acts of right government.

12-14. The call to survey Zion, or the Church, as a fortified city, is designed to suggest "how well our God secures His fold."

This security is perpetual, and its pledge is His guidance through this life.

PSALM 49

Vss. 1-20. This Psalm instructs and consoles. It teaches that earthly advantages are not reliable for permanent happiness, and that, however prosperous worldly men may be for a time, their ultimate destiny is ruin, while the pious are safe in God's care.

1-3. All are called to hear what interests all. **world**—lit., "duration of life," the present time.

ADAM CLARKE

10. *According to thy name*. As far as Thou art known, so far art Thou praised; and where Thou art known, Thou wilt have praise to the end of the earth. And why? *Thy right hand is full of righteousness*. Thou art continually dispensing Thy blessings to the children of men.

11. *Let Mount Zion rejoice*. The Temple is restored in majesty, which was threatened with total destruction; it is again repaired. *Let the daughters of Judah be glad*. That Thou hast turned her captivity, and poured out Thy judgments upon her oppressors.

12. *Walk about Zion*. Consider the beauty and magnificence of the Temple, count *the towers* by which it is fortified.

13. *Mark ye well her bulwarks*. See the redoubts by which she is defended. *Consider her palaces*. See her courts, chambers, altars; make an exact register of the whole, that you may have to tell to your children how Jerusalem was built in troublesome times; how God restored you; and how He put it into the hearts of the heathen to assist to build, beautify, and adorn the temple of our God.

PSALM 49

The title, "To the chief Musician, A Psalm for the sons of Korah," has nothing particular in it.

1. *Hear this, all ye people*. The first four verses contain the author's exordium or introduction, delivered in a very pompous style, and promising the deepest lessons of wisdom and instruction.

MATTHEW HENRY

of wisdom; what he had to say is wisdom and understanding; it will make those wise and intelligent that receive it. It was what he had himself well digested.

II. He engages his own attention (*v.* 4): *I will incline my ear to a parable.* It is called a *parable,* not because it is figurative and obscure, but because it is a wise discourse and very instructive. It is the same word that is used concerning Solomon's proverbs. Those that undertake to teach others must first learn themselves.

III. He promises to make the matter as plain and as affecting as he could: *I will open my dark saying upon the harp.* Some understood it not, it was a riddle to them; tell them of the vanity of the things that are seen, and of the reality and weight of invisible things, and they say, *Ah Lord God! doth he not speak parables?* Others understood it well enough, but they were not moved by it, it never affected them, and for their sake he would open it upon the harp, and try that expedient to work upon them, to win upon them. *A verse may find him whom a sermon flies.* Herbert.

IV. He begins with the application of it to himself. *Wherefore should I fear?* he means, *Wherefore should I fear their fear* (Isa. viii. 12), the fears of worldly people. "Wherefore should I fear in the days of trouble and persecution, *when the iniquity of my heels,* or of my supplanters that endeavour to trip up my heels, *shall compass me about,* and they shall surround me with their mischievous attempts? Why should I be afraid of those whose power lies in their wealth? I will not fear their power, for it cannot enable them to ruin me." *The iniquity of our heels* (or of our steps, our past sins) will compass us about, will be set in order before us. In these days worldly wicked people will be afraid; nothing more dreadful to those that have set their hearts upon the world than to think of leaving it; but wherefore should a good man fear death, who has God with him? (xxiii. 4).

Verses 6–14

I. A description of the spirit and way of worldly people, whose portion is in this life, xvii. 14. A man may have abundance of the wealth of this world and be made better by it, may thereby have his heart enlarged in love, and thankfulness, and obedience, and may do that good with it which will be fruit abounding to his account; and therefore it is not men's having riches that denominates them worldly, but their setting their hearts upon them as the best things; and so these worldly people are here described. *They trust in their wealth* (*v.* 6); they depend upon it as their portion and happiness. Their gold is their hope (Job xxxi. 24), and so it becomes their God. Thus our Saviour explains the difficulty of the salvation of rich people (Mark x. 24): *How hard is it for those that trust in riches to enter into the kingdom of God!* See 1 Tim. vi. 17. *They call their lands after their own names,* hoping thereby to perpetuate their memory, and, if their lands do retain the names by which they called them, it is but a poor honour; but they often change their names when they change their owners. *Their inward thought is that their houses shall continue for ever,* and with this thought they please themselves.

II. A demonstration of their folly herein. In general (*v.* 13), *This their way is their folly.* God himself pronounced him *a fool* who thought his goods were laid up for many years, and that they would be a portion for his soul, Luke xii. 19, 20. The love of the world is a disease that runs in the blood; men have it by kind, till the grace of God cures it. With all their wealth they cannot save the life of the dearest friend they have in the world, nor purchase a reprieve for him when he is under the arrest of death (*v.* 7–9). Everlasting life is a jewel of too great a value to be purchased by the wealth of this world. We are *not redeemed with corruptible things, such as silver and gold,* 1 Pet. i. 18, 19. Christ did that for us which all the riches of the world could not do; well therefore may he be dearer to us than any worldly things. Christ did that for us which a brother, a friend, could not do for us, no, not one of the best estate or interest; and therefore those that *love father or brother more than him are not worthy of him.* Some rich people are wise, they are politicians, but they cannot outwit death, nor evade his stroke, with all their art and management; others are fools and brutish. These, though they do no good, yet perhaps do no great hurt in the world: but that shall not excuse them; they shall perish, and be taken away by death, as well as the wise that did mischief with their craft. As their wealth will stand them in no stead in a dying hour, so neither will their honour (*v.* 12): *Man, being in honour, abides not.* We will suppose

JAMIESON, FAUSSET, BROWN

4. **incline**—to hear attentively (Ps. 17:6; 31:2). **parable**—In *Hebrew* and *Greek* "parable" and "proverb" are translations of the same word. It denotes a *comparison,* or form of speech, which under one image includes many, and is expressive of a general truth capable of various illustrations. Hence it may be used for the *illustration* itself. For the former sense, "proverb" (i.e., one word for several) is the usual English term, and for the latter, in which comparison is prominent, "parable" (i.e., one thing laid by another). The distinction is not always observed, since here, and in Psalm 78:2; "proverb" would better express the style of the composition (cf. also Prov. 26:7, 9; Hab. 2:6; John 16:25, 29). Such forms of speech are often very figurative and also obscure (cf. Matt. 13:12-15). Hence the use of the parallel word—**dark saying**—or, riddle (cf. Ezek.17: 2). **open**—is to explain. **upon the harp**—the accompaniment for a lyric.

5. **iniquity**—or, calamity (Ps. 40:12). **of my heels**—lit., "my supplanters" (Gen. 27:36), or oppressors: "I am surrounded by the evils they inflict."

6. They are vainglorious—

13. Though their way is folly, others follow the same course of life.

7-9.—yet unable to save themselves or others. **it ceaseth for ever**—i.e., the ransom fails, the price is too precious, costly. **corruption**—lit., "pit," or, "grave," thus showing that "soul" is used for life. **10. For he seeth**—i.e., corruption; then follows the illustration. **wise . . . fool**—(Ps. 14:1; Prov. 1:32; 10:1). **likewise**—alike altogether—(Ps 4:8)—die—all **meet the same fate. 11.** Still infatuated and flattered with hopes of perpetuity, they call their lands, or "celebrate their names on account of (their) lands."

12. Contrasted with this vanity is their frailty. However honored, man **abideth not**—lit., "lodgeth not," remains not till morning, but suddenly perishes as (wild) beasts, whose lives are taken without warning.

ADAM CLARKE

4. *I will incline mine ear to a parable.* This was the general method of conveying instruction among the Asiatics. They used much figure and metaphor to induce the reader to study deeply in order to find out the meaning. Reflect deeply; and thus in some measure taught them the use, government, and managment of their minds.

5. *The iniquity of my heels.* Perhaps *akebai,* which we translate *my heels,* should be considered the contracted plural of *akebim,* "supplanters." The verse would then read thus: "Wherefore should I fear in the days of evil, though the iniquity of my supplanters should compass me about?"

13. *Their posterity approve their sayings.* Go the same way; adopt their maxims.

8. *For the redemption of their soul is precious.* It is of too high a price to be redeemed with corruptible things, such as silver or gold, and has required the sacrificial death of Christ. *And it ceaseth for ever.* This is very obscure, and may apply to the ransom which riches could produce. That ransom must be forever unavailable, because of the value of the soul. Or this clause should be added to the following verse, and read thus: "And though he cease to be during the hidden time, yet he shall live on through eternity, and not see corruption." This is probably the "dark saying" which it was the design of the author to utter in a parable, and leave it to the ingenuity of posterity to find it out.

11. *Their inward thought is, that their houses shall continue for ever.* Thus, by interpolation, we have endeavored to patch up a sense to this clause. Instead of *kirbam,* their "inward part," the Septuagint appear to have used a copy in which the second and third letters have been transposed, *kibram,* "their sepulchres"; for they translate: "For their graves are their dwellings for ever." So six or seven feet long, and two or three wide, is sufficient to hold the greatest conqueror in the universe!

12. *Man being in honour abideth not.* However rich, wise, or honorable, they must die; and if they die not with a sure hope of eternal life, they die like beasts.

MATTHEW HENRY

a man advanced to the highest pinnacle of preferment, as great and happy as the world can make him, man in splendour, yet then he abides not. His honour does not continue; that is a fleeting shadow. Their condition on the other side death will be very miserable. While a saint can ask proud Death, *Where is thy sting?* Death will ask the proud sinner, *Where is thy wealth, thy pomp?* The beauty of holiness is that which the grave, that consumes all other beauty, cannot touch, or do any damage to.

Verses 15–20

Good reason is here given to good people,

I. Why they should not be afraid of death. There is no cause for that fear if they have such a comfortable prospect as David here has of a happy state on the other side death, *v.* 15. The believing hopes of the soul's redemption from the grave, and reception to glory, are the great support and joy of the children of God in a dying hour. They hope,

1. That God will redeem their souls from the power of the grave, which includes, (1) The preserving of the soul from going to the grave with the body. The grave has a power over the body, by virtue of the sentence (Gen. iii. 19), and it is cruel enough in executing that power (Cant. viii. 6); but it has no such power over the soul. It has power to silence, and imprison, and consume the body; but the soul then moves, and acts, and converses, more freely than ever (Rev. vi. 9, 10); it is immaterial and immortal. When death breaks the dark lantern, yet it does not extinguish the candle that was pent up in it. (2) The reuniting of the soul and body at the resurrection. "*God shall redeem my soul from the sheol of hell*" (*v.* 15), and therefore the first death has no sting and the grave no victory.

2. That he will receive them to himself. He redeems their souls, that he may receive them. Ps. xxxi. 5, *Into thy hands I commit my spirit, for thou hast redeemed it.* He will receive them into his favour, will admit them into his kingdom, into the mansions that are prepared for them (John xiv. 2, 3), those everlasting habitations, Luke xvi. 9.

II. Why they should not be afraid of the prosperity and power of wicked people in this world.

1. He supposes the temptation very strong to envy the prosperity of sinners, for he supposes, they are made rich, and so are enabled to give law to all about them and have everything at command. They are very easy and secure in themselves and in their own minds (*v.* 18): *In his life-time he blessed his soul;* that is, he thought himself a very happy man because he prospered in the world. Believers *bless themselves in the God of truth* (Isa. lxv. 16), and think themselves happy if he be theirs; carnal people bless themselves in the wealth of the world, and think themselves happy if they have abundance of that. They applaud that in themselves which God condemns, and speak peace to themselves when God denounces war against them. "The worldling magnified himself; but thou that dost not, like him, speak well of thyself, but do well for thyself, in securing thy eternal welfare, thou shalt be praised, if not of men, yet of God, which will be thy everlasting honour."

2. He suggests that which is sufficient to take off the strength of the temptation, by directing us to look forward to the end of prosperous sinners (lxxiii. 17). *When he dies* it is taken for granted that he goes into another world himself, but *he shall carry nothing away with him* of all that which he has been so long heaping up. Grace is glory that will ascend with us, but no earthly glory will descend after us. *The soul shall go to the generation of his fathers,* his worldly wicked fathers, whose sayings he approved and whose steps he trod in, his fathers who would not hearken to the word of God, Zech. i. 4. A fool, a wicked man, in honour, is really as despicable an animal as any under the sun; he is *like the beasts that perish* (*v.* 20); nay, it is better to be a beast than to be a man that makes himself like a beast.

PSALM 50

A psalm of Asaph.

Verses 1–6

It is probable that Asaph was not only the chief musician, who put a tune to this psalm, but that he was himself the penman of it; in Hezekiah's time they praised God *in the words of David and Asaph the seer,* 2 Chron. xxix. 30.

I. The court called, in the name of the King of kings (*v.* 1): *The mighty God, even the Lord, hath spoken*—El, Elohim, Jehovah, the God of infinite power, justice, and mercy, Father, Son, and Holy Ghost. God is the Judge, the Son of God came for judgment into the world, and the Holy Ghost is

JAMIESON, FAUSSET, BROWN

14. Like sheep—(cf. vs. 12) unwittingly, they—**are laid**—or, put., etc. **death shall feed on** [or, better, "shall rule"] **them**—as a shepherd (cf. "feed," Ps. 28:9, *Margin*). **have dominion over** [or, subdue] **them in the morning**—suddenly, or in their turn. **their beauty**—lit., "form" or shape. **shall consume**—lit., "is for the consumption" i.e., of the grave. **from their dwelling**—lit., "from their home (they go) to it," i.e., the grave.

15. The pious, delivered from the—**power**—lit., "the hand," of death, are taken under God's care.

16-19. applies this instruction. Be not anxious (Ps. 37:1, etc.), since death cuts off the prosperous wicked whom you dread. **Though . . . lived . . .**—lit., "For in his life he blessed his soul," or, himself (Luke 12:19, 16:25); yet (vs. 19); he has had his portion. **men will praise . . . thyself**—Flatterers enhance the rich fool's self-complacency; the form of address to him strengthens the emphasis of the sentiment.

20. (Cf. vs. 12.) The *folly* is more distinctly expressed by *understandeth not,* substituted for *abideth not.*

PSALM 50

Vss. 1-23. In the grandeur and solemnity of a divine judgment, God is introduced as instructing men in the nature of true worship, exposing hypocrisy, warning the wicked, and encouraging the pious. **1-4.** The description of this majestic appearance of God resembles that of His giving the law (cf. Exod. 19:16; 20:18; Deut. 32:1).

ADAM CLARKE

14. *Like sheep they are laid in the grave.* "Into sheol," the place of separate spirits. *Death shall feed on them.* "Death shall feed them!" What an astonishing change! All the good things of life were once their portion, and they lived only to eat and drink; **and now they live in** sheol, and Death himself feeds them! and with what? Damnation.

15. *But God will redeem my soul from the power of the grave.* "From the hand of sheol." That is, by the plainest construction, I shall have a resurrection from the dead, and an entrance into His glory; and death shall have no dominion over me."

19. *They shall never see light.* Rise again they shall; but they shall never see the light of glory, for there is prepared for them the "blackness of darkness" forever.

PSALM 50

In the title this is said to be "A Psalm of Asaph." There are twelve that go under his name; and most probably he was author of each, for he was of high repute in the days of David, and is mentioned second to him as a composer of psalms: "Moreover Hezekiah the king and the princes commanded the Levites to sing praise unto the Lord with the words of David, and of Asaph the seer." His band, sons or companions, were also eminent in the days of David, as we learn from 1 Chronicles xxv, etc. Asaph himself

MATTHEW HENRY

the Spirit of judgment. All the earth is called to attend.

II. The judgment set, and the Judge taking his seat. As, when God gave the law to Israel in the wilderness, it is said, *He came from Sinai, and rose up from Seir, and shone forth from Mount Paran, and then from his right hand went a fiery law* (Deut. xxxiii. 2), so when God comes to reprove them for their hypocrisy, and to send forth his gospel to supersede the legal institutions, it is said here, 1. That *he shall shine out of Zion*, as then from the top of Sinai, *v.* 2. Because in Zion his oracle was now fixed, thence his judgments upon that provoking people were denounced, and God, who always dwells in Zion, may be said to *shine out of Zion*. The gospel, which set up spiritual worship, was to *go forth from Mount Zion* (Isa. ii. 3, Mic. iv. 2), and the preachers of it were to *begin at Jerusalem* (Luke xxiv. 47). Zion is here called *the perfection of beauty*, because it was the holy hill; and holiness is indeed the perfection of beauty. 2. That he *shall come, and not keep silence*, but shall show his displeasure at them, and the partition-wall of the ceremonial law should be taken down; this shall now no longer be concealed. In the great day *our God shall come and shall not keep silence*, but shall make those to hear his judgment that would not hearken to his law. 3. That his appearance should be majestic and terrible: *A fire shall devour before him*. The fire of his judgments shall make way for the rebukes of his word, that the sinners in Zion might be startled out of their sins. When his gospel kingdom was to be set up Christ *came to send fire on the earth*, Luke xii. 49. The Spirit was given in cloven tongues as of fire, introduced by a rushing mighty wind, which was very tempestuous, Acts ii. 2, 3. And in the last judgment Christ shall come in flaming fire, 2 Thess. i. 8. 4. That as on Mount Sinai he came with *ten thousands of his saints*, so he shall now *call to the heavens from above*, to take notice of this solemn process (*v.* 4).

III. The parties summoned (*v.* 5): *Gather my saints together unto me*. This may be understood either, 1. Of saints indeed. When God will reject the services of those that only offered sacrifice, resting in the outside of the performance, he will graciously accept those who, in sacrificing, *make a covenant with him*, and so attend to and answer the end of the institution of sacrifices. It is only by sacrifice, by Christ the great sacrifice (from whom all the legal sacrifices derived what value they had), that we poor sinners can covenant with God so as to be accepted of him. Or, 2. It may be understood of saints in profession, such as the people of Israel were, who are called *a kingdom of priests* and *a holy nation*, Exod. xix. 6.

IV. The issue of this solemn trial foretold (*v.* 6): *The heavens shall declare his righteousness*, those heavens that were called to be witnesses to the trial (*v.* 4); the *people in heaven shall say, Hallelujah. As the heavens declare the glory*, the wisdom and power, of God the *Creator* (xix. 1), so they shall no less openly declare the glory, the justice and righteousness, of God the *Judge*; and so loudly do they proclaim both that *there is no speech nor language where their voice is not heard*, as it follows there, *v.* 3.

Verses 7–15

God is here dealing with those that placed all their religion in the observances of the ceremonial law, and thought those sufficient.

I. He lays down the original contract between him and Israel.

II. He puts a slight upon the legal sacrifices, *v.* 8.

1. This may be considered as looking back to the use of these under the law. God had a controversy with the Jews; but what was the ground of the controversy? They thought God was mightily beholden to them for the many sacrifices they had brought to his altar; but God here shows them he did not need their sacrifices. What occasion had he for their bullocks and goats who has the command of all *the beasts of the forest*, and the *cattle upon a thousand hills* (*v.* 9, 10). God's infinite self-sufficiency proves our utter insufficiency to add anything to him. He could not be benefited by their sacrifices. *Will I eat the flesh of bulls?* It is as absurd to think that their sacrifices could, of themselves, and by virtue of any innate excellency in them, add any pleasure or praise to God, as it would be to imagine that an infinite Spirit could be supported by meat and drink, as our bodies are. No; *to obey is better than sacrifice*, and to love God and our neighbour *better than all burnt-offerings*.

2. This may be considered as looking forward to the abolishing of these by the gospel of Christ. When God shall set up the kingdom of the Messiah he shall abolish the old way of worship by sacrifice and offerings; he will no more have those to be *continually*

JAMIESON, FAUSSET, BROWN

CHARLES H. SPURGEON:

"The mighty God, even the Lord"—El, Elohim, Jehovah, three glorious names for the God of Israel. To render the address the more impressive, these august titles are mentioned, just as in royal decrees the names and dignities of monarchs are placed in the forefront. Here the true God is described as Almighty, as the only and perfect object of adoration and as the self-existent one, "Hath spoken, and called the earth from the rising of the sun until the going down thereof." The dominion of Jehovah extends over the whole earth, and therefore to all mankind is his decree directed. The east and the west are bidden to hear the God who makes his sun to rise on every quarter of the globe. Shall the summons of the great King be despised? Will we dare provoke him to anger by slighting his call?—*The Treasury of David*

4. from above—lit., "above" (Gen. 1:7). **heavens . . . earth**—For all creatures are witnesses (Deut. 4:26; 30:19; Isa. 1:2). **5. my saints**—(Ps. 4:3)

—**made**—[lit., "cut"] **a covenant . . .**—alluding to the dividing of a victim of sacrifice, by which covenants were ratified, the parties passing between the divided portions (cf. Gen. 15: 10, 18).

6. The inhabitants of heaven, who well know God's character, attest His righteousness as a judge.

7. I will testify against—i.e., for failure to worship aught. **thy God**—and so, by covenant as well as creation, entitled to a pure worship.

8-15. However scrupulous in external worship, it was offered as if they conferred an obligation in giving God His own, and with a degrading view of Him as needing it.

ADAM CLARKE

was one of the musicians who sounded with cymbals of brass, 1 Chron. xv. 19. And he is mentioned with great respect, Neh. xii. 46: "For in the days of David and Asaph of old there were chief of the singers, and songs of praise and thanksgiving unto God." He was certainly a prophetic man; he is called a seer—one on whom the Spirit of God rested; and seems from this, his education, and natural talent, to be well qualified to compose hymns or psalms in the honor of God. Persons capable of judging, on a comparison of those psalms attributed to Asaph with those known to be of David, have found a remarkable difference in the style. The style of David is more polished, flowing, correct, and majestic than that of Asaph, which is more stiff and obscure.

1-6. *The mighty God, even the Lord, hath spoken*. Here the essential names of God are used: *El, Elohim, Yehovah, hath spoken*. The first six verses of this psalm seem to contain a description of the great judgment. In this light I shall consider this part of the psalm, and show—*First*, The preparatives to the coming of the great Judge. "El Elohim Jehovah *hath spoken, and called the earth*," all the children of men. *Out of Zion, the perfection of beauty* (the beauty where all perfection is comprised), *God hath shined*, vv. 1-2. (1) He has sent His Spirit to convince men of sin, righteousness, and judgment. (2) He has sent His Word. *Secondly*, The accompaniments. (1) His approach is proclaimed, v. 3: *Our God shall come*. (2) The trumpet proclaims his approach: "He *shall not keep silence*." (3) Universal nature shall be shaken, and the earth and its works be burnt up: *A fire shall devour before him, and it shall be very tempestuous round about him*, v. 3. *Thirdly*, The witnesses are summoned and collected from all quarters; some from heaven, and some from earth. (1) Guardian angels. (2) Human associates. *He shall call to the heavens from above, and to the earth, that he may judge his people*, v. 4. *Fourthly*, The procedure. As far as it respects the righteous, orders are issued: *Gather my saints*, those who are saved from their sins and made holy, *together unto me*. And that the word *saints* might not be misunderstood, it is explained by *those that have made a covenant with me by sacrifice;* those who have entered into union with God, through the sacrificial offering of the Lord Jesus Christ. *Fifthly*, The final issue: all the angelic host and all the redeemed of the Lord join in applauding acclamation at the decision of the Supreme Judge.

7. *Hear, O my people*. As they were now amply informed concerning the nature and certainty of the general judgment, and were still in a state of probation, Asaph proceeds to show them the danger to which they were exposed, and the necessity of repentance and amendment, that when that great day should arrive, they might be found among those who had made a covenant with God by sacrifice. And he shows them that the sacrifice with which God would be well pleased was quite different from the bullocks, he-goats, etc., which they were in the habit of offering. In short, he shows here that God has intended to abrogate those sacrifices, as being no longer of any service. For when the people began to trust in them, without looking to the thing signified, it was time to put them away.

8. *I will not reprove thee*. I do not mean to find fault with you for not offering sacrifices. You have offered them; they *have been continually before me*. But you have not offered them in the proper way.

MATTHEW HENRY

before him (*v.* 8); he will no more require of his worshippers to bring him their bullocks and their goats, to be burnt upon his altar, *v.* 9.

III. He directs to the best sacrifices of prayer and praise as those which, under the law, were preferred before all burnt-offerings and sacrifices, and on which then the greatest stress was laid, and which now, under the gospel, come in the room of those carnal ordinances which were imposed until the times of reformation. He shows us here (*v.* 14, 15) what is good, and what the Lord our God requires of us, and will accept, when sacrifices are slighted and superseded. 1. We must make a penitent acknowledgment of our sins: *Offer to God confession. A broken and contrite heart* is the sacrifice which *God will not despise*, li. 17. If the sin was not abandoned the sin-offering was not accepted. 2. We must give God thanks for his mercies to us: *Offer to God thanksgiving*, every day, often every day (*seven times a day will I praise thee*): and *this shall please the Lord*, if it come from a humble thankful heart, *better than an ox or bullock that has horns and hoofs*, lxix. 30, 31. 3. We must make conscience of performing our covenants with him: *Pay thy vows to the Most High*, forsake thy sins, and do thy duty better. Dr. Hammond applies this to the great gospel ordinance of the eucharist, in which we are to give thanks to God for his great love in sending his Son to save us. Instead of all the Old Testament types of a Christ to come, we have that blessed memorial of a Christ already come. 4. In the day of distress we must address ourselves to God by faithful and fervent prayer (*v.* 15): *Call upon me in the day of trouble.*

Verses 16–23

God, by the psalmist, having instructed his people in the right way of worshipping him, here directs his speech to the wicked.

I. The charge drawn up against them. 1. They are charged with invading and usurping the honours and privileges of religion (*v.* 16): *What hast thou to do*, O wicked man! *to declare my statutes?* This is a challenge to those that are really profane, but seemingly godly, to show what title they have to the cloak of religion. Some think it points prophetically at the scribes and Pharisees that were the teachers and leaders of the Jewish church at the time when the kingdom of the Messiah, and that evangelical way of worship spoken of in the foregoing verses, were to be set up. They violently opposed that great revolution, and used all the power and interest which they had by sitting in Moses's seat to hinder it; but the account which our blessed Saviour gives of them (Matt. xxiii), and St. Paul (Rom. ii. 21, 22), makes this expostulation here agree very well to them. They took on them to declare God's statutes, but they hated Christ's instruction; and therefore what had they to do to expound the law, when they rejected the gospel? But it is applicable to all those that are practisers of iniquity, and yet professors of piety, especially if withal they be preachers of it. 2. They are charged with transgressing and violating the laws and precepts of religion. *Thou hatest instruction.* They loved to give instruction, and to tell others what they should do, for this fed their pride; but they hated to receive instruction from God himself, for that would be a mortification to them. *Thou castest my words behind thee.* 1, A close confederacy with the worst of sinners (*v.* 18): "*When thou sawest a thief*, instead of reproving him, *thou consentedst with him*, didst approve of his practices, and desire to share in the profits of his cursed trade; *and thou hast been partaker with adulterers*." 2. A constant persisting in the worst of tongue-sins (*v.* 19): "*Thou givest thy mouth to evil*, not only allowest thyself in, but addictest thyself wholly to, all manner of evil-speaking." Lying: *Thy tongue frames deceit.* Slandering (*v.* 20): "*Thou sittest, and speakest against thy brother*, dost basely abuse and misrepresent him; *thou sittest* and doest this, as a judge upon the bench, with authority; thou sittest in the seat of the scornful, to deride and backbite those whom thou oughtest to respect and be kind to."

II. The proof of this charge (*v.* 21): "*These things thou hast done;* the fact is too plain to be denied, the fault too bad to be excused; these things God knows, and thy own heart knows, thou hast done."

III. The Judge's patience, and the sinner's abuse of that patience: *I kept silence*, did not give thee any disturbance in thy sinful way, but let thee alone to take thy course; sentence against thy evil works was respited, and not executed speedily." His patience is the more wonderful because the sinner makes such an ill use of it. Sinners take God's silence for consent and his patience for connivance; and therefore the longer they are reprieved the more are their hearts hardened.

JAMIESON, FAUSSET, BROWN

Reproving them for such foolish and blasphemous notions, He teaches them to *offer*, or lit., "sacrifice," thanksgiving, and pay, or perform, their vows—i.e., to bring, with the external symbolical service, the homage of the heart, and faith, penitence, and love.

To this is added an invitation to seek, and a promise to afford, all needed help in trouble.

16-20. the wicked—i.e., the formalists, as now exposed, and who lead vicious lives (cf. Rom. 2:21, 23).

They are unworthy to use even the words of God's law. Their hypocrisy and vice are exposed by illustrations from sins against the seventh, eighth, and ninth commandments.

ADAM CLARKE

JOSEPH PARKER:

Then the Lord, even in the lips and visions of Asaph, doubly poet, becomes condescending, gentle, and kind, saying, "And call upon me in the day of trouble: I will deliver thee, and thou shalt glorify me." Literally, "My glory is in thy salvation; when I glorify myself, it is by saving thy people." The Lord is not glorified by having infinite tribute paid to him because he is majestic; he is glorified when we say to him, "Lord, I was little, and you made me great; I was lost, and you found me; I was a poor blind wanderer in the wilderness, and you came after me and saved me; and this I will tell to all the world, saying, 'Come, all ye that fear God, and I will declare what he has done for my soul.' " Thus is God glorified; not in being offered the bouquets of his universe, but by living so as to show men that all we are and have that is holy and good is from the Lord.—*The People's Bible*

From the sixteenth to the twenty-second verse Asaph appears to refer to the final rejection of the Jews from having any part in the true covenant sacrifice.

16. *But unto the wicked.* The bloodthirsty priests, proud Pharisees, and ignorant scribes of the Jewish people.

17. *Seeing thou hatest instruction.* All these rejected the counsel of God against themselves, and refused to receive the instructions of Christ.

MATTHEW HENRY

IV. The fair warning given of the dreadful doom of hypocrites (*v.* 22): "*Now consider this, you that forget God*, consider that God knows and keeps account of all your sins, patience abused will turn into the greater wrath, for if these things be not considered, and the consideration of them improved, he will *tear you in pieces, and there will be none to deliver*."

V. Full instructions given to us all how to prevent this fearful doom. 1. Man's chief end is to glorify God, and we are here told that *whoso offers praise glorifies him*; whether he be Jew or Gentile, those spiritual sacrifices shall be accepted from him. We must praise God, direct it to God, as every sacrifice was directed; see that it be made by fire, sacred fire, that it be kindled with the flame of holy and devout affection. 2. Man's chief end, in conjunction with this, is to enjoy God; and we are here told that those who *order their conversation aright shall see his salvation*. Thanksgiving is good, but thanks-living is better.

JAMIESON, FAUSSET, BROWN

21, 22. God, no longer (even in appearance) disregarding such, exposes their sins and threatens a terrible punishment. **forget God**—This denotes unmindfulness of His true character.

23. offereth praise—(vs. 14), so that the external worship is a true index of the heart.

ordereth . . . aright—acts in a straight, right manner, opposed to turning aside (Ps. 25:5). In such, pure worship and a pure life evince their true piety, and they will enjoy God's presence and favor.

ADAM CLARKE

23. *Whoso offereth praise*. These are the very same words as those in v. 14, and should be read the same way, "Sacrifice the thank offering." Jesus is the great eucharistic Sacrifice; offer Him up to God in your faith and prayers. *Ordereth his conversation*. "Disposeth his way." *Will I shew the salvation of God*. I will cause him to see into the salvation of God, into God's method of saving sinners by Christ.

MATTHEW HENRY

PSALM 51

To the chief musician. A psalm of David, when Nathan the prophet came unto him, after he had gone in to Bathsheba.

Verses 1–6

The title has reference to a very sad story, that of David's fall. 1. The sin which, in this psalm, he laments, was the folly and wickedness he committed with his neighbour's wife. This sin of David's is recorded for warning to all, that he who thinks he stands may take heed lest he fall. 2. The repentance which, in this psalm, he expresses, was brought through the ministry of Nathan, who was sent of God to convince him of his sin. But those that have been overtaken in any fault ought to reckon a faithful reproof the greatest kindness that can be done them and a wise reprover their best friend. *Let the righteous smite me, and it shall be excellent oil*. 3. David, being convinced of his sin, poured out his soul to God in prayer for mercy and grace. 4. He drew up, by divine inspiration, the workings of his heart towards God, upon this occasion, into a psalm.

In these words we have,

I. David's humble petition, *v.* 1, 2. His prayer is much the same with that which our Saviour puts into the mouth of his penitent publican in the parable: *God be merciful to me a sinner!* Luke xviii. 13. David does not balance his evil deeds with his good deeds, nor can he think that his services will atone for his offences; but he flies to God's infinite mercy, and depends upon that only for pardon and peace: *Have mercy upon me, O God!*

1. What his plea is for this mercy: "*Have mercy upon me, O God!* Have mercy upon me for mercy's sake. I have nothing to plead with thee but," (1) "The freeness of thy mercy, according to thy lovingkindness, thy clemency, the goodness of thy nature, which inclines thee to pity the miserable." (2) "The fulness of thy mercy."

2. What is the particular mercy that he begs—the pardon of sin. *Blot out my transgressions*, as a debt is blotted or crossed out of the book, when either the debtor has paid it or the creditor has remitted it. "*Wash me thoroughly from my iniquity. Cleanse me from my sin*." Nathan had assured David, upon his first profession of repentance, that his sin was pardoned. *The Lord has taken away thy sin; thou shalt not die*, 2 Sam. xii. 13. Yet he prays, *Wash me, cleanse me, blot out my transgressions*. God had forgiven him, but he could not forgive himself; and therefore he is thus importunate for pardon.

II. David's penitential confessions, *v.* 3–5.

1. He was very free to own his guilt before God: *I acknowledge my transgressions;* this he had formerly found the only way of easing his conscience, xxxii. 4, 5. Nathan said, *Thou art the man. I am*, says David; *I have sinned*.

2. He had such a deep sense of it that he was continually thinking of it with sorrow and shame. "*My sin is ever before me*. It is *ever against me*."

(1) He confesses his actual transgressions (*v.* 4): *Against thee, thee only, have I sinned*. The best men, if they sin, should give the best example of repentance. David published his confession of sin that when hereafter he should come into trouble none might say God had done him any wrong; for he owns the Lord is righteous: thus will all true penitents justify God by condemning themselves. *Thou art just in all that is brought upon us*.

(2) He confesses his original corruption (*v.* 5): *Behold, I was shapen in iniquity*. David elsewhere speaks of the admirable structure of his body (cxxxix. 14, 15); it was *curiously wrought*; and yet here he

JAMIESON, FAUSSET, BROWN

PSALM 51

Vss. 1-19. On the occasion, cf. II Samuel 11:12. The Psalm illustrates true repentance, in which are comprised conviction, confession, sorrow, prayer for mercy, and purposes of amendment, and it is accompanied by a lively faith.

1-4. A plea for mercy is a confession of guilt. **blot out**—as from a register. **transgressions**—lit., "rebellions" (Ps. 19:13; 32:1).

Wash me—Purity as well as pardon is desired by true penitents.

For . . . before me—Conviction precedes forgiveness; and, as a gift of God, is a plea for it (II Sam. 12:13; Ps. 32:5; I John 1:9). **Against thee**—chiefly, and as sins against others are violations of God's law, in one sense *only*. **that . . . judgest**—i.e., all palliation of his crime is excluded; it is the design in making this confession to recognize God's justice, however severe the sentence.

5, 6. His guilt was aggravated by his essential, native sinfulness, which is as contrary to God's requisitions of inward purity as are outward sins to those for right conduct.

ADAM CLARKE

PSALM 51

The title is long: "To the chief Musician, A Psalm of David, when Nathan the prophet came unto him, after he had gone in to Bath-sheba."

1. *Have mercy upon me, O God*. Without mercy I am totally, finally ruined and undone. *According to thy lovingkindness*. Mark the gradation in the sense of these three words, *Have mercy on me; thy lovingkindness; thy tender mercies*, here used to express the divine compassion. *Blot out my transgressions*. "Wipe out." There is a reference here to an indictment. The Psalmist knows what it contains; he pleads guilty, but begs that the writing may be defaced.

2. *Wash me throughly*. "Wash me again and again—cause my washings to be multiplied."

4. *Against thee, thee only, have I sinned*. This verse is supposed to show the impropriety of affixing the above title to this psalm. It could not have been composed on account of the matter with Bath-sheba and the murder of Uriah, for surely these sins could not be said to have been committed against God only. *That thou mightest be justified when thou speakest*. Perhaps, to save the propriety of the title, we might understand the verse thus: David, being king, was not liable to be called to account by any of his subjects; nor was there any authority in the land by which he could be judged and punished. In this respect, God alone was greater than the king; and to Him alone, as king, he was responsible.

5. *Behold, I was shapen in iniquity*. A genuine penitent will hide nothing of his state; he sees and bewails, not only the acts of sin which he has committed, but the disposition that

MATTHEW HENRY

says it was shapen in inqiuity, sin was twisted in with it; not as it came out of God's hands. It is to be sadly lamented by everyone of us that we brought into the world with us a corrupt nature, wretchedly degenerated from its primitive purity and rectitude. This is what we call *original sin*, because it is as ancient as our original, and because it is the original of all our actual transgressions. It is a bent to backslide from God.

III. David's acknowledgment of the grace of God (*v.* 6), both his goodwill towards us (*thou desirest truth in the inward parts*, thou wouldst have us all honest and sincere, and true to our profession") and his good work in us—"*In the hidden part thou hast made*," or shalt make, "*me to know wisdom*." Truth and wisdom will go very far towards making a man a good man. What God requires of us he himself works in us, and he works it in the regular way, enlightening the mind, and so gaining the will. David was conscious of the uprightness of his heart towards God in his repentance, and therefore doubted not but God would accept him. He hoped that God would enable him to make good his resolutions, that in the hidden part, in the new man, which is called the *hidden man of the heart* (1 Pet. iii. 4), he would make him to know wisdom so as to discern and avoid the designs of the tempter another time.

Verses 7–13

I. See here what David prays for. Many petitions he here puts up, to which if we do but add, "for Christ's sake," they are as evangelical as any other.

1. He prays that God would cleanse him from his sins and the defilement he had contracted by them (*v.* 7): *Purge me with hyssop.* The expression here alludes to a ceremonial distinction, that of cleansing the leper, or those that were unclean by the touch of a body by sprinkling water, or blood, or both upon them with a bunch of hyssop, by which they were, at length, discharged from the restraints they were laid under by their pollution. "Lord, let me be as well assured of my restoration to thy favour, and to the privilege of communion with thee, as they were thereby assured of their re-admission to their former privileges." But it is founded upon gospel-grace: *Purge me with hyssop*, that is, with the blood of Christ applied to my soul by a lively faith, as water of purification was sprinkled with a bunch of hyssop. It is the blood of Christ (which is therefore called *the blood of sprinkling*, Heb. xii. 24), that purges the conscience from dead works, from that guilt of sin and dread of God which shut us out of communion with him, as the touch of a dead body, under the law, shut a man out from the courts of God's house.

2. He prays that, his sins being pardoned, he might have the comfort of that pardon. He asks not to be comforted till first he is cleansed; but if sin, the bitter root of sorrow, be taken away, he can pray in faith, "*Make me to hear joy and gladness* (*v.* 8), that is, let me have a well-grounded peace, of thy creating, thy speaking." The pain of a heart truly broken for sin may well be compared to that of a broken bone; and it is the same Spirit who as a Spirit of bondage smites and wounds and as a Spirit of adoption heals and binds up.

3. He prays for a complete and effectual pardon. This is that which he is most earnest for as the foundation of his comfort (*v.* 9): "*Hide thy face from my sins*, that is, be not provoked by them to deal with me as I deserve; they are ever before me, let them be cast behind thy back. *Blot out all my iniquities* out of the book of thy account; blot them out, as a cloud is blotted out and dispelled by the beams of the sun," Isa. xliv. 22.

4. He prays for sanctifying grace. His great concern is to get his corrupt nature changed, and therefore he prays, *Create in me a clean heart, O God!* "*Lord, renew a right spirit within me*"; repair the decays of spiritual strength. Renew a *constant* spirit within me, so some. He had, in this matter, discovered much inconstancy and inconsistency with himself, and therefore he prays, "Lord, fix me for the time to come, that I may never in like manner depart from thee."

5. He prays for the continuance of God's goodwill towards him and the progress of his good work in him, *v.* 11. "*Cast me not away from thy presence*, as one whom thou abhorrest and canst not endure to look upon." *Take not thy Holy Spirit from me.* We are undone if God take his Holy Spirit from us. Saul was a sad instance of this. How exceedingly sinful, how exceedingly miserable, was he, when the Spirit of the Lord had departed from him! David knew it, and therefore begs thus earnestly: "Lord, whatever thou take from me, my children, my crown, my life, yet *take not thy Holy Spirit from me*."

JAMIESON, FAUSSET, BROWN

thou shalt make . . .—may be taken to express God's gracious purpose in view of His strict requisition; a purpose of which David might have availed himself as a check to his native love for sin, and, in not doing so, aggravated his guilt. **truth . . . and . . . wisdom**—are terms often used for piety (cf. Job 28:28; Ps. 119:30).

7-12. A series of prayers for forgiveness and purifying. **Purge . . . hyssop**—The use of this plant in the ritual (Exod. 12:22; Num. 19:6, 18) suggests the idea of atonement as prominent here; "purge" refers to vicarious satisfaction (Num. 19: 17-20).

Make . . . joy—by forgiving me, which will change distress to joy.

Hide . . .—Turn from beholding.

Create—a work of almighty power. **in me**—lit., "to me," or, "for me"; bestow as a gift, a heart free from taint of sin (Ps. 24:4; 73:1). **renew**—implies that he had possessed it; the essential principle of a new nature had not been lost, but its influence interrupted (Luke 22:32); for vs. 11 shows that he had not lost God's presence and Spirit (I Sam. 16:13), though he had lost the "joy of his salvation" (vs. 12), for whose return he prays. **right spirit**—lit., constant, firm, not yielding to temptation. **free spirit**—"thy" ought not to be supplied, for the word "free" is, lit., "willing," and "spirit" is that of David. "Let a willing spirit uphold me," i.e., with a soul willingly conformed to God's law, he would be preserved in a right course of conduct.

ADAM CLARKE

led to those acts. He deplores, not only the transgression, but the carnal mind, which is enmity against God.

6. *Behold, thou desirest truth.* I am the very reverse of what I should be. Thou desirest truth in the heart, but in me there is nothing but sin and falsity. *Thou shalt make me to know wisdom.* Thou wilt teach me to restrain every inordinate propensity, and to act according to the dictates of sound wisdom, the rest of my life.

7. *Purge me with hyssop.* "Thou shalt make a sin offering for me," probably alluding to the cleansing of the leper, Lev. xiv. 1, etc.

9. *Hide thy face from my sins.* The sentiment here is nearly the same as that in v. 3. His sin was ever before his own face; and he knew that the eye of God was constantly upon him, and that His purity and justice must be highly incensed on the account. He therefore, with a just horror of his transgressions, begs God to turn away His face from them, and to blot them out, so that they may nevermore be seen.

10. *Create in me a clean heart.* Mending will not avail; my heart is altogether corrupted. It must be new made, made as it was in the beginning. This is exactly the sentiment of St. Paul: "Neither circumcision availeth any thing, nor uncircumcision, but a new creature [creation]"; and the salvation given under the gospel dispensation is called a being "created anew in Christ Jesus." *A right spirit within me.* A constant, steady, determined spirit; called in v. 12 a noble spirit; a free, generous, princely spirit; cheerfully giving up itself to thee; no longer bound and degraded by the sinfulness of sin.

MATTHEW HENRY

6. He prays for the restoration of divine comforts and the perpetual communications of divine grace, *v.* 12. *Restore unto me the joy of thy salvation.* A child of God knows no true nor solid joy but the joy of God's salvation, joy in God his Saviour and in the hope of eternal life. "*Uphold me with thy free Spirit:* I am ready to fall, either into sin or into despair; Lord, sustain me; my own spirit is not sufficient; if I be left to myself, I shall certainly sink."

II. David here promises, *v.* 13, *I will teach transgressors thy ways.* He had been himself a transgressor, and therefore could speak experimentally to transgressors, and having found mercy with God in the way of repentance, could teach others God's ways. Penitents should be preachers. *Sinners shall be converted unto thee.*

Verses 14–19

I. David prays against the guilt of sin, and prays for the grace of God, enforcing both petitions from a plea taken from the glory of God, which he promises with thankfulness to show forth. The particular sin he prays against is blood-guiltiness, the sin he had now been guilty of, having slain Uriah with the sword of the children of Ammon. He promises that, if God would deliver him, *his tongue should sing aloud of his righteousness*; God should have the glory both of pardoning mercy and of preventing grace. He prays for the grace of God and promises to improve that grace to his glory (*v.* 15): "*O Lord! open thou my lips,* not only that I may teach and instruct sinners, but *that my mouth shall show forth thy praise,* that I may have a heart enlarged in praise." Guilt had closed his lips, and therefore he had little confidence towards God. To those that are tongue-tied by reason of guilt the assurance of the forgiveness of their sins says effectually, *Ephphatha—Be opened*; and, when the lips are opened, what should they speak but the praises of God.

II. David offers the sacrifice of a penitent contrite heart. He knew that the sacrificing of beasts was in itself of no account with God (*v.* 16). As they cannot make satisfaction for sin, so God cannot take any sactisfaction in them, any otherwise than as the offering of them is expressive of love and duty to him. He knew also how acceptable true repentance is to God (*v.* 17): *The sacrifices of God are a broken spirit.* It is a sharp work wrought there, no less than the breaking of the heart; not in despair but in necessary humiliation and sorrow for sin. It is a heart pliable to the word of God, a heart subdued and brought into obedience; it is a heart that is tender, like Josiah's, and trembles at God's word. The breaking of Christ's body for sin is the only sacrifice of atonement, for no sacrifice but that could take away sin; but the breaking of our hearts for sin is a sacrifice of acknowledgment.

III. David intercedes for Zion and Jerusalem.

1. For the good of the church of God (*v.* 18): *Do good in thy good pleasure unto Zion,* that is, "To all the particular worshippers in Zion, to all that love and fear thy name; keep them from falling into such wounding wasting sins as these of mine; defend and succour all that fear thy name." Those that have been in spiritual troubles themselves know how to pity and pray for those that are in like manner afflicted. We must not forget to pray for the church of God; nay, our Master has taught us in our daily prayers to begin with that, *Hallowed be thy name, Thy kingdom come.*

2. For the honour of the churches of God, *v.* 19. They will come to his tabernacle with whole burnt-offerings, which were intended purely for the glory of God, and they shall offer, not lambs and rams only, but bullocks, the costliest sacrifices, upon his altar. "*Thou shalt he pleased with them,* that is, we shall have reason to hope so when we perceive the sin taken away which threatened to hinder thy acceptance." It is a great comfort to think of the communion that is between God and his people in their public assemblies, how he is honoured by their humble attendance on him and they are happy in his gracious acceptance of it.

JAMIESON, FAUSSET, BROWN

13. Then—Such will be the effect of this gracious work. **ways**—of providence and human duty (Ps. 18:21, 30; 32:8; Luke 22:32).

14. Deliver—or, Free me (Ps. 39:8) from the *guilt* of murder (II Sam. 12:9, 10; Ps. 5:6). **righteousness**—as in Psalm 7:17; 31:1.

15. open . . . lips—by removing my sense of guilt.

16. Praise is better than sacrifice (Ps. 50:14), and implying faith, penitence, and love, glorifies God. In true penitents the joys of pardon mingle with sorrow for sin.

18. Do good . . .—Visit not my sin on Thy Church. **build . . . walls**—is to show favor; cf. Psalm 89:40, for opposite form and idea.

19. *God reconciled,* material sacrifices will be acceptable (Ps. 4:5; cf. Isa. 1:11-17).

ADAM CLARKE

14. *Deliver me from bloodguiltiness.* This is one of the expressions that gives most color to the propriety of the title affixed to this psalm. Here he may have in view the death of Uriah, and consider that his blood cries for vengeance against him, and nothing but the mere mercy of God can wipe this blood from his conscience. The prayer here is earnest and energetic: *O God! thou God of my salvation,* deliver me!

16. *For thou desirest not sacrifice.* This is the same sentiment which he delivers in Ps. xl. 6, etc.

17. *The sacrifices of God are a broken spirit.* I have the *broken spirit, ruach nishbarah,* and the *broken and contrite heart, leb nishbar venidkeh.* These words are very expressive. *Shabar* signifies exactly the same as our word "shiver," to break into pieces, to reduce into splinters; and *dakah* signifies to "beat out thin," to beat out masses of metal into thin plates. The spirit broken all to pieces, and the heart broken all to pieces, stamped and beaten out, are the sacrifices which, in such cases, Thou requirest; and these *thou wilt not despise.* We may now suppose that God had shone upon his soul, healed his broken spirit, and renewed and removed his broken and distracted heart; and that he had now received the answer to the preceding prayers. And here the psalm properly ends, as in the following two verses there is nothing similar to what we find in the rest of this most important composition.

18. *Do good in thy good pleasure unto Zion.* This and the following verse most evidently refer to the time of the Captivity, when the walls of Jerusalem were broken down and the Temple service entirely discontinued; and, consequently, are long posterior to the times of David. Hence it has been concluded that the psalm was not composed by David, nor in his time, and that the title must be that of some other psalm inadvertently affixed to this. The fourth verse has also been considered as decisive against this title; but the note on that verse has considerably weakened, if not destroyed, that objection. I have been long of opinion that, whether the title be properly or improperly affixed to this psalm, these two verses make no part of it. The subject is totally dissimilar; and there is no rule of analogy by which it can be interpreted as belonging to the psalm, to the subject, or to the person. I think they oiginally made a psalm of themselves, a kind of ejaculatory prayer for the redemption of the captives from Babylon, the rebuilding of Jerusalem, and the restoration of the Temple worship. And, taken in this light, they are very proper and very expressive.

PSALM 52 (MATTHEW HENRY)

To the chief musician, Maschil. *A psalm* of David, when Doeg the Edomite came and told Saul, and said unto him, David has come to the house of Ahimelech.

Verses 1–5

The title is a brief account of the story to which the psalm refers, 1 Sam. xxii. 1-23.

I. David argues the case fairly with this proud and mighty man, *v.* 1. Doeg was, by his office, a

PSALM 52 (JAMIESON, FAUSSET, BROWN)

Vss. 1-9. Cf. I Samuel 21:1-10; 22:1-10, for the history of the title. The first verse gives the theme; the boast of the wicked over the righteous is vain, for God constantly cares for His people. This is expanded by describing the malice and deceit, and then the ruin, of the wicked, and the happy state of the pious.

1. mighty man—lit., hero. Doeg may be thus addressed, ironically, in respect of his might in slander.

PSALM 52 (ADAM CLARKE)

The title is, "To the chief Musician, and instructive Psalm of David, when Doeg the Edomite came and informed Saul, and said to him, David is come to the house of Ahimelech." The history to which this alludes is the following: David, having learned that Saul was determined to destroy him, went to take refuge with Achish, king of Gath. In his journey he passed by Nob, where the Tabernacle then was, and took thence

MATTHEW HENRY

mighty man, for he was set over the servants of Saul, chamberlain of the household. This was he that boasted himself, not only in the power he had to do mischief, but in the mischief he did. It is uncertain how the following words come in: *The goodness of God endures continually.* The patience and forbearance of God are abused by sinners to the hardening of their hearts in their wicked ways. Because God is continually doing them good, therefore they boast in mischief. But it is rather to be taken to show the sinfulness of his sin: "God is continually doing good, and those that therein are like him have reason to glory in their being so; but thou art continually doing mischief, and therein art utterly unlike him, and contrary to him, and yet gloriest in being so."

II. He draws up a high charge against him in the court of heaven, *v.* 2–4. He accuses him of the wickedness of his tongue and the wickedness of his heart. Four things he charges him with:—1. Malice. His tongue does *mischief*, not only pricking like a needle, but cutting *like a sharp razor*. 2. Falsehood. It was a *deceitful tongue* that he did this mischief with (*v.* 4); he loved lying (*v.* 3), and this sharp razor did *work deceitfully* (*v.* 2). He told the truth, but not all the truth. It will not save us from the guilt of lying to be able to say, "There was some truth in what we said," if we pervert it, and make it to appear otherwise than it was. 3. Subtlety in sin: "*Thy tongue devises mischiefs;* that is, it speaks the mischief which thy heart devises." 4. Affection to sin: "*Thou lovest evil more than good;* that is, thou lovest evil. Thou wouldst rather please Saul by telling a lie than please God by speaking truth." Those are of Doeg's spirit who, instead of being pleased with an opportunity of doing a man a kindness, are glad when they have a fair occasion to do a man a mischief.

III. He reads his doom and denounces the judgments of God against him for his wickedness (*v.* 5): "Thou hast destroyed the priests of the Lord and cut them off, and therefore *God shall likewise destroy thee for ever.*" Doeg is here condemned, 1. To be driven out of the church: *He shall pluck thee out of the tabernacle*, not thy dwelling-place, but God's." Justly was he deprived of all the privileges of God's house who had been so mischievous to his servants. 2. To be driven out of the world: "*He shall root thee out of the land of the living*, in which thou thoughtest thyself so deeply rooted."

Verses 6–9

David was at this time in great distress; the mischief Doeg had done him was but the beginning of his sorrows; and yet here we have him triumphing in tribulation.

I. In the fall of Doeg. They shall observe God's judgments on Doeg, and speak of them, 1. To the glory of God: *They shall see and fear* (*v.* 6); that is, they shall reverence the justice of God. 2. To the shame of Doeg. They shall laugh at him, not with a ludicrous, but a rational serious laughter, as *he that sits in heaven shall laugh at him*, ii. 4. He shall appear ridiculous, and worthy to be laughed at. *Lo, this is the man that made not God his strength.* Now that which ruined Doeg's prosperity was, (1) That he did not build it upon a rock: *He made not God his strength.* Those wretchedly deceive themselves that think to support themselves in their power and wealth without God and religion. (2) That he did build it upon the sand. He thought his wealth would support itself: *He trusted in the abundance of his riches*, which, he imagined, were *laid up for many years.*

II. In his own stability, *v.* 8, 9. "This mighty man is plucked up by the roots; *but I am like a green olive-tree*, planted and rooted, fixed and flourishing; he is turned out of God's dwelling-place, but I am established in it." Now what must we do that we may be as green olive-trees? 1. We must live a life of faith and holy confidence in God and his grace: *I trust in the mercy of God for ever and ever.* 2. We must live a life of thankfulness and holy joy in God (*v.* 9): "*I will praise thee for ever, because thou hast done it*, hast performed thy promise to me." 3. We must live a life of expectation and humble dependence upon God: "*I will wait on thy name;* I will attend upon thee in all those ways wherein thou hast made thyself known, hoping for the discoveries of thy favour to me and willing to tarry till the time appointed for them; *for it is good before thy saints.*"

JAMIESON, FAUSSET, BROWN

2. tongue—for self. **mischiefs**—evil to others (Ps. 5:9; 38:12). **working deceitfully**—(Ps. 10:7), as a keen, smoothly moving razor, cutting quietly, but deeply. **3, 4. all-devouring**—lit., swallowing, which utterly destroy (cf. Ps. 21:9; 35:25).

5. likewise—or, so, also, as you have done to others God will do to you (Ps. 18:27). The following terms describe the most entire ruin.

6. shall . . . fear—regard with religious awe. **laugh at him**—for his folly;

7. for trusting in riches and being strong in—**wickedness**—lit., mischief (vs. 2), instead of trusting in God. **the man**—lit., the mighty man, or hero (vs. 1).

8. The figure used is common (Ps. 1:3; Jer. 11:16). **green**—fresh. **house . . .**—in communion with God (cf. Ps. 27:4, 5).

for ever and ever—qualifies mercy. **9. hast done**—i.e., what the context supplies, preserved me (cf. Ps. 22:31).

wait . . . name—hope in Thy perfections, manifested for my good (Ps. 5:11; 20:1). **for it is good**—i.e., Thy name, and the whole method or result of its manifestation (Ps. 54:6; 69:16).

ADAM CLARKE

the sword of Goliath; and, being spent with hunger, took some of the shewbread. Doeg, an Edomite, one of the domestics of Saul, being there, went to Saul and informed him of these transactions. Saul immediately ordered Ahimelech into his presence, upbraided him for being a partisan of David, and ordered Doeg to slay him and all the priests. Doeg did so, and there fell by his hand eighty-five persons. And Saul sent and destroyed Nob and all its inhabitants, old and young, with all their property; none escaping but Abiathar, the son of Ahimelech, who immediately joined himself to David. The account may be found 1 Sam. xxi. 1-7; xxii. 9-23.

5. *God shall likewise destroy thee.* God shall set himself to destroy you; "He will pull down thy building"; He shall unroof it, dilapidate, and dig up your foundation.

7. *In the abundance of his riches.* Literally, in the "multiplication of his riches." He had got much, he hoped to get more, and expected that his happiness would multiply as his riches multiplied. And this is the case with most rich men. *Strengthened himself in his wickedness.* Loved money instead of God; and thus his depravity, being increased, was *strengthened.*

MATTHEW HENRY

PSALM 53

To the chief musician upon Mahalath, Maschil. *A psalm* of David.

Verses 1–6

1. The fact of sin. Is that proved? Yes, God is a witness to it. All the sinfulness of their hearts and lives is naked and open before him. 2. The fault of sin. It is that which makes this world such an evil world as it is; it is going back from God, *v.* 3. 3. The fountain of sin. How comes it that men are so bad? Surely it is because *there is no fear of God before their eyes.* Men's bad practices flow from their bad principles. 4. The folly of sin. He is a fool that harbours corrupt thoughts. Atheists, whether in opinion or practice, are the greatest fools in the world. Those that do not seek God do not understand; they are like brute-beasts, for man is distinguished from the brutes, not so much by the powers of reason as by a capacity for religion. *The workers of iniquity* may truly be said to know nothing that do not know God, *v.* 4. 5. The filthiness of sin. Sinners are corrupt (*v.* 1); their nature is vitiated and spoiled, and the more noble the nature is the more vile it is when it is depraved. 6. The fruit of sin. See to what a degree of barbarity it brings men at last; when men's hearts are hardened through the deceitfulness of sin see their cruelty to their brethren, that are bone of their bone—because they will not *run with them to the same excess of riot,* they *eat them up as they eat bread*; as if they had not only become beasts, but beasts of prey. 7. The fear and shame that attend sin (*v.* 5): *There were those in great fear* who had made God their enemy. *The wicked flees when none pursues.* See the ground of this fear; it is because God has formerly *scattered the bones of those that encamped against* his people, not only broken their power and dispersed their forces, but slain them. 8. The faith of the saints, and their hope and power touching the cure of this great evil, *v.* 6. There will come a Saviour, a great salvation, a salvation from sin.

PSALM 54

To the chief musician on Neginoth, Maschil. *A psalm* of David, when the Ziphim came and said to Saul, Doth not David hide himself with us?

Verses 1–3

1. The great distress that David was now in. The Ziphim came of their own accord, and informed Saul where David was, with a promise to deliver him into his hand. Never let a good man expect to be safe and easy till he comes to heaven. How treacherous, how officious, were these Ziphim! 2. His prayer to God for succour and deliverance, *v.* 1, 2. David has no other plea to depend upon than God's name, no other power to depend upon than God's strength, and those he makes his refuge and confidence. Even in his flight, when he had not opportunity for solemn address to God, he was ever and anon lifting up to heaven: *Hear my prayer,* which comes from my heart, and *give ear to the words of my mouth.* 3. His plea which is taken from the character of his enemies, *v.* 3. They are *strangers*; such were the Ziphites, unworthy the name of Israelites. "They have used me more basely and barbarously than the Philistines themselves would have done." They are *oppressors*; such was Saul, who, as a king, should have used his power for the protection of all his good subjects, but abused it for their destruction. They were very formidable and threatening; they not only hated him and wished him ill, but they rose up against him in a body, joining their power to do him a mischief. They were very spiteful and malicious: *They seek after my soul. They have not set God before them,* that is, they have quite cast off the thoughts of God; they do not consider that in fighting against his people, they fight against him.

Verses 4–7

David's faith in his prayer.

I. He was sure that he had God on his side, *Behold, God is my helper.* Though men and devils aim to be our destroyers, they shall not prevail while God is our helper: *The Lord is with those that uphold my soul.* Compare cxviii. 7, "*The Lord taketh my part with those that help me.*"

II. God taking part with him, he doubted not but his enemies should fall before him (*v.* 5): "*He shall reward evil unto my enemies that observe me.* The evil they designed against me the righteous God will return upon their own heads." David would not render evil to them, but he knew God would: *I as a deaf man heard not, for thou wilt hear.* We must not

JAMIESON, FAUSSET, BROWN

PSALM 53

Vss. 1-6. *Upon Mahalath*—(cf. Ps. 88, title). Why this repetition of Psalm 14 is given we do not know.

1-4, with few verbal changes, correspond with Psalm 14:1-4.

5. Instead of assurances of God's presence with the pious, and a complaint of the wicked, Psalm 14:5, 6 portrays the ruin of the latter, whose "bones" even "are scattered" (cf. Ps. 141:7), and who are put to shame as contemptuously rejected of God.

PSALM 54

Vss. 1-7. Cf. title of Psalms 4 and 32; for the history, I Samuel 23:19, 29; 26:1-25. After an earnest cry for help, the Psalmist promises praise in the assurance of a hearing.

1. by thy name—(Ps. 5:11), specially, power. **judge me**—as in Psalm 7:8; 26:1. **2.** (Cf. Ps. 4:1; 5:1.)

3. strangers—perhaps Ziphites. **oppressors**—lit., "terrible ones" (Isa. 13:11; 25:3). Such were Saul and his army.

not set . . . them—acted as atheists, without God's fear (cf. Ps. 16:8).

4. (Cf. Ps. 30:10.) **with them**—on their side, and for me (cf. Ps. 46:11).

5. He shall . . . evil—or. Evil *shall return* on (Ps. 7:16) my enemies or watchers, i.e., to do me evil (Ps. 6:7). **in thy truth**—Thy verified promise.

ADAM CLARKE

PSALM 53

The title, "To the chief Musician upon Mahalath, an instructive Psalm of David." The word *mahalath,* some translate the "president"; others, "hollow instruments." A flute pipe, or wind instrument with holes, appears to be what is intended. "To the chief player on the flute"; or, "To the master of the band of pipers."

1. *The fool hath said in his heart.* The whole of this psalm, except a few inconsiderable differences, is the same as the fourteenth. By referring to the fourteenth, the reader will find the subject of it explained. *Have done abominable iniquity.* Instead of *avel,* "evil" or "iniquity," eight of Kennicott's and De Rossi's MSS. have *alilah,* "work," which is nearly the same as in Psalm xiv.

4. *Have the workers of iniquity.* For *workers* seventy-two of Kennicott's and De Rossi's MSS., with several ancient editions, add the word "all"—"all the workers of iniquity," which is the reading in the parallel place in Psalm xiv.

5. *For God hath scattered the bones of him that encampeth against thee: thou hast put them to shame, because God hath despised them.* The reader will see, on comparing this with the fifth and sixth verses of Psalm xiv, that the words above are mostly added here to what is said there; and appear to be levelled against the Babylonians, who sacked and ruined Jerusalem, and who were now sacked and ruined in their turn . . . *Oh that the salvation of Israel were come out of Zion!* I have already shown that the proper translation is, "Who shall give from Zion salvation to Israel?" The word *salvation* is in the plural here, "deliverances."

PSALM 54

The title is, "To the chief Musician upon Neginoth, an instructive Psalm of David, when the Ziphites came to Saul, and said, Doth not David conceal himself among us?"

Ziph was a village in the southern part of Palestine. David having taken refuge in the mountains of that country, the Ziphites went to Saul, and informed him of the fact. Saul, with his army, immediately went thither, and was on one side of a mountain while David was on the other. Just when he was about to fall into the hands of his merciless pursuer, an express came to Saul that the Philistines had invaded Israel, on which he gave up the pursuit and returned to save his country, and David escaped to En-gedi. See the account in 1 Sam. xxiii. 19-29. *Neginoth,* from *nagan,* to "strike" or "play" on some kind of instrument, probably signifies stringed instruments, such as were played on with a plectrum.

1. *Save me, O God, by thy name.* Save me by thyself alone; so *name* here may be understood. The name of God is often God himself. David was now in such imminent danger of being taken and destroyed that no human means were left for his escape; if God therefore had not interfered, he must have been destroyed.

2. *Hear my prayer.* In his straits he had recourse to God; for from Him alone, for the reasons alleged above, his deliverance must proceed.

3. *Strangers are risen up against me.* The Ziphites. *And oppressors.* Saul, his courtiers, and his army.

MATTHEW HENRY

avenge ourselves, because God has said, *Vengeance is mine.* But he prays, *Cut them off in thy truth.* This is not a prayer of malice, but a prayer of faith; for it has an eye to the word of God, and only desires the performance of that.

III. He promises to give thanks to God for all the experiences he had had of his goodness to him (*v.* 6): *I will sacrifice unto thee. I will praise thy name.* A thankful heart, and our lips giving thanks to his name, are the sacrifices God will accept.

IV. He speaks of his deliverance as a thing done (*v.* 7): I will praise thy name, and say, "*He has delivered me*; this shall be my song then." *My eye has seen its desire upon my enemies*, not seen them cut off and ruined, but forced to retreat, tidings being brought to Saul that the Philistines were upon him, 1 Sam. xxiii. 27, 28. All David desired was to be himself safe; when he saw Saul draw off his forces he saw his desire. This may perhaps point at Christ, of whom David was a type; God would deliver him out of all the troubles of his state of humiliation, and he was perfectly sure of it; and all things are said to be put under his feet; for, though we see not yet all things put under him, yet we are sure he shall reign till all his enemies be made his footstool, and he shall see his desire upon them.

PSALM 55

To the chief musician on Neginoth, Maschil. *A psalm* of David.

Verses 1–8

I. David praying. Prayer is a salve for every sore and a relief to the spirit under every burden: *Give ear to my prayer, O God! v.* 1. *Hide not thyself from my supplication.* If we, in our prayers, sincerely lay open ourselves, our case, our hearts to God, we have reason to hope that he will not hide himself, his favours, his comforts, from us.

II. David weeping; for in this he was a type of Christ that he was a man of sorrows and often in tears (*v.* 2): "*I mourn in my complaint*" (or in my *meditation*, my *melancholy musings*), "and I make a noise; I cannot forbear such sighs and groans, and other expressions of grief, as discover it to those about me." It is *because of the voice of the enemy*, the menaces and insults of Absalom's party, that swelled, and hectored, and stirred up the people to cry out against David, and shout him out of his palace and capital city, as afterwards the chief priests stirred up the mob to cry out against the Son of David, *Away with him—Crucify him. They cast iniquity upon me.* They hated him themselves, and therefore they studied to make him odious, that others also might hate him. This made him mourn, and the more because he could remember the time when he was the darling of the people, and answered to his name, *David—a beloved one.*

III. David trembling, and in great consternation. We may well suppose him to be so upon the breaking out of Absalom's conspiracy and the general defection of the people. David was a man of great boldness, and in some very eminent instances had signalized his courage, and yet, when the danger was surprising and imminent, his heart failed him. Now David's *heart is sorely pained within him*; *the terrors of death have fallen upon him, v.* 4. Fearfulness of mind and trembling of body came upon him, and horror covered and overwhelmed him, *v.* 5. Sometimes David's faith made him, in a manner, fearless, and he could boldly say, when surrounded with enemies, *I will not be afraid what man can do unto me.* But at other times his fears prevail and tyrannize; for the best men are not always alike strong in faith. How desirous he was, in this fright, to retire into a desert, anywhere to be far enough from hearing the voice of the enemy and seeing their oppressions. He said (*v.* 6), to God in prayer, to himself in meditation, to his friends in complaint, *O that I had wings like a dove!* He was so surrounded with enemies that he saw not how he could escape but upon the wing, and therefore he wishes, *O that I had wings!* not like a hawk that flies strongly, but *like a dove* that flies swiftly; he wishes for wings, not to fly upon the prey, but to fly from the birds of prey, for such his enemies were. The dove flies low, and takes shelter as soon as she can, and thus would David fly. He would make his escape *—from the wind, storm, and tempest*, the tumult and ferment that the city was now in, and the danger to which he was exposed. "*I would fly away and be at rest, v.* 6. I would fly anywhere, if it were to a barren frightful wilderness, ever so far off, so I might be quiet," *v.* 7.

Verses 9–15

David here complains of his enemies, whose wicked

JAMIESON, FAUSSET, BROWN

6. I will freely . . .—or, present a *free-will* offering (Lev. 7:16; Num. 15:3).

7. mine eye . . . desire—(cf. Ps. 59:10; 112:8), expresses satisfaction in beholding the overthrow of his enemies as those of God, without implying any selfish or unholy feeling (cf. Ps. 52:6, 7).

PSALM 55

Vss. 1-23. In great terror on account of enemies, and grieved by the treachery of a friend, the Psalmist offers an earnest prayer for relief. He mingles confident assurances of divine favor to himself with invocations and predictions of God's avenging judgments on the wicked. The tone suits David's experience, both in the times of Saul and Absalom, though perhaps neither was exclusively before his mind.

1. hide not thyself . . .—(cf. Ps. 13:1; 27:9), withhold not help. **2.** The terms of the last clause express full indulgence of grief.

3. oppression—lit., "persecution." **they . . . iniquity**—lit., "they make evil doings slide upon me."

4, 5. express great alarm. **come upon** [or lit., "into"] **me.**

6. be at rest—lit., "dwell," i.e., permanently. **7, 8.** Even a wilderness is a safer place than exposure to such evils, terrible as storm and tempest.

ADAM CLARKE

6. *I will freely sacrifice unto thee.* Or, "I will sacrifice nobly unto Thee." Not only with a willing mind, but with a liberal hand will I bring sacrifice unto Thee.

7. *For he hath delivered me.* Saul had now decamped, and was returned to save his territories; and David in the meanwhile escaped to En-gedi. God was most evidently the Author of this deliverance. *Mine eye hath seen his desire upon mine enemies.* It is not likely that this psalm was written after the death of Saul, and therefore David could not say that he had seen his desire. The words might be translated, "My eye hath seen my enemies"—they have been so near that I could plainly discover them. Thus almost all the versions have understood the text. I have seen them, and yet they were not permitted to approach me. God has been my Deliverer.

PSALM 55

The title, "To the chief Musician upon Neginoth, A Psalm of David, giving instruction." This is the same as the preceding.

1. *Give ear to my prayer.* The frequency of such petitions shows the great earnestness of David's soul.

2. *I mourn in my complaint.* "In my sighing"; a strong guttural sound, expressive of the natural accents of sorrow. *And make a noise.* I am in a "tumult"—I am strongly agitated.

3. *They cast iniquity upon me.* They charge me with horrible crimes.

4. *The terrors of death are fallen upon me.* I am in hourly expectation of being massacred.

5. *Fearfulness.* How natural is this description! He is in distress—he mourns—makes a noise; sobs and sighs; his heart is wounded; he expects nothing but death; this produces fear; this produces tremor, which terminates in that deep apprehension of approaching and inevitable ruin that overwhelms him with horror. No man ever described a wounded heart like David.

7. *Would I wander far off.* He did escape, and yet his enemies were so near as to throw stones at him; but he escaped beyond Jordan, 2 Sam. xvii. 22-23.

8. *The windy storm.* From the sweeping wind and tempest—Absalom and his party, and the mutinous people in general.

MATTHEW HENRY

plots had brought him, though not to his faith's end, yet to his wits' end.

I. The character he gives of the enemies. They were of the worst sort of men, and his description of them agrees very well with Absalom and his accomplices. He complains of the city of Jerusalem, which strangely fell in with Absalom and fell off from David: *How has that faithful city become a harlot!* David did himself see nothing but *violence and strife in the city* (*v.* 9). He saw that violence and strife went about it day and night, and mounted its guards, *v.* 10. *Wickedness*, all manner of wickedness, *is in the midst thereof.* Deceit and guile, and all manner of treacherous dealing, *departed not from her streets, v.* 11. Is Jerusalem, the headquarters of God's priests, so ill taught? Can Jerusalem be ungrateful to David himself, its own illustrious founder, and be made too hot for him, so that he cannot reside in it? He complains of one of the ringleaders of the conspiracy, that had been very industrious to foment jealousies, to misrepresent him and his government, and to incense the city against him. Who was most active in it? "Not a sworn enemy, not Shimei, nor any of the nonjurors; then I could have borne it, for I should not have expected better from them." *But it was thou, a man, my equal, v.* 13. The Chaldee-paraphrase names Ahithophel as the person here meant. "*We took counsel together*, spent many an hour together, with a great deal of pleasure, in religious discourse," or, as Dr. Hammond reads it, "*We joined ourselves together to the assembly;* I gave him the right hand of fellowship in holy ordinances, and then *we walked to the house of God in company*, to attend the public service." There always has been, and always will be, a mixture of good and bad, sound and unsound, in the visible church. We must not wonder if we be sadly deceived in some that have made great pretensions to those two sacred things, religion and friendship; David himself, though a very wise man, was thus imposed upon, which may make similar disappointments the more tolerable. to us

II. His prayers against them. He prays, 1. That God would disperse them, as he did the Babel-builders (*v.* 9): "*Destroy, O Lord! and divide their tongues*; by making them to disagree among themselves, and clash with one another." God often destroys the church's enemies by dividing them; nor is there a surer way to the destruction of any people than their division. 2. That God would destroy them, as he did Dathan and Abiram, Num. xvi. 30. "*Let death seize upon them* by divine warrant, and *let them go down quickly into hell*; let them be dead, and buried, and so utterly destroyed, in a moment; for wickedness is wherever they are; it is in the midst of them."

Verses 16–23

In these verses,

I. David perseveres in his resolution to call upon God, being well assured that he should not seek him in vain (*v.* 16): "*As for me*, let them take what course they please to secure themselves, let violence and strife be their guards, prayer shall be mine; this I have found comfort in, and therefore this will I abide by: *I will call upon God*, and commit myself to him, and *the Lord shall save me*." "*I will pray and cry aloud. I will meditate*" (so the former word signifies). He will pray frequently, every day, and three times a day—*evening, and morning, and at noon.* Those that think three meals a day little enough for the body ought much more to think three solemn prayers a day little enough for the soul, and to count it a pleasure, not a task. It was Daniel's practice to pray three times a day (Dan. vi. 10), and noon was one of Peter's hours of prayer, Acts x. 9.

II. He assures himself that God would in due time give an answer of peace to his prayers.

1. That he himself should be delivered and his fears prevented. He begins to rejoice in hope (*v.* 18): *God has delivered my soul in peace*, that is, he will deliver it; David is as sure of the deliverance as if it were already wrought. With an eye of faith he now sees himself surrounded, as Elisha was, with chariots of fire and horses of fire, and therefore triumphs thus, *There are many with me*, more *with me than against me*, 2 Kings vi. 16, 17.

2. That his enemies should be reckoned with, and brought down.

(1) David here gives their character as the reason why he expected God would bring them down. They stand in no awe of God (*v.* 19): "*Because they have no changes* (no afflictions, no interruption to the constant course of their prosperity, no crosses to empty them from vessel to vessel) *therefore they fear not God.*" They are treacherous and false, and will not be held by the most sacred and solemn engage-

JAMIESON, FAUSSET, BROWN

the city—perhaps Jerusalem, the scene of anarchy. **10, 11,** which is described in detail (cf. Ps. 7:14-16). **Wickedness**—lit., "Mischief," evils resulting from others (Ps. 5:9; 52:2, 7). **streets**—or lit., "wide places," markets, courts of justice, and any public place.

12-14. This description of treachery does not deny, but aggravates, the injury from enemies. **guide**—lit., "friend" (Prov. 16:28: 17: 9). **acquaintance**—in *Hebrew*, a yet more intimate associate. **in company**—lit., "with a crowd," in a festal procession.

9. Destroy—lit., "swallow" (Ps. 21:9). **divide their tongues**—or, confound their speech, and hence their counsels (Gen. 11:7).

15. Let death . . .—or, "Desolations are on them." **let them go**—(lit., "they will go"). **quick**—or, living in the midst of life, death will come (cf. Num. 16:33). **among them**—or, within them, in their hearts (Ps. 5:9; 49:11).

16-18. God answers his constant and repeated prayers. **many with me**—i.e., by the context, fighting with me.

19. God hears the wicked in wrath. **abideth** [or, sitteth] **of old**—enthroned as a sovereign. **Because . . . no changes**—Prosperity hardens them (Ps. 73:5).

ADAM CLARKE

12. *It was not an enemy.* It is likely that in all these three verses Ahithophel is meant, who, it appears, had been at the bottom of the conspiracy from the beginning.

14. *Walked unto the house of God in company.* Or with haste; for the rabbins teach that we should walk hastily to the Temple, but slowly from it.

9. *Destroy, O Lord.* "Swallow them up"—confound them. *Divide their tongues.* Let his counsellors give opposite advice. And the prayer was heard. Hushai and Ahithophel gave opposite counsel. Absalom followed that of Hushai; and Ahithophel, knowing that the steps advised by Hushai would bring Absalom's affairs to ruin, went and hanged himself. See 2 Samuel xv; xvi; and xvii.

15. *Let death seize upon them.* This is a prediction of the sudden destruction which should fall on the ringleaders in this rebellion. And it was so. Ahithophel, seeing his counsel rejected, hanged himself. Absalom was defeated; and, fleeing away, he was suspended by the hair in a tree, under which his mule had passed; and being found thus by Joab, he was dispatched with three darts; and the people who espoused his interests were almost all cut off. *Let them go down quick into hell.* Let them go down alive into the pit. Let the earth swallow them up! And something of this kind actually took place. Absalom and his army were defeated; 20,000 of the rebels were slain on the field; and "the wood devoured more people that day than the sword devoured," 2 Sam. xviii. 7-8.

17. *Evening, and morning, and at noon, will I pray.* This was the custom of the pious Hebrews. See Dan. vi. 10. The Hebrews began their day in the evening, and hence David mentions the evening first.

19. *Because they have no changes.* At first Absalom, Ahithophel, and their party carried all before them. There seemed to be a very general defection of the people; and as in their first attempts they suffered no "reverses," therefore they feared not God. Most of those who have few or no afflictions and trials in life have but little religion. They become sufficient to themselves, and call not upon God.

MATTHEW HENRY

ments (*v.* 20). They are base and hypocritical, pretending friendship while they design mischief (*v.* 21): "*The words of his mouth*" (probably, he means Ahithophel particularly) "*were smoother than butter and softer than oil*, yet, at the same time, *war was in his heart*, and those very words had such a mischievous design in them that they were as *drawn swords* designed to stab."

(2) David here foretells their ruin. *God shall hear and afflict them.* God shall *bring them down.* They were bloody men, and cut others off, and therefore God will justly cut them off: they were deceitful men, and defrauded others of the one-half perhaps of what was their due, and now God will cut them short.

III. He encourages himself and all good people to commit themselves to God, with confidence in him. "*I will trust in thee*, in thy providence, and power, and mercy, and not in my own prudence, strength, or merit; when bloody and deceitful men are cut off in the midst of their days I shall still live by faith in thee." And this he will have others to do (*v.* 22): "*Cast thy burden upon the Lord*, whoever thou art that art burdened, and whatever the burden is." *Cast thy care upon the Lord*, so the LXX, to which the apostle refers, 1 Pet. v. 7. Care is a burden; it makes the heart stoop (Prov. xii. 25). To cast our burden upon God is to stay ourselves on his providence and promise. If we do so, it is promised, 1. That he will sustain us. He has not promised to free us immediately from that trouble which gives rise to our cares and fears; but he will provide that we be not tempted above what we are able. 2. That he will never suffer the righteous to be moved, to be so shaken by any troubles as to quit either their duty to God, or their comfort in him.

JAMIESON, FAUSSET, BROWN

20, 21. The treachery is aggravated by hypocrisy. The changes of number, vss. 15, 23, and here, enliven the picture, and imply that the chief traitor and his accomplices are in view together.

22. thy burden—lit., "gift," what is assigned you. **he shall sustain**—lit., "supply food," and so all need (Ps. 57:25; Matt. 6:11). **to be moved**—from the secure position of His favor (cf. Ps. 10:6). **23. bloody . . . days**—(cf. Ps. 5:6; 51:14), deceit and murderous dispositions often united. The threat is directed specially (not as a general truth) against the wicked, then in the writer's view.

ADAM CLARKE

20. *He hath put forth his hands.* A further description of Ahithophel. He betrayed his friends, and he broke his covenant with his king.

21. *Were smoother than butter.* He was a complete courtier, and a deep, designing hypocrite besides. His words "were as soft as butter, and as smooth as oil," while he meditated war; and the fair words which were intended to deceive were intended also to destroy—they were *drawn swords.* This is a literal description of the words and conduct of Absalom, as we learn from the inspired historian, 2 Sam. xv. 2, etc. He was accustomed to wait at the gate, question the persons who came for justice and judgment, throw out broad hints that the king was negligent of the affairs of his kingdom and had not provided an effective magistracy to administer justice among the people; and added that if he were appointed judge in the land justice should be done to all. He bowed also to the people, and kissed them; and thus "he stole the hearts of the men of Israel." See the passages referred to above.

MATTHEW HENRY — PSALM 56

To the chief musician, upon Jonath-elem-rechokim, Michtam of David, when the Philistines took him to Gath.

Verses 1–7

David, in this psalm, by his faith throws himself into the hands of God, even when he had by his fear and folly thrown himself into the hands of the Philistines. 1 Sam. xxi. 10, 11. This is called *Michtam—a golden psalm.* So some other psalms are entitled, but this has something peculiar in the title; it is upon *Jonath-elem-rechokim*, which signifies *the silent dove afar off.* Some apply this to David himself, who wished for the wings of a dove on which to fly away. He was forced to wander afar off, to seek for shelter in distant countries; there he was like the doves of the valleys, mourning and melancholy; but silent, neither murmuring against God nor railing at the instruments of his trouble.

I. He complains to God the malice of his enemies, to show what reason he had to fear them (*v.* 1): *Be merciful unto me, O God!* That petition includes all the good we come to the throne of grace for. He prays that he might find mercy with God, for with men he could find no mercy. When he fled from the cruel hands of Saul he fell into the cruel hands of the Philistines. "Lord" (says he), "be thou merciful to me now, or I am undone." "*They are many that fight against me*, and think to overpower me with numbers; take notice of this, *O thou Most High!* and make it to appear that wherein they deal proudly thou art above them." They were very barbarous: they would *swallow him up*, *v.* 1 and again *v.* 2. They were very unanimous (*v.* 6): *They gather themselves together*; though they were many, and of different interests among themselves, yet they united and combined against David, as Herod and Pilate against the Son of David. They were very powerful, quite too hard for him if God did not help him: "*They fight against me* (*v.* 2); *they oppress me*, *v.* 1. I am almost overcome and borne down by them, and reduced to the last extremity." They were very subtle and crafty (*v.* 6): "*They hide themselves;* they cover their designs, that they may the more effectually prosecute and pursue them. They hide themselves as a lion in his den, that they may mark my steps"; that is, "they observe everything I say and do with a critical eye, that they may have something to accuse me of." They were very spiteful and malicious. "*They wrest my words*, put them upon the rack, to extort that out of them which was never in them." They were very restless and unwearied. They continually waited for his soul; it was the life, the precious life, they hunted for; it was his death they longed for, *v.* 6.

II. He encourages himself in God, and in his promises, power, and providence, *v.* 3, 4. "*What time I am afraid*, in the day of my fear, when I am

JAMIESON, FAUSSET, BROWN — PSALM 56

Vss. 1-13. *Upon Jonath-elem-rechokim*—lit., "upon the dove of silence" of distant places; either denoting a melody (cf. on Ps. 9) of that name, to which this Psalm was to be performed; or it is an enigmatical form of denoting the subject, as given in the history referred to (I Sam. 21:11, etc.), David being regarded as an uncomplaining, meek dove, driven from his native home to wander in exile. Beset by domestic and foreign foes, David appeals confidently to God, recites his complaints, and closes with joyful and assured anticipations of God's continued help.

1, 2. would swallow—lit., "pants as a raging beast" (Acts 9:1). **enemies**—watchers (Ps. 54:5). **most High**—As it is not elsewhere used absolutely for God, some render the word here, arrogantly, or proudly, as qualifying "those who fight," etc.

5, 6. A vivid picture of the conduct of malicious enemies.

ADAM CLARKE — PSALM 56

The title of this psalm is very long: "To the conqueror, concerning the dumb dove in foreign places: golden Psalm of David." If the title be at all authentic, David may mean himself and his companions by it, when he escaped from the hands of the Philistines; particularly from the hands of Achish, king of Gath. *Elem* signifies to "compress" or "bind together"; also, a "small band or body of men." And *yonath*, from *yanah*, to "oppress" or "afflict," is properly applied to the dove because of its being so defenseless, and often becoming the prey of ravenous birds. It is possible, therefore, that the title may imply no more than—"A prayer to God in behalf of himself and the oppressed band that followed him, and shared his misfortunes in distant places."

2. *O thou most High. Marom.* I do not think that this word expresses any attribute of God, or indeed is at all addressed to Him. It signifies, literally, "from on high," or "from a high or elevated place": "For the multitudes fight against me from the high or elevated place"; the place of authority—the court and cabinet of Saul.

MATTHEW HENRY

most terrified from without and most timorous within, then *I will trust in thee*, and thereby my fears shall be silenced." He resolves to make God's promises the matter of his praises, *In God I will praise*, not only his work which he has done, but *his* word which he has spoken. Some understand by *his word* his providences, every event that he orders and appoints: "When I speak well of God I will with him speak well of everything that he does." Thus supported, he will bid defiance to all adverse powers: "*When in God I have put my trust*, I am safe, I am easy, and *I will not fear what flesh can do unto me*." As we must not trust to an arm of flesh when it is engaged for us, so we must not be afraid of an arm of flesh when it is stretched out against us.

III. He foresees and foretells the fall of those that fought against him (*v.* 7): *Shall they escape by iniquity?* They hope to escape God's judgments, as they escape men's, by violence and fraud, and the arts of injustice and treachery; but shall they escape? No, certainly they shall not. The sin of sinners will never be their security.

Verses 8–13

Several things David here comforts himself with in the day of his distress and fear.

I. That God took particular notice of all his grievances and all his griefs, *v.* 8. *Thou tellest my wanderings*, my *flittings*, so the old translation. David was now but a young man (under thirty) and yet he had had many removes, from his father's house to the court, thence to the camp, and now he was hunted like a partridge upon the mountains; but this comforted him, that God kept a particular account of all his motions, and numbered all the weary steps he took, by night or by day. When he was wandering he was often weeping, and therefore prays, "*Put thou my tears into thy bottle*, to be preserved and looked upon: nay, I know they are *in thy book*, the book of thy remembrance." God has a bottle and a book for his people's tears, both those for their sins and those for their afflictions. He observes them with compassion and tender concern; he is afflicted in their afflictions, and knows their souls in adversity. Paul was mindful of Timothy's tears (2 Tim. i. 4), and God will not forget the sorrows of his people. God will comfort his people according to the time wherein he has afflicted them, and give to those to reap in joy who sowed in tears. What was sown a tear will come up a pearl.

II. That his prayers would be powerful for the defeat and discomfiture of his enemies, as well as for his own support and encouragement (*v.* 9): "*When I cry unto thee, then shall my enemies turn back;* I need no other weapons than prayers and tears; *this I know, for God is for me*, to plead my cause, to protect and deliver me; and, if God be for me, who can be against me so as to prevail?" We fight best upon our knees, Eph. vi. 18.

III. That his faith in God would set him above the fear of man, *v.* 10, 11. Here he repeats, with a strong pathos, what he had said (*v.* 4), "*In God will I praise his word;* that is, I will firmly depend upon the promise for the sake of him that made it." *In God have I put my trust*, and in him only, and therefore "*I will not be afraid what man can do unto me* (*v.* 11), though I know very well what he would do if he could," *v.* 1, 2.

IV. That he was in bonds to God (*v.* 12): "*Thy vows are upon me, O God!*—not upon me as a burden which I am loaded with, but as a badge which I glory in. It ought to be the matter of our consideration and joy that *the vows of God are upon us*—our baptismal vows renewed at the Lord's table, our occasional vows under convictions, under corrections, by these we are bound to live to God.

V. That he should still have more and more occasion to praise him: *I will render praises unto thee.* This is part of the performance of his vows; for vows of thankfulness properly accompany prayers for mercy, and when the mercy is received must be made good. "*Thou hast delivered my soul*, my life, *from death*, which was just ready to seize me." If God have delivered us from sin, either from the commission of it by preventing grace or from the punishment of it by pardoning mercy, we have reason to own that he has thereby delivered our souls from death, which is the wages of sin. "*Thou* wilt *deliver my feet from falling*; thou hast done the greater, and therefore thou wilt do the less; thou hast begun a good work, and therefore thou wilt carry it on and perfect it." Those that think they stand must take heed lest they fall, because the best stand no longer than God is pleased to uphold them. God never brought his people out of Egypt to slay them in the wilderness. He that in conversion delivers the soul from so great a death as sin is will not fail *to preserve it to his heavenly kingdom.*

JAMIESON, FAUSSET, BROWN

3. in [or lit., "unto"] **thee**—to whom he turns in trouble. **4. in God . . . his word**—By His grace or aid (Ps. 60:12; 108:13), or, "I will boast in God as to His word"; in either case His word is the special matter and cause of praise.

flesh—for mankind (Ps. 65:2; Isa. 31:3), intimating frailty.

7. Shall they escape . . . ?—or better, "Their escape is by iniquity." **cast . . . people**—humble those who so proudly oppose Thy servant.

8. God is mindful of his exile and remembers his tears. The custom of *bottling the tears* of mourners as a memorial, which has existed in some Eastern nations, may explain the figure.

9. God is for me—or, on my side (Ps. 118:6; 124:1, 2); hence he is sure of the repulse of his foes.

12. I will render praises—will pay what I have vowed.

13. The question implies an affirmative answer, drawn from past experience. **falling**—as from a precipice. **before God**—in His favor during life.

ADAM CLARKE

4. *In God I will praise his word. Belohim* may mean here "through God," or "by the help of God," *I will praise his word.* And that he should have cause to do it, he says, *In God I have put my trust*, and therefore he says, *I will not fear what flesh can do unto me.* He repeats this sentiment in the tenth and eleventh verses.

8. *Thou tellest my wanderings.* Thou seest how often I am obliged to shift the place of my retreat. I am hunted everywhere; but Thou "numberest all my hiding-places," and seest how often I am in danger of losing my life.

Put thou my tears into thy bottle. Here is an allusion to a very ancient custom, which we know long obtained among the Greeks and Romans, of putting the tears which were shed for the death of any person into small phials, and offering them on the tomb of the deceased. *Are they not in thy book?* Thou hast taken an exact account of all the tears I have shed in relation to this business, and Thou wilt call my enemies to account for every tear.

10-11. See on v. 4, where the same words occur.

MATTHEW HENRY

PSALM 57

To the chief musician, Al-taschith, Michtam of David, when he fled from Saul in the cave.

Verses 1–6

The title of this psalm has one word new in it, *Al-taschith—Destroy not.* Some make it to be only some known tune to which this psalm was set; others apply it to the occasion and matter of the psalm. *Destroy not;* that is, David would not let Saul be destroyed, when now in the cave there was a fair opportunity of killing him, and his servants would fain have done so. No, says David, *destroy him not,* 1 Sam. xxiv. 4, 6. Or, rather, God would not let David be destroyed by Saul; he suffered him to persecute David, but still under his limitation, *Destroy him not.*

I. He supports himself with faith and hope in God, and prayer to him, *v.* 1, 2. *Be merciful to me, O Lord!* It was the publican's prayer, Luke xviii. 13. To recommend himself to God's mercy, he here professes,

1. That all his dependence is upon God: *My soul trusteth in thee, v.* 1. At the footstool of the throne of his grace, he humbly professes his confidence in him: *In the shadow of thy wings will I make my refuge,* as the chickens take shelter under the wings of the hen when the birds of prey are ready to strike at them, *until these calamities be over-past.* He was confident his troubles would end well, in due time; *these calamities will be over-past.* He comforted himself in the goodness of God's nature, by which he is inclined to succour and protect his people, as the hen is by instinct to shelter her young ones.

2. That all his desire is towards God (*v.* 2): "*I will cry unto God most high,* for succour and relief; to him that is most high will I lift up my soul, and pray earnestly, even *unto God that performs all things for me.*"

3. That all his expectation is from God (*v.* 3): *He shall send from heaven, and save me.* Those that make God their only refuge, and fly to him by faith and prayer, may be sure of salvation, in his way and time. Look which way he will, on this earth, refuge fails, no help appears; but he looks for it from heaven. Those that lift up their hearts to things above may thence expect all good. *God shall send forth his mercy and truth.* We need no more to make us happy than to have the benefit of the mercy and truth of God, xxv. 10.

II. He represents the power and malice of his enemies (*v.* 4): *My soul is among lions.* He describes their malicious projects against him (*v.* 6) and shows the issue of them: "*They have prepared a net for my steps,* in which to take me, and I might not again escape out of their hands; *they have digged a pit before me,* that I might, ere I am aware, run headlong into it." But let us see what comes of it. 1. It is indeed some disturbance to David: *My soul is bowed down.* But, 2. It was destruction to themselves; they dug a pit for David, *into the midst whereof they have fallen.*

III. He prays to God to glorify himself and his own great name (*v.* 5): "Whatever becomes of me and my interest, *be thou exalted, O God! above the heavens, and let thy glory be above* or over *all the earth;* let all the inhabitants of this earth be brought to know and praise thee." Thus God's glory should lie nearer our hearts, and we should be more concerned for it, than for any particular interests of our own. When David was in the greatest distress and disgrace he did not pray, *Lord, exalt me,* but, *Lord, exalt thy own name.* Thus the Son of David, when his soul was troubled, and he prayed, *Father, save me from this hour,* immediately withdrew that petition, and presented this in the room of it, *For this cause came I to this hour; Father, glorify thy name,* John xii. 27, 28.

Verses 7–11

How strangely is the tune altered here! David's prayer and complaints, by the lively actings of faith, are here, all of a sudden, turned into praises and thanksgivings. Observe,

I. How he prepares himself for the duty of praise (*v.* 7): *My heart is fixed, O God! my heart is fixed.* My heart is *erect,* or *lifted up* (so some), which was bowed down, *v.* 6. *My heart is fixed,* it is prepared for every event, being *stayed upon God,* cxii. 7; Isa. xxvi. 3. *My heart is fixed* to *sing and give praise, attending on the Lord without distraction.*

II. How he excites himself to the duty of praise (*v.* 8): *Awake up my glory,* that is, my tongue (our tongue is our glory, and never more so than when it is employed in praising God), or my soul, that must be first awakened; dull and sleepy devotions will never be acceptable to God.

III. How he pleases himself, and even prides him-

JAMIESON, FAUSSET, BROWN

PSALM 57

Vss. 1-11. *Al-taschith*—"Destroy not." This is perhaps an enigmatical allusion to the critical circumstances connected with the history, for which cf. I Samuel 22:1; 26:1-3. In Moses' prayer (Deut. 9:26) it is a prominent petition deprecating God's anger against the people. This explanation suits the 58th and 59th also. Asaph uses it for the 75th, in the scope of which there is allusion to some emergency. *Michtam*—(Cf. Ps. 16). To an earnest cry for divine aid, the Psalmist adds, as often, the language of praise, in the assured hope of a favorable hearing.

1. my soul—or self, or life, which is threatened.

shadow of thy wings—(Ps. 17:8; 36:7). **calamities**—lit., "mischiefs" (Ps. 52:2; 55:10).

2. performeth—or, completes what He has begun. **3. from . . . swallow me up**—that pants in rage after me (Ps. 56:2).

mercy and . . . truth—(Ps. 25:10; 36:5), as messengers (Ps. 43:3) sent to deliver him.

4. The mingled figures of wild beasts (Ps. 10:9; 17:12) and weapons of war (Ps. 11:2) heighten the picture of danger. **whose . . . tongue**—or slanders.
6. (Cf. Ps. 7:15; 9:15, 16.)

5. This doxology illustrates his view of the connection of his deliverance with God's glory.

7. I will . . . praise—both with voice and instrument.

8. Hence—he addresses his glory, or tongue (Ps. 16:9; 30:12), and his psaltery, or lute and harp. **I myself . . . early**—lit., "I will awaken dawn," poetically expressing his zeal and diligence.

ADAM CLARKE

PSALM 57

The title is, "To the chief Musician, Al-taschith [destroy not], a golden Psalm of David (or one to be engraven), when he fled from Saul in the cave." It is very likely that this psalm was made to commemorate his escape from Saul in the cave of En-gedi, where Saul had entered without knowing that David was there, and David cut off the skirt of his garment. And it is not improbable that, when he found that Saul was providentially delivered into his hand, he might have formed the hasty resolution to take away his life, as his companions counselled him to do; and in that moment the divine monition came, *al tascheth!* "Destroy not! lift not up thy hand against the Lord's anointed!" Instead, therefore, of taking away his life, he contented himself with taking away his skirt, to show him that he had been in his power. When, afterwards, he composed the psalm, he gave it for title the words which he received as a divine warning. See the history, 1 Samuel xxiv.

1. *Be merciful unto me.* To show David's deep earnestness, he repeats this twice; he was in great danger, surrounded by implacable enemies, and he knew that God alone could deliver him. *In the shadow of thy wings.* A metaphor taken from the brood of a hen taking shelter under her wings when they see a bird of prey, and there they continue to hide themselves till their enemy disappears. In a storm, or tempest of rain, the mother covers them with her wings to afford them shelter and defense.

2. *I will cry unto God most high.* He is the Most High, and therefore far above all my enemies, though the prince of the power of the air be at their head. *Unto God, lael,* unto the "strong God," One against whom no human or diabolic might can prevail. David felt his own weakness, and he knew the strength of his adversaries; and therefore he views God under those attributes and characters which were suited to his state. *That performeth all things for me.* Who *works* for me; *gomer,* He who "completes" for me, and will bring all to a happy issue.

3. *God shall send forth his mercy and his truth* Here *mercy* and *truth* are personified. They are the messengers that God will send from heaven to save me. His *mercy* ever inclines Him to help and save the distressed. This He has promised to do; and His *truth* binds Him to fulfill the promises or engagements His mercy has made, to both saints and sinners.

4. *My soul is among lions.* I agree with Dr. Kennicott that this should be translated, "My soul dwells in parched places."

6. *They have prepared a net for my steps.* A gin such as huntsmen put in the places which they know the prey they seek frequents. *They have digged a pit.* Another method of catching game and wild beasts. They dig a pit, cover it over with weak sticks and turf. The beasts, not suspecting danger where none appears, in attempting to walk over it, fall through and are taken. Saul digged a pit, laid snares for the life of David, and fell into one of them himself, particularly at the cave of En-gedi; for he entered into the very pit or cave where David and his men were hidden, and his life lay at the generosity of the very man whose life he was seeking!

7. *My heart is fixed.* My heart is prepared to do and suffer Thy will. It is *fixed*—it has made the firmest purpose through His strength, by which I can do all things.

8. *Awake up, my glory.* I think the Syriac likely to be the true reading: "Awake up, my harp; awake, psaltery and harp: I will awake early." The last five verses of this psalm are nearly the same with the first five verses of Psalm cviii. Rabbi Solomon Jarchi tells us that David had a harp at his bed's head, which

MATTHEW HENRY

self, in the work of praise. He resolves to *praise him among the people* and to *sing unto him among the nations*, *v.* 9. This intimates, 1. That he would even make the earth ring with his sacred songs, that all might take notice how much he thought himself indebted to the goodness of God. 2. That he desires to bring others in to join with him in praising God. He will publish God's praises *among the people*. David, in his psalms, which fill the universal church, and will to the end of time, may be said to be still *praising God among the people* and *singing to him among the nations;* for all good people make use of his words in praising God.

IV. How he furnishes himself with matter for praise, *v.* 10. *Thy mercy is great unto the heavens*, great beyond conception and expression; and *thy truth unto the clouds*, great beyond discovery, for what eye can reach that which is wrapped up in the clouds?

V. How he leaves it at last to God to glorify his own name (*v.* 11): *Be thou exalted, O God!*

JAMIESON, FAUSSET, BROWN

9, 10. As His mercy and truth, so shall His praise, fill the universe.

ADAM CLARKE

played of itself when the north wind blew on it; and then David arose to give praise to God.

9. *Among the people.* The Israelites. *Among the nations.* The Gentiles at large.

10. *Thy mercy is great unto the heavens.* It is as far above all human description and comprehension as the heavens are above the earth. See Ps. xxxvi. 5-6, where nearly the same words occur.

11. *Be thou exalted, O God, above the heavens.* The same sentiments and words which occur in v. 5.

MATTHEW HENRY

PSALM 58

To the chief musician, Al-taschith, Michtam of David.

Verses 1–5

We have reason to think that this psalm refers to the malice of Saul against David.

In these verses David, not as a king, for he had not yet come to the throne, but as a prophet, in God's name arraigns and convicts his judges. Two things he charges them with:—

I. The corruption of their government. They were a congregation, a bench of justices. One would not have thought a congregation of such could be bribed and biassed with pensions, and yet, it seems, they were, because the son of Kish could do that for them which the son of Jesse could not, 1 Sam. xxii. 7. The judges would not do right, would not protect or vindicate oppressed innocency (*v.* 1): "*Do you indeed speak righteousness, or judge uprightly?* No; your own consciences cannot but tell you that you do not discharge the trust reposed in you as magistrates, by which you are bound to be *a terror to evildoers and a praise to those that do well.* Remember you are sons of men; mortal and dying, and that you stand upon the same level before God with the meanest of those you trample upon, and must yourselves be called to an account and judged. *In heart you work wickedness.* The more there is of the heart in any act of wickedness the worse it is, Eccles. viii. 11. And what was their wickedness? "*You weigh the violence of your hands in the earth*" (or *in the land*), "the peace of which you are appointed to be the conservators of." They did all the vioence and injury they could, either to enrich or avenge themselves, and they weighed it. They did it with a great deal of craft and caution: "*You frame it by rule and lines*" (so the word signifies). They did it under colour of justice.

II. The corruption of their nature. This was the root of bitterness from which that gall and wormwood sprang (*v.* 3): *The wicked*, who in heart work wickedness, *are estranged from the womb*, estranged from God and all good, *alienated from the divine life*, and its principles, powers, and pleasures, Eph. iv. 18. They are called, and not miscalled, *transgressors from the womb*; one can therefore expect no other than that they will *deal very treacherously*; see Isa. xlviii. 8. They go astray from God and their duty as soon as they are born (that is, as soon as possibly they can); the foolishness that is bound up in their hearts appears with the first operations of reason. Three instances are here given of the corruption of nature:—1. Falsehood. They soon learn to speak lies, and *bend their tongues, like their bows*, for that purpose, Jer. ix. 3. 2. Malice. *Their poison* (that is, their ill-will, and the spite they bore to goodness and all good men, particularly to David) was *like the poison of a serpent*, innate, venomous, and very mischievous, and that which they can never be cured of. 3. Untractableness. They are malicious, and nothing will work upon them, no reason, no kindness, to mollify them, and bring them to a better temper. *They are like the deaf adder that stops her ear*, *v.* 4, 5. David compares them to the deaf adder or viper, concerning which there was then this tradition, that whereas, by music or some other art, they had a way of charming serpents, to destroy them or at least disable them to do mischief, this deaf adder would lay one ear to the ground and stop the other with her tail, so that she could not hear the voice of the enchantment, and so defeated the intention of it and secured herself.

JAMIESON, FAUSSET, BROWN

PSALM 58

Vss. 1-11. David's critical condition in some period of the Sauline persecution probably occasioned this Psalm, in which the Psalmist teaches that the innate and actual sinfulness of men deserves, and shall receive, God's righteous vengeance, while the pious may be consoled by the evidence of His wise and holy government of men.

1. O congregation—lit., "Oh, dumb"—the word used is never translated "congregation." "Are ye dumb? ye should speak righteousness," may be the translation. In any case, the writer remonstrates with them, perhaps a council, who were assembled to try his cause, and bound to give a right decision.

2. This they did not design; but **weigh . . . violence**—or give decisions of violence. *Weigh* is a figure to express the acts of judges. **in the earth**—publicly.

3-5. describe the wicked generally, who sin naturally, easily, malignantly, and stubbornly.

stoppeth her [or, lit., "his"] **ear**—i.e., the wicked man (the singular used collectively), who thus becomes like the deaf adder which has no ear.

ADAM CLARKE

PSALM 58

The title seems to have no reference to the subject of the psalm. See the introduction to the preceding.

2. *Yea, in heart ye work wickedness.* With their tongues they had spoken maliciously, and given evil counsel. In their hearts they meditated nothing but wickedness. And though in their *hands* they held the scales of justice, yet in their use of them they were balances of injustice and violence. This is the fact to which the Psalmist alludes, and the figure which he uses is that of Justice with her scales or balances, which, though it might be the emblem of the court, yet it did not prevail in the practice of these magistrates and counsellors.

3. *The wicked are estranged from the womb.* "This," says Dr. Kennicott, "and the next two verses, I take to be the answer of Jehovah to the question in the two first verses, as the 6th, 7th, and 8th, are the answer of the psalmist, and the remainder contains the decree of Jehovah."

4. *Their poison is like the poison of a serpent.* When they bite, they convey poison into the wound, as the serpent does. They not only injure you by outward acts, but by their malevolence they poison your reputation. Such is the slanderer, and such his influence in society.

MATTHEW HENRY

Verses 6–11

In these verses we have,

I. David's prayers against his enemies, and all the enemies of God's church and people. 1. He prays that they might be disabled to do any further mischief (*v.* 6): *Break their teeth, O God!* Not so much that they might not feed themselves as that they might not be able to make prey of others, iii. 7. He does not say, "Break their necks" (no; let them live to repent, *slay them not, lest my people forget*), but, "Break their teeth, for they are lions, they are young lions, that live by rapine." 2. That they might be disappointed in the plots they had already laid, and might not gain their point: "*When he bends his bow*, and takes aim *to shoot his arrows* at the upright in heart, *let them be as cut in pieces*, *v.* 7. Let them fall at his feet, and never come near the mark." 3. That they and their interest might waste and come to nothing, that they might *melt away as waters that run continually*; that is, as *water spilt upon the ground, which cannot be gathered up again*, but gradually dries away and disappears. He prays (*v.* 8) that they might *melt as a snail*, which wastes by its own motion, in every stretch it makes leaving some of its moisture behind, which, by degrees, must needs consume it, though it makes a path to shine after it. And he prays that they might be *like the untimely birth of a woman*, which dies as soon as it begins to live and never *sees the sun*.

II. His prediction of their ruin (*v.* 9): "*Before your pots can feel the* heat of a fire of *thorns* made under them." 1. The proverbial expressions are somewhat difficult, but the sense is plain, that the judgments of God often surprise wicked people in the midst of their jollity, and hurry them away of a sudden. 2. There are two things which the psalmist promises himself as the effects of sinners' destruction: (1) That saints would be encouraged and comforted by it (*v.* 10): *The righteous shall rejoice when he sees the vengeance*. The prosperity and success of the wicked are a discouragement to the righteous; they sadden their hearts, and are sometimes a strong temptation to them to question their foundations, lxxiii. 2, 13. But when they see the judgments of God they rejoice in the confirmation thereby given to their faith in the providence of God and his justice and righteousness in governing the world. (2) That sinners would be convinced and converted by it, *v.* 11. The vengeance God sometimes takes on the wicked in this world will bring men to say, *Verily, there is a reward for the righteous*. Some shall have their minds so changed that they shall willingly own it, and see with satisfaction, That God is, and, [1] That he is the bountiful rewarder of his saints and servants: *Verily* (*however it be*, so it may be read) *there is a fruit to the righteous*. Even in this world there is a reward for the righteous. [2] That he is the righteous governor of the world, and will surely reckon with the enemies of his kingdom. *He is a God* (so we read it), not a weak man, not an angel, not a mere name, not (as the atheists suggest) a creature of men's fear and fancy, not a deified hero, not the sun and moon, as idolaters imagined, but a God, a self-existent perfect Being; he it is that judges the earth.

JAMIESON, FAUSSET, BROWN

6. He prays for their destruction, under the figure of ravenous beasts (Ps. 3:7; 7:2).

7. which run continually—lit., "they shall go to themselves, utterly depart, as rapid mountain torrents. **he bendeth . . . his arrows**—prepares it. The term for preparing a bow applied to arrows (Ps. 64:3). **let them . . . pieces**—lit., "as if they cut themselves off"—i.e., become blunted and of no avail.

8, 9. Other figures of this utter ruin; the last denoting rapidity. In a shorter time than pots feel the heat of thorns on fire—**he shall take them away as with a whirlwind**—lit., "blow him (them) away." **both living, . . . wrath**—lit., "as the living" or fresh as the heated or burning—i.e., thorns—all easily blown away, so easily and quickly the wicked. The figure of the "snail" perhaps alludes to its loss of saliva when moving. Though obscure in its clauses, the general sense of the passage is clear. **10, 11. wash . . . wicked**—denoting great slaughter. The joy of triumph over the destruction of the wicked is because they are God's enemies, and their overthrow shows that He reigneth (cf. Ps. 52:5-7; 54:7). In this assurance let heaven and earth rejoice (Ps. 96:10; 97:1, etc.).

ADAM CLARKE

8. *As a snail which melteth*. The Chaldee reads the verse thus: "They shall melt away in their sins as water flows off; as the creeping snail that smears its track; as the untimely birth and the blind mole, which do not see the sun."

9. *Before your pots can feel the thorns*. Ye shall be destroyed with a sudden destruction. So very short will be the time that it may be likened to the heat of the first blaze of dry thorns under a pot, that has not as yet been able to penetrate the metal, and warm what is contained in it.

10. *The righteous shall rejoice when he seeth the vengeance*. He shall have a strong proof of the divine providence. *He shall wash his feet in the blood of the wicked*. This can only mean that the slaughter would be so great, and at the same time so very nigh to the dwelling of the righteous, that he could not go out without dipping his feet in the blood of the wicked. The Syriac, Vulgate, Septuagint, Aethiopic, Arabic, and Anglo-Saxon read "hands" instead of *feet*. Everything that is vindictive in the psalms must be considered as totally alien from the spirit of the gospel, and not at all, under our dispensation, to be imitated.

11. *So that a man shall say*. That is, people, seeing these just judgments of God, shall say, *There is a reward* ("fruit") to the *righteous* man. He has not sown his seed in vain; he has not planted and watered in vain. He has the fruit of his labours; he eats the fruit of his doings.

MATTHEW HENRY — PSALM 59

To the chief musician, Al-taschith, Michtam of David, when Saul sent and they watched the house to kill him.

Verses 1–7

Saul sent a party of his guards to beset David's house in the night, that they might seize him and kill him; we have the story 1 Sam. xix. 11. It was when his hostilities against David were newly begun, and he had but just before narrowly escaped Saul's javelin. These first eruptions of Saul's malice could not but put David into disorder and be both grievous and terrifying, and yet he kept up his communion with God, and such a composure of mind as that he was never out of frame for prayer and praises.

I. David prays to be delivered out of the hands of his enemies, "*Deliver me from my enemies, O my God!* thou art *God*, and canst deliver me, *my* God, under whose protection I have put myself. Set me on high out of the power and malice of those that rise up against me. O deliver me! and save me." He prays (*v.* 4), "*Awake to help me*, take cognizance of my case, behold that with an eye of pity, and exert thy power for my relief." Thus the disciples, in the storm, awoke Christ, saying, *Master, save us, we perish*. And thus earnestly should we pray daily to be defended and delivered from our spiritual enemies, the temptations of Satan, and the corruptions of our own hearts, which war against

JAMIESON, FAUSSET, BROWN — PSALM 59

Vss. 1-17. Cf. Psalm 57, and for history, I Sam. 19:11, etc. The scope is very similar to that of the 57th: prayer in view of malicious and violent foes, and joy in prospect of relief.

1. defend—(Cf. *Margin*). **rise up . . . me**—(Cf. Ps. 17:7).

ADAM CLARKE — PSALM 59

The title, "To the chief Musician, Al-taschith, Michtam of David," has already occurred, and perhaps means no more than that the present psalm is to be sung as Psalm lvii, the first which bears this title. But there is here added the supposed occasion on which David made this psalm; it was "when Saul sent, and they watched the house to kill him." When the reader considers the whole of this psalm carefully, he will be convinced that the title does not correspond to the contents. The psalm most evidently agrees to the time of Nehemiah, when he was endeavoring to rebuild the walls of Jerusalem, when the enterprise was first mocked; then opposed by Sanballat the Horonite, Tobiah the Ammonite, and Geshem the Arabian, who watched day and night that they might cause the work to cease, and laid ambuscades for the life of Nehemiah himself. Every part of the psalm agrees to this, and I am therefore of Calmet's opinion, that the psalm was composed in that time, and probably by Nehemiah, or by Esdras.

1. *Deliver me from mine enemies, O my God.*

MATTHEW HENRY

our spiritual life.

II. He pleads for deliverance. Our God gives us leave to plead, not to move him, but to move ourselves. David does so here.

1. He pleads the bad character of his enemies. They are *workers of iniquity*, and therefore not only his enemies, but God's enemies; they are *bloody men*, and therefore not only his enemies, but enemies to all mankind.

2. He pleads their malice against him, and the imminent danger he was in from them, *v.* 3. "*They lie in wait*, taking an opportunity to do me a mischief. They are united by league, and actually *gathered* together *against me*. They are very ingenious in their contrivances and (*v.* 4): *They run and prepare themselves*, with the utmost speed and fury, to do me a mischief." He takes particular notice of the brutish conduct of the messengers that Saul sent to take him (*v.* 6): "*They return at evening* from the posts assigned them in the day, to apply themselves to their works of darkness, and then *they make a noise like a hound* in pursuit of the hare." *They belch out with their mouth* the malice that boils in their hearts, *v.* 7. *Swords are in their lips;* that is, reproaches that wound my heart with grief (xlii. 10), and slanders that stab and wound my reputation.

3. He pleads his own innocency, not as to God (he was never backward to own himself guilty before him), but as to his persecutors, "*Not for my transgression, nor for my sin, O Lord!* thou knowest, who knowest all things." And again (*v.* 4), *without my fault*. The innocency of the godly will not secure them from the malignity of the wicked. Though our innocency will not secure us from troubles, yet it will greatly support and comfort us under our troubles. If we are conscious to ourselves of our innocency, we may with humble confidence appeal to God and beg of him to plead our injured cause.

4. He pleads that his enemies were profane and atheistical, and bolstered themselves up in their enmity to David, with the contempt of God: *For who*, say they, *doth hear? v.* 7. Not God himself, x. 11; xciv. 7.

III. He refers himself and his cause to the just judgment of God, *v.* 5. *Be not merciful to any wicked transgressors. Selah—Mark that.* Though he had transgressed, he was a penitent transgressor, and did not obstinately persist in what he had done amiss. Therefore he could appeal to God in this way.

Verses 8–17

David here encourages himself, in reference to the threatening power of his enemies, with a pious resolution to wait upon God.

I. He resolves to wait upon God (*v.* 9): "*Because of his strength*." It is our wisdom and duty, in times of danger and difficulty, to wait upon God; for he is our defence. He hopes God will be to him a God of mercy (*v.* 10): "*The God of my mercy shall prevent me* with the blessings of his goodness and the gifts of his mercy, and be better to me than my own expectations." Whatever mercy there is in God, it is laid up for us; and is ready to be laid out upon us. Here are several things which he foretells concerning his enemies. He foresees that God would expose them to scorn, as they had indeed made themselves ridiculous, *v.* 8. "They think *God does not hear them, but thou, O Lord! shalt laugh at them* for their folly, to think that he who planted the ear shall not hear, and *thou shalt have* all such other heathenish people that live without God in the world, *in derision*." God would make them standing monuments of his justice (*v.* 11): *Slay them not;* let them not be killed outright, *lest my people forget*. Thus Cain himself, though a murderer, was not slain, lest the vengeance should be forgotten, but was sentenced to be *a fugitive and a vagabond*. "So scatter them that they may never again unite to do mischief, *bring them down, O Lord, our shield!*" *For the sin of their mouth, even for the words of their lips, let them* for this *be taken in their pride*, even for their cursing others and themselves (a sin Saul was subject to, 1 Sam. xiv. 28, 44), and lying. Saul and his party think to rule and carry all before them, but they shall be made to know that there is a higher than they, that there is one who does and will overrule them. He *rules in Jacob*; for there he keeps his court; there he is known, and his name is great. But he *rules to the end of the earth*; for all nations are within the territories of his kingdom. Their sin was their hunting for David to make a prey of him; their punishment should be that they should be reduced to such extreme poverty that they should hunt about for meat to satisfy their hunger. Thus they should be, not cut off at once, but scattered (*v.* 11). He foretells that they should be forced to beg their bread from door to door. *They shall make a noise like a dog*. When they were

JAMIESON, FAUSSET, BROWN

2. (Cf. Ps. 5:5; 6, 8.)

4, 5. prepare, etc.—lit., "set themselves as in array." **awake**—(Cf. Ps. 3:7; 7:6), appeals to God in His covenant relation to His people (Ps. 9:18). **6, 7.** They are as ravening dogs seeking prey, and as such, "belch out"—i.e., slanders, their impudent barkings.

for who, say they—For the full expression with the supplied words, cf. Psalm 84:5.

9. By judicious expositors, and on good grounds, this is better rendered, "O my strength, on Thee will I wait" (vs. 17). **defence**—(Cf. Ps. 18:3). **10. prevent me**—(Ps. 21:3). **see my desire**—in their overthrow (Ps. 54:7). **enemies**—as in Psalm 5:8.

8. (Cf. Ps. 2:4; 37:13.)

11. Slay them not—at once (Judg. 2:21-23); but perpetuate their punishment (Gen. 4:12; Num. 32:13), by scattering or making them wander, and humble them.

12. let them even be . . . taken in their pride—while evincing it—i.e., to be punished for their lies, etc.

13. Though delayed for wise reasons, the utter destruction of the wicked must come at last, and God's presence and power in and for His Church will be known abroad (I Sam. 17:46; Ps. 46:10, 11).

ADAM CLARKE

A very proper prayer in the mouth of Nehemiah, when resisted in his attempts to rebuild the walls of Jerusalem by Sanballat, Tobiah, and Geshem, who opposed the work, and endeavored to take away the life of the person whom God had raised up to restore and rebuild Jerusalem. I conceive the psalm to have been made on this occasion, and on this hypothesis alone I think it capable of consistent explanation.

2. *The workers of iniquity*. Principally Sanballat the Horonite, Tobiah the Ammonite, and Geshem the Arabian, who were the chief enemies of the poor returned captives. *Bloody men*. The above, who sought the destruction of the Israelites; and particularly that of Nehemiah, whom four times they endeavored to bring into an ambush, that they might take away his life. See Neh. vi. 1-4.

3. *For, lo, they lie in wait for my soul*. For my "life."

4. *They run and prepare themselves*. They leave no stone unturned that they may effect my destruction and prevent the building.

5. *O Lord God of hosts*. This was a proper view to take of God, when Israel, a handful of poor, distressed captives, were surrounded and oppressed by the heathen chiefs above mentioned, and their several tribes. But Jehovah, *God of hosts*, was the *God of Israel;* and hence Israel had little to fear. *Be not merciful to any wicked transgressors*. Do not favor the cause of these wicked men. They are "changers of iniquity"; they go through the whole round of evil, find out and exercise themselves in all the varieties of transgression. How exactly does this apply to Nehemiah's foes! They sought, by open attack, wiles, flattery, foul speeches, fair speeches, threats, and ambuscades to take away his life. Do not show them favor, that they may not succeed in their wicked designs. The prayer here is exactly the same in sentiment with that of Nehemiah, chap. iv. 4-5. "Hear, O our God; for we are despised: and turn their reproach upon their own head . . . cover not their iniquity, and let not their sin be blotted out."

6. *They return at evening*. When the beasts of prey leave their dens and go prowling about the cities and villages, these come about the city to see if they may get an entrance, destroy the work, and those engaged in it.

7. *They belch out with their mouth*. They use the lowest insult, the basest abuse. They deal in sarcasm, ridicule, slander, and lies.

8. *Thou, O Lord, shalt laugh at them*. They have mocked us; God will turn them and their schemes into ridicule and contempt. "Thou shalt have all these heathenish nations in derision."

9. *Because of his strength will I wait upon thee*. With this reading, I can make no sense of the passage. But instead of *uzzo*, "his strength," *uzzi*, "my strength," is the reading of fourteen of Kennicott's and De Rossi's MSS., of the Vulgate, Septuagint, Chaldee. "To thee I commit all my strength."

10. *The God of my mercy shall prevent me*. The mercy of God shall "go before me." *God shall let me see my desire*. The sentence is short, "God will let me see concerning my enemies," i.e., how He will treat them.

11. *Slay them not, lest my people forget*. I believe the Chaldee gives the true sense of this verse: "Do not slay them suddenly, lest my people should forget. Drive them from their habitations by thy power, and reduce them to poverty by the loss of their property."

MATTHEW HENRY

in quest of David they made a noise like an angry dog snarling and barking; now, when they are in quest of meat, they shall make a noise like a hungry dog howling and wailing. Those that repent of their sins *mourn*, when in trouble, *like doves*; those whose hearts are hardened make a noise, when in trouble, like dogs, *like a wild bull in a net, full of the fury of the Lord. If they be not satisfied, they will tarry all night*, so that what people do give them is not with goodwill, but only to get rid of them, lest by their continual coming they weary them. It is not poverty, but discontent, that makes a man unhappy.

II. He expects to praise God, that God's providence would find him matter for praise and that God's grace would work in him a heart for praise, *v.* 16, 17.

1. He would praise his power and his mercy; both should be the subject-matter of his song. Power, without mercy, is to be dreaded; mercy, without power, is not what a man can expect much benefit from; but God's power by which he is able to help us, and his mercy by which he is inclined to help us, will justly be the everlasting praise of all the saints. He would praise him because he had, many a time, found him his defence and his refuge in the day of trouble.

2. He would *sing aloud*, as one much affected with the glory of God, that was not ashamed to own it, and that desired to affect others with it.

JAMIESON, FAUSSET, BROWN

14, 15. Meanwhile let the rapacious dogs prowl, they cannot hurt the pious; yea, they shall wander famished and sleepless. **grudge if . . .**—lit., "they shall stay all night," i.e., obtain nothing.

16, 17. Contrast the lot of God's servant, who employs his time in God's praise.

sing aloud . . . in the morning—when *they* retire famishing and disappointed, or it may denote delightful diligence in praise, as in Psalm 30:5.

ADAM CLARKE

14. *At evening let them return.* He had mentioned before, v. 6, that these persons came like beasts of prey round the city striving to get in, that they might take possession. Now, being fully assured of God's protection, and that they shall soon be made a public example, he says, "Let them return and make a noise like a dog," like dogs, jackals, and other famished creatures, who come howling about the city walls for something to eat, and wander up and down for meat, grumbling because they are not satisfied, v. 15. Nehemiah had made up all the breaches, and had the city guarded so well day and night that there was no longer any fear of being taken by surprise.

17. *Unto thee, O my strength.* A similar sentiment to that expressed in v. 9. But the words are very emphatic: "God is my strength; God is my elevation. My God is my mercy."

MATTHEW HENRY

PSALM 60

To the chief musician, upon Shushan-eduth, Michtam of David, to teach, when he strove with Aram-naharaim, and with Aramzobah, when Joab returned and smote of Edom in the valley of salt 12,000.

Verses 1–5

The general design of the psalm. It is *Michtam—David's jewel*, and it is *to teach*. The Levites must teach it to the people, and by it teach them both to trust in God and to triumph in him. He was at war with the Syrians, and still had a conflict with them, both those of Mesopotamia and those of Zobah. He had gained a great victory over the Edomites, by his forces, under the command of Joab, who had left 12,000 of the enemy dead upon the spot. He is in care about his strife with the Assyrians, and in reference to that he prays.

In these verses, which begin the psalm, we have,

I. A melancholy memorial of the many disgraces and disappointments which God had, for some years past, put the people under. 1. He complains of *hard things* which they had seen (that is, which they had suffered), while the Philistines and other ill-disposed neighbours took all advantages against them, *v.* 3. 2. He owns God's displeasure to be the cause of all the hardships they had undergone: *"Thou hast been displeased* by us, displeased against us (*v.* 1), and in thy displeasure hast cast us off and scattered us, else our enemies could not have prevailed thus against us." 3. He laments the ill effects and consequences of the miscarriages of the late years. The whole nation was in a convulsion: *Thou hast made the earth* (or *the land*) *to tremble*, *v.* 2. The good people themselves were in a consternation: *"Thou hast made us to drink the wine of astonishment* (*v.* 3); we were like men intoxicated, and at our wits' end, not knowing how to reconcile these dispensations with God's promises; we can do nothing, nor know we what to do." When God is turning his hand in our favour, it is good to remember our former calamities. Our calamities serve as foils to our joys.

II. A thankful notice of the encouragement God had given them to hope that, though things had been long bad, they would now begin to mend (*v.* 4): *"Thou hast given a banner to those that fear thee* (for, as bad as the times are, there is a remnant among us that desire to fear thy name, for whom thou hast a tender concern), *that it may be displayed* by thee, *because of the truth of* thy promise which thou wilt perform, and to be displayed by them, in defence of truth and equity," xlv. 4. This banner was David's government, the establishment and enlargement of it over all Israel. It united them, as soldiers are gathered together to their colours. It animated them, and put life and courage into them. It struck a terror upon their enemies, to whom they could now hang out a flag of defiance. Christ, the Son of David, is given *for an ensign of the people* (Isa. xi. 10), for a banner to those that fear God; in him, as the centre of their unity, they glory and take courage. His love is the banner over them; in his name and strength they wage war with the powers of darkness, and under him the church becomes terrible as an army with banners.

III. A humble petition for seasonable mercy. *O turn thyself to us again!* (*v.* 1); smile upon us, be at peace with us, and in that peace we shall have peace.

JAMIESON, FAUSSET, BROWN

PSALM 60

Vss. 1-12. *Shushan-eduth*—Lily of testimony. The lily is an emblem of beauty (cf. Ps. 45, title). As a description of the Psalm, those terms combined may denote a beautiful poem, witnessing—i.e., for God's faithfulness as evinced in the victories referred to in the history cited. *Aram-naharaim*—Syria of the two rivers, or Mesopotamia beyond *the river* (Euphrates) (II Sam. 10:16). *Aram-zobah*—Syria of Zobah (II Sam. 10:6), to whose king the king of the former was tributary. The war with Edom, by Joab and Abishai (II Chron. 18:12, 25), occurred about the same time. Probably, while doubts and fears alternately prevailed respecting the issue of these wars, the writer composed this Psalm, in which he depicts, in the language of God's people, their sorrows under former disasters, offers prayer in present straits, and rejoices in confident hope of triumph by God's aid.

1-3. allude to disasters. **cast . . . off**—in scorn (Ps. 43:2; 44:9). **scattered**—broken our strength (cf. II Sam. 5:20).

drink . . . wine of astonishment—lit., "of staggering"—i.e., made us weak (cf. Ps. 75:8; Isa. 51:17, 22).

4, 5. Yet to God's banner they will rally, and pray that, led and sustained by His power (right hand, Ps. 17: 7; 20:6), they may be safe. **hear me**—or, hear us.

Oh, turn thyself—or, restore to us (prosperity). The figures of physical, denote great civil, commotions (Ps. 46:2, 3).

ADAM CLARKE

PSALM 60

The title, "To the chief Musician upon the hexachord, or lily of the testimony, a golden Psalm of David, for instruction; when he strove with Aram Naharaim, Syria of the two rivers (Mesopotamia) and Aram-Zobah, Syria of the watchmen (Coelosyria), when Joab returned, and smote twelve thousand Edomites in the Valley of Salt." I have only to remark here that there is nothing in the contents of this psalm that bears any relation to this title. According to the title it should be a song of victory and triumph, instead of which the first part of it is a tissue of complaints of disaster and defeat, caused by the divine desertion. Besides, it was not Joab that slew 12,000 men in the Valley of Salt; it was Abishai, the brother of Joab; and the number 12,000 here is not correct; for there were 18,000 slain in that battle, as we learn from 1 Chron. xviii. 12. The Valley of Salt or salt pits is in Idumea. To reconcile the difference between the numbers, various expedients have been hit on; but still the insuperable objection remains: the contents of this psalm and this title are in opposition to each other. That the psalm deplores a defeat is evident from the first three and last two verses. This is the last of the six psalms to which *michtam* is prefixed; the others are Psalms xvi; lvi; lvii; lviii; and lix. I have said something relative to this word in the introduction to Psalm xvi.

1. *O God, thou hast cast us off.* Instead of being our General in the battle, Thou hast left us to ourselves.

3. *Thou hast made us to drink the wine of astonishment.* We reel as drunken men; we are giddy, like those who have drunk too much wine; but our giddiness has been occasioned by the astonishment and dismay that have taken place in consequence of the prevalence of our enemies, and the unsettled state of the land.

4. *Thou hast given a banner.* "A sign," something that was capable of being fixed on a pole. *That it may be displayed.* "That it may be unfurled." *Because of the truth.* "From the face of truth"; which has been thus paraphrased: If we have displayed the ensign of Israel, and gone forth against these our enemies, who have now made such a terrible breach among us (vv. 1-3), it was because of Thy truth—the promises of victory which we supposed would attend us at all times.

MATTHEW HENRY

"*Heal the breaches of our land* (*v.* 2), not only the breaches made upon us by our enemies, but the breaches made among ourselves by our unhappy divisions." Thus they might be preserved out of the hands of their enemies (*v.* 5): "*That thy beloved may be delivered, save with thy right hand,* and by such instruments as thou art pleased to make the men of thy right hand, *and hear me.*" God's praying people may take the general deliverances of the church as answers to their prayers in particular.

Verses 6–12

David is here rejoicing in hope and praying in hope (*v.* 6): "*God has spoken in his holiness* (that is, he has given me his word of promise, has *sworn by his holiness, and he will not lie unto David,* lxxxix. 35), therefore *I will rejoice* with the hopes of the performance of the promise, which was intended for more than a pleasing promise."

I. David here rejoices in prospect of two things:—

1. The perfecting of this revolution in his own kingdom. God having *spoken in his holiness* that David shall be king, he doubts not but the kingdom is all his own, as sure as if it were already in his hand: *I will divide Shechem* (a pleasant city in Mount Ephraim) *and mete out the valley of Succoth,* as my own. *Gilead is mine, and Manasseh is mine,* and both are entirely reduced, *v.* 7. Ephraim would furnish him with soldiers for his lifeguards and his standing forces; Judah would furnish him with able judges for his courts of justice; and thus Ephraim would be *the strength of his head* and Judah *his lawgiver.* Thus may an active believer triumph in the promises, for they are all yea and amen in Christ. "*God has spoken in his holiness,* and then pardon is mine, peace mine, grace mine, Christ mine, heaven mine, God himself mine." *All is yours, for you are Christ's,* 1 Cor. iii. 22, 23.

2. The conquering of the neighbouring nations, which had been vexatious to Israel, and which were still dangerous, and opposed to David, *v.* 8. Moab shall be enslaved, and put to the meanest drudgery. *The Moabites became David's servants,* 2 Sam. viii. 2. Edom shall be made a dunghill to throw old shoes upon; at least David shall take possession of it as his own, which was signified by *drawing off his shoe* over, it, Ruth iv. 7. As for the Philistines, let them, if they dare, triumph over him as they had done; he will soon force them to change their note. But the war is not yet brought to an end; there is a *strong city,* Rabbah (perhaps) of the children of Ammon, which yet holds out; Edom is not yet subdued. Now David is here enquiring for help to carry on the war: "*Who will bring me into the strong city? Wilt not thou, O God?* For thou hast *spoken in thy holiness*; and wilt not thou be as good as thy word?" He takes notice of the frowns of Providence they had been under: *Thou hadst,* in appearance, *cast us off; thou didst not go forth with our armies.* At the same time that they own God's justice in what was past they hope in his mercy for what was to come.

II. He prays in hope. His prayer is, *Give us help from trouble, v.* 11. Even in the day of their triumph they see themselves in trouble, because still in war, which is troublesome even to the prevailing side. Though now they were conquerors yet (so uncertain are the issues of war), unless God gave them help in the next engagement, they might be defeated; therefore, *Lord, send us help from the sanctuary. Help from trouble* is rest from war, which they prayed for, as those that contended for equity, not for victory. "*Through God we shall do valiantly,* and so we shall do victoriously; for *he it is,* and he only, *that shall tread down our enemies,* and shall have the praise of doing it." Though *it is God that performs all things for us,* yet there is something to be done by us. Hope in God is the best principle of true courage. Those that do their duty under his conduct may afford to do it valiantly; for what need those fear who have God on their side?

JAMIESON, FAUSSET, BROWN

6-10. God hath spoken in [or, "by"] **his holiness**—(Ps. 89:35; Amos 4:2), on the pledge of His attributes (Ps. 22:3; 30:4). Taking courage from God's promise to give them possession (Exod. 23:31; Deut. 11:24) (and perhaps renewed to him by special revelation), with triumphant joy he describes the conquest as already made.

Shechem, and . . . Succoth—as widely separated points, and—**Gilead . . . and Manasseh**—as large districts, east and west of Jordan, represent the whole land. **divide . . . and mete out**—means to have entire control over. **Ephraim**—denotes the military (Deut. 33:17); and—**Judah**—(the lawgiver, Gen. 49:10), the civil power. Foreign nations are then presented as subdued.

8. Moab—is a washpot—the most ordinary vessel. **over** [or, at] **Edom**—(as a slave) he casts his shoe.

Philistia, triumph . . . [or, rather, shout] **for me**—acknowledges subjection (cf. Ps. 108:9, "over Philistia will I triumph").

9, 10. He feels assured that, though once angry, God is now ready to favor His people. **who will lead me**—or, *who has led me,* as if the work were now begun. **Wilt not thou**—or, Is it not Thou?

11, 12. Hence he closes with a prayer for success, and an assurance of a hearing.

ADAM CLARKE

6. *God hath spoken.* Judah shall not only be reestablished in Jerusalem, but shall possess Samaria, where *Shechem* is, and the country beyond Jordan, in which is situated the *valley of Succoth.* Dividing and meting out signify possession.

7. *Gilead is mine.* This country was also beyond Jordan, and *Manasseh* and *Ephraim* are put for the tribes that formed the kingdom of Israel. All these, after the return from the Captivity, formed but one people, the Jews and Israelites being united. *The strength of mine head.* It shall be the principal support of the newfound kingdom, when all distinctions shall be buried. *Judah is my lawgiver.* This tribe was chief of all those who returned from the Captivity; and Zerubbabel, who was their leader, was chief of that tribe, and of the family of David. As this part of the psalm appears to relate to the return of the captives from Babylon, and their repossession of their own land, the Psalmist may refer, not only to the promises of their restoration, but also to the principal person under whose superintendence they returned.

8. *Moab is my washpot.* The Moabites shall be reduced to the meanest slavery. *Over Edom will I cast out my shoe.* I will make a complete conquest of Idumea, and subject the Edomites to the meanest offices, as well as the Moabites. *Philistia, triumph thou because of men.* John Hyrcanus subdued the Idumeans, and caused them to receive circumcision, and profess the Jewish religion. The words here seem to predict their entire subjugation.

In an essay for a new translation of the Bible, there is what appears to me a correct paraphrase of the seventh and eighth verses: "Gilead and Manasseh have submitted unto me; Ephraim furnishes me with valiant men, and Judah with men of prudence and wisdom. I will reduce the Moabites to servitude; I will triumph over the Edomites, and make them my slaves; and the Philistines shall add to my triumph."

PSALM 61

MATTHEW HENRY

To the chief musician upon Neginah. *A psalm* of David.

Verses 1–4

I. David's close adherence and application to God by prayer in the day of his distress and trouble: "Whatever comes, *I will cry unto thee* (*v.* 2), as one that will not let thee go except thou bless me." This he will do, "*From the end of the earth,* or of *the land,* from the most remote and obscure corner of the country, *will I cry unto thee.* Though *my heart is overwhelmed,* it is not so sunk, so burdened, but that it may be lifted up to God in prayer. Nay, because my heart is ready to be overwhelmed, therefore *I will*

JAMIESON, FAUSSET, BROWN

Vss. 1-8. *Neginah*—or, Neginoth (cf. Ps. 4, title). Separated from his usual spiritual privileges, perhaps by Absalom's rebellion, the Psalmist prays for divine aid, and, in view of past mercies, with great confidence of being heard.

1-3. From the end—i.e., places remote from the sanctuary (Deut. 28:64). **heart is overwhelmed**—lit., "covered over with darkness," or, distress.

ADAM CLARKE

The title, "To the chief Musician upon Neginah." The verb *nagan* signifies to "strike or play on a musical instrument," especially one of the stringed kind. The psalm appears to have been written about the close of the Captivity, and the most judicious interpreters refer it to that period.

2. *From the end of the earth. Arets* should be here translated "land," not *earth,* and so it

MATTHEW HENRY

cry unto thee, for by that means it will be supported and relieved." Weeping must quicken praying, and not deaden it.

II. The particular petition he put up to God when his heart was overwhelmed and he was ready to sink: *Lead me to the rock that is higher than I;* that is, "To the rock which is too high for me to get up to unless thou help me to it. To the rock on the top of which I shall be set further out of the reach of my troubles, and nearer the serene and quiet region, than I can be by any power or wisdom of my own." This rock is Christ; those are safe that are in him.

III. His desire and expectation of an answer of peace. He begs in faith (*v.* 1): "*Hear my cry, O God! attend unto my prayer;* that is, let me have the present comfort of knowing that I am heard (xx. 6), and in due time let me have that which I pray for."

IV. The ground of this expectation, and the plea he uses to enforce his petition (*v.* 3): "*Thou hast been a shelter for me;* I have found in thee a rock higher than I: therefore I trust thou wilt still lead me to that rock."

V. His resolution to continue in the way of duty to God and dependence on him, *v.* 4. David was now banished from the tabernacle, which was his greatest grievance, but he is assured that God by his providence would bring him back. He speaks of abiding in it *for ever* because that tabernacle was a type and figure of heaven, Heb. ix. 8, 9, 24. Those that dwell in God's tabernacle, as it is a house of duty, during their short *ever* on earth, shall dwell in that tabernacle which is the house of glory during an endless *ever. I will make my refuge in the covert of his wings*, as the chickens seek both warmth and safety under the wings of the hen.

Verses 5–8

I. With what pleasure David looks back upon what God had done for him formerly (*v.* 5): *Thou, O God! hast heard my vows.* God is a witness to all our vows, all our good purposes, and all our solemn promises of new obedience. "The prayers thou hast graciously heard and answered," encouraged him now to pray, *O God! hear my cry.* "Thou hast heard my vows, and given a real answer to them; for *thou hast given me a heritage of those that fear thy name.*" We need desire no better heritage than that of those who fear God.

II. With what assurance he looks forward to the continuance of his life (*v.* 6): *Thou shalt prolong the king's life.* His resolution was to abide in God's tabernacle for ever (*v.* 4), in a way of duty; and now his hope is that he shall abide before God for ever, in a way of comfort.

III. With what importunity he begs of God to take him and keep him always under his protection: *O prepare mercy and truth which may preserve him!* David is sure that God will prolong his life, and therefore prays that he would preserve it, not that he would prepare him a strong lifeguard, or a well-fortified castle, but that he would prepare mercy and truth for his preservation. We need not desire to be better secured than under the protection of God's mercy and truth.

IV. With what cheerfulness he vows the grateful returns of duty to God (*v.* 8): *So will I sing praise unto thy name for ever. That I may daily perform my vows.* His praising God was itself the performance of his vows.

JAMIESON, FAUSSET, BROWN

to the rock (Ps. 18:2; 40:2). **higher than I**—which otherwise I cannot ascend.

shelter . . . and strong tower—repeat the same sentiment.

4. I will abide—So I desire to do (cf. Ps. 23:6). **trust in the covert . . .**—*make* my refuge in the shadow (cf. Ps. 17:8; 36:7).

5. the heritage—or, part in the spiritual blessings of Israel (Ps. 21:2-4). **vows**—implies prayers. **6, 7. the king**—himself and his royal line ending in Christ. Mercy and truth personified, as in Psalm 40:11; 57:3. **abide before God**—lit., "sit as a king in God's presence," under His protection.

8. Thus for new blessings will new vows of praise ever be paid.

ADAM CLARKE

should be in numerous places besides. But here it seems to mean the country beyond the Euphrates, as it is thought to do in Ps. lxv. 5, 8, called there also "the ends of the earth" or land.

1. *Hear my cry, O God.* In the midst of a long and painful captivity, oppressed with suffering, encompassed with cruel enemies and isolent masters, I address my humble prayer to Thee, O my God.

4. *I will abide in thy tabernacle.* The greater portion of those psalms which were composed during and after the Captivity, says Calmet, had Levites and priests for their authors. Hence we find the ardent desire so frequently expressed of seeing the Temple; of praising God there; of spending their lives in that place, performing the functions of their sacred office.

6. *Thou wilt prolong the king's life.* The words are very emphatic, and can refer to no ordinary person. Literally, "Days upon days Thou wilt add to the king; and his years shall be like the generations of this world, and the generations of the world to come." I am persuaded no earthly king is intended; and it is Christ, as Mediator, that "shall abide before God for ever," v. 7.

7. *He shall abide before God for ever.* Literally, "He shall sit forever before the faces of God." He shall ever appear in the presence of God for us. *Prepare mercy and truth, which may preserve him.* As Mediator, His attendants will ever be *mercy* and *truth.* He will dispense the *mercy* of God, and thus fulfill the *truth* of the various promises and predictions which had preceded His incarnation.

MATTHEW HENRY

PSALM 62

To the chief musician, to Jeduthun. A psalm of David.

Verses 1–7

I. David's profession of dependence upon God, and upon him only, for all good (*v.* 1): *Truly my soul waiteth upon God. Nevertheless* (so some) or "*However it be*, whatever difficulties or dangers I may meet with, though God frown upon me and I meet with discouragements in my attendance on him, yet still my soul waits upon God" (or *is silent to God*, as the word is), "says nothing against what he does, but quietly expects what he will do." "From him I know it will come, and therefore on him will I patiently wait till it does come, for his time is the best time."

II. The ground and reason of this dependence (*v.* 2): *He only is my rock and my salvation; he is my defence.* Creatures are insufficient; they are nothing without him, and therefore I will look above them to him.

III. The improvement he makes of his confidence in God. "If God is my strength and mighty deliverer, *I shall not be greatly moved* (that is, I shall not be undone and ruined); I may be shocked, but I shall not be sunk." His enemies are slighted, and all their attempts against him looked upon by him with con-

JAMIESON, FAUSSET, BROWN

PSALM 62

Vss. 1-12. *To Jeduthun*—(cf. Ps. 39, title). The general tone of this Psalm is expressive of confidence in God. Occasion is taken to remind the wicked of their sin, their ruin, and their meanness. **1. waiteth**—lit., "is silent," trusts submissively and confidently as a servant.

2. The titles applied to God often occur (Ps. 9:9; 18:2). **be greatly moved**—(Ps. 10:6). No injury shall be permanent, though devised by enemies.

ADAM CLARKE

PSALM 62

The title, "To the chief Musician, to Jeduthan," may mean that the psalm was sent to him who was the chief or leader of the band of the family of Jeduthun. It appears that Asaph, Jeduthun, and Heman were chief singers in the time of David; that they, with their families, presided over different departments of the vocal and instrumental worship in the Tabernacle, 1 Chron. xxv. 1, etc.

1. *Truly my soul waiteth upon God.* I do not think that the original will warrant this translation, "Surely to God only is my soul dumb." I am subject to God Almighty. He has a right to lay on me what He pleases; and what He lays on me is much less than I deserve; therefore am I "dumb" before God.

MATTHEW HENRY

tempt, *v.* 3, 4. "*How long will you* do it? Will you never be convinced of your error? Will your malice never have spent itself?" Envy was at the bottom of their malice; they were grieved at David's advancement, and therefore plotted, by diminishing his character, to hinder his preferment. *They delight in lies. They bless with their mouth* (they compliment David to his face), *but they curse inwardly;* in their hearts they wish him all mischief, and privately they are carrying on some evil design or other, by which they hope to ruin him. It is dangerous putting our trust in men who are thus false; but God is faithful. *You shall be slain all of you,* by the righteous judgments of God. Saul and his servants were slain by the Philistines on Mount Gilboa, according to this prediction. God's church is built upon a rock which will stand, but those that fight against it shall be *as a bowing wall and a tottering fence,* which, having a rotten foundation, falls of a sudden, and buries those in the ruins of it that put themselves under the shadow and shelter of it. David is himself encouraged to continue waiting upon God (*v.* 5–7). "If God will save my soul, as to everything else let him do what he pleases with me, and I will acquiesce in his disposals, knowing they shall *all turn to my salvation,*" Phil. i. 19. He repeats (*v.* 6) what he had said concerning God (*v.* 2), as one that dwelt much upon it in his thoughts: *He only is my rock and my salvation; he is my defence,* I know he is; but there he adds, *I shall not be greatly moved,* here, *I shall not be moved at all.* And, as David's faith in God advances to an unshaken stayedness, so his joy in God improves itself into a holy triumph (*v.* 7): *In God is my salvation and my glory.*

Verses 8–12

Here we have David's exhortation to others to trust in God and wait upon him.

I. He counsels all to wait upon God, as he did, *v.* 8. *You people* (that is, all people); all shall be welcome to trust in God, for he is *the confidence of all the ends of the earth,* lxv. 5. "*Trust in him;* depend upon him to perform all things for you, upon his wisdom and goodness, his power and promise, his providence and grace. Do this *at all times.*" *Pour out your heart before him.* The expression seems to allude to the pouring out of the drink-offerings before the Lord. When we make a penitent confession of sin our hearts are therein *poured out before God,* 1 Sam. vii. 6. But here it is meant of prayer, which, if it be as it should be, is the pouring out of the heart before God. We must lay our grievances before him, offer up our desires to him with all humble freedom, patiently submitting our wills to his: this is pouring out our hearts. *God is a refuge for us,* not only my refuge (*v.* 7), but a refuge for us all, even as many as will flee to him and take shelter in him.

II. He cautions us to take heed of misplacing our confidence. Let us not trust in the men of this world, for they are broken reeds (*v.* 9): *Surely men of low degree are vanity,* utterly unable to help us, and *men of high degree are a lie,* that will deceive us if we trust to them. But lay them *in the balance,* the balance of the scripture, or rather make trial of them, see how they will prove, whether they will answer your expectations from them or no, and you will write *Tekel* upon them; they are alike *lighter than vanity.* Let us not trust in the wealth of this world, let not that be made our strong city (*v.* 10): *Trust not in oppression;* that is, in riches got by fraud and violence. Nay, because it is hard to have riches and not to trust in them, if they increase, though by lawful and honest means, we must take heed lest we let out our affections inordinately towards them: "*Set not your heart upon them;* be not eager for them." This we are most in danger of doing when riches increase.

III. He gives a very good reason why we should make God our confidence, because he is a God of infinite power, mercy, and righteousness, *v.* 11, 12. "God has spoken it, and I have heard it, once, yea, twice. He has spoken it, and I have heard once, yea, twice (that is, many a time), by the events that have concerned me in particular. He has spoken it and I have heard it by the light of revelation, by dreams and visions (Job iv. 15), by the glorious manifestation of himself upon Mount Sinai" (to which, some think, it does especially refer), "and by the written word." To some God speaks twice and they will not hear once; but to others he speaks but once, and they hear twice. Compare Job xxxiii. 14. Now what is it which is thus spoken and thus heard? *Power belongs to God;* he is almighty, and can do everything; with him nothing is impossible. He is a God of infinite goodness. Here the psalmist turns his speech to God himself, as being desirous to give him the glory of his goodness, which is his glory: *Also unto thee, O Lord! belongeth mercy.* He is merciful in a way peculiar to himself; he is the *Father of mercies,*

JAMIESON, FAUSSET, BROWN

3. Their destruction will come; as a tottering wall they already are feeble and failing. **bowing wall shall ye be**—better supply "are." Some propose to apply these phrases to describe the condition of "a man"—i.e., the pious suffer: thus, "Will ye slay him," etc.; but the other is a good sense. **4. his excellency**—or, elevation to which God had raised him (Ps. 4:2). This they try to do by lies and duplicity (Ps. 5:9).

5, 6. (Cf. Ps. 1:2.) **not be moved**—not at all; his confidence has increased. **7. rock of my strength**—or strongest support (Ps. 7:10; 61:3).

8. pour out your heart—give full expression to feeling (I Sam. 1:15; Job 30:16; Ps. 42:4). **ye people**—God's people.

9. No kind of men are reliable, compared with God (Isa. 2:22; Jer. 17:5). **altogether**—alike, one as the other (Ps. 34:3).

10. Not only are oppression and robbery, which are wicked means of wealth, no grounds of boasting; but even wealth, increasing lawfully, ought not to engross the heart.

11. once; twice—(as in Job 33:14; 40:5), are used to give emphasis to the sentiment. God's power is tempered by His mercy, which it also sustains.

12. for thou renderest—lit., "that Thou renderest," etc., connected with "I heard this," as the phrase—**"that power . . ."**—teaching that by His power He can show both mercy and justice.

ADAM CLARKE

3. *How long will ye imagine mischief?* The original word has been translated variously; "rush upon, rage against, stir yourselves up, thrust against." The root is *hathath* or *hathah,* "to rush violently upon, to assault." It points out the disorderly, riotous manner in which this rebellion was conducted. *As a bowing wall . . . a tottering fence.* Ye are just ready to fall upon others and destroy them; and in that fall yourselves shall be destroyed: "Ye shall be slain the whole of you."

4. *To cast him down from his excellency.* They are consulting to dethrone me, and use treachery and falsehood in order to bring it about: *They delight in lies.*

7. *In God is my salvation. Al Elohim,* "Upon God is my salvation"; He has taken it upon himself.

9. *Men of low degree are vanity. Beney Adam,* which we here translate *men of low degree,* literally, "sons of Adam," are put in opposition to *beney ish, men of high degree,* literally, the "sons of substance," or children of substantial men. *Adam* was the name of the first man when formed out of the earth; *Ish* was his name when united to his wife, and they became one flesh. Before, he was the incomplete man; after, he was the complete man. *Enosh* is another name given to man; but this concerns him in his low, fallen, wretched estate; it properly signifies "weak, poor, afflicted, wretched man." *To be laid in the balance.* "In the balances they ascend." *They are altogether lighter than vanity.* Literally, "Both of them united are vanity."

10. *Trust not in oppression.* Do not suppose that my unnatural son and his partisans can succeed. *Become not vain in robbery.* If you have laid your hands on the spoils of my house, do not imagine that these ill-gotten riches will prosper. God will soon scatter them to all the winds of heaven. All oppressors come to an untimely end, and all property acquired by injustice has God's curse on it.

11. *God hath spoken once.* God has *once* addressed His people in giving the law on Mount Sinai. *Twice have I heard this.* Except some of the ancient versions, almost every version, translation, and commentary has missed the sense and meaning of this verse. The true version is this: "Once hath God spoken; these two things have I heard." Now what are the two things he had heard? (1) "That strength is the Lord's"; that is, He is the Origin of power. (2) "And to thee, Lord, is mercy"; that is, He is the Fountain of mercy. These, then, are the two grand truths that the law, yea, the whole revelation of God, declares through every page. He is the Almighty; He is the most merciful; and hence the inference: The powerful, just, and holy God, the most merciful and compassionate Lord, will by and by judge the world, and will render to man according to his works. How this beautiful meaning should have been unseen by almost every interpreter is hard to say; these verses contain one of the most instructive truths in the Bible.

MATTHEW HENRY

2 Cor. i. 3. He never did, nor ever will do, any wrong to any of his creatures: *For thou renderest to every man according to his work.*

PSALM 63

A psalm of David, when he was in the wilderness of Judah.

Verses 1–2

The title tells us when the psalm was penned, when David was *in the wilderness of Judah*; that is, *in the forest of Hareth* (1 Sam. xxii. 5) or in *the wilderness of Ziph*, 1 Sam. xxiii. 15. Even in Canaan, though a fruitful land and the people numerous, yet there were wildernesses, places less fruitful and less inhabited than other places. It will be so in the world, in the church, but not in heaven; there *the wilderness shall blossom as the rose*. The best and dearest of God's saints and servants may sometimes have their lot cast in a wilderness. There are psalms proper for a wilderness, and we have reason to thank God that it is the wilderness of Judah we are in, not the wilderness of Sin.

David, in these verses, *stirs up himself to take hold on God*,

I. By a lively active faith: *O God! thou art my God.* We must acknowledge that God is, that we speak to one that really exists and is present with us, when we say, *O God!* which is a serious word; pity it should ever be used as a by-word.

II. By pious and devout affections,

1. He resolves to seek God, and his favour and grace: *Thou art my God*, and therefore *I will seek thee;* for *should not a people seek unto their God*? Isa. viii. 19. *Early will I seek thee.* "*My soul thirsteth for thee* and *my flesh longeth for thee* (that is, my whole man is affected with this pursuit) here *in a dry and thirsty land*."

2. He longs to enjoy God. What is it that he does so passionately wish for? What is his petition and what is his request? It is this (*v.* 2), *To see thy power and thy glory, so as I have seen thee in the sanctuary*. That is, "To see it here in this wilderness as I have seen it in the tabernacle, to see it in secret as I have seen it in the solemn assembly." He longs to be brought out of the wilderness, not that he might see his friends again and be restored to the pleasures and gaieties of the court, but that he might have access to the sanctuary, not to see the priests there, and the ceremony of the worship, but *to see thy power and glory*. He does not say, as I have seen them, but "as I have seen *thee*." We cannot see the essence of God, but we see him in seeing by faith his attributes and perfections. Those were precious minutes which he spent in communion with God; he loved to think them over again.

Verses 3–6

How soon are David's complaints and prayers turned into praises and thanksgivings! David was now in a wilderness, and yet had his heart much enlarged in blessing God.

I. What David will praise God for (*v.* 3): *Because thy loving kindness is better than life.* It is our spiritual life, and that is better than temporal life, xxx. 5. We have better provisions and better possessions than the wealth of this world can afford us, and in the service of God, and in communion with him, we have better employments and better enjoyments than we can have in the business and converse of this world.

II. How he will praise God, and how long, *v.* 4. "*Thus will I bless thee*, thus as I have now begun; the present devout affections shall not pass away, like the morning cloud, but shine more and more, like the morning sun." *I will bless thee while I live.* Praising God must be the work of our whole lives. *I will lift up my hands in thy name.* In all our prayers and praises we are taught to begin with,—*Hallowed be thy name*, and to conclude with,—*Thine is the glory*.

III. With what pleasure and delight he would praise God, *v.* 5. *My soul shall be satisfied as with marrow and fatness*, not only as with bread, which is nourishing, but as with marrow, which is pleasant and delicious, Isa. xxv. 6. There is that in a gracious God, and in communion with him, which gives abundant satisfaction to a gracious soul, xxxvi. 8; lxv. 4. And there is that in a gracious soul which takes abundant satisfaction in God and communion with him. He will praise God *with joyful lips*. When with the heart man believes and is thankful with the mouth confession must be made of both, to the glory of God; not that the performances of the mouth are accepted without the heart (Matt. xv. 8), but out of the abundance of the heart the mouth must speak

JAMIESON, FAUSSET, BROWN

PSALM 63

Vss. 1-11. The historical occasion referred to by the title was probably during Absalom's rebellion (cf. II Sam. 15:23, 28; 16:2). David expresses an earnest desire for God's favor, and a confident expectation of realizing it in his deliverance and the ruin of his enemies.

1. early . . . seek thee—earnestly (Isa. 26:9). The figurative terms—dry and thirsty—lit., "weary," denoting moral destitution, suited his outward circumstances. **soul—and—flesh**—the whole man (Ps. 16:9, 10).

2. The special object of desire was God's perfections as displayed in his worship (Ps. 27:4).

3. Experiencing God's mercy, which exceeds all the blessings of life, his lips will be opened for his praise (Ps. 51:15).

4. Thus—lit., "Truly." **will I bless**—praise Thee (Ps. 34:1).

lift up my hands—in worship (cf. Ps. 28:2). **in thy name**—in praise of Thy perfections.

5-8. Full spiritual blessings satisfy his desires, and acts of praise fill his thoughts and time.

ADAM CLARKE

PSALM 63

The title of this psalm is, "A Psalm of David, when he was in the wilderness of Judah." It is most probable that the psalm was written when David took refuge in the forest of Hareth, in the wilderness of Ziph, when he fled from the court of Achish.

1. *O God, thou art my God.* He who can say so, and feels what he says, need not fear the face of any adversary. He has God, and all sufficiency in Him.

Early will I seek thee. From the dawn of day. What first lays hold of the heart in the morning is likely to occupy the place all the day.

2. *To see thy power and thy glory . . . in the sanctuary.* In His public ordinances God had often showed His *power* in the judgments He executed, in the terror He impressed, and in awakening the sinful; and His glory in delivering the tempted, succoring the distressed, and diffusing peace and pardon through the hearts of His followers. God shows His *power* and *glory* in His *ordinances;* therefore *public worship* should never be neglected. *We must see God*, says the old Psalter, *that he may see us.* In His temple He dispenses His choicest blessings.

3. *Thy lovingkindness is better than life. Thy lovingkindness, chasdecha,* "thy effusive mercy," *is better, mechaiyim,* "than lives; it is better than," or "good beyond," countless ages of human existence.

MATTHEW HENRY

(xlv. 1). Praising lips must be joyful lips.

IV. How he would entertain himself with thoughts of God when he was most retired (*v.* 6): I will praise thee *when I remember thee upon my bed.* God was in all his thoughts, which is the reverse of the wicked man's character, x. 4. The thoughts of God were ready to him: "*I remember thee;* that is, when I go to think, I find thee at my right hand, present to my mind." And they were fixed in him: "*I meditate on thee.*" Thoughts of God must not be transient thoughts, passing through the mind, but abiding thoughts, dwelling in the mind. David was now wandering and unsettled, but, wherever he came, he brought his religion along with him. When sleep departs from our eyes (through pain, or sickness of body, or any disturbance in the mind) our souls, by remembering God, may be at ease, and repose themselves. Perhaps an hour's pious meditation will do us more good than an hour's sleep would have done. See xvi. 7; xvii. 3; iv. 4; cxix. 62.

Verses 7–11

David here expresses his confidence in God and his joyful expectations from him (*v.* 7): *In the shadow of thy wings I will rejoice,* alluding either to the wings of the cherubim stretched out over the ark of the covenant, between which God is said to dwell, or to the wings of a fowl, under which the helpless young ones have shelter, as the eagle's young ones (Exod. xix. 4; Deut. xxxii. 11), which speaks the divine power, and the young ones of the common hen (Matt. xxiii. 37), which speaks more of divine tenderness. It is a phrase often used in the psalms (xvii. 8; xxxvi. 7; lvii. 1; lxi. 4; xci. 4), and nowhere else in this sense, except Ruth ii. 12, where Ruth, when she became a proselyte, is said to *trust under the wings of the God of Israel.* It is our duty to *rejoice in the shadow of God's wings,* which denotes our recourse to him by faith and prayer, as naturally as the chickens, when they are cold or frightened, run by instinct under the wings of the hen.

I. What were the supports and encouragements of David's confidence in God.

1. His former experiences of God's power in relieving him: "*Because thou hast been my help* when other helps and helpers failed me, therefore I will still rejoice in thy salvation, will trust in thee for the future, and will do it with delight and holy joy."

2. The present sense he had of God's grace carrying him on in these pursuits (*v.* 8): *My soul follows hard after thee,* which speaks a very earnest desire and a serious vigorous endeavour to keep up communion with God. David owns, to the glory of God, *Thy right hand upholds me.*

II. David triumphed in the hope,

1. That his enemies should be ruined, *v.* 9, 10. There were those that *sought his soul to destroy it,* not only his life (which they struck at, both to prevent his coming to the crown and because they envied and hated him for his wisdom, piety, and usefulness), but his soul, which they sought to destroy by banishing him from God's ordinances. But they shall *go into the lower parts of the earth,* to the grave, to hell; their enmity to David would be their death. *They shall be a portion for foxes;* either their dead bodies shall be a prey to ravenous beasts or their houses and estates shall be a habitation for wild beasts, Isa. xxxiv. 14.

2. That he himself should gain his point at last (*v.* 11), that he should be advanced to the throne to which he had been anointed: *The king shall rejoice in God.* David's advancement would be the consolation of his friends. *Every one that swears to him* (that is, to David), that comes into his interest and takes an oath of allegiance to him, *shall glory* in his success. *Those that fear thee will be glad when they see me.* Those that heartily espouse the cause of Christ shall glory in its victory at last. *If we suffer with him, we shall reign with him.* It would be the confutation of his enemies: *The mouth of those that speak lies,* of Saul, and Doeg, and others that misrepresented David, *shall be* quite *stopped.*

JAMIESON, FAUSSET, BROWN

night—as well as day.

Past favors assure him of future, and hence he presses earnestly near to God, whose power sustains him (Ps. 17:8; 60:5).

9, 10. those . . . to destroy it—or lit., "to ruin," or, "for ruin"—i.e., such as seek to injure me (are) *for* ruin—appointed to it (cf. Ps. 35:8).

shall go . . . earth—into the grave, or, to death; as their bodies are represented as a portion for—**foxes**—lit., "jackals."

11. the king—i.e., David himself, and all who reverence God, "shall share a glorious part," while treacherous foes shall be for ever silenced (Ps. 62:4).

ADAM CLARKE

7. *Therefore in the shadow of thy wings.* I will get into the very secret of Thy presence, into the holy of holies, to the mercy seat, over which the cherubs extend their wings. If the Psalmist does not allude to the overshadowing of the mercy seat by the extended wings of the cherubim, he may have in view, as a metaphor, the young of fowls, seeking shelter, protection, and warmth under the wings of their mothers. See the same metaphor, Ps. lxi. 4.

8. *My soul followeth hard after thee.* "My soul cleaves (or) is glued after thee."

10. *They shall fall by the sword.* "They shall be poured out by the hand of the sword." That is, their life's blood shall be shed either in war or by the hand of justice. *They shall be a portion for foxes.* They shall be left unburied, and the "jackals" shall feed upon their dead bodies.

11. *But the king shall rejoice.* David shall come to the kingdom according to the promise of God. *That sweareth by him.* It was customary to swear by the life of the king. The Egyptians swore by the life of Pharaoh; and Joseph conformed to this custom, as may be seen in the Book of Genesis, chap. xlii. 15-16. But here it may refer to God. He is the King, and swearing by His name signifies binding themselves by His authority.

MATTHEW HENRY

PSALM 64

To the chief musician. A psalm of David.

Verses 1–6

David, in these verses, puts in before God a representation of his own danger and of his enemies' character.

I. He earnestly begs of God to preserve him (*v.* 1, 2): *Hear my voice, O God! in my prayer;* that is, grant me the thing I pray for, and this is it, *Lord, preserve my life from fear of the enemy.* He prays, "*Hide me from the secret counsel of the wicked,* from the mis-

JAMIESON, FAUSSET, BROWN

PSALM 64

Vss. 1-10. A prayer for deliverance from cunning and malicious enemies, with a confident view of their overthrow, which will honor God and give joy to the righteous.

1. preserve . . . fear—as well as the danger producing it.

ADAM CLARKE

PSALM 64

The title, "To the chief Musician, or conqueror, A Psalm of David."

MATTHEW HENRY

chief which they secretly consult among themselves to do against me, and *from the insurrection of the workers of iniquity*, who join forces, as they join counsels, to do me a mischief."

II. He complains of the great malice and wickedness of his enemies.

1. They are very spiteful in their calumnies and reproaches, *v.* 3, 4. They are described as military men, with their sword and bow, archers that take aim exactly, secretly, and suddenly, and shoot at the harmless bird that apprehends not herself in any danger. Their tongues are their swords. The tongue is a little member, but, like the sword, it is a dangerous weapon. *Bitter words* are *their arrows*—scurrilous reflections, opprobrious nicknames, false representations, slanders, and calumnies. The upright man is their mark. The better any man is the more he is envied by those that are themselves bad, and the more ill is said of him. They *shoot in secret*, that those they shoot at may not discover them and avoid the danger, for *in vain is the net spread in the sight of any bird*. And *suddenly do they shoot*, without giving a man lawful warning or any opportunity to defend himself. Herein *they fear not*, that is, they are confident of their success.

2. They are very close and very resolute in their malicious projects, *v.* 5. They consult with themselves and one another how to do the most mischief and most effectually: *They commune of laying snares privily*. All their communion is in sin and all their communication is how to sin securely. *They say, Who shall see them?* A practical disbelief of God's omniscience is at the bottom of all the wickedness of the wicked.

3. They are very industrious in putting their projects in execution (*v.* 6): "*They search out iniquity;* they take a great deal of pains to find out some iniquity or other to lay to my charge; they dig deep, and look far back, and put things to the utmost stretch, that they may have something to accuse me of." Half the pains that many take to damn their souls would serve to save them.

Verses 7–10

I. The judgments of God upon these malicious persecutors of David. The punishments answer the sin. 1. They shot at David secretly and suddenly, to wound him; but God shall shoot at them, for he *ordains his arrows against the persecutors* (vii. 13), against the face of them, xxi. 12. And God's arrows will hit surer, and fly swifter, and pierce deeper, than theirs do or can. 2. Their tongues fell upon him, but God shall *make their tongues to fall upon themselves*. Those that love cursing, it shall come unto them. Sometimes men's secret wickedness is brought to light by their own confession, and then their own tongue falls upon them.

II. The influence which these judgments should have upon others.

1. Their neighbours shall shun them and shift for their own safety. They *shall flee away*, for fear of being involved in their ruin.

2. Spectators shall reverence the providence of God therein, *v.* 9. *They shall wisely consider his doing*. They shall be affected with a holy awe of God upon the consideration of it. They shall speak to one another and to all about them of the justice of God in punishing persecutors. *This is the finger of God*.

3. Good people shall in a special manner take notice of it, *v.* 10. *The righteous shall be glad in the Lord*, not glad of the misery and ruin of their fellow-creatures, but glad that God is glorified, and his word fulfilled, and the cause of injured innocency pleaded effectually. It shall encourage their faith.

PSALM 65

To the chief musician. A psalm *and* song of David.

Verses 1–5

The psalmist here has no particular concern of his own at the throne of grace, but begins with an address to God, as the mouth of a congregation.

I. How he gives glory to God, *v.* 1. 1. By humble thankfulness: *Praise waiteth for thee, O God! in Zion*, waits in expectation of the mercy desired, waits till it arrives, that it may be received with thankfulness at its first approach. "Praise waits, with an entire satisfaction in thy holy will and dependence on thy mercy." *Praise is silent unto thee* (so the word is), as wanting words to express the great goodness of God. As there are holy *groanings which cannot be uttered*, so there are holy adorings which cannot be uttered. 2. By sincere faithfulness: *Unto thee shall the vow be performed*, that is, the sacrifice shall be offered up which was vowed. Better it is not to vow

JAMIESON, FAUSSET, BROWN

2. insurrection—lit., "uproar," noisy assaults, as well as their secret counsels.

3, 4. Similar figures for slander (Ps. 57:4; 59:7). **bend**—lit., "tread," or, prepared. The allusion is to the mode of bending a bow by treading on it; here, and in Psalm 58:7, transferred to arrows.

the perfect—one innocent of the charges made (Ps. 18:23). **and fear not**—(Ps. 55:19), not regarding God.

5. A sentiment here more fully presented, by depicting their deliberate malice.

6. This is further evinced by their diligent efforts and deeply laid schemes.

7. The contrast is heightened by representing God as using weapons like theirs.

8. their . . . tongue to fall . . .—i.e., the consequences of their slanders, etc. (cf. Ps. 10:2; 31:16).

all that see . . . away—Their partners in evil shall be terrified.

9, 10. Men, generally, will acknowledge God's work, and the righteous, rejoicing in it, shall be encouraged to trust Him (Ps. 58:10).

PSALM 65

Vss. 1-13. This is a song of praise for God's spiritual blessings to His people and His kind providence over all the earth.

1. Praise waiteth for thee—lit., "To Thee silence praise," or (cf. Ps. 62:1), To Thee silence is praise—i.e., Praise is waiting as a servant—it is due to Thee.

So the last clause expresses the duty of paying vows. These two parts of acceptable worship, mentioned in Psalm 50:14, are rendered in Zion, where God chiefly displays His mercy and receives homage.

ADAM CLARKE

4. *That they may shoot in secret*. They lurk, that they may take their aim the more surely, and not miss their mark. *Suddenly*. When there is no fear apprehended, because none is seen.

5. *They commune of laying snares*. They lay snares to entrap those whom they cannot slay by open attack or private ambush.

6. *They search out iniquities; they accomplish a diligent search*. The word *chaphash*, which is used three times, as a noun and a verb, in this sentence, signifies "to strip off the clothes." They investigate iniquities; they perfectly investigate an investigation."

7. *But God shall shoot at them with an arrow*. They endeavor to trace me out, that they may shoot me; but God will shoot at them. This, if the psalm refer to the times of David, seems to be prophetic of Saul's death. The archers pressed upon him, and sorely wounded him with their arrows (1 Sam. xxxi. 3).

8. *Their own tongue to fall upon themselves*. All the plottings, counsels, and curses they have formed against me shall come upon themselves.

9. *And all men shall fear*. They endeavored to hide their mischief; but God shall so punish them that all shall see it, and shall acknowledge in their chastisement the just judgment of God. The wicked, in consequence, shall fear, and

10. *The righteous shall be glad*. They shall see that God does not abandon His followers to the malice of bad men.

PSALM 65

1. *Praise waiteth for thee*. Praise is "silent" or "dumb" for Thee. Thou alone art worthy of praise.

MATTHEW HENRY

than to vow and not to pay.

II. What he gives him glory for.

1. For hearing prayer (*v.* 2): *Praise waits for thee;* and why is it so ready? (1) "Because thou art ready to grant our petitions. *O thou that hearest prayer!* thou canst answer every prayer, for thou art able to do for us more than we are able to ask or think (Eph. iii. 20), and thou wilt answer every prayer of faith, either in kind or kindness." (2) Because, for that reason, we are ready to run to him when we are in our straits. "*Therefore,* because thou art a God hearing prayer, *unto thee shall all flesh come.*"

2. For pardoning sin. In this *who is a God like* unto him? Micah vii. 18. "Our sins reach to the heavens, *iniquities prevail against us,* our own consciences accuse us and we have no reply to make; and yet, *as for our transgressions, thou shalt purge them away,* so that we shall not come into condemnation for them."

3. For the kind entertainment he gives to those that attend upon him and the comfort they have in communion with him. Iniquity must first be purged away (*v.* 3) and then we are welcome to compass God's altars, *v.* 4.

(1) They are blessed. Not only blessed is the nation (xxxiii. 12), but *blessed is the man,* the particular person, how mean soever, *whom thou choosest, and causest to approach unto thee, that he may dwell in thy courts.* To come into communion with God is to converse with him as one we love and value. It is to dwell in his courts, as the priests and Levites did, that were at home in God's house; it is to be constant in the exercises of religion. We come into communion with God, not recommended by any merit of our own, but by God's free choice: "*Blessed is the man whom thou choosest,* and so distinguishest from others who are left to themselves."

(2) They shall be satisfied. Here the psalmist changes the person, not, *He* shall be satisfied (the man whom thou choosest), but, *We* shall, which teaches us to apply the promises to ourselves: *We shall be satisfied with the goodness of thy house, even of thy holy temple.* God keeps a good house. There is abundance of goodness in his house, righteousness, grace, and all the comforts of the everlasting covenant; there is enough for all, enough for each; it is ready, always ready; and all on free cost, without money and without price.

4. For the operations of his power on their behalf (*v.* 5): *By terrible things in righteousness wilt thou answer us, O God of our salvation!* This may be understood of the rebukes which God in his providence sometimes gives to his own people; he often answers them by terrible things, for the awakening and quickening of them, but always in righteousness; he neither does them any wrong nor means them any hurt, for even then he is the God of their salvation. See Isa. xlv. 15.

5. For the care he takes of all his people. He is *the confidence of all the ends of the earth* that is, of all the saints all the world over, and not theirs only that were of the seed of Israel; for he is the God of the Gentiles as well as of the Jews.

Verses 6–13

His power and sovereignty as the God of nature.

I. He establishes the earth and it abides, cxix. 90. *By his own strength he setteth fast the mountains* (*v.* 6). Hence they are called *everlasting mountains,* Hab. iii. 6. Yet God's covenant with his people is said to stand more firmly than they, Isa. liv. 10.

II. He stills the sea, and it is quiet, *v.* 7. The sea in a storm makes a great noise, but, when God pleases, he commands silence among the waves and billows, and lays them to sleep, turns the storm into a calm quickly, cvii. 29. And by the sea, as well as by the unchangeableness of the earth, it appears that he whose the sea and the dry land are is girded with power. And by this our Lord Jesus gave a proof of his divine power, that he *commanded the winds and waves, and they obeyed him.* To this quieting of the sea he adds, as a thing much of the same nature, that he stills *the tumult of the people.*

III. He renews the morning and evening, *v.* 8. This regular succession of day and night may be considered, 1. As an instance of God's great power, and so it strikes an awe upon all: *Those that dwell in the uttermost parts of the earth are afraid at thy* signs or *tokens*; they are by them convinced that there is a supreme deity, a sovereign monarch, before whom they ought to fear and tremble. 2. As an instance of God's great goodness, and so it brings comfort to all: *Thou makest the outgoings of the morning,* before the sun rises, *and of the evening,* before the sun sets, *to rejoice.* As it is God that scatters the light of the morning and draws the curtains of the evening, so he gives occasion to us to rejoice in both. We are to

JAMIESON, FAUSSET, BROWN

2. All are encouraged to pray by God's readiness to hear.

3. God's mercy alone delivers us from the burden of iniquities, by purging or expiating by an atonement the transgressions with which we are charged, and which are denoted by—**Iniquities**—or lit., "Words of iniquities."

4. dwell in thy courts; ... [and] satisfied with the goodness ... temple—denote communion with God (Ps. 15:1; 23:6; cf. Ps. 5:7). This is a blessing for all God's people, as denoted by the change of number.

5. terrible things—i.e., by the manifestation of justice and wrath to enemies, accompanying that of mercy to His people (Ps. 63:9-11; 64:7-9).

the confidence—object of it. **of all ... earth**—the whole world—i.e., deservedly such, whether men think so or not.

6-13. God's great power and goodness are the grounds of this confidence. These are illustrated in His control of the mightiest agencies of nature and nations affecting men with awe and dread (Ps. 26:7; 98:1, etc.), and in His fertilizing showers, causing the earth to produce abundantly for man and beast.

outgoings of ... rejoice—*all* people from east to west.

ADAM CLARKE

3. *Iniquities prevail against me.* This is no just rendering of the original, "Iniquitous words have prevailed against me," or, "The words of iniquity are strong against me." All kinds of calumnies, lies, and slanders have been propagated, to shake my confidence and ruin my credit. *Our transgressions, thou shalt purge them away.* Whatsoever offenses we have committed against Thee, Thou wilt pardon; *tecapperem,* Thou wilt "make atonement" for them, when with hearty repentance and true faith we turn unto Thee.

4. *Blessed is the man whom thou choosest.* This is spoken in reference to the priests, who were chosen of God to minister at the Tabernacle; and who were permitted to *approach,* "draw nigh," to the Divine Majesty by the various offerings and sacrifices which they presented.

F. B. MEYER:

"Blessed is the man whom thou choosest, and causest to approach unto thee" (65:4). I would be one of those favored ones, my Savior. There is nothing that the heart can conceive which is to be compared with this blessedness. The light of nature, the joy of friendship, the fascination of art and books, can give no such delight as this approach to you, this dwelling in your courts. But the longer I know myself, the surer I am that you must cause me to approach, that you must put forth extraordinary means for making me dwell. So cause me to approach that I may dwell.

When thy soul has put up such a prayer as this, be sure that an answer will come. You may be brought nigh by an invisible but all-penetrating attraction, as when the sun draws the earth, or the magnet the needle: or perhaps God will answer you by terrible things in righteousness. There will be deep humiliations, solemn heart searchings, sharp crucifixions, cherished purposes thwarted, the keenest pain, the most searching fire. But through all, there will come a growing tenderness and desire.

—*Great Verses Through the Bible*

8. *Are afraid at thy tokens.* Thunder and lightning, storms and tempests, eclipses and meteors, tornadoes and earthquakes, are proofs to all who dwell even in the remotest parts of the earth that there is a Supreme Being who is wonderful and terrible in His acts. From this verse to the end of the psalm there is a series of the finest poetic imagery in the world. *The outgoings of the morning.* The rising and setting sun, the morning and evening twilight, the invariable succession of day and night, are all

MATTHEW HENRY

look upon our daily worship, alone and with our families to be both the most needful of our daily occupations and the most delightful of our daily comforts.

IV. He waters the earth and makes it fruitful. How much the fruitfulness of this lower part of the creation depends upon the influence of the upper is easy to observe; if the heavens be as brass, the earth is as iron, which is a sensible intimation to a stupid world that every good and perfect gift is from above. All God's blessings, even spiritual ones, are expressed by his raining righteousness upon us. The common blessing of rain from heaven and fruitful seasons is here described.

1. How much there is in it of the power and goodness of God. God that made the earth hereby visits it, sends to it, gives proof of his care of it, *v.* 9. God that made it dry land, hereby waters it, in order to its fruitfulness. Though the productions of the earth flourished before God had caused it to rain, yet even then there was a mist which answered the intention, and *watered the whole face of the ground,* Gen. ii. 5, 6. Our hearts are dry and barren unless God himself be as the dew to us and water us; and the plants of his own planting he will water and make them to increase. Rain is *the river of God, which is full of water.* This river of God enriches the earth, which without it would quickly be a poor thing. The riches of the earth are abundantly more useful to man than those which are hidden in its bowels; we might live well enough without silver and gold, but not without corn and grass.

2. How much benefit is derived from it to the earth and to man upon it. (1) To the earth itself. The rain in season gives it a new face. Even *the ridges* of the earth, off which the rain seems to slide, are watered *abundantly,* for they drink in the rain which comes often upon them; *the furrows* of it, which are turned up by the plough, are settled by the rain and made fit to receive the seed (*v.* 10); they are settled by being made soft. That which makes the soil of the heart tender settles it; for the heart is established with that grace. Thus the spring is an earnest of a blessing upon the whole year, which God is therefore said to *crown with his goodness* (*v.* 11). And his paths are said to *drop fatness.* These communications of God's goodness to this lower world are very extensive (*v.* 12): *They drop upon the pastures of the wilderness,* and not merely upon the pastures of the inhabited land. The deserts, which man takes no care of and receives no profit from, are under the care of the divine Providence, and we ought to be thankful not only for that which serves us, but for that which serves any part of the creation. So extensive are the gifts of God's bounty that in them the hills, *the little hills, rejoice on every side,* even the north side, that lies most from the sun. Hills are not above the need of God's providence; little hills are not below the cognizance of it. (2) To man upon the earth. *As for the earth, out of it comes bread* (Job xxviii. 5), for out of it comes corn; but every grain of corn that comes out of it God himself prepared; and therefore he provides rain for the earth, that thereby he may prepare corn for man, under whose feet he has put the rest of the creatures and for whose use he has fitted them. The yearly produce of the corn is not only an operation of the same power that raises the dead, but an instance of that power not much unlike it (as appears by that of our Saviour, John xii. 24), and the constant benefit we have from it is an instance of that goodness which endures for ever. Corn and cattle are the two staple commodities, and both are owing to the divine goodness in watering the earth, *v.* 13. The valleys are so fruitful that they seem to be *covered over with corn,* in the time of harvest. The lowest parts of the earth are commonly the most fruitful, and one acre of the humble valleys is worth five of the lofty mountains. But both corn-ground and pasture-ground, answering the end of their creation, are said to *shout for joy and sing,* because they are serviceable to the honour of God and the comfort of man.

JAMIESON, FAUSSET, BROWN

visitest—in mercy (cf. Ps. 8:4). **river of God**—His exhaustless resources.

thy paths—ways of providence (Ps. 25:4, 10). **wilderness**—places, though not inhabited by men, fit for pasture (Lev. 16:21, 22; Job 24:5). **pastures**—(In vs. 12) is lit., "folds," or "enclosures for flocks"; and in vs. 13 it may be "lambs"—the same word used and so translated in Psalm 37:20; so that "the flocks are clothed with lambs" (a figure for abundant increase) would be the form of expression.

ADAM CLARKE

ordained by Thee, and contribute to the happiness and continuance of man and beast. Or, All that fear Thee praise Thee in the morning, when they go to their work, and in the evening, when they return home, for Thy great goodness manifested in the continuance of their strength, and the success of their labor.

9. *Thou visitest the earth.* God is represented as going through the whole globe, and examining the wants of every part, and directing the clouds how and where to deposit their fertilizing showers, and the rivers where to direct their beneficial courses.

The river of God. Some think the Jordan is meant, and the visiting and watering refer to rain after a long drought. But the clouds may be thus denominated which properly are the origin of rivers.

10. *Thou waterest the ridges.* In seedtime Thou sendest that measure of rain that is necessary, in order to prepare the earth for the plough; and then, when the *ridges* are thrown into furrows, thou makest them *soft with showers,* so as to prepare them for the seed. *Thou blessest the springing thereof.* Literally, "Thou wilt bless its germinations"—its springing buds.

11. *Thou crownest the year.* A full and plentiful harvest is the crown of the year, and this springs from the unmerited goodness of God. "Thou encirclest," as with a diadem.

12. *The pastures of the wilderness.* Even the places which are not cultivated have their sufficiency of moisture, so as to render them proper places of pasturage for cattle. The terms "wilderness" and "desert," in the Sacred Writings, mean, in general, places not inhabited and uncultivated, though abounding with timber, bushes, and herbage. *The little hills rejoice.* Literally, "The hills gird themselves with exultation." The metaphor appears to be taken from the frisking of lambs, bounding of kids, and dancing of shepherds and shepherdesses, in the joy-inspiring summer season.

PSALM 66 (MATTHEW HENRY)

To the chief musician. A song *or* psalm.

Verses 1–7

I. In these verses the psalmist calls upon all people to praise God, *all lands, all the earth, v.* 1. This speaks the glory of God for he is good to all. 2. The duty of man, that all are obliged to praise God; it is part of the law of creation, and therefore is required of every creature. 3. A prediction of the conversion of the Gentiles to the faith of Christ; the time should come when all lands should praise God. 4. The psalmist will abound in it himself, and wishes that

PSALM 66 (JAMIESON, FAUSSET, BROWN)

Vss. 1-20. The writer invites all men to unite in praise, cites some striking occasions for it, promises special acts of thanksgiving, and celebrates God's great mercy.

1. Make . . . noise—or, Shout.

PSALM 66 (ADAM CLARKE)

MATTHEW HENRY

God might have his tribute paid him by all the nations of the earth and not by the land of Israel only. We must be hearty and zealous, open and public, as those that are not ashamed of our Master. And both these are implied in making a noise, a joyful noise. In praising God we must do it so as to glorify him. *Reckon it your greatest glory to praise God*, so some.

II. He had called upon all lands to praise God (*v.* 1), and he foretells (*v.* 4) that they shall do so: *All the earth shall worship thee.* They shall *sing to God*, that is, *sing to his name*, for it is only to his declarative glory, that by which he has made himself known, not to his essential glory, that we can contribute anything by our praises.

III. We are here called upon *to come and see the works of God*; for *his own works praise him*, whether we do or no; and the reason why we do not praise him more and better is because we do not duly and attentively observe them. Let us therefore see God's works (*v.* 5), and then speak of them, and speak of them to him (*v.* 3): *Say unto God, How terrible art thou in thy works, terrible in thy doings!* 1. God's works are wonderful in themselves. God *is terrible* (that is, admirable) in his works. In all his doings towards the children of men he is terrible, and to be eyed with a holy awe. Much of religion lies in a reverence for the divine Providence. 2. They are formidable to his enemies, and have many a time forced and frightened them into a feigned submission (*v.* 3): *Through the greatness of thy power*, before which none can stand, *shall thy enemies submit themselves unto thee; they shall lie unto thee* (so the word is), that is, they shall be compelled, sorely against their wills, to make their peace with thee upon any terms. 3. They are comfortable and beneficial to his people, *v.* 6. When Israel came out of Egypt, *he turned the sea into dry land* before them, which encouraged them to follow God's guidance through the wilderness; and, when they were to enter Canaan, for their encouragement in their wars Jordan was divided before them, and *they went through that flood on foot*. The joys of our fathers were our joys, and we ought to look upon ourselves as sharers in them. 4. They are commanding to all. God by his works keeps up his dominion in the world (*v.* 7): *He rules by his power for ever; his eyes behold the nations.* He has a commanding arm. *Strong is his hand, and high is his right hand.* Hence he infers, *Let not the rebellious exalt themselves;* let not those that have revolting and rebellious hearts dare to rise up in any acts of rebellion against God.

Verses 8–12

Two things we have reason to bless God for:—

I. Common protection (*v.* 9): *He holdeth our soul in life. He puts our soul in life*, so the word is. He that gave us our being, by a constant renewed act upholds us in our being, and his providence is a continued creation. *It is not existence, but happiness, that deserves the name of life.* He *suffers not our feet to be moved*, preventing many unforeseen evils.

II. Special deliverance from great distress.

1. How grievous the distress and danger were, *v.* 11, 12. What particular trouble of the church this refers to does not appear; it might be the trouble of some private persons or families only. But, whatever it was, they were pressed down with it, and kept under as with a load *upon their loins*, *v.* 11. Is anything more dangerous than fire and water? *We went through both*, that is, afflictions of different kinds. When men rose up against us, that was fire and water. That was the case here: "*Thou hast caused men to ride over our heads*, to trample upon us and insult over us, to hector and abuse us, nay, and to make perfect slaves of us; they have said to our souls, *Bow down, that we may go over*," Isa. li. 23.

2. How gracious God's design was in bringing them into this distress and danger. See what the meaning of it is (*v.* 10): *Thou, O God! hast proved us, and tried us.* By afflictions we are proved as silver in the fire. Our graces, by being exercised, may be made more strong and active, and so we may be improved, as silver when it is refined by the fire and made more clear from its dross; and this will be to our unspeakable advantage, for thus we are made partakers of God's holiness, Heb. xii. 10.

3. How glorious the issue was at last. The troubles of the church will certainly end well. They are in fire and water, but they get through them: "*We went through fire and water*, and did not perish in the flames or floods." Whatever the troubles of the saints are, blessed be God, there is a way through them. *Thou broughtest us out into a wealthy place* into a *well-watered* place (so the word is), *like the gardens of the Lord*, and therefore fruitful.

JAMIESON, FAUSSET, BROWN

2. his name—as in Psalm 29:2. **make his praise glorious**—lit., "place honor, His praise," or, "as to His praise"—i.e., let His praise be such as will glorify Him, or, be honorable to Him.

3, 4. A specimen of the praise. **How terrible**—(Cf. Ps. 65:8).

submit—(Cf. *Margin*), show a forced subjection (Ps. 18:44), produced by terror.

5, 6. The terrible works illustrated in Israel's history (Exod. 14:21). By this example let rebels be admonished.

7. behold the nations—watch their conduct.

8, 9. Here is, perhaps, cited a case of recent deliverance. **holdeth . . . in life**—lit., "putteth our soul in life"—i.e., out of danger (Ps. 30:3; 49:15). **to be moved** (Cf. Ps. 10:6; 55:22).

10-12. Out of severe trials, God had brought them to safety (cf. Isa. 48:10; I Pet. 1:7). **affliction**—lit., "pressure," or, as in Psalm 55:3, oppression, which, laid on the —**loins**—the seat of strength (Deut. 33:11), enfeebles the frame.

men to ride over our heads [made us to pass] **through fire . . .**—figures describing prostration and critical dangers (cf. Isa. 43:2; Ezek. 36:12).

wealthy—lit., "overflowing," or, irrigated, and hence fertile.

ADAM CLARKE

3. *How terrible art thou!* Consider the plagues with which He afflicted Egypt before He brought your fathers from their captivity, which obliged all His enemies to submit.

Thine enemies submit themselves. Literally, "lie unto Thee." This was remarkably the case with Pharaoh and the Egyptians. They promised again and again to let the people go, when the hand of the Lord was upon them; and they as frequently falsified their word.

9. *Which holdeth our soul in life.* Literally, "he who placeth our soul in lives." We are preserved alive, have health of body, and feel the life of God in our hearts. *And suffereth not our feet to be moved.* Keeps us steadfast in His testimonies.

11. *Thou broughtest us into the net.* This refers well to the case of the Israelites when, in their departure from Egypt, pursued by the Egyptians, having the Red Sea before them and no method of escape, Pharaoh said, "The wilderness hath shut them in . . . they are entangled," comparing their state to that of a wild beast in a net.

10. *For thou, O God, hast proved us.* This is a metaphor taken from melting and refining metals; afflictions and trials of various kinds are represented as a furnace where ore is melted, and a crucible where it is refined.

MATTHEW HENRY

Verses 13–20

The psalmist, having before stirred up all people to bless the Lord, here stirs up himself.

I. In his devotions to his God, *v.* 13–15. 1. By costly sacrifices (*v.* 13): *I will go into thy house with burnt-offerings.* His sacrifices should be public, in the place which God had chosen: "I will go into thy house with them." Christ is our temple, to whom we must bring our spiritual gifts, and by whom they are sanctified. They should be the best of the kind—*burnt-sacrifices,* which were wholly consumed upon the altar. He will *offer bullocks with goats with the incense of rams.* Or *rams with incense.* The incense typifies Christ's intercession, without which the fattest of our sacrifices will not be accepted. 2. By a conscientious performance of his vows. This was the psalmist's resolution (*v.* 13, 14), *I will pay thee my vows, which my lips have uttered when I was in trouble.*

II. In his declarations to his friends, *v.* 16. He calls together a congregation of good people to hear his thankful narrative of God's favours to him: "*Come and hear, all you that fear God.*" God's people should communicate their experiences to each other. We should take all occasions to tell one another of the great things which God has done for our souls, the spiritual blessings with which he has blessed us. Now what was it that God had done for his soul? (1) He had wrought in him a love to the duty of prayer, and had by his grace enlarged his heart in that duty (*v.* 17): *I cried unto him with my mouth.* God has given us leave to pray, a command to pray, encouragements to pray, and (to crown all) a heart to pray. By crying to him we do indeed extol him. He is pleased to reckon himself honoured by the humble believing prayers of the upright. In seeking our own welfare, we seek his glory. *His exaltation was under my tongue* (so it may be read); that is, I was considering in my mind how I might exalt and magnify his name. When prayers are in our mouths praises must be in our hearts. (2) He had wrought in him a dread of sin as an enemy to prayer (*v.* 18): *If I regard iniquity in my heart,* I know very well *the Lord will not hear me.* The sense of this place is plain: *If I regard iniquity in my heart,* that is, **"If I have favourable thoughts of it, if I love it, indulge it, and allow myself in it, God will not hear my prayer, nor can I expect an answer of peace to it."** (3) He had graciously granted him an answer of peace to his prayers (*v.* 19). This God did for his soul, by answering his prayer, he gave him a token of his favour. And therefore he concludes (*v.* 20), *Blessed be God.* What we win by prayer we must wear with praise. Lest it should be thought that the deliverance was granted for the sake of some worthiness in his prayer, he ascribes it to God's mercy. "It was not my prayer that fetched the deliverance, but his mercy that sent it."

PSALM 67

To the chief musician on Negonoth. A psalm *or* song.

Verses 1–7

The psalmist was elevated to receive the spirit of prophecy concerning the enlargement of God's kingdom.

I. He begins with a prayer for the welfare and prosperity of the church then in being, *v.* 1. Our Saviour, in teaching us to say, *Our Father,* has intimated that we ought to pray with and for others; so the psalmist here prays not, *God be merciful to me, and bless me,* but to *us,* and bless *us.* We are here taught, 1. That all our happiness comes from God's mercy and takes rise in that; and therefore the first thing prayed for is, *God be merciful to us,* to us sinners. 2. *God bless us;* that is, give us an interest in his promises, and confer upon us all the good contained in them. *God bless us* is a comprehensive prayer. 3. *God cause his face to shine upon us*; that is, God by his grace qualify us for his favour and then give us the tokens of his favour. *To shine with us* (so the margin reads it); *with us* doing our endeavour, and let it crown that endeavour with success.

II. He passes from this to a prayer for the conversion of the Gentiles (*v.* 2): *That thy way may be known upon earth.* Thus public-spirited must we be in our prayers. *Father in heaven, hallowed be thy name, thy kingdom come.*

1. These verses, which point at the conversion of the Gentiles, may be taken, (1) As a prayer; and so it speaks the desire of the Old Testament saints. They desired nothing more than the throwing down of the enclosure and the laying open of the advantages. See then how the spirit of the Jews, in the days of Christ and his apostles, differed from the spirit of

JAMIESON, FAUSSET, BROWN

13-15. These full and varied offerings constitute the payment of vows (Lev. 22:18-23). **I will offer**—lit., "make to ascend"—alluding to the smoke of burnt offering, which explains the use of—**incense**—elsewhere always denoting the fumes of aromatics.

16-20. With these he unites his public thanks, inviting those who fear God (Ps. 60:4; 61:5, His true worshippers) to hear. He vindicates his sincerity, inasmuch as God would not hear hypocrites, but had heard him.

he was extolled with my tongue—lit., exaltation (was) under my tongue," as a place of deposit, whence it proceeded—i.e., honoring God was habitual. **If I regard iniquity**—lit., "see iniquity with pleasure."

PSALM 67

Vss. 1-7. A prayer that, by God's blessing on His people, His salvation and praise may be extended over the earth.

1. cause his face to shine—show us favor (Num. 6:24, 25; Ps. 31:16).

2. thy way—of gracious dealing (Isa. 55:8), as explained by—**saving health**—or lit., "salvation."

ADAM CLARKE

14. *When I was in trouble.* This is generally the time when good resolutions are formed, and vows made; but how often are these forgotten when affliction and calamity are removed!

18. *If I regard iniquity in my heart.* "If I have seen iniquity in my heart," if I have known it was there, and encouraged it.

PSALM 67

The title here is the same with that of Psalm iv, where see the notes. It is supposed to have been written at the return from the Babylonish captivity, and to foretell the conversion of the Gentiles to the Christian religion. The prayer for their salvation is very energetic.

1. *God be merciful unto us.* This is nearly the same form of blessing as that used Num. vi. 25.

2. *That thy way may be known.* That Thy will, Thy gracious designs towards the children of men, Thy way of reconciling them to thyself, of justifying the ungodly, and sanctifying the unholy, may be known to all the nations upon the earth! *Thy saving health.* "Thy salvation."

MATTHEW HENRY

their fathers. The Israelites indeed that were of old desired that God's name might be known among the Gentiles; those counterfeit Jews were enraged at the preaching of the gospel to the Gentiles. (2) As a prophecy that it shall be as he here prays.

2. Three things are here prayed for, with reference to the Gentiles:—

(1) That divine revelation might be sent among them, *v.* 2. "Let them all know, as well as we do, *what is good and what the Lord our God requires of them;* let them be blessed and honoured with the same righteous statutes and judgments which are so much the praise of our nation and the envy of all its neighbours," Deut. iv. 8. If God make known his way to us, and we walk in it, he will show us his saving health, l. 23. Those that have themselves experimentally known the pleasantness of God's ways, and the comforts of his salvation, cannot but desire and pray that they may be known to others, even among all nations.

(2) That divine worship may be set up among them, as it will be where divine revelation is received and embraced (*v.* 3): "*Let the people praise thee, O God!* let them have matter for praise, let them have hearts for praise; yea, let not only some, but *all the people, praise thee.*" It is a prayer, [1] That the gospel might be preached to them, and then they would have cause enough to praise God, as for the day-spring after a long and dark night. [2] That they might be converted and brought into the church, and then they would have a disposition to praise God. [3] That they might be incorporated into solemn assemblies, that they might all together praise him with one mind and one mouth.

(3) That the divine government may be acknowledged (*v.* 4): *O let the nations be glad, and sing for joy!* The joy he wishes to the nations is holy joy; for it is joy that *God has taken to himself his great power and has reigned.* Let them be glad that *thou shalt judge the people righteously.* Let us all be glad that we are not to be one another's judges, but that he that judges us is the Lord, whose judgment we are sure is according to truth.

III. He concludes with a joyful prospect of all good when God shall do this, when the nations shall be converted and brought to praise God.

1. The lower world shall smile upon them, and they shall have the fruits of that (*v.* 6): *Then shall the earth yield her increase.* Not but that God gave rain from heaven and fruitful seasons to the nations when they *sat in darkness* (Acts xiv. 17); but when they were converted the earth yielded its increase to God; and then it was fruitful to some good purpose. Then it yielded its increase more than before to the comfort of men, who through Christ acquired a covenant-title to the fruits of it and had a sanctified use of it.

2. The upper world shall smile upon them, and they shall have the favours of that, which is much better: *God, even our own God, shall bless us, v.* 6. And again (*v.* 7), *God shall bless us.* We receive the increase of the earth as a mercy indeed when with it God, even our own God, gives us his blessing.

3. All the world shall hereby be brought to do like them: *The ends of the earth shall fear him,* that is, worship him, which is to be done with a godly fear.

JAMIESON, FAUSSET, BROWN

3-5. *Thanks* will be rendered for the blessings of His wise and holy government (cf. Isa. 2:3, 4; 11:4).

6, 7. The blessings of a fruitful harvest are mentioned as types of greater and spiritual blessings, under which all nations shall fear and love God.

ADAM CLARKE

When or by whom this psalm was written cannot be ascertained. It seems to be simply a prophecy concerning the calling of the Gentiles, the preaching of the apostles, and the diffusion and influence of Christianity in the world. It is a fine piece of devotion, and it would be nearly impossible to read or repeat it with a cold and unaffected heart.

CHARLES H. SPURGEON:

"O let the nations be glad and sing for joy" (67:4), or, they shall joy and triumph. When men know God's way and see his salvation, it brings to their hearts much happiness. Nothing creates gladness so speedily, surely, and abidingly as the salvation of God. Nations never will be glad till they follow the leadership of the great Shepherd; they may shift their modes of government from monarchies to republics, and from republics to communes, but they will retain their wretchedness till they bow before the Lord of all. What a sweet word is that "to sing for joy!" Some sing for form, others for show, some as a duty, others as an amusement, but to sing from the heart because overflowing joy must find a vent, this is to sing indeed. Whole nations will do this when Jesus reigns over them in the power of his grace. We have heard hundreds and even thousands sing in chorus, but what will it be to hear whole nations lifting up their voices, as the noise of many waters and like great thunders. When shall the age of song begin? When shall groans and murmurs be exchanged for holy hymns and joyful melodies?

"For thou shalt judge the people righteously." Wrong on the part of governors is a fruitful source of national woe, but where the Lord rules, rectitude is supreme. He does ill to none. His laws are righteousness itself. He rights all wrongs and releases all who are oppressed. Justice on the throne is a fit cause for national exultation.

—The Treasury of David

PSALM 68

To the chief musician. A psalm *or* song of David.

Verses 1–6

I. David prays that God would appear in his glory,

1. For the confusion of his enemies (*v.* 1, 2): "*Let God arise,* as a judge to pass sentence upon them, as a general to take the field and do execution upon them; *and let them be scattered.* Let God arise, as the sun when he goes forth in his strength; and the children of darkness shall be scattered, as the shadows of the evening flee before the rising sun." Thus does David comment upon Moses's prayer, and not only repeats it with application to himself and his own times, but enlarges upon it, to direct us how to make use of scripture-prayers. Though we are to pray for our enemies as such, yet we are to pray against God's enemies as such, against their enmity to him and all their attempts upon his kingdom.

2. For the comfort and joy of his own people (*v.* 3): "*Let the righteous be glad,* that are now in sorrow; *let them rejoice before God,* let them rejoice with gladness."

II. He praises God for his glorious appearances,

1. As a great God, infinitely great (*v.* 4): He *rides upon the heavens, by his name JAH.* He is the spring of all the motions of the heavenly bodies, as he that

PSALM 68

Vss. 1-35. This is a *Psalm-song* (cf. Psalm 30, title), perhaps suggested by David's victories, which secured his throne and gave rest to the nation. In general terms, the judgment of God on the wicked, and the equity and goodness of His government to the pious, are celebrated. The sentiment is illustrated by examples of God's dealings, cited from the Jewish history and related in highly poetical terms. Hence the writer intimates an expectation of equal and even greater triumphs and summons all nations to unite in praises of the God of Israel. The Psalm is evidently typical of the relation which God, in the person of His Son, sustains to the Church (cf. vs. 18).

1-3. Cf. Numbers 10:35; Psalm 1:4; 22:14, on the figures here used. **before him**—as in vs. 2, *from* His presence, as dreaded; but in vs. 3, *in* His presence, as under His protection (Ps. 61:7). **the righteous**—all truly pious, whether of Israel or not. **4. extol him . . . heavens**—lit., "cast up for Him who rideth in the deserts," or "wilderness" (cf. vs. 7), alluding to the poetical representation of His leading His people in the wilderness as a conqueror, before whom a way is to be prepared, or "cast up" (cf. Isa. 40:3; 62:

PSALM 68

It is probable that this psalm, or a part of it at least, might have been composed by Moses, to be recited when the Israelites journeyed (see Num. x. 35); and that David, on the same model, constructed this psalm. It might have been sung also in the ceremony of transporting the ark from Kirjath-jearim to Jerusalem, or from the house of Obed-edom to the Tabernacle erected at Sion.

I know not how to undertake a comment on this psalm; it is the most difficult in the whole Psalter. There are customs here referred to which I do not fully understand; there are words whose meaning I cannot, to my own satisfaction, ascertain; and allusions which are to me inexplicable. Yet of the composition itself I have the highest opinion. It is sublime beyond all comparison; it is constructed with an art truly admirable; it possesses all the dignity of the sacred language. None but David could have composed it.

1. *Let God arise.* This was sung when the Levites took up the ark upon their shoulders; see Num. x. 35-36.

MATTHEW HENRY

rides in the chariot sets it a-going, has a supreme command of the influences of heaven. He rules these by his name, *Jah*, or *Jehovah*, a self-existent self-sufficient being, the fountain of all being, power, motion, and perfection; this is his name for ever.

2. As a gracious God, a God of mercy and tender compassion. He is great, but being a God of great power, he uses his power for the relief of those that are distressed, *v.* 5, 6. The fatherless, the widows, the solitary, find him a God all-sufficient to them. He that *rides on the heavens* glories that he is *a Father of the fatherless. Though God be high, yet has he respect unto the lowly.* He is *a Father of the fatherless*, to pity them, to bless them, to teach them, to provide for them, to portion them. They have liberty to call him Father, and to plead their relation to him as their guardian, cxlvi. 9; x. 14, 18. He is a patron of the widows, to give them counsel and to redress their grievances, to own them and plead their cause, Prov. xxii. 23. He has an ear open to all their complaints and a hand open to all their wants. He is so *in his holy habitation*; let them go to his holy habitation, to his word and ordinances; there they may find him and find comfort in him. When families are to be built up he is the founder of them: *God sets the solitary in families*, brings those into comfortable relations that were lonely, he *makes those dwell at home that were* forced to *seek* for relief *abroad* (so Dr. Hammond), putting those that were destitute into a way of getting their livelihood.

3. As a righteous God, (1) In relieving the oppressed. He *brings out those that are bound with chains*, and sets those at liberty who were unjustly imprisoned and brought into servitude. No chains can detain those whom God will make free. (2) In reckoning with the oppressors: *The rebellious dwell in a dry land* and have no comfort in that which they have got by fraud and injury.

Verses 7–14

Fresh mercies should put us in mind of former mercies and revive our grateful sense of them. Let it never be forgotten.

I. That God himself was the guide of Israel through the wilderness, *v.* 7. It was not a journey, but a march, for they went as soldiers, as an army with banners.

II. That he manifested his glorious presence with them at Mount Sinai, *v.* 8. Never did any people see the glory of God, nor hear his voice, as Israel did, Deut. iv. 32, 33. Never had any people such an excellent law given them, so expounded, so enforced. *Sinai itself*, that vast mountain, that long ridge of mountains, *was moved at the presence of God*; see Judges v. 4, 5; Deut. xxxiii. 2; Hab. iii. 3. It would encourage their faith in him and dependence upon him. Whatever mountains of difficulty lay in the way of their happy settlement, he that could move Sinai itself could remove them.

III. That he provided very comfortably for them both in the wilderness and in Canaan (*v.* 9, 10): *Thou didst send a plentiful rain and hast prepared of thy goodness for the poor.* This may refer, 1. To the victualling of their camp with manna in the wilderness, which was rained upon them, as were also the quails (lxxviii. 24, 27). Or, 2. To the seasonable supplies granted them in Canaan, that land *flowing with milk and honey*, which is said to *drink water of the rain of heaven*, Deut. xi. 11. This looks further to the spiritual provision made for God's Israel; the Spirit of grace and the gospel of grace are the plentiful rain with which God confirms his inheritance, and from which their fruit is found, Isa. xlv. 8.

IV. That he often gave them victory over their enemies. *The Lord gave the word*, as general of their armies. He raised up judges for them, gave them their commissions and instructions, and assured them of success. God gave them his word (*the word of the Lord* came unto them) and then *great was the company of the preachers*—prophets and *prophetesses*, for the word is feminine. *Kings of armies did flee*, retired without striking a stroke; they fled apace, fled and never rallied again. *She that tarried at home divided the spoil.* Not only the men, the soldiers that abode by the stuff, who were to share the prey (1 Sam. xxx. 24), but even the women that tarried at home had a share, which intimates the abundance of spoil that should be taken. *When the Almighty scattered kings for her* (for the church) *she was white as snow in Salmon*, purified and refined by the mercies of God; *when the host went forth against the enemy they kept themselves from every wicked thing*, and so the host returned victorious, and Israel by the victory were confirmed in their purity and piety. By the resurrection of Christ our spiritual enemies were made to flee, they were for ever disabled to hurt any of God's people.

JAMIESON, FAUSSET, BROWN

10). **by his name JAH**—or, Jehovah, of which it is a contraction (Exod. 15:3; Isa. 12:2) (*Hebrew*). **name**—or, perfections (Ps. 9:10; 20:1), which—

5, 6. are illustrated by the protection to the helpless, vindication of the innocent, and punishment of rebels, ascribed to Him.

setteth the solitary in families—lit., "settleth the lonely" (as wanderers) "at home." Though a general truth, there is perhaps allusion to the wandering and settlement of the Israelites.

rebellious dwell in a dry land—removed from all the comforts of home.

7, 8. (Cf. Exod. 19:16-18.) **thou wentest**—in the pillar of fire. **thou didst march**—lit., "in Thy tread," Thy majestic movement.

even Sinai itself—lit., "that Sinai," as in Judg. 5:5.

9, 10. a plentiful rain—a rain of gifts, as manna and quails. **Thy congregation**—lit., "troop," as in II Sam. 23:11, 13—the military aspect of the people being prominent, according to the figures of the context. **therein**—i.e., in the land of promise. **the poor**—Thy humble people (vs. 9; cf. Ps. 10:17; 12:5).

11. gave the word—i.e., of triumph.

company—or, choir of females, celebrating victory (Exod. 15:20). **12. Kings of armies**—i.e., with their armies. **she that . . . at home**—Mostly women so remained, and the ease of victory appears in that such, without danger, quietly enjoyed the spoils.

ADAM CLARKE

4. *Extol him that rideth upon the heavens by his name JAH. Baaraboth*, which we render "in the high heavens," is here of doubtful signification. Probably it may mean the gloomy desert, through which God, in the chariot of His glory, led the Israelites. *By his name JAH. Yah*, probably a contraction of the word *Yehovah*. It might be translated "the Self-existent."

7. *O God, when thou wentest forth.* This and the following verse most manifestly refer to the passage of the Israelites through the wilderness.

9. *Didst send a plentiful rain.* "A shower of liberality." I believe this to refer to the manna by which God refreshed and preserved alive the weary and hungry Israelites.

10. *Thy congregation hath dwelt therein.* "Thy living creature." Does not this refer to the quails that were brought to the camp of the Israelites, and *dwelt*, as it were, round about it?

11. *Great was the company of those that published it. Hammebasseroth tsaba rab;* "Of the female preachers there was a great host." Such is the literal translation of this passage; the reader may make of it what he pleases. But the publication of good news, or of any joyful event, belonged to the women. It was they who announced it to the people at large; and to this universal custom, which prevails to the present day, the Psalmist alludes.

MATTHEW HENRY

V. That from a low and despised condition they had been advanced to splendour and prosperity. When they were bond-slaves in Egypt, and afterwards when they were oppressed sometimes by one potent neighbour and sometimes by another, they did, as it were, *lie among the pots* or rubbish, as despised broken vessels. But God, at length, *delivered them from the pots* (lxxxi. 6), and in David's time they were in a fair way to be one of the most prosperous kingdoms in the world, *like the wings of a dove covered with silver, v.* 13. "And so," says Dr. Hammond, "under Christ's kingdom, the heathen idolaters worshipping wood and stone, and given up to the vilest lusts, should from that detestable condition be advanced to the service of Christ, and the practice of all Christian virtues, the greatest inward beauties in the world."

Verses 15–21

David here comes to give him praise as Zion's God in a special manner; compare ix. 11. *Sing praises to the Lord who dwelleth in Zion*, for which reason Zion is called *the hill of God.*

I. He compares it with the hill of Bashan and other high and fruitful hills, and prefers it before them, *v.* 15, 16. It is true, Zion was but little and low in comparison with them, yet it has the pre-eminence above them all, that it is *the hill of God.* "Why do you insult over poor Zion, and boast of your own height? This is the hill which God has chosen." Zion was especially honourable because it was a type of the gospel church, which is therefore called Mount Zion (Heb. xii. 22), and this is intimated here, when he said, *The Lord will dwell in it for ever.*

II. He compares it with Mount Sinai, of which he had spoken (*v.* 8), and shows that it has the Shechinah or divine presence in it as really, though not as sensibly, as Sinai itself had, *v.* 17. Angels are *the chariots of God.* They are vastly numerous: *Twenty thousands*, even thousands multiplied. There is an *innumerable company of angels* in the heavenly Jerusalem, Heb. xii. 22. Some read the last words of the verse, *Sinai is in the sanctuary;* that is, the sanctuary was to Israel instead of Mount Sinai, whence they received divine oracles.

III. The glory of Mount Zion was the King whom God *set on that holy hill* (ii. 6). Of his ascension the psalmist here speaks, and to it his language is expressly applied (Eph. iv. 8): *Thou hast ascended on high* (*v.* 18); compare xlvii. 5, 6. Christ's ascending on high is spoken of to his honour. He then triumphed over the gates of hell. He led *captivity captive;* that is, he led his captives in triumph, as great conquerors used to do, Col. ii. 15. He led those captive who had led us captive, and who, if he had not interposed, would have held us captive for ever. Nay, he *led captivity itself captive*, having quite broken the power of sin and Satan. This intimates the complete victory which Jesus Christ obtained over our spiritual enemies; it was such that through him *we also are more than conquerors*, that is, triumphers, Rom. viii. 37. He then opened the gates of heaven to all believers: *Thou hast received gifts for men.* He *gave gifts to men*, so the apostle reads it, Eph. iv. 8. And he gave what he had received; having received power to give eternal life, he bestows it upon *as many as were given him*, John xvii. 2. *Thou hast received gifts in man* (so the margin), that is, in the human nature which Christ was pleased to clothe himself with, that he might be a *merciful and faithful high priest in things pertaining to God.* To magnify the kindness and love of Christ to us in receiving these gifts for us, he received them for the *rebellious also*, for those that had been rebellious. Perhaps it is especially meant of the Gentiles, that had been *enemies in their minds by wicked works*, Col. i. 21. This magnifies the grace of Christ exceedingly that through him rebels are, upon their submission, not only pardoned, but preferred. Christ came to a rebellious world, not to condemn it, but that through him it might be saved. He *received gifts for the rebellious*, that *the Lord God might dwell among them*, that he might set up a church in a rebellious world.

IV. The glory of Zion's King is that he is a Saviour and benefactor to all his willing people and a consuming fire to all those that persist in rebellion against him, *v.* 19–21. We have here good and evil, life and death, the blessing and the curse, set before us (Mark xvi. 16). So many, so weighty, are the gifts of God's bounty to us that he may be truly said to *load us* with them; he *pours out blessings till there is no room to receive them*, Mal. iii. 10. *He is our God*, and therefore he will be the God of eternal salvation to us; for that only will answer the vast extent of his covenant-relation to us as our God. Those that persist in their enmity to him will certainly be ruined (*v.* 21): *God shall wound the head of his enemies,*—of

JAMIESON, FAUSSET, BROWN

13. Some translate this, "When ye shall lie between the borders, ye shall . . . ," comparing the peaceful rest in the borders or limits of the promised land to the proverbial beauty of a gentle dove. Others understand by the word rendered "pots," the smoked sides of caves, in which the Israelites took refuge from enemies in the times of the judges; or, taking the whole figuratively, the rows of stones on which cooking vessels were hung; and thus that a contrast is drawn between their former low and afflicted state and their succeeding prosperity. In either case, a state of quiet and peace is described by a beautiful figure. **14.** Their enemies dispersed, the contrast of their prosperity with their former distress is represented by that of the snow with the dark and somber shades of Salmon.

15, 16. Mountains are often symbols of nations (Ps. 46:2; 65:6). That of Bashan, northeast of Palestine, denotes a heathen nation, which is described as a "hill of God," or a great hill. Such are represented as envious of the hill (Zion) on which God resides;

17. and, to the assertion of God's purpose to make it His dwelling, is added evidence of His protecting care. He is described as in the midst of His heavenly armies—**thousands of angels**—lit., "thousands of repetitions," or, thousands of thousands—i.e., of chariots. The word—**angels**—was perhaps introduced in our version, from Deuteronomy 33:2, and Galations 3:19. They are, of course, implied as conductors of the chariots. **as . . . Sinai, in the holy place**—i.e., He has appeared in Zion as once in Sinai. **18.** From the scene of conquest He ascends to His throne, leading—**captivity** [or, many captives (Judg. 5:12)] **captive. received gifts for men**—accepting their homage, even when forced, as that of rebels. **that the Lord God might dwell**—or lit., "to dwell, O LORD God" (cf. vs. 16)—i.e., to make this hill, His people or Church, His dwelling. This Psalm typifies the conquests of the Church under her divine leader, Christ. He, indeed, "who was with the Church in the wilderness" (Acts 7:38) is the ***Lord***, described in this ideal ascension. Hence Paul (Eph. 4:8) applies this language to describe His real ascension, when, having conquered sin, death, and hell, the Lord of glory triumphantly entered heaven, attended by throngs of adoring angels, to sit on the throne and wield the scepter of an eternal dominion. The phrase—**received gifts for** [or lit., "among"] **men**—is by Paul, "gave gifts to men." Both describe the acts of a conqueror, who receives and distributes spoils. The Psalmist uses "receiving" as evincing the success, Paul "gave" as the act, of the conqueror, who, having subdued his enemies, proceeds to reward his friends. The special application of the passage by Paul was in proof of Christ's exaltation. What the Old Testament represents of His descending and ascending corresponds with His history. He who descended is the same who has ascended. As then ascension was an element of His triumph, so is it now; and He, who, in His humiliation, must be recognized as our vicarious sacrifice and the High Priest of our profession, must also be adored as Head of His Church and author of all her spiritual benefits.

19-21. God daily and fully supplies us. The issues or escapes from death are under His control, who is the God that saves us, and destroys His and our enemies.

wound the head—or, violently destroy (Num. 24:8; Ps. 110:6).

ADAM CLARKE

15. *The hill of God is as the hill of Bashan.* This and the following verse should be read thus: "Is Mount Bashan the craggy mount, Mount Bashan, the mount of God? Why envy ye, ye craggy mounts? This is the mount of God in which He has desired to dwell."

17. *The chariots of God are twenty thousand.* "Two myriads of thousands doubled." Does not this mean simply 40,000? A myriad is 10,000; two myriads, 20,000; these doubled, 40,000.

18. *Thou hast ascended on high.* When the ark had reached the top of Sion, and was deposited in the place assigned for it, the singers joined in the following chorus. This seems to be an allusion to a military triumph. The conqueror was placed on a very elevated chariot. *Led captivity captive.* The conquered kings and generals were usually tied behind the chariot of the conqueror—bound to it, bound together, and walked after it, to grace the triumph of the victor.

Thou hast received gifts for men. "And *gave* gifts *unto* men," Eph. iv. 8. At such times the conqueror threw money among the crowd. *Yea, for the rebellious also.* Even to the rebellious, those who were his enemies.

That the Lord God might dwell among them. Yah Elohim, "the self-existing God"; see v. 4. The conqueror now coming to fix his abode among the conquered people to organize them under his laws, to govern and dispense justice among them. The whole of this is very properly applied by St. Paul, Eph. iv. 5, to the resurrection and glory of Christ.

19. *Blessed be the Lord, who daily loadeth us.* "With benefits" is not in the text. Perhaps it would be better to translate the clause thus: "Blessed be Adonai, our Prop day by day, who supports us." Or, "Blessed be the Lord, who supports us day by day." Or as the Vulgate, Septuagint, and Arabic: "Blessed be the Lord daily, our God who makes our journey prosperous; even the God of our salvation." The word *amas*, which we translate "to load," signifies "to lift, bear up, support," or "to bear a burden for another." Hence it would not be going far from the ideal meaning to translate: "Blessed is the Lord day by day, who bears our burdens for us."

20. *The issues from death.* The "going out" or "exodus" from death—from the land of Egypt and house of bondage. Or the expression may mean, Life and death are in the hand of God. "He can create, and he destroys."

MATTHEW HENRY

Satan the old serpent (of whom it was by the first promise foretold that *the seed of the woman* should *break his head,* Gen. iii. 15). He will *wound the hairy scalp of such a one as goeth on still in his trespasses.* In calling the head *the hairy scalp* perhaps there is an allusion to Absalom, whose bushy hair was his halter. Or it denotes the most fierce and barbarous of his enemies, who let their hair grow, to make themselves look the more frightful.

Verses 22–31

In these verses we have three things:—

I. The gracious promise which God makes of the redemption of his people, and their victory over his and their enemies (*v.* 22, 23): *The Lord said,* "I will do great things for my people, as the God of their salvation," *v.* 20. "I will *again bring them from the depths of the sea,*" as he did Israel when he brought them out of the slavery of Egypt into the ease and liberty of the wilderness; "and *I will again bring them from Bashan,*" as he did Israel when he brought them from their wants and wanderings in the wilderness into the fulness and settlement of the land of Canaan; for the land of Bashan was on the other side Jordan, where they had wars with Sihon and Og, and whence their next removal was into Canaan. But this is not all. He will make them victorious over their enemies (*v.* 23): *That thy feet may be dipped,* as thou passest along, *in the blood of thy enemies,* and the *tongue of thy dogs* may lap *in the same.* Dogs licked the blood of Ahab; and, in the destruction of the anti-christian generation, we read of blood up *to the horses' bridles,* Rev. xiv. 20.

II. The welcome which God's own people shall give to these glorious discoveries of his grace. "*They have seen,* thy people have seen, *thy goings, O God!* While others regard not the work of the Lord, they have seen *the goings of my God, my King, in the sanctuary.*" An active faith appropriates God; he is God and King; but that is not all, he is *my* God and *my* King. God's most remarkable outgoings are, even in the sanctuary, in and by his word and ordinances, and among his people in the gospel church especially. When we see *his goings in his sanctuary,* those that are immediately employed in the service of the temple praise him, *v.* 25. It was expected that the Levites should lead in his praises. And, it being a day of extraordinary triumph, *among them were damsels playing with timbrels.* "Thus (says Dr. Hammond) when Christ has gone up to heaven the apostles shall celebrate and publish it to all the world, and even the women that were witnesses of it shall affectionately join with them in divulging it." Let all the people of Israel in their solemn religious assembly give glory to God: *Bless God,* not only in temples, but in the synagogues, or schools of the prophets, or wherever there is a congregation of those that *come forth from the fountain of Israel.* Public mercies, which we jointly share in, call for public thanksgivings, which all should join in. Let those among them who are the most eminent go before the rest in praising God, *v.* 27. There was *little Benjamin* (that was the royal tribe in Saul's time) *with their rulers, the princes of Judah* (that was the royal tribe in David's time), and *their council,* their captains or leaders. We depend upon him, for the perfecting of what he has begun, *v.* 28. In the former part of the verse the psalmist speaks to Israel: "*Thy God has commanded thy strength;* that is, whatever is done for thee, or whatever strength thou hast to help thyself, it comes from God, his power and grace, and the word which he has commanded." In the latter part he speaks to God, encouraged by his experiences: "*Strengthen, O God! that which thou hast wrought for us.* Lord, confirm what thou hast commanded, perform what thou hast promised, and bring to a happy end that good work which thou hast so gloriously begun."

III. The powerful invitation and inducement which would hereby be given to those that are without to come in and join themselves to the church, *v.* 29–31. This was in part fulfilled by the accession of many proselytes to the Jewish religion in the days of David and Solomon; but it was to have its full accomplishment in the conversion of the Gentile nations to the faith of Christ, Eph. iii. 6. Some shall submit for fear (*v.* 30): "*The company of spearmen,* that stand it out against Christ and his gospel, that are furious and outrageous as a multitude of bulls, fat and wanton as the calves of the people" (which is a description of those Jews and Gentiles that opposed the gospel of Christ and did what they could to prevent the setting up of his kingdom in the world), "Lord, rebuke them, abate their pride and confound their devices, till, conquered by the convictions of their consciences, they be every one of them brought, to *submit themselves with pieces of silver,* as being glad

JAMIESON, FAUSSET, BROWN

goeth on still in . . . trespasses—perseveringly impenitent.

22. Former examples of God's deliverance are generalized: as He has done, so He will do. **from Bashan**—the farthest region; and—**depths of the sea**—the severest afflictions. Out of all, God will bring them.

The figures of vs. 23 denote the completeness of the conquest, not implying any savage cruelty (cf. II Kings 9:36; Isa. 63:1-6; Jer. 15:3).

24-27. The triumphal procession, after the deliverance, is depicted. **They have seen**—impersonally, "There have been seen." **the goings of my God**—as leading the procession; the ark, the symbol of His presence, being in front.

The various bands of music (vs. 25) follow, and all who are—**from** [or lit., "of"] **the fountain of Israel**—i.e., lineal descendants of Jacob, are invited to unite in the doxology. Then by one of the nearest tribes, one of the most eminent, and two of the most remote, are represented the whole nation of Israel, passing forward (Num. 7).

28, 29. Thanks for the past, and confident prayer for the future victories of Zion are mingled in a song of praise.

30. The strongest nations are represented by the strongest beasts (cf. *Margin*).

ADAM CLARKE

22. *From the depths of the sea.* All this seems to speak of the defeat of the Egyptians and the miraculous passage of the Red Sea.

27. *There is little Benjamin.* This is a description of another part of the procession.

28. *Thy God hath commanded.* This and the following verses are what they sang.

30. *Rebuke the company of spearmen.* "The wild beast of the reed"—the crocodile or hippopotamus, the emblem of Pharaoh and the Egyptians; thus all the versions. Our translators have mistaken the meaning, but they have put the true sense in the margin.

MATTHEW HENRY

to make their peace with the church upon any terms." Many, by being rebuked, have been happily saved from being ruined. But as for those that will not submit, he prays for their dispersion, which amounts to a prophecy of it: *Scatter thou the people that delight in war.* This may refer to the unbelieving Jews, who delighted in making war upon the holy seed, and would not submit themselves, and were therefore scattered over the face of the earth. David had himself been a man of war, but could appeal to God that he never delighted in war and bloodshed for its own sake. Others shall submit willingly (*v.* 29, 31): *Because of thy temple at Jerusalem* (this David speaks of in faith, for the temple of Jerusalem was not built in his time, only the materials and model were prepared) *kings shall bring presents unto thee.* He mentions *Egypt* and *Ethiopia*, two countries out of which subjects and suppliants were least to be expected (*v.* 31): *Princes shall come out of Egypt* as ambassadors to seek God's favour and submit to him; and they shall be accepted, for *the Lord of hosts shall* thereupon *bless them, saying, Blessed be Egypt my people*, Isa. xix. 25. Even Ethiopia, that had stretched out her hands against God's Israel (2 Chron. xiv. 9), should now *stretch out her hands unto God*, in prayer, in presents, and to take hold on him, and that soon.

Verses 32–35

The psalmist, having prayed for the Gentiles, here invites them to come in and join with the devout Israelites in praising God, intimating that their accession to the church would be the matter of their joy and praise (*v.* 32): Let the *kingdoms of the earth sing praises to the Lord.*

I. Because of his supreme and sovereign dominion: *He rides upon the heavens of heavens which were of old* (*v.* 33); compare *v.* 4. He has from the beginning, nay, from before all time, prepared his throne; he sits on the circuit of heaven, and dispenses the influences of his power and goodness to this lower world.

II. Because of his awful and terrible majesty: *He sends out his voice, and that a mighty voice.* This may refer either generally to the thunder, which is called *the voice of the Lord* and is said to be *powerful and full of majesty* (xxix. 3, 4), or in particular to that thunder in which God spoke to Israel at Mount Sinai.

III. Because of his mighty power: *Ascribe you strength unto God* (*v.* 34). *Thine is the kingdom and power*, and therefore *thine is the glory.* We must acknowledge his power. In the kingdom of grace: *His excellency is over Israel;* he shows his sovereign care in protecting and governing his church. In the kingdom of providence: *His strength is in the clouds*, whence comes the thunder of his power, the *small rain, and the great rain of his strength.*

IV. Because of the glory of his sanctuary and the wonders wrought there (*v.* 35): *O God! thou art terrible out of thy holy places.* God is to be admired and adored with reverence and godly fear by all those that attend him in his holy places, that receive his oracles. Nor is any attribute of God more dreadful to sinners than his holiness.

V. Because of the grace bestowed upon his people: *The God of Israel is he that gives strength and power unto his people*, which the gods of the nations, that were vanity and a lie, could not give to their worshippers; how should they help them, when they could not help themselves? If it be the God of Israel that gives strength and power unto his people, they ought to say, *Blessed be God.* If all be from him, let all be to him.

JAMIESON, FAUSSET, BROWN

thy temple at [or lit., "over"] **Jerusalem**—His palace or residence (Ps. 5:7) symbolized His protecting presence among His people, and hence is the object of homage on the part of others.

31 Princes—or, lit., "fat ones," the most eminent from the most wealthy, and the most distant nation, represent the universal subjection.

stretch out [or, make to run] **her hands**—denoting haste.

32-36. To Him who is presented as riding in triumph through His ancient heavens and proclaiming His presence—to Him who, in nature, and still more in the wonders of His spiritual government, out of His holy place (Ps. 43:3), is terrible, who rules His Church, and, by His Church, rules the world in righteousness—let all nations and kingdoms give honor and power and dominion evermore.

ADAM CLARKE

31. *Ethiopia shall soon stretch out her hands unto God.* There were Egyptians at Jerusalem on the Day of Pentecost, who, St. Hilary tells us, on their return to their own country proclaimed what they had seen, and became in that country the ambassadors of Christ. The Ethiopian eunuch was one of the first among the Gentiles who received the gospel. Thus *princes* or chief men came out of Egypt, and Ethiopia stretched out her hands to God. The Hebrew is very emphatic: "Cush will cause her hands to run out to God."

34. *His strength is in the clouds.* This refers to the bursting, rattling, and pounding of thunder and lightning.

35. *O God, thou art terrible out of thy holy places.* The sanctuary and heaven. Out of the former He had often shone forth with consuming splendor; see the case of Korah and his company. Out of the latter He had often appeared in terrible majesty in storms, thunder, lightning. *He that giveth strength and power unto his people.* Therefore that people must be invincible who have this strong and irresistible God for their Support.

MATTHEW HENRY

PSALM 69

To the chief musician upon Shoshannim. *A psalm* of David.

Verses 1–12

In these verses David complains of his troubles.

I. His complaints are very sad, and he pours them out before the Lord, as one that hoped thus to ease himself of a burden that lay very heavy upon him.

1. He complains of the deep impressions that his troubles made upon his spirit (*v.* 1, 2): "The *waters of affliction*, those bitter waters, *have come unto my soul*, not only threaten my life, but disquiet my mind, so that I cannot enjoy God and myself as I used to do." *The spirit of a man will sustain his infirmity;* but what shall we do when the spirit is wounded? That was David's case here. This points at Christ's sufferings in his soul, and the inward agony he was in when he said, *Now is my soul troubled;* and, *My soul is exceedingly sorrowful;* for it was his soul that he made an offering for sin.

2. He complains of the long continuance of his troubles (*v.* 3): *I am weary of my crying.* He cried

JAMIESON, FAUSSET, BROWN

PSALM 69

Vss. 1-36. *Upon Shoshannim*—(cf. Ps. 45, title). Mingling the language of prayer and complaint, the sufferer, whose condition is here set forth, pleads for God's help as one suffering in His cause, implores the divine retribution on his malicious enemies, and, viewing his deliverance as sure, promises praise by himself, and others, to whom God will extend like blessings. This Psalm is referred to seven times in the New Testament as prophetical of Christ and the gospel times. Although the character in which the Psalmist appears to some in vs. 5 is that of a sinner, yet his *condition* as a *sufferer* innocent of alleged crimes sustains the *typical* character of the composition, and it may be therefore regarded throughout, as the 22d, as typically expressive of the feelings of our Saviour in the flesh.

1, 2—(Cf. Psalm 40:2.) **come in unto my soul**—lit., "come even to my soul," endanger my life by drowning (Jonah 2:5).

ADAM CLARKE

PSALM 69

The title is: "To the chief Musician upon Shoshannim, A Psalm of David." See this title explained on Psalm xlv.

The psalm is supposed to have been written during the Captivity, and to have been the work of some Levite divinely inspired. It is a very fine composition, equal to most in the Psalter. Several portions of it seem to have a reference to our Lord; to His advent, passion, resurrection, the vocation of the Gentiles, the establishment of the Christian Church, and the reprobation of the Jews. The ninth verse is quoted by St. John, chap. ii. 17. The twenty-first verse is quoted by St. Matthew, chap. xxvii. 34, 48; by St. Mark, chap. xv. 23; by St. John, chap. xix. 29; and applied to the sufferings of our Lord, in the treatment He received from the Jews. St. Paul quotes the twenty-second as a prophecy of the wickedness of the Jews, and the punishment

MATTHEW HENRY

to his God, and the more death was in his view the more life was in his prayers; yet he had not immediately an answer of peace given. *My eyes fail while I wait for my God.* Yet his pleading this with God is an indication that he is resolved not to give up believing and praying. His throat is dried, but his heart is not; his eyes fail, but his faith does not. Thus our Lord Jesus, on the cross, cried out, *Why hast thou forsaken me?* yet, at the same time, he kept hold of his relation to him: *My God, my God.*

3. He complains of the malice and multitude of his enemies, their injustice and cruelty, and the hardships they put upon him, *v.* 4. "*They hate me without a cause;* I never did them the least injury, that they should bear me such ill-will." Our Saviour applies this to himself (John xv. 25): *They hated me without a cause.* These enemies were not to be despised, but were very formidable both for their number —*They are more than the hairs of my head*—and for their strength—They *are mighty* in authority and power. *Then I restored that which I took not away.* Applying this to David, it was what his enemies compelled him to, and it was what he consented to, that, if possible, he might pacify them and make them to be at peace with him. But, applying it to Christ, it is an observable description of the satisfaction which he made to God for our sin by his blood: *Then he restored that which he took not away;* he underwent the punishment that was due to us, paid our debt, suffered for our offence. God's glory, in some instances of it, was taken away by the sin of man; man's honour, and peace, and happiness, were taken away; it was not he that took them away, and yet by the merit of his death he restored them.

4. He complains of the unkindness of his friends and relations (*v.* 8): "*I have become a stranger to my brethren;* they make themselves strange to me and are shy of conversing with me and ashamed to own me." This was fulfilled in Christ, whose *brethren did not believe on him* (John vii. 5), who *came to his own and his own received him not* (John i. 11), and who was forsaken by his disciples.

5. He complains of the contempt that was put upon him and the reproach with which he was continually loaded. And in this especially his complaint points at Christ, who for our sakes submitted to the greatest disgrace and made himself of no reputation. David here takes notice of aggravations of the indignities done him. They ridiculed him for that by which he both humbled himself and honoured God. When David, purely in devotion to God and to testify his respect to him, *wept, and chastened his soul with fasting,* and *made sackcloth his garment,* as humble penitents used to do, instead of commending his devotion, they did all they could to prevent others from following his good example; for *that was to his reproach.* They laughed at him as a fool for mortifying himself thus; and even for this he *became a proverb to them.* Even the gravest and the most honourable, from whom better was expected: *Those that sit in the gate speak against me.* He was the song of the drunkards; they made themselves and their companions merry with him. See what is commonly the lot of the best of men: those that are the praise of the wise are the song of fools. But it is easy to those that rightly judge of things to despise being thus despised.

II. His confessions of sin are very serious (*v.* 5): "*O God! thou knowest my foolishness,* both what is and what is not; and therefore thou knowest how innocent I am of those crimes which they charge upon me." This is the genuine confession of a penitent, who knows that he cannot prosper in covering his sin, and that *therefore* it is his wisdom to acknowledge it, because it is naked and open before God. He knows the corruption of our nature: *Thou knowest the foolishness* that is bound up in my heart. He knows the transgressions of our lives, even those that are committed most secretly. They are all done in his sight, and are never cast behind his back till they are repented of and pardoned.

III. His supplications are very earnest. "*Save me, O God!* save me from sinking, from despairing." *Let not those that wait on thee, O Lord God of hosts! and that seek thee, O God of Israel! be ashamed and confounded for my sake.* This intimates his fear that if God did not appear for him it would be a discouragement to all other good people and would give their enemies occasion to triumph over them. If Jesus Christ had not been owned and accepted of his Father in his sufferings, all that seek God, and wait for him, would have been ashamed and confounded; but they have confidence towards God, and in his name come boldly to the throne [of grace.

IV. His plea is very powerful, *v.* 7, 9. "Lord, roll away the reproach, and plead my cause. *For thy*

JAMIESON, FAUSSET, BROWN

3—(Cf. Psalm 6:6.) **mine eyes fail**—in watching (Ps. 119:82).

4. hate me . . .—(Cf. John 15:25). On the number and power of his enemies (cf. Ps. 40:12).

then I restored . . . away—i.e., he suffered wrongfully under the imputation of robbery.

wept (and chastened) my soul—lit., "wept away my soul," a strongly figurative description of deep grief.

sit in the gate— public place (Prov. 31:31).

5. This may be regarded as an appeal, vindicating his innocence, as if he had said, "If sinful, thou knowest," etc. Though *David's condition* as a *sufferer* may *typify* Christ's, without requiring that a parallel be found *in character.*

6. for my sake—lit., "in me," in my confusion and shame.

ADAM CLARKE

they were to receive. He quotes the twenty-third verse in the same way. Those portions which the writers of the New Testament apply to our Lord, we may apply also; of others we should be careful.

1. *The waters are come in unto my soul.* I am in the deepest distress. The waters have broken their dikes, and are just ready to sweep me away! In the first, second, third, fourteenth, and fifteenth verses the Psalmist, speaking in the person of the captives in Babylon, compares their captivity to an abyss of waters, breaking all bounds, and ready to swallow them up; to a deep mire, in which there was no solid bottom, and no standing; and to a pit, in which they were about to be enclosed forever. This is strongly figurative, and very expressive.

3. *I am weary of my crying.* A pathetic description of the state of the poor captives for about seventy years.

4. *Then I restored that which I took not away.* I think, with Calmet, that this is a sort of proverbial expression, like such as these, "Those who suffered the wrong, pay the costs."

12. *They that sit in the gate.* At the gates were the courts for public justice.

MATTHEW HENRY

sake I have borne reproach." Those that are evil spoken of for well-doing may with a humble confidence leave it to God to *bring forth their righteousness as the light. The zeal of thy house has eaten me up.* Those that hate thee and thy house for that reason hate me, because they know how zealously affected I am to it. It is this that has eaten up all the love and respect I had among them. Or it may be construed as an instance of David's zeal for God's house, that he resented all the indignities done to God's name as if they had been done to his own name. He laid to heart all the contempt cast upon religion. Both the parts of this verse are applied to Christ. 1. It was an instance of his love to his Father that *the zeal of his house did even eat him up* when he whipped the buyers and sellers out of the temple, which reminded his disciples of this text, John ii. 17. 2. It was an instance of his self-denial, and that he pleased not himself, that the *reproaches of those that reproached God fell upon him* (Rom. xv. 3), and therein he set us an example.

Verses 13–21

They spoke ill of him for his fasting and praying, and for that he was made the song of the drunkards; but, notwithstanding that, he resolves to continue praying. Though we may be jeered for well-doing, we must never be jeered out of it. *As for me, my prayer is unto thee, O Lord!*

I. What his requests are. *Hear me* (*v.* 13), and again, *Hear me, O Lord!* (*v.* 16), *Hear me speedily* (*v.* 17), not only hear what I say, but grant what I ask. *Deliver me out of the mire;* let me not stick in it, so some, but help me out, and *set my feet on a rock,* xl. 2. "*Let me be delivered from those that hate me,* as a lamb from the paw of a lion, *v.* 14. Though I have come into deep waters (*v.* 2), let not the water-flood overflow me, *v.* 15. Let me not fall into the gulf of despair; let not that deep swallow me up; let not that pit shut her mouth upon me, for then I am undone." He prayed that God would turn to him (*v.* 16), that he would smile upon him, and not hide his face from him, *v.* 17.

II. What his pleas are to enforce these petitions. 1. He pleads God's mercy and truth (*v.* 13): *In the multitude of thy mercy hear me.* He repeats his argument taken from the mercy of God: "*Hear me,* for *thy lovingkindness is good.* It is so in itself; it is rich and plentiful and abundant. Turn to me, *according to the multitude of thy tender mercies,*" *v.* 16. 2. He pleads his own distress and affliction: "*Hide not thy face* from me, *for I am in trouble* (*v.* 17), and therefore need thy favour; therefore it will come seasonably, and therefore I shall know how to value it." *Thou hast known my reproach, my shame, and my dishonour.* The psalmist speaks the language of an ingenuous nature when he says (*v.* 20): *Reproach has broken my heart; I am full of heaviness;* for it bears hard upon one that knows the worth of a good name to be put under a bad character; but when we consider what an honour it is to be dishonoured for God, and to be counted worthy to suffer shame for his name (as they deemed it, Acts v. 41), we shall see there is no reason at all why it should be any heart-breaking to us. 3. He pleads the insolence and cruelty of his enemies (*v.* 18): "*My adversaries are all before thee* (*v.* 19); thou knowest what danger I am in from them, what enemies they are to thee, in what they do and design against me." One instance of their barbarity is given (*v.* 21): *They gave me gall for my meat* (the word signifies a bitter herb, and is often joined with wormwood) *and in my thirst they gave me vinegar to drink.* 4. He pleads the unkindness of his friends and his disappointment in them (*v.* 20): *I looked for some to take pity, but there was none;* they all failed him like the brooks in summer. This was fulfilled in Christ, for in his sufferings all his disciples forsook him and fled.

Verses 22–29

These imprecations are not David's prayers against his enemies, but prophecies of the destruction of Christ's persecutors, especially the Jewish nation, which our Lord himself foretold with tears, and which was accomplished about forty years after the death of Christ. The first two verses of this paragraph are expressly applied to the judgments of God upon the unbelieving Jews by the apostle (Rom. xi. 9, 10), and therefore the whole must look that way.

I. The judgments which should come upon the crucifiers of Christ; not upon all of them, for there were those who had a hand in his death and yet repented and found mercy (Acts ii. 23; iii. 14, 15), but upon those of them and their successors who justified it by an obstinate infidelity and rejection of his gospel, and by an inveterate enmity to his disciples and followers. See 1 Thess. ii. 15, 16. It

JAMIESON, FAUSSET, BROWN

7-12. This plea contemplates his relation to God as a sufferer in His cause. Reproach, domestic estrangement (Mark 3:21; John 7:5), exhaustion in God's service (John 2:17), revilings and taunts of base men were the sufferings.

13-15. With increasing reliance on God, he prays for help, describing his distress in the figures of vss. 1, 2.

16-18. These earnest terms are often used, and the address to God, as indifferent or averse, is found in Psalm 3:7; 22:24; 27:9, etc.

19, 20. Calling God to witness his distress, he presents its aggravation produced by the want of sympathizing friends (cf. Isa. 63:5; Mark 14:50). **21.** Instead of such, his enemies increase his pain by giving him most distasteful food and drink. The Psalmist may have thus described by figure what Christ found in reality (cf. John 19:29, 30).

ADAM CLARKE

9. *The zeal of thine house hath eaten me up.* The strong desire to promote Thy glory has absorbed all others. This verse is very properly applied to our Lord, John ii. 17.

13. *My prayer is unto thee, O Lord, in an acceptable time.* This seems to refer to the end of the Captivity, which Jeremiah had said should last seventy years, Jer. xxv. 11-12.

16. *Thy lovingkindness is good.* The word *chesed* signifies "exuberance of kindness"; and the word *rachamim,* which we translate *tender mercies,* signifies such affection as mothers bear to their young.

21. *They gave me also gall for my meat.* This is applied to our Lord, Matt. xxvii. 34.

MATTHEW HENRY

is here foretold,

1. That their sacrifices and offerings should be a mischief and prejudice to them (*v.* 22): *Let their table become a snare.* This may be understood of the altar of the Lord, which is called *his table and theirs* because in feasting upon the sacrifices they were partakers of the altar. Or it may be understood of their common creature-comforts, even their necessary food; they had given Christ gall and vinegar, and therefore justly shall their meat and drink be made gall and vinegar to them.

2. That they should never have the comfort either of that knowledge or of that peace which believers are blessed with in the gospel of Christ (*v.* 23). *Let their eyes be darkened,* that they see not the glory of God in the face of Christ. Their sin was that they would not see, but shut their eyes against the light. "Let them be driven to despair, and filled with constant confusion." This was fulfilled in the desperate counsels of the Jews when the Romans came upon them.

3. That they should fall and lie under God's anger and fiery indignation (*v.* 24): *Pour out thy indignation upon them.*

4. That their place and nation should be utterly taken away, the very thing they were afraid of, and to prevent which, as they pretended, they persecuted Christ (John xi. 48): *Let their habitation be desolate* (*v.* 25), which was fulfilled when their country was laid waste by the Romans, and *Zion, for their sakes, was ploughed as a field,* Mic. iii. 12. The temple was the house which they were in a particular manner proud of, but this was *left unto them desolate,* Matt. xxiii. 38. *Let none dwell in their tents,* which was remarkably fulfilled in Judah and Jerusalem, for after the destruction of the Jews it was long ere the country was inhabited to any purpose.

5. That their way to ruin should be downhill, and nothing should stop them (*v.* 27): "Lord, leave them to themselves, to *add iniquity to iniquity.*" *Let them not come into thy righteousness.* Not that God shuts out any from that righteousness, for the gospel excludes none that do not by their unbelief exclude themselves.

6. That they should be cut off from all hopes of happiness (*v.* 28): *Let them be blotted out of the book of the living;* let them not be suffered to live any longer, since, the longer they live, the more mischief they do. Multitudes of the unbelieving Jews fell by sword and famine. The nation, as a nation, was blotted out, and became not a people.

II. What the sin is for which these dreadful judgments should be brought upon them (*v.* 26): *They persecute him whom thou hast smitten, and talk to the grief of thy wounded.* Christ was he whom God had smitten, for *it pleased the Lord to bruise him,* and he was esteemed *stricken, smitten of God, and afflicted,* and therefore men *hid their faces from him,* Isa. liii. 3, 4, 10. They persecuted him with a rage reaching up to heaven; they cried, *Crucify him, crucify him.*

III. What the psalmist thinks of himself in the midst of all (*v.* 29): "*But I am poor and sorrowful;* that is the worst of my case, under outward afflictions, yet *written among the righteous,* and not under God's indignation as they are."

Verses 30–36

The psalmist here, both as a type of Christ and as an example to Christians, concludes a psalm with holy joy and praise which he began with complaints and remonstrances of his griefs.

I. He resolves to praise God himself (*v.* 30, 31): "*I will praise the name of God,* not only with my heart, but with my song, and *magnify him with thanksgiving.*" And *this shall please the Lord,* through Christ the Mediator of our praises as well as of our prayers, better than the most valuable of the legal sacrifices (*v.* 31), *an ox or bullock.* This is a plain intimation that in the days of the Messiah an end should be put, not only to the sacrifices of atonement, but to those of praise and acknowledgment which were instituted by the ceremonial law; and, instead of them, spiritual sacrifices of praise and thanksgiving are accepted. It is a great comfort to us that humble and thankful praises are more pleasing to God than the most costly pompous sacrifices are or ever were.

II. He encourages other good people to rejoice in God and continue seeking him (*v.* 32, 33): *The humble shall see this and be glad.* They shall see 1. How ready God is to hear the poor when they cry to him, and to give them that which they call upon him for. 2. The exaltation of the Saviour, for of him the psalmist had been speaking, and of himself as a type of him.

III. He calls upon all the creatures to praise God, the heaven, and earth, and sea, and the inhabitants of each, *v.* 34. The praises of the world must be

JAMIESON, FAUSSET, BROWN

22, 23. With unimportant verbal changes, this language is used by Paul to describe the rejection of the Jews who refused to receive the Saviour (Rom. 11:9, 10). The purport of the figures used is that blessings shall become curses, the "table" of joy (as one of food) a "snare," their "welfare," lit., "peaceful condition," or security, a "trap."

Darkened eyes and failing strength complete the picture of the ruin falling on them under the invoked retribution. **continually to shake**—lit., "to swerve" or bend in weakness.

24, 25. An utter desolation awaits them. They will not only be driven from their homes, but their homes—or lit., "palaces," indicative of wealth—shall be desolate (cf. Matt. 23:38).

27, 28. iniquity—or, punishment (Ps. 40:12). **come . . . righteousness**—partake of its benefits.

book of the living—or "life," with the next clause, a figurative mode of representing those saved, as having their names in a register (cf. Exod. 32:32; Isa. 4:3).

26. Though smitten of God (Isa. 53:4), men were not less guilty in persecuting the sufferer (Acts 2:23). **talk to the grief**—in respect to, about it, implying derision and taunts. **wounded**—or, lit., "mortally wounded."

29. poor and sorrowful—the afflicted pious, often denoted by such terms (cf. Ps. 10:17; 12:5). **set me . . . high**—out of danger.

30, 31. Spiritual are better than mere material offerings (Ps. 40:6; 50:8); hence a promise of the former, and rather contemptuous terms are used of the latter.

32, 33. Others shall rejoice. "Humble" and poor, as in vs. 29. **your heart . . .**—address to such (cf. Ps. 22:26). **prisoners**—peculiarly liable to be despised.

ADAM CLARKE

22. *Let their table become a snare.* The execrations here and in the following verses should be read in the future tense, because they are predictive; and not in the imperative mood, as if they were the offspring of the Psalmist's resentment.

27. *Add iniquity unto their iniquity.* "Give iniquity," that is, the reward of it, "upon" or "for their iniquity." Or, as the original signifies "perverseness," treat their perverseness with perverseness.

28. *Let them be blotted out.* They *shall* be blotted out from the land of the living. They shall be cut off from life, which they have forfeited by their cruelty and oppression. The Psalmist is speaking of retributive justice, and in this sense all these passages are to be understood.

29. *I am poor and sorrowful.* Literally, "I am laid low, and full of pain or grief." Hence the prayer, *Let thy salvation, O God, set me up on high.* My oppression has laid me low; Thy salvation shall make me high!

33. *For the Lord heareth the poor.* "The beggars." He perhaps refers here to the case of the captives, many of whom were reduced to the most abject state. *His prisoners.* The captives, shut up by His judgments in Chaldea, without any civil liberty, like culprits in a prison.

MATTHEW HENRY

offered for God's favours to his church, *v.* 35, 36. for God will save Zion, the holy mountain, where his service was kept up. *The cities of Judah shall be built*, particular churches shall be formed and incorporated according to the gospel model, that there may be a remnant to *dwell there* and to *have it in possession.* Those that love his name, that have a kindness for religion in general, shall embrace the Christian religion, and take their place in the Christian church; they shall dwell therein, as citizens; and of the household of God. David shall never want a man to stand before him. The Redeemer shall see his seed, and prolong his days in them, till the mystery of God shall be finished and the mystical body completed.

PSALM 70

To the chief musician. *A psalm* of David, to bring to remembrance.

Verses 1–5

The title tells us that this psalm was designed to bring to remembrance; that is, to put God in remembrance of his mercy and promises. We may in prayer use the words we have often used before: our Saviour in his agony prayed thrice, saying the same words; so David here uses the words he had used before.

I. David here prays that God would make haste to relieve and succour him (*v.* 1, 5): *I am poor and needy*, in want and distress, and much at a loss within myself. "*Make haste unto me*, for the longing desire of my soul is towards thee; I shall perish if I be not speedily helped. I have no other to expect relief from: *Thou art my help and my deliverer*. Thou hast engaged to be so to all that seek thee; I depend upon thee to be so to me; I have often found thee so; and thou art sufficient, all-sufficient, to be so; therefore make haste to me."

II. He prays that God would fill the faces of his enemies with shame, *v.* 2, 3. "*Let them be ashamed;* let them be brought to repentance, so filled with shame as that they may seek thy name (lxxxiii. 16); let them see their folly in fighting against those whom thou dost protect. However, let their designs against me be frustrated and then they will be ashamed and confounded, and *much cast down in their own eyes*," Neh. vi. 16.

III. He prays that God would fill the hearts of his friends with joy (*v.* 4). Let us make the service of God our great business and the favour of God our great delight and pleasure, for that is seeking him and loving his salvation. Let us then be assured that, if it be not our own fault, the joy of the Lord shall fill our minds and the high praises of the Lord shall fill our mouths. All who wish well to the comfort of the saints, and to the glory of God, cannot but say a hearty *amen* to this prayer, that those who love God's salvation may say continually, *Let God be magnified.*

PSALM 71

Verses 1–13

I. He prays that he might never be made ashamed of his dependence upon God nor disappointed in his believing expectations from him. With this petition every true believer may come boldly to the throne of grace.

1. David professes his confidence in God, and repeats his profession of that confidence, still presenting the profession of it to God and pleading it with him. We praise God by telling him (if it be indeed true) what an entire confidence we have in him (*v.* 1): "*In thee, O Lord!* and in thee only, *do I put my trust.* Whatever others do, I choose the God of Jacob for my help." *Thou art my rock and my fortress* (*v.* 3); and again, "*Thou art my refuge, my strong refuge*" (*v.* 7); that is, "I fly to thee, and am sure to be safe in thee, and under thy protection. If thou secure me, none can hurt me. *Thou art my hope and my trust*" (*v.* 5); that is, "thou hast proposed thyself to me in thy word as the proper object of my hope and trust; I have hoped in thee, and never found it in vain to do so."

2. His confidence in God is supported and encouraged by his experiences (*v.* 5, 6): "*Thou hast been my trust from my youth;* ever since I was capable of discerning between my right hand and my left, I stayed myself upon thee, for *by thee have I been holden up from the womb.*" He that was our help from our birth ought to be our hope from our youth. If we received so much mercy from God before we were capable of doing him any service, we should lose no time when we are capable. "Thou art he that took me into the arms of thy grace, under the shadow of

JAMIESON, FAUSSET, BROWN

34-36. The call on the universe for praise is well sustained by the prediction of the perpetual and extended blessings which shall come upon the covenant people of God. Though, as usual, the imagery is taken from terms used of Palestine, the whole tenor of the context indicates that the spiritual privileges and blessings of the Church are meant.

PSALM 70

Vss. 1-5. This corresponds to Psalm 40:13-17 with a very few variations, as "turn back" (vs. 3) for "desolate," and "make haste unto me" (vs. 5) for "thinketh upon me." It forms a suitable appendix to the preceding, and is called "a Psalm to bring to remembrance," as the 38th.

PSALM 71

Vss. 1-24. The Psalmist, probably in old age, appeals to God for help from his enemies, pleading his past favors, and stating his present need; and, in confidence of a hearing, he promises his grateful thanks and praise.

1-3. (Cf. Psalm 30:1-3.) **given commandment**–lit., "ordained," as in Psalm 44:4; 68:28. **rock . . . fortress–(Ps. 18:2).**

4, 5. cruel man–corrupt and ill-natured–lit., "sour." **trust**–place of trust. **6-9.** His history from early infancy illustrated God's care, and his wonderful deliverances were at once occasions of praise and ground of confidence for the future.

ADAM CLARKE

35. *God will save Zion.* This fixes the psalm to the time of the Captivity. There was no Zion belonging to the Jews in the time of Saul, when those suppose the psalm to be written who make David the author; for David, after he came to the throne, won the stronghold of Zion from the Jebusites (2 Sam. v. 7; 1 Chron. xi. 5). *Will build the cities of Judah.* This refers to the return from the Captivity, when all the destroyed cities should be rebuilt, and the Jews repossess their forfeited heritages.

PSALM 70

The title in the Hebrew is, "To the chief Musician, A Psalm of David, to bring to remembrance." It is almost word for word the same with the last five verses of Psalm xl, to the notes on which the reader is referred.

5. *But I am poor and needy.* I am a poor man, and a beggar—an afflicted beggar.

3. *That say, Aha, aha. Heach! heach!* a note of supreme contempt. See on Ps. xl. 15.

PSALM 71

There is no title to this psalm in either the Hebrew or Chaldee; and the reason is, it was written as a part of the preceding psalm, as appears by about twenty-seven of Kennicott's and De Rossi's MSS. For the first, second, and third verses, see their parallels, Ps. xxxi. 1-3.

4. *Out of the hand of the wicked.* Probably his unnatural son *Absalom,* called here *rasha, the wicked,* because he had violated all laws, human and divine. *The unrighteous and cruel man.* Probably Ahithophel, who was the iniquitous counsellor of a wicked and rebellious son.

MATTHEW HENRY

thy wings, into the bond of thy covenant. I have reason to hope that thou wilt protect me; thou that hast held me up hitherto wilt not let me fall now; thou that helpedst me when I could not help myself wilt not abandon me now that I am as helpless as I was then. *My praise shall therefore be continually of thee*."

3. His requests to God are,

(1) That he might *never be put to confusion* (*v.* 1), that he might not be disappointed of the mercy he expected and so made ashamed of his expectation.

(2) That he might be delivered out of the hand of his enemies (*v.* 2): "*Deliver me in thy righteousness.* As thou art the righteous Judge of the world, pleading the cause of the injured, cause me in some way or other to escape. *Incline thy ear unto my prayers,* and, answer to them, save me out of my troubles," *v.* 4. *Thou hast given commandment to save me* (*v.* 3); that is, thou hast promised to do it, and such efficacy is there in God's promises that they are often spoken of as commands, like that. The many eyes that were upon him (*v.* 7): "*I am as a wonder unto many;* every-one waits to see what will be the issue of such extraordinary troubles as I have fallen into and such extraordinary confidence as I profess to have in God." Or, "I am looked upon as a monster, whom everybody shuns, and therefore am undone if the Lord be not my refuge. Men abandon me, but God will not."

(3) That he might always find rest and safety in God (*v.* 3): *Be thou my strong habitation;* be thou to me *a rock of repose, whereto I may continually resort.* Those that are at home in God, that live a life of communion with him and confidence in him, that continually resort unto him by faith and prayer, may promise themselves a strong habitation, such as will never fall of itself nor can ever be broken through by any invading power. "*Let my mouth be filled with thy praise,* as now it is with my complaints, and then I shall not be ashamed of my hope, but my enemies will be ashamed of their insolence."

(4) That he might not be neglected now in his declining years (*v.* 9): *Cast me not off* now *in the time of* my *old age; forsake me not when my strength fails.* Observe here. The infirmities of age: *My strength fails.* Where there was strength of body and vigour of mind, strong sight, a strong voice, strong limbs, alas! in old age they fail. 2. God's presence with him under these infirmities: *Lord, cast me not off;* do *not then forsake me.* To be cast off and forsaken of God is a thing to be dreaded at any time, especially in the time of old age and when our strength fails us; for it is God that is the strength of our heart. But that the faithful servants of God may be comfortably assured that he will not cast them off in old age, nor forsake them when their strength fails them. He is a Master that is not wont to cast off old servants. In this confidence David here prays again (*v.* 12): "*O God! be not far from me; O my God! make haste for my help,* lest I perish before help come."

II. He prays that his enemies might be made ashamed of their designs against him. *They lay wait for my soul* (*v.* 10), and are adversaries to that, *v.* 13. *They take counsel together.* They say, *God has forsaken him; persecute and take him.* Here their premises are utterly false. All are not forsaken of God who think themselves so or whom others think to be so. And, as their premises were false, so their inference was barbarous. But *rejoice not against me, O my enemy! though I fall, I shall rise.* He that seems to forsake for a small moment will gather with everlasting kindness. "*Let them be confounded and consumed that are adversaries to my soul.* If they will not be confounded by repentance, and so saved, let them be confounded with everlasting dishonour, and so ruined."

Verses 14–24

David is here in a holy transport of joy and praise, arising from his faith and hope in God; we have both together, *v.* 14, where there is a sudden and remarkable change of his voice; his fears are all silenced, his hopes raised, and his prayers turned into thanksgivings. "Let my enemies say what they will, to drive me to despair, *I will hope continually*, hope in all conditions, in the most cloudy and dark day; I will live upon hope and will hope to the end."

I. His heart is established in faith and hope. "*I will go in the strength of the Lord God,* not sit down in despair, but stir up myself, will go forth and go on, not in any strength of my own, but in God's strength, and in the strength of his grace. *I will make mention of thy righteousness,* that is, thy faithfulness to every word which thou hast spoken, the equity of thy disposals, and thy kindness to thy people that trust in thee. This I will make mention of as my plea

JAMIESON, FAUSSET, BROWN

my praise . . . of thee—lit., "in" or "by Thee" (Ps. 22:25).

10, 11. The craft and malicious taunts of his enemies now led him to call for aid (cf. on the terms used, II Sam. 17:12; Ps. 3:2; 7:2). **12.** (Cf. Ps. 22:19; 40:4.) **13.** (Cf. Ps. 35:4; 40:14.)

14-16. The ruin of his enemies, as illustrating God's faithfulness, is his deliverance, and a reason for future confidence. **for I know . . . thereof**—innumerable, as he had not time to count them.

in the strength . . .—or, relying on it. **thy righteousness**—or, faithful performance of promises to the pious (Ps. 7:17; 31:1).

F. B. MEYER:

My trust from my youth. Some commentators ascribe this psalm to Jeremiah. His pensive, plaintive tone is certainly present in it. But whoever the author, he must have written in his old age (vv. 9, 17, 18). One keynote is "great" and "greatly" (vv. 19–21, 23); another is "all the day" (vv. 8, 15, 24).

Old men need have no failure in their buoyancy and gladness if they will fix their thoughts where the psalmist fixed his. Other subjects will soon wear out, but they who make God's righteousness and salvation their theme will ever have material for meditation and praise. We have here an inexhaustible subject, and one which will keep us young. Let us ask for help that we may disappoint the calculations of those who hate us, whether men or demons. It is a piteous spectacle when apparently prosperous careers are overclouded and age is overwhelmed in catastrophes which there is no time to surmount. But such is not God's way with his loyal servants. His rivers do not end in swamps and marshes, but broaden and deepen till they kiss the mighty ocean. —*Bible Commentary*

ADAM CLARKE

7. ***I am as a wonder unto many.*** **I am "as a portent," or "type."**

9. ***Cast me not off in the time of old age.*** **The original might be translated and paraphrased thus: "Thou wilt not cast me off till the time of old age; and according to the failure of my flesh, Thou wilt not forsake me."**

13. ***Let them be confounded.*** **They *shall* be confounded: these are prophetic denunciations.**

16. ***I will go. Abo,*** **I will enter, i.e., into the Tabernacle, *in the strength* or "mightinesses" of *Adonai Jehovah,* the supreme God, who is my Prop, Stay, and Support.**

MATTHEW HENRY

in prayer for thy mercy." He hopes that God will not leave him in his old age, but will be the same to him to the end that he had been all along, *v.* 17, 18. *Thou hast taught me from my youth.* The good education and good instructions which his parents gave him when he was young he owns himself obliged to give God thanks for as a great favour. When he was middle-aged he had *declared all God's wondrous works.* Those that have got good when they are young must be doing good when they are grown up, and must continue to communicate what they have received. *Now that I am old and grey-headed,* dying to this world and hastening to another, *O God! forsake me not.* Those that have been taught of God from their youth, and have made it the business of their lives to honour him, may be sure that he will not leave them when they are old and grey-headed, but will make the evil days of old age their best days. "I will not only *show thy strength,* by my own experience of it, *to this generation,* but I will leave my observations upon record for the benefit of posterity, and so show it *to everyone that is to come.*" It is a debt which the old disciples of Christ owe to the succeeding generations to leave behind them a solemn testimony to the power, pleasure, and advantage of religion, and the truth of God's promises. He hopes that God would revive him and raise him up out of his present low and disconsolate condition (*v.* 20): *Thou who hast made me to see and feel great and sore troubles,* above most men, *shalt quicken me again.* He does not say, "Thou hast burdened me with those troubles," but "shown them to me," as the tender father shows the child. If we have a due regard to the hand of God in our troubles, we may promise ourselves, in due time, a deliverance out of them. "Thou shalt not only restore me to *my greatness* again, but shalt *increase* it, and give me a better interest, after this shock, than before; thou shalt not only comfort me, but *comfort me on every side,* so that I shall see nothing black or threatening on any side." Sometimes God makes his people's troubles contribute to the increase of their greatness, and their sun shines the brighter for having been under a cloud. He hopes that all his enemies would be put to confusion, *v.* 24. *They are confounded, they are brought to shame, that seek my hurt.*

II. Let us now see how his heart is enlarged in joy and praises, how he rejoices in hope, and sings in hope; for we are saved by hope. *My mouth shall show forth thy righteousness and thy salvation;* and again (*v.* 24), *My tongue shall talk of thy righteousness,* and this *all the day.* God's righteousness, which David seems here to be in a particular manner affected with, includes a great deal: the rectitude of his nature, the equity of his providential disposals, the righteous laws he has given us to be ruled by, the righteous promises he has given us to depend upon, and the everlasting righteousness which his Son has brought in for our justification. God's righteousness and his salvation are here joined together. "*I know not the numbers thereof* (*v.* 15). Though I cannot give a particular account of thy favours to me, they are so many, yet, knowing them to be numberless, I will be still speaking of them, for in them I shall find new matter," *v.* 19. This is praising God, acknowledging his perfections and performances to be so high that we cannot apprehend them, so great that we cannot comprehend them. *O God! who is like unto thee?* None in heaven, none on earth, no angel, no king. God is a non-such; we do not rightly praise him if we do not own him to be so. *I will praise thee, even thy truth.* God is made known by his word; if we praise that, and the truth of that, we praise him. It is God's honour that he is a Holy One; it is his people's honour that he is the Holy One of Israel. He will express his joy and exultation in sacred music—*with the psaltery, with the harp;* at these David excelled, and the best of his skill shall be employed in setting forth God's praises to such advantage as might affect others. "*Unto thee will I sing,* to thy honour, and with a desire to be accepted of thee. *My lips shall greatly rejoice when I sing unto thee,* knowing they cannot be better employed. *My soul* shall rejoice *which thou hast redeemed.*" We do not make melody to the Lord, in singing his praises, if we do not do it with our hearts. My lips shall rejoice, but that is nothing; lip-labour, though ever so well laboured, if that be all, is but lost labour in serving God; the soul must be at work, and with all that is within us we must bless his holy name.

JAMIESON, FAUSSET, BROWN

17-21. Past experience again encourages. **taught me . . .**—by providential dealings.

depths of the earth—debased, low condition.

increase . . .—i.e. the great things done for me (vs. 19; cf. Ps. 40: 5).

is very high—distinguished (Ps. 36:5; Isa. 55:9).

22-24. To the occasion of praise he now adds the promise to render it. **will . . . praise**—lit., "will thank." **even thy truth**—as to Thy truth or faithfulness.

ADAM CLARKE

F. B. MEYER:

"Thou who hast shown me many and sore troubles, shalt quicken me again" (71:20). God shows us the troubles. We stand beside Him, and the mighty billows break around, but are shivered into myriads of drops. As we ride beside Him in the chariot of salvation, He points out to us the forms of dreaded evils, the ravines, the glaciers, the awful steeps; but it is as though we were cradled in some soft golden cloud which fringes the edge of the precipice, and glides along splintered cliffs where the chamois could not find footing. Look at this, saith our Guide. These are the troubles that overwhelm souls and drain their life! Behold them, but thou shalt not suffer them! I show you them that you may know how to comfort and help those who have been overwhelmed. Sometimes, as this part of our education is being carried forward, we have to descend into "the lower parts of the earth," pass through subterranean passages, lie buried among the dead. But never for a moment is the cord of fellowship and union between God and us strained to breaking; and from the depths God will bring us up again.

Never doubt God. Never say that He has forsaken or forgotten. Never think that He is unsympathetic. He will quicken again. There is always a smooth piece in every skein, however tangled. The longest day at last rings out the evensong. The winter snow lies long, but it goes at last. Be steadfast; your labor is not in vain. God turns again, and comforts. And when He does, the heart which had forgotten its psalmody breaks out in jubilant song, as does the psalmist's.—*Great Verses Through the Bible*

24. ***Talk of thy righteousness.*** **The righteousness of God is frequently used in this psalm, and in other places, to signify His justice, judgments, faithfulness, truth, mercy. There are few words of more general import in the Bible.**

19. ***Thy righteousness . . . is very high. Ad marom*****—is up to the exalted place, reaches up to heaven.**

22. ***I will also praise thee with the psaltery. Bichli nebel,*** **"with the instrument nebel."** ***Unto thee will I sing with the harp; bechinnor,*** **"with the kinnor." Both were stringed instruments.**

MATTHEW HENRY

PSALM 72

A psalm for Solomon.

Verse 1

This verse is a prayer for the king, even the king's son.

I. We may apply it to Solomon: *Give him thy judgments, O God! and thy righteousness;* make him a man, a king; make him a good man, a good king. 1. It is the prayer of a father for his child, a dying blessing, such as the patriarchs bequeathed to their children. Solomon learned to pray for himself as his father had prayed for him, not that God would give him riches and honour, but a wise and understanding heart. Parents cannot give grace to their children, but may by prayer bring them to the God of grace. 2. It is the prayer of a king for his successor. David had executed judgment and justice during his reign, and now he prays that his son might do so too. Such a concern as this we should have for posterity. 3. It is the prayer of subjects for their king. It should seem, David penned this psalm for the use of the people, that they, in singing, might pray for Solomon. Those who would live quiet and peaceable lives must pray for kings and all in authority, that God would give them his judgments and righteousness.

II. We may apply it to Christ; not that he who intercedes for us needs us to intercede for him; but, 1. It is a prayer of the Old Testament church for sending the Messiah. 2. It is an expression of the satisfaction which all true believers take in the authority which the Lord Jesus has received from the Father: "Let him have all power both in heaven and earth, and be the Lord our righteousness; let him be the great trustee of divine grace for all that are his."

Verses 2–17

This is a prophecy of the prosperity and perpetuity of the kingdom of Christ under the shadow of the reign of Solomon. 1. As a plea to enforce the prayer: "Lord, *give him thy judgments and thy righteousness*" (*v.* 1). 2. As an answer of peace to the prayer. That this prophecy must refer to the kingdom of the Messiah is plain, because there are many passages in it which cannot be applied to the reign of Solomon. The kingdom here spoken of is to last as long as the sun, but Solomon's was soon extinct. Therefore even the Jewish expositors understand it of the kingdom of the Messiah.

I. That it should be a *righteous government* (*v.* 2): *He shall judge thy people with righteousness.* Compare Isa. xi. 4. All the laws of Christ's kingdom are consonant to the eternal rules of equity. The peace of his kingdom shall be supported by righteousness (*v.* 3).

II. That it should be a peaceable government: *The mountains shall bring peace, and the little hills* (*v.* 3); that is (says Dr. Hammond), both the superior and the inferior courts of judicature in Solomon's kingdom. There shall be *abundance of peace*, *v.* 7. Solomon's name signifies *peaceable*, and such was his reign. But peace is, in a special manner, the glory of Christ's kingdom; for, as far as it prevails, it reconciles men to God, to themselves, and to one another, and slays all enmities; for he is our peace.

III. That the poor and needy should be, in a particular manner, taken under the protection of this government: *He shall judge thy poor*, *v.* 2. *The poor of the people*, and *the children of the needy*, he will be sure so to judge as to save, *v.* 4. This is insisted upon again (*v.* 12, 13), intimating that Christ will be sure to carry his cause on behalf of his injured poor. *He will deliver the needy* that lie at the mercy of their oppressors. *He will spare the needy* that throw themselves on his mercy, he will *save their souls*, and that is all they desire. *Blessed are the poor in spirit, for theirs is the kingdom of heaven.* Christ is the poor man's King.

IV. That proud oppressors shall be reckoned with: *He shall break them in pieces* (*v.* 4). The devil is the great oppressor, whom Christ will break in pieces and of whose kingdom he will be the destruction. So *precious shall their blood be unto him* that not a drop of it shall be shed, by the deceit or violence of Satan or his instruments, without being reckoned for. Christ is a King, who, though he calls his subjects sometimes to resist unto blood for him, yet is not prodigal of their blood.

V. That religion shall flourish under Christ's government (*v.* 5): *They shall fear thee as long as the sun and moon endure.* Solomon indeed built the temple, but it did not last long; this therefore must point at Christ's kingdom. Faith in Christ will set up, and keep up, the fear of God; and therefore this is the everlasting gospel that is preached.

JAMIESON, FAUSSET, BROWN

PSALM 72

Vss. 1-19. *For,* or lit., "of Solomon." The closing verse rather relates to the 2d book of Psalms, of which this is the last, and was perhaps added by some collector, to intimate that the collection, to which, as chief author, David's name was appended, was closed. In this view, these may consistently be the productions of others included, as of Asaph, sons of Korah, and Solomon; and a few of David's may be placed in the latter series. The fact that here the usual mode of denoting authorship is used, is strongly conclusive that Solomon was the author, especially as no stronger objection appears than what has been now set aside. The Psalm, in highly wrought figurative style, describes the reign of a king as "righteous, universal, beneficent, and perpetual." By the older Jewish and most modern Christian interpreters, it has been referred to Christ, whose reign, present and prospective, alone corresponds with its statements. As the imagery of Psalm 2 was drawn from the martial character of David's reign, that of this is from the peaceful and prosperous state of Solomon's.

1. Give the king . . .—a prayer which is equivalent to a prediction. **judgments**—the acts, and (figuratively) the principles of a right government (John 5:22; 9:39). **righteousness**—qualifications for conducting such a government. **king's son**—same person as a king—a very proper title for Christ, as such in both natures.

2, etc. The effects of such a government by one thus endowed are detailed. **thy people . . . and thy poor**—or, meek, the pious subjects of his government.

3. As **mountains** and **hills** are not usually productive, they are here selected to show the abundance of peace, being represented as —**bringing**—or, lit., "bearing" it as a produce. **by righteousness**—i.e., by means of his eminently just and good methods of ruling.

children of the needy—for the needy (cf. sons of strangers, Ps. 18:45).

4. That peace, including prosperity, as an eminent characteristic of Christ's reign (Isa. 2:4; 9:6; 11:9), will be illustrated in the security provided for the helpless and needy, and the punishment inflicted on oppressors, whose power to injure or mar the peace of others will be destroyed (cf. Isa. 65:25; Zech. 9:10).

5. as long as . . . endure—lit., "with the sun," coeval with its existence, and *before,* or, *in presence of the moon,* while it lasts (cf. Gen. 11:28, "before Terah," lit., "in presence of," while he lived).

ADAM CLARKE

PSALM 72

The title *lishelomoh,* we translate, "A Psalm for Solomon." The Chaldee says, "By the hand of Solomon, spoken prophetically." The Syriac, "A Psalm of David, when he had constituted Solomon king." All the other versions attribute it to Solomon himself. But in the conclusion of the psalm it appears to be attributed to David. "The prayers of David the son of Jesse are ended." It is most probably a psalm of David, composed in his last days, when he had set this beloved son on the throne of the kingdom.

1. *Give the king thy judgments.* Let Solomon receive Thy law, as the civil and ecclesiastical code by which he is to govern the kingdom. *And thy righteousness unto the king's son.* Solomon is called here *the king,* because now set upon the Jewish throne; and he is called *the king's son,* to signify his right to that throne on which he now sat.

3. *The mountains shall bring peace.* Perhaps *mountains* and *hills* are here taken in their figurative sense, to signify princes and petty governors. But what is the meaning of *the little hills, by righteousness?* Why, it has no meaning; and it has none because it is a false division of the verse. The word *bitsedakah,* "in righteousness," at the end of v. 3, should begin v. 4, and then the sense will be plain. V. 3: "The mountains and the hills shall bring prosperity to the people." V. 4: "In righteousness *he shall judge the poor of the people, he shall save the children of the needy, and shall break in pieces the oppressor.*"

5. *They shall fear thee.* There is no sense in which this can be spoken of Solomon, nor indeed of any other man; it belongs to Jesus Christ, and to Him alone.

MATTHEW HENRY

And, as Christ's government promotes devotion towards God, so it promotes both justice and charity among men (*v.* 7): *In his days shall the righteous flourish.* The law of Christ, written in the heart, disposes men to be honest and just, and to render to all their due; it likewise disposes men to live in love, and so it produces abundance of peace and beats swords into ploughshares. Both holiness and love shall be perpetual in Christ's kingdom, and shall never go to decay, for the subjects of it shall *fear God as long as the sun and moon endure*; Christianity, having got footing in the world, shall keep its ground till the end of time, and having got footing in the heart, it will continue there till, by death, the sun, and the moon, and the stars (that is, the bodily senses) are darkened.

VI. That Christ's government shall be very comfortable to all his faithful loving subjects (*v.* 6): *He shall*, by the graces and comforts of his Spirit, *come down like rain upon the mown grass*; not on that which is cut down, but that which is left growing, that it may spring again, though it was beheaded.

VII. That Christ's kingdom shall be greatly enlarged.

1. The extent of his territories (*v.* 8): *He shall have dominion from sea to sea* (from the South Sea to the North, or from the Red Sea to the Mediterranean) *and from the river* Euphrates, or Nile, *to the ends of the earth.* Solomon's dominion was very large (1 Kings iv. 21), according to the promise, Gen. xv. 18. But no sea, no river, is named, that it might, by these proverbial expressions, intimate the universal monarchy of the Lord Jesus. His gospel has been, or shall be, preached *to all nations* (Matt. xxiv. 14). His territories shall be extended to those countries, (1) That were strangers to him: *Those that dwell in the wilderness*, that seldom hear news, shall hear the glad tidings of the Redeemer, *shall bow before him*, shall believe in him, worship him, and take his yoke upon them. (2) That were enemies to him, and had fought against him: *They shall lick the dust.*

2. The dignity of his tributaries. He shall not only reign over those that dwell in the wilderness, the peasants and cottagers, but over those that dwell in the palaces (*v.* 10): *The kings of Tarshish, and of the isles*, that lie most remote from Israel and are *the isles of the Gentiles* (Gen. x. 5), *shall bring presents* to him as their sovereign Lord. This was literally fulfilled in Solomon (for *all the kings of the earth sought the wisdom of Solomon, and brought every man his present*, 2 Chron. ix. 23, 24), and in Christ too, when the wise men of the east came to worship him and *brought him presents*, Matt. ii. 11.

VIII. That he shall be honoured and beloved by all his subjects (*v.* 15): *He shall live;* his subjects shall desire his life (*O king! live for ever*) and with good reason; for he has said, *Because I live, you shall live also.* Presents shall be made to him. Though he shall be able to live without them, for he needs neither the gifts nor the services of any, yet to him *shall be given of the gold of Sheba.* He that is best must be served with the best. Prayers shall be made for him, and that continually. The people prayed for Solomon, and that helped to make him and his reign so great a blessing to them. But how is this applied to Christ? He needs not our prayers, nor can have any benefit by them. But the Old Testament saints prayed for his coming, prayed continually for it; for they called him, *He that should come.* And now that he has come we must pray for the success of his gospel and the advancement of his kingdom, which he calls praying for him. Praises shall be made of him. *Daily shall he be praised.*

IX. That under his government there shall be a wonderful increase both of meat and mouths. The country shall grow rich. Sow but a *handful of corn on the top of the mountains*, whence one would expect but little, and yet *the fruit of it shall shake like Lebanon*; it shall come up like a wood, so thick, and tall, and strong, like the cedars of Lebanon. This is applicable to the wonderful productions of the seed of the gospel in the days of the Messiah. A handful of that seed, sown in the mountainous and barren soil of the Gentile world, produced a wonderful harvest gathered in to Christ. The fields were *white unto harvest*, John iv. 35; Matt. ix. 37. The towns shall grow populous: *Those of the city shall flourish like grass*, for number, for verdure.

X. That his government shall be perpetual, both to his honour and to the happiness of his subjects. The Lord Jesus shall reign for ever, and of him only this must be understood, and not at all of Solomon. It is Christ only that shall *be feared throughout all generations* (*v.* 5) and *as long as the sun and moon endure*, *v.* 7. 1. The honour of the prince is immortal and shall never be sullied (*v.* 17): *His name shall endure for ever.* As the names of earthly princes are

JAMIESON, FAUSSET, BROWN

7, and, carrying out the figure, the results are described in an abundant production. **the righteous**—lit., "righteousness." **flourish**—lit., "sprout," or, "spring forth."

6. A beautiful figure expresses the *grateful* nature of His influence;

8. The foreign nations mentioned (vss. 9, 10) could not be included in the limits, if designed to indicate the boundaries of Solomon's kingdom. The terms, though derived from those used (Exod. 23:31; Deut. 11:24) to denote the possessions of Israel, must have a wider sense. Thus, "ends of the earth" is never used of Palestine, but always of the world (cf. *Margin*).

9-11. The extent of the conquests. **They that dwell in the wilderness**—the wild, untutored tribes of deserts. **bow . . . dust**—in profound submission. The remotest and wealthiest nations shall acknowledge Him (cf. Ps. 45:12).

15. In his prolonged life he will continue to receive the honorable gifts of the rich, and the prayers of his people shall be made for him, and their praises given to him.

12-14. They are not the conquests of arms, but the influences of humane and peaceful principles (cf. Isa. 9:7; 11:1-9; Zech. 9:9, 10).

16. The spiritual blessings, as often in Scripture, are set forth by material, the abundance of which is described by a figure, in which a "handful" (or lit., "a piece," or small portion) of corn in the most unpropitious locality, shall produce a crop, waving in the wind in its luxuriant growth, like the forests of Lebanon. **they of the city . . . earth**—This clause denotes the rapid and abundant increase of population—**of** [or, "from"] **the city**—Jerusalem, the center and seat of the typical kingdom. **flourish**—or, glitter as new grass—i.e., bloom. This increase corresponds with the increased productiveness. So, as the gospel blessings are diffused, there shall arise increasing recipients of them, out of the Church in which Christ resides as head.

17. His name—or, glorious perfections. **as long as the sun**—(Cf. vs. 5). **men shall be blessed**—(Gen. 12:3; 18:18).

ADAM CLARKE

7. *In his days shall the righteous flourish.* There was nothing but peace and prosperity all the days of Solomon. For in his days "Judah and Israel dwelt safely, every man under his vine and under his fig tree, from Dan even to Beer-sheba," 1 Kings iv. 25. *So long as the moon endureth.* "Till there be no more moon."

6. *He shall come down like rain upon the mown grass.* The word which we translate *mown grass* more properly means "pastured grass" or "pastured land," for the dew of the night is intended to restore the grass which has been eaten in the course of the day.

8. *He shall have dominion also from sea to sea.* The best comment on this, as it refers to Solomon, may be found in 1 Kings iv. 21, 24. *Unto the ends of the earth*, or "land," must mean the tract of country along the Mediterranean Sea, which was the boundary of the land on that side. But, as the words may refer to Christ, everything may be taken in its utmost latitude and extent.

9. *They that dwell in the wilderness.* It is likely that those who dwell by the seacoasts, and support themselves by navigation and fishing, are here intended.

10. *The kings of Tarshish and of the isles shall bring presents. Minchah* signifies a gratitude or friendly offering. *The kings of Sheba and Seba.* Both countries of Arabia. From the former came the queen of Sheba, to hear the wisdom of Solomon. And she brought exceeding great gifts. *Eshcar* signifies "a compensative present, made on account of benefits received."

11. *All kings shall fall down before.* They shall reverence him on account of his great wisdom, riches, etc. *All nations shall serve him.* All the surrounding nations. This and the preceding verses are fully explained by 1 Kings x. 23-25. If we take these expressions to mean literally all the habitable globe, then they cannot be applied to Solomon; but if we take them as they are most evidently used by the sacred writer, then they are literally true.

16. *There shall be a handful of corn.* The earth shall be exceedingly fruitful. Even a handful of corn sown on the top of a mountain shall grow up strong and vigorous; and it shall be, in reference to crops in other times, as the cedars of Lebanon are to common trees or shrubs; and as the earth will bring forth in handfuls, so the people shall be multiplied who are to consume this great produce.

17. *His name shall endure for ever.* Hitherto this has been literally fulfilled. Solomon is celebrated in the east and in the west, in the

MATTHEW HENRY

continued in their posterity, so Christ's in himself. 2. The happiness of the people is universal, too; *Men shall be blessed*, truly and for ever blessed, *in him*.

Verses 18–20

I. The psalmist is here enlarged in thanksgivings for the prophecy and promise, *v*. 18, 19. So sure is every word of God that we have reason enough to give thanks for what he has said, though it be not yet done. We must own that for all the great things he has done for the world God is worthy to be praised; *Blessed be the Lord*, that is, *blessed be his glorious name*. We are here taught to bless the name of Christ, and to bless God in Christ. 1. As the Lord God, as a self-existent self-sufficient Being, and our sovereign Lord. 2. As the God of Israel, in covenant with that people and worshipped by them. 3. As the God *who only does wondrous things*, in creation and providence, and especially this work of redemption, which excels them all.

II. He is earnest in prayer for the accomplishment of this prophecy and promise: *Let the whole earth be filled with his glory*. David shuts up the prayer with a double seal: "*Amen and amen*." He even shuts up his life with this prayer, *v*. 20. This was the last psalm that ever he penned, though not placed last in this collection. With this he breathes his last: "Let God be glorified, let the kingdom of the Messiah be set up, and I desire no more. With this let *the prayers of David the son of Jesse* be *ended*. Even so, come, Lord Jesus, come quickly."

PSALM 73

A psalm of Asaph.

Verses 1–14

This psalm begins somewhat abruptly: *Yet God is good to Israel* (so the margin reads it). Though wicked people receive many of the gifts of his providential bounty, yet we must own that he is, in a peculiar manner, good to Israel.

The psalmist designs an account of a temptation to envy the prosperity of the wicked.

I. He lays down, in the first place, that great principle which he is resolved to abide by while he was parleying with this temptation, *v*. 1. Job, when he was entering into such a temptation, fixed for his principle the omniscience of God: *Times are not hidden from the Almighty*, Job xxiv. 1. Jeremiah's principle is the justice of God: *Righteous art thou, O God! when I plead with thee*, Jer. xii. 1. Habakkuk's principle is the holiness of God: *Thou art of purer eyes than to behold iniquity*, Hab. i. 13. The psalmist's, here, is the goodness of God. He had had many thoughts in his mind concerning the providences of God, but this word, at last, settled him: "For all this, God is good, *good to Israel, even to those that are of a clean heart*." Those are the Israel of God that are of a clean heart. God, who is good to all, is in a special manner good to his church and people, as he was to Israel of old.

II. He comes now to relate the shock that was given to his faith in God's distinguishing goodness to Israel, by a strong temptation to think that the Israel of God are no happier than other people and that God is no kinder to them than to others.

1. He speaks of it as a very narrow escape that he had not been overthrown by this temptation (*v*. 2): "*But as for me*, though I was so well satisfied in the goodness of God to Israel, yet *my feet were almost gone* (the tempter had almost tripped up my heels), *my steps had well-nigh slipped, for I was envious at the foolish*." There are storms that will try the firmest anchors. Many a precious soul, that shall live for ever, had once a very narrow turn for its life.

2. The psalmist's temptation. He *saw*, with grief, *the prosperity of the wicked, v*. 3. They seem to have the least share of the troubles and calamities of this life (*v*. 5): *They are not in the troubles of other men*, even of wise and good men, *neither are they plagued like other men*, but seem as if by some special privilege they were exempted from the common lot of sorrows. They seem to have the greatest share of the comforts of this life. They live at ease so that *their eyes stand out with fatness, v*. 7. There are many who have a great deal of this life in their hands, but nothing of the other life in their hearts. They are ungodly, and yet they prosper and *increase in riches, v*. 12. *They are the prosperous of the age*, so some read it. Their end seems to be peace. This is mentioned first, as the most strange of all (*v*. 4): *There are no bands in their death*. They are not taken off by a violent death. Nay, they are not bound by the terrors of conscience in their dying moments. We cannot judge of men's state on the other side death. Men may die like lambs,

JAMIESON, FAUSSET, BROWN

18, 19. These words close the Psalm in terms consistent with the style of the context, while **20** is evidently, from its prosaic style, an addition for the purpose above explained.

ended—lit., "finished," or completed; the word never denotes fulfilment, except in a very late usage, as in Ezra 1:1; Daniel 12:7.

PSALM 73

Vss. 1-28. *Of Asaph* *God is good to His people.* For although the prosperity of the wicked, and the afflictions of the righteous, tempted the Psalmist to misgivings of God's government, yet the sudden and fearful ruin of the ungodly, seen in the light of God's revelation, reassures his heart; and, chiding himself for his folly, he is led to confide renewedly in God, and celebrate His goodness and love.

1. The abrupt announcement of the theme indicates that it is the conclusion of a perplexing mental conflict, which is then detailed (cf. Jer. 12:1-4). **Truly**—or, Surely it is so.

clean heart—(Ps. 18: 26) describes the true Israel.

2. The figures express his wavering faith, by terms denoting tottering and weakness (cf. Ps. 22:5; 62:3).

3-9. The prosperous wicked are insolently proud (cf. Ps. 5:5). They die, as well as live, free from perplexities: pride adorns them, and violence is their clothing; indeed they are inflated with unexpected success.

ADAM CLARKE

north and in the south. *All nations shall call him blessed*. Because of the extraordinary manner in which he was favored by the Most High. I well know that all these things are thought to belong properly to Jesus Christ; and, in reference to Him, they are all true, and ten thousand times more than these. But I believe they are all properly applicable to Solomon.

20. *The prayers of David the son of Jesse are ended*. This was most probably the last psalm he ever wrote.

PSALM 73

This is the commencement of the Third Book of the Psalter; and the psalm before us has for title, "A Psalm of Asaph"; or, as the margin has it, "A Psalm for Asaph." The title in the Hebrew is *mizmor leasaph;* "A Psalm of Asaph," and it is likely that this *Asaph* was the composer of it; that he lived under the Babylonish captivity; and that he published this psalm to console the Israelites under bondage, who were greatly tried to find themselves in such outward distress and misery, while a people much more wicked and corrupt than they were in great prosperity, and held them in bondage.

2. *My feet were almost gone*. I had nearly given up my confidence. I was ready to find fault with the dispensations of providence, and thought the Judge of all the earth did not do right.

3. *I was envious at the foolish*. I saw persons who worshipped not the true God, and others who were abandoned to all vices, in possession of every temporal comfort, while the godly were in straits, difficulties, and affliction.

4. *No bands in their death*. Many of the godly have sore conflicts at their death. Their enemy then thrusts sore at them that they may fall, or that their confidence in their God may be shaken. But of this the ungodly know nothing. Satan will not molest *them;* he is sure of his prey. They are entangled, and cannot now break their nets. Their consciences are seared; they have no sense of guilt. If they think at all of another world, they presume on that mercy which they never sought, and of which they have no distinct notion. Perhaps, "they die without a sigh or a groan; and thus go off as quiet as a lamb" —to the slaughter.

MATTHEW HENRY

and yet have their place with the goats. They made a very bad use of their outward prosperity and were hardened by it in their wickedness. It made them very proud and haughty. Because they live at ease, *pride compasses them as a chain*, *v.* 6. *Pride ties on their chain*, or necklace; so Dr. Hammond reads it. It is no harm to wear a chain or necklace; but when it is worn to gratify a vain mind, it ceases to be an ornament. And, as the pride of sinners appears in their dress, so it does in their talk: *They speak loftily* (*v.* 8); they affect *great swelling words of vanity* (2 Pet. ii. 18). It made them oppressive to their poor neighbours (*v.* 6): *Violence covers them as a garment. They speak wickedly concerning oppression;* they oppress, and justify themselves in it. *They are corrupt*, that is, dissolved in pleasures and everything that is luxurious (so some). It made them very insolent in their demeanour towards both God and man (*v.* 9): *They set their mouth against the heavens*, putting contempt upon God himself. They cannot reach the heavens with their hands, to shake God's throne, but they show their ill-will by setting their mouth against the heavens. *Their tongue* also *walks through the earth*, and they take liberty to abuse all that come in their way. They could not have been thus wicked if they had not learned to say (*v.* 11), *How doth God know? And is there knowledge in the Most High?* What an affront is it to the God of infinite knowledge, from whom all knowledge is, to ask, *Is there knowledge in him?* Well may he say (*v.* 12), *Behold, these are the ungodly*. He observed that while wicked men thus prospered in their impiety, good people were in great affliction, and he himself in particular. He looked abroad and saw many of God's people greatly at a loss (*v.* 10): "Because the wicked are so very daring *therefore his people return hither*; they know not what to say to it any more than I do, and the rather because *waters of a full cup are wrung out to them*; they are not only made to drink of the bitter cup of affliction, but to drink all. Care is taken that they lose not a drop of that unpleasant potion; the waters are wrung out unto them, that they may have the dregs of the cup." These are the waters wrung out to them: "For my part," says he, "*all the day long have I been plagued* with one affliction or another, *and chastened every morning*, as duly as the morning comes." From all this arose a very strong temptation to cast off his religion. There are those, even among God's professing people, that say, "*How does God know?* Surely all things are left to blind fortune, and not disposed of by an all-seeing God." Though the psalmist's feet were not so far gone as to question God's omniscience, yet he was tempted to question the benefit of religion, and to say (*v.* 13), *Verily, I have cleansed my heart in vain*, and have, to no purpose, *washed my hands in innocency*. But when the pure in heart, those blessed ones, shall see God (Matt. v. 8), they will not say that they cleansed their hearts in vain.

Verses 15–20

How he kept his footing and got the victory.

I. He kept up a respect for God's people, and restrained himself from speaking what he had thought amiss, *v.* 15. He got the victory by degrees, and this was the first point he gained; he was ready to say, *Verily, I have cleansed my heart in vain*, but he kept his mouth with this consideration, "*If I say, I will speak thus, behold, I should* give the greatest offence imaginable to *the generation of thy children*." Though he thought amiss, he took care not to utter that evil thought which he had conceived. If therefore thou hast been so foolish as to think evil, *lay thy hand upon thy mouth*, and let it go no further, Prov. xxx. 32. We must think twice before we speak once, both because some things may be thought which may not be spoken and because the second thoughts may correct the mistakes of the first. There is nothing that can give more general offence to the generation of God's children than to say that *we have cleansed our heart in vain* or that it is vain to serve God.

II. He foresaw the ruin of wicked people. "I endeavoured to understand the meaning of this unaccountable dispensation of Providence; but *it was too painful for me*. I could not conquer it by the strength of my own reasoning." If there were not another life after this, we could not fully reconcile the prosperity of the wicked with the justice of God. But (*v.* 17) *he went into the sanctuary of God;* he consulted the scriptures, and he prayed to God to make this matter plain to him, and, at length, he understood wicked people were rather to be pitied than envied, for they were but ripening for ruin. The sanctuary must be the resort of a tempted soul. All is well that ends well, everlastingly well; but nothing well that ends ill, everlastingly ill. The prosperity of the wicked is short and uncertain. The high places in which Providence sets them are *slippery places*

JAMIESON, FAUSSET, BROWN

With all this—**They are corrupt**—or, lit., "they deride," they speak maliciously and arrogantly and invade even heaven with blasphemy (Rev. 13:6), and cover earth with slanders (Job 21:7-14).

10-12. Hence God's people are confounded, turned hither (or back) and thither, perplexed with doubts of God's knowledge and care, and filled with sorrow. **prosper in the world**—lit., "secure for ever."

13, 14. The Psalmist, partaking of these troubles, is especially disturbed in view of his own case, that with all his diligent efforts for a holy life, he is still sorely tried.

15. Freed from idiomatic phrases, this verse expresses a supposition, as, "Had I thus spoken, I should," etc., intimating that he had kept his troubles to himself. **generation of thy children**—Thy people (I John 3:1). **offend**—lit., "deceive, mislead."

16, 17. Still he—**thought**—lit., "studied," or, pondered this riddle; but in vain; it remained a toil (cf. *Margin*), till he—**went into the sanctuary**—to inquire (cf. Exod. 25:22; Ps. 5:7; 27:4).

ADAM CLARKE

6. *Pride compasseth them about as a chain.* Perhaps there is an allusion here to the office which some of them bore. Chains of gold were ensigns of magistracy and civil power.

7. *Their eyes stand out with fatness.* "Their countenance is changed because of fatness."—Chaldee. *They have more than heart could wish.* It would be more literal to say, "They surpass the thoughts of their heart." They have more than they expected, though not more than they wish.

8. *They are corrupt.* "They mock, act dissolutely."

9. *Set their mouth against the heavens.* They blaspheme God, ridicule religion, mock at Providence, and laugh at a future state. *Their tongue walketh through the earth.* They find fault with everything; they traduce the memory of the just in heaven, and ridicule the saints that are upon earth. They criticize every dispensation of God.

10. *Therefore his people return hither.* "Therefore shall my people be converted, where they shall find abundance of waters." That is. The people, seeing the iniquity of the Babylonians, and feeling their oppressive hand, shall be converted to Me; and I shall bring them to their own land, where they shall find an abundance of all the necessaries of life.

15. *If I say, I will speak thus.* I have at last discovered that I have reasoned incorrectly, and that I have the uniform testimony of all Thy children against me. From generation to generation they have testified that the Judge of all the earth does right.

17. *Until I went into the sanctuary.* That this psalm was written during the Captivity there is little room to doubt. How then can the Psalmist speak of *the sanctuary?* There was none at Babylon, and at Jerusalem it had been long since destroyed. There is no way to solve this difficulty but by considering that *mikdeshey* may be taken in the sense of "holy places"—places set apart for prayer and meditation.

18. *Thou didst set them in slippery places.* Affluence is a slippery path; few have ever walked in it without falling.

MATTHEW HENRY

(*v.* 18). Their destruction is sure, and sudden, and very great. They flourish for a time, but are undone for ever. He speaks of it as God's doing, and therefore it cannot be resisted: *Thou castest them down.* It is swift; for *how are they brought into desolation as in a moment! v.* 19. It is a total and final ruin: *They are utterly consumed with terrors.* Their prosperity is therefore not to be envied at all, but despised. *As a dream when one awaketh, so, O Lord! when thou awakest*, or when they awake (as some read it), *thou shalt despise their image*, their shadow, *and make it to vanish. In the day of the great judgment* (so the Chaldee paraphrase reads it), *they shall rise to shame and everlasting contempt.* They shall be made to awake out of the sleep of their carnal security, and then God shall despise their image. How did God despise that rich man's image when he said, *Thou fool, this night thy soul shall be required of thee!* Luke xii. 19, 20.

Verses 21–28

An account of the good improvement which the psalmist made of that sore temptation with which he had been assaulted and by which he was almost overcome.

I. He learned to think very humbly of himself and to abase and accuse himself before God (*v.* 21, 22); *My heart was grieved, and I was pricked in my reins;* temptation was to Paul as a thorn in the flesh, 2 Cor. xii. 7. The working of envy and discontent is as painful as any. The psalmist owns it was his ignorance to vex himself at this: "So ignorant was I of that which I might have known. *I was as a beast* (*Behemoth—a great beast*) *before thee.* Beasts mind present things only, and never look before at what is to come; and so did I. To be ready to wish myself one of them, and to think of changing conditions with them! *So foolish was I.*"

II. He took occasion hence to own his dependence on the grace of God (*v.* 23): "*Nevertheless*, foolish as I am, *I am continually with thee* and in thy favour; *thou hast holden me by my right hand.*" He had said, in the hour of temptation (*v.* 14), *All the day long have I been plagued;* but here he corrects himself for that passionate complaint: "Though God has chastened me, he has not cast me off; notwithstanding all the crosses of my life, *I have been continually* with thee. Though God has sometimes written bitter things against me, yet he has still *holden me by my right hand* to prevent my losing my way in the wildernesses through which I have walked." If he has thus maintained the spiritual life, the earnest of eternal life, we ought not to complain. "*My feet were almost gone*, and they would have quite gone, past recovery, but that thou hast holden me by my right hand and so kept me from falling."

III. He encouraged himself to hope that the same God who had delivered him from this evil work would *preserve him to his heavenly kingdom*, as St. Paul does (2 Tim. iv. 18): "I am now upheld by thee, therefore *thou shalt guide me with thy counsel*, leading me, as thou hast done hitherto, and thou *shalt afterwards receive me to glory*," *v.* 24. The psalmist had like to have paid dearly for following his own counsels in this temptation and therefore resolves for the future to take God's advice. If God direct us in the way of our duty, he will afterwards reconcile us to all the dark providences that now puzzle and perplex us, and ease us of the pain we have been put into by some threatening temptations.

IV. He was hereby quickened to cleave the more closely to God, and very much confirmed and comforted in the choice he had made of him, *v.* 25, 26. He had complained of his afflictions (*v.* 14); but this makes them very light and easy, *All is well if God be mine.* We have here the breathings of a sanctified soul towards God, and its repose in him. *Whom have I in heaven but thee?* There is scarcely a verse in all the psalms more expressive than this of the pious and devout affections of a soul to God. God alone, that made the soul, can make it happy. If God be our felicity we must have him (*Whom have I but thee?*), we must choose him. Our desires must not only be offered up to God, but they must all terminate in him, desiring nothing more than God, but still more and more of him. "*There is none in heaven but thee. I desire none on earth besides thee;* not only none in heaven, which we have but little acquaintance with, but none on earth, where we have many friends and where much of our present interest and concern lie." *My flesh and my heart fail.* Others have experienced and we must expect, the failing both of flesh and heart. The body will fail by sickness, age, and death. *But God is the strength of my heart and my portion for ever.* He speaks as one careless of the body (let that fail, there is no remedy), but as one concerned about the soul, to be *strengthened in the*

JAMIESON, FAUSSET, BROWN

18-20. their end—future (Ps. 37:37, 38), which is dismal and terribly sudden (Prov. 1:27; 29:1), aggravated and hastened by terror. As one despises an unsubstantial dream, so God, waking up to judgment (Ps. 7:6; 44:23), despises their vain shadow of happiness (Ps. 39:6; Isa. 29:7). They are thrown into ruins as a building falling to pieces (Ps. 74:3).

21, 22. He confesses how—**foolish**—lit., "stupid," and —**ignorant**—lit., "not discerning," had been his course of thought. **before thee**—lit., "with Thee," in conduct respecting Thee.

23. Still he was *with God*, as a dependent beneficiary, and so kept from falling (vs. 2).

24. All doubts are silenced in confidence of divine guidance and future glory. **receive me to glory**—lit., "take for (me) glory" (cf. Ps. 68:18; Eph. 4:8).

25, 26. God is his only satisfying good. **strength**—lit., "rock" (Ps. 18:2). **portion**—(Ps. 16:5; Lam. 3:24).

ADAM CLARKE

21. *Thus my heart was grieved.* The views which I got of this subject qu[illegible] founded me; I was equally astonished [illegible] sudden overthrow and my own igno[illegible] felt as if I were a beast in stupidity.

25. *Whom have I in heaven but thee?* The original is more emphatic: "Who is there to me in the heavens? And with thee I have desired nothing in the earth."

26. *My flesh . . . faileth.* I shall soon die: *and my heart*—even my natural courage, will fail; and no support but what is supernatural will then be available. Therefore, he adds, *God is the strength of my heart.* Literally, "the Rock of my heart."

CHARLES H. SPURGEON:

"So foolish was I" (v. 22). He, though a [illegible] of God, had acted as if he had been one o[illegible] fools whom God abhors. Had he not even [illegible]vied them?—and what is that but to aspire [illegible] be like them? The wisest men have enough foll[illegible] in them to ruin them unless grace prevents. "And ignorant." He had acted as if he knew nothing, had babbled like an idiot, had uttered the very drivel of a witless loon. He did not know how sufficiently to express his sense of his own fatuity. "I was as a beast before thee." Even in God's presence he had been brutish and worse than a beast. As the grass-eating ox has but this present life, and can only estimate things thereby, and by the sensual pleasure which they afford, even so had the Psalmist judged happiness by this mortal life—by outward appearances and by fleshly enjoyments. Thus he had, for the time, renounced the dignity of an immortal spirit, and, like a mere animal, judged after the sight of the eyes. We should be very loath to call an inspired man a beast, and yet, penitence made him call himself so; nay, he uses the plural, by way of emphasis, and as if he were worse than any one beast. It was but an evidence of his true wisdom that he was so deeply conscious of his own folly.

—*The Treasury of David*

MATTHEW HENRY

inner man.

V. He was fully convinced of the miserable condition of all wick... people. This he learned in the sanctuary upon ...s occasion, and he would never forget it (*v.* 2)...o, *those that are far from thee,* in a state of ...nce and estrangement, that desire the Almight... depart from them, *shall* certainly *perish.*

VI. He ... greatly encouraged to cleave to God and to ...m him, *v.* 28. Our drawing near to God takes ...ng that makes the bliss. Here is a great happ...own, That it is good to draw near to God; trut... of it lies in the application, "It is good but ... If wicked men, notwithstanding all their fo..., shall perish and be destroyed, then let ...n the Lord God, in him, not in them (see ...5), in him, and not in our worldly prosperity; ...rust in God, and neither fret at them nor be of them.

PSALM 74

Maschil of Asaph.

...ses 1-11

This psalm is entitled *Maschil—a psalm to give* ...*truction,* for it was penned in a day of affliction, ...hich is intended for instruction.

I. The displeasure of God against the people of ...od was the cause and bitterness of all their calamities. They expostulate with God (*v.* 1). Christ himself, upon the cross, cried out, *My God, my God, why hast thou forsaken me?* So the church here, *O God! why hast thou forsaken us for ever?* Here they speak according to their present dark and melancholy apprehensions. The people of God must not think that because they are cast down they are therefore cast off, that because men cast them off therefore God does. This expostulation intimates that they dreaded God's casting them off more than anything. *Why does thy anger smoke?* that is, why does it rise up to such a degree that all about us take notice of it. They plead their relation to him: "We are *the sheep of thy pasture.* That the wolves worry the sheep is not strange; but was ever any shepherd thus displeased at his own sheep? *Remember,* we are *thy congregation* (*v.* 2), and devoted to thy praise; we are *the rod,* or tribe, *of thy inheritance,* from whom thou hast received praise and worship more than from the neighbouring nations. We are pleading for *Mount Zion, wherein thou hast dwelt,* which has been the place of thy peculiar delight and residence, thy demesne and mansion. It is *thy congregation,* which thou hast *purchased of old* by many miracles of mercy when they were first formed into a people; it is *thy inheritance, which thou hast redeemed* when they were sold into servitude. Now, Lord, wilt thou now abandon a people that cost thee so dear, and has been so dear to thee?" Much more reason have we to hope that God will not cast off any whom Christ has redeemed with his own blood. "*Lift up thy feet;* that is, come with speed to repair the desolations that are made in thy sanctuary, which otherwise will be perpetual and irreparable."

II. They complain of the outrage and cruelty of their enemies, but only what they had done against the sanctuary and the synagogue. The temple at Jerusalem was the *dwelling-place of God's name,* and therefore the *sanctuary,* or *holy place, v.* 7. In this the enemies did wickedly (*v.* 3), for they destroyed it in downright contempt of God and affront to him. They *roared in the midst of God's congregations, v.* 4, where God's faithful people attended on him with a humble reverent silence. *They set up their ensigns for signs.* The banners of their army they set up in the temple. This daring defiance of God and his power touched his people in a tender part. Men took a pride in destroying *the carved work* of the temple, *v.* 5, 6. Some read it thus: *They show themselves, as one that lifts up axes on high in a thicket of trees,* for so do they break down the carved work of the temple; they make no more scruple of breaking down the rich wainscot of the temple than woodcutters do of hewing trees in the forest. They set fire to it, and so violated or *destroyed it to the ground, v.* 7. The Chaldeans burnt the house of God, 2 Chron. xxxvi. 19. And the Romans *left not there one stone upon another* (Matt. xxiv. 2), till Zion, the holy mountain, was by Titus Vespasian ploughed as a field. He complains of the desolations of the synagogues, or schools of the prophets. *Let us destroy them together;* not only the temple, but all the places of religious worship and the worshippers with them. They *burnt up all the synagogues of God in the land* and laid them all waste.

III. The great aggravation of all these calamities

JAMIESON, FAUSSET, BROWN

27, 28. The lot of apostates, described by a figure of frequent use (Jer. 3:1, 3; Ezek. 23:35), is contrasted with his, who finds happiness in nearness to God (Jas. 4:8), and his delightful work the declaration of His praise.

PSALM 74

Vss. 1-23. If the historical allusions of vss. 6-8, etc., be referred, as is probable, to the period of the captivity, the author was probably a descendant and namesake of Asaph, David's contemporary and singer (cf. II Chron. 35:15; Ezra 2:41). He complains of God's desertion of His Church, and appeals for aid, encouraging himself by recounting some of God's mighty deeds, and urges his prayer on the ground of God's covenant relation to His people, and the wickedness of His and their common enemy.

1. cast . . . off—with abhorrence (cf. Ps. 43:2; 44: 9). There is no disavowal of guilt implied. The figure of fire to denote God's anger is often used; and here, and in Deuteronomy 29:20, by the word "smoke," suggests its continuance. **sheep . . . pasture**—(Cf. Ps. 80:1; 95:7).

2. The terms to denote God's relation to His people increase in force: "congregation"—"purchased"—"redeemed"—"Zion," His dwelling.

3. Lift . . . feet—(Gen. 29:1)—i.e., Come (to behold) the desolations (Ps. 73:19).

roar—with bestial fury. **congregations**—lit., "worshipping assemblies." **ensigns**—lit., "signs"—substituted their idolatrous objects, or tokens of authority, for those articles of the temple which denoted God's presence. **5, 6.** Though some terms and clauses here are very obscure, the general sense is that the spoilers destroyed the beauties of the temple with the violence of woodmen. **was famous**—lit., "was known." **carved work**—(I Kings 6:29). **thereof**—i.e., of the temple, in the writer's mind, though not expressed till vs. 7, in which its utter destruction by fire is mentioned (II Kings 25:9; Isa. 64:11). **7. defiled**—or, profaned, as in Psalm 89:39.

8. together—at once, all alike. **synagogues**—lit., "assemblies," for places of assembly, whether such as schools of the prophets (II Kings 4:23), or "synagogues" in the usual sense, there is much doubt.

ADAM CLARKE

PSALM 74

The title is, Maschil of Asaph, or, "A Psalm of Asaph, to give instruction." That this psalm was written at a time when the Temple was ruined, Jerusalem burnt, and the prophets scattered or destroyed, is evident.

CHARLES H. SPURGEON:

God is never weary of his people so as to abhor them; and even when his anger is turned against them, it is but for a small moment and with a view to their eternal good. Grief in its distraction asks strange questions and surmises impossible terrors. It is a wonder of grace that the Lord has not long ago put us away as men lay aside cast-off garments, but he hates putting away, and will still be patient with his chosen. "Why doth thine anger smoke against the sheep of thy pasture?" They are thine, they are the objects of thy care, they are poor, silly, and defenseless things: pity them, forgive them, and come to their rescue. They are but sheep; do not continue to be wroth with them. It is a terrible thing when the anger of God smokes, but it is an infinite mercy that it does not break into a devouring flame. It is proper to pray the Lord to remove every sign of his wrath, for it is to those who are truly the Lord's sheep a most painful thing to be the objects of his displeasure. To vex the Holy Spirit is no mean sin, and yet how frequently are we guilty of it; hence it is no marvel that we are often under a cloud.

—*The Treasury of David*

4. *Thine enemies roar.* Thy people, who were formerly a distinct and separate people, and who would not even touch a Gentile, are now obliged to mingle with the most profane. Their boisterous mirth, their cruel mockings, their insulting commands are heard everywhere in all our assemblies. *They set up their ensigns for signs.* They set up their standards in the place of ours. The fifth, sixth, and seventh verses give a correct historical account of the ravages committed by the Babylonians, as we may see from 2 Kings xxv. 4, 7-9 and Jer. lii. 7, 18-19.

8. *Let us destroy them.* Their object was totally to annihilate the political existence of the Jewish people. *They have burned up all the synagogues of God in the land.* It is supposed that there were no *synagogues* in the land till after the Babylonish captivity. How then could the Chaldeans burn up any in Judea? The word *moadey,* which we translate *synagogues,* may be

MATTHEW HENRY

was that they had no prospect at all of relief, nor could they foresee an end of them (*v.* 9): "We see our enemy's sign set up in the sanctuary, but *we see not our signs. There is no more any prophet* to tell us how long the trouble will last and when things concerning us shall have an end, that hope may support us under our troubles." *How long shall the adversary reproach and blaspheme thy name?* Not "How long shall we be troubled?" but "How long shall God be blasphemed? *Why withdrawest thou thy hand*, and dost not stretch it out, to deliver thy people and destroy thy enemies?"

Verses 12–17

Two things quiet the minds of those that are here sorrowing for the solemn assembly:—

I. That God is the God of Israel, a God in covenant with his people (*v.* 12): *God is my King of old.* This comes in both as a plea in prayer to God and as a prop to their own faith and hope, to encourage themselves to expect deliverance, considering the *days of old*, lxxvii. 5. Several things are here mentioned which God had done for his people as their King of old, which encouraged them to commit themselves to him and depend upon him.

1. He had divided the sea before them when they came out of Egypt, not by the strength of Moses or his rod, but by his own strength; and he that could do that could do anything.

2. He had destroyed Pharaoh and the Egyptians. Pharaoh was the *leviathan*; the Egyptians were *the dragons*, fierce, and cruel. God crushed their powers, though complicated, and at last drowned them all in the Red Sea. This was typical of Christ's victory over Satan and his kingdom, pursuant to the first promise, that the seed of the woman should break the serpent's head. This providence was meat to their faith and hope, to encourage them in the other difficulties they were likely to meet in the wilderness.

3. God had both ways altered the course of nature, both in fetching streams out of the rock and turning streams into rock, *v.* 15. He had dissolved the rock into waters: *Thou didst bring out the fountain and the flood* out of the rock, out of the flinty rock. Let this never be forgotten, but let it especially be remembered that the rock was Christ, and the waters out of it were spiritual drink. He had congealed the waters into rock: *Thou driedst up mighty* rapid *rivers*, Jordan particularly at the time when it overflowed all its banks. He that did these things could now deliver his oppressed people.

II. That the God of Israel is the God of nature, *v.* 16, 17. It is he that orders the regular successions and revolutions, day and night. He is the Lord of all time. It is he that opens the eyelids of the morning light, and draws the curtains of the evening shadow. *He has prepared the moon and the sun.* "Thou hast *appointed all the bounds of the earth*, and the different climates of its several regions, for *thou hast made summer and winter*, the frigid and the torrid zones; or, rather, the constant revolutions of the year and its several seasons." He that had power at first to settle, and still to preserve, this course of nature by the diurnal and annual motions of the heavenly bodies, has certainly all power both to save and to destroy. He that is faithful to his covenant with the day and with the night, will certainly make good his promise to his people. His covenant with Abraham and his seed is as firm as that with Noah and his sons, Gen. viii. 21.

Verses 18–23

The psalmist here, in the name of the church, most earnestly begs that God would appear for them against their enemies, and put an end to their present troubles. *Arise, O God! plead thy own cause.*

I. The persecutors are God's sworn enemies: "Lord, they have not only abused us, they have directly and immediately reproached thee, and *blasphemed thy name*," *v.* 18. The psalmist insists much upon this: "We dare not answer their reproaches; Lord, do thou answer them. Remember that the *foolish people have blasphemed thy name* (*v.* 18) and that still *the foolish man reproaches thee daily.*" Those that reproach God are foolish. As atheism is folly (xiv. 1), profaneness and blasphemy are no less so. Perhaps those are cried up as the wits of the age that ridicule religion and sacred things; but really they are the greatest fools. They do not hide their blasphemous thoughts in their own bosoms, but proclaim them with a loud voice (*forget not the voice of thy enemies*, *v.* 23). God needs not to be put in remembrance by us of what he has to do, but thus we must show our concern for his honour and believe that he will vindicate us.

II. The persecuted are his covenant-people. They have fallen into the hands of *the multitude of the*

JAMIESON, FAUSSET, BROWN

9. **signs**—of God's presence, as altar, ark, etc. (cf. vs. 4; II Chron. 36:18, 19; Dan. 5:2). **no more any prophet**—(Isa. 3:2; Jer. 40:1; 43:6). **how long**—this is to last. Jeremiah's prophecy (25:11), if published, may not have been generally known or understood. To the bulk of the people, during the captivity, the occasional and local prophetical services of Jeremiah, Ezekiel, and Daniel would not make an exception to the clause, "there is no more any prophet." **10.** (Cf. Ps. 31:1.) **how long . . . reproach**—us as deserted of God. **blaspheme thy name**—or, perfections, as power, goodness, etc. (Ps. 29:2). **11.** Why cease to help us? (Cf. Ps. 3:7; 7:6; 60:5).

12. For—lit., "And," in an adversative sense.

13-15. Examples of the "salvation wrought" are cited. **divide the sea**—i.e., Red Sea. **brakest . . . waters**—Pharaoh and his host (cf. Isa. 51:9, 10; Ezek. 29:3, 4).

heads of leviathan—The word is a collective, and so used for many. **the people . . . wilderness**—i.e., wild beasts, as conies (Prov. 30:25, 26), are called a people. Others take the passages literally, that the sea monsters thrown out on dry land were food for the wandering Arabs.

cleave the fountain—i.e., the rocks of Horeb and Kadesh—for fountains.

driedst up—Jordan, and, perhaps, Arnon and Jabbok (Num. 21:14).

16, 17. The fixed orders of nature and bounds of earth are of God.

18. (Cf. vs. 10; Deut. 32:6.) The contrast is striking—that such a God should be thus insulted!

ADAM CLARKE

taken in a more general sense, and mean any places where religious assemblies were held. This is the only place in the Old Testament where we have the word synagogue. Indeed, wherever there was a place in which God met with patriarch or prophet, and any memorial of it was preserved, there was a *moed*, or place of religious meeting; and all such places the Chaldeans would destroy, pursuant to their design to extinguish the Jewish religion, and blot out all its memorials from the earth.

13. *Thou didst divide the sea.* When our fathers came from Egypt.

Thou brakest the heads of the dragons in the waters. Pharaoh, his captains, and all his hosts were drowned in the Red Sea, when attempting to pursue them.

15. *Thou didst cleave the fountain.* Thou didst cleave the rock in the wilderness, of which all the congregation drank.

Thou driedst up mighty rivers. Does not this refer to the cutting off the waters of the Jordan, so that the people passed over dry-shod?

CHARLES H. SPURGEON:

"Remember this, that the enemy hath reproached, O Lord" (74:18). Against thee, the ever-glorious Maker of all things, have they spoken; thine honor have they assailed, and defied even thee. This is forcible pleading indeed, and reminds us of Moses and Hezekiah in their intercessions: "What wilt thou do unto thy great name?" "It may be that the Lord thy God will hear the words of Rabshakeh, who hath reproached the living God." Jehovah is a jealous God, and will surely glorify his own name; here our hope finds foothold. "And that the foolish people have blasphemed thy name." The meanness of the enemy is here pleaded. Sinners are fools, and shall fools be allowed to insult the Lord and oppress his people; shall the abjects curse the Lord and defy him to his face? When error grows too bold its day is near, and its fall certain. Arrogance foreshadows ripeness of evil, and the next step is rottenness. Instead of being alarmed when bad men grow worse and more audacious, we may reasonably take heart, for the hour of their judgment is evidently near.—*The Treasury of David*

MATTHEW HENRY

wicked, v. 19. *The dark places of the earth are full of the habitations of cruelty.* The land of the Chaldeans where there was none of the light of the knowledge of the true God (though otherwise it was famed for learning and arts), was indeed a dark place; the inhabitants of it were *alienated from the life of God through the ignorance that was in them,* and therefore they were cruel: where there was no true divinity there was scarcely to be found common humanity. The psalmist pleads with God: "It is *thy turtle-dove* that is ready to be swallowed up by the multitude of the wicked," *v.* 19. The church is a dove for harmlessness and mildness, a dove for mournfulness in a day of distress, a turtle-dove for fidelity and the constancy of love. "Shall thy turtle-dove, that is true to thee and devoted to thy honour, be delivered into the *hand of the multitude of the wicked?* Lord, it will be thy honour to help the weak, especially thy own. Wilt thou not perform the promises thou hast, in thy covenant, made to them? Appear, Lord, for those that will praise thy name, against those that blaspheme it."

PSALM 75

To the chief musician, Al-taschith. A psalm *or* song of Asaph.

Verses 1–5

I. The psalmist gives to God the praise of the great things he had done for him and for his people Israel (*v.* 1): *Unto thee, O God! do we give thanks.* Not only *I* do give thanks, but *we* do, I and all my friends. There are many works which God does for his people that may truly be called *wondrous works,* out of the common course of providence. These wondrous works declare the nearness of his name.

II. He lays himself under an obligation to use his power well (*v.* 2): *When I shall receive the congregation I will judge uprightly.* Here he takes it for granted that God would, in due time, perfect that which concerned him. "When I am a judge I will judge, and *judge uprightly;* not as those that went before me, who either neglected judgment or perverted it." Public trusts are to be managed with great integrity; those that judge must judge uprightly, according to the rules of justice, without respect of persons.

III. He promises himself that his government would be a public blessing to Israel, *v.* 3. The present state of the kingdom was very bad: *The earth and all the inhabitants thereof are dissolved;* and no marvel, when the former reign was so dissolute that all went to rack and ruin. They were all to pieces, two against three and three against two, crumbled into factions and parties, which was likely to issue in their ruin; but *I bear up the pillars of it.* The fabric would have sunk if David had not held up the pillars of it. This may well be applied to Christ and his government.

IV. He checks those that opposed his government, that were against his accession to it and obstructed the administration of it. *I said unto the fools, Deal not foolishly.* As soon as he came to the crown he issued a proclamation against vice and profaneness, and here we have the contents of it. 1. To the simple sneaking sinners, the fools in Israel, that corrupted themselves, he said, "*Deal not foolishly;* do not act so directly contrary both to your reason and to your interest." 2. To the proud daring sinners, the wicked, that set God himself at defiance, he says, "*Lift not up the horn;* boast not of your power and prerogatives; *lift not up your horn on high,* as though you could have what you will and do what you will; *speak not with a stiff neck,* in which is an iron sinew, that will never bend to the will of God in the government; for those that will not bend shall break."

Verses 6–10

I. Here are two great truths laid down concerning God's government of the world.

1. That from God alone kings receive their power (*v.* 6, 7), and therefore to God alone David would give the praise of his advancement. We see strange revolutions in states and kingdoms, and are surprised at the sudden disgrace of some and elevation of others. *Promotion comes not from the east, nor from the west, nor from the desert.* Men cannot gain promotion either by the wisdom or wealth of the children of the east, nor by the numerous forces of the isles of the Gentiles, that lay westward, nor those of Egypt or Arabia, that lay south; no concurring smiles of second causes will raise men to preferment without the first cause. The learned Bishop Lloyd (*Serm. in loc.*) gives this gloss upon it: "All men took the original of power to be from heaven, but from whom there many knew not; the eastern nations, who were gener-

JAMIESON, FAUSSET, BROWN

19. multitude—lit., "beast," their flock or company of men (Ps. 68:10).

turtle-dove—i.e., the meek and lonely Church. **congregation**—lit., "company," as above—thus the Church is represented as the spoiled and defeated remnant of an army, exposed to violence. **20.** And the prevalence of injustice in heathen lands is a reason for invoking God's regard to His promise (cf. Num. 14:21; Ps. 7:16; 18:48). **21. oppressed**—broken (Ps. 9:9). **return**—from seeking God. **ashamed**—(Ps. 35:4). **22, 23.** (Cf. Ps. 3:7; 7:6.) God hears the wicked to their own ruin (Gen. 4:10; 18:20).

PSALM 75

Vss. 1-10. *Al-taschith*—(Cf. Ps. 57, title). In impending danger, the Psalmist, anticipating relief in view of God's righteous government, takes courage and renders praise.

1. God's name or perfections are set forth by His wondrous works.

2, 3. These verses express the purpose of God to administer a just government, and in a time of anarchy that He sustains the nation. Some apply the words to the Psalmist. **receive the congregation**—lit., "take a set time" (Ps. 102:13; Hos. 2:3), or an assembly at a set time—i.e., for judging.

Pillars of it—(I Sam. 2:8).

4-8. Here the writer speaks in view of God's declaration, warning the wicked.

Lift . . . up the horn—to exalt power, here, of the wicked himself—i.e., to be arrogant or self-elated. **speak . . . neck**—insolently.

promotion—lit., "a lifting up." God is the only right judge of merit.

ADAM CLARKE

PSALM 75

The title is, "To the chief Musician, or conqueror, Al-taschith, destroy not, A Psalm or Song of Asaph." See this title Al-taschith explained Psalm lvii. The psalm seems to have been composed during the Captivity, and appears to be a continuation of the subject in the preceding.

1. *Unto thee, O God, do we give thanks.* The numerous manifestations of Thy providence and mercy show that Thou art not far off, but near; this *thy wondrous works declare.* These words would make a proper conclusion to the preceding psalm, which seems to end very abruptly. The second verse is the commencement of the divine answer to the prayer of Asaph.

F. B. MEYER:

"God is near" (vv. 1–3). There are high moments in life when we realize how real and near God is. The ground on which we stand is holy. We know that we are safe in the pavilion of our Father's care. Then we give repeated thanks (v. 1). Presently God speaks and assures us that when the earth and its inhabitants dissolve, he will sustain its pillars. What an encouragement is this when the whole world seems about to be dissolved!

Turning from God to man, the psalmist rebukes his enemies and bids them cease their arrogant talk and behavior (v. 4). The horn is the strength of certain beasts and is a symbol of power (Deut. 33:17; Dan. 7:7). But God is the supreme ruler of men. Our position or promotion in life is his arrangement, to be held as a sacred trust for him. Let us, amid a world in arms, be lighthearted and sing. God will take care of those who trust him.

—*Bible Commentary*

6. *For promotion cometh neither from the east,* etc. As if the Lord had said, speaking to the Babylonians, None of all the surrounding powers shall be able to help you; none shall pluck you out of My hand. I am the Judge; I will pull you down, and set My afflicted people up, v. 7.

MATTHEW HENRY

ally given to astrology, took it to come from their stars, especially the sun, their god. No, says David, it comes neither from the east nor from the west, neither from the rising nor from the setting of such a planet, or such a constellation, nor from the south, nor from the exaltation of the sun or any star in the mid-heaven." He mentions not the north because the same word that signifies the north signifies the secret place, and from the secret of God's counsel it does come, or from the oracle in Zion, which lay on the north side of Jerusalem. *God is the judge*, the governor or umpire. When parties contend for the prize, he *puts down one and sets up another* as he sees fit, so as to serve his own purposes and bring to pass his own counsels. He, who is infinitely wise, holy, and good, has power to set up and put down whom, and when, and how he pleases.

2. That from God alone all must receive their doom (*v.* 8): *In the hand of the Lord there is a cup*, which he puts into the hands of the children of men, a cup of providence, mixed up of many ingredients. The sufferings of Christ are called a *cup*, Matt. xx. 22; John xviii. 11. *The wine is red*, denoting the wrath of God, which is infused into the judgments executed on sinners. It is red as fire for it burns. It is *full of mixture*. There are mixtures of mercy and grace in the cup of affliction when it is put into the hands of God's own people, mixtures of the curse when it is put into the hands of the wicked; it is wine mingled with gall. Some drops of this wrath may light on good people; they have their share in common calamities; but the dregs of the cup are reserved for the wicked. The calamity itself is but the vehicle into which the curse is infused, the top of which has little of the infusion; but the sediment is pure wrath, and that shall fall to the share of sinners. They shall *wring them out*, that not a drop of the wrath may be left behind.

II. Here are two practical inferences. 1. He will praise God, and give him glory, for the power to which he has advanced him (*v.* 9): *I will declare for ever* that which *thy wondrous works declare*, *v.* 1. He will give glory to God, as the God of Jacob, knowing it was for Jacob his servant's sake, and because he loved his people Israel, that he made him king over them. 2. He will use the power with which he is entrusted for the great ends for which it was put into his hands, *v.* 10, as before, *v.* 2, 4. "Though not all the heads, yet *all the horns, of the wicked will I cut off*, with which they push their poor neighbours; I will disable them to do mischief."

JAMIESON, FAUSSET, BROWN

CHARLES H. SPURGEON:

"For in the hand of the Lord there is a cup" (75:8). The punishment of the wicked is prepared, God himself holds it in readiness; he has collected and concocted woes most dread, and in the chalice of his wrath he holds it. They scoffed his feast of love; they shall be dragged to his table of justice, and made to drink their due deserts.

"And the wine is red." The retribution is terrible—it is blood for blood, foaming vengeance for foaming malice. The very color of divine wrath is terrible; what must the taste be? "It is full of mixture." Spices of anger, justice, and incensed mercy are there. Their misdeeds, their blasphemies, their persecutions have strengthened the liquor as with potent drugs. Ten thousand woes are burning in the depths of that fiery cup, which to the brim is filled with indignation.
—The Treasury of David

in the hand . . . a cup . . . red—God's wrath often thus represented (cf. Isa. 51:17; Jer. 25: 15).

but the dregs—lit., "surely the dregs, they shall drain it."

9, 10. Contrasted is the lot of the pious who will praise God, and, acting under His direction, will destroy the power of the wicked, and exalt that of the righteous.

ADAM CLARKE

8. *It is full of mixture.* Alluding to that mingled potion of stupefying drugs given to criminals to drink previously to their execution. See a parallel passage to this, Jer. xxv. 15-26.

10. *All the horns of the wicked.* All their power and influence will I cut off, and will exalt and extend the power of the *righteous*. All was punctually fulfilled: the *wicked*—the Babylonians—were all cut off; the *righteous*—the Jews—were delivered and *exalted*.

MATTHEW HENRY

PSALM 76

To the chief musician on Neginoth. A psalm *or* song of Asaph.

Verses 1–6

The psalmist triumphs here in God, the centre of all our triumphs.

I. In the revelation God had made of himself to them, *v.* 1. It is the honour and privilege of Judah and Israel that among them *God is known*, and where he is known *his name* will be *great*.

II. In the tokens of God's special presence with them in his ordinances, *v.* 2. In the whole land of Judah and Israel God was known, but *in Salem, in Zion*, were *his tabernacle* and *his dwelling-place*. There he kept court; there he received the homage of his people by their sacrifices; thither they came to address themselves to him, and of that place he said, *Here will I dwell, for I have desired it.*

III. In the victories they had obtained over their enemies (*v.* 3): *There broke he the arrows of the bow.* 1. Here are bow and arrows, shield and sword, and all for battle; but all are broken and rendered useless. In the tabernacle and dwelling-place in Zion, there he broke the arrows of the bow; it was done in the field of battle, and yet it is said to be done in the sanctuary, because done in answer to the prayers which God's people there made to him. Public successes are owing as much to what is done in the church as to what is done in the camp. Now,

2. This victory redounded very much to the immortal honour of Israel's God (*v.* 4): *"Thou art*, and hast manifested thyself to be, *more glorious and excellent than the mountains of prey.* Than the great and mighty ones who think themselves firmly fixed like mountains, but are really mountains of prey, oppressive to all about them. It is their glory to destroy; it is thine to deliver." *The stouthearted have despoiled and disarmed themselves* (so some read it); when God pleases he can make his enemies to weaken and destroy themselves. *They have slept*, not the sleep of the righteous, but *their sleep*, the sleep of sinners, that shall awake to everlasting shame. The men of might can no more *find their hands* than the stout-hearted can their spirit. As the bold men are

JAMIESON, FAUSSET, BROWN

PSALM 76

Vss. 1-12. *On Neginoth*—(Cf. Ps. 4, title). This Psalm commemorates what the preceding anticipates: God's deliverance of His people by a signal interposition of power against their enemies. The occasion was probably the events narrated in II Kings 19:35; Isaiah 37. (Cf. Ps. 46.)

1, 2. These well-known terms denote God's people and Church and His intimate and glorious relations to them. **Salem**—(Gen. 14:18) is Jerusalem.

3. brake . . . the arrows—lit., "thunderbolts" (Ps. 78: 48), from their rapid flight or ignition (cf. Ps. 18:14; Eph. 6:16). **the battle**—for arms (Hos. 2:18).

4. Thou—God. **mountains of prey**—great victorious nations, as Assyria (Isa. 41:15; Ezek. 38:11, 12; Zech. 4:7).

5. slept their sleep—died (Ps. 13:3). **none . . . found . . . hands**—are powerless. **6. chariot and horse**—for those fighting on them (cf. Ps. 68: 17).

ADAM CLARKE

PSALM 76

The title, "To the chief Musician on Neginoth, a Psalm or Song of Asaph." See the titles to Psalms iv and vi. If Asaph was its author, it could not be the Asaph that flourished in the days of David but some other gifted and divinely inspired man of the same name, by whom several others of the psalms appear to have been composed during the Captivity.

2. *In Salem also is his tabernacle. Salem* was the ancient name of Jebus, afterward called Jerusalem. Here was the *tabernacle* set up; but afterwards, when the Temple was built on Mount Zion, there was His habitation. The psalm was evidently composed after the building of Solomon's Temple.

3. *There brake he the arrows of the bow.* "The fiery arrows."

5. *The stouthearted are spoiled.* The boasting blasphemers, such as Rab-shakeh, and his master, Sennacherib, the king of Assyria. *They have slept their sleep.* They were asleep in their tent when the destroying angel, the suffocating wind, destroyed the whole; they over whom it passed never more awoke.

cowed, so the strong men are lamed, and cannot so much as find their hands, to save their own heads, much less to hurt their enemies.

Verses 7–12

This victory is here made to speak three things:—

I. Terror to God's enemies (*v.* 7–9): *Thou, even thou, art to be feared.* Let all the world learn by this event to stand in awe of the great God. *Who may stand in thy sight from the minute that thou art angry?* God's people are the *meek of the earth* (Zeph. ii, 3) that can bear any wrong, but do none. Though the meek of the earth are by their meekness exposed to injury, yet God will, sooner or later, appear for their salvation. When God comes to save *all the meek of the earth,* he will *cause judgment to be heard from heaven.* The righteous God long seems to keep silence, yet, sooner or later he will make judgment to be heard. When God is speaking judgment from heaven it is time for the earth to compose itself into an awful and reverent silence: *The earth feared and was still.*

II. Comfort to God's people, *v.* 10. *Surely the wrath of man shall praise thee,* not only by the checks given to it, when it shall be forced to confess its own impotency, but even by the liberty given to it for a time. The more *the heathen rage* and plot *against the Lord and his anointed* the more will God be praised for setting *his King upon his holy hill of Zion* in spite of them, ii. 1, 6. What will not turn to his praise shall not be suffered to break out: *The remainder of wrath shalt thou restrain.*

III. Duty to all, *v.* 11, 12. Let all submit themselves to this great God and become his loyal subjects. We are commanded to do homage to the King of kings: *Vow and pay;* that is, take an oath of allegiance to him and make conscience of keeping it. And, having taken him for our King, let us bring presents to him. Not that God needs any present we can bring, but prayers and praises, and especially our hearts, are the presents we should bring to the Lord our God. He ought to be feared: *He is the fear* (so the word is); his name is glorious and with him is terrible majesty. He shall *cut off the spirit of princes;* he shall slip it off as easily as we slip off a flower from the stalk or a bunch of grapes from the vine; so the word signifies.

7. may . . . sight—contend with Thee (Deut. 9: 4; Josh. 7:12).

8, 9. God's judgment on the wicked is His people's deliverance (Ps. 9:12; 10:7).

10. Man's wrath praises God by its futility before His power.

restrain—or, gird—i.e., Thyself, as with a sword, with which to destroy, or as an ornament to Thy praise. **11, 12.** Invite homage to such a God (II Chron. 32:23), who can stop the breath of kings and princes when He wills (Dan. 5:23).

7. *Thou, even thou, art to be feared.* The Hebrew is simple, but very emphatic: *attah nora attah,* "Thou art terrible; Thou art." The repetition of the pronoun deepens the sense. *When once thou art angry.* Literally, "From the time thou art angry." In the moment Thy wrath is kindled, in that moment judgment is executed.

9. *The meek of the earth.* The humbled or oppressed people of the land. The poor Jews, now utterly helpless, and calling upon the Lord for succor.

10. *Surely the wrath of man shall praise thee.* The rage of Sennacherib shall only serve to manifest Thy glory. The stronger he is, and the more he threatens, and the weaker Thy people, the more shall Thy majesty and mercy appear in his destruction and their support. *The remainder of wrath shalt thou restrain.* The Hebrew gives rather a different sense: "Thou shalt gird thyself with the remainder of wrath." Even after Thou hast sent this signal destruction upon Sennacherib and his army, Thou wilt continue to pursue the remnant of the persecutors of Thy people; their wrath shall be the cause of the excitement of Thy justice to destroy them. As a man girds himself with his girdle, that he may the better perform his work, so Thou wilt gird thyself with wrath, that Thou mayest destroy Thy enemies.

11. *Vow, and pay unto the Lord.* Bind yourselves to Him, and forget not your obligations. *That ought to be feared.* "To the terrible One."

PSALM 77

To the chief musician, to Jeduthun. A psalm of Asaph.

Verses 1–10

We have here the lively protraiture of a good man under prevailing melancholy. Drooping saints, that are of a sorrowful spirit, may here as in a glass see their own faces. The griefs and fears seem to have been over when he penned this record, for he says (*v.* 1), *I cried unto God, and he gave ear unto me.* He inserts it in the beginning of his narrative as an intimation that his trouble did not end in despair.

I. His melancholy prayers. *My voice was unto God, and I cried, even with my voice unto God.* Thus he gave vent to his grief and gained some ease; and thus he took the right way in order to relief (*v.* 2): *In the day of my trouble I sought the Lord.* Those that are under trouble of mind must not think to drink it away, or laugh it away, but must pray it away.

II. His melancholy grief. *My sore,* or wound, *ran in the night,* and bled inwardly, and it ceased not, no, not in the time appointed for rest and sleep. *My soul refused to be comforted;* he had no mind to hearken to those that would be his comforters. Those that are in sorrow affront God, if they refuse to be comforted.

III. His melancholy musings. When he remembered God his thoughts fastened only upon his justice, and wrath, and dreadful majesty, and thus God himself became a terror to him. He could not enjoy sleep, which, if it be quiet and refreshing, is a parenthesis to our griefs and cares: "*Thou holdest my eyes waking* with thy terrors, which make me full of *tossings to and fro until the dawning of the day.*" He was so troubled that he could not speak and refresh himself. Grief never preys so much upon the spirits as when it is thus smothered and pent up.

IV. His melancholy reflections (*v.* 5, 6): "*I have considered the days of old,* and compared them with the present days; and our former prosperity does but aggravate our present calamities: for we see not the wonders that our fathers told us of." But *say not thou* that *the former days were better than these.* Neither let the remembrance of the comforts we have lost make us unthankful for those that are left. Particularly he *called to remembrance his song in the night,* but he was out of tune, and the remembrance

PSALM 77

Vss. 1-20. *To Jeduthun*—(Cf. Ps. 39, title). In a time of great affliction, when ready to despair, the Psalmist derives relief from calling to mind God's former and wonderful works of delivering power and grace.

1, expresses the purport of the Psalm;

2, his importunacy. **my sore ran . . . night**—lit., "my hand was spread," or, stretched out (cf. Ps. 44:20). **ceased not**—lit., "grew not numb," or, feeble (Gen. 45:26; Ps. 38:8). **my soul . . . comforted**—(cf. Gen. 37:35; Jer. 31:15).

3-9. His sad state contrasted with former joys. **was troubled**—lit., "violently agitated," or disquieted (Ps. 39:6; 41:5).

holdest . . . waking—or, fast, that I cannot sleep. Thus he is led to express his anxious feelings in several earnest questions indicative of impatient sorrow.

PSALM 77

The title, "To the chief Musician (or conqueror), to Jeduthun, A Psalm of Asaph." On this title we may observe that both Asaph and Jeduthun were celebrated singers in the time of David, and no doubt were masters or leaders of bands which long after their times were called by their names. Hence psalms composed during and after the Captivity have these names prefixed to them. But there is reason to believe also that there was a person of the name of Asaph in the captivity at Babylon. The author must be considered as speaking in the persons of the captive Israelites. It may however be adapted to the case of any individual in spiritual distress through strong temptation, or from a sense of the divine displeasure in consequence of backsliding.

2. *My sore ran in the night, and ceased not.* This is a most unaccountable translation; the literal meaning of *yadi niggerah,* which we translate *my sore ran,* is, "my hand was stretched out," i.e., in prayer. He continued during the whole night with his voice and hands lifted up to God, and ceased not.

3. *My spirit was overwhelmed.* As the verb is in the *hithpael* conjugation, the word must mean, "My spirit was overpowered in itself." It purposed to involve itself in this calamity.

4. *Thou holdest mine eyes waking.* Literally, "Thou keepest the watches of mine eyes"—my grief is so great that I cannot sleep. *I am so troubled that I cannot speak.* This shows an increase of sorrow and anguish. At first he felt his misery, and called aloud. "Small troubles are loquacious; the great are dumb."

5. *I have considered the days of old.* "I have counted up"; I have reckoned up the various dispensations of Thy mercy in behalf of the distressed, marked down in the history of our fathers.

6. *I call to remembrance my song in the night.* I do not think that *neginathi* means *my song.*

MATTHEW HENRY

did but *pour out his soul in him*, xlii. 4. See Job xxxv. 10.

V. His melancholy fears and apprehensions: "*I communed with my own heart, v.* 6. Come, my soul, what will be the issue of these things? And thus I began to reason, *Will the Lord cast off for ever*, as he does for the present? His *tender mercies* have been withheld, but *are they shut up*, shut up *in anger*?" (*v.* 7-9). This is the language of a disconsolate deserted soul, not uncommon even with those that *fear the Lord*, Isa. l. 10. Spiritual trouble is of all trouble most grievous to a gracious soul; nothing wounds and pierces it like the apprehensions of God's being angry. God's own people, in a cloudy and dark day, may be tempted to make desperate conclusions about their own spiritual state and the condition of God's church and kingdom in the world, and, as to both, to give up all for gone. But we must not give way to such suggestions as these. Let faith answer them from the Scripture: *Will the Lord cast off for ever?* God forbid, Rom. xi. 1. *Is his mercy clean gone for ever?* No; his *mercy endures for ever*, ciii. 17. *Doth his promise fail for evermore?* No; *it is impossible for God to lie*, Heb. vi. 18. *Has he in anger shut up his tender mercies?* No; they are *new every morning* (Lam. iii. 23); and therefore, *How shall I give thee up, Ephraim?* Hos. xi. 8, 9. On a sudden, he checked himself with that word, *Selah*, "Stop there; go no further," and he then chid himself (*v.* 10): *I said, This is my infirmity.* He is soon aware that it is not well said, and therefore, "*Why art thou cast down, O my soul? I said, This is my affliction;* everyone has his affliction, his trouble in the flesh; and this is mine, the cross I must take up." Despondency of spirit, and distrust of God, under affliction, are too often the infirmities of good people. When at any time it is working in us we must thus suppress the rising of it. We must argue down the insurrections of unbelief, *But I will remember the years of the right hand of the Most High.* He had been considering the *years of ancient times* (*v.* 5), the blessings formerly enjoyed, but now he considered them as *the years of the right hand of the Most High*, that those blessings of ancient times came from the sovereign disposal of his right hand who is *over all, God blessed for ever*, and this satisfied him.

Verses 11-20

The psalmist here recovers himself. He tried again, and, upon this second trial, found it not in vain. "*I will remember, surely I will*, what God has done for his people of old, till I can thence infer a happy issue of the present dark dispensations," *v.* 11, 12. The due remembrance of the works of God will be a powerful antidote against distrust of his promise, for he is God and changes not.

Two things, in general, satisfied him:

I. That *God's way is in the sanctuary, v.* 13. It is *in holiness*, so some. He has holy ends in all he does. His way is according to his promise, which he has made known in the sanctuary. All he does is intended for the good of his church.

II. That God's *way is in the sea.* Though God is holy, just, and good, yet we cannot give an account of the reasons of his proceedings. *His path is in the great waters and his footsteps are not known, v.* 19. God's ways are like the deep waters which cannot be fathomed (xxxvi. 6), like the way of a ship in the sea, which cannot be tracked, Prov. xxx. 18, 19. *Who is so great a God as our God?* Let us first give to God the glory of the great things he has done for his people, and acknowledge him, herein, great above all comparison. "*Thou art the God that* alone *doest wonders*, above the power of any creature; *thou hast* visibly, and beyond any contradiction, *declared thy strength among the people.*" God brought Israel out of Egypt, *v.* 15. This was the beginning of mercy to them. Though they were delivered by power, yet they are said to be redeemed, as if it had been done by price, because it was typical of the great redemption, which was to be wrought out, in the fulness of time, both by price and power. He divided the Red Sea before them (*v.* 16): *The waters* gave way, and a lane was made through. Not only the surface of the waters, but *the depths, were troubled*, and opened to the right and to the left. He destroyed the Egyptians (*v.* 17): *The skies sent out a sound; thy arrows also went abroad*, which is explained (*v.* 18): *The voice of thy thunder was heard in the heaven* (that was the sound which the skies sent forth); *the lightnings lightened the world*—those were the arrows which went abroad, by which the host of the Egyptians was discomfited, and yet when the waters returned to their place *his footsteps were not known* (*v.* 19); there was no mark set upon the place. He took his people Israel under his own guidance and protection (*v.* 20): *Thou leddest thy people like a flock.* God went before them with

JAMIESON, FAUSSET, BROWN

my spirit was overwhelmed—or, fainted (Ps. 107:5; Jonah 2:7).

10. Omitting the supplied words, we may read, "This is my affliction—the years of," etc.—years being taken as parallel to affliction (cf. Ps. 90: 15), as of God's ordering.

11, 12. He finds relief in contrasting God's former deliverances. Shall we receive good at His hands, and not evil? Both are orderings of unerring mercy and unfailing love.

13. Thy way . . . in the sanctuary—God's ways of grace and providence (Ps. 22:3; 67:2), ordered on holy principles, as developed in His worship; or implied in His perfections, if "holiness" be used for "sanctuary," as some prefer translating (cf. Exod. 15:11). **14-20.** Illustrations of God's power in His special interventions for His people (Exod. 14), and, in the more common, but sublime, control of nature (Ps. 22:11-14; Hab. 3:14) which may have attended those miraculous events (Exod. 14:24). **Jacob and Joseph**—representing all.

water . . . , footsteps—may refer to His actual leading the people through the sea, though also expressing the mysteries of providence.

ADAM CLARKE

We know that *neginath* signifies some stringed musical instrument that was struck with a plectrum, but here it possibly might be applied to the psalm that was played on it. But it appears to me rather that the Psalmist here speaks of the circumstances of composing the short ode contained in the seventh, eighth, and ninth verses, which it is probable he sung to his harp as a kind of dirge, if indeed he had a harp in that distressful captivity. *My spirit made diligent search.* The verb *chaphas* signifies such an investigation as a man makes who is obliged to strip himself in order to do it; or, to lift up coverings, to search fold by fold, or in our phrase, to leave no stone unturned.

7. *Will the Lord cast off for ever?* Will there be no end to this captivity?

8. *For evermore?* "To generation and generation."

10. *And I said, This is my infirmity.* The Hebrew is very obscure, and has been differently translated: "And I said, Is this my weakness? Years the right hand of the Most High."

13. *Thy way . . . is in the sanctuary.* See Ps. lxxiii. 17.

16. *The waters saw thee.* What a fine image! He represents God approaching the Red Sea; and the waters, seeing Him, took fright, and ran off before Him, dividing to the right and left to let Him pass. I have not found anything more majestic than this.

17. *The clouds poured out water.* It appears from this that there was a violent tempest at the time of the passage of the Red Sea. There was a violent storm of thunder, lightning, and rain.

MATTHEW HENRY

all the care and tenderness of a shepherd. Moses and Aaron led them; they could not do it without God, but God did it with and by them. Moses was their governor, Aaron their high priest. The two great ordinances of magistracy and ministry is, though not so great a miracle, yet as great a mercy to any people as the pillar of cloud and fire was to Israel in the wilderness.

PSALM 78

Maschil of Asaph.

Verses 1–8

These verses contain the preface to this history. It is indeed *Maschil—a psalm to give instruction.*

I. The psalmist demands attention (*v.* 1): *Give ear, O my people! to my law.* Some make these the psalmist's words. He calls his instructions his *law* or *edict;* such was their commanding force in themselves. David was a king, and he would interpose his royal power for the edification of his people. Or the psalmist, being a prophet, speaks as God's mouth, and so calls them *his people,* and demands subjection to what was said as to a law.

II. Several reasons are given why we should diligently attend. 1. The things here discoursed of are weighty (*v.* 2): *I will open my mouth in a parable, I will utter dark sayings,* which challenge your most serious regard. These are called *dark sayings,* not because they are hard to be understood, but because they are carefully to be looked into. 2. They are the monuments of antiquity—*dark sayings of old which our fathers have told us, v.* 3. They are things of undoubted certainty. The honour we owe to our parents and ancestors obliges us to attend to that which our fathers have told us. 3. They are to be transmitted to posterity, and it lies as a charge upon us carefully to hand them down (*v.* 4); because our fathers told them to us *we will not hide them from their children.* Our care must be for posterity in general. That which we are to transmit to our children is not only the knowledge of languages, arts and sciences, liberty and property, but especially the praises of the Lord, and the wonderful works he has done. Our great care must be to lodge our religion, that great deposit, pure and entire in the hands of those that succeed us. (1) The law of God was given with a particular charge to teach it diligently to their children (*v.* 5): *He established a testimony* or covenant, and enacted a law, in Jacob and Israel, which he *commanded them to make known to their children,* Deut. vi. 7, 20. The church of God, as the historian says of the Roman commonwealth, was not to be *a thing of one age,* but was to be kept up from one generation to another. (2) The providences of God concerning them. God gave order that his laws should be made known to posterity. It is requisite that with them his works also should be made known. Let these be told to our children and our children's children, *that, not forgetting the works of God* wrought in former days, *they* might *set their hope in God and keep his commandments.* Those only may with confidence hope for God's salvation that make conscience of doing his commandments. They may take warning (*v.* 8): *That they might not be as their fathers, a stubborn and rebellious generation.* Though they were the seed of Abraham, taken into covenant with God, their *spirit was not steadfast with him,* but upon every occasion they flew off from him.

Verses 9–39

In these verses,

I. The psalmist observes the rebukes that the people of Israel had brought upon themselves by their dealing treacherously with God, *v.* 9–11. *The children of Ephraim,* in which tribe Shiloh was, though they were well armed and shot with bows, yet *turned back in the day of battle.* This seems to refer to that shameful defeat which the Philistines gave them in Eli's time, when they took the ark prisoner, 1 Sam. iv. 10, 11. Well might that event be thus fresh in mind in David's time, above forty years after, for the ark, which in that memorable battle was seized by the Philistines, though it was quickly brought out of captivity, was never brought out of obscurity till David fetched it from Kirjath-jearim to his own city. Note: the shameful cowardice of the children of Ephraim. Sin dispirits men and takes away the heart. They were basely treacherous and perfidious, for *they kept not the covenant of God.* They *forgot his works and his wonders.* Our forgetfulness of God's works is at the bottom of our disobedience to his laws.

II. He takes occasion hence to consult precedents. The narrative in these verses is very remarkable, for it relates a kind of struggle between God's goodness and man's badness, and mercy, at length, rejoices against judgment.

JAMIESON, FAUSSET, BROWN

PSALM 78

Vss. 1-72. This Psalm appears to have been occasioned by the removal of the sanctuary from Shiloh in the tribe of Ephraim to Zion in the tribe of Judah, and the coincident transfer of pre-eminence in Israel from the former to the latter tribe, as clearly evinced by David's settlement as the head of the Church and nation. Though this was the execution of God's purpose, the writer here shows that it also proceeded from the divine judgment on Ephraim, under whose leadership the people had manifested the same sinful and rebellious character which had distinguished their ancestors in Egypt.

1. my people . . . my law—the language of a religious teacher (vs. 2; Lam. 3:14; Rom. 2:16, 27; cf. Ps. 49:4). The history which follows was a "dark saying," or riddle, if left unexplained, and its right apprehension required wisdom and attention. **3-8.** This history had been handed down (Exod. 12:14; Deut. 6:20) for God's honor, and that the principles of His law might be known and observed by posterity.

This important sentiment is reiterated in (vss. 7, 8) negative form. **testimony**—(Ps. 19:7.)

stubborn and rebellious—(Deut. 21:18.) **set not their heart**—on God's service (II Chron. 12:14).

9-11. The privileges of the first-born which belonged to Joseph (I Chron. 5:1, 2) were assigned to Ephraim by Jacob (Gen. 48:1). The supremacy of the tribe thus intimated was recognized by its position (in the marching of the nation to Canaan) next to the ark (Num. 2:18-24), by the selection of the first permanent locality for the ark within its borders at Shiloh, and by the extensive and fertile province given for its possession. Traces of this prominence remained after the schism under Rehoboam, in the use, by later writers, of *Ephraim* for *Israel* (cf. Hos. 5:3-14; 11:3-12). Though a strong, well-armed tribe, and, from an early period, emulous and haughty (cf. Josh. 17:14; Judg. 8:1-3; II Sam. 19:41), it appears, in this place, that it had rather led the rest in cowardice than courage; and had incurred God's displeasure, because, diffident of His promise, though often heretofore fulfilled, it had failed as a leader to carry out the terms of the covenant, by not driving out the heathen (Exod. 23:24; Deut. 31:16; II Kings 17:15).

ADAM CLARKE

PSALM 78

2. *In a parable.* Or, I will give you instruction by numerous examples; see Ps. xlix. 1-4, which bears a great similarity to this. The term *parable,* in its various acceptations, has already been sufficiently explained; but *mashal* may here mean "example," as opposed to *torah,* "law" or "precept," v. 1.

4. *We will not hide them.* In those ancient times there was very little reading, because books were exceedingly scarce; tradition was therefore the only, or nearly the only, means of preserving the memory of past events. They were handed down from father to son by parables or pithy sayings, and by chronological poems. This very psalm is of this kind, and must have been very useful to the Israelites, as giving instructions concerning their ancient history, and recounting the wonderful deeds of the Almighty in their behalf.

9. *The children of Ephraim . . . turned back.* This refers to some defeat of the Ephraimites; and some think to that by the men of Gath. mentioned in 1 Chron. vii. 21.

MATTHEW HENRY

1. God did great things for his people Israel when he first incorporated them and formed them into a people: *Marvellous things did he in the sight of their fathers.* He made a lane for them through the Red Sea, and caused them, gave them courage, to pass through, though the waters stood over their heads as a heap, *v.* 13. He provided a guide for them through the untrodden paths of the wilderness (*v.* 14); he led them step by step, *in the day time by a cloud,* which also sheltered them from the heat, and *all the night with a light of fire,* which made the darkness of night less frightful, and perhaps kept off wild beasts, Zech. ii. 5. He furnished their camp with fresh water in a dry and thirsty land by broaching a rock (*v.* 15, 16): *He clave the rocks in the wilderness.* Out of the dry and hard rock he gave them drink, not distilled as out of an alembic, drop by drop, but in streams *running down like rivers,* and as out of the great depths. God gives abundantly, and is rich in mercy.

2. When God began thus to bless them they began to affront him (*v.* 17): *They sinned yet more against him.* They bore the miseries of their servitude better than the difficulties of their deliverance, and never murmured at their taskmasters so much as they did at Moses and Aaron. *They provoked the Most High.* In the wilderness they said and did that which they knew would provoke him: *They tempted God in their heart, v.* 18. (1) By desiring, or rather demanding, that which he had not thought fit to give them: *They asked meat for their lust.* God had given them the manna, wholesome pleasant food and in abundance. But this would not serve; they must have meat for their lust, dainties and varieties. (2) By distrusting his power to give them what they desired. They challenged him to give them flesh; and, if he did not, they would say it was because he could not (*v.* 19): *They spoke against God.* It was as injurious a reflection as could be cast upon God to say, *Can God furnish a table in the wilderness?* What an unreasonable insatiable thing is luxury! Such a mighty thing did these epicures think a table well furnished to be that they thought it was more than God himself could give them in that wilderness. And which is easier, to furnish a table in the wilderness, which a rich man can do, or to fetch water out of a rock, which the greatest potentate on the earth cannot do? Be it ever so great a thing that we ask, it becomes us to own, ***Lord, if thou wilt, thou canst.***

3. God justly resented the provocation and was much displeased with them (*v.* 21): *The Lord heard this, and was wroth.* God thus resented the provocation (*v.* 22): *Because* by this it appeared that *they believed not in God. They trusted not in the salvation* he had begun to work for them; for then they would not thus have questioned its progress. He *commanded the clouds from above.* Usually by their showers they contribute to the earth's producing corn; but now, when God so commanded them, they showered down corn themselves, which is therefore called here *the corn of heaven.* Everyone, even the least child in Israel, did *eat the bread of the mighty* (so the margin reads it); and yet it was strong meat for strong men. They were not stinted, for *he sent them meat to the full.* The daily provision God makes for us has no less of mercy. He expressed his resentment of the provocation, not in denying them what they so inordinately lusted after, but in granting it to them. *He caused an east wind to blow and a south wind,* either a south-east wind, or an east wind first to bring in the quails from that quarter and then a south wind to bring in more from that quarter; so that *he rained flesh upon them;* an abundance of it, *as dust, as the sand of the sea* (*v.* 27), so that the meanest Israelite might have sufficient; and it cost them nothing, no, not the pains of fetching it from the mountains, for *he let it fall in the midst of their camp, round about their habitation, v.* 28. We have the account, Num. xi. 31, 32. He made them pay dearly for their quails; for, though he *gave them their own desire, they were not estranged from their lust* (*v.* 29, 30); their appetite was insatiable; they were well filled and yet they were not satisfied. Such is the nature of lust; the more it is humoured the more humoursome it grows. There were some contented Israelites, that did eat moderately of the quails and were never the worse; for it was not the meat that poisoned them, but their own lust.

4. The judgments of God upon them did not reform them any more than his mercies (*v.* 32): *For all this, they sinned still;* they murmured and quarrelled with God and Moses as much as ever. Those hearts are hard indeed that will neither be melted by the mercies of God nor broken by his judgments.

5. They persisting in their sins, God proceeded in his judgments, but they were judgments of another nature, which wrought not suddenly, but slowly.

JAMIESON, FAUSSET, BROWN

12-14. A record of God's dealings and the sins of the people is now made. The writer gives the history from the exode to the retreat from Kadesh; then contrasts their sins with their reasons for confidence, shown by a detail of God's dealings in Egypt, and presents a summary of the subsequent history to David's time. **Zoan**—for Egypt, as its ancient capital (Num. 13:22; Isa. 19:11).

15, 16. There were two similar miracles (Exod. 17:6; Num. 20:11). **great depths**—and—**rivers**—denote abundance.

17-20. yet more—lit., "added to sin," instead of being led to repentance (Rom. 2:4).

in their heart—(Matt. 15:19.) **for their lust**—lit., "soul," or, desire.

provoking—and—**tempted**—illustrated by their absurd doubts, **19, 20,** in the face of His admitted power.

21. fire—the effect of the "anger" (Num. 11:1). **22.** (Cf. Heb. 8:8, 9.)

23-29. (Cf. Exod. 16; Num. 11.) **angels' food**—lit., "bread of the mighty" (cf. Ps. 105:40); so called, as it came from heaven. **meat**—lit., "victuals," as for a journey.

their . . . desire—what they longed for. **30, 31. not estranged . . . lust**—or, desire—i.e., were indulging it. **slew . . . fattest**—or, among the fattest; some of them—**chosen**—the young and strong (Isa. 40:31), and so none could resist.

ADAM CLARKE

12. *The field of Zoan.* "Tanis" was the capital of Pharaoh, where Moses wrought so many miracles. It was situated in the Delta, on one of the most easterly branches of the Nile.

18. *By asking meat for their lust.* "For their souls," i.e., "for their lives"; for they said in their hearts that the light bread, the manna, was not sufficient to sustain their natural force, and preserve their lives.

25. *Man did eat angels' food.* "Man did eat the bread of the mighty ones." They ate such bread as could be expected only at the tables of the rich and great; the best, the most delicate food.

26. *He caused an east wind to blow.* See Num. xi. 31.

32. *For all this they sinned still.* How astonishing is this! They were neither drawn by mercies nor awed by judgments!

MATTHEW HENRY

Therefore their days did he consume in vanity in the wilderness *and their years in trouble.* They were condemned to wear out thirty-eight tedious years in the wilderness, which indeed were consumed in vanity; for in all those years there was not a step taken nearer Canaan, but they were turned back again, and wandered to and fro as in a labyrinth. Those that sin still must expect to be in trouble still. And the reason why we spend our days in so much vanity and trouble, why we live with so little comfort and to so little purpose, is because we do not live by faith.

6. Under these rebukes they professed repentance, but they were not sincere in this profession. Their profession was plausible enough (*v.* 34, 35): *When he slew them,* or condemned them to be slain, *then they sought him.* In a fright they cried to God for mercy, and promised they would reform and be very good; then *they returned to God, and enquired early after him.* They were not sincere in this profession (*v.* 36, 37): *They did but flatter him with their mouth,* as if they thought by fair speeches to prevail with him to revoke the sentence. They thawed in the sun, but froze in the shade. They did but *lie to God wtih their tongues, for their heart was not with him.*

7. God hereupon, in pity to them, put a stop to the judgments which were threatened and in part executed (*v.* 38, 39): *But he, being full of compassion, forgave their iniquity.* He spared their lives till they had reared another generation which should enter into the promised land. Because he was *full of compassion,* he said, *How shall I give thee up, Ephraim? How shall I deliver thee, Israel?* Hos. xi. 8. Though they did not rightly remember that he was their rock, he *remembered that they were but flesh.* He considered what an easy thing it would be to crush them: *They are as a wind that passeth away and cometh not again.* It were easy to argue they may justly be cut off, but God argues, on the contrary, therefore he will not destroy them; for the true reason is, *He is full of compassion.*

Verses 40–72

The matter and scope of this paragraph are the same with the former, showing what great mercies God had bestowed upon Israel, how provoking they had been, what judgments he had brought upon them for their sins, and yet how, in judgment, he remembered mercy at last.

I. The sins of Israel in the wilderness again reflected on (*v.* 40, 41): *How often did they provoke him in the wilderness!* God kept an account, Num. xiv. 22, *They have tempted me these ten times.* By provoking him they did not so much anger him as grieve him, for he looked upon them as his children (*Israel is my son, my first-born*). They grieved him because they put him under a necessity of afflicting them, which he did not willingly. After they had humbled themselves before him they *turned back and tempted God,* prescribing to him what proofs he should give of his power and presence with them and what methods he should take in leading them and providing for them. It is presumption for us to limit *the Holy One of Israel*; for, being *the Holy One of Israel,* he will do what is most for our good. That which occasioned their limiting God was their forgetting his former favours (*v.* 42). There are some days made remarkable by signal deliverances, which ought never to be forgotten.

II. The mercies of God to Israel, and this catalogue of the works of wonder which God wrought for them begins higher, and is carried down further, than that before, *v.* 12, &c.

1. This begins with their deliverance out of Egypt, and the plagues with which God compelled the Egyptians to let them go. Several of the plagues of Egypt are here specified, which speak aloud the power of God and his favour to Israel. The turning of the waters into blood; they had made themselves drunk with the blood of God's people, even the infants, and now God gave them blood to drink, *for they were worthy, v.* 44. The flies and frogs infested them, *v.* 45. The plague of locusts, which devoured their increase, and that for which they had laboured, *v.* 46. The *hail,* which *destroyed* their trees, especially *their vines,* the weakest of trees (*v.* 47), and *their cattle,* especially *their flocks* of sheep, the weakest of their cattle (*v.* 48), and the *frost,* or congealed rain (as the word signifies), was so violent that it destroyed even the *sycamore-trees.* The death of the first-born was the last and sorest of the plagues of Egypt, and that which perfected the deliverance of Israel; it was first in intention (Exod. iv. 23), but last in execution; for, if gentler methods would have done the work, this would have been prevented. Pharaoh's heart having been often hardened after less judgments had softened it, God now *stirred up all his wrath. He made a way,* or (as the word is) *he weighed a*

JAMIESON, FAUSSET, BROWN

33-39. Though there were partial reformations after chastisement, and God, in pity, withdrew His hand for a time, yet their general conduct was rebellious, and He was thus provoked to waste and destroy them, by long and fruitless wandering in the desert.

lied . . . tongues—a feigned obedience (Ps. 18:44). **heart . . . not right**—or, firm (cf. vs. 8; Ps. 51:10).

a wind . . . again—lit., "a breath," thin air (cf. Ps. 103:16; Jas. 4:14).

40, 41. There were ten temptations (Num. 14:22). **limited**—as in vss. 19, 20. Though some prefer "grieved" or "provoked."

The retreat from Kadesh (Deut. 1:19-23) is meant, whether—**turned**—be for turning back, or to denote repetition of offense.

43. wrought—set or held forth.

45. The dog-fly or the mosquito. **46. caterpillar**—the *Hebrew* name, from its voracity, and that of—**locust**—from its multitude. **47, 48.** The additional effects of the storm here mentioned (cf. Exod. 9:23-34) are consistent with Moses' account. **gave . . . cattle**—lit., "shut up" (cf. Ps. 31:8).

ADAM CLARKE

33. *Their days did he consume in vanity.* By causing them to wander forty years in the wilderness, vainly expecting an end to their labor, and the enjoyment of the promised rest, which, by their rebellions, they had forfeited.

35. *That God was their rock.* They recollected in their affliction that Jehovah was their *Rock,* the Source, not only of their being, but of all their blessings; or that He was their sole Protector. *And the high God their redeemer. Veel elyon goalam,* "And the strong God, the Most High, their kinsman." That one who possessed the right of redemption. The Hebrew word *goel* answers to the Greek *Soter,* a "savior"; and is given to the Lord Jesus Christ, the strong God, the Most High, the Redeemer of a lost world. After this verse there is the following Masoretic note: "The middle of the book." And thus the reader has arrived at the middle of the Psalter.

36. *Nevertheless they did flatter him with their mouth.* I think the Vulgate gives the true sense of the Hebrew: "They loved him with their mouth; and they lied unto him with their tongue."

38. *But he, being full of compassion.* Feeling for them as a father for his children. *Forgave their iniquity. Yechapper,* "made an atonement" for their iniquity. *And did not stir up all his wrath.* The punishment was much less than the iniquity deserved.

39. *He remembered that they were but flesh.* Weak mortals. *A wind that passeth away, and cometh not again.* I believe this to be a bad translation, and may be productive of error; as if when a man dies his being were ended, and death were an eternal sleep. The translation should be, "The spirit goeth away, and it doth not return." The Arabic takes away all ambiguity: "He remembered that they were flesh; and a spirit which, when it departs, does not again return." The human being is composed of flesh and spirit, or body and soul; these are easily separated, and, when separated, the body turns to dust, and the spirit returns no more to animate it in a state of probation.

41. *Limited the Holy One of Israel.* The Chaldee translates, "And the Holy One of Israel they signed with a sign." Here it most obviousiy means an insult offered to God.

44. *Turned their rivers into blood.* See Exod. vii. 20.

45. *He sent . . . flies . . . and frogs.* See Exod. viii. 6, 24.

46. *The caterpiller, and . . . the locust.* See Exod. x. 13.

48. *He gave up their cattle.* See Exod. ix. 23.

MATTHEW HENRY

path, to his anger. He did not cast it upon them uncertainly, but by weight. His anger was weighed with the greatest exactness in the balances of justice; for, in his greatest displeasure, he never did, nor ever will do, any wrong to any of his creatures: the path of his anger is always weighed. *He sent evil angels among them*, not evil in their own nature, but in respect to the errand upon which they were sent; they were destroying angels, or angels of punishment. The execution itself was very severe. *He smote all the first-born in Egypt* (*v*. 51) *the chief of their strength*, the hopes of their respective families. God made a way for *his own people to go forth like sheep*, not knowing whither they went, and *guided them in the wilderness*, as a shepherd guides his flock, with all possible care and tenderness, *v*. 52. *He led them on safely*, though in dangerous paths, so that *they feared not*, that is, they needed not to fear. *But the sea overwhelmed their enemies* that ventured to pursue them into it, *v*. 53. It was a lane to them, but a grave to their persecutors.

2. It is carried down as far as their settlement in Canaan (*v*. 54): *He brought them to the border of his sanctuary*, to that land in the midst of which he set up his sanctuary. That is a happy land which is the border of God's sanctuary. The whole land in general, and Zion in particular, was *the mountain which his right hand had purchased*. He *made them to ride on the high places of the earth*, Isa. lviii. 14; Deut. xxxii. 13. They found the Canaanites in the full possession of that land, but God made his people *Israel tread upon their high places, dividing* each tribe *an inheritance by line*.

III. The sins of Israel after they were settled in Canaan, *v*. 56–58. The children were *like their fathers*, and brought their old corruptions into their new habitations. They seemed sometimes devoted to God, but they presently *turned aside*, and *provoked him to anger with their high places and their graven images*. Idolatry was the sin that did most easily beset them, and which, though they often professed their repentance for, they as often relapsed into.

IV. The judgments God brought upon them for these sins. Idolatry is winked at among the Gentiles, but not in Israel (*v*. 59): *When God heard this*, when he heard the cry of their iniquity, which came up before him, *he was wroth*. He deserted his tabernacle among them, and removed the defence which was upon that glory, *v*. 60. God never leaves us till we leave him. The *tabernacle at Shiloh* was *the tent God had placed among men*, in which God would *in very deed dwell with men upon the earth*; but, when his people treacherously forsook it, he justly forsook it, and then all its glory departed. He gave up all into the hands of the enemy. Those whom God forsakes become an easy prey to the destroyer. God permits them to take the ark prisoner, and carry it off as a trophy of their victory, to show that he had not only forsaken the tabernacle, but even the ark itself (*v*. 61): *He delivered his strength into captivity*, as if it had been weakened and overcome, *and his glory* fell under the disgrace of being abandoned *into the enemy's hand*. We have the story, 1 Sam. iv. 11. He suffers the armies of Israel to be routed by the Philistines (*v*. 62, 63): *He gave his people over unto the sword*, for he *was wroth with his inheritance*; and that wrath of his was the *fire which consumed their young men*, in the prime of their time, and made such a devastation of them that *their maidens were not praised*, that is, *were not given in marriage* because there were no young men for them to be given to. Even *their priests*, who attended the ark, *fell by the sword*, Hophni and Phinehas. Justly they fell, for they made themselves vile, and were sinners before the Lord. When the priests fell *their widows made no lamentation*, *v*. 64. The widow of Phinehas, instead of lamenting her husband's death, died herself, when she had called her son *Ichabod*, 1 Sam. iv. 19, &c.

V. God's return, in mercy, to them, and his gracious appearances for them after this. God was *grieved for the miseries of Israel* (Judges x. 16). And therefore *then the Lord awaked as one out of sleep* (*v*. 65), *and like a mighty man that shouteth by reason of wine*, like one that is refreshed with sleep, and whose heart is made glad by the sober and moderate use of wine, and is therefore the more vigorous.

1. He plagued the Philistines who held the ark in captivity, *v*. 66. He smote them with emerods, *in the hinder parts*. Sooner or later God will glorify himself by putting disgrace upon his enemies, even when they are most elevated with their successes.

2. He provided a new settlement for his ark after it had been some months in captivity and some years in obscurity. He did indeed *refuse the tabernacle of Joseph*; he never sent it back to Shiloh, in the tribe of Ephraim, *v*. 67. The ruins of that place were standing monuments of divine justice. *Go, see what*

JAMIESON, FAUSSET, BROWN

49. evil angels—or, **angels of evil**—many were perhaps employed, and other evils inflicted.

50, 51. made a way—removed obstacles, gave it full scope. **chief of their strength**—lit., "first-fruits," or, "first-born" (Gen. 49:3; Deut. 21:17). **Ham**—one of whose sons gave name (*Mizraim, Hebrew*) to Egypt. **52-54. made his . . . forth**—or, brought them by periodical journeys (cf. Exod. 15:1).

border of his sanctuary—or, holy border—i.e., region of which—**this mountain**—(Zion) was, as the seat of civil and religious government, the representative, used for the whole land, as afterwards for the Church (Isa. 25:6, 7). **purchased**—or, procured by His right hand or power (Ps. 60:5).

55. by line—or, the portion thus measured. **divided them**—i.e., the heathen, put for their possessions, so **tents**—i.e., of the heathen (cf. Deut. 6:11). **56, 57. a deceitful bow**—which turns back, and so fails to project the arrow (II Sam. 1:22; Hos. 7:16). They relapsed. **58.** Idolatry resulted from sparing the heathen (cf. vss. 9-11).

59, 60. heard—perceived (Gen. 11:7). **abhorred**—but not utterly. **tent . . . placed**—lit., "caused to dwell," set up (Josh. 18:1).

61. his strength—the ark, as symbolical of it (Ps. 96:6).

62. gave—or, shut up. **his people**—(vs. 48; I Sam. 4:10-17). **63. fire**—either figure of the slaughter (I Sam. 4:10), or a literal burning by the heathen. **given to marriage**—lit., "praised"—i.e., as brides.

64. (Cf. I Sam. 4:17); and there were, doubtless, others. **made no lamentation**—either because stupefied by grief, or hindered by the enemy.

65. (Cf. Ps. 22:16; Isa. 42:13.)

66. And he smote . . . part—or, struck His enemies' back. The Philistines never regained their position after their defeats by David.

ADAM CLARKE

49. *By sending evil angels.* This is the first mention we have of *evil angels*. There is no mention of them in the account we have of the plagues of Egypt in the Book of Exodus, and what they were we cannot tell. An angel or "messenger" may be either animate or inanimate, a disembodied spirit or human being, any thing or being that is an instrument sent of God for the punishment or support of mankind.

54. *The border of his sanctuary.* "Of his holy place," that is, the land of Canaan, called afterwards *the mountain, which his right hand had purchased*, because it was a mountainous country, widely differing from Egypt, which was a long, continued, and almost perfect level.

60. *He forsook the tabernacle of Shiloh.* The Lord, offended with the people, and principally with the priests, who had profaned His holy worship, gave up His ark into the hands of the Philistines. And so true it is that he *forsook the tabernacle of Shiloh* that He never returned to it again. See 1 Sam. vi. 1; 2 Samuel vi; 1 Kings viii. 1; where the several removals of the ark are spoken of, and which exp'ain the remaining part of this psalm. Because God suffered the Philistines to take the ark, it is said, v. 61: He "delivered his strength into captivity, and his glory into the enemy's hand"; and v. 67, that "he refused the tabernacle of Joseph, and chose not the tribe of Ephraim." For Shiloh was in the tribe of Ephraim, the son of Joseph; and God did not suffer His ark to return thither, but to go to Kirjath-jearim, which was in the tribe of Benjamin; from thence to the house of Obed-edom; and so to Zion in the tribe of Judah, as it follows, v. 68.

63. *Their maidens were not given to marriage. Hullalu,* were not celebrated with marriage songs.

64. *Their priests fell by the sword.* Hophni and Phinehas, who were slain in that unfortunate battle against the Philistines in which the ark of the Lord was taken, 1 Sam. iv. 11.

65. *Then the Lord awaked.* He seemed as if He had totally disregarded what was done to His people, and the reproach that seemed to fall on himself and His worship by the capture of the ark. *Like a mighty man. Kegibbor,* "like a hero" *that shouteth by reason of wine.* One who, going forth to meet his enemy, having taken a sufficiency of wine to refresh himself, and become a proper stimulus to his animal spirits, shouts—gives the war signal for the onset; impatient to meet the foe, and sure of victory. The idea is not taken from the case of a drunken man. A person in such a state would be very unfit to meet his enemy, and could have little prospect of conquest.

66. *He smote his enemies in the hinder parts.* This refers to the hemorrhoids with which he afflicted the Philistines. See 1 Sam. v. 6-10.

67. *He refused the tabernacle of Joseph.* See the note on v. 60.

MATTHEW HENRY

I did to Shiloh, Jer. vii. 12. The moving of the ark is not the removing of it. Shiloh has lost it, but Israel has not. God will have a church in the world, and a kingdom among men, though this or that place may have its candlestick removed. When God *chose not the tribe of Ephraim*, of which tribe Joshua was, he *chose the tribe of Judah* (*v.* 68), because of that tribe Jesus was to be, who is greater than Joshua. Kirjath-jearim, the place to which the ark was brought after its rescue out of the hands of the Philistines, was in the tribe of Judah. Thence it was removed to Zion, *that Mount Zion which he loved* (*v.* 68), which *was beautiful for situation, the joy of the whole earth;* there it was that he *built his sanctuary like high palaces* and *like the earth*, *v.* 69. David indeed erected only a tent for the ark, but a temple was then designed and prepared for, and finished by his son. Solomon built it, and yet here it is said *God built it*, for his father had taught him, perhaps with reference to this undertaking, that *except the Lord build the house those labour in vain* that build it, cxxvii. 1. It was not finally destroyed till the gospel temple was erected, which is to continue *as long as the sun and moon endure* (lxxxix. 36, 37) and against which the *gates of hell shall not prevail.*

3. He set a good government over them, a monarchy, and a monarch after his own heart: *He chose David his servant* out of all the thousands of Israel, and put the sceptre into his hand, from whom Christ was to come, and who was to be a type of him, *v.* 70. Concerning David, he descended from the prince of the tribe of Judah, but his education was poor. He was bred not a scholar, not a soldier, but a shepherd. He was *taken from the sheepfolds*, as Moses was; for God delights to put honour upon the humble and diligent, and sometimes he finds those most fit for public action that have spent the beginning of their time in solitude and contemplation. The son of David was upbraided with the obscurity of his original: *Is not this the carpenter?* David was taken, he does not say from leading the rams, but *from following the ewes*, especially those *great with young*, which intimated that of all the good properties of a shepherd he was most remarkable for his tenderness and compassion to those of his flock that most needed his care. It was a great honour that God put upon him, in advancing him to be a king, especially to be king over Jacob and Israel, God's peculiar people, near and dear to him; but withal it was a great trust. David, having so great a trust put into his hands, obtained mercy of the Lord to be found both skilful and faithful in the discharge of it (*v.* 72): *So he fed them;* he ruled them and taught them, guided and protected them, *according to the integrity of his heart*, aiming at nothing but the glory of God and the good of the people committed to his charge. He was not only very sincere in what he designed, but very prudent in what he did. Happy the people that are under such a government! With good reason does the psalmist make this the finishing crowning instance of God's favour to Israel, for David was a type of Christ the great and good Shepherd.

JAMIESON, FAUSSET, BROWN

67, 68. tabernacle of Joseph—or, home, or, tribe, to which—**tribe of Ephraim**—is parallel (cf. Rev. 7:8). Its pre-eminence was, like Saul's, only permitted. Judah had been the choice (Gen. 49:10).

69. Exalted as—high palaces—or, mountains, and abiding as—**the earth.**

70-72. God's sovereignty was illustrated in this choice. The contrast is striking—humility and exaltation—and the correspondence is beautiful. **following . . . ewes . . .**—lit., "ewes giving suck" (cf. Isa. 40:11). On the pastoral terms, cf. Ps. 79:13.

ADAM CLARKE

69. *He built his sanctuary like high palaces.* The temple of God at Jerusalem was the only one in the land. And there He *established* His ark, to go no more out as long as the Temple should last. Before this time it was frequently in a migratory state, not only in the wilderness, but afterwards in the Promised Land. See the notes on v. 60.

70. *He chose David.* See the account, 1 Sam. xvi. 11, etc.

MATTHEW HENRY

PSALM 79

A psalm of Asaph.

Verses 1-5

We have here a sad complaint exhibited in the court of heaven.

I. They complain here of the outrageous fury of the oppressor, exerted against places, *v.* 1. They did all the mischief they could to the holy land; they invaded that, and made inroads into it: "*The heathen have come into thy inheritance*, to plunder that, and lay it waste." Canaan was dearer to the pious Israelites as God's inheritance than as their own. Injuries done to religion should grieve us more than even those done to common right, nay, to our own right. This psalmist had mentioned it in the foregoing psalm as an instance of God's great favour to Israel that he had *cast out the heathen before them*, lxxviii. 55. But see what a change sin made; now the heathen are suffered to pour in upon them. *They have laid Jerusalem on heaps.* The inhabitants were buried in the ruins of their own houses. That sanctuary which God had built and which was thought to be established as the earth, was now laid level with the ground: *Thy holy temple have they defiled*, by entering into it and laying it waste. God's own people had defiled it by their sins, and therefore God suffered their enemies to defile it by their insolence. They were prodigal of blood, and killed God's people without mercy; nor did they give any quarter (*v.* 3): *Their blood have they shed like water*, wherever they met with them, *round about Jerusalem*, in all the avenues of the city; whoever *went out or*

JAMIESON, FAUSSET, BROWN

PSALM 79

Vss. 1-13. This Psalm, like the 74th, probably despicts the desolations of the Chaldeans (Jer. 52:12-24). It comprises the usual complaint, prayer, and promised thanks for relief.

1. (Cf. Ps. 74:2-7.)

2, 3. (Cf. Jer. 15:3; 16:4.)

ADAM CLARKE

PSALM 79

The title, "A Psalm of Asaph," must be understood as either applying to a person of the name of Asaph who lived under the Captivity, or else to the family of Asaph, or to a band of singers still bearing the name of that Asaph who flourished in the days of David; for most undoubtedly the psalm was composed during the Babylonish captivity, when the city of Jerusalem lay in heaps, the Temple was defiled, and the people were in a state of captivity. Some think it was composed by Jeremiah; and it is certain that the sixth and seventh verses are the same with Jer. x. 25: "Pour out thy fury upon the heathen that know thee not, and upon the families that call not on thy name: for they have eaten up Jacob, and devoured him, and consumed him, and have made his habitation desolate."

1. *The heathen are come into thine inheritance.* Thou didst cast them out, and take Thy people in; they have cast us out, and now taken possession of the land that belongs to Thee. They have defiled the Temple, and reduced Jerusalem to a heap of ruins, and made a general slaughter of Thy people.

MATTHEW HENRY

came in was *waited for of the sword.* Even the *dead bodies of God's servants, the flesh of his saints,* whose names and memories they had a particular spite at, they dug up again, and *gave them to be meat to the fowls of the heaven and to the beasts of the earth;* they hung them in chains, which was grievous to the Jews, because God had given them an express law against this, as a barbarous thing, Deut. xxi. 23. "*We that survive have become a reproach to our neighbours;* they all study to abuse us and load us with contempt, so that we have become *a scorn and derision to those that are round about us.*" If God's professing people degenerate from what themselves and their fathers were, they must expect to be told of it.

II. They wonder more at God's anger, *v.* 5. This they discern in the anger of their neighbours. *How long, Lord, wilt thou be angry?* Shall it be *for ever?* This intimates that they desired no more than that God would be reconciled to them, and then the remainder of men's wrath would be restrained.

Verses 6–13

The petitions here put up to God are very suitable to the present distresses of the church.

I. They pray that God would so turn away his anger from them as to turn it upon those that persecuted and abused them (*v.* 6). This prayer is in effect a prophecy, in which the *wrath of God is revealed from heaven against all ungodliness and unrighteousness of men.* The reason why men do not call upon God is because they do not know him, how able and willing he is to help them. Those that persist in ignorance of God, and neglect of prayer, are the ungodly, who live *without God in the world. They have devoured Jacob, v.* 7. They have not only disturbed, but devoured, Jacob, not only encroached upon his dwelling-place, the land of Canaan, but laid it waste by plundering and depopulating it. "*Pour out thy wrath* upon them; not only restrain them from doing further mischief, but reckon with them for the mischief they have done."

II. They pray for the pardon of sin, which they own to be the cause of all their calamities. "Remember not against us our first sins," which some make to look as far back as the golden calf. If the children by repentance cut off the entail of the parents' sin, they may in faith pray that God will not *remember them against them.* When God pardons sin he blots it out and remembers it no more. *Deliver us, and purge away our sins, v.* 9. Then deliverances from trouble are granted in love, and are mercies indeed.

III. They pray that God would bring their troubles to a good end and that speedily: *Let thy tender mercies speedily prevent us, v.* 8. Unless divine mercy did speedily interpose to prevent their ruin, they were undone. This whets their importunity: "*Lord, help us; Lord, deliver us;* help us under our troubles, that we may bear them well. Deliver us from sin, from sinking. *We are brought very low,* and, being low, shall be lost if thou help us not." Those who make God the God of their salvation shall find him so. They plead no merit of theirs; they pretend to none; but, "*Help us for the glory of thy name;* pardon us for thy name's sake. *Wherefore should the heathen say, Where is their God?* He has forsaken them, and forgotten them; and this they get by worshipping a God whom they cannot see." "Lord," say they, "make it to appear that thou art by making it to appear that thou art with us, and for us, that when we are asked, *Where is your God?* we may be able to say, He is nigh unto us and you see he is so by what he does for us."

IV. They pray that God would avenge them on their adversaries. "Let the avenging of our blood" (according to the ancient law, Gen. ix. 6) "be known among the heathen; and by this means *let God be known among the heathen* as *the God to whom vengeance belongs* (xciv. 1) and the God that espouses his people's cause." The reproach wherewith they have blasphemed God himself we may in faith pray that God would render seven-fold into their bosoms, to humble them, and bring them to repentance.

V. They pray that God would find out a way for the rescue of his poor prisoners, *v.* 11. Their brethren who had fallen into the hands of the enemy, were kept close prisoners, and, because they durst not be heard to bemoan themselves, they vented their griefs in deep and silent sighs. "*Let their sighs come up before thee,* and be thou pleased to take cognizance of their moans." They promise the returns of praise for the answers of prayer (*v.* 13): *So we will give thee thanks for ever.* They oblige themselves not only to give God thanks at present, but to *show forth his praise unto all generations.*

JAMIESON, FAUSSET, BROWN

4. (Cf. Ps. 44:13; Jer. 42:18; Lam. 2:15.)

5. How long–(Ps. 13:1). **be angry**–(Ps. 74:1-10). **jealousy burn**–(Deut. 29:20).

6, 7. (Cf. Jer. 10:25.) Though we deserve much, do not the heathen deserve more for their violence to us (Jer. 51:3-5; Zech. 1:14)? The singular denotes the chief power, and the use of the plural indicates the combined confederates. **called upon** [or, by] **thy name**–proclaimed Thy attributes and professed allegiance (Isa. 12:4; Acts 2:21).

8. former iniquites–lit., "iniquities of former times." **prevent** [lit., "meet"] **us**–as in Psalm 21:3.

purge . . . sins–lit., "provide atonement for us." Deliverance from sin and suffering, for their good and God's glory, often distinguish the prayers of Old Testament saints (cf. Eph. 1:7).

9. for . . . glory of thy name [and for] **thy name's sake**–both mean for illustrating Thy attributes, faithfulness, power, etc.,

10. This ground of pleading often used (Exod. 32:12; Num. 14:13-16). **blood . . . shed**–(vs. 3).

11. prisoner–the whole captive people. **power**–lit., "arm" (Ps. 10:15). **12. into their bosom**–The lap or folds of the dress is used by Eastern people for receiving articles. The figure denotes retaliation (cf. Isa. 65:6, 7). They reproached God as well as His people. **13. sheep . . . pasture** (Cf. Ps. 74:1; 78:70).

ADAM CLARKE

2. *The dead bodies of thy servants.* It appears that in the destruction of Jerusalem the Chaldeans did not bury the bodies of the slain, but left them to be devoured by birds and beasts of prey. This was the grossest inhumanity.

4. *We are become a reproach to our neighbours.* The Idumeans, Philistines, Phoenicians, Ammonites, and Moabites, all gloried in the subjugation of this people; and their insults to them were mixed with blasphemies against God.

8. *Remember not against us former iniquities.* Visit us not for the sins of our forefathers. *We are brought very low.* Literally, "We are greatly thinned." Few of us remain.

9. *Purge away our sins. Capper,* "be propitiated," or "receive an atonement" on account of our sins.

10. *Where is their God?* Show where Thou art by rising up for our redemption, and the infliction of deserved punishment upon our enemies.

11. *The sighing of the prisoner.* The poor captive Israelites in Babylon, who sigh and cry because of their bondage. *Those that are appointed to die.* "Sons of death." Either those who were condemned to death because of their crimes or condemned to be destroyed by their oppressors. Both these senses apply to the Israelites. They were sons of death, i.e., worthy of death because of their sins against God; they were condemned to death or utter destruction by their Babylonish enemies.

12. *Sevenfold into their bosom.* That is, Let them get in this world what they deserve for the cruelties they have inflicted on us. Let them suffer in captivity who now have us in bondage. Probably this is a prediction.

MATTHEW HENRY

PSALM 80

To the chief musician upon Shoshannim, Eduth. A psalm of Asaph.

Verses 1–7

The psalmist here applies to God by prayer, with reference to the present afflicted state of Israel.

I. He entreats God's favour for them (*v*. 1, 2), as the Shepherd of Israel, under whose guidance and care Israel was. He *leads Joseph like a flock*, to the best pastures and out of the way of danger. He *dwells between the cherubim*, where he is ready to receive petitions and to give directions. The mercy-seat was between the cherubim; and it is very comfortable in prayer to look up to God as sitting on a throne of grace. He desires from God, that he would give ear to the cry of their miseries and of their prayers, that he would *stir up his strength*. It had seemed to slumber: "Lord, awaken it. Lord, be to thy people a powerful help and a present help; Lord, do this *before Ephraim, Benjamin and Manasseh*." Perhaps these three tribes are named because they were the tribes which formed that squadron of the camp of Israel that in their march through the wilderness followed next after the tabernacle; so that before them the ark of God's strength rose to scatter their enemies.

II. He complains of God's displeasure. God was angry, and he dreads that more than anything, *v*. 4. He apprehended that God was *angry against the prayers of his people*. That God should be angry at the sins of his people and at the prayers of his enemies is not strange; but that he should be angry at the prayers of his people is strange indeed. If he be really angry at the prayers of his people, we may be sure it is because they ask amiss, James iv. 3. But perhaps it is only in their own apprehension; he seems angry with their prayers when really he is not; for thus he will try their perseverance in prayer, as Christ tried the woman of Canaan when he said: *It is not meet to take the children's bread and cast it to dogs*. Now the tokens of God's displeasure which they had been long under were both their sorrow and shame. *Thou feedest them with the bread of tears;* they eat their meat from day to day in tears; this is the vinegar in which they *dipped their morsel*, xlii. 3. Many that spend their time in sorrow shall spend their eternity in joy. It is to their shame, *v*. 6. Their enemies laughed among themselves to see the frights they were in, and the disappointments they met with.

III. He prays earnestly for converting grace in order to their salvation: *Turn us again, O God! v*. 3. *Turn us again, O God of hosts!* (*v*. 7) and then *cause thy face to shine and we shall be saved*. It is the burden of the song, for we have it again, *v*. 19. "Lord, turn us to thee in a way of repentance and reformation, and then, no doubt, thou wilt return to us in a way of mercy and deliverance." Observe, 1. No salvation but from God's favour. 2. No obtaining favour with God unless we be converted to him. 3. No conversion to God but by his own grace. *Turn thou me, and I shall be turned*. The prayer here is for a national conversion. National holiness would secure national happiness.

Verses 8–19

The psalmist is here presenting his suit for the Israel of God, and pressing it home at the throne of grace. The church is here represented as a vine (*v*. 8, 14) and a vineyard, *v*. 15. The root of this vine is Christ, Rom. xi. 18. The branches are believers, John xv. 5. The church is like a vine, weak and needing support, unsightly and having an unpromising outside, but spreading and fruitful, and its fruit most excellent. The church is a choice and noble vine; we have reason to acknowledge the goodness of God that he has planted such a vine in the wilderness of this world, and preserved it to this day.

I. How the vine of the Old Testament church was planted at first. It was *brought out of Egypt* with a high hand; *the heathen were cast out* of Canaan to make room for it, seven nations to make room for that one.

II. How it spread and flourished. 1. The land of Canaan itself was fully peopled. At first they were not so numerous as to replenish it, Exod. xxiii. 29. But in Solomon's time *Judah and Israel were many as the sand of the sea*. Israel not only had abundance of men, but those mighty men of valour. 2. They extended their conquests and dominion to the neighbouring countries (*v*. 11): *She sent out her boughs to the sea*, the great sea westward, and *her branches to the river*, to the river of Egypt southward, the river of Damascus northward, or rather the river Euphrates eastward, Gen. xv. 18. But it is observable here concerning this vine that it is praised for its *shadow*, its *boughs*, and its *branches*, but not a word

JAMIESON, FAUSSET, BROWN

PSALM 80

Vss. 1-19. *Shoshannim*—Lilies (Ps. 45, title). *Eduth*—Testimony, referring to the topic as a testimony of God to His people (cf. Ps. 19:7). This Psalm probably relates to the captivity of the ten tribes, as the former to that of Judah. Its complaint is aggravated by the contrast of former prosperity, and the prayer for relief occurs as a refrain through the Psalm.

1, 2. Joseph—for Ephraim (I Chron. 7:20-29; Ps. 78:67; Rev. 7:8), for Israel. **Shepherd**—(Cf. Gen. 49:24). **leadest . . .**—(Ps. 77:20). **dwellest . . . cherubim**—(Exod. 25:20); the place of God's visible glory, whence He communed with the people (Heb. 9:5). **shine forth**—appear (Ps. 50:2; 94:1). **Before Ephraim . . .**—These tribes marched next the ark (Num. 2:18-24). The name of Benjamin may be introduced merely in allusion to that fact, and not because that tribe was identified with Israel in the schism (I Kings 12:16-21; cf. also Num. 10:24).

5. bread of tears—still an Eastern figure for affliction. **6. strife**—object or cause of (Isa. 9:11). On last clause cf. Psalm 79:4; Ezekiel 36:4.

3. Turn us—i.e., from captivity. **thy face to shine**—(Num. 6:25).

a vine—(Ps. 78:47). The figure (Isa. 16:8) represents the flourishing state of Israel, as predicted (Gen. 28:14), and verified (I Kings 4:20-25).

8-11. brought—or plucked up, as by roots, to be replanted.

ADAM CLARKE

PSALM 80

The title: see Psalms xlv; lx; and lxix, where everything material is explained. This psalm seems to have been written on the same occasion with the former. One ancient MS. in the public library in Cambridge writes the eightieth and the seventy-ninth all as one psalm; the subject matter is precisely the same—was made on the same occasion, and probably by the same author.

1. *O Shepherd of Israel*. The subject continued from the last verse of the preceding psalm. *That dwellest between the cherubims*. It was between the cherubim, over the cover of the ark, called the mercy seat, that the glory of the Lord, or symbol of the Divine Presence, appeared. *Shine forth*. Restore Thy worship; and give us such evidences of Thy presence now as our fathers had under the first Tabernacle, and afterwards in the Temple built by Solomon.

2. *Before Ephraim and Benjamin and Manasseh*. It is supposed that these three tribes represent the whole, Benjamin being incorporated with Judah, Manasseh comprehending the country beyond Jordan, and Ephraim all the rest.

5. *Thou feedest them with the bread of tears*. They have no peace, no comfort, nothing but continual sorrow. *In great measure*. "Threefold." Some think it was a certain measure used by the Chaldeans, the real capacity of which is not known. Others think it signifies "abundance" or "abundantly."

3. *Turn us again*. "Convert" or "restore" us. There are four parts in this psalm, three of which end with the above words; see the third, seventh, and nineteenth verses; and one with words similar, v. 14.

8. *Thou hast brought a vine out of Egypt*. This is a most elegant metaphor, and everywhere well-supported. The same similitude is used by Isaiah, chap. v. 1, etc.; by Jeremiah, chap. ii. 21; by Ezekiel, chap. xvii. 5-6; by Hosea, chap. x. 1; by Joel, chap. i. 7; by Moses, Deut. xxxii. 32-33; and often by our Lord himself, Matt. xx. 1, etc; xxi. 33, etc.; Mark xii. 1, etc. And this was the ordinary figure to represent the Jewish church. We may remark several analogies here: (1) This vine was brought out of Egypt that it might be planted in a better and more favorable soil. (2) When the husbandman has marked out a proper place for his vineyard, he hews down and roots up all other trees; gathers out the stones, brambles, etc. So God cast out the heathen nations from the land of Canaan, that His pure worship might be established, and that there might not remain there any incitements to idolatry.

9. *Thou preparedst . . . before it*. (3) When the ground is properly cleared, the vines are placed in the ground at proper distances. So when God had cast out the heathen, He caused the land to be divided by lot to the different tribes, and then to the several families of which these tribes were composed. *And didst cause it to take deep root*. (4) By sheltering, propping up, and loosening the ground about the tender plants, they are caused to take a deep and firm rooting in the ground. Thus did God, by especial manifestations of His kind providence, support and protect the Israelites in Canaan. *It filled the land*. (5) To multiply vines, the gardener cuts off a shoot from the old tree, then plants it in proper soil. Thus God so carefully, tenderly, and abundantly blessed the Israelites that they increased and multiplied and, in process of time, filled the whole land of Canaan.

10. *The hills were covered*. (6) The vine, carefully cultivated in a suitable soil, may be spread to any extent. In the land of Judea it formed shades under which the people not only sheltered and refreshed themselves in times of sultry heats; but it is said they even ate, drank, and dwelt under the shelter of their vines. See 1 Kings iv. 25; Mic. iv. 4; 1 Mac. xiv. 12.

11. *She sent out her boughs unto the sea, and her branches unto the river*. The Israelitish empire extended from the river Euphrates on the east to the Mediterranean Sea on the west.

MATTHEW HENRY

of its fruit, for *Israel was an empty vine*, Hos. x. 1. God came looking for grapes, but, behold, wild grapes, Isa. v. 2. And, if a vine do not bring forth fruit, no tree so useless, so worthless, Ezek. xv. 2, 6.

III. How it was wasted and ruined: "Lord, thou hast done great things for this vine, and why shall it be all undone again? Will God desert and abandon that which he himself gave being to?" *v.* 12. *Why hast thou then broken down her hedges?* There was a good reason. This noble vine had become *the degenerate plant of a strange vine* (Jer. ii. 21). As soon as ever God *broke down their hedges* and left them exposed troops of enemies presently broke in. Those that passed by the way plucked at them; the *boar out of the wood* and the *wild beast of the field* were ready to ravage it, *v.* 13. But till God had *broken down their hedges* they could not pluck a leaf of this vine. The deplorable state of Israel is described (*v.* 16): *It is burnt with fire; it is cut down;* the people are treated like thorns and briers, that are nigh unto cursing and whose end is to be burned, and no longer like vines that are protected and cherished.

IV. Their requests to God hereupon. 1. That God would help the vine (*v.* 14, 15). "*Look down from heaven,* that place of prospect, that place of power, whence thou canst send effectual relief—thence make a gracious visit, to this vine. Lord, it is formed by thyself and for thyself, and therefore it may with a humble confidence be committed to thyself and to thy own care." What we read the *branch*, in the Hebrew is the *son* (*Ben*), whom in thy counsel thou hast made strong for thyself. That branch was to come out of the stock of Israel (*my servant the branch,* Zech. iii. 8), and therefore, till he should come, Israel in general, and the house of David in particular, must be preserved. *He is the true vine,* John xv. i; Isa. xi. 1. "*Let thy hand be upon the man of thy right hand,*" that king (whoever it was) of the house of David that was now to go in and out before them; "let thy hand be upon him, not only to protect and cover him, but to own him, and strengthen him, and give him success." *So will not we go back from thee.* Adding also this prayer, "*Quicken us,* put life into us, and then *we will call upon thy name.*" We cannot call upon God's name in a right manner unless he quicken us. But many interpreters, both Jewish and Christian, apply this to the Messiah, the Son of David, the protector and Saviour of the church and the keeper of the vineyard. He is the man of God's right hand, to whom he has *sworn by his right hand* (so the Chaldee), whom he has exalted to his right hand, and who is indeed his right hand, the arm of the Lord, for all power is given to him. The stability and constancy of believers are entirely owing to the grace and strength which are laid up for us in Jesus Christ, lxviii. 28.

JAMIESON, FAUSSET, BROWN

12. hedges—(Isa. 5: 5).

13. The boar—may represent the ravaging Assyrian and the "wild beast" other heathen.

16. it—[the vine] or **they**—[the people] are suffering from Thy displeasure.

14, 15. visit this vine—favorably (Ps. 8:4). **And the vineyard**—or, "And protect or guard what thy right hand," etc. **the branch**—lit., "over the Son of man," preceding this phrase, with "protect" or "watch." **for thyself**—a tacit allusion to the plea for help; for

17. thy hand . . . upon—i.e., strengthen (Ezra 7:6; 8:22). **man of . . . hand**—may allude to Benjamin (Gen. 35:18). The terms in the latter clause correspond with those of vs. 15, from "and the branch," etc., literally, and confirm the exposition given above. **18.** We need quickening grace (Ps. 71:20; 119:25) to persevere in Thy right worship (Gen. 4:26; Rom. 10:11). **19.** (Cf. vs. 3, O God; vs. 7, O God of hosts.)

ADAM CLARKE

12. *Why hast thou . . . broken down?* (7) When a vineyard is planted, it is properly fenced to preserve it from being trodden down. So God protected Jerusalem and His temple by His own almighty arm, and none of their enemies could molest them as long as they had that protection. As it was now spoiled, it was a proof that that protection had been withdrawn.

13. *The boar out of the wood.* Nebuchadnezzar, king of Babylon, who was a fierce and cruel sovereign.

14. *Return . . . O God of hosts.* Thou hast abandoned us, and therefore our enemies have us in captivity. Come back to us, and we shall again be restored.

15. *The vineyard which thy right hand hath planted.* Thy holy and pure worship, which Thy almighty power had established in this city. *And the branch . . . thou madest strong for thyself.* The original is *veal ben*, "and upon the Son whom thou hast strengthened for thyself." Many have thought that the Lord Jesus is meant.

17. *The man of thy right hand.* The only person who can be said to be at the right hand of God as intercessor is Jesus, the Messiah. Let Him become our Deliverer.

18. *So will not we go back from thee.* We shall no more become idolaters; and it is allowed on all hands that the Jews were never guilty of idolatry after their return from the Babylonish captivity. *Quicken us.* "Make us alive," for we are nearly as good as dead.

19. *Turn us again.* Redeem us from this captivity. *O Lord God of hosts.* Thou who hast all power in heaven and earth, the innumerable hosts of both worlds being at Thy command. *Cause thy face to shine.* Let us know that thou art reconciled to us. Smile upon Thy poor rebels, weary of their sins, and prostrate at Thy feet, imploring mercy. *And we shall be saved.* From the power and oppression of the Chaldeans, from the guilt and condemnation of our sins, and from Thy wrath and everlasting displeasure.

MATTHEW HENRY — PSALM 81

To the chief musician upon Gittith. *A psalm* of Asaph.

Verses 1-7

When the people of God were gathered together in *the solemn day, the day of the feast of the Lord,* they must be told that they had business to do, for we do not go to church to sleep nor to be idle.

I. The worshippers of God are excited to their work, and are taught, by singing this psalm, to stir up both themselves and one another, to it *v.* 1-3. In doing this we must eye God as *our strength*, and as *the God of Jacob*, *v.* 1. To him, as our strength, we must pray, and we must sing praise to him as the God of all the wrestling seed of Jacob, with whom we have a spiritual communion. We must do this by all the expressions of holy joy and triumph. It was then to be done by musical instruments, the *timbrel, harp, and psaltery*; and by blowing *the trumpet*, some think in remembrance of the sound of the trumpet on Mount Sinai, which waxed louder and louder. Singing aloud intimates that we must be warm and affectionate in praising God. No time is amiss for praising God, but some are times appointed, not for God to meet us (he is always ready), but for us to meet one another, that we may join together in praising God.

II. They are here directed in their work. *This was a statute for Israel*, for the keeping up of a face of religion among them; it was *a law of the God of Jacob*, which all the seed of Jacob are bound by, and must be subject to. This solemn service was *ordained for a testimony* (*v.* 5), a standing traditional evidence, that they might know and remember what God had done for their fathers. When God went out against the land of Egypt, that he might force Pharaoh to let Israel go, then he ordained solemn feast-days to

JAMIESON, FAUSSET, BROWN — PSALM 81

Vss. 1-16. *Gittith*—(Cf. Ps. 8, title). A festal Psalm, probably for the passover (cf. Matt. 26:30), in which, after an exhortation to praise God, He is introduced, reminding Israel of their obligations, chiding their neglect, and depicting the happy results of obedience.

1. our strength—(Ps. 38:7).

2. unites the most joyful kinds of music, vocal and instrumental.

3. the new moon—or the month. **the time appointed**—(Cf. Prov. 7:20).

5. a testimony—The feasts, especially the passover, attested God's relation to His people. **Joseph**—for *Israel* (Ps. 80:1). **went out through**—or over, i.e., Israel in the exodus. **I heard**—change of person. The writer speaks for the nation. **language**—lit., "lip" (Ps. 14:1). An aggravation or element of their distress that their oppressors were foreigners (Deut. 28:49).

ADAM CLARKE — PSALM 81

The title is the same as to Psalm xiii, which see. There are various opinions concerning the occasion and time of this psalm, but it is pretty generally agreed that it was either written for or used at the celebration of the Feast of Trumpets (see on Lev. xxiii. 24), which was held on the first day of the month Tisri, which was the beginning of the Jewish year; and on that day it is still used in the Jewish worship. The psalm may have been used in celebrating the Feast of Trumpets on the first day of Tisri, the Feast of Tabernacles on the fifteenth of the same month, the creation of the world, the Feasts of the New Moons, and the deliverance of the Israelites from Egypt—to all which circumstances it appears to refer.

1. *Sing aloud unto God our strength.* Their is much meaning here. As God is our Strength, let that strength be devoted to His service; therefore, sing aloud! This is principally addressed to the priests and Levites.

2. *Take a psalm. Zimrah.* I rather think that this was the name of a musical instrument. *Bring hither the timbrel. Toph;* some kind of drum or tom-tom. *The pleasant harp. Kinnor.* A stringed instrument. *With the psaltery. Nebel.* The cithara.

3. *Blow up the trumpet. Shophar,* a species of horn. Certainly a wind instrument, as the last two were stringed instruments. The feast of the *new moon* was always proclaimed by sound of trumpet. For want of astronomical knowledge,

MATTHEW HENRY

be observed by a statute for ever in their generations, as a memorial of it, particularly the passover, which perhaps is meant by the *solemn-feast-day* (*v.* 3). Here he changes the person, *v.* 6. God speaks by him, saying, *I removed the shoulder from the burden.* Let him remember this on the feast-day, God had brought them out of the house of bondage, had removed their shoulder from the burden of oppression under which they were ready to sink, *had delivered their hands from the pots,* or panniers, or baskets, in which they carried clay or bricks. God had delivered them at the Red Sea. He answered them with a real answer, out of *the secret place of thunder.* It may be meant of the giving of the law at Mount Sinai, which was the secret place, for it was death to gaze (Exod. xix. 21), and it was in thunder that God then spoke. God had borne their manners in the wilderness: "*I proved thee at the waters of Meribah;* thou didst there show thy temper, what an unbelieving murmuring people thou wast, and yet I continued my favour to thee." Now if they, on their solemn feast-days, were thus to call to mind their redemption out of Egypt, much more ought we, on the Christian sabbath, to call to mind a more glorious redemption wrought out for us by Jesus Christ from worse than Egyptian bondage.

Verses 8-16

God, by the psalmist, here speaks to Israel, and in them to us.

I. He demands their diligent and serious attention to what he was about to say (*v.* 8): "*Hear, O my people!* Hear what is said with the greatest solemnity, for it is what *I will testify unto thee.* Do not only give me the hearing, but *hearken unto me,* that is, be advised by me, be ruled by me."

II. He puts them in mind of their obligation to him as the Lord their God and Redeemer (*v.* 10): *I am the Lord thy God, who brought thee out of the land of Egypt;* this is the preface to the ten commandments, and a powerful reason for the keeping of them.

III. He gives them an abstract both of the precepts and of the promises which he gave them, as the Lord and their God, upon their coming out of Egypt. The great command was that they should have no other gods before him (*v.* 9): *There shall no strange god be in thee,* none besides thy own God. The great promise was that God himself, as a God all-sufficient, would be nigh unto them (Deut. iv. 7), that, if they would adhere to him as their powerful protector and ruler, they should always find him their bountiful benefactor: "*Open thy mouth wide and I will fill it,* as the young ravens that cry open their mouths wide and the old ones fill them." We cannot look for too little from the creature nor too much from the Creator. The pleasures of sense will surfeit and never satisfy (Isa. lv. 2); divine pleasures will satisfy and never surfeit.

IV. He charges them with a high contempt of his authority, *v.* 11. He had done much for them, and designed to do more; but all in vain: "*My people would not hearken to my voice,* but turned a deaf ear to all I said." *They would none of me. They acquiesced not in my word* (so the Chaldee); God was willing to be to them a God, but they were not willing to be to him a people. "Israel, the seed of Jacob my friend, set me at nought, and *would* have *none of me.*" All the wickedness of the wicked world is owing to the wilfulness of the wicked will.

V. He justifies himself with this in the spiritual judgments he had brought upon them (*v.* 12): *So I gave them up unto their own hearts' lusts,* which would be more dangerous enemies and more mischievous oppressors to them than any of the neighbouring nations ever were. God withdrew his Spirit from them, took off the bridle of restraining grace, left them to themselves. *Ephraim is joined to idols; let him alone.* Let them take their course. And see what follows: *They walked in their own counsels.* "I left them to do as they would, and then they did all that was ill."

VI. He testifies his goodwill to them. He saw how sad their case was, and how sure their ruin, when they were delivered up to their own lusts. Now here God looks upon them with pity, and shows that it was with reluctance that he thus abandoned them to their folly and fate. *O that my people had hearkened!* See Isa. xlviii. 18. Thus Christ lamented the obstinacy of Jerusalem, *If thou hadst known,* Luke xix. 42. The expressions here are very affecting (*v.* 13-16), designed to show how unwilling God is that any should perish and desirous that all should come to repentance.

1. The great mercy God had in store for his people, and which he would have wrought for them if they had been obedient. *I should have subdued their enemies;* and it is God only that is to be depended on for the subduing of our enemies. He would *soon*

JAMIESON, FAUSSET, BROWN

6. God's language alludes to the burdensome slavery of the Israelites.

7. secret place—the cloud from which He troubled the Egyptians (Exod. 14:24).

proved thee—(Ps. 7:10; 17:3)—tested their faith by the miracle.

8. (Cf. Ps. 50:7.) The reproof follows to vs. 12. **if thou wilt hearken**—He then propounds the terms of His covenant: they should worship Him alone, who (vs. 10) had delivered them, and would still confer all needed blessings.

11, 12. They failed, and He gave them up to their own desires and hardness of heart (Deut. 29:18; Prov. 1:30; Rom. 11:25).

13-16. Obedience would have secured all promised blessings and the subjection of foes. In this passage, "should have," "would have," etc., are better, "should" and "would" expressing God's intention at the time, i.e., when they left Egypt.

ADAM CLARKE

the Jews were put to sad shifts to know the real time of the new moon. They generally sent persons to the top of some hill or mountain about the time which the new moon should appear. The first who saw it was to give immediate notice to the Sanhedrin; they closely examined the reporter as to his credibility, and whether his information agreed with their calculations. If all was found satisfactory, the president proclaimed the new moon by shouting out, "*Mikkodesh!*" "It is consecrated!" This word was repeated twice aloud by the people, and was then proclaimed everywhere by blowing of horns, or what is called the sound of trumpets.

4. *This was a statute for Israel.* See the statute, Num. x. 10 and Lev. xxiii. 24.

5. *I heard a language that I understood not.* All the versions, except the Chaldee, read the pronoun in the third person, instead of the first. "He heard a language that he understood not."

7. *Thou calledst in trouble.* They had cried by reason of their burdens, and the cruelty of their taskmasters; and God heard that cry, and delivered them. See Exod. iii. 7, etc. *In the secret place of thunder.* On Mount Sinai, where God was heard but not seen. *At the waters of Meribah.* See this transaction, Exod. xvii. 1, etc.

8. *Hear, O my people.* These are nearly the same words with those spoken at the giving of the law, Exod. xx. 2.

11. *Israel would none of me.* "They willed Me not"; they would not have Me for their God.

12. *Unto their own hearts' lust.* To the obstinate wickedness of their heart.

13. *Oh that my people had hearkened unto me . . . Israel had walked in my ways!* Nothing can be more plaintive than the original; sense and sound are surprisingly united.

MATTHEW HENRY

have done it. If he but turn his hand, the *haters of the Lord will submit themselves to him* (*v.* 15). In spite of all the attempts of their enemies against them, ***their time should have endured for ever***, and they should never have been disturbed in the possession of the good land God had given them. He would have given them great plenty of all good things (*v.* 16): *He should have fed them with the finest of the wheat*, with the best grain and the best of the kind. Wheat was the staple commodity of Canaan. He would not only have provided for them the best sort of bread, but *with honey out of the rock would he have satisfied them*. In short, God designed to make them every way easy and happy.

2. The duty God required from them as the condition of all this mercy. He expected no more than that they should *hearken to him*, as a scholar to his teacher, to receive his instructions—as a servant to his master, to receive his commands; and that they should *walk in his ways*.

3. Observe how the reason of the withholding of the mercy is laid in their neglect of the duty: If they had *hearkened to me, I would soon have subdued their enemies*. National sin or disobedience is the great and only thing that retards and obstructs national deliverance. It is sin that makes our troubles long and salvation slow.

JAMIESON, FAUSSET, BROWN

CHARLES H. SPURGEON:

"He should have fed them also with the finest of the wheat" (81:16). Famine would have been an unknown word; they would have been fed on the best of the best food, and have had abundance of it as their every day diet. "And with honey out of the rock should I have satisfied thee." Luxuries as well as necessaries would be forthcoming, the very rocks of the land would yield abundant and sweet supplies; the bees would store the clefts of the rocks with luscious honey, and so turn the most sterile part of the land to good account. The Lord can do great things for an obedient people. When his people walk in the light of his countenance and maintain unsullied holiness, the joy and consolation which he yields them are beyond conception. To them the joys of heaven have begun even upon earth. They can sing in the ways of the Lord.—*The Treasury of David*

ADAM CLARKE

15. *Their time should have endured for ever.* That is, Their prosperity should have known no end.

16. *With the finest of the wheat.* Literally, "with the fat of wheat."

PSALM 82 (Matthew Henry)

A psalm of Asaph.

Verses 1–5

I. God's supreme presidency and power in all councils and courts (*v.* 1): *God stands*, as chief director, *in the congregation of the mighty*, the mighty One, *in the councils of the prince*, the supreme magistrate, and he judges among the gods, the inferior magistrates; both the legislative and the executive power of princes is under his eye and his hand. The magistrates are the *mighty*. They are so in authority, for the public good. They are, in the Hebrew dialect, called *gods*; the same word is used for these subordinate governors that is used for the sovereign ruler of the world. They are *elohim*. Angels are so called because God is pleased to make use of their service in the government of this lower world; and magistrates in an inferior capacity are likewise the ministers for the keeping of order and peace, and particularly of his justice in punishing evil-doers and protecting those that do well. Good magistrates are God's vicegerents, and great blessings to any people. In a mixed monarchy, the sovereign, and his congregation, his privy-council, his parliament, his bench of judges. *God stands*, he *judges among them*; they have their power from him and are accountable to him. *By him kings reign*. God has their hearts in his hands, and his counsels shall stand, whatever devices are in men's hearts. Let magistrates consider this and be awed by it; God is with them in the judgment, 2 Chron. xix. 6; Deut. i. 17. Let subjects consider this and be comforted with it; for good princes and good judges are under a divine direction, and bad ones are under a divine restraint.

II. A charge given to all magistrates to do good with their power, as they will answer it to him by whom they are entrusted with it, *v.* 3, 4. *Defend the poor*, who have no money wherewith to fee counsel, *and the fatherless*, who, while they are young and unable to help themselves, have lost those who would have been the guides of their youth. Magistrates must be fathers to their country in general. They are to administer justice impartially, and do *right to the afflicted and needy*. They are to rescue those who have already fallen into the hands of oppressors (*v.* 4): *Rid them out of the hand of the wicked*. These are clients whom there is nothing to be got by, yet these are those whose cause they must espouse.

III. A charge drawn up against bad magistrates, *v.* 2, 5. They *judge unjustly*, contrary to the rules of equity and the dictates of their consciences. To do unjustly is bad, but to judge unjustly is much worse, because it is doing wrong under colour of right. They were told plainly enough that it was their office and duty to protect and deliver the poor; yet they judge unjustly, for *they know not, neither will they understand*. They have baffled their own consciences, and so they walk on in darkness. What were the consequences of this sin: *All the foundations of the earth* (or *of the land*) *are out of course*. The miscarriages of public persons are public mischiefs.

Verses 6–8

The dignity of their character is acknowledged (*v.* 6): *I have said, You are gods*. He called them *gods* because they had a commission from God, and were

PSALM 82 (Jamieson, Fausset, Brown)

Vss. 1-8. Before the great Judge, the judges of the earth are rebuked, exhorted, and threatened.

1. congregation—(Cf. Exod. 12:3; 16:1). **of the mighty**—i.e., of God, of His appointment.

the gods—or judges (Exod. 21:6; 22:9), God's representatives.

3, 4. So must good judges act (Ps. 10:14; 29:12). **poor and needy**—(Cf. Ps. 34:10; 41:1).

2. accept the persons—lit., "lift up the faces," i.e., from dejection, or admit to favor and communion, regardless of merit (Lev. 19:15; Prov. 18:5).

5. By the wilful ignorance and negligence of judges, anarchy ensues (Ps. 11:3; 75:3). **out of course**—(Cf. *Margin*; Ps. 9:6; 62:2).

PSALM 82 (Adam Clarke)

This psalm, which, in the title, is attributed to Asaph, was probably composed in the time when Jehoshaphat reformed the courts of justice throughout his states; see 2 Chron. xix. 6-7, where he uses nearly the same words as in the beginning of this psalm.

1. *God standeth in the congregation of the mighty.* The Hebrew should be translated, "God standeth in the assembly of God."

3. *Defend the poor.* You are their natural protectors under God.

2. *Accept the persons of the wicked.* "Lift up their faces," encourage them in their oppressions.

5. *They know not.* The judges are not acquainted with the law of God, on which all their decisions should be founded. *Neither will they understand.* They are ignorant, and do not wish to be instructed. *All the foundations of the earth.* "All the civil institutions of the land totter."

6. *Ye are gods.* Or, with the prefix of *ke*, the particle of similitude, *keelohim*, "like God."

MATTHEW HENRY

delegated and appointed by him to be the conservators of the public peace. God has put some of his honour upon them, and employs them in his providential government of the world. It is a hard thing for men to have so much honour put upon them by the hand of God, and so much honour paid them, as ought to be by the children of men, and not to be proud of it and puffed up with it. But here follows a mortifying consideration: *You shall die like men.* This may be taken either, 1. As the punishment of bad magistrates, such as judged unjustly, and by their misrule put the *foundations of the earth out of course.* They shall die like other wicked men, *and fall like one of the* heathen *princes.* Or, 2. As the period of the glory of all magistrates in this world. "You are called gods, but you have no patent for immortality; *you shall die like men,* like common men; and *like one of them, you, O princes! shall fall.*" *Death mingles sceptres with spades.*

The God of heaven exalted, *v.* 8. The psalmist finds it to little purpose to reason with these proud oppressors; and therefore he looks up to God and begs of him *to take unto himself his great power*; *Arise, O God! judge the earth; Thou shalt inherit all nations.* In this faith we must pray, "*Arise, O God! judge the earth,* appear against those that judge unjustly, and set shepherds over thy people after thy own heart." It is a prayer that Christ would come, who is to judge the earth, and that God shall *give him the heathen for his inheritance.*

JAMIESON, FAUSSET, BROWN

6, 7. Though God admitted their official dignity (John 10:34), He reminds them of their mortality. **fall like . . .**—be cut off suddenly (Ps. 20:8; 91:7).

8. As rightful sovereign of earth, God is invoked personally to correct the evils of His representatives.

ADAM CLARKE

7. *But ye shall die like men. Keadam,* "ye shall die like Adam," who fell from his high perfection and dignity as ye have done.

8. *Arise, O God, judge the earth.* Justice is perverted in the land; take the sceptre, and rule thyself. *For thou shalt inherit all nations.* Does not this last verse contain a prophecy of our Lord, the calling of the Gentiles, and the prevalence of Christianity over the earth? Thus several of the fathers have understood the passage.

MATTHEW HENRY

PSALM 83

A song *or* psalm of Asaph.

Verses 1–8

The Israel of God were in danger and great distress.

I. The psalmist here begs of God to appear on the behalf of his threatened people (*v.* 1): "*Keep not thou silence, O God!* but give judgment for us against those that do us an apparent wrong." Sometimes God holds his peace, as if he would observe an exact neutrality, and let them fight it out. Then he gives us leave to call upon him, as here, "*Keep not thou silence, O God!* Lord, speak to us by the prophets for our encouragement against our fears. Lord, speak for us by thy providence and speak against our enemies; speak deliverance to us and disappointment to them."

II. An account of the grand alliance of the neighbouring nations against Israel, which he begs of God to break.

This confederacy is formed against the Israel of God, and so, in effect, against the God of Israel. They hated the religious worshippers of God, because they hated God's holy religion and the worship of him. *They are confederate against thee, v.* 5. "Lord," says the psalmist, "they are thy enemies, for they consult against thy hidden ones." God's people are his hidden ones. Their life is *hid with Christ in God.* God takes them under his special protection, hides them in the hollow of his hand. They resolve to destroy those whom God resolves to preserve. *Thy enemies make a tumult, v.* 2. They are noisy in their clamours. This comes in as a reason why God should not keep silence: "The enemies talk big and talk much; Lord, let them not talk all, but do thou *speak to them in thy wrath,*" ii. 5. *They have lifted up the head.* In confidence of their success, they are so elevated as if they could overpower the Almighty. They have *taken crafty counsel, v.* 3. Whatever separate clashing interest they have among themselves, against the people of God they *consult with one consent* (*v.* 5). It is no less than the utter ruin and extirpation of Israel that they design (*v.* 4): "*Come, let us cut them off from being a nation, that the name of Israel may be no more in remembrance,* no, not in history." It is the secret wish of many wicked men that the church of God might not have a being in the world, that there might be no such thing as religion among mankind. Having banished the sense of it out of their own hearts, they would gladly see the whole earth rid of it. But *he that sits in heaven shall laugh at them.* The nations that entered into this alliance are here mentioned (*v.* 6–8); the Edomites and Ishmaelites, both descendants from Abraham, lead the van. These were allied to Israel in blood and yet in alliance against Israel. There are no bonds of nature so strong but the spirit of persecution has broken through them. *The brother shall betray the brother to death.* The Philistines were long a thorn in Israel's side, and very vexatious. *Assur* (that is, the Assyrian) *also is joined with them.*

JAMIESON, FAUSSET, BROWN

PSALM 83

Vss. 1-18. *Of Asaph*—(Cf. Ps. 74, title). The historical occasion is probably that of II Chronicles 20:1, 2 (cf. Psalms 47, 48). After a general petition, the craft and rage of the combined enemies are described, God's former dealings recited, and a like summary and speedy destruction on them is invoked.

1. God addressed as indifferent (cf. Ps. 35:22; 39:12). **be not still**—lit., "not quiet," as opposed to action.

3. hidden ones—whom God specially protects (Ps. 27:5; 91:1).

2. thine enemies—as well as ours (Ps. 74:23; Isa. 37:23).

5. they have consulted—with heart, or cordially. **together**—all alike.

4. from being a nation—utter destruction (Isa. 7:8; 23:1). **Israel**—here used for Judah, having been the common name.

6-8. tabernacles—for people (Ps. 78:67). **they**—all these united with the children of Lot, or Ammonites and Moabites (cf. II Chron. 20:1).

ADAM CLARKE

PSALM 83

The title, "A Song or Psalm of Asaph," contains nothing particular. Among a multitude of conjectures relative to the time and occasion of this psalm, that which refers it to the confederacy against Jehoshaphat, king of Judah, mentioned in 2 Chronicles xx, is the most likely.

1. *Keep not thou silence.* A strong appeal to God just as the confederacy was discovered.

2. *Thine enemies make a tumult.* They are not merely the enemies of Thy people, but they are the enemies of thyself, Thy worship, ordinances, and laws. They *make a tumult;* they throng together. *They . . . have lifted up the head.* They have made an irruption into the land of Judea, and encamped at En-gedi, by the Dead Sea, 2 Chron. xx. 1-2.

4. *Let us cut them off.* Let us exterminate the whole race, that there may not be a record of them on the face of the earth. And their scheme was well laid. Eight or ten different nations united themselves in a firm bond to do this; and they had kept their purpose so secret that the king of Judah does not appear to have heard of it till his territories were actually invaded, and the different bodies of this coalition had assembled at En-gedi. Never was Judah before in greater danger.

5. *They have consulted together with one consent.* With a united heart, *leb yachdav. They are confederate against thee.* "They have made a covenant," *berith yachrithu,* "they have cut the covenant sacrifice." They have slain an animal, divided him in twain, and passed between the pieces of the victim; and have thus bound themselves to accomplish their purpose.

6. *The tabernacles of Edom.* The "tents" of these different people are seen in the grand encampment. *Hagarenes.* These people dwelt on the east of Gilead; and were nearly destroyed in the days of Saul, being totally expelled from their country, 1 Chron. v. 10, but afterwards recovered some strength and consequence; but where they dwelt after their expulsion by the Israelites is not known.

7. *Gebal.* The Giblites, who were probably the persons here designed, were a tribe of the ancient inhabitants of the land of Canaan, and are mentioned as unconquered at the death of Joshua, chap. xiii. 5. They are called stone-squarers or Giblites, 1 Kings v. 18, and were of considerable assistance to Hiram, king of Tyre, in preparing timber and stones for the building of the Temple. They appear to have been eminent in the days of Ezekiel, who terms them "the ancients of Gebal and the wise men thereof," who were shipbuilders, chap. xxvii. 9. *Ammon* and *Moab* were the descendants of the children of Lot. Their bad origin is sufficiently

MATTHEW HENRY | JAMIESON, FAUSSET, BROWN | ADAM CLARKE

CHARLES H. SPURGEON:

"Do unto them as unto the Midianites" (83:9). Faith delights to light upon precedents and quote them before the Lord; in the present instance, Asaph found a very appropriate one, for the nations in both cases were very much the same and the plight of the Israelites very similar. Yet Midian perished, and the Psalmist trusted that Israel's present foes would meet with the like overthrow from the hand of the Lord. "As to Sisera, as to Jabin, at the brook of Kishon." The hosts were swept away by the suddenly swollen torrent and utterly perished; which was a second instance of divine vengeance upon confederated enemies of Israel. When God wills it, a brook can be as deadly as a sea. Kishon was as terrible to Jabin as was the Red Sea to Pharaoh. How easily can the Lord smite the enemies of his people. God of Gideon and of Barak, wilt thou not again avenge thine heritage of their bloodthirsty foes?—*The Treasury of David*

Verses 9–18

The psalmist prays for the destruction of those confederate forces, and, in God's name, foretells it. This prophecy reaches to all the enemies of the gospel-church.

I. The defeat and discomfiture of former combinations may be pleaded in prayer to God, because God is the same still to his people and the same against his and their enemies; with him is no variableness. *Do to them as to the Midianites;* let them be routed by their own fears, for so the Midianites were, more than by Gideon's 300 men. Do to them as to the army under the command of Sisera (who was general under Jabin king of Canaan) which God discomfited (Judges iv. 15). *They became as dung on the earth;* their dead bodies were thrown like dung laid in heaps by Barak's small but victorious army. *So let all thy enemies perish, O Lord!* that is, So they shall perish. He prays that their leaders might be destroyed as they had been formerly, *v.* 11, 12. They said, *Let us take to ourselves the houses of God in possession* (*v.* 12), the *pleasant places* of God (so the word is), by which we may understand the land of Canaan, which was a pleasant land and was Immanuel's land, or the temple, which was indeed God's pleasant place (Isa. lxiv. 11), or (as Dr. Hammond suggests) the pleasant pastures, which these Arabians, who traded in cattle, did in a particular manner seek after. They shall be made *like Oreb and Zeeb* (Judges vii. 25), and *like Zeba and Zalmunna* (Judges viii. 21).

II. He prays that God would *make them like a wheel* (*v.* 13), that they might be in continual motion, unsettled and giddy in all their counsels, that they might roll down easily and speedily to their own ruin. Or, as some think, that they might be broken by the judgments of God, as the corn is broken, or beaten out, by the wheel which was then used in threshing. "The wheel, though it continually turn round, is fixed on its own axis; but let them have no more fixation than the light stubble has, which the wind hurried away." When the stubble is driven by the wind it will rest, at last, under some hedge, in some ditch or other; but he prays that they might not only be driven away as stubble, but burnt up as stubble. The application of these comparisons we have (*v.* 15): *So persecute them with thy tempest,* persecute them to their utter ruin, and make *them afraid with thy storm.*

III. He illustrates it by the good consequences of their confusion, *v.* 16–18. They did what they could to put God's people to shame, but the shame will at length return upon themselves. The beginning of this shame might be a means of their conversion: "Let them be broken and baffled in their attempts, *that they may seek thy name, O Lord!*" That which we should earnestly desire and beg of God for our enemies and persecutors is that God would bring them to repentance, and we should desire no other confusion to them than what may be a step towards their conversion. If they will not be ashamed and repent, let them be put to shame, that other men may know and own, if they themselves will not, *that thou, whose name alone is JEHOVAH* (that incommunicable, though not ineffable name) *art the Most High over all the earth.*

9-11. Compare the similar fate of these (II Chron. 20:23) with that of the foes mentioned in Judges 7:22, here referred to. They destroyed one another (Judg. 4:6-24; 7:25). Human remains form manure (cf. II Kings 9:37; Jer. 9:22).

12. The language of the invaders. **houses**—lit., "residences," enclosures, as for flocks (Ps. 65:12). **of God**—as the proprietors of the land (II Chron. 20:11; Isa. 14:25).

13. like a wheel—or, whirling of any light thing (Isa. 17:13), as stubble or chaff (Ps. 1:4).

14, 15. Pursue them to an utter destruction.

16. that they may seek—or as vs. 18, supply "men," since vss. 17, 18 amplify the sentiment of vs. 16, expressing more fully the measure of destruction, and the lesson of God's being and perfections (cf. II Chron. 20:29) taught to all men.

known. See Gen. xix. 30, etc. *Amalek.* The Amalekites are well-known as the ancient and inveterate enemies of the Israelites. They were neighbors to the Idumeans. *The Philistines.* These were tributaries to Jehoshaphat, 2 Chron. xvii. 11; but it seems they took advantage of the present times to join in the great confederacy against him. *The inhabitants of Tyre.* These probably joined the confederacy in hopes of making conquests and extending their territory on the mainland.

8. *Assur also is joined.* The Ammonites might have got those auxiliaries from beyond the Euphrates, against Jehoshaphat, as formerly they were brought against David. See 2 Sam. x. 16. *They have holpen the children of Lot.* The Ammonites, who appear to have been the chief instigators in this war.

9. *Do unto them as unto the Midianites.* Who were utterly defeated by Gideon, Judg. vii. 21-22. *As to Sisera.* Captain of the army of Jabin, king of Canaan, who was totally defeated by Deborah and Barak, near Mount Tabor, by the river Kishon; and himself, after having fled from the battle, slain by Jael, the wife of Heber, the Kenite. See Judg. iv. 15, etc.

10. *Perished at En-dor.* This refers to the defeat of the Midianites by Gideon, who were encamped in the Valley of Jezreel, at the foot of Mount Gilboa, and near to Tabor, Judg. vi. 33; vii. 1, and consequently in the environs of Endor.

11. *Make their nobles like Oreb, and like Zeeb.* They were two of the chiefs, or generals, of the Midianites; and were slain in the pursuit of the Midianites, by the men of Ephraim; and their heads brought to Gideon on the other side of Jordan. Judg. vii. 24-25. *Yea, all their princes as Zebah, and as Zalmunna.* These were kings of Midian who were encamped at Karkor with 15,000 men, whom Gideon attacked there, and defeated, and took the kings prisoners; and finding that they had killed his own brothers, slew them both. See Judg. viii. 10-21.

12. *Let us take to ourselves the houses of God in possession.* Nearly the words spoken by the confederates when they came to attack Jehoshaphat. See 2 Chron. xx. 11.

13. *O my God, make them like a wheel.* Alluding to the manner of threshing corn in the East. A large, broad wheel was rolled over the grain on a threshing floor, which was generally in the open air; and the grain being thrown up by a shovel against the wind, the chaff was thus separated from it, in the place where it was threshed.

14. *The flame setteth the mountains on fire.* This may refer to the burning of the straw and chaff, after the grain was threshed and winnowed.

15. *So persecute them.* In this and the two following verses we find several awful execrations; and all this seems to be done in reference to that ancient custom, "pouring execrations on an enemy previously to battle." The reader is particularly requested to refer to the case of Balaam being hired by the king of Moab to curse Israel previously to his intended attack; see Numbers xxii.

16. *That they may seek thy name.* Let them be confounded in all their attempts on Israel, and see so manifestly that Thou hast done it that they may invoke Thy name and be converted to Thee.

17. *Let them . . . perish.* That is, in their present attempts. Some have objected to the execrations in this psalm, without due consideration. None of these execrations refer either to their souls or to their eternal state, but merely to their discomfiture in their present attempts.

18. *That men may know.* That they may acknowledge, and be converted to Thee. Here is no malice; all is self-defense.

PSALM 84

To the chief musician upon Gittith. A psalm for the sons of Korah.

Verses 1–7

The psalmist here, being by force restrained from waiting upon God in public ordinances, is brought under a more sensible conviction than ever of the worth of them.

PSALM 84

Vss. 1-12. Cf. on titles of Psalms 8, 42. The writer describes the desirableness of God's worship and prays for a restoration to its privileges.

PSALM 84

The title here is the same as that of Psalm lxxxi, only that was for Asaph, this for the sons of Korah. This person was one of the chief rebels against Moses and Aaron; there were

MATTHEW HENRY

I. The wonderful beauty he saw in holy institutions (*v.* 1): *How amiable are thy tabernacles. O Lord of hosts!* The tabernacle is spoken of as more than one (*thy tabernacles*) because there were several courts in which the people attended, and because the tabernacle itself consisted of a holy place and a most holy. How lovely is the sanctuary in the eyes of all that are truly sanctified! Gracious souls see a wonderful, an inexpressible, beauty in holiness, and in holy work. A tabernacle was a mean habitation, but the beauty of holiness is spiritual, and the glory is within.

II. The longing desire he had to return to the enjoyment of public ordinances, or rather of God in them, *v.* 2. It was an entire desire; body, soul, and spirit. It was an intense desire. He longed, he fainted, he cried out. Yet it was not so much the courts of the Lord that he coveted, but he cried out, in prayer, *for the living God* himself. Ordinances are empty things if we meet not with God in the ordinances.

III. His grudging the happiness of the little birds that made their nests in the buildings that were adjoining to God's altars, *v.* 3. *The sparrow has found a house and the swallow a nest for herself.* These little birds, by the instinct and direction of nature, provide habitations for themselves in houses, as other birds do in the woods: some such David supposes there were in the buildings about the courts of God's house, and wishes himself with them. He would rather live in a bird's nest nigh God's altars than in a palace at a distance from them. He sometimes wished for *the wings of a dove*, on which to *fly into the wilderness* (*v.* 6); here for the wings of a sparrow, that he might fly undiscovered into God's courts. The word for a sparrow signifies any little bird, and (if I may offer a conjecture) perhaps when, in David's time, music was introduced so much into the sacred service, to complete the harmony they had singing-birds in cages hung about the courts of the tabernacle (for we find the singing of birds taken notice of to the glory of God, civ. 12), and David envies the happiness of these, and would gladly change places with them. David envies the happiness not of those birds that flew over the altars, but of those that had nests for themselves there. David will not think it enough to sojourn in God's house *as a wayfaring man to tarry for a night*; but let this be his rest, his home; here he will dwell. And he takes notice that these birds not only have nests for themselves there, but that there they lay their young; for those who have a place in God's courts themselves cannot but desire that their children also may have in God's house, a place and a name. Observe how he eyes God in this address: Thou art the *Lord of hosts, my King and my God.* Where should a poor, distressed subject seek for protection but with his king? *And should not a people seek unto their God?* My King, my God, is Lord of hosts; by him and his altars let me live and die.

IV. His acknowledgment of the happiness both of the ministers and of the people that had liberty of attendance on God's altars. Blessed are the ministers, the priests and Levites, who have their residence about the tabernacle and are in their courses employed in the service of it (*v.* 4). *They will be still praising thee;* and, if there be a heaven upon earth, it is in praising God, in continually praising him. Apply this to his house above; blessed are those that dwell there, angels and glorified saints, for they *rest not day nor night from praising God.* Blessed are the people, the inhabitants of the country, who, though they do not constantly dwell in God's house as the priests do, yet have liberty of access to it, *v.* 5–7. *Blessed is the man whose strength is in thee*, who makes thee his strength and strongly stays himself upon thee. They are such as have a love for holy *ordinances*: *In whose heart are the ways of them*, that is, who, having placed their happiness in God as their end, rejoice in all the ways that lead to him. They are such as will break through difficulties and discouragements in waiting upon God in holy ordinances, *v.* 6. When they come up out of the country to worship at the feasts their way lies through many a dry and sandy valley (so some), in which they are ready to perish for thirst; but they dig little pits to receive and keep the rain-water for their refreshments. Their way lay through many a weeping valley, so Baca signifies, that is (as others understand it), many watery valleys, which in wet weather, when *the rain filled the pools*, were impassable; but, by draining and trenching them, they made a road through them for the benefit of those who went up to Jerusalem. Care should be taken to keep those roads in repair that lead to church, as well as those that lead to market. But all this is intended to show they had a good will to the journey. Our way to heaven lies through a valley of Baca, but even that may be made a well if we make a due improvement of the comforts God has

JAMIESON, FAUSSET, BROWN

1. amiable—not lovely, but beloved. **tabernacles**—(Ps. 43:3).

2. longeth—most intensely (Gen. 31:30; Ps. 17:12). **fainteth**—exhausted with desire. **courts**—as tabernacles (vs. 1)—the whole building. **crieth out**—lit., "sings for joy"; but here, and Lamentations 2:19, expresses an act of sorrow as the corresponding noun (Ps. 17:1; 61:2). **heart and . . . flesh**—as in Psalm 63:1.

3. thine altars—i.e., of burnt offering and incense, used for the whole tabernacle. Its structure afforded facilities for sparrows and swallows to indulge their known predilections for such places. Some understand the statement as to the birds as a comparison: "as they find homes, so do I desire *thine altars,*" etc.

4. This view is favored by the language here, which, as in Psalms 15:1; 23:6, recognizes the blessing of membership in God's family by terms denoting a *dwelling in His house.*

5. (Cf. Ps. 68:28.) **in whose heart . . . ways**—i.e., who knows and loves the way to God's favor (Prov. 16:17; Isa. 40:3, 4).

6. valley of Baca—or weeping. Through such, by reason of their dry and barren condition, the worshippers often had to pass to Jerusalem. As they might become wells, or fountains, or pools, supplied by refreshing rain, so the grace of God, by the exercises of His worship, refreshes and revives the hearts of His people, so that for sorrows they have "rivers of delight" (Ps. 36:8; 46:4).

ADAM CLARKE

three, Korah, Dathan, and Abiram, who made an insurrection; and the earth opened, and swallowed up them and their partisans, Numbers xvi. The children of Dathan and Abiram perished with their fathers; but by a particular dispensation of providence the children of Korah were spared. See Num. xxvi. 11. The family of Korah was continued in Israel; and it appears from 1 Chron. xxvi. 1-19 that they were still employed about the Temple, and were porters or keepers of the doors. They were also singers in the Temple; see 2 Chron. xx. 19. This psalm might have been sent to them to be sung, or one of themselves might have been its author.

1. *How amiable are thy tabernacles!* In this plural noun he appears to include all the places in or near the Temple where acts of divine worship were performed.

2. *My soul longeth.* It is a Levite that speaks, who ardently longs to regain his place in the Temple, and his part in the sacred services.

3. *Yea, the sparrow hath found an house.* It is very unlikely that sparrows and swallows, or birds of any kind, should be permitted to build their nests, and hatch their young, in or about altars which were kept in a state of the greatest purity, and where perpetual fires were kept up for the purpose of sacrifice, burning incense, etc. Without altering the text, if the clause be read in a parenthesis, the absurdity will be avoided, and the sense be good. "My heart crieth out for the living God (even the sparrow hath found a house, and the ring-dove, a nest for herself, where she may lay her young), for thine altars, O Lord of hosts!" Or read the parenthesis last: "My heart crieth out for the living God; for thine altars, O Lord of hosts, my King and my God. Even the sparrow hath found out a house, and the swallow (ring-dove) a nest for herself, where she may lay her young"; but I have no place, of either rest or worship, understood.

4. *Blessed are they that dwell in thy house.* They who have such a constant habitation in Thy temple as the sparrow or the swallow has in the house wherein it has built its nest.

5. *In whose heart are the ways of them.* This is no sense. The original, however, is obscure: "The high ways are in their hearts"; that is, the roads winding to Thy temple.

6. *Passing through the valley of Baca make it a well.* I believe *Baca* to be the same here as Bochim, Judg. ii. 1-5, called "The Valley of Weeping." *The rain also filleth the pools.* The Hebrew may be translated differently, and has been differently understood by all the versions. "Yea, the instructor is covered or clothed with blessings."

MATTHEW HENRY

provided for the pilgrims to the heavenly city. They are such as are still pressing forward till they come to their journey's end at length (*v.* 7): *They go from strength to strength.* Instead of being fatigued with the tediousness of their journey and the difficulties they met with, the nearer they came to Jerusalem the more lively and cheerful they were. Those that press forward in their Christian course shall find God adding grace to their graces, John i. 16.

Verses 8–12

I. The psalmist prays for audience and acceptance with God. He prays (*v.* 8, 9), only that God would hear his prayer and give ear. He calls himself (as many think) *God's anointed,* for David was anointed by him and anointed for him. He has an eye to God under several of his glorious titles—as *the Lord God of hosts,* who has all the creatures at his command, as the *God of Jacob,* a God in covenant with his own people, and as *God our shield,* who takes his people under his special protection.

II. He pleads his love to God's ordinances and his dependence upon God himself.

1. God's courts were his choice, *v.* 10. *A day spent in thy courts,* in attending on the services of religion, wholly abstracted from all secular affairs, *is better than a thousand,* anywhere else in this world. *I would rather be a doorkeeper,* rather be in the meanest place and office, *in the house of my God, than dwell* in state, as Master, *in the tents of wickedness.* I would rather be a porter in God's house than a prince in those tents where wickedness reigns, rather lie at the threshold (so the word is); that was the beggar's place (Acts iii. 2): "no matter" (says David), "let that be my place rather than none."

2. God himself was his hope, and joy, and all. *The Lord God is a sun and shield.* We are here in darkness, but, if God be our God, he will be to us a sun, to enlighten and enliven us, to guide and direct us. We are here in danger, but he will be to us a shield to secure us. *The Lord will give grace and glory.* Grace signifies both the goodwill of God towards us and the good work of God in us; glory signifies both the honour which he now puts upon us, in giving us the adoption of sons, and that which he has prepared for us in the inheritance of sons. God will give them grace in this world as a preparation for glory, and glory in the other world as the perfection of grace; both are God's gift, his free gift. *No good thing will be withheld from those that walk uprightly.* This is a comprehensive promise, and is such an assurance of the present comfort of the saints that, whatever they desire, and think they need, they may be sure that either Infinite Wisdom sees it is not good for them or Infinite Goodness will give it to them in due time. Those are blessed who have the privileges of God's house. If we cannot go to the house of the Lord, we may go by faith to the Lord of the house, and in him we shall be happy and may be easy.

JAMIESON, FAUSSET, BROWN

7. The figure of the pilgrim is carried out. As such daily refit their bodily strength till they reach Jerusalem, so the spiritual worshipper is daily supplied with spiritual strength by God's grace till he appears before God in heaven. **appeareth . . . God**—the terms of the requisition for the attendance on the feasts (cf. Deut. 16:16).

9. God is addressed as a shield (cf. vs. 11). **thine anointed**—David (1 Sam. 16:12).

10. I had . . . doorkeeper—lit., "I choose to sit on the threshold," the meanest place.

11, 12. As a sun God enlightens (Ps. 27:1); as a shield He protects.

grace—God's favor, its fruit—**glory**—the honor He bestows.

uprightly—(Ps. 15:2; 18:23). **that trusteth**—constantly.

ADAM CLARKE

7. *They go from strength to strength.* They proceed from one degree of grace to another, gaining divine virtue through all the steps of their probation. *Every one of them in Zion appeareth before God.* This is a paraphrase, and a bad one, but no translation. They shall proceed *from strength to strength.* "The God of gods shall be seen in Zion." God shall appear in their behalf, as often as they shall seek Him, in consequence of which they shall increase in spiritual strength.

11. *For the Lord God is a sun and shield.* To illuminate, invigorate, and warm; to protect and defend all such as prefer Him and His worship to everything the earth can produce. It is remarkable that not one of the versions understands the *shemesh,* as signifying *sun,* as we do. They generally concur in the following translation: "For the Lord loveth mercy and truth, and he will give grace and glory." The Chaldee says, "The Lord is as a high wall and a strong shield; grace and glory will the Lord give, and will not deprive those of blessedness who walk in perfection."

MATTHEW HENRY

PSALM 85

To the chief musician. A psalm for the sons of Korah.

Verses 1–7

The people of God, in a very low and weak condition, are here taught how to address themselves to God.

I. They are to acknowledge with thankfulness the great things God had done for them (*v.* 1-3). God had shown himself propitious to their land, and had smiled upon it as his own: "*Thou hast been favourable to thy land,* as thine, with distinguishing favours." He had not dealt with them according to the desert of their provocations (*v.* 2): "*Thou hast forgiven the iniquity of thy people,* and not punished them as in justice thou mightest. *Thou hast covered all their sin.*" The bringing back of their captivity was *then* an instance of God's favour to them, when it was accompanied with the pardon of their iniquity. "Having *covered all their sin,* thou hast *taken away all thy wrath*"; for when sin is set aside God's anger ceases; God is pacified if we are purified.

II. They are taught to pray to God for grace and mercy, in reference to their present distress; this is inferred from the former: "Thou hast done well for our fathers; do well for us, for we are the children of the same covenant." 1. They pray for converting grace: "*Turn us, O God of our salvation!*" 2. They pray for the removal of the tokens of God's displeasure: "*Cause thine anger towards us to cease.*" Observe the method, "First turn us to thee, and then cause thy anger to turn from us." 3. They pray for the manifestation of God's goodwill to them (*v.* 7):

JAMIESON, FAUSSET, BROWN

PSALM 85

Vss. 1-13. On the ground of former mercies, the Psalmist prays for renewed blessings, and, confidently expecting them, rejoices.

1. captivity—not necessarily the Babylonian, but any great evil (Ps. 14:7). **2, 3.** (Cf. Ps. 32:1-5.) To turn from the "fierceness," implies that He was reconcilable, though **(4-7)** having still occasion for the anger which is deprecated.

ADAM CLARKE

PSALM 85

The title of this psalm we have seen before, Psalm xlii. As to the time, it seems to have been written during, or even after, the return from the Babylonish captivity. In the first three verses the Psalmist acknowledges the goodness of God in bringing the people back to their own land; he next prays to God to restore them to their ancient prosperity. In the spirit of prophecy, he waits on God, and hears Him promise to do it; and then exults in the prospect of so great a good. The whole psalm seems also to have a reference to the redemption of the world by Jesus Christ.

1. *Lord, thou hast been favourable.* Literally, "Thou hast been well pleased with Thy land." *Thou hast brought back the captivity.* This seems to fix the time of the psalm to be after the return of the Jews from Babylon.

2. *Thou hast forgiven the iniquity.* "Thou hast borne, or carried away, the iniquity." An allusion to the ceremony of the scapegoat.

3. *Thou hast taken away.* "Thou hast gathered up all Thy wrath." This carries on the metaphor in the second verse: "Thou hast collected all Thy wrath, and carried it away with all our iniquities."

MATTHEW HENRY

"*Show us thy mercy, O Lord!* let us know that thou hast mercy on us and mercy in store for us." 4. They pray that God would appear on their behalf: "*Grant us thy salvation;* grant it by thy promise, and then, no doubt, thou wilt work by it thy providence."

III. They are taught humbly to expostulate with God concerning their present troubles, *v.* 5, 6. "*Wilt thou be angry with us for ever? Wilt thou draw out thy anger unto all generations?* Thou wast not angry with our fathers for ever, but didst soon turn thyself from the fierceness of thy wrath; why then wilt thou be angry with us for ever? *Wilt thou not revive us again* (*v.* 6), revive us with deliverances wrought for us?" God had granted to the children of the captivity *some reviving in their bondage*, Ezra ix. 8. Their return out of Babylon was as *life from the dead*, Ezek. xxxvii. 11, 12. Now, Lord (say they), *wilt thou not revive us again*, and *put thy hand again the second time* to gather us in? Isa. xi. 11; Ps. cxxvi. 1, 4. *Revive thy work in the midst of the years*, Hab. iii. 2. "Revive us again." If God be the fountain of all our mercies, he must be the centre of all our joys.

Verses 8–13

We have here an answer to the prayers and expostulations.

I. In general, it is an answer of peace. The psalmist (*v.* 8), *stands upon his watch-tower* to *hear what God will say unto him.* "Compose thyself, O my soul! in a humble silence to attend upon God and wait his motions. I have spoken enough; now I will hear what God will speak, and welcome his holy will. *What saith my Lord unto his servant?*" *He will speak peace to his people, and to his saints.* Sooner or later, God will speak peace to them; if he do not command outward peace, yet he will suggest inward peace, speaking that to their hearts by his Spirit which he has spoken to their ears by his word and ministers and making them to hear joy and gladness. He takes the comfort of it; and so must we: "*I will hear what God the Lord will speak*, hear the assurances he gives of peace, in answer to prayer." *But let them not turn again to folly;* for it is on these terms, and no other, that peace is to be expected.

II. Here are the particulars of this answer of peace. He gives us the pleasing prospect of the flourishing estate of the church in the last five verses of the psalm, which describe the peace and prosperity God blessed the children of the captivity with, when at length they gained a settlement in their own land. But it may be taken both as a promise also to all who fear God and work righteousness, that they shall be easy and happy, and as a prophecy of the kingdom, of the Messiah and the blessings with which that kingdom should be enriched.

1. Help at hand (*v.* 9): "*Surely his salvation is nigh.*" When the tale of bricks is doubled, then Moses comes. When trouble is nigh salvation is nigh, for God is a very present help in time of trouble to all who are his.

2. Honour secured: "*That glory may dwell in our land*, that we may have the worship of God settled and established among us; for that is the glory of a land. When that goes, *Ichabod—the glory has departed*; when that stays glory dwells."

3. Graces meeting, and happily embracing (*v.* 10, 11): *Mercy and truth, righteousness and peace, kiss each other.* This may be understood, (1) Of the reformation of the people and of the government. When in every congress mercy and truth meet, in every embrace righteousness and peace kiss, and common honesty is indeed common, then glory dwells in a land. (2) Of the return of God's favour. When a people return to God he will return to them and abide with them in a way of mercy. So some understand this, man's truth and God's mercy, man's righteousness and God's peace, meet together. If *truth spring out of the earth*, that is (as Dr. Hammond expounds it), out of the hearts of men, the proper soil for it to grow in, righteousness (that is, God's mercy) shall look down from heaven, as the sun does upon the world when it sheds its influences on the productions of the earth and cherishes them. (3) Of the harmony of the divine attributes in the Messiah's undertaking. Our salvation is so well contrived, so well concerted, that God may have mercy upon poor sinners, and be at peace with them, without any wrong to his truth and righteousness.

4. Great plenty of everything desirable (*v.* 12): *The Lord shall give that which is good*, everything that he sees to be good for us. When the glory of the gospel dwells in our land, then it shall yield its increase.

5. A sure guidance in the good way (*v.* 13): *The righteousness* of his promise assuring us of happiness, and the righteousness of sanctification, shall go before him to prepare his way; and these shall be our guide to *set us in the way of his steps*, that we may go forth to meet him when he is coming towards us in ways of mercy.

JAMIESON, FAUSSET, BROWN

draw out—or, prolong (Ps. 36:10).

8. He is confident God will favor His penitent people (Ps. 51:17; 80:18). **saints**—as in Psalm 4:3, the "godly."

9. They are here termed **"them that fear him"**; and grace produces glory (Ps. 84:11).

10. God's promises of "mercy" will be verified by His "truth" (cf. Ps. 25:10; 40:10); and the "work of righteousness" in His holy government shall be "peace" (Isa. 32:17). There is an implied contrast with a dispensation under which God's truth sustains His threatened wrath, and His righteousness inflicts misery on the wicked. **11.** Earth and heaven shall abound with the blessings of this government; **12-13,** and, under this, the deserted land shall be productive, and men be "set," or guided in God's holy ways. Doubtless, in this description of God's returning favor, the writer had in view that more glorious period, when Christ shall establish His government on God's reconciled justice and abounding mercy.

ADAM CLARKE

8. *I will hear what God the Lord will speak.* The Psalmist goes as a prophet to consult the Lord; and, having made his request, waits an answer from the spirit of prophecy. He is satisfied that the answer will be gracious; and having received it, he relates it to the people. *He will speak peace.* He will give prosperity to the people in general; and to *his saints*, His followers, in particular.

But let them not turn again to folly. Let them not abuse the mercy of their God, by sinning any more against Him.

10. *Mercy and truth are met together.* Where did these meet? In Christ Jesus. When were they reconciled? When He poured out His life on Calvary.

11. *Truth shall spring out of the earth.* In consequence of this wonderful reconciliation, the truth of God shall prevail among men. The seeds of it shall be so plentifully sown by the preaching of Christ and His apostles that true religion shall be diffused over the world.

13. *Righteousness shall go before him.* Perhaps this verse may receive its best solution from Rom. iii. 25: "Whom God hath set forth to be a propitiation through faith in his blood, to declare his righteousness for the remission of sins that are past." This term the apostle uses to point out God's method of justifying or saving mankind. And this, in the preaching of the pure gospel, is ever going before to point out the Lord Jesus, and the redemption that is in His blood.

MATTHEW HENRY

PSALM 86

A prayer of David.

Verses 1–7

This psalm was published under the title of *a prayer of David.*

I. The petitions he puts up to God. *Unto thee, O Lord! do I lift up my soul,* as he had said xxv. 1. In all the parts of prayer the soul must ascend upon the wings of faith and holy desire. 1. He begs that God would give a gracious audience to his prayers (*v.* 1): *Bow down thy ear, O Lord! hear me.* When God hears our prayers it is fitly said that he *bows down his ear* to them, for it is admirable condescension in God that he is pleased to take notice of such mean creatures as we are and such defective prayers as ours are. 2. He begs that God would take him under his special protection (*v.* 2): *Preserve my soul; save thy servant.* "Preserve my soul from that one evil and dangerous thing to souls, even from sin; preserve my soul, and so save me." All those whom God will save he preserves, and will preserve them to his heavenly kingdom. 3. He begs that God would look upon him with an eye of pity and compassion (*v.* 3): *Be merciful to me, O Lord!* "Men show no mercy; we ourselves deserve no mercy; but, Lord, for mercy-sake, be *merciful unto me.*" 4. He begs that God would fill him with inward comfort (*v.* 4): *Rejoice the soul of thy servant.* It is God only that can *put gladness into the heart and make the soul to rejoice,* and, as it is the duty of those who are God's servants to *serve him with gladness,* so it is their privilege to be *filled with joy and peace in believing,* and in faith to pray. Prayer is the nurse of spiritual joy.

II. The pleas with which he enforces these petitions. 1. He pleads his relation to God: "Thou art my God, to whom I have devoted myself, and on whom I depend, and I am thy servant (*v.* 2)." 2. He pleads his distress: "*Hear me, for I am poor and needy.*" 3. He pleads God's goodwill towards all that seek him (*v.* 5): "To thee do I *lift up my soul* in desire and expectation; *for thou, Lord, art good.*" 4. He pleads God's good work in himself, by which he had qualified him for the tokens of his favour. *I am holy,* therefore preserve my soul. He does not say this in pride and vain glory, but with humble thankfulness to God. *I am one whom thou favourest* (so the margin reads it), whom thou hast *set apart for thyself. I am holy* (*v.* 2), and yet needy, *poor in the world, but rich in faith. I cry unto thee daily, and all the day, v.* 3. It is comfortable if an affliction finds the wheels of prayer a-going, and that they are not then to be set a-going. "*In the day of my trouble,* whatever others do, *I will call upon thee,* and commit my case to thee, for thou wilt hear and answer me.

Verses 8–17

David is here going on in his prayer.

I. He gives glory to God. *Among the gods,* the false gods, whom the heathens worshipped, the angels, the kings of the earth, among them all, *there is none like unto thee, O Lord!* none so wise, so mighty, so good; *neither are there any works like unto thy works,* which is an undeniable proof that there is none like him. As the fountain of all being and the centre of all praise (*v.* 9): "*Thou hast made all nations,* made them all of one blood; they all derive their being from thee, and have a constant dependence on thee, and therefore *they shall come and worship before thee and glorify thy name.*" This was to have its full accomplishment in the days of the Messiah. "Therefore all nations shall worship before thee, because as King of nations *thou art great,* thy sovereignty absolute, and, for the proof of this, *thou doest wondrous things,* thou art God alone, not only none like thee, but none besides thee." Man is bad, very wicked and vile (*v.* 14); no mercy is to be expected from him; *but thou, O Lord! art a God full of compassion, and gracious, v.* 15. Men are barbarous, but God is gracious; men are false, but God is faithful. God is not only compassionate, but full of compassion, and in him *mercy rejoiceth against judgment.* It is some satisfaction to a good man to think that others shall praise and glorify God, but it is his greatest care and pleasure to do it himself. "Whatever others do" (says David), "*I will praise thee, O Lord my God!* not only as the Lord, but as my God. I will do it as long as I live, and hope to be doing it to eternity." With good reason does he resolve to be thus praising God: *For great is thy mercy towards me. Thou hast delivered my soul from the lowest hell.*

II. He prays earnestly for mercy and grace from God. He complains of the restless and implacable malice of his enemies against him (*v.* 14): "They were *proud men, violent men.* They *rise up against me* in open rebellion; and the design is not only to depose me, but to destroy me. Lord, appear against them,

JAMIESON, FAUSSET, BROWN

PSALM 86

Vss. 1-17. This is a prayer in which the writer, with deep emotion, mingles petitions and praises, now urgent for help, and now elated with hope, in view of former mercies. The occurrence of many terms and phrases peculiar to David's Psalms clearly intimates its authorship.

1, 2. poor and needy—a suffering child of God, as in Psalm 10:12, 17; 18:27. **I am holy**—or, godly, as in Psalm 4:3; 85:8. **4. lift up my soul**—with strong desire (Ps. 25:1).

5-7. unto all . . . that call upon thee—or, worship Thee (Ps. 50:15; 91:15) however undeserving (Exod. 34:6; Lev. 11:9-13).

8. neither . . . works—lit., "nothing like thy works," the "gods" have none at all.

9, 10. The pious Jews believed that God's common relation to all would be ultimately acknowledged by all men (Ps. 45:12-16; 47: 9).

13, 14. The reason: God had delivered him from death and the power of insolent, violent, and godless persecutors (Ps. 54:3; Ezek. 8: 12). **15.** Contrasts God with his enemies (cf. vs. 5).

ADAM CLARKE

PSALM 86

The title attributes this psalm to David, and in this all the versions agree; but in its structure it is the same with those attributed to the sons of Korah, and was probably made during the Captivity. It is a very suitable prayer for a person laboring under affliction from persecution or calumny.

1. *Bow down thine ear.* Spoken after the manner of men: I am so low, and so weak, that, unless Thou stoop to me, my voice cannot reach Thee.

2. *For I am holy. Ki chasid ani,* "for I am merciful."

5. *For thou, Lord, art good.* I found my expectations of help on Thy own goodness, through which Thou art always ready to forgive. And I found it also on Thy well-known character, to which all Thy followers bear testimony, viz., that Thou art *plenteous in mercy unto all them that call upon thee.*

10. *For thou art great.* Almighty, infinite, eternal. *And doest wondrous things.* Thou art the "Worker of miracles." This appears to be a prophecy of the calling of the Gentiles to the faith of Christ, and the evidence to be given to His divine mission by the miracles which He should work. *Thou art God alone.* Septuagint, "Thou art the only, the great God."

14. *The assemblies of violent men.* "The congregation of the terrible ones."

12. *I will praise thee . . . with all my heart.* When my heart is united to fear Thy name, then shall I praise Thee with my whole heart.

MATTHEW HENRY

for they are thy enemies as well as mine." His petitions are,

1. For the operations of God's grace in him, *v.* 11. "*Teach my thy way, O Lord!* the way that thou hast appointed me to walk in; when I am in doubt concerning it, make it plain to me what I should do; let me hear the voice saying, *This is the way*." *Teach me thy way; I will walk in thy truth.* One would think it should be, *Teach me thy truth, and I will walk in thy way;* but it comes all to one; it is the way of truth that God teaches and that we must choose and walk in, Ps. cxix. 30. Christ is the way and the truth, and we must both learn Christ and walk in him. "*Unite my heart to fear thy name.* Make me sincere in religion. A hypocrite has a double heart; let mine be single and entire for God, not divided between him and the world, not straggling from him."

2. For the tokens of God's favour to him, *v.* 16, 17. Three things he here prays for:—(1) That God would speak peace and comfort to him: "*O turn unto me,* as to one thou lovest." (2) That God would work deliverance for him, and set him in safety: "Give me *thy strength*; put strength into me, that I may help myself, and put forth thy strength for me, that I may be saved out of the hands of those that seek my ruin." (3) That God would put a reputation on him: "*Show me a token for good.* Let me have some instances of thy favour to me, *that those who hate me may see it, and be ashamed* of their enmity to me, as they will have reason to be when they perceive that *thou, Lord, hast helped me and comforted me*."

JAMIESON, FAUSSET, BROWN

11. Teach—Show, point out. **the way**—of Providence. **walk in thy truth**—according to its declarations.

unite my heart—fix all my affections (Ps. 12: 2; Jas. 4:8). **to fear thy name**—(cf. vs. 12) to honor Thy perfections.

16. son . . . handmaid—home-born servant (cf. Luke 15:17). **17. Show me**—lit., "Make with me a token," by Thy providential care. Thus in and by his prosperity his enemies would be confounded.

ADAM CLARKE

11. *Teach me thy way.* Instruct me in the steps I should take, for without Thy teaching I must go astray.

Unite my heart. Yached lebabi, "join" all the purposes, resolutions, and affections of my heart "together," *to fear* and to glorify *thy name.* This is a most important prayer.

MATTHEW HENRY

PSALM 87

A psalm *or* song for the sons of Korah.

Verses 1–3

Some make the first words of the psalm to be part of the title; it is a psalm or song whose subject is the holy mountains—the temple built in Zion upon Mount Moriah. Three things are here observed, in praise of the temple:—1. That it was founded on the holy mountains, *v.* 1. It is built high; the *mountain of the Lord's house is established upon the top of the mountains,* Isa. ii. 2. It is built firmly upon the everlasting mountains and the perpetual hills; for sooner shall the mountains depart, and the hills be removed, than the covenant of God's peace shall be disannulled, and on that the church is built, Isa. liv. 10. Holiness is the strength and stability of the church: it is this that will support it and keep it from sinking; not so much that it is built upon mountains as that it is built upon holy mountains—upon the promise of God. 2. That God had expressed a particular affection for it (*v.* 2): *The Lord loveth the gates of Zion,* of the temple, of *the houses of doctrine* (so the Chaldee), *more than all the dwellings of Jacob,* whether in Jerusalem or anywhere else in the country. 3. That there was much said concerning it in the word of God (*v.* 3): *Glorious things are spoken of thee, O city of God!* God said of the temple, *My eyes and my heart shall be there perpetually; I have sanctified this house, that my name may be there for ever,* 2 Chron. vii. 16. Yet more glorious things are spoken of the gospel-church. It is the spouse of Christ, the purchase of his blood; it is a *peculiar people, a holy nation, a royal priesthood,* and the *gates of hell shall not prevail against it.*

Verses 4–7

Zion is here compared with other places, and preferred before them; the church of Christ is more glorious and excellent than the nations of the earth. 1. It is owned that other places have their glories (*v.* 4): "*I will make mention of Rahab*" (that is, *Egypt*) "*and Babylon, to those that know me; behold Philistia and Tyre, with Ethiopia,* we will observe that *this man was born there*; here and there one famous man, eminent for knowledge and virtue, may be produced, that was a native of these countries; here and there one that becomes a proselyte and a worshipper of the true God." But some give another sense of it, supposing that it is a prophecy. God says, "*I will reckon Egypt and Babylon with those that know me.* I will reckon them my people as much as Israel when they shall receive the gospel of Christ, and own them as born in Zion, born again there, and admitted to the privileges of Zion as freely as a true-born Israelite." Those that were strangers and foreigners became *fellow-citizens with the saints,* Eph. ii. 19. 2. It is proved that the glory of Zion outshines them all, upon many accounts; for, (1) Zion shall produce many great and good men, many prophets and kings, who should be greater favourites of heaven and greater blessings to the earth, than ever were bred in Egypt or Babylon. *A man, a man*

JAMIESON, FAUSSET, BROWN

PSALM 87

Vss. 1-7. This triumphal song was probably occasioned by the same event as the 46th. The writer celebrates the glory of the Church, as the means of spiritual blessing to the nation.

1. His [i.e., God's] **foundation**—or, what He has founded, i.e., Zion (Isa. 14:32). **is in the holy mountains**—the location of Zion, in the wide sense, for the capital, or Jerusalem, being on several hills.

2. gates—for the enclosures, or city to which they opened (Ps. 9:14; 122:2; cf. Ps. 132:13, 14).

3. spoken of [or *in*] **thee**—i.e., the city of God (Ps. 46:4; 48: 2).

4. This is what is spoken by God. **to them . . . me**—lit., "for My knowers," they are true worshippers (Ps. 36:10; Isa. 19:21). These are mentioned as specimens. **this** [i.e., nation] . . . **was born there**—Of each it is said, "This was born," or is a native of Zion, spiritually.

ADAM CLARKE

PSALM 87

The title, "A Psalm or Song for the sons of Korah," gives us no light into the author or meaning of this psalm. It begins and ends so abruptly that many have thought it to be only a fragment of a larger psalm. This opinion is very likely. Those who suppose it to have been made when Jerusalem was rebuilt and fortified imagine it to have been an exclamation of the author on beholding its beauty and contemplating its privileges. If this opinion be allowed, it will account for the apparent abruptness in the beginning and end.

1. *His foundation is in the holy mountains.* Jerusalem was founded on the mountains or hills of Zion and Moriah.

4. *I will make mention of Rahab.* The meaning seems to be, *Rahab;* i.e., "Egypt, Babylon, Tyre, Philistia, and Ethiopia" are not so honorable as Jerusalem.

MATTHEW HENRY

was born in her, by which some understand Christ, born at Bethlehem near Zion. The greatest honour that ever was put upon the Jewish nation was, that of them, *as concerning the flesh, Christ came*, Rom. xi. 5. (2) Zion's interest shall be strengthened and settled by an almighty power. *The Highest himself shall* undertake to *establish her* upon an everlasting foundation, whatever convulsions and revolutions there are of states and kingdoms, and however heaven and earth may be shaken, these are things which cannot be shaken, but must remain. (3) Zion's sons shall be registered with honour (*v.* 6): *The Lord shall count, when he writes up the people*, and takes a catalogue of his subjects, *that this man was born there*, and so is a subject by birth, by the first birth, being born in his house—by the second birth, being born again of his Spirit. (4) Zion's songs shall be sung with joy and triumph: *As well the singers as the players on instruments shall be there* to praise God, *v.* 7. It was much to the honour of Zion, and is to the honour of the gospel-church, that there God is served and worshipped with rejoicing: his work is done, and done cheerfully; see lxviii. 25. *All my springs are in thee*, O Zion!

JAMIESON, FAUSSET, BROWN

5. The writer resumes—**This and that man**—lit., "man and man," or many (Gen. 14:10; Exod. 8:10, 14), or all (Isa 44:5; Gal. 3:28). **the highest . . . her**—God is her protector.

6. The same idea is set forth under the figure of a register made by God (cf. Isa. 4:3).

7. As in a great procession of those thus *written up*, or registered, seeking Zion (Isa. 2:3; Jer. 50:5), "the singers" and "players," or pipers, shall precede. **all my springs**—So each shall say, "All my sources of spiritual joy are in Thee" (Ps. 46:4; 84:6).

ADAM CLARKE

5. *This and that man was born in her.* It will be an honor to any person to have been born in Zion. But how great is the honor to be born from above, and be a citizen of the Jerusalem that is from above!

6. *The Lord shall count, when he writeth up the people.* "In the register of the people." When He takes account of those who dwell in Jerusalem, He will particularly note those who were born in Zion. This has an easy spiritual meaning. When God takes an account of all professing Christians, He will set apart those for inhabitants of the New Jerusalem who were born in Zion, who were born again, received a new nature, and were fitted for heaven.

7. *As well the singers.* Perhaps this may mean no more than, The burden of the songs of all the singers and choristers shall be, "All my fountains (ancestors and posterity) are in Thee," and consequently entitled to all Thy privileges and immunities.

PSALM 88 (MATTHEW HENRY)

A song *or* psalm for the sons of Korah, to the chief musician upon Mahalath Leannoth, Maschil of Heman the Ezrahite.

Verses 1–9

The very first words are the only words of comfort in all the psalm. But, before he begins his complaint, the psalmist calls God *the God of his salvation*, which intimates that, bad as things were, he looked up to God for salvation and depended upon him to be the author of it.

I. A man of prayer. It is his comfort that he had prayed; it is his complaint that, notwithstanding his prayer, he was still in affliction. "*I have cried unto thee* (*v.* 1), and have *stretched out my hands unto thee* (*v.* 9), as one that would take hold on thee, and even catch at the mercy, with a holy fear of coming short and missing of it." He was very frequent and constant in prayer: *I have called upon thee daily* (*v.* 9), nay, *day and night*, *v.* 1. He directed his prayer to God, and from him expected and desired an answer (*v.* 2): "*Let my prayer come before thee*, to be accepted of thee."

II. He was a man of sorrows, and therefore some make him, in this psalm, a type of Christ. He cries out (*v.* 3): *My soul is full of troubles;* so Christ said, *Now is my soul troubled;* and, in his agony, *My soul is exceedingly sorrowful even unto death*, like the psalmist's here, for he says, *My life draws nigh unto the grave.*

III. He looked upon himself as a dying man, whose heart was ready to break with sorrow (*v.* 5): *Free among the dead like the slain that lie in the grave*, whom thou rememberest no more, to protect or provide for the dead bodies. "*Thou hast laid me in the lowest pit*, as low as possible, my condition low, my spirits low, *in darkness, in the deep* (*v.* 6)." Thus greatly may good men be afflicted through the power of melancholy and the weakness of faith.

IV. He complained most of God's displeasure against him (*v.* 7): *Thy wrath lies hard upon me.* Could he have discerned the favour and love of God in his affliction, it would have lain light upon him; but it lay hard, very hard, upon him, so that he was ready to sink and faint under it.

V. It added to his affliction that his friends deserted him. When we are in trouble it is some comfort to have those about us that love us, and sympathize with us; but this good man had none such (*v.* 8): *Thou hast put away my acquaintance far from me.* "*Thou hast made me an abomination to them;* they are not only shy of me, but sick of me, and I am looked upon by them, not only with contempt, but with abhorrence."

VI. He looked upon his case as helpless and deplorable: "*I am shut up, and I cannot come forth*, a prisoner, and no way open of escape." Thus he bemoans himself (*v.* 9): *My eye mourneth by reason of affliction.* Yet weeping must not hinder praying; we must sow in tears: *My eye mourns*, but *I cry unto thee daily.*

Verses 10–18

I. The psalmist expostulates with God concerning the present deplorable condition he was in (*v.* 10–12): "*Wilt thou do a miraculous work to the dead*, and raise them to life again? Shall those that are dead and buried *rise up to praise thee*? Departed souls may indeed know God's wonders and declare his faithfulness, justice, and lovingkindness; but deceased bodies cannot; they can neither receive God's favours in

PSALM 88 (JAMIESON, FAUSSET, BROWN)

Vss. 1-18. *Upon Mahalath*—either an instrument, as a lute, to be used as an accompaniment (*Leannoth*, for singing) or, as others think, an enigmatic title (cf. Ps. 5:22 and 45, titles), denoting the subject—i.e., "sickness or disease, for humbling," the idea of spiritual maladies being often represented by disease (cf. Ps. 6:5, 6; 22:14, 15, etc.). On the other terms, cf. Psalm 42:32. Heman and Ethan (Ps. 89, title) were David's singers (I Chron. 6:18, 33; 15:17), of the family of Kohath. If the persons alluded to (I Kings 4:31; I Chron. 2:6), they were probably adopted into the tribe of Judah. Though called a song, which usually implies joy (Ps. 83 :1), both the style and matter of the Psalm are very despondent; yet the appeals to God evince faith, and we may suppose that the word "song" might be extended to such compositions.

1, 2. Cf. on the terms used, Psalms 22:2; 31:2. **3. grave**—lit., "hell" (Ps. 16:10), death in wide sense. **4. go . . . pit**—of destruction (Ps. 28:1). **as a man**—lit., "a stout man," whose strength is utterly gone.

5. Free . . . dead—Cut off from God's care, as are the slain, who, falling under His wrath, are left, no longer sustained by His hand. **6.** Similar figures for distress in Psalms 63:9; 69:3.

7. Cf. Psalm 38:2, on first, and Psalm 42:7, on last clause.

8. Both cut off from sympathy and made hateful to friends (Ps. 31:11).

9. Mine eye mourneth—lit., "decays," or fails, denoting exhaustion (Ps. 6:7; 31:9). **I . . . called**—(Ps. 86:5, 7). **stretched out**—for help (Ps. 44:20).

10. shall the dead [the remains of ghosts] **arise**—lit., "rise up," i.e., as dead persons. **11, 12** amplify the foregoing, the whole purport (as Ps. 6:5) being to contrast death and life as seasons for praising God.

PSALM 88 (ADAM CLARKE)

Perhaps the title of this psalm, which is difficult enough, might be thus translated: "A poem to be sung to the conqueror, by the sons of Korah, responsively, in behalf of a distressed person; to give instruction to Heman the Ezrahite." Heman and Ethan, whose names are separately prefixed to this and the following psalm, are mentioned as the grandsons of Judah by his daughter-in-law Tamar, 1 Chron. ii. 6. If these were the same persons mentioned in 1 Kings iv. 31, they were eminent in wisdom; for it is there said that Solomon's wisdom "excelled the wisdom of all the children of the east country, and all the wisdom of Egypt. For he was wiser than all men; than Ethan the Ezrahite, and Heman, and Chalcol, and Darda, the sons of Mahol," vv. 30-31.

5. *Free among the dead*, I rather think, means "stripped among the dead." Both the fourth and fifth verses seem to allude to a field of battle. The slain and the wounded are found scattered over the plain; the spoilers come among them and strip, not only the dead, but those also who appear to be mortally wounded, and cannot recover, and are so feeble as not to be able to resist. *They are cut off from thy hand.* An allusion to the roll in which the general has the names of all that compose his army under their respective officers. And when one is killed, he is erased from this register, and remembered no more, as belonging to the army.

8. *Thou hast made me an abomination.* This verse has been supposed to express the state of a leper, who, because of the infectious nature of his disease, is separated from his family, is abominable to all, and at last shut up in a separate house, whence he does not come out to mingle with society.

10. *Wilt thou shew wonders to the dead? Methim*, "dead men." *Shall the dead? Rephaim*, "departed spirits." *Arise and praise thee?* Anymore in this life? The interrogations in this and the following two verses imply the strongest negations.

11. *Or thy faithfulness in destruction?* Faithfulness in God refers as well to His fulfilling His threatenings as to His keeping His promises.

12. *The land of forgetfulness.* The place of separate spirits, or the invisible world.

MATTHEW HENRY

comfort nor return them in praise." But he thus pleads with God for speedy relief: "Lord, thou art good, thou art faithful, thou art righteous; these attributes of thine will be made known in my deliverance, but, if it be not hastened, it will come too late."

II. He resolves to continue instant in prayer, because the deliverance was deferred (*v.* 13): "*Unto thee have I cried* many a time, and found comfort in so doing, and therefore I will continue to do so; *in the morning shall my prayer prevent thee.*" How could he say, *My prayer shall prevent thee?* It intimates that he would be up earlier than ordinary to pray, would *prevent* (that is, go before) his usual hour of prayer. "My prayer shall not stay for the encouragement of the beginning of mercy, but reach towards it with faith and expectation even before the day dawns."

III. He sets down what he will say to God in prayer. He will humbly reason (*v.* 14): "*Lord, why castest thou off my soul?* What is it that provokes thee to treat me as one abandoned? *Show me wherefore thou contendest with me.*" Nothing grieves a child of God so much as God's hiding his face from him, nor is there anything he so much dreads as God's casting off his soul. If the sun be clouded, that darkens the earth; but if the sun should abandon the earth, and quite cast it off, what a dungeon would it be! *I suffer thy terrors, v.* 15. The psalmist here explains himself, and tells us what he means by God's terrors, even his *fierce wrath.* "*I am* so *afflicted* with them that I am *ready to die,* and" (as the word is) "*to give up the ghost. Thy terrors have cut me off,*" *v.* 16. They had almost taken away the use of his reason: *When I suffer thy terrors I am distracted.* This had continued long: *From my youth up I suffer thy terrors.* He had been from his childhood afflicted with melancholy. Sometimes those whom God designs for eminent services are prepared for them by exercises of this kind. No friend was a comfort to him (*v.* 18): *Lover and friend hast thou put far from me.* Next to the comforts of religion are those of friendship and society; therefore to be friendless is (as to this life) almost to be comfortless.

PSALM 89

Maschil of Ethan the Ezrahite.

Verses 1–4

The psalmist has a very sad complaint to make of the deplorable condition of the family of David at this time, and yet he begins the psalm with songs of praise. Let our complaints be turned into thanksgivings. 1. However it be, the everlasting God is good and true, *v.* 1. God's mercies are inexhaustible and his truth is inviolable; and these must be the matter of our joy and praise: "*I will sing of the mercies of the Lord for ever,* sing a praising song to God's honour, a pleasant song for my own solace, an instructive song, for the edification of others." 2. However it be, the everlasting covenant is firm and sure, *v.* 2–4. "Things now look black, and threaten the utter extirpation of the house of David; but *I have said,* and I have warrant from the word of God to say it, that *mercy shall be built up for ever.*" If mercy shall be built for ever, then the *tabernacle of David, which has fallen down,* shall *be raised out of its ruins,* and *built up as in the days of old,* Amos ix. 11. An abstract of the covenant upon which this faith and hope are built: *I have said it,* says the psalmist, for *God hath sworn it.* He brings in God speaking (*v.* 3), owning, to the comfort of his people, "*I have made a covenant,* and therefore will make it good." The covenant is made with David, representing the covenant of grace made with Christ as head of the church and with all believers as his spiritual seed. It was promised that his family should continue—*Thy seed will I establish for ever. I will build up thy throne to all generations.* This has its accomplishment only in Christ, of the seed of David, who lives for ever.

Verses 5–14

These verses are full of the praises of God.

I. Where, and by whom, God is to be praised. *The heavens shall praise thy wonders, O Lord! v.* 5. The works of God are wonders even to those that are best acquainted and most intimately conversant with them; the more God's works are known the more they are admired and praised. God is praised by the assemblies of his saints on earth. "Thy faithfulness and the truth of thy promise, that rock on which the church is built, shall be praised in the congregation of the saints, who owe their all to that faithfulness, and whose constant comfort it is that there is a promise, and that he is faithful who has promised."

JAMIESON, FAUSSET, BROWN

13. prevent—meet—i.e., he will diligently come before God for help (Ps. 18:41).

14. On the terms (Ps. 27:9; 74:1; 77:7).

15. from . . . youth up—all my life. With **16, 17** the extremes of anguish and despair are depicted.

18. into darkness—Better omit "into"—mine acquaintances (are) darkness, the gloom of death, etc. (Job 17:13, 14).

PSALM 89

Vss. 1-52. *Of Ethan*—(see Ps. 88, title). This Psalm was composed during some season of great national distress, perhaps Absalom's rebellion. It contrasts the promised prosperity and perpetuity of David's throne (with reference to the great promise of II Sam. 7), with a time when God appeared to have forgotten His covenant. The picture thus drawn may typify the promises and the adversities of Christ's kingdom, and the terms of confiding appeal to God provided appropriate prayers for the divine aid and promised blessing.

1. mercies—those promised (Isa. 55:3; Acts 13:34), and—**faithfulness**—i.e., in fulfilling them. **2. I have said**—expressed, as well as felt, my convictions (II Cor. 4:13).

3, 4. The object of this faith expressed in God's words (II Sam. 7:11-16). **with** [or lit., "to"] **my chosen**—as the covenant is in the form of a promise.

ADAM CLARKE

13. *Shall my prayer prevent thee?* It shall "get before" Thee. I will not wait till the accustomed time to offer my morning sacrifice; I shall call on Thee long before others come to offer their devotions.

18. *Lover and friend.* I have no comfort, and neither friend nor neighbor to sympathize with me. *Mine acquaintance into darkness.* "Darkness is my companion."

PSALM 89

It is most probable that this psalm was composed during the Captivity. Of Ethan and Heman we have already seen something in the introduction to the preceding psalm. The title should probably be translated, "To give instruction to Ethan the Ezrahite."

The psalm divides itself into two grand parts. The first extends from v. 1 to 37, in which the Psalmist shows God's mercy to the house of David, and the promises which He has given to it of support and perpetuity. The second part begins with v. 38, and ends with the psalm; and in it the author complains that, notwithstanding these promises, the kingdom of Judah is overthrown and the royal family ruined; and he entreats the Lord to remember His covenant made with that family, and restore them from their captivity.

4. *Thy seed will I establish for ever, and build up thy throne to all generations.* And this covenant had most incontestably Jesus Christ in view. This is the *seed,* or posterity, that should sit on the throne, and reign for ever and ever. David and his family are long since become extinct; none of his race has sat on the Jewish throne for more than two thousand years. But the Christ has reigned invariably since that time, and will reign till all His enemies are put under His feet.

MATTHEW HENRY

In religious assemblies God has promised the presence of his grace, but we must also, in them, have an eye to his glorious presence, that the familiarity we are admitted to may not breed the least contempt. A holy awe of God must fall upon us, and fill us, in all our approaches to God, even in secret.

II. What it is to praise God; it is to acknowledge that there is none like him, *v.* 6. *To whom will you liken me, or shall I be equal? saith the Holy One,* Isa. xl. 25. This is insisted on again (*v.* 8): *Who is a strong Lord like unto thee?* Among men it is too often found that those who are most able to break their word are least careful to keep it; but God is both strong and faithful; he can do everything, and yet will never do an unjust thing.

III. What we ought, in our praises, to give God the glory of. 1. The command God has of the most ungovernable creatures (*v.* 9) *Thou rulest the raging of the sea.* This coming in here as an act of omnipotence, what manner of man then was the Lord Jesus, whom the *winds and seas obeyed?* 2. The victories God has obtained over the enemies of his church. *Thou hast broken Rahab,* many a *proud enemy* (so it signifies), Egypt in particular, which is sometimes called *Rahab,* broken it in pieces, as one that is slain and utterly unable to make head again. The remembrance of the breaking of Egypt in pieces is a comfort to the church, in reference to the present power of Babylon; for God is still the same. 3. The incontestable property he has (*v.* 11, 12): "Men are honoured for their large possessions; but *the heavens are thine, O Lord! the earth also is thine. The world and the fulness thereof,* all the riches contained in it, all the inhabitants of it, both the tenements and the tenants, are all thine; for *thou hast founded them,"* He specifies (1) The remotest parts of the world: *"Thou hast created them,* and therefore knowest them, takest care of them, and hast tributes of praise from them." The north is said to be *hung over the empty place;* yet what fulness there is there God is the owner of it. (2) The highest parts of the world. He mentions the two highest hills in Canaan—*"Tabor and Hermon,* these shall rejoice in thy name, and they produce offerings for thy altar." Tabor is commonly supposed to be that high mountain in Galilee on the top of which Christ was transfigured. 4. The power and justice, the mercy and truth, with which he governs the world and rules in the affairs of the children of men, *v.* 13, 14. God is able to do everything; for he is the Lord God Almighty. He never did, nor ever will do, anything that is either unjust or unwise; for *righteousness and judgment are the habitation of his throne.* He always does that which is kind to his people and consonant to the word which he has spoken: *"Mercy and truth shall go before thy face,* truth in being as good as thy word, mercy in being better."

Verses 15–18

The psalmist, having largely shown the blessedness of the God of Israel, here shows the blessedness of the Israel of God. As *there is none like unto the God of Jeshurun, so, happy art thou, O Israel! there is none like unto thee, O people!* especially as a type of the gospel-Israel, consisting of all true believers, whose happiness is here described.

I. Glorious discoveries are made to them, and glad tidings of good brought to them; they hear, *they know the joyful sound, v.* 15. This may allude 1. To the shout of a victorious army. Israel have the tokens of God's presence with them in their wars. Or, 2. To the sound that was made over the sacrifices and on the solemn feastdays, lxxxi. 1–3. This was the happiness of Israel, that they had among them the free and open profession of God's holy religion. Or, 3. To the sound of the jubilee-trumpet; a joyful sound it was to servants and debtors, to whom it proclaimed release. The gospel is indeed a joyful sound, a sound of victory, of liberty, of communion with God; blessed are the people that hear it, and know it, and bid it welcome.

II. Special tokens of God's favour are granted them: *"They shall walk, O Lord! in the light of thy countenance;* they shall govern themselves by thy directions, shall be guided by thy eye; and they shall delight themselves in thy consolations."

III. They never want matter for joy. Those that rejoice in Christ Jesus have enough to counterbalance their grievances and silence their griefs; and therefore their joy is full (1 John i. 4).

IV. Their relation to God is their honour and dignity. "In *thy righteousness shall they be exalted,* and not in any righteousness of their own. In thy favour, which through Christ we hope for, *our horn shall be exalted.* The horn denotes beauty, plenty, and power."

V. Their relation to God is their protection and safety (*v.* 18): *"For our shield is of the Lord"* (so the

JAMIESON, FAUSSET, BROWN

6, 7. This is worthy of our belief, for His faithfulness (is praised) by the congregation of saints or holy ones; i.e., angels (cf. Deut. 33:2; Dan. 8:13). **sons of the mighty**—(cf. Ps. 29:1). So is He to be admired on earth.

8-14. To illustrate His power and faithfulness examples are cited from history. His control of the sea (the most mighty and unstable object in nature), and of Egypt (Ps. 87:4), the first great foe of Israel (subjected to utter helplessness from pride and insolence), are specimens.

At the same time, the whole frame of nature founded and sustained by Him, Tabor and Hermon for east and west, and "north and south," together representing the whole world, declare the same truth as to His attributes. **rejoice in thy name**—praise Thy perfections by their very existence.

15. His government of righteousness is served by "mercy" and "truth" as ministers (Ps. 85:10-13). **know the joyful sound**—understand and appreciate the spiritual blessings symbolized by the feasts to which the people were called by the trumpet (Lev. 25:9, etc.).

walk . . . countenance—live in His favor (Ps. 4:6; 44:3).

16, 17. in [or, "by"] **thy righteousness**—Thy faithful just rule. **glory** [or, "beauty"] **of their strength**—They shall be adorned as well as protected. **our horn**—exalt our power (Ps. 75:10; Luke 1:69).

18. Thus is introduced the promise to "our shield," "our king," David.

ADAM CLARKE

6. *For who in the heaven? Shachak* signifies the ethereal regions, all visible or unbounded space; the universe. Who is like Jesus? Even in His human nature none of *the sons of the mighty* can be compared with Him. He atones for the sin of the world, and saves to the uttermost all who come unto God through Him.

7. *God is greatly to be feared.* In all religious assemblies the deepest reverence for God should rest upon the people. Where this does not prevail, there is no true worship.

8. *Thy faithfulness round about thee?* Or, more properly, "Thy faithfulness is round about thee." Thou still keepest Thy promises in view.

10. *Thou hast broken Rahab.* Thou hast destroyed the power of Egypt, having overthrown the king and its people when they endeavored to prevent Thy people from regaining their liberty. *As one that is slain.* The whole clause in the original is, "Thou, like a hero, hast broken down Egypt."

12. *The north and the south.* It is generally supposed that by these four terms all the four quarters of the globe are intended. *Tabor,* a mountain of Galilee, was on the west of Mount *Hermon,* which was beyond Jordan, to the east of the source of that river.

14. *Justice and judgment are the habitation of thy throne.* The throne—the government—of God is founded in righteousness and judgment. *Mercy and truth shall go before thy face.* These shall be the heralds that shall announce the coming of the Judge. His *truth* binds Him to fulfill all His declarations, and His *mercy* shall be shown to all those who have fled for refuge to the hope that is set before them in the gospel.

15. *Blessed is the people.* "Oh, the blessednesses of that people that know the joyful sound; they shall walk vigorously in the light of Thy countenance."

16. *In thy name shall they rejoice.* Or "greatly exult."

MATTHEW HENRY	JAMIESON, FAUSSET, BROWN	ADAM CLARKE

margin), "and *our king is from the Holy One of Israel.* If God be our ruler, he will be our defender; and who is he then that can harm us?"

Verses 19–37

The covenant God made with David and his seed was mentioned before (*v.* 3, 4); but in these verses it is enlarged upon. Certainly it looks at Christ, and has its accomplishment in him much more than in David. The comforts of our redemption flow from the covenant of redemption; all our springs are in that, Isa. lv. 3. *I will make an everlasting covenant with you, even the sure mercies of David,* Acts xiii. 34.

I. What assurance we have of the truth of the promise, which may encourage us to build upon it. *Thou didst speak in vision to thy Holy One.* God's promise to David, which is especially referred to here, was spoken in vision to Nathan the prophet, 2 Sam. vii. 12–17. *Then,* when the *Holy One of Israel was their king* (*v.* 18), he appointed David to be his viceroy. How it was sworn to and ratified (*v.* 35): *Once have I sworn by my holiness.* His swearing once is enough; he needs not swear again, as David did (1 Sam. xx. 17); for his word and oath are two immutable things.

II. The choice made of the person to whom the promise is given, *v.* 19, 20. David was a king of God's own choosing, so is Christ, and therefore both are called *God's kings,* Ps. ii. 6. David was mighty, a man chosen out of the people. God exalted him, and ordered Samuel to anoint him. But this is to be applied to Christ. 1. He is mighty, *able to save to the uttermost,* for he is the Son of God—mighty in love. 2. He is *chosen out of the people,* one of us, bone of our bone, that takes part with us of flesh and blood. 3. God has found him. He is a Saviour of God's own providing. 4. God has *laid help upon him.* He has exalted him, by constituting him the prophet, priest, and king of his church, clothing him with power, raising him from the dead, and setting him at his own right hand. He is called *Messiah,* or *Christ,* the *Anointed.*

III. The promises made to this chosen one, to David in the type and the Son of David in the antitype.

1. With reference to himself, as king and God's servant, it is here promised, (1) That God would stand by him and strengthen him in his undertaking (*v.* 21): "*With him my hand* not only shall be, but *shall be established,* by promise. *My arm also shall strengthen him* to break through and bear up under all his difficulties." (2) That he should be victorious over his enemies, that they should not encroach upon him (*v.* 22): *The son of wickedness shall not exact upon him,* nor afflict him. Christ became a surety for our debt, and thereby Satan and death thought to gain advantage against him; but he satisfied the demands of God's justice, and then they could not exact upon him. *The prince of this world cometh, but he has nothing in me,* John xiv. 30. *I will beat down his foes before his face;* the prince of this world shall be cast out, principalities and powers spoiled, and he shall be the death of death itself, and the destruction of the grave, Hos. xiii. 14. (3) *My faithfulness and my mercy shall be with him.* They were with David; God continued merciful to him, and so approved himself faithful. They were with Christ; God made good all his promises to him. But that is not all; God's mercy to us, and his faithfulness to us, are with Christ; and it is in him that all the promises of God are yea and amen. So that if any poor sinners hope for benefit by the faithfulness and mercy of God, let them know it is with Christ, and to him they must apply for it (*v.* 28): *My mercy will I keep for him, for evermore;* in the channel of Christ's mediation all the streams of divine goodness will for ever run. And, as the mercy of God flows to us through him, so the promise of God is, through him, firm to us: *My covenant shall stand fast with him,* both the covenant of redemption made with him and the covenant of grace made with us in him. (4) That his kingdom should be greatly enlarged (*v.* 25): *I will set his hand in the sea* (he shall have the dominion of the seas, and the isles of the sea), and *his right hand in the rivers,* the inland countries that are watered with rivers. David's kingdom extended itself to the Great Sea, and the Red Sea, to the river of Egypt and the river Euphrates. But it is in the kingdom of the Messiah that this has its full accomplishment, and shall have more and more, when *the kingdoms of this world shall become the kingdoms of the Lord and of his Christ* (Rev. xi. 15). (5) That he should own God as his Father, and God would own him as his Son, his firstborn, *v.* 26, 27. This is a comment upon these words in Nathan's message concerning Solomon (for he also was a type of Christ as well as David), *I will be his Father and he shall be my Son* (2 Sam. vii. 14), and the relation shall be

CHARLES H. SPURGEON:

"Then thou spakest in vision to thy holy one" (89:19). The Psalmist returns to a consideration of the covenant made with David. The holy one here may be either David or Nathan the prophet, but most probably the latter, for it was to him that the word of the Lord came by night (2 Sam. 7:4, 5). God condescends to employ his gracious ministers to be the means of communication between himself and his favored ones—even to King David, the covenant was revealed by Nathan the prophet; thus the Lord puts honor upon his ministers.

"I have laid help upon one that is mighty." The Lord had made David a mighty man of valor, and now he covenants to make him the helper and defender of the Jewish state. In a far fuller sense the Lord Jesus is essentially and immeasurably mighty, and on him the salvation of his people rests by divine appointment, while his success is secured by divine strength being engaged to be with him. Let us lay our faith where God has laid our help.—*The Treasury of David*

19-37. Then—when the covenant was established, of whose execution the exalted views of God now given furnish assurance. **thou . . . to thy holy one**—or godly saint, object of favor (Ps. 4:3). *Nathan* is meant (II Sam. 7:17; I Chron. 17:3-15). **laid help**—lit., "given help." David was chosen and then exalted. **20. I have found**—having sought and then selected him (I Sam. 16:1-6),

21, will protect and sustain (Isa. 41:10),

22-25, by restraining and conquering his enemies, and performing My gracious purpose of extending his dominion

—hand [and] **right hand**—power (Ps. 17:7; 60:5). **sea, and . . . rivers**—limits of his empire (Ps. 72:8).

26, 27. first-born—one who is chief, most beloved or distinguished (Exod. 4:22; Col. 1:15). In God's sight and purposes he was the first among all monarchs, and specially so in his typical relation to Christ.

20. *I have found David my servant.* This is the sum of what God had said in prophetic visions to His saints or holy persons, Samuel, Nathan, and Gad. Here the Psalmist begins to reason with God relative to David, his posterity, and the perpetuity of his kingdom; which promises appear now to have utterly failed, as the throne had been overturned and all the people carried into captivity. But all these things may have reference to Christ and His kingdom, for we are assured that David was a type of the Messiah.

22. *The enemy shall not exact upon him.* None of his enemies shall be able to prevail against him. It is worthy of remark that David was never overthrown; he finally conquered every foe that rose up against him.

25. *I will set his hand also in the sea.* This was literally fulfilled in David. *Hand* signifies power or authority; he set his hand on the sea in conquering the Philistines, and extending his empire along the coast of the Mediterranean Sea. All the coasts of the Red Sea, the Persian Gulf, and the Arabic Ocean might be said to have been under his government, for they all paid tribute to him or his son Solomon.

27. *I will make him my firstborn.* I will deal with him as a father by his firstborn son, to whom a double portion of possessions and honors belong. *Firstborn* is not always to be understood literally in Scripture. It often signifies simply a well-beloved or best beloved son; one

MATTHEW HENRY

owned on both sides. *He shall cry unto me, Thou art my Father.* Christ did so, in the days of his flesh, when he offered up strong cries to God, and taught us to address ourselves to him as *our Father in heaven. I will make him my firstborn.* It is Christ's prerogative to be *the firstborn of every creature*, and, as such, the *heir of all things*, Col. i. 15; Heb. i, 2, 6.

2. With reference to his seed. God's covenants always took in the seed of the covenanters (*v.* 29, 36): *His seed shall endure for ever*, and with it his throne. Now this will be differently understood according as we apply it to Christ or David.

(1) If we apply it to David, by his seed we are to understand his successors, Solomon and the following kings of Judah. It is supposed that they might degenerate; in such a case they must expect to come under divine rebukes. But though they were corrected, they should not be disinherited. This refers to that part of Nathan's message (2 Sam. vii. 14, 15), *If he commit iniquity, I will chasten him*, but *my mercy shall not depart from him.* Thus far David's seed and throne did endure. The family of David continued a family of distinction till that Son of David came whose throne should endure for ever; see Luke i. 27, 32; ii. 4, 11.

(2) If we apply it to Christ, by his seed we are to understand his subjects, all believers, his spiritual seed, the children which God has given him, Heb. ii. 13. This is that seed which shall be made to endure for ever, and his throne in the midst of them, in the church in the heart, *as the days of heaven.* To the end Christ shall have a people in the world to serve and honour him. *He shall see his seed; he shall prolong his days.* Thus Christ's throne and kingdom shall be perpetuated: the kingdom of his grace shall continue through all the ages of time and the kingdom of his glory to the endless ages of eternity. It is here supposed that there will be much amiss in the subjects of Christ's kingdom. His children may *forsake God's law* (*v.* 30) by omissions, and *break his statutes* (*v.* 31) by commissions. Many corruptions there are in the church, as well as in the hearts of those who are the members of it. They are here told that they must smart for it (*v.* 32): *I will visit their transgressions with a rod.* Their being related to Christ shall not excuse them from being called to an account. But observe what affliction is to God's people. 1. It is but a rod, not an axe, not a sword; it is for correction, not for destruction. 2. It is a rod in the hand of God (*I will visit them*). *If they break my law, then I will visit their transgression with the rod*, but not else. The continuance of Christ's kingdom is made certain by the inviolable promise and oath of God, notwithstanding all this (*v.* 23): *Nevertheless, my kindness will I not* totally and finally *take from him.* Afflictions are not only consistent with covenant-love, but to the people of God they flow from it. For Christ's sake, in him the mercy is laid up for us, and God says, *I will not take it from him* (*v.* 33), *I will not lie unto David*, *v.* 35. *My faithfulness shall not fail, my covenant will I not break.* That which is said and sworn is that God will have a church in the world as long as sun and moon endure, *v.* 36, 37. The *seed of Christ shall be established for ever*, as *lights of the world* while the world stands, to shine in it, and, when it is at an end, they shall be established lights shining in the firmament of the Father.

Verses 38–52

I. A very melancholy complaint of the present deplorable state of David's family, which the psalmist thinks hard to be reconciled to the covenant God made with David. "Thou saidst thou wouldst not *take away thy lovingkindness, but thou hast cast off.*" Sometimes, it is no easy thing to reconcile God's providences with his promises, and yet God's works fulfil his word and never contradict it. 1. David's house seemed to have lost its interest in God. God had been pleased with his anointed, but now he was *wroth with him* (*v.* 38). 2. The honour of the house of David was lost and laid in the dust: *Thou hast profaned his crown* (which was always looked upon as sacred) by *casting it to the ground*, to be trampled on, *v.* 39. 3. It was exposed and made a prey to all the neighbours (*v.* 40): *Thou hast broken down all his hedges* (all those things that were a defence to them, and particularly that hedge of protection which they thought God's covenant and promise had made about them) and thou *hast made even his strongholds a ruin. He is a reproach to his neighbours*, who triumph in his fall from so great a degree of honour. Everyone helps forward the calamity (*v.* 42): "*Thou hast set up the right hand of his adversaries*, not only given them power, but inclined them to turn their power this way." 4. It was disabled to help itself (*v.* 43): "*Thou hast turned the edge of his sword*, and made it blunt, that it cannot do execution as it has done; and (which

JAMIESON, FAUSSET, BROWN

28-37. This relation is perpetual with David's descendants, as a whole typical in official position of his last greatest descendant. Hence though in personal relations any of them might be faithless and so punished, their typical relation shall continue. His oath confirms His promise, and the most enduring objects of earth and heaven illustrate its perpetual force (Ps. 72:5, 7, 17).

Once—one thing (Ps. 27:4). **by my holiness**—as a holy God. **that I will not lie**—lit., "if I lie"—part of the form of swearing (I Sam. 24:6; II Sam. 3:35). **It shall . . . moon . . . heaven**—lit., "*As the moon,* and the witness in the sky is sure, i.e., the moon."

38-52 present a striking contrast to these glowing promises, in mournful evidences of a loss of God's favor. **38. cast off**—and *rejected* (cf. Ps. 15:4; 43:2; 44:9).

39. An insult to the "crown," as of divine origin, was a profanation. **40-45.** The ruin is depicted under several figures—a vineyard whose broken "hedges," and "strongholds," whose ruins invite spoilers and invaders; a warrior, whose enemies are aided by God, and whose sword's "edge"—lit., rock or strength (Josh. 5:2) is useless; and a youth prematurely old.

ADAM CLARKE

preferred to all the rest, and distinguished by some eminent prerogative. Thus God calls Israel His son, His firstborn, Exod. iv. 22.

29. *His seed also will I make to endure for ever.* This can apply only to the spiritual David.

34. *My covenant will I not break.* My determination to establish a spiritual Kingdom, the Head of which shall be Jesus, the Son of David, shall never fail.

36. *His throne as the sun.* Splendid and glorious! dispensing light, heat, life, and salvation to all mankind.

38. *But thou hast cast off.* Hitherto the Psalmist has spoken of the covenant of God with David and his family, which led them to expect all manner of prosperity, and a perpetuity of the Jewish throne. Now he shows what appears to him a failure of the promise, and what he calls in the next verse the making void the covenant of His servant. God cannot lie to David; how is it then that His crown is profaned, that it is cast down to the ground; the land being possessed by strangers, and the twelve tribes in the most disgraceful and oppressive captivity?

40. *Thou hast broken down all his hedges.* Thou hast permitted the land to be stripped of all defense; there is not even one strong place in the hands of Thy people.

41. *All that pass by the way spoil him.* The land is in the condition of a vineyard, the hedge of which is broken down, so that they who pass by may pull the grapes, and dismantle or tear down the vines. The Chaldeans and the Assyrians began the ravage; the Samaritans on the one hand, and the Idumeans on the other, have completed it.

F. B. MEYER:

"Nevertheless my lovingkindness will I not utterly take from him" (89:32, 33). I was asked the other day if I believed, as an increasing number were said to do, that each man bears his own sin, and that there is no such thing as the vicarious imputation of the sins of the world to the Lamb of God. I said at once that this idea, so growingly prevalent, would not avail to help men and women like many of those with whom I come in contact, and are deeply dyed. Tell them that they must bear their own sin, and they turn from you in despair. This is what conscience has been reading to them hourly from the stony book of the law. The soul dreads to have to bear its sin, and cries out for propitiation and covering. A dying man said recently, "I have been into the valley of death, and where is my covering?" Men need a covering. It is requisite that help should be laid upon One that is mighty (v. 19).

We used to distinguish between guilt and secondary consequences of sin. For guilt we must have the transference of the black load of sin to our Savior. But it is also perfectly true that the nervous or physical system of the drunkard will never be what it might have been. The consequences of wrongdoing must be reaped. God will forgive you, and his lovingkindness will not depart; but He will visit your transgression with the rod, and your iniquity with stripes. But even here his mercy will avail to transform the curse into a blessing, and make myrtles bloom where thistles had flourished. God's love can so transmute these results of sin that where sin reigned unto death, grace shall reign unto eternal life. But never forget that when once God has entered into covenant with a soul, He will stand to it till the heavens be no more.—*Great Verses Through the Bible*

MATTHEW HENRY

is worse) thou hast turned the edge of his spirit, and taken off his courage, *and hast not made him to stand* as he used to do *in the battle.*" 5. It was upon the brink of an inglorious exit (*v.* 45): *The days of his youth hast thou shortened.* This seems to intimate that the psalm was penned in Rehoboam's time, when the house of David was but in the days of its youth, and yet waxed old and began to decay already. When posterity degenerates, it falls into disgrace, and iniquity stains their glory. How apt we are to place the happiness of the church in something external, and to think the promise fails. Our Master has so expressly told us that his kingdom is not of this world.

II. A very pathetic expostulation with God upon this. *How long, O Lord! wilt thou hide thyself? For ever?* That which grieved them most was that God himself had kept them long in the dark. It seemed an eternal night, when God had withdrawn: *Thou hidest thyself for ever.* He pleads the shortness and vanity of life (*v.* 47): *Remember how short my time is, how transitory I am* (say some), therefore unable to bear the power of thy wrath, and therefore a proper object of thy pity. *Wherefore hast thou made all men in vain?* or, *Unto what vanity hast thou created all the sons of Adam!* If the ancient lovingkindnesses spoken of (*v.* 49) be forgotten (those relating to another life), man is indeed made in vain. Considering man as mortal, if there were not a future state on the other side of death, we might be ready to think that man was made in vain. If we think that God has made men in vain because so many have short lives, it is true that God has made them so, but it is not true that *therefore* they are made in vain. For those whose days are few may yet glorify God and do some good, may keep their communion with God and get to heaven. If we think that God has made men in vain because most men neither serve him nor enjoy him, it is true that, as to themselves, they were made in vain, but it was not owing to God that they were made in vain; it was owing to themselves. He pleads the universality of death (*v.* 48): "*What man*" (what *strong man*, so the word is), "*is he that liveth and shall not see death?* The king himself is not exempted. Lord, since he is under a fatal necessity of dying, let not his whole life be made miserable. Let him not therefore be delivered into the hand of the grave by the miseries of a dying life, till his time shall come." It concerns us therefore to make sure of happiness on the other side of death, that, *when we fail, we may be received into everlasting habitations.* The next plea is taken from the kindness God had for his servant David (*v.* 49): *Lord, where are thy former lovingkindnesses*, which thou showedst, nay, *which thou swaredst*, to *David in thy truth*? Wilt thou fail of doing what thou hast promised? God's unchangeableness and faithfulness assure us that God will not cast off those whom he has chosen and covenanted with. The last plea is taken from the indignity done to God's anointed (*v.* 50, 51). "They are thy enemies who do thus reproach us; and wilt thou not appear against them as such? *They have reproached the footsteps of thy anointed.*" They reflected upon all the steps which the king had taken in the course of his administration, tracked him in all his motions. Or, if we apply it to Christ, the Lord's Messiah, they reproached the Jews with the slowness of his coming. They called him, *He that should come;* but, because he had not yet come, they told them he would never come, they must give over looking for him.

III. The psalm concludes with praise, even after this sad complaint (*v.* 52): *Blessed be the Lord for evermore, Amen, and amen.* Thus he confronts the reproaches of his enemies. The more others blaspheme God the more we should bless him. Thus he corrects his own complaints. He began the psalm with thanksgiving, before he made his complaint (*v.* 1); and now he concludes it with a doxology.

JAMIESON, FAUSSET, BROWN

days of his youth—or, youthful vigor, i.e., of the royal line, or promised perpetual kingdom, under the figure of a man.

46. How long . . .—(Cf. Ps. 13:1; 88:14; Jer. 4:4.)

47. These expostulations are excited in view of the identity of the prosperity of this kingdom with the welfare of *all mankind* (Gen. 22:18; Ps. 72:17; Isa. 9:7; 11:1-10); for if such is the fate of this chosen royal line.

48. What man—lit., "strong man—shall live?" and, indeed, have not all men been made in vain, as to glorifying God?

49-51. The terms of expostulation are used in view of the actual appearance that God had forsaken His people and forgotten His promise, and the plea for aid is urged in view of the reproaches of His and His people's enemies (cf. Isa. 37: 17-35).

bear in my bosom—as feeling the affliction of the people (Ps. 69:9). **footsteps**—ways (Ps. 56:6).

Blessed . . .—denotes returning confidence (Ps. 34: 1-3). **Amen, and Amen**—closes the third book of Psalms.

ADAM CLARKE

CHARLES H. SPURGEON:

"The days of his youth hast thou shortened" (89:45). The time of the king's energy was brief; he grew feeble before his time. "Thou hast covered him with shame." Shame was heaped upon him because of his premature decay and his failure in arms. This was very grievous to the writer of the Psalm, who was evidently a most loyal adherent of the house of David. In this our day we have to bemoan the lack of vigor in religion—the heroic days of Christianity are over, her raven locks are sprinkled with untimely gray. Is this according to the covenant? Can this be as the Lord has promised? Let us plead with the righteous Judge of all the earth, and beseech him to fulfill his word wherein he has promised that those who wait upon him shall renew their strength.

Selah. The interceding poet takes breath amid his lament, and then turns from describing the sorrows of the kingdom to pleading with the Lord.

46. "How long, Lord?" The appeal is to Jehovah, and the argument is the length of the affliction endured. Chastisement with a rod is not a lengthened matter; therefore he appeals to God to cut short the time of tribulation. "Wilt thou hide thyself for ever?" Hast thou not promised to appear for thy servant—wilt thou then forever forsake him? "Shall thy wrath burn like fire?" Shall it go on and on evermore till it utterly consume its object? Be pleased to set a bound! How far wilt thou go? Wilt thou burn up the throne which thou hast sworn to perpetuate? Even thus we would entreat the Lord to remember the cause of Christ in these days. Can he be so angry with his church as to leave her much longer? How far will he suffer things to go? Shall truth die out, and saints exist no more? How long will he leave matters to take their course? Surely he must interpose soon, for, if he does not, true religion will be utterly consumed, as it were, with fire.—*The Treasury of David*

52. *Blessed be the Lord for evermore.* Let Him treat us as He will, His name deserves eternal praises; our affliction, though great, is less than we have deserved.

This verse concludes the **Third Book** of the Psalter; and, I think, has been added by a later hand, in order to make this distinction, as every Masoretic Bible has something of this kind at the end of each book.

PSALM 90

A prayer of Moses the man of God.

Verses 1–6

This psalm is entitled *a prayer of Moses.* Moses taught the people of Israel to pray, and put words into their mouths which they might make use of in turning to the Lord. In these verses we are taught,

I. To give God the praise of his care concerning his people at all times (*v.* 1): *Lord, thou hast been to us a habitation*, or *dwelling-place*, *a refuge* or *help*, *in all generations.* They plead his former kindnesses to their ancestors. Canaan was a land of pilgrimage to their fathers the patriarchs, who dwelt there in tabernacles; but then God was their habitation, and, wherever they went, they were at home, at rest, in

PSALM 90

Vss. 1-17. Contrasting man's frailty with God's eternity, the writer mourns over it as the punishment of sin, and prays for a return of the divine favor. *A Prayer* [mainly such] *of Moses the man of God*—(Deut. 33:1; Josh. 14:6); as such he wrote this (cf. titles of Psalm 18 and Psalm 36).

1. dwelling-place—home (cf. Ezek. 11:16), as a refuge (Deut. 33:27).

PSALM 90

The title of this psalm is, "A Prayer of Moses the man of God." The Chaldee has, "A prayer which Moses the prophet of the Lord prayed when the people of Israel had sinned in the wilderness." All the versions ascribe it to Moses; but that it could not be of Moses the lawgiver is evident from this consideration, that the age of man was not then seventy or eighty years, which is here stated to be its almost universal limit, for Joshua lived one hundred and ten years, and Moses himself one hundred and twen-

MATTHEW HENRY

him. Egypt had been a land of bondage for many years, but even then God was their refuge.

II. To give God the glory of his eternity (*v.* 2): *Before the mountains were brought forth, before he made the highest part of the dust of the world* (as it is expressed, Prov. viii. 26), *before the earth fell in travail*, or, as we may read it, *before thou hadst formed the earth and the world* (that is, before the beginning of time) thou hadst a being; *even from everlasting to everlasting thou art God.* Again at all the grievances that arise from our own mortality, we may take comfort from God's immortality.

III. To own God's absolute sovereign dominion over man, and his power to dispose of him as he pleases (*v.* 3): *Thou turnest man to destruction*, to the destruction of the body, of the earthly house; *and* thou *sayest*, *Return, you children of men.* He does thereby call men to repent of their sins and live a new life. Sometimes he wonderfully restores them, and says, as the old translation reads it, *Again thou sayest, Return* to life and health again. Though God turns all men to destruction, yet he will again say, *Return, you children of men*, at the general resurrection, when, though a man dies, yet he shall live again.

IV. To acknowledge the infinite disproportion there is between God and men, *v.* 4. "A thousand years, to us, are a long period, which we cannot expect to survive; but it is, *in thy sight, as yesterday*, as one day; nay, it is but as a *watch of the night*," which was but three hours. Betwixt a minute and a million of years there is some proportion, but betwixt time and eternity there is none. But it might be objected against the doctrine of the resurrection that it is a long time since it was expected and it has not yet come. Let that be no difficulty, for a thousand years, in God's sight, are but as one day.

V. To see the frailty of man, and his vanity even at his best estate (*v.* 5, 6); look upon all the children of men, and we shall see their life is a dying life: *Thou carriest them away as with a flood.* As soon as we are born we begin to die, and every day of our life carries us so much nearer death. Men are carried away as with a flood and yet *they are as a sleep.* They consider not their own frailty. Like men asleep, they imagine great things to themselves, till death wakes them. Time passes unobserved by us, as it does with men asleep. It is a short and transient life, like that of the grass which grows up and flourishes, in the morning looks green and pleasant, but in the evening the mower cuts it down, and it withers and loses all its beauty. Death will change us shortly, perhaps suddenly; and it is a great change that death will make with us in a little time. Man, in his prime, does but flourish as the grass.

Verses 7–11

Moses had, in the foregoing verses, lamented the frailty of human life in general. But here he teaches the people of Israel to confess before God that righteous sentence of death which by their sins they had brought upon themselves.

I. They are here taught to acknowledge the wrath of God to be the cause of all their miseries. *We are consumed, we are troubled*, and it is *by thy anger*, by *thy wrath* (*v.* 7); *our days have passed away in thy wrath*, *v.* 9. We are too apt to look upon death as no more than a debt owing to nature; whereas it is not so; if the nature of man had continued in its primitive purity, there would have been no such debt owing to it. It is a debt to the justice of God, a debt to the law. *Sin entered into the world, and death by sin.*

II. They are taught to confess their sins (*v.* 8): *Thou hast set our iniquities before thee, even our secret sins.* God had herein an eye to their unbelief and murmuring, their distrusting his power and their despising the pleasant land. *"Thou hast set our secret sins* (those which go no further than the heart, and which are at the bottom of all the overt acts) *in the light of thy countenance*; that is, thou hast discovered these, and brought these also to the account, and made us to see them, who before overlooked them."

III. They are taught to look upon themselves as dying and passing away, and not to think either of a long life or of a pleasant one (*v.* 9). Though we are not quite deprived of the residue of our years, yet we are likely to *spend* them *as a tale that is told.* The thirty-eight years they wore away in the wilderness, for little or nothing is recorded of that which happened to them from the second years to the fortieth. Their joyful prospect of a prosperous glorious life in Canaan was turned into the melancholy prospect of a tedious death in the wilderness. That is applicable to the state of every one of us in the wilderness of this world: *We spend our years, we bring them to an end*, each year, and all at last, *as a tale that is told.* Some of our years are as a pleasant

JAMIESON, FAUSSET, BROWN

2. brought forth [and] **formed**—both express the idea of production by birth.

3. to destruction—lit., "even to dust" (Gen. 3:19), which is partly quoted in the last clause.

4. Even were our days now 1000 years, as Adam's, our life would be but a moment in God's sight (II Pet. 3:8). **a watch**—or, third part of a night (cf. Exod. 14:24).

5, 6. Life is like grass, which, though changing under the influence of the night's dew, and flourishing in the morning, is soon cut down and withereth (Ps. 103:15; I Peter 1:24).

7, 8. For—A reason, this is the infliction of God's wrath. **troubled**—lit., "confounded by terror" (Ps. 2:5).

Death is by sin (Rom. 5:12). Though "secret," the light of God's countenance, as a candle, will bring sin to view (Prov. 20:27; I Cor. 4:5).

9. are passed—lit., "turn," as to depart (Jer. 6:4). **spend**—lit., "consume." **as a tale**—lit., a thought," or, "a sigh" (Ezek. 2:10).

ADAM CLARKE

ty. Therefore the psalm cannot at all refer to such ancient times.

3. *Thou turnest man to destruction.* Literally, "Thou shalt turn dying man, *enosh*, to the small dust, but Thou wilt say, Return, ye children of Adam." This appears to be a clear and strong promise of the resurrection of the human body, after it has long slept, mingled with the dust of the earth.

4. *For a thousand years in thy sight.* As if he had said, Though the resurrection of the body may be a thousand (or any indefinite number of) years distant, yet, when these are past, they are *but as yesterday*, or a single *watch in the night*.

5. *Thou carriest them away as with a flood.* On the whole, life is represented as a stream; youth, as morning; old age, as evening; death, as sleep; and the resurrection as the return of the flowers in spring. All these images appear in these curious and striking verses, 3–6.

8. *Thou hast set our iniquities before thee.* Every one of our transgressions is set before Thee, noted down in Thy awful register!

9. *We spend our years as a tale.* "We consume our years like a groan."

MATTHEW HENRY

story, others as a tragical one, most mixed, but all short and transient: that which was long in the doing may be told in a short time. Every year passed *as a tale that is told*; but what was the number of them? As they were vain, so they were few (*v.* 10), seventy or eighty at most, which may be understood either 1. Of the lives of the Israelites in the wilderness; all those that were numbered when they came out of Egypt, above twenty years old, were to die within thirty-eight years; they numbered those only that *were able to go forth to war*, most of whom, we may suppose, were between twenty and forty, who therefore must have all died before eighty years old, and many before sixty. See what work sin made. Or, 2. Of the lives of men in general, ever since the days of Moses. It may be taken thus: *Our years are seventy, and the years of some, by reason of strength, are eighty; but the breadth of our years* (for so the latter word signifies, rather than strength), *the whole extent of them, from infancy to old age, is but labour and sorrow.* In the sweat of our face we must eat bread.

IV. They are taught by all this to stand in awe of the wrath of God (*v.* 11): *Who knows the power of thy anger?* The psalmist speaks as one afraid of God's anger, and amazed at the greatness of the power of it. *Who knows it*, so as to improve the knowledge of it? Those who make a mock at sin, and make light of Christ, surely do not know the power of God's anger.

Verses 12–17

These are the petitions of this prayer, grounded upon the foregoing meditations and acknowledgments. Four things they are here directed to pray for:—

I. For a sanctified use of the sad dispensation they were now under. "*Lord, teach us to number our days* (*v.* 12); Lord, give us grace duly to consider how few they are, and how little a while we have to live in this world." We must so number our days as to compare our work with them, and mind it accordingly with a double diligence, as those that have no time to trifle. Those that would learn this arithmetic must pray for divine instruction.

II. For the turning away of God's anger from them, "*Yet return, O Lord!* be thou reconciled to us, and *let it repent thee concerning thy servants* (*v.* 13); send us tidings of peace to comfort us again after these heavy tidings. *We are thy servants, thy people* (Isa. lxiv. 9); when wilt thou change thy way towards us?" In answer to this prayer, and upon their profession of repentance (Num. xiv. 39, 40), God, in the next chapter, proceeded with the laws concerning sacrifices (Num. xv. 1, &c.), which was a token that it repented him concerning his servants; for, *if the Lord had been pleased to kill them, he would not have shown them such things as these.*

III. For comfort and joy in the returns of God's favour to them, *v.* 14, 15. They pray for the mercy of God; for they pretend not to plead any merit of their own. *Have mercy upon us, O God! Early in the morning* of our days, when we are young and flourishing, *v.* 6. "*O satisfy us with thy mercy*, not only that we may be easy and at rest within ourselves, which we can never be while we lie under thy wrath, but that we *may rejoice and be glad*, not only for a time, upon the first indications of thy favour, but *all our days*, though we are to spend them in the wilderness. *Make us glad according to the days wherein thou hast afflicted us;* let the days of our joy in thy favour be as many as the days of our pain for thy displeasure have been and as pleasant as those have been gloomy. Now put into our hands the cup of salvation."

IV. For the progress of the work of God among them notwithstanding, *v.* 16, 17. "*Let thy work appear upon thy servants;* let it appear that thou hast wrought upon us, to bring us home to thyself and to fit us for thyself. Let thy work appear, and in it thy glory will appear to us and those that shall come after us." Perhaps, in this prayer, they distinguish between themselves and their children, for so God distinguished in his late message to them (Num. xiv. 31, *Your carcases shall fall in this wilderness, but your little ones will I bring into Canaan*): "Lord," say they, "let *thy work appear upon us*, to reform us, and bring us to a better temper, and then *let thy glory appear to our children*, in performing the promise to them which we have forfeited." *Let the beauty of the Lord our God be upon us;* let it appear that God favours us. Let the grace of God in us, and the light of our good works, make our faces to shine, and let divine consolations put gladness into our hearts, and a lustre upon our countenances, and that also will be the beauty of the Lord upon us. *Establish thou the work of our hands upon us.* God's working upon us (*v.* 16) does not discharge

JAMIESON, FAUSSET, BROWN

10. Moses' life was an exception (Deut. 34:7). **it is . . . cut off**—or, driven, as is said of the quails in using the same word (Num. 11:31). In view of this certain and speedy end, life is full of sorrow.

11. The whole verse may be read as a question implying the negative, "No one knows what Thy anger can do, and what Thy wrath is, estimated by a true piety."

12. This he prays we may know or understand, so as properly to number or appreciate the shortness of our days, that we may be wise.

13. (Cf. Ps. 13:2.) **let it repent**—a strong figure, as in Exodus 32:12, imploring a change in His dealings.

14. early—promptly. **15.** As have been our sorrows, so let our joys be great and long.

16. thy work—or, providential acts. **thy glory**—(Ps. 8:5; 45:3), the honor accruing from Thy work of mercy to us.

17. let the beauty—or sum of His gracious acts, in their harmony, be illustrated in us, and favor our enterprise.

ADAM CLARKE

10. *Threescore years and ten.* This psalm could not have been written by Moses, because the term of human life was much more extended when he flourished than eighty years at the most.

12. *So teach us to number our days.* Let us deeply consider our own frailty, and the shortness and uncertainty of life, that we may live for eternity, acquaint ourselves with Thee, and be at peace; that we may die in Thy favor, and live and reign with Thee eternally.

13. *Return, O Lord, how long?* Wilt Thou continue angry with us forever? *Let it repent thee.* "Be comforted," rejoice over them to do them good. Be glorified rather in our salvation than in our destruction.

14. *O satisfy us early.* Let us have Thy mercy soon (literally, "in the morning").

15. *Make us glad according to the days.* Let Thy people have as many years of prosperity as they have had of adversity. We have now suffered seventy years of a most distressful captivity.

17. *And let the beauty of the Lord.* Let us have Thy presence, blessing, and approbation, as our fathers had. *Establish thou the work of our hands.* This is supposed, we have already seen, to relate to their rebuilding the Temple, which the surrounding heathens and Samaritans wished to hinder.

MATTHEW HENRY | JAMIESON, FAUSSET, BROWN | ADAM CLARKE

us from using our utmost endeavours in serving him and working out our salvation. But, when we have done all, we must wait upon God for the success.

PSALM 91

Verses 1–8

I. A great truth laid down in general, That all those who live a life of communion with God are constantly safe under his protection, and may therefore preserve a holy serenity of mind at all times (*v.* 1). It is the character of a true believer that he *dwells in the secret place of the Most High*; he is at home in God, returns to God, and reposes in him as his rest; he acquaints himself with inward religion, and makes heart-work of the service of God, worships within the veil. It is the privilege and comfort of those that do so that they *abide under the shadow of the Almighty*; he shelters them. They shall have a residence, under God's protection.

II. The psalmist's comfortable application of this to himself (*v.* 2): *I will say of the Lord*, whatever others say of him, *He is my refuge*. Idolaters called their idols *Mahuzzim*, their *most stronghold* (Dan. xi. 39), but therein they deceived themselves; those only secure themselves that make the Lord their God, their fortress. There being no reason to question his sufficiency, fitly does it follow, *In him will I trust*.

III. The great encouragement he gives to others to do likewise, not only from his own experience but from the truth of God's promise (*v.* 3, 4, &c.): *Surely he shall deliver thee*. Now here it is promised,

1. That believers shall be kept from imminent danger which would be fatal to them (*v.* 3). This promise protects, (1) The natural life, and is often fulfilled in our preservation from these dangers which are very threatening and very near. (2) The spiritual life, which is protected by divine grace from the temptations of Satan.

2. That God himself will be their protector. *He shall cover thee with his feathers, under his wings*, which alludes to the hen *gathering her chickens under her wings*, Matt. xxiii. 37. By natural instinct she not only protects them, but calls them under that protection when she sees them in danger, not only keeps them safe, but cherishes them and keeps them warm. To this the great God is pleased to compare his care of his people. Wings and feathers, though spread with the greatest tenderness, are yet weak, and easily broken through, and therefore it is added, *His truth shall be thy shield and buckler*, a strong defence. God is as willing to guard his people as the hen is to guard the chickens, and as able as a man of war in armour.

3. That he will not only keep them from evil, but from the fear of evil, *v.* 5, 6. God by his grace will keep thee from disquieting distrustful fear (that fear which hath torment) in the midst of the greatest dangers. Wisdom shall keep thee from being causelessly afraid, and faith shall keep thee from being inordinately afraid. Thou shalt not be afraid of the arrow, as knowing that though it may hit thee it cannot hurt thee; if it take away the natural life, yet it shall be so far from doing any prejudice to the spiritual life that it shall be its perfection.

4. That they shall be preserved in common calamities, in a distinguishing way (*v.* 7): "When *thousands and ten thousands* fall, fall by sickness, or fall by the sword in battle, *fall at thy side, at thy right hand, yet it shall not come nigh thee*, the fear of death shall not." When multitudes die round about us, though thereby we must be awakened to prepare for our own death, yet we must not be *afraid with any amazement*, nor make ourselves subject to bondage, as many do all their life-time, *through fear of death*, Heb. ii. 15. *Only with thy eyes shalt thou behold and see the just reward of the wicked*, which perhaps refers to the destruction of the first-born of Egypt by the pestilence.

Verses 9–16

More promises to the same purport with those in the foregoing verses.

I. The psalmist assures believers of divine protection, from his own experience. The character of those who shall have the benefit and comfort of these promises. They are such as make *the Most High their habitation* (*v.* 9), as dwell in love and so dwell in God. It is our duty to be at home in God, to make our choice of him, and then to live our life in him as our habitation. We shall be welcome to him as a man to his own habitation. To encourage us to make the Lord our habitation, and to hope for safety and satisfaction in him, the psalmist intimates the comfort he had had in doing so: "He whom thou makest thy *habitation is my refuge*; and I have found him firm and faithful, and in him there is room enough, and shelter enough,

PSALM 91

Vss. 1-16. David is the most probable author; and the pestilence, mentioned in II Sam. 24, the most probable of any special occasion to which the Psalm may refer. The changes of person allowable in poetry are here frequently made.

1. dwelleth in the secret place (Ps. 27:5; 31:20) denotes nearness to God. Such as do so abide or lodge secure from assaults, and can well use the terms of trust in vs. 2.

3. snares . . . [and] **. . . noisome pestilence**—lit., "plagues of mischiefs" (Ps. 5:9; 52:7), are expressive figures for various evils.

4. For the first figure cf. Deuteronomy 32:11; Mark 23:37.

buckler—lit., "surrounding"—i.e., a kind of shield covering all over.

5. terror—or, what causes it (Prov. 20:2). **by night**—then aggravated. **arrow**—i.e., of enemies.

7-8. The security is more valuable, as being special, and, therefore, evidently of God; and while ten thousands of the wicked fall, the righteous are in such safety that they only see the calamity.

PSALM 91

CHARLES H. SPURGEON:

"He that dwelleth in the secret place of the most High" (91:1). The blessings here promised are not for all believers, but for those who live in close fellowship with God. Every child of God looks towards the inner sanctuary and the mercy seat, yet all do not *dwell* in the most holy place; they run to it at times, and enjoy occasional approaches, but they do not habitually reside in the mysterious presence. Into the secret place those only come who know the love of God in Christ Jesus, and those only *dwell* there to whom to live is Christ. To them the veil is rent, the mercy seat is revealed, the covering cherubs are manifest, and the awful glory of the Most High is apparent: these, like Simeon, have the Holy Ghost upon them, and like Anna they depart not from the temple; they are the courtiers of the Great King, the valiant men who keep watch around the bed of Solomon, the virgin souls who follow the Lamb whithersoever he goeth.—*The Treasury of David*

4. ***He shall cover thee with his feathers.*** **He shall act towards thee as the hen does to her brood—take thee under His wings when birds of prey appear, and also shelter thee from chilling blasts.**

His truth shall be thy shield and buckler. **His revelation; His Bible. That truth contains promises for all times and circumstances, and these will be invariably fulfilled to him that trusts in the Lord. The fulfillment of a promise relative to defense and support is to the soul what the best shield is to the body.**

5. *The terror by night.* The Chaldee translates this verse, "Thou shalt not fear the demons that walk by night; nor the arrow of the angel of death which is shot in the daytime." Thou needest not to fear a sudden and unprovided-for death.

7. *A thousand shall fall at thy side.* It is a promise of perfect protection, and the utmost safety.

ALEXANDER MACLAREN:

This cry of the devout soul suggests to me that our response ought to be the establishment of a close personal relation between us and God. "Thou, O Lord! art *my* refuge." The Psalmist did not content himself with saying, "Lord! thou hast been *our* dwelling place in all generations," or as one of the other psalmists has it, "God is *our* refuge and *our* strength." That thought was blessed, but it was not enough for the Psalmist's present need, and it is never enough for the deepest necessities of any soul. We must isolate ourselves and stand, God and we, alone together—at heart grips—we grasping His hand and He giving himself to us—if the promises which are sent down into the world for all who will make them theirs can become ours.—*Expositions of Holy Scripture*

MATTHEW HENRY

both for thee and me." The promises are sure to all those who have thus made *the Most High* their *habitation.* Whatever happens to them, nothing shall hurt them (*v.* 10). Though trouble or affliction befall thee, yet there shall be no real evil in it, for it shall come from the love of God and shall be sanctified; it shall come, not for thy hurt, but for thy good; and though, for *the present, it be not joyous but grievous* yet, in the end, it shall yield so well that thou thyself shalt own *no evil befell thee.* He who is the Lord of the angels, who gave them their being and gives laws to them, whose they are and whom they were made to serve, *he shall give his angels a charge over thee,* not only over the church in general, but over every particular believer. The charge is *to keep thee in all thy ways*; here is a limitation of the promise: They *shall keep thee in thy ways.* Wherever the saints go the angels are charged with them, as the servants are with the children. *Thou shalt tread upon the lion and adder.* The devil is called *a roaring lion,* the old *serpent, the red dragon*; so that to this promise the apostle seems to refer (Rom. xvi. 20), *The God of peace shall tread Satan under your feet.* Christ has broken the serpent's head, spoiled our spiritual enemies (Col. ii. 15). It may be applied to that care of the divine Providence by which we are preserved from ravenous noxious creatures (*the wild beasts of the field shall be at peace with thee,* Job v. 23); yea, and have ways and means of taming them, James iii. 7.

II. He brings in God himself speaking words of comfort to the saints, and declaring the mercy he had in store for them, *v.* 14–16. Observe,

1. To whom these promises do belong; they are described by three characters:—(1) They are such as know God's name. His nature we cannot fully know; but by his name he has made himself known. (1) They are such as have set their love upon him; those who rightly know him will love him. (3) They are such as by prayer keep up a constant correspondence with him.

2. What the promises are which God makes to the saints. (1) That he will, in due time, deliver them out of trouble: *I will deliver him* (*v.* 14 and again *v.* 15), denoting a double deliverance, living and dying, a deliverance in trouble and a deliverance out of trouble. (2) That he will, in the mean time, *be with them in trouble, v.* 15. If he does not immediately put a period to their afflictions, yet they shall have his gracious presence with them in their troubles. (3) That herein he will answer their prayers: *He shall call upon me;* I will pour upon him the spirit of prayer, *and* then *I will answer,* by providences, and answer by graces, *strengthening them with strength in their souls* (cxxxviii. 3); thus he answered Paul with *grace sufficient,* 2 Cor. xii. 9. (4) That he will exalt and dignify them: *I will set him on high,* out of the reach of trouble, above the stormy region, on a rock *above the waves,* Isa. xxxiii. 16. They shall be enabled, by the grace of God, to look down upon the things of this world with a holy contempt and indifference, to look up to the things of the other world with a holy ambition and concern. (5) That they shall have a sufficiency of life in this world (*v.* 16). *With length of days will I satisfy him.* They shall live long enough: they shall be continued in this world till they have done the work they were sent into this world for and are ready for heaven, and that is long enough. A man may die young, and yet die full of days, *satur dierum—satisfied with living.* (6) That they shall have an eternal life in the other world. This crowns the blessedness: *I will show him my salvation.* It is probable that the word refers to the better country, that is, the heavenly.

JAMIESON, FAUSSET, BROWN

9-12. This exemption from evil is the result of trust in God, who employs angels as ministering spirits (Heb. 1:14). **13.** Even the fiercest, strongest, and most insidious animals may be trampled on with impunity. **14-16.** God Himself speaks (cf. Ps. 46:10; 75:2, 3). All the terms to express safety and peace indicate the most undoubting confidence (cf. Ps. 18:2; 20:1; 22:5). **set his love**—that of the most ardent kind. **show him**—lit., "make him see" (Ps. 50:23; Luke 2:30).

ADAM CLARKE

11. *He shall give his angels charge over thee.* The angels of God shall have an especial charge to accompany, defend, and preserve thee; and against their power, the influence of evil spirits cannot prevail. *To keep thee in all thy ways.* The path of duty is the way of safety.

12. *They shall bear thee up in their hands.* Take the same care of thee as a nurse does of a weak and tender child; lead thee, teach thee to walk, lift thee up out of the way of danger, *lest thou dash thy foot against a stone,* receive any kind of injury, or be prevented from pursuing thy path with safety and comfort.

13. *Thou shalt tread upon the lion and adder.* Even the king of the forest shall not be able to injure thee. And even the "asp," one of the most venomous of serpents, shall not be able to injure thee.

14. *Because he hath set his love upon me.* Here the Most High is introduced as confirming the word of His servant. He has fixed his love, his heart and soul, on Me. *I will set him on high.* I will place him out of the reach of all his enemies.

15. *He shall call upon me.* He must continue to pray; all his blessings must come in this way. When he calls, I will answer him. *I will be with him in trouble.* Literally, "I am with him." *And honour him.* "I will glorify him."

16. *With long life.* Literally, "With length of days will I fill him up."

And shew him my salvation. "I will make him see (or contemplate) My salvation."

MATTHEW HENRY

PSALM 92

A psalm or song for the sabbath day.

Verses 1–6

This psalm was appointed to be sung, at least it usually was sung, in the house of the sanctuary on the sabbath day. The sabbath day must be a day, not only of holy rest, but of holy work. The proper work of the sabbath is praising God; every sabbath day must be a thanksgiving day. One of the Jewish writers refers it to the kingdom of the Messiah, and calls it, *A psalm or song for the age to come,* which shall be all sabbath.

I. We are called upon and encouraged to praise God (*v.* 1–3): *It is a good thing to give thanks unto the Lord.* Praising God is good work: it is good in itself and good for us. 1. How we must praise God. We must do it by *showing forth his lovingkindness and his faithfulness.* We must show forth, not only his greatness and majesty, his holiness and justice, which magnify him and strike an awe upon us, but

JAMIESON, FAUSSET, BROWN

PSALM 92

Vss. 1-15. *A Psalm-song*—(Cf. Ps. 30, title.) The theme: God should be praised for His righteous judgments on the wicked and His care and defense of His people. Such a topic, at all times proper, is specially so for the reflections of the Sabbath-day.

1. sing . . . name—celebrate Thy perfections. **2. in the morning, . . . every night**—diligently and constantly (Ps. 42:8). **loving-kindness**—lit., "mercy." **faithfulness**—in fulfilling promises (Ps. 89:14).

ADAM CLARKE

PSALM 92

The title, "A Psalm or Song for the Sabbath," gives no information concerning the time, occasion, or author.

2. *To shew forth thy lovingkindness. Chasdecha,* Thy abundant mercy, *in the morning*—that has preserved me throughout the night, and brought me to the beginning of a new day; *and thy faithfulness every night,* that has so amply fulfilled the promise of preservation during the course of the day. This verse contains a general plan for morning and evening prayer.

MATTHEW HENRY

his lovingkindness and his faithfulness; for his goodness is his glory (Exod. xxxiii. 18, 19), and by these he proclaims his name. His mercy and truth are the great supports of our faith and hope, and the great encouragements of our love and obedience. This was then done, not only by singing, but by music joined with it, *upon an instrument of ten strings* (*v.* 3). 2. When we must praise God—*in the morning and every night*, not only on sabbath days, but every day; not only in public assemblies, but in secret, and in our families. We must begin and end every day with praising God.

II. We have an example set before us in the psalmist himself (*v.* 4): *Thou, Lord, hast made me glad through thy work. I will triumph in the works of thy hands.* From a joyful remembrance of what God has done for us we may raise a joyful prospect of what he will do. We cannot comprehend the greatness of God's works, and therefore must reverently and awfully wonder at them. "Men's works are little and trifling, for their thoughts are shallow; but, Lord, *thy works are great* and such as cannot be measured; for *thy thoughts are very deep* and such as cannot be fathomed." The greatness of God's works shall lead us to consider the depth of his thoughts.

III. We are admonished not to neglect the works of God, by the character of those who do so, *v.* 6. Those are fools who will not acquaint themselves with them, nor give him the glory of them.

Verses 7–15

The psalmist had said (*v.* 4) that from the works of God he would take occasion to triumph; and here he does so.

I. He triumphs over God's enemies (*v.* 7, 9, 11). When they are flourishing (*v.* 7) as *the grass* in spring (so thickly sown, so green, and growing so fast), *and all the workers of iniquity do flourish* in pomp, and power, one would think that it was a certain evidence of God's favour; but it is quite otherwise. The very *prosperity of fools shall slay them*, Prov. i. 32. Though they are daring, *v.* 9. They are thy enemies, and they fight against God. They shall perish: for *who ever hardened his heart against God and prospered*? Though they had a particular malice against the psalmist, yet he triumphs over them (*v.* 11): "*My eye shall see my desire on my enemies that rise up against me;* I shall see them not only disabled from doing me any further mischief, but reckoned with for the mischief they have done me, and brought either to repentance or ruin."

II. He triumphs in God, and his glory and grace. 1. In the glory of God (*v.* 8). 2. In the grace of God, his favour and the fruits of it (*v.* 10). *My horn shall thou exalt*, when *thy enemies perish;* for *then shall the righteous shine forth as the sun*, when the wicked shall be doomed to *shame and everlasting contempt*. He adds, *I shall be anointed with fresh oil*, which denotes a fresh confirmation in his office to which he had been anointed, or abundance of plenty, so that he should have fresh oil as often as he pleased, or renewed comforts to revive him when his spirits drooped. Grace is the anointing of the Spirit. The saints are here represented as *trees of righteousness*, Isa. lxi. 3; Ps. i. 3. They are *planted in the house of the Lord*, *v.* 13. The trees of righteousness do not grow of themselves; they are *planted*, not in common soil, but *in the house of the Lord*. Trees are not usually planted in a house; but God's trees are said to be planted in his house because it is from his grace, by his word and Spirit, that they receive all the sap and virtue that keep them alive and make them fruitful. It is here promised that they shall grow, *v.* 12. Where God gives true grace he will give more grace. God's trees shall grow higher, like the tall cedars in Lebanon; they shall grow nearer heaven; they shall grow stronger, like the cedars, and fitter for use. They shall be cheerful and respected by all about them. *They shall flourish like the palm-tree*, which has a stately body and large boughs. Dates, the fruit of it, are very pleasant, and it is ever green. The wicked flourish as the grass (*v.* 7), which is soon withered, but the righteous as the palm-tree, which is long-lived and which the winter does not change. It has been said of the palm-tree, *Sub pondere crescit—The more it is pressed down the more it grows;* so the righteous flourish under their burdens. They shall be fruitful. The products of sanctification, all the instances of a lively devotion, good works, by which God is glorified and others are edified, these are the fruits of righteousness, in which it is the privilege of the righteous to abound. It is promised that they shall bring forth fruit in old age. Other trees, when they are old, leave off bearing, but in God's trees the strength of grace does not fail with the strength of nature. The last days of the saints are sometimes their best days, and their last work is their best work. As it is by the

JAMIESON, FAUSSET, BROWN

3. In such a work all proper aid must be used. **with a . . . sound**—or, *on Higgaion* (cf. Ps. 9:16), perhaps an instrument of that name, from its sound resembling the muttered sound of meditation, as expressed also by the word. This is joined with the harp.

4. thy work—i.e. of providence (Ps. 90:16, 17). **5. great . . . works**—correspond to *deep* or vast *thoughts* (Ps. 40:5; Rom. 11:23).

6. A brutish man knoweth not i.e., God's works, so the Psalmist describes himself (Ps. 73:22) when amazed by the prosperity of the wicked, now understood and explained.

11. see . . . [and] **. . . hear my desire**—or, lit., "look on" my enemies and hear of the wicked (cf. Ps. 27:11; 54:7)—i.e., I shall be gratified by their fall.

8. This he does in part, by contrasting their ruin with God's exaltation and eternity. **most high**—as occupying the highest place in heaven (Ps. 7:7; 18:16). **9, 10.** A further contrast with the wicked, in the lot of the righteous, safety and triumph. **horn . . . exalt**—is to increase power (Ps. 75:5). **anointed . . . fresh** [or, new] **oil**—(Ps. 23:5) a figure for refreshment (cf. Luke 7:46). Such use of oil is still common in the East.

12-14. The vigorous growth, longevity, utility, fragrance, and beauty of these noble trees, set forth the life, character, and destiny of the pious;

15, and they thus declare God's glory as their strong and righteous ruler.

ADAM CLARKE

F. B. MEYER:

"I am anointed with fresh oil" (92:10). There is perennial freshness in God—in the works of nature, in his love, and in the renewal of the soul. Does the eye ever tire of the changeful beauty of the clouds? Though we look out from childhood to old age on the same landscape, there is always something fresh to captivate the roving eye. Think of the unfailing freshness in love—love of woman to man, of mother to child. Think of the freshness of each returning day, of earth in her springtime robe, with the myriads of sweet children, whose laughter is as ringing and their eyes as bright as if the earth were young, instead of being old and weary. And if God can do this for the works of his hands, is there any limit in the freshness which He will communicate to his children?

Each morning bend your heads, ye priests of the Most High, for fresh anointing for the new ministries that await you. The former grace and strength will not suffice; old texts must be rejuvenated and reminted; old vows must be respoken; the infilling of the Holy Spirit must be as vivid, and may be as definite, as at the first. See to it that you do not rise from your knees till you can say, "I have been, and am, anointed with fresh oil." And the anointing that ye receive from Him shall abide on you, teaching you how to abide in Him. So you shall bring forth fruit in old age, and in life's winter be full of sap and fervor.—*Great Verses Through the Bible*

12. ***The righteous shall flourish like the palm tree.*** Very different from the wicked, v. 7, who are likened to grass. These shall have a short duration, but those shall have a long and useful life. They are compared also to the cedar of Lebanon, an incorruptible wood, and extremely long-lived.

13. *Those that be planted in the house of the Lord.* I believe the Chaldee has the true meaning here: "His children shall be planted in the house of the sanctuary of the Lord, and shall flourish in the courts of our God."

14. *They shall still bring forth fruit in old age.* They shall continue to grow in grace, and be fruitful to the end of their lives. It is a rare case to find a man in old age full of faith, love, and spiritual activity.

MATTHEW HENRY

promises that believers first partake of a divine nature, so it is by the promises that that divine nature is preserved and kept up. All that ever trusted in God found him faithful and all-sufficient, and none were ever made ashamed of their hope in him.

PSALM 93

Verses 1–5

The Lord reigns. It is the song of the gospel church, of the glorified church (Rev. xix. 6), *Hallelujah;* the Lord *God omnipotent reigns.* Here we are told how he reigns.

I. The Lord reigns gloriously: *He is clothed with majesty.*

II. He reigns powerfully. He is not only clothed with majesty, as a prince in his court, but he is *clothed with strength,* as a general in the camp. He has wherewithal to support his greatness and to make it truly formidable. See him not only clad in robes, but clad in armour. With this power *he has girded himself;* it is not derived from any other, nor does the executing of it depend upon any other. The world is established by the creating power of God, when he founded it upon the seas; it is so still, by that providence which upholds all things and is a continued creation. Though God clothes himself with majesty, yet he condescends to take care of this lower world and to settle its affairs; and, if he established the world, much more will he establish his church, that it cannot be moved.

III. He reigns eternally (*v.* 2): *Thy throne is established of old.* The whole administration of his government was settled in his eternal counsels before all worlds. Because God himself was from everlasting, his throne and all the determinations of it were so too; for in an eternal mind there could not but be eternal thoughts.

IV. He reigns triumphantly, *v.* 3, 4. *The floods have lifted up, O Lord!* (to God himself the remonstrance is made) *the floods have lifted up their voice,* which speaks terror. It alludes to a tempestuous sea. The church is said to *be tossed with tempests* (Isa. liv. 11). We may apply it to the tumults that are sometimes in our own bosoms, but, if the Lord reign there, even the winds and seas shall obey him. An immovable anchor is cast in this storm (*v.* 4): *The Lord himself is mightier.* The power of the church's enemies is but *as the noise of many waters*; there is more of sound than substance in it. *Pharaoh king of Egypt is but a noise,* Jer. xlvi. 17. The unlimited sovereignty and irresistible power of the great Jehovah are very encouraging to the people of God, in reference to all the noises and hurries they meet with in this world, Ps. xlvi. 1, 2.

V. He reigns in truth and holiness, *v.* 5. All his promises are inviolably faithful: *Thy testimonies are very sure.* As God is able to protect his church, so he is true to the promises he has made of its safety and victory. God's church is his house. The holiness of it is its beauty. and it is its strength and safety; it is the holiness of God's house that secures it against the many waters and their noise. Where there is purity there shall be peace.

PSALM 94

Verses 1–11

I. A solemn appeal to God against the cruel oppressors of his people, *v.* 1, 2.

1. The titles they give to God for the encouraging of their faith in this appeal: *O God! to whom vengeance belongeth;* and *thou Judge of the earth.* He is judge, supreme judge, judge alone, from whom every man's judgments proceeds. He that gives law gives sentence upon every man according to his works, by the rule of that law. His throne is the last refuge (the *dernier ressort,* as the law speaks) of oppressed innocency. He is *judge of the earth,* of the whole earth. As he has authority to avenge wrong, so it is his nature, and property. *O God! to whom vengeance belongs,* who wilt not suffer might always to prevail against right. This is a good reason why we must not avenge ourselves, because God has said, *Vengeance is mine;* and it is daring presumption to usurp his prerogative and step into his throne, Rom. xii. 19.

2. What is it they ask of God. "Lord," say they, "show thyself; make them know that thou art and that thou art ready to *show thyself strong on the behalf of those whose hearts are upright with thee.*" The enemies thought God was conquered because his people were. *Render a reward to the proud;* that is, "Reckon with them for all their insolence, and the injuries they have done to thy people."

II. A humble complaint to God of the pride and

JAMIESON, FAUSSET, BROWN

PSALM 93

Vss. 1-5. This and the six following Psalms were applied by the Jews to the times of the Messiah. The theme is God's supremacy in creation and providence.

1. God is described as a King entering on His reign, and, for robes of royalty, investing Himself with the glorious attributes of His nature. The result of His thus reigning is the durability of the world.

2-4. His underived power exceeds the most sublime exhibitions of the most powerful objects in nature (Ps. 89:9).

5. While His power inspires dread, His revealed will should secure our confidence (cf. Ps. 19:7; 25:10), and thus fear and love combined, producing all holy emotions, should distinguish the worship we offer in His house, both earthly and heavenly.

PSALM 94

Vss. 1-23. The writer, appealing to God in view of the oppression of enemies, rebukes them for their wickedness and folly, and encourages himself, in the confidence that God will punish evildoers, and favor His people.

1, 2. God's revenge is His judicial infliction of righteous punishment.

Lift up thyself—or, "Arise," both figures representing God as heretofore indifferent (cf. Ps. 3:7; 22:16, 20).

ADAM CLARKE

PSALM 93

1. *The Lord reigneth.* He continues to govern everything He has created; and He is every way qualified to govern all things, for *he is clothed with majesty,* and, *with strength*—dominion is His, and He has supreme power to exercise it; and He has so established the world that nothing can be driven out of order; all is ruled by Him. Nature is His agent, or rather, nature is the sum of the laws of His government; the operations carried on by the divine energy, and the effects resulting from those operations.

3. *The floods have lifted up.* Multitudes of people have confederated against Thy people, and troop succeeds troop as the waves of the sea succeed each other.

4. *The Lord . . . is mightier than the noise of many waters.* Greater in strength than all the peoples and nations that can rise up against Him. *Mighty waves of the sea.* Even the most powerful empires can prevail nothing against Him; therefore those who trust in Him have nothing to fear.

5. *Thy testimonies are very sure.* Thou wilt as surely fulfil Thy word as Thou wilt keep possession of Thy throne. *Holiness becometh thine house.* Thy nature is holy, all Thy works are holy, and Thy word is holy; therefore Thy *house*—Thy Church—should be holy.

PSALM 94

1. *O Lord God, to whom vengeance belongeth.* God is the Author of retributive justice, as well as of mercy. What is here referred to is that simple act of justice which gives to all their due.

2. *Lift up thyself.* Exert Thy power. *Render a reward to the proud.* To the Babylonians, who oppress and insult us.

MATTHEW HENRY

cruelty of the oppressors, *v.* 3. They are wicked; they are *workers of iniquity*; and therefore they hate and persecute those whose goodness shames and condemns them. They are insolent, and take a pleasure in magnifying themselves. Those that speak highly of themselves, that triumph and boast, are apt to speak hardly of others. "*They break in pieces thy people, O Lord!* and do all they can to afflict thy heritage, to grieve them, to crush them, to run them down, to root them out." God's people are his heritage. They are inhuman, and take a pleasure in wronging those that are least able to help themselves (*v.* 6). "Lord, *how long* shall they do thus?"

III. A charge of atheism exhibited against the persecutors. Their atheistical thoughts are here discovered (*v.* 7): *They say, The Lord shall not see.* They have the confidence to say, "*The Lord shall not see;* he will not only wink at small faults, but shut his eyes at great ones too." He that says either that Jehovah the living God shall not see or that the God of Jacob shall not regard the injuries done to his people, *Nabal* is his name and folly is with him (*v.* 8): "*Understand, you brutish among the people,* and let reason guide you." God sees and regards all you sav and do. None are so bad but means are to be used for the reclaiming and reforming of them, none so brutish, so foolish, but it should be tried whether they may not yet be made wise; while there is life there is hope. The works of creation (*v.* 9), the formation of human bodies, prove that there is a God, prove also that God has infinitely and transcendently in himself all those perfections that are in any creature. *He that planted the ear shall he not hear? He that formed the eye shall he not see?* Could he give, would he give, that perfection to a creature which he has not in himself? By the knowledge of ourselves we may be led a great way towards the knowledge of God—if by the knowledge of our own bodies, and the organs of sense, so as to conclude that if we can see and hear much more can God, then certainly by the knowledge of our own souls. The gods of the heathen had eyes and saw not, ears and heard not; our God has no eyes nor ears, as we have, and yet we must conclude he both sees and hears, because we have our sight and hearing from him. *He that chastises the heathen* for their polytheism and idolatry, *shall not he* much more *correct* his own people for their atheism and profaneness? Dr. Hammond gives another very probable sense of this: "*He that instructs the nations* (that is, gives them his law), *shall not he correct*, that is, shall not he judge them according to that law, and call them to an account for their violations of it?" The same word signifies to chastise and to instruct, because chastisement is intended for instruction and instruction should go along with chastisement. *He that teaches man knowledge, shall he not know?* He not only, as the God of nature, has given the light of reason, but, as the God of grace, has given the light of revelation, has shown man what is true wisdom and understanding; and he that does this, shall he not know? Job xxviii. 23, 28. God will take cognizance even of what we think (*v.* 11): *The Lord knows the thoughts of man, that they are vanity.* Even in good thoughts there is a fickleness and inconstancy which may well be called *vanity*. Thoughts are words to God, and vain thoughts are provocations.

Verses 12–23

The psalmist speaks comfort to suffering saints from God's promises and his own experience.

I. From God's promises, which are such as not only save them from being miserable, but secure a happiness to them (*v.* 12): *Blessed is the man whom thou chastenest.* Here he looks above the instruments of trouble, and eyes the hand of God, which puts quite another colour upon it. The enemies break in pieces God's people (*v.* 5); but God by them chastens his people, as the father the son in whom he delights, and the persecutors are only the rod he makes use of. Now it is here promised,

1. That God's people shall get good by their sufferings. When he chastens them he will teach them, and blessed is the man who is thus taken under a divine discipline, for *none teaches like God.* When we are chastened we must pray to be taught, and look into the law as the best expositor of Providence. It is not the chastening itself that does good, but the teaching that goes along with it and is the exposition of it.

2. That they shall see through their sufferings (*v.* 13): *That thou mayest give him rest from the days of adversity.* The days of their adversity shall not last always. God *therefore* teaches his people by their troubles, that he may prepare them for deliverance, and so give them rest from their troubles, that the affliction, having done its work, may be removed.

JAMIESON, FAUSSET, BROWN

3, 4. In an earnest expostulation he expresses his desire that the insolent triumph of the wicked may be ended.

5, 6. people [and] **heritage**—are synonymous, the people being often called God's heritage. As justice to the weak is a sign of the best government, their oppression is a sign of the worst (Deut. 10:18; Isa. 10:2).

7. Their cruelty is only exceeded by their wicked and absurd presumption (Ps. 10:11; 59:7).

8. ye brutish—(Cf. Ps. 73:22; 92: 6).

9-11. The evidence of God's providential government is found in His creative power and omniscience, which also assure us that He can punish the wicked in regard to all their vain purposes.

12, 13. On the other hand He favors though He chastens, the pious, and will teach and preserve them till the prosperous wicked are overthrown.

ADAM CLARKE

3. *How long shall the wicked triumph?* The wicked are often in prosperity; and this only shows us of how little worth riches are in the sight of God, when He bestows them on the most contemptible of mortals.

5. *They break in pieces thy people.* This was true of the Babylonians. Nebuchadnezzar slew many; carried the rest into captivity; ruined Jerusalem; overturned the Temple; sacked, pillaged, and destroyed all the country.

6. *They slay the widow.* Nebuchadnezzar carried on his wars with great cruelty.

8. *Understand, ye brutish.* These are the same expressions as in Ps. xcii. 6.

9. *He that planted the ear, shall he not hear?* This is allowed to be an unanswerable mode of argumentation. Whatever is found of excellence in the creature must be derived from the Creator, and exist in Him in the plenitude of infinite excellence.

10. *He that chastiseth the heathen, shall not he correct?* You, who are heathens, and heathens of the most abandoned kind.

He that teacheth man knowledge. We here supply *shall not he know?* But this is not acknowledged by the original, nor by any of the versions. Indeed it is not necessary; for either the words contain a simple proposition, "It is He who teacheth man knowledge," or this clause should be read in connection with v. 11: "Jehovah, who teacheth man knowledge, knoweth the devices of man, that they are vanity."

12. *Blessed is the man whom thou chastenest.* "Whom thou instructest," *and teachest him out of thy law.* Two points here are worthy of our most serious regard: (1) God gives knowledge to man, gives him understanding and reason. (2) He gives him a revelation of himself; He places before that reason and understanding His divine law.

13. *That thou mayest give him rest.* He whom God instructs is made wise unto salvation; and he who is thus taught has rest in his soul, and peace and confidence in adversity.

MATTHEW HENRY

3. That they shall see the ruin of those that are the instruments of their sufferings.

4. That, though they may be cast down, yet certainly they shall not be cast off, *v.* 14. Whatever their friends do, God will not cast them off, nor throw them out of his covenant or out of his care. St. Paul comforted himself with this, Rom. xi. 1.

5. That, bad as things are, they shall mend (*v.* 15): *Judgment shall return unto righteousness;* the seeming disorders of Providence (for real ones there never were) shall be rectified. Then *all the upright in heart shall be after it;* they shall return to a prosperous and flourishing condition, and shine forth out of obscurity; they shall accommodate themselves to the dispensations of divine Providence with suitable affections. Dr. Hammond thinks this was most eminently fulfilled in the destruction of Jerusalem first, and afterwards of heathen Rome, the crucifiers of Christ and persecutors of Christians, and the rest which the churches had thereby.

II. From his own experiences and observations.

1. He and his friends had been oppressed by cruel and imperious men, that had power in their hands and abused it by abusing all good people with it. They were *evil-doers* and *workers of iniquity* (*v.* 16); they abandoned themselves to all manner of impiety and immorality, and then their throne was a *throne of iniquity, v.* 20. Iniquity is daring enough even when human laws are against it, which often prove too weak to give an effectual check to it; but how insolent, how mischievous, is it when it is backed by a law! These workers of iniquity *condemn the innocent blood* for violating their decrees. See an instance in Daniel's enemies; they *framed mischief by a law* when they obtained an impious edict against prayer (Dan. vi. 7), and, when Daniel would not obey it, *condemned his innocent blood* to the lions. The best benefactors of mankind have often been thus treated, under colour of law and justice, as the worst of malefactors.

2. The oppression they were under bore very hard upon them. The psalmist *had almost dwelt in silence* (*v.* 17); he was at his wits' end, and knew not what to say or do; he was ready to drop into the grave, that land of silence. (St. Paul, in a like case, *received a sentence of death within himself,* 2 Cor. i. 8, 9). He said, "*My foot slippeth* (*v.* 18); I must *fall.* I *shall one day perish by the hand of Saul.* My hope fails me; I do not find such firm footing for my faith as I have sometimes found." See Ps. lxxiii. 2. He had a multitude of perplexed entangled thoughts within him concerning the course he should take and what was likely to be the issue of it.

3. In this distress they sought for help, and succour, and some relief (*v,* 16): "*Who will rise up for me against the evil-doers?* Have I any friend who, in love to me will appear for me?" He looked, but there was none to save, there was none to uphold. When St. Paul was brought before Nero's throne of iniquity *no man stood by him,* 2 Tim. iv. 16. They cried out: "Lord, *shall the throne of iniquity have fellowship with thee?* Wilt thou countenance and support these tyrants in their wickedness? We know thou wilt not." A throne has fellowship with God when it is a throne of justice and answers the end of the erecting of it; but, when it becomes a *throne of iniquity,* it has no longer fellowship with God.

4. They found succour and relief in God, and in him only. *Unless I had* made him *my help,* by putting my trust in him and expecting relief from him, I could never have kept possession of my own soul; but living by faith in him has kept my head above water, has given me breath, and something to say. We are beholden not only to God's power, but to his pity, for spiritual supports: *Thy mercy,* the gifts of thy mercy and my hope in thy mercy, *held me up.* "*In the multitude of my thoughts within me,* crowding and jostling one another like a multitude, *thy comforts delight my soul;* silence my unquiet thoughts and keep my mind easy." God's comforts will reach the soul, and not the fancy only, and will bring with them that peace and that pleasure which the smiles of the world cannot give and which the frowns of the world cannot take away.

5. God is, and will be, as a righteous Judge, the protector of right and the punisher of wrong; this the psalmist had both the assurance of and the experience of. "When none else will, nor can, nor dare, shelter me, *the Lord is my defence,* to preserve me from the evil of my troubles, from sinking under them and being ruined by them; and he is *the rock of my refuge,* in the clefts of which I may take shelter, and on the top of which I may set my feet, to be out of the reach of danger."

JAMIESON, FAUSSET, BROWN

14, 15. This results from His abiding love (Deut. 32:15), which is further evinced by His restoring order in His government, whose right administration will be approved by the good.

20. throne—power, rulers. **iniquity** [and] **mischief**—both denote evils done to others, as **21** explains.

16. These questions imply that none other than God will help (Ps. 60:9), **17-19,** a fact fully confirmed by his past experience. **dwelt in silence**—as in the grave (Ps. 31:17). **my thoughts**—or, anxious cares.

22, 23. Yet he is safe in God's care. **defence**—(Ps. 59:9). **rock of . . . refuge**—(Ps. 9:9; 18:2). **bring . . . iniquity**—(Cf. Ps. 5:10; 7:16). **in their . . . wickedness**—while they are engaged in evil-doing.

CHARLES H. SPURGEON:

"Unless the Lord had been my help, my soul had almost dwelt in silence" (v. 17). Without Jehovah's help the Psalmist declares that he should have died outright, and gone into the silent land, where no more testimonies can be borne for the living God. Or he may mean that he would not have had a word to speak against his enemies, but would have been wrapped in speechless shame. Blessed be God, we are not left to that condition yet, for the Almighty Lord is still the helper of all those who look to him. Our inmost soul is bowed down when we see the victories of the Lord's enemies—we cannot brook it, we cover our mouths in confusion; but he will yet arise and avenge his own cause; therefore have we hope.

—The Treasury of David

ADAM CLARKE

15. ***But judgment shall return unto righteousness.*** **If we read *yosheb,* "shall sit," for *yashub,* "shall return," we have the following sense: "Until the just one shall sit in judgment, and after him all the upright in heart." Cyrus has the epithet "the just one" in different places in the Prophet Isaiah. See Isa. xli. 2, 10; xlv. 8; li. 5.**

18. ***When I said, My foot slippeth.*** **When I found myself weak and my enemy strong.** ***Thy mercy, O Lord, held me up.*** **"Propped me." It is a metaphor taken from anything falling, that is propped, shored up, or buttressed. How often does the mercy of God thus prevent the ruin of weak believers!**

16. ***Who will rise up for me?*** **Who is he that shall be the deliverer of Thy people? Who will come to our assistance against these wicked Babylonians?**

17. ***Unless the Lord had been my help.*** **Had not God in a strange manner supported us while under His chastising hand, we had been utterly cut off.** ***My soul had almost dwelt in silence.*** **The Vulgate has *in inferno;* the Septuagint, "in the invisible world."**

MATTHEW HENRY

PSALM 95

Verses 1–7

The psalmist here, as often elsewhere, stirs up himself and others to praise God.

I. How God is to be praised. The praising song must be *a joyful noise, v.* 1 and again *v.* 2. Spiritual joy is the heart and soul of thankful praise. *Rejoice in him* as our Father and King, and a God in covenant with us. With humble reverence, and holy awe (*v.* 6): "*Let us worship, and bow down, and kneel before him*, as becomes those who know what an infinite distance there is between us and God, how much we are in danger of his wrath and in need of his mercy." We must speak forth, sing forth, his praises out of the abundance of a heart filled with love, and joy, and thankfulness—*Sing to the Lord; make a noise, a joyful noise to him, with psalms.* We must praise God in concert, in the solemn assemblies: "*Come, let us sing;* let us join in singing to the Lord. *Let us come* together *before his presence*, where his people are wont to expect his manifestations of himself."

II. Why God is to be praised.

1. Because he is *a great God*, and sovereign Lord of all, *v.* 3. (1) He has great power: *He is a great King above all gods*, above all deputed deities, all magistrates, to whom he said, *You are gods* above all counterfeit deities. (2) He has great possessions. This lower world is here particularly specified. How great is that God whose *the whole earth is, and the fulness thereof*, in whose hand it is, as he has the actual directing and disposing of all (*v.* 4); even *the deep places of the earth are in his hand*; and *the height of the hills*, whatever grows or feeds upon them, *is his also.* Whatever strength is in any creature it is derived from God and employed for him (*v.* 5): *The sea is his* for *he made it*, gathered its waters and fixed its shores; *the dry land* is his, for *his hands formed* it, when his word made *the dry land* appear. His being the Creator of all makes him, without dispute, the owner of all. This being a gospel psalm, we may very well suppose that it is the Lord Jesus whom we are here taught to praise. As Mediator, he is *a great King above all gods; by him*, as the eternal Word, *all things were made* (John i. 3), and it was fit he should be the restorer and reconciler of all who was the Creator of all, Col. i. 16, 20.

2. Because he is our God, not only has he dominion over us, as he has over all the creatures, but stands in special relation to us (*v.* 7): *He is our God.* He is our Creator; we must *kneel before the Lord our Maker*, *v.* 6. Idolaters kneel before gods which they themselves made; we kneel before a God who made us. He is our Saviour, and the author of our blessedness. He is here called *the rock of our salvation* (*v.* 1). We are therefore his, under all possible obligations: *We are the people of his pasture and the sheep of his hand.* We must praise him, because he preserves and maintains us. All the church's children are in a special manner so; Israel *are the people of his pasture and the sheep of his hand*; and therefore he demands their homage in a special manner. The gospel church is his flock. Christ is the great and good Shepherd of it, and therefore to him must be *glory in the churches throughout all ages*, Eph. iii. 21.

Verses 7–11

The latter part of this psalm is an exhortation to those who sing gospel psalms to live gospel lives.

I. The duty required of all those that *are the people of* Christ's *pasture and the sheep of his hand.* He expects that they *hear his voice*, for he has said, *My sheep hear my voice*, John x. 27. If you call him *Master*, or *Lord*, then *do the things which he says*, and be his willing obedient people. Hearing the voice of Christ is the same with believing.

II. The sin they are warned against is hardness of heart. *If you will hear his voice*, and profit by what you hear, then do *not harden your hearts*; for the seed sown on the rock never brought any fruit to perfection.

III. The example of the Israelites in the wilderness.

1. "Take heed of sinning as they did, lest you be shut out of the everlasting rest as they were out of Canaan." So often did they provoke God by their distrusts and murmurings that the whole time of their continuance in the wilderness might be called a *day of temptation*, or *Massah*, the other name given to that place (Exod. xvii. 7), because they tempted the Lord, saying, *Is the Lord among us or is he not?* The more experience we have had of the power and goodness of God the greater is our sin if we distrust him.

2. The charge drawn up, in God's name, against the unbelieving Israelites, *v.* 9, 10. Their sin was unbelief: they *tempted* God and *proved* him, Num. xiv. 3, 4. This is called *rebellion*, Deut. i. 26, 32. The aggravation of this sin was that they *saw God's*

JAMIESON, FAUSSET, BROWN

PSALM 95

Vss. 1-11. David (Heb. 4:7) exhorts men to praise God for His greatness, and warns them, in God's words, against neglecting His service.

1. The terms used to express the highest kind of joy.

2. come . . . presence—lit., "approach," or, meet Him (Ps. 17:13).

3. above . . . gods—esteemed such by men, though really nothing (Jer. 5:7; 10:10-15).

4, 5. The terms used describe the world in its whole extent, subject to God.

6. come—or, "enter," with solemn forms, as well as hearts.

rock—a firm basis, giving certainty of salvation (Ps. 62:7).

7. This relation illustrates our entire dependence (cf. Ps. 23:3; 74:1). The last clause is united by Paul (Heb. 3:7) to the following (cf. Ps. 81:8),

8-11, warning against neglect; and this is sustained by citing the melancholy fate of their rebellious ancestors, whose provoking insolence is described by quoting the language of God's complaint (Num. 14:11) of their conduct at *Meribah* and *Massah*, names given (Exod. 17:7) to commemorate their strife and contention with Him (Ps. 78:18, 41).

ADAM CLARKE

PSALM 95

This psalm is also without a title, in both the Hebrew and Chaldee; but is attributed to David by the Vulgate, Septuagint, Aethiopic, Arabic, and Syriac, and by the author of the Epistle to the Hebrews, chap. iv. 3-7. Houbigant, and other learned divines, consider this psalm as composed of three parts: (1) The part of the people, v. 1 to the middle of v. 7. (2) The part of the priest or prophet, from the middle of v. 7 to the end of v. 8. (3) The part of Jehovah, vv. 9-11.

2. *Let us come before his presence.* "His faces," with thanksgiving, "with confession," or "with the confession offering."

3. *For the Lord is a great God.* The Supreme Being has three names here: El, Jehovah, Elohim. The first implies His strength; the second, His being and essence; the third, His covenant relation to mankind. In public worship these are the views we should entertain of the Divine Being.

6. *O come, let us worship.* Three distinct words are used here to express three different acts of adoration: (1) *Let us worship,* let us "prostrate" ourselves, the highest act of adoration by which the supremacy of God is acknowledged. (2) *Let us . . . bow down, nichraah,* let us "crouch down, bending the legs under," as a dog in the presence of his master, which solicitously waits to receive his commands. (3) *Let us kneel,* "let us put our knees to the ground," and thus put ourselves in the posture of those who supplicate.

7. *For he is our God.* Here is the reason for this service. He has condescended to enter into a covenant with us, and He has taken us for His own; therefore *we are the people of his pasture.* Or rather, as the Chaldee, Syriac, Vulgate, and Aethiopic read, "We are his people, and the sheep of the pasture of his hand." We are His own; He feeds and governs us, and His powerful hand protects us.

To day if ye will hear his voice. This should commence the eighth verse, as it begins what is supposed to be the part of the priest or prophet who now exhorts the people; as if he had said: Seeing you are in so good a spirit, do not forget your own resolutions, and harden not your hearts, as your fathers did in Meribah and Massah, in the wilderness. The same fact and the same names as are mentioned in Exod. xvii. 7, when the people murmured at Rephidim, because they had no water; hence it was called *Meribah*, contention or provocation, and *Massah*, temptation.

9. *When your fathers tempted me.* "Tried me," by their insolence, unbelief, and blasphemy. They *proved me*—they had full proof of My power to save and to destroy. There they *saw my work*—they saw that nothing was too hard for God.

MATTHEW HENRY

work; they saw what he had done for them in bringing them out of Egypt, what he was now doing for them every day in the bread he rained from heaven, and the water out of the rock, than which they could not have more unquestionable evidences of God's presence with them. *It is a people that do err in their hearts, and they have not known my ways.* Men's unbelief and distrust of God, their murmurings and quarrels with him, are the effect of their ignorance. They saw his work (*v.* 9) and he *made known his acts to them* (ciii. 7); and yet they *did not know* the ways of his providence, or the ways of his commandments. The reason why people slight and forsake the ways of God is because they do not know them. *They do err in their heart;* they wander out of the way; in heart they turn back. The sins of God's professing people do not only anger him, but grieve him, especially their distrust of him. See the patience of God towards provoking sinners; he was grieved with them forty years, and yet those years ended in a triumphant entrance into Canaan made by the next generation. The sentence passed upon them for their sin (*v.* 11). He *swore solemnly in his wrath*, his just and holy wrath. God is not subject to such passions as we are; but he is said to be angry at sin and sinners, to show the malignity of sin and the justice of God's government. *That they should not enter into his rest*, the rest which he had prepared for them, a settlement for them and theirs.

Now this case of Israel may be applied to those of their posterity that lived in David's time, when this psalm was penned. But it must be applied to us Christians, because so the apostle applies it. There is a spiritual and eternal rest set before us, and promised to us, of which Canaan was a type. Those that, like Israel, distrust God, will justly be shut out from his rest: they themselves have decided it, Heb. iv. 1.

JAMIESON, FAUSSET, BROWN

err in their heart—Their wanderings in the desert were but types of their innate ignorance and perverseness.

that they should not—lit., "if they . . . ," part of the form of swearing (cf. Num. 14:30; Ps. 89:35).

ADAM CLARKE

10. *Forty years long.* They did nothing but murmur, disbelieve, and rebel, from the time they began their journey at the Red Sea till they passed over Jordan, a period of *forty* years. *They have not known my ways.* The verb *yada*, "to know," is used here, as in many other parts of Scripture, to express approbation. They knew God's ways well enough, but they did not like them, and would not walk in them.

MATTHEW HENRY

PSALM 96

Verses 1–9

The call here given us to praise God is very lively.

I. We are here required to honour God,

1. With songs, *v.* 1, 2. Three times we are here called to *sing unto the Lord*; that is, "*Bless his name*, speak well of him, that you may bring others to think well of him." *Sing a new song*, the product of new affections. A new song is a song for new favours. A new song is a New Testament song, a song of praise for the new covenant and the precious privileges of that covenant. A new song is a song that shall be ever new. This is a prophecy of the calling of the Gentiles; all the earth shall have this *new song put into their mouths.* Let the subject-matter of this song be *his salvation*, the great salvation which was to be wrought out by the Lord Jesus.

2. With sermons (*v.* 3): *Declare his glory among the heathen*, even *his wonders among all people.* Salvation by Christ is here spoken of as a work of wonder. This salvation was, in the Old Testament times, as heaven's happiness is now, *a glory to be revealed.*

3. With religious services, *v.* 7–9. Hitherto, though in every nation those that feared God and wrought righteousness were accepted of him, yet instituted ordinances were the peculiarities of the Jewish religion. All the earth is here summoned to fear before the Lord, to worship him. The acts of devotion to God are here described. We must *give unto the Lord.* It is what must be paid, and, if not, will be recovered, and yet, if it come from holy love, God is pleased to accept it as a gift. We must *give unto the Lord the glory due unto his name.* We must *bring an offering into his courts.* We must bring ourselves in the first place, the *offering up of the Gentiles*, Rom. xv. 16. We must *worship him in the beauty of holiness*, with holy hearts, sanctified by the grace of God, devoted to the glory of God. All the acts of worship must be performed with a holy awe and reverence.

II. Glorious things are here said of him; *The Lord is great, and* therefore *greatly to be praised* (*v.* 4) and *to be feared.* Even the new song proclaims God great as well as good. He is great in his sovereignty over all that pretend to be deities; *feared above all gods*—all princes, who were often deified after their deaths. He is great in his right, even to the noblest part of the creation; for it is his own work and derives its being from him. *Splendour and majesty are before him*, in his immediate presence above, where the angels cover their faces, as unable to bear the dazzling lustre of his glory. *Strength and beauty are in his sanctuary*, both that above and this below. If we attend him in his sanctuary, we shall behold his beauty, for *God is love*, and experience his strength for *he is our rock.*

JAMIESON, FAUSSET, BROWN

PSALM 96

Vss. 1-13. The substance of this Psalm, and portions of the 97th, 98th, and 100th, are found in I Chronicles 16, which was used by David's directions in the dedication of the tabernacle on Mount Zion. The dispensation of the Messiah was typified by that event, involving, as it did, a more permanent seat of worship, and the introduction of additional and more spiritual services. Hence the language of these Psalms may be regarded as having a higher import than that pertinent to the occasion on which it was thus publicly used.

1-3. All nations are invited to unite in this most joyful praise. **new song**—lit., "fresh," or new mercies (Ps. 33:3; 40:3). **2. show forth**—lit., "declare joyful tidings." **salvation**—illustrates His glory in its wonders of love and mercy.

7-9. Give—or, ascribe (Ps. 29:1) due honor to Him, by acts of appointed and solemn worship in His house.

offering—of thanks. **beauty of holiness**—(Ps. 29:2.) **fear . . . him**—(Ps. 2:11.)

4, 5. For He is not a local God, but of universal agency, while idols are nothing.

6. Honour and majesty—are His attendants, declared in His mighty works, while power and grace are specially seen in His spiritual relations to His people.

ADAM CLARKE

PSALM 96

This psalm has no title, in either the Hebrew or Chaldee. We have seen in 1 Chron. xvi. 23-33 a psalm nearly like this, composed by David, on bringing the ark to Sion, from the house of Obed-edom. But the psalm, as it stands in the Chronicles, has thirty verses; and this is only a section of it, from the twenty-third to the thirty-third. It is very likely that this part was taken from the psalm above mentioned, to be used at the dedication of the second Temple. The one hundred and fifth psalm is almost the same as that in Chronicles, but much more extensive.

1. *Sing unto the Lord a new song.* A song of peculiar excellence, for in this sense the term *new* is repeatedly taken in the Scriptures.

2. *Shew forth his salvation from day to day.* The original is very emphatic, "Preach the gospel of His salvation from day to day."

3. *Declare his glory among the heathen.* The heathen do not know the true God; as His being and attributes are at the foundation of all religion, these are the first subjects of instruction for the Gentile world. *Declare,* "detail, number out" *his glory,* His "splendour and excellence." *His wonders among all people.* Declare also to the Jews His wonders, "his miracles."

8. *Come into his courts.* Probably referring to the second Temple.

9. *Worship the Lord in the beauty of holiness.* I think *behadrath kodesh* signifies "holy ornaments," such as the high priest wore in his ministrations. These were given him for glory and beauty; and the Psalmist calls on him to put on his sacerdotal garments, to bring his offering, *minchah,* and come into the courts of the Lord, and perform his functions, and make intercession for the people.

4. *He is to be feared above all gods.* I think the two clauses of this verse should be read thus: Jehovah is great, and greatly to be praised. Elohim is to be feared above all. I doubt whether the word *Elohim* is ever, by fair construction, applied to false gods or idols. The contracted form in the following verse appears to have this meaning.

5. *All the gods of the nations are idols. Elohey.* All those reputed or worshipped as gods among the heathens are *elilim,* "vanities, emptinesses, things of nought." Instead of being *Elohim,* they are *elilim;* they are not only not God, but they are nothing.

MATTHEW HENRY

Verses 10–13

Instructions given to those who were to preach the gospel to the nations.

I. Let it be told *that the Lord reigns,* the Lord Christ reigns, that King whom God determined to set upon his holy hill of Zion. See how this was first said *among the heathen* by Peter, Acts x. 42. Some of the ancients added a gloss to this, which by degrees crept into the text, *The Lord reigneth from the tree* (so Justin Martyr, Austin, and others, quote it), meaning the cross, when he had this title written over him, *The King of the Jews.*

II. Let it be told that Christ's government will be the world's happy settlement: *The world also shall be established, that it shall not be moved.* Sin had given it a shock, and still threatens it; but Christ, as Redeemer, upholds all things, and preserves the course of nature. The Christian religion, as far as it is embraced, shall establish states and kingdoms, and preserve good order among men.

III. Let them be told that Christ's government will be just and righteous, *v.* 13. He says himself, *For judgment have I come into this world* (John ix. 39, xii. 31), and declares that *all judgment was committed to him,* John v. 22, 27. He shall rule in the hearts and consciences of men by the commanding power of truth and the Spirit of righteousness and sanctification. When Pilate asked our Saviour, *Art thou a king?* he answered, *For this cause came I into the world, that I should bear witness unto the truth* (John xviii. 37).

IV. Let them be told that his coming draws nigh, that this King, this Judge, standeth before the door. Between this and his first coming the revolutions of many ages intervened, and yet he came at the set time, and so sure will his second coming be.

V. Let them be called upon to rejoice in the Messiah, and this great trust that is to be lodged in his hand (*v.* 11, 12): *Let heaven and earth rejoice, the sea, the field,* and *all the trees of the wood.* The meaning is, 1. That the days of the Messiah will be joyful days. When Samaria received the gospel *there was great joy in that city* (Acts viii. 8), and, when the eunuch was baptized, *he went on his way rejoicing, v.* 39. 2. That it is the duty of every one of us to bid Christ and his kingdom welcome; for, though he comes conquering and to conquer, yet he comes peaceably. 3. That the whole creation will have reason to rejoice in the setting up of Christ's kingdom, even *the sea* and *the field.* There will, in the first place, be *joy in heaven, joy in the presence of the angels of God.*

JAMIESON, FAUSSET, BROWN

10. Let all know that the government of the world is ordered in justice, and they shall enjoy firm and lasting peace (cf. Ps. 72:3, 7; Isa. 9:6, 7).

11-13. For which reason the universe is invoked to unite in joy, and even inanimate nature (Rom. 8:14-22) is poetically represented as capable of joining in the anthem of praise.

ADAM CLARKE

F. B. MEYER:

"Say among the nations, The Lord reigneth" (96:10). Tell it out! The message is too good to warrant silence. That the Lord is King is the secret of jubilation and blessing for all the world.

Nature is glad, because his rule will emancipate her from the thraldom under which she has groaned too long. When the kingdom is established in the hand of the Son of Man, the long travail of creation will be over; the new heavens and earth will have emerged. Therefore the psalmist depicts the outburst of thanksgiving from seas, and fields, and trees. The world of men may be glad also, because the reign of Jesus means equity for the oppressed, equal-handed justice for the poor, peace among the nations.

But, above all, gladness becomes the saints. If the Lord Jesus has become king of your heart, and has brought blessing to you, do not hesitate to give voice to your allegiance. In private, sing unto Him a new song; in public, show forth his salvation and declare his glory. Tell it out, tell it out! Have you ever seriously considered whether it may not be God's will for you to give up your life to going forth to distant lands, to tell it out that God has made Jesus King, and that He must reign, and that His reign is blessedness?

—Great Verses Through the Bible

11-13. The Psalmist here in the true spirit of poetry gives life and intelligence to universal nature, producing them all as exulting in the reign of the Messiah, and the happiness which should take place in the earth when the gospel should be universally preached.

MATTHEW HENRY

PSALM 97

Verses 1–7

What was to be said among the heathen in the foregoing psalm (*v.* 10) is here said again (*v.* 1) and is made the subject of this psalm, and of psalm xcix. *The Lord reigns;* that is the great truth here laid down. The Lord Jesus reigns.

I. *Let the earth rejoice,* for hereby it is *established* (xcvi. 10). Not only let the people of Israel rejoice in him as King of the Jews, and the daughter of Zion as her King, but let all the earth rejoice. *Let the multitude of isles,* the many or great isles, *be glad thereof.* All have reason to rejoice in Christ's government. Sometimes indeed *clouds and darkness are round about him;* his dispensations are altogether unaccountable; *his way is in the sea and his path in the great waters.* There is a depth in his counsels, which we must not pretend to fathom. But still *righteousness and judgment are the habitation of his throne;* a golden thread of justice runs through the whole web of his administration. In this he resides, for it is his habitation. In this he rules, for it is *the habitation of his throne. His commandments are,* and will be, *all righteous.* Who can contradict or dispute what the *heavens declare? All the people see his glory,* or may see it. The glory of God, in the face of Christ, was made to shine in distant countries. *Worship him, all you gods.* The words in Heb. i. 6, "*Let all the angels of God worship him,*" are a key to this whole psalm, and show us that it must be applied to the exalted Redeemer. All power is given him both in heaven and earth, *angels, authorities, and powers, being made subject unto him,* 1 Pet. iii. 22.

II. Christ's government, though it may be matter of joy to all, will yet be matter of terror to some, and it is their own fault that it is so, *v.* 3–5, 7. He that reigns, to the *joy of the whole earth,* yet, as he has his subjects, so he has *his enemies* (*v.* 3). These enemies are here called *hills* (*v.* 5), for their height, and strength, and immovable obstinacy. Their persecuting the apostles, and *forbidding them to speak*

JAMIESON, FAUSSET, BROWN

PSALM 97

Vss. 1-13. The writer celebrates the Lord's dominion over nations and nature, describes its effect on foes and friends, and exhorts and encourages the latter.

1-2. This dominion is a cause of joy, because, even though our minds are oppressed with terror before the throne of the King of kings (Exod. 19:16; Deut. 5:22), we know it is based on righteous principles and judgments which are according to truth.

6. heavens—or, their inhabitants (Ps. 50:6), as opposed to "nations" in the latter clause (cf. Isa. 40:5; 66:18).

3-5. The attending illustrations of God's awful justice on enemies (Ps. 83:14) are seen in the disclosures of His almighty power on the elements of nature (cf. Ps. 46:2; 77:17; Hab. 3:6, etc.).

ADAM CLARKE

The psalm has no title in either the Hebrew or Chaldee. The author of the Epistle to the Hebrews, chap. i. 6, quotes a part of the seventh verse of this psalm, and applies it to Christ. Who the author was is uncertain; it is much in the spirit of David's finest compositions, and yet

PSALM 97

many learned men suppose it was written to celebrate the Lord's power and goodness in the restoration of the Jews from the Babylonish captivity.

1. *The Lord reigneth.* Here is a simple proposition, which is a self-evident axiom, and requires no proof. Jehovah is infinite and eternal; is possessed of unlimited power and unerring wisdom, as He is the Maker, so He must be the Governor, of all things. His authority is absolute, and His government therefore universal. In all places, on all occasions, and in all times, Jehovah reigns.

2. *Clouds and darkness are round about him.* There must be *clouds and darkness*—an impenetrable obscurity—round about Him; and we can no more comprehend Him in the eternity that passed before time commenced than we can in the eternity that is to come, when time shall be no more.

Righteousness and judgment are the habitation of his throne. Righteousness, tsedek, the principle that acts according to justice and equity; that gives to all their due, and ever holds in all things an even balance. *And judgment, mishpat,* the principle that discerns, orders, directs, and determines everything according to truth and justice. These form *the habitation of his throne;* that is, His government and management of the world are according to these.

3. *A fire goeth before him. Fire* is generally represented as an accompaniment of the appear-

MATTHEW HENRY

to the Gentiles, filled up their sin, and brought *wrath upon them to the uttermost*, 1 Thess. ii. 15, 16. That wrath is here compared to consuming fire, which will not only burn the rubbish upon the hills, but will even *melt the hills* themselves *like wax*, *v.* 5. The most resolute and daring opposition will be baffled *at the presence of the Lord. The earth saw and trembled*, and the ears of all that heard were made to tingle. This was fulfilled in the destruction of Jerusalem and the Jewish nation by the Romans, about forty years after Christ's resurrection, which, like fire, and like lightning, astonished all their neighbours (Deut. xxix. 24). Idolaters also would be put to confusion by the setting up of Christ's kingdom (*v.* 7): *Confounded be all those who serve graven images*, the Gentile world, who *did service to those that by nature are no gods* (Gal. iv. 8). This is a prayer for the conversion of the Gentiles, that those who have been so long serving dumb idols may be convinced of their error, ashamed of their folly, and may, by the power of Christ's gospel, be brought to serve the only living and true God. The destruction of Paganism in the Roman empire was fulfilled about 300 years after Christ.

Verses 8–12

I. The reasons that are given for Zion's joy in the government of the Redeemer. God is glorified, and whatever redounds to his honour is his people's pleasure. *Thou, Lord, art high above all the earth* (*v.* 9). The exaltation of Christ, and the advancement of God's glory among men thereby, are the rejoicing of all the saints. *He preserves the souls of the saints;* he preserves their lives as long as he has any work for them to do. But something more is meant than their lives; for those that will be his disciples must be willing to lay down their lives. It is the *immortal soul* that Christ preserves, the *inward man*, which may be renewed more and more when the *outward man decays*. *Light is sown for the righteous*, that is, *gladness for the upright in heart*. The subjects of Christ's kingdom are told to expect tribulation in the world, yet let them know, to their comfort, that *light is sown* for them. What is sown will come up again in due time; though, like winter seed, it may lie long under the clods, yet it will return in a rich and plentiful increase. Christ told his disciples, at parting (John xvi. 20), *You shall be sorrowful, but your sorrow shall be turned into joy*.

II. The rules that are given for Zion's joy. Let it be a pure and holy joy. You that love the Lord Jesus, that *love his appearing* and kingdom, that love his word and his exaltation, see that you hate evil. A true love to God will show itself in a real hatred of all sin, as that abominable thing which he hates. Let the joy terminate in God (*v.* 12): *Rejoice in the Lord, you righteous*. All the lines of joy must meet in him as in the centre. See Phil. iii. 3; iv. 4. Let it express itself in praise and thanksgiving: *Give thanks at the remembrance of his holiness*.

JAMIESON, FAUSSET, BROWN

7. Idolaters are utterly put to shame, for if angels must worship Him, how much more those who worshipped them. **all ye gods**—lit., "all ye angels" (Ps. 8:5; 138:1; Heb. 1:6, 2:7). Paul quotes, not as a prophecy, but as language used in regard to the Lord Jehovah, who in the Old Testament *theophania* is the second person of the Godhead.

8, 9. The exaltation of Zion's king is joy to the righteous and sorrow to the wicked. **daughters of Judah**—(Cf. Ps. 48:11). **above all gods**—(Ps. 95:3).

10-13. Let gratitude for the blessings of providence and grace incite saints (Ps. 4:3) to holy living. Spiritual blessings are in store, represented by light (Ps. 27:1) and gladness. **sown**—to spring forth abundantly for such, who alone can and well may rejoice in the holy government of their sovereign Lord (cf. Ps. 30:4; 32:11).

ADAM CLARKE

ances of the Supreme Being. He appeared on Mount Sinai in the midst of fire, thunder, and lightnings, Exod. xix. 16-18. St. Paul tells us (2 Thess. i. 7-8) that "the Lord Jesus shall be revealed from heaven with His mighty angels, in flaming fire"; and St. Peter (2 Epist. iii. 7, 10-11), that when the Lord shall come to judgment the heavens and the earth shall be destroyed by fire.

5. *The Lord of the whole earth. Adon col haarets*, the Director, Stay, and Support of the whole earth.

7. *Confounded be all they*. Rather, "They shall be confounded that boast themselves in idols." *Worship him*. Who? Jesus; so says the apostle, Heb. i. 6. *All ye gods*. "His angels"; so the Septuagint and the apostle: "Let all the angels of God worship him." And the words are most certainly applied to the Saviour of the world by the author of the Epistle to the Hebrews.

8. *Zion heard, and was glad*. All the land of Israel, long desolated, heard of the judgments which God had shown among the enemies of His people. *And the daughters of Judah*. All the villages of the land—Zion as the mother, and all the villages in the country as her *daughters*—rejoice in the deliverance of God's people.

10. *Ye that love the Lord, hate evil*. Because it is inconsistent with His love to you, as well as your love to Him. *He preserveth the souls of his saints*. The *saints, chasidaiv*, "His merciful people"; their *souls*, lives, are precious in his sight. He preserves them; keeps them from every evil, and every enemy.

12. *Rejoice in the Lord, ye righteous*. It is your privilege to be happy. Exult in Him through whom ye have received the atonement. *Rejoice;* but let it be *in the Lord*. *At the remembrance of his holiness*. But why should you give thanks at the remembrance that God is holy? Because He has said, "Be ye holy; for I am holy"; and in holiness alone true happiness is to be found.

MATTHEW HENRY

PSALM 98

Verses 1–3

A song of praise for redeeming love is a *new song*. Converts sing a *new song*; they change their wonder and change their joy, and therefore change their note.

I. The wonders he has wrought: *He has done marvellous things*, *v.* 1. The work of our salvation by Christ is a work of wonder. The more it is known the more it will be admired.

II. The conquests he has won: *His right hand and his holy arm have gotten him the victory*. Our Redeemer has surmounted all the difficulties that lay in the way of our redemption. He got his victory by his own power.

III. The discoveries he has made to the world of the work of redemption. What he has wrought for us he has revealed to us, and both by his Son; the gospel-revelation is that on which the gospel-kingdom is founded—*the word which God sent*, Acts x. 36.

IV. The accomplishment of the prophecies and promises of the Old Testament. God is said, in sending Christ, to *perform the mercy promised to our fathers, and to remember the holy covenant*, Luke i. 72. It was in consideration of that, and not of their merit.

Verses 4–9

The setting up of the kingdom of Christ is here represented as a matter of joy and praise.

I. Let all the children of men rejoice in it, for they all have, or may have, benefit by it. Again and again we are here called upon by all ways and means possible to express our joy in it and give God praise for it. Let sacred songs attend the new King. Let these be

JAMIESON, FAUSSET, BROWN

PSALM 98

Vss. 1-9. In view of the wonders of grace and righteousness displayed in God's salvation, the whole creation is invited to unite in praise.

1. gotten . . . victory—lit., "made salvation," enabled Him to save His people. **right hand, and . . . arm**—denote power. **holy arm**—or, arm of holiness, the power of His united moral perfections (Ps. 22:3; 32:11). **2. salvation**—the result of His **righteousness** (Ps. 7:17; 31:1, and both are publicly displayed.

3. The union of **mercy** and **truth** (Ps. 57:3; 85:10) secure the blessings of the promise (Gen. 12:3; 18:18) to all the world (Isa. 52:10).

ADAM CLARKE

PSALM 98

In the Hebrew this is simply termed *mizmor*, "a psalm." The psalm in its subject is very like the ninety-sixth. It was probably written to celebrate the deliverance from the Babylonish captivity, but is to be understood prophetically of the redemption of the world by Jesus Christ.

1. *A new song*. "A song of excellence." Give Him the highest praise. See on Ps. xcvi. 1. *Hath done marvellous things*. "Miracles"; the same word as in Ps. xcvi. 3, where we translate it "wonders." *His holy arm*. His almighty power. *Hath gotten him the victory*. "Hath made salvation to himself."

2. *Made known his salvation*. He has delivered His people in such a way as to show that it was supernatural, and that their confidence in the unseen God was not in vain.

3. *He hath remembered his mercy*. His gracious promises to their forefathers. *And his truth*. Faithfully accomplishing what He had promised. All this was fulfilled under the gospel.

5. *With . . . the voice of a psalm*. I think *zimrah*, which we translate "psalm," means either a musical instrument or a species of ode modulated by different voices.

MATTHEW HENRY

music, not only with the soft and gentle melody of *the harp*, but since it is a victorious King whose glory is to be celebrated, let him be proclaimed with the martial sound of the *trumpet* and *cornet*, *v.* 6.

II. Let the inferior creatures rejoice in it, *v.* 7–9. This is to the same purport with what we had before (xcvi. 11–13): *Let the sea roar*, and let that be called, not as it used to be, a *dreadful noise*, but a *joyful noise*; for the coming of Christ, and the salvation wrought out by him, have quite altered the property of the troubles and terrors of this world, so that when the floods *lift up their voice*, *lift up their waves*, we must not construe that to be the sea roaring against us, but rather rejoicing with us. One would think that Virgil had these psalms in his eye, as well as the oracles of the Cumean Sibyl, in his fourth eclogue, where he either ignorantly or basely applies to Asinius Pollio the ancient prophecies, which at that time were expected to be fulfilled; for he lived in the reign of Augustus Caesar, a little before our Saviour's birth. He owns they looked for the birth of a child from heaven that should be a great blessing to the world, and restore the golden age:—

A new race descends from the lofty sky;
Thy influence shall efface every stain of corruption,
And free the world from alarm.

Many other things he says of this long-looked-for child, which Ludovicus Vives thinks applicable to Christ; and he concludes, as the psalmist here, with a prospect of the rejoicing of the whole creation herein:

See how this promis'd age makes all rejoice.

And, if all rejoice, why should not we?

PSALM 99

Verses 1–5

The foundation of all religion is laid in this truth, That *the Lord reigns*. God governs the world by his providence, governs the church by his grace, and both by his Son. We are to believe not only that *the Lord lives*, but that *the Lord reigns*. This is the triumph of the Christian church, and here it was the triumph of the Jewish church, that Jehovah was their King; and hence it is inferred, *Let the people tremble*. The Old Testament dispensation had much of terror in it. But we are not now come to *that mount that burned with fire*, Heb. xii. 18. Now that *the Lord reigns let the earth rejoice*. Then he ruled more by the power of holy fear; now he rules by the power of holy love. *The Lord reigns, let the earth be moved*. Those that submit to him shall be established, and not *moved* (xcvi. 10); but those that oppose him will be moved. The kingdom of Christ cannot be moved; the *things which cannot be shaken shall remain*, Heb. xii. 27. *In these is continuance*, Isa. lxiv. 5.

God's kingdom, set up in Israel, is here the subject of the psalmist's praise.

I. Two things the psalmist affirms:—1. God presided in the affairs of religion: *He sitteth between the cherubim* (*v.* 1), to give law by the oracles thence delivered. This was the honour of Israel, that they had among them the Shechinah, or special presence of God. *The Lord is great in Zion* (*v.* 2); there he is known and praised (lxxvi. 1, 2). *He is high* there *above all people*; so in Zion the perfections of the divine nature appear more illustrious than anywhere else. Therefore *let those* that dwell in Zion, and worship there, *praise thy great and terrible name, for it is holy*. 2. He was all in all in their civil government, *v.* 4. As in Jerusalem was the testimony of Israel, so *there were set thrones of judgment*, cxxii. 4, 5. Their government was a theocracy. God raised up David to rule over them. and he is *the king* whose *strength loves judgment*. He is strong; all his strength he has from God. The people of Israel had a good king; but they are here taught to look up to God as he by whom their king reigns: *Thou dost establish equity* (that is, God gave them those excellent laws by which they were governed), and *thou executest judgment and righteousness in Jacob*.

II. Putting these two things together, we see what was the happiness of Israel above any other people (*v.* 5): "*Exalt you the Lord our God, and worship at his footstool;* give him the glory of the good government you are under, as it is now established, both in church and state."

Verses 6–9

The happiness of Israel in God's government is here further made out by some particular instances of his administration, especially with reference to those that were the most useful governors of that

JAMIESON, FAUSSET, BROWN

4-6 make a loud noise—or, burst forth (Isa. 14:7; 44:23). **before . . . King**—hail Him as your sovereign; and while, with every aid to demonstrate zeal and joy, intelligent creatures are invited to praise, as in Psalm 96:11-13, inanimate nature is also summoned to honor Him who triumphs and rules in righteousness and equity.

PSALM 99

Vss. 1-9. God's government is especially exercised in and for His Church, which should praise Him for His gracious dealings.

tremble . . . be moved—inspired with fear by His judgments on the wicked.

1. sitteth . . . cherubim—(cf. I Sam. 4:4; Ps. 80:1).

2. great in Zion—where He dwells (Ps. 9:11).

3. thy . . . name—perfections of justice, power, etc. **great and terrible**—producing dread (Deut. 10:17), and to be praised by those over whom He is exalted (Ps. 97:9). **it is holy**—or, He is holy (vss. 5, 9; Isa. 6:3). **4, 5.** To His wise and righteous government all nations should render honor. **king's . . . judgment**—His power is combined with justice. **he is holy**—(cf. Ps. 22:3).

ADAM CLARKE

6. *With trumpets.* Some kind of tubular instruments, of the form and management of which we know nothing. *And sound of cornet. Shophar*, the word commonly used for what we call "trumpet."

7. *Let the sea roar.* These are either fine poetic images or, if we take them as referring to the promulgation of the gospel, by *the sea* all maritime countries and commercial nations may be intended.

8. *Let the floods clap their hands.* Properly "the rivers"—possibly meaning immense continents, where only large rivers are found.

9. *For he cometh to judge the earth.* He comes to make known His salvation, and show His merciful designs to all the children of men. *With righteousness shall he judge the world.* See the notes on Psalm xcvi. There is a very great similarity between this psalm and the Magnificat of the Blessed Virgin.

PSALM 99

The Hebrew and Chaldee have no title; all the versions but the Chaldee attribute it to David.

1. *The Lord reigneth.* See the note on Ps. xcvii. 1.

Let the people tremble. He will establish His kingdom in spite of His enemies; let those who oppose Him tremble for the consequences.

He sitteth between the cherubims. This is in reference to the ark, at each end of which was a cherub of glory; and the Shechinah, or symbol of the Divine Presence, appeared on the lid of the ark, called also the "mercy seat," between the cherubim. Sitting between the cherubim implies God's graciousness and mercy.

2. *The Lord is great in Zion.* It is among His own worshippers that He has manifested His power and glory in an especial manner. There He is known, and there He is worthily magnified.

3. *Let them praise thy great and terrible name.* Let them confess Thee to be great and terrible; let them tremble before Thee. *For it is holy. Kadosh hu.* As this not only ends this verse but the fifth also, and in effect the ninth, it seems to be a species of chorus which was sung in a very solemn manner at the conclusion of each of these parts. His holiness—reason why He should be exalted, praised, and worshipped.

4. *The king's strength.* If this psalm were written by David, he must mean by it that he was God's vicegerent or deputy, and that, even as king, God was his Strength, and the Pattern according to which equity, judgment, and righteousness should be executed in Jacob.

5. *Worship at his footstool.* Probably meaning the ark on which the divine glory was manifested. Sometimes the earth is called God's footstool, Matt. v. 35; Isa. lxvi. 1; sometimes Jerusalem; sometimes the Temple, Lam. ii. 1; sometimes the Tabernacle, Ps. xxxii. 7; and sometimes the ark, 1 Chron. xxviii. 2.

MATTHEW HENRY

people—Moses, Aaron, and Samuel, in the two former of whom the theocracy or divine government began, and in the last of whom that form of government, in a great measure, ended.

I. The intimate communion they had with God. None of all the nations of the earth could produce three such men as these, that had such an intercourse with Heaven, and whom God *knew by name*, Exod. xxxiii. 17. Samuel, though not among his priests, yet was *among those that called on his name*; and for *this* they were all famous, *They called upon the Lord*. By their obedience: *They kept his testimonies, and the ordinances that he gave them;* they made conscience of their duty. Moses did all according to the pattern shown him; it is often repeated, *According to all that God commanded Moses, so did he*. Aaron and Samuel did likewise. They all wonderfully prevailed with God in prayer; miracles were wrought at their special instance and request. He communed with them as one friend familiarly converses with another (*v.* 7).

II. The good offices they did to Israel. They interceded for the people, and for them also they obtained many an answer of peace. *Moses stood in the gap*, and *Aaron between the living and the dead*; and, when Israel was in distress, Samuel cried unto the Lord for them, 1 Sam. vii. 9. This is here referred to (*v.* 8): "*Thou answeredst them, O Lord our God! thou wast a God that forgavest*" the people they prayed for. The people are again called upon to praise God (*v.* 9): "*Exalt the Lord our God*, on account of what he has done for us formerly, as well as of late, *and worship at his holy hill* of Zion."

JAMIESON, FAUSSET, BROWN

6-8. The experience of these servants of God is cited for encouragement. **among . . . priests, among . . . upon the Lord** [and] **He spake . . . pillar**—may be referred to all three (cf. Exod. 18:19; Lev. 8:15; Deut. 5:5; I Sam. 9:13). **cloudy pillar**—the medium of divine intercourse (Exod. 33:9; Num. 12:5). Obedience was united with worship. God answered them as intercessors for the people, who, though forgiven, were yet chastened (Exod. 32:10, 34).

ADAM CLARKE

7. *He spake unto them in the cloudy pillar*. That is, He directed all their operations, marchings, and encampments by this cloudy pillar. See Exod. xxxiii. 9.

8. *Thou . . . forgavest them*. When the people had sinned, and wrath was about to descend on them, Moses and Aaron interceded for them, and they were not destroyed. *Tookest vengeance of their inventions*. God spared them, but showed his displeasure at their misdoings. He chastised, but did not consume them. This is amply proved in the history of this people.

9. *Worship at his holy hill*. Worship Him publicly in the Temple.

MATTHEW HENRY

PSALM 100

Verses 1–5

The psalm does indeed answer to the title, *A psalm of praise*. If we take the foregoing psalm to be a call to the Jewish church to rejoice in the administration of God's kingdom, which they were under (as the four psalms before it were calculated for the days of the Messiah), this psalm, perhaps, was intended for proselytes, that came over out of all lands to the Jews' religion.

I. A strong invitation to worship God. In all acts of religious worship, whether in secret or in our families, we come into God's presence, and serve him; but it is in public worship especially that we *enter into his gates and into his courts. Serve the Lord with gladness*. By holy joy we do really serve God. Gospel-worshippers should be joyful worshippers. We must *come before his presence with singing*, not only songs of joy, but songs of praise. *Enter into his gates with thanksgiving, v.* 4. We must take it as a favour to be admitted into his service, and that we have ordinances instituted and opportunity continued of waiting upon God in those ordinances.

II. The matter of praise, and motives to it, are very important, *v.* 3, 5. Know you what God is in himself and what he is to you. Knowledge is the mother of devotion and of all obedience: blind sacrifices will never please a seeing God. Let us know then these six things concerning the Lord Jehovah:—1. *That the Lord he is God*, the only living and true God—that he is a Being infinitely perfect, self-existent, and self-sufficient, and the fountain of all being. He is an eternal Spirit, incomprehensible and independent, the first cause and last end. 2. That he is our Creator: *It is he that has made us, and not we ourselves*. He gave us being, he gave us this being; he is both the former of our bodies and the Father of our spirits. We did not, we could not, make ourselves. 3. That therefore he is our rightful owner. The Masorites, by altering one letter in the Hebrew, read it, *He made us, and his we are*, or *to him we belong*. Put both the readings together, and we learn that because God *made us, and not we ourselves*, therefore we are not our own, but his. 4. That he is our sovereign ruler: *We are his people*. 5. That he is our bountiful benefactor. We are *the sheep of his pasture*, whom he takes care of; the *flock of his feeding* (so it may be read). 6. That he is a God of infinite mercy and goodness (*v.* 5).

JAMIESON, FAUSSET, BROWN

PSALM 100

Vss. 1-5. As closing this series (cf. on Ps. 94), this Psalm is a general call on all the earth to render exalted praise to God, the creator, preserver, and benefactor of men.

1, 2. With thankful praise, unite service as the subjects of a king (Ps. 2:11, 12).

3. To the obligations of a creature and subject is added that of a beneficiary (Ps. 95:7).

4. Join joyfully in His public worship. The terms are, of course, figurative (cf. Ps. 84:2; 92:13; Isa. 66:23). **Enter**—or, Come with solemnity (Ps. 95:6).

5. The reason: God's eternal mercy and truth (Ps. 25:8; 89:7).

ADAM CLARKE

PSALM 100

This psalm is entitled in the Hebrew *mizmor lethodah*, not "A Psalm of praise," as we have it, but "A Psalm for the confession, or for the confession offering," very properly translated by the Chaldee: "Praise for the sacrifice (or offering) of confession." The Vulgate, Septuagint, and Aethiopic have followed this sense.

1. *Make a joyful noise. Hariu*, "exult, triumph, leap for joy." *All ye lands*. Not only Jews, but Gentiles, for the Lord bestows His benefits on all with a liberal hand.

2. *Serve the Lord with gladness*. It is your privilege and duty to be happy in your religious worship. The religion of the true God is intended to remove human misery, and to make mankind happy. He whom the religion of Christ has not made happy does not understand that religion, or does not make a proper use of it.

3. *Know ye that the Lord he is God*. Acknowledge in every possible way, in both public and private, that Jehovah, the uncreated, self-existent, and eternal Being, is *Elohim*, the God who is in covenant with man, to instruct, redeem, love, and make him finally happy. *It is he that hath made us*. He is our Creator and has consequently the only right in and over us. *And not we ourselves*. I can never think that this is the true reading, though found in the present Hebrew text, in the Vulgate, Septuagint, Aethiopic, and Syriac. In twenty-six of Kennicott's and De Rossi's MSS. we have "and his we are." This is the reading of the Targum, or Chaldee paraphrase, "and his we are," and is the reading of the text in the Complutensian Polyglot, of both the Psalters which were printed in 1477, and is the *keri*, or marginal reading in most Masoretic Bibles. Every person must see, from the nature of the subject, that it is the genuine reading.

4. *Enter into his gates with thanksgiving*. Publicly worship God; and when ye come to the house of prayer, be thankful that you have such a privilege; and when you *enter his courts*, praise Him for the permission. The word which we render *with thanksgiving* is properly "with the confession offering or sacrifice."

5. *For the Lord is good*. Goodness, the perfect, eternal opposition to all badness and evil, is essential to God. Mercy and compassion are modifications of His goodness; and as His nature is eternal, so His mercy, springing from His goodness, must be everlasting. And as truth is an essential characteristic of an infinitely intelligent and perfect nature, therefore God's truth must endure from generation to generation. Whatsoever He has promised must be fulfilled, through all the successive generations of men, as long as sun and moon shall last.

MATTHEW HENRY

PSALM 101

Verses 1–8

David here cuts out to himself and others a pattern both of a good magistrate and a good master of a family.

I. The chosen subject of the psalm (*v.* 1): *I will sing of mercy and judgment*, that is, David since he was first anointed to be king, had met with many a rebuke and much hardship on the one hand, and yet, on the other hand, had had many wonderful deliverances wrought for him and favours bestowed upon him; of these he will sing unto God. God's providences concerning his people are commonly mixed —*mercy and judgment;* God has set the one over-against the other, and appointed them April-days, showers and sunshine. Whatever our outward condition neither the laughter of a prosperous condition nor the tears of an afflicted condition must put us out of tune for sacred songs. It may be understood of David's mercy and judgment; he would, in this psalm, promise to be merciful, and just. Family-mercies and family-afflictions are both of them calls to family-religion.

II. The general resolution David took up to conduct himself carefully and conscientiously in his court, *v.* 2. We have here,

1. A good purpose concerning his conversation; he would live by rule. In his family particularly, he would *walk within his house*, where he was more out of the eye of the world, but where he still saw himself under the eye of God. He resolves to *walk in a perfect way*, in the way of God's commandments. *I will behave myself wisely.*

2. A good prayer: *O when wilt thou come unto me?* It is a desirable thing, when a man has a house of his own, to have God come to him and dwell with him in it. David, as he purposed, *behaved himself wisely in all his ways; and*, as he prayed, *the Lord was with him.*

III. His particular resolution to practise no evil himself (*v.* 3): "*I will set no wicked thing before my eyes;* I will not design nor aim at anything but what is for the glory of God and the public welfare."

IV. His further resolution not to keep bad servants, nor to employ those about him that were vicious. He will have nothing to do with spiteful malicious people, who care not what mischief they do to those they have a pique against (*v.* 4): "*A froward heart* (one that delights to be cross and perverse) *shall depart from me*, as not fit for society, the bond of which is love, *I will not know*." "*Whoso privily slanders his neighbour*, either raises or spreads false stories, to the prejudice of his good name, *him will I cut off* from my family and court." David will prevent the preferment of those that hope to curry favour with him. "Therefore him *that has a high look and a proud heart will I not suffer*; I will have no patience with those that are still grasping at all preferments, for it is certain that they do not aim at doing good, but only at aggrandizing themselves and their families." God resists the proud, and so will David. "*He that worketh deceit*, though he may insinuate himself into my family, yet, as soon as he is discovered, *shall not dwell within my house*." David will make use of no such persons as agents for him.

V. His resolution to put those in trust under him that were honest and good (*v.* 6): *My eyes shall be upon the faithful in the land.* The kingdom must be searched for honest men to make courtiers of; and, if any man is better than another, he must be preferred. Saul chose servants for their goodliness (1 Sam. viii. 16), but David for their goodness.

VI. His resolution to extend his zeal to the reformation of the city and country, as well as of the court (*v.* 8). He would be forward and zealous in promoting the reformation of manners and suppression of vice. That which he aimed at was not only the securing of his own government and the peace of the country, but the honour of God in the purity of his church, *That I may cut off all wicked doers from the city of the Lord.*

PSALM 102

A prayer of the afflicted, when he is overwhelmed, and poureth out his complaint before the Lord.

Verses 1–11

The title of this psalm is *a prayer of the afflicted.* Here is a prayer put into the hands of the afflicted: let them set, not their hands, but their hearts to it, and present it to God. When our state and our spirits are overwhelmed, it is our duty by prayer to *pour out our complaints before the Lord*, which intimates the leave God gives us to be free with him and the

JAMIESON, FAUSSET, BROWN

PSALM 101

Vss. 1-8. In this Psalm the profession of the principles of his domestic and political government testifies, as well as actions in accordance with it, David's appreciation of God's mercy to him, and His judgment on his enemies: and thus he sings or celebrates God's dealings.

2. He avows his sincere purpose, by God's aid, to act uprightly (Gen. 17:1; Ps. 18:30).

3. set . . . eyes—as an example to be approved and followed. **no wicked thing**—lit., "word," plan or purpose of Belial (Ps. 41:8). **work of . . . aside**—apostates. **not cleave to me**—I will not be implicated in it (cf. Ps. 1:1-3).

4. A froward [or, perverse] **heart**—(Ps. 18:26). Such a temper I will not indulge, nor even know evil or wickedness.

7. not dwell—lit., "not sit," or tarry, or be established.

5, 6. The slanderers and haughty persons, so mischievous in society, I will disown; but—**Mine eyes . . . upon**—or, I will select reliable and honest men for my servants.

8. will early—or, diligently. **city of the Lord**—or, holy place (Ps. 48:2), where wicked men shall not be tolerated.

PSALM 102

Vss. 1-28. *A prayer of the afflicted . . .*—The general terms seem to denote the propriety of regarding the Psalm as suitably expressive of the anxieties of any one of David's descendants, piously concerned for the welfare of the Church. It was probably David's composition, and, though specially suggested by some peculiar trials, descriptive of fu-

ADAM CLARKE

PSALM 101

The Hebrew and all the versions attribute this psalm to David. It shows us the resolutions he formed when he came to the throne, and it is a perfect model according to which a wise prince should regulate his conduct and his government.

1. *I will sing of mercy and judgment.* David might say, Adverse and prosperous providences have been of the utmost use to my soul; therefore I will thank God for both. Or, as he was probably now called to the government of all the tribes, he might make a resolution that he would show *chesed*, incessant benevolence, to the upright; and *mishpat*, the execution of judgment, to the wicked; and would make the conduct of God the model of his own.

2. *I will behave myself wisely.* God's law prescribes a perfect way of life; in this perfect way I have professed to walk, and I must act wisely in order to walk in it. *When wilt thou come unto me?* I can neither walk in this way nor grow wise unto salvation unless Thou come unto me by Thy grace and Spirit. *I will walk within my house.* It is easier for most men to walk with a perfect heart in the church, or even in the world, than in their own families. How many are as meek as lambs among others, when at home they are wasps or tigers! The man who, in the midst of family provocations, maintains a Christian character, being meek, gentle, and long-suffering to his wife, his children, and his servants, has got a perfect heart, and adorns the doctrine of God his Saviour in all things. The original is very emphatic: "I will set myself to walk"; I will make it a determined point thus to walk.

4. *A froward heart.* Rash and headstrong men shall not be employed by me. *I will not know a wicked person.* I will give no countenance to sinners of any kind, and whatever is *evil* shall be an object of my abhorrence.

5. *Whoso privily slandereth his neighbour.* The Chaldee gives a remarkable meaning to the Hebrew, "He who speaks with the triple tongue against his neighbour." That is, the tongue by which he slays three persons, viz., (1) The man whom he slanders; (2) Him to whom he communicates the slander; and, (3) Himself, the slanderer. Every slanderer has his triple tongue, and by every slander inflicts those three deadly wounds. Such a person deserves to be *cut off.*

6. *Mine eyes.* My approbation. *Upon the faithful.* The humble, upright followers of God. *That they may dwell with me.* Be my confidants and privy counsellors.

PSALM 102

The Hebrew, and nearly all the versions, give the following title to this psalm: "A prayer of the afflicted, when he is overwhelmed, and pours out his sighing before the Lord." There seems to be little doubt that this is the prayer of the captives in Babylon when, towards the end of the Captivity, they were almost worn out with

MATTHEW HENRY

liberty of speech we have before him. It intimates also what an ease it is to an afflicted spirit to unburden itself by a humble representation of its grievances and griefs.

I. The psalmist humbly begs of God to take notice of his affliction, and of his prayer in his affliction, *v.* 1, 2. Let us *lift up the prayer*, and our souls with it. If we put up a *prayer in faith*, we may in faith say, *Hear my prayer, O Lord!* "Manifest thyself for me; not only hear me, but answer me; grant me the deliverance I am in want of and in pursuit of; answer me speedily, even *in the day when I call.*"

II. He makes a lamentable complaint of the low condition to which he was reduced by his afflictions. His body was emaciated. As prosperity and joy are represented by *making fat the bones*, so great trouble and grief are here represented by the contrary: *My bones are burnt as a hearth* (*v.* 3); they *cleave to my skin* (*v.* 5); nay, *my heart is smitten, and withered like grass* (*v.* 4). *I am withered like grass* (*v.* 11), scorched with the burning heat of my troubles. He was so taken up with the thoughts of his troubles that he *forgot to eat his bread* (*v.* 4); he had no appetite. He affected solitude, as melancholy people do. His friends deserted him and were shy of him (*v.* 6, 7): "*I am like a pelican of the wilderness*, or a *bittern* (so some) that makes a doleful noise; *I am like an owl*, that affects to lodge in deserted ruined buildings; *I watch, and am as a sparrow upon the house-top.* I live in a garret, and there spend my hours in poring on my troubles and bemoaning myself." When his friends went off from him his foes set themselves against him (*v.* 8). When they could not otherwise reach him they shot arrows at him, even *bitter words*. He fasted and wept under the tokens of God's displeasure (*v.* 9, 10). It was not so much the trouble itself that troubled him as the wrath of God which he was under the apprehensions of as the cause of the trouble. *My days are consumed like smoke* (*v.* 3), which vanishes away quickly. They are *like a shadow that declines* (*v.* 11), like the evening-shadow. Now all this is properly a prayer for a particular person afflicted, yet is supposed to be a description of the afflictions of the church of God, with which the psalmist sympathizes, making public grievances his own.

Verses 12–22

Many exceedingly great and precious comforts are here to balance the foregoing complaints; for *unto the upright there arises light in the darkness.*

I. We are dying creatures, and our interests and comforts are dying, but God is an everliving everlasting God (*v.* 12): "*My days are like a shadow;* there is no remedy; night is coming upon me; but, *thou, O Lord! shalt endure for ever.*" God *endures for ever*, his church's faithful protector; and we may be confident that they shall not be neglected.

II. Poor Zion is now in distress, but there will come a time for her relief and succour (*v.* 13). The hope of deliverance is built upon the goodness of God and upon the power of God. There is a time set for the deliverance of the church, which will come at the time which Infinite Wisdom has appointed (and therefore it is the best time) and which Eternal Truth has fixed it to, and therefore it is a certain time, and shall not be forgotten nor further adjourned. Zion was now in ruins, that is, the temple that was built in the city of David: the favouring of Zion is the building of the temple up again, as it is explained, *v.* 16. *Thy servants take pleasure* even in *the stones* of the temple, though they were thrown down and scattered, and *favour the dust*, the very rubbish and ruins of it, *v.* 14. When the temple was ruined, yet the stones of it were to be had for a new building, and there were those who encouraged themselves with that. *The heathen shall fear the name of the Lord*, shall have better thoughts of the church of God than they have had, when God by his providence thus puts an honour upon it. They shall say, We will go with you, for we have *seen that God is with you*, Zech. viii. 23. All that have made his glory their highest end desire it and pray for it.

III. The prayers of God's people now seem to be slighted and no notice taken of them, but they will be reviewed and greatly encouraged (*v.* 17): *He will regard the prayer of the destitute.* They are the *destitute*. It is an elegant word that is here used, which signifies the heath in the wilderness, a low shrub, or bush, like the hyssop of the wall. They are in a low and broken state, enriched with spiritual blessings, but destitute of temporal good things. When we consider our own meanness, our darkness and deadness, and the manifold defects in our prayers, we have cause to suspect that our prayers will be received with disdain in heaven; but we are here assured of the contrary, for we have an advocate with the

JAMIESON, FAUSSET, BROWN

ture times. *overwhelmed*—(cf. Ps. 61:2). *complaint*—(Ps. 55:2). *pouring out the soul*—(Ps. 62:8). The tone of complaint predominates, though in view of God's promises and abiding faithfulness, it is sometimes exchanged for that of confidence and hope.

1-3. The terms used occur in Psalms 4:1; 17:1, 6; 18:6; 31:2, 10; 37:20.

4. (Cf. Ps. 121:6.) **so that I forget**—or, have forgotten, i.e., in my distress (Ps. 107:18), and hence strength fails. **5. voice . . . groaning**—effect put for cause, my agony emaciates me.

6, 7. The figures express extreme loneliness.

8. sworn against me—or lit., "by me," wishing others as miserable as I am (Num. 5:21).

9. ashes—a figure of grief, my bread; weeping or tears, my drink (Ps. 80:5). **10. lifted . . . cast me down**—or, cast me away as stubble by a whirlwind (Isa. 64:6). **11. shadow . . . declineth**—soon to vanish in the darkness of night.

12. Contrast with man's frailty (cf. Ps. 90:1-7). **thy remembrance**—that by which Thou art remembered, Thy promise.

13, 14. Hence it is here adduced. **for** [or, "when"] **. . . the set time . . .**—the time promised, the indication of which is the interest felt for Zion by the people of God.

15-17. God's favor to the Church will affect her persecutors with fear. **When the Lord shall build**—or better, *Because* the Lord hath built, etc., as a reason for the effect on others; for in thus acting and hearing the humble, He is most glorious.

ADAM CLARKE

oppression, cruelty, and distress. The author of the Epistle to the Hebrews has applied the twenty-fifth, twenty-sixth, and twenty-seventh verses to our Lord, and the perpetuity of His kingdom.

1. *Hear my prayer.* The chief parts of the psalm answer well to the title; it is the language of the deepest distress, and well directed to Him from whom alone help can come.

3. *My days are consumed like smoke.* He represents himself (for the Psalmist speaks in the name of the people) under the notion of a pile of combustible matter, placed upon a fire, which soon consumes it, part flying away in smoke, and the residue lying on the hearth in the form of charred coal and ashes. The Chaldeans were the fire, and the captive Jews the fuel, thus converted into smoke and ashes.

4. *My heart is smitten, and withered like grass.* The metaphor here is taken from grass cut down in the meadow. It is first *smitten* with the scythe, and then *withered* by the sun.

6. *I am like a pelican of the wilderness.* It may be the pelican or the bittern. The original, *kaath*, is mentioned in Lev. xi. 18, and is there described.

8. *They that are mad against me are sworn against me.* The Chaldeans are determined to destroy us, and they have bound themselves by oath to do it.

11. *My days are like a shadow that declineth.* Or rather, "My days decline like the shadow."

13. *Thou shalt arise, and have mercy upon Zion.* While he is humbled at the footstool of mercy, and earnestly praying for mercy, an answer of peace is given. He is assured, not only that they shall be delivered, but that the time of deliverance is at hand. The *set time*—the seventy years predicted by Jeremiah—was ended, and God gave him to see that He was ever mindful of His promises.

14. *Thy servants take pleasure in her stones.* Though Jerusalem was at this time in a heap of ruins, yet even her rubbish was sacred in the eyes of the pious, for this had been the city of the great King.

17. *The prayer of the destitute. Haarar* of him who is laid in utter ruin, who is entirely wasted.

MATTHEW HENRY

Father, and are under grace, not under the law. *This shall be written for the generation to come, that none may despair*, though they be destitute, nor think their prayers forgotten because they have not an answer to them immediately. Many that are now unborn, shall, by reading the history of the church, praise the Lord for his answers to prayer.

IV. The prisoners under condemnation unjustly seem as sheep appointed for the slaughter, but care shall be taken for their discharge (*v.* 19, 20): God has *looked down from the height of his sanctuary, from heaven*, to do acts of grace, *to hear the groaning of the prisoners, to loose those that are appointed to death.* God takes notice not only of the prayers of his afflicted people, which are the language of grace, but even of their groans, which are the language of nature. We have an instance in Peter, Acts xii. 6. If God by his providences declare his name, we must by our acknowledgments of them declare his praise, which ought to be the echo of his name. God will discharge his people that were prisoners and captives in Babylon, *that they may declare his name in Zion*, the place he has chosen to put his name, *and his praise in Jerusalem*, at their return thither. They will help to draw in others to the worship of God (*v.* 22): *When the people of God are gathered together* at Jerusalem (as they were after their return out of Babylon) many out of the kingdoms joined with them *to serve the Lord* (Ezra vi. 21). But look further, at the conversion of the Gentiles to the faith of Christ in the latter days. Christ has proclaimed *liberty to the captives*, and *the opening of the prison to those that were bound*, that they may declare the name of the Lord in the gospel-church, in which Jews and Gentiles shall unite.

Verses 23–28

I. The imminent danger that the Jewish church was in of being quite extirpated and cut off by the captivity in Babylon (*v.* 23): *He weakened my strength in the way.* This the psalmist speaks of as in his own person, and it is very applicable to common afflictions. Bodily distempers soon *weaken our strength in the way.* When in the midst of our days our strength is weakened, what can we expect but that the *number of our months should be cut off in the midst?* It has often been the lot of those that have used their strength well to have it weakened, and of those that could very ill be spared to have their days shortened.

II. A prayer for continuance (*v.* 24): "*O my God! take me not away in the midst of my days.*" This is a prayer for the afflicted, that God would not *take us away in the midst of our days*, but that, if it be his will, he would spare us to do him further service and to be made riper for heaven.

III. A plea to enforce this prayer taken from the eternity of the Messiah promised, *v.* 25–27. The apostle quotes these verses (Heb. i. 10–12). It is very comfortable, in reference to all the changes and all the dangers that *Jesus Christ is the same yesterday, to-day, and for ever. Thy years are throughout all generations*, and cannot be shortened. It is comfortable in reference to the death of our own bodies, and the removal of our friends from us, that God is an ever living God, and that therefore, if he be ours, in him we may have everlasting consolation. Earth and heaven, the universe and its fulness, derive their being from God by his Son (*v.* 25): "*Of old hast thou laid the foundation of the earth*, which is founded *on the seas* and *on the floods* and yet *it abides*; much more shall the church, which is *built upon a rock.*" God will unmake the world again (*v.* 26, 27): *They shall perish*, for *thou shalt change them* by the same almighty power that made them, and *thou shalt endure*; *thou art the same.* God and the world, Christ and the creature, are rivals for the innermost and uppermost place in the soul of man, the immortal soul. 1. A portion in the creature is fading and dying: *They shall perish;* they will not last so long as we shall last. Heaven and earth shall *wax old as a garment. As a vesture shalt thou change them, and they shall be changed*, altered, so that they shall be *new heavens and a new earth.* See God's sovereign dominion over heaven and earth. He can change them as he pleases and when he pleases; and the revolutions of day and night, summer and winter, are earnests of their last and final change, when *the heavens* and *time* (which is measured by them) *shall be no more.* 2. A portion in God is perpetual and everlasting: *Thou art the same*, subject to no change; and *thy years have no end*, *v.* 27. Christ will be the same in the performance that he was in the promise, the same to his church in captivity that he was to his church at liberty. Let not the church fear the weakening of her strength, or the shortening of her days, while Christ himself is both her strength and her life; he is the same, and has said, *Because I live you shall live also.*

JAMIESON, FAUSSET, BROWN

18. people . . . created—(cf. Ps. 22:31), an organized body, as a Church.

19-22. A summary of what shall be written. **For**—or, "That," as introducing the statement of God's condescension. **to loose . . . appointed**—or, deliver them (Ps. 79:11).

To declare . . .—or, that God's name may be celebrated in the assemblies of His Church, gathered from all nations (Zech. 8:20-23), and devoted to His service.

23-28. The writer, speaking for the Church, finds encouragement in the midst of all his distresses. God's eternal existence is a pledge of faithfulness to His promises. **in the way**—of providence. **weakened**—lit., "afflicted," and made fearful of a premature end, a figure of the apprehensions of the Church, lest God might not perform His promise, drawn from those of a person in view of the dangers of early death (cf. Ps. 89:47).

Paul (Heb. 1:10) quotes vss. 26-28 as addressed to Christ in His divine nature. The scope of the Psalm, as already seen, so far from opposing, favors this view, especially by the sentiments of vss. 12-15 (cf. Isa. 60:1). The association of the Messiah with a day of future glory to the Church was very intimate in the minds of Old Testament writers; and with correct views of His nature it is very consistent that He should be addressed as the Lord and Head of His Church, who would bring about that glorious future on which they ever dwelt with fond delightful anticipations.

ADAM CLARKE

18. *The people which shall be created.* "The Gentiles, who shall be brought to the knowledge of salvation by Christ," as the Syriac states in its inscription of this psalm.

19. *For he hath looked down.* This, with the three following verses, seems to me to contain a glorious prophecy of the incarnation of Christ, and the gathering in of the Jews and the Gentiles to Him.

24. *I said, O my God.* This and the following verses seem to be the form of prayer which the captives used previously to their deliverance.

Thy years are throughout all generations. This was a frequent argument used to induce God to hear prayer. We are frail and perishing; Thou art everlasting; deliver us, and we will glorify Thee.

27. *But thou art the same.* "But thou art He," that is, the Eternal. *Thy years shall have no end.* "They shall not be completed."

MATTHEW HENRY

IV. A comfortable assurance of an answer to this prayer (*v.* 28): *The children of thy servants shall continue;* since Christ is the same, the church shall continue from one generation to another; from the eternity of the head we may infer the perpetuity of the body, though often weak and distempered, and even at death's door. Those that hope to *wear out the saints of the Most High* will be mistaken.

PSALM 103

Verses 1–5

David is here communing with his own heart, and he is no fool that thus talks to himself.

I. How he stirs up himself to the duty of praise, *v.* 1, 2. It is the Lord that is to be blessed. It is the soul that is to be employed in blessing God, *and all that is within* us. The work requires the inward man, the whole man, and all little enough.

II. How he furnishes himself with abundant matter for praise: "Come, my soul, consider what God has done for thee." 1. "He has pardoned thy sins (*v.* 3); he has forgiven, and *does forgive, all thy iniquities.*" This is mentioned first because by the pardon of sin that is taken away which kept good things from us, and we are restored to the favour of God, which bestows good things on us. He is still forgiving, as we are still sinning and repenting. 2. "He has cured thy sickness." Our crimes were capital, but God saves our lives by pardoning them; our diseases were mortal, but God saves our lives by healing them. These two go together; for, as for God, his work is perfect and not done by halves; if God take away the guilt of sin by pardoning mercy, he will break the power of it by renewing grace. 3. "He has rescued thee from danger." *The redemption of the soul is precious;* we cannot compass it, and therefore are the more indebted to divine grace that has wrought it out, to him who has *obtained eternal redemption for us.* See Job xxxiii. 24, 28. 4. "He has not only saved thee from death and ruin, but has made thee truly and completely happy, with honour, pleasure, and long life." *He crowns thee with his lovingkindness and tender mercies*, and what greater dignity is a poor soul capable of than to be advanced into the love and favour of God? "He has given thee a prospect and pledge of long life: *Thy youth is renewed like the eagle's.*" The eagle is long-lived, and, as naturalists say, when she is old, casts all her feathers (as indeed she changes them every year at moulting time), and fresh ones come, so that she becomes young again. When God, by the graces and comforts of his Spirit, recovers his people from their decays, and fills them with new life and joy, an earnest of eternal life and joy, then they may be said to *return to the days of their youth*, Job xxxiii. 25.

Verses 6–18

I. Truly God is good to all (*v.* 6): He *executes righteousness and judgment for all that are oppressed.*

II. He is in a special manner good to Israel.

1. He has revealed himself and his grace to us (*v.* 7): *He made known his ways unto Moses*, and by him *his acts to the children of Israel.* Divine revelation is one of the greatest of divine favours, for God restores us to himself by revealing himself to us, and gives us all good by giving us knowledge.

2. He has never been rigorous and severe with us, but always tender, full of compassion, and ready to forgive.

(1) It is in his nature to be so (*v.* 8): *The Lord is merciful and gracious.* He is not soon angry, *v.* 8. He is *slow to anger*, bears long with those that are very provoking, defers punishing, that he may give space to repent, and does not speedily execute the sentence of his law. Though he signify his displeasure against us for our sins by the rebukes of Providence, and the reproaches of our own consciences, yet he will not always keep us in pain and terror, but, after the spirit of bondage, will give the spirit of adoption.

(2) We have found him so; *he has not dealt with us after our sins*, *v.* 10. He has not inflicted the judgments which we have merited; *God's patience should lead us to repentance*, Rom. ii. 4.

3. He has pardoned our sins, not only my *iniquity* (*v.* 3), but *our transgressions*, *v.* 12. *As the heaven is high above the earth* (*v.* 11) (so high that the earth is but a point to the vast expanse), so God's mercy is above the merits of those that fear him most, so much above and beyond them that there is no proportion at all between them. The fulness of his pardons, an evidence of the riches of his mercy (*v.* 12): *As far as the east is from the west so far has he removed our transgressions from us*, so that they shall never be laid to our charge, nor rise up in judgment against

JAMIESON, FAUSSET, BROWN

PSALM 103

Vss. 1-22. A Psalm of joyous praise, in which the writer rises from a thankful acknowledgment of personal blessings to a lively celebration of God's gracious attributes, as not only intrinsically worthy of praise, but as specially suited to man's frailty. He concludes by invoking all creatures to unite in his song.

1. Bless . . .—when God is the object, praise. **my soul**—myself (Ps. 3:3; 25:1), with allusion to the act, as one of intelligence. **all . . . within me**—(Deut. 6: 5). **his holy name**—(Ps. 5:11), His complete moral perfections. **2. forget not all**—not any, none of His benefits.

3. diseases—as penal inflictions (Deut. 39:2; II Chron. 21:19).

4. redeemeth—Cost is implied. **destruction**—lit., "pit of corruption" (Ps. 16: 10).

crowneth—or, adorneth (Ps. 65:11). **tender mercies**—compassions (cf. Ps. 25:6; 40:11).

5. By God's provision, the saint retains a youthful vigor like the eagles (Ps. 92:14; cf. Isa. 40:31).

6. Lit., "righteousness and judgments," denoting various acts of God's government. **7. ways**—of providence, etc., as usual (Ps. 25:4; 67:2). **acts**—lit., "wonders" (Ps. 7:11; 78:17).

8-10. God's benevolence implies no merit. He shows it to sinners, who also are chastened for a time (Exod. 34:6). **keep (anger)**—in Leviticus 19:18, bear a grudge (Jer. 3:5, 12).

11. great—efficient. **12. removed . . . from us**—so as no longer to affect our relations to Him.

ADAM CLARKE

28. *The children of thy servants shall continue.* Thy Church shall be permanent, because founded on Thee; it shall live throughout all the revolutions of time.

PSALM 103

The inscription in the Hebrew, and in all the versions, gives this psalm to David; and yet many of the ancients believed it to refer to the times of the Captivity, or rather to its conclusion, in which the redeemed Jews give thanks to God for their restoration.

3. *Who forgiveth.* The benefits are the following, (1) Forgiveness of sin. (2) Restoration of health: *Who healeth all thy diseases.*

4. *Who redeemeth.* (3) Preservation from destruction. *Haggoel*, properly, redemption of life by the kinsman; possibly looking forward, in the spirit of prophecy, to Him who became Partaker of our flesh and blood, that He might have the right to redeem our souls from death by dying in our stead. (4) Changing and ennobling his state; weaving a crown for him out of *lovingkindness and tender mercies.*

5. *Who satisfieth thy mouth.* (5) For continual communications of spiritual and temporal good, so that the vigor of his mind was constantly supported and increased. *Thy youth is renewed like the eagle's.* He refers to the molting of birds, which, in most, takes place annually, in which they cast their old feathers and get a new plumage.

12. *As far as the east is from the west.* As the east and the west can never meet in one point, but be forever at the same distance from each other, so our sins and their decreed punishment are removed to an eternal distance by His mercy.

MATTHEW HENRY

us. If we thoroughly forsake them, God will thoroughly forgive them.

4. He has pitied our sorrows, *v.* 13, 14. God is a Father to those that fear him and owns them for his children, and he is tender of them as a father. The father pities his children that are weak in knowledge and instructs them, pities them when they are froward and bears with them, pities them when they are sick and comforts them (Isa. lxvi. 13), pities them when they have fallen and helps them up again, pities them when they have offended, and, upon their submission, forgives them, pities them when they are wronged and gives them redress; thus *the Lord pities those that fear him.* He has reason to know our frame, for he framed us; and, having himself made man of the dust, *he remembers that he is dust.*

5. He has perpetuated his covenant-mercy and thereby provided relief for our frailty, *v.* 15–18. *As for man, his days are as grass,* which grows out of the earth, rises but a little way above it, and soon withers. Man, in his best estate, is but *like a flower of the field,* which, though distinguished a little from the grass, will wither with it. The flower of the garden is commonly more choice and valuable, and, though in its own nature withering, will last the longer for its being sheltered by the garden wall and the gardener's care; but the flower of the field (to which life is here compared) is not only withering in itself, but exposed to the cold blasts, and liable to be cropped and trodden on by the beasts of the field. Man's life is not only wasting of itself, but its period may be anticipated by a thousand accidents. God considers this, and pities him; let him consider it himself, and be humble. How long and lasting God's mercy is to his people (*v.* 17, 18): it will continue longer than their lives, and will survive their present state. Those only shall have the benefit of God's promises that make conscience of his precepts. The continuance of the mercy which belongs to such as these; it will last them longer than their lives on earth, and therefore they need not be troubled though their lives be short, since death itself will be no abridgement, no infringement, of their bliss. God's mercy is better than life, for it will out-live it.

Verses 19–22

I. The doctrine of universal providence laid down, *v.* 19. He has secured the happiness of his peculiar people by promise and covenant, but the order of mankind, and the world in general, he secures by common providence. *The Lord has a throne* of his own, a throne of glory, a throne of government. But though God's throne is in heaven, and there he keeps his court, and thither we are to direct to him (*Our Father who art in heaven*), yet *his kingdom rules over all.* He takes cognizance of all the inhabitants, and all the affairs, of this lower world. *His kingdom rules over all.*

II. The duty of universal praise inferred from it: if all are under God's dominion, all must do him homage.

1. Let the holy angels praise him (*v.* 20, 21): not as if they needed any excitement of ours to praise God, they do it continually; but thus David expresses his high thoughts of God as worthy of the adorations of the holy angels.

2. Let *all his works* praise him (*v.* 22), that is, all the children of men, in all parts of the world, let them all praise God; yea, and the inferior creatures too, which are God's works also; let them praise him objectively, though they cannot praise him actually, cxlv. 10. He began with *Bless the Lord, O my soul!* and, when he had penned and sung this excellent hymn to his honour, David does not say, Now, O my soul! thou hast blessed the Lord, sit down, and rest thee, but, *Bless the Lord, O my soul!* yet more and more.

JAMIESON, FAUSSET, BROWN

13. pitieth—lit., "has compassion on." **14. he** [who formed, Ps. 94:9] **knoweth our frame**—lit., "our form." **we are dust**—made of and tending to it (Gen. 2:7).

15, 16. So short and frail is life that a breath may destroy it. **it is gone**—lit., "it is not." **know it no more**—no more recognize him (Ps. 90:6; Isa. 40:6-8).

17, 18. For similar contrast cf. Psalms 90:2-6; 102:27, 28. **such . . . covenant**—limits the general terms preceding. **righteousness**—as usual (Ps. 7:17; 31:1).

19. God's firm and universal dominion is a pledge that He will keep His promises (Ps. 11:4; 47:8).

20-22. do his commandments . . . word—or, lit., "so as to hearken," etc., i.e., their acts of obedience are prompt, so that they are ever ready to hear, and know, and follow implicitly His declared will (cf. Deut. 26:17; Luke 1:19). **ye his hosts**—myriads, or armies, as corresponding to *angels* of *great power:* denoting multitudes also. **all his works**—creatures of every sort, everywhere.

ADAM CLARKE

13. *Like as a father pitieth his children.* This is a very emphatic verse, and may be thus translated: "As the tender compassions of a father towards his children, so the tender compassions of Jehovah towards them that fear Him."

14. *For he knoweth our frame.* "Our formation"; the manner in which we are constructed, and the materials of which we are made.

15. *His days are as grass.* See the note on Ps. xc. 5.

17. *The mercy of the Lord is from everlasting to everlasting. Chesed* signifies more particularly the "exuberant goodness of God." This is an attribute of His nature, and must be from everlasting to everlasting; and hence His righteousness (*tsidketh*), His merciful mode of justifying the ungodly, is extended from one generation to another.

PSALM 104

MATTHEW HENRY

Verses 1–9

When we are addressing ourselves to any religious service we must *stir up ourselves to take hold on God* in it (Isa. lxiv. 7); so David does here.

I. The psalmist looks up to the divine glory shining in the upper world, of which, though it is one of the things not seen, faith is the evidence. With what reverence and holy awe does he begin his meditation: *O Lord my God! thou art very great!* Princes appear great, 1. In their robes; and what are God's robes? *Thou art clothed with honour and majesty, v.* 1. Thou *coverest thyself with light as with a garment, v.* 2. God *dwells in light* (1 Tim. vi. 16); he clothes himself with it. 2. In their palaces or pavilions; and what is God's palace and his pavilion? He *stretches out the*

JAMIESON, FAUSSET, BROWN

Vss. 1-35. The Psalmist celebrates God's glory in His works of creation and providence, teaching the dependence of all living creatures; and contrasting the happiness of those who praise Him with the awful end of the wicked.

1. God's essential glory, and also that displayed by His mighty works, afford ground for praise.

2. light—is a figurative representation of the glory of the invisible God (Matt. 17:2; I Tim. 6:16). Its use in this connection may refer to the first work of creation (Gen. 1:3). **stretchest out the heavens**—

ADAM CLARKE

This psalm has no title in either the Hebrew or Chaldee. It is properly a poem on the works of God in the creation and government of the world; and some have considered it a sort of epitome of the history of the creation, as given in the Book of Genesis.

2. *Who coverest thyself with light.* Light, insufferable splendor, is the robe of the Divine Majesty. Light and fire are generally the accompaniments of the Supreme Being, when He manifests His presence to His creatures.

MATTHEW HENRY

heavens like a curtain, *v.* 2. So he did at first, when he made the firmament, which in the Hebrew has its name from its being expanded, or *stretched out*, Gen. i. 7. God *covers himself with light*, yet, in compassion to us, *he makes darkness his pavilion. Thick clouds are a covering to him.* The vastness of this pavilion may lead us to consider how great, how very great, he is that *fills heaven and earth.* Though air and water are fluid bodies, yet, by the divine power, they are kept as tight and as firm in the place assigned them as a chamber is with beams and rafters. How great a God is he whose presence-chamber is thus reared, thus fixed! 3. In their coaches of state, with their stately horses, which add much to the magnificence of their entries; but God *makes the clouds his chariots.* He descended in a cloud, as in a chariot, to Mount Sinai, to give the law, and to Mount Tabor, to proclaim the gospel (Matt. xvii. 5), and he *walks* (a gentle pace indeed, yet stately) *upon the wings of the wind.* 4. In their retinue or train of attendants; and here also God is very great, for (*v.* 4) he *makes his angels spirits.*

II. He looks down, and looks about, to the power of God shining in this lower world.

1. He has founded the earth, *v.* 5. Though he has *hung it upon nothing* (Job xxvi. 2), yet it is as immovable as if it had been laid upon the surest foundations. Though it has received a dangerous shock by the sin of man, and the malice of hell strikes at it, yet *it shall not be removed for ever*, that is, not till the end of time, when it must give way to the new earth.

2. He has set bounds to the sea; for that also is his. (1) He brought it within bounds in the creation. God said, *Let the waters under the heaven be gathered to one place, and let the dry land appear*, Gen. i. 9. This command of God is here called his *rebuke*, as if he gave it because he was displeased that the earth was not fit for man to dwell on. Power went along with this word, and therefore it is also called here *the voice of his thunder*, *v.* 7. *At thy rebuke*, as if they were made sensible that they were out of their place, *they fled.* As it is said on another occasion (lxxvii. 16), *The waters saw thee, O God! the waters saw thee; they were afraid.* So here; God rebuked the waters for man's sake, to prepare room for him. (2) He keeps it within bounds, *v.* 9. The waters are forbidden to pass over the limits set them; they may not, and therefore they do not, *turn again to cover the earth.*

Verses 10–18

I. He provides fresh water: *He sends the springs into the valleys*, *v.* 10. It is God that *sends the springs into the* brooks, *which* walk by easy steps between *the hills*, and receive increase from the rain-water that descends from them. These *give drink*, not only to man, and those creatures that are immediately useful to him, but *to every beast of the field* (*v.* 11); for where God has given life he provides a livelihood.

II. He provides food convenient for them, both for man and beast: ***He waters the hills from his chambers*** (**v. 13**), **from those chambers spoken of (*v.* 3), *the beams of which he lays in the waters*, those store-chambers, the clouds that distil fruitful showers. It is a satisfaction to the earth to bear the fruit of God's works for the benefit of man, for thus it answers the end of its creation.**

1. For the cattle there is grass, and the beasts of prey, that live not on grass, feed on those that do; for man there is herb, *wine, and oil, and bread*, *v.* 15. We have a necessary dependence upon God for all the supports of this life. Let us also consider that we are in this respect fellow-commoners with the beasts; the same earth, the same spot of ground, that brings grass for the cattle, brings corn for man.

2. The divine providence not only furnishes animals with their proper food, but vegetables also with theirs (*v.* 16): *The trees of the Lord are full of sap*, not only men's trees, which they take care of and have an eye to, in their orchards, and parks, and other enclosures, but God's trees, which grow in the wildernesses, and are taken care of only by his providence: they *are full of sap* and want no nourishment. Even *the cedars of Lebanon* have enough from the earth; they are trees *which he has planted*, and which therefore he will protect and provide for. We may apply this to the trees of righteousness, which are the planting of the Lord, planted in his vineyard; these *are full of sap*, for what God plants he will water, and those that *are planted in the house of the Lord shall flourish in the courts of our God*, xcii. 13.

III. He takes care that they shall have suitable habitations to dwell in. To men God has given discretion to build for themselves and for the cattle that are serviceable to them; but there are some creatures which God more immediately provides a settlement for. 1. The birds. Some birds, by instinct, make their nests in the bushes near rivers (*v.* 12):

JAMIESON, FAUSSET, BROWN

the visible heavens or sky which cover the earth as a curtain (Isa. 40:12).

3. in the waters—or, it may be "with"; using this fluid for the beams, or frames, of His residence accords with the figure of clouds for chariots, and wind as a means of conveyance. **walketh**—or, moveth (cf. Ps. 18:10, 11; Amos 9:6). **4.** This is quoted by Paul (Heb. 1:7) to denote the subordinate position of angels; i.e., they are only messengers as other and material agencies. **spirits**—lit., "winds." **flaming fire**—(Ps. 105:32) being here so called. **5.** The earth is firmly fixed by His power.

6-9. These verses rather describe the wonders of the flood than the creation (Gen. 7:19, 20; II Pet. 3:5, 6). God's method of arresting the flood and making its waters subside is poetically called a "rebuke" (Ps. 76:6; Isa. 50:2), and the process of their subsiding by undulations among the hills and valleys is vividly described.

10-13. Once destructive, these waters are subjected to the service of God's creatures. In rain and dew from His chambers (cf. vs. 3), and fountains and streams, they give drink to thirsting animals and fertilize the soil.

14, 15, so that men and beasts are abundantly provided with food. **for the service**—lit., "for the culture," etc., by which he secures the results. **oil . . . shine**—lit., "makes his face to shine more than oil," i.e., so cheers and invigorates him, that outwardly he appears better than if anointed. **strengtheneth . . . heart**—gives vigor to man (cf. Judg. 19:5).

Trees thus nourished supply homes to singing birds, and the earth teems with the productions of God's wise agencies,

ADAM CLARKE

CHARLES H. SPURGEON:

"Who coverest thyself with light as with a garment" (104:2): wrapping the light about him as a monarch puts on his robe. The conception is sublime: but it makes us feel how altogether inconceivable the personal glory of the Lord must be: if light itself is but his garment and veil, what must be the blazing splendor of his own essential being! We are lost in astonishment, and dare not pry into the mystery lest we be blinded by its insufferable glory.

"Who stretchest out the heavens like a curtain"—within which he might dwell. Light was created on the first day and the firmament upon the second, so that they fitly follow each other in this verse. Oriental princes put on their glorious apparel and then sit in state within curtains, and the Lord is spoken of under that image: but how far above all comprehension the figure must be lifted, since the robe is essential light, to which suns and moons owe their brightness, and the curtain is the azure sky studded with stars for gems.—*The Treasury of David*

7. *At thy rebuke they fled.* When God separated the waters which were above the firmament from those below, and caused the dry land to appear. He commanded the separation to take place; and the waters, as if instinct with life, hastened to obey.

13. *From his chambers.* The clouds, as in v. 3.

MATTHEW HENRY

By the springs that *run among the hills* some of the *fowls of heaven have their habitation, which sing among the branches.* They sing, according to their capacity, to the honour of their Creator and benefactor, and their singing may shame our silence. Our *heavenly Father feeds them* (Matt. vi. 26). Those that fly heavenward shall not want resting-places. *The stork* is particularly mentioned; *the fir-trees,* which are very high, *are her house,* her castle. 2. The smaller sorts of beasts (*v.* 18): *The wild goats* are guided by instinct to *the high hills,* which are a refuge to them; and *the rabbits,* which are also helpless animals, find shelter in *the rocks,* where they can set the beasts of prey at defiance. Does God provide thus for the inferior creatures; and will he not himself be a refuge and dwelling-place to his own people?

Verses 19–30

We are here taught to praise and magnify God,

I. For the constant revolutions and succession of day and night, and the dominion of sun and moon over them. The heathen worshipped them as deities; and therefore the scripture takes all occasions to show that the gods they worshipped are the creatures and servants of the true God (*v.* 19). 1. The shadows of the evening befriend the repose of the night (*v.* 20): *Thou makest darkness and it is night,* which, though black, contributes to the beauty of nature, and is as a foil to the light of the day; and under the protection of the night *all the beasts of the forest creep forth* to feed, which they are afraid to do in the day. 2. The light of the morning befriends the business of the day (*v.* 22, 23): *The sun arises* (for, as he *knows his going down,* so, thanks be to God, he knows his rising again), and then the wild beasts betake themselves to their rest. The beasts of prey creep forth with fear; man goes forth with boldness, as one that has dominion.

II. For the replenishing of the ocean (*v.* 25, 26): As *the earth is full of God's riches, so is this great and wide sea.* God has appointed it its place and made it serviceable to man both for navigation, and also to be his storehouse for fish. God made not the sea in vain, any more than the earth.

III. For the seasonable and plentiful provision which is made for all the creatures, *v.* 27, 28. God is a bountiful benefactor to them: He *gives them their meat*; he *opens his hand and they are filled with good.* Even the meanest creatures are not below his cognizance. They *all wait upon him.* They seek their food, according to the natural instinct God has put into them and in the proper season for it.

IV. For the absolute power and sovereign dominion which he has over all the creatures, by which every species is still continued, though the individuals of each are daily dying and dropping off. *Thou takest away their breath,* which is in thy hand, and then, and not till then, *they die and return to their dust,* to their first principles. The *spirit of the beast, which goes downward,* is at God's command, as well as *the spirit of a man, which goes upward.* Though one generation of them passes away, another comes, and from time to time they are created; new ones rise up instead of the old ones, and this is a continual creation. Thus the *face of the earth is renewed* from day to day by the light of the sun (which beautifies it anew every morning), from year to year by the products of it, which enrich it anew every spring and put quite another face upon it from what it had all winter.

In the midst of this discourse the psalmist breaks out into wonder at the works of God (*v.* 24): *O Lord! how manifold are thy works! in wisdom hast thou made them all.*

Verses 31–35

The psalmist concludes this meditation with:

I. Praise to God: *The glory of the Lord shall endure for ever, v.* 31. It shall endure to the end of time in his works of creation and providence; it shall endure to eternity in the felicity and adorations of saints and angels. Man's glory is fading; God's glory is everlasting. *The Lord shall rejoice in his works.* We often do that which, upon review, we cannot rejoice in, but are displeased at, and wish undone again. But God always *rejoices in his works,* because they are all done in wisdom. As a God of almighty power (*v.* 32): *He looks on the earth, and it trembles,* as unable to bear his frowns—trembles, as Sinai did, *at the presence of the Lord. He touches the hills, and they smoke.* The volcanoes, or burning mountains, such as Etna, are emblems of the power of God's wrath, fastening upon proud unhumbled sinners. *Who knows the power of his anger?* Who then dares set it at defiance? Because we have our being from God, and depend upon him for the support and continuance of it, as long as we live and have our being we must continue to praise God; and when

JAMIESON, FAUSSET, BROWN

16-19. God's care of even wild animals and uncultivated parts of the earth.

20-23. He provides and adapts to man's wants the appointed times and seasons.

24-26. From a view of the earth thus full of God's blessings, the writer passes to the sea, which, in its immensity, and as a scene and means of man's activity in commerce, and the home of countless multitudes of creatures, also displays divine power and beneficence. The mention of **leviathan**—(Job 40:20) heightens the estimate of the sea's greatness, and of His power who gives such a place for sport to one of His creatures. **27-30.** The entire dependence of this immense family on God is set forth.

With Him, to kill or make alive is equally easy. To hide His face is to withdraw favor (Ps. 13:1). By His spirit, or breath, or mere word, He gives life. It is His constant providence which repairs the wastes of time and disease.

31-34. While God could equally glorify His power in destruction, that He does it in preservation is of His rich goodness and mercy, so that we may well spend our lives in grateful praise, honoring to Him, and delightful to pious hearts (Ps. 147: 1).

ADAM CLARKE

17. *Where the birds make their nests. Tsipporim* signifies swallows, sparrows, and small birds in general; here opposed to the *chasidah* or *stork.* Perhaps the heron may be understood, which is said to be the first of all birds to build her nest, and she builds it on the very highest trees. The general meaning is that God has provided shelter and support for the greatest and smallest birds; they are all objects of His providential regard.

25. *This great and wide sea.* The original is very emphatic: "This very sea, great and extensive of hands." Its waters, like arms, encompassing all the terrene parts of the globe. I suppose the Psalmist was within sight of the Mediterranean when he wrote these words.

26. *There go the ships.* He appears at this time to have seen the ships under sail. *That leviathan.* This may mean the whale, or any of the large marine animals.

30. *Thou sendest forth thy spirit, they are created.* "They are created again."

MATTHEW HENRY

we have no life, no being, on earth, we hope to have a better life and better being in a better world and there to be doing this work in a better manner and in better company.

II. Joy to himself (*v.* 34): *My meditation of him shall be sweet;* it shall be fixed and close; it shall be affecting and influencing; and therefore it shall be sweet. "*I will be glad in the Lord;* it shall be a pleasure to me to praise him; I will be glad of all opportunities to set forth his glory; and I will *rejoice in the Lord always* and in him only."

III. Terror to the wicked (*v.* 35): *Let the sinners be consumed out of the earth; and let the wicked be no more.* None can prosper that harden themselves against the Almighty. When *the wicked are no more* I hope to be praising God world without end; and therefore, *Praise you the Lord*; let all about me join with me in praising God. *Hallelujah;* sing praise to Jehovah. This is the first time that we meet with *Hallelujah.*

JAMIESON, FAUSSET, BROWN

35. Those who refuse such a protector and withhold such a service mar the beauty of His works, and must perish from His presence. The Psalm closes with an invocation of praise, the translation of a Hebrew phrase, which is used as an English word, "Hallelujah," and may have served the purpose of a chorus, as often in our psalmody, or to give fuller expression to the writer's emotions. It is peculiar to Psalms composed after the captivity, as "Selah" is to those of an earlier date.

ADAM CLARKE

33. *I will sing unto the Lord.* I will sing unto the Lord "with my lives," the life that I now have and the life that I shall have hereafter. *I will sing praise to my God.* "In my eternity"; my going on, my endless progression.

MATTHEW HENRY

PSALM 105

Verses 1–7

I. Give unto God the glory due unto his name. 1. We must *give thanks to him*, as one who has always been our bountiful benefactor. 2. *Call upon his name*, as one whom you depend upon for further favours. Praying for further mercies is an acknowledgement of former mercies. 3. *Make known his deeds* (*v.* 1), that others may join with you in praising him. *Talk of all his wondrous works* (*v.* 2), as we talk of things that we are full of. We should talk of them *as we sit in the house and as we go by the way* (Deut. vi. 7). 4. *Sing psalms to* God's honour, as those that rejoice in him, and desire to testify that joy and to transmit it to posterity, as memorable things anciently were handed down by songs, when writing was scarce. 5. *Glory in his holy name;* glory not of their own achievements, but of their acquaintance with God and their relation to him, Jer. ix. 23, 24. 6. *Seek him;* place your happiness in him, and then pursue that happiness. *Seek his strength*, that is, his grace, the strength of his Spirit to work in you that which is good, which we cannot do but by strength derived from him. "*Seek his face evermore.* Seek it while you live in this world, and you shall have it while you live in the other world, and even there shall be for ever seeking it in an infinite progression, and be ever satisfied." 7. *Let the hearts of those rejoice that do seek him* (*v.* 3); for they have chosen well. If those have reason to rejoice that *seek the Lord*, much more those that have *found him.*

II. Some arguments to quicken us to these duties. 1. "Consider both what he has said and what he has done to engage us for ever to him. Remember the wonders of his providence which he has *wrought for you* and those who are gone before you—the wonders of his law, which he has written to you, and entrusted you with, *the judgments of his mouth*, as well as the judgments of his hand," *v.* 5. 2. "Consider the relation you stand in to him (*v.* 6): *You are the seed of Abraham his servant; the children of Jacob his chosen, chosen* and *beloved* for the fathers' sake, and therefore ought to tread in the steps of those whose honours you inherit. You are the children of godly parents; do not degenerate. You are God's church upon earth, and, if you do not praise him, who should?"

Verses 8–24

We are here taught, in praising God, to look a great way back, and to give him the glory of what he did for his church in former ages, especially when it was in the founding and forming. We may fetch proper matter for praise from the histories of the gospels and the acts of the apostles, which relate the birth of the Christian church, as the psalmist here does from the histories of Genesis and Exodus, which relate the birth of the Jewish church.

I. God's promise to the patriarchs, that he would give to their seed the land of Canaan for an inheritance, was a type of the promise of eternal life made in Christ to all believers. In all the marvellous works which God did for Israel *he remembered his covenant* (*v.* 8) and he will remember it *for ever.* In the parallel place it is expressed as our duty (1 Chron. xvi. 15), *Be you mindful always of his covenant.* The promise is here called a *covenant*, because there was something required on man's part as the condition of the promise. See to whom God *swore by himself*, Heb. vi. 13, 14. The covenant itself: *Unto thee will I give the land of Canaan, v.* 11. The patriarchs had a right to it, not by providence, but by promise; and their seed should be put in possession of it, as *the lot of their inheritance*, a sure title, by virtue of their birth; it shall come to them by the favour of God, and not

JAMIESON, FAUSSET, BROWN

PSALM 105

Vss. 1-45. After an exhortation to praise God, addressed especially to the chosen people, the writer presents the special reason for praise, in a summary of their history from the calling of Abraham to their settlement in Canaan, and reminds them that their obedience was the end of all God's gracious dealings.

1. call . . . name—(Ps. 79:6; Rom. 10:13). Call on Him, according to His historically manifested glory. After the example of Abraham, who, as often as God acquired for Himself a name in guiding him, *called* in solemn worship upon the name of the Lord (Gen. 12:8, 13:4). **among the people**—or, peoples (Ps. 18:49). **deeds**—or, wonders (Ps. 103:7). **3, 4.** Seeking God's favor is the only true mode of getting true happiness, and *His strength* is the only true source of protection (cf. Ps. 32:11; 40:16). **Glory . . . name**—boast in His perfections. The world glories in its horses and chariots against the Church of God lying in the dust; but *our* hope is in the name, i.e., the power and love of God to His people, manifested in past deliverances.

5, 6. judgments . . . mouth—His judicial decisions for the good and against the wicked. **chosen**—rather qualifies "children" than "Jacob," as a plural. **7.** Rather, "He, Jehovah, is our God." His title, JEHOVAH, implies that He, the unchangeable, self-existing Being, makes things to be, i.e., fulfils His promises, and therefore will not forsake His people. Though specially of His people, He is God over all.

8-11. The covenant was often ratified. **commanded**—or, ordained (Ps. 68:28). **word**—answering to "covenant" in the parallel clause, viz., the word of promise, which, according to vs. 10, He set forth for an inviolable law. **to a thousand generations**—perpetually. A verbal allusion to Deuteronomy 7:9 (cf. Exod. 20:6). **9. Which covenant**—or, "Word" (vs. 8). **10, 11.** Alluding to God's promise to Jacob (Gen. 28:13). Out of the whole storehouse of the promises of God, only one is prominently brought forward, namely, that concerning the possession of Canaan. Everything revolves around this. The wonders and judgments have all for their ultimate design the fulfilment of this promise.

ADAM CLARKE

PSALM 105

We find several verses of this psalm in 1 Chronicles xvi, from which it is evident that David was the author of the principal part of it; but it was probably enlarged and sung at the restoration of the people from the Babylonish captivity.

2. *Talk ye of all his wondrous works.* "Of his miracles." Who have so many of these to boast of as Christians! Christianity is a tissue of miracles, and every part of the work of grace on the soul is a miracle.

7. *He is the Lord our God.* He is *Jehovah*, the self-existent and eternal God. He is *our God*, He is our Portion; has taken us for His people, and makes us happy in His love.

The following abstract of the history of the Israelites presents but few difficulties. See the notes on Psalm lxxviii.

MATTHEW HENRY

any merit of their own. Heaven is the inheritance we have obtained, Eph. i. 11. And *this is the promise which God has promised us* (as Canaan was the promise he promised them), *even eternal life*, 1 John ii. 25; Tit. i. 2.

II. His providences concerning the patriarchs while they were waiting for the accomplishment of this promise, which represent to us the care God takes of his people in this world, while they are yet on this side the heavenly Canaan; for these things *happened unto them for examples* and encouragements to all the heirs of promise, that live by faith as they did.

1. They were wonderfully protected and sheltered, and (as the Jewish masters express it) *gathered under the wings of the divine Majesty*. This is accounted for, *v.* 12–15. They were exposed to injuries from men. To the three renowned patriarchs, Abraham, and Isaac, and Jacob, God's promises were very rich; again and again he told them he would be their God. Even in this world he was not wanting to them, but that he might appear, to do uncommon things for them, he exercised them with uncommon trials. (1) They were few, *very few*. Abraham was called alone (Isa. li. 2). (2) They were strangers, and therefore were the most likely to be abused. Their religion made them to be looked upon as strangers (1 Pet. iv. 4) and to be hooted at as *speckled birds*, Jer. xii. 9. (3) They were unsettled (*v.* 13): *They went from one nation to another*, from one part of that land to another, *from one kingdom to another people*, from Canaan to Egypt, from Egypt to the land of the Philistines, forced to it by famine. They were guarded by the special providence of God, *v.* 14, 15. They were not able to help themselves and yet, (4) No men were suffered to wrong them, but even those that hated them, had their hands tied, and could not do what they would. This may refer to Gen. xxxv. 5, where we find that *the terror of God was upon the cities that were round about them*, so that, though provoked, *they did not pursue after the sons of Jacob*. (5) Even crowned heads, that did offer to wrong them, were controlled and baffled. *He reproved kings for their sakes* in dreams and visions, *saying, "Touch not my anointed; do my prophets no harm."* Pharaoh king of Egypt was plagued (Gen. xii. 17) and Abimelech king of Gerar was sharply rebuked (Gen. xx. 6) for doing wrong to Abraham.

2. They were wonderfully provided for and supplied. To try the faith of the patriarchs, God *broke the whole staff of bread*, even in that good land. God graciously took care for their relief. It was in obedience to his precept, and in dependence upon his promise, that they were now sojourners in Canaan, and therefore he could not in honour suffer any good thing to be wanting to them. As he restrained one Pharaoh from doing them wrong, so he raised up another to do them a kindness, by preferring and entrusting Joseph, of whose story we have here an abstract. Many years before the famine began, he was sent before them, to nourish them in the famine. He went not so much as a factor or commissary; but *he was sold* thither *for a servant*, a slave for term of life, without any prospect of being ever set at liberty. And yet he was brought lower; he was made a prisoner (*v.* 18): *His feet they hurt with fetters*. Being unjustly charged with a rape upon his mistress, *the iron entered into his soul*, that is, was very painful to him; yet all this was the way to his preferment. He continued a prisoner, neither tried nor bailed, *until the time* appointed of God for his release (*v.* 19), when *his word came*, that is, his interpretations of dreams came to pass, and the report thereof came to Pharaoh's ears by the chief butler. And then *the word of the Lord cleared him*; that is, the power God gave him to foretell things to come rolled away the reproach his mistress had loaded him with; for it could not be thought that God would give such a power to so bad a man as he was represented to be. *God's word tried him*, tried his faith and patience, and then it came in power to give command for his release. There is a time set when God's word will come for the comfort of all that trust in it, Hab. ii. 3. *At the end it shall speak, and not lie*. God gave the word, and then *the king sent and loosed him*. Pharaoh, finding him to be a favourite of Heaven, *let him go free*. He advanced him to the highest posts of honour, *v.* 21, 22, lord high chamberlain of his household. He made him prime minister of state. In all this Joseph was designed to save the house of Israel from perishing by the famine. Joseph being thus sent before, and put into a capacity of maintaining all his father's house, *Israel also came into Egypt* (*v.* 23), where he and all his were comfortably provided for many years.

3. They were wonderfully multiplied, according to the promise made to Abraham that his seed should be as the sand of the sea for multitude, *v.* 24.

JAMIESON, FAUSSET, BROWN

12-15. few . . . in number—alluding to Jacob's words (Gen. 34:30), "I being *few in number*." **yea, very few**—lit., "as a few," i.e., like fewness itself (cf. Isa. 1:9). **strangers**—sojourners in the land of their future inheritance, as in a strange country (Heb. 11:9).

13. from one nation to another—and so from danger to danger; now in Egypt, now in the wilderness, and lastly in Canaan. Though a few strangers, wandering among various nations, God protected them.

14. reproved kings—Pharaoh of Egypt and Abimelech of Gerar (Gen. 12:17; 20:3). **Touch not**—referring to Genesis 26:11, where Abimelech says of Isaac, "He that *toucheth* this man or his wife shall surely be put to death." **mine anointed**—as specially consecrated to Me (Ps. 2:2). The patriarch was the prophet, priest, and king of his family. **my prophets**—in a similar sense, cf. Genesis 20:7. The "anointed" are those vessels of God, consecrated to His service, "in whom (as Pharaoh said of Joseph, Gen. 41:38) the Spirit of God is" [HENGSTENBERG]. **16.** God ordered the famine. God **called for a famine**—as if it were a *servant*, ready to come at God's bidding. Cf. the centurion's words, as to disease being God's servant (Matt. 8:8, 9). **upon the land**—viz., Canaan (Gen. 41:54). **staff of bread**—what supports life ((Lev. 26:26; Ps. 104:15; Isa. 3:1). **17-21.** Joseph was sent of God (Gen. 45:5).

hurt with fetters—(Gen. 40:3). **was laid in iron**—lit., "his soul," or, he (Ps. 16:10) came into iron, or, he was bound to his grief (cf. Ps. 3:2; 11:1). Joseph is referred to as being an appropriate type of those "bound in affliction and iron" (Ps. 107:10). The "soul" is put for the whole person, because the soul of the captive suffers still more than the body. **his word came**—His prophecy (Gen. 41:11-20) to the officers came to pass, or was fulfilled (Judg. 13:12, 17; I Sam. 9:6, explain the form of speech).

the word [or, saying, or decree] **of the Lord tried** [or, proved] **him**—by the afflictions it appointed him to endure before his elevation (cf. Gen. 41:40-43). **22. To bind**—Not literally *bind;* but *exercise over them absolute control,* as the parallel in the second clause shows; also Genesis 41:40, 44, in which not literal *fettering*, but *commanding obedience,* is spoken of. It refers to vs. 18. The soul that was once *bound* itself now *binds* others, even princes. The same moral *binding* is assigned to the saints (Ps. 149:8). **teach . . . senators wisdom**—the ground of his exaltation by Pharaoh was his *wisdom* (Gen. 41:39); viz., in state policy, and ordering well a kingdom. **23-25. Israel . . . and Jacob**—i.e., Jacob himself is meant, as vs. 24 speaks of "his people." Still, he came with his whole house (Gen. 46:6, 7). **sojourned**—(Gen. 47:4). **land of Ham**—or, Egypt (Ps. 78:51).

ADAM CLARKE

F. B. MEYER:

"He was laid in chains of iron" (105:18). The margin of the R.V. suggests another rendering: "His soul entered into the iron." May we not yet again turn the sentence round, and say that the iron entered into his soul? When we first meet him, Joseph is a tender, yielding lad, with dreams of rule, but no conspicuous power. Yet he emerges from his captivity well qualified to take the helm of Egypt, just then sore driven and tossed by tempest. How can this striking transformation be accounted for, save that he had taken iron into his moral nature through his painful experiences?

The physician often prescribes an iron tonic for anemic patients: and what iron is to the outer man that also the captivity of circumstances, deferred hope, and anguish of soul are to the inner. You have been fickle and uncertain of late; dreaming of power, but powerless; yearning for the only good, but greedy of trifles; you must have a course of iron. God wants Iron Dukes, and Iron souls. And there is a process also by which He can turn Iron into Steel. It means high temperature, sudden transitions, and blasts of heavenly air.

"If call'd, like Abraham's child, to climb
The hill of sacrifice,
Some angel may be there in time—
Deliverance shall arise!
Or if some darker lot be good,
Oh, teach us to endure
The sorrow, pain, or solitude
That make the spirit pure!

Life is very mysterious. Indeed, it would be inexplicable unless we believed that God was preparing us for scenes and ministries that lie beyond the vail of sense in the eternal world, where highly tempered spirits will be required for special service.

—*Great Verses Through the Bible*

19. *Until the time that his word came.* This appears to refer to the completion of Joseph's interpretation of the dreams of the chief butler and baker.

The word of the Lord tried him. This seems to refer to the interpretation of Pharaoh's dreams, called *imrath Yehovah,* "the oracle of the Lord," because sent by Him to Pharaoh.

MATTHEW HENRY

Verses 25–45

After the history of the patriarchs follows the history of the people of Israel, when they grew into a nation.

I. Their affliction in Egypt (*v.* 25): *He turned* the *heart* of the Egyptians, who had protected them, *to hate* them and *deal subtilely* with them. God's goodness to his people exasperated the Egyptians against them. They *dealt subtilely* with them, to find out ways and means to weaken them and prevent their growth; they made their burdens heavy and their lives bitter, and slew their male children as soon as they were born.

II. Their deliverance out of Egypt, that it might never be forgotten, is put into the preface to the ten commandments.

1. The instruments employed in that deliverance (*v.* 26): *He sent Moses his servant* on this errand and joined Aaron in commission with him. Moses was designed to be their lawgiver and chief magistrate, Aaron to be their chief priest.

2. The means of accomplishing that deliverance; these were the plagues of Egypt. *They showed the words of his signs* (so it is in the original), for every plague had an exposition going along with it; they spoke loud. They are all or most of them here specified, though not in the order in which they were inflicted. (1) The plague of darkness, *v.* 28. This was one of the last, though here mentioned first. *They were not obedient to his word*, which may be applied to Pharaoh and the Egyptians, who, notwithstanding the terror of this plague, *would not let the people go*. (2) The turning of the river Nilus (which they idolized) *into blood*, which *slew their fish* (*v.* 29), Num. xi. 5. (3) The frogs, shoals of which their land brought forth. (4) Flies of divers sorts swarmed in their air, and lice in their clothes, *v.* 31; Exod. viii. 17, 24. (5) Hail-stones shattered their trees, even the strongest timber-trees in *their coasts*, and killed their vines, and their other fruit-trees, *v.* 32, 33; Exod. ix. 23. (6) *Locusts and caterpillars* destroyed *all the* herbs which were made for the service of man and ate the bread out of their mouths, *v.* 34, 35. (7) Having mentioned all the plagues but those of the murrain and boils, he concludes with that which gave the conquering stroke, and that was the death of *the first-born*, *v.* 36.

3. The mercies that accompanied this deliverance. They had been impoverished, and yet they came out rich and wealthy. God not only brought them forth, but he *brought them forth with silver and gold*, *v.* 37. Their lives had been made bitter to them, and their bodies and spirits broken by their bondage; and yet, when God brought them forth, *there was not one feeble person*, none sick, none so much as sickly, *among their tribes*. They had been trampled upon and insulted over; and yet they were brought out with honour (*v.* 38). They had spent their days in sorrow and in sighing, by reason of their bondage; but now he brought them forth *with joy and gladness*, *v.* 43.

4. The special care God took of them in the wilderness. He *spread a cloud for a covering* (*v.* 39), which was to them not only a screen and umbrella, but a cloth of state. A cloud was often God's pavilion (xviii. 11) and now it was Israel's. He appointed a pillar of *fire to give light in the night*. He fed them both with necessaries and dainties (*v.* 40). *He opened the rock, and the waters gushed out*, *v.* 41.

5. Their entrance, at length, into Canaan (*v.* 44): *He gave them the lands of the heathen.*

6. The reasons why God did all this for them. (1) Because he would himself perform the promises of the world, *v.* 42. *Because he remembered the word of his holiness* (that is, his covenant) *with Abraham his servant*, he would not suffer one iota or tittle of that to fall to the ground. See Deut. vii. 8. (2) Because he would have them to perform the precepts of the word, to bind them to which was the greatest kindness he could put upon them. God having thus done them good, they might the more cheerfully receive his law, designed for their good, and might be sensible of their obligations in gratitude to live in obedience to him. We are *therefore* made, maintained, and redeemed, that we may live in obedience to the will of God; and the hallelujah with which the psalm concludes may be taken as a thankful acknowledgment of God's favours.

JAMIESON, FAUSSET, BROWN

turned their heart—God controls men's free acts (cf. I Sam. 10:9). "When Saul had turned his back to go from (God's prophet) Samuel, God *turned* (*Margin*) him to another heart" (see Exod. 1:8, etc.). Whatever evil the wicked man plots against God's people, God holds bound even his heart, so as not to lay a single plan except what God permits. Thus Isaiah (43:17) says it was *God* who *brought forth the army* of Pharaoh to pursue Israel to their own destruction (Exod. 4:21; 7:3). **26. Moses . . . chosen**—both what they were by divine choice (Psalm 78:70). **27. signs**—lit., "words of signs," or rather, as "words" in *Hebrew* means "things," "things of His signs," i.e., His marvellous tokens of power (Ps. 145:5, *Margin*). Cf. the same Hebraism (Ps. 65:3, *Margin*). **28-36.** The ninth plague is made prominent as peculiarly wonderful. **they rebelled not**—Moses and Aaron promptly obeyed God (Heb. 11:27); (cf. Exod. 7-11 and Ps. 78:44-51, with which this summary substantially agrees). Or, rather, the "darkness" here is figurative (Jer. 13:16), the literal plague of darkness (Exod. 10:22, 23) being only *alluded* to as the symbol of God's wrath which overhung Egypt as a dark cloud during all the plagues. Hence, it is placed first, out of the historical order. Thus, "They rebelled not (i.e., no longer) against His word," refers to *the Egyptians*. Whenever God sent a plague on them, *they were ready to let Israel go*, though refusing when the plague ceased. **His word**—His command to let Israel go [HENGSTENBERG]. Of the ten plagues, only eight are mentioned, the fifth, the murrain of beasts, and the sixth, the boils, being omitted. **29, 30.** He deprived them of their favorite "fish," and gave them instead, out of the water, loathsome "frogs," and (vs. 31) upon their land tormenting "flies" (the dog-fly, according to MAURER) and "lice" (gnats, HENGSTENBERG). **32. hail for rain**—instead of fertilizing showers, hail destructive to trees. This forms the transition to the vegetable kingdom. The locusts in vs. 34 similarly are destructive to plants. **gave them**—referring to Leviticus 26:4. "I *give* you rain in due season." His "gift" to Israel's foes is one of a very different kind from that bestowed on His people. **33. their coasts**—all their land (Ps. 78:54). **34. caterpillars**—lit., "the lickers up," devouring insects; probably the hairy-winged locust. **36. the chief**—lit., "the firstlings." The ascending climax passes from the food of man to man himself. The language here is quoted from Ps. 78:51. **37. with silver and gold**—*presented* them by the Egyptians, as an acknowledgment due for their labors in their bondage (cf. Exod. 12:35). **one feeble person**—or, stumbler, unfit for the line of march. Cf. "harnessed," i.e., accoutred and marshalled as an army on march (Exod. 13:18; Isa 5:27). **38**—(Cf. Exod. 12:33; Deut. 11:25.) **39. covering**—in sense of protection (cf. Exod. 13:21; Num. 10:34). In the burning sands of the desert the cloud protected the congregation from the heat of the sun; an emblem of God's protecting favor of His people, as interpreted by Isaiah (Isa. 4:5, 6; cf. Num. 9:16). **42-45.** The reasons for these dealings: (1) God's faithfulness to His covenant, "His holy promise" of Canaan, is the fountain whence flowed so many acts of marvellous kindness to His people (cf. vss. 8, 11). Exodus 2:24 is the fundamental passage [HENGSTENBERG]. (2) That they might be obedient. The observance of God's commands by Abraham was the object of the covenant with him (Gen. 18:19), as it was also the object of the covenant with Israel, that they might observe God's statutes. **remembered . . . and Abraham**—or, "remembered His holy word (i.e., covenant confirmed) *with* Abraham." **inherited the labour**—i.e., the fruits of their labor; their corn and vineyards (Josh. 21:43-45).

ADAM CLARKE

25. *He turned their heart.* "Their heart was turned." So the Syriac and Arabic.

27. *They shewed his signs.* Here is a reference to the plagues with which God afflicted the Egyptians.

28. *They rebelled not against his word.* Instead of *velo maru*, "They rebelled," some think that it should be read *velo shamru*, "They did not observe or keep His word." Or the words may be spoken of Moses and Aaron; they received the commandment of God, and they did not rebel against it. It could not be spoken of the Egyptians, for they rebelled against His words through the whole course of the transactions.

33. *He smote their vines also and their fig trees.* This is not mentioned in Exodus; but we have had it before, Ps. lxxviii. 47.

41. *He opened the rock, and the waters gushed out.* See Exod. xvii. 6.

PSALM 106

MATTHEW HENRY

Verses 1–5

I. Bless God (*v.* 1, 2). Give him thanks for his goodness. Give him the glory of his greatness, his *mighty acts*. When we have said the most we can of the mighty acts of the Lord, the one half is not told.

II. Bless the people of God, account them happy

JAMIESON, FAUSSET, BROWN

Vss. 1-48. This Psalm gives a detailed confession of the sins of Israel in all periods of their history, with special reference to the terms of the covenant as intimated (Ps. 105:45). It is introduced by praise to God for the wonders of His mercy, and concluded by a supplication for His favor to His afflicted

ADAM CLARKE

As a part of the preceding psalm is found in 1 Chronicles xvi, so the first and last two verses of this are found in the same place (vv. 34-36); and yet it is supposed by eminent commentators to be a prayer of the captives in Babylon, who acknowledge the mercies of God,

MATTHEW HENRY

(*v.* 3). God's people are those whose principles are sound—*They keep judgment;* they do *righteousness,* are just to God and to all men, and herein they are steady and constant.

III. Bless ourselves in the favour of God, place our happiness in it, and seek it, accordingly, with all seriousness, *v.* 4, 5. As there are a people in the world who are in a peculiar manner God's people, so there is a peculiar favour which God bears to that people, which all gracious souls desire an interest in. *O visit me with thy salvation.* That salvation be my portion for ever (*v.* 5): *"That I may see the good of thy chosen* and be as happy as the saints are; and happier I do not desire to be."

Verses 6–12

A penitential confession of sin, which was in a special manner seasonable now that the church was in distress; thus we must justify God in all that he brings upon us, acknowledging that *therefore* he has done right, because *we have done wickedly.*

I. God's afflicted people here own themselves guilty before God (*v.* 6): "*We have sinned with our fathers. We have committed iniquity,* that which is in its own nature sinful, and we have sinned with a high hand presumptuously."

II. They bewail the sins of their fathers when they were first formed into a people.

1. The strange stupidity of Israel in the midst of the favours God bestowed upon them (*v.* 7): *They understood not thy wonders in Egypt.* They thought the plagues of Egypt were intended for their deliverance, whereas they were intended also for their instruction and conviction, not only to force them out of their Egyptian slavery, but to cure them of their inclination to Egyptian idolatry. We lose the benefit of providences for want of understanding them. And, as their understandings were dull, so their memories were treacherous; *they remembered not the multitude of* God's *mercies* in them.

2. Their perverseness arising from this stupidity: *They provoked him at the sea, even at the Red Sea.* The provocation was, despair of deliverance and wishing they had been left in Egypt still, Exod. xiv. 11, 12. They reproach him, as if all that power had no mercy in it, but he had brought them out of Egypt on purpose to *kill them in the wilderness.*

3. The great salvation God wrought for them notwithstanding their provocations, *v.* 8–11. He forced a passage for them through the sea. He interposed between them and their pursuers, and prevented them from cutting them off, as they designed. The Red Sea, which was a lane to them, was a grave to the Egyptians (*v.* 11) (Exod. xiv. 30). Though they did not deserve this favour, he designed it; and their undeservings should not alter his designs, nor make him withdraw his promise, or fail in the performance of it. Moses prays (Num. xiv. 17, 19), *Let the power of my Lord be great and pardon the iniquity of this people.* The power of the God of grace in pardoning sin and sparing sinners is as much to be admired as the power of the God of nature in dividing the waters.

4. The good impression this made upon them for the present (*v.* 12): *Then believed they his words,* and acknowledged that God was with them of a truth, and had, in mercy to them, brought them out of Egypt, and not with any design to slay them in the wilderness. Then *they sang his praise,* in that song of Moses penned on this great occasion, Exod. xv. 1.

Verses 13–33

This is an abridgment of the history of Israel's provocations in the wilderness, and this abridgment is abridged by the apostle, with application to us Christians (1 Cor. x. 5, &c.).

I. The cause of their sin was disregard to the works and word of God, *v.* 13. 1. They minded not what he had done for them: *They soon forgot his works. They made haste;* their expectations anticipated God's promises; they expected to be in Canaan shortly, and because they were not they questioned whether they should ever be there. Again (*v.* 21, 22): *They forgot God their Saviour.* Those that forget the works of God forget God himself, who makes himself known by his works. 2. They minded not what God had said to them nor would they depend upon it: *They waited not for his counsel.* They had not patience to tarry God's time. The difficulties were looked upon as insuperable.

II. Many of their sins are here mentioned, together with the tokens of God's displeasure which they fell under for those sins.

1. They would have flesh, and yet would not believe that God would give it to them (*v.* 14). They were also, in all probability, within a step of Canaan, yet had not patience to stay for dainties till they came

JAMIESON, FAUSSET, BROWN

people, and a doxology.

1. Praise . . .—(Ps. 104:24), begins and ends the Psalm, intimating the obligations of praise, however we sin and suffer. I Chron. 16:34-36 is the source from which the beginning and end of this Psalm are derived. **2.** His acts exceed our comprehension, as His praise our powers of expression (Rom. 11:33). Their unutterable greatness is not to keep us back, but to urge us the more to try to praise Him as best we can (Ps. 40:5; 71:15). **3.** The blessing is limited to those whose principles and acts are right. How "blessed" Israel would be now, if he had "observed God's statutes" (Ps. 105:45). **4, 5.** In view of the desert of sins to be confessed, the writer invokes God's covenant mercy to himself and the Church, in whose welfare he rejoices. The speaker, *me, I,* is not the Psalmist himself, but the people, the present generation (cf. vs. 6). **visit**—(Cf. Ps. 8:4.) **see the good**—participate in it (Ps. 37:13.) **thy chosen**—viz., Israel, God's elect (Isa. 43:20; 45:4). As God seems to have *forgotten* them, they pray that He would "remember" them with the favor which *belongs* to His own people, and which once they had enjoyed. **thine inheritance**—(Deut. 9:29; 32:9.) **6.** Cf. I Kings 8:47; Daniel 9:5, where the same three verbs occur in the same order and connection, the original of the two later passages being the first one, the prayer of Solomon in dedicating the temple. **sinned . . . fathers**—like them, and so partaking of their guilt. The terms denote a rising gradation of sinning (cf. Ps. 1:1). **with our fathers**—we and they together forming one mass of corruption. **7-12.** Special confession. Their rebellion at the sea (Exod. 14:11) was because they had not remembered nor understood God's miracles on their behalf.

That God saved them in their unbelief was of His mere mercy, and for His own glory. **the sea . . . the Red Sea**—the very words in which Moses' song celebrated the scene of Israel's deliverance (Exod. 15:4). Israel began to rebel against God at the very moment and scene of its deliverance by God!

8. for his name's sake—(Ezek. 20:14.) **9. rebuked**—(Ps. 104:7.) **as through the wilderness**—(Isa. 63:11-14.)

12. believed . . . his words—This is said not to praise the Israelites, but God, who constrained even so unbelieving a people momentarily to "believe" while in immediate view of His wonders, a faith which they immediately afterwards lost (vs. 13; Exod. 14:31; 15:1).

13-15. The faith induced by God's display of power in their behalf was short lived, and their new rebellion and temptation was visited by God with fresh punishment, inflicted by leaving them to the result of their own gratified appetites, and sending on them spiritual poverty (Num. 11:18). **They soon forgat**—lit., "They hasted, they forgat" (cf. Exod. 32:8). "They have turned aside *quickly* (or *hastily*) out of the way." The haste of our desires is such that we can scarcely allow God one day. Unless He immediately answers our call, instantly then arise impatience, and at length despair. **his works**—(Deut. 11:3, 4; Dan. 9:14.) **his counsel**—They waited not for the development of God's counsel, or *plan for their deliverance,* at His own time, and in His own way.

14. Lit., "lusted a lust" (quoted from Num. 11:4, *Margin*). Previously, there had been impatience as to *necessaries* of life; here it is *lusting* (Ps. 78:18).

ADAM CLARKE

confess their own sins and those of their forefathers, and implore the Lord to gather them from among the heathen, and restore them to their own country.

6. *We have sinned.* Here the confession begins; what preceded was only the introduction to what follows: Our forefathers sinned, and suffered; we, like them, have sinned, and do suffer.

7. *Our fathers understood not.* They did not regard the operation of God's hands, and therefore they understood neither His designs nor their own interest.

At the sea, even at the Red sea. They *provoked, (al yam) at the sea; beyam suph,* "in the sea *Suph,*" or Red Sea. They provoked Him at it and in it.

8. *He saved them for his name's sake.* "On account of His name"; to manifest His own power, goodness, and perfections.

10. *The hand of him that hated them.* Pharaoh.

12. *Then believed they.* Just while the miracle was before their eyes.

13. *They soon forgat his works.* Three days afterwards, at the waters of Marah, Exod. xv. 24.

They waited not for his counsel. They were impatient, and would not wait till God should in His own way fulfill His own designs.

MATTHEW HENRY

thither. Now how did God show his displeasure against them for this. We are told how (*v.* 15): *He gave them their request,* but gave it them in anger, and with a curse, for he *sent leanness into their soul;* he filled them with uneasiness of mind, and terror of conscience, and a self-reproach. Or this is put for that great plague with which the Lord smote them, *while the flesh was yet between their teeth,* as we read, Num. xi. 33.

2. They quarrelled with the government which God had set over them both in church and state (*v.* 16): *They envied Moses* his authority *in the camp,* as generalissimo and chief justice; they envied *Aaron* his power, as *saint of the Lord,* consecrated to the office of high priest, and Korah would needs put in for the pontificate, while Dathan and Abiram, as princes of the tribe of Reuben, Jacob's eldest son, would claim to be chief magistrates. How did God show his displeasure for this? We are told how (*v.* 17, 18); we have the story, Num. xvi. 32, 35. Those that flew in the face of the civil authority were punished by *the earth,* which *opened and swallowed them up.* Those that would usurp the ecclesiastical authority in things pertaining to God suffered the vengeance of heaven, and the pretending sacrificers were themselves sacrificed to divine justice.

3. They made and worshipped the golden calf, and this in Horeb, where the law was given, and where God had expressly said, *Thou shalt* neither *make any graven image* nor *bow down* to it; they did both: *They made a calf and worshipped* it, *v.* 19. Herein they put an affront upon the two great lights which God has made to rule the moral world: That of human reason; for *they changed their glory,* their God, *into the similitude of* Apis, one of the Egyptian idols, *an ox that eateth grass,* than which nothing could be more grossly and scandalously absurd, *v.* 20. That of divine revelation, which was afforded to them, not only in the words God spoke to them, but in the works he wrought for them, *v.* 21, 22. For this God showed his displeasure by declaring the decree that he would cut them off from being a people, as they had, as far as lay in their power, in effect cut him off from being a God; he *spoke of destroying them* (*v.* 23), and certainly he would have done it if *Moses, his chosen, had not stood before him in the breach* (*v.* 23). See the power of prayer, and the interest which God's chosen have in heaven. See a type of Christ, God's *chosen,* his elect, *in whom his soul delights,* who *stood before him in the breach* to *turn away* his wrath from a provoking world, and ever lives, for this end, making intercession.

4. They gave credit to the report of the evil spies concerning the land of Canaan, in contradiction to the promise of God (*v.* 24), and therefore were for making a captain and returning to Egypt again, basely charging God with a design upon them in bringing them thither that they might become a prey to the Canaanites, Num. xiv. 2, 3. And, when they were reminded of God's power and promise, they were so far from hearkening to that voice of the Lord that they attempted to stone those who spoke to them, Num. xiv. 10. This also was displeasing to God, for he swore in his wrath that they should not enter into his rest (xcv. 11; Num. xiv. 28); and he threatened that their children also should be *overthrown and scattered* (*v.* 26, 27), and the whole nation dispersed; but Moses prevailed for mercy for their seed, that they might enter Canaan.

5. They were guilty of a great sin in the matter of Peor; and this was the sin of the new generation, when they were within a step of Canaan (*v.* 28): *They joined themselves to Baal-peor,* and so were entangled both in idolatry and in adultery, in corporeal and in spiritual whoredom, Num. xxv. 1–3. Those that did often partake of the altar of the living God now *ate the sacrifices of the dead,* of the idols of Moab (that were dead images, or dead men canonized or deified), or sacrifices to the infernal deities on the behalf of their dead friends. *Thus they provoked God to anger with their inventions* (*v.* 29). A plague among them, in a little time swept away 24,000 of those impudent sinners. God stirred up Phinehas to use his power as a magistrate for the suppressing of the sin and checking the contagion of it. He stood up in his zeal for the Lord of hosts, and executed judgment upon Zimri and Cozbi, a service so pleasing to God that upon it *the plague was stayed, v.* 30. But, Phinehas herein signalizing himself, a special mark of honour was put upon him, for what he did was *counted to him for righteousness to all generations* (*v.* 31).

6. Their continued murmurings to the very last of their wanderings; for in the fortieth year they *angered God at the waters of strife* (*v.* 32), which refers to that story, Num. xx. 3–5. *It went ill with Moses for*

JAMIESON, FAUSSET, BROWN

15. but sent leanness—rather, "*and* sent," i.e., *and thus, even in doing so,* the punishment was inflicted at the very time their request was granted. So Ps. 78:30, "While their meat was yet in their mouths, the wrath of God came upon them." **soul**—the animal soul, which craves for food (Num. 11:6; Ps. 107:18). This soul got its wish, and with it and in it its own punishment. The place was therefore called *Kibroth-hattaavah,* "the graves of lust," because there they buried the people who had lusted. Animal desires when gratified mostly give only a hungry craving for more (Jer. 2:13). **16-18.** All the congregation took part with Dathan, Korah, etc., and their accomplices (Num. 16:41). **Aaron the saint**—lit., "the holy one," as consecrated priest; not a moral attribute, but one designating his office as *holy* to the Lord. The rebellion was followed by a double punishment: (1) (vs. 17) of the *non-Levitical* rebels, the Reubenites, Dathan and Abiram, etc. (Deut. 11:6; Num. 26:10); these were swallowed up by the earth. **covered**—"closed upon them" (Num. 16:33). (2) Of the *Levitical* rebels, with Korah at their head (vs. 18; Num. 16:35; 26:10); these had *sinned* by fire, and were punished by fire, as Aaron's (being high priest) sons had been (Lev. 10:2; Num. 16:1-35). **19-23.** From indirect setting God at naught, they pass to direct. **made**—though prohibited in Exod. 20:4, 5 to *make a likeness,* even of the true God. **calf**—called so in contempt. They would have made an ox or bull, but their idol turned out but a *calf;* an imitation of the divine symbols, the cherubim; or of the sacred bull of Egyptian idolatry. The idolatry was more sinful in view of their recent experience of God's power in Egypt and His wonders at Sinai (Exod. 32:1-6). Though intending to worship Jehovah under the symbol of the calf, yet as this was incompatible with His nature (Deut. 4:15-17), they in reality gave up Him, and so were given up by Him. Instead of the Lord of heaven, they had as their glory the image of an ox that does nothing but eat grass. **23. he said**—viz., to Moses (Deut. 9:13). With God, *saying* is as certain as *doing;* but His purpose, while full of wrath against sin, takes into account the mediation of Him of whom Moses was the type (Exod. 32:11-14; Deut. 9:18, 19). **Moses his chosen**—i.e., to be His servant (cf. Ps. 105:26). **in the breach**—as a warrior covers with his body the broken part of a wall or fortress besieged, a perilous place (Ezek. 13:5; 22:30). **to turn away** [or, prevent] **his wrath**—(Num. 25:11; Ps. 78:38.) **24-27.** The sin of refusing to invade Canaan, "the pleasant land" (Jer. 3:19; Ezek. 20:6; Dan. 8:9), "the land of beauty," was punished by the destruction of that generation (Num. 14:28), and the threat of dispersion (Deut. 4:25; 28:32) afterwards made to their posterity, and fulfilled in the great calamities now bewailed, may have also been then added. **despised**—(Num. 14:31.) **believed not his word**—by which He promised He would give them the land; but rather the word of the faithless spies (cf. Ps. 78:22). **lifted up his hand**—or, swore, the usual form of swearing (cf. Num. 14:30, *Margin*). **27. To overthrow**—lit., "To make them fall"; alluding to the words (Num. 14:39). **among . . . nations . . . lands**—The "wilderness" was not more destructive to the *fathers* (vs. 26) than residence among the heathen ("nations") shall be to the children. Lev. 26:33, 38 is here, before the Psalmist's mind, the determination against the "seed" when rebellious, being not *expressed* in Num. 14:31-33, but *implied* in the determination against the fathers. **28-30. sacrifices of the dead**—i.e. of lifeless idols, contrasted with "the living God" (Jer. 10:3-10; cf. Ps. 115:4-7; I Cor. 12:2). On the words, "joined themselves to Baal-peor," see Numbers 25:2, 3, 5. Baal-peor, i.e. the possessor of Peor, the mountain on which *Chemosh,* the idol of Moab, was worshipped, and at the foot of which Israel at the time lay encamped (Num. 23:28). The name never occurs except in connection with that locality and that circumstance. **provoked**—excited grief and indignation (Ps. 6:7; 78:58). **stood**—as Aaron "stood between the living and the dead, and the plague was stayed" (Num. 16:48). **executed judgment**—lit., "judged," including sentence and act. **31. counted . . . righteousness**—"a just and rewardable action." **for**—or, "unto," to the procuring of righteousness, as in Romans 4:2; 10:4. Here it was a particular act, not faith, nor its object Christ; and *what was procured* was not justifying righteousness, or what was to be rewarded with eternal life; for no one act of man's can be taken for complete obedience. But it was that which God approved and rewarded with a perpetual priesthood to him and his descendants (Num. 25:13; I Chron. 6:4, etc.). **32, 33.** (Cf. Num. 20:3-12; Deut. 1:37; 3:26). **went ill with** [lit., "was bad for"] **Moses**—His conduct, though under great

ADAM CLARKE

16. *They envied Moses.* A reference to the case of Korah and his company. *Aaron the saint.* The anointed, the high priest of the Lord.

20. *Thus they changed their glory.* That is, their God, who was their Glory; and they worshipped an ox in His stead. See the use St. Paul makes of this, Rom. i. 23.

22. *Wondrous works in the land of Ham.* Egypt is called *the land of Ham* or Cham, because it was peopled by Misraim, the son of Cham.

28. *Ate the sacrifices of the dead. Methim,* of "dead men." Most of the heathen idols were men who had been deified after their death.

MATTHEW HENRY

their sakes; for, though he was the meekest of all the men in the earth, yet their clamours at that time were so peevish and provoking that they put him into a passion, and, having now grown very old and off his guard, *he spoke unadvisedly with his lips* (*v.* 33). For he said in a heat, *Hear now, you rebels, must we fetch water out of this rock for you?* God shows his displeasure against this sin of theirs by shutting Moses and Aaron out of Canaan for their misconduct upon this occasion. If he deals thus severely with Moses for one unadvised word, what does their sin deserve who have spoken so many presumptuous wicked words? God deprived them of the blessing of Moses's guidance and government at a time when they most needed it, so that his death was more a punishment to them than to himself.

Verses 34–48

I. The narrative concludes with an account of Israel's conduct in Canaan, which was of a piece with that in the wilderness, and God's dealings with them, wherein, as all along, both justice and mercy appeared.

1. They were very provoking to God. By the time they were just settled in Canaan they corrupted themselves, and forsook God. They spared the nations which God had doomed to destruction (*v.* 34). They promised themselves that, notwithstanding this, they would not join in any dangerous affinity with them. The next news we hear is, They were *mingled among the heathen,* made leagues with them and contracted an intimacy with them, so that they *learned their works, v.* 35. They thought they would never join with them in their worship; but by degrees they learned that too (*v.* 36). That sin drew on many more, and brought the judgments of God upon them. When they joined with them in some of their idolatrous services, they little thought that ever they should be guilty of that barbarous and inhuman piece of idolatry the sacrificing of their living children to their dead gods; but they came to that at last (*v.* 37, 38). *They sacrificed their sons and daughters,* pieces of themselves, to devils, and added the most unnatural murder to their idolatry. They *shed innocent blood,* the most innocent, for it was infant-blood, nay, it was the *blood of their sons and daughters.* Their sin was, in part, their own punishment; for by it *The land was polluted with blood, v.* 38. They wronged their consciences (*v.* 39), and so debauched their own minds, and were rendered odious in the eyes of the holy God.

2. God brought his judgments upon them; and what else could be expected? He was angry with them, for from them he took it as more ungrateful than from the heathen that never knew him. *He abhorred his own inheritance.* This is the worst thing in sin, that it makes us loathsome to God; and the nearer any are to God in profession the more loathsome are they if they rebel against him, like a dunghill at our door. Their enemies then fell upon them, and their defence having departed, made an easy prey of them (*v.* 41, 42): *He gave them into the hands of the heathen.* The punishment answered to the sin. They *mingled with the heathen and learned their works;* and therefore God justly made use of them as the instruments of their correction. The heathen hated them. Apostates lose all the love on God's side, and get none on Satan's; and when those that *hated them ruled over them,* no marvel that they oppressed them. When God granted them some relief, yet they went on in their sins, and their troubles also were continued, *v.* 43. This refers to the days of the Judges, when God often raised up deliverers and wrought deliverances for them, and yet they relapsed to idolatry. Those that will not by repentance humble themselves, are justly debased. At length they cried unto God, and God returned in favour to them, *v.* 44–46. They were chastened for their sins, but not destroyed, cast down, but not cast off. God *heard their cry* with tender compassion (Exod. iii. 7) and overlooked their provocations. Though he is not a *man that he should repent,* so as to change his mind, yet he is a gracious God, who pities us, and changes his way. Bad as they were, he would not break with them, because he would not break his own promise. He not only restrained the remainder of their enemies' wrath, but he infused compassion even into their stony hearts, and made them relent, which was more than any art of man could have done.

II. The psalm concludes with prayer and praise. 1. Prayer for the completing of his people's deliverance. Many who were forced into foreign countries, in the times of the Judges (as Naomi was, Ruth i. 1), had not returned in the beginning of David's reign, and therefore it was seasonable to pray, Lord, gather the dispersed Israelites *from among the heathen, to give thanks to thy holy name,* in the Lord's house, from which they were now banished. 2. Praise for

JAMIESON, FAUSSET, BROWN

provocation, was punished by exclusion from Canaan.

34-39. They not only failed to expel the heathen, as God "commanded" (Exod. 23:32, 33), lit., "said (they should)," but conformed to their idolatries, and thus became spiritual adulterers (Ps. 73:27).

unto devils—*Septuagint,* demons (cf. I Cor. 10:20), or evil spirits.

polluted with blood—lit., "blood," or "murder" (Ps. 5:6; 26:9).

40-43. Those nations first seduced and then oppressed them (cf. Judg. 1:34; 2:14; 3:30). Their apostasies ungratefully repaid God's many mercies till He finally abandoned them to punishment (Lev. 26:39).

44-46. If, as is probable, this Psalm was written at the time of the captivity, the writer now intimates the tokens of God's returning favor. **repented**—(cf. Ps. 90:13). **made . . . pitied**—(I Kings 8:50; Dan. 1:9).

These tokens encourage the prayer and the promise of praise (Ps. 30:4), which is well closed by a doxology.

ADAM CLARKE

33. *They provoked his spirit. Himru,* from *marah,* "to rebel." They brought it into a rebellious state; he was soured and irritated, and was off his guard. *So that he spake unadvisedly with his lips.* For this sentence we have only these two words in the Hebrew, *vayebatte bisephathaiv,* "He stuttered or stammered with his lips," indicating that he was transported with anger. See Num. xx. 10-12.

36. *They served their idols. Atsabbeyhem,* their "labors" or "griefs"—idols, so called because of the pains taken in forming them, the labor in worshipping them, and the grief occasioned by the divine judgments against the people for their idolatry.

37. *They sacrificed their sons and their daughters unto devils.* "To demons." Devil is never in Scripture used in the plural; there is but one devil, though there are many demons.

43. *Many times did he deliver them.* See the Book of Judges; it is a history of the rebellions and deliverances of the Israelites.

46. *He made them also to be pitied.* This was particularly true as to the Babylonish captivity. For Cyrus gave them their liberty; Darius favored them, and granted them several privileges; and Artaxerxes sent back Nehemiah, and helped him to rebuild Jerusalem and the Temple. See the Books of Ezra and Nehemiah.

48. *Blessed be the Lord God of Israel.* Here both gratitude and confidence are expressed; gratitude for what God had already wrought, and confidence that He would finish the great work of their restoration. *From everlasting to everlasting.* "From the hidden term to the hidden

MATTHEW HENRY

the beginning and progress of it (*v.* 48): *Blessed be the Lord God of Israel from everlasting to everlasting.* Let the priests say this, and then *let all the people say, Amen, Hallelujah.*

PSALM 107

Verses 1–9

I. A general call to all to give thanks to God, *v.* 1.

II. A particular demand hereof from *the redeemed of the Lord*, which may well be applied spiritually to the *children of God that were scattered abroad*, whom Christ died to *gather together in one*, out of all lands, John xi. 52; Matt. xxiv. 31. But it seems here to be meant of a temporal deliverance, wrought for them when *they cried unto the Lord, v.* 6. 1. They were in an enemy's country, but God wrought out their rescue: *He redeemed them from the hand of the enemy* (*v.* 2), it may be *by the Spirit of God* working on the spirits of men. 2. They were dispersed as outcasts, but God gathered them out of all the countries whither they were scattered, *v.* 3. God knows those that are his, and where to find them. 3. They were bewildered, had no road to travel in, no dwelling place to rest in, *v.* 4. *They wandered in the wilderness.* But *God led them forth by the right way* (*v.* 7), directed them *that they might go to a city of habitation*, which they themselves should inhabit. This may refer to poor travellers in general, those particularly whose way lay through the wilds of Arabia, where they were often at a loss. Or it has an eye to the wanderings of the children of Israel in the wilderness for forty years. 4. They were ready to perish for hunger (*v.* 5). Israel's wants were seasonably supplied. The same God that has led us has fed us all our life long unto this day. Now for all this those who receive mercy are called upon to return thanks (*v.* 8): *Oh that men* (it is meant especially of those men whom God has graciously relieved) *would praise the Lord for his goodness* to them in particular, *and for his wonderful works to* others of *the children of men!*

Verses 10–16

The goodness of God towards prisoners and captives. Prisoners are said to *sit in darkness* (*v.* 10), desolate and disconsolate; they sit *in the shadow of death*, which intimates great danger. They are *bound in affliction, and* many times *in iron, because they rebelled against the words of God. They contemned the counsel of the Most High*, and thought they neither needed it nor could be the better for it; and those that will not be counselled cannot be helped. For this they are bound in affliction. The design of this affliction is to bring *down their heart* (*v.* 12), to humble them for sin. The duty of this afflicted state is to pray (*v.* 13). Prisoners have time to pray, who, when they were at liberty, could not find time; they see they have need of God's help, though formerly they thought they could do well enough without him. *They cried unto the Lord, and he saved them, v.* 13. *He brought them out of darkness into light*, and their liberty was to them life from the dead, *v.* 14. Were they *fettered?* He broke their bands asunder. Were they imprisoned in strong castles? *He broke the gates of brass* and the *bars of iron* wherewith those gates were made fast; he did not put back, but *cut in sunder.*

Verses 17–22

Bodily sickness is another of the calamities of this life which gives us an opportunity of experiencing the goodness of God.

I. If we knew no sin, we should know no sickness. Sinners are fools; they wrong themselves, and all against their own interest, not only their spiritual, but their secular interest. They prejudice their bodily health by intemperance and endanger their lives by indulging their appetites. Those that dote most on the meat that perishes, when they come to be sick are sick of it, and the dainties they love are loathed. And when the appetite is gone the life is as good as gone: *Then they cry unto the Lord, v.* 19. Is any sick? Let him pray; let him be prayed for. Prayer is a salve for every sore.

II. It is by the power and mercy of God that we are recovered from sickness, and then it is our duty to be thankful. *He sent his word and healed them, v.* 20. This may be applied to the miraculous cures which Christ wrought when he was upon earth; he said, *Be clean, Be whole*, and the work was done. It may also be applied to the spiritual cures which the Spirit of grace works in regeneration; he sends his word, and heals souls. In the common instances of recovery from sickness God in his providence does but speak, and it is done. When those that have

JAMIESON, FAUSSET, BROWN

PSALM 107

Vss. 1-43. Although the general theme of this Psalm may have been suggested by God's special favor to the Israelites in their restoration from captivity, it must be regarded as an instructive celebration of God's praise for His merciful providence to all men in their various emergencies. Of these several are given—captivity and bondage, wanderings by land and sea, and famine; some as evidences of God's displeasure, and all the deliverances as evidence of His goodness and mercy to them who humbly seek Him.

1, 2. This call for thankful praise is the burden or chorus (cf. vs. 8, 15, etc.). **redeemed of the Lord**—(cf. Isa. 35:9, 10). **say**—i.e., that His mercy, etc. **hand of**—or, power of enemy. **3. gathered**—alluding to the dispersion of captives throughout the Babylonian empire. **from the south**—lit., "the sea," or, Red Sea (Ps. 114:3), which was on the south. **4-7.** A graphic picture is given of the sufferings of those who from distant lands returned to Jerusalem; or, **city of habitation** may mean the land of Palestine. **fainted**—was overwhelmed (Ps. 61:3; 77:3).

8, 9. To the chorus is added, as a reason for praise, an example of the extreme distress from which they had been delivered—extreme hunger, the severest privation of a journey in the desert.

10-16. Their sufferings were for their rebellion against (Ps. 105: 28) the words, or purposes, or promises, of God for their benefit.

When humbled they cry to God, who delivers them from bondage, described as a dark dungeon with doors and bars of metal, in which they are bound in iron—i.e., chains and fetters. **shadow of death**—darkness with danger (Ps. 23:4). **broken**—lit., "shivered" (Isa. 45:2).

17-22. Whether the same or not, this exigency illustrates that dispensation of God according to which sin brings its own punishment. **are afflicted**—lit., "afflict themselves," i.e., bring on disease, denoted by loathing of food, and drawing **near unto** [lit., "even to"] **the gates** [or, domains, Ps. 9:16] **of death.**

sent his word—i.e., put forth His power. **their destructions**—i.e., that which threatened them.

ADAM CLARKE

term," from the beginning of time to the end of time, from eternity and on to eternity.

This is the end of the fourth book of the Psalms.

PSALM 107

This psalm has no title, either in the Hebrew or in any of the versions. The author is unknown; but it was probably like Psalms cv and cvi, made and sung at the dedication of the second Temple. The three psalms seem to be on the same subject. In them the author has comprised the marvellous acts of the Lord towards his people; the transgressions of this people against God; the captivities and miseries they endured in consequence; and finally God's merciful kindness to them in their restoration from captivity, and reestablishment in their own land. This psalm seems to have been sung in parts: the 8th, 15th, 21st, and 31st verses, with the 6th, 13th, 19th, and 28th, forming what may be called the burden of the song, in singing of which the whole chorus joined.

4. *They wandered in the wilderness.* Here begins the first comparison: the Israelites in captivity are compared to a traveller in a dreary, uninhabited, and barren desert, spent with hunger and thirst, as well as by the fatigues of the journey, v. 5.

8. *Oh that men would praise the Lord!* This is the burden of each part of this responsive song; see the introduction.

9. *For he satisfieth the longing soul.* "The soul that pushes forward in eager desire" after salvation.

10. *Such as sit in darkness.* Here begins the second similitude, which he uses to illustrate the state of the captives in Babylon, viz., that of a prisoner in a dreary dungeon.

13. *Then they cried unto the Lord in their trouble.* This was the salutary effect which their afflictions produced; they began to cry to God for mercy and help.

15. *Oh that men!* This is the burden of the second part, as it was of the first. See v. 8.

16. *For he hath broken.* This is the reason given for thanks to God for His deliverance of the captives. It was not a simple deliverance; it was done so as to manifest the irresistible power of God. He tore the prison in pieces, and *cut the bars of iron* asunder.

17. *Fools because of their transgression.* This is the third comparison, the Captivity being compared to a person in a dangerous malady. Our version does not express this clause well: "Fools, because of the way of their transgressions, are afflicted."

18. *Their soul abhorreth all manner of meat.* A natural description of a sick man; appetite is gone, and all desire for food fails. See a similar image, Job xxxiii. 20.

19. *Then they cry.* The effect produced by affliction as before.

MATTHEW HENRY

been sick are restored they must return to God an answer of praise (*v.* 21, 22): *Let all men praise the Lord for his goodness,* and let those, particularly, to whom God has thus granted a new life, spend it in his service; *let them sacrifice with thanksgiving,* not only bring a thank-offering to the altar, but a thankful heart to God.

Verses 23–32

The psalmist here calls upon those to give glory to God who are delivered from dangers at sea. Though the Israelites dealt not much in merchandise, yet their neighbours the Tyrians and Zidonians did, and for them perhaps this part of the psalm was especially calculated.

I. The power of God appears at all times in the sea, *v.* 23, 24. It appears to those *that go down to the sea in ships,* as mariners, merchants, fishermen, or passengers, *that do business in great waters. These see the works of the Lord, and his wonders.* The deep itself is a wonder, its vastness, its saltness, its ebbing and flowing. The great variety of living creatures in the sea is wonderful. Let those that go to sea be led, by all the wonders they observe there, to consider and adore the infinite perfections of that God whose the sea is, for he made it and manages it.

II. It especially appears in storms at sea. *Then* wonders begin to appear in the deep, when God *commands and raises the* strong *wind,* which *fulfils his word,* cxlviii. 8. A stranger, who had never seen it, would not think it possible for a ship to live at sea, as it will in a storm, and ride it out, and yet God taught man to make ships that should so strangely keep above water. When the storm is very high, even those that are used to the sea can neither shake off nor dissemble their fears, but are quite *at their wits' end* (*v.* 27), not knowing what to do more for their preservation. Those that go to sea must expect such perils and the best preparation for them is liberty of access to God by prayer. We have a saying, "Let those that would learn to pray go to sea"; I say, Let those that will go to sea learn to pray. Those that have the Lord for their God have a present help in every time of need, so that when they are at their wits' end they are not at their faith's end. God sometimes appears for those that are in distress at sea, in answer to their prayers: *He brings them out* of the danger. *He makes the storm a calm, v.* 29. The seamen are made easy. The voyage becomes prosperous and successful: *So he brings them to their desired haven, v.* 30. Thus he carries his people safely through all the storms and tempests that they meet with in their voyage heaven-ward, and lands them, at length, in the desired harbour.

Verses 33–43

The psalmist, having given God the glory of the providential reliefs granted to persons in distress, here gives him the glory of the revolutions of providence, and the surprising changes it sometimes makes in the affairs of the children of men.

I. He gives some instances of these revolutions.

1. Fruitful countries are made barren and barren countries are made fruitful. Much of the comfort of this life depends upon the soil in which our lot is cast. The sin of man has often marred the fruitfulness of the soil, *v.* 33, 34. The goodness of God has often mended the barrenness of the soil, and turned a *wilderness,* a land of drought, *into water-springs, v.* 35.

2. Necessitous families are raised and enriched, while prosperous families are impoverished and go to decay. We see many greatly increasing whose beginning was small, *v.* 36–38. Those that were *hungry* are made to *dwell* in fruitful lands; there they take root, and gain a settlement. Providence puts good land under their hands, and they build upon it. But lodgings, though ever so convenient, will not serve without lands, and therefore they must *sow the fields, and plant vineyards* (*v.* 37). Man's industry must attend God's blessing, and then God's blessing will crown man's industry. The fruitfulness of the soil should engage, for it does encourage, diligence; and, ordinarily, *the hand of the diligent,* by the blessing of God, *makes rich, v.* 38. We see many that have suddenly risen as suddenly sunk and brought to nothing (*v.* 39) by adverse providences, and end their days as low as they began them; or their families after them lose as fast as they got, and scatter what they heaped together. Those that were high and great in the world are abased, and those that were mean and despicable are advanced to honour, *v.* 40, 41. Those that exalt themselves God will abase. He makes *them to wander in the wilderness, where there is no way.* Those that were afflicted and trampled on are not only delivered, but set on high out of the reach of their troubles. God is to be acknowledged both in setting up families and in building them up. Let

JAMIESON, FAUSSET, BROWN

To the chorus is added the mode of giving thanks, by a sacrifice and joyful singing (Ps. 50:14).

23-32. Here are set forth the perils of seafaring, futility of man's, and efficiency of God's, help. **go ... sea**—alluding to the elevation of the land at the coast. **These see ... deep**—illustrated both by the storm He raises and the calm He makes with a word (Ps. 33:9). **waves thereof**—lit., "His waves" (God's, Ps. 42:7).

are ... end—lit., "all their wisdom swallows up itself," destroys itself by vain and contradictory devices, such as despair induces.

He maketh ... calm—or, to stand to stillness, or in quiet. Instead of acts of temple worship, those of the synagogue are here described, where the people with the **assembly,** or session of elders, convened for reading, singing, prayer, and teaching.

33-41. God's providence is illustriously displayed in His influence on two great elements of human prosperity, the earth's productiveness and the powers of government. He punishes the wicked by destroying the sources of fertility, or, in mercy, gives fruitfulness to deserts, which become the homes of a busy and successful agricultural population.

By a permitted misrule and tyranny, this scene of prosperity is changed to one of adversity. He rules rulers, setting up one and putting down another. **wander ... wilderness**—reduced to misery (Job 12:24).

ADAM CLARKE

21. *Oh that men!* The intercalary verse, or burden, as before.

22. *And let them sacrifice.* For their healing they should bring a sacrifice; and they should offer the life of the innocent animal unto God, as He has spared their lives; and let them thus confess that God has spared them when they deserved to die; and let them declare also *his works with rejoicing;* for who will not rejoice when he is delivered from death?

23. *They that go down to the sea in ships.* This is the fourth comparison. Their captivity was as dangerous and alarming as a dreadful tempest at sea to a weather-beaten mariner.

26. *They mount up to the heaven.* This is a most natural and striking description of the state of a ship at sea in a storm: when the sea appears to run mountains high, and the vessel seems for a moment to stand on the sharp ridge of one most stupendous, with a valley of a frightful depth between it and a similar mountain, which appears to be flying in the midst of heaven, that it may submerge the hapless bark, when she descends into the valley of death below. *Their soul is melted because of trouble.* This is not less expressive than it is descriptive. The action of raising the vessel to the clouds, and precipitating her into the abyss, seems to dissolve the very soul. The whole mind seems to melt away, so that neither feeling, reflection, nor impression remains, nothing but the apprehension of inevitable destruction! When the ship is buffeted between conflicting waves, which threaten either to tear her asunder or crush her together; when she reels to and fro, and staggers like a drunken man, not being able to hold any certain course, then indeed are they *at their wit's end;* or, as the inimitable original expresses it, "and all their skill is swallowed up"—seems to be gulped down by the frightful abyss into which the ship is about to be precipitated.

31. *Oh that men!* The intercalary verse, or burden, as before. See v. 8.

MATTHEW HENRY

not princes be envied, nor the poor despised, for God has many ways of changing the condition of both.

II. Such surprising turns as these are of use, 1. For the solacing of saints. They observe these dispensations with pleasure (*v.* 42). It is a great comfort to a good man to see how God manages the children of men, as the potter does the clay, to see despised virtue advanced and impious pride brought low, to see it evinced that *verily there is a God that judges in the earth.* 2. For the silencing of sinners. When sinners see how their punishment answers to their sin, and how justly God deals with them in taking away from them those gifts of his which they had abused, they shall not have one word to say for themselves. 3. For the satisfying of all concerning the divine goodness (*v.* 43): *Whoso is wise, and will observe these things,* these various dispensations of divine providence, *even they shall understand the lovingkindness of the Lord.* A prudent observance of the providences of God will contribute very much to the accomplishing of a good Christian.

PSALM 108

A song or psalm of David.

Verses 1–5

We may here learn how to praise God from the example of one who was master of the art. 1. We must praise God with fixedness of heart. Wandering straggling thoughts must be gathered in, and kept close to the business. 2. We must praise God with freeness of expression: I will praise him *with my glory*, that is, with my tongue. Our tongue is our glory, and never more so than when it is employed in praising God. David's skill in music was his glory, it made him famous, and this should be consecrated to the praise of God. Whatever gift we excel in we must praise God with. 3. We must praise God with affection, and must stir up ourselves that it may be done in a lively manner and not carelessly (*v.* 2): *Awake, psaltery and harp;* let it not be done with a dull and sleepy tune, but let the airs be all lively. Warm devotions honour God. 4. We must praise God publicly, as those that are not ashamed to own our obligations to him. 5. We must, in our praises, magnify the mercy and truth of God (*v.* 4). We cannot see further than the heavens and clouds; whatever we see of God's mercy and truth there is still more to be seen, more reserved to be seen, in the other world.

Verses 6–13

We must be public-spirited in prayer, and bear upon our hearts the concerns of the church of God, *v.* 6. It is God's *beloved,* and therefore must be ours; and therefore we must pray for its deliverance. An active faith can rejoice in what God has said, though it be not yet done; for with him saying and doing are not two things, whatever they are with us. God had promised David to give him the hearts of his subjects; and therefore he surveys the several parts of the country as his own already: "*Shechem* and *Succoth, Gilead* and *Manassah, Ephraim* and *Judah*, are all my own," *v.* 8. He will, without fail, give him the heathen for his *inheritance and the utmost parts of the earth for his possessions.* David looks upon *Moab*, and *Edom*, and *Philistia*, as his own already (*v.* 9). We must take encouragement from the beginnings of mercy to pray and hope for the perfecting of it (*v.* 10, 11): "*Who will bring me into the strong cities* that are yet unconquered? Who will make me master of the country of *Edom*, which is yet unsubdued?" The question was probably to be debated in a council of war, what methods they should take to subdue the Edomites; but he brings it into his prayers, *Wilt not thou, O God?* We must not be discouraged in prayer, nor beaten off from our hold of God, though Providence has in some instances frowned upon us. We must seek help from God, renouncing all confidence in the creature (*v.* 12). *Vain is the help of man.* "It is really so, and therefore we are undone if thou do not help us; we apprehend it to be so, and therefore depend upon thee for help and have the more reason to expect it." We must do our part, but we can do nothing of ourselves; it is only *through God that we shall do valiantly.*

PSALM 109

To the chief Musician. A psalm of David.

Verses 1–5

It is the unspeakable comfort of all good people that, whoever is against them, God is for them.

I. David refers himself to God's judgment (*v.* 1):

JAMIESON, FAUSSET, BROWN

42, 43. In this providential government, good men will rejoice, and the cavils of the wicked will be stopped (Job 5:16; Isa. 52:15), and all who take right views will appreciate God's unfailing mercy and unbounded love.

PSALM 108

Vss. 1-13. This Psalm is composed of vss. 1-5 of Psalm 57:7-11; and vss. 6-12 of Psalm 60:5-12. The varieties are verbal and trivial, except that in vs. 9, "over Philistia will I triumph," differs from Psalm 60:8, the interpretation of which it confirms. Its altogether triumphant tone may intimate that it was prepared by David, omitting the plaintive portions of the other Psalms, as commemorative of God's favor in the victories of His people.

PSALM 109

Vss. 1-31. The writer complains of his virulent enemies, on whom he imprecates God's righteous punishment, and to a prayer for a divine interposition in his behalf appends the expression of his con-

ADAM CLARKE

PSALM 108

This psalm is compounded of two psalms which we have had already under review. Verses 1-5 are the same with the vv. 7-11 of Psalm lvii. And vv. 6-13 are the same with vv. 5-12 of Psalm lx. That the psalms referred to were made by David, and were applicable to the then state of his affairs, has been the opinion of many; and it is probable that the captives in Babylon composed this out of two above, and applied it to the state of their affairs. Their captivity being now ended, or nearly at an end, they look and pray for their restoration to their own land, as amply as it was possessed in the most prosperous days of David.

3. *Among the people.* The Jews. *Among the nations.* The Gentiles. Wherever this psalm is sung or read, among either Jews or Gentiles, David may be said to sing praise to God.

PSALM 109

The title of this psalm, "To the chief Musician, A Psalm of David," has already often occurred, and on it the versions offer nothing new. The Syriac says it is "a Psalm of David,

CHARLES H. SPURGEON:

"Through God we shall do valiantly: for he it is that shall tread down our enemies." God's help shall inspire us to help ourselves. Faith is neither a coward nor a sluggard: she knows that God is with her, and therefore she does valiantly; she knows that he will tread down her enemies, and therefore she arises to tread them down in his name. Where praise and prayer have preceded the battle, we may expect to see heroic deeds and decisive victories. *"Through God"* is our secret support; from that source we draw all our courage, wisdom, and strength. *"We shall do valiantly."* This is the public outflow from that secret source: our inward and spiritual faith proves itself by outward and valorous deeds. *"He shall tread down our enemies."* They shall fall before him, and as they lie prostrate he shall march over them, and all the hosts of his people with him. This is a prophecy. It was fulfilled to David, but it remains true to the Son of David and all who are on his side. The church shall yet arouse herself to praise her God with all her heart, and then with songs and hosannas she will advance to the great battle; her foes shall be overthrown and utterly crushed by the power of her God, and the Lord's glory shall be above all the earth. Send it in our time, we beseech thee, O Lord.—*The Treasury of David*

MATTHEW HENRY

"*Hold not thy peace*, but *let my sentence come forth from thy presence*, xvii. 2. Delay not to give judgment upon the appeal made to thee." The title he gives to God is: "*O God of my praise!* the God in whom *I glory*, and not in any wisdom or strength of my own."

II. He complains of his enemies. They are *wicked*; they delight in doing mischief (*v.* 2); their words are *words of hatred*, *v.* 3. "They are *deceitful* in their protestations and professions of kindness, while at the same time they speak against me behind my back, *with a lying tongue*." They were restless in their designs. They were unjust; their accusations of him, and sentence against him, were all groundless: "*They have fought against me without a cause;* I never gave them any provocation." They were very ungrateful, and *rewarded him evil for good*, *v.* 5. *For my love they are my adversaries*. The more he endeavoured to gratify them the more they hated him.

III. He resolves to keep close to his duty and take the comfort of that: *But I give myself unto prayer* (*v.* 4). When David's enemies falsely accused him, and misrepresented him, he applied to God and by prayer committed his cause to him. Though they were his adversaries for his love, yet he continued to pray for them; if others are abusive and injurious to us, yet let not us fail to do our duty to them, nor *sin against the Lord in ceasing to pray for them*, 1 Sam. xii. 23. Now herein David was a type of Christ, who was compassed about with *words of hatred*, and yet *gave himself to prayer*, to pray for them. *Father, forgive them.*

Verses 6–20

David here fastens upon one particular person worse than the rest of his enemies, and in a holy zeal for God and against sin and the enemies of Christ, particularly Judas who betrayed him, he imprecates and predicts his destruction, and such a one as our Saviour calls him, *A son of perdition.* Calvin speaks of it as a detestable piece of sacrilege, common in his time among Franciscan friars and other monks, that if anyone had malice against a neighbour he might hire some of them to curse him every day, which he would do in the words of these verses. Greater impiety can scarcely be imagined than to vent a devilish passion in the language of sacred writ.

I. The imprecations here are very terrible in full force against the implacable enemies and persecutors of God's church and people, that *will not repent, to give him glory*. It is here foretold concerning this bad man,

1. That he should be sentenced as a criminal (*v.* 6, 7): *Set thou a wicked man over him*, to be as cruel and oppressive to him as he has been to others. Set his own wicked heart over him, set his own conscience against him; let that fly in his face.

2. That, being condemned, he should be executed as a most notorious malefactor. He should lose his life, and the number of his months be cut off in the midst, by the sword of justice. Such bloody and *deceitful men shall not live out half their days*. Consequently all his places should be disposed of to others. His family should be beheaded and beggared, *his wife* should be made *a widow* and *his children fatherless*, by his untimely death, *v.* 9. They shall be *vagabonds and shall beg*, because they are conscious to themselves that all mankind have reason to hate them for their father's sake. His estate should be ruined, as the estates of malefactors are confiscated (*v.* 11). This wicked man having never shown mercy there shall *be none to extend mercy to him*, by *favouring his fatherless children* when he is gone, *v.* 12. The children of wicked parents often fare the worse for their parents' wickedness in this way that the bowels of men's compassion are shut up from them, which yet ought not to be, for why should children suffer for that which was not their fault, but their infelicity?

What hurries some to shameful deaths, and brings the families and estates of others to ruin, makes them and theirs despicable and odious, and entails poverty, and shame, and misery, upon their posterity. It is sin, that mischievous destructive thing.

II. The ground of these imprecations bespeaks them just, though they sound very severe. 1. To justify the imprecations of vengeance upon the sinner's posterity, the sin of his ancestors is here brought into the account (*v.* 14, 15), *the iniquity of his fathers* and *the sin of his mother*. All the innocent blood that had been shed upon the earth, from that of righteous Abel, was required from that persecuting generation, who, by putting Christ to death, *filled up the measure of their fathers*. 2. To justify the imprecations of vengeance upon the sinner himself, his own sin is here charged upon him, which called aloud for it. He had loved cruelty, persecuted the poor, whom he should have protected and relieved, and *slew the broken in heart*, whom he should have comforted and healed. Here is a barbarous man indeed, not fit to live. He had

JAMIESON, FAUSSET, BROWN

fidence and a promise of his praises. This Psalm is remarkable for the number and severity of its imprecations. Its evident typical character (cf. vs. 8) justifies the explanation of these already given, that as the language of David respecting his own enemies, or those of Christ, it has respect not to the penitent, but to the impenitent and implacable foes of good men, and of God and His cause, whose inevitable fate is thus indicated by inspired authority.

1. God of my praise—its object, thus recognizing God as a certain helper. *Be not silent* (cf. Ps. 17: 13; 28:1). **2. For the mouth . . . opened** [or, They have opened a wicked mouth] **against me**—lit., "with me," i.e., Their intercourse is living, or, they slander me to my face (Matt. 26:59). **3.** (Cf. Ps. 35:7; 69:4.)

4, 5. They return evil for good (cf. Ps. 27:12; Prov. 17:13). **I give myself unto prayer**—or lit., "I (am) prayer," or, as for me, prayer, i.e., it is my resource for comfort in distress.

6. over him—one of his enemies prominent in malignity (Ps. 55:12). **let Satan stand**—as an accuser, whose place was the right hand of the accused (Zech. 3:1, 2).

7. The condemnation is aggravated when prayer for relief is treated as a sin.

8. The opposite blessing is long life (Ps. 91:16; Prov. 3:2). The last clause is quoted as to Judas by Peter (Acts 1:20). **office**—lit., "charge," *Septuagint*, and Peter, "oversight." **9, 10.** Let his family share the punishment, his children be as wandering beggars to prowl in their desolate homes, a greedy and relentless creditor grasp his substance, his labor, or the fruit of it, enure to strangers and not his heirs, and his unprotected, fatherless children fall in want, so that his posterity shall utterly fail.

13. posterity—lit., "end," as in Psalm 37:38, or, what comes after; i.e., reward, or success, or its expectation, of which posterity was to a Jew a prominent part.

14, 15. Added to the terrible overthrow following his own sin, let there be the imputation of his parents' guilt, that it may now come before God, for His meting out its full consequences, in cutting off the memory of them (i.e., the parents) from the earth (Ps. 34:16).

16. Let God remember guilt, because he (the wicked) did not remember mercy. **poor and needy . . . broken in heart**—i.e., pious sufferer (Ps. 34:18; 35:10; 40:17).

ADAM CLARKE

when the people, without his knowledge, made *Absalom* king; on which account he was slain: but to us (Christians) he details the passion of Christ." That it contains a prophecy against *Judas* and the enemies of our Lord is evident from Acts i. 20. Probably, in its primary meaning (for such a meaning it certainly has), it may refer to *Ahithophel*. The execrations in it should be rendered in the *future* tense, as they are mere prophetic denunciations of God's displeasure against sinners. Taken in this light, it cannot be a stumbling block to any person. God has a right to denounce those judgments which He will inflict on the workers of iniquity. But perhaps the whole may be the execrations of *David's* enemies against himself. See on v. 20. *Ahithophel*, who gave evil counsel against *David*, and being frustrated hanged himself, was no mean prototype of *Judas*, the traitor; it was probably on this account that *St. Peter*, Acts i. 20, applied it to the case of *Judas*, as a prophetic declaration concerning him, or at least a subject that might be accommodated to his case.

1. *Hold not thy peace.* Be not silent; arise and defend my cause.

4. *But I give myself unto prayer.* "And I prayer." The Chaldee: "but I pray."

6. *Let Satan stand at his right hand.* As the word *satan* means an "adversary" simply, though sometimes it is used to express the evil spirit *Satan*, I think it best to preserve here its grammatical meaning: "Let an adversary stand at his right hand"; i.e., Let him be opposed and thwarted in all his purposes.

7. *Let him be condemned.* "Let him come out a wicked man"; that is, let his wickedness be made manifest. *Let his prayer become sin.* I once more apprise the reader that if these are not the words of David's enemies against himself (see on v. 20) they are prophetic denunciations against a rebellious and apostate person or people, hardened in crime, and refusing to return to God.

8. *Let another take his office.* The original literally means "superintendence, oversight, inspection from actual visitations."

MATTHEW HENRY

loved cursing, and therefore let the curse come upon his head, *v.* 17–19. Let God's cursing him be his shame, as his cursing his neighbour was his pride. This points at the utter ruin of Judas, and the spiritual judgments which fell on the Jews for crucifying Christ. The psalmist concludes his imprecations with a terrible *Amen.*

Verses 21–31

David takes God's comforts to himself, but in a very humble manner.

I. "*I am poor and needy*, and one that needs and craves thy help." He was troubled in mind (*v.* 22): *My heart is wounded within me*, not only broken with outward troubles, but wounded with a sense of guilt; and *a wounded spirit who can bear*? He was unsettled, *tossed up and down like the locust*, his mind unsteady, hunted like a partridge on the mountains. His body was wasted, and almost worn away (*v.* 24): *My knees are weak through fasting*, either forced fasting or voluntary fasting, when he chastened his soul. But it is better to have this leanness in the body, while the soul prospers and is in health, than, like Israel, to have leanness sent into the soul, while the body is feasted. In all this David was a type of Christ, who in his humiliation was thus weakened, thus reproached.

II. He prays for mercy for himself. "Lord, do for me what seems good in thy eyes. Do that which thou knowest will be for me, really for me, in the issue for me, though for the present it may seem to make against me." More particularly, he prays (*v.* 26): "*Help me, O Lord my God! O save me!* Save me from sin, help me to do my duty." He prays (*v.* 28), Though they *curse, bless thou.* If God bless us, we need not care who curses us.

III. He prays that his enemies might *be ashamed* (*v.* 28), *clothed with shame* (*v.* 29), that they might *cover themselves with their own confusion*, that they might be left to themselves, to do that which would expose them and *manifest their folly before all men.* In this he prays that they might be brought to repentance which is the chief thing we should beg of God for our enemies.

IV. He pleads God's glory, the honour of his name. "*Deliver me, because thy mercy is good;* let that be the measure, of my salvation." He concludes the psalm with joy, the joy of faith. He promises God that he will praise him (*v.* 30). He promises himself that he shall have cause to praise God (*v.* 31). God was David's protector in his sufferings, and was present also with the Lord Jesus in his, saved his soul from those that pretended to be the judges of it, and received it into his own hands.

JAMIESON, FAUSSET, BROWN

17-19. Let his loved sin, cursing, come upon him in punishment (Ps. 35:8), thoroughly fill him as water and oil, permeating to every part of his system (cf. Num. 5:22-27), and become a garment and a girdle for a perpetual dress. **20. Let this . . . reward**—or, wages, pay for labor, the fruit of the enemy's wickedness. **from the Lord**—as His judicial act.

21, 22. do . . . for me—i.e., kindness. **wounded**—lit., "pierced" (Ps. 69:16, 29).

23. like the shadow—(Cf. Ps. 102:11). **tossed up and down**—or, driven (Exod. 10:19). **24, 25.** Taunts and reproaches aggravate his afflicted and feeble state (Ps. 22:6, 7).

26, 27. Let my deliverance glorify Thee (cf. Ps. 59:13). **28-31.** In confidence that God's blessing would come on him, and confusion and shame on his enemies (Ps. 73:13), he ceases to regard their curses, and anticipates a season of joyful and public thanksgiving; for God is near to protect (Ps. 16:8, 34:6) the poor from all unrighteous judges who may condemn him.

ADAM CLARKE

20. *Let this be the reward of mine adversaries from the Lord, and of them that speak evil against my soul.* Is not this verse a key to all that preceded it? The original, fairly interpreted, will lead us to a somewhat different meaning: "This is the work of my adversaries before the Lord, and of those who speak evil against my soul," or "life." That is, all that is said from the sixth to the twentieth verse consists of the evil words and imprecations of my enemies against my soul, laboring to set the Lord, by imprecations, against me, that their curses may take effect. This, which is a reasonable interpretation, frees the whole psalm from every difficulty. Surely the curses contained in it are more like those which proceed from the mouth of the wicked than from one inspired by the Spirit of the living God. Taking the words in this sense, which I am persuaded is the best, and which the original will well bear and several of the versions countenance, then our translation may stand just as it is; only let the reader remember that at the sixth verse David begins to tell how his enemies cursed him, while he prayed for them.

21. *But do thou for me.* While they use horrible imprecations against me, and load me with their curses, act Thou for me, and deliver me from their maledictions. While they curse, do Thou bless. This verse is a further proof of the correctness of the interpretation given above.

22. *I am poor and needy.* I am afflicted and impoverished; and my heart is wounded—my very life is sinking through distress.

23. *I am gone like the shadow.* "I have walked like the declining shadow"—I have passed my meridian of health and life; and as the sun is going below the horizon, so am I about to go under the earth. *I am tossed up and down as the locust.* When swarms of locusts take wing, and infest the countries in the East, if the wind happen to blow briskly, the swarms are agitated and driven upon each other, so as to appear to be heaved to and fro, or tossed up and down.

25. *When they looked upon me they shaked their heads.* Thus was David treated by Shimei, 2 Sam. xvi. 5-6, and our blessed Lord by the Jews, Matt. xxvii. 39.

28. *Let them curse, but bless thou.* See on v. 20. Of the mode of interpretation recommended there, this verse gives additional proof.

MATTHEW HENRY — PSALM 110

Verses 1–4

Some have called this psalm *David's creed*, almost all the articles of the Christian faith being found in it, the title calls it *David's psalm*, for in the believing foresight of the Messiah he both praised God and solaced himself. Much more may we, in singing it, to whom that is fulfilled, which is here foretold. Glorious things are here spoken of Christ.

I. He is David's Lord. We must take special notice of this because he himself does. Matt. xxii. 43, *David, in spirit, calls him Lord.*

II. He is constituted a sovereign Lord by the counsel and decree of God himself: *The Lord*, Jehovah, *said unto him, Sit* as a king. He *receives of the Father* this honour and glory (2 Pet. i. 17).

III. He was to be advanced to the highest honour, and entrusted with absolute sovereign power. *Sit thou at my right hand.* Sitting is a resting posture; after his services and sufferings, he entered into rest. It is a ruling posture; he sits to give law, to give judgment.

IV. All his enemies were in due time to be made his footstool. Even Christ himself has enemies that fight against his kingdom. There are those that will not have him to reign over them, and thereby they join themselves to Satan, who will not have him to reign at all. These enemies will *be made his footstool.* It will not be done immediately. This the apostle observes. Heb. ii. 8, *We see not yet all things put under him.* Christ himself shall wait till it is done.

V. He should have a kingdom set up in the world, beginning at Jerusalem (*v.* 2). The kingdom of Christ took rise from Zion, the city of David, for he was the Son of David, and was to have *the throne of his father David.* By the rod of his strength, or his strong rod, is meant his everlasting gospel, and the power of the Holy Ghost. This strong rod God sent forth; he poured out the Spirit, and gave both commissions and qualifications to those that preached the word, and *ministered the Spirit*, Gal. iii. 5. It was sent out of Zion, for there the Spirit was given, and there

JAMIESON, FAUSSET, BROWN — PSALM 110

Vss. 1-7. The explicit application of this Psalm to our Saviour, by Him (Matt. 22:42-45) and by the apostles (Acts 2:34; I Cor. 15:25; Heb. 1:13), and their frequent reference to its language and purport (Eph. 1:20-22; Phil. 2:9-11; Heb. 10:12, 13), leave no doubt of its purely prophetic character. Not only was there nothing in the position or character, personal or official, of David or any other descendant, to justify a reference to either, but utter severance from the royal office of all priestly functions (so clearly assigned the subject of this Psalm) positively forbids such a reference. The Psalm celebrates the exaltation of Christ to the throne of an eternal and increasing kingdom, and a perpetual priesthood (Zech. 6:13), involving the subjugation of His enemies and the multiplication of His subjects, and rendered infallibly certain by the word and oath of Almighty God.

1. The Lord said—lit., "A saying of the Lord," (cf. Ps. 36:1), a formula, used in prophetic or other solemn or express declarations. **my Lord**—That the Jews understood this term to denote the Messiah their traditions show, and Christ's mode of arguing on such an assumption (Matt. 22:44) also proves. **Sit . . . at my right hand**—not only a mark of honor (I Kings 2:19), but also implied participation of power (Ps. 45:9; Mark 16:19; Eph. 1:20). **Sit**—as a king (Ps. 29:10), though the position rather than posture is intimated (cf. Acts. 7:55, 56). **until I make . . .**—The dominion of Christ over His enemies, as commissioned by God, and entrusted with all power (Matt. 28:18) for their subjugation, will assuredly be established (I Cor. 15:24-28). This is neither His government as God, nor that which, as the incarnate Saviour, He exercises over His people, of whom He will ever be Head. **thine enemies thy footstool**—an expression taken from the custom of Eastern conquerors (cf. Josh. 10:24; Judg. 1:7) to signify

ADAM CLARKE — PSALM 110

The Hebrew, and all the versions except the Arabic, attribute this psalm to David; nor can this be doubted, as it is thus attributed in the New Testament. We have in it the celebration of some great potentate's accession to the crown; but the subject is so grand, the expressions so noble, and the object raised so far above what can be called human, that no history has ever mentioned a prince to whom a literal application of this psalm can be made. To Jesus Christ alone, to His everlasting priesthood and government, as King of Kings and Lord of Lords, can it be applied.

1. *The Lord said unto my Lord. Jehovah* said unto my *Adoni.* That David's Lord is the Messiah is confirmed by our Lord himself and by the apostles Peter and Paul.

Sit thou at my right hand. This implies the possession of the utmost confidence, power, and preeminence.

Until I make thine enemies. Jesus shall reign till all His enemies are subdued under Him.

MATTHEW HENRY

the preaching of the gospel among all nations must begin, at Jerusalem.

VI. That his kingdom, being set up, should be maintained and kept up in the world, in spite of all the opposition of the power of darkness. He shall rule *in the midst of his enemies.* He sits in heaven in the midst of his friends; he rules on earth in the midst of his enemies.

VII. He should have a great number of subjects, who should be to him for a name and a praise, *v.* 3.

1. They are given to him by the Father. *Thine they were and thou gavest them me,* John xvii. 6. They are redeemed by him, Tit. ii. 14. They are his by right, antecedent to their consent.

2. They should be *a willing people,* servants that choose their service, soldiers that are volunteers and not pressed men.

3. That they should be so *in the day of his power, in the day of thy muster. In the day of thy armies* (so some); "when the first preachers of the gospel shall be sent forth, as Christ's armies, then all that are *thy people shall be willing*; that will be thy time of setting up thy kingdom."

4. They should be so *in the beauty of holiness*; they shall be charmed into a subjection to Christ by the sight given them of his beauty, who is the holy Jesus. They shall be admitted by him into the beauty of holiness, as spiritual priests, to minister in his sanctuary in the beautiful attire or ornaments of grace and sanctification. Holiness is the livery of Christ's family and that which *becomes his house for ever.* Christ's soldiers are all thus clothed; these are the colours they wear.

5. He should have great numbers of people devoted to him. In the early days of the gospel, in the morning of the New Testament, the youth of the church, great numbers flocked to Christ, and there were *multitudes that believed,* a *remnant of Jacob,* that was as a *dew from the Lord,* Mic. v. 7; Isa. lxiv. 4, 8. *The dew of the youth* is a numerous, illustrious, hopeful show of young people flocking to Christ, which would be to the world as dew to the ground, to make it fruitful.

6. He should be not only a king, but a priest, *v.* 4. Our Lord Jesus Christ is God's minister to us, and our advocate with God, and so is a Mediator between us and God. He is said to be *a priest for ever,* not only because we are never to expect any other dispensation of grace than this by the priesthood of Christ, but because the blessed fruits and consequences of it will remain to eternity. He is a priest, not of the order of Aaron, but of that of Melchizedek, which, as it was prior, so it was upon many accounts superior. The apostle comments largely upon these words (Heb. vii) and builds on them his discourse of Christ's priestly office, which he shows was no new notion, but built upon this most sure word of prophecy. For, as the New Testament explains the Old, so the Old Testament confirms the New, and Jesus Christ is the Alpha and Omega of both.

Verses 5–7

Here we have our great Redeemer.

I. Conquering his enemies (*v.* 5, 6): Our Lord Jesus will certainly bring to nought all the opposition made to his kingdom.

1. The conqueror: *The Lord—Adonai,* the Lord Jesus, he to whom all judgment is committed, he shall make his own part good against his enemies. Christ's sitting at the right hand of God speaks as much terror to his enemies as happiness to his people.

2. The time fixed for this victory: *In the day of his wrath,* that is, the time appointed for it, when the measure of their iniquities is full, and they are ripe for ruin.

3. The extent of this victory. He *shall strike through kings.* Satan is the prince of this world, Death the king of terrors, and we read of kings that make war with the Lamb; but they shall all be brought down and broken. The trophies of Christ's victories will be set up *among the heathen,* and in many countries, wherever any of his enemies are.

4. The equity of this victory: *He shall judge among them.* It is not a military execution, which is done in fury, but a judicial one.

5. The effect of this victory; it shall be the complete and utter ruin of all his enemies. He shall *wound the heads,* which seems to refer to the first promise of the Messiah (Gen. iii. 15), that he should *bruise the serpent's head.* He shall *fill the places with the dead bodies.* The slain of the Lord shall be many.

II. We have here the Redeemer saving his friends and comforting them (*v.* 7). 1. He shall be humbled: *He shall drink of the brook in the way,* that bitter cup which the Father put into his hand. Christ drank of this brook when he was made a curse for us, and therefore, when he entered upon his suffering, he

JAMIESON, FAUSSET, BROWN

a complete subjection. **2. the rod of thy strength**—the rod of correction (Isa. 9:4; 10:15; Jer. 48:12), by which Thy strength will be known. This is His Word of truth (Isa. 2:3; 11:4), converting some and confounding others (cf. II Thess. 2:8). **out of Zion**—or, the Church, in which God dwells by His Spirit, as once by a visible symbol in the tabernacle on Zion (cf. Ps. 2:6). **rule thou . . .**—over enemies now conquered. **in the midst**—once set upon, as by ferocious beasts (Ps. 22:16), now humbly, though reluctantly, confessed as Lord (Phil. 2:10, 11). **3. Thy people . . . willing**—lit., "Thy people (are) free-will offerings"; for such is the proper rendering of the word "willing," which is a plural noun, and not an adjective (cf. Exod. 25:2; Ps. 54:6), also a similar form (Judg. 5:2-9). **in the day of thy power**—Thy people freely offer themselves (Rom. 12:1) in Thy service, enlisting under Thy banner. **in the beauties of holiness**—either as in Psalm 29:2, the loveliness of a spiritual worship, of which the temple service, in all its material splendors, was but a type; or more probably, the appearance of the worshippers, who, in this spiritual kingdom, are a nation of kings and priests (I Peter 2:9; Rev. 1:5), attending this Priest and King, clothed in those eminent graces which the beautiful vestments of the Aaronic priests (Lev. 16:4) typified. The last very obscure clause—**from the womb . . . youth**—may, according to this view, be thus explained: The word "youth" denotes a period of life distinguished for strength and activity (cf. Eccles. 11:9)—the "dew" is a constant emblem of whatever is refreshing and strengthening (Prov. 19:12; Hos. 14:5). The Messiah, then, as leading His people, is represented as continually in the vigor of youth, refreshed and strengthened by the early dew of God's grace and Spirit. Thus the phrase corresponds as a member of a parallelism with "the day of thy power" in the first clause. "In the beauties of holiness" belongs to this latter clause, corresponding to "Thy people" in the first, and the colon after "morning" is omitted. Others prefer: Thy youth, or youthful vigor, or body, shall be constantly refreshed by successive accessions of people as dew from the early morning; and this accords with the New Testament idea that the Church is Christ's body (cf. Micah 5:7). **4.** The perpetuity of the priesthood, here asserted on God's oath, corresponds with that of the kingly office just explained.

after the order—(Heb. 7:15) after the similitude of Melchisedek, is fully expounded by Paul, to denote not only perpetuity, appointment of God, and a royal priesthood, but also the absence of priestly descent and succession, and superiority to the Aaronic order.

5. at thy right hand—as Psalm 109:31, upholding and aiding, which is not inconsistent with vs. 1, where the figure denotes participation of power, for here He is presented in another aspect, as a warrior going against enemies, and sustained by God.

strike through—smite or crush. **kings**—not common men, but their rulers, and so all under them (Ps. 2:2, 10).

6. The person is again changed. The Messiah's conquests are described, though His work and God's are the same. As after a battle, whose field is strewn with corpses, the conqueror ascends the seat of empire, so shall He judge or rule among many nations, and subdue **the head** [or (as used collectively for many) the heads] **over many lands. wound**—lit., "smite," or "crush" (cf. vs. 5).

7. As a conqueror, "faint, yet pursuing," He shall be refreshed by **the brook in the way,** and pursue to completion His divine and glorious triumphs.

ADAM CLARKE

2. *The rod of thy strength.* The gospel—the doctrine of Christ crucified.

3. *Thy people shall be willing in the day of thy power.* This verse has been woefully perverted. It has been supposed to point out the irresistible operation of the grace of God on the souls of the elect, thereby making them willing to receive Christ as their Saviour. Now whether this doctrine be true or false, it is not in this text, nor can it receive the smallest countenance from it. There has been much spoken against the doctrine of what is called "free will" by persons who seem not to have understood the term. "Will" is a free principle. "Free will" is as absurd as "bound will"; it is not "will" if it be not free. Volition is essential to the being of the soul, and to all rational and intellectual beings. This is the most essential discrimination between matter and spirit. Let us examine the text. The Hebrew words literally translated are, "Thy princely people, or free people, in the day of thy power." It merely expresses the character of the people who shall constitute the kingdom of Christ. *Am nedaboth* is the people of liberality—the princely, noble, and generous people.

In the beauties of holiness. "In the splendid garments of holiness." An allusion to the beautiful garments of the high priest. *From the womb of the morning.* As the dew flows from the womb of the morning, so shall all the godly from Thee. They are *the dew of thy youth;* they are the offspring of Thy own nativity. As the human nature of our Lord was begotten by the creative energy of God in the womb of the Virgin, so the followers of God are "born, not of blood, nor of the will of the flesh," but by the Divine Spirit.

4. *The Lord hath sworn.* Has most firmly purposed, and will most certainly perform it. *And will not repent.* Will never change this purpose.

After the order of Melchizedek. For the elucidation of this point the reader is requested to refer to Gen. xiv. 18-19.

6. *He shall judge among the heathen.* David shall greatly extend his dominion, and rule over the Idumeans, Moabites, Philistines, etc. *He shall fill . . . with the dead bodies.* He shall fill pits—make heaps of slain; there shall be an immense slaughter among his enemies.

MATTHEW HENRY

went over the brook Kidron, John xviii. 1. 2. He shall be exalted: *Therefore shall he lift up the head.* When he died he *bowed the head* (John xix. 30), but he soon lifted up the head by his own power in his resurrection. He lifted up the head as a conqueror. Because he drank of the brook in the way therefore he lifted up his own head, and so lifted up the heads of all his faithful followers, who, *if they suffer with him, shall also reign with him.*

PSALM 111

Verses 1–5

The title of the psalm being *Hallelujah*, the psalmist keeps to his text.

I. He resolves to praise God himself, *v.* 1. We must praise God both in private and in public, in less and greater assemblies, in our own families and in the courts of the Lord's house.

II. He recommends to us the *works of the Lord* as the proper subject of our meditations when we are praising him—the dispensations of his providence towards the world, towards the church, and towards particular persons. 1. God's works are great like himself; there is nothing in them that is mean or trifling: they are the products of infinite wisdom and power. 2. They are entertaining and exercising to the inquisitive—*sought out of all those that have pleasure therein.* Those that have pleasure in the works of God will not take up with a superficial transient view of them, but will diligently search into them and observe them. In studying both natural and political history we discover the greatness and glory of God's works. 3. They are all just and holy: *His righteousness endures for ever.* 4. They are memorable, fit to be registered and kept on record. Much that we do is so trifling that the greatest kindness is to forget it. But notice is to be taken of God's works, and an account to be kept of them (*v.* 4). *He has made his wonderful works to be remembered.* 5. In them the Lord shows that he is *gracious and full of compassion. He will be ever mindful of his covenant;* so that they can taste covenant-love even in common mercies. Some refer this to the manna with which God fed his people Israel in the wilderness.

Verses 6–10

Glory to God,

I. For the great things he has done for his people, for his people Israel, of old and of late: *He has shown his people the power of his works* (*v.* 6). 1. The possession God gave to Israel in the land of Canaan. This he did in Joshua's time, when the seven nations were subdued, and in Davids' time, when the neighbouring nations became tributaries to David. 2. The many deliverances which he wrought for his people when by their iniquities they had sold themselves into the hand of their enemies (*v.* 9). These redemptions were typical of the great redemption which in the fulness of time was to be wrought out by the Lord Jesus.

II. For the stability both of his word and of his works, which assure us of the great things he will do for them. 1. What God has done shall never be undone. He will not undo it himself, and men and devils cannot (*v.* 7): *The works of his hand are verity and judgment* (*v.* 8), that is, they *are done in truth and uprightness.* Upon the beginning of his works we may depend for the perfecting of them. 2. What God has said shall never be unsaid: *All his commandments are sure*, all straight and therefore all steady.

III. For the setting up and establishing of religion among men. Because the discoveries of religion tend so much to his honour. Review what he has made known of himself in his word and in his works, and you will see, and say, that God is great. Because the dictates of religion tend so much to man's happiness. Reverence of him and obedience to him are as much our interest as they are our duty. Men can never begin to be wise till they begin to fear God; all true wisdom takes its rise from true religion, and has its foundation in it. *A good understanding have all those that do his commandments.* Where the fear of the Lord rules in the heart there will be a constant conscientious care to keep his commandments, not to talk of them, but to do them; and such have a good understanding. Their obedience is a plain indication of their mind that they do indeed fear God. We have reason to praise God, to praise him for ever, for putting man into such a fair way to happiness.

JAMIESON, FAUSSET, BROWN

PSALM 111

Vss. 1-10. The Psalmist celebrates God's gracious dealings with His people, of which a summary statement is given.

1. Praise ye the Lord—or, *Hallelujah* (Ps. 104:35). This seems to serve as a title to those of the later Psalms, which, like this, set forth God's gracious government and its blessed fruits. This praise claims the **whole heart** (Ps. 86:12), and is rendered publicly. **upright**—a title of the true Israel (Ps. 32: 11).

2. His **works,** i.e., of providence and grace, are **sought**—or, carefully studied, by all desiring to know them.

3, 4. honourable and glorious—lit., "honor and majesty," which illustrate His glorious perfections. **righteousness**—(Ps. 7:17; 31:1), which He has made memorable by wonders of love and mercy, in supplying the wants of His people according to covenant engagements.

6-8. His power was shown especially in giving them the promised land, and His faithfulness and justice thus displayed are, like His precepts, reliable and of permanent obligation.

9. The deliverance He provided accorded to His established covenant. Thus He manifested Himself in the sum of His perfections (Ps. 20:1, 7; 22:3) worthy of reverence.

10. And hence love and fear of such a God is the chief element of true wisdom (cf. Prov. 1:7; 9:10).

ADAM CLARKE

PSALM 111

This is one of the alphabetical or acrostic psalms; but it is rather different from those we have already seen, as the first eight verses each contain two members, and each member commences with a consecutive letter of the Hebrew alphabet. But the last two verses are composed of three members each, characterized the same way, making twenty-two members or hemistichs in the whole, to each of which a consecutive letter of the alphabet is prefixed.

1. *I will praise the Lord with my whole heart.* If we profess to "sing to the praise and glory of God," the heart, and the *whole heart,* without division and distraction, must be employed in the work. *In the assembly. Besod,* in the "secret assembly"—the private religious meetings for the communion of saints. *And in the congregation, edah,* the "general assembly"—the public congregation.

2. *The works of the Lord are great. Gedolim,* "vast in magnitude."

5. *He hath given meat. Tereph,* "prey." This may allude to the quails in the wilderness.

6. *The power of his works.* They have seen that these things did not arrive in the common course of nature; it was "not by might, nor by power," but by the Spirit of the Lord of hosts they were done. And it required a display of the power of God to give them the heritage of the heathen.

8. *They stand fast for ever.* "They are propped up, buttressed, for ever." They can never fail; for God's power supports His works, and His providence preserves the record of what He has done.

9. *He sent redemption.* He sent Moses to redeem them out of Egypt; various judges to deliver them out of the hands of their oppressors; Ezra, Nehemiah, and Zerubbabel to deliver them from Babylon; and the Lord Jesus to redeem a whole lost world from sin, misery, and death. *Holy and reverend is his name.* The word *reverend* comes to us from the Latin *reverendus* and is compounded of *re,* intensive, and *vereor,* "to be feared." But *reverend* is not applied to God in this way; nor does the word *nora* bear this signification. It rather means "terrible": "Holy and terrible," or, "Holy and tremendous is his name." This title belongs not to man; nor does any minister, in assuming the title reverend, assume this.

10. *The fear of the Lord is the beginning of wisdom.* The original stands thus: "The beginning of wisdom is the fear of Jehovah." Wisdom itself begins with this fear. A *good understanding have all they that do his commandments.* These last words we add as necessary to make up the sense; but there is no need of this expedient, as the words of the original literally read thus: "The beginning of wisdom is the fear of Jehovah; good discernment to the doers."

MATTHEW HENRY

PSALM 112

Verses 1–5

The psalmist begins with a call to us to praise God, but immediately applies himself to praise the people of God. We have reason to praise the Lord that there are a people in the world who fear him and serve him, and that they are a happy people, both which are owing entirely to the grace of God.

I. A description of those who are here pronounced blessed, and to whom these promises are made.

1. They are well-principled, well affected to his government, such as stand in awe of God and have a constant reverence for his majesty and deference to his will. He *that fears the Lord*, as a Father, with the disposition of a child, not of a slave, *delights greatly in his commandments*. They are written in his heart and he calls them an easy, a pleasant, yoke. He delights not only in God's promises, but in his precepts.

2. They are honest and sincere in their professions and intentions. They are called *the upright* (*v.* 2, 4), who are really as good as they seem to be, and deal faithfully both with God and man. There is no true religion without sincerity; that is gospel-perfection.

3. They are both just and kind in all their dealings. One instance is given of his beneficence (*v.* 5): He *shows favour and lends*. Sometimes there is as much charity in lending as in giving, as it obliges the borrower both to industry and honesty.

II. The blessedness that is here entailed upon those that answer to these characters. Happiness, all happiness, to *the man that feareth the Lord*.

1. The posterity of good men shall fare the better for his goodness (*v.* 2): *His seed shall be mighty on earth*. Religion has been the raising of many a family, if not so as to advance it high, yet so as to fix it firmly. When good men themselves are happy in heaven their seed perhaps are considerable on earth, and will themselves own that it is by virtue of a blessing descending from them. *The generation of the upright shall be blessed;* if they tread in their steps, they shall be the more blessed for their relation to them.

2. They shall prosper in the world, and especially their souls shall prosper, *v.* 3. They shall be blessed with outward prosperity as far as is good for them. But, which is much better, is that they shall be blessed with spiritual blessings, which are the true riches. Grace is better than gold, for it will outlast it. He shall have wealth and riches, and yet shall keep up his religion. When this endures in the family, and the heirs of the father's estate inherit his virtues too, that is a happy family indeed.

3. They shall have comfort in affliction (*v.* 4): *Unto the upright there arises light in the darkness*. They shall have their share in the common calamities of human life; but, *when they sit in darkness, the Lord shall be a light to them*, Mic. vii. 8.

4. They shall have wisdom for the management of all their concerns, *v.* 5. It is part of the character of a good man that he will use his discretion in managing his affairs, in getting and saving, that he may have to give.

Verses 6–10

I. The satisfaction of saints, and their stability. It is the happiness of a good man that *he shall not be moved for ever*, *v.* 6.

1. A good man will have a settled reputation. A good name with God and good people: *The righteous shall be in everlasting remembrance* (*v.* 6). There are those that do all they can to sully his reputation and to load him with reproach; but his integrity shall survive him. Some that have been eminently righteous are *had in a lasting remembrance* on earth; but in heaven their remembrance shall be truly everlasting. Those that are forgotten on earth, and despised, are remembered there, and honoured, and *their righteousness found unto praise, and honour, and glory* (1 Pet. i. 7). That which shall especially turn to the honour of good men is their liberality to the poor: *He has dispersed, he has given to the poor;* he has not suffered his charity to run all in one channel, or directed it to some few objects that he had a particular kindness for, but he has dispersed it.

2. A good man shall have a settled spirit, for *he shall not be afraid; his heart is established*, *v.* 7, 8. It is their endeavour to keep their minds stayed upon God, and so to keep them calm and God has promised them both cause to do so and grace to do so. The fixedness of the heart is a sovereign remedy against the disquieting fear of evil tidings. Trusting in the Lord is the best and surest way of fixing and establishing the heart. *He shall not be afraid, till he see his desire upon his enemies*, that is, till he come to heaven, where he shall see Satan, and all his spiritual enemies, trodden under his feet. *Till he look upon his oppressors*, look boldly in their faces, as being now no

JAMIESON, FAUSSET, BROWN

PSALM 112

Vss. 1-10. **This Psalm may be regarded as an exposition of Psalm 111:10, presenting the happiness of those who fear and obey God, and contrasting the fate of the ungodly.**

1. True fear produces obedience and this happiness.

2, 3. Temporal blessings follow the service of God, exceptions occurring only as they are seen by God to be inconsistent with those spiritual blessings which are better.

4. light–figurative for relief (Ps. 27:1; 97:11). The **upright** are like God (Lev. 6:36; Ps. 111:4).

5-9. Generosity, sound judgment in God, form a character which preserves from fear of evil and ensures success against enemies. While a man thus truly pious is liberal, he increases in substance. **not be moved**–(cf. Ps. 13:4; 15:5.)

heart is established–or, firm in right principles. **see his desire**–(Ps. 50:23; 54:7.)

ADAM CLARKE

PSALM 112

This is another of the acrostic or alphabetical psalms, under the title *Hallelujah*. It is formed exactly as the preceding in the division of its verses. It has ten verses in the whole. The first eight each contain two hemistichs, beginning with a consecutive letter of the alphabet; the ninth and tenth verses, three each, making twenty-two in the whole. It is understood to have been written after the Captivity, and probably by Zechariah and Haggai; to them it is ascribed by the Vulgate.

1. *Blessed is the man that feareth the Lord*. This seems to be the continuation of the preceding psalm. There it was asserted that the beginning of wisdom was the fear of the Lord, and here the blessedness of the man who thus fears is stated. *That delighteth greatly*. It is not enough to fear God; we must also love Him. Fear will deter us from evil; love will lead us to obedience. And the more a man fears and loves God, the more obedient will he be, till at last he will delight greatly in the commandments of his Maker.

2. *His seed shall be mighty*. His "posterity." So the word should always be understood in this connection.

3. *Wealth and riches shall be in his house*. This is often the case; a godly man must save both time and money. Before he was converted he lost much time, and squandered his money.

8. *His heart is established*. "His heart is propped up"; he is buttressed up by the strength of his Maker.

9. *He hath dispersed*. He has scattered abroad his munificence; he has given particularly *to the poor; his righteousness*—his almsgiving, his charity—*remaineth for ever*. See v. 3. *His horn* —his power and authority—*shall be exalted with honour*. He shall rise to influence only through his own worth, and not by extortion or flattery.

MATTHEW HENRY

longer under their power.

II. The vexation of sinners, *v.* 10. Two things shall fret them:—1. The felicity of the righteous. It will vex them to see those whom they hated and despised, and whose ruin they sought and hoped to see, the favourites of Heaven, and advanced to have *dominion over them* (xlix. 14).

PSALM 113

Verses 1–9

I. Glory to God,

1. The invitation is very pressing: *Praise you the Lord*, and again and again, *Praise him, praise him; blessed be his name*, for it is to be praised, *v.* 1–3.

2. The invitation is very extensive. God has praise —from his own people. They have most reason to praise him. The angels are the servants of the Lord; they praise God, and praise him better than we can. Let God be praised through all the generations of time. *Blessed be his name now and always. From the rising of the sun to the going down of the same*, that is, throughout the habitable world. It ought to be praised by all nations; for in every place, from east to west, there appear the manifest proofs and products of his wisdom, power, and goodness.

II. We are here directed what to give him the glory of. Let us look up with an eye of faith, and see how high his glory is in the upper world, and mention that to his praise, *v.* 4, 5. Put all the nations together, and he is above them all; they are before him as the *drop of the bucket and the small dust of the balance*, Isa. xl. 15, 17. The throne of his glory is in the highest heavens. *His glory is above the heavens*, that is, above the angels; he is above what they are—above what they do, for they are under his command—and above what even they can speak him to be. He is a God *who exalts himself to dwell, who humbles himself, in heaven, and in earth.* God is said to *exalt himself* and to *humble himself*, both are his own act and deed. God's condescending goodness appears in the cognizance he takes of the world below him. His glory is *above the nations* and *above the heavens*, and yet neither is neglected by him. *God is great*, yet *he despises not any*, Job xxxvi. 5. *He humbles himself to behold* all his creatures. Considering the infinite perfection, sufficiency, and felicity of the divine nature, it must be acknowledged as an act of wonderful condescension that God is pleased to take into the thoughts of his eternal counsel, and into the hand of his universal Providence, both the armies of heaven and the inhabitants of the earth (Dan. iv. 35); even in this dominion he humbles himself. If it be such condescension for God to behold things in heaven and earth, what an amazing condescension was it for the Son of God to come from heaven to earth and take our nature upon him, that he might *seek and save those that were lost*! He not only beholds the great things in the earth, but the meanest, and does wonders for them, out of the common road of providence and chain of causes, which shows that the world is governed, not by a course of nature, for that would always run in the same channel, but by a God of nature, who delights in doing things we looked not for. Sometimes, on a sudden (*v.* 7, 8): *He raises up the poor out of the dust, that he may set him with princes.* Gideon is fetched from threshing, Saul from seeking the asses, and David from keeping the sheep; the apostles are sent from fishing to be *fishers of men.* The treasure of the gospel is put into earthen vessels, and the weak and foolish ones of the world are pitched upon to be preachers of it, to confound the *wise and mighty* (1 Cor. i. 27, 28), that the excellency of the power may be of God. When Joseph's virtue was tried and manifested he was raised from the prison-dust and *set with princes.* Those that have been long barren are sometimes, on a sudden, made fruitful, *v.* 9. This may look back to Sarah and Rebecca, Rachel, Hannah, and Samson's mother, or forward to Elizabeth; and many such instances there have been, in which God has looked on the affliction of his handmaids and taken away their reproach. *He makes the barren woman to keep house*, not only builds up the family, but thereby finds the heads of the family something to do.

JAMIESON, FAUSSET, BROWN

10. Disappointed in their malevolent wishes by the prosperity of the pious, the wicked are punished by the working of their evil passions, and come to naught.

PSALM 113

Vss. 1-9. God's majesty contrasted with His condescension and gracious dealings towards the humble furnish matter and a call for praise. The Jews, it is said, used this and Psalms 114-118 on their great festivals, and called them the *Greater Hallel, or Hymn.*

1-3. Earnestness and zeal are denoted by the emphatic repetitions. **servants**—or, all the people of God. **name of the Lord**—perfections (Ps. 5:11; 111: 9). **From the rising . . .**—all the world.

4-6. God's exaltation enhances His condescension:

7, 8, which is illustrated as often in raising the worthy poor and needy to honor (cf. I Sam. 2:8; Ps. 44:25).

9. On this special case, cf. I Sam. 2:21. Barrenness was regarded as a disgrace, and is a type of a deserted Church (Isa. 54:1).

the barren woman . . . house—lit., "the barren of the house," so that the supplied words may be omitted.

ADAM CLARKE

10. *The wicked shall see it. Rasha,* "the wicked one." Some think Satan is meant. It is distinguished from *reshaim,* "wicked men," in the conclusion of the verse. *Shall gnash with his teeth.* Through spite and ill will. *And melt away.* Through envy and hopeless expectation of similar good; for his *desire* in reference to himself, and in reference to him who is the object of his envy, *shall perish*—shall come to nothing.

PSALM 113

Psalms cxiii; cxiv; cxv; cxvi; cxvii; and cxviii form the great *Hallel,* and were sung by the Jews on their most solemn festivals, and particularly at the Passover. To these reference is made by the Evangelists, Matt. xxvi. 30 and Mark xiv. 26, there called the "hymn" which Jesus and His disciples sung at the Passover, for the whole of the psalms were considered as one grand hymn of thanksgiving. It was probably composed after the return from the Captivity. It has no title but *Hallelujah* in the Hebrew and ancient versions.

1. *Praise, O ye servants.* Probably an address to the Levites.

3. *From the rising of the sun.* From morning to evening be always employed in the work. Or it may be a call on all mankind to praise God for His innumerable mercies to the human race. Praise Him from one end of the world unto the other. And therefore the Psalmist adds,

4. *The Lord is high above all nations.* He governs all, He provides for all; therefore let all give Him praise.

5. *Who is like unto the Lord?* Those who are highly exalted are generally unapproachable; they are proud and overbearing; or so surrounded with magnificence that to them the poor have no access, but God, though infinitely exalted, humbleth himself to behold even heaven itself, and much more does He humble himself when He condescends to behold earth and her inhabitants (v. 6).

9. *He maketh the barren woman to keep house.* This is a figure to point out the desolate, decreasing state of the captives in Babylon, and the happy change which took place on their return to their own land. These are nearly the words of Hannah, 1 Sam. ii. 5.

MATTHEW HENRY

PSALM 114

Verses 1-8

The psalmist is here remembering *the days of old,* and the wonders which their fathers told them of (Judges vi. 13), for time, as it does not wear out the guilt of sin, so it should not wear out the sense of mercy.

I. God brought Israel out of the house of bondage with a high hand and a stretched-out arm: *Israel went out of Egypt, v.* 1. They did not steal out clandestinely, but marched out with all the marks of honour.

II. God himself framed their civil and sacred constitution (*v.* 2): *Judah and Israel were his sanctuary, his dominion.* When he delivered them out of the hand of their oppressors it was *that they might serve him* in the duties of religious worship and in obedience to the moral law. He set up his sanctuary among them, in which he gave them the special tokens of his presence with them and promised to receive their homage and tribute. He was himself their lawgiver and their judge, and their government was a theocracy: *The Lord was their King.*

III. The Red Sea was divided before them at their coming out of Egypt, both for their rescue and the ruin of their enemies; and the river Jordan, when they entered into Canaan (*v.* 3). The psalmist asks, in a poetical strain (*v.* 5), *What ailed thee, O thou sea! that thou fleddest?* And furnishes the sea with an answer (*v.* 7); it was *at the presence of the Lord.* This is designed to express that it was not from any natural cause, but it was *at the presence of the Lord,* who gave the word. Israel are taught to triumph over the sea, and Jordan. There is no sea, no Jordan, so deep, so broad, but, when God's time shall come for the redemption of his people, it shall be divided and driven back if it stand in their way. Apply this, (1) To the planting of the Christian church in the world. What ailed Satan and the powers of darkness, that they trembled and truckled as they did? Mark i. 34. What ailed the heathen oracles, that they were silenced, struck dead? What ailed their idolatries, and witchcrafts, that they died away before the gospel. What ailed the persecutors and opposers of the gospel, that they gave up their cause, and called to rocks and mountains for shelter? It was *at the presence of the Lord,* and that power which went along with the gospel. (2.) To the work of grace in the heart. What turns the stream in a regenerate soul? What ails the lusts and corruptions, that they fly back, that the prejudices are removed and the whole man has become new? It is at the presence of God's Spirit that imaginations are *cast down,* 2 Cor. x. 5.

IV. The earth shook and trembled when God came down on Mount Sinai to give the law (*v.* 4): *The mountains skipped like rams, and* then *the little hills* might well be excused if they skipped *like lambs,* either when they are frightened or when they sport themselves.

V. God supplied them with water out of the rock, which followed them through the dry and sandy deserts. The same almighty power that turned waters into a rock to be a wall to Israel (Exod. xiv. 22) turned the rock into waters to be a well to Israel: as they were protected, so they were provided for, by miracles; for such was the standing water, that fountain of waters into which the rock, the flinty rock, was turned, *and that rock was Christ,* 1 Cor. x. 4.

PSALM 115

Verses 1-8

I. Boasting is here for ever excluded, *v.* 1. Let no opinion of our own merits have any room either in our prayers or in our praises, but let both centre in God's glory. All the good we do is done by the power of his grace, and all the good we have is the gift of his mere mercy, and therefore he must have all the praise. All our songs must be sung to this humble tune, *Not unto us, O Lord!* and again, *Not unto us, but to thy name,* let all the glory be given. This must be our highest and ultimate end in our prayers, and therefore it is made the first petition in the Lord's prayer, as that which guides all the rest, *Hallowed be thy name*; and, in order to that, *Give us our daily bread, &c.*

II. The reproach of the heathen is here for ever silenced.

1. The psalmist complains of the reproach of the heathen (*v.* 2): *Wherefore should they say, Where is now their God?* Do they not know that our God is everywhere by his providence and always nigh to us by his promise and grace?

2. He gives a direct answer to their question, *v.* 3. "Do they ask where is our God? *Our God is in the*

JAMIESON, FAUSSET, BROWN

PSALM 114

Vss. 1-8. The writer briefly and beautifully celebrates God's former care of His people, to whose benefit nature was miraculously made to contribute.

1-4. of strange language—(cf. Ps. 81:5).

Judah is put as a parallel to **Israel,** because of the destined, as well as real, prominence of that tribe.

5-8. The questions place the implied answers in a more striking form. **at the presence of**—lit., "from before," as if affrighted by the wonderful display of God's power. Well may such a God be trusted, and great should be His praise.

skipped . . . rams—(Ps. 29:6), describes the waving of mountain forests, poetically representing the *motion* of the mountains. The poetical description of the effect of God's presence on the sea and Jordan alludes to the history (Exod. 14:21; Josh. 3:14-17).

PSALM 115

Vss. 1-18. The Psalmist prays that God would vindicate His glory, which is contrasted with the vanity of idols, while the folly of their worshippers is contrasted with the trust of God's people, who are encouraged to its exercise and to unite in the praise which it occasions.

1-3. The vindication of God's mercy and faithfulness (Ps. 25:10; 36:6) is the "glory" of His "name," which is desired to be illustrated in the deliverance of His people, as the implied mode of its manifestation.

In view of the taunts of the heathen, faith in His dominion as enthroned in the heaven (Ps. 2:4; 11:4) is avowed. **Where is now . . .**—"now" is "not a particle of time, but of entreaty," as in our forms of speech, "Come now," "See now," etc.

ADAM CLARKE

PSALM 114

This psalm has no title. The word *Hallelujah* is prefixed in all the versions except the Chaldee and Syriac. It seems like a fragment, or a part of another psalm. In many MSS. it is only the beginning of the following, both making but one psalm in all the versions except the Chaldee.

1. *A people of strange language.* The language of the Egyptians in the time of Joseph was so different from that of the Hebrews that they could not understand each other. See Gen. xlii. 23.

2. *Judah was his sanctuary.* He set up His true worship among the Jews, and took them for His peculiar people.

5. *What ailed thee, O thou sea?* The original is very abrupt; and the personification very fine and expressive:

What to thee, O sea, that thou fleddest away!
O Jordan, that thou didst roll back!
Ye mountains, that ye leaped like rams!
And ye hills, like the young of the fold!

After these very sublime interrogations God appears, and the Psalmist proceeds as if answering his own questions:

At the appearance of the Lord, O earth, thou didst tremble;
At the appearance of the strong God of Jacob.
Converting the rock into a pool of waters;
The granite into water springs.

I know the present Hebrew text reads *chuli,* "tremble thou," in the imperative; but almost all the versions understood the word in past tense, and read as if the Psalmist was answering his own questions, as stated in the translation above.

PSALM 115

2. *Wherefore should the heathen say?* This appears to refer to a time in which the Israelites had suffered some sad reverses, so as to be brought very low, and to be marked by the heathen.

MATTHEW HENRY | JAMIESON, FAUSSET, BROWN | ADAM CLARKE

heavens, where the gods of the heathen never were, *in the heavens*, and therefore out of sight; but, though his majesty be unapproachable, it does not therefore follow that his being is questionable. In the lower world are the products of his power. Do you ask where he is? He is at the beginning and end of everything, *and not far from any of us*.

3. He returns their question upon themselves. He does in effect ask, What are the gods of the heathen? He shows that their gods, though they are not shapeless things, are senseless things. Idolaters, at first, worshipped the sun and moon (Job xxxi. 26), which was bad enough, but not so bad as that which they were now come to, which was the worshipping of images, *v.* 4. The matter of them was *silver and gold*, dug out of the earth (*man found them poor and dirty in a mine*), proper things to make money of, but not to make gods of. The make of them was from the artificer; they are creatures of men's vain imaginations and *the works of men's hands*, and therefore can have no divinity in them. *The workmen made it, therefore it is not God*, Hos. viii. 6. These idols are represented here as the most ridiculous things, a mere jest, fitter for a toy-shop than a temple, for children to play with than for men to pray to. The painter, the carver, the statuary, did their part well enough; they made them with *mouths* and *eyes*, *ears* and *noses*, *hands* and *feet*, but they could put no life into them and therefore no sense. They had better have worshipped a dead carcase (for that had life in it once) than a dead image, which neither has life nor can have. *They speak not*, in answer to those that consult them; the crafty priest must speak for them. In Baal's image there was *no voice, neither any that answered. They see not* the prostrations of their worshippers before them, much less their burdens and wants. *They hear not* their prayers, though ever so loud; *they smell not* their incense, though ever so strong, ever so sweet; *they handle not* the gifts presented to them, much less have they any gifts to bestow on their worshippers; they cannot *stretch forth their hands to the needy*. *They walk not*, they cannot stir a step for the relief of those that apply to them. Nay, they do not so much as *breathe through their throat*; they have not the least sign or symptom of life. He thence infers the sottishness of their worshippers (*v.* 8): *Those that make them* images show their ingenuity, and doubtless are sensible men; *but those that make them* gods show their stupidity and folly. *They see not* the invisible things of the true and living God in the works of creation; *they hear not* the voice of the day and the night, which in every speech and language declare his glory, xix. 2, 3. By worshipping these foolish puppets, they make themselves more and more foolish like them, and set themselves at a greater distance from everything that is spiritual, sinking themselves deeper into the mire of sense.

Verses 9–18

I. We are earnestly exhorted, all of us, to repose our confidence in God, and not suffer our confidence in him to be shaken by the heathens' insulting over us upon the account of our present distresses. It is folly to trust in dead images, but it is wisdom to trust in the living God, for he is a *help and a shield* to those that do *trust in them*. Therefore, let Israel trust in the Lord; the body of the people, as to their public interests, and every particular Israelite, as to his own private concerns. Let the priests, the Lord's ministers, and all the families of the *house of Aaron, trust in the Lord* (*v.* 10). They ought to be examples to others of a cheerful confidence in God in the worst of times. Let the proselytes, who are not of the seed of Israel, but *fear the Lord*, who worship him and make conscience of their duty to him, let them *trust in him*, for he will not fail nor forsake them, *v.* 11.

II. We are greatly encouraged to trust in God. *The Lord has been mindful of us.* All our comforts are derived from God's *thoughts to us-ward*; he *has been mindful of us*, though we have forgotten him. From what he has done for us we may infer, *He will bless us;* he that has been our *help and our shield* will be so; so that we have reason to hope that he who has delivered, and does, will yet deliver. *He will bless us;* he has promised that he will. God's blessing us is not only speaking good to us, but doing well for us. Nay (*v.* 13), *he will bless those that fear the Lord*, though they be not of the house of Israel or the house of Aaron; for it was a truth, before Peter perceived it, *That in every nation he that fears God is accepted of him*, and blessed, Acts x. 34, 35. Both the weak in grace and the strong shall be blessed of God, the lambs and the sheep of his flock. It is promised (*v.* 14), *The Lord shall increase you*, especially increase in spiritual blessings, with the increasings of God. He will bless you with the increase of knowledge and wisdom, of grace, holiness and joy. "*He*

CHARLES H. SPURGEON:

"Their idols are silver and gold" (v. 4). Mere dead inert matter; at the best only made of precious metal, but that metal quite as powerless as the commonest wood or clay. The value of the idol shows the folly of the maker in wasting his substance, but certainly does not increase the power of the image, since there is no more life in silver and gold than in brass or iron. "The work of men's hands." Inasmuch as the maker is always greater than the thing that he has made, these idols are less to be honored than the artificers who fashioned them. How irrational that men should adore that which is less than themselves! How strange that a man should think that he can make a god! Can madness go further? Our God is a spirit, and his hands made the heavens and the earth: well may we worship him, and we need not be disturbed at the sneering question of those who are so insane as to refuse to adore the living God and yet bow their knees before images of their own carving. We may make an application of all this to the times in which we are now living. The god of modern thought is the creation of the thinker himself, evolved out of his own consciousness or fashioned according to his own notion of what god should be. Now, it is evident that such a being is no God. It is impossible that there should be a God at all except the God of revelation. A god who can be fashioned by our own thoughts is no more a god than the image manufactured or produced by our own hands. The true God must of necessity be his own revealer. It is clearly impossible that a being who can be excogitated and comprehended by the reason of man should be the infinite and incomprehensible God. Their idols are blinded reason and diseased thought, the product of men's muddled brains, and they will come to nought.—*The Treasury of David*

4-7. (Cf. Isa. 40:18-20; 44:9-20.) **speak ... throat**—lit., "mutter," not even utter articulate sounds.

8. every one that trusteth—they who trust, whether makers or not.

9-13. The repetitions imply earnestness.

14. Opposed to the decrease pending and during the captivity.

12. *The Lord hath been mindful.* He has never yet wholly abandoned us to our enemies. There is a great deal of emphasis in this verse; several words are redoubled to make the subject the more affecting. I give a literal translation:

"V. 12. The Lord has been mindful of us; He will bless the house of Israel; He will bless the house of Aaron. V. 13: He will bless them that fear Jehovah, the small with the great.

V. 14: Jehovah will add upon you, upon you and upon all your children.

MATTHEW HENRY

shall increase you more and more; so that, as long as you live, you shall be still increasing, till you come to perfection, as the shining light," Prov. iv. 18. "*You and your children;* you in your children." For (*v.* 15), *You are blessed of the Lord*, you and your children are so; *all that see them shall acknowledge them, that they are the seed which the Lord has blessed*, Isa. lxi. 9.

III. We are stirred up to praise God by the psalmist's example, who concludes with a resolution to persevere in his praises. God is to be praised, *v.* 16. See how stately his palace is, and the throne he has prepared in the heavens: *The heaven, even the heavens are the Lord's. The earth he has given to the children of men*, having designed it, when he made it, for their use, to find them meat, drink, and lodging. The dead are not capable of praising him (*v.* 17), nor *any that go into silence.* The soul indeed lives in a state of separation from the body and is capable of praising God; and *the souls of the faithful, after they are delivered from the burdens of the flesh*, do praise God, are still praising him; for they go up to the land of perfect light and constant business. Therefore it concerns us to praise him (*v.* 18): *But we*, we that are alive, *will bless the Lord from this time forth* and to eternity. *Hallelujah.*

JAMIESON, FAUSSET, BROWN

15-17. They were not only God's peculiar people, but as living inhabitants of earth, assigned the work of His praise as monuments of divine power, wisdom, and goodness.

18. Hence let us fulfil the purpose of our creation, and evermore show forth His praise.

ADAM CLARKE

V. 15: Blessed are ye of the Lord, the Maker of heaven and earth. V. 16: The heavens of heavens are the Lord's: but the earth He hath given to the sons of Adam."

MATTHEW HENRY

PSALM 116

Verses 1–9

I. A general account of David's experience, and his pious resolutions (*v.* 1, 2), which are as the contents of the whole psalm, and give an idea of it. He had experienced God's goodness to him in answer to prayer. *He has inclined his ear to me.* It is wonderful condescension in God to hear prayer; it is bowing his ear. He begins the psalm somewhat abruptly with a profession of that which his heart was full of: *I love the Lord* (as xviii. 1); and fitly does he begin with this, in compliance with the first and great commandment. *Therefore I will call upon him.* Why should we glean in any other field when we have been so well treated in this? Nay, *I will call upon him as long as I live* (Heb., *In my days*), every day, to the last day.

II. A more particular narrative of God's gracious dealings with him. Let us review David's experiences. He was in great distress and trouble (*v.* 3): *The sorrows of death compassed me*, that is, such sorrows as were likely to be his death. Perhaps the extremity of bodily pain, or trouble of mind, is called here *the pains of hell.* In his trouble he had recourse to God by faithful and fervent prayer, *v.* 4. He tells us that he prayed: *Then called I upon the name of the Lord.* He tells us what his prayer was; it was short, but to the purpose: "*O Lord! I beseech thee, deliver my soul;* save me from death, and save me from sin, for that is it that is killing to the soul." He found by experience that God is gracious and merciful, and in his compassion *preserves the simple*, *v.* 6. Because they are simple (that is, sincere, and upright, and without guile) therefore God preserves them, as he preserved Paul, who had his conversation in the world *not with fleshly wisdom, but in simplicity and godly sincerity.* Let David speak his own experience. "*I was brought low*, was plunged into the depth of misery, and then *he helped me*, helped me both to bear the worst and to hope the best, helped me to pray, else desire had failed, helped me to wait, else faith had failed. I was one of the simple ones whom God preserved, the poor man who *cried and the Lord heard him*", xxxiv. 6. God graciously delivered, *First*, His *soul from death.* It is God's great mercy to us that we are alive; and the mercy is the more sensible if we have been at death's door and yet have been spared and raised up. The deliverance of the soul from spiritual death is especially to be acknowledged by all those who are now sanctified and shall be shortly glorified. *Secondly*, His *eyes from tears*, that is, his heart from inordinate grief. *Thirdly*, His *feet from falling*, from falling into sin and so into misery. God had done all this for him, and therefore he will live a life of delight in God (*v.* 7): *Return unto thy rest, O my soul!* God has dealt kindly with thee, and therefore thou needest not fear that ever he will deal hardly with thee. God is the soul's rest; in him only it can *dwell at ease*; to him therefore it must retire, and rejoice in him. Return to that rest which Christ gives to *the weary and heavy-laden*, Matt. xi. 28. He will live a life of devotedness to God (*v.* 9): *I will walk before the Lord in the land of the living*, that is, in this world, as long as I continue to live in it. The *land of the living* is a land of mercy, which we ought to be thankful for; it is a land of opportunity, which we should improve.

JAMIESON, FAUSSET, BROWN

PSALM 116

Vss. 1-19. The writer celebrates the deliverance from extreme perils by which he was favored, and pledges grateful and pious public acknowledgments.

1, 2. A truly grateful love will be evinced by acts of worship, which *calling on God* expresses (vs. 13: Ps. 55:16; 86:7; cf. Ps. 17:6; 31:2).

3, 4. For similar figures for distress see Psalm 18:4, 5. **gat hold upon me**—Another sense ("found") of the same word follows, as we speak of disease *finding us*, and of our finding or catching disease.

5-8. The relief which he asked is the result not of his merit, but of God's known pity and tenderness, which is acknowledged in assuring himself (his soul, Ps. 11:1; 16:10) of rest and peace.

All calamities are represented by *death, tears*, and *falling of the feet* (Ps. 56:13).

9. **walk before the Lord**—act, or live under His favor and guidance (Gen. 17:1; Ps. 61:7). **land of the living**— (Ps. 27:13).

ADAM CLARKE

PSALM 116

This psalm is also without a title, and its author is unknown. It appears to have been written after the Captivity, and to be a thanksgiving to God for that glorious event. The Psalmist compares this captivity to "death" and the "grave"; and shows the happy return to the Promised Land, called here "the land of the living." The people recollect the vows of God which were upon them, and purpose to fulfill them. They exult at being enabled to worship God in the Temple at Jerusalem.

3. *The sorrows of death.* The "cables" or "cords of death," alluding to their bonds and fetters during their captivity; or to the cords by which a criminal is bound, who is about to be led out to execution. *The pains of hell.* "The straitnesses of the grave."

6. *The Lord preserveth the simple. Pethaim*, which all the versions render "little ones." Those who are meek and lowly of heart, who feel the spirit of little children, these He preserves, as He does little children.

8. *Thou hast delivered my soul from death.* Thou hast rescued my "life" from the destruction to which it was exposed.

Mine eyes from tears. Thou hast turned my sorrow into joy.

9. *I will walk before the Lord.* "I will set myself to walk." I am determined to walk.

MATTHEW HENRY

Verses 10–19

The Septuagint and some other ancient versions make these verses a distinct psalm separate from the former; and some have called it the *Martyr's psalm*, for the sake of *v.* 15. Three things David here makes confession of:—

I. His faith (*v.* 10): *I believed, therefore have I spoken.* This is quoted by the apostle (2 Cor. iv. 13) with application to himself and his fellow-ministers, who, though they suffered for Christ, were not ashamed to own him. David believed the being, providence, and promise of God, particularly the assurance God had given him by Samuel that he should exchange his crook for a sceptre: a great deal of hardship he went through in the belief of this, and therefore he spoke, spoke to God by prayer (*v.* 4), by praise, *v.* 12.

II. His fear (*v.* 11): *I was greatly afflicted,* and then *I said in my haste*—in my *amazement* (so some)—*in my flight* (so others), when Saul was in pursuit of me, *All men are liars,* all with whom he had to do, Saul and all his courtiers; his friends, who he thought would stand by him, deserted him and disowned him when he fell into disgrace at court. What we speak amiss, in haste, we must by repentance unsay again (as David, xxxi. 22), and then it shall not be laid to our charge.

III. His gratitude, *v.* 12, &c. God had been better to him than his fears, and had graciously delivered him out of his distresses. *What shall I render unto the Lord for all his benefits towards me?* Here he speaks, sensible of many mercies received from God—*all his benefits.* Not as if he thought he could render anything proportionable, for what he had received; but he desired to render something acceptable, as the acknowledgment of a grateful mind. He will in the most devout and solemn manner offer up his praises and prayers to God, *v.* 13, 17. "*I will take the cup of salvation,* that is, I will offer the drink-offerings appointed by the law, in token of my thankfulness to God, and rejoice with my friends in God's goodness to me"; this is called *the cup of deliverance* because drunk in memory of the deliverance. "God, having bestowed so many benefits upon me, whatever cup he shall put into my hands I will readily take it, and not dispute it; but welcome his holy will." David spoke the language of the Son of David. John xviii. 11, *The cup that my Father has given me, shall I not* take it and *drink it?* We must first *give our own selves* to God as *living sacrifices* (Rom. xii. 1, 2 Cor. viii. 5), and then lay out of what we have for his honour in works of piety and charity. Why should we offer that to God which costs us nothing? He will always entertain thoughts of God, as very tender of the lives and comforts of his people (*v.* 15): *Precious in the sight of the Lord is the death of his saints,* so precious that he will not gratify any of David's enemies, with his death. This truth David had comforted himself with in the depth of his distress and danger; and, the event having confirmed it, he comforts others with it. Having asked, *What shall I render?* here he surrenders himself, which was *more than all burnt-offerings and sacrifices* (*v.* 16): *O Lord! truly I am thy servant.* I choose to be so; I resolve to be so; I will live and die in thy service. He had called God's people, who are dear to him, *his saints*; but, when he comes to apply it to himself, he does not say, *Truly I am thy saint,* but, *I am thy servant.* David was a king, and yet he glories in this, that he was God's servant. Two ways men came to be servants:—*First,* By birth. "Lord, I was born in thy house; I am *the son of thy handmaid,* and therefore thine." It is a great mercy to be the children of godly parents, as it obliges us to duty and is pleadable with God for mercy. *Secondly,* By redemption. He that procured the release of a captive took him for his servant. "*Lord, thou hast loosed my bonds;* and therefore *I am thy servant,* and entitled to thy protection as well as obliged to thy work." *The very bonds which thou hast loosed shall tie me faster unto thee.* He will make conscience of paying his vows and making good what he had promised. Vows are debts that must be paid, for it is better not to vow than to vow and not pay. He will pay his vows in the courts of the tabernacle, *in the midst of Jerusalem* that he might bring devotion into more reputation.

PSALM 117

Verses 1–2

There is a great deal of gospel in this psalm. The apostle has furnished us with a key to it (Rom. xv. 11), where he quotes it as a proof that the gospel was to be preached to the Gentile nations, which yet was so great a stumbling-block to the Jews. Why should that offend them when it is said, and

JAMIESON, FAUSSET, BROWN

10, 11. Confidence in God opposed to distrust of men, as not reliable (Ps. 68:8, 9). He speaks from an experience of the result of his faith.

in my haste—lit., "terror," or "agitation," produced by his affliction (cf. Ps. 31:22).

12-14. These are modes of expressing acts of worship (cf. vs. 4; Ps. 50:14; Jonah 2:9). **the cup of salvation**—the drink offering which was part of the thank offering (Num. 15:3-5). **now**—(cf. Ps. 115:2). "Oh, that (I may do it)" in the presence, etc.

15, 16. By the plea of being a home-born servant, he intimates his claim on God's covenant love to His people.

17-19. An ampler declaration of his purpose, designating the place, the Lord's house, or earthly residence in Jerusalem.

PSALM 117

ADAM CLARKE

11. *All men are liars.* "The whole of man is a lie."

12. *What shall I render?* "What shall I return?" *For all his benefits.* "His retributions," the returns He had made to my prayers and faith.

13. *I will take the cup of salvation.* Literally, "The cup of salvation, or deliverance, will I lift up." Alluding to the action in taking the cup of blessing among the Jews, which, when the person or master of the family lifted up, he said these words, "Blessed be the Lord, the Maker of the world, who has created the fruit of the vine!"

14. *I will pay my vows unto the Lord now in the presence of all his people.* He was probably now bringing his offering to the Temple. These words are repeated, v. 18.

15. *Precious in the sight of the Lord.* Many have understood this verse as meaning, "The saints are too precious in the Lord's sight lightly to give them over to death."

17. *I will offer to thee.* As it is most probable that this psalm celebrates the deliverance from Babylon, it is not wonder that we find the Psalmist so intent on performing the rites of his religion in the Temple at Jerusalem, which had been burnt with fire, and was now reviving out of its ruins, the Temple service having been wholly interrupted for nearly fourscore years.

19. *In the midst of thee, O Jerusalem.* He speaks as if present in the city, offering his vowed sacrifices in the Temple to the Lord.

PSALM 117

This is the shortest psalm in the whole collection; it is written as a part of the preceding in thirty-two of Kennicott's and De Rossi's MSS., and is found thus printed in some ancient editions.

MATTHEW HENRY

they themselves had often sung it, *Praise the Lord, all you Gentiles, and laud him, all you people.* Some of the Jewish writers confess that this psalm refers to the kingdom of the Messiah; nay, one of them has a fancy that it consists of two verses to signify that in the days of the Messiah God should be glorified by two sorts of people, by the Jews, according to the law of Moses, and by the Gentiles, according to the seven precepts of the sons of Noah, which yet should make one church, as these two verses make one psalm.

I. The vast extent of the gospel church, *v.* 1. Here *all nations* are called to praise the Lord, which could not be applied to the Old Testament times, because, unless the people of the land became Jews and were circumcised, they were not admitted to praise God with them. But the gospel of Christ is ordered to be preached to all nations, and by him the partition-wall is taken down, and those that were *afar off* are *made nigh.* Who should be admitted into the church? *All nations* and *all people.* The original words are the same that are used for the *heathen that rage* and *the people that imagine* against Christ (ii. 1); those that had been enemies to his kingdom should become his willing subjects. The gospel of the kingdom was to be preached *to all the world, for a witness to all nations,* Matt. xxiv. 14; Mark xvi. 15. The tidings of the gospel, being sent to all nations, should give them cause to praise God; the institution of gospel-ordinances would give them opportunity to praise God; and the power of gospel-grace would give them hearts to praise him.

II. The unsearchable riches of gospel-grace, which are to be the matter of our praise, *v.* 2. In the gospel those celebrated attributes of God, his mercy and his truth, shine most brightly in themselves and most comfortably to us. Things for which the Gentiles should glorify God (Rom. xv. 8, 9), for *the truth of God* and for *his mercy.* God's mercy is the fountain of all our comforts and his truth the foundation of all our hopes, and therefore for both we must praise the Lord.

JAMIESON, FAUSSET, BROWN

Vss. 1, 2. This may be regarded as a doxology, suitable to be appended to any Psalm of similar character, and prophetical of the prevalence of God's grace in the world, in which aspect Paul quotes it (Rom. 15:11; cf. Ps. 47:2; 66:8).

2. is great toward us—lit., "prevailed over or protected us."

ADAM CLARKE

F. B. MEYER:

Psalm 117 is the shortest chapter in the Bible and its center; but small as it is, it breathes a worldwide spirit and reaches out to all nations. "It is a dewdrop reflecting the universe." The apostle quotes it in Rom. 15:11 as foretelling the call of the Gentiles. Here, as in Isa. 11:10 and elsewhere, the spirit of the singer overleaps all national exclusiveness and comprehends *all* people and *all* time.

Let us learn to exercise the spirit of praise in our daily sphere. Surely we also can say that God's loving-kindness has been, and is, "great toward us." "Where sin abounded, grace did much more abound." The permanence of this love is guaranteed by God's faithfulness; for his truth is his troth. The shortest prayer of praise should find room for Hallelujah!

—Bible Commentary

2. *For his merciful kindness is great. Gabar,* is "strong." *And the truth of the Lord endureth for ever.* Whatsoever He has promised, that He will most infallibly fulfill.

MATTHEW HENRY — PSALM 118

Verses 1–18

It appears here, as often elsewhere, that David had his heart full of the goodness of God.

I. He celebrates God's mercy in general, and calls upon others to acknowledge it, from their own experience of it (*v.* 1). Priests and people, Jews and proselytes, must all own God's goodness, and all join in the same thankful song; if they can say no more, let them say this for him, that *his mercy endures for ever,* that they have had experience of it all their days.

II. He preserves an account of God's gracious dealings with him in particular. David had, in his time, waded through a great deal of difficulty, which gave him great experience of God's goodness. There are many who, when they are lifted up, care not for speaking of their former depressions; but David takes all occasions to remember his own low estate. He was *in distress* (*v.* 5), there were many that *hated him* (*v.* 7), and this could not but be a great grief to one of an ingenuous spirit, that strove to gain the good affections of all. *All nations compassed me about, v.* 10. All the nations adjacent to Israel set themselves to give disturbance to David, when he had newly come to the throne, Philistines, Moabites, Syrians, Ammonites, &c. They were confederate against him. They were virulent and violent, and, for a time, prevalent, in their attempts against him. *They compassed me about like bees,* came upon him in swarms, set upon him with their malignant stings; but it was to their own destruction, as the bee, they say, loses her life with her sting. Two ways David was brought into trouble:—(1) By the injuries that men did him (*v.* 13): *Thou* (O enemy!) *hast thrust sore at me. Thrusting thou hast thrust at me* (so the word is), so that I was *ready to fall.* (2) By the afflictions which God laid upon him (*v.* 18): *The Lord has chastened me sore.* Men thrust at him for his destruction; God chastened him for his instruction. They thrust at him with the malice of enemies; God chastened him with the love and tenderness of a Father. God heard his prayer (*v.* 5): "*He answered me* with enlargements; he did more for me than I was able to ask; he enlarged my heart in prayer and yet gave more largely than I desired." God baffled the designs of his enemies against him: They are *quenched as the fire of thorns* (*v.* 12), which burns furiously for a while, makes a great noise and a great blaze, but is presently out, and cannot do the mischief that it threatened. God preserved his life when there was but a step between him and death (*v.* 18): "He has *chastened me,* but he

JAMIESON, FAUSSET, BROWN — PSALM 118

Vss. 1-29. After invoking others to unite in praise, the writer celebrates God's protecting and delivering care towards him, and then represents himself and the people of God as entering the sanctuary and uniting in solemn praise, with prayer for a continued blessing. Whether composed by David on his accession to power, or by some later writer in memory of the restoration from Babylon, its tone is joyful and trusting, and, in describing the fortune and destiny of the Jewish Church and its visible head, it is typically prophetical of the Christian Church and her greater and invisible Head.

1-4. The trine repetitions are emphatic (cf. vss. 10-12, 15, 16; Ps. 115:12, 13). **Let . . . say**—Oh! that Israel may say. **now**—as in Psalm 115:2; so in vss. 3, 4. After "now say" supply "give thanks." **that his mercy**—or *for* His mercy. **5. distress**—lit., "straits," to which **large place** corresponds, as in Psalm 4:1; 31:8.

10-12. Though as numerous and irritating as bees, by God's help his enemies would be destroyed. **as the fire of thorns**—suddenly. **in the name . . .**—by the power (Ps. 20:5; 124:8).

ADAM CLARKE — PSALM 118

Most probably David was the author of this psalm, though many think it was written after the Captivity. It partakes of David's spirit, and everywhere shows the hand of a master. The style is grand and noble; the subject, majestic.

10. *All nations compassed me about.* This is by some supposed to relate to David, at the commencement of his reign, when all the neighboring Philistine nations endeavored to prevent him from establishing himself in the kingdom. Others suppose it may refer to the Samaritans, Idumeans, Ammonites, and others who endeavored to prevent the Jews from rebuilding their city and their Temple after their return from captivity in Babylon.

MATTHEW HENRY

has not *given me over unto death*, for he has not given me over to the will of my enemies." From his own experience he can say, *It is better*, and more safe, there is more reason *to trust in the Lord, than to put confidence in man*, yea, though it be *in princes*, *v.* 8, 9. It enabled him to triumph in that trust. *The Lord is on my side.* If we are on God's side, he is on ours; if we be for him and with him, he will be for us and with us (*v.* 7): "*The Lord takes my part*, and stands up for me, *with those that help me.* If God be our strength, he must be our song; if he work all our works in us, he must have all praise and glory from us. If he be our strength and our song, he has become not only our Saviour, but our salvation. He triumphs in an assurance of the continuance of his comfort, his victory, and his life. *First*, Of his comfort (*v.* 15): *The voice of rejoicing and salvation is in the tabernacles of the righteous*, and in mine particularly, in my family. The dwellings of the righteous in this world are but tabernacles, mean and movable; here we have no city, *no continuing city*. But these tabernacles are more comfortable to them than the palaces of the wicked are to them; for in the house where religion rules, 1. There is salvation. 2. Where there is salvation there is cause for rejoicing, for continual joy in God. 3. Where there is rejoicing there ought to be *the voice* of rejoicing, that is, praise and thanksgiving. *Secondly*, Of his victory: *The right hand of the Lord does valiantly* (*v.* 15) and *is exalted*; for (as some read it) *it has exalted me. Thirdly*, Of his life (*v.* 17): "*I shall not die* by the hands of my enemies that seek my life, *but live and declare the works of the Lord*; I shall live a monument of God's mercy and power; his works shall be declared in me, and I will make it the business of my life to praise and magnify God, looking upon that as the end of my preservation."

Verses 19–29

An illustrious prophecy of the humiliation and exaltation of our Lord Jesus, his sufferings, and the glory that should follow. Peter thus applies it directly to the chief priests and scribes, and none of them could charge him with misapplying it, Acts iv. 11.

I. The preface with which this precious prophecy is introduced, *v.* 19–21. 1. The psalmist desires admission into the sanctuary of God, there to celebrate the glory of him *that cometh in the name of the Lord: Open to me the gates of righteousness.* So the temple gates are called. And when the gates of righteousness are opened to us we must *go into them*, must enter into the holiest, as far as we have leave, *and praise the Lord.* 2. He sees admission granted him (*v.* 20): *This is the gate of the Lord*, the gate of his appointing, *into which the righteous shall enter.* Some by this gate understand Christ, by whom we are taken into fellowship with God and our praises are accepted; he is *the way*; there is no coming to the Father but by him (John xiv. 6). The psalmist triumphs in the discovery that the gate of righteousness, which had been so long shut, and so long knocked at, was now at length opened. 3. He promises to give thanks to God for this favour (*v.* 21): *I will praise thee.* Those that saw Christ's day at so great a distance saw cause to praise God for the prospect; for in him they saw that God had heard them, had heard the prayers of the Old Testament saints for the coming of the Messiah, and would be their salvation.

II. The prophecy itself, *v.* 22, 23. This may have some reference to David's preferment; he was the stone which Saul and his courtiers rejected, but was by the wonderful providence of God advanced to be the headstone of the building. But its principal reference is to Christ; and here we have, 1. His humiliation. He is *the stone which the builders refused*; he is the *stone cut out of the mountain without hands*, Dan. ii. 34. This stone was *rejected by the builders*, by the rulers and people of the Jews (Acts iv. 8, 10, 11); they refused to own him as the Messiah. They *denied him in the presence of Pilate* (Acts iii. 13) when they said, *We have no king but Cæsar*. 2. His exaltation. He *has become the headstone of the corner*; he is advanced to the highest degree both of honour and usefulness, to be above all, and all in all. He is the chief-corner-stone in the foundation, in whom Jew and Gentile are united, that they may be built up one holy house. He is the chief top-stone in the corner, in whom the building is completed, and who must in all things have the pre-eminence, as the *author and finisher of our faith*. 3. The hand of God in all this: His hand went with him throughout his whole undertaking, and from first to last he did his Father's will; and this ought to be *marvellous in our eyes.* Christ's name is *Wonderful*; and the redemption he wrought out is the most amazing of all God's works of wonder.

III. The joy wherewith it is entertained and the

JAMIESON, FAUSSET, BROWN

8, 9. Even the most powerful men are less to be trusted than God.

6, 7. Men are helpless to hurt him, if God be with him (Ps. 56:9), and, if enemies, they will be vanquished (Ps. 54:7).

13-16. The enemy is triumphantly addressed as if present. **rejoicing and salvation**—the latter as cause of the former.

right hand . . . is exalted—His power greatly exerted. **17, 18.** He would live, because confident his life would be for God's glory.

19-21. Whether an actual or figurative entrance into God's house be meant, the purpose of solemn praise is intimated, in which only the righteous would or could engage.

22, 23. These words are applied by Christ (Matt. 21:42) to Himself, as the foundation of the Church (cf. Acts 4:11; Eph. 2:20; I Pet. 2:4, 7). It may here denote God's wondrous exaltation to power and influence of him whom the rulers of the nation despised. Whether (see above) David or Zerubbabel (cf. Hag. 2:2; Zech. 4:7-10) be primarily meant, there is here typically represented God's more wonderful doings in exalting Christ, crucified as an impostor, to be the Prince and Saviour and Head of His Church.

ADAM CLARKE

7. *The Lord taketh my part with them that help me.* Literally, "The Lord is to me among my helpers." *Therefore shall I see my desire upon them that hate me.* Literally, "And I shall look among them that hate me." As God is on my side, I fear not to look the whole of them in the face. I shall see them defeated.

19. *Open to me the gates.* Throw open the doors of the Temple, that I may enter and perform my vows unto the Lord.

20. *This gate of the Lord.* Supposed to be the answer of the Levites to the request of the king.

21. *I will praise thee.* He is now got within the gates, and breaks out into thanksgivings for the mercies he had received. He is *become my salvation*—He himself hath saved me from all mine enemies.

22-23. *The stone which the builders refused.* See a full elucidation of these two verses in the notes on Matt. xxi. 42.

MATTHEW HENRY

acclamations which attend this prediction.

1. Let the day be solemnized to the honour of God with great joy (*v.* 24): *This is the day the Lord has made.* Or it may very fitly be understood of the Christian sabbath, which we sanctify in remembrance of Christ's resurrection, when the rejected stone began to be exalted. Here is the doctrine of the Christian sabbath: *It is the day which the Lord has made*, has made remarkable, made holy, has distinguished from other days; he has made it for man. *We will rejoice and be glad in it*, not only in the institution of the day, but in the occasion of it, Christ's becoming the *head of the corner*. Sabbath days must be rejoicing days.

2. Let the exalted Redeemer be met, and attended, with joyful hosannas, *v.* 25, 26. This is like *Vivat rex —Long live the king*, and expresses a hearty joy for his accession to the crown. *Hosanna* signifies, *Save now, I beseech thee.* "Lord, save me, I beseech thee; let this Saviour be my Saviour, and, in order to that, my ruler; let me be taken under his protection and owned as one of his willing subjects. Let me have victory over those lusts *that war against my soul*, and let divine grace go on in my heart *conquering and to conquer*." "Lord, preserve even the Saviour himself. Let his name be sanctified, his *kingdom come*, his *will be done*." Thus *let prayer be made for him continually*, lxxii. 15. On the Lord's day, when we rejoice in his kingdom, we must pray for the advancement of it more and more. Let the priests, the Lord's ministers, do their part in this great solemnity, *v.* 26. Let them bless the prince with their praises: *Blessed is he that cometh in the name of the Lord.* We must bid him welcome into our hearts, saying, "Come in, thou blessed of the Lord; come in by thy grace and Spirit, and take possession of me for thy own." We must pray for the enlargement and edification of his church, for the ripening of things for his second coming and then that he who has said, *Surely I come quickly*, would *even so come*. Christ's ministers are not only warranted, but appointed to pronounce a blessing, in his name, upon all his loyal subjects that love him, and his government in sincerity, Eph. vi. 24.

3. Let sacrifices of thanksgiving be offered to his honour who offered for us the great atoning sacrifice, *v.* 27. *He has shown us light*, that is, he has given us the knowledge of himself and his will. He *has shined upon us* (so some); he has given us occasion for joy and rejoicing, which is light to the soul, by giving us a prospect of everlasting light in heaven. The duty which this privilege calls for: *Bind the sacrifice with cords*, that, being killed, the blood of it may be sprinkled *upon the horns of the altar*, according to the law. Or this may have a peculiar significancy here; the sacrifice we are to offer to God, in gratitude for redeeming love, is ourselves, not to be slain upon the altar, but *living sacrifices* (Rom. xii. 1), to be bound to the altar, spiritual sacrifices of prayer and praise.

4. The psalmist concludes with his own thankful acknowledgments of divine grace, in which he calls upon others to join with him, *v.* 28, 29. He will have all about him to give thanks to God for these glad tidings of great joy to all people, that there is a Redeemer, even Christ the Lord. In him it is that God *is good* to man and that *his mercy endures for ever.* He concludes this psalm as he began it (*v.* 1), for God's glory must be the Alpha and Omega, the beginning and the end, of all our addresses to him.

JAMIESON, FAUSSET, BROWN

24. This is the day—or period distinguished by God's favor of all others.

25. Save now—*Hebrew, Hosannah* (cf. Ps. 115:2, etc., as to *now*) a form of prayer (Ps. 20:9), since, in our use, of praise.

26. he that cometh . . . Lord—As above intimated, this may be applied to the visible head of the Jewish Church entering the sanctuary, as leading the procession; typically it belongs to Him of whom the phrase became an epithet (Mal. 3:1; Matt. 21:9).

27-29. showed us light—or favor (Ps. 27:1; 97:11). With the sacrificial victim brought bound to the altar is united the more spiritual offering of praise (Ps. 50: 14, 23), expressed in the terms with which the Psalm opened.

ADAM CLARKE

24. *This is the day which the Lord hath made.* As the Lord hath called me to triumph, this is the day which He hath appointed for that purpose. This is a gracious opportunity; I will improve it to His glory.

25. *Save now, I beseech thee.* These words were sung by the Jews on the Feast of Tabernacles, when carrying green branches in their hands; and from the *hoshiah nna*, we have the word *hosanna*. This was sung by the Jewish children when Christ made His public entry into Jerusalem. See Matt. xxi. 9.

26. *We have blessed you.* The answer of the Levites to the king.

27. *God is the Lord. El Yehovah*, "the strong God Jehovah." *Which hath shewed us light.* "And He will illuminate us." Perhaps at this time a divine splendor shone upon the whole procession, a proof of God's approbation.

29. *O give thanks unto the Lord.* This is the general doxology or chorus. All join in thanksgiving, and they end as they began: *His mercy endureth for ever.*

MATTHEW HENRY

PSALM 119

1. Aleph

Verses 1–3

The psalmist here shows that godly people are happy people. What we must do and be that we may attain to it, we are here told. Those are happy, 1. Who make the will of God the rule of all their actions, *v.* 1. God's word is a law to them. They walk in the paths of that law. This is *walking in God's ways* (*v.* 3), the ways which he has marked out to us. 2. Who are upright and honest in their religion —*undefiled in the way*, not only who keep themselves *unspotted from the world*, but who are habitually sincere in their intentions, *in whose spirit there is no guile*, who are really as good as they seem to be and row the same way as they look. 3. Who are true to the trust reposed in them as God's professing people. Those who would *walk in the law of the Lord* must *keep his testimonies*, that is, his truths. Or *his testimonies* may denote his covenant; the ark of the covenant is called *the ark of the testimony*. Those do not keep covenant with God who do not keep the commandments of God. 4. Who have a single eye to God as their chief good and highest end in all they do in religion (*v.* 2): They *seek him with their whole*

JAMIESON, FAUSSET, BROWN

PSALM 119

Vss. 1-176. This celebrated Psalm has several peculiarities. It is divided into twenty-two parts or stanzas, denoted by the twenty-two letters of the Hebrew alphabet. Each stanza contains eight verses, and the first letter of each verse is that which gives name to the stanza. Its contents are mainly praises of God's Word, exhortations to its perusal, and reverence for it, prayers for its proper influence, and complaints of the wicked for despising it. There are but two verses (122, 132) which do not contain some term or description of God's Word. These terms are of various derivations, but here used, for the most part, synonymously, though the use of a variety of terms seems designed, in order to express better the several aspects in which our relations to the revealed word of God are presented. The Psalm does not appear to have any relation to any special occasion or interest of the Jewish Church or nation, but was evidently "intended as a manual of pious thoughts, especially for instructing the young, and its peculiar artificial structure was probably adopted to aid the memory in retaining the language."

ADAM CLARKE

PSALM 119

This is another of the alphabetical or acrostic psalms. It is divided into twenty-two parts, answering to the number of letters in the Hebrew alphabet. Every part is divided into eight verses; and each verse begins with that letter of the alphabet which forms the title of the part, e.g.: The first eight verses have *aleph* prefixed, the second eight *beth*, each of the eight verses beginning with that letter; and so of the rest. It is not easy to give any general analysis of this psalm; it is enough to say that it treats in general on the privileges and happiness of those who observe the law of the Lord. That law is exhibited by various names and epithets tending to show its various excellences. Earnest prayers are offered to God for wisdom to understand it, and for grace to observe it faithfully. The words which express that revelation which God had then given to men, or some particular characteristic of it, are generally reckoned to be the ten following: (1) testimonies; (2) commandments; (3) precepts; (4) word; (5) law; (6) ways;

MATTHEW HENRY

heart. 5. Who carefully avoid all sin (*v.* 3): *They do no iniquity.* They are conscious of much that clogs them in the ways of God, but not of that iniquity which draws them out of those ways.

Verses 4–6

We must own ourselves under the highest obligations to walk in God's law (*v.* 4): *Thou hast commanded us to keep thy precepts,* to make religion our rule, and look up to God for wisdom and grace to do so (*v.* 5). "Thou wouldest have me keep thy precepts, and, Lord, I fain would keep them." *This is the will of God, even our sanctification;* and it shall be our will. Every good man has a *respect to all* God's *commandments,* those that concern both the inward and the outward man, both the head and the heart. Those who have a sincere *respect to all* God's *commandments shall not be ashamed.* They shall have clearness and courage in their own souls.

Verses 7–8

I. David's endeavour to perfect himself in his religion. He hopes to *learn* God's *righteous judgments.* He knew much, but he was still pressing forward and desired to know more. As long as we live we must be scholars in Christ's school, and sit at his feet.

II. The use he would make of his divine learning. *I will praise thee when I have learned thy judgments,* intimating that he could not learn unless God taught him, and that divine instructions are special blessings. Those have well learned God's statutes who have come up to a full resolution, in the strength of his grace, to keep them.

III. His prayer to God not to leave him. Good men see themselves undone if God forsakes them; for then the tempter will be too hard for them.

2. Beth

Verse 9

1. A weighty question asked. By what means may the next generation be made better than this? *Wherewithal shall a young man cleanse his way?* 2. A satisfactory answer given to this question. Young men may effectually *cleanse their way by taking heed thereto according to* the *word* of God. Young men must make the word of God their rule; that will do more towards the cleansing of young men than the laws of princes or the morals of philosophers. They must carefully apply that rule as a standard, and steer by that chart and compass.

Verse 10

David's experience: "*I have sought thee.* If I have not yet found thee, *I have sought thee,* and thou never saidst, Seek in vain, nor wilt say so to me, for *I have sought thee with my whole heart.* Thou that hast inclined me to seek thy precepts, never suffer me to wander from them."

Verse 11

The close application which David made of the word of God to himself: *He hid it in his heart* that it might be ready to him whenever he had occasion to use it. God's word is a treasure worth laying up, and there is no laying it up safely but in our hearts; if we have it only in our heads, our memories may fail us: but if our hearts be delivered into the mould of it, and the impressions of it remain on our souls, it is safe.

Verse 12

David gives glory to God: "*Blessed art thou, O Lord!* He asks grace from God: *Teach me thy statutes;* give me to know and do my duty in everything."

Verses 13–16

I. David had edified others with what he had been taught out of the word of God (*v.* 13). This he did, not only as a king in making orders, and giving judgment, according to the word of God, nor only as a prophet, by his psalms, but in his common discourse.

II. He looks forward with a holy resolution never to cool in his affection to the word of God; (*v.* 15): *I will meditate in thy precepts.* He not only discoursed of them to others but he communed with his own heart about them. David took more delight in God's statutes than in the pleasures of his court or the honours of his camp, more than in his sword or in his harp. When the law is written in the heart duty becomes a delight.

3. Gimel

Verse 17

David prays, ***Deal bountifully with me, that I may*** *live.* It was God's bounty that gave us life, that gave us this life; and the same bounty that gave it

JAMIESON, FAUSSET, BROWN

1. undefiled—lit., "complete," perfect, or sincere (cf. Ps. 37:37). **in** [or "of"] **the way**—course of life. **walk** [act] **in the law**—according to it (cf. Luke 1:6). **law**—from a word meaning "to teach," is a term of rather general purport, denoting the instruction of God's Word. **2. testimonies**—The word of God is so called, because in it He *testifies* for truth and against sin. **seek him**—i.e., a knowledge of Him, with desire for conformity to His will. **3. his ways**—the course He reveals as right. **4-6. precepts**—are those directions which relate to special conduct, from a word meaning "to inspect." **statutes**—or ordinances, positive laws of permanent nature. Both words originally denote rather positive than moral laws, such as derive force from the divine appointment, whether their nature or the reasons for them are apprehended by us or not. **commandments**—or institutions. The term is comprehensive, but rather denotes fundamental directions for conduct, both enjoining and forbidding. **have respect unto**—or regard carefully as to their whole purport. **7. judgments**—rules of conduct formed by God's judicial decisions; hence the wide sense of the word in the Psalms, so that it includes decisions of approval as well as condemnation.

8. Recognizes the need of divine grace.

9. The whole verse may be read as a question; for, **by taking heed**—is better, "for" taking heed, i.e., so as to do it. The answer is implied, and inferable from vss. 5, 10, 18, etc., i.e., by God's grace.

10-16.

We must carefully treasure up the word of God, declare it to others, meditate on it, and heartily delight in it; and then by His grace we shall act according to it.

ADAM CLARKE

(7) truth; (8) judgments; (9) righteousness; (10) statutes. I believe it is almost universally asserted that in every verse of this psalm one or other of those ten words is used, except in v. 122; but on a closer inspection we shall find that none of them is used in the above sense in the 84th, 90th, 121st, 122nd, and 132nd.

Letter *Aleph*—First Division

1. *Blessed are the undefiled in the way.* "Oh, the blessedness of the perfect ones in the way! This psalm begins something like the first, By the *perfect,* which is the proper meaning of the original word, we are to understand those who sincerely believe what God has spoken, religiously observe all the rules and ceremonies of His religion, and have their lives and hearts regulated by the spirit of love, fear, and obedience. This is further stated in the second verse.

4. *Thy precepts diligently. Meod,* "superlatively, to the uttermost." God has never given a commandment the observance of which He knew to be impossible.

5. *O that my ways were directed!* "I wish that my way may be confirmed to keep Thy statutes."

8. *O forsake me not utterly. Ad meod,* "to utter dereliction."

Letter *Beth*—Second Division

9. *A young man cleanse his way. Orach,* which we translate *way* here, signifies a "track," a "rut," such as is made by the wheel of a cart or chariot. A young sinner has no broad, beaten path; he has his private ways of offense, his secret pollutions.

16. *I will delight myself.* The word is very emphatic: *eshtaasha,* "I will skip about and jump for joy." He must exult in God's word as his treasure, live in the spirit of obedience as his work, and ever glory in God, who has called him to such a state of salvation.

Letter *Gimel*—Third Division

17. *Deal bountifully. Gemol,* "reward" Thy servant. Let him have the return of his faith and prayers, that the divine *life* may be preserved

MATTHEW HENRY

continues it, and gives all the supports and comforts of it. Therefore we ought to spend our lives in God's service.

Verse 18

There are *wondrous things* in God's *law*, not only strange things, which are unexpected, but excellent things, which are to be valued, and things which were long *hidden from the wise and prudent*, but are now *revealed unto babes*. If there were wonders in the law, much more in the gospel. We are by nature blind to the things of God, till his grace cause the scales to fall from our eyes. And the more God opens our eyes the more wonders we see in the word of God.

Verse 19

The acknowledgment which David makes of his own condition: *I am a stranger in the earth*. All good people confess themselves to be so; for heaven is their home, and the world is but their inn, the land of their pilgrimage. David was a man that knew as much of the world, and was as well known in it, as most men. He had a name like the names of the great men, and yet he calls himself a stranger. "Lord, show thy commandments to me; as long as I live, give me to be growing in my acquaintance with it. *I am a stranger*, and therefore stand in need of a guide, a guard, a companion, a comforter; let me have thy commandments always in view, for they will be all this to me, all that a poor stranger can desire."

Verse 20

David had prayed that God would open his eyes (*v.* 18) and open the law (*v.* 19); now here he pleads the earnestness of his desire for knowledge and grace.

Verse 21

The wretched character of wicked people. The temper of their minds is bad. They are *proud*; they magnify themselves above others. And yet that is not all: they magnify themselves against God, and set up their wills in opposition to the will of God. There is something of pride at the bottom of every wilful sin. They *do err from thy commandments*, and embrace principles contrary to thy commandments, and then no wonder that they err in practice. They are certainly cursed, for *God resists the proud*; and those that throw off the commands of the law lay themselves under its curse (Gal. iii. 10).

Verse 22

David prays against the reproach and contempt of men, that they might be *removed*, or (as the word is) *rolled, from off him*. This intimates that they lay upon him, and that neither his greatness nor his goodness could secure him from being libelled and lampooned. He was not jeered out of well-doing: "Lord, remove it from me, *for I have kept thy testimonies* notwithstanding." If in a day of trial we still retain our integrity, we may be sure it will end well.

Verse 23

David was abused even by great men, who should have known better his character and his case. Herein David was a type of Christ, for they were the princes of this world that vilified and *crucified the Lord of glory*, 1 Cor. ii. 8. Under these abuses: he *meditated in God's statutes*, went on in his duty, and did not regard them. When they spoke against him, he found that in the word of God which spoke for him, and spoke comfort to him, and then none of these things moved him.

Verse 24

Here David explains his meditating in God's statutes (*v.* 23), which was of such use to him when princes sat and spoke against him. God's statutes were *his counsellors*, and they counselled him to bear it patiently and commit his cause to God.

4. DALETH

Verse 25

I. David's complaint. *My soul cleaves to the dust*, which is a complaint either, 1. Of his corruptions, his inclination to the world, and a deadness to holy duties. David's complaint here is like St. Paul's of a body of death that he carried about with him. Or, 2. Of his afflictions, either trouble of mind or outward trouble, and both together brought him even to the *dust of death*.

II. His petition for relief: "*Quicken thou me according to thy word*. By thy providence put life into my affairs, by thy grace put life into my affections; cure me of my spiritual deadness and make me lively in my devotion."

Verses 26–27

David had opened his case, opened his very heart to God: "*I have declared my ways*, and acknowledged

JAMIESON, FAUSSET, BROWN

17-20. Life is desirable in order to serve God; that we may do so aright, we should seek to have our eyes opened to behold His truth, and earnestly desire fully to understand it.

21-24. God will rebuke those who despise His word and deliver His servants from their reproach, giving them boldness in and by His truth, even before the greatest men.

25-27. Submitting ourselves in depression to God, He will revive us by His promises, and lead us to declare His mercy to others.

ADAM CLARKE

in his soul! Then he will keep Thy word. From *gamal*, "to reward," comes the name of *gimel*, the third letter in the Hebrew alphabet, which is prefixed to every verse in this part, and commences it with its own name. This is a stroke of the Psalmist's art and ingenuity.

18. *Open thou mine eyes. Gal*, "reveal my eyes," illuminate my understanding, take away the veil that is on my heart, and then shall I see wonders in Thy law. The Holy Scriptures are plain enough; but the heart of man is darkened by sin. The Bible does not so much need a comment as the soul does the light of the Holy Spirit.

20. *My soul breaketh*. We have a similar expression: "It broke my heart." It expresses excessive longing, grievous disappointment, hopeless love, accumulated sorrow.

23. *Princes also did sit*. It is very likely that the nobles of Babylon did often, by wicked misrepresentations, render the minds of the kings of the empire evil affected towards the Jews.

24. *Thy testimonies also are . . . my counsellors*. "The men of my counsel." I sit with them; and I consider every testimony Thou hast given as a particular counsellor, one whose advice I especially need.

Letter *Daleth*—Fourth Division

25. *My soul cleaveth unto the dust*. It would be best to translate *naphshi*, "my life," and then cleaving to the dust may imply an apprehension of approaching death; and this agrees best with the petition, *Quicken thou me*. "Make me alive." Keep me from going down into the dust.

MATTHEW HENRY

thee in them all, have taken thee along with me in all my designs and enterprises." It is an unspeakable comfort to a gracious soul to think with what tenderness all its complaints are received by a gracious God, 1 John v. 14, 15. "Let me have a good understanding of *the way of thy precepts; so shall I talk* with the more assurance *of thy wondrous works*."

Verses 28–29

1. David's representation of his own griefs: *My soul melteth for heaviness*, which is to the same purport with *v*. 25, *My soul cleaveth to the dust*. Heaviness in the heart of man makes it to melt, to drop away like a candle that wastes. 2. His request for God's grace: "*Strengthen thou me* with strength in my soul, *according to thy word*. (Deut. xxxiii. 25): *Remove from me the way of lying*. David had, in a strait, cheated Ahimelech (1 Sam. xxi. 2), and Achish, *v*. 13 and *ch*. xxvii. 10. Great difficulties are great temptations to palliate a lie with the colour of a pious fraud and a necessary self-defence; therefore David prays that God would prevent him from falling into this sin any more. *Grant me thy law graciously;* grant me that to keep me from the *way of lying*. David had the law written with his own hand, for the king was obliged to transcribe a copy of it for his own use (Deut. xvii. 18); but he prays that he might have it written in his heart. "Grant it me *graciously*"; he begs it as a special token of God's favour.

Verses 30–32

Those who will make anything to purpose of their religion must first make it their deliberate choice; so David did: *I have chosen the way of truth. Thy judgments have I laid before me*, as he who learns to write lays his copy before him, that he may write according to it, as the workman lays his model and platform before him, that he may do his work exactly. We must have the word in our heart by an habitual conformity to it, that we may walk by rule. Those who make religion their choice and rule are likely to adhere to it faithfully. The choosing Christian is likely to be the steady Christian; while those that are Christians by chance tack about if the wind turn. "*Lord, put me not to shame;* do not reject my services, which will put me to the greatest confusion." The more comfort God gives us the more duty he expects from us, *v*. 32. God by his Spirit, enlarges the hearts of his people when he gives them wisdom (for that is called *largeness of heart*, 1 Kings iv. 29), when he *sheds abroad the love of God* in the heart, and puts gladness there. The joy of our Lord should be wheels to our obedience.

5. He

Verses 33–34

I. David begs to be taught of God, as knowing that *none teaches like him*, Job xxxvi. 22. Teach me the way of my duty in such a way as no man could teach: *Lord, give me understanding*.

II. He promises faithfully that he would be a good scholar. If God would teach him, he was sure he should learn to good purpose: "*I shall keep the law*, which I shall never do unless I be taught of God."

Verses 35–36

He had before prayed to God to enlighten his understanding, that he might know his duty; here he prays to God to bow his will, and quicken the active powers of his soul, that he might do his duty; for *it is God that works in us both to will and to do*, as well as to understand, what is good, Phil. ii. 13. "*Make me to do;* strengthen me for every good work." *Incline my heart to thy testimonies*, to those things which thy testimonies prescribe; not only make me willing to do my duty, as that which I must do, but make me desirous to do my duty. Duty is done with delight when the heart is inclined to it: it is God's grace that inclines us. "Restrain and mortify the inclination there is in me to *covetousness*." That is a sin which stands opposed to all God's testimonies. Those that would have the love of God rooted in them must get the love of the world rooted out of them.

Verse 37

David prays for restraining grace: *Turn away my eyes from beholding vanity*. The honours, pleasures, and profits of the world are the vanities, the prospect of which draw multitudes away from the paths of religion and godliness. The eye, when fastened on these, infects the heart with the love of them, and so it is alienated from God and divine things; so we ought to pray that God by his providence would keep vanity out of our sight and that by his grace he would keep us from being enamoured with the sight of it.

JAMIESON, FAUSSET, BROWN

28-32. In order to adhere to His word, we must seek deliverance from temptations to sin as well as from despondency.

enlarge [or expand] **my heart**—with gracious affections.

33-38. To encourage us in prayer for divine aid in adhering to His truth, we are permitted to believe that by His help we shall succeed. **the way of thy statutes**—i.e., the way or manner of life prescribed by them.

The help we hope to obtain by *prayer* is to be the basis on which our *resolutions* should rest.

Turn away mine eyes—lit., "Make my eyes to pass, not noticing evil." **vanity**—lit., "falsehood;" all other objects of trust than God; idols, human power, etc. (Ps. 31:6; 40:4; 60:11; 62:9). **quicken . . . in thy way**—make me with *living* energy to pursue the way marked out by Thee. *Revive* me from the *death* of spiritual helplessness (vss. 17, 25, 40, 50; Ps. 116:3).

ADAM CLARKE

26. *I have declared my ways*. "I have numbered my ways"; I have searched them out; I have investigated them. And that he had earnestly prayed for pardon of what was wrong in them is evident, for he adds, *Thou heardest me*.

28. *My soul melteth. Dalaph* signifies "to distill, to drop as tears from the eye." As my distresses cause the tears to distil from my eyes, so the overwhelming load of my afflictions causes my life to ebb and leak out.

Truth, *emunah*, from *aman*, "to make steady, constant, to settle, trust, believe." The law that is established, steady, confirmed, and ordered in all things, and sure; which should be believed on the authority of God, and trusted to as an infallible testimony from Him who cannot lie nor deceive.

31. *I have stuck*. "I have cleaved to, been glued to," them—the same word as in v. 25.

32. *I will run*. The particle which we translate *when* should be translated "because."

Letter *He*—Fifth Division

33. *Teach me, O Lord, the way of thy statutes*. To understand the spiritual reference of all the statutes under the law required a teaching which could come only from God.

34. *With my whole heart*. I will not trifle with my God, I will not divide my affections with the world; God shall have all.

Testimonies, *edoth*, from *ad*, denoting "beyond, farther, all along, to bear witness, or testimony." The rites and ceremonies of the law; because they point out matters beyond themselves, being types and representations of the good things that were to come.

MATTHEW HENRY

Verse 38

A good man is *God's servant*, subject to his law and employed in his work, that is, *devoted to his fear*, given up to his direction and disposal, and taken up with high thoughts of him and all those acts of devotion which have a tendency to his glory. Those that are God's servants may, in faith and with humble boldness, pray that God would *establish his word to them*, that is, that he would fulfil his promises to them in due time. What God has promised we must pray for; we need not be so aspiring as to ask more; we need not be so modest as to ask less.

Verse 39

David prays against *reproach*, as before, *v.* 22. He had done that which might give *occasion to the enemies of the Lord to blaspheme*; now he prays that God, who has all men's hearts and tongues in his hands, would be pleased to prevent this, to *deliver him from all his transgressions*, that he *might not be the reproach of the foolish*, which he feared (xxxix. 8). "Lord, thou sittest in the throne, and *thy judgments are right* and *good*, just and kind, to those that are wronged, and therefore to thee I appeal from the unjust and unkind censures of men."

Verse 40

David professes the ardent affection he had to the word of God: "*I have longed after thy precepts*, not only loved them, but I have earnestly desired to know them more. Thou hast wrought in me this languishing desire, put life into me, that I may prosecute it; *quicken me in thy righteousness*, in thy righteous ways, according to thy righteous promise."

6. Vau

Verses 41–42

1. David's prayer for the salvation of the Lord. "Lord, thou art my Saviour; I am miserable in myself, and thou only canst make me happy; *let thy salvation come to me*. Hasten temporal salvation to me from my present distresses, and hasten me to the eternal salvation, by giving me the necessary qualifications for it." Dependence upon the grace and promise of God for that salvation are the two pillars on which our hope is built, and they will not fail us.

Verses 43–44

David's humble petition for the tongue of the learned, that he might know how to *speak a word in season* for the glory of God: *Take not the word of truth utterly out of my mouth*. He means, "Lord, let the word of truth be always in my mouth; let me have the wisdom and courage which are necessary to enable me both to use my knowledge for the instruction of others, and to make profession of my faith whenever I am called to it." He professes his resolution to adhere to his duty in the strength of God's grace: "*So I shall keep thy law continually*. If I have thy word not only in my heart, but in my mouth, I shall do all I should do, stand complete in thy whole will."

Verses 45–48

What David experienced of an affection to the law of God: "*I seek thy precepts, v.* 45. I do all I can to *understand what the will of the Lord is* and to discover his mind. *I seek thy precepts*, for *I have loved them, v.* 47, 48. I not only give consent to them as good, but as good for me." Five things he promises himself in the strength of God's grace:—(1) That he should be free and easy in his duty: "*I will walk at liberty*, freed from that which is evil, and free to that which is good, doing it not by constraint but willingly." (2) That he should be bold and courageous in his duty: *I will speak of thy testimonies also before kings*. We must never be afraid to our own religion, though it should expose us to the wrath of kings, but speak of it as that which we will live and die by, like the three children before Nebuchadnezzar, Dan. iii. 16; Acts iv. 20. (3) That he should be cheerful and pleasant in his duty (*v.* 47): "*I will delight myself in thy commandments*, in conversing with them, in conforming to them. I will never be so well pleased with myself as when I do that which is pleasing to God." (4) That he should be diligent and vigorous in his duty: *I will lift up my hands to thy commandments*. "I will lay my hands to the command, not only to praise it, but practise it; nay, I will lift up my hands to it, that is I will put forth all the strength I have to do it." (5) That he should be thoughtful and considerate in his duty (*v.* 48): "*I will meditate in thy statutes*."

7. Zain

Verse 49

David here pleads with God in prayer for that mercy and grace which he hoped for. God had given him the promise on which he hoped: "Lord,

JAMIESON, FAUSSET, BROWN

who is devoted to thy fear—or better, "which (i.e., Thy word) is for Thy fear," for producing it. "Which is to those who fear Thee." God's word of promise belongs peculiarly to such (cf. Gen. 18:19; I Kings 2:4; 8:25) [Hengstenberg].

39, 40. Our hope of freedom from the *reproach of inconsistency* is in God's power, quickening us to live according to His Word, which He leads us to love. **for thy judgments are good**—The time must therefore be at hand when Thy justice will turn the "reproach" from Thy Church upon the world (Isa. 25:8; 66:5, Zeph. 2:8-10).

41-44. The sentiment more fully carried out. God's mercies and salvation, as revealed in His Word, provide hope of forgiveness for the past and security in a righteous course for the future. **42.** The possession of God's gift of "salvation" (vs. 41) will be the Psalmist's answer to the foe's "reproach," that his hope was a fallacious one.

45-48. To freedom from reproach, when imbued with God's truth, there is added "great boldness in the faith," accompanied with increasing delight in the holy law itself, which becomes an element of happiness.

48. **My hands . . . lift up unto . . . commandments**—i.e., I will *prayerfully* (Ps. 28:2) direct my heart to keep Thy commandments.

49-51. Resting on the promises consoles under affliction and the tauntings of the insolent.

ADAM CLARKE

38. *Stablish thy word.* Fulfill the promises Thou hast made to me.

Letter *Vau*—Sixth Division

41. *Let thy mercies come.* Let me speedily see the accomplishment of all my prayers! Let me have *thy salvation*—such a deliverance as it becomes Thy greatness and goodness to impart. Let it be *according to thy word*—Thy exceeding great and precious promises.

Word, *dabar*, "to discourse, utter one's sentiments, speak consecutively and intelligibly." Any prophecy or immediate communication from heaven, as well as the whole body of divine revelation.

Precepts, *pikkudim*, from *pakad*, "to take notice or care of a thing, to attend, have respect to, to appoint, to visit"; because they take notice of our way, have respect to the whole of our life and conversation, superintend, overlook, and visit us in all the concerns and duties of life.

MATTHEW HENRY

I desire no more than that thou wouldst *remember thy word unto thy servant*, and *do as thou hast said*"; see 1 Chron. xvii. 23. Thou art faithful, and therefore wilt perform what thou hast promised, and not break thy word. He that did by his Spirit work faith in us, will, according to our faith, work for us, and will not disappoint us.

Verse 50

David's experience of benefit by the word. "*Thy word has quickened me.* It made me alive when I was dead in sin; it has many a time made me lively when I was dead in duty; it has quickened me to that which is good when I was backward and averse to it, and it has quickened me in that which is good when I was cold and indifferent."

Verse 51

David had been jeered for his religion. Though he had done eminent services to his country, yet, because he was a devout conscientious man, *the proud had him greatly in derision*; they laughed at him for his praying, and called it *cant*, for his seriousness, and called it *mopishness*, for his strictness, and called it *needless preciseness*. Yet he had not been jeered out of his religion. The traveller goes on his way though the dogs bark at him. Those can bear but little for Christ that cannot bear a hard word for him.

Verse 52

When David was derided for his godliness he not only held fast his integrity, but comforted himself. He not only bore reproach, but bore it cheerfully. It was a comfort to him to think that it was for God's sake that he bore reproach. Those that are derided for their adherence to God's law may comfort themselves with this, that *the reproach of Christ* will prove, in the end, *greater riches* to them *than the treasures of Egypt*.

Verse 53

Those that are openly and grossly wicked: *They forsake thy law.* The impression which the wickedness of the wicked made upon David: it frightened him. He trembled to think of the dishonour done to God, the gratification given to Satan, and the mischiefs done to the souls of men. He dreaded the consequences of it both to the sinners themselves and to the interests of God's kingdom among men.

Verse 54

This world is the house of our pilgrimage, the house in which we are pilgrims. We must confess ourselves *strangers and pilgrims upon earth*, who are not at home here, nor must be here long. Even David's palace is but the house of his pilgrimage. "*Thy statutes have been my songs*, with which I here entertain myself," as travellers are wont to divert the thoughts of their weariness, and take off something of the tediousness of their journey, by singing a pleasant song now and then. David was the sweet singer of Israel, and here we are told whence he fetched his songs; they were all borrowed from the word of God.

Verses 55–56

When others were sleeping David was remembering God's name, and, by repeating that lesson, increasing his acquaintance with it; in the night of affliction this he called to mind. *I remembered thy name in the night*, and therefore was careful to *keep thy law* all day. "I had the comfort of keeping thy law because I kept it." God's work is its own wages. A heart to obey the will of God is a most valuable reward of obedience.

8. Cheth

Verse 57

David can appeal to God in this matter: "Lord, thou knowest that I have chosen thee for my portion, and depend upon thee to make me happy." He makes the law of God his rule: *I have said that I would keep thy words;* and what I have said by thy grace I will do, and will abide by it to the end." Those that take God for their portion must take him for their prince.

Verse 58

David, having in the foregoing verse reflected upon his covenants with God, here reflects upon his prayers to God, and renews his petition. He prays, "*Be merciful to me*, in the forgiveness of what I have done amiss, and in giving me grace to do better for the future." He prayed—*with his whole heart*.

Verses 59–60

He *thought on his ways*. The word signifies a fixed

JAMIESON, FAUSSET, BROWN

49. upon which—rather, "Remember Thy word unto Thy servant, *because*," etc. So the *Hebrew* requires [Hengstenberg].

50. for—rather, "This is my comfort . . . *that*," etc. [Maurer]. **hath quickened**—What the Word *has already done* is to faith a pledge of what *it shall yet do*.

52-56. The pious take comfort, when harassed and distressed by wickedness of men who forsake God's law, in remembering that the great principles of God's truth will still abide; and also God's "judgments of old" (vs. 52), i.e., His past interpositions in behalf of His people are a pledge that He will again interpose to deliver them; and they become the theme of constant and delightful meditation. The more we keep the more we love the law of God.

53. Horror—rather, "vehement wrath" [Hengstenberg].

54. songs—As the exile sings songs of his home (Ps. 137:3), so the child of God, "a stranger on earth," sings the songs of heaven, his true home (Ps. 39:12). In ancient times, laws were put in verse, to imprint them the more on the memory of the people. So God's laws are the believer's songs. **house of my pilgrimage**—present life (Gen. 17:8; 47:9; Heb. 11:13).

56. Rather, "This is peculiarly mine (*lit., to me*), *that* I keep Thy precepts" [Hengstenberg and Maurer].

57-60. Sincere desires for God's favor, penitence, and activity in a new obedience, truly evince the sincerity of those who profess to find God a portion (Num. 18:20; Ps. 16:5; Lam. 3:24).

58. favour— Hebrew, "face" (Ps. 45:12).

ADAM CLARKE

49. *Remember the word.* Thou hast *promised* to redeem us from our captivity; on that *word* we have built our *hope. Remember* that Thou hast thus promised, and see that we thus *hope.*

50. *This is my comfort.* While enduring our harsh captivity, we anticipated our enlargement; and thy *word of promise* was the *means* of keeping our souls *alive.*

51. *The proud have had me.* We have been treated, not only with oppressive cruelty, but also with contempt, because we still professed to trust in Thee, the living God, who because of our transgressions hadst been greatly displeased with us; yet we have *not declined from thy law.*

52. *I remembered thy judgments of old.* The word *judgments* is here taken for providential dealing, and indeed kind treatment, that which God showed to the Hebrews in bearing with and blessing them. And it was the recollection of these judgments that caused him to comfort himself.

54. *Thy statutes have been my songs.* During our captivity all our consolation was derived from singing Thy praises, and chanting among our fellow captives portions of Thy law, and the precepts it contains.

Letter *Cheth*—Eighth Division

57. *Thou art my portion, O Lord.* From the fifty-seventh to the sixtieth verse may be seen the progress of the work of grace on the human heart, from the first dawn of heavenly light till the soul is filled with the fullness of God. The author has been obliged, for the support of his acrostic plan, to interchange circumstances, putting that sometimes behind which in the order of grace comes before; I shall therefore follow what I conceive to be its order in the connection of grace.

57. Sixthly—To keep himself firm in his present resolutions, he binds himself unto the Lord. *I have said that I would keep thy words.* Seventhly—He did not seek in vain; God reveals himself in the fullness of blessedness to him, so that he is enabled to exclaim, *Thou art my portion, O Lord.*

58. *Fourthly*—Being determined in his heart, he tells us *I intreated favour with my whole heart.* He found he had sinned, that he needed mercy, that he had no time to lose, that he must be importunate; and therefore he sought that mercy with all his soul. Fifthly—Feeling that he deserved nothing but wrath, that he had no right to any good, he cries for mercy in the way that God had promised to convey it: *Be merciful unto me.* And to this he is encouraged only by the promise of God; and therefore prays, *Be merciful unto me according to thy word.*

MATTHEW HENRY

abiding thought. Some make it an allusion to those who work embroidery, who are very exact and careful to cover the least flaw, or to those who cast up their accounts, who reckon with themselves, What do I owe? What am I worth? He *turned his feet to God's testimonies*. He determined to make the word of God his rule, and to walk by that rule. He did this immediately and without demur (*v.* 60): *I made haste and delayed not*. Now this account which David here gives of himself may refer either to his constant practice every day, or it may refer to his first acquaintance with God and religion, when he began to throw off the vanity of childhood and youth, and to remember his Creator.

Verse 61

David's enemies were wicked men, who hated him for his godliness and tried to take away his good name. But here are the testimonies of David's conscience for him that he had held fast his religion when he was stripped of everything else, as Job did when the bands of the Chaldeans and Sabeans had robbed him: *But I have not forgotten thy law*.

Verse 62

Though David is, in this psalm, much in prayer, yet he did not neglect the duty of thanksgiving; for those that pray much will have much to give thanks for. He does not say, "*I will give thanks* because of thy favours to me," but, "*Because of thy righteous judgments*, all the disposals of thy providence in wisdom and equity." David's heart was set upon his thanksgivings. He would *rise at midnight to give thanks* to God. Public worship will not excuse us from secret worship. He did not lie still and give thanks, but rose out of his bed, perhaps in the cold and in the dark, to do it the more solemnly.

Verse 63

David had often expressed the great love he had to God; here he expresses the great love he had to the people of God. He loved them; not so much because they were his best friends, and most forward to serve him, but because they were such as *feared God* and *kept his precepts*. He was *a companion of them*. He joined with them in holy ordinances in the courts of the Lord, where rich and poor, prince and peasant, meet together. He sympathized with them in their joys and sorrows (Heb. x. 33).

Verse 64

David pleads that God is good to all the creatures according to their necessities and capacities; as the heaven is full of God's glory, so *the earth is full of his mercy*. Not only the children of men upon the earth, but even the inferior creatures, taste of God's goodness. He therefore prays that God would be good to him according to his necessity and capacity.

9. Teth

Verses 65–66

David makes a thankful acknowledgment of God's gracious dealings with him all along: *Thou hast dealt well with thy servant*. However God has dealt with us, we must own he has dealt *well* with us, better than we deserve, and all in love and with design to work for our good. Upon these experiences he grounds a petition for divine instruction: "*Teach me good judgment and knowledge*." Teach me *a good taste* (so the word signifies), a good relish, to discern things that differ, to distinguish between truth and falsehood, good and evil; for *the ear tries words, as the mouth tastes meat*. Many have knowledge who have little judgment. Where God has given a good heart a good head too may in faith be prayed for.

Verse 67

David tells: 1. Of the temptations of a prosperous condition: "*Before I was afflicted*, while I lived in peace and plenty, and knew no sorrow, *I went astray* from God and my duty." Prosperity is the unhappy occasion of much iniquity; it makes people conceited of themselves, indulgent of the flesh, forgetful of God, in love with the world, and deaf to the reproofs of the word. See xxx. 6. 2. Of the benefit of an afflicted state: "*Now have I kept thy word*, and so have been recovered from my wanderings." God often makes use of afflictions as a means to reduce those to himself who have wandered from him. The prodigal's distress brought him to himself first and then to his father.

Verse 68

David praises God's goodness and gives him the glory of it: *Thou art good and doest good*. "Lord, thou doest good to all, art the bountiful benefactor of all the creatures; this is the good I beg thou wilt do to me,—Instruct me in my duty, incline me to it, and enable me to do it.

JAMIESON, FAUSSET, BROWN

59. So the prodigal son, when reduced to straits of misery (Luke 15:17, 18).

61, 62. This the more, if opposition of enemies, or love of ease is overcome in thus honoring God's law. **have robbed me**—better, surrounded me, either as forcible constraints like fetters, or as the cords of their nets. Hengstenberg translates, "snares."

62. At midnight—Hengstenberg supposes a reference to the time when the Lord went forth to slay the Egyptian first-born (Exod. 11:4; 12: 29; cf. Job 34:20). But it rather refers to the Psalmist's own praises and prayers in the night-time. Cf. Paul and Silas (Acts 16:25; cf. Ps. 63:6).

63. The communion of the saints. Delight in their company is an evidence of belonging to them (Ps. 16:3; Amos 3:3; Mal. 3:16).

64. While opposed by the wicked, and opposing them, the pious delight in those who fear God, but, after all, rely for favor and guidance not on merit, but mercy.

65-67. The reliance on promises (vs. 49) is strengthened by experience of past dealings according with promises, and a prayer for guidance, encouraged by sanctified affliction. **66. Teach me good judgment and knowledge**–viz., in Thy word (so as to fathom its deep spirituality); for the corresponding expression (vss. 12, 64, 68), is, "Teach me Thy statutes."

67. Referred by Hengstenberg to the chastening effect produced on the Jews' minds by the captivity (Jer. 31:18, 19). The truth is a general one (Job 5:6; John 15:2; Heb. 12:11).

Cf. as to the Lord Jesus (Acts 10:38).

ADAM CLARKE

59. First—*I thought on my ways*. I deeply pondered them; I turned them upside down; I viewed my conduct on all sides. The word, as used here, is a metaphor taken from embroidering, where the figure must appear the same on the one side as it does on the other; therefore, the cloth must be turned on each side every time the needle is set in, to see that the stitch be fairly set. Thus narrowly and scrupulously did the Psalmist examine his conduct; and the result was a deep conviction that he had departed from the way of God and truth. Secondly—*And turned my feet unto thy testimonies*. Having made the above discovery, and finding himself under the displeasure of God, he abandoned every evil way, took God's word for his directory, and set out fairly in the way of life and salvation.

60. Thirdly—*I made haste, and delayed not*. He did this with the utmost speed, and did not trifle with his convictions, nor seek to drown the voice of conscience. The original word, which we translate *delayed not*, is amazingly emphatic, *velo hithmahmahti*, "I did not stand what-what-what-ing"; or, as we used to express the same sentiment, "shilly-shallying" with myself. I was determined, and so set out.

61. *The bands of the wicked have robbed me. Chebley*, the "cables," "cords," or "snares" of the wicked.

66. *Teach me good judgment and knowledge*. "Teach me [to have] a good taste and discernment." Let me see and know the importance of divine things, and give me a relish for them.

67. *Before I was afflicted I went astray*. Many have been humbled under affliction, and taught to know themselves and humble themselves before God, that probably without this could never have been saved; after this, they have been serious and faithful.

As the letter *teth* begins but few words, not forty, in the Hebrew language, there is less variety under this division than under any of the preceding.

MATTHEW HENRY

Verses 69–70

Those that were proud envied David's reputation, because it eclipsed them, and therefore did all they could to blemish him. They therefore persuaded themselves it was no sin to tell a deliberate lie if it might but expose him to contempt. David bore it patiently; he kept that precept which forbade him to render railing for railing. He did not envy their prosperity. *Their heart is as fat as grease.* The proud are *at ease* (cxxiii. 4); they are full of the world, and the wealth and pleasures of it; and this makes them secure, and stupid; they are past feeling. They roll themselves in the pleasures of sense. I would not change conditions with them. *I delight in thy law;* I build my security upon the promises of God's word. The children of God, who are acquainted with spiritual pleasures, need not envy the children of this world their carnal pleasures.

Verse 71

The proud and the wicked lived in pomp and pleasure, while David, though he kept close to God and his duty, was still in affliction. David could speak experimentally: *It was good for me;* many a good lesson he had learnt by his afflictions. The afflictions had contributed to the improvement of his knowledge and grace. He that chastened him taught him.

Verse 72

God's *law*, which he got acquaintance with by his affliction, was *better* to him than all the *gold and silver* which he lost by his affliction. David had but a little of the word of God in comparison with what we have, yet see how highly he valued it. We have both the Old and New Testament complete. He valued the law, because it is *the law of God's mouth*, the revelation of his will. His riches increased, and yet he did not set his heart upon them, but upon the word of God.

10. Jod

Verse 73

David adores God as the author of his being, Job x. 8. Every man is as truly the work of God's hands as the first man was, Ps. cxxxix. 15, 16. "*Thy hands have* not only *made me*, but *fashioned me*, and given me this being, this noble and excellent being, endued with these powers and faculties." He addresses himself to God as the God of grace, and begs he will be the author of his new and better being. "Lord, make me anew by thy grace, that I may answer the ends of my creation and live to some purpose: *Give me understanding, that I may learn thy commandments.*"

Verse 74

The confidence of this good man in the hope of God's salvation: "*I have hoped in thy word.* It is a hope that *maketh not ashamed*; but is present satisfaction, and fruition at last." The comforts which some of God's children have in God, and the favours they have received from him, should be matter of joy to others of them.

Verse 75

Still David is in affliction, and owns his sin was justly corrected: *I know, O Lord! that thy judgments are right*, are righteousness itself. We know that God is holy in his nature and wise and just in all the acts of his government, and therefore we cannot but know, in the general, that his *judgments are right*, though, in some particular instances, there may be difficulties which we cannot easily resolve. Afflictions are in the covenant, and therefore they are not meant for our hurt, but are intended for our good.

Verses 76–77

An earnest petition to God for his favour. Those that own the justice of God in their afflictions (as David had done, *v.* 75) may, in faith, and with humble boldness, be earnest for the mercy of God, and the tokens and fruits of that mercy, in their affliction. He prays for God's *merciful kindness* (*v.* 76), his *tender mercies*, *v.* 77. "Let these *come to me*," that is, "the evidence of them and the effects of them; let them work my relief and deliverance. That will comfort me when nothing else will; that will comfort me whatever grieves me."

Verses 78–79

There were those that dealt perversely with him and misconstrued all he said and did, but David regarded it not. He knew it was *without cause.* The causeless reproach, like the curse causeless, does not hurt us, and therefore should not move us. He could pray, in faith: "*Let* them *be ashamed*, that is, let them be brought either to repentance or to ruin." He valued the goodwill of saints. *Let those that fear thee turn to me.* Good men desire the friendship and

JAMIESON, FAUSSET, BROWN

69, 70. The crafty malice of the wicked, in slandering him, so far from turning him away, but binds him closer to God's Word, which they are too stupid in sin to appreciate. Hengstenberg refers the "lie" (vs. 69) to such slanders against the Jews during the captivity, as that in Ezra 4, of sedition. **fat as grease**—spiritually insensible (Ps. 17:10; 73:7; Isa. 6:10).

71, 72. So also affliction of any kind acts as a wholesome discipline in leading the pious more highly to value the truth and promises of God.

73. As God made, so He can best control, us. So as to Israel, he owed to God his whole internal and external existence (Deut. 32:6).

74. So when He has led us to rely on His truth, He will "make us to the praise of His grace" by others. "Those who fear Thee will be glad at my prosperity, as they consider my cause their cause" (Ps. 34:2; 142:7).

75-78. in faithfulness—i.e., without in the least violating Thy faithfulness; because my sins deserved and needed fatherly chastisement.

Enduring chastisement with a filial temper (Heb. 12:6-11), God's promises of mercy (Rom. 8:28) will be fulfilled, and He will give comfort in sorrow (Lam. 3:22; II Cor. 1:3, 4). **77. Let thy tender mercies come unto me**—As I am not able to come unto them. But the wicked will be confounded.

ADAM CLARKE

The Law, *torah*, from *yarah*, to "direct, guide, teach, make straight, or even, point forward"; because it guides, directs, and instructs in the way of righteousness; makes our path straight, shows what is even and right, and points us onward to peace, truth, and happiness.

Commandments, *mitsvoth*, from *tasvah*, "to command, order, ordain"; because they show us what we should do, and what we should leave undone, and exact our obedience.

76. *Thy merciful kindness.* Let me derive my comfort and happiness from a diffusion of Thy love and mercy, *chasdecha*, "thy exuberant goodness," through my soul.

77. *Let thy tender mercies.* "Thy fatherly and affectionate feelings."

MATTHEW HENRY

society of those that are good. Some think it intimates that when David had been guilty of that foul sin in the murder of Uriah, those that feared God turned from him, for they were ashamed of him; this troubled him, and therefore he prays, Lord, let them *turn to me* again.

Verse 80

David's prayer for sincerity. His dread of the consequences of hypocrisy: "*Let my heart be sound*, that I may come *boldly to the throne of grace*, and may lift up my face without spot at the great day."

11. Caph

Verses 81–82

He longs *for the salvation of the Lord* and *for his word*, that is, salvation according to the word. He is eager for the objects of faith, salvation from the present calamities and doubts and fears. It may be understood of the coming of the Messiah; the souls of the faithful even *fainted to see* that salvation of which the prophets testified. (1 Pet. i. 10); their eyes failed for it. Abraham saw it at a distance, and so did others, but at such a distance that they could not steadfastly see it. David cried out, "*When wilt thou comfort me?*" When the *eyes fail* yet the faith must not; for *the vision is for an appointed time, and at the end it shall speak and shall not lie.*

Verse 83

David begs God would make haste to comfort him, *for I have become like a bottle in the smoke*, a leathern bottle, which, if it hung any while in the smoke, was not only blackened with soot, but dried, and parched, and shrivelled up. David was thus wasted by age, and sickness, and sorrow. David had been of a ruddy countenance, but now he is withered, his colour is gone, his cheeks are furrowed. A bottle, when it is thus wrinkled with the smoke, is thrown by, and there is no more use of it. Thus was David, in his low estate, looked upon *as a despised broken vessel.* Though his affliction was great, yet it had not driven him from his duty, and therefore he was within the reach of God's promise: *Yet do I not forget thy statutes.*

Verse 84

David prays against the instruments of his troubles. He prays not for power to avenge himself (he bore no malice to any), but that God would take to himself the vengeance that belonged to him. "*The days of my affliction are many;* thou seest, Lord, how many they be; when wilt thou return in mercy to me? O let the days of my trouble be shortened."

Verses 85–87

David's state was *herein* a type and figure of the state both of Christ and Christians grievously persecuted. His persecutors were *proud.* They were unjust. *They dug pits for him*, which intimates that they were deliberate in their designs against him. They herein showed their enmity to God himself. The pits they *dug for him* were *not after God's law*; he means they were very much against his law, which forbids to *devise evil to our neighbour*. The law appointed that, if a man dug a pit which occasioned any mischief, he should answer for the mischief (Exod. xxi. 33, 34), much more when it was dug with a mischievous design. He begs that God would stand by him, and succour him: "*They persecute me; help thou me;* help me under my troubles, that I may bear them patiently, and in due time help me out of my troubles." *God help me* is an excellent comprehensive prayer; it is a pity that it should ever be used lightly and as a by-word.

Verse 88

David at prayer for divine grace: "*Quicken me after thy lovingkindness; so shall I keep thy testimonies.*" He had prayed before, *Quicken me in thy righteousness* (*v.* 40); but here, *Quicken me after thy lovingkindness.* The surest token of God's goodwill toward us is his good work in us.

12. Lamed

Verses 89–91

The psalmist acknowledges the unchangeableness of the word of God and of all his counsels: "*For ever, O Lord! thy word is settled. Thou art for ever thyself* (so some read it); thou art the same, and with thee there is no variableness and this is a proof of it. *Thy word*, by which the heavens were made, *is settled* there in the abiding products of it." *Thy faithfulness is unto all generations.* He produces, for proof of it, the constancy of the course of nature: *Thou hast established the earth for ever and it abides.* It is by virtue of God's promise to Noah (Gen. viii. 22) that *day and night, summer and winter*, observe a steady course. All the creatures are, in their places, and

JAMIESON, FAUSSET, BROWN

78. but I will meditate in thy precepts—and so shall not be "ashamed," i.e., put to shame (vs. 80). **79, 80.** Those who may have thought his afflictions an evidence of God's rejection will then be led to return to Him; as the friends of Job did on his restoration, having been previously led through his afflictions to doubt the reality of his religion. **Let my . . . be sound**—i.e., perfect, sincere. **ashamed**—disappointed in my hope of salvation.

81-83. In sorrow the pious heart yearns for the comforts of God's promises (Ps. 73:26; 84:2).

82. Mine eyes fail for thy word—i.e., with yearning desire for Thy word. When the eyes fail, yet faith must not.

83. bottle in the smoke—as a skin bottle dried and shriveled up in smoke, so is he withered by sorrow. Wine bottles of skin used to be hung up in smoke to dry them, before the wine was put in them [Maurer].

84-87. The shortness of my life requires that the relief afforded to me from mine enemies should be speedy.

85. pits—plots for my destruction. **which**—rather, "who," i.e., "the proud"; "pits" is not the antecedent. **87. consumed me upon earth**—Hengstenberg translates, "in the land"; understanding "me" of the *nation* Israel, of which but a small remnant was left. But *English Version* is simpler; either, "They have consumed me so as to leave almost nothing of me on earth"; or, "They have almost destroyed and prostrated me on the earth" [Maurer]. **87. I forsook not**—Whatever else I am forsaken of, I forsake not Thy precepts, and so am not mistaken of Thee (Ps. 39:5, 13; II Cor. 4:8, 9), and the injuries and insults of the wicked increase the need for it.

But, however they act regardless of God's law, the pious, adhering to its teaching, receive quickening grace, and are sustained steadfast.

89-91. In all changes God's Word remains firm (I Pet. 1:25). Like the heavens, it continually attests God's unfailing power and unchanging care (Ps. 89:2). **is settled in**—i.e., stands as firmly as the heaven in which it dwells, and whence it emanated. **90.** (Ps. 33:9.) **91. They**—the heaven (vs. 89) and the earth (vs. 90). Hengstenberg translates, "They stand *for* thy judgment," i.e., ready, as obedient servants, to execute them. The usage of this Psalm favors this view. But see Jeremiah 33:25.

ADAM CLARKE

82. *Mine eyes fail.* With looking up for the fulfillment of Thy promise, as my heart fails in longing after Thy presence.

83. *Like a bottle in the smoke.* In the Eastern countries their *bottles* are made of skins; one of these hung in the smoke must soon be parched and shrivelled up. This represents the exhausted state of his body and mind by long bodily affliction and mental distress.

85. *The proud have digged pits.* The Vulgate, Septuagint, Aethiopic, and Arabic translate this verse thus: "They have recited to me unholy fables, which are not according to thy law."

Letter *Lamed*—Twelfth Division

89. *For ever, O Lord, thy word is settled in heaven.* Thy purposes are all settled above, and they shall all be fulfilled below.

90. *Thy faithfulness.* That which binds Thee to accomplish the promise made.

91. *They continue this day.* This verse should be thus read: "All are Thy servants; therefore they continue this day according to Thy ordinances."

MATTHEW HENRY

according to their capacities, serviceable to their Creator, and answer the ends of their creation; and shall man be the only rebel, the only revolter from his allegiance, and the only unprofitable burden of the earth?

Verse 92

David was in affliction, and ready to *perish in his affliction*, not likely to die, so much as likely to despair; he therefore admires the goodness of God to him, that he had kept the possession of his own soul, was enabled to keep close to his God and was not driven from his religion. God's law was his delight in his affliction; it afforded him abundant matter of comfort. His meditations on it, were his delightful entertainment in solitude and sorrow. A Bible is a pleasant companion at any time.

Verse 93

The best evidence of our love to the word of God is never to forget it. See here what is the best help for bad memories, namely, good affections.

Verse 94

David claims relation to God: "*I am thine*, devoted to thee and owned by thee, thine in covenant." He proves his claim: "*I have sought thy precepts*." This will be the best evidence that we belong to God.

Verse 95

David complains of the malice of his enemies. He comforts himself in the word of God as his protection: "While they are contriving my destruction, *I consider thy testimonies*, which secure to me my salvation."

Verse 96

David's testimony: *I have seen an end of all perfection*. Poor perfection which one sees an end of! Yet such are all those things in this world which pass for perfections. David, in his time, had seen Goliath, the strongest, overcome, Asahel, the swiftest, overtaken, Ahithophel, the wisest, befooled, Absalom, the fairest, deformed; and, in short, he had *seen an end of perfection*, of *all perfection*. The glory of man is but as the flower of the grass. *But thy commandment is broad, exceedingly broad*. The word of God reaches to all cases, to all times.

13. MEM

Verse 97

David's inexpressible love to the word of God: *O how love I thy law!* He not only loved the promises, but loved the law, and delighted in it after the inner man. What we love we love to think of; by *this* it appeared that David loved the word of God that it was his *meditation*.

Verses 98–100

An account of David's learning. In his youth he minded business in the country as a shepherd; from his youth he minded business in the court and camp. Which way then could he get any great stock of learning? He had it from God as the author: *Thou hast made me wise*. He had it by the word of God as the means, by *his commandments* and *his testimonies*. A good man, wherever he goes, carries his Bible along with him, if not in his hands, yet in his head and in his heart. The best way to improve in knowledge is to abide and abound in all the instances of serious godliness; for, *if any man do his will, he shall know of the doctrine* of Christ, shall know more and more of it, John vii. 17. The love of the truth prepares for the light of it; the *pure in heart shall see God* here. He outwitted his enemies; God, by these means, made him wiser to baffle and defeat their designs. He outstripped his *teachers*, and had more understanding than all of them. He may mean those who had been his teachers when he was young; he built so well upon the foundation which they had laid that, with the help of his Bible, he became able to teach them. It is no reflection upon our teachers, but rather an honour to them, to improve so as to excel them. He outdid *the ancients, either those of his day* or those of former days. In short, the written word is a surer guide to heaven than all the doctors and fathers, the teachers and ancients, of the church; and the sacred writings kept, and kept to, will teach us more wisdom than all their writings.

Verse 101

David's care to avoid the ways of sin: "*I have refrained my feet from the evil ways* they were ready to step aside into. I checked myself and drew back as soon as I was aware that I was entering into temptation." His abstaining from sin was evidence that he did conscientiously aim to keep God's word and had made that his rule.

JAMIESON, FAUSSET, BROWN

92-94. Hence the pious are encouraged and inclined to seek a knowledge of it, and persevere amidst the efforts of those planning and *waiting* to destroy them. **92. my delights**—plural, **not** merely *delight*, but equal to all other delights.

93. The bounds of created perfection may be defined, but those of God's law in its nature, application, and influence, are infinite. There is no human thing so perfect but that something is wanting to it; its limits are narrow, whereas God's law is of infinite breadth, reaching to all cases, perfectly meeting what each requires, and to all times (Ps. 19:3, 6, 7-11; Eccles. 3:11). It cannot be cramped within any definitions of man's dogmatical systems. Man never outgrows the Word. It does not shock the ignorant man with declared anticipations of discoveries which he had not yet made; while in it the man of science finds his newest discoveries by tacit anticipations provided for.

97. This characteristic love for God's law (cf. Ps. 1:2) ensures increase.

98-100, of knowledge, both of the matter of all useful, moral truth, and an experience of its application. **98. wiser than mine enemies**—with all their carnal cunning (Deut. 4:6, 8). **they are ever with me**—The *Hebrew* is, rather *singular*, "it is ever with me"; the commandments forming ONE *complete whole*, Thy law.

100. more than the ancients—Antiquity is no help against stupidity, where it does not accord with God's word [LUTHER] (Job 32:7-9). The Bible is the key of all knowledge, the history of the world, past, present, and to come (Ps. 111:10). He who does the will of God shall know of the doctrine (John 7:17). **understanding**—is practical skill (Ps. 2:10; 32:8).

101-104. Avoidance of sinful courses is both the effect and means of increasing in divine knowledge (cf. Ps. 19:10).

ADAM CLARKE

CHARLES H. SPURGEON:

"Unless thy law had been my delights, I should then have perished in mine affliction" (119:92). That word which has preserved the heavens and the earth also preserves the people of God in their time of trial. With that word we are charmed; it is a mine of delight to us. We take a double and treble delight in it, and derive a multiplied delight from it, and this stands us in good stead when all other delights are taken from us. We should have felt ready to lie down and die of our griefs if the spiritual comforts of God's word had not uplifted us; but by their sustaining influence we have been borne above all the depressions and despairs which naturally grow out of severe affliction. Some of us can set our seal to this statement. Our affliction, if it had not been for divine grace, would have crushed us out of existence, so that we should have perished. In our darkest seasons nothing has kept us from desperation but the promise of the Lord: yea, at times nothing has stood between us and self-destruction save faith in the eternal Word of God.—*The Treasury of David*

96. *I have seen an end of all perfection.* Literally, "Of all consummations I have seen the end"; as if one should say, Everything of human origin has its limits and end, howsoever extensive, noble, and excellent.

Letter *Mem*—Thirteenth Division

97. *O how love I thy law!* This is one of the strongest marks of a gracious and pious heart, cast in the mold of obedience.

100. *I understand more than the ancients.* God had revealed to him more of that hidden wisdom which was in His law than He had done to any of his predecessors. And this was most literally true of David, who spoke more fully about Christ than any who had gone before him; or, indeed, followed after him.

MATTHEW HENRY

Verse 102

David's constancy in his religion. He had *not departed from God's judgments*; he had not chosen any other rule than the word of God, nor had he wilfully deviated from that rule. "It was divine grace in my heart that enabled me to receive those instructions."

Verses 103–104

The pleasure and delight which David took in the word of God; it was *sweet to his taste, sweeter than honey*. There is such a thing as a spiritual taste, an inward savour and relish of divine things. The word of God helped him to a good head: "*Through thy precepts I get understanding* to discern between truth and falsehood, good, and evil, so as not to mistake either in the conduct of my own life or in advising others." It helped him to a good heart: "*Therefore*, because I have got understanding of the truth, *I hate every false way*, and am steadfastly resolved not to turn aside into it."

14. Nun

Verse 105

The nature of the word of God, and the great intention of giving it to the world; it is a *lamp and a light*. It discovers to us, concerning God and ourselves, that which otherwise we could not have known. The commandment is a lamp kept burning with the oil of the Spirit; it is like the lamps in the sanctuary, and the pillar of fire to Israel. It must be not only a *light to our eyes*, to gratify them, but a *light to our feet* and *to our path*, to direct us in the choice of our way in general and in the particular steps we take in that way.

Verse 106

The notion David had of religion; it is *keeping God's righteous judgments*. God's commands are his judgments. It is good for us to bind ourselves with a solemn oath to be religious. We must swear to the Lord as subjects swear allegiance to their sovereign, promising fealty, appealing to God concerning our sincerity in this promise.

Verse 107

David laboured under many discouragements. The recourse he has to God in this condition; he prays for his grace: "*Quicken me, O Lord!* make me lively, make me cheerful; quicken me by afflictions to greater diligence in my work."

Verse 108

What David here earnestly prays for are the acceptance of the *free-will-offerings*, not of his purse, but of his *mouth*, his prayers and praises. They must be *free-will-offerings*, for we must offer them abundantly and cheerfully, and it is this willing mind that is accepted.

Verses 109–110

David in danger of losing his life. There is but a step between him and death, for the *wicked have laid a snare* for him; Saul did so many a time, because he hated him for his piety. What they could not effect by open force they hoped to compass by treachery, which made him say, *My soul is continually in my hand*. In the multitude of his cares for his own safety he finds room in his head and heart for the word of God, and has that in his mind as fresh as ever; and where that dwells richly it will be a *well of living water*.

Verses 111–112

The psalmist resolves to stick to the word of God and to live and die by it. "*Thy testimonies* (the truths, the promises, of thy word) *have I taken as a heritage for ever, for they are the rejoicing of my heart*." He expected an eternal happiness in God's testimonies. The covenant God had made with him was an everlasting covenant, and therefore he took it as *a heritage for ever*. He resolves to govern himself by it: *I have inclined my heart to do thy statutes*. Those that would have the blessings of God's testimonies must come under the bonds of his statutes.

15. Samech

Verse 113

David's dread of the risings of sin, and the first beginnings of it: *I hate* vain *thoughts*. Though David could not say that he was free from vain thoughts, yet he could say that he hated them; he did not countenance them, nor give them any entertainment, but did what he could to keep them out, at least to keep them under. *But thy law do I love*, which forbids those vain thoughts, and threatens them. The more we love the law of God the more we shall get the mastery of our vain thoughts, the more hateful they will be to us.

JAMIESON, FAUSSET, BROWN

105. Not only does the Word of God inform us of His will, but, as a light on a path in darkness, it shows us how to follow the right and avoid the wrong way. The lamp of the Word is not the sun. He would blind our eyes in our present fallen state; but we may bless God for the light shining as in a dark place, to guide us until the Sun of Righteousness shall come, and we shall be made capable of seeing Him (II Peter 1:19; Rev. 22:4). The lamp is fed with the oil of the Spirit. The allusion is to the lamps and torches carried at night before an Eastern caravan.

106-108. Such was the national covenant at Sinai and in the fields of Moab.

108. free-will offerings—the spontaneous expressions of his gratitude, as contrasted with the *appointed* "offerings" of the temple (Hos. 14:2; Heb. 13:15). He determines to pursue this way, relying on God's quickening power (vs. 50) in affliction, and a gracious acceptance of his "spiritual sacrifices of prayer and praise" (Ps. 50:5; 14, 23). **109, 110.** In the midst of deadly perils (the phrase is drawn from the fact that what we carry in our hands may easily slip from them, Judg. 12:3; I Sam. 28:21; Job 13:14; cf. I Sam. 19:5), and exposed to crafty enemies, his safety and guidance is in the truth and promises of God.

111, 112. These he joyfully takes as his perpetual heritage, to perform the duties and receive the comforts they teach, evermore.

113. vain thoughts—better, unstable persons, lit., "divided men," those of a *divided*, doubting mind (Jas. 1:8); "a double-minded man" [Hengstenberg], skeptics, or, skeptical notions as opposed to the certainty of God's word.

ADAM CLARKE

Judgments, *mishpatim*, from *shaphat*, "to judge, determine, regulate, order, and discern," because they judge concerning our words and works; show the rules by which they should be regulated; and cause us to discern what is right and wrong, and decide accordingly.

Letter *Nun*—Fourteenth Division

105. *Thy word is a lamp*. This is illustrated thus by Solomon, Prov. vi. 23: "The commandment is a lamp; and the law is light; and reproofs of instruction are the way of life."

107. *I am afflicted very much. Ad meod*, "to extremity, excessively." *Quicken me*. Deliver us from our bondage.

108. *The freewill offerings of my mouth*. "The voluntary offerings which I have promised." Or, As we are in captivity, and cannot sacrifice to Thee, but would if we could, accept the praises of our mouth, and the purposes of our hearts, instead of the sacrifices and offerings which we would bring to Thy altar, but cannot.

109. *My soul is continually in my hand. Naphshi*, "my life." The expression signifies to be in continual danger.

Letter *Samech*—Fifteenth Division

113. *I hate vain thoughts*. I have hated *seaphim*, "tumultuous, violent men."

MATTHEW HENRY

Verse 114

David, when Saul pursued him, often betook himself to close places for shelter; in war he guarded himself with his shield. Now God was both these to him, a hiding-place to preserve him from danger and a shield to preserve him in danger, his life from death and his soul from sin.

Verse 115

I will keep the commandments of my God. Bravely resolved! like a saint, like a soldier; for true courage consists in a steady resolution against all sin and for all duty. Those that resolve to keep the commandments of God must have no society with evil-doers; for bad company is a great hindrance to a holy life. We must not choose wicked people for our companions, Ps. i. 1; Eph. v. 11.

Verses 116–117

David prays for sustaining grace; for this grace sufficient he besought the Lord twice: *Uphold me;* and again, *Hold thou me up.* He sees himself not only unable to go on in his duty by any strength of his own, but in danger of falling into sin unless he was prevented by divine grace. We stand no longer than God holds us and go no further than he carries us. Those that hope in God's word may be sure that the word will not fail them, and therefore their hope will not make them ashamed.

Verses 118–120

God's judgment on wicked people, on those that *wander from his statutes,* that will not have God to reign over them. Now see how God deals with them, that you may neither fear them nor envy them. He *puts them all away like dross.* Wicked people are as dross, which, though it be mingled with the good metal in the ore, and seems to be of the same substance with it, must be separated from it. God casts them off because they *err from his statutes* and because *their deceit is falsehood,* that is, because they deceive themselves by setting up false rules, in opposition to God's statutes, and because they go about to deceive others with their hypocritical pretences. David's fear of the wrath of God: *My flesh trembles for fear of thee.* Instead of insulting over those who fell under God's displeasure, he humbled himself.

16. AIN

Verses 121–122

David had not done wrong; he could truly say, "*I have done judgment and justice,* I have made conscience of rendering to all their due, and have not by force or fraud hindered any of their right." He is sensible that he cannot make his part good himself, and therefore begs that God would appear for him. Christ is our surety with God; and, if he be so, Providence shall be our surety against all the world.

Verse 123

David, being oppressed, is here waiting and wishing for the salvation of the Lord. He cannot but think that it comes slowly. He was sometimes ready to despair and to think that, because the salvation did not come when he looked for it, it would never come. Though our eyes fail, yet God's word does not, and therefore those that build upon it, though now discouraged, shall in due time see his salvation.

Verses 124–125

David's petition for divine instruction: "*Teach me thy statutes*; give me to know all my duty." In difficult times we should desire more to be told what we must do than what we may expect, and should pray more to be led into the knowledge of scripture-precepts than of scripture-prophecies. He pleads his relation to God: "*I am thy servant,* and have work to do for thee; therefore *teach me* to do it and to do it well."

Verse 126

A complaint of the daring impiety of the wicked. A desire that God would appear, for the vindication of his own honour: "*It is time for thee, Lord, to work,* to do something for the effectual confutation of atheists and infidels, and the silencing of those that set their mouth against the heavens." Some read it, and the original will bear it, *It is time to work for thee, O Lord!* it is time for everyone in his place to appear on the Lord's side—against the threatening growth of profaneness and immorality.

Verses 127–128

David here, as often in this psalm, professes the great love he had to the word and law of God. David saw that the word of God answers all purposes better than money does, for it enriches the soul towards God; and therefore he loved it better than

JAMIESON, FAUSSET, BROWN

114. hiding-place—(Cf. Ps. 27:5). **shield**—(Ps. 3:3; 7-10). **hope in thy word**—confidently rest on its teachings and promises.

115-117. Hence he fears not wicked men, nor dreads disappointment, sustained by God in making His law the rule of life. **Depart from me**—Ye can do nothing with me; *for,* etc. (Ps. 6:8).

118-120. But the disobedient and rebellious will be visited by God's wrath, which impresses the pious with wholesome fear and awe.

their deceit is falsehood—i.e., all their cunning deceit, wherewith they seek to entrap the godly, *is in vain.* **120.** The "judgments" are those on the wicked (vss. 119). Joyful hope goes hand in hand with fear (Hab. 3:16-18).

121-126. On the grounds of his integrity, desire for God's word, and covenant relation to Him, the servant of God may plead for His protecting care against the wicked, gracious guidance to the knowledge of truth, and His effective vindication of the righteous and their cause, which is also His own. **Be surety**—Stand for me against my oppressors (Gen. 43:9; Isa. 38:14).

127, 128. Therefore [i.e., In view of these benefits, or, Because of the glory of Thy law, so much praised in the previous parts of the Psalm] **I love . . .,** [and] **Therefore** (repeated)—All its precepts, on all subjects, are estimable for their

ADAM CLARKE

Statutes, *chukkim,* from *chak,* "to mark, trace out, describe, and ordain"; because they mark out our way, describe the line of conduct we are to pursue, and order or ordain what we are to observe.

122. *Be surety for thy servant.* Give a pledge or token that Thou wilt help me in times of necessity. Or, "Be bail for Thy servant." What a word is this! Pledge thyself for me, that Thou wilt produce me safely at the judgment of the great day. Then sustain and keep me blameless till the coming of Christ. Neither of these two verses has any of the ten words in reference to God's law or attributes. The *judgment* and the *justice* refer to the Psalmist's own conduct in v. 121. Verse 122 has no word of the kind.

126. *It is time for thee, Lord, to work.* The *time* is fulfilled in which Thou hast promised deliverance to Thy people.

127. *Above gold. Mizzahab,* more than "resplendent gold"; gold without any strain or rust. *Yea, above fine gold. Umippaz,* "above solid gold"; gold separated from the dross, perfectly refined.

MATTHEW HENRY

gold, for it had done that for him which gold could not do, and would stand him in stead when the wealth of the world would fail him.

17. PE

Verse 129

The word of God gives us admirable discoveries of God, and Christ, and another world; admirable proofs of divine love and grace. The majesty of the style, the purity of the matter, the harmony of the parts, are all wonderful. Its effects upon the consciences of men, both for conviction and comfort, are wonderful.

Verse 130

The great use for which the word of God was intended, to give light, that is, to give understanding. Even *the entrance of God's word gives light.* If we begin at the beginning, and take it before us, we shall find that the very first verses of the Bible give us surprising and yet satisfying discoveries of the origin of the universe. We find we begin to see when we begin to study the word of God. Some understand it of the New Testament, which is the opening or unfolding of the Old, which would give light concerning life and immortality. It shows us a way to heaven so plain that the *wayfaring men, though fools, shall not err therein.*

Verse 131

When Christ is formed in the soul there are gracious longings. *I opened my mouth and panted,* as one overcome with heat, or almost stifled, pants for a mouthful of fresh air.

Verse 132

David's request for God's favour to himself: "*Look* graciously *upon me; and be merciful to me.*" How humble his petition is! He asks not for the operations of God's hand, only for the smiles of his face; and for that he does not plead merit, but implores mercy. "Lord, I am one of *those that love thy name,* love thee and thy word, and thou usest to be kind to those that do so." The dealings of God with those that love him are such that a man needs not desire to be any better dealt with, 1 Cor. x. 13.

Verse 133

David is, in this verse, as earnest for the good work of God in him, as in the verse before, for the goodwill of God towards him. "*Order my steps in thy word;* having led me into the right way, let every step I take in that way be under the guidance of thy grace." "*Let no iniquity have dominion over me* that I should be led captive by it."

Verse 134

David prays that he might live a quiet and peaceable life, and might not be harassed and discomposed by those that studied to be vexatious. "Let me be delivered out of the hands of my enemies, so shall I keep thy precepts more cheerfully."

Verse 135

David here, as often elsewhere, writes himself God's servant, a title he gloried in, though he was a king. He is very ambitious of his Master's favour, accounting that his happiness and chief good. "*Make thy face to shine upon thy servant;* let me be accepted of thee, and let me know that I am so. If the world frown upon me, yet do thou smile."

Verse 136

David in sorrow, to such a degree that he weeps *rivers of tears.* David had prayed for comfort in God's favour (*v.* 135); now he pleads that he was qualified for that comfort, and had need of it, for he was one of those that mourned in Zion, Isa. lxi. 3. He wept not for his troubles, though they were many, but for the dishonour done to God: *Because they keep not thy law,* that is, those about me, *v.* 139.

18. TZADDI

Verses 137–138

The righteousness of God. He rules the world by his providence, according to the principles of justice and never did, nor ever can do, any wrong to any of his creatures. As he acts like himself, so his law requires that we act like ourselves and like him, that we be just to ourselves and to all we deal with, true to all the engagements we lay ourselves under both to God and man.

Verse 139

The great contempt which wicked men put upon religion: *My enemies have forgotten thy words.*

JAMIESON, FAUSSET, BROWN

purity, and lead one imbued with their spirit to hate all evil (Ps. 19:10). The Word of God admits of no eclecticism; its least title is perfect (Ps. 12:6; Matt. 5:17-19).

129. **wonderful**—lit., "wonders," i.e., of moral excellence.

130. The entrance—lit., "opening"; God's words, as an open door, let in light, or knowledge. Rather, as HENGSTENBERG explains it, "*The opening up,*" or, "*explanation* of thy word." To the natural man the doors of God's Word are shut. Luke 24: 27, 31; Acts 17:3; Eph. 1:18, confirm this view," "opening (i.e., explaining) and alleging," etc. **unto the simple**—those needing or desiring it (cf. Ps. 19: 7).

131-135. An ardent desire (cf. Ps. 56:1, 2) for spiritual enlightening, establishment in a right course, deliverance from the wicked, and evidence of God's favor is expressed. **I opened my mouth, and panted**—as a traveller in a hot desert pants for the cooling breeze (Ps. 63:1; 84:2).

Look . . . upon me—opposed to hiding or averting the face (cf. Ps. 25:15; 86:6; 102:17). **as thou usest to do**—or, "as it is *right* in regard to those who love Thy name." Such have a *right* to the manifestations of God's grace, resting on the nature of God as faithful to His promise to such, not on their own merits.

Order my steps—*Make firm,* so that there be no halting (Ps. 40:2). **any iniquity**—vs. 34 (favors HENGSTENBERG, "any iniquitous man," any "oppressor." But the parallel first clause in this (vs. 33) favors *English Version* (Ps. 19:13). His hope of deliverance from *external* oppression of man (vs. 34) is founded on his deliverance from the *internal* "dominion of iniquity," in answer to his prayer (vs. 33).

136. Zealous himself to keep God's law, he is deeply afflicted when others violate it (cf. vs. 53). Lit., "Mine eyes come down (dissolved) like waterbrooks" (Lam. 3:48; Jer. 9:1). **because . . .**—(Cf. Ezek. 9:4; Jer. 13:17).

137-139. God's justice and faithfulness in His government aggravate the neglect of the wicked, and more excite the lively zeal of His people.

139. (Ps. 69:9.)

ADAM CLARKE

130. *The entrance of thy words giveth light. Pethach,* the "opening" of it. When I open my Bible to read, light springs up in my mind.

131. *I opened my mouth, and panted.* A metaphor taken from an animal exhausted in the chase. He runs, open-mouthed, to take in the cooling air, the heart beating high, and the muscular force nearly expended through fatigue.

133. *Order my steps.* Make them "firm"; let me not walk with a halting or unsteady step. *Have dominion over me. Bi,* "in me." Let me have no governor but God; let the throne of my heart be filled by Him, and none other.

135. *Make thy face to shine.* Give me a sense of Thy approbation. Let me know, by the testimony of Thy Spirit in my conscience, that Thou art reconciled to me.

Righteousness, *tsedakah,* from *tsadak,* "to do justice, to give full weight." That which teaches a man to give to all their due. This word is applied to God's judgments, testimonies, and commandments; they are all righteous, give to all their due, and require what is due from everyone.

MATTHEW HENRY

David reckoned those his enemies who forgot the words of God because they were enemies to religion, therefore his *zeal consumed him*, when he observed their impieties. Zeal against sin should constrain us to do what we can against it in our places, at least to do so much the more in religion ourselves.

Verse 140

Every good man, being a servant of God, loves the word of God, because it lets him know his Master's will and directs him in his Master's work.

Verse 141

God has chosen the foolish things of the world, and it has been the common lot of his people to be a despised people. David poor and yet pious, would not throw off his religion, though it exposed him to contempt, for he knew that was designed to try his constancy.

Verse 142

God's word is a law, and that law is truth. We are reasonable creatures, and as such we must be ruled by truth. If the principles be true, the practices must be agreeable to them, else we do not act rationally. We are creatures, and therefore subjects, and must be ruled by our Creator; and whatever he commands we are bound to obey as a law. Here is truth brought to the understanding, there to sit chief, and direct the motions of the whole man; but, lest the authority of that should become weak through the flesh, here is a law to bind the will and bring that into subjection.

Verses 143–144

David finds himself not only mean, but miserable, as far as this world could make him so: *Trouble and anguish have taken hold on me*—trouble without, anguish within. *Yet thy commandments are my delights*. There are delights, variety of delights, in the word of God, which the saints have often the sweetest enjoyment of when they are in trouble and anguish, 2 Cor. i. 5. He does not say, "Give me a further revelation," but, *Give me a further understanding.*

19. KOPH

Verses 145–146

David's good prayers. He *cried with his whole heart*; we are likely to speed when we thus strive and wrestle in prayer. He cried unto God. Whither should the child go but to his father when anything ails him? The great thing he prayed for was salvation: *Save me*. We need desire no more than God's salvation (l. 23) and the *things that accompany it*, Heb. vi. 9.

Verses 147–148

Hope in God's word encouraged him to continue instant in prayer, though the answer did not come immediately: *"I hoped in thy word*, which I knew would not fail me." The more intimately we converse with the word of God, and the more we dwell upon it in our thoughts, the better able we shall be to speak to God. Reading the word will not serve, but we must meditate in it. David began the day with God. The first thing he did in the morning, before he admitted any business, was to pray. If our first thoughts in the morning be of God they will help to keep us in his fear all the day long. Even in *the night-watches*, when he awaked from his first sleep, he would rather meditate and pray than turn himself and go to sleep again.

Verse 149

David applies to God for grace and comfort with much solemnity. *"Lord, quicken me;* stir me up to that which is good, and make me vigorous, and lively, and cheerful in it. Let habits of grace be drawn out into act."

Verses 150–151

David was in danger from his enemies. They followed him closely and he was just ready to fall into their hands: *They draw nigh*. They were at his heels. God sometimes suffers persecutors to prevail very far against his people, so that, as David said (1 Sam. xx. 3), *There is but a step between them and death*. It is the happiness of the saints that, when trouble is near, God is near, and no trouble can separate between them and him. He is never far to seek, but he is within our call, Deut. iv. 7.

Verse 152

This confirms the foregoing verse, *All thy commandments are truth;* he means the covenant, the word which God has commanded to a thousand generations. The promises are *founded for ever*, so that when heaven and earth shall have passed away every iota and tittle of the promise shall stand firm, 2 Cor. i. 20. David

JAMIESON, FAUSSET, BROWN

140. very pure—lit., "refined," shown pure by trial.

141. The pious, however despised of men, are distinguished in God's sight by a regard for His law.

142-144. The principles of God's government are permanent and reliable, and in the deepest distress His people find them a theme of delightful meditation and a source of reviving power (vss. 17, 116). **law is the truth**—It therefore cannot deceive as to its promises. **everlasting**—(Ps. 111:3), though to outward appearance seeming dead.

145-149. An intelligent devotion is led by divine promises and is directed to an increase of gracious affections, arising from a contemplation of revealed truth.

prevented—lit., "came before," anticipated not only the *dawn*, but even the usual periods of *the night;* when the nightwatches, which might be expected to find me asleep, come, they find me awake (Ps. 63:6; 77:4; Lam. 2:19). Such is the earnestness of the desire and love for God's truth.

quicken me—revive my heart according to those principles of justice, founded on Thine own nature, and revealed in Thy law, which specially set forth Thy mercy to the humble as well as justice to the wicked (cf. vs. 30).

150-152. Though the wicked are *near* to injure, because *far* from God's law, He is *near* to help, and faithful to His word, which abides for ever.

ADAM CLARKE

140. *Thy word is very pure.* It is "purification." It is not a purified thing, but a thing that purifies. "Now ye are clean," said Christ, by "the word which I have spoken unto you." God's Word is a Fire to purify as well as a Hammer to break.

142. *Thy righteousness is an everlasting righteousness.* The word *tsedek* is a word of very extensive meaning in the Bible. It signifies, not only God's inherent righteousness and perfection of nature, but also His method of treating others, His plan of redemption, His method of saving others.

147. *I prevented the dawning.* "I went before the dawn or twilight."

148. *Mine eyes prevent.* "Go before the watches." Before the watchman proclaims the hour, I am awake, meditating on Thy words. The Jews divided the night into three watches, which began at what we call six o'clock in the evening, and consisted each of four hours. The Romans taught them afterwards to divide it into four watches of three hours each.

152. *Concerning thy testimonies, I have known of old.* "Long ago I have known concerning thy testimonies."

MATTHEW HENRY

knew of old, from the days of his youth, ever since he began to look towards God, that the word of God is what one may venture one's all upon.

20. Resh

Verses 153–154

David has an eye to God's pity, and prays, "*Consider my affliction.*" He has an eye to God's power and prays, "*Deliver me;*" and again, "*Deliver me.*" He has an eye to God's righteousness, and prays, "*Plead my cause;* and take me for thy client." He has an eye to God's grace, and prays, "*Quicken me.* Lord, Revive and comfort me, till the deliverance is wrought!"

Verse 155

How can those expect to seek God's favour with success, when they are in adversity, who never sought his statutes when they were in prosperity? But eternal salvation is certainly far from them. They thrust it from them by thrusting the Saviour from them; it is so far from them that they cannot reach it, and the longer they persist in sin the further it is.

Verse 156

David had spoken of the misery of the wicked (*v.* 155); but God is good notwithstanding; there were tender mercies sufficient in God to have saved them, if they had not *despised the riches of those mercies.*

Verse 157

David, being a public person, had many enemies, but withal he had many friends, who loved him and wished him well; let him set the one over-against the other. In this David was a type both of Christ and his church. The enemies, the persecutors, of both, are many. A man who is steady in the way of his duty, though he may have many enemies, needs fear none.

Verse 158

David *beheld the transgressors,* and it *grieved* him to see them dishonour God, serve Satan, debauch the world, and ruin their own souls.

Verse 159

David does not say, "Consider how I fulfil thy precepts"; he was conscious to himself that in many things he came short; but, "Consider how I love them." Our obedience is pleasing to God, and pleasant to ourselves, only when it comes from a principle of love.

Verse 160

David here comforts himself with the faithfulness of God's word. *It is true from the beginning.* Ever since God began to reveal himself to the children of men all he said was true and to be trusted. The church, from its beginning, was built upon this rock. It has not gained its validity by lapse of time. But the *beginning of God's word was true* (so some read it); his government was laid on a sure foundation. It will be found faithful to the end.

21. Schin

Verse 161

It has been the common lot of the best men to be persecuted; and the case is the worse if princes be the persecutors, for they have not only the sword in their hand, but they have the law on their side, and can do it with reputation and a colour of justice. It is sad that the power which magistrates have from God, and should use for him, should ever be employed against him. David never gave them provocation. "They would make me stand in awe of them and their word, and do as they bid me; but *my heart stands in awe of thy word,* and I am resolved to please God, and keep in with him, whoever is displeased and falls out with me."

Verse 162

He had just now said that his heart stood in awe of his word, and yet here he declares that he rejoiced in it. The more reverence we have for the word of God the more joy we shall find in it.

Verse 163

Love and hatred are the leading affections of the soul; if those be fixed aright, the rest move accordingly. Here we have them fixed aright in David. 1. He had a rooted antipathy to sin; he could not endure to think of it: *I hate and abhor lying,* which may be taken for all sin. Hypocrisy is lying; false doctrine is lying; breach of faith is lying. Lying, in commerce or conversation, is a sin which every good man hates. 2. He had a rooted affection to the word of God: *Thy law do I love.* And the reason why he loved the law of God was because of the truth of it.

JAMIESON, FAUSSET, BROWN

153-155. Though the remembering of God's law is not meritorious, yet it evinces a filial temper and provides the pious with promises to plead, while the wicked in neglecting His law, reject God and despise His promises (cf. Ps. 9:13; 43:1; 69:18). **154. Plead . . .**–Hengstenberg translates, "Fight my fight." (See Ps. 35:1; 43:1; Micah 7:9.)

156. (Cf. vs. 149.)

157. (Cf. vss. 86, 87, 95.)

158. (Cf. vs. 136.) **transgressors**–or, lit., "traitors," who are faithless to a righteous sovereign and side with His enemies (cf. Ps. 25:3, 8).

159. (Cf. vss. 121-126; 153-155.) **quicken . . .**–(vs. 88.) This prayer occurs here for the ninth time, showing a deep sense of frailty.

160. God has been ever faithful, and the principles of His government will ever continue worthy of confidence. **from the beginning**–i.e., "every word *from Genesis* (called so by the Jews from its first words, 'In the beginning') to the end of the Scriptures is true." Hengstenberg translates more literally, "The *sum* of thy words is truth." The sense is substantially the same. The whole body of revelation is truth. "Thy Word is nothing but truth" [Luther].

161-165. (Cf. vss. 46, 86.) **161. awe**–reverential, not slavish fear, which could not coexist with love (vs. 163; I John 4:8). Instead of fearing his persecutors, he fears God's Word alone (Luke 12:4, 5). The Jews inscribe in the first page of the great Bible (Gen. 28), "How dreadful is this place! This is none other but the house of God, and this is the gate of heaven!" **162.** (Cf. Matt. 13:44, 45.) Though persecuted by the mighty, the pious are not turned from revering God's authority to seek their favor, but rejoice in the possession of this "pearl of great price," as great victors in spoils. Hating falsehood and loving truth, often, every day, praising God for it, they find peace and freedom from temptation.

163. lying–i.e., as in vs. 29, unfaithfulness to the covenant of God with His people; apostasy.

ADAM CLARKE

154. *Plead my cause. Ribah ribi.* "Be my Advocate in my suit."

156. *Great are thy tender mercies.* They are *rabbim,* "multitudes." They extend to all the wretchednesses of all men.

158. *I beheld the transgressors, and was grieved.* Literally, "I was affected with anguish."

160. *Thy word is true from the beginning. Rosh,* "the head or beginning of Thy word, is true." Does he refer to the first word in the Book of Genesis, *bereshith,* "in the beginning"? The learned reader knows that *rash,* or *raash,* is the root in that word. Every word Thou hast spoken from the first in *Bereshith* (Genesis) to the end of the law and prophets, and all Thou wilt yet speak, must be true; and all such shall have, in due time, their fulfillment.

Letter *Schin*—Twenty-first Division

161. *Princes have persecuted me.* This may refer to what was done by prime ministers, and the rulers of provinces, to sour the king against the unfortunate Jews, in order still to detain them in bondage. In reference to David, the plotting against him in Saul's court, and the dangers he ran in consequence of the jealousies of the Philistine lords while he sojourned among them, are well-known.

163. *I . . . . abhor lying.* Perhaps they might have made the confessions which the Chaldeans required, and by mental reservation have kept an inward firm adherence to their creed; but this, in the sight of the God of truth, must have been *lying;* and at such a sacrifice they would not purchase their enlargement, even from their captivity.

MATTHEW HENRY

Verse 164

Many think that once a week will serve, or once or twice a day, but David would praise God seven times a day at least. We must praise God at every meal, in everything give thanks. We must praise God for his precepts, for his promises, even for our afflictions, if through grace we get good by them.

Verse 165

Good men, who are governed by a principle of love to the word of God are easy, and have a holy serenity; none enjoy themselves more than they do. They may be in great troubles without and yet enjoy great peace within, *sat lucis intus—abundance of internal light*. They will make the best of that which is, and not quarrel with anything that God does.

Verse 166

Here is the whole duty of man; to keep our eye upon God's favour as our end: "*Lord, I have hoped for thy salvation.*" To keep our eye upon God's word as our rule: *I have done thy commandments.* God has joined these two together, and let no man put them asunder. We cannot, upon good grounds, hope for God's salvation, unless we set ourselves to do his commandments, Rev. xxii. 14.

Verses 167–168

Our love to the word of God must be a superlative love, and it must be a victorious love, such as will subdue and mortify our lusts. Bodily exercise profits little in religion; we must make heart-work of it or we make nothing of it.

22. TAU

Verses 169–170

We must come to God as beggars come to our doors for an alms. He is concerned that his prayer might come before God, might come near before him, that is, that he might have grace and strength by faith and fervency to lift up his prayers, that no guilt might interpose to shut out his prayers and to separate between him and God, and that God would graciously receive his prayers and take notice of them.

Verse 171

A great favour which David expects from God, that he will teach him his *statutes*. This he had often prayed for in this psalm, and now that he is drawing towards the close of the psalm he speaks of it as taken for granted. *My lips shall utter praise when thou hast taught me*. Then he shall have cause to praise God. Then he shall know how to praise God, and have a heart to do it.

Verse 172

The more we see of God's commandments the more industrious we should be to bring others acquainted with them. We should always make the word of God the governor of our discourse, so as never to transgress it by sinful speaking or sinful silence; and we should often make it the subject-matter of our discourse, that it may feed many and *minister grace to the hearers*.

Verses 173–174

David prays that divine grace would work for him: *Let thy hand help me*. He looks up to God in hopes that the hand that had made him would help him; for, if the Lord do not help us, whence can any creature help us? Three things he pleads:—(1) That he had made religion his serious and deliberate choice: "*I have chosen thy precepts*." (2) That his heart was upon heaven: "*I have longed for thy salvation*." (3) That he took pleasure in doing his duty: "*Thy law is my delight*."

Verse 175

"Let me live that, in doing this, I may praise God here in this world of conflict and opposition." *Let my soul live*, that is, let me be sanctified and comforted, for sanctification and comfort are the life of the soul, *and* then *it shall praise thee*.

Verse 176

As unconverted sinners are like lost sheep (Luke xv. 4), so weak unsteady saints are like lost sheep, Matt. xviii. 12, 13. We are apt to wander like the sheep, and very unapt, when we have gone astray, to find the way again. "Lord, seek me, as I used to seek my sheep when they went astray"; for David had been himself a tender shepherd. "Lord, own me for one of thine; for, though I am a stray sheep, I have thy mark." Thus he concludes the psalm with a penitent sense of his own sin and a believing dependence on God's grace.

JAMIESON, FAUSSET, BROWN

nothing shall offend them—or, *cause them* to offend

166-168. As they keep God's law from motives of love for it, and are free from slavish fear, the are ready to subject their lives to His inspection.

168. all my ways are before thee—I wish to order my ways as before Thee, rather than in reference to man (Gen. 19:1; Ps. 73:23). All men's ways are under God's eye (Prov. 5:21); the godly alone realize the fact, and live accordingly.

169, 170. The prayer for *understanding* of the truth precedes that for *deliverance*. The fulfilment of the first is the basis of the fulfilment of the second (Ps. 90:11-17). On the terms "cry" and "supplication" (cf. Ps. 6:9; 17:1).

171, 172. shall utter—or, *pour* out praise (cf. Ps. 19:2); shall cause Thy praises to stream forth as from a bubbling, overflowing fountain.

My tongue shall speak of thy word—lit., "answer Thy Word," i.e., with praise, *respond to Thy word*. Every expression in which we praise God and His Word is a response, or acknowledgment, corresponding to the perfections of Him whom we praise.

173, 174. (Cf. vss. 77, 81, 92.) **I have chosen**—in preference to all other objects of delight. **175.** Save me that I may praise Thee. **thy judgments**—as in vss. 149, 156. **176.** Though a wanderer from God, the truly pious ever desires to be drawn back to Him; and, though for a time negligent of duty, he never forgets the commandments by which it is taught. **lost**—therefore utterly helpless as to recovering itself (Jer. 50:6; Luke 15:4). Not only the sinner before conversion, but the believer after conversion, is unable to recover himself; but the latter, after temporary wandering, knows to whom to look for restoration. These last two verses seem to sum up the petitions, confessions, and professions of the Psalm. The writer desires God's favor, that he may praise Him for His truth, confesses that he has erred, but, in the midst of all his wanderings and adversities, professes an abiding attachment to the revealed Word of God, the theme of such repeated eulogies, and the recognized source of such great and unnumbered blessings. Thus the Psalm, though more than usually didactic, is made the medium of both parts of devotion—prayer and praise.

ADAM CLARKE

164. *Seven times a day do I praise thee*. We have often seen that seven was a number expressing perfection, completion, among the Hebrews; and that it is often used to signify many, or an indefinite number, see Prov. xxiv. 16; Lev. xxvi. 28. And here it may mean no more than that his soul was filled with the spirit of gratitude and praise, and that he very frequently expressed his joyous and grateful feelings in this way.

Way, *derech*, "to proceed, go on, walk, tread." The way in which God goes in order to instruct and save man; the way in which man must tread in order to be safe, holy, and happy.

Letter *Tau*—Twenty-second Division

169. *Let my cry come near before thee*. Here the Psalmist's cry for deliverance is personified; made an intelligent being, and sent up to the throne of grace to negotiate in his behalf.

171. *My lips shall utter praise*. *Tehillah*, a song of praise.

175. *Let my soul live*. Let my "life" be preserved, and my soul quickened!

There is one extraordinary perfection in this psalm: Begin where you will, you seem to be at the commencement of the piece; end where you will, you seem to close with a complete sense. And yet it is not like the Book of Proverbs, a tissue of detached sentences. It is a whole composed of many parts, and all apparently as necessary to the perfection of the psalm as the different alphabetical letters under which it is arranged are to the formation of a complete alphabet.

MATTHEW HENRY

PSALM 120

A song of degrees.

Verses 1–4

David brought into distress by *lying lips and a deceitful tongue*. There were those that sought his ruin, and had almost effected it. They flattered him that they might without suspicion carry on their designs against him. They smiled in his face and kissed him, even when they were aiming to smite him under the fifth rib. David was herein a type of Christ, who was distressed by lying lips and deceitful tongues. Having no fence against false tongues, he appealed to him who has all men's hearts in his hand, and can, when he pleases, bridle their tongues. His prayer was, "*Deliver my soul, O Lord! from lying lips.*" He obtained a gracious answer to this prayer. Let liars consider what shall be given to them: *God shall shoot at them with an arrow; suddenly shall they be wounded.* They set God at a distance from them, but from afar his arrows can reach them. They will strike deep into the hardest heart. His wrath is compared to burning coals of juniper, which do not flame or crackle, like thorns under a pot, but have a vehement heat, and keep fire very long even when they seem to be gone out.

Verses 5–7

The psalmist here complains of the bad neighbourhood into which he was driven; and some apply the two foregoing verses to this: "What shall the deceitful tongue do to those that lie open to it? What shall a man get by living among such malicious deceitful men? Nothing but *sharp arrows* and *coals of juniper*." *Woe is me*, says David, *that I sojourn in Mesech and Kedar*. Not that David dwelt in the country of Mesech or Kedar; but he dwelt among rude and barbarous people, like the inhabitants of Mesech and Kedar. While he was in banishment, he looked upon himself as a sojourner, never at home. A good man cannot think himself at home while he is banished from God's ordinances. It is a great grief to all that love God to be without the means of grace and of communion with God. He *dwelt in the tents of Kedar*, where the shepherds were probably in an ill name for being litigious, like the herdsmen of Abraham and Lot. Those that David dwelt with were such as not only hated him, but hated peace. Perhaps Saul's court was the Mesech and Kedar in which David dwelt, and Saul was the man he meant that hated peace. *I peace* (so it is in the original); "I love peace and pursue peace; *I am for peace*, and have made it to appear that I am so."

PSALM 121

A song of degrees.

Verses 1–8

This psalm teaches us to stay ourselves upon God as a God all-sufficient for us. "*Shall I lift up my eyes to the hills?*"—so some read it. "Does my help come thence? Shall I depend upon the powers of the earth, upon the strength of princes, who hold up their heads towards heaven? No; I never expect help to come from them; my confidence is in God only." *We must lift up our eyes above the hills* (so some read it); we must look beyond instruments to God, who makes them that to us which they are. "*My help comes from the Lord;* in his own way and time." We must encourage our confidence in God with this that he *made heaven and earth*, and he who did that can do anything. God himself has undertaken to be our protector: *The Lord is thy keeper, v.* 5. The same that is the protector of the church in general is engaged for the preservation of every particular believer, the same wisdom, the same power, the same promises. *He that keepeth Israel* (*v.* 4) *is thy keeper, v.* 5. The shepherd of the flock is the shepherd of every sheep, and will take care that not one, even of the little ones, shall perish. He is a wakeful watchful keeper: "*He that keepeth Israel*, that keepeth thee, O Israelite! *shall neither slumber nor sleep*." He not only protects those whom he is the keeper of, but he refreshes them: He *is their shade*. He is always near to his people for their protection and refreshment, and never at a distance; he *is* their *keeper* and *shade on their right hand*; so that he is never far to seek. The right hand is the working hand; let them but turn themselves dexterously to their duty, and they shall find God ready to them, to assist them and give them success, Ps. xvi. 8. *The sun shall not smite thee* with his heat *by day nor the moon* with her cold and moisture *by night*. He will keep them *night and day* (Isa. xxvii. 3). It may be understood figuratively: "Thou shalt not be

JAMIESON, FAUSSET, BROWN

PSALM 120

Vss. 1-7. This is the first of fifteen Psalms (120-134) entitled "A Song of Degrees" (121st—lit., A song *for* the degrees), or *ascents*. It seems most probable they were designed for the use of the people when *going up* (cf. I Kings 12:27, 28) to Jerusalem on the festival occasions (Deut. 16:16), three times a year. David appears as the author of four, Solomon of one (127), and the other ten are anonymous, probably composed after the captivity. In this Psalm the writer acknowledges God's mercy, prays for relief from a malicious foe, whose punishment he anticipates, and then repeats his complaint.

2, 3. Slander and deceit charged on his foes implies his innocence. **tongue**—as in Psalm 52:2, 4. **4. Sharp arrows of the mighty**—destructive inflictions.

coals of juniper—which retain heat long. This verse may be read as a description of the wicked, but better as their punishment, in reply to the question of vs. 3.

5. A residence in these remote lands pictures his miserable condition.

6, 7. While those who surrounded him were maliciously hostile, he was disposed to peace. This Psalm may well begin such a series as this, as a contrast to the promised joys of God's worship.

PSALM 121

Vss. 1-8. God's guardian care of His people celebrated.

1. I will lift up mine eyes—expresses desire (cf. Ps. 25:1), mingled with expectation. The last clause, read as a question, is answered,

2, by avowing God to be the helper, of whose ability His creative power is a pledge (Ps. 115:15), to which,

3, 4, His sleepless vigilance is added. **to be moved**—(Cf. Ps. 38:16; 66:9).

5. upon thy right hand—a protector's place (Ps. 109:31; 110:5).

6-8. God keeps His people at all times and in all perils. **nor the moon by night**—poetically represents the dangers of the night, over which the moon presides (Gen. 1:16).

ADAM CLARKE

PSALM 120

This psalm, and all the rest that follow it, to the end of Psalm cxxxiv, fifteen in number, are called Psalms of Degrees; for thus the Hebrew title *hammaaloth* is generally translated, as coming from the root *alah*, "to ascend or mount upwards." Hence *maaloth*, "steps or stairs for ascending," 1 Kings x. 19-20; 2 Kings ix. 13. But as the word may be applied to elevation in general, hence some have thought that it may here signify the elevation of voice, "these psalms being sung with the highest elevations of voice and music." Others have thought the word expresses rather the matter of these psalms, as being of peculiar excellence.

1. *In my distress*. Through the causes afterwards mentioned. *I cried unto the Lord*. Made strong supplication for help. *And he heard me*. Answered my prayer by comforting my soul. It appears to be a prayer of the captives in Babylon for complete liberty, or perhaps he recites the prayer the Israelites had made previously to their restoration.

4. *Sharp arrows*. The Chaldee has, "The strong, sharp arrows are like lightning from above, with coals of juniper kindled in hell beneath."

5. *That I sojourn in Mesech*. The Chaldee has it, "Woe is me that I am a stranger with the Asiatics and that I dwell in the tents of the Arabs."

PSALM 121

This appears to be a prayer of the Jews in their captivity, who are solicitous for their restoration. It is in the form of a dialogue. Vv. 1-2. The person who worships God speaks the two first verses, "I will lift up mine eyes . . . my help cometh." V. 3. The ministering priest answers him, "He will not suffer thy foot to be moved: He that keepeth thee will not slumber." To which the worshipper answers that he knows that "he that keepeth Israel shall neither slumber nor sleep," v. 4; but he seems to express a doubt whether he shall be an object of the divine attention. Vv. 5, etc. The priest resumes; and, to the conclusion of the psalm, gives him the most positive assurances of God's favor and protection.

1. *Unto the hills*. Jerusalem was built upon a mountain; and Judea was a mountainous country.

4. *He that keepeth Israel*. The Divine Being represents himself as a Watchman, who takes care of the city and its inhabitants during the night watches, and who is never overtaken with slumbering or sleepiness.

MATTHEW HENRY

hurt either by the open assaults of thy enemies, which are as visible as the scorching beams of the sun, or by their secret treacherous attempts, which are like the insensible insinuations of the cold by night." "*The Lord shall preserve thee from all evil*, the evil of sin and the evil of trouble. Even that which kills shall not hurt." It is the spiritual life, especially, that God will take under his protection: *He shall preserve thy soul.* He will keep us in all our ways: "*He shall preserve thy going out and thy coming in.* Thou shalt be under his protection in all thy journeys and voyages, outward-bound or homeward-bound. He will keep thee in life and death, thy going out and going on while thou livest and thy coming in when thou diest, going out to thy labour in the morning of thy days and coming home to thy rest when the evening of old age calls thee in," civ. 23. He will continue his care over us *from this time forth and even for evermore.*

PSALM 122

A song of degrees of David.

Verses 1–5

We ought to worship God in our own houses, but that is not enough; we must *go into the house of the Lord*, to pay our homage to him there, and *not forsake the assembling of ourselves together.* Those that rejoice in God will rejoice in calls and opportunities to wait upon him. We should desire our Christian friends, when they have any good work in hand, to call for us and take us along with them. Those that came out of the country, when they found the journey tedious, comforted themselves with this, that they should be in Jerusalem shortly, and that would make amends for all the fatigues of their journey. It is the beautiful city, not only for situation, but for building. It is built uniform, *compact together*, the houses strengthening and supporting one another. It was a type of the gospel-church, which is compact together in holy love and Christian communion, so that it is all as one city. It is the holy city, *v.* 4, the place where all Israel meet one another: *Thither the tribes go up*, from all parts of the country, to their general rendezvous; and they come together to hear what God has to say to them. It is the royal city (*v.* 5): *There are set thrones of judgment. Therefore* the people had reason to be in love with Jerusalem, because justice was administered there by a man after God's own heart.

Verses 6–9

David calls upon others to wish well to Jerusalem, *v.* 6, 7. *Pray for the peace of Jerusalem*, for the welfare of it, for all good to it, particularly for the uniting of the inhabitants among themselves. The peace and welfare of the gospel church, particularly in our land, is to be earnestly desired and prayed for by every one of us. Words are put into our mouths (*v.* 7): *Peace be within thy walls*, for all the inhabitants in general, all within the walls, from the least to the greatest. Peace be in thy fortifications; let them never be attacked, or, if they be, let them never be taken, but be an effectual security to the city. Let *prosperity* be *in the palaces* of the great men that sit at the helm and have the direction of public affairs. He resolved that whatever others do he will say, *Peace be within thee.* He did not say, "Let others pray for the public peace, the priests and the prophets, whose business it is, and the people, that have nothing else to do, and I will fight for it and rule for it." No; " I will pray for it too." It is *for my brethren and companions' sakes*, that is, for the sake of all true-hearted Israelites, whom I look upon as my brethren (so he calls them, 1 Chron. xxviii. 2) and who have often been my companions in the worship of God, which has knit my heart to them. Our concern for the public welfare is right when it is the effect of a sincere love to God's institutions and his faithful worshippers.

PSALM 123

A song of degrees.

Verses 1–4

The title here given to God: *O thou that dwellest in the heavens.* Our Lord Jesus has taught us, in prayer, to have an eye to God as *our Father in heaven.* Heaven is a place of prospect and a place of power; he that dwells there beholds thence all the calamities of his people and thence can send to save them. In every prayer we lift up our soul, the eye of our soul, to God, especially in trouble, which was the case here. Our eyes must wait upon God as *the Lord*,

JAMIESON, FAUSSET, BROWN

thy going out . . .—all thy ways (Deut. 28:19; Ps. 104: 23).

evermore—includes a future state.

PSALM 122

Vss. 1-9. This Psalm might well express the sacred joy of the pilgrims on entering the holy city, where praise, as the religious as well as civil metropolis, is celebrated, and for whose prosperity, as representing the Church, prayer is offered.

1, 2. Our feet shall stand—lit., "are standing." **gates**—(Cf. Ps. 9:14; 87:2).

3-5. compact together—all parts united, as in David's time.

testimony—If "unto" is supplied, this may denote the ark (Exod. 25:10-21); otherwise the *act of going* is denoted, called a **testimony** in allusion to the requisition (Deut. 16:16), with which it was a compliance. **there are set thrones**—or, *do sit, thrones* used for the occupants, David's sons (II Sam. 8:18).

6, 7. Let peace, including prosperity, everywhere prevail.

8, 9. In the welfare of the city, as its civil, and especially the religious relations, was involved that of Israel. **now**—as in Psalm 115:2. Let me say—**house of . . . God**—in wider sense, the Church, whose welfare would be promoted by the good of Jerusalem.

PSALM 123

Vss. 1-4. An earnest and expecting prayer for divine aid in distress.

1. (Cf. Ps. 121:1.) **thou that dwellest**—lit., "sittest as enthroned" (cf. Ps. 2:4; 113:4, 5).

ADAM CLARKE

8. *Thy going out and thy coming in.* Night and day—in all your business and undertakings; and this through the whole course of your life: *for evermore.*

PSALM 122

In the preceding psalms we find the poor captives crying to God for deliverance; here they are returning thanks that they find they are permitted to return to their own land and to the ordinances of their God.

1. *I was glad when they said.* When Cyrus published an edict for their return, the very first object of their thanksgiving was the kindness of God in permitting them to return to His ordinances.

2. *Our feet shall stand.* For seventy years we have been exiled from our own land; our heart was in Jerusalem, but our feet were in Chaldea. Now God has turned our captivity, and our feet shall shortly stand within the gates of Jerusalem.

5. *There are set thrones of judgment.* There were the public courts, and thither the people went to obtain justice.

6. *Pray for the peace of Jerusalem. Shalom* signifies both peace and "prosperity."

7. *Peace be within thy walls.* This is the form of prayer that they are to use: "May prosperity ever reside within they walls, on all the people that dwell there; and tranquility within thy palaces or high places, among the rulers and governors of the people."

PSALM 123

This psalm is probably a complaint of the captives in Babylon relative to the contempt and cruel usage they received. The author is uncertain.

MATTHEW HENRY

and *our God, until that he have mercy upon us.* This is illustrated (*v.* 2) by a similitude: Our eyes are to God as *the eyes of a servant,* and *handmaid, to the hand of their master and mistress.* The eyes of a servant are to his master's directing hand, expecting that he will appoint him his work. Servants look to their master, or their mistress, for their portion of meat in due season, Prov. xxxi. 15. And to God must we look for daily bread, for grace sufficient. If the servant meet with opposition in his work, if he be questioned for what he does, who should bear him out and right him, but his master that set him on work? The people of God, when they are persecuted, may appeal to their Master, *We are thine; save us.* The people of God were now under his rebukes; and whither should they turn but to him that smote them? Isa. ix. 13. They submit themselves to and humble themselves under God's mighty hand. The servant expects his wages, his *well-done,* from his master. Hypocrites have their eye to the world's hand; thence *they have their reward* (Matt. vi. 2); but true Christians have their eye to God as their rewarder. The humble address which God's people present to him in their calamitous condition (*v.* 3, 4): *Have mercy upon us, O Lord! have mercy upon us.* They set forth their grievances: *We are exceedingly filled with contempt.* Reproach is the wound. Some translate the words which we render, *those that are at ease,* and *the proud,* so as to signify the persons that are scorned and contemned. "Our soul is troubled to see how those that are at peace, and the excellent ones, are scorned and despised." Taking the words as we read them, they were the epicures who lived at ease, carnal sensual people, Job xii. 5. They trampled on God's people, thinking they magnified themselves by vilifying them.

PSALM 124

A song of degrees of David.

Verses 1–5

The people of God were reduced to the very brink of ruin. The more desperate the disease appears to have been the more does the skill of the Physician appear in the cure. *Men rose up against us,* creatures of our own kind, and yet bent upon our ruin. No less would serve than the destruction of those they had conceived a displeasure against. "God was on our side; he took our part, espoused our cause, and appeared for us. That God was Jehovah; there the emphasis lies. If it had not been Jehovah himself, a God of infinite power and perfection, that had undertaken our deliverance, our enemies would have overpowered us." Happy the people, therefore, whose God is all-sufficient.

Verses 6–8

The psalmist further magnifies the great deliverance God had lately wrought for them. They were delivered like a lamb out of the very jaws of a beast of prey. They were rescued like *a bird,* a little bird (the word signifies a sparrow), *out of the snare of the fowler.* God's people are taken in the snare, and are as unable to help themselves out as any weak and silly bird is; and *then* God breaks the snare, and turns the counsel of the enemies into foolishness. *Our help is in the name of the Lord.* David had directed us (cxxi. 2) to depend upon God for help as to our personal concerns—here as to the concerns of the public. It is a comfort that Israel's God is the same that made the world, and therefore will have a church in the world, and can secure that church in times of the greatest danger and distress.

PSALM 125

A song of degrees.

Verses 1–3

Three very precious promises made to the people of God.

I. The character of God's people, to whom these promises belong. 1. Who are *righteous* (*v.* 3), righteous before God, righteous to God, and righteous

JAMIESON, FAUSSET, BROWN

2. Deference, submission, and trust, are all expressed by the figure. In the East, servants in attending on their masters are almost wholly directed by *signs,* which require the closest observance of the hands of the latter. The servants of God should look (1) to His directing hand, to appoint them their work; (2) to His supplying hand (Ps. 104:28), to give them their portion in due season; (3) to His protecting hand, to right them when wronged; (4) to His correcting hand (Isa. 9:13; I Pet. 5:6; cf. Gen. 16:6); (5) to His rewarding hand.

3. contempt—was that of the heathen, and, perhaps, Samaritans (Neh. 1:3; 2:19). **4. of those that are at ease**—self-complacently, disregarding God's law, and despising His people.

PSALM 124

Vss. 1-8. The writer, for the Church, praises God for past, and expresses trust for future, deliverance from foes.

1, 2. on our side—for us (Ps. 56:9). **now**—or, "oh! let Israel . . ." **rose . . . against . . .**—(Ps. 3:1; 56:11). **3. Then**—i.e., the time of our danger. **quick**—lit., "living" (Num. 16:32, 33), description of ferocity.

4. 5. (Cf. Ps. 18:4, 16.) The epithet **proud** added to **waters** denotes insolent enemies. **6, 7.** The figure is changed to that of a rapacious wild beast (Ps. 3:7), and then of a fowler (Ps. 91:3), and complete escape is denoted by breaking the net.

8. (Cf. Ps. 121:2.) **name**—in the usual sense (Ps. 5:11; 20:1.) He thus places over against the great danger the omnipotent God, and drowns, as it were in an anthem, the wickedness of the whole world and of hell, just as a great fire consumes a little drop of water [LUTHER].

PSALM 125

Vss. 1-5. God honors the confidence of His people, by protection and deliverance, and leaves hypocrites to the doom of the wicked.

1, 2. Mount Zion—as an emblem of permanence, and locality of Jerusalem as one of security, represent the firm and protected condition of God's

ADAM CLARKE

2. *As the eyes of servants.* We now wait for Thy commands, feeling the utmost readiness to obey them when made known to us.

4. *Those that are at ease.* The Babylonians, who, having subdued all the people of the neighboring nations, lived *at ease,* had none to contend with them, and now became luxurious, indolent, and insolent; they were contemptuous and proud.

PSALM 124

In our present Hebrew copies this psalm is attributed to David; but this inscription is wanting in three of Kennicott's and De Rossi's MSS., as also in the Septuagint, Syriac, Vulgate, Aethiopic, and Arabic; and in most of the ancient fathers, Greek and Latin, who found no other inscription in their copies of the text than "A Psalm of degrees." It was composed long after David's days, and appears to be a thanksgiving either for their deliverance from the Babylonish captivity or for a remarkable deliverance from some potent and insidious enemy after their return to Judea. Or, what appears to be more likely, it is a thanksgiving of the Jews for their escape from the general massacre intended by Haman, prime minister of Ahasuerus, king of Persia.

1. *If it had not been the Lord.* This might refer to the plot against the whole nation of the Jews by Haman, in the days of Mordecai and Esther, when by his treacherous schemes the Jews, wheresoever dispersed in the provinces of Babylon, were all to have been put to death in one day.

5. *Then the proud waters.* The proud Haman had nearly brought the flood of desolation over our lives.

7. *Our soul is escaped as a bird out of the snare.* This is a fine image, and at once shows the weakness of the Jews and the cunning of their adversaries. Haman had laid the snare completely for them; humanly speaking there was no prospect of their escape. But the Lord was on their side; and the providence that induced Ahasuerus to call for the book of the records of the kingdom to be read to him, as well indeed as the once very improbable advancement of Esther to the throne of Persia, was the means used by the Lord for the preservation of the whole Jewish people from extermination. God thus broke the snare, and the bird escaped, while the poacher was caught in his own trap, and executed. See the Book of Esther, which is probably the best comment on this psalm.

PSALM 125

This psalm is without a title; it belongs most probably to the times after the Captivity and has been applied, with apparent propriety, to the opposition which Sanballat the Horonite, Geshem the Arabian, and Tobiah the Ammonite gave to the Jews while employed in rebuilding

MATTHEW HENRY

to all men. 2. Who *trust in the Lord*, who depend upon his care and devote themselves to his honour. The closer our expectations are confined to God the higher our expectations may be raised from him.

II. The promises themselves.

1. That their hearts shall be established by faith: those minds shall be truly stayed that are stayed on God. Their faith shall be their fixation, Isa. vii. 9. *They shall be as Mount Zion*, which is firm as it is a mountain supported by providence, much more as a holy mountain supported by promise.

2. That, committing themselves to God, they shall be safe, under his protection, from all the insults of their enemies, as Jerusalem had a natural fastness and fortification in the *mountains* that *were round about* it, *v.* 2.

3. That their troubles shall last no longer than their strength will serve to bear them up under them, *v.* 3. It is promised that, though it may come upon their lot, it shall not rest there; it shall not continue so long as the enemies design, and as the people of God fear, but God will cut the work short in righteousness, so short that even *with the temptation he will make a way for them to escape*.

Verses 4–5

The prayer the psalmist puts up for the happiness of those that are sincere and constant (*v.* 4): *Do good, O Lord! unto those that are good.* He does not say, Do good, O Lord! to those that are perfect, that are sinless and spotless, but to those that are sincere and honest. God's promises should quicken our prayers. The prospect he has of the ruin of hypocrites and deserters; he does not pray for it but he predicts it. The last words, *Peace upon Israel*, may be taken as a prayer: "God preserve his Israel in peace, when his judgments are abroad reckoning with evil-doers." We read them as a promise: *Peace shall be upon Israel.*

JAMIESON, FAUSSET, BROWN

people (cf. Ps. 46:5), supported not only by Providence, but by covenant promise. Even the mountains shall depart, and the hills be removed, but God's kindness shall not depart, nor His covenant of peace be removed (Isa. 54:10). **They that trust**—(vs. 1) are "His people," (vs. 2). **3.** Though God may leave them for a time under the rod, or power (Ps. 2:9), and oppression of the wicked for a time, as a chastisement, He will not suffer them to be tempted so as to fall into sin (I Cor. 10:13). The wicked shall only prove a correcting rod to them, not a destroying sword; even this rod shall not *remain* ("rest") on them, lest they be tempted to despair and apostasy (Ps. 73:13, 14). God may even try His people to the uttermost: when nothing is before our eyes but pure despair, then He delivers us and gives life in death, and makes us blessed in the curse (II Cor. 1:8, 9) [LUTHER]. **the lot**—the possession, lit., "Canaan," spiritually, the heavenly inheritance of holiness and bliss which is appointed to the righteous. Sin's dominion shall not *permanently* come between the believer and his inheritance.

4. (Cf. Ps. 7:10; 84:11.) **5.** Those who turn aside (under temptation) permanently show that they are hypocrites, and their lot or portion shall be with the wicked (Ps. 28:3). **crooked ways**—(Cf. Deut. 9:16; Mal. 2:8, 9). **their**—is emphatic; the "crooked ways" proceed from *their own* hearts. The true Israel is here distinguished from the false. Scripture everywhere opposes the Jewish delusion that mere outward descent would save (Rom. 2:28, 29; 9:6, 7; Gal. 6:16). The byways of sin from the way of life.

ADAM CLARKE

the walls of Jerusalem and restoring the Temple.

3. *For the rod of the wicked shall not rest upon the lot of the righteous. Rod*, here, may be taken for persecution, or for rule; and then it may be thus interpreted: "The wicked shall not be permitted to persecute always, nor to have a permanent rule."

MATTHEW HENRY

PSALM 126

Verses 1–3

While the people of Israel were captives in Babylon their harps were hung upon the willow-trees, but now that their captivity is turned they resume their harps; Providence pipes to them, and they dance. The long want of mercies greatly sweetens their return. Cyrus, for reasons of state, proclaimed liberty to God's captives, and yet it was *the Lord's doing*, according to his word many years before. God sent them into captivity, not as dross is put into the fire to be consumed, but as gold to be refined. It came so suddenly that at first they were in confusion, not knowing what to make of it, nor what it was tending to: "We thought ourselves *like men that dream*; we thought it too good news to be true." The surprise of it put them into such an ecstasy and transport of joy that they could scarcely contain themselves within the bounds of decency in the expressions of it: *Our mouth was filled with laughter and our tongue with singing.* The notice which their neighbours took: *They said among the heathen*, Jehovah, the God of Israel, *has done great things* for that people, such as our gods cannot do for us. The heathen were but spectators, and spoke of it only as matter of news; they had no part nor lot in the matter; but the people of God spoke of it as sharers in it. Thus it is comfortable speaking of the redemption Christ has wrought out as wrought out for us. *Who loved me, and gave himself for me.*

Verses 4–6

These verses look forward to the mercies that were yet wanted. Those that had come out of captivity were still in distress, even in their own land (Neh. i. 3) and many yet remained in Babylon. "*Turn again our captivity.* Let those that have returned to their own land be eased of the burdens which they are yet groaning under. Let those that remain in Babylon have their hearts stirred up, as ours were, to take the benefit of the liberty granted." The beginnings of mercy are encouragements to us to pray for the completing of it. All the saints may comfort themselves with this confidence, that their tears will certainly end in a harvest of joy at last, *v.* 5, 6. Weeping must not hinder sowing; when we suffer ill we must be doing well. Yea, as the ground is by the rain prepared for the seed. There are tears which are themselves the seed that we must sow, tears of sorrow for sin, our own and others, tears of sympathy with the afflicted church, and tears of tenderness in prayer and under the word. Job, and Joseph, and David, and many others, had harvests of joy after sorrow. Those that sow in the tears of godly sorrow shall reap in the joy of a sealed pardon and a settled peace.

JAMIESON, FAUSSET, BROWN

PSALM 126

Vss. 1-6. To praise for God's favor to His people is added a prayer for its continued manifestation.

1-3. The joy of those returned from Babylon was ecstatic, and elicited the admiration even of the heathen, as illustrating God's great power and goodness. **turned again the captivity**—i.e., restored from it (Job 39:12; Ps. 14:7; Prov. 12:14). HENGSTENBERG translates: "When the Lord turned Himself to the turning of Zion" (see *Margin*), God returns to His people when they return to Him (Deut. 30:2, 3).

4. All did not return at once; hence the prayer for repeated favors. **as the streams in the south**—or, the torrents in the desert south of Judea, dependent on rain (Josh. 15:9), reappearing after dry seasons (cf. Job 6:15; Psalm 68:9). The point of comparison is joy at the reappearing of what has been so painfully missed. **5, 6.** As in husbandry the sower may cast his seed in a dry and parched soil with desponding fears, so those shall reap abundant fruit who toil in tears with the prayer of faith. (Cf. the history, Ezra 6:16, 22). **He that goeth forth**—lit., better, "He goes—he comes, he comes," etc. The repetition implies there is no end of weeping here, as there shall be no end of joy hereafter (Isa. 35:10). **precious seed**—rather, seed to be drawn from the seed-box for sowing; lit., "seed-draught." Cf. on this Psalm, Jer. 31:9, etc.

ADAM CLARKE

PSALM 126

This psalm is not of David, has no title in the Hebrew or any of the versions, and certainly belongs to the close of the Captivity.

1. *When the Lord turned again the captivity.* When Cyrus published his decree in favor of the Jews, giving them liberty to return to their own land, and rebuild their city and Temple. *We were like them that dream.* The news was so unexpected that we doubted for a time the truth of it. We believed it was too good news to be true, and thought ourselves in a dream or illusion.

4. *Turn again our captivity.* This is either a recital of the prayer they had used before their deliverance, or it is a prayer for those who still remained in the provinces beyond the Euphrates. The Jewish captives did not all return at once; they came back at different times, and under different leaders, Ezra, Nehemiah, Zerubbabel, etc.

6. *He that goeth forth and weepeth, bearing precious seed.* The metaphor seems to be this: A poor farmer has had a very bad harvest; a very scanty portion of grain and food has been gathered from the earth. The seedtime is now come, and is very unpromising. Out of the famine a little seed has been saved to be sown, in hopes of another crop; but the badness of the present season almost precludes the entertainment of hope. He carries his all, his *precious seed*, with him in his seed basket; and with a sorrowful heart commits it to the furrow, watering it in effect with his tears, and earnestly imploring the blessing of God upon it. The appointed weeks of harvest come, and the grain is very productive. He fills his arms, his carriages with the sheaves and shocks; and returns to his large, expecting family in triumph, praising God for the wonders He has wrought. So shall it be with this handful of returning Israelites. They also are to be sown—scattered all over the land; the blessing of God shall be upon them, and their faith and numbers shall be abundantly increased.

MATTHEW HENRY

PSALM 127

A song of degrees for Solomon.

Verses 1–5

Solomon would be apt to lean to his own understanding and forecast, and therefore his father teaches him to look higher, and to take God along with him in his undertakings. We must depend upon God's blessing and not our own contrivance, 1. For the raising of a family: *Except the Lord build the house*, by his providence and blessing, *those labour in vain*, though ever so ingenious, *that build it*. We may understand it of the material house: except the Lord bless the building it is to no purpose for men to build. If the model and design be laid in pride and vanity, or if the foundations be laid in oppression and injustice (Hab. ii. 11, 12), God certainly does not build there; nay, if God be not acknowledged, we have no reason to expect his blessing, and without his blessing all is nothing. Or it is to be understood of the making of a family considerable that was mean: men labour to do this by advantageous matches, offices, employments, purchases; but all in vain, unless God build up the family. If the guards of the city cannot secure it without God, much less can the good man of the house save his house from being broken up. 2. For the enriching of a family; this is a work of time and thought, but cannot be effected without the favour of Providence. "*It is vain for you to rise up early and sit up late*, and so to deny yourselves your bodily refreshments, in the eager pursuit of the wealth of the world." All this is to get money, and all in vain except God prosper them, for *riches are* not always *to men of understanding*, Eccles. ix. 11. Those that love God, and are beloved of him, have their minds easy and live very comfortably without this ado. God gives us sleep as he gives it to his beloved when with it he gives us grace to lie down in his fear (our souls returning to him and reposing in him as our rest), and when we awake to be still with him and to use the refreshment we have by sleep in his service. *He gives his beloved sleep*, that is, quietness and contentment of mind, a comfortable enjoyment of what is present and a comfortable expectation of what is to come. Children are *God's gift*, *v.* 3, and they are to us what he makes them, comforts or crosses. *Children are a heritage*, and a *reward*, and are so to be accounted, blessings and not burdens; for he that sends mouths will send meat if we trust in him. Children are a heritage for the Lord, as well as from him. The family that has a large stock of children is like a quiver full of arrows, of different sizes we may suppose, but all of use one time or other; children of different capacities and inclinations.

PSALM 128

A song of degrees.

Verse 1–6

Godliness has the promise of the life that now is and of that which is to come. In every nation he that fears God and works righteousness is accepted of him, and therefore is blessed whether he be high or low, rich or poor, in the world; if religion rule him, it will protect and enrich him. "*Happy shalt thou be;* if thou *fear God and walk in his ways. It shall be well with thee;* whatever befalls thee, good shall be brought out of it; it shall be well with thee while thou livest, better when thou diest, and best of all to eternity." *Thou shalt eat the labour of thy hands.* Here is a double promise, (1) That they shall have something to do (for an idle life is a miserable uncomfortable life) and shall have capacity to do it, and shall not be forced to be beholden to others for necessary food, and to live upon the labours of other people. (2) That they shall succeed in their employments, and they and theirs shall enjoy what they get. As the sleep, so the food, of a labouring man is sweet. They shall have comfort in their family-relations. As a wife and children are very much a man's care, so, if by the grace of God they are such as they should be, they are very much a man's delight. The *wife* shall be *as a vine by the sides of the house*, not only as a spreading vine which serves for an ornament, but as a fruitful vine, and with the fruit whereof both God and man are honoured, Judges ix. 13. The vine is a weak and tender plant, and needs to be supported and cherished, but it is a very valuable plant. The wife's place is the husband's house; there her business lies, and that is her castle. *Where is Sarah thy wife? Behold, in the tent;* where should she be else? Her place is *by the sides of the house*, not under-foot to be trampled on, nor yet upon the house-top to domineer. The *children* shall be *as olive plants*, likely in time to be olive-trees. It is pleasant to parents who have a

JAMIESON, FAUSSET, BROWN

PSALM 127

Vss. 1-5. The theme of this Psalm, *that human enterprises only succeed by the divine blessing*, was probably associated with the building of the temple by Solomon, its author. It may have been adopted in this view, as suited to this series especially, as appropriately expressing the sentiments of God's worshippers in relation to the erection of the second temple.

1, 2 suggest the view of the theme given.

so he giveth his beloved sleep—i.e., His providential care gives sleep which no efforts of ours can otherwise procure, and this is a reason for trust as to other things (cf. Matt. 6:26-32). **3-5.** Posterity is often represented as a blessing from God (Gen. 30:2, 18; I Samuel 1:19, 20).

Children are represented as the defenders (arrows) of their parents in war, and in litigation. **adversaries in the gate**—or place of public business (cf. Job. 5:4; Ps. 69:12).

PSALM 128

Vss. 1-6. The temporal blessings of true piety. The 8th chapter of Zechariah is a virtual commentary on this Psalm. Cf. vs. 3 with Zechariah 8:5; and vs. 2 with Leviticus 26:16; Deuteronomy 28:33; Zechariah 8:10; and vs. 6 with Zechariah 8:4.

1. (Cf. Ps. 1:1.)

2. For thou shalt eat—i.e., It is a blessing to live on the fruits of one's own industry.

3. by the sides—or, within (Ps. 48:2).

olive plants—are peculiarly luxuriant (Ps. 52:8).

ADAM CLARKE

PSALM 127

The Hebrew, Chaldee, and Vulgate attribute this psalm to Solomon. The Septuagint, Aethiopic, Arabic, and Anglo-Saxon have no title, but simply "A Psalm of Degrees." It was most likely composed for the building of the second Temple, under Nehemiah, and by some prophet of that time.

1. *Except the Lord build the house.* To build a house is taken in three different senses in the sacred writings. (1) To build the temple of the Lord, which was called *the house*, by way of eminence. (2) To build any ordinary house, or place of dwelling. (3) To have a numerous offspring. *Ben*, "a son," and *bath*, "a daughter," and *beith*, "a house," come from the same root *banah*, "to build"; because sons and daughters build up a household. Now it is true that unless the good hand of God be upon us we cannot prosperously build a place of worship for His name. Unless we have His blessing, a dwelling house cannot be comfortably erected. And if His blessing be not on our children, the house (the family) may be built up, but instead of its being the house of God, it will be the synagogue of Satan.

Except the Lord keep the city. When the returned Jews began to restore the walls of Jerusalem, and rebuild the city, Sanballat, Tobiah, and others formed plots to prevent it. Nehemiah, being informed of this, set up proper watches and guards. To this the Psalmist alludes; and in effect says, Though you should watch constantly, guard every place, and keep on your armor ready to repel every attack, yet remember the success of all depends upon the presence and blessing of God. While, therefore, you are not slothful in business, be fervent in spirit, serving the Lord; for there is no success in either spiritual or secular undertakings but in consequence of the benediction of the Almighty.

PSALM 128

This psalm has no title, either in the Hebrew or in any of the versions. It seems to be a continuation of the preceding psalm, or rather the second part of it. The man who is stated to have a numerous offspring, in the preceding psalm, is here represented as sitting at table with his large family. A person in the meanwhile coming in sees his happy state, speaks of his comforts, and predicts to him and his all possible future good. And why? Because the man and his family fear God, and walk in His ways.

2. *Thou shalt eat the labour of thine hands.* You shall not be exempted from *labour*. You shall work; but God will bless and prosper that work, and you and your family shall eat of it.

MATTHEW HENRY	JAMIESON, FAUSSET, BROWN	ADAM CLARKE

table spread, though but with ordinary fare, to see their children round about it, and not scattered, or the parents forced from them. Parents love to have their children at table, to keep up the pleasantness of the table-talk, to have them in health, craving food and not physic, to have them like *olive-plants*, straight and green, sucking in the sap of their good education. "Thy family shall be built up and continued, and thou shalt have the pleasure of seeing it." *Children's children*, if they be good children, *are the crown of old men* (Prov. xvii. 6), who are apt to be fond of their grandchildren. "Thou shalt *see the good of Jerusalem* as long as thou shalt live, though thou shouldest live long, and shalt not have thy private comforts allayed and embittered by public troubles."

5. In temporal blessings the pious do not forget the richer blessings of God's grace, which they shall ever enjoy. **6.** Long life crowns all other temporal favors. As Psalm 125:5, this Psalm closes with a prayer for peace, with prosperity for God's people.

5. *The Lord shall bless thee out of Zion.* In all your approaches to Him in His house by prayer, by sacrifice, and by offering, you shall have His especial blessing. You shall thrive everywhere, and in all things.

6. *And peace upon Israel.* This is the same conclusion as in Psalm cxxv, and should be translated, "Peace be upon Israel!"

PSALM 129

A song of degrees.

Verses 1–4

The church of God here speaks, as one single person, now old and grey-headed, but calling to remembrance the former days. 1. The church has been often greatly distressed by its enemies on earth. God's people have always had many enemies, and the state of the church, from its infancy, has frequently been an afflicted state. *The ploughers ploughed upon my back*, *v.* 3. The enemies of God's people have all along used them very barbarously. They tore them, as the husbandman tears the ground with his ploughshare. When God permitted them to plough thus he intended it for his people's good, that, their fallow ground being thus broken up, he might sow the seeds of his grace upon them, and reap a harvest of good fruit from them: howbeit, the enemies meant not so; *they made long their furrows*, never knew when to have done, aiming at the destruction of the church. Many by the *furrows* they made on the backs of God's people understand the stripes they gave them. *The cutters cut upon my back*, so they read it. The saints have often *had trials of cruel scourgings*, and so it was fulfilled in Christ, who *gave his back to the smiters*, Isa. l. 6. 2. The church has been always graciously delivered by her friend in heaven. The enemies' projects have been defeated. Christ has built his church upon a rock, and the gates of hell have not prevailed against it, nor ever shall. God *has cut asunder the cords of the wicked*, has cut their gears, their traces, and so spoiled their ploughing, has cut their scourges, and so spoiled their lashing, has cut the bands of captivity in which they held God's people.

Verses 5–8

The psalmist concludes his psalm as Deborah did her song, *So let all thy enemies perish, O Lord!* Judges v. 31. The confusion predicted is illustrated by a similitude; while God's people shall flourish as the loaded palm-tree, or the green and fruitful olive, their enemies shall *wither as the grass upon the house-top.* As they are enemies to Zion they are so certainly marked for ruin that they may be looked upon as the grass on the house-tops, which is little, and short, and sour, and good for nothing. It *withers before it grows up* to any maturity, having no root; and the higher its place is, which perhaps is its pride, the more it is exposed to the scorching heat of the sun, and consequently the sooner does it wither. Mowing the grass on the house-top would be a jest, and therefore those that have a reverence for the name of God will not prostitute to it the usual forms of salutation, which savoured of devotion.

PSALM 129

Vss. 1-8. The people of God, often delivered from enemies, are confident of His favor, by their overthrow in the future.

1, 2. may Israel now say—or, oh! let Israel say (Ps. 124:1). Israel's youth was the sojourn in Egypt (Jer. 2:2; Hos. 2:15). **prevailed**—lit., "been able," i.e., to accomplish their purpose against me (Ps. 13:4). **3, 4.** The *ploughing* is a figure of scourging, which most severe physical infliction aptly represents all kinds.

the cords—i.e., which fasten the plough to the ox; and *cutting* denotes God's arresting the persecution.

5, 6. The ill-rooted roof grass, which withers before it grows up and procures for those gathering it no harvest blessing (Ruth 2:4), sets forth the utter uselessness and the rejection of the wicked.

PSALM 129

This psalm was written after the Captivity. It has no title in any of the versions, nor in the Hebrew text, except the general one of "A Psalm of Degrees."

1. *Many a time have they afflicted me.* The Israelites had been generally in affliction or captivity from the earliest part of their history, here called their *youth.* So Hos. ii. 15: "She shall sing . . . as in the days of her youth . . when she came up out of the land of Egypt." See Jer. ii. 2 and Ezek. xvi. 4.

2. *Yet they have not prevailed.* They endeavored to annihilate us as a people, but God still preserves us as His own nation.

5. *Let them all be confounded.* They shall be confounded.

6. *As the grass upon the house tops.* As in the East the roofs of the houses were flat, seeds of various kinds falling upon them would naturally vegetate; and, because of the want of proper nourishment, would necessarily dry and wither away.

8. *Neither do they which go by say.* There is a reference here to the salutations which were given and returned by the reapers in the time of the harvest. We find that it was customary, when the master came to them into the field, to say unto the reapers, "The Lord be with you"; and for them to answer, "The Lord bless thee" (Ruth ii. 4).

PSALM 130

A song of degrees.

Verses 1–4

The best men may sometimes be in *the depths*, in great trouble and affliction. But, in the greatest depths, it is our privilege that we may cry unto God and be heard. To cry unto God is the likeliest way both to prevent our sinking lower and to recover us out of the *horrible pit and miry clay*, xl. 1, 2. *If thou, Lord, shouldst mark iniquities, O Lord! who shall stand?* His calling God *Lord* twice, in so few words, *Jah* and *Adonai*, is very emphatic, and intimates a very awful sense of God's glorious majesty and a dread of his wrath. We cannot justify ourselves before God, or plead Not guilty. If God deal with us in strict justice, we are undone. *It is of his mercy that we are not consumed* by his wrath. It is our unspeakable comfort, in all our approaches to God, that there is forgiveness with him, for that is what we need. He has promised to forgive the sins

PSALM 130

Vss. 1-8. The penitent sinner's hope is in God's mercy only.

1, 2. depths—for great distress (Ps. 40:2; 69:3).

3. shouldest mark—or, take strict account (Job 10:14; 14:16), implying a confession of the existence of sin. **who shall stand**—(Ps. 1:6). *Standing* is opposed to the guilty sinking down in fear and self-condemnation (Mal. 3:2; Rev. 6:15, 16). The question implies a negative, which is thus more strongly stated. **4.** Pardon produces filial fear and love. Judgment without the hope of pardon creates fear and dislike. The sense of forgiveness, so far from producing licentiousness, produces holiness (Jer. 33:9; Ezek. 16:62, 63; I Pet. 2:16). "There is for-

PSALM 130

This psalm has no author's name, either in the Hebrew or in any of the versions. It was most probably composed during the Captivity; and contains the complaint of the afflicted Jews, with their hopes of the remission of those sins which were the cause of their sufferings, and their restoration from captivity to their own land. This is one of those called "penitential psalms."

3. *If thou . . . shouldest mark iniquities.* If Thou shouldest set down every deviation in thought, word, and deed from Thy holy law; and if Thou shouldest call us into judgment for all our infidelities, of both heart and life, O Lord, who could stand? Who could stand such a trial, and who could stand acquitted in the judgment?

MATTHEW HENRY

of those that do repent. *There is a propitiation with thee*, so some read it. Jesus Christ is the great propitiation, and through him we hope to obtain forgiveness. But this encourages us to come into his service that we shall not be turned off for every misdemeanour; no, nor for any, if we truly repent.

Verses 5–8

"*I wait for the Lord;* from him I expect relief and comfort, believing it will come, longing till it does come, but patiently bearing the delay of it, and resolving to look for it from no other hand. *My soul doth wait. In his word do I hope.*" We must hope for that only which he has promised in his word, and not for the creatures of our own fancy and imagination. "Well-assured that the morning will come; so am I that God will return in mercy to me, for God's covenant is more firm than the ordinances of day and night, for they shall come to an end, but that is everlasting." Those that watch with sick people, and travellers that are abroad upon their journey, long before day wish to see the dawning of the day; but more earnestly does this good man long for the tokens of God's favour and the visits of his grace. *Mercy is with* him in all his works, in all his counsels. Jesus Christ *saves his people from their sins* (Matt. i. 21), *redeems them from all iniquity* (Tit. ii. 14), and *turns away ungodliness from Jacob*, Rom. xi. 26. Redemption from sin includes redemption from all other evils, and therefore is a plenteous redemption.

PSALM 131

A song of degrees of David.

Verses 1–3

This was David's rejoicing, that his heart could witness for him that he had walked humbly with his God. He aimed not at a high condition, but, if God had so ordered, could have been well content to spend all his days in the sheepfolds. His own brother, in a passion, charged him with pride (1 Sam. xvii. 28), but the charge was groundless and unjust. He had neither a scornful nor an aspiring look: "*My eyes are not lofty*, either to look with envy upon those that are above me or to look with disdain upon those that are below me." As he had not proudly aimed at the kingdom, so, since God had appointed him to it, he had been as humble as a little child. Our Saviour has taught us humility by this comparison (Matt. xviii. 3); we must *become as little children*. Our hearts are naturally as desirous of worldly things as the babe of the breast. But, by the grace of God, a soul that is sanctified, is weaned from those things. Thus does a gracious soul quiet itself under the loss of that which it loved, and lives comfortably, upon God and the covenant-grace.

PSALM 132

A song of degrees.

Verses 1–10

Solomon's address to God for his favour to him, and his acceptance of his building a house to God's name. What he had done was in pursuance of the pious vow which his father David had made to build a house for God. Solomon pleads not any merit of his own: "I am not worthy, for whom thou shouldst do this; but, *Lord, remember David*, with whom thou madest the covenant." He especially pleads the solemn vow that David had made as soon as ever he was settled in his government, and before he was well settled in a house of his own, that he would build a house for God. He had observed in the law frequent mention of the *place that God would choose to put his name there*, to which all the tribes should resort. When he came to the crown there was no such place; Shiloh was deserted, and no other place was pitched upon, for want of which the feasts of the Lord were not kept with due solemnity. "Well," says David, "I will find out such a place for the general rendezvous of all the tribes, a place of *habitation for the Mighty One of Jacob*, a place for the ark, where there shall be room both for the priests and people to attend upon it." The thing had been long talked of, and nothing done, till at last David when he went out one morning about public business, made a vow that before night he would determine the place either where the tent should be pitched for the reception of the ark, at the beginning of his reign, or rather where Solomon should build the temple, which was

JAMIESON, FAUSSET, BROWN

giveness with thee, not that thou mayest be presumed upon, but feared."

5, 6. wait for the Lord—in expectation (Ps. 27:14). **watch for . . .**—in earnestness and anxiety.

7, 8. Let Israel . . .—i.e., All are invited to seek and share divine forgiveness. **from all his iniquities**—or, punishments of them (Ps. 40, 12, etc.).

PSALM 131

Vss. 1-3. This Psalm, while expressive of David's pious feelings on assuming the royal office, teaches the humble, submissive temper of a true child of God.

1. eyes lofty—a sign of pride (Ps. 18:27). **exercise myself**—lit., "walk in," of "meddle with." **2. Surely . . .**—The form is that of an oath or strongest assertion. Submission is denoted by the figure of a weaned child. As the child weaned by his mother from the breast, so I still the motions of pride in me (Matt. 18:3, 4; Isa. 11:8; 28:9). Hebrew children were often not weaned till three years old. **soul**—may be taken for desire, which gives a more definite sense, though one included in the idea conveyed by the usual meaning, *myself*.

PSALM 132

Vss. 1-18. The writer, perhaps Solomon (cf. vss. 8, 9), after relating David's pious zeal for God's service, pleads for the fulfilment of the promise (II Sam. 7:16), which, providing for a perpetuation of David's kingdom, involved that of God's right worship and the establishment of the greater and spiritual kingdom of David's greater Son. Of Him and His kingdom both the temple and its worship, and the kings and kingdom of Judah, were types. The congruity of such a topic with the tenor of this series of Psalms is obvious.

1-5. This vow is not elsewhere recorded. It expresses, in strong language, David's intense desire to see the establishment of God's worship as well as of His kingdom. **remember David**—lit., "remember for David," i.e., all his troubles and anxieties on the matter.

habitation—lit., "dwellings," generally used to denote the sanctuary.

ADAM CLARKE

This is a most solemn saying; and if we had not the doctrine that is in the next verse, who could be saved?

4. *But there is forgiveness with thee.* Thou canst forgive; mercy belongs to Thee, as well as judgment.

5. *I wait for the Lord.* The word *kavah*, which we translate "to wait," properly signifies the "extension of a cord from one point to another." This is a fine metaphor: God is one point, the human heart is the other; and the extended cord between both is the earnest, believing desire of the soul. This desire, strongly extended from the heart to God, is the active, energetic waiting which God requires, and which will be successful.

6. *More than they that watch for the morning.* I believe the original should be read differently from what it is here. The Chaldee has, "More than they who observe the morning watches, that they may offer the morning oblation." This gives a good sense and is, perhaps, the true meaning.

7. *Let Israel hope in the Lord.* What *reason* is there for this *hope?* A twofold reason: (1) *With the Lord there is mercy. Hachesed*, "that mercy," the fund, the essence of mercy. (2) *And with him is plenteous redemption.* "That abundant redemption."

8. *He shall redeem Israel.* "He will make a ransom for Israel."

PSALM 131

Some think that David composed this psalm as a vindication of himself, when accused by Saul's courtiers that he affected the crown, and was laying schemes and plots to possess himself of it. Others think the psalm was made during the Captivity, and that it contains a fair account of the manner in which the captives behaved themselves under the domination of their oppressors.

1. *Lord, my heart is not haughty.* The principle of pride has no place in my heart; and consequently the high, lofty, and supercilious look does not appear in my eyes. I neither look up, with desire to obtain, to the state of others, nor look down with contempt to the meanness or poverty of those below me. And the whole of my conduct proves this; for "I have not exercised myself," walked, "in high matters," nor associated myself with the higher ranks of the community, nor *in great matters*, "wonderful" or sublime things; *too high for me*, "alien from me," and that do not belong to a person in my sphere and situation in life.

PSALM 132

Some attribute this psalm to David, but without sufficient ground; others, to Solomon, with more likelihood; and others, to some inspired author at the conclusion of the Captivity, which is, perhaps, the most probable. It refers to the building of the second Temple, and placing the ark of the covenant in it.

2. *How he sware unto the Lord.* It is only in this place that we are informed of David's vow to the Lord relative to the building of the Temple but we find he had fully purposed the thing.

3. *Surely I will not come.* This must refer to the situation of the Temple; or, as we would express it, he would not pass another day till he had found out the ground on which to build the Temple, and projected the plan, and devised ways and means to execute it.

5. *The mighty God of Jacob.* "The Mighty One of Jacob." We have this epithet of God for the first time in Gen. xlix. 24.

MATTHEW HENRY

not fixed till the latter end of his reign. *Then David said, This is the house of the Lord.* It is good in the morning to cut out work for the day, binding ourselves that we will do it before we sleep, only with submission to Providence. The people of Israel, *v.* 6, 7, were inquisitive after the ark; for they lamented its obscurity, 1 Sam. vii. 2. They *heard of it at Ephratah* (that is, at Shiloh, in the tribe of Ephraim); there they were told it had been, but it was gone. They *found it*, at last, *in the fields of the wood*, that is, in Kirjath-jearim, which signifies *the city of woods.* Thence all Israel fetched it, with great solemnity, in the beginning of David's reign (1 Chron. xiii. 6), so that in building this house for the ark Solomon had gratified all Israel. They were resolved to attend it: "Let us but have a convenient place, and *we will go into his tabernacle*, to pay our homage there; *we will worship at his footstool* as subjects and suppliants, which we neglected to do, for want of such a place, *in the days of Saul*," 1 Chron. xiii. 3. He prays, *v.* 8–10. God would vouchsafe, not only to take possession of, but to take up his residence in, this temple which he had built. *Let thy priests be clothed with righteousness.* "They are *thy priests*, and will therefore discredit their relation to thee if they *be not clothed with righteousness.*" Let the people of God have the comfort of the due administration of holy ordinances among them. *"Turn not away the face of thy anointed*, that is, deny me not the things I have asked of thee, send me not away ashamed."

Verses 11–18

These promises relate to the establishment both in church and state, both to the throne of the house of David and to the testimony of Israel fixed on Mount Zion. The promises concerning Zion's hill are as applicable to the gospel-church as these concerning David's seed are to Christ, and therefore both pleadable by us and very comfortable to us.

I. The choice God made of David's house and Zion hill. Both were of divine appointment.

1. God chose David's family for the royal family and confirmed his choice by an oath, *v.* 11, 12. A long succession of kings should descend from his loins: *Of the fruit of thy body will I set upon thy throne*, which was fulfilled in Solomon; David himself lived to see it with great satisfaction, 1 Kings i. 48. The crown was also entailed conditionally upon his heirs for ever: *If thy children*, in following ages, *will keep my covenant and my testimony that I shall teach them.* The issue of this was that they did not keep God's covenant, and so the entail was at length cut off, and *the sceptre departed from Judah* by degrees. An everlasting successor, a king, should descend from his loins of *the increase of whose government and peace there shall be no end.* St. Peter applies this to Christ, nay, he tells us that David himself so understood it (Acts ii. 30).

2. God chose Zion hill for the holy hill, and confirmed his choice by the delight he took in it, *v.* 13, 14. God said, *Here will I dwell*, and therefore David said, *Here will I dwell*, for here he adhered to his principle, *It is good for me to be near to God.* Zion must be here looked upon as a type of the gospel-church, which is called *Mount Zion* (Heb. xii. 22), and in it what is here said of Zion has its full accomplishment. Zion was long since ploughed as a field, but the church of Christ *is the house of the living God* (1 Tim. iii. 15), and it is his *rest for ever*, and shall be blessed with his presence always, even to the end of the world.

II. The blessings God has in store for David's house and Zion hill. Whom God chooses he will bless.

1. The blessings of the life that now is; for godliness has the promise of them, *v.* 15. The earth shall yield her increase; where religion is set up there shall be provision. God's people have a special blessing upon common enjoyments, and that blessing puts a peculiar sweetness into them. The promise goes further: *I will satisfy her poor with bread.* They shall have provision enough. If there be scarcity, the poor are the first that feel it, so that it is a sure sign of plenty if they have sufficient. And this may be understood spiritually of the provision that is made for the soul in the word and ordinances; God will abundantly bless that for the nourishment of the new man, and satisfy the poor in spirit with the bread of life. The blessings of the life that is to come, things pertaining to godliness (*v.* 16), which is an answer to the prayer, *v.* 9. It was desired that the priests might be *clothed with righteousness*; it is here promised that God will *clothe them with salvation.* They shall both *save themselves and those that hear them*, and *add those to the church that shall be saved.*

2. God, having chosen David's family, here promises to bless that also with suitable blessings. *There*, in Zion, *will I make the horn of David to bud*, *v.* 17. The royal dignity shall increase more and

JAMIESON, FAUSSET, BROWN

6. These may be the "words of David" and his pious friends, who, at Ephratah, or Bethlehem (Gen. 48:7), where he once lived, may have heard of the ark, which he found for the first time **in the fields of the wood**–or, *Jair*, or *Kirjath-jearim* (City of woods) (I Sam. 7:1; II Sam. 6:3, 4), whence it was brought to Zion.

7. The purpose of engaging in God's worship is avowed.

8, 9. The solemn entry of the ark, symbolical of God's presence and power, with the attending priests, into the sanctuary, is proclaimed in the words used by Solomon (II Chron. 6:41). **10-12. For thy servant David's sake** [i.e., On account of the promise made to him] **turn . . . anointed**–Repulse not him who, as David's descendant, pleads the promise to perpetuate his royal line.

After reciting the promise, substantially from II Sam. 7:12-16 (cf. Acts 2:30, etc.), an additional plea,

13, is made on the ground of God's choice of Zion (here used for Jerusalem) as His dwelling, inasmuch as the prosperity of the kingdom was connected with that of the Church (Ps. 122:8, 9). **14-18.** That choice is expressed in God's words, ***I will sit*** or ***dwell,*** or sit enthroned

The joy of the people springs from the blessings of His grace, conferred through the medium of the priesthood.

ADAM CLARKE

6. *Lo, we have heard of it at Ephratah.* This may be considered as a continuation of David's vow; as if he had said: As I had determined to build a temple for the ark, and heard that it was at Ephratah, I went and found it in the "fields of Jaar"—not the wood, but Kirjath Jaar or Jearim, where the ark was then lodged—and having found it, he entered the Tabernacle, v. 7; and then, adoring that God whose presence was in it, he invited Him to arise and come to the place which he had prepared for Him.

8. *Arise, O Lord, into thy rest; thou, and the ark of thy strength.* Using the same expressions which Solomon used when he dedicated the Temple, 2 Chron. vi. 41-42. If we take vv. 6-8, not as the continuation of David's vow, but as the words of the captives in Babylon, the explanation will be plain and easy: "We have heard, O Lord, from our fathers, that Thy tabernacle was formerly a long time at Shiloh, in the tribe of Ephraim. And our history informs us that it has been also at Kirjath-jearim, *the fields of the wood;* and afterwards it was brought to Jerusalem, and there established; but Jerusalem is now ruined, the Temple destroyed, and Thy people in captivity. Arise, O Lord, and re-establish Thy dwelling place in Thy holy city!"

11. *The Lord hath sworn.* As David sware to the Lord, so the Lord swears to David, that He will establish his throne, and place his posterity on it; and that He had respect to David's Antitype, we learn from St. Peter, Acts ii. 30.

13. *The Lord hath chosen Zion.* Therefore neither Shiloh nor Kirjath-jearim is the place of his rest.

14. *This is my rest for ever.* Here the Christian Church is most indubitably meant. This is God's place forever.

CHARLES H. SPURGEON:

"This is my rest forever" (v. 14). Oh, glorious words! It is God himself who here speaks. Think of rest for God! A Sabbath for the Eternal and a place of abiding for the Infinite. He calls Zion *my rest.* Here his love remains and displays itself with delight. "He shall rest in his love." And this *forever.* He will not seek another place of repose, nor grow weary of his saints. In Christ the heart of Deity is filled with content, and for his sake he is satisfied with his people, and will be so world without end. These august words declare a distinctive choice—*this* and no other; a certain choice—this which is well known to me; a present choice—*this* which is here at this moment. God had made his election of old, he has not changed it, and he never will repent of it: his church was his rest and *is* his rest still. As he will not turn from his oath, so he will never turn from his choice. Oh, that we may enter into *his* rest, may be part and parcel of his church, and yield by our loving faith a delight to the mind of him who taketh pleasure in them that fear him, in them that hope in his mercy.

—The Treasury of David

MATTHEW HENRY

more, and constant additions be made to the lustre of it. Christ is the *horn of salvation* which God has raised up, and made to bud, *in the house of his servant David. I have ordained a lamp for my anointed.* Thou wilt *light my candle,* xviii. 28. That lamp is likely to burn brightly which God ordains. A lamp is a successor, for, when a lamp is almost out, another may be lighted by it; it is a succession, for by this means David shall not want a man to stand before God. Christ is the lamp and the light of the world. "*His enemies,* who have formed designs against him, *will I clothe with shame,* when they shall see their designs baffled." *Upon himself shall his crown flourish,* that is, his government shall be more and more his honour. The crowns of earthly princes *endure not to all generations* (Prov. xxvii. 24), but Christ's crown shall endure to all eternity and the crowns reserved for his faithful subjects are such as *fade not away.*

PSALM 133

A song of degrees of David.

Verses 1–3

Sometimes it is chosen, as the best expedient for preserving peace, that brethren should live asunder and at a distance from each other; that indeed may prevent enmity and strife (Gen. xiii. 9), but the goodness and pleasantness are *for brethren to dwell together* and so *to dwell in unity, to dwell even as one* (so some read it), as having one heart, one soul, one interest.

The tribes of Israel had long had separate interests during the government of the Judges; but now they were united under one common head, now the ark was fixed, and with it the place of their rendezvous for public worship and the centre of their unity. Now let them live in love. It is a rare thing, and therefore admirable. It is fragrant as the holy anointing oil, which was strongly perfumed, and diffused its odours, when it was poured upon the head of Aaron, or his successor the high priest, so plentifully that it ran down the face, even to the collar or binding of the garment, *v.* 2. So must our brotherly love be. with a pure heart, devoted to God. Holy love, is in the sight of God, of great price. Christ's love to mankind was part of that *oil of gladness* with which he was *anointed above his fellows.* Aaron and his sons were not admitted to minister unto the Lord till they were anointed with this ointment, nor are our services acceptable to God without this holy love; if we have it not we are nothing, 1 Cor. xiii. 1, 2. It is profitable as well as pleasing; it is *as the dew;* it brings abundance of blessings along with it, as numerous as the drops of dew. It cools the scorching heat of men's passions, as the evening dews cool the air and refresh the earth. It moistens the heart, and makes it tender and fit to receive the good seed of the word. It is *as the dew of Hermon,* a common hill (for brotherly love is the beauty and benefit of civil societies), *and as the dew that descended upon the mountains of Zion,* a holy hill, for it contributes greatly to the fruitfulness of sacred societies. Loving people are blessed people. They are blessed of God, and therefore blessed indeed. The blessing which God commands on those that dwell in love is *life for evermore;* that is the blessing of blessings. Those that dwell in love not only dwell in God, but do already dwell in heaven.

PSALM 134

A song of degrees.

Verses 1–3

I. Our blessing God, that is, speaking well of him, which here we are taught to do, *v.* 1, 2. 1. It is a call to the *Levites* to do it. Some of them did *by night stand in the house of the Lord,* to guard the holy things of the temple, that they might not be profaned, and the rich things of the temple, that they might not be plundered. While the ark was in curtains there was the more need of guards upon it. They attended likewise to see that neither the fire on the altar nor the lamps in the candlestick went out. Probably it was usual for some devout and pious Israelites to sit up with them; we read of one that *departed not from the temple night or day,* Luke ii. 37. Now these are here called upon to *bless the Lord.* 2. It is a call to us to do it, who, as Christians, are made priests to our God, and Levites, Isa. lxvi. 21. We are the *servants of the Lord;* we have a place and a name in his house, in his sanctuary; we stand before him to minister to him. Let us therefore *bless the Lord.* Let us *lift up* our *hands* in prayer, in praise, in vows; let us do our work with diligence and cheerfulness, and an elevation of mind.

JAMIESON, FAUSSET, BROWN

make the horn . . . to bud—enlarge his power. **a lamp**—the figure of prosperity (Ps. 18:10, 28; 89:17).

With the confounding of his enemies is united his prosperity and the unceasing splendor of his crown.

PSALM 133

Vss. 1-3. The blessings of fraternal unity.

1, 2. As the fragrant oil is refreshing, so this affords delight. The holy anointing oil for the high priest was olive oil mixed with four of the best spices (Exod. 30:22, 25, 30). Its rich profusion typified the abundance of the Spirit's graces.

As the copious dew, such as fell on Hermon, falls in fertilizing power on the mountains of Zion, so this unity is fruitful in good works.

3. there—i.e., in Zion, the Church; the material Zion, blessed with enriching dews, suggests this allusion the source of the influence enjoyed by the spiritual Zion. **commanded the blessing**—(Cf. Ps. 68:28).

PSALM 134

Vss. 1-3. **1, 2.** The pilgrim bands arriving at the sanctuary call on the priests, who **stand in the house of the Lord** at the time of the evening sacrifice, to unite in praising God in their name and that of the people, using appropriate gestures, to which the priests reply, pronouncing the Mosaic blessing which they alone could pronounce. A fit epilogue to the whole pilgrim-book, Psalms 120-134. **1. by night**—the *evening* service **(Ps. 141:2)**, as opposed to *morning* (Ps. 92:2). **2. Lift up your hands**—(Cf. Ps. 28:2).

ADAM CLARKE

18. *His enemies will I clothe with shame.* Every opponent of the Christian cause shall be confounded. *But upon himself shall his crown flourish.* There shall be no end of the government of Christ's kingdom. From v. 11 to the end, the spiritual David and his posterity are the subjects of which the psalm treats.

PSALM 133

There are different opinions concerning this psalm; the most probable is that it represents the priests and Levites returned from captivity, and united in the service of God in the sanctuary. This, the preceding, and the following appear to make one subject. In the one hundred and thirty-second, the Lord is entreated to enter His temple, and pour out His benediction; in the one hundred and thirty-third, the beautiful order and harmony of the Temple service is pointed out; and in the one hundred and thirty-fourth, all are exhorted to diligence and watchfulness in the performance of their duty.

1. *Behold, how good and how pleasant!* Unity is, according to this scripture, a *good* thing and a *pleasant;* and especially among *brethren*—members of the same family, of the same Christian community, and of the same nation.

2. *Like the precious ointment.* The composition of this holy anointing oil may be seen, Exod. xxx. 23; sweet cinnamon, sweet calamus, *cassia lignea,* and olive oil. The odor of this must have been very agreeable, and serves here as a metaphor to point out the exquisite excellence of brotherly love. *Ran down upon the beard.* The oil was poured upon the head of Aaron so profusely as to run down upon his garments. It is customary in the East to pour out the oil on the head so profusely as to reach every limb.

3. *As the dew of Hermon, and as the dew that descended upon the mountains of Zion.* This was not Mount Zion in Jerusalem, but "Sion," which is a part of Hermon. See Deut. iv. 48: "Mount Sion, which is Hermon." On this mountain the dew is very copious.

PSALM 134

This is the last of the fifteen psalms called "psalms of degrees." It is intimately connected with the preceding two psalms, and is an exhortation to the priests and Levites who kept nightly watch in the Temple to be assiduous in praising the Lord. It seems to consist of two parts: First, An exhortation, probably from the high priest, to those priests and Levites who kept watch in the Temple by night, to spend their time profitably, and duly celebrate the praises of God, vv. 1-2. The second part, which is contained in the third verse, is the prayer of the priests and Levites for the high priest, who seems now to be going to his rest.

1. *Behold, bless ye the Lord.* I believe *hinneh* should be taken here in the sense of "take heed." *Which by night stand.* Who minister during the night.

2. *Lift up your hands in the sanctuary. Kodesh,* "in holiness." The expression seems very similar to that of St. Paul, 1 Tim. ii. 8: "Lifting up holy hands, without wrath and doubting."

MATTHEW HENRY

II. God's blessing us, and that is doing well for us, which we are here taught to desire, *v.* 3. We need desire no more to make us happy than to be blessed of the Lord, for those whom he blesses are blessed indeed.

PSALM 135

Verses 1–4

1. The duty we are called to—to *praise the Lord*, to *praise his name*; *praise him*, and again *praise him*. We must not only thank him for what he has done for us, but praise him for what he is in himself and has done for others. 2. The persons that are called upon to do this—the *servants of the Lord*, the priests and Levites *that stand in his house*, and all the devout and pious Israelites that stand *in the courts of his house* to worship there, *v.* 2. Who should praise him if they do not? 3. The reasons why we should praise God. He is good to all. His goodness is his glory, and we must make mention of it to his glory. The work is its own wages.

Verses 5–14

The psalmist had suggested to us the goodness of God, as the proper nature of our cheerful praises; here he suggests to us the greatness of God as the proper matter of our praises.

I. He asserts the doctrine of God's greatness (*v.* 5): *The Lord is great*, great indeed, who knows no limits of time or place.

II. He proves him to be a great God by the greatness of his power, *v.* 6. He has an absolute power, and may do what he will. This absolute almighty power is of universal extent; he does what he will *in heaven, in earth, in the seas*, and in *all the deep places* that are in the bottom of the sea or the bowels of the earth.

III. He gives instances of his great power,

1. In the kingdom of nature, *v.* 7. All the powers of nature prove the greatness of the God of nature, from whom they are derived and on whom they depend. The chain of natural causes was not only framed by him at first, but is preserved by him. It is by his power that exhalations are drawn up from the terraqueous globe. The heat of the sun raises them, but it has that power from God. It is he who, out of those vapours so raised, forms the rain. They are returned with advantage in fruitful showers. He *makes lightnings for the rain*; by them he shakes the clouds, that they may water the earth. Here are fire and water thoroughly reconciled by divine omnipotence. Winds blow where they list, from what point of the compass they will, and we are so far from directing them that we cannot tell whence they come nor whither they go, but God *brings them out of his treasuries* with exactness and design.

2. In the kingdoms of men. Observe God's sovereign dominion and irresistible power, (1) In bringing Israel out of Egypt, humbling Pharaoh by many plagues, and so forcing him to let them go. (2) In destroying the kingdoms of Canaan before them, *v.* 10. No power of hell or earth can prevent the accomplishment of the promise of God when the time, the set time, for it has come. (3) In settling them in the land of promise. He that gives kingdoms to whomsoever he pleases gave Canaan to be a heritage to Israel his people.

IV. He triumphs in the perpetuity of God's glory and grace. *Thy name, O God! endures for ever.* This seems to refer to Exod. iii. 15, where, when God had called himself *the God of Abraham, Isaac, and Jacob*, he adds, *This is my name for ever and this is my memorial unto all generations.* He will be kind to his people. He will plead their cause against others that contend with them. *He will judge his people*, that is, he will judge for them, and will not suffer them to be run down.

Verses 15–21

These verses design:—

I. To arm the people of God against idolatry and all false worships, by showing what sort of gods they were that the heathen worshipped, as we had it before, cxv. 4, &c. They were gods of their own making; being so, they could have no power but what their makers gave them. They had the shape of animals, but could not perform the least act, no, not of the *animal* life. Their worshippers were therefore as stupid and senseless as they were, both those that made them to be worshipped and those that trusted in them when they were made, *v.* 18.

JAMIESON, FAUSSET, BROWN

3. After the manner directed (Num. 6:23). **out of Zion**—the Church, as His residence, and thus seat of blessings. Thus close the songs of degrees.

PSALM 135

Vss. 1-21. A Psalm of praise, in which God's relations to His Church, His power in the natural world, and in delivering His people, are contrasted with the vanity of idols and idol worship.

1-3. In the general call for praise, the priests, **that stand in the house of the Lord,** are specially mentioned.

4-7. God's choice of Israel is the first reason assigned for rendering praise; the next, His manifested greatness in creation and providence. **heaven, and ... seas, and all ... ends of the earth**—denote universality.

8, 9. The last plague is cited to illustrate His "tokens and wonders."

10-12. The conquest of Canaan was by God's power, not that of the people. **heritage**—or, possession.

13. name ... memorial—Each denote that by which God is made known. **14. will judge**—do justice (Ps. 72:2). **repent himself**—change His dealings (Ps. 90:13).

15-18. (Cf. Ps. 115:4-8.) **are like unto them**—or, shall be like, etc. Idolaters become spiritually stupid and perish with their idols (Isa. 1:31).

ADAM CLARKE

3. *Bless thee out of Zion.* As if they had said, "We will attend to your orders; go in peace, and may God shower down His blessings upon you!" The blessing pronounced by the priests was the following: "The Lord bless thee, and keep thee: the Lord make his face shine upon thee, and be gracious unto thee: the Lord lift up his countenance upon thee, and give thee peace" (Num. vi. 24-26).

PSALM 135

This psalm is intimately connected with the preceding. It is an exhortation addressed to the priests and Levites, and to all Israel, to publish the praises of the Lord. The conclusion of this psalm is nearly the same with Psalm cxv; and what is said about idols, and the effects of the power of God, seems to be taken from it and the tenth chapter of Jeremiah; and from these and other circumstances it appears the psalm was written after the Captivity; and might, as Calmet conjectures, have been used at the dedication of the second Temple.

1. *Praise ye the Lord.* This may be considered as the title, for it has none other. *Praise ye the name of the Lord.* Perhaps the original, *halelu eth shem Yehovah*, should be translated, "Praise ye the name Jehovah"; that is, Praise God in His infinite essence of being, holiness, goodness, and truth.

2. *Ye that stand.* Priests and Levites. For which he gives several reasons.

3. *The Lord is good.* Here is the first reason why He should be praised; and a second is subjoined—*for it is pleasant.* It is becoming to acknowledge this infinite Being, and our dependence on Him.

4. *For the Lord hath chosen Jacob.* This is a third reason. He has taken the Israelites for His peculiar people, "his peculiar treasure."

5. *The Lord is great.* Unlimited in His power —another reason. *Is above all gods.* Every class of being, whether idolized or not; because he is the Fountain of existence. This is a fifth reason.

15. *The idols of the heathen.* This verse and the following, to the end of the eighteenth, are almost word for word the same as vv. 4-8 of Psalm cxv.

MATTHEW HENRY

II. To stir up the people of God to true devotion in the worship of the true God, *v.* 19–21. In the parallel place (cxv. 9–11), by way of inference from the impotency of idols, the duty thus pressed upon us is to *trust in the Lord*; here to bless him; by putting our trust in God we give glory to him.

PSALM 136

Verses 1–9

The duty we are here again and again called to is to *give thanks*, to *offer the sacrifice of praise continually*, not the fruits of our ground or cattle, but *the fruits of our lips, giving thanks to his name*, Heb. xiii. 15. We must give thanks *to the Lord*, Jehovah, Israel's God (*v.* 1), *the God of gods*, the God whom angels adore, from whom magistrates derive their power (*v.* 2), *to the Lord of lords*, the Sovereign of all sovereigns, *v.* 3. We must give thanks to God for his goodness and mercy (*v.* 1): *Give thanks to the Lord*, not only because he does good, but because he is good. Not only for that mercy which is now handed out to us here on earth, but for that which shall endure for ever in the glories and joys of heaven. We must give God thanks for the instances of his power and wisdom. He made the heavens, and stretched them out, and in them we not only see his wisdom and power, but we taste his mercy in their benign influences; as long as the heavens endure the mercy of God endures in them, *v.* 5. *The earth hath he given to the children of men*, and all its products. The sun, moon, and stars, he placed in the firmament of heaven, to shed their light and influences upon this earth, *v.* 7–9.

Verses 10–22

The great things God did for Israel, when he formed them into a people, and set up his kingdom among them, are here mentioned, as often elsewhere in the psalms, as instances both of the power of God and of the particular kindness he had for Israel. He brought them out of Egypt, *v.* 10–12. He forced them a way through the Red Sea, which obstructed them at their first setting out. He not only divided the sea, but gave his people courage to go through it when it was divided, which was an instance of God's power over men's hearts, as the former of his power over the waters. He conducted them through a vast howling wilderness (*v.* 16); there he led them and fed them. He destroyed kings before them, to make room for them (*v.* 17, 18). It is good to enter into the detail of God's favours and not to view them in the gross, and in each instance to observe, and own, that God's *mercy endureth for ever*. He put them in possession of a good land, *v.* 21, 22. As he said to the Egyptians, *Let my people go*, so to the Canaanites, *Let my people in*, that they may serve me. In this *God's mercy* to them *endureth for ever*, because it was a figure of the heavenly Canaan, the *mercy of our Lord Jesus Christ unto eternal life*.

Verses 23–26

God's everlasting mercy is here celebrated in the redemption of his church, *v.* 23, 24. In the many redemptions wrought for the Jewish church out of the hands of their oppressors (when, in the years of their servitude, their estate was very low, God remembered them, and raised them up saviours, the judges, and David), but especially in the great redemption of the universal church, of which these were types, we have a great deal of reason to say, "*He remembered us in our low estate*, in our lost estate, *for his mercy endureth for ever*; he sent his Son to redeem us from sin, and death, and hell, and all our spiritual enemies, *for his mercy endureth for ever*." It is an instance of the mercy of God's providence that wherever he has given life he gives food agreeable and sufficient; and he is a good housekeeper that provides for so large a family. In all his glories, and all his gifts (*v.* 26): *Give thanks to the God of heaven*. This and that particular mercy may perhaps endure but a while, but the mercy that is in God *endures for ever*; it is an inexhaustible fountain.

PSALM 137

Verses 1–6

I. The people of God in tears, but sowing in tears. They were posted *by the rivers of Babylon*, in a strange land, a great way from their own country, whence they were brought as prisoners of war. The land of Babylon was now a house of bondage to that people, as Egypt had been in their beginning. Their conquerors quartered them *by the rivers*, with design to

JAMIESON, FAUSSET, BROWN

19-21—(Cf. Ps. 115:9-11.) There we have "trust" for "bless" here. **out of Zion**—(Cf. Ps. 110:2; 134:3.) From the Church, as a center, His praise is diffused throughout the earth.

PSALM 136

Vss. 1-26. The theme is the same as that of Psalm 135. God should be praised for His works of creation and providence, His deliverance and care of His people, and judgments on their enemies, and His goodness to all. The chorus to every verse is in terms of that of Psalm 106:1; 118:1-4, and was perhaps used as the *Amen* by the people, in worship (cf. I Chron. 16:36; Ps. 105:45).

1-3. The divine titles denote supremacy. **4. alone**—excluding all help.

5, 6. by [or, "in"] **wisdom**—(Ps. 104:24). **made**—lit., "maker of." **above** [or, higher than] **the waters**—(Ps. 24:2).

12. Cf. similar expressions (Exod. 3:20; Deut. 4:34, etc.). **15. overthrew**—lit., "shook off," as in Exodus 14:27, as a contemptuous rejection of a reptile.

23. remembered us—or, for us (Ps. 132:1). **our low estate**—i.e., captivity. **24. And hath redeemed** [or, lit., "snatched"] **us**—alluding to the sudden deliverance effected by the overthrow of Babylon. **25.** To the special favors to His people is added the record of God's goodness to all His creatures (cf. Matt. 6:30).

26. God of heaven—occurs but once (Jonah 1:9) before the captivity. It is used by the later writers as specially distinguishing God from idols.

PSALM 137

Vss. 1-9. This Psalm records the mourning of the captive Israelites, and a prayer and prediction respecting the destruction of their enemies.

1. rivers of Babylon—the name of the city used for the whole country.

ADAM CLARKE

19. *Bless the Lord, O house.* See similar verses, Ps. cxv. 9-13.

PSALM 136

This psalm is little else than a repetition of the preceding, with the burden, "because his mercy endureth for ever," at the end of every verse. It seems to have been a responsive song; the first part of the verse sung by the Levites, the burden by the people. It has no title in the Hebrew, nor in any of the versions. It was doubtless written after the Captivity. The author is unknown.

1. *O give thanks unto the Lord; for he is good.* This sentiment often occurs: the goodness of the divine nature, as a ground both of confidence and of thanksgiving. *For his mercy endureth for ever.* These words, which are the burden of every verse, *ki leolam chasdo*, might be translated: "For His tender mercy is to the coming age"; meaning, probably, if the psalm be prophetic, that peculiar display of His compassion, the redemption of the world by the Lord Jesus. These very words were prescribed by David as an acknowledgment, to be used continually in the divine worship, see 1 Chron. xvi. 41: also by Solomon, 2 Chron. vii. 3, 6; and observed by Jehoshaphat, 2 Chron. xx. 21; all acknowledging that, however rich in mercy God was to them, the most extensive displays of His goodness were reserved for the age to come; see 1 Pet. i. 10-12.

2. *The God of gods. Ladonai haadonim.* As *adonai* signifies "director," it may apply here, not to idols, for God is not their God, but to the priests and spiritual rulers; as Lord of lords may apply to kings and magistrates, etc. He is God and Ruler over all the rulers of the earth, whether in things sacred or civil.

4. *Who alone doeth great wonders.* "Miracles."

6. *Stretched out the earth above the waters.* Or "upon the waters."

25. *Giveth food to all flesh.* By whose universal providence every intellectual and animal being is supported and preserved. The appointing every living thing food, and that sort of food which is suited to its nature, is an overwhelming proof of the wondrous providence, wisdom, and goodness of God.

PSALM 137

Neither the Hebrew nor Chaldee has any title. Some think it was sung when they returned from Babylon; others, while they were there. It was evidently composed during or at the close of the Captivity.

1. *By the rivers of Babylon.* In their captivity

MATTHEW HENRY

employ them there. We find some of them by the *river Chebar* (Ezek. i. 3). There they *sat down* to indulge their grief by poring on their miseries. Thoughts of Zion drew tears from their eyes; but they were deliberate tears (we *sat down and wept*), tears with consideration—*we wept when we remembered Zion*, the holy hill on which the temple was built. Their affection to God's house swallowed up their concern for their own houses. They laid by their instruments of music (*v.* 2): *We hung our harps upon the willows.* They did not hide their harps in the bushes, or the hollows of the rocks; but hung them up in view, that the sight of them might affect them with this deplorable change. Yet perhaps they were faulty in doing this; for praising God is never out of season.

II. The abuses which their enemies put upon them when they were in this melancholy condition, *v.* 3. They had *carried them away captive* from their own land and then *wasted them* in the land of their captivity. To complete their woes they insulted over them: They *required of us mirth and a song.* It argues a base and sordid spirit to upbraid those that are in distress either with their former joys or with their present griefs, or to challenge those to be merry who, we know, are out of tune for it. No songs would serve them but the *songs of Zion*, with which God had been honoured; so that in this demand they reflected upon God himself as Belshazzar, when he drank wine in temple-bowls.

III. The patience wherewith they bore these abuses, *v.* 4. They had laid by their harps, and would not resume them. Profane scoffers are not to be humoured. The reason they gave is very mild and pious: *How shall we sing the Lord's song in a strange land?* "It is the *Lord's song*; it is a sacred thing; it is peculiar to the temple-service, and therefore we dare not sing it in the land of a stranger, among idolaters."

IV. The constant affection they retained for Jerusalem, the city of their solemnities, even now that they were in Babylon. It was always in their minds; they remembered it; many of them had never seen it. In their daily prayers they opened their windows towards Jerusalem; and how then could they forget it. "*Let my right hand forget her art*" (which the hand of an expert musician never can, unless it be withered), "nay, *let my tongue cleave to the roof of my mouth*, if I have not a good word to say for Jerusalem wherever I am."

Verses 7–9

The pious Jews in Babylon, having afflicted themselves with the thoughts of the ruins of Jerusalem, here please themselves with the prospect of the ruin of her impenitent implacable enemies; but this not from a spirit of revenge, but from a holy zeal for the glory of God and the honour of his kingdom. And all this was a fruit of the old enmity of Esau against Jacob, because he got the birthright and the blessing. *Lord, remember* them, says the psalmist, which is an appeal to his justice against them. Far be it from us to avenge ourselves, if ever it should be in our power, but we will leave it to him who has said, *Vengeance is mine. O daughter of Babylon!* proud and secure as thou art, we know well thou *art to be destroyed*, or (as Dr. Hammond reads it) *who art the destroyer.* The destroyers shall be destroyed. "Thou shalt be served *as thou hast served us*, as barbarously used by the destroyers as we have been by thee." Let not those expect to find mercy who, when they had power, did not show mercy. None escape if the little ones perish. Those are the seed of another generation; so that, if they be cut off, the ruin will be not only total, as Jerusalem's was, but final.

JAMIESON, FAUSSET, BROWN

remembered Zion—or, Jerusalem, as in Psalm 132:13.

2. upon the willows—which may have grown there then, if not now; as the palm, which was once common, is now rare in Palestine.

3, 4. Whether the request was in curiosity or derision, the answer intimates that a compliance was incongruous with their mournful feelings (Prov. 25:20).

5, 6. For joyful songs would imply forgetfulness of their desolated homes and fallen Church.

The solemn imprecations on the **hand** and **tongue,** if thus forgetful, relate to the cunning or skill in playing, and the power of singing.

7-9. Remember . . . the children of Edom—(Cf. Ps. 132:1), i.e., to punish. **the day of Jerusalem**—its downfall (Lam. 4:21, 22; Obad. 11-13). **daughter of Babylon**—the people (Ps. 9:13). Their destruction had been abundantly foretold (Isa. 13:14; Jer. 51:23). For the terribleness of that destruction, God's righteous judgment, and not the passions of the chafed Israelites, was responsible.

ADAM CLARKE

and dispersion, it was customary for the Jews to hold their religious meetings on the banks of rivers. Mention is made of this Acts xvi. 13, where we find the Jews of Philippi resorting to "a river side, where prayer was wont to be made."

2. *We hanged our harps upon the willows.* The *willows* were very plentiful in Babylon. The great quantity of them that were on the banks of the Euphrates caused Isaiah, chap. xv. 7, to call it "the brook [or river] of the willows." This is a most affecting picture. Perhaps resting themselves after toil, and wishing to spend their time religiously, they took their harps, and were about to sing one of the songs of Zion; but, reflecting on their own country, they became so filled with distress that they unstrung their harps with one consent, and hung them on the willow bushes, and gave a general loose to their grief. Some of the Babylonians, who probably attended such meetings for the sake of the music, desired them to sing one of Zion's songs. This is affectingly told.

3. *They that carried us away captive required of us a song.* This was as unreasonable as it was insulting.

4. *How shall we sing the Lord's song? Eich! nashir;* "Oh, we sing!" Who does not hear the deep sigh in the strongly guttural sound of the original *eich!* wrung, as it were, from the bottom of the heart? Can we, in this state of slavery—we, exiles, from our country—we sing, or be mirthful in these circumstances?

7. *Remember . . . the children of Edom.* It appears from Jer. xii. 6; xxv. 14; Lam. iv. 21-22; Ezek. xxv. 12; Obad. 11-14, that the Idumeans joined the army of Nebuchadnezzar against their brethren the Jews; and that they were main instruments in razing the walls of Jerusalem even to the ground.

8. *O daughter of Babylon, who art to be destroyed.* Or, "O thou daughter of Babylon, the destroyer." *Rewardeth thee as thou hast served us.* This was Cyrus, who was chosen of God to do this work, and is therefore called *happy*, as being God's agent in its destruction.

9. *Happy . . . that taketh and dasheth thy little ones.* That is, So oppressive have you been to all under your domination as to become universally hated and detested; so that those who may have the last hand in your destruction, and the total extermination of your inhabitants, shall be reputed *happy*—shall be celebrated and extolled as those who have rid the world of a curse so grievous. These prophetic declarations contain no excitement to any person or persons to commit acts of cruelty and barbarity, but are simply declarative of what would take place in the order of the retributive providence and justice of God, and the general opinion that should in consequence be expressed on the subject.

MATTHEW HENRY — PSALM 138

A psalm of David.

Verses 1–5

I. He would praise God with sincerity and zeal—"*With my heart, with my whole heart*, with that which is within me and with all that is within me, inward impressions agreeing with outward expressions." *Before the gods will I sing praise unto thee*, before the princes, and judges, and great men. *I will worship towards thy holy temple.* The priests alone went into the temple; the people, at the nearest, did but worship towards it, and that they might do at a distance. Christ is our temple, and towards him we must look as Mediator between us and God, in all our praises of him. Heaven is God's holy temple, and thitherward we must lift up our eyes in all our addresses to God. *Our Father in heaven.*

II. He would praise God for the fountain of his comforts—*for thy lovingkindness and for thy truth. For thou hast magnified thy word* (thy promise, which is truth) *above all thy name.* God has made

JAMIESON, FAUSSET, BROWN — PSALM 138

Vss. 1-8. David thanks God for His benefits, and anticipating a wider extension of God's glory by His means, assures himself of His continued presence and faithfulness.

1. (Cf. Ps. 9:1.) **before the gods**—whether *angels* (Ps. 8:5); or *princes* (Exod. 21:6, Ps. 82:6; or *idols* (Ps. 97:7); denotes a readiness to worship the true God alone, and a contempt of all other objects of worship.

2. (Cf. Ps. 5:7.) **thy word above all thy name**—i.e.,God's promise (II Sam. 7), sustained by

ADAM CLARKE — PSALM 138

The Hebrew and all the versions attribute this psalm to David, and it is supposed to have been made by him when, delivered from all his enemies, he was firmly seated on the throne of Israel.

1. *Before the gods will I sing. Neged Elohim,* "in the presence of Elohim"; most probably meaning before the ark, where were the sacred symbols of the Supreme Being.

2. *For thy lovingkindness.* Thy "tender mercy" shown to me; and for the fulfillment of *thy truth*—the promises Thou hast made. *Thou hast magnified thy word above all thy name.*

MATTHEW HENRY

himself known to us in many ways in creation and providence, but most clearly by his word. Some good interpreters understand it of Christ, the essential Word, and of his gospel, which are magnified above all the discoveries God had before made of himself to the fathers. He had been in affliction, and he remembers. *Thou strengthenedst me with strength in my soul.* If God give us strength in our souls to bear the burdens, resist the temptations, and do the duties of an afflicted state, if he strengthen us to keep hold of himself by faith, to maintain the peace of our own minds and to wait with patience for the issue, we must own that he has answered us, and we are bound to be thankful.

III. David was himself a king, and therefore he hoped that kings would be wrought upon by his experiences, and his example, to embrace religion. This may have reference to the kings that were neighbours to David, as Hiram and others. "They shall all praise thee." When they visited David, and, after his death, Solomon (as *all the kings of the earth* are expressly said to have done, 2 Chron. ix. 23), they readily joined in the worship of the God of Israel. It may look further, to the calling of the Gentiles and the disciplining of all nations by the gospel of Christ, of whom it is said that *all kings shall fall down before him*, Ps. lxxii. 11. They shall *sing in the ways of the Lord*, in the ways of his providence and grace towards them.

Verses 6–8

David here comforts himself with three things:—

I. The favour God bears to his humble people (*v.* 6): *Though the Lord be high, yet has he respect unto the lowly*, smiles upon them as well pleased with them, and, sooner or later, he will put honour upon them, while *he knows the proud afar off*, knows them, but disowns them.

II. The care God takes of his afflicted oppressed people, *v.* 7. David, though a great and good man, expects to *walk in the midst of trouble*, but encourages himself with hope. "When my spirit is ready to sink and fail, *thou* shalt *revive me*, and make me easy and cheerful under my troubles." He would protect him: "*Thou shalt stretch forth thy hand*, though not against my enemies to destroy them, yet *against the wrath of my enemies*, to restrain that and set bounds to it." He would in due time work deliverance for him: *Thy right hand shall save me.* Christ is the right hand of the Lord, that shall save all those who serve him.

III. Whatever good work God has begun for his people he will perform it (*v.* 8): *The Lord will perfect that which concerns me*, which is most needful for me. Every good man is most concerned about his duty to God and his happiness in God, that the former may be faithfully done and the latter effectually secured; and if indeed these are the things that our hearts are most upon, there is a good work begun in us, and he that has begun it will perfect it, Phil. i. 6. Our hopes that we shall persevere must be founded, not upon our own strength, for that will fail us, but upon the mercy of God, for that will not fail. It is well pleaded, "*Lord, thy mercy endures for ever;* let me be for ever a monument of it." He turns his expectation into a petition: "*Forsake not*, do not let go, *the work of thy own hands.* Lord, I am the work of thy own hands, my soul is so, do not forsake me."

JAMIESON, FAUSSET, BROWN

His mercy and truth, exceeded all other manifestations of Himself as subject of praise.

3-5. That promise, as an answer to his prayers in distress, revived and strengthened his faith; and, as the basis of other revelations of the Messiah, it will be the occasion of praise by all who hear and receive it (Ps. 68:29, 31; Isa. 4:3).

for great [is] the glory—or, when the glory shall be great, in God's fulfilling His purposes of redemption.

6, 7. On this general principle of God's government (Isa. 2:11; 57:15; 66: 2), he relies for God's favor in saving him, and overthrowing his enemies. **knoweth afar off**—their ways and deserts (Ps. 1:6).

8. God will fulfil His promise.

ADAM CLARKE

All the versions read this sentence thus: "For thou hast magnified above all the name of thy holiness." Thou hast proved that Thou hast all power in heaven and in earth, and that Thou art true in all Thy words. The original I think might be thus translated: "For Thou hast magnified Thy name and Thy word over all," or, "on every occasion."

CHARLES H. SPURGEON:

"All the kings of the earth shall praise thee, O Lord, when they hear the words of thy mouth" (v. 4). Kings have usually small care to hear the word of the Lord; but King David feels assured that if they do hear it, they will feel its power. A little piety goes a long way in courts; but brighter days are coming, in which rulers will become hearers and worshipers: may the advent of such happy times be hastened. What an assembly!—"all the kings of the earth!" What a purpose! Gathered to hear the words of Jehovah's mouth. What a preacher! David himself rehearses the words of Jehovah. What praise! when they all in happy union lift up their songs unto the Lord. Kings are as gods below, and they do well when they worship the God above. The way of conversion for kings is the same as for ourselves: faith to them also cometh by hearing, and hearing by the word of God. Happy are those who can cause the word of the Lord to penetrate palaces; for the occupants of thrones are usually the last to know the joyful sounds of the gospel. David, the king, cared for king's souls, and it will be wise for each man to look first after those who are of his order.

—*The Treasury of David*

8. *The Lord will perfect.* **Whatever is further necessary to be done, He will do it.**

MATTHEW HENRY — PSALM 139

To the chief musician. A psalm of David.

Verses 1–6

God with whom we have to do has a perfect knowledge of us, and all the motions and actions both of our inward and of our outward man are open before him.

I. David lays down this doctrine of address to God; acknowledging it to him, and giving him the glory. When we speak to God of himself we shall find ourselves concerned to speak with the utmost degree both of sincerity and reverence.

II. He lays it down in a way of application to himself, not "Thou hast known *all*," but, "Thou hast known *me*." So here, "*Thou hast searched me, and known me.*" David was a king, and *the hearts of kings are unsearchable* to their subjects (Prov. xxv. 3), but they are not so to their Sovereign.

III. He descends to particulars: "Thou knowest me wherever I am and whatever I am doing, me and all that belongs to me. *Thou knowest* me and all my motions, *my down-sitting* to rest, *my up-rising* to work. Thou knowest me when I come home, how I walk before my house, and when I go abroad, on what errands I go. Thou knowest all my imaginations. It is often unobserved by ourselves, and yet *thou*

JAMIESON, FAUSSET, BROWN — PSALM 139

Vss. 1-24. After presenting the sublime doctrines of God's omnipresence and omniscience, the Psalmist appeals to Him, avowing his innocence, his abhorrence of the wicked, and his ready submission to the closest scrutiny. Admonition to the wicked and comfort to the pious are alike implied inferences from these doctrines.

ADAM CLARKE — PSALM 139

The title of this psalm in the Hebrew is, "To the chief Musician [or, To the Conqueror], A Psalm of David." The versions in general follow the Hebrew. And yet, notwithstanding these testimonies, there appears internal evidence that the psalm was not written by David, but during or after the time of the Captivity, as there are several Chaldaisms in it. See vv. 2-3, 7, 9, 19-20, collated with Dan. ii. 29-30; iv. 16; vii. 28; some of these will be noticed in their proper places.

1. *O Lord, thou hast searched me.* "Thou hast investigated me"; Thou hast thoroughly acquainted thyself with my whole soul and conduct.

2. *My downsitting and mine uprising.* Even these inconsiderable and casual things are under Thy continual notice. I cannot so much as take a seat, or leave it, without being marked by Thee.

MATTHEW HENRY

understandest my thoughts afar off." Or, "*Thou understandest them afar off*, even before I think them, and long after I have thought them and have myself forgotten them." Or "*Thou understandest them from afar;* from the height of heaven thou seest into the depths of the heart," xxxiii. 14. "*Thou compassest* every particular *path*, so as thoroughly to distinguish between the good and evil of what I do. "*Thou knowest* me in all my retirements; thou knowest *my lying down*; when I am reflecting upon what has passed all day, thou knowest what I have in my heart and with what thoughts I go to bed." *There is not a word in my tongue*, not a vain word, nor a good word, *but thou knowest it altogether. When there is not a word in my tongue, O Lord! thou knowest all* (so some read it); for thoughts are words to God. *Thou hast beset me behind and before.* Wherever we are we are under the eye and hand of God. God knows us as we know not only what we see, but what we feel.

IV. He speaks of it with admiration (*v.* 6): *It is too wonderful for me; it is high.* We cannot by searching find out how God searches and finds out us; nor do we know how we are known.

Verses 7–16

David is sure that God perfectly knows him and all his ways,

I. Because he is always under his eye. If God is omnipresent, he must needs be omniscient. Heaven and earth include the whole creation, and the Creator fills both (Jer. xxiii. 24); he not only knows both, and governs both, but he fills both. Every part of the creation is under God's influence. No flight can remove us out of God's presence: "*Whither shall I go from thy Spirit, from thy presence*, that is, from thy spiritual presence, from thyself, who art a Spirit?" *God is a Spirit*, and therefore it is folly to think that because we cannot see him he cannot see us: *Whither shall I flee from thy presence?* (*Quocunque te flexeris, ibi Deum videbis occurrentem tibi—Whithersoever thou turnest thyself, thou wilt see God meeting thee*, said Seneca.) David specifies the most remote and distant places, and counts upon meeting God in them. (1) In heaven: "*If I ascend* thither, as I hope to do shortly, *thou art there*, and it will be my eternal bliss to be with thee there." (2) *In hell*—in *Sheol*, which may be understood of the depth of the earth, the very centre of it. Should we dig as deep as we can underground, and think to hide ourselves there, we should be mistaken. Or it may be understood of the state of the dead. When we are removed out of the sight of all living, we are not out of sight of the living God; from his eye we cannot hide ourselves. Or it may be understood of the place of the damned: *If I make my bed in hell* (an uncomfortable place to make a bed in) *behold, thou art there*, in thy power and justice. In the remotest corners of this world: "*If I take the wings of the morning*, the rays of the morning-light (called the wings of the sun, Mal. iv. 2), than which nothing more swift, and flee upon them to *the uttermost parts of the sea*, or of the earth, should I flee to the most distant and obscure islands (the *ultima Thule*, the *Terra incognita*), I should find thee there; *there shall thy hand lead me*, as far as I go, *and thy right hand shall hold me*, that I can go no further, that I cannot go out of thy reach."

2. No veil can hide us from God's eye, *v.* 11, 12. "*If I say*, Yet *the darkness shall cover me*, when nothing else will, I find myself deceived; the curtains of the evening will stand me in no more stead than the wings of the morning; *even the night shall be light about me*." No hypocritical mask or disguise, how specious soever, can save any person or action from appearing in a true light before God.

II. Because he is the work of his hands. He that framed the engine knows all the motions of it. God made us, and therefore he knows us. "*Thou hast possessed my reins.* The possession thou hast of my reins is a rightful possession, *for thou coveredst me in my mother's womb*, that is, thou madest me (Job x. 11), thou madest me in secret." The soul is concealed from all about us. It was God himself that thus covered us, and therefore he can, when he pleases, discover us. "*I will praise thee*, the author of my being; my parents were only the instruments of it." We were his work, according to the divine model: *In thy book all my members were written.* Eternal wisdom formed the plan. We are *fearfully and wonderfully made*; we may justly be astonished at these living temples, the composition of every part, and the harmony of all together. As a great mercy all our members *in continuance were fashioned*, according as they were written in the book of God's wise counsel, *when as yet there was none of them.*

JAMIESON, FAUSSET, BROWN

CHARLES H. SPURGEON:

Verse 7. Here omnipresence is the theme—a truth to which omniscience naturally leads up. "Whither shall I go from thy spirit?" Not that the Psalmist wished to go from God, or to avoid the power of the divine life; but he asks this question to set forth the fact that no one can escape from the all-pervading being and observation of the great invisible Spirit. Observe how the writer makes the matter personal to himself—"Whither shall I go?" It were well if we all thus applied truth to our own cases. It were wise for each one to say: The spirit of the Lord is ever around *me*: Jehovah is omnipresent *to me.* "Or whither shall I flee from thy presence?" If full of dread, I hastened to escape from that nearness of God which had become my terror, which way could I turn? "Whither?" "Whither?" He repeats his cry. No answer comes back to him. The reply to his first "Whither?" is its echo—a second "Whither?" From the sight of God he cannot be hidden, but that is not all—from the immediate, actual, constant presence of God, he cannot be withdrawn. We must be, whether we will it or not, as near to God as our soul is to our body. This makes it dreadful work to sin; for we offend the Almighty to his face, and commit acts of treason at the very foot of his throne. Go from him, or flee from him we cannot: neither by patient travel nor by hasty flight can we withdraw from the all-surrounding Deity. His mind is in our mind; himself within ourselves. His spirit is over our spirit; our presence is ever in his presence.

Verse 8. "If I ascend into heaven, thou art there." Filling the loftiest region with his yet loftier presence, Jehovah is in the heavenly place, at home, upon his throne. The ascent, if it were possible, would be unavailing for purposes of escape; it would, in fact, be a flying into the center of the fire to avoid the heat. There would he be immediately confronted by the terrible personality of God. Note the abrupt words: "Thou, there." "If I make my bed in hell, thou art there." Descending into the lowest imaginable depths among the dead, there should we find the Lord. Thou! says the Psalmist, as if he felt that God was the one great existence in all places. Whatever Hades may be, or whoever may be there, one thing is certain, Thou, O Jehovah, art there. Two regions, the one of glory and the other of darkness, are set in contrast, and this one fact is asserted of both—"thou art there." Whether we rise up or lie down, take our wing or make our bed, we shall find God near us. A "behold" is added to the second clause, since it seems more a wonder to meet with God in hell than in heaven, in Hades than in Paradise. Of course the presence of God produces very different effects in these places, but it is unquestionably in each; the bliss of one, the terror of the other. What an awful thought, that some men seem resolved to take up their night's abode in hell, a night which shall know no morning.

—*The Treasury of David*

ADAM CLARKE

Thou understandest my thought.* "My Cogitation." This word is Chaldee, see Dan. ii. 29-30. *Afar off.* While the figment is forming that shall produce them.

3. *Thou compassest my path. Zeritha*—thou dost winnow, ventilate, or "sift" my path; *and my lying down, ribi*, my "bed." *And art acquainted.* Thou treasurest up—this is the import of *sachan.* Thou hast the whole number of *my ways*, and the steps I took in them.

4. *There is not a word in my tongue.* "Although [*ki*] there be not a word in my tongue, behold, O Jehovah, Thou knowest the whole of it"; that is, Thou knowest all my words before they are uttered, as Thou knowest all my thoughts while as yet they are unformed.

5. *Thou hast beset me behind and before.* "The hereafter and the past, Thou hast formed me."

7. *Whither shall I go from thy spirit?* Surely *ruach* in this sense must be taken personally; it certainly cannot mean either breath or wind. To render it so would make the passage ridiculous. *From thy presence?* "From thy faces." Why do we meet with this word so frequently in the plural number when applied to God? And why have we His *spirit*, and His "appearances" or "faces," both here? A Trinitarian would at once say, "The plurality of persons in the Godhead is intended"; and who can prove that he is mistaken?

15. *My substance was not hid from thee.* My "bones" or "skeleton." *Curiously wrought.* Embroidered, made of needlework. These two words, says Bishop Horsley, describe the two principal parts of which the human body is composed: the bony skeleton, the foundation of the whole; and the external covering of muscular flesh, tendons, veins, arteries, nerves, and skin —a curious web of fibers.

16. *Thine eyes did see my substance.* My "embryo state."

MATTHEW HENRY

Verses 17–24

Here the psalmist makes application of the doctrine of God's omniscience,

I. He acknowledges, with wonder and thankfulness, the care God had taken of him all his days, *v.* 17, 18. God, who knew him, thought of him, and his thoughts towards him were thoughts of love. God's omniscience has watched over us to do us good, Jer. xxxi. 28. Providence has had a vast reach in its dispensations concerning us, and has brought things about for our good quite beyond our contrivance and foresight. We cannot conceive the multitude of God's compassions, which are all new every morning. "*When I awake*, every morning, *I am still with thee*, under thy eye and care, safe and easy under thy protection."

II. He concludes from this doctrine that ruin will certainly be the end of sinners. God knows all the wickedness of the wicked, and therefore he will reckon for it. God will punish them, because they set him at defiance (*v.* 20): *They speak against thee wickedly*. They are his *enemies*, and declare their enmity by *taking his name in vain*. Some make it to be a description of hypocrites: "They speak of thee for mischief; they talk of God, pretending to piety, and, being enemies to God, while they pretend friendship, they *take* his *name in vain*; they swear falsely." 1. He defies them: "*Depart from me, you bloody men ;* you shall not debauch me, for I will not admit your friendship nor have fellowship with you; and you cannot destroy me. David detests them *v.* 21, 22: "Lord, thou knowest the heart, and canst witness for me; *do not I hate those that hate thee*, because they hate thee? I hate them because I love thee, and hate to see such indignities put upon thy blessed name. *Am not I grieved with those that rise up against thee*, grieved to see their rebellion and to foresee their ruin, which it will certainly end in?" Sin is hatred, and sinners are lamented, by all that fear God. "*I hate them*" (that is, *I hate the work of them that turn aside*, ci. 3).

III. He appeals to God concerning his sincerity, *v.* 23, 24. "Lord, I hope I am not in a wicked way, but *see if there be any wicked way in me*, any corrupt inclination remaining; let me see it; and root it out of me, for I do not allow it." *Lead me in the way everlasting*.

PSALM 140

To the chief musician. A psalm of David.

Verses 1–7

In *this*, as in other things, David was a type of Christ, that he suffered before he reigned, was humbled before he was exalted, and that as there were many who loved and valued him, and sought to do him honour, so there were many who hated and envied him, and sought to do him mischief.

I. He gives a character of his enemies. There was one that seems to have been the ring-leader of them, whom he calls *the evil man* and *the man of violences* (*v.* 1, 4), probably he means Saul. But there were many besides this one who were confederate against David. They are very subtle (*v.* 2), have laid the scheme with all the cunning imaginable. *They have*, like mighty hunters, *hidden a snare*, and *spread a net*, and *set gins* (*v.* 5), that he might fall into their hands ere he was aware. Great persecutors have often been great politicians, which has indeed made them the more formidable; but *the Lord preserves the simple. They have sharpened their tongues like a serpent*, that infuses his venom with his tongue; and there is so much malignity in all they say that one would think there was nothing *under their lips* but *adders' poison*, *v.* 3. They are all *gathered together* against me *for war*, *v.* 2. Those who can agree in nothing else can agree to persecute a good man. Herod and Pilate will unite in this, and in this they resemble Satan, who is not divided against himself, all the devils agreeing in Beelzebub. The pride of persecutors may be the encouragement of the persecuted, for the more haughty they are the faster are they ripening for ruin.

II. He prays: "Lord, *deliver me, preserve me, keep me* (*v.* 1, 4); let them not prevail to take away my life, my reputation, my interest, my comfort, and to prevent my coming to the throne. *Keep me* from doing as they do, or as they promise themselves I shall do."

III. He triumphs in God, and thereby, in effect, he triumphs over his persecutors, *v.* 6, 7. "*I said, Thou art my God;* and, if my God, then my shield and mighty protector." In his access to God, it comforted him, that he was not only taken into covenant with God, but into communion with him. He had help from God and happiness in him: "*O God the Lord—*

JAMIESON, FAUSSET, BROWN

F. B. MEYER:

"See if there be any way of grief in me" (139:24). The A.V. says "wicked way"; but the R.V. margin gives "way of grief." We may be in a way that causes God grief, even though it is not what men might term a way of wickedness. We may be grieving our blessed Lord more than we know, substituting an ideal religious standard, or absorption in his work, or the conception which our friends persist in holding concerning us, for that direct personal fellowship with Himself, which alone is religion. Ah! How much we may have grieved the Spirit of Christ! Not always consciously. Often in pleading for us, the Lord must needs say, "Forgive; they know not what they do." But we are unwilling that his tender heart should suffer, or his face be overcast with grief, because of our waywardness; therefore we say, "Search us and know us; try us and show us the ways of grief." Be prepared for his revelations, searching and startling.

Lord, that is what we want! We have been going in ways of grief. We desire to go in the way everlasting—the way of eternal life; the way which we shall never need to retrace; the way that touches the deepest life possible to the creature. But we cannot find it for ourselves, nor even see the next step; therefore we stretch out poor, groping hands, and cry, "Lead us, as a woman may lead her blind child. We do not ask to see the distant way. Show us the next thing, and the next, and the next, till thy grief is turned to gladness."—*Great Verses Through the Bible*

PSALM 140

Vss. 1-13. The style of this Psalm resembles those of David in the former part of the book, presenting the usual complaint, prayer, and confident hope of relief.

1. evil man—Which of David's enemies is meant is not important.

2-5. This character of the wicked, and the devices planned against the pious, correspond to Psalm 10:7; 31:13; 58:4, etc. **sharpened . . . like a serpent**—not like a serpent does, but they are thus like a serpent in cunning and venom. **snare** [and] **net**—for threatening dangers (cf. Ps. 38:12; 57: 6).

6. (Cf. Ps. 5:1-12; 16:2).

ADAM CLARKE

17. *How precious also are thy thoughts!* "Thy cogitations"; a Chaldaism, as before. *How great is the sum of them!* "How strongly rational are the heads or principal subjects of them!"

18. *If I should count them.* I should be glad to enumerate so many interesting particulars, but they are beyond calculation. *When I awake.* Thou art my Governor and Protector night and day.

19. *Surely thou wilt slay the wicked.* The remaining part of this psalm has no visible connection with the preceding. I rather think it a fragment or a part of some other psalm. *Ye bloody men.* "Men of blood," men guilty of death.

21. *Do not I hate them?* I hold their conduct in abomination.

22. *With perfect hatred.* Their conduct, their motives, their opposition to Thee, their perfidy and idolatrous purposes, I perfectly abhor.

23. *Search me, O God.* Investigate my conduct, examine my heart, put me to the test, and examine my thoughts.

24. *If there be any wicked way.* "A way of idolatry, or of error." *Lead me in the way everlasting.* "In the old way"—the way in which our fathers walked, who worshipped Thee.

PSALM 140

The Hebrew and all the versions attribute this psalm to David; and it is supposed to contain his complaint when persecuted by Saul.

1. *From the evil man.* Saul, who was full of envy, jealousy, and cruelty against David, to whom both himself and his kingdom were under the highest obligations, endeavored by every means to destroy him.

2. *They gathered together.* He and his courtiers form plots and cabals against my life.

3. *They have sharpened their tongues.* They employ their time in forging lies and calumnies against me, and those of the most virulent nature.

5. *Have hid a snare for me.* They hunted David as they would a dangerous wild beast.

4. *Preserve me from the violent man.* Saul again, who was as headstrong and violent in all his measures as he was cruel, and inflexibly bent on the destruction of David.

MATTHEW HENRY

Jehovah Adonai! as *Jehovah* thou art self-existent and self-sufficient, an infinitely perfect being; as *Adonai* thou art my stay and support, my ruler and governor, and therefore *the strength of my salvation,* my strong Saviour. *Thou hast covered my head in the day of battle.*"

Verses 8–13

David prays: "*Grant not, O Lord! the desires of the wicked,* but frustrate them; *hear the voice of my supplications.*" He prays: "*O further not his wicked device;* let not Providence favour any of his designs, but cross them; suffer *not his wicked device* to proceed, but chain his wheels, and stop him in the career of his pursuits." He foretells the ruin of his enemies: "*The mischief of their own lips* shall *cover* their heads (*v.* 9); the evil they have wished to me shall come upon themselves, their curses shall be blown back into their own faces, and the very designs which they have laid against me shall turn to their own ruin," vii. 15, 16. The judgments of God shall *fall upon them,* compared here to *burning coals,* in allusion to the destruction of Sodom. Evil speakers must expect to be shaken, for they shall never *be established in the earth.* What is got by fraud and falsehood, by calumny and unjust accusation, will not prosper. "*I know that the Lord will maintain the* just and injured *cause of* his *afflicted* people, and will not suffer might always to prevail against right, though it be but *the right of the poor.*" The closing words, *The upright shall dwell in thy presence,* denote both God's favour to them ("Thou shalt admit them to dwell in thy presence in grace here, in glory hereafter, and it shall be their safety and happiness") and their duty to God.

JAMIESON, FAUSSET, BROWN

7. day of battle—lit., "of armor," i.e., when using it.

8. (Cf. Ps. 37:12; 66:7.) **lest they exalt themselves**—or, they will be exalted if permitted to prosper. **9.** Contrasts his head covered by God (vs. 7) with theirs, or (as head may be used for persons) with them, covered with the results of their wicked deeds (Ps. 7:16).

10. (Cf. Ps. 11:6; 120:4.) **cast into the fire; into deep pits**—figures for utter destruction. **11. an evil speaker**—or, slanderer will not be tolerated (Ps. 101: 7). The last clause may be translated: "an evil (man) He (God) shall hunt," etc. **12.** (Cf. Ps. 9:4.)

13. After all changes, the righteous shall have cause for praise. Such **shall dwell**—sit securely, under God's protection (Ps. 21:6; 41:12).

ADAM CLARKE

11. *Let not an evil speaker be established.* "A man of tongue."

MATTHEW HENRY

PSALM 141

A psalm of David.

Verses 1–4

I. David loved prayer, and he begs of God that his prayers might be heard and answered, *v.* 1, 2. *David cried unto God.* His crying denotes fervency in prayer. "*Give ear to my voice;* let me have a gracious audience." Those that cry in prayer may hope to be heard in prayer, not for their loudness, but their liveliness. *Make haste unto me.* He that believes does not make haste, but he that prays may be earnest with God to make haste. His *praying* and the *lifting up of his hands in prayer* denotes both the elevation of his desire and the out-goings of his hope and expectation, the lifting up of the hand signifying the lifting up of the heart, and being used instead of lifting up the sacrifices which were heaved and waved before the Lord. Prayer is a spiritual sacrifice; it is the offering up of the soul, and its best affections, to God. Prayer is of a sweet-smelling savour to God, as incense, which yet has no savour without fire; nor has prayer without the fire of holy love and fervour.

II. David begs that he might be kept from sin, knowing that his prayers would not be accepted unless he took care to watch against sin. We must be as earnest for God's grace in us as for his favour towards us. "*Set a watch, O Lord! before my mouth,* and, nature having made my lips to be a door to my words, let grace keep that door, that no word may be suffered to go out which may in any way tend to the dishonour of God or the hurt of others. *Incline not my heart to any evil thing;* whatever inclination there is in me to sin, let it be not only restrained, but mortified, by divine grace." While we live in such an evil world, and carry about with us such evil hearts, we have need to pray that we may neither be drawn in by any allurement nor driven on by any provocation. "*Let me not eat of their dainties.* Let me not join with them, lest thereby I be inveigled into their sins." Good men will pray even against the sweets of sin.

Verses 5–10

I. David desires to be told of his faults. *Let the righteous smite me; it shall be a kindness.* We are here taught how to receive the reproofs of the righteous and wise. If my own heart does not *smite me,* as it ought, let my friend do it; let me never fall under that dreadful judgment of being let alone in sin. We must account it a piece of friendship. We must not only bear it patiently, but take it as a kindness. Though reproofs cut, it is in order to a cure, and therefore they are much more desirable than the kisses of an enemy (Prov. xxvii. 6) or the song of fools, Eccles. vii. 5. It *shall be as an excellent oil* to a wound, to mollify it and close it up; *it shall not break my head,* as some reckon it to do, who could as well bear to have their heads broken as to be told of their

JAMIESON, FAUSSET, BROWN

PSALM 141

Vss. 1-10. This Psalm evinces its authorship as the preceding, by its structure and the character of its contents. It is a prayer for deliverance from sins to which affliction tempted him, and from the enemies who caused it.

CHARLES H. SPURGEON:

We are not to look upon prayer as easy work requiring no thought, it needs to be "set forth"; what is more, it must be set forth "before the Lord," by a sense of his presence and a holy reverence for his name: neither may we regard all supplication as certain of divine acceptance, it needs to be set forth before the Lord "as incense," concerning the offering of which there were rules to be observed, otherwise it would be rejected by God. "And lifting up of my hands as the evening sacrifice." Whatever form his prayer might take his one desire was that it might be accepted of God. Prayer is sometimes presented without words by the very motions of our bodies: bended knees and lifted hands are the tokens of earnest, expectant prayer. Certainly work, or in lifting up of the hands in labor, is prayer if it be done in dependence upon God and for his glory: there is a hand-prayer as well as a heart-prayer, and our desire is that this may be sweet unto the Lord as the sacrifice of eventide. Holy hope, lifting up of hands that hang down, is also a kind of worship: may it ever be acceptable with God. The Psalmist makes a bold request: he would have his humble cries and prayers to be as much regarded of the Lord as the appointed morning and evening sacrifices of the holy place. Yet the prayer is by no means too bold; for, after all, the spiritual is in the Lord's esteem higher than the ceremonial, and the calves of the lips are a truer sacrifice than the calves of the stall.—*The Treasury of David*

ADAM CLARKE

PSALM 141

This psalm is generally attributed to David, and considered to have been composed during his persecution by Saul. Some suppose that he made it at the time that he formed the resolution to go to Achish, king of Gath; see 1 Sam. xxvi. It is generally thought to be an evening prayer, and has long been used as such in the service of the Greek church.

1. *Lord, I cry unto thee.* Many of David's psalms begin with complaints, but they are not those of habitual plaint and peevishness. He was in frequent troubles and difficulties, and he always sought help in God.

2. *As incense.* Incense was offered every morning and evening before the Lord, on the golden altar, before the veil of the sanctuary (Exod. xxix. 39 and Num. xxviii. 4). *As the evening sacrifice. Minchah,* which is generally taken for a gratitude offering or unbloody sacrifice. The literal translation of the passage is, "Let my prayer be established for incense before Thy faces; and the lifting up of my hands for the evening oblation."

4. *Let me eat not of their dainties.* This may refer to eating things forbidden by the law, or to the partaking in banquets or feasts in honor of idols.

5. *Let the righteous smite me.* This verse is extremely difficult in the original. The following translation, in which the Syriac, Vulgate, Septuagint, Aethiopic, and Arabic nearly agree, appears to me to be the best: "Let the righteous chastise me in mercy, and instruct me; but let not the oil of the wicked anoint my head. It shall not adorn my head; for still my prayer shall be against their wicked works." The oil of the wicked may here mean his smooth, flattering speeches; and the Psalmist intimates that he would rather suffer the cutting reproof of the righteous than the oily talk of the flatterer.

MATTHEW HENRY

faults; but, says David, "I am not of that mind; it is my sin that has broken my head, that has broken my bones, Ps. li. 8. The reproof is an excellent oil, to cure the bruises sin has given me. It shall not *break my head*, if it may but help to break my heart."

II. David hopes his persecutors will, some time or other, bear to be told of their faults, as he was willing to be told of his (*v.* 6). Some think this refers to the relentings that were in Saul's breast when he said, with tears, *Is this thy voice, my son David?* 1 Sam. xxiv. 16; xxvi. 21.

III. David complains of the great extremity to which he and his friends were reduced (*v.* 7): *Our bones are scattered at the grave's mouth*, out of which they are thrown up, so long have we been dead; and they are as little regarded as chips among the hewers of wood, which are thrown in neglected heaps.

IV. David casts himself upon God, and depends upon him for deliverance: "*But my eyes are unto thee* (*v.* 8). From thee I expect relief, bad as things are, and in *thee is my trust*."

JAMIESON, FAUSSET, BROWN

ADAM CLARKE

6. *When their judges are overthrown in stony places.* "In the hands of the rock." *They shall hear my words; for they are sweet.* Some think there is here an allusion to David's generous treatment of Saul in the cave of En-gedi, and afterwards at the hill of Hachilah, in this verse, which might be translated: "Their judges have been dismissed in the rocky places; and have heard my words, that they were sweet."

PSALM 142

MATTHEW HENRY

Maschil of David. A prayer when he was in the cave.

Verses 1–3

Whether it was in the cave of *Adullam*, or that of *Engedi*, that David prayed this prayer, is not material; it is plain that he was in distress. When he durst not stretch forth his hands against his prince, he lifted them up to his God. There is no cave so deep, so dark, but we may out of it send up our souls in prayer, to God. He calls this prayer *Maschil—a psalm of instruction*, because of the good lessons he had himself learnt in the cave on his knees.

I. How David complained to God, *v.* 1, 2. When the danger was over he was not ashamed to own (as great spirits sometimes are) the fright he had been in. Let not men think it any disparagement to them, when they are in affliction, to cry to God, and to cry like children to their parents when anything frightens them. *He cried unto the Lord with his voice*, with the voice of his mind (so some think), for, being hidden in the cave, he durst not speak with an audible voice, lest that should betray him; but mental prayer is vocal to God, and he hears the groanings which cannot, or dare not, be uttered, Rom. viii. 26. *I showed before him my trouble.* As one that put a confidence in God he unbosomed himself to him and then cheerfully left it with him. We are apt to show our trouble too much to ourselves, aggravating it, and poring upon it, whereas by showing it to God we might cast the care upon him who careth for us.

II. What he complained of: "*In the way wherein I walked*, suspecting no danger, *have they privily laid a snare for me*, to entrap me." Saul gave Michal his daughter to David on purpose that she might be *a snare to him*, 1 Sam. xviii. 21.

III. What comforted him in the midst of these complaints (*v.* 3): "*When my spirit was overwhelmed within me*, and ready to sink under the burden of grief and fear, *then thou knewest my path*, that is, then it was a pleasure to me to think that thou knewest it. Thou knewest it, that is, thou didst protect, preserve, and secure it," Ps. xxi. 7; Deut. ii. 7.

Verses 4–7

He was disowned and deserted by his friends, *v.* 4. When he was made an outlaw, then *no man would know him*, but everybody was shy of him. He looked *on his right hand* for an advocate (cix. 31), but, since Jonathan's appearing for him had like to have cost him his life, nobody was willing to venture in defence of his innocency. How many good men have been deceived by such swallow-friends, who are gone when winter comes! Herein he was a type of Christ, who was forsaken of all men, even of his own disciples, and trod the wine-press alone. David tells us what he said to God in the cave: "*Thou art my refuge and my portion in the land of the living.* The cave I am in is but a poor refuge. Lord, *thy name* is the *strong tower* that *I run into*. Thou art *my refuge*, in whom alone I shall think myself safe." Those who in sincerity take the Lord for their God shall find him all-sufficient and they may humbly claim their interest: "*Lord, thou art my refuge in the land of the living*, that is, while I live and have my being, whether in this world or in a better." He addressed himself to God (*v.* 6, 7): "Lord, *deliver me from my persecutors*, either tie their hands or turn their hearts, break their power or blast their projects, restrain them or rescue me, *for they are stronger than I.* Lord, *bring my soul out of prison*, not only bring me safe out of this cave, but bring me out of all my perplexities."

JAMIESON, FAUSSET, BROWN

Vss. 1-7. *Maschil*—(cf. Ps. 32, title). *When he was in the cave*, either of Adullam (I Sam. 22:1), or En-gedi (I Sam. 24:3). This does not mean that the Psalm was composed *in the cave*, but that the precarious mode of life, of which his refuge in caves was a striking illustration, occasioned the complaint, which constitutes the first part of the Psalm and furnishes the reason for the prayer with which it concludes, and which, as the prominent characteristic, gives its name.

1. with my voice—audibly, because earnestly.

(Cf. Ps. 62:8.) **complaint**—or, a sad musing.

3. **thou knewest . . . path**—The appeal is indicative of conscious innocence; knowest it to be right, and that my affliction is owing to the snares of enemies, and is not deserved (cf. Ps. 42:4; 61:2).

4. Utter desolation is meant. **right hand**—the place of a protector (Ps. 110:5). **cared for**—lit., "sought after," to do good.

5. (Cf. Ps. 31:14; 62:7.)

6. (Cf. Ps. 17:1.)

7. (Cf. Ps. 25:17.) **that I may praise**—lit., "for praising," or that Thy name may be praised, i.e., by the righteous, who shall surround me with sympathizing joy (Ps. 35:27).

ADAM CLARKE

The title says, "An Instruction of David," or a Psalm of David giving instruction; "A Prayer when he was in the cave." David was twice in great peril in caves: (1) At the cave of Adullam, when he fled from Achish, king of Gath, 1 Samuel xxii; (2) When he was in the cave of En-gedi, where he had taken refuge from the pursuit of Saul; and the latter, without knowing that David was in it, had gone into it on some necessary occasion, 1 Samuel xxiv. If the inscription can be depended on, the cave of En-gedi is the most likely of the two, for the scene laid here.

3. *Then thou knewest my path.* When Saul and his army were about the cave in which I was hidden, *thou knewest my path*—that I had then no way of escape but by miracle; but Thou didst not permit them to know that I was wholly in their power.

7. *Bring my soul out of prison.* Bring *naphshi*, "my life," out of this cave in which it is now imprisoned, Saul and his men being in possession of the entrance. *The righteous shall compass me about.* They "shall crown me"; perhaps meaning that the pious Jews, on the death of Saul, would cheerfully join together to make him king, being convinced that God, by His bountiful dealings with him, intended that it should be so.

MATTHEW HENRY

PSALM 143

A psalm of David.

Verses 1–6

I. David is a suppliant to his God, an appellant against his persecutors, and he begs that God will give judgment upon it, in his faithfulness as the Judge of right and wrong. We have no righteousness of our own to plead, and therefore must plead God's righteousness, the word of promise which he has freely given us and caused us to hope in.

II. He humbly begs not to be proceeded against in strict justice, *v.* 2. He seems here, if not to correct, yet to explain, his plea (*v.* 1), Deliver me *in thy righteousness*; "I mean," he says, "the righteous promises of the gospel, not the righteous threatenings of the law." His petition is, "*Enter not into judgment with thy servant;* do not deal with me in strict justice, as I deserve to be dealt with." David, before he prays for the removal of his trouble, prays for the pardon of his sin, and depends upon mere mercy for it.

III. He complains of his enemies (*v.* 3): "Saul, that great enemy, *has persecuted my soul,* sought my life, with a restless malice. He has forced me to *dwell in darkness,* not only in dark caves, but in dark thoughts and apprehensions, in the clouds of melancholy, *as* helpless, and hopeless as *those that have been long dead.* Lord, let me find mercy with thee, for I find no mercy with men."

IV. He bemoans the oppression of his mind, occasioned by his outward troubles (*v.* 4): *Therefore is my spirit* overpowered and *overwhelmed within me.*

V. He applies himself to the use of proper means for the relief of his troubled spirit. If he can keep possession of nothing else, he will do what he can to keep possession of his own soul and to preserve his inward peace. He looks back, and *remembers the days of old* (*v.* 5), God's former appearances for his afflicted people and for him in particular. He looks round, and takes notice of the works of God in the visible creation, and the providential government of the world: *I meditate on all thy works. I muse on,* or (as some read it) *I discourse of, the* operation *of thy hands,* how great, how good, it is! The more we consider the power of God the less we shall fear the face or force of man, Isa. li, 12, 13. He looks up with earnest desires towards God and his favour (*v.* 6): *I stretch forth my hands unto thee. My soul thirsteth after thee; it is to thee* (so the word is), entire for thee, intent on thee; it is *as a thirsty land,* which, being parched with excessive heat, gapes for rain.

Verses 7–12

Three things David here prays for:—

I. The manifestations of God's favour towards him. He dreads God's frowns: "Lord, *hide not thy face from me.*" Disconsolate saints have sometimes cried out of the wrath of God, as if they had been damned sinners, Job vi. 4; Ps. lxxxviii. 6. He entreats God's favour (*v.* 8): *Cause me to hear thy lovingkindness in the morning.* God speaks to us by his word and by his providence, and in both we should desire and endeavour to *hear his lovingkindness* (cvii. 43).

II. The operations of God's grace in him. *Cause me to know the way wherein I should walk.* A good man does not ask what is the way in which he must walk, or in which is the most pleasant walking, but what is the right way, the way in which he should walk. He pleads, "*I lift up my soul unto thee,* to be moulded and fashioned according to thy will." "*Teach me to do thy will,* not only show me what thy will is, but teach me how to do it." *Lead me into the land of uprightness,* into a settled course of holy living, which will lead to heaven. We cannot find the way that will bring us to that land unless God show us, nor go in that way unless he take us by the hand and lead us, as we lead those that are weak, or lame, or timorous, or dim-sighted. The plea is, "*Thy Spirit is good,* and able to make me good," good and willing to help those that are at a loss. *Let thy good Spirit lead me,* so some read it. He prays that he might be enlivened to do his will (*v.* 11): "*Quicken me, O Lord!* quicken my graces, that they may be active—quicken my devotions, that they may be lively."

III. The appearance of God's providence for him (*v.* 9): "*Deliver me, O Lord! from my enemies,* that they may not have their will against me; *for I flee unto thee to hide me.*" He prays: "Deliver me from my outward trouble, from the trouble of my soul, the trouble that threatens to overwhelm my spirit."

JAMIESON, FAUSSET, BROWN

PSALM 143

Vss. 1-12. In structure and style, like the preceding (Psalms 104-142), this Psalm is clearly evinced to be David's. It is a prayer for pardon, and for relief from enemies; afflictions, as usual, producing confession and penitence.

1. in thy faithfulnes . . . and . . . righteousness—or, God's regard to the claims which He has permitted His people to make in His covenant. **2. enter . . . judgment**—deal not in strict justice. **shall no . . . justified**—or, is no man justified, or innocent (Job 14: 3; Rom. 3:20).

3, 4. The exciting reason for his prayer—his afflictions—led to confession as just made: he now makes the complaint. **as those that have been long dead**—deprived of life's comforts (cf. Ps. 40:15; 88:3-6).

5, 6. The distress is aggravated by the contrast of former comfort (Ps. 22: 3-5), for whose return he longs.

a thirsty land—which needs rain, as did his spirit God's gracious visits (Ps. 28:1; 89:17).

7. spirit faileth—is exhausted.

8. (Cf. Ps. 25:1-4; 59;16). **the way . . . walk**—i.e., the way of safety and righteousness (Ps. 142:3-6).

10. (Cf. Ps. 5:8; 27:11.) **land of uprightness**—lit., "an even land" (Ps. 26:12).

11. (Cf. Ps. 23:3; 119:156). **12.** God's mercy to His people is often wrath to His and their enemies (cf. Ps. 31:17). **thy servant**—as chosen to be such, entitled to divine regard.

9. (Cf. Ps. 31:15-20.)

ADAM CLARKE

PSALM 143

The Hebrew and all the versions attribute this psalm to David; and the Vulgate, Septuagint, Aethiopic, and Arabic state that it was composed on the rebellion of his son Absalom. Nor is there anything in the psalm that positively disagrees with this inscription. This is the last of the seven psalms styled "penitential."

3. *He hath made me to dwell in darkness.* Literally, "in dark places." This may be understood of David's taking refuge in caves and dens of the earth, to escape from his persecuting son.

6. *I stretch forth my hands.* This is a natural action. All in distress, or under the influence of eager desire, naturally extend their hands and arms, as if to catch at help and obtain succor. *As a thirsty land,* parched and burned by the sun, longs for rain, so does my thirsty soul for the living God.

7. *Hear me speedily.* "Make haste" to answer me. A few hours, and my state may be irretrievable. In a short time my unnatural son may put an end to my life.

8. *Cause me to hear thy lovingkindness in the morning.* This petition was probably offered in the night season. David had dispatched his messengers in all directions, and prays to God that he might by the morning get some good news. *Cause me to know the way wherein I should walk.* Absalom and his partisans are in possession of all the country. I know not in what direction to go, that I may not fall in with them; point out by Thy especial providence the path I should take.

10. *Teach me to do thy will.* "Thy pleasure." To be found doing the will of God is the only safe state for man.

MATTHEW HENRY

PSALM 144

A psalm of David.

Verses 1–8

I. David acknowledges his dependence upon God and his obligations to him, *v.* 1, 2. *Blessed be the Lord my rock* (*v.* 1), *my goodness my fortress.* He multiplies words to express the satisfaction he had in God. "He is *my strength*, on whom I stay. *My goodness*, not only good to me, but the author of all the goodness that is in me, and *from whom comes every good and perfect gift.*" David had formerly sheltered himself in strongholds at En-gedi (1 Sam. xxiii. 29), which perhaps were natural fastnesses. He had lately made himself master of the stronghold of Zion, which was fortified by art, and he *dwelt in the fort* (2 Sam. v. 7, 9), but he depends not on these. "Lord," says he, "thou art *my fortress* and *my high tower. My shield*, not only *my fortress* at home, but *my shield* abroad in the field of battle." Wherever a believer goes he carries his protection along with him. He was bred a shepherd, and seems not to have been designed by his parents or himself for anything more. But God had made him a soldier. His hands had been used to the crook and his fingers to the harp, but God *taught his hands to war and his fingers to fight*, because he designed him for Israel's champion. God had made him a sovereign prince, had taught him to wield the sceptre as well as the sword. He *subdueth my people under me.*

II. He admires God's condescension to man and to himself in particular (*v.* 3, 4): "*Lord, what is man*, what a poor little thing is he, *that thou takest knowledge of him, that thou makest account of him.*" The meanness and mortality of man, notwithstanding the dignity put upon him (*v.* 4): *Man is like to vanity;* so frail is he, so weak, so helpless, compassed about with so many infirmities, and his continuance here so very short and uncertain, that he is as like as may be to vanity itself.

III. He begs of God to give him success against the enemies that invaded him, *v.* 5–8. He does not specify who they were that he was in fear of, but says, *Scatter them, destroy them.* But afterwards he describes them (*v.* 7, 8): "They are *strange children*, Philistines, bad neighbours to Israel. One cannot take their word, for their *mouth speaketh vanity*; nay, if they give their hand upon it, or offer their hand to help you, there is no trusting them; for *their right hand is a right hand of falsehood.*" David prays that God would appear. "*Bow thy heavens, O Lord!* and make it evident that they are indeed thine, and that thou art the Lord of them, Isa. lxiv. 1. *Touch the mountains*, our strong and stately enemies, *and* let them *smoke.* Show thyself as thou didst upon Mount Sinai."

Verses 9–15

In this latter part of the psalm as in the former; David first gives glory to God and then begs mercy from him.

I. He praises God for the experiences he had had of his goodness to him, *v.* 9, 10. In the midst of his complaints concerning the power and treachery of his enemies, here is a holy exultation in his God: *I will sing a new song to thee, O God!* a song of praise for new mercies. He tells us what this new song shall be (*v.* 10): *It is he that giveth salvation unto kings.* Kings are the protectors of their people, but it is God that is *their* protector. How much service do they owe him then with their power who gives them all their salvations! He has engaged to give salvation to those kings that are his subjects and rule for him; witness the great things he had done for *David his servant.* This may refer to Christ the Son of David, and then it is a new song indeed, a New Testament song.

II. He prays for the continuance of God's favour.

1. That he might be delivered from the public enemies, *v.* 11. Here he repeats his prayer and plea, *v.* 7, 8.

2. That he might see the public peace and prosperity: "Lord, let us have victory, that we may have quietness, which we shall never have while our enemies have it in their power to do us mischief." David desired for his people (*v.* 12): "*That our sons and our daughters may be* in all respects such as we could wish." It is desirable to see *our daughters as cornerstones*, or corner-pillars, *polished after the similitude of a palace*, or temple. By daughters families are united and connected, to their mutual strength, as the parts of a building are by the cornerstones; and when they are graceful and beautiful both in body and mind they are then polished after the similitude of a nice structure. When we see our daughters well-established and stayed with wisdom and discretion—when we see them by faith united to Christ—

JAMIESON, FAUSSET, BROWN

PSALM 144

Vss. 1-15. David's praise of God as his all-sufficient help is enhanced by a recognition of the intrinsic worthlessness of man. Confidently imploring God's interposition against his enemies, he breaks forth into praise and joyful anticipations of the prosperity of his kingdom, when freed from vain and wicked men.

F. B. MEYER:

"My. . ." (144:1, 2). Notice that repeated *my.* David had learned that nothing can take the place of personal dealings with God. Surely he had realized the fulfillment of his own thoughts about dwelling in the house of the Lord all the days of his life and beholding his beauty. There is a great fear lest many of God's most earnest and devoted children may be losing sight of Jesus in these active days. We allow our work for Christ, our doctrines about Him, and our rules for becoming like Him to intercept our view of Him. Too seldom do we get so near Him as to be able to talk to Him face to face; or pile word on word in our ineffectual effort to tell Him what we think of Him. One who loved much sang:

"Jesus, Jesus, dearest Lord,
Forgive me if I say
For very love, thy dearest name,
A thousand times a day."

After all, it is not thoughts about Christ but Christ himself that we all need. To know Him in all the various aspects of his character, as Loving-kindness, Fortress, Shield, and Conqueror! Jesus can be the supply of your every need; and as the days pass, you will probably find yourself put into situations which will force you to discover in Him some new aspect, some fresh characteristics, something that would never have appeared to view, till the awful exigency had arisen. Then put out your hand and say *my.*

Always distinguish between the words attain and obtain. We can never earn his gracious help, either by prayer, or service; but we may claim, appropriate, and take. Learn to put your hand on all spiritual blessings in Christ, and say, *mine.*
—*Great Verses Through the Bible*

ADAM CLARKE

PSALM 144

The Hebrew, and all the versions, attribute this psalm to David. Calmet thinks, and with much probability, that it was composed by David after the death of Absalom, and the restoration of the kingdom to peace and tranquility. From a collation of this with Psalm xviii, of which it appears to be an abridgment, preserving the same ideas and the same forms of expression, there can be no doubt of both having proceeded from the same pen, and that David was the author.

2. *Who subdueth my people.* Who has once more reduced the nation to a state of loyal obedience. This may refer to the peace after the rebellion of Absalom.

4. *Man is like to vanity.* Literally, "Adam is like to Abel," exposed to the same miseries, accidents, and murderers; for in millions of cases the hands of brothers are lifted up to shed the blood of brothers.

9. *I will sing a new song.* A song of peculiar excellence. I will pour forth all my gratitude, and all my skill, on its composition. See Ps. xxxiii. 2-3.

MATTHEW HENRY

when we see them purified and consecrated to God as living temples, we think ourselves happy in them. He prays for a growing estate with a growing family. *First*, That their storehouses might be well-replenished with the fruits and products of the earth: that, having abundance, we may be thankful to God, generous to our friends, and charitable to the poor. *Secondly*, That their flocks might greatly increase: *That our sheep may bring forth thousands, and ten thousands, in our* folds. Much of the wealth of their country consisted in their flocks. *Thirdly*, That their beasts designed for service might be fit for it: *That our oxen may be strong to labour* in the plough. "Let not our enemies break in upon us; let us not have occasion to march out against them." War brings with it abundance of mischiefs, whether it be offensive or defensive. Let there be no oppression nor faction—*no complaining in our streets*, that the people may have no cause to complain either of their government or of one another. It is desirable thus to dwell in quiet habitations. His reflection upon this description of the prosperity of the nation, which he so much desired (*v.* 15): *Happy are the people that are in such a case* (but it is seldom so, and never long so), *yea, happy are the people whose God is the Lord.*

JAMIESON, FAUSSET, BROWN

CHARLES H. SPURGEON:

"Yea, happy is that people, whose God is the Lord" (v. 15). This comes in as an explanation of their prosperity. Under the Old Testament Israel had present earthly rewards for obedience; when Jehovah was their God they were a nation enriched and flourishing. This sentence is also a sort of correction of all that had gone before, as if the poet would say, "All these temporal gifts are a part of happiness, but still the heart and soul of happiness lies in the people being right with God, and having a full possession of him. Those who worship the happy God become a happy people." Then if we have not temporal mercies literally, we have something better: if we have not the silver of the earth, we have the gold of heaven, which is better still.
—*The Treasury of David*

ADAM CLARKE

13. *That our garners*, etc. "Our garners are full." These are not prayers put up by David for such blessings, but assertions that such blessings were actually in possession. All these expressions should be understood in the present tense. *Ten thousands in our streets.* "In our pens or sheep-walks."

14. *Our oxen may be strong to labour.* We have not only an abundance of cattle, but they are of the most strong and vigorous breed. *No breaking in.* So well-ordered is the police of the kingdom that there are no depredations, no robbers, housebreakers, or marauding parties in the land.

15. *Happy is that people.* "Oh, how happy are the people!"

MATTHEW HENRY

PSALM 145

David's *psalm* of praise.

Verses 1-9

The entitling of this *David's psalm of praise* may intimate that he took a particular pleasure in it and sung it often; it was his companion wherever he went. In this former part of the psalm God's glorious attributes are praised, as, in the latter part of the psalm, his kingdom and the administration of it.

I. Who shall be employed in giving glory to God. Whatever others do, the psalmist will himself be much in praising God. It was his duty; it was his delight. He would give glory to God, not only in his solemn devotions, but in his common conversation. He will be constant to this work: *Every day will I bless thee.* No day must pass, though ever so busy a day, though ever so sorrowful a day, without praising God. God is every day blessing us, doing well for us; there is therefore reason that we should be every day blessing him, speaking well of him. He doubts not but others also would be forward to this work. David's zeal would provoke many, and it has done so. They shall keep it up in an uninterrupted succession (*v.* 4): "*One generation shall praise thy works to another.*"

II. What we must give to God the glory of: his greatness and his great works. We must declare, *Great is the Lord, and*, if great, then *greatly to be praised*, with all that is within us, to the utmost of our power. His greatness indeed cannot be comprehended. When we cannot, by searching, find the bottom, we must sit down at the brink, and adore the depth, Rom. xi. 33. We must see God acting and working in all the affairs of this lower world.

His goodness is his glory, Exod. xxxiii. 19. *They shall abundantly utter the memory of thy great goodness, v.* 7. It can never be exhausted, for he ever will be as rich in mercy as he ever was. But, whenever we utter God's great goodness, we must not forget, at the same time, to *sing of his righteousness*; for, as he is gracious in rewarding those that serve him faithfully, so he is righteous in punishing those that rebel against him. There is a fountain of goodness in God's nature (*v.* 8): *The Lord is gracious* to those that serve him; he is *full of compassion* to those that need him, *slow to anger* to those that have offended him, *and of great mercy* to all that seek him and sue to him. He is ready to give, and ready to forgive.

Verse 10-21

The greatness and goodness of God were celebrated in the former part of the psalm; in these verses we are taught to give him *the glory of his kingdom*, in the administration of which his greatness and goodness shine so clearly, so very brightly. Praise is expected (*v.* 10): *All* God's *works shall praise* him. All God's works do praise him, as the beautiful building praises the builder or the well-drawn picture praises the painter; but the saints bless him as the children of prudent tender parents rise up and call them blessed.

They shall speak of thy kingdom. His kingdom is great indeed, for all the kings and kingdoms of the earth are under his control. The courts of Solomon and Ahasuerus were magnificent; but, compared with the glorious majesty of God's kingdom, they were but as glow-worms to the sun.

JAMIESON, FAUSSET, BROWN

PSALM 145

Vss. 1-21. A Psalm of praise to God for His mighty, righteous, and gracious government of all men, and of His humble and suffering people in particular.

1, 2. (Cf. Ps. 30:1.) **bless thy name**—celebrate Thy perfections (Ps. 5:11). God is addressed as king, alluding to His government of men.

4. **shall declare**—lit., "they shall declare," i.e., all generations. **5. I will speak**—or, muse (Ps. 77:12; 119:15). **thy wondrous works**—or, words of thy wonders, i.e., which described them (Ps. 105: 27, *Margin*. **6. terrible acts**—which produce dread or fear.

3. (Cf. Ps. 18:3; 48:1.) **greatness**—as displayed in His works.

7. **memory**—(Ps. 6:5), remembrance, or what causes to be remembered.

righteousness—as in Psalm 143:1, goodness according to covenant engagement.

8, 9. (Cf. 103:8; 111:4.) **over all . . .**—rests on all His works.

10. **bless**—as in vs. 1, to praise with reverence, more than merely to praise.

ADAM CLARKE

PSALM 145

This psalm is attributed to David by the Hebrew and all the versions. It is the last of the acrostic psalms, and should contain twenty-two verses, as answering to the twenty-two letters of the Hebrew alphabet. But the verse between the thirteenth and fourteenth, beginning with the letter *nun*, is lost out of the present Hebrew copies; but a translation of it is found in the Syriac, Septuagint, Vulgate, Aethiopic, Arabic, and Anglo-Saxon. It is an incomparable psalm of praise.

4. *One generation.* Thy creating and redeeming acts are recorded in Thy word; but Thy wondrous providential dealings with mankind must be handed down by tradition, from generation to generation, for they are in continual occurrence, and consequently innumerable.

3. *His greatness is unsearchable.* Literally, "To His mightinesses there is no investigation." All in God is unlimited and eternal.

10. *All thy works shall praise thee.* The God who is good to all. *Thy saints. Chasideycha*, "Thy compassionate ones"; those who are partakers of Thy great mercy, v. 8.

MATTHEW HENRY

When *they speak of the glory of* God's *kingdom* they must *talk of* his *power* (*v.* 11); and, as a proof of it, let them *make known his mighty acts* (*v.* 12). Note the perpetuity of it, *v.* 13. The thrones of princes totter, and the flowers of their crowns wither, monarchies come to an end; but, Lord, *thy kingdom is an everlasting kingdom.* His royal style and title are, *The Lord God, gracious and merciful;* and his government answers to his title. The goodness of God appears in what he does, for all the creatures in general (*v.* 15, 16): He *provides food for all flesh.* All the creatures live upon God, and, as they had their being from him at first, so on him they depend for the continuance of it. The inferior creatures indeed have not the knowledge of God, nor are capable of it, and yet they are said to *wait upon God,* because they seek their food according to the instinct which the God of nature has put into them. *Thou givest them their meat in due season.* The children of men, in particular, he governs as reasonable creatures. In all the acts of government he is just, injurious to none, but administering justice to all. *The ways of the Lord are equal,* though ours are unequal. He supports those that are sinking, and it is his honour to help the weak, *v.* 14. He *upholds all that fall,* in that, though they fall, they are not utterly cast down. If those who were *bowed down* by oppression and affliction are *raised up,* it was God that raised them. And, with respect to all those *that are heavy-laden* under the burden of sin, if they come to Christ by faith, he will ease them, he will raise them. He is very ready to hear and answer the prayers of his people, *v.* 18, 19. In this appears the grace of his kingdom, that his subjects have not only liberty, of petitioning but all the encouragement that can be to petition. It was said (*v.* 16) that he *satisfies the desire of every living thing,* much more *will he fulfil the desire of those that fear him;* for he that feeds his birds will not starve his babes. *He will hear their call and will save them;* that is hearing them to purpose, as he heard David (that is, saved him) *from the horn of the unicorn,* xxii. 21. He will hear and help us if we worship and serve him with a holy awe of him. In all devotions inward impressions must be answerable to the outward expressions, else they are not performed in truth. He takes those under his special protection who have confidence in him (*v.* 20): *The Lord preserves all those that love him.* The psalmist concludes (*v.* 21): *My mouth shall speak the praise of the Lord.* When we have said what we can, in praising God, still there is more to be said. As the end of one mercy is the beginning of another, so should the end of one thanksgiving be. While I have breath to draw, my mouth shall still speak God's praises. *Let all flesh, all mankind, bless his holy name for ever and ever.*

JAMIESON, FAUSSET, BROWN

11, 12. The declaration of God's glory is for the extension of His knowledge and perfections in the world. **13.** (Cf. Dan. 4:3, 34.)

15, 16, eyes of . . . thee—or, look with expecting faith (Ps. 104:27, 28).

14. (Cf. Ps. 37:17; 54:4.)

17. holy . . . works—lit., "merciful" or "kind, goodness" (Ps. 144:2) is the corresponding noun. **righteous**—in a similar relation of meaning to "righteousness" (vs. 7). **18, 19.** (Cf. Ps. 34:7, 10.)

20. Those who fear Him (vs. 19) are those who are here said to love Him. **21.** (Cf. Ps. 23:21.) **all flesh**—(Ps. 65:2).

The Psalm ends, as it began, with ascriptions of praise, in which the pious will ever delight to join.

ADAM CLARKE

13. *Thy dominion endureth.* There is neither age nor people in and over which God does not manifest His benignly ruling power. As the above verse begins with the letter *mem,* the next in the order of the alphabet should begin with *nun;* but that verse is totally wanting. To say it never was in is false, because the alphabet is not complete without it; and it is an unanswerable argument to prove the careless manner in which the Jews have preserved the divine records. One MS., now in Trinity College, Dublin, has it thus, I suppose by correction, in the bottom of the page: "The Lord is faithful in all his words; and merciful in all his works." The Septuagint and Vulgate are the same with the Hebrew given above.

15. *The eyes of all wait upon thee.* What a fine figure! God is here represented as the universal Father, providing food for every living creature. *In due season.* The kind of food that is suited to every animal, and to all the stages of life in each animal.

16. *Thou openest thine hand.* What a hand is this that holds in it all the food that meets the desires and necessities of the universe of creatures!

14. *The Lord upholdeth all that fall.* "The falling," or those who are not able to keep their feet; the weak. He shores them up; he is their Prop.

17. *The Lord is righteous.* It was the similarity of this to the omitted verse, which should have been the fourteenth, that caused it to be omitted.

20. *The Lord preserveth.* He is the Keeper of all them that love Him. *But all the wicked will he destroy.* There is something curious in the *shomer,* the Keeper or Guardian of the pious; He is *shamid,* the Destroyer of the wicked. The first word implies. He is continually keeping them; the second, that He *causes* the others to be destroyed.

MATTHEW HENRY — PSALM 146

Verses 1–4

David, himself a prince, considered his dignity as so far from excusing him from praise that it rather obliged him to lead in it; therefore he stirred up himself to it: *Praise the Lord, O my soul!* and he resolved to abide by it: "*I* will praise him with my heart, *I will sing praises* to him as *the Lord,* infinitely blessed and glorious in himself, and as *my God,* in covenant with me." It might be thought that he himself, having been so great a blessing to his country, should be adored, according to the usage of the heathen nations, who deified their heroes, that they should all come and *trust in his shadow.* "No," says David, "*Put not your trust in princes* (*v.* 3), not in me, not in any other; do not repose your confidence in them. Be not too sure of their constancy and fidelity; it is possible they may both change their minds and break their words." We cannot be sure of their continuance. Suppose he has it in his power to help us while he lives, yet he may be suddenly taken off when we expect most from him (*v.* 4). Princes are mortal, as well as other men, and therefore we cannot have that assurance of help from them which we may have from that Potentate who hath immortality.

Verses 5–10

The psalmist encourages us to put our confidence in God: *Happy is he that has the God of Jacob for his help, whose hope is in the Lord his God.* Those shall have God for their help who take him for their God, and serve and worship him, have their hope in him, and live a life of dependence upon him. Every believer may look upon him as the God of Jacob, of the church in general, and therefore may expect relief from him, in reference to public distresses, and as his God in particular, and therefore may depend upon him in all personal wants and straits.

JAMIESON, FAUSSET, BROWN — PSALM 146

Vss. 1-10. An exhortation to praise God, who, by the gracious and faithful exercise of His power in goodness to the needy, is alone worthy of implicit trust.

ADAM CLARKE — PSALM 146

This is the first of the psalms called *Hallelujah* Psalms, of which there are five, and which conclude the book. No author's name is prefixed to this, in either the Hebrew or Chaldee. It was probably written after the Captivity, and may refer to the time when Cyrus, prejudiced by the enemies of the Jews, withdrew his order for the rebuilding of the walls of Jerusalem, to which revocation of the royal edict the third verse may refer: *Put not your trust in princes.*

F. B. MEYER:

"In that very day his thoughts perish" (146:4). Who among us has not bitterly reproached himself for the evanescence of noble resolution—the dying down of earnest purpose? Too often they have been like the early dew and the morning cloud. In the day in which we made them our purposes they have perished.

What is the remedy? It is suggested in those memorable words of Jesus, "The water that I shall give him shall become in him a well of water, springing up unto eternal life." When once Jesus has been allowed to do his chosen work in the soul, He opens a subterranean passage to the reservoirs of eternity, along and through which the supplies from God's own heart begin to enter and rise up within the soul. Abide in Him, and the sap of his life will suggest, renew, and reinforce, the purposes of the holy life. Rise up, O well, for ever rise, within hearts that desire a fixed purpose to love God! Infirm of purpose we need never be, while God waits to create in us a steadfast spirit (Ps. 51:10). We must be rooted and grounded in Him. Then will be manifest in us the fruit of the Spirit, which is "love, joy, peace, longsuffering, gentleness, goodness, faith, meekness, self-control" (Gal. 5:22, 23).—*Great Verses Through the Bible*

MATTHEW HENRY

Dr. Hammond quotes one of the rabbis, who says of *v.* 10 that it belongs to the days of the Messiah. And that it does so he thinks will appear by comparing *v.* 7, 8, with the characters Christ gives of the Messiah (Matt. xi. 5, 6), *The blind receive their sight, the lame walk;* and the closing words there, *Blessed is he whosoever shall not be offended in me,* he thinks may very well be supposed to refer to *v.* 5. *The Lord our God* is the *Maker of the world,* and therefore has all power in himself, and the command of the powers of all the creatures (*v.* 6). It is very applicable to Christ, by whom God made the world, and *without whom was not anything made that was made.* It is a great support to faith that the Redeemer of the world is the same that was the Creator of it, and therefore has a goodwill to it. He is a God of inviolable fidelity. Our Lord Jesus is the Amen, *the faithful witness,* as well as *the beginning,* the author and principle, *of the creation of God,* Rev. iii. 14. He is the patron of injured innocency: *He pleads the cause of the oppressed,* and (as we read it) he *executes judgment* for them. The Messiah came to rescue the children of men out of the hands of Satan the great oppressor, and, all judgment being committed to him, the executing of judgment upon persecutors is so among the rest, Jude 15. He is a bountiful benefactor to the necessitous: *He gives food to the hungry;* so God does in an ordinary way for the answering of the cravings of nature; so he has done sometimes in an extraordinary way, as when ravens fed Elijah; so Christ did more than once when he fed thousands miraculously. This encourages us to hope in him as the nourisher of our souls with the bread of life. He is the author of liberty to those that were bound: *The Lord looseth the prisoners.* He brought Israel out of the house of bondage in Egypt and afterwards in Babylon. The miracles Christ wrought, in making the dumb to speak and the deaf to hear with that one word, *Ephphatha—Be opened,* his cleansing lepers, and so discharging them from their confinement, and his raising the dead out of their graves, may all be included in this one of *loosing the prisoners;* and we may take encouragement from those to hope in him for that spiritual liberty which he came to proclaim, Isa. lxi. 1, 2. He gives sight to those that have been long deprived of it: *The Lord can open the eyes of the blind,* and has often given to his afflicted people to see that comfort which before they were not aware of; witness Gen. xxi. 19, and the prophet's servant, 2 Kings vi. 17. But this has special reference to Christ; for *since the world began was it not heard that any man opened the eyes of one that was born blind* till Christ did it (John ix. 32) and thereby encouraged us to hope in him for spiritual illumination. He *raises those that are bowed down* by supporting them under their burdens, and, in due time, removing their burdens. This was literally performed by Christ when he made a poor woman straight that had been *bowed together, and could in no wise lift up herself* (Luke xiii. 12); and he still does it by his grace, giving rest to those that were weary and heavily laden, and raising up with his comforts those that were humbled and cast down. *The Lord loveth the righteous.* He has a tender concern for those that stand in special need of his care: *The Lord preserves the strangers.* It is the glory of the Messiah that he will subvert all the counsels of hell and earth that militate against his church. His kingdom shall continue through all the revolutions of time, to the utmost ages of eternity, *v.* 10. Let *this* encourage us to trust in God at all times that *the Lord shall reign for ever,* in spite of all the malignity of the powers of darkness, *even thy God, O Zion! unto all generations.*

JAMIESON, FAUSSET, BROWN

CHARLES H. SPURGEON:

8. "The Lord openeth the eyes of the blind." Jesus did this very frequently, and hereby proved himself to be Jehovah. He who made the eye can open it, and when he does so it is to his glory. How often is the mental eye closed in moral night! And who can remove this dreary effect of the Fall but the Almighty God? This miracle of grace he has performed in myriads of cases, and it is in each case a theme for loftiest praise. "The Lord raiseth them that are bowed down." This also Jesus did literally, thus doing the work peculiar to God. Jehovah consoles the bereaved, cheers the defeated, solaces the despondent, comforts the despairing. Let those who are bowed to the ground appeal to him, and he will speedily upraise them. "The Lord loveth the righteous." He gives to them the love of complacency, communion, and reward. Bad kings affect the licentious, but Jehovah makes the upright to be his favored ones. This is greatly to his glory. Let those who enjoy the inestimable privilege of his love magnify his name with enthusiastic delight. Loved ones, you must never be absent from the choir! You must never pause from his praise whose infinite love has made you what you are.

9. "The Lord preserveth the strangers." Many monarchs hunted aliens down, or transported them from place to place, or left them as outlaws unworthy of the rights of man; but Jehovah made special laws for their shelter within his domain. In this country the stranger was, a little while ago, looked upon as a vagabond—a kind of wild beast to be avoided if not to be assaulted; and even to this day there are prejudices against foreigners which are contrary to our holy religion. Our God and King is never strange to any of his creatures, and if any are left in a solitary and forlorn condition, he has a special eye to their preservation. "He relieveth the fatherless and widows." These excite his compassion, and he shows it in a practical way by upraising them from their forlorn condition. The Mosaic law made provision for these destitute persons. When the secondary fatherhood is gone the child falls back upon the primary fatherhood of the Creator; when the husband of earth is removed the godly widow casts herself upon the care of her Maker.—*The Treasury of David*

ADAM CLARKE

7. *Which executeth judgment for the oppressed.* For those who suffer by violence or calumny. This may refer to the Israelites, who suffered much by oppression from the Babylonians, and by calumny from the Samaritans, who had prejudiced the king of Persia against them. *Giveth food to the hungry.* No doubt He fed the poor captives by many displays of His peculiar providence. *The Lord looseth the prisoners.* And as He has sustained you so long under your captivity, so will He bring you out of it.

9. *Preserveth the strangers.* He has preserved you strangers in a strange land, where you have been in captivity for seventy years; and though in an enemy's country, He has provided for the widows and orphans as amply as if He had been in the Promised Land. *The way of the wicked he turneth upside down.* He "subverts, turns aside."

PSALM 147

Verses 1–11

I. The duty of praise is recommended to us. We are called to it again and again: *Praise you the Lord* (*v.* 1), and again (*v.* 7), *Sing unto the Lord with thanksgiving, sing praise upon the harp to our God* (let all our praises be directed to him and centre in him), *for it is good* to do so; it is our duty, and therefore good in itself. In giving honour to God we really do ourselves a great deal of honour.

II. God is the proper object of our praises. Is Jerusalem to be raised out of small beginnings? Is it to be recovered out of its ruins? In both cases, *The Lord builds up Jerusalem.* The gospel-church, the Jerusalem that is from above, is of his building. Are any of his people outcasts? Have they made themselves so by their own folly? He gathers them by giving them repentance and bringing them again into the communion of saints. They are *broken in heart,* humbled, and troubled, for sin, inwardly

PSALM 147

Vss. 1-20. This and the remaining Psalms have been represented as specially designed to celebrate the rebuilding of Jerusalem (cf. Neh. 6:16; 12:27). They all open and close with the stirring call for praise. This one specially declares God's providential care towards all creatures, and particularly His people.

1. (Cf. Ps. 92:1; 135:3.)

2. (Cf. Ps. 107:3; Isa. 11:12.) **3.** Though applicable to the captive Israelites, this is a general and precious truth.

PSALM 147

This psalm, which is without title in the Hebrew, Chaldee, and Vulgate, is attributed by the other versions to Haggai and Zechariah. It was probably penned after the Captivity, when the Jews were busily employed in rebuilding Jerusalem, as may be gathered from the second and thirteenth verses. It may be necessary to remark that all the versions, except the Chaldee, divide this psalm at the end of the eleventh verse, and begin a new psalm at the twelfth. By this division the numbers of the psalms agree in the versions with the Hebrew; the former having been, till now, one behind.

1. *Praise is comely.* It is decent, befitting, and proper that every intelligent creature should acknowledge the Supreme Being; and as He does nothing but good to the children of men, so they

MATTHEW HENRY

pained at the remembrance of it. Their very hearts are rent, under the sense of the dishonour they have done to God and the injury they have done to themselves by sin. To those whom God heals with the consolations of his Spirit he speaks peace. The stars are innumerable, but *he calleth them all by their names*. They are his servants, he musters them; they come and go at his bidding, and all their motions are under his direction. He mentions this as one instance of many, to show that *great is our Lord and of great power* (he can do what he pleases), and of *his understanding there is no computation.* Man's knowledge is soon drained. But God's knowledge is a depth that can never be fathomed. *The Lord lifts up the meek*, who abase themselves before him, and whom men trample on; but *the wicked*, who conduct themselves insolently towards God and scornfully towards all mankind, who lift themselves in pride and folly, he *casteth down to the ground*. Though he is so great as to command the stars, he is so good as not to forget even the fowls *v.* 8, 9. *He covereth the heaven with clouds.* Clouds look melancholy, and yet without them we could have no rain and consequently no fruit. Thus afflictions, for the present, look black, and dark, and unpleasant, but from these clouds of affliction come those showers that make the harvest to *yield the peaceable fruits of righteousness* (Heb. xii. 11). By the rain which distils on the earth he *makes grass to grow upon the mountains*, even the high mountains, which man neither takes care of nor reaps the benefit of. This grass he *gives* to *the beast* for *his food*, the beast of the mountains which runs wild, which man makes no provision for. And even the *young ravens*, which, being forsaken by their old ones, *cry*, are heard by him, and ways are found to feed them. God will delight to honour, not the strength of armies, but the strength of grace. *He delighteth not in the strength of the horse*, the warhorse, nor in infantry, for he *taketh no pleasure in the legs of a man.* If one king, making war with another king, goes to God to pray for success, it will not avail him to plead, "Lord, I have a gallant army, the horse and foot in good order." But God is pleased to own the strength of grace. The Lord accepts and *takes pleasure* in those that *fear him and that hope in his mercy*. Our fear must save our hope from swelling into presumption, and our hope must save our fear from sinking into despair.

Verses 12–20

Jerusalem, and Zion, the holy city, the holy hill, are here called upon to *praise God*, *v.* 12. Jerusalem and Zion must praise God, 1. For their common safety. They had gates, and kept their gates barred in times of danger; but that would not have been an effectual security to them if God had not *strengthened the bars of their gates* and fortified their fortifications. 2. For the increase of their people. This strengthens the bars of the gates as much as anything. 3. For the public tranquillity, that they were delivered from the terrors and desolations of war: *He makes peace in thy borders*, by putting an end to the wars that were, and preventing the wars that were threatened and feared. 4. For great plenty, the common effect of peace: He *filleth thee with the finest of the wheat*. Canaan abounded with the best wheat (Deut. xxxii. 14) and exported it to the countries abroad, as appears, Ezek. xxvii. 17. The land of Israel was not enriched with precious stones nor spices, but with *the finest of the wheat*, with bread, which strengthens man's heart. He that protects Zion and Jerusalem is that God of power from whom all the powers of nature are derived and on whom they depend. As the world was at first made, so it is still upheld and governed, by a word of almighty power. *God speaks and it is done.* With him are the *treasures of the snow and the hail* (Job xxxviii. 22, 23), and out of these treasures he draws as he pleases. It falls silently, and makes no more noise than the fall of a lock of wool; it covers the earth, and keeps it warm like a fleece of wool, and so promotes its fruitfulness. God can work by contraries, and bring meat out of the eater, can warm the earth with cold snow. When he pleases (*v.* 18) *he sends out his word and melts them;* the frost, the snow, the ice, are all dissolved quickly, in order to which he *causes the wind*, the *south wind, to blow*, and *the waters*, which were frozen, *flow* again as they did before. This thawing word may represent the gospel of Christ, and this thawing wind the Spirit of Christ (for the Spirit is compared to the wind, John iii. 8); both are sent for the melting of frozen souls. Converting grace, like the thaw, softens the heart that was hard, moistens it, and melts it into tears of repentance; it warms good affections, and makes them to flow, which, before, were chilled and stopped up. It is very evident, and yet how it is done is unaccountable:

JAMIESON, FAUSSET, BROWN

4, 5. God's power in nature (Isa. 40: 26-28, and often) is presented as a pledge of His power to help His people. **telleth . . . stars**—what no man can do (Gen. 15:5).

6. That power is put forth for the good of the meek and suffering pious, and confusion of the wicked (Ps. 146:8, 9).

7-9. His providence supplies bountifully the wild animals in their mountain homes. **Sing . . . Lord**—lit., "Answer the Lord," i.e., in grateful praise to His goodness, thus declared in His acts.

10, 11. The advantages afforded, as in war by the strength of the horse or the agility of man, do not incline God to favor any; but those who fear and, of course, trust Him, will obtain His approbation and aid.

12-14. strengthened . . . gates—or, means of defense against invaders,

maketh . . . borders—or, territories (Gen. 23:17; Isa. 54:12).

15-18. God's Word, as a swift messenger, executes His purpose, for with Him to command is to perform (Gen. 1:3; Ps. 33:9), and He brings about the wonders of providence as easily as men cast crumbs. **morsels**—used as to food (Gen. 18:5), perhaps here denotes hail.

ADAM CLARKE

should speak good of His name.

2. *The Lord doth build up.* The Psalmist appears to see the walls rising under his eye, because the outcasts of Israel, those who had been in captivity, are now gathered together to do the work.

3. *He healeth the broken in heart.* "The shivered in heart." From the root *shabar*, "to break in pieces," we have our word "shiver," to break into splinters, into shivers.

4. *He telleth the number of the stars.* He whose knowledge is so exact as to tell every star in heaven can be under no difficulty to find out and collect all the scattered exiles of Israel.

5. *His understanding is infinite.* "To his intelligence there is no number"; though He numbers the stars, His understanding is without number. It is infinite; therefore He can know, as He can do, all things.

6. *The Lord lifteth up the meek.* The humbled, the afflicted.

7. *Sing unto the Lord. Enu*, sing a responsive song, sing in parts, answer one another.

8. *Who covereth the heaven with clouds.* Collects the vapors together, in order to cause it to rain upon the earth. Even the direction of the winds, the collection of the clouds, and the descent of the rain are under the especial management of God. These things form a part of His providential management of the world. *Maketh grass to grow upon the mountains.* After this clause the Vulgate, the Septuagint, Aethiopic, Arabic, and Anglo-Saxon add, "and herb for the service of man." It appears that a hemistich, or half-line, has been lost from the Hebrew text; which, according to the above versions, must have stood thus: as in Ps. civ. 14: "And herbage for the service of mankind."

11. *The Lord taketh pleasure in them that fear him.* That are truly religious. *In those that hope is his mercy.* Even the cry of the penitent is pleasing in the ear of the Lord. With this verse the hundred and forty-sixth psalm ends in all the versions, except the Chaldee. And the hundred and forty-seventh commences with the twelfth verse. I believe these to be two distinct psalms. The subjects of them are not exactly the same, though something similar; and they plainly refer to different periods.

13. *He hath strengthened the bars of thy gates.* He has enabled you to complete the walls of Jerusalem. From the former part of the psalm it appears the walls were then in progress; from this part, they appear to be completed, and provisions to be brought into the city to support its inhabitants.

17. *He casteth forth his ice* (probably hailstones) like crumbs.

18. *He sendeth out his word.* He gives a command; the south wind blows; the thaw takes place; and the ice and snow being liquefied, *the waters flow*, where before they were bound up by the ice.

MATTHEW HENRY

such is the change wrought in the conversion of a soul, when God's word and Spirit are sent to melt it and restore it to itself. Jacob and Israel had God's statutes and judgments among them. They were under his peculiar government; the municipal laws of their nation were of his framing and enacting, and their constitution was a theocracy. They had the benefit of divine revelation; the great things of God's law were written to them. They did not find out God's statutes and judgments of themselves, but *God showed his word unto Jacob*, and by that word he made known to them his *statutes and judgments*. Other nations had plenty of outward good things; some nations were very rich, others had pompous powerful princes and polite literature, but none were blessed with God's statutes and judgments as Israel were. Let *Israel* therefore *praise the Lord* in the observance of these statutes.

PSALM 148

Verses 1–6

We, in this dark and depressed world, know but little of the world of light and exaltation. But this we know,

I. That there is above us a world of blessed angels by whom God is praised, an innumerable company of them. The psalmist has an eye here, *v.* 1, 2, to *the heavens*, to *the heights*. The heavens are the heights, and therefore we must lift up our souls above the world unto God in *the heavens*, and *on things above* we must *set our affections*. It is his delight to think that God is praised *in the heights*. When, in singing this psalm, we call upon the angels to praise God (as we did, ciii. 20), we mean that we desire God may be praised by the ablest hands and in the best manner, that we have a spiritual communion with those that dwell in his house above, and that we have come by faith, and hope, and holy love, to the *innumerable company of angels*, Heb. xii. 22.

II. That there is above us not only an assembly of blessed spirits, but a system of vast bodies too, and those bright ones, in which God is praised. There are the *sun, moon*, and *stars*, which continually, either day or night, present themselves to our view, as looking-glasses, in which we may see a faint shadow (for so I must call it, not a resemblance) of the glory of him that is *the Father of lights, v.* 3. *The heavens of heavens are the Lord's* (cxv. 16) and yet *they cannot contain him*, 1 Kings viii. 27. The Chaldee paraphrase reads it, *Praise him, you heavens of heavens, and you waters that depend on the word of him who is above the heavens. Let them praise the name of the Lord*, that is, let us praise the name of the Lord for them, and observe what constant and fresh matter for praise may be fetched from them. *He commanded* them (great as they are) out of nothing, *and they were created* at a word's speaking. He still upholds and preserves them (*v.* 6): *He hath established them for ever and ever*, that is, to the end of time, a short ever, but it is their ever; they shall last as long as there is occasion for them.

Verses 7–14

Even in this world God is praised: *Praise you the Lord from the earth, v.* 7.

I. Even those creatures that are not dignified with the powers of reason are summoned into this concert, because God may be glorified in them, *v.* 7–10. Let the *dragons* or *whales*, that sport themselves in the mighty waters (civ. 26), dance before the Lord, to his glory. *All deeps*, and their inhabitants, praise God. *Out of the depths* God may be praised. There are fiery meteors; lightning is fire. There are watery meteors, *hail*, and *snow*, and the *vapours* of which they are gendered. There are *stormy winds*; be they ever so strong, so stormy, they *fulfil God's word*; and by *this* Christ showed himself to have a divine power, that he *commanded even the winds and the seas*, and *they obeyed him*. There are *mountains and all hills*, from which we may fetch matter for praise; there are plants, some exalted by their usefulness, as the *fruitful trees*, for the fruits of which God is to be praised, others by their stateliness, as *all cedars*, those *trees of the Lord*, civ. 16. In the animal kingdom we find God glorified, even by the *beasts* that run wild, *and all cattle* that are tame and in the service of man, *v.* 10. Even the *creeping things* have not sunk so low, nor do the *flying fowl* soar so high, as not to be called upon to *praise the Lord*. Much of the wisdom, power, and goodness of the Creator appears in the several capacities and instincts of the creatures, in the provision made for them and the use made of them. Surely we cannot but acknowledge God with wonder and thankfulness.

II. Much more those creatures that are dignified

JAMIESON, FAUSSET, BROWN

19, 20. This mighty ruler and benefactor of heaven and earth is such especially to His chosen people, to whom alone (Deut. 4:32-34) He has made known His will, while others have been left in darkness. Therefore unite in the great hallelujah.

PSALM 148

Vss. 1-14. The scope of this Psalm is the same as that of the preceding.

1. heavens [and] **heights**—are synonymous.

hosts—(cf. Ps. 103:21).

4. heavens of heavens—the very highest. **waters**—clouds, resting above the visible heavens (cf. Gen. 1:7). **5. praise the name**—as representing His perfections.

he commanded—*He* is emphatic, ascribing creation to God alone. **6.** The perpetuity of the frame of nature is, of course, subject to Him who formed it. **a decree . . . pass**—His ordinances respecting them shall not change (Jer. 36:31), or perish (Job 34:20; Ps. 37:36).

7-10. The call on the earth, as opposed to heaven, includes *seas* or *depths*, whose inhabitants the dragon, as one of the largest (cf. on leviathan, Ps. 104:26), is selected to represent. The most destructive and ungovernable agents of inanimate nature are introduced **fulfilling his word**—or, law, may be understood of each. Next the most distinguished productions of the vegetable world. **fruitful trees**—or, trees of fruit, as opposed to forest trees. Wild and domestic, large and small animals are comprehended.

ADAM CLARKE

PSALM 148

This psalm has no title, but by the Syriac it is attributed to Haggai and Zechariah; and the Septuagint and the Aethiopic follow it. As a hymn of praise, this is the most sublime in the whole book.

1. *Praise ye the Lord from the heavens. Min hashshamayim* signifies whatever belongs to the heavens, all their inhabitants; as *min haarets*, v. 7, signifies all that belongs to the earth, all its inhabitants and productions.

3. *Praise ye him, sun and moon.* The meaning of this address and all others to inanimate nature is this: Every work of God's hand partakes so much of His perfections that it requires only to be studied and known in order to show forth the manifold wisdom, power, and goodness of the Creator.

7. *Praise the Lord from the earth.* As, in the first address, he calls upon the heavens and all that belong to them, so here, in this second part, he calls upon the earth and all that belong to it. *Ye dragons. Tanninim*, whales, porpoises, sharks, and sea monsters of all kinds. *And all deeps.* Whatsoever is contained in the sea, the astonishing flux and reflux of the ocean.

9. *Fruitful trees.* Fruit trees of all kinds. *And all cedars.* Every kind of forest tree.

10. *Beasts.* "Wild beasts" of every kind. *All cattle.* All domestic animals.

MATTHEW HENRY

with the powers of reason ought to employ them in praising God: *Kings of the earth and all people, v.* 11, 12. God is to be praised in the order and constitution of kingdoms, the *pars imperans—the part that commands*, and the *pars subdita—the part that is subject: Kings of the earth and all people.* God is to be praised also in the constitution of families, for he is the founder of them; and for all the comfort of relations, the comfort that parents and children, brothers and sisters, have in each other, God is to be praised. Let all manner of persons praise God. Those on whom God has put honour must honour him with it, and the power they are entrusted with puts them in a capacity of bringing more glory to God and doing him more service than others. Yet the praises of the people are expected also. Christ despised not the hosannas of the multitude. *Young men and maidens*, let them turn their mirth into this channel. *Old men* must not think that either the gravity or the infirmity of their age will excuse them from it; *and children* too must begin betimes to praise God. *His glory is above* both *the earth and the heaven*, and let all the inhabitants both of earth and heaven praise him and yet acknowledge his name to be exalted *far above all blessing and praise.*

III. Most of all his own people, who are dignified with peculiar privileges, must in a peculiar manner give glory to him, *v.* 14. They had him *nigh to them in all that which they called upon him for.* This blessing has now come upon the Gentiles, through Christ, for those that *were afar off are* by *his blood made nigh*, Eph. ii. 13. Let those whom God honours honour him.

JAMIESON, FAUSSET, BROWN

11, 12. Next all rational beings, from the highest in rank to little children. **princes**—or, military leaders.

13. Let them—all mentioned. **excellent**—or, exalted (Isa. 12:4). **his glory**—majesty (Ps. 45:3). **above the earth and heaven**—*Their united* splendors fail to match His.

14. exalteth the horn—established power (Ps. 75:5, 6). **praise of** [or lit., "for"] **his saints**—i.e., occasions for them to praise Him. They are further described as His people, and near Him, sustaining by covenanted care a peculiarly intimate relation.

ADAM CLARKE

13. *Let them*, all already specified, *praise the name of Jehovah*, because He excels all beings; and *his glory*, as seen in creating, preserving, and governing all things, is *al*, "upon" or "over" *the earth and heaven.* All space and place as well as the beings found in them, show forth the manifold wisdom and goodness of God.

14. *He also exalteth the horn.* Raises to power and authority *his people. The praise.* Jehovah is the Subject of the praise of all His *saints.*

MATTHEW HENRY

PSALM 149

Verses 1–5

I. The calls given to God's Israel to praise. *All his works* were, in the foregoing psalm, excited to *praise him*; but here his saints in a particular manner are required to bless him. *Israel* in general, the body of the church (*v.* 2), *the children of Zion* particularly, the inhabitants of that holy hill, who are nearer to God than other Israelites; those that have the word and ordinances of God near to them, are justly expected to do more in praising God than others. All true Christians may call themselves *the children of Zion*, for in faith and hope *we have come unto Mount Zion*, Heb. xii. 22. *Let Israel rejoice*, and *the children of Zion be joyful*, and *the saints be joyful in glory.* Much of the power of godliness in the heart consists in making God our chief joy and solacing ourselves in him; and ourfaith in Christ is described by our rejoicing in him. We must sing a *new song*, sing with new affections, which make the song new, though the words have been used before. The gospel-canon for psalmody is to *sing with the spirit* and *with the understanding.* We must praise God in public, in the *solemn assembly* (*v.* 1), *in the congregation of saints.* Thus God's name must be owned before the world. We must praise him in private. *Let the saints* be so transported with their joy in God as to *sing aloud upon their beds*, when they awake in the night, full of the praises of God, as David, cxix. 62.

II. The cause given to God's Israel for praise. He gave us our being as men, and we have reason to praise him for that, for it is a noble and excellent being. He gave Israel their being as a people, as a church. If he made them, he is their King; he that gave being no doubt may give law. He is a king that rules by love, and therefore to be praised; for *the Lord takes pleasure in his people*, in their services, in their prosperity, in communion with them, and in the communications of his favour to them. He has prepared for their future glory: *He will beautify the meek*, the lowly, and contrite in heart, that are patient under their afflictions and *show all meekness towards all men.* They shall appear comely, before all the world, with the comeliness that he puts upon them. The righteous shall be beautified in that day when they *shine forth as the sun.* In the hopes of this, let them now, in the darkest day, *sing a new song.*

Verses 6–9

The Israel of God are here represented triumphing over their enemies, which is both the matter of their praise (let them give to God the glory of those triumphs) and the recompence of their praise; those that are truly thankful to God for their tranquillity shall be blessed with victory. The many victories over the nations of Canaan and other nations that were devoted to destruction began in Moses and Joshua, who, when they taught Israel *the high praises of the Lord*, did withal put a *two-edged sword in their hand*; David did so too, for he was the captain of

JAMIESON, FAUSSET, BROWN

PSALM 149

Vss. 1-9. This Psalm sustains a close connection with the foregoing. The chosen people are exhorted to praise God, in view of past favors, and also future victories over enemies, of which they are impliedly assured.

1. (Cf. Ps. 96:1.) **2.** God had signalized His relation as a sovereign, in restoring them to their land. **3. in the dance**—(Ps. 30:11). The dance is connected with other terms, expressive of the great joy of the occasion. The word may be rendered *lute*, to which the other instruments are joined. **sing praises**—or, sing and play.

5. in glory—the honorable condition to which they are raised. **upon their beds**—once a place of mourning (Ps. 6:6).

4. taketh pleasure—lit., "accepts," alluding to acceptance of propitiatory offerings (cf. Ps. 7:18). **beautify . . .**—adorn the humble with faith, hope, joy, and peace.

6. high (praise)—or, deeds. They shall go forth as religious warriors, as once religious laborers (Neh. 4:17).

ADAM CLARKE

PSALM 149

This seems to be a song of triumph after some glorious victory, probably in the time of the Maccabees. It has been also understood as predicting the success of the gospel in the nations of the earth. It has no title in the Hebrew, nor in any of the versions, and no author's name.

1. *Sing unto the Lord a new song.* That is, as we have often had occasion to remark, an "excellent song," the best we can possibly pronounce. So the word *chadash* is often understood; and so the word *novus*, "new," was often used among the Latin writers.

3. *Let them praise his name in the dance. Bemachol*, "with the pipe," or some kind of wind music, classed here with *toph*, the drum, and *kinnor*, the *harp*. I know no place in the Bible where *machol* and *machalath* mean *dance* of any kind; they constantly signify some kind of pipe.

4. *The Lord taketh pleasure in his people.* The pleasure or goodwill of God is in His people; He loves them ardently, and will load them with His benefits while they are humble and thankful; for *he will beautify*, "He will make fair," *the meek*, "the lowly," the humble, *with salvation.*

6. *Let the high praises of God.* Let them sing songs the most sublime, with the loudest noise consistent with harmony. *And a twoedged*

MATTHEW HENRY

their hosts, and taught the children of Judah the use of the bow (2 Sam. i. 18). They *executed vengeance upon the heathen* (the Philistines, Moabites, Ammonites, and others, 2 Sam. viii. 1, &c.) *and punishments upon the people*, for all the wrong they had done to God's people, *v.* 7. Their kings and nobles were taken prisoners (*v.* 8). Some apply it to the time of the Maccabees, when the Jews sometimes gained great advantages against their oppressors. And if it seem strange that the meek should, notwithstanding that character, be thus severe, they do not do it from any personal malice and revenge, or any bloody politics that they govern themselves by, but by commission from God, according to his direction, and in obedience to his command. But, since now no such special commissions can be produced, this will by no means justify the violence either of subjects against their princes or of princes against their subjects, or both against their neighbours, under pretence of religion; for Christ never intended that his gospel should be propagated by fire and sword or his righteousness wrought by the wrath of man. When the high praises of God are in our mouth with them we should have an olive-branch of peace in our hands. Christ's victories are by the power of his gospel and grace over spiritual enemies, in which all believers are more than conquerors. The word of God is the *two-edged sword* (Heb. iv. 12), the *sword of the Spirit* (Eph. vi. 17). With this two-edged sword the first preachers of the gospel obtained a glorious victory over the powers of darkness; vengeance was executed upon the gods of the heathen, by the conviction and conversion of those that had been long their worshippers. The strongholds of Satan were cast down (2 Cor. x. 4, 5); great men were made to tremble at the word, as Felix; Satan, the god of this world, was cast out, according to the judgment given against him. With this two-edged sword believers fight against their own corruptions, and, through the grace of God, subdue and mortify them; self, that once sat king, is bound with chains and brought into subjection to the yoke of Christ. *This honour have all the saints.*

JAMIESON, FAUSSET, BROWN

7. The destruction of the incorrigibly wicked attends the propagation of God's truth, so that the military successes of the Jews, after the captivity, typified the triumphs of the Gospel.

9. the judgment written–either in God's decrees, or perhaps as in Deuteronomy 32:41-43.

this honour–i.e., to be thus employed, will be an honorable service, to be assigned **his saints**–or, godly ones (Ps. 16:3).

ADAM CLARKE

sword in their hand. Perhaps there is an allusion here to the manner in which the Jews were obliged to labor in rebuilding the walls of Jerusalem: "Every one with one of his hands wrought in the work, and with the other hand held a weapon," Neh. iv. 17.

7. *To execute vengeance upon the heathen.* This may refer simply to their purpose of defending themselves to the uttermost, should their enemies attack them while building their wall. *Punishments upon the people.* The unfaithful and treacherous Jews; for we find that some, even of their nobles, had joined with Sanballat and Tobiah (see Neh. vi. 17-19); and it appears also that many of them had formed alliances with those heathens, which were contrary to the law; see Neh. xiii. 15-29.

9. *To execute upon them the judgment written.* In Deut. vii. 1, God promises His people complete victory over all their enemies, and over the heathen. God repeatedly promises such victories to His faithful people; and this is, properly speaking, the *judgment written,* i.e., foretold.

MATTHEW HENRY

PSALM 150

Verses 1–6

If, as some suppose, this psalm was primarily intended for the Levites, to stir them up in the house of the Lord, as singers and players on instruments, yet we must take it as speaking to us, who are made to our God spiritual priests.

I. This tribute of praise comes, 1. From *his sanctuary*; praise him there. Let his priests, let his people, attend there with their praises. Where should he be praised, but there where he does, in a special manner, both manifest his glory and communicate his grace? 2. From *the firmament of his power. Praise him* because of his power and glory which appear in the firmament, its vastness, its brightness, and because of the powerful influences it has upon this earth.

II. Upon what account this tribute of praise is due, 1. The works of his power (*v.* 2): *Praise him for his mighty acts;* for *his mightinesses* (so the word is), for all the instances of his might, the power of his providence, the power of his grace, what he has done in the creation, government, and redemption of the world, for the children of men in general, for his own church and children in particular. 2. The glory and majesty of his being: *Praise him according to his excellent greatness.* Not that our praises can bear any proportion to God's greatness, for it is infinite. Be not afraid of saying too much in the praises of God, all the danger is of saying too little.

III. In what manner this tribute must be paid, with all the kinds of musical instruments that were then used in the temple-service, *v.* 3–5. In serving God we should spare no cost nor pains. The best music in God's ears is devout and pious affections, *not a melodious string, but a melodious heart.* Praise God with a strong faith; praise him with holy love and delight; praise him with an entire confidence in Christ; praise him with a believing triumph over the powers of darkness; praise him by a universal respect to all his commands; praise him by promoting the interests of the kingdom of his grace; praise him by a lively hope and expectation of the kingdom of his glory. Various instruments being used in praising God, it should yet be done with perfect harmony; they must not hinder, but help one another. The New Testament concert, is *with one mind and one mouth to glorify God,* Rom. xv. 6.

IV. Who must pay this tribute (*v.* 6): *Let everything that has breath praise the Lord.* He began with a call to those that had a place in his sanctuary and were

JAMIESON, FAUSSET, BROWN

PSALM 150

Vss. 1-6. This is a suitable doxology for the whole book, reciting the "place, theme, mode, and extent of God's high praise."

1. in his sanctuary–on earth.

firmament . . .– which illustrates His power.

2. mighty acts–(Ps. 145:4).

excellent greatness–or, abundance of greatness.

3, 4. trumpet–used to call religious assemblies; the **organs**–or pipe, a wind instrument, and the others were used in worship. **5. cymbals**–suited to loud praise (Neh. 12:27).

ADAM CLARKE

PSALM 150

This psalm is without title and author in the Hebrew, and in all the ancient versions. It is properly the full chorus of all voices and instruments in the Temple, at the conclusion of the grand *Hallelujah,* to which the five concluding psalms belong.

1. *Praise God in his sanctuary.* In many places we have the compound word *halelu-yah,* "praise ye Jehovah"; but this is the first place in which we find *halelu-el,* "praise God," or "the strong God." Praise Him who is Jehovah, the infinite and self-existent Being; and praise Him who is God, *El* or *Elohim,* the great God in covenant with mankind, to bless and save them unto eternal life. *In his sanctuary*—in the Temple; in whatever place is dedicated to His service. Or, "in his holiness"—through His own holy influence in your hearts. *The firmament of his power.* Through the whole expanse, to the utmost limits of His power. As *rakia* is the firmament of vast expanse that surrounds the globe, and probably that in which all the celestial bodies of the solar system are included, it may have that meaning here. Praise Him whose power and goodness extend through all worlds; and let the inhabitants of all those worlds share in the grand chorus, that it may be universal.

2. *For his mighty acts.* Whether manifested in creation, government, mercy, or justice. *His excellent greatness.* According to the multitude of His magnitude, or of His majesty.

3. *The sound of the trumpet. Sophar,* from its noble, cheering, and majestic sound; for the original has this ideal meaning. *With the psaltery. Nebel;* the nabla, a hollow stringed instrument; perhaps like the guitar. *And harp. Kinnor,* another stringed instrument, played on with the hands or fingers.

4. *Praise him with the timbrel. Toph,* drum, tabret, or tympanum, or tom-tom of the ancients; a skin stretched over a broad hoop; perhaps something like the tambourine. *And dance. Machol,* the "pipe." It never means *dance;* see the note on Ps. cxlix. 3. *Stringed instruments. Minnim.* This literally signifies "strings put in order"; perhaps a triangular kind of hollow in-

MATTHEW HENRY

employed in the temple-service; but he concludes with a call to all the children of men, in prospect of the time when the Gentiles should be taken into the church, and *in every place*, as acceptably as at Jerusalem, *this incense should be offered*, Mal. i. 11. The singing of birds is a sort of praising God. The brutes do in effect say to man, "We would praise God if we could; do you do it for us." Now that the gospel is ordered to be preached *to every creature*, to every human creature, it is required that every human creature praise the Lord. Prayers are called *our breathings*, Lam. iii. 56. Let everyone that breathes towards God in prayer, breathe forth his praises too. While we have breath let us praise the Lord, and when death runs us out of breath, we shall remove to a better state to breathe God's praises in a freer better air.

The first three of the five books of psalms (according to the Hebrew division) concluded with *Amen and Amen*, the fourth with *Amen, Hallelujah*, but the last, and in it the whole book, concludes with only *Hallelujah*, because the last six psalms are wholly taken up in praising God and there is not a word of complaint or petition in them. Let us often take a pleasure in thinking what glorified saints are doing in heaven, what those are doing whom we have been acquainted with on earth, but who have gone before us thither; and let it quicken us to do this part of the will of God on earth as those do it that are in heaven. *Hallelujah* is the word there; let us echo to it now, *Hallelujah, praise you the Lord.*

JAMIESON, FAUSSET, BROWN

6. LIVING VOICES SHALL TAKE UP THE FAILING SOUNDS OF DEAD INSTRUMENTS, AND AS THEY CEASE ON EARTH, THOSE OF INTELLIGENT RANSOMED SPIRITS AND HOLY ANGELS, AS WITH THE SOUND OF MIGHTY THUNDERS, WILL PROLONG ETERNALLY THE PRAISE, SAYING: "ALLELUIA! SALVATION, AND GLORY, AND HONOR, AND POWER, UNTO THE LORD OUR GOD"; ALLELUIA! FOR THE LORD GOD OMNIPOTENT REIGNETH." AMEN!

ADAM CLARKE

strument on which the strings were regularly placed, growing shorter and shorter till they came to a point. This would give a variety of sounds, from a deep bass to a high treble. *Organs. Ugab.* Very likely the mouth organ.

5. *Loud cymbals. Tseltselim.* Two hollow plates of brass, which, being struck together, produced a sharp clanging sound. This instrument is still in use. What the *high sounding cymbals* meant I know not, unless those of a larger make, struck above the head, and consequently emitting a louder sound.

6. *Let every thing that hath breath.* Either to make a vocal noise, or a sound by blowing into pipes, fifes, flutes, trumpets, etc. Let all join together, and put forth all your strength and all your skill in sounding the praises of Jehovah; and then let a universal burst with HALLELUJAH! close the grand ceremony. It is evident that this psalm has no other meaning than merely the summoning up all the voices, and all the instruments, to complete the service in full chorus.

Of such peculiar importance did the Book of Psalms appear to our blessed Lord and His apostles that they have quoted nearly fifty of them several times in the New Testament. There is scarcely a state in human life that is not distinctly marked in them; together with all the variety of experience which is found, not merely among pious Jews, but among Christians, the most deeply acquainted with the things of Christ.

THE BOOK OF PROVERBS

I. Introduction (1:1-7)
A. The purpose (1:1-5)
B. The method (1:6, 7)

II. Instructions on wisdom (1:8-9:18)
A. Parental counsel (1:8-19)
1. Wisdom—true friends (1:8, 9)
2. Folly—false friends (1:10-19)
B. Wisdom's call (1:20-33)
1. The announcement (1:20, 21)
2. The call (1:22-33)
C. Parental counsels (2:1-7:27)
1. On wisdom (2:1-3:35)
2. A personal testimony (4:1-9)
3. Exhortations (4:10-7:27)
D. Wisdom's call (8:1-36)
1. The announcement (8:1-3)
2. The call (8:4-36)
E. A contrast (9:1-18)
1. Wisdom (9:1-12)
2. Folly (9:12-18)

III. Proverbs—first collection (10:1-24:34)
A. Proverbs (10:1-22:16)
B. A series of proverbial discourses (22:17-24:34)
1. Social admonition (22:17-23:14)
2. Parental counsels (23:15-24:22)
3. Concerning social order (24:23-34)

IV. Proverbs—second collection (25:1-29:27)
A. Title (25:1)
B. A posthumous collection of picturesque proverbs (25:2-29:27)

V. Appendix (30:1-31:31)
A. The words of Agur (30:1-33)
1. Title (30:1)
2. Human incompleteness in wisdom (30:2-6)
3. Prayer (30:7-9)
4. Conduct (30:10-33)
B. The oracles of Lemuel (31:1-31)
1. His mother's counsel (31:1-9)
2. His mother's picture (31:10-31)

I. A new author, made use of by the Holy Ghost for making known the mind of God to us, is Solomon; through his hand came this book of Scripture and the two that follow it, Ecclesiastes and Canticles, a sermon and a song. Some think he wrote Canticles when he was very young, Proverbs in the midst of his days, and Ecclesiastes when he was old.

A. He was a king, and a king's son. The penmen of Scripture, hitherto, were most of them men of rank in the world, as Moses and Joshua, Samuel and David, and now Solomon; but, after him, the inspired writers were generally poor prophets, men of no figure in the world, because that dispensation was approaching in which God would choose the "weak and foolish things of the world to confound the wise and mighty" and the poor should be employed to evangelize. Solomon was a very rich king, and his dominions were very large, and yet he was a prophet and a prophet's son.

B. He was one whom God endued with extraordinary measures of wisdom and knowledge, in answer to his prayers at his accession to the throne. His prayer was exemplary: "Give me a wise and an understanding heart"; the answer to it was encouraging: he had what he desired and "all other things were added to him."

C. He was one who had his faults, and in his latter end turned aside from those good ways of God. But let those who are most eminently useful take warning by this not to be proud or secure; and let us all learn not to think the worse of good instructions though we have them from those who do not themselves altogether live up to them.

II. A new way of writing, in which divine wisdom is taught us by Proverbs, or short sentences, which contain their whole design within themselves and are not connected with one another. We have had divine *laws, histories,* and *songs,* and now divine *proverbs*; such various methods has Infinite Wisdom used for our instruction. Teaching by proverbs was:

A. An ancient way of teaching. It was the most ancient way among the Greeks; each of the seven wise men of Greece had one saying that he valued himself upon, and that made him famous. These sentences were inscribed on pillars, and had in great veneration.

B. It was a plain and easy way of teaching. A proverb, which carries both its sense and its evidence in a little compass, is quickly apprehended and easily retained.

C. It was a very profitable way of teaching, and served admirably well to answer the end. The world is governed by proverbs. "As saith the proverb of the ancients" (1 Sam. 24:13), or (as we commonly express it), "As the old saying is," goes very far with most men in forming their notions and fixing their resolves.

Some think we may judge of the temper and character of a nation by the complexion of its vulgar proverbs. Yet there are many corrupt proverbs, which tend to debauch men's minds and harden them in sin. The devil has his proverbs, and the world and the flesh have their proverbs, which reflect reproach on God and religion (as Ezek. 12:22; 18:2). These proverbs of Solomon were not merely a collection of the wise sayings that had been formerly delivered, as some have imagined, but were the dictates of the Spirit of God in Solomon. The very first of them (1:7) agrees with what God said to man in the beginning (Job 28:28, "Behold, the fear of the Lord, that is wisdom"); so that though Solomon was great, and his name may serve as much as any man's to recommend his writings, yet, behold, "a greater than Solomon is here." It is God, by Solomon, that here speaks to us.

MATTHEW HENRY

CHAPTER 1

Verses 1–6

An introduction to this book, which some think was prefixed by the collector Ezra; but it is rather supposed to have been penned by Solomon himself, who, in the beginning of his book, proposes his end in writing it.

I. Who wrote these wise sayings, *v.* 1. They are *the proverbs of Solomon.* His name signifies *peaceable,* and the character both of his spirit and of his reign were peaceable. David, whose life was full of troubles, wrote a book of devotion; for *is any afflicted? let him pray.* Solomon, who lived quietly, wrote a book of instruction; for when the *churches had rest they were edified.* In times of peace we should learn ourselves, and teach others, that which in troublous times we must practise. He was *the son of David.* He had been blessed with a good education, and

JAMIESON, FAUSSET, BROWN

CHAPTER 1

Vss. 1-33. After the title the writer defines the design and nature of the instructions of the book. He paternally invites attention to those instructions and warns his readers against the enticements of the wicked. In a beautiful personification, wisdom is then introduced in a most solemn and impressive manner, publicly inviting men to receive its teachings, warning those who reject, and encouraging those who accept, the proffered instructions.

ADAM CLARKE

CHAPTER 1

MATTHEW HENRY

many a prayer had been put up for him (Ps. lxxii. 1), the effect of both appeared in his wisdom and usefulness. He was *king of Israel.* All the earth sought to Solomon *to hear his wisdom* (1 Kings iv. 30; x. 24). His servants had collected 3000 proverbs of his, but these, of his own writing, do not amount to a thousand. In these he was divinely inspired.

II. They were written (*v.* 2–4) for the use and benefit of all. This book will help us, 1. To form right notions of things, and to possess our minds with clear and distinct ideas, that we may know both how to speak and act wisely. 2. To distinguish between truth and falsehood, good and evil—*to perceive the words of understanding.* 3. To order our conversation aright, *v.* 3. This book will give that knowledge which will dispose us to render to all their due, to God the things that are God's, in all the exercises of religion, and to all men what is due to them.

III. They are of use to all, but are designed especially, 1. For *the simple, to give subtlety to them.* The instructions here given are plain, and those are likely to receive benefit by them who are sensible of their own ignorance and their need to be taught, and those who receive these instructions, though they be simple, will hereby be made subtle, to know the sin they should avoid and the duty they should do. 2. For young people, to give them *knowledge and discretion.* Youth is the learning age, receives impressions, and retains what is then received. Youth is rash, and heady, and inconsiderate; *man is born like the wild ass's colt,* and therefore needs to be broken by the restraints and managed by the rules we find here. Solomon had an eye to posterity in writing this book, hoping by it to season the minds of the rising generation with the generous principles of wisdom and virtue. Those who are young and simple may by them be made wise, and are not excluded from Solomon's school, as they were from Plato's, *v.* 5, 6. Even wise men must hear, and not think themselves too wise to learn. A wise man, by increasing in learning, is profitable to others, 1. As a counsellor. *A man of understanding* in these precepts of wisdom, *shall* by degrees *attain unto wise counsels*; he shall come to *sit at the helm,* so the word signifies. Those whom God has blessed with wisdom must study to do good with it. It is more dignity indeed to be counsellor to the prince, but it is more charity to be counsellor to the poor. 2. As an interpreter (*v.* 6)—*to understand a proverb.* Solomon was himself famous for expounding riddles and resolving hard questions, which was of old the celebrated entertainment of the eastern princes. Here he undertakes to furnish his readers with that talent. "They shall *understand a proverb,* even *the interpretation,* without which the proverb is a nut uncracked; when they hear a wise saying, though it be figurative, they shall take the sense of it, and know how to make use of it."

Verses 7–9

Solomon, having undertaken to *teach a young man knowledge and discretion,* here lays down two general rules, to fear God and honour his parents.

I. Let them have regard to God as their supreme.

1. He lays down this truth, that *the fear of the Lord is the beginning of knowledge* (*v.* 7); it is *the principal part of knowledge* (so the margin). We are not qualified to profit by the instructions that are given us unless our minds be possessed with a holy reverence of God, and every thought within us be brought into obedience to him.

2. To confirm this truth, he observes, *Fools* (atheists, who have no regard to God) *despise wisdom and instruction.* Those are fools who do not fear God and value the scriptures; and though they may pretend to be admirers of wit they are really strangers and enemies to wisdom.

II. Let them have regard to their parents (*v.* 8, 9): *My son, hear the instruction of thy father.* He means, not only that he would have his own children to be observant of him, nor only that he would have his pupils to look upon him as their father and attend to his precepts, but that he would have all children to be dutiful and respectful to their parents.

1. He takes it for granted that parents will, with all the wisdom they have, instruct their children, and, with all the authority they have, give law to them for their good. They are reasonable creatures, and when we tell them what they must do we must tell them why. But they are wilful, and therefore with the instruction there is need of a law.

2. He charges children both to receive and to retain the good lessons and laws their parents give them. "*Hear the instruction of thy father,* and be thankful for it, and subscribe to it. *Forsake not their law;* think not that when thou art grown up, and no longer under tutors and governors, thou mayest live at large;

JAMIESON, FAUSSET, BROWN

To know . . . instruction—lit., "for knowing," i.e., such is the design of these writings. **wisdom**—or the use of the best means for the best ends, is generally employed in this book for true piety. **instruction**—discipline, by which men are trained. **to perceive** [lit., "for perceiving," the design (as above)] . . . **understanding**—i.e., words which enable one to discern good and evil. **To receive . . . of wisdom**—For receiving that discipline which *discretion* imparts. The *Hebrew* for wisdom differs from that of vs. 2, and denotes rather discreet counsel. Cf. the opposite traits of the fool (ch. 16:22). **justice . . . equity**—all the attributes of one upright in all his relations to God and man. **simple**—one easily led to good or evil; so the parallel. **young man**—one inexperienced. **subtilty**—or prudence (ch. 3:21; 5:21).

discretion—lit., "device," both qualities, either good or bad, according to their use. Here good, as they imply wariness by which to escape evil and find good.

5, 6. Such writings the wise, who pursue right ends by right means, will value. **learning**—not the act, but matter of it. **wise counsels**—or the art and principles of governing.

To understand—so as to . . . such will be the result. **interpretation**—(Cf. *Margin*). **words of the wise**—(Cf. vs. 2). **dark sayings**—(Cf. Ps. 49: 4; John 16:25; and *Introduction,* I).

7. The fear of the Lord—the principle of true piety (cf. ch. 2:5; 14: 26, 27; Job 28:28; Ps. 34:11; 111:10; Acts 9:31). **beginning**—first part, foundation.

fools—the stupid and indifferent to God's character and government; hence the wicked.

8. My son—This paternal form denotes a tender regard for the reader. Filial sentiments rank next to piety towards God, and ensure most distinguished rewards (cf. ch 6:20; Eph. 6:2, 3).

ADAM CLARKE

2. *To know wisdom.* That is, this is the design of parabolical writing in general; and the particular aim of the present work. This and the two following verses contain the interpretation of the term "parable," and the author's design in the whole book. The first verse is the title, and the next three verses are an explanation of the nature and design of this very important tract. *Wisdom. Chochmah* may mean here, and in every other part of this book, not only that divine science by which we are enabled to discover the best end and pursue it by the most proper means, but also the whole of that heavenly teaching that shows us both ourselves and God, directs us into all truth, and forms the whole of true religion. *And instruction. Musar,* the "teaching" that discovers all its parts.

3. *To receive the instruction. Haskel,* the deliberate "weighing" of the points contained in the teaching, so as to find out their importance. *Equity. Mesharim,* "rectitude."

4. *To give subtilty to the simple.* The word *simple,* from *simplex,* compounded of *sine,* "without," and *plica,* "a fold," properly signifies "plain and honest."

5. *A wise man will hear.* I shall not only give such instructions as may be suitable to the youthful and inexperienced, but also to those who have much knowledge and understanding.

6. *Dark sayings. Chidoth,* enigmas or riddles, in which the Asiatics abounded.

7. *The fear of the Lord.* In the preceding verses Solomon shows the advantage of acting according to the dictates of wisdom; in the following verses he shows the danger of acting contrary to them. *The fear of the Lord* signifies that religious reverence which every intelligent being owes to his Creator. This fear or religious reverence is said to be *the beginning of knowledge; reshith,* the principle, the first moving influence, begotten in a tender conscience by the Spirit of God. No man can ever become truly wise who does not begin with God, the Fountain of knowledge; and he whose mind is influenced by the fear and love of God will learn more in a month than others will in a year. *Fools despise. Evilim,* evil men. Men of bad hearts, bad heads, and bad ways.

8. *My son, hear.* "Father" was the title of preceptor, and "son" that of disciple, among the Jews. But here the reference appears to be to the children of a family; the *father* and the *mother* have the principal charge, in the first instance, of their children's instruction.

MATTHEW HENRY

no, *the law of thy mother* was according to the law of thy God, and therefore it must never be forsaken." Some observe that whereas the laws of the Persians and Romans, provided only that children should pay respect to their father, the divine law secures the honour of the mother also. "The instructions and laws of thy parents, carefully observed, *shall be an ornament of grace unto thy head* (*v.* 9), and shall make thee look as those that wear gold *chains about their necks*."

Verses 10–19

Here Solomon gives another general rule to young people to take heed of the snare of bad company (*v.* 10): "*My son*, whom I love, and have a tender concern for, *if sinners entice thee, consent thou not*." Sinners love company in sin; the angels that fell were tempters almost as soon as they were sinners. They do not threaten or argue, but entice with flattery and fair speech. "*Consent thou not;* and then, though they entice thee, they cannot force thee. Have no fellowship with them." To enforce this caution,

I. He represents the fallacious reasonings which sinners use in their enticements, for the beguiling of unstable souls. He specifies highwaymen, who do what they can to draw others into their gang, *v.* 11–14. "*Come with us* (*v.* 11); let us have thy company." At first they pretend to ask no more; but the courtship rises higher (*v.* 14): "*Cast in thy lot among us;* let us resolve to live and die together: and *let us all have one purse*, that what we get together we may spend merrily together." They thirst after blood, and hate those that are innocent, because by their honesty and industry they shame and condemn them: "*Let us* therefore *lay wait for* their *blood*, and *lurk privily* for them; they travel unarmed; therefore we shall make easy prey of them. And, O how sweet it will be to *swallow them up alive*!" (*v.* 12). They hope to get a good booty by it (*v.* 13): "We shall *find all precious substance* by following this trade. What though we venture our necks by it? we shall *fill our houses with spoil*." They call it *precious substance*; whereas it is neither substance nor precious; it is a shadow; it is vanity, especially that which is got by robbery, Ps. lxii. 10.

II. He shows the perniciousness of these ways (*v.* 15): "*My son, walk not thou in the way with them; refrain thy foot from their path;* do not take example by them, nor do as they do." Consider their way (*v.* 16): *Their feet run to evil*, to that which is displeasing to God and hurtful to mankind, for they *make haste to shed blood*. The way of sin is down-hill; men not only cannot stop themselves, but, the longer they continue in it, the faster they run, and make haste in it. They are plainly told that this wicked way will certainly end in their own destruction, and yet they persist in it. They are like the silly bird, that sees the net spread to take her, and yet she is decoyed into it by the bait, and does not take the warning which her own eyes give her, *v.* 17. Their greediness of gain hurries them upon those practices which will not suffer them to live out half their days.

Now, though Solomon specifies only the temptation to rob on the highway, yet he intends hereby to warn us against all other evils which sinners entice men to. Such are the ways of the drunkards and unclean.

Verses 20–33

Solomon, having shown how dangerous it is to hearken to the temptations of Satan, here shows how dangerous it is not to hearken to the calls of God.

I. By whom God calls to us—by *wisdom*. It is *wisdom* that *crieth without*. The word is plural—*wisdoms*, for, as there is infinite wisdom in God, so there is the *manifold wisdom of God*, Eph. iii. 10. God speaks to the children of men by all the kinds of wisdom. 1. Human understanding is wisdom, the light and law of nature, the powers and faculties of reason, and the office of conscience, Job xxxviii. 36. 2. Civil government is wisdom; magistrates are his vicegerents. 3. Divine revelation is wisdom; all its dictates, all its laws, are wise as wisdom itself. God does, by the written word, by his servants the prophets, and all the ministers of this word, declare his mind to sinners. 4. Christ himself is Wisdom, is Wisdoms, for *in him are hidden all the treasures of wisdom and knowledge*, and he is the centre of all divine revelation, not only the *essential Wisdom*, but the *eternal Word*, by whom God speaks to us and to whom he has *committed all judgment*. He calls himself *Wisdom*, Luke vii. 35.

II. He calls to us, 1. Very publicly, that whosoever hath ears to hear may hear. The rules of wisdom are published *without in the streets*, not in the schools

JAMIESON, FAUSSET, BROWN

On the figures of vs. **9**, cf. Genesis 41:42; Song of Solomon 1:10; 4:9.

10-19. A solemn warning against temptation. **10. entice**—lit., "open the way." **consent . . . not**—Sin is in consenting or yielding to temptation, not in being tempted.

11-14. Murder and robbery are given as specific illustrations. **lay wait . . . lurk privily**—express an effort and hope for successful concealment. **swallow . . . grave**—utterly destroy the victim and traces of the crime (Num. 16:33; Ps. 55:15). Abundant rewards of villainy are promised as the fruits of this easy and safe course.

15, 16. The society of the wicked (way or path) is dangerous. Avoid the beginnings of sin (ch. 4:14; Ps. 1:1; 119:101).

17-19. Men warned ought to escape danger as birds instinctively avoid visibly spread nets. But stupid sinners rush to their own ruin (Ps. 9:16), and, greedy of gain, succeed in the very schemes which destroy them (I Tim. 6:10), not only failing to catch others, but procuring their own destruction.

20-33. Some interpreters regard this address as the language of the Son of God under the name of Wisdom (cf. Luke 11:49). Others think that wisdom, as the divine attribute specially employed in acts of counsel and admonition, is here personified, and represents God. In either case the address is a most solemn and divine admonition, whose matter and spirit are eminently evangelical and impressive (cf. *Note* on ch. 8). **20. Wisdom**—lit., "Wisdoms," the plural used either because of the unusual sense, or as indicative of the great excellency of wisdom (cf. ch. 9:1).

streets—or most public places, not secretly.

ADAM CLARKE

18. *They lay wait for their own blood.* I believe it is the innocent who are spoken of here, for whose *blood* and *lives* these *lay wait* and *lurk privily;* certainly not their own, by any mode of construction.

16. *For their feet run to evil.* The whole of this verse is wanting in the Septuagint, and in the Arabic.

17. *Surely in vain the net is spread in the sight of any bird.* The wicked are represented as lurking privily for the innocent.

20. *Wisdom crieth.* Here wisdom is again personified, as it is frequently, throughout this book; where nothing is meant but the teachings given to man, either by divine revelation or the voice of the Holy Spirit in the heart. And this voice of *wisdom* is opposed to the seducing language of the wicked mentioned above.

MATTHEW HENRY

only, or in the palaces of princes, but among the common people that pass and repass *in the opening of the gates* and *in the city.* 2. Very pathetically; she *cries,* she *utters her words* with all possible clearness and affection. God is desirous to be heard and heeded.

III. What the call of God and Christ is.

1. He reproves sinners for their folly and their obstinately persisting in it, *v.* 22. In general, they are such as are *simple. Simple ones love simplicity.* They do foolishly, and are in their element, sporting themselves in their own deceivings and flattering themselves in their wickedness. *Scorners delight in scorning,* and make a jest of everything that comes in their way. Scoffers at religion are especially meant. *Fools hate knowledge.* Those are enemies to religion that do not understand it aright. And those are the worst of fools that hate to be instructed. The God of heaven desires the conversion and reformation of sinners and not their ruin, is much displeased with their dilatoriness, he waits to be gracious, and is willing to reason the case with them, *v.* 22.

2. He invites them to repent and become wise, *v.* 23. *Turn you at my reproof,* that is, return to your right mind, turn to God, turn to your duty, turn and live. Those that love simplicity find themselves under a moral impotency to change their own mind and way; they cannot turn by any power of their own. To this God answers, "*Behold, I will pour out my Spirit unto you;* set yourselves to do what you can, and the grace of God shall work in you both to will and to do that good which, without that grace, you could not do." *I will pour out my Spirit unto you.* The means of this grace is the word. It is therefore promised, "*I will make known my words unto you,* not only speak them to you, but give you to understand them."

3. He reads the doom of those that continue obstinate against all these means and methods of grace, *v.* 24–32. The crime is, in short, rejecting Christ and the offers of his grace, and refusing to submit to the terms of his gospel, which would have saved them both from the curse of the *law of God* and from the dominion of the *law of sin.* Christ *stretched out his hand* to offer them mercy, but they *refused* and *no man regarded.* Christ not only reproved them for what they did amiss, but counselled them to do better (those are *reproofs of instruction* and evidences of love and goodwill), but they *set at nought all his counsel* as not worth heeding, and *would none of his reproof, v.* 25. This is repeated (*v.* 30): "They *would none of my counsel,* but rejected it with disdain, *they despised all my reproof,* as if it were all a jest, and not worth taking notice of." They were exhorted to submit to the government of right reason and religion, but they rebelled against both. Reason should not rule them, for *they hated knowledge* (*v.* 29), because it discovered to them the evil of their deeds. Religion could not rule them, for they *did not choose the fear of the Lord,* but chose to walk in the way of *their heart and in the sight of their eyes.* They would not take the benefit of God's mercy when it was offered them, and therefore justly fall as victims to his justice, *ch.* xxix. 1. Their *calamity will come* (*v.* 26); troubles will come, in mind, in estate, which will convince them of their folly in setting God at a distance. Their *fear shall come* (the thing they were afraid of shall befall them); it shall *come as desolation,* as a mighty deluge bearing down all before it; and it shall come *as a whirlwind,* which suddenly and forcibly drives away all the chaff. *Distress and anguish shall come upon them,* for they shall see no way to escape, *v.* 27. Now God pities their folly, but he will then *laugh at their calamity* (*v.* 26). Those that ridicule religion will thereby but make themselves ridiculous before all the world. Now God is ready to hear their prayers and to meet them with mercy, if they would but seek to him for it; but then the door will be shut, and they shall cry in vain (*v.* 28): "*Then shall they call upon me* when it is too late, *Lord, Lord, open to us,* but *I will not answer,* because, when I called, they would not answer." But, ordinarily, while there is life there is room for prayer and hope of speeding, and therefore this must refer to the inexorable justice of the last judgment. They shall *eat the fruit of their own way;* their wages shall be according to their work. Now they value themselves upon their worldly prosperity; but then that shall help to aggravate their ruin, *v.* 32. They are now proud of their own security and sensuality; but *the ease of the simple* (so the margin reads it) *shall slay them;* the more secure they are the more certain and the more dreadful will their destruction be, *and the prosperity of fools shall* help to *destroy them,* by puffing them up with pride, glueing their hearts to the world, furnishing them with fuel for their lusts, and hardening their hearts in their evil ways.

JAMIESON, FAUSSET, BROWN

21. The publicity further indicated by terms designating places of most common resort.

22. simple ones–(Cf. vs. 4.) **simplicity**–implying ignorance. **scorners**–(Ps. 1:1) –who despise, as well as reject, truth. **fools**–Though a different word is used from that of vs. 7, yet it is of the same meaning.

23. reproof–implying conviction deserving it (cf. John 16:8, *Margin*).

pour out–abundantly impart. **my spirit**–whether of wisdom personified, or of Christ, a divine agent.

24. stretched . . . hand–Earnestness, especially in beseeching, is denoted by the figure (cf. Job 11:13; Ps. 68:31; 88:9).

25. set at naught–rejected as of no value. **would none of**–lit., "were not willing or inclined to it."

29, 30. The sinner's infatuated rejection brings his ruin.

26, 27. In their extreme distress He will not only refuse help, but aggravate it by derision. **fear**–the object of it. **desolation**–lit., "a tumultuous noise," denoting their utter confusion. **destruction**–or calamity (vs. 26) compared to a whirlwind, as to fatal rapidity. **distress**–(Ps. 4:1; 44:11). **anguish**–a state of inextricable oppression, the deepest despair.

28. Now no prayers or most diligent seeking will avail (ch. 8:17).

31. fruit . . . way–result of conduct (Isa. 3:10; Ezek. 11:21; Rom. 6:21; Gal. 6:7, 8). **be filled**–even to repletion (Ps. 123:4).

32, turning away–i.e., from the call of vs. 23. **simple**–as in vs. 22. **prosperity**–quiet, implying indifference.

ADAM CLARKE

22. *Ye simple ones. Pethayim,* ye who have been seduced and deceived.

23. *Turn you at my reproof.* At my "convincing mode of arguing."

24. *Because I have called.* These and the following words appear to be spoken of the persons who are described, vv. 11-19, who have refused to return from their evil ways till arrested by the hand of justice; and here the wise man points out their deplorable state.

32. *For the turning away of the simple.* This difficult place seems to refer to such a case as we term "turning king's evidence," where an accomplice saves his own life by impeaching the rest of his gang. This is called his "turning" or "repentance," *meshubah;* and he was the most likely to turn, because he was of the *pethayim,*

MATTHEW HENRY

4. He concludes with an assurance of safety and happiness to all those that submit to the instructions of wisdom (*v.* 33): "*Whoso hearkeneth unto me,* and will be ruled by me, he *shall dwell* under the special protection of Heaven, so that nothing shall do him any real hurt. He shall have no disquieting apprehensions of danger; he shall not only be safe from evil, but *quiet from the fear of* it."

CHAPTER 2

Verses 1–9

Solomon tells us where we may find wisdom, and how we may get it.

I. What means we must use that we may obtain wisdom.

1. We must closely attend to the word of God, for that is the word of wisdom, *which is able to make us wise unto salvation, v.* 1, 2. The words of God are the fountain and standard of wisdom and understanding. Many wise things may be found in human compositions, but divine revelation, and true religion built upon it, are all wisdom.

2. We must be much in prayer, *v.* 3. We must *cry after knowledge.* We must *lift our voice for understanding,* lift it up to heaven; thence these good and perfect gifts must be expected. We must *give our voice to understanding* (so the word is), speak for it, vote for it, submit the tongue to the command of wisdom.

3. We must be willing to take pains (*v.* 4); we must *seek it as silver,* preferring it far before all the wealth of this world, and labouring in search of it as those who dig in the mines.

II. What success we may hope for in the use of these means. Our labour shall not be in vain; for, "*Thou shalt understand the fear of the Lord* (*v.* 5). that is, thou shalt know how to worship him aright." *Thou shalt find the knowledge of God,* which is necessary to our fearing him aright. We shall know how to conduct ourselves aright towards all men (*v.* 9): "*Thou shalt understand,* by the word of God, *righteousness, and judgment, and equity,* shalt learn those principles of justice, and charity, and fair dealing, which shall make thee fit for every relation, and faithful to every trust. It shall give thee not only a right notion of justice, but a disposition to practise it, and to render to all their due."

III. What ground we have to hope for this success in our pursuits of wisdom; we must take our encouragement herein from God only, *v.* 6–8.

1. God has wisdom to bestow, *v.* 6. *The Lord* not only is wise himself, but he *gives wisdom.*

2. He has blessed the world with a revelation of his will. *Out of his mouth,* by the law and the prophets, by the written word and by his ministers, *come knowledge and understanding,* such a discovery of truth and good as will make us truly knowing and intelligent.

3. He has particularly provided that good men, who are sincerely disposed to do his will, shall have that *knowledge and* that *understanding, v.* 7, 8. *The righteous,* and those who *walk uprightly,* are *his saints,* devoted to his honour, and set apart for his service. The means of wisdom are given to all, but wisdom itself, *sound wisdom,* is laid *up for the righteous,* laid up in Christ their head. The same that is the Spirit of revelation in the word is a Spirit of wisdom in the souls of those that are sanctified. Some read it, He *lays up substance for the righteous,* not only substantial knowledge, but substantial happiness and comfort, Prov. viii. 21. Even those who *walk uprightly* may be brought into danger for the trial of their faith, but God is *a buckler to them,* so that nothing that happens to them shall do them any real hurt. If we depend upon God, and seek to him for wisdom, he will uphold us in our integrity, will enable us to *keep the paths of judgment*; for he *preserves the way of his saints. Work out your salvation,* for *God works in you.*

Verses 10–22

True wisdom will keep us from the paths of sin, and do us a greater kindness than if it enriched us with all the wealth of the world.

I. Our preservation from the evil of sin, and, consequently, from trouble that attends it. "When wisdom has entire possession of thee, it will *keep thee.*" When it *enters into the heart* as the leaven into the dough, then it is likely to do us good. "When thou callest the practice of virtue, not a slavery and a task, but *liberty* and *pleasure,* then thou wilt find the benefit of it." More particularly, wisdom will preserve us from men of corrupt principles, atheistical profane men, who make it their business to debauch young men's judgments, and instil into their minds

JAMIESON, FAUSSET, BROWN

33. dwell safely—lit., "in confidence" (Deut. 12:10). **be quiet**—or at ease, in real prosperity. **from fear**—without fear.

CHAPTER 2

Vss. 1-22. Men are invited to seek wisdom because it teaches those principles by which they may obtain God's guidance and avoid the society and influence of the wicked, whose pernicious courses are described.

1-5. Diligence in hearing and praying for instruction must be used to secure the great principle of godliness, the fear of God. **1. hide . . . with thee**—lay up in store (cf. ch. 7:1). **2.** Listen attentively and reflect seriously (ch. 1:24; Ps. 130:2). **understanding**—right perception of truth. **3. Yea, if**—lit., "When if," i.e., in such a case. **knowledge**—or, discrimination. **understanding**—as in vs. 2.

There must be earnest prayer and effort.

5. understand—or, perceive intelligently. **find**—obtain.

9. Then—emphatic, in such a case. **righteousness . . . path**—all parts of duty to God and man.

6. For—God is ready (Jas. 1:5; 4:8). **out of his mouth**—by revelation from Him.

7. sound wisdom—lit., "substance," opposed to what is fictitious. According to the context, this may be assistance, as here corresponding with **buckler,** or safety, or wisdom, which procures it (cf. ch: 3:21; 8:14; 18:1; Job 6:13; 12:13). **layeth up**—provides, ever ready. **8. keepeth . . . way**—God defends the right way, and those in it. **saints**—objects of favor (cf. Ps. 4:3, etc.). He guides and guards them.

10, 11. Idea of vs. 9, amplified; on terms cf vs. 2 and vs. 4.

ADAM CLARKE

seduced or deceived persons. And this evidence was given against them when they were in their prosperity, *shalvah,* their "security," enjoying the fruits of their depredations; and being thus in a state of fancied security, they were the more easily taken and brought to justice.

CHAPTER 2

JOSEPH PARKER:

Verses 2, 3. Man must listen to Wisdom if he would be wise; his attitude must be one of attention; he must turn his ear towards the heavens, and listen for every whisper that may proceed from the skies; and while his ear is listening, his heart must be applied with unbroken attention to understanding. Everything depends upon our spirit as to the results of our study in the school of Wisdom. Few men really listen, or incline their ear unto Wisdom; they think they are listening, while they are only hearing imperfectly; they do not store every little word in their hearts; they do not combine the word with the tone in which it is spoken. They leap to conclusions without anxiously and carefully passing through the whole process of exposition and exhortation. Not only is there to be listening to, there is to be crying after knowledge, and a lifting up of the voice for understanding. These terms may be regarded as equivalent to an exercise in prayer. If we personate knowledge and individualize understanding, then the attitude of the seeker is that of a suppliant; he prays to the genius of knowledge, he wishes the spirit of understanding; he begs them to be gracious to him, and to withhold nothing from him that can enrich his mind or edify his character.

—*The People's Bible*

7. *He layeth up sound wisdom. Tushiyah.* We have met with this word in Job; see chap. v. 12; vi. 13; xi. 6; xii. 16; especially Job xi. 6.

MATTHEW HENRY

prejudices against religion and arguments for vice: "It will *deliver thee from the way of the evil man* (*v.* 12), *from the way* in which he walks, and in which he would persuade thee to walk." They *speak froward things*; they say all they can against religion. *They leave the paths of uprightness*, which they were trained up in, *to walk in the ways of darkness*, which hate the light, in which men are led blindfold by ignorance and error, and which lead men into utter darkness. They take a pleasure in sin, both in committing it themselves and in seeing others commit it (*v.* 14). They *rejoice* in an opportunity *to do evil.* It is sport to fools to do mischief; to see those that are hopeful drawn into the ways of sin, and then to see them hardened and confirmed in those ways. Their *ways are crooked*, a great many windings and turnings to escape the pursuit of their convictions. Women of corrupt practices lead to *fleshly lusts*, which defile the body, that living temple, but withal *war against the soul.* The adulteress is here called *the strange woman*, to be shunned by every Israelite as if she were a heathen, and a stranger to that sacred commonwealth. She is false to him whom she entices. She speaks fair, tells him how much she admires him above any man, but she *flatters with her words*; she has no true affection for him, nor any desire of his welfare, any more than Delilah had of Samson's. All she designs is to pick his pocket and gratify a base lust of her own. She is false to her husband, and violates the sacred obligation she lies under to him. She is false to God himself: She *forgets the covenant of her God*, the marriage-covenant (*v.* 17), to which God is not only a witness, but a party, for, he having instituted the ordinance, both sides vow to him to be true to each other. Take heed of the sin of whoredom. It is a sin that has a direct tendency to the killing of the soul, the extinguishing of all good affections and dispositions in it. Let discretion preserve every man, not only from the evil woman, but from the evil house, for the *house inclines to death*; *and her paths unto Rephaim*, to the *giants* (so some read it), the sinners of the old world, who, living in luxury and excess of riot, were cut down out of time, and their foundation was overthrown with a flood. *None*, or next to none, *that go unto her, return again.* It is very rare that any who are caught in this snare of the devil recover themselves, so much is the heart hardened, and the mind blinded, by the deceitfulness of this sin. Many interpreters think that this caution against the *strange woman*, besides the literal sense, is to be understood figuratively, as a caution against idolatry, which is spiritual whoredom. Wisdom will keep thee from all familiarity with the worshippers of images. Wisdom will keep thee from being captivated by the carnal mind, and from subjecting the spirit to the dominion of the flesh.

II. This wisdom will be of use to guide and direct us in that which is good (*v.* 20): *That thou mayest walk in the way of good men.* It will be our wisdom to walk in that way, to ask for the good old way and walk therein, Jer. vi. 16; Heb. vi. 12; xii. 1. *The paths of the righteous* are the paths of life. "That thou mayest imitate those excellent persons, the patriarchs and prophets, and be preserved in *the paths of those righteous* men who followed after them." *The upright shall dwell in the land*, peaceably and quietly, as long as they live.

JAMIESON, FAUSSET, BROWN

12-15. To deliver—as from great danger (ch. 6:5). **way . . . man**—(Ps. 1:1). **froward things**—perversity (ch. 6:14; 23:23), what is opposed to truth. **paths of uprightness**—or, plainness. **walk**—habitually act; **14,** and that with pleasure, in ignorance of good and pursuit of evil. **frowardness**—Not only their own perversity, but that of others is their delight. They love most the worst things. **15. crooked**—tortuous, unprincipled. **froward**—lit., (they) are going back, not only aside from right, but opposite to it.

16-19. Deliverance from another danger. **the strange woman**—This term is often used for harlot, or loose woman (Judg. 11:1, 2), married (ch. 7:5, 19) or not (I Kings 11:1), so called, because such were, perhaps at first, foreigners, though "strange" may also denote whatever is opposed to right or proper, as *strange fire* (Num. 3:4); *strange incense* (Exod. 30:9). **flattereth**—lit., "smooths." **her words**—(Ps. 5:9).

17. guide . . . youth—lawful husband (Jer. 3:4). **covenant . . . God**—of marriage made in God's name.

18. inclineth—sinks down (cf. Num. 13:31). **the dead**—or shades of the departed (Ps. 88:10). **19.** i.e., such as remain impenitent (cf. Eccles. 7:26). **paths of life**—(Ps. 16:11), opposed to paths unto the dead.

20. That . . . way of good—i.e., Such is the object of these warnings.

21, 22. (Cf. Ps. 37:3, 9, 22, 27.) **transgressors**—or impious rebels (cf. Jer. 9:2). **rooted out**—utterly destroyed, as trees plucked up by the roots.

ADAM CLARKE

12. *The man that speaketh froward things. Tahpuchoth*, things of "subversion"; from *taphach*, "to turn or change the course of a thing."

16. *The stranger which flattereth with her words.* She that "smooths" with her words. The original intimates the glib, oily speeches of a prostitute.

22. *Transgressors. Bogedim.* The "garment men," the hypocrites; those who act borrowed characters, who go under a cloak.

MATTHEW HENRY — CHAPTER 3

Verses 1-6

A life of communion with God will be of unspeakable advantage.

I. We must have a continual regard to God's precepts, *v.* 1, 2. Fix God's law, and his commandments, as our rule. Not only our heads, but our hearts, must *keep God's commandments.* To encourage us to submit ourselves to all the restraints and injunctions of the divine law, we are assured (*v.* 2) that it is the certain way to long life and prosperity. Even the days of old age shall not be evil days, but days in which thou shalt have pleasure: *Peace shall they* be continually *adding to thee. Great* and growing *peace have those that love the law.*

II. We must have a continual regard to God's promises, which go along with his precepts (*v.* 3): '*Let not mercy and truth forsake thee*, God's mercy in promising, and his truth in performing. *Bind them about thy neck*, as the most graceful ornament." It is the greatest honour we are capable of in this world to have an interest in the mercy and truth of God. "*Write them upon the table of thy heart*, as dear to thee; take a pleasure in applying them and thinking them over." To encourage us to do this we are assured (*v.* 4) that this is the way to recommend our-

JAMIESON, FAUSSET, BROWN — CHAPTER 3

Vss. 1-35. The study of truth commended. God must be feared, honored, and trusted, and filial submission, under chastisement, exhibited. The excellence of wisdom urged and illustrated by its place in the divine counsels. Piety enforced by a contrast of the destiny of the righteous and the wicked.

1. law [and] **commandments**—all divine instructions (cf. Ps. 119). **let thine heart keep**—or sincerely observe (ch. 4:13; 5:2). **2. length . . . life**—often promised as blessings (Ps. 21:4; 91:16). **peace**—includes prosperity (Ps. 125:5). **add**—abound to thee.

3. mercy and truth—God's faithfulness to His promises is often expressed by these terms (Ps. 25:10; 57:3). As attributes of men, they express integrity in a wide sense (ch. 16:6; 20:28). **bind . . . write . . . heart**—outwardly adorn and inwardly govern motives.

ADAM CLARKE — CHAPTER 3

2. *For length of days.* Three eminent blessings are promised here: (1) long days; (2) years of lives; (3) *shalom*, prosperity; i.e., health, long life, and abundance.

3. *Let not mercy and truth forsake thee.* Let these be your constant companions through life.

MATTHEW HENRY

selves both to our Creator and fellow-creatures: *So shalt thou find favour and good understanding.* A good man seeks the favour of God in the first place. He shall be owned as one of Wisdom's children, and shall have praise with God. He wishes to have favour with men also, to be *accepted of the multitude of his brethren* (Esther x. 3); they shall understand him aright.

III. We must have a continual regard to God's providence, must depend upon it in all our affairs, both by faith and prayer. We must therefore *trust in the Lord with all our hearts* (*v.* 5); we must believe that he is able to do what he will, wise to do what is best, and good, according to his promise, to do what is best for us, if we love him, and serve him. By prayer (*v.* 6): *In all thy ways acknowledge God.* We must ask his leave, and not design anything but what we are sure is lawful. We must ask his advice and beg direction from him. We must ask success of him, as those who know *the race is not to the swift.* For our encouragement to do this, it is promised, "*He shall direct thy paths,* so that thy way shall be safe and good and the issue happy at last."

Verses 7–12

Three exhortations, each enforced with a good reason:—

I. We must live in a humble and dutiful subjection to God and his government (*v.* 7): "*Fear the Lord,* as your sovereign Lord and Master; be ruled in everything by your religion and subject to the divine will." *Be not wise in thy own eyes.* There is not a greater enemy to the power of religion, and the fear of God in the heart, than conceitedness of our own wisdom. *Fear the Lord, and depart from evil;* take heed of doing anything to offend him and to forfeit his care. For our encouragement thus to live in the fear of God it is here promised (*v.* 8) that it shall be as serviceable even to the outward man as our necessary food. *It shall be health to thy navel.* It will be strengthening: It shall be *marrow to thy bones.* The prudence, temperance, and sobriety, the calmness and composure of mind, and the good government of the appetites and passions, which religion teaches, tend very much not only to the health of the soul, but to a good habit of body.

II. We must make a good use of our estates, and that is the way to increase them, *v.* 9, 10. *Honour the Lord with thy substance.* Worldly wealth is but poor substance, yet, such as it is, we must honour God with it, and then, if ever, it becomes substantial. We must honour God *with our increase.* It is meant of the increase of the earth, for we live upon annual products, to keep us in constant dependence on God. God, who is the first and best, must have the first and best of everything. *So shall thy barns be filled with plenty.* "God shall bless thee with an increase of that which is for use, not for show or ornament—for spending and laying out, not for hoarding and laying up." What we gave we have.

III. We must conduct ourselves aright under our afflictions, *v.* 11, 12. We must not despise an affliction, be it ever so light and short, as if it were not worth taking notice of, or as if it were not sent on an errand and therefore required no answer. We must not be stocks, and stones, and stoics, under our afflictions, hardening ourselves under them, and concluding we can easily get through them without God. We must not be weary of an affliction, not be dispirited, dispossessed of our own souls, or driven to despair. A divine correction is *the chastening of the Lord.* It is from God, and therefore we must not be weary of it, for he knows our frame, both what we need and what we can bear. A fatherly correction comes not from his vindictive justice as a Judge, but his wise affection as a Father. The father corrects *the son whom he* loves, nay, and because he loves him and desires he may be wise and good.

Verses 13–20

Happy is the man that findeth wisdom, that true wisdom which consists in the knowledge and love of God, and an entire conformity to all his truths, providences, and laws.

I. What it is to find wisdom so as to be made happy by it. He is the happy man who, having found it, makes it his own, who *draws out understanding* (so the word is). Having it not in himself, he draws it with the bucket of prayer from the fountain of all wisdom, *who gives liberally.* He takes pains for it, as he does who draws ore out of the mine. That is well got, and to good purpose, that is thus used to good purpose. We read here of the merchandise of wisdom, which intimates, we must make it our business, and not a by-business, as the merchant bestows the main of his thoughts and time upon his merchandise. This is that pearl of great

JAMIESON, FAUSSET, BROWN

4. favour—grace, amiability (ch. 22:11; Ps. 45:2); united with this, **a good understanding**—(cf. *Margin*), a discrimination, which secures success. **in the sight . . . man**—such as God and man approve.

5. Trust . . . heart—This is the center and marrow of true wisdom (ch. 22:19; 28:25). The positive duty has its corresponding negation in the admonition against self-confidence. **6. ways**—(Ps. 1:1.) **acknowledge**—by seeking His wise aid (ch. 16:3; Ps. 37:5; Jer. 9:23, 24). **direct**—lit., "make plain" (cf. Heb. 12:13).

7. (Cf. ch. 27:2; Rom. 12:16.) **fear . . . evil**—reverentially regarding His law.

8. It—This conduct. **health**—(Cf. *Margin*). **to thy navel**—for all the organs of nourishment. **marrow**—(Cf. *Margin*). **bones**—frame of body. True piety promotes bodily health.

9, 10. (Cf. ch. 11:25; Exod. 23:19; Deut. 18:4; Isa. 32:8; II Cor. 9:13.) **presses**—or wine fats (Joel 2:24; 3:13).

11, 12. The true intent of afflictions considered; they do not contradict the assertion of the blessed state of the pious (Job 5:17; Heb. 12:5, 6).

he delighteth—or receiveth as denoting reconciliation regarding the offense which produced chastisement.

13. findeth—lit., "reaches," or "obtains by seeking." **getteth**—lit., "draws out," as metals by digging.

ADAM CLARKE

6. *In all thy ways acknowledge him.* Begin, continue, and end every work, purpose, and device with God. Earnestly pray for His direction at the commencement; look for His continual support in the progress; and so begin and continue that all may terminate in His glory. And then it will certainly be to your good, for we never honor God without serving ourselves.

11. *Despise not the chastening of the Lord.* The word *musar* signifies "correction, discipline, and instruction."

12. *Whom the Lord loveth.* To encourage thee to bear correction, know that it is a proof of God's love to thee; and thereby He shows that He treats thee as a father does his son, even that one to whom he bears the fondest affection. The last clause the Septuagint translate, "And chasteneth every son whom he receiveth"; and Heb. xii. 6 quotes this *literatim.*

MATTHEW HENRY

price which, when we have found it, we must willingly sell all for the purchase of, Matt. xiii. 45, 46. *Buy the truth* (Prov. xxiii. 23); he does not say at what rate, because we must buy it at any rate rather than miss it. It is not enough to lay hold of wisdom, but we must keep our hold, hold it fast, with a resolution never to let it go, but to persevere in the ways of wisdom to the end.

II. The happiness of those who find it is a transcendent happiness, more than can be found in the wealth of this world, if we had ever so much of it, *v.* 14, 15. All would not purchase heavenly wisdom; it *cannot be gotten for gold,* Job xxviii. 15, &c. All would not countervail the want of heavenly wisdom nor be the ransom of a soul lost by its own folly. All would not make a man half so happy as those are who have true wisdom, though they have none of all these things. True happiness is inclusive of all those things which are supposed to make men happy, *v.* 16, 17. Wisdom is here represented as a bright and bountiful queen, reaching forth gifts to her faithful and loving subjects. She offers life *in her right hand.* Religion puts us into the best methods of prolonging life, and, though our days on earth should be no more than our neighbour's, yet it will secure to us everlasting life in a better world. Riches and honour she reaches out with *her left hand.* True piety has in it the greatest true pleasure. *Her ways are ways of pleasantness.* All the enjoyments and entertainments of sense are not comparable to the pleasure which gracious souls have in communion with God and doing good. The way of religion, as it is the right way, so it is a pleasant way; it is smooth and clean, and strewed with roses: *All her paths are peace.* There is not only peace in the end, but peace in the way. It is the happiness of paradise (*v.* 18): *She is a tree of life.* True grace is that to the soul which the tree of life would have been, from which our first parents were shut out for eating of the forbidden tree. Those that feed on this heavenly wisdom shall find an antidote against age and death; they shall *eat and live for ever.* It is a participation of the happiness of God himself, for wisdom is his everlasting glory and blessedness, *v.* 19, 20. *Happy is the man that finds wisdom,* for he will thereby be *thoroughly furnished for every good word and work.* He has wherewithal to make good all the foregoing promises of long life, riches, and honour; for all the wealth of heaven, earth, and seas, is his.

Verses 21–26

I. The exhortation is, to have religion's rules always in view and always at heart, *v.* 21. "*My son, let them not depart from thy eyes;* let not thy eyes ever depart from them to wander after vanity. Have them always in mind, and as long as thou livest, keep up and cultivate thy acquaintance with them." Have them always at heart; for it is in that treasury, the hidden man of the heart, that we must *keep sound wisdom and discretion.*

II. The argument to enforce this exhortation is taken from the unspeakable advantage which wisdom, thus kept, will be of to us. "It will be *life to thy soul* (*v.* 22); it will quicken thee to thy duty; it will revive thee under thy troubles when thou beginnest to droop and despond. It will be thy spiritual life, an earnest of life eternal." It shall be *grace to thy neck,* as a chain of gold, or a jewel. *Grace to thy jaws* (so the word is), grateful to thy *taste and relish* (so some); it shall infuse *grace into all thou sayest* (so others), shall furnish thee with acceptable words, which shall gain thee credit. Good people are taken under God's special protection, and are safe and may be easy, *v.* 23. If our religion be our companion, it will be our convoy: "*Then shalt thou walk in thy way safely.* The natural life, and all that belongs to it, shall be under the protection of God's providence; the spiritual life, and all its interests, are under the protection of his grace; so that thou shalt be kept from falling into sin or trouble." The way of duty is the way of safety. "We are in danger of falling, but wisdom will keep thee, that *thy foot shall not stumble* at those things which overthrow many, but which thou shalt know how to get over." By night, *v.* 24, we lie exposed and are most subject to frights. "But keep up communion with God, and keep a good conscience, and then *when thou liest down thou shalt not be afraid* of fire, or thieves, or spectres, or any of the terrors of darkness, knowing that when we, and all our friends, are asleep, yet *he that keeps Israel neither slumbers nor sleeps.*" The way to have a good night is to keep a good conscience; and the sleep, as of the labouring man, so of the wise and godly man, is sweet. Integrity and uprightness will preserve us, so that we need *not be afraid of sudden fear, v.* 25. But let not the wise and good man fear the *desolation of the wicked, when*

JAMIESON, FAUSSET, BROWN

14, 15. The figure of vs. 13 carried out. **it**—i.e., wisdom. **merchandise**—acquisition by trading. **fine gold**—dug gold, solid as a nugget. **rubies**—gems, or pearls.

16, 17. Wisdom personified as bringing the best blessings (cf. Matt. 6:33; I Tim. 4:8).

Her ways—such as she directs us to take.

18. Wisdom allegorized as **a tree of life**—(Gen. 2:9; 3:22,) whose fruit preserves life, gives all that makes living a blessing.

19, 20. The place of wisdom in the economy of creation and providence commends it to men, who, in proportion to their finite powers, may possess this invaluable attribute, and are thus encouraged by the divine example of its use to seek its possession.

21. sound wisdom—(cf. ch. 2:7). **let . . . eyes**—i.e., these words of instruction.

22-24, assign reasons in their value for happiness and ornament, guidance and support in dangers, both when waking and sleeping.

25. Be not—or, You shall not be. **sudden fear**—what causes it (ch. 1:27), any unlooked-for evil (Ps. 46:3; 91:12; I Pet. 3:14). **desolation**—(ch. 1:27). **26.** The reason; such as are objects of God's favor. **be thy confidence**—lit., "in thy confidence," in the source of thy strength (cf. Nah. 3:9, for the same construction, *Hebrew*).

ADAM CLARKE

JOSEPH PARKER:

Verse 14. The idea of trading suggests that wisdom and understanding are to be obtained in the way in which merchandise is produced for market uses, involving every type of calculation, effort, arrangement, and legitimate adventure. Sometimes wisdom is as merchandise which is brought from afar, through much toil of shipping and much risk of sailing, yet so determined is the merchant that he will be deterred by nothing that threatens to overwhelm him. Silver and gold are set down as types by which we are to understand and appreciate the varying degrees of value: in the case of wisdom and understanding even these types of things most precious are left behind. All history shows how truly the world has been devoted to money-getting; when the wise man wanted a simile by which to indicate the eagerness which should characterize the studious disposition, he turned to the marketplace for his metaphor.

—*The People's Bible*

18. *She is a tree of life.* "The tree of lives," alluding most manifestly to the tree so called which God in the beginning planted in the garden of paradise.

19. *The Lord by wisdom hath founded the earth.* Here wisdom is taken in its proper acceptation, for that infinite knowledge and skill which God has manifested in the creation and composition of the earth, and in the structure and economy of the heavens.

21. *Keep sound wisdom and discretion. Tushiyah umezimmah.* We have met with both these words before. *Tushiyah* is the "essence" or "substance" of a thing; *mezimmah* is the "resolution" or "purpose" formed in reference to something good or excellent. To acknowledge God as the Author of all good is the *tushiyah,* the "essence," of a godly man's creed. To resolve to act according to the directions of His wisdom is the *mezimmah,* the "religious purpose," that will bring good to ourselves and glory to God.

24. *When thou liest down.* In these verses (23-26) the wise man describes the confidence, security, and safety which proceed from a consciousness of innocence.

MATTHEW HENRY

it comes, that is, the desolation which the wicked ones make of religion and the religious.

Verses 27–35

Precepts of wisdom which relate to our neighbour.

I. We must render to all their due, both in justice and charity, and not delay to do it (*v.* 27, 28): "*Withhold not good from those to whom it is due, when it is in the power of thy hand to do it*, but it was thy great fault if thou didst, by thy extravagances, disable thyself to do justly and show mercy. If thou hast it by thee today, say not to thy neighbour, *Go thy way for this time*, and come at a more convenient season, and I will then see what will be done; *tomorrow I will give;* whereas thou art not sure that thou shalt live till tomorrow, or that tomorrow thou shalt *have it by thee*. Make not excuses to shift off a duty that must be done, nor delight to keep thy neighbour in pain and in suspense, nor to show the authority which the giver has over the beggar; but readily and cheerfully, and from a principle of conscience towards God, give good to *those to whom it is due*," to the *lords and owners of it* (so the word is), to those who upon any account are entitled to it. This requires us, 1. To pay our just debts without fraud or delay. 2. To give wages to those who have earned them. 3. To provide for our relations, and those that have dependence on us, for to them it is due. 4. To render dues both to church and state, magistrates and ministers. 5. To be ready to all acts of friendship and humanity, and in everything to be neighbourly; for these are things that are due by the law of doing as we would be done by. 6. To be charitable to the poor and necessitous.

II. We must never design any hurt or harm to anybody (*v.* 29): "*Devise not evil against thy neighbour;* and the rather because *he dwells securely by thee*, and entertains no jealousy or suspicion of thee, and therefore is off his guard."

III. We must not be quarrelsome and litigious (*v.* 30): "Do not *strive with a man without cause*; contend not for that which thou hast no title to; resent not that as a provocation which peradventure was but an oversight. Never trouble thy neighbour with frivolous complaints and accusations, or vexatious law-suits, when thou mightest right thyself in a friendly way." Law must be the last refuge.

IV. We must not envy the prosperity of evil-doers, *v.* 31. "*Envy not the oppressor;* though he be rich and great. *Choose none of his ways;* do not imitate him. Never think of doing as he does, though thou wert sure to get by it all that he has, for it would be dearly bought." Now, to show what little reason saints have to envy sinners, Solomon here, in the last four verses of the chapter, compares the condition of sinners and saints together. Saints are beloved, *v.* 32. The froward sinners, whose lives are a perverse contradiction to his will, are *abomination to the Lord*. He that hates nothing that he has made yet abhors those who have thus marred themselves. The righteous therefore have no reason to envy them, for he communicates to them the secret tokens of his love; they know his mind, and the meanings and intentions of his providence, better than others can. Saints are under his blessing, they and their habitation, *v.* 33. The just have a habitation, a poor cottage (the word is used for sheep-cotes), a very mean dwelling; but God blesses it from the beginning of the year to the end of it. Those who exalt themselves shall certainly be abased: *Surely he scorns the scorners*. Those who scorn to submit to the discipline of religion, who scoff at godliness and godly people, God will lay them open to scorn before all the world. Those who humble themselves shall be exalted, for *he gives grace to the lowly*; he works that in them which puts honour upon them and for which they are *accepted of God and approved of men*. The end of sinners will be everlasting shame, the end of saints endless honour, *v.* 35.

JAMIESON, FAUSSET, BROWN

27, 28. Promptly fulfil all obligations both of justice and charity (cf. Jas. 2:15, 16).

29, 30. Do not abuse confidence and avoid litigation.

31. oppressor—or man of mischief. The destiny of successful evildoers warns against desiring their lot (Ps. 37:1, 2, 35, 36).

32-35. Reasons for the warning. **froward**—(ch. 2:15). **secret . . . righteous**—in their communion (Amos 3:7).

33. curse . . . wicked—It abides with them, and will be manifested. **34.** The retribution of sinners, as in Ps. 18:26.

35. inherit—as a portion. **shame**—or disgrace, as opposed to honor. **promotion**—(cf. *Margin*); as honor for well-doing makes men conspicuous, so fools are signalized by disgrace.

ADAM CLARKE

27. *Withhold not good from them to whom it is due.* "From the lords of it." But who are they? The poor.

31. *Envy thou not the oppressor.* Oh, how bewitching is *power!* Every man desires it; and yet all hate *tyrants.* But query, if all had *power*, would not the major part be *tyrants?*

32. *But his secret. Sodo, his secret assembly;* godly people meet there, and God dwells there.

33. *The curse of the Lord.* No godly people meet in such a house, nor is God ever an inmate there. *But he blesseth the habitation of the just.* He considers it as His own temple. There He is worshipped in spirit and in truth; and hence God makes it His dwelling place.

34. *Surely he scorneth the scorners: but he giveth grace unto the lowly.* The Septuagint has, "The Lord resisteth the proud; but giveth grace to the humble." These words are quoted by St. Peter, 1st Epist. v. 5, and by St. James, chap. iv. 6, just as they stand in the Septuagint, with the change of "God," for "the Lord."

MATTHEW HENRY

CHAPTER 4

Verses 1–13

I. The invitation which Solomon gives to his children (*v.* 1, 2): *Hear, you children, the instruction of a father*. "Let my own children, in the first place, receive those instructions which I set down for the use of others also." Magistrates and ministers are concerned to take a more than ordinary care for the instruction of their own families. Let all young people, in the days of their childhood and youth, take pains to get knowledge and grace, for then their minds are formed and seasoned. He does not say, *My* children, but *You* children. Let all that would receive instruction come with the disposition of children, though they be grown persons. Let all prejudices be laid aside, and the mind be as white

JAMIESON, FAUSSET, BROWN

CHAPTER 4

Vss. 1-27. To an earnest call for attention to his teachings, the writer adds a commendation of wisdom, preceded and enforced by the counsels of his father and teacher. To this he adds a caution (against the devices of the wicked), and a series of exhortations to docility, integrity, and uprightness.

ADAM CLARKE

CHAPTER 4

MATTHEW HENRY

paper. Let them be dutiful, tractable, and self-diffident, and take the word as the word of a father, which comes both with authority and with affection. We must see it coming from God as *our Father in heaven*, to whom we pray, from whom we expect blessings, the Father of our spirits. We must look upon our teachers as our fathers, who love us and seek our welfare. We are told (*v.* 1), not only that it is the *instruction of a father*, but that it is *understanding*, and therefore should be welcome to intelligent creatures. Religion has reason on its side, and we are taught it by fair reasoning. It is a law indeed (*v.* 2), but that law is founded upon unquestionable principles of truth, upon *good doctrine*, which is worthy of all acceptation. *If* we admit the doctrine, we cannot but submit to the law.

II. The instructions he gives them. He had them from his parents, and teaches his children the same that they taught him, *v.* 3, 4. His parents loved him, and therefore taught him: *I was my father's son.* David had many sons, but Solomon was his son *indeed*, as Isaac is called (Gen. xvii. 19) and for the same reason, because on him the covenant was entailed. He was *tender, and only beloved, in the sight of his mother*. Though he was a prince, and heir-apparent to the crown, yet they did not let him live at large; they tutored him. And perhaps David was the more strict with Solomon in his education because he had seen the ill effects of undue indulgence in Adonijah, whom he had not *crossed in anything* (1 Kings i. 6). What his parents taught him he teaches others. When Solomon was grown up he not only remembered, but took a pleasure in repeating, the good lessons his parents taught him when he was a child. Though Solomon was a wise man himself, and divinely inspired, yet, when he was to teach wisdom, he did not think it below him to quote his father. Those that would teach well, in religion, must not look with contempt upon the knowledge of their predecessors; if we must keep to the good old way, why should we scorn the good old words? Jer. vi. 16. Solomon enforces his exhortations with the authority of his father David, a man famous in his generation. These instructions were, *v.* 4–13, precept and exhortation. David, in teaching his son, expressed himself with great warmth and importunity, and inculcated the same thing again and again. He recommends to him his Bible, his father's *words* (*v.* 4), the *words of his mouth* (*v.* 5), his *sayings* (*v.* 10), all the good lessons he had taught him; and perhaps he means particularly the book of Psalms, many of which were *Maschils—psalms of instruction*, and two of them are expressly said to be *for Solomon.* He must *hear and receive them* (*v.* 10). He must *hold fast the form of sound words* which his father gave him (*v.* 4): *Let thy heart retain my words;* and except the word be hid in the heart, lodged in the will and affections, it will not be retained. He must govern himself by them: *Keep my commandments.* He must stick to them and abide by them: "*Decline not from the words of my mouth* (*v.* 5), as fearing they will be too great a check upon thee, but *take fast hold of instruction* (*v.* 13), as being resolved to keep thy hold and never let it go." A principle of religion in the heart is the one thing needful; therefore, Get this *wisdom*, get this *understanding*, *v.* 5. And again, "*Get wisdom*, and, *with all thy getting, get understanding*, *v.* 7. Get wisdom by experience, get it *above all thy getting*; be more in care and take more pains to get this than to get the wealth of this world." True wisdom is God's gift. God gives it to those that labour for it. *Forget her not* (*v.* 5), *forsake her not* (*v.* 6), *let her not go* (*v.* 13) *but keep her. Love her* (*v.* 6), and *embrace her* (*v.* 8), as worldly men love their wealth and set their hearts upon it. If we cannot be great masters of wisdom, yet let us be true lovers of it; let us embrace it with a sincere affection, as those that admire its beauty. *Exalt her*, *v.* 8. Always keep up high thoughts of religion, and do all thou canst to maintain the credit of it among men. Let *Wisdom's* children not only justify her, but magnify her, honouring those that fear the Lord, though they are low in the world, and in regarding a *poor wise man*, we exalt wisdom. It is the main matter (*v.* 7): *Wisdom is the principal thing;* other things which are solicitous to get and keep are nothing to it. It is that which recommends us to God, which beautifies the soul, which enables us to live to some good purpose in the world, and to get to heaven at last; and therefore it is the principal thing. It has reason and equity on its side (*v.* 11): "*I have taught thee in the way of wisdom*, and so it will be found to be at last. *I have led thee in right paths*, agreeable to the eternal rules and reasons of good and evil." David not only taught his son by good instructions, but led him both by a good example and by applying general instructions to particular cases. *Keep my*

JAMIESON, FAUSSET, BROWN

1, 2. (Cf. ch. 1:8.) **to know**—in order to know. **doctrine**—the matter of learning (ch. 1:5), such as he had received (Lam. 3:1).

3. father's son—emphatic, a son specially regarded, and so called **tender,** as an object of special care (cf. I Chron. 22:7; 29:1); **an** idea further expressed by **only beloved**—(or, as an only son), (Gen. 22:2), though he had brothers (I Chron. 3:5).

4. He taught—or directed me. **retain**—as well as receive. **keep . . . and live**—observe, that you may live (ch. 7:2).

5. Get—as a possession not to be given up. **neither decline**—i.e., from obeying my word.

7. (Cf. Job 28:28.) **getting**—or possession; a desire for wisdom is wise.

6. Not only accept but love wisdom, who will keep thee from evil, and evil from thee.

8. As you highly esteem her, she will raise you to honor. **embrace her**—with fond affection.

11, 12. way of wisdom—which it prescribes. **led thee**—lit., "caused thee to tread," as a path (Ps. 107:7). **not be straitened**—have ample room (Ps. 18:36).

ADAM CLARKE

JOSEPH PARKER:

"For I was my father's son, tender and only beloved in the sight of my mother. He taught me also, and said unto me, Let thine heart retain my words: keep my commandments, and live" (vv. 3, 4).

Solomon knew youth because he had himself been young. He knew also the advantage of instruction, for he himself had enjoyed it. Thus one generation may benefit another, and increase its years by preventing a repetition of its errors. We save a man's time by saving him from mistakes, and thus we actually add to the length of his life. It is today that men may compress centuries within the span of the allotted term: if we were wise we, though so modern, would be the true patriarchs of history. What wisdom is stored for us! How easy now is the ascent to the temple of understanding! Every father can leave his son the fortune of a noble example. That is more than gold, more than acres, more than fame. Here it is that virtue has its splendid opportunity! Men may have been looking in the wrong direction for a heritage for their children. Let that heritage be a vivid recollection of a home sanctified by prayer, a life devoted to good doing, an example of industry and justice, a spirit of hopefulness and charity, and that memory will be an inheritance and a refuge in life's most painful hours. The man in the text was an only son, and therefore was in a trying position; yet his father and his mother were wise, so they enriched him with wisdom, and kept not from him the advantages of discipline. Fools are they who ruin their children under the hypocrisy of being kind to them. In after years the victims of such kindness will be the bitterest of its critics.—*The People's Bible*

7. *Wisdom is the principal thing. Reshith chochmah,* "Wisdom is the principle." *Wisdom* prescribes the best end, and the means best calculated for its attainment. *Understanding* directs to the ways, times, places, and opportunities of practicing the lessons of wisdom.

MATTHEW HENRY

commandments and live, v. 4. That of our Saviour agrees with this, *If thou wilt enter into life, keep the commandments,* Matt. xix. 17. "Receive wisdom's sayings, *and the years of thy life shall be many* (*v.* 10), as many in this world as Infinite Wisdom sees fit, and in the other world thou shalt live that life the years of which shall never be numbered. *Keep her* therefore, whatever it cost thee, *for she is thy life,*" *v.* 13. "Love wisdom, and cleave to her, and she shall *preserve thee, she shall keep thee* (*v.* 6) from sin, the worst of evils; she shall keep thee from hurting thyself, and then none else can hurt thee." As we say, "Keep thy shop, and thy shop will keep thee"; so, "Keep thy wisdom, and thy wisdom will keep thee. It will be thy honour and reputation (*v.* 8): *Exalt* wisdom and though she needs not thy service she will abundantly recompence it, *she shall promote thee, she shall bring thee to honour.*" This he insists on (*v.* 9): "*She shall give to thy head an ornament of grace* in this world, and in the other world *a crown of glory shall she deliver to thee,* a crown that shall never wither."

Verses 14–19

Some make David's instructions to Solomon, which began *v.* 4, to continue to the end of the chapter; but it is more probable that Solomon begins here again. In these verses he cautions us against the path of the wicked.

I. The caution itself, *v.* 14, 15. We must take heed of falling in with sin and sinners; *Enter not into the paths of the wicked.* "If, ere thou wast aware, thou didst enter in at the gate, because it was wide, *go not* on *in the way of evil men.* As soon as thou art made sensible of thy mistake, retire immediately, take not a step more, stay not a minute longer, in the way that certainly leads to destruction." It intimates likewise at what a distance we should keep from sin and sinners; he does not say, Keep at a due distance, but at a great distance, the further the better; never think you can get far enough from it.

II. The reasons to enforce this caution. "Consider the character of the men whose way thou art warned to shun." They are mischievous men (*v.* 16, 17). They are continually endeavouring to *cause some to fall,* to ruin them body and soul. Mischief is rest and sleep to them. Mischief is meat and drink to them; they feed and feast upon it. *They eat the bread of wickedness and drink the wine of violence* (*v.* 17). All they eat and drink is got by rapine and oppression. "Shun those that delight to do mischief, for whatever friendship they may pretend, they will do thee mischief; thou wilt ruin thyself if thou dost concur with them (*ch.* i. 18) and they will ruin thee if thou dost not." The way of righteousness is light (*v.* 18): *The path of the just,* which they have chosen, and in which they walk, *is as light*; the *light shines on their ways* (Job xxii. 28). Christ is *their way* and he is *the light.* They are guided by the word of God and that is *a light to their feet*; they themselves are *light in the Lord* and they *walk in the light as he is in the light.* It is as the morning-light, which *shines out of obscurity* (Isa. lviii. 8, 10) and puts an end to the *works of darkness.* It is a growing light; it *shines more and more,* not like the light of a meteor, which soon disappears, or that of a candle, which burns dim and burns down, but like that of the rising sun, which mounts upward shining. It will arrive, in the end, at *the perfect day.* The *way of* sin *is as darkness, v.* 19. The works he had cautioned us not to have fellowship with are *works of darkness.* What true pleasure and satisfaction can those have who know no pleasure and satisfaction but what they have in doing mischief? *The way of the wicked is dark,* and therefore dangerous; for they stumble, and yet *know not at what they stumble.*

Verses 20–27

Solomon, having warned us not to do evil, here teaches us how to do well.

I. We must have a continual regard to the word of God.

1. The sayings of wisdom must be our principles by which we must govern ourselves, our monitors to warn us of duty and danger; therefore, "*Incline thy ear to them* (*v.* 20); humbly bow to them; diligently listen to them." We must retain them carefully (*v.* 21); we must lay them before us as our rule: "*Let them not depart from thy eyes;* view them, review them, and in everything aim to conform to them." We must lodge them within us, as a commanding principle: "*Keep them in the midst of thy heart,* as things dear to thee, and which thou art afraid of losing."

2. The reason why we must thus make much of the words of wisdom is because they will be both food and physic to us, like *the tree of life,* Rev. xxii. 2.

JAMIESON, FAUSSET, BROWN

13–(Cf. ch. 3:18.) The figure of laying hold with the hand suggests earnest effort.

9. ornament–such as the chaplet or wreath of conquerors. **deliver**–(Cf. Gen. 14:20.) The allusion to a shield, contained in the *Hebrew,* suggests protection as well as honor (cf. vs. 6).

14. (Cf. Ps. 1:1.) Avoid all temptations to the beginning of evil.

16, 17. The reason is found in the character of sinners, whose zeal to do evil is forcibly depicted (ch. 6:4; Ps. 36:5). They live by flagrant vices (ch. 1:13). Some prefer to render, "Their bread is wickedness, their drink violence" (cf. Job 15:16; 34:7).

18, 19. As shining light increases from twilight to noonday splendor, so the course of the just increases in purity, but that of the wicked is as thickest darkness, in which one knows not on what he stumbles.

20-22. (Cf. vss. 10, 13; ch. 3:8, etc.).

ADAM CLARKE

13. *Take fast hold. Hachazek,* "Seize it strongly," and keep the hold; and do this as for life.

17. *For they eat the bread of wickedness.* By privately stealing. *And drink the wine of violence.* By highway robbery.

18. *But the path of the just.* The path of the wicked is gloomy, dark, and dangerous; that of the righteous is open, luminous, and instructive. This verse contains a fine metaphor; it refers to the sun rising above the horizon, and the increasing twilight, till his beams shine full upon the earth. The original may be translated, "going and illuminating unto the prepared day."

MATTHEW HENRY

(1) Food: *For they are life unto those that find them*, *v.* 22. As the spiritual life was begun by the word, so by the same word it is still nourished and maintained. (2) Physic. They are *health to all their flesh*, to the whole man, both body and soul; they help to keep both in good plight. They are *a medicine to all their flesh* (so the word is), to all their corruptions, for they are called flesh. There is in the word of God a proper remedy for all our spiritual maladies.

II. We must keep a watchful eye and a strict hand upon all the motions of our inward man, *v.* 23. *Keep thy heart with all diligence.* God, who gave us these souls, gave us a strict charge with them. We must set a strict guard, accordingly, upon all the avenues of the soul; keep our hearts from doing hurt and getting hurt, from being defiled by sin and disturbed by trouble; keep out bad thoughts; keep up good thoughts; keep the affections upon right objects and in due bounds. *Keep them with all keepings* (so the word is); there are many ways of keeping things—by care, by strength, by calling in help, and we must use them all in keeping our hearts. A good reason is given for this care, because *out of it are the issues of life.* Out of a heart well kept will flow living issues, good products, to the glory of God and the edification of others.

III. We must set a *watch before the door of our lips*, that we offend not with our tongue (*v.* 24): *Put away from thee a froward mouth and perverse lips.* We must conceive a great detestation of all manner of evil words, cursing, swearing, lying, slandering, brawling, filthiness, and foolish talking, all which come from a *froward mouth and perverse lips*, that will not be governed either by reason or religion, but contradict both, and which are as unsightly and ill-favoured before God as a crooked distorted mouth drawn awry is before men.

IV. We must make a covenant with our eyes: "Let them *look right on and straight before thee*, (*v.* 25). Let the eye be fixed and not wandering; let it not rove after every thing that presents itself, for then it will be diverted from good and ensnared in evil. Let thy intentions be sincere and uniform, and look not asquint at any by-end." We must keep our eye upon our Master, and be careful to approve ourselves to him; keep our eye upon our rule, and conform to that; keep our eye upon our mark, the *prize of the high calling*, and direct all towards that. *Oculum in metam—The eye upon the goal.*

V. We must act considerately in all we do (*v.* 26): *Ponder the path of thy feet, weigh it* (so the word is); "put the word of God in one scale, and what thou hast done, or art about to do, in the other, and see how they agree. Do nothing rashly."

VI. We must act with steadiness, caution, and consistency: "*Let all thy ways be established* (*v.* 26) and be not unstable in them."

JAMIESON, FAUSSET, BROWN

22. health . . . flesh—by preserving from vices destructive of health.

23. with all diligence—or, above, or more than all, *custody* (cf. *Margin*), all that is kept (cf. Ezek. 38:7), because the heart is the depository of all wisdom and the source of whatever affects life and character (Matt. 12:35; 15:19).

24. a froward mouth—i.e., a mouth, or words of ill nature. The *Hebrew* word differs from that used (ch. 2:15; 3:32). **perverse**—or, quarreling. **lips**—or, words.

25. Let . . . before thee—i.e., pursue a sincere and direct purpose, avoiding temptations.

26. Ponder—Consider well; a wise course results from wise forethought.

27. (Cf. vs. 25.) Avoid all by-paths of evil (Deut. 2:27; 17:11). A life of integrity requires attention to heart, speech, eyes, and conduct.

ADAM CLARKE

23. *Keep thy heart with all diligence.* "Above all keeping," guard your heart. He who knows anything of himself knows how apt his affections are to go astray. *For out of it are the issues of life.* "The goings out of lives."

24. *A froward mouth.* Beware of hastiness, anger, and rash speeches. *And perverse lips.* Do not delight in nor acquire the habit of contradicting and gainsaying; and beware of calumniating and backbiting your neighbor.

MATTHEW HENRY

CHAPTER 5

Verses 1–14

I. A solemn preface, to introduce the caution which follows, *v.* 1, 2. Solomon here addresses himself to his son, that is, to all young men, as unto his children. "It is *my wisdom, my understanding*; I undertake to teach thee wisdom, which is to be learned in my school." Solomon's lectures are not designed to fill our heads with matters of nice speculation, or doubtful disputation, but to guide us in the government of ourselves.

II. The caution itself is to abstain from fleshly lusts, from adultery, fornication, and all uncleanness. Some apply this figuratively, and by the adulterous woman here understand idolatry, or false doctrine, which tends to debauch men's minds and manners, but the primary scope of it is plainly to warn us against seventh-commandment sins. It is true *the lips of a strange woman drop as a honey-comb* (*v.* 3); the kisses of its mouth, the words of its mouth, are *smoother than oil*, that the poisonous pill may go down glibly and there may be no suspicion of harm in it. But consider: It *is bitter as wormwood, v.* 4. What was luscious in the mouth rises in the stomach and turns sour there. If some that have been guilty of this sin have repented and been saved, yet the direct tendency of the sin is to destruction of body and soul; the *feet* of it *go down to death, v.* 5. Consider how false the charms are. The adulteress flatters and speaks fair, her words are honey and oil, but she will deceive those that hearken to her: *Her ways are movable, that thou canst not know them.* **Proteus-like, she puts on many shapes, that she may keep in with** those whom she has a design upon. And what does she aim at with all this art and management? Nothing but to keep them from *pondering the path of life*,

JAMIESON, FAUSSET, BROWN

CHAPTER 5

Vss. 1-23. A warning against the seductive arts of wicked women, enforced by considering the advantages of chastity, and the miserable end of the wicked.

1. This connection of **wisdom** and **understanding** is frequent (ch. 2:2; 3:7); the first denotes the use of wise means for wise ends; the other, the exercise of a proper discrimination in their discovery. **2. regard**—or, observe. **keep**—preserve constantly.

3. (Cf. ch. 2:16.) Her enticing promises are deceitful.

4. her end—lit., "her future," in sense of reward, what follows (cf. Ps. 37:37; 73:17). Its nature is evinced by the use of figures, opposite those of vs. 3. The physical and moral suffering of the deluded profligate are notoriously terrible. **5. feet . . . , steps**—i.e, course of life ends in death.

6. her ways . . . know—Some prefer, "that she may not ponder the path of life," etc.; but perhaps a better sense is, "her ways are varied, so as to prevent your knowledge of her true character, and so of true happiness."

ADAM CLARKE

CHAPTER 5

4. *Bitter as wormwood.* Something as excessive in its bitterness as honey is in its sweetness.

MATTHEW HENRY

for she knows that, if they once come to do that, she shall certainly lose them. Those are *ignorant of Satan's devices* who do not understand that the great thing he drives at in all his temptations is to keep them from choosing the path of life, to prevent them from being religious. The caution itself is very pressing (*v.* 7, 8): "*Remove thy way far from her;* if thy way should happen to lie near her, change thy way, rather than expose thyself to danger; *come not nigh the door of her house;* go on the other side of the street, nay, go through some other street, though it be about." Such tinder there is in the corrupt nature that it is madness, upon any pretence whatsoever, to come near the sparks. This sin blasts the reputation. "Thou wilt *give thy honour unto others* (*v.* 9); thou wilt lose it thyself; thou wilt put into the hand of each of thy neighbours a stone to throw at thee, for they will cry shame on thee as a foolish man." It wastes the time, gives *the years*, the years of youth, the flower of men's time, *unto the cruel*. Those years that should be given to the honour of a gracious God are spent in the service of a cruel sin. It ruins the estate (*v.* 10): "*Strangers* will be *filled with thy wealth*, which thou art but entrusted with as a steward for thy family; and the fruit of *thy labours*, which should be provision for thy own house, will be in *the house of a stranger*, that neither has right to it nor will ever thank thee for it." It is destructive to the health, and shortens men's days: *Thy flesh and thy body* will be *consumed* by it, *v.* 11. The lusts of uncleanness not only *war against the soul*, which the sinner neglects and is in no care about, but they war against the body too, which he is so indulgent of and is in such care to pamper. "Though thou art merry now, *sporting thyself in thy own deceivings*, yet thou wilt certainly *mourn at the last*," *v.* 11. Solomon brings in the convinced sinner reproaching himself because he hated to be reformed and therefore hated to be informed, and could not endure either to be taught his duty or to be told of his faults—*My heart despised reproof*, *v.* 12. He cannot but own that parents and ministers had given him good counsel and fair warning (*v.* 13). He had not taken their counsel, had not *obeyed their voice*, for indeed he *never inclined his ear to those that instructed him.* By the frequent acts of sin the habits of it were so rooted and confirmed that his heart was fully set in him to commit it (*v.* 14): *I was almost in all evil in the midst of the congregation and assembly.*

Verses 15–23

Solomon, having shown the great evil that there is in adultery and fornication, prescribes remedies against them.

I. Enjoy with satisfaction the comforts of lawful marriage, which was ordained for the prevention of uncleanness. Let none complain that God has dealt unkindly with them in forbidding them those pleasures which they have a natural desire of, for he has graciously provided for the regular gratification of them. "Thou mayest not indeed eat of every tree of the garden, but choose thee out one, which thou pleasest, and of that thou mayest freely eat; nature will be content with that, but lust with nothing." Let young men marry, marry and not burn. Have a *cistern, a well of thy own* (*v.* 15), even the wife *of thy youth*, *v.* 18. *Wholly abstain, or wed.*—Herbert. Let him that is married take delight in his wife, and let him be very fond of her, not only because she is the wife that he himself has chosen and he ought to be pleased with his own choice, but because she is the wife that God in his providence appointed for him. *Let thy fountain be blessed* (*v.* 18); think thyself very happy in her, look upon her as a blessed wife, let her have thy blessing, pray daily for her, and then *rejoice with her*. Mutual delight is the bond of mutual fidelity. Let him be fond of his wife and love her dearly (*v.* 19). If thou wilt suffer thy love to run into an excess, let it be only of thy own wife. Let him take delight in his children and look upon them with pleasure (*v.* 16, 17). Let him then scorn the offer of forbidden pleasures when he is *always ravished with the love* of a faithful virtuous wife; let him consider what an absurdity it will be for him to be *ravished with a strange woman* (*v.* 20). If the dictates of reason may be heard, the laws of virtue will be obeyed.

II. "See the eye of God always upon thee and let his fear rule in thy heart," *v.* 21. *The ways of man*, all his motions, all his actions, are *before the eyes of the Lord*. God sees it in a true light, and knows it with all its causes, circumstances, and consequences. He not only sees, but *ponders all his goings*, judges concerning them, as one that will shortly judge, the sinner for them.

III. "Foresee the certain ruin of those that go on

JAMIESON, FAUSSET, BROWN

8, 9. Avoid the slightest temptation. **thine honour**—in whatever consisting, strength (ch. 3:13) or wealth.

thy years—by cutting them off in dissipation. **unto the cruel**—for such the sensual are apt to become.

10. wealth—lit., "strength," or the result of it. **labours**—the fruit of thy painful exertions (Ps. 127:2). There may be a reference to slavery, a commuted punishment for death due the adulterer (Deut. 22: 22).

11. at the last—the end, or reward (cf. vs. 4). **mourn**—roar in pain. **flesh and . . . body**—the whole person under incurable disease.

12-14. The ruined sinner vainly laments his neglect of warning and his sad fate in being brought to public disgrace. **evil**—for affliction, as in Genesis 19:20; 49:15.

15-20. By figures, in which **well, cistern, and fountain,** represent the wife, and **rivers of waters** the children, men are exhorted to constancy and satisfaction in lawful conjugal enjoyments. In vs. 16, **fountains** (in the plural) rather denote the produce or waters of a spring, lit., "what is from a spring," and corresponds with "rivers of waters." **only thine own**—harlots' children have no known father. **wife . . . youth**—married in youth.

loving . . . roe—other figures for a wife from the well-known beauty of these animals. **breasts**—(Cf. Song of Sol. 1:13; Ezek. 23: 3, 8). **ravished**—lit., "intoxicated," i.e., fully satisfied.

21. The reason, God's eye is on you,

ADAM CLARKE

7. *Hear me . . . O ye children. Banim,* "sons," young men in general, for these are the most likely to be deceived and led astray.

11. *When thy flesh and thy body are consumed.* The word *shear,* which we render "body," signifies properly the remains, residue, or remnant of a thing; and is applied here to denote the breathing carcass, putrid with the concomitant disease of debauchery. The mourning here spoken of is of the most excessive kind; the word *naham* is often applied to the growling of a lion, and the hoarse, incessant murmuring of the sea.

15. *Drink waters out of thine own cistern.* Be satisfied with thy own wife; and let the wife see that she reverence her husband, and not tempt him by inattention or unkindness to seek elsewhere what he has a right to expect, but cannot find at home.

MATTHEW HENRY	JAMIESON, FAUSSET, BROWN	ADAM CLARKE

still in their trespasses." Those that live in this sin promise themselves impunity, but they deceive themselves; their sin will find them out, *v.* 22, 23. As their own iniquities do arrest them in the reproaches of conscience and present rebukes (Jer. vii. 19), so their own iniquities shall arrest them and bind them over to the judgments of God. There needs no prison, no chains; they shall be *holden in the cords of their own sins.*

22, 23, and He will cause sin to bring its punishment. **without instruction**—lit., "in want of instruction," having refused it (cf. Job 13:18; Heb. 11:24). **go astray**—lit., "be drunken." The word "ravished" (vs. 19) here denotes fulness of punishment.

MATTHEW HENRY — CHAPTER 6

Verses 1–5

It is the excellency of the word of God that it teaches us not only divine wisdom for another world, but human prudence for this world, that we may order our affairs with discretion; and this is one good rule. To avoid suretiship, because by it poverty and ruin are often brought into families. 1. We must look upon suretiship as a snare and decline it accordingly, *v.* 1, 2. "It is dangerous enough for a man to be bound for his friend, though it be one whose circumstances he is well acquainted with, and well assured of his sufficiency, but much more to *strike the hands with a stranger*, to become surety for one whom thou dost not know to be either able or honest." If thou hast rashly entered into such engagements, either wheedled into them or in hopes to have the same kindness done for thee another time, know that *thou art snared with the words of thy mouth.* If we have been drawn into this snare, it will be our wisdom by all means, with all speed, to get out of it, *v.* 3–5. It sleeps for the present; we hear nothing of it. The debt is not demanded; the principal says, "Never fear, we will take care of it." But still the bond is in force, interest is running on, the creditor may come upon thee when he will and perhaps may be hasty and severe. Therefore *deliver thyself*; rest not till either the creditor give up the bond or the principal give thee counter-security. Leave no stone unturned till thou hast agreed with thy adversary and compromised the matter, so that thy bond may not come against thee or thine.

But how are we to understand this? We are not to think it is unlawful in any case to become surety, or bail, for another; it may be a piece of justice or charity. Paul became bound for Onesimus, Philem. 19. We may help a young man into business that we know to be honest, and gain him credit by passing our word for him, and so do him a great kindness without any detriment to ourselves. But, 1. It is every man's wisdom to keep out of debt as much as may be, for it is an incumbrance upon him, entangles him in the world, puts him in danger of doing wrong or suffering wrong. The *borrower is servant to the lender*, and makes himself very much a slave to the world. A man ought never to be bound as surety for more than he is both able and willing to pay, and can afford to pay without wronging his family.

Verses 6–11

Solomon addresses himself to the sluggard who loves his ease, lives in idleness, sticks to nothing, and in a particular manner is careless in the business of religion.

I. By way of instruction, *v.* 6–8, he sends him to school, for sluggards must be schooled. The sluggard is not willing to come to school to him (dreaming scholars will never love wakeful teachers) and therefore he has found him out another school, as low as he can desire. *Go to the ant, to the bee*, so the LXX. Man is taught more than the beasts of the earth, and made wiser than the fowls of heaven, and yet is so degenerated that he may learn wisdom from the meanest insects and be shamed by them. When we observe the wonderful sagacities of the inferior creatures we must receive instruction to ourselves; by spiritualizing common things, we may make the things of God ready to us, and converse with them daily. *Consider her ways.* The sluggard is so because he does not consider. In particular, learn to *provide meat in summer.* We must prepare for hereafter, and not eat up all, and lay up nothing, but in gathering time, treasure up for a spending time. Lay in for winter, for straits and wants that may happen, and for old age; much more in the affairs of our souls. In the enjoyment of the means of grace provide for the want of them, in life for death, in time for eternity. Even *in summer*, when the weather is hot, the ant is busy in *gathering food* and laying it up, and does not indulge her ease, nor take her pleasure, as the grasshopper, that sings and sports in the summer and then perishes in the winter. The ants help one another; if one have a grain of corn too big for her to carry home, her neighbours will come in to her assistance. It is our wisdom to im-

JAMIESON, FAUSSET, BROWN — CHAPTER 6

Vss. 1-35. After admonitions against suretyship and sloth (cf. vss. 6-8), the character and fate of the wicked generally are set forth, and the writer (vss. 20-35) resumes the warnings against incontinence, pointing out its certain and terrible results. This train of thought seems to intimate the kindred of these vices.

1, 2. if—The condition extends through both verses. **be surety**—art pledged.

stricken . . . hand—bargained (cf. Job 17:3). **with a stranger**—i.e., for a friend (cf. ch. 11:15; 17:18).

3. come . . . friend—in his power. **humble . . . sure thy friend**—urge as a suppliant; i.e., induce the friend to provide otherwise for his debt, or secure the surety. **4, 5.** The danger requires promptness.

6-8. The improvident sluggards usually want sureties. Hence, such are advised to industry by the ant's example.

ADAM CLARKE — CHAPTER 6

1. *If thou be surety for thy friend.* "For thy neighbor"; i.e., any person. If you pledge yourself in behalf of another, you take the burden off him, and place it on your own shoulders; and when he knows he has got one to stand between him and the demands of law and justice, he will feel little responsibility. Striking or shaking hands when the mouth had once made the promise was considered as the ratification of the engagement, and thus the man became ensnared with the words of his mouth.

3. *Do this . . . deliver thyself.* Continue to press him for whom you are become surety, to pay his creditor; give him no rest till he do it, else you may fully expect to be left to pay the debt.

5. *Deliver thyself as a roe.* The antelope. If you are got into the snare, get out if you possibly canst; make every struggle and exertion, as the antelope taken in the net, and the bird taken in the snare would, in order to get free from your captivity.

6. *Go to the ant, thou sluggard.* The *ant* is a remarkable creature for foresight, industry, and economy.

MATTHEW HENRY

prove the season while that favours us. *Walk while you have the light.* The ant has *no guides* and *rulers*, but does it of herself, following the instinct of nature. We have parents, masters, ministers, magistrates, to put us in mind of our duty, to direct us in it.

II. By way of reproof, *v.* 9–11.

1. He expostulates with the sluggard: "*How long wilt thou sleep, O sluggard? When wilt thou* think it time to *arise?*" Sluggards should be roused in the duties of their particular calling as men or their general calling as Christians. "*How long wilt thou* waste thy time, and *when wilt thou* be a better husband? *How long wilt thou* love thy ease, and *when wilt thou* learn to deny thyself, and to take pains? *How long wilt thou* delay, and put off, and trifle away thy opportunities; and *when wilt thou* stir up thyself to do what thou hast to do, which, if it be not done, will leave thee for ever undone?"

2. He exposes the frivolous excuses he makes for himself. When he is roused he stretches himself, and begs for more *sleep*, more *slumber*; he is well in his warm bed, and cannot endure to think of rising, especially of rising to work. He promises himself and his master that he will desire but *a little* more *sleep, a little* more *slumber*, and then he will get up and go to his business. But herein he deceives himself; the more a slothful temper is indulged the more it prevails. Thus men's great work is left undone by being put off yet a little longer—*from day to day.* A little more sleep proves an everlasting sleep.

3. He gives him fair warning of the fatal consequences of his slothfulness, *v.* 11. *Poverty and want* will certainly come upon those that are slothful in their business. He that leaves his concerns at sixes and sevens will soon see them go to wreck and ruin, and bring his noble to nine-pence. Spiritual poverty comes upon those that are slothful in the service of God. *It will leave thee as naked as if thou wert stripped by a highwayman;* so Bishop Patrick.

Verses 12–19

I. If the slothful are to be condemned, that do nothing, much more those that do ill, and contrive to do all the ill they can. It is a *naughty person* that is here spoken of, Heb. *A man of Belial.* A man of Belial is here described. He is *a wicked man*, that makes a trade of doing evil, especially with his tongue, for he *walks* and works his designs *with a froward mouth* (*v.* 12), by lying and perverseness. He has the subtlety of the serpent, and carries on his projects with a great deal of craft (*v.* 13), *with his eyes, with his feet, with his fingers.* Those whom he makes use of as the tools of his wickedness, understand the ill meaning of a wink of his eye, a stamp of his feet, for the least motion of his fingers. He gives orders for evil-doing so that he may not be suspected. It is not so much ambition or covetousness that *is in his heart*, as downright *frowardness*, malice, and ill nature. He aims not so much to enrich and advance himself as to do an ill turn to those about him. *His calamity shall come* and *he shall be broken;* he that devised mischief shall fall into mischief. *Suddenly shall he be broken*, to punish him for all the wicked arts he had to surprise people into his snares.

II. A catalogue of those things which are in a special manner odious to God, all which are generally to be found in men of Belial. God hates every sin. But there are some sins which he does in a special manner hate; and all those here mentioned are such as are injurious to our neighbour. Those things which God hates we must hate in ourselves. 1. Haughtiness and contempt of others—*a proud look.* Pride is the first, because it is at the bottom of much sin. When the show of men's countenance witnesses against them that they overvalue themselves and undervalue all about them, this is in a special manner hateful to him. 2. Falsehood, and fraud, and dissimulation. Next to a *proud look*, nothing is more an abomination to God than *a lying tongue*; nothing more sacred than truth, nor more necessary to conversation than speaking truth. 3. Cruelty and blood-thirstiness. The devil was, from the beginning, a liar and a murderer (John viii. 44), so *hands that shed innocent blood* are hateful to God, because they have in them the devil's image and do him service. 4. Subtlety in the contrivance of sin, *a heart that* designs and a head that *devises wicked imaginations.* The more there is of craft and management in sin the more it is an abomination to God. 5. Vigour and diligence in the prosecution of sin—*feet that are swift in running to mischief.* The eagerness and industry, of sinners, in their sinful pursuits, may shame us who go about that which is good so awkwardly and so coldly. 6. False-witness bearing: There cannot be a greater affront to God, nor a greater injury to our neighbour, than knowingly to give a false testimony. 7. Making mischief between

JAMIESON, FAUSSET, BROWN

9, 10. Their conduct graphically described; **11,** and the fruits of their self-indulgence and indolence presented. **as . . . travelleth**—lit., "one who walks backwards and forwards," i.e., a highwayman. **armed man**—i.e.. one prepared to destroy.

12. A naughty person—lit., "A man of Belial," or of worthlessness, i.e., for good, and so depraved, or wicked (cf. I Sam. 25:25; 30:22, etc.). Idleness and vice are allied. Though indolent in acts, he actively and habitually (**walketh**) is ill-natured in speech (ch. 4:24). **13, 14.** If, for fear of detection, he does not speak, he uses signs to carry on his intrigues. These signs are still so used in the East.

deviseth—lit., "constructs, as an artisan." **mischief**—evil to others. **Frowardness**—as in ch. 2:14. **discord**—especially litigation. Cunning is the talent of the weak and lazy. **15.** *Suddenness* aggravates evil (cf. vs. 11; ch. 29:1). **calamity**—lit., "a crushing weight." **broken**—shivered as a potter's vessel; utterly destroyed (Ps. 2:9).

16-19. six . . . seven—a mode of speaking to arrest attention (ch. 30:15, 18; Job 5:19). **proud look**—lit., "eyes of loftiness" (Ps. 131:1). Eyes, tongue, etc., for persons.

speaketh—lit., "breathes out," habitually speaks (Ps. 27:12; Acts 9:1).

ADAM CLARKE

F. B. MEYER:

The ants swarm in the woods and fields, and rebuke our laziness and thriftlessness. They work day and night, storing their galleries with food, building mounds which relative to the size of the builders are three or four times larger than the pyramids. In sickness they nurse one another; in the winter they feed on their supplies. Learn from the ceaseless industry of Nature, and do something worthy before sundown!

—Bible Commentary

11. *So shall thy poverty come as one that travelleth.* That is, with slow but surely approaching steps. *Thy want as an armed man.* That is, with irresistible fury; and you are not prepared to oppose it.

14. *He deviseth mischief.* He plots schemes and plans to bring it to pass. *He soweth discord.* Between men and their wives, by seducing the latter from their fidelity.

15. *Suddenly shall he be broken.* Probably alluding to some punishment of the adulterer, such as being stoned to death.

MATTHEW HENRY

relations and neighbours, and using all wicked means possible, not only to alienate their affections one from another, but to irritate their passions one against another. The God of love and peace hates *him that sows discord among brethren.*

Verses 20–35

I. A general exhortation faithfully to adhere to the word of God and to take it for our guide in all our actions.

1. We must look upon the word of God both as a light (*v.* 23) and as a law, *v.* 20, 23. It is a light, which our understandings must subscribe to; it *is a lamp* to our eyes for discovery, and so to our feet for direction. The word of God reveals to us truths of eternal certainty. Scripture-light is the sure light. It is a law, which our wills must submit to.

2. We must receive it as *our father's commandment* and *the law of our mother, v.* 20. It is God's commandment and his law. Our parents directed us to it, trained us up in the knowledge and observance of it. We believe indeed, not for their saying, for we have tried it ourselves and find it to be of God; but we were beholden to them for recommending it to us. The cautions, counsels, and commands which our parents gave us agree with the word of God, and therefore we must hold them fast.

3. We must retain the word of God and the good instructions which our parents gave us out of it. "*Keep thy father's commandment*, keep it still, and never forsake it." We must never lay them by (*v.* 21): *Bind them continually*, not only *upon thy hand* (as Moses had directed, Deut. vi. 8) but *upon thy heart.* Phylacteries upon the hand were of no value at all, any further than they occasioned pious thoughts and affections in the heart. *Tie them about thy neck*, as an ornament—*about thy throat* (so the word is); let them be a guard that no forbidden fruit may be suffered to go in nor any evil word suffered to go out through the throat. If we bind it continually upon our hearts, we must follow its direction. "*When thou goest, it shall lead thee* (*v.* 22); it shall lead thee in the good and right way. It will say unto thee, when thou art ready to turn aside, *This is the way; walk in it.* Let it be thy rule, and then thou shalt be led by the Spirit; he will be thy monitor and support." It will be our guard: "*When thou sleepest*, and liest exposed to the malignant powers of darkness, *it shall keep thee*; thou shalt be safe, and shalt think thyself so." It will be our companion: "*When thou awakest* in the night, and knowest not how to pass thy waking minutes, *it shall talk with thee*, with pleasant meditations in the night-watches; *when thou awakest* in the morning, and art contriving the work of the day, *it shall talk with thee* about it, and help thee to contrive for the best," Ps. i. 2.

II. A particular caution against the sin of uncleanness.

1. When we consider how much this iniquity abounds we shall not wonder that the cautions against it are so often repeated. "The reproofs of instruction are *the way of life* to thee, because they are designed *to keep thee from the evil woman*, who will be certain death to thee, from being enticed by *the flattery of the tongue of a strange woman*, who pretends to love thee, but intends to ruin thee." The greatest kindness we can do ourselves, is to keep at a distance from this sin (*v.* 25): "*Lust not after her beauty*, no, not *in thy heart*, for, if thou dost, thou hast *there* already *committed adultery with her.* Talk not of the charms in her face; *let her* not *take thee with her eye-lids.* Her looks are arrows and fiery darts; they call it a pleasing captivity, but it is a destroying one, it is worse than Egyptian slavery."

2. Divers arguments Solomon here urges to enforce this caution. It is a sin that impoverishes men, wastes their estates, and reduces them to beggary (*v.* 26): *By means of a whorish woman a man is brought to a piece of bread.* It threatens death; it kills men: *The adulteress will hunt for the precious life*, perhaps designedly, as Delilah for Samson's. It brings guilt upon the conscience. He that *touches his neighbour's wife*, with an immodest touch, cannot be *innocent*, *v.* 29. The bold presumptuous sinner says, "I may sin and yet escape punishment." He might as well say, I will *take fire into my bosom and not burn my clothes.* It is a much more scandalous sin than stealing is, *v.* 30–33. When Nathan would convict David of the evil of his adultery he did it by a parable concerning the most aggravated theft, which, in David's judgment, deserved to be punished with death (2 Sam. xii. 5), and then showed him that his sin was *more exceedingly sinful* than that. It is a greater reproach to a man's reason, for he cannot excuse it, as a thief may, by saying that it was to satisfy his hunger. Therefore *whoso commits adultery with a woman lacks understanding*, and deserves to be stigmatized as an arrant fool. It will be *a wound*

JAMIESON, FAUSSET, BROWN

20-23. Cf. ch. 1:8; 3:3, etc.). **it**—(cf. vs. 23); denotes the instruction of parents (vs. 20), to which all the qualities of a safe guide and guard and ready teacher are ascribed. It prevents the ingress of evil by supplying good thoughts, even in dreams (ch. 3:21-23; Ps. 19:9; II Pet. 1:19).

reproofs—(ch. 1:23) the convictions of error produced by instruction. **24.** A specimen of its benefit. By appreciating truth, men are not affected by lying flattery.

25. One of the cautions of this instruction, avoid alluring beauty. **take** [or, ensnare] **. . . eyelids**—By painting the lashes, women enhanced beauty.

26. The supplied words give a better sense than the old version: "The price of a whore is a piece of bread." **adulteress**—(cf. *Margin*), which the parallel and context (29-35) sustain. Of similar results of this sin, cf. ch. 5:9-12. **will hunt**—alluding to the snares spread by harlots (cf. ch. 7:6-8). **precious life**—more valuable than all else. **27-29.** The guilt and danger most obvious. **30, 31.** Such a thief is pitied, though heavily punished. **sevenfold**—(cf. Exod. 22:1-4), for many, ample (cf. Gen. 4:24; Matt. 18:21), even if all his wealth is taken.

32. lacketh understanding—or, heart; destitute of moral principle and prudence.

ADAM CLARKE

F. B. MEYER:

"Bind them continually upon thine heart, tie them about thy neck" (Prov. 6:21). If the son addressed here is bidden to thus care for the words of his parents, how much more should we ponder those of God as given us in God's blessed Book.

"When thou walkest, it shall lead thee." There is a little circle of friends whom I know of who read this book of Proverbs through every month for practical direction on the path of life. A West-countryman said of this collection of wise words, "If any man shall maister the Book of Proverbs, no man shall maister he." Take for instance the weighty counsels of the first five verses. How many lives would have been saved from bitter anguish and disappointment if only they had been ruled by them! Let every young man also ponder the closing verses. Let us all meditate more constantly on the Word of God.

"When thou sleepest, it shall watch thee." The man who meditates on the Word of God by day will not be troubled by evil dreams at night. Whatever unholy spirits may prowl around his bed, they will be restrained from molesting him whose head is pillowed on some holy word of God. And on awakening, the Angel of Revelation will whisper words of encouragement and love.

"And when thou awakest, it shall talk with thee." The heart is accustomed to commune with itself about many things, but when the mind is full of God through his Word, it seems as though the monologue becomes a dialogue. To all our wonderings, fears, questionings, answers come back from the infinite glory in words of Scripture. Some wear amulets about their necks to preserve them; but the Word of God is both a safeguard and choice treasure.

—*Great Verses Through the Bible*

22. ***When thou goest, it shall lead thee.*** **Here the law is personified; and is represented as a nurse, teacher, and guardian, by night and day.**

MATTHEW HENRY

to his good name, a *dishonour* to his family, and, though the guilt of it may be done away by repentance, the *reproach* of it never will. David's sin in the matter of Uriah was not only a perpetual blemish upon his own character, but gave occasion to the enemies of the Lord to blaspheme his name too. He that touches his neighbour's wife, and is familiar with her, gives him occasion for jealousy, much more he that debauches her, which, if kept ever so secret, might then be *discovered by the waters of jealousy*, Num. v. 12, etc.

CHAPTER 7

Verses 1–5

These verses are an introduction to his warning against fleshly lusts, much the same with that, *ch.* vi. 20, &c., and ending (*v.* 5) as that did (*v.* 24), *To keep thee from the strange woman.* He speaks in God's name; for it is God's *commandments* that we are to *keep*, his *words*, his *law*. We must keep it as our life: *Keep my commandments and live* (*v.* 2). Keep *my law as the apple of thy eye.* A little thing offends the eye, and therefore nature has so well guarded it. We pray, with David, that God would keep us as the apple of his eye (Ps. xvii. 8), that our lives and comforts may be precious in his sight; and they shall be so (Zech. ii. 8) if we be in like manner tender of his law and afraid of the least violation of it. "*Bind them upon thy fingers;* let them be precious to thee; look upon them as the *signet on thy right hand*; wear them continually as thy wedding-ring, the badge of thy espousals to God." Look upon the word of God as putting an honour upon thee, as an ensign of thy dignity. *Write them upon the table of thy heart*, as the names of the friends we dearly love, we say, are written in our hearts. "*Say unto wisdom, Thou art my sister*, whom I dearly love and take delight in; *and call understanding thy kinswoman*, to whom thou art nearly allied, and for whom thou hast a pure affection; call her thy friend, whom thou courtest." We must make the word of God familiar to us, for our defence and armour, to keep us *from the strange woman*, from sin, particularly from the sin of uncleanness, *v.* 5.

Verses 6–23

Solomon here, to enforce the caution he had given against the sin of whoredom, tells a story of a young man that was ruined to all intents and purposes by the enticements of an adulterous woman. Such a story as this would serve the lewd profane poets of our age to make a play of, and the harlot with them would be a heroine; nothing would be so entertaining to the audience, as her arts of beguiling the young gentleman. Her conquests would be celebrated as the triumphs of wit and love, and the comedy would conclude very pleasantly; and every young men that saw it acted would covet to be so picked up. Thus *fools make a mock at sin.* But Solomon here relates it, and all wise and good men read it, as a very melancholy story. The impudence of the adulterous woman is very justly looked upon with the highest indignation, and the easiness of the young man with the tenderest compassion. It is supposed to be a parable, or imagined case, but I doubt it was too true, and it is still too often true.

Solomon was a magistrate, and, as such, inspected the manners of his subjects. But here he writes as a minister, a prophet, who is by office a watchman, to give warning, that we may not be ignorant of Satan's devices, but may know where to double our guard.

I. The person tempted was a *young man*, *v.* 7. Fleshly lusts are called *youthful lusts* (2 Tim. ii. 22). Young people ought in a special manner to fortify their resolutions against this sin. He was a young man *void of understanding*, that went abroad into the world, not principled as he ought to have been with wisdom and the fear of God, and so ventured to sea without ballast, without pilot, cord, or compass. He kept bad company. He was sauntering, and had nothing to do, but *passed through the street* as one that knew not how to dispose of himself. One of the sins of filthy Sodom was *abundance of idleness*, Ezek. xvi. 49. He was a night-walker. Having fellowship with the unfruitful works of darkness, he begins to move *in the twilight in the evening*, *v.* 9. He steered his course towards the house of one that he thought would entertain him, and that he might be merry with; he went *near her corner*, the *way to her house* (*v.* 8), contrary to Solomon's advice (*ch.* v. 8), *Come not nigh the door of her house.*

II. The person tempting, not a common prostitute, was a married wife (*v.* 19), not suspected of any such wickedness, and yet, in the *twilight of the evening*, when her husband was abroad, abominably impudent.

JAMIESON, FAUSSET, BROWN

33. dishonour—or, shame, as well as hurt of body (ch. 3:35). **reproach . . . away**—No restitution will suffice; **34, 35,** nor any terms of reconciliation be admitted. **regard** [or, accept] **any ransom.**

CHAPTER 7

Vss. 1-27. The subject continued, by a delineation of the arts of strange women, as a caution to the unwary.

1-4. Similar calls (ch. 3:1-3; 4:10, etc.). **apple . . . eye**—pupil of eye, a custody (ch. 4:23) of special value.

Bind . . . fingers—as inscriptions on rings.

5. The design of the teaching (cf. ch.: 2:16; 6:24).

6. For—or, "Since," introducing an example to illustrate the warning, which, whether a narrative or a parable, is equally pertinent. **window** [or, opening of the] . . . **casement**—or lattice. **looked**—lit., "watched earnestly" (Judg. 5:28).

7. simple—as in ch. 1:4. **void of . . .**—(Cf. ch. 6:32.)

8. her corner—where she was usually found. **went . . . house**—implying, perhaps, confidence in himself by his manner, as denoted in the word **"went"**—lit., "tread pompously." **9.** The time, **twilight**, ending in darkness. **black . . . night**—lit., "pupil," or, "eye," i.e., middle of night.

ADAM CLARKE

CHAPTER 7

2. *As the apple of thine eye.* As the pupil of the eye, which is of such essential necessity to sight, and so easily injured.

F. B. MEYER:

"Say unto Wisdom, Thou art my sister; and call Understanding thy kinswoman" (Prov. 7:4). This wisdom might seem to be too unearthly and ethereal to engage our passionate devotion, unless we remember that she was incarnated in Jesus Christ, who, throughout this book, seems forthshadowed in the majestic conception of wisdom. And who shall deny that the most attractive and lovable traits are blended in his matchless character as Son of Man and exalted Redeemer.

With what sensitive purity He bent his face to the ground and wrote on the dust, when her accusers brought to Him a woman taken in the act of sin! With what thoughtfulness He sent word to Peter that he was risen, and provided the meal for his weary and wave-drenched sailor friends on the shores of the lake! With what quick intuition He read Mary's desire to anoint Him for the burying!

It was this combination of what is sweet in woman and strong in man, which so deeply satisfied men like Bernard, Rutherford, Fenelon, and thousands more, who have been shut out from the delights of human love, but have found in Jesus the complement of their need, the satisfaction of their hunger and thirst. In Him, for them, was restored the vision of the sweet mother of early childhood; of the angel-sister who went to be with God; of the early love that was never destined to be realized.

Women find in Jesus strength on which to lean their weakness; and men find Him the tender, thoughtful sympathy to which they can confidently entrust themselves. We are born for the infinite and divine; earthy loves, at their best, are only patterns of things in the heavens. They are priceless; but let us look into them and through them, to behold the unseen and eternal that lie beneath.

—*Great Verses Through the Bible*

7. *Among the simple ones.* The inexperienced, inconsiderate young men. *A young man void of understanding.* "Destitute of a heart." He had not wisdom to discern the evil intended, nor courage to resist the flatteries of the seducer.

MATTHEW HENRY

She had the *attire of a harlot* (*v.* 10), gaudy and flaunting. She is *subtle of heart*, mistress of all the arts of wheedling, and knowing how by all her caresses to serve her own base purposes. *She is loud and stubborn*, talkative and self-willed, noisy and troublesome, wilful and headstrong, and cannot bear to be counselled, much less reproved, by husband or parents, ministers or friends. She is a *daughter of Belial*, that will endure no yoke. She is all for gadding abroad, changing place and company. She is here, and there, and everywhere but where she should be. She *lies in wait at every corner*, to pick up such as she can make a prey of. Virtue is a penance to those to whom home is a prison.

III. She met the young spark. Perhaps she knew him; however she knew by his fashions that he was such a son as she wished for; so she *caught him about* the neck and *kissed* him, contrary to all the rules of modesty (*v.* 13), and *with an impudent face* invited him not only to *her house*, but to *her bed*. She courted him to sup with her (*v.* 14, 15): *I have peace-offerings with me.* Hereby she gives him to understand that she was compassed about with so many blessings that she had occasion to offer peace-offerings, in token of joy and thankfulness; so that he needed not fear having his pocket picked. She had been today at the temple, and was as well respected there as any that worshipped in the courts of the Lord. She had paid her vows, and, as she thought, made all even with God Almighty, and therefore might venture upon a new score of sins. It is sad that a show of piety should become the shelter of iniquity. The Pharisees made long prayers, that they might the more plausibly carry on their covetous and mischievous designs. The greatest part of the flesh of the peace-offerings was by the law returned back to the offerers, to feast upon with their friends, Lev. vii. 15. "Come," says she, "come home with me, for I have good cheer enough, and only want good company to help me off with it." She pretends to have a very great affection for him above any man: "*Therefore*, because I have a good supper upon the table, *I came forth to meet thee*, for no friend in the world shall be so welcome to it as thou shalt," *v.* 15. They will sit down to eat and drink, and then play the wanton. The bed is *decked with coverings of tapestry* and *carved works.* The sheets are of *fine linen of Egypt*, *v.* 16. It is *perfumed* with the sweetest scents, *v.* 17. Come, therefore, and *let us take our fill of love*, *v.* 18. Of *love*, does she say? Of *lust* she means, but it is a pity that the name of love should be thus abused. True love is from heaven. "Never fear," says she, "the *good man is not at home*" (*v.* 19); she does not call him her *husband*, but "the *good man* of the house, of whom I am weary." But will he not return quickly? No: "he has *gone a long journey*, and cannot return on a sudden; he *appointed the day* of his return, and he never comes home sooner than he says he will. *He has taken a bag of money with him*—either to buy goods and he will not return till he has laid it all out, or to revel." Whether justly or not, she insinuates that he was a bad husband; so she would represent him, because she was resolved to be a bad wife, and must have that for an excuse; it is often groundlessly suggested, but is never a sufficient excuse.

IV. Promising the young man everything that was pleasant, and impunity in the enjoyment she gained her point, *v.* 21. It should seem, the youth, though very simple, had no ill design, else a word, a beck, a wink, would have served and there would have been no need of all this harangue; but though he did not intend any such thing, nay, had something in his conscience that opposed it, yet *with her much fair speech she caused him to yield.* His corruptions at length triumphed over his convictions. *With the flattery of her lips she forced him;* he could not stop his ear against such a charmer, but surrendered. With what pity does Solomon here look upon this foolish young man, when he sees him follow the adulterous woman! He gives him up for gone. Going without his breast-plate, he will receive his death's wound, *v.* 23. That which makes his case the more piteous is that he is not himself aware of his misery and danger; he goes laughing to his ruin.

We have here the application of the foregoing story: "*Hearken to me therefore*, and not to such seducers (*v.* 24); give ear to a father, and not to an enemy." *Let not thy heart decline to her ways* (*v.* 25); never leave the paths of virtue. Do not only keep thy feet from those ways, but let not so much as thy heart incline to them. Let reason, and conscience, and the fear of God ruling in the heart, check the inclinations of the sensual appetite. Thousands have been undone by this sin; and those not only the weak and simple youths, such as he was of whom he had now spoken, but *many strong men have been slain by her*, *v.* 26. Therefore *stand in awe and sin not.*

JAMIESON, FAUSSET, BROWN

10. attire—that of harlots was sometimes peculiar. **subtile**—or, wary, cunning. **11, 12. loud**—or, noisy, bustling. **stubborn**—not submissive.

without . . . streets, . . . corner—(Cf. I Tim. 5:13; Titus 2:5.)

13-15. The preparations for a feast do not necessarily imply peculiar religious professions. The offerer retained part of the victim for a feast (Lev. 3:9, etc.).

This feast she professes was prepared for him whom she boldly addresses as one sought specially to partake of it. **16, 17. my bed**—or, couch, adorned in the costliest manner. **bed**—in vs. 17, a place for sleeping.

18-20. There is no fear of discovery. **the day appointed**—perhaps, lit., "a full moon," i.e., a fortnight's time (cf. vs. 19).

21. caused . . . yield—or, inclines. **flattering**—(Cf. ch. 5:3). **forced him**—by persuasion overcoming his scruples. **22. straightway**—quickly, either as ignorant of danger, or incapable of resistance.

23. Till —He is now caught (ch. 6:26).

24. The inferential admonition is followed, **26, 27,** by a more general allegation of the evils of this vice. Even the mightiest fail to resist her deathly allurements.

ADAM CLARKE

11. *She is loud and stubborn.* She is never at rest, always agitated.

13. *And with an impudent face.* "She strengthened her countenance," assumed the most confident look she could.

14. *I have peace offerings with me.* More literally, "The sacrifices of the peace offerings are with me." *Peace offerings* were offerings the spiritual design of which was to make peace between God and man, to make up the breach between them which sin had occasioned. *Have I payed my vows.* She seems to insinuate that she had made a vow for the health and safety of this young man; and having done so, and prepared the sacrificial banquet, came actually out to seek him, that he might partake of it with her, v. 15.

16. *I have decked my bed. Arsi*, "my couch or sofa"; distinguished from *mishcabi*, "my bed," v. 17, the place to sleep on, as the other was the place to recline on at meals.

18. *Come, let us take our fill of love.* "Let us revel in the breasts"; and then it is added, *Let us solace ourselves with loves;* "Let us gratify each other with loves, with the utmost delights."

19. *For the good man.* Literally, "For the man is not in his house."

20. *He hath taken.* Literally, "The money bag he hath taken in his hand." He is gone a journey of itinerant merchandising. This seems to be what is intended. *And will come home at the day appointed.* The time fixed for a return from such a journey.

MATTHEW HENRY

CHAPTER 8

Verses 1–11

I. The things revealed are easy to be known, for they *belong to us and to our children* (Deut. xxix. 29), for they are proclaimed in some measure by the works of the creation (Ps. xix. 1), more fully by the consciences of men and the eternal reasons and rules of good and evil, but most clearly by Moses and the prophets. The precepts of wisdom are proclaimed aloud (*v.* 1): *Does not Wisdom cry?* Yes, she cries aloud, and does not spare (Isa. lviii. 1). The curses and blessings were read with a loud voice by the Levites, Deut. xxvii. 14. And men's own hearts sometimes speak aloud to them; there are clamours of conscience, as well as whispers. They are proclaimed from on high (*v.* 2): *She stands in the top of high places;* it was from the top of Mount Sinai that the law was given, and Christ expounded it in a sermon upon the mount. Wisdom speaks openly; truth seeks no corners, but gladly appeals to the light, *in the places of concourse,* where multitudes are gathered together. Wisdom's discoveries and directions are given to all promiscuously. They are proclaimed where they are most needed, and therefore are published *in the places of the paths,* where many ways meet. The foolish man *knows not how to go to the city* (Eccles. x. 15), and therefore Wisdom stands ready to direct him, stands *at the gates, at the entry of the city,* ready to tell him where the seer's house is, 1 Sam. ix. 18. Nay, she follows men to their own houses, and cries to them *at the coming in at the doors,* saying, *Peace be to this house.* Wisdom speaks to us: "*Unto you, O men! I call* (*v.* 4), not to angels (they need not these instructions), not to devils (they are past them), not to the brute-creatures (they are not capable of them), but *to you, O men!*" They are designed to make them wise (*v.* 5); they are calculated not only for men that are capable of wisdom, but for sinful men, fallen men, foolish men, that need it, and are undone without it: "*O you simple ones! understand wisdom.* Though you are ever so simple, Wisdom will undertake to give you *an understanding heart.*"

II. The things revealed are worthy of all acceptation. They are *excellent things* (*v.* 6), *princely things,* so the word is. Things which relate to an eternal God, an immortal soul, and an everlasting state, must needs be *excellent things.* They are *right things* (*v.* 6), *all in righteousness* (*v.* 8), and *nothing froward or perverse in them.* There is nothing in them that puts any hardship upon us, that lays us under any undue restraints, unbecoming the dignity and liberty of the human nature. They are of unquestionable truth. *My mouth shall speak truth* (*v.* 7). Every word of God is true. His word to us is *yea, and amen;* never then let ours be *yea and nay.* They are all *plain,* and not hard to be understood. If the book is sealed, it is to those who are willingly ignorant.

III. The right knowledge of those things is to be preferred before all the wealth of this world (*v.* 10, 11): *Receive my instruction, and not silver. Wisdom is* in itself, and therefore must be in our account, *better than rubies.* It will bring us in a better price, and it will be a better ornament than jewels.

Verses 12–21

Wisdom here is Christ, *in whom are hidden all the treasures of wisdom and knowledge;* it is Christ in the word and Christ in the heart, not only Christ revealed to us, but Christ revealed in us.

I. Divine wisdom gives men good heads (*v.* 12): *I Wisdom dwell with prudence,* not with carnal policy, for prudence is the product of religion and an ornament to religion; and there are more *witty inventions* found out with the help of the scripture, both for the right understanding of God's providences and for the doing of good in our generation, than were ever discovered by the learning of the philosophers or the politics of statesmen. We may apply it to Christ himself. We had found out many inventions for our ruin; he found out one for our recovery.

II. It gives men good hearts, *v.* 13. True religion, consisting in *the fear of the Lord,* teaches men, 1. To hate all sin, as displeasing to God and destructive to the soul: *The fear of the Lord is to hate evil, the evil way.* 2. Particularly to hate pride and passion, those two common and dangerous sins.

III. It has a great influence upon public affairs, *v.* 14. Christ, as God, has strength and wisdom; as Redeemer, he is *the wisdom of God and the power of God.* He is the wonderful counsellor and gives that grace which alone is *sound wisdom.* True religion gives men the best counsel in all difficult cases, and helps to make their way plain. And therefore Wisdom says, *By me kings reign* (*v.* 15, 16). They reign by him, and therefore ought to reign for him. Re-

JAMIESON, FAUSSET, BROWN

CHAPTER 8

Vss. 1-36. Contrasted with sensual allurements are the advantages of divine wisdom, which publicly invites men, offers the best principles of life, and the most valuable benefits resulting from receiving her counsels. Her relation to the divine plans and acts is introduced, as in ch. 3:19, 20, though more fully, to commend her desirableness for men, and the whole is closed by an assurance that those finding her find God's favor, and those neglecting ruin themselves. Many regard the passage as a description of the Son of God by the title, Wisdom, which the older Jews used (and by which He is called in Luke 11:49), as John 1:1, etc., describes Him by that of *Logos,* the Word. But the passage may be taken as a personification of wisdom: for, (1) Though described as with God, wisdom is not asserted to be God. (2) The use of personal attributes is equally consistent with a *personification,* as with the description of a real person. (3) The personal pronouns used accord with the gender (fem.) of wisdom constantly, and are never changed to that of the person meant, as sometimes occurs in a corresponding use of *spirit,* which is neuter in Greek, but to which masculine pronouns are often applied (John 16:14), when the acts of the Holy Spirit are described. (4) Such a personification is agreeable to the style of this book (cf. chs. 1:20; 3:16, 17; 4:8; 6:20-22; 9:1-4), whereas no prophetical or other allusions to the Saviour or the new dispensation are found among the quotations of this book in the New Testament, and unless this be such, none exist. (5) Nothing is lost as to the importance of this passage, which still remains a most ornate and also solemn and impressive teaching of inspiration on the value of wisdom.

1-4. The publicity and universality of the call contrast with the secrecy and intrigues of the wicked (ch. 7:8, etc.). **5. wisdom**—lit., "subtilty" in a good sense, or, prudence. **fools**—as ch. 1:22.

6. excellent things—or, plain, manifest. **opening . . . things**—upright words.

8. in righteousness—or, righteous (Ps. 9:8: 11:7). **froward**—lit., "twisted," or contradictory, i.e., to truth.

7. For . . . truth—lit., "My palate shall meditate," or (as Orientals did) "mutter," my thoughts expressed only to myself are truth. **wickedness**—specially falsehood, as opposed to truth.

9. plain . . . understandeth—easily seen by those who apply their minds. **that find**—implying search. **10. not silver**—preferable to it, so last clause implies comparison. **11.** (Cf. ch. 3:14, 15.)

12. prudence—as in vs. 5. The connection of "wisdom" and "prudence" is that of the dictates of sound wisdom and its application. **find . . . inventions**—or, devices, discreet ways (ch. 1:4).

13. For such is the effect of the fear of God, by which hatred to evil preserves from it. **froward mouth**—or, speech (ch. 2:12; 6:14).

14. It also gives the elements of good character in counsel. **sound wisdom**—(Ch. 2:7). **I . . . strength**—or, "As for me, understanding is strength to me," the source of power (Eccles. 9:16); good judgment gives more efficiency to actions; **15, 16,** of which a wisely conducted government is an example.

ADAM CLARKE

CHAPTER 8

1. *Doth not wisdom cry?* Here wisdom is again personified. It is represented in this chapter in a twofold point of view: (1) Wisdom, the power of judging rightly, implying the knowledge of divine and human things. (2) As an attribute of God, particularly displayed in the various and astonishing works of creation.

2. *In the places of the paths.* "The constituted house of the paths." Does not this mean the house of public worship?

4. *Unto you, O men. Ishim,* men of wealth and power, "will I call"; and not to you alone, for my voice is *al beney Adam,* "to all the descendants of Adam," to the whole human race.

5. *O ye simple. Pethaim,* you that are deceived, and with flattering words and fair speeches deluded and drawn away. *Ye fools. Kesilim,* ye stupid, stiff-necked, senseless people.

8. *All the words . . . are in righteousness. Betsedek,* in justice and equity, testifying what man "owes" to his God, to his neighbor, and to himself; giving to each his "due." This is the true import of *tsadak. There is nothing froward. Niphtal,* tortuous, involved, or difficult. *Or perverse. Ikkesh,* distorted, leading to obstinacy. On the contrary,

9. *They are all plain. Nechochim,* straightforward, over against every man, level to every capacity.

10. *Receive my instruction, and not silver.* A Hebrew idiom: "Receive my instruction in preference to silver."

12. *I wisdom dwell with prudence.* Prudence is defined, "wisdom applied to practice"; so wherever true wisdom is, it will lead to action, and its activity will be always in reference to the accomplishment of the best ends by the use of the most appropriate means. Hence comes what is here called *knowledge of witty inventions,* "I have found out knowledge and contrivance."

14. *Counsel is mine. Tushiyah,* "substance, reality, essence," all belong to me.

15. *By me kings reign.* In this and the following verse five degrees of civil power and authority are mentioned: (1) *melachim,* kings; (2) *rozenim,* consuls; (3) *sarim,* princes, chiefs

MATTHEW HENRY

ligion is very much the strength and support of the civil government; it teaches subjects their duty, and so *by it kings reign* over them the more easily; it teaches kings their duty, and so *by it kings reign* as they ought; they *decree justice*, while they *rule in the fear of God*. Those rule well whom religion rules.

IV. It will make all those happy that receive it. They shall be happy in the love of Christ; for he it is that says, *I love those that love me*, *v.* 17. "*Those that seek me early*, that is, seek me earnestly, seek me first before anything else, that begin betimes in the days of their youth to seek me, they shall find what they seek." Christ shall be theirs, and they shall be his. They shall have as much riches and honour as Infinite Wisdom sees good for them (*v.* 18). They are *riches and righteousness*, riches honestly got, not by fraud and oppression, but in regular ways, and riches charitably used, for alms are called *righteousness*. Therefore they are *durable riches*. That which is well got will wear well and will be left to the children's children, and that which is well spent in works of piety and charity is put out to the best interest and so will be durable. They shall have that which is infinitely better, if they have not riches and honour in this world (*v.* 19): "*My fruit is better than gold*, and will turn to a better account, will be of more value in less compass, *and my revenue better than the choicest silver*, will serve a better trade." They shall be happy in the grace of God now; that shall be their guide in the good way, *v.* 20. This is that fruit of wisdom which is *better than gold, than fine gold*, it *leads us in the way of righteousness*, shows us that way and goes before us in it, the way that God would have us walk in and which will certainly bring us to our desired end. They shall be happy in the glory of God hereafter, *v.* 21. It is a happiness which will subsist of itself, and stand alone, without the accidental supports of outward conveniences. Spiritual and eternal things are the only real and substantial things. Joy in God is substantial joy, solid and well-grounded. The promises are their bonds, Christ is their surety, and both substantial. It is satisfying; it will not only fill their hands, but *fill their treasures*, *v.* 21. The things of this world may fill men's bellies (Ps. xvii. 14), but not their treasures, for they cannot in them secure to themselves *goods for many years*.

Verses 22–31

Wisdom here has personal properties and actions; and that intelligent divine person can be no other than the Son of God himself, to whom the principal things here spoken of wisdom are attributed in other scriptures. The best exposition of these verses we have in the first four verses of St. John's gospel. *In the beginning was the Word*, &c. Concerning the Son of God observe,

I. His personality and distinct subsistence, one with the Father and of the same essence, and yet a person of himself, whom *the Lord possessed* (*v.* 22), *who was set up* (*v.* 23) *was brought forth* (*v.* 24, 25), *was by him* (*v.* 30), for he was *the express image of his person*, Heb. i. 3.

II. His eternity; he was begotten of the Father, for *the Lord possessed* him, as his own Son, his beloved Son, laid him in his bosom; he was *brought forth as the only-begotten of the Father*, and this *before all worlds*. The Word was eternal, and had a being before the world, before the beginning of time; and therefore it must follow that it was from eternity. *The Lord possessed him in the beginning of his way*, of his eternal counsels, for those were *before his works*. This way indeed had no beginning, for God's purposes in himself are eternal like himself, but God speaks to us in our own language. Wisdom explains herself (*v.* 23): *I was set up from everlasting, Before the earth was*, and before man was made. Before the sea was (*v.* 24), *when there were no depths* in which the waters were gathered together, *no fountains* from which those waters might arise, none of that deep on which the Spirit of God moved for the production of the visible creation, Gen. i. 2. Before the mountains were, *v.* 25, the eternal Word *brought forth*. Before the habitable parts of the world, which men cultivate (*v.* 26), *the fields* in the valleys, to which the mountains are as a wall, which are *the highest part of the dust of the world;* the *first part of the dust* (so some), the atoms which compose the several parts of the world; the *chief or principal part of the dust*, so it may be read, and understood of man, the principal part of the dust, dust enlivened, dust refined—the eternal Word had a being, *in him was the life of men*.

III. His agency in making the world. He not only had a being before the world, but he was present, not as a spectator, but as the architect, when the world was made. *By him God made the worlds*, Eph. iii. 9; Heb. i. 2; Col. i. 16. When, on the first

JAMIESON, FAUSSET, BROWN

17. early—or, diligently, which may include the usual sense of early in life.

18. durable riches . . . righteousness—Such are the "riches," enduring sources of happiness in moral possessions (cf. ch. 3: 16).

19. (Cf. vs. 11, 3:16).

20, 21. The courses in which wisdom leads conduct to a true present prosperity (ch. 23:5).

22-31. Strictly, God's attributes are part of Himself. Yet, to the poetical structure of the whole passage, this commendation of wisdom is entirely consonant. In order of time all His attributes are coincident and eternal as Himself. But to set forth the importance of wisdom as devising the products of benevolence and power, it is here assigned a precedence. As it has such in divine, so should it be desired in human, affairs (cf. ch. 3:19).

22. possessed—or, created; in either sense, the idea of precedence. **in the beginning**—or simply, "beginning," in apposition with "me." **before . . . of old**—preceding the most ancient deeds. **23. I was set up**—ordained, or inaugurated (Ps. 2:6). The other terms carry out the idea of the earliest antiquity, and **24-29** illustrate it by the details of creation.

brought forth—(Cf. Ps. 90:2). **abounding**—or, laden with water. **settled**—i.e., sunk in foundations. **fields**—or, out-places, deserts, as opposite to (habitable) **world. highest part**—or, sum, all particles together,

ADAM CLARKE

of the people; (4) *nedibim*, nobles; and (5) *shophetim*, judges or civil magistrates. Instead of *shophetey arets, judges of the earth*, *shophetey tsedek*, "righteous judges," or "judges of righteousness," is the reading of 162 of Kennicott's and De Rossi's MSS., both in the text and in the margin, and of several ancient editions. And this is the reading of the Vulgate, the Chaldee, and the Syriac; and should undoubtedly supersede the other.

17. *And those that seek me early shall find me.* Not merely betimes in the morning, though he who does so shall find it greatly to his advantage (see on Psalm iv.), but early in life.

ALEXANDER MACLAREN:

Verse 21. "Those who love wisdom" might be a Hebrew translation of "philosopher" and possibly the Jewish teachers of wisdom were influenced by Greece, but their conception of wisdom has a deeper source than the Greek had, and what they meant by loving it was a widely different attitude of mind and heart from that of the Greek philosopher. It could never be said of the disciples of a Plato that their quest was sure to end in finding what they sought. Many a man has "followed knowledge, like a sinking star," and has only caught a glimmer of a far-off and dubious light. There is only one search which is certain always to find what it seeks, and that is the search which knows where the object of it is, and seeks not as for something the locality of which is unknown, but as for that which the place of which is certain. The heart that truly and supremely affects God is never condemned to seek in vain. The Wisdom of this book herself is presented as proclaiming, "They that seek me earnestly shall find me," and humble souls in every age since then have set to their seal that the word is true to their experience. For there are two seekers in every such case, God and man. "The Father seeketh such to worship Him," and His love goes through the world, yearning and searching for hearts that will turn to Him. The shepherd seeks for the lost sheep, and lays it on his shoulders to bear it back to the fold. Jesus Christ is the incarnation of the seeking love of God. And the human seeker finds God, or rather is found by God, for no aspiration after Him is vain, no longing unresponded to, no effort to find Him unresponded to. We have as much of God as we wish, as much as our desires have fitted us to receive. The all-penetrating atmosphere enters every chink open to it, and no seeking soul has ever had to say, "I sought Him but found Him not."

—*Expositions of Holy Scripture*

23. *I was set up from everlasting.* I was diffused or "poured out," Isa. xxix. 10.

24. *When there were no depths. Tehomoth*, before the original chaotic mass was formed. See Gen. i. 2. *I was brought forth.* "I was produced as by laboring throes."

26. *The highest part of the dust of the world.* "The first particle of matter."

MATTHEW HENRY

day of the creation, God said, *Let there be light*, and with a word produced it, this eternal Wisdom was that almighty Word: Then *I was there, when he prepared the heavens.* He was no less active when, on the second day, he stretched out the firmament, the vast expanse, and *set* that as *a compass upon the face of the depth* (*v.* 27), surrounded it on all sides with that canopy, that curtain. He was also employed in the third day's work, when the *waters above the heavens* were gathered together by *establishing the clouds above*, and those under the heavens by *strengthening the fountains of the deep*, which send forth those waters (*v.* 28), and by preserving the bounds of the sea, which is the receptacle of those waters, *v.* 29.

IV. The infinite complacency which the Father had in him, and he in the Father (*v.* 30): *I was by him, as one brought up with him.* As by an eternal generation he was brought forth of the Father, so by an eternal counsel he was brought up with him. He did what he saw the Father do (John v. 19), pleased his Father, did according to the commandment he received from his Father, and all this *as one brought up with him.* He was *daily his Father's delight* (*my elect, in whom my soul delighteth*, says God, Isa. xlii. 1). This may be understood of the satisfaction they had in each other, with reference to the great work of man's redemption.

V. The gracious concern he had for mankind, *v.* 31. Wisdom *rejoiced*, not so much in the rich products of the earth, but in the redemption and salvation of man.

Verses 32–36

The application of Wisdom's discourse; the design and tendency of it is to bring us all into an entire subjection to the laws of religion, and to rectify what is amiss in our hearts and lives.

I. An exhortation to hear and obey the voice of Wisdom, to discern the voice of Christ, as the sheep know the shepherd's voice. "*Hearken unto me, O you children!*" *v.* 32. "Read the word written, sit under the word preached, bless God for both, and hear him in both speaking to you." Let Wisdom's children justify Wisdom by hearkening to her. Hear Wisdom's words with a willing heart (*v.* 33): "*Hear instruction, and refuse it not*, either as that which you need not or as that which you like not; it is offered you as a kindness, and it is at your peril if you refuse it." We must hear Wisdom so as to *watch daily at her gates*, as beggars to receive an alms, as clients and patients to receive advice, and as servants, with humility, and patience *at the posts of her doors.* We must watch and wait, as Christ's hearers, that *hanged on him* to hear him, as the word in the original is (Luke xix. 48 and *ch.* xxi. 38) *came early in the morning to hear him.*

II. An assurance of happiness to all those that do hearken to Wisdom. They shall find what they seek. But will it make them amends if they do find it? Yes (*v.* 35): *Whoso finds me finds life*, that is, all happiness, all that good which he needs or can desire. Christ is Wisdom, and he that finds Christ, *finds life;* for Christ is life to all believers.

III. The doom passed upon all those that reject Wisdom and her proposals, *v.* 26. They ruin themselves, and Wisdom will not hinder them, because they have set at nought all her counsel. They *sin against Christ*; they act in contempt of his authority, and in contradiction to all the purposes of his life and death. Those that offend Christ do the greatest wrong to themselves; they *wrong their own souls. O Israel! thou hast destroyed thyself.*

JAMIESON, FAUSSET, BROWN

when he set . . . depth—marked out the circle, according to the popular idea of the earth, as circular, surrounded by depths on which the visible concave heavens rested. **established . . . deep**—i.e., so as to sustain the waters above and repress those below the firmament (Gen. 1:7-11; Job 26:8). **commandment**—better, the shore, i.e., of the sea. **foundations**—figuratively denotes the solid structure (Job 38:4; Ps. 24:2). **30, 31. one brought up**—an object of special and pleasing regard. The bestowal of wisdom on men is represented by its finding a delightful residence and pleasing God.

32-36. Such an attribute men are urged to seek. **watching . . . waiting**—lit., "so as to watch"; wait, denoting a most sedulous attention. **sinneth . . . me**—or better, missing me, as opposed to finding.

35. (Cf. Luke 13:23, 24.) **love death**—act as if they did (cf. ch. 17:9).

ADAM CLARKE

28. *The clouds above.* "The ethereal regions."

30. *Then I was by him, as one brought up.* A "nursling," a darling child.

34. *Watching daily at my gates.* Wisdom is represented as having a school for the instruction of men; and seems to point out some of the most forward of her scholars coming, through their intense desire to learn, even before the gates were opened, and waiting there for admission, that they might hear every word that was uttered, and not lose one accent of the heavenly teaching. Blessed are such.

36. *Wrongeth his own soul.* It is not Satan, it is not sin, properly speaking, that hurts him; it is himself.

MATTHEW HENRY — CHAPTER 9

Verses 1–12

Wisdom is here introduced as a magnificent and munificent queen, great and generous; that Word of God is this Wisdom in which God makes known his goodwill towards men; God the Word is this Wisdom, to whom the Father has committed all judgment. The word is plural, *Wisdoms*; for in Christ are hid treasures of wisdom.

I. The rich provision which Wisdom has made for the reception of all those that will be her disciples. This is represented under the similitude of a sumptuous feast. 1. Here is a stately palace provided, *v.* 1. Wisdom, not finding a house capacious enough for all her guests, has built one on purpose, and, has *hewn out her seven pillars.* Heaven is the house which Wisdom has built to entertain all her guests that are called to the marriage-supper of the Lamb; that is her Father's house, where there are many mansions, and whither she has gone to prepare places for us. 2. Here is a splendid feast got ready (*v.* 2): *She has killed her beasts; she has mingled her wine. She has killed her sacrifice* (so the word is); it is a sumptuous

JAMIESON, FAUSSET, BROWN — CHAPTER 9

Vss. 1-18. The commendation of wisdom is continued, under the figure of a liberal host, and its provisions under that of a feast (cf. Luke 14:16-24). The character of those who are invited is followed by a contrasted description of the rejectors of good counsel; and with the invitations of wisdom are contrasted the allurement of the wicked woman.

1. house—(cf. ch. 8:34). **her**—or, "its" (the house). **seven pillars**—the number seven for many, or a sufficiency (ch. 6:31).

2. mingled—to enhance the flavor (ch. 23:30; Isa. 5:22).

ADAM CLARKE — CHAPTER 9

The same Wisdom speaks here who spoke in the preceding chapter. There she represented herself as manifest in all the works of God in the natural world, all being constructed according to counsels proceeding from an infinite understanding. Here she represents herself as the great potentate who was to rule all that she had constructed; and having an immense family to provide for, had made an abundant provision, and calls all to partake of it.

MATTHEW HENRY

but a sacred feast, a feast upon a sacrifice. *She has* completely *furnished her table* with all the satisfactions that a soul can desire—righteousness and grace, peace and joy, the assurances of God's love, the consolations of the Spirit, and all the pledges and earnests of eternal life.

II. The gracious invitation she has given, not to some particular friends, but to all in general. *She has sent forth her maidens*, *v.* 3. The ministers of the gospel are commissioned to give notice of the preparations which God has made, in the everlasting covenant, for all those that are willing to come up to the terms of it; and they, with maiden purity, not corrupting themselves or the word of God, and with an exact observance of their orders, are to call upon all they meet with, even in *the highways and hedges*, to come and feast with Wisdom, for *all things are now ready*, Luke xiv. 23. She herself *cries upon the highest places of the city*, as one earnestly desirous of the welfare of the children of men. The invitation is given: *Whoso is simple* and *wants understanding*, *v.* 4. Wisdom invites such, because what she has to give is what they must need. He that is simple is invited, that he may be made wise, and he that *wants a heart* (so the word is) let him come hither, and he shall have one. Her preparations are designed for the cure of the mind. We are invited to Wisdom's house: *Turn in hither*. I say *we* are, for which of us is there that must not own the character of the invited, that are *simple and want understanding?* We are invited to her table (*v.* 5): *Come, eat of my bread*, that is, taste of the true pleasures that are to be found in the knowledge and fear of God. By faith acting on the promises of the gospel we feed, we feast, upon the provisions Christ has made for poor souls. We must break off from all bad company: "*Forsake the foolish*, converse not with them." The first step towards virtue is to shun vice, and therefore to shun the vicious. "Live not a mere animal-life, but the life of men. *Live* and you *shall live*; live spiritually, and you shall live eternally," Eph. v. 14.

III. The instructions which Wisdom gives to the ministers and others, who in their places are endeavouring to serve her designs. Their work must be, not only to tell in general what preparation is made for souls, but they must address themselves to particular persons, tell them of their faults, *reprove*, *rebuke*, *v.* 7, 8. They must instruct them how to amend—*teach*, *v.* 9. The word of God is intended, and therefore so is the ministry of that word, *for reproof, for correction, and for instruction in righteousness*. They would meet with some *scorners* and *wicked men* who would mock the messengers of the Lord, and misuse them. And, though they are not forbidden to invite those simple ones to Wisdom's house, yet they are advised not to pursue the invitation by reproving and rebuking them. Thus Christ said of the Pharisees, *Let them alone*, Matt. xv. 14. They would meet with others, who are wise, and good, and just; thanks be to God, all are not scorners. We meet with some who are so wise as to be willing and glad to be taught. If there be occasion, we must reprove them; for wise men are not so perfectly wise but there is that in them which needs a reproof. The more wisdom a man has the more desirous he should be to have his weaknesses shown him. With our reproofs we must *give* them *instruction*, and must *teach* them, *v.* 9. It is as great an instance of wisdom to take a reproof well as to give it well. A *wise man* will be made wiser by the reproofs; he *will increase in learning*, will grow in knowledge, and so grow in grace.

IV. The instructions she gives to those that are invited, which her maidens must inculcate upon them.

1. Let them know wherein true wisdom consists, *v.* 10. The *fear of God is the beginning of wisdom*. A reverence of God's majesty, and a dread of his wrath, are the first steps towards true religion. *The knowledge of holy things* (the word is plural) *is understanding*, the things pertaining to the service of God (those are called *holy things*), that pertain to our own sanctification.

2. Let them know what will be the advantages of this wisdom (*v.* 11): "*By me thy days shall be multiplied*. It will contribute to the health of thy body, and so *the years of thy life* on earth *shall be increased*. It will bring thee to heaven, and there the *years of thy life shall be increased without end*."

3. Let them know what will be the consequence of their choosing or refusing this fair offer, *v.* 12. "*If thou be wise, thou shalt be wise for thyself;* thou wilt be the gainer by it, not Wisdom. *If thou scornest* Wisdom's proffer, *thou alone shalt bear it*."

Verses 13–18

How industrious the tempter is to seduce unwary souls into the paths of sin!

I. Who is the tempter—*a foolish woman*, Folly

JAMIESON, FAUSSET, BROWN

furnished—lit., "set out," "arranged."

3. maidens—servants to invite (cf. Ps. 68:11; Isa. 40:9). **highest places**—ridges of heights, conspicuous places. **4-6.** (Cf. ch. 1:4; 6:32.) Wisdom not only supplies right but forbids wrong principles.

7, 8. shame—(Cf. ch. 3:35.) **a blot**—or, stain on character. Bot terms denote the evil done by others to one whose faithfulness secures a wise man's love.

9. The more a wise man learns, the more he loves wisdom.

10. (Cf. ch. 1:7.) **of the holy**—lit., "holies," persons or things, or both. This knowledge gives right perception.

11. (Cf. ch. 3:16-18; 4:10.)

12. You are mainly concerned in your own conduct.

ADAM CLARKE

4. *Whoso is simple*. Let the young, heedless, and giddy attend to my teaching. *Him that wanteth understanding*. Literally, "he that *wanteth understanding*. Literally, "he that wanteth a heart"; who is without courage, is feeble and fickle, and easily drawn aside from the holy commandment.

5. *Come, eat of my bread*. Not only receive my instructions, but act according to my directions. *Drink of the wine . . . I have mingled*. Enter into my counsels; be not contented with superficial knowledge on any subject, where anything deeper may be attained.

7. *He that reproveth a scorner*. The person who "mocks" at sacred things.

9. *Give instruction to a wise man*. Literally, "Give to the wise, and he will be wise."

MATTHEW HENRY

herself, in opposition to Wisdom. Carnal sensual pleasure I take to be especially meant by this *foolish woman* (*v.* 13); for that defiles the mind and stupefies conscience. This tempter is here described to be ignorant: *She is simple and knows nothing*, that is, she has no sufficient solid reason to offer. *Whoredom, and wine, and new wine, take away the heart;* they besot men, and make fools of them. The less she has to offer that is rational the more violent and pressing she is, and carries the day often by dint of impudence. She *is clamorous* and noisy (*v.* 13). *She sits at the door of her house* (*v.* 14), watching for a prey. *She sits on a seat* (*on a throne*, so the word signifies) *in the high places of the city*, as if she had authority, and perhaps she gains more by pretending to be fashionable than by pretending to be agreeable.

II. Who are the tempted—young people who have been well educated. They are *passengers that go right on their ways* (*v.* 15), that have been trained up in the paths of religion and virtue and set out very hopefully and well, and are not (as that young man, *ch.* vii. 8) *going the way to her house*. Such as these she lays snares for, and uses all her charms, to pervert them. She calls them *simple*, and *wanting understanding*, and therefore courts them to her school, that they may be cured of the restraints and formalities of their religion.

III. What the temptation is (*v.* 17): *Stolen waters are sweet.* It is to water and bread, whereas Wisdom invites to the beasts she has killed, and the wine she has mingled; however, bread and water are acceptable enough to those that are hungry and thirsty; and this is pretended to be more *sweet* and *pleasant* than common, for it is *stolen water and bread eaten in secret*, with a fear of being discovered. The pleasures of prohibited lusts are boasted of as more relishing than those of prescribed love; and dishonest gain is preferred to that which is justly gotten.

IV. An effectual antidote against the temptation, *v.* 18. He that so far wants understanding as to be drawn aside by these enticements is led on, ignorantly, to his own inevitable ruin: *He knows that the dead are there*, that those who live in pleasure are *dead while they live, dead in trespasses and sins. Her guests*, that are treated with these *stolen waters*, are led captive by Satan at his will.

JAMIESON, FAUSSET, BROWN

13. foolish woman—or lit., "woman of folly," specially manifested by such as are described.

clamorous—or, noisy (ch. 7:11). **knoweth nothing**—lit., "knoweth not what," i.e., is right and proper. **14. on a seat**—lit., "throne," takes a prominent place, impudently and haughtily.

15,
16. to allure those who are right-minded, and who are addressed as in vs. 4, as **simple**—i.e., easily led (ch. 1:4) and unsettled, though willing to do right.

17. The language of a proverb, meaning that forbidden delights are sweet and pleasant, as fruits of risk and danger.

18. (Cf. ch. 2:18, 19; 7:27.)

ADAM CLARKE

16. *Whoso is simple, let him turn in hither.* Folly or Pleasure, here personified, uses the very same expressions as employed by Wisdom, v. 4. Wisdom says, "Let the simple turn in to me." No, says Folly, "Let the simple turn in to me." If he turn in to Wisdom, his folly shall be taken away, and he shall become wise; if he turn in to Folly, his darkness will be thickened, and his folly will remain. Wisdom sets up her school to instruct the ignorant: Folly sets her school up next door, to defeat the designs of Wisdom.

17. *Stolen waters are sweet.* I suppose this to be a proverbial mode of expression, importing that "illicit pleasures are sweeter than those which are legal." The meaning is easy to be discerned; and the conduct of multitudes shows that they are ruled by this adage. On it are built all the *adulterous intercourses* in the land.

CHAPTER 10 (Matthew Henry)

Verse 1

The comfort of parents, natural, political, and ecclesiastical, depends upon the good behaviour of those under their charge. Children should conduct themselves wisely, and live up to their good education, that they may gladden the hearts of their parents. It adds to the comfort of young people that thereby they do something towards recompensing their parents for all the care they have taken with them, and occasion pleasure to them in old age; and it is the duty of parents to rejoice in their children's wisdom and well-doing.

Verses 2–3

These two verses speak to the same purport. Wealth which men get unjustly will do them no good, because God will blast it: *Treasures of wickedness profit nothing*, *v.* 2. When profit and loss come to be balanced the profit gained by the treasures will by no means countervail the loss sustained by the wickedness, Matt. xvi. 26. They do not profit the soul. God *casts away the substance of the wicked* (*v.* 3). We often see that scattered by the justice of God which has been gathered together by the injustice of men. That which is honestly got will turn to a good account, for God will bless it. *Righteousness delivers from death*, that is, wealth gained, and kept, and used, in a right manner, answers the end of wealth, which is to keep us alive and be a defence to us.

Verse 4

Those are in a fair way to *become poor who deal with a slack hand*, who are careless and remiss in their business. Those *who deal with a deceitful hand* (so it may be read); who think to enrich themselves by fraud, will, in the end, impoverish themselves, not only by bringing the curse of God on what they have, but by forfeiting their reputation with men. Those who are diligent and honest, who are careful about their affairs, are likely to increase what they have. This is true in the affairs of our souls as well as in our worldly affairs; slothfulness and hypocrisy lead to spiritual poverty, but those who are *fervent in spirit, serving the Lord*, are likely to be *rich in faith* and *rich in good works*.

CHAPTER 10 (Jamieson, Fausset, Brown)

Vss. 1-32. Here begins the second part of the book, chs. 10-22:16, which, with the third, ch. 22: 16-ch. 25, contains series of proverbs whose sense is complete in one or two verses, and which, having no logical connection, admit of no analysis. The parallelisms of chs. 10-15 are mostly antithetic; and those of chs. 16-22:16, synthetic. The evidences of art in the structure are very clear, and indicate, probably, a purpose of facilitating the labor of memorizing.

1. wise [and] **foolish**—as they follow or reject the precepts of wisdom. **maketh . . . father**—or, gladdens a father. **heaviness**—or, grief.

2. Treasures . . . nothing—i.e., Ill-gotten gains give no true happiness (cf. ch. 4:17; Matt. 6:19).

3. (Cf. Ps. 37:16-20.) The last clause is better: "He will repel the greedy desires of the wicked."

righteousness—especially *beneficence* (Ps. 112:9). **death**—the greatest of all evils.

4. slack—lit., "deceitful." failing of its purpose (cf. Hos. 7:16). **maketh rich**—(cf. vs. 22).

CHAPTER 10 (Adam Clarke)

1. *The proverbs of Solomon.* Some ancient MSS. of the Vulgate have, "The second book of the Proverbs."

A wise son maketh a glad father. The parallels in this and several of the succeeding chapters are those which Bishop Lowth calls the antithetic: when two lines correspond with eath other by an opposition of terms and sentiments; when the second is contrasted with the first—sometimes in expression, sometimes in sense only.

MATTHEW HENRY

Verse 5

Those who improve their opportunities, who provide for hereafter while provision is to be made, *gather in summer*, which is gathering time. He who does so *is a wise son.* He acts wisely for his parents, whom, if there be occasion, he ought to maintain. *He who sleeps* idles away his time, and neglects his work, especially *who sleeps in harvest*, when he should be laying in for winter, *is a son that causes shame*; for he is a foolish son; he prepares shame for himself when winter comes. He who gets wisdom in the days of his youth *gathers in summer*, and he will have the credit of his industry; but he who idles away the days of his youth will bear the shame of his indolence when he is old.

Verse 6

Variety of blessings shall descend from above, and visibly abide on the head of good men. Blessings shall be on their head as a coronet to dignify them and as a helmet to protect them. *The mouth of the wicked is covered* with *violence.* Their mouths shall be stopped with shame for the violence which they have done.

Verse 7

Both the just and the wicked, when their days are fulfilled, must die. Between their bodies in the grave there is no visible difference; between the souls of the one and the other, in the world of spirits, there is a vast difference. Blessed men leave behind them blessed memories. Those that honour God he will thus honour, Ps. cxii. 3, 6, 9. It is part of the duty of the survivors: *Let the memory of the just be blessed*, so the Jews read it, and observe it as a precept, not naming an eminently just man that is dead without adding, *Let his memory be blessed.* Bad men are and shall be forgotten, or spoken of with contempt.

Verse 8

The obedient will take it as a privilege to be under government; and to be told their duty. And this is their wisdom; those are *wise in heart* who are tractable, and shall stand and be established. The disobedient, that will not be governed, nor endure any yoke, that will not be taught, nor take any advice, are fools, for they act against themselves and their own interest. They are commonly *prating fools*, full of talk, but full of nonsense, boasting of themselves.

Verse 9

Men's integrity will be their security: *He that walks uprightly* towards God and man, that is faithful to both and means as he says, *walks surely*; he is safe under a divine protection. He goes on his way with a humble boldness, being well armed against the temptations of Satan, the troubles of the world, and the reproaches of men. Men's dishonesty will be their shame: *He that perverts his way*, that dissembles with God and man, though he may for a time pass current, *shall be known* to be what he is.

Verse 10

Mischief is here said to attend designing, self-disguising sinners: *He that winks with the eye*, as if he took no notice of you, when he is watching an opportunity to do you an ill turn, that makes signs to his accomplices to assist him in executing his wicked projects, *causes sorrow* both to others and to himself. A *prating fool shall fall*, as was said before, *v.* 8. But his case is less dangerous of the two. He does not create so much sorrow to others as *he that winks with his eyes.* The dog that bites is not always the dog that barks.

Verse 11

How industrious a good man is, by communicating his goodness! *His mouth*, the outlet of his mind, *is a well of life*; it is a constant spring, whence issues good discourse for the edification of others. How industrious a bad man is, by concealing his badness: to do hurt with it: *The mouth of the wicked covers violence*, disguises the designed mischief with professions of friendship. *Violence covers the mouth of the wicked;* what he got by violence shall by violence be taken from him, Job v. 4, 5.

Verse 12

The great mischief-maker is malice. Even where there is no manifest occasion of strife, yet *hatred* seeks occasion and so *stirs it up.* Those are spiteful ill-natured people who take a pleasure in setting their neighbours by the ears, by tale-bearing, evil surmises, and misrepresentations, blowing up the sparks of contention into a flame, at which, with an unaccountable pleasure, they warm their hands. The great peace-maker, is *love*, which *covers all sins*, that is,

JAMIESON, FAUSSET, BROWN

5. son—as ch. 1:8, 10, and often. **sleepeth**—in indolence, and not for rest. **causeth shame**—lit., "is base" (cf. ch. 14:35; 17:2).

6. Blessings—lit., "Praises." The last clause is better: "The mouth of the wicked covereth, or concealeth, violence, or mischievous devices," to be executed in due time (Ps. 5:9; 10:7; Rom. 3:14), and hence has no praises (cf. vs. 11).

7. blessed—lit., "for a blessing," or praise. **shall rot**—lit., "be worm-eaten," useless and disgusting.

8. wise . . .—(cf. ch. 9:8, 9, 16), opposed to **prating fool**—or, fool of lips of wicked language. **fall**—headlong, suddenly.

9. perverteth his ways—acts deceitfully. **known**—discovered and punished.

10. Two vices contrasted; hypocrisy, or insinuating evil against one (ch. 6:13; Ps. 35:19), and rashness of speech. In each case, the results are on the evil-doers.

11. a well—or, source of good to himself and others (John 7:37, 38). On last clause cf. vs. 6.

12. strifes—or, litigations. **covereth**—by forgiveness and forbearance.

ADAM CLARKE

7. *The memory of the just is blessed.* Or "is a blessing." *But the name of the wicked shall rot.* This is another antithesis.

8. *A prating fool shall fall.* This clause is repeated in the tenth verse.

JOSEPH PARKER:

"The wise in heart will receive commandments: but a prating fool shall fall" (v. 8).

The wise in heart will look out for the word of authority, and will not consider it an indignity to submit to God's rule. This, indeed, is the very perfectness of Christian education—to know that we are ignorant, and that we are under guidance, and that the true counsel and direction can come only from heaven. The consummation of all prayer is—"Not my will, but thine, be done." This is not only the consummation of prayer, it is the last attainment of wisdom. We have to work faithfully and arduously in order to realize this remote conclusion. When a man has come to find that he knows nothing, and that he is in the hands of God, waiting for everything, and that his utmost might can only enable him to cooperate with God, never to go before, but always to toil behind with a willing heart, he is approaching the close of his earthly education—he is getting ready for the school of heaven, where the lessons are deeper, and where the opportunity of advancement is enlarged.

The prating fool is nowhere well spoken of; he is doomed to fall. Fools despise wisdom and instruction. By "fools" we are to understand persons who are self-conceited, headstrong, who will listen to no counsel, but who insist that they know everything, and are independent of every one. They prate, they talk loudly, they vex others by their criticism, they will always be heard; it is not for them to sit still and in a passive mood receive instruction; they will be instructors, leaders, loud speakers, not knowing that while they are holding their heads so high their feet are steadily moving down to the pit. A companion of fools shall be destroyed.

—*The People's Bible*

MATTHEW HENRY

the offences among relations which occasion discord. Love, instead of proclaiming and aggravating the offence, extenuates it as far as it is capable of being extenuated. Love will excuse the offence; when we are able to say that there was no ill intended, but it was an oversight, and we love our friend notwithstanding. It will also overlook the offence that is given us, and cover it, and by this means strife is prevented.

Verse 13

Wisdom and grace are the honour of good men. It is a man's honour to have wisdom, but much more to be instrumental to make others wise. Folly and sin are the shame of bad men: *A rod is for the back of him that is void of understanding—of him that wants a heart;* he exposes himself to the lashes of his own conscience, to the censures of the magistrate, and to the righteous judgments of God.

Verse 14

Observe, 1. It is the wisdom of the wise that they treasure up a stock of useful knowledge, which will be their preservation: *Wisdom is* therefore *found in their lips* (*v.* 13), because it is laid up in their hearts. 2. It is the folly of fools that they lay up mischief in their hearts. Their *mouth is near destruction,* having the *sharp arrows of bitter words* always at hand to throw about.

Verse 15

Rich people think themselves happy because they are rich; but it is their mistake: *The rich man's wealth is,* in his own conceit, *his strong city,* whereas the worst of evils it is utterly insufficient to protect them from. Poor people think themselves undone because they are poor; but it is their mistake. It sinks their spirits, whereas a man may live very comfortably, though he has but a little to live on, if he be but content, and keep a good conscience, and live by faith.

Verse 16

A righteous man eats only *the labour of his hands,* but that *labour tends to life;* he aims at nothing but to get an honest livelihood, to live and maintain his family. Nor does it tend only to his own life, but he would enable himself to do good to others; he labours *that he may have to gain* (Eph. iv. 28). A wicked man's wealth tends *to sin.* He makes it the food and fuel of his lusts, his pride and luxury; he does hurt with it and not good.

Verse 17

Those are in the right that do not only receive instruction, but retain it, keep it for their own use, that they may govern themselves by it, keep it for the benefit of others, that they may instruct them. Those are in the wrong that do not receive instruction, but wilfully and obstinately refuse it. They will not be taught their duty because it discovers their faults to them. The traveller that has missed his way, and cannot bear to be shown the right way, must needs err; he certainly misses *the way of life.*

Verse 18

Malice is folly and wickedness when it is concealed by flattery and dissimulation: He *is a fool,* though he may think himself a politician. *Lying lips* are bad enough of themselves, but have a peculiar malignity in them when they are made *a cloak of maliciousness. He that utters slander is a fool* too, for God will sooner or later bring forth that righteousness as the light which he endeavours to cloud.

Verse 19

Usually, those that speak much speak amiss, and among many words there cannot but be many idle words. Those that love to hear themselves talk do not consider what work they are making for repentance. It is therefore good to *keep our mouth as with a bridle: He that refrains his lips,* that often checks himself, is a wise man.

Verses 20–21

Value men, not by their wealth and preferment in the world, but by their virtue. Good men are good for something. As long as they have a mouth to speak, that will make them valuable and useful. *The tongue of the just is as choice silver;* they are sincere, freed from the dross of guile and evil design. They will enrich those that hear them with wisdom. It makes them useful: *The lips of the righteous feed many;* for they are full of the word of God, which is the bread of life, wherewith souls are nourished up. Bad men are good for nothing. *The heart of the wicked is little worth.* His principles, his notions, his thoughts, his purposes, and all the things that fill him, and affect him, are worldly and carnal, and

JAMIESON, FAUSSET, BROWN

13. In the lips . . . found—hence, not beaten, as the wicked-speaking fool. **void of understanding**—(ch. 6:32; 7:7).

14. lay up knowledge—i.e., as treasures for good use. **mouth . . . destruction**—or, as to the mouth, etc., destruction is near; they expose themselves to evil by prating.

15. Both by trusting in "uncertain riches" (I Tim. 6:17), or by the evils of poverty (ch. 30:9), men, not fearing God, fall into dangers.

16. The industry of the righteous is alone truly successful, while the earnings of the wicked tempt and lead to sin.

17. keepeth—observes (ch. 3:18; 4:22). **refuseth**—or, turns from reproof, which might direct him aright.

18. Both vices must one day be known and punished, and hence their folly.

19. Much speech involves risk of sin; hence the wisdom of restraining the tongue (Ps. 39:1; Jas. 1:26).

20. Right speech is the fruit of a good heart, but the wicked show theirs to be useless.

21. Fools not only fail to benefit others, as do the righteous, but procure their own ruin (cf. vss. 11, 17; Hos. 4:6).

ADAM CLARKE

13. *A rod is for the back of him.* **The rod is a most powerful instrument of knowledge.**

14. *Wise men lay up knowledge.* **They keep secret everything that has a tendency to disturb domestic or public peace; but the foolish man blabs all out, and produces much mischief. Think much, speak little, and always think before you speak. This will promote your own peace and that of your neighbor.**

19. *In the multitude of words.* **It is impossible to speak much and yet speak nothing but truth, and injure no man's character in the meanwhile.**

20. *The heart of the wicked is little worth.* **Kimat, is like little or nothing.**

MATTHEW HENRY

therefore of no value. *He that is of the earth speaks of the earth*, and neither understands nor relishes the things of God, John iii. 31; 1 Cor. ii. 14.

Verse 22

Worldly wealth is that which most men have their hearts very much upon, but they generally mistake both the nature of the thing they desire and the way by which they hope to obtain it. Desirable wealth is to be expected, not by making ourselves drudges to the world (Ps. cxxvii. 2), but by *the blessing of God*. It is this that *makes rich and adds no sorrow*; what comes from the love of God has the sign of God, to preserve the soul from those turbulent lusts and passions of which the increase of riches is commonly the incentive.

Verse 23

It *is as laughter to a fool to do mischief.* He makes a laughing matter of sin. When he is warned not to sin, he makes a jest of the admonition. When he has sinned, he ridicules reproofs, and laughs away the convictions of his own conscience, *ch.* xiv. 9. Wisdom carries along with it the evidence of its own excellency. You need say no more in praise of *a man understanding* than this, "He is an *understanding man*; he *has wisdom*."

Verses 24–25

I. It shall be as ill with the wicked as they can fear, and as well with the righteous, as they can desire. The wicked, it is true, buoy themselves up sometimes in their wickedness with vain hopes which will deceive them, but at other times they cannot but be haunted with just fears, and those *fears shall come upon them.* The righteous it is true, sometimes have their fears, but their desire is towards the favour of God and a happiness in him, and that *desire shall be granted.* According to their faith, not according to their fear, it shall be *unto them*, Ps. xxxvii. 4.

II. The prosperity of the wicked shall quickly end, but the happiness of the righteous shall never end, *v.* 25.

Verse 26

Those that are of a slothful disposition are not fit to be sent on an errand. Such therefore are very unmeet to be ministers, Christ's messengers. A slothful servant is to his master as uneasy and troublesome as *vinegar to the teeth* and *smoke to the eyes*; he provokes his passion, as vinegar sets the teeth on edge, and occasions him grief to see his business neglected and undone, as smoke sets the eyes a-weeping.

Verses 27–28

Religion lengthens men's lives and crowns their hopes. *What man is he that would see good days?* Let him be religious, and then his days shall not only be many, but happy, for *the hope of the righteous shall be gladness.* Wickedness shortens men's lives, and frustrates their hopes.

Verses 29–30

Strength and stability are entailed upon integrity: *The way of the Lord is strength to the upright*, confirms him in his uprightness. All God's dealings with him, merciful and afflictive, serve to quicken him to his duty and animate him against his discouragements. A good conscience, kept pure from sin, gives a man boldness in a dangerous time. That *joy of the Lord* which is to be found only in the *way of the Lord* will be our strength (Neh. viii. 10), and therefore *the righteous shall never be removed.* Ruin and destruction are the certain consequences of wickedness. God's judgments will root them out.

Verses 31–32

It is both the proof and the praise of a man's wisdom and goodness that he speaks wisely and well. A good man, in his discourse, *brings forth wisdom* for the benefit of others. He *knows what is acceptable*, what discourse will be pleasing to God. It is the sin, and will be the ruin, of a wicked man, that he speaks wickedly.

CHAPTER 11

Verse 1

Nothing is more offensive to God than deceit in commerce. *A false balance* is here put for all manner of unjust and fraudulent practices in dealing with any person, which are all an *abomination to the Lord.* Men make light of such frauds, and think there is no sin in that which there is money to be got by. Nothing is more pleasing to God than fair and honest dealing, nor more necessary to make us and our devotions acceptable to him: *A just weight is his delight.*

JAMIESON, FAUSSET, BROWN

22. it maketh . . . "it" is emphatic. Riches from God are without the sorrow of ill-gotten wealth (cf. Eccles. 2:21-23; I Tim. 6:9, 10, 17).

23. Sin is the pleasure of the wicked; wisdom that of the good.

24. it—the very thing. The wicked get dreaded evil; the righteous, desired good.

25. (Cf. Ps. 1:4; 37:9, 10, 36.) **righteous . . . foundation**—well laid and firm (Matt. 7:24, 25).

26. i.e., causes vexation.

27. (Cf. ch. 9:11; Ps. 55:23.) **28. gladness**—in confidence of realizing it. **expectation . . . perish**—in disappointment.

29. The way . . . i.e., God's providence sustains the righteous and overthrows the wicked (Hos. 14:9). **30.** (Cf. ch. 12:3; Ps. 37:9-11; 102:28.) **earth**—or, land of promise.

31. bringeth forth—lit., "germinates" as a plant. **froward**—(Cf. ch. 2:12, 14). **cut off**—as an unproductive plant. **32. know**—regard and provide for (Ps. 1:6). **frowardness**—all kinds of deceit and ill-nature. The word is plural.

CHAPTER 11

Vss. 1-31. **1.** (Cf. *Margin.*) The Hebrews used stones for weights. **just**—complete in measure.

ADAM CLARKE

22. *The blessing of the Lord, it maketh rich.* **Whatever we receive in the way of providence has God's blessing in it, and will do us good.**

ALEXANDER MACLAREN:

Verse 29. "The way of the Lord" means, sometimes in the Old Testament and sometimes in the New, religion, considered as the way in which God desires a man to walk. So we read in the New Testament of "the way" as the designation of the profession and practice of Christianity; and "the way of the Lord" is often used in the Psalms for the path which He traces for man by His sovereign will.

But that, of course, is not the meaning here. Here it means, not the road in which God prescribes that we should walk, but that road in which He Himself walks; or, in other words, the sum of the divine action, the solemn footsteps of God through creation, providence, and history. "His goings forth are from everlasting." "His way is in the sea." "His way is in the sanctuary." Modern language has a whole set of phrases which mean the same thing as the Jew meant by "the way of the Lord," only that God is left out. They talk about the "current of events," "the general tendency of things," "the laws of human affairs," and so on. I, for my part, prefer the old fashioned "Hebraism." To many modern thinkers the whole drift and tendency of human affairs affords no sign of a person directing these. They hear the clashing and grinding of opposing forces, the thunder as of falling avalanches, and the moaning as of a homeless wind, but they hear the sounds of no footfalls echoing down the ages. This ancient teacher had keener ears. Well for us if we share his faith, and see in all the else distracting mysteries of life and history, "the way of the Lord!"

—*Expositions of Holy Scripture*

CHAPTER 11

1. *A false balance is abomination.* **This refers to the balance itself deceitfully constructed, so that it is sooner turned at one end than at the other. This is occasioned by one end of the beam being longer than the other.** *But a just weight.* **The "perfect stone," probably because weights were first made of stone; see the law, Deut. xxv. 13-35.**

MATTHEW HENRY

Verse 2

Pride is a shame to a man who springs out of the earth, who lives upon alms, depends upon God, and has forfeited all he has, to be proud. He that is haughty makes himself contemptible; it is a sin for which God often brings men down, as he did Nebuchadnezzar and Herod, whose ignominy immediately attended their vain-glory. As with the proud there is folly, and will be shame, so *with the lowly there is wisdom*, and will be honour, for a man's wisdom gains him respect and makes his face to shine before men.

Verse 3

The integrity of an honest man will itself be his guide. His principles are fixed, his rule is certain, and therefore his way is plain; his sincerity keeps him steady, and he need not tack about every time the wind turns, having no other end to drive at than to keep a good conscience. The iniquity of a bad man will itself be his ruin. The perverseness of sinners will be their destruction, though they think themselves ever so well fortified.

Verse 4

Riches will stand men in no stead in that day. They will neither put by the stroke nor ease the pain, much less take out the sting; what profit will this world's birthrights be then? A good conscience will make death easy. It is the privilege of the righteous not to be hurt of the second death, and so not much hurt by the first.

Verses 5–6

These two verses are to the same purport with *v.* 3. The ways of religion are plain and safe, and in them we may enjoy a holy security. *The righteousness of the upright* shall be armour of proof to them, to deliver them from the allurements of the devil and the world, and from their menaces. The ways of wickedness are dangerous and destructive: *The wicked shall fall* into misery and ruin *by their own wickedness.* Their sin will be their punishment.

Verse 7

It will be the great aggravation of the misery of wicked people that their hopes will sink into despair just when they expect them to be crowned with fruition. When a godly man dies his expectations are outdone, and all his fears vanish; but when a wicked man dies his hopes vanish.

Verse 8

Good people are helped out of the distresses which they thought themselves lost in, and their feet are set in a large room, Ps. lxvi. 12; xxxiv. 19. God has found out a way to deliver his people even when they have despaired. The wicked have fallen into the distresses which they thought themselves far from. Mordecai is saved from the gallows, Daniel from the lion's den, and Peter from the prison; and their persecutors *come in their stead.* The Israelites are delivered out of the Red Sea and the Egyptians drowned in it.

Verse 9

It is not only the murderer with his sword, but the *hypocrite with his mouth,* that *destroys his neighbour,* decoying him into sin, or into mischief, by the specious pretences of kindness and goodwill. *Death and life are in the power of the tongue,* but no tongue more fatal than the flattering tongue.

Verses 10–11

Good men are generally well-beloved by their neighbours. *When it goes well with the righteous,* when they are advanced and put into a capacity of doing good according to their desire, it is so much the better for all about them, and *the city rejoices.* Wicked people may perhaps have here and there a well-wisher, but among the generality of their neighbours they get ill-will; they may be feared, but they are not loved, and therefore *when they perish there is shouting.* There is good reason for this, because those that are good do good. *Good men are public blessings. By the blessing of the upright,* the blessings with which they are blessed, which enlarge their sphere of usefulness,—by the blessings with which they bless their neighbours, their advice, their examples, their prayers,—by the blessings with which God blesses others for their sake,—by these *the city is exalted.* Wicked men are public nuisances.

Verses 12–13

Silence is recommended as an instance of true friendship. *A man of understanding,* that has rule over his own spirit, if he be provoked, *holds his peace,*

JAMIESON, FAUSSET, BROWN

2. Self-conceit is unteachable; the humble grow wise (cf. ch. 16:18; 18:12).

3. guide—to lead, as a shepherd (ch. 6:37; Ps. 78:52). **perverseness**—ill-nature. **destroy**—with violence.

4. (Cf. ch. 10:2.) **wrath**—i.e., of God.

5. direct—or, make plain; wicked ways are not plain (ch. 13:17). **6. deliver them**—i.e., from evil, which the wicked suffer by their own doings (ch. 5:22; Ps. 9:16).

7. expectation . . . perish—for death cuts short all his plans (Luke 16:25). **hope of unjust**—better, "hope of wealth," or power (cf. Isa. 40:29, *Hebrew*). This gives an advance on the sentiment of the first clause. Even hopes of gain die with him.

8. Perhaps the *trouble* prepared by the wicked, and which he inherits (cf. vs. 6).

9. (Cf. Ps. 35:16; Dan. 11:32.) The just is saved by superior discernment.

10, 11. The last may be a reason for the first. Together, they set forth the relative moral worth of good and bad men. **By the blessing**—implying active benevolence.

ADAM CLARKE

2. *When pride cometh.* The proud man thinks much more of himself than any other can do; and, expecting to be treated according to his own supposed worth, which treatment he seldom meets with, he is repeatedly mortified, ashamed, confounded, and rendered indignant. *With the lowly.* The "humble," the "modest," as opposed to the *proud,* referred to in the first clause. The humble man looks for nothing but justice, expects nothing in the way of commendation or praise, and can never be disappointed but in receiving praise.

JOSEPH PARKER:

Pride has a short day in which to live; immediately behind red and blustering pride comes pale-faced, cowering shame. No pride can stand that is not based on reason and sanctioned by morality: without these guarantees it is mere ostentation, vanity, irrational and unseasonable boasting, exploding by its own energy, and coming to nothing because of its irregularity. There is nothing to be proud of upon the earth. We cannot be proud of our strength, for in our highest estate we are but like the grass, which today is, and tomorrow is cast into the oven. We cannot be proud even of intellectual abilities, for we have nothing that we have not received, and indeed the higher our intellectual power the more modest will be our whole feeling in relation to ourselves. Partial power is more likely to be proud than is complete strength. It is while we grow that we are a surprise to ourselves, but when we have come to something like maturity we begin to feel how little there is on earth that is to be accounted of, and how true it is that he that glorieth should glory in the Lord. With the lowly is wisdom, with the modest, with the simple in heart, with the unselfish: they may not have the wisdom of letters, but they have that deeper wisdom which is before letters and which will survive all literature—the wisdom of an open heart, an unprejudiced understanding, a loving and obedient will, a disposition whose mute prayer is continually, Lord, give me light, and show me what is true. God himself will dwell with the lowly man as in a chosen habitation; he will come to him by night and tarry with him to the break of day, and if he leave him it is but for a small moment, that his return may be marked by an intenser desire and adoration.

—The People's Bible

9. *An hypocrite with his mouth. Chaneph* might be better translated "infidel" than *hypocrite.* The latter is one that pretends to religion. The former is one who disbelieves divine revelation, and accordingly is polluted, and lives in pollution.

MATTHEW HENRY

that he may neither give vent to his passion nor kindle the passion of others by any opprobrious language or peevish reflections. *He that is void of wisdom* discovers his folly by this; he *despises his neighbour*, calls him *Raca*, and *Thou fool*, upon the least provocation. *A tale-bearer*, that carries all the stories he can pick up, true or false, from house to house, to make mischief and sow discord, *reveals secrets* which he has been entrusted with, and so breaks the laws, and forfeits all the privileges, of friendship and conversation.

Verse 14

Where no counsel is, no consultation, but everything done rashly, only caballing for parties and divided interests, *the people fall*, crumble into factions, fall to pieces. Councils of war are necessary to the operations of war; two eyes see more than one; and mutual advice is mutual assistance. *In the multitude of counsellors*, that see their need one of another, and act in concert and with concern for the public welfare, *there is safety*.

Verse 15

Our estates are not our own; we are but stewards. There is a good husbandry which is good divinity, part of the character of a good man, Ps. cxii. 5. Every man must be just to his family, else he is not true to his stewardship. In particular, we must not enter rashly into suretiship. There is danger of bringing ourselves into trouble by it, and our families too when we are gone: *He that is surety for a stranger*, he *shall smart for it. He shall be sadly crushed and broken by it*, and perhaps become a bankrupt.

Verse 16

Strong men retain riches. Men of spirit and interest are able to make good against all who stand in their way, are likely to keep what they have and to get more. *A gracious woman* is as solicitous to preserve her reputation for wisdom and modesty, humility and courtesy, and all those other graces that are the true ornaments of her sex, as strong men are to secure their estates; and those women who are truly gracious will secure their honour by their good conduct.

Verse 17

A *merciful*, tender, good-humoured *man, does good to his own soul*, makes and keeps himself easy. He has the pleasure of doing his duty, and contributing to the comfort of those that are to him as *his own soul*; for *we are members one of another*. We may by the *soul* understand the *inward man*, as the apostle calls it, and then it teaches us that the first and great act of mercy is to provide well for our own souls the necessary supports of the spiritual life. A *cruel*, froward, ill-natured man, *troubles his own flesh*, and so his sin becomes his punishment.

Verse 18

The wicked works a deceitful work, builds himself a house upon the sand, which will deceive him when the storm comes. *Sin deceived me, and by it slew me.* He *that sows righteousness* shall have *a sure reward*; it is made as sure to him as eternal truth can make it.

Verse 19

True holiness is true happiness; it is a preparative for it, a pledge and earnest of it. *Righteousness* inclines, disposes, and leads, the soul *to life*. Those that indulge themselves in sin are fitting themselves for destruction.

Verse 20

It concerns us to know what God hates and what he loves, that we may govern ourselves accordingly. Nothing is more offensive to God than hypocrisy and double-dealing, for these are signified by the word which we translate *frowardness*, pretending justice, but intending wrong, walking in crooked ways, to avoid discovery. Nothing is more pleasing to God than sincerity and plain-dealing.

Verse 21

Confederacies in sin shall certainly be broken, and shall not avail to protect the sinners: *Though hand join in hand*, though there are many that concur by their practice to keep wickedness in countenance, though they are in league for the support and propagation of it, though wicked children tread in the steps of their wicked parents, they shall not be held guiltless; it will not excuse them to say that they did as the most did and as their company did. *The seed of the righteous*, that follow the steps of their righteousness, though they may fall into trouble, shall, in due time, *be delivered*.

JAMIESON, FAUSSET, BROWN

12. despiseth—or, reviles, a course contrasted with the prudent silence of the wise. **holdeth his peace**—as if neither hearing nor telling. **13. tale-bearer**—(cf. *Margin*), one trading as a peddler in scandal, whose propensity to talk leads him to betray confidence.

14. counsel—the art of governing (ch. 1:5). **counsellors**—lit., "one giving counsel"; the participle used as a collective.

15. (Cf. ch. 6:1.) **suretiship**—(Cf. *Margin*), the actors put for the action, which may be lawfully hated.

16. retaineth—or lit., "lay hold of as a support." Honor is to a feeble woman thus as valuable as riches to men.

17. merciful—kind to others; opposed to cruel. Such benefit themselves by doing good to others (cf. ch. 24:5), while the cruel injure themselves as well as others. **flesh**—i.e., his body, by penuriousness (Col. 2:23).

18. a deceitful work—or, wages, which fail to satisfy, or flee away (ch. 10:2; 23:5). **sure reward**—or, gain, as from trading (Hos. 10:12; Gal. 6:8, 9).

19. Inference from vs. 18 (cf. vss. 5, 6; ch. 10:16).

20. (Cf. vs. 5.) **froward**—as in ch. 2:15, opposed to the simplicity and purity of the **upright. in their way**—or, conduct.

21. The combined power of the wicked cannot free them from just punishment, while the unaided children of the righteous find deliverance by reason of their pious relationship (Ps. 37:25, 26).

ADAM CLARKE

13. *A talebearer.* The walking busybody, the trader in scandal.

15. *He that is surety for a stranger shall smart for it.* He shall find evil upon evil in it. See chap. vi. 1.

16. *A gracious woman retaineth honour.* Instead of this the Septuagint have, "A gracious woman raiseth up honour to the man; but she that hateth righteous things is a throne of dishonour." A good wife is an honor to her husband, and a bad wife is her husband's reproach. If this be so, how careful should a man be whom he marries!

JOSEPH PARKER:

Verse 16. Here the sexes are put in beautiful apposition: woman is gracious, man is strong. Graciousness dissociated from strength has indeed an influence all its own; strength dissociated from graciousness is mere strength, and is wanting in all those attributes which excite and satisfy the deepest confidences of the world. A woman can work miracles by her graciousness. She knows how to enter the sick chamber noiselessly. She knows how to enter the room without violence, ostentation, or impressiveness, which signifies vanity and display. Woman can speak the gentle word, and look the gracious look, and use the magical touch of friendship and trust, and, in short, can carry her own way without appearing to do so by the very force of tenderness, sympathy, and persuasiveness. Who would raise the foolish question whether grace or strength is the more desirable attribute? Each is desirable in its own way; a combination that is the very perfection of character. Strength and beauty are in the house of the Lord. The great column looks all the better for the beautiful capital which crowns and enriches it. Men should endeavor to cultivate grace, tenderness, all that is charmful in spirit, disposition, and action: this cannot be done by mere mimicry; it is to be done by living continually with Christ, studying his spirit, entering into all his purposes, and reproducing, not mechanically, but spiritually, as much as possible of all that was distinctive of his infinite character. The Bible has ever given honor to woman. He is a fool and an unjust man who wishes to keep women in silence, obscurity, and in a state of unimportance; and she is a foolish woman who imagines that she cannot be gracious without being strong, and who wishes to sacrifice her graciousness to some empty reputation for worthless energy.—*The People's Bible*

MATTHEW HENRY

Verse 22

By *discretion* here understand *religion* and *grace*, a true relish (so the word signifies) of the honours and pleasures that attend an unspotted virtue; so that *a woman without discretion* is a woman of a loose and dissolute conversation. Beauty or comeliness of body is *as a jewel of gold*, and, where there is wisdom and grace to guard against the temptations of it, it is a great ornament. A foolish wanton woman, of a light carriage, is fitly compared to a swine, though she be ever so handsome, wallowing in the mire of filthy lusts, with which the mind and conscience are defiled, and, though washed, returning to them. It is lamented that beauty should be so abused. It is quite misplaced, *as a jewel in a swine's snout*, with which he roots in the dunghill.

Verse 23

The righteous would have *good, only good*; all they desire is that it may go well with all about them; they wish no hurt to any, but happiness to all; as to themselves, their desire is to obtain the favour of a good God and to preserve the peace of a good conscience; and good they shall have, that good which they desire, Ps. xxxvii. 4. *The wicked* expect and desire mischief to others, but it shall return upon themselves; as they loved cursing, they shall have enough of it.

Verse 24

A man may grow rich by prudently spending what he has, may scatter in works of piety, charity, and generosity, and yet may increase; nay, by that means may increase, as the corn is increased by being sown. But it is especially to be ascribed to God; he blesses the giving hand, and so makes it a getting hand, 2 Cor. ix. 10. A man may grow poor by meanly sparing what he has, *withholding more than is meet*, not paying just debts, not relieving the poor, not providing what is convenient for the family. This *tends to poverty*, and forfeits the blessing of God.

Verse 25

The liberal soul that prays for the afflicted and provides for them, that scatters blessings with gracious lips and generous hands, that soul *shall be made fat* with true pleasure and enriched with more grace. *He that waters* others with the streams of his bounty *shall be also watered himself;* God will certainly return plentiful showers of his blessing. *He that waters, even he shall be as rain* (so some read it); he shall be recruited as the clouds are which return after the rain, and shall be further useful.

Verse 26

It is a sin, when corn is dear and scarce, to withhold it, in hopes that it will grow dearer, so to keep up and advance the market, when it is already so high that the poor suffer by it; and at such a time it is the duty of those that have stocks of corn by them to consider the poor, and to be willing to sell at the market-price, to be content with moderate profit.

Verse 27

He that rises early to that which is good (so the word is), that seeks opportunities of serving his friends and relieving the poor, and lays out himself therein, *procures favour*. All about him love him, and, which is better than life, he has God's loving-kindness. Those that are industrious to do mischief ruin themselves.

Verse 28

Our righteousness will stand us in stead when our riches fail us: *The righteous shall* then *flourish as a branch*, the branch of righteousness, like a tree whose leaf shall not wither, Ps. i. 3. When those that take root in the world wither those that are grafted into Christ shall be fruitful and flourishing.

Verse 29

Two extremes in the management of family-affairs are here condemned. 1. Carefulness and carnal policy, on the one hand. There are those that by their anxiety about their business and fretfulness about their losses, and their niggardliness towards their families, *trouble their own houses*; while others think, by supporting factions and feuds in their families, to serve some turn for themselves. But they will both be disappointed; they will *inherit the wind*. All they will get by these arts will be empty and worthless as the wind. 2. Carelessness and want of common prudence, on the other. He that is a fool in his business, that minds it not, that has no contrivance and consideration, not only loses his reputation, but becomes a *servant to the wise in heart*. He is impoverished, while those that manage wisely

JAMIESON, FAUSSET, BROWN

22. Jewels were often suspended from the nose (Gen. 24:47; Isa. 3:21). Thus adorned, a hog disgusts less than a fair and indiscreet woman.

23. (Cf. ch. 10:28.) The wrath is that of God.

24-31. The scope of the whole is a comment on vs. 23. Thus liberality (vs. 24), by God's blessing, secures increase, while penuriousness, instead of expected gain, procures poverty.

25. liberal soul—(Cf. *Margin*). **made fat**—prospers (ch. 28:25; Deut. 32:15; Luke 6:38).

watereth . . . watered—a common figure for blessing.

26. Another example of the truth of vs. 23; the miser loses reputation, though he saves corn. **selleth it**—i.e., at a fair price.

27. good [and] **mischief**—i.e., of others. **procureth . . . seeketh**—implying success.

28. (Cf. ch. 10:15; Ps. 49:6; I Tim. 6:17.) **righteous . . . branch**—(Ps. 1:3; Jer. 17:8.)

29. troubleth—as ch. 15:27 explains, by greediness for gain (cf. vs. 17). **inherit . . . wind**—Even successful, his gains are of no real value. So the fool, thus acting, either comes to poverty, or heaps up for others.

ADAM CLARKE

22. *A jewel of gold in a swine's snout.* That is, beauty in a woman destitute of good breeding and modest carriage is as becoming as a gold ring on the snout of a swine.

24. *There is that scattereth, and yet increaseth.* The bountiful man who gives to the poor, never turning away his face from anyone in distress, the Lord blesses his property, and the bread is multiplied in his hand.

25. *The liberal soul shall be made fat.* He who gives to the distressed, in the true spirit of charity, shall get a hundredfold from God's mercy. How wonderful is the Lord! He gives the property, gives the heart to use it aright, and recompenses the man for the deed, though all the fruit was found from himself! *He that watereth.* A man who distributes in the right spirit gets more good himself than the poor man does who receives the bounty. Thus "it is more blessed to give than to receive."

26. *He that withholdeth corn.* Who refuses to sell because he hopes for a dearth, and then he can make his own price.

MATTHEW HENRY

raise themselves, and come to have dominion over him.

Verse 30

The righteous are as *trees of life*; the fruits of their piety and charity, their instructions, reproofs, examples, and prayers, their interest in heaven, and their influence upon earth, are like the fruits of that tree, contributing to the nourishment of the spiritual life in many; they are the ornaments of paradise, God's church on earth. The wise are something more; they are as trees of knowledge, commanded to have knowledge. *He that is wise*, by communicating his wisdom, *wins souls*, wins them over into the interests of God's kingdom among men. Those that would win souls have need of wisdom to know how to deal with them.

Verse 31

This is the only one of Solomon's proverbs that has that note of attention prefixed to it, *Behold!* which intimates that it contains not only an evident truth, but an eminent truth. Some understand both parts of "recompence" as displeasure: *The righteous*, if they do amiss, shall be punished for their offences in this world; much more shall wicked people be punished for theirs, which are committed, not through infirmity, but with a high hand. Others understand it of a "recompence" of reward to the righteous and punishment to sinners. There are some recompences *in the earth*, in this world; but many sins go unpunished in the earth, and services unrewarded, which indicates that there is a judgment to come. Many times *the righteous* are *recompensed* for their righteousness here *in the earth*, though that is not the only reward intended for them, but whatever the word of God has promised them, or the wisdom of God sees good for them, they shall have *in the earth*. *The wicked* also, are sometimes remarkably punished in this life, nations, families, particular persons.

CHAPTER 12

Verse 1

Those that have grace will delight in all the instructions that are given them by the word or providence of God; they will value a good education, and think it not a hardship, but a happiness, to be under a strict and prudent discipline. Those show themselves not only void of grace, but void of common sense, that take it as an affront to be told of their faults, and an imposition upon their liberty to be put in mind of their duty. Those that desire to live in loose families and societies, where they may be under no check, are the *brutish*.

Verse 2

Our Father judges of his children very much by their conduct one to another; and therefore *a good man*, that is merciful, and charitable, and does good, *draws out favour from the Lord* by his prayers; but a malicious man, that devises wickedness against his neighbours, *he will condemn*, as unworthy of a place in his kingdom.

Verse 3

Though men may advance themselves by sinful arts, they cannot by such arts settle and secure themselves. *A man shall not be established by wickedness;* it may set him in high places, but they are slippery places, Ps. lxxiii. 18. Though good men may have but little of the world, yet what is honestly got will wear well.

Verse 4

He that is blessed with a good wife is as happy as if he were upon the throne, for she is no less than *a crown* to him. A virtuous woman is pious and prudent, active for the good of her family, makes conscience of her duty, a woman that can bear crosses without disturbance. She is faithful to him and by her example teaches his children and servants to be so too. A bad wife is no better than *rottenness in his bones*, an incurable disease, besides that *she makes him ashamed*. She that is silly and slothful, wasteful and wanton, passionate and ill-tongued, ruins both the credit and comfort of her husband.

Verse 5

We mistake if we imagine that thoughts are free; they are under the divine cognizance. A good man may have in his mind bad suggestions, but he does not indulge them and harbour them. It is a man's honour to mean honestly, though a word or action may be misplaced, or mistimed, or at least misinterpreted. But it is a man's shame to act with deceit, with trick and design, not only with a long reach, but with an overreach.

JAMIESON, FAUSSET, BROWN

30. a tree of life—Blessings to others proceed from the works of the righteous (ch. 3:18). **winneth souls**—(Cf. *Margin*), to do them good as opposed to ch. 6:25; Ezek. 13:18 (cf. Luke 5:10).

31. Behold—Thus calling attention to the illustrations (cf. vs. 23), the sentiment of which is confirmed even in time, not excluding future rewards and punishments.

CHAPTER 12

Vss. 1-28. **1. loveth knowledge**—as the fruit of instruction or training (ch. 1:2). **hateth reproof**—(Ch. 10:17.) **brutish**—stupid, regardless of his own welfare (Ps. 49:10; 73:22).

3. Wickedness cannot give permanent prosperity. **root . . . not be moved**—firm as a flourishing tree—(Ps. 1:3; 15:5; Jer. 17:8).

4. A virtuous woman—in the wide sense of well disposed to all moral duties (ch. 31:10). **maketh ashamed**—i.e., by misconduct. **rottenness**—an incurable evil.

5. thoughts—or, purposes. **are right**—lit., "are judgment," i.e., true decisions. **counsels**—(Cf. ch. 11:14.) **deceit**—contrary to truth and honesty.

ADAM CLARKE

30. *The fruit of the righteous is a tree of life.* "The tree of lives."

31. *Behold, the righteous shall be recompensed in the earth,* etc. The Septuagint, Syriac, and Arabic read this verse as follows: "And if the righteous scarcely be saved, where shall the ungodly and the sinner appear?" And this St. Peter quotes *literatim*, 1st Epist. iv. 18.

CHAPTER 12

1. *Whoso loveth instruction. Musar,* discipline or correction, *loveth knowledge;* for correction is the way to knowledge. *But he that hateth reproof is brutish. Baar,* he is a bear.

4. *A virtuous woman is a crown to her husband.* "A strong woman." Our word "virtue" (*virtus*) is derived from *vir*, a "man"; and as man is the noblest of God's creatures, virtue expresses what is becoming to man; that is noble, courageous, and dignified; and as *vir*, a "man," comes from *vis*, "power" or "strength," so it implies what is strong and vigorous in **principle**.

MATTHEW HENRY

Verse 6

In the foregoing verse the *thoughts* of the wicked and righteous were compared. Wicked indeed those are whose *words* are to *lie in wait for blood*; their tongues are swords to those that stand in their way, to good men whom they hate and persecute. See an instance, Luke xx. 20, 21. Good men speak help to their neighbours: The *mouth of the upright* is ready to be opened in the cause of those that are oppressed (*ch.* xxxi. 8).

Verse 7

Turn the wicked, and they are not; they stand in such a slippery place that the least touch of trouble brings them down, like the apples of Sodom, which look fair, but touch them and they go to dust. The prosperity of the righteous will endure. Death will remove them, but their *house* shall *stand*, their families shall be kept up.

Verse 8

The best reputation is that which attends virtue and the prudent conduct of life: *A man shall be commended* not according to his riches or preferments, his craft and subtlety, but *according to his wisdom*, the honesty of his designs. The worst reproach is that which follows wickedness, that turns aside to crooked ways.

Verse 9

It is the folly of some that they covet to make a great figure abroad, and yet want necessaries at home, and, if their debts were paid, would not be worth a morsel of bread, nay, perhaps, pinch their bellies to put it on their backs, that they may appear very gay, because fine feathers make fine birds. The character of those is every way better who content themselves in a lower sphere, where they are despised for the plainness of their dress, that they may be able to afford themselves, not only necessaries, but conveniences, in their own houses, not only bread, but a servant.

Verse 10

A good man will be merciful. He regards even *the life of his beast*, not only because it is his servant, but because it is God's creature. The beasts that are under our care must be provided for, must have convenient food and rest. Balaam was checked for beating his ass. The law took care for oxen. A wicked man will be unmerciful; even his *tender mercies* are *cruel*; natural compassion is turned into hard-heartedness.

Verse 11

It is men's wisdom to mind their business and follow an honest calling, for that is the way, by the blessing of God, to get a livelihood. Be busy, and that is the true way to be easy. Keep thy shop and thy shop will keep thee. It is men's folly to neglect their business, for then they come to want bread, and make themselves burdensome to others, eating the bread out of other people's mouths.

Verse 12

The care and aim of a wicked man. "Oh that I were but as cunning as such a man, that I had but his art of over-reaching, that I could but take my revenge on one I have spite to as effectually as he can!" A good man desires, to do good and to be fixed and confirmed in doing good. The wicked desires only a net wherewith to fish for himself; the righteous desires to yield fruit for the benefit of others and God's glory, Rom. xiv. 6.

Verse 13

Many a man has paid dearly in this world for the transgression of his lips, and has felt the lash on his back for want of a bridle upon his tongue, Ps. lxiv. 8. The righteous extricate themselves out of trouble by their own wisdom, when God in mercy comes in for their succour.

Verse 14

Even good words will turn to a good account (*v.* 14): *A man* shall gain present comfort, inward pleasure which is truly satisfying, by the good he does with his pious discourse and prudent advice. Good works: much more, will be abundantly rewarded.

Verse 15

A fool thinks he is in the right in everything he does, and *therefore* asks no advice. A wise man is willing to be advised, desires to have counsel given him, and *hearkens to counsel*, being diffident of his own judgment.

JAMIESON, FAUSSET, BROWN

6. The words—or, expressed designs of the wicked are for evil purposes. **the mouth**—or, words of the righteous delivering instead of ensnaring men.

7. Such conduct brings a proper return, by the destruction of the wicked and well-being of the righteous and his family.

8. despised—as opposed to **commended** (ch. 11:12). **perverse heart**—or, wicked principles, as opposed to one of wisdom.

9. despised—held in little repute, obscure (I Sam. 18: 23; Isa. 3:5). **hath a servant**—implying some means of honest living. **honoureth himself**—is self-conceited.

10. regardeth—lit., "knoweth" (Ps. 1:6). **mercies . . . cruel**—as acts of compassion ungraciously rendered to the needy. The righteous more regards a beast than the wicked a man.

11. The idler's fate is the result of indolence and want of principle (ch. 6:32; 7:7).

12. the wicked . . . evil—They love the crafty arts of deception. **the root . . . (fruit)**--their own resources supply them; or, it may be rendered: "He (God) giveth, or sets (Ezek. 17:22) the root of the righteous," and hence it is firm: or, the verb is impersonal; "As to the root, (etc.), it is firm" (ch. 17:19).

13, 14. The sentiment expanded. While the wicked, such as liars, flatterers, etc., fall by their own words, the righteous are unhurt. Their good conduct makes friends, and God rewards them.

15. The way . . . eyes—The fool is self-conceited (cf. vs. 1; ch. 1:32; 10:17; Jas. 3:17).

ADAM CLARKE

9. *He that is despised, and hath a servant.* I believe the Vulgate gives the true *sense* of this verse: "Better is the poor man who provides for himself, than the proud who is destitute of bread." The versions in general agree in this sense.

10. *A righteous man regardeth the life of his beast.* One principal characteristic of a holy man is mercy. I once in my travels met with the Hebrew of this clause on the signboard of a public inn, which, being very appropriate, reminded me that I should feed my horse. *The tender mercies of the wicked are cruel.* Are "violent, without mercy, ruthless."

MATTHEW HENRY

Verse 16

Passion is folly: a wise man may be angry when there is just cause for it, but then he has his anger under check, is *lord of his anger*, whereas a fool's anger lords it over him. Those that are soon angry, that are quickly put into a flame by the least spark, have not that rule which they ought to have over their own spirits. Meekness is wisdom: *A prudent man covers shame.* He covers the passion that is in his own breast; he keeps his mouth as with a bridle. It is a kindness to ourselves, and contributes to the repose of our own minds, to extenuate and excuse the injuries and affronts that we receive, instead of aggravating them and making the worst of them.

Verse 17

Here is, 1. A faithful witness representing everything fairly, to the best of his knowledge, whether in judgment or in common conversation, whether he be upon his oath or no, makes it to appear that he is governed and actuated by the principles and laws of righteousness, and he promotes justice by doing honour to it. 2. A false witness condemned for a cheat; he *shows forth deceit*, and is possessed by a lying spirit.

Verse 18

The tongue is death or life, poison or medicine, as it is used. Slanders, like a sword, wound the reputation of those of whom they are uttered. Whisperings and evil surmises, like a sword, divide and cut asunder the bonds of love and friendship, and separate those that have been dearest to each other. There are words that are curing and healing, closing up those wounds which the backbiting tongue had given, restoring peace, and persuading to reconciliation.

Verse 19

If truth be spoken, it will hold good. What is true will be always true; we may abide by it. A *lying tongue* will be disproved. The liar, when he comes to be examined, will be found not consistent with himself as he is that speaks truth. Truth may be eclipsed, but it will come to light.

Verse 20

Those that devise mischief deceive themselves. Let them imagine it ever so artfully, deceivers will be deceived. Those that study the things which make for peace and give peaceable advice, promote healing and further the public welfare, will have not only the credit, but the comfort of it. *Blessed are the peacemakers.*

Verse 21

If men be sincerely righteous, God has engaged that no evil shall happen to them. He will, by the power of his grace in them, keep them so that, though they be tempted, yet they shall not be overcome by the temptation, and though they come into trouble, yet those troubles shall have no evil in them (Ps. xci. 10), for they shall be overruled to work for their good. Those that live in contempt of God and man shall be made miserable with the mischiefs that shall come upon them. Those that delight in mischief shall have enough of it.

Verse 22

Lying is an abomination to the Lord, not only because it is a breach of his law, but because it is destructive to human society. Those that *deal truly* and sincerely in all their dealings are *his delight*, and he is well pleased with them.

Verse 23

He that is wise communicates his knowledge when it may turn to the edification of others, but he conceals it when the showing of it would only tend to his own commendation. Prudent men will carefully avoid everything that savours of ostentation. He that is foolish cannot avoid proclaiming his folly.

Verse 24

Industry is the way to preferment. Solomon advanced Jeroboam because he saw that he was an industrious young man, and minded his business, 1 Kings xi. 28. Those that are diligent when they are young will get that which will enable them to rule, and so to rest, when they are old. Knavery is the way to slavery. Those that, because they will not take pains in an honest calling, live by their shifts and arts of dishonesty, are paltry and beggarly, and will be kept under.

Verse 25

The cause and consequence of melancholy is *heaviness in the heart*; it is a load of care, and fear,

JAMIESON, FAUSSET, BROWN

16. prudent . . . shame—He is slow to denounce his insulters (Jas. 1:19).

18. speaketh—lit., "speaketh hastily," or indiscreetly (Ps. 106:33), as an angry man retorts harsh and provoking invectives. **tongue . . . health**—by soothing and gentle language.

19. Words of truth are consistent, and stand all tests, while lies are soon discovered and exposed.

20. that imagine—or, plan (ch. 3:29). They design a deceitful course, to which, with all its evils and dangers to others and themselves, the happiness of peacemakers is opposed (cf. Matt. 5:9; Rom. 12:18).

21. no evil—(as in Ps. 91:10), under God's wise limitations (Rom. 8:28). **mischief**—as penal evil.

22. deal truly—or, faithfully, i.e., according to promises (cf. John 3:21).

23. concealeth—by his modesty (ch. 10:14; 11:13). **heart . . . proclaimeth**—as his lips speak his thoughts (cf. Eccles. 10:3).

24. slothful—(cf. *Margin*), so called because he fails to meet his promises. **under tribute**—not denoting legal taxes, but the obligation of dependence.

ADAM CLARKE

16. *A fool's wrath is presently known.* We have a proverb very like this, and it will serve for illustration: A fool's bolt is soon shot.

18. *There is that speaketh. Boteh,* "blabbing out, blustering."

21. *There shall no evil happen to the just.* No, for all things work together for good to them that love God.

MATTHEW HENRY

and sorrow, upon the spirits; it makes them stoop, prostrates and sinks them. The cure of it: *A good word* from God, applied by faith, *makes it glad*: *Cast thy burden upon the Lord, and he shall sustain thee;* the good word of God, particularly the gospel, is designed to make the hearts glad that are weary and heavy laden, Matt. xi. 28.

Verse 26

The righteous is more abundant than his neighbour (so the margin); he is richer, though not in this world's goods, yet in the graces and comforts of the Spirit, which are the true riches. There is a true excellency in religion; it ennobles men, inspires them with generous principles. His neighbour may make a greater figure in the world, but the righteous man has the intrinsic worth. Wicked men walk in a way which *seduces them*. It seems to them to be a pleasant way, but it is all a cheat.

Verse 27

That which may make us hate slothfulness and deceit, for the word here signifies both: *The slothful* deceitful *man* has roast meat, but that which he roasts is not what he himself *took in hunting*. Or, if slothful deceitful men have taken anything by hunting, yet they do not roast it when they have taken it. The *substance of a diligent man*, though it be not great perhaps, *is* yet *precious*. It comes from the blessing of God; he has comfort in it; it does him good, and his family. It is his own daily bread, not bread out of other people's mouths.

Verse 28

Religion is a *pathway*, a way which God has cast up for us (Isa. xxxv. 8); it is a highway, the king's highway, the King of kings' highway, a way which is tracked before us by all the saints, the good old way, full of the footsteps of the flock. There is not only life at the end, but there is life in the way. In it *there is no death*, none of that sorrow of the world which works death.

JAMIESON, FAUSSET, BROWN

25. a good word—one of comfort.

26. more excellent—(cf. *Margin*); or, more successful, while the wicked fail; or, we may read it: "The righteous guides his friend, but," etc., i.e., The ability of the righteous to aid others is contrasted with the ruin to which the way of the wicked leads themselves.

27. (Cf. vs. 24.) **took in hunting**—or, his venison. He does not improve his advantages. **the substance . . . precious**—or, the wealth of a man of honor is being diligent, or diligence. **precious**—lit., "honor" (Eccles. 10:1).

28. (Cf. ch. 8:8, 20, etc.) A sentiment often stated; here first affirmatively, then negatively.

ADAM CLARKE

JOSEPH PARKER:

How true it is that "heaviness in the heart of man maketh it stoop"; burdens it like a weight that cannot be borne; takes out of it all energy and lithesomeness and hope, all spring and fire, and depresses it to the earth with cruelty of weight. How true it is that "A good word maketh the heart glad"; the speaker is looked upon as an apostle from heaven; he is hailed as a friend who is able to drive away the lowering clouds, and turn the desert into a garden: a place for the good word must always be found in life; even the gladdest souls have times of depression; and those who lead the world sometimes fall into the rear, and the song dies upon their lips. The church should be the place where the good word is always spoken—a word that cheers men, enlivens, elevates, inspires, and ennobles them; the great broad word that comes down from heaven, rich with everything that the human soul can need in all the moments which make a mystery of its existence. How true it also is that "The righteous is more excellent than his neighbor"; has about him a peculiarity of quality; he is not only equal to his neighbor, as wise and generous and genial and kind, but there is a point at which he rises above his merely worldly neighbor; he can go further into the darkness of human life, speak more tenderly to its sorrow, and kindle the light of hope where other men flee away because of a darkness that may be felt.—*The People's Bible*

MATTHEW HENRY

CHAPTER 13

Verse 1

There is great hope of those that have a reverence for their parents, and are willing to be advised and admonished by them. There is little hope of those that will not so much as *hear rebuke*, but scorn to submit to government and scoff at those that deal faithfully with them. How can those mend a fault who will not be told of it.

Verse 2

Inward comfort and satisfaction will be daily bread. Violence done will recoil in the face of him that does it: *The soul of the transgressors* that plots mischief, and vents it by word and deed, *shall eat violence*; they shall have their belly full of it. Every man shall drink as he brews, eat as he speaks; for by our words we must be justified or condemned.

Verse 3

A guard upon the lips is a guard to the soul. He that is cautious, that thinks twice before he speaks once, *keeps his soul* from a great deal of guilt and grief and saves himself the trouble of many bitter reflections. There is many a one ruined by an ungoverned tongue.

Verse 4

The slothful desire the gains which the diligent get, but they hate the pains which the diligent take; they covet everything that is to be coveted, but will do nothing that is to be done; and therefore it follows, They have nothing; for he that will not labour let him hunger, and let him not *eat*, 2 Thess. iii. 10. The happiness and honour of the diligent: they shall have abundance. This is especially true in spiritual affairs.

Verse 5

It is the undoubted character of every *righteous man* that he *hates lying* (that is, all sin, for every sin is a lie, and particularly all fraud and falsehood in commerce and conversation), not only that he will not tell a lie, but he abhors lying, from a rooted reigning principle of love to truth and justice, and conformity to God. If the wicked man's eyes were opened, and his conscience awakened, he would *abhor himself and repent in dust and ashes*.

Verse 6

Those that are *upright in their way* deal sincerely both with God and man, their integrity will keep

JAMIESON, FAUSSET, BROWN

CHAPTER 13

Vss. 1-25. **1.** (Cf. ch. 6:1-5; 10:1, 17.)

2. shall eat—i.e., obtain (ch. 12:14). **transgressors**—as in ch. 2:22. **violence**—or, mischief to themselves.

3. He . . . mouth . . . life—because evil speeches may provoke violence from others. On last clause cf. ch. 10:14.

4. (Cf. ch. 12:11, 27.)

5. loathsome . . . shame—better, causeth shame and reproach (cf. ch. 19:26), by slander, etc., which the righteous hates.

6. A sentiment of frequent recurrence, that piety benefits and sin injures.

ADAM CLARKE

CHAPTER 13

1. ***A wise son heareth his father's instruction.*** The child that has had a proper nurturing will profit by his father's counsels, but the child that is permitted to fulfill its own will and have its own way will jest at the reproofs of its parents.

3. ***He that keepeth his mouth keepeth his life.*** It has often been remarked that God has given us two eyes, that we may see much; two ears, that we may hear much; but has given us but one tongue, and that fenced in with teeth, to indicate that we should speak but little.

MATTHEW HENRY

them from the temptations of Satan, which shall not prevail over them. Those that are wicked, even their wickedness will be their overthrow at last, and they are held in the cords of it in the meantime.

Verse 7

The world is a great cheat. Some that are really poor would be thought to be rich and are thought to be so; they trade and spend as if they were rich, make a great show when perhaps, if all their debts were paid, they are not worth a groat. This is sin, and shame. Some that are really rich would be thought to be poor, because they sordidly and meanly live below what God has given them. In this there is an ingratitude to God, injustice to the family and neighbourhood, and uncharitableness to the poor. There are many presuming hypocrites, that are really poor and empty of grace and yet pretend themselves rich, and will not own their poverty. There are many timorous trembling Christians, that are spiritually rich, and full of grace, and yet think themselves poor, and by their doubts and fears, their complaints and griefs, *make themselves poor.*

Verse 8

We are apt to judge of men's blessedness, at least in this world, by their wealth, but Solomon shows what a gross mistake it is. Those that are rich, if by some they are respected for their riches, yet by others they are envied and brought in danger of their lives, which therefore they are forced to ransom with their riches. How little is a man beholden to his wealth when it only serves to redeem that life which otherwise would not have been exposed! Those that are poor, if by some, that should be their friends, they are despised and overlooked, yet are despised and overlooked by others that would be their enemies if they had anything to lose.

Verse 9

The light of the righteous rejoices, that is, it increases, and makes them glad. Even their outward prosperity is their joy, and much more those gifts, graces, and comforts, with which their souls are illuminated. *The lamp of the wicked* burns dimly and faint; it looks melancholy, like a taper in an urn and it will shortly *be put out.*

Verse 10

Foolish pride is the great make-bate. Would you know *whence come wars and fightings*? They come from this root of bitterness. Pride makes men impatient of contradiction, impatient of competition, impatient of contempt, or anything that looks like a slight, and hence arise quarrels among relations and neighbours, quarrels in states and kingdoms, in churches and Christian societies. Men will not forgive, because they are proud. Those that are humble and peaceable will ask and take advice, will consult their own consciences, their Bibles, their ministers, their friends, to preserve quietness and prevent quarrels.

Verse 11

That which is won ill will never wear well. That which is got by such employments as are not lawful, or not becoming Christians, that which is got by gaming, may as truly be said to be *gotten by vanity* as that which is got by fraud and lying, and *will be diminished.* That which is got by industry and honesty will grow more, instead of growing less; it will be a maintenance; it will be an inheritance; it will be an abundance.

Verse 12

Nothing is more grievous than the disappointment of a raised expectation, though not in the thing itself by a denial, yet in the time of it by a delay. Nothing is more grateful than to enjoy that, at last, which we have long wished and waited for: It puts men into a sort of paradise, a garden of pleasure, for *it is a tree of life.* It will make the happiness of heaven the more welcome to the saints that it is what they have earnestly longed for as the crown of their hopes.

Verse 13

Those that prefer the rules of carnal policy before divine precepts, and the allurements of the world and the flesh before God's promises and comforts, despise his word. *He that fears the commandment,* that stands in awe of God, has a reverence for his word, is afraid of displeasing God and incurring the penalties annexed to the commandment, *shall be rewarded* for his godly fear.

Verse 14

By *the law of the wise* we may understand the principles and rules by which they govern themselves: They will be constant springs of comfort, as *a*

JAMIESON, FAUSSET, BROWN

7. In opposite ways men act hypocritically for gain of honor or wealth.

8. Riches save some from punishment, while others suffer because they will not heed the rebuke of sloth, which makes and keeps them poor.

9. light . . . lamp—prosperity; the first, the greater, and it **rejoiceth**—burns brightly, or continues, while the other, at best small, soon fails.

10. The obstinacy which attends self-conceit, produces contention, which the well-advised, thus evincing modesty, avoid.

11. by vanity—or, nothingness, i.e., which is vain or useless to the public (as card playing or similar vices). **gathereth . . . labour**—(cf. *Margin*), little by little, laboriously.

12. desire cometh—is realized. **a tree of life**—or, cause of happiness.

13. the word—i.e., of advice, or, instruction (cf. ch. 10:27; 11:31).

ADAM CLARKE

8. *The ransom of a man's life.* In despotic countries, a rich man is often accused of some capital crime, and to save his life though he may be quite innocent, is obliged to give up his riches; but the poor, in such countries, are put to no trouble.

9. *The light of the righteous rejoiceth.* They shall have that measure of prosperity which shall be best for them. *Light* and *lamp* in both cases may signify posterity.

10. *By pride cometh contention.* Perhaps there is not a quarrel among individuals in private life, nor a war among nations, that does not proceed from pride and ambition.

14. *The law of the wise is a fountain of life.* Perhaps it would be better to translate, "The law is to the wise man a fountain of life."

MATTHEW HENRY

fountain of life; the closer we keep to those rules the more effectually we secure our own peace. Those that follow the dictates of this law will escape *the snares of death* which those run into that forsake *the law of the wise.*

Verse 15

Those that conduct themselves prudently, and *serve Christ*, are *accepted of God and approved of men*, Rom. xiv. 17, 19. The way of sinners is rough and uneasy. It is *hard*, hard upon others, who complain of it, hard to the sinner himself, who can have little enjoyment of himself while he is doing that which is disobliging to all mankind.

Verse 16

It is wisdom to be cautious: *Every prudent* discreet *man* acts with deliberation and is careful not to meddle with that which he has not some knowledge of. It is folly to be rash, as the *fool* is, who is forward to undertake that which he is no way fit for, and so makes himself ridiculous.

Verse 17

The ill consequences of betraying a trust. *A wicked messenger*, who, being sent to negotiate any business, is false to him that employed him, will be discovered and punished. The happy effects of fidelity: An *ambassador* who *faithfully* discharges his trust, and serves the interests of those who employ him, is health to those by whom and for whom he is employed, heals differences between them; he is health to himself, for he secures his own interest. This is applicable to ministers, Christ's messengers.

Verse 18

He that is so proud that he scorns to be taught will certainly be abased. He that is so humble that he takes it well to be told of his faults shall certainly be exalted: *He that regards a reproof*, gains respect.

Verse 19

There are in man strong desires of happiness; God has provided for the accomplishment of those desires. *The desire* of good men towards the favour of God and spiritual blessings brings that which *is sweet to their souls*, Ps. iv. 6, 7. Yet evil men will not be happy; for *it is* an *abomination to* them *to depart from evil*, which is necessary to their being happy.

Verse 20

Those that would be good must keep good company, which is an evidence for them that they would be good (men's character is known by the company they choose). Multitudes are brought to ruin by bad company.

Verse 21

Whom God pursues he is sure to overtake. They may prosper for a while and grow very secure, but their damnation slumbers not, though they do. *The righteous* shall be abundantly recompensed for all the good they have done, and all the ill they have suffered, in this world.

Verse 22

A good man's estate lasts. It is part of his praise that he is thoughtful for posterity. He is careful, both by justice and charity, to obtain the blessing of God upon what he has, and to entail that blessing upon his children. If he should not leave them much of this world's goods, his prayers, his instructions, his good example, will be the best entail, and the promises of the covenant will be an inheritance to his *children's children*, Ps. ciii. 17. God, in his providence, often brings into their hands that which wicked people had laid up for themselves.

Verse 23

A small estate may be improved by industry, so that a man, by making the best of everything, may live comfortably upon it. The less compass the field is of the more left the skill and labour of the owner be employed about it, and it will turn to a very good account. Let him dig, and he need not beg. A great estate may be ruined by indiscretion. Men overbuild themselves or over-buy themselves, keep a better table, or more servants, than they can afford.

Verse 24

To the education of children in that which is good there is necessary a due correction for what is amiss. It is *his* rod that must be used, the rod of a parent, directed by wisdom and love, and designed for good, not the rod of a servant. It is good to begin the necessary restraints before vicious habits are confirmed. Those really hate their children, though they pretend to be fond of them, that do not keep them under a strict discipline.

JAMIESON, FAUSSET, BROWN

14. (Cf. ch. 10:11.) **fountain**—or, source of life. **to depart**—(cf. ch. 1:2-4), or, for departing, etc., and so gives life.

15. Right perception and action secure good will, while evil ways are difficult as a stony road. The wicked left of God find punishment of sin in sinning. **hard**—or, harsh (cf. Hebrew: Deut. 21:4; Jer. 5:15).

16. dealeth—acts with foresight. **a fool . . . folly**—for want of caution.

17. A wicked [or, unfaithful] **messenger falleth into mischief**—or, by mischief, or evil, and so his errand fails. Contrasted is the character of the faithful, whose faithfulness benefits others.

18. (Cf. ch. 10:17; 12:1.)

19. Self-denial, which fools will not endure, is essential to success.

20. The benefits of good and evil of bad society are contrasted.

21. (Cf. ch. 11:31.) **good . . . repaid**—or, He (God) will repay good.

22. wealth . . . just—While good men's estates remain in their families, God so orders that the gains of sinners enure to the just (cf. ch. 28:8; Ps. 37:18, 22, 26, etc.).

23. The laboring poor prosper more than those who injudiciously or wickedly strive, by fraud and violence, to supersede the necessity of lawful labor.

24. spareth—or, withholds. **rod**—of correction. **hateth**—or, acts as if he hated him (cf. ch. 3: 12; 8:36). **chasteneth . . . betimes**—or, diligently seeks for him all useful discipline.

ADAM CLARKE

15. *The way of transgressors is hard.* Never was a truer saying; most sinners have more pain and difficulty to get their souls damned than the righteous have, with all their cross-bearings, to get to the kingdom of Heaven.

ALEXANDER MACLAREN:

Verse 23. The inventor of this proverb had looked carefully and sympathetically at the way in which the little peasant proprietors worked; and he saw in that a pattern for all life. It is not always the case, of course, that a little holding means good husbandry, but it is generally so; and you will find few waste corners and few unweeded patches on the ground of a man whose whole ground is measured by rods instead of by miles. There will usually be little wasted time, and few neglected opportunities of working in the case of the peasant whose subsistence, with that of his family, depends on the diligent and wise cropping of the little patch that does belong to him.

And so, dear brethren! if you and I have to take our place in the ranks of the one-talented men, the commonplace run of ordinary people, the more reason for us to enlarge our gifts by a sedulous diligence, by an unwearied perseverance, by a keen look-out for all opportunities of service, and above all by a prayerful dependence upon Him from whom alone comes the power to toil, and who alone gives the increase. The less we are conscious of large gifts the more we should be bowed in dependence on Him from whom cometh "every good and perfect gift"; and who gives according to His wisdom; and the more earnestly should we use that slender possession which God may have given us. Industry applied to small natural capacity will do far more than larger power rusted away by sloth. You all know that it is so in regard to daily life, and common business, and the acquisition of mundane sciences and arts. It is just as true in regard to the Christian race, and to the Christian Church's work of witness.

Who are they who have done the most in this world for God and for men? The largely endowed men? "Not many wise, not many mighty, not many noble are called." The coral insect is microscopic, but it will build up from the profoundest depth of the ocean a reef against which the whole Pacific may dash in vain. It is the small gifts that, after all, are the important ones. So let us cultivate them the more earnestly, the more humbly we think of our own capacity. "Play well thy part; there all the honor lies." God, who has builded up some of the towering Alps out of micaflakes, builds up His Church out of infinitesimally small particles—slenderly endowed men touched by the consecration of His love.

—*Expositions of Holy Scripture*

24. *He that spareth his rod hateth his son.* That is, if he *hated* him, he could not do him a greater disservice than not to correct him when his obstinacy or disobedience requires it. We have met with this subject already, and it is a favorite with Solomon.

MATTHEW HENRY

Verse 25

It is the happiness of the righteous that they shall have enough and that they know when they have enough. Those that feed on the bread of life, eat, and are filled. It is the misery of the wicked that, through the insatiableness of their own desires, they are always needy; even their *belly shall want*; their sensual appetite is always craving.

CHAPTER 14

Verse 1

A good wife is a great blessing to a family. By a prudent wife, one that is pious, industrious, and considerate, the affairs of the family are made to prosper, debts are paid, the children well educated and the family has comfort within doors and credit without; thus is the house built. Many a family is brought to ruin by ill housewifery, as well as by ill husbandry. A *foolish* woman, that has no fear of God, that is wilful, and wasteful, and is all for jaunting and feasting, cards and the playhouse, will as certainly be the ruin of her house as if she *plucked it down with her hands*.

Verse 2

Grace reigning is a reverence of God, and gives honour to him. Sin reigning is no less than a contempt of God.

Verse 3

Where there is pride in the heart, and no wisdom in the head to suppress it, it commonly shows itself in the words: *In the mouth there is pride*, proud boasting, proud scorning; this is the *rod*, or branch, *of pride*; the word is used only here and Isa. xi. 1. It grows from that root of bitterness which is in the heart. The root must be plucked up, or we cannot conquer this branch. Or it is meant of a smiting beating rod, a *rod of pride* which strikes others. *The lips of the wise shall preserve them* from doing that mischief to others which proud men do with their tongues, and from bringing that mischief on themselves which haughty scorners are often involved in.

Verse 4

The neglect of husbandry is the way to poverty: *Where no oxen are*, to till the ground and tread out the corn, *the crib* is empty, *is clean*; there is no straw for the service of the cattle, and consequently no bread for the service of man. *The crib* indeed *is clean* from dung, which pleases the neat and nice, that cannot endure husbandry because there is so much dirty work in it, and therefore will sell their oxen to keep the crib clean. This shows the folly of those who addict themselves to the pleasures of the country, but do not mind the business of it, who (as we say) keep more horses than kine, more dogs than swine; their families must needs suffer by it. Those who take pains about their ground are likely to reap the profit of it.

Verse 5

In the administration of justice much depends upon the witnesses, and therefore it is necessary to the common good that witnesses be principled. A witness that is conscientious will not dare to give in a testimony that is in the least untrue. But a witness that will be bribed, and biassed, and browbeaten, *will utter lies* with as much assurance as if what he said were all true.

Verse 6

The reason why some people seek wisdom, and do not find it, is because they do not seek it from a right principle. They are scorners, and it is in scorn that they ask instruction, that they may ridicule what is told them. He *that understands*, so as to *depart from evil* (for *that is understanding*), to quit his prejudices, to lay aside all corrupt dispositions and affections, will easily apprehend instruction and receive the impressions of it.

Verse 7

A wicked man is *a foolish man*. We must decline such a one and depart from him. Sometimes the only way we have of reproving wicked discourse is by leaving the company and going out of the hearing of it.

Verse 8

It is not the wisdom of the learned, which consists only in speculation, that is here recommended, but *the wisdom of the prudent*, which is practical, and is of use to direct our actions. It *is to understand our own way*, not to be critics and busybodies in other men's matters, but to look well to ourselves and

JAMIESON, FAUSSET, BROWN

25. The comparative temporal prosperity of the righteous and wicked, rather than contentment and discontent, is noted.

CHAPTER 14

Vss. 1-35. **1. Every wise . . .**—lit., "The wisdoms" (cf. ch. 9:1) "of women," plural, a distributive form of speech. **buildeth . . . house**—increases wealth, which the foolish, by mismanagement, lessen.

2. uprightness—is the fruit of fearing God, as falsehood and ill-nature (ch. 2:15; 3:32) of despising Him and His law.

3. rod of pride—i.e., the punishment of pride, which they evince by their words. The words of the wise procure good to them.

4. crib is clean—empty; so "cleanness of teeth" denotes want of food (cf. Amos 4:6). Men get the proper fruit of their doings (Gal. 6:7).

5. A faithful witness . . .—one tested to be such. **utter** [or, breathe out] **lies**—i.e., habitually lies (ch. 6:19; cf. Acts 9:1). Or the sense is, that habitual truthfulness, or lying, will be evinced in witness-bearing.

6. An humble, teachable spirit succeeds in seeking (ch. 8:9; John 7:17; Jas. 1:5, 6).

7. Avoid the society of those who cannot teach you.

8. Appearances deceive the thoughtless, but the prudent discriminate.

ADAM CLARKE

CHAPTER 14

1. *Every wise woman buildeth her house.* By her prudent and industrious management she increases property in the family, furniture in the house, and food and raiment for her household.

3. *The mouth of the foolish is a rod of pride.* The reproofs of such a person are ill-judged and ill-timed, and generally are conveyed in such language as renders them not only ineffectual, but displeasing, and even irritating.

6. *A scorner seeketh wisdom. I believe the scorner* means, in this book, the man that despises the counsel of God.

MATTHEW HENRY

to understand the directions of our way. The bad conduct of a bad man; he puts a cheat upon himself. He does not rightly understand his way; he thinks he does, and so misses his way.

Verse 9

Wicked people are hardened in their wickedness: they *make a mock at sin.* They make a laughing matter of the sins of others, and they make a light matter of their own sins. Those that make light of sin make light of Christ. Good people, if they in anything offend, presently repent and obtain the favour of God. They have goodwill one to another; and, in their societies, there is mutual charity and compassion in cases of offences, and no mocking.

Verse 10

Every man feels his own burden, especially a burden upon the spirits. We must not censure the griefs of others, for we know not what they feel; their stroke perhaps is heavier than their groaning. Many enjoy divine consolations, which others are not aware of, much less are sharers in.

Verse 11

Sin is the ruin of great families. Righteousness is the rise and stability even of mean families: Even *the tabernacle of the upright,* though movable and despicable as a tent, *shall flourish,* if Infinite Wisdom see good.

Verse 12

The way of ignorance and carelessness, the way of sensuality and flesh-pleasing, seem right to those that walk in them, much more the way of hypocrisy in religion, external performances, partial reformations, and blind zeal; this they imagine will bring them to heaven. They will perish with a lie in their right hand. Self-deceivers will prove in the end self-destroyers.

Verse 13

Sometimes when sinners are under convictions, or some great trouble, they dissemble their grief by a forced mirth, because they will not seem to yield. When men really are merry, yet at the same time there is something that casts a damp upon it, their consciences tell them they have no reason to be merry (Hos. ix. 1); they cannot but see the vanity of it. Spiritual joy is seated in the soul; the joy of the hypocrite is but from the teeth outward. *The end of that mirth is heaviness.*

Verse 14

The *backslider in heart,* who for fear of suffering, or in hope of profit or pleasure, forsakes God and his duty, shall be *filled with his own ways;* God will give him enough of them. *He that is filthy shall be filthy still. A good man shall be* abundantly *satisfied from himself,* from what God has wrought in him. As sinners never think they have sin enough till it brings them to hell, so saints never think they have grace enough till it brings them to heaven.

Verse 15

It is folly to be credulous, to heed every flying report, to take things upon trust from common fame, and give credit to everyone that will promise payment. *The prudent man* will try before he trusts.

Verse 16

Holy fear is an excellent guard upon every holy thing, and against everything that is unholy. It is wisdom to depart *from evil,* to be afraid of coming near the borders of sin or dallying with the beginnings of it. Presumption is folly. He who, when he is warned of his danger, *rages and is confident,* furiously pushes on, persists in his rebellion, and plays upon the precipice, is a fool.

Verse 17

Men who are peevish and touchy, and are *soon angry,* say and do that which is ridiculous, and so expose themselves to contempt. *A man of wicked devices,* who stifles his resentments till he has an opportunity of being revenged, is hated by all mankind. An angry man through the surprise of a temptation disgraces himself, but it is soon over, and he is sorry for it. But that of a spiteful revengeful man is odious; there is no fence against him nor cure for him.

Verse 18

Sin is the shame of sinners: *The simple,* who love simplicity, get nothing by it; they *inherit folly.* What they value themselves upon is really foolish. They will for ever rue their own foolish choice. Wisdom is the honour of the wise: *The prudent crown* them-

JAMIESON, FAUSSET, BROWN

9. Fools . . . sin—or, Sin deludes fools. **righteous . . . favour**—i.e., of God, instead of the punishment of sin.

10. Each one best knows his own sorrows or joys.

11. (Cf. ch. 12:7.) The contrast of the whole is enhanced by that of **house** and **tabernacle**, a permanent and a temporary dwelling.

12. end thereof—or, reward, what results (cf. ch. 5:4). **ways of death**—leading to it.

13. The preceding sentiment illustrated by the disappointments of a wicked or untimely joy.

14. filled . . . ways—receive retribution (ch. 1:31). **a good man . . . himself**—lit., "is away from such," will not associate with him.

15. The simple . . . word—He is credulous, not from love, but heedlessness (ch. 13:16).

16. (Cf. ch. 3:7; 28:14.) **rageth**—acts proudly and conceitedly.

17. He . . . angry—lit., "short of anger" (cf. vs. 29, opposite idea). **man . . . hated**—i.e., the deliberate evildoer is more hated than the rash.

18. inherit—as a portion (cf. 3:35). **are crowned**—lit., "are surrounded with it," abound in it.

ADAM CLARKE

9. *Fools make a mock at sin.* And only fools would do so. But he that makes a sport of sinning will find it no sport to suffer the vengeance of an eternal fire.

10. *The heart knoweth his own bitterness. Morrath naphsho,* "The bitterness of its soul."

CHARLES H. SPURGEON:

"The backslider in heart shall be filled with his own ways; and a good man shall be satisfied from himself" (Prov. 19:14). A common principle is here laid down and declared to be equally true in reference to two characters, who in other respects are a contrast. Men are affected by the course which they pursue; for good or bad their own conduct comes home to them. The backslider and the good man are very different, but in each of them the same rule is exemplified—they are both filled by the result of their lives. The backslider becomes filled by that which is within him, as seen in his life, and the good man also is filled by that which grace implants within his soul. The evil leaven in the backslider leavens his entire being and sours his existence, while the gracious fountain in the sanctified believer saturates his whole manhood and baptizes his entire life. In each case the fulness arises from that which is within the man, and is in its nature like the man's character; the fullness of the backslider's misery will come out of his own ways, and the fullness of the good man's content will spring out of the love of God which is shed abroad in his heart.

The meaning of this passage will come out better if we begin with an illustration. Here are two pieces of sponge, and we wish to fill them: you shall place one of them in a pool of foul water, it will be filled, and filled with that which it lies in; you shall put the other sponge into a pure crystal stream, and it will also become full, full of the element in which it is placed. The backslider lies in the dead sea of his own ways, and the brine fills him; the good man is plunged like a pitcher into "Siloa's brook, which flows hard by the oracle of God," and the river of the water of life fills him to the brim. A wandering heart will be filled with sorrow, and a heart confiding in the Lord will be satisfied with joy and peace.—*The Treasury of the Old Testament*

17. *He that is soon angry.* "Short of nostrils"; because, when a man is angry, his nose is contracted.

MATTHEW HENRY

selves *with knowledge*. Wise heads shall be respected as if they were crowned heads. Wisdom is not only justified, but glorified, of all her children.

Verse 19

The wicked are oftentimes impoverished and brought low, so that they are forced to beg, their wickedness having reduced them to straits; while good men, by the blessing of God, are enriched, and enabled to give, and do give, even to the evil; for where God grants life we must not deny a livelihood.

Verse 20

The poor, who should be pitied, and relieved, *is hated*, and kept at a distance, even *by his own neighbour*. Most are swallow-friends, that are gone in winter. It is good having God our friend, for he will not desert us when we are poor. *The rich have many friends* in hope to get something out of them.

Verse 21

Men's character and condition are measured by their conduct towards their poor neighbours. *He that despises his neighbour* because he is of a mean extraction, rustic education, and makes but a mean figure, that thinks it below him to take notice of him, *is a sinner*, and shall be dealt with as a sinner. *He that has mercy on the poor*, is ready to do all the good offices he can to him, and does that which is pleasing to God.

Verse 22

Those are that not only do evil, but devise it, think that by sinning with craft and carrying on their intrigues with more artifice than others, shall come off better. But they are mistaken. God's justice cannot be outwitted. Those that devise evil against their neighbours greatly err, for it will end in their own ruin. Those that are so liberal as to devise liberal things, that seek opportunities of doing good, and contrive how to make their charity most extensive and most acceptable to those that need it, *by liberal things they shall stand*, Isa. xxxii. 8.

Verse 23

Industrious people are generally thriving people. *The stirring hand gets a penny*. Those that love to boast of their business and make a noise about it, and that waste their time in tittle-tattle, waste what they have, and the course they take *tends to penury*. It is true in the affairs of our souls; those that take pains in the service of God, that strive earnestly in prayer, will find profit in it. But if men's religion runs all out in talk and noise, they will be spiritually poor, and come to nothing.

Verse 24

If men be wise and good, riches make them so much the more honourable and useful, and give them more influence. Those that have wealth, and wisdom to use it, will have a great opportunity of honouring God and doing good in the world. If men be wicked and corrupt, their wealth will but the more expose them.

Verse 25

A faithful witness *delivers the souls* of the innocent, who are falsely accused, and their good names, which are as dear to them as their lives. A false witness forges *lies*, and yet pours them out with the greatest assurance imaginable. It is the interest of a nation to detect and punish false-witness-bearing, for truth is the cement of society.

Verses 26–27

The *fear of the Lord* is here put for all gracious principles, producing gracious practices. Where this resigns it produces security and serenity of mind. It enables a man still to hold fast his peace, and gives him boldness before God and the world. It entails a blessing upon posterity. The children of religious parents often do the better for their parents' instructions and example and fare the better for their faith and prayers. "*Our fathers trusted in thee*, therefore we will." It is an over-flowing ever-flowing spring of comfort and joy. It is a sovereign antidote against sin and temptation.

Verse 28

Here are two maxims in politics: 1. That it is much for the honour of a king to have a populous kingdom; it is a sign that he rules well, since strangers are hereby invited to come and settle under his protection and his own subjects live comfortably. It is therefore the wisdom of princes, by a mild and gentle government, by encouraging trade and husbandry, to promote the increase of their people.

JAMIESON, FAUSSET, BROWN

19. Describes the humbling of the wicked by the punishment their sins incur.

20. This sad but true picture of human nature is not given approvingly, but only as a fact.

21. For such contempt of the poor is contrasted as sinful with the virtuous compassion of the good.

22. As usual, the interrogative negative strengthens the affirmative. **mercy and truth**—i.e., God's (Ps. 57:3; 61:7).

23. labour—painful diligence. **talk . . . penury**—idle and vain promises and plans.

24. (Cf. ch. 3:16.) **foolishness . . . folly**—Folly remains, or produces folly; it has no benefit.

25. *Life* often depends on truth-telling. **a deceitful . . . lies**—He that breathes out lies is deceit, not to be trusted (vs. 5).

26. The blessings of piety descend to children (ch. 13:22; 20:7; Exod. 20:6). **27.** (Cf. ch. 13:14.) **fear of the Lord**—or, *law of the wise,* is wisdom (Ps. 111:10).

28. The teaching of a true political economy.

ADAM CLARKE

JOSEPH PARKER:

Verse 26. Such is the testimony of the ages. The Bible is full of illustrations of the action of this doctrine. In no book probably is the fear of the Lord so elaborately described as to its nature and its application as in the Book of Proverbs. Throughout the whole of the Bible the fear of the Lord is declared to be the beginning of wisdom. It is not a servile fear; the worshiper is not a croucher, waiting in an abject position in order to be noticed by a tyrannical despot: fear means reverence, veneration, awe, a sense of the grandeur and majesty of the Lord, not only as that term stands for infinity, brilliance, and attributes of an intellectual kind, but as it stands for holiness, truth, purity, justice, and every expression that indicates moral supremacy. He who fears the Lord is strong in the confidence of ultimate justice; he is confident also in the final exposition of providence, being assured that the way of God to man will be so revealed at last that it will be seen to have been the right way, the only true way, notwithstanding the varieties of the road, the steep hills, the bleak deserts, the stony paths, the cold rivers that had to be crossed in the dark night, the afflictions that had to be endured when the heart and flesh had failed and strength had been exhausted—at the last it will be seen that God has not given one stroke too much, taken away one treasure too many, or dug one grave too deep; the righteous will be the first to confess that God has done all things wisely, well, and lovingly.

A beautiful expression is "his children." Here in the very midst of the Proverbs we find the sublime doctrine of the fatherhood of God. Here too we find that God's children need a place of refuge; they have often to flee from the storm, from the wrath of man, and from an apparently angry nature, for every law seems to fight against them: blessed be God, when all outward things are marked by an excitement of an apparently uncontrollable kind, are heaving and tossing as if shaken by an earthquake, the children of God can go not to law but to the Lawmaker himself, yea, to the very heart of God, and there can rest in hope and confidence, and while the storm howls without around the rock of the sanctuary that holy place can be filled with sacred and triumphant song. Have we really endeavored to find a refuge in God?—*The People's Bible*

MATTHEW HENRY

2. That when the people are lessened the prince is weakened: *In the want of people is the leanness of the prince* (so some read it); trade lies dead, the ground lies untilled, the army wants to be recruited, the navy to be manned, and all because there are not hands sufficient.

Verse 29

Meekness is wisdom. *He* rightly understands himself, and the infirmities of human nature, who *is slow to anger*, and knows how to excuse the faults of others as well as his own, so as by no provocation to be put out of the possession of his own soul. Unbridled passion is folly proclaimed: *He that is hasty of spirit*, whose heart is tinder to every spark of provocation, that is all fire and tow, thinks to magnify himself, whereas really he *exalts his own folly*.

Verse 30

Our health depends on the government of our passions and the preserving of the temper of the mind. A healing spirit, made up of love and meekness, a hearty, friendly, cheerful disposition, is *the life of the flesh*; it contributes to a good constitution of body; people grow fat with good humour. A fretful, envious, discontented spirit, makes the countenance pale, and is the *rottenness of the bones*.

Verse 31

Whosoever he be that wrongs a poor man, let him know that he puts an affront upon his Maker. God made him, and gave him his being. We have all one Father, one Maker. He reckons himself honoured in the kindnesses that are done them; he takes them as done to himself, and will show himself accordingly pleased with them. *I was hungry, and you gave me meat*.

Verse 32

A wicked man cleaves so closely to the world that he cannot find in his heart to leave it, but is driven away out of it; his soul is required, is forced from him. He *is driven away in his wickedness*, dies in his sins. A godly man when he finishes his course, *has hope in his death* of a happiness on the other side death, of better things in another world than ever he had in this.

Verse 33

Modesty is the badge of wisdom. His *wisdom rests in his heart*; he digests what he knows, and has it ready to him, but does not make a noise with it. If fools have a little smattering of knowledge, they take all occasions to produce it.

Verse 34

Justice, reigning in a nation, puts an honour upon it. A righteous administration of the government, equity between man and man, public countenance given to religion, charity and compassion to strangers, uphold the throne, elevate the people's minds, and qualify a nation for the favour of God. Vice in a nation puts disgrace upon it: *Sin is a reproach to any* city or kingdom. The people of Israel were great when they were good, but when they forsook God all about them insulted them and trampled on them.

Verse 35

In a well-ordered court and government smiles and favours are dispensed among those in public trusts according to their merits. Those who behave themselves wisely shall be respected and preferred. No man's services shall be neglected to please a party or a favourite. Those who are selfish and false, who betray their country, oppress the poor, and sow discord, shall be displaced.

CHAPTER 15

Verse 1

Peace may be kept by soft words. If wrath be risen like a threatening cloud, pregnant with storms and thunder, *a soft answer* will disperse it and turn it away. Reason will be better spoken, and a righteous cause better pleaded, with meekness than with passion; hard arguments do best with soft words. Nothing stirs up anger, and sows discord, like *grievous words*, calling foul names, upbraiding men with their infirmities, or anything that lessens them and makes them mean.

Verse 2

He that has knowledge is not only to enjoy it, for his own entertainment, but use it aright, for the edification of others; and it is *the tongue* that must make use of it. A wicked heart by the tongue becomes very hurtful; for *the mouth of fools belches*

JAMIESON, FAUSSET, BROWN

29. slow . . . understanding—(Cf. vs. 17). **hasty**—(Cf. vs. 17). **exalteth folly**—makes it conspicuous, as if delighting to honor it.

30. A sound heart—both literally and figuratively, a source of health; in the latter sense, opposed to the known effect of evil passions on health.

31. reproacheth his Maker—who is the God of such, as well as of the rich (ch. 22:2; Job 31:15; and specially I Sam. 2:8; Ps. 113:7).

32. driven—thrust out violently (cf. Ps. 35:5, 6). **hath hope**—trusteth (ch. 10:2; 11:4; Ps. 2: 12), implying assurance of help.

33. resteth—preserved in quietness for use, while fools blazon their folly (ch. 12:23; 13:16).

34. Righteousness—just principles and actions. **exalteth**—raises to honor. **is a reproach**—brings on them the ill-will of others (cf. ch. 13:6).

35. wise—discreet or prudent. **causeth shame**—(ch. 10:5; 12:4) acts basely.

CHAPTER 15

Vss. 1-33. **1. soft**—tender or gentle. **turneth . . . wrath**—from any one. **stir up**—as a smouldering fire is excited.

2. useth . . . aright—commends knowledge by its proper use. **poureth out**—utters abundantly (ch. 12:23), and so disgusts others.

ADAM CLARKE

29. *That is hasty of spirit. Ketsar ruach*, "the short of spirit"; one that is easily irritated; and, being in a passion, he is agitated so as to be literally short of breath.

34. *But sin is a reproach to any people*. I am satisfied this is not the sense of the original, *vechesed leummim chattath;* which would be better rendered, "And mercy is a sin offering for the people."

CHAPTER 15

1. *A soft answer*. Gentleness will often disarm the most furious, where positive derangement has not taken place. One angry word will always beget another, for the disposition of one spirit always begets its own likeness in another. Thus kindness produces kindness, and rage produces rage. Universal experience confirms this proverb.

2. *Useth knowledge aright*. This is very difficult to know: when to speak, and when to be silent; what to speak, and what to leave unspoken; the manner that is best and most suitable to the occasion, the subject, the circumstances, and the persons. All these are difficulties, often even to the wisest men.

MATTHEW HENRY

out foolishness, whilst filthiness, and foolish talking, corrupt good manners.

Verse 3

The eyes of the Lord are in every place; for he not only sees all from on high (Ps. xxxiii. 13), but he is everywhere present. Secret sins, services, and sorrows, are under his eye. He is displeased with the evil and approves of the good. This speaks as much comfort to saints as terror to sinners.

Verse 4

A good tongue is healing to sin-sick souls by convincing them, and reconciling parties at variance; this is the healing of the tongue, which *is a tree of life*, the leaves of which have a sanative virtue, Rev. xxii. 2. He that knows how to discourse will make the place he lives in a paradise. An evil tongue is wounding.

Verse 5

Let superiors give instruction and reproof to those that are under their charge. They must not only instruct with the light of knowledge, but reprove with zeal; and both these must be done with the authority and affection of a father. It is indeed against the grain with good-humoured men to find fault, and make those about them uneasy; but better so than to suffer them to go on the way to ruin. He that slights his good education is a fool and is likely to live and die one.

Verse 6

Where righteousness is riches are, and the comforts of them. If there be not much of this world's goods, yet where there is grace there is true treasure; and those who have but little, if they have a heart to be therewith content, and to enjoy the comfort of that little, it is enough; it is all riches. Where wickedness is, though there may be riches, yet there is vexation of spirit.

Verse 7

We use knowledge aright when we disperse it, not confine it to a few of our intimates. We must take pains to spread and propagate useful knowledge, must teach some that they may teach others.

Verse 8

God has sacrifices brought him even by wicked men, but their sacrifices, though ever so costly, are not accepted of God, because not offered in sincerity nor from a good principle. God has such a love for upright good people that their *prayer is a delight* to him.

Verse 9

The sacrifices of the wicked are an abomination to God, not for want of some nice points of ceremony, but because the whole course and tenor of their conversation, is wicked.

Verse 10

This shows that those who cannot bear to be corrected must expect to be destroyed. Of all sinners, reproofs are worst resented by apostates.

Verse 11

This confirms what was said (*v.* 3) concerning God's omnipresence, in order to his judging of evil and good. God knows all things, even those things that are hidden from the eyes of all living. The word here used for *destruction* is *Abaddon*, which is one of the devil's names, Rev. ix. 11. That destroyer, though he deceives us, cannot evade or elude the divine cognizance. God sees through all his disguises, Job xxvi. 6. If he sees through the depths and wiles of Satan himself, *much more* can he search men's hearts. *God is greater than our hearts*, and knows them better than we know them ourselves, and therefore is an infallible Judge of every man's character, Heb. iv. 13.

Verse 12

A scorner is one that not only makes a jest of God and religion, but bids defiance to the methods employed for his conviction and reformation. He cannot endure to retire into his own heart and commune seriously, nor let his own heart smite him, if he can help it. That man's case is sad who is afraid of arguing with himself. He cannot endure the advice and admonitions of his friends.

Verse 13

Harmless mirth is recommended to us, as that which contributes to the health of the body, making

JAMIESON, FAUSSET, BROWN

3. beholding—watching (cf. ch. 5:21; Ps. 66:7).

4. A wholesome tongue—(cf. *Margin*), pacifying and soothing language. **tree of life**—(ch. 3:18; 11:30). **perverseness therein**—cross, ill-natured language. **breach . . . spirit**—(cf. Isa. 65:14, *Hebrew*), grieves, instead of appeasing.

5. (Cf. ch. 4:1; 10:17; 13:1-18.) **is prudent**—acts discreetly.

6. treasure—implying utility. **trouble**—vexation and affliction.

7. (Cf. ch. 10:20, 21.) **heart . . . not so**—not right, or vain.

8, 9. The sacrifice [and] **prayer**—are acts of worship. **way . . . followeth . . . righteousness**—denote conduct. God's regard for the worship and deeds of the righteous and wicked respectively, so stated in Psalm 50:17; Isaiah 1:11.

10. (Cf. ch. 10:17.) **the way**—that in which God would have him to go (ch. 2:13; Ps. 119:1).

11. Hell—(Ps. 16:10.) **destruction**—or, Abaddon, the place of the destroyer. All the unseen world is open to God, much more men's hearts.

12. (Cf. ch. 9:8.) **go unto the wise**—to be instructed.

ADAM CLARKE

F. B. MEYER:

"The prayer of the upright is his delight" (Prov. 15:8). We too seldom consider the pleasure that the prayer of His people gives to God. Often we go to Him with no other thought than to find relief from the pressure of anxiety or sin. We hardly realize that He is looking for our coming because He loves us. Thus nothing delights Him more than the time we consecrate for heartfelt fellowship with Him. Think, O child of God, when next the hour of prayer comes round, that God is waiting for you. Would you cause Him disappointment by curtailing it, and by passing cursorily through a form, when He looks for the fellowship of the soul? Remember how Jesus said, "The Father seeketh such to worship Him."

The prayer which gives God delight is one which is characterized thus: (1) It must be an identification with the prayer of the Lord Jesus. In Him alone can the Father take delight, and in us only as far as we are in the Beloved, and He in us. (2) We must come in full assurance of faith, our hearts sprinkled from an evil conscience, and our lives rid of all known inconsistency and impurity. (3) We must give time for God to speak to us. Rev. Andrew Murray says, "Bow quietly before Him in humble faith and adoration. God is. God is near. God is love, longing to make Himself known." (4) Lie very low before God. Sink down before Him in the lowest dust of self-abasement, reckoning yourself to be nothing. (5) Present yourself to God that He may fulfill through you his own loving purposes.

In the Book of Revelation, we are bidden to behold the Angel of the Covenant mingling much incense with the prayers of all the saints. That incense is the merit of Jesus, which makes our prayers delightful (Rev. 8:3–5).

—Great Verses Through the Bible

11. *Hell and destruction. Sheol vaabaddon. Hades,* the invisible world, the place of separate spirits till the resurrection, and *Abaddon,* the place of torment, are ever under the eye and control of the Lord.

MATTHEW HENRY

men lively and fit for business, making the face to shine and rendering us pleasant one to another. A cheerful spirit under the government of wisdom and grace, is a great ornament to religion, puts a further lustre upon the beauty of holiness, and makes men the more capable of doing good. Hurtful melancholy is what we are cautioned against, as a great enemy to us, when it has dominion and plays the tyrant. *The spirit is broken*, and becomes unfit for the service of God.

Verse 14

Here are two things to be wondered at:—A wise man not satisfied with his wisdom, but still seeking the increase of it; the more he has the more he would have. A fool well satisfied with his folly and not seeking the cure of it.

Verse 15

Some are much in affliction, and of a sorrowful spirit, and all their days are evil days. Such are not to be censured or despised, but pitied and prayed for, succoured and comforted. Others are of a cheerful spirit; and they have not only good days, but have *a continual feast*; and if they serve God with gladness of heart, and it is oil to the wheels of their obedience (all this, and heaven too), then they serve a good Master.

Verses 16–17

Christian contentment, and joy in God, make life easy and pleasant. Cheerfulness of spirit will furnish a man with *a continual feast*, though he has but little in the world—holiness and love. A *little*, if we keep a good conscience, and serve God faithfully with the little we have, will be more comfortable, *than great treasure and trouble therewith*. Those that have *great treasure* have often great *trouble therewith*. If those that have great estates would do their duty with them, and then trust God with them, their treasure would not have so much trouble attending it. It is therefore far better to have but a little of the world, to keep up communion with God, and enjoy him in it, and live by faith, than to have the greatest plenty and live without God in the world. If *brethren dwell together in unity*, if they are friendly, and hearty, and pleasant, that will make *a dinner of herbs* a feast sufficient. Love will sweeten it and they may be as merry over it as if they had all dainties. If there be mutual enmity and strife, though there be a whole ox for dinner, a fat ox, there can be no comfort in it; the leaven of malice, of hating and being hated, is enough to sour it all.

Verse 18

Anger strikes the fire which sets cities and churches into a flame: *A wrathful man*, with his peevish passionate reflections, gives occasion to others to quarrel. *He that is slow to anger* not only *prevents* strife, but if it be already kindled, brings water to the flame, unites those again that have fallen out, and by gentle methods brings them to mutual concessions for peace-sake.

Verse 19

Those that have no heart to their work pretend that they cannot do their work without a great deal of hardship and danger; and therefore they go about it with as much reluctance as if they were to go barefoot through a thorny hedge. An honest desire and endeavour to do our duty will, by the grace of God, make it easy, and we shall find it strewed with roses.

Verse 20

Good children are the joy of their parents, who ought to have joy of them, having taken so much care and pains about them. And it adds much to the satisfaction of those that are good if they have reason to think that they have been a comfort to their parents in their declining years. Wicked children put contempt upon their parents, slight their authority, and make an ill requital for their kindness.

Verse 21

A wicked man sins, not only without regret, but with delight. A fool walks by no rule, acts with no sincerity or steadiness; *but a man of understanding*, the eyes of whose understanding are enlightened by the Spirit, *walks uprightly*, lives a regular life, and studies in everything to conform himself to the will of God.

Verse 22

If men will not take time and pains to deliberate with themselves, or are so confident of their own judgment that they scorn to consult with others, they are not likely to bring anything considerable to pass; circumstances defeat them which, with a little consultation, might have been foreseen and obviated.

JAMIESON, FAUSSET, BROWN

13. maketh . . . countenance—or, benefits the countenance. **spirit is broken**—and so the countenance is sad.

14. (Cf. ch. 10:21, 22.) The wise grow wiser, the fools more foolish (ch. 9: 9).

15. The state of the heart governs the outward condition. **evil**—sad, contrasted with the cheerfulness of a feast.

16. trouble—agitation, implying the anxieties and perplexities attending wealth held by worldlings (ch. 16:18; I Tim. 6:6).

17. dinner [or, allowance (II Kings 25:30)] **of herbs**—and that the plainest. **and hatred**—(cf. ch. 10:12, 18).

18. (Cf. ch. 14:29; 16:32.)

19. The difficulties of the slothful result from want of energy; the righteous find a **plain** [and open] **way**—lit., "a highway," by diligence (I Sam. 10:7; Ps. 1:3).

20. (Cf. ch. 10:1.)

21. walketh uprightly—and so finds his joy (ch. 3:6; 10: 23).

22. Without counsel—or, deliberation, implying a wise deference to the opinions of the wise and good, contrasted with rashness.

ADAM CLARKE

CHARLES H. SPURGEON:

A slothful man is the opposite of a righteous man. In the text they are set in opposition. "The way of the slothful man" is placed in contrast, not with the way of the diligent man, but with "the way of the righteous"; as if to show that the slothful man is the very opposite of being a righteous man. A sluggard is not a righteous man, and he cannot be; he misses a main part of rightness. It is very seldom that a sluggard is honest: he owes at least more labor to the world than he pays. He is guilty of sins of omission, for he fails in obedience to one of the laws laid upon manhood since the fall: "In the sweat of thy face shalt thou eat bread." He aspires to eat his bread without earning it: he would, if he could, eat bread for nought, or eat the bread for which others toil; and this verges upon coveting and stealing, and generally leads up to one or both of these sins. The sluggard evades the common law of society; and equally does he offend against the rule which our apostle promulgated in the Church: "If any would not work, neither should he eat." The sluggard is not righteous, for he does not render to God according to the strength lent to him, nor to man according to the work assigned him. A slothful man is a soldier who would let others fight the battle of life while he lies under the baggage wagon asleep, until rations are served out. He is a husbandman who only husbands his own strength, and would eat the grapes while others trim the vines. He would, if possible, be carried on his bed into the kingdom of heaven; he is much too great a lover of ease to go on pilgrimage over rough and weary ways. If the kingdom of heaven suffereth violence from others, it will never suffer violence from him. He is too idle to be importunate, too slothful to be earnest.

He cannot be a righteous man, for slothfulness leads to the neglect of duty in many ways, and very soon it leads to lying about those neglects of duty, and no liar can have a portion in heaven. Idleness is selfishness, and this is not consistent with the love of our neighbor, nor with any high degree of virtue. Every good thing withers in the drought of idleness. In fact, all kinds of vices are comprehended in the one vice of sloth; and, if you tell me that a man is a sluggard, I have his whole character before me in the blackest of letters. His fallow fields are well adapted for evil seed; and, no doubt, Satan will raise a fine crop of weeds in every corner of his life.—*The Treasury of the Old Testament*

---

19. ***The way of the slothful man is as an hedge of thorns.*** **Because he is slothful, he imagines ten thousand difficulties in the way which cannot be surmounted; but they are all the creatures of his own imagination, and that imagination is formed by his sloth.**

MATTHEW HENRY

Verse 23

We speak wisely when we speak seasonably: when it is needed, and, as we say, hits the joint. Many a good word comes short of doing the good it might have done, for want of being well-timed.

Verse 24

The way of wisdom and holiness is *the way of life*, the way that leads to eternal life. Be wise and live. It is the way to escape *from hell beneath*. A good man sets his *affections on things above*, and deals in those things. His *conversation is in heaven*; his way leads directly thither; there his treasure is, *above*, out of the reach of enemies, above the changes of this lower world.

Verse 25

The proud, that magnify themselves, and trample on all about them, are such as God *will destroy*, not them only, but *their houses*. Those that are dejected God delights to support. *He will establish the border* which the poor widow is not herself able to defend and make good.

Verse 26

The thoughts of wicked men, for the most part, are such as God hates, and are an offence to him, who not only knows the heart and all that passes and repasses there, but requires the innermost and uppermost place in it. The thoughts and *words of the pure* may be understood both of their devotions to God and of their discourses with men. Both are pleasant when they come from a pure, a purified, heart.

Verse 27

He that is greedy of gain, and makes himself a slave to the world, hurries, and puts himself and all about him upon the stretch, frets and vexes at every loss and disappointment, and quarrels with everybody that stands in the way of his profit—is a burden and vexation to his children and servants. Those that are generous entail a blessing upon their families; *He that* abhors all sinful indirect ways of getting money—that hates to be paltry and mercenary, and is willing, if there be occasion, to do good gratis—he shall have the comfort of life; his name and family shall live and continue.

Verse 28

It is the character of a righteous man that being convinced of the account he must give of his words, and of the good and bad influence of them upon others, he makes conscience of speaking truly (it is his *heart* that *answers*, he speaks as he thinks, Ps. xv. 2), and of speaking pertinently and profitably, and therefore he *studies to answer*, that his speech may be with grace, Neh. ii. 4; v. 7. A wicked man never heeds what he says, but his *mouth pours out evil things*, to the dishonour of God and religion.

Verse 29

God sets himself at a distance from those that set him at defiance. He will draw nigh to those in a way of mercy who draw nigh to him in a way of duty.

Verse 30

It is pleasant to have a good prospect, to see the light of the sun (Eccles. xi. 7) and by it to see the wonderful works of God, with which this lower world is beautiful and enriched. The consideration of this should make us thankful for our eyesight. It is also very comfortable to hear (as some understand it) *a good report* concerning others; a good man has no greater joy than to hear that his friends walk in the truth.

Verse 31

The ear that can take *the reproof* will love the reprover. Faithful friendly reproofs are here called *the reproofs of life* because they are means of spiritual life. Those that learn well, and obey well, are likely in time to teach well and rule well.

Verse 32

Those who *refuse correction* (margin) *despise their own souls*. The fundamental error of sinners is undervaluing their own souls; therefore they wrong the soul to please the body. *He that hears reproof*, and amends the faults, *gets understanding*, by which his soul is secured from bad ways and directed in good ways.

Verse 33

An awe of God upon our spirits will put us upon the wisest counsels and chastise us when we say or do unwisely. Where there is humility there is a happy presage of honour and preparative for it.

JAMIESON, FAUSSET, BROWN

23. Good advice blesses the giver and receiver.

24. (Cf. Col. 3:2.) Holy purposes prevent sinning, and so its evils.

25. The most desolate who have God's aid have more permanent good than the self-reliant sinner (ch. 2:22; 12:7). **border**—or, boundary for possessions (Ps. 78:54).

26. are pleasant words—i.e., pleasing to God (ch. 8:8, 9).

27. (Cf. ch. 11:17.) Avarice brings trouble to him and his. **hateth gifts**—or, bribes (Exod. 23:8; Ps. 15:5), and is not avaricious.

28. (Cf. vs. 14; ch. 10:11.) Caution is the fruit of wisdom; rashness of folly.

29. far . . . wicked—in His love and favor (Ps. 22:11; 119:155).

30. light of the eyes—(ch. 13:9). What gives light rejoiceth the heart, by relieving from anxiety as to our course; so **good report**—or, doctrine (Isa. 28:9; 53:1), **maketh . . . fat**—or, gives prosperity (ch. 3:13-17; 9:11). The last clause is illustrated by the first.

31, 32. (Cf. ch. 10:17.) **reproof of life**—which leads to life. **abideth . . . wise**—is numbered among them. **refuseth**—or, neglects, passes by (ch. 1:25; 4:15). **despiseth . . . soul**—so acts as if esteeming its interests of no value.

33. The fear . . . wisdom—Wisdom instructs in true piety. **before . . . humility**—(cf. Luke 24:26; I Pet. 1:11); opposite (cf. ch. 16:18).

ADAM CLARKE

24. ***The way of life is above to the wise.*** **There is a treble antithesis here: (1) the way of the wise, and that of the fool. (2) The one is above, the other below. (3) The one is of life, the other is of death.**

27. ***He that is greedy of gain***—**he who** ***will*** **be rich.** ***Troubleth his own house***—**he is a torment to himself and his family by his avariciousness and penury, and a curse to those with whom he deals.** ***But he that hateth gifts***—**whatever is given to pervert judgment.**

28. ***The heart of the righeous studieth to answer.*** **His tongue never runs before his wit; he never speaks rashly, and never unadvisedly; because he** ***studieth***, **ponders, his thoughts and his words.**

31. ***The ear that heareth the reproof.*** **That receives it gratefully and obeys it. "Advice is for them that will take it"; so says one of our own old proverbs.**

MATTHEW HENRY

CHAPTER 16

Verse 1

In short, 1. *Man purposes.* He has a freedom of thought and a freedom of will permitted him; let him form his projects, and lay his schemes, as he thinks best: but, after all, 2. *God disposes.* Man cannot go on with his business without the assistance and blessing of God, who *made man's mouth* and teaches us what we shall say.

Verse 2

We are all apt to be partial in judging of ourselves. The judgment of God concerning us is according to truth: He *weighs the spirits* in a just and unerring balance, knows what is in us, and passes a judgment upon us accordingly, and by his judgment we must stand or fall.

Verse 3

The only way to have our *thoughts established* is to *commit our works to the Lord.* The great concerns of our souls must be committed to the grace of God. All our outward concerns must be committed to the providence of God, and to the sovereign, wise, and gracious disposal of that providence. *Roll thy works upon the Lord* (so the word is); roll the burden of thy care from thyself upon God.

Verse 4

God is the first cause. Even the wicked are his creatures, though they are rebels; he gave them those powers with which they fight against him. God is the last end. All is of him and from him, and therefore all is to him and for him.

Verse 5

The pride of sinners sets God against them. The power of sinners cannot secure them against God, though they strengthen themselves with both hands. Though they strengthen one another with their confederacies and combinations, joining forces against God, they shall not escape his righteous judgment.

Verse 6

The guilt of sin is taken away from us—by the *mercy and truth* of God, in Jesus Christ the Mediator, and not by the legal sacrifices, Mic. vi. 7, 8. The power of sin is broken in us. The corrupt inclinations are purged out. *By the fear of the Lord,* and the influence of that fear, *men depart from evil;* those will not dare to sin against God who keep up in their minds a holy dread and reverence of him.

Verse 7

God can turn foes into friends when he pleases. He that has all hearts in his hand can make *a man's enemies to be at peace with him.* He will do it for us when we please him. God made Esau to be at peace with Jacob, Abimelech with Isaac.

Verse 8

A small estate, honestly come by, which a man is content with, serves God with cheerfully, and puts to a right use, is much more valuable than a great estate ill-got, and then ill-kept or ill-spent. It carries with it more inward satisfaction, a better reputation with all that are wise and good; it will last longer, and will turn to a better account in the great day, when men will be judged, not according to what they had, but what they did.

Verse 9

Man is a reasonable creature, that has the faculty of contriving for himself. But as a depending creature, he is subject to the direction and dominion of his Maker. If men *devise their way,* so as to make God's glory their end and his will their rule, they may expect that he will *direct their steps* by his Spirit and grace, so that they shall not miss their way nor come short of their end. *Lord, direct my way,* 1 Thess. iii. 11.

Verse 10

It may be read as a precept to the kings and judges of the earth to be wise and instructed. Let them be just, and rule in the fear of God. It may be taken as a promise to all good kings, that if they sincerely aim at God's glory, and seek direction from him, he will qualify them with wisdom and grace above others, in proportion to the eminency of their station and the trusts lodged in their hands.

Verse 11

The administration of public justice by the magistrates is an ordinance of God; in it the scales are held, and ought to be held by a steady and impartial hand. The observance of justice in commerce between man and man is likewise a divine appointment.

JAMIESON, FAUSSET, BROWN

CHAPTER 16

Vss. 1-33. **1. preparations**—schemes. **in man**—or lit., "to man," belonging, or pertaining to him. **the answer . . . Lord**—The efficient ordering is from God: "Man proposes; God disposes."

2. clean—or, faultless. **weigheth**—or, tries, judges, implying that they are faulty (ch. 21:2; 24:12).

3. (Cf. *Margin.*) Rely on God for success to your lawful purposes.

4. for himself—"for its answer, or purpose," i.e., according to God's plan; the wicked are for the day of evil (Ps. 49:5; Jer. 17:18); sinning and suffering answer to each other, are indissolubly united.

5. (Cf. ch. 3:32.)

6. By mercy and truth—i.e., God's (Ps. 85:10); He effects the atonement, or covering of sin; and the principles of true piety incline men to depart from evil; or, "mercy" and "truth" may be man's, indicative of the gracious tempers which work instrumentally in procuring pardon. **purged**—expiated (as in Lev. 16:33; Isa. 27:9, *Hebrew*).

7. Persecutions, of course, excepted.

8. (Cf. ch. 15:6, 16, 17.)

9. (Cf. vs. 3.) **directeth**—establisheth.

10. The last clause depends on the first, expressing the importance of equity in decisions, so authoritative.

11. are the Lord's . . . his work—i.e., what He has ordered, and hence should be observed by men.

ADAM CLARKE

CHAPTER 16

1. ***The preparations of the heart in man.*** The Hebrew is literally, "To man are the dispositions of the heart; but from the Lord is the answer of the tongue." Man proposes his wishes, but God answers as He thinks proper. The former is the free offspring of the heart of man; the latter, the free volition of God.

3. *Commit thy works unto the Lord.* See that what you do is commanded; and then begin, continue, and end all in His name. *And thy thoughts shall be established*—these schemes or arrangements, though formed in the heart, are agreeable to the divine will, and therefore shall be established.

4. *Even the wicked for the day of evil.* The whole verse is translated by the Chaldee thus: "All the works of the Lord are for those who obey him; and the wicked is reserved for the evil day."

6. *By mercy and truth iniquity is purged.* This may be misunderstood, as if a man, by showing mercy and acting according to truth, could atone for his own iniquity. The Hebrew text is not ambiguous: "By mercy and truth he shall atone for iniquity." He, God, by His *mercy,* in sending His Son, Jesus, into the world," "shall make an atonement for iniquity" according to His *truth*—the word which He declared by His holy prophets since the world began.

11. *All the weights of the bag are his.* Alluding, probably, to the *standard weights* laid up in a bag in the *sanctuary,* and to which all weights in common use in the land were to be referred, in order to ascertain whether they were just.

MATTHEW HENRY

Verse 12

A good king not only does justice, but it is *an abomination* to him to do otherwise. He hates the thought of doing wrong and perverting justice. He that makes conscience of using his power aright shall find that to be the best security of his government, and it will obtain the blessing of God, a basis to the throne and a strong guard about it.

Verse 13

Good kings hate parasites and those that flatter them. They not only do righteousness themselves, but take care to employ those under them that do righteousness too. A good king will therefore put those in power who are conscientious, and will say that which is righteous and discreet.

Verse 14–15

These two verses show the power of kings, which is everywhere great, but was especially so in those eastern countries, where they were absolute and arbitrary. We have reason to bless God for the happy constitution of the government we live under, which maintains the prerogative of the prince without any injury to the liberty of the subject. But here it is intimated. 1. How formidable *the wrath of a king is*: It is *as messengers of death*; the wrath of Ahasuerus was so to Haman. An angry word from an incensed prince has been to many a *messenger of death.* He must be a very *wise man* that knows how to *pacify* the wrath of a king with a world fitly spoken, as Jonathan once pacified his father's rage against David, 1 Sam. xix. 6. 2. How valuable and desirable the king's favour is to those that have incurred his displeasure; it is life from the dead if the king be reconciled to them. To others it is *as a cloud of the latter rain*, very refreshing to the ground. Those are fools who to escape the wrath, and obtain the favour, of an earthly prince, will throw themselves out of God's favour.

Verse 16

Heavenly wisdom is better than worldly wealth, and to be preferred before it. Grace is more valuable than gold. Grace is the gift of God's peculiar favour; gold only of common providence. Grace is for the soul and eternity; gold only for the body and time. Grace will stand us in stead in a dying hour, when gold will do us no good. There is vanity and vexation of spirit in getting wealth, but joy and satisfaction of Spirit in getting wisdom. *Great peace have those that love it.*

Verse 17

It is *the way of the upright* to avoid sin, and this is a highway marked out by authority, tracked by many that have gone before us. It is the care of the upright to preserve their souls. Those that adhere to their duty secure their felicity. Keep thy way and God will keep thee.

Verse 18

Pride will have a fall. It is the act of justice that those who have lifted up themselves should be laid low. Pharaoh, Sennacherib, Nebuchadnezzar, were instances of this. When proud men set God's judgments at defiance, it is a sign that they are at the door, witness the case of Benhadad and Herod. Therefore let us not fear the pride of others, but greatly fear pride in ourselves.

Verse 19

Those that are proud and will put forth themselves that thrust, and shove, and scramble, for preferment, are the men that commonly *divide the spoil* and share it among them. Humility, while it recommends us to the favour of God, qualifies us for his gracious visits, secures us from many temptations, and preserves the quiet and repose of our own souls, is much better than that high-spiritedness which, though it carry the honour and wealth of the world, makes God a man's enemy and the devil his master.

Verse 20

Prudence gains men respect and success: but it is piety only that will secure men's true happiness. Some read the former part of the verse as of piety, which is indeed true wisdom: *He that attends to the word* (the word of God, *ch.* xiii. 13) shall *find good* in it and good by it. And whoso *trusts in the Lord* is happy.

Verse 21

Those that have solid wisdom will have the credit of it; and a deference will be paid to their judgment. Those that with their wisdom deliver their sentiments easily and with a good grace, *increase learning*; they diffuse and propagate knowledge to others, and do

JAMIESON, FAUSSET, BROWN

12. Rulers are rightly expected, by their position, to hate evil; for their power is sustained by righteousness.

13. A specification of the general sentiment of vs. 12.

14. This wrath, so terrible and certain, like **messengers of death** (I Kings 2:25), can be appeased by the **wise.**

15. light of . . . countenance—favor (Ps. 4:6). **life**—preserves it, or gives blessings which make it valuable. **the latter rain**—fell just before harvest and matured the crop; hence specially valuable (Deut. 11:14).

16. (Cf. ch. 3:16; 4:5.)

17. The highway—A common, plain road represents the habitual course of the righteous in departing from evil. **keepeth**—observes.

18, 19. (Cf. ch. 15:33.) Haughtiness and pride imply self-confidence which produces carelessness, and hence the fall—lit., "sliding."

divide the spoil—i.e., conquer. Avoid the society of the proud (Jas. 4:6).

20. handleth a matter—wisely considers *the word,* i.e., of God (cf. ch. 13:13). **trusteth**—(Cf. Ps. 2:12; 118:8, 9.)

21. wise in heart—who rightly consider duty. **sweetness of the lips**—eloquent discourse, persuades and instructs others.

ADAM CLARKE

JOSEPH PARKER:

Verse 16. Solomon returns to the very doctrine on which his book is based, and the very doctrine which he himself had proved in all the earlier processes of his better life. Gold changes in value; gold sometimes flies away like a frightened bird from the nest which it has warmed; but wisdom abides in winter and in summer; it is at once the most silent and the most eloquent of companions: it takes up no room, yet it fills the whole horizon of life; it can sing as well as speak; it has a key for every lock, it has an answer to every enigma; it loves to bow down in loving homage before the eternal throne, and to increase its volume and its quality by cultivating vital communion with the only wise God. Gold can remain with us in this world only; even suppose we can keep it to the very last day, and enjoy the very last luxury it can buy, we know of a certainty that it is the last luxury, that it is the last day, that it is the final effort; but wisdom is not something which the soul possesses, it is something which is transformed into the very nature of the soul; it gives the soul its highest and divinest qualities. What is it to have much silver, and to have no understanding? "Understanding" means sagacity, farsightedness, power of balancing one event against another, and especially that patient power which can wait until seed has grown, and until the mystery of growth has consummated itself. All human experience corroborates this text. There is nothing in gold, there is nothing in silver, that is not terminable; there is nothing in wisdom that is not of the nature of seed, which requires only to be sown in the right soil, administered to by the right agencies of nature, to grow up, some bearing thirty, some sixty, and some an hundredfold.

Verse 18. Sentences of this kind can only have come after great experience. As we have before said, these proverbs are not speculations, but conclusions drawn from actual processes. We understand a statement of this kind best when we figure the writer as a man who has been watching the ways of life, and who has seen in a thousand instances ten times told how pride eventuates, and how a haughty spirit comes to fruition. The wise man tells us that pride yields the fruit of destruction, and a haughty spirit bears the fruit of humiliation. Pride can only grow for a certain time, strutting forth in all emptiness and vanity, as if it were a figure that deserved attention, and, behold, all the time it is walking along the level road to the pit of destruction: and a haughty spirit—that is, a spirit full of self-conceit and contempt for others—becomes so inflated and exaggerated and intolerable that at last it falls over the brink, and no man utters a cry of distress because it has sunk into the abyss. Only modesty is safe. Modesty is the first condition of true moral prosperity. When we come to know that we are nothing and have nothing in ourselves, and that we depend for everything upon the living God, we shall be saved from pride and from haughtiness.—*The People's Bible*

MATTHEW HENRY

good with it, and by that means increase their own stock. *To him that has, and uses what he has, more shall be given.*

Verse 22

There is always some good to be gotten by a wise and good man. His understanding is a *spring of life* to himself; within his own thoughts he entertains and edifies himself, if not others. There is nothing that is good to be gotten by a fool.

Verse 23

Solomon had commended eloquence, or *the sweetness of the lips* (*v.* 21), and seemed to prefer it before wisdom; but here he corrects himself, as it were, and shows that unless there be a good treasure within to support the eloquence it is worth little. Wisdom in *the heart* is the main matter. Quaint expressions please the ear, and humour the fancy, but it is learning that must convince the judgment and sway that, to which wisdom in the heart is necessary.

Verse 24

The *pleasant words* here commended must be those which *the heart of the wise teaches, and adds learning to* (*v.* 23), words of seasonable advice, instruction, and comfort, words taken from God's word, for that is it which Solomon had learned from his father to account *sweeter than honey and the honey-comb*, Ps. xix. 10. Many things are pleasant that are not profitable, but these *pleasant words are health to the bones*, to the inward man, as well as *sweet to the soul.*

Verse 25

This we had before (*ch.* xiv. 12), but here it is repeated, 1. By way of caution to us all to be impartial in self-examination. 2. By way of terror to those whose way is not right, however it may seem to themselves or others.

Verse 26

This is designed to engage us to diligence, and quicken us, both in our worldly business and in the work of religion; for in the original it is, *The soul that labours for itself.* It is heart-work which is here intended, the labour of the soul. If we make religion our business, God will make it our blessedness.

Verses 27–28

There are those that are not only vicious themselves, but spiteful and mischievous to others, and they are the worst of men. They *dig up evil*; they take a great deal of pains to find out something or other on which to ground a slander. If none appear above ground they will dig for it, by diving into what is secret, or looking a great way back, or by evil suspicions and surmises, and forced innuendos. In the lips of a slanderer and backbiter *there is as a fire*, to brand his neighbour's reputation. *A froward man*, that cannot find in his heart to love anybody but himself, is vexed to see others live in love, and therefore makes it his business to *sow strife*, by telling lies, and carrying ill-natured stories between *chief friends*, so as to *separate* them one from another. Those are bad men, and bad women, too, that do such ill offices; they are doing the devil's work.

Verse 29

Evil men described to us, that we may neither do like them nor have anything to do with them. They are *violent men*, that do all by rapine and oppression, that *shut their eyes*, meditating with the closest application *to devise froward things*, to contrive how they may do the greatest mischief to their neighbour. Then *moving their lips*, giving the word of command to their agents, they *bring the evil to pass.* Such do all they can to *entice* others to join in doing mischief, *leading them in a way that is not good*, but offensive to God.

Verse 31

Let old people be old disciples. If old people *be found in the way of righteousness*, their age will be their honour. Old age, as such, is honourable, and commands respect but, if it be found in the way of wickedness, its honour is forfeited, its crown laid in the dust, Isa. lxv. 20. Grace is the glory of old age.

Verse 32

The grace of meekness is to be *slow to anger*, not easily put into a passion, nor apt to resent provocation, so slow in our motions towards anger that we may be quickly stopped and pacified. It is to have the rule of our own spirits, particularly our passions. He that gets and keeps the mastery of his passions *is better than the mighty*. Behold, a greater than Alexander or Cæsar is here. The conquest of our own unruly passions, requires more true wisdom, and a more steady management, than the obtaining of a

JAMIESON, FAUSSET, BROWN

22. Understanding—or, discretion, is a constant source of blessing (ch. 13:14), benefiting others; but fools' best efforts are folly.

23. The heart is the source of wisdom flowing from the mouth.

24. (Cf. ch. 15:26.) Gentle, kind words, by soothing the mind, give the body health.

25. (Cf. ch. 14:2.)

26. Diligence is a duty due to one's self, for his wants require labor.

27. ungodly man—(Cf. ch. 6: 12.) **diggeth up evil**—labors for it.

in his lips . . . fire—His words are calumniating (Jas. 3:6). **28.** (Cf. ch. 6:14; 10-31.) **whisperer**—prater, tale-bearer (ch. 18:8; 26:20).

29. violent man—or, man of mischief (ch. 3:31).

enticeth—(ch. 1:10.) **30. He shutteth his eyes**—denoting deep thought (Ps. 64:6). **moving** [or, biting] **his lips**—a determined purpose (ch. 6:13).

31. (Cf. ch. 20:29.) **if**—or, *which* may be supplied properly, or without it the sense is as in ch. 3:16; 4:10, that piety is blessed with long life.

32. (Cf. ch. 14:29.) **taketh a city**—i.e., by fighting.

ADAM CLARKE

ALEXANDER MACLAREN:

A slight thread of connection may be traced in some of the proverbs in this passage. Verse 22, with its praise of "Wisdom," introduces one instance of Wisdom's excellence in verse 23, and that again, with its reference to speech, leads on to verse 24 and its commendation of "pleasant words." Similarly, verses 27–30 give four pictures of vice, three of them beginning with "a man." We may note, too, that, starting with verse 26, every verse till verse 30 refers to some work of "the mouth" or "lips."

The passage begins with one phase of the contrast between Wisdom and Folly, which this book is never weary of emphasizing and underscoring. We shall miss the force of its most characteristic teaching unless we keep well in mind that the two opposites of Wisdom and folly do not refer only or chiefly to intellectual distinctions. The very basis of "Wisdom," as this book conceives it, is the "fear of the Lord," without which the man of biggest, clearest brain, and most richly stored mind, is, in its judgment, "a fool." Such "understanding," which apprehends and rightly deals with the deepest fact of life, our relation to God and to His law, is a "well-spring of life." The figure speaks still more eloquently to Easterns than to us. In those hot lands the cool spring, bursting through the baked rocks or burning sand, makes the difference between barrenness and fertility, the death of all green things and life. So where true Wisdom is deep in a heart, it will come flashing up into sunshine, and will quicken the seeds of all good as it flows through the deeds. "Everything liveth whithersoever the river cometh." Productiveness, refreshment, the beauty of the sparkling waves, the music of their ripples against the stones, and all the other blessings and delights of a perpetual fountain, have better things corresponding to them in the life of the man who is wise with true Wisdom which begins with the fear of God. Just as it is active in the life, so is Folly. But its activity is not blessing and gladdening, but punitive. For all sin automatically works its own chastisement, and the curse of Folly is that, while it corrects, it prevents the "fool" from profiting by the correction. Since it punishes itself, one might expect that it would cure itself, but experience shows that, while it wields a rod, its subjects "receive no correction." That insensibility is the paradox and the Nemesis of "Folly."

—Expositions of Holy Scripture

32. *He that ruleth his spirit than he that taketh a city.* It is much easier to subdue an enemy without than one within. There have been many kings who had conquered nations and yet were slaves to their own passions.

MATTHEW HENRY

victory over an enemy. No lives or treasures are sacrificed to it. It is harder to quash an insurrection at home than to resist an invasion from abroad; such are the gains of meekness that by it *we are more than conquerors.*

Verse 33

Nothing comes to pass by chance, nor is an event determined by a blind fortune, but everything by the will and counsel of God. All the disposals of Providence concerning our affairs we must look upon to be the directing of our lot, the determining of what we referred to God, and we must be reconciled to them accordingly.

CHAPTER 17

Verse 1

These words recommend family-love and peace, as conducing very much to the comfort of human life. Those that live in unity and quietness, and that study to make themselves obliging to one another, live very comfortably, though they work hard and fare hard, though they have but each of them *a morsel*, and that *a dry morsel.* There may be peace and quietness where there are not three meals a day, provided there be a joint satisfaction in God's providence and a mutual satisfaction in each other's prudence. Holy love may be found in a cottage. Those that live in contention, that are always jarring and brawling, though they have plenty of dainties, live uncomfortably; they cannot expect the blessing of God upon them. Love will sweeten a *dry morsel*, but strife will sour and embitter *a house full of sacrifices.*

Verse 2

True merit does not go by dignity. Sometimes it so happens that the servant is wise, and a blessing and credit to the family, when the son is a fool, and a shame to the family. True dignity will go by merit. A prudent servant may perhaps come to have such an interest in his master as to be taken in for a child's share of the estate and to *have part of the inheritance among the brethren.*

Verse 3

As *the fining-pot is for silver*, both to prove it and to improve it, so *the Lord tries the hearts*; he searches whether they are standard or no, and those that are he refines and makes purer, Jer. xvii. 10. God tries the heart by affliction (Ps. lxvi. 10, 11), and often chooses his people in that furnace (Isa. xlviii. 10) and makes them choice. It is God only that *tries the hearts.* Men have no such way of trying one another's hearts.

Verse 4

Those that design to do ill support themselves by falsehood and lying: *A wicked doer gives ear*, with a great deal of pleasure, *to false lips*, that will justify him in the ill he does. Sinners will strengthen one another's hands.

Verse 5

Those who trample upon the poor, who ridicule their wants, *reproach their Maker*, who owns them, and takes care of them, and can, when he pleases, reduce us to that condition. *He that is glad at calamities*, that he may be built up upon the ruins of others, and regales himself with the judgments of God when they are abroad, let him know that he *shall not go unpunished.*

Verse 6

It is an honour to a man to live so long as to see his children's children (Ps. cxxviii. 6; Gen. l. 23), to see his house built up in them, and to see them likely to serve their generation according to the will of God. This crowns and completes their comfort in this world. It is an honour to children to have wise and godly parents, and to have them continued to them even after they have themselves grown up and settled in the world.

Verse 7

A fool, in Solomon's proverbs, signifies a wicked man, whom *excellent speech* does not become, because his conversation gives the lie to his excellent speech. If it is unbecoming a despicable man to presume to speak as a philosopher or politician, much more unbecoming is it for a prince, for a man of honour, to take advantage from the confidence that is put in him to lie, and dissemble, and make no conscience of breaking his word.

JAMIESON, FAUSSET, BROWN

33. Seemingly the most fortuitous events are ordered by God.

CHAPTER 17

Vss. 1-28. **1. sacrifices**—or, feasts made with part of them (cf. 7:14; Lev. 2:3; 7:31). **with**—lit., "of." **strife**—its product, or attendant.

2. (Cf. ch. 14:35.) **causeth shame**—(ch. 10:5.) **shall . . . inheritance**—i.e., share a brother's part (cf. Num. 27:4, 7).

3. God only knows, as He tries (Ps. 12:6; 66:10) the heart.

4. Wicked doers and speakers alike delight in calumny.

5. (Cf. ch. 14:31.) **glad at calamities**—rejoicing in others' evil. Such are rightly punished by God, who knows their hearts.

6. Prolonged posterity is a blessing, its cutting off a curse (ch. 13:22; Ps. 109:13-15), hence children may glory in virtuous ancestry.

7. Excellent speech—(Cf. *Margin*). Such language as ill suits a fool, as lying (ought to suit) a prince (ch. 16:12, 13).

ADAM CLARKE

33. *The lot is cast into the lap.* On the *lot*, see Num. xxvi. 55. How far it may be proper now to put difficult matters to the lot, after earnest prayer and supplication, I cannot say. *Formerly*, it was both lawful and efficient; for after it was solemnly cast, the decision was taken as coming immediately from the Lord. But those who need most to have recourse to the lot are those who have not piety to pray nor faith to trust to God for a positive decision.

CHAPTER 17

1. *Better is a dry morsel.* Peace and contentment, and especially domestic peace, are beyond all other blessings.

JOHN GILL:

Verse 3. "The fining-pot is for silver, and furnace for gold." Refiners of silver have their fining-pots, in which they purify the silver from the dross; and goldsmiths have their crucibles to melt and purify their gold, by which assays of the worth and value of it may be made. "But the Lord trieth the hearts"; there is no vessel, as Gersom observes, in which they can be put and tried by creatures; a man does not know, nor can he thoroughly search and try his own heart, and much less the hearts of others; God only knows and tries them (Jer. 17:9, 10). The Septuagint, Vulgate Latin, and Arabic versions, render it by way of similitude, "as the fining-pot is for silver," as silver is refined in the pot, and gold in the furnace, so are the hearts of God's people, and their graces tried and purified by him in the furnace of affliction; the variety of troubles they are exercised with are made useful for the purging away of the dross of sin and corruption, and for the brightening of their graces (1 Pet. 1:7).

Verse 4. "A wicked doer giveth heed to false lips." A man of an ill spirit, of a mischievous disposition, that delights in doing wickedness; he carefully attends to such as speak falsehood; he listens to lies and calumnies, loves to hear ill reports of persons, and takes pleasure in spreading them to the hurt of their characters; and men of bad hearts and lives give heed to seducing spirits, to false teachers, to such as speak lies in hypocrisy, who sooth and harden them in their wickedness. And "a liar giveth ear to a naughty tongue": or, "to a tongue of destruction"; a calumniating, backbiting tongue, which destroys the good name and reputation of men; and he that is given to lying is made up of lying, or is a lie itself, as the word signifies; who loves and makes a lie, as antichrist and his followers; such a one hearkens diligently to every thing that may detract from the character of those he especially bears an ill will to: or it may be better rendered, "he that hearkens to a lie" gives heed "to a naughty tongue"; for a lying tongue is a naughty one, evil in itself, pernicious in its effects and consequences.

—*Gill's Commentary*

7. *Excellent speech becometh not a fool.* This proverb is suitable to those who affect, in public speaking, fine language which comports neither with their ordinary conversation nor with their education.

MATTHEW HENRY

Verse 8

Rich men value a little money as if it were a *precious stone*, and value themselves on it as if it gave them not only ornament, but power, and everyone were bound to be at their beck, even justice itself. Whithersoever they turn this sparkling diamond they expect it should dazzle the eyes of all, and make them do just what they would have them do in hopes of it.

Verse 9

The way to preserve peace among relations and neighbours is to make the best of everything, not to tell others what has been said or done against them when it is not necessary to their safety, nor to take notice of what has been said or done against ourselves, but to excuse both, and put the best construction upon them. "It was an oversight; therefore overlook it. It was done through forgetfulness; therefore forget it."

Verse 10

A word is enough to the wise. Stripes are not enough for a fool, to make him sensible of his errors, that he may repent of them.

Verse 11

He is an evil man indeed that seeks all occasions to rebel against God, and the government God has set over him, and to contradict and quarrel with those about him. *A rebellious man seeks mischief* (so some read it), watches all opportunities to disturb the public peace. Because he will not be reclaimed by mild and gentle methods, *a cruel messenger shall be sent against him*, some dreadful judgment or other, as a messenger from God.

Verse 12

A passionate man is a brutish man in his passion ungoverned, and a *fool in his folly*. He is a dangerous man, falls foul of everyone that stands in his way, even the innocent. A bear robbed of her whelps sets upon the first man she meets as the robber. *Ira furor brevis est—Anger is temporary madness.* One may more easily guard against an enraged bear, than an outrageous angry man.

Verse 13

A malicious mischievous man is ungrateful to his friends. To render evil for evil is brutish, but to render evil for good is devilish. He is unkind to his family, for he entails a curse upon it.

Verse 14

The danger in *the beginning of strife*. One hot word begets another, and so on, till it proves like the cutting of a dam; when the water has got a little passage it does itself widen the breach, and there is then no stopping it. Take heed of the first spark of contention and put it out as soon as it appears.

Verse 15

When those that are entrusted with the administration of public justice, do either acquit the guilty or condemn those that are not guilty, this defeats the end of government, which is to protect the good and punish the bad.

Verse 16

God's great goodness to foolish men, in putting *a price into his hand to get wisdom*. We have rational souls, the means of grace, the strivings of the Spirit, access to God by prayer; we have time and opportunity. Good parents, relations, ministers, friends, are helps to get wisdom. It is *a price*, therefore of value. We have reason to wonder that God should entrust us with such advantages. Man's neglect of God's favour and his own interest, is absurd and unaccountable: ***He has no part to it.***

Verse 17

Friends must be constant to each other *at all times*. That is not true friendship which is not constant. Swallow-friends fly to you in summer, but are gone in winter. But if I love my friend because he is wise, and good, though he fall into poverty and disgrace, still I shall love him. Christ is a friend that loves at all times (John xiii. 1) and we must so love him, Rom. viii. 35. Relations must in a special manner be tender of one another in affliction: *A brother is born* to succour a brother or sister in distress. Some take it thus: *A friend that loves at all times is born* (that is, becomes) a *brother in adversity*, and is so to be valued.

Verse 18

It is wisdom to keep out of debt as much as may be, especially to dread suretiship. Those that are

JAMIESON, FAUSSET, BROWN

8. One so corrupt as to take a bribe evinces his high estimate of it by subjection to its influence (ch. 18:16; 19:6).

9. seeketh love—(Cf. *Margin*). The contrast is between the peacemaker and talebearer.

10. Reproof more affects the wise than severe scourging, fools.

11. Such meet just retribution (I Kings 2:25). **a cruel messenger**—one to inflict it.

12. They are less rational in anger than wild beasts.

13. (Cf. Ps. 7:4; 35:12.) **evil**—injury to another (ch. 13:21).

14. letteth . . . water—as a breach in a dam. **before . . . meddled with**—before strife has become sharp, or, by an explanation better suiting the figure, before it *rolls on*, or increases.

15. abomination . . . Lord—as reversing His method of acting (ch. 3:32; 12:2).

16. Though wealth cannot buy wisdom for those who do not love it, yet wisdom procures wealth (ch. 3:16; 14:24).

17. To the second of these parallel clauses, there is an accession of meaning, i.e., that a brother's love is specially seen in adversity.

18. (Cf. ch. 6:1-5; 11:15.) **in the presence . . .**—i.e., he either fails to consult his friend, or to follow his advice.

ADAM CLARKE

8. *A gift is as a precious stone.* It both enriches and ornaments. In the latter clause there is an evident allusion to cut stones. Whithersoever you turn them, they reflect the light, are brilliant and beautiful.

12. *Let a bear robbed of her whelps.* At which times such animals are peculiarly fierce.

13. *Whoso rewardeth evil for good.* Here is a most awful warning. As many persons are guilty of the sin of ingratitude, and of paying kindness with unkindness, and good with evil, it is no wonder we find so much wretchedness among men; for God's word cannot fail. Evil shall not depart from the houses and families of such persons.

14. *The beginning of strife is as when one letteth out water.* As soon as the smallest breach is made in the dike or dam, the water begins to press from all parts towards the breach. The resistance becomes too great to be successfully opposed, so that dikes and all are speedily swept away. Such is the beginning of contentions, quarrels, lawsuits. *Leave off contention, before it be meddled with.* As you see what an altercation must lead to, therefore do not begin it. Before it be "mingled together," before the spirits of the contending parties come into conflict, are joined together in battle, and begin to deal out mutual reflections and reproaches. When you see that the dispute is likely to take this turn, leave it off immediately.

17. *A friend loveth at all times.* Equally in adversity as in prosperity. And a *brother*, according to the ties and interests of consanguinity, is *born* to support and comfort a brother in distress.

18. *Striketh hands.* Striking each other's hands, or shaking hands, was anciently the form in concluding a contract. See chap. vi. 1.

MATTHEW HENRY

void of understanding are commonly taken in this snare, to the prejudice of their families.

Verse 19

He that loves strife, that in his worldly business loves to go to law, in religion loves controversies, and in common conversation loves to fall out, *he loves transgression.* He pretends to stand up for truth, and for his right, but really he loves sin. Those that are ambitious expose themselves to trouble. *He that exalts his gate*, builds a stately house, at least a fine frontispiece, that he may outshine his neighbours, seeks his own destruction.

Verse 20

He that has a froward heart, that sows discord and is full of resentment, cannot take any rational satisfaction in it; he *finds no good. He that has a perverse tongue*, spiteful and abusive, scurrilous or backbiting, loses his friends, provokes his enemies, and pulls trouble upon his own head.

Verse 21

There was *joy when a man-child was born into the world*, and yet, if he prove vicious, his own father will wish he had never been born. The name of Absalom signifies his *father's peace*, but he was his greatest trouble. *The father of a fool* lays that so much to heart that he *has no joy* of anything else.

Verse 22

It is healthful to be cheerful. The Lord is for the body, and has provided for it, not only meat, but medicine, and has here told us that the best medicine is *a merry heart*, not a heart addicted to vain, carnal, sensual mirth. God gives us leave to be cheerful and cause to be cheerful, especially if by his grace he gives us hearts to be cheerful. This *does good to a medicine* (so some read it); it will make physic more efficient. Or *it does good as a medicine* to the body, making it easy and fit for business. The sorrows of the mind often contribute to the sickliness of the body: *A broken spirit*, sunk by the burden of afflictions, and especially a conscience wounded with the sense of guilt, *dries the bones.*

Verse 23

He is *a wicked man* that will *take a gift* to engage him to give a false testimony, verdict, or judgment; he is ashamed of it, for he takes it, with all the secrecy imaginable, *out of the bosom* where he knows it is laid ready for him; it is industriously concealed. The course of justice is not only obstructed but turned into injustice.

Verse 24

An intelligent man lays his *wisdom before him*, as his card and compass which he steers by, has his eye always upon it. He that has a roving rambling fancy, will never be fit for any solid business, and cannot fix his thoughts to one subject nor pursue any one purpose with steadiness.

Verse 25

Wicked children are an affliction to both their parents. They are an occasion of *anger* to the father (so the word signifies), because they contemn his authority, but of sorrow and *bitterness* to the mother, because they abuse her tenderness.

Verse 26

Let magistrates see to it that they never *punish the just.* When princes become tyrants and persecutors their thrones will be neither easy nor firm. Let subjects not find fault with the government for doing its duty, for it is a wicked thing *to strike princes for equity*, by defaming their administration.

Verse 27

A gracious spirit is a precious spirit, and renders a man amiable and *more excellent than his neighbour.* He is of a *cool spirit* (so some read it), not heated with passion. A cool head with a warm heart is an admirable composition. *He that has knowledge*, and aims to do good with it, is careful, when he does speak to speak to the purpose. He *spares his words*, because they are better spared than ill-spent.

CHAPTER 18

Verse 1

The original here is difficult. Some take it as a rebuke to an affected singularity. When men take a pride in *separating themselves* from the sentiments and society of others, in contradicting all that has been said and advancing new notions of their own,

JAMIESON, FAUSSET, BROWN

19. **strife**—contention is, and leads to, sin. **he that exalteth his gate**—gratifies a vain love of costly building. **seeketh**—or, findeth, as if he sought (cf. "loveth death," ch. 8:36).

20. The second clause advances on the first. The ill-natured fail of good, and the cavilling and fault-finding incur evil.

21. (Cf. ch. 23:24.) Different words are rendered by **fool,** both denoting stupidity and impiety.

22. (Cf. ch. 14:30; 15:13.) The effect of the mind on the body is well known. **drieth**—as if the marrow were exhausted. **medicine**—or, body, which better corresponds with bone.

23. a gift . . . bosom—Money and other valuables were borne in a fold of the garment, called the bosom. **to pervert**—i.e., by bribery.

24. Wisdom . . . him—ever an object of regard, while a fool's affections are unsettled.

25. a grief—or cross, vexation (cf. vs. 21; ch. 10:1).

26. Also—i.e., Equally to be avoided are other sins: punishing good subjects, or resisting good rulers.

27, 28. Prudence of speech is commended as is an excellent or calm spirit, not excited to vain conversation.

CHAPTER 18

ADAM CLARKE

19. *He that exalteth his gate.* The exalting of the gate may mean proud boasting and arrogant speaking, such as has a tendency to kindle and maintain strife.

22. *A merry heart doeth good like a medicine.* Instead of *gehah, a medicine,* it appears that the Chaldee and Syriac had read in their copies *gevah,* the "body," as they translate in this way. This makes the apposition here more complete: "A merry heart doeth good to the body; but a broken spirit drieth the bones."

23. *A gift out of the bosom.* Out of his purse; as in their bosoms, above their girdles, the Asiatics carry their purses.

CHAPTER 18

1. *Through desire a man, having separated himself.* The original is difficult and obscure. The Vulgate, Septuagint, and Arabic read as follows: "He who wishes to break with his friend, and seeks occasions or pretenses, shall at all times be worthy of blame." The nearest

MATTHEW HENRY

it is to gratify a desire of vain-glory, and they are seekers and meddlers and pretend to pass a judgment upon every man's matter. Our translation seems to take it as an excitement to diligence in the pursuit of wisdom. If we would get knowledge or grace, we must desire it, and must *separate ourselves* from all those things which would retard us in the pursuit, retire out of the noise of this world's vanities, and then *seek and intermeddle with all* the means and instructions of *wisdom,* and be acquainted with a variety of opinions, that we may prove all things and hold fast that which is good.

Verse 2

A fool may pretend to understanding but he has no true delight in it. He does not love his book, nor his business, nor his Bible, nor his prayers; he would rather be playing the fool with his sports. He has no good design in it, only *that his heart may discover itself,* that he may have something to make a show with, because he loves to hear himself talk.

Verse 3

This may include a double sense: 1. Wicked people are scornful people, and put *contempt* upon others. *When the wicked comes* into any company, into schools of wisdom or into assemblies for worship, *then comes contempt* of God, of his people and ministers, and of everything that is said and done. 2. Wicked people are shameful people, and bring *contempt* upon themselves, for God has said that those *who despise him shall be lightly esteemed.*

Verse 4

An intelligent man has in him a treasure of useful things, which furnishes him with something to say that is pertinent and profitable. This is as *deep waters,* which make no noise, but never run dry The words of such *a man's mouth are as a flowing brook.* What he sees cause to speak flows naturally. It is clean and fresh.

Verse 5

This justly condemns those who, being employed in the administration of justice, pervert judgment, conniving at men's crimes because of their dignity or wealth. The merits of the cause must be regarded, not the person.

Verses 6–7

A fool's lips enter into contention by advancing foolish notions which others oppose, and so a quarrel is begun. Proud, and passionate men, and drunkards, are fools, whose lips *enter into contention.* The *fool's mouth* does, in effect, *call for strokes*; he has said that which deserves to be punished with strokes. They involve themselves in ruin: A *fool's mouth,* which has been, or would have been, the destruction of others, proves at length *his own destruction.*

Verse 8

Tale-bearers are those who secretly carry stories from house to house, told with design to blast reputation, to break friendship, to make mischief between relations. Now the words of such are here said to be, *Like as when men are wounded* (so the margin reads it); they pretend that it is with the greatest grief and reluctance that they speak of them. They look as if they themselves were wounded by it, whereas really they are fond of the story, and tell it with pride and pleasure. Thus their words seem; but they *go down as poison into the innermost parts of the belly.* The words of the tale-bearer wound him of whom they are spoken, his credit and interest, and him to whom they are spoken, his love and charity.

Verse 9

Those are justly branded as fools who are wasters of their estates, who live above what they have. Idleness is no better. He that is remiss in his work, whose *hands hang down* (so the word signifies), that stands, as we say, with his thumbs in his mouth, is own brother to him that is a prodigal. One scatters what he has, the other lets it run through his fingers.

Verse 10

Here is God's sufficiency for the saints: His *name is a strong tower* for them, in which they may take rest when they are weary and take sanctuary when they are pursued. The wealth laid up in this tower is enough to enrich them. The strength of this tower is enough to protect them.

Verse 11

The rich man has his portion and treasure in the things of this world. His wealth is as much his confidence, and he expects as much from it, as a

JAMIESON, FAUSSET, BROWN

Vss. 1-24. **1. Through desire . . . seeketh**—i.e., seeks selfish gratification. **intermeddleth . . . wisdom**—or, rushes on (ch. 17:14) against all wisdom, or what is valuable (ch. 2:7).

2. that his heart . . . itself—i.e., takes pleasure in revealing his folly (ch. 12:23; 15:2).

3. So surely are sin and punishment connected (ch. 16:4). **wicked,** for "wickedness," answers to **ignominy,** or the state of such; and **contempt,** the feeling of others to them; and to **reproach,** a manifestation of contempt.

4. Wise speech is like an exhaustless stream of benefit.

5. accept the person—(Cf. Psalm 82:2). "It is not good" is to be supplied before **to overthrow.**

6, 7. The quarrelsome bring trouble on themselves. Their rash language ensnares them (ch. 6:2).

8. (Cf. ch. 16: 28). **as wounds**—not sustained by the *Hebrew;* better, as "sweet morsels," which men gladly swallow. **innermost . . . belly**—the mind, or heart (cf. ch. 20:27 -30; Ps. 22:14).

9. One by failing to get, the other by wasting wealth, grows poor. **waster**—lit., "master of washing," a prodigal.

10. name of the Lord—manifested perfections (Ps. 8:1; 20:2), as faithfulness, power, mercy, etc., on which men rely. **is safe**—lit., "set on high, out of danger" (Ps. 18:2; 91: 4).

11. contrasts with vs. 10 (cf. ch. 10:15). Such is a vain trust (cf. Ps. 73:6).

ADAM CLARKE

translation to the Hebrew is perhaps the following: "He who is separated shall seek the desired thing [i.e., the object of his desire] and shall intermeddle [mingle himself] with all realities or all essential knowledge." He finds that he can make little progress in the investigation of divine and natural things, if he have much to do with secular or trifling matters. He therefore separates himself as well from unprofitable pursuits as from frivolous company, and then enters into the spirit of his pursuit; is not satisfied with superficial observances, but examines the substance and essence, as far as possible, of those things which have been the objects of his desire. This appears to me the best meaning.

2. *But that his heart may discover itself.* It is a fact that most vain and foolish people are never satisfied in company but in showing their own nonsense and emptiness. But this verse may be understood as confirming the view already given of the preceding, and may be translated thus: "But a fool doth not delight in understanding, though it should even manifest itself."

3. *When the wicked cometh.* Would it not be better to read this verse thus? "When the wicked cometh contempt cometh; and with ignominy cometh reproach."

4. *The words of a man's mouth.* That is, the wise sayings of a wise man are like *deep waters;* howsoever much you pump or draw off, you do not appear to lessen them. *The wellspring of wisdom.* Where there is a sound understanding, and a deep, well-informed mind, its wisdom and its counsels are an incessant stream, *mekor chochmah,* "the vein of wisdom," ever throwing out its healthy streams.

8. *The words of a talebearer.* "The words of the whisperer," the busybody, the busy, meddling croaker.

9. *He also that is slothful.* A slothful man neglects his work, and the materials go to ruin; the waster, he destroys the materials. They are both destroyers.

10. *The name of the Lord is a strong tower. The name of the Lord* may be taken for the Lord himself; He is *a strong tower,* a refuge, and place of complete safety, to all that trust in Him.

11. *The rich man's wealth.* See chap. x. 15.

MATTHEW HENRY

godly man from his God. He makes his *wealth his city*, where he rules, with a great deal of self-complacency, and sets danger at defiance, as if nothing could hurt him. *His scales are his pride;* his wealth is his wall, and he thinks it a *high wall*, which cannot be scaled. Herein he cheats himself. It is a *strong city*, and a *high wall*, but it is so only *in his own conceit*.

Verse 12

Pride is the presage of ruin, and ruin will at last be the punishment of pride. Humility is the presage of honour, and honour shall at length be the reward of humility.

Verse 13

Some take a pride in being quick. They *answer a matter before they hear it*. When they have heard one side, they think the matter so plain that they need not trouble themselves to hear the other. Whereas, though a ready wit is an agreeable thing to play with, it is solid judgment and sound wisdom that do business. It is folly for a man to pass sentence upon a matter which he has not patience to make a strict enquiry into.

Verse 14

Many infirmities, many calamities, we are liable to in this world, in body, name, and estate, which a man may bear if he have but good courage, and act with reason and resolution, especially if he have a good conscience. If the *spirit of a man* will *sustain the infirmity*, much more will the spirit of a Christian, or rather the Spirit of God witnessing and working with our spirits in a day of trouble.

Verse 15

The more prudent a man is the more inquisitive will he be after knowledge, the knowledge of God and his duty, and the way to heaven, for that is the best knowledge. We must get knowledge, not only into our heads, but into our hearts.

Verse 16

A man's gift, if he be in prison, may procure his enlargement. Or, if a mean man know not how to get access to a great man, he may do it by a fee to his servants or a present to himself; those will make room for him. It will bring him to sit among *great men*, in honour and power. See how corrupt the world is when men's gifts will do that for them which their merits will not do, though ever so great.

Verse 17

This shows that one tale is good till another is told. He that speaks first will be sure to tell a story so that his cause shall appear good, whether it really be so or no. The defendant should be heard and perhaps may make the matter appear quite otherwise than it did. We must therefore remember that we have two ears, to hear both sides before we give judgment.

Verse 18

Contentions commonly happen among the mighty, that are confident of their being able to make their part good and therefore will hardly condescend to the necessary terms of an accommodation; whereas those that are poor are forced to be peaceable, and sit down losers. Even the contentions of the mighty may be ended by lot if they cannot otherwise be compromised.

Verse 19

Great care must be taken to prevent quarrels among relations, and those that are under special obligation to each other, because they are most unnatural and unbecoming. Great pains must be taken to compromise matters in variance between relations, with all speed, because it is a work of much difficulty.

Verse 20

Our comfort depends very much upon the testimony of our own consciences, for us or against us. The *belly* is here put for the conscience, as *ch.* xx. 27. The testimony of our consciences will be for us, or against us, according as we have or have not governed our tongues well. According as *the fruit of the mouth* is good or bad, so the character of the man is, and consequently the testimony of his conscience concerning him.

Verse 21

Many a one has been his own death by a foul tongue, or the death of others by a false tongue; and, on the contrary, many a one has saved his life by a prudent gentle tongue, and saved the lives of others by intercession for them.

JAMIESON, FAUSSET, BROWN

12. (Cf. ch. 15:33; 16

13. Hasty speech evinces self-conceit, and ensures shame (ch. 26:12).

14. infirmity—bodily sickness, or outward evil. The **spirit,** which sustains, being **wounded,** no support is left, except, as implied, in God.

15. (Cf. ch: 1:5,15, 31.)

16. (Cf. ch. 17:8, 23.) Disapproval of the fact stated is implied.

17. One-sided statements are not reliable. **searcheth**—thoroughly (ch. 17:9, 19).

18. The lot—whose disposal is of God (ch. 16:13), may, properly used, be a right mode of settling disputes.

19. No feuds so difficult of adjustment as those of relatives; hence great care should be used to avoid them.

20. (Cf. ch. 12:14; 13:2.) Men's words are the **fruit,** or, **increase of his lips,** and when good, benefit them. **satisfied with**—(Cf. ch. 1:31; 14:14.)

21. Death and life—or, the greatest evil and good. **that love it**—i.e., the tongue, or its use for good or evil. **eat . . . fruit**—(Cf. vs. 19; Jas. 1:19.)

ADAM CLARKE

12. *Before destruction.* See chap. xi. 2 and xvi. 18.

16. *A man's gift maketh room for him.* It is, and ever has been, a base and degrading practice in Asiatic countries to bring a gift or present to the great man into whose presence you come. Without this there is no audience, no favor, no justice.

18. *The lot causeth contentions to cease.* See chap. xvi. 33.

19. *A brother offended is harder to be won than a strong city.* Almost all the versions agree in the following reading: "A brother assisted by a brother, is like a fortified city; and their decisions are like the bars of a city." Coverdale is both plain and terse: "The unitie of brethren is stronger then a castell, and they that holde together are like the barre of a palace."

21. *Death and life are in the power of the tongue.* This may apply to all men. Many have lost their lives by their tongue, and some have saved their lives by it. But it applies most forcibly to *public pleaders;* on many of their tongues hangs *life* or *death*.

MATTHEW HENRY

Verse 22

A good wife is a great blessing to a man. He that *finds a wife* (that is, a wife indeed; a bad wife does not deserve to be called by a name of so much honour), that finds a help meet for him (that is a wife in the original acceptation of the word), has found that which will not only contribute more than anything to his comfort in this life, but will forward him in the way to heaven. God is to be acknowledged in it with thankfulness.

Verse 23

Poverty, though many inconveniences to the body attend it, has often a good effect upon the spirit, for it makes men humble. It teaches them to *use entreaties.* It tells them they must take what is given them and be thankful. At the throne of God's grace we are all poor, and must use entreaties. A prosperous condition, though it has many advantages, has often this mischief attending it, that it makes men proud, haughty and imperious. It is very foolish humour of some rich men, especially those who have risen from little, that they think it becomes them to answer roughly, whereas gentlemen ought to be gentle, James iii. 17.

Verse 24

Would we have friends and keep them, we must not only not affront them, but we must love them. We may promise ourselves a great deal of comfort in a true friend. Sometimes *there is a friend,* that is nothing akin to us, the bonds of whose esteem and love prove stronger than those of nature. Christ is a friend to all believers that *sticks closer than a brother.*

JAMIESON, FAUSSET, BROWN

22. The old versions supply "good" before the "wife," as the last clause and ch. 19:14 imply (cf. ch. 31:10).

23. the rich . . . roughly—He is tolerated because rich, implying that the estimate of men by wealth is wrong.

24. A man . . . friendly—better, "A man . . . (is) to, or may triumph (Ps. 108:9), or, shout for joy (Ps. 5:11), i.e., may congratulate himself." Indeed, there is a Friend who is better than a brother; such is the "Friend of sinners," who may have been before the writer's mind.

ADAM CLARKE

22. *Whoso findeth a wife findeth a good thing.* Marriage, with all its troubles and embarrassments, is a blessing from God; and there are few cases where a wife of any sort is not better than none, because celibacy is an evil; for God himself hath said, "It is not good for man to be alone."

24. *There is a friend that sticketh closer than a brother.* In many cases the genuine friend has shown more attachment, and rendered greater benefits, than the natural brother. Some apply this to God; others, to Christ; but the text has no such meaning.

MATTHEW HENRY

CHAPTER 19

Verse 1

1. The credit and comfort of a poor man: Let him be honest and *walk in integrity,* let him keep a good conscience, let him speak and act with sincerity when he is under the greatest temptations to break his word, and then let him value himself upon that, for all wise and good men will value him. 2. The shame of a rich man, notwithstanding all his pomp. If he have a shallow head and an evil tongue he *is a fool.*

Verse 2

To be without the knowledge of the soul is not good, so some read it. *He that hastes with his feet* (that does things inconsiderately and with precipitation, and will not take time to ponder the path of his feet) *sins.* As good not know as not consider.

Verse 3

The foolishness of man perverts his way. Men meet with crosses and disappointments in their affairs, and it is owing to themselves and their own folly; it is their own iniquity that corrects them. When they have done so they lay the blame upon God, and their hearts fret against him, as if he had done them wrong, whereas really they wrong themselves.

Verse 4

Wealth enables a man to send many presents, and do many good offices, and so gains him many friends, who flatter him, but really love what he has. He, who while he prospered, was beloved and respected, if he fall into poverty is *separated from his neighbour,* is not owned nor looked upon, is bidden to keep his distance and told he is troublesome.

Verse 5

Men *teach their tongues to speak lies,* Jer. ix. 5. Those that will take a liberty to tell lies in discourse are in a fair way to be guilty of the greater wickedness of false-witness-bearing, whenever they are tempted to it, though they seemed to detest it. But it *shall not escape* the righteous judgment of God, who is jealous, and will not suffer his name to be profaned.

Verses 6–7

The prince that has power in his hand, and preferments at his disposal, has his antechamber thronged with petitioners, ready to adore him for what they can get. How earnest then should we be for the favour of God, which is far beyond that of any earthly prince. But, it should seem, liberality will go further than majesty itself to gain respect, for *every man is a friend to him that gives gifts.* Those that are accounted benefactors exercise an authority which may give them an opportunity of doing good, Luke xxii. 25. Those that are poor and low are slighted

JAMIESON, FAUSSET, BROWN

CHAPTER 19

Vss. 1-29. **1.** (Cf. ch. 28:6.) "Rich" for **fool** here. Integrity is better than riches (ch. 15:16, 17; 16:8).

2. The last illustrates the first clause. Rashness, the result of ignorance, brings trouble.

3. perverteth . . . way—turns him back from right (ch. 13:6; Jas. 1:13); and he blames God for his failures.

4. (Cf. ch. 14:20.) Such facts are often adduced with implied disapprobation.

5. Cf. vs. 9, where **perish** explains **not escape** here (cf. Ps. 88:9, 10).

ADAM CLARKE

CHAPTER 19

1. *Better is the poor.* The upright, poor man is always to be preferred to the rich or self-sufficient fool.

2. *Also, that the soul be without knowledge, it is not good.* Would it not be plainer, as it is more literal, to say, "Also, to be without knowledge, is not good for the soul"?

JOHN GILL:

Verse 3. "The foolishness of man perverteth his way." The sinfulness of his heart and nature: the folly which is bound up in it causes him to go astray out of the way in which he should go, or makes things go cross with him; so that the ways he takes do not prosper, nor his schemes succeed; but every thing goes against him, and he is brought into straits and difficulties. "And his heart fretteth against the Lord"; laying all the blame on him; and ascribing his ill success, not to his own sin and folly, but to divine Providence, which works against him; and therefore frets and murmurs at him; and, instead of charging his own ways with folly, charges the ways of God with inequality (Ezek. 18:25; Jude 16).

—Gill's Commentary

MATTHEW HENRY

and despised. It should not be so; we must honour all men, even under their greatest abasements. *All the brethren of the poor do hate him;* even his own relations look upon him as a blemish to their family; and then others of his friends, that were nothing akin to him, *go far from him,* to get out of his way. *He pursues them with words,* hoping to prevail with them by his importunity to be kind to him, but all in vain; they have nothing for him. Let poor people therefore make God their friend, pursue him with their prayers, and he will not be wanting to them.

Verse 8

Get wisdom, get knowledge, and grace, and acquaintance with God; those that do so, show that they *love their own souls,* and will be found to have done themselves the greatest kindness imaginable. He that *keeps understanding* shall certainly *find good,* all good.

Verse 9

We have need to be again and again warned of the danger of the sin of lying and false-witness-bearing. His punishment shall be such as will be his destruction: he *shall perish.* It is a damning destroying sin.

Verse 10

Pleasure and liberty ill become a fool. A man that has not wisdom and grace has no right nor title to true joy, and therefore it is unseemly. Power and honour ill become a man of a servile spirit. None are so insolent and intolerable as a beggar on horseback, *a servant when he reigns, ch.* xxx. 22.

Verse 11

A wise man will observe these two rules about his anger: 1. Not to be over-hasty in his resentments: *Discretion* teaches us to *defer our anger* till we have thoroughly considered all the merits of the provocation, and then to defer the prosecution of it till there be no danger of running into any indecencies. Plato said to his servant, "I would beat thee, but that I am angry." 2. Not to be over-critical in his resentments. It is here made a man's *glory to pass over a transgression,* or, if he sees fit to take notice of it, yet to forgive it.

Verse 12

Kings are not common persons; their frowns are very terrible and their smiles very comfortable, and therefore it concerns them that they never frighten a good man from doing well with their frowns, nor ever give countenance to a wicked man in doing ill with their smiles, for then they abuse their influence, Rom. xiii. 3. To make subjects faithful and dutiful let them be encouraged in all good services to the public by the hopes of the favour of their prince.

Verse 13

A foolish son is a great affliction. A son that will apply himself to no study or business, that will take no advice, that lives a lewd, loose, rakish life, and spends what he has extravagantly, games it away, or that is proud, foppish, and conceited, such a one is the grief *of his father.* A cross peevish wife is as great an affliction: Her *contentions are continual.* Those that are accustomed to chide never want something or other to chide at; but it is *a continual dropping,* that is, a continual vexation, as it is to have a house so much out of repair that it rains in and a man cannot lie dry in it.

Verse 14

A discreet and virtuous wife is a choice gift of God's providence to a man—a wife that is *prudent,* in opposition, to one that is contentious, *v.* 13. *A prudent wife* makes the best of everything. If a man has such a wife let him ascribe it to the goodness of God, who made him a helpmeet for him, and perhaps by some hits and turns of providence that seemed casual brought her to him. A good estate may be *the inheritance of fathers,* which, by the common direction of Providence, comes in course to a man; but no man has a good wife by descent or entail.

Verse 15

A sluggish slothful disposition stupefies men, and makes them mindless of their own affairs, as if they were *cast into a deep sleep,* dreaming much, but doing nothing. Even their souls are idle and lulled asleep, their rational powers chilled and frozen. Those that will not labour cannot expect to eat, but must *suffer hunger.* One that is idle in the affairs of his soul, that takes no care or pains to work out his salvation, shall perish for want of that which is necessary to the life and happiness of the soul.

JAMIESON, FAUSSET, BROWN

8. (Cf. *Margin;* ch. 15:32.) **loveth . . . soul**—or, himself, which he evinces by regarding his best interests. **keepeth**—or, regards.

10. (Cf. ch. 17:7.) The fool is incapable of properly using pleasure as knowledge, yet for him to have it is less incongruous than the undue elevation of servants. Let each abide in his calling (I Cor. 7:20).

11. (Cf. ch. 14:29; 16:32.) This inculcation of a forgiving spirit shows that true religion is always the same (Matt. 5:22-24).

12. (Cf. ch. 16:14, 15; 20:2.) A motive to submission to lawful authority.

13. calamity—lit., "calamities," varied and many. **continual dropping**—a perpetual annoyance, wearing out patience.

14. A contrast of men's gifts and God's, who, though author of both blessings, confers the latter by His more special providence. **and**—or, "but," implying that the evils of vs. 13 are only avoided by His care.

15. a deep sleep—a state of utter indifference. **idle soul**—or, person (cf. ch. 10:4; 12:24).

ADAM CLARKE

F. C. COOK:

Verse 7. It seems best to follow the Vulgate in taking the last clause as a separate maxim, "He who pursues words, nought are they;" i.e. the fair speeches and promises of help come to nothing. A various reading in the Hebrew gives, "he pursues after words, and these he shall have"—i.e. these, and nothing else.

This and other like maxims do not in reality cast scorn and shame on a state which Christ has pronounced "blessed." Side by side with them is verse 1, setting forth the honor of an upright poverty. But as there is an honorable poverty, so there is one which is altogether inglorious, caused by sloth and folly, leading to shame and ignominy, and it is well that the man who wishes to live rightly should avoid this.

—*Barnes' Notes*

10. *Delight is not seemly for a fool. Taanug,* splendid or luxurious living, rank, equipage. These sit ill on a *fool,* though he be by birth a lord.

13. *The contentions of a wife are a continual dropping.* The man who has got such a wife is like a tenant who has got a cottage with a bad roof, through every part of which the rain either drops or pours. He can neither sit, stand, work, nor sleep, without being exposed to these droppings.

14. *A prudent wife is from the Lord.* One who has a good understanding; who avoids complaining, though she may often have cause for it.

MATTHEW HENRY

Verse 16

Those that make conscience of *keeping the commandment* in everything, that live by rule, *keep their own souls*; they secure their present peace and future bliss. If we keep God's word, God's word will keep us from everything really hurtful.

Verse 17

The duty of charity includes two things: 1. Compassion, which is the inward principle of charity in the heart; it is to *have pity on the poor*, 1 Cor. xiii. 3. 2. Bounty and liberality. We must not only pity the poor, but give, according to their necessity and our ability, James ii. 15, 16. It is charity to do for the poor, as well as to give. What is given to the poor, or done for them, God will place it to account as lent to him, *lent upon interest* (so the word signifies); he takes it kindly, as if it were done to himself. *He will pay him again*, in temporal, spiritual, and eternal blessings.

Verse 18

As soon as ever there appears a corrupt disposition in them check it immediately, before it is hardened into a habit. If the point can be gained without correction, well and good; but if you find that your forgiving them once, upon a dissembled repentance and promise of amendment, does but embolden them to offend again, put on resolution. It is better that he should cry under thy rod than under the sword of the magistrate, or of divine vengeance.

Verse 19

Angry men never want woe. Those that are of headstrong passions, commonly bring themselves and their families into trouble by vexatious suits and quarrels. All which troubles to themselves and others would be prevented if they would get the rule of their own spirits. It may be read, *He that is of great wrath* (meaning the child that is to be corrected and is impatient of rebuke, cries and makes a noise) *deserves to be punished; for, if thou deliver him* for the sake of that, thou wilt be forced to punish him the more the next time.

Verse 20

It is well with those that are *wise in their latter end*, wise for their future state, wise for another world. Those that would *be wise in their latter end* must be willing to be taught, advised and reproved, when they are young.

Verse 21

God knows the *many devices that are in men's hearts* (as those, Ps. ii. 1–3, Micah iv. 11). His counsel often breaks men's measures and baffles their devices; but their devices cannot in the least alter his counsel, nor disturb the proceedings of it. Politic designing men think they can outwit all mankind, but there is a God in heaven that laughs at them! Ps. ii. 4. All God's purposes, which we are sure are right and good, shall be accomplished in due time!

Verse 22

It cannot but be *the desire of a man*, if he have any spark of virtue in him, to be kind. It is far better to have a heart to do good and want ability for it than to have ability for it and want a heart to it. *A poor man*, who wishes you well, but can promise you nothing, because he has nothing to be kind with, *is better than a liar*, who makes you believe he will do mighty things, but, when it comes to the setting, will do nothing.

Verse 23

Those that live in the fear of God *shall not be visited with evil*; they may be visited with afflictions, but there shall be nothing to hurt the soul, whereas all the satisfactions of sense are transient and soon gone. He shall have true and complete happiness. Serious godliness has a direct tendency *to life*, to all good, to eternal life.

Verse 24

A sluggard is here exposed as a fool. All his care is to save himself from labour and cold. He *hides his hand in his bosom*; his hands are cold, and he must warm them in his bosom. He is resolved against labour and hardship. He will not be at pains to feed himself, to take his hand out of his bosom, no, not to put meat into his own mouth.

Verse 25

The punishment of scorners will be a means of good to others. If it cure not the infected, it may prevent the spreading of the infection. The reproof of wise men will be a means of good to themselves.

JAMIESON, FAUSSET, BROWN

16. (Cf. ch. 10:17; 13:13.) **despiseth . . . ways**—opposed to keeping or observing, neglects (ch. 16:17) (as unworthy of regard) his moral conduct.

17. (Cf. ch. 14:21; Ps. 37:26). **hath pity**—shown by acts (cf. *Margin*).

18. (Cf. ch. 13:24; 23:13.) **let not . . . spare**—lit., "do not lift up thy soul" (Ps. 24:4; 25:1), i.e., do not desire to his death; a caution to passionate parents against angry chastisement.

19. Repeated efforts of kindness are lost on ill-natured persons.

20. (Cf. ch. 13:18-20.) **latter end**—(Ch. 5:11.) In youth prepare for age.

21. (Cf. ch. 16:1, 9; Ps. 33:10, 11.) The failure of man's devices is implied.

22. desire—i.e., to do good, indicates a kind disposition (ch. 11:23); and the poor thus affected are better than liars, who say and do not.

23. The fear . . . life—(Cf. ch. 3:2). **abide**—or, remain contented (I Tim. 4:8). **not visited with evil**—(ch. 10:3; Ps. 37:25), as a judgment, in which sense *visit* is often used (Ps. 89:32; Jer. 6:15).

24. bosom—lit., a wide dish in which the hand was plunged in eating (Matt. 26:23). Cf. ch. 26:15, the sentiment expressed with equal irony and less exaggeration.

25. Such is the benefit of reproof; even the simple profit, much more the wise.

ADAM CLARKE

17. *Lendeth unto the Lord.* Oh, what a word is this! God makes himself debtor for everything that is given to the *poor!* Who would not advance much upon such credit?

18. *Let not thy soul spare for his crying.* This is a hard precept for a parent. Nothing affects the heart of a parent so much as a child's cries and tears. But it is better that the child may be caused to cry, when the correction may be healthful to his soul, than that the parent should cry afterwards, when the child is grown to man's estate and his evil habits are sealed for life.

21. *There are many devices.* The same sentiment as in chap. xvi. 1.

MATTHEW HENRY

Do but *reprove one that has understanding and he will* so far understand himself, so kindly does he take reproof and so wisely improve it.

Verse 26

The sin of a prodigal son is injurious to his parents, and basely ungrateful to those that were the instruments of his being and have taken so much care about him: ***He wastes his father***, wastes his estate which he should have to support him in his old age, and breaks his heart. He ***chases away his mother***, makes her weary of the house, with his rudeness and insolence, and glad to retire for a little quietness; and, when he has spent all, he turns her out of doors.

Verse 27

There is that which seems designed for the instruction, but really tends to the destruction of young men. The factors for vice will undertake to teach them how to palliate sins and stop the mouth of their own consciences, how to get clear of restraints. It is the wisdom of young men to turn a deaf ear to such instructions.

Verse 28

An ungodly witness is one that bears false witness against his neighbour, and will forswear himself to do another a mischief, in which there is great injustice, great impiety. Tell him of law and equity, that the scriptures and an oath are sacred things, that there will come a reckoning day; he laughs at it all. They are greedy, and glad of that which gives them an opportunity to sin.

Verse 29

Scorners are fools. Those that ridicule things sacred and serious do but make themselves ridiculous.

JAMIESON, FAUSSET, BROWN

26. Unfilial conduct often condemned (ch. 17:21-25; 20: 20; Deut. 21:18, 21).

27. Avoid whatever leads from truth.

28. ungodly witness—(cf. *Margin*), one false by bad principles (cf. ch. 6:12). **scorneth judgment**—sets at naught the dictates of justice. **devoureth**—lit., swalloweth, as something delightful.

29. Their punishment is sure, fixed, and ready (cf. ch. 3:34; 10:13).

ADAM CLARKE

JOSEPH PARKER:

Verse 27. The instruction of bad men can only tend to badness. It may have all the form of philosophical teaching, but its moral inspiration is bad, and therefore it must come to darkness and confusion in the end. The passage might be rendered, "Cease to hear instruction if you are going to err afterwards." That gives another view of the exhortation. Do not attend church if you mean to turn your religious service into an excuse for immorality: do not read books if you are simply seeking for a key that will enable you to open gates that are forbidden: better not appear to care for instruction than to accept it as an instrument which is perverted to mischievous purposes: be honest, be sincere—on no account pretend to love the right and yet do the wrong, because you add to the wrong the aggravation of hypocrisy. Get instruction for the purpose of being stronger. Pursue knowledge that you may have both hands filled with instruments which will enable you to do a great and useful work in society.

—*The People's Bible*

MATTHEW HENRY — CHAPTER 20

Verse 1

Wine is a mocker; strong drink is raging. It smiles upon him at first, but *at the last it bites.* It rages in his conscience. It is raging in the body. *When the wine is in the wit is out*, and then the man, according as his natural temper is, either mocks like a fool or rages like a madman. Drunkenness, which pretends to be a sociable thing, renders men unfit for society. A drunkard is a fool, and a fool he is likely to be.

Verse 2

Those princes that rule by wisdom and love, rule like God himself, but those that rule merely by terror, and with a high hand, do but rule like a lion in the forest, with a brutal power. How unwise therefore those are that quarrel with them! They *sin against their own lives.* Much more do those do so that provoke the King of kings to anger.

Verse 3

He thinks himself a wise man that is quick in resenting affronts, that stands upon every nicety of honour and right, but he that thus meddles creates needless vexation to himself. Really *it is an honour for a man to cease from strife*, to drop a controversy, to forgive an injury, and to be friends.

Verse 4

Slothfulness keeps men from ploughing and sowing when the season is: some excuse or other he has to shift it off, but the true reason is that it is *cold* weather. Thus careless are many in the affairs of their souls. Those that *will not plough* in seedtime cannot expect to reap in harvest. They must beg their bread when the diligent are bringing home their sheaves with joy.

Verse 5

Though men's counsels and designs are carefully concealed by them, so that they are as *deep water* which one cannot fathom, yet there are those who by sly insinuations and questions will get out of them both what they have done and what they intend to do. Some are very able and fit to give counsel, but they are reserved; they have a great deal in them, but it is loth to come out. *A man of understanding will draw it out*, as wine out of a vessel.

Verse 6

Most men will talk a great deal of their charity, hospitality, and piety. But it is hard to find those that really are kind and liberal, that have done more than they care to hear spoken of, that will be true friends in a strait.

JAMIESON, FAUSSET, BROWN — CHAPTER 20

Vss. 1-30. **1. mocker**—scorner. Such men are made by wine. **strong drink**—made by spicing wine (cf. Isa. 5:11, 22); and it may include wine. **raging**—or, boisterous as a drunkard. **deceived**—lit., "erring," or reeling.

2. (Cf. ch. 19:12.) Men who resist authority injure themselves (Rom. 13:2).

3. to cease from strife—or, better, "to dwell from or without strife," denoting the habit of life. **fool . . . meddling**—(Ch. 17:14).

4. shall . . . beg—lit., "ask" (in this sense, Ps. 109:10).

5. Counsel . . . water—i.e., deeply hidden (ch. 18:4; Ps. 13:2). The wise can discern well.

6. Boasters are unreliable. **goodness**—or, kind disposition.

ADAM CLARKE — CHAPTER 20

1. *Wine is a mocker.* It deceives by its fragrance, intoxicates by its strength, and renders the intoxicated ridiculous. *Strong drink. Shechar,* any strong, fermented liquor, whether of the vine, date, or palm species.

2. *The fear of a king.* Almost the same with chap. xix. 12.

3. *It is an honour for a man.* The same sentiment as chap. xix. 11.

MATTHEW HENRY

Verse 7
A good man keeps a good conscience, and has the comfort of it, for *it is his rejoicing*. He is not liable to those uneasinesses which those are liable to that walk in deceit. He does well for his family. God has mercy in store for the seed of the faithful.

Verse 8
He is *a king* that deserves to be called so who *sits in the throne*, not as a throne of honour, to take his ease and oblige men to keep their distance, but as a *throne of judgment*, that he may do justice, give redress to the injured. If he inspect his affairs himself, those that are employed will be restrained from doing wrong. If great men be good men, and will use their power as they may and ought, what good may they do and what evil may they prevent!

Verse 9
This question is not only a challenge to any man to prove himself sinless, but a lamentation of the corruption of mankind. Here, in this imperfect state, no person whatsoever can pretend to be without sin. Those that think themselves as good as they should be cannot, and those that are really good will not, dare not, say this.

Verse 10
In paying and receiving money, which was then commonly done by the scale, they had *divers weights*, an underweight for what they paid and an overweight for what they received; and *divers measures*, a scanty measure to sell by and a large measure to buy by. Under these is included all manner of fraud and deceit in commerce and trade. They are all *alike an abomination to the Lord*. He hates those that thus break the common faith by which justice is maintained.

Verse 11
The tree is known by its fruits, even a young tree, and *a child by his* childish things. Children will discover themselves. One may soon see what their temper is. Parents should observe their children, that they may discover their disposition and genius, and manage them accordingly, drive the nail that will go and draw out that which goes amiss.

Verse 12
God is the God of nature, and *formed the eye* and *planted the ear* (Ps. xciv. 9). Hearing and seeing are the learning senses, and we must particularly own God's goodness in them. It is he that gives the ear that hears God's voice, the eye that sees his beauty, for it is he that opens the understanding.

Verse 13
Though thou must sleep yet *love not sleep*, as those do that hate business. Love not sleep for its own sake, but only as it fits for further work. And, when thou art awake, look up, and do not let slip thy opportunities; apply thy mind closely to thy business.

Verse 14
What arts men use to get a good bargain and to buy cheap! They vilify and run down that which they know to be of value; they cry, "*It is naught, it is naught;* it has this and the other fault, and it is too dear; we can have better and cheaper elsewhere, or have bought better and cheaper." But the seller does as extravagantly commend his goods and justify the price he sets on them, and so there is a fault on both sides. When the buyer has beaten down the seller he goes his way, and boasts what excellent goods he has got at his own price.

Verse 15
The *lips of knowledge* (a good understanding to guide the lips and to diffuse the knowledge) are to be preferred before gold and rubies. They are more rare in themselves, more scarce and hard to be got. They make us rich towards God, rich in good works, 1 Tim. ii. 9, 10.

Verse 16
Those that will be bound for anybody that will ask them, in rash suretiship to oblige their idle companions, cannot hold out long. Those that are in league with abandoned women will be beggars in a little time; never give them credit without a good pledge.

Verse 17
All the pleasures and profits of sin are *bread of deceit*. They are stolen, for they are forbidden fruit; and they will deceive men, for they are not what they promise. For a time, however, they are *rolled under the tongue as a sweet morsel*. Afterwards the sinner's

JAMIESON, FAUSSET, BROWN

7. The conduct of good men proclaims their sound principles. God's covenant and their good example secure blessing to their children (ch. 4:26; Ps. 112:1, 2).

8. As in ch. 14:35; 16:10, 15, this is the character of a good king, not of all kings.

9. The interrogation in the affirmative strengthens the implied negation (cf. Job. 15:14; Eccles. 7:20).

10. Various measures, implying that some are wrong (cf. ch. 11:1; 16:11).

11. The conduct of children even is the best test of principle (cf. Matt. 7:16).

12. Hence, of course, God will know all you do (Ps. 94:9).

13. Activity and diligence contrasted with sloth (ch. 6:9; 10:11). **lest . . . poverty**—lit., "be deprived of inheritance."

14. when . . . his way—implying that he goes about boasting of his bargains.

15. The contrast denotes the greater value of knowledge (cf. ch. 3:14-16).

16. Take his garment implies severe exaction, justified by the surety's rashness. **a strange woman**—by some readings "strangers," but the former here, and in ch. 27:13, is allowable, and strengthens the sense. The debauchee is less reliable than the merely careless.

Bread . . . sweet—either as unlawfully (ch. 9:17) or easily obtained.

ADAM CLARKE

9. *Who can say, I have made my heart clean?* No man. But thousands can testify that the blood of Jesus Christ has cleansed them from all unrighteousness. And he is *pure from* his *sin* who is justified freely through the redemption that is in Jesus.

10. *Divers weights, and divers measures.* Hebrew: "A stone and a stone; an ephah and an ephah." One the standard, the other below it; one to buy with, the other to sell by.

12. *The hearing ear, and the seeing eye.* Every *good* we possess comes from God; and we should neither use our eyes, nor our ears, nor anything we possess, but in strict subserviency to His will.

13. *Love not sleep, lest thou come to poverty.* Sleep is an indescribable blessing; but how often is it turned into a curse! It is like food; a certain measure of it restores and invigorates exhausted nature; more than that oppresses and destroys life. A lover of sleep is a paltry, insignificant character.

14. *It is naught, it is naught, saith the buyer.* How apt are men to decry the goods they wish to purchase, in order that they may get them at a cheaper rate; and, when they have made their bargain and carried it off, boast to others at how much less than its value they have obtained it!

16. *Take his garment that is surety for a stranger.* I suppose the meaning to be, If a stranger or unknown person become surety in a case, greater caution should be used, and such security taken from this stranger as would prevent him from running away from his engagements.

17. *Bread of deceit is sweet.* Property acquired by falsehood, speculation, etc., without labor, is pleasant to the unprincipled, slothful man; but there is a curse in it, and the issue will prove it.

MATTHEW HENRY

mouth shall be filled with gravel. Some nations have punished malefactors by mingling gravel with their bread.

Verse 18

Ask counsel of God, and beg direction from him. What is done hastily and with precipitation is repented of at leisure. It is especially our wisdom to be cautious in making war. Consider, and take advice, whether the war should be begun or no, and, when it is begun, consider how and by what arts it may be prosecuted, for management is as necessary as courage.

Verse 19

Tale-bearers are unprincipled people that go about carrying stories, make mischief among neighbours and relations, sow in the minds of people jealousies of their governors, of their ministers, and of one another, and reveal secrets. "Be not familiar with such; do not give them hearing for you may be sure that they will betray your secrets too and tell tales of you." Flatterers are commonly tale-bearers.

Verse 20

An undutiful child becomes very wicked by degrees. He began with despising his father and mother, but at length he arrives at such a pitch as to curse them, in defiance of God and his law, which has made this a capital crime (Exod. xxi. 17, Matt. xv. 4). An undutiful child becomes very miserable at last: *His lamp shall be put out in obscure darkness;* all his honour shall be laid in the dust.

Verse 21

There are those who will be rich, by right or wrong, who will cheat their own father, grudging themselves and their families food. An estate that is suddenly raised is often as suddenly ruined. It proves *soon ripe and soon rotten.*

Verse 22

We must not avenge ourselves. *"Say not thou I will recompense evil* for evil. Do not wish revenge. Never say that thou wilt do a thing which thou canst not in faith pray to God to assist thee in, and *that* thou canst not do in meditating revenge." We must refer ourselves to God, and leave it to him to plead our cause, to maintain our right, and reckon with those that do us wrong in such a way and manner as he thinks fit and in his own due time.

Verse 23

This is to the same purport with what was said *v.* 10. It is here added, *A false balance is not good,* to intimate that it is not only abominable to God, but unprofitable to the sinner himself; there is really no good to be got by it, for a bargain made by fraud will prove a losing bargain in the end.

Verse 24

We have a constant dependence upon God. All our natural actions depend upon his providence, all our spiritual actions upon his grace. The best man is no better than God makes him. We have no foresight of future events, and therefore *How can a man understand his own way?* We so little understand own own way that we know not what is good for ourselves, and therefore we must commit our way unto the Lord.

Verse 25

Sacrilege, men's alienating holy things and converting them to their own use, is here called *devouring* them. What is devoted to the service of God ought to be conscientiously preserved to the purposes designed. Those that hurry over religious offices (their praying and preaching) may be said to *devour that which is holy. It is a snare to a man, after* he has made *vows* to God, *to enquire* how he may evade them or contrive excuses for the violating of them. If the matter of them was doubtful, and the expressions were ambiguous, that was his fault; he should have made them with more caution and consideration.

Verse 26

Magistrates must *scatter the wicked,* who are linked in confederacies, and there is no doing this but by *bringing the wheel over them,* that is, putting the laws in execution against them, crushing their power and quashing their projects.

Verse 27

The great soul of man is a divine light; it is the *candle of the Lord,* a candle of his lighting. Con-

JAMIESON, FAUSSET, BROWN

mouth . . . gravel—well expresses the pain and grief given at last.

18. (Cf. ch. 15:22.) Be careful and considerate in important plans.

19. Those who love to tell news will hardly keep secrets. **flattereth . . . lips**—(cf. *Margin*; ch. 1:10). **meddle . . . him**— lit., "join," or "associate with."

20. his lamp—(Cf. ch. 13:9; 24:20).

21. gotten hastily—contrary to God's providence (ch. 28:20), implying its unjust or easy attainment; hence the man is punished, or spends freely what he got easily (cf. vs. 17).

22. (Cf. Ps. 27:14; Rom. 12:17-19.)

23. (Cf. vs. 10; ch. 11:1.)

24. Man's goings—lit., "Stately steppings of a strong man." **a man**—any common man. **understand** [or, perceive] **his . . . way.**

25. devoureth . . . holy—or, better, who rashly speaks promises, or devotes what is holy, consecrating any thing. This suits better the last clause, which expresses a similar view of the results of rashly vowing.

26. (Cf. vs. 8.) **bringeth . . . over them**—The wheel was used for threshing grain. The figure denotes severity (cf. Amos 1:3).

ADAM CLARKE

20. *Whoso curseth his father.* Such persons were put to death under the law; see Exod. xxi. 17; Lev. xx. 9; and here it is said, *Their lamp shall be put out*—they shall have no posterity; God shall cut them off both root and branch.

21. *An inheritance . . . gotten hastily.* Gotten by speculation; by lucky hits; not in the fair, progressive way of traffic, in which money has its natural increase. All such inheritances are short-lived; God's blessing is not in them, because they are not the produce of industry; and they lead to idleness, pride, fraud, and knavery.

25. *Who devoureth that which is holy.* It is a sin to take that which belongs to God, His worship, or His work, and devote it to one's own use. *And after vows to make enquiry.* That is, if a man be inwardly making a rash vow, the fitness or unfitness, the necessity, expediency, and propriety of the thing should be first carefully considered. But how foolish to make the vow first, and afterwards to inquire whether it was right in the sight of God to do it!

26. *Bringeth the wheel over them.* He threshes them in his anger, as the wheel does the grain on the threshing floor.

MATTHEW HENRY

science, that noble faculty, is God's deputy in the soul; it is a candle not only lighted by him, but lighted for him. By the help of conscience we come to know ourselves. The spirit of a man has a self-consciousness (1 Cor. ii. 11); it searches into the dispositions and affections of the soul, praises what is good, condemns what is otherwise.

Verse 28

A good king must be strictly faithful to his word, must abhor all dissimulation, must support and countenance truth. He must likewise rule with clemency, and compassion. These virtues will make him easy and safe, beloved by his people.

Verse 29

Both young and old have their advantages and neither of them must despise nor envy the other. The young are strong and fit for action, able to break through difficulties. The old are grave, and fit for counsel, and, though they have not the strength that young men have, yet they have more wisdom and experience.

Verse 30

Many need severe rebukes. Some criminals must feel the rigour of the law and public justice; gentle methods will not work upon them; they must be beaten black and blue. Severe rebukes sometimes do a great deal of good, as corrosives contribute to the cure of a wound, eating out the proud flesh.

JAMIESON, FAUSSET, BROWN

27. The spirit . . . Lord—Men's minds are God's gifts, and thus able to search one another (cf. vs. 5; ch. 18:8, 17; I Cor. 2:11).

28. (Cf. ch. 3:3; 16:6, 12.)

29. Each age has its peculiar excellence (ch. 16:31).

30. blueness—lit., "joining," the process of uniting the edges of a wound throws off purulent matter. **stripes . . . belly**—So punishment provides healing of soul (ch. 18:8), by deterring from evil courses.

ADAM CLARKE

27. *The spirit of man is the candle of the Lord.* God has given to every man a mind, which He so enlightens by His own Spirit that the man knows how to distinguish good from evil; and conscience, which springs from this, searches the inmost recesses of the soul.

28. *Mercy and truth preserve the king.* These are the brightest jewels in the royal crown, and those kings who are most governed by them have the stablest government.

29. *The glory of young men is their strength.* Scarcely any young man affects to be wise, learned, etc.; but all delight to show their strength and to be reputed strong. *And the beauty of old men is the gray head.* They no longer affect strength and agility, but they affect wisdom, experience, prudent counsels, and are fond of being reputed wise, and of having respect paid to their understanding and experience.

30. *The blueness of a wound. Chabburoth,* from *chabar,* "to unite, to join together." Does it not refer to the cicatrix of a wound when, in its healing, the two lips are brought together? By this union the wound is healed.

MATTHEW HENRY

CHAPTER 21

Verse 1

Even the *hearts* of men are in God's hand. God can change men's minds, can turn them from that which they seemed most intent upon, as the husbandman, by canals and gutters, turns the water through his grounds, which does not alter the nature of the water, nor put any force upon it, any more than God's providence does upon the native freedom of man's will, but directs the course of it to serve his own purpose.

Verse 2

We are all apt to think too favourably of our own character. The proud heart is very ingenious in making that appear right to itself which is far from being so, to stop the mouth of conscience. God looks at the heart, and judges men according to their actions, their principles and intentions.

Verse 3

Many deceive themselves that, if they offer sacrifice, that will procure them a dispensation for unrighteousness. Living a good life (doing justly and loving mercy) is more pleasing to God than the most pompous devotion. Sacrifices were of divine institution, and were acceptable to God if they were offered in faith and with repentance, otherwise not, Isa. i. 11, &c. But even then moral duties were preferred before them (1 Sam. xv. 22).

Verse 4

He that carries himself insolently and scornfully towards both God and man, and that is always ploughing and plotting some mischief, is indeed a wicked man.

Verse 5

If we would live plentifully and comfortably we must be diligent in our business, and not shrink from the toil and trouble of it.Those that are rash and inconsiderate in their affairs, that are greedy of gain, by right or wrong, and make haste to be rich by unjust practices, are in the road to poverty.

Verse 6

Those that hope to enrich themselves by dishonest practices may perhaps heap up treasures, but will not meet with the satisfaction they expect. It is a *vanity tossed to and fro*; disappointment and vexation of spirit to them. They lay themselves open to the envy and ill-will of men and to the wrath of God.

Verse 7

Getting money by lying (*v.* 6) is no better than downright robbery. Cheating is stealing. Men *refuse to do judgment*; they will not render to all their due, but withhold it, and omissions make way for commissions; they come at length to robbery itself.

Verse 8

The froward man, the man of deceit, that acts by craft and trick, his way is strange, contrary to all the rules of honour and honesty. It is strange, for

JAMIESON, FAUSSET, BROWN

CHAPTER 21

Vss. 1-31. **1. rivers**—irrigating channels (Ps. 1:3), whose course was easily turned (cf. Deut. 11:10). God disposes even kings as He pleases (ch. 16:9; Ps. 33:15).

2. (Cf. ch. 14:2; 16:2-25.)

3. (Cf. Ps. 50:7-15; Isa. 1:11, 17.)

4. high look—(Cf. *Margin*: Ps. 131:1). **proud heart**—or, heart of breadth, one that is swollen (cf. Ps. 101:5). **ploughing**—better "lamp," a frequent figure for prosperity (ch. 20:20); hence joy or delight.

5. The contrast is between steady industry and rashness (cf. ch. 19:2).

6. The getting—or, what is obtained (cf. Job 7:2; Jer. 22:13, *Hebrew*). **vanity . . . to and fro**—as fleeting as chaff or stubble in the wind (cf. ch. 20:17-21; Ps. 62:10). Such gettings are unsatisfactory. **them . . . death**—act as if they did (ch. 8:36; 17:19).

7. robbery—or, destruction, especially oppression, of which they are authors. **shall destroy**—lit., "cut with a saw" (I Kings 7:9), i.e., utterly ruin them. Their sins shall be visited on them in kind. **to do judgment**—what is just and right.

8. of man—any one; his way is opposed to truth, and also estranged from it.

ADAM CLARKE

CHAPTER 21

1. *The king's heart is in the hand of the Lord.* The Lord is the only Ruler of princes. He alone can govern and direct their counsels. But there is an allusion here to the Eastern method of watering their lands. Several canals are dug from one stream; and by opening a particular sluice, the husbandman can direct a stream to whatever part he pleases. So the king's heart, wherever it turns; i.e., to whomsoever he is disposed to show favor.

3. *To do justice and judgment.* The words of Samuel to Saul. See 1 Sam. xv. 23.

4. *An high look.* The evidence of pride, self-conceit, and vanity. *A proud heart,* from which the high look, etc., come. *And the plowing.* "The lamp," the prosperity and posterity of the wicked; *is sin*—it is evil in the seed, and evil in the root, evil in the branch, and evil in the fruit.

MATTHEW HENRY

you know not when you have him. Men that are pure are proved to be such by their work, for it *is right*, it is just and regular; and they are accepted of God and approved of men.

Verse 9

What a great affliction it is to a man to have a brawling scolding woman for his wife, who is fretful to herself and furious to her children and servants. If a man has a wide house, spacious and pompous, this will embitter the comfort of it to him. He finds it his best way to retire *into a corner of the house-top*, and sit alone there, out of the hearing of her clamour.

Verse 10

A very wicked man desires that evil may be done and that he may have the pleasure of having a hand in it. *His neighbour*, his friend, his nearest relation, cannot gain from him the least kindness.

Verse 11

Let the law be executed upon a scorner, and even he that is simple will be awakened and alarmed by it, and will discern the evil of sin. *When the wise is instructed* by the preaching of the word *he* (not only the wise himself, but the simple that stands by) *receives knowledge*.

Verse 12

The righteous man (the judge or magistrate) *examines the house of the wicked*, searches it for arms or for stolen goods, makes a diligent enquiry concerning his family, that he may *overthrow the wicked for their wickedness* and prevent their doing any further mischief.

Verse 13

An uncharitable man *stops his ears at the cry of the poor*, turns them away from his door, and *shuts up the bowels of his compassion*, Acts vii. 57. He shall himself be reduced to straits, which will make him *cry*. Men will not hear him, but reward him as he has rewarded others. God will not hear him; for he that *showed no mercy shall have judgment without mercy* (James ii. 13).

Verse 14

A handsome present, prudently managed, will turn away some men's wrath when it seemed implacable. If it be a bribe to pervert justice, that is so scandalous that those who are fond of it are shamed of it.

Verse 15

It is a pleasure and satisfaction to good men to see justice administered by the government they live under, and also to practise it themselves. It is a terror to wicked men to see the laws put in execution against vice and profaneness.

Verse 16

The sinner *wanders out of the way of understanding*, and when once he has left that good way he wanders endlessly. The way of religion is *the way of understanding*; those that are not truly pious are not truly intelligent; and they go astray like lost sheep.

Verse 17

An epicure *loves pleasure*. God allows us to use the delights of sense soberly and temperately, *wine to make glad the heart*, and *oil to make the face to shine* and beautify the countenance; but he that sets his heart upon them is impatient of everything that crosses him in his pleasures. *He shall be a poor man* who once could not live without dainties and varieties. Many a beau becomes a beggar.

Verse 18

The wicked, that are the troublers of a land, ought to be punished, for the preventing of those national judgments which otherwise will be inflicted. God will rather leave many wicked people to be cut off than abandon his own people.

Verse 19

Unbridled passions embitter and spoil the comfort of all relations. Those cannot dwell in peace and happiness that cannot dwell in peace and love.

Verse 20

Those that are wise will increase what they have and live plentifully; their wisdom will teach them to proportion their expenses to their income and to lay up a good stock of all things convenient, particularly of *oil*, one of the staple commodities of Canaan. It is better to have an old-fashioned house, and have it well furnished, than a fine modern one, with sorry housekeeping.

Verse 21

We must do justly and love mercy, and, though

JAMIESON, FAUSSET, BROWN

The pure proves himself such by his right conduct.

9. corner—a turret or arbor on the roof. **brawling**—or contentious. **wide house**—lit., "house of fellowship," large enough for several families.

10. So strongly does he desire to do evil (Psalm 10:3; Eccles. 8:11), that he will not even spare his friend if in his way.

11. (Cf. ch. 19:25.) That which the simple learn by the terrors of punishment, the wise learn by teaching.

12. (Cf. Psalm 37:35-38; 73:17, 20.) **house**—family or interests. **overthroweth**—either supply "God" (cf. ch. 10:24), or the word is used impersonally.

13. The principles of retribution, often taught (cf. Ps. 18:26; Matt. 7:1-12).

14. The effect of bribery (ch. 17:23) is enhanced by secrecy, as the bribed person does not wish his motives made known.

15. But the just love right and need no bribes. The wicked at last meet destruction, though for a time happy in concealing corruption.

16. the way of understanding—(Cf. ch. 12:26; 14:22). **remain**—i.e., rest as at a journey's end; death will be his unchanging home.

17. Costly luxuries impoverish.

18. (Cf. ch. 11:8.) By suffering what they had devised for the righteous, or brought on them, the wicked became their ransom, in the usual sense of substitutes (cf. Josh. 7:26; Esther 7:9).

19. (Cf. vs. 9.) **wilderness**—pasture, though uninhabitable ground (Ps. 65:12).

20. The wise, by diligence and care, lay up and increase wealth, while fools "spend" lit., "swallow it up," greedily.

ADAM CLARKE

9. *In a corner of the house top.* A shed raised on the flat roof; *a wide house; beith chaber*, "a house of fellowship"; what we should call a lodging house, or a house occupied by several families.

12. *The righteous man wisely considereth.* This verse is understood as implying the pious concern of a righteous man for a wicked family, whom he endeavors by his instructions to bring into the way of knowledge and peace.

JOSEPH PARKER:

Verse 12. The "righteous man" should rather be the "righteous one," and by that one we are to understand the Almighty himself. The text would then read: "The righteous God marks the house of the wicked, and God throws down the wicked for their destruction." Here is the solemn principle of judgment applied to individual life and individual habitation. The picture is that of God seated in the heavens, and marking the house of the wicked man, noting all that goes on under its roof, marking all the history that is enclosed by its walls, and at the right time bringing upon the roof of the wicked man's house the rod of lightning, so that it is cleft in twain, and the wicked are overthrown even in the midst of their orgies and the very madness of their delight. For a long time the house of the wicked seems to be secure; every window is aflame with a rosy light through the long night time, and through the open door are heard noises of music and of dancing; the rejoicing is for a time only; God is watching the whole process, and at the right moment he will overthrow the house and plough up its foundations. Better to be in a little house of honesty and righteousness and truth than in a great palace of dishonesty and unrighteousness and falsehood. He that is righteous lives in a rock that cannot be overthrown, a pavilion within which there can be no fear of the violence of raging storms. How is this to be obtained? What is the rock within which the heart of man can safely live? Has it been named? Has it not been called the Rock of Ages? And have not they who have fled to it been assured day by day of ever-increasing security? That rock is open to us all—the very granite bears upon it an inscription indicative of hospitality and welcome. Blessed are they who flee to it that they may find rest and sustenance.

—*The People's Bible*

MATTHEW HENRY

we cannot attain to perfection, yet it will be a comfort to us if we aim at it. Those that do *follow after righteousness* shall *find righteousness*.

Verse 22

Those that have wisdom, though they are so modest as not to promise much, often perform great things, even against those that are so confident of their strength. A stratagem, well managed, may effectually *scale the city of the mighty and cast down the strength* it had such a confidence in. *A wise man* will gain upon the affections of people and conquer them by strength of reason, which is a more noble conquest than that obtained by strength of arms.

Verse 23

Those that would keep their souls must keep a watch before the door of their lips, must *keep the mouth* by temperance, that nothing be eaten or drunk to excess; they must *keep the tongue* also, that no forbidden word go out of the door of the lips, no corrupt communication. Keep thy heart, and that will keep thy tongue from sin; keep thy tongue, and that will keep thy heart from trouble.

Verse 24

Most of the wrath that inflames the spirits and societies of men is *proud wrath*. Men cannot bear the least slight, nor in anything to be crossed or contradicted, but they are in a heat, immediately. It makes them scornful when they are angry.

Verses 25–26

The slothful are as fit for labour as other men. They are enemies to themselves; for their slothfulness starves them, their desires at the same time stab them. Though their hands refuse to labour, their hearts cease not to covet riches, and pleasures, and honours. They expect everybody should do for them. Many that must have money with which to make provision for the flesh, and would not be at pains to get it honestly, have turned highwaymen, and that has killed them. The righteous and industrious have their desires satisfied, and enjoy not only that satisfaction, but the further satisfaction of doing good to others. The slothful are always gaping to receive, *but the righteous* are always contriving to give.

Verse 27

Sacrifices were of divine institution; and when they were offered in faith, and with repentance and reformation, God was well-pleased. They were an *abomination* when they were brought by wicked men, who did not repent of their sins, mortify their lusts, and amend their lives. *Much more when* they were brought with *wicked minds*, when their sacrifices were made serviceable to their wickedness. When men make a show of devotion, when holiness is pretended, but some wickedness intended, then the performance is an abomination, Isa. lxvi. 5.

Verse 28

A man may tell a lie perhaps in his haste; but he that gives in a false testimony does it with deliberation and solemnity, and it cannot but be a presumptuous sin. The vengeance he imprecated upon himself, when he took the false oath, will come upon him. He *who hears* (that is, obeys) the command of God, which is to *speak every man truth with his neighbour*, testifies nothing but what he knows to be true, *speaks constantly* (that is, consistently with himself).

Verse 29

A wicked man *hardens his face*—brazens it, that he may not blush—steels it, that he may not tremble when he commits the greatest crimes; he bids defiance to the terrors of the law and the checks of his own conscience. A good man does not say, What *would* I do? but, What *should* I do? And so he *directs his way* by a safe and certain rule.

Verse 30

There can be no success against God. Though men think they have *wisdom*, and *understanding*, and *counsel*, the best politics and politicians, on their side, yet if it be *against the Lord*, it cannot prosper long. There can be no success without God. Be the cause ever so good and the means of carrying it on ever so probable, still men must acknowledge God and take him along with them. Means indeed are to be used; *the horse* must be *prepared against the day of battle*, and the foot too. *But*, after all, *safety* and salvation *are of the Lord*; he can save without armies, but armies cannot save without him.

JAMIESON, FAUSSET, BROWN

21. He who tries to act justly and kindly (Ps. 34:14) will prosper and obtain justice and honor.

22. "Wisdom is better than strength" (Eccles. 7:19; 9:15). **strength . . . thereof**—that in which they confide.

23. (Cf. ch. 13:2, 3; Jas. 3:6-10.)

24. The reproachful name is deserved by those who treat others with anger and contempt.

25. desire—i.e. of ease and idleness brings him to starvation. **26.** The sin of covetousness marks the sluggard, as the virtue of benevolence the righteous.

27. God regards the heart, and hypocrisy is more odious than open inconsistency. **wicked mind—or design** (ch. 1:4).

28. (Cf. ch. 19:5.) **that heareth**—or heeds instruction, and so grows wise. **speaketh constantly**—or sincerely (cf. Hab. 1:5), and hence is believed (ch. 12:19; Jas. 1:19).

29. hardeneth his face—is obstinate. **directeth . . . way**—considers it, and acts advisedly.

30, 31. Men's best devices and reliances are vain compared with God's, or without His aid (ch. 19:21; Ps. 20:7; 33:17).

ADAM CLARKE

JOHN GILL:

Verse 21. "He that followeth after righteousness and mercy" is eager, diligent, and fervent in his pursuit of these things: "after righteousness"; not a legal righteousness, such as the Jews followed after, but did not attain to; because they sought it not by faith, but as it were by the works of the law (Rom. 9:31, 32), by which there is no righteousness, or justification before God: but an evangelical righteousness, the righteousness of Christ (Isa. 51:1). To follow after it is to seek, desire, and thirst after it (Matt. 5:6—6:32), which supposes a want of righteousness, a sense of that want; a view of a righteousness apart from themselves, even in Christ; a love and liking of it, and therefore following after it; it being pure, perfect, agreeable to the law and justice of God, which justifies now, and will answer for them in time to come. And such follow after "mercy" or "grace"; seeing themselves miserable by sin, and having no merit of their own, apply to God for pardoning grace and mercy; and seek for righteousness in a way of grace, as a free gift: it may be understood, in consequence of the former, of a diligent and eager performance of works of righteousness and mercy, and an earnest desire after both. And such a man "findeth life, righteousness, and honor"; which is more than he is said to follow after: spiritual "life," which he has from Christ by his Spirit, and in whom all the blessings of life come; who has it in his hands to give, and does give it to all his people; "righteousness" also he finds, not in himself, but in Christ; and an excellent finding this is; a robe of righteousness, which he lays hold upon, puts on, and rejoices in: and likewise "honor," through relation to God and Christ; through grace received from them; by enjoying the presence of them, and being made a king and priest to God; and hereafter will be placed at Christ's right hand, inherit the kingdom of glory, sit on the same throne with Christ, and wear the crown of life and righteousness.

Verse 22. "A wise man scaleth the city of the mighty." Which makes good what is elsewhere said, that "wisdom is better than strength" (Eccles. 9:16); and sometimes more is done by prudence and wisdom, by art and cunning, by schemes and stratagems, than by power and force; especially in military affairs, and particularly in besieging and taking fortified cities; when one wise man, by his wisdom, may so order and manage things, as to be able, with a few under his command, to mount the walls of a city and take it, though defended by a mighty garrison in it. This may be applied to our Lord Jesus Christ entering into the city of a man's heart, possessed by the strong man armed; overcoming him, taking from him his armor and dividing his spoil (Luke 11:21, 22). "And casteth down the strength of the confidence thereof"; the strong walls, bulwarks, and such fortifications, in which the mighty in the city placed their confidence: and the like does Christ, when he enters into the heart of a sinner by his word and Spirit; he destroys all its former strong confidences, and brings it into subjection to himself (2 Cor. 10:4, 5).—*Gill's Commentary*

MATTHEW HENRY

CHAPTER 22

Verse 1

We should be more careful to do that by which we may get and keep a good name than that by which we may raise and increase a great estate. By great riches we may relieve the bodily wants of others, but by a good name we may recommend religion to them. To be well beloved, to have an interest in the esteem and affections of all about us; this is better *than silver and gold.*

Verse 2

The greatest man in the world must acknowledge God to be his Maker, and is under the same obligations to be subject to him that the meanest is; and the poorest has the honour to be the work of God's hands as much as the greatest. *Rich and poor meet together* at the bar of God's justice, all guilty before God; and they meet at the throne of God's grace; the poor are as welcome there as the rich. There is the same Christ, the same scripture, the same Spirit, the same covenant of promises, for them both. There is the same heaven for poor saints that there is for rich.

Verse 3

A prudent man will *foresee an evil* before it comes and stand on his guard. When the clouds are gathering for a storm he takes the warning, and flies to the name of the Lord as his strong tower. *The simple*, who believe every word that flatters them, will believe none that warns them, and so they *pass on and are punished.* See an instance of both these, Exod. ix. 20, 21.

Verse 4

Religion does very much consist—in *humility and the fear of the Lord*; that is, walking humbly with God. What is to be gotten by it—*riches, and honour*, and comfort, *and* long *life*, in this world, as far as God sees good, and the privileges of the covenant of grace, *and* eternal *life* at last.

Verse 5

In the way of the froward, that crooked way, *which* is contrary to the will and word of God, *thorns and snares are* found, thorns of grief for past sins and snares entangling them in further sin. *He that keeps his soul*, that watches carefully over his own heart and ways, is *far from* those *thorns and snares*, for his way is both plain and pleasant.

Verse 6

Train up children in that learning age. *Catechise* them; initiate them. *Train* them as soldiers, who are taught to handle their arms, keep rank, and observe the word of command. *Train* them up *in the way they should go*, the way in which, if you love them, you would have them go. *Train up a child according as he is capable* (so some take it), with a gentle hand, as nurses feed children, little and often, Deut. vi. 7. Good impressions made upon them then will abide upon them all their days.

Verse 7

The rich rule over the poor, and too often with pride and rigour, unlike to God, who, though he be great, yet despises not any. *The borrower is servant to the lender*, and must sometimes beg, *Have patience with me.* Some sell their liberty to gratify their luxury.

Verse 8

Ill-gotten gains will not prosper. *He that sows iniquity*, that does an unjust thing in hopes to get by it, *shall reap vanity.* If the rod of authority turn into a *rod of anger*, if men rule by passion instead of prudence, instead of the public welfare, their power shall not bear them out, Isa. x. 24, 25.

Verse 9

A charitable man has a *bountiful eye*, opposed to the evil eye (*ch.* xxiii. 6) and the same with the *single eye* (Matt. vi. 22),—an eye that seeks out objects of charity, that, upon the sight of one in want and misery, affects the heart with compassion,—an eye that with the alms gives a pleasant look, which makes the alms doubly acceptable. He has also a liberal hand: *He gives of his bread*, the bread appointed for his own eating. God himself will bless him.

Verse 10

The scorner sows discord. Much of the *strife and contention* which disturb the peace is owing to *the evil interpreter* (as some read it), that construes everything into the worst, and takes a pride in bantering all mankind. Those that would secure the peace must exclude the scorner.

JAMIESON, FAUSSET, BROWN

CHAPTER 22

Vss. 1-29. **1. A good name**—(Job 30:8, *Hebrew*); "good" is supplied here from Ecclesiastes 7:1. **loving favour**—kind regard, i.e., of the wise and good.

2. Before God all are on the same footing (ch. 14:31; 17:5).

3. are punished—i.e., for their temerity; for the **evil** is not necessarily punitive, as the **prudent** might otherwise be its objects.

4. humility and the fear of the Lord—are in apposition; one produces the other. On the results, cf. ch. 3:16; 8:18.

5. he that . . . them—Those who properly watch over their own souls are thus preserved from the dangers which attend the way of perverse men (ch. 16:17).

6. Train—initiate, or early instruct. **the way**—lit., "his way," that selected for him in which he should go; for early training secures habitual walking in it.

7. The influence of wealth sets aside moral distinctions is implied, and, of course, disapproved (cf. ch. 19:6; 21:14, etc.).

8. (Cf. ch. 11:18; Ps. 109:16-20; Gal. 6:7, 8.) **the rod . . . fail**—His power to do evil will be destroyed.

9. a bountiful eye—i.e., a beneficent disposition. **for he giveth . . . poor**—His acts prove it.

10. Cast out—or drive away. Scorners foster strife by taunts and revilings.

ADAM CLARKE

CHAPTER 22

1. *A good name. Shem*, a "name," put for reputation, credit, fame. Used nearly in the same way that we use it: "He has got a name."

2. *The rich and poor meet together. Ashir*, the "opulent," whether in money, land, or property; *rash*, the man that is destitute of these, and lives by his labor, whether a handicraftsman, or one that tills the ground. In the order of God, the rich and the poor live together, and are mutually helpful to each other. Without the poor, the rich could not be supplied with the articles which they consume; for the poor include all the laboring classes of society: and without the rich, the poor could get no vent for the produce of their labor, nor, in many cases, labor itself.

5. *Thorns and snares.* Various difficulties, trials, and sufferings.

6. *Train up a child in the way he should go.* The Hebrew of this clause is curious: "Initiate the child at the opening (the mouth) of his path." *Chanac*, which we translate *train up* or "initiate," signifies also "dedicate"; and is often used for the consecrating anything, house, or person, to the service of God. Dedicate, therefore in the first instance, your child to God; and nurse, teach, and discipline him as God's child, whom He has entrusted to your care.

MATTHEW HENRY

Verse 11

A complete gentleman, fit to be employed in public business, must be an honest man, a man *that loves pureness of heart* and hates all impurity, free from all deceit, all selfishness and sinister designs, that is just and delights in keeping his own conscience clean. He must also speak with a good grace, not to daub and flatter, but to deliver his sentiments decently, in language as clean as his spirit. *The king*, if he be wise and good, and understand his own and his people's interest, *will be his friend.*

Verse 12

God takes special care to *preserve knowledge*, that is, to keep up religion in the world by keeping up among men the knowledge of himself and of good and evil. He preserves *men of knowledge*, wise and good men (2 Chron. xvi. 9), particularly faithful witnesses, who speak what they know. *He overthrows the words of the transgressor*, and *preserves knowledge* in spite of him.

Verse 13

Many frighten themselves from real duties by imaginary difficulties: *The slothful man* has work to do *without* in the fields, but he fancies *there is a lion* there. He talks of *a lion without*, but considers not his real danger from the devil, that *roaring lion*, which is in bed with him, and from his own slothfulness, which kills him.

Verse 14

This is designed to warn all young men against the lusts of uncleanness. As they regard the welfare of their souls, let them take heed of *the mouth of strange women*, of the kisses of their lips (*ch.* vii. 13), their charms and enticements. Dread them; have nothing to do with them. Those who abandon themselves to that sin are abandoned of God: who takes off the bridle of his restraining grace.

Verse 15

Sin is *foolishness*; it is contrary both to our reason and to our true interest. It *is in the heart*; there is an inward inclination to sin, to speak and act foolishly. It is not only *found* there, but it is *bound* there; it is annexed to the heart (so some); vicious dispositions cleave closely to the soul. Correction is necessary to the cure of it. There must be strictness and severity, which will cause grief. Children need to be corrected, and kept under discipline, by their parents; and we all need to be corrected by our heavenly Father (Heb. xii. 6, 7), and under the correction we must kiss the rod.

Verse 16

Rich men sometimes *oppress the poor and give to the rich*. They will not in charity relieve the poor, but they will make presents *to the rich*, and give them great entertainments, either in vain-glory, that they may look great, or in policy, that they may receive it again with advantage. Such *shall surely come to want*. Many have been beggared by a foolish generosity, but never any by a prudent charity. Christ bids us invite the poor, Luke xiv. 12, 13.

Verses 17–21

Solomon here changes his style. Since the beginning of *ch.* x, he had laid down doctrinal truths, leaving us to make the application as we went along; but here, to the end of *ch.* xxiv, he directs his speech to his son, his pupil, his reader, his hearer, speaking as to a particular person. Hitherto, for the most part, his sense was comprised in one verse, but here usually it is drawn out further. Here is,

I. An earnest exhortation to get wisdom and grace, by attending to *the words of the wise* men, both written and preached. To these *words*, to this *knowledge*, the ear must be *bowed down* and the *heart applied* by faith, and love, and close consideration. The ear will not serve without the heart.

II. Arguments to enforce this exhortation. Consider,

1. The worth and weight of the things themselves which Solomon in this book gives us. They are not trivial, jocular proverbs. They are *excellent things*, which concern the glory of God, the holiness and happiness of our souls, the welfare of mankind, *princely things* (so the word is), fit for kings to speak and senates to hear.

2. The clearness of these things and the directing of them to us in particular. The emphasis here is that they are *made known to thee, even to thee*, and *written to thee*, as if it were a letter directed to thee by name. It is suited to thee and to thy case. If we make use of them in our discourse, they will be very becoming. *They shall be fitted in thy lips.*

JAMIESON, FAUSSET, BROWN

11. (Cf. *Margin.*) **pureness of heart**—and gentle, kind words win favor, even from kings.

12. preserve—or guard. **knowledge**—its principles and possessors. **overthroweth**—utterly confounds and destroys the wicked.

13. Frivolous excuses satisfy the indolent man's conscience.

14. The mouth—or flattering speeches (ch. 5:3; 7:5) ensnare man, *as pits*, beasts. God makes their own sin their punishment.

15. is bound—or firmly fixed. Chastisement deters from crime and so leads to reformation of principle.

16. These two vices pertain to the same selfish feeling. Both are deservedly odious to God and incur punishment.

17. Here begins another division of the book, marked by those encouragements to the pursuit of wisdom, which are found in the earlier chapters. It will be observed that from vs. 22 to ch. 24:12, the proverbs are generally expressed in two verses instead of one

18. These lessons must be laid up in the mind, and **fitted,** or better, fixed in the lips so as to be ever ready.

19. That . . . Lord—This is the design of the instruction. **20. excellent things**—or probably of former times. **counsels and knowledge**—both advice and instruction.

ADAM CLARKE

CHARLES H. SPURGEON:

Verse 13. This slothful man seems to cherish that one dread of his about the lions as if it were his favorite aversion, and he felt it to be too much trouble to invent another excuse. Perhaps he hugs it to his soul all the more because it is a home-born fear, conjured up by his own imagination; and as mothers are said to love their weakest children best, so is he fondest of this most imbecile of excuses: at any rate, it serves him for a passable excuse for laziness, and that is what he wants. If you can get the king of beasts to apologize for your idleness there is a sort of royalty about your pretences: he hopes his sloth will appear the less disgraceful if he can paint a lion rampant upon its shield.

—*The Treasury of the Old Testament*

14. *The mouth of strange women is a deep pit.* In chap. xxiii. 27, he says, "A whore is a deep ditch; and a strange woman is a narrow pit."

17. *Bow down thine ear.* From this to the end of v. 21 are contained, not proverbs, but directions how to profit by that which wisdom has already delivered; the nature of the instruction, and the end for which it was given.

MATTHEW HENRY

3. The advantage designed us by them. The *excellent things* which God has *written to* us are not like the commands which the master gives his servant, which are all intended for the benefit of the master, but like those which the master gives his scholar, which are all intended for the benefit of the scholar. We cannot trust in God except in the way of duty; we are *therefore* taught our duty, that we may have reason to trust in God. It is a desirable thing to know, not only *the words of truth*, but *the certainty of* them, that our faith may be intelligent and rational, and may grow up to a full assurance. *If any man do his will, he shall know* for certain that the doctrine is of God, John vii. 17. Knowledge is given us to do good with, that others may light their candle at our lamp, and that we may in our place serve our generation according to the will of God.

Verses 22–23

After this solemn preface, one would have expected something new and surprising; but no; here is a plain but very needful caution against the inhuman practice of oppressing poor people. The sin itself is *robbing the poor* and making them poorer. It is bad to rob any man, but most absurd to rob the poor, whom we should relieve. *To oppress the afflicted*, and so to add affliction to them is not only a base and cowardly thing, to take advantage against a man because he is helpless, but it is unnatural, and proves men worse than beasts. He that robs and oppresses the poor does it at his peril. The oppressed will find God their powerful patron.

Verse 24

A good caution against being intimate with a passionate man. A man who is easily provoked, touchy, and apt to resent affronts, who, when he is in a passion, grows outrageous, is not fit to be made a friend, for he will be angry with us, and he will expect that we should, like him, be angry with others, and that will be our sin. It is dangerous conversing with those that throw about the sparks of their passion, "Lest thou imitate him, to humour him, and so contract an ill habit."

Verses 26–27

We must not cheat people of their money, by *striking hands* ourselves, or *becoming surety for others*, when we *have not to pay*. If a man is disabled to pay his debts, he ought to be pitied and helped; but he that takes up money or goods himself, or is bound for another, when he knows that he has not wherewithal to pay, does in effect pick his neighbour's pocket, and though, in all cases, compassion is to be used, yet he may thank himself if the law have its course and his *bed* be *taken from under him*, which might not be taken for a pledge to secure a debt, Exod. xxii. 26, 27. For, if a man appeared to be so poor that he had nothing else to give for security, he ought to be relieved, but, for the recovery of a debt, it seems it might be taken by the *strict operation of law*.

Verse 28

The land-marks, or meer-stones, are standing witnesses to every man's right; let not those be removed quite away, for thence come wars, and fightings, and endless disputes; let them not be removed so as to take from thy neighbour's lot to thy own, for that is downright robbing him and entailing the fraud upon posterity. Deference is to be paid, in all civil matters, to usages that have prevailed time out of mind.

Verse 29

A truly ingenious industrious man is here commended who lays out himself to get business, though it be but in a very low and narrow sphere. A man of despatch knows how to bring a deal of business into a little compass. Though now he *stands before mean men*, is employed by them, yet he will rise, and is likely enough to *stand before kings*, as an ambassador or prime-minister.

CHAPTER 23

Verses 1–3

We are in most danger of falling into this sin: "When thou hast great plenty before thee, varieties and dainties, such a table spread as thou hast seldom seen." The temptation may be stronger to one that is not used to such entertainments. We must alarm ourselves into temperance and moderation: "*Put a knife to thy throat*, that is, restrain thyself, as it were with a sword hanging over thy head. But that is

JAMIESON, FAUSSET, BROWN

21. Specially he desires to secure accuracy, so that his pupil may teach others.

22, 23. Here follow ten precepts of two verses each. Though men fail to defend the poor, God will (ch. 17:5; Ps. 12:5). **in the gate**—place of public gathering (Job 5:4; Ps. 69:12).

24, 25. (Cf. ch. 2:12-15; 4:14.) **a snare . . . soul**—The unsuspecting are often misled by bad company.

26, 27. (Cf. ch. 6:1; 17:18.) **should he take . . .**—(i.e., the creditor.

28. (Cf. ch. 23:10.) Do not entrench on others (Deut. 19:14; 27:17).

29. Success rewards diligence (ch. 10:4; 21:5).

CHAPTER 23

Vss. 1-35. **1-3.** Avoid the dangers of gluttony. **put a knife**—an Eastern figure for putting restraint on the appetite. **are deceitful meat**—though well tasted, injurious.

ADAM CLARKE

JOHN GILL:

Verse 23. "For the Lord will plead their cause." If counselors at the bar will not, he will; if judges on the bench will not do them justice, he will; he will judge the poor of the people; he will plead their cause, and plead it thoroughly, till he has brought forth judgment unto victory: woe to the man against whom Jehovah pleads; happy the poor on whose side he is; for their Redeemer is mighty, the Lord of hosts is his name (Ps. 72:4; Jer. 50:24). "And spoil the soul of those that spoiled them"; they could only spoil the poor of their goods, but the Lord can and will spoil and destroy the souls of the spoilers in hell: or, "spoil them that spoiled their soul or life"; that is, who spoiled them of their goods, and took away that small pittance they had, which was their life or livelihood; they shall be spoiled themselves that spoil others; the same measure they have meted out shall be measured out to them again; God will destroy them and destroy the earth, even antichrist and his followers, the oppressors of Christ's poor on earth (Rev. 11:18).—*Gill's Commentary*

24. *Make no friendship with an angry man.* Spirit has a wonderful and unaccountable influence upon spirit. From those with whom we associate we acquire habits, and learn their ways, imbibe their spirit, show their tempers, and walk in their steps. We cannot be too choice of our company, for we may soon learn ways that will be a snare to our souls.

27. *If thou hast nothing to pay.* Should any man give security for more than he is worth? If he does, is it not a fraud on the very face of the transaction?

28. *Remove not the ancient landmark.* Do not take the advantage, in ploughing or breaking up a field contiguous to that of your neighbor, to set the dividing stones farther into his field that you may enlarge your own. Let all ancient divisions, and the usages connected with them, be held sacred. Bring in no new dogmas, nor rites, nor ceremonies, into religion, or the worship of God, that are not clearly laid down in the sacred writings.

CHAPTER 23

1. *When thou sittest to eat with a ruler.* When invited to the table of your betters, eat moderately. Do not appear as if half starved at home. Eat not of delicacies to which you are not accustomed; they are deceitful meat; they please, but they do not profit. They are pleasant to the sight, the taste, and the smell; but they are injurious to health.

MATTHEW HENRY

not enough: lay the axe to the root; mortify that appetite which has such a power over thee."

Verses 4–5

Some are given to appetite (*v.* 2), others to covetousness. We must endeavour to live comfortably, and provide for our children and families, but we must not seek great things. Be not of those that will be rich, that design it as their highest end, 1 Tim. vi. 9. What thou hast, or doest, be master of it, and not a slave to it as those that *rise up early, sit up late,* and *eat the bread of carefulness,* and all to be rich. The things of this world are a show, a shadow, a sham upon the soul that trusts to them. Wilt thou do a thing so absurd in itself? What thou, a reasonable creature, wilt thou dote upon shadows? Riches are very uncertain things; *They make themselves wings, and fly away.* The wings they fly away upon are of their own making. They have in themselves the principles of their own corruption. They go irresistibly and irrecoverably, as *an eagle towards heaven,* that flies strongly, and flies out of sight and out of call (there is no bringing her back); thus do riches leave men in grief and vexation if they set their hearts upon them.

Verses 6–8

There are those that pretend to bid their friends welcome that are not hearty and sincere in it. They have a fair tongue, and know what they should say: *Eat and drink, saith he,* because it is expected that the master of the feast should so compliment his guests; but they have *an evil eye,* and grudge their guests every bit they eat. If a man be so mean that he cannot find in his heart to bid his friends welcome to what he has, he ought not to add to that the guilt of dissimulation by inviting them. "*Eat not thou the bread* of such a man; let him keep it to himself. Do not sponge upon those that are bountiful, but especially scorn to be beholden to those that are paltry and not sincere."

Verse 9

It is our duty to take all fit occasions to speak of divine things; but, some will make a jest of everything. A wise man is advised not to *speak in the ears* of such fools. If what a wise man says in his wisdom will not be heard, let him hold his peace, and try whether the wisdom of that will be regarded.

Verses 10–11

The fatherless are taken under God's special protection. He is *their Redeemer*, their *Goël,* their near kinsman, that will take their part and stand up for them. Every man therefore must be careful not to injure them in anything, or to invade their rights, either by a clandestine removal of the old landmarks or by a forcible entry into their fields.

Verses 12–16

A parent should persuade his child to attend to the words of knowledge so that he may learn what is his duty. A tender parent finds it hard to administer correction but, for his child's good, he beats *him with the rod,* gives him a gentle correction, the *stripes of the sons of men,* not such as we give to beasts. The rod will not kill him; it will prevent his killing himself by those vicious courses which the rod will restrain him from. It is to be hoped that those will do *right things* when they grow up who learn to *speak right things* when they are young. "Children, if you be wise and good, devout and conscientious, we shall think our labour in instructing you well bestowed. We shall rejoice in hope that you will be a credit and comfort to us, if we should live to be old, that you will bear up the name of Christ in your generation, that you will live comfortably in this world and happily in another."

Verses 17–18

"*Let not thy heart envy sinners;* do not grudge them either the liberty they take to sin or the success they have in sin; it will cost them dearly and they are to be pitied rather than envied." We must be in the fear of the Lord, taking a pleasure in contemplating God's glory and complying with his will. *There will be an end of the prosperity of the wicked,* therefore *do not envy them* (Ps. lxxiii. 17); there will be an end of thy afflictions, *perfect love will shortly cast out fear,* and *thy expectation* of the reward not only will be *not cut off,* or disappointed, but it will be infinitely outdone.

Verses 19–28

"*Hearken unto thy father who begat thee,* and who therefore has an authority over thee and an affection for thee, and can have no other design than thy own

JAMIESON, FAUSSET, BROWN

4, 5. (Cf. I Tim. 6:9, 10.) **thine own wisdom**—which regards riches intrinsically as a blessing. **Wilt . . . eyes**—As the eyes fly after or seek riches, they are not, i.e., either become transitory or unsatisfying; fully expressed by their flying away.

6-8. Beware of deceitful men, whose courtesies even you will repent of having accepted. **evil eye**—or purpose (ch. 22:9; Deut. 15:9; Matt. 6:23). **The morsel . . . words**—i.e., disgusted with his true character, all pleasant intercourse will be destroyed.

9. (Cf. ch. 9:8.) "Cast not your pearls . . . " (Matt. 7:6).

10, 11. (Cf. ch. 22:22, 23.) **redeemer**—or avenger (Lev. 25:25, 26; Num. 35:12), hence advocate (Job. 19:25). **plead . . . thee**—(Cf. Job 31:21; Ps. 35:1; 68:5).

12. Here begins another series of precepts. **13, 14.** While there is little danger that the use of the "divine ordinance of the rod" will produce bodily harm, there is great hope of spiritual good. **15. 16.** The pleasure afforded the teacher by the pupil's progress is a motive to diligence. **my reins**—(Cf. Ps. 7:9.)

17, 18. (Cf. *Margin.*) The prosperity of the wicked is short. **an end**—or hereafter, another time, when apparent inequalities shall be adjusted (cf. Ps. 37:28-38).

19-21. guide . . . way—or direct thy thoughts to a right course of conduct (cf. ch. 4:4; 9:6).

ADAM CLARKE

4. *Labour not to be rich.* Let not this be your object. *Cease from thine own wisdom.* Your own "understanding" or "prudence."

6. *Of him that hath an evil eye.* Never eat with a covetous or stingy man; if he entertains you at his own expense, he grudges every morsel you put in your mouth. This is well-marked by the wise man in the next verse: "Eat and drink, saith he . . . but his heart is not with thee."

8. *The morsel which thou hast eaten.* On reflection you will even blame yourself for having accepted his invitation.

10. *Remove not the old landmark.* See the preceding chapter, v. 28. *Enter not into the fields of the fatherless.* Take nothing that belongs to an orphan. The heaviest curse of God will fall upon them that do so.

11. *For their redeemer is mighty. Goalam,* their "kinsman." The word means the person who has a right, being next in blood, to redeem a field or estate, alienated from the family.

14. *Thou shalt beat him with the rod.* A proper correction of children was a favorite point of discipline with Solomon. We have already seen how forcibly he speaks on this subject.

18. *Surely there is an end.* There is another life; and *thine expectation* of the enjoyment of a blessed immortality *shall not be cut off.*

MATTHEW HENRY

good." We ought to *give reverence to the fathers of our flesh*, who were the instruments of our being; much more ought we to obey and be in subjection to the *Father of our spirits*, who made us and is the author of our being. And since *the mother* also, from a sense of duty to God and from love to her child, gives him good instructions, let him not *despise her*, nor her advice, *when she is old. Buy the truth and sell it not* (*v.* 23). Truth is that by which the heart must be guided and governed, for without truth there is no goodness. We must buy it whatever it costs us, we shall not repent the bargain. Riches should be employed for the getting of knowledge, rather than knowledge for the getting of riches. When we are at pains in searching after truth, then we buy it. *Heaven concedes everything to the laborious.* We must not sell it. Do not part with it for pleasures, honours, riches, anything in this world. God, in this exhortation, speaks to us as unto children: "Son, Daughter, *Give me thy heart." Thou shalt love the Lord thy God with all thy heart.* To this call we must readily answer, "*My father, take my heart*, such as it is, and make it such as it should be; take possession of it, and set up thy throne in it." *Be not a wine-bibber. Be not an* excessive *eater of flesh.* Intemperance must be avoided in meat as well as drink. He fetches an argument against this sin from the expensiveness of it. *The drunkard and the glutton* hate to be reformed, though they are told they *shall come to poverty.* Drunkenness is the cause of *drowsiness*; it stupefies men, and makes them inattentive to business, and then all goes to wreck and ruin. Whoredom is a sin which bewitches men to their ruin: *The adulteress lies in wait as a robber*, pretending friendship, but designing to strip them both of their armour and of their ornaments. It is a sin that contributes more than any other to the spreading of vice and immorality in a kingdom. One adulteress may be the ruin of many a precious soul and may help to debauch a whole town. Houses of uncleanness are therefore such pest-houses as ought to be suppressed by those whose office it is to take care of the public welfare.

Verses 29–35

Solomon here gives fair warning against the sin of drunkenness, to confirm what he had said, *v.* 20. *Look not thou upon the wine when it is red.* Red wine was in Canaan looked upon as the best wine; it is therefore called *the blood of the grape.* Covet not that which pleases the eye, but let thy serious thoughts convince thee that that which seems delightful is really hurtful. The pernicious consequences of the sin of drunkenness: *At the last it bites*, *v.* 32. The drunkard is made sick by his surfeit, beggared and ruined in his estate, especially when his conscience is awakened and he cannot reflect upon it without horror and indignation at himself. It embroils men in quarrels. Many have woe and sorrow, and cannot help it; but drunkards wilfully create woe and sorrow to themselves. The wounds which men receive in defence of their country and its just rights are their honour; but *wounds without cause*, received in the service of their lusts, are marks of their infamy. Drunkenness makes men impure and insolent, *v.* 33. The *eyes* grow unruly and *behold strange women* to lust after them, and so let in adultery into the heart. The tongue also grows unruly and talks extravagantly; by it the *heart utters perverse things*, contrary to reason, religion, and common civility. What ridiculous incoherent nonsense men will talk when they are drunk! It stupefies and besots men, *v.* 34. Their judgments are clouded, and they have no more steadiness and consistency than he that sleeps *upon the top of a mast.* Set a drunkard in the stocks, and he is not sensible of the punishment. *"They have stricken me, and I was not sick; I felt it not."* Drunkenness turns men into stocks and stones; they are scarcely to be reckoned animals; they are dead while they live. *Look not upon the wine when it is red.*

CHAPTER 24

Verses 1–2

"Let not such a thought ever come into thy mind, O that I could shake off the restraints of religion and conscience, and take as great a liberty to indulge the sensual appetite, as I see such and such do! No; *desire not to be with them*, to do as they do and fare *as they fare*, and to *cast in thy lot among* them." Do not think with them, *for their heart studies destruction* to others, but it will prove destruction to themselves. It is therefore thy wisdom to have nothing to do with them. Nor hast thou any reason to look upon them with envy, but with pity rather, or a just indignation at their wicked practices.

JAMIESON, FAUSSET, BROWN

riotous . . . flesh—prodigal, or eating more than necessary. Instead of "their flesh" (cf. *Margin*), better, "flesh to them," i.e., used for pleasure. **drowsiness**—the dreamy sleep of the slothful. **22. Hearken**—i.e., obey (ch. 1:8; Eph. 6:1). **despise . . . old**—Adults revere the parents whom, as children, they once obeyed.

23. Buy—lit., "get" (ch. 4:5). **truth**—generally and specially as opposed to errors of all kinds. **24, 25.** (Cf. ch. 10:1; 17:21, 25.)

26-35. A solemn warning against whoredom and drunkenness (Hos. 4:11). **26. give . . . heart**—This is the address of that divine wisdom so often presented (ch. 8:1; 9:3, etc.). **heart**—confidence. **observe**—keep. **my ways**—such as I teach you (ch. 3:17; 9:6). **27, 28. deep ditch**—a narrow pit, out of which it is hard to climb. **lieth in wait**—to ensnare men into the pit, as hunters entrap game (cf. ch. 22:14). **increaseth . . . transgressors**—(ch. 5:8-10). The vice alluded to is peculiarly hardening to the heart.

29, 30. This picture is often sadly realized now. **mixed wine**—(Cf. ch. 9:2; Isa. 5:11.) **31. when . . . red**—the color denoting greater strength (cf. Gen. 49:11; Deut. 32:14). **giveth . . . cup**—lit., "gives its eye,)" i.e., sparkles. **moveth . . . aright**—Perhaps its foaming is meant.

32. The acute miseries resulting from drunkenness contrasted with the temptations.

33, 34. The moral effects: it inflames passion (Gen. 19:31, 35), lays open the heart, produces insensibility to the greatest dangers, and debars from reformation, under the severest sufferings.

35. awake—i.e., from drunkenness (Gen. 9: 24). This is the language rather of acts than of the tongue.

CHAPTER 24

Vss. 1-34. **1, 2.** (Cf. ch. 23:3, 17; Ps. 37:1.)

studieth—meditateth. **talk . . . mischief**—Their expressed purposes are to do evil.

ADAM CLARKE

20. *Be not among winebibbers.* There is much of this chapter spent in giving directions concerning eating, drinking, and entertainments in general. (1) The pupil is directed relative to the manner in which he is to conduct himself in his visits to the tables of the rich and great. (2) Relative to the covetous, and his intercourse with them. And (3) To public entertainments, where there were generally riot and debauch.

22. *Despise not thy mother when she is old.* A very necessary caution, as very old women are generally helpless, useless, and burdensome; yet these circumstances do not at all lessen the child's duty. And this duty is strengthened by the divine command here given.

23. *Buy the truth.* Acquire the knowledge of God at all events; and in order to do this, too much pains, industry, and labor cannot be expended. *And sell it not.* When once acquired, let no consideration deprive you of it.

26. *My son, give me thine heart.* This is the speech of God to every human soul. Give your affections to God, so as to love Him with all your heart, soul, mind, and strength.

28. *Increaseth the transgressors among men.* More iniquity springs from this one source of evil than from any other cause in the whole system of sin. Women and strong drink cause many millions to transgress.

29-30. *Who hath woe?* I believe Solomon refers here to the natural effects of drunkenness. And perhaps *oi*, which we translate *woe*, and *aboi*, which we translate *sorrow*, are mere natural sounds or vociferations that take place among drunken men, either from illness or the nauseating effects of too much liquor. As to *contentions* among such; *babbling* on a variety of subjects, which they neither understand nor are fit to discuss; *wounds*, got by falling out about nothing; and *redness of eyes*, bloodshot with excess of drink, or black and blue eyes with fighting—these are such common and general effects of these compotations as naturally to follow from them. So that they who *tarry long at wine*, and use *mixed wine* to make it more inebriating, are the very persons who are most distinguished by the circumstances enumerated above.

31. *Look not thou upon the wine.* Let neither the color, the odor, the sparkling of the wine, when poured out, induce you to drink of it. However good and pure it may be, it will to you be a snare, because you are addicted to it, and have no self-command.

33. *Thine eyes shall behold strange women.* Evil concupiscence is inseparable from drunkenness.

CHAPTER 24

MATTHEW HENRY

Verses 3–6

A man, with prudent management, may raise his estate and family by lawful and honest means, with the blessing of God upon his industry; and, if the other be raised a little sooner, yet these will last a great deal longer. True wisdom will make men's outward affairs prosperous and successful. It will *build a house and establish it, v.* 3. Men may by unrighteous practices build their houses, but they cannot establish them, for the foundation is rotten (Hab. ii. 9, 10). It will enrich a house and furnish it, *v.* 4. *By knowledge the chambers* of the soul are filled with the graces and comforts of the Spirit, those *precious and pleasant riches.* It will fortify a house and turn it into a castle: *Wisdom is better than weapons of war,* offensive or defensive. The spirit is strengthened both for the spiritual work and the spiritual warfare by true wisdom. Wisdom will erect a college, or council of state. Wisdom will be of use, to make an advantageous peace.

Verses 7–9

It is no easy thing to get wisdom; those that have natural parts good enough, yet if they be foolish, that is, if they be slothful and will not take pains, if they be viciously inclined and keep bad company, it *is too high* for them; they are not likely to reach it. And, for want of it, they are unfit for the service of their country: They *open not their mouth in the gate*; they are not admitted into the council or magistracy, or, if they are, they are dumb statues, they say nothing, because they have nothing to say. This *devising evil* is *the thought of foolishness, v.* 9. It is bad to do evil, but it is worse to devise it; for that has in it the subtlety and poison of the old serpent. But it may be taken more generally. We contract guilt, not only by the act of foolishness, but by the thought of it, though it go no further; the first risings of sin in the heart are sin, offensive to God, and must be repented of or we are undone. *The scorner,* who takes a pleasure in affronting people and reflecting upon them, *is an abomination to men.*

Verse 10

In *the day of adversity* we are apt to *faint,* to droop and be discouraged, to desist from our work, and to despair of relief. "It is a sign that thou art not a man of any resolution, any firmness of thought, any consideration, any faith (for that is the strength of a soul), if thou canst not bear up under an afflictive change of thy condition." *Be of good courage* therefore, *and God shall strengthen thy heart.*

Verses 11–12

A great duty required of us is to appear for the relief of oppressed innocency. Though the persons be not such as we are under any particular obligation to, we must help them, out of a general zeal for justice. It is easy to make an excuse when we say, *We knew it not,* or, *We forgot.* It is not easy with such excuses to evade the judgment of God. God *ponders the heart and keeps the soul*; keeps an eye upon it. We should be tender of the lives of others, and do all we can to preserve them, because our lives have been precious in the sight of God and he has graciously kept them. He will *render to every man according to his works,* not only the commission of evil works, but the omission of good works.

Verse 13–14

The study of wisdom will be very pleasant. We *eat honey because it is sweet to the taste,* and upon that account we call it *good,* especially that which runs first from the *honeycomb.* Canaan was said to flow with milk and honey, and honey was the common food of the country (Luke xxiv. 41, 42), even for children, Isa. vii. 15. Thus should we feed upon wisdom, and relish the good instructions of it. Those that have experienced the power of truth and godliness are abundantly satisfied of the pleasure of both; they have tasted the sweetness of them, and all the atheists in the world with their sophistry, and the profane with their banter, cannot alter their sentiments.

Verses 15–16

The designs of the wicked against the righteous; the plot is laid deeply: They *lay wait against the dwelling of the righteous.* They doubt not but to *spoil his dwelling-place* because his condition is low and distressed, and he is almost down already. The righteous man, whose ruin was expected, recovers himself. The *just man falls,* sometimes *falls seven times* perhaps, sins of infirmity, through the surprise of temptation; but he *rises again* by repentance, finds mercy with God, and regains his peace. *The wicked* man, who expected to see his ruin and to help it forward, is undone.

JAMIESON, FAUSSET, BROWN

3, 4. (Cf. ch. 14:1; Isa. 54:14.) **house**—including the family. **by knowledge . . . riches**—(ch. 8:18; 21:20.) **5, 6.** The general statement (Eccles. 9:16, 18) is specially illustrated (cf. ch. 21:22; Ps. 144:1).

7. (Cf. ch. 14:16.) **in the gate**—(Cf. ch. 22:22.) **8.** So called even if he fails **to do evil. 9.** Same thought varied.

10. Lit., "If thou fail in the day of straits (**adversity**), strait (or small) is thy strength," which is then truly tested.

11, 12. Neglect of known duty is sin (Jas. 4:17). **ready** [lit., "bowing down"] **to be slain**—i.e., unjustly. God's retributive justice cannot be avoided by professed ignorance.

13, 14. As delicious food whets the appetite, so should the rewards of wisdom excite us to seek it. **reward**—lit., "after part," the proper result (cf. ch. 23:18; Ps. 37:37, 38).

15, 16. The plots of the wicked against the good, though partially, shall not be fully successful (Ps. 37:24); while the wicked, falling under penal evil, find no help. **seven times**—often, or many (ch. 6:16, 31; 9: 1).

ADAM CLARKE

3. *Through wisdom is an house builded.* That is, a family; household affairs. See chap. ix. 1.

9. *The thought of foolishness is sin.* "The device of folly is transgression"; or, "An evil purpose is sinful"; or, perhaps more literally, "The device of the foolish is sin."

13. *And the honeycomb.* I have often had occasion to remark how much finer the flavor of honey is in the honeycomb than it is after it has been expressed from it, and exposed to the action of the air. See 1 Sam. xiv. 27; Ps. xix. 10; Prov. v. 3; xvi. 24; xxvii. 7; Cant. iv. 11; v. 1

14 *So shall the knowledge of wisdom be unto thy soul.* True religion shall be to your soul as the honeycomb is to your mouth. *Then there shall be a reward, and thy expectation shall not be cut off.* This is precisely the same with that in the preceding chapter, v. 18. The word *acharith* we translate in the former place "an end," and here we translate it "a reward"; but there is no place I believe in the sacred writings in which it has any such acceptation; nor can such a meaning be deduced from the root *achar,* which always refers to "behind, after, extremity, latter part, time," but never carries the idea of "recompense, compensation," or suchlike. There is another state or life, and your expectation of happiness in a future world shall not be cut off. In this sense the versions all understood it.

15. *The dwelling of the righteous. Tsaddik,* the man who is walking unblamably in all the testimonies of God, who is rendering to every man his due.

16. *For a just man. Tsaddik,* the "righteous," the same person mentioned above. *Falleth seven times.* Gets very often into distresses through his resting place being spoiled by the wicked man, the robber, the spoiler of the desert, lying in wait for this purpose, v. 15. *And riseth up again.* Though God permit the hand of violence sometimes to spoil his tent, temptations to assail his mind, and afflictions to press down his body, he constantly emerges; and every time he passes through the furnace, he comes out brighter and more refined. *But the wicked shall fall into mischief.* And there they shall lie, having no strong arm to uphold them.

MATTHEW HENRY

Verses 17–18

If any have done us an ill turn, or if we bear them ill-will only because they stand in our way, when any damage comes to them (suppose they fall), our corrupt hearts are too apt to conceive a secret delight and satisfaction in it. "Men hope in the ruin of their enemies or rivals to wreak their revenge or to find their account; but be not thou so inhuman; *rejoice not when* the worst *enemy* thou hast *falls.*" *The Lord* will *see it*, though it be hidden in the heart only, *and it* will *displease him*, as it will displease a prudent father to see one child triumph in the correction of another, which he ought to take warning by, not knowing how soon it may be his own case, he having so often deserved it.

Verses 19–20

Even that which grieves us must not *fret* us; nor must our eye be evil against any because God is good. If wicked people prosper, we must not therefore incline to do as they do. Envy not their prosperity. There is no true happiness in it. *He has his reward*, Matt. vi. 2. Those are not to be envied that have their portion in this life and must out-live it, Ps. xvii. 14. Their *candle* shines brightly, but it shall presently *be put out.*

Verses 21–22

Religion and loyalty must go together. As men, it is our duty to honour our Creator, to worship and reverence him; as members of a community, incorporated for mutual benefit, it is our duty to be faithful and dutiful to the government God has set over us, Rom. xiii. 1, 2. Those are not truly loyal that are not religious. How should he be true to his prince that is false to his God? And, if they come in competition, it is an adjudged case, we must *obey God rather than men.* Those that are of restless, factious, turbulent spirits, commonly pull mischief upon their own heads ere they are aware: *Their calamity shall rise suddenly.*

Verses 23–26

As subjects must do their duty, and be obedient to magistrates, so magistrates must do their duty in administering justice to their subjects. They must always weigh the merits of a cause, and not be swayed by any regard, one way or other, to the parties concerned. A good judge will know the truth, not know faces, so as to countenance a friend and help him out in a bad cause, or so much as omit anything that can be said or done in favour of a righteous cause, when it is the cause of an enemy. They must discountenance and give check to all fraud, violence, injustice, and immorality. Let magistrates and ministers, and private persons too that are capable of doing it, *rebuke* the wicked, that they may bring them to repentance or put them to shame, and they shall have the comfort of it in their own bosoms: *To them shall be delight*, when their consciences witness for them that they have been witnesses for God. They must *give a right answer*, that is, give their opinion and pass sentence according to law and the true merits of the cause; and *everyone shall kiss his lips that* does so, that is, shall love and honour him with a kiss of allegiance. He that in common conversation speaks pertinently and with sincerity is beloved and respected by all.

Verse 27

This is a rule of prudence in the management of household affairs. We must prefer necessaries before conveniences, and not lay that out for show which should be expended for the support of the family. We must not think of building till we can afford it: "First apply thyself to *thy work without in the field*; look after thy husbandry, for it is that by which thou must get; and, when thou hast got well by that, then, and not till then, thou mayest think of rebuilding and beautifying *thy house*."

Verses 28–29

As *a witness:* "Never bear a testimony against any man *without cause*, unless what thou sayest thou knowest to be punctually true and thou hast a clear call to testify it. Never bear a false testimony against anyone"; As a plaintiff or prosecutor: If there be occasion to bring an action or information against thy neighbour, let it not be from a spirit of revenge. Even a righteous cause becomes unrighteous when it is prosecuted with malice.

Verses 30–34

The view which Solomon took of *the field and vineyard of the slothful* man. He cast his eye upon a *field* and a *vineyard* unlike all the rest; for, though the soil was good, yet there was nothing growing in them but *thorns and nettles*; and, if there had been any fruit, it would have been eaten up by the beasts, for there was no fence. He paused a little *and considered it, looked* again *upon it, and received instruction.*

JAMIESON, FAUSSET, BROWN

17, 18. Yet let none rejoice over the fate of evildoers, lest God punish their wrong spirit by relieving the sufferer (cf. ch. 17:5; Job 31:29).

19, 20. (Ps. 37:1, 38; 18:28.) **candle**–or, prosperity; it shall come to an end (ch. 13:9; 20:20).

21, 22. A warning against impiety and resistance to lawful rule (Rom. 13:1-7; I Pet. 2:17). **meddle . . . change** –(Cf. *Margin*), lit., "mingle yourself," avoid the society of restless persons. **their calamity . . .**–either what God and the king inflict, or what *changers* and their company suffer; better the first.

23. These . . . wise–lit., "are of the wise," as authors (cf. "Psalms of David," *Hebrew*). "These" refers to the verses following, to ch. 25. **to have respect**–lit., "to discern faces," show partiality, **24, 25,** of which an example is justifying the wicked, to which is opposed, rebuking him, which has a blessing.

26. kiss his lips–love and obey, do homage (Ps. 2:12; Song of Sol. 8:1). **right answer**–lit., "plain (ch. 8: 9) words," opposed to deceptive, or obscure.

27. Prepare . . . in the field–Secure, by diligence, a proper support, and then build; provide necessaries, then comforts, to which a house rather pertained, in a mild climate, permitting the use of tents.

28. Do not speak even truth needlessly against any, and never falsehood. **29.** Especially avoid retaliation (Matt. 5:43-45; Rom. 12:17).

30, 31. A striking picture of the effects of sloth. **32-34.** From the folly of the sluggard learn wisdom (ch. 6:10, 11).

ADAM CLARKE

18. *And he turn away his wrath from him.* Wrath is here taken for the effect of wrath, punishment; and the meaning must be—lest he take the punishment from him, and inflict it upon you.

20. *For there shall be no reward to the evil man. Acharith.* There shall not be the future state of blessedness to the wicked. See the note on v. 14. His *candle . . . shall be put out;* his prosperity shall finally cease, or he shall have no posterity.

23. *These things also belong to the wise.* "These also to wise." This appears to be a new section; and perhaps what follows belongs to another collection. Probably fragments of sayings collected by wise men from the Proverbs of Solomon.

26. *Kiss his lips.* Shall treat him with affection and respect.

MATTHEW HENRY	JAMIESON, FAUSSET, BROWN	ADAM CLARKE

He did not break out into any passionate censures of the owner, but he endeavoured himself to get good by the observation. Plutarch relates a saying of Cato Major, "That wise men profit more by fools than fools by wise men; for wise men will avoid the faults of fools, but fools will not imitate the virtues of wise men." What a scandalous thing slothfulness is, and how injurious to the family, and to the affairs of our souls! Our souls are our fields and vineyards, which we are every one of us to take care of, to dress, and to keep. They are capable of being improved with good husbandry. These fields and vineyards are often in a very bad state, not only no fruit brought forth, but all overgrown with *thorns* and *nettles* (scratching, stinging, inordinate lusts and passions, pride, covetousness, sensuality, malice, those are the thorns and nettles, the wild grapes, which the unsanctified heart produces), no guard kept against the enemy, but the *stone-wall broken down.* Where it is thus it is owing to the sinner's own slothfulness and folly.

CHARLES. H. SPURGEON:

We may find instruction everywhere. To a spiritual mind nettles have their use, and weeds have their doctrine. Are not all thorns and thistles meant to be teachers to sinful men? Are they not brought forth of the earth on purpose that they may show us what sin has done, and the kind of produce that will come when we sow the seed of rebellion against God? "I went by the field of the slothful, and by the vineyard of the man void of understanding," says Solomon; "I saw, and considered it well: I looked upon it, and received instruction." Whatever you see, take care to consider it well, and you will not see it in vain. You shall find books and sermons everywhere, in the land and in the sea, in the earth and in the skies, and you shall learn from every living beast, and bird, and fish, and insect, and from every useful or useless plant that springs out of the ground.
—*The Treasury of the Old Testament*

MATTHEW HENRY — CHAPTER 25

Verse 1
This verse is the title of this latter collection of Solomon's proverbs. The publishers were Hezekiah's servants, who, it is likely, herein acted as his servants, being appointed by him to do this good service to the church, among other good offices that he did *in the law and in the commandments,* 2 Chron. xxxi. 21. They copied out these proverbs from the records of Solomon's reign, and published them as an appendix to the former edition of this book. It may be a piece of very good service to the church to publish other men's works that have lain hidden in obscurity.

Verses 2–3
An instance given of the honour of God: *It is his glory to conceal a matter.* There is an unfathomable depth in his counsels, Rom. xi. 33. We see what he does, but we know not the reasons. It is God's glory that he needs not *search into a matter,* because he knows it without search; but it is the honour of kings to search out the matters that are brought before them, to take pains in examining offenders and not to give judgment hastily.

Verses 4–5
The vigorous endeavour of a prince to suppress vice, and reform the manners of his people, is the most effectual way to support his government. The duty of magistrates is to use their power for the terror of evil works and evil workers, not only to banish those that are vicious, but so to frighten them that they may not spread the infection of their wickedness among their subjects. This is called *taking away the dross from the silver,* which is done by the force of fire. The reformation of the court will promote the reformation of the kingdom, Ps. ci. 3, 8.

Verses 6–7
Religion is so far from destroying good manners that it teaches us to give place to those to whom it belongs. Religion teaches us humility and self-denial, which is a better lesson than that of good manners. This is really the way to advancement, as our Saviour shows in a parable that seems to be borrowed from this, Luke xiv. 9. It is better, more for a man's satisfaction and reputation, to be advanced above his pretensions and expectations, than to be thrust down below them.

Verses 8–10
"Be not hasty in bringing an action, before thou hast thyself considered it, and consulted with thy friends about it. Bring not an action before thou hast tried to end the matter amicably (*v.* 9): *Debate thy cause with thy neighbour* privately, and perhaps you will understand one another better and see that there is no occasion to go to law." *Reveal not the secret of another,* so some read it. "Do not, in revenge, to disgrace thy adversary, disclose that which should be kept private and which does not at all belong to the cause." Be thus cautious in going to law, otherwise the cause will be in danger of going against thee. It will turn very much to thy reproach if thou fall under the character of being litigious.

Verses 11–12
Instruction, advice, or comfort, given seasonably, and in apt expressions, adapted to the case of the person spoken to and agreeing with the character of the person speaking—*is like golden* balls resembling *apples,* brought to table in a silver network basket, or in a silver box of that which we call *philligree*-work, through which the golden apples might be seen.

JAMIESON, FAUSSET, BROWN — CHAPTER 25

Vss. 1-28. **1.** The character of these proverbs sustains the title **also**—refers to the former part of the book. **copied out**—lit., "transferred," i.e., from some other book to this; not given from memory. **2.** God's unsearchableness impres-

2. God's unsearchableness impresses us with awe (cf. Isa. 45:15; Rom. 11:33). But kings, being finite, should confer with wise counsellors; **3.** Ye wisely keeping state secrets, which to common men are as inaccessible heights and depths.

4, 5. As separating impurities from ore leaves pure silver, so taking from a king wicked counsellors leaves a wise and beneficent government. **before**—or, "in presence of," as courtiers stood about a king.

6, 7. Do not intrude into the presence of the king, for the elevation of the humble is honorable, but the humbling of the proud disgraceful (Luke 14:8-10).

8. (Cf. ch. 3:30.) **lest . . . shame**—lest you do what you ought not, when shamed by defeat, or "lest thou art shut out from doing any thing." **9, 10.** (Cf. Matt. 5:25; *Margin.*) **secret**—i.e., of your opponent, for his disadvantage, and so you be disgraced, not having discussed your difficulties with him.

11. a word fitly—lit., "quickly," as wheels roll, just in time. The comparison **as apples . . . silver** gives a like sense. **apples . . .**—either real apples of golden color, in a silver network basket, or imitations on silver embroidery.

ADAM CLARKE — CHAPTER 25

1. *These are also proverbs of Solomon.* It seems that the remaining part of this book contains proverbs which had been collected by the order of King Hezekiah, and were added to the preceding book as a sort of supplement, having been collected from traditionary sayings of Solomon.

2. *It is the glory of God to conceal a thing.* This has been understood as referring to the revelation of God's will in His Word, where there are many things concealed in parables, allegories, metaphors, similitudes. And it is becoming the majesty of God so to publish His will that it must be seriously studied to be understood, in order that the truth may be more prized when it is discovered. And if it be God's glory thus partially to conceal his purposes, it is the glory of a king to search and examine this Word, that he may understand how by Him kings reign and princes decree judgment.

3. *The heaven for height.* The simple meaning of this is, the reasons of state, in reference to many acts of the executive government, can no more be fathomed by the common people than the height of the heavens and the depth of the earth.

7. *Come up hither.* Our Lord refers to this; see Luke xiv. 8.

8. *Go not forth hastily to strive.* To enter into a lawsuit.

11. *A word fitly spoken.* "Upon its wheels." An observation, caution, reproof, or advice that comes in naturally, runs smoothly along, is not forced nor dragged in, that appears to be without design, to rise out of the conversation, and though particularly relative to one point, will appear to the company to suit all. *Is like apples of gold in pictures of silver.* Is like the refreshing orange or beautiful citron, served up in open-work or filigree baskets, made of silver. The Asiatics excel in filigree silver work.

MATTHEW HENRY

Doubtless it was some ornament of the table, then well known. A reproof with discretion, well given, by *a wise reprover*, and well taken, by an *obedient ear*, it is an *ear-ring of gold* and an *ornament of fine gold*, very graceful and well becoming both the reprover and the reproved.

Verse 13

A servant ought to be *faithful to him that sends him*, and to see to it that he does not, by mistake or with design, falsify his trust. This will be the satisfaction of the master; it will *refresh his soul* as much as ever the *cold of snow* (which in hot countries they preserve by art all the year round) refreshed the labourers in the harvest, that *bore the burden and heat of the day*.

Verse 14

Who pretends to have received or given that which he never had, which he never gave, makes a noise of his great accomplishments and his good services, but it is all false; he is not what he pretends to be. Such a one is like the morning-cloud, that passes away, and disappoints those who looked for rain from it to water the parched ground (Jude 12), *clouds without water*.

Verse 15

Two things recommended in dealing with others, 1. Patience, to bear a present heat without being put into a heat by it, and to wait for a fit opportunity to offer our reasons and to give persons time to consider them. By this means even a *prince* may be *persuaded*. 2. Mildness, to speak without passion or provocation: *A soft tongue breaks the bone;* it mollifies the roughest spirits and overcomes those that are most morose, like lightning, which, they say, has sometimes broken the bone, and yet not pierced the flesh.

Verse 16

"*Hast thou found honey?*" It is not forbidden fruit to thee, as it was to Jonathan; thou mayest eat of it with thanksgiving to God. *Eat as much as is sufficient*, and no more. We must use all pleasures as we do honey, with a check upon our appetite. The pleasures of sense lose their sweetness by the excessive use of them and become nauseous, as honey, which turns sour in the stomach.

Verse 17

It is a piece of civility to visit our neighbours sometimes. It is wisdom, as well as good manners, not to be troublesome to our friends in visiting them too often, nor stay too long, nor contrive to come at meal-time, nor make ourselves busy in the affairs of their families. *After the third day fish and company become distasteful.* Familiarity breeds contempt. How much better a friend then is God than any other friend; the oftener we come to him the better and the more welcome.

Verse 18

A false testimony is everything that is dangerous; it *is a maul* (or *club* to knock a man's brains out with), a flail, which there is no fence against; it is *a sword* to wound near at hand and a *sharp arrow* to wound at a distance; we have therefore need to pray, *Deliver my soul, O Lord! from lying lips*, Ps. cxx. 2.

Verse 19

Confidence in an unfaithful man (so we read it), in a man whom we thought trusty but who proves otherwise, proves not only unserviceable, but painful and vexatious, like a *broken tooth, or a foot out of joint*.

Verse 20

The absurdity here censured is *singing songs to a heavy heart*. Those that are in great sorrow are to be comforted by sympathizing with them, but we take a wrong course if we think to relieve them by being merry with them, and endeavouring to make them merry. *Taking away a garment* from a man in *cold weather*, makes him colder, and pouring *vinegar upon nitre* puts it into a ferment; so incongruous, is it to sing pleasant songs to one that is of a sorrowful spirit. Some read it in a contrary sense: *As he that puts on a garment in cold weather* warms the body, or as *vinegar upon nitre* dissolves it, so he that *sings songs* of comfort to a person in sorrow refreshes him and dispels his grief.

Verses 21–22

However the scribes and Pharisees had corrupted the law the commandment of loving our brethren, even that of loving our enemies, was not only a new,

JAMIESON, FAUSSET, BROWN

12. Those who desire to know and do rightly, most highly esteem good counsel (ch. 9:9; 15:31). The listening ear is better than one hung with gold.

13. Snow from mountains was used to cool drinks; so refreshing is a faithful messenger (ch. 13:17).

14. **clouds**—lit., "vapors" (Jer. 10:13), clouds only in appearance. **a false gift**—promised, but not given.

15. Gentleness and kindness overcome the most powerful and obstinate. **long forbearing**—or, slowness to anger (ch. 14:29; 15:18).

16, 17. A comparison, as a surfeit of honey produces physical disgust, so your company, however agreeable in moderation, may, if excessive, lead your friend to hate you.

18. **A false witness** is as destructive to reputation, as such weapons to the body (ch. 24:28). **beareth . . . witness**—lit., "answereth questions," as before a judge, against his **neighbor.**

19. *Treachery* annoys as well as de-ceives.

20. Not only is the incongruity of songs (i.e., joyful) and sadness meant, but an accession of sadness, by want of sympathy, is implied.

ADAM CLARKE

12. *As an earring of gold.* I believe *nezem* to mean the nose ring with its pendants; the left nostril is pierced, and a ring put through it, as in the ear.

14. *A false gift.* "A lying gift," one promised but never bestowed.

17. *Withdraw thy foot.* Another proverb will illustrate this: "Too much familiarity breeds contempt."

20. *As vinegar upon nitre.* The original word *nather* is what is known among chemists as the *natron* of the ancients and of the Scriptures, and carbonate of soda. It is used in the East for the purposes of washing. If vinegar be poured on it, Dr. Shaw says a strong fermentation immediately takes place, which illustrates what Solomon says here: "The singing of songs to a heavy heart is like vinegar upon natron"; that is, "there is no affinity between them."

MATTHEW HENRY

but also an old commandment, an Old Testament commandment, though our Saviour has given it to us with the new enforcement of his own great example in loving us when we were enemies. We shall mollify them as the refiner melts the metal in the crucible, not only by putting it over the fire, but by heaping coals of fire upon it. The way to turn an enemy into a friend is to act towards him in a friendly manner.

Verse 23

Slanders would not be so readily spoken as they are if they were not readily heard; but good manners would silence the slanderer if he saw that his tales displeased the company. If we cannot otherwise reprove, we may do it by our looks. Who knows but it may silence and drive away a *backbiting tongue*? Many abuse those they speak of only in hopes to curry favour with those they speak to.

Verse 24

This is the same with what he had said, *ch.* xxi. 9. Those are to be pitied that are unequally yoked, especially with such as are brawling and contentious, whether husband or wife; for it is equally true of both.

Verse 25

It is sometimes with impatience that we expect to hear from abroad; our souls thirst after it. How acceptable good news will be when it does come, as refreshing as cold water to one that is thirsty. Heaven is a country afar off; how refreshing is it to hear good news thence, both in the everlasting gospel, which signifies glad tidings, and in the witness of the Spirit with our spirits that we are God's children.

Verse 26

For the righteous to fall into sin in the sight of the wicked *troubles the fountains* by grieving some, and *corrupts the springs* by infecting others and emboldening them to do likewise. For the righteous to be oppressed and trampled upon, by the violence or subtlety of evil men, this is the troubling of the fountains of justice and corrupting the very springs of government, *ch.* xxviii. 12, 28; xxix. 2. For the righteous to be cowardly, to truckle to the wicked, this is a reflection upon religion, and so is like a *troubled fountain* and a *corrupt spring*.

Verse 27

It is true of all the delights of the children of men that they will surfeit, but never satisfy, and they are dangerous to those that allow themselves the liberal use of them. *For men to search their own glory*, to court applause is not their glory, but their shame; everyone will laugh at them for it. Some give another sense of this verse: *To eat much honey is not good*, but to search into glorious and excellent things is a great commendation, it is true glory; we cannot therein offend by excess.

Verse 28

A wise and virtuous man is one that has *rule over his own spirit*. A vicious man, who has not this rule over his own spirit, is *like a city that is broken down and without walls*. He lies exposed to all the temptations of Satan and becomes an easy prey.

JAMIESON, FAUSSET, BROWN

21, 22. (Cf. Matt. 5:44; Rom. 12:20.) As metals are melted by heaping coals upon them, so is the heart softened by kindness.

23. Better, "As the north wind bringeth forth (Ps. 90:2) or produces rain, so does a concealed or slandering tongue produce anger."

25. (Cf. vs. 13.) **good news**—i.e., of some loved interest or absent friend, the more grateful as coming from afar.

26. From troubled fountains and corrupt springs no healthy water is to be had, so when the righteous are oppressed by the wicked, their power for good is lessened or destroyed.

27. Satiety surfeits (vs. 16); so men who are self-glorious find shame. **is not glory**—"not" is supplied from the first clause, or "is grievous," in which sense a similar word is used (ch. 27:2).

28. Such are exposed to the incursions of evil thoughts and successful temptations.

ADAM CLARKE

22. *Thou shalt heap coals of fire upon his head.* Not to consume, but to melt him into kindness.

23. *The north wind driveth away rain.* The margin has, "The north wind bringeth forth rain." It is said that the "north wind brings forth rain at Jerusalem, because it brings with it the vapours arising from the sea that lies north of it." *A backbiting tongue.* "A hidden tongue."

24. *It is better to dwell in the corner.* See chap. xxi. 9.

27. *It is not good to eat much honey.* He that searches too much into mysteries is likely to be confounded by them. I really think this is the meaning of the place.

MATTHEW HENRY

CHAPTER 26

Verse 1

Bad men, who have neither wit nor grace, are sometimes preferred by princes, and applauded and cried up by the people. It is very absurd and unbecoming. It is as incongruous *as snow in summer*, as injurious *as rain in harvest*, which hinders the labourers and spoils the fruits of the earth when they are ready to be gathered.

Verse 2

He that is cursed without cause, whether by furious imprecations or solemn anathemas, the curse shall do him no more harm than the bird that flies over his head, than Goliath's curses did to David, 1 Sam. xvii. 43.

Verse 3

Wicked men are compared to *the horse* and *the ass*, so brutish are they, and not to be governed but by force or fear, so low has sin sunk men, so much below themselves. A *horse* unbroken needs *a whip* for correction, and an *ass a bridle* for direction and to check him when he would turn out of the way; so a vicious man, who will not be under the guidance and restraint of religion and reason, ought to be whipped and bridled, to be rebuked severely, and to be restrained from offending any more.

JAMIESON, FAUSSET, BROWN

CHAPTER 26

Vss. 1-28. **1.** The incongruities of nature illustrate also those of the moral world. The fool's unworthiness is also implied (ch. 17:7; 19:10).

2. Though not obvious to us, **the bird**—lit., "sparrow"—and **swallow**—have an object in their motions, so penal evil falls on none without a reason.

3. The rod is as much needed by fools and as well suited to them, as whips and bridles are for beasts.

ADAM CLARKE

CHAPTER 26

2. *As the bird.* As the "sparrow" flies about the house, and the "swallow" emigrates to strange countries, so an undeserved malediction may flutter about the neighborhood for a season; but in a short time it will disappear as the bird of passage.

MATTHEW HENRY

Verses 4–5

The scripture-style seems to contradict itself, but really does not. Wise men have need to be directed how to deal with fools; and they have need of wisdom in dealing with such, to know when to keep silence and when to speak, for there may be a time for both In some cases a wise man will not set his wit to that of a fool so far as to *answer him according to his folly.* "If he boast of himself, do not answer him by boasting of thyself. If he rail and talk passionately, do not thou rail and talk passionately too. If he tell one great lie, do not thou tell another to match it. If he banter, do not answer him in his own language, *lest thou be like him.*" Yet, in other cases, a wise man will use his wisdom for the conviction of a fool, when, by taking notice of what he says, there may be hopes of doing good. "If thou have reason to think that thy silence will be deemed an evidence of weakness, in such a case *answer him,* and let it be an answer *to the man,* beat him at his own weapons, and that will be an answer *to the point.* If he offer anything that looks like an argument, then give him an answer, *lest he be wise in his own conceit* and boast of a victory."

Verses 6–9

Solomon here shows that fools are fit for nothing; they are either sottish men, who will never think and design at all, or vicious men, who will never think and design well. They are not fit to be entrusted with any business, not fit to go on an errand (*v.* 6): *He that* does but *send a message by the hand of a fool,* of a careless heedless person, will find his message misunderstood, and so many blunders made that he might as well have *cut off his legs,* that is, never have sent him. He will *drink damage*; it will be very much to his prejudice to have employed such a one. People will be apt to judge of the master by his messenger. To *give honour to a fool* is to put a sword in a madman's hand, with which we know not what mischief he may do, even to those that put it into his hand. *A parable in the mouth of fools* ceases to be a parable, and becomes a jest. As *the legs of the lame are not equal,* by reason of which their going is unseemly, so unseemly is it for a fool to pretend to speak apophthegms, and give advice. His good words raise him up, but then his bad life takes him down, and so his *legs are not equal.* He does but do mischief with it to himself and others, as a drunkard does with a thorn, or any other sharp thing which he takes in his hand, with which he tears himself and those about him, because he knows not how to manage it.

Verse 10

Our translation gives this verse a different reading in the text and in the margin; and accordingly it expresses either, 1. The equity of a good God. *The great God that formed all things* at first, and still governs them in infinite wisdom, renders to every man according to his work. He *rewards the fool,* who sinned through ignorance, *with few stripes*; and he *rewards the transgressor,* who sinned presumptuously, *with many stripes.* Or, 2. The iniquity of a bad prince (so the margin reads it): *A great man grieves all, and he hires the fool; he hires also the transgressors.* When a wicked man gets power in his hand, by himself, and by the fools and knaves whom he employs under him, he grieves all who are under him and is vexatious to them.

Verse 11

What an abominable thing sin is! When his conscience is convinced, or he feels smart from his sin, he is sick of it, he seems then to detest it and to be willing to part with it. Sinners, who have been convinced only and not converted, return to sin again, forgetting how sick it made them.

Verse 12

A spiritual disease is self-conceit. Many a one, *wise in his own conceit,* has some little sense, but is proud of it, has such a conceit of his own abilities as makes him opinionative, dogmatical, and censorious. *There is more hope of a fool,* that knows and owns himself to be such, *than of* such a one.

Verse 13

The slothful man dreads *the way, the streets,* the place where work is to be done and a journey to be gone. He dreams of, and pretends to dread—*a lion in the way.* When he is pressed to be diligent, either in his worldly affairs or in religion, this is his excuse: *There is a lion in the way,* some insuperable difficulty or danger which he cannot pretend to grapple with. It is a foolish thing to frighten ourselves from real duties by fancied difficulties, Eccles. xi. 4.

JAMIESON, FAUSSET, BROWN

4, 5. Answer not—i.e., approvingly by like folly. **Answer**—by reproof.

6. A fool fails by folly as surely as if he were maimed. **drinketh damage**—i.e., gets it abundantly (Job 15:16; 34:7).

7. legs . . . equal—or, "take away the legs," or the legs . . . are weak. In any case the idea is that they are the occasion of an awkwardness, such as the fool shows in using a parable or proverb (cf. *Introduction;* ch. 17:7). **8.** A stone, bound in a sling, is useless; so honor, conferred on a fool, is thrown away. **9.** As vexatious and unmanageble as a thorn in a drunkard's hand is a parable to a fool. He will be as apt to misuse is as to use it rightly.

10. Various versions of this are proposed (cf. *Margin*). Better perhaps—"Much He injures (or lit., "wounds") all who reward," etc., i.e., society is injured by encouraging evil men. **transgressors**—may be rendered vagrants. The word *God* is improperly supplied.

11. returneth . . . folly—Though disgusting to others, the fool delights in his folly.

12. The self-conceited are taught with more difficulty than the stupid.

13. (Cf. ch. 22:13.)

ADAM CLARKE

F. C. COOK:

Verses 4, 5. Two sides of a truth. To "answer a fool according to his folly" is in v. 4 to bandy words with him, to descend to his level of coarse anger and vile abuse; in v. 5 it is to say the right word at the right time, to expose his unwisdom and untruth to others and to himself, not by a teaching beyond his reach, but by words that he is just able to apprehend. The apparent contradiction between the two verses led some of the Rabbis to question the canonical authority of the Book. The Pythagoreans had maxims expressing a truth in precepts seemingly contradictory.—*Barnes' Notes*

6. *Cutteth off the feet.* Sending by such a person is utterly useless.

8. *As he that bindeth a stone in a sling, so is he that giveth honour to a fool.* It is entirely thrown away. This, however, is a difficult proverb; and the versions give but little light on the subject. The Hebrew may be translated, "As a piece of precious stone among a heap of stones, so is he that giveth honor to a fool." On this interpretation the meaning would rather be, "It is as useless to throw a jewel among a heap of stones to increase its bulk as to give honor to a fool."

11. *As a dog returneth to his vomit.* See 2 Pet. ii. 22.

MATTHEW HENRY

Verse 14

Having seen the slothful man in fear of his work, here we find him in love with his ease; he lies in his bed on one side till he is weary of that, and then turns to the other, but still in his bed, when it is far in the day and work is to be done, as the door is moved, but not removed. The sluggard is one that does not care to get out of his bed, but seems to be hung upon it, *as the door upon the hinges*. He does not care to get forward with his business; in that he stirs to and fro a little, but to no purpose; he is where he was.

Verse 15

The sluggard has now, with much ado, got out of his bed, but he might as well have lain there still. He *hides his hand in his bosom* for fear of cold; next to his warm bed is his warm bosom. Or he pretends that he is lame, as some do that make a trade of begging; something ails his hand; he would have it thought that it is blistered with yesterday's hard work. He himself is the loser by it, for he starves himself: *It grieves him to bring his hand to his mouth*, that is, he cannot find in his heart to feed himself. It is an elegant hyperbole, aggravating his sin, that he cannot endure to take the least pains. Those that are slothful in religion will not be at pains to feed their own souls with the word of God, the bread of life, nor to fetch in promised blessings by prayer.

Verse 16

The sluggard thinks himself *wiser than seven men*, than seven wise men, for they are such as *can render a reason*. He that takes pains in religion can render a good reason for it; he knows that he is working for a good Master and that *his labour shall not be in vain*. But *the sluggard* thinks himself *wiser than seven* such. It is *the sluggard*, above all men, that is thus self-conceited. His good opinion of himself is the cause of his slothfulness; he will not take pains to get wisdom because he thinks he is wise enough already. His slothfulness is the cause of his good opinion of himself. If he would but take pains to examine himself he would have other thoughts of himself.

Verse 17

That which is here condemned is *meddling with strife that belongs not to us*. If we can be instrumental to make peace between those that are at variance we must do it; but to make ourselves busy in other men's matters, and parties in other men's quarrels, is to court trouble. It is like taking a snarling cur *by the ears*, that will snap at you and bite you.

Verses 18–19

Those that make no scruple of *deceiving their neighbours* are *as madmen that cast firebrands, arrows, and death*. They value themselves as cunning men, but really they are *as madmen*. There is not a greater madness in the world than a wilful sin. The excuse which men commonly make for the mischief they do is that they did it in jest; *Am I not in sport?* But it will prove dangerous playing with fire and jesting with edge-tools. He that sins in jest must repent in earnest, or his sin will be his ruin. Truth is too valuable a thing to be sold for a jest, and so is the reputation of our neighbour.

Verses 20–22

Contention is as a fire; it heats the spirit, burns up all that is good, and puts families and societies into a flame. We must not give ear to *tale-bearers*, for they feed the fire of contention with fuel; nay, they spread it with combustible matter; the tales they carry are fireballs. Those who by insinuating base characters, revealing secrets, and misrepresenting words and actions, are to be banished, and then strife will as surely cease as the fire will go out when it has no fuel. Whisperers and backbiters are incendiaries not to be suffered. They wound love and charity and give a fatal stab to friendship and Christian fellowship. We must not associate with peevish passionate people. These are *contentious men* that *kindle strife, v.* 21. The less we have to do with such the better, for it will be very difficult to avoid quarrelling with those that are quarrelsome.

Verse 23

This may be meant either, 1. Of *a wicked heart* showing itself in *burning lips*, furious words, burning in malice; ill words and ill-will agree as well together as *a potsherd* and the *dross of silver*, which, now that the pot is broken and the dross separated from the silver, are fit to be thrown to the dunghill. Or 2. Of *a wicked heart* disguising itself with *burning lips*, burning with professions of love and friendship.

JAMIESON, FAUSSET, BROWN

14. (Cf. ch. 6:10; 24:33.) He moves but does not leave his place.

15. (Cf. ch. 19:24.)

16. The thoughtless being ignorant of their ignorance are conceited.

17. meddleth—as in ch. 20:19; 24:21; as either holding a dog by the ears or letting him go involves danger, so success in another man's strife or failure involves a useless risk of reputation, does no good, and may do us harm.

18, 19. Such are reckless of results.

20, 21. The talebearers foster (ch. 16:28), and the contentious excite, strife. **22.** (Cf. ch. 18:8.)

23. *Warm professions* can no more give value to insincerity than silver coating to rude earthenware.

ADAM CLARKE

JOSEPH PARKER:

Verses 13, 14. As the fool has no friends in the Book of Proverbs, so the sluggard or the slothful man is everywhere encountered with contempt and disgust. Creation has no room for sluggards. The whole economy of life is constructed, as we know it, for the proper exercise of our faculties, for the development of industry, for the completion of beneficent service. Every man should be up early in the morning and take advantage of the dawn; every man should have a distinct plan in life, and should patiently and gratefully realize that plan, line by line; to be without a policy of life is to be without sufficient inspiration and impulse, is to be the sport of every chance, and is to be the prey of every temptation.—*The People's Bible*

16. *Than seven men that can render a reason. Seven* here only means perfection, abundance, or multitude. He is wiser in his own eyes than a multitude of the wisest men.

17. *He that passeth by.* This proverb stands true ninety-nine times out of a hundred, where people meddle with domestic broils, or differences between men and their wives.

20. *Where no wood is, there the fire goeth out.* The tale-receiver and the talebearer are the agents of discord. If none received the slander in the first instance, it could not be propagated. Hence our proverb, "The receiver is as bad as the thief."

22. *The words of a talebearer.* The same with chap. xviii. 8.

23. *Burning lips and a wicked heart.* Splendid, shining, smooth lips; that is, lips which make great professions of friendship are like a vessel plated over with base metal to make it resemble silver; but it is only a vile pot, and even the outside is not pure.

MATTHEW HENRY

This is *like a potsherd covered with* the scum or *dross of silver*, but a wise man is soon aware of the cheat.

Verses 24–26

The want of sincerity in men's profession of friendship, and the making of it subservient to the most malicious intentions is here spoken of as a common thing (*v.* 24): *He that hates* his neighbour, and is contriving to do him a mischief, yet *dissembles with his lips*, talks kindly with him, as Cain with Abel, this man *lays up deceit within him*, that is, he keeps in his mind the mischief he intends to do his neighbour. Remember to distrust when a man *speaks fair*; be not too forward to *believe him* unless you know him well, for it is possible there may be *seven abominations in his heart*. Though the fraud may be carried on plausibly awhile, it will be brought to light, *v.* 26. He *whose hatred is covered by deceit* will one time or other be discovered. Love (says one) is the best armour, but the worst cloak and will serve dissemblers as the disguise which Ahab put on and perished in.

Verse 27

What pains men take to do mischief to others, concealing their design with a profession of friendship! It is *digging a pit*, it is *rolling a stone*, hard work, and yet men will stick at it to gratify their passion and revenge. Their violent dealing will return upon their own heads; they shall themselves *fall into the pit they digged*, and the stone they rolled *will return upon them*, Ps. vii. 15, 16; ix. 15, 16.

Verse 28

There are two sorts of lies equally detestable: 1. A slandering lie: *A lying tongue hates those that are afflicted by it;* it afflicts them by calumnies and reproaches because it hates them. The mischief of this is obvious; it afflicts, it hates, and owns it, and everybody sees it. 2. A flattering lie secretly works ruin. It is little suspected, and men betray themselves by being credulous of the compliments that are passed upon them. A wise man therefore will be more afraid of a flatterer that kisses and kills than of a slanderer that proclaims war.

CHAPTER 27

Verse 1

Boast not thyself, no, not *of tomorrow*, much less of many days or years to come. This does not forbid preparing for tomorrow, but presuming upon tomorrow. We must not put off the great work of conversion, that one thing needful, till tomorrow, as if we were sure of it, *but today, while it is called today*, hear God's voice. *We know not what a day may bring forth*, what event may be in the teeming womb of time. God has wisely kept us in the dark concerning future events, that he may train us up in a dependence upon himself and a continued readiness for every event, Acts i. 7.

Verse 2

Let our own works be such as will praise us, even *in the gates*, Phil. iv. 8. When we have done it we must not commend ourselves, for that is an evidence of pride. There may be a just occasion for us to vindicate ourselves, but it does not become us to applaud ourselves.

Verses 3–4

The wrath of a fool, who when he is provoked cares not what he says and does, is more grievous than a great stone or a load of sand. Those who have no command of their passions sink under the load of them. The wrath of a fool lies heavily upon those he is enraged at. It is therefore our wisdom not to give provocation to a fool, but, if he be in a passion, to get out of his way. Rooted malice is much worse. *Wrath is cruel*, and does many a barbarous thing, but secret enmity of another, envy at his prosperity, and a desire of revenge for some affront, are much more mischievous. One may avoid a sudden heat, as David escaped Saul's javelin, but when it grows, as Saul's did, to a settled envy, there is no *standing before it*.

Verses 5–6

It is good for us to be reproved, and told of our faults, by our friends. *Faithful are the reproofs of a friend*, though for the present they are painful as *wounds*. The physician's care is to cure the patient's disease, not to please his palate. It is dangerous to be caressed and flattered by *an enemy*, whose *kisses are deceitful*. Joab's kiss and Judas's were deceitful. Some read it: *The Lord deliver us from an enemy's kisses, from lying lips, and from a deceitful tongue.*

JAMIESON, FAUSSET, BROWN

24. dissembleth—though an unusual sense of the word (cf. *Margin*), is allowable, and better suits the context, which sets forth hypocrisy.

25. Sentiment of vs. 24 carried out. **seven . . . heart**—i.e., very many (cf. ch. 24:16). **26, 27.** Deceit will at last be exposed, and the wicked by their own arts often bring on retribution (cf. ch. 12:13; Ps. 17:16; 9:17, etc.).

28. Men hate those they injure. **lying tongue**—*lips* for the persons (cf. ch. 4:24; Ps. 12:3).

CHAPTER 27

Vss. 1-27. **1.** Do not confide implicitly in your plans (ch. 16:9; 19:21; Jas. 4:13-15).

2. Avoid self-praise.

3. The literal sense of **heavy,** applied to material subjects, illustrates its figurative, *grievous,* applied to moral. **a fool's wrath**—is unreasonable and excessive.

4. envy—or, jealousy (cf. *Margin;* ch. 6:34), is more unappeasable than the simpler bad passions.

5, 6. love—not manifested in acts is useless; and even, if its exhibition by rebukes wounds us, such love is preferable to the frequent (cf. *Margin*), and hence deceitful, kisses of an enemy.

ADAM CLARKE

25. *For there are seven abominations in his heart.* That is, he is full of abominations.

27. *Whoso diggeth a pit.* See Ps. vii. 15.

28. *A lying tongue hateth those that are afflicted by it.* He that injures another hates him in proportion to the injury he has done him.

CHAPTER 27

1. *Boast not thyself of to morrow.* See Jas. iv. 13, etc.

2. *Let another man praise thee, and not thine own mouth.* We have a similar proverb, which illustrates this: "Self-praise is no commendation."

MATTHEW HENRY

Verse 7

Solomon here, as often in this book, shows that the poor have in some respects the advantage of the rich; for, 1. They have a better relish of their enjoyments. Hunger is the best sauce. Coarse fare, with a good appetite to it, has a sensible pleasantness in it. Those that fare sumptuously every day nauseate even delicate food. Those that have no more than their necessary food, though it be such as *the full soul* would call *bitter*, to them it *is sweet*; they eat it with pleasure, digest it, and are refreshed by it. They are more thankful: *The hungry* will bless God for bread and water, while those that are *full* think the greatest dainties scarcely worth giving thanks for.

Verse 8

There are many that do not know when they are well off; they love to wander, they are glad of a pretence to go abroad, and do not care for staying long at a place. Those that thus desert the post assigned to them are like *a bird that wanders from her nest*. They are always wavering, like the wandering bird that hops from bough to bough and rests nowhere. When the bird wanders from her nest the eggs and young ones there are neglected. Those that love to be abroad leave their work at home undone.

Verses 9–10

A charge given to be faithful and constant to our friends, our old friends. It is good to have a bosom-friend, whom we can be free with. It is good also to have a special respect to those who have been friends to our family: "*Thy own friend*, especially if he have been *thy father's friend, forsake not*. He is a tried friend; he knows thy affairs; therefore be advised by him." It is a duty we owe to our parents, when they are gone, to love their friends. Solomon's son undid himself by forsaking the counsel of his father's friends. There is a great deal of *sweetness* in conversing with a cordial friend. It is like *ointment and perfume*, which exhilarate the spirits. It *rejoices the heart*; the burden of care is made lighter by unbosoming ourselves to our friend. *The sweetness of* friendship lies not in hearty mirth, but in *hearty counsel*, faithful advice, sincerely given and without flattery, *by counsel of the soul* (so the word is). We are here advised not to go into a *brother's house*, not to expect relief from a kinsman merely for kindred-sake, but rather to apply ourselves to our neighbours, who are at hand, and will be ready to help us at an exigence. It is wisdom to oblige them by being neighbourly.

Verse 11

Children may be a comfort to their parents and may *make their hearts glad*, even when *the evil days come*, and so recompense them for their care, *ch.* xxiii. 15. They may be a credit to them: "*That I may answer him that reproaches me* with having been over-strict and severe in bringing up my children." Those that have been blessed with a religious education should conduct themselves so as to silence those who say, *A young saint, an old devil;* and to prove the contrary, *A young saint, an old angel.*

Verse 12

Evil may be foreseen. Where there is temptation, it is easy to foresee that if we thrust ourselves into it there will be sin, and there will follow the evil of punishment; and, commonly, God warns before he wounds. The *prudent man, foreseeing the evil*, forecasts accordingly, *and hides himself, but the simple* is either so dull that he does not foresee it or so wilful and slothful that he will take no care to avoid it.

Verse 13

Those are hastening to poverty that have so little consideration as to be bound for everybody that will ask them and those that are given to women. Such as these will take up money as far as ever their credit will go, but they will certainly cheat their creditors at last, nay, they are cheating them all along.

Verse 14

It is our duty to give everyone his due praise, to applaud those who excel in knowledge, virtue, and usefulness, and to acknowledge the kindnesses we have received with thankfulness; but not to do this *with a loud voice, rising early in the morning*, to be always harping on this string, in all companies, even to our friend's face, to magnify the merits of our friend above measure. It is a greater folly to be fond of being ourselves extravagantly praised. Modest praises invite such as are present to add to the commendation, but immoderate praises tempt them to detract rather and to censure one that they hear over-commended. Over-praising a man makes him the object of envy.

JAMIESON, FAUSSET, BROWN

7. The luxury of wealth confers less happiness than the healthy appetite of labor.

8. Such are not only out of place, but out of duty and in danger.

9. rejoice the heart—the organ of perceiving what pleases the senses. **sweetness . . . counsel**— or, wise counsel is also pleasing. **10.** Adhere to tried friends. The ties of blood may be less reliable than those of genuine friendship.

11. The wisdom of children both reflects credit on parents and contributes to their aid in difficulties.

12, 13. (Cf. ch. 20:16; 22:3).

14. Excessive zeal in praising raises suspicions of selfishness.

ADAM CLARKE

F. B. MEYER:

"The full soul loatheth an honeycomb" (Prov. 27:7). Honey was not used in sacrifices made by fire unto the Lord. Its luscious taste may have made it an emblem of the pleasures of the world. As bees roam from flower to flower, sipping nectar here and there, so does the heart of the worldling roam over the world for satisfaction; settling nowhere for long, but extracting sweets from a variety of attractive sources.

The best way of combatting worldliness is by satisfying the heart with something better. The full soul loatheth even the honeycomb. When the prodigal gets the fatted calf, he has no further hankering after the husks which the swine eat. The girl who gets real jewels throws away her shams; and the child who has become a man has no taste for childish toys that once seemed all-important. This is the meaning of the old proverb: Love God, and do as you like. Whenever the spirit of worldliness gets into a congregation, you may be sure that the teaching has been defective, and that souls have not been made to sit at the rich banquet of the divine providing.

We are reminded of the words which the psalmist applied to the Word of God: "Sweeter than honey, or the honeycomb." Fill your heart with God and his sacred truth, and the things of the world will lose their charm. Do you know this absorbing love of Jesus? We can at least choose to know it, and present ourselves to the Holy Spirit, that He may shed it abroad in our hearts. Oh to be full! Full of the more abundant life of which the Lord spoke, of the unspeakable joy, of the peace that passeth understanding—in a word, of Jesus, as the chief and best.

—*Great Verses Through the Bible*

10. *Thine own friend.* A well and long tried friend is invaluable. Him that has been a friend to your family never forget, and never neglect. And, in the time of adversity, rather apply to such a one than go to your nearest relative who keeps himself at a distance.

12. *A prudent man foreseeth the evil.* The very same as chap. xxii. 3.

13. *Take his garment.* The same as chap. xx. 16.

14. *He that blesseth his friend.* He who makes loud and public protestations of acknowledgments to his friend for favors received subjects his sincerity to suspicion.

MATTHEW HENRY

And the greatest danger of all is that it is a temptation to pride, 2. Cor. xii. 6.

Verses 15–16

Here, as before, Solomon laments the case of him that has a peevish passionate wife. It is a grievance that there is no avoiding, for it is like *a continual dropping in a very rainy day.* The contentions of a neighbour may be like a sharp shower, troublesome for the time, yet, while it lasts, one may take shelter; but *the contentions of a wife* are like a constant soaking rain, for which there is no remedy but patience. See *ch.* xix. 13. A wise man would hide it if he could, but he cannot, any more than he can conceal the noise of the wind when it blows or the smell of a strong perfume. Those that are froward and brawling will proclaim their own shame, even when their friends, in kindness to them, would cover it.

Verse 17

Wise and profitable discourse sharpens men's wits; and those that have ever so much knowledge may by conference have something added to them. Good men's graces are sharpened by converse with those that are good, and bad men's lusts and passions are sharpened by converse with those that are bad, as iron is sharpened by its like, especially by the file. Men are filed, made smooth, and bright, and fit for business (who were rough, and dull, and inactive), by conversation.

Verse 18

Though the calling be laborious and despicable, yet those who keep to it will find there is something to be got by it. Let not a poor gardener, who *keeps the fig-tree,* be discouraged; though it require constant care and attendance to nurse up fig-trees, and, when they have grown to maturity, to keep them in good order, and gather the figs in their season, yet he shall be paid for his pains: He *shall eat the fruit* of it, 1 Cor. ix. 7. A poor servant if he be diligent in *waiting on his master,* if *he keep his master* (so the word is), if he do all he can that his estate be not wasted, such a one *shall be honoured,* be preferred and rewarded. God is a Master who has engaged to put an honour on those that serve him faithfully, John xii. 26.

Verse 19

As the water is a looking-glass in which we may see our faces by reflection, so there are mirrors by which the *heart of a man* is discovered to *a man,* that is, to himself. Let a man examine his own conscience, his thoughts, affections, and intentions. Let him behold his *natural face in the glass* of the divine law (Jas. i. 23), and he may discern what kind of man he is and what is his true character, which it will be of great use to every man rightly to know. As there is a similitude between the face of a man and the reflection of it in the water, so there is between one man's heart and another's; for God has fashioned men's hearts alike.

Verse 20

Two things are insatiable, and near of kin—death and sin. Men labour for that which surfeits, but satisfies not. Those whose eyes are ever towards the Lord in him are satisfied, and shall for ever be so.

Verse 21

Silver and gold are tried by putting them into the furnace and fining-pot; so is a man tried by praising him. If a man be made, by the applause that is given him, proud and scornful,—if he take the glory to himself which he should transmit to God, thereby it will appear that he is a vain foolish man, and has nothing in him truly praise-worthy. If, on the contrary, a man is made by his praise more thankful to God, more respectful to his friends, more diligent to do good to others, by this it will appear that he is a wise and good man, 2 Cor. vi. 8.

Verse 22

Solomon had said (*ch.* xxii. 15), *The foolishness* which *is bound in the heart of a child may be driven out by the rod of correction,* for then the mind is to be moulded, the vicious habits not having taken root. Here he shows that, if it be not done then, it will be next to impossible to do it afterwards. Some are so bad that rough and severe methods must be used with them, after gentle means have been tried in vain; they must be *brayed in a mortar.* God will take this way with them by his judgments; the magistrates must take this way with them by the rigour of the law. Force must be used with those that will not be ruled by reason, and love, and their own interest.

Verses 23–27

A command given us to be diligent in our callings

JAMIESON, FAUSSET, BROWN

15. (Cf. ch. 19:13.) **very . . . day**—lit., "a day of showers." **16. hideth**—or, restrains (i.e., tries to do it); is as fruitless an effort, as that of holding the wind. **the ointment . . . right hand**—the organ of power (Ps. 17:7; 18:35). His right hand endeavors to repress perfume, but vainly. Some prefer: "His right hand comes on oil, i.e. cannot take hold." Such a woman cannot be tamed.

17. a man sharpeneth . . . friend—i.e., conversation promotes intelligence, which the face exhibits.

18. Diligence secures a reward, even for the humble servant.

19. We may see our characters in the developed tempers of others.

20. Men's cupidity is as insatiable as the grave.

21. Praise tests character. **a man to his praise**—according to his praise, as he bears it. Thus vain men seek it, weak men are inflated by it, wise men disregard it, etc.

22. The obstinate wickedness of such is incurable by the heaviest inflictions.

ADAM CLARKE

15. *A continual dropping.* See chap. xix. 13.

16. *Whosoever hideth her hideth the wind.* You may as well attempt to repress the blowing of the wind as the tongue of a scold; and to conceal this unfortunate propensity of a wife is as impossible as to hush the storm, and prevent its sound from being heard. *The ointment of his right hand.* You can no more conceal such a woman's conduct than you can the smell of the aromatic oil with which your hand has been anointed.

17. *Iron sharpeneth iron.* As hard iron, viz., steel, will bring a knife to a better edge when it is properly whetted against it, so one friend may be the means of exciting another to reflect, dive deeply into, and illustrate a subject, without which whetting or excitement this had never taken place.

19. *As in water face answereth to face.* As a man sees his face perfectly reflected by the water, when looking into it, so the wise and penetrating man sees generally what is in the heart of another by considering the general tenor of his words and actions.

F. C. COOK:

19. As we see our own face when we look on the mirror-like surface of the water, so in every heart of man we may see our own likeness. In spite of all diversities we come upon the common human nature in which we all alike share. Others see in the reference to the reflection in the water the thought that we judge others by ourselves, find them faithful or the reverse, as we ourselves are.

20. Hades, the world of the dead, and Destruction (Death, the destroying power, personified) have been at all times and in all countries thought of as all-devouring, insatiable. Yet one thing is equally so, the lust of the eye, the restless craving which grows with what it feeds on (Eccles. 1:8).

21. Better, "So let a man be to his praise," let him purify it from all the alloy of flattery and baseness with which it is too probably mixed up.

22. "Bray." To pound wheat in a mortar with a pestle, in order to free the wheat from its husks and impurities, is to go through a far more elaborate process than threshing. But the folly of the fool is not thus to be got rid of. It sticks to him to the last; all discipline, teaching, experience seem to be wasted on him.

—*Barnes' Notes*

MATTHEW HENRY

is directed to husbandmen and shepherds, but it is to be extended to all other lawful callings. We ought not to live in idleness. We ought to understand our business, and not meddle with that which we do not understand. We should, with our own eyes, inspect the *state of our flocks*; it is the master's eye that makes them fat. *Riches are not for ever.* "*Look well to thy flocks and herds*, thy estate in the country and the stock upon that, for these are staple commodities, which, in a succession, will be for ever, whereas riches in trade and merchandise will not be so; the *crown* itself may perhaps not be so sure to thy family as thy flocks and herds." *The hay appears.* In taking care of the *flocks and herds*, "There needs no great labour, no ploughing or sowing; the food for them is the spontaneous product of the ground; thou hast nothing to do but to turn them into it in the summer, *when the grass shows itself*, and to *gather the herbs of the mountains* for them against winter. God has done his part; thou art ungrateful to him, and unjustly refusest to serve his providence, if thou dost not do thine." Good husbandry is profitable in a family: "Keep thy sheep, and thy sheep will help to keep thee; thou shalt have food for thy children and servants, *goats' milk enough* (*v.* 27); and *enough is as good as a feast.* Thou shalt have raiment likewise: the *lambs' wool shall be for thy clothing.* Thou shalt have money to pay thy rent; the goats thou shalt have to sell shall be *the price of thy field*"; nay, as some understand it, "*Thou shalt become a purchaser*, and buy land to leave to thy children," *v.* 26. Plain food and plain clothing, if they be but competent, are all we should aim at. "Reckon thyself well done to if thou be clothed with home-spun cloth, with the fleece of thy own lambs, and fed with goats' milk; let that serve for thy food which serves for the *food of thy household and the maintenance of thy maidens.* Be not desirous of dainties, *far-fetched and dear-bought.*"

CHAPTER 28

Verse 1

Guilt in the conscience makes men a terror to themselves, so that they are ready *to flee when none pursues*; like one that absconds for debt, who thinks everyone he meets a bailiff. Sin makes men cowards. *The righteous are bold as a lion*, as a young lion; in the greatest dangers they have a God of almighty power to trust to. *Therefore will not we fear though the earth be removed.*

Verse 2

National sins bring national disorders. *For the transgression of a land*, and a general defection from God and religion to idolatry, profaneness, or immorality, *many are the princes thereof*, many at the same time pretending to the sovereignty, by which the people are crumbled into parties and factions, one cutting off another, or soon cut off by the hand of God or of a foreign enemy. The government sometimes suffers for the sins of the people. Wisdom will prevent or redress these grievances: *By a man* or by a people, *of understanding*, that come again to their right mind, things are kept in a good order. We cannot imagine what a great deal of service one wise man may do to a nation in a critical juncture.

Verse 3

Those who know by experience the miseries of poverty should be compassionate to those who suffer the like, but they are inexcusably barbarous if they be injurious to them. How imperious those commonly are who, being indigent and necessitous, get into power. If a prince promote a poor man, he forgets that ever he was poor, and none shall be so oppressive to the poor as he, nor squeeze them so cruelly. He *is like a sweeping rain*, which washes away the corn in the ground, and lays and beats out that which has grown, so that it *leaves no food.*

Verse 4

Those that *praise the wicked* make it to appear that they do themselves *forsake the law*, and go contrary to it, for that condemns the wicked. Wicked people will speak well of one another, and so strengthen one another's hands in their wicked ways, hoping thereby to silence the clamours of their own consciences and to serve the interests of the devil's kingdom. Those that do indeed make conscience of the law of God themselves will, in their places, vigorously oppose sin.

Verse 5

As the prevalency of men's lusts is owing to the

JAMIESON, FAUSSET, BROWN

23, 24. flocks—constituted the staple of wealth. It is only by care and diligence that the most solid possessions can be perpetuated (ch. 23:5).

25-27. The fact that providential arrangements furnish the means of competence to those who properly use them is another motive to diligence (cf. Ps. 65:9-13). **The hay appeareth**—lit., "Grass appeareth" (Job 40:15; Ps. 104:14).

household—lit., "house," the family (Acts 16:15; I Cor. 1:16).

CHAPTER 28

Vss. 1-28. A bad conscience makes men timid; the righteous are alone truly bold (ch. 14:26; Ps. 27:1).

2. Anarchy producing contending rulers shortens the reign of each. **but by a man . . . prolonged**—or, "by a man of understanding—i.e., a good ruler—he who knows or regards the right, i.e., a good citizen, shall prolong (his days)." Good rulers are a blessing to the people. Bad government as a punishment for evil is contrasted with good as blessing to the good.

3. A poor man . . .—Such, in power, exact more severely, and so leave subjects bare.

4. They that forsake . . . wicked—Wrongdoers encourage one another.

ADAM CLARKE

23. *The state of thy flocks.* The directions to the end of the chapter refer chiefly to pastoral and agricultural affairs. Do not trust your flocks to the shepherd merely; number them yourself; look into their condition; see how they are tended; and when, and with what, and in what proportion, they are fed.

24. *For riches are not for ever.* All other kinds of property are very transitory. Money and the highest civil honors are but for a short season. Flocks and herds, properly attended to, may be multiplied and continued from generation to generation. The *crown* itself is not naturally so permanent.

CHAPTER 28

3. *A poor man that oppresseth the poor.* Our Lord illustrates this proverb most beautifully by the parable of the two debtors, Matt. xviii. 23.

MATTHEW HENRY

darkness of their understandings, so the darkness of their understandings is very much owing to the dominion of their lusts. *Men understand not judgment*, because they are *evil men*. As men's *seeking the Lord* is a good sign that they do understand much, so it is a good means of their understanding more, even of their understanding all things needful for them. If a man *do his will*, he shall *know his doctrine*, John vii. 17.

Verse 6

It is maintained as a paradox to a blind world that an honest, godly, poor man, is better than a wicked, ungodly, rich man, has a better character, is in a better condition, has more comfort in himself, is a greater blessing to the world, and is worthy of much more honour and respect. It is not only certain that his case will be better at death, but it is better in life.

Verse 7

Religion is true wisdom, and it makes men wise in every relation. Wickedness is not only a reproach to the sinner himself, but to all that are akin to him.

Verse 8

That which is ill-got, though it may increase much, will not last long. A man may perhaps raise a great estate, in a little time, by usury and fraud, but it will not continue; he gathers it for himself, but another man's shall be raised out of the ruins of it. Sometimes God in his providence so orders it that that which one got unjustly another uses charitably.

Verse 9

God speaks to us by his law, and expects we should hear him and heed him; *we* speak to him by prayer, to which we wait for an answer of peace.

Verse 10

The seducers, who attempt to draw good people into sin and mischief, shall not gain their point; they shall *fall themselves into their own pit*; and having been not only sinners, but tempters, their condemnation will be so much the greater, Matt. xxiii. 14, 15. The sincere shall not only be preserved from the evil way which the wicked would decoy them into, but they shall have the graces and comforts of God's Spirit.

Verse 11

Those that are rich are apt to think themselves wise, because, whatever else they are ignorant of, they know how to get and save; and expect that all they say should be regarded as an oracle and a law. A *poor man*, who has taken pains to get wisdom, having no other way (as the rich man has) to get a reputation, *searches him out*, and makes it to appear that he is not such a scholar, nor such a politician, as he is taken to be.

Verse 12

The comfort of the people of God is the honour of the nation in which they live. There is a *great glory* dwelling in the land when *the righteous do rejoice*, when they have their liberty, the free exercise of their religion, and are not persecuted. The advancement of the wicked is the eclipsing of the beauty of a nation: *When the wicked rise* and get head they make head against all that is sacred, and then *a man is hidden*, a good man is thrust into obscurity.

Verse 13

The folly of indulging sin, of palliating and excusing it, denying or extenuating it, diminishing it, dissembling it, or throwing the blame of it upon others: *He that* thus *covers his sins shall not prosper*. David owns himself to have been in a constant agitation while he *covered his sins*, Ps. xxxii. 3, 4. While the patient conceals his distemper he cannot expect a cure. *He that confesses* his guilt to God, and is careful not to return to sin again, shall *find mercy* with God. His conscience shall be eased and his ruin prevented. See 1 John i. 9; Jer. iii. 12, 13.

Verse 14

Most people think that those are happy who never fear; but there is a fear which is so far from having torment in it that it has in it the greatest satisfaction. Happy is the man who always keeps up in his mind a holy awe and reverence of God, who is always afraid of incurring his displeasure, who keeps conscience tender and has a dread of the appearance of evil. *He that hardens his heart*, that mocks at fear, and sets God and his judgments at defiance, his presumption will be his ruin.

JAMIESON, FAUSSET, BROWN

5. (Cf. John 7:17.) Ignorance of moral truth is due to unwillingness to know it.

6. (Cf. ch. 10:6.) Riches cannot compensate for sin, nor the want of them affect integrity.

7. (Cf. ch. 17:25.) **riotous men**—or, gluttons (ch. 23:20, 21).

8. usury . . . unjust gain—(cf. *Margin*). The two terms, meaning nearly the same, may denote excessive interest. God's providence directs the proper use of wealth.

9. (Cf. ch. 15:8; 21:27.) **hearing**—i.e., obeying. God requires sincere worshippers (Ps. 66:18; John 4:24).

10. (Cf. ch. 26:27.)

11. A poor but wise man can discover (and expose) the rich and self-conceited.

12. great glory—or, cause for it to a people, for the righteous rejoice in good, and righteousness exalts a nation (ch. 14:34). **a man . . . hidden**—i.e., the good retire, or all kinds try to escape a wicked rule.

13. (Cf. Ps. 32:3-5.) Concealment of sin delivers none from God's wrath, but He shows mercy to the humble penitent (Ps. 51:4).

14. feareth—i.e., God, and so repents. **hardeneth his heart**—makes himself insensible to sin, and so will not repent (ch. 14:16; 29:1).

ADAM CLARKE

8. *He that by usury . . . increaseth his substance.* By taking unlawful interest for his money; lending to a man in great distress money, for the use of which he requires an exorbitant sum.

F. B. MEYER:

"He that covereth his transgressions shall not prosper" (Prov. 28:13). There must be confession before forgiveness. This is clearly taught everywhere in God's Word. "If thy brother trespass against thee seven times a day, and seven times a day turn to thee, saying, I repent, thou shalt forgive him." But he must turn and say, I repent. This is the clear condition. You may and must use every method of inducing him to say this; but he must be brought to say it, before it is right to pronounce the gracious formula of absolution. There may be the disposition to forgive, but there cannot be the declaration of forgiveness, until the wrongdoer perceives the wrong and expresses his regret and sorrow.

The prodigal must say to his father, "I have sinned." It is only as we confess our sins, that our merciful High Priest can forgive us our sins and cleanse us from all unrighteousness. Confession is to take God's side against sin. It is the lifting out of one thing after another from heart and life, and holding them for a moment before God, with the acknowledgment that it is our fault, our grievous fault.

There is only one way in which transgressions can be covered: that of which the psalmist speaks, when he says, Blessed is the man whose iniquity is forgiven, whose sin is covered, because hidden under the propitiation of the blood. In Hood's poem, Eugene Aram sought to cover his sin under the leaves of the forest, and beneath the waters of the river. But in vain. So sinners try to cover their sins in vain. But God hath set forth Christ Jesus to be a propitiation—a word which denoted the mercy seat—the lid that covered the stone slabs on which the finger of God had written the Law.

—*Great Verses Through the Bible*

MATTHEW HENRY

Verse 15
It is written indeed, *Thou shalt not speak evil of the ruler of thy people;* but if he be a wicked ruler, that oppresses the people, this scripture calls him *a roaring lion and a ranging bear.* He is brutish, barbarous, and blood-thirsty, to be put among the beasts of prey.

Verse 16
A ruler that is covetous will neither do justly nor love mercy, but the people under him shall be bought and sold. *He that hates covetousness shall prolong* his government and peace, shall be happy in the affections of his people and the blessing of his God.

Verse 17
This agrees with that ancient law, *Whoso sheddeth man's blood, by man shall his blood be shed* (Gen. ix. 6). He that has committed murder, though he flees for his life, shall be continually haunted with terrors, shall himself *flee to the pit,* betray himself, and torment himself like Cain. Those that acquit the murderer, or do anything to help him off, come in sharers in the guilt of blood.

Verse 18
Those that are honest are always safe. He that acts with sincerity, that speaks as he thinks, has a single eye to the glory of God and the good of his brethren, *shall be saved* hereafter. They shall be safe now. Integrity and unrightness will give them a holy security in the worst of times. They may be injured, but they cannot be hurt. Those that are false and dishonest are never safe.

Verse 19
He that *tills his land,* and tends his shop, and minds his business, whatever it is, he *shall have plenty of bread,* of that which is necessary for himself and his family and with which he may be charitable to the poor; he shall *eat the labour of his hands.* Those that are idle, and careless, and company-keepers, though they indulge themselves in living (as they think) easily and pleasantly, they take the way to live miserably.

Verse 20
We are directed in the true way to be happy, and that is to be holy and honest. He that is *faithful* to God and man shall be blessed of the Lord. Usefulness shall be the reward of faithfulness, and it is a good reward. We are cautioned against a false way to happiness, and that is, right or wrong, raising an estate suddenly. He shall not be accounted innocent by his neighbours, but shall have their ill will and ill word. He does not say that he *cannot be innocent,* but there is probability that he will not prove so: *He that hasteth with his feet sinneth,* stumbleth, falleth.

Verse 21
It is a fundamental error in the administration of justice to consider the parties concerned more than the merits of the cause, so as to favour one because he is a gentleman, my countryman, my own acquaintance, or is of my party and persuasion, and to bear hard on the other party because he is a stranger, a poor man, or has been my rival, or has voted against me. Those that are partial will be paltry. Those that have once broken through the bonds of equity, though, at first, it must be some great bribe, when they have debauched their consciences, they will, at length, be so sordid that *for a piece of bread* they will give judgment against their consciences.

Verse 22
Solomon shows the sin and folly of those that will *be rich;* they will be so with all speed. They *have an evil eye,* that is, they are always grieving at those that have more than they. *Poverty shall come upon* them.

Verse 23
Flatterers may please those for a time who, upon second thoughts, will detest and despise them. Reprovers may displease those at first who yet afterwards, when the passion is over and the bitter physic begins to work well, will love and respect them. He that cries out against his surgeon for hurting him when he is searching his wound will yet pay him well, and thank him too, when he has cured it.

Verse 24
As Christ shows the wickedness of those children who think it is no duty to maintain their parents (Matt. xv. 5), so Solomon here shows the wickedness of those who think it is no sin to rob their parents, either by force or by wheedling them or threatening them, or by running into debt and leaving them to pay it. He that does it *is the companion of a destroyer,* no better than a robber on the highway.

JAMIESON, FAUSSET, BROWN

15. The rapacity and cruelty of such beasts well represent some wicked men (cf. Ps. 7:2; 17:12).

16. The prince . . . understanding—i.e., He does not perceive that oppression jeopards his success. Covetousness often produces oppression, hence the contrast.

17. doeth violence . . . blood . . .—or, that is oppressed by the blood of *life* (Gen. 9:6), which he has taken. **to the pit**—the grave or destruction (ch. 1:12; Job 33:18-24; Ps. 143:7). **stay him**—sustain or deliver him.

18. (Cf. ch. 10:9; 17:20.) Double dealing is eventually fatal.

19. (Cf. ch. 10:4; 20:4.) **vain persons**—idle, useless drones, implying that they are also wicked (ch. 12:11; Ps. 26:14).

20. maketh haste . . . rich—implying deceit or fraud (ch. 20:21), and so opposed to **faithful** or reliable.

21. respect of persons—(ch. 24:23). Such are led to evil by the slightest motive.

22. (Cf. vs. 20.) **evil eye**—in the general sense of ch. 23:6, here more specific for covetousness (cf. ch. 22:9; Matt. 20:15). **poverty . . . him**—by God's providence.

23. (Cf. ch. 9:8, 9; 27:5.) Those benefited by reproof will love their monitors.

24. (Cf. Matt. 15:4-6.) Such, though heirs, are virtually thieves, to be ranked with highwaymen.

ADAM CLARKE

JOHN GILL:

Verse 15. "As a roaring lion, and a ranging bear." Which are both terrible; the lion that roars for want of food, or when it is over its prey; and the bear, when it runs from place to place in quest of provision, being hungry and very desirous of food, has a keen appetite, as some think the word signifies. The Targum and Jarchi take it to be expressive of the cry and roaring it makes at such a time, as well as the lion (Isa. 59:11); so the Tigurine version. Roaring is the proper epithet of a lion, and is frequently given it in Scripture, and in other writers; and the bear, it is thought to have its name, in the Oriental language, from the growling and murmuring noise it makes when hungry. So is "a wicked ruler over the poor people"; one that rules over them in a tyrannical manner, sadly oppresses them, takes away the little from them they have, which is very cruel and barbarous; when he ought to protect and defend them, and against whom they cannot stand, and whom they dare not resist; and who therefore must be as terrible to them, being as cruel and voracious as the above animals. Tyrants are frequently compared to lions (Jer. 4:7; 50:7; 2 Tim. 4:17); and the man of sin, the wicked ruler and great oppressor of God's poor people, is compared to both; his feet are as the feet of a bear, and his mouth as the mouth of a lion (Rev. 12:2).

—Gill's Commentary

19. *He that tilleth his land.* See chap. xii. 11.

20. *He that maketh haste to be rich.* See chap. xiii. 11; xx. 21.

24. *Whoso robbeth his father.* The father's property is as much his own, in reference to the child, as that of the merest stranger. He who robs his parents is worse than a common robber; to the act of dishonesty and rapine he adds ingratitude, cruelty, and disobedience. Such a person is *the companion of a destroyer;* he may be considered as a murderer.

MATTHEW HENRY

Verse 25

Those make themselves lean, and continually unquiet, that are haughty and quarrelsome, for they are opposed to those that *shall be made fat.* Those make themselves fat, and always easy, that live in a continual dependence upon God and his grace: *He who puts his trust in the Lord,* who, instead of struggling for himself, commits his cause to God, *shall be made fat.*

Verse 26

A fool *trusts to his own heart,* to his own wisdom, his own strength, his own merit and righteousness, and the good opinion he has of himself. He that *walks wisely,* that trusts not to his own heart, but is humble and self-diffident, and goes on in the strength of the Lord God, *he shall be delivered.*

Verse 27

He that gives to the poor shall himself be never the poorer for so doing; he *shall not lack. He that hides his eyes,* that he may not see the miseries of the poor lest his eye should affect his heart and extort some relief from him, he *shall have many a curse,* both from God and man.

Verse 28

This is to the same purport with what we had, *v.* 12. When power is put into the hands of *the wicked, men hide themselves;* wise men retire into privacy, and decline public business, not caring to be employed under them; rich men get out of the way, for fear of being squeezed for what they have; and good men abscond, despairing to do good and fearing to be ill-treated. When bad men are disgraced, and their power taken from them, then *the righteous increase;* for, *when they perish,* good men will be put in their room.

CHAPTER 29

Verse 1

The obstinacy of many wicked people is to be greatly lamented. They are *often reproved* by parents and friends, by magistrates and ministers, but they *harden their necks.* Perhaps they fling away, and will not so much as give the reproof a patient hearing. Those that go on in sin, in spite of admonition, *shall be destroyed;* if the rods answer not the end, expect the axes. They *shall be destroyed, and no healing,* so the word is.

Verse 2

This is what was said before, *ch.* xxviii. 12, 28. 1. *The people* will have cause to *rejoice* or *mourn* according as their rulers are *righteous* or *wicked;* for, if *the righteous* be in *authority,* sin will be punished and restrained; *but,* if *the wicked* get power, religion and religious people will be persecuted, and so the ends of government will be perverted. *The people* will actually *rejoice* or *mourn* according as their rulers are *righteous* or *wicked.*

Verse 3

A virtuous young man *loves wisdom,* he is *a philosopher* (*a lover of wisdom*), for religion is the best philosophy; he avoids bad company, and especially the company of lewd women. A vicious young man hates *wisdom; he keeps company with* scandalous women, who will be his ruin, both in soul and body.

Verse 4

A prince should *establish the land,* maintain its laws, settle the minds of his subjects, secure their liberties, and properties from hostilities and for posterity. This he must do *by judgment* and by the steady administration of justice, without respect of persons. *A man of oblations* (so it is in the margin) *overthrows the land;* a man that is either sacrilegious or superstitious, or a man that will, for a bribe, connive at the most guilty, and, in hope of one, persecute the innocent—such governors as these will ruin a country.

Verse 5

Those may be said to *flatter their neighbours* who applaud good in them, which really either is not or is not such as they represent it. These *spread a net for their* neighbours' feet. It has an ill effect on those who are flattered; it puffs them up with pride, and so proves a net that entangles them in sin. He that flatters others, in expectation that they will return his compliments and flatter him, does but make himself ridiculous and odious even to those he flatters.

JAMIESON, FAUSSET, BROWN

25. of a proud heart—lit., "puffed up of soul"—i.e., self-confident, and hence overbearing and litigious. **made fat**—or, prosperous (ch. 11:25; 16:20).

26. (Cf. ch. 3:6-8.) **walketh wisely**—i.e., trusting in God (ch. 22:17-19).

27. (Cf. ch. 11:24-26.) **hideth his eyes**—as the face (Ps. 27:9; 69:17), denotes inattention.

28. The elevation of the wicked to power drives men to seek refuge from tyranny (cf. vs. 12; ch. 11:10; Ps. 12:8).

CHAPTER 29

Vss. 1-27. **1. hardeneth . . . neck**—obstinately refuses counsel (II Kings 17:14; Neh. 9:16). **destroyed**—lit., "shivered" or "utterly broken to pieces." **without remedy**—lit., "without healing" or repairing.

2. (Cf. ch. 11:10; 28:28.) **in authority**—(Cf. *Margin*), increased in power.

3. (Cf. ch. 4:6, 7; 10:1, etc.)

4. by judgment—i.e., righteous decisions, opposed to those procured by gifts (cf. ch. 28:21), by which good government is perverted. **land**—for nation.

5. (Cf. ch. 26:28.) **spreadeth . . . feet**—By misleading him as to his real character, the flatterer brings him to evil, prepared by himself or others.

ADAM CLARKE

25. *Shall be made fat.* Shall be prosperous.

26. *He that trusteth in his own heart is a fool.* For his heart, which is deceitful and desperately wicked, will infallibly deceive him.

CHAPTER 29

1. *Hardeneth his neck.* Becomes stubborn and obstinate.

JOHN GILL:

Verse 1. "He that being often reproved hardeneth his neck." Or "a man of reproofs"; either a man that takes upon him to be a censurer and reprover of others, and is often at that work, and yet does those things himself which he censures and reproves in others; and therefore must have an impudent face and a hard heart, a seared conscience, and a stiff neck; his neck must be an iron sinew, and his brow brass: or rather a man that is often reproved by others, by parents, by ministers of the Gospel, by the Lord himself, by the admonitions of his word and Spirit, and by the correcting dispensations of his providence; and yet despises and rejects all counsel and admonition, instruction and reproofs of every kind, and hardens himself against them, and shows no manner of regard unto them. The metaphor is taken from oxen, which kick and toss about, and will not suffer the yoke to be put upon their necks. Such an one "shall suddenly be destroyed"; or "broken"; as the potter's vessel is broken to pieces with an iron rod, and can never be put together again; so such persons shall be punished with everlasting destruction, which shall come upon them suddenly, when they are crying Peace to themselves, notwithstanding the reproofs of God and men. "And that without remedy"; or, "and there is no healing"; no cure of their disease, which is obstinate; no pardon of their sins; no recovery of them out of their miserable and undone state and condition; they are irretrievably lost; there is no help for them, having despised all advice and instruction.—*Gill's Commentary*

MATTHEW HENRY

Verse 6

One sin is a temptation to another, and there are troubles which, as *a snare*, come suddenly upon evil men in the midst of their transgressions. The snare that is *in the transgression of evil men* spoils all their mirth, *but righteous* men are kept from those snares, or delivered out of them; they walk at liberty, and therefore they *sing and rejoice*.

Verse 7

A *righteous* judge *considers the cause of the poor*. It is every man's duty to consider the poor (Ps. xli. 1), but the judgment of the poor is to be considered by those that sit in judgment. Sense of justice must make both judge and advocate as solicitous and industrious in the poor man's cause as if they hoped for the greatest advantage. A *wicked* man, because it is a poor man's cause, which there is nothing to be got by, *regards not to know it*, for he cares not which way it goes, right or wrong. See Job xxix. 16.

Verse 8

Scornful men employed in the business of the state do things with precipitation, because they scorn to deliberate. They scorn to be hampered by laws and constitutions; break their faith, because they scorn to be bound by their word. Thus they *bring a city into a snare* by their ill conduct, or (as the margin reads it) they *set a city on fire*; they sow discord among the citizens and run them into confusion. *Wise men* by promoting religion, which is true wisdom, *turn away the wrath* of God, and by prudent counsels, reconcile contending parties.

Verse 9

If a wise man contend with a wise man, he may hope to be understood, and, as far as he has reason and equity on his side, to carry his point and make it issue amicably; but, if he *contend with a foolish man, there is no rest;* he will see no end of it. Whether the foolish man take angrily or scornfully what is said to him, whether he rail at it or mock at it, there will be *no rest*. The wisest man must expect to be either scolded or ridiculed if he *contend with a fool*. Whether the wise man himself *rage or laugh*, whether he take the serious or the jocular way of dealing with the fool, no good is done.

Verse 10

Bad men hate their best friends: *The bloodthirsty*, all the seed of the old serpent, who *was a murderer from the beginning, hate the upright*. Bloody men do especially *hate upright* magistrates, who would restrain and reform them. *The just*, whom the bloody men hate, *seek their soul*, pray for their conversion, and would gladly do anything for their salvation. This Christ taught us. *Father, forgive them*.

Verse 11

He is *a fool* who *utters all his mind*, who, whatever is started in discourse, quickly shoots his bolt,— who, when he is provoked, will say anything that comes uppermost, whoever is reflected upon by it. *A wise man* will not *utter all his mind* at once, but will take time for a second thought, or reserve the present thought for a fitter time. He will not deliver himself in a continued speech, or starched discourse, but with pauses, that he may hear what is to be objected and answer it.

Verse 12

Lies will be told to those that will hearken to them; but the receiver, in this case, is as bad as the thief. Those that do so will have *all their servants wicked*, for they will have lies told of them; and they will be wicked, for they will tell lies to them.

Verse 13

This shows how wisely the great God serves the designs of his providence by persons of very different tempers. Some are *poor*, and honest, and laborious; others are rich, slothful, and *deceitful*. They *meet together* in the business of this world, and *the Lord enlightens both their eyes*. To some of both sorts he gives his grace. He enlightens the eyes of the poor by giving them patience, and of the deceitful by giving them repentance, as Zaccheus. *The poor and the deceitful* we are ready to look upon as blemishes of Providence, but God makes even them to display the beauty of Providence.

Verse 14

The rich will look to themselves, but *the poor* and needy the prince must *defend* (Ps. lxxxii. 3) and plead for, Prov. xxxi. 9. Those magistrates that do their duty *shall be established for ever*.

JAMIESON, FAUSSET, BROWN

6. In [or, By] **the transgression**—he is brought into difficulty (ch. 12:13), but the righteous go on prospering, and so sing or rejoice.

7. considereth—lit., "knows," as Ps. 1:6. **the cause**—i.e., in courts of justice (cf. vs. 14). The voluntary neglect of it by the wicked (ch. 28:27) occasions oppression.

8. Scornful men—those who contemptuously disregard God's law. **bring**—(Cf. *Margin*), kindle strife. **turn away** [i.e., abate] **wrath.**

9. contendeth—i.e., in law. **whether ... laugh**—The fool, whether angry or good-humored, is unsettled; or referring the words to the wise man, the sense is, that all his efforts, severe or gentle, are unavailing to pacify the fool.

10. bloodthirsty—(Cf. *Margin*), murderers (Ps. 5:6; 26:9). **hate . . .** (ch. 1:11; Gen. 3:4.) **seek . . . soul**—i.e.,) to preserve it.

11. (Cf. ch. 12:16; 16:32.) **mind**—or spirit, for anger or any ill passion which the righteous restrain.

12. His servants imitate him.

13. (Cf. ch. 22:2.) **deceitful man**—lit., "man of vexations," an exactor. **the Lord . . . their eyes**—sustains their lives (I Sam. 14:27; Ps. 13:3); i.e., both depend on Him, and He will do justice.

14. (Cf. ch. 20:28; 25:5.) Such is the character of the King of kings (Ps. 72:4, 12).

ADAM CLARKE

JOSEPH PARKER:

"If a wise man contendeth with a foolish man, whether he rage or laugh, there is no rest" (v. 9). Wise men should therefore leave the strife before it is begun. Whether the wise man treat the fool with haughty disdain, or with good nature, the result will be the same, that is to say, the fool will not cease from his strife or folly. Everything is thrown away upon the fool. Possibly the sense may be that the fool himself rages and laughs: it is impossible for him to listen judicially to any arguments that may be offered: he laughs without reason and he denounces without reason; his laughter is madness: in short, he is a fool, a dull, stupid person, headstrong in his own way, lying quite beyond the line of reasoning or persuasion. Always let a fool alone.

"The poor and the deceitful man meet together: the Lord lighteneth both their eyes" (v. 13). The rich and the poor meet together, but the Lord is the maker of them both. We see the Lord both in men and in their circumstances. It is practical atheism to regard God as the Creator of the man and as having nothing to do with the man's surroundings. "The Lord lighteneth both their eyes," that is to say, each of them, whether rich or poor, oppressor or oppressed, owes his life to the living God, and from that living God each shall receive due judgment in the end. Whatever may be said of the circumstances of each as to their origin or explanation, it is certain that the life of each is derived from heaven, and an account of it is due to the divine Giver.—*The People's Bible*

13. *The poor and the deceitful man.* It is difficult to fix the meaning of *techachim*, which we here render *the deceitful man*. I suppose the meaning may be the same as in chap. xxii. 2: "The rich and poor meet together: the Lord is the maker of them all."

MATTHEW HENRY

Verse 15
Parents must not only tell their children what is good and evil, but they must chide them, and correct them too, if need be. If a *reproof* will serve without *the rod*, it is well, but *the rod* must never be used without a rational and grave *reproof*; and then it will *give wisdom. A child* that is not restrained or reproved, but is *left to himself*, as Adonijah was, may do well if he will, but, if he take to ill courses, he proves a disgrace to his family, and *brings his mother to shame.*

Verse 16
The more sinners there are the more sin there is. In the old world, when *men began to multiply*, they began to degenerate and corrupt themselves and one another. The more sin there is the nearer is the ruin threatened. Let not *the righteous* have their faith and hope shocked by the increase of sin and sinners. Let them not say that *God has forsaken the earth*, but wait with patience; the transgressors shall fall into disgrace and destruction.

Verse 17
It is a pleasure to parents, which none know but those that are blessed with it, to see the happy fruit of the good education they have given their children, and to have a prospect of their well-doing for both worlds. Children must be trained and not suffered to do what they will and to go without rebuke when they do amiss.

Verse 18
Where there is no vision, no prophet to expound the law, no priest or Levite to teach the good knowledge of the Lord, no means of grace, the word of the Lord is scarce, there is *no open vision* (1 Sam. iii. 1), where it is so *the people perish*; the word has many significations. 1. *The people are made naked*, stripped of their ornaments and so exposed to shame, stripped of their armour and so exposed to danger. How bare does a place look without Bibles and ministers, and what an easy prey it is to the enemy of souls! 2. *The people rebel*, not only against God, but against their prince; good preaching would make people good subjects, but, for want of it, they are turbulent and factious. 3. *The people are idle*, or *they play*, as the scholars are apt to do when the master is absent. 4. *They are scattered as sheep having no shepherd*, for want of the masters of assemblies to call them and keep them together, Mark vi. 34. 5. *They perish;* they are *destroyed for lack of knowledge*, Hos. iv. 6.

Verse 19
Unprofitable, slothful, wicked servants serve not from conscience, or love, but purely from fear. No rational words will work upon them; they *will not be corrected* and reformed by fair means, no, nor by foul *words.* No rational words will be got from them. They are dogged and sullen; and, *though they understand* the questions you ask them, they *will not* give you an *answer.*

Verse 20
Seest thou a man that is hasty in his matters, that is of a light desultory wit, gallops over a book, but takes no time to digest it? *There is more hope of* making a scholar and a wise man of one that is dull and heavy, and slow in his studies, than of one that has such a mercurial genius and cannot fix. *Seest thou a man that is* forward to speak to every matter that is started, as if he were an oracle? *There is more hope of a* modest *fool*, who is sensible of his folly, than of such a self-conceited one.

Verse 21
It is an ungrateful thing in a servant to behave insolently because he has been used tenderly. The humble prodigal thinks himself unworthy *to be called a son*, and is content to be a servant; the pampered slave thinks himself too good to be called *a servant*, and will be *a son at the length*, will be on a par with his master, and perhaps pretend to the inheritance.

Verse 22
An angry, passionate, furious disposition makes men provoking to one another. It makes men provoking to God. Undue anger is a sin which is the cause of many sins.

Verse 23
Those that think to gain respect by lifting up themselves, talking big, appearing fine, and applauding themselves, will expose themselves to contempt, lose their reputation, and provoke God by humbling providences to bring them down and lay them *low*. Those who *humble themselves shall be exalted*, and shall be established in their dignity.

JAMIESON, FAUSSET, BROWN

15. (Cf. ch. 13:24; 23:13.)

16. (Cf. vss. 2, 12; Ps. 12:1-8.) **shall see . . . fall**—and triumph in it (Ps. 37:34-38; 58:10, 11).

17. (Cf. vss. 3, 15; ch. 19:18.) **give thee rest**—peace and quiet (cf. vs. 9).

18. no vision—instruction in God's truth, which was by prophets, through visions (I Sam. 3:1). **people perish**—(Cf. *Margin*), are deprived of moral restraints. **keepeth the law**—has, and observes, instruction (ch. 14:11, 34; Ps. 19:11).

19. A servant—who lacks good principle. **corrected**—or discovered. **will not answer**—i.e., will not obey.

20. (Cf. ch. 21:5.) **hasty in . . . words**—implying self-conceit (ch. 26:12).

21. become his son—assume the place and privileges of one.

22. (Cf. ch. 15:18.) Such are delighted by discord and violence.

23. (Cf. ch. 16:18; 18:12.) **honour . . . spirit**—or, such shall lay hold on honor (ch. 11:16).

ADAM CLARKE

F. B. MEYER:

"Where there is no vision" (Prov. 29:18). What a difference it makes to our teaching and preaching where there is no vision! The people perish for want of seers of those who can say with the apostle, "That which we have seen and heard, declare we unto you also, that ye may have fellowship with us." It is not difficult to know whether a poet or painter has a vision. If he have, there is glow and passion in his work. And it is not more difficult to detect in the accent of the speaker on divine things, whether he is speaking at second-hand, or as the result of direct vision.

This vision of God was vouchsafed to Moses and Elijah and the apostle Paul. Concerning the latter God said, "He shall be a minister and a witness of things which he has seen." This is our only qualification for teaching others; not intellect, nor imagination, nor rhetoric, but to have seen the King and beheld the pattern on the mount. For such a vision, on our part, there must be humility, patience, and faith, a definite withdrawal from the life of sense, and a definite fixedness of gaze on the things that are unseen and eternal. But on God's part there must be revelation. "It pleased God," said the apostle, "to reveal his Son in me, that I might preach Him."

The apostle said, "I could not see for the glory of that light." A party of tourists was divided one dull morning in Switzerland; the majority thought that it was useless to attempt the mountains. A few started, soon got beyond the low hanging clouds, spent a day in the heights under marvelous skies, and returned at night, radiant, and overflowing with what they had seen. Ah, speaking is easy when one has seen!

—Great Verses Through the Bible

18. *Where there is no vision.* Where divine revelation and the faithful preaching of the sacred testimonies are neither reverenced nor attended, the ruin of that land is at no great distance. *But he that keepeth the law, happy is he.* So our Lord: "Blessed are they that hear the word of God, and keep it."

22. *An angry man stirreth up strife.* His spirit begets its like wherever he goes. *And a furious man aboundeth in transgression.* His furious spirit is always carrying him into extremes, and each of these is a transgression.

23. *A man's pride shall bring him low.* A proud man is universally despised, and such are often exposed to great mortifications.

MATTHEW HENRY

Verse 24

Those who are drawn away by the enticement of sinners incur guilt: *He* does so that goes *partner with* such as rob and defraud. The receiver is as bad as the thief; and, being drawn in to join with him in the commission of the sin, he cannot escape joining with him in the concealment of it, though it be with the most horrid perjuries and execrations. They even *hate their own souls*, for they wilfully do that which will be the inevitable destruction of them.

Verse 25

We are cautioned not to dread the power of man. Slavish fear *brings a snake*, that is, exposes men to many insults, or rather to many temptations. Abraham, for *fear of man*, denied his wife, and Peter his Master, and many a one his God and religion. *Whoso puts his trust in the Lord shall be* set on high, above the power of man and above the fear of that power.

Verse 26

Men, to advance and enrich themselves, *seek the ruler's favour*. Solomon was himself a *ruler*, and knew with what sedulity men made their application to him, some on one errand, others on another, but all for his *favour*. Haman had *the ruler's favour*, and yet it availed him nothing. Look up to God, and seek the favour of the Ruler of rulers; for *every man's judgment proceeds from the Lord*. It is not with us as the ruler pleases, it is as God pleases.

Verse 27

This expresses not only the innate contrariety that there is between virtue and vice, but the old enmity that has always been between the seed of the woman and the seed of the serpent, Gen. iii. 15. All that are sanctified have a rooted antipathy to wickedness and wicked people. They have a good will to the souls of all, but they hate the ways and practices of those that are impious. Thus *an unjust* man makes himself odious *to the just*, and it is one part of his present shame and punishment that good men cannot endure him. All that are unsanctified have a like rooted antipathy to godliness and godly people.

JAMIESON, FAUSSET, BROWN

24 hateth . . . soul—(Cf. ch. 8:36.) **heareth cursing**—(Lev. 5:1), risks the punishment, rather than reveal truth.

25. The fear . . . snare—involves men in difficulty (cf. vs. 6). **shall be safe**—(Cf. *Margin;* ch. 18:10.)

26. (Cf. *Margin;* Ps. 27:8.) God alone will and can do exact justice.

27. (Cf. ch. 3:32.) On last clause, cf. vs. 16; Psalm 37:12.

ADAM CLARKE

24. *Hateth his own soul. Naphsho*, his "life," as the outraged law may at any time seize on and put him to death. *He heareth cursing.* "The execration," or adjuration, "but he will not tell it." He has no fear of God, nor reverence for an oath, because his heart is hardened through the deceitfulness of sin.

25. *The fear of man bringeth a snare.* How often has this led weak men, though sincere in their general character, to deny their God, and abjure His people! See the case of Peter.

MATTHEW HENRY

CHAPTER 30

Verses 1-6

Agur was a *collector* (so it signifies), a gatherer, one that collected the wise sayings and observations of others (*v.* 3), "*I* have not *learned wisdom* myself, but have been a scribe, or amanuensis, to other wise and learned men." *Ithiel and Ucal* are mentioned: 1. As the names of his pupils, whom he instructed. Probably they wrote what he dictated, as Baruch wrote from the mouth of Jeremiah. Or, 2. As the subject of his discourse. *Ithiel* signifies *God with me*, the application of *Immanuel, God with us. Ucal* signifies *the Mighty One*, for it is upon one that is mighty that help is laid for us.

Three things the prophet here aims at:—

I. To abase himself. Before he makes confession of his faith he makes confession of his folly and the weakness and deficiency of reason, which make it so necessary that we be guided and governed by faith.

Agur, when he was applied to by others as wiser than most, acknowledged himself more foolish than any. Whatever high opinion others may have of us, it becomes us to have low thoughts of ourselves. He speaks of himself as wanting a revelation to guide him in the ways of truth and wisdom. The natural man, the natural powers, perceive not, nay, they *receive not, the things of the Spirit of God.*

II. To advance Jesus Christ, and the Father in him (*v.* 4): *Who hath ascended up into heaven*, &c. Some understand this of God and of his works, which are both incomparable and unsearchable. Others refer it to Christ, to Ithiel and Ucal, the Son of God, for it is the Son's name, as well as the Father's, that is here enquired after, and a challenge given to any to vie with him. What is *his Son's name*, by whom he does all these things? The Old Testament saints expected the Messiah to be the *Son of the Blessed*, and he is here spoken of as a person distinct from the Father, but his name as yet secret.

III. To assure us of the truth of the word of God, and to recommend it to us, *v.* 5, 6. Agur's pupils expect to be instructed by him in the things of God. "Alas!" says he, "I cannot undertake to instruct you; go to the word of God. *Every word of God is pure;* there is not the least mixture of falsehood and corruption in it." God in his word, God in his promise, is *a shield*, a sure protection, to all those that *put their trust in him*. It is sufficient, and therefore we must not add to it (*v.* 6). We must be content

JAMIESON, FAUSSET, BROWN

CHAPTER 30

Vss. 1-33. **1.** This is the title of this chapter **the prophecy**—lit., "the burden" (cf. Isa. 13:1; Zech. 9:1), used for any divine instruction; not necessarily a prediction, which was only a kind of prophecy (I Chron. 15:27, *a song*). Prophets were inspired men, who spoke for God to man, or for man to God (Gen. 20:7; Exod. 7:14, 15, 16). Such, also, were the New Testament prophets. In a general sense, Gad, Nathan, and others were such, who were divine teachers, though we do not learn that they ever predicted. **the man spake**—lit., "the saying of the man"; an expression used to denote any solemn and important announcement (cf. II Sam. 23:1; Ps. 36:1; 110:1; Isa. 1:24, etc.). Ithiel and Ucal were perhaps pupils. **2-4. brutish**—stupid, a strong term to denote his lowly self-estimation; or he may speak of such as his natural condition, as contrasted with God's all-seeing comprehensive knowledge and almighty power.

The questions of the last clause emphatically deny the attributes mentioned to be those of any creature, thus impressively strengthening the implied reference of the former to God (cf. Deut. 30:12-14; Isa. 40:12; Eph. 4:8).

5. (Cf. Ps. 12:6; 119:140.) **6. Add . . . words**—implying that his sole reliance was on God's all-sufficient teaching. **reprove** [convict] **thee**—and so the falsehood will appear.

ADAM CLARKE

CHAPTER 30

1. *The words of Agur the son of Jakeh.* The words *Agur, Jakeh, Ithiel,* and *Ucal* have been considered by some as proper names; by others, as descriptive characters. With some, *Agur* is Solomon; and *Jakeh*, David; and *Ithiel* and *Ucal* are epithets of Christ. From this introduction, from the names here used, and from the style of the book, it appears evident that Solomon was not the author of this chapter; and that it was designed to be distinguished from his work by this very preface, which specifically distinguishes it from the preceding work. Nor can the words in verses 2, 3, 8, and 9 be at all applied to Solomon, they suit no part of Solomon's life nor of his circumstances. We must, therefore, consider it an appendix or supplement to the preceding collection.

3. *I neither learned wisdom.* I have never been a scholar in any of those schools of the wise men, nor *have the knowledge of the holy, kedoshim*, of the saints or holy persons.

4. *What is his name?* Show me the nature of this Supreme Being. Point out His eternity, omniscience, omnipresence, omnipotence; comprehend and describe Him, if you can. *What is his son's name?* Many are of opinion that Agur refers here to the first and second persons of the ever-blessed Trinity. It may be so; but who would venture to rest the proof of that most glorious doctrine upon such a text, to say nothing of the obscure author? The doctrine is true, sublimely true; but many doctrines have suffered in controversy by improper texts being urged in their favor. Every lover of God and truth should be very choice in his selections when he comes forward in behalf of the more mysterious doctrines of the Bible. Quote nothing that is not clear; advance nothing that does not tell. When we are obliged to spend a world of critical labor in order to establish the sense of a text which we intend to allege in favor of the doctrine we wish to support, we may rest assured that we are going the wrong way to work. Those who indiscriminately amass every text of Scripture they think bears upon the sub-

MATTHEW HENRY

with what God has thought fit to make known to us of his mind, and not covet to be *wise above what is written.*

Verses 7–9

After Agur's confession and creed, here follows his litany,

I. The preface to his prayer: *Two things have I required* (that is, *requested*) of thee, O God! Before we go to pray it is good to consider what we need, and what the things are which we have to ask of God.

II. The prayer itself. The *two things* he requires are grace sufficient and food convenient. 1. Grace sufficient for his soul: *Remove from me vanity and lies.* Some understand it as a prayer for the pardon of sin, for, when God forgives sin, he removes it, he takes it away. 2. Food convenient for his body. "*Feed me with the bread of my allowance,* such bread as thou thinkest fit to allow me." Our Saviour seems to refer to this when he teaches us to pray, *Give us this day our daily bread.* He prays against the extremes of abundance and want: *Give me neither poverty nor riches.* He hereby intends to express the value which wise and good men have for a middle state of life, and, with submission to the will of God, desires that that might be his state, neither great honour nor great contempt. He gives a pious reason for his prayer, *v.* 9. "*Lest I be rich* and sin, or *poor* and sin." Sin is that which a good man is afraid of in every condition and under every event. Prosperity makes people proud and forgetful of God, as if they had no need of him. A good man also dreads the temptations of a poor condition: *Lest I be poor and steal.* Poverty is a strong temptation to dishonesty. Agur dreads this lest he should dishonour God by it.

Verses 10–14

I. A caution not to abuse other people's servants any more than our own, nor to make mischief between them and their masters. *Hurt not a servant with thy tongue* (so the margin reads it); for it argues a sordid disposition to smite anybody secretly with the scourge of the tongue, especially a servant, who is not a match for us.

II. An account of some wicked generations of men, that are justly abominable to all that are virtuous and good. 1. Such as are abusive to their parents. *There is a generation* of such; young men of that black character commonly herd together, and irritate one another against their parents, because they cannot endure the yoke. 2. Such as are conceited of themselves, and yet *are not cleansed from their filthiness,* the filthiness of their hearts, which they pretend to be the best part of them. 3. Such as are haughty and scornful to those about them, *v.* 13. There is a generation of such, on whom he that *resists the proud* will pour contempt. 4. Such as are cruel to the poor and barbarous to all that lie at their mercy (*v.* 14); their teeth are iron and steel, *swords and knives,* instruments of cruelty, with which they *devour the poor* with the greatest pleasure imaginable, and as greedily as hungry men cut their meat and eat it.

Verses 15–17

He had spoken before of those that devoured the poor (*v.* 14), now here he speaks of their insatiableness in doing this. Now those are *two daughters* of the *horse-leech,* its genuine offspring, that still cry, "*Give, give,* give more blood, give more money"; for the bloody are still blood-thirsty; being drunk with blood, they add thirst to their drunkenness, and will seek it yet again.

I. He specifies four other things which are insatiable, 1. The grave, into which multitudes fall, and yet still more will fall, and it swallows them all up, and returns none. 2. The *barren womb,* which is impatient of its affliction in being barren, and cries, as Rachel did, *Give me children.* 3. The *parched ground* in time of drought (especially in those hot countries), which still soaks in the rain that comes in abundance upon it and in a little time wants more. 4. The *fire,* which, when it has consumed abundance of fuel, yet still devours all the combustible matter that is thrown into it. So insatiable are the corrupt desires of sinners, and so little satisfaction have they even in the gratification of them.

II. He adds a terrible threatening to disobedient children (*v.* 17). Those that dishonour their parents shall be hanged in chains, as it were, for the birds of prey to pick out their eyes, those eyes with which they looked so scornfully on their good parents. The dead bodies of malefactors were not to hang all night, but before night the ravens would have picked out their eyes.

Verses 18–23

I. An account of four things that are *too wonderful*

JAMIESON, FAUSSET, BROWN

7-9. A prayer for exemption from wickedness, and the extremes of poverty and riches, the *two things* mentioned. Contentment is implied as desired.

vanity—all sorts of sinful acts (Job 11:11; Isa. 5:18).

be full . . . deny—i.e., puffed up by the pride of prosperity. **take the name . . . vain**—This is not (*Hebrew*) the form (cf. Exod. 20:7), but "take" rather denotes laying violent hold on any thing; i.e. lest I assail God's name or attributes, as justice, mercy, etc., which the poor are tempted to do.

10. Accuse not—Slander not (Ps. 10:7). **curse . . . guilty**—lest, however lowly, he be exasperated to turn on thee, and your guilt be made to appear.

11-14. Four kinds of hateful persons—(1) graceless children, (2) hypocrites, (3) the proud, (4) cruel oppressors (cf. on vs. 14, Ps. 14:4; 52:2)—are now illustrated; (1) vss. 15, 16, the insatiability of prodigal children and their fate; (2) vs. 17, hypocrisy, or the concealment of real character; (3 and 4) vs. 18-20, various examples of pride and oppression.

15, 16. horse-leech—supposed by some to be the vampire (a fabulous creature), as being literally insatiable; but the other subjects mentioned must be taken as this, comparatively insatiable. The use of a fabulous creature agreeably to popular notions is not inconsistent with inspiration. **There are three . . . yea, four**—(Cf. ch. 6:16).

17. The eye—for the person, with reference to the use of the organ to express mockery and contempt, and also as that by which punishment is received. **the ravens . . . eagles . . . eat**—either as dying unnaturally, or being left unburied, or both.

ADAM CLARKE

ject they defend give their adversaries great advantage against them. I see many a sacred doctrine suffering through the bad judgment of its friends every day.

5. *Every word of God is pure.* "Every oracle of God is purified." A metaphor taken from the purifying of metals. Everything that God has pronounced, every inspiration which the prophets have received, is pure, without mixture of error, without dross. *He is a shield unto them.* And this oracle among the rest. He is the Defense of all *them that put their trust in him.*

6. *Add not thou unto his words.* You can no more increase their value by any addition than you can that of gold by adding any other metal to it.

7. *Two things have I required of thee.* These two petitions are mentioned in the next verse.

8. *Remove far from me vanity and lies* (1) All false shows, all false appearances of happiness, every vain expectation. Let me not set my heart on anything that is not solid, true, durable, and eternal. (2) Lies, all words of deception, empty pretensions, false promises, uncertain dependences, and words that fail; promises which, when they become due, are like bad bills. From the import of the original, I am satisfied that Agur prays against idolatry, false religion, and false worship of every kind. *Give me neither poverty nor riches.* Here are three requests: (1) Give me not poverty. The reason is added: Lest, being poor, I shall get into a covetous spirit, and, impelled by want, distrust my Maker, and take my neighbor's property; and, in order to excuse, hide, or vindicate my conduct, *I take the name of my God in vain; taphasti,* "I catch at the name of God." Or, by swearing falsely, endeavor to make myself pass for innocent.

(2) *Give me* not *riches.* For which petition he gives a reason also: *Lest I be full,* and addict myself to luxurious living, pamper the flesh and starve the soul, and so *deny thee,* the Fountain of goodness; and. if called on to resort to first principles, I say, *Who is the Lord [Jehovah]?*

(3) The third request is, *Feed me with food convenient for me;* the meaning of which is, "Give me as prey my statute allowance of bread," i.e., my daily bread, a sufficient portion for each day.

11. *There is a generation.* There are such persons in the world. In this and the following three verses the wise man points out four grand evils that prevailed in his time.

The *first,* Those who not only did not honor, but who evil-treated, their parents.

12. The *second,* Those who were self-righteous, supposing themselves *pure,* and were not so.

13. The *third,* Those who were full of vanity, pride, and insolence.

14. The *fourth,* The greedy, cruel, and oppressive, and especially oppressive to the poor.

15. *The horseleech hath two daughters, crying, Give, give.* The word *alukah,* which we here translate *horseleech,* is read in no other part of the Bible. May it not, like Agur, Jakeh, Ithiel, and Ucal, be a proper name, belonging to some well-known woman of his acquaintance, and well-known to the public, who had two daughters notorious for their covetousness and lechery?

MATTHEW HENRY

to be fully known,

1. The first three are natural things, and are only designed as comparisons for the illustration of the last. We cannot trace *An eagle in the air*. Which way she has flown cannot be discovered, nor can we account for the wonderful swiftness of her flight. *A serpent upon a rock*. The way of a serpent in the sand we may find by the track, but not of a serpent upon the hard rock. *A ship in the midst of the sea* leaves no mark behind it. The kingdom of nature is full of wonders *past finding out*.

2. The fourth is a mystery of iniquity, more accountable than any of these; it belongs to the depths of Satan. The cursed arts which a vile adulterer has to debauch a maid, and to persuade her to yield to his wicked and abominable lust. The cursed arts which a vile adulteress has to conceal her wickedness; so close are her intrigues that it is as impossible to discover her as to track an *eagle in the air*. She eats the forbidden fruit, and then *wipes her mouth*, that it may not betray itself, and with a bold and impudent face says, *I have done no wickedness*. To her own conscience she denies the fault. Thus multitudes ruin their souls by calling evil good and out-facing their convictions with a self-justification.

II. An account of four things that are intolerable, that is, four sorts of persons that are very troublesome. 1. *A servant* when he is entrusted with power is most insolent and imperious. 2. *A fool*, a silly, rude, boisterous, vicious man, when he has grown rich, and is partaking of the pleasures of the table, will disturb all the company with his extravagant talk. 3. An ill-natured, cross-grained, *woman*, when she gets a husband, having made herself odious by her pride and sourness, so that one would not have thought anybody would ever love her, yet, if at last she be married, that honourable estate makes her more intolerably scornful and spiteful than ever. A gracious woman, when she is married, will be yet more obliging. 4. An old maid-servant that has prevailed with her mistress to leave her what she has will be intolerably proud and malicious, and think herself wronged if anything be left from her. Let those therefore whom Providence has advanced to honour from mean beginnings carefully watch against pride and haughtiness.

Verses 24–28

I. Agur, having specified four things that seem great and yet are really contemptible, here specifies four things that are little and yet are very admirable, great in miniature. They teach us, 1. Not to admire bodily bulk, or beauty, or strength, but to judge of men by their wisdom and conduct, their industry and application to business. 2. To admire the wisdom and power of the Creator in the smallest and most despicable animals, in an ant as much as in an elephant. 3. To blame ourselves who do not act so much for our own true interest as the meanest creatures do for theirs. 4. Not to despise the weak things of the world; there are those that are *little upon the earth*, and yet *are exceedingly wise*. Margin, *They are wise, made wise* by the special instinct of nature. All that are wise to salvation are made wise by the grace of God.

II. Those he specifies are, 1. The *ants*, minute and very weak, and yet they are very industrious in gathering proper food in the summer, the proper time. This is so great a piece of wisdom that we may learn of them to be wise for futurity, *ch.* vi. 6. 2. The *conies*, the Arabian mice, weak creatures, and very timorous, have so much wisdom as to *make their houses in the rocks*, where they are well guarded. Sense of our own indigence and weakness should drive us to him that is a *rock higher than we* for shelter and support. 3. The *locusts* are little also, and *have no king*, as the bees have, but *they go forth all of them by bands*, like an army in battle-array (Joel ii. 25). *They go forth all of them gathered together* (so the margin); sense of weakness should engage us to keep together, that we may strengthen the hands of one another. 4. The *spider*. Spiders are very ingenious in weaving their webs with a fineness and exactness such as no art can pretend to come near: They *take hold with their hands*, and spin a fine thread out of their own bowels, with a great art; and they are not only in poor men's cottages, but in *kings' palaces*.

Verses 29–33

I. An enumeration of four things which are majestic and stately in their going: 1. *A lion*, the king of beasts, because *strongest among beasts*. The lion *turns not away*, nor alters his pace, for fear of any pursuers. 2. *A greyhound* that is girt in the loins and fit for running; or (as the margin reads it) *a horse*. 3. *A he-goat*, the comeliness of whose going is when he goes first and leads the flock. It is the comeliness of a

JAMIESON, FAUSSET, BROWN

18-20. Hypocrisy is illustrated by four examples of the concealment of all methods or traces of action, and a pertinent example of double dealing in actual vice is added, i.e., the **adulterous woman. she eateth . . . mouth**—i.e., she hides the evidences of her shame and professes innocence.

21-23. Pride and cruelty, the undue exaltation of those unfit to hold power, produce those vices which disquiet society (cf. ch. 19:10; 28:3). **heir . . . mistress**—i.e., takes her place as a wife (Gen. 16:4).

24-31. These verses provide two classes of apt illustrations of various aspects of the moral world, which the reader is left to apply. By the first, diligence and providence are commended; the success of these insignificant animals being due to their instinctive sagacity and activity, rather than strength.

conies— mountain mice, or rabbits.

spider—tolerated, even in palaces, to destroy flies. **taketh . . . hands**—or, uses with activity the limbs provided for taking prey.

The other class provides similes for whatever is majestic or comely, uniting efficiency with gracefulness.

ADAM CLARKE

JOSEPH PARKER:

Verses 24–28. These words distinctly teach that wisdom is not measurable by physical magnitude. The large man may be a little man. The little boy may shelter a great soul. The elephantine and prodigious body may hardly have a soul at all. These things are perfectly well known, yet we require to be reminded of them with some frequency, because so many appeals are addressed to our senses. We are not called upon to admire mere bigness, bulk, surface, and weight. The same terms do not always mean the same thing. Sometimes little is not merely little. Sometimes greatness is greatness *minus*. Some pounds have sixteen ounces in them, others have only twelve. Butchers and silversmiths do not reckon by the same arithmetical tables. In a prosperous condition of society, a single diamond may be worth more money than all the beasts in a cattle market; but in times of famine one lamb will be more precious than all the diamonds in kings' houses. Value varies according to circumstances. He is the wise man who knows the one thing whose value never changes, which overbalances and reduces to insignificance the pomp of unintelligent creation. If we lay hold of these things and estimate values correctly, it will help in the adjustment of social relations and in the appreciation of those virtues which ought ever to be uppermost in a true condition of society. We are called upon to remember that wisdom, and wisdom alone, is the true standard of measurement; that the humblest life is greater than the sublimest art, and that one spark of intellect is infinitely more precious than the most crushing animal strength.

It is possible to be little and yet to be exceeding wise. Let us gather round these little wise creatures and learn what we may from them. "Ask now the beasts, and they shall teach thee; and the fowls of the air, and they shall tell thee." He makes a wise use of nature who regards it as a book of divine instruction. Everything has its lesson. Everywhere we find the signature, the autograph of God, and he will never deny his own handwriting. God hath set his tabernacle in the dewdrop as surely as in the sun. Man can no more create the smallest polyp than he could create the greatest world. We are surrounded by instructors; we are in a great schoolhouse; it is full of letters, lessons, illustrations, and appeals. If, then, we be found fools after all, how bitter, how terrible must be our condemnation! Blame not the savage in the lonely forest for his ignorance of letters; but the man who has had every opportunity of attaining scholarship, and after all remains in ignorance, rightly deserves concentrated bitterness of human contempt. Let us beware of setting up precedents and inaugurating analogies and instituting seats of judgment; because God will gather them all together one day, and his great white throne will be the more terrible for the precedents we ourselves have perpetrated.

—*The People's Bible*

MATTHEW HENRY

Christian's going to go first in a good work and to lead others in the right way. 4. *A king*, who, when he appears in his majesty, is looked upon with reverence and awe, and *there is no rising up against* him. And, if *there is no rising up* against an earthly prince, *woe to him* then *that strives with his Maker*. It is intended that we should learn courage and fortitude in all virtuous actions from the *lion* and *not to turn away for any* difficulty we meet with; from the *greyhound* we may learn quickness and despatch, from the *he-goat* the care of our family and those under our charge, and from *a king* to have our children in subjection with all gravity, and from them all to *go well*, so that we may not only be safe, but *comely, in going*.

II. A caution to us to keep our temper at all times and under all provocations. We must take shame to ourselves, whenever we are justly charged with a fault, and not insist upon our own innocency: If we have *lifted up ourselves* in peevish opposition, we have therein *done foolishly*. If we have but *thought evil*, if we are conscious to ourselves that we have harboured an ill design in our minds, we must *lay our hand upon our mouth*, that is humble ourselves for what we have done amiss. We must keep the evil thought we have conceived in our minds from breaking out in evil speeches. It is bad to think ill, but it is much worse to speak it, for that implies a consent to the evil thought. We must not irritate the passions of others. Some are so very provoking in their words and conduct that they even *force wrath*, and where that *is there is confusion and every evil work*. As the violent agitation of the cream fetches all the good out of the milk, and the hard *wringing of the nose* will extort blood from it, so this *forcing of wrath* wastes both the body and spirits of a man, and robs him of all the good that is in him. The spirit is heated by degrees with strong passions; one angry word begets another, and so it goes on till it ends in irreconcilable feuds.

JAMIESON, FAUSSET, BROWN

32. As none can hope, successfully, to resist such a king, suppress even the thought of an attempt. **lay . . . hand upon thy mouth**—"lay" is well supplied (Judg. 18:19; Job 29:9; 40:4).

33. i.e., strife—or other ills, as surely arise from devising evil as natural effects from natural causes.

ADAM CLARKE

JOHN GILL:

Verse 32. "If thou hast done foolishly in lifting up thyself." Against a king, against whom there is no rising up; by speaking evil of him, or rebelling against him; which is acting a foolish part, since it brings a man into troubles and difficulties inextricable; or by self-commendation, which is the height of folly, and the fruit of pride; or carried it in such a haughty and overbearing manner to others, as to provoke to wrath and anger. "Or if thou hast thought evil"; purposed and designed it, and contrived the scheme of doing it, though not yet put in execution; though folly is not actually committed, yet since the thought of it is sin, care should be taken to prevent it. Lay "thine hand upon thy mouth"; think again before the thing resolved on is done; as studious and thoughtful men put their hand to their mouth, when they are deeply considering any affair before them: or put a stop to the design, let it go no further; what has been thought of in the mind, let it never come out of the mouth, nor be carried into execution; stifle it in the first motion: or if this respects a foolish action done, as it also may, since it stands connected with both clauses, then the sense is, be silent; do not pretend to deny the action, nor to excuse it.—*Gill's Commentary*

MATTHEW HENRY

CHAPTER 31

Verses 1-9

Most interpreters are of opinion that Lemuel is Solomon; the name signifies one that is *for God*, or *devoted to God*. Lemuel is supposed to be a fond, endearing name, by which his mother used to call him. One would the rather incline to think it is Solomon that here tells us what *his mother taught him* because he tells us (*ch.* iv. 4) what his father taught him. But some think that Lemuel was a prince of some neighbouring country, whose mother was a daughter of Israel. It is the duty of mothers, as well as fathers, to teach their children what is good, that they may do it, and what is evil, that they may avoid it; when they are young and tender they are most under the mother's eye, and she has then an opportunity of moulding their minds well.

I. Her expostulation with the young prince, by which she speaks as one considering what advice to give him: "Thou art descended from me; thou art *the son of my womb*, and therefore what I say comes from the authority and affection of a parent. Thou art a piece of myself. Be wise and good, and then I am well paid. Thou art *the son of my vows*, the son I prayed to God to give me and promised to give back to God." Our children that by baptism are dedicated to God, for whom and in whose name we covenanted with God, may well be called *the children of our vows*.

II. The caution she gives him against those two destroying sins of *uncleanness* and *drunkenness*: *Give not thy strength unto women*, unto strange women. He must not be soft and effeminate. It lessens the honour of kings and makes them mean. Are those fit to govern others that are themselves slaves to their own lusts? If they would preserve their people from the unclean spirit, they must themselves be patterns of purity. The king must not *drink wine* or *strong drink* to excess; *it is not for kings, to* allow themselves that liberty; it is a disparagement to their dignity, and profanes their crown, by confusing the head that wears it. All Christians are *made to our God kings and priests*. *It is not for* Christians *to drink* to excess; it ill becomes the heirs of the kingdom and the spiritual priests, Lev. x. 9. It is a sad complaint which is made of the priests and prophets (Isa. xxviii. 7), that *they have erred through wine, and through strong drink they are out of the way*; and tumble in judgment.

III. The counsel she gives him to do good with his wealth. "Thou hast wine or strong drink at command; instead of doing thyself hurt with it, do others good with it; let those have it that need it,

JAMIESON, FAUSSET, BROWN

CHAPTER 31

Vss. 1-31. **1.** On the title of this, the 6th part of the book, cf. *Introduction*. **prophecy**—as in ch. 30: 1.

2. What, my son?—i.e., What shall I say? Repetitions denote earnestness. **son . . . womb**—as our phrase, "my own son," a term of special affection. **son. . . vows**—as one dedicated to God; so the word *Lemuel* may mean.

3-9. Succinct but solemn warnings against vices to which kings are peculiarly tempted, as carnal pleasures and oppressive and unrighteous government are used to sustain sensual indulgence. **3. strength**—mental and bodily resources for health and comfort. **thy ways**—or course of life.

to that . . . kings—lit., "to the destroying of kings," avoid destructive pleasures (cf. ch. 5:9; 7:22, 27; Hos. 4:11).

4, 5. Stimulants enfeeble reason, pervert the heart, and do not suit rulers, who need clear and steady minds, and well-governed affections (cf. ch. 20:1; 22:29). **pervert . . . afflicted**—They give unrighteous decisions against the poor.

ADAM CLARKE

CHAPTER 31

1. *The words of king Lemuel. Dibrey lemuel melech*, "The words to Muel the king." So the Syriac; and so I think it should be read, the *lamed* being the article or preposition. There is no evidence whatever that *Muel* or *Lemuel* means Solomon; the chapter seems to be much later than his time, and the several Chaldaisms which occur in the very opening of it are no mean proof of this. If Agur was not the author of it, it may be considered as another supplement to the Book of Proverbs. Most certainly Solomon did not write it. *The prophecy that his mother taught him. Massa* may here signify the "oracle," the subject that came by divine inspiration. From this and some other circumstances it is probable that both these chapters were written by the same author.

2. *What, my son?* The Chaldee *bar* is used twice in this verse, instead of the Hebrew *ben*, "son." This verse is very elliptical; and commentators, according to their different tastes, have inserted words, indeed some of them a whole sentence, to make up the sense. Perhaps Coverdale has hit the sense as nearly as any other: "These are the wordes of Kynge Lemuel; and the lesson that his mother taughte him. My sonne, thou son of my body, O my deare beloved sonne!" *The son of my vows?* A child born after vows made for offspring is called the child of a person's vows.

MATTHEW HENRY

through sickness or pain. We must deny ourselves in the gratifications of sense, that we may have to spare for the relief of the miseries of others. Wine is a cordial, and therefore to be used for want and not for wantonness, by those only that need cordials, as Timothy, who is advised to *drink a little wine*, only *for his stomach's sake and his often infirmities*, 1 Tim. v. 23. He must do good with his power, his knowledge, and must administer justice with care, courage, and compassion, *v.* 8, 9. He must *judge righteously*, and, without fear of the face of man, boldly pass sentence according to equity: *Open thy mouth*, which denotes the liberty of speech that princes and judges ought to use in passing sentence. He must especially look upon himself as obliged to be the patron of oppressed innocency, especially of those that were *dumb*, and knew not how to speak for themselves, either through fear, or being over-talked by the prosecutor or overawed by the court.

Verses 10–31

This description of the *virtuous woman* is designed to show what wives the women should make and what wives the men should choose; it consists of twenty-two verses, each beginning with a letter of the Hebrew alphabet in order, which makes some think it was a poem by itself, written by some other hand, and perhaps commonly repeated for the ease of which it was made alphabetical. We have the abridgment of it in the New Testament (1 Tim. ii. 9, 10, 1 Pet. iii. 1–6), where the duty prescribed to wives agrees with this description of a good wife.

I. A general enquiry after such a one (*v.* 10). *A virtuous woman—a woman of strength* (so the word is), though the weaker vessel, yet made strong by wisdom and grace, and the fear of God: it is the same word that is used in the character of good judges (Exod. xviii. 21). *A virtuous woman* is a woman of spirit, who has the command of her own spirit and knows how to manage other people's. *A virtuous woman* is a woman of resolution, who, having espoused good principles, is firm and steady to them. *Who can find* her? Good women are very scarce. But he that designs to marry ought to take heed that he be not biassed by beauty or gaiety, wealth or parentage, dressing well or dancing well; for all these may be and yet the woman not be virtuous. The more rare good wives are the more they are to be valued.

II. A particular description of her and of her excellent qualifications.

1. She is very industrious to recommend herself to her husband's esteem and affection. She conducts herself so that he may repose an entire confidence in her. He trusts in her chastity. He trusts in her conduct, that she will act in all affairs with prudence and discretion. He trusts in her fidelity to his interests. When he goes abroad, to attend the concerns of the public, he can confide in her to order all his affairs at home. She contributes so much to his content *that he shall have no need of spoil*; he need not be griping and scraping abroad, as those must be whose wives are proud and wasteful at home. He thinks himself so happy in her that he envies not those who have most of the wealth of this world; he needs it not, he has enough, having such a wife. She shows her love to him, not by a foolish fondness, but by prudent endearments, giving him good words, and not bad ones, no, not when he is out of humour, studying to provide what is fit for him both in health and sickness. And this is her care *all the days of her life*; not at first only, or now and then, when she is in a good humour, but perpetually. If she survive him, still she is doing him good in her care of his children, his estate, and good name. She adds to his reputation in the world (*v.* 23): *Her husband is known in the gates*, known to have a good wife. By his cheerful countenance and pleasant humour it appears that he has an agreeable wife at home. One may know he has a good wife at home, that takes care of his clothes.

2. She is one that takes pains in the duty of her place and takes pleasure in it. She hates to sit still and do nothing: *She eats not the bread of idleness*, *v.* 27. She is careful to fill up time, that none of that be lost. When daylight is done her business lying within-doors, and her work worth candle-light, with that she lengthens out the day; and *her candle goes not out by night*, *v.* 18. *She rises* early, *while it is yet night* (*v.* 15), to give her servants their breakfast, that they may be ready to go cheerfully about their work. She is none of those who sit up playing cards, or dancing, till midnight, till morning, and then lie in bed till noon. She applies herself to the business that is proper for her. It is not in scholar's business, or statesman's business, or husbandman's business, that she employs herself, but in woman's business. *She seeks wool and flax*, where she may have the best of each, cheapest; she has a stock of both, and with

JAMIESON, FAUSSET, BROWN

6, 7. The proper use of such drinks is to restore tone to feeble bodies and depressed minds (cf. Ps. 104:15).

8, 9. Open . . . cause—Plead for those who cannot plead for themselves, as the orphan, stranger, etc. (cf. Ps. 72:12; Isa. 1:17). **appointed to destruction**—who are otherwise ruined by their oppressors (cf. ch. 29:14, 16).

10-31. This exquisite picture of a truly lovely wife is conceived and drawn in accordance with the customs of Eastern nations, but its moral teachings suit all climes. In *Hebrew* the verses begin with the letters of the *Hebrew* alphabet in order (cf. *Introduction* to Poetical Books).

10. Who . . . woman?—The question implies that such are rare, though not entirely wanting (cf. ch. 18:22; 19:14). **virtuous**—lit., "of strength," i.e., moral courage (cf. ch. 12:4; Ruth 3:11). **her price . . .**—(cf. ch. 3:15).

11. heart . . . trust in her—He relies on her prudence and skill.

no need of spoil—does not lack profit or gain, especially, that obtained by the risk of war. **12. do . . . good**—contribute good to him.

23. in the gates—(cf. ch. 22:22). His domestic comfort promotes his advancement in public dignity.

27. (Cf. I Tim. 5:14; Titus 2:5.) She adds to her example a wise management of those under her control. **17, 18.** To energy she adds a watchfulness in bargains, and a protracted and painful industry. The last clause may figuratively denote that her prosperity (cf. ch. 24:20) is not short lived.

15. She diligently attends to expending as well as gathering wealth;

13, 14. Ancient women of rank thus wrought with their hands; and such, indeed, were the customs of Western women a few centuries since. In the East also, the fabrics were articles of merchandise.

ADAM CLARKE

6. *Give strong drink unto him that is ready to perish.* We have already seen that inebriating drinks were mercifully given to condemned criminals, to render them less sensible of the torture they endured in dying. This is what was offered to our Lord; but He refused it.

8. *Open thy mouth for the dumb.* For such accused persons as have no counsellors, and cannot plead for themselves. *Are appointed to destruction. Beney chaloph,* variously translated, "children of passage"—indigent travellers; "children of desolation"—those who have no possessions, or orphans. I believe it either signifies those who are strangers, and are travelling from place to place, or those who are ready to perish in consequence of want or oppression.

10. *Who can find a virtuous woman?* This and the following verses are acrostic, each beginning with a consecutive letter of the Hebrew alphabet: v. 10, *aleph*; v. 11, *beth;* v. 12, *gimel;* and so on to the end of the chapter, the last verse of which has the letter *tau.* From this to the end of the chapter we have the character of a woman of genuine worth laid down; first, in general, vv. 10-12; secondly, in its particular or component parts, vv. 13-29; and, thirdly, the summing up of the character, vv. 30-31.

Her general character. (1) She is a *virtuous woman*—a woman of power and strength. (2) She is invaluable; her *price is far above rubies*—no quantity of precious stones can be equal to *her* worth.

11. *The heart of her husband.* (3) She is an unspotted wife. *The heart of her husband doth safely trust in her*—he knows she will take care that a proper provision is made for his household, and will not waste anything. He *has no need for spoil*—he is not obliged to go out on predatory excursions, to provide for his family, at the expense of the neighboring tribes.

12. *She will do him good.* (4) She has her husband's happiness in view constantly.

23. *Her husband is known in the gates.* (14) She is a loving wife, and feels for the respectability and honor of her husband. He is an elder among his people, and he sits as a magistrate in the gate.

27. *She looketh well to the ways of her household.* (18) She is a moral manager; she takes care that all shall behave themselves well, that none of them shall keep bad company or contract vicious habits. *And eateth not the bread of idleness.* (19) She knows that idleness leads to vice; and therefore everyone has his work, and everyone has his proper food.

18. *She perceiveth that her merchandise is good.* (8) She takes care to manufacture the best articles of the kind, and to lay on a reasonable price that she may secure a ready sale. (9) She is *watchful* and careful. *Her candle*—her "lamp"—burns all night, which is of great advantage in case of sudden alarms.

15. *She riseth also while it is yet night.* (4) She is an economist of time.

13. *She seeketh wool, and flax, and worketh willingly.*

MATTHEW HENRY

this she does not only set the poor on work, which is a very good office, but does herself *work willingly with her hands. She lays her* own *hands to the spindle*, or spinning-wheel, *and her hands hold the distaff* (*v.* 19), and she does not reckon it an abridgment of her liberty. The spindle and the distaff are here mentioned as her honour, while the ornaments of the daughters of Zion are reckoned up to their reproach, Isa. iii. 18, &c. She does not employ herself in sitting work only, or in that which is only the nice performance of the fingers (there are works that are scarcely one remove from doing nothing); but, if there be occasion, she will go through with work that requires all the strength she has, which she will use as one that knows it is the way to have more.

3. She is one that makes what she does to turn to a good account. She perceives that she can make things herself better and cheaper than she can buy them. She brings in provisions of all things necessary and convenient for her family, *v.* 14. She purchases lands, and enlarges the demesne of the family (*v.* 16): *She considers a field, and buys it*. She considers what an advantage it will be to the family. Though she have ever so much mind to it she will not buy it till she has first considered whether it be worth her money, whether the ground will answer the character given of it, and whether she has money at command to pay for it. *She* also *plants a vineyard*, but it is *with the fruit of her hands*. She furnishes her house well and has good clothing for herself and her family (*v.* 22): *She makes herself coverings of tapestry* to hang her rooms, and they are of her own making. *Her* own *clothing* is rich and fine: it is *silk and purple*. She has rich clothes and puts them on well. The senator's robes which her husband wears are of her own spinning, and they look better and wear better than any that are bought. She also gets good warm clothing for her children. She needs not fear the cold of the most pinching winter, for she and her family are well provided with clothes. *All her household are clothed in scarlet*, strong cloth and fit for winter, and yet making a good appearance. She makes more than she and her household have occasion for; and therefore, when she has sufficiently stocked her family, *she sells fine linen and girdles to the merchants* (*v.* 24), who carry them to Tyre, the mart of the nations, or some other trading city. She lays up for hereafter: *She shall rejoice in time to come*, having laid in a good stock for her family.

4. She takes care of her family and all the affairs of it, *gives meat to her household* (*v.* 15). *She looks well to the ways of her household* (*v.* 27).

5. She is charitable *to the poor*, *v.* 20. She is as intent upon giving as she is upon getting. *She reaches forth her hands to the needy* that are at a distance.

6. She is discreet, not talkative, censorious, nor peevish. When she does speak, it is with prudence and very much to the purpose. *In her tongue is the law of kindness*. The law of love and kindness is written in the heart, but it shows itself in the tongue. She is full of religious discourse, which shows how full her heart is of another world even when her hands are most busy about this world.

7. That which completes and crowns her character is that she *fears the Lord*, *v.* 30. With all those good qualities she lacks not that *one thing needful*. The fear of God reigning in the heart is the beauty of the soul; it recommends those that have it to the favour of God, and is, in his sight, of great price; it will last for ever, and bid defiance to death itself, which consumes the beauty of the body, but consummates the beauty of the soul.

III. The happiness of this virtuous woman.

1. She has the comfort and satisfaction of her virtue in her own mind (*v.* 25). She enjoys a firmness and constancy of mind, has spirit to bear up under many crosses and disappointments, and this is her clothing, for defence as well as decency. She deals honourably with all, *and shall rejoice in time to come*; she shall reflect upon it with comfort, when she comes to be old, that she was not idle or useless when she was young. Nay, *she shall rejoice* with *fulness of joy and pleasures for evermore*.

2. She is a great blessing to her relations, *v.* 28. *Her children* grow up in her place, *and* they *call her blessed*. *Her husband* thinks himself so happy in her that he takes all occasions to speak well of her.

3. She gets the good word of all her neighbours. A woman that fears the Lord, shall have praise *of God* (Rom. ii. 29). She shall be highly praised (*v.* 29): *Many have done virtuously*, *she excels them all*. Those ought to be praised the fruit of whose hands is praise-worthy. If her children be dutiful and respectful to her, they then *give her of the fruit of her hands*; she reaps the benefit of all the care she has taken of them.

JAMIESON, FAUSSET, BROWN

19. No work, however mean, if honest, is disdained.

16., and hence has means to purchase property.

22. coverings of tapestry—or, coverlets, i.e., for beds. **silk** [or, linen (cf. Exod. 26:1; 27:9)] **and purple**—i.e., the most costly goods.

21. scarlet—or, purple, by reason of the dyes used, the best fabrics; as a matter of taste also; the color suits cold.

24. fine linen—or, linen shirts, or the material for them. **girdles**—were often costly and highly valued (II Sam. 18:11). **delivereth**—or, giveth as a present or to sell.

20. Industry enables her to be charitable.

30. Favour—or, Grace of personal manner. **beauty**—of face, or form (cf. ch. 11:22). True piety alone commands permanent respect and affection (I Pet. 3:3).

25. Strength and honour—*Strong* and *beautiful* is her clothing; or, figuratively, for moral character, vigorous and honorable. **shall rejoice...come**—in confidence of certain maintenance. **26.** Her conversation is wise and gentle.

28. She is honored by those who best know her.

29. The words are those of her husband, praising her. **virtuously**—(Cf. vs. 10.)

31. The result of her labor is her best eulogy.

Nothing can add to the simple beauty of this admirable portrait. On the measure of its realization in the daughters of our own day rest untold results, in the domestic, and, therefore, the civil and religious, welfare of the people.

ADAM CLARKE

19. *She layeth her hands to the spindle*. (10) She gives an example of skill and industry to her household. She takes *the distaff*, that on which the wool or flax was rolled; and *the spindle*, that by twisting of which she twisted the thread with the right hand, while she held the distaff in the guard of the left arm, and drew down the thread with the fingers of the left hand.

17. *She girdeth her loins with strength*. (7) She takes care of her own health and strength, not only by means of useful labor, but by healthy exercise.

14. *She is like the merchants' ships*. (3) She acts like merchants. If she buys anything for her household, she sells sufficient of her own manufactures to pay for it.

16. *She considereth a field, and buyeth it*. (5) She provides for the growing wants of her family. (6) She does not restrict herself to the bare necessaries of life; she is able to procure some of its comforts.

22. *She maketh herself coverings of tapestry*. (13) She has tapestry, *marbaddim*, either tapestry, carpeting, or quilted work for her beds; and her own *clothing* is *shesh*, fine flax, or linen cloth, and *purple;* probably for a cloak or mantle.

21. *She is not afraid of the snow*. (12) She is not anxious relative to the health and comfort of her family in the winter season, having provided clothes sufficient for each in the cold weather, in addition to those which they wore in the warm season. *For all her household are clothed with scarlet*. Not *scarlet*, for the color can avail nothing in keeping off the cold. But *shanim*, from *shanah*, "to double," signifies not only *scarlet*, so called from being twice or doubly dyed, but also "double garments."

24. *She maketh fine linen, and selleth it*. (15) She is here remarkable for carrying on a traffic of splendid and ornamental dresses.

20. *She stretcheth out her hand to the poor*. (11) She is truly charitable.

30. *Favour is deceitful, and beauty is vain*.

Here is the *summing up* of the character. (1) *Favour, chen*, "grace" of manner, may be *deceitful;* many a fair appearance of this kind is put on, assumed for certain secular or more unworthy purposes. (2) *Beauty, haiyophi*, elegance of shape, symmetry of features, dignity of mien, and beauty of countenance, are all *hebel*, "vanity"; (3) *But a woman that feareth the Lord*, that possesses true religion, has that grace that harmonizes the soul, that purifies and refines all the tempers and passions, and that ornament of beauty, a meek and quiet mind, which in the sight of God is of great price. *She shall be praised*. This is the lasting grace, the unfading beauty.

25. *Strength and honour are her clothing*. (16) All the articles manufactured by herself or under her care have a double perfection: (1) They are strong. (2) They are elegant. *Strength and honour are her clothing*.

26. *She openeth her mouth with wisdom*. (17) He comes now to the moral management of her family. *In her tongue is the law of kindness*. This is the most distinguishing excellence of this woman. There are very few of those who are called managing women who are not lords over their husbands, tyrants over their servants, and insolent among their neighbors.

28. *Her children arise up, and call her blessed*. (20) She considers a good education next to divine influence; and she knows also that if she train up a child in the way he should go, when he is old he will not depart from it.

29. *Many daughters have done virtuously*. This is undoubtedly the speech of the husband, giving testimony to the excellence of his wife. But high as the character of this Jewish matron stands in the preceding description, I can say that I have met at least her equal in a daughter of the Rev. Dr. Samuel Annesly, the wife of Samuel Wesley, Sr., rector of Epworth in Lincolnshire, and mother of the late extraordinary brothers, John and Charles Wesley.

THE BOOK OF ECCLESIASTES

I. Theme (1:1-11)
A. Inclusive statement—vapor of vapors (1:2-3)
B. Elaboration (1:4-11)

II. The evidence (1:12-8:17)
A. Personal (1:12-2:26)
1. Knowledge (1:12-18)
2. Mirth (2:1-3)
3. Wealth (2:4-11)
4. Life (2:12-26)

B. Relative (3:1-8:17)
1. The mechanism of the universe (3:1-22)
2. Sociological oppressions (4:1-16)
3. Religion (5:1-7)
4. Poverty and prosperity (5:8-6:12)
5. Indifference (7:1-8:17)

III. The effect (9:1-11:8)
A. Worldly wisdom extolled (9:1-16)
1. One event to all (9:1-6)
2. Enter into life (9:7-10)
3. Advantages are of little worth (9:11-12)
4. Wisdom under the sun (9:13-16)

B. Worldly wisdom exemplified (9:17-11:8)
1. Discretion (9:17-10:20)
2. Diligence (11:1-7)
3. Darkness (11:8)

IV. The correction (11:9-12:14)
A. Stated (11:9-10)
B. Urged (12:1-12)
C. Summarized (12:13-14)

The account we have of Solomon's apostasy from God, in the latter end of his reign (1 Kings 11:1), is the tragical part of his story; we may suppose that he spoke his *Proverbs* in the prime of his time, while he kept his integrity, but delivered his *Ecclesiastes* when he had grown old (for of the burdens and decays of age he speaks with great feeling, ch. 12), and was, by the grace of God, recovered from his backslidings. There he dictated his observations; here he wrote his own experiences; this is what days speak and wisdom which the multitude of years teaches.

I. It is a sermon in print; the text is (1:2), "Vanity of vanities, all is vanity"; that is the doctrine too; it is proved at large by many arguments and various objections are answered, and in the close we have the application, by way of exhortation, to "remember our Creator," to "fear him," and to "keep his commandments." There are indeed many things in this book which are dark and hard to be understood, and some things which men "wrest to their own destruction," for want of distinguishing between Solomon's arguments and the objections of atheists; but there is enough easy and plain to convince us of the vanity of the world and its utter insufficiency to make us happy, the vileness of sin and its certain tendency to make us miserable, and of the wisdom of being religious, and the solid comfort and satisfaction that are to be had in doing our duty both to God and man.

II. It is a penitential sermon; it is a recantation sermon, in which the preacher sadly laments his own folly in promising himself satisfaction in the things of this world, and even in the forbidden pleasures of sense, which now he finds more bitter than death. His fall is a proof of the weakness of man's nature: "Let not the wise man glory in his wisdom," when Solomon himself, the wisest of men, played the fool so egregiously; nor "let the rich man glory in his riches," since Solomon's wealth was so great a snare to him and did him a great deal more hurt than Job's poverty did him.

III. It is a practical, profitable sermon. Solomon, being brought to repentance, resolves, like his father, to "teach transgressors God's way" (Ps. 51:13). The fundamental error of the children of men is the same with that of our first parents, hoping to be "as gods" by entertaining themselves with that which seems "good for food, pleasant to the eyes, and desirable to make one wise." Now the scope of this book is to show that this is a great mistake, that our happiness consists not in being as gods to ourselves to have what we will and do what we will, but in living in harmony with God's purposes for us. Solomon, in this book, assures us that "to fear God and to keep his commandments is the whole of man." He shows the vanity of those things in which men commonly look for happiness, as human learning and policy, sensual delight, honor and power, riches and great possessions. He prescribes remedies. Though we cannot cure them of their vanity, we may prevent the trouble they give us, by sitting loose to them, but laying our expectations low from them, and acquiescing in the will of God, especially by remembering God in the days of our youth, and continuing in his fear and service all our days.

MATTHEW HENRY

CHAPTER 1

Verses 1–3

I. An account of the penman of this book; it was Solomon, for no other son of David was king of Jerusalem; but he conceals his name *Solomon, peaceable*, because by his sin he had brought trouble upon himself and his kingdom, had broken his peace with God, and therefore was no more worthy of that name. Call me not *Solomon*, call me *Marah*, for, *behold, for peace I had great bitterness*. But he calls himself,

1. *The preacher*, which intimates his present character. He is *Koheleth*, which comes from a word which signifies *to gather*.

(1) Koheleth is a *penitent soul*, or one *gathered*, one that had gone astray like a lost sheep, but was now gathered in from his wanderings. The spirit that was dissipated after a thousand vanities is now collected and made to centre in God. It is only the penitent soul that God will accept, the heart that is broken, not the head that is bowed down like a bulrush only for a day. And it is only the gathered soul that comes back from its by-paths.

(2) A *preaching soul* is one *gathering*. Being himself *gathered*, and being reconciled to the church, he endeavours to gather others to it that had gone astray like him. God by his Spirit made him a preacher, in token of his being reconciled to him; a commission is a tacit pardon. Christ sufficiently testifies his forgiving Peter by committing his lambs and sheep to his trust.

2. *The son of David*. He looked upon it as a great aggravation of his sin that he had such a father. His being the son of David encouraged him to repent

JAMIESON, FAUSSET, BROWN

CHAPTER 1

Vss. 1-18. Introduction. **1. the Preacher**—and *Convener of assemblies* for the purpose. See my Preface. *Koheleth* in *Hebrew*, a symbolical name for *Solomon*, and of *Heavenly Wisdom* speaking through and identified with him. Verse 12 shows that "king of Jerusalem" is in apposition, not with "David," but "Preacher."

ADAM CLARKE

CHAPTER 1

1. *The words of the Preacher*. Literally, "The words of Choheleth, son of David, king of Jerusalem." The word *Koheleth* is a feminine noun, from the root *kahal*, to collect, gather together, assemble; and means, "she who assembles or collects a congregation"; translated by the Septuagint, "a public speaker, a speaker in an assembly"; and hence translated by us "a preacher."

MATTHEW HENRY

and hope for mercy, for David had fallen into sin, but repented, and therein he took example from him and found mercy as he did.

3. *King of Jerusalem.* God had done much for him, in raising him to the throne, and yet he had so ill requited him. He thought it no disparagement to him, as a king, to be a preacher; but the people would regard him the more as a preacher because he was a king.

II. The general scope and design of the book is, for the making of us truly religious, to take down our esteem of and expectation from the things of this world. In order to this, he shows,

1. That they are *all vanity, v.* 2. It is *all vanity*, not only in the abuse of it, when it is perverted by the sin of man, but even in the use of it. It is expressed here very emphatically; not only, *All is vain*, but in the abstract, *All is vanity;* as if vanity were the *proprium quarto modo—property in the fourth mode*, of the things of this world, that which enters into the nature of them. They are not only *vanity*, but *vanity of vanities*, the vainest vanity, vanity in the highest degree. Many speak contemptuously of the world because they are hermits, and know it not, or beggars, and have it not; but Solomon knew it. He had dived into nature's depths (1 Kings iv. 33), and he had it, more of it perhaps than ever any man had. He spoke in God's name, and was divinely inspired to say it, deliberately, and laid it down as a fundamental principle, on which he grounded the necessity of being religious. One main thing he designed was to show that the everlasting throne and kingdom must be of another world; for all things in this world are subject to vanity, and therefore have not in them sufficient to answer the extent of that promise.

2. That they are insufficient to make us happy. *What profit has a man of all the pains he takes? v.* 3. The business of this world is *labour*; the word signifies both care and toil. It is work that wearies men. *What profit has a man of all that labour?* Solomon says (Prov. xiv. 23), *In all labour there is profit;* and yet here he denies that there is any profit. As to our present condition in the world, it is true that by labour we get that which we call *profit*; we *eat the labour of our hands*; but here he determines that it is not a real benefit. In short, the wealth and pleasure of this world, if we had ever so much of them, are not sufficient to make us happy. As goods are increased care about them is increased, and *those are increased that eat of them*, and a little thing will embitter all the comfort of them; and then *what profit has a man* of all his labour? As to the soul, and the life that is to come, we may much more truly say, *What profit has a man of all his labour?* All he gets by it will not supply the wants of the soul, will not atone for the sin of the soul, nor cure its diseases.

Verses 4–8

To prove the vanity of all things under the sun Solomon here shows the time of our enjoyment of these things is very short. We continue in the world but for one generation, which is continually passing away to make room for another, and we are passing with it. While the stream of mankind is continually flowing, how little enjoyment has one drop of that stream of the pleasant banks between which it glides! We may give God the glory of that constant succession of generations, but as to our own happiness, let us not expect it within such narrow limits, but in an eternal rest and consistency. It is well for mankind in general that the earth endures to the end of time, when it and all the works in it shall be burnt up; but what is that to particular persons, when they remove to the world of spirits? Man abides upon the earth but a little while. The sun sets indeed every night, yet it rises again in the morning, as bright and fresh as ever. *But man lies down and rises not*, Job xiv. 7, 12. All things in this world are movable and mutable, constant in nothing but inconstancy, still going, never resting. And can we expect rest in a world where all things are thus full of labour (*v.* 8), on a sea that is always ebbing and flowing, and her waves continually working and rolling? Man's mind is as restless in its pursuits as the sun, and wind, and rivers, but never satisfied, never contented; the more it has of the world the more it would have; and it would be no sooner filled with the streams of outward prosperity, than the sea is with *all the rivers that run into it*; it is still as it was, *a troubled sea that cannot rest.* The earth is where it was; the sun, and winds, and rivers, keep the same course. We must therefore look above the sun for satisfaction, and for a new world. Our senses are unsatisfied, and the objects of them unsatisfying. Curiosity is still inquisitive, because still unsatisfied, and the more it is humoured the more nice and peevish it grows, crying, *Give, give.*

JAMIESON, FAUSSET, BROWN

of Jerusalem—rather, *in* Jerusalem, for it was merely his metropolis, not his whole kingdom.

2. The theme proposed of the first part of his discourse. **Vanity of vanities**—Hebraism for the most utter vanity. So "holy of holies" (Exod. 26); "servant of servants" (Gen. 9:25). The repetition increases the force. **all**—*Hebrew, "the* all"; all without exception, viz., earthly things. **vanity**—not in themselves, for God maketh nothing in vain (I Tim. 4:4, 5), but vain when put in the place of God and made the *end*, instead of the *means* (Ps. 39:5, 6; 62:9; Matt. 6:33); vain, also, because of the "vanity" to which they are "subjected" by the fall (Rom. 8:20).

3. What profit . . . labour—i.e., "What profit" as to the chief good (Matt. 16:26). Labor is profitable *in its proper place* (Gen. 2:15; 3:19; Prov. 14:23). **under the sun**—i.e., *in this life,* as opposed to the future world. The phrase often recurs, but only in Ecclesiastes.

4. earth . . . for ever—(Ps. 104:5). While the *earth* remains the same, the generations of *men* are ever changing; what lasting profit, then, can there be from the toils of one whose sojourn on earth, as an individual, is so brief? The "for ever" is comparative, not absolute (Ps. 102:26). **5.** (Ps. 19:5, 6.) "Panting" as the *Hebrew* for "hasteth"; metaphor, from a runner (Ps. 19:5, "a strong man") in a "race." It applies rather to the *rising* sun, which seems *laboriously* to mount up to the meridian, than to the setting sun; the accents too favor MAURER, "And (that too, returning) to his place, where panting he riseth." **6. according to his circuits**—i.e., it returns afresh to its former circuits, however many be its previous veerings about. The north and south winds are the two prevailing winds in Palestine and Egypt. **7.** By subterraneous cavities, and by evaporation forming rain-clouds, the fountains and rivers are supplied from the sea, into which they then flow back. The connection is: *Individual* men are continually changing, while the *succession of the race* continues; just as the sun, wind, and rivers are ever shifting about, while the cycle in which they move is invariable; they return to the point whence they set out. Hence is man, as in these objects of nature which are his analogue, with all the seeming changes "there is no new thing" (vs. 9). 8. MAURER translates, "All *words* are wearied out," i.e., are inadequate, as also, "man cannot express" all the things in the world which undergo this ceaseless, changeless cycle of vicissitudes: "The eye is not satisfied with seeing them," etc. But it is plainly a return to the idea (vs. 3) as to *man's* "labor," which is only wearisome and profitless; "no new" good can accrue from it (vs. 9); for as the sun, etc., so man's laborious works move in a changeless cycle. The **eye** and **ear** are two of the taskmasters for which man toils. But these are never "satisfied" (ch. 6:7; Prov. 27:20). Nor can they be so hereafter, for there will be nothing "new." Not so the chief good, Jesus Christ (John 4:13, 14; Rev. 21:5).

ADAM CLARKE

2. *Vanity of vanities.* As the words are an exclamation, it would be better to translate, "O vanity of vanities!" Emptiness of emptinesses!

5 and 6. These verses are confused by being falsely divided. The first clause of the sixth should be joined to the fifth verse. "The sun also ariseth, and the sun goeth down, and hasteth to his place where he ariseth; going to the south, and circulating to the north."

6. "The wind is continually whirling about, and the wind returneth upon its whirlings." It is plain, from the clause which I have restored to the fifth verse, that the author refers to the approximations of the sun to the northern and southern tropics. All the versions agree in applying the first clause of the sixth verse to the sun, and not to the wind. Our version alone has mistaken the meaning. The author points out two things here: (1) Day and night, marked by the appearance of the sun above the horizon; proceeding apparently from east to west; where he sinks under the horizon, and appears to be lost during the night. (2) His annual course through the twelve signs of the zodiac, when, from the equinoctial, he proceeds southward to the Tropic of Capricorn; and thence turneth about towards the north, till he reaches the Tropic of Cancer.

7. *All the rivers run into the sea; yet the sea is not full.* The reason is, nothing goes into it either by the rivers or by rain that does not come from it; and to the place whence the rivers come, whether from the sea originally by evaporation or immediately by rain, thither they return again. For the water exhaled from the sea by evaporation is collected in the clouds, and in rain falls upon the tops of the mountains; and produces streams, several of which, uniting, make rivers, which flow into the sea.

MATTHEW HENRY

Verses 9–11

How grateful it is to think that none ever made such advances in knowledge, and such discoveries by it, as we, that none ever made such improvements. We boast of new fashions, new hypotheses, new methods, new expressions, which jostle out the old, and put them down. But this is all a mistake. What is there in the kingdom of nature of which we may say, *This is new?* The powers of nature and the links of natural causes are still the same that ever they were. Men's hearts, and the corruptions of them, are still the same; their desires, and pursuits, and complaints, are still the same. Tatianus the Assyrian, showing the Grecians how all the arts which they valued themselves upon owed their original to those nations which they counted barbarous, thus reasons with them: "For shame, do not call those things *εὑρήσεις—inventions,* which are but *μίμησεις—imitations.*" What reason have we to think that the world should be any kinder to us than it has been to those that have gone before us, since there is nothing in it that is new, and our predecessors have made as much of it as could be made? If we would be entertained with new things, we must acquaint ourselves with the things of God, get a new nature; then *old things pass away, and all things become new,* 2 Cor. v. 17. The gospel puts *a new song into our mouths.* Many think they have found satisfaction that their names shall be perpetuated, that posterity will celebrate the actions they have performed. How many *former things* and persons were there, which in their day looked very great and made a mighty figure, and yet *there is no remembrance* of them. Here and there one person or action that was remarkable met with a kind historian, and had the good hap to be recorded, when at the same time there were others, no less remarkable, that were dropped.

Verses 12–18

That which bids fairest to be the happiness of a reasonable creature is knowledge and learning; if this be vanity, everything else must needs be so. Now as to this,

I. Solomon tells us here what trial he had made of it, and that with such advantages that, if true satisfaction could have been found in it, he would have found it. He had his royal seat *in Jerusalem,* which then deserved, better than Athens ever did, to be called *the eye of the world.* Solomon's great wealth and honour put him into a capacity of making his court the centre of learning and the rendezvous of learned men. He made it his business to acquaint himself with *all the things that are done under the sun,* that are done by the providence of God or by the art and prudence of man. Though he was a prince, he made himself a drudge to learning, was not discouraged by its knots, nor took up short of its depths. And this he did not merely to gratify his own genius, but to qualify himself for the service of God and his generation, and to make an experiment how far the enlargement of the knowledge would go towards the settlement and repose of the mind. He *saw all the works that were done under the sun* (*v.* 14), works of nature in the upper and lower world, works of art, the product of men's wit, in a personal or social capacity. He had as much satisfaction in the success of his searches as ever any man had. Solomon must be acknowledged a competent judge of this matter, for he had not only got his head full of notions, but his *heart had great experience of wisdom and knowledge,* of the power and benefit of knowledge, as well as the entertainment of it; what he knew he had digested, and knew how to use. So industrious was Solomon to improve himself in knowledge that he gained instruction both by the wisdom of prudent men and by the madness of foolish men, by *the field of the slothful,* as well as of *the diligent.*

II. He tells us what was the result of this trial, to confirm what he had said, that *all is vanity.* He found that his searches after knowledge were very toilsome, and a weariness to the mind (*v.* 13). As bread for the body, so that for the soul, must be got and eaten *in the sweat of our face.* "*I have seen all the works* of a world full of business, have observed what the children of men are doing; *and behold,* whatever men think of their own words, I see *all is vanity and vexation of spirit.*" The more we see of the world the more we see to make us uneasy, and, with Heraclitus, to look upon all with weeping eyes. Solomon especially perceived that the knowledge of *wisdom and folly* was *vexation of spirit, v.* 17. It vexed him to see many that had wisdom not use it, and many that had folly not strive against it. He found that when he had got some knowledge he could neither gain that satisfaction to himself, nor do that good to others with it which he expected, *v.* 15. The minds and manners of men are crooked and perverse.

JAMIESON, FAUSSET, BROWN

9. Rather, "no new thing *at all*"; as in Numbers 11:6. This is not meant in a general sense; but there is no new source of happiness (the subject in question) which can be devised; the same round of petty pleasures, cares, business, study, wars, etc., being repeated over and over again [HOLDEN].

10. old time–[*Hebrew,* "ages"]. **which was**–The *Hebrew plural* cannot be joined to the verb *singular.* Therefore translate: "It hath been in the ages before; certainly it hath been before us" [HOLDEN]. Or, as MAURER: "That which has been (done) before us (in our presence, I Chron. 16:33), has been (done) already in the old times." **11.** The reason why some things are thought "new," which are not really so, is the imperfect record that exists of preceding ages among their successors. **those that . . . come after**–i.e., those that live *still later* than the "things, rather the *persons* or generations, vs. 4, with which this verse is connected, the six intermediate verses being merely illustrations of vs. 4 [WEISS], that are to come" (ch. 2:16; 9:5).

12. Resumption of vs. 1, the intermediate verses being the introductory statement of his thesis. Therefore, "the Preacher" (*Koheleth*) is repeated. **was king**–instead of "am," because he is about to give the results of his *past* experience during his long reign. **in Jerusalem**–specified, as opposed to David, who reigned both in Hebron and Jerusalem; whereas Solomon reigned only in Jerusalem. "King of Israel in Jerusalem," implies that he reigned over *Israel and Judah combined;* whereas David, at Hebron, reigned only over *Judah,* and not, until he was settled in Jerusalem, over both Israel and Judah.

13. this sore travail–viz., that of "searching" out all things done under heaven." Not human wisdom in general, which comes afterwards (ch. 2:12, etc.), but laborious inquiries into, and speculations about, the works of men; e.g., political science. As man is doomed to get his bread, so his knowledge, by the sweat of his brow (Gen. 3:19) [GILL]. **exercised**–i.e., disciplined; lit., "that they may thereby *chastise* or *humble* themselves." **14.** The reason is here given why investigation into man's "works" is only "sore travail" (vs. 13); viz., because all man's ways are vain (vs. 18) and cannot be mended (vs. 15). **vexation of** ["a preying upon" the] **spirit**–MAURER translates; "the pursuit of wind," as in ch. 5:16; Hosea 12:1, "Ephraim feedeth on wind." But old versions support the *English Version.* **15.** Investigation (vs. 13) into human ways is vain labor, for they are hopelessly "crooked" and "cannot be made straight" by it (ch. 7:13). God, the chief good, alone can do this (Isa. 40:4; 45:2). **wanting**–(Dan. 5:27). **numbered**–so as to make a complete number; so equivalent to "supplied" [MAURER]. Or, rather, man's state is *utterly wanting;* and that which is wholly defective cannot be numbered or calculated. The investigator thinks he can draw up, in accurate *numbers,* statistics of man's wants; but these, including the defects in the investigator's labor, are not partial, but total. **16. communed with . . . heart**–(Gen. 24:45.) **come to great estate**–Rather, "I *have magnified* and gotten" (lit., "added," increased), etc. **all . . . before me in Jerusalem**–viz., the priests, judges, and two kings that preceded Solomon. His wisdom exceeded that of all before

ADAM CLARKE

10. *Is there any thing?* The original is beautiful. "Is there anything which will say, See this! it is new?"

11. *There is no remembrance.* I believe the general meaning to be this: Multitudes of ancient transactions have been lost, because they were not recorded; and of many that have been recorded, the records are lost. And this will be the case with many others which are yet to occur.

12. *I the Preacher was king.* This is a strange verse, and does not admit of an easy solution. It is literally, "I, Choheleth, have been king over Israel, in Jerusalem."

13. *And I gave my heart to seek and search.* While Solomon was faithful to his God, he diligently cultivated his mind. His giving himself to the study of natural history, philosophy, poetry, etc., are sufficient proofs of it. He had not intuitive knowledge from God, but he had a capacity to obtain every kind of knowledge useful to man. *This sore travail.* This is the way in which knowledge is to be acquired; and in order to investigate the operations of nature, the most laborious discussions and perplexing experiments must be instituted, and conducted to their proper results. It is God's determination that knowledge shall be acquired in no other way.

14. *Behold, all is vanity.* After all these discussions and experiments, when even the results have been the most successful, I have found only rational satisfaction, but not that supreme good by which alone the soul can be made happy.

15. *That which is crooked cannot be made straight.* There are many apparent irregularities and anomalies in nature for which we cannot account, and there are many defects that cannot be supplied. This is the impression from a general view of nature; but the more we study and investigate its operations, the more we shall be convinced that all is a consecutive and well-ordered whole; and that in the chain of nature not one link is broken, deficient, or lost.

16. *I communed with mine own heart.* Liter-

MATTHEW HENRY

Solomon thought, with his wisdom and power together, thoroughly to reform his kingdom, but he was disappointed. All the philosophy and politics in the world will not restore the corrupt nature of man. Learning will not alter men's natural tempers, nor cure them of their sinful distempers. *That which is wanting* in our knowledge is so much that it *cannot be numbered.* The more we know the more we see of our own ignorance. Upon the whole, therefore, he concluded that great scholars do but make themselves great mourners; *for in much wisdom is much grief, v.* 18. Those *that increase knowledge* have so much the more quick and sensible perception of the calamities of this world. Let us not therefore be driven off from the pursuit of any useful knowledge, but put on patience to break through the sorrow of it; but let us despair of finding true happiness in this knowledge, and expect it only in the knowledge of God and the careful discharge of our duty to him.

JAMIESON, FAUSSET, BROWN

Jesus Christ, the antitypical *Koheleth*, or "*Gatherer* of men," (Luke 13:34), and "Wisdom" incarnate (Matt. 11:19; 12:42). **had . . . experience**—lit., "had *seen*" (Jer. 2:31). Contrast with this glorying in worldly wisdom Jeremiah 9:23, 24. **17. wisdom . . . madness**—i.e., their effects, the works of human wisdom and folly respectively. "Madness," lit., "vaunting extravagance"; ch. 2:12; 7:25, etc., support *English Version* rather than DATHE, "splendid matters." "Folly is read by *English Version* with some MSS., instead of the present *Hebrew* text, "prudence." If *Hebrew* be retained, understand "prudence," *falsely so called* (I Tim. 6:20), "craft" (Dan. 8:25). **18. wisdom . . . knowledge**—not in general, for wisdom, etc., are most excellent in their place; but *speculative knowledge of man's ways* (vss. 13, 17), which, the farther it goes, gives one the more pain to find how "crooked" and "wanting" they are (vs. 15; ch. 12:12).

ADAM CLARKE

ally, "I spoke, I, with my heart, saying."

17. *To know madness and folly. Holloth vesichluth.* "Parables and science."—Septuagint. So the Syriac; nearly so the Arabic. "What were error and foolishness."—Coverdale. Perhaps "gaiety" and "sobriety" may be the better meaning for these two difficult words. I can scarcely think they are taken in that bad sense in which our translation exhibits them.

18. *For in much wisdom is much grief.* The more we know of ourselves, the less satisfied shall we be with our own hearts; and the more we know of mankind, the less willing shall we be to trust them, and the less shall we admire them. *He that increaseth knowledge increaseth sorrow.* And why so? Because, independently of God, the principal objects of knowledge are natural and moral evils.

MATTHEW HENRY — CHAPTER 2

Verses 1–11

Solomon here, in pursuit of the *summum bonum—the felicity* of man, adjourns out of his study, where he had in vain sought for it, into the park and his garden; he exchanges the company of the philosophers and grave senators for that of the wits and gallants, to try if he could find true satisfaction and happiness among them. Here he takes a great step downward, from the noble pleasures of the intellect to the brutal ones of sense.

I. He resolved to try what mirth would do and the pleasures of wit. "*Enjoy pleasure*, and take thy fill of it; cast away care, and resolve to be merry." Many that are poor are very merry; beggars in a barn are so to a proverb. Mirth comes short of the solid delights of the rational powers, yet it is to be preferred before those that are merely carnal and sensual. Some distinguish man from the brutes, not only as *animal rationale—a rational animal*, but as *animal risibile—a laughing animal.* "Try therefore," says Solomon, "to laugh and be fat, to laugh and be happy." The judgment he passed upon this experiment: *I said of laughter, It is mad*, or, *Thou art mad, and of mirth, What doeth it?* Innocent mirth, soberly, seasonably, and moderately used, is a good thing, fits for business, and helps to soften the toils of human life; but, when it is excessive and immoderate, it is foolish and fruitless. It is but a palliative cure to the grievances of this present time.

II. Finding himself not happy in that which pleased his fancy, he resolved next to try that which would please the palate, *v.* 3. *I sought in my heart to give myself unto wine*, that is, to good meat and good drink. Solomon applied himself to it critically, and only to make an experiment. He sought *to lay hold on folly*, to see the utmost that that folly would do towards making men happy. He resolved that the folly should not take hold of him, not get the mastery of him. He took care at the same time to *acquaint* himself *with wisdom*, to manage himself wisely in the use of his pleasures, so that they should not do him any prejudice nor disfit him to be a competent judge of them. This Solomon proposed to himself, but he found it *vanity. Wine is a mocker;* and it will be impossible for any man to say that thus far he will give himself to it and no further. That which he aimed at was not to gratify his appetite, but to find out man's happiness. Observe the description he gives of man's happiness—it is *that good for the sons of men which they should do under the heaven all their days. Good Master, what good thing shall I do?* Our happiness consists not in being idle, but in doing aright, in being well employed. But that any man should give himself to wine, in hopes to find out in that the best way of living in this world, was an absurdity which Solomon here, in the reflection, condemns.

III. Perceiving quickly that it was folly to give himself to wine, he next tried the most costly entertainments and amusements.

1. He gave himself much to building, both in the city and in the country; and, having been at such vast expense in the beginning of his reign to build a house for God, he was the more excusable if afterwards he pleased his own fancy in building for himself. In building, he had the pleasure of employing the poor and doing good to posterity. We read of Solomon's buildings (1 Kings ix. 15–19), and they were all *great works.* See his mistake; he enquired after the *good* works he should do (*v.* 3), and, in pursuit of the enquiry, applied himself to *great* works. *Good* works indeed are truly great, but many are reputed great works which are far from being good.

2. He took to love a garden, which is to some as

JAMIESON, FAUSSET, BROWN — CHAPTER 2

Vss. 1-26. He next tries pleasure and luxury, retaining however, his worldly "wisdom" (ch. 3:9), but all proves "vanity" in respect to the chief good.

1. I said . . . heart—(Luke 12:19). **thee**—my heart, I will test whether thou canst find that solid good in pleasure which was not in "worldly wisdom." But this also proves to be "vanity" (Isa. 50:11).

2. laughter—including *prosperity*, and *joy* in general (Job 8:21). **mad**—i.e., *when made the chief good;* it is harmless in its proper place. **What doeth it?**—Of what avail is it in giving solid good? (ch. 7:6; Prov. 14:13).

3-11. Illustration more at large of vss 1, 2. **3. sought**—I resolved, after search into many plans. **give myself unto**—lit., "to draw my flesh (body) to" wine (including all banquetings). Image from a captive drawn after a chariot in triumph (Rom. 6:16, 19; I Cor. 12:2); or, one "allured" (II Pet. 2:18, 19). **yet acquainting . . . wisdom**—lit., and my heart (still) *was behaving*, or *guiding itself*, with wisdom [GESENIUS]. MAURER translates: "*was weary of* (worldly) wisdom." But the end of vs. 9 confirms *English Version.*

folly—viz., pleasures of the flesh, termed "mad," vs. 2. **all the days . . .**—(See *Margin* and ch. 6:12; Job. 15:20).

ADAM CLARKE — CHAPTER 2

2. *I said of laughter, It is mad.* Literally, "To laughter I said, O mad one! and to mirth, What is this one doing?"

3. *To give myself unto wine, yet acquainting* (*noheg*, "guiding") *mine heart with wisdom.* I did not run into extremes.

4. *I builded me houses.* Palace after palace; the house of the forest of Lebanon, 1 Kings vii. 1, etc.; a house for the queen; the Temple, etc., 2 Chron. viii. 1, etc; 1 Kings ix. 10, etc.; besides many other buildings of various kinds.

MATTHEW HENRY

bewitching as building. He *planted himself vineyards*; he *made himself* fine *gardens and orchards* (*v.* 5). He had not only forests of timber-trees, but *trees of all kinds of fruit*, which he himself had planted.

3. He laid out a great deal of money in water-works, ponds, and canals, not for sport and diversion, but for use, *to water the wood that brings forth trees* (*v.* 6); he not only planted, but watered, and then left it to God to give the increase.

4. When he proposed to himself to do *great works* he must employ many hands, and therefore procured *servants and maidens*, and of those he *had servants born in his house, v.* 7.

5. He *had large possessions of great and small cattle*, herds and flocks, as his father had before him (1 Chron. xxvii. 29, 31).

6. He grew very rich, and was not at all impoverished by his building and gardening.

7. He had all sorts of melody and music, vocal and instrumental. These are called *the delights of the sons of men*.

8. He enjoyed, more than ever any man did, a composition of rational and sensitive pleasures at the same time. In the midst of these entertainments *his wisdom remained with him, v.* 9. Yet his judgment and conscience gave no check to his pleasures, nor hindered him from extracting the very quintessence of the delights of sense, *v.* 10. He had as much pleasure in his business as ever any man had: *My heart rejoiced in all my labour*. It sweetened his business that he enjoyed the success of it, and it sweetened his enjoyments that they were the product of his business; so that, upon the whole, he was certainly as happy as the world could make him.

9. We have, at length, the judgment he deliberately gave of all this, *v.* 11. When Solomon reviewed *all his works that his hands had wrought* with the utmost cost and care, *and the labour that he had laboured to do* in order to make himself easy and happy, nothing answered his expectation; *behold, all was vanity and vexation of spirit; there was no profit under the sun*, neither by the employments nor by the enjoyments of this world.

Verses 12–16

Solomon having tried what satisfaction was to be had in learning, and in the pleasures of sense, here compares them and passes judgment upon them.

I. He sets himself to consider both wisdom and folly. He here turns himself again to behold them, to see if, upon a second view and second thoughts, he could gain more satisfaction. Let us acquiesce in Solomon's judgment of the things of this world, and not think of repeating the trial; for we can never have such advantages as he had to make the experiment nor be able to make it with equal application of mind.

II. He gives the preference to wisdom far before folly. I soon *saw* (says he) *that there is an excellency in wisdom more than in folly*, as much as there is in light above darkness. The pleasures of wisdom, though they suffice not to make men happy, yet vastly transcend the pleasures of wine. Wisdom enlightens the soul with surprising discoveries and necessary directions for the right government of itself; but sensuality clouds the mind, and is as darkness to it. *The wise man's eyes are in his head* (*v.* 14), where they should be, ready to discover both the dangers that are to be avoided and the advantages that are to be improved. *The fool walks in darkness*, and is ever and anon either at a loss, or at a plunge.

III. Yet he maintains that, in respect of lasting happiness and satisfaction, the wisdom of this world gives a man very little advantage. The same sickness, the same sword, devours wise men and fools. Solomon applies this mortifying observation to himself (*v.* 15). Why should I take so much pains to get wisdom, when, as to this life, it will stand me in so little stead? *Then I said in my heart that this also is vanity*. Wise men and fools are forgotten alike (*v.* 16): *There is no remembrance of the wise more than of the fool*. It is promised to the righteous that they *shall be had in everlasting remembrance*, and *their memory shall be blessed*, and they shall shortly *shine as the stars*; but there is no such promise made concerning the wisdom of this world, that that shall perpetuate men's names, for those names only are perpetuated that are *written in heaven*. Between the death of a godly and a wicked man there is a great difference, but not between the death of a wise man and a fool.

Verses 17–26

Solomon after a contemplative life and a voluptuous life, betook himself to an active life, and found no more satisfaction in it than in the other; still it is all *vanity and vexation of spirit*.

JAMIESON, FAUSSET, BROWN

4. (I Kings 7:1-8; 9:1, 19; 10:18, etc.) **vineyards**—(Song of Sol. 8:11.) **5. gardens**—*Hebrew*, "paradises," a foreign word; *Sanscrit*, "a place enclosed with a wall"; *Armenian* and *Arabic*, "a pleasure-ground with flowers and shrubs near the king's house, or castle." An earthly paradise can never make up for the want of the heavenly (Rev. 2:7). 6. **pools**—artificial, for irrigating the soil (Gen. 2:10; Neh. 2:14; Isa. 1:30). Three such reservoirs are still found, called Solomon's cisterns, a mile and a half from Jerusalem. **wood that bringeth forth**—rather, "the grove that *flourisheth with* trees" [LOWTH]. **7. born in my house**—These were esteemed more trustworthy servants than those bought (Gen. 14:14; 15:2, 3; 17:12, 13, 27; Jer. 2:14), called *songs of* one's *handmaid* (Exod. 23:12; cf. Gen. 12:16; Job 1:3). **8.** (I Kings 10:27; II Chron. 1:15; 9:20). **peculiar treasure of kings and ... provinces**—contributed by them, as tributary to him (I Kings 4:21, 24) a poor substitute for the wisdom whose "gain is better than fine gold" (Prov. 3:14, 15). **singers**—so David (II Sam. 19:35). **musical instruments ... of all sorts**—introduced at banquets (Isa. 5:12; Amos 6:5, 6); rather, "a princess and princesses," from an *Arabic* root. One regular wife, or queen (Esther 1:9); Pharaoh's daughter (I Kings 3:1); other secondary wives, "princesses," distinct from the "concubines" (I Kings 11:3; Ps. 45:10; Song of Sol. 6:8) [WEISS, GENENIUS]. Had these been omitted, the enumeration would be incomplete. **9. great**—opulent (Gen. 24:35; Job. 1:3; see I Kings 10:23). **remained**—(vs. 3). **10. my labour**—in procuring pleasures. **this**—evanescent "joy" was my only "portion out of all my labor" (ch. 3:22; 5:18; 9:19; I Kings 10:5). **11.** But all these I felt were only "vanity," and of no "profit" as to the chief good. "Wisdom" (worldly *common sense*, sagacity), which still "remained with me" (vs. 9), showed me that these could not give solid happiness.

12. He had tried (wordly) wisdom (ch. 1:12-18) and folly (foolish pleasure) (vs. 1-11); he now compares them (vs. 12), and finds that while (worldly) **wisdom excelleth folly** (vss. 13, 14), yet the one event, death, befalls both (vs. 14-16), and that thus the wealth acquired by the wise man's "labor" may descend to a "fool" that hath not labored (vss. 18, 19, 21); therefore all his labor is vanity (vss. 22, 23). **what can the man do ... already done**—(ch. 1:9.) Parenthetical. A future investigator can strike nothing out "new," so as to draw a different conclusion from what I draw by comparing "wisdom and madness." HOLDEN, with less ellipsis, translates, "What, O man, shall come after the king?" etc. Better, GROTIUS, "What man can come after (compete with) the king in the things which are done?" None ever can have the same means of testing what all earthly things can do towards satisfying the soul; namely, worldly wisdom, science, riches, power, longevity, all combined. **13, 14.** (Prov. 17:24.) The worldly "wise" man has *good sense* in managing his affairs, *skill* and *taste* in building and planting, and keeps within *safe* and *respectable* bounds in pleasure, while the "fool" is wanting in these respects ("darkness," equivalent to *fatal error, blind infatuation*), yet one event, death, happens to both (Job 21:26). **15. why was I**—so anxious to become, etc. (II Chron. 1:10). **Then**—Since such is the case. **this**—viz., pursuit of (worldly) wisdom; it can never fill the place of the true wisdom (Job. 28:28; Jer. 8:9). **16. remembrance**—a great aim of the worldly (Gen. 11:4). The righteous alone attain it (Ps. 112:6; Prov. 10:7). **for ever**—no *perpetual* memorial. **that which now is**—MAURER, "In the days to come all things shall be *now long ago* forgotten."

ADAM CLARKE

5. *I made me gardens and orchards. Pardesim*, "paradises." How well Solomon was qualified to form gardens, orchards, vineyards, conservatories, etc., may be at once conceived when we recollect his knowledge of natural history; and that he wrote treatises on vegetables and their properties, from the cedar to the hyssop.

7. *Great and small cattle*. And multitudes of most of these he needed, when we are told that his household consumed daily ten stall-fed oxen, with twenty from the pasture, with a hundred sheep; besides harts, roebucks, fallow deer, fatted fowls, and other kinds of provision.

8. *The peculiar treasure of kings and of the provinces*. (1) The *taxes* levied off his subjects. (2) The *tribute* given by the neighboring potentates. *Men singers and women singers*. This includes all instrumental and vocal performers. These may be called the delights of the sons of men. *Musical instruments, and that of all sorts*. For these seven words, there are only two in the original, *shiddah veshiddoth*. These words are acknowledged on all hands to be utterly unknown, if not utterly inexplicable. *Sadeh*, in Hebrew, is a "field," and occurs in various parts of the Bible. *Sadoth* is "fields," 1 Sam. xxii. 7. May not Solomon be speaking here of "farms upon farms" or "estates upon estates," which he had added by purchase to the common regal portion?

11. *And, behold, all was vanity*. Emptiness. *And vexation of spirit*. Because it promised the good I wished for, but did not, could not, perform the promise; and left my soul discontented and chagrined.

15. *As it happeneth to the fool*. Literally, "According as the event is to the fool, it happens to me, even me." There is a peculiar beauty and emphasis in the repetition of *me*.

16. *There is no remembrance*. The wise and the fool are equally subject to death; and, in most instances, they are equally forgotten.

MATTHEW HENRY

I. The business of which he made trial was business *under the sun* (*v.* 17–20), about the things of this world; it was the business of a king. It is *labour under the sun*, labour for the *meat that perishes* (John vi. 27; Isa. lv. 2), that Solomon here speaks of with so little satisfaction. It was the better sort of business *in wisdom, and knowledge, and equity*, *v.* 21. It was rational business, which related to the government of his kingdom. It was labour wherein he *showed himself wise* (*v.* 19), which many people have in their eye more than anything else in the prosecution of their worldly business.

II. He soon grew weary of it. He *hated all his labour*. After he had had his fine houses, and gardens, awhile, he began to look upon them with contempt. This expresses not a gracious hatred of these things, which is our duty, to love them less than God and religion (Luke xiv. 26), nor a sinful hatred of them, which is our folly, to be weary of the place God has assigned us and the work of it, but a natural hatred of them, arising from a surfeit and a sense of disappointment in them. Have we so often bored into this earth for some rich mine of satisfaction, and found not the least sign of it, but been always frustrated in the search, and shall we not at length despair of ever finding it? At length he *hated life itself* (*v.* 17), because it is subject to so many toils and troubles, and a constant series of disappointments.

III. Two things made him weary:

1. His business was so great a toil to himself: The *work that he had wrought under the sun was grievous unto him*, *v.* 17. A man of business is described to be uneasy both in his *going out* and his *coming in*, *v.* 23. He is deprived of his pleasure by day. He is disturbed in his repose *by night*. See what fools those are that make themselves drudges to the world, and do not make God their rest; night and day they cannot but be uneasy. So that, upon the whole matter, it is *all vanity*, *v.* 17.

2. The gains of his business must all be left to others. To a gracious soul this is no uneasiness at all; why should we not rather be pleased that, when we are gone, those that come after us shall fare the better for our wisdom and industry? He knows not what *he* will prove to whom he leaves it, whether *a wise man or a fool*, a wise man that will make it more or a fool that will bring it to nothing. It is probable that Solomon wrote this very feelingly, being afraid what Rehoboam would prove.

IV. The best use which is therefore to be made of the wealth of this world is to use it cheerfully and do good with it. With this he concludes the chapter, *v.* 24–26. That good which is here recommended to us is the utmost pleasure and profit we can expect or extract from the business of this world, and the furthest we can go to rescue it from its *vanity* and *vexation*. We must be more in care to use an estate well, for the ends for which we were entrusted with it, than how to increase it. He would not have us to give up business, and take our ease, that we may *eat and drink*; we must *enjoy good in our labour*; we must use these things, not to excuse us from, but to make us diligent and cheerful in, our worldly business. We must herein *acknowledge God*; we must see that *it is from the hand of God*. A heart to enjoy them is the gift of God's grace. Solomon himself, with all his possessions, could aim at no more and desire no better (*v.* 25). Yet Solomon could not obtain it by his own wisdom, without the special grace of God, and therefore directs us to expect it from the hand of God and pray to him for it. Riches are a blessing or a curse to a man according as he has or has not a heart to make good use of them. God makes them a reward to a good man, if with them he give him *wisdom, and knowledge, and joy*, to enjoy them cheerfully himself and to communicate them charitably to others. He makes them a punishment to a bad man if he denies him a heart to take the comfort of them, for they do but tantalize him and tyrannize over him. *Godliness, with contentment, is great gain.* Ungodliness is commonly punished with discontent and an insatiable covetousness, which are sins that are their own punishment.

JAMIESON, FAUSSET, BROWN

17. Disappointed in one experiment after another, he is weary of life. The backslider ought to have rather reasoned as the prodigal (Hos. 2:6, 7; Luke 15:17, 18). **grievous unto me**—(Job. 10:1.) **18, 19.** One hope alone was left to the disappointed worldling, the perpetuation of his name and riches, laboriously gathered, through his successor. For selfishness is mostly at the root of worldly parents' alleged providence for their children. But now the remembrance of how he himself, the piously reared child of David, had disregarded his father's dying charge (I Chron. 28:9), suggested the sad misgivings as to what Rehoboam, his son by an idolatrous Ammonitess, Naamah, should prove to be; a foreboding too fully realized (I Kings 12; 14:21-31). **20.** *I gave up as desperate all* hope of solid fruit from *my labor*. **21.** Suppose "there is a man. . . ." **equity**—rather "with success," as the *Hebrew* is rendered (ch. 11:6), "prosper," though *Margin* gives "right" [Holden and Maurer]. **evil**—not in itself, for this is the ordinary course of things, but "evil," as regards the chief good, that one should have toiled so fruitlessly. **22.** Same sentiment as in vs. 21, interrogatively. **23.** The only fruit he has is, not only sorrows *in* his days, but *all* his days are sorrows, and his travail (not only *has* griefs connected with it, but *is* itself), grief. **24.** *English Version* gives a seemingly Epicurean sense, contrary to the general scope. The *Hebrew*, lit. is, "It is *not good* for man that he should eat," etc., "and should make his soul see good" (or "*show* his soul, i.e., himself, happy"), etc. [Weiss]. According to Holden and Weiss, ch. 3:12, 22 differ from this verse in the text and meaning; here he means, "It is not good that a man should feast himself, and falsely make as though his soul were happy"; he thus refers to a false *pretending* of happiness *acquired by and for one's self*; in ch. 3:12, 22 and 5: 18, 19, to *real seeing*, or *finding* pleasure *when God gives it*. There it is said to be *good* for a man to enjoy with satisfaction and thankfulness the blessings which God gives; here it is said *not* to be *good* to take an unreal pleasure to one's self by feasting, etc. **This also I saw**—I perceived by experience that good (real pleasure) is not to be taken at will, but comes only from the hand of God [Weiss] (Ps. 4:6; Isa. 57:19-21). Or as Holden, "It is the appointment from the hand of God, that the sensualist has no solid satisfaction" (good). **25. hasten**—after indulgences (Prov. 7:23; 19:2), *eagerly pursue* such enjoyments. None can compete with me in this. If I, then, with all my opportunities of enjoyment, failed utterly to obtain solid pleasure of my own making, apart from God, who else can? God mercifully spares His children the sad experiment which Solomon made, by denying them the goods which they often desire. He gives them the fruits of Solomon's experience, without their paying the dear price at which Solomon bought it. **26.** True, literally, in the Jewish theocracy; and in some measure in all ages (Job 27:16,17; Prov. 13:22, 28:8). Though the retribution be not so visible and immediate now as then, it is no less real. Happiness even here is more truly the portion of the godly (Ps. 84:11; Matt. 5:5; Mark 10:29, 30; Rom. 8:28; I Tim. 4:8). **that he** [the sinner] **may give**—i.e., unconsciously and in spite of himself. The godly Solomon had satisfaction in his riches and wisdom, when God gave them (II Chron. 1). The backsliding Solomon had no happiness when he sought it in them apart from God; and the riches which he heaped up became the prey of Shishak (II Chron. 12).

ADAM CLARKE

17. *Therefore I hated life.* "The lives," of both the wise, the madman, and the fool. Also all the stages of life, the child, the man, and the sage.

18. *I hated all my labour.* Because (1) It has not answered the end for which it was instituted; (2) I can enjoy the fruits of it but a short time; (3) I must leave it to others, and know not whether a wise man, a knave, or a fool will possess it.

19. *A wise man or a fool?* Alas! Solomon, the wisest of all men, made the worst use of his wisdom, had 300 wives and 700 concubines, and yet left but one son behind him to possess his estates and his throne, and that one was the silliest of fools!

21. *For there is a man.* Does he not allude to himself? As if he had said, "I have labored to cultivate my mind in wisdom and in science, in knowledge of men and things, and have endeavored to establish equity and dispense justice. And now I find I shall leave all the fruits of my labor to a man that hath not labored therein, and consequently cannot prize what I have wrought." Does he not refer to his son Rehoboam?

23. *His days are sorrows.* What a picture of human life where the heart is not filled with the peace and love of God! All his days are sorrows, all his labors griefs, all his nights restless.

25. *For who can eat . . . more than I?* But instead of *chuts mimmenni*, "more than I," *chuts mimmennu*, "without him," is the reading of eight of Kennicott's and De Rossi's MSS., as also of the Septuagint, Syriac, and Arabic. "For who maye eat, drynke, or bring enythinge to pass without him?"—Coverdale. I believe this to be the true reading. No one can have a true relish of the comforts of life without the divine blessing. This reading connects all the sentences: "This also I saw, that it was from the hand of God—for who can eat, and who can relish without him? For God giveth to man that is good." It is through His liberality that we have anything to eat or drink; and it is only through His blessing that we can derive good from the use of what we possess.

26. *Giveth . . . wisdom, and knowledge, and joy.* (1) God gives *wisdom*—the knowledge of himself, light to direct in the way of salvation. (2) *Knowledge*—understanding to discern the operation of His hand. (3) *Joy*.

MATTHEW HENRY

CHAPTER 3

Verses 1–10

We live in a world of changes. The several events of time, and conditions of human life, are vastly different from one another, and we are continually passing and repassing between them. In the *wheel of nature* (James iii. 6) sometimes one spoke is uppermost and by and by the contrary; there is a constant ebbing and flowing, waxing and waning from one extreme to the other. When we are in prosperity, we should be easy, and yet not secure—not to be secure

JAMIESON, FAUSSET, BROWN

CHAPTER 3

Vss. 1-22. Earthly pursuits are no doubt lawful in their proper time and order (vss. 1-8), but unprofitable when out of time and place; as for instance, when pursued as the solid and chief good (vss. 9, 10); whereas God makes everything beautiful in its season, which man obscurely comprehends (vs. 11). God allows man to enjoy moderately and virtuously His earthly gifts (vss. 12, 13). What consoles us amidst the instability of earthly bless-

ADAM CLARKE

CHAPTER 3

MATTHEW HENRY

because we live in a world of changes, and yet to be easy, and, as he had advised (*ch.* ii. 24), *to enjoy the good of our labour*, in a humble dependence upon God, neither lifted up with hopes, nor cast down with fears, but with evenness of mind.

I. A general proposition is laid down: *To every thing there is a season, v.* 1. Those things which seem most contrary the one to the other will, in the revolution of affairs, each take their turn and come into play. The day will give place to the night and the night again to the day. Is it summer? It will be winter. Is it winter? Stay a while, and it will be summer. Every purpose has its time.

II. Some of these changes are purely the act of God, others depend more upon the will of man. Everything *under heaven* is thus changeable, but in heaven there is an unchangeable state. 1. There is *a time to be born and a time to die*. But, as there is *a time to be born and a time to die*, so there will be a time to rise again. 2. There is *a time* for men *to plant*, a time of the year, a time of their lives; but, when *that which was planted* has grown fruitless and useless, it is *time to pluck it up*. 3. *A time to kill*, when the judgments of God are abroad in a land and lay all waste; but, when he returns in ways of mercy, then is *a time to heal* what *he has torn* (Hos. vi. 1, 2), to comfort a people after the time that he has *afflicted them*, Ps. xc. 15. 4. *A time to break down* a family, an estate, a kingdom, when it has ripened itself for destruction; but God will find *a time*, if they return and repent, to rebuild what he has broken down. 5. *A time* when God's providence calls *to weep and mourn*, but, on the other hand, there is a time when God calls to cheerfulness, *a time to laugh and dance*, and then he expects we should *serve him with joyfulness and gladness of heart*. 6. *A time to cast away stones*, by breaking down fortifications, when God gives peace in the borders, but there is *a time to gather stones together*, for the making of strongholds, *v.* 5. 7. *A time to embrace* a friend when we find him faithful, but *a time to refrain from embracing* when we find he is unfair or unfaithful. It is commonly applied to conjugal embraces, and explained by 1 Cor. vii. 3–5; Joel ii. 16. 8. *A time to get* money, preferment, good bargains, when opportunity smiles, a time when a wise man will *seek* (so the word is); when he is setting out in the world and has a growing family, when he is in his prime, then it is time for him to be busy and make hay when the sun shines. There will come *a time to lose*, when what has been soon got will be soon scattered. 9. *A time to keep*, when we have use for what we have got, but there may come *a time to cast away*, when love to God may oblige us to cast away what we have, because we must deny Christ and wrong our consciences if we keep it (Matt. x. 37, 38). 10. *A time to rend* the garments, as upon occasion of some great grief, *and a time to sew* them again, in token that the grief is over. 11. *A time* when it is our duty *to keep silence*, when it is an *evil time* (Amos v. 13), or when we are in danger of speaking amiss (Ps. xxxix. 2); but there is also *a time to speak* for the glory of God when silence would be the betraying of a righteous cause. 12. *A time to love*, and to show ourselves friendly, to be free and cheerful, but there may come *a time to hate*, when we shall see cause to break off all familiarity with some that we have been fond of, and to be upon the reserve. 13. *A time of war*, when God draws the sword for judgment, when men draw the sword for justice, but we may hope for *a time of peace*, when the sword of the Lord shall be sheathed and he shall *make wars to cease* (Ps. xlvi. 9). War shall not last always, nor is there any peace to be called lasting on this side the everlasting peace.

III. If our present state be subject to such vicissitude, *What profit has he that works?* We must look upon ourselves as upon our probation in it. There is indeed no profit *in that wherein we labour*; the thing itself, when we have it, will do us little good; but, if we make a right use of the disposals of Providence about it, there will be profit in that (*v.* 10): *I have seen the travail which God has given to the sons of men*, not to make up a happiness by it, but *to be exercised in it*, to have various graces exercised by the variety of events, to have their dependence upon God tried by every change, and to be trained and taught. Every change cuts us out some new work, which we should be more solicitous about, than about the event.

Verses 11–15

Solomon shows the hand of God in all those changes.

I. We must make the best of *that which is*, and must believe it best for the present, and accommodate ourselves to it: *He has made everything beautiful in his time* (*v.* 11). Cold is as becoming in winter as

JAMIESON, FAUSSET, BROWN

ings is, God's counsels are immutable (vs. 14).

1. Man has his appointed cycle of seasons and vicissitudes, as the sun, wind, and water (ch. 1:5-7). **purpose**—as there is a fixed "season" in God's "purposes" (e.g., He has fixed the "time" when man is "to be born," and "to die," vs. 2), so there is a lawful "time" for man to carry out his "purposes" and inclinations. God does not condemn, but approves of, the *use* of earthly blessings (vs. 12); it is the *abuse* that He condemns, the making them the chief end (I Cor. 7:31). The earth, without human desires, love, taste, joy, sorrow, would be a dreary waste, without water; but, on the other hand, the misplacing and excess of them, as of a flood, need control. Reason and revelation are given to control them. **2. time to die**—(Ps. 31:15; Heb. 9:27). **plant**—A man can no more reverse the times and order of "planting," and of "digging up," and transplanting, than he can alter the times fixed for his "birth" and "death." To try to "plant" *out of season* is vanity, however good *in season;* so to make earthly things *the chief end* is vanity, however good they be in order and season. GILL takes it, not so well, figuratively (Jer. 18:7, 9; Amos 9:15; Matt. 15:13). **3. time to kill**—viz., judicially, criminals; or, in wars of self-defense; not in malice. Out of this time and order, killing is murder. **to heal**—God has His times for "healing" (lit., Isa. 38:5, 21; fig., Deut. 32:39; Hos. 6:1; spiritually, Ps. 147:3; Isa. 57:19). To *heal* spiritually, before the sinner feels his *wound,* would be out of time, and so injurious. **time to break down**—cities, as Jerusalem, by Nebuchadnezzar. **build up**—as Jerusalem, in the time of Zerubbabel; spiritually (Amos 9:11), "the set time" (Ps. 102:13-16). **4. mourn**—viz., for the dead (Gen. 23:2). **dance**—as David before the ark (II Sam. 6:12-14; Ps. 30:11); spiritually (Matt. 9:15; Luke 6:21; 15:25). The Pharisees, by requiring sadness *out of time,* erred seriously. **5. cast away stones**—as out of a garden or vineyard (Isa. 5:2). **gather**—for building; fig., the Gentiles, once castaway stones, were in due time made parts of the spiritual building (Eph. 2:19, 20), and children of Abraham (Matt. 3:9); so the restored Jews hereafter (Ps. 102:13, 14; Zech. 9:16). **refrain. . . . embracing**—(Joel 2:16: I Cor. 7:5, 6.) **6. time to get**—e.g., to gain honestly a livelihood (Eph. 4:23). **lose**—When God wills losses to us, then is our time to be content. **keep**—not to give to the idle beggar (II Thess. 3:10). **cast away**—in charity (Prov. 11:24); or to part with the dearest object, rather than the soul (Mark 9:43). To be careful is right in its place, but not when it comes between us and Jesus Christ (Luke 10:40-42). **7. rend**—garments, in mourning (Joel 2:13); fig., nations, as Israel from Judah, already foretold, in Solomon's time (I Kings 11:30, 31), to be "sewed" together hereafter (Ezek. 37:15, 22). **silence**—(Amos 5:13), in a national calamity, or that of a friend (Job. 2:13); also not to murmur under God's visitation (Lev. 10:3; Ps. 39:1, 2, 9). **8. hate**—e.g., sin, lusts (Luke 14:26); i.e., to love *God* so much more as to seem in comparison to *hate* "father or mother," when coming between us and God. **time of war . . . peace**—(Luke 14:31).

9. But these earthly pursuits, while lawful in their season, are "unprofitable" when made by man, what God never intended them to be, the chief good. Solomon had tried to create an artificial forced joy, at times when he ought rather to have been serious; the result, therefore, of his labor to be happy, out of God's order, was disappointment. "A time to plant" (vs. 2) refers to his *planting* (ch. 2:5); "laugh" (vs. 4), to ch. 2:1, 2. "his mirth," "laughter"; "build up," "gather stones" (vss. 3, 5), to his "building" (ch. 2:4); "embrace," "love," to his "princess" (*Note,* ch. 2:8); "get" (perhaps also "gather," vss. 5, 6), to his "gathering" (ch. 2:8). All these were of no "profit," because not in God's time and order of bestowing happiness. **10.** (Ch. 1:13.)

11. his time—i.e. ***in its*** proper *season* (Ps. 1:3), opposed to worldlings putting earthly pursuits *out of their proper time and place* (*Note,* vs. 9).

ADAM CLARKE

1. *To every thing there is a season, and a time to every purpose.* Two general remarks may be made on the first eight verses of this chapter. (1) God by His providence governs the world, and has determined particular things and operations to particular times. In those times such things may be done with propriety and success; but if we neglect the appointed seasons, we sin against this providence, and become the authors of our own distresses. (2) God has given to man that portion of duration called time—the space in which all the operations of nature, of animals, and intellectual beings are carried on. But while nature is steady in its course, and animals faithful to their instincts, man devotes it to a great variety of purposes; but very frequently to that for which God never made time, space, or opportunity.

JOSEPH PARKER:

There is a time to dance as surely as there is a time to die. It is not a dial of cloud on which the hands move; it is now and again bright like the very sun. Every man dances—must dance; every man cries in bitterness of soul—must cry, for his sorrow is very great. Is it right to dance? You may well ask, Is it right to breathe? It is not a question of right or wrong, it is a question of necessity. Whether you will turn dancing into an art or not, please yourself, but you *must* dance when joy blows her trumpet and sunshine warms the blood. There is a time to cast away stones—to uproot, abolish, tear down, and destroy; and there is a time to construct, to build, and to make strong. The great thing is to know the time, and to say the right word at the right moment. There is a time to dance, but he who would dance in the house of mourning is a foolish man and one not to be endured. There is a time to mourn, but he who would mourn at a wedding would be as one that shut out the sun and shortened the road to the grave. We are not to mix the seasons. We are not to pluck sour fruit for our eating. If possible, we are to meet the conditions that are around us. "Rejoice with them that do rejoice, and weep with them that weep." If we are not in wedding mood, then turn aside from the wedding banquet, lest a cloud fall on the bride's gladness; if we are lifted up with great joy, then escape from the path of the mourner, lest we grieve him with unseasonable mirth. "To every thing there is a season," and he is the wise man who puts away his sickle in seed time, nor makes the wedding bells clash when the heart is made poor by death. The turning of one season into another is often the direct work of God: "Thou hast turned for me my mourning into dancing: thou hast put off my sackcloth, and girded me with gladness."

—*The People's Bible*

11. *Beautiful in his time.* God's works are well done; there are order, harmony, and beauty in them all. Even the caterpillar is a finished beauty in all the changes through which it

MATTHEW HENRY

heat in summer; and the night, in its turn, is a black beauty, as the day, in its turn, is a bright one. There is a wonderful harmony in the divine Providence and all its disposals, so that events considered in their relations and tendencies, together with the seasons of them, appear very beautiful, to the glory of God and the comfort of those that trust in him. Though we see not the complete beauty of Providence, yet we shall see it, and a glorious sight it will be, when the mystery of God shall be finished. Deut. xxxii. 4; Ezek. i. 18.

II. We must wait with patience for the full discovery of that which to us seems intricate and perplexed, acknowledging that we *cannot find out the work that God makes from the beginning to the end,* and therefore must judge nothing before the time. While the picture is in drawing, and the house in building, we see not the beauty of either; but when the artist has given them their finishing strokes, then all appears very good. We see but the middle of God's works, not from the beginning of them (then we should see how admirably the plan was laid in the divine counsels), nor to the end of them, which crowns the action (then we should see the product to be glorious); but we must wait till the veil be rent. Those words, *He has set the world in their hearts,* are differently understood. 1. Some make them to be a reason why we may know more of God's works than we do. If men did but give themselves to the exact observation of things, they might in most of them perceive an admirable order and contrivance. 2. Others make them to be a reason why we do not know so much of God's works as we might: "We have the world so much in our hearts, are so taken up with thoughts and cares of worldly things, that we have neither time nor spirit to eye God's hand in them."

III. *There is no* certain lasting, *good in* these things (*v.* 12, 13). All the *good* there is *in them* is *to do good* with them, to our families, to our neighbours, to the poor, to the public, to its civil and religious interests. What have we our beings, capacities, and estates for, but to be some way serviceable to our generation? It is *in this life,* where we are in a state of trial and probation for another life. Every man's life is his opportunity of doing that which will make for him in eternity. Let us make ourselves easy, *rejoice, and enjoy the good of our labour,* as *it is the gift of God,* and so enjoy God in it, and return him thanks.

IV. We must be satisfied in the disposals of the divine Providence, both as to personal and public concerns. "Let it be as God wills", for, how cross soever it may be to our designs and interests, God's will is his wisdom. That counsel needs not to be altered. If we could see it altogether at one view, we should see it so perfect that *nothing can be put to it,* for there is no deficiency in it, *nor anything taken from it,* for there is nothing in it unnecessary, or that can be spared.

V. We must study to answer God's end in all his providences. Whatever changes we see or feel in this world, we must acknowledge the inviolable steadiness of God's government. With the events of Providence (*v.* 15): *That which has been is now.* The world, as it has been, is and will be constant in inconstancy; for *God requires that which is past,* that is, repeats what he has formerly done. There has no change befallen us, *but such as is common to men.*

Verses 16–22

Solomon is still showing that everything in this world, without piety and the fear of God, is vanity. In these verses he shows that power and life itself are nothing without the fear of God.

I. Here is the vanity of man, mighty upon the throne, man upon the judgment-seat, where, if he be governed by the laws of religion, he is God's viceregent. But without the fear of God it *is vanity,* for, set that aside, and,

1. The judge will not judge aright. Solomon perceived that there was *wickedness in the place of judgment. Man being in honour, and not understanding* what he ought to do, *becomes like the beasts that perish,* like the beasts of prey. It would have been better for the people to have had no judges than to have had such. It would have been better for the judges to have had no power than to have used it to such ill purposes.

2. The judge will himself be judged for not judging aright. *I said in my heart* that this unrighteous judgment is not conclusive, for there will be a review of the judgment; *God shall judge* between *the righteous and the wicked,* shall judge for the righteous and plead their cause. It is an unspeakable comfort to the oppressed that their cause will be heard over again. Let them therefore wait with patience, for there is another *Judge* that *stands before the door. There is a time* for the re-hearing of causes, redressing of

JAMIESON, FAUSSET, BROWN

set the world in their heart—given them capacities to understand *the world* of nature as reflecting God's wisdom in its beautiful order and times (Rom. 1:19,20). "Everything" answers to "world," in the parallelism. **so that**—i.e., but in such a manner that man only sees a portion, not the whole "from beginning to end" (ch. 8:17; Job 26:14; Rom. 11:33; Rev. 15:4). PARKHURST, for "world," translates: "Yet He hath put *obscurity in the midst of them,*" lit., "a secret," so man's mental *dimness of sight* as to the full mystery of God's works. So HOLDEN and WEISS. This incapacity for "finding out" (comprehending) God's work is chiefly the fruit of the fall. The worldling ever since, not knowing God's time and order, labors in vain, because out of time and place. **12. in them**—in God's works (vs. 11), as far as relates to man's duty. Man cannot fully comprehend them, but he ought joyfully to receive ("rejoice in") God's gifts, and "do good" with them to himself and to others. This is never out of season (Gal. 6:9, 10). Not sensual joy and self-indulgence (Phil. 4:4; Jas. 4:16, 17). **13.** Lit., "And also as to every man who eats," etc., "this is the gift of God" (vs. 22; ch. 5:18). When received as God's gifts, and to God's glory, the good things of life are enjoyed in their due time and order (Acts 2:46; I Cor. 10:31; I Tim. 4:3, 4). **14.** (I Sam. 3:12; II Sam. 23:5; Ps. 80:34; Matt. 24:35; Jas. 1:17.) **for ever**—as opposed to man's perishing labors (ch. 2:15-18). **any thing taken from it**—opposed to man's "crooked and wanting" works (ch. 1:15; 7:13). The event of man's labors depends wholly on God's immutable purpose. Man's part, therefore, is to do and enjoy every earthly thing *in its proper season* (vss. 12, 13), not setting aside God's order, but observing deep reverence towards God; for the mysteriousness and unchangeableness of God's purposes are designed to lead "man to fear before Him." Man knows not the event of each act; otherwise he would think himself independent of God. **15.** Resumption of ch. 1:9. Whatever changes there be, the succession of events is ordered by God's "everlasting" laws (vs. 14), and returns in a fixed cycle. **requireth that . . . past**—After many changes, God's law *requires* the return of the same cycle of events, as in *the past,* lit., "that which is driven on." LXX and *Syriac* translate: "God requireth (i.e., avengeth) the p*ersecuted* man"; a transition to vss. 16, 17. The parallel clauses of the verse support *English Version.*

16. Here a difficulty is suggested. If God "requires" events to move in their perpetual cycle, why are the wicked allowed to deal unrighteously in the place where injustice ought least of all to be; viz., "the place of judgment" (Jer. 12:1)? **17.** Solution of it. There is a coming judgment in which God will vindicate His righteous ways. The sinner's "time" of his unrighteous "work" is short. God also has His "time" and "work" of judgment; and, meanwhile, is overruling, for good at last, what seems now dark. Man cannot now "find out" the plan of God's ways (vs. 11; Ps. 97:2). If judgment instantly followed every sin, there would be no scope for free-will, faith, and perseverance of saints in spite of difficulties. The previous darkness will make the light at last the more glorious. **there**—(Job 3:17-19) in eternity, in the presence of the Divine Judge, opposed to the "there," in the human place of judgment (vs. 16): so "from *thence*" (Gen. 49:24).

ADAM CLARKE

passes, when its structure is properly examined, and the end kept in view in which each change is to issue. Nothing of this kind can be said of the works of man. The most finished works of art are bungling jobs, when compared with the meanest operation of nature.

He hath set the world in their heart. Haolam, that "hidden time"—the "period beyond" the present—eternity. The proper translation of this clause is the following: "Also that eternity hath he placed in their heart, without which man could not find out the work which God hath made from the commencement to the end." God has deeply rooted the idea of eternity in every human heart, and every considerate man sees that all the operations of God refer to that endless duration. See v. 14. And it is only in eternity that man will be able to discover what God has designed by the various works He has formed.

14. *I know that, whatsoever God doeth, it shall be for ever. Leolam,* "for eternity"; in reference to that grand consummation of men and things intimated in v. 11. *Nothing can be put to it.* No new order of beings, whether animate or inanimate, can be produced. God will not create more; man cannot add. *Nor any thing taken from it.* Nothing can be annihilated; no power but that which can create can destroy.

15. *And God requireth that which is past,* i.e., that it may return again in its proper order.

MATTHEW HENRY

grievances, and reversing of unjust decrees, though as yet we see it not here, Job xxiv. 1.

II. Here is the vanity of man as mortal. He now comes to speak more generally *concerning the estate of the sons of men* in this world, and shows that their reason, without religion and the fear of God, advances them but little above the beasts. Lay no blame on God; let them not say that he made this world to be man's prison and life to be his penance. God made man *little lower than the angels*; if he be mean and miserable, it is his own fault. It is no easy matter to convince proud men that *they are but men* (Ps. ix. 20), much more to convince bad men *that they are beasts*, being destitute of religion. A worldly, carnal, earthly-minded *man, has no pre-eminence above the beast, for all* that which he sets his heart upon *is vanity, v.* 19. *That which befalls the sons of men* is no other than that which *befalls beasts*; death makes much the same change with a beast that it does with a man. As to their bodies, the change is altogether the same, except the different respects that are paid to them by the survivors. Solomon here observes that *all go unto one place*; the dead bodies of men and beasts putrefy alike; *all turn to dust again* in their corruption.

As to their spirits there is indeed a vast difference, but not a visible one, *v.* 21. It is certain that *the spirit of* the sons of men at death *goes upwards* to the Father of spirits, who made it; it dies not with the body, but *is redeemed from the power of the grave*, Ps. xlix. 15. The soul of a man is then like a candle taken out of a dark lantern, which leaves the lantern useless indeed, but does itself shine brighter. Those that live by sense, as all carnal sensualists do, that *walk in the sight of their eyes*, have no *pre-eminence above the beasts*. It is not strange that those live like beasts who think they shall die like beasts, but on such the noble faculties of reason are lost. An inference drawn from it (*v.* 22): *There is nothing better*, as to this world, *than that a man should rejoice in his own works*, that is, Keep a clear conscience, and never admit *iniquity* into *the place of righteousness*. Live a cheerful life. If God has prospered the work of our hands unto us, let us rejoice in it, and not make it a burden.

JAMIESON, FAUSSET, BROWN

estate—The estate of fallen man is so ordered (these wrongs are permitted), that God might "manifest," i.e., thereby *prove* them, and that they might themselves see their mortal frailty, like that of the beasts. **sons of men**—rather, *sons of Adam,* a phrase used for *fallen men*. The toleration of injustice until the judgment is designed to "manifest" men's characters in their fallen state, to see whether the oppressed will bear themselves aright amidst their wrongs, knowing that the time is short, and there is a coming judgment. The oppressed share in death, but the comparison to "beasts" applies especially to *the ungodly oppressors* (Ps. 49:12, 20). They too need to be "manifested" (proved), whether, considering that they must soon die as the "beasts," and fearing the judgment to come, they will repent (Dan. 4:27). **19.** Lit., "For the sons of men (Adam) *are a mere chance,* as also the beast is a mere chance." These words can only be the sentiments of the skeptical oppressors. God's delay in judgment gives scope for the "manifestation" of their infidelity (ch. 8:11; Ps. 55:19; II Pet. 3:3, 4). They *are* "brute *beasts,*" morally (vs. 18; Jude 10); and they end by maintaining that man, physically, has no pre-eminence over the beast, both alike being "fortuities." Probably this was the language of Solomon himself in his apostasy. He answers it in vs. 21. If vss. 19, 20 be *his* words, they express only that *as regards liability to death,* excluding the future judgment, as the skeptic oppressors do, man is on a level with the beast. Life is "vanity," if regarded independently of religion. But vs. 21 points out the vast difference between them in respect to the future destiny; also (vs. 17) beasts have no "judgment" to come. **breath**—vitality. **21. Who knoweth**—Not *doubt* of the destination of man's spirit (ch. 12:7); but "*how few*, by reason of the outward mortality to which man is as liable as the beast and which is the ground of the skeptic's argument, comprehend the wide difference between man and the beast" (Isa. 53:1). The *Hebrew* expresses the difference strongly, "The spirit of man that ascends, it belongeth to on high; but the spirit of the beast that descends, it belongeth to below, even to the earth." Their destinations and proper element differ utterly [WEISS]. **22.** (Cf. vs. 12; ch. 5:18.) Inculcating a thankful enjoyment of God's gifts, and a cheerful discharge of man's duties, founded on fear of God; not as the sensualist (ch. 11:9); not as the anxious money-seeker (ch. 2:23; 5:10-17). **his portion**—in the present life. If it were made his *main* portion, it would be "vanity" (ch. 2:1; Luke 16:25). **for who . . .**—Our ignorance as to the future, which is God's "time" (vs. 11), should lead us to use the present time in the best sense and leave the future to His infinite wisdom (Matt. 6:20, 25, 31-34).

ADAM CLARKE

21. The word *ruach,* which is used in this and the nineteenth verse, has two significations, "breath" and "spirit." It signifies *spirit,* or an incorporeal substance, as distinguished from flesh, or a corporeal one, 1 Kings xxii. 21-22 and Isa. xxxi. 3. And it signifies the spirit or soul of man, Ps. xxxi. 6; Isa. lvii. 16; in this book, chap. xii. 7, and in many other places. In this book it is used also to signify the breath, spirit, or soul of a beast. While it was said in v. 19, "They have all one breath," i.e., the man and the beast live the same kind of animal life, in this verse a proper distinction is made between the *ruach,* or "soul" of man, and the *ruach,* or "soul" of the beast: the one *goeth upward,* the other *goeth downward.* The literal translation of these important words is this: "Who considereth the [*ruach*] immortal spirit of the sons of Adam, which ascendeth? it is from above; [*hi lemalah*] and the spirit or breath of the cattle which descendeth? it is downwards unto the earth," i.e., it tends to the earth only.

22. *A man should rejoice in his own works.* Do not turn God's blessings into sin by perverseness and complaining; make the best of life. God will sweeten its bitters to you, if you be faithful. Remember this is the state to prepare for glory, and the evils of life may be so sanctified to you as to work for your good.

MATTHEW HENRY

CHAPTER 4

Verses 1–3

Solomon had a large soul (1 Kings iv. 29) and it appeared by this, among other things, that he had a very tender concern for the miserable and the afflicted. He had taken the oppressors to task (*ch.* iii. 16, 17); now he observes the oppressed and here he does it as a preacher:

I. The troubles of their condition (*v.* 1) grieved him. Servants and labourers were oppressed by their masters, debtors by cruel creditors and creditors too by fraudulent debtors, tenants by hard landlords and orphans by treacherous guardians, and, worst of all, subjects oppressed by arbitrary princes and unjust judges. He *beheld the tears of such as were oppressed*, unable to help themselves: *On the side of their oppressors there was power*, when they had done wrong, to stand to it and make good what they had done, so that the poor were born down with a strong hand and had no way to obtain redress.

II. Being thus hardly used, they are tempted to envy those that are dead and in their graves, and to wish they had never been born (*v.* 2, 3); and Solomon is ready to agree with them. "*I praised the dead that are already dead* before they had well begun to live. I concluded that it is better with them than with *the living that are yet alive*, and that is all, dragging the long and heavy chain of life, and wearing out its tedious minutes." Better never to have been born than be born to *see the evil work that is done under the sun*, and not only to be in no capacity to mend the matter, but to suffer ill for doing well. A good man, how calamitous a condition soever he is in in this world, cannot have cause to wish he had never been born, since he is glorifying the Lord even in the fires.

JAMIESON, FAUSSET, BROWN

CHAPTER 4

Vss. 1-16. **1. returned**—viz., to the thought set forth (ch. 3:16; Job 35:9).

power—MAURER, not so well, "violence." **no comforter**—twice said to express *continued* suffering without any to give comfort (Isa. 53:7). **2.** A profane sentiment if severed from its connection; but just in its bearing on Solomon's scope. If religion were not taken into account (ch. 3:17, 19), to die as soon as possible would be desirable, so as not to suffer or witness "oppressions"; and still more so, not to be born at all (ch. 7:1). Job (3:12; 21:7), David (Ps. 73:3, etc.), Jeremiah (12:1), Habakkuk (1:13), all passed through the same perplexity, until they went into the sanctuary, and looked beyond the present to the "judgment" (Ps. 73:17; Hab. 2:20; 3:17, 18). Then they saw the need of delay, before completely punishing the wicked, to give space for repentance, or else for accumulation of wrath (Rom. 2:15); and before completely rewarding the godly, to give room for faith and perseverance in tribulation (Ps. 92:7-12). Earnests, however, are often even now given, by partial judgments of the future, to assure us, in spite of difficulties, that God governs the earth. **3. not seen**—nor *experienced.*

ADAM CLARKE

CHAPTER 4

1. *Considered all the oppressions. Ashukim* signifies any kind of "injury" which a man can receive in his person, his property, or his good fame.

2. *Wherefore I praised the dead.* I considered those happy who had escaped from the pilgrimage of life to the place where the wicked cease from troubling, and where the weary are at rest.

3. *Which hath not yet been.* Better never to have been born into the world than to have seen and suffered so many miseries.

MATTHEW HENRY

Verses 4–6

I. If a man be acute, and dexterous, and successful in his business, he gets the ill-will of *his neighbours* (*v.* 4), and the more for the reputation he has got by his honesty. Cain envied Abel, Esau Jacob and Saul David, and all for their right works. This is downright diabolism. Those that excel in virtue will always be an eye-sore to those that exceed in vice, which should not discourage us from any right work, but drive us to expect the praise of it, not from men, but from God.

II. If a man be stupid and blundering in his business, he does ill for himself (*v.* 5): *The fool* that goes about his work as if *his hands* were muffled and *folded together*, that does everything awkwardly, *the sluggard* that loves his ease and *folds his hands together* to keep them warm, *eats his own flesh*, is a cannibal to himself, brings himself into such a poor condition that he has nothing to eat but his own flesh. The following words (*v.* 6), *Better is a handful with quietness than both the hands full with travail and vexation of spirit*, may be taken either, 1. As the sluggard's excuse of himself in his idleness, as if a little with idleness is better than abundance with honest labour. But, 2. I rather take it as Solomon's advice to keep the mean between *travail* and slothfulness. Let us by honest industry lay hold on the handful, that we may not want necessaries, but not grasp at both the hands full, which will but create us vexation of spirit. Moderate pains and moderate gains will do best.

Verses 7–12

Solomon fastens upon another instance of the vanity of this world, that frequently the more men have of it the more they would have; and on this they are so intent that they have no enjoyment of what they have.

I. Selfishness is the cause of this evil (*v.* 7, 8): *There is one alone*, that minds none but himself, cares for nobody; *there is not a second*, nor does he desire there should be: one mouth he thinks enough in a house. He makes himself a slave to his business. Though *he has neither child nor brother*, none to take care of but himself, nor dares he marry, for fear of the expense of a family, *yet is there no end to his labour*. He never thinks he has enough: *His eye is not satisfied with riches*. He has enough for his back, for his belly, for his calling, for his family, for his living decently in the world, but he has not enough for his eyes. He denies himself the comfort of what he has: He *bereaves his soul of good*. He has no excuse for doing this: *He has neither child nor brother*, none that are poor or dear to him. It is wisdom for those that take pains about this world to consider whom they take all this pains for, and whether it be really worth while. If men do not consider this, it *is vanity, and a sore travail*; they shame and vex themselves to no purpose.

II. Sociableness is the cure of this evil. Men are thus sordid because they are all for themselves. Solomon shows, by divers instances, that *it is not good for man to be alone* (Gen. ii. 18); he designs to recommend to us both marriage and friendship. *Two are better than one*, and more happy jointly than either of them could be separately. *They have a good reward of their labour*. He that serves himself has himself only for his paymaster. But he that is kind to another has *a good reward*; the pleasure and advantage of holy love will be an abundant recompence for all the *work and labour of love*. He proves it by divers instances of the benefit of friendship and good conversation. It is good for two to travel together, *for if* one happen to *fall*, the other will be ready *to help him up*. If a man fall *into sin*, his friend will help to *restore him with the spirit of meekness*. Virtuous and gracious affections are excited by good society, and Christians warm one another by *provoking one another to love and to good works*. If an enemy find a man alone, he is likely to *prevail against him*; but, if he have a second, he may do well enough: *two shall withstand him*. As was said of the ancient Britons, when the Romans invaded them, *Dum singuli pugnant, universi vincuntur—While they fight in detached parties, they sacrifice the general cause*. In our spiritual warfare we may be helpful to one another as well as in our spiritual work; next to the comfort of communion with God, is that of the communion of saints. He concludes with this proverb, *A threefold cord is not easily broken*, any more than a bundle of arrows, though each single thread, and each single arrow, is. Two together he compares to *a threefold cord*; for where two are closely joined in holy love and fellowship, Christ will by his Spirit come to them, and make the third, as he joined himself to the two disciples going to Emmaus, and then there is *a threefold cord* that can never be *broken*.

JAMIESON, FAUSSET, BROWN

4. right—rather (as in ch. 2:21, *Note*), prosperous. Prosperity, which men so much covet, is the very source of provoking oppression (vs. 1) and "envy," so far is it from constituting the chief good.

5. Still the **fool,** the *wicked* oppressor who "folds his hands together" *in idleness* (Prov. 6:10; 24:33), living on the means he wrongfully wrests from others, is not to be envied even in this life; for such a one "eateth his own flesh," i.e., is a *self-tormentor*, never satisfied, his spirit preying on itself (Isa. 9:20; 49:26). **6.** *Hebrew;* "One *open hand (palm) full of* quietness, than both *closed hands full of* travail." "Quietness" (mental tranquillity flowing from honest labor), opposed to "eating one's own flesh" (vs. 5), also opposed to anxious labor to gain (vs. 8; Prov. 15:16, 17; 16:8).

7. A vanity described in vs. 8. **8. not a second**—no partner.

child—"son or brother," put for any heir (Deut. 25:5-10).

eye—(ch. 1:8.) The miser would not be able to give an account of his infatuation.

9. Two—opposed to "one" (vs. 8). Ties of union, marriage, friendship, religious communion, are better than the selfish solitariness of the miser (Gen. 2:18). **reward**—Advantage accrues from their efforts being conjoined. TALMAN says, "A man without a companion is like a left hand without the right."

10. if they fall—if *the one or other* fall, as may happen to *both*, viz., into any distress of body, mind, or soul. **11.** (I Kings 1:1.) The image is taken from man and wife, but applies universally to the *warm* sympathy derived from social ties. So Christian ties (Luke 24:32; Acts 28:15).

12. one—enemy. **threefold cord**—proverbial for a *combination of many*—e.g., husband, wife, and children (Prov. 11:14); so Christians (Luke 10:1; Col. 2:2,19). Untwist the cord, and the separate threads are easily "broken."

ADAM CLARKE

4. *For this a man is envied.* If a man act uprightly and properly in the world, he soon becomes the object of his neighbor's envy and calumny too. Therefore the encouragement to do good, to act an upright part, is very little. This constitutes a part of the vain and empty system of human life.

6. *Better is an handful with quietness.* These may be the words of the slothful man, and spoken in vindication of his idleness. Or the words may contain Solomon's reflection on the subject.

8. *There is one alone, and there is not a second.* Here covetousness and avarice are characterized. The man who is the center of his own existence—has neither wife, child, nor legal heir—and yet is as intent on getting money as if he had the largest family to provide for. This is not only *vanity,* the excess of foolishness, but it is also *sore travail.*

9. *Two are better than one.* Married life is infinitely to be preferred to this kind of life, for the very reasons alleged below, and which require no explanation.

MATTHEW HENRY

Verses 13–16

I. A king is not happy unless he have wisdom, *v.* 13, 14. If he be *foolish* he will not suffer any counsel or admonition to be given him. Folly and wilfulness commonly go together, and those that most need admonition can worst bear it; but neither age nor titles will secure men respect if they have not true wisdom and virtue to recommend them; while wisdom and virtue will gain men honour even under the disadvantages of youth and poverty.

II. A king is not likely to continue if he have not a confirmed interest in the affections of the people. He that is king must have a successor, a *second*, a *child that shall stand up in his stead*, his own, suppose, or perhaps that *poor and wise child* spoken of, *v.* 13. People are never long easy and satisfied: *There is no end*, no rest, *of all the people;* they are continually fond of changes, and know not what they would have. As it has been, so it is likely to be still: *Those that come after* will be of the same spirit, and *shall not* long *rejoice in him* whom at first they seemed extremely fond of. To-day, *Hosanna*—tomorrow, *Crucify. This is vanity and vexation of spirit.*

JAMIESON, FAUSSET, BROWN

13. The "threefold cord" of social ties suggests the subject of *civil government*. In this case too, he concludes that kingly power confers no lasting happiness. The "wise" child, though a supposed case of Solomon, answers, in the event foreseen by the Holy Ghost, to Jeroboam, then a poor but valiant youth, once a "servant" of Solomon, and (I Kings 11:26-40) appointed by God through the prophet Ahijah to be heir of the kingdom of the ten tribes about to be rent from Rehoboam. The "old and foolish king" answers to Solomon himself, who had lost his wisdom, when, in defiance of two warnings of God (I Kings 3:14; 9:2-9), he forsook God. **will no more be admonished**—knows not yet how to take warning (see *Margin*). God had by Ahijah already intimated the judgment coming on Solomon (I Kings 11:11-13). **14. out of prison**—Solomon uses this phrase of a supposed case; e.g., Joseph raised from a dungeon to be lord of Egypt. His words are at the same time so framed by the Holy Ghost that they answer virtually to Jeroboam, who fled to escape a "prison" and death from Solomon, to Shishak of Egypt (I Kings 11:40). This unconscious presaging of his own doom, and that of Rehoboam, constitutes the irony. David's elevation from poverty and exile, under Saul (which may have been before Solomon's mind), had so far their counterpart in that of Jeroboam. **whereas . . . becometh poor**—rather, "though he (the youth) was born poor in his kingdom" (in the land where afterwards he was to reign). **15.** "I considered all the living," the present generation, in relation to ("with") the "*second* youth" (the *legitimate* successor of the "old king," as opposed to the "poor youth," the one *first* spoken of, about to be raised from poverty to a throne), i.e., Rehoboam. **in his stead**—the old king's. **16.** Notwithstanding their now worshipping the rising sun, the heir-apparent, I reflected that "there were no bounds, no stability (II Sam. 15:6; 20:1), no check on the love of innovation, of all that have been before them," i.e., the past generation; so "also they that come after," i.e., the next generation, "shall not rejoice in him," viz., Rehoboam. The parallel, "shall not rejoice," fixes the sense of "no bounds," *no permanent adherence,* though now men *rejoice* in *him*.

ADAM CLARKE

JOSEPH PARKER:

"Better is a poor and a wise child than an old and foolish king, who will no more be admonished" (v. 13). What of the label if the bottle be empty? Sad indeed is it when the man's name is the greater part of him! A king without kingliness—is there any irony so mocking and tormenting? Better be a good hearer than a bad preacher. Whatever we are, let us be that well. A jackdraw has some respectability as such, but not a whit when he steals the peacock's feathers. "A live dog is better than a dead lion." What disastrous possibilities there are in life! Imagine the possibility of a man being described as "an old and foolish king"! The word "king" represents eternal youthfulness, energy, and influence; the possibility described in the text is that the term "king" may remain when all its kingliness has departed. We are manifestly called to progress in life, so that in old age we should be wiser, purer, and gentler than ever; but there stares us in the face the ghastly possibility that the years may but increase our weakness, and the multitude of days may but make our folly the more apparent. Christianity calls upon us to make our old age into an aspect of youth. There is to be no old age in the sense of spiritual exhaustion, or moral decrepitude, or misanthropic isolation; old age is to be equivalent to increase of kingliness and bounty and holy influence.—*The People's Bible*

MATTHEW HENRY — CHAPTER 5

Verses 1–3

Solomon's design, in driving us off from the world, by showing us its vanity, is to drive us to God and to our duty.

I. He here sends us to *the house of God*, to the place of public worship. Let our disappointments in the creature turn our eyes to the Creator. In the word and prayer there is a balm for every wound.

II. He charges us to behave ourselves well there. Religious exercises are not vain things, but, if we mismanage them, they become vain to us. "*Keep thy foot*, not keep it back from the house of God (as Prov. xxv. 17), but *look well to thy goings, ponder the path of thy feet*, lest thou take a false step. Address thyself to the worship of God with a solemn pause, and take time to compose thyself, not going about it with precipitation, which is called *hasting with the feet*, Prov. xix. 2. Keep thy thoughts from roving and wandering; keep thy affections from running out towards wrong objects." Some think it alludes to the charge given to Moses and Joshua to *put off their shoes* (Exod. iii. 5, Joshua v. 15). We must take heed that the sacrifice we bring be not *the sacrifice of fools* —that we rest not in the sign and ceremony, and the outside of the performance, without regarding the sense and meaning of it, for that is the *sacrifice of fools*. Men may be doing evil even when they do not know it, when they do not consider it. Wicked minds cannot choose but sin, even in the acts of devotion. We must be *ready to hear*; must diligently *attend* to the word of God read and preached. *Hearing* is often put for *obeying*, and that is it that is *better than sacrifice*, 1 Sam. xv. 22; Isa. i. 15, 16. *Let the word of the Lord come* (said a good man), *and if I had* 600 *necks I would bow them all to the authority of it.* We must be very cautious in all approaches to God (*v.* 2): *Be not rash with thy mouth*, in making prayers, or protestations, or promises; *let not thy heart be hasty to utter anything before God.* If we come without an errand, we shall go away without any advantage. What we *utter before God* must come from *the heart*, and therefore we must never let our tongue outrun our thoughts in our devotions. Thoughts are words to God. It is not enough that what we say comes from the heart, but it must come from a composed heart, and not from a sudden heat or passion. *God is in heaven*, where he is *far exalted above all our*

JAMIESON, FAUSSET, BROWN — CHAPTER 5

Vss. 1-20. **1.** From vanity connected with kings, he passes to vanities (vs. 7) which may be fallen into convinced of the vanity of the creature, wish to worship the Creator.

Keep thy foot—In going to worship, go with considerate, circumspect, reverent feeling. The allusion is to the taking off the shoes, or sandals, in entering a temple (Exod. 3:5; Josh. 5: 15, which passages perhaps gave rise to the custom). WEISS needlessly reads, "Keep thy *feast days*" (Exod. 23:14, 17; the three great feasts). **hear**—rather, "To be ready (to draw nigh with the desire) to hear (obey) is a better sacrifice than the offering of fools" [HOLDEN]. *(Vulgate: Syriac.)* (Ps. 51:16, 17; Prov. 21:3; Jer. 6:20; 7:21-23; 14:12; Amos 5:21-24). The warning is against mere ceremonial self-righteousness, as in ch. 7:12. *Obedience* is the spirit of the law's requirements (Deut.10:12). Solomon sorrowfully looks back on his own neglect of this (cf. I Kings 8:63 with 11:4, 6). *Positive* precepts of God must be kept, but will not stand instead of obedience to His *moral* precepts. The last provided no sacrifice for *wilful* sin (Num. 15:30, 31; Heb. 10:26-29). **2. rash**—opposed to the *considerate reverence* ("keep thy foot," vs. 1). This verse illustrates vs. 1, as to *prayer* in the house of God ("before God," Isa. 1:12); so vss. 4-6 as to *vows*. The remedy to such vanities is stated (vs. 6). "Fear thou God." **God is in heaven**—Therefore He ought to be approached with carefully weighed words, by thee, a frail creature of earth. **3.** As much "business," engrossing the mind, gives birth to incoherent "dreams," so many words, uttered inconsiderately in prayer, give birth to and betray "a fool's speech" (ch. 10:14), [HOLDEN and WEISS]. But vs. 7 implies that the "dream" is not a comparison, but the *vain thoughts of the fool* (sinner, Ps. 73:20), arising from multiplicity of (worldly) "business." His "dream" is that God hears him for his much speaking (Matt. 6:7), independently of the frame of mind [*English Version* and MAURER]. "Fool's voice" answers to "dream" in the parallel; it comes by the many "words" flowing from the fool's "dream."

ADAM CLARKE — CHAPTER 5

1. *Keep thy foot.* This verse the Hebrew and all the versions join to the preceding chapter. Solomon, having before intimated, though very briefly, that the only cure against human vanity is a due sense of religion, now enters more largely on this important subject, and gives some excellent directions with regard to the right performance of divine service, the nature of vocal and mental prayer, the danger of rash vows. The whole verse might be more literally translated thus: "Guard your steps as you are going to the house of God; and approach to hearken, and not to give the sacrifice of fools, for none of them have knowledge about doing evil."

3. *For a dream cometh.* That is, as dreams are generally the effect of the business in which we have been engaged during the day, so a multitude of words evidence the feeble workings of the foolish heart.

MATTHEW HENRY

blessing and praise. We are on earth, the footstool of his throne, unworthy to have any communion with him. Therefore we must be grave, humble, serious, and reverent in speaking to him.

Verses 4–8

Four things we are exhorted to in these verses:

I. To be conscientious in paying our vows.

1. A vow is a bond upon the soul (Num. xxx. 2). When, under the sense of some affliction (Ps. lxvi. 14), or in the pursuit of some mercy (1 Sam. i. 11), thou hast vowed a vow *unto God*, know that *thou hast opened thy mouth unto the Lord and thou canst not go back*; therefore perform what thou hast promised. *Pay that which thou hast vowed;* pay it in full and *keep not back any part of the price.* Have we vowed to *give our own selves unto the Lord?* Let us then be as good as our word. *Defer not to pay it.*

2. Two reasons are here given why we should speedily and cheerfully pay our vows: (1) Because otherwise we affront God; we play the fool with him, as if we designed to put a trick upon him; and *God has no pleasure in fools.* (2) Because otherwise we wrong ourselves, we incur the penalty for the breach of it; so that it would have been better a great deal *not to have vowed.* Not to have *vowed* would have been but an omission, but to *vow and not pay* incurs the guilt of treachery, and perjury; it is *lying to God,* Acts v. 4.

II. To be cautious in making our vows. We must take heed that we never vow anything that is sinful, or that may be an occasion of sin, for such a vow is ill-made and must be broken. *Suffer not thy mouth,* by such a vow, *to cause thy flesh to sin,* as Herod's rash promise caused him to cut off the head of John the Baptist. "When thou hast made a *vow*, do not seek to evade it; *say not before the priest,* who is called the *angel or messenger of the Lord of hosts,* that, upon second thoughts, thou hast changed thy mind, and desirest to be absolved from the obligation of thy vow; but stick to it, and do not seek a hole to creep out at." If we treacherously cancel the words of our mouths, and revoke our vows, God will justly overthrow our projects.

III. To keep up the fear of God, *v.* 7. Many, of old, pretended to know the mind of God by *dreams*, and almost made God's people forget his name by their *dreams* (Jer. xxiii. 25, 26); and many now perplex themselves with their frightful or odd dreams, as if they foreboded disaster. Those that heed dreams shall have a multitude of them; but in them all *there are divers vanities.* Therefore never heed them; instead of repeating them lay no stress upon them, draw no disquieting conclusions from them, but *fear thou God.*

IV. Every good man that has a sense of justice and a concern for mankind, is angry to see *the oppression of the poor*, and the *violent perverting of judgment and justice in a province*, oppression under colour of law and backed with power. The kingdom in general may have a good government, and yet it may so happen that a particular province may be committed to a bad man. When things look thus dismal we may satisfy ourselves that, though oppressors be *high*, God is *higher than the highest* of creatures, than the highest of princes. God is the *Most High over all the earth*, and his *glory is above the heavens.* Though oppressors be secure, God has his eye upon them, and will reckon for all their violent perverting of judgment.

Verses 9–17

Solomon shows that there is as much vanity in great riches, and the *lust of the eye* about them, as there is in the *lusts of the flesh* and the *pride of life*, and a man can make himself no more happy by hoarding an estate than by spending it.

I. He grants that the products of the earth, for the support and comfort of human life, are valuable things (*v.* 9). There is *profit to be got out of the earth*, and it is *for all*; all need it; it is appointed for all; there is enough for all. The earth is our storehouse and the beasts are fellow-commoners with us. *The king himself is served of the field*, and would be starved, without its products. This puts a great honour upon the husbandman's calling, that it is the most necessary of all to the support of man's life.

II. He maintains that the riches that are more than these, that are for hoarding, not for use, are *vain things*, and will not make a man easy or happy. The more men have the more they would have, *v.* 10. Natural desires are at rest when that which is desired is obtained, but corrupt desires are insatiable. There are bodily desires which silver itself will not satisfy; if a man be hungry ingots of silver will do no more to satisfy his hunger than clods of clay. Much less will worldly abundance satisfy spiritual desires. *When*

JAMIESON, FAUSSET, BROWN

4. Hasty words in *prayer* (vss. 2, 3) suggest the subject of hasty *vows.* A vow should not be hastily made (Judg. 11:35; I Sam. 14:24). When made, it must be kept (Ps. 76:11), even as God keeps His word to us (Exod. 12:41, 51; Josh. 21:45). **5.** (Deut. 23:21, 23.)

6. thy flesh—Vow not with "thy mouth" a vow (e.g., fasting), which the lusts of the flesh (body, *Margin*, ch. 2:3) may tempt thee to break (Prov. 20: 25). **angel**—the "messenger" of God (Job 33:23); minister (Rev. 1:20); i.e., the priest (Mal. 2:7) "before" whom a breach of a vow was to be confessed (Lev. 5:4, 5). We, Christians, in our vows (e.g., at baptism, the Lord's Supper, etc.) vow in the presence of Jesus Christ, "the angel of the covenant" (Mal. 3:1), and of ministering angels as witnesses (I Cor. 11:10; I Tim. 5:21). Extenuate not any breach of them as a slight error. **7.** (*Note*, vs. 3.) God's service, which ought to be our chief good, becomes by "dreams" (foolish fancies as of God's requirements of us in worship), and random "words," positive "vanity." The remedy is, whatever fools may do, "Fear *thou* God" (ch. 12:13).

8. As in ch. 3:16, so here the difficulty suggests itself. If God is so exact in even punishing hasty words (vss. 1-6), why does He allow gross injustice? In the remote "provinces," the "poor" often had to put themselves for protection from the inroads of Philistines, etc., under chieftains, who oppressed them even in Solomon's reign (I Kings 12:4). **the matter**—lit., "the pleasure," or purpose (Isa. 53:10). Marvel not at this *dispensation of God's will,* as if He had abandoned the world. Nay, there is coming a capital judgment at last, and an earnest of it in partial punishments of in serving the King of kings, even by those who, sinners meanwhile. **higher than the highest**—(Dan. 7:18.) **regardeth**—(II Chron. 16:9.) **there be higher**—*plural*, i.e., the three persons of the Godhead, or else, "regardeth (not only the 'highest' kings, than whom He 'is higher,' but even the petty tyrants of the provinces, viz., the high ones who are above them" (the poor) [WEISS].

9. "The profit (produce) of the earth is (ordained) for (the common good of) all: even the king himself is served by (the fruits of) the field" (II Chron. 26:10). Therefore the common Lord of all, high and low, will punish at last those who rob the "poor" of their share in it (Prov. 22:22, 23; Amos 8:4-7). **10.** Not only will God punish at last, but meanwhile the oppressive gainers of "silver" find no solid "satisfaction" in it. **shall not be satisfied**—so the oppressor "eateth his own flesh" (ch. 4:1, 5, *Note*). **with increase**—is not satisfied with the gain that he makes.

ADAM CLARKE

4. *When thou vowest a vow.* When in distress and difficulty, men are apt to promise much to God if He will relieve them, but generally forget the vow when the distress or trouble is gone by.

6. *Neither say thou before the angel, that it was an error.* I believe by the *angel* nothing else is intended than the priest, whose business it was to take cognizance of vows and offerings. See Lev. v. 4-5. In Mal. ii. 7 the priest is called the angel of the Lord of hosts.

7. *In . . . dreams . . . are . . . divers vanities; but fear thou God.* If, by the disturbed state of your mind during the day, or by Satanic influence, you dream of evil, do not give way to any unreasonable fears or gloomy forebodings of any coming mischief; fear God. Fear neither the dream nor its interpretation; God will take care of and protect you.

8. *Marvel not at the matter. Hachephets,* the "will," i.e., of God, which permits such evils to take place; for all things shall work together for good to them that love Him.

9. *The profit of the earth is for all.* The earth, if properly cultivated, is capable of producing food for every living creature; and without cultivation none has a right to expect bread. *The king himself is served by the field.* Without the field he cannot have supplies for his own house; and, unless agriculture flourish, the necessary expenses of the state cannot be defrayed.

MATTHEW HENRY

goods increase, they are increased that eat them, v. 11. *The more meat the more mouths.* Does the estate thrive? And does not the family at the same time grow more numerous and the children grow up to need more? The more men have the better house they must keep. The owner sees that as his own, which those about him enjoy as much of the real benefit of as he; only he has the satisfaction of doing good to others, which indeed is a satisfaction to one who believed what Christ said, that *it is more blessed to give than to receive.* The more men have the more care they have about it, which perplexes them and disturbs their repose, *v.* 12. Refreshing sleep is as much the support and comfort of this life as food is. Those commonly sleep best that work hard and have but what they work for: *The sleep of the labouring man is sweet.* Those that have everything else often fail to secure a good night's sleep. The more men have the more danger they are in both of doing mischief and of having mischief done them (*v.* 13): *There is an evil, a sore evil, riches kept for the owners thereof* (who have been industrious to hoard them and keep them safely) to *their hurt*; they would have been better without them. They *do hurt with their riches,* which not only put them into a capacity of gratifying their own lusts but give them an opportunity of oppressing others and dealing hardly with them. Often they sustain *hurt by their riches.* They would not be envied, would not be robbed, if they were not rich. Those riches that have been laid up with a great deal of pains *perish by evil travail,* by the very pains and care which they take to secure and increase them. Many a one has lost all by catching at all. How much soever men have when they die, they must leave it all behind them (*v.* 15, 16): *As he came forth of his mother's womb naked, so shall he return.* In respect of the body we must go as we came; the dust shall return to the earth as it was. But sad is our case if the soul return as it came, unsanctified. This is a *sore evil; he* thinks it so whose heart is glued to the world, that he *shall take nothing of his labour which he may carry away in his hand*; his riches will not go with him into another world nor stand him in any stead there. If we labour in religion, the grace and comfort we get by that labour we may carry away in our hearts, and shall be the better for it to eternity; that is meat that endures. Men will see that they have *laboured for the wind* when at death they find the profit of their labour is all gone, gone like the wind, they know not whither. Those that have much, if they set their hearts upon it, have not only uncomfortable deaths, but uncomfortable lives too, *v.* 17. This covetous worldling, that is so bent upon raising an estate, *all his days eats in darkness and much sorrow, and it is his sickness and wrath*; he has not only no pleasure of his estate, nor any enjoyment of it himself, for he *eats the bread of sorrow* (Ps. cxxvii. 2), but a great deal of vexation to see others eat of it.

Verse 18–20

Solomon, from the vanity of riches hoarded up, here infers that the best course we can take is to use well what we have, to serve God with it, to do good with it, and take the comfort of it to ourselves and our families; this he had pressed before, *ch.* ii. 24; iii. 22. Life is God's gift, and he has appointed us *the number of the days* of our life (Job xiv. 5); let us therefore spend those days in *serving the Lord our God with joyfulness and gladness of heart.* We must not do the business of our calling as a drudgery, and make ourselves slaves to it, but we must *rejoice in our labour,* not grasp at more business than we can go through without perplexity and disquiet. Those that cheerfully use what God has given them thereby honour the giver, answer the intention of the gift, act rationally and generously, do good in the world, and make what they have turn to the best account, and this is both their credit and their comfort; *it is good and comely*; there is duty and decency in it. A heart to do thus is such a gift of God's grace as crowns all the gifts of his providence. This is the way to relieve ourselves against the many toils and troubles which our lives on earth are incident to (*v.* 20): *He shall not much remember the days of his life,* the days of his sorrow and sore travail, his working days, his weeping days. He shall either forget them or remember them as waters that pass away; he shall not much lay to heart his crosses, nor long retain the bitter relish of them, *because God answers him in the joy of his heart,* balances all the grievances of his labour with the joy of it and recompenses him for it by giving him to *eat the labour of his hands.*

JAMIESON, FAUSSET, BROWN

11. they . . . that eat them—the rich man's dependents (Ps. 23:5).

12. Another argument against anxiety to gain riches. "Sleep . . . sweet" answers to "quietness" (ch. 4:6); "not suffer . . . sleep," to "vexation of spirit." Fears for his wealth, and an overloaded stomach without "laboring" (cf. ch. 4:5), will not suffer the rich oppressor to sleep.

13, 14. Proofs of God's judgments even in this world (Prov. 11:31). The rich oppressor's wealth provokes enemies, robbers, etc. Then, after having kept it for an expected son, he loses it beforehand by misfortune ("by evil travail"), and the son is born to be heir of poverty. Ch. 2:19, 23 gives another aspect of the same subject.

16. Even supposing that he loses not his wealth before death, *then* at last he must go stripped of it all (Ps. 49:17). **laboured for . . . wind**—(Hos. 12:1; I Cor. 9:26).

17. eateth—appropriately put for "liveth" in general, as connected with vss. 11, 12, 18. **darkness**—oppposed to "light (joy) of countenance" (ch. 8:1; Prov. 16:15). **wrath**—fretfulness, lit., "His sorrow is much, and his infirmity (of body) and wrath."

18. Returns to the sentiment (ch. 3:12, 13, 22); translate: "Behold the good which I have seen, and which is becoming" (in a man). **which God giveth**—viz., both the good of his labor and his life. **his portion**—legitimately. **It** is God's gift that makes it so when regarded as such. Such a one will use, not abuse, earthly things (I Cor. 7:31). Opposed to the anxious life of the covetous (vss. 10, 17). **19.** As vs. 18 refers to the "laboring" man (vs. 12), so vs. 19 to the "rich" man, who gets wealth not by "oppression" (vs. 8), but by "God's gift." He is distinguished also from the "rich" man (ch. 6:2) in having received by God's gift not only "wealth," but also "power to eat thereof," which that one has not. "To take his portion" limits him to the lawful use of wealth, not keeping back from God *His* portion while enjoying *his own.* **20.** He will not remember much, looking back with disappointment, as the ungodly do (ch. 2:11), on the days of his life. **answereth . . . in the joy**—God *answers* his prayers in giving him "power" to *enjoy* his blessings. GESENIUS and *Vulgate* translate, "For God (so) *occupies* him with joy," etc., that he thinks not much of the shortness and sorrows of life. HOLDEN, "Though God gives not much (as to real enjoyment), yet he remembers (with thankfulness) the days; for (he knows) God *exercises* him by the joy," etc. (tries him by prosperity), so *Margin,* but *English Version* is simplest.

ADAM CLARKE

11. *When goods increase.* An increase of property always brings an increase of expense, by a multitude of servants; and the owner really possesses no more, and probably enjoys much less, than he did when every day provided its own bread, and could lay up no store for the next.

12. *The sleep of a labouring man is sweet.* His labor is healthy exercise. He is without possessions, and without cares; his sleep, being undisturbed, is sound and refreshing.

13. *Riches kept for the owners thereof to their hurt.* This may be the case through various causes: (1) He may make an improper use of them, and lose his health by them. (2) He may join in an unfortunate partnership and lose all. (3) His riches may excite the desire of the robber; and he may spoil him of his goods, and even take away his life. (4) Or he may leave them to his son, who turns profligate, spends the *whole,* and ruins both his body and soul. I have seen this again and again.

14. *And he begetteth a son, and there is nothing in his hand.* He has been stripped of his property by unfortunate trade or by plunderers, and he has nothing to leave to his children.

15. *As he came forth.* However it may be, he himself shall carry nothing with him into the eternal world. If he die worth millions, those millions are dead to him forever; so he has had no real profit from all his labors, cares, anxieties, and vast property!

17. *All his days also he eateth in darkness.* Even his enjoyments are embittered by uncertainty. He fears for his goods; the possibility of being deprived of them fills his heart with anguish. But instead of *yochel,* "he shall eat," *yelech,* "he shall walk," is the reading of several MSS. *He* "walks" *in darkness*—he has no evidence of salvation. *And wrath with his sickness.* His last hours are awful.

MATTHEW HENRY

CHAPTER 6

Verses 1–6

Solomon now shows the evil of having and not using. This *is an evil which* Solomon himself saw *under the sun, v.* 1. Solomon, as a king, took notice of this evil as a prejudice to the public, who are damaged not only by men's prodigality on the one hand, but by their penuriousness on the other. As it is with the blood in the natural body, so it is with the wealth of the body politic, if, instead of circulating, it stagnates, it will be of ill consequence. Solomon as a preacher observed the evils that were done that he might reprove them and warn people against them.

I. The abundant reason the miser has to serve God. *Riches* and *wealth* commonly gain people *honour* among men. *Riches, wealth, and honour,* are God's gifts, the gifts of his providence. Yet they are given to many that do not make a good use of them. *He wants nothing for his soul of all that he desires.* He does not desire grace for his soul, the better part; all he desires is enough to gratify the sensual appetite, and that he has. He is supposed to have a numerous family, to *beget a hundred children,* which are the stay and strength of his house and in whom he has the prospect of having his name built up. To complete his happiness, he is supposed to *live many years, a thousand years twice told.*

II. The little heart he has to use this which God gives him, for the ends and purposes for which it was given him. This is his fault. He cannot find in his heart to take the comfort of what he has himself. He has meat before him, but he has *not power to eat thereof.* His sordid niggardly temper will not suffer him to lay it out, no, not upon himself. Because he has not the will to serve God with it, God denies him the power to serve himself with it. God orders it so that *a stranger eats it.* This may be well called *vanity, and an evil disease.* Our worst diseases are those that arise from the corruption of our own hearts. He deprives himself of the good that he might have had of his worldly possessions. *His soul is not filled with good, v.* 3. *He has no burial,* none agreeable to his rank, no decent burial, but *the burial of an ass.*

III. *An untimely birth,* a child that is carried from the womb to the grave, *is better than he.* Solomon here pronounces *an untimely birth,* upon many accounts, to be very sad (*v.* 4, 5): *He comes in with vanity* and he *departs in darkness*; little or no notice is taken of him; being an abortive, he has no *name,* or, if he had, it would soon be forgotten and buried in oblivion; it would *be covered with darkness,* as the body is with the earth. Nay (*v.* 5), *he has not seen the sun,* but from the darkness of the womb he is hurried immediately to that of the grave, and, which is worse than not being known to any, he has not *known anything.*

Verses 7–10

The preacher here further shows the vanity and folly of heaping up worldly wealth and expecting happiness in it.

I. How much soever we toil about the world, and get out of it, we can have for ourselves no more than a maintenance (*v.* 7). A little will serve to sustain us comfortably and a great deal can do no more.

II. Those that have ever so much are still craving; let a man labour ever so much *for his mouth, yet the appetite is not filled.* The desires of the soul find nothing in the wealth of the world to give them any satisfaction. *The soul is not filled,* so the word is.

III. A fool may have as much worldly wealth, and may enjoy as much of the pleasure of it, as a wise man; nay, and perhaps not be so sensible of the vexation of it: *What has the wise more than the fool?* (*v.* 8). A fool can fare as well, can dress as well, and make as good a figure in any public appearance, as a wise man; so that if there were not pleasures and honour peculiar to the mind, which *the wise man has more than the fool,* as to this world they would be upon a level.

IV. Even a poor man, who has business, and is discreet, diligent, in the management of it, may get as comfortably through this world as he that is loaded with an overgrown estate. Why, he is better beloved and more respected among his neighbours, and has a better interest than many a rich man that is griping and haughty.

V. The enjoyment of what we have cannot but be acknowledged more rational than a greedy grasping at more (*v.* 9): *Better is the sight of the eyes,* making the best of that which is present, *than the wandering of the desire.* He is much happier that is always content, though he has ever so little, than he that is always coveting, though he has ever so much. We cannot say, *Better is the sight of the eyes than the* fixing *of the desire* upon God, and the resting of the

JAMIESON, FAUSSET, BROWN

CHAPTER 6

Vss. 1-12. **1. common**—or else more literally, —"great upon man," falls heavily upon man.

2. for his soul—i.e., his enjoyment.

God giveth him not power to eat—This distinguishes him from the "rich" man in ch. 5:19. "God hath given" distinguishes him also from the man who got his wealth by "oppression" (ch. 5:8, 10). **stranger**—those not akin, nay, even hostile to him (Jer. 51:51; Lam. 5:2; Hos. 7:9). He seems to have it in his "power" to do as he will with his wealth, but an unseen power gives him up to his own avarice: God wills that he should toil for "a stranger" (ch. 2:26), who has found favor in God's sight. **3.** Even if a man (of this character) have very many (equivalent to "a hundred," II Kings 10:1) children, and not have a "stranger" as his heir (vs. 2), and live long ("days of years" express the *brevity* of life *at its best,* Gen. 47:9), yet enjoy no real "good" in life, and lie unhonored, without "burial," at death (II Kings 9:26, 35), the embryo is better than he. In the East to be without burial is the greatest degradation. "Better the fruit that drops from the tree before it is ripe than that left to hang on till rotten" [HENRY]. **4. he**—rather "it," "the untimely birth." So "its" not "*his* name." **with vanity**—to no purpose; a type of the driftless existence of him who makes riches the chief good. **darkness**—of the abortive; a type of the unhonored death and dark future beyond the grave of the avaricious. **5. this**—*yet* "it has more rest than" the toiling, gloomy miser. **6.** If the miser's length of "life" be thought to raise him above the abortive, Solomon answers that long life, without enjoying real good, is but lengthened misery, and riches cannot exempt him from going whither "all go." He is fit neither for life, nor death, nor eternity. **7. man**—rather, "the man," viz., the miser (vss. 3-6). For not *all* men labor for the mouth, i.e., for selfish gratification. **appetite**—*Hebrew,* "the soul." The insatiability of the desire prevents that which is the only end proposed in toils, viz., self-gratification; "the man" thus gets no "good" out of his wealth (vs. 3). **8. For**—However [MAURER]. The "for" means (in contrast to the insatiability of the miser), *For what* else is the advantage which *the wise man hath above the fool?*" *What* (advantage, i.e., superiority, above him who knows not how to walk uprightly) *hath the poor who knoweth to walk before the living?* i.e., to use and enjoy life aright (ch. 5:18, 19), a cheerful, thankful, godly "walk" (Ps. 116:9).

9. Answer to the question in vs. 8. This is the advantage: "Better is the sight of the eyes (the wise man's godly enjoyment of present *seen* blessings) than the (fool's) wandering, lit., *walking* (Ps. 73:9), of the desire," i.e., vague, insatiable desires for what he has not (vs. 7; Heb. 13:5). **this**—restless wandering of desire, and not enjoying contentedly the present (I Tim. 6:6, 8).

ADAM CLARKE

CHAPTER 6

2. *A man to whom God hath given riches.* A man may possess much earthly goods and yet enjoy nothing of them.

F. B. MEYER:

"Under the sun" (Eccles. 6:1). The Preacher constantly refers to what is done under the sun; and is not this the clue to so much that is puzzling in this book? If your horizon is limited to what the sun shines on, it is impossible to get the true standpoint of vision, or discover the real policy of life. If this world and the time-day are all, we are entangled in an inexplicable maze. It is impossible to believe in the existence of a benign and wise Creator unless there is more than we can see, larger than we can grasp. We have no choice but blank materialism, unless we believe there is someone and something over and above the sun, and that the sun and his attendant train of worlds is but a speck in the vastness of his existence.

O Christian soul, let you and me get beyond the sun, which one day will be no more, to the Lord, who is an everlasting light. Let us sit with Him in the heavenlies, and thence look down upon man and his little life. What inconsiderable atoms do kings and empires appear; even our affliction seems to be but light, and for a moment! Not on this side of the sun, but on that lies our true portion and home, our enduring substance.

In order to live as we should, the sun must be under our feet, a position which is only possible to those who are in Christ Jesus. "I knew a man in Christ," says the Apostle, "caught up into the third heaven, and he heard unspeakable things." Would you be unworldly, seek to become otherworldly. Do you want the sun to grow dim?—ask for the light which is above the brightness of the sun.

Set your affections on those things which are above, where Christ sits at the right hand of God.—*Great Verses Through the Bible*

9. *Better is the sight of the eyes than the wandering of the desire.* This is translated by the Vulgate as a sort of adage: "It is better to see what one desires than to covet what one knows not." It is better to enjoy the present than to feed oneself with vain desires of the future. What we translate *the wandering of the desire, mehaloch nephesh,* is "the travelling of the soul." It shows the soul to be in a restless state, and consequently to be unhappy.

MATTHEW HENRY

soul in him.

VI. Whatever we attain to in this world, still we are but men, and the greatest possessions cannot set us above the common accidents of human life. That busy animal that makes such a stir and such a noise in the world, *is named already*. He that made him gave him his name, *and it is known that it is man*; and it is a humbling name, Gen. v. 2. He *called their name Adam*; and all theirs have the same character, *red earth*. It is good for rich and great men to know and consider that they are *but men*, Ps. ix. 20.

Verses 11–12

There be many things that increase vanity; even that which pretends to increase wealth and pleasure does but increase vanity and make it more vexatious. We do not know what to wish for, because that which we promise ourselves most satisfaction in often proves most vexatious to us. Thoughtful people are in care to do everything for the best, if they knew it; but it is an instance of the corruption of our hearts that we are apt to desire that as good for us which is really hurtful. Since everything is vanity, *Who can tell a man what shall be after him under the sun?* He can no more please himself with the hopes of *what shall be after him*, to his children and family, than with the relish of what is with him, since he can neither foresee himself, nor can anyone else foretell to him, *what shall be after him.*

JAMIESON, FAUSSET, BROWN

10. Part II begins here. Since man's toils are vain, what is the chief good? (vs. 12). The answer is contained in the rest of the book. "That which hath been (man's various circumstances) is named already (not only has existed, ch. 1:9; 3:15, but has received its just *name*, 'vanity,' long ago), and it is known that it (vanity) is man" (*Hebrew*, "Adam," equivalent to man "of *red* dust," as his Creator appropriately named him from his frailty). **neither may he contend . . .**—(Rom. 9:20.) **11.** "Seeing" that man cannot escape from the "vanity," which by God's "mighty" will is inherent in earthly things, and cannot *call in question* God's wisdom in these dispensations (equivalent to "contend," etc.), "what is man the better" of these vain things as regards the chief good? None whatever. **12. For who knoweth . . .**—The ungodly know not what is really "good" during life, nor "what shall be after them," i.e., what will be the event of their undertakings (ch. 3: 22; 8:7). The godly might be tempted to "contend with God" (vs. 10) as to His dispensations; but they cannot fully know the wise purposes served by them now and hereafter. Their sufferings from the oppressors are more really good for them than cloudless prosperity; sinners are being allowed to fill up their measure of guilt. Retribution in part vindicates God's ways even now. The judgment shall make all clear. In ch. 7, he states what is good, in answer to this verse.

ADAM CLARKE

10. *That which hath been is named already.* The Hebrew of this verse might be translated, "Who is he who is? His name has been already called. And it is known that he is Adam; and that he cannot contend in judgment with him who is stronger than he."

12. *For who knoweth what is good for man in this life?* Those things which we deem good are often evil. And those which we think evil are often good.

MATTHEW HENRY

CHAPTER 7

Verses 1–6

In these verses Solomon lays down some great truths which seem paradoxes.

I. That the honour of virtue is really more valuable and desirable than all the wealth and pleasure in this world (*v.* 1): *A good name is before good ointment* (so it may be read). *Good ointment* is here put for all the profits of the earth (among the products of which oil was reckoned one of the most valuable), for all the delights of sense (it is called *the oil of gladness*), and for the highest titles of honour, for kings are anointed. *A good name is* better *than* all *riches* (Prov. xxii. 1). Christ paid Mary for her ointment with a *good name*, a name in the gospels (Matt. xxvi. 13).

II. If we have lived so as to merit a *good name, the day of our death*, which will put a period to our cares, and toils, and sorrows, and remove us to rest, and joy, and eternal satisfaction, *is better than the day of our birth.*

III. That it will do us more good to go to a funeral than to go to a festival (*v.* 2). We may possibly glorify God, and do good, and get good, in the house of feasting; but, considering how apt we are to be vain and frothy, proud and secure, and indulgent of the flesh, *it is better* for us *to go to the house of mourning*, not to see the pomp of the funeral, but to share in the sorrow of it. The uses to be gathered from *the house of mourning* are by way of information: *That is the end of all men.* By way of admonition: *The living will lay it to his heart.* Nothing is more easy and natural than by the death of others to be put in mind of our own. Some perhaps *will lay that to heart*, and *consider their latter end*, who would not lay a good sermon to heart. *The house of mourning* is the wise man's school, where he has learned many a good lesson. It is the character of a fool that his *heart is in the house of mirth.* If he be at any time in *the house of mourning*, he is under a restraint; his heart at the same time *is in the house of mirth.*

IV. The common proverb says, "An ounce of mirth is worth a pound of sorrow"; but the preacher teaches us a contrary lesson: *Sorrow is better than laughter. By the sadness* that appears in *the countenance, the heart is* often *made better.*

V. It is much better for us to have our corruptions mortified by the *rebuke of the wise* than to have them gratified by *the song of fools, v.* 5. And what an absurd thing it is for a man to dote so much upon such a transient pleasure as *the laughter of a fool*, which may fitly be compared to the burning *of thorns under a pot*, which makes a great noise and a great blaze, for a little while, but presently scatters its ashes, and contributes scarcely anything to the production of a boiling heat, for that requires a constant fire! *The laughter of a fool* is noisy and flashy, and is not an instance of true joy. *This is also vanity.*

Verses 7–10

Solomon had often complained before of *oppressions* which were a great discouragement to virtue and piety.

JAMIESON, FAUSSET, BROWN

CHAPTER 7

Vss. 1-29. **1.** (See *Note*, ch. 6:12.) **name**—character; a godly mind and life; not mere *reputation* with man, but what a man *is* in the eyes of God, with whom the *name* and *reality* are one thing (Isa. 9:6). This alone is "good," while all else is "vanity" when made the chief end. **ointment**—used lavishly at costly banquets and peculiarly refreshing in the sultry East. The *Hebrew* for "name" and for "ointment," have a happy paronomasia, *Sheem, Shemen.* "Ointment" is fragrant only in the place where the person is whose head and garment are scented, and only for a time. The "name" given by God to His child (Rev. 3:12) is for ever and in all lands. So in the case of the woman who received an everlasting name from Jesus Christ, in reward for her precious ointment (Isa. 56:5; Mark 14:3-9). Jesus Christ Himself hath such a name, as the Messiah, equivalent to Anointed (Song of Sol. 1:3). **and the day of** [his] **death . . .**—not a general censure upon God for creating man; but, connected with the previous clause, death is to him, who hath a godly name, "better" than the day of his birth; "far better," as Philippians 1:23 has it. **2.** Proving that it is not a *sensual* enjoyment of earthly goods which is meant in ch. 3:13; 5:18. A thankful use of these is right, but frequent feasting Solomon had found dangerous to piety in his own case. So Job's fear (ch. 1:4, 5). The house of feasting often shuts out thoughts of God and eternity. The sight of the dead in the "house of mourning" causes "the living" to think of their own "end."

3. Sorrow—such as arises from serious thoughts of eternity. **laughter**—reckless mirth (ch. 2:2). **by the sadness . . . better**—(Ps. 126: 5, 6; II Cor. 4:17; Heb. 12:10, 11). MAURER translates: "In sadness of countenance there is (may be) a good (*cheerful*) heart." So *Hebrew*, for "good," equivalent to "cheerful" (ch. 11:19); but the parallel clause supports *English Version.* **5.** (Ps. 141:4, 5). Godly reproof offends the flesh, but benefits the spirit. Fools' songs in the house of mirth please the flesh, but injure the soul. **6. crackling**—answers to the loud merriment of fools. It is the very fire consuming them which produces the seeming merry noise (Joel 2:5). Their light soon goes out in the black darkness. There is a paronomasia in the *Hebrew, Sirim* (thorns), *Sir* (pot). The wicked are often compared to "thorns" (II Sam. 23:6; Nah. 1: 10). Dried cow-dung was the common fuel in Palestine; its slowness in burning makes the quickness of a fire of thorns the more graphic, as an image of the sudden end of fools (Ps. 118:12).

ADAM CLARKE

CHAPTER 7

1. *A good name.* Unsatisfactory as all sublunary things are, yet still there are some which are of great consequence, and among them a good name. The place is well paraphrased in the following verses:

"*A spotless name,*
By virtuous deeds acquired, is sweeter far
Than fragrant balms, whose odours round diffused
Regale the invited guests. Well may such men
Rejoice at death's approach, and bless the hours
That end their toilsome pilgrimage; assured
That till the race of life is finish'd none
Can be completely blest."

2. *It is better to go to the house of mourning.* It is much more profitable to visit the house of mourning for the dead than the house of festivity. In the former we find occasion for serious and deeply edifying thoughts and reflections; from the latter we seldom return with one profitable thought or one solid impression.

3. *Sorrow is better than laughter.* The reason is immediately given; for by the sorrow *of the countenance*—the grief of heart that shows itself in the countenance—*the heart is made better.* In such cases, most men try themselves at the tribunal of their own consciences, and resolve on amendment of life.

4. *The heart of the wise is in the house of mourning.* A wise man loves those occasions from which he can derive spiritual advantage; and therefore prefers visiting the sick, and sympathizing with those who have suffered privations by death. But the fool—the gay, thoughtless, and giddy—prefers places and times of diversion and amusement.

6. *For as the crackling of thorns.* They make a great noise, a great blaze, and are extinguished in a few moments. Such, indeed, comparatively, are the joys of life: they are noisy, flashy, and transitory.

MATTHEW HENRY

I. He grants the temptation to be strong (*v.* 7): *Surely* it is often too true that *oppression makes a wise man mad.* If a wise man be much and long oppressed, he is apt to speak and act unlike himself, to break out into indecent complaints against God and man. *It destroys the heart of a gift* (so the latter clause may be read); even the generous heart is destroyed by being oppressed. We should therefore make great allowances to those that are abused; we know not what we should do if it were our own case.

II. The character of oppressors is very bad, so some understand, *v.* 7. If he that had the reputation of *a wise man* becomes an *oppressor*, he becomes a *madman*; and *the gifts* he takes do but *destroy his heart* and extinguish the poor remains of sense and virtue in him, and he is rather to be pitied than envied; let him alone, and in a little time he will ruin himself. The issue, at length, will be good: *Better is the end of a thing than the beginning thereof. Better was the end of* Moses's treaty with Pharaoh, that proud oppressor, when Israel was brought forth with triumph, *than the beginning* of it, when the tale of bricks was doubled, and everything looked discouraging.

III. If we would not be driven mad by oppression, we must be clothed with humility; *for the proud in spirit* are those that grow outrageous when they are hardly bestead. We must put on patience, *bearing* patience, to submit to the will of God in the affliction, and *waiting* patience to expect the issue in God's due time. We must govern our passion with wisdom and grace (*v.* 9): *Be not hasty in thy spirit to be angry;* those that cannot brook delays are apt to be angry if they be not immediately gratified. "Be not long angry"; for though anger may come into the bosom of a wise man, and pass through it as a wayfaring man, it *rests* only *in the bosom of fools.* We must make the best of that which is (*v.* 10): "Take it not for granted *that the former days were better than these,* nor enquire *what is the cause* that they were so, for therein *thou does not enquire wisely*; thou art so much a stranger to the times past, and such an incompetent judge even of the present times, that thou canst not expect a satisfactory answer to the enquiry. It is folly to cry up the goodness of former times, so as to derogate from the mercy of God to us in our own times; as if God had been unjust and unkind to us in casting our lot in an iron age, compared with the golden ages that went before us; this arises from nothing but fretfulness and discontent, and an aptness to pick quarrels with God himself. We are not to think there is any universal decay in nature, or degeneracy in morals. God has been always good, and men always bad; and if, in some respects, the times are now worse than they have been, perhaps in other respects they are better.

Verses 11–22

I. The praises of wisdom. Wisdom is necessary to the managing and improving of our worldly possessions: *Wisdom is good with an inheritance,* that is, an inheritance is good for little without wisdom. Wisdom is not only good for the poor, but it is good for the rich too, good with riches to keep a man from getting hurt by them, and to enable a man to do good with them. *Wisdom is good* of itself, and makes a man useful; but, if he have a good estate with it, that will put him into a greater capacity of being useful, and with his wealth he may be more serviceable to his generation than he could have been without it. Wisdom contributes to our safety, and is a shelter to us from the storms of trouble and its scorching heat; it *is a shadow* (so the word is), *as the shadow of a great rock in a weary land. Wisdom is a defence, and money* (that is, as *money*) *is a defence.* As a rich man makes his wealth, so a wise man makes his wisdom, a *strong city.* It is joy and true happiness to a man. This is *the excellency of knowledge,* divine knowledge, not only above money, but above wisdom too, human wisdom, *the wisdom of this world,* that it *gives life to those that have it. The fear of the Lord, that is wisdom,* and that is life; it prolongs life. It will put strength into a man, and be his stay and support (*v.* 19): *Wisdom strengthens the wise,* strengthens their spirits, and makes them bold and resolute, by keeping them always on sure grounds.

II. Some of the precepts of wisdom.

1. *Consider the work of God.* To silence our complaints concerning cross events, let us consider the hand of God in them and not open our mouths against that which is his doing. Consider that every work of God is wise, just, and good, and there is an admirable beauty and harmony in his works, and all will appear at last to have been for the best. *Who can make that straight which he has made crooked?* Who can change the nature of things from what is settled by the God of nature.

JAMIESON, FAUSSET, BROWN

7. oppression—recurring to the idea (ch. 3:16; 5:8). Its connection with vss. 4-6 is, the sight of "oppression" perpetrated by "fools" might tempt the "wise" to call in question God's dispensations, and imitate the folly (equivalent to "madness") described (vss. 5:6). WEISS, for "oppression," translates, "distraction," produced by merriment. But ch. 5:8 favors *English Version.* **a gift**—i.e., the sight of *bribery* in "places of judgment" (ch. 3:16) might cause the wise to lose their wisdom (equivalent to "heart"), (Job 12:6; 21: 6, 7; 24:1, etc.). This suits the parallelism better than "a heart of gifts"; a benevolent heart, as WEISS.

8. connected with vs. 7. Let the "wise" wait for "the end," and the "oppressions" which now (in "the beginning") perplex their faith, will be found by God's working to be overruled to their good. "Tribulation worketh *patience*" (Rom. 5:3), which is infinitely better than "the proud spirit" that prosperity might have generated in them, as it has in fools (Ps. 73:2, 3, 12-14, 17-26; Jas. 5:11).

9. angry—impatient at adversity befalling thee, as Job was (ch. 5:2; Prov. 12:16).

10. Do not call in question God's ways in making thy former days better than thy present, as Job did (ch. 29:2-5). The very putting of the question argues that heavenly "wisdom" (*Margin*) is not as much as it ought made the chief good with thee.

11. Rather, "Wisdom, *as compared* with an inheritance, is good," i.e., is as good as an inheritance; "yea, better (lit., "and a profit") to them that see the sun" (i.e., *the living,* ch. 11:7; Job 3:16; Ps. 49:19).

12. Lit., (To be) in (i.e., under) the *shadow* (Isa. 30:2) of wisdom (is the same as to be) in (under) the *shadow* of money; wisdom no less *shields* one from the ills of life than money does. **is, that**—rather, "the excellency of the knowledge *of* wisdom giveth life," i.e., life in the highest sense, here and herafter (Prov. 3:18; John 17:3; II Pet. 1:3). Wisdom (religion) cannot be lost as money can. It *shields* one in adversity, as well as prosperity; money, only in prosperity. The question in vs. 10 implies a want of it.

13. *Consider* as to *God's work,* that it is impossible to alter His dispensations; *for who can,* etc. **straight . . . crooked**—Man cannot amend what God wills to be "wanting" and "adverse" (ch. 1:15; Job 12:14).

ADAM CLARKE

7. *Oppression maketh a wise man mad.* This has been translated with good show of reason, "Surely oppression shall give lustre to a wise man: but a gift corrupteth the heart." The chief difference here is in the word *yeholel,* which, from the root *halal,* signifies "to glister, irradiate," as well as "to move briskly, to be mad, furious, in a rage"; and certainly the former meaning suits this place best.

8. *Better is the end.* We can then judge of the whole, and especially if the matter relate to the conduct of Divine Providence. At the beginning we are often apt to make very rash conjectures, and often suppose that such and such things are against us, and that everything is going wrong.

9. *Anger resteth in the bosom of fools.* A wise man, off his guard, may feel it for a moment, but in him it cannot rest; it is a fire which he immediately casts out of his breast. But the fool—the man who is under the dominion of his own tempers—harbors and fosters it, till it takes the form of malice, and then excited him to seek full revenge on those whom he deems enemies.

10. *The former days were better than these.* This is a common saying, and it is as foolish as it is common. There is no weight nor truth in it. "In former times men might be more religious, use more self-denial, be more exemplary." This is all false. In former days men were wicked as they are now, and religion was unfashionable. God also is the same now as He was then.

11. *Wisdom is good with an inheritance.* In this chapter Solomon introduces many observations which appear to be made by objectors against his doctrine; and as he was satisfied of their futility, he proposes them in their own full strength, and then combats and destroys them. It is quite necessary to attend to this; else we shall take the objector's words for those of Solomon and think, as some have done, that the wise man contradicts and refutes himself. Here an objector, who had listened to the wise man declaiming in favor of wisdom, suddenly interrupts him, and says in effect, "I grant the truth of what you have said. Wisdom is very good in its place; but what is it without property? A man who has a good inheritance may be profited by wisdom, because it will show him how to manage it to the best advantage."

12. *Wisdom is a defence.* To whom Solomon answers: All true wisdom is most undoubtedly a great advantage to men in all circumstances; and money is also of great use, but it cannot be compared to wisdom. *Knowledge* of divine and human things is a great blessing. Money is the means of supporting our animal life; but *wisdom*—the religion of the true God—gives *life to them that have it.*

13. *Consider the work of God.* Such is the nature of His providence that it puts money into the hands of few, but wisdom is within the reach of all. The former can rarely be acquired, for God puts it out of the reach of most men, and you cannot *make that straight, which he has made crooked;* the latter may be easily attained by every person who carefully and seriously seeks it from God.

MATTHEW HENRY

2. We must accommodate ourselves to the various dispensations of Providence that respect us, and do the work and duty of the day in its day, *v.* 14. Day and night, summer and winter, are set *the one over-against the other*, that in prosperity we may rejoice *as though we rejoiced not*, and in adversity may weep *as though we wept not*, and it is *to the end that man may find nothing after him*, that he may live in a dependence upon Providence and be ready for whatever happens. Our religion, in general, must be the same in all conditions, but the particular instances and exercises of it must vary, as our outward condition does. *In a day of prosperity* we must *be joyful*, be doing good, and getting good, maintain a holy cheerfulness, *and serve the Lord with gladness of heart. In a day of adversity consider.* We cannot answer God's end in afflicting us unless we consider why and wherefore he contends with us.

3. We must not be offended at the greatest prosperity of wicked people, nor at the saddest calamities that may befall the godly in this life, *v.* 15. Wisdom will teach us how to construe those dark chapters of Providence so as to reconcile them with the wisdom, holiness, goodness, and faithfulness of God. *All things have I seen in the days of my vanity.* Though Solomon was so wise a man, he calls the days of his life *the days of his vanity*, for the best days on earth are so, in comparison with the days of eternity. The calamities of the righteous are preparing them for their future blessedness, and the wicked are but ripening for ruin. There is a judgment to come, which will rectify this seeming irregularity, and we must wait with patience till then.

4. Wisdom will be of use both for caution to saints in their way, and for a check to sinners in their way. *A just man may perish in his righteousness*, but let him not, by his own imprudence and rash zeal, pull trouble upon his own head, and then reflect upon Providence as dealing hardly with him. "*Be not righteous overmuch*," *v.* 16. Self-denial and mortification of the flesh are good; but if we prejudice our health by them, and unfit ourselves for the service of God, we are *righteous overmuch*. Be not opinionative, and conceited of thy own abilities. Set not up for a critic, to find fault with everything that is said and done. As to sinners: It is true *there is a wicked man that prolongs his life in his wickedness* (*v.* 15); but let none say that therefore they may safely be as wicked as they will; no, *be not overmuch wicked* (*v.* 17); " be not so foolish as to lay thyself open to the law, *why shouldst thou die before thy time?* "

5. Wisdom will direct us in the mean between two extremes, and keep us always in the way of our duty, which we shall find a plain and safe way (*v.* 18): "*It is good that thou shouldst take hold of this,* this wisdom, this care, not to run thyself into snares. *Yea, also from this withdraw not thy hand.* Take hold of the bridle by which thy headstrong passions must be held in, as *the horse and mule that have no understanding*; and, having taken hold of it, keep thy hold. Be conscientious, and yet be cautious, and to this exercise thyself.

6. Wisdom will teach us how to conduct ourselves in reference to others. Wisdom teaches us not to expect that those we deal with should be faultless; we ourselves are not so, none are so. This *wisdom strengthens the wise* and arms them against provocation (*v.* 19), so that they are not put into any disorder by it. Those they have dealings with are not incarnate angels, but sinful sons and daughters of Adam: even the best are so, insomuch that *there is not a just man upon earth, that doeth good and sinneth not, v.* 20. Wisdom teaches us not to be quick-sighted in resenting affronts, but to wink at many of the injuries that are done us, and act as if we did not see them (*v.* 21): "*Take no heed to all words that are spoken; set not thy heart to them.* Be not solicitous or inquisitive to know what people say of thee. Approve thyself to God and thy own conscience, and then heed not what men say of thee. If thou heed every word that is spoken, perhaps *thou wilt hear thy own servant curse thee* when he thinks thou dost not hear him. It is easier to pass by twenty such affronts than to avenge one. Wisdom puts us in mind of our own faults (*v.* 22): "Be not enraged at those that speak ill of thee, *for oftentimes*, if thou retire into thyself, thy own conscience will tell thee *that thou thyself hast cursed others*, spoken ill of them, and thou art paid in thy own coin." If we be truly angry with ourselves, as we ought to be, for backbiting and censuring others, we shall be the less angry with others for backbiting and censuring us.

Verses 23–29

Solomon had hitherto been proving the vanity of the world and its utter insufficiency to make men happy; now here he comes to show the vileness of sin,

JAMIESON, FAUSSET, BROWN

14. consider—resumed from vs. 13. "Consider," i.e., regard it as "the work of God"; for "God has made (*Hebrew*, for 'set') this (adversity) also as well as the other" (prosperity). "Adversity" is one of the things which "God has made crooked," and which man cannot "make straight." He ought therefore to be "patient" (vs. 8). **after him**—equivalent to "that man may not find anything (to blame) after God" i.e., *after* "considering God's work," vs. 13). *Vulgate* and *Syriac*, "*against* Him" (cf. vs. 10; Rom. 3:4).

15. An objection entertained by Solomon "in the days of his vanity" (apostasy) (ch. 8:14; Job 21:7). **just . . . perisheth**—(I Kings 21:13.) *Temporal* not eternal death (John 10:28). But see *Note*, vs. 16; "*just*" is probably a *self-justiciary*. **wicked . . . prolongeth**—See the antidote to the abuse of this statement in ch. 8:12. **16.** HOLDEN makes vs. 16 the scoffing inference of the objector, and vs. 17 the answer of Solomon, now repentant. So (I Cor. 15:32) the skeptic's objection; (vs. 33) the answer. However, "Be not righteous over much," may be taken as Solomon's words, forbidding a *self-made* righteousness of outward performances, which would wrest salvation from God, instead of receiving it as the gift of His *grace*. It is a fanatical, pharisaical righteousness, separated from God; for the "fear of God" is in antithesis to it (vs. 18; ch. 5:3, 7; Matt. 6:1-7; 9:14; 23:23, 24; Rom. 10:3; I Tim. 4:3). **over wise**—(Job 11:12; Rom. 12:3, 16), presumptuously self-sufficient, as if acquainted with the whole of divine truth. **destroy thyself**—expose thyself to needless persecution, austerities and the wrath of God; hence to an untimely death. "Destroy thyself" answers to "perisheth" (vs. 15); "righteous over much," to "a just man." Therefore in vs. 15 it is *self-justiciary*, not a truly righteous man, that is meant. **17. over much wicked**—so worded, to answer to "righteous *over much*." For if not taken thus, it would seem to imply that we *may* be wicked *a little*. "Wicked" refers to "wicked man" (vs. 15); "die before thy time," to "prolongeth his life," antithetically. There may be a wicked man spared to "live long," owing to his avoiding gross excesses (vs. 15). Solomon says, therefore, Be not so foolish (answering antithetically to "over wise," vs. 16), as to run to such excess of riot, that God will be provoked to cut off prematurely thy day of grace (Rom. 2:5). The precept is addressed to a *sinner*. Beware of aggravating thy sin, so as to make thy case desperate. It refers to the days of Solomon's "vanity" (apostasy, vs. 15), when only such a precept would be applicable. By LITOTES it includes, "Be not wicked *at all*." **18. this . . . this**—the two opposite excesses (vs. 16, 17), fanatical, self-wise righteousness, and presumptuous, foolhardy wickedness. **he that feareth God shall come forth of them all**—shall escape all such extremes (Prov. 3:7). **19.** *Hebrew*, "The wisdom," i.e., the true wisdom, religion (II Tim. 3:15). **than ten mighty**—i.e., able and valiant generals (vs. 12; ch. 9:13-18; Prov. 21:22; 24:5). These "watchmen wake in vain, except the Lord keep the city" (Ps. 127:1). **20.** Referring to vs. 16. Be not self-righteous, seek not to make thyself "*just*" before God by a superabundance of self-imposed performances; "for true 'wisdom,' or 'righteousness,' shows that there is not a *just* man," etc. **21.** As therefore thou being far from perfectly "just" thyself, hast much to be forgiven by God, do not take too strict account, as the *self-righteous* do (vs. 16; Luke 18:9, 11), and thereby shorten their lives (vss. 15, 16), of words spoken against thee by others, e.g., thy servant: Thou art their "fellow servant" before God (Matt. 18:32-35). **22.** (I Kings 2:44.)

ADAM CLARKE

15. *There is a just man that perisheth.* This is another objection; as if he had said, "I also have had considerable experience; and I have not discovered any marked approbation of the conduct of the righteous, or disapprobation of that of the wicked. On the contrary, I have seen a righteous man perish, while employed in the work of righteousness; and a wicked man prosperous, and even exalted, while living wickedly."

16. *Why shouldest thou destroy thyself?* "Make thyself desolate," so that thou shalt be obliged to stand alone. *Neither make thyself over wise;* "Do not pretend to abundance of wisdom." In other words, and in modern language, "There is no need of all this watching, fasting, praying, self-denial; you carry things to extremes." To this the man of God answers:

17. *Be not over much wicked, neither be thou foolish: why shouldest thou die before thy time?* Do not multiply wickedness; do not add direct opposition to godliness to the rest of your crimes. Why should you provoke God to destroy you before your time?

19. *Wisdom strengtheneth the wise.* One wise, thoroughly learned, and scientific man may be of more use in fortifying and defending a city than ten "princes."

20. *There is not a just man upon earth, that doeth good, and sinneth not. Lo yechta,* that "may not sin." There is not a man upon earth, however just he may be, and habituated to do good, but is liable to commit sin; and therefore should continually watch and pray, and depend upon the Lord. But the text does not say, "The just man does commit sin," but simply that he "may sin"; and so our translators have rendered it in 1 Sam. ii. 25, twice in 1 Kings viii. 31, 46; and 2 Chron. vi. 36.

21. *Thy servant curse thee.* Make light of you, speak evil of you.

22. *Thou thyself . . . hast cursed others. Kalalta;* you have spoken evil; have vilified others.

MATTHEW HENRY

and its certain tendency to make men miserable; and this, as the former, he proves from his own experience, and it was a dear-bought experience. He is here, more than anywhere in all this book, putting on the habit of a penitent.

I. He owns and laments the deficiencies of his wisdom.

1. His searches were industrious. God had given him a capacity for knowledge above any. He resolved, if it were possible, to gain his point: *I said, I will be wise.* He resolved to spare no pains (*v.* 25): "*I applied my heart.* I set *myself to know, and to search, and to seek out wisdom,* to accomplish myself in all useful learning, philosophy, and divinity."

2. Yet his success was not answerable or satisfying: "*I said, I will be wise, but it was far from me;* I could not compass it. After all the more I know the more I see there is to be known, and the more sensible I am of my own ignorance. *That which is far off, and exceedingly deep, who can find it out?*" He means God himself, his counsels and his works; when he searched into these he presently found himself puzzled and run aground. Blessed be God, there is nothing which we have to do which is not plain and easy; *the word is nigh us* (Prov. viii. 9); but there is a great deal which we would wish to know which is *far off.*

II. He owns and laments the instances of his folly in which he had exceeded, as, in wisdom, he came short.

1. His enquiry concerning the evil of sin. He *applied his heart to know the wickedness of folly, even of foolishness and madness.* Sin has many disguises, as being loth to appear sin, and it is very hard to strip it of these and to see it in its true nature and colours. It is necessary to our repentance for sin that we be acquainted with the evil of it, as it is necessary to the cure of a disease to know its nature, causes, and malignity. Solomon, who, in the days of his folly, had set his wits on work to invent pleasures and was ingenious in making provision for the flesh, now that God had opened his eyes is as industrious to find out the aggravations of sin and so to put an edge upon his repentance. Ingenious sinners should be ingenious penitents. Solomon lays the greatest stress upon *the wickedness of folly,* by which perhaps he means his own iniquity, the sin of uncleanness, for that was commonly called *folly in Israel,* Gen. xxxiv. 7; Deut. xxii. 21; Judges xx. 6; 2 Sam. xiii. 12. When he indulged himself in it, he made a light matter of it; but now he desires to see the *wickedness* of it. As there is a wickedness in folly, so there is a folly in wickedness, even foolishness and madness.

2. The result of this enquiry. He now discovered the evil of that great sin which he himself had been guilty of, the *loving of many strange women,* 1 Kings xi. 1. He found the remembrance of the sin very grievous. *I find it more bitter than death.* The heart of the adulterous woman is *snares and nets.* The unwary souls are enticed into them by the bait of pleasure. Her hands are as bands, with which, under colour of fond embraces, she holds those fast that she has seized. *He that pleases God shall escape from her.* He now endeavoured to find out the number of his actual transgressions (*v.* 27). He desired to find them out as a penitent, that he might the more particularly acknowledge them. He soon found himself at a loss, and perceived that they were innumerable (*v.* 28): *Which yet my soul seeks;* I am still counting, but I cannot count them all. I still make new discoveries of the wickedness that there is in my own heart, Jer. xvii. 9, 10. This he illustrates by comparing the corruption of his own heart and life with the corruption of the world, where he scarcely found one good man among a thousand. He found (*v.* 20) that he had sinned even in doing good. The source of all the folly and madness that are in the world is in man's apostasy from God and his degeneracy from his primitive rectitude (*v.* 29). Man, as he came out of God's hands, was (as we may say) a little picture of his Maker, who is *good and upright.* He was marred, and in effect unmade, by his own folly and badness: *They have sought out many inventions*—they, our first parents, or the whole race, all in general and every one in particular. Instead of being for God's institutions, he was for his own inventions.

JAMIESON, FAUSSET, BROWN

23. All this—resuming the "all" in vs. 15; vss. 15-22 is therefore the fruit of his dearly bought experience in the days of his "vanity." **I will be wise**—I tried to "be wise," independently of God. But true wisdom was then "far from him," in spite of his *human* wisdom, which he retained by God's gift. So "over wise" (vs. 16).

24. That . . . far off . . . deep—True wisdom is so when sought independently of "fear of God" (vs. 18; Deut. 30:12, 13; Job 11:7, 8; 28:12-20, 28; Ps. 64:6; Rom. 10:6, 7).

25. Lit., "I turned myself and mine heart to." A phrase peculiar to Ecclesiastes, and appropriate to the penitent *turning* back to *commune with his heart* on his past life.

wickedness of folly—He is now a step further on the path of penitence than in ch. 1: 17; 2:12, where "folly" is put without "wickedness" prefixed. **reason**—rather, *the right estimation* of things. HOLDEN translates also "foolishness (i.e., sinful folly, answering to 'wickedness' in the parallel) of madness" (i.e., of man's mad pursuits). **26.** "I find" that, of all my sinful follies, none has been so ruinous a snare in seducing me from God as idolatrous women (I Kings 11:3; 4; Prov. 5:3, 4; 22: 14). As "God's favor is better than life," she who seduces from God is "more bitter than death." **whoso pleaseth God**—as Joseph (Gen. 39:2, 3, 9). It is God's *grace* alone that keeps any from falling. **27. this**—viz., what follows in vs. 28. **counting one by one**—by comparing one thing with another [HOLDEN and MAURER]. **account**—a right estimate. But vs. 28 more favors GESENIUS. "Considering *women one by one.*" **28.** Rather, referring to his *past* experience, "Which my soul *sought* further, but I *found* not." **one man**—i.e., worthy of the name, "man," "upright"; not more than one in a thousand of my courtiers (Job 33:23; Ps. 12:1). Jesus Christ alone of men fully realizes the perfect ideal of "man." "Chiefest among ten thousand" (Song of Sol. 5:10). No *perfect* "woman" has ever existed, not even the Virgin Mary. Solomon, in the word "thousand," alludes to his three hundred wives and seven hundred concubines. Among these it was not likely that he should find the fidelity which *one* true wife pays to *one* husband. Connected with vs. 26, not an unqualified condemnation of the sex, as Proverbs 12:4; 31:10, etc., prove. **29.** The "only" way of accounting for the scarcity of even comparatively upright men and women is that, whereas God made man upright, they (men) have, etc. The only account to be "found" of the origin of evil, the great mystery of theology, is that given in Holy Writ (Gen. 2, 3). Among man's "inventions" was the one especially referred to in vs. 26, the bitter fruits of which Solomon experienced, the breaking of God's primeval marriage law, joining one man to *one* woman (Matt. 19:4, 5, 6). "Man" is *singular,* viz., Adam; "they," *plural,* Adam, Eve, and their posterity.

ADAM CLARKE

JOHN GILL:

Verse 23. "All this have I proved by wisdom." Referring either to all that he had been discoursing of hitherto in this book, concerning the vanity of natural wisdom and knowledge, of pleasure, power, and riches; or to the several useful instructions given in this chapter, particularly concerning patiently bearing everything from the hands of God or men (vv. 8–22). This, by the help and use of that wisdom which God had given him, he had made trial of, and found it to be right, and therefore recommended it to others; though he acknowledges that, with all his wisdom, he was far from perfection. "I said, I will be wise; but it was far from me"; he determined, if possible, to attain to the perfection of wisdom, and made use of all means to come at it; that he might know all the works of God in creation, the nature, use, and excellency of them; in providence, his different dispensations towards the sons of men, and the causes of them; and in grace, the redemption and salvation of men, and the mysteries thereof; but the more he knew, the more he was convinced of his own ignorance, and seemed further off from the summit of knowledge than he was before; and plainly saw, that perfection in wisdom is not attainable in this life.

—*Gill's Commentary*

25. *I applied mine heart.* I cast about, *sabbothi,* I made a circuit; I circumscribed the ground I was to traverse; and all within my circle I was determined to *know,* and to "investigate," *and to seek out wisdom, and the reason of things.* Has man reason and understanding? If so, then this is his work. God as much calls him to use these powers in this way as to believe on the Lord Jesus that he may be saved. Every doctrine of God is a subject for both reason and faith to work on.

26. *And I find more bitter than death the woman.* After all his investigation of the "wickedness of folly" and the "foolishness of madness," he found nothing equally dangerous and ruinous with the blandishments of cunning women.

27. *Counting one by one.* I have compared one thing with another; man with woman, his wisdom with her wiles; his strength with her blandishments; his influence with her ascendancy; his powers of reason with her arts and cunning; and in a thousand men, I have found one thoroughly upright man; but among a thousand women I have not found one such. This is a lamentable account of the state of morals in Judea, in the days of the wise King Solomon.

29. *Lo, this only have I found, that God hath made man upright.* Whatever evil may be now found among men and women, it is not of God, for God made them all upright. This is a singular verse, and has been most variously translated. I doubt much whether the word *chishbonoth* should be taken in a bad sense. It may signify the whole of human devices, imaginations, inventions, artifice, with all their products; arts, sciences, schemes, plans, and all that they have found out for the destruction or melioration of life. God has given man wondrous faculties; and of them he has made strange uses, and they have been at one time his help, and at another his bane.

MATTHEW HENRY

CHAPTER 8

Verses 1–5

I. An encomium of *wisdom* (*v.* 1), that is, of true piety, guided in all its exercises by prudence and discretion. The wise man is the good man, that knows God and glorifies him. *Who is as the wise man?* Heavenly wisdom will make a man an incomparable man. No man without grace, though he be learned,

JAMIESON, FAUSSET, BROWN

CHAPTER 8

Vss. 1-17. **1.** Praise of true wisdom continued (ch. 7:11, etc.). "Who" is to be accounted "equal to the wise man?"

ADAM CLARKE

CHAPTER 8

MATTHEW HENRY

or noble, or rich, is to be compared with a man that has true grace and is therefore accepted of God. It makes him useful among his neighbours: *Who* but the *wise man knows the interpretation of a thing,* that is, understands the times and events. *It makes his face to shine,* as Moses's did when he came down from the mount; it puts honour upon a man and a lustre on his whole conversation. *The strength of his face,* the sourness and severity of his *countenance* (so some understand the last clause), *shall be changed* by it into that which is sweet and obliging. Even those whose natural temper is rough and morose, by *wisdom* are strangely altered. It emboldens a man against his adversaries. *The boldness of his face shall be* doubled by wisdom; it will add to his courage when he not only has an honest cause to plead, but by his wisdom knows how to manage it.

II. A particular instance of wisdom is subjection to authority. We must be observant of the laws. In all those things wherein the civil power is to interpose, whether legislative or judicial, we ought to submit to its order. *I counsel thee; I charge thee,* not only as a prince but as a preacher: "I recommend it to thee as a piece of wisdom; I say, whatever those say that are given to change, *keep the king's commandment. Observe the mouth of a king*" (so the phrase is). Some understand the following clause as a limitation of this obedience: *Keep the king's commandment,* yet so as to have a *regard to the oath of God,* that is, so as to keep a good conscience and not to violate thy obligations to God, which are prior and superior to thy obligations to the king. We must not be forward to find fault with the public administration (*v.* 3): "*Be not hasty to go out of his sight,* when he is displeased at thee (*ch.* x. 4), or when thou art displeased at him; fly not off in a passion, nor forsake the kingdom." "*Stand not in an evil thing;* in any offence thou hast given to thy prince humble thyself, and do not justify thyself, for that will make the offence much more offensive." We must prudently accommodate ourselves to our opportunities, both for our own relief, if we think ourselves wronged, and for the redress of public grievances: *A wise man's heart discerns both time and judgment* (*v.* 5). We *must needs be subject, for conscience-sake.* "*Keep the king's commandments,* for he has sworn to rule thee in the fear of God, and thou hast sworn, in that fear, to be faithful to him." It is called *the oath of God* because he is a witness to it and will avenge the violation of it.

Verses 6–8

Solomon here shows that even the wisest may yet be surprised by a calamity which they had not any foresight of, and therefore it is our wisdom to expect and prepare for sudden changes. Man *knows not that which shall be* himself; and *who can tell him when* or how *it shall be?* (*v.* 7). The stars cannot foretell a man what shall be, or any of the arts of divination. God has, in wisdom, concealed from us the knowledge of future events, that we may be always ready for changes. *Because to every purpose there is* but one way, one method, one proper opportunity, *therefore the misery of man is great upon him.* Men are miserable because they are not sufficiently sagacious and attentive. Whatever other evils may be avoided, we are all under a fatal necessity of dying (*v.* 8). When the soul is required it must be resigned. *There is no man that has power over* his own *spirit, to retain it,* when it is summoned to return to God who gave it. Death is an enemy that we must all enter the lists with, sooner or later: *There is no discharge in that war.* Men's wickedness, by which they often evade or outface the justice of the prince, cannot secure them from the arrest of death, nor can the most obstinate sinner harden his heart against those terrors.

Verses 9–13

Solomon, in these verses, encourages us, in reference to the mischief of tyrannical and oppressive rulers. He had observed that many a time *one man rules over another to his hurt.* It is sad with a people when those that should protect their religion and rights aim at the destruction of both. To the hurt of the rulers (so we render it), *to their own hurt. What hurt men do to others will return, in the end, to their own hurt.* He had observed them to prosper and flourish in the abuse of their power (*v.* 10): *I saw* those *wicked* rulers *come and go from the place of the holy,* go in state to and return in pomp from the place of judicature (which is called *the place of the Holy One* because *the judgment is the Lord's,* Deut. i. 17), and they continued all their days in office, were never reckoned with for their maladministration, but died in honour and were buried magnificently. *And they were forgotten in the city where they had so done;* their wicked practices were not remembered against them when they were gone. He had observed that

JAMIESON, FAUSSET, BROWN

"Who (like him) knoweth the interpretation" of God's providences (e.g., ch. 7:8, 13, 14), and God's word (e.g., ch. 7:29, *Note;* Prov. 1:6)? **face to shine**—(ch. 7:14; Acts 6:15.) *A sunny countenance,* the reflection of a tranquil conscience and serene mind. Communion with God gives it (Exod. 34:29, 30).

boldness—austerity. **changed**—into a benign expression by true wisdom (religion) (Jas. 3:17). MAURER translates, "The *shining* (brightness) of his face is *doubled,*" arguing that the *Hebrew* noun for "boldness" is never used in a bad sense (Prov. 4:18). Or as *Margin,* "strength" (ch. 7:19; Isa. 40:31; II Cor. 3:18). But the adjective is used in a bad sense (Deut. 28:50). **2. the king's**—Jehovah, peculiarly the king of Israel in the theocracy; vss. 3, 4, prove it is not the earthly king who is meant. **the oath of God**—the covenant which God made with Abraham and renewed with David; Solomon remembered Ps. 89:35, "I have *sworn,*" etc. (vs. 36), and the penalties if David's children should forsake it (vss. 30-32); inflicted on Solomon himself; yet God not "utterly" forsaking him (vss. 33, 34). **3. hasty**—rather, "Be not *terror-struck* so as to go out of His sight." Slavishly "terror-struck" is characteristic of the sinner's feeling toward God; he vainly tries to flee out of His sight (Ps. 139:7); opposed to the "shining face" of filial confidence (vs. 1; John 8:33-36; Rom. 8:2; I John 4:18). **stand not**—persist not. **for he doeth**—God inflicts what punishment He pleases on persisting sinners (Job 23:13; Ps. 115:3). True of none save God. **4.** God's very "word" is "power." So the gospel word (Rom. 1:16; Heb. 4:12). **who may say . . .**—(Job 9:12; 33:13; Isa. 45:9; Dan. 4:35.) Scripture does not ascribe such arbitrary power to earthly kings. **5. feel**—experience. **time**—the neglect of the right "times" causes much of the sinful folly of the spiritually unwise (3:1-11). **judgment**—the right manner [HOLDEN]. But as God's future "judgment" is connected with the "time for every purpose" in ch. 3:17, so it is here. The punishment of persisting sinners (vs. 3) suggests it. The wise man realizes the fact, that as there is a fit "time" for every purpose, so for the "judgment." This thought cheers him in adversity (ch. 7:14; 8:1). **6. therefore the misery . . .**—because the foolish sinner does not think of the right "times" and the "judgment." **7. he**—the sinner, by neglecting times (e.g., "the accepted *time,* and the day of salvation, II Cor. 6:2), is taken by surprise by the judgment (ch. 3:22; 6:12; 9:12). The godly wise observe the due times of things (ch. 3:1), and so, looking for the judgment, are not taken by surprise, though not knowing the precise "when" (I Thess. 5:2-4); they "know the time" to all saving purposes (Rom. 13:11). **8. spirit**—"breath of life" (ch. 3:19), as the words following require. Not "wind," as WEISS thinks (Prov. 30:4). This verse naturally follows the subject of "times" and "judgment" (vss. 6, 7). **discharge**—alluding to the liability to military service of all above twenty years old (Num. 1:3), yet many were exempted (Deut. 20:5-8). But in *that* war (death) there is no exemption. **those . . . given to**—lit,, the *master* **of it.** Wickedness can get money for the sinner, but cannot deliver him from the death, temporal and eternal, which is its penalty (Isa. 28:15, 18). **9. his own hurt**—The tyrannical ruler "hurts" not merely his subjects, but *himself;* so Rehoboam (I Kings 12); but the "time" of "hurt" chiefly refers to eternal ruin, incurred by "wickedness," at "the *day* of death" (vs. 8), and the "*time*" of "judgment" (vs. 6; Prov. 8:36). **10. the wicked**—viz., rulers (vs. 9). **buried**—with funeral pomp by man, though little meriting it (Jer. 22:19); but this only formed the more awful contrast to their death, temporal and eternal, inflicted by God (Luke 16:22, 23). **come and gone from the place of the holy**—went to and came from *the place of judicature,* where they sat as *God's representatives* (Ps. 82:1-6), with pomp [HOLDEN]. WEISS translates, "Buried and *gone* (utterly), even from the holy place they departed." As Joab, by Solomon's command, was sent to the grave from the "holy place" *in the temple,* which was not a sanctuary to murderers (Exod. 21:14; I Kings 2:28, 31). The use of the very word "bury" there makes this view likely; still "who had come and gone" may be retained. Joab *came* to the altar, but had to *go* from it; so the "wicked rulers" (vs. 9) (including *high priests*) came to, and went from, *the temple,* on occasions of solemn worship, but did not thereby escape their doom. **forgotten**—(Prov. 10:7.)

ADAM CLARKE

1. *Who knoweth the interpretation? Pesher,* a pure Chaldee word, found nowhere else in the Bible but in the Chaldee parts of Daniel. *A man's wisdom maketh his face to shine.* Every state of the heart shines through the countenance.

The boldness of his face shall be changed. The verse might be read, "The wisdom of a man shall illuminate his face; and the strength of his countenance shall be doubled."

2. *To keep the king's commandment.* This sentence would be better translated, "I keep the mouth of the king"; I take good heed not to meddle with state secrets; and if I know, to hide them. Or, I am obedient to the commands of the laws; I feel myself bound by whatever the king has decreed. *In regard of the oath of God.* You have sworn obedience to him; keep your oath, for the engagement was made in the presence of God. It appears that the Jewish princes and chiefs took an oath of fidelity to their kings. This appears to have been done to David, 2 Sam. v. 1-3; to Joash, 2 Kings xi. 17; and to Solomon, 1 Chron. xxix. 24.

3. *Be not hasty.* I consider the first five verses here as directions to courtiers, and the more immediate servants of kings.

F. B. MEYER:

"The King's word hath power" (v. 4). When our King speaks it is done. He spoke in creation, and power went with his word to call all things out of nothing. He spoke in his earthly ministry, and power accompanied every word, in giving eyes to the blind and life to the dead. He spoke, and the paralyzed had power to walk. He spoke, and the winds dropped, while the tumultuous waves were hushed to rest. He spoke, and men knew their sins were forgiven, to be remembered against them no more for ever. He spoke, and the dying thief passed into Paradise.

Whatever He bids you do by his word, be sure that He will enable you to do it by his power. He works in us to will and to work of his good pleasure; that is, He never directs us in any path of obedience or service without furnishing a sufficient supply of grace. Does He bid you renounce some evil habit? The power to renounce it awaits you. Claim it. Does He bid you walk on the water? The power by which to walk only waits for you to claim it. Does He bid you perform irksome duty? There is such transforming power issuing from Him as to make duty a delight, if only you avail yourself of it. Whenever you are called to stand up to speak the word of your King, be sure to seek and obtain the power—that shall prove your best credential. Take the power of the King with you: it is his signet ring, by which men will be convinced that you have been entrusted with his word.—*Great Verses Through the Bible*

MATTHEW HENRY

their prosperity hardened them in their wickedness, *v.* 11. It is true of all sinners in general, and particularly of wicked rulers, that, *because sentence against their evil works is not executed speedily*, they think it will never be executed, and therefore they set the law at defiance and *their hearts are full in them to do evil*; they venture to do more mischief, and commit iniquity with a high hand. Sentence is passed against evil works and evil workers by the righteous Judge of heaven and earth, even against the evil works of princes and great men. The execution of this sentence is often delayed, and the sinner goes on, not only unpunished, but prosperous and successful. Sinners herein deceive themselves, for, though the *sentence* be *not executed speedily*, it will be executed the more severely at last. We should not be discouraged. "*It shall be well with those that fear God*, I say with all those, and those only, *who fear before him*." When they lie at the mercy of proud oppressors they fear God more than they fear them. And therefore "*surely I know*, I know it by the promise of God, and the experience of all the saints, *that*, however it goes with others, *it shall go well with them*." A good man's days have some substance in them; he lives to a good purpose. A wicked man's days are all *as a shadow*, empty and worthless. These days *shall not be prolonged* to what he promised himself. Though they may be *prolonged* (*v.* 12) beyond what others expected, yet his day shall come to fall. He shall fall short of everlasting life, and then his long life on earth will be worth little.

Verses 14–17

Wise and good men, have, of old, been perplexed with this difficulty, how the prosperity of the wicked and the troubles of the righteous can be reconciled with the holiness and goodness of the God that governs the world. Concerning this Solomon here gives us his advice.

I. He would not have us to be surprised at it, as though some strange thing happened, for he himself saw it in his days, *v.* 14. 1. He saw *just men to whom it happened according to the work of the wicked*, who, notwithstanding their righteousness, suffered very hard things. He saw *wicked men to whom it happened according to the work of the righteous*, who prospered as remarkably as if they had been rewarded for some good deed. We see the just troubled and perplexed in their own minds, the wicked easy, fearless, and secure.

II. He would have us not to charge God with iniquity, but to charge the world with vanity. No fault is to be found with God; but, as to the world, *This is vanity upon the earth*, and again, *This is also vanity*, that is, it is a certain evidence that the things of this world are not the best things nor were ever designed to make happiness for us, for, if they had, God would not have allotted so much of this world's wealth to his worst enemies and so much of its troubles to his best friends; there must therefore be another life after this the joys and griefs of which must be real and substantial.

III. He would have us not to fret ourselves about it, but cheerfully to enjoy what God has given us in the world, and make the best of it, though it be much better with others, and such as we think very unworthy (*v.* 15): *Then I commended joy*, a holy security and serenity of mind, arising from a confidence in God, and his power, and promise, *because a man has no better thing under the sun than to eat and drink*, that is, soberly and thankfully to make use of the things of this life, *and to be cheerful, whatever happens, for that shall abide with him of his labour*. Our present life is a life *under the sun*, but we look for *the life of the world to come*, which will commence and continue when *the sun shall be turned into darkness* and shine no more.

IV. He would not have us undertake to give a reason for that which God does, for *his way is in the sea and his path in the great waters*, past finding out, *v.* 16, 17. Both he himself and many others had very closely studied the point, and searched far into the reasons of the prosperity of the wicked and the afflictions of the righteous. It was all labour in vain, *v.* 17. When we look upon *all the works of God* and his providence, and compare one part with another, we *cannot find* that there is any certain method by which *the work that is done under the sun* is directed. God's ways are above ours, nor is he tied to his own former ways, but *his judgments are a great deep*.

JAMIESON, FAUSSET, BROWN

11. The reason why the wicked persevere in sin: God's delay in judgment (Matt. 24:48-51; II Pet. 3:8, 9). "They see not the smoke of the pit, therefore they dread not the fire" [SOUTH], (Ps. 55:19). Joab's escape from the punishment of his murder of Abner, so far from "leading him to repentance," as it ought (Rom. 2:4), led him to the additional murder of Amasa.

12. He says this, lest the sinner should abuse the statement (ch. 7:15), "A wicked man *prolongeth* his life." **before him**—lit., "at His presence"; reverently serve Him, realizing His continual presence. **13. neither shall he prolong**—not a contradiction to vs. 12. The "prolonging" of his days there is only *seeming*, not *real*. Taking into account his eternal existence, his present days, however seemingly long, are really short. God's delay (vs. 11) exists only in man's short-sighted view. It gives scope to the sinner to repent, or else to fill up his full measure of guilt; and so, in either case, tends to the final vindication of God's ways. It gives exercise to the faith, patience, and perseverance of saints. **shadow**—(ch. 6:12; Job 8:9).

14. An objection is here started (entertained by Solomon in his apostasy), as in ch. 3:16; 7:15, to the truth of retributive justice, from the fact of the just and the wicked not now receiving always according to their respective deserts; a cavil, which would seem the more weighty to men living under the Mosaic covenant of temporal sanctions. The objector adds, as Solomon had said, that the worldling's pursuits are "vanity" (vs. 10), "I *say* (not 'said') *this* also is vanity. Then I commend mirth," etc. [HOLDEN]. Vss. 14, 15 may, however, be explained as teaching a cheerful, thankful use of God's gifts "under the sun," i.e., not making them the *chief* good, as sensualists do, which ch. 2:2; 7:2, forbid; but in "the fear of God," as ch. 3:12; 5:18; 7:18; 9:7, opposed to the abstinence of the self-righteous ascetic (ch. 7:16), and of the miser (ch. 5:17).

15. no better thing . . .—viz., for the "just" man, whose *chief* good is religion, not for the worldly. **abide**—*Hebrew*, "adhere"; not *for ever*, but it is the only sure good to be enjoyed from *earthly labors* (equivalent to "of his labor the days of his life"). Still, the language resembles the skeptical precept (I Cor. 15:32), introduced only to be refuted; and "abide" is too strong language, perhaps, for a religious man to apply to "eating" and "mirth." **16.** Reply to vss. 14, 15. When I applied myself to observe man's toils after happiness (some of them so incessant as not to allow sufficient time for "sleep"), then (vs. 17, the apodosis) I saw that man cannot find out (the reason of) God's inscrutable dealings with the "just" and with the "wicked" here (vs. 14; ch. 3:11; Job 5:9; Rom. 11:33); his duty is to acquiesce in them as good, because they are *God's*, though he *sees* not all the reasons for them (Ps. 73:16). It is enough to know "the righteous are in God's hand" (ch. 9:1). "Over wise" (ch. 7:16); i.e., Speculations above what is written are vain.

ADAM CLARKE

11. *Because sentence. Pithgam*, a "divine decree or declaration." This is no Hebrew, but a mere Chaldee word, and occurs only in the later books of the Bible, Esther, Ezra, and Daniel, and nowhere else but in this place.

14. *There be just men.* See chap. vii. 16.

16. *When I applied mine heart to know wisdom.* This is the reply of the wise man: "I have also considered these seeming contradictions. God governs the world; but we cannot see the reasons of His conduct, nor know why He does this, omits that, or permits a third thing. We may study night and day, and deprive ourselves of rest and sleep, but we shall never fathom the depths that are in the divine government; but all is right and just."

MATTHEW HENRY

CHAPTER 9

Verses 1–3

It has been observed concerning those who have pretended to search for the philosophers' stone that, though they could never find what they sought for, yet in the search they have hit upon many other useful discoveries and experiments. Thus Solomon, when, in the close of the foregoing chapter, he *applied his heart to know the work of God*, he found out that which abundantly recompensed him for the search, and therefore *he considered all this in his heart*, and weighed it deliberately, that he might *declare* it for the good of others.

The great difficulty which Solomon met with in studying providence was the little difference that is made between good men and bad in the distribution of comforts and crosses. This has perplexed the minds of many wise men. Solomon says that which may prevent its being a stumbling-block to us.

I. Before he describes the temptation in its strength he lays down a great and unquestionable truth. Job lays down the doctrine of God's omniscience (Job xxiv. 1), Jeremiah the doctrine of his righteousness (Jer. xii. 1), another prophet that of his holiness (Hab. i. 13), the psalmist that of his goodness and peculiar favour to his own people (Ps. lxxiii. 1), and that is it which Solomon here resolves to abide by, that, though good and evil seem to be dispensed promiscuously, yet God has a particular care of and concern for his own people: *The righteous and the wise, and their works, are in the hand of God*, under his special protection and guidance; all their affairs are managed by him for their good; to be recompensed in the other world, though not in this. Whatever happens all God's saints are in his hand, Deut. xxxiii. 3; John x. 29; Ps. xxxi. 15.

II. He lays this down for a rule, that the love and hatred of God are not to be measured and judged of by men's outward condition. *No man knows either love or hatred* by those things that are the objects of sense. These we may know by that which is within us if we love God with all our heart. These will be known by that which shall be hereafter, by men's everlasting state.

III. Having laid down these principles, he acknowledges that *all things come alike to all*. Some make this, and all that follows to *v.* 13, to be the perverse reasoning of the atheists against the doctrine of God's providence; but I rather take it to be Solomon's concession, when he had fixed those truths which are sufficient to guard against any ill use that may be made of what he grants.

1. The great difference that there is between the characters of the righteous and the wicked. (1) The righteous are *clean*, have *clean hands and pure hearts*; the wicked are *unclean*, under the dominion of unclean lusts. God will certainly put a difference *between the clean and the unclean* in the other world, though he does not seem to do so in this. (2) The righteous *sacrifice* both with inward and outward worship: the wicked *sacrifice not*, that is, they neglect God's worship and grudge to part with any thing for his honour. (3) The righteous do good in the world. (4) The wicked man *swears*, has no veneration for the name of God; but the righteous man *fears an oath* with great reverence.

2. The little difference there is between the conditions of the righteous and the wicked in this world: *There is one event to* both. Is David rich? So is Nabal. Is Ahab killed in a battle? So is Josiah. There is a vast difference between the nature of the same event to the one and to the other; the effects of it are likewise vastly different; the same providence to the one is *a savour of life unto life*, to the other *of death unto death*, though, to outward appearance, it is the same.

IV. He owns this to be a grievance to those that are wise and good: "*This is an evil*, the greatest perplexity, *among all things that are done under the sun*" (*v.* 3). It hardens atheists, and strengthens the hands of evildoers. When they see that *there is one event to the righteous and the wicked* they wickedly infer thence that it is all one to God whether they are righteous or wicked.

V. For the further clearing of this great difficulty he concludes with the doctrine of the misery of the wicked; however they may prosper, *madness is in their heart while they live, and after that they go to the dead.*

Verses 4–10

Solomon, in a fret, had *praised the dead more than the living* (*ch.* iv. 2); but here, considering the advantages of life to prepare for a better life, he seems to be of another mind

I. He shows the advantages which the living have

JAMIESON, FAUSSET, BROWN

CHAPTER 9

Vss. 1-18. **1. declare**—rather, explore; the result of my exploring is this, that "the righteous, etc., are in the hand of God.

No man knoweth either the love or hatred (of God to them) by all that is before them," i.e., by what is *outwardly* seen in His present dealings (ch. 8:14, 17). However, from the sense of the same words, in vs. 6, "love and hatred" seem to be the feelings *of the wicked towards the righteous*, whereby they caused to the latter comfort or sorrow. Translate: "Even the love and hatred" (exhibited towards the righteous, are in God's hand) (Ps. 76:10; Prov. 16:7). "No man knoweth all that is before them." **2. All things . . . alike**—not universally; but as to *death*. Vss. 2-10 are made by HOLDEN the objection of a skeptical sensualist. However, they may be explained as Solomon's language. He repeats the sentiment already implied in ch. 2:14; 3:20; 8:14.

good—morally. **clean**—ceremonially. **sacrificeth**—alike to Josiah who sacrificed to God, and to Ahab who made sacrifice to Him cease. **sweareth**—rashly and falsely.

one event—not eternally; but *death* is common to all.

3. Translate, "There is an evil above all (evils) that are done," etc., viz., that not only "there is one event to all," but "also the heart of the sons of men" makes this fact a reason for "madly" persisting in "evil while they live, and after that," etc., sin is "madness." **the dead**—(Prov. 2:18; 9:18.)

ADAM CLARKE

CHAPTER 9

1. *The righteous, and the wise, and their works, are in the hand of God.* This is a continuation of the preceding subject; and here the wise man draws a conclusion from what he had seen, and from the well-known character of God, that the righteous, the wise, and their conduct were all in the hand of God, protected by His power, and safe in His approbation. But we cannot judge from the occurrences which take place in life who are the objects of God's love or displeasure.

2. *All things come alike to all.* This is very generally true; but God often makes a difference, and His faithful followers witness many interventions of divine providence in their behalf. But there are general blessings, and general natural evils, that equally affect the just and the unjust. But in this all is right; the evils that are in nature are the effects of the fall of man, and God will not suspend general laws, or alter them, to favor individual cases.

MATTHEW HENRY

above those that are dead, *v.* 4-6. If a man's condition be, upon any account, bad, *there is hope* it will be amended. If *the heart be full of evil, and madness be in it,* yet while there is life *there is hope* that by the grace of God there may be a blessed change wrought. *The living know they shall die;* it is a thing yet to come, and therefore provision may be made for it. *The dead know not anything. They have no more a reward* for their toils about the world, but all they got must be left to others; they have a reward for their holy actions, but not for their worldly ones. The things of this world will not be a portion for the soul. The world can only be an annuity for life, not a *portion for ever*. There is an end of their affections, their friendships and enmities: *Their love, and their hatred, and their envy have now perished.*

II. Hence he infers that it is our wisdom to make the best use of life while it does last. Solomon, having been ensnared by the abuse of delights, warns others of the danger, not by a total prohibition of them, but by directing to the moderate use of them. "Let thy spirit be easy and pleasant; then let there be *joy* and *a merry heart* within." We must enjoy ourselves, enjoy our friends, enjoy our God, and be careful to keep a good conscience. We must serve God with gladness, in the use of what he gives us, and be liberal in communicating it to others, and not suffer ourselves to be oppressed with inordinate care about the world. "Make use of the comforts and enjoyments which God has given thee. Evidence thy cheerfulness (*v.* 8): *Let thy garments be always white.* Be neat, wear clean linen, and be not slovenly." "Make thyself agreeable to thy relations: *Live joyfully with the wife whom thou lovest.* Do not engross thy delights, not caring what becomes of those about thee, but let them share with thee and make them easy too. Keep to thy wife, to one, and do not multiply wives. *Live joyfully with her*, and be most cheerful when thou art with her. Take pleasure in thy family, thy vine and thy olive plants." Those whose works God has accepted have reason to be cheerful and ought to be so. God loves to have his servants sing at their work. "Live joyfully. Let a gracious serenity of mind be a powerful antidote against the vanity of the world." *That is thy portion in* the things of *this life*. In God, and another life, thou shalt have a better portion. "Therefore *eat with joy* and *a merry heart* that thy soul may take the more pains and the joy of the Lord may be its strength and oil to its wheels," *v.* 10. This is the world of service; that to come is the world of recompence. This is the world of probation and preparation for eternity. Harvest-days are busy days; and we must make hay while the sun shines. Serving God and working out our salvation must be done with *all that is within us,* and all little enough.

Verses 11–12

The preacher had exhorted us (*v.* 10) to do what we have to do *with all our might*; but here he reminds us that, when we have done all, we must leave the issue with God.

I. We are often disappointed of the good we had great hopes of, *v.* 11. Events, both in public and private affairs, do not always agree even with the most rational prospects and probabilities. One would think that the lightest of foot should, in running, win the prize; and yet *the race is not* always *to the swift*; some accident happens to retard them, or they are too secure, and let those that are slower get the start of them. One would think that, in fighting, the most numerous and powerful army should be always victorious, and, in single combat, that the mighty champion should win; but *the battle is not* always *to the strong*; a host of Philistines was once put to flight by Jonathan and his man; the goodness of the cause has often carried the day against the most formidable power. One would think that men of sense should always be men of substance, and get great estates; and yet it does not always prove so; even *bread is not* always *to the wise*, much less *riches* always *to men of understanding.* One would think that those who understand men, and have the art of management, should always get preferment; but many ingenious men have spent their days in obscurity. All these disappointments to us seem casual, and we call them *chance*, but really they are according to the counsel of God, here called *time*, in the language of this book, *ch.* iii. 1; Ps. xxxi. 15. *Time and chance happen to them all.*

II. We are often surprised with evils (*v.* 12): *Man knows not his time*, the time of his calamity. It is *not for us to know the times*, no, not our own time, when or how we shall die. God has, in wisdom, kept us in the dark, that we may be always ready. We may meet with trouble in that very thing wherein we promise ourselves satisfaction, as the fishes and

JAMIESON, FAUSSET, BROWN

4. For–rather, "Nevertheless." *English Version* rightly reads as the *Margin, Hebrew,* "that is joined," instead of the text, "who is to be chosen?" **hope**–not of mere temporal good (Job 14:7); but of yet repenting and being saved. **dog**–metaphor for the vilest persons (I Sam. 24:14). **lion**–the noblest of animals (Prov. 30:30). **better**–as to hope of salvation; the noblest who die unconverted have no hope; the vilest, so long as they have life, have hope. **5. know that they shall die**–and may thereby be led "so to number their days, that they may apply their hearts to wisdom" (ch. 7:1-4; Ps. 90:12). **dead know not anything**–i.e., so far as their *bodily* senses and *worldly* affairs are concerned (Job 14:21; Isa. 63:16); also, they know no door of repentance open to them, such as is to all on earth. **neither . . . reward**–no advantage from their worldly labors (ch. 2:18-22; 4:9). **memory**–not of the righteous (Ps. 112:6; Mal. 3:16), but *the wicked,* who with all the pains to perpetuate their names (Ps. 49:11) are soon "forgotten" (ch. 8:10). **6. love, and . . . hatred . . .** –(referring to vs. 1, where see the *Note*). Not that these cease in a future world absolutely (Ezek. 32:27; Rev. 22:11); but as the end of this verse shows, relatively to persons and things in this world. Man's love and hatred can no longer be exercised for good or evil in the same way as here; but the fruits of them remain. What he is at death he remains for ever. "Envy," too, marks the wicked as referred to, since it was therewith that they assailed the righteous (vs. 1, *Note*). **portion**–Their "portion" was "in this life" (Ps. 17:14), that they now "cannot have any more." **7.** Addressed to the "righteous wise," spoken of in vs. 1. Being "in the hand of God," who now accepteth "thy works" in His service, as He has previously accepted thy person (Gen. 4:4), thou mayest "eat . . . with a cheerful (not sensually 'merry') heart" (ch. 3:13; 5:18; Acts 2:46). **8. white**–in token of joy (Isa. 61:3). Solomon was clad in *white* (JOSEPHUS, *Antiquities,* 8:7, 3); hence his attire is compared to the "*lilies*" (Matt. 6:29), typical of the spotless righteousness of Jesus Christ, which the redeemed shall wear (Rev. 3:18; 7:14). **ointment**–(Ps. 23:5), opposed to a gloomy exterior (II Sam. 14:2; Ps. 45:7; Matt. 6:17); typical, also (ch. 7:1; Song of Sol. 1:3). **9. wife . . . lovest**–godly and true love, opposed to the "snares" of the "thousand" concubines (ch. 7:26, 28), "among" whom Solomon could not find the true love which joins one man to *one* woman (Prov. 5:15, 18, 19; 18:22; 19:14). **10.** "Whatsoever," viz., in the service of God. This and last verse plainly are the language of Solomon, not of a skeptic, as Holden would explain it. **hand . . .**–(*Margin,* Lev. 12:8; *Margin,* I Sam. 10:7.) **thy might**–diligence (Deut. 6:5; *Margin,* Jer. 48:10). **no work . . . in the grave**–(John 9:4; Rev. 14:13.) "The soul's playday is Satan's work-day; the idler the man the busier the tempter" [SOUTH]. **11.** This verse qualifies the sentiment, vss. 7-9. Earthly "enjoyments," however lawful in their place (ch. 3:1), are to give way when any work to be done for God requires it. Reverting to the sentiment (ch. 8:17), we ought, therefore, not only to work God's work "with might" (vs. 10), but also with the feeling that the event is wholly "in God's hand" (vs. 1). **race . . . not to the swift**–(II Sam. 18:23); spiritually (Zeph. 3:19; Rom. 9:16).

nor . . . battle to . . . strong–(I Sam. 17:47; II Chron. 14:9, 11, 15; Ps. 33:16.)

bread–livelihood. **favour**–of the great.

chance–seemingly, really Providence. But as man cannot "find it out" (ch. 3:11), he needs "with all might" to use opportunities. Duties are ours; events, God's.

12. his time–viz., of death (ch. 7:15; Isa. 13:22). Hence the danger of delay in doing the work of God, as one knows not when his opportunity will end (vs. 10).

ADAM CLARKE

4. *For to him that is joined to all the living there is hope.* While a man lives he hopes to amend, and he hopes to have a better lot; and thus life is spent, hoping to grow better, and hoping to get more. *A living dog is better than a dead lion.* I suppose this was a proverb.

6. *Also their love, and their hatred.* It is evident that he speaks here of the ignorance, want of power, etc., of the dead, in reference only to this life. And though they have no more a *portion . . . under the sun,* yet he does not intimate that they have none anywhere else.

7. *Go thy way, eat thy bread with joy.* Do not vex and perplex yourselves with the dispensations and mysteries of providence; enjoy the blessings which God has given you, and live to His glory, and then God will accept your works.

8. *Let thy garments be always white.* The Jews wore white garments on festal occasions, as emblems of joy and innocence. Be always pure, and always happy.

9. *Live joyfully with the wife whom thou lovest.* Marry prudently, keep faithfully attached to the wife you have chosen, and rejoice in the labor of your hands.

11. *But time and chance. Eth,* time or opportunity, and *pega,* incident or occurrence—*happeneth to them all.* Every man has what may be called time and space to act in, and opportunity to work.

MATTHEW HENRY

the birds are drawn into the snare and net by the bait. Men often find their bane where they sought their bliss. Let us be always ready for changes, that, though they may be sudden, they may be no terror to us.

Verses 13–18

Solomon still recommends wisdom to us as necessary to the preserving of our peace. This wisdom which enables a man to serve his country out of pure affection, when he himself gains no advantage by it, is the wisdom which, Solomon says, *seemed great unto him, v.* 13.

I. Solomon here gives an instance, probably a case in fact, of a *poor man* who with his wisdom did great service in a time of public distress and danger (*v.* 14): *There was a little city;* there were but *few men within it*, and ready to give up their city as not tenable. Against this little city a *great king* came with a numerous army, and besieged it. Did victory and success attend the *strong*? No; there was found in this little city, among the few men that were in it, *one poor wise man*—not preferred to any place of profit or power in the city. Being wise, he served the city, though he was poor. In their distress they found him out (Judges xi. 7) and begged his advice and assistance; and *he by his wisdom delivered the city*, either by prudent instructions given to the besieged, directing them to some unthought-of stratagem for their own security, or by a prudent treaty with the besiegers, as the woman at Abel, 2 Sam. xx. 16. *No man remembered that same poor man;* no recompence was made him, no marks of honour put upon him, but he lived in as much poverty and obscurity as he had done before.

II. From this instance he draws some useful inferences. He observes: *Wisdom is better than strength, v.* 16, *better than weapons of war*, offensive or defensive, *v.* 18. *The words of wise men are heard in quiet;* what they speak, being rational and to the purpose, spoken calmly and with deliberation, will gain respect, and sway with men more than the imperious clamour of him that *rules among fools*, who chose him to be their ruler, for his noise and blustering. A few close arguments are worth a great many big words. Wise and good men, notwithstanding this, must often content themselves with the satisfaction of having done good when they cannot have the praise they should have. Wisdom capacitates a man to serve his neighbours. Many a man is buried alive in poverty and obscurity who, if he had but fit encouragement given him, might be a great blessing to the world; many a pearl is lost in its shell. But there is a day coming when wisdom and goodness shall be in honour, and the *righteous shall shine forth.* From what he had observed of the great good which one wise and virtuous man may do he infers what a great deal of mischief one wicked man may do. A sinful condition is a wasteful condition. How many of the good gifts both of nature and Providence does one sinner destroy. One sinner, who makes its his business to debauch others, may defeat and frustrate the intentions of a great many good laws.

JAMIESON, FAUSSET, BROWN

evil net—fatal to them. The unexpected suddenness of the capture is the point of comparison. So the second coming of Jesus Christ, "as a snare" (Luke 21:35). **evil time**—as an "evil net," fatal to them.

13. Rather, "I have seen wisdom of this kind also," i.e., exhibited in the way which is described in what follows [MAURER].

14, 15. (II Sam. 20:16-22.) **bulwarks**—military works of besiegers. **15. poor**—as to the temporal advantages of true wisdom, though it often saves others. It receives little reward from the world, which admires none save the rich and great.

no man remembered—(Gen. 40:23.) **16.** Resuming the sentiment (ch. 7:19; Prov. 21:22; 24:5). **poor man's wisdom is despised**—not the poor man mentioned in vs. 15; for *his* wisdom could not have saved the city, had "his words not been heard"; but poor men in general. So Paul (Acts 27:11). **17.** Though generally the poor wise man is not heard (vs. 16), yet "the words of wise men, when heard in quiet (when calmly given heed to, as in vs. 15), are more serviceable than," etc.

ruleth—as the "great king" (vs. 14). Solomon reverts to "the rulers to their own hurt" (ch. 8:9). **18. one sinner,** etc.—(Josh. 7:1, 11, 12.) Though wisdom excels folly (vs. 16; ch. 7:19), yet a "little folly (equivalent to *sin*) can destroy much good," both in himself (ch. 10:1; Jas. 2:10) and in others. "Wisdom" must, from the antithesis to "sinner," mean religion. Thus typically, the "little city" may be applied to *the Church* (Luke 12:32; Heb. 12:22); the great king to *Satan* (John 12:31); the despised poor wise man, Jesus Christ (Isa. 53:2, 3; Mark 6:3; II Cor. 8:9; Eph. 1:7, 8; Col. 2:3).

ADAM CLARKE

JOSEPH PARKER:

Verses 14, 15. The incident is but small as compared with what has already been said regarding the pomp and boast of wickedness; yet the smallness of the incident is the smallness of its seed, not the smallness of a pebble. "The kingdom of heaven is like unto a grain of mustard seed;" so is this incident. "By the blessing of the upright the city is exalted." Ten righteous men would have saved the cities of the plain. It is surely discouraging that the poor man was not remembered, though he delivered the little city when a great king came against it, and besieged it, and built great bulwarks against it. Nevertheless the wise man will not give up his wisdom, for he finds a secret delight in its enjoyment. "Wisdom strengtheneth the wise more than ten mighty men which are in the city." It was the wisdom of Jesus Christ that astounded his contemporaries, and made them marvel concerning his origin and his resources. From whence hath this man these things? and what wisdom is this that is given unto him, that even such mighty works are wrought by his hands? It is important to notice that the poor man's wisdom is despised and his words are not heard. As this is true in the common walks of life, we are prepared to believe it true in those higher relations which Jesus Christ sustained to the world. He was despised and rejected of men. We are prone to say, Show true wisdom, and the world will instantly recognize it and obey its commands. History gives a flat contradiction to this supposition. The world has not known wisdom when it has seen it, nor answered the voice of eloquence when it has heard it, nor bowed before the presence of beauty when it has been most openly revealed. Yet the wise man must not be discouraged, for his time is yet to come. It is still true that wisdom is better than weapons of war.—*The People's Bible*

MATTHEW HENRY

CHAPTER 10

Verses 1–3

I. *A little folly* is a great blemish to him that *is in reputation for wisdom and honour*, and is as hurtful to his good name as *dead flies* are to a sweet perfume. True wisdom will gain a man a reputation, which is like a box of precious ointment. The reputation that is got by a great deal of wisdom, may be easily lost, by a *little folly*, because envy fastens upon eminency, and makes the worst of the mistakes of those who are cried up for wisdom.

II. *A wise man's heart is at his right hand*, so that he goes about his business with dexterity. But a *fool's heart is at his left hand*; it is always to seek when he has anything to do that is of importance, and therefore he goes awkwardly about it.

III. How apt fools are at every turn to proclaim their own folly, and expose themselves; he that is either silly or wicked *says to everyone he meets that he is a fool* (*v.* 3), that is, he discovers his folly as plainly as if he had told them so.

Verses 4–11

The scope of these verses is to keep subjects loyal and dutiful to the government.

I. Let not subjects carry on a quarrel with their prince upon any private personal disgust (*v.* 4): "*If the spirit of the ruler rise up against thee*, if he is displeased at thee, yet *leave not thy place*, forget not the duty of a subject, revolt not from thy allegiance, do not, in a passion, quit thy post in his service."

JAMIESON, FAUSSET, BROWN

CHAPTER 10

Vss. 1-20. **1.** Following up ch. 9:18. **him that is in reputation**—e.g., David (II Sam. 12:14); Solomon (I Kings 11); Jehoshaphat (II Chron. 18; 19:2); Josiah (II Chron. 35:22). The more delicate the perfume, the more easily spoiled is the ointment. Common oil is not so liable to injury. So the higher a man's religious character is, the more hurt is caused by a sinful folly in him. Bad savor is endurable in oil, but not in what professes to be, and is compounded by the perfumer ("apothecary") for, fragrance. "Flies" answer to "a little folly" (sin), appropriately, being *small* (I Cor. 5:6); also, "Beelzebub" means *prince of flies.* "Ointment" answers to "reputation" (ch. 7:1; Gen. 34:30). The verbs are *singular,* the noun *plural,* implying that *each* of the flies causes the stinking savor. **2.** (Ch. 2:14.) **right**—The right hand is more expert than the left. The godly wise is more on his guard than the foolish sinner, though at times he slip. Better a diamond with a flaw, than a pebble without one. **3. by the way**—in his ordinary *course;* in his simplest acts (Prov. 6:12-14). That he "saith," *virtually,* "that he" himself, etc. [LXX]. But *Vulgate,* "He thinks that *every one* (*else* whom he meets) is a fool." **4. spirit**—anger. **yielding pacifieth**—(Prov. 15:1.) This explains "leave not thy place"; do not in a *resisting* spirit withdraw from thy post of duty (ch. 8:3).

ADAM CLARKE

CHAPTER 10

4. *If the spirit of the ruler rise up against thee.* If the king gets incensed against you. *Leave not thy place.* Humble yourself before him; that is *thy place* and duty.

MATTHEW HENRY

II. Let not subjects commence a quarrel with their prince. He grants *there is an evil often seen under the sun*, an evil which the king only can cure, for *it is an error which proceeds from the ruler* (*v.* 5); it is a mistake which rulers, consulting their personal affections, are too often guilty of, that men are not preferred according to their merit, but *folly is set in great dignity*. It is ill with a people when vicious men are advanced and men of worth are kept under hatches. This is illustrated *v.* 7. "*I have seen servants upon horses*, men not so much of mean extraction, but of sordid, servile, mercenary dispositions."

1. Let neither prince nor people violently attempt changes. Let not princes invade the rights and liberties of their subjects; let not subjects mutiny and rebel against their princes; for, (1) *He that digs a pit* for another, it is ten to one but he *falls into it* himself. If princes become tyrants, or subjects become rebels, all histories will tell both what is likely to be their fate. (2) *Whoso breaks a hedge*, an old hedge, that has long been a land-mark, let him expect that a *serpent*, or *adder*, such as harbour in rotten hedges, will *bite him*. (3) *Whoso removes stones*, to pull down a wall, or building, does but pluck them upon himself; he shall be *hurt therewith*. Those that go about to alter a well-modelled well-settled government, will quickly perceive that it is easier to find fault than to mend. (4) *He that cleaves the wood*, especially if, as it follows, he has sorry tools (*v.* 10), *shall be endangered thereby*; the chips, or his own axe-head, will fly in his face. If we meet with knotty pieces of timber, men of perverse and ungovernable spirits, and we think to master them by force and violence, the attempt may turn to our own damage.

2. Rather let both prince and people act towards each other with prudence, mildness, and good temper: *Wisdom is profitable to direct* the ruler how to manage a people that are inclined to be turbulent, so as neither, by a supine negligence to embolden them, nor by rigour and severity to provoke them to seditious practices. It is likewise profitable to direct the subjects how to act towards a prince that is inclined to bear hard upon them, so as not to alienate his affections, but to win upon him by humble remonstrances and peaceable expedients. Let wisdom direct to gentle methods and forbear violent ones. Wisdom will teach us to whet the tool we are to make use of, rather than, by leaving it blunt, oblige ourselves to exert so much the *more strength*, *v.* 10. Whet before we cut, that is, consider and premeditate what is fit to be said and done in every difficult case. The mower loses no time when he is whetting his scythe. Wisdom will teach us to enchant the serpent we are to contend with, rather than think to out-hiss it (*v.* 11): *The serpent will bite* if he be not by singing and music charmed. *A babbler is no better. He that is lord of the tongue* may say what he will, it is as dangerous dealing with him as with a serpent uncharmed. To those that may say anything it is wisdom to say nothing that is provoking.

Verses 12–15

Solomon here shows the mischief of folly.

I. Fools talk a great deal to no purpose, and they show their folly by the impertinence of their words: whereas *the words of a wise man's mouth are gracious*, and do good to all about him, *the lips of a fool* not only expose him to reproach, but *will swallow up himself* and bring him to ruin. A fool's talk takes rise from his own weakness and wickedness: *The beginning of the words of his mouth is foolishness*, the foolishness in his heart is the corrupt spring out of which all these polluted streams flow. *The end of his talk is madness. A fool also is full of words*, a passionate fool especially, that never knows when to leave off. He will have the last word, though it be but the same with that which was the first. Many who are empty of sense are *full of words*; and the least solid are the most noisy. He is *full of words*, for if he do but speak the most trite and common thing, *a man cannot tell what shall be*, because he loves to hear himself talk, he will say it again, *what shall be after him who can tell him*?

II. Fools toil a great deal to no purpose (*v.* 15); *The labour of the foolish*, to accomplish their designs, *wearies everyone of them*. All their labour is for the world and the body, and the meat that perishes. The foolish never bring anything to pass, *because they know not how to go to the city*, that is, because they have not capacity to apprehend the plainest thing, such as the entrance into a great city, where one would think it were impossible for a man to miss his road.

Verses 16–20

I. The happiness of a land depends upon the char-

JAMIESON, FAUSSET, BROWN

5. **as**—rather, "*by reason of* an error" [MAURER and HOLDEN]. 6. **rich**—not in mere wealth, but in *wisdom*, as the antithesis to "folly" (for "foolish men") shows. So *Hebrew*, rich, equivalent to "liberal," in a good sense (Isa. 32:5). Mordecai and Haman (Esther 3:1, 2; 6:6-11). 7. **servants upon horses**—the worthless exalted to *dignity* (Jer. 17:25); and vice versa (II Sam. 15:30).

8. The fatal results to kings of such an unwise policy; the wrong done to others recoils on themselves (ch. 8:9); they fall into the pit which they dug for others (Esther 7:10; Ps. 7:15; Prov. 26:27). Breaking through the wise fences of their throne, they suffer unexpectedly themselves; as when one is stung by a serpent lurking in the stones of his neighbor's garden wall (Ps. 80:12), which he maliciously pulls down (Amos 5:19). 9. **removeth stones**—viz., of an ancient building [WEISS]. His neighbor's landmarks [HOLDEN]. *Cuts out* from the quarry [MAURER]. **endangered**—by the splinters, or by the head of the hatchet, flying back on himself. Pithy aphorisms are common in the East. The sense is: Violations of true wisdom recoil on the perpetrators. 10. **iron . . . blunt**—in "cleaving wood" (vs. 9), answering to the "fool set in dignity" (vs. 6), who wants sharpness. More force has then to be used in both cases; but force without judgment "endangers" one's self. Translate, "If one hath blunted his iron" [MAURER]. The preference of rash to judicious counsellors, which entailed the pushing of matters by *force*, proved to be the "hurt" of Rehoboam (I Kings 12). **wisdom is profitable to direct**—to a prosperous issue. Instead of forcing matters by main "strength" to one's own hurt (ch. 9:16, 18).

11. A "serpent will bite" if "enchantment" is not used; "and a babbling calumniator is no better." Therefore, as one may escape a serpent by charms (Ps. 58:4, 5), so one may escape the sting of a calumniator by discretion (vs. 12), [HOLDEN]. Thus, "without enchantment" answers to "not whet the edge" (vs. 10), both expressing, figuratively, *want of judgment*. MAURER translates, "There is no gain to the enchanter" (*Margin*, "*master of the tongue*") from his enchantments, because the serpent bites before he can use them; hence the need of continual caution. Vss. 8-10, caution in acting; vs. 11 and following verses, caution in speaking.

12. **gracious**—Thereby he takes precaution against sudden injury (vs. 11). **swallow up himself**—(Prov. 10:8, 14, 21, 32; 12:13; 15:2; 22:11). 13. Illustrating the *folly* and *injuriousness* of the fool's words; last clause of vs. 12.

14. **full of words**—(ch. 5:2.) **a man cannot tell what shall be**—(ch. 3:22; 6:12; 8:7; 11:2; Prov. 27:1.) If man, universally (including the wise man), cannot foresee the future, much less can the fool; his "many words" are therefore futile. 15. **labour . . . wearieth**—(Isa. 55:2; Hab. 2:13.) **knoweth not how to go to the city**—proverb for *ignorance of the most ordinary matters* (vs. 3); spiritually, *the heavenly city* (Ps. 107:7; Matt. 7:13, 14). MAURER connects vs. 15 with the following verses. The labor (vexation) caused by the foolish (injurious princes, vss. 4-7) harasses him who "knows not how to go to the city," to ingratiate himself with them there. *English Version* is simpler.

ADAM CLARKE

5. *An error which proceedeth from the ruler.* What this error in the ruler is, the two following verses point out: it is simply this—an injudicious distribution of offices, and raising people to places of trust and confidence who are destitute of merit.

8. *Whoso breaketh an hedge, a serpent shall bite him.* While spoiling his neighbor's property, he himself may come to greater mischief; while pulling out the sticks, he may be bit by a serpent, who has his nest there.

9. *Whoso removeth stones.* This verse teaches care and caution. Whoever pulls down an old building is likely to be hurt by the stones; and in cleaving wood, many accidents occur for want of sufficient caution.

10. *If the iron be blunt.* If the axe have lost its edge, and the owner do not sharpen it, he must apply the more strength to make it cut. But the *wisdom* that *is profitable to direct* will teach him that he should *whet* his axe, and spare his *strength.*

11. *The serpent will bite without enchantment. Belo lachash,* "without hissing." as a snake may bite before it hisses, so also will the babbler, talkative person, or calumniator. Without directly speaking evil, he insinuates things injurious to the reputation of his neighbor.

14. *A man cannot tell what shall be.* A foolish babbling man will talk on every subject, though he can say as little on the past as he can on the future.

15. *He knoweth not how to go to the city.* I suppose this to be a proverb: "He knows nothing; he does not know his way to the next village."

MATTHEW HENRY

acter of its rulers. 1. The people cannot be happy when their princes are childish and voluptuous (*v.* 16): *Woe unto thee, O land!* when *thy king is a child*, not so much in age as in understanding; when the prince is weak and foolish as a child, fickle, fretful and humoursome, it is ill with the people. Nor is it much better with a people when their princes *eat in the morning*, that is, make a god of their belly and make themselves slaves to their appetites. If the princes and privy-counsellors are wise the land may do the better; but if they addict themselves to their pleasures, before the despatch of the public business, by eating and drinking *in a morning*, when judges are epicures, and do not eat to live, but live to eat, what good can a nation expect! The people cannot but be happy when their rulers are generous and active, sober and temperate, and men of business, *v.* 17. Wisdom, virtue, and the fear of God, beneficence, and a readiness to do good to all mankind, these ennoble the royal blood. When the subordinate magistrates are more in care to discharge their trusts than to gratify their appetites; when they *eat in due season*, that is, when they have despatched their business, the land is blessed. Magistrates should *eat for strength*, that their bodies may be fitted to serve their souls in the service of God and their country. It is well with a people when their princes are examples of temperance, when those that have most to spend upon themselves know how to deny themselves.

II. Of what ill consequence slothfulness is both to private and public affairs (*v.* 18): *By much slothfulness and idleness of the hands*, the neglect of business, and the love of ease and pleasure, *the building decays, drops through* first, and by degrees drops down. If the king be *a child* and will take no care, if the *princes eat in the morning* and will take no pains, the affairs of the nation suffer loss, and all its foundations are out of course through the slothfulness and self-seeking of those that should be the *repairers of its breaches*.

III. How industrious generally all are, both princes and people, to get money, because that serves for all purposes, *v.* 19. He seems to prefer money before mirth: *A feast is made for laughter*, not the laughter of the fool, which is madness, but that of wise men, by which they fit themselves for business and severe studies. Money of itself answers nothing; it will neither feed nor clothe; but, as it is the instrument of commerce, it answers all the occasions of this present life. But it answers nothing to the soul; it will not procure the pardon of sin, the favour of God, the peace of conscience.

IV. How cautious subjects have need to be that they harbour not any disloyal purposes in their minds, nor keep up any factious cabals or consultations against the government. "*Curse not the king, no, not in thy thought*, do not wish ill to the government in thy mind." "*Curse not the rich*, the princes and governors, *in thy bedchamber*, in a conclave or club of persons disaffected to the government; associate not with such; *come not into their secret;* join not with them in plotting against it. Though the design be carried on ever so closely, *a bird of the air shall carry the voice* to the king, who has more spies about than thou art aware of, *and that which has wings shall tell the matter*, to thy confusion and ruin."

JAMIESON, FAUSSET, BROWN

16. a child—given to pleasures; behaves with childish levity. Not *in years;* for a nation may be happy under a young prince, as Josiah. **eat in the morning**—the usual time for dispensing *justice* in the East (Jer. 21:12); here, given to feasting (Isa. 5:11; Acts 2:15).

17. son of nobles—not merely in blood, but in virtue, the true nobility (Song of Sol. 7:1; Isa. 32:5, 8).

in due season—(ch. 3:1), not until duty has first been attended to. **for strength**—to refresh the body, not for *revelry* (included in "drunkenness").

18. building—lit., "the joining of the rafters," viz., the kingdom (vs. 16; Isa. 3:6; Amos 9:11). **hands**—(ch. 4:5; Prov. 6:10.) **droppeth**—By neglecting to repair the roof in time, the rain gets through.

19. Referring to vs. 18. Instead of repairing the breaches in the commonwealth (equivalent to "building"), the princes "make a feast for laughter (vs. 16), and wine maketh their *life* glad (Ps. 104:15), and (but) money supplieth (answereth their wishes by supplying) all things," i.e., they take bribes to support *their extravagance;* and hence arise the wrongs that are perpetrated (vss. 5, 6; ch. 3:16; Isa. 1:23; 5:23). MAURER takes "all things" of *the wrongs* to which princes are instigated by "money"; e.g., the heavy taxes, which were the occasion of Rehoboam losing ten tribes (I Kings 12:4, etc.).

20. thought—lit., "consciousness." **rich**—the great. The language, as applied to earthly princes knowing the "thought," is figurative. But it literally holds good of the King of kings (Ps. 139), whose consciousness of every evil thought we should ever realize. **bed-chamber**—the most secret place (II Kings 6:12). **bird of the air . . .**—proverbial (cf. Hab. 2:11; Luke 19:40); in a way as marvellous and rapid, as if birds or some winged messenger carried to the king information of the curse so uttered. In the East superhuman sagacity was attributed to birds (see my *Note*, Job 28:21; hence the proverb).

ADAM CLARKE

16. *Thy princes eat in the morning!* They do nothing in order; turn night into day, and day into night; sleep when they should wake, and wake when they should sleep; attending more to chamberings and banquetings than to the concerns of the state.

JOHN GILL:

Verse 17. "Blessed art thou, O land, when thy king is the son of nobles." Or "heroes," called *Hhorim* in the Hebrew, which signifies "white"; either from the white garment they wore, or rather from the purity and ingenuity of their minds and manners; being illustrious persons, not only by birth and education, but in their lives and actions. Now a land is happy when it is governed by a king that is not only descended from a race of heroes and illustrious men, and has a princely and liberal education; but that imitates his ancestors, and treads in their steps, and is famous himself for wisdom, virtue, and real piety, in which true nobilty consists; and so the Vulgate Latin version renders it, "whose king is noble"; who is of an ingenuous mind, his princely virtues and qualifications; who is wise and prudent, skillful in the affairs of government, and assiduous and industrious therein; for as, on the one hand, kings may, as they commonly do, descend from illustrious progenitors, and yet be base and wicked, ignoble and infamous, in their administration; and, on the other hand, persons may be raised from a low estate to royal dignity, as David and others, and yet behave with great prudence and ingenuity. The Targum applies this to the land of Israel also, and instances of Hezekiah, a man mighty in the law. "And thy princes eat in due season, for strength, and not for drunkenness"; that is, eat their meals at proper times, and that after they have been at business; to refresh nature, and recruit their strength, that they may be fit for further service; and do not indulge themselves, and spend their time, in rioting and drunkenness.—*Gill's Commentary*

MATTHEW HENRY — CHAPTER 11

Verses 1–6

Solomon presses rich people to abound in liberality to the poor.

I. The duty itself is recommended to us, *v.* 1. *Cast thy bread upon the waters, thy bread-corn upon the low places* (so some understand it), alluding to the husbandman, who *goes forth, bearing precious seed*, sparing bread-corn from his family for the seed, knowing that without that he can have no harvest another year; thus the charitable man takes from his bread-corn for seed-corn, to supply the poor, that he may *sow beside all waters* (Isa. xxxii. 20), because as he sows so he must *reap*, Gal. vi. 7. Give freely to the poor, though it may seem thrown away and lost, as that which is *cast upon the waters*. Send it a voyage, send it as a venture, as merchants that trade by sea. Trust it *upon the waters*; it shall not sink. "*Give a portion to seven and also to eight*, that is, be free and liberal in works of charity." Give not a pittance, but *a portion*, a meal. Give to many, *to seven, and also to eight*; if thou meet with seven objects of charity, give to them all, and then, if thou meet with an eighth, give to that, and, if with eight more, give to them all too. God is rich in mercy to all, to us, though unworthy; he *gives liberally, and upbraids not* with former gifts.

II. The reasons with which it is pressed upon us.

JAMIESON, FAUSSET, BROWN — CHAPTER 11

Vss. 1-10. **1.** Vs. 2 shows that *charity* is here inculcated. **bread**—bread-corn. As in the Lord's prayer, *all things needful for the body and soul.* Solomon reverts to the sentiment (ch. 9:10). **waters**—image from the custom of sowing seed by casting it from boats into the overflowing waters of the Nile, or in any marshy ground. When the waters receded, the grain in the alluvial soil sprang up (Isa. 32:20). "Waters" express *multitudes,* so vs. 2; Revelation 17:15; also the seemingly *hopeless* character of the recipients of the charity; but it shall prove at last to have been not thrown away (Isa. 49:4).

2. portion—of thy bread. **seven**—the perfect number. **eight**—even *to more than seven:* i.e., to *many* (so "waters," vs. 1), nay, even to *very many* in need (Job 5:19; Micah 5:5).

ADAM CLARKE — CHAPTER 11

1. *Cast thy bread upon the waters.* An allusion to the sowing of rice, which was sown upon muddy ground, or ground covered with water, and trodden in by the feet of cattle. It thus took root and grew, and was found after many days in a plentiful harvest. Give alms to the poor, and it will be as seed sown in good ground.

2. *Give a portion to seven.* Never cease giving while you see a person in distress, and have werewithal to relieve him.

MATTHEW HENRY

"Though thou *cast it upon the waters*, and it seem lost, yet *thou shalt find it after many days*, as the husbandman finds his seed again in a plentiful harvest. The return may be slow, but it is sure and will be so much the more plentiful." Wheat, the most valuable grain, lies longest in the ground. Our opportunity for well-doing is very uncertain: "*Thou knowest not what evil may be upon the earth*, which may deprive thee of thy estate, and put thee out of a capacity to do good. Many make use of this as an argument against giving to the poor, because they know not what hard times may come when they may want themselves; whereas we should therefore the rather be charitable, that, when *evil days come*, we may have the comfort of having done good while we were able.

III. The excuses of the uncharitable.

1. Some will say that what they have is their own, and will ask, Why should we *cast* it thus *upon the waters*? Look up, man, and consider how soon thou wouldest be starved in a barren ground, *if the clouds* over thy head should plead thus, that they have their waters for themselves. Are the heavens thus bountiful to the poor earth, that is so far below them, and wilt thou grudge thy bounty to thy poor brother, who is *bone of thy bone*?

2. Some will say that their sphere of usefulness is low and narrow; they cannot do the good that they see others can, who are in more public stations, and therefore they will sit still and do nothing. Nay, says he, *in the place where the tree falls*, or happens to be, *there it shall be*, for the benefit of those to whom it belongs; every man must labour to be a blessing to that place, whatever it is, where the providence of God casts him; wherever we are we may find good work to do if we have but hearts to do it.

3. Some will object to the many discouragements they have met with in their charity. They have been reproached for it as proud and pharisaical; they shall be despised if they do not give as others do; they have taxes to pay and they know not what use will be made of their charity; these, and a hundred such objections, he answers, in one word (*v.* 4): *He that observes the wind shall not sow*, which signifies doing good; *and he that regards the clouds shall not reap*, which signifies getting good. If we stand thus magnifying every little difficulty, starting objections and fancying hardship where there is none, we shall never go on with our work. If the husbandman should decline, or leave off, sowing for the sake of every flying cloud, and reaping for the sake of every blast of wind, he would make but an ill account of his husbandry at the year's end.

4. Some will say, "We do not see in which way what we expend in charity should ever be made up to us. To this he answers, "*Thou knowest not the work of God*, nor is it fit thou shouldst. Thou mayest be sure he will make good his word of promise, though he does not tell thee how." Our ignorance of the work of God he shows, in two instances:—(1) We *know not what is the way of the Spirit*, of *the wind* (so some), we *know not whence it comes, or whither it goes*, or when it will turn; yet the seamen lie ready waiting for it, till it turns about in favour of them; so we must do our duty, in expectation of the time appointed for the blessing. Or it may be understood of the human soul; we know that God made us, and gave us these souls, but how they entered into these bodies, animate them, and operate upon them, we know not; the soul is a mystery to itself, no marvel then that *the work of God* is so to us. (2) We know not *how the bones are fashioned in the womb of her that is with child*. We cannot describe the manner either of the formation of the body or of its information with a soul; both, we know, are *the work of God*, and we acquiesce in his work. Let him therefore that has done the greater for us be cheerfully depended upon to do the less.

5. Some say, "We have been charitable, and never yet saw any return for it; many days are past, and we have not *found it again*," to which he answers (*v.* 6), Yet go on, proceed and persevere in well-doing. *In the morning sow thy seed and in the evening do not withhold thy hand. In the morning* of youth lay out thyself to do good; give out of the little thou hast; *and in the evening* of old age yield not to the common temptation of old people to be penurious; even then *withhold not thy hand*, but do good to the last, *for thou knowest not* which work of charity *shall prosper*, both as to others and as to thyself, *this or that*, but hast reason to hope that *both shall be alike good.*

Verses 7–10

Having by many excellent precepts taught us how to live well, the preacher comes now to teach us how to die well.

JAMIESON, FAUSSET, BROWN

evil—The day may be near, when you will need the help of those whom you have bound to you by kindnesses (Luke 16:9). The very argument which covetous men use against liberality (viz., that bad times may come), the wise man uses for it.

3. clouds—answering to "evil" (vs. 2), meaning, When the times of evil are fully ripe, evil *must* come; and speculations about it beforehand, so as to prevent one sowing seed of liberality, are vain (vs. 4).

tree—Once the storm uproots it, it lies either northward or southward, according as it fell. So man's character is unchangeable, whether for hell or heaven, once that death overtakes him (Rev. 22:11, 14, 15). *Now* is his time for liberality, before the evil days come (ch. 12:1).

4. Therefore sow thy charity in faith, without hesitancy or speculation as to results, because they may not seem promising (ch. 9:10). So in vs. 1, man is told to "cast his bread-corn" on the seemingly unpromising "waters" (Ps. 126:5, 6). The farmer would get on badly, who, instead of sowing and reaping, spent his time in watching the wind and clouds.

5. spirit—How the *soul* animates the body! Thus the transition to the formation of the *body* "in the womb" is more natural, than if with MAURER we translate it "wind" (ch. 1:6; John 3:8).

bones . . . grow—(Job 10:8, 9; Ps. 139:15, 16.) **knowest not the works of God**—(ch. 3:11; 8:17; 9:12.)

6. morning . . . evening—early and late; when young and when old; in sunshine and under clouds. **seed**—of godly works (Hos. 10:12; II Cor. 9:10; Gal. 6:7).

prosper—(Isa. 55: 10, 11.) **both . . . alike**—Both the unpromising and the promising sowing may bear good fruit in *others*: certainly they shall to the faithful *sower*.

ADAM CLARKE

Thou knowest not what evil. Such may be the change of times that you may yet stand in need of similar help yourself. Do as you would be done by.

3. *If the clouds be full of rain.* Act as the clouds; when they are full they pour out their water on the field and on the desert.

Where the tree falleth, there it shall be. Death is at no great distance; you have but a short time to do good. Acquire a heavenly disposition while here, for there will be no change after this life.

4. *He that observeth the wind shall not sow.* The man that is too scrupulous is never likely to succeed in anything. If a man neither plough nor sow till the weather is entirely to his mind, the season will in all probability pass before he will have done anything. So if you are too nice in endeavoring to find out who are the impostors among those who profess to be in want, the real object may perish whom otherwise you might have relieved, and whose life might have been thereby saved.

5. *As thou knowest not . . . the way of the spirit.* Why God should have permitted such and such persons to fall into want, and how they came into all their distresses, you cannot tell, no more than you can how the soul is united to the body.

6. *In the morning sow thy seed.* Be ready at all times to show mercy; begin in the *morning*, continue till the *evening*. You do not know the most worthy object. It is enough that God knows; and if your motive be good, He will applaud and reward you.

MATTHEW HENRY

I. He applies himself to the aged: *Truly the light is sweet;* the light of *the sun* is so; it is *a pleasant thing for the eyes to behold* it. It is pleasant to see the light; the heathen were so charmed with the pleasure of it that they worshipped the sun. It is pleasant by it to see other things. It cannot be denied that life is sweet. It is sweet to all men; nature says it is so; nor can death be desired for its own sake unless as a period to present evils or a passage to future good. *If a man live many years, yet let him remember the days of darkness* are coming. Here is, (1) A summer's day supposed to be enjoyed—that life may continue long, even many years, and that, by the goodness of God, it may be made comfortable and a man may *rejoice in them all.* However, some rejoice in their many years more than others; if these two things meet, a prosperous state and a cheerful spirit, these two indeed may do much towards enabling a man to *rejoice in them all,* and yet the most cheerful spirit has its damps; jovial sinners have their melancholy qualms, and cheerful saints have their gracious sorrows; so that it is but a supposition, not a case in fact, that a man should *live many years and rejoice in them all.* But, (2) Here is a winter's night to be expected after this summer's day: *Yet let* this hearty old man *remember the days of darkness, for they shall be many.* They are many, but they are not infinite. As the longest day will have its night, so the longest night will have its morning. *The days of darkness* will come with much the less terror if we have thought of them before.

II. He applies himself to the young to awaken them to think of death (*v.* 9, 10).

1. An ironical concession to the vanities and pleasures of youth: *Rejoice, O young man! in thy youth.* Solomon speaks thus ironically to the young man to expose his folly, and the absurdity of a voluptuous vicious course of life.

2. A powerful check given to these vanities and pleasures: *Know thou that for all these things God shall bring thee into judgment.*

3. A word of caution and exhortation inferred from all this, *v.* 10. Let young people look to themselves and manage well both their souls and their bodies. **Let them take care that their minds be not lifted up with pride, nor disturbed with anger, or any sinful** passion: *Remove sorrow,* or anger, *from thy heart;* the word signifies any disorder or perturbation of the mind. Young people are apt to be impatient of check and control, to fret at anything that is humbling, and their proud hearts rise against everything that crosses and contradicts them. Let them keep at a distance from everything which will be sorrow in the reflection. Let them take care that their bodies be not defiled by intemperance, uncleanness, or any fleshly lusts: *Put away evil from the flesh,* and let not the members of thy body be instruments of unrighteousness.

III. The preacher urges that which is the great argument of his discourse, the vanity of all present things, their uncertainty and insufficiency. 1. He reminds old people of this (*v.* 8): *All that comes is vanity;* yea, though *a man live many years and rejoice in them all.* 2. He reminds young people of this: *Childhood and youth are vanity.* The pleasures and advantages of childhood and youth are passing away; these flowers will wither, and these blossoms fall; let them therefore be knit into good fruit, which will continue and abound to a good account.

JAMIESON, FAUSSET, BROWN

7. light—of life (ch. 7:11; Ps. 49:19). Life is enjoyable, especially to the godly.

8. But while man thankfully enjoys life, "let him remember" it will not last for ever. The "many days of darkness," i.e., the unseen world (Job 10:21, 22; Ps. 88:12), also days of "evil" in this world (vs. 2), are coming; therefore sow the good seed while life and good days last, which are not too long for accomplishing life's duties. **All that cometh**—i.e., All that followeth in the *evil* and *dark days* is vain, as far as *work for God* is concerned (ch. 9:10).

9. Rejoice—not *advice,* but *warning.* So I Kings 22:15, is irony; if thou dost rejoice (*carnally,* ch. 2:2; 7:2, not *moderately,* as in ch. 5:18), etc., then "know that . . . God will bring thee into judgment" (ch. 3:17; 12:14). **youth . . . youth**—distinct *Hebrew* words, *adolescence* or boyhood (before vs. 13), and full-grown *youth.* It marks the gradual progress in self-indulgence, to which the young especially are prone; they see the roses, but do not discover the thorns, until pierced by them. Religion will cost self-denial, but the want of it infinitely more (Luke 14: 28). **10. sorrow**—i.e., *the lusts* that end in "sorrow," opposed to "rejoice," and "heart cheer thee" (vs. 9), *Margin,* "anger," i.e., all "ways of thine heart"; "remove," etc., is thus opposed to "walk in," etc. (vs. 9).

flesh—the bodily organ by which the sensual *thoughts* of the "heart" are embodied in *acts.*

childhood—rather, "boyhood"; the same *Hebrew* word as the first, "youth" in vs. 9. A motive for self-restraint; the time is coming when the vigor of youth on which thou reliest, will seem vain, except in so far as it has been given to God (ch. 12:1). **youth**—lit., *the dawn* of thy days.

ADAM CLARKE

ALEXANDER MACLAREN:

Verse 9. I take these words to be said in good faith, as a frank recognition of the fact that, after all we have been hearing about vanity and vexation of spirit, life is worth living, and that God means young people to be glad and to make the best of the fleeting years that will never come back with the same buoyancy and elasticity all their lives long. And then I take it that the words added are not meant to destroy or neutralize the concession of the first sentence, but only to purify and ennoble a gladness which, without them, would be apt to be strained by many a corruption, and to make permanent a joy which, without them, would be sure to die down into the miserable, peevish, and feeble old age of which the grim picture follows, and to be quenched at last in death. So there are three words that I take out of this text of mine, and that I want to bring before my young friends as exhortations which it is wise to follow. These are Rejoice, Reflect, Remember. Rejoice—the fitting gladness of youth; reflect—the solemn thought that will guard the gladness from stain; remember—the religion which will make these things ever last.

—*Expositions of Holy Scripture*

10. *Therefore remove sorrow.* "Anger"; every kind of violent passion.

MATTHEW HENRY — CHAPTER 12

Verses 1–7

I. A call to young people to think of God, and mind their duty to him, when they are young: *Remember now thy Creator in the days of thy youth.* "You that are young flatter yourselves with expectations of great things from the world, but it yields no solid satisfaction to a soul; therefore *remember your Creator,* and so guard yourselves against the mischiefs that arise from the vanity of the creature." It is the royal physician's antidote against the particular diseases of youth, the indulgence of sensual pleasures, the vanity which childhood and youth are subject to; to prevent and cure this, *remember thy Creator.* God is our Creator, he *made us and not we ourselves,* and is therefore our rightful Lord. We must pay him the honour and duty which we owe him as our Creator. *Remember thy Creators;* the word is plural, as it is Job xxxv. 10. For God said, *Let us make man,* us, Father, Son, and Holy Ghost. "Begin in the beginning of thy days to remember him from whom thou hadst thy being. Call him to mind through all the days of thy youth, and never forget him. Guard thus against the temptations of youth, and thus improve the advantages of it."

II. A reason to enforce this command: *While the*

JAMIESON, FAUSSET, BROWN — CHAPTER 12

Vss. 1-14. **1.** As ch. 11:9, 10 showed what youths are to shun, so this verse shows what they are to follow. **Creator**—"Remember" that thou art not thine own, but God's property; for He has created thee (Ps. 100:3). Therefore serve Him with thy "all" (Mark 12:30), and with thy *best* days, not with the dregs of them (Prov. 8:17; 22:6; Jer. 3:4; Lam. 3:27). The *Hebrew* is "Creators," plural, implying the plurality of persons, as in Genesis 1:26; so *Hebrew,* "Makers" (Isa. 54:5).

ADAM CLARKE — CHAPTER 12

MATTHEW HENRY

evil days come not, and the years of which thou shalt say I have no pleasure in them.

1. Do it quickly, "Before sickness and death come." Before old age comes, *years of which we shall say, We have no pleasure in them,*—when our *strength* shall be *labour and sorrow,*—when there will be *no pleasure* but in the reflection of a good life on earth and the expectation of a better life in heaven.

2. These two arguments he enlarges upon in the following verses, only inverting the order. It is the greatest absurdity and ingratitude imaginable to give the cream and flower of our days to the devil, and reserve the bran, and refuse, and dregs of them for God. If the calamities of age will be such as are here represented, we shall have need of something to support and comfort us then, and nothing will be more effectual than the testimony of our consciences that we began betimes to remember our Creator. How can we expect God should help us when we are old, if we will not serve him when we are young? The infirmities of old age are here elegantly described in figurative expressions. Then *the sun* and *the light* of it, *the moon* and *the stars*, and the light which they borrow from it, will *be darkened.* They look dim to old people, in consequence of the decay of their sight; their intellectual powers and faculties, which are as lights in the soul, are weakened; their understanding and memory fail them. Then *the clouds return after the rain*; no sooner has one cloud blown over than another succeeds it, so it is with old people, when they have got free from one pain or ailment, they are seized with another. Then *the keepers of the house tremble.* The head, which is as the watchtower, shakes, and the arms and hands, which are ready for the preservation of the body, shake too, and grow feeble. Then *the strong men shall bow themselves*; the legs cannot serve for travelling as they have done, but are soon tired. Then the *grinders cease because they are few*; the teeth cease to do their part, *because they are few. Those that look out of the windows are darkened.* Moses was a rare instance of one who, when 120 years old, had good eyesight. *The doors are shut in the streets.* Old people keep within doors, and care not for going abroad to entertainments. Old people *rise up at the voice of the bird.* They have no sound sleep as young people have, but a little thing disturbs them, even the chirping of a bird. With them *all the daughters of music* are *brought low.* Old people grow hard of hearing, and unapt to distinguish sounds and voices. They are *afraid of that which is high*, afraid to go to the top of any high place, either because, for want of breath, they cannot reach it, or, their heads being giddy, they dare not venture to it. *The almond-tree flourishes.* The old man's hair has grown white, so that his head looks like an almond-tree in the blossom. *The grasshopper is a burden and desire fails.* Old men can bear nothing; the lightest thing sits heavily upon them, both on their bodies and on their minds, a little thing sinks and breaks them. It is probable that Solomon wrote this when he was himself old, and could speak feelingly of the infirmities of age, which perhaps grew the faster upon him for the indulgence he had given himself in sensual pleasures. All this makes a good reason why we should *remember our Creator in the days of our youth*, that he may remember us when *evil days come*, and his comforts may delight our souls when the delights of sense are in a manner worn off. Death will fix us in an unchangeable state: *Man* shall then *go to his long home.* He has gone to his rest, to the place where he is to fix. He has gone *to his house of eternity.* This should make us willing to die, that, at death, we must *go home*; and why should we not long to go to our Father's house? Death will be an occasion of sorrow to our friends that love us. When *man goes to his long home the mourners go about the streets*—the real mourners, and the mourners for ceremony, that were hired to weep for the dead, both to express and to excite the real mourning. Death will dissolve the frame of nature and take down the earthly house of this tabernacle, which is elegantly described, *v.* 6. Then shall *the silver cord*, by which soul and body were wonderfully fastened together, *be loosed*, that sacred knot untied; *the golden bowl*, which held the waters of life for us, *be broken*; then shall *the pitcher* with which we used to fetch up water, for the constant support of life and the repair of its decays, *be broken*, even *at the fountain*, so that it can fetch up no more; and *the wheel* (all those organs that serve for the collecting and distributing of nourishment) shall be *broken*, and disabled to do their office any more. The body shall become like a watch when the spring is broken, the motion of all the wheels is stopped and they all stand still. Death will resolve us into our first principles, *v.* 7. Man is a strange sort of creature, a ray of heaven united to a clod of earth; at death

JAMIESON, FAUSSET, BROWN

while . . . not–i.e., *before that* (Prov. 8:26) the evil days come; viz., calamity and old age, when one can no longer serve God, as in youth (ch. 11:2, 8). **no pleasure**–of a sensual kind (II Sam. 19:35; Ps. 90:10). Pleasure in God continues to the godly old (Isa. 46:4).

2. Illustrating "the evil days" (Jer. 13:16). "Light," "sun," etc., express *prosperity;* "darkness," *pain* and *calamity* (Isa. 13:10; 30:26). **clouds . . . after . . . rain**–After rain sunshine (comfort) might be looked for, but only a brief glimpse of it is given, and the gloomy clouds (pains) return. **3. keepers of the house**–viz., *the hands and arms* which *protected* the body, as guards do a palace (Gen. 49:24; Job 4:19; II Cor. 5:1), are now palsied. **strong men . . . bow**–(Judg. 16:25, 30.) Like supporting pillars, *the feet and knees* (Song of Sol. 5:15); the *strongest* members (Ps. 147:10). **grinders**–the molar teeth. **cease**–are idle. **those that look out of the windows**–the eyes; the powers of vision, looking out from beneath the eyelids, which open and shut like the casement of a window. **4. doors**–*the lips,* which are closely *shut* together as *doors,* by old men in eating, for, if they did not do so, the food would drop out (Job 41:14; Ps. 141:3; Micah 7:5). **in the streets**–i.e., toward the street, "the *outer* doors" [MAURER and WEISS]. **sound of . . . grinding**–The teeth being almost gone, and the lips "shut" in eating, the sound of mastication is scarcely heard. **the bird**–the cock. In the East all mostly rise with the dawn. But the old are glad to rise from their sleepless couch, or painful slumbers still earlier, viz., when the cock crows, before dawn (Job. 7:4) [HOLDEN]. The least noise awakens them [WEISS]. **daughters of music**–the organs that produce and that enjoy music; the *voice* and *ear.* **5. that which is high**–The old are afraid of ascending a *hill.* **fears . . . in the way**–Even on the level *highway* they are full of fears of falling, etc. **almond . . . flourish**–In the East the hair is mostly dark. *The white head* of the old among the dark-haired is like *an almond tree,* with its white blossoms, among the dark trees around [HOLDEN]. The almond tree *flowers* on a leafless stock in *winter* (answering to *old age,* in which all the powers are dormant), while the other trees are flowerless. GESENIUS takes the *Hebrew* for *flourishes* from a different root, *casts off;* when the old man *loses* his gray hairs, as the almond tree *casts* its white flowers. **grasshoppers**–the dry, shrivelled, old man, his backbone sticking out, his knees projecting forwards, his arms backwards, his head down, and the apophyses enlarged, is like that insect. Hence arose the fable, that Tithonus in very old age was changed into a grasshopper [PARKHURST]. "The locust *raises itself* to fly"; the old man about to leave the body is like a locust when it is assuming its winged form, and is about to fly [MAURER]. **a burden**–viz., to himself. **desire shall fail**–satisfaction shall be abolished. For "desire," *Vulgate* has "the caper tree," provocative of lust; not so well. **long home**–(Job 16:22; 17:13.) **mourners**–(Jer. 9:17-20), hired for the occasion (Matt. 9:23). **6.** A double image to represent *death,* as in vss. 1-5, *old age:* (1) A *lamp* of frail material, but *gilded* over, often in the East hung from roofs by a *cord* of silk and *silver* interwoven; as the lamp is dashed down and broken, when the cord breaks, so man at death; the golden bowl of the lamp answers to *the skull,* which, from the vital preciousness of its contents, may be called "golden"; "the silver cord" is *the spinal marrow,* which is white and precious as silver, and is attached to the brain. (2) *A fountain,* from which water is drawn by *a pitcher* let down by a rope wound round *a wheel;* as, when the pitcher and wheel are broken, water can no more be drawn, so life ceases when the vital energies are gone. The "fountain" *may* mean the right ventricle of the heart; the "cistern," the left; the pitcher, the veins; the wheel the aorta, or great artery [SMITH]. The circulation of the blood, whether known or not to Solomon, *seems* to be implied in the language put by the Holy Ghost into his mouth. This gloomy picture of old age applies to those who have not "remembered their Creator in youth." They have none of the consolations of God, which they might have obtained in youth; it is now too late to seek them. A good old age is a blessing to the godly (Gen. 15:15; Job 5:26; Prov. 16:31; 20:29).

ADAM CLARKE

2. *While the sun, or the light, or the moon, or the stars, be not darkened.* I.e., in the spring, prime, and prosperity of life. *Nor the clouds return.* The infirmities of old age, of which winter is a proper emblem, as spring is of youth in the former clause of this verse.

3. *In the day when the keepers of the house.* The body of man is here compared to a house; mark the metaphors and their propriety. (1) *The keepers shall tremble*—the hands become paralytic. (2) *The strong men shall bow.* The legs become feeble, and unable to support the weight of the body. (3) *The grinders cease because they are few.* The teeth decayed and mostly lost, and *few* that remain being incapable of properly masticating hard substances or animal food. And so they cease. (4) *Those that look out of the windows.* The optic nerves, which receive impressions, through the medium of the different humors of the eye, from surrounding objects—they *are darkened.*

4. *And the doors shall be shut in the streets.* (5) The *doors*—the lips, which are the doors by which the mouth is closed. (6) *Be shut in the streets.* The *doors* or lips are *shut* to hinder the food in chewing from dropping out; as the teeth, which prevented that before, are now lost. (7) *The sound of the grinding is low.* Little noise is now made in eating, because the teeth are either lost or become so infirm as not to suffer their being pressed close together; and the mouth being kept shut to hinder the food from dropping out, the sound in eating is scarcely heard. (8) *He shall rise up at the voice of the bird.* His sleep is not sound, as it used to be, and the crowing of the cock awakes him. And so much difficulty does he find to respire while in bed that he is glad of the dawn to rise up and get some relief. The chirping of the sparrow is sufficient to awake him. (9) *All the daughters of musick shall be brought low.* The voice becomes feeble and squeaking, and merriment and pleasure are no more.

5. *When they shall be afraid of that which is high.* (10) Being so feeble, they are afraid to trust themselves to ascend steps, stairs, etc., without help. (11) *Fears shall be in the way.* They dare not walk out, lest they should meet some danger which they have not strength to repel nor agility to escape. (12) *The almond tree shall flourish.* Not *flourish*, but "fall off." The hair falls off. The almond tree, having white flowers, is a fit emblem of a hoary head. (13) *The grasshopper shall be a burden.* Even such an inconsiderable thing as a locust, or a very small insect, shall be deemed burdensome, their strength is so exceedingly diminished. (14) *Desire shall fail.* Both relish and appetite for food, even the most delicate, that to which they were formerly so much attached, now fails. (15) *Because man goeth to his long home. El beith olamo,* "to the house of his age"; the place destined to receive him when the whole race or course of life shall be finished, for *olam* takes in the whole course or duration of a thing. (16) He is just departing into the invisible world, and this is known by *the mourners* going *about the streets.*

6. *Or ever the silver cord be loosed.* We have already had all the external evidences of old age, with all its attendant infirmities; next follow what takes place in the body, in order to produce what is called death, or the separation of body and soul. (1) *The silver cord.*—The spinal marrow, from which all the nerves proceed, as itself does from the brain. This is said to be *loosed;* as the nervous system became a little before, and at the article of death, wholly debilitated. (2) *The golden bowl be broken.* The brain contained in the cranium, or skull. *Broken*—be rendered unfit to perform its functions. (3) *Or the pitcher be broken at the fountain.* The *vena cava,* which brings back the blood to the right ventricle of the heart, here called the *fountain,* the "spring" whence the water gushes up; properly applied here to the heart. (4) *The wheel broken at the cistern.* The great aorta, which receives the blood from the *cistern,* the left ventricle of the heart, and distributes it to the different parts of the system. These may be said, as in the case of the brain above, to be *broken,* i.e., rendered useless.

MATTHEW HENRY

these are separated, and each goes to the place whence it came. The body, that clod of clay, *returns to* its own *earth.* The soul, that beam of light, *returns to* that *God* who, when he *made man of the dust of the ground, breathed into him the breath of life,* to make him *a living soul* (Gen. ii. 7).

Solomon is here drawing towards a close. He repeats his text (*v.* 8). He recommends what he had written upon this subject by divine direction and inspiration to our serious consideration.

1. They are the words of one that was a convert, a penitent, that could speak by dear-bought experience of the vanity of the world and the folly of expecting great things from it. He was *Coheleth,* one gathered in from his wanderings. *Vanity of vanities, saith the* penitent.

2. They are the words of one that was wise, endued with extraordinary measures of wisdom, famous for it among his neighbours, who all sought unto him *to hear his wisdom,* and therefore a competent judge of this matter.

3. He was one that made it his business to do good, and to use wisdom aright.

4. He took a great deal of pains and care to do good, designing to *teach the people knowledge.* He chose the most profitable way of preaching, by proverbs or short sentences.

5. He put what he had to say in such a dress as he thought would be most pleasing: *He sought to find out acceptable words,* words of delight (*v.* 10); that good matter might not be spoiled by a bad style.

6. *That which was written was upright* and sincere, even *words of truth.* Most are for smooth things, that flatter them, rather than right things, that direct them (Isa. xxx. 10), but to those that understand themselves, and their own interest, *words of truth* will always be *acceptable words.*

7. That which he and other holy men wrote will be of great advantage to us, especially by the exposition of it, *v.* 11. The words are *as nails* to those that are wavering and inconstant, to fix them to that which is good. They are *as goads* to such as are dull and draw back, and *nails* to such as are desultory and draw aside, that what good there is in us may be *as a nail fastened in a sure place,* Ezra ix. 8. Solemn assemblies for religious worship are an ancient divine institution, intended for the honour of God and the edification of his church. There must be masters of these assemblies, who are Christ's ministers. Their business is to fasten the *words of the wise,* and drive them as *nails* to the head, in order to which the word of God is likewise as *a hammer,* Jer. xxiii. 29.

8. That which is written, and thus recommended to us, is of divine origin. Though it comes to us through various hands (many *wise men,* and many *masters of assemblies*), yet it is *given by one* and the same *shepherd,* the *shepherd of Israel, that leads Joseph like a flock,* Ps. lxxx. 1.

9. The sacred inspired writings, if we will but make use of them, are sufficient to guide us in the way to true happiness. "*And further,* nothing now remains but to tell thee that *of making many books there is no end.*" Let men write ever so many books for the conduct of human life, write till they have tired themselves with much study, they cannot give better instructions than those we have from the word of God.

The great enquiry which Solomon prosecutes in this book is, *What is that good which the sons of men should do? ch.* ii. 3. What is the true way to true happiness, the certain means to attain our great end? He had found it, by the help of that discovery which God anciently made to man (Job. xxviii. 28), that serious godliness is the only way to true happiness: *Let us hear the conclusion of the whole matter.*

I. The summary of religion. Setting aside all matters of doubtful disputation, to be religious is to *fear God and keep his commandments.* 1. The root of religion is the fear of God reigning in the heart, a reverence of his majesty, a deference to his authority, and a dread of his wrath. 2. The rule of religion is the law of God revealed in the scriptures. Our fear towards God must be taught by his commandments (Isa. xxix. 13), and those we must keep and carefully observe.

II. The vast importance of it: *This is the whole of man;* it is all his business and all his blessedness; our whole duty is summed up in this and our whole comfort is bound up in this.

III. A powerful inducement to this, *v.* 14. We shall see of what vast consequence it is to us that we be religious if we consider the account we must every one of us shortly give of himself to God. *God shall bring every work into judgment.* The great thing to be then judged concerning *every work* is whether it be good or evil.

JAMIESON, FAUSSET, BROWN

7. **dust**—the dust-formed body. **spirit**—surviving the body; implying its immortality (ch. 3:11). **8-12.** A summary of the first part.

13, 14. A summary of the second. **Vanity . . .**—Resumption of the sentiment with which the book began (ch. 1:2; I John 2:17).

9. **gave good heed**—lit., "he weighed." The "teaching the people" seems to have been *oral;* the "proverbs," *in writing.* There must then have been auditories *assembled to hear* the inspired *wisdom of the Preacher.* See the explanation of *Koheleth* in the *Introduction* and ch. 1 (I Kings 4:34). **that which is written . . .**—rather, (he sought) "*to write down* uprightly (or 'aright') words of truth" [HOLDEN and WEISS]. "Acceptable" means an agreeable style; "uprightly . . . truth," correct sentiment. 11. **goads**—piercing deeply into the mind (Acts 2:37; 9:5; Heb. 4:12); evidently *inspired words,* as the end of the verse proves.

fastened—rather, on account of the *Hebrew* genders, (The words) "are fastened (in the memory) like nails" [HOLDEN].

masters of assemblies—rather, "the masters of collections (i.e., collectors of inspired sayings, Prov. 25:1), are given ('have published them as proceeding' [HOLDEN]) from one Shepherd," viz., the Spirit of Jesus Christ [WEISS], (Ezek. 37:24). However, the mention of "goads" favors the *English Version,* "masters of assemblies," viz., *under-shepherds,* inspired by *the Chief Shepherd* (I Pet. 5:2-4). SCHMIDT translates, "The masters of assemblies are fastened (made sure) as nails," so Isa. 22:23. **12.** (*Note,* ch. 1:18.) **many books**—of mere *human* composition, opposed to "by these"; these *inspired* writings are the only sure source of "admonition." **(over much) study**—in mere human books, wearies the body, without solidly profiting the soul.

13. The grand inference of the whole book. **Fear God**—The antidote to following creature-idols, and "vanities," whether self-righteousness (ch. 7:16, 18), or wicked oppression and other evils (ch. 8:12, 13), or mad mirth (ch. 2:2; 7:2-5), or self-mortifying avarice (ch. 8:13, 17), or youth spent without God (ch. 11:9; 12:1).

this is the whole duty of man—lit., "this is the whole man," the full ideal of man, as originally contemplated, realized wholly by Jesus Christ alone; and, through Him, by saints now in part, hereafter perfectly (I John 3:22-24; Rev. 22:14). **14.** The future judgment is the test of what is "vanity," what solid, as regards the chief good, the grand subject of the book.

ADAM CLARKE

7. *Then shall the dust return to the earth as it was: and the spirit shall return unto God.* (5) Putrefaction and solution take place; the whole mass becomes decomposed, and in process of time is reduced to dust, from which it was originally made; while *the spirit, haruach,* "that spirit," which God at first breathed into the nostrils of man, returns *to God who gave it.*

8. This affecting and minute description of old age and death is concluded by the author with the same exclamation by which he began this book: *Vanity of vanities,* saith Koheleth; *all is vanity.* Now that man, the masterpiece of God's creation, the delegated sovereign of this lower world, is turned to dust, what is there stable or worthy of contemplation besides?

9. *Because the preacher was wise, he still taught the people knowledge.* And in order to do this he took *good heed*—considered what would be most useful. *He set in order*—collected and arranged, many parables, probably alluding to the book over which we have already passed.

10. *He sought to find out acceptable words. Dibrey chephets,* "words of desire," words of will; the best, the most suitable words; those which the people could best understand. But these words were not such as might merely please the people; they were *words of truth,* such as came from God and might lead them to Him.

11. *The words of the wise.* Doctrines of faith, illustrated by suitable language, are *as nails fastened by the masters of assemblies,* the "masters of collections," those who had made the best collections of this kind, the matter of which was of the most excellent nature.

12. *And further, by these, my son, be admonished.* Hear such teachers, and receive their admonitions, and do not receive the grace of God in vain. *Of making many books there is no end.* Two thousand years have elapsed since this was written; and since that time some millions of treatises have been added, on all kinds of subjects, to those which have gone before.

THE BOOK OF SONG OF SOLOMON

I. The marriage (1:1-2:7)
A. The Shulammite and the virgins (1:1-6)
1. The bride awaiting the wedding (1:1-4a)
2. The virgins to the bride (1:4b)
3. The bride, in the bridegroom's house (1:4c)
4. The virgins to the bridegroom (1:4d)
5. The bride (1:4e-6)
a. To the bridegroom (1:4e)
b. To the virgins (1:5-6)

B. The bride and the bridegroom (1:7-2:6)
1. The bride (1:7)
2. The bridegroom (1:8-10)
3. The virgins to the bride (1:11)
4. The bride (1:12-14)
5. The bridegroom (1:15)
6. The bride (1:16-2:1)
7. The bridegroom (2:2)
8. The bride (2:3-6)

C. The singer (2:7)

II. The betrothal (2:8-7:9)
A. Memories of the wooing (2:8-3:5)
1. The bride—how the beloved came (2:8-14)
2. The brothers—interrupting the wooing (2:15)
3. The bride—answering the wooer (2:16, 17)
4. The bride—her dreams after the wooing (3:1-4)
5. The singer (3:5)

B. The betrothal (3:6-5:1)
1. The singer—the coming of Solomon (3:6-11)
2. Solomon—the proposal (4:1-15)
3. The bride—the acceptance (4:16)
4. Solomon (5:1)
a. To the bride (5:1a)
b. To his retinue (5:1b)

C. Experiences following betrothal (5:2-7:9)
1. The bride—the maiden's troubled dream (5:2-6:3)
a. The coming of the beloved in the night (5:2-5)
b. The door opened, but the beloved vanished (5:6a)
c. Her search (5:6b-6:2)
(1) Out in the streets (5:6b)
(2) The ill-treatment of the watchmen (5:7)
(3) Appeal to the women of Jerusalem (5:8)
(4) Their answer (5:9)
(5) Her description of her beloved (5:10-16)
(6) Inquiry of the women (6:1)
(7) Her answer (6:2)
d. She awakes (6:3)
2. Solomon (6:4-7:9)
a. Description of the Shulammite (6:4-9a)
b. Effect upon the virgins of the vision of her (6:9b-13)
c. Continued description (7:1-9)

III. The united life (7:10-8:14)
A. The bride—her desire to visit her home with her bridegroom (7:10-8:3)
B. The singer (8:4-5a)
C. The bride and bridegroom together (8:5b-14)
1. The bridegroom (8:5b)
2. The bride (8:6-12)
a. Quotations from the brothers (8:6-9)
b. Answer of the bride (8:10-12)
3. The bridegroom (8:13)
4. The bride (8:14)

In our belief both of the divine extraction and of the spiritual exposition of this book, we are confirmed by the concurring testimony both of the Jews and of the Christian church. This *Song of Solomon's* is very unlike the songs of his father David; there is not the name of God in it; it is never quoted in the New Testament; we find no expressions of natural religion or pious devotion, nor any of the marks of immediate revelation. It seems as hard as any part of Scripture to be made "a savour of life unto life," and to those who come to the reading of it with carnal minds and corrupt affections, it is in danger of being made a "savour of death unto death"; and therefore, the Jewish doctors advised their young people not to read it till they were thirty years old, lest by the abuse of that which is most pure and sacred, the flames of lust should be kindled. But, on the other hand, with the help of the many faithful guides we have for the understanding of this book it appears to be a bright and powerful ray of heavenly light, admirably fitted to excite pious and devout affections in holy souls, and improve their acquaintance and communion with God.

It is an allegory, the letter of which kills those who look no further, but the spirit of which gives life. It is a parable, which makes divine things more difficult to those who do not love them, but more plain and pleasant to those who do. Experienced Christians here find a counterpart of their experiences, and to them it is intelligible. It is an *Epithalamium*, or nuptial song, wherein, by the expressions of love between a bridegroom and his bride, are set forth and illustrated the mutual affections that pass between God and a remnant of mankind. It is a pastoral; the bride and bridegroom are brought in as a shepherd and his shepherdess.

This song might easily be taken in a spiritual sense by the Jewish church, for whose use it was first composed. God betrothed the people of Israel to himself; he entered into covenant with them, and it was a marriage covenant. He had given abundant proofs of his love to them and required of them that they should love him with all their heart and soul. Idolatry was often spoken of as spiritual adultery, to prevent which this song was penned.

It may be more easily taken in a spiritual sense by the Christian church, because the condescensions and communications of divine love appear more rich and free under the gospel than they did under the law, and the communion between heaven and earth more familiar. God sometimes spoke of himself as the husband of the Jewish church (Isa. 54:5; Hos. 2:16, 19), and rejoiced in it as his bride (Isa. 62:4, 5). But more frequently is Christ represented as the bridegroom of his church (Matt. 25:1; Rom. 7:4; 2 Cor. 11:2; Eph. 5:32), and the church as the bride, the Lamb's wife (Rev. 19:7; 21:2, 9). The best key to this book is the 45th Psalm, which we find applied to Christ in the New Testament.

MATTHEW HENRY

CHAPTER 1

Verse 1

This book is a *song* to stir up the affections. It is evangelical; and gospel-times should be times of joy, for gospel-grace puts *a new song* into our mouths, Ps. xcviii. 1. The penman is Solomon. It is not the song of fools, as many of the songs of love are, but the song of the wisest of men; nor can any man give a better proof of his wisdom than to celebrate the love of God to mankind. Solomon's songs were a

JAMIESON, FAUSSET, BROWN

CHAPTER 1

VSS. 1-17. CANTICLE I.—THE BRIDE SEARCHING FOR AND FINDING THE KING. Ch. 1:2-2:7. **1. The song of songs**—The most excellent of all songs, *Hebrew* idiom (Exod. 29:37; Deut. 10:14). A foretaste on earth of the "new song" to be sung in glory (Rev. 5:9; 14:3; 15:2-4). **Solomon's**—"King of Israel," or "Jerusalem," is not added, as in the opening of Proverbs and Ecclesiastes, not because Solomon

ADAM CLARKE

CHAPTER 1

1. *The song of songs.* A song of peculiar excellence.

MATTHEW HENRY

thousand and five (1 Kings iv. 32); those that were of other subjects are lost, but this of seraphic love remains. Solomon, like his father, was addicted to poetry, and, which way soever a man's genius lies, he should endeavour to honour God and edify the church with it. It is not certain when Solomon penned this sacred song. Some think that he penned it after he recovered himself by the grace of God from his backslidings. It is more probable that he penned it in the beginning of his time, while he kept close to God and kept up his communion with him. It is here fitly placed after *Ecclesiastes*; for when by that book we are thoroughly convinced of the vanity of the creature, and its insufficiency to satisfy us and make a happiness for us, we shall be quickened to seek for happiness in the love of Christ, and that transcendent pleasure which is to be found only in communion with God through him.

Verses 2–6

The spouse, in this dramatic poem, is here first introduced addressing herself to the bridegroom and then to the daughters of Jerusalem.

I. To the bridegroom, not giving him any name or title, but beginning abruptly: *Let him kiss me.* Two things the spouse desires,

1. The bridegroom's friendship (*v.* 2): "*Let him kiss me with the kisses of his mouth*, that is, be reconciled to me, and let me know that he is so; let me have the tokens of his favour." Thus the Old Testament church desired Christ's manifesting himself in the flesh. "Let him no longer send to me, but come himself, no longer speak by angels and prophets, but let me have the word of his own mouth, those *gracious words* (Luke iv. 22), which will be to me as the *kisses of his mouth*, sure tokens of reconciliation, as Esau's kissing Jacob was." All gospel-grace is summed up in his kissing us, as the father of the prodigal kissed him when he returned a penitent. It is a kiss of peace. She gives several reasons for this desire. (1) Because of the great esteem she has for his love: *Thy love is better than wine.* Gracious souls take more pleasure in loving Christ and being beloved of him, in the fruits and gifts of his love, than any man ever took in the most exquisite delights of sense.

(2) Because of the fragrancy of his love and the fruits of it (*v.* 3): "*Because of the savour of thy good ointment* (the agreeableness and acceptableness of thy graces and comforts to all that rightly understand both them and themselves), *thy name is as ointment poured forth*; thy very name is precious to all the saints; it is an ointment and perfume which rejoice the heart."

(3) Because of the general affection that all holy souls have to him: *Therefore do the virgins love thee.* It is Christ's *love shed abroad in our hearts* that draws out all that are pure from the corruptions of sin. Those are the virgins that love Jesus Christ and *follow him whithersoever he goes*, Rev. xiv. 4. Christ is the darling of all the *pure in heart*.

2. The bridegroom's fellowship, *v.* 4.

(1) Her petition for divine grace: *Draw me.* "Draw me to thyself, draw me nearer, draw me home to thee." Christ has told us that none come to him but such as the Father draws, John vi. 44.

(2) Her promise to improve that grace: *Draw me*, and then *we will run after thee.* The flowing forth of the soul after Christ, and its ready compliance with him, are the effect of his grace; we could not run after him if he did not draw us, 2 Cor. iii. 5; Phil. iv. 13. When Christ pours out his Spirit upon the church in general, which is his bride, all the members of it do thence receive enlivening quickening influences.

(3) The immediate answer that was given to this prayer: *The King has* drawn me, has *brought me into his chambers.* It is not so much an answer fetched by faith from the word of Christ's grace as an answer fetched by experience from the workings of his grace. Those that are drawn to Christ are brought, not only into his courts, into his palaces (Ps. xlv. 15), but into his presence-chamber.

JAMIESON, FAUSSET, BROWN

had not yet ascended the throne [MOODY STUART], but because his personality is hid under that of Christ, the true Solomon (equivalent to *Prince of Peace*). The earthly Solomon is not introduced, which would break the consistency of the allegory. Though the bride bears the chief part, the Song throughout is not hers, but that of her "Solomon." He animates her. He and she, the Head and the members, form but one Christ [ADELAIDE NEWTON]. Aaron prefigured Him as priest; Moses, as prophet; David, as a suffering king; Solomon, as the triumphant prince of peace. The camp in the wilderness represents the Church in the world; the peaceful reign of Solomon, after all enemies had been subdued, represents the Church in heaven, of which joy the Song gives a foretaste. **2. him**—abruptly. She names him not, as is natural to one whose heart is full of some much desired friend: so Mary Magdalene at the sepulchre (John 20:15), as if everyone must know whom she means, the *one* chief object of her desire (Ps. 73:25; Matt. 13:44-46; Phil. 3:7, 8). **kiss**—the token of *peace* from the Prince of Peace (Luke 15:20); "our Peace" (Ps. 85:10; Col. 1:21; Eph. 2:14). **of his mouth**—marking the tenderest affection. For a king to permit his hands, or even garment, to be kissed, was counted a great honor; but that he should himself kiss another *with his mouth* is the greatest honor. God had in times past spoken by *the mouth* of His prophets, who had declared the Church's betrothal; the bride now longs for contact with *the mouth of the Bridegroom Himself* (Job 23:12; Luke 4:22; Heb. 1:1, 2). True of the Church before the first advent, longing for "the hope of Israel," "the desire of all nations"; also the awakened soul longing for the kiss of *reconciliation;* and further, the kiss that is the token of the *marriage contract* (Hos. 2:19, 20), and of *friendship* (I Sam. 20:41; John 14:21; 15:15). **thy love**—*Hebrew*, "loves," viz., tokens of love, loving blandishments. **wine**—which makes glad "the heavy heart" of one ready to perish, so that he "remembers his misery no more" (Prov. 31:6, 7). So, in a "better" sense, Christ's love (Hab. 3:17, 18). He gives the same praise to the bride's love, with the emphatic addition, "How much" (ch. 4:10). Wine was created by His first miracle (John 2), and was the pledge given of His love at the last supper. The spiritual wine is His blood and His spirit, the "new" and better wine of the kingdom (Matt. 26:29), which we can never drink to "excess," as the other (Eph. 5:18; cf. Ps. 23:5; Isa. 55:1). 3. Rather, "As regards the savor of thy ointments, it is good" [MAURER]. In ch. 4:10, 11, the Bridegroom reciprocates the praise of the bride in the same terms. **thy name**—Christ's *character and office* as the "Anointed" (Isa. 9:6; 61:1), as "the savor of ointments" are the graces that surround His *person* (Ps. 45:7, 8). Ecclesiastes 7:1, in its fullest sense, applies to Him. The holy anointing oil of the high priest, which it was death for anyone else to make (so Acts 4:12), implies the exclusive preciousness of Messiah's name (Exod. 30:23-28, 31-38). So Mary brake the box of precious ointment over Him, appropriately (Mark 14:5), the broken box typifying His body, which, when broken, diffused all grace: compounded of various spices, etc. (Col. 1:19; 2:9); of sweet odor (Eph. 5:2). **poured**—(Isa. 53:12; Rom. 5:5.) **therefore**—because of the manifestation of God's character in Christ (I John 4:9, 19). So the penitent woman (Luke 7:37, 38, 47). **virgins**—the pure in heart (II Cor. 11:2; Rev. 14:4). The same *Hebrew* is translated, "thy hidden ones" (Ps. 83:3). The "ointment" of the Spirit "poured forth" produces the "love of Christ" (Rom. 5:5). **4.** (1) The cry of ancient Israel for Messiah, e.g., Simeon, Anna, etc. (2) The cry of an awakened soul for the drawing of the Spirit, after it has got a glimpse of Christ's loveliness and its own helplessness. **Draw me**—The Father draws (John 6:44). The Son draws (Jer. 31:3; Hos. 11:4; John 12:32). "Draw" here, and "Tell" (vs. 7), reverently qualify the word "kiss" (vs. 2). **me, we**—No believer desires to go to heaven alone. We are converted as *individuals;* we follow Christ as joined in a *communion* of saints (John 1:41, 45). Individuality and community meet in the bride. **run**—Her earnestness kindles as she prays (Isa. 40:31; Ps. 119:32, 60). **after thee**—not before (John 10:4). **king . . . brought me into**—(Ps. 45:14, 15; John 10:16). He is the anointed *Priest* (vs. 3); *King* (vs. 4). **chambers**—Her prayer is answered even beyond her desires. Not only is she permitted to *run* after Him, but is brought into the inmost pavilion, where Eastern kings admitted none but the most intimate friends (Esther 4:11; 5:2; Ps. 27:5). The erection of the temple of Solomon was the first bringing of the bride into permanent, instead of migratory, chambers of the King. Christ's body on earth was the next (John

ADAM CLARKE

2. *Let him kiss me.* She speaks of the bridegroom in the third person, to testify her own modesty, and to show him the greater respect.

3. *Thy name is as ointment poured forth.* Your name is as refreshing to my heart, as the best perfumes diffused through a chamber are to the senses of the guests.

4. *Draw me.* Let me have the full assurance of your affection.

We will run after thee. Speaking in the plural through modesty, while still herself is meant. *The king hath brought me.* My spouse is a mighty *king*, no ordinary person. *Into his chambers.* He has favored me with his utmost confidence.

MATTHEW HENRY

(4) Being *brought into the chamber*, "We have what we would have. Our desires are crowned with unspeakable delights; all our griefs vanish, and *we will be glad and rejoice*." All our joy shall centre in God: "*We will rejoice*, not in the ointments, or the chambers, but *in thee*. It is God only that is our *exceeding joy*, Ps. xliii. 4. We have no joy but in Christ."

(5) The communion which a gracious soul has with all the saints in this communion with Christ. In the chambers to which we are brought we not only meet with him, but meet with one another. Whatever differences of apprehension and affection there may be among Christians in other things, this they are all agreed in, Jesus Christ is precious to them.

II. To *the daughters of Jerusalem*, *v.* 5, 6. The believer speaks to those that were in the church, but not of it, or to weak Christians, babes in Christ, willing to be taught in the things of God. She observed these by-standers look disdainfully upon her because of her blackness, in respect both of sins and sufferings, upon account of which they thought she had little reason to expect the kisses she wished for (*v.* 2) or to expect that they should join with her in her joys, *v.* 4. She owns she is *black*. Guilt blackens; the heresies, scandals, and offences, that happen in the church, make her *black*; and the best saints have their failings. Sorrow blackens; that seems to be especially meant; the church is often mean, and poor, and despicable, her beauty sullied with weeping. She asserts her own comeliness notwithstanding (*v.* 5): *I am black*, *but comely*, black *as the tents of Kedar*, in which the shepherds lived, which were very coarse, and never whitened, weatherbeaten and discoloured by long use, but comely *as the curtains of Solomon*. The church is sometimes *black* with persecution, *but comely* in patience, constancy, and consolation. True believers are *black* in themselves, *but comely* in Christ, with the comeliness that he puts upon them, *black* outwardly, for the *world knows them not*, but *all glorious within*, Ps. xlv. 13.

The blackness was not natural, but contracted, and was owing to the hard usage that had been given her: *Look not upon me* so scornfully *because I am black*.

(1) *I am black* by reason of my sufferings: *The sun has looked upon me*. She was fair and comely; whiteness was her proper colour; but she got this blackness by *the burden and heat of the day*, which she was forced to bear. But what was the matter? She fell under the displeasure of those of her own house: *My mother's children were angry with me*. She was *in perils by false brethren*. The Samaritans, who claimed kindred to the Jews, were vexed at anything that tended to the prosperity of Jerusalem, Neh. ii. 10. They dealt very hardly with her: *They made me the keeper of the vineyards*, that is, "They seduced me to sin, drew me into false worships, to serve their gods, which was like dressing their vineyards." These are the grievances which good people complain most of in a time of persecution, that their consciences are forced. "They brought me into trouble, imposed that upon me which was toilsome, and very disgraceful." Keeping the vineyards was base servile work. Her mother's children made her the drudge of the family.

(2) "My sufferings are such as I have deserved; for *my own vineyard have I not kept*."

Verses 7–11

I. The humble petition which the spouse presents to her beloved, the shepherdess to the shepherd, the church and every believer to Christ, for a more free and intimate communion with him. She turns from the *daughters of Jerusalem* and looks up to heaven for relief, *v.* 7. 1. The title she gives to Christ: *O thou whom my soul loveth*. 2. The opinion she has of him as the good shepherd of the sheep; she doubts not but he *feeds his flock* and *makes them rest at noon*. Jesus Christ graciously provides both repast and repose for his sheep. Is it with God's people a noon-time of outward troubles, inward conflicts? Christ has rest for them. 3. Her request to him that she might be admitted into his society: *Tell me, where thou feedest*. "Tell me where to find thee, where I may have conversation with thee, *where thou feedest* and tendest thy flock, that there I may have some of thy company." 4. The plea she uses for the enforcing of this request: "*For why should I be as one that turns aside by* (or after) *the flocks of thy companions*, that pretend to be so, but are really thy competitors, and rivals with thee." Turning aside from Christ after other lovers is that which gracious souls dread. Good Christians will be afraid of giving any occasion to those about them to question their faith in Christ and their love to him.

II. The gracious answer which the bridegroom gives to this request, *v.* 8. See how ready God is to

JAMIESON, FAUSSET, BROWN

2:21), whereby believers are brought within the veil (Eph. 2:6; Heb. 10:19, 20). Entrance into the closet for prayer is the first step. The earnest of the future bringing into heaven (John 14:3). *His* chambers are the bride's also (Isa. 26:20). There are various *chambers, plural* (John 14:2). **be glad and rejoice**—*inward* and *outward* rejoicing. **in thee**—(Isa. 61:10; Phil. 4:1, 4). Not in *our* spiritual frames (Ps. 30:6, 7). **remember**—rather, "commemorate with praises" (Isa. 63:7). The mere *remembrance* of spiritual joys is better than the *present enjoyment* of carnal ones (Ps. 4:6, 7). **upright**—rather, "uprightly," "sincerely" (Ps. 58:1; Rom. 12:9); so Nathanael (John 1:47); Peter (John 21:17); or "deservedly" [MAURER]. **5. black**—viz., "as the tents of Kedar," equivalent to *blackness* (Ps. 120:5). She draws the image from the black goatskins with which the Scenite Arabs ("Kedar" was in Arabia Petræa) cover their tents (contrasted with the splendid state tent in which *the King* was awaiting His bride according to Eastern custom); typifying the darkness of man's natural state. To feel this, and yet also feel one's self in Jesus Christ "comely as the curtains of Solomon," marks the believer (Rom. 7:18, etc.; 8:1); I Tim. 1:15, "I *am* chief"; so she says not merely, "I was," but "I am"; *still* black in herself, but comely through *His* comeliness put upon her (Ezek. 16:14). **curtains**—first, the hangings and veil in the temple of Solomon (Ezek. 16:10); then, also, the "fine linen which is the righteousness of saints" (Rev. 19:8), the white wedding garment provided by Jesus Christ (Isa. 61:10; Matt. 22:11; I Cor. 1:30; Col. 1:28; 2:10; Rev. 7:14). *Historically*, the dark tents of Kedar represent the Gentile Church (Isa. 60:3-7, etc.). As the vineyard at the close is transferred from the Jews, who had not kept their own, to the Gentiles, so the Gentiles are introduced at the commencement of the Song; for they were among the earliest inquirers after Jesus Christ (Matt. 2): the wise men from the East (Arabia, or Kedar). **daughters of Jerusalem**—professors, not the bride, or "the virgins," yet not enemies; invited to gospel blessings (ch. 3:10, 11); so near to Jesus Christ as not to be unlikely to find Him (ch. 5:8); desirous to seek Him with her (ch. 6:1; cf. ch. 6:13; 7:1, 5, 8). In ch. 7:8, 9, the bride's Beloved becomes *their* Beloved; not, however, of *all* of them (ch. 8:4; cf. Luke 23:27, 28). **6.** She feels as if her blackness was so great as to be gazed at by all. **mother's children**—(Matt. 10:36.) She is to forget "her own people and her father's house," i.e., the worldly connections of her unregenerate state (Ps. 45:10); they had maltreated her (Luke 15:15, 16). Children of the same mother, but not the same father [MAURER], (John 8:41-44). They made her a common keeper of vineyards, whereby the sun looked upon, i.e., burnt her; thus she did "not keep her own" vineyard, i.e., fair beauty. So the world, and the soul (Matt. 16:26; Luke 9:25). The believer has to watch against the same danger (I Cor. 9:27). So he will be able, instead of the self-reproach here, to say as in ch. 8:12. **7. my soul loveth**—more intense than "the virgins" and "the upright love thee" (vss. 3, 4; Matt. 22:37). To carry out the design of the allegory, the royal encampment is here represented as moving from place to place, in search of green pastures, under the *Shepherd King* (Ps. 23). The bride, having first enjoyed communion with him in the pavilion, is willing to follow Him into labors and dangers; arising from all absorbing love (Luke 14:26); this distinguishes her from the formalist (John 10:27; Rev. 14:4). **feedest**—tendest thy flock (Isa. 40:11; Heb. 13:20; I Peter 2:25; 5:4; Rev. 7:17.) No *single* type expresses *all* the office of Jesus Christ; hence arises the variety of *diverse* images used to portray the manifold aspects of Him: these would be quite incongruous, if the Song referred to the earthly Solomon. Her intercourse with Him is peculiar. She hears His voice, and addresses none but Himself. Yet it is through a veil; she sees Him not (Job 23:8, 9). If we would be fed, we must follow the Shepherd through the *whole* breadth of His Word, and not stay on *one* spot alone. **makest . . . to rest**—distinct from "feedest"; periods of rest are vouchsafed after labor (Isa. 4:6; 49:10; Ezek. 34:13-15). Communion in private must go along with public following of Him. **turneth aside**—rather one *veiled*, i.e., as a *harlot*, not His true bride (Gen. 38:15), [GESENIUS]; or as a *mourner* (II Sam. 15:30), [WEISS]; or as one *unknown* [MAURER]. All imply estrangement from the Bridegroom. She feels estranged even among Christ's true servants, answering to "thy companions" (Luke 22:28), so long as she has not Himself present. The opposite spirit to I Corinthians 3:4. **8. If**—she ought to have *known* (John 14:8, 9). The confession of her ignorance and *blackness* (vs. 5) leads Him to call her "fairest" (Matt. 12:20). Her

ADAM CLARKE

The upright love thee. The most perfect and accomplished find you worthy of their highest esteem.

5. *I am black, but comely*. This is literally true of many of the Asiatic women; though black or brown, they are exquisitely beautiful. *As the tents of Kedar*. I am tawny, like the tents of the Arabians.

6. *Because the sun hath looked upon me*. The bride gives here certain reasons why she was dark-complexioned. *The sun hath looked upon me*. I am sunburnt, tanned by the sun; being obliged, perhaps, through some domestic jealousy or uneasiness, to keep much without: *My mother's children were angry with me; they made me keeper of the vineyards*.

8. *If thou know not*. This appears to be the reply of the virgins. They know not exactly; and therefore direct the bride to the shepherds, who would give information.

MATTHEW HENRY

answer prayer. How affectionately he speaks to her: *O thou fairest among women!* Believing souls are fair, in the eyes of the Lord Jesus, above any other. How mildly he checks her for her ignorance, in these words, *If thou know not.* What! dost thou not know where to find me and my flock? Compare Christ's answer to a like address of Philip's (John xiv. 9), *Have I been so long time with you, and yet hast thou not known me, Philip?* With what tenderness he acquaints her where she might find him. Follow the track, ask for the good old way, observe *the footsteps of the flock*, and *go forth by* them. Sit under the direction of good ministers: "*Feed* thyself *and thy kids beside the tents of the under-shepherds.* Bring thy charge with thee; they shall all be welcome; *the shepherds* will be helpers, therefore abide by their tents." Those that would have acquaintance and communion with Christ must adhere to holy ordinances, must join themselves to his people. Those that have the charge of families must bring them with them to religious assemblies; let their *kids*, their children, their servants, have the benefit of *the shepherds' tent.*

III. The high encomiums which the bridegroom gives of his spouse. 1. He calls her his *love* (*v.* 9); it is an endearing compellation often used in this book: "My friend, my companion, my familiar." 2. He compares her to a set of strong and stately *horses in Pharaoh's chariots.* Egypt was famous for the best horses. The church had complained of her own weakness, and the danger of being made a prey by her enemies: "Fear not," says Christ; "*I have made thee like a company of horses;* I have put strength into thee, so that thou shalt *mock at fear. I have compared thee to my company of horses* which triumphed over *Pharaoh's chariots*, the holy angels, *horses of fire.*" 3. He admires the beauty and ornaments of her countenance (*v.* 10): *Thy cheeks are comely with rows of jewels*, the attire of the head, curls of hair, or knots of ribbons; *thy neck also with chains*, such as persons of the first rank wear, *chains of gold.* The ordinances of Christ are the ornaments of the church. The graces, gifts, and comforts of the Spirit, are the adorning of every believing soul, and beautify it.

IV. His gracious purpose to add to her ornaments; for where God has given true grace he will give more grace. She shall be yet further beautified (*v.* 11): *We will make thee borders of gold*, inlaid, or enamelled, *with studs of silver.* The same that is the author will be the finisher of the good work; and it cannot miscarry.

Verses 12–17

Between Christ and his spouse endearments are exchanged.

I. Believers in communion with him.

1. The humble reverence believers have for Christ as their Sovereign, *v.* 12. He has fellowship with them and rejoices in them; he *sits at his table* to bid them welcome. When good Christians, in any religious duty, especially in the ordinance of the Lord's supper, where the King is pleased to *sit* with us *at his* own *table*, have their graces exercised, their hearts broken by repentance, healed by faith, and inflamed with holy love, then the *spikenard sends forth the smell thereof.*

2. The strong affection they have for Christ as their *beloved*, their *well-beloved*, *v.* 13. Christ is not only *beloved* by all believing souls, but is their *well-beloved*, their best-beloved, their only beloved. Christ is accounted *a bundle of myrrh* and *a cluster of camphire*, everything, that is pleasant and delightful. The doctrine of his gospel, and the comforts of his Spirit, are very refreshing to them, and they rest in his love.

The word translated *camphire* is *copher*, the same word that signifies *atonement* or *propitiation.* Christ is *a cluster of* merit and righteousness to all believers; *he is the propitiation for their sins. He shall lie all night between my breasts*, near my heart. Christ lays the beloved disciples in his bosom; why then should not they lay their beloved Saviour in their bosoms?

JAMIESON, FAUSSET, BROWN

jealousy of letting even "His companions" take the place of Himself (vs. 7) led her too far. He directs her to follow them, as they follow Him (I Cor. 11:1; Heb. 6:10, 12); to use ordinances and the ministry; where *they* are, *He* is (Jer. 6:16; Matt. 18:19, 20; Heb. 10:25). Indulging in isolation is not the way to find Him. It was thus, literally, that Zipporah found her bridegroom (Exod. 2:16). The bride unhesitatingly asks the watchmen afterwards (ch. 3:3). **kids**—(John 21:15). Christ is to be found in active ministrations, as well as in prayer (Prov. 11:25). **shepherds' tents**—ministers in the sanctuary (Ps. 84: 1). **9. horses in Pharaoh's chariots**—celebrated for *beauty, swiftness*, and *ardor*, at the Red Sea (Exod. 14:15). These qualities, which *seem* to belong to the ungodly, *really* belong to the saints [MOODY STUART]. The allusion may be to the horses brought at a high price by Solomon out of Egypt (II Chron. 1:16, 17). So the bride is redeemed out of spiritual Egypt by the true Solomon, at an infinite price (Isa. 51:1; I Pet. 1:18, 19). But the deliverance from *Pharaoh at the Red Sea* accords with the allusion to the tabernacle (ch. 1:5; 3:6, 7); it rightly is put at the beginning of the Church's call. The *ardor* and *beauty* of the bride are the point of comparison; (vs. 4) "run"; (vs. 5) "comely." Also, like Pharaoh's horses, she forms a great company (Rev. 19:7, 14). As Jesus Christ is both Shepherd and Conqueror, so believers are not only His *sheep*, but also, as a Church *militant* now, His *chariots and horses* (ch. 6:4). **10. rows of jewels**—(Ezek. 16:11, 12, 13). OLERIUS says, Persian ladies wear two or three rows of pearls round the head, beginning on the forehead and descending down to the cheeks and under the chin, so that their faces seem to be set in pearls (Ezek. 16:11). The comparison to the horses (vs. 9) implies the vital energy of the bride; this verse, her superadded graces (Prov. 1:9; 4:9; I Tim. 2:9; II Pet. 1:5). **11. We**—the Trinity implied by the Holy Ghost, whether it was so by the writer of the Song or not (Gen. 1:26; Prov. 8:30; 30:4). "The Jews acknowledged God as king, and Messiah as king, in interpreting the Song, but did not know that these two are one" [LEIGHTON]. **make**—not merely *give* (Eph. 2:10). **borders of gold, with studs** [i.e., spots] **of silver**—Jesus Christ delights to give more "to him that hath" (Matt. 25:29). He crowns *His own work* in us (Isa. 26:12). The "borders" here are equivalent to "rows" (vs. 10); but here, the King seems to give the finish to her attire, by adding a *crown* (*borders*, or circles) of gold studded with silver spots, as in Esther 2:17. Both the *royal* and *nuptial* crown, or chaplet. The *Hebrew* for "spouse" (ch. 4:8) is *a crowned one* (Ezek. 16:12; Rev. 2:10). The crown is given at once upon conversion, in title, but in sensible possession afterwards (II Tim. 4:8). **12. While**—It is the presence of the Sun of Righteousness that draws out the believer's odors of grace. It was the sight of Him at table that caused the two women to bring forth their ointments for Him (Luke 7:37, 38; John 12:3; II Cor. 2:15). Historically fulfilled (Matt. 2:11); spiritually (Rev. 3:20); and in church worship (Matt. 18:20); and at the Lord's Supper especially, for here *public* communion with Him at table amidst His friends is spoken of, as vs. 4 refers to *private* communion (I Cor. 10:16, 21); typically (Exod. 24:9-11); the future perfect fulfilment (Luke 22:30; Rev. 19:9). The allegory supposes the King to have stopped in His movements and to be seated with His friends on the divan. What grace that a table should be prepared for us, while still militant (Ps. 23:5)! **my spikenard**—**not boasting, but** *owning* the Lord's grace to and in her. The spikenard is a lowly herb, the emblem of humility. She rejoices that *He* is well pleased with her graces, His own work (Phil. 4:18). **13. bundle of myrrh**—abundant *preciousness (Greek)*, (I Pet. 2:7). Even a *little* myrrh was costly; much more a *bundle* (Col. 2:9). BURROWES takes it of *a scent-box filled with liquid myrrh;* the liquid obtained by incision gave the tree its chief value. **he**—rather, "it"; it is the myrrh that lies in the bosom, as the cluster of camphire is in the vineyards (vs. 14). **all night**—an undivided heart (Eph. 3:17; contrast Jer. 4:14; Ezek. 16:15, 30). Yet on account of the everlasting covenant, God restores the adulteress (Ezek. 16:60, 62; Hos. 2:2, etc.). The night is the whole present dispensation till the everlasting day dawns (Rom. 13:12). Also, lit., "night" (Ps. 119:147, 148), the night of *affliction* (Ps. 42:8). **14. cluster**—Jesus Christ is one, yet *manifold* in His graces. **camphire**—or, "cypress." The hennah is meant, whose odorous flowers grow in clusters, of a color white and yellow softly blended; its bark is dark, the foliage light green. Women deck their persons with them. The loveliness of Jesus Christ. **vineyards**—appropriate in respect to Him who is "the vine." The spikenard was for the

ADAM CLARKE

9. I have compared thee . . . to a company of horses. This may be translated, more literally, "I have compared you to my mare, in the chariots or courses of Pharaoh"; and so the versions understood it. Mares, in preference to horses, were used both for riding and for chariots in the East.

12. While the king sitteth at his table. "In his circle," probably meaning the circle of his friends at the marriage festivals, or a round table.

MATTHEW HENRY

II. Jesus Christ has a great love for his church and every true believer; they are amiable in his eyes (*v.* 15): *Behold, thou art fair, my love;* and again, *Behold, thou art fair.* He says this to show that there is a real beauty in holiness, that all who are sanctified are thereby beautified; they are truly fair. One instance of the beauty of the spouse is here mentioned, that she *has doves' eyes,* as *ch.* iv. 1. Those are fair, in Christ's account, who have, not the piercing eye of the eagle, but the pure and chaste eye of the *dove,* not like the hawk, who, when he soars upwards, still has his eye upon the prey on earth, but a humble modest eye, such an eye as discovers a simplicity and godly sincerity and a dove-like innocency, lightened and guided by the Holy Spirit.

III. The church expresses her value for Christ, and returns esteem for esteem (*v.* 16): *Behold, thou art fair.* Lord, saith the church, "Dost thou call me fair? I am fair no otherwise than as I have thy image stamped upon me. Thou art *pleasant* to all that are thine." Having expressed her esteem of her husband's person, she next, like a loving spouse, applauds the accommodations he had for her entertainment, his *bed,* his *house,* his *rafters* or *galleries* (*v.* 16), which may fitly be applied to those holy ordinances in which believers have fellowship with Jesus Christ, receive the tokens of his love and return their devout affections to him. These she calls *ours,* Christ and believers having a joint-interest in them. They are his institutions and their privileges; in them Christ and believers meet. All is *ours* if we are Christ's. Does the colour of the bed, and the furniture belonging to it, help to set it off? *Our bed is green,* a colour which, in a pastoral, is preferred before any other, because it is the colour of the fields and groves. *The beams of our house are cedar* (*v.* 17), which probably refers to the temple Solomon had lately built for communion between God and Israel, which was of *cedar,* a strong sort of wood, sweet, durable, and which will never rot, typifying the firmness and continuance of the church. The galleries for walking are of *fir,* or *cypress,* wood that was pleasing both to the sight and to the smell, intimating the delight which the saints take in walking with Christ. Everything in the covenant of grace is very firm, very fine, and very fragrant.

JAMIESON, FAUSSET, BROWN

banquet (vs. 12); the myrrh was in her bosom continually (vs. 13); the camphire is in the midst of natural beauties, which, though lovely, are eclipsed by the one cluster, Jesus Christ, preëminent above them all. **En-gedi**—in South Palestine, near the Dead Sea (Josh. 15:62; Ezek. 47:10), famed for aromatic shrubs. **15. fair**—He discerns beauty in her, who had said, "I am black" (vs. 5), because of the everlasting covenant (Ps. 45:11; Isa. 62:5; Eph. 1:4, 5). **doves' eyes**—large and beautiful in the doves of Syria. The prominent features of her beauty (Matt. 10:16), gentleness, innocence, and constant love, emblem of the Holy Ghost, who changes us to *His own* likeness (Gen. 8:10, 11; Matt. 3:16). The opposite kind of eyes (Ps. 101:5; Matt. 20:15; II Pet. 2:14). **16.** *Reply of the Bride.* She presumes to call Him beloved, because He called her so first. Thou callest me "fair"; if I am so, it is not in myself; it is all from Thee (Ps. 90:17); but *Thou* art fair in Thyself (Ps. 45:2). **pleasant**—(Prov. 3:17) towards Thy friends (II Sam. 1:26). **bed . . . green**—the couch of green grass on which the King and His bride sit to "rest at noon." Thus her prayer in vs. 7 is here granted; a green oasis in the desert, always found near waters in the East (Ps. 23:2; Isa. 41:17-19). The scene is a kiosk, or summerhouse. *Historically,* the literal resting of the Babe of Bethlehem and his parents on the *green* grass provided for cattle (Luke 2). In this verse there is an incidental allusion, in vs. 15, to the offering (Luke 2:24). So the "cedar and fir" ceiling refers to the temple (I Kings 5:6-10; 6-15-18); type of the heavenly temple (Rev. 21:22). **17. our house**—see *Note,* vs. 16; but *primarily,* the kiosk (Isa. 11:10), "His rest." Cedar is pleasing to the eye and smell, hard, and never eaten by worms. **fix**—rather, cypress, which is hard, durable, and fragrant, of a reddish hue [GENSIUS, WEISS, and MAURER]. Contrasted with the shifting "tents" (vs. 5), *His* house is "*our* house" (Ps. 92:13; Eph. 2:19; Heb. 3:6). Perfect oneness of Him and the bride (John 14:20; 17:21). There is the shelter of a princely roof from the sun (Ps. 121:6), without the confinement of walls, and amidst rural beauties. The carved ceiling represents the wondrous excellencies of His divine nature.

ADAM CLARKE

15. *Thou hast doves' eyes.* The large and beautiful dove of Syria is supposed to be here referred to, the eyes of which are remarkably fine.

MATTHEW HENRY

CHAPTER 2

Verses 1–2

I. He that is the Son of the Highest calls and owns himself *the rose of Sharon, and the lily of the valleys,* to express his presence with his people in this world, the easiness of their access to him, and the beauty and sweetness which they find in him. *The rose,* for beauty and fragrancy, is the chief of flowers, and our Saviour prefers the clothing of *the lily* before that of *Solomon in all his glory.* Christ is *the rose of Sharon,* where the best roses grew, *the rose of the field* (so some), denoting that the gospel salvation lies open to all. He is not a rose locked up in a garden. He is a *lily* for whiteness, a *lily of the valleys* for sweetness. He is a *lily of the valleys,* or *low places,* in his humiliation. Humble souls see most beauty in him. To those that are in the *valleys* he is a *lily.*

II. His church is *as a lily;* he himself is *the lily* (*v.* 1). The beauty of believers consists in their resemblance to Jesus Christ. They are as lilies, for those are made like Christ in whose hearts his *love is shed abroad.* The church of Christ as far excels all other societies as a bed of roses excels a bush of thorns. *As a lily,* compassed with *thorns.* The wicked, *the daughters* of this world, such as have no love to Christ, are as *thorns,* worthless and useless, noxious and hurtful. God's people are *as lilies among* them, scratched and torn, shaded and obscured, by them; they are dear to Christ, and yet exposed to hardships and troubles.

Verses 3–7

I. The spouse commends her beloved and prefers him before all others: *As the apple-tree among the trees of the wood,* useful and serviceable to man, yielding pleasant and profitable fruit, while the other trees are of little use, no, not the cedars themselves. till they are cut down, *so is my beloved among the sons,*

II. She remembers the abundant comfort she has had in communion with him: She *sat down* by him *with great delight,* as shepherds sometimes repose themselves. A double advantage she found in sitting down so near the Lord Jesus:—1. A refreshing shade: *I sat down under his shadow.* Christ is to believers *as the shadow* of a great tree. Those that *are weary and heavily laden* may find *rest* in Christ. We must *sit down under this shadow with delight,* must put an entire confidence in the protection of it. 2. Pleasing nourishing food. This tree drops its fruits to those

JAMIESON, FAUSSET, BROWN

CHAPTER 2

Vss. 1-17. **1. rose**—if applied to Jesus Christ, it, with the white lily (lowly, II Cor. 8:9), answers to "white and ruddy" (ch. 5:10). But it is rather the *meadow-saffron:* the *Hebrew* means radically a plant with a *pungent bulb,* inapplicable to the *rose.* So *Syriac.* It is of a white and violet color [MAURER, GESENIUS, and WEISS]. The bride thus speaks of herself as lowly though lovely, in contrast with the lordly "apple" or citron tree, the bridegroom (vs. 3); so the "lily" is applied to her (vs. 2). **Sharon**—(Isa. 35:1, 2.) In North Palestine, between Mount Tabor and Lake Tiberias (I Chron. 5:16). LXX and *Vulgate* translate it, "a plain"; though they err in this, the *Hebrew* Bible not elsewhere favoring it, yet the parallelism to *valleys* shows that, in the proper name Sharon, there is here a tacit reference to its meaning of lowliness. Beauty, delicacy, and lowliness, are to be in her, as they were in Him (Matt. 11:29). **2.** *Jesus Christ to the Bride* (Matt. 10:16; John 15:19; I John 5:19). Thorns, equivalent to the wicked (II Sam. 23:6; Ps. 57:4). **daughters**—of men, not of God; not "the virgins." "If thou art the lily of Jesus Christ, take heed lest by impatience, rash judgments, and pride, thou thyself become a thorn" [LUTHER]. **3.** *Her reply.* **apple**—generic including the golden citron, pomegranate, and orange apple (Prov. 25:11). He combines the *shadow* and fragrance of the citron with the *sweetness* of the orange and pomegranate fruit. The foliage is perpetual; throughout the year a succession of blossoms, fruit, and perfume (Jas. 1:17). **among the sons**—parallel to "among the daughters" (vs. 2). He alone is ever fruitful among the fruitless wild trees (Ps. 89:6; Heb. 1:9). **I sat . . . with . . . delight**—lit., "I eagerly desired and sat" (Ps. 94:19; Mark 6:31; Eph. 2:6; I Pet. 1:8). **shadow**—(Ps. 121:5; Isa. 4:6; 25:4; 32:2). Jesus Christ interposes the shadow of His cross between the blazing rays of justice and us sinners. **fruit**—Faith plucks it (Prov. 3:18). Man lost the tree of life (Gen. 3). Jesus Christ regained it for him; he eats it partly now (Ps. 119:103; John 6:55, 57; I Pet. 2:3); fully hereafter (Rev. 2:7; 22:2, 14); not earned by the sweat of his brow, or by his righteousness (Rom. 10). Contrast the worldling's fruit (Deut. 32:32; Luke 15:16). **4.** Historically fulfilled in the joy of Simeon and Anna in the temple, over the infant Saviour (Luke 2), and that of Mary,

ADAM CLARKE

CHAPTER 2

1. *I am the rose of Sharon.* Sharon was a very fruitful place, where David's cattle were fed, 1 Chron. xxvii. 29. It is mentioned as a place of excellence, Isa. xxxv. 2, and as a place of flocks, Isa. lxv. 10. Perhaps it would be better, with almost all the versions, to translate, "I am the rose of the field." The bridegroom had just before called her fair; she, with a becoming modesty, represents her beauty as nothing extraordinary, and compares herself to a common flower of the field. This, in the warmth of his affection, he denies, insisting that she as much surpasses all other maidens as the flower of the lily does the bramble, v. 2.

3. *As the apple tree.* The bride returns the compliment, and says, As the apple or citron tree is *among the trees of the wood,* so is the bridegroom among all other men.

I sat down under his shadow. I am become his spouse, and my union with him makes me indescribably happy.

MATTHEW HENRY

that *sit down under its shadow*, and they will find them *sweet unto their taste.* Promises are sweet to a believer. Pardons are sweet, and peace of conscience is sweet, assurances of God's love, joys of the Holy Ghost, the hopes of eternal life, and the present foretastes of it are sweet, all sweet to those that have their spiritual senses exercised.

III. She owns herself obliged to Jesus Christ for all the benefit and comfort she had in communion with him (*v.* 4): "*I sat down under* the apple-tree, but he admitted me to a more intimate communion with him." *He brought me to the house* of wine. One of the rabbin by *the banqueting-house* understands *the tabernacle of the congregation*; surely then we may apply it to Christian assemblies, where the gospel is preached and gospel-ordinances are administered, particularly the Lord's supper, that *banquet of wine.* We should never have come *into the banqueting-house*, never have been acquainted with spiritual pleasures, if Christ had not brought us. *His banner over me was love; he brought me* in with a banner displayed over my head. The gospel is compared to a *banner* or *ensign* (Isa. xi. 12), and that which is represented in this banner is *love, love*; and this is the entertainment in *the banqueting-house.*

IV. She professes her strong affection and most passionate love to Jesus Christ (*v.* 5): *I am sick of love*, overcome, overpowered, by it. She cries out: "Oh *stay me with flagons*, or *ointments*, or *flowers*, anything that is reviving; *comfort me with apples*, with the fruits of that *apple-tree*, Christ (*v.* 3), with the merit and mediation of Christ and the sense of his love to my soul."

V. She experiences the power and tenderness of divine grace, relieving her in her present faintings, *v.* 6. Though he seemed to have withdrawn, yet he was even then a very present help. "*His left hand is under my head*, to bear it up, nay, as a pillow to lay it easy. For, in the meantime, *his right hand embraces me*, and thereby gives me an unquestionable assurance of his love." Believers owe all their strength and comfort to the supporting left hand and embracing right hand of the Lord Jesus.

VI. Finding her beloved thus nigh unto her she is in great care that her communion with him be not interrupted (*v.* 7): *I charge you, O you daughters of Jerusalem.* She gives them this charge *by the roes and the hinds of the field*, that is, by everything that is amiable in their eyes, and dear to them, *as the loving hind and the pleasant roe.* Those that experience the sweetness of communion with Christ cannot but desire the continuance of these blessed visits.

Verses 8–13

The church is here pleasing herself with the thoughts of her further communion with Christ.

I. She rejoices in his approach, *v.* 8. She hears

JAMIESON, FAUSSET, BROWN

too (cf. Luke 1:53); typified (Exod. 24:9-11). Spiritually, the bride or beloved is led (vs. 4) first *into the King's chambers*, thence is *drawn* after Him in answer to her prayer; is next received on a grassy couch under a cedar kiosk; and at last in a "banqueting hall," such as, Josephus says, Solomon had in his palace, "wherein all the vessels were of gold" (*Antiquities*, 8:5, 2). The transition is from holy retirement to *public* ordinances, church-worship, and the Lord's Supper (Ps. 36:8). The bride, as the queen of Sheba, is given "all her desire" (I Kings 10:13; Ps. 63:5; Eph. 3:8, 16-21; Phil. 4:19); type of the heavenly feast hereafter (Isa. 25:6, 9). **his banner . . . love**—After having rescued us from the enemy, our victorious captain (Heb. 2:10) seats us at the banquet under a banner inscribed with *His name*, "love" (I John 4:8). His love conquered us to Himself; this banner rallies round us the forces of Omnipotence, as our protection; it marks to what country we belong, heaven, the abode of love, and in what we most glory, the cross of Jesus Christ, through which we triumph (Rom. 8:37; I Cor. 15:57; Rev. 3:21). Cf. with "*over* me," "*underneath* are the everlasting arms" (Deut. 33:27). **5. flagons**—MAURER prefers translating, "dried raisin cakes"; from the *Hebrew* root "fire," viz., dried by heat. But the "house of *wine*" (*Margin*, vs. 4) favors "flagons"; the "new wine" of the kingdom, the Spirit of Jesus Christ. **apples**—from the tree (vs. 3), so sweet to her, the promises of God. **sick of love**—the highest degree of sensible enjoyment that can be attained here. It may be at an early or late stage of experience. Paul (II Cor. 12:7). In the last sickness of J. Welch, he was overheard saying, "Lord, hold thine hand, it is enough; thy servant is a clay vessel, and can hold no more" [FLEMING, *Fulf. Script.*]. In most cases this intensity of joy is reserved for the heavenly banquet. Historically, Israel had it, when the Lord's glory filled the tabernacle, and afterwards the temple, so that the priests could not stand to minister; so in the Christian Church, on Pentecost. The bride addresses *Christ* mainly, though in her rapture she uses the *plural*, "Stay (*ye*) me," speaking generally. So far from asking the withdrawal of the manifestations which had overpowered her, she asks for more: so ""*fainteth for*" (Ps. 84:2); also Peter, on the mount of transfiguration (Luke 9:33), "Let us make . . . . *not knowing what he said.*" **6.** The "stay" she prayed for (vs. 5) is granted (Deut. 33:12, 27; Ps. 37:24; Isa. 41:16). None can pluck from that *embrace* (John 10:28-30). His hand keeps us from falling (Matt. 14:30, 31); to it we may commit ourselves (Ps. 31:5). **left hand**—is the inferior hand, by which the Lord less signally manifests His love, than by the right; the secret hand of ordinary providence, as distinguished from that of manifested grace (the "right"). They really go together, though sometimes they seem divided; here both are felt at once. THEODORET takes the left hand, equivalent to *judgment and wrath;* the right, equivalent to *honor and love.* The hand of justice no longer is lifted to smite, but is under the head of the believer to support (Isa. 42:21); the hand of Jesus Christ pierced by justice for our sin supports us. The charge not to disturb the beloved occurs thrice; but the sentiment here, "His left hand . . . ," nowhere else fully; which accords with the intensity of joy (vs. 5) found nowhere else; in ch. 8:3, it is only conditional, "*should* embrace," not "doth." **7. by the roes**—not an oath but a solemn charge, to act as cautiously as the hunter would with the wild roes, which are proverbially timorous; he must advance with breathless circumspection, if he is to take them; so he who would not lose Jesus Christ and His Spirit, which is easily grieved and withdrawn, must be tender of conscience and watchful (Ezek. 16:43; Eph. 4:30; 5:15; I Thess. 5:19). In *Margin*, title of Psalm 22, Jesus Christ is called the "*Hind* of the morning," hunted to death by the dogs (cf. vss. 8, 9, where He is represented as bounding on the hills, Ps. 18:33). Here He is *resting*, but with a repose easily broken (Zeph. 3:17). It is thought a gross rudeness in the East to awaken one sleeping, especially a person of rank. **my love**—in *Hebrew*, *Feminine* for *Masculine*, the abstract for concrete, Jesus Christ being the embodiment of *love* itself (ch. 3:5; 8:7), where, as here, the context requires it to be applied to Him, not her. She too is "love" (ch. 7:6), for His love calls forth her love. Presumption in the convert is as grieving to the Spirit as despair. The *lovingness* and *pleasantness* of the hind and roe (Prov. 5:19) is included in this image of Jesus Christ.

CANTICLE II.—Ch. 2:8-3:5.—JOHN THE BAPTIST'S MINISTRY. **8. voice**—an exclamation of joyful surprise, evidently after a long silence. The restlessness of sin and fickleness in her had disturbed His

ADAM CLARKE

F. C. COOK:

4. "His banner." As the standard is the rallying point and guide of the individual soldier, so the bride, transplanted from a lowly station to new scenes of unwonted splendor, finds support and safety in the known attachment of her beloved. His "love" is her "banner." The thought is similar to that expressed in the name "Jehovah-nissi" (Ex. 17:15).

5. "Flagons." More probably "cakes of raisins" or dried grapes (2 Sam. 6:19; 1 Chron. 16:3; Hos. 3:1). For an instance of the reviving power of dried fruit, see 1 Sam. 30:12.

6. Render as a wish or prayer: "O that his left hand were under my head, and that his right hand did embrace me!" Let him draw me to him with entire affection.

—*Barnes' Notes*

F. B. MEYER:

"The voice of my Beloved" (S. of Sol. 2:8). There are times when winter rules within, and the atmosphere is full of rain, and the birds are mute. It does not necessarily argue that we have backslidden; only that the rich, emotional life has for a little died down, as the sap sinks to the earth during the winter's pause.

The first symptom of returning joy is the voice of the Beloved Master. We do not seek Him, but He us. We do not call, but He calls. The voice of spring is heard sounding through our soul. The sweet, clear, tender notes of the Savior ring melodiously around us, and as we hear them we know that our winter is past, the rain is over and gone, and the flowers and birds are at hand.

Rise up, my love! Rise up from lethargy and sloth; from the low levels on which you have lived; from the earth with its attractions, and the grave with its fetters. And as the command issues from his lips, He gives rising grace. Come away, He cries. There is richer life and wider upon the mountains. Let us climb the heights that beckon us. The voice of Christ is constantly summoning us to fuller experiences, to leave what is behind and below, to press up and on, so that we may know Him and the power of his resurrection.

How appropriate these words are as we may conceive of them being spoken to the expectant Church! After centuries of waiting she shall hear the archangel's trump, and it will be the call of her Beloved to rise up and come away. Then her winter will be past forever; the unwithering flowers will appear; the time of singing will have come; and the voice of the turtledove, significant of affection, will be heard throughout Emmanuel's Land.

—*Great Verses Through the Bible*

MATTHEW HENRY

him speak: "It is *the voice of my beloved*, calling to me to tell me he is coming." She sees him come. This may very well be applied to the prospect which the Old Testament saints had of Christ's coming in the flesh. *Abraham saw his day* at a distance, *and was glad*. Those that waited for the consolation of Israel with an eye of faith saw him come, and triumphed in the sight. He comes cheerfully; he comes leaping and skipping *like a roe* and like *a young hart* (*v*. 9), as one pleased and that had his delights with the sons of men. He comes surmounting all the difficulties that lay in his way; he comes *leaping over the mountains, skipping over the hills*, making nothing of discouragements. The curse of the law, the death of the cross, must be undergone, all the powers of darkness must be grappled with, but, before the resolutions of his love, these great mountains become plains. Whatever opposition is given at any time to the deliverance of God's church, Christ will break through it. He comes speedily, *like a roe* or *a young hart*; they thought the time long, but really he hastened.

II. She pleases herself with the glimpses she has of him: "He *stands behind our wall*; I know he is there, for sometimes *he looks forth at the window*, and displays *himself through the lattice*." Such was the state of the Old Testament church while it was in expectation of the coming of the Messiah. They had him near them; they had him with them, though they could not see him clearly. They saw him looking through the windows of the ceremonial institutions and smiling through those lattices; in their sacrifices and purifications Christ discovered himself to them, and gave them intimations and earnests of his grace. In the sacraments Christ is near us, but it is *behind the wall* of external signs, through *those lattices* he manifests himself to us; but we shall shortly *see him as he is*.

III. She repeats the gracious invitation he had given her to come walking with him, *v*. 10–13.

1. He called her his love and his fair one. Those that take Christ for their beloved, he will own as his; never was any love lost that was bestowed upon Christ.

2. He called her to *rise and come away*, *v*. 10, and again, *v*. 13.

3. He gave for a reason the return of the spring, and the pleasantness of the weather. The season is elegantly described. *The winter is past*, the dark, cold, and barren winter; they do not endure always. And the spring would not be so pleasant as it is if it did not succeed the winter, which is a foil to its beauty, Eccles. vii. 14. *The rain is over and gone*, the winter-rain, the cold stormy rain; it is over now, and *the dew is as the dew of herbs*.

Thy flowers appear on the earth. All winter they are dead and buried in their roots, and there is no sign of them; but in the spring they revive, and show themselves in a wonderful variety and verdure.

The time of the singing of birds has come. The little birds, which all the winter lie hid in their retirements and scarcely live, when the spring returns forget all the calamities of the winter, and to the best of their capacity chant forth the praises of their Creator. Doubtless he who understands the birds that cry for want (Ps. cxlvii. 9) takes notice of those that *sing for joy*, Ps. civ. 12. *The voice of the turtle is heard in our land*, which is one of the season-birds mentioned Jer. viii. 7, that observe the time of their coming and the time of their singing, and so

JAMIESON, FAUSSET, BROWN

rest with her, which she had professed not to wish disturbed "till He should please." He left her, but in sovereign grace unexpectedly heralds His return. She awakes, and at once recognizes His voice (I Sam. 3:9, 10; John 10:4); her sleep is not so sinfully deep as in ch. 5:2. **leaping**—bounding, as the roe does, over the roughest obstacles (II Sam. 2:18; I Chron. 12:8); as the father of the prodigal "had compassion and *ran*" (Luke 15:20). **upon the hills**—as the sunbeams glancing from hill to hill. So *Margin*, title of Jesus Christ (Ps. 22), "Hind of the *morning*" (type of His resurrection). Historically, the coming of the kingdom of heaven (the gospel dispensation), announced by John Baptist, is meant; *it* primarily is the garden or vineyard; the bride is called so in a secondary sense. "The voice" of Jesus Christ is indirect, through "the friend of the bridegroom" (John 3:29), John the Baptist. Personally, He is silent during John's ministration, who awoke the long slumbering Church with the cry. "Every *hill* shall be made low," in the spirit of Elias, on the "rent mountains" (I Kings 19:11; cf. Isa. 52:7). Jesus Christ is implied as coming with intense desire (Luke 22:15; Heb. 10:7), disregarding the mountain hindrances raised by man's sin. **9. he standeth**—after having bounded over the intervening space like a roe. He often stands near when our unbelief hides Him from us (Gen. 28:16; Rev. 3:14-20). His usual way; long promised and expected; sudden at last; so, in visiting the second temple (Mal. 3:1); so at Pentecost (Acts 2:1, 2); so in visiting an individual soul, Zaccheus (Luke 19:5, 6; John 3:8); and so, at the second coming (Matt. 24:48, 50; II Pet. 3:4, 10). So it shall be at His second coming (I Thess. 5:2, 3). **wall**—over the cope of which He is first seen; next, He looks *through* (not *forth;* for He is outside) at the windows, *glancing* suddenly and stealthily (not as *English Version*, "showing Himself") through the lattice. The prophecies, types, etc., were lattice glimpses of Him to the Old Testament Church, in spite of the *wall* of separation which sin had raised (John 8:56); clearer glimpses were given by John Baptist, but not unclouded (John 1:26). The legal wall of partition was not to be removed until His death (Eph. 2:14, 15; Heb. 10:20). Even now, He is only seen by *faith*, through the windows of His Word and the lattice of ordinances and sacraments (Luke 24:35; John 14:21); not full vision (I Cor. 13:12); an incentive to our looking for His second coming (Isa. 33:17; Titus 2:13). **10, 11.** Loving reassurance given by Jesus Christ to the bride, lest she should think that He had ceased to love her, on account of her unfaithfulness, which had occasioned His temporary withdrawal. He allures her to brighter than worldly joys (Micah 2:10). Not only does the saint wish to depart to be with Him, but He still more desires to have the saint with Him above (John 17:24). Historically, the vineyard or garden of the King, here first introduced, is "the kingdom of heaven preached" by John the Baptist, before whom "the law and the prophets were" (Luke 16:16). **11. the winter**—the law of the covenant of works (Matt. 4:16). rain is over—(Heb. 12:18-24; I John 2:8). Then first the Gentile Church is called "beloved, which was not beloved" (Rom. 9:25). So "the winter" of estrangement and sin is "past" to the believer (Isa. 44:22; Jer. 50:20; II Cor. 5:17; Eph. 2:1). The rising "Sun of righteousness" dispels the "rain" (II Sam. 23:4; Ps. 126:5, Mal. 4:2). The winter in Palestine is past by April, but all the showers were not over till May. The time described here is that which comes directly after these last showers of winter. In the highest sense, the coming resurrection and deliverance of the earth from the *past* curse is here implied (Rom. 8:19; Rev. 21:4; 22:3). No more "clouds" shall then "return after the rain" (Eccles. 12:2; Rev. 4:3; cf. Gen. 9:13-17); "the rainbow round the throne" is the "token" of this. **12. flowers**—tokens of anger past, and of grace come. "The summoned bride is welcome," say some fathers, "to weave from them garlands of beauty, wherewith she may adorn herself to meet the King." Historically, the flowers, etc., only give promise; the fruit is not ripe yet; suitable to the preaching of John the Baptist, "The kingdom of heaven is *at hand*"; not yet fully come. **the time of . . . singing**—the rejoicing at the advent of Jesus Christ. GREGORY NYSSENUS refers the *voice* of the turtledove to John the Baptist. It with the olive branch announced to Noah that "the rain was over and gone" (Gen. 8:11). So John the Baptist, spiritually. Its *plaintive* "voice" answers to his preaching of *repentance* (Jer. 8:6, 7). *Vulgate* and LXX translate, "The time of *pruning*," viz., spring (John 15:2). The mention of the "turtle's" cooing better accords with our text. The turtledove is migratory (Jer. 8:7), and "comes" early in May; emblem of love, and

ADAM CLARKE

8. *Behold, he cometh leaping.* This appears to be highly characteristic of the gambols of the shepherds, and points out the ecstasy with which those who were enamored ran to their mates.

CHARLES H. SPURGEON:

Verses 10–13. The things which are seen are types of the things which are not seen. The works of creation are pictures to the children of God of the secret mysteries of grace. God's truths are the apples of gold, and the visible creatures are the baskets of silver. The very seasons of the year find their parallel in the little world of man within. We have our winter—dreary, howling winter—when the north wind of the law rushes forth against us, when every hope is nipped, when all the seeds of joy lie buried beneath the dark clods of despair, when our soul is fast fettered like a river bound with ice, without waves of joy, or flowings of thanksgiving. Thanks be to God, the soft south wind breathes upon our soul, and at once the waters of desire are set free, the spring of love comes on, flowers of hope appear in our hearts, the trees of faith put forth their young shoots, the time of the singing of birds comes in our hearts, and we have joy and peace in believing through the Lord Jesus Christ.

That happy springtide is followed in the believer by a rich summer, when his graces, like fragrant flowers, are in full bloom, loading the air with perfume; and fruits of the Spirit like citrons and pomegranates swell into their full proportion in the genial warmth of the Sun of Righteousness. Then comes the believer's autumn, when his fruits grow ripe, and his fields are ready for the harvest; the time has come when his Lord shall gather together His "pleasant fruits," and store them in heaven; the feast of ingathering is at hand—the time when the year shall begin anew, an unchanging year, like the years of the right hand of the Most High in heaven.

Now, beloved, each particular season has its duty. The husbandman finds that there is a time to plough, a time to sow, a time to reap; there is a season for vintage, and a period for pruning of the vine; there is a month for planting of herbs, and for the ingathering of seeds. To everything there is a time and a purpose, and every season has its special labor. It seems from the text, that whenever it is springtime in our hearts, then Christ's voice may be heard saying, "Arise, My love, My fair one, and come away." Whenever we have been delivered from a dreary winter of temptation or affliction, or tribulation, whenever the fair spring of hope cometh upon us, and our joys begin to multiply, then we should hear the Master bidding us seek after something higher and better, and we should go forth in His strength to love Him more, and serve Him more diligently than aforetime. This I take to be the truth taught in the text, and to any with whom the time of the singing of birds is come, in whom the flowers appear—to any such I hope the Master may speak till their souls shall say, "*My* beloved spake, and said unto *me*, rise up, My love, My fair one, and come away."

—*The Treasury of the Old Testament*

MATTHEW HENRY

shame us who understand not the times, nor sing in singing time. *The fig-tree puts forth her green figs*, by which *we know that summer is nigh.* Now this description of the returning spring, as a reason for coming away with Christ, is applicable to the introducing of the gospel in the room of the Old Testament dispensation, during which it had been winter time with the church. Christ's gospel warms that which was cold, makes that fruitful which before was dead and barren; when it comes to any place it puts a beauty and glory upon that place (2 Cor. iii. 7, 8). Springtime is pleasant time, and so is gospel-time. The delivering of the church from the power of persecuting enemies is like spring after a winter of suffering and restraint. When the storms of trouble are over and gone, when the *voice of the turtle*, the joyful sound of the gospel of Christ, is again heard, and ordinances are enjoyed with freedom, then *arise and come away*, sing in the ways of the Lord. When the churches had rest, then were they edified, Acts ix. 31. The conversion of sinners from a state of nature to a state of grace is like the return of the spring, a universal change, a new creation; being born again. The soul that was hard, and cold, and frozen, and unprofitable, like the earth in winter, becomes fruitful, like the earth in spring, and by degrees, like it, brings its fruits to perfection. This blessed change is owing purely to the approaches and influences of the sun of righteousness. A child of God, under doubts and fears, is like the earth in winter, its nights long, its days dark. But comfort will return; the birds shall sing again, and the flowers appear. Arise therefore, poor drooping soul, and *come away.* The bones that lay in the grave, as the roots of plants in the ground during the winter, shall at the resurrection *flourish as a herb*, Isa. lxvi. 14; xxvi. 19. That will be an eternal farewell to winter and a joyful entrance upon an everlasting spring.

Verses 14-17

I. The invitation which Christ gives to the church, and every believing soul, to come into communion with him, *v.* 14.

1. David had called the church God's *turtle-dove* (Ps. lxxiv. 19), and so she is here called; a dove for beauty, for innocence and inoffensiveness; a gracious spirit is a dove-like spirit, loving quietness and cleanliness, and faithful to Christ, as the turtle to her mate. The Spirit descended *like a dove* on Christ, and so he does on all Christians, making them of a *meek and quiet spirit.*

2. This dove is *in the clefts of the rock and in the secret places of the stairs.* Christ is the rock, to whom she flies for shelter, as a dove in the hole of a rock, when struck at by the birds of prey, Jer. xlviii. 28. She retires *into the secret places of the stairs*, where she may be alone, and may the better commune with her own heart. Christ often withdrew to a mountain *himself alone, to pray.*

3. Christ calls her out of her retirements: Come, *let me see thy countenance, let me hear thy voice.*

4. For her encouragement, he tells her: *Sweet is thy voice;* thy praying voice is music in God's ears.

II. The charge which Christ gives to his servants to suppress that which is a terror to his church (*v.* 15): *Take us the foxes, the little foxes*, that creep in insensibly; for, though they are little, they *spoil the vines*, especially now when our vines have *tender grapes* that must be preserved, or the vintage will fail. Believers are as vines; their fruits are as *tender grapes* at first, which must have time to come to maturity. This charge to *take the foxes* is, 1. A charge to believers to mortify their own sinful appetites and passions, which are *as foxes, little foxes*, that destroy their graces, crush good beginnings, and prevent their coming to perfection. Seize the *little foxes*, the first risings of sin, those sins that seem little, for they often prove very dangerous. 2. A charge to all to oppose and prevent the spreading of such opinions and practices as tend to corrupt men's judgments, debauch their consciences, perplex their minds, and discourage their inclinations to virtue. Persecutors are foxes (Luke xiii. 32); false prophets are foxes, Ezek. xiii. 4. Those that sow the tares of heresy or schism, and obstruct the progress of the gospel, they are the *foxes, the little foxes*, which must be tamed, or restrained from doing mischief.

III. The profession which the church makes of her relation to Christ, and her interest in him and communion with him, *v.* 16. He had called her to *rise* and *come away* with him. Now this is her answer to that call:

1. She comforts herself with the thoughts of the relation between her and her beloved: *My beloved is mine;* this denotes propriety. Believers are partakers of Christ; they are taken not only into covenant, but into communion with him. All he has promised in

JAMIESON, FAUSSET, BROWN

so of the Holy Ghost. Love, too, shall be the keynote of the "new *song*" hereafter (Isa 35:10; Rev. 1:5; 14:3; 19:6). In the individual believer now, joy and love are here set forth in their *earlier* manifestations (Mark 4:28). **13. putteth forth**—rather, ripens, lit., "makes red" [MAURER]. The unripe figs, which grow in winter, begin to ripen in early spring, and in June are fully matured [WEISS]. **vines with the tender grape**—rather, "the vines *in flower*," lit., "a flower," in apposition with "vines" [MAURER]. The vine flowers were so sweet that they were often put, when dried, into new wine to give it flavor. Applicable to the first manifestations of Jesus Christ, "the true Vine," both to the Church and to individuals; as to Nathanael under *the fig tree* (John 1:48). **Arise . . .**—His call, described by the bride, ends as it began (vs. 10); it is a consistent whole; "love" from first to last (Isa. 52:1, 2; II Cor. 6:17, 18). "Come," in the close of Revelation 22:17, as at His earlier manifestation (Matt. 11:28). **14. dove**—here expressing endearment (Ps. 74:19). Doves are noted for *constant attachment;* emblems, also, in their soft, plaintive note, of *softened penitents* (Isa. 59:11; Ezek. 7:16); other points of likeness are their *beauty;* "their wings covered with silver and gold" (Ps. 68:13), typifying the change in the converted; the *dovelike spirit*, breathed into the saint by the Holy Ghost, whose emblem is the dove; *the messages of peace* from God to sinful men, as Noah's dove, with the olive branch (Gen. 8), intimated that the flood of wrath was past; *timidity*, fleeing with fear from sin and self to the cleft Rock of Ages (*Margin*, Isa. 26:4; Hos. 11:11); *gregarious*, flocking together to the kingdom of Jesus Christ (Isa. 60:8); *harmless simplicity* (Matt. 10:16). **clefts**—the refuge of doves from storm and heat (Jer. 48:28; see Jer. 49:16). GESENIUS translates the *Hebrew* from a different root, "the refuges." But see, for "clefts," Exodus 33:18-23. It is only when we are *in* Christ Jesus that our "voice is *sweet* (in prayer, ch. 4:3, 11; Matt. 10:20; Gal. 4:6, because it is *His* voice *in* us; also in speaking *of* Him, Mal. 3:16); and our countenance comely" (Exod. 34:29; Ps. 27:5; 71:3; Isa. 33:16; II Cor. 3:18). **stairs**—(Ezek. 38:29). *Margin*, a steep rock, broken into stairs or terraces. It is in "secret places" and rugged scenes that Jesus Christ woos the soul from the world to Himself (Mic. 2:10; 7:14). So Jacob amid the stones of Bethel (Gen. 28:11-19); Moses at Horeb (Exod. 3); so Elijah (I Kings 19:9-13); Jesus Christ with the three disciples on a "high mountain apart," at the transfiguration (Matt. 17:1); John in Patmos (Rev. 1). "Of the eight beatitudes, five have an afflicted condition for their subject. As long as the waters are on the earth, we dwell in the ark; but when the land is dry, the dove itself will be tempted to wander" [JEREMY TAYLOR]. Jesus Christ does not invite her to leave the rock, but *in it* (Himself), yet in holy freedom to lay aside the timorous spirit, look up boldly as accepted in Him, pray, praise, and confess Him (in contrast to her shrinking from being *looked at*, ch. 1:6), (Eph. 6:19; Heb. 13:15; I John 4:18); still, though trembling, the voice and countenance of the soul in Jesus Christ are pleasant to Him. The Church found no cleft in the Sinaitic legal rock, though good in itself, wherein to hide; but in Jesus Christ stricken by God for us, as the rock smitten by Moses (Num. 20:11), there is a hiding-place (Isa. 32:2). *She* praised His "voice" (vss. 8, 10); it is thus that her voice also, though tremulous, is "sweet" to Him here. **15.** Transition to the vineyard, often formed in "stairs" (vs. 14), or terraces, in which, amidst the vine leaves, foxes hid. **foxes**—generic term, including jackals. They eat only grapes, not the vine flowers; but they need to be driven out *in time* before the grape is ripe. She had failed in watchfulness before (ch. 1:6); now when converted, she is the more jealous of *subtle* sins (Ps. 139:23). In spiritual winter certain evils are frozen up, as well as good; in the spring of revivals these start up unperceived, crafty, false teachers, spiritual pride, uncharitableness, etc. (Ps. 19:12; Matt. 13:26; Luke 8:14; II Tim. 2:17; Heb. 12:15). "Little" sins are parents of the greatest (Eccles. 10:1; I Cor. 5:6). Historically, John the Baptist spared not the *foxlike* Herod (Luke 13:32), who gave vinelike promise of fruit af first (Mark 6:20), at the cost of his life; nor the viper-Sadducees, etc.; nor the varied subtle forms of sin (Luke 3:7-14). **16. mine . . . his**—rather, "is *for me . . . for Him*" (Hos. 3:3), where, as here, there is the assurance of indissoluble union, in spite of temporary absence. Next verse, entreating Him to return, shows that He has gone, perhaps through her want of guarding against the "little sins" (vs. 15). The order of the clauses is reversed in ch. 6:3, when she is riper in faith; there she rests more on *her being His;* here, on *His being hers;* and no doubt her sense of love to

ADAM CLARKE

JOSEPH PARKER:

Is it then all sunshine? Do we leave behind us all discipline? Let us read these words: "Take us the foxes, the little foxes, that spoil the vines: for our vines have tender grapes" (2:15). There is nothing fanciful in regarding these "foxes" and "little foxes" as representing spiritual enemies or difficulties peculiar to our situation and capacity. The little foxes spoil the vines, the grapes. What are these little foxes? Which of us is guilty of some great heresy? who can stand up and say he belongs to the party of the great and violent apostasy? who will rank himself with those who openly blaspheme against heaven? Not a man. Who will charge himself with glaring crimes, with obvious and intentional rebellion against God? We do no err in that direction. These would indeed be great foxes, great displays of depravity—a depravity that overleaps itself by its very extravagance and vulgarity. We need have little fear of ourselves along that line; we have lived too long and seen too much to commit ourselves to such gross profanity. But what of the little foxes—the irregularities, the nameless indulgences, the self-consideration, the endless omissions? Who makes some great speech infamous in its conception and its rhetoric? No man at all connected with the sanctuary of God. But what about the little bitter speeches that spoil family communion, the petty criticisms, the malignant, half-concealed allusions, the reminiscences that are all sting, the odd sentences that give the hearer heartache all day? and what of concealed selfishness—that worst kind of all, that gloves its hand, that cloaks its personality, that apes the attitude and speech of generosity; a calculated selfishness that touches and retires, that asks as if not asking, that claims as if not asserting, but persistently pursues its own policy and its own advantage? There, if the question be pressed severely, we shall fall at one stroke, and be taken captive instantly and completely.

Have we got rid of the larger evils? Then attention must be directed to what are known as minor evils—the little foxes, the little blotches upon the character, the small aberrations that require an eye of spiritual criticism to see that they are aberrations at all. We can draw a rough circle with a practiced hand, but lay the compass upon it, and then see how defective it is when brought under the judgment of a true geometry. So we may in life do many things tolerably well, wonderfully well, so well as to attract attention and elicit commendations, but when the compasses of the sanctuary are laid upon our circles, the best of them is but a rough polygon; it is no circle at all. Yet to the eye it looks quite right. But what is the eye of the body? What can it see? What can it judge? It is dependent upon atmosphere and distance, and at the very best it is a lame judge of straight lines or circular lines. We must be judged by the spirit of the sanctuary, by the genius of the altar, by the Holy Spirit, and then so judged there is fire enough in the criticism to burn us with the scorching of hell.—*The People's Bible*

16. *My beloved is mine.* The words of the bride on his entering: "I am your own; you are wholly mine."

MATTHEW HENRY

the gospel, all he has prepared in heaven, all is yours.
2. She comforts herself with the thoughts of the communications of his grace to his people: *He feeds among the lilies.* He *feeds* among believers, that is, he takes pleasure in them and their assemblies.

IV. The church's hope and expectation of Christ's coming. 1. She doubts not but that the *day will break* and the *shadows* will *flee away.* The gospel-day will dawn, and the shadows of the ceremonial law will flee away. This was the comfort of the Old Testament church. Or it may refer to the second coming of Christ, and the eternal happiness of the saints.

2. She begs the presence of her beloved, in the meantime, to support and comfort her: "*Turn, my beloved,* come and visit me, *be with me always to the end of the age.* Come over even *the mountains of division,* with some gracious anticipations of that light and love."

JAMIESON, FAUSSET, BROWN

Him is a pledge that she is His (John 14:21, 23; I Cor. 8:3); this is her consolation in His withdrawal now. **I am his**—by creation (Ps. 100:3), by redemption (John 17:10; Rom. 14:8; I Cor. 6:19). **feedeth**—as a "roe," or gazelle (vs. 17); instinct is sure to lead him back to his feeding-ground, where the lilies abound. So Jesus Christ, though now withdrawn, the bride feels sure will return to His favorite resting-place (ch. 7:10; Ps. 132:14). So hereafter (Rev. 21:3). Psalm 45, title, terms his lovely bride's "lilies" [HENGSTENBERG] pure and white, though among thorns (vs. 2). **17. Night** is the image of the present world (Rom. 13:12). "Behold men as if dwelling in subterranean cavern" [PLATO *Republic*, vii. 1]. **Until**—i.e., "Before that," etc. **break**—rather, "breathe"; referring to the refreshing breeze of dawn in the East; or to the air of *life,* which distinguishes morning from the deathlike stillness of night. MAURER takes this verse of the *approach of night,* when the breeze arises after the heat of day (cf. *Margin,* Gen. 3:8, with Gen. 18:1), and the "shadows" are lost in night (Ps. 102:11); thus our life will be the *day;* death, the *night* (John 9:4). The *English Version* better accords with (ch. 3:1). "By *night*" (Rom. 13:12). **turn**—to me. **Bether**—Mountains of Bithron, separated from the rest of Israel by the Jordan (II Sam. 2:29), not far from Bethabara, where John baptized and Jesus was first manifested. Rather, as *Margin,* "of divisions," and LXX, *mountains intersected* with deep gaps, hard to pass over, separating the bride and Jesus Christ. In ch. 8:14 the mountains are *of spices,* on which the roe feeds, not *of separation;* for at His first coming He had to overpass the gulf made by sin between Him and us (Zech. 4:6, 7); in His second, He will only have to come down from the fragrant hill above to take home His prepared bride. Historically, in the ministry of John the Baptist, Christ's call to the bride was not, as later (ch. 4:8), "Come *with* me," but "Come away," viz., to meet Me (vss. 2, 10, 13). Sitting in darkness (Matt. 4:16), she "waited" and "looked" eagerly for Him, the "great light" (Luke 1:79; 2:25, 38); at His rising, the shadows of the law (Col. 2:16, 17; Heb. 10:1) were to "flee away." So we wait for the second coming, when means of grace, so precious now, shall be superseded by the Sun of righteousness (I Cor. 13:10, 12; Rev. 21:22, 23). The Word is our light until then (II Pet. 1:19).

ADAM CLARKE

He feedeth among the lilies. The odor with which he is surrounded is as fine as if he passed the night among the sweetest-scented flowers.

17. *Until the day break.* Literally, "until the day breathe"; until the first dawn, which is usually accompanied with the most refreshing breezes. *The shadows flee away.* Referring to the evening or setting of the sun, at which all shadows vanish.

The mountains of Bether. Translated also "mountains of division," supposed to mean the mountains of Beth-horon.

MATTHEW HENRY — CHAPTER 3

Verses 1–5

It was hard to the Old Testament church to find Christ in the ceremonial law. Long was the consolation of Israel looked for before it came. At length Simeon had *him* in his arms *whom his soul loved.* It is applicable to the case of particular believers, who often walk in darkness, but those that seek Christ to the end shall find him at length.

I. How the spouse sought him in vain *upon her bed* (*v.* 1). She wanted the communion she used to have with him, as David when he *thirsted for God, for the living God.* She sought him, but she saw not her signs, and yet she sought them. She failed in her endeavour.

II. How she sought him in vain abroad, *v.* 2. And yet she is not driven off by the disappointment. She resolves, "*I will rise now;* I will not lie here if I cannot find my beloved here. *I will rise now* without delay, and seek him immediately, lest he withdraw further from me." Those that seek Christ must not startle at difficulties. "*I will rise, and go about the city,* the holy city, in the streets, and the broad-ways"; for she knew he was not to be found in any blind by-ways. We must seek in the city, in Jerusalem, which was a type of the gospel-church, in holy ordinances. She had a good purpose when she said, *I will arise now,* but the good performance was all in all. How heavy is the accent on this repeated complaint: *I sought him, but I found him not!*

JAMIESON, FAUSSET, BROWN — CHAPTER 3

Vss. 1-11. **1. By night**—lit., "By nights." Continuation of the longing for the dawn of the Messiah (ch. 2:17; Ps. 130:6; Mal. 4:2). The spiritual desertion here (ch. 2:17; 3:5) is not due to indifference, as in ch. 5:2-8. "As nights and dews are better for flowers than a continual sun, so Christ's absence (at times) giveth sap to humility, and putteth an edge on hunger, and furnisheth a fair field to faith to put forth itself" [RUTHERFORD]. Contrast ch. 1:13; Psalm 30:6, 7. **on . . . bed**—the secret of her failure (Isa. 64:7; Jer. 29:13; Amos 6:1, 4; Hos. 7:14). **loveth**—no want of sincerity, but of diligence, which she now makes up for by leaving her bed to seek Him (Ps. 22:2; 63:8; Isa. 26:9; John 20:17). Four times (vss. 1-4) she calls Jesus Christ, "Him whom my soul loveth," designating Him as *absent;* language of desire: "He loved me," would be language of *present* fruition (Rev. 1:5). In questioning the watchmen (vs. 3), she does not even name Him, so full is her heart of Him. Having found Him at dawn (for throughout *He* is the *morning*), she charges the daughters not to abridge by intrusion the period of His stay. Cf. as to the thoughtful seeking for Jesus Christ in the time of John the Baptist, in vain at first, but presently after successful (Luke 3:15-22; John 1:19-34). **found him not**—Oh, for such honest dealings with ourselves (Prov. 25:14; Jude 12)! **2.** Wholly awake for God (Luke 14:18-20; Eph. 5:14). "An honest resolution is often to (the doing of) duty, like a needle that draws the thread after it" [DURHAM]. Not a mere wish, that counts not the cost—to leave her easy bed, and wander in the dark night seeking Him (Prov. 13:4; Matt. 21:30; Luke 14:27-33). **the city**—Jerusalem, literally (Matt. 3:5; John 1:19), and spiritually the *Church* here (Heb. 12:22), in glory (Rev. 21:2). **broad ways**—open spaces at the gates of Eastern cities, where the public assembled for business. So, the assemblies of worshippers (ch. 8:2, 3; Prov. 1:20-23; Heb. 10:25). She had in her first awakening shrunk from them, seeking Jesus Christ alone; but she was desired to seek the footsteps of the flock (ch. 1:8), so now in her second trial she goes forth to them of herself. "The more the soul grows in

ADAM CLARKE — CHAPTER 3

1. *By night on my bed I sought him.* It appears that the bridegroom saw the bride only by night, that on the night referred to here he did not come as usual. The bride, troubled on the account, rose and sought him, inquired of the city guards, and continued to seek till at last she found him, and brought him to her apartment, vv. 2-4.

MATTHEW HENRY

III. How she enquired of the watchmen concerning him, *v.* 3. In the night the watchmen *go about the city,* for the preservation of its peace and safety; these met her in her walks, and she asked them if they could give her any tidings of her beloved. Gracious souls press through crowds of other delights in pursuit of Christ. *Saw you him whom my soul loveth?* We must search the scriptures, be much in prayer, keep close to ordinances, and all with this upon our heart, *Saw you him whom my soul loveth?* Those only who have seen Christ themselves are likely to direct others to a sight of him.

IV. How she found him at last, *v.* 4. She *passed from* the watchmen as soon as she perceived they could give her no tidings of her beloved. But soon after she parted from the watchmen she found him whom she sought. Those that continue seeking Christ shall find him at last, and when perhaps they were almost ready to despair of finding him. See Ps. xlii. 7, 8; lxxvii. 9, 10; Isa. liv. 7, 8.

V. How close she kept to him when she had found him. She is now as much in fear of losing him as before she was in care to find him. Those that hold Christ fast in the arms of faith and love shall *not let him go*; he will abide with them.

VI. How desirous she was to make others acquainted with him: "*I brought him to my mother's house,* that all my relations, all who are dear to me, might have the benefit of communion with him." Wherever we find Christ we must take him home with us to our houses, especially to our hearts. The church is our mother, and we should be concerned for her interests, that she may have Christ present with her.

VII. What care she was in that no disturbance might be given him (*v.* 5); she repeats the charge she had before given (*ch.* ii. 7) to the *daughters of Jerusalem* not to *stir up or awake her love.* Let all *clamour and bitterness be put* far *from you,* for that *grieves the Holy Spirit of God,* Eph. iv. 30, 31. Some make this to be Christ's charge not to disturb his church, nor trouble the minds of the disciples.

Verse 6

These are the words of the *daughters of Jerusalem,* to whom the charge was given, *v.* 5. They had looked shyly upon the bride because she was black (*ch.* i. 6); but now they admire her, and speak of her with great respect: *Who is this?* How beautiful she looks! Who would have expected such a person to *come out of the wilderness?* This is applicable to the Jewish church, when, after forty years' wandering in the wilderness, they came out of it, to take possession of the land of promise. Balaam said when he stood admiring them: *From the top of the rocks I see him. How goodly are thy tents, O Jacob!* Num. xxiii. 9; xxiv. 5. It is also applicable to the recovery of a gracious soul out of a state of desertion and despondency. She ascends *out of the wilderness,* the dry and barren land, *like pillars of smoke,* like a cloud of incense ascending from the altar. This intimates a fire of pious and devout affections in the soul. Christ's return to the soul gives life to its devotion, and its communion with God is most reviving when it ascends *out of a wilderness.* She is *perfumed with myrrh and frankincense.* She is replenished with the graces of God's Spirit, which are as sweet spices, or as the holy incense. *Who is this?* What a monument of mercy is this! The graces and comforts with which she is *perfumed* are called the *powders of the merchant,* for they are dear-bought, by our Lord Jesus, that blessed merchant, who took a long voyage, and was at vast expense, no less than that of his own blood, to purchase them for us.

Verses 7–11

The daughters of Jerusalem stood admiring the spouse and commending her, but she transfers all the glory to Christ, and directs them to look from her to him. Here he is three times called *Solomon.* It is Christ that is here meant, who is greater than Solomon, and of whom Solomon was an illustrious type for his wisdom and especially his building the temple.

Three things she admires:

I. The safety of his bed (*v.* 7): *Behold his bed,* even *Solomon's,* very rich and fine; for such *the curtains of Solomon* were. Christ's bed, though he had *not where to lay his head,* is better than Solomon's. The church is his bed, for he has said of it, *This is my rest for ever; here will I dwell.* The hearts of believers are his bed, for he lies all night between their breasts, Eph. iii. 17. That which she admires his bed for is

JAMIESON, FAUSSET, BROWN

grace, and the less it leans on ordinances, the more it prizes and profits by them" [MOODY STUART] (Ps. 73:16, 17). **found him not**—Nothing short of Jesus Christ can satisfy her (Job 23:8-10; Ps. 63:1, 2). **3. watchmen**—ministers (Isa. 62:6; Jer. 6:17; Ezek. 3:17; Heb. 13:17), fit persons to consult (Isa. 21:11; Mal. 2:7). **found me**—the general ministry of the Word "finds" individually souls in quest of Jesus Christ (Gen. 24:27, end of verse; Acts 16:14); whereas formalists remain unaffected. **4.** Jesus Christ is generally "found" near the watchmen and means of grace; but they are not Himself; the star that points to Bethlehem is not the Sun that has risen there; she hastens past the guideposts to the goal [MOODY STUART]. Not even angels could satisfy Mary, instead of Jesus Christ (John 20:11-16). **found him**—(Isa. 45:19; Hos. 6:1-3; Matt. 13:44-46). **held him . . .**—willing to be held; not willing, if not held (Gen. 32:26; Matt. 28:9; Luke 24:28, 29; Rev. 3:11). "As a little weeping child will hold its mother fast, not because it is stronger than she, but because her bowels constrain her not to leave it; so Jesus Christ yearning over the believer *cannot go,* because He *will* not" [DURHAM]. In ch. 1:4 it is He who leads the bride into His chambers; here it is she who leads Him into her mother's. There are times when the grace of Jesus Christ seems to draw us to Him; and others, when we with strong cries draw Him to us and ours. In the East one large apartment often serves for the whole family; so the bride here speaks of her mother's apartment and her own together. The mention of the "mother" excludes impropriety, and imparts the idea of heavenly love, pure as a sister's, while ardent as a bride's; hence the frequent title, "my sister—spouse." Our mother after the Spirit, is *the Church,* the new Jerusalem (John 3:5-8; Gal. 4:19, 26); for her we ought to pray continually (Eph. 3:14-19), also for the *national* Jerusalem (Isa. 62:6, 7; Rom. 10:1), also for the *human family,* which is our mother and kindred after the flesh; these our mother's children have evilly treated us (ch. 1:6); but, like our Father, we are to return good for evil (Matt. 5:44, 45), and so bring Jesus Christ home to them (I Pet. 2:12). **5.** So ch. 2:7; but *there* it was for the non-interruption of her own fellowship with Jesus Christ that she was anxious; *here* it is for the not grieving of the Holy Ghost, on the part of the daughters of Jerusalem. Jealously avoid levity, heedlessness, and offenses which would mar the gracious work begun in others (Matt. 18:7; Acts 2:42, 43; Eph. 4:30).

CANTICLE *III.*—Ch. 3:6-5:1.—THE BRIDEGROOM WITH THE BRIDE. Historically, the ministry of Jesus Christ on earth. **6.** New scene (vss. 6-11). The friends of the Bridegroom see a cortege approach. His palanquin and guard. **cometh out**—rather, "up from"; the wilderness was lower than Jerusalem [MAURER]. **pillars of smoke**—from the perfumes burned around Him and His bride. Image from Israel and the tabernacle (answering to "bed," vs. 7) marching through the desert with the pillar of smoke by day and fire by night (Exod. 14:20), and the pillars of smoke ascending from the altars of incense and of atonement; so Jesus Christ's righteousness, atonement, and ever-living intercession. Balaam, the last representative of patriarchism, was required to curse the Jewish Church, just as *it* afterwards would not succumb to Christianity without a struggle (Num. 22:41), but he had to bless in language like that here (Num. 24:5, 6). Angels too joyfully ask the same question, when Jesus Christ with the tabernacle of His body (answering to *His bed,* vs. 7; John 1:14, "dwelt," *Greek* "tabernacled," John 2:21) ascends into heaven (Ps. 24:8-10); also when they see His glorious bride with Him (Ps. 68:18; Rev. 7:13-17). Encouragement to her; amid the darkest trials (vs. 1), she is still on the road to glory (vs. 11) in a palanquin "paved with love" (vs. 10); she is now in soul spiritually "coming," exhaling the sweet graces, faith, love, joy, peace, prayer, and praise; (the fire is lighted *within,* the "smoke" is seen *without,* Acts 4:13); it is in the *desert* of trial (vss. 1-3) she gets them; she is the "merchant" buying from Jesus Christ without money or price (Isa. 55:1; Rev. 3:18); just as myrrh and frankincense are got, not in Egypt, but in the Arabian sands and the mountains of Palestine. Hereafter she shall "come" (vss. 6, 11) in a glorified body, too (Phil. 3:21). Historically, Jesus Christ returning from the wilderness, full of the Holy Ghost (Luke 4:1, 14). The same, "Who is this," etc. (Isa. 63:1, 5). **7.** In vs. 6 the *wilderness* character of the Church is portrayed; in vss. 7, 8, its *militant* aspect. In vs. 9, 10, Jesus Christ is seen dwelling in believers, who are His "chariot" and "body." In vs. 11, the consummation in glory. **bed**—palanquin. His body, lit., guarded by a definite number of angels, *threescore,*

ADAM CLARKE

4. *Into my mother's house.* The women in the East have all separate apartments, into which no person ever attempts to enter except the husband. We find Isaac bringing Rebecca into his mother's tent, when he made her his wife, Gen. xxiv. 67.

5. *I charge you.* The same adjuration as before, chap. ii. 7.

F. C. COOK:

3:6—5:2. The principal and central action of the Song; the bride's entry into the city of David, and her marriage there with the king. Jewish interpreters regard this part of the poem as symbolizing the "first" entrance of the Church of the Old Testament into the land of promise, and her spiritual espousals, and communion with the King of kings, through the erection of Solomon's Temple and the institution of its acceptable worship. Christian Fathers, in a like spirit, make most things here refer to the espousals of the Church with Christ in the Passion and Resurrection, or the communion of Christian souls with Him in meditation thereon.

6–11. Two or more citizens of Jerusalem, or the Chorus of youths, companions of the bridegroom, describe the magnificent appearance of the bride borne in a royal litter, and then that of the king in festive joy wearing a nuptial crown.

6. "Wilderness" is here pasture land in contrast with the cultivated districts and garden enclosures round the city. Cp. Jer. 23:10; Joel 2:22; Isa. 42:11; Ps. 65:12.

"Pillars of smoke." Here an image of delight and pleasure. Frankincense and other perfumes are burned in such abundance round the bridal equipage that the whole procession appears from the distance to be one of moving wreaths and columns of smoke.

"All powders of the merchant." Every kind of spice forming an article of commerce.

7. "Bed." Probably the royal litter or palanquin in which the bride is borne, surrounded by his own bodyguard consisting of "sixty mighties of the mighty men of Israel."

—*Barnes' Notes*

MATTHEW HENRY

the guard that surrounded it. Those that rest in Christ not only dwell at ease (many do so who yet are in the greatest danger) but they dwell in safety. This bed had *threescore valiant men about it*, as yeoman of the guard, well armed: *They all hold swords*, and know how to hold them; they are *expert in war.* They are in a posture of defence, *every man* with *his sword upon his thigh* and his hand upon his sword, ready to draw upon the first alarm, and this *because of fear in the night*, and the apprehension which the spouse may have of danger. These guards are set for her satisfaction, that she may be *quiet from the fear of evil*, which believers themselves are subject to, when they are under a cloud as to their spiritual state. Christ himself was under the special protection of his Father; he had legions of angels at his command. The church is well guarded; more are with her than against her. All the attributes of God are engaged for the safety of believers; his peace protects those in whom it rules (Phil. iv. 7). Our danger is from *the rulers of the darkness of this world*, but we are safe in the *armour of light*.

II. The splendour of his chariot, *v.* 9, 10. This chariot was of Solomon's own contriving and making, the materials very rich, *silver*, and *gold*, and *cedar*, and *purple*. Some by this *chariot* (the word is nowhere else used in scripture) understand the human nature of Christ, in which the divine nature rode as in an open chariot. It was a divine workmanship (*A body hast thou prepared me*); the structure was very fine, but that which was at the bottom of it was love, pure love to the children of men. Others make it to represent the everlasting gospel, in which, as in an open chariot, Christ shows himself. *The pillars* are of *silver*, for the words of the Lord are *as silver tried* (Ps. xii. 6). It is hung with *purple*, a princely colour; all the adornings of it are dyed in the precious blood of Christ. But that which completes the glory of it is *love*; *It is paved with love*, it is lined with love, *love of the daughters of Jerusalem*, a holy *love*. Silver is better than cedar, gold than silver, but love is better than gold, better than all, and it is put last, for nothing can be better than that. The gospel is all *love*.

III. The lustre of his royal person, when he appears in his greatest pomp, *v.* 11. The call that is given to the *daughters of Zion*: *Go forth, and behold* him. Christ, in his gospel, manifests himself. Let each of us add to the number of those that give honour to him. Look with pleasure upon Christ in his glory. Look upon him with an eye of faith, with a fixed eye. Take notice of his *crown*, either the crown of gold, adorned with jewels, which he wore on his coronation-day, or the garland or crown of flowers and green tied with ribbons which his mother made for him, to adorn the solemnity of his nuptials. Applying this to Christ: *Go forth*, and see king Jesus, *with the crown wherewith his* Father *crowned him*, when he declared him his *beloved Son, in whom* he was *well-pleased*, when he *set him as King upon his holy hill of Zion*. Some apply it to the *crown of thorns* with which *his mother*, the Jewish church, *crowned him* on the day of his death, which was *the day of his espousals* to his church, when he *loved it, and gave himself for it* (Eph. v. 25). It seems especially to mean the honour done him by his church, as his mother, and by all true believers. When believers accept of him as theirs, and join themselves to him in an everlasting covenant, it is his coronation-day in their souls. Before conversion they were crowning themselves, but then they begin to crown Christ, and continue to do so from that day forward. It is *the day of his espousals*, in which he betroths them to him for ever in loving-kindness and in mercies. It is *the day of the gladness of his heart*; he is pleased with the honour that his people do him.

CHAPTER 4

Verses 1–7

I. A particular account of the beauties of the church, and of gracious souls on whom the image of God is renewed, consisting *in the beauty of holiness*. Those that honour Christ he will honour, 1 Sam. ii. 30.

1. He does not flatter her, but encourages her under her present dejections. She was espoused to him, and that made her beautiful.

JAMIESON, FAUSSET, BROWN

or sixty (Matt. 26:53), from the wilderness (Matthew 4:1, 11), and continually (Luke 2:13; 22:43; Acts 1:10, 11); just as 600,000 of Israel guarded the Lord's tabernacle (Num. 2:17-32), one for every 10,000. In contrast to the "bed of sloth" (vs. 1). **valiant**—(Josh. 5:13, 14.) Angels guarding His *tomb* used like words (Mark 16:6). **of Israel**—true subjects, not mercenaries. **8. hold**—not actually grasping them, but having them girt on the thigh ready for use, like their Lord (Ps. 45:3). So believers too are guarded by angels (Ps. 91:11; Heb. 1:14), and they themselves need "every man" (Neh. 4:18) to be armed (Ps. 144:1, 2; II Cor. 10:4; Eph. 6:12, 17; I Tim. 6:12), and "expert" (II Cor. 2:11). **because of fear in the night**—Arab marauders often turn a wedding into mourning by a night attack. So the bridal procession of saints in the night of this wilderness is the chief object of Satan's assault. **9. chariot**—more elaborately made than the "bed" or travelling litter (vs. 7), from a *Hebrew* root, "to elaborate" [EWALD]. So the temple of "cedar of Lebanon," as compared with the temporary tabernacle of shittim wood (II Sam. 7:2, 6, 7; I Kings 5: 14; 6:15-18). Jesus Christ's body is the antitype, "made" by the Father for Him (I Cor. 1:30; Heb. 10:5), the wood answering to His human nature, the gold, His divine; the two being but one Christ. 10. pillars—supporting the canopy at the four corners; curtains at the side protect the person within from the sun. Pillars with silver sockets supported the veil that enclosed the holy of holies; emblem of Jesus Christ's *strength* (I Kings 7:21), *Margin*, "silver," emblem of His *purity* (Ps. 12:6); so the saints hereafter (Rev. 3:12). **bottom**—rather, *the back for resting or reclining on* (*Vulgate* and LXX) [MAURER]. So the floor and mercy seat, the *resting-place* of God (Ps. 132:14) in the temple, was gold (I Kings 6:30). covering—rather, *seat* as in Leviticus 15:9. Hereafter the saints shall share His *seat* (Rev. 3:21). **purple**—the veil of the holiest, partly purple, and the *purple* robe put on Jesus Christ, accord with *English Version*, *"covering."* "Purple" (including scarlet and crimson) is the emblem of *royalty*, and of *His blood;* typified by the passover lamb's blood, and the wine when the twelve *sat* or *reclined* at the Lord's table. **paved**—tesselated, like mosaic pavement, with the various acts and promises of love of Father, Son, and Holy Ghost (Zeph. 3: 17; I John 4:8, 16), in contrast with the tables of stone in the "midst" of the ark, covered with writings of stern command (cf. John 19:13); *this* is all grace and love to believers, who answer to "the daughters of Jerusalem" (John 1:17). The exterior silver and gold, cedar, purple, and guards, may deter, but when the bride enters *within*, she rests on a pavement of love. **11. Go forth**—(Matt. 25:6). **daughters of Zion**—spirits of saints, and angels (Isa. 61:10; Zech. 9:9). **crown**—nuptial (Ezek. 16:8-12), (the Hebrews wore costly crowns or chaplets at weddings) (Ps. 2:6; Rev. 19:12). The crown of thorns was once His nuptial chaplet, His blood the wedding wine-cup (John 19:5). "His mother," that so crowned Him, is the *human race,* for He is "the Son of *man,*" not merely the son of Mary. The same mother reconciled to Him (Matt. 12:50), as the Church, travails in birth for souls, which she presents to Him as a crown (Phil. 4:1; Rev. 4:10). Not being ashamed to call the children brethren (Heb. 2:11-14), He calls *their* mother *His* mother (Ps. 22:9; Rom. 8:29; Rev. 12:1, 2). **behold**—(II Thess. 1:10.) **day of his espousals**—chiefly final marriage, when the number of the elect is complete (Rev. 6:11). **gladness**—(Ps. 45:15; Isa. 62:5; Rev. 19:7). MOODY STUART observes as to this Canticle (ch. 3:6-5:1), the center of the Book, these characteristics: (1) The bridegroom takes the chief part, whereas elsewhere the bride is the chief speaker. (2) Elsewhere He is either "King" or "Solomon"; here He is twice called "King Solomon." The bride is six times here called the "spouse"; never so before or after; also "sister" four times, and, except in the first verse of the next Canticle, nowhere else. (3) He and she are never separate; no absence, no complaint, which abound elsewhere, are in this Canticle.

CHAPTER 4

Vss. 1-16. 1. Contrast with the bride's state by nature (Isa. 1:6) *her state by grace* (vss. 1-7), "perfect through His comeliness put upon her" (Ezek. 16: 14; John 15:3). The praise of Jesus Christ, unlike that of the world, hurts not, but edifies; as His, not ours, is the glory (John 5:44; Rev. 4:10, 11). Seven features of beauty are specified (vss. 1-5) ("lips" and "speech" are but one feature, vs. 3), the number for

ADAM CLARKE

7. *Threescore valiant men.* These were the guards about the pavilion of the bridegroom, who were placed there because of fear in the night. The security and state of the prince required such a guard as this, and the passage is to be literally understood.

9. *Of the wood of Lebanon.* Of the cedar that grew on that mount. It is very likely that a "nuptial bed," not a *chariot,* is intended by the original word.

10. *The pillars . . . of silver.* The bedposts were made of silver. *The bottom thereof of gold.* This may refer to cords made of gold thread, or to the mattress, which was made of cloth ornamented with gold. *The covering . . . of purple.* Most probably the canopy.

The midst . . . paved with love. The counterpane, superb piece of embroidery, wrought by some of the noble maids of Jerusalem, and, as a proof of their affection, respect, and love, presented to the bride and bridegroom on their nuptial day.

CHAPTER 4

MATTHEW HENRY

2. As to the representation here made of the beauty of the church, the images are certainly very bright, the shades strong, and the comparisons bold. Seven particulars are specified, a number of perfection, for the church is enriched with manifold graces by *the seven spirits* that *are before the throne*, Rev. i. 4; 1 Cor. i. 5, 7.

(1) Her *eyes*. A good eye contributes much to beauty: *Thou hast doves' eyes*, clear and chaste, and often cast up towards heaven. Wisdom and knowledge are the eyes of the new man; they must be clear, but not haughty, *not exercised in things too high for us*. When our aims and intentions are sincere and honest, then we have *doves' eyes*. The *doves' eyes* are *within the locks*, which are as a shade upon them. They cannot fully see. As long as we are here in this world we *know but in part*.

(2) Her *hair*; it is compared to *a flock of goats*, which looked white, and were, on the top of the mountains, like a fine head of hair. Some by the *hair* here understand the outward conversation of a believer, which ought to be comely, and decent, and agreeable to the holiness of the heart.

(3) Her *teeth*, *v.* 2. Ministers are the church's teeth; like nurses, they chew the meat for the babes of Christ. These are here compared to *a flock of sheep*. Christ called his disciples and ministers a *little flock*. It is the praise of teeth to be *even*, to be white, and kept clean, *like sheep from the washing*.

(4) Her *lips*; these are compared to *a thread of scarlet*, *v.* 3. Red lips are comely, and a sign of health, as the paleness of the lips is a sign of faintness and weakness. When we praise God with *our lips*, *and with the mouth make confession* of him *to salvation*, then they are as *a thread of scarlet*. All our good works and good words must be *washed in the blood of Christ*, dyed like the *scarlet thread*, and then they are acceptable to God.

(5) Her *temples*, or cheeks, which are here compared to *a piece of a pomegranate*, a fruit which, when cut in two, has rich veins or specks in it, like a blush in the face. Humility and modesty, blushing at the remembrance of sin and in a sense of our unworthiness of the honour put upon us, will beautify us very much in the eyes of Christ.

(6) Her *neck*; this is here compared to *the tower of David*, *v.* 4. This is generally applied to the grace of faith, by which we are united to Christ, as the body is united to the head by the neck; this *is like the tower of David*, furnishing us with weapons of war, especially *bucklers* and *shields*, as the soldiers were supplied with them out of that tower, for *faith* is our *shield* (Eph. vi. 16): those that have it never want a *buckler*, for God will compass them *with his favour as with a shield*.

(7) Her *breasts*; these *are like two young roes that are twins*, *v.* 5. The church's breasts are the *breasts of her consolation* (Isa. lxvi. 11). Some apply these to the two Testaments; others to the two sacraments, the seals of the covenant of grace; others to ministers, who are to be spiritual nurses to the children of God and to give out to them the *sincere milk of the word*, *that they may grow thereby*, and, in order to that, are themselves to *feed among the lilies* where Christ feeds (*ch.* ii. 16).

II. The bridegroom's resolution hereupon to retire *to the mountain of myrrh* (*v.* 6) and there to make his residence. This *mountain of myrrh* is supposed to signify Mount Moriah, on which the temple was built, where incense was daily burnt to the honour of God. Christ's parting promise to his disciples, as the representatives of the church, answers to this: *Lo, I am with you always, even to the end of the world.* Where the ordinances of God are duly administered there Christ will be. The holy hill (as some observe) is here called both a *mountain of myrrh*, which is bitter, and a *hill of frankincense*, which is sweet, for there we have occasion both to mourn and rejoice; repentance is a bitter sweet. But in heaven it will be all frankincense, and no myrrh.

JAMIESON, FAUSSET, BROWN

perfection. To each of these is attached a comparison from nature: the resemblances consist not so much in outward likeness, as in the combined sensations of delight produced by contemplating these natural objects. **doves**—the large melting eye of the Syrian dove appears especially beautiful amid the foliage of its native groves: so the bride's "eyes within her locks" (Luke 7:44). MAURER for "locks," has "veil"; but locks suit the connection better: so the *Hebrew* is translated (Isa. 47:2). The dove was the only bird counted "clean" for sacrifice. Once the heart was "the cage of every unclean and hateful bird." Grace makes the change. **eyes**—(Matt. 6: 22; Eph. 1:18; contrast Matt. 5:28; Eph. 4:18; I John 2:16.) Chaste and guileless (Matt. 10:16, *Margin;* John 1:47). John the Baptist, historically, was the "turtledove" (ch. 2:12), with eye directed to the coming Bridegroom: his Nazarite unshorn hair answers to "locks" (John 1:29, 36). **hair . . . goats**—The hair of goats in the East is fine like silk. As long hair is her glory, and marks her subjection to man (I Cor. 11:6-15), so the Nazarite's hair marked his subjection and separation unto God. (Cf. 16:17, with II Cor. 6:17; Titus 2:14; I Pet. 2:9.) Jesus Christ cares for the minutest concerns of His saints (Matt. 10:30). **appear from**—lit., "*that lie down* from"; lying along the hillside, they seem to *hang from* it: a picture of the bride's hanging tresses. **Gilead**—beyond Jordan: there stood "the heap of witness" (Gen. 31:48). **2. even shorn**—is translated (I Kings 6:25), "of one size"; so the point of comparison to *teeth* is their *symmetry* of form; as in "came up from the washing," the *spotless whiteness;* and in "twins," the *exact correspondence of the upper and lower teeth:* and in "none barren," *none wanting,* none without its fellow. Faith is the tooth with which we eat the living bread (John 6:35, 54). Contrast the teeth of sinners (Ps. 57:4; Prov. 30:14); also their end (Ps. 3:7; (Matt. 25:30). Faith leads the flock to the washing (Zech. 13:1; I Cor. 6:11; Titus 3:5). **none . . . barren**—(II Pet. 1:8.) He who is begotten of God begets instrumentally other sons of God. **3. thread**—like a delicate fillet. Not thick and white as the leper's lips (type of sin), which were therefore to be "covered," as "unclean" (Lev. 13:45). **scarlet**—The blood of Jesus Christ (Isa. 6:5-9) cleanses the leprosy, and unseals the lips (Isa. 57:19; Hos. 14:2; Heb. 13:15). Rahab's scarlet thread was a type of it (Josh. 2:18). **speech**—not a separate feature from the *lips* (Zeph. 3:9; Col. 4:6). Contrast "uncircumcised lips" (Exod. 6:12). MAURER and BURROWES translate, "thy mouth." **temples**—rather, *the upper part of the cheek* next the temples: the seat of shamefacedness; so, "within thy locks," no display (I Cor. 11:5, 6, 15). Mark of true penitence (Ezra 9:6; Ezek. 16:63). Contrast Jer. 3:3; Ezek. 3:7. **pomegranate**—When cut, it displays in rows seeds pellucid, like crystal, tinged with red. Her modesty is not on the surface, but within, which Jesus Christ can see into. **4. neck**—stately: in beautiful contrast to the blushing temples (vs. 3); not "stiff" (Isa. 48:4; Acts 7:51), as that of unbroken nature; nor "stretched forth" wantonly (Isa. 3:16); nor burdened with the legal yoke (Lam. 1:14; Acts 15:10); but erect in gospel freedom (Isa. 52:2). **tower of David**—probably on Zion. He was a man of war, preparatory to the reign of Solomon, the king of peace. So warfare in the case of Jesus Christ and His saints precedes the coming rest. Each soul won from Satan by Him is a trophy gracing the bride (Luke 11:22); (each hangs on Him, Isa. 22:23, 24); also each victory of her faith. As shields adorn a temple's walls (Ezek. 27:11), so necklaces hang on the bride's neck (Judg. 5:30; I Kings 10:16). **5. breasts**—The bust is left open in Eastern dress. The breastplate of the high priest was made of "two" pieces, folded one on the other, in which were the Urim and Thummim (*lights* and *perfection*). "Faith and love" are the double breastplate (I Thess. 5:8), answering to "hearing the word" and "keeping it," in a similar connection with breasts (Luke 12:27, 28). **roes**—He reciprocates her praise (ch. 2:9). Emblem of *love* and *satisfaction* (Prov. 5:19). **feed**—(Ps. 23:2.) **among the lilies**—shrinking from thorns of strife, worldliness, and ungodliness (II Sam. 23:6; Matt. 13:7). Roes feed *among,* not *on* the lilies: where these grow, there is moisture producing green pasturage. The lilies represent her white dress (Ps. 45:14; Rev. 19:8). **6.** Historically, *the hill of frankincense* is Calvary, where, "through the eternal Spirit He offered Himself"; the mountain of myrrh is His embalmment (John 19:39) till the resurrection "day-break." The 3d Canticle occupies the one cloudless day of His presence on earth, beginning from the night (ch. 2: 17) and ending with the night of His departure (ch. 4:6). His promise is almost exactly in the words of

ADAM CLARKE

1. *As a flock of goats.* Because it was black and sleek, as the hair of the goats of Arabia and Palestine is known to be. The mountains of Gilead were beyond Jordan.

2. *Thy teeth are like a flock.* This comparison appears to be founded on the evenness, neatness, and whiteness of the newly shorn and newly washed sheep.

3. *Thy lips are like a thread of scarlet.* Both lips and cheeks were ruddy. "Like the section of a pomegranate," that side cut off on which is the finest blush. She had beautiful hair, beautiful eyes, beautiful cheeks and lips, and a most pleasing and dulcet voice.

JOHN GILL:

Verse 4. "Thy neck is like the tower of David, builded for an armory." This was either the stronghold of Zion; or some tower erected by David for an armory, wherein his worthies or mighty men hung up their shields; Mr. Sandys says it stood aloft in the utmost angle of a mountain, whose ruins are yet extant: though the neck is compared to this, not for its height, seeing a high and stretched out neck is a token of pride and haughtiness with the Jews (Isa. 3:16; Ps. 74:5); and so the phrase is used in Latin writers; but for its being ornamented with spoils hung up in it, as golden shields after mentioned, as the neck is with pearls, jewels, and chains of gold (ch. 1:10). The word for "armory" is from *alaph,* to teach; not as being a pattern to teach artificers, as Jarchi; nor to show passengers their way, as R. Jonah and others, who think this tower was built as a *pharus,* for such a purpose; but it was as an arsenal, in which young learners of the art of war laid up their weapons, as well as what were taken from an enemy; or what were made and laid up here, as a store in time of need.—*Gill's Commentary*

MATTHEW HENRY

III. His repeated commendation of the beauty of his spouse (*v.* 7): *Thou art all fair, my love.* The particulars, as of those of the creation, he pronounces *all very good.* There is nothing amiss in thee, and thou hast all beauties in thee; thou art *sanctified wholly* in every part; *all things have become new* (2 Cor. v. 17); there is not only a new face and a new name, but a new man, a new nature.

Verses 8–14

These are still the words of Christ to his church, expressing his affection to her.

I. The endearing names and titles by which he calls her, to express his love to her, to assure her of it, and to engage and excite her love to him. Twice here he calls her *My spouse* (*v.* 8, 11) and three times *My sister, my spouse, v.* 9, 10, 12. Mention was made (*ch.* iii. 11) of *the day of his espousals,* and, after that, she is called his *spouse,* not before. There is a marriage-covenant between Christ and his church, between Christ and every true believer. Christ calls his church his *spouse.* Because no one relation among men is sufficient to set forth Christ's love to his church, and to show that all this must be understood spiritually, he owns her in two relations, *My sister, my spouse.* His calling her *sister* is grounded upon his taking our nature upon him in his incarnation.

II. The gracious call he gives her to come along with him as a faithful bride. 1. All that have by faith come to Christ must come with Christ, in holy obedience to him and compliance with him. Being joined to him, we must walk with him. This is his command to us daily: "*Come with me, my spouse;* come with me to God as a Father; come with me onward, heavenward; *come with me from Lebanon, from the top of Amana, from the lions' dens.*" These mountains are to be considered, (1) As seemingly delightful places. Lebanon is called *that goodly mountain,* Deut. iii. 25. We read of the pleasant *dew of Hermon* (Ps. cxxxiii. 3) and the *joy of Hermon* (Ps. lxxxix. 12). This is Christ's call to his spouse to come off from the world, to sit loose to all the delights of sense. They must *come away* and live above the tops of the highest hills on earth, that they may have *their conversation in heaven. From the tops of Shenir and Hermon,* which were on the other side Jordan, as from Pisgah, they could see the land of Canaan; from this world we must look forward to the better country. (2) These hills indeed are pleasant enough, but there are in them *lions' dens;* they are *mountains of the leopards,* mountains of prey, though they seem *glorious and excellent,* Ps. lxxvi. 4. On the tops of these mountains there are many dangerous temptations. *Come with me from* the temples of idolaters, and the societies of wicked people; *come out from among them, and be you separate. Come from* under the dominion of your own lusts, which are as *lions* and *leopards.*

2. It may be taken as a promise: Thou shalt *come with me from Lebanon, from the lions' dens;* that is, "Many shall be brought home to me, as living members of the church, from every point, from Lebanon in the north, Amana in the west, Hermon in the east, Shenir in the south, from all parts, to *sit down with Abraham, Isaac and Jacob,* Matt. viii. 11. See Isa. xlix. 11, 12.

III. The great delight Christ takes in his church. 1. No expressions of love can be more passionate than these here, in which Christ manifests his affection to his church; and yet that great proof of his love, his dying for it, goes far beyond them all. A spouse so dearly bought and paid for could not but be dearly loved. *Thou hast ravished my heart;* the word is used only here. *Thou hast hearted me,* or *Thou hast unhearted me.* New words are coined to express the inexpressibleness of Christ's surprising love to his church. *Thou hast ravished my heart with one of thy eyes,* those *doves' eyes,* clear and chaste (which were commended, *v.* 1). The ornaments she has from him, that is, the obedience she yields to him, for that is the *chain of her neck,* the graces that enrich her soul. Having shaken off the *bands of our neck,* by which we were tied to this world (Isa. lii. 2), we are bound with the *cords of love,* as *chains of gold,* to Jesus Christ, and our necks are brought under his sweet and easy yoke. *How fair is thy love!* how beautiful is it! How well does it become a believer thus to love Christ. Nothing recommends us to Christ as this does. The ointments, the odours wherewith she is perfumed, that is to say, the gifts and graces of the Spirit, her good works, are *an odour of a sweet smell, a sacrifice acceptable, well-pleasing to God,* Phil. iv. 18. Love and obedience to God are more pleasing to Christ than sacrifice or incense. *The smell of her garments* too, the visible profession she makes of religion, and relation to Christ, is as *the smell of Lebanon.* Likewise, her words are sweet (*v.* 11):

JAMIESON, FAUSSET, BROWN

her prayer (ch. 2:17), (the same Holy Ghost breathing in Jesus Christ and His praying people), with the difference that she then looked for His visible coming. He now tells her that when He shall have gone from sight, He still is to be met with spiritually in prayer (Ps. 68:16; Matt. 28:20), until the everlasting day break, when we shall see face to face (I Cor. 13:10, 12). **7.** Assurance that He is going from her in love, not in displeasure (John 16:6, 7). **all fair**—still stronger than ch. 1:15; vs. 1. **no spot**—our privilege (Eph. 5:27; Col. 2:10); our duty (II Cor. 6:17; Jude 23; Jas. 1:27).

9. sister . . . spouse—This title is here first used, as He is soon about to institute the Supper, the pledge of the nuptial union. By the term "sister," carnal ideas are excluded; the ardor of a spouse's love is combined with the purity of a sister's (Isa. 54:5; cf. Mark 3:35).

8. Invitation to her to leave the border mountains (the highest worldly elevation) between the hostile lands north of Palestine and the Promised Land (Ps. 45:10; Phil. 3:13). **Amana**—south of Anti-Libanus; the river Abana, or Amana, was near Damascus (II Kings 5:12). **Shenir**-The whole mountain was called *Hermon;* the part held by the Sidonians was called *Sirion;* the part held by the Amorites, *Shenir* (Deut. 3:9). Infested by the devouring lion and the stealthy and swift leopard (Ps. 76:4; Eph. 6:11; I Pet. 5:8). Contrasted with the mountain of myrrh, etc. (vs. 6; Isa. 2:2); the good land (Isa. 35:9). **with me**—twice repeated emphatically. The presence of Jesus Christ makes up for the absence of all besides (Luke 18:29, 30; II Cor. 6:10). Moses was permitted to see Canaan from Pisgah; Peter, James, and John had a foretaste of glory on the mount of transfiguration.

one—Even *one* look is enough to secure His love (Zech. 12: 10; Luke 23:40-43). Not merely the Church collectively, but each *one* member of it (Matt. 18:10, 14; Luke 15:7, 24, 32). **chain**—necklace (Isa. 62:3; Mal. 3:17), answering to the "shields" hanging in the tower of David (vs. 4). Cf. the "ornament" (I Pet. 3:4); "chains" (Prov. 1:9; 3:22). **10. love**—*Hebrew,* "loves"; manifold tokens of thy love. **much better**—answering to her "better" (ch. 1:2), but with *increased* force. An Amœbean pastoral character pervades the Song, like the classic Amœbean idylls and eclogues. **wine**—The love of His saints is a more reviving cordial to Him than wine; e.g., at the feast in Simon's house (Luke 7:36, 47; John 4:32; cf. Zech. 10:7). **smell of . . . ointments than all spices**—answering to her praise (ch. 1:3) with increased force. Fragrant, as being fruits of *His* Spirit in us (Gal. 5:22). **11. drop**—always ready to fall, being full of honey, though not always (Prov. 10:19) actually *dropping* (ch. 5:13; Deut. 32: 2; Matt. 12:34). **honeycomb**—(Prov. 5:3; 16:24). **under thy tongue**—not always *on,* but *under,* the tongue, ready to fall (Ps. 55:21). Contrast her former state (Ps. 140:3; Rom. 3:13). "Honey and milk" were the glory of the good land. The change is illustrated in the penitent thief. Contrast Matthew 27:44 with Luke 23:39, etc. It was literally with "one" eye, a sidelong glance of love "better than wine," that he refreshed Jesus Christ (vss. 9, 10). "To-day shalt thou be *with Me* (cf. vs. 8) in Paradise" (vs. 12), is the only joyous sentence of His seven utterances on the cross. **smell of . . . garments**—which are often perfumed in the East (Ps. 45:8). The perfume comes from Him on us (Ps. 133:2). We draw nigh to God in the perfumed garment of our elder brother (Gen. 27:27; see Jude 23). **Lebanon**—abounding in odoriferous trees (Hos. 14: 5-7).

ADAM CLARKE

JOSEPH PARKER:

Verse 8. What is the idea? The text is orientally picturesque, but what is the spiritual notion of it which can be carried through all the ages of human spiritual civilization? The idea is that the native home of the bride is situated in Northern Palestine, here set forth in image by four peaks or hills. Lebanon represents the western range which overlooks the Mediterranean, and is here used as representing the whole mountain system, where wild beasts lodge and roam. The whole idea is that the Shulamite Virgin who is sought as a bride lives in high, craggy, cavernous regions—amid inhospitable scenes—and close to the mountain haunts of beasts of prey. Such words as Amana, Shenir, Hermon, and Lebanon are used to typify a region of mountain, rock, fastness, forest, and jungle. There the fair Shulamite has her native home. That is one side of the picture. On the other side is the king, who lives in Jerusalem, the royal city, the city of peace, far away from the haunts of leopards; and he goes forth to invite the bride to leave the crag and the den, the forest and the danger, saying: Come to Jerusalem, to the center of civilization, to the home of beauty, to the king's palace, to the splendid and inviolable home,—no lion shall be there, nor any ravenous beast go up thereon—come, O my dove, that art in the clefts of the rock, whose lips drop as the honeycomb, and the smell of whose garments is as the smell of Lebanon,—come! That is the attitude of the figures in this oriental word picture. This is the action of Christ in relation to the Church, which is his Bride; and the picture in every line corresponds with the ministry of Christ as set forth in the New Testament. This is the center of the song—the Shulamite far away on the crags and in the desert places of her native land, and the king sighing for her, calling her to come away from the desert, and all its inhospitableness, to the city and all its abundance of peace and joy.

—The People's Bible

9. *Thou hast ravished my heart. Libbabtini,* "Thou hast hearted me," i.e., taken away my heart. *With one of thine eyes. Beachad meeynayich.* "Even one of your eyes, or one glance of your eyes, has been sufficient to deprive me of all power; it has completely overcome me."

MATTHEW HENRY

Thy lips O my spouse! drop as the honeycomb. If what God speaks to us be *sweeter* to us *than the honey and the honeycomb* (Ps. xix. 10), what we say to him in prayer and praise shall also be pleasing to him. In the word of God there is sweet and wholesome nourishment, milk for babies, honey for those that are grown up.

2. The church is fitly compared to a *garden*, to a garden which, as was usual, had *a fountain in it* (*v.* 12–14). This garden is *a garden enclosed*, a paradise separated from the common earth. It is appropriated to God; he has *set it apart for himself*; Israel is God's portion. It is enclosed for secrecy; the saints are God's hidden ones. Christ walks in his garden unseen. It is enclosed for safety; a hedge of protection is made about it, which all the powers of darkness cannot find. It has a spring in it, and a fountain, but it is *a spring shut up* and *a fountain sealed*, that it may not by any injurious hand he muddied or polluted. The souls of believers are as *gardens enclosed*; grace in them is as *a spring shut up* there in *the hidden man of the heart*, where the water that Christ gives is *a well of living water*, John iv. 14; vii. 38. The Old Testament church was *a garden enclosed* by the partition wall of the ceremonial law. The Bible was then *a spring shut up* and *a fountain sealed*; it was confined to one nation; but now the wall of separation is removed, the gospel preached to every nation, and *in Jesus Christ there is neither Greek nor Jew. Thy plants*, or plantations, *are an orchard of pomegranates with pleasant fruits, v.* 13. Here are *fruits, pleasant fruits, all trees of frankincense*, and *all the chief spices, v.* 14. Here is great plenty of fruits, the best of the kind. Their *chief spices* were much more valuable than the choicest of our flowers. Saints in the church, and graces in the saints, are very fitly compared to these *fruits and spices*; for *the trees of righteousness* are the *planting of the Lord* (Isa. lxi. 3). Saints are the blessings of this earth. They are permanent, and will be preserved to good purpose, when flowers are withered and good for nothing. Grace, ripened into glory, will last for ever.

Verses 15–16

These seem to be the words of the spouse, the church, in answer to the commendations which Christ, the bridegroom, had given of her as a pleasant fruitful garden.

I. She owns her dependence upon Christ himself to make this garden fruitful. To him she has an eye (*v.* 15) as the *fountain of gardens*. To him she gives all the glory of her fruitfulness, as being nothing without him. The church transmits the praise to Christ, and says to him, *All my springs are in thee;* thou art *the well of living waters* (Jer. ii. 13). Those that are gardens to Christ must acknowledge him a fountain to them, from whose fulness they receive and to whom it is owing that their souls are as *a watered garden*, Jer. xxxi. 12.

II. She implores the influences of the blessed Spirit to make this garden fragrant (*v.* 16): *Awake, O north wind! and come, thou south.* This is a prayer for the church in general, that there may be a plentiful effusion of the Spirit. This prayer was answered in the pouring out of the Spirit on *the day of pentecost* (Acts ii. 1), ushered in by a *mighty wind*; then the apostles, who were bound up before, flowed forth, and were *a sweet savour to God*, 2 Cor. ii. 15. Sanctified souls are as gardens, gardens of the Lord, enclosed for him. Graces in the soul are as spices in these gardens. The blessed Spirit, in his operations upon the soul, is as the *north and the south wind.* There is the north wind of convictions, and the south wind of comforts. The flowing forth of the spices of grace depends upon the gales of the Spirit.

III. She invites Christ to the best entertainment the garden affords: *Let my beloved* then *come into his garden and eat his pleasant fruits*; let him have the honour of all the products of the garden, and let me have the comfort of his acceptance of them. The believer can take little pleasure in his garden, unless Christ, the beloved of his soul, come to him, nor have any jot of the fruits of it, unless they redound some way or other to the glory of Christ.

JAMIESON, FAUSSET, BROWN

12. The *Hebrew* has no "is." Here she is distinct from the garden (ch. 5:1), yet identified with it (vs. 16) as being one with Him in His sufferings. Historically the Paradise, into which the soul of Jesus Christ entered at death; and the tomb of Joseph, in which His body was laid amid "myrrh," etc. (vs. 6), situated in *a nicely kept* garden (cf. "gardener," John 20:15); "sealed" with a stone (Matt. 27:66); in which it resembles "wells" in the East (Gen. 29:3, 8). It was in a garden of light Adam fell; in a garden of darkness, Gethsemane, and chiefly that of the tomb, the second Adam retrieved us. Spiritually the garden is the gospel kingdom of heaven. Here all is ripe; previously (ch. 2:13) it was "the *tender* grape." The garden is His, though He calls the plants hers (vs. 13) by His gift (Isa. 61:3, end). **spring . . . fountain**—Jesus Christ (John 4:10) sealed, while He was in the sealed tomb: it poured forth its full tide on Pentecost (John 7:37-39). Still He is a sealed fountain until the Holy Ghost opens it to one (I Cor. 12:3). The Church also is "a garden enclosed" (Ps. 4:3; Isa. 5: 1, etc.). Contrast Psalm 80: 9-12. So "a spring" (Isa. 27:3; 58:11); "sealed" (Eph. 4:30; II Tim. 2: 19). As wives in the East are secluded from public gaze, so believers (Ps. 83:3; Col. 3:3). Contrast the open streams which "pass away" (Job. 6:15-18; II Pet. 2:17). **13. orchard**—*Hebrew*, "a paradise," i.e., a pleasure-ground and orchard. Not only flowers, but fruit trees (John 15:8; Phil. 1:11). **camphire**—not camphor (ch. 1:14), *hennah*, or cypress blooms. **14. calamus**—"sweet cane" (Exod. 30:23; Jer. 6:20). **myrrh and aloes**—Ointments are associated with His death, as well as with feasts (John 12:7). The bride's ministry of "myrrh and aloes" is recorded (John 19:39).

15. of—This pleasure-ground is not dependent on mere reservoirs; it has a fountain *sufficient to water* many "gardens" (*plural*). **living**—(Jer. 17:8; John 4:13, 14; 7:38, 39.) **from Lebanon**—Though the fountain is lowly, the source is lofty; fed by the perpetual snows of Lebanon, refreshingly cool (Jer. 18:14), fertilizing the gardens of Damascus. It springs upon earth; its source is heaven. It is now not "sealed," but open "streams" (Rev. 22: 17). **16. Awake**—lit., "arise." All besides is ready; one thing alone is wanted—the breath of God. This follows rightly after His death (ch. 6:12; Acts 2). It is His call to the Spirit to come (John 14:16); in John 3:8, compared to "the wind"; quickening (John 6:63; Ezek. 27:9). Saints offer the same prayer (Ps. 85:6; Hab. 3:2). The north wind "*awakes*," or *arises* strongly, viz., the Holy Ghost as a reprover (John 16:8-11); the south wind "*comes*" gently, viz., the Holy Ghost as the comforter (John 14:16). The west wind brings rain from the sea (I Kings 18:44, 45; Luke 12:54). The east wind is tempestuous (Job 27:21; Isa. 27:8) and withering (Gen. 41:23). These, therefore, are not wanted; but first the north wind clearing the air (Job 37:22; Prov. 25:23), and then the warm south wind (vs. 17); so the Holy Ghost first clearing away mists of gloom, error, unbelief, sin, which intercept the light of Jesus Christ, then infusing spiritual warmth (II Cor. 4:6), causing the graces to exhale their odor. **Let my beloved . . .**—*the bride's reply*. The fruit was now at length ripe; the last passover, which He had so desired, is come (Luke 22:7, 15, 16, 18), the only occasion in which He took charge of the preparations. **his**—answering to Jesus Christ's "My." She owns that the garden is His, and the fruits in her, which she does not in false humility deny (Ps. 66:16; Acts 21: 19; I Cor. 15:10) are His (John 15:8; Phil. 1:11).

ADAM CLARKE

12. *A garden inclosed . . . a spring shut up, a fountain sealed.* Different expressions to point out the fidelity of the bride, or of the Jewish queen.

F. B. MEYER:

"Awake, O north wind; and come, thou south; blow upon my garden" (S. of Sol. 4:16). The garden of the heart is like one of those old-fashioned gardens, surrounded by high brick walls, prepared for fruit trees. I have one in my eye as I write, on the south wall of which old apple trees have bloomed and fruited for generations. The garden is filled with all manner of spices, "spikenard and saffron, calamus and cinnamon, and with all trees of frankincense." Sometimes, however, the spices hang heavily upon the air. They are present, but hardly discernable to the quickest sense. Then the wind is needed to blow through the garden path, that the spices may flow out and pass beyond the barriers to the passers-by.

How often it has happened in the history of the children of God, that those who have known them have never realized the intrinsic excellence and loveliness of their characters until the north wind of sorrow and pain has broken with blustering force upon them. Then suddenly spices of rarest odor have exhaled and been carried afar. How the delicate trees dread the north wind! What a tremor goes through the crowded garden walks when they hear the husbandman calling to the north wind to awake! We all choose the south wind. But remember that the Euroclydon that swept down the ravines of Crete upon the Alexandrian corn ship brought out spices which had slumbered unknown in the heart of the great apostle. His courage! His patience! His power of inspiring hope amid despair, and breaking bread with thanksgiving! Ah, north wind, thy ministry has been of incalculable worth to all of us. We shiver before thy searching power, but the spices will repay. A vane in Leicestershire is inscribed with "God is love." He is so, from whatever quarter the wind blows.

—*Great Verses Through the Bible*

MATTHEW HENRY — CHAPTER 5

Verse 1

These words are Christ's answer to the church's prayer in the close of the foregoing chapter, *Let my beloved come into his garden;* here he has come. She called him *her beloved* because she loved him; in return he called her his *sister and spouse*. Those that make Christ their best beloved shall be owned by him in the nearest and dearest relations. She invited him to *come into his garden*, and he says, *I have come.*

JAMIESON, FAUSSET, BROWN — CHAPTER 5

Vss. 1-16. **1.** Answer to her prayer (Isa. 65:24; Rev. 3:20). **am come**—already (ch. 4:16); "come" (Gen. 28:16). **sister . . . spouse**—As Adam's was created of his flesh, out of his opened side, there being none on earth on a level with him, so the bride out of the pierced Saviour (Eph. 5:30-32). **have gathered . . . myrrh**—His course was already complete; the myrrh, etc. (Matt. 2:11; 26:7-12; John 19: 39), emblems of the indwelling of the anointing

ADAM CLARKE — CHAPTER 5

1. *I am come into my garden. Bathi*, "I came, or have come"; this should be translated in the past tense, as the other preterite verbs in this clause.

MATTHEW HENRY

Those that throw open the door of their souls to Jesus Christ shall find him ready to come into them; and in every place where he records his name he will meet his people, and bless them, Exod. xx. 24. She only desired him to *eat the fruits* of the garden, but he brought along with him something more, *honey*, and *wine*, and *milk*, which yield substantial nourishment, and which were the products of Canaan, Immanuel's land. The great work of man's redemption, and the riches of the covenant of grace, are a feast to the Lord Jesus and they ought to be so to us.

Verses 2–8

In this song of loves and joys we have here a melancholy scene; the spouse here speaks, not to her beloved, but of him, and it is a sad story she tells of her own folly and ill conduct.

I. Listlessness that had seized her. *She slept*, that is, pious affections cooled, she neglected her duty and grew remiss in it. True Christians are not always alike lively and vigorous in religion. But Grace was remaining, notwithstanding: "*My heart wakes;* my own conscience reproaches me for it, and ceases not to rouse me out of my sluggishness. I sleep, but it is not a dead sleep; I strive against it; I cannot be easy under this indisposition." We ought to take notice of our own spiritual slumbers and distempers, and to reflect upon it with sorrow and shame that we have fallen asleep when Christ has been nigh us in his garden.

II. The call that Christ gave to her, when she was under this indisposition: *It is the voice of my beloved;* she knew it to be so, which was a sign that her heart was awake. Like the child Samuel, she heard at the first call, but did not, like him, mistake the person; she knew it to be the voice of Christ. He knocks, to awaken us to come and let him in, knocks by his word and Spirit, knocks by afflictions and by our own consciences. Those whom he loves he will not let alone in their carelessness, but will find some way or other to awaken them, to rebuke and chasten them. Observe how moving the call is: *Open to me, my sister, my love.* He sues for entrance who may demand it; he knocks who could easily knock the door down. He gives her all the most endearing titles imaginable: *My sister, my love, my dove, my undefiled;* he gives her no hard names. *His loving-kindness he will not utterly take away. Open to me.* Can we deny entrance to such a friend, to such a guest? He begs to be admitted *under the character of a poor traveller* that wants a lodging: "*My head is wet with the dew*, consider what hardships I have undergone, to merit thee, which surely may merit from thee so small a kindness as this." When Christ was crowned with thorns, then was his head *wet with the dew.* Do we thus requite him for his love?

III. The excuse she made to put off her compliance with this call (*v.* 3): *I have put off my coat; How shall I put it on again?* She is half asleep; she knows the voice of her beloved, but cannot find in her heart to open to him. She was undressed, she had *washed her feet*, and would not have occasion to wash them again. Frivolous excuses are the language of prevailing slothfulness in religion; Christ calls to us to open to him, but we pretend we have no mind, or we have no strength, or we have no time. Those put a great contempt upon Christ that cannot find in their hearts to bear a cold blast for him, or get out of a warm bed.

IV. The powerful influences of divine grace, by which she was made willing to rise and open to her beloved. When he could not prevail with her by persuasion he *put in his hand by the hole of the door*, to unbolt it, as one weary of waiting, *v.* 4. This intimates a work of the Spirit upon her soul. The conversion of Lydia is represented by the *opening of her heart* (Acts xvi. 14).

V. Her compliance with these methods of divine grace at last: *My bowels were moved for him.* She was moved with compassion to her beloved, because his *head was wet with the dew.* Did Christ redeem us in his pity? Let us in pity receive him, and for his sake, those that are his, when at any time they are in distress. He made her ashamed of her dullness and slothfulness (*v. 5, I rose up, to open to my beloved*). It was her own act, and yet he wrought it in her. And now her *hands dropped with myrrh upon the handles of the lock.* Either, 1. She found it there when she applied her hand to the lock, to shoot it back; he that *put in his hand by the hole of the door* left it there as an evidence that he had been there. When Christ has wrought powerfully upon a soul he leaves a blessed sweetness in it. 2. She brought it thither. When she came to open to him she prepared to anoint his head, and so to refresh and comfort him; she was in such haste to meet him that she would not stay to make the usual preparation, but dipped

JAMIESON, FAUSSET, BROWN

Holy Ghost, were already gathered. **spice**—lit., "balsam." **have eaten**—answering to her "eat" (ch. 4:16). **honeycomb**—distinguished here from liquid "honey" dropping from trees. The last supper, here set forth, is one of *espousal,* a pledge of the future *marriage* (ch. 8:14; Rev. 19:9). Feasts often took place in gardens. In the absence of sugar, then unknown, honey was more widely used than with us. His eating honey with milk indicates His true, yet spotless, human nature from infancy (Isa. 7:15); and after His resurrection (Luke 24:42). **my wine**—(John 18:11)—a cup of wrath to Him, of mercy to us, whereby God's Word and promises become to us "milk" (Ps. 19:10; I Pet. 2:2). "My" answers to "His" (ch. 4:16). The "myrrh (emblem, by its bitterness, of *repentance*), honey, milk (*incipient faith*), wine" (*strong faith*), in reference to believers, imply that He accepts all their graces, however various in degree. **eat**—He desires to make us partakers in His joy (Isa. 55:1, 2; John 6:53-57; I John 1:3). **drink abundantly**—so as to be *filled* (Eph. 5:18; as Hag. 1:6). **friends**—(John 15:15).

CANTICLE IV.—CH. 5:2-8:4—FROM THE AGONY OF GETHSEMANE TO THE CONVERSION OF SAMARIA. **2.** Sudden change of scene from evening to midnight, from a betrothal feast to cold repulse. He has gone from the feast alone; night is come; He knocks at the door of His espoused; she hears, but in sloth does not shake off half-conscious drowsiness; viz., the disciples' torpor (Matt. 26:40-43), "the spirit willing, the flesh weak" (cf. Rom. 7; Gal. 5). Not *total* sleep. The lamp was burning beside the *slumbering* wise virgin, but wanted trimming (Matt. 25:5-7). It is *His* voice that rouses her (Jonah 1:6; Eph. 5:14; Rev. 3:20). Instead of bitter reproaches, He addresses her by the most endearing titles, "my sister, my love," etc. Cf. His thought of *Peter* after the denial (Mark 16:7). **dew**—which falls heavily in summer nights in the East (see Luke 9:58). **drops of the night**—(Ps. 22:2; Luke 22:44.) His death is not *expressed,* as unsuitable to the allegory, a song of love and joy; vs. 4 refers to the scene in the judgment hall of Caiaphas, when Jesus Christ employed the cock-crowing and look of love to awaken Peter's sleeping conscience, so that his "bowels were moved" (Luke 22:61, 62); vss. 5, 6, the disciples with "myrrh," etc. (Luke 24:1, 5), seeking Jesus Christ in the tomb, but finding Him not, for He has "withdrawn Himself" (John 7:34; 13:33); vs. 7, the trials by watchmen extend through the whole night of His withdrawal from Gethsemane to the resurrection; they took off the "veil" of Peter's disguise; also, literally the linen cloth from the young man (Mark 14:51); vs. 8, the sympathy of friends (Luke 23:27). **undefiled**—not polluted by spiritual adultery (Rev. 14:4; Jas. 4:4). **3.** Trivial excuses (Luke 14:18). **coat**—rather, the inmost vest, next the skin, taken off before going to bed. **washed . . . feet**—before going to rest, for they had been soiled, from the Eastern custom of wearing sandals, not shoes. Sloth (Luke 11:7) and despondency (Deut. 7:17-19).

4. A key in the East is usually a piece of wood with pegs in it corresponding to small holes in a wooden bolt within, and is put through a hole in the door, and thus draws the bolt. So Jesus Christ "puts forth His hand (viz., His Spirit, Ezek. 3:14), by (*Hebrew*, 'from,' so in ch. 2:9) the hole"; in "chastening" (Ps. 38:2; Rev. 3:14-22, singularly similar to this passage), and other unexpected ways letting Himself in (Luke 22:61, 62). **bowels . . . moved for him**—It is His which are first troubled for us, and which cause ours to be troubled for Him (Jer. 31:20; Hos. 11:8). **5. dropped with myrrh**—The best proof a bride could give her lover of welcome was to anoint herself (the back of the hands especially, as being the coolest part of the body) *profusely* with the *best* perfumes (Exod. 30:23; Esther 2:12; Prov. 7:17); "sweet-smelling" is in the *Hebrew* rather, "spontaneously exuding" from the tree, and therefore the *best.* She designed also to anoint Him, whose "head was filled with the drops of night" (Luke 24:1). The myrrh typifies *bitter* repentance, the fruit of the Spirit's unction (II Cor. 1:21, 22). **handles of the lock**—sins which closed the heart against Him.

ADAM CLARKE

JOSEPH PARKER:

Look at the case. The Church which goes into such rhapsodies of admiration as we find in the Canticles breaks down at one point. Whose love is it that gives way? It is not the love of Christ. When a break does occur in the holy communion, where does that break take effect? Look at the image in the fifth chapter. The Church is there represented as having gone to rest, and in the deep darkness a knock is heard at the door, and a well-known voice says: "Open to me, my sister, my love, my dove, my undefiled: for my head is filled with dew, and my locks with the drops of the night" (v. 2). What is the response of the Shulamite—or, as we should say, the Church? The answer is: "I have put off my coat; how shall I put it on? I have washed my feet; how shall I defile them?" Thus we are caught at unexpected times, and in ways we have never calculated. It is when we are asked to do unusual things that we find out the scope and the value of our Christian profession. How difficult it is to be equally strong at every point! How hard, how impossible, to have a day-and-night religion; a religion that is in the light and in the darkness the same, as watchful at midnight as at midday; as ready to serve in the snows of winter as amid the flowers of the summertime! So the Shulamite breaks down. She has been sentimentalizing, rhapsodizing, calling to her love that he would return to her; and now that he has come she says: "I have put off my coat; how shall I put it on?" How hard for human nature to be divine! How difficult for the finite even to urge itself in the direction of the infinite! How impossible to keep awake all night even under the inspiration of love, unless that inspiration be constantly renewed by intercourse with heaven! Keep my eyes open at midnight, O thou coming One, and may I be ready for you when you come, though it be at midnight, or at the crowing of the cock, or at noonday: may I by your grace be ready for your coming!

The whole subject of excuses is here naturally opened up. "I have put off my coat; how shall I put it on?" What a refrain to all the wild rhapsody! When the Shulamite cries that her loving and loved one may return, always add, I have put off my coat: how shall I put it on? I have laid myself down; how can I rise again to undo the door?—Oh that he would come at regular times, in the ordinary course of things, that he would not put my love to these unusual and exceptional tests: for twelve hours in the day I should be ready, but having curtained myself round, and lain down to sleep, how can I rise again? Thus all rhapsody goes down, all mere sentiment perishes in the using; it is undergoing a continual process of evaporation. Nothing stands seven days a week and four seasons in the year but reasoned love, intelligent apprehension of great principles, distinct inwrought conviction that without Christ life is impossible, or were it possible it would be vain, painful, and useless. Have we any such excuses, or are these complaints historical noises, unknown to us in their practical realization? Let the question find its way into the very middle of the heart. There is an ingenuity of self-excusing, a department in which genius can find ample scope for all its resources.—*The People's Bible*

MATTHEW HENRY

her hand in her box of ointment, that she might readily anoint his head. Those that open the doors of their hearts to Christ, those *everlasting doors*, must meet him with the lively exercises of faith and other graces, and with these must anoint him.

VI. Her sad disappointment when she did open to her beloved. *I opened to my beloved*, as I intended, but, alas! *my beloved had withdrawn himself, and was gone. My beloved was gone, was gone*, so the word is.

1. She did not open to him at his first knock, and now she came too late. Christ will be sought while he may be found; if we slip our time, we may lose our passage. Christ justly rebukes our delays and suspends the communications of comfort from those that are remiss.

2. She still calls him her *beloved*, being resolved, how cloudy and dark soever the day be, she will not quit her relation to him. She now remembers the words he said to her when he called her: "*My soul failed when he spoke;* his words melted me when he said, *My head is wet with the dew;* and yet I lay still, and made excuses, and did not open to him." She went in pursuit of him: *I sought him; I called him. I could not find him; he gave me no answer.* There are those who have a true love for Christ, and yet have not immediate answers to their prayers for his smiles; but he gives them an equivalent if he strengthens them with strength in their souls to continue seeking him, Ps. cxxxviii. 3. St. Paul could not prevail for the removing of the *thorn in the flesh*, but was answered with grace sufficient for him. She was ill-treated by the watchmen: *They found me; they smote me; they wounded me, v.* 7. They took her for a lewd woman and beat her accordingly. Disconsolate saints are taken for sinners, and are censured and reproached as such. When she was disabled to prosecute her enquiry herself she gave charge to those about her to assist her (*v.* 8): *I charge you, O you daughters of Jerusalem!* all my friends and acquaintance, *if you find my beloved*, "Speak a good word for me; tell him that *I am sick of love.*" It is better to be sick of love to Christ than at ease in love to the world.

Verses 9–16

I. The daughters of Jerusalem answer to the charge she had given them, *v.* 9. Observe the respectful title they give to the spouse: *O thou fairest among women!* The church is the most excellent society in the world, and the beauty of the sanctuary a transcendent beauty. Holiness is the symmetry of the soul. Even those that have little acquaintance with Christ, as those daughters of Jerusalem, cannot but see beauty in those that bear his image. Their enquiry concerning her beloved: "*What is thy beloved more than another beloved?*" Some take it for a scornful question, blaming her for making such ado about him. Carnal hearts see nothing excellent or extraordinary in the Lord Jesus, in his person or offices, in his doctrine or in his favours. Others rather take it for a serious question, and suppose that those who put it intended to comfort the spouse, who, they knew would recover new spirits if she did but talk awhile of her beloved. They wondered what moved the spouse to charge them concerning her beloved with so much concern, and concluded there must be something more in him than in another. There begin to be hopes of people when they begin to enquire concerning Christ. And sometimes the extraordinary zeal of one, in enquiring after Christ, may be a means to provoke many (2 Cor. ix. 2).

II. The account which the spouse gives of her beloved in answer to this question. She assures them, in general, that he is one of incomparable perfections and unparalleled worth (*v.* 10). He has everything in him that is lovely: *My beloved is white and ruddy*. This points not at any extraordinary beauty of his body, when he should be incarnate, but at his divine glory, in the eyes of those that are enlightened to discern spiritual things. In him we may behold the *beauty of the Lord*; he was the *holy child Jesus*; that was his fairness. His love to us renders him lovely. He is *white* in the spotless innocency of his life, *ruddy* in the bloody sufferings he went through at his death,—*white*, in his glory, as God, *ruddy* in his assuming the nature of man, *Adam—red earth.* He has that loveliness in him which is not to be found in any other: He is *the chief among ten thousand.* She gives a particular detail of his accomplishments, conceals not his power or comely proportion. Ten instances she here gives of his beauty. The design, in general, is to show that he is every way qualified for his undertaking, and has all that in him which may recommend him to our esteem, love, and confidence. Christ's appearance to John (Rev. i. 13, &c.) may be compared with the description which the spouse gives of him here, the

JAMIESON, FAUSSET, BROWN

6. withdrawn—He *knocked* when she was sleeping; for to have left her *then* would have ended in the death sleep; He *withdraws* now that she is roused, as she needs correction (Jer. 2:17, 19), and can appreciate and safely bear it now, which she could not then. "The strong He'll strongly try" (I Cor. 10:13). **when he spake**—rather, *because of His speaking;* at the remembrance of His tender words (Job 29:2, 3, Ps. 27:13; 142:7), or *till He should speak.* **no answer**—(Job. 23:3-9; 30:20; 34:29; Lam. 3:44.) Weak faith receives immediate comfort (Luke 8:44, 47, 48); strong faith is tried with delay (Matt. 15:22, 23). **7. watchmen**—historically, the Jewish priests, etc. (see *Note*, vs. 2); spiritually, ministers (Isa. 62:6; Heb. 13:17), faithful in "smiting" (Ps. 141:5), but (as she leaves them, vs. 8) too harsh; or, perhaps, unfaithful; disliking her zeal wherewith she sought Jesus Christ, first, with spiritual prayer, "opening" her heart to Him, and then in charitable works "about the city"; miscalling it fanaticism (Isa. 66:5), and taking away her veil (the greatest indignity to an Eastern lady), as though she were positively immodest. She had before sought Him by night in the streets, under strong affection (ch. 3:2-4), and so without rebuff from "the watchmen," found Him immediately; but now after sinful neglect, she encounters pain and delay. God forgives believers, but it is a serious thing to draw on His forgiveness; so the *growing reserve* of God towards Israel observable in Judges, as His people repeat their demands on His grace. **8.** She turns from the unsympathizing watchmen to humbler persons, not yet themselves knowing Him, but in the way towards it. Historically, His secret friends in the night of His withdrawal (Luke 23:27, 28). Inquirers *may* find ("*if* ye find") Jesus Christ before she who has grieved His Spirit finds Him again. **tell**—in prayer (Jas. 5:16). **sick of love**—from an opposite cause (ch. 2:5) than through excess of delight at His *presence;* now excess of pain at His *absence*. **9.** Her own beauty (Ezek. 16:14), and lovesickness for Him, elicit now their inquiry (Matt. 5:16); heretofore "other lords besides Him had dominion over them"; thus they had seen "no beauty in Him" (Isa. 26:13; 53:2). **10.** (I Peter 3:15.) **white and ruddy**—health and beauty. So David (equivalent to *beloved*), His forefather after the flesh, and type (I Sam. 17:42). "The Lamb" is at once His nuptial and sacrificial name (I Pet. 1:19; Rev. 19:7), characterized by white and red; *white*, His spotless manhood (Rev. 1:14). The *Hebrew* for *white* is properly "illuminated by the sun," white as the light" (cf. Matt. 17:2); *red*, in His blood-dyed garment as slain (Isa. 63:1-3; Rev. 5:6; 19:13). Angels are white, not red; the blood of martyrs does not enter heaven; His alone is seen there. **chiefest**—lit., "a standard-bearer"; i.e., as conspicuous above all others, as a standard-bearer is among hosts (Ps. 45:7; 89:6; Isa. 11:10; 55:4; Heb. 2:10; cf. II Sam. 18:3; Job 33:23; Phil. 2:9-11; Rev. 1:5). The chief of sinners needs the "chiefest" of Saviours. **11. head . . . gold**—*the Godhead* of Jesus Christ, as distinguished from His *heel*, i.e., His manhood, which was "bruised" by Satan; both together being one Christ (I Cor. 11:3). Also His sovereignty, as Nebuchadnezzar, the supreme king was "the head of gold" (Dan. 2:32-38; Col. 1:18), the highest creature, compared with Him, is brass, iron, and clay. "Preciousness" (*Greek*, I Pet. 2:7). **bushy**—*curled,* token of Headship. In contrast with her *flowing* locks (ch. 4:1), the token of her subjection to Him (Ps. 8:4-8; I Cor. 11:3, 6-15). The *Hebrew* is (pendulous as) the *branches of a palm,* which, when in leaf, resemble waving plumes of feathers. **black**—implying youth; no "gray hairs" (Ps. 102:27; 110:3, 4; Hos. 7:9). Jesus Christ was crucified in the prime of vigor and manliness. In heaven, on the other hand, His hair is "white," He being the Ancient of days (Dan. 7:9). These contrasts often concur in Him (vs. 10), "white and ruddy"; here the "raven" (vs. 12), the "dove," as both with Noah in the ark (Gen. 8); emblems of judgment and mercy. **12. as the eyes of doves**—rather, "as doves" (Ps. 68:13); bathing in "the rivers"; so combining in their "silver" feathers the *whiteness* of milk with the *sparkling brightness* of the water trickling over them (Matt. 3:16). The "milk" may allude to the white around the pupil of the eye. The "waters" refer to the eye as the fountain of *tears of sympathy* (Ezek. 16:5, 6; Luke 19:41). Vivacity, purity, and love, are the three features typified. **fitly set**—as a gem in a ring; as the precious stones in the high priest's breastplate. Rather, translate as *Vulgate* (the doves), *sitting at the fulness* of the stream; by the full stream; or, as MAURER (the eyes) "*set in fulness,* not sunk in their sockets (Rev. 5:6), ("seven," expressing *full* perfection), (Zech. 3:9; 4:10). **13.**

ADAM CLARKE

7. *Took away my veil.* They tore it off rudely, to discover who she was. To tear the veil signifies, in Eastern phrase, to dishonor a woman.

8. *I am sick of love.* "I am exceedingly concerned for his absence, and am distressed on account of my thoughtless carriage towards him."

9. *What is thy beloved more than another beloved?* This question gives the bride an opportunity to break out into a highly wrought description of the beauty and perfections of her spouse.

10. *My beloved is white and ruddy.* Red and white, properly mixed, are essential to a fine complexion, and this is what is intimated. He has the finest complexion *among ten thousand* persons; not one in that number is equal to him. Literally, "He bears the standard among ten thousand men."

11. *His head is as the most fine gold.* He has the most beautiful head, fine and majestic. Gold is here used to express excellence.

His locks are bushy. Crisped or curled. *Black as a raven.* His hair is black and glossy.

12. *His eyes are as the eyes of doves.* See chap. iv. 1. *Washed with milk.* The white of the eye, exceedingly white.

MATTHEW HENRY

scope of both being to represent him transcendently glorious. (1) *His head is as the most fine gold. The head of Christ is God* (1 Cor. xi. 3). Christ's head bespeaks his sovereign dominion over all and his vital influence upon his church and all its members. (2) *His locks are bushy and black, black as a raven,* whose blackness is his beauty; *black and bushy,* denoting that he is ever young and that there is in him nothing that waxes old. (3) *His eyes are as the eyes of doves,* fair and clear, and chaste and kind (4) *His cheeks are as a bed of spices,* and *as sweet flowers,* or towers of sweetness. The half discoveries Christ makes of himself to the soul are reviving and refreshing, fragrant above the richest flowers and perfumes. (5) *His lips are like lilies,* sweet and pleasant. Such are *the words of his lips* to all that are sanctified; *grace is poured into his lips,* and those that heard him *wondered at the gracious words which proceeded out of his mouth.* (6) *His hands are as gold rings set with the beryl,* a noted precious stone, *v.* 14. Great men had their hands adorned with gold rings on their fingers, set with precious stones, but, in her eye, *his hands* themselves were *as gold rings*; all the instances of his power, the works of his hands, all the performances of his providence and grace, are all precious, as gold, *as the precious onyx and the sapphire,* all fitted to the purpose for which they were designed, and all beautiful, *as rings set with beryl.*

(7) *His bowels are as bright ivory.* It denotes his tender compassion and affection for his spouse. This love of his is like *bright ivory,* finely polished, and richly *overlaid with sapphires.* The love itself is strong and firm, bright and sparkling.

(8) *His legs are as pillars of marble, v.* 15. This bespeaks his stability and steadfastness; he is able to bear all the weight of the government that is upon his shoulders. (9) *His countenance* (his port and mien) *is as Lebanon,* that stately hill; his aspect beautiful and charming, *excellent as the cedars.* (10) *His mouth is most sweet;* it is *sweetness* (so the word is), *v.* 16. The words of his mouth are all sweet to a believer. The tokens of his love, have a transcendent sweetness in them, and are most delightful to those who have their *spiritual senses exercised. To you that believe he is precious.* She concludes with a full assurance both of faith and hope, and so gets the mastery of her trouble. Here is a full assurance of faith concerning the complete beauty of the Lord Jesus: "*He is altogether lovely.*" Here is a full assurance of hope concerning her own interest in him: "*This is my beloved, and this is my friend;* and therefore wonder not that I thus long after him. He is mine, *my Lord and my God* (John xx. 28), mine according to the tenor of the gospel-covenant, mine in all relations, bestowed upon me, to be all that to me that my poor soul stands in need of." It is spoken of here with an air of triumph: "This is he whom I have chosen, and to whom I have given up myself. None but Christ, none but Christ. This is he on whom my heart is, for he is my best-beloved; this is he in whom I trust, and from whom I expect all good, for *this is my friend.*"

JAMIESON, FAUSSET, BROWN

cheeks—the seat of beauty, according to the *Hebrew* meaning [GESENIUS]. Yet men smote and spat on them (Isa. 50:6). **bed**—full, like the raised surface of the garden bed; fragrant with ointments, as beds with aromatic plants (lit., "balsam"). **sweet flowers**—rather, "*terraces* of aromatic herbs"—"*high-raised* parterres of sweet plants," in parallelism to "bed," which comes from a *Hebrew* root, meaning "elevation." **lips**—(Ps. 45:2; John 7:46.) **lilies**—red lilies. Soft and gentle (I Pet. 2:22, 23). How different lips were man's (Ps. 22:7)! **dropping . . . myrrh**—viz., His lips, just as the sweet dewdrops which hang in the calyx of the lily. **14. rings set with . . . beryl**—*Hebrew, Tarshish,* so called from the city. The ancient chrysolite, gold in color (LXX), our topaz, one of the stones on the high priest's breastplate, also in the foundation of New Jerusalem (Rev. 21; also Dan. 10:6). "Are as," is plainly to be supplied, see in vs. 13 a similiar ellipsis; not as MOODY STUART: "*have* gold rings." The hands bent in are compared to beautiful rings, in which beryl is set, as the nails are in the fingers. BURROWES explains the rings as *cylinders* used as signets, such as are found in Nineveh, and which resemble fingers. A ring is the token of sonship (Luke 15:22). A slave was not allowed to wear a *gold* ring. He imparts His sonship and freedom to us (Gal. 4:7); also of authority (Gen. 41:42; cf. John 6:27). He seals us in the name of God with His signet (Rev. 7:2-4), cf. below, ch. 8:6, where she desires to be herself *a signet ring* on His arms; so "graven on the palms," etc., i.e., on the signet ring in His hand (Isa. 49:16; contrast Hag. 2:23, with Jer. 22:24). **belly**—BURROWES and MOODY STUART translate, "body." NEWTON, as it is elsewhere, "bowels"; viz., His compassion (Ps. 22:14; Isa. 63:15; Jer. 31:20; Hos. 11:8). **bright**—lit., "elaborately wrought so as to shine," so His "prepared" body (Heb. 10:5); the "ivory palace" of the king (Ps. 45:8); spotless, pure, so the bride's "neck is as to tower of *ivory*" (ch. 7:4). **sapphires**—spangling in the girdle around Him (Dan. 10:5). "To the pure all things are pure." As in statuary to the artist the partly undraped figure is suggestive only of beauty, free from indelicacy, so to the saint the personal excellencies of Jesus Christ, typified under the ideal of the noblest human form. As, however, the bride and bridegroom are in public, the usual robes on the person, richly ornamented, are presupposed (Isa. 11:5). Sapphires indicate His *heavenly* nature (so John 3:13, "*is* in heaven"), even in His humiliation, *overlaying* or cast "over" His ivory human body (Exod. 24:10). Sky-blue in color, the *height* and *depth* of the love of Jesus Christ (Eph. 3:18). **15. pillars**—strength and steadfastness. Contrast man's "legs" (Eccles. 12:3). Allusion to the temple (I Kings 5:8, 9; 7:21), the "cedars" of "Lebanon" (Ps. 147:10). Jesus Christ's "legs" were not broken on the cross, though the thieves' were; on them rests the weight of our salvation (Ps. 75:3). **sockets of fine gold**—His sandals, answering to the bases of the pillars; "set up from everlasting" (Prov. 8:22, 23). From the head (vs. 11) to the feet, "of fine gold." He was tried in the fire and found without alloy. **countenance**—rather, *His aspect,* including both *mien* and *stature* (cf. *Margin,* II Sam. 23:21 with I Chron. 11:23). From the several *parts,* she proceeds to the general effect of the *whole* person of Jesus Christ. **Lebanon**—so called from its *white* limestone rocks. **excellent**—lit., "choice," i.e., fair and tall as the cedars on Lebanon (Ezek. 31:3, etc.). Majesty is the prominent thought (Ps. 21:5). Also the cedars' *duration* (Heb. 1:11); *greenness* (Luke 23:31), and refuge afforded by it (Ezek. 17:22, 23). **16.** Lit., "His *palate* is *sweetness,* yea, all over *loveliness,*" i.e, He is the *essence* of these qualities. **mouth**—so ch. 1:2, not the same as "lips" (vs. 13), His breath (Isa. 11:4; John 20:22). "All over," all the beauties scattered among creatures are transcendently concentrated in Him (Col. 1:19; 2:9). **my beloved**—for I love Him. **my friend**—for He loves me (Prov. 18:24). Holy boasting (Ps. 34:2; I Cor. 1:31).

ADAM CLARKE

CHARLES H. SPURGEON:

"Yea, He is altogether lovely" (v. 16). Looking at my text I felt much humbling of spirit, and I hesitated to preach upon it, for I said in my heart, "It is high, I cannot attain unto it." These deep texts show us the shortness of our plumb line; these ocean verses are so exceeding broad that our skills are apt to be driven far out of sight of land where our timid spirits tremble to spread the sail. Then I comforted myself by the thought that though I could not comprehend this text in a measure, nor weigh its mountains in scales, or its hills in a balance, yet it was all mine own, by the gift of divine grace, and therefore I need not fear to enter upon the meditation of it. If I cannot grasp the ocean in my span, yet may I bathe therein with sweet content; if I cannot describe the King in His beauty, yet may I gaze upon Him, since the old proverb says, "A beggar may look at a prince." Though I pretend not so to preach from such a heavenly Word as that before us, as to spread before you all its marrow and fatness, yet may I gather up a few crumbs which fall from its table. Poor men are glad of crumbs, and crumbs from such a feast are better than loaves from the tables of the world. Better to have a glimpse of Jesus, than to see all the glory of the earth all the days of our life. If we fail on this subject we may do better than if we succeeded upon another; so we will pluck up courage, seek divine help, and draw near to this wondrous text, with our shoes from off our feet like Moses when he saw the bush aglow with God.

This verse has been translated in another way: "He is all desires"; and so indeed Jesus is. He was the desire of the ancients, He is the desire of all nations still. To His own people He is their all in all; they are complete in Him; they are filled out of His fullness. He is the delight of His servants, and fills their expectations to the full. But we will not dispute about translations, for, after all, with such a text, so full of unutterable spiritual sweetness, every man must be his own translator, and into his own soul must the power of the message come, by the enforcement of the Holy Spirit. Such a text as this is very like manna which fell in the wilderness, of which the rabbis say it tasted after each man's liking. If the flavor in a man's mouth was very sweetness, the angel's food which fell around the camp was luscious as any dainty he had conceived; whatever he might be, the manna was to him as he was. So shall this text be. To you with low ideas of Christ the words shall but glide over your ears, and be meaningless; but if your spirit be ravished with the precious love of Jesus there shall be songs of angels, and more than that, the voice of God's own Spirit to your soul.

—*The Treasury of the Old Testament*

MATTHEW HENRY — CHAPTER 6

Verses 1–3

I. The enquiry which the daughters of Jerusalem made concerning Christ, *v.* 1. They still continue their high thoughts of the church, and call her, as before, the *fairest among women.* And now they raise their thoughts higher concerning Christ: *Whither has thy beloved gone, that we may seek him with thee?* This would be but an unacceptable compliment, if the song were not to be understood spiritually; for love is jealous of a rival; but those that truly love Christ are desirous that others should love him too.

JAMIESON, FAUSSET, BROWN — CHAPTER 6

Vss. 1-13. **1.** Historically, at Jesus Christ's crucifixion and burial, Joseph of Arimathea, and Nicodemus, and others, joined with His professed disciples. By speaking of Jesus Christ, the bride does good not only to her own soul, but to others (*Note,* ch. 1:4; Mal. 3:16; Matt. 5:14-16). Cf. the hypocritical use of similar words (Matt. 2:8).

ADAM CLARKE — CHAPTER 6

1. ***Whither is thy beloved gone?*** **These words are supposed to be addressed to the bride by her own companions, and are joined to the preceding chapter by the Hebrew and all the versions.**

MATTHEW HENRY

JAMIESON, FAUSSET, BROWN

ADAM CLARKE

The spouse had described him and had expressed her own love to him, and that flame in her breast scattered sparks into theirs. As sinful lusts, when they break out, defile many, so the pious zeal of some may *provoke many*, 2 Cor. ix. 2.

II. The answer which the spouse gave to this enquiry, *v.* 2, 3. Now she knows very well where he is (*v.* 2): "*My beloved* is not to be found in the streets of the city, and the crowd and noise that are there, but he *has gone down to his garden*, a place of retirement." The more we withdraw from the hurry of the world the more likely we are to have acquaintance with Christ, who took his disciples into a garden, there to be witnesses of the agonies of his love. Christ's church is a garden enclosed, *his garden*, which he has planted. Those that would find Christ may expect to meet with him in *his garden* the church; they must attend upon him in the ordinances which he has instituted, the word, sacraments, and prayer, wherein he will be with us *always, even to the end of the world.* When Christ comes down to his church it is to feed his flock, which he feeds not, as other shepherds, in the open fields, but in his garden. He comes to feed his friends, and entertain them, *for the Lord takes pleasure in those that fear him.* He has many gardens, many particular churches of different sizes and shapes; but, while they are his, he manifests himself among them, and is well pleased with them. He picks the lilies one by one, and gathers them to himself; and there will be a general harvest of them at the great day. She had acted unkindly to her beloved, and he had justly withdrawn himself from her, and therefore there was occasion to take fresh hold of the covenant, which continues firm between Christ and believers, notwithstanding their failings and his frowns, Ps. lxxxix. 30–35. "I have been careless and wanting in my duty, and yet *I am my beloved's*. He has justly hidden his face from me and yet *my beloved is mine*." When we have not a full assurance of Christ's love we must live by a faithful adherence to him. "Though I have not the sensible consolation I used to have, yet I will cleave to this, *Christ is mine and I am his*."

Verses 4–10

Now we must suppose Christ graciously returned to his spouse, having forgiven and forgotten all her unkindness, for he speaks very tenderly and respectfully to her.

I. He pronounces her truly amiable (*v.* 4): *Thou art beautiful, O my love! as Tirzah*, a city in the tribe of Manasseh, whose name signifies *pleasant*, or *acceptable. Thou art comely as Jerusalem*, a city *compact together* (Ps. cxxii. 3), and which Solomon had built and beautified. It was the holy city, and that was the greatest beauty of it; and fitly is the church compared to it. The gospel-church is *the Jerusalem that is above* (Gal. iv. 26), *the heavenly Jerusalem* (Heb. xii. 22); in it God has *his sanctuary*, and is, in a special manner, present; therefore it is *comely as Jerusalem*, and, being so, is *terrible as an army with banners.*

II. He owns himself in love with her, *v.* 5, though, for a small moment, he had hid his face from her. *Turn thy eyes towards me* (so some read it), "turn the eyes of faith and love towards me, *for they have lifted me up*; look unto me, and be comforted." When we are calling to God to turn the eye of his favour towards us he is calling to us to turn the eye of our obedience towards him.

III. He repeats, almost word for word, part of the description, he had given of her beauty (*ch.* iv. 1–3), her *hair*, her *teeth*, her *temples* (*v.* 5–7), to show that he had still the same esteem for her that he had before.

IV. He sees all the beauties and perfections of others meeting and centring in her (*v.* 8, 9): "*There are*, it may be, *threescore queens*, who, like Esther, have by their beauty attained to the royal state and dignity, *and fourscore concubines, virgins without number*, but *my dove, my undefiled, is but one*, a holy one." She excels them all. Go through all the world, and view the societies of men that reckon themselves wise and happy, kingdoms, courts, senates, councils, they are none of them to be compared with the church of Christ. There are particular persons who are famed for their accomplishments, the beauties of their language, and performances, but the beauty of holiness is beyond all other beauty. "Though there are many particular churches, some of greater dignity, others of less, some of longer, others of shorter, standing, and many particular believers, of different gifts and attainments, yet they all constitute but one catholic church, are all but parts of that whole, and that is *my dove, my undefiled*." Christ is the centre of the church's unity.

V. He shows how much she was esteemed, not by him only, but by all that had acquaintance with her.

2. gone down—Jerusalem was on a hill (answering to its *moral* elevation), and the gardens were at a little distance in the valleys below. **beds of spices**—(balsam) which He Himself calls the "mountain of myrrh," etc. (ch. 4:6), and again (ch. 8:14), the resting-place of His body amidst spices, and of His soul in paradise, and now in heaven, where He stands as High Priest for ever. Nowhere else in the Song is there mention of mountains of spices. **feed in . . . gardens**—i.e., in the churches, though He may have withdrawn for a time from the individual believer: she implies an invitation to the daughters of Jerusalem to enter His spiritual Church, and become lilies, made white by His blood. He is gathering some lilies now to plant on earth, others to transplant into heaven (ch. 5:1; Gen. 5:24; Mark 4:28, 29; Acts 7:60). **3.** In speaking of Jesus Christ to others, she regains her own assurance. Lit., "I am *for* my beloved . . . *for me*." Reverse order from ch. 2:16. She *now*, after the season of darkness, grounds her convictions on His love towards her, more than on hers towards Him (Deut. 33:3). *There*, it was the young believer concluding that she was His, from the sensible assurance that He was hers.

4. Tirzah—meaning *pleasant* (Heb. 13:21); "well-pleasing" (Matt. 5:14); the royal city of one of the old Canaanite kings (Josh. 12:24); and after the revolt of Israel, the royal city of its kings, before Omri founded Samaria (I Kings 16:8, 15). No ground for assigning a later date than the time of Solomon to the Song, as Tirzah was even in his time the capital of the north (Israel), as Jerusalem was of the south (Judah). **Jerusalem**—residence of the kings of *Judah*, as Tirzah, of *Israel* (Ps. 48:1, etc.; 122:1-3; 125:1, 2). Loveliness, security, unity, and loyalty; also the union of Israel and Judah in the Church (Isa. 11:13; Jer. 3:18; Ezek. 37:16, 17, 22; cf. Heb. 12:22; Rev. 21:2, 12). **terrible**—awe-inspiring. Not only armed as a city on the defensive, but as an army on the offensive. **banners**—(*Note*, ch. 5:10; Ps. 60:4); Jehovah-nissi (II Cor. 10:4).

5. (Ch. 4:9; Gen. 32:28; Exod. 32:9-14; Hos. 12:4.) This is the way "the army" (vs. 4) "overcomes" not only enemies, but Jesus Christ Himself, with eyes fixed on Him (Ps. 25:15; Matt. 11:12). Historically. vss. 3, 4, 5 represent the restoration of Jesus Christ to His Church at the resurrection; His sending her forth as an army, with new powers (Mark 16:15-18, 20); His rehearsing the *same* instructions (cf. vs. 6, *Note*) as when with them (Luke 24:44). **5. overcome**—lit., "have taken me by storm." **6.** Not vain repetition of ch. 4:1, 2. The use of the same words shows His love unchanged after her temporary unfaithfulness (Mal. 3:6). **8. threescore**—indefinite number, as in ch. 3:7. Not queens, etc., *of Solomon*, but witnesses of the espousals, rulers of the earth contrasted with the saints, who, though many, are but "one" bride (Isa. 52:15; Luke 22:25, 26; John 17:21; I Cor. 10:17). The one bride is contrasted with the many wives whom Eastern kings had in violation of the marriage law (I Kings 11:1-3).

2. *My beloved is gone down into his garden.* The answer of the bride to her companions.

4. *Beautiful . . . as Tirzah.* This is supposed to be the address of Solomon to the bride. Tirzah was a city in the tribe of Ephraim (Josh. xii. 24) and the capital of that district. It appears to have been beautiful in itself, and beautifully situated, for Jeroboam made it his residence before Samaia was built; and it seems to have been the ordinary residence of the kings of Israel, 1 Kings xiv. 17; xv. 53. Its name signifies "beautiful" or "delightful." *Comely as Jerusalem.* This was called "the perfection of beauty" Ps. xlviii. 2-3; l. 2. And thus the poet compares the bride's beauty to the two finest places in the land of Palestine, and the capitals of the two kingdoms of Israel and Judah.

5. *Thy hair is as a flock of goats.* See chap. iv. 1.

6. *Thy teeth.* See chap. iv. 2.

7. *As a piece of a pomegranate.* See chap. iv. 3.

8. *There are threescore queens.* Though there be sixty queens, and eighty concubines, or secondary wives, and virgins innumerable, in my harem, yet you, my dove, my undefiled, are *achath, one*, the only one, she in whom I delight beyond all.

MATTHEW HENRY

As Solomon himself is said to have been *tender and an only one in the sight of his mother* (Prov. iv. 3), so was she *the only one of her mother*, as dear as if she had been an only one, *the choice one of her that bore her.* All the kingdoms of the world, and the glory of them, are nothing, in Christ's account, compared with the church. She was admired by all her acquaintance, not only *the daughters*, her juniors, but even *the queens and the concubines*, who might have reason to be jealous of her as a rival; *they* all *blessed her*, *praised her*, and spoke well of her. Those that have any correct sense of things cannot but be convinced in their consciences (whatever they say) that godly people are excellent people; many will give them their good word, and more their goodwill. Jesus Christ is well pleased with those that honour such as fear the Lord, and takes it ill of those that *offend any of his little ones.*

VI. He produces the encomium that was given of her, and makes it his own (*v.* 10): *Who is she that looks forth as the morning?* This is applicable both to the church in the world and to grace in the heart. Christians are, or should be, the lights of the world. The patriarchal church *looked forth as the morning* when the promise of the Messiah was first made known, and *the day-spring from on high visited* this dark world. The Jewish church was *fair as the moon*; the ceremonial law was an imperfect light; it shone by reflection; did not make day, nor had *the sun of righteousness yet risen.* But the Christian church is *clear as the sun*, exhibits a great *light to those that sat in darkness.* The beauty of the church and of believers is *awful as an army with banners.* The church, in this world, is *as an army*, as the camp of Israel in the wilderness; its state is militant; it is in the midst of enemies, and is engaged in a constant conflict with them. Believers are soldiers in this army. It has its *banners*; the gospel of Christ is an ensign (Isa. xi. 12). It is marshalled, and kept in order and under discipline. It is *terrible* to its enemies. When the church preserves her purity she secures her honour and victory; when she is *fair as the moon*, and *clear as the sun*, she is truly great and formidable.

Verses 11–13

Christ having now returned to his spouse, and the breach being entirely made up, here gives an account of the distance and of the reconciliation.

I. When he had withdrawn from his church as his spouse, yet even then he had his eye upon it as his garden, which he took care of (*v.* 11): "*I went down into the garden of nuts*, or nutmegs, *to see the fruits of the valley*, with concern, to see them as my own." When he was out of sight he was no further off than the garden, observing *how the vine flourished*, that he might do all which was necessary to promote its flourishing. He went to see whether *the pomegranates budded.* Christ observes the first beginnings of the good work of grace in the soul and the early buddings of devout affections and inclinations there, and is well pleased with them, as we are with the blossoms of the spring.

II. Yet he could not long content himself with this, but suddenly felt a powerful inclination to return to his church, being moved with her lamentations after him (*v.* 12): "*Or ever I was aware, my soul made me like the chariots of Ammi-nadib;* I could not any longer keep at a distance; and I presently resolved to fly back to my love." And now the spouse perceives that he *heard the voice of her supplications*, and became *like the chariots of Ammi-nadib*, which were noted for their beauty and swiftness. Christ's people ought to be a willing people. If they continue seeking Christ and longing after him, even when he seems to withdraw from them, he will return to them in due time.

III. He, having returned to her, kindly courted her return to him, notwithstanding the discouragements she laboured under. Let her take the comfort of the return of her beloved, *v.* 13. Here the church is called the *Shulamite*, referring to *Salem*, the place of her birth and residence, as the woman of *Shunem* is called the *Shunamite.* Heaven is the Salem whence the saints have their birth, and where they have their citizenship. She is invited to return. As revolting sinners have need to be called to again and again (*Turn you, turn you, why will you die?*) so disquieted saints have need to be called to again and again, *Turn you, turn you*, why will you droop; *Why art thou cast down, O my soul?* Having returned, she is desired to show her face: *That we may look upon thee.* Go no longer with thy face covered like a mourner. Christ is pleased with the cheerfulness and humble confidence of his people and would have them look pleasant. A short account is given of what is to be seen in her. The question is asked, *What will you see in the Shulamite?* And it is answered, *As it were the*

JAMIESON, FAUSSET, BROWN

9. Hollow professors, like half wives, have no part in the one bride. **only one of her mother**—viz., "Jerusalem above" (Gal. 4:26). The "little sister" (ch. 8:8) is not inconsistent with her being "the only one"; for that sister is one with herself (John 10:16). **choice**—(Eph. 1:4; II Thess. 2:13.) As she exalted Him above all others (ch. 5:10), so He now her. **daughters . . . blessed her**—(Isa 8:18; 61:9; Ezek. 16:14; II Thess. 1:10.) So at her appearance after Pentecost (Acts. 4:13; 6:15; 24:25; 26:28).

10. The words expressing the admiration of the daughters. Historically (Acts 5:24-39.) **as the morning**—As yet she is not come to the fulness of her light (Prov. 4:18). **moon**—shining in the night, by light borrowed from the sun; so the bride, in the darkness of this world, reflects the light of the Sun of righteousness (II Cor. 3:18). **sun**—Her light of justification is perfect, for it is His (II Cor. 5:21; I John 4:17). The moon has less light, and has only one half illuminated; so the bride's sanctification is as yet imperfect. Her future glory (Matt. 13:43). **army**—(vs. 4). The climax requires this to be applied to the starry and angelic hosts, from which God is called Lord of Sabaoth. Her final glory (Gen. 15:5; Dan. 12:3; Rev. 12:1). The Church Patriarchal, "the morning"; Levitical, "the moon"; Evangelical, "the sun"; Triumphant, "the bannered army" (Rev. 19:14).

11. The bride's words; for she everywhere is the narrator, and often soliloquizes, which He never does. The first garden (ch. 2:11-13) was that of spring, full of flowers and grapes not yet ripe; the second, autumn, with spices (which are always connected with the person of Jesus Christ), and nothing unripe (ch. 4:13, etc.). The third here, of "nuts," from the previous autumn; the end of winter, and verge of spring; the Church in the upper room Acts 1:13, etc.), when one dispensation was just closed, the other not yet begun; the hard shell of the old needing to be broken, and its inner sweet kernel extracted [ORIGEN] (Luke 24:27, 32); waiting for the Holy Ghost to usher in spiritual spring. The *walnut* is meant, with a bitter outer husk, a hard shell, and sweet kernel. So the Word is distasteful to the careless; when awakened, the sinner finds the letter hard, until the Holy Ghost reveals the sweet inner spirit. **fruits of the valley**—MAURER translates, "the *blooming products* of the *river*," i.e., the plants growing on the margin of the river flowing through the garden. She goes to watch the *first* sproutings of the various plants. **12.** Sudden outpourings of the Spirit on Pentecost (Acts 2), while the Church was using the means (answering to "the garden," vs. 11; John 3:8). **Ammi-nadib**—supposed to me one proverbial for swift driving. Similarly (ch. 1:9). Rather, *my willing people* (Ps. 110:3). A willing chariot bore a "willing people"; or Nadib is *the Prince*, Jesus Christ (Ps. 68:17). She is borne in a moment into His presence (Eph. 2:6). **13.** Entreaty of the daughters of Jerusalem to her, in her chariot-like flight from them (cf. II Kings 2:12; II Sam. 19:14). **Shulamite**—new name applied to her now for the first time. *Feminine* of Solomon, Prince of Peace; His bride, daughter of peace, accepting and proclaiming it (Isa. 52:7; John 14:27; Rom. 5:1; Eph. 2:17). Historically, this name answers to the time when, not without a divine design in it, the young Church met in *Solomon's* porch (Acts 3:11, 5:12). The entreaty, "Return, O Shulamite," answers to the people's desire to keep Peter and John, after the lame man was healed, when they were about to enter the temple. Their reply attributing the glory not to themselves, but to Jesus Christ, answers to the bride's reply here,

ADAM CLARKE

10. *Looketh forth as the morning.* The bride is as lovely as the dawn of day.

F. C. COOK:

10. "As the morning." The glorious beauty of the bride bursts upon them like a second "dawn," as she comes forth to meet them at the commencement of another day. Peculiar poetical words are used for "sun" (burning heat) and "moon" (white one). The same terms are applied to sun and moon in Isaiah 24:23; 30:26.

11, 12. The bride's words may be paraphrased: "You speak of me as a glorious beauty: I was lately but a simple maiden engaged in rustic toils. I went down one day into the walnut garden" (the walnut abounded on the shores of Lake Gennesaret, and is still common in Northern Palestine) "to inspect the young plants of the vale" (i.e. the wady, or watercourse, with verdant banks in the early spring after the rainy season), "and to watch the budding and blossoming of vine and pomegranate." "Then, suddenly, ere I was myself aware, my soul" (the love-bound heart) "had made me the chariot of a lordly people" (i.e. an exalted personage, one who resides on the high places of the earth; compare 2 Kings 2:12; 8:14, where Elijah and Elisha, as the spiritual leaders of the nation, are "the chariot and horsemen of Israel"). This last clause is another instance of the love for military similitudes in the writer of the Song.

"Ammi-nadib." Lit. "my people a noble one." The reference is either to Israel at large as a wealthy and dominant nation, under Solomon, or to the bride's people (the Shulamites) in particular, to the chief place among whom, by her union with the king, she is now exalted.

—*Barnes' Notes*

12. *The chariots of Ammi-nadib.* Probably for their great speed these chariots became proverbial.

13. *Return, O Shulamite.* This appears to be addressed to the bride, as now the confirmed, acknowledged wife of Solomon. *The company of two armies.* Or the "musicians of the camps."

MATTHEW HENRY

company of two armies. (1) Some think she gives this account of herself. Alas! says she, *What will you see in the Shulamite?* nothing that is worth your looking upon, nothing but *as it were the company of two armies* actually engaged, where nothing is to be seen but blood and slaughter. The watchmen had wounded her, and she carried in her face the marks of those wounds, looked as if she had been fighting. She had said (*ch.* i. 6), *Look not upon me because I am black;* here she says, "Look not upon me because I am bloody." (2) Others think her beloved gives this account of her. "I will tell you what you shall *see in the Shulamite*; you shall see as noble a sight as that of two armies, or two parts of the same army, drawn out in rank and file; not only *as an army with banners*, but as *two armies*, with a majesty double to what was before. She is as *Mahanaim*, as the two hosts which Jacob saw (Gen. xxxii. 1, 2), a host of saints and a host of angels ministering to them; the church militant, the church triumphant."

CHAPTER 7

Verses 1–9

The title which Jesus Christ here gives to the church is new: *O prince's daughter!* agreeing with Ps. xlv. 13, where she is called *the king's daughter*. She is so in respect of her new birth, born from above, begotten of God, and his workmanship, bearing the image of the King of kings, and guided by his Spirit. She is so by marriage; Christ, by betrothing her to himself, though he found her mean and despicable, has made her a *prince's daughter*.

I. A copious description of the beauty of the spouse, which seems to be given by Christ himself, and to be designed to express his love to her as before, *ch.* iv. 1, &c., and *ch.* vi. 5, 6. The similitudes are here different from before, to show that the beauty of holiness is such as nothing in nature can reach. That commendation of the spouse, *ch.* iv, was immediately upon the espousals (*ch.* iii. 11), this upon her return from a by-path (*ch.* vi. 13); yet this exceeds that, to show the constancy of Christ's love to his people; *he loves them to the end.* The spouse had described the beauty of her beloved in ten particulars (*ch.* v. 11, &c.); and now he describes her in as many. The beauties of the church are reckoned from foot to head. 1. Her *feet* are here praised; the feet of Christ's ministers are beautiful in the eyes of the church (Isa. lii. 7), and her feet are here said to be beautiful in the eyes of Christ. *How beautiful are thy feet with shoes!* When believers, being made free from the captivity of sin (Acts xii. 8), have *their feet shod with the preparation of the gospel of peace*, and walk steadily according to the rule of the gospel, then their *feet are beautiful with shoes*; they tread firmly. 2. *The joints of the thighs are* here said to be *like jewels*, and those curiously wrought by *a cunning workman.* This is explained by Eph. iv. 16 and Col. ii. 19, where the mystical body of Christ is said to be held together by *joints and bands*, as the hips and knees (both which are *the joints of the thighs*) serve the natural body in its strength and motion. The church is *then* comely in Christ's eyes when those joints are kept firm by holy love and unity. 3. The *navel* is here compared to a round cup or *goblet*. The fear of the Lord is said to be *health to the navel.* See Prov. iii. 8. 4. The *belly is like a heap of wheat* in the storechamber, which perhaps was sometimes adorned with flowers. The *wheat* is useful, the *lilies* are beautiful; there is everything in the church which may be to the members of that body either for use or for ornament. All the body is nourished from the *belly*; it denotes the spiritual prosperity of a believer and the healthful constitution of the soul. 5. The *breasts are like two young roes that are twins*, *v.* 3. This comparison we had before, *ch.* iv. 5. 6. The *neck*, which before was compared to *the tower of David* (*ch.* iv. 4), is here compared to *a tower of ivory*, so white, so precious; such is the faith of the saints, by which they are joined to Christ their head. 7. The *eyes are* compared to *the fishpools in Heshbon*, or the artificial fish-ponds, *by a gate*, either of Jerusalem or of Heshbon, which is called *Bath-rabbim*, the daughter of a multitude, because a great thoroughfare. The understanding, the intentions of a believer, are clean and clear as these ponds. 8. The *nose* is like *the tower of Lebanon*, the forehead or face set *like a flint* (Isa. l. 7), undaunted as that tower was impregnable. So it denotes the magnanimity and holy bravery of the church, or (as others) a spiritual sagacity to discern things that differ, as animals strangely distinguish by the smell. This tower *looks towards Damascus*, the head city of Syria, denoting the boldness of the church in facing its enemies. 9. The *head like Carmel*, a very high hill near the sea, *v.* 5. The head of a be-

JAMIESON, FAUSSET, BROWN

"What will ye see" in me? "As it were," etc. She accepts the name Shulamite, as truly describing her. But adds, that though "one" (vs. 9), she is nevertheless "two." Her glories are her Lord's, beaming through her (Eph. 5:31, 32). The two armies are the family of Jesus Christ in heaven, and that on earth, joined and one with Him; the one militant, the other triumphant. Or Jesus Christ and His ministering angels are one army, the Church the other, both being one (John 17:21, 22). Allusion is made to Mahanaim (meaning *two hosts*), the scene of Jacob's victorious conflict by prayer (Gen. 32:2, 9, 22-30). Though she is peace, yet she has warfare here, between flesh and spirit within and foes without; her strength, as Jacob's at Mahanaim, is Jesus Christ and His host enlisted on her side by prayer; whence she obtains those graces which raise the admiration of the daughters of Jerusalem.

CHAPTER 7

Vss. 1-13. **thy feet**—rather, thy goings" (Ps. 17: 5). Evident allusion to Isaiah 52:7: *"How beautiful . . . are the feet* of him . . . that publisheth *peace"* (Shulamite, ch. 6:13). shoes—Sandals are richly jewelled in the East (Luke 15:22; Eph. 6:15). She is evidently "on the mountains," whither she was wafted (ch. 6:12), *above* the daughters of Jerusalem, who therefore portray her *feet* first. daughter—of God the Father, with whom Jesus Christ is one (Matt. 5:9), "children of (the) God" (of *peace*), equivalent to Shulamite (Ps. 45:10-15; II Cor. 6:18), as well as bride of Jesus Christ. **prince's**—therefore princely herself, freely giving the word of life to others, not sparing her "feet," as in ch. 5:3; Exod. 12:11. To act on the offensive is defensive to ourselves. **joints**—rather, "the rounding"; the full graceful curve of the hips in the female figure; like the *rounding* of a *necklace* (as the *Hebrew* for "jewels" means). Cf. with the *English Version,* Eph. 4:13-16; Col. 2:19. Or, applying it to the girdle binding together the robes round the hips (Eph. 6:14). **cunning workman**—(Ps. 139:14-16; Eph. 2:10, 22: 5:29, 30, 32). **2. navel**—rather, "girdle-clasp," called from the part of the person underneath. The "shoes" (vs. 1) prove that *dress* is throughout presupposed on all parts where it is usually worn. She is "a bride adorned for her husband"; the "uncomely parts," being most adorned (I Cor. 12:23). The girdle-clasp was adorned with red rubies resembling the "round goblet" (crater or *mixer)* of spice-mixed wine (not "liquor," ch. 8:2; Isa. 5:22). The wine of the "New Testament in His blood" (Luke 22:20). The spiritual exhilaration by it was mistaken for that caused by new wine (Acts 2:13-17; Eph. 5:18). **belly**—i.e., *the vesture* on it. As in Psalm 45:13, 14, gold and needlework compose the bride's attire, so golden-colored "wheat" and white "lilies" here. The ripe grain, in token of harvest joy, used to be decorated with lilies; so the accumulated spiritual food (John 6:35; 12:24), free from chaff, not fenced with thorns, but made attractive by lilies (believers, ch. 2:2; Acts 2:46, 47; 5:13, 14, in common partaking of it). Associated with the exhilarating wine-cup (Zech. 9:17), as here. **3.** The daughters of Jerusalem describe her in the same terms as Jesus Christ in ch. 4:5. The testimonies of heaven and earth coincide. **twins**—faith and love. **4. tower of ivory**—In ch. 4:4, Jesus Christ saith, "a tower of David builded for an armory." Strength and conquest are the main thought in His description; here, beauty and polished whiteness; contrast ch. 1. **fishpools**—seen by BURCKHARDT, clear (Rev. 22:1), deep, quiet, and full (I Cor. 2:10, 15). **Heshbon**—east of Jordan, residence of the Amorite king, Sihon (Num. 21:25, etc.), afterwards held by Gad. **Bath-rabbim**—"daughter of a multitude"; a crowded thoroughfare. Her eyes (ch. 4:1) are called by Jesus Christ, "doves' eyes," waiting on Him. But here, looked on by the daughters or Jerusalem, they are compared to a placid lake. She is calm even amidst the crowd (Prov. 8:2; John 16:33). **nose**—or, face. **tower of Lebanon**—a border fortress, watching the hostile Damascus. Towards Jesus Christ her face was full of holy shame (ch. 4:1, 3, *Notes*); towards spiritual foes, like a watchtower (Hab. 2:1; Mark 13:37; Acts 4:13), elevated, so that she looks not up from earth to heaven, but down from heaven to earth. If we retain "nose," discernment of spiritual fragrance is meant. **5. upon thee**—the head-dress "upon" her. **Carmel**—signifying a well-cultivated field (Isa. 35:2). In ch. 5:15 He is compared to

ADAM CLARKE

CHAPTER 7

1. *How beautiful are thy feet with shoes!* "How graceful is your walking!" In the sixth chapter the bridegroom praises the Shulamite, as we might express it, from head to foot. Here he begins a new description, taking her from foot to head.

JOHN GILL:

Verse 1. "How beautiful are thy feet with shoes." It is no unusual thing to describe the comeliness of women by their feet, and the ornaments of them; so Hebe is described by Homer as having beautiful feet, and Juno by her golden shoes: particular care was taken of, and provision made for, the shoes of queens and princesses in the eastern countries; Herodotus tells us that the city of Anthylla was given peculiarly to the wife of the king of Egypt, to provide her with shoes; which custom, he says, obtained when Egypt became subject to Persia (Esther 2:18). Shoes of a red, or scarlet, or purple color, were in esteem with the Jews; and so the Targum here is, "purple shoes": the word used is thought by some to signify a color between scarlet and purple. That this is said of the church is plain from the appellation of her, "O Prince's daughter!" the same with the King's daughter (Ps. 45:13); the daughter of the King of kings; for, being espoused to Christ, his Father is her Father, and his God her God: besides, she is born of him who is the Prince of the kings of the earth (1 John 2:28); she is both a Prince's wife and a Prince's daughter. It may be rendered, "O noble," or "princely daughter"; being of a free princely spirit, in opposition to a servile one (Ps. 51:12); of a bountiful and liberal spirit, as in Isaiah 32:5–8; in distributing temporal things to the necessities of the poor; and in communicating spiritual things to the comfort and edification of others.

—Gill's Commentary

MATTHEW HENRY

liever is *lifted up above his enemies* (Ps. xxvii. 6), above the storms of the lower region, as the top of Carmel was, pointing heavenward. 10. *The hair of the head* is said to be *like purple.* This denotes the amiableness of a believer in the eyes of Christ, even to *the hair*, or (as some understand it) the pins with which *the hair* is dressed.

II. The church thus beautified and adorned is lovely indeed if she be so in his eyes. His love makes this comeliness truly valuable. 1. He delighted to look upon his church. *The king is held in the galleries,* and cannot leave them. And, if Christ has such delight *in the galleries* of communion with his people, much more reason have they to delight in them. 2. He was struck with admiration at the beauty of his church (*v.* 6): *How fair and how pleasant art thou, O love! How art thou made fair!* (so the word is), "not born so, but made so with the comeliness which I have put upon thee." 3. He determined to keep up communion with his church. He compares her *stature to a palm-tree* (*v.* 7), so straight, so strong, does she appear. The *palm-tree* is observed to flourish most when it is loaded; so the church, the more it has been afflicted, the more it has multiplied; and the branches of it are emblems of victory. Christ says, "*I will go up to the palm-tree,* to entertain myself with the shadow of it (*v.* 8) and *I will take hold of its boughs* and observe the beauty of them." He compares her *breasts* (her pious affections towards him) *to clusters of grapes,* a most pleasant fruit (*v.* 7), and he repeats it (*v.* 8): They *shall be* (that is, they shall be to me) *as clusters of the vine,* which *make glad the heart.* "Now that I come *up to the palm-tree* thy graces shall be exerted and excited." *The smell of* their nostrils is *like the smell of apples,* or oranges, which is pleasing and reviving. And, *lastly, the roof of her mouth is like the best wine* (*v.* 9); her spiritual taste and relish, of the words she speaks to God and man, which come from *the roof of the mouth,* these are pleasing to God. *The prayer of the upright is his delight.* It is like that wine which is palatable and grateful to the taste. It *goes down sweetly.* Nothing *goes down* so *sweetly* with a gracious soul as the wine of God's consolations. The presence of Christ by his Spirit with his people shall be reviving and refreshing to them, as that strong wine which makes *the lips* even *of those that are asleep* (that are ready to faint away in a delirium), *to speak.* Unconverted sinners are asleep; saints are often drowsy, and listless, and half asleep; but the word and Spirit of Christ will put life and vigour into the soul, and *out of the abundance of the heart* that is thus filled *the mouth* will *speak.*

Verses 10–13

These are the words of the spouse, the church, the believing soul.

I. She here triumphs in her relation to Christ. With what holy exultation does she say (*v.* 10), "*I am my beloved's,* not my own, but entirely devoted to him and owned by him." Glorying in this, that she is his, to serve him, she comforts herself with this, that his *desire is towards her.* Christ's desire was strongly towards his chosen remnant, when he came from heaven to earth to seek and save them. This is a comfort to believers that, whosoever slights them, Christ has a desire towards them, such a desire as will again bring him from heaven to earth to receive them to himself.

II. She humbly and earnestly desires communion with him (*v.* 11, 12): "*Come, my beloved,* let us take a walk together, that I may receive counsel, instruction, and comfort from thee, and may make known my wants and grievances to thee, with freedom, and without interruption." Thus Christ walked with the two disciples that were going to the village called *Emmaus,* and talked with them, till he made their *hearts burn within them.* She desires to go forth into the fields and villages to have this communion with him. Those that would converse with Christ must go forth from the world, must avoid everything that would divert the mind and be a hindrance to it when it should be wholly taken up with Christ. *Let us get up early to the vineyards.* It intimates her care to improve opportunities of conversing with her beloved. She will be content to take up her lodging in the villages. His presence will make them fine and pleasant. A gracious soul can reconcile itself to the poorest accommodations, if it may have communion with God in them.

III. She desires to be better acquainted with the state of her own soul and the present posture of its affairs (*v.* 12): *Let us see if the vine flourish.* Our own souls are our vineyards. We are made keepers of these vineyards, and therefore are concerned often to look into them, to examine the state of our own souls, to seek whether the *vine flourishes,* whether we be fruitful in the fruits of righteousness. And especi-

JAMIESON, FAUSSET, BROWN

majestic Lebanon; she here, to *fruitful* Carmel. Her head-dress, or crown (II Tim. 4:8; I Pet. 5:4). Also the souls won by her (I Thess. 2:19, 20), a token of her fruitfulness. **purple**—royalty (Rev. 1:6). As applied to hair, it expresses the glossy splendor of black hair (lit., "pendulous hair") so much admired in the East (ch. 4:1). While the King compares her hair to the flowering hair of goats (the token of her *subjection*), the daughters of Jerusalem compare it to *royal* purple. **galleries**—(so ch. 1:17. *Margin;* Rev. 21:3.) But MAURER translates here, "flowing ringlets"; with these, as with "thongs" (so LEE, from the *Arabic* translates it) "the King is held" bound (ch. 6:5; Prov. 6:25). Her purple crowns of martyrdom especially captivated the King, appearing from His galleries (Acts 7:55, 56). As Samson's strength was in his locks (Judg. 16:17). Here first the daughters see the King themselves. **6.** Nearer advance of the daughters to the Church (Acts 2:47; 5:13, end). Love to her is the first token of love to Him (I John 5:1, end). **delights**—fascinating charms to them and to the King (vs. 5; Isa. 62:4, Hephzibah). Hereafter, too (Zeph. 3:17; Mal. 3:12; Rev. 21:9). **7. palm tree**—(Ps. 92:12.) The sure sign of *water near* (Exod. 15:27; John 7:38). **clusters**—not of dates, as MOODY STUART thinks. The parallelism (vs. 8), "clusters of the vine," shows it is here clusters of grapes. Vines were often trained (termed "wedded") on other trees. **8.** The daughters are no longer content to admire, but resolve to lay hold of her fruits, high though these be. The palm stem is bare for a great height, and has its crown of fruit-laden boughs at the summit. It is the symbol of triumphant joy (John 12:13); so hereafter (Rev. 7:9). **breasts**—(Isa. 66:11.) **the vine**—Jesus Christ (Hos. 14:7, end; John 15:1). **nose**—i.e., breath; the Holy Ghost breathed into her *nostrils* by Him, whose "mouth is most sweet" (ch. 5:16). **apples**—citrons, off the tree to which He is likened (ch. 2:3). **9. roof of thy mouth**—thy voice (Prov. 15:23). **best wine**—the *new* wine of the gospel kingdom (Mark 14:25), poured out at Pentecost (Acts 2:4, 13, 17). **for my beloved**—(Ch. 4:10). Here first the daughters call Him theirs, and become one with the bride. The steps successively are (ch. 1:5) where they misjudge her (ch. 3:11); ch. 5:8, where the possibility of their finding Him, before she regained Him, is expressed; ch. 5:9 (ch. 6:1; 7:6, 9), (John 4:42). **causing . . . asleep to speak**—(Isa. 35:6; Mark 5:19, 20; Acts 2:47; Eph. 5:14.) Jesus Christ's first miracle turned water into "good wine kept until now" (John 2); just as the Gospel revives those asleep and dying under the law (Prov. 31:6; Rom. 7:9, 10, 24, 25; 8:1).

10. Words of the daughters of Jerusalem and the bride, now united into one (Acts 4:32). They are mentioned again distinctly (ch. 8:4), as fresh converts were being added from among inquirers, and these needed to be charged not to grieve the Spirit. **his desire is toward me**—strong assurance. He so desires us, as to give us sense of His desire toward us (Ps. 139:17, 18; Luke 22:15; Gal. 2:20; I John 4:16).

11. field—the country. "The tender grape (MAURER translates, flowers) and vines" occurred before (ch. 2:13). But here she prepares for Him all kinds of fruit old and new; also, she anticipates, in going forth to seek them, communion with Him in "loves." "Early" implies immediate earnestness. "The villages" imply distance from Jerusalem. At Stephen's death the disciples were scattered from it through Judea and Samaria, preaching the word (Acts 8). Jesus Christ was with them, confirming the word with miracles. They gathered the *old* fruits, of which Jesus Christ had sown the seed (John 4), as well as *new* fruits. **lodge**—forsaking *home* for Jesus Christ's sake (Matt. 19:29). **12.** (Mark 1:35; John 9:4; Gal. 6:10.) Assurance fosters diligence, not indolence.

ADAM CLARKE

7. *Like to a palm tree.* Which is remarkably straight, taper, and elegant.

F. B. MEYER:

"I am my Beloved's, and his desire is toward me" (S. of Sol. 7:10). This is the thankful recognition of the Bride. She knows that she belongs to, that she is loved by, the Bridegroom—that his desire is turned towards her with ineffable longing.

Dear soul, do you realize the desire of your Beloved towards you? You love Him; but He loves you ever so much more. You desire Him; but his desire towards you is as much greater than yours towards Him, as sunlight is more brilliant than moonlight. Know ye not, says James, that the Spirit which He has caused to dwell in us longeth even to envy? Jesus desires all our love, all our energy, all our possessions, that we should be only, always, all for Him. How have we responded to his great desire? Alas, our response has been very uncertain and unsatisfactory. Sometimes we have felt a pure flame answering affection; but it has soon been obscured with clouds of smoke, or has died down for want of oil.

The Lord desires more of our time, that we should withdraw ourselves from the busy rush of the world and the absorbing interests of life, in order to allow Him to commune with us. He desires more of our affection, that He may teach us how to respond to his love. He desires to teach us how to share his riches, as his joint-heirs; how to sit with Him in heavenly places; how to work in the energy of his Spirit. Let us yield ourselves to his desires, and allow Him to effect in us and for us all He desires for us, so that we may give Him delight. "As the bridegroom rejoiceth over the bride, so shall thy God rejoice over thee." If, as Zephaniah says, He is silent in his love, because his love is too strong for speech, we may yield ourselves to it without misgiving.—*Great Verses Through the Bible*

11. *Let us go forth into the field.* It has been conjectured that the bridegroom arose early every morning, left the bride's apartment, and withdrew to the country; often leaving her asleep, and commanding her companions not to disturb her till she should awake of herself. Here the bride wishes to accompany her spouse to the country, and spend a night at his country house.

12. *Let us get up early to the vineyards.* When in the country, we shall have the better opportunity to contemplate the progress of the spring vegetation; and there she promises to be peculiarly affectionate to him.

MATTHEW HENRY

ally let us enquire whether *the tender grape appear* and whether *the pomegranates bud forth*, what good motions and dispositions there are in us that are yet but young and tender, that they may be protected and cherished with particular care, that they may bring forth fruit unto perfection. And, if we would be acquainted with ourselves, we must beg of him to search and try us, to help us in the search, and discover us to ourselves.

IV. She promises to her beloved the best entertainment she can give him; for he will come in to us, and sup with us, Rev. iii. 20. 1. She promises him her best affections. 2. She promises him her best provision, *v.* 13. "There we shall find pleasant odours, for *the mandrakes give a smell.* We shall also find that which is good for food, as well as pleasant to the eye: *At our gates are all manner of pleasant fruits.*" The fruits and exercises of grace are pleasant to the Lord Jesus. These must be carefully devoted to his service and honour, must be always ready, as that is which is laid up at our gates. There is a great variety of these pleasant fruits, with which our souls should be well stocked; we must have grace for all occasions. Those that truly love Christ will think all they have even their most *pleasant fruits*, and what they have treasured up most carefully, too little to be bestowed upon him.

JAMIESON, FAUSSET, BROWN

13. mandrakes—*Hebrew, audaim,* from a root meaning "to love"; love-apples, supposed to exhilarate the spirits and excite love. Only here and Genesis 30:14-16. *Atropa mandragora* of Linnaeus; its leaves like lettuce, but dark green, flowers purple, root forked, fruit of the size of an apple, ruddy and sweet-smelling, gathered in wheat harvest, **i.e., in May** (*Mariti*, ii. 195). **gates**—the **entrance to** the kiosk or summerhouse. Love "lays up" the best of everything for the person beloved (I Cor. 10:31; Phil. 3:8; I Pet. 4:11), thereby really, though unconsciously, laying up for itself (I Tim. 6:18, 19).

ADAM CLARKE

TODAY'S DICTIONARY OF THE BIBLE:

Mandrakes—Hebrew *dudâîm*; i.e., "love plants"—occurs only in Gen. 30:14–16 and Song of Sol. 7:13. Many interpretations have been given this word *dudâîm.* It has been rendered "violets," "lilies," "jasmines," "truffles or mushrooms," "flowers," the "citron," etc. The weight of authority is in favor of its being regarded as the *Mandragora officinalis* of botanists—"a near relative of the nightshades, the 'apple of Sodom' and the potato plant." It possesses stimulating and narcotic properties (Gen. 30:14–16). The fruit of this plant resembles the potato apple in size, and is of a pale orange color. It has been called the "love apple." The Arabs call it "Satan's apple." It still grows near Jerusalem and in other parts of Palestine.

MATTHEW HENRY — CHAPTER 8

Verses 1–4

1. The spouse wishes for a constant intimacy and freedom with the Lord Jesus. She was obliged to be shy and to keep at some distance; she therefore wishes she may be taken for his sister, he having called her so (*ch.* v. 1), and that she might have the same chaste and innocent familiarity with him that a sister has with a brother. It is the wish of all believers for a more intimate communion with him, that they might *receive the Spirit of sanctification*, and so Christ might be as their brother, that is, that they might be as his brethren, which *then* they are when by grace they are made partakers of a divine nature, Heb. ii. 11, &c. 2. She promises herself then the satisfaction of making a more open profession of her relation to him than at present she could make: "*When I should find thee without*, anywhere, even before company, *I would kiss thee*, as a sister does her own brother." The church, since Christ's incarnation, can better own him than she could before, when she would have been laughed at for being so much in love with one that was not yet born. Christ has become as our brother; wherever we find him, therefore, let us be ready to own our relation to him and affection for him. 3. She promises to improve the opportunity she should then have for cultivating an acquaintance with him (*v.* 2): "*I would lead thee*, as my brother. I would bring *thee into my mother's house*, into the church, into the solemn assemblies (*ch.* iii. 4), and *there thou wouldst instruct me.*" It is the presence of Christ in and with his church that makes the word and ordinances instructive to her children, who shall all be taught of God. 4. She promises him to bid him welcome to the best she had; she would *cause him to drink of her spiced wine and the juice of her pomegranate.* The exercise of grace and the performance of duty are to the Lord Jesus, very acceptable to him, as expressive of a grateful sense of his favours. 5. She doubts not but to experience his tender care of her, that she should be supported by his power. (*His left hand shall be under my head*) and that she should be comforted with his love—*His right hand should embrace me.* While we are following hard after Christ his *right hand sustains* Ps. lxiii. 8. *Underneath are the everlasting arms.* 6. She charges those about her to take heed of doing anything to interrupt the pleasing communion she now had with her beloved (*v.* 4). The church, our common mother, charges all her children that they never do anything to provoke Christ to withdraw.

Verses 5–7

I. The spouse is much admired by those about her. It comes in in a parenthesis, but in it gospel-grace lies as plain, and as much above ground, as anywhere in this mystical song: *Who is this that comes up from the wilderness, leaning upon her beloved?* They are the words of the daughters of Jerusalem, to whom she spoke (*v.* 4); they see her, and bless her. The Jewish church came up from the wilderness supported by the divine power and favour, Deut. xxxii. 10, 11. The Christian church was raised up from a low and desolate condition by the grace of Christ relied on, Gal. iv. 27. Particular believers are admirable, and divine grace is to be admired in them, when by the

JAMIESON, FAUSSET, BROWN — CHAPTER 8

Vss. 1-14. **1.** He had been a brother already. Why, then, this prayer here? It refers to the time after His resurrection, when the previous *outward* intimacy with Him was no longer allowed, but it was implied it should be renewed at the second coming (John 20:17). For this the Church here prays; meanwhile she enjoys *inward* spiritual communion with Him. The last who ever "kissed" Jesus Christ on earth was the traitor Judas. The bride's return with the King to her mother's house answers to Acts 8:25, after the mission to Samaria. The rest spoken of (vs. 4) answers to Acts 9:31. **that sucked . . . mother**—a brother born of the same mother; the closest tie.

2. Her desire to bring Him into her home circle (John 1:41). **who would instruct me**—rather, "thou wouldest instruct me," viz., how I might best please thee (Isa. 11:2, 3; 50:4; Luke 12: 12; John 14:26; 16:13).

spiced wine—seasoned with aromatic perfumes. Jesus Christ ought to have our choicest gifts. Spices are never introduced in the song in His absence; therefore the time of His return from "the mountain of spices" (vs. 14) is contemplated. The cup of betrothal was given by Him at the last supper; the cup or marriage shall be presented by her at His return (Matt. 26:29). Till then the believer often cannot feel towards, or speak of, Him as he would wish. **3, 4.** The "left and right hand," etc., occurred only once actually (ch. 2:6), and here optatively. Only at His first manifestation did the Church palpably embrace Him; at His second coming there shall be again sensible communion with Him. The rest in vs. 4, which is a *spiritual* realization of the wish in vs. 3 (I Pet. 1:8), and the charge not to disturb it, close the 1st, 2d, and 4th canticles; not the 3d, as the bridegroom there takes charge Himself; nor the 5th, as, if *repose* formed its close, we might mistake the present state for our rest. The broken, longing close, like that of the whole Bible (Rev. 22:20), reminds us we are to be waiting for a Saviour to come. On "daughters of Jerusalem," see *Note*, ch. 7:10.

CANTICLE V.—Ch. 8:5-14.—FROM THE CALL OF THE GENTILES TO THE CLOSE OF REVELATION. **5. Who is this**—Words of the daughters of Jerusalem, i.e., the churches of Judea; referring to Paul, on his return from Arabia ("the wilderness"), whither he had gone after conversion (Gal. 1:15-24).

ADAM CLARKE — CHAPTER 8

1. *O that thou wert as my brother!* The bride, fearing that her fondness for her spouse might be construed into too great a familiarity, wishes that he were her little brother; and then she might treat him in the most affectionate manner, and kiss him even in the streets without suspicion, and without giving offense to anyone.

CHARLES H. SPURGEON:

Verse 5. Careful readers will have noticed that in the verses which precede, the spouse had been particularly anxious that her communion with her Lord might not be disturbed. Her language is intensely earnest, "I charge you, O daughters of Jerusalem, that ye stir not up, nor awake my love, until He please." She valued much the fellowship with which her Beloved solaced her; she was jealously alarmed lest she should endanger the continuance of it; lest any sin on her part or on the part of her companions should cause the Beloved to withdraw Himself in anger. Now it is a very striking fact that immediately after we read a verse so full of solicitous care concerning the maintenance of communion, we immediately fall upon another verse in which the upward progress of that selfsame spouse is the theme of admiration; she who would not have her Beloved disturbed is the selfsame bride who cometh up from the wilderness, leaning herself upon Him; from which it is clear that there is a most intimate connection between communion with Christ and progress in grace, and therefore the more careful we are to maintain fellowship with our Lord, the more successful shall we be in going from strength to strength in all those holy graces which are landmarks on the road to glory. The well-head and fountain of growth in grace is well-sustained communion and manifest oneness with Christ; we may strive after moral virtue if we will, but we shall be like those foolish children who pluck flowers and thrust them into their little gardens without roots; but if we strive after increasing faith in Jesus, we shall be as wise men, who plant choice bulbs and living seeds, from which shall in due time uprise the golden cups or the azure bells of lovely flowers.
—*The Treasury of the Old Testament*

MATTHEW HENRY

power of that grace they are brought *up from the wilderness, leaning* with a holy confidence *upon* Jesus Christ *their beloved.* This bespeaks the beauty of a soul, and the wonders of divine grace.

II. She addresses herself to her beloved.

1. She puts him in mind of the former experience which she and others had had of comfort in applying to him. (1) For her own part: "*I raised thee up under the apple tree*, that is, I have many a time wrestled with thee by prayer and have prevailed. When I was alone in the acts of devotion, retired in the orchard, under *the apple-tree*, meditating and praying, then *I raised thee up*, to help me and comfort me," as the disciples raised him up in the storm, saying, *Master, carest thou not that we perish?* (Mark iv. 38). (2) Others also had had like experience of comfort in Christ. There *thy mother brought thee forth*, the universal church, or believing souls, in whom Christ was formed, Gal. iv. 15. Those that had *travailed* in convictions at last *brought forth* in consolations, and the *pain was forgotten* for joy of the Saviour's birth.

2. She begs of him that her union with him might be confirmed, and her communion with him continued and made more intimate (*v.* 6): *Set me as a seal upon thy heart, as a seal upon thy arm.* "Let me have a place in thy heart, an interest in thy love. Be thou my high priest; let my name be written on thy breast-plate, nearer thy heart. Let thy power be engaged for me, as an evidence of thy love to me; let me be not only a *seal upon thy heart*, but a *seal upon thy arm*; let me be ever borne up in thy arms, and know it to my comfort."

3. To enforce this petition, she pleads the power of love.

(1) Love is a vigorous passion. It is *strong as death.* Christ's love to us was *strong as death*, for it broke through death itself. *He loved us, and gave himself for us.* The love of true believers to Christ is *strong as death*, for it makes them dead to everything else. *Jealousy is cruel as the grave*, which swallows up and devours all; those that truly love Christ are jealous of everything that would draw them from him. *The coals thereof* burn with incredible fury and irresistible force, as the *coals of fire that have a most vehement flame*, a *flame of the Lord* (so some read it). Holy love is a fire that begets a vehement heat in the soul, and consumes the dross and chaff that are in it.

(2) Love is a valiant victorious passion. Holy love is so; the reigning love of God in the soul is constant and firm, and will not be drawn off from him by *life or death*, Rom. viii. 38. Death, and all its terrors, will not frighten a believer from loving Christ: *Many waters*, though they will quench fire, *cannot quench this love*, no, nor the *floods drown it*, *v.* 7. No waters could quench Christ's love to us, nor any floods drown it; he waded through the greatest difficulties, even seas of blood.

Verses 8–12

Christ and his spouse having sufficiently confirmed their love to each other, *strong as death* and inviolable, they are here, in these verses, consulting together about their affairs. Yoke-fellows, having laid their hearts together, lay their heads together.

I. They are here consulting about their sister, their little sister, and the disposing of her.

1. The spouse proposes her case with a compassionate concern (*v.* 8): *We have a little sister and she has no breasts* (she has not grown up to maturity); *what shall we do for* this *little sister* of *ours in the day that she shall be spoken for?* (1) This may be understood as spoken by the Jewish church concerning the Gentile world. God had espoused the church of the Jews, and she was richly endowed, but what shall become of the poor Gentiles. Their condition (say the pious Jews) is very forlorn; they are *sisters*, but they are *little*, because not dignified with the knowledge of God; they *have no breasts*, no divine revelation, no scriptures, no ministers, no breasts of consolation, being *strangers to the covenants of promise. What shall we do for* them? We can but pity them, and pray for them. Now the tables are turned; the Gentiles are betrothed to Christ, and ought to return the kindness by an equal concern for the bringing in of the Jews again, our eldest sister, that once had breasts, but now has none.

2. Christ soon determines what to do in this case, and his spouse agrees with him in it (*v.* 9): "*If she be a wall*, if the good work be once begun with the Gentiles, with the souls that are to be called in, if the *little sister, when she shall be spoken for* by the gospel, will but receive the word, and build herself upon Christ the foundation, *we will build upon her a palace of silver*, we will carry on the good work that is begun, till the wall become a palace, the wall of stone a palace of silver." This *little sister*, when once she is joined to the Lord, shall be made to *grow into a holy*

JAMIESON, FAUSSET, BROWN

I raised thee . . . she . . . bare thee—(Acts 26:14-16.) The first words of Jesus Christ to the bride since her going to the garden of nuts (ch. 6:9, 10); so His appearance to Paul is the only one since His ascension, vs. 13 is not an address of Him as *visible:* her reply implies He is not visible (I Cor. 15:8). Spiritually, she was found in the moral wilderness (Ezek. 16:5, Hos. 13: 5); but now she is "coming up from" it (Jer. 2:2; Hos. 2:14), especially in the last stage of her journey, her conscious weakness casting itself the more wholly on Jesus Christ (II Cor. 12:9). "Raised" (Eph. 2:1-7). Found ruined under the forbidden tree (Gen. 3); restored under the shadow of Jesus Christ crucified, "the green tree" (Luke 23:31), fruit-"bearing" by the cross (Isa. 53:11; John 12:24). Born again by the Holy Ghost" "there" (Ezek. 16:3-6). In this verse, *her dependence,* in the similar verse, ch. 3:6, etc., *His omnipotence to support her,* are brought out (Deut. 33:26). **6.** Implying approaching absence of the Bridegroom. **seal**—having her name and likeness engraven on it. His Holy Priesthood also in heaven (Exod. 28:6-12, 15-30); Heb. 4:14); "his heart" there answering to "thine heart" here, and "two shoulders" to "arm." (Cf. Jer. 22:24, with Hag. 2:23.) But the Holy Ghost (Eph. 1:13, 14). As in vs. 5, she was "leaning" on Him, i.e., her arm on His *arm,* her head on His *bosom;* so she prays now that before they part, her impression may be engraven both on His *heart* and His *arm,* answering to His *love* and His *power* (Ps. 77:15; see Gen. 38:18; Isa. 62:3). **love is strong as death**—(Acts 21:13; Rom. 8:35-39; Rev. 12:11.) This their love unto death flows from His (John 10:15; 15:13). **jealousy . . . the grave**—*Zealous love,* jealous of all that would come between the soul and Jesus Christ (I Kings 19:10; Ps. 106:30, 31; Luke 9:60; 14:26; I Cor. 16:22). **cruel**—rather, "unyielding" hard, as the grave will not let go those whom it once holds (John 10:28). **a most vehement flame**—lit., "the fire-flame of Jehovah" (Ps. 80:16; Isa. 6:6). Nowhere else is *God's* name found in the Song. The zeal that burnt in Jesus Christ (Ps. 69:9; Luke 12:49, 50) kindled in His followers (Acts 2:3; Rom. 15:30; Phil. 2:17). **7. waters**—in contrast with the "coals of fire" (vs. 6; I Kings 18:33-38). Persecutions (Acts 8:1) cannot quench love (Heb. 10:34; Rev. 12:15, 16). Our many provocations have not quenched His love (Rom. 8:33-39). **if . . . give all the substance . . . contemned**—Nothing short of Jesus Christ Himself, not even heaven without Him, can satisfy the saint (Phil. 3:8). Satan offers the world, as to Jesus Christ (Matt. 4: 8), so to the saint, in vain (I John 2:15-17; 5:4). Nothing but our love in turn can satisfy Him (I Cor. 13:1-3). **8.** The Gentile Church (Ezek. 16:48). "We," i.e., the Hebrew Church, which heretofore admitted Gentiles to communion, only by becoming *Judaic proselytes.* Now first *idolatrous* Gentiles are admitted *directly* (Acts 11:17-26). Generally, the saint's anxiety for other souls (Mark 5:19; John 4:28, 29). **no breasts**—neither faith nor love as yet (*Note,* ch. 4:5), which "come by hearing" of Him who first loved us. Not yet fit to be His bride, and mother of a spiritual offspring. **what shall we do**—the chief question in the early Church at the first council (Acts 15). How shall "the elder brother" treat the "younger," already received by the Father (Luke 15:25-32)? Generally (II Sam. 15:15; John 9:4; Acts 9:6; Gal. 6:10). **In the day . . . spoken for**—i.e., when she shall be *sought in marriage* (Judg. 14:7), viz., by Jesus Christ, the heavenly bridegroom.

9. wall . . . door—the very terms employed as to the Gentile question (Acts 14:27; Eph. 2:14). If she be a wall in Zion, founded on Jesus Christ (I Cor. 3:11), we will not "withstand God" (Acts 11:17; 15:8-11). But if so, we must not "build" (Acts 15:14-17) on her "wood, hay, stubble" (I Cor. 3:12), i.e., Jewish rites, etc., but "a palace of silver," i.e., all the highest privileges of church communion (Gal. 2:11-18; Eph. 2:11-22). Image from the splendid turrets "built" on the "walls" of Jerusalem, and flanking the

ADAM CLARKE

5. *That cometh up from the wilderness.* Perhaps the words of the daughters of Jerusalem, who, seeing the bride returning from the country, leaning on the arm of her beloved, are filled with admiration at her excellent carriage and beauty.

6. *A most vehement flame.* "The flame of God."

8. *We have a little sister.* This young girl belonged most probably to the bride.

She hath no breasts. She is not yet marriageable.

What shall we do for our sister? How shall we secure her comfort and welfare?

In the day when she shall be spoken for? When any person shall demand her in marriage.

9. *If she be a wall.* All these expressions, says Calmet, show that it was necessary to provide a husband for this young sister. For a woman without a husband is like a wall without towers, and without defense; is like a gate or door without bar or lock; and like a city without walls.

MATTHEW HENRY

temple, a habitation of God through the Spirit, Eph. ii. 21, 22. *If she be a door*, when this palace comes to be finished, then *we will enclose her with boards of cedar*. Though the beginnings of grace be small, the latter end shall greatly increase.

3. The spouse takes this occasion to acknowledge with thankfulness his kindness to her, *v.* 10. She is very willing to trust him with her *little sister*, for she herself had had great experience of his grace, and, for her part, she owed her all to him: *I am a wall, and my breasts like towers. Then was I in his eyes as one that found favour*. With what joy and triumph we ought to speak of God's grace towards us, and with what satisfaction we should look back upon the special times and seasons when *we were in his eyes as those that find favour*; these were days never to be forgotten.

II. They are here consulting about *a vineyard* they had in the country, the church of Christ on earth considered under the notion of *a vineyard* (*v.* 11, 12): *Solomon had a vineyard at Baal-hamon*; his vineyard was a type of the church of Christ. Our Saviour has given us a key to these verses in the parable of the vineyard let out to unthankful husbandmen, Matt. xxi. 33. The bargain was that, every one of the tenants having so much of the vineyard assigned him as would contain 1000 vines, he was to pay the annual rent of 1000 *pieces of silver*; for we read (Isa. vii. 23) that in a fruitful soil there were 1000 *vines at* 1000 *silverlings*. 1. Christ's church is his vineyard, a pleasant place; he delights to walk in it, and is pleased with its fruits. 2. He has entrusted each of us with his vineyard, as *keepers* of it. The privileges of the church are that good thing which he has committed to us, to be kept as a sacred trust. The service of the church is to be our business. 3. He expects rent from those that are employed in his vineyard and entrusted with it. *He comes, seeking fruit*, and requires gospel-duty of all those that enjoy gospel-privileges. 4. Though Christ has *let out his vineyard to keepers*, yet still it is his, and he has his eye always upon it for good. Some take these for Christ's words (*v.* 12): *My vineyard, which is mine, is before me;* and they observe how he dwells upon his property in it: It is *my vineyard, which is mine*; so dear is his church to him, it is *his own in the world* (John xiii. 1), and therefore he will always have it under his protection. 5. The church, that enjoys the privileges of the vineyard, must have them always before her. The keeping of the vineyard requires constant care and diligence. They are rather the words of the spouse: *My vineyard, which is mine, is before me*. She had lamented her fault and folly in not keeping her *own vineyard* (*ch.* i. 6), but now she resolves to reform. Our hearts are our vineyards, which we must *keep with all diligence*.

Verses 13–14

Christ and his spouse are here parting for a while; she must stay below *in the gardens* on earth, where she has work to do for him; he must remove to *the mountains of spices* in heaven, where he has business to attend for her, as *an advocate with the Father*.

I. He desires to hear often from her. "*Thou that*, for the present, *dwellest in the gardens*, dressing and keeping them till thou remove from the garden below to the paradise above—*thou*, O believer! *that dwellest in the gardens* of solemn ordinances, *in the gardens* of church-fellowship and communion, *the companions* are so happy as to hear *thy voice, cause me to hear it* too." *The communion of saints* is an article of our covenant, as well as an article of our creed, *to exhort one another daily. Hearken to the voice* of the church, as far as it agrees with the voice of Christ. In the midst of our communion with one another we must not neglect our communion with Christ; he here bespeaks it: "*The companions hearken to thy voice;* it is a pleasure to them; *cause me to hear it*. Pour out thy heart to me." We *cause him to hear* our prayers when we not only pray, but wrestle and strive in prayer.

II. She desires his speedy return to her (*v.* 14): *Make haste, my beloved*, to come again, and receive me to thyself; *be thou like a roe, or a young hart, upon the mountains of spices. Even so, come, Lord Jesus, come quickly*. True believers, as they are looking for, so they are hastening to, the coming of that *day of the Lord*. The spouse, after an endearing conference with her beloved, finding it must break off, concludes with this affectionate request for the perfecting and perpetuating of this happiness in the future state. It is good to conclude our devotions with a joyful expectation of the glory to be revealed, and holy humble breathings towards it. We should not part but with the prospect of meeting again. It is good to conclude every sabbath with thoughts of the everlasting sabbath, which shall have no night at the end of it, nor any week-day to come after it.

JAMIESON, FAUSSET, BROWN

"door," or gateway. The Gentile Church is the "door," the type of catholic accessibleness (I Cor. 16:9); but it must be not a mere thoroughfare but furnished with a wooden framework, so as not merely to admit, but also to safely enclose: cedar is fragrant, beautiful, and enduring. **10.** The Gentile Church's joy at its free admission to gospel privileges (Acts 15:30, 31). She is one wall in the spiritual temple of the Holy Ghost, the Hebrew Church is the other; Jesus Christ, the common foundation, joins them (Eph. 2:11-22). **breasts . . . towers**—alluding to the silver palace, which the bridal virgins proposed to build on her (vs. 9). "Breasts" of consolation (Isa. 66:11); faith and love (I Thess. 5:8); opposed to her previous state, "no breasts" (vs. 8; II Thess. 1:3). Thus Ezekiel 16:46, 61 was fulfilled, both Samaria and the Gentiles being joined to the Jewish gospel Church. **favour**—rather, *peace*. The Gentile Church too is become the Shulamite (ch. 6: 13), or *peace*-enjoying bride of Solomon, i.e., Jesus Christ, the Prince of Peace (Rom. 5:1; Eph. 2:14). Reject not those whom God accepts (Num. 11:28; Luke 9:49; Acts 15:8, 9). Rather, superadd to such every aid and privilege (vs. 9). **11.** The joint Church speaks of Jesus Christ's vineyard. Transference of it from the Jews, who rendered not the fruits, as is implied by the silence respecting any, to the Gentiles (Matt. 21:33-43). **Baal-hamon**—equivalent to *the owner of a multitude;* so Israel in Solomon's day (I Kings 4:20); so Isa. 5:1, "*a very fruitful hill*" abounding in *privileges*, as in *numbers*. **thousand pieces**—viz., silverlings, or shekels. The vineyard had 1000 vines probably; a vine at a silverling (Isa. 7:23), referring to this passage. **12.** "mine" by grant of the true Solomon. Not merely "let out to keepers," as in the Jewish dispensation of *works*, but "mine" by *grace*. This is "before me," i.e., *in my power* [MAURER]. But though no longer under constraint of "keeping" the law as a mere letter and covenant of works, *love* to Jesus Christ will constrain her the more freely to render all to Solomon (Rom. 8:2-4; I Cor. 6:20; Gal. 5:13; I Pet. 2:16), after having paid what justice and His will require should be paid to others (I Cor. 7:29-31; 9:14). "Before me" may also mean "I will never lose sight of it" (contrast ch. 1:6) [MOODY STUART]. She will not keep it for herself, though so freely given to her, but for His use and glory (Luke 19:13; Rom. 6:15; 14:7-9); I Cor. 12:7). Or the "two hundred" may mean a *double tithe* (two-tenths of the whole paid back by Jesus Christ) as the reward of grace for our surrender of *all* (the thousand) to Him (Gal. 6:7; Heb. 6:10); then she and "those that keep" are the same [ADELAIDE NEWTON]. But Jesus Christ pays back not merely *two tithes*, but *His all* for our all (I Cor. 3:21-23).

13. Jesus Christ's address to her; now no longer visibly present. Once she "had not kept" her vineyard (ch. 1:6); now she "dwells" in it, not as its owner, but its superintendent under Jesus Christ, with vine-dressers ("companions"), e.g., Paul, etc. (Acts 15:25, 26), under her (vss. 11, 12); these ought to obey her when she obeys Jesus Christ. Her voice in prayer and praise is to be heard continually by Jesus Christ, if her voice before men is to be effective (ch. 2:14, end; Acts 6:4; 13:2, 3). **14.** (See *Note*, ch. 2:17.) As she began with longing for His first coming (ch. 1:2), so she ends with praying for His second coming (Ps. 130:6; Phil. 3:20, 21; Rev. 22:20). MOODY STUART makes the roe upon spices to be the musk-deer. As there are four gardens, so four mountains, which form not mere images, as Gilead, Carmel, etc., but part of the structure of the Song: (1) Bether, or *division* (ch. 2:17), God's justice *dividing* us from God. (2) Those "of leopards" (ch. 4:8), sin, the world, and Satan. (3) That "of myrrh and aloes" (ch. 4:6, 14), the sepulchre of Calvary. (4) Those "of spices," here answering to "the hill of frankincense" (ch. 4:6), where His *soul* was for the three days of His death, and heaven, where He is a High Priest now, offering incense for us on the fragrant mountain of His own finished work (Heb. 4:14, 7:25; Rev. 8:3, 4); thus He surmounts the other three mountains, God's justice, our sin, death. The mountain of spices is as much greater than our sins, as heaven is higher than earth (Ps. 103:11). The abrupt, unsatisfied close with the yearning prayer for His *visible* coming shows that the marriage is future, and that to wait eagerly for it is our true attitude (I Cor. 1:7; I Thess. 1:10; Titus 2:13; II Pet. 3:12).

ADAM CLARKE

CHARLES H. SPURGEON:

Verse 14. The Song of Songs describes the love of Jesus Christ to His people, and it ends with an intense desire on the part of the Church that the Lord Jesus should come back to her. The last word of the lover to the Beloved One is, "Speed Thy return; make haste and come back." Is it not somewhat singular that, as the last verse of the Book of love has this note in it, so the last verses of the whole Book of God, which I may also call the Book of love, have that same thought in them? At the twentieth verse of the last chapter of the Revelation, we read, "He that testifieth these things saith, Surely I come quickly. Amen. Even so, come, Lord Jesus." The Song of love and the Book of love end in almost the selfsame way, with a strong desire for Christ's speedy return.

Are your hearts, dear friends, in tune with that desire? They ought to be, yet have not some of you almost forgotten that Jesus is to come a second time? Refresh your memories. Others of you, who know that He will come, have you not thought of it as a doctrine that might be laid by on the shelf? Have you not been without any desire for His glorious appearing? Is this right? If you have no longings for Christ's appearance, no desires for His speedy return, surely your heart is sick, and your love is faint. I fear that you are getting into a lukewarm state.

Christ is our "Beloved." This is a word of affection; and our Lord Jesus Christ is the object of affection to us. If you read the Bible, especially if you read the New Testament, and study the life of Christ, and yet you only admire it, and say to yourself, "Jesus Christ was a wonderful being," you do not know Him yet; you have but a very indistinct idea of Him. If, after reading that life, you sit down, and dissect it, and say to yourself, coolly, calmly, deliberately, "So far as is practicable, I will try and imitate Christ," you do not know Him, you have not come near to the real Christ as yet. If any man should say, "I am near the fire," and yet he is not warm, I should question the truth of his words; and though he might say, "I can see the fire; I can tell you the appearance of the coals," yet if he were not warmed at all, I should still think that he was mistaken.

But when you really come to see Jesus, and to say, "I love Him; my heart yearns towards Him; my delight is in Him; He has won my love, and holds it in His own heart," then you begin to know Him. Brethren, true religion is practical, it is also contemplative; but it is not true religion at all if it is not full of love and affection. Jesus must reign in your heart, or else, though you may give Him what place you like in your head, you have not truly received Him. To Jesus, beyond all others, is applicable this title of the Beloved, for they who know Him love Him.

—*The Treasury of the Old Testament*

THE BOOK OF ISAIAH

I. Prophecies of judgment (1:1-35:10)
A. First circle—public ministry (1:1-7:25)
1. During the reign of Uzziah (1:1-5:30)
2. During reigns of Jotham and Ahaz (6:1-7:25)
B. Second circle—private ministry (8:1-27:13)
1. Signs of the prophet and his children (8:1-12:6)
2. Burdens of the nations (13:1-23:18)
a. Babylon (Assyria) (13:1-14:27)
b. Philistia (14:28-32)
c. Moab (15:1-16:14)
d. Damascus (17:1-11)
e. Parenthetical soliloquy (17:12-18:7)
f. Egypt (19:1-20:6)
g. Babylon (21:1-10)
h. Dumah (21:11-12)
i. Arabia (21:13-17)
j. Jerusalem (22:1-25)
k. Tyre (23:1-18)
3. The vision of the Day of the Lord (24:1-27:13)
C. Third circle—public ministry (28:1-35:10)
1. Concerning the chosen (28:1-33:24)
a. Five woes against the chosen (28:1-32:20)
b. The woe against Assyria (33:1-24)
2. Concerning the world (34:1-35:10)

II. Historical interlude (36:1-39:8)
A. Hezekiah's trouble (36:1-22)
B. Hezekiah's prayer (37:1-38)
C. Hezekiah's sickness (38:1-22)
D. Hezekiah's folly (39:1-8)

III. Prophecies of peace (40:1-66:24)
A. The purpose of peace (40:1-48:22)
1. Prologue (40:1-11)
2. The Majesty of Jehovah (40:12-31)
3. The manifesto of Jehovah (41:1-42:25)
4. The messages of Jehovah (43:1-45:25)
5. The might of Jehovah (46:1-47:15)
6. The Mercy of Jehovah (48:1-22)
B. The prince of peace (49:1-57:21)
1. Sustained through suffering (49:1-53:12)
a. Jehovah's call (49:1-50:3)
b. His servant's answer (50:4-53:12)
2. Singing in triumph (54:1-57:21)
a. The son of assurance (54:1-17)
b. The great appeal (55:1-13)
c. The administration (56:1-57:21)
C. The program of peace (58:1-65:25)
1. The declaration of conditions (58:1-59:21)
2. The ultimate realization (60:1-62:12)
3. The principle of discrimination (63:1-65:25)
D. Epilogue (66:1-24)

A prophet is one that has a great intimacy with heaven and a great interest there, and consequently a commanding authority upon earth. Prophecy was most commonly by dreams, voices, or visions, communicated to prophets first, and by them to the children of men (Num. 12:6). Before the sacred canon of the Old Testament began to be written there were prophets, who were like Bibles to the church. Our Savior seems to reckon Abel among the prophets (Matt. 23:31, 35). Enoch was a prophet; Noah was a preacher of righteousness. God said of Abraham, He "is a prophet" (Gen. 20:7). Jacob foretold things to come (Gen. 49:1). Moses was, beyond all comparison, the most illustrious of all the Old Testament prophets, for with him the Lord spoke "face to face" (Deut. 34:10). But after the death of Moses, for some ages, the Spirit of the Lord appeared and acted in the church of Israel more as a martial spirit than as a spirit of prophecy, and inspired men more for acting than speaking in the time of the judges. We find the Spirit of the Lord coming upon Othniel, Gideon, Samson and others, for the service of their country, with their swords, not with their pens. In all the book of Judges there is never once mention of a prophet, only Deborah is called a prophetess. Then the word of the Lord was precious; there was no open vision (1 Sam. 3:1). But in Samuel prophecy revived, and in him a famous period of the church began, a time of great light in a constant, uninterrupted succession of prophets, till some time after the captivity, when the canon of the Old Testament was completed. Then prophecy ceased for nearly 400 years. We read of prophets raised up for special public services, among whom the most famous were Elijah and Elisha in the kingdom of Israel. There was nothing of their own writing but one epistle of Elijah's, 2 Chron. 21:12. But, towards the latter end of the kingdoms of Judah and Israel, it pleased God to direct his servants the prophets to write some of their sermons. The dates of many of their prophecies are uncertain, but the earliest of them was in the days of Uzziah king of Judah, and Jeroboam the second, his contemporary, king of Israel, about 200 years before the captivity. If they begin to murder the prophets, yet they shall not murder their prophecies; these shall remain as witnesses against them. Hosea was the first of the writing prophets; and Joel, Amos, and Obadiah, published then prophecies about the same time. Isaiah began some time after, but his prophecy is placed first, because it is the largest of them all, and has most in it of Him to whom all the prophets bore witness; and indeed so much of Christ that he is justly styled the "Evangelical Prophet," and, by some of the ancients, "a fifth Evangelist."

I. Concerning the prophet himself. He was (if we may believe the tradition of the Jews) of the royal family, his father being (they say) brother to King Uzziah. He was certainly much at court, especially in Hezekiah's time. The Spirit of God sometimes served his own purpose by the particular genius of the prophet; for prophets were not speaking trumpets through which the Spirit spoke, but speaking men by whom the Spirit spoke, making use of their natural powers, in respect both of light and flame, and advancing them above themselves.

II. Concerning the prophecy. It is transcendently useful; serving for conviction of sin, direction in duty, and consolation in trouble. Two great distresses of the church are here referred to, Sennacherib's invasion, which happened in his own time, and the captivity in Babylon, which happened long after; and in encouragements laid up for these times of need we find abundance of the grace of the gospel. There are not so many quotations in the gospels out of any, perhaps not out of all, the prophecies of the Old Testament, as out of this; nor such express testimonies concerning Christ, witness that of his being born of a virgin (ch. 7) and that of his sufferings (ch. 53). The beginning of this book abounds most with reproofs for sin and threatenings of judgment; the latter end of it is full of good words and comfortable words. This method the Spirit of Christ took formerly in the prophets and does still, first to convince and then to comfort; and those that would be blessed with the comforts must submit to the convictions.

MATTHEW HENRY

CHAPTER 1

Verse 1

I. The name of the prophet, *Isaiah*, which, in the New Testament, is read *Esaias*. His name signifies *the salvation of the Lord*—a proper name, especially for this prophet, who prophesies so much of Jesus the Saviour and of the great salvation wrought out by him. He is said to be *the son of Amoz*, the brother,

JAMIESON, FAUSSET, BROWN

CHAPTER 1

Vss. 1-31. **1.** THE GENERAL TITLE OR PROGRAM applying to the entire book: this discountenances the Talmud tradition, that he was sawn asunder by Manasseh. **Isaiah**—equivalent to *"The Lord shall save"*; significant of the subject of his prophecies. On "vision," see I Sam. 9:9; Num. 12:6;

ADAM CLARKE

CHAPTER 1

The kingdom of Judah seems to have been in a more flourishing condition during the reigns of Uzziah and Jotham than at any other time after the revolt of the ten tribes. The former recovered the port of Elath on the Red Sea, which the Edomites had taken in the

MATTHEW HENRY

or son, of Amaziah king of Judah, a tradition as uncertain as that rule, that, where a prophet's father is named, he also was himself a prophet.

II. The nature of the prophecy. It is a vision. The prophets were called *seers*, and therefore their prophecies are fitly called *visions*. It was what he saw with the eyes of his mind, and foresaw as clearly by divine revelation, as if he had seen it with his bodily eyes.

III. The subject of the prophecy. Some chapters there are in this book which relate to Babylon, Egypt, Tyre, and other neighbouring nations; but it takes its title from that which is the main substance of it, and is therefore said to be *concerning Judah and Jerusalem*. Isaiah brings to them in a special manner, 1. Instruction; for to them pertain the oracles of God. 2. Reproof and threatening; for if in Judah, if in Salem, iniquity be found, they, sooner than any other, shall be reckoned with for it. 3. Comfort and encouragement in evil times; for the children of Zion shall be joyful in their king.

IV. The date of the prophecy. Isaiah prophesied *in the days of Uzziah, Jotham, Ahaz, and Hezekiah*. By this it appears, 1. That he prophesied long, especially if (as the Jews say) he was at last put to death by Manasseh, being sawn asunder, to which some suppose the apostle refers, Heb. xi. 37. From the year that king Uzziah died (*ch.* vi. 1) to Hezekiah's sickness and recovery was forty-seven years; how much before, and after, he prophesied, is not certain. 2. That he passed through variety of times. Jotham was a good king, and Hezekiah a better, and no doubt took advice from this prophet; but between them, and when Isaiah was in the prime of his time, the reign of Ahaz was very profane and wicked.

Verses 2–9

I. The prophet, though he speaks in God's name, despairing to gain audience with the children of his people, addresses himself to the heavens and the earth (*v.* 2): *Hear, O heavens! and give ear, O earth!* Sooner will the inanimate creatures hear, who observe the law and answer the end of their creation, than this stupid senseless people. Let the lights of heaven shame their darkness, and the fruitfulness of the earth their barrenness, and the strictness of each to its time their irregularity. Moses begins thus in Deut. xxxii. 1.

II. He charges them with base ingratitude. Let heaven and earth hear and wonder at, 1. God's gracious dealings with such a peevish provoking people: "I have nourished and brought them up as children; they have been well fed and well taught" (Deut. xxxii. 6). 2. Their ill-natured conduct towards him, who was so tender of them: "*They have rebelled against me.*"

III. He attributes this to their ignorance and inconsideration (*v.* 3): *The ox knows, but Israel does not.* Observe, 1. The sagacity of the ox and the ass, creatures of the dullest sort; yet the ox has such a sense of duty as to know his owner and to serve him. The ass has such a sense of interest as to know his master's crib, where he is fed, and to abide by it. Man is shamed in knowledge by these silly animals, and is not only sent to school to them (Prov. vi. 6, 7), but set in a form below them (Jer. viii. 7). 2. The sottishness and stupidity of Israel. God is their owner and proprietor. He made us, and has provided well for us; yet many that are called the people of God ask, "*What is the Almighty, that we should serve him?*" They do not know, they do not consider. They know; but their knowledge does them no good, because they do not consider what they know; they do not apply it to their case, nor their minds to it. Inconsideration of what we do know is as great an enemy to us in religion as ignorance of what we should know. *Therefore* men revolt from God, and rebel against him.

IV. He laments the corruption of their church and kingdom. The disease of sin was epidemic, and all orders and degrees of men were infected with it: *Ah sinful nation! v.* 4.

1. The wickedness was universal. They were a sinful nation; the generality of the people were vicious and profane. Their wickedness was upon them as *a talent of lead*, Zech. v. 7, 8. They came of a bad stock, were a *seed of evil-doers*. Treachery ran in the blood. They were a race and family of rebels. They were not only corrupt children, but *children that were corrupters*, that propagated vice, and infected others with it. *They have provoked the Holy One of Israel unto anger* wilfully and designedly; they knew what would anger him, and that they did.

2. He illustrates it by a comparison taken from a sick and diseased body, all overspread with leprosy, or, like Job's, with sore boils, *v.* 5, 6. The distemper has seized the vitals, and so threatens to be mortal.

JAMIESON, FAUSSET, BROWN

Judah and Jerusalem—Other nations also are the subjects of his prophecies; but only in their relation to the Jews (chs. 13-23); so also the ten tribes of Israel are introduced only in the same relation (chs. 7-9). Jerusalem is particularly specified, being the site of the temple, and the center of the theocracy, and the future throne of Messiah (Ps. 48:2, 3, 9; Jer. 3:17). Jesus Christ is the "Lion of the tribe of Judah" (Rev. 5:5). **Uzziah**—called also Azariah (II Kings 14:21; II Chron. 26). The Old Testament prophecies spiritually interpret the histories, as the New Testament Epistles interpret the Gospels and Acts. Study them together, to see their spiritual relations. Isaiah prophesied for only a few years before Uzziah's death; but his prophecies of that period (chs. 1-6) apply to Jotham's reign also, in which he probably *wrote* none; for ch. 7 enters immediately on Ahaz' reign, after Uzziah in ch. 6; the prophecies under Hezekiah follow next.

2. The very words of Moses (Deut. 32); this implies that the *law was the charter and basis of all prophecy* (ch. 8:20). **Lord**—*Jehovah;* in *Hebrew,* "the self-existing and promise-fulfilling, unchangeable One." The Jews never pronounced this holy name. but substituted Adonai. The *English Version,* LORD in capitals, marks the *Hebrew* Jehovah, though *Lord* is rather equivalent to Adonai than Jehovah.

children—(Exod. 4:22.) **rebelled**—as sons (Deut. 21: 18) and as subjects, God being king in the theocracy (ch. 63:10). "Brought up," lit., "elevated," viz., to peculiar privileges (Jer. 2:6-8; Rom. 9:4, 5). **3.** (Jer. 8:7.) **crib**—the stall where it is fed (Prov. 14:4). Spiritually the word and ordinances. **Israel**—The whole nation, Judah as well as Israel, in the restricted sense. God regards His covenant people in their designed unity. **not know**—viz.. his Owner, as the parallelism requires; i.e., *not recognize* Him as such (Exod. 19:5, equivalent to "my people," John 1:10, 11). **consider**—*attend to* his Master (ch. 41:8), notwithstanding the spiritual *food* which He provides (answering to "crib" in the parallel clause).

4. people—the peculiar designation of God's elect nation (Hos. 1:10), that *they* should be "laden with iniquity" is therefore the more monstrous. Sin is a *load* (Ps. 38:4; Matt. 11:28). **seed**—another appellation of God's elect (Gen. 12:7; Jer. 2:21), designed to be a "holy seed" (ch. 6:13), but, awful to say, "evildoers!" **children**—by adoption (Hos. 11:1), yet "evildoers"; not only so, but "corrupters" of others (Gen. 6:12); the climax. So "nation—people—seed—children." **provoked**—lit., "despised," viz., so as to provoke (Prov. 1:30, 31). **Holy One of Israel**—the peculiar heinousness of their sin, that it was against *their* God (Amos 3:2). **gone . . . backward**—lit., "estranged" (Ps. 58:3). **5. Why**—rather, as *Vulgate,* "On what part." Image from a body covered all over with marks of blows (Ps. 38: 3). There is no part in which you have not been smitten. **head . . . sick . . .**—not referring, as it is commonly quoted, to their *sins,* but to the univer-

ADAM CLARKE

reign of Joram. He was successful in his wars with the Philistines, and took from them several cities; as likewise against some people of Arabia Deserta, and against the Ammonites, whom he compelled to pay him tribute. He repaired and improved the fortifications of Jerusalem; and had a great army, well appointed and disciplined. He was no less attentive to the arts of peace; and very much encouraged agriculture and the breeding of cattle. Jotham maintained the establishments and improvements made by his father; added to what Uzziah had done in strengthening the frontier places; conquered the Ammonites, who had revolted; and exacted from them a more stated and probably a larger tribute. However, at the latter end of his time, the league between Pekah, king of Israel, and Rezin, king of Syria, was formed against Judah; and they began to carry their designs into execution.

But in the reign of Ahaz, his son, not only all these advantages were lost, but the kingdom of Judah was brought to the brink of destruction. Pekah, king of Israel, overthrew the army of Ahaz, who lost in battle 120,000 men; and the Israelites carried away captives 200,000 women and children, who however were released and sent home again upon the remonstrance of the prophet Oded. After this, as it should seem, the two kings of Israel and Syria, joining their forces, laid siege to Jerusalem; but in this attempt they failed of success. In this distress Ahaz called in the assistance of Tiglath-pileser, king of Assyria, who invaded the kingdoms of Israel and Syria, and slew Rezin. But he was more in danger than ever from his too powerful ally; to purchase whose forbearance, as he had before bought his assistance, he was forced to strip himself and his people of all the wealth he could possibly raise from his own treasury, from the Temple, and from the country. About the time of the siege of Jerusalem the Syrians took Elath, which was never after recovered. The Edomites likewise, taking advantage of the distress of Ahaz, ravaged Judea, and carried away many captives. The Philistines recovered what they had before lost; and took many places in Judea, and maintained themselves there. Idolatry was established by the command of the king in Jerusalem, and throughout Judea; and the service of the Temple was either intermitted or converted into an idolatrous worship.

Hezekiah, his son, on his accession to the throne, immediately set about the restoration of the legal worship of God, both in Jerusalem and through Judea. He cleansed and repaired the Temple, and held a solemn Passover. He improved the city, repaired the fortification, erected magazines of all sorts, and built a new aqueduct. In the fourth year of his reign Shalmaneser, king of Assyria, invaded the kingdom of Israel, took Samaria, and carried away the Israelites into captivity, and replaced them by different people sent from his own country; and this was the final destruction of that kingdom, in the sixth year of the reign of Hezekiah.

Hezekiah was not deterred by this alarming example from refusing to pay the tribute to the king of Assyria, which had been imposed on Ahaz. This brought on the invasion of Sennacherib in the fourteenth year of his reign, an account of which is inserted among the prophecies of Isaiah. After a great and miraculous deliverance from so powerful an enemy, Hezekiah continued his reign in peace. He prospered in all his works, and left his kingdom in a flourishing state to his son Manasseh—a son in every respect unworthy of such a father.

2. *Hear, O heavens*—"Hear, O ye heavens." God is introduced as entering into a public action, or pleading, before the whole world, against His disobedient people. The prophet, as herald or officer to proclaim the summons to the court, calls upon all created beings, celestial and terrestrial, to attend and bear witness to the truth of His plea and the justice of His cause. By the same bold figure, Micah calls upon the mountains, that is, the whole country of Judea, to attend to him, chap. vi. 1-2. With the like invocation, Moses introduces his sublime song: "Give ear, O ye heavens, and I will speak; and hear, O earth, the words of my mouth" (Deut. xxxii. 1). *I have nourished.* The Septuagint have, "I have begotten."

MATTHEW HENRY

They had become corrupt in their judgment: the leprosy was in their head. It has overspread the whole body, and so becomes exceedingly noisome. There is *no soundness*, no good principles, no religion (for that is the health of the soul), nothing but *wounds and bruises*, guilt and corruption. No attempts were made for reformation, or, if they were, they proved ineffectual: The wounds *have not been closed, nor bound up, nor mollified with ointment.* While sin remains unrepented of, the wounds are not mollified or closed up, nor anything done towards the healing of them.

V. He sadly bewails the judgments of God which they had brought upon themselves. Their kingdom was almost ruined, *v.* 7. "Look and see how it is; *your country is desolate*; as for the fruits of your land, which should be food for your families, *strangers devour them before your eyes*, and you cannot prevent it; you starve while your enemies surfeit." Jerusalem, which was as the daughter of Zion (the temple built on Zion was a mother to Jerusalem), was now lost, deserted, and exposed *as a cottage in a vineyard*, which, when the vintage is over, nobody dwells in, and every person is afraid of coming near it as if it were *a besieged city*, *v.* 8. Probably this sermon was preached in the reign of Ahaz, when Judah was invaded by the kings of Syria and Israel, the Edomites and the Philistines, who slew many, and carried many away into captivity, 2 Chron. xxviii. 5, 17, 18. National impiety and immorality bring national desolation. Yet they were not at all reformed, and therefore God threatens to take another course with them (*v.* 5). God sometimes, in a way of righteous judgment, ceases to correct those who have been long incorrigible, and whom therefore he designs to destroy.

VI. He comforts himself with the consideration of a remnant that should be the monuments of divine grace and mercy, notwithstanding this general corruption and desolation, *v.* 9. *The Lord of hosts left unto them a very small remnant*, that were kept pure from the common apostasy and kept safe and alive from the common calamity. This is quoted by the apostle (Rom. ix. 27), and applied to those few of the Jewish nation who in his time embraced Christianity. This remnant is often a very small one. Multitude is no mark of the true church. Christ's is a little flock. It is good for a people that have been saved from utter ruin to look back and see how near they were to it, to see how much they owed to a few good men that stood in the gap, and that that was owing to a good God, who left them these good men.

Verses 10–15

I. God calls to them (but calls in vain) to hear his word, *v.* 10. 1. The title he gives them is very strange: *You rulers of Sodom*, and *people of Gomorrah.* This intimates what a righteous thing it would have been with God to make them like Sodom and Gomorrah (*v.* 9). The rulers are boldly attacked here by the prophet as rulers of Sodom; for he knew not how to give flattering titles. The tradition of the Jews is that for this he was long after put to death. His demand upon them is very reasonable: "*Hear the word of the Lord*, and *give ear to the law of our God;* attend to that which God has to say to you, and let his word be a law unto you."

II. He justly refuses to hear their prayers and accept their services, their sacrifices and burnt-offerings, the fat and blood of them (*v.* 11), their attendance in his courts (*v.* 12), their oblations, their incense, and their solemn assemblies (*v.* 13), their new moons and their appointed feasts (*v.* 14), their devoutest addresses (*v.* 15); they are all rejected, because their hands were full of blood.

1. There are many who are strangers, nay, enemies, to the power of religion, and yet seem very zealous for the show and shadow and form of it. This sinful nation brought to the altar of the God of Israel, sacrifices, peace-offerings and burnt-offerings, which were wholly consumed to the honour of God. They prayed, prayed often, made many prayers, thinking they should be heard for their much speaking. Their hearts were empty of true devotion. They came to *appear* before God (*v.* 12), *to be seen* before him (so the margin reads it). Their hands were full of blood. They were guilty of murder, rapine, and oppression, under colour of law and justice. Malice is heart-murder in the account of God; he that hates his brother in his heart has, in effect, his hands full of blood.

2. When sinners are under the judgments of God they will more easily be brought to fly to their devotions than to forsake their sins and reform their lives.

3. The most pompous and costly devotions of wicked people, without a thorough reformation of

JAMIESON, FAUSSET, BROWN

sality of their *punishment.* However, sin, the moral disease of the *head* or intellect, and the *heart,* is doubtless made its own punishment (Prov. 1:31; Jer. 2:19; Hos. 8:11). "Sick," lit., is in a state of sickness [GESENIUS]; "has *passed into* sickness" [MAURER]. **6.** From the lowest to the highest of the people; "the ancient and honorable, the *head;* the prophet that teacheth lies, the tail." See Isaiah 9: 13-16. He first states their wretched condition, obvious to all (vss. 6-9); and then, not previously, their irreligious state, the cause of it. **wounds**—judicially inflicted (Hos. 5:13). **mollified with ointment**—The art of medicine in the East consists chiefly in external applications (Luke 10:34; Jas. 5:14). **7.** Judah had not in Uzziah's reign recovered from the ravages of the Syrians in Joash's reign (II Chron. 24:24), and of Israel in Amaziah's reign (II Chron. 25:13, 23, etc.). Compare Isaiah's contemporary (Amos 4:6-11), where, as here (vss. 9, 10), Israel is compared to "Sodom and Gomorrah," because of the judgments on it by "fire." **in your presence**—before your eyes: without your being able to prevent them. **desolate . . .**—lit., "there is desolation, such as one might look for from foreign" invaders. **8. daughter of Zion**—the city (Ps. 9:14), Jerusalem and its inhabitants (II Kings 19:21): "daughter," *feminine, singular* being used as a neuter collective noun, equivalent to *sons* (see below, *Margin,* ch. 12:6) [MAURER]. Metropolis or "mother-city" is the corresponding term. The idea of youthful beauty is included in "daughter." **left**—as a *remnant* escaping the general destruction. **cottage**—a hut, made to give temporary *shelter* to the caretaker of the vineyard. **lodge**—not permanent. **besieged**—rather, as "left," and vs. 9 require, *preserved,* viz., from the desolation all round [MAURER]. **9.** Jehovah of Sabaoth, i.e., God of the angelic and starry hosts (Ps. 59:5; 147:4; 148:2). The latter were objects of idolatry, called hence *Sabaism* (II Kings 17:16). God is above even them (I Chron. 16:26). "The groves" were symbols of these starry hosts; it was their worship of Sabaoth instead of the Lord of Sabaoth, which had caused the present desolation (II Chron. 24:18). It needed no less a power than His, to preserve even a "remnant." Condescending grace for the elect's sake, since He has no need of us, seeing that He has countless hosts to serve Him.

10. Sodom—spiritually (Gen. 19; Jer. 23:14; Ezek. 16:46; Rev. 11:8).

11. God does not here absolutely disparage sacrifice, which is as old and universal as sin (Gen. 3:21; 4:4), and sin is almost as old as the world; but sacrifice, unaccompanied with obedience of heart and life (I Sam. 15:22; Ps. 50:9-13; 51:16-19; Hos. 6:6). *Positive* precepts are only means; *moral* obedience is the end. A foreshadowing of the gospel, when the One real sacrifice was to supersede all the shadowy ones, and "bring in everlasting righteousness" (Ps. 40:6, 7; Dan. 9:24-27; Heb. 10:1-14). **full**—to satiety; weary of **burnt offerings**—burnt whole, except the blood, which was sprinkled about the altar. **fat**—not to be eaten by man, but burnt on the altar (Lev. 3:4, 5, 11, 17). **12. appear before me**—in the temple where the Shekinah, resting on the ark, was the symbol of God's presence (Exod. 23:15; Ps. 42:2).

ADAM CLARKE

3. *The ox knoweth.* An amplification of the gross insensibility of the disobedient Jews, by comparing them with the most heavy and stupid of all animals, yet not so insensible as they.

4. *Ah sinful nation*—"Degenerate." *Are corrupters*—"Are estranged." *They are gone away backward*—"They have turned their backs upon Him."

5. *Why should ye be stricken any more?*—"On what part?"

6. *They have not been closed*—"It hath not been pressed." The pharmaceutical art in the East consists chiefly in external applications; accordingly the prophet's images in this place are all taken from surgery.

7-9. *Your country is desolate.* The description of the ruined and desolate state of the country in these verses does not suit any part of the prosperous times of Uzziah and Jotham. It very well agrees with the time of Ahaz, when Judea was ravaged by the joint invasion of the Israelites and Syrians, and by the incursions of the Philistines and Edomites. The day of this prophecy is therefore generally fixed to the time of Ahaz. But on the other hand it is said, 2 Kings xv. 37, that in Jotham's time "the Lord began to send against Judah Rezin . . . and Pekah." If we may suppose any invasion from that quarter to have been actually made at the latter end of Jotham's reign, I should choose to refer this prophecy to that time.

8. *As a cottage in a vineyard*—"As a shed in a vineyard." A little, temporary hut covered with boughs, straw, turf, or the like materials, for a shelter from the heat by day and the cold and dews by night, for the watchman that kept the garden or vineyard during the short season the fruit was ripening (see Job xxvii. 18), and presently removed when it had served that purpose. *As a lodge.* That is, after the fruit was gathered, the lodge being then permitted to fall into decay. Such was the desolate, ruined state of the city.

9. *The Lord of hosts.* As this title of God, *Yehovah tsebaoth,* "Jehovah of hosts," occurs here for the first time, I think it proper to note that I translate it always, "Jehovah God of hosts," taking it as an elliptical expression for *Yehovah Elohey tsebaoth.* This title imports that Jehovah is the God or Lord of hosts or armies. *We should have been as Sodom.* As completely and finally ruined as *that* and the cities of the plain were, no vestige of which remains at this day.

10. *Ye rulers of Sodom*—"Ye princes of Sodom." The incidental mention of Sodom and Gomorrah in the preceding verse suggested to the prophet this spirited address to the rulers and inhabitants of Jerusalem, under the character of princes *of Sodom* and *people of Gomorrah.* Two examples of a sort of elegant turn of the like kind may be observed in St. Paul's Epistle to the Romans, chap. xv. 4-5, 12-13.

11. *To what purpose?*—"What have I to do?" The prophet Amos has expressed the same sentiments with great elegance—Amos v. 21-24. *The fat of fed beasts.* The fat and the blood are particularly mentioned because these were in all sacrifices set apart to God. The fat was always burnt upon the altar, and the blood was partly sprinkled, differently on different occasions, and partly poured out at the bottom of the altar. See Leviticus iv.

12. *When ye come to appear.* The appearing before God here refers chiefly to the three solemn annual festivals. See Exod. xxiii. 14. *Tread my courts* (no more). So the Septuagint divide the sentence, joining the end of this verse to the beginning of the next: "To tread my court ye shall not add . . . ye shall not be again accepted in worship."

MATTHEW HENRY

the heart and life, are so far from being acceptable to God that really they are an abomination to him. It is here shown in a great variety of expressions that *to obey is better than sacrifice*; nay, that sacrifice, without obedience, is a jest, an affront and provocation to God. Their sacrifices are here represented as fruitless and insignificant: *To what purpose is the multitude of your sacrifices? v.* 11. They are *vain oblations, v.* 13. Their attention to God's institutions was all lost labour, and served not to answer any good intention: *Who has required these things at your hands? v.* 12. They pray, but God will not hear, for, though they make many prayers, none of them come from an upright heart. "They are *your* sacrifices, they are none of mine; I am full of them, even surfeited with them." Their coming into his courts he calls *treading them*, or trampling upon them. Their incense, though ever so fragrant, was an abomination to him, for it was burnt in hypocrisy and with an ill design. Their solemn assemblies he could not *away with*, could not see with any patience. God is never weary of hearing the prayers of the upright, but soon weary of the costly sacrifices of the wicked. Sin is hateful to God, so hateful that it makes even men's prayers and their religious services hateful to him. Dissembled piety is double iniquity.

Verses 16–20

I. A call to repentance and reformation: "If you would have your sacrifices accepted, and your prayers answered, you must begin your work at the right end: *Be converted to my law* else expect not to be accepted in the acts of your devotion." As justice and charity will never atone for atheism and profaneness, so prayers and sacrifices will never atone for fraud and oppression.

1. They must *cease to do evil*, must do no more wrong, shed no more innocent blood. This is the meaning of washing themselves and *making themselves clean, v.* 16. We must put away not only the evil of our doings by refraining from the gross acts of sin, but the roots and habits of sin, that are in our hearts.

2. They must *learn to do well*. This was necessary to the completing of their repentance. We must be doing good, the good which the Lord our God requires. We must learn to do well; take pains to get the knowledge of our duty. He urges them particularly to second-table duties: "*Seek judgment;* enquire what is right, that you may do it. *Relieve the oppressed.* Avenge those that suffer wrong, the fatherless and the widow, whom, because they are weak and helpless, proud men trample upon and abuse. Speak for those that know not how to speak for themselves and that have not wherewithal to gratify you for your kindness."

II. A demonstration, at the bar of right reason, of the equity of God's proceedings with them: "*Come now, and let us reason together* (*v.* 18); while your hands are full of blood I will have nothing to do with you, though you bring me a multitude of sacrifices; but if you wash, and make yourselves clean, you are welcome to draw nigh to me; come now, and let us talk the matter over." Religion has reason on its side; there is all the reason in the world why we should do as God would have us do. The case needs only to be stated and it will determine itself.

1. They could not in reason expect any more than that, if they repented and reformed, they should be restored to God's favour, notwithstanding their former provocations. Here is no penance imposed, nor the yoke made heavier. He does not say, "If you be *perfectly* obedient", but, "If you be *willingly* so"; for, if there be a willing mind, it is accepted. All their sins should be pardoned, and should not be mentioned against them. Though our sins have been as scarlet and crimson, a deep dye, though we have been often dipped, by our many backslidings, into sin, and though we have lain long soaking in it, as the cloth does in the scarlet dye, yet pardoning mercy will thoroughly discharge the stain. If we make ourselves clean by repentance and reformation (*v.* 16), God will make us white by a full remission. "Be but willing and obedient, and *you shall eat the good of the land*, the land of promise." If sin be pardoned, creature-comforts become comforts indeed.

2. They could not in reason expect any other than that, if they continued obstinate in their disobedience, the sentence of the law should be executed upon them (*v.* 20).

Verses 21–30

I. The woeful degeneracy of Judah and Jerusalem is sadly lamented. The royal city had been a faithful city, faithful to God and the interests of his kingdom among men, faithful to the nation and its public interests. *It was full of judgment;* justice was duly administered. *Righteousness lodged in it.* That beauteous virtuous spouse was now become an

JAMIESON, FAUSSET, BROWN

who hath required this—as if you were doing God a service by such hypocritical offerings (Job 35:7). God did require it (Exod. 23:17), but not in this spirit (Micah 6:6, 7). **courts**—areas, in which the worshippers were. None but priests entered the temple itself. **13. oblations**—unbloody; "meat (old English sense, not *flesh*) offerings," i.e., of flour, fruits, oil, etc. (Lev. 2:1-13). *Hebrew, mincha.* **incense**—put upon the sacrifices, and burnt on the altar of incense. Type of prayer (Ps. 141:2; Rev. 8:3). **new moons**—observed as festivals (Num. 10:10; 28:11, 14) with sacrifices and blowing of silver trumpets. **sabbaths**—both the seventh day and the beginning and closing days of the great feasts (Lev. 23:24-39). **away with**—bear, MAURER translates, "I cannot *bear iniquity and* the solemn meeting," i.e., the meeting associated with iniquity—lit., the *closing* days of the feasts; so the great days (Lev. 23:36; John 7:37). **14. appointed**—the sabbath, passover, pentecost, day of atonement, and feast of tabernacles [HENGSTENBERG]; they alone were fixed to certain times of the year. **weary**—(ch. 43:24.) **15.** (Ps. 66:18; Prov. 28:9; Lam. 3:43, 44.) **spread . . . hands**—in prayer (I Kings 8:22). *Hebrew*, "bloods," for *all* heinous sins, persecution of God's servants especially (Matt. 23:35). It was the vocation of the prophets to dispel the delusion, so contrary to the law itself (Deut. 10:16), that outward ritualism would satisfy God.

16. God saith to the sinner, "Wash *you*," etc., that he, finding his inability to "make" himself "clean," may cry to *God*, Wash me, cleanse me (Ps. 51:2, 7, 10). **before mine eyes**—not mere outward reformation before *man's* eyes, who cannot, as God, see into the heart (Jer. 32:19).

17. seek judgment—*justice*, as magistrates, instead of *seeking* bribes (Jer. 22:3, 16). **judge**—vindicate (Ps. 68:5; Jas. 1:27).

18. God deigns to argue the case with us, that all may see the just, nay, loving principle of His dealings with men (ch. 43:26). **scarlet**—the color of Jesus Christ's robe when bearing our "sins" (Matt. 27:28). So Rahab's thread (Josh. 2:18; cf. Lev. 14:4). The rabbins say that when the lot used to be taken, a *scarlet* fillet was bound on the scapegoat's head, and after the high priest had confessed his and the people's sins over it, the fillet became *white:* the miracle ceased, according to them, forty years before the destruction of Jerusalem, i.e., exactly when Jesus Christ was crucified; a remarkable admission of adversaries. *Hebrew* for "scarlet" radically means *double-dyed;* so the *deep-fixed permanency* of sin in the heart, which no mere tears can wash away. **snow**—(Ps. 51:7.) Repentance is presupposed, before sin can be made white as snow (vss. 19, 20); *it* too is God's gift (Jer. 31:18, end; Lam. 5:21; Acts 5:31). **red**—refers to "blood" (vs. 15). **as wool**—restored to its original undyed whiteness. This verse shows that the old fathers did not look only for transitory promises (Article VII, BOOK OF COMMON PRAYER). For sins of ignorance, and such like, alone had trespass offerings appointed for them; greater guilt therefore needed a greater sacrifice, for, "without shedding of blood there was no remission"; but none such was appointed, and yet forgiveness was promised and expected; therefore spiritual Jews must have looked for the One Mediator of both Old Testament and New Testament, though dimly understood. **19, 20.** *Temporal* blessings in "the land of their possession" were prominent in the Old Testament promises, as suited to the childhood of the Church (Exod. 3:17). New Testament *spiritual* promises derive their imagery from the former (Matt. 5:5). **Lord hath spoken it**—Isaiah's prophecies rest on the law (Lev. 26:33). God alters not His word (Num. 23:19) **21. faithful**—as a wife (ch. 54:5; 62:5; Hos. 2: 19, 20). **harlot**—(Ezek. 16:28-35.) **righteousness lodged**—(II Pet. 3:13.)

ADAM CLARKE

13. ***The new moons and sabbaths*—"The fast and the day of restraint." The prophet Joel (chap. i. 14 and ii. 15) twice joins together the fast and the day of restraint. *Atsarah,* "the restraint," is rendered, both here and in other places of our English translation, "the solemn assembly." Certain holy days ordained by the law were distinguished by a particular charge that "no servile work" should be done therein (Lev. xxiii. 36; Num. xxix. 35; Deut. xvi. 8). This circumstance clearly explains the reason of the name "the restraint," or "the day of restraint," given to those days.**

16. ***Wash you.* Referring to the preceding verse, "Your hands are full of blood," and alluding to the legal washing commanded on several occasions. See Lev. xiv. 8-9, 47.**

19. ***Ye shall eat the good of the land.* Referring to v. 7: it shall not be "devoured by strangers."**

20. ***Ye shall be devoured with the sword*—"Ye shall be food for the sword."**

MATTHEW HENRY

adulteress; righteousness no longer dwelt in Jerusalem, even murderers lived undisturbed there; the princes themselves were so cruel and oppressive that they had become no better than murderers. The degeneracy of Jerusalem is illustrated (*v.* 22): *Thy silver has become dross.* This degeneracy of the magistrates is as great a reproach and injury to the kingdom as the debasing of their coin would be and the turning of their silver into dross. *Thy wine is mixed with water,* and so has become flat and sour. Dross may shine like silver, and the wine that is mixed with water may retain the colour of wine, but neither is worth anything. Thus they retained a show and pretence of virtue and justice, but had no true sense of either. "Thy princes, that should keep others in their allegiance to God and subjection to his law, are themselves rebellious, and set God and his law at defiance. Those that should restrain thieves, are themselves companions of thieves; they share with the thieves they protect in their unlawful gain. The profit of their places is all their aim, to make the best hand they can of them, right or wrong. They ought to protect those that are injured. But *they judge not the fatherless,* take no care to guard the orphans, *nor does the cause of the widow come unto them,* because the poor widow has no bribe to give, with which to bring her cause on."

II. A resolution is taken up to redress these grievances (*v.* 24): *Therefore saith the Lord, the Lord of hosts, the Mighty One of Israel*—who has power to make good what he says—*Ah! I will ease me of my adversaries.* God will find out a time and a way to ease himself of this burden. If God's professing people conform not to his image, as the Holy One of Israel (*v.* 4), they shall feel the weight of his hand as the Mighty One of Israel. Though the church has a great deal of dross in it, yet it shall not be thrown away, but refined (*v.* 25): "*I will purely purge away thy dross.* Vice shall be suppressed and oppressors deprived of their power to do mischief." The reformation of a people is God's own work: "*I will turn my hand upon thee;* I will do that for the reviving of religion which I did at first for the planting of it." He does it by blessing them with good magistrates and good ministers of state (*v.* 26): "*I will restore thy judges as at the first,* to put the laws in execution against evildoers, *and thy counsellors,* to transact public affairs, *as at the beginning.*" He does it (*v.* 27), by planting in men's minds principles of justice and governing their lives by those principles. Men may do much by external restraints; but God does it effectually by the influences of *his Spirit.* All the redeemed of the Lord shall be converts, and their conversion is their redemption: "*Her converts,* or *those that return of her* (so the margin), shall be redeemed with righteousness." The reviving of a people's virtue is the restoring of their honour: *Afterwards thou shalt be called the city of righteousness, the faithful city.* Those that hate to be reformed shall be destroyed and not chastened only. The openly profane that have quite cast off all religion, and the hypocrites that live wicked lives under the cloak of a religious profession shall both be destroyed together. *And those that forsake the Lord,* to whom they had formerly joined themselves, *shall be consumed,* as the water in the conduit-pipe is soon consumed when it is cut off from the fountain. Their idols shall not be able to help them, *the oaks which they have desired, and the gardens which they have chosen;* that is, the images which they have worshipped in their groves and under the green trees, for which they forsook the true God, and which they worshipped privately in their own gardens. This was the practice of the transgressors and the sinners; but they shall be ashamed of it, not with a show of repentance, but of despair, *v.* 29. They shall be ashamed of their idols; for the idols themselves *shall go into captivity, ch.* xlvi. 1, 2. They shall not be able to help themselves (*v.* 31): "*Even the strong man shall be as tow,* not only soon broken and pulled to pieces, but easily catching fire; and *his work* (so the margin reads it), shall be as a spark to his own tow."

Now all this is applicable to, 1. The blessed work of reformation which was wrought in Hezekiah's time after the abominable corruptions of the reign of Ahaz. 2. To their return out of their captivity in Babylon. 3. To the gospel-kingdom and the pouring out of the Spirit, by which the New Testament church should be made a new Jerusalem, a city of righteousness. 4. To the second coming of Christ, when he shall thoroughly purge his floor.

JAMIESON, FAUSSET, BROWN

murderers—murderous *oppressors,* as the antithesis requires (*Note,* vs. 15; I John 3:15). **22.** Thy princes and people are degenerate in *solid worth,* equivalent to "silver" (Jer. 6; 28, 30; Ezek. 22:18, 19), and in their use of *the living Word,* equivalent to "wine" (Song of Sol. 7:9). **mixed**—lit., "circumcised." So the *Arabic,* "to murder" wine, equivalent to dilute it.

23. companions of thieves—by connivance (Prov. 29:24). **gifts**—(Ezek. 22:12.) A nation's corruption begins with its rulers.

24. Lord . . . Lord—*Adonai,* JEHOVAH. **mighty One of Israel**—mighty to take vengeance, as before, to save. **Ah**—indignation. **ease me**—My long tried patience will *find relief* in at last punishing the guilty (Ezek. 5:13). God's language condescends to human conceptions. **25. turn . . . hand**—not in wrath, but in *grace* (Zech. 13:7), "upon *thee,*" as vss. 26, 27 show; contrasted with the *enemies,* of whom He will *avenge* Himself (vs. 24). **purely**—lit., "as alkali purifies." **dross . . . tin**—not *thy sins,* but the sinful *persons* (Jer. 6:29); "enemies" (vs. 24); degenerate princes (*Note,* vs. 22), intermingled with the elect "remnant" of grace. **tin**—*Hebrew, bedil,* here the alloy of lead, tin, etc., separated by smelting from the silver. The pious Bishop Bedell took his motto from this. **26.** As the degeneracy had shown itself most in the *magistrates* (vss. 17-23), so, at the "restoration," these shall be such as the theocracy "at the first" had contemplated, viz., after the Babylonish restoration in part and typically, but fully and antitypically under Messiah (ch. 32:1; 52:8; Jer. 33:7; Matt. 19:28). **faithful**—no longer "an harlot." **27. redeemed**—temporarily, civilly, and morally; type of the spiritual *redemption* by the *price* of Jesus Christ's blood (I Pet. 1:18, 19), the foundation of "judgment" and "righteousness," and so of pardon. The *judgment* and *righteousness* are God's first (ch. 42:21; Rom. 3: 26); so they become man's when "converted" (Rom. 8:3, 4); typified in the display of God's "justice," then exhibited in delivering His covenant people, whereby justice or "righteousness" was produced in them. **converts**—so MAURER. But *Margin,* "they that return of her," viz., the remnant that return from captivity. However, as Isaiah had not yet expressly foretold the Babylonian captivity, the *English Version* is better. **28. destruction**—lit., "breaking into shivers" (Rev. 2:27). The prophets hasten forward to the final extinction of the ungodly (Ps. 37:20; Rev. 19:20; 20:15); of which antecedent judgments are types. **29. ashamed**—(Rom. 6:21.) **oaks**—Others translate the "terebinth" or "turpentine tree." Groves were dedicated to idols. Our Druids took their name from the *Greek* for "oaks." A sacred tree is often found in Assyrian sculpture; symbol of the starry hosts, Saba. **gardens**—planted enclosures for idolatry; the counterpart of the garden of Eden. **30. oak**—Ye shall be like the "oaks," the object of your "desire" (vs. 29). People become like the gods they worship; they never rise above their level (Ps. 135:18). So men's sins become their own scourges (Jer. 2:9). The leaf of the idol oak fades by a law of necessary consequence, having no living sap or "water" from God. So "garden" answers to "gardens" (vs. 29). **31. strong**—powerful rulers (Amos 2:9), **maker of it**—rather, his work. He shall be at once the fuel, "tow," and the cause of the fire, by kindling the first "spark." **both**—the wicked ruler, and "his work," which "is as a spark."

ADAM CLARKE

24. *Ah, I will ease me*—"Aha! I will be eased." Anger, arising from a sense of injury and affront, especially from those who, from every consideration of duty and gratitude, ought to have behaved far otherwise, is an uneasy and painful sensation; and revenge, executed to the full on the offenders, removes that uneasiness, and consequently is pleasing and quieting, at least for the present. Ezekiel v. 13 introduces God expressing himself in the same manner: "And mine anger [shall] be [fully] accomplished, and I will cause my fury to rest upon them, and I will" give myself ease.

This is a strong instance of the metaphor called anthropopathism, by which throughout the Scriptures the sentiments, sensations, and affections, the bodily faculties, qualities, and members, of men are attributed to God. The foundation of this is obvious; it arises from necessity. We have no idea of the natural attributes of God, of His pure essence, of His manner of existence, of His manner of acting. When therefore we would treat on these subjects, we find ourselves forced to express them by sensible images.

25. *I will turn my hand upon thee.* This seems to be a metaphor taken from the custom of those who, when the metal is melted, strike off the scoriae with their hands previously to its being poured out into the mould.

27. *With judgment*—"In judgment."

29. *For they shall be ashamed of the oaks.* Sacred groves were a very ancient and favorite appendage of idolatry. They made a principal part of the religion of the old inhabitants of Canaan; and the Israelites were commanded to destroy their groves, among other monuments of their false worship. The Israelites themselves became afterwards very much addicted to this species of idolatry.

29. *For they shall be ashamed*—"For ye shall be ashamed."

MATTHEW HENRY

CHAPTER 2

Verses 1–5

The particular title of this sermon (*v.* 1) is the same with the general title of the book (*ch.* i. 1), only that what is there called the *vision* is here called *the word which Isaiah saw.*

This sermon begins with the prophecy relating to the last days, the days of the Messiah, when his kingdom should be set up in the world, at the latter end of the Mosaic economy. In the last days of the earthly Jerusalem, just before the destruction of it, this heavenly Jerusalem should be erected, Heb. xii. 22; Gal. iv. 26. Gospel times are the last days. For, 1. They were a great while waited for by the Old Testament saints, and came at last. 2. We are not to look for any dispensation of divine grace but what we have in the gospel, Gal. i. 8, 9. 3. We are to look for the second coming of Jesus Christ at the end of time, 1 John ii. 18.

The prophet here foretells,

I. The planting of the Christian religion in the world. Christianity shall then be the mountain of the Lord's house. The gospel church shall then be the rendezvous of all the spiritual seed of Abraham. Now it is here promised, 1. That Christianity shall be openly preached and professed; it shall be *prepared* (so the margin reads it) in the top of the mountains, in the view and hearing of all. What the apostles did was not *done in a corner*, Acts xxvi. 26. It was the lighting of a beacon, the setting up of a standard. 2. That it shall be firmly fixed and rooted; it shall be established on the top of the everlasting mountains, built upon a *rock*, so that the *gates of hell shall not prevail against it*, unless they could pluck up mountains by the roots. 3. That it shall not only overcome all opposition, but overtop all competition; it shall be *exalted above the hills.* This *wisdom of God in a mystery* shall outshine all the wisdom of this world, all its philosophy and all its politics.

II. The bringing of the Gentiles into it. 1. The nations shall be admitted into it, even the uncircumcised, who were forbidden to come into the courts of the temple at Jerusalem. 2. *All nations shall flow into it;* having liberty of access, multitudes shall embrace the Christian faith.

III. The mutual assistance and encouragement which this confluence of converts shall give to one another. "*Come, and let us go up to the mountain of the Lord;* though it be uphill and against heart, yet it is *the mountain of the Lord*, who will assist the ascent of our souls towards him." The gospel church is here called, not only *the mountain of the Lord*, but *the house of the God of Jacob*; for in it God's covenant with Jacob and his praying seed is kept up and has its accomplishment. It is worth while to take pains to go up to his holy mountain to be taught his ways, and those who are willing to take that pains shall never find it labour in vain. "If he will *teach us his ways*, we will *walk in his paths*; if he will let us know our duty, we will by his grace make conscience of doing it."

IV. The means by which this shall be brought about: *Out of Zion shall go forth the law*, the New Testament law, the law of Christ, as of old the law of Moses from Mount Sinai, even *the word of the Lord from Jerusalem.* The gospel is a law, a law of faith; it is the *word of the Lord.* And in the temple on Mount Zion the disciples preached the gospel, Acts v. 20. And it was by this gospel, which took rise from Jerusalem, that the gospel church was *established on the top of the mountains.*

V. The erecting of the kingdom of the Redeemer in the world: *He shall judge among the nations.* By his Spirit working on men's consciences he shall judge, and try men and check them; his kingdom is spiritual, *and not of this world.*

VI. The great peace which should be the effect of the success of the gospel in the world (*v.* 4): *They shall beat their swords into ploughshares. Nation shall then not lift up sword against nation,* as now they do, *neither shall they learn war any more*, for they shall have no more occasion for it. The design and tendency of the gospel are to make peace and to slay all enmities. It has in it the most powerful obligations and inducements to peace. The gospel of Christ, as far as it prevails, disposes men to be peaceable, softens men's spirits, and sweetens them; and the love of Christ, shed abroad in the heart, constrains men to love one another. The primitive Christians were famous for brotherly love; their very adversaries took notice of it. Here is a practical inference drawn from all this (*v.* 5): *O house of Jacob! come you, and let us walk in the light of the Lord.* By the house of Jacob is meant either Israel according to the flesh, or spiritual Israel, all that are brought to the God of Jacob. Will God teach us his ways? Will he show

JAMIESON, FAUSSET, BROWN

CHAPTER 2

Vss. 1-22. **1.** The inscription. **The word**—the revelation.

2. Same as Micah 4. As Micah prophesied in Jotham's reign, and Isaiah in Uzziah's, Micah rests on Isaiah, whom he confirms: not vice versa. HENGSTENBERG on slight grounds makes Micah 4 the original. **last days**—i.e., Messiah's: especially the days yet to come, to which all prophecy hastens, when "the house of the God *of Jacob,*" viz., at Jerusalem, shall be the center to which the converted nations shall flock together (Matt. 13:32; Luke 2:31, 32; Acts 1:6, 7); where "the kingdom" of Israel is regarded as certain and the *time* alone uncertain (Ps. 68:15, 16; 72:8, 11).

mountain of the Lord's house . . . in the top . . .—the temple on Mount Moriah: type of the Gospel, beginning at Jerusalem, and, like an object set on the highest hill, made so conspicuous that all nations are attracted to it. **flow**—as a broad stream (ch. 66:12).

3. If the curse foretold against Israel has been literally fulfilled, so shall the promised blessing be literal. We Gentiles must not, while giving them the curse, deny them their peculiar blessing by spiritualizing it. The Holy Ghost shall be poured out for *a general* conversion then (Jer. 50:5; Zech. 8:21, 23; Joel 2:28). **from Jerusalem**—(Luke 24:47) an earnest of the future relations of Jerusalem to Christendom (Rom. 11:12, 15).

4. judge—as a sovereign umpire, settling all controversies (cf. ch. 11:4). LOWTH translates work, conviction.

plowshares—in the East resembling a short sword (ch. 9:6, 7; Zech. 9:10).

5. The connection is: As Israel's high destiny is to be a blessing to all nations (Gen. 12:3), let Israel's children walk worthy of it (Eph. 5:8).

ADAM CLARKE

CHAPTER 2

The prophecy contained in the second, third, and fourth chapters makes one continued discourse. The first five verses of chap. ii foretell the kingdom of Messiah, the conversion of the Gentiles, and their admission into it. From the sixth verse to the end of the second chapter is foretold the punishment of the unbelieving Jews for their idolatrous practices, their confidence in their own strength, and distrust of God's protection; and moreover the destruction of idolatry, in consequence of the establishment of Messiah's kingdom. The whole of the third chapter, with the first verse of the fourth, is a prophecy of the calamities of the Babylonian invasion and captivity; with a particular amplification of the distress of the proud and luxurious daughters of Sion; chap. iv. 2-6 promises to the remnant, which shall have escaped this severe purgation, a future restoration to the favor and protection of God.

This prophecy was probably delivered in the time of Jotham, or perhaps in that of Uzziah, as Isaiah is said to have prophesied in his reign; to which time not any of his prophecies is so applicable as that of these chapters. The seventh verse of the second and the latter part of the third chapter plainly point out times in which riches abounded, and luxury and delicacy prevailed. Plenty of silver and gold could arise only from their commerce, particularly from that part of it which was carried on by the Red Sea. This circumstance seems to confine the prophecy within the limits above mentioned, while the port of Elath was in their hands. It was lost under Ahaz, and never recovered.

2. *In the last days.* "Wherever the latter times are mentioned in Scripture, the days of the Messiah are always meant," says Kimchi on this place.

And *the mountain of the Lord's house,* says the same author, is Mount Moriah, on which the Temple was built. The prophet Micah, chap. iv. 1-4, has repeated this prophecy of the establishment of the kingdom of Christ, and of its progress to universality and perfection, in the same words; for as he did not begin to prophesy till Jotham's time, and this seems to be one of the first of Isaiah's prophecies, I suppose Micah to have taken it from hence.

MATTHEW HENRY

us his glory in the face of Christ? Let us walk comfortably in the light of this peace. Shall there be no more war? Let us then go on our way rejoicing.

Verses 6–9

I. Israel's doom. This is set forth in two words, the first and the last of this paragraph; but they are two dreadful words. 1. Their case (*v.* 6): *Therefore thou hast forsaken thy people.* Miserable is the condition of that people whom God has forsaken. This was the deplorable case of the Jewish church after they had rejected Christ. *Your house is left unto you desolate,* Matt. xxiii. 38. 2. Their case desperate, wholly desperate (*v.* 9): *Therefore forgive them not.* This prophetical prayer amounts to a threatening that they should not be forgiven. This refers not to particular persons (many of them repented and were pardoned), but to the body of that nation.

II. Israel's doom, and the reasons upon which it is grounded. In general, it is sin that provokes God to forsake his people. The particular sins which the prophet specifies are such as abounded among them at that time. There was a partial and temporary rejection of them by the captivity in Babylon, which was a type of their final destruction by the Romans, and which the sins here mentioned brought upon them.

1. God set them apart for himself, as a peculiar people, dignified above all other people (Num. xxiii. 9); but they were *replenished from the east;* they *naturalized* foreigners, and encouraged them to settle among them, and mingled with them, Hos. vii. 8. Their country was peopled with Syrians and Chaldeans, Moabites and Ammonites, and with them they admitted the fashions and customs of those nations, and *pleased themselves in the children of strangers.* Thus did they profane their crown and their covenant.

2. God gave them his oracles, the scriptures and the seers, but they slighted these, and became soothsayers like the Philistines, introduced their arts of divination, and hearkened to those who by the stars, or the clouds, or the flight of birds, or the entrails of beasts, pretended to discover things secret or foretell things to come. The Philistines were noted diviners, 1 Sam. vi. 2.

3. God assured them that he would be their wealth and strength; but, distrusting his power and promise, they made gold their hope, and furnished themselves with horses and chariots, and relied upon them for their safety, *v.* 7. It is not having silver and gold, horses and chariots, that is a provocation to God, but desiring them insatiably.

4. God himself was their God, and instituted ordinances of worship for them; but they slighted both him and his institutions, *v.* 8. Their land was full of idols; every city had its god (Jer. xi. 13). Those that love idols will multiply them; so sottish were they that they *worshipped the work of their own hands.* God had enriched them with silver and gold, and yet of that silver and gold they made idols.

5. God had put honour upon them; but they basely diminished themselves (*v.* 9): *The mean man boweth down to his idol,* a thing below the meanest that has any spark of reason left. Nor is it only the illiterate that do this, but even the *great man* forgets his grandeur and humbles himself to worship idols, deifies men no better than himself, and consecrates stones so much baser than himself.

Verses 10–22

The prophet here goes on to show what a desolation would be brought upon their land when God should have forsaken them. This may refer particularly to their destruction by the Chaldeans first, and afterwards by the Romans.

I. To startle and awaken sinners, who bid defiance to God and his judgments (*v.* 10): "*Enter into the rock;* God will attack you with such terrible judgments that you shall be forced to *enter into the rock, and hide yourself in the dust, for fear of the Lord.* You shall lose all your courage, and tremble at the shaking of a leaf." To the same purport, *v.* 19. *They shall go into the holes of the rocks, and into the caves of the earth,* the darkest the deepest places. It was so particularly at the destruction of Jerusalem by the Romans (Luke xxiii. 30) and of the persecuting pagan powers, Rev. vi. 16. And all *for fear of the Lord, and of the glory of his majesty.* Those that will not fear God and flee to him will be forced to fear him and flee from him to a refuge of lies. It will be in vain to think of finding refuge in the caves of the earth when the earth itself is shaken; there will be no shelter then but in God and in things above.

II. To humble and abase proud sinners, *v.* 11: *The lofty looks of man shall be humbled.* It is repeated (*v.* 17), *The loftiness of man shall be bowed down.* Men's haughtiness will be brought down, either by

JAMIESON, FAUSSET, BROWN

6. Therefore—rather, "For": reasons why there is the more need of the exhortation in vs. 5. **thou**—transition to Jehovah: such rapid transitions are natural, when the mind is full of a subject.

replenished—rather, filled, viz., with the superstitions of the East, Syria, and Chaldea. **soothsayers**—forbidden (Deut. 18:10-14). **Philistines**—southwest of Palestine: antithesis to "the east." **please themselves**—rather, join hands with, i.e., enter into alliances, matrimonial and national: forbidden (Exod. 23:32; Neh. 13:23, etc.).

7. gold—forbidden to be heaped together (Deut. 17:17). Solomon disobeyed (I Kings 10:21, 27). **horses . . . chariots**—forbidden (Deut. 17:16). But Solomon disobeyed (I Kings 20:26). Horses could be used effectively for war in the plains of Egypt; not so in the hilly Judea. God designed there should be as wide as possible a distinction between Israel and the Egyptians. He would have His people wholly dependent on Him, rather than on the ordinary means of warfare (Ps. 20:7). Also horses were connected with idolatry (II Kings 23:11); hence His objection: so the transition to "idols" (vs. 8) is natural. **8.** (Hos. 8:4.) Not so much public idolatry, which was not sanctioned in Uzziah's and Jotham's reign, but (see II Kings 15:4, 35) as *private.* **9. mean—in rank: not morally base: opposed to "the great man." The** former is in *Hebrew, Adam,* the latter, *ish.* **boweth**—viz., to idols. *All* ranks were idolaters. **forgive . . . not**—a threat expressed by an imperative. Isaiah so identifies himself with God's will, that he prays for that which he knows God purposes. So Revelation 18:6.

10. Poetical form of expressing that, such were their sins, they would be obliged by God's judgments to seek a hiding-place from His wrath (Rev. 6:15, 16). **dust**—equivalent to "caves of the earth," or dust (vs. 19). **for fear . . .**—lit., "from the face of the terror of the Lord."

11. lofty looks—lit., "eyes of pride" (Ps. 18:27). **humbled**—by calamities. God will so vindicate His honor "in that day" of judgments, that none else "shall be exalted" (Zech. 14:9).

ADAM CLARKE

JOSEPH PARKER:

Verse 6. "Therefore thou hast forsaken thy people." The term is logical. God never forsakes his people in any whimsical way: he is not a man, or a son of man, that he should treat his creatures arbitrarily, moodily—now full of sunshine in relation to them, and now covered with great clouds, without giving any reason for change. It is a most noticeable feature in Biblical revelation that when God forsakes men he gives the reason for abandoning them. The reason is always moral. God never leaves man because he is little, or weak, or self-distrustful, or friendless, or homeless, or brokenhearted; when God forsakes man it is because man has first forsaken him, broken his laws, defied his sword, challenged his judgment, forsaken with ungrateful abandonment the altar at which the life has received its richest blessing. So, never let us neglect the word "therefore" in reading concerning divine judgments.

—*The People's Bible*

6. *They be replenished*—"And they multiply." *And are soothsayers*—"They are filled with diviners."

7. *Their land is also full of horses*—"And his land is filled with horses." This was in direct contradiction to God's command in the law: "But he [the king] shall not multiply horses to himself, nor cause the people to return to Egypt, to the end that he should multiply horses . . . neither shall he greatly multiply to himself silver and gold," Deut. xvii. 16-17. Uzziah seems to have followed the example of Solomon (see 1 Kings x. 26-29), who first transgressed in these particulars. He recovered the port of Elath on the Red Sea, and with it that commerce which in Solomon's days had "made silver and gold at Jerusalem as plenteous as stones," 2 Chron. i. 15. He had an army of 307,500 men, in which, as we may infer from the testimony of Isaiah, the chariots and horses made a considerable part.

8. *Their land also is full of idols*—"And his land is filled with idols." Uzziah and Jotham are both said, 2 Kings xv. 3-4, 34-35, to have done "that which was right in the sight of the Lord"; that is, to have adhered to and maintained the legal worship of God, in opposition to idolatry and all irregular worship; "save that the high places were not removed: [where] the people sacrificed and burned incense still." There was hardly any time when they were quite free from this irregular and unlawful practice, which **they seem to have** looked upon as very consistent with the true worship of God. Even after the conversion of Manasseh, when he had removed the strange gods, and commanded Judah to serve Jehovah the God of Israel, it is added, "Nevertheless the people did sacrifice still in the high places, yet unto the Lord [Jehovah] their God only," 2 Chron. xxxiii. 17. The worshipping on the high places therefore does not necessarily imply idolatry; and from what is said of these two kings, Uzziah and Jotham, we may presume that the public exercise of idolatrous worship was not permitted in their time. The idols therefore here spoken of must have been such as were designed for a private and secret use.

9. *Boweth down*—"Shall be bowed down." This has reference to the preceding verse. They bowed themselves down to their idols; therefore shall they be bowed down and brought low under the avenging hand of God. *Therefore forgive them not.* "And thou wilt not forgive them."

MATTHEW HENRY

the grace of God convincing them of the evil of their pride, and clothing them with humility, or by the providence of God depriving them of all those things they were proud of and laying them low. This shall be done: because the *Lord alone will be exalted.* This shall be done: by humbling judgments, that shall mortify men, and bring them down (*v.* 12): *The day of the Lord of hosts*, the day of his wrath and judgment, *shall be upon everyone that is proud.* This day of the Lord is here said to be upon *all the cedars of Lebanon, that are high and lifted up.* Here the day of the Lord is said to be *upon the cedars*, those of Lebanon, that were the straightest and stateliest,—upon the oaks, those of Bashan, that were the strongest and sturdiest, —upon the natural elevations, *the high mountains and the hills that are lifted up* (*v.* 14), that overtop the valleys and seem to push the skies,—and upon the artificial fastnesses, *every high tower and every fenced wall, v.* 15. Understand these, 1. As representing the proud people themselves, that are in their own apprehensions like the cedars and the oaks, firmly rooted, and not to be stirred by any storm, and looking on all around them as shrubs. *The highest hills are most exposed to lightning.* These vaunting men, who are as high towers in which the noisy bells are hung,—these fenced walls, that fortify themselves with their native hardiness, and intrench themselves in their fastnesses—shall be brought down. 2. As particularizing the things they are proud of, and of which they make their boast. He will *take from them all their armour wherein they trusted.* They were proud of their trade abroad; but the day of the Lord shall be *upon all the ships of Tarshish*; they shall founder at sea or be ship-wrecked in the harbour. The day of the Lord shall be *upon all pleasant pictures*, the curious painting they brought home in their ships from other countries.

III. To make idolaters ashamed of their idols, and of the respect they have paid to them (*v.* 18): ***The idols he shall utterly abolish.*** **When the Lord alone shall be exalted (*v.* 17) he will not only pour contempt upon proud men, but much more upon all pretended deities. Their friends shall desert them; their enemies shall destroy them. They cannot secure themselves, so far are they from being able to secure their worshippers. Their worshippers shall abandon them, either from a conviction of their falsehood or from a sad experience of their inability to help them, *v.* 20. When men are themselves frightened by the judgments of God into the holes of the rocks, they shall cast their idols, which they have made their gods and hoped to make their friends in the time of need, to the moles and to the bats. God can make men sick of those idols that they have been most fond of. Covetous men make silver and gold their idols, money their god; but the time may come when they may feel it as much their burden as ever they made it their confidence. There was a time when the mariners threw the wares, and even the *wheat, into the sea* (Jonah i. 5; Acts xxvii. 38). The darkest holes, where the moles and the bats lodge, are the fittest places for idols, that have eyes and see not. It is possible that sin may be both loathed and left and yet not truly repented of out of any love to God, but only from a slavish fear of his wrath.**

IV. To make those that have trusted in an arm of flesh ashamed of their confidence (*v.* 22): "*Cease from man.* How weak man is: *His breath is in his nostrils*, puffed out every moment, soon gone for good and all. *Put not your trust in man.* Let not him be your fear, let not him be your hope; but look up to the power of God, to which all the powers of men are subject and subordinate; let your *hope be in the Lord your God.*"

JAMIESON, FAUSSET, BROWN

God will so vindicate His honor "in that day" of judgments, that none else "shall be exalted" (Zech. 14:9). **12.** Man has had many days: "the day of the Lord" shall come at last, beginning with judgment, a never-ending day in which God shall be "all in all" (I Cor. 15:28; II Pet. 3:10). **every**—not merely *person*, as *English Version* explains it, but every *thing* on which the nation prided itself. **13. cedars . . . oaks**—image for haughty nobles and princes (Amos 2:9; Zech. 11:1, 2; cf. Rev. 19:18-21). **Bashan**—east of Jordan, north of the river Jabbok, famous for fine oaks, pasture, and cattle. Perhaps in "oaks" there is reference to their idolatry (ch. 1: 29). **14. high . . . hills**—referring to the "high places" on which sacrifices were unlawfully offered, even in Uzziah's (equivalent to Azariah) reign (II Kings 15:4). Also, *places* of strength, fastnesses in which they trusted, rather than in God; so **15. tower . . . wall**—*Towers* were often made on the walls of cities. **fenced**—strongly fortified. **16. Tarshish**—*Tartessus* in southwest Spain, at the mouth of the Guadalquivir, near Gibraltar. It includes the adjoining region: a Phœnician colony; hence its connection with Palestine and the Bible (II Chron. 9:21). The name was also used in a wide sense for *the farthest west*, as our West Indies (ch. 66:19; Ps. 48:7; 72:10). "Ships of Tarshish" became a phrase for *richly laden* and *far-voyaging* vessels. The judgment shall be on all that minister to man's luxury (cf. Rev. 18:17-19). **pictures**—ordered to be destroyed (Num. 33:52). Still to be seen on the walls of Nineveh's palaces. It is remarkable that whereas all other ancient civilized nations, Egypt, Assyria, Greece, Rome, have left monuments in the fine arts, Judea, while rising immeasurably above them in the possession of "the living oracles," has left none of the former. The fine arts, as in modern Rome, were so often associated with polytheism, that God required His people in this, as in other respects, to be separate from the nations (Deut. 4:15-18). But *Vulgate* translation is perhaps better, "All that is beautiful to the sight"; not only paintings, but all luxurious ornaments. One comprehensive word for all that goes before (cf. Rev. 18:12, 14, 16). **17.** Repeated from vs. 11, for emphatic confirmation. **18. idols**—lit., "vain things," "nothings" (I Cor. 8:4). Fulfilled to the letter. *Before* the Babylonian captivity the Jews were most prone to idolatry; in no instance, *ever since.* For the future fulfilment, see Zechariah 13:2; Revelation 13:15; 19:20. **19.** The fulfilment answers exactly to the threat (vs. 10). they—the idol-worshippers. **caves**—abounding in Judea, a hilly country; hiding-places in times of alarm (I Sam. 13:6). **shake . . . earth**—and the heavens also (Heb. 12:26). Figure for severe and universal judgments. **20. moles**—Others translate "mice." The sense is, *under ground*, in darkness. **bats**—unclean birds (Lev. 11:19), living amidst tenantless ruins (Rev. 11:13).

22. The high ones (vss. 11, 13) on whom the people trust, shall be "brought low" (ch. 3:2); therefore "cease from" depending on them, instead of on the Lord (Ps. 146:3-5).

ADAM CLARKE

13-16. *And upon all the cedars*—"Even against all the cedars." Princes, potentates, rulers, captains, rich men. These verses afford us a striking example of that peculiar way of writing which makes a principal characteristic of the parabolical or poetical style of the Hebrews, and in which the prophets deal so largely, namely, their manner of exhibiting things divine, spiritual, moral, and political by a set of images taken from things natural, artificial, religious, historical, in the way of metaphor or allegory. Of these nature furnishes much the largest and the most pleasing share; and all poetry has chiefly recourse to natural images, as the richest and most powerful source of illustration. ***Ships of Tarshish.*** **This term is in Scripture frequently used by a metonymy for ships in general, especially such as are employed in carrying on traffic between distant countries,** as Tarshish was the most celebrated mart of those times, frequented of old by the Phoenicians, and the principal source of wealth to Judea and the neighboring countries. The learned seem now to be perfectly well agreed that Tarshish is Tartessus, a city of Spain, whence the Phoenicians, who first opened this trade, brought silver and gold (Jer. x. 9; Ezek. xxvii. 12), in which that country then abounded. Tarshish is celebrated in Scripture (2 Chron. viii. 17-18; ix. 21) for the trade which Solomon carried on thither, in conjunction with the Tyrians. Jehoshaphat (1 Kings xxii. 48; 2 Chron. xx. 36) attempted afterwards to renew their trade.

19-21. *Into the holes of the rocks*—"Into caverns of rocks." The country of Judea, being mountainous and rocky, is full of caverns, as appears from the history of David's persecution under Saul. At En-gedi, in particular, there was a cave so large that David with 600 men hid themselves in the sides of it; and Saul entered the mouth of the cave without perceiving that anyone was there, (1 Samuel xxiv). Josephus, *Antiq.* xiv. 15, and Bell. *Jud.* 1. 16, tell us of a numerous gang of banditti, who, having infested the country, and being pursued by Herod with his army, retired into certain caverns almost inaccessible, near Arbela in Galilee, where they were with great difficulty subdued.

20. *Which they made each one for himself to worship*—"Which they have made to worship." *To the moles.* They shall carry their idols with them into the dark caverns, old ruins, or desolate places, to which they shall flee for refuge; and so shall give them up, and relinquish them to the filthy animals that frequent such places, and have taken possession of them as their proper habitation.

22. *Cease ye from man.* Trust neither in him, nor in the gods that he has invented. Neither he, nor they, can either save or destroy.

MATTHEW HENRY

CHAPTER 3

Verses 1-8

God was now about to ruin all their creature-confidences, so that they should meet with nothing but disappointments in all their expectations from them (*v.* 1): *The stay and the staff* shall be taken away, all their supports. Their church and kingdom had now grown old and were going to decay, and they were (after the manner of aged men, Zech. viii. 4) leaning on a staff: now God threatens to take away their staff. St. Jerome refers this to the sensible decay of the Jewish nation after they had crucified our Saviour Rom. xi. 9, 10. I rather take it as a warning to all nations not to provoke God.

I. Bread is the staff of life: but God can *take away the whole stay of bread and the whole stay of water*; and it is just with him to do so when that which was given to be provision for the life is made provision for the lusts. He can take away the bread and the

JAMIESON, FAUSSET, BROWN

CHAPTER 3

Vss. 1-26. **1. For**—continuation of ch. 2:22. **Lord of hosts**—therefore able to do as He says. **doth**—present for future, so certain is the accomplishment. **stay . . . staff**—the same *Hebrew* word, the one masculine, the other feminine, an *Arabic* idiom for *all kinds of support.* What a change from the previous luxuries (ch. 2:7)! Fulfilled in the siege by Nebuchadnezzar and afterwards by Titus (Jer. 37: 21; 38:9).

ADAM CLARKE

CHAPTER 3

1. *The stay and the staff*—"Every stay and support." Hebrew, "the support masculine, and the support feminine"; that is, every kind of support, whether great or small, strong or weak.

MATTHEW HENRY

water by withholding the rain, Deut. xxviii. 23, 24. He can take away the stay of bread and the stay of water by withholding his blessing, by which man lives. Christ is the bread of life and the water of life; if he be our stay, we shall find that this is a good part not to be taken away, John iv. 14; vi. 27.

II. Their army—their generals, and commanders shall be taken away. *The mighty man, and the man of war*, and even the inferior officer, *the captain of fifty*, shall be removed. Let not the strong man therefore glory in his strength, nor any people trust too much to their mighty men.

III. Their ministers of state, their learned men, their politicians, their clergy, also should be taken away—*the judges, the prophets, the prudent*, who were assistants to the judges, *the diviners*, who used unlawful arts, *the ancients*, elders in age, in office. When the whole stay is to be broken, *the cunning artificer* too shall be taken away; and the last is *the eloquent orator*, the man skilful of speech, who in some cases may do good service. Moses cannot speak well, but Aaron can.

IV. It is the business of the sovereign to bear up the pillars of the land, Ps. lxxv. 3. But it is here threatened that this stay should fail them. When the mighty men and the prudent are removed *children shall be their princes*—children in age, who must be under tutors and governors, children in understanding and disposition, childish men, no more fit to rule than a child in the cradle. These shall rule over them, with all the folly, fickleness, and frowardness, of a child.

V. The union of the subjects among themselves, their good order and the good understanding is here threatened. God would send an evil spirit among them too (as Judges ix. 23), which would make them unneighbourly one towards another (*v.* 5): "*The people shall be oppressed every one by his neighbour*, and their princes, being children, will take no care to restrain the oppressors or relieve the oppressed." It is as ill an omen to a people as can be when the rising generation are untractable and ungovernable.

VI. The government shall go a-begging, *v.* 6. It is taken for granted that there is no way of redressing all these grievances, and bringing things into order again, but by good magistrates, who shall be invested with power by common consent, and shall exert that power for the good of the community. The case is represented as very deplorable, and things as having come to a sad pass; for children being their princes, every man will think himself fit to prescribe who shall be a magistrate. *A man shall take hold* by violence of one to make him a ruler; he shall urge it upon his brother. It will be looked upon as ground sufficient for the preferring of a man to be a ruler that he has clothing better than his neighbours. It would have been some sense to have said, "Thou hast wisdom, integrity, experience; be thou our ruler." But it was a jest to say, *Thou hast clothing; be thou our ruler*. Those who are thus pressed to come into office will swear themselves off, because they know themselves unable to bear the charges of the office (*v.* 7): *He shall swear* (shall lift up the hand, the ancient ceremony used in taking an oath) *I will not be a healer; make not me a ruler*. Rulers must be healers, and good rulers will be so; they must study to unite their subjects, and not widen the differences that are among them. But why will he not be a ruler? Because *in my house is neither bread nor clothing*. It was a sign that the case of the nation was very bad when nobody was willing to accept a place in the government of it. God brought things to this sad pass, not for want of goodwill to the country. *Jerusalem is ruined* and *Judah is fallen*; and they may thank themselves. They have brought their destruction upon their own heads, for *their tongue and their doings are against the Lord*; in word and action they broke the law of God. They provoked him to his face, as if the more they knew of his glory the greater pride they took in slighting it.

Verses 9–15

God proceeds in his controversy with his people.

I. It was for sin that God contended with them; if they vex themselves they will see that they must *thank* themselves: *Woe unto their souls! For they have rewarded evil unto themselves. Alas for their souls!* (so it may be read, in a way of lamentation), *for they have procured evil to themselves, v.* 9. They had grown impudent, *v.* 9. This hardens men against repentance as much as anything. Those that are past shame (we say) are past grace, and then past hope (*v.* 12): "*Those who lead thee* (the princes, priests, and prophets) mislead thee; they *cause thee to err*." Their judges, who should have patronised and protected the oppressed, were themselves the greatest oppressors, *v.* 14, 15. The elders of the people, and the princes *have eaten up the vineyard.* God's vine-

JAMIESON, FAUSSET, BROWN

2. Fulfilled (II Kings 24:14). **prudent**—the *Hebrew* often means a "soothsayer" (Deut. 18: 10-14); thus it will mean, the diviners, on whom they rely, shall in that day fail. It is found in a good sense (Prov. 16:10), from which passage the Jews interpret it *a king;* "without" whom Israel long has been (Hos. 3:4). **ancient**—old and experienced (I Kings 12:6-8). **3. captain of fifty**—not only captains of thousands, and centurions of a hundred, but even semi-centurions of fifty, shall fail. **honourable**—lit., "of dignified aspect." **cunning**—skilful. The mechanic's business will come to a standstill in the siege and subsequent desolation of the state; artisans are no mean "stay" among a nation's safeguards. **eloquent orator**—rather, as *Vulgate*, "skilled in whispering," i.e., incantation (Ps. 58:5). See ch. 8:19 below; and *Note* on "prudent" (vs. 2) above. **4. children**—in ability for governing; antithesis to the "ancient" (see vs. 12; Eccles. 10:16). **babes**—in warlike might; antithesis to "the mighty" and "man of war."

5. The anarchy resulting under such imbecile rulers (vs. 4); unjust exactions mutually; the forms of respect violated (Lev. 19:32). **base**—low-born. Compare the marks of "the last days" (II Tim. 3:2).

6. Such will be the want of men of wealth and ability, that they will "take hold of" (ch. 4:1) the first man whom they meet, having any property, to make him "ruler." **brother**—one having no better hereditary claim to be ruler than the "man" supplicating him. **Thou hast clothing**—which none of us has. Changes of raiment are wealth in the East (II Kings 5:5). **ruin**—Let our ruined affairs be committed to thee to retrieve.

7. **swear**—lit., "lift up," viz., his hand; the gesture used in solemn attestation. Or, his voice, i.e., answer; so *Vulgate*. **healer**—of the body politic, incurably diseased (ch. 1:6). **neither . . . clothing**—so as to relieve the people and maintain a ruler's dignity. A nation's state must be bad indeed, when none among men, naturally ambitious, is willing to accept office. 8. Reason given by the prophet, why all shrink from the government. **eyes of his glory**—to provoke His "glorious" Majesty before His "eyes" (cf. ch. 49: 5; Hab. 1:13). The *Syriac* and LOWTH, by a slight change of the *Hebrew*, translate, "the *cloud* of His glory," the Shekinah. **9. show**—The *Hebrew* means, "that which may be *known* by their countenances" [GESENIUS and WEISS]. But MAURER translates, "Their respect for person"; so *Syriac* and *Chaldee*. But the parallel word "declare" favors the other view. KIMCHI, from the *Arabic*, translates "their hardness" (Job 19:3, *Margin*), or impudence of countenance (Jer. 3:3). They have lost not only the substance of virtue, but its color. **witness**—lit., "corresponds" to them; their look answers to their inner character (Hos. 5:5). **declare**—(Jude 13). "Foaming *out* their own shame"; so far from making it a secret, "glorying" in it (Phil. 3:19). **unto themselves**—Cf. "in themselves" (Prov. 1:31; 8:36; Jer. 2:19; Rom. 1:27). **10.** The faithlessness of many is no proof that *all* are faithless. Though nothing but croaking of frogs is heard on the surface of the pool, we are not to infer there are no fish beneath [BENGEL]. (See ch. 1:19, 20.) **fruit of doings**—(Prov. 1:31) in a good sense (Gal. 6:8; Rev. 22:14). Not salvation by works, but by fruit-bearing faith (ch. 45:24; Jer. 23:6). GESENIUS and WEISS translate, *Declare as to* the righteous that, etc. MAURER, "Say that *the righteous is blessed.*" **11. ill**—antithesis to "well" (vs. 10); emphatic ellipsis of the words italicized. "Ill!" **hands**—his conduct; "hands" being the instrument of acts (Eccles. 8:12, 13). **12.** (See vs. 4.) **oppressors**—lit., "exactors," i.e., exact-

ADAM CLARKE

The following two verses, 2-3, are very clearly explained by the sacred historian's account of the event, the captivity of Jehoiachin by Nebuchadnezzar, king of Babylon: "And he carried away all Jerusalem, and all the princes, and all the mighty men of valour, even ten thousand captives, and all the craftsmen and smiths: none remained, save the poorest sort of the people of the land," 2 Kings xxiv. 14.

4. *I will give children to be their princes*—"I will make boys their princes." This also was fully accomplished in the succession of weak and wicked princes, from the death of Josiah to the destruction of the city and Temple, and the taking of Zedekiah, the last of them, by Nebuchadnezzar.

6. *Of the house of his father*—"Of his father's house." *Thou hast clothing*—"Take by the garment." That is, shall entreat him in an humble and supplicating manner. "Ten men . . . shall take hold of the skirt of him that is a Jew, saying, We will go with you: for we have heard that God is with you," Zech. viii. 23. And so in Isa. iv. 1, the same gesture is used to express earnest and humble entreaty. *And let this ruin be under thy hand*—"And let thy hand support."

7. *In that day shall he swear*—"Then shall he openly declare." *For in my house is neither bread nor clothing.* "It is customary through all the East," says Sir J. Chardin, "to gather together an immense quantity of furniture and clothes; for their fashions never alter." Princes and great men are obliged to have a great stock of such things in readiness for presents upon all occasions. A great quantity of provision for the table was equally necessary. This explains the meaning of the excuse made by him that is desired to undertake the government. He alleges that he has not wherewithal to support the dignity of the station, by such acts of liberality and hospitality as the law of custom required of persons of superior rank.

9. *The shew of their countenance.* Bishop Lowth has it "the steadfastness of their countenance"—they appear to be bent on iniquity; their eyes tell the wickedness of their hearts. *They declare their sin as Sodom.* Impure propensities are particularly legible in the eyes. *They have rewarded evil unto themselves.* Every man's sin is against his own soul.

MATTHEW HENRY

yard, which they were appointed to be the dressers and keepers of, they burnt (so the word signifies). God reasons with these great men (*v.* 15): "*What mean you, that you beat my people in pieces?* Do you think you had power given you for such a purpose as this?" *You grind the faces of the poor;* you put them to as much pain and terror as if they were ground in a mill.

II. In this controversy God himself is the prosecutor (*v.* 13): *The Lord stands up to plead,* and he *stands to judge the people,* for those that were oppressed; and he will *enter into judgment with the princes, v.* 14. The greatest of men cannot exempt themselves from the scrutiny and sentence of God's judgment. The indictment is proved: "Look upon the oppressors, and the *show of their countenance witnesses against them* (*v.* 9); look upon the oppressed, and you see how their faces are battered and abused," *v.* 15. To punish those that had abused their power God sets those over them that had not sense to use their power: *Children are their oppressors, and women rule over them* (*v.* 12), men that have as weak judgments and strong passions as women and children. Had they been righteous, it would have been well with them; but, if it be ill with them, it is because they are wicked and will be so (*v.* 10, 11). When the whole *stay of bread is taken away,* yet in the *day of famine the righteous shall be satisfied*; they *shall eat the fruit of their doings*—they shall have the testimony of their consciences that they kept themselves pure from iniquity, and therefore the common calamity is not to them what it is to others. There is a woe to wicked people, and it shall be ill with them.

Verses 16–26

The prophet's business was to show all sorts of people what they had contributed to the national guilt and what share they must expect in the national judgments that were coming. Here he reproves and warns the daughters of Zion.

I. The sin charged upon the daughters of Zion, *v.* 16. Two things they here stand indicted for—haughtiness and wantonness. They discovered the disposition of their mind by their gait and gesture. They are haughty, for they *walk with stretched-forth necks,* that they may seem tall. Their eyes are wanton, *deceiving* (so the word is). They affect a formal starched way of going, *mincing,* or nicely tripping. They make a *tinkling with their feet,* having, as some think, little bells upon their shoes. These were the daughters of Zion who should have behaved with the gravity that becomes women professing godliness.

II. The punishments threatened for this sin; and they answer the sin as face answers to face in a glass, *v.* 17, 18. 1. They *walked with stretched-forth necks,* but God will *smite with a scab the crown of their head,* which shall make them ashamed to show their heads, being obliged to cut off their hair. 2. They cared not what they laid out in great variety of fine clothes; but God will reduce them to such poverty and distress that they shall not have clothes sufficient to cover their nakedness. 3. They were extremely proud of their ornaments; but God will strip them of those ornaments, when their houses shall be plundered, their treasures rifled, and they themselves led into captivity. It is not at all material to enquire what sort of ornaments these were. Fashions alter and so do the names of them. Many of these things, we may suppose, were ridiculous, and, if they had not been in fashion, would have been hooted at. Those things that were decent and convenient, as *the linen, the hoods, and the veils,* needed not to be provided in such abundance and variety.

III. They were very nice about their clothes; but God would make those bodies of theirs a reproach and burden to them (*v.* 24): *Instead of sweet smell* (those tablets, or boxes, of perfume, *houses of the soul* or *breath,* as they are called, *v.* 20, *margin*) *there shall be stink,* garments grown filthy with being long worn. *Instead of a* rich embroidered *girdle* used to make the clothes sit tight, there shall be *a rent*; old rotten clothes rent into rags. *Instead of well-set hair,* there shall be *baldness,* the hair being plucked off or shaven, as was usual in times of great affliction (*ch.* xv. 2; Jer. xvi. 6), or in great servitude, Ezek. xxix. 18. *Instead of a stomacher,* or sash, there shall be *a girding of sackcloth,* in token of deep humiliation; *and burning instead of beauty.* Those that had a good complexion when they are carried into captivity shall be tanned and sunburnt; the best faces are soonest injured by the weather. From all this let us learn not to affect that which is gay and costly. There shall be none to be charmed by them (*v.* 25): *Thy men shall fall by the sword, and thy mighty in the war.* And, when Zion's guards are cut off, no marvel that Zion's gates *lament and mourn* (*v.* 26). The city itself, being desolate, shall *sit upon the ground* like a disconsolate widow.

JAMIESON, FAUSSET, BROWN

ing princes (ch. 60:17). They who *ought* to be *protectors* are *exactors;* as unqualified for rule as "children," as effeminate as "women." Perhaps it is also implied that they were under the influence of their harem, the women of their court. **lead**—*Hebrew,* "call thee blessed"; viz., the false *prophets,* who flatter the people with promises of safety in sin; as the political "rulers" are meant in the first clause. **way of thy paths**—(Jer. 6:16.) The right way set forth in the law. "Destroy"—*Hebrew,* "Swallow up," i.e., cause so utterly to disappear that not a vestige of it is left. **13. standeth up**—no longer *sitting* in silence. **plead**—indignant against a wicked people (ch. 66:16; Ezek. 20:35). **14. ancients**—Hence they are spoken of as "taken away" (vss. 1, 2). **vineyard**—the Jewish theocracy (ch. 5:1-7; Ps. 80:9-13). **eaten up**—"burnt"; viz., by "oppressive exactions" (vs. 12). Type of the crowning guilt of the husbandmen in the days of Jesus Christ (Matt. 21:34-41). **spoil . . . houses**—(Matt. 23:14.) **15.** What right have ye to beat, etc. (Ps. 94:5; Mic. 3:2, 3). **grind**—by exactions, so as to leave them nothing. **faces**—persons; with the additional idea of it being *openly* and *palpably* done. "Presence," equivalent to (*Hebrew*) "face." **16.** Luxury had become great in Uzziah's prosperous reign (II Chron. 26:5). **stretched forth**—proudly elevated (Ps. 75:5). **wanton**—rather, "making the eyes to glance about," viz., wantonly (Prov. 6:13) [MAURER]. But LOWTH, "falsely setting off the eyes with paint." Women's eyelids in the East are often colored with stibium, or powder of lead (*Note,* Job 42:14; Jer. 4:30, *Margin*). **mincing**—tripping with short steps. **tinkling**—with their ankle-rings on both feet, joined by small chains, which sound as they walk, and compel them to take short steps; sometimes little bells were attached (vss. 18, 20). **17. smite with a scab**—lit., "make bald," viz., by disease. **discover**—cause them to suffer the greatest indignity that can befall female captives, viz. to be stripped naked, and have their persons exposed (ch. 47:3; cf. with ch. 20:4). **18. bravery**—the finery. **tinkling**—(See vs. 16.) **cauls**—network for the head. Or else, from an *Arabic* root, "little suns," answering to the "tires" or neck-ornaments, "like the moon" (Judg. 8:21). The *chumarah* or crescent is also worn in front of the head-dress in West Asia. **19. chains**—rather, pendants, hanging about the neck, and dropping on the breast. **mufflers**—veils covering the face, with apertures for the eyes, close above and loosely flowing below. The word radically means "tremulous," referring to the changing effect of the spangles on the veil. **20. bonnets**—turbans. **ornaments of the legs**—the short stepping-chains from one foot to another, to give a measured gait; attached to the "tinkling ornaments" (vs. 16). **headbands**—lit., "girdles." **tablets**—rather, houses of the breath, i.e., smelling-boxes [*Vulgate*]. **earrings**—rather, amulets suspended from the neck or ears, with magic formulæ inscribed; the root means to "whisper" or "conjure." **21. nose jewels**—The cartilage between the nostrils was bored to receive them; they usually hung from the left nostril. **22.** Here begin *entire* articles of apparel. Those before were single ornaments. **changeable**—from a root, "to put off"; not worn commonly; put on and off on special occasions. So, dress-clothes (Zech. 3:4). **mantles**—fuller tunics with sleeves, worn over the common one, reaching down to the feet. **wimples**—i.e., mufflers, or hoods. In Ruth 3:15, veils; perhaps here, a broad cloak, or shawl, thrown over the head and body. **crisping pins**—rather, money bags (II Kings 5:23). **23. glasses**—mirrors of polished metal (Exod. 38:8). But LXX, a transparent, gauzelike, garment. **hoods**—miters, or diadems (ch. 62:3; Zech. 3:5). **veils**—large enough to cover the head and person. Distinct from the smaller veils ("mufflers") above (Gen. 24:65). Token of woman's subjection (I Cor. 11:10). **24. stink**—arising from ulcers (Zech. 14:12). **girdle**—to gird up the loose Eastern garments, when the person walked. **rent**—LXX, better, a "rope," an emblem of poverty; the poor have nothing else to gird up their clothes with. **well-set hair**—(I Pet. 3:3, 4.) **baldness**—(vs. 17.) **stomacher**—a broad plaited girdle. **sackcloth**—(II Sam. 3:31.) **burning**—a sunburnt countenance, owing to their hoods and veils being stripped off, while they had to work as captives under a scorching sun (Song of Sol. 1:6). **25. Thy men**—of Jerusalem. **26. gates**—The place of concourse personified is represented mourning for the loss of those multitudes which once frequented it. **desolate . . . sit upon . . . ground**—the very figure under which Judea was represented on medals after the destruction by Titus: a *female sitting* under a palm tree in a posture of grief; the motto, *Judæa capta* (Job 2:13; Lam. 2:10, where, as here primarily, the destruction by Nebuchadnezzar is alluded to).

ADAM CLARKE

13. *The people*—"His people."

14. *The vineyard*—"My vineyard."

15. *And grind the faces.* The expression and the image is strong, to denote grievous oppression, but is exceeded by the prophet Micah, chap. iii. 1-3.

16. *And wanton eyes*—"And falsely setting off their eyes with paint." Hebrew, "falsifying" their eyes.

17. *The Lord will smite*—"Will the Lord humble." *Will discover their secret parts*—"Expose their nakedness." It was the barbarous custom of the conquerors of those times to strip their captives naked, and to make them travel in that condition. This is always mentioned as the hardest part of the lot of captives. Nahum, chap. iii. 5-6, denouncing the fate of Nineveh, paints it in very strong colors.

18. *Ornaments about their feet*—"The ornaments of the feet rings." *And their cauls*—"the net-works."

20. *The tablets.* The words which we translate *tablets,* and Bishop Lowth, "perfume boxes," literally signify "houses of the soul"; and may refer to strong-scented bottles used for pleasure and against fainting.

23. *And the veils.*—"The transparent garments."

24. *Instead of sweet smell*—"perfume." *Burning instead of beauty*—"A sunburnt skin."

26. *Sit upon the ground.* Sitting on the ground was a posture that denoted mourning and deep distress. The prophet Jeremiah (Lam. ii. 8) has given it the first place among many indications of sorrow.

MATTHEW HENRY

CHAPTER 4

Verse 1

Here we have the effect and consequence of that great slaughter of men. Providence has so wisely ordered that, *on an average of years*, there is nearly an equal number of males and females born into the world, yet, through the devastations made by war, there should scarcely be one man in seven left alive. As there are deaths attending the bringing forth of children, which are peculiar to the woman, there are deaths peculiar to men, those by the sword perhaps devour more than child-bed does. It is foretold that there should be *seven women to one man.* By reason of the scarcity of men, whereas men ordinarily make their court to the women, the women should now take hold of the men. Seven should now, by consent, become the wives of one man,—and that whereas by the law the husband was obliged to provide food and raiment for his wife (Exod. xxi. 10), these women will be bound to support themselves; they will *eat bread of their own earning, and wear apparel of their own working*, and the man they court shall be at no expense, only they desire to be called his wives, to *take away the reproach* of a single life. They are willing to be wives upon any terms. All their care was to get husbands—modesty was forgotten, and with them the reproach of vice was nothing to the reproach of virginity.

Verses 2–6

By the foregoing threatenings everything looks melancholy. But here the sun breaks out from behind the cloud. Many exceedingly great and precious promises we have in these verses, giving assurance of comfort, and these certainly point at the kingdom of the Messiah, and the great redemption to be wrought out by him, under the figure of the restoration of Judah and Jerusalem by the reforming reign of Hezekiah after Ahaz and the return out of their captivity in Babylon; to both these events the passage may have some reference, but chiefly to Christ.

I. God will raise up a righteous branch, which shall produce fruits of righteousness (*v.* 2): *In that day*, when Jerusalem shall be destroyed, and the Jewish nation dispersed, the kingdom of the Messiah shall be set up.

1. Christ himself shall be exalted. He is the *branch of the Lord*; it is one of his prophetical names, *my servant the branch* (Zech. iii. 8; vi. 12), a *rod out of the stem of Jesse and a branch out of his roots* (*ch.* xi. 1). The ancient Chaldee paraphrase here reads, *The Christ, or Messiah, of the Lord.* He shall himself be advanced to the glory which he had with the Father before the world was.

2. His gospel shall be embraced. The success of the gospel is the fruit of the branch of the Lord; all the graces and comforts of the gospel spring from Christ. But it is called *the fruit of the earth* because it sprang up in this world. We may understand it of both the persons and the things that are the products of the gospel. If the branch of the Lord be beautiful and glorious in our eyes, even the fruit of the earth also will be excellent and comely, because then we may take it as the fruit of the promise, Ps. xxxvii. 16; 1 Tim. iv. 8.

II. God will reserve to himself a holy seed, *v.* 3. When the generality shall be cut off as withered branches, by their own unbelief, yet some shall be left. 1. This is a remnant such as are written among the living. Those that are kept alive in killing times were written for life in the book of divine Providence, *written in the Lamb's book of life*, Rev. xiii. 8. All that were *written among the living* shall be found among the living, every one; for of all that were given to Christ he will lose none. 2. It is a remnant *under the dominion of grace*; for everyone that is *written among the living* shall be called *holy*, and shall be accepted of God accordingly.

III. God will reform his church and will rectify and amend whatever is amiss in it, *v.* 4. Then the remnant shall be *called holy, when the Lord shall have washed away their filth*, washed it from among them by cutting off the wicked persons, washed it from within them by purging out the wicked thing. Jerusalem, though the holy city, needed reformation. By the daughters of Zion may be meant the country towns and villages, which were related to Jerusalem as the mother-city, and which needed reformation. The filth shall be washed away; for wickedness is filthiness, particularly blood-shed. *The Lord shall do it.* Reformation-work is God's work. But how? By the judgment of his providence the sinners were destroyed; but it is by the Spirit of his grace that they are reformed and converted. The Spirit herein acts, enlightening the mind, convincing the conscience, guiding us, separating between the precious and the

JAMIESON, FAUSSET, BROWN

CHAPTER 4

Vss. 1-6. **1. that day**—the calamitous period described in previous chapter.

seven—indefinite number among the Jews. So many men would be slain, that there would be very many more women than men; e.g., seven women, contrary to their natural bashfulness, would sue to (equivalent to "take hold of," ch. 3:6) one man to marry them.

eat . . . own bread—foregoing the privileges, which the law (Exod. 21:10) gives to wives, when a man has more than one. **reproach**—of being unwedded and childless; especially felt among the Jews, who were looking for "the seed of the woman," Jesus Christ, described in vs. 2; ch. 54:1, 4; Luke 1:25.

2. In contrast to those on whom vengeance falls, there is a manifestation of Jesus Christ to the "escaped of Israel" in His characteristic attributes, *beauty* and *glory*, typified in Aaron's garments (Exod. 28:2). Their *sanctification* is promised as the fruit of their being "written" in the book of life by sovereign love (vs. 3); the means of it are the "spirit of judgment" and that of "burning" (vs. 4). Their "defense" by the special presence of Jesus Christ is promised (vss. 5, 6). **branch**—the sprout of JEHOVAH. Messiah (Jer. 23:5; 33:15; Zech. 3:8; 6:12; Luke 1:78, *Margin*). The parallel clause does not, as MAURER objects, oppose this; for "fruit of the earth" answers to "branch"; He shall not be a dry, but a *fruit-bearing branch* (ch. 27:6; Ezek. 34:23-27). He is "of the *earth*" in His birth and death, while He is also "of the *Lord*" (*Jehovah*) (John 12:24). His name, "the Branch," chiefly regards His descent from David, *when the family was low and reduced* (Luke 2:4, 7, 24); a sprout with more than David's glory, springing as from a decayed tree (ch. 11:1; 53: 2; Rev. 22:16). **excellent**—Heb. 1:4; 8:6). **comely**—(Song of Sol. 5:15, 16; Ezek. 16:14). **escaped of Israel**—the elect remnant (Rom. 11:5); (1) in the return from Babylon; (2) in the escape from Jerusalem's destruction under Titus; (3) in the still future assault on Jerusalem, and deliverance of "the third part"; events mutually analogous, like concentric circles (Zech. 12:2-10; 13:8, 9, etc.; 14:2; Ezek. 39: 23-29; Joel 3). **3. left in Zion**—equivalent to the "escaped of Israel" (vs. 2). **shall be called**—shall *be* (ch. 9:6). **holy**—(ch. 52:1; 60:21; Rev. 21:27.) **written**—in the book of life, antitypically (Phil. 4:3; Rev. 3:5; 17:8). Primarily, in the *register* kept of *Israel's* families and tribes. **living**—not "blotted out from the registry, as *dead;* but written there as among the "escaped of Israel" (Dan. 12:1; Ezek. 13: 9). To the *elect of Israel,* rather than the saved in general, the *special* reference is here (Joel 3:17). **4. When**—i.e., After. **washed**—(Zech. 13:1). **filth**—moral (ch. 1:21-25). **daughters of Zion**—same as in ch. 3:16. **purged**—purified by judgments; destroying the ungodly, correcting and refining the godly. **blood**—(ch. 1:15.) **spirit**—Whatever God does in the universe, He does by His *Spirit,* "without the hand" of man (Job 34:20; Ps. 104:30). Here He is represented using His power as *Judge.* **burning**—(Matt. 3:11, 12). The same Holy Ghost, who sanctifies believers by the fire of affliction (Mal. 3:2, 3), dooms unbelievers to the fire of perdition (I Cor. 3:13-15).

ADAM CLARKE

CHAPTER 4

1. *And . . . seven women.* The division of the chapters has interrupted the prophet's discourse, and broken it off almost in the midst of the sentence. "The numbers slain in battle shall be so great that seven women shall be left to one man."

2. *The branch of the Lord*—"The branch of Jehovah." The Branch is an appropriate title of the Messiah; and *the fruit* of the land means the great Person to spring from the house of Judah, and is only a parallel expression signifying the same, or perhaps the blessings consequent upon the redemption procured by Him.

3. *Written among the living.* That is, whose name stands in the enrollment or register of the people; or every man living, who is a citizen of Jerusalem.

4. *The spirit of burning* means the fire of God's wrath, by which He will prove and purify His people; gathering them into His furnace, in order to separate the dross from the silver, the bad from the good. The severity of God's judgments, the fiery trial of His servants, Ezekiel (chap. xxii. 18-22) has set forth at large, after his manner, with great boldness of imagery and force of expression. God threatens to gather them into the midst of Jerusalem, as into the furnace; to blow the fire upon them, and to melt them. Malachi, chap. iii. 2-3, treats the same subject, and represents the same event, under the like images.

MATTHEW HENRY

vile, quickening and invigorating the affections, and making men zealous in good work.

IV. God will protect his church, and all that belong to it (*v.* 5, 6). Those that are sanctified are well fortified.

1. Their tabernacles shall be defended, *v.* 5, tabernacles of their rest, their houses, where they worship God with their families. God takes particular care of the dwelling-places of his people, the poorest cottage as well as the stateliest palace. Their assemblies or tabernacles of meeting for religious worship—all the congregations of Christians, though but two or three met together in Christ's name, shall be taken under the special protection of heaven. This writ of protection is drawn up in a similitude taken from the safety of the camp of Israel when they marched through the wilderness. God will give to the Christian church as real proofs of his care of them, as he then gave to Israel. Though miracles have ceased, yet God is the same to the New Testament church that he was to Israel of old. A similitude is taken from the outside cover of rams' skins and badgers' skins that was upon the curtains of the tabernacle, as if every dwelling-place and every assembly were as dear to God as that tabernacle was: *Upon all the glory shall be a defence*, to save it from wind and weather. Gospel truths and ordinances, the scriptures and the ministry, are the church's glory; and upon all this glory there is a defence. If God himself be the glory in the midst of it, he will himself be a wall of fire round about it, impenetrable and impregnable. Grace in the soul is the glory of it, and those that have it are *kept by the power of God* as in a stronghold, 1 Pet. i. 5. The divine power and goodness shall be a tabernacle to all the saints. God himself will be their hiding-place (Ps. xxxii. 7); they shall be at home in him, Ps. xci. 9. God is a refuge to his people in all weathers.

JAMIESON, FAUSSET, BROWN

5. create—The "new creation" needs as much God's creative omnipotence, as the material creation (II Cor. 4:6; Eph. 2:10). So it shall be in the case of the Holy Jerusalem to come (ch. 65:17, 18). **upon**—The pillar of cloud stood over the tabernacle, as symbol of God's favor and presence (Exod. 13:21, 22; Ps. 91:1). Both on *individual families* ("every dwelling") and on the *general* sacred "assemblies" (Lev. 23:2). The "cloud" became a "fire" by night in order to be seen by the Lord's people. **upon all the glory**—"upon the glorious whole"; viz., the Lord's people and sanctuary [MAURER]. May it not mean, "Upon whatever the glory (the *Shekinah* spoken of in the previous clause) shall rest, there shall be a defense." The symbol of His presence shall ensure also safety. So it was to Israel against the Egyptians at the Red Sea (Exod. 14:19, 20). So it shall be to literal Jerusalem hereafter (Zech. 2:5). Also to the Church, the spiritual "Zion" (ch. 32:18; 33:15-17; Heb. 12:22). **tabernacle**—Christ's body (John 1:14). "The Word 'tabernacled' (*Greek* for 'dwelt') among us" (John 2:21; Heb. 8:2). It is a "shadow from the heat" and "refuge from the storm" of divine wrath against man's sins (ch. 25:4). Heat and storms are violent in the East; so that a portable tent is a needful part of a traveller's outfit. Such shall be God's wrath hereafter, from which the "escaped of Israel" shall be sheltered by Jesus Christ (ch. 26:20, 21; 32:2). **covert**—answering to "defense" (vs. 5). The *Hebrew* for *defense* in vs. 5, is "covering"; the lid of the ark or mercy seat was named from the same *Hebrew* word, *caphar;* the *propitiatory;* for it, being sprinkled with blood by the high priest once a year, on the day of atonement, *covered* the people typically from wrath. Jesus Christ is the true Mercy Seat, on whom the Shekinah rested, the *propitiatory*, or atonement, beneath whom the law is kept, as it was literally within the ark, and man is *covered* from the storm. The redeemed Israel shall also be, by union with Him, a tabernacle for God's glory, which, unlike that in the wilderness, shall not be taken down (ch. 38:20).

ADAM CLARKE

5. *A cloud and smoke by day.* This is a manifest allusion to the pillar of a cloud and of fire which attended the Israelites in their passage out of Egypt, and to the glory that rested on the Tabernacle, Exod. xiii. 21; xl. 38. The prophet Zechariah, chap. ii. 5, applies the same image to the same purpose: And I "will be unto her a wall of fire round about, and I will be the glory in the midst of her." That is, the visible presence of God shall protect her.

MATTHEW HENRY

CHAPTER 5

Verses 1–7

God, to awaken sinners to repentance, speaks sometimes in plain terms and sometimes in parables, sometimes in prose and sometimes in verse, as here. God the Father dictates it to the honour of Christ his well beloved Son, whom he has constituted Lord of the vineyard. The prophet sings it to the honour of Christ. The Old Testament prophets were friends of the bridegroom. Christ is God's beloved Son and our beloved Saviour. This parable was put into a song that it might be the more moving and the more easily learned, remembered, and transmitted to posterity. It is an exposition of the song of Moses (Deut. xxxii), showing that what he then foretold was now fulfilled.

I. The great things which God had done for the Jewish church and nation. The soil they were planted in was *a very fruitful hill, the horn of the son of oil*: so it is in the margin. There was plenty, and there was dainty: they did there eat the fat and drink the sweet. Observe further what God did for this vineyard. 1. He fenced it. If they had not thrown down their fence, no inroad could have been made upon them, Ps. cxxv. 2; cxxi. 4. 2. He gathered the stones out of it. He proffered his grace to take away the stony heart. 3. He planted it with the choicest vine, set up a pure religion among them. 4. He built a tower in the midst of it for defence. The temple was this tower. 5. He made a wine-press therein, set up his altar, to which the sacrifices, as the fruits of the vineyard, should be brought.

II. The disappointment of his just expectations: *He looked that it should bring forth grapes.* God expects vineyard-fruit from those that enjoy vineyard-privileges. Good purposes and good beginnings are good things, but not enough; there must be fruit, a good heart and a good life, vineyard fruit, thoughts and affections, words and actions, agreeable to the Spirit. His expectations are frustrated: *It brought forth wild grapes.* 1. Wild grapes are the fruits of the corrupt nature. 2. Wild grapes are hypocritical performances in religion, that look like grapes.

JAMIESON, FAUSSET, BROWN

CHAPTER 5

Vss. 1-30. PARABLE OF JEHOVAH'S VINEYARD. A new prophecy; entire in itself. Probably delivered about the same time as chs. 2 and 3, in Uzziah's reign. Cf. vss. 15, 16 with ch. 2:17; and vs. 1 with ch. 3:14. However, the close of the chapter alludes *generally* to the still distant invasion of Assyrians in a later reign (cf. vs. 26 with ch. 7:18; and vs. 25 with ch. 9:12). When the time drew nigh, according to the ordinary prophetic usage, he handles the details *more particularly* (chs. 7, 8); viz., the calamities caused by the Syro-Israelitish invasion, and subsequently by the Assyrians whom Ahaz had invited to his help. **1. to**—rather, "concerning" [GESENIUS], i.e., in the person of My beloved, as His representative [VITRINGA]. Isaiah gives a hint of the distinction and yet unity of the Divine Persons (cf. *He* with *I*, vss. 2, 3). **of my beloved**—inspired by Him; or else, a tender song [CASTALIO]. By a slight change of reading "a song of His love" [HOUBIGANT]. "The Beloved" is Jehovah, the Second Person, the "Angel" of God the Father, not in His character as incarnate *Messiah,* but as *God of the Jews* (Exod. 23:20, 21; 32:34; 33:14). **vineyard**—ch. 3:14; Ps. 80:8, etc.). The Jewish covenant people, separated from the nations for His glory, as the object of His peculiar care (Matt. 20:1; 21:33). Jesus Christ in the "vineyard" of the New Testament Church is the same as the Old Testament Angel of the Jewish covenant. **fruitful hill**—lit., "a horn" ("peak," as the Swiss *shreckhorn*) *of the son of oil;* poetically, for *very fruitful.* Suggestive of isolation, security, and a sunny aspect. Isaiah alludes plainly to the Song of Solomon (Song of Sol. 6:3; 8:11, 12), in the words "*His* vineyard" and "*my* Beloved" (cf. ch. 26:20; 61:10, with Song of Solomon 1:4; 4:10). The transition from "branch" (ch. 4:2) to "vineyard" here is not unnatural. **2. fenced**—rather, "digged and trenched" the ground to prepare it for planting the vines [MAURER]. **choicest vine**—*Hebrew, sorek;* called still in Morocco, *serki;* the grapes had scarcely perceptible seeds; the Persian *kishmish* or *bedana,* i.e., without seed (Gen. 49:11). **tower**—to watch the vineyard against the depredations of man or beast, and for the use of the owner (Matt. 21:33). **winepress**—including the winefat; both hewn, for coolness, out of the rocky undersoil of the vineyard. **wild grapes**—The *Hebrew* expresses offensive putrefaction, answering to the corrupt state of the Jews. Fetid fruit of the wild vine [MAURER], instead of "choicest" grapes. Of the poisonous monk's hood

ADAM CLARKE

CHAPTER 5

1. *Now will I sing to my wellbeloved a song of my beloved*—"Let me sing now a song." *A song of my beloved*—"A song of loves."

In a very fruitful hill—"On a high and fruitful hill." Hebrews, "on a horn the son of oil."

2. *Wild grapes*—"Poisonous berries."

MATTHEW HENRY

III. An appeal to themselves whether God must not be justified and they condemned, *v.* 3, 4. *O inhabitants of Jerusalem, and men of Judah! judge, I pray you, betwixt me and my vineyard.* Here is a challenge to show wherein God had been wanting to them: *What could have been done more to my vineyard, that I have not done in it?* They had everything requisite. "Wherefore, what reason can be given why it should bring forth wild grapes, when I looked for grapes?"

IV. Their doom read, and sentence passed upon them (*v.* 5, 6): "*And now go to,* since nothing can be offered in excuse of the crime or arrest of the judgment, *I will tell you what I am now determined to do to my vineyard.* I will be troubled with it no more; in short, it shall cease to be a vineyard, and be turned into a wilderness: the church of the Jews shall be unchurched. *I will take away the hedge thereof,* and then it will become bare." God will remove all their defences and they will become an easy prey to their enemies. They shall no longer have the face of a vineyard, the form and shape of a church and commonwealth, but shall be levelled and laid waste. Those who would not bring forth good fruit should bring forth none. The curse of barrenness is the punishment of the sin of barrenness. This had its partial accomplishment in the destruction of Jerusalem by the Chaldeans, its full accomplishment in the final rejection of the Jews, and has its frequent accomplishment in the departure of God's Spirit from those who have long resisted him.

V. The explanation of this parable, or a key to it (*v.* 7). The vineyard is *the house of Israel,* the body of the people, incorporated in one church and commonwealth, and the vines are *the men of Judah*; these he had dealt graciously with, and from them he expected suitable returns. The grapes that were expected and the wild grapes that were produced: *He looked for judgment and righteousness,* that the people should be honest and the magistrates strictly administer justice. This might reasonably be expected; but the fact was quite otherwise; instead of judgment there was the cruelty of the oppressors, and instead of righteousness the cry of the oppressed.

Verses 8–17

Eagerness of the world, and indulgence of the flesh, are the two sins against which the prophet, in God's name, here denounces woes. These were sins which then abounded among the men of Judah, some of the wild grapes they brought forth (*v.* 4).

I. Here is a woe to those who set their hearts upon the wealth of the world (*v.* 8), who *join house to house and lay field to field, till there be no place,* no room for anybody to live by them. If they could succeed, they monopolize possessions and preferments. They are inordinate in their desires to enrich themselves. They are herein careless of others. They care not what hardships they put upon those that they have power over, nor what wicked arts they use to heap up treasure to themselves. The punishment of this sin is that neither the houses nor the fields should turn to any account, *v.* 9, 10. The houses they were so fond of should be untenanted, should stand long empty: *Many houses shall be desolate,* the people that should dwell in them, being cut off by sword, famine, or pestilence, or carried into captivity. We have a saying, That fools build houses for wise men to live in; but sometimes, as the event proves, they are built for no man to live in. The fields they were so fond of should be unfruitful (*v.* 10): *Ten acres of vineyard shall yield* only such grapes as will make but *one bath* of wine (about eight gallons), *and the seed of a homer,* a bushel's sowing, shall yield but an ephah, the tenth part of a homer; so that they should not have more than a tenth part of their seed again.

II. Here is a woe to those that dote upon the pleasures of sense, *v.* 11, 12. Sensuality ruins men as certainly as worldliness and oppression. The sinners against whom this woe is denounced are such as are given to drink. They sit at their cups all day, *and continue till night, till wine inflame them*—inflame their lusts. They are such as never give their mind to anything that is serious: *They regard not the work of the Lord;* they observe not his power, wisdom, and goodness, in those creatures which they abuse, nor the bounty of his providence in giving them those good things which they make the food and fuel of their lusts. It is here foretold they should be dislodged; the land should spew out these drunkards (*v.* 13): *My people* have therefore *gone into captivity, because they have no knowledge*; how should they have knowledge when by their excessive drinking they make sots and fools of themselves? They should be impoverished, and come to want that which they had wasted and abused to excess: Even *their glory are men of famine,* subject to it and slain by it; and *their multitude are dried up*

JAMIESON, FAUSSET, BROWN

[GESENIUS]. The Arabs call the fruit of the nightshade "wolf-grapes" (Deut. 32:32, 33; II Kings 4:39-41). Jerome tries to specify the details of the parable; the "fence," *angels;* the "stones gathered out," *idols;* the "tower," the *temple* "in the midst" of Judea; the "winepress," the *altar.* **3. And now . . .**—appeal of God to themselves, as in ch. 1:18; Mic. 6:3. So Jesus Christ, in Matthew 21:40, 41, alluding in the very form of expression to this, makes them pass sentence on themselves. God condemns sinners "out of their own mouth" (Deut. 32:6; Job 15:6; Luke 19: 22; Rom. 3:4). 4. God has done all that could be done for the salvation of sinners, consistently with His justice and goodness. The God of nature is, as it were, amazed at the unnatural fruit of so well-cared a vineyard. **5. go to**—i.e., attend to me. **hedge . . . wall**—It had both; a proof of the care of the owner. But now it shall be trodden down by wild beasts (enemies) (Ps. 80:12, 13). **6. I will . . . command**—The parable is partly dropped and Jehovah, as in vs. 7, is implied to be the Owner: for He alone, not an ordinary husbandman (Matt. 21:43; Luke 17:22), could give such a "command." **no rain**—antitypically, *the heaven-sent teachings of the prophets* (Amos 8:11). Not accomplished in the Babylonish captivity; for Jeremiah, Ezekiel, Daniel, Haggai, and Zechariah prophesied during or after it. But in gospel times. **7.** Isaiah here applies the parable. It is no mere *human* owner, nor *a literal* vineyard that is meant. **vineyard of the Lord**—His *only* one (Exod. 19:5; Amos 3:2). **pleasant**—"the plant of his delight"; just as the husbandman was at pains to select the *sorek,* or "choicest vine" (vs. 2); so God's election of the Jews. **judgment**—justice. The play upon words is striking in the *Hebrew,* "He looked for *mishpat,* but behold *mispat* (bloodshed); for *tsedaqua,* but behold *tseaqua* (the cry that attends anarchy, covetousness, and dissipation, vs. 8, 11, 12; compare the cry of the rabble by which justice was overborne in the case of Jesus Christ, Matt. 27:23, 24).

8-23. SIX DISTINCT WOES AGAINST CRIMES. **8.** (Lev. 25:13; Mic. 2:2.) The jubilee restoration of possessions was intended as a guard against avarice. **till there be no place**—left for any one else. **that they may be**—rather, and ye be. **the earth**—the land.

9. In mine ears . . . the Lord—viz., has revealed it, as in ch. 22:14. **desolate**—lit., "a desolation," viz., on account of the national sins. **great and fair**—houses. **10. acres**—lit., "yokes"; as much as one yoke of oxen could plow in a day. **one**—only. **bath**—of wine; seven and a half gallons. **homer . . . ephah**—Eight bushels of seed would yield only three pecks of produce (Ezek. 45:11). The ephah and bath, one-tenth of an homer. **11.** Second **Woe**—against intemperance. **early**—when it was regarded especially shameful to drink (Acts 2:15; I Thess. 5:7). Banquets for revelry began earlier than usual (Eccles. 10:16, 17). **strong drink**—*Hebrew, sichar,* implying intoxication. **continue**—drinking all day till evening. **12.** Music was common at ancient feasts (ch. 24:8, 9; Amos 6:5, 6). **viol**—an instrument with twelve strings (JOSEPHUS, *Antiquities* 8. 10). **tabret**—*Hebrew, toph,* from the use of which in drowning the cries of children sacrificed to Moloch, *Tophet* received its name. *Arabic, duf.* A kettle drum, or tambourine. **pipe**—flute or flageolet: from a *Hebrew* root "to bore through"; or else, "to dance" (cf. Job 21; 11-15). **regard not . . . Lord**—a frequent effect of feasting (Job 1:5; Ps. 28:5). **work . . . operation**—in punishing the guilty (vs. 19; ch. 10:12). **13. are gone**—The prophet sees the *future* as if it were before his eyes. **no knowledge**—because of their foolish recklessness (vs. 12; ch. 1:3; Hos. 4:6; Luke 19:44). **famished**—awful contrast to their luxurious feasts (vss. 11, 12). **multitude**—plebeians in contradistinction to the "honorable men," or nobles. **thirst**—(Ps. 107:4, 5.) Contrast to their drinking (vs. 11). In their deportation and exile, they shall hunger and thirst.

ADAM CLARKE

F. B. MEYER:

"What could have been done more to my vineyard, that I have not done in it?" (Isa. 5:4). This is what the Owner of all souls will say of his dealings with each when the discipline and husbandry of time are over. Each of us is God's vineyard, and for each God has done the best possible. At the end of all things God will have no reason to feel that had He adopted some other method the barren waste of some heart would have brought forth fruit. It will be seen then, Omniscience itself being witness, that every soul of man had the chance of becoming a fruitful vineyard; and if he became the reverse, it was due to no failure in either the wisdom or grace of God.

—Great Verses Through the Bible

7. *And he looked for judgment.* The play on the words in this place is very remarkable: *mishpat, mishpach, tsedakah, tseakah.* There are many examples of it in the other prophets, but Isaiah seems peculiarly fond of it.

9. *Many houses.* This has reference to what was said in the preceding verse: "In vain are ye so intent upon joining house to house, and field to field; your houses shall be left uninhabited, and your fields shall become desolate and barren; so that a vineyard of ten acres shall produce but one bath (not eight gallons) of wine, and the husbandman shall reap but a tenth part of the seed which he has sown." This means such an extent of vineyard as would require ten yoke of oxen to plough in one day.

11. *Woe unto them that rise up early!* There is a likeness between this and the following passage of the prophet Amos, chap. vi. 3-6.

13. *And their honourable men*—"And the nobles."

MATTHEW HENRY

with thirst. Multitudes should be cut off by famine and sword (*v.* 14): *Therefore hell has enlarged herself.* Tophet, the common burying-place, proves too little; so many are there to be buried that they shall be forced to enlarge it. They should be humbled and abased, and all their honours laid in the dust. God shall be glorified, *v.* 16. He shall be exalted in the judgment and righteousness of these dispensations. Good people shall be relieved and succoured (*v.* 17): *Then shall the lambs feed after their manner;* the meek ones of the earth, who followed the Lamb, who were persecuted and put into fear by those proud oppressors, shall feed quietly, and there shall be none to make them afraid. The country shall be laid waste, and become a prey to the neighbours: *The waste places of the fat ones,* the possessions of those rich men that lived at their ease, shall be eaten by strangers that were nothing akin to them.

Verses 18–30

I. Sins described which will bring judgments upon the men of Judah who lived at that time, and though it may relate primarily to them, is intended for warning to all people, in all ages. Those are here said to be in a woeful condition,

1. Who are violent in their sinful pursuits (*v.* 18), who *draw iniquity with cords of vanity,* who take as much pains to sin as the cattle do that draw in a team. They think themselves as sure of compassing their wicked project as if they were pulling it towards them with strong cart-ropes; but they will prove cords of vanity, which will break when they come to any stress. Those that sin through infirmity are drawn away by sin; those that sin presumptuously draw iniquity to them, in spite of the oppositions of Providence and the checks of conscience. Some by sin pull God's judgments upon their own heads, as it were, with cart-ropes.

2. Who set the justice of God at defiance, and challenge the Almighty to do his worst (*v.* 19): *They say, Let him make speed, and hasten his work.* They ridicule the prophets, and banter them. They will not believe the revelation of God's wrath from heaven unless they see it executed. If God should appear against them, as he has threatened, yet they think themselves able to make their part good with him. **"We have heard his word, but it is all talk; let him hasten his work, we shall shift for ourselves well enough."**

3. Who confound the distinctions between moral good and evil, *who call evil good and good evil* (*v.* 20). Those do a great deal of wrong to God, and religion, and conscience, to their own souls, and to the souls of others, who call drunkenness good fellowship, and covetousness good husbandry, and on the other hand, call seriousness ill-nature, and who say all manner of evil falsely concerning godliness.

4. Who though they are guilty of such gross mistakes have a great opinion of their own judgments (*v.* 21): They are *wise in their own eyes*; they think they can outwit Infinite Wisdom and countermine Providence itself.

5. Who glory that they are able to bear a great deal of strong liquor without being overcome by it (*v.* 22), *who are mighty to drink wine,* and use their strength in the service of their lusts. Drunkards ungratefully abuse their bodily strength, which God has given them for good purposes, and by degrees cannot but weaken it.

6. Who, as judges, pervert justice, *v.* 23. They *justify the wicked for reward,* and find some pretence or other to clear him from his guilt and shelter him from punishment; and they condemn the innocent, and *take away their righteousness from them.*

II. The judgments described, which these sins would bring upon them. The righteous God will take vengeance, *v.* 24–30. He had compared this people to a vine (*v.* 7), which, it was hoped, would be fruitful; but the grace of God was received in vain, and the root became rottenness, being dried up from beneath, and the blossom would blow off as dust. Sin weakens the strength, the root, of a people, so that they are easily rooted up; it defaces the beauty, the blossoms, of a people, and takes away the hopes of fruit. Sinners make themselves as stubble and chaff. *As the fire devours the stubble,* chaff is consumed, unhelped and unpitied. God does not reject men for every transgression of his law and word; but, when his word is despised and his law cast away, what can they expect but that God should utterly abandon them? The justice of God appoints it; for that is *the anger of the Lord* which is *kindled against his people,* his necessary vindication. *He has stretched forth his hand against them.* That hand which had many a time been stretched out for them against their enemies is now stretched out against them. When God comes forth in wrath against a people the hills

JAMIESON, FAUSSET, BROWN

14. hell—the grave; *Hebrew, sheol; Greek, hades;* the unseen world of spirits. Not here, the place of torment. Poetically, it is represented as enlarging itself immensely, in order to receive the countless hosts of Jews, which should perish (Num. 16:30). **their**—i.e., of the Jewish people. **he that rejoiceth**—the drunken reveller in Jerusalem. **15.** (Cf. ch. 2:9, 11, 17.) *All* ranks, "mean" and "mighty" alike; so "honorable" and "multitude" (vs. 13). **16.** God shall be "exalted" in man's view, because of His manifestation of His "justice" in punishing the guilty. **sanctified**—*regarded as holy* by reason of His "righteous" dealings. **17. after their manner**—lit., according to their own word, i.e., *at will.* Otherwise, *as in their own pasture* [GESENIUS]: so the *Hebrew* in Micah 2:12. The lands of the Scenite tent-dwellers (Jer. 35:7). Arab shepherds in the neighborhood shall roam at large, the whole of Judea being so desolate as to become a vast pasturage. **waste . . . fat ones**—the *deserted* lands of *the rich* (Ps. 22:29, "fat"), then gone into captivity; "strangers," i.e., nomad tribes shall make their flocks to feed on [MAURER]. Figuratively, "the lambs" are the pious, "the fat ones" the impious. So tender disciples of Jesus Christ (I John 21:15) are called "lambs"; being meek, harmless, poor, and persecuted. Cf. Ezekiel 39:18, where the fatlings are the rich and great (I Cor. 1:26, 27). The "strangers" are in this view the "other sheep not of" the Jewish "fold (John 10:16), the *Gentiles* whom Jesus Christ shall "bring" to be partakers of the rich privileges (Rom. 11:17) which the Jews ("fat ones," Ezek. 34:16) fell from. Thus "after their (own) manner" will express that the Christian Church should worship God in freedom, released from legal bondage (John 4:23; Gal. 5:1). **18.** Third **Woe**—against obstinate perseverance in sin, as if they wished to provoke divine judgments. **iniquity**—guilt, incurring punishment [MAURER]. **cords . . . cart rope**—Rabbins say, "An evil inclination is at first like a fine *hair-string,* but the finishing like a *cart-rope.*" The antithesis is between the slender *cords* of sophistry, like the spider's web (ch. 59:5; Job 8:14), with which one sin *draws* on another, until they at last bind themselves with great guilt as with a *cart-rope.* They strain every nerve in sin. **vanity**—wickedness. **sin**—substantive, not a verb: they draw on themselves "sin" and its penalty recklessly. **19. work**—vengeance (vs. 12). Language of defiance to God. So Lamech's boast of impunity (Gen. 4:23, 24; cf. Jer. 17:15; II Pet. 3:3, 4). **counsel**—God's threatened purpose to punish. **20.** Fourth **Woe**—against those who confound the distinctions of right and wrong (cf. Rom. 1:28), "reprobate," *Greek,* "undiscriminating: the moral perception darkened." **bitter . . . sweet**—sin is *bitter* (Jer. 2:19; 4:18; Acts 8:23; Heb. 12:15); though it seem sweet for a time (Prov. 9:17, 18). Religion is *sweet* (Ps. 119:103) **21.** Fifth **Woe**—against those who were so "wise in their own eyes" as to think they knew better than the prophet, and therefore rejected his warnings (ch. 29:14, 15).

22, 23. Sixth **Woe**—against corrupt judges, who, "mighty" in drinking "wine" (a boast still not uncommon), if not in defending their country, obtain the means of self-indulgence by taking bribes ("reward"). The two verses are closely joined [MAURER]. **mingle strong drink**—not with *water,* but *spices* to make it intoxicating (Prov. 9:2, 5; Song of Sol. 8:2). **take away the righteousness**—set aside the just claims of those having a righteous cause.

24. Lit., "tongue of fire eateth" (Acts 2:3). **flame consumeth the chaff**—rather, withered grass falleth before the flame (Matt. 3:12). **root . . . blossom**—*entire* decay, both the hidden *source* and outward *manifestations* of prosperity, perishing (Job 18:16; Mal. 4:1). **cast away . . . law**—in its spirit, while retaining the letter. **25. anger . . . kindled**—(II Kings 22:13, 17.) **hills . . . tremble**—This probably fixes the date of this chapter, as it refers to the *earthquake in the days of Uzziah* (Amos 1:1; Zech. 14:5). The earth trembled as if conscious of the presence of God (Jer. 4:24; Hab. 3:6).

ADAM CLARKE

17. *The lambs.* The meaning is, Their luxurious habitations shall be so entirely destroyed as to become a pasture for flocks. *After their manner*—"Without restraint."

18. *With a cart rope*—"As a long cable." "An evil inclination," says Kimchi on this place, from the ancient rabbins, "is at the beginning like a fine hair-string, but at the finishing like a thick cart-rope."

CHARLES H. SPURGEON:

Verse 18. The text begins with "Woe"; but when we get a woe in this book of blessings it is sent as a warning, that we may escape from woe. God's woes are better than the devil's welcomes. God always means man's good, and only sets ill before him that he may turn from the dangers of a mistaken way, and so may escape the ill which lies at the end of it. Think me not unkind at this time because my message sounds harshly, and has a note in it of sorrow rather than joy. It may be most for your pleasure for ages to come to be for a while displeased. It may make the bells ring in your ears forever if instead of the dulcet sound of the harp, you hear the shrill clarion startling you to thoughtfulness. Mayhap "Woe, woe, woe," though it should sound with a dreadful din in your ear, may be the means of leading you to seek and find your Savior, and then throughout eternity no woe shall ever come near to you. May the good Spirit of all grace put power into my warning, that you may profit by it.

—The Treasury of the Old Testament

25. *The hills did tremble*—"And the mountains trembled." Probably referring to the great earthquakes in the days of Uzziah, king of Judah, in or not long before the time of the prophet himself, recorded as a remarkable era in the title of the prophecies of Amos, chap. i. 1, and by Zechariah, chap. xiv. 5.

MATTHEW HENRY

tremble, fear seizes even their great men. What sight can be more frightful than the carcases of men thrown *as dung* (so the margin reads it) *in the midst of the streets*? This intimates that multitudes should be slain, not only soldiers in battle, but the inhabitants of their cities put to the sword in cold blood, and that the survivors should neither have hands nor hearts to bury them. This ruin should be done by a foreign enemy, that should lay all waste. Those who know him are not made use of to fulfil his counsel. If God set up his standard, he can incline men's hearts to enlist themselves under it, though perhaps they know not why or wherefore. *Behold, they shall come with speed swiftly*. This is described here in elegant and lofty expressions, *v.* 27–30. Though their marches be long, yet *none among them shall be weary*. Though the way be rough, yet none among them shall *stumble*. Though they be forced to keep constant watch, yet *none shall slumber nor sleep*. They shall not desire any rest or relaxation; they shall not put off their clothes, nor *loose the girdle of their loins*, but shall always have their belts on and swords by their sides. Not a *latchet of their shoes shall be broken* which they must stay to mend, as Joshua ix. 13. Their arms and ammunition shall all be fixed, and in good posture; *their arrows sharp, and all their bows bent*, none unstrung. Their horses and chariots of war shall all be fit for service; their horses so strong, that *their hoofs shall be like flint*, and the wheels of their chariots not broken, or battered, but swift *like a whirlwind*. All the soldiers shall be bold and daring (*v.* 29): *Their roaring shall be like a lion*, who with his roaring animates himself, and terrifies all about him. *They shall roar like the roaring of the sea* in a storm. There shall not be the least prospect of relief or succour. If the light is darkened in the heavens, how great is that darkness! If God hide his face, no marvel the heavens hide theirs and appear gloomy, Job xxxiv. 29.

JAMIESON, FAUSSET, BROWN

torn—rather, were as dung (Ps. 83:10). **For all this . . .**—This burden of the prophet's strains, with dirge-like monotony, is repeated at ch. 9:12, 17, 21; 10:4. With all the past calamities, still heavier judgments are impending; which he specifies in the rest of the chapter (Lev. 26:14, etc.). **26. lift . . . ensign**—to call together the hostile nations to execute His *judgments* on Judea (ch. 10:5-7; 45:1). But for *mercy* to it, in ch. 11:12; 18:3. **hiss**—(cf. 7:18.) Bees were drawn out of their hives by the sound of a flute, or *hissing*, or *whistling* (Zech. 10:8). God will collect the nations round Judea like bees (Deut. 1:44; Ps. 118:12). **end of the earth**—the widely distant subject races of which the Assyrian army was made up (ch. 22:6). The ulterior fulfilment took place in the siege under Roman Titus. Cf. "end of the earth" (Deut. 28:49, etc.). So the pronoun is *singular* in the *Hebrew*, for "them," "their," "whose" (him, his, etc.), vss. 26, 27, 28, 29; referring to some *particular* nation and person [HORSLEY]. **27. weary**—with long marches (Deut. 25:18). **none . . . slumber**—requiring no rest. **girdle**—with which the ancient loose robes used to be girded for action. Ever ready for march or battle. **nor the latchet . . . broken**—The soles were attached to the feet, not by upper leather as with us, but by straps. So securely clad that not even a strap of their sandals gives way, so as to impede their march. **28. bent**—ready for battle. **hoofs . . . flint**—The ancients did not shoe their horses: hence the value of hard hoofs for long marches. **wheels**—of their chariots. The Assyrian army abounded in cavalry and chariots (ch. 22:6, 7; 36:8). **29. roaring**—their battle cry. **30. sorrow, and the light is darkened**—Otherwise, *distress and light* (i.e., hope and fear) alternately succeed (as usually occurs in an unsettled state of things), *and darkness arises in*, etc. [MAURER]. **heavens**—lit., "clouds," i.e., its sky is rather "clouds" than sky. Otherwise from a different *Hebrew* root, "in its destruction" or ruins. HORSLEY takes "sea . . . look unto the land" as a new image taken from mariners in a coasting vessel (such as all ancient vessels were), *looking for the* nearest *land*, which the *darkness* of the storm conceals, so that *darkness and distress* alone may be said to be visible.

ADAM CLARKE

27. *None . . . among them.* Kimchi has well illustrated this continued exaggeration or hyperbole, as he rightly calls it, to the following effect: "Through the greatness of their courage, they shall not be fatigued with their march; nor shall they stumble though they march with the utmost speed: they shall not slumber by day, nor sleep by night; neither shall they ungird their armour, or put off their sandals to take their rest. Their arms shall be always in readiness, their arrows sharpened, and their bows bent. The hoofs of their horses are hard as a rock. They shall not fail, or need to be shod with iron: the wheels of their carriages shall move as rapidly as a whirlwind."

CHAPTER 6 (Matthew Henry)

Verses 1–4

The vision which Isaiah saw when he was, as is said of Samuel, *established to be a prophet of the Lord* (1 Sam. iii. 20), was intended to confirm his faith. Thus God appeared at first as a God of glory to Abraham (Acts vii. 2), and to Moses, Exod. iii. 2. Ezekiel's prophecies, and St. John's, begin with visions of the divine glory. Those who are to teach others the knowledge of God ought to be well acquainted with him themselves.

The vision was *in the year that king Uzziah died*, who had reigned as well as any of the kings of Judah, above fifty years. About the time that he died Isaiah saw this vision of God upon a throne. Israel's king dies, but Israel's God still lives. King Uzziah died a leper in an hospital, but the King of kings still sits upon his throne.

I. See God upon his throne, and that throne *high and lifted up*, not only above other thrones, as it transcends them, but over other thrones, as it rules them. Isaiah saw not *Jehovah*—the essence of God (no man has seen that, or can see it), but *Adonai*—his dominion. He saw the Lord Jesus; so this vision is explained John xii. 41, that Isaiah now saw Christ's glory. See the sovereignty of the Eternal Monarch: he sits *upon a throne*—a throne of glory, before which we must worship,—a throne of government, under which we must be subject,—and a throne of grace, to which we may come boldly.

II. See his temple, his church on earth, filled with the manifestations of his glory. His *train*, the skirts of his robes, *filled the temple*, the whole world (for it is all God's temple), or rather the Church, which is filled, enriched, and beautified with the tokens of God's special presence.

III. See the bright and blessed attendants on his throne (*v.* 2): *Above the throne the seraphim stood*, the holy angels, who are called *seraphim—burners*; for he *makes his ministers a flaming fire*, Ps. civ. 4. They burn in love to God, and zeal for his glory and against sin. It is the glory of the angels that they are seraphim, have heat proportionable to their light, have abundance, not only of divine knowledge, but of holy love. They had *each of them six wings*, not stretched upwards (as those whom Ezekiel saw, *ch.* i. 11), but, 1. Four were for covering; with the two upper wings they covered their faces, and with the two lowest wings they covered their feet. This

CHAPTER 6 (Jamieson, Fausset, Brown)

Vss. 1-13. VISION OF JEHOVAH IN HIS TEMPLE. Isaiah is outside, near the altar in front of the temple. The doors are supposed to open, and the veil hiding the Holy of Holies to be withdrawn, unfolding to his view a vision of God represented as an Eastern monarch, attended by seraphim as His ministers of state (I King 22:19), and with a robe and flowing train (a badge of dignity in the East), which filled the temple. This assertion that he had seen God was, according to tradition (not sanctioned by ch. 1:1; see *Introduction*), the pretext for sawing him asunder in Manasseh's reign (Heb. 11:37). Visions often occur in the other prophets: in Isaiah there is only this one, and it is marked by characteristic clearness and simplicity. **In . . . year . . . Uzziah died**—Either *literal* death, or *civil* when he ceased as a leper to exercise his functions as king [CHALDEE], (II Chron. 26:19-21). 754 B.C. [CALMET]; 578 [COMMON CHRONOLOGY.] This is not the first beginning of Isaiah's prophecies, but his inauguration to a higher degree of the prophetic office: vs. 9, etc., implies the tone of one who had already experience of the people's obstinacy. **Lord**—here *Adonai; Jehovah* in vs. 5; *Jesus Christ* is meant as speaking in vs. 10, according to John 12:41. Isaiah could only have "seen" *the Son*, not the divine essence (John 1:18). The words in vs. 10 are attributed by Paul (Acts 28:25, 26) to the *Holy Ghost*. Thus the Trinity in unity is implied; as also by the thrice "Holy" (vs. 3). Isaiah mentions the robes, temple, and seraphim, but not the form of God Himself. Whatever it was, it was different from the usual Shekinah: that was on the mercy seat, this on a throne; that a cloud and fire, of this no form is specified: over that were the cherubim, over this the seraphim; that had no clothing, this had a flowing robe and train. **2. stood**—not necessarily the posture of *standing;* rather, *were in attendance on Him* [MAURER], hovering on expanded wings. **the**—not in the *Hebrew*. **seraphim**—nowhere else applied to God's attendant angels; but to *the fiery flying* (not winged, but *rapidly moving*) serpents, which bit the Israelites (Num. 21:6), called so from the poisonous *inflammation* caused by their bites. *Seraph* is to burn; implying the *burning* zeal, dazzling *brightness* (II Kings 2:11; 6:17; Ezek. 1:13; Matt. 28:3) and serpent-like *rapidity* of the seraphim in God's service. Perhaps Satan's form as a *serpent* (*nachash*) in his appearance to

CHAPTER 6 (Adam Clarke)

As this vision seems to contain a solemn designation of Isaiah to the prophetic office, it is by most interpreters thought to be the first in order of his prophecies. But this perhaps may not be so; for Isaiah is said, in the general title of his prophecies, to have prophesied in the time of Uzziah, whose acts, first and last, he wrote, 2 Chron. xxvi. 22, which is usually done by a contemporary prophet; and the phrase *in the year that Uzziah died* probably means after the death of Uzziah, as the same phrase (chap. xiv. 28) means after the death of Ahaz.

In this vision the ideas are taken in general from royal majesty, as displayed by the monarchs of the East; for the prophet could not represent the ineffable presence of God by any other than sensible and earthly images. The particular scenery of it is taken from the Temple. God is represented as seated on His throne above the ark, in the most holy place, where the glory appeared above the cherubim, surrounded by His attendant ministers. The veil, separating the most holy place from the holy or outermost part of the Temple, is here supposed to be taken away; for the prophet, to whom the whole is exhibited, is manifestly placed by the altar of burnt offering, at the entrance of the Temple (compare Ezek. xliii. 5-6,) which was filled with the train of the robe, the spreading and overflowing of the divine glory.

2. *Above it stood the seraphims.* From *seraph*, "to burn." He saw, says Kimchi, the angels as flames of fire, that the depravity of that generation might be exhibited, which was worthy of being totally burnt up.

MATTHEW HENRY

bespeaks their great humility and reverence. They not only cover their feet, but even their faces. Two were made use of for flight; when they are sent on God's errands they fly swiftly (Dan. ix. 21). This teaches us to do the work of God with cheerfulness and expedition.

IV. Hear the song of praise, which the angels sing to the honour of him that sits on the throne, *v.* 3. With zeal and fervency—*they cried* aloud; and with unanimity—*they cried one to another,* without the least jarring voice to interrupt the harmony. The song was the same which is sung by the four living creatures, Rev. iv. 8. The church above is the same in its praises; there is no change of times or notes there. Here is one of his most glorious titles praised: he is *the Lord of hosts,* and one of his most glorious attributes, his holiness. Power, without purity to guide it, would be a terror to mankind. God's power was spoken twice (Ps. lxii. 11), but his holiness thrice, *Holy, holy, holy.* It may refer to the three persons in the Godhead, Holy Father, Holy Son, and Holy Spirit (for it follows, *v.* 8, *Who will go for us?*) or perhaps to *that which was, and is, and is to come. The earth is full of his glory,* of the glory of his power and purity; for he is holy in all his works, Ps. cxlv. 17.

V. Observe the tokens of terror with which the temple was filled, upon this vision of the divine glory, *v.* 4. The house was *shaken*; even *the posts of the door,* which were firmly fixed, *moved at the voice of him that cried,* at the voice of God, who called to judgment (Ps. l. 4). The house was *darkened*; it was *filled with smoke*, which was as a *cloud spread* upon *the face of his throne* (Job xxvi. 9). In the temple above, everything will be seen clearly. There God dwells in light; here he *makes darkness his pavilion,* 2 Chron. vi. 1.

Verses 5–8

I. The consternation that the prophet was put into by the vision which he saw of the glory of God (*v.* 5): *Then said I, Woe is me!* One would think, he should have said, "Happy am I, nothing now shall trouble me"; but, on the contrary, he cries out, "*Woe is me! for I am undone.*"

1. What the prophet reflected upon in himself which terrified him: "*I am undone because I am a man of unclean lips.*" Some think he refers particularly to some rash word he had spoken, or to his sinful silence in not reproving sin with boldness. But it may be taken more generally: *I am a sinner;* particularly, *I have offended in word.* We all have reason to bewail it before the Lord, (1) That we are of unclean lips ourselves; our lips are not consecrated to God. We are unworthy to take God's name into our lips. The impurity of our lips ought to be the grief of our souls, for by our words we shall be justified or condemned. (2) That we dwell among those who are so too. The disease is hereditary and epidemic, which is so far from lessening our guilt that it should rather increase our grief, considering that we have not done what we might have done for the cleansing of the pollution of other people's lips; we have rather learned their way and spoken their language, as Joseph in Egypt learned the courtier's oath, Gen. xlii. 16.

2. What gave occasion for these sad reflections: *My eyes have seen the King, the Lord of hosts.* We are undone if there be not a Mediator between us and this holy God, 1 Sam. vi. 20. Isaiah was thus humbled, to prepare him for the honour he was now to be called to as a prophet.

II. The silencing of the prophet's fears by the comfortable words, with which the angel answered him, *v.* 6, 7. One of the seraphim immediately flew to him, to purify him. Those that are struck down with the visions of God's glory shall soon be raised up again with the visits of his grace. Here was one of the seraphim dismissed, for a time, from the throne of God's glory, to be a messenger of his grace to a good man; and he came flying to him. To our Lord Jesus himself, in his agony, there *appeared an angel from heaven, strengthening him,* Luke xxii. 43. The seraph *brought a live coal from the altar,* and touched his lips with it to cleanse them. The blessed Spirit works as fire, Matt. iii. 11. The seraph put life into the prophet, for the way to purge the lips from the uncleanness of sin is to fire the soul with the love of God. "*Lo, this has touched thy lips,* to assure thee of this, that *thy iniquity is taken away and thy sin purged.* The guilt of thy sin is removed by pardoning mercy, the guilt of thy tongue-sins. Thy corrupt disposition to sin is removed by renewing grace; and therefore nothing can hinder thee from being accepted with God as a worshipper, or from being employed for God as a messenger to the children of men."

III. The renewing of the prophet's mission, *v.* 8. Here is a communication between God and Isaiah.

JAMIESON, FAUSSET, BROWN

man has some connection with his original form as a seraph of light. The head of the serpent was the symbol of *wisdom* in Egypt (cf. Num. 21:8; II Kings 18:4). The seraphim, with six wings and one face, can hardly be identified with the cherubim, which had four wings (in the temple only *two)* and four faces (Ezek. 1:5-12). (But cf. Rev. 4:8.) The "face" and "feet" imply a human form; something of a serpentine form (perhaps a basilisk's head, as in the temples of Thebes) may have been mixed with it: so the cherub was compounded of various animal forms. However, seraph may come from a root meaning "princely," applied in Daniel 10:13 to Michael [MAURER]; just as cherub comes from a root (changing *m* into *b*), meaning "noble." **twain** —Two wings alone of the six were kept ready for instant flight in God's service; two veiled their faces as unworthy to look on the holy God, or pry into His secret counsels which they fulfilled (Exod. 3:6; Job 4:18; 15:15); two covered their feet, or rather the whole of the *lower parts* of their persons—a practice usual in the presence of Eastern monarchs, in token of reverence (cf. Ezek. 1:11, *their bodies).* Man's service *a fortiori* consists in reverent waiting on, still more than in active service for, God. **3.** (Rev. 4:8.) The Trinity is implied (see *Note* on "Lord." vs. 1). God's *holiness* is the keynote of Isaiah's whole prophecies. **whole earth**—the *Hebrew* more emphatically, *the fulness of the whole earth* is His *glory* (Ps. 24:1; 72:19). **4. posts of . . . door**—rather, foundations of the thresholds. **house** —temple. **smoke**—the Shekinah cloud (I Kings 8: 10; Ezekiel 10:4.)

undone—(Exod. 33:20.) The same effect was produced on others by the presence of God (Judg. 6:22; 13:22; Job 42:5, 6; Luke 5:8; Rev. 1:17). **lips**—appropriate to the context which describes the praises of the *lips,* sung in alternate responses (Exod. 15:20, 21; vs. 3) by the seraphim: also appropriate to the office of *speaking* as the prophet of God, about to be committed to Isaiah (vs. 9).

seen—not strictly Jehovah Himself (John 1:18; I Tim. 6:16), but the symbol of His presence. **Lord**—*Hebrew,* JEHOVAH.

6. unto me— The seraph had been in the temple, Isaiah *outside of it.* **live coal**—lit., "a hot stone," used, as in some countries in our days, to roast meat with, e.g., the meat of the sacrifices. Fire was a symbol of purification, as it takes the dross out of metals (Mal. 3:2, 3). **the altar**—of burnt offering, in the court of the priests before the temple. The fire on it was at first kindled by God (Lev. 9:24), and was kept continually burning. **7. mouth . . . lips**—(Cf. *Note,* vs. 5). The *mouth* was touched because it was the part to be used by *the prophet* when inaugurated. So "*tongues* of fire" rested on the disciples (Acts. 2:3, 4) when they were being set apart to *speak* in various languages of Jesus. **iniquity**—conscious unworthiness of acting as God's messenger. **purged**—lit., "covered," i.e., expiated, not by any physical effect of fire to cleanse from sin, but in relation to the *altar sacrifices,* of which Messiah, who here commissions Isaiah, was in His death to be the antitype: it is implied hereby that it is only by sacrifice sin can be pardoned.

ADAM CLARKE

He covered his feet. "It is a great mark of respect in the East to cover the feet, and to bow down the head in the presence of the king."

3. *Holy, holy, holy.* This hymn, performed by the seraphim, divided into two choirs, the one singing responsively to the other, is formed upon the practice of alternate singing, which prevailed in the Jewish church from the time of Moses, whose ode at the Red Sea was thus performed (see Exod. xv. 20, 32), to that of Ezra, under whom the priests and Levites sung alternately, "O praise Jehovah, for he is gracious; for his mercy endureth for ever," Ezra iii. 11.

5. *Woe is me! for I am undone.* "I am become dumb." There is something exceedingly affecting in this complaint. I am a man of unclean lips; I cannot say, Holy, holy, holy! which the seraphs exclaim. They are holy; I am not so: they see God, and live; I have seen Him, and must die, because I am unholy. Only the pure in heart shall see God, and they only can live in His presence forever.

6. *A live coal.* The word of prophecy which was put into the mouth of the prophet. *From off the altar.* That is, from the altar of burnt offerings, before the door of the Temple, on which the fire that came down at first from heaven (Lev. ix. 24; 2 Chron. vii. 1) was perpetually burning. It was never to be extinguished, Lev. vi. 12-13.

MATTHEW HENRY

How can we expect that God should speak by us if we never heard him speaking to us? God is here deliberating with himself: *Whom shall I send? And who will go for us?* Thus he would teach us that the sending forth of ministers is a work not to be done but upon mature deliberation. It puts an honour upon the ministry that, when God would send a prophet to speak in his name, he appeared in all the glories of the upper world. *Whom shall I send?* intimating that he would send them a *prophet from among their brethren*, Heb. ii. 17. God is pleased to send us his mind by men like ourselves, who are themselves concerned in the messages they bring. Those who are workers together with God are sinners and sufferers together with us. Who is sufficient? Such a degree of courage and concern for the souls of men, and withal such an insight into the mysteries of the kingdom of heaven, are seldom to be met with. None are allowed to go for God but those who are sent by him, Rom. x. 15. It is Christ's work to put men into the ministry, 1 Tim. i. 12. The office seemed to go a-begging, yet Isaiah offered himself: "I will go, and leave the success to God. Here am I; send me." What he says denotes readiness: "Here am I, a volunteer, not pressed into the service." *Behold me;* so the word is. "*Here I am*, ready to encounter the greatest difficulties. *I have set my face as a flint*."

Verses 9–13

God takes Isaiah at his word, and here sends him on a strange errand—to foretell the ruin of his people and even to ripen them for that ruin. And this was to be a type of the state of the Jewish church in the days of the Messiah, when they should obstinately reject the gospel, and should thereupon be rejected of God. These verses are quoted in part, or referred to, six times, in the New Testament. Isaiah is here given to understand these four things:

1. That the generality of the people to whom he was sent would turn a deaf ear to his preaching, and wilfully shut their eyes against all the discoveries of the mind and will of God which he had to make to them (*v.* 9).

2. That, as they would not be made better by his ministry, they should be made worse by it; those that were wilfully blind should be judicially blinded (*v.* 10): "They will not understand or perceive thee, and therefore thou shalt be instrumental to *make their heart fat*, senseless, and sensual, and so to *make their ears* yet more *heavy*, and to *shut their eyes* the closer; so that, at length, their recovery and repentance will become utterly impossible." Even the word of God oftentimes proves a means of hardening sinners.

3. That the consequence of this would be their *utter ruin, v.* 11, 12. The prophet asks, "*Lord, how long?*" (an abrupt question): "Shall it always be thus? Must I and other prophets always labour in vain among them, and will things never be better?" In answer to this he is told that it should issue in the final destruction of the Jewish church and nation. "Their cities shall be uninhabited, and the land shall be untilled, *desolate with desolation* (as it is in the margin)." Spiritual judgments often bring temporal judgments upon persons and places. This was in part fulfilled in the destruction of Jerusalem by the Chaldeans, but, the foregoing predictions being so expressly applied in the New Testament to the Jews in our Saviour's time, doubtless this points at the final destruction of that people by the Romans.

4. That yet a remnant should be reserved to be the monuments of mercy, *v.* 13. *But in it shall be a tenth*, a certain number, but a very small number in comparison with the multitude that shall perish in their unbelief. Concerning this tithe, this saved remnant, we are here told, (1) That they shall return (*ch.* vi. 13; x. 21), shall return from sin to God and duty, shall return out of captivity to their own land. (2) That they shall be eaten, that is, shall be accepted of God as the tithe was, which was meat in God's house, Mal. iii. 10. (3) That they shall be like a timber-tree in winter, which has life, though it has no leaves: *As a teil-tree and as an oak, whose substance is in them even when they cast their leaves*, so this remnant, though they may be stripped of their outward prosperity, shall yet recover themselves, as a tree in the spring, and flourish again. (4) That this distinguished remnant shall be the stay and support of the public interests. *The holy seed* in the soul is the substance of the man; a principle of grace reigning in the heart will keep life there; he that is *born of God* has *his seed remaining in him*, 1 John iii. 9. As the trees that grow on either side of the causeway (the raised way, or terrace-walk, that leads from the king's palace to the temple (1 Kings x. 5), support the causeway by keeping up the earth, which would otherwise be crumbling away, so the small residue

JAMIESON, FAUSSET, BROWN

8. I . . us—The change of number indicates the Trinity (cf. Gen. 1:26; 11:7). Though not a sure *argument* for the doctrine, for the *plural may* indicate merely majesty, it *accords* with that truth proved elsewhere.

Whom . . . who—implying that *few* would be willing to bear the self-denial which the delivering of such an unwelcome message to the Jews would require on the part of the messenger (cf. I Chron. 29:5).

Here am I—prompt zeal, now that he has been specially qualified for it (vs. 7; ch. I Sam. 3:10, 11; Acts 9:6).

9. Hear . . . indeed—*Hebrew,* "In hearing hear," i.e., *Though ye hear* the prophet's warnings *again and again,* ye are doomed, because of your perverse will (John 7:17), *not to understand.* Light enough is given in revelation to guide those sincerely seeking to *know,* in order that they may *do,* God's will; darkness enough is left to confound the wilfully blind (ch. 43:8). So in Jesus' use of parables (Matt. 13:14). **see . . . indeed**—rather, "though ye *see again and again,*" yet, etc. **10. Make . . . fat**—(Ps. 119:17.) "Render them the more hardened by thy warnings" [MAURER]. This effect is the fruit, not of *the truth* in itself, but of the corrupt state of *their hearts,* to which God here judicially gives them over (ch. 63: 17). GESENIUS takes the imperatives as futures. "Proclaim truths, the *result* of which proclamation *will be* their becoming the more hardened" (Rom. 1:28; Eph. 4:18); but this does not so well as the former set forth God as *designedly* giving up sinners to *judicial* hardening (Rom. 11:8; II Thess. 2:11). In the first member of the sentence, the order is, *the heart, ears, eyes;* in the latter, the reverse order, *the eyes, ears, heart.* It is from the *heart* that corruption flows into the *ears and eyes* (Mark 7:21, 22); but through *the eyes and ears healing* reaches the *heart* (Rom. 10:17), [BENGEL]. (Jer. 5:21; Ezek. 12: 2; Zech. 7:11; Acts 7:57; II Tim. 4:4.) In Matthew 13:15, the words are quoted in the *indicative,* "*is* waxed gross" (so the LXX), not the *imperative,* "make fat"; God's word as to the future is as certain as if it were already fulfilled. To *see with one's eyes* will not convince a will that is opposed to the truth (cf. John 11:45, 46; 12:10, 11). "One must *love* divine things in order to *understand* them" [PASCAL]. **be healed**—of their spiritual malady, sin (ch. 1:6; Ps. 103:3; Jer. 17:14). **11. how long**—will this wretched condition of the nation being hardened to its destruction continue? **until**—(ch. 5:9)—fulfilled primarily at the Babylonish captivity, and more fully at the dispersion under the Roman Titus. **12.** (II Kings 25:21.) **forsaking**—abandonment of dwellings by their inhabitants (Jer. 4:29). **13. and it shall return, and . . . be eaten**—Rather, *but it shall be again* given over *to be consumed:* if even a tenth survive the first destruction, it shall be destroyed by a second (ch. 5:25; Ezek. 5:1-5, 12), [MAURER and HORSLEY]. In *English Version,* "return" refers to the poor remnant left in the land at the Babylonish captivity (II Kings 24:14; 25:12), which afterwards fled to Egypt in fear (II Kings 25:26), and subsequently *returned* thence along with others who had fled to Moab and Edom (Jer. 40:11, 12), and suffered under further divine judgments. **teil**—rathser, *terebinth or turpentine tree* (ch. 1:29). **substance . . . when . . . cast . . . leaves**—rather, "As a *terebinth* or *oak in which, when they are cast down* (not 'cast their leaves,' Job 14:7), *the trunk* or *stock* remains, *so the holy seed* (Ezra 9:2) *shall be the stock of that* land." The seeds of vitality still exist in both the land and the scattered people of Judea, waiting for the returning spring of God's favor (Rom. 11:5, 23-29). According to Isaiah, not all Israel, but the *elect remnant alone,* is destined to salvation. God shows unchangeable severity towards sin, but covenant faithfulness in preserving a remnant, and to it Isaiah bequeaths the prophetic legacy of the second part of his book (ch. 40-66).

ADAM CLARKE

CHARLES H. SPURGEON:

Brethren, the heathen are perishing, and there is but one way of salvation for them, for there is but one name given under heaven among men whereby they must be saved. God in the glorious unity of His divine nature is calling for messengers who shall proclaim to men the way of life. Out of the thick darkness my ear can hear that sound mysterious and divine, "Whom shall I send?" If you will but listen with the ear of faith you may hear it today—"Whom shall I send?" While the world lies under the curse of sin the living God, who willeth not that any should perish but that they should come to repentance, is seeking for heralds to proclaim His mercy; He is asking even in pleading terms for some who will go forth to the dying millions and tell the wondrous story of His love—"Whom shall I send?" As if to make the voice more powerful by a threefold utterance we hear the sacred Trinity enquire, "Who will go for us?" The Father asks, "Who will go for Me and invite My far-off children to return?" The Son enquires, "Who will seek for Me My redeemed but wandering sheep?" The Holy Spirit demands, "In whom shall I dwell, and through whom shall I speak that I may convey life to the perishing multitudes?" God in the unity of His nature crieth, "Whom shall I send?" and in the trinity of His persons He asks, "Who will go for us?"

—*The Treasury of the Old Testament*

10. *Make the heart of this people fat*—"Gross." The prophet speaks of the event, the fact as it would actually happen, not of God's purpose and act by his ministry. Or the words may be understood thus, according to the Hebrew idiom: "Ye certainly hear, but do not understand; ye certainly —, but do not acknowledge." Seeing this is the case, make the heart of this people fat—declare it to be stupid and senseless; and remove from them the means of salvation, which they have so long abused.

13. *A tenth.* This passage, though somewhat obscure, and variously explained by various interpreters, has, I think, been made so clear by the accomplishment of the prophecy that there remains little room to doubt of the sense of it. When Nebuchadnezzar had carried away the greater and better part of the people into captivity, there was yet *a tenth* remaining in the land, the poorer sort left to be vinedressers and husbandmen, under Gedaliah, 2 Kings xxv. 12, 22, and the dispersed Jews gathered themselves together, and returned to him, Jer. xl. 12; yet even these, fleeing into Egypt after the death of Gedaliah, contrary to the warning of God given by the prophet Jeremiah, miserably perished there.

MATTHEW HENRY

of religious, serious, praying people, are the support of the state, and help to keep things together and save them from going to decay.

CHAPTER 7

Verses 1–9

The prophet Isaiah had his commission renewed in the year that king Uzziah died, *ch.* vi. 1. Jotham his son reigned, and reigned well, sixteen years. All that time, no doubt, Isaiah prophesied as he was commanded, and yet we have not in this book any of his prophecies dated in the reign of Jotham; but this, which is put first, was in the days of Ahaz the son of Jotham.

I. A formidable design laid against Jerusalem by Rezin king of Syria and Pekah king of Israel, who had made descents upon Judah severally, 2 Kings xv. 37. But now, in the second or third year of the reign of Ahaz, they entered into an alliance against Judah. Because Ahaz, though he found the sword over his head, began his reign with idolatry, *God delivered him into the hand of the king of Syria and of the king of Israel* (2 Chron. xxviii. 5). **Flushed with this victory, they went up towards Jerusalem to besiege it.**

II. The great distress that Ahaz and his court were in when they received advice of this design: *It was told the house of David* that Syria and Ephraim had signed a league against Judah, *v.* 2. News being brought that the two armies of Syria and Israel had taken the field. *The heart of Ahaz was moved with fear*, and then no wonder that *the heart of his people was so, as the trees of the wood are moved with the wind.* Now that which caused this fright was the sense of guilt and the weakness of their faith. They had made God their enemy, and knew not how to make him their friend.

III. The orders given to Isaiah to encourage Ahaz in his distress, because he was a son of David and king of Judah. God had kindness for him for his father's sake, who must not be forgotten, and for his people's sake, who must not be abandoned. He ordered Isaiah to take his little son with him, because he carried a sermon in his name, *Shear-jashub—A remnant shall return.* This son was so called for the encouragement of those of God's people who were carried captive, assuring them that they should return. He directed him where he should find Ahaz, *at the end of the conduit of the upper pool*, where he was contriving how to order the water-works, so as to secure them to the city (*ch.* xxii. 9–11; 2 Chron. xxxii, 3, 4), or giving some necessary directions for the fortifying of the city. He put words in his mouth, else the prophet would not have known how to bring a message of good to such a bad man, but God intended it for the support of faithful Israelites. The prophet must rebuke their fears (*v.* 4): *Take heed, and be quiet.* Pluck up thy spirits and be courageous. He must teach them to despise their enemies, not in pride, or security, but in faith and dependence upon God. Ahaz's fear called them two powerful politic princes, for either of whom he was an unequal match. "No," says the prophet, "they are *two tails of smoking firebrands*; they are angry, they are fierce, as fireballs, and they make one another worse by being in a confederacy, as sticks of fire put together burn the more violently. But they are only smoking firebrands, *tails* of smoking firebrands, in a manner burnt out already; their force is spent; you may put your foot on them, and tread them out." He must assure them that the present design of these high allies (so they thought themselves) against Jerusalem should certainly be defeated and come to nothing, *v.* 5–7. Judah had done them no wrong; they had no pretence to quarrel with Ahaz; but, without any reason, they said, *Let us go up against Judah, and vex it.* They count upon dividing the kingdom into two parts, one

JAMIESON, FAUSSET, BROWN

CHAPTER 7

Chapters 7, 8, and 9:1-7. PREDICTION OF THE ILL SUCCESS OF THE SYRO-ISRAELITISH INVASION OF JUDAH—AHAZ' ALLIANCE WITH ASSYRIA, AND ITS FATAL RESULTS TO JUDEA—YET THE CERTAINTY OF FINAL PRESERVATION AND OF THE COMING OF MESSIAH. In the Assyrian inscriptions the name of Rezin, king of Damascus, is found among the tributaries of Tiglath-pileser, of whose reign the annals of seventeen years have been deciphered. For the historical facts in this chapter, cf. II Kings 15:37-16:9. Rezin of Syria and Pekah of Israel, as confederates, advanced against Jerusalem. In the first campaign (II Chron. 28) they "smote Ahaz with a great slaughter." Their object was probably to unite the three kingdoms against Assyria. Egypt seems to have favored the plan, so as to interpose these confederate kingdoms between her own frontier and Assyria (cf. vs. 18, "Egypt"; and II Kings 17:4, Hoshea's league with Egypt). Rezin and Pekah may have perceived Ahaz' inclination towards Assyria rather than towards their own confederacy; this and the old feud between Israel and Judah (I Kings 12:16) occasioned their invasion of Judah. Ahaz, at the *second* inroad of his enemies (cf. II Chronicles 28 and II Kings 15:37, with ch. 16:5), smarting under his former defeat, applied to Tiglath-pileser, in spite of Isaiah's warning in this chapter, that he should rather rely on God; that king accordingly attacked Damascus, and slew Rezin (II Kings 9); and probably it was at the same time that he carried away part of Israel captive (II Kings 15: 29), unless there were *two* assaults on Pekah—that in II Kings 15:29, the earlier, and that in which Tiglath helped Ahaz subsequently [G. V. SMITH]. Ahaz was saved at the sacrifice of Judah's independence and the payment of a large tribute, which continued till the overthrow of Sennacherib under Hezekiah (ch. 37; II Kings 16:8, 17, 18; II Chron. 28:20). Ahaz' reign began about 741 B.C., and Pekah was slain in 738 [WINER]. **1. Ahaz**—In the first years of his reign the design of the two kings against Judah was carried out, which was formed in Jotham's reign (II Kings 15:37). **Syria**—*Hebrew, Aram* (Gen. 10: 22, 23), originally the whole region between the Euphrates and Mediterranean, including *Assyria,* of which *Syria* is an abbreviation; here the region round Damascus, and along Mount Libanus. **Jerusalem**—An actual siege of it took place, but was foiled (II Kings 16:5). **2. is confederate with**—rather, *is encamped upon* the territory of Ephraim [MAURER], or better, as Rezin was encamped against *Jerusalem, "is supported by"* [LOWTH] Ephraim, whose land lay between Syria and Judah. The mention of "David" alludes, in sad contrast with the present, to the time when David made Syria subject to him (II Sam. 8:6). **Ephraim**—the ten tribes. **as . . . trees of . . . wood**—a simultaneous agitation. **3. Go forth**—out of the city, to the place where Ahaz was superintending the works for defense and the cutting off of the water supply from the enemy, and securing it to the city. So ch. 22:9; II Chron. 32:4. **Shearjeshub**—i.e., A remnant shall return (ch. 6:13). His very name (cf. vs. 14; ch. 8:3) was a standing memorial to Ahaz and the Jews that the nation should not, notwithstanding the general calamity (vss. 17-25; ch. 8:6-8), be utterly destroyed (ch. 10:21, 22). **conduit**—an aqueduct from the pool or reservoir for the supply of the city. At the foot of Zion was Fount Siloah (ch. 8:6; Neh. 3:15, John 9:7), called also Gihon, on the west of Jerusalem (II Chron. 32:30). Two pools were supplied from it, *the Upper,* or *Old* (ch. 22:11), or *King's* (Neh. 2:14), and *the Lower* (ch. 22:9), which received the superfluous waters of the upper. The upper pool is still to be seen, about seven hundred yards from the Jaffa gate. The highway leading to the fullers' field, which was in a position near water for the purposes of washing, previous to drying and bleaching, the cloth, was probably alongside the aqueduct. **4. Take heed,** etc.—i.e., *See that* thou be quiet (not seeking Assyrian aid in a fit of panic). **tails**—mere *ends* of firebrands, almost consumed themselves (about soon to fall before the Assyrians, vs. 8), therefore harmless. **smoking**—as about to go out; not *blazing.* **son of Remaliah**—Pekah, a usurper (II Kings 15:25). The Easterners express contempt by designating one, not by his own name, but by his father's, especially when the father is but little known (I Sam. 20:27, 31). **6. vex**—rather, "throw into consternation" [GESENIUS]. **make a breach**—

ADAM CLARKE

CHAPTER 7

The confederacy of Rezin, king of Syria, and Pekah, king of Israel, against the kingdom of Judah, was formed in the time of Jotham; and perhaps the effects of it were felt in the latter part of his reign; see 2 Kings xv. 37. However, in the very beginning of the reign of Ahaz they jointly invaded Judah with a powerful army, and threatened to destroy or to dethrone the house of David. The king and royal family being in the utmost consternation on receiving advices of their designs, Isaiah is sent to them to support and comfort them in their present distress, by assuring them that God would make good His promises to David and his house. This makes the subject of this, and the following, and the beginning of the ninth chapters.

Chapter vii begins with a historical account of the occasion of this prophecy; and then follows, vv. 4-16, a prediction of the ill success of the designs of the Israelites and Syrians against Judah; and from thence to the end of the chapter, a denunciation of the calamities to be brought upon the king and people of Judah by the Assyrians, whom they had now hired to assist them. Chapter viii has a pretty close connection with the foregoing; it contains a confirmation of the prophecy before given of the approaching destruction of the kingdoms of Israel and Syria by the Assyrians, of the denunciation of the invasion of Judah by the same Assyrians. Verses 9-10 give a repeated general assurance that all the designs of the enemies of God's people shall be in the end disappointed, and brought to naught; vv. 11, etc., admonitions and threatenings, concluding with an illustrious prophecy, chap. ix. 1-6, of the manifestation of Messiah, the transcendent dignity of His character, and the universality and eternal duration of His kingdom.

JOSEPH PARKER:

When the news was told to the house of David, saying, Syria leans upon Ephraim, or Syria is confederated with Ephraim, the two are one, the heart of Ahaz "was moved, and the heart of his people, as trees of the wood are moved with the wind." And yet the true Davidic spirit that was within Jerusalem felt no flutter of panic. The Spirit of the indwelling God is not represented even by the men who inhabit Jerusalem: they are of the flesh, their days are a handful, they are quailing under great infirmity, they are disturbed by something within themselves, and all this concurring with an outward untowardness of circumstance, eventuates in panic, in heart-fluttering, in heart-melting, so that even strong men say, Alas! what shall we do in face of this tremendous confederacy? God is the keeper of Jerusalem. The battle is not yours, but God's.

—*The People's Bible*

MATTHEW HENRY

for the king of Israel, the other for the king of Syria, who had agreed in one viceroy—*a king* to be *set in the midst of it, even the son of Tabeal*, some obscure person, it is uncertain whether a Syrian or an Israelite. So sure were they of gaining their point that they divided the prey before they had caught it. God himself gives them his word that the attempt should not take effect (*v.* 7): *Thus saith the Lord God, It shall not stand, neither shall it come to pass.* They should neither of them enlarge their dominions, nor push their conquests any further: *The head city of Syria is Damascus, and the head man of Damascus is Rezin;* this he glories in, and this let him be content with, *v.* 8. *The head city of Ephraim* has long been *Samaria, and the head man in Samaria is* now Pekah *the son of Remaliah.* These shall be made to know their own; their bounds are fixed, and they shall not pass them, to make themselves masters of the cities of Judah, much less to make Jerusalem their prey. Ephraim, which perhaps was the more malicious and forward enemy of the two, should shortly be quite rooted out, and should be so far from seizing other people's lands that they should not be able to hold their own. It was the greatest folly in the world for those to be ruining their neighbours who were themselves marked for ruin, and so near to it.

He must urge them to mix faith with assurances (*v.* 9): "*If you will not believe* what is said to you, *surely you shall not be established.* The things told you are encouraging, yet they will not be so to you, unless you be willing to take God's word."

Verses 10–16

I. God, by the prophet, makes a gracious offer to Ahaz, to confirm the foregoing predictions by such sign or miracle as he should choose (*v.* 10, 11): *Ask thee a sign of the Lord thy God.* He considers our frame, and that, living in a world of sense, we are apt to require proofs, which he has favoured us with in sacramental signs and seals. See how gracious God is even to the evil and unthankful; Ahaz is bidden to choose his sign, as Gideon about the fleece (Judges vi. 37).

II. Ahaz rudely refuses this gracious offer (*v.* 12): *I will not ask.* The true reason why he would not ask for a sign was because, having a dependence upon the Assyrians, their forces, and their gods, for help, he would not thus far be beholden to the God of Israel. Yet he pretends a pious reason: *I will not tempt the Lord.*

III. The prophet reproves him and his court for their contempt of prophecy (*v.* 13): "*Is it a small thing for you to weary men* by your oppression and *will you weary my God also* with the affronts you put upon him? In affronting the prophets, you think you put a slight only upon men like yourselves, and consider not that you affront God himself, whose messengers they are."

IV. The prophet, in God's name, gives them a sign (*v.* 14), a sign in general of his goodwill to Israel and to the house of David. Of your nation, of your family, the Messiah is to be born, and you cannot be destroyed while that blessing is in you. You have been told that he should be born among you, I am now further to tell you that he shall be born of a virgin, which will signify both the divine power and the divine purity with which he shall be brought into the world. This, though it was to be accomplished above 500 years after, was a most encouraging sign to the house of David, and an assurance that God would not cast them off.

JAMIESON, FAUSSET, BROWN

rather, "cleave it asunder." Their scheme was to divide a large portion of the territory between themselves, and set up a vassal king of their own over the rest. **son of Tabeal**—unknown; a Syrian-sounding name, perhaps favored by a party in Jerusalem (ch. 3:6, 9, 12). **7.** (Ch. 8:10; Prov. 21:30.) **8. head**—i.e., in both Syria and Israel the *capital* shall remain as it is; they shall not conquer Judah, but each shall possess only his own dominions. **threescore and five . . . not a people**—As these words break the symmetry of the parallelism in this verse, either they ought to be placed after "Remaliah's son," in vs. 9, or else they refer to some older prophecy of Isaiah, or of Amos (as the Jewish writers represent), parenthetically; to which, in vs. 8, the words, "If ye will not believe . . . not be established," correspond in parallelism. *One* deportation of Israel happened within one or two years from this time, under Tiglath-pileser (II Kings 15:29). *Another* in the reign of Hoshea, under Shalmaneser (II Kings 17:1-6), was about twenty years after. But the final one which utterly "broke" up Israel so as to be "not a people," accompanied by a colonization of Samaria with foreigners, was under Esar-haddon, who carried away Manasseh, king of Judah, also, in the twenty-second year of his reign, sixty-five years from the utterance of this prophecy (cf. Ezra 4:2, 3, 10, with II Kings 17:24; II Chron. 33:11) [USHER]. The event, though so far off, was enough to assure the people of Judah that as God, the Head of the theocracy, would *ultimately* interpose to destroy the enemies of His people, so they might rely on Him *now*. **9. believe, . . . be established**—There is a paronomasia, or play on the words, in the *Hebrew:* "if ye will not *confide*, ye shall not *abide*." Ahaz brought distress on himself by distrust in the Lord, and trust in Assyria. **11. Ask thee**—since thou dost not credit the prophet's words. **sign**—a miraculous token to assure thee that God will fulfil His promise of saving Jerusalem (ch. 37:30; 38:7, 8). "Signs," facts then present or near at hand as pledges for the more distant future, are frequent in Isaiah. **ask . . . in . . . depth**—lit., "Make deep, . . . ask it," i.e., Go to the depth of the earth or of *Hades* [*Vulgate* and LOWTH], or, Mount high for it (lit., "Make high"). So in Matthew 16:1. Signs in *heaven* are contrasted with the signs on earth and below it (raising the dead) which Jesus Christ had wrought (cf. Rom. 10:6, 7). He offers Ahaz the widest limits within which to make his choice. **12. neither . . . tempt**—hypocritical pretext of keeping the law (Deut. 6:16); "tempt," i.e., put God to the proof, as in Matthew 4:7, by seeking His miraculous interposition without warrant. But here there *was* the warrant of the prophet of God; to have asked a sign, when thus offered, would not have been a *tempting* of God. Ahaz' true reason for declining was his resolve not to do God's will, but to negotiate with Assyria, and persevere in his idolatry (II Kings 16:7, 8, 3, 4, 10). Men often excuse their distrust in God, and trust in their own devices, by *professed* reverence for God. Ahaz may have fancied that though Jehovah was the God of Judea and could work a sign there, that was no proof that the local god of Syria might not be more powerful. Such was the common heathen notion (ch. 10:10, 11:36:18-20). **13. Is it a small thing?**—Is it not enough for you (Num. 16:9)? The allusion to "David" is in order to contrast *his* trust in God with his degenerate descendant Ahaz' distrust. **weary**—try the patience of. **men**—prophets. Isaiah as yet had given no outward proof that he was from God; but now God has offered a sign, which Ahaz publicly rejects. The sin is therefore *now* not merely against "men," but openly against "God." Isaiah's manner therefore changes from mildness to bold reproof. **14. himself**—since thou wilt not ask a sign, nay, rejectest the offer of one. **you**—for the sake of the house of believing "David" (God remembering His everlasting covenant with David), not for unbelieving Ahaz' sake. **Behold**—arresting attention to the extraordinary prophecy. **virgin**—from a root, "to lie hid," virgins being closely kept from men's gaze in their parents' custody in the East. The *Hebrew,* and LXX here, and *Greek* (Matt. 1: 23), have the article, *the* virgin, some definite one known to the speaker and his hearers; primarily, the woman, then a virgin, about immediately to become the second wife, and bear a child, whose attainment of the age of discrimination (about three years) should be preceded by the deliverance of Judah from its two invaders; its fullest significancy is realized in "*the* woman" (Gen. 3:15), whose seed should bruise the serpent's head and deliver captive man (Jer. 31: 22; Mic. 5:3). Language is selected such as, while *partially* applicable to the immediate event, receives its *fullest,* most appropriate, and exhaustive accom-

ADAM CLARKE

8. *Threescore and five years.* It was sixty-five years from the beginning of the reign of Ahaz, when this prophecy was delivered, to the total depopulation of the kingdom of Israel by Esarhaddon, who carried away the remains of the ten tribes which had been left by Tiglath-pileser, and Shalmaneser, and who planted the country with new inhabitants.

9. *If ye will not believe.* That is, unless ye believe this prophecy of the destruction of Israel, ye Jews also, as well as the people of Israel, shall not remain established as a kingdom and people; ye also shall be visited with punishment at the same time.

14-15. At the time referred to, the kingdom of Judah, under the government of Ahaz, was reduced very low. Pekah, king of Israel, had slain in Judea 120,000 persons in one day; and carried away captives 200,000, including women and children, together with much spoil. To add to their distress, Rezin, king of Syria, being confederate with Pekah, had taken Elath, a fortified city of Judah, and carried the inhabitants away captive to Damascus. In this critical conjuncture, need we wonder that Ahaz was afraid that the enemies who were now united against him must prevail, destroy Jerusalem, end the kingdom of Judah, and annihilate the family of David? To meet and remove this fear, apparently well-grounded, Isaiah is sent from the Lord to Ahaz, swallowed up now both by sorrow and by unbelief, in order to assure him that the counsels of his enemies should not stand; and that they should be utterly discomfited. To encourage Ahaz, he commands

MATTHEW HENRY

The Messiah shall be introduced on a glorious errand, wrapped up in his glorious name: They *shall call his name Immanuel—God with us*, God in our nature, God at peace with us, in covenant with us. This was fulfilled in their calling him *Jesus—a Saviour* (Matt. i. 21–25), for, if he had not been *Immanuel—God with us*, he could not have been *Jesus—a Saviour*. The promised seed shall be Immanuel, *God with us*; let that word comfort you (*ch.* viii. 10), that *God is with us*, and (*v.* 8) that your land is Immanuel's land. Let not *the heart of the house of David* be moved thus (*v.* 2), nor let Judah fear the setting up of the son of Tabeal (*v.* 6), for nothing can cut off the entail on the Son of David that shall be Immanuel. The strongest consolations, in time of trouble, are those which are borrowed from Christ, our relation to him, our interest in him, and our expectations of him and from him. Of this child it is further foretold (*v.* 15), he shall be truly man, and shall be nursed and brought up like other children: *Butter and honey shall he eat*. Here is another sign in particular of the speedy destruction of these princes now a terror to Judah, *v.* 16. "Before *this* child (so it should be read), this child which I have now in my arms"—not Immanuel, but Shearjashub, his own son—*v.* 3, "*shall know how to refuse the evil and choose the good*, before this child be three or four years older, *the land that thou abhorrest*, these confederate forces of Israelites and Syrians *shall be forsaken of both their kings*, both Pekah and Rezin." This was fully accomplished; for, within two or three years after this, Hoshea conspired against Pekah, and slew him (2 Kings xv. 30), and, before that, the king of Assyria took Damascus, and slew Rezin, 2 Kings xvi. 9. Nay, there was a present event, which happened immediately. *Shearjashub* signifies *The remnant shall return*, which doubtless points at the wonderful return of those 200,000 captives whom Pekah and Rezin had carried away, who were brought back, by the Spirit of the Lord of hosts. Read the story, 2 Chron. xxviii. 8–15. The prophetical naming of this child having thus had its accomplishment, no doubt this should have its accomplishment likewise. Syria and Israel should be deprived of both their kings.

Verses 17–25

After the comfortable promises made to Ahaz as a branch of the house of David, here follow terrible threatenings against him, as a degenerate branch of that house. His iniquity shall be *chastened with the rod*.

I. The judgment threatened is great, *v.* 17, brought upon the prince himself and upon the people, and upon the royal family, *upon* all *thy father's house*.

II. The enemy employed as the instrument of this judgment is the king of Assyria. Ahaz reposed great confidence in that prince for help against the confederate powers of Israel and Syria, 2 Kings xvi. 7, 8. Now God threatens that that king of Assyria whom he made his stay instead of God should become a scourge to him. Henceforward the kings of Assyria were, for a long time, grieving thorns to Judah. 1. Summons given to the invaders (*v.* 18): *The Lord shall whistle for the fly and the bee*. See *ch.* v. 26. Enemies that seem as contemptible as a fly or a bee and are as easily crushed, shall yet, when God pleases, do his work as effectually as lions and young lions. 2. Possession taken by them, *v.* 19. It should seem as if the country were in no condition to make resistance. They find no difficulties in forcing their way, but *come and rest all of them in the desolate valleys*, which the inhabitants had deserted upon the first alarm. They shall come and rest in the low grounds like swarms of flies and bees, and shall render themselves impregnable by taking shelter in the holes of the rocks, as bees often do, and show themselves formidable by appearing openly upon all thorns and all bushes; so generally shall the land be overspread with them.

JAMIESON, FAUSSET, BROWN

plishment in Messianic events. The New Testament application of such prophecies is not a strained "accommodation"; rather the temporary fulfilment of an adaptation of the far-reaching prophecy to the present passing event, which foreshadows typically the great central end of prophecy, Jesus Christ (Rev. 19:10). Evidently the wording is such as to apply more fully to Jesus Christ than to the prophet's son; "virgin" applies, in its simplest sense, to the Virgin Mary, rather than to the prophetess who ceased to be a *virgin* when she "conceived"; "Immanuel," *God with us* (John 1:14; Rev. 21:3), cannot in a strict sense apply to Isaiah's son, but only to Him who is presently called expressly (ch. 9:6), "the Child, the Son, Wonderful (cf. ch. 8:18), the mighty *God*." Local and temporary features (as in vss. 15, 16) are added in every type; otherwise it would be no type, but the thing itself. There are resemblances to the great Antitype sufficent to be recognized by those who seek them; dissimilarities enough to confound those who do not desire to discover them. **call**—i.e., *she* shall, or as *Margin, thou, O Virgin, shalt call;* mothers often named their children (Gen. 4:1, 25; 19:37; 29:32). In Matthew 1:23 the expression is strikingly changed into, "*They* shall call"; when the prophecy received its *full* accomplishment, no longer is the name Immanuel restricted to the *prophetess'* view of His character, as in its partial fulfilment in her son; *all* shall then call (i.e., not literally), or *regard* Him as *peculiarly and most fitly characterized by the descriptive name,* "Immanuel" (I Tim. 3:16; Col. 2:9). **name**—not mere appellation, which neither Isaiah's son nor Jesus Christ bore literally; but what describes His manifested attributes; His *character* (so ch. 9:6). The name in its proper destination was not arbitrary, but characteristic of the individual; sin destroyed the faculty of perceiving the internal being; hence the severance now between the name and the character; in the case of Jesus Christ and many in Scripture, the Holy Ghost has supplied this want [OLSHAUSEN]. **15. Butter**—rather, curdled milk, the acid of which is grateful in the heat of the East (Job 20:17). **honey**—abundant in Palestine (Judg. 14:8; I Sam. 14:25; Matt. 3:4). Physicians directed that the first food given to a child should be honey, the next milk [BARNAB. Ep.]. HORSLEY takes this as implying the real humanity of the Immanuel Jesus Christ, about to be fed as other infants (Luke 2:52). Verse 22 shows that besides the fitness of milk and honey for children, a state of *distress* of the inhabitants is *also* implied, when, by reason of the invaders, milk and honey, things produced *spontaneously*, shall be the only abundant articles of food [MAURER]. **that he may know**—rather, until He shall know. **evil . . . choose . . . good**—At about three years of age moral consciousness begins (cf. ch. 8:4; Deut. 1:39; Jonah 4:11). **16. For**—The deliverance implied in the name "Immanuel," and the cessation of distress as to food (vss. 14, 15), shall last only till the child grows to know good and evil; for. . . . **the land that . . . abhorrest . . . forsaken of . . . kings**—rather, desolate shall be the land, before whose two kings thou art alarmed [HENGSTENBERG and GENESIUS]. **the land**—viz., Syria and Samaria regarded as one (II Kings 16:9; 15:30), just *two* years after this prophecy, as it foretells. HORSLEY takes it, "The land (Judah and Samaria) of (the former of) which thou art the plague (lit., "thorn") shall be forsaken," etc.; a prediction thus, that Judah and Israel (appropriately regarded as *one* "land") should cease to be kingdoms (Luke 2:1; Gen. 49:10) before Immanuel came.

17-25. FATAL CONSEQUENCES OF AHAZ' ASSYRIAN POLICY. Though temporary deliverance (ch. 7:16; 8:4) was to be given then, and final deliverance through Messiah, sore punishment shall follow the former. After subduing Syria and Israel, the Assyrians shall encounter Egypt (II Kings 23:29), and Judah shall be the battlefield of both (vs. 18), and be made tributary to that very Assyria (II Chron. 28:20; II Kings 16:7, 8) now about to be called in as an ally (ch. 39:1-6). Egypt, too, should prove a fatal ally (ch. 36:6; 31:1, etc.). **18. hiss**—whistle, to bring bees to settle (*Note*, ch. 5:26). **fly**—found in numbers about the arms of the Nile and the canals from it (ch. 19:5-7; 23:3), here called "rivers." Hence arose the plague of flies (Exod. 8:21). Figurative, for *numerous* and *troublesome* foes from the remotest parts of Egypt, e.g., Pharaoh-necho. **bee**—(Deut. 1:44; Ps. 118:12.) As numerous in Assyria as the fly in marshy Egypt. Sennacherib, Esarhaddon, and Nebuchadnezzar fulfilled this prediction. **19. rest**—image of flies and bees kept up. The enemy shall overspread the land *everywhere*, even in "desolate valleys." **thorns**—wild, contrasted with "bushes," which were *valued* and objects of

ADAM CLARKE

him to ask a sign or miracle, which should be a pledge in hand that God should, in due time, fulfill the predictions of His servant, as related in the context.

On Ahaz humbly refusing to ask any sign, it is immediately added, "Therefore the Lord himself shall give you a sign; Behold, a virgin shall conceive, and bear a son, and shall call his name Immanuel. Butter and honey shall he eat." Both the divine and human nature of our Lord, as well as the miraculous conception, appear to be pointed out in the prophecy quoted here by the evangelist: He shall be called *Immanuel;* literally, "The strong God with us": similar to those words in the New Testament: "The word [which] was God . . . was made flesh, and dwelt among us . . . full of grace and truth," John i. 1, 14. And "God was manifest in the flesh," 1 Tim. iii. 16. So that we are to understand *God with us* to imply God incarnated—God in human nature. This seems further evident from the words of the prophet, v. 15: *Butter and honey shall he eat*—He shall be truly man—grow up and be nourished in a human natural way, which refers to His being with us, i.e., incarnated. To which the prophet adds, *That he may know to refuse the evil, and choose the good;* or rather, "According to His knowledge, reprobating the evil, and choosing the good." This refers to Him as God, and is the same idea given by this prophet, chap. liii. 11: "By his knowledge [the knowledge of Christ crucified] shall my righteous servant justify many; for he shall bear their iniquities [offences]." Now this union of the divine and human nature is termed a *sign* or "miracle," i.e., something which exceeds the power of nature to produce. And this miraculous union was to be brought about in a miraculous way: *Behold, a virgin shall conceive.* The word is very emphatic, *haalmah, the virgin;* the only one that ever was, or ever shall be, a mother in this way.

But how could that be a sign to Ahaz, which was to take place so many hundreds of years after? I answer, the meaning of the prophet is plain: not only Rezin and Pekah should be unsuccessful against Jerusalem at that time, which was the fact; but Jerusalem, Judea, and the house of David should be both preserved, notwithstanding their depressed state, and the multitude of their adversaries, till the time should come when a virgin should bear a son. This is a most remarkable circumstance—the house of David could never fail, till a virgin should conceive and bear a son—nor did it. But when that incredible and miraculous fact did take place, the kingdom and house of David became extinct!

18. *Egypt, and . . . Assyria.* Sennacherib, Esarhaddon, Pharaoh-necho, and Nebuchadnezzar, who one after another desolated Judea.

MATTHEW HENRY

3. Great desolations made, and the country generally depopulated (*v.* 20): *The Lord shall shave the hair of the head, and beard, and feet;* he shall sweep all away. God will make that to be an instrument of his destruction which he hired into his service. Many are beaten with that arm of flesh which they trusted to rather than to the arm of the Lord.

4. The consequences of this general depopulation: The flocks of cattle shall be all destroyed, so that a man shall with much ado save for his own use a young cow and two sheep—a poor stock (*v.* 21). The few cattle that are left shall have such a large compass of ground to feed in that *they shall give abundance of milk*, such as shall produce butter enough, *v.* 22. There shall also be such want of men that the milk of one cow and two sheep shall serve a whole family, which used to keep servants and consume a great deal. The country shall be so depopulated that there shall be butter and honey enough, for the few that are left in it. Good land, that used to be let well, shall be all overrun with briers and thorns (*v.* 23).

The implements of husbandry shall be turned into instruments of war, *v.* 24, with arrows and bows, to hunt for wild beasts in the thickets, or to defend themselves from robbers. There shall be briers and thorns in abundance where they should not be, but none where they should be, *v.* 25. *The hills that shall be digged with the mattock*, for special use, from which the cattle used to be kept off with the fear of briers and thorns, shall now be thrown open, the *hedges broken down for the boar out of the wood* to waste it, Ps. lxxx. 12, 13.

JAMIESON, FAUSSET, BROWN

care (see *Margin*). **20. razor**—The Assyrians are to be God's *instrument* of devastating Judea, just as a razor sweeps away all hair before it (ch. 10:5; Ezek. 29:19, 20). **hired**—alluding to Ahaz' hiring (II Kings 16:7, 8) Tiglath-pileser against Syria and Israel; namely, **by them beyond the river**—viz., the Euphrates; the eastern boundary of Jewish geographical knowledge (Ps. 72:8); the river which Abram crossed; the Nile also may be included (vs. 18) [G. V. SMITH]. GESENIUS translates, "With a razor *hired in the parts beyond the river.*" **head . . . feet**—the *whole* body, including the most honored parts. To cut the "beard" is the greatest indignity to an Easterner (ch. 50:6; II Sam. 10: 4, 5; Ezek. 5:1). **21-25.** THE COMING DESOLATE STATE OF THE LAND OWING TO THE ASSYRIANS AND EGYPTIANS. **nourish**—i.e., own. **young cow** —a heifer giving milk. *Agriculture* shall cease, and the land become one great *pasturage.* **22. abundance**—by reason of the wide range of land lying desolate over which the cows and sheep (including goats) may range. **butter**—thick milk, or *cream.* **honey**—(*Note,* vs. 15). Food of *spontaneous* growth will be the resource of the *few* inhabitants left. Honey shall be abundant as the bees will find the wild flowers abounding everywhere. **23. where there were . . .**—where up to that time there was so valuable a vineyard as to have in it 1000 vines, worth a silverling *(shekel,* about 50 cents; *a large price*) each, there shall be only briers (Song of Sol. 8:11). Vineyards are estimated by the number of the vines, and the goodness of the kind of vine. Judea admits of a high state of cultivation, and requires it, in order to be productive; its present barrenness is due to neglect. **24.** It shall become a vast hunting ground, abounding in wild beasts (cf. Jer. 49:19). **25. shall be**—rather, were once. **digged**—in order to plant and rear vines (ch. 5:6). **there shall not come**—i.e., none shall come who fear thorns, seeing that thorns shall abound on all sides [MAURER]. Otherwise, "Thou shalt not come *for fear of thorns*" [GESENIUS]. Only cattle shall be able to penetrate the briery ground. **lesser cattle**—sheep and goats.

ADAM CLARKE

20. *The river.* That is, the Euphrates. *Shall the Lord shave with a razor that is hired.* To shave with the hired razor the head, the feet, and the beard is an expression highly parabolical, to denote the utter devastation of the country from one end to the other; and the plundering of the people, from the highest to the lowest, by the Assyrians, whom God employed as His instrument to punish the Jews. Ahaz himself, in the first place, hired the king of Assyria to come to help him against the Syrians, by a present made to him of all the treasures of the Temple, as well as his own. And God himself considered the great nations whom He thus employed as His mercenaries, and paid them their wages. Thus He paid Nebuchadnezzar for his services against Tyre, by the conquest of Egypt, Ezek. xxix. 18-20. The hairs of the head are those of the highest order in the state; those of the feet, or the lower parts, are the common people; the beard is the king, the high priest, the very supreme in dignity and majesty.

The remaining verses of this chapter, 21-25, contain an elegant and very expressive description of a country depopulated, and left to run wild, from its adjuncts and circumstances: the vineyards and cornfields, before well-cultivated, now overrun with briers and thorns; much grass, so that the few cattle that are left, *a young cow, and two sheep,* have their full range, and abundant pasture, so as to yield milk in plenty to the scanty family of the owner; the thinly scattered people living, not on corn, wine, and oil, the produce of cultivation, but on milk and honey, the gifts of nature; and the whole land given up to the wild beasts, so that the miserable inhabitants are forced to go out armed with bows and arrows, either to defend themselves against the wild beasts or to supply themselves with necessary food by hunting.

MATTHEW HENRY — CHAPTER 8

Verses 1–8

In these verses we have a prophecy of the successes of the king of Assyria against Damascus, Samaria, and Judah, that the two former should be laid waste by him, and the last greatly frightened.

I. Orders given to the prophet to write this prophecy, to be read of all men, that when the thing came to pass they might know that God had sent him; for that was one end of prophecy, John xiv. 29. He must *take a great roll*, and he must write in it all that he had foretold concerning the king of Assyria's invading the country; he must *write it with a man's pen*, in the usual way. The prophet is directed to call his book *Maher-shalal-hash-baz—Make speed to the spoil, hasten to the prey*, intimating that the Assyrian army should come upon them with great speed and make great spoil.

II. The care of the prophet to get this record well attested (*v.* 2): *I took unto me faithful witnesses to record;* he wrote the prophecy in their presence that they might be ready to make oath of it, that the prophet had so long before foretold the descent which the Assyrians made upon that country. He names his witnesses. One was Uriah the priest; he is mentioned in the story of Ahaz (2 Kings xvi. 10, 11).

III. The making of the title of his book the name of his child. His wife (because the wife of a prophet) is called *the prophetess*; she *conceived and bore a son*, another son, who must carry a sermon in his name, as the former had done (*ch.* vii. 3), but with this difference, that spoke mercy, *Shearjashub—The remnant shall return;* but, that being slighted, this speaks judgment, *Maher-shalal-hash-baz—In making speed to the spoil he shall hasten, or he has hastened, to the prey*. Every time the child was called by his name, or any part of it, it would serve as a memorandum of the judgments approaching.

IV. The prophecy itself, which explains this mystical name.

1. That Syria and Israel, who were now in confederacy against Judah, should in a little time become an easy prey to the king of Assyria (*v.* 4): "*Before the child*, now newly born and named, shall have *knowledge to cry, My father, and, My mother*", that is, "in about a year or two, *the riches of Damascus, and the spoil of Samaria*, those cities that are now so secure, *shall be taken away before the king of Assyria*, who shall plunder both city and country as trophies of his victory."

JAMIESON, FAUSSET, BROWN — CHAPTER 8

Chapters 8 and 9:1-7. The first seven verses of ch. 9 belong to this section. Ch. 8 continues the subject of ch. 7, but at a later preiod (cf. ch. 8:4 with ch. 7:16); implying that the interval till the accomplishment is shorter now than then. The tone of ch. 8:17, 21, 22, expresses calamity more immediate and afflictive than ch. 7:4, 15, 22. **1. great**—suitable, for letters large enough to be read by all. **roll**—rather, *tablet* of wood, metal, or stone (ch. 30: 8; Hab. 2:2); sometimes coated with wax, upon which characters were traced with a pointed instrument, or iron stylus; skins and papyrus were also used (ch. 19:7). **man's pen**—i.e., in ordinary characters which the humblest can read (so Hab. 2:2). *Hebrew, enosh* means a "common man," is contrasted with the *upper ranks* (Rev. 21:17; Rom. 3:5). Not in hieroglyphics. The object was that, after the event, all might see that it had been predicted by Isaiah. **concerning**—the title and subject of the prophecy. **Maher-shalal-hash-baz**—"They (i.e., the Assyrians) hasten to the spoil (viz., to spoil Syria and Samaria), they speed to the prey" [GESENIUS]. Otherwise, "The spoil (i.e., spoiler) hastens, the rapine speeds forward" [MAURER]. **2. I took**—rather, "The Lord said to me, that I should take," etc. [MAURER]. **Uriah**—an accomplice of Ahaz in idolatry, and therefore a witness not likely to assist the prophet of God in getting up a *prophecy after the event* (II Kings 16:10). The witnesses were in order that when the event should come, they might testify that the tablet containing the prophecy had been inscribed with it at the time that it professed. **Zechariah**—(II Chron. 29:13.) **3. prophetess**—perhaps the same as the "virgin" (ch. 7:14), in the interim married as Isaiah's second wife: this is in the primary and temporary sense. Immanuel is even in this sense distinct from Maher-shalal-hash-baz. Thus nineteen months at least intervene from the prophecy (ch. 7:14), nine before the birth of Immanuel, and ten from that time to the birth of Maher-shalal-hash-baz: adding eleven or twelve months *before* the latter could cry, "Father" (ch. 8:4), we have about three years in all, agreeing with ch. 7:15, 16. **4. before . . .**—within a year.

ADAM CLARKE — CHAPTER 8

The prophecy of the foregoing chapter relates directly to the kingdom of Judah only. The first part of it promises them deliverance from the united invasion of the Israelites and Syrians; the latter part, from v. 17, denounces the desolation to be brought upon the kingdom of Judah by the Assyrians. The sixth, seventh, and eighth verses of this chapter seem to take in both the kingdoms of Israel and Judah. "This people refuseth the waters of Shiloah" may be meant of both: the Israelites despised the kingdom of Judah, which they had deserted, and now attempted to destroy; the people of Judah, from a consideration of their own weakness and a distrust of God's promises, being reduced to despair, applied to the Assyrians for assistance against the two confederate kings. But how could it be said of Judah that they rejoiced in Rezin and the son of Remaliah, the enemies confederated against them? This, therefore, must be understood of Israel. The prophet denounces the Assyrian invasion, which should overwhelm the whole kingdom of Israel under Tiglath-pileser and Shalmaneser; and the subsequent invasion of Judah by the same power under Sennacherib, which would bring them into the most imminent danger, like a flood reaching to the neck, in which a man can but just keep his head above water. The two next verses, 9 and 10, are addressed by the prophet, as a subject of the kingdom of Judah, to the Israelites and Syrians, and perhaps to all the enemies of God's people, assuring them that their attempts against that kingdom shall be fruitless, for that the promised Immanuel, to whom he alludes by using His name to express the signification of it, "for God is with us" shall be the Defense of the house of David, and deliver the kingdom of Judah out of their hands. He then proceeds to warn the people of Judah against idolatry, divination, and the like forbidden practices; to which they were much inclined, and which would soon bring down God's judgments upon Israel. The prophecy concludes at the sixth verse of chap. ix with promises of blessings in future times by the coming of the great Deliverer already pointed out by the name of Immanuel, whose person

MATTHEW HENRY

2. That forasmuch as there were many in Judah that were secretly in the interests of Syria and Israel, and were disaffected to the house of David, God would chastise them also by the king of Assyria. What was the sin of the discontented party in Judah (*v.* 6): *This people*, whom the prophet here speaks to, *refuse the waters of Shiloah that go softly*, despise their own country and love to run it down, because it does not make so great a noise in the world, as some other kings and kingdoms do. They refuse the comforts which God's prophets offer them from the word of God, but *they rejoice in Rezin and Remaliah's son*, who were the enemies of their country, and were now actually invading it. Such vipers does many a state foster in its bosom, that eat its bread, and yet adhere to its enemies, and are ready to quit its interests if they but seem to totter. The same king of Assyria that should lay Ephraim and Syria waste should be a scourge and terror to those of their party in Judah, *v.* 7, 8. Because they *refuse the waters of Shiloah the Lord brings upon them the waters of the river, strong and many*, the river Euphrates. They slighted the land of Judah, because it had no river to boast of comparable to that. "Well," says God, "if you be such admirers of Euphrates, you shall have enough of it; the king of Assyria, whose country lies upon that river, shall come with his great army. God shall bring that army upon you." Let us be best pleased with the waters of Shiloah, that go softly, for rapid streams are dangerous. It is threatened that the Assyrian army should break in upon them like a deluge, bearing down all before it. *He shall reach even to the neck*, that is, he shall advance so far as to lay siege to Jerusalem. In the greatest deluge of trouble God can and will keep the head of his people above water. Though the stretching out of the wings of the Assyrian, that bird of prey, though the right and left wing of his army, should fill the breadth of the land of Judah, yet still it is *thy land, O Immanuel!* It was to be Christ's land; for there he was to be born.

Verses 9–15

The prophet here returns to speak of the present distress that Ahaz and his court and kingdom were in upon account of the threatening confederacy of the ten tribes and the Syrians against them.

I. He triumphs over the invading enemies, and, in effect, bids them do their worst (*v.* 9, 10): "*O you people, you of far countries*, give ear to what the prophet says to you in God's name. We doubt not but you will now make your utmost efforts against Judah and Jerusalem. You *associate yourselves* in alliance. You *gird yourselves*, and again you *gird yourselves*. You *take counsel together. You speak the word;* you determine what to do, and are confident that the matter will be accomplished with a word's speaking. All your efforts will be ineffectual. *You shall be broken in pieces.* Not only shall your attempts be ruined, but your attempts shall be your ruin; you shall be broken by those designs you have formed against Jerusalem. *For God is with us:* he is on our side, to take our part and fight for us; and, *if God be for us, who can be against us?*"

II. He comforts and encourages the people of God with the same comforts and encouragements which he himself had received.

1. The prophet tells us how he was himself taught of God not to give way to such amazing fears (*v.* 11): "*The Lord spoke to me with a strong hand not to walk in the way of this people*, not to say as they say nor do as they do, not to approve of making peace upon any terms, or calling in the help of the Assyrians." God instructed the prophet not to go down the stream. There is a proneness in the best of men to be frightened at threatening clouds, especially when fears are epidemic.

2. Now what is it that he says to God's people?

(1) He cautions them against a sinful fear, *v.* 12. It seems it was the way of this people at this time, and fear is catching. He whose heart fails him makes his brethren's heart to fail, like his heart (Deut. xx. 8); therefore *Say you not, A confederacy, to all those to whom this people shall say, A confederacy.* Do not join with those that are for making a league with the Assyrians, through unbelief, and distrust of God and their cause. Do not, when any little thing is amiss, cry out, There is a plot, a plot. When they talk what dismal news there is, *Syria is joined with Ephraim*, what will become of us? do not you fear their fear.

(2) He advises them to a gracious religious fear: *But sanctify the Lord of hosts himself*, *v.* 13. The believing fear of God is a special preservative against the disquieting fear of man; see 1 Pet. iii. 14, 15, where this is quoted, and applied to suffering Christians.

(3) He assures them of a holy security and serenity

JAMIESON, FAUSSET, BROWN

6. waters of Shiloah . . . softly—Their source is on the southeast of Zion and east of Jerusalem. It means "sent," the water being *sent* through an aqueduct (John 9:7). Figurative for the mild, though now weak, sway of the house of David; in the highest sense Shiloah expresses the benignant sway of Jehovah in the theocracy, administered through David. Contrast to the violent Euphrates, "the river" that typifies Assyria (vs. 7; Rev. 17:15). "This people" refers both to *Israel*, which preferred an alliance with Rezin of Syria to one with the kings of Judah, and to *Judah*, a party in which seems to have favored the pretentions of the son of Tabeal against David's line (ch. 7:6; also to *Judah's desire to seek an Assyrian alliance* is included in the censure (cf. ch. 7:17). Verse 14 shows that both nations are meant; both alike rejected the divine Shiloah. Not "*My* people," as elsewhere, when God expresses favor, but "this people" (ch. 6:9). **7. therefore**—for the reason given in vs. 6, the Assyrian flood, which is first to overflood Syria and Samaria, shall rise high enough to reach rebel Judah also (vs. 8). **the river**—Euphrates swollen in spring by the melting of the snow of the Armenian mountains (cf. vs. 6; ch. 7:20). **all his glory**—Eastern kings travel with a gorgeous retinue. **channels**—natural and artificial in the level region, Mesopotamia. **8. pass through**—The flood shall not stop at Syria and Samaria, but shall *penetrate into* Judea. **the neck**—When the waters reach to the neck, a man is near drowning; still the *head* is not said to be overflowed. Jerusalem, elevated on hills, is the head. The danger shall be so imminent as to reach near it at Sennacherib's invasion in Hezekiah's reign; but it shall be spared (ch. 30:28). **wings**—the extreme bands of the Assyrian amies, fulfilled (ch. 36:1; 37:25). **thy land, O Immanuel**—Though temporarily applied to Isaiah's son, in the *full* sense this is applicable only to Messiah, that Judea is *His*, was, and still is, a pledge that, however sorely overwhelmed, it shall be saved at last; the "head" is safe even now, waiting for the times of restoration (Acts 1:6); at the same time these words imply that, notwithstanding the temporary deliverance from Syria and Israel, implied in "Immanuel," the greatest calamities are to follow to Judah. **9. Associate yourselves**—rather, "Raise tumults," or, Rage, i.e., Do your worst [Maurer], referring perhaps to the attack of Rezin and Pekah on Jerusalem. **and . . . be broken in pieces**—rather, "yet ye shall be thrown into consternation." *Imperative* in the *Hebrew*, according to the idiom whereby the second of two imperatives implies the *future*, viz., the consequence of the action contained in the first (so ch. 6:9). The name "Immanuel" in vs. 8 (cf. vs. 10) suggests the thought of the ultimate safety of *Immanuel's land*, both from its present two invaders, and even from the Assyrians, notwithstanding the grievous flood wherewith the previous verses foretell they shall deluge it. The succession of the house of David cannot be set aside in Judah, for Immanuel Messiah is to be born in it as heir of David, of whom Isaiah's son is but a type (ch. 9:4, 6). **give ear . . . far countries**—witness the discomfiture of Judah's enemies. The prophecy probably looks on *also* to the final conspiracy of Antichrist and his supporters against the Heir of David's throne in the latter days and their utter overthrow [Horsley]. **gird yourselves . . . gird yourselves**—The repetition expresses vehemently the *certainty* of their being *thrown into consternation* (not as *English Version*, "broken in pieces"). **10. the word**—of command, for the assault of Jerusalem. **God is with us**—"Immanuel implies this (Num. 14:9; Ps. 46:7). **11. with a strong hand**—or else, "when He grasped me with His hand" [Horsley]. Maurer, as *English Version*, "with the impetus of His hand," i.e., the felt impulse of His inspiration in my mind (Jer. 15:17; Ezek. 1:3; 3:14, 22; 37:1). **way of . . . people**—their distrust of Jehovah, and the panic which led them and Ahab to seek Assyrian aid. **12-16.** The words of Jehovah. **12. confederacy**—rather, a conspiracy; an appropriate term for the *unnatural* combination of *Israel* with *Syrian* foreigners against Judea and the theocracy, to which the former was bound by ties of blood and hereditary religion [Maurer]. **to all . . . say**—rather, of all which this people calleth a conspiracy [G. V. Smith]. **their fear**—viz., object of fear: the hostile conspiracy. **be afraid**—rather [Maurer], "nor make others to be afraid."

13. Sanctify—*Honor* His *holy* name by regarding Him as your only hope of safety (ch. 29:23; Num. 20:12). **him . . . fear**—"fear" lest you provoke His wrath by your fear of man and distrust of Him.

ADAM CLARKE

and character are set forth in terms the most ample and magnificent.

And here it may be observed that it is almost the constant practice of the prophet to connect in like manner deliverances temporal with spiritual. Thus the eleventh chapter, setting forth the kingdom of Messiah, is closely connected with the tenth, which foretells the destruction of Sennacherib. So likewise the destruction of nations, enemies to God, in the thirty-fourth chapter, introduces the flourishing state of the kingdom of Christ in the thirty-fifth. And thus the chapters from xl to xlix inclusive, plainly relating to the deliverance from the captivity of Babylon, do in some parts plainly relate to the greater deliverance by Christ.

1. *Take thee a great roll.* In this manner he was to record the prophecy of the destruction of Damascus and Samaria by the Assyrians, the subject and sum of which prophecy is here expressed with great brevity in four words, *maher shalal hash baz*; i.e., "to hasten the spoil, to take quickly the prey"; which are afterwards applied as the name of the prophet's son, who was made a sign of the speedy completion of it—Maher-shalal-hash-baz: *Haste-to-the-spoil, Quick-to-the-prey.* And that it might be done with the greater solemnity, and to preclude all doubt of the real delivery of the prophecy before the event, he calls witnesses to attest the recording of it.

4. *Before the child.* The prophecy was accordingly accomplished within three years; when Tiglath-pileser, king of Assyria, went up against Damascus and took it, and carried the people of it captive to Kir, and slew Rezin, and also took the Reubenites and the Gadites, and the half-tribe of Manasseh, and carried them captive to Assyria, 2 Kings xv. 29; xvi. 9; 1 Chron. v. 26.

6. *Forasmuch as this people refuseth.* The gentle *waters of Shiloah,* a small fountain and brook just without Jerusalem, which supplied a pool within the city for the use of the inhabitants, is an apt emblem of the state of the kingdom and house of David, much reduced in its apparent strength, yet supported by the blessing of God; and is finely contrasted with the waters of the Euphrates, great, rapid, and impetuous—the image of the Babylonian empire, which God threatens to bring down like a mighty flood upon all these apostates of both kingdoms, as punishment for their manifold iniquities, and their contemptuous disregard of His promises.

8. *He shall reach even to the neck.* He compares Jerusalem, says Kimchi, to the head of the human body. As when the waters come up to a man's neck, he is very near drowning, so the king of Assyria coming up to Jerusalem was like a flood reaching to the neck—the whole country was overflowed, and the capital was in imminent danger.

9. *Associate yourselves*—"Know ye this." God by His prophet plainly declares to the confederate adversaries of Judah, and bids them regard and attend to His declaration, that all their efforts shall be in vain.

11. *With a strong hand.* That is, with a strong and powerful influence of the prophetic Spirit.

MATTHEW HENRY

of mind in so doing (*v.* 14): *He shall be for a sanctuary;* make him your fear, and you shall find him your hope, your help, your defence, and your mighty deliverer. He will be your sanctuary, to which you may flee for safety, and where you shall not need to fear any evil.

III. He threatens the ruin of the ungodly and unbelieving, both in Judah and Israel. They have no part nor lot in the foregoing comforts. The prophet foresees that the greatest part of both the houses of Israel would not *sanctify the Lord of hosts.* What was a savour of life unto life to others would be a savour of death unto death to them. "So that *many among them shall stumble and fall.*"

Verses 16–22

I. The unspeakable privilege which the people of God enjoy in being entrusted with the sacred writings. That they may sanctify the Lord of hosts, may make him their fear and find him their sanctuary, *bind up the testimony*, *v.* 16. 1. It is a *testimony* and a *law*; God has attested it, and he has enjoined it. As a testimony it directs our faith; as a law it directs our practice; and we ought both to subscribe to the truths of it and to submit to the precepts of it. 2. This testimony and this law are bound up and sealed, for we are not to add to them nor diminish from them. 3. They are lodged as a sacred deposit in the hands of the disciples of *the children of the prophets and the covenant*, Acts iii. 25. This is the good thing which is committed to them, 2. Tim. i. 13, 14.

II. The good use which we ought to make of this privilege. This we are taught,

1. By the prophet's own practice and resolutions, *v.* 17, 18. He specifies two discouragements: (1) The frowns of God upon his people, whose interests lay very near his heart: "He *hides his face from the house of Jacob*, and seems at present to neglect them, and lay them under the tokens of his displeasure." (2) The contempt and reproaches of men, not only upon himself, but upon his disciples, among whom the law and the testimony were sealed: *I and the children whom the Lord has given me are for signs and wonders;* we are gazed at as outlandish people. Christ looks upon believers as his children, whom the Father gave him (John xvii. 6), and both he and they are for signs and wonders, spoken against (Luke ii. 34), everywhere spoken against, Acts xxviii. 22. He saw the hand of God in all that which was discouraging to him, and kept his eye upon that. He therefore resolved to wait upon the Lord and to look for him; to attend even while he hid his face, and to expect with a humble assurance his return in mercy.

2. By the counsel and advice which he gives to his disciples, to whom were committed the lively oracles. He supposes they would be tempted, in the day of their distress, to consult *those that had familiar spirits.* Thus Saul, when he was in straits, made his application to the witch of Endor (1 Sam. xxviii. 7, 15), and Ahaziah to the god of Ekron, 2 Kings i. 2. These conjurors *peeped and muttered.* The words here may refer to their voice and manner of speaking. They spoke not with boldness and plainness, but as those who desire to amuse people rather than to instruct them. There were express laws against this wickedness (Lev. xix. 31; xx. 27), and yet it was found in Israel, is found even in Christian nations. Dread the use of spells and charms, and consulting those that by hidden arts pretend to tell fortunes, cure diseases. He furnishes them with an answer to this temptation, "If any go about thus to ensnare you, give them this reply: *Should not a people seek to their God?* What! *for the living to the dead!* Tell them that a people ought to seek unto their God; now Jehovah is our God, and therefore we ought to consult with him, and not with those that have familiar spirits, Mic. iv. 5. Should not a people under guilt, and in trouble, seek to their God for pardon and peace? Should not a people in doubt, in want, and in danger, seek to their God for direction, supply, and protection?" What can be more absurd than to expect that our friends that are dead should do that for us, when we deify them and pray to them, which our living friends cannot do? Necromancers consulted the dead, as the witch of Endor, and so proclaimed their own folly. He directs them to consult the oracles of God. If the prophets that were among them did not speak directly to every case, yet they had the written word, and to that they must have recourse. Those will never be drawn to consult wizards that know how to make a good use of their Bibles. Make God's statutes your counsellors, and you will be counselled aright. We must *speak according to that word*, that is, we must make this our standard (1 Tim. vi. 3). We must make this use of the law and the testimony because those that concur not with the word of God do thereby evince that *there is no light*,

JAMIESON, FAUSSET, BROWN

14. sanctuary—inviolable asylum, like the altar of the temple (I Kings 1:50; 2:28; Ezek. 11:16; cf. Prov. 18:10); viz., to those who fear and trust in Him. **but . . . offence**—i.e., a rock over which they should fall to their hurt; viz., those who would not believe. **both . . . houses**—Israel and Judah. Here again the prophecy expands beyond the temporary application in Ahaz' time. The very stone, Immanuel, which would have been a *sanctuary* on belief, becomes a fatal *stumbling block* through unbelief. Jesus Christ refers to this in Matthew 21:44. (Cf. Deut. 32:4, 15, 18, 30, 31, 37; Dan. 2:34; Rom. 9:33; I Pet. 2:8.) **gin**—trap, in which birds are unexpectedly caught (Luke 21:35; I Thess. 5:2). So at the destruction of Jerusalem under Titus. **15. stumble . . . taken**—images from the means used in taking wild animals. **16. Bind up . . . seal**—What Isaiah had before briefly noted by inscribing *Maher-shalal-hash-baz* in a *tablet,* fixed up in some public place, he afterwards wrote out more in detail in a *parchment roll* (ch. 30:8); this he is now to *seal up,* not merely in order that nothing may be added to, or taken from it, as being complete, but to imply that it relates to distant events, and is therefore to be a *sealed* and *not understood* testimony (ch. 6:9, 10), except in part among God's disciples," i.e., those who "sanctify the Lord" by obedient trust (Ps. 25:14). Subsequent revelations would afterwards clear up what now was dark. So the Apocalypse explains what in Daniel was left unexplained (cf. Dan. 8:26; 12:9). "The words are closed up and *sealed* till the time of the end"; but Revelation 22:10, "*Seal not* the sayings of the prophecy . . . for the time is at hand" (cf. Rev. 5:1, 5, 9), **testimony**—attested by Uriah and Zechariah (vs. 2). **law**—the revelation just given, having the force of a law. **disciples**—not as MAURER, Uriah and Zechariah (cf. John 7:17; 15:15). **17. I**—Whatever the rest of the nation may do, I will look to Jehovah alone. **that hideth . . . face**—*though* He seems now to *withdraw His countenance* from *Judah* (the then representive of "the house of Jacob"). Let us *wait* and trust in, though we cannot see, Him (ch. 50:10; 54:8; Hab. 2:3; Luke 2:25, 38). **18. I and the children**—Isaiah means "salvation of Jehovah"; His children's names, also (ch. 7:3; 7:14; 8:3), were "signs" suggestive of the coming and final deliverance. **wonders**—i.e., symbols of the future (ch. 20:3; Zech. 3:8). "Behold I . . . me" is quoted in Hebrews 2:13 to prove *the manhood of the Messiah.* This is the *main* and *ultimate* fulfilment of the prophecy; its *temporary* meaning is applied to Ahaz' time. Isaiah typically, in vss. 17, 18, personates Messiah, who is at once "Father" and "Son," *Isaiah* and *Immanuel,* "Child" and "Mighty God," and is therefore called here a "wonder," as in ch. 9:6, "Wonderful." Hence in Hebrews 2:13, believers are called His "children"; but in vss. 11, 12, His 'brethren." On "the LORD hath given me," see John 6:37, 39; 10:29; 17:12. **which dwelleth in . . . Zion**—and will therefore protect *Jerusalem.* **19. Seek unto**—Consult in your national difficulties. **them . . . familiar spirits**—necromancers, spirit-charmers. So Saul, when he had forsaken God (I Sam. 28:7, etc.), consulted the witch of Endor in his difficulties. These follow in the wake of idolatry, which prevailed under Ahaz (II Kings 16:3, 4, 10). He copied the soothsaying as he did the idolatrous "altar" of Damascus (cf. Lev. 20:6, which forbids it, ch. 19:3). **wizards**—men claiming supernatural *knowledge;* from the old English, "*to wit,*" i.e., know. **peep**—rather "chirp faintly," as young birds do; this sound was generally ascribed to departed spirits; by ventriloquism the soothsayers caused a low sound to proceed as from a grave, or dead person. Hence the LXX renders the *Hebrew* for necromancers here "ventriloquists" (cf. ch. 29:4). **mutter**—moan. **should not . . .**—The answer which Isaiah recommends to be given to those advising to have recourse to necromancers. **for the living . . .**—"should one, *for the safety* of the living, seek unto (consult) the dead?" [GESENIUS]. LOWTH renders it, "*In place of* (consulting) the living, should one consult the dead?" **20. To the law . . .** the revelation of God by His prophet (vs. 16), to which he directs them to refer those who would advise necromancy. **if they speak not . . . it is because** *English Version* understands "they" as the necromancers. But the *Hebrew* rendered "because" is not this but "who"; and "if not," ought rather to be "shall they not"; or, *truly they shall* speak according to this word, *who* have no *morning light* (so the *Hebrew,* i.e., prosperity after the night of sorrows) *dawning* on them [MAURER and G. V. SMITH]. They who are in the dark night of trial, without a dawn of hope, shall surely say so, Do not seek, as we did, to necromancy, but to the law," etc. *The law* perhaps includes here the *law of Moses,* which was the

ADAM CLARKE

CHARLES H. SPURGEON:

Verse 18. We might possibly have had some difficulty in explaining this verse, or we might have referred it to the prophet Isaiah and his sons, had not inspiration been its own expositor. Turn to the New Testament and the text will be no mystery to you; its key hangs on its proper nail. In Hebrews 2:11–13 we read—"For both he that sanctifieth and they who are sanctified are all of one: for which cause he is not ashamed to call them brethren, saying, I will declare thy name unto my brethren, in the midst of the church will I sing praise unto thee. And again, I will put my trust in him. And again, Behold, I and the children which God hath given me." We have thus from divine revelation assured evidence that it is our Lord who speaks, and speaks of His people as His children. This clue we will follow.

The context sets forth the different results which result from the appearance of the Savior. He is rejected by many, and accepted by others. He was set for the fall and rise of many in Israel. To those who receive Him He is a glory and a defence, but to others "a stone of stumbling and a rock of offence." Even now His gospel is a "savor of death unto death" as well as a "savor of life unto life." The election of grace is always being worked out, the separating process continues, and will continue, until the eternal purpose has been completely fulfilled. There are those who respond in faith to the Savior, and come to Him; while others willfully and wickedly close their eyes to His brightness and reject Him, and He leaves them in their willing unbelief. "He came unto his own, and his own received him not. But to as many as received him, to them gave he power to become the sons of God, even to them that believe on his name."

Of those who received the Lord, we find it written that the testimony of God would be left in their charge. "Bind up the testimony; seal the law among my disciples." The outside world rejects the testimony of God; its own thoughts and opinions are much more pleasant to it; but among the Lord's disciples His commands are prized, and His teachings sacredly preserved. They see the seal of the living God upon the gospel, and they also set to it their seal that God is true; they accept the gospel of Jesus as very truth, and hold it, and mean to hold it against all comers.

—*The Treasury of the Old Testament*

20. *To the law and to the testimony*—"Unto the command, and unto the testimony." *Because there is no light in them*—"In which there is no obscurity." Kimchi says this was the form of an oath: "By the law and by the testimony such and such things are so." Now if they had sworn this falsely, it is because there is *no light,* no "illumination," no scruple of conscience, *in them.*

MATTHEW HENRY

no morning light (so the word is) *in them*. Those that reject divine revelation have not human understanding; nor do those rightly admit the oracles of reason who will not admit the oracles of God. Some read it as a threatening: "If they speak not according to this word, there shall be no light to them, but they shall be driven to darkness and despair"; as it follows here, *v.* 21, 22. What light had Saul when he consulted the witch? 1 Sam. xxviii. 18, 20. He reads the doom of those that seek familiar spirits and regard not God's law and testimony; they may expect all horror and misery, *v.* 21, 22. They shall *pass through* the land, unfixed, unsettled; they shall be *hardly bestead* whither to go for the necessary supports of life. Those who used to be fed to the full shall be hungry. Those that go away from God go out of the way of all good. These people *when they shall be hungry shall fret themselves*, and shall be very provoking to all about them; they will forget all the rules of duty and decency, and will treasonably *curse their king* and blasphemously curse *their God*. When they have broken the bonds of their allegiance, no marvel if those of their religion do not hold them long: they next curse their God, curse him, and die. They shall look upward, but heaven shall frown upon them and look gloomy; and how can it be otherwise when they curse their God? They shall look to the earth, but what comfort can that yield to those with whom God is at war?

CHAPTER 9

Verses 1–7

The first words of this chapter plainly refer to the close of the foregoing chapter, where everything looked black and melancholy: *Behold, trouble, and darkness, and dimness*—but *to the upright there shall arise light in the darkness* (Ps. cxii. 4). *Nevertheless it shall not be such dimness* as sometimes there has been. In the worst of times God's people have a *nevertheless* to allay and balance their troubles; they are persecuted, but not forsaken (2 Cor. iv. 9), sorrowful yet always rejoicing, 2 Cor. vi. 10. And it is matter of comfort to us, when things are at the darkest, that he who *forms the light and creates the darkness* (*ch.* xlv. 7) has appointed to both their bounds and set the one over against the other, Gen. i. 4.

I. Three things are here promised, and they all point ultimately at the grace of the gospel, with which the saints were to comfort themselves in every cloudy and dark day.

1. A glorious light, which shall by degrees dispel the dimness, that it shall not be as it sometimes has been: *Not such as was in her vexation; when at first he lightly afflicted the land of Zebulun and Naphtali* (which lay remote and most exposed to the inroads of the neighbouring enemies), *and afterwards he more grievously afflicted the land by the way of the sea and beyond Jordan* (*v.* 1), 2 Kings x. 32. If a light affliction do not humble and reform us, we must expect to be afflicted more grievously. *Israel has been without the true God and a teaching priest, and in those times there was no peace.* But the dimness threatened (*ch.* viii. 22) shall not prevail to such a degree; for (*v.* 2) *the people that walked in darkness have seen a great light.* At this time when the prophet lived, there were many prophets in Judah and Israel, whose prophecies were a great light both for direction and comfort to the people of God, who adhered to the law and the testimony. This was to have its full accomplishment when our Lord Jesus began to appear as a prophet, and to preach the gospel in the land of Zebulun and Naphtali, and in Galilee of the Gentiles.

2. A glorious increase, and a universal joy arising from it (*v.* 3) "*Thou*, O God! *hast multiplied the nation*; it has been diminished by one sore judgment after another, yet now thou hast begun to multiply it again." Yet it follows, "*Thou hast not increased the joy*—the carnal joy and mirth. But, notwithstanding that, *they joy before thee*; there is a great deal of serious spiritual joy among them, joy in the presence of God." This is very applicable to the times of gospel light, spoken of *v.* 2. "And to him" (so the Masorites read it) "thou hast magnified the joy, to everyone that receives the light." The following words favour this reading: "*They joy before thee;* they come before thee in holy ordinances with great joy; their mirth is not like that of Israel under their vines and fig-trees (thou hast not increased that joy) but it is in the favour of God and in the tokens of his grace." It is holy joy: *They joy before thee;* they rejoice in spirit (as Christ did, Luke x. 21), and that is before God. It is a great joy; *according to the joy in harvest*, when those who have with patience waited for the precious fruits of the earth, reap in

JAMIESON, FAUSSET, BROWN

"Magna Charta" on which prophetism commented [KITTO]. **21, 22.** More detailed description of the despair, which they shall fall into, who sought necromancy instead of God; vs. 20 implies that *too late* they shall see how much better it would have been for them to have sought "to the law," etc. (Deut. 32:31). But now they are given over to despair. Therefore, while seeing the truth of God, they only "curse their King and God"; foreshadowing the future, like conduct of those belonging to the "kingdom of the beast," when they shall be visited with divine plagues (Rev. 16:11; cf. Jer. 18:12). **through it**—viz., the land. **hardly bestead**—oppressed with anxiety. **hungry**—a more grievous famine than the temporary one in Ahaz' time, owing to Assyria; *then* there was *some* food, but *none now* (ch. 7:15, 22; Lev. 26:3-5, 14-16, 20). **their king . . . God**—Jehovah, King of the Jews (Ps. 5:2; 68:24). **look upward . . . unto the earth**—Whether they look up to heaven, or down towards *the land of Judea*, nothing but despair shall present itself. **dimness of anguish**—darkness of distress (Prov. 1:27). **driven to darkness**—rather, *thick darkness* (Jer. 23:12). Driven onward, as by a sweeping storm. The Jewish rejection of "their King and God," Messiah, was followed by all these awful calamities.

CHAPTER 9

VSS. 1-7. CONTINUATION OF THE PROPHECY IN CHAPTER 8. **1. Nevertheless . . .**—rather, "*For* darkness shall not (continually) be on it (i.e., the land) on which there is (now) distress" [HENGSTENBERG and MAURER]. The "for" refers, not to the words immediately preceding, but to the consolations in ch. 8:9, 10, 17, 18. Do not despair, *for*, etc. **when at the first . . .**—rather, "as the former time has brought contempt on the land of Zebulun and Naphtali (viz., the deportation of their inhabitants under Tiglath-pileser, II Kings 15:29, a little before the giving of this prophecy); so shall the after-coming time bring honor to the way of the sea (the district around the lake of Galilee), the land beyond [but HENGSTENBERG, "by the side of"] Jordan (*Perea*, east of Jordan, belonging to Reuben, Gad, and half-Manasseh), the circle [but HENGSTENBERG, "Galilee"] (i.e., region) of the "Gentiles" [MAURER, HENGSTENBERG, etc.]. *Galil* in *Hebrew* is a "circle," "circuit," and from it came the name Galilee. North of Naphtali, inhabited by a mixed race of Jews and Gentiles of the bordering Phœnician race (Judg. 1:30; I Kings 9:11). Besides the recent deportation by Tiglath-pileser, it had been sorely smitten by Benhadad of Syria, 200 years before (I Kings 15:20). It was after the Assyrian deportation colonized with heathens, by Esar-haddon (II Kings 17:24). Hence arose the contempt for it on the part of the southern Jews of purer blood (John 1:46; 7:52). The same region which was so darkened once, shall be among the first to receive Messiah's light (Matt. 4:13, 15, 16). It was in despised Galilee that He first and most publicly exercised His ministry; from it were most of His apostles. Foretold in Deuteronomy 33:18, 19; Acts 2:7; Psalm 68:27, 28, Jerusalem, the theocratic capital, might readily have known Messiah; to compensate less favored Galilee, He ministered mostly there; Galilee's very debasement made it feel its need of a Saviour, a feeling not known to the self-righteous Jews (Matt. 9:13). It was appropriate, too, that He who was both "the Light to lighten the Gentiles, and the Glory of His people Israel," should minister chiefly on the border land of *Israel*, near the *Gentiles*. **2. the people**—the whole nation, Judah and Israel. **shadow of death**—the darkest misery of captivity. **3. multiplied . . . nation**—primarily, the rapid *increase* of Israelites after the return from Babylon; more fully and exhaustively the rapid spread of Christianity at first. **not increased the joy**—By a slight change in the *Hebrew*, *its* (joy) is substituted by some for *not*, because "not increased the joy" seems opposite to what immediately follows, "the joy," etc. HENGSTENBERG, retains *not* thus: "Whose joy thou hadst not increased," (i.e., hadst *diminished*). Others, "Hast thou not increased the joy?" The very difficulty of the reading, *not*, makes it less likely to be an interpolation. HORSLEY best explains it: The prophet sees in vision a shifting scene, comprehending at one glance the history of the Christian Church to remotest times—a land dark and thinly peopled—lit up by a sudden light—filled with new inhabitants—then struggling with difficulties, and again delivered by the utter and final overthrow of their enemies. The influx of Gentile converts

ADAM CLARKE

21. *Hardly bestead*—"Distressed." Instead of *niksheh*, "distressed," the Vulgate, Chaldee, and Symmachus manifestly read *nichshal*, "stumbling, tottering through weakness, ready to fall," a sense which suits very well with the place. *And look upward*—"And he shall cast his eyes upward."

CHAPTER 9

1. *Dimness*—"Accumulated darkness." *The land of Zebulun*. Zebulun, Naphtali, Manasseh, that is, the country of Galilee all round the Sea of Gennesareth, were the parts that principally suffered in the first Assyrian invasion under Tiglath-pileser; see 2 Kings xv. 29; 1 Chron. v. 26. And they were the first that enjoyed the blessings of Christ's preaching the gospel, and exhibiting His miraculous works among them.

3. *And not increased the joy*—"Thou hast increased their joy."

MATTHEW HENRY

joy; and as in war men rejoice when, after a hazardous battle, *they divide the spoil.* The gospel brings with it plenty and victory.

3. A glorious liberty and enlargement (*v.* 4, 5): "They shall rejoice before thee, and with good reason, *for thou hast broken the yoke of his burden,* for he shall no longer be in servitude; and thou hast broken *the staff of his shoulder and the rod of his oppressor,* as the Midianites' yoke was broken from off the neck of Israel by the agency of Gideon." *Do unto them as to the Midianites.* What temporal deliverance this refers to is not clear, probably the preventing of Sennacherib from making himself master of Jerusalem, which was done, *as in the day of Midian,* by the immediate hand of God; done silently and without noise. But doubtless it looks further, to that great light which should visit those that sat in darkness; it would bring *deliverance to the captives,* Luke iv. 18. The design of the gospel is to break the yoke of sin and Satan, to remove the burden of guilt and corruption, that we might be brought into the glorious liberty of the children of God. Christ broke the yoke of the ceremonial law (Acts xv. 10; Gal. v. 1), and delivered us *out of the hand of our enemies,* that we might *serve him without fear,* Luke i. 74, 75. This is done by the Spirit working like fire (Matt. iii. 11), not as the battle of the warrior is fought, with confused noise; no, the weapons of our warfare are not carnal.

II. But who, where, is he that shall undertake and accomplish these great things for the church? The prophet tells us (*v.* 6, 7) they shall be done by the Messiah, *Immanuel* (*ch.* vii. 14), and now speaks of it, in the prophetic style, as a thing already done: the *child is born,* because the church before his incarnation reaped great benefit and advantage. As he was the Lamb slain, so he was the child born, *from the foundation of the world,* Rev. xiii. 8. All the great things that God did for the Old Testament church were done by him as the eternal Word, and for his sake as the Mediator. The Jewish nation, and particularly the house of David, were preserved many a time from imminent ruin only because that blessing was in them. The Chaldee paraphrast understands it of the man that shall endure for ever, even Christ:

1. See him in his humiliation. The same that is *the mighty God* is *a child born*; thus did he humble and empty himself, to exalt and fill us. He is born into our world. *The Word was made flesh, and dwelt among us.* God so loved the world that he gave him. He is born *to us,* he is given to us.

2. See him in his exaltation. This child, this Son of God, this Son of man, is invested with the highest honour and power so that we cannot but be happy if he be our friend. He shall be called *Wonderful, Counsellor, &c.* His people shall know him and worship him by these names. He is *wonderful, counsellor.* Justly is he called *wonderful,* for he is both God and man. He is the *counsellor,* for he was intimately acquainted with the counsels of God from eternity, and he gives counsel to the children of men. He is the wisdom of the Father, and is made of God to us wisdom. He is *the mighty God—God, the mighty One.* As he has wisdom, so he has strength. He is able to save to the utmost. He is *the everlasting Father,* or *the Father of eternity*; he is God, one with the Father, who is from everlasting to everlasting. He is the author of everlasting life and happiness to them, and so is the Father of a blessed eternity to them. He is *the prince of peace.* As a King, he preserves, commands, creates peace, in his kingdom. He is our peace. His throne is above every throne (*v.* 6): *The government shall be upon his shoulder*—his only. He shall not only wear the badge of it upon his shoulder (the *key of the house of David, ch.* xxii. 22), but he shall bear the burden of it. Glorious things are here spoken of Christ's government, *v.* 7. It shall be multiplied; the lustre of it shall increase, and it shall shine more and more brightly in the world. It shall be a peaceable government, agreeable to his character as the prince of peace. He shall rule by love, and as his government increases the peace shall increase. It shall be administered with prudence and equity: *He shall order it, and settle it, with justice and judgment.* It shall be an everlasting kingdom: *There shall be no end of the increase of his government.* God himself has undertaken to bring all this about: "*The Lord of hosts,* who has all power in his hand and all creatures at his beck, *shall perform this.*"

Verses 8–21

Here are terrible threatenings directed primarily against Israel, the kingdom of the ten tribes, Ephraim and Samaria, the ruin of which is here foretold, all which came to pass within a few years, but they look further and read the doom of all the nations that

JAMIESON, FAUSSET, BROWN

(represented here by "Galilee of the Gentiles") soon was to be followed by the growth of corruption, and the final rise of Antichrist, who is to be destroyed, while God's people is delivered, as in the case of Gideon's victory over Midian, not by man's prowess, but by the special interposition of God. **before thee**—a phrase taken from sacrificial feasts; the tithe of harvest was eaten *before God* (Deut. 12:7; 14:26). **as men rejoice . . . divide . . . spoil**—referring to the judgments on the enemies of the Lord and His people, which usually accompany revelations of His grace. **4.** The occasion of the "joy," the deliverance not only of Ahaz and Judah from the Assyrian tribute (II Kings 16:8), and of Israel's ten tribes from the oppressor (II Kings 15:19), but of the Jewish Christian Church from its last great enemy. **hast**—the past time for the future, in prophetic vision; it expresses the *certainly* of the event. **yoke of his burden**—the yoke with which he was burdened. **staff of . . . shoulder**—the staff which strikes his shoulder [MAURER]; or the wood, like a yoke, on the neck of slaves, the badge of servitude [ROSENMULLER]. **day of Midian**—(Judg. 7:8-22). As Gideon with a handful of men conquered the hosts of Midian, so Messiah the "child" (vs. 6) shall prove to be the "Prince of peace," and the small Israel under Him shall overcome the mighty hosts of Antichrist (cf. Mic. 5:2-5), containing the same contrast, and alluding also to "the Assyrian," the then enemy of the Church, as here in Isaiah, the type of the last great enemy. For further analogies between Gideon's victory and the Gospel, cf. II Corinthians 4:7, with Judges 7:22. As the "dividing of the spoil" (vs. 3) was followed by that which was "not joy," the making of the idolatrous ephod (Judg. 8:24-27), so the gospel victory was soon followed by apostasy at the first, and shall be so again after the millennial overthrow of Antichrist (Rev. 20:3, 7-9), previous to Satans' last doom (Rev. 20:10). **5. every battle . . .**—rather, "every greave of (the warrior who is) armed with greaves in the din of battle, and the martial garment (or cloak, called by the Latins *sagum*) rolled in blood, shall be for burning, (and) fuel for fire" [MAURER]. All warlike accoutrements shall be destroyed, as no longer required in the new era of peace (ch. 2:4, 11:6, 7; Ps. 46:9; Ezek. 39:9; Mic. 5: 5, 10; Zech. 9:9, 10). Cf. Malachi 4:1, as to the previous *burning* up of the wicked. **6. For**—the ground of these great expectations, **unto us**—for the benefit of the Jews first, and then the Gentiles (cf. "unto *you*" (Luke 2:11). **son . . . given**—(Ps. 2: 7.) God's gratuitous gift, on which man had no claim (John 3:16; Rom. 6:23). **government . . . upon . . . shoulder**—The ensign of office used to be worn *on the shoulder,* in token of *sustaining* the government (ch. 22:22). Here *the government on* Messiah's *shoulder* is in marked antithesis to the "yoke and staff" of the oppressor on Israel's "shoulder" (vs. 4). He shall receive the kingdom of the earth from the Father, to vindicate it from the misrule of those to whom it was entrusted to hold it for and under the Most High, but who sought to hold it in defiance of His right; the Father asserts His right by the Son, the "Heir of all things," who will hold it for Him (Dan. 7:13, 14). **name . . . called**—His *essential characteristics shall be.* **Wonderful**—(*Note,* ch. 8:18; Judg. 13:18; *Margin,* I Tim. 3:16.) **Counsellor**—(Ps. 16:7; Rom. 11:33, 34; I Cor. 1:24; Col. 2:3.) **mighty God**—(ch. 10:21; Ps. 24:8; Titus 2:13.) HORSLEY translates: "God the mighty man." "Unto us . . . God" is equivalent to "Immanuel" (ch. 7:14). **everlasting Father**—This marks Him as "Wonderful," that He is "a child," yet the "everlasting *Father*" (John 10:30; 14:9). Earthly kings leave their people after a short reign; He will reign over and bless them *for ever* [HENGSTENBERG]. **Prince of Peace**—(*Note,* vs. 5; Gen. 49:10; *Shiloh,* "The Tranquillizer.") Finally (Hos. 2:18). Even already He is "our peace" (Luke 2:14; Eph. 2: 14). **7. Of . . . increase . . . no end**—His princely rule shall perpetually increase and be unlimited (Dan. 2:44). **throne of David**—(I Kings 8:25; Ps. 2:6; 132:11; Jer. 3:17, 18; Ezek. 34:23-26; 37: 16, 22; Luke 1:32, 33; Acts 2:30). **judgment . . . justice**—It is not a kingdom of mere might, and triumph of force over enemies, but of righteousness (ch. 42:21 Ps. 45:6, 7), attainable only in and by Messiah. **zeal . . .**—including not only Christ's hidden spiritual victory over Satan at the first coming, but the open one accompanied with "judgments" on Antichrist and every enemy at the second coming (ch. 59:17; Ps. 9:6-8).

Vss. 8-21, and chap. 10:1-4. PROPHECY AS TO THE TEN TRIBES. Delivered a little later than the previous one. The chapters 9 and 10 ought to have been so divided. The present division into *chapters* was made by Cardinal Hugo, in A.D. 1250; and into

ADAM CLARKE

JOSEPH PARKER:

"As in the day of Midian" (v. 4). What day was that? We have read about it, and we ought to know the reference. The victory of Gideon over the Midianites was one of the most conspicuous instances of valor and military success in all Biblical history, the record of which is to be found in Judges 8:24–27. Great historical events should abide thus; old history should not be lost. Men make little phrases of this kind like refrains to a song—"As in the day of Midian." That is the right use of history. The God that enabled me to kill the lion and the bear will make this uncircumcised Philistine a child in my hands: the Lord that gave me victory in the day of Midian will enable me to set my foot upon the neck of every foe. Turn history into music; turn solemn memories into joyous inspirations, and thus make yesterday supply bread for today's hunger.—*The People's Bible*

5. *Every battle of the warrior*—"The greaves of the armed warrior." I take it to mean that part of the armor which covered the legs and feet. The burning of heaps of armor, gathered from the field of battle, as an offering made to the god supposed to be the giver of victory, was a custom that prevailed among some heathen nations; and the Romans used it as an emblem of peace, which perfectly well suits with the design of the prophet in this place. A medal struck by Vespasian on finishing his wars both at home and abroad represents the goddess Peace holding an olive branch in one hand, and, with a lighted torch in the other, setting fire to a heap of armor. Ezekiel, chap. xxxix. 8-10, in his bold manner, describes the burning of the arms of the enemy, in consequence of the complete victory to be obtained by the Israelites over God and Magog.

6. *The government shall be upon his shoulder.* That is, the ensign of government; the sceptre, the sword, the key, or the like, which was borne upon or hung from the shoulder. *The everlasting Father*—"The Father of the everlasting age," or "the Father of eternity." *Prince of Peace.* The Prince of prosperity, the Giver of all blessings.

7. This is an illustrious prophecy of the incarnation of Christ, with an enumeration of those characters in which He stands most nearly related to mankind as their Saviour, and of others by which His infinite majesty and Godhead are shown. He shall appear as a child, born of a woman, born as a Jew, under the law, but not in the way of ordinary generation. He is *a Son . . . given*—the human nature, in which the fullness of the Godhead was to dwell, being produced by the creative energy of the Holy Ghost in the womb of the Virgin. See Matt. i. 20-21, 23, 25, and Luke i. 35, and Isa. vii. 14, and the notes on those passages. As being God manifested in the flesh, He was wonderful in His conception, birth, preaching, miracles, sufferings, death, resurrection, and ascension; wonderful in His person, and wonderful in His working. He is the *Counsellor* that expounds the law; shows its origin, nature, and claims; instructs, pleads for the guilty; and ever appears in the presence of God for men. He is the *mighty God;* God essentially and efficiently prevailing against His enemies, and destroying ours. He is the *Father* of eternity; the Origin of all being, and the Cause of the existence, and particularly the Father of the spirits of all flesh. The *Prince of Peace*—not only the Author of peace, and the Dispenser of peace, but also He that rules by peace, whose rule tends always to perfection, and produces prosperity.

MATTHEW HENRY

forget God, and will not have Christ to reign over them.

I. The preface to this prediction (*v.* 8): *The Lord sent a word into Jacob*, sent it by his servants the prophets. He warns before he wounds, but they took no care to turn away his wrath. It fell upon them as a storm of rain and hail from on high, which they could not avoid.

II. The sins charged upon the people of Israel, which provoked God to bring these judgments upon them. 1. Their insolent defiance of the justice of God, thinking themselves a match for him: "They *say, in the pride and stoutness of their heart*, Let God himself do his worst. If he ruin our houses, we will repair them, and make them stronger. If the houses that were built of bricks be demolished in the war, we will rebuild them with hewn stones. If the enemy cut down the sycamores, we will plant cedars." 2. Their incorrigibleness under all the rebukes of Providence hitherto (*v.* 13): *The people turn not unto him that smiteth them, neither do they seek the Lord of hosts;* either they are atheists, and have no religion, or idolators, and seek those gods that are the creatures of their own fancy and the works of their own hands. 3. Their general corruption of manners and abounding profaneness. Those that should have reformed them helped to debauch them (*v.* 16): *The leaders of this people* mislead them, and *cause them to err*. But it is ill with a people when their physicians are their worst disease. "*Those, that bless this people*, or *call them blessed* (so the margin reads it), that flatter them, and soothe them in their wickedness, and cry *Peace, peace, to them*, cause them to err." We have reason to be afraid of those that speak well of us when we do ill; see Prov. xxiv. 24; xxix. 5. Wickedness was universal, and all were infected with it (*v.* 17): *Every one is a hypocrite and an evil doer*. Everyone is profane towards God (so the word properly signifies) and an evil doer towards man. These two commonly go together: those that fear not God regard not man.

III. The judgments threatened against them for this wickedness of theirs.

1. In general, hereby they exposed themselves to the wrath of God. It should devour as fire (*v.* 18): *Wickedness shall burn as the fire*. The briers and thorns, when the fire consumes them, shall *mount up like the lifting up of smoke*, so that the whole land shall be darkened by it; they shall be in trouble, and see no way out (*v.* 19): *The people shall be as the fuel of the fire*.

2. God would arm the neighbouring powers against them, *v.* 11, 12. At this time Israel was in league with Syria against Judah; but the Assyrians, who were adversaries to the Syrians, when they had conquered them should invade Israel, and God would join the enemies of Israel together in alliance. Those that partake with each other in sin, as Syria and Israel in invading Judah, must expect to share in the punishment of sin. The Syrians themselves, whom they were now in league with, should be a scourge to them, they before and the Philistines behind. They should be surrounded with enemies on all sides, who should *devour them with open mouths*, *v.* 12. The Philistines were not now looked upon as formidable enemies, and the Syrians were looked upon as firm friends; and yet these shall devour Israel.

3. God would take from the midst of them those they confided in, *v.* 14, 15. *The Lord will cut off head and tail, branch and rush*, which is explained in the next verse. (1) Their magistrates, who were honourable by birth and office were *the head*, these were the branch; but because these caused them to err they should be cut off. (2) Their false prophets, were *the tail* and the *rush*, the most despicable of all. A wicked minister is the worst of men. *Corruptio optimi est pessima—The best things become when corrupted the worst.*

4. The desolation should be as general as the corruption had been, and none should escape it, *v.* 17. *The Lord shall have no joy in their young men*, that were in the flower of their youth; nor will he say, *Deal gently with the young men for my sake*. He *shall not have mercy on their fatherless and widows*, though he is, in a particular manner, the patron and protector of such. They had corrupted their way like all the rest.

5. Every one should help forward the common ruin, *No man shall spare his brother.* Civil wars soon bring a kingdom to desolation. Such there were in Israel. In these broils, men *snatched on the right hand, and yet were hungry* still, and did eat the *flesh of their own arms*, preyed upon themselves for hunger, *v.* 20. This bespeaks famine and scarcity. These broils should be not only among particular persons and private families, but among the tribes (*v.* 21): *Manasseh shall devour Ephraim, and Ephraim Manasseh.* Those that could unite against Judah could not unite with one another. Mutual enmity and animosity

JAMIESON, FAUSSET, BROWN

verses, by Robert Stephens, the famous printer of Paris, in 1551. After the Assyrian invasion of Syria, that of Ephraim shall follow (II Kings 16:9); verses 8-11, 17-20, foretell the intestine discords in Israel after Hoshea had slain Pekah (A.D. 739), i.e., just after the Assyrian invasions, when for seven years it was stripped of magistrates and torn into factions. There are four strophes, each setting forth Ephraim's *crime* and consequent *punishment*, and ending with the formula, "For all this His anger is not turned away," etc. (vss. 12, 17, 21, and ch. 10:4). **8.** *Heading of the prophecy;* (vss. 8-12), the *first* strophe. **unto Jacob**–*against* the ten tribes [LOWTH]. **lighted upon**–fallen from heaven by divine revelation (Dan. 4:31). **9. know**–to their cost: experimentally (Hos. 9:7). **Samaria**–the capital of Ephraim (cf. as to phrase, ch. 1:1). **10. bricks**–in the East generally sun-dried, and therefore soon dissolved by rain. Granting, say the Ephraimites to the prophet's threat, that our affairs are in a ruinous state, we will restore them to more than their former magnificence. Self-confident unwillingness to see the judgments of God (ch. 26:11). **hewn stones**–(I Kings 5:17.) **sycamores**–growing abundantly on the low lands of Judea, and though useful for building on account of their antiseptic property (which induced the Egyptians to use them for the cases of their mummies), not very valuable. The *cedar*, on the other hand, was odorous, free from knots, durable, and precious (I Kings 10:27). "We will replace cottages with palaces." **11. adversaries of Rezin**–the Assyrians, who shall first attack Damascus, shall next advance "against *him*" (Ephraim). This is the punishment of Ephraim's pride in making light (vs. 10) of the judgment already inflicted by God through Tiglath-pileser (II Kings 15:29). A *second* Assyrian invasion (*Note* on the beginning of ch. 7) shall follow. The reading "princes" for "adversaries" in uncalled for. **join**–rather, "arm"; cover with armor [MAURER]. **his**–Rezin's. **12. Syrians**–Though now allies of Ephraim, after Rezin's death they shall join the Assyrians against Ephraim. "Together," in vs. 11, refers to this. Conquering nations often enlist in their armies the subject races (ch. 22:6; cf. II Kings 16:9; Jer 35:11), [ABEN-ERZA, GESENIUS]. HORSLEY less probably takes "Syrians before," as *the Syrians to the east*, i.e., not Rezin's subjects, but the *Assyrians:* "Aram" being the common name of Syrians and Assyrians. **Philistines**–of Palestine. **behind**–from the *west:* in marking the points of the compass, Orientalists face the east, which is *before* them: the west is *behind*. *The right hand* is the south: *the left*, the north. **devour**–as a ravenous beast (ch. 1:20; Jer. 10:25; 30:16; Num. 14:9). **For all this . . .**–The burden of each strophe. **13-17.** Second strophe. **turneth not**–the design of God's chastisements; not fulfilled in their case; a new cause for punishment (Jer. 2:20; 5:3). **14. head and tail**–proverbial for *the highest and lowest* (Deut. 28: 13, 44). **branch and rush**–another image for the same thought (ch. 19:15). The branch is *elevated* on the top of the tree: the rush is coarse and *low*. **15. ancient**–the older. **honourable**–the man of rank. **prophet . . . lies, . . . tail**–There were many such in Samaria (I Kings 22:6, 22, 23; cf. as to "tail," Rev. 9:19). **16. leaders . . .**–See *Margin,* and *Note*, ch. 3:12. **17. no joy**–the parallelism, "neither . . . mercy," shows that this means, He shall have *no such delight* in their youthful warriors, however much they be the nation's delight and reliance, as to *save* them from the enemy's sword (ch. 31:8; cf. Jer. 18:21). **fatherless,** etc.–not even the usual objects of His pity (Ps. 10:14, 18; 68:5; Jer. 49:11; Hos. 14:3) shall be spared. **hypocrite**–rather, a libertine, polluted [HORSLEY]. **folly**–wickedness (Ps. 14:1). **still**–Notwithstanding all these judgments, more remain. **18-21.** Third strophe. **burn**-not only *spreading* rapid-**eth**–maketh consumption, ly, but also *consuming* like fire; sin is its own punishment. **briers . . . thorns**–emblem of the wicked; especially those of low rank (ch. 27:4; II Sam. 23:6). **forest**–from the humble *shrubbery* the flame spreads to the vast *forest;* it reaches *the high*, as well as *the low*. **mount up like . . . smoke**–rather. "They (*the thickets of the forest*) shall *lift themselves proudly aloft* [the *Hebrew* is from a *Syriac* root, *a cock*, expressing stateliness of motion, from his strutting gait, HORSLEY], in (in passing into) volumes of ascending smoke" [MAURER]. **19. darkened**–viz., with smoke (vs. 18). LXX and *Chaldee* render it, "is burnt up," so MAURER, from an *Arabic* root meaning "suffocating heat." **no man . . . spare . . . brother**–intestine discord snapping asunder the dearest ties of nature. **20. hungry**–not literally. Image from unappeasable hunger, to picture internal factions, reckless of the most tender ties (vs. 19), and insatiably spreading misery and death on every side (Jer. 19:9). **eat**–

ADAM CLARKE

10. *The bricks.* "The eastern bricks," says Sir John Chardin, "are only clay well moistened with water, and mixed with straw, and dried in the sun." These bricks are properly opposed to hewn stone, so greatly superior in beauty and durableness. *The sycomores,* which, as Jerome on the place says, are timber of little worth, with equal propriety are opposed to the *cedars.* By this *mashal*, or figurative and sententious speech, they boast that they shall easily be able to repair their present losses, suffered perhaps by the first Assyrian invasion under Tiglath-pileser, and to bring their affairs to a more flourishing condition than ever.

11. *The adversaries of Rezin against him*—"The princes of Retsin against him." The princes of Retsin, the late ally of Israel, that is, the Syrians, expressly named in the next verse, shall now be excited against Israel.

12. *With open mouth*—"On every side."

18. *For wickedness.* Wickedness rageth like a fire, destroying and laying waste the nation; but it shall be its own destruction, by bringing down the fire of God's wrath, which shall burn up *the briers and the thorns;* that is, the wicked themselves. Briers and thorns are an image frequently applied in Scripture, when set on fire, to the rage of the wicked; violent, yet impotent, and of no long continuance.

MATTHEW HENRY

among the tribes of God's Israel is a sin that ripens them for ruin, and a sad symptom of ruin hastening on apace.

6. Though they should be followed with all these judgments, yet God would not let fall his controversy with them. It is the burden of this song (*v.* 12, 17, 21): *For all this his anger is not turned away, but his hand is stretched out still.* They do not repent and reform. His anger therefore continues to burn against them and *his hand is stretched out still. The people turn not to him that smites them,* and therefore he continues to smite them.

CHAPTER 10

Verses 1–4

Whether they were the princes and judges of Israel or Judah, or both, that the prophet denounced this woe against, is not certain. Here is,

I. The indictment drawn up against these oppressors, *v.* 1, 2. They are charged, 1. With making wicked laws and edicts: They *decree unrighteous decrees.* Woe to the superior powers that devise these decrees! And woe to the inferior officers that draw them up, and enter them upon record—*the writers that write the grievousness.* 2. With perverting justice in the execution of the laws that were made. 3. With enriching themselves by oppressing those that lay at their mercy. They *rob the fatherless* of the little that is left them, because they have no friend to appear for them.

II. A challenge given them with all their pride and power to outface the judgments of God (*v.* 3): "*What will you do? To whom will you flee?* You can trample upon the widows and fatherless; but *what will you do when God riseth up?*" Job xxxi. 14. "*Where will you leave your glory,* to find it again when the storm is over?" The wealth they had got was their glory, and they had no place of safety in which to deposit it.

III. Sentence passed upon them, by which they are doomed, some to imprisonment and captivity (*they shall bow down among the prisoners,* or *under them*) others to death. Those that had trampled upon the widows and fatherless shall themselves be trodden down, *v.* 4. "This it will come to," says God, "*without me,* that is, because you have deserted me and driven me away from you."

Verses 5–19

The destruction of the kingdom of Israel by Shalmaneser king of Assyria was foretold in the foregoing chapter, and it had its accomplishment in the sixth year of Hezekiah, 2 Kings xviii. 10. It was total and final, head and tail were all cut off. Now the correction of the kingdom of Judah by Sennacherib king of Assyria is foretold in this chapter; and this prediction was fulfilled in the fourteenth year of Hezekiah (2 Kings xviii. 13, 17). It ended in the confusion of the Assyrians and the great encouragement of Hezekiah and his people in their return to God.

I. God, in his sovereignty, deputed the king of Assyria to be his servant, and made use of him as a tool (*v.* 5, 6): "*O Assyrian!* know this, that thou art *the rod of my anger*; and I will send thee to be a scourge to *the people of my wrath.*" The Jews though they appeared very good, were *a hypocritical nation,* that made a profession of religion, and at this time particularly of reformation, but were not truly religious, not truly reformed. Hezekiah had in a great measure cured them of their idolatry, and now they ran into profaneness; hypocrisy is profaneness. Being a profane hypocritical nation, they are the people of God's wrath. See what a change sin made: those that had been God's chosen and hallowed people, had now become the *people of his wrath,* Amos iii. 2. The Assyrian, though he appeared very great, was but *the rod of God's anger,* an instrument God was pleased to make use of for the chastening of his people. *The staff in their hand,* wherewith they smite his people, *is his indignation*; it is his wrath that puts the staff into their hand. Sometimes God makes an idolatrous nation, that serves him not at all, a scourge to a hypocritical nation, that serves him not in sincerity and truth. The Assyrian is called the *rod of God's anger. I will send him; I will give him a charge.* The Assyrian is *to take the spoil and to take the prey,* not to shed any blood. He is to plunder the country, rifle the houses, drive away the cattle, strip the people of all their wealth and ornaments, and *tread them down like the mire of the streets.* But why must the Assyrian prevail thus against them? Not that they might be ruined, but that they might be reformed.

II. The king of Assyria, in his pride, pretended to be absolute and to act for his own honour. *God ordained him for judgment* to be an instrument of bringing his people to repentance, *howbeit he means*

JAMIESON, FAUSSET, BROWN

not literally, but *destroy* (Ps. 27:2; Job 19:22). **flesh of . . . arm**—those nearest akin: their former support (helper) (ch. 32:2) [MAURER]. **21. Manasseh, Ephraim**—the two sons of Joseph. So closely united as to form between them but one tribe; but now about to be rent into factions, thirsting for each other's blood. Disunited in all things else, but united "together against their brother Judah" (II Kings 15: 10, 30).

CHAPTER 10

Vss. 1-4. Fourth strophe. **1. them that decree**—viz., unrighteous judges. **write grievousness . . .** not the scribes, but the magistrates *who caused unjust decisions* (lit., "injustice" or "grievousness") *to be recorded* by them (ch. 65:6) [MAURER], (ch. 1:10, 23). **2. To turn aside . . .**—The effect of their conduct is to pervert the cause of the needy [HORSLEY]. In *English Version* "from judgment" means "from *obtaining justice.*" **take away the right**—"make plunder of the right" (rightful claim) [HORSLEY].

3. what will ye do—what way of escape will there be for you? **visitation**—of God's wrath (ch. 26:14; Job 35:15; Hos. 9:7). **from far**—from Assyria. **leave . . . glory**—rather, "deposit (for safekeeping) your *wealth*" [LOWTH]. So Psalm 49:17. **4. Without me**—not having Me to "flee to" (vs. 3). **bow down**—Bereft of strength they shall fall; or else, they shall lie down fettered. **under . . . under**—rather, "among" (lit., in the place of) [HORSLEY]. The "under" may be, however, explained, "trodden *under the* (feet of the) *prisoners* going into captivity," and "overwhelmed *under the* heaps of *slain* on the battlefield" [MAURER].

Chapters 10:5-34, and 11:12. DESTRUCTION OF THE ASSYRIANS; COMING OF MESSIAH; HYMN OF PRAISE. Verses 9, 11 show that Samaria was destroyed before this prophecy. It was written when Assyria proposed (a design which it soon after tried to carry out under Sennacherib) to destroy Judah and Jerusalem, as it had destroyed Samaria. This is the first part of Isaiah's prophecies under Hezekiah. Probably between 722 and 715 B.C. (see vs. 27).

5. O Assyrian . . .—rather, "What, ho [but MAURER, *Woe to the*], Assyrian! He is the rod and staff of Mine anger (*My instrument in punishing;* Jer. 51:20; Ps. 17:13). In their hands is Mine indignation" [HORSLEY, after JEROME]. I have put into the Assyrians' hands the execution of Mine indignation against My people. **6. send him**—"Kings' hearts are in the hand of the Lord" (Prov. 21:1). **hypocritical**—polluted [HORSLEY]. **nation**—Judah, against whom Sennacherib was forming designs. **of my wrath**—objects of My wrath.

give . . . charge—(Jer. 34:22.) **and to tread . . .**—HORSLEY translates: "And then to make *him* (the Assyrian) a trampling under foot like the mire of the streets" (so vs. 12; ch.33:1; Zech. 10:5). But see ch. 37:26.

ADAM CLARKE

20. *The flesh of his own arm*—"The flesh of his neighbor." Jeremiah has the very same expression: "And every one shall eat the flesh of his neighbour" (see chap. xix. 9); that is, they shall harass and destroy one another. "Manasseh [shall destroy] Ephraim; and Ephraim, Manasseh," which two tribes were most closely connected in both blood and situation as brothers and neighbors; "and both of them in the midst of their own dissensions shall agree in preying upon Judah."

CHAPTER 10

4. *Without me.* That is, without my aid; they shall be taken captive even by the captives, and shall be subdued even by the vanquished.

5. *O Assyrian*—"Ho to the Assyrian." Here begins a new and distinct prophecy, continued to the end of the twelfth chapter; and it appears from vv. 9-11 of this chapter that this prophecy was delivered after the taking of Samaria by Shalmaneser, which was in the sixth year of the reign of Hezekiah. And as the former part of it foretells the invasion of Sennacherib, and the destruction of his army, which makes the whole subject of this chapter, it must have been delivered before the fourteenth of the same reign. *The staff in their hand*—"The staff in whose hand."

MATTHEW HENRY

not so, nor does his heart think so, v. 7. He does not think that he is either God's servant or Israel's friend. God designs to correct his people, and to cure them of their hypocrisy, and bring them nearer to himself; but was that Sennacherib's design? He designs nothing but *to destroy and to cut off nations not a few,* and to make himself master of them. He designs to gratify his own covetousness and to set up for a universal monarch. By his general's letter to Hezekiah, written in his name, vainglory and arrogance seem to have entered into the spirit of the man. His haughtiness and presumption are here described, partly to represent him as ridiculous and partly to assure the people of God that he would be brought down. He boasts of the great things he had done to other nations. He had made their kings his courtiers (*v.* 8): "*My princes are altogether kings.* Those that are now my princes are such as have been kings." Or those that were absolute princes in their own dominions held their crowns under him, and did him homage. He had made himself master of cities. He names several (*v.* 9) that were all alike reduced by him. *Calno* soon yielded *as Carchemish* did, *Hamath* could not hold out any more than *Arpad,* and *Samaria* had become his as well as *Damascus.* He *found out the kingdoms of the idols* and found out ways to make them his own, *v.* 10. Sennacherib vainly imagined that every conquest of a kingdom was the conquest of a god. He had enlarged his own dominions, and *removed the bounds of the people* (*v.* 13), enclosing many large territories within the limits of his own kingdom. *I have robbed their treasures.* Great conquerors are often no better than great robbers. "*I have put down the inhabitants as a valiant man.* Those that sat high I have humbled." He boasts he had done all this by his own policy and power (*v.* 13): "*By the strength of my hand,* for I am valiant; *and by my wisdom, for I am prudent.*" He had done all this with ease, and had made but a diversion of it, as if he had been taking birds' nests (*v.* 14): *My hand has found as a nest the riches of the people.* "*As one gathers the eggs that are left* in the nest by the dam, so easily *have I gathered all the earth.*" Like Alexander, he thought he had conquered the world. He threatens what he will do to Jerusalem, which he was now about to lay siege to, *v.* 10, 11. He blasphemously calls the God of Israel an *idol,* and sets him on a level with the false gods of other nations, as if none were the true God but Mithras, the sun, whom he worshipped. He might have known that the worshippers of the God of Israel were expressly forbidden to make any graven images, and if any did it must be by stealth, and therefore they could not be so rich and pompous as those of other nations. If he means the ark and the mercy-seat, he speaks like himself, very foolishly. Those who make external pomp and splendour a mark of the true church go by the same rule. Because he had conquered Samaria he concluded Jerusalem would fall. But it did not follow; for Jerusalem adhered to her God, whereas Samaria had forsaken him.

III. God, in his justice, rebukes his pride and reads his doom.

1. He shows the vanity of his insolent and audacious boasts (*v.* 15): *Shall the axe boast itself against him that hews therewith? or shall the saw magnify itself against him that shaketh it?* "O what a dust do I make!" said the fly upon the cart-wheel in the fable. "What destruction do I make among the trees!" says the axe. Two ways the axe may be said to *boast itself against him that hews with it*: By way of resistance and opposition. Sennacherib blasphemed God, threatened to serve him as he had served the gods of the nations; now this was as if the axe should fly in the face of him that hews with it. The tool striving with the workman is no less absurd than the clay striving with the potter; and as it is a thing not to be justified that men should fight against God with the wit, and wealth, and power, which he gives them, so it is a thing not to be suffered. By way of competition. Shall the axe take to itself the praise of the work it is employed in? So absurd was it for Sennacherib to say, *By the strength of my hand I have done it, and by my wisdom, v.* 13. It is as if the rod, when it is shaken, should boast that it guides the hand which shakes it; whereas, *when the staff is lifted up, is it not wood still?*

2. He foretells his fall and ruin. When God had done his work by him he would then do his work upon him, *v.* 12. In reference to Sennacherib's invasion, God designed to do good to Zion and Jerusalem by this providence. When God brings his people into trouble it is to bring sin to their remembrance, and to awaken them to a sense of their duty, to teach them to pray and to love and help one another. When these points are, in some measure, gained by the affliction, it shall be removed, in mercy (Lev. xxvi. 41,

JAMIESON, FAUSSET, BROWN

7. meaneth not so—He is only thinking of his own schemes, while God is overruling them to *His* purposes. **think**—intend. Sinners' plans are no less culpable, though they by them unconsciously fulfil God's designs (Ps. 76:10; Mic. 4:12). So Joseph's brethren (Gen. 50:20; Prov. 16:4). The *sinner's motive,* not the *result* (which depends on God), will be the test in judgment. **heart to destroy . . . not a few**—Sennacherib's ambition was not confined to Judea. His plan was also to conquer Egypt and Ethiopia (ch. 20; Zech. 1:15).

8-11. Vauntings of the Assyrians. Illustrated by the self-laudatory inscriptions of Assyria deciphered by HINCKS. **princes . . . kings**—Eastern satraps and governors of provinces often had the title and diadem of kings. Hence the title, "King of kings," implying the greatness of Him who was *over* them (Ezek. 26:7; Ezra 7:12). **9. Is not . . . as**—Was there any one of these cities able to withstand me? Not one. So Rabshakeh vaunts (ch. 36:19). **Calno**—Calneh, built by Nimrod (Gen. 10:10), once his capital, on the Tigris. **Carchemish**—Circesium, on the Euphrates. Taken afterwards by Necho, king of Egypt; and retaken by Nebuchadnezzar: by the Euphrates (Jer. 46:2). **Hamath**—in Syria, north of Canaan (Gen. 10:18). Taken by Assyria about 753 B.C. From it colonists were planted by Assyria in Samaria. **Arpad**—near Hamath. **Samaria**—now overthrown. **Damascus**—(ch. 17). **10, 11. found**—unable to resist me: *hath overcome* (so Ps. 21:8). **and whose**—rather, "and their." This clause, down to "Samaria," is parenthetical. **excel**—were more powerful. He regards Jerusalem as idolatrous, an opinion which it often had given too much ground for: Jehovah was in his view the mere *local* god of Judea, as Baal of the countries where it was adored, nay, inferior in power to some national gods (ch. 36:19, 20, 37:12). See in opposition, ch. 37:20; 46:1. **As my hand . . . shall I not,** *as* **I have**—a double protasis. Agitation makes one accumulate sentences.
13. I am prudent—He ascribes his success to his own prudence, not to God's providence. **removed the bounds**—set aside old, and substituted new boundaries of kingdoms at will. A criminal act, as Jehovah Himself had appointed the boundaries of the nations (Deut. 32:8). **treasures**—"hoarded treasures" [HORSLEY]. **put down . . . inhabitants like . . .** —rather, "as a valiant man, I have brought down *(from their seats)* those *seated*" (viz., on thrones; as in Ps. 2:4; 29:10; 55:19. The *Hebrew* for "He that abideth," is *He that sitteth on a throne*); otherwise, "I have *brought down* (as *captives into Assyria,* which lay *lower* than Judea; therefore 'brought *down,'* cf. ch. 36:1, 10), *the inhabitants*" [MAURER].
14. nest—implying the ease with which he carried off all before him. **left**—by the parent bird. **none . . . moved . . . wing**—image from an angry bird resisting the robbery of its "nest." **peeped**—chirped even low (ch. 8:19). No resistance was offered me, of deed, or even *word.* **15.** Shall the instrument boast against Him who uses it? Through *free* in a sense, and carrying out his own plans, the Assyrian was unconciously carrying out *God's* purposes. **shaketh it**—moves it back and forward. **staff . . . lift . . . itself . . . no wood**—rather, "as if the staff (*man,* the instrument of God's judgments on his fellow man) should set aside (Him who is) not wood" (*not* a mere instrument, as *man*). On "no wood" cf. Deut. 32:21, "that which is *not God*"; ch. 31:8 shows that God is meant here by "not wood" [MAURER].

12. whole work—His entire plan is regard to the *punishment* of the Jews (vss. 5-7). **Zion**—the royal residence, the court, princes and nobles; as distinguished from "Jerusalem," the *people* in general. **fruit**—the result of, i.e., the plants emanating from. **stout**—*Hebrew,* "greatness of," i.e., pride of. **glory**—haughtiness.

ADAM CLARKE

F. B. MEYER:

"Shall the axe boast itself against him that heweth therewith?" (v. 15). The Assyrian thought that he was acting on his own impulse, and in his pride congratulated himself on his exploits. The prophet reminded him that it was not so. He was only an axe, a saw, a rod, in the hand of the Eternal God whose supremacy he was inclined to challenge and set at nought.

This thought underlay the apostle's reply to those who magnified him against Apollos or Cephas. What are we, he cries, but ministers through whom ye believed, even as God granted to each of us? We are only instruments of God's husbandry, implements through which He fulfills his plans (1 Cor. 3). It dates an era in the life, when we cease to work for God, and allow God to work through us.

Thoughts like these correct alike pride and despondency. Pride, because whatever is the result of our work, we can no more take the credit of it than the pen that wrote the "Paradise Lost" could take to itself the credit of its production. At the best, it is not you, but the grace of God that was with you. You are only a pipe in the organ, but the breath that educed your music was divine. And in despondency it is very helpful to remember that if we are nothing, God is all-sufficient; if we have failed, it is the more needful for Him to exert more power. Throw back the responsibility of all results on God. Only see to it that you are a polished shaft, an unblunted saw, and leave Him to do through you what He will.—*Great Verses Through the Bible*

15. *No wood*—"Its master."

MATTHEW HENRY

42). The rod shall *accomplish that for which God sends it.* When God had wrought this work of grace for his people he would work a work of wrath upon their invaders: *I will punish the fruit of the stout heart of the king of Assyria.* This attempt upon Zion and Jerusalem should certainly be baffled, and come to nothing, *v.* 16, 19. God himself will do it, as *the Lord of hosts,* and as *the light of Israel.* We are sure he can do it, for he is *the Lord of hosts,* of all the hosts of heaven and earth. We have reason to hope he will do it, for he is *the light of Israel, and his Holy One.* This destruction shall be as a consumption of the body by a disease: *The Lord shall send leanness among his fatnesses,* or *his fat ones.* His numerous army, that was like a body covered with fatness, shall be diminished, and waste away, and become like a skeleton. *Under his glory he will kindle a burning, as the burning of a fire,* which shall lay his army in ruins as suddenly as a raging fire lays a stately house in ashes. *The light of Israel shall be for a fire* to the Assyrians, as the same pillar of cloud was a light to the Israelites and a terror to the Egyptians in the Red Sea. *It shall burn and devour its thorns and briers,* his officers and soldiers, as thorns and briers. "Even *the glory of his forest* (*v.* 18), the choice troops of his army, that he valued as men do their timber-trees (the glory of their forest) or their fruit-trees (the glory of their Carmel), shall be put as briers and thorns before the fire." The prophet tells us the army would hereby be reduced to a very small number: *The rest of the trees of his forest shall be few.* Those few who remained should be quite dispirited: *They shall be as when a standard-bearer fainteth.*

Verses 20–23

The prophet had said (*v.* 12) that *the Lord would perform his whole work upon Mount Zion and upon Jerusalem,* by Sennacherib's invading the land.

I. The conversion of some, to whom this providence should yield the peaceable fruit of righteousness, though for the present it was not joyous, but grievous; these are but a remnant (*v.* 22), *the remnant of Israel* (*v.* 20), *the remnant of Jacob* (*v.* 21). This remnant of Israel are said to be *such as had escaped of the house of Jacob,* such as escaped the corruptions of the house of Jacob, and kept their integrity in times of common apostasy. "They *shall no more again stay upon him that smote them,* shall never depend upon the Assyrians for help against their other enemies, finding that they are themselves their worst enemies." "*The remnant shall return* (that was signified by the name of the prophet's son, *Shearjashub, ch.* vii. 3), *even the remnant of Jacob.* They shall return, after the raising of the siege of Jerusalem, not only to the quiet possession of their houses and lands, but to God and to their duty; they shall repent, and pray, and seek his face, and reform their lives." This promise of the conversion and salvation of a remnant of Israel is applied by the apostle (Rom. ix. 27) to the remnant of the Jews which at the first preaching of the gospel received and entertained it.

II. The consumption of others: *The Lord God of hosts shall make a consumption, v.* 23. This meant the consumption of the estates and families of many of the Jews by the Assyrian army. It is *determined,* not only that there shall be such a consumption, but it is *cut out* (so the word is); it is particularly appointed how far it shall extend and how long it shall continue. God will justly bring this consumption upon a provoking people, but he will wisely and graciously set bounds to it.

Verses 24–34

The prophet, in his preaching, distinguishes between the precious and the vile. He speaks terror, in Sennacherib's invasion, to the hypocrites, who were the *people of God's wrath, v.* 6. But here he speaks comfort to the sincere, who were the people of God's love.

I. An exhortation to God's people not to be frightened at this threatening calamity. *Let the sinners in Zion be afraid* (*ch.* xxxiii. 14); but *O my people, that dwellest in Zion, be not afraid of the Assyrian, v.* 24.

II. The silencing of their fear. The Assyrian shall do nothing against them but what God has appointed and determined. The storm shall soon blow over (*v.* 25): *Yet a very little while—a little, little while* (so the word is), *and the indignation shall cease, even my anger,* which is *the staff in their hand* (*v.* 5). The enemy that threatens them shall himself be reckoned with. He *lifted up his staff* against Zion, but God *shall stir up a scourge for him* (*v.* 26); he is a terror to God's people, but God will be a terror to him. The prophet, for the encouragement of God's people, quotes precedents. The destruction of the Assyrian shall be *According to the slaughter of Midian* (which was effected by an invisible power), and as,

JAMIESON, FAUSSET, BROWN

16. fat ones—(ch. 5:17.) The robust and choice soldiers of Assyria (Ps. 78:31, where "fattest" answers in the parallelism to "chosen," or "young men," *Margin*). **leanness**—carrying out the image on "fat ones." *Destruction* (Ps. 106:15). Fulfilled (ch. 37:36). **his glory**—Assyria's *nobles.* So in ch. 5:13 *Margin;* ch. 8:7. **kindle**—a new image from *fire* consuming quickly dry materials (Zech. 12:6). **17, 18. light of Israel**—carrying out the image in the end of vs. 16. *Jehovah,* who is a *light* to *Israel,* shall be the "fire" (Deut. 4:24; Heb. 12:29) that shall ignite the "thorns," (the Assyrians, like dry fuel, a ready prey to flame). **18. glory of his forest**—The *common* soldiers, the *princes, officers,* etc., all alike *together,* shall be consumed (*Note,* ch. 9:18). **in one day**—(ch. 37:36.) **fruitful field**—lit., "Carmel," a rich mountain in the tribe of Asher. Figurative for Sennacherib's mighty army. Perhaps alluding to his own boasting words about to be uttered (ch. 37:24), "I will enter the forest of his Carmel." **soul and body**—proverbial for utterly; the *entire* man is made up of *soul and body.* **as when a standard-bearer fainteth**—rather, "they shall be as when a *sick man* (from a *Syriac* root) wastes away." Cf. "leanness," i.e., wasting destruction (vs. 16) [MAURER]. Or, "there shall be an entire *dissipation,* like a perfect *melting*" (viz., of the Assyrian army) [HORSLEY]. **19. rest**—those who shall survive the destruction of the host. **his forest**—same image as in vs. 18, for the once dense army. **child . . . write**—so few that a child might count them.

20-22. The effect on the "remnant" (contrasted with the Assyrian remnant, vs. 19); viz., those who shall be left after the invasion of Sennacherib, will be a return from dependence on external idolatrous nations, as Assyria and Egypt (II Kings 18:21; 16:7-9), to the God of the theocracy; fulfilled in part in the pious Hezekiah's days; but from the *future* aspect under which Paul, in Rom. 9:27, 28 (cf. "short work" with "whole work," vs. 12, here), regards the whole prophecy, the "remnant," "who stay upon the Lord," probably will receive their fullest realization in the portion of Jews left after that Antichrist shall have been overthrown, who shall "return" unto the Lord (ch. 6:13; 7:3; Zech. 12:9, 10; 14:2, 3; Zeph. 3:12). **21. mighty God**—(ch. 9:6) the God who shall have evinced such *might* in destroying Israel's enemies. As the Assyrians in Sennacherib's reign did not carry off *Judah* captive, the returning "remnant" cannot *mainly* refer to this time. **22. yet**—rather in the sense in which Paul quotes it (Rom. 9:27), "Though Israel be now numerous as the sand, a remnant *only* of them shall return"—the great majority shall perish. The reason is added, Because "the consumption (fully completed destruction) *is* decreed (lit., *decided on, brought to an issue*), it overfloweth (ch. 30:28; 8:8) with *justice*"; i.e., the infliction of just punishment (ch. 5:16) [MAURER]. **23. even determined**—"A consumption, *and whatever is determined,*" or *decreed* [MAURER]. **midst**—Zion, the central point of the earth as to Jehovah's presence. **land**—Israel. But LXX, "in the whole *habitable world.*" So *English Version* (Rom. 9:28), "upon the *earth.*"

24. Therefore—Return to the main proposition, Assyria's ultimate punishment, though employed as God's "rod" to chastise Judea for a time. **O my people**—God's tenderness towards His elect nation. **after the manner of Egypt**—as Egypt and Pharaoh oppressed thee. Implying, too, as Israel was nevertheless *delivered* from them, so now it would be from the Assyrian Sennacherib. The antithesis in vs. 26 requires this interpretation [MAURER]. **25. For**—Be not afraid (vs. 24), *for . . .*—**indignation . . . cease**—The punishments of God against Israel shall be consummated and ended (ch. 26:20; Dan. 11:36). "Till the indignation be accomplished," etc. **mine anger**—shall turn to their (the Assyrians') destruction. **26. slaughter of**—"stroke upon." **Midian**—(ch. 9:4; Judg. 7:25). **as his rod was upon the sea**—rather, understanding "stroke" from the previous clause, "according to the stroke of His rod upon the

ADAM CLARKE

16. *And under his glory.* That is, all that he could boast of as great and strong in his army, expressed afterwards, v. 18, by "the glory of his forest, and of his fruitful field."

17. *And it shall burn and devour his thorns*—"And he shall burn and consume his thorn." The *briers* and *thorns* are the common people; "the glory of his forest" is the nobles and those of highest rank and importance. See note on chap. ix. 17, and compare Ezek. xx. 47. The fire of God's wrath shall destroy them, both great and small; it shall consume them "from the soul to the flesh," a proverbial expression—*soul and body,* as we say. It shall consume them entirely and altogether; and the few that escape shall be looked upon as having escaped from the most imminent danger; "as a firebrand plucked out of the fire," Amos iv. 11.

21. *The remnant shall return . . . unto the mighty God. El gibbor,* the mighty or conquering God; the Messiah, the same Person mentioned in v. 6 of the preceding chapter.

24. *After the manner of Egypt*—"In the way of Egypt." Sennacherib, soon after his return from his Egyptian expedition, which, I imagine, took him up three years, invested Jerusalem. He is represented by the prophet as lifting up his rod in his march from Egypt, and threatening the people of God, as Pharaoh and the Egyptians had done when they pursued them to the Red Sea. But God in His turn will lift up His rod over the sea, as He did at that time, in the way, or after the manner, of Egypt. And as Sennacherib has imitated the Egyptians in his threats, and came full of rage against them from the same quarter, so God will act over again the same part that He had taken formerly in Egypt, and overthrow their enemies in as signal a manner.

25. *The indignation*—"Mine indignation."

26. *And as his rod was upon the sea*—"And like His rod which He lifted up over the sea."

MATTHEW HENRY

at the rock of Oreb, one of the princes of Midian, after the battle, was slain, so shall Sennacherib be after the defeat of his forces. *As his rod was upon the sea*, the Red Sea, to divide it for the escape of Israel and then to close it for the destruction of their pursuers so shall his rod now be *lifted up, after the manner of Egypt*, for the deliverance of Jerusalem and the destruction of the Assyrian. They shall be wholly delivered from the power of the Assyrian, and from the fear of it, *v.* 27. The yoke shall not only be taken away, but it *shall be destroyed, because of the anointing:* (1) For Hezekiah's sake, the anointed of the Lord, an active reformer, dear to God. (2) For David's sake. This is why God would defend Jerusalem from Sennacherib (*ch.* xxxvii. 35). (3) For his people Israel's sake, the good people among them. (4) For the sake of the Messiah, the Anointed of God.

III. The terror of the enemy and the terror with which many were struck, *v.* 28.

1. How formidable the Assyrians were! Here is a particular description of the march of Sennacherib, what swift advances he made: *He has come to Aiath*, &c. *At Michmash he has laid up his carriages*, as if he had no further occasion for his heavy artillery, so easily was every place reduced; or the store-cities of Judah, fortified, had now become his magazines. Some remarkable pass he had taken: *They have gone over the passage.*

2. How cowardly the men of Judah were, the degenerate seed of that lion's whelp. They *fled* upon the first alarm. And *poor Anathoth*, a priests' city, that should have been a pattern of courage, shrieks louder than any, *v.* 30. With respect to those that *gathered themselves* together, it was not to fight, but to flee by consent, *v* 31. This shows how fast the news of the enemy's progress flew through the kingdom: *He has come to Aiath*, says one, nay, says another, *He has passed to Migron*, &c.

3. How impotent his attempt upon Jerusalem shall be: *He shall remain at Nob*, whence he may see Mount Zion, and there *he shall shake his hand* against it, *v.* 32. He shall threaten it, and that shall be all.

4. How fatal it would prove to himself. When he ***shakes his hand at Jerusalem, the Lord shall lop the bough with terror and cut down the thickets of the forest***, *v.* 33, 34. The high and stately trees shall be hewn down; that is, the haughty shall be humbled. *The thickets of the forest he shall cut down.* The Assyrian soldiers under arms, their spears erect, looked like a forest, like Lebanon; but, when in one night they all became as dead, Lebanon was of a sudden cut down *by a mighty one*, by the destroying angel, and, if this be the exit of that proud invader, let not God's people be afraid of him.

JAMIESON, FAUSSET, BROWN

Red Sea" (Exod. 14:16, 26). His "rod" on the Assyrian (vss. 24, 26) stands in bold contrast to the Assyrian used as a "rod" to strike others (vs. 5). **after the manner of Egypt**—as He lifted it up against Egypt at the Red Sea. **27. his burden**—the Assyrians' oppression (ch. 9:3). Judah was still tributary to Assyria; Hezekiah had not yet revolted, as he did in the beginning of Sennacherib's reign. **because of**—(Hos. 10:15.) **the anointing**—viz., Messiah (Dan. 9:24). Just as in ch. 9:4-6, the "breaking of the yoke of" the enemies' "burden and staff" is attributed to *Messiah, "For* unto us a child is born," etc., so it is here. MAURER not so well translates, "Because of the fatness"; an image of the Assyrians' fierce and wanton pride drawn from a well-fed bull tossing off the yoke (Deut. 32:15). So vs. 16 above, and ch. 5:17, "*fat* ones." **28-32.** Onward gradual march of Sennacherib's army towards Jerusalem, and the panic of the inhabitants vividly pictured before the eyes. **come to**—*come upon* as a sudden invader (Gen. 34:27). **Aiath**—same as Ai (Josh. 7:2; Neh. 7:32). In the north of Benjamin; so the other towns also; all on the line of march to Jerusalem. **Michmash**—nine miles northeast of Jerusalem. **laid up . . . carriages**—He has left his heavier *baggage* (so "carriages" for the *things carried,* Acts 21:15) at Michmash, so as to be more lightly equipped for the siege of Jerusalem. So I Sam. 17:22; 25:13; 30:24 [JEROME and MAURER]. **29. passage**—the jaws of the wady or defile at Michmash (I Sam. 13:23; 14: 4, 5). **lodging**—their quarters for the night, after having passed the defile which might have been easily guarded against them. **Ramah**—near Geba; seven miles from Jerusalem. **Gibeah of Saul**—his birthplace and residence, in Benjamin (I Sam. 11:4), distinct from Gibeah *of Judah* (Josh. 15:57). **30. daughter of Gallim**—*Gallim and her sons* (*Note,* ch. 1:8; II Kings 19:21). "Cry aloud in consternation." **Laish**—not the town in Dan (Judg. 18:7), but one of the same name near Jerusalem (I Maccabees 9:9). **Anathoth**—three miles from Jerusalem in Benjamin; the birthplace of Jeremiah. "Poor" is applied to it in pity, on account of the impending calamity. Others translate, Answer her, O Anathoth. **31. Madmenah**—not the city in Simeon (Josh. 15:31), but a village near Jerusalem. **removed**—fled from fear. **gather themselves to flee**—"put their goods in a place of safety" [MAURER]. **32. that day**—lit., "As yet *this* (one only) day (is allowed to the soldiers) for remaining (halting for rest) at Nob"; northeast of Jerusalem on Olivet; a town of the priests (Neh. 11: 32). **daughter**—rightly substituted for the Chetib reading, *house*. His "shaking his hand" in menace implies that he is now at Nob. *within sight of* Jerusalem. **33. bough**—lit., the "beauty" of the tree; "the beautiful branch." **high ones of stature**—"the upright *stem,"* as distinguished from the previous "boughs" [HORSLEY]. **34.** This verse and vs. 33 describe the sudden arrest and overthrow of Sennacherib in the height of his success; vss. 18, 19; Ezek. 31:3, etc., 14, etc., contain the same image; "Lebanon" and its forest are the Assyrian army; the "iron" axe that fells the forest refers to the stroke which destroyed the one hundred and eighty-five thousand Assyrians (II Kings 19:35). The "Mighty One" is Jehovah (vs. 21; ch. 9:6).

ADAM CLARKE

28. *He is come to Aiath.* A description of the march of Sennacherib's army approaching Jerusalem in order to invest it, and of the terror and confusion spreading and increasing through the several places as he advanced; expressed with great brevity, but finely diversified. The places here mentioned are all in the neighborhood of Jerusalem, from *Ai* northward, to *Nob* westward of it; from which last place he might probably have a prospect of Mount *Zion. Anathoth* was within three Roman miles of Jerusalem, according to Eusebius, Jerome, and Josephus. *Nob* was probably still nearer. And it should seem from this passage of Isaiah that Sennacherib's army was destroyed near the latter of these places.

29. *They are gone over the passage*—"They have passed the strait." The strait here mentioned is that of Michmas, a very narrow passage between two sharp hills or rocks (see 1 Sam. xiv. 4-5), where a great army might have been opposed with advantage by a very inferior force.

MATTHEW HENRY — CHAPTER 11

Verses 1-9

The prophet had before spoken of a child that should be born, on whose shoulders the government should be. He had said (*ch.* x. 27) that *the yoke should be destroyed because of the anointing*; now here he tells us on whom that anointing should rest.

I. The Messiah should, in due time, arise out of the house of David, as that *branch* of the Lord which he had said (*ch.* iv. 2) should be glorious. This branch should arise—from *Jesse*. He should be the son of David, with whom the covenant of royalty was made. David is often called *the son of Jesse*, and Christ is called so. He is called a *rod*, and a *branch*; both the words here used signify a small, tender product, a *twig* and a *sprig*, such as is easily broken off. The enemies of God's church were just before compared to stately boughs (*ch.* x. 33), but Christ to a tender branch (*ch.* liii. 2); yet he shall be victorious over them. He is said to come out of Jesse rather than David, because Jesse lived and died in meanness and obscurity; his family was of small account (1 Sam. xviii. 18). He comes forth out of the *stem*, or *stump*, of Jesse. The house of David was reduced and brought very low at the time of Christ's birth, witness the obscurity and poverty of Joseph and Mary. The Chaldee paraphrase reads this, *There shall come forth a King from the sons of Jesse, and the Messiah* (or

JAMIESON, FAUSSET, BROWN — CHAPTER 11

Vss. 1-16. From the local and temporary national deliverance the prophet passes by the law of suggestion in an easy transition to the end of all prophecy—the everlasting deliverance under Messiah's reign, not merely His first coming, but chiefly His second coming. The *language* and illustrations are still drawn from the temporary national subject, with which he began, but the glories described pertain to Messiah's reign. Hezekiah cannot, as some think, be the subject; for he was already come, whereas the "stem of Jesse" was yet future ("shall come") (cf. Mic. 4:11, etc.; 5:1, 2; Jer. 23:5, 6; 33:15, 16; Rom. 15:12). **1. rod**—When the proud "boughs" of "Lebanon" (ch. 10:33, 34, the Assyrians) are lopped, and the vast "*forests* cut down" amidst all this rage, a seemingly humble *rod* shall come out of Jesse (Messiah), who shall retrieve the injuries done by the Assyrian "*rod*" to Israel (ch. 10:5, 6, 18, 19). **stem**—lit., "the stump" of a tree cut close by the roots: happily expressing the *depressed* state of the royal house of David, owing to the hostile storm (ch. 10:18, 19), when Messiah should arise from it, to raise it to more than its pristine glory. Luke 2:7 proves this (ch. 53:2; *Note,* ch. 8:6; cf. Job 14:7, 8). **Branch**—Scion. He is nevertheless also the "root" (vs. 10; Rev. 5:5; 22:16. "Root and offspring" combines both, Zech. 3:8; 6:12).

ADAM CLARKE — CHAPTER 11

The prophet had described the destruction of the Assyrian army under the image of a mighty forest, consisting of flourishing trees growing thick together, and of a great height; of Lebanon itself crowned with lofty cedars, but cut down and laid level with the ground by the axe wielded by the hand of some powerful and illustrious agent. In opposition to this image he represents the great Person who makes the subject of this chapter as a slender twig shooting out from the trunk of an old tree, cut down, lopped to the very root, and decayed; which tender plant, so weak in appearance, should nevertheless become fruitful and prosper. This contrast shows plainly the connection between this and the preceding chapter, which is moreover expressed by the connecting particle; and we have here a remarkable instance of that method so common with the prophets, and particularly with Isaiah, of taking occasion, from the mention of some great temporal deliverance, to launch out into the display of the spiritual deliverance of God's people by the Messiah. For that this prophecy relates to the Messiah we have the express authority of St. Paul, Rom. xv. 12. Thus in the latter part of Isaiah's

MATTHEW HENRY

Christ) *shall be anointed out of his sons' sons.*

II. He should be every way qualified for that great work to which he was designed. This tender branch should be so watered with the dews of heaven as to become a strong rod for a sceptre to rule, *v.* 2. *The Spirit of the Lord shall rest upon him.* He shall have the Spirit not by measure, but without measure, the fulness of the Godhead dwelling in him, Col. i. 19; ii. 9. He began his preaching with this (Luke iv. 18), *The Spirit of the Lord is upon me.* He shall have *the spirit of wisdom and understanding, of counsel and knowledge.* He shall know how to administer the affair of his spiritual kingdom to the glory of God and the welfare of men. He was famed for courage in his teaching the way of God in truth, and not caring for any man, Matt. xxii. 16.

III. He should be accurate, and exact in the administration of his government and the exercise of the power committed to him (*v.* 3): The Spirit wherewith he shall be clothed *shall make him of quick understanding in the fear of the Lord.* Jesus Christ had the spirit without measure, that he might perfectly understand his undertaking.

IV. He should be just and righteous in all the acts of his government. *He shall not judge after the sight of his eyes,* with respect of persons (Job xxxiv. 19), nor *reprove after the hearing of his ears,* by the representations of others, as men commonly do; nor by the fair words they speak, *calling him, Lord, Lord;* but he will judge by the hidden man of the heart, and the inward principles men are governed by, of which he is an infallible witness. He will judge righteous judgment (*v.* 5): *Righteousness shall be the girdle of his loins.* It shall constantly compass him and shall be his honour; he shall gird himself for every action, shall gird on his sword for war in righteousness. *With righteousness shall he judge the poor;* he shall judge in favour and defence of those that have right on their side, though they are poor in the world, and because they are poor in spirit. Christ is the poor man's King, Ps. lxxii. 2, 4. He shall *debate with evenness for the meek of the earth,* or of the land. Some read it, *He shall reprove or correct the meek of the earth with equity.* If his own people, the meek of the land, do amiss, he will *visit their transgression with the rod. But he shall smite the earth,* the man of the earth, that doth oppress (Ps. x. 18) *with the rod of his mouth,* the word of his mouth, speaking terror and ruin to them. *With the breath of his lips,* by the operation of his Spirit, according to his word, *he shall slay the wicked.*

V. That there should be great peace and tranquillity under his government (*ch.* ix. 6). Peace signifies two things:

1. Unity or concord, intimated in these figurative promises, that even *the wolf shall dwell* peaceably *with the lamb;* men of the most fierce and furious dispositions shall have their temper so strangely altered by the grace of Christ that they shall live in love even with the weakest and such as formerly were an easy prey. Christ, who is our peace, came to slay all enmities and to settle lasting friendships among his followers, particularly between Jews and Gentiles. *The leopard shall* not only not tear the kid, but shall *lie down with her:* even *their young ones shall lie down together,* and shall be trained up in blessed amity. *The lion* shall cease to be ravenous and *shall eat straw like the ox,* as some think all the beasts of prey did before the fall. *The asp* and *the cockatrice* shall cease to be venomous, so that parents shall let their children *play* with them. A generation of vipers shall become a seed of saints. This is fulfilled in the wonderful effect of the gospel upon the minds of those that sincerely embrace it; it changes the nature, and makes those that trampled on the meek of the earth, not only meek like them, but affectionate towards them. Some hope it shall yet have a further accomplishment in the latter days, when *swords shall be beaten into ploughshares.*

2. Safety or security. Christ, the great Shepherd, shall take such care of his flock that they shall not only not destroy one another, but no enemy from without shall be permitted to give them any molestation. God's people shall be delivered, not only from evil, but from the fear of it. The effect of it shall be tractableness, and a willingness to receive instruction: *A little child shall lead those* who formerly scorned to be controlled by the strongest man. The cause of it shall be the knowledge of God. The more there is of that the more there is of a disposition to peace. *The earth shall be full of the knowledge of the Lord,* which shall extinguish men's heats and animosities. There is much more of the knowledge of God to be got by the gospel of Christ than could be got by the law of Moses.

JAMIESON, FAUSSET, BROWN

2. Spirit of the Lord—JEHOVAH. The Spirit by which the prophets spake: for Messiah was to be a *Prophet* (ch. 61:1; Deut. 18:15, 18). *Seven* gifts of the Holy Spirit are specified, to imply that the *perfection* of them was to be in Him. Cf. "the *seven* Spirits" (Rev. 1:4), i.e., the Holy Ghost in His *perfect fulness: seven* being the sacred number. The prophets had only a portion out of the "*fulness*" in the Son of God (John 1: 16; 3:34; Col. 1:19). **rest**—permanently; not merely *come* upon Him (Num. 11:25, 26). **wisdom**—(I Cor. 1:30; Eph. 1:17; Col. 2:3.) **understanding**—coupled with "wisdom," being its fruit. Discernment and discrimination (Matt. 22:18; John 2:25). **counsel . . . might**—the faculty of *forming* counsels, and that of *executing* them (ch. 28:29). Counsellor (ch. 9:6). **knowledge**—of the deep things of God (Matt. 11:27). The knowledge of Him gives us true knowledge (Eph. 1:17). **fear of the Lord**—reverential, obedient fear. The first step towards true "knowledge" (Job 28:28; Ps. 111:10). **3. make him of quick understanding**—lit., *quick-scented* in the fear of Jehovah"; endowed with a singular sagacity in discerning the genuine principle of religious fear of God, when it lies dormant in the yet unawakened sinner (Matt. 12:20; Acts 10; 16:14) [HORSLEY]. But MAURER, "He shall *delight* in the fear of God." The *Hebrew* means "to delight in the odors" of anything (Exod. 30:38; Amos 5:21); "smell," i.e., "delight in." **after . . . sight**—according to mere external appearances (John 7:24; 8:15; Jas. 2:1; I Sam. 16:7). Herein Messiah is represented a just Judge and Ruler (Deut. 1:16, 17). **reprove**—"decide," as the parallelism shows. **after . . . ears**—by mere plausible hearsays, but by the true merits of each case (John 6:64; Rev. 2:23). **4. judge**—see that impartial justice is done them. **reprove**—"decide." But LOWTH, "work conviction in." "Judge" may mean here "rule," as in Psalm 67:4. Cf. "meek . . . earth" with Matthew 5:5, and Revelation 11:15. **earth**—its *ungodly* inhabitants, answering to "the wicked" in the parallel, and in antithesis to the "poor" and "meek," viz., in spirit, the humble pious (Matt. 5:3). It is at the same time implied that "the earth" will be extraordinarily wicked when He shall come to judge and reign. His reign shall therefore be ushered in with judgments on the apostates (Ps. 2:9-12; Luke 18:8; Rev. 2:27). **rod of . . . mouth**—condemning sentences which proceed from His mouth against the wicked (Rev. 1:16; 2:16; 19:15, 21). **breath of . . . lips**—his judicial decisions (ch. 30:28; Job 15:30; Rev. 19:20; 20:9-12). He as the Word of God (Rev. 19:13-15) comes to strike that blow which shall decide His claim to the kingdom, previously usurped by Satan, and "the beast" to whom Satan delegates his power. It will be a day of judgment to the Gentile dispensation, as the first coming was to the Jews. Cf. a type of the "rod" (Num. 17:2-10). **5. righteousness . . . girdle**—(Rev. 1:13; 19:11.) The antitypical High Priest (Exod. 28:4). The *girdle* secures firmly the rest of the garments (I Peter 1:13). So "truth" gives firm consistency to the whole character (Eph. 5:14). In ch. 59:17, "righteousness" is His *breastplate.* **6. wolf . . . lamb**—Each animal is coupled with that one which is its natural prey. A fit state of things under the "Prince of Peace" (ch. 65:25; Ezek. 34: 25; Hos. 2:18). These may be figures for *men* of corresponding animal-like characters (Ezek. 22:27; 38:13; Jer. 5:6; 13:23; Matt. 7:15; Luke 10:3). Still a *literal* change in the relations of animals to man and each other, restoring the state in Eden, is a more likely interpretation. Cf. Genesis 2:19, 20, with Psalm 8:6-8, which describes the restoration to man, in the person of "the Son of man," of the lost dominion over the animal kingdom of which he had been designed to be the merciful vicegerent under God, for the good of his animal subjects (Rom. 8: 19-22). **7. feed**—viz., "together"; taken from the second clause. **straw**—no longer *flesh and blood.* **8. play**—lit., "delight" himself in sport. **cockatrice**—a fabulous serpent supposed to be hatched from the egg of a cock. The *Hebrew* means a kind of adder, more venomous than the asp; BOCHART supposes the basilisk to be meant, which was thought to poison even with its breath. **9. my holy mountain**—Zion, i.e., Jerusalem. The seat of government and of Messiah's throne is put for the whole earth (Jer. 3:17). **sea**—As the waters find their way into every cavern of *its depths,* so Christianity shall pervade every recess of the earth (Hab. 2:14). As vss. 1-5 describe the *personal* qualities of *Messiah,* and vss. 6-9 the regenerating effects of His coming on *creation,* so vss. 10-16 the results of it in the restoration of His people, *the Jews,* and the conversion through them of *the Gentiles.*

ADAM CLARKE

prophecies the subject of the great redemption, and of the glories of the Messiah's kingdom, arises out of the restoration of Judah by the deliverance from the captivity of Babylon, and is all along connected and intermixed with it.

ALEXANDER MACLAREN:

The main point as to the character of the Messiah which this prophesy sets forth is that, whatever He was to be, He was to be by reason of the resting on Him of the Spirit of Jehovah. The directness, fullness, and continuousness of His inspiration are emphatically proclaimed in that word "shall rest," which can scarcely fail to recall John's witness, "I have beheld the Spirit descending as a dove out of heaven; and it abode upon him." The humanity on which the Divine Spirit uninterruptedly abides, ungrieved and unrestrained, must be free from the stains which so often drive that heavenly visitant from our breasts. The whitebreasted Dove of God cannot brood over foulness. There has never been but one manhood capable of receiving and retaining the whole fullness of the Spirit of God.

The gifts of that Spirit, which become qualities of the Messiah in whom He dwells, are arranged (if we may use so cold a word) in three pairs; so that, if we include the introductory designation, we have a sevenfold characterization of the Spirit, recalling the seven lamps before the throne and the seven eyes of the Lamb in the Apocalypse, and symbolizing by the number the completeness and sacredness of that inspiration. The resulting character of the Messiah is a fair picture of one who realizes the very ideal of a strong and righteous ruler of men. "Wisdom and understanding" refer mainly to the clearness of intellectual and moral insight; "counsel and might," to the qualities which give sound practical direction and vigor to follow, and carry through, the decisions of practical wisdom; while "the knowledge and fear of the Lord" define religion by its two parts of acquaintance with God founded on love, and reverential awe which prompts to obedience. The fulfillment, and far more than fulfillment, of this ideal is in Jesus, in whom were "hid all the treasures of wisdom and knowledge," to whom no circumstances of difficulty ever brought the shadow of perplexity, who always saw clearly before Him the path to tread, and had always "might" to tread it, however rough, who lived all His days in unbroken fellowship with the Father and in lowly obedience.

—*Expositions of Holy Scripture*

4. *With the rod of his mouth*—"By the blast of his mouth."

MATTHEW HENRY

Verses 10–16

A further prophecy of the enlargement and advancement of the kingdom of the Messiah, under the figure of Judah in the latter end of Hezekiah's reign, after the defeat of Sennacherib.

I. This prediction was in part accomplished when the great things God did for Hezekiah and his people proved as an ensign, inviting the neighbouring nations to them *to enquire of the wonders done in the land,* on which errand the king of Babylon's ambassadors came. To them the Gentiles sought; and Jerusalem was then glorious, *v.* 10. Then many of the Israelites of the ten tribes, who were forced by the king of Assyria to flee for shelter into all the countries about, were encouraged to return to their own country and put themselves under the protection of the king of Judah. This is said to be a recovery of them *the second time* (*v.* 11), such an instance of the power of God as their first deliverance out of Egypt. Then the *outcasts of Israel* should be brought home, and those of Judah too. Then the old feud between Ephraim and Judah shall be forgotten, and they shall join against the Philistines and their other common enemies, *v,* 13, 14. When God's time has come for the deliverance of his people mountains of opposition shall become plain before him. Let us not despair therefore when the interests of the church seem to be brought very low; God can soon turn gloomy days into glorious ones.

II. It had a further reference to the days of the Messiah and the accession of the Gentiles to his kingdom; for to these the apostle applies *v.* 10, of which the following verses are a continuation. Rom. xv. 12, *There shall be a root of Jesse; and he that shall rise to reign over the Gentiles, in him shall the Gentiles trust.* That is a key to this prophecy, which speaks of Christ as the root of Jesse, or *a branch out of his roots* (*v.* 1), *a root out of a dry ground, ch.* liii. 2.

1. *He shall stand,* or be set up, *for an ensign of the people.* When he was crucified he was *lifted up from the earth,* that, as an ensign or beacon, he might *draw* the eyes and the hearts of *all men unto him,* John xii. 32. He is set up as an ensign in the preaching of the everlasting gospel, in which the ministers are as standard-bearers.

2. *To him shall the Gentiles seek.* We read of Greeks that did so (John xii. 21, *We would see Jesus*).

3. *His rest shall be glorious.* Some understand this of the death of Christ (the triumphs of the cross made even that glorious), others of his ascension, when he sat down to rest at the right hand of God. Or rather it is meant of the gospel church.

4. Both Jews and Gentiles shall be gathered to him, *v.* 11. A remnant of both, a little remnant in comparison, recovered with great difficulty. There shall be a remnant of the Jews gathered in: *The outcasts of Israel and the dispersed of Judah* (*v.* 12), many of whom, at the time of the bringing of them in to Christ, were *Jews of the dispersion.*

5. There shall be a happy accommodation between Judah and Ephraim, and both shall be safe from their adversaries and have dominion over them, *v.* 13, 14. The coalescence between Judah and Israel at that time was a type and figure of the uniting of Jews and Gentiles.

For they shall fly upon the shoulders of the Philistines, as an eagle strikes at her prey, and shall extend their conquests eastward over the Edomites, Moabites, and Ammonites. Some of all nations shall become obedient to the faith.

JAMIESON, FAUSSET, BROWN

10. root—rather, "shoot from the root" (cf. *Note,* vs. 1; ch. 53: 2; Rev. 5:5; 22:16). **stand**—permanently and prominently, as a banner lifted up to be the rallying point of an army or people (ch. 5:26; John 12:32). **the people**—*peoples,* answering to "the Gentiles" in the parallel member. **to it . . . seek**—diligently (Job 8: 5). They shall give in their allegiance to the Divine King (ch. 2:2; 60:5; Zech. 2:11). HORSLEY translates, "Of *Him* shall the Gentiles *inquire;* viz., in a religious sense, *resort as to an oracle for consultation* in difficulties (Zech. 14:16). Cf. Romans 15:12, which quotes this passage, "In *Him* shall the Gentiles trust." **rest**—resting-place (ch. 60:13; Ps. 132:8, 14; Ezek. 43:7). The sanctuary in the temple of Jerusalem was "the resting-place of the ark and of Jehovah." So the glorious Church which is to be is described under the image of an oracle to which all nations shall resort, and which shall be filled with the visible glory of God. **11. set . . . hand**—take in hand the work. **the second time**—Therefore the coming restoration of the Jews is to be distinct from that after the Babylonish captivity, and yet to resemble it. The first restoration was *literal,* therefore so shall the second be; the latter, however, it is implied here, shall be much more universal than the former (ch. 43:5-7; 49:12, 17, 18; Ezek. 37:21; Hos. 3:5; Amos 9:14, 15; Mic. 4:6, 7; Zeph. 3:19, 20; Zech. 10:10; Jer. 23:8). **Pathros**—one of the three divisions of Egypt, Upper Egypt. **Cush**—either Ethiopia, south of Egypt, now Abyssinia, or the southern parts of Arabia, along the Red Sea. **Elam**—Persia, especially the southern part of it now called Susiana. **Shinar**—Babylonian Mesopotamia, the plain between the Euphrates and the Tigris: in it Babel was begun (Gen. 10:1). In the Assyrian inscriptions RAWLINSON distinguishes three periods: 1. The Chaldean; from 2300 B.C. to 1500, in which falls Chedorlaomer (Gen. 14), called in the cuneiform characters Kudur of Hur, or Ur of the Chaldees, and described as the conqueror of Syria. The seat of the first Chaldean empire was in the south, towards the confluence of the Tigris and Euphrates. 2. The Assyrian, down to 625 B.C. 3. The Babylonian, from 625 to 538 B.C., when Babylon was taken by the Persian Cyrus. **islands of . . . sea**—the far western regions beyond the sea [JEROME]. As to the "remnant" destined by God to survive the judgments on the nation, cf. Jeremiah 46:28. **12.** In the first restoration Judah alone was restored, with perhaps some few of Israel (the ten tribes): in the future restoration *both* are expressly specified (Ezek. 37:16-19; Jer. 3:18). To Israel are ascribed the "outcasts" (masculine); to Judah the "dispersed" (feminine), as the former have been longer and more utterly castaways (though not finally) than the latter (John 7:52). The masculine and feminine conjoined express the *universality* of the restoration. **13. envy . . . of Ephraim . . . Judah**—which began as early as the time (Judg. 8:1; 12:1, etc.) Joshua had sprung from, and resided among the Ephraimites (Num. 13:9; Josh. 19:50); the sanctuary was with them for a time (Josh. 18:1). The *jealousy* increased subsequently (II Sam. 2:8, etc.; 19:41; 20:2; 3:10); and even before David's time (I Sam. 11:8; 15:4), they had appropriated to themselves the national name Israel. It ended in disruption (I Kings 11:26, etc.; 12; cf. II Kings 14:9; Ps. 78:56-71). **adversaries of Judah**—rather, "the adversaries *from* Judah"; those of Judah *hostile to the Ephraimites* [MAURER]. The parallelism "the envy of Ephraim," viz., against Judah, requires this, as also what follows; viz., "Judah shall not vex Ephraim" (Ezek. 37: 15, 17, 19). **14.** With united forces they shall subdue their foes (Amos 9:12). **fly**—as a bird of prey (Hab. 1:8). **upon the shoulders**—This expresses an attack made unexpectedly on one *from behind.* The image is the more apt, as the *Hebrew* for "shoulders" in Numbers 34:11 is used also of a maritime coast. They shall make a sudden victorious descent *upon their borders* southwest of Judea. **them of the east**-*Hebrew,* children of the East, the Arabs, who, always hostile, are not to be reduced under regular government, but are only to be despoiled (Jer. 49:28, 29). **lay . . . hand upon**—take possession of (Dan. 11:42). **Edom**—south of Judah, from the Dead Sea to the Red Sea. **Moab**—east of Jordan and the Dead Sea. **Ammon**—east of Judea, north of Moab, between the Arnon and Jabbok. **15.** There shall be a second exodus, destined to eclipse even the former one from Egypt in its wonders. So the prophecies elsewhere (Ps. 68:22; Exod. 14:22; Zech. 10:11). The same deliverance furnishes the imagery by which the return from Babylon is described (ch. 48:20, 21). **destroy**—lit., "devote," or "doom," i.e., dry up; for what God dooms, perishes (Ps. 106:9; Nah. 1:4). **tongue**

ADAM CLARKE

10. *A root of Jesse, which shall stand*—"The root of Jesse, which standeth." St. John hath taken this expression from Isaiah, Rev. v. 5 and xxii. 16, where Christ hath twice applied it to himself. The one hundred and tenth psalm is a good comment on this verse.

11. *And it shall come to pass in that day.* This part of the chapter contains a prophecy which certainly remains yet to be accomplished.

KEIL-DELITZSCH:

Asshur and Egypt stand here in front, and side by side, as the two great powers of the time of Isaiah (7:18–20). As appendices to Egypt, we have (1) *Pathros,* the southland, i.e. Upper Egypt, so that Mizraim in the stricter sense is Lower Egypt (see, on the other hand, Jer. 44:15); and (2) *Cush,* the land which lies still farther south than Upper Egypt on both sides of the Arabian Gulf; and as appendices to Asshur, (1) *'Elam,* i.e. Elymais, in southern Media, to the east of the Tigris; and (2) *Shinar,* the plain to the south of the junction of the Euphrates and Tigris. Then follow the Syrian *Hamath* at the northern foot of the Lebanon; and lastly, *"the islands of the sea,"* i.e. the islands and coastland of the Mediterranean, together with the whole of the insular continent of Europe. There was no such *diaspora* of Israel at the time when the prophet uttered this prediction, nor indeed even after the dissolution of the northern kingdom; so that the specification is not historical, but prophetic. The redemption which the prophet here foretells is a second, to be followed by no third; consequently the banishment out of which Israel is redeemed is the ultimate form of that which is threatened in 6:12 (cf. Deut. 30:1 sqq.). It is the second redemption, the counterpart of the Egyptian. He will then stretch out His hand again; and as He once delivered Israel out of Egypt, so will He now redeem it—purchase it back out of all the countries named. Observe how, in the prophet's view, the conversion of the heathen becomes the means of the redemption of Israel. The course which the history of salvation has taken since the first coming of Chirst, and which it will continue to take to the end, as described by Paul in the Epistle to the Romans, is distinctly indicated by the prophet. At the word of Jehovah the heathen will set His people free, and even escort them (49:22; 62:10); and thus He will gather again (*âsaph,* with reference to the one gathering point; *kibbētz,* with reference to the dispersion of those who are to be gathered together) from the utmost ends of the four quarters of the globe, "the outcasts of the kingdom of Israel, and the dispersed of the kingdom of Judah," both men and women.

—Commentary on the Old Testament

MATTHEW HENRY

6. Everything that might hinder the progress and success of the gospel shall be taken out of the way, so when Jews and Gentiles are to be brought together into the gospel church all obstructions shall be removed (*v.* 15, 16), difficulties that seemed insuperable shall be strangely got over, *the blind shall be led by a way that they knew not*. See *ch.* xlii. 15, 16; xliii. 19, 20. Converts shall be brought in chariots and in litters, *ch.* lxvi. 20.

CHAPTER 12

Verses 1–3

This is the former part of the hymn of praise prepared for the use of the Jewish church when God would work great deliverances for them, and of the Christian church when the kingdom of the Messiah should be set up in the world. The scattered church, being united into one body, shall, as one man, thus praise God.

I. The promise is sure, and the blessings contained when they are bestowed, will furnish the church with abundant matter for thanksgiving.

II. *Thou shalt say*, that is, thou oughtest to say so. *In that day*, when many are brought home to Jesus Christ and flock to him as doves to their windows, *thou shalt say, O Lord! I will praise thee. O Lord! I will praise thee, though thou wast angry with me.* Even God's frowns must not put us out of tune for praising him. By Jesus Christ, the root of Jesse, God's anger against mankind was turned away; for *he is our peace*. Those whom God is reconciled to he comforts. God sometimes brings his people into a wilderness that there he may *speak comfortably to them*, Hosea ii. 14. They are taught to triumph in God (*v.* 2): "*Behold*, and wonder; *God is my salvation;* not only my Saviour, by whom I am saved, but my salvation, in whom I am safe." We have work to do and temptations to resist, and we may depend upon him to enable us for both. We have many troubles to undergo, and we may depend upon him to comfort us in all our tribulations, for he *giveth songs in the night*. Observe the title here given to God: *Jah, Jehovah*. Jah is the contraction of Jehovah, and both signify his eternity and unchangeableness, which are a great comfort to those that depend upon him as their strength and their song. "*Therefore*, because the Lord Jehovah is your strength and song and will be your salvation, *out of the wells of salvation* in God, who is the fountain of all good to his people, *you shall draw water with joy*. God's promises revealed, ratified, and given out to us, in his ordinances, are wells of salvation.

Verses 4–6

This is the second part of this evangelical song, and believers stir up themselves to praise God and here invite and encourage one another to do it.

I. *The inhabitants of Zion* and Jerusalem, whom God had protected from Sennacherib's violence, *v.* 6, ought to be most forward and zealous in praising him. *Thou inhabitress of Zion;* the word is feminine. Let women be strong in the Lord, and out of their mouth praise shall be perfected.

II. Praise the Lord by prayer: *Call upon his name*. We must not only speak to God, but speak to others concerning him, *proclaim his name. Declare his doings among the people*, among the heathen, that they may be brought into communion with Israel and the God of Israel. When the apostles preached the gospel to all nations, beginning at Jerusalem, then this scripture was fulfilled. "*Cry out and shout;* welcome the gospel to yourselves and publish it to others with huzzas and loud acclamations, as those that *shout for victory* (Exod. xxxii. 18) or for the coronation of a king," Num. xxiii. 21. *Great is the Holy One*, for he is glorious in holiness; *therefore* great, because holy. It is the happiness of Israel that the God who is in covenant with them, and in the midst of them, is infinitely great.

JAMIESON, FAUSSET, BROWN

of the Egyptian Sea—the Bubastic branch of the Nile [VITRINGA]; but as the *Nile* was not the obstruction to the exodus, it is rather the west tongue or Heroöpolite fork of the *Red Sea*. **with . . . mighty wind**—such as the "strong east wind" (Exod. 14:21), by which God made a way for Israel through the Red Sea. The *Hebrew* for "mighty" means *terrible*. MAURER translates, "With the terror of His *anger*"; i.e., *His terrible anger*. **in the seven streams**—rather, "shall smite it (*divide it by smiting*) *into* seven (*many*) streams, so as to be easily crossed" [LOWTH]. So Cyrus divided the river Gyndes, which retarded his march against Babylon, into 360 streams, so that even a woman could cross it (HERODOTUS, 1. 189). "The river" is the Euphrates, the obstruction to Israel's return "from Assyria" (vs. 16), a type of all future impediments to the restoration of the Jews. **dry shod**—*Hebrew*, "in shoes." Even in sandals they should be able to pass over the once mighty river without being wet (Rev. 16:12). **16. highway**—clear of obstructions (ch. 19:23; 35:8). **like as . . . Israel . . . Egypt**—(ch. 51:10, 11; 63:12, 13.)

CHAPTER 12

VSS. 1-6. THANKSGIVING HYMN OF THE RESTORED AND CONVERTED JEWS. Just as Miriam, after the deliverance of the Red Sea (ch. 11:16), celebrated it with an ode of praise (Exod. 15). **2. Lord** JEHOVAH—*Jah, Jehovah*. The *repetition* of the name denotes emphasis, and the unchangeableness of God's character. **strength . . . song . . . salvation**—derived from Exodus 15:2; Psalm 118:14. The idea of *salvation* was peculiarly associated with the feast of *tabernacles* (see vs. 3). Hence the cry "Hosanna," "*Save, we beseech thee,*" that accompanied Jesus' triumphal entry into Jerusalem on that day (the fifteenth of the seventh month) (Matt. 21:9; cf. with Ps. 118:25, 26); the earnest of the perfected "salvation" which He shall bring to His people at His glorious second appearance at Jerusalem (Heb. 9:28). "He shall appear the second time without sin unto *salvation*." Cf. Revelation 21:3, "The *tabernacle* of God is with men." Cf. Luke 9:33, "three tabernacles: one for *thee* . . ." (the transfiguration being a pledge of the future kingdom), (Ps. 118:15; Zech. 14:16). As the Jew was reminded by the feast of tabernacles of his wanderings in tents in the wilderness, so the Jew-Gentile Church to come shall call to mind, with thanksgiving, the various past ways whereby God has at last brought them to the heavenly "city of habitation" (Ps. 107:7). **3. draw water . . . salvation**—an expressive image in a hot country. On the last day of the feast of tabernacles the Jews used to bring water in a golden pitcher from the fountain of Siloam, and pour it, mingled with wine, on the sacrifice on the altar, with great rejoicing. This is the allusion in Jesus' words on "the last day of the feast" (John 7:2, 37-39). The pouring out of water indicated *repentance* (I Sam. 7:6; cf., as to the *Jews'* repentance hereafter, Zech. 12:10). There shall be a *latter* outpouring of the Spirit like the *former* one on pentecost (Joel 2:23). **wells**—not mere *streams*, which may run dry, but ever-flowing *fountains* (John 4:14; 7:38), "Out of his belly (i.e., in and from himself)—*living* water" (ch. 42:18; Ps. 84:6; Zech. 13:1; Rev. 7:17).

6. inhabitant of Zion—*Hebrew*, "inhabitress"; so "daughter of Zion," i.e., Zion and its people.

4. make mention—*Hebrew*, "cause it to be remembered." **5. Sing . . .**—alluding to Exod. 15:21.

in the midst of thee—of Jerusalem literally (Jer. 3:17; Ezek. 48:35; Zeph. 3:15, 17; Zech. 2:10).

ADAM CLARKE

15. *The Lord . . . shall smite it in the seven streams*—"Smite with a drought." Here is a plain allusion to the passage of the Red Sea. And the Lord's shaking His hand over the river with His vehement wind refers to a particular circumstance of the same miracle: for He "caused the sea to go back by a strong east wind all that night, and made the sea dry land," Exod. xiv. 21. The *tongue;* a very apposite and descriptive expression for a bay such as that of the Red Sea. It is used in the same sense, Josh. xv. 2, 5; xviii. 19.

CHAPTER 12

This hymn seems, by its whole tenor, and by many expressions in it, much better calculated for the use of the Christian Church than for the Jewish, in any circumstances, or at any time that can be assigned. The Jews themselves seem to have applied it to the times of Messiah. On the last day of the Feast of Tabernacles they fetched water in a golden pitcher from the fountain of Shiloah, springing at the foot of Mount Sion without the city. They brought it through the water gate into the Temple, and poured it, mixed with wine, on the sacrifice as it lay upon the altar, with great rejoicing. They seem to have taken up this custom, for it is not ordained in the law of Moses, as an emblem of future blessings, in allusion to this passage of Isaiah, "Ye shall draw waters with joy from the fountains of salvation," expressions that can hardly be understood of any benefits afforded by the Mosaic dispensation. Our Saviour applied the ceremony, and the intention of it, to himself, and the effusion of the Holy Spirit, promised, and to be given, by Him. The sense of the Jews in this matter is plainly shown by the following passage of the Jerusalem Talmud: "Why is it called the place or house of drawing?" (for that was the term for this ceremony, or for the place where the water was taken up) "Because from thence they draw the Holy Spirit; as it is written, And ye shall draw water with joy from the fountains of salvation."

1. *Though thou wast angry*—"For though thou hast been angry." The Hebrew phrase is exactly the same with that of St. Paul, Rom. vi. 17: "But thanks be to God, that ye were the slaves of sin; but have obeyed from the heart"; that is, "that whereas, or though, ye were the slaves of sin, yet ye have now obeyed from the heart the doctrine on the model of which ye were formed."

6. *Thou inhabitant of Zion*. Not only the Jewish people, to whom His word of salvation was to be sent first, but also all members of the Church of Christ; as in them, and in His Church, the Holy One of Israel dwells.

MATTHEW HENRY

CHAPTER 13

INTRODUCTION BY ADAM CLARKE:

This and the following chapter—striking off the last five verses of the latter, which belong to a quite different subject—contain one entire prophecy, foretelling the destruction of Babylon by the Medes and Persians; delivered probably in the reign of Ahaz, about two hundred years before its accomplishment. The captivity itself of the Jews at Babylon, which the prophet does not expressly foretell, did not fully take place till about one hundred and thirty years after the delivery of this prophecy; and the Medes, who are expressly mentioned in chap. xiii. 17 as the principal agents in the overthrow of the Babylonian monarchy, by which the Jews were released from that captivity, were at this time an inconsiderable people.

The former part of this prophecy is one of the most beautiful examples that can be given of elegance of composition, variety of imagery, and sublimity of sentiment and diction, in the prophetic style; and the latter part consists of an ode of supreme and singular excellence.

The prophecy opens with the command of God to gather together the forces which He had destined to this service, vv. 2-3. Upon which the prophet immediately hears the tumultuous noise of the different nations crowding together to His standard; he sees them advancing, prepared to execute the divine wrath, vv. 4-5. He proceeds to describe the dreadful consequences of this visitation, the consternation which will seize those who are the objects of it; and, transferring unawares the speech from himself to God, v. 11, sets forth, under a variety of the most striking images, the dreadful destruction of the inhabitants of Babylon which will follow, vv. 11-16, and the everlasting desolation to which that great city is doomed, vv. 17-22.

The deliverance of Judah from captivity, the immediate consequence of this great revolution, is then set forth, without being much enlarged upon, or greatly amplified, chap. xiv. 1-2. This introduces, with the greatest ease and the utmost propriety, the triumphant song on that subject, vv. 4-28.

A chorus of Jews is introduced, expressing their surprise and astonishment at the sudden downfall of Babylon; and the great reverse of fortune that had befallen the tyrant, who, like his predecessors, had oppressed his own, and harassed the neighboring kingdoms. These oppressed kingdoms, or their rulers, are represented under the image of the fir trees and the cedars of Libanus, frequently used to express anything in the political or religious world that is supereminently great and majestic: the whole earth shouteth for joy; the cedars of Libanus utter a severe taunt over the fallen tyrant, and boast their security, now he is no more.

The scene is immediately changed, and a new set of persons is introduced. The regions of the dead are laid open, and Hades is represented as rousing up the shades of the departed monarchs. They rise from their thrones to meet the king of Babylon at his coming, and insult him on his being reduced to the same low estate of impotence and dissolution with themselves.

The Jews now resume the speech; they address the king of Babylon as the morning star fallen from heaven, as the first in splendor and dignity in the political world, fallen from his high state. They introduce him as uttering the most extravagant vaunts of his power and ambitious designs in his former glory. These are strongly contrasted in the close with his present low and abject condition.

Immediately follows a different scene, and a most happy image, to diversify the same subject, to give it a new turn, and an additional force. Certain persons are introduced who light upon the corpse of the king of Babylon, cast out and lying naked on the bare ground, among the common slain, just after the taking of the city; covered with wounds, and so disfigured that it is some time before they know him. They accost him with the severest taunts; and bitterly reproach him with his destructive ambition, and his cruel usage of the conquered; which have deservedly brought him this ignominious treatment, so different from that which those of his rank usually meet with, and which shall cover his posterity with disgrace.

To complete the whole, God is introduced, declaring the fate of Babylon, the utter extirpation of the royal family, and the total desolation of the city; the deliverance of His people, and the destruction of their enemies; confirming the irreversible decree by the awful sanction of His oath.

Verses 1–5

The general title of this book was, *The vision of Isaiah the son of Amoz, ch.* i. 1, but the particular inscription of this sermon is *the burden of Babylon.* It is a burden, a lesson they were to learn (so some understand it), but it would be a load which should lie heavily upon them. It is the burden of Babylon or Babel, which at this time was a dependent upon the Assyrian monarchy (the metropolis of which was Nineveh), but soon after revolted and became a monarchy of itself, a very potent one, in Nebuchadnezzar. This prophet afterwards foretold the captivity of the Jews in Babylon, *ch.* xxxix. 6. In these verses a summons is given to those powerful nations whom God would use as instruments for the destruction of Babylon: he names them (*v.* 17) the *Medes,* who, in conjunction with the Persians, under the command of Darius and Cyrus, were the ruin of the Babylonian monarchy.

I. Babylon is here called *the gates of the nobles* (*v.* 2), because of the abundance of noblemen's houses that were in it. But *the whole land* is doomed to destruction (*v.* 5); for, though the nobles were the leaders in persecuting, yet the whole land concurred with them in it.

II. The persons brought together to lay Babylon waste are here called God's *sanctified ones* (*v.* 3), designed for this service and set apart to it by the purpose and providence of God. It intimates that in God's intention, though not in theirs, it was a holy war; they designed the enlargement of their own empire, but God designed the release of his people. Cyrus, the person principally concerned, was justly called *a sanctified one,* for he was God's anointed (*ch.* xlv. 1) and a figure of him that was to come. They are called God's *mighty ones,* because they had their might from God and were now to use it for him. It is said of Cyrus that in this expedition *God held his right hand, ch.* xlv. 1. Though Cyrus did not know God, yet God used him as his servant (*ch.* xlv. 4, *I have surnamed thee* as my servant, though *thou hast not known me*). They are very numerous, *a multitude, a great people, kingdoms of nations* (*v.* 4), not rude and barbarous, but regular troops. *They come from a far country, from the end of* heaven. The vast country of Assyria lay between Babylon and Persia.

III. The summons given them is effectual, *A banner is lifted up upon the high mountain, v.* 2. It is the *Lord of hosts that musters the host of the battle, v.* 4.

Verses 6–18

We have here a description of the terrible desolation which should be made in Babylon by the Medes and Persians. Those that were now secure were bidden to *howl* and lament for,

JAMIESON, FAUSSET, BROWN

CHAPTER 13

VSS. 1-22. CHAPTERS 13-23 CONTAIN PROPHECIES AS TO FOREIGN NATIONS.—CHAPTERS 13, 14, AND 27, AS TO BABYLON AND ASSYRIA. The predictions as to foreign nations are for the sake of the covenant people, to preserve them from despair, or reliance on human confederacies, and to strengthen their faith in God: also in order to extirpate narrow-minded nationality: God is Jehovah to Israel, not for Israel's sake alone, but that He may be thereby Elohim to the nations. These prophecies are in their right chronological place, in the beginning of Hezekiah's reign; then the nations of Western Asia, on the Tigris and Euphrates, first assumed a most menacing aspect. **1. burden**—*weighty* or *mournful* prophecy [GROTIUS]. Otherwise, simply, *the prophetical declaration,* from a *Hebrew* root *to put forth with the voice* anything, as in Numbers 23:7 [MAURER]. **of Babylon**—*concerning* Babylon. **2. Lift . . . banner**—(ch. 5:26; 11:10.) **the high mountain**—rather, "*a bare* (lit., bald, i.e., without trees) mountain"; from it the banner could be seen afar off, so as to rally together the peoples against Babylon. **unto them**—unto the Medes (vs. 17), the assailants of Babylon. It is remarkable that Isaiah does not *foretell* here the Jews' captivity in Babylon, but *presupposes* that event, and throws himself *beyond,* predicting *another* event still more future, the overthrow of the city of Israel's oppressors. It was now 174 years before the event. **shake . . . hand**—*beckon* with the hand—wave the hand to direct the nations to march against Babylon. **nobles**—Babylonian. Rather, in a bad sense, *tyrants;* as in ch. 14:5, "rulers" in parallelism to "the wicked"; and Job 21: 28 [MAURER]. **3. sanctified ones**—the Median and Persian soldiers *solemnly set apart* by Me for the destruction of Babylon, not *inwardly* "sanctified," but *designated* to fulfil God's *holy* purpose (Jer. 51: 27, 28; Joel 3:9, 11; where the *Hebrew* for *prepare* war is "sanctify" war). **for mine anger**—to execute it. **rejoice in my highness**—"Those who are *made to triumph for* My honor" [HORSLEY]. The heathen Medes could not be said to "rejoice in God's highness" MAURER translates, "My haughtily exulting ones" (Zeph. 3:11); a special characteristic of the Persians (HERODOTUS, 1. 88). They *rejoiced in their own highness,* but it was *His* that they were unconsciously glorifying. **4. the mountains**—viz., which separate Media and Assyria, and on one of which the banner to rally the hosts is supposed to be reared. **tumultuous noise**—The Babylonians are vividly depicted as hearing some unwonted sound like the din of a host; they try to distinguish the sounds, but can only perceive a *tumultuous noise.* **nations**—Medes, Persians, and Armenians composed Cyrus' army. **5. They**—viz., "Jehovah," and the armies which are

ADAM CLARKE

CHAPTER 13

1. *The burden of Babylon.* The prophecy that foretells its destruction by the Medes and Persians.

3. *I have commanded my sanctified ones.* The persons "consecrated" to this very purpose. Nothing can be plainer than that the verb *kadash,* "to make holy," signifies also to "consecrate" or "appoint" to a particular purpose. Bishop Lowth translates, "my enrolled warriors." This is the sense.

4. *Of the battle*—"For the battle." Cyrus' army was made up of many different nations. Jeremiah calls it "an assembly of great nations from the north country," chap. l. 9.

5. *From the end of heaven.* Kimchi says, Media, "the end of heaven," in Scripture phrase, means the east.

MATTHEW HENRY

I. *The day of the Lord is at hand* (*v.* 6), a little day of judgment, when God will act as a just avenger of his own and his people's injured cause. *The day of the Lord cometh, v.* 9. God will deal in severity with them for the severities they exercised upon God's people.

II. Their hearts shall fail them, and they shall have neither courage nor comfort left, *v.* 7, 8. Those that in the day of peace were *proud*, and *haughty*, and *terrible* (*v.* 11), shall, when trouble comes, be dispirited and at their wits' end: *All hands shall be faint*, and unable to hold a weapon, *and every man's heart shall melt, they shall be amazed one at another*. In frightening themselves, they shall frighten one another. *Their faces shall be as flames*, pale as flames, through fear, or red as flames, blushing at their cowardice.

III. All hope shall fail them (*v.* 10): *The stars of heaven shall not give their light*, but shall be clouded and *the sun shall be darkened in his going forth*, a certain sign of foul weather.

IV. God will visit them *for their iniquity*, particularly the sin of pride, *v.* 11. That pride must now have its fall: *The haughtiness of the terrible* must now be *laid low*, particularly of Nebuchadnezzar and his son Belshazzar, who had, in their pride, trampled upon the people of God.

V. So great a slaughter will produce a scarcity of men (*v.* 12): *I will make a man more precious than fine gold*. Populous countries are soon depopulated by war.

VI. Such a confusion of their affairs shall be like the *shaking of the heavens* with thunders and the *removing of the earth* by earthquakes. All shall go to rack and ruin *in the day of the wrath of the Lord of hosts*, *v.* 13. Babylon, which used to be like a roaring lion and a raging bear shall become *as a chased roe and as a sheep that no man takes up*, *v.* 14. The army consisting of troops of divers nations, shall be so dispirited and dispersed, that they shall *turn every man to his own people*.

VII. There shall be a scene of blood and horror, as is usual where the sword devours. The conqueror gives no quarter, but puts all to the sword. Those of other nations that come in to their assistance shall be cut off with them. Since the most sacred laws of nature, and of humanity itself are silenced by the fury of war, the conquerors shall, in the most barbarous manner, *dash the children to pieces, and ravish the wives*, *v.* 16.

VIII. The enemy shall be inexorable. These Medes, in conjunction with the Persians, shall take no bribes, *v.* 17. The Medes *shall not regard silver*. They shall show no pity (*v.* 18), not to *the young men* that are in the prime; nor to the age of innocency—*they shall have no pity on the fruit of the womb, nor spare little children.*

Verses 19–22

The great havoc and destruction which it was foretold should be made by the Medes and Persians in Babylon here end in final destruction. Babylon was a noble city. It was *the glory of kingdoms and the beauty of the Chaldees' excellency;* it was that *head of gold* (Dan. ii. 37, 38); it was called *the lady of kingdoms* (ch. xlvii. 5), *the praise of the whole earth* (Jer. li. 41), *like a pleasant roe* (so the word signifies); but it shall be as a *chased roe*, *v.* 14. It is foretold that it should be wholly destroyed, like Sodom and Gomorrah. Babylon was taken when Belshazzar was in his revels; and, though Cyrus and Darius did not demolish it, yet by degrees it went to ruin. It is foretold here (*v.* 20) *that it shall never be inhabited*: in Adrian's time nothing remained but the wall. And whereas it is prophesied concerning Nineveh, that when it should be deserted and left desolate yet flocks should lie down in the midst of it, it is here said concerning Babylon that *the Arabians*, who were *shepherds*, *should not make their folds there*; the country should be so barren that there would be no grazing for sheep. It shall be the receptacle of *wild beasts*, that affect solitude; the houses of Babylon *shall be full of doleful creatures, owls and satyrs*, that are themselves frightened thither, and by whom all others are frightened thence. Benjamin Bar-Jona, in his Itinerary, speaking of Babel, has these words:

JAMIESON, FAUSSET, BROWN

"the weapons of His indignation." **far country**—Media and Persia, stretching to the far north and east. **end of heaven**—the far east (Ps. 19:6). **destroy**—rather, "to seize" [HORSLEY]. **6. day of the Lord**—day of His vengeance on Babylon (ch. 2:12). Type of the future "day of wrath" (Rev. 6:17). **destruction**—lit., "a devastating tempest." **from the Almighty**—not from mere man; therefore irresistible. "Almighty," *Hebrew, Shaddai*. **7. faint . . . melt**—So Jeremiah 50:43; cf. Joshua 7:5. Babylon was taken by surprise on the night of Belshazzar's impious feast (Dan. 5:30). Hence the sudden *fainting and melting of hearts*. **8. pangs**—The *Hebrew* means also a "messenger." HORSLEY, therefore, with LXX translates, "The *heralds* (who bring word of the unexpected invasion) *are terrified*." MAURER agrees with *English Version*, lit., "they shall take hold of pangs and sorrows." **woman . . . travaileth**—(I Thess. 5:3.) **amazed**—the stupid, bewildered gaze of consternation. **faces . . . flames**—"their visages have the livid hue of flame" [HORSLEY]; with anguish and indignation. **9. cruel**—not strictly, but *unsparingly just;* opposed to *mercy*. Also answering to the cruelty (in the strict sense) of Babylon towards others (ch. 14:17) now about to be visited on itself. **the land**—"the earth" [HORSLEY]. The language from vs. 9 to vs. 13 can only primarily and *partially* apply to Babylon; fully and *exhaustively*, the judgments to come, hereafter, on the whole earth. Cf. vs. 10 with Matt. 24:29; Rev. 8:12. The sins of Babylon, *arrogancy* (vs. 11; ch. 4:11; 47:7, 8), *cruelty, false worship* (Jer. 50:38), *persecution of the people of God* (ch. 47:6), are peculiarly characteristic of the Antichristian world of the latter days (Dan. 11:32-37; Rev. 17:3, 6; 18:6, 7, 9-14, 24). **10. stars . . .**—fig. for *anarchy, distress*, and *revolutions* of kingdoms (ch. 34:4; Joel 2:10; Ezek. 32:7, 8; Amos 8:9; Rev. 6:12-14). There may be a *literal* fulfilment *finally*, shadowed forth under this imagery (Rev. 21:1). **constellations—*Hebrew***, "a fool," or "impious one"; applied to the constellation *Orion*, which was represented as an impious giant (Nimrod deified, the founder of Babylon) chained to the sky. See *Note*, Job. 38:31. **11. world**—*the impious* of the world (cf. ch. 11:4). **arrogancy**—Babylon's besetting sin (Dan. 4:22, 30). **the terrible**—rather, tyrants [HORSLEY]. **12. man . . . precious**—I will so cut off Babylon's defenders, that *a single man* shall be as rare and precious as the finest gold. **13.** Image for mighty revolutions (ch. 24:19; 34:4; Hab. 3:6, 10; Hag. 2:6, 7; Rev. 20:11). **14. it**—Babylon. **roe**—gazelle; the most timid and easily startled. **no man taketh up**—sheep defenseless, *without a shepherd* (Zech. 13:7). **every man . . . to his own people**—The "mingled peoples" of foreign lands shall flee out of her (Jer. 50:16, 28, 37; 51:9). **15. found**—in the city. **joined**—"intercepted" [MAURER]. "Every one that has *withdrawn himself*," viz., to hide in the houses [GESENIUS]. **16.** (Ps. 137:8, 9.) **17. Medes**—(Ch. 21:2; Jer. 51:11, 28.) At that time they were subject to Assyria; subsequently Arbaces, satrap of Media, revolted against the effeminate Sardanapalus, king of Assyria, destroyed Nineveh, and became king of Media, in the ninth century B.C. **not regard silver**—In vain will one try to buy his life from them for a ransom. The heathen Xenophon (*Cyrop.* 5, 1, 10) represents Cyrus as attributing this characteristic to the Medes, *disregard of riches*. A curious confirmation of this prophecy. **18. bows**—in the use of which the Persians were particularly skilled. **19. glory of kingdoms**—(Ch. 14:4; 47:5; Jer. 51:41.) **beauty of . . . excellency**—*Hebrew*, "the glory of the pride" of the Chaldees; it was their glory and boast. **as . . . Gomorrah**—as utterly (Jer. 49:18; 50:40; Amos 4:11). Taken by Cyrus, by clearing out the canal made for emptying the superfluous waters of the Euphrates, and directing the river into this new channel, so that he was able to enter the city by the old bed in the night. **20.** literally fulfilled. **neither . . . Arabian pitch tent**—Not only shall it not be a permanent residence, but not even a *temporary* resting-place. The Arabs, through dread of evil spirits, and believing the ghost of Nimrod to haunt it, will not pass the night there (cf. vs. 21). **neither . . . shepherds**—The region was once most fertile; but owing to the Euphrates being now no longer kept within its former channels, it has become a stagnant marsh, unfit for flocks; and on the wastes of its ruins (bricks and cement) no grass grows. **21. wild beasts**—*Hebrew, tsiyim*, animals dwelling in arid wastes. Wild cats, remarkable for their howl [BOCHART]. **doleful creatures**—"howling beasts," lit., "howlings" [MAURER]. **owls**—rather, ostriches; a timorous creature, delighting in solitary deserts and making a hideous noise [BOCHART]. **satyrs**—sylvan demi-gods—half man, half goat—believed by the Arabs to haunt these ruins; probably

ADAM CLARKE

10. *For the stars of heaven*—"Yea, the stars of heaven." The Hebrew poets, to express happiness, prosperity, the advancement of states, kingdoms, and potentates, make use of images taken from the most striking parts of nature, from the heavenly bodies, from the sun, moon, and stars—which they describe as shining with increased splendor, and never setting. On the contrary, the destruction of kingdoms is represented by opposite images. The stars are obscured, the moon withdraws her light, and the sun shines no more! The earth quakes, and the heavens tremble; and all things seem tending to their original chaos. See Joel ii. 10; iii. 15-16; Amos viii. 9; Matt. xxiv. 29.

And the moon shall not cause her light to shine. This in its further reference may belong to the Jewish polity, in both church and state, which should be totally eclipsed, and perhaps shine no more in its distinct state forever.

11. *I will punish the world*—"I will visit the world." That is, the Babylonish empire.

12. *I will make a man more precious than fine gold . . . wedge of Ophir*. The Medes and Persians will not be satisfied with the spoils of the Babylonians. They seek either to destroy or enslave them; and they will accept no ransom for any man—either for *enosh*, the poor man, or for *adam*, the more honorable person. All must fall by the sword, or go into captivity together; for the Medes (*v.* 17) regard not silver, and delight not in gold.

14. "And the remnant." Here is plainly a defect in this sentence, as it stands in the Hebrew text; the subject of the proposition is lost. What is it that shall be like a roe chased? The Septuagint happily supply it, "the remnant." *They shall . . . turn*—"They shall look." That is, the forces of the king of Babylon, destitute of their leader, and all his auxiliaries, collected from Asia Minor, and other distant countries, shall disperse and flee to their respective homes.

15. *Every one that is found*—"Everyone that is overtaken." That is, none shall escape from the slaughter; neither they who flee singly, dispersed and in confusion, nor they who endeavor to make their retreat in a more regular manner, by forming compact bodies; they shall all be equally cut off by the sword of the enemy.

17. *Which shall not regard silver*—"Who shall hold silver of no account." That is, who shall not be induced, by large offers of gold and silver for ransom, to spare the lives of those whom they have subdued in battle; their rage and cruelty will get the better of all such motives.

18. *Their bows also shall dash.* Both Herodotus, i. 61, and Xenophon, *Anab.* iii., mention that the Persians used large bows, and the latter says particularly that their bows were three cubits long, *Anab.* iv. They were celebrated for their archers, see chap. xxii. 6; Jer. xlix. 35. Probably their neighbors and allies, the Medes, dealt much in the same sort of arms.

19. *And Babylon.* The great city of Babylon was at this time rising to its height of glory, while the prophet Isaiah was repeatedly denouncing its utter destruction. From the first of Hezekiah to the first of Nebuchadnezzar, under whom it was brought to the highest degree of strength and splendor, are about one hundred and twenty years. It was, according to the lowest account given of it by ancient historians, a regular square, 45 miles in compass, enclosed by a wall 200 feet high and fifty broad, in which there were 100 gates of brass. Its principal ornaments were the temple of Belus, in the middle of which was a tower of eight stories of building, upon a base of a quarter of a mile square, a most magnificent palace, and the famous hanging gardens, which were an artificial mountain, raised upon arches, and planted with trees of the largest as well as the most beautiful sorts. Cyrus took the city by diverting the waters of the Euphrates, which ran through the midst of it, and entering the place at night by the dry channel. The river, being never restored afterward to its proper course, overflowed the whole country, and made it little better than a great morass. This and the great slaughter of the inhabitants, with other bad consequences of the taking of the city, was the first step to the ruin of the place. The

MATTHEW HENRY

"This is that Babel which was thirty miles in breadth; it is now laid waste. There are the ruins of a palace of Nebuchadnezzar, but men dare not enter in, for fear of serpents and scorpions, which possess the place."

It is intimated that this destruction should come shortly (*v.* 22): *Her time is near to come.* This prophecy of the destruction of Babylon was intended for the support and comfort of the people of God when they were captives there and grievously oppressed; and the accomplishment of the prophecy was nearly 200 years after the time when it was delivered.

JAMIESON, FAUSSET, BROWN

animals of the goat-ape species [VITRINGA]. *Devil-worshippers*, who *dance* amid the ruins on a certain night [J. WOLFF]. **22. wild beasts of the islands**—rather, jackals; called by the Arabs "sons of howling"; an animal midway between a fox and a wolf [BOCHART and MAURER]. **cry**—rather, "answer," "respond" to each other, as wolves do at night, producing a most dismal effect. **dragons**—serpents of various species, which hiss and utter dolorous sounds. Fable gave them wings, because they stand with much of the body elevated and then dart swiftly. MAURER understands here another species of jackal. **her time . . . near**—though 174 years distant, yet "near" to Isaiah, who is supposed to be speaking to the Jews as if now captives *in* Babylon (ch. 14:1, 2).

ADAM CLARKE

Persian monarchs ever regarded it with a jealous eye; they kept it under, and took care to prevent its recovering its former greatness. Darius Hystaspes not long afterward most severely punished it for a revolt, greatly depopulated the place, lowered the walls, and demolished the gates. Xerxes destroyed the temples.

MATTHEW HENRY — CHAPTER 14

Verses 1–3

Babylon must be ruined, because God has mercy in store for his people. The injuries done to them must be revenged upon their persecutors. The yoke which Babylon had long laid on their necks must be broken and they must be set at liberty.

I. The ground of these favours to Jacob and Israel—the kindness God had for them and the choice he had made of them (*v.* 1): "*The Lord will have mercy on Jacob*, the seed of Jacob now captives in Babylon; and *will yet choose them*, though he has seemed for a time to refuse and reject them."

II. The particular favours he designed them. The *Lord will set them in their own land*, out of which they were driven—the holy land, the land of promise. *Strangers shall be joined with them*, saying, *We will go with you, for we have heard that God is with you*, Zech. viii. 23. These proselytes should be very helpful to them in their return home: *The people* among whom they live *shall take them*, take care of them, and *bring them to their place*—as friends—as servants, willing to do them all the good offices they could. In the return of the captives from Babylon, all that were about them, pursuant to Cyrus's proclamation, contributed to their removal (Ezra i. 4, 6), not as the Egyptians, because they were sick of them, but because they loved them. Many would of choice go with them. They *shall possess them in the land of the Lord for servants and handmaids.* The advantages of that land made it the paradise of those servants that had been strangers to the covenants of promise, for there was *one law to the stranger and to those that were born in the land.* They that would not be reconciled should be reduced and humbled by them: *They shall take those captives whose captives they were and shall rule over their oppressors*, righteously, but not revengefully. They should see a happy termination of all their grievances (*v.* 3): *The Lord shall give thee rest from thy sorrow and thy fear, and from thy hard bondage.* God himself undertakes to work a blessed change.

Verses 4–23

The kings of Babylon, successively, were oppressors of God's people. The Babylonian monarchy bade fair to be an absolute, universal, and perpetual one, and, in these pretensions, vied with the Almighty; it is therefore very justly brought down and the last monarch, Belshazzar, *was slain on that night* that Babylon was taken (Dan. v. 30).

I. The fall of the king of Babylon: a most curious composition is here prepared. It gives us an account of the life and death of this mighty monarch, how he *went down slain to the pit*, though he had been *the terror of the mighty in the land of the living*, Ezek. xxxii. 27.

1. The prodigious height of wealth and power at which this monarch and monarchy arrived. Babylon was a *golden city*, *v.* 4. The king of Babylon, having so much wealth, by the help of that *ruled the nations* (*v.* 6), gave them law, and at his pleasure *weakened the nations* (*v.* 12), that they might not be able to make head against him. Such vast armies did he bring into the field, that he *made the earth to tremble, and shook kingdoms* (*v.* 16); all his neighbours were afraid of him, and were forced to submit to him.

2. The wretched abuse of all this wealth and power,

(1) Great oppression and cruelty. He is known by the name of the *oppressor* (*v.* 4); he has *the sceptre of the rulers* (*v.* 5), but it is *the staff of the wicked. He smote the people*, not in justice, for their correction and reformation, but *in wrath* (*v.* 6), *with a continual stroke.* He ruled them *in anger*, so that he who had the government of all about him had no government of himself. He *made the world as a wilderness*, *v.* 17. He was severe to his captives (*v.* 17). He *opened not*

JAMIESON, FAUSSET, BROWN — CHAPTER 14

VSS. 1-3. THE CERTAINTY OF DELIVERANCE FROM BABYLON. 4-23. THE JEWS' TRIUMPHAL SONG THEREAT. "It moves in lengthened elegiac measure like a song of lamentation for the dead, and is full of lofty scorn" [HERDER] 24-27. CONFIRMATION OF THIS BY THE HEREFORETOLD DESTRUCTION OF THE ASSYRIANS UNDER SENNACHERIB; a pledge to assure the captives in Babylon that He who, with such ease, overthrew the Assyrian, could likewise effect His purpose as to Babylon. The Babylonian king, the subject of this prediction, is Belshazzar, as representative of the kingdom (Dan. 5). **1. choose**—"set His choice upon." A deliberate predilection [HORSLEY]. Their restoration is grounded on their *election* (see Ps. 102:13-22). **strangers**—proselytes (Esther 8:17; Acts 2:10; 17:4, 17). Tacitus, a heathen (*Hist.* 5. 5), attests the fact of numbers of the Gentiles having become Jews in his time. An earnest of the future effect on the heathen world of the Jews' spiritual restoration (ch. 60:4, 5, 10; Mic. 5:7; Zech. 14:16; Rom. 11:12). **2. the people**—of Babylon, primarily. Of the whole Gentile world ultimately (ch. 49:22; 66:20; 60:9). **their place**—Judea (Ezra 1). **possess**—receive in possession. **captives**—not by physical, but by moral might; the force of love, and regard to Israel's God (ch. 60:14). **3. rest**—(Ch. 28:12; Ezek. 28:25, 26.)

4-8. A CHORUS OF JEWS EXPRESS THEIR JOYFUL SURPRISE AT BABYLON'S DOWNFALL:—The whole earth rejoices; the cedars of Lebanon taunt him. **4. proverb**—The Orientals, having few books, embodied their thoughts in weighty, figurative, briefly expressed gnomes. Here a taunting song of triumph (Mic. 2:4; Hab. 2:6). **the king**—the ideal representative of Babylon; perhaps Belshazzar (Dan. 5). The mystical Babylon is ultimately meant. **golden city**—rather, "the exactress of gold" [MAURER]. But the old translators read differently in the *Hebrew*, "oppression," which the parallelism favors (cf. ch. 3:5). **5. staff**—not the scepter (Ps. 2:9), but the staff with which one strikes others, as he is speaking of more tyrants than one (ch. 9:4; 10:24; 14:29) [MAURER]. **rulers**—tyrants, as the parallelism "the wicked" proves (cf. *Note*, ch. 13:2). **6. people**—the peoples subjected to Babylon. **is persecuted**—the *Hebrew* is rather *active*, "which persecuted them, without any to hinder him" [VULGATE, JEROME, and HORSLEY]. **7. they**—the once subject nations of the whole earth. HOUBIGANT places the stop after "fir trees" (vs. 8), "The very fir trees break forth," etc. But the parallelism is better in *English Version*. **8. the fir trees**—now left undisturbed. Probably a kind of evergreen. **rejoice at thee**—(Ps. 96: 12). *At thy fall* (Ps. 35:19, 24). **no feller**—as formerly, when thou wast in power (ch. 10:34; 37: 24).

9-11. THE SCENE CHANGES FROM EARTH TO HELL. Hades (the *Amenthes* of Egypt), the unseen abode of the departed; some of its tenants, once mighty monarchs, are represented by a bold personification as rising from their seats in astonishment at the descent among them of the humbled king of Babylon. This proves, in opposition to WARBURTON, *Div. Leg.*, that the belief existed among the Jews that there was a Sheol or Hades, in which the "Rephaim" or manes of the departed abode. **9. moved**—put into agitation. **for thee**—i.e., "at thee"; towards thee; explained by "to meet thee at thy coming" [MAURER]. **chief ones**—lit., "goats"; so rams, leaders of the flock; princes (Zech. 10:3). The idea of *wickedness* on a *gigantic* scale is included (Ezek. 34:17; Matt. 25:32, 33). MAGEE derives Rephaim (*English Version*, "the dead") from a *Hebrew* root, "to resolve into first elements"; so *the deceased* (ch. 26:14) *ghosts* (Prov. 21:16). These being magnified by the imagination of the living into gigantic stature, gave their name to *giants* in general (Gen. 6:4; 14:5;

ADAM CLARKE — CHAPTER 14

1. *And will yet choose Israel.* That is, will still regard Israel as His chosen people, however He may seem to desert them, by giving them up to their enemies and scattering them among the nations. Judah is sometimes called Israel; see Ezek. xiii. 16; Mal. i. 1; ii. 11. But the name of Jacob and of Israel, used apparently with design in this place, each of which names includes the twelve tribes, and the other circumstances mentioned in this and the next verse, which did not in any complete sense accompany the return from the captivity of Babylon, seem to intimate that this whole prophecy extends its views beyond that even.

4. *This proverb*—"This parable." *Mashal.* I take this to be the general name for poetic style among the Hebrews, including every sort of it, as ranging under one or other, or all of the characters, of sententious, figurative, and sublime; which are all contained in the original notion, or in the use and application of the word *mashal.* Parables or proverbs, such as those of Solomon, are always expressed in short, pointed sentences; frequently figurative, being formed on some comparison; generally forcible and authoritative, in both the matter and the form. And such in general is the style of the Hebrew poetry. The verb *mashal* signifies to rule; to exercise authority; to make equal; to compare one thing with another; to utter parables or acute, weighty, and powerful speeches, in the form and manner of parables, though not properly such. *The golden city ceased. Madhebah,* which is here translated *golden city*, is a Chaldee word. Probably it means that golden coin which was given to the Babylonians by way of tribute. So the word is understood by the Vulgate, where it is rendered *tributum.*

9. *Hell from beneath is moved for thee to meet thee.* That is, Nebuchadnezzar. Tyrannical kings who have oppressed and spoiled mankind are here represented as enthroned in hell, and as taking a Satanic pleasure in seeing others of the same description enter those abodes of misery!

MATTHEW HENRY

the house of his prisoners; he *did not let them loose homeward* (so the margin reads it); he kept them in close confinement, and never would suffer any to return to their own land. This refers especially to the people of the Jews. He was oppressive to his own subjects (*v.* 20): *Thou hast destroyed thy land, and slain thy people.*

(2) Great pride and haughtiness. Notice is here taken of his *pomp*, the extravagancy of his retinue, *v.* 11. But it was the temper of his mind that ripened him for ruin (*v.* 13, 14): *Thou hast said in thy heart*, like Lucifer, *I will ascend into heaven.* The king of Babylon here promises himself he shall surpass all his neighbours, and to be as far above those about him as the heaven is above the earth. He called for the vessels of the temple at Jerusalem, to profane them; see Dan. v. 2. In the same humour he here said, *I will sit upon the mount of the congregation in the sides of the north*; so Mount Zion is said to be situated, Ps. xlviii. 2. Perhaps Belshazzar was projecting an expedition to Jerusalem at the time when God cut him off. He would vie with the God of Israel, of whom he had heard that he had his residence *above the heights of the clouds.* "But thither," says he, "*will I ascend*, and be as great as he; I will be like him whom they call *the Most High*." Some of the first founders of the Assyrian monarchy were deified and stars had their names from them. "But," says he, "*I will exalt my throne above them* all."

3. The utter ruin that should be brought upon him. It is foretold his wealth and power should be broken. He has been long an oppressor, but he shall cease to be so, *v.* 4. Those that will not cease to sin God will make to cease. *The Lord*, the righteous God, *has broken the staff of that wicked prince. He is persecuted* (*v.* 6); violent hands are laid upon him. It is the common fate of tyrants to be deserted by their flatterers. Tiberius and Nero thus saw themselves abandoned. He should be slain, and be *weak as the dead* are, and *like unto them, v.* 10. His *pomp is brought down to the grave* (*v.* 11), that is, it perishes with him. This mighty prince, that used to lie on a bed of down, now shall have the *worms spread under him and the worms covering him*, which, though he fancied himself a god, proved him to be made of the same mould with other men. *The kings of the nations lie in glory* (*v.* 18), *everyone in his own house*, that is, his own burying-place. But this king of Babylon is *cast out* and has no grave (*v.* 19); his dead body is thrown, like that of a beast, into the ditch *like an abominable branch* of some noxious poisonous plant, which nobody will touch, or as the clothes of malefactors put to death and by the hand of justice *thrust through with a sword*, on whose dead bodies heaps of stones are raised. The king of Babylon's dead body shall be *trodden under feet* by the horses and soldiers and crushed to pieces. Thus he *shall not be joined with his ancestors in burial, v.* 20. Now that he is gone *the whole earth is at rest and is quiet*, for he was the great disturber of the peace; now they all *break forth into singing*; the fir-trees and cedars of Lebanon now think themselves safe; there is no danger now of their being cut down, to furnish him with timber. The neighbouring princes who are compared to fir-trees and cedars (Zech. xi. 2), may now be easy, and out of fear of being dispossessed of their rights. The dead will bid him welcome, especially those whom he had barbarously hastened thither (*v.* 9, 10): *Hell from beneath is moved for thee, to meet thee at thy coming. The chief ones of the earth*, who when they were alive were kept in awe by him shall scoffingly rise from their thrones and ask him if he will please to sit down in them, as he used to do in their thrones on earth? "*Hast thou also become weak as we?* Who would have thought it? Thou that didst rank thyself among the immortal gods, art thou come to take thy fate among us poor mortal men? *How hast thou fallen from heaven, O Lucifer! son of the morning! v.* 11, 12. Has such a star become a clod of clay? Did ever any man fall from such a height of honour and power into such an abyss of shame and misery?" *Those that see him shall narrowly look upon him, and consider him* (*v.* 15, 16). "Never was death so great a change to any man as it is to him. Is it possible that a man, who a few hours ago looked so great, should now look so ghastly, so despicable, and neglected? *Is this the man that made the earth to tremble and shook kingdoms?* Who could have thought he should ever come to this?" Ps. lxxxii. 7.

JAMIESON, FAUSSET, BROWN

Ezek. 32:18, 21). "Rephaim," translated in LXX, "giants" (cf. *Note,* Job 26:5, 6). Thence, as the giant Rephaim of Canaan were notorious even in that guilty land, *enormous wickedness* became connected with the term. So the Rephaim came to be *the wicked spirits* in Gehenna, the lower of the two portions into which Sheol is divided. **10.** They taunt him and derive from his calamity consolation under their own (Ezek. 31:16). **weak**—as a shade bereft of blood and life. **Rephaim, "the dead,"** may come from a *Hebrew* root, meaning similarly "feeble," "powerless." The speech of the departed closes with the next verse. **11.** "Pomp" and music, the accompaniment of Babylon's former feastings (ch. 5:12; 24:8), give place to the corruption and the stillness of the grave (Ezek. 32:27). **worm**—that is bred in putridity. **worms**—properly **those** from which the crimson dye is obtained. Appropriate here; instead of the *crimson* coverlet, *over* thee shall be "worms." Instead of the gorgeous couch, "*under* thee" shall be the maggot.

12-15. The Jews Address Him Again as a Fallen Once-bright Star. The language is so framed as to apply to the Babylonian king primarily, and at the same time to shadow forth through him, the great final enemy, the man of sin, Antichrist, of Daniel, St. Paul, and St. John; he alone shall fulfil exhaustively all the lineaments here given. **12. Lucifer**—"day star." A title truly belonging to Christ (Rev. 22:16), "the bright and morning star," and therefore hereafter to be assumed by Antichrist. Gesenius, however, renders the *Hebrew* here as in Ezek. 21:12; Zech. 11:2, "howl." **weaken**—"prostrate"; as in Exodus 17:13, "discomfit." **13. above . . . God**—In Daniel 8:10, "stars" express *earthly potentates.* "The stars" are often also used to express *heavenly principalities* (Job 38:7). **mount of the congregation**—the place of solemn *meeting* between God and His people in the temple at Jerusalem. In Daniel 11:37, and II Thessalonians 2:4, this is attributed to Antichrist. **sides of the north**—viz., the sides of Mount Moriah on which the temple was built; *north* of Mount Zion (Ps. 48:2). However, the parallelism supports the notion that the Babylonian king expresses himself according to his own, and not Jewish opinions (so in ch. 10:10) that "mount of the congregation" will mean the *northern* mountain (perhaps in Armenia) fabled by the Babylonians to be *the common meeting-place of their gods.* "Both sides" imply *the angle* in which the sides meet; and so the expression comes to mean "*the extreme parts* of the north." So the Hindoos place the Meru, the dwelling-place of their gods, in the north, in the Himalayan mountains. So the Greeks, in the *northern* Olympus. The Persian followers of Zoroaster put the Ai-bordsch in the Caucasus north of them. The allusion to the stars harmonizes with this; viz., that those near the *North* Pole, the region of the aurora borealis (cf. *Note,* Job 23:9; 37:22 [Maurer, LXX, Syriac]. **14. clouds**—rather, "the cloud," singular. Perhaps there is a reference to the cloud, the symbol of the divine presence (ch. 4:5; Exod. 13:21). So this tallies with II Thess. 2:4, "*above* all that is called God"; as here "*above* . . . the cloud"; and as the Shekinah-*cloud* was connected with the *temple,* there follows, "he *as God* sitteth in the *temple* of God," answering to "I will be *like the Most High*" here. Moreover, Revelation 17:4, 5, represents Antichrist as seated in Babylon, to which city, literal and spiritual, Isaiah refers here. **15. to hell**—to Sheol (vs. 6), thou who hast said, "I will ascend into *heaven*" (Matt. 11:23). **sides of the pit**—antithetical to the "sides of the north" (vs. 13). Thus the reference is to the *sides* of the sepulcher round which the dead were arranged in niches. But Maurer here, as in vs. 13, translates, "the *extreme,*" or innermost *parts* of the sepulchre: as in Ezek. 32:23 (cf. I Sam. 24:3).

16-20. The Passers-by Contemplate with Astonishment the Body of the King of Babylon Cast Out, instead of Lying in a Splendid Mausoleum, and Can Hardly Believe Their Senses that It Is He. **16. narrowly look**—to be certain they are not mistaken. **consider**—"meditate upon" [Horsley]. **17. opened not . . . house . . . prisoners**—But Maurer, as *Margin,* "Did not let his captives loose *homewards.*" **18. All**—i.e., This is the *usual* practice. **in glory**—in a grand mausoleum. **house**—i.e., "sepulchre," as in Ecclesiastes 12:5; "grave" (vs. 19). To be excluded from the family sepulcher was a mark of infamy (ch. 34:3; Jer. 22:19; I Kings 13:22; II Chron. 21:20; 24:25; 28:27). **19. cast out of**—not that he had lain *in* the grave and was then *cast out of* it, but "cast out *without* a grave," *such as might have been expected by thee* ("thy"). **branch**—a useless *sucker* starting up from the root of a tree, and cut away by the husbandman. **raiment of**

ADAM CLARKE

12. *O Lucifer, son of the morning!* The versions in general agree in this translation, and render *heilel* as signifying *Lucifer,* the morning star, whether Jupiter or Venus; as these are both bringers of the morning light, or morning stars, annually in their turn. And although the context speaks explicitly concerning Nebuchadnezzar, yet this has been, I know not why, applied to the chief of the fallen angels, who is most incongruously denominated Lucifer (the bringer of light!), an epithet as common to him as those of Satan and Devil. But the truth is, the text speaks nothing at all concerning Satan nor his fall, nor the occasion of that fall. Besides, I doubt much whether our translation be correct. *Heilel,* which we translate *Lucifer,* comes from *yalal,* "yell, howl, or shriek," and should be translated, "Howl, son of the morning"; and so the Syriac has understood it.

13. *I will ascend into heaven.* I will get the empire of the whole world. *I will exalt my throne above the stars of God*—above the Israelites, who are here termed the stars of God. This chapter speaks not of the ambition and fall of Satan, but of the pride, arrogance, and fall of Nebuchadnezzar. *The mount of the congregation*—"The mount of the Divine Presence." It appears plainly from Exod. xxv. 22 and xxix. 42-43 (where God appoints the place of meeting with Moses, and promises to meet with him before the ark to commune with him, and to speak unto him, and to meet the children of Israel at the door of the Tabernacle) that the Tabernacle, and afterwards the door of the Tabernacle, and Mount Zion whereon it stood, were called the Tabernacle, and the mount of convention or of appointment,* not from the people's assembling there to perform the services of their religion (which is what our translation expresses by calling it "the tabernacle of the congregation"), but because God appointed that for the place where He himself would meet with Moses and commune with him, and would meet with the people.

19. *Like an abominable branch*—"Like the tree abominated." That is, as an object of abomination and detestation, such as the tree is on which a malefactor has been hanged.

MATTHEW HENRY

4. Here is an inference drawn from all this (*v.* 20): *The seed of evil-doers shall never be renowned.* The princes of the Babylonian monarchy were evildoers, and therefore they had this infamy entailed upon them. There is no credit in a sinful way.

II. The utter ruin of the royal family is here foretold, together with the royal city.

1. The royal family is to be wholly extirpated. The Medes and Persians, that are to be employed in this destroying work, are ordered, when they have slain Belshazzar, to *prepare slaughter for his children* (*v.* 21). Nebuchadnezzar had slain Zedekiah's sons (Jer. lii. 10), and, for that iniquity of his, his seed are paid in the same coin, that they *may not rise up to possess the land* and do as much mischief in their day as their fathers had done in theirs. The providence of God consults the welfare of nations more than we are aware of by cutting off some who, if they had lived, would have done mischief.

2. The royal city is to be demolished and deserted, *v.* 23. It shall be a possession for solitary frightful birds, particularly *the bittern,* joined with the cormorant and the owl, *ch.* xxxiv. 11.

Verses 24–32

It was almost 200 years from this prediction of Babylon's fall to the accomplishment of it. The people to whom Isaiah prophesied might ask, "What is this to us?" To the question he answers by a prediction of the ruin both of the Assyrians and of the Philistines, shortly. These would be a pledge of future deliverance.

I. Assurance given of the destruction of the Assyrians (*v.* 25): *I will break the Assyrian in my land.* Sennacherib brought a formidable army into the land of Judah, but there God broke it. "*I will break the Assyrian;* let me alone to do it." The breaking of the power of the Assyrian would be the breaking of the yoke from off the neck of God's people: *His burden shall depart from off their shoulders,* the burden of quartering that vast army and paying contribution. This prophecy is here ratified and confirmed by an oath (*v.* 24): *The Lord of hosts hath sworn.* What is here said of this particular intention is true of all God's purposes. The breaking of the Assyrian power is made a specimen of what God would do with all the nations engaged against him and his church (*v.* 26), not only upon the Assyrian empire which was then reckoned to be all the world, as afterwards the Roman empire was (Luke ii. 1) for with it many nations fell that had dependence upon it. It is still true, and will ever be so. God will be an enemy to his people's enemies, Exod. xxiii. 22. All the powers on earth are defied to change God's plan (*v.* 27): "*The Lord of hosts has purposed* to break the Assyrian's yoke, *and who has power* enough *to turn it back* or to stay the course of his judgments?"

II. Assurance is likewise given of the destruction of the Philistines and their power. This came *in the year that king Ahaz died,* which was the first year of Hezekiah's reign, *v.* 28. The Philistines are rebuked for triumphing in the death of king Uzziah. He had been as a serpent to them (*v.* 29), had brought them very low, 2 Chron. xxvi. 6. He *warred against the Philistines, broke down their walls, and built cities among them.* But when Uzziah abdicated, it was told with joy in Gath and *published in the streets of Ashkelon.* They made reprisals upon Ahaz, and took many cities of Judah (2 Chron. xxviii. 18), yet *out of the root* of Uzziah *should come a cockatrice,* a more formidable enemy than Uzziah, even Hezekiah, the fruit of whose government should be to them *a fiery flying serpent,* for he should fall upon them with incredible swiftness and fury. *He smote the Philistines even to Gaza* (2 Kings xviii. 8). "When the people of God, whom the Philistines had wasted, and distressed, and impoverished, shall enjoy plenty again, and *the first-born of their poor shall feed* (the poorest among them shall have food convenient), then, as for the Philistines, God will kill *their root with famine*" (*v.* 30). When the *needy* of God's people *shall lie down in safety,* delighting in the songs of peace, then every gate and every city of the Philistines shall be howling and crying (*v.* 31), and there shall be a total dissolution of their state; for from Judea, which lay north of the Philistines, *there shall come a smoke* (a vast army raising a great dust, the indication of a devouring fire at hand), *and none* of all that army *shall be alone in his appointed times;* none shall straggle or be missing when they are to engage.

III. The good use that should be made of all these events for the encouragement of the people of God (*v.* 32): *What shall one then answer the messengers of the nations?*

1. This implies that the great things God does for his people are noticed by their neighbours. Messengers will be sent to enquire concerning them. It concerns

JAMIESON, FAUSSET, BROWN

those . . . slain—covered with gore, and regarded with abhorrence as unclean by the Jews. Rather, "*clothed* i.e., covered) *with* the slain"; as in Job 7:5, "My flesh is clothed with worms and clods of dust" [MAURER]. **thrust through**—i.e., "the slain who have been thrust through," etc. **stones of . . . pit**—whose bodies are buried in sepulchers excavated amidst stones, whereas the king of Babylon is an *unburied* "carcass trodden under foot." **20. not . . . joined with them**—whereas the princes slain with thee shall be buried, thou shalt not. **thou . . . destroyed . . . land**—Belshazzar (or *Naboned*) oppressed his land with wars and tyranny, so that he was much hated (Xenophon, *Cyrop.* 4. 6, 3; 7. 5, 32). **seed . . . never be renowned**—rather, "shall not be named for ever"; the Babylonian dynasty shall end with Belshazzar; his family shall not be perpetuated [HORSLEY].

21-23. GOD'S DETERMINATION TO DESTROY BABYLON. **21. Prepare . . .**—charge to the Medes and Persians, as if they were God's *conscious* instruments. **his children**—Belshazzar's (Exod. 20:5). **rise**—to occupy the places of their fathers. **fill . . . with cities**—MAURER translates, "enemies," as the *Hebrew* means in I Samuel 28:16; Psalm 139:20; viz., lest they inundate the world with their armies. VITRINGA translates, "disturbers." In *English Version* the meaning is, "lest they fill the land with *such* cities" of pride as Babylon was. **22. against them**—the family of the king of Babylon. **name**—all the *male* representatives, so that the name shall become extinct (ch. 56:5; Ruth 4:5). **remnant**—all that is left of them. The dynasty shall cease (Dan. 5:28-31). Cf. as to Babylon in general, Jeremiah 51:62. **23. bittern**—rather, the hedgehog [MAURER and GESENIUS]. Strabo (16:1) states that enormous hedgehogs were found in the islands of the Euphrates. **pools**—owing to Cyrus turning the waters of the Euphrates over the country. **besom**—sweepnet [MAURER], (I Kings 14:10; II Kings 21:13.)

24-27. A FRAGMENT AS TO THE DESTRUCTION OF THE ASSYRIANS UNDER SENNACHERIB. This would comfort the Jews when captives in Babylon, being a pledge that God, who had *by that time* fulfilled the promise concerning Sennacherib (though now still future), would also fulfil His promise as to destroying Babylon, Judah's enemy. In this vs. 24 *the Lord's thought* (purpose) stands in antithesis to *the Assyrians' thoughts* (ch. 10:7). (See ch. 46:10, 11; I Sam. 15:29; Mal. 3:6.) **25. That**—My purpose, namely, "that." **break . . . yoke**—(Ch. 10:27). **my mountains**—Sennacherib's army was destroyed on the mountains near Jerusalem (ch. 10:33, 34). God regarded Judah as peculiarly His. **26. This is . . . purpose . . . whole earth**—A hint that the prophecy embraces the present world of all ages in its scope, of which the purpose concerning Babylon and Assyria, the then representatives of the world power, is but a part. **hand . . . stretched out upon**—viz., in punishment (ch. 5:25). **27.** (Dan. 4:35.)

28-32. PROPHECY AGAINST PHILISTIA. To comfort the Jews, lest they should fear that people; not in order to call the Philistines to repentance, since the prophecy was probably never circulated among them. They had been subdued by Uzziah or Azariah (II Chron. 26:6); but in the reign of Ahaz (II Chron. 28:18), they took several towns in south Judea. Now Isaiah denounces their final subjugation by Hezekiah. **28. In . . . year . . . Ahaz died**—726 B.C. Probably it was in this year that the Philistines threw off the yoke put on them by Uzziah. **29. Palestina**—lit., "the land of sojourners." **rod . . . broken**—The *yoke* imposed by Uzziah (II Chron. 26:6) was thrown off under Ahaz (II Chron. 28:18). **serpent's root**—the stock of Jesse (ch. 11:1). Uzziah was doubtless regarded by the Philistines as a biting "serpent." But though the effects of his bite have been got rid of, a more deadly *viper,* or "cockatrice" (lit., "viper's offspring," as Philistia would regard him), viz., Hezekiah awaits you (II Kings 18:8). **30. first-born of . . . poor**—Hebraism, for the *most abject poor; the first-born* being the foremost of the family. Cf. "first-born of death" (Job 18:13), for the most *fatal death.* The Jews, heretofore exposed to Philistine invasions and alarms, shall be in safety. Cf. Psalm 72:4, "Children of the needy," expressing those "needy in *condition.*" **feed**—image from a flock feeding in safety. **root**—radical destruction. **He shall slay**—Jehovah shall. The change of person, He after I, is a common Hebraism. **31. gate**—i.e., ye who throng the gate; the chief place of concourse in a city. **from . . . north**—Judea, north and east of Palestine. **smoke**—from the signal-fire, whereby a hostile army was called together (the *Jews'* signal-fire is meant here, the "pillar of cloud and fire," (Exod. 13:21; Neh. 9:19); or else from the region devastated by fire [MAURER]. GESENIUS less

ADAM CLARKE

KEIL-DELITZSCH:

Verse 20. "Thou art not united with them in burial, for thou hast destroyed thy land, murdered thy people: the seed of evil-doers will not be named for ever." In this way is vengeance taken for the tyrannical manner in which he has oppressed and exhausted his land, making his people the involuntary instruments of his thirst for conquest, and sacrificing them as victims to that thirst. For this reason he does not meet with the same compassion as those who have been compelled to sacrifice their lives in his service. And it is not only all over forever with him, but it is so with his dynasty also. The prophet, the messenger of the penal justice of God, and the mouthpiece of that Omnipotence which regulates the course of history, commands this.

Verse 21. "Prepare a slaughter-house for his sons, because of the iniquity of their fathers! They shall not rise and conquer lands, and fill the face of the earth with cities." The exhortation is addressed to the Medes, if the prophet had any particular persons in his mind at all. After the nocturnal storming of Babylon by the Medes, the new Babylonian kingdom and royal house which had been established by Nabopolassar vanished entirely from history. The last shoot of the royal family of Nabopolassar was slain as a child of conspirators. The second Nebuchadnezzar deceived the people (as Darius says in the great inscription of Behistan), declaring, "I am Nabukudracara the son of Nabunita." Let no Babylonian kingdom ever arise again! Nimrod, the first founder of a Babylonion-Assyrian kingdom, built cities to strengthen his monarchy. The king of Asshur built cities for the Medes, for the purpose of keeping them better in check. And it is to this building of cities, as a support to despotism, that the prophet here refers.—*Commentary on the Old Testament*

28. *In the year that king Ahaz died was this burden.* Uzziah had subdued the Philistines, 2 Chron. xxvi. 6-7; but, taking advantage of the weak reign of Ahaz, they invaded Judea, and took, and held in possession, some cities in the southern part of the kingdom. On the death of Ahaz, Isaiah delivers this prophecy, threatening them with the destruction that Hezekiah, his son, and great-grandson of Uzziah, should bring upon them; which he effected, for "he smote the Philistines, even unto Gaza, and the borders thereof," 2 Kings xviii. 8. Uzziah, therefore, must be meant by the rod that smote them, and by the serpent from whom should spring the *fiery flying serpent,* v. 29, that is, Hezekiah, a much more terrible enemy than even Uzziah had been.

31. *There shall come from the north a smoke*—"From the north cometh a smoke." That is, a cloud of dust raised by the march of Hezekiah's army against Philistia, which lay to the southwest from Jerusalem.

MATTHEW HENRY

us always to be ready to give a reason of the hope that we have in the providence of God *with meekness and fear*, 1 Pet. iii. 15.

2. The answer which is to be given to the messengers: God is and will be a faithful friend to his church and people. Tell them that *the Lord has founded Zion.* God, in all the revolutions of states and kingdoms, is founding Zion; he is aiming at the advancement of his church's interests. The messengers of the nations, when they sent to enquire concerning Hezekiah's successes against the Philistines, expected to learn of politics, and arts of war, but they are told that these successes were not owing to anything of that nature, but to the care God took of his church. *The poor of his people shall trust in it*, his poor people who have lately been brought very low. The *poor receive the gospel*, Matt. xi. 5. They shall trust to this, to this great truth, that the Lord has founded Zion; on this they shall build their hopes, and not on an arm of flesh. However it may go with particular parties, the church, having God himself for its founder and Christ the rock for its foundation, cannot but stand firm. They will not fear what man can do unto them.

JAMIESON, FAUSSET, BROWN

probably refers it to the *cloud of dust* raised by the invading army. **none . . . alone . . . in . . . appointed times**—Rather, "There shall not be *a straggler* among his (the enemy's) *levies.*" The Jewish host shall advance on Palestine in close array; none shall fall back or lag from weariness (ch. 5:26, 27), [LOWTH]. MAURER thinks the *Hebrew* will not bear the rendering "levies" or "armies." He translates, "There is not one (of the Philistine watch-guards) who will remain *alone* (exposed to the enemy) *at his post,"* through fright. On "alone," cf. Psalm 102:7; Hosea 8:9. **32. messengers of the nation**—When messengers come from Philistia to inquire as to the state of Judea, the reply shall be, that the Lord . . . (Ps. 87:1, 5; 102:16). **poor**—(Zeph. 3:12).

ADAM CLARKE

32. *The messengers of the nation*—"The ambassadors of the nations." The ambassadors of the neighbouring nations, that send to congratulate Hezekiah on his success; which in his answer he will ascribe to the protection of God. See 2 Chron. xxxii. 23. Or if the reading of the text be preferred, the ambassadors sent by the Philistines to demand peace.

CHAPTER 15

Verses 1-5

The country of Moab was of small extent, but very fruitful. It bordered upon the lot of Reuben on the other side Jordan and upon the Dead Sea. Naomi went to sojourn there when there was a famine in Canaan. This is the country which (it is here foretold) should be wasted and grievously harassed. We find another prophecy of its ruin (Jer. xlviii), which was accomplished by Nebuchadnezzar. This prophecy here was to be fulfilled *within three years* (*ch.* xvi. 14), and therefore was fulfilled, either by the army of Shalmaneser, about the time of the taking of Samaria, in the fourth year of Hezekiah, or by the army of Sennacherib, which, ten years after, invaded Judah. The prophet delivered this prophecy to his own people to show them that there is a providence which governs the world and all the nations of it—and that to the God of Israel the worshippers of false gods were accountable. The accomplishment of this prophecy shortly *(within three years)* might be a confirmation of the prophet's mission and of the truth of all his other prophecies. Concerning Moab it is here foretold,

I. That their chief cities should be surprised and taken in a night by the enemy (*v.* 1): Therefore there shall be great grief, *because in the night Ar of Moab is laid waste and Kir of Moab*, the two principal cities of that kingdom. *In the night that they were taken*, or sacked, *Moab was cut off.* The seizing of them laid the whole country open, and made the wealth of it an easy prey. As the country feeds the cities, so the cities protect the country, and neither can say to the other, *I have no need of thee.*

II. That the Moabites should have recourse to their idols for relief (*v.* 2): *He* (that is, the king of Moab) *has gone up to Bajith* (or rather to the house or temple of Chemosh), *and Dibon*, the inhabitants of Dibon, *have gone up to the high places*, where they worshipped their idols, there to make their complaints.

III. That there should be universal grief all the country over. It is described here very affectingly. Moab shall be a vale of tears—a little map of this world, *v.* 2. The Moabites shall lament the loss of Nebo and Medeba, two considerable cities which, it is likely, were plundered and burnt. They shall tear their hair for grief to such a degree that *on all their heads shall be baldness, and they shall cut off their beards*, according to the customary expressions of mourning in those times and countries. *In the streets they shall gird themselves with sackcloth* (*v.* 3). They shall go up to *the tops of their houses* which were flat-roofed, and there they shall *weep abundantly*, shall *howl*, crying to their gods. *They shall come down with weeping* (so the margin reads it) from the tops of their houses weeping as much as they did when they went up.

IV. That the courage of their militia should fail them. Though they were bred soldiers, they *shall cry out* and shriek for fear, and every one of them shall have *his life become grievous to him*, *v.* 4.

V. That the outcry for these calamities should propagate grief to all the adjacent parts, *v.* 5. The prophet himself has impressions made upon his spirit by the prediction of it: *My heart shall cry out for Moab;* though they are enemies to Israel, they are our fellow-creatures. It becomes God's ministers to be of a tender spirit, to be like their master, who wept over Jerusalem even when he gave her up to ruin, like their God, *who desires not the death of sinners.* All

CHAPTER 15

VSS. 1-9. CHAPS. 15 and 16 FORM ONE PROPHECY ON MOAB. LOWTH thinks it was delivered in the first years of Hezekiah's reign and fulfilled in the fourth when Shalmaneser, on his way to invade Israel, may have seized on the strongholds of Moab. Moab probably had made common cause with Israel and Syria in a league against Assyria. Hence it incurred the vengeance of Assyria. Jeremiah has introduced much of this prophecy into his 48th chapter.

1. Because—rather, "Surely"; lit., (I affirm) that [MAURER]. **night**—the time best suited for a hostile incursion (ch. 21:4; Jer. 39:4). **Ar**—meaning in *Hebrew*, "the city"; the metropolis of Moab, on the south of the river Arnon. **Kir**—lit., a citadel; not far from Ar, towards the south. **2. He**—Moab personified. **Bajith**—rather, "to the *temple"* [MAURER]; answering to the "sanctuary" (ch. 16:12), in a similar context. **to Dibon**—Rather, as Dibon was in *a plain* north of the Arnon, "Dibon (is gone up) to the high places," the usual places of sacrifice in the East. Same town as Dimon (vs. 9). **to weep**—at the sudden calamity. **over Nebo**—rather "in Nebo"; not "on account of" Nebo (cf. vs. 3) [MAURER]. The town Nebo was adjacent to the mountain, not far from the northern shore of the Dead Sea. There it was that Chemosh, the idol of Moab, was worshipped (cf. Deut. 34:1). **Medeba**—south of Heshbon, on a hill east of Jordan. **baldness . . . beard cut off**—The Orientals regarded the beard with peculiar veneration. To cut one's beard off is the greatest mark of sorrow and mortification (cf. Jer. 48:37). **3. tops of . . . houses**—flat; places of resort for prayer, etc., in the East (Acts 10:9). **weeping abundantly**—"melting away in tears." HORSLEY prefers "descending to weep." Thus there is a "parallelism by alternate construction" [LOWTH], or *chiasmus;* "howl" refers to "tops of houses." "Descending to weep" to "streets" or squares, whither they descend from the housetops. **4. Heshbon**—an Amorite city, twenty miles east of Jordan; taken by Moab after the carrying away of Israel (cf. Jer. 48). **Elealeh**—near Heshbon, in Reuben. **Jahaz**—east of Jordan, in Reuben. Near it Moses defeated Sihon. **therefore**—because of the sudden overthrow of their cities. Even the armed men, instead of fighting in defense of their land, shall join in the general cry. **life . . .** rather, "his soul is grieved" (I Sam. 1:8) [MAURER]. **5. My**—The prophet himself is moved with pity for Moab. Ministers, in denouncing the wrath of God against sinners, should do it with tender sorrow, not with exultation. **fugitives**—fleeing from Moab, wander as far as to Zoar, on the extreme boundary south of the Dead Sea. HORSLEY translates, "her nobility," (Hos. 4:18). **heifer . . .**—i.e., raising their voices

CHAPTER 15

This and the following chapter, taken together, make one entire prophecy, very improperly divided into two parts. The time of its delivery, and consequently of its accomplishment, which was to be in three years from that time, is uncertain; the former not being marked in the prophecy itself, nor the latter recorded in history. But the most probable account is that it was delivered soon after the foregoing, in the first year of Hezekiah; and that it was accomplished in his fourth year, when Shalmaneser invaded the kingdom of Israel. He might probably march through Moab; and to secure everything behind him, possess himself of the whole country, by taking their principal strong places, Ar and Kirhares.

Jeremiah has happily introduced much of this prophecy of Isaiah into his own larger prophecy against the same people in his forty-eighth chapter, denouncing God's judgment on Moab, subsequent to the calamity here foretold, and to be executed by Nebuchadnezzar, by which means several mistakes of transcribers in the present text of both prophets may be rectified.

2. *He is gone up to Bajith, and to Dibon. Alah habbayith* should be rendered, "He is gone to the house," i.e., to their chief temple, where they practiced idolatry. Dibon was the name of a tower where also was an idolatrous temple; thither they went to weep and pray before their idols, that they might interpose and save them from their calamities.

On all their heads shall be baldness. Herodotus, ii. 36, speaks of it as a general practice among all men, except the Egyptians, to cut off their hair as a token of mourning. "Cut off thy hair . . . and cast it away," says Jeremiah, vii. 29, "and take up a lamentation."

4. *The armed soldiers*—"The very loins." So the Septuagint and the Syriac. They cry out violently, with their utmost force.

5. *My heart shall cry out for Moab*—"The heart of Moab crieth within her." *An heifer of three years old*—"A young heifer." In full strength.

MATTHEW HENRY

the neighbouring cities shall echo to the lamentations of Moab. *The fugitives*, who are making the best of their way to shift for their own safety, shall carry the cry *to Zoar*, the city to which their ancestor Lot fled for shelter from Sodom's flames and which was spared for his sake. They shall make as great a noise with their cry *as a heifer of three years old* does when she goes *lowing* for her calf, as 1 Sam. vi. 12. They shall go up the hill of *Luhith* (as David went up the ascent of Mount Olivet, many a weary step and all in tears, 2 Sam. xv. 30), and *in the way of Horonaim* (a dual termination), the way that leads to the two Beth-horons, the upper and the nether, which we read of, Joshua xvi. 3, 5.

Verses 6–9

"By this time *the cry has gone round about all the borders of Moab*," *v.* 8. It has reached to *Eglaim*, a city at one end of the country, and to *Beer-elim*, a city as far the other way.

I. *The waters of Nimrim are desolate* (*v.* 6), that is, the country is plundered and impoverished. Famine is usually the sad effect of war. Look into the houses, and they are stripped too (*v.* 7): *The abundance* of wealth that *they had gotten* with a great deal of industry, and *that which they had laid up* with a great deal of care, *shall they carry away to the brook of the willows*. Either the owners shall carry it thither to hide it or the enemies shall pack it up and send it home, by water perhaps, to their own country.

II. *The waters of Dimon are turned into blood* (*v.* 9), that is, the inhabitants of the country are slain in great numbers. *Dimon* signifies *bloody*; the place shall answer to its name. *I will bring additions upon Dimon* (so the word is), additional plagues; I have yet more judgments in reserve for them. *For all this, God's anger is not turned away*. Some make their escape, others are overlooked, and are as a remnant of the land; but upon both God *will bring lions*, beasts of prey.

JAMIESON, FAUSSET, BROWN

"like a heifer" (cf. Jer. 48:34, 36). The expression "three years old," implies one at its full vigor (Gen. 15:9), as yet not brought under the yoke; as Moab heretofore unsubdued, but now about to be broken. So Jeremiah 31:18; Hosea 4:13. MAURER translates, "Eglath (in *English Version*, "a heifer") *Shelishijah*" (i.e., *the third*, to distinguish it from two others of the same name). **by the mounting up**—up the ascent. **Luhith**—a mountain in Moab. **Horonaim**—a town of Moab not far from Zoar (Jer. 48:5). It means "the two poles," being near caves. **cry of destruction**—a cry appropriate to the destruction which visits their country. **6. For**—the cause of their flight southwards (II Kings 3:19, 25). "For" the northern regions and even the city Nimrim (the very name of which means "limpid waters," in Gilead near Jordan) are without water or herbage. **7. Therefore**—because of the devastation of the land. **abundance**—lit., "that which is over and above" the necessaries of life. **brook of . . . willows**—The fugitives flee from Nimrim, where the waters have failed, to places better watered. *Margin* has "valley of Arabians"; i.e., to the valley on the boundary between them and Arabia Petrea; now Wady-el Arabah. Arabia means a "desert." **8. Eglaim**—(Ezek. 47:10), *En-eglaim*. Not the Agalum of Eusebius, eight miles from Areopolis towards the south; the context requires a town on the very borders of Moab or beyond them. **Beer-elim**—lit., "the well of the Princes"—(so Num. 21:16-18). Beyond the east borders of Moab. **9. Dimon**—same as Dibon (vs. 2). Its waters are the Arnon. **full of blood**—The slain of Moab shall be so many. **bring more**—fresh calamities, viz., the "lions" afterwards mentioned (II Kings 17:25; Jer. 5:6; 15:3). VITRINGA understands Nebuchadnezzar as meant by "the lion"; but it is *plural*, "lions." The "more," or in *Hebrew*, "additions," he explains of the addition made to the waters of Dimon by the streams of *blood* of the slain.

ADAM CLARKE

7. *To the brook of the willows*—"To the valley of willows." That is, to Babylon.

MATTHEW HENRY — CHAPTER 16

Verses 1–5

God has made it to appear that he delights not in the ruin of sinners by telling them what they may do to prevent the ruin; so he does here to Moab.

I. He advises them to be just to the house of David, and to pay the tribute they had formerly covenanted to pay (*v.* 1): *Send you the lamb to the ruler of the land*. David made the Moabites tributaries to him, 2 Sam. viii. 2. Afterwards they paid their tribute to the kings of Israel (2 Kings iii. 4), and paid it in lambs. Now the prophet requires them to pay it to Hezekiah. Let it be levied from all parts of the country, *from Selah*, a frontier city of Moab on the one side, *to the wilderness*, a boundary of the kingdom on the other side: and let it be sent *to the mount of the daughter of Zion*, the city of David. Some think it is spoken ironically. I rather take it as good advice seriously given, like that of Daniel to Nebuchadnezzar when he was reading him his doom, Dan. iv. 27. And it is applicable to the great gospel duty of submission to Christ, as the ruler of the land, and our ruler. When you come to God, the great ruler, come in the name of the Lamb, the Lamb of God. *The daughters of Moab* (the country villages, or the women of your country) shall flutter about the *fords of Arnon*, attempting that way to make their escape to some other land, *like a wandering bird thrown out of the nest* half-fledged.

II. He advises them to be *kind to the seed of Israel* (*v.* 3): Take counsel, reverse all the unrighteous decrees you have made, by which you have put hardships upon the people of God.

1. The prophet foresaw some storm coming upon the people of God, who, by the merciful providence of God, escaped the fury of the Assyrian army, but were put to the utmost extremity to shift for their own safety. The danger and trouble they were in were like the scorching heat at noon.

2. He bespeaks a shelter for them in the land of Moab, when their own land was made too hot for them. Thus kindly must they deal with the people of God. If they would continue in their habitations, let them now open their doors to the dispersed members of God's church, and be to them like a cool shade to those that *bear the burden and heat of the day*. "*Betray not him that wandereth*, nor deliver him up" (as the Edomites did, Obad. 13, 14), "but *hide the outcasts*." "Nay, do not only hide them for a time, but, if there be occasion, let them be naturalized: *Let my outcasts dwell with thee, Moab* (*v.* 4); find a lodging for them and *be thou a covert to them*." They are *outcasts*, but they are *my outcasts*. The Lord knows those that are his wherever he finds them, even

JAMIESON, FAUSSET, BROWN — CHAPTER 16

Vss. 1-14. CONTINUATION OF THE PROPHECY AS TO MOAB. **1. lamb**—advice of the prophet to the Moabites who had fled southwards to Idumea, to send to the king of Judah the tribute of lambs, which they had formerly paid to *Israel*, but which they had given up (II Kings 3:4, 5). David probably imposed this tribute before the severance of Judah and Israel (II Sam. 8:2). Therefore Moab is recommended to gain the favor and protection of *Judah*, by paying it to the Jewish king. Type of the need of submitting to Messiah (Ps. 2:10-12; Rom. 12:1). **from Sela to**—rather, "from Petra *through* (lit., 'towards') the wilderness" [MAURER]. Sela means "a rock," *Petra* in *Greek;* the capital of Idumea and Arabia Petrea; the dwellings are mostly hewn out of the rock. The country around was a vast common ("wilderness") or open pasturage, to which the Moabites had fled on the invasion from the west (ch. 15:7). **ruler of the land**—viz., of *Idumea,* i.e., the king of Judah; Amaziah had become master of Idumea and Sela (II Kings 14:7). **2. cast out of . . . nest**—rather, "as a *brood* cast out" (in apposition with "a wandering bird," or rather, *wandering birds),* viz., a brood just fledged and expelled from the nest in which they were hatched [HORSLEY]. Cf. ch. 10:14; Deuteronomy 32:11. **daughters of Moab**—i.e., the inhabitants of Moab. So II Kings 19:21; Psalm 48:11; Jeremiah 46:11; Lamentations 4:22 [MAURER]. **at the fords**—trying to cross the boundary river of Moab, in order to escape out of the land. EWALD and MAURER make "fords" a poetical expression for "*the dwellers* on Arnon," answering to the parallel clause of the same sense, "daughters of Moab." **3-5**. GESENIUS, MAURER, etc., regard these verses as an address of the fugitive Moabites to the Jews for protection; they translate vs. 4, "Let mine outcasts *of Moab* dwell with thee, Judah"; the protection will be refused by the *Jews*, for the pride of Moab (vs. 6). VITRINGA makes it an additional advice *to Moab,* besides paying tribute. Give shelter to the Jewish outcasts who take refuge in thy land (vss. 3, 4); so "mercy" will be shown thee in turn by whatever king sits on the "throne" of "David" (vs. 5). Isaiah foresees that Moab will be too *proud* to pay the tribute, or conciliate Judah by sheltering its outcasts (vs. 6); therefore judgment shall be executed. However, as Moab just before is represented as itself an *outcast* in Idumea, it seems incongruous that it should be called on to *shelter* Jewish outcasts. So that it seems rather to foretell the ruined state of Moab *when its people should beg the Jews for shelter,* but be refused for their pride. **make . . . shadow as . . . night . . . in . . . noonday**—

ADAM CLARKE — CHAPTER 16

1. *Send ye the lamb.*—"I will send forth the son." Both the reading and the meaning of this verse are still more doubtful than those of the preceding. The Septuagint and Syriac read, "I will send"; the Vulgate and Talmud Babylon. read "send," singular imperative. The Syriac, for *car,* "a lamb," reads *bar,* "a son," which is confirmed by five MSS. of Kennicott and De Rossi. The first two verses describe the distress of Moab on the Assyrian invasion, in which even the son of the prince of the country is represented as forced to flee for his life through the desert, that he may escape to Judea; and the young women are driven forth like young birds cast out of the nest, and endeavoring to wade through the fords of the river Arnon. Perhaps there is not so much difficulty in this verse as appears at first view. "Send ye the lamb to the ruler of the land" may receive light from 2 Kings iii. 4-5: "And Mesha king of Moab was a sheepmaster, and rendered unto the king of Israel an hundred thousand lambs [with their wool], and an hundred thousand rams . . . But . . . when Ahab was dead . . . the king of Moab rebelled against . . . Israel." Now the prophet exhorts them to begin paying the tribute as formerly, that their punishment might be averted or mitigated.

3. *Take counsel*—"Impart counsel."

MATTHEW HENRY

where no one else knows them. He will himself be their dwelling-place if they have no other, and in him they shall be at home.

3. He assures them of the mercy God had in store for his people. They should not long need their kindness, or be troublesome to them: *For the extortioner is almost at an end* already, *and the spoiler ceases.* They should, ere long, be in a capacity to return their kindness (*v.* 5): "Though the throne of the ten tribes be overturned, yet *the throne of David shall be established in mercy,* and by the same methods may your throne be established if you please. Make Hezekiah your friend. He *shall sit upon the throne in truth.* Then he shall sit *judging,* and will then be a protector to those that have been a shelter to the people of God." And see in him the character of a good magistrate. He shall *seek judgment*; that is, he shall seek occasions of doing right to those that are wronged. He shall *hasten righteousness,* and not delay to do justice. Let the Moabites take example by this, and then assure themselves that their state shall be established.

Verses 6–14

I. The sins with which Moab is charged, *v.* 6. The prophet seems to check himself for going about to give good counsel to the Moabites. He would have healed them, but they would not be healed. Perhaps there are more precious souls ruined by pride than by any one lust whatsoever. The Moabites were notorious for this: "*We have heard* in both ears *of the pride of Moab.* They think themselves too wise to be advised; therefore they will not take example by Hezekiah to do justly and love mercy. We have heard of *his wrath* too (for those that are very proud are commonly very passionate), particularly his wrath against the people of God, whom he will rather persecute than protect. It is with *his lies* that he gains the gratifications of his pride and his passion; *but his lies shall not be so*; he shall not compass his proud and angry projects as he hoped he should."

II. The sorrows with which Moab is threatened (*v.* 7): *Therefore shall Moab howl for Moab. For the foundations of Kir-hareseth shall you mourn.* That great and strong city, which had held out against a mighty force (2 Kings iii. 25), should now be levelled with the ground. Moab was famous for its fields and vineyards; but those shall all be laid waste by the invading army, *v.* 8, 10. It was planted with choice and noble vines, with *principal plants,* which reached *even to Jazer,* and wound themselves along the ranges on which they were spread, even *through the wilderness* of Moab. There were vineyards there, *stretched out,* even to *the sea,* the Dead Sea. Many a time they had shouted *for their summer fruits, and for their harvest.* They had had *joy and gladness* in their fields and vineyards, *singing* and *shouting at the treading of their grapes.* Nothing is said of their praising God for their abundance, and giving him the glory of it. They made it the food and fuel of their lusts, therefore they should be stripped of all. "The fields shall *languish.* The soldiers, called here *the lords of the heathen,* shall break down all the plants, *principal plants,* the choicest that could be got. The joy of harvest has ceased; there is no more singing; the ruin of their country has marred their mirth." Destroy the vines and the fig-trees, and you make all the mirth of a carnal heart to cease, Hos. ii. 11, 12. But a gracious soul can rejoice in the Lord as the God of its salvation even when the fig-tree does not blossom and there is no fruit in the vine, Hab. iii. 17, 18. The concurrence of the prophet with them in this sorrow: "*I will with weeping bewail Jazer, and the vine of Sibmah,* and look with a compassionate concern upon the desolations of such a pleasant country. *I will water thee with my tears, O Heshbon!* and mingle them with thy tears;" nay (*v.* 11), it appears to be an inward grief: *My bowels shall sound like a harp for Moab.* The afflictions of the world, as well as those of the church, should be afflictions to us. See *ch.* xv. 5.

III. In the close of the chapter we see the insufficiency of the gods of Moab to help them, *v.* 12. "Moab shall be soon *weary of the high place.* He shall spend his spirits and strength in vain in praying to his idols; they cannot help him, and he shall be convinced that they cannot." But when he is weary of his high places, he will not go, as he should, to God's sanctuary, but to *his* sanctuary, to the temple of Chemosh, the principal idol of Moab (so it is generally understood); and he shall pray there to as little purpose. The thing itself was long since determined (*v.* 13): *This is the word,* this is the thing, *that the Lord has spoken concerning Moab, since the time* that he began to be so proud, and insolent, and abusive to God's people. The country was long ago doomed to ruin. Now it was made known when it should be

JAMIESON, FAUSSET, BROWN

emblem of a thick shelter from the glaring noonday heat (ch. 4:6; 25:4; 32:2). **bewray . . . wandereth**—Betray not the fugitive to his pursuer. **4.** Rather, "Let the outcasts of Moab dwell with thee" (Judah) [HORSLEY]. **4. for the extortioner . . .**—The Assyrian *oppressor* probably. **is at an end**—By the time that Moab begs Judah for shelter, Judah shall be in a condition to afford it, *for* the Assyrian oppressor shall have been "consumed out of the land." **5.** If Judah shelters the suppliant Moab, allowing him to remain in Idumea, a blessing will redound to Judah itself and its "throne." **truth . . . judgment . . . righteousness**—language so divinely framed as to apply to "the latter days" under King Messiah, when "the Lord shall bring again the captivity of Moab" (Ps. 72:2; 96:13; 98:9; Jer. 48:47; Rom. 11: 12). **hasting**—"prompt in executing."

6. We—Jews. We reject Moab's supplication for his pride.

lies—false boasts. **not be so**—rather, "not right"; shall prove vain (ch. 25:10; Jer. 48:29, 30; Zeph. 2: 8). "It shall not be so; his lies shall not so effect it." **7. Therefore**—all hope of being allowed shelter by the Jews being cut off. **foundations**—i.e., "ruins"; because, when houses are pulled down, the "foundations" alone are left (ch. 58:12). Jeremiah, in the parallel place (Jer. 48:31), renders it "men," who are the moral foundations or stay of a city. **Kir-hareseth**—lit., "a citadel of brick." **surely they are stricken**—rather, joined with "mourn"; "Ye shall mourn *utterly* stricken" [MAURER and HORSLEY]. **8. fields**—vine-fields (Deut. 32:32). **vine of Sibmah**—near Heshbon: viz., languishes. **lords of . . . heathen**—The heathen princes, the Assyrians, etc., who invaded Moab, destroyed his vines. So Jeremiah in the parallel place (Jer. 48:32, 33). MAURER thinks the following words require rather the rendering, "Its (the vine of Sibmah) shoots (the wines got from them) overpowered (by its generous flavor and potency) the lords of the nations" (Gen. 49:11, 12, 22). **come . . ., Jazer**—They (the vine-shoots) reached even to Jazer, fifteen miles from Heshbon. **wandered**—They overran in wild luxuriance the wilderness of Arabia, encompassing Moab. **the sea**—the Dead Sea; or else some lake near Jazer now dry; in Jeremiah 48:32 called the sea of Jazer; but see *Note* there (Ps. 80:8-11). **9. I**—will bewail for its desolation, though I belong to another nation (*Note,* ch. 15:5). **with . . . weeping of Jazer**—as Jazer weeps. **shouting for . . . fallen—rather,** "*Upon* thy summer fruits and upon thy *luxuriant vines* the shouting (*the battle shout,* instead of the *joyous shout* of the grape-gatherers, usual at the vintage) is fallen" (vs. 10; Jer. 25:30; 51:14). In the parallel passage (Jer. 48:32) the words substantially express the same sense. "The *spoiler* is fallen upon thy summer fruits." **10. gladness**—such as is felt in gathering a rich harvest. There shall be *no harvest* or vintage owing to the desolation; therefore no "gladness." **11. bowels**—in Scripture the seat of yearning compassion. It means the inward seat of emotion, the heart, etc. (ch. 63:15; cf. ch. 15:5; Jer. 48:36.) **sound . . . harp**—as its strings vibrate when beaten with the plectrum or hand. **12. when it is seen that**—rather, "When Moab shall have *appeared* (before his gods; cf. Exod. 23:15), *when* he is weary (i.e., when he shall have fatigued himself with observing burdensome rites; I Kings 18:26, etc.), on the high place (cf. ch. 15:2), *and* shall come to his sanctuary (of the idol Chemosh on Mount Nebo) to pray, he shall not prevail"; he shall effect nothing by his prayers [MAURER]. **13. since that time**—rather, "respecting that time" [HORSLEY]. BARNES translates it, "*formerly*" in contrast to "but *now*" (vs. 14): heretofore former prophecies (Exod. 15:15; Num. 21:29) have been given as to Moab, of which Isaiah has given the substance: *but now* a definite and steady *time* also is fixed.

ADAM CLARKE

4. *Let mine outcasts dwell with thee, Moab*—"Let the outcasts of Moab sojourn with thee, O Zion." *The oppressors*—"The oppressor." Perhaps the Israelites, who in the time of Ahaz invaded Judah, defeated his army, slaying 120,000 men, and brought the kingdom to the brink of destruction. Judah, being now in a more prosperous condition, is represented as able to receive and to protect the fugitive Moabites. And with those former times of distress the security and flourishing state of the kingdom under the government of Hezekiah is contrasted.

5. *In mercy shall the throne be established.* May not this refer to the throne of Hezekiah? Here we have the character of such a king as cannot fail to be a blessing to the people.

6. *We have heard of the pride of Moab*—"We have heard the pride of Moab." Zephaniah, chap. ii. 8-10, in his prophecy against Moab, the subject of which is the same with that of Jeremiah in his forty-eighth chapter, enlarges much on the pride of Moab, and their insolent behavior towards the Jews.

7. *For the foundations of Kir-hareseth*—"For the men of Kirhares." A palpable mistake in this place is happily corrected by the parallel text of Jer. xlviii. 31. In the same place of Jeremiah, and in v. 36, and here in v. 11, the name of the city is Kirheres, not Kir-hareseth.

8. *Languish*—"Are put to shame." The meaning of this verse is that the wines of Sibmah and Heshbon were greatly celebrated, and in high repute with all the great men and princes of that and the neighboring countries, who indulged themselves even to intemperance in the use of them; so that their vines were so much in request as not only to be propagated all over the country of Moab to the sea of Sodom, but to have scions of them sent even beyond the sea into foreign countries.

9. *With the weeping*—"As with the weeping." *For thy summer fruits and for thy harvest is fallen*—"And upon thy vintage the destroyer hath fallen."

10. *Neither shall there be shouting*—"An end is put to the shouting."

12. *When it is seen that Moab*—"When Moab shall see."

MATTHEW HENRY

done. *The Lord has spoken* that it shall be *within three years*, v. 14. God makes known his mind by degrees; the light of divine revelation shone more and more, and so does the light of divine grace in the heart. *The glory of Moab shall be contemned*, that is, it shall be contemptible, when all those things they have gloried in shall come to nothing. It was the glory of Moab that their country was very populous and their forces were courageous; but the little remnant that is left shall be *very small and feeble. Within three years, as the years of a hireling*, it shall be at the three years' end exactly, for a servant that is hired for a certain term keeps account to a day. Fair warning is given, and with it space to repent, which if they had improved, as Nineveh did, we have reason to think the judgments threatened would have been prevented.

JAMIESON, FAUSSET, BROWN

14. three years . . . hireling—Just as a hireling has his fixed term of engagement, which neither he nor his master will allow to be added to or to be taken from, so the limit within which Moab is to fall is unalterably fixed (ch. 21:16). Fulfilled about the time when the Assyrians led Israel into captivity. The ruins of Elealeh, Heshbon, Medeba, Dibon, etc., still exist to confirm the inspiration of Scripture. The accurate *particularity of specification* of the places 3000 years ago, confirmed by modern research, is a strong testimony to the truth of prophecy.

ADAM CLARKE

MATTHEW HENRY — CHAPTER 17

Verses 1–5

We have here the burden of Damascus; the Chaldee paraphrase reads it, *The burden of the cup of the curse to drink to Damascus in;* and, the ten tribes being in alliance they must expect to pledge Damascus in this cup of trembling. 1. Damascus itself, the head city of Syria, must be destroyed; the houses will be burnt, the walls, and gates, and fortifications demolished, and the inhabitants carried away captive, so that it is *taken away from being a city*, and is reduced to *a ruinous heap*, v. 1. The country towns are abandoned by their inhabitants. *The cities of Aroer* (a province of Syria so called) *are forsaken* (v. 2); so that the places which should be for men to live in are for *flocks to lie down in.* Stately houses are converted into sheep-cotes. The strongholds of Israel, the kingdom of the ten tribes, will be brought to ruin: *The fortress shall cease from Ephraim* (v. 3). The Syrians were the ring-leaders in that confederacy against Judah, and therefore they are punished first and sorest; and, now that Israel is weakened, *The remnant of Syria shall be as the glory of the children of Israel;* those few that remain of the Syrians shall be in as mean and despicable a condition as the children of Israel are. The glory of Jacob is wasted like a man in a consumption, v. 4. *The glory of Jacob* was their numbers, but this glory *shall be made thin*, when many are cut off, and few left. Israel died of a lingering disease; the kingdom of the ten tribes wasted gradually. It is all gathered and carried away by the Assyrian army, v. 5. And the victorious army, like the careful husbandmen in the valley of Rephaim, where the corn was extraordinary, would not, if they could help it, leave an ear behind.

Verses 6–8

Mercy is here reserved, in a parenthesis in the midst of judgment, for a remnant that should escape the common ruin of the kingdom of the ten tribes. The meek of the earth were hidden in the day of the Lord's anger, and had their lives made comfortable to them by their retirement to the land of Judah. 1. They shall be but a small remnant, who shall be marked for preservation (*v.* 6): *Gleaning grapes shall be left in it.* The body of the people were carried into captivity. Those that are left are but like the poor remains of an olive tree when it has been carefully shaken: if there be *two or three berries in the top of the uppermost bough* (out of the reach of those that shook it), that is all. They shall be a sanctified remnant, *v.* 7, 8. These had repented of their sins and returned their lives, and therefore were snatched thus as brands out of the burning. They shall look up to their Creator, shall acknowledge his hand in all the events concerning them, merciful and afflictive, and shall submit to his hand. They shall look from their idols, the creatures of their own fancy, shall no longer worship them, and expect relief from them. He that looks to his Maker must not *look to the altars, the work of his hands*, must not retain the least respect for *that which his fingers have made*, but break it to pieces.

Verses 9–11

Here the prophet returns to foretell the desolations that should be made in Israel by the army of the Assyrians. Even the strong cities, which should have protected the country, shall not be able to protect themselves: They *shall be as a forsaken bough and an uppermost branch* of an old tree, which has gone to decay, is bare, and dry, and dead. As the Canaanites fled before Israel, so Israel should now flee before the Assyrians. The country should be laid waste, *v.* 10, 11. "It is *because thou hast forgotten the God of thy salvation* and all the great salvations he has wrought for thee, and *hast not been mindful of the rock of thy*

JAMIESON, FAUSSET, BROWN — CHAPTER 17

Vss. 1-11. Prophecy concerning Damascus and Its Ally Samaria, i.e., Syria and Israel, which had leagued together (chs. 7 and 8). Already, Tiglath-pileser had carried away the people of Damascus to Kir, in the fourth year of Ahaz (II Kings 16:9); but now in Hezekiah's reign a *farther* overthrow is foretold (Jer. 49:23; Zech. 9:1). Also, Shalmaneser carried away Israel from Samaria to Assyria (II Kings 17:6; 18:10, 11) in the *sixth* year of Hezekiah of Judah (the ninth year of Hoshea of Israel). This prophecy was, doubtless, given previously in the *first* years of Hezekiah when the foreign nations came into nearer collision with Judah, owing to the threatening aspect of Assyria. **Damascus**—put before *Israel* (Ephraim, vs. 3), which is chiefly referred to in what follows, because it was the prevailing power in the league; with it Ephraim either stood or fell (ch. 7). **2. cities of Aroer**—i.e., the cities round Aroer, and under its jurisdiction [Gesenius]. So "cities with their villages" (Josh. 15:44); "Heshbon and all her cities" (Josh. 13:17). Aroer was near Rabbah-ammon, at the river of Gad, an arm of the Jabbok (II Sam. 24:5), founded by the Gadites (Num. 32:34). **for flocks**—(Ch. 5:17). **3. fortress . . . cease**—The strongholds shall be pulled down (*Samaria* especially: Hos. 10:14; Mic. 1:6; Hab. 1:10). **remnant of Syria**—all that was left after the overthrow by Tiglath-pileser (II Kings 16:9). **as the glory of . . . Israel**—They shall meet with the same fate as Israel, their ally. **4. glory of Jacob**—the kingdom of Ephraim and all that they rely on (Hos. 12:2; Mic. 1:5). **fatness . . . lean**—(*Note*, ch. 10:16.) **5. harvestman . . .**—The inhabitants and wealth of Israel shall be swept away, and but few left behind just as the husbandman gathers the corn and the fruit, and leaves only a few gleaning ears and grapes (II Kings 18:9-11). **with his arm**—He collects the standing grain with one arm, so that he can cut it with the sickle in the other hand. **Rephaim**—a fertile plain at the southwest of Jerusalem toward Bethlehem and the country of the Philistines (II Sam. 5:18-22). **6. in it**—i.e., in the land of Israel. **two or three . . . in the top**—A few poor inhabitants shall be left in Israel, like the two or three olive berries left on the topmost boughs, which it is not worth while taking the trouble to try to reach. **7. look to his Maker**—instead of trusting in their *fortresses*—(vs. 3; Mic. 7:7). **8. groves**—A symbolical tree is often found in Assyrian inscriptions, representing *the hosts of heaven* (Saba), answering to Asteroth or Astarte, the queen of heaven, as Baal or Bel is the king. Hence the expression, "image of the grove," is explained (II Kings 21:7). **images**—lit., "images to the sun," i.e., to Baal, who answers to the sun, as Astarte to the hosts of heaven (II Kings 23:5; Job 31:26).

9. forsaken bough—rather "the leavings of woods," what the axeman leaves when he cuts down the grove (cf. vs. 6). **which they left because of**—rather, "which (the enemies) shall leave for the children of Israel"; lit., "shall leave (in departing) *from before the face* of the children of Israel [Maurer]. But a few cities out of many shall be left to Israel, by the purpose of God, executed by the Assyrian. **10. forgotten . . . God of . . . salvation . . . rock**—(Deut. 32:15, 18). **plants**—rather, nursery grounds, pleasure-grounds [Maurer]. **set**

ADAM CLARKE — CHAPTER 17

This prophecy by its title should relate only to Damascus; but it fully as much concerns, and more largely treats of, the kingdom of Samaria and the Israelites, confederated with Damascus and the Syrians against the kingdom of Judah. It was delivered probably soon after the prophecies of the seventh and eighth chapters, in the beginning of the reign of Ahaz; and was fulfilled by Tiglath-pileser's taking Damascus, and carrying the people captives to Kir (2 Kings xvi. 9) and overrunning a great part of the kingdom of Israel, and carrying a great number of the Israelites also captives to Assyria; and still more fully in regard to Israel, by the conquest of the kingdom, and the captivity of the people, effected a few years after by Shalmaneser.

1. *The burden of Damascus.* If we credit *Midrash*, the Damascenes were the most extensive and flagrant of all idolaters. "There were in Damascus three hundred and sixty-five streets, in each of these was an idol, and each idol had his peculiar day of worship; so that the whole were worshipped in the course of the year." This, or anything like this, was a sufficient reason for this city's destruction.

2. *The cities of Aroer are forsaken*—"The cities are deserted forever."

4. *In that day.* That is, says Kimchi, the time when the ten tribes of Israel, which were *the glory of Jacob*, should be carried into captivity.

5. *As when the harvestman gathereth.* That is, the king of Assyria shall sweep away the whole body of the people, as the reaper strippeth off the whole crop of corn; and the remnant shall be no more in proportion than the scattered ears left to the gleaner. *The valley of Rephaim* near Jerusalem was celebrated for its plentiful harvest; it is here used poetically for any fruitful country.

10. *Strange slips*—"Shoots from a foreign soil." The pleasant plants and shoots from a

MATTHEW HENRY

strength, who has been thy strength many a time, or thou wouldst have been broken long since." They had taken great care to improve their land and to make it more pleasant. It was like a garden and a vineyard; replenished with plants, the choicest of its own growth; and not content with them, they sent to all the neighbouring countries for strange slips. This instance seems to be put in general for their great industry in cultivating their ground; they doubt not but their plants will grow and flourish. But *the harvest shall be a heap*, all in confusion, *in the day of grief and of desperate sorrow.* The harvest had sometimes been a day of grief, if the crop was thin; and yet in that case there was hope that the next would be better. But this shall be desperate sorrow, for they shall see not only this year's products carried off, but the property of the ground altered and their conquerors lords of it.

Verses 12–14

These verses read the doom of those that rob the people of God. If the Assyrians and Israelites invade and plunder Judah, if the Assyrian army take God's people captive and lay their country waste, let them know that ruin will be their lot. The Assyrian army was made up out of divers nations: it was *the multitude of many people* (*v.* 12), by which weight they hoped to carry the cause. They were noisy, like the roaring of the seas, to frighten God's people from resisting them. Sennacherib and Rabshakeh, in their speeches and letters, made a mighty noise to strike terror upon Hezekiah and his people; the nations that followed them *made a rushing like the rushing of many waters.* They thought to carry their point by dint of noise; but (*v.* 12), he *shall rebuke them*, that is, God shall, *and* then *they shall flee afar off.* Sennacherib, and Rabshakeh, and the remains of their forces, shall be chased by their own terrors, *as the chaff of the mountains* which stand bleak *before the wind, and like a rolling thing before the whirlwind*, like thistle-down (so the margin). God will make *them like a wheel* or rolling thing, and *make them afraid with his storm*, Ps. lxxxiii. 13, 15. This shall be done suddenly (*v.* 14): *At evening-tide* they are very troublesome, and threaten trouble to the people of God; but *before the morning they are not.* At sleeping time they are cast into a deep sleep, Ps. lxxvi. 5, 6. It was in the night that the angel routed the Assyrian army.

JAMIESON, FAUSSET, BROWN

in—rather, "set them," the pleasure-grounds. **strange slips**—cuttings of plants from far, and therefore valuable. **11. In the day . . . thy plant**—rather, "In the day of *thy planting*" [HORSLEY]. **shalt . . . make . . . grow**—MAURER translates, "Thou didst *fence* it," viz., the pleasure-ground. The parallel clause, "Make . . . flourish," favors *English Version.* As soon as thou plantest, it grows. **in the morning**—i.e., immediately after; so in Psalm 94:14, the *Hebrew*, "in the morning," is translated "early." **but . . . shall be a heap**—rather, "but (promising as was the prospect) the harvest *is gone*" [HORSLEY]. **in . . . day of grief**—rather, "in the day of (expected) *possession*" [MAURER]. "In the day of *inundation*" [HORSLEY]. **of desperate sorrow**—rather, "And the sorrow shall be desperate or irremediable." In *English Version* "heap" and "sorrow" may be taken together by hendiadys. "The heap of the harvest shall be desperate sorrow" [ROSENMULLER].

Chap. 17:12-18:7. SUDDEN DESTRUCTION OF A GREAT ARMY IN JUDEA (viz., that of the Assyrian Sennacherib), AND ANNOUNCEMENT OF THE EVENT TO THE ETHIOPIAN AMBASSADORS. The connection of this fragment with what precedes is: notwithstanding the calamities coming on Israel, the people of God shall not be utterly destroyed (ch. 6:12, 13); the Assyrian spoilers shall perish (ch. 17:13, 14). **12. Woe . . . multitude**—rather, "*Ho* (Hark)! *a noise* of," etc. The prophet in vision perceives the vast and mixed Assyrian hosts (*Hebrew*, "many *peoples*," see *Note*, ch. 5:26): on the hills of Judah (so "mountains," vs. 13): but at the "rebuke" of God, they shall "flee as chaff." **to the rushing . . . that make**—rather, "the roaring . . . roareth" (cf. ch. 8:7; Jer. 6:23). **13. shall . . . shall**—rather, "God rebuketh (Ps. 9:5) them, and they *flee—are chased*"; the event is set before the eyes as actually present, not future. **chaff of . . . mountains**—Threshing-floors in the East are in the open air on *elevated* places, so as to catch the wind which separates the chaff from the wheat (Ps. 88:13; Hos. 13:3). **rolling thing**—anything that rolls: *stubble.* **14. eventide . . . before morning**—fulfilled to the letter in the destruction "before morning" of the vast host that "at evening-tide" was such a *terror* ("trouble") to Judah; on the phrase see Psalm 90:6; 30:5. **he is not**—viz., the enemy. **us**—the Jews. A general declaration of the doom that awaits the foes of God's people (ch. 54:17).

ADAM CLARKE

foreign soil are allegorical expressions for strange and idolatrous worship; vicious and abominable practices connected with it; reliance on human aid, and on alliances entered into with the neighboring nations, especially Egypt; to all which the Israelites were greatly addicted, and in their expectations from which they should be grievously disappointed.

12. *Woe to the multitude!* The last three verses of this chapter seem to have no relation to the foregoing prophecy, to which they are joined. It is a beautiful piece, standing singly and by itself, for neither has it any connection with what follows. Whether it stands in its right place or not, I cannot say. It is a noble description of the formidable invasion and the sudden overthrow of Sennacherib, which is intimated in the strongest terms and the most expressive images, exactly suitable to the event.

14. *He is not*—"He is no more." Though God may permit the wicked to prevail for a time against His people, yet in the end those shall be overthrown, and the glory of the Lord shall shine brightly on them that fear Him; for the earth shall be subdued, and the universe filled with His glory.

MATTHEW HENRY — CHAPTER 18

Verses 1–7

Interpreters are very much at a loss where to find this land that lies beyond the rivers of Cush. Some take it to be Egypt, but against this it is objected that the next chapter is distinguished by the title of *the burden of Egypt.* Others take it to be Ethiopia, of which Tirhakah was king. He thought to protect the Jews, as it were, under *the shadow of his wings*, by giving a powerful diversion to the king of Assyria, when he was attacking Jerusalem, 2 Kings xix. 9. But though by his ambassadors he bade defiance to the king of Assyria, God will take another course to protect Jerusalem. But from a hint of Dr. Lightfoot's, in his Harmony of the Old Testament, I incline to understand this chapter as a prophecy against Assyria, and so a continuation of the last three verses of the foregoing chapter. That was against the army of the Assyrians which rushed in upon Judah; this is against the land of Assyria itself, which lay beyond the rivers Euphrates and Tigris.

JAMIESON, FAUSSET, BROWN — CHAPTER 18

Isaiah announces the overthrow of Sennacherib's hosts and desires the Ethiopian ambassadors, now in Jerusalem, to bring word of it to their own nation; and he calls on the whole world to witness the event (vs. 3). As ch. 17:12-14 announced the presence of the foe, so ch. 18 foretells his overthrow. The heading in *English Version*, "God will destroy the Ethiopians," is a mistake arising from the wrong rendering "Woe," whereas the *Hebrew* does not express a threat, but is an *appeal* calling attention (ch. 55:1; Zech. 2:6): "Ho." He is not speaking *against* but *to* the Ethiopians, calling on them to hear his prophetical announcement as to the destruction of their enemies. **1. shadowing with wings**—rather, "land *of the winged bark*"; i.e., "barks with wing-like sails, answering to vessels of bulrushes" in vs. 2; the word "rivers," in the parallelism, also favors it; so LXX and *Chaldee* [EWALD]. "Land of the clanging sound of *wings*," i.e., armies, as in ch. 8:8; the rendering "bark," or "ship," is rather dubious [MAURER]. The armies referred to are those of Tirhakah, advancing to meet the Assyrians (ch. 37:9). In *English Version*, "shadowing" means *protecting*—stretching out its *wings* to defend a feeble people, viz., the Hebrews [VITRINGA]. The *Hebrew* for "wings" is the same as for the idol *Cneph*, which was represented in temple sculptures with wings (Ps. 91:4). **beyond**—Meroe, the island between the "rivers" Nile and Astaboras is meant, famed for its commerce, and perhaps the seat of the Ethiopian government, hence addressed here as representing the whole empire: remains of temples are still found, and the name of "Tirhakah" in the inscriptions. This island region was probably the chief part of Queen Candace's kingdom (Acts 8:27). For "beyond" others translate less literally "which borderest on." **Ethiopia**—lit., Cush. HORSLEY is probably right that the *ultimate* and *fullest* reference of the prophecy is to the restoration of the Jews in the Holy Land through the instrumentality of some *distant* people skilled in navigation (vs. 2; ch. 60:9, 10; Ps. 45:15; 68:31; Zeph. 3:10). Phœnician voyagers coasting along would speak of all Western *remote* lands as "beyond" the Nile's mouths. "Cush," too,

ADAM CLARKE — CHAPTER 18

This is one of the most obscure prophecies in the whole Book of Isaiah. The subject of it, the end and design of it, the people to whom it is addressed, the history to which it belongs, the person who sends the messengers, and the nation to whom the messengers are sent, are all obscure and doubtful.

1. *Woe to the land! Hoi arets!* This interjection should be translated "Ho!" for it is properly a particle of calling: Ho, land! Attend! Give ear!

Shadowing with wings—"The winged cymbal." The Egyptian sistrum is expressed by a periphrasis.

Which is beyond the rivers of Ethiopia—"Which borders on the rivers of Cush."

MATTHEW HENRY

I. The attempt made by this land (whatever it is) upon *a nation scattered and peeled, v.* 2. Whether this refer to the Ethiopians waging war with the Assyrians, or the Assyrians with Judah, it teaches us that a people which have been terrible from their beginning, and borne a mighty sway, may yet become scattered and peeled, and may be spoiled even by their own rivers, that should enrich both the husbandman and the merchant. "It is a nation that has been terrible, and is now a nation scattered and peeled, meted out and trodden down, and therefore an easy prey for us."

II. The alarm sounded to the nations about, by which they are summoned to take notice of what God is about to do, *v.* 3. *He lifts up an ensign upon the mountains, and blows a trumpet,* by which he proclaims war against the enemies of his church, and calls in all her friends. He is about to do some great work, as *Lord of hosts.*

III. The assurance God gives to his prophet, by him to be given to his people, that, though he might seem for a time to sit by as an unconcerned spectator, yet he would certainly appear for the comfort of his people and the confusion of his and their enemies (*v.* 4): *So the Lord said unto me.* He will take care of his people, and be a shelter to them. He will regard his *dwelling-place*; Zion is his rest for ever, and he will *look after it* (so some read it). He will be as a clear heat after rain (so the margin), like a dew and *a cloud in the heat of harvest*, which are very welcome, the dew to the ground and the cloud to the labourers. Great men have their winter-house and their summer-house (Amos iii. 15); but those that are at home with God have both in him. He will reckon with his and their enemies, *v.* 5, 6. When the Assyrian army promises itself a plentiful harvest in the taking of Jerusalem, God shall destroy that army as easily as the husbandman cuts off the sprigs of the vine with pruning hooks, or *takes away and cuts down the branches.* This seems to point at the dead bodies of the soldiers scattered like the branches of a wild vine,

JAMIESON, FAUSSET, BROWN

has a wide sense, being applied not only to Ethiopia, but Arabia Deserta and Felix, and along the Persian Gulf, as far as the Tigris (Gen. 2:13). **2. ambassadors**—messengers sent to Jerusalem at the time that negotiations passed between Tirhakah and Hezekiah against the expected attack of Sennacherib (ch. 37:9). **by . . . sea**—on the *Nile* (ch. 19:5): as what follows proves. **vessels of bulrushes**—light canoes, formed of papyrus, daubed over with pitch: so the "ark" in which Moses was exposed (Exod. 2: 3). **Go**—Isaiah tells them to take back the tidings of what God is about to do (vs. 4) against the common enemy of both Judah and Ethiopia. **scattered and peeled**—rather, "strong and energetic" [MAURER]. The *Hebrew* for "strong" is lit., drawn out (*Margin,* Ps. 36:10; Eccles. 2:3). "Energetic," lit., sharp (Hab. 1:8; *Margin,* the verb means to "sharpen" a sword, Ezek. 21:15, 16); also "polished." As HERODOTUS (3:20, 114) characterizes the Ethiopians as "the tallest and fairest of men," G. V. SMITH translates, "tall and comely"; lit., extended (ch. 45: 14, "men of stature") *and polished* (the Ethiopians had *smooth, glossy skins*). In *English Version* the reference is to the Jews, *scattered* outcasts, and loaded with indignity (lit., "having their hair torn off" HORSLEY). **terrible**—the *Ethiopians* famed for warlike prowess [ROSENMULLER]. The *Jews* who, because of God's plague, made others to fear the like (Deut. 28:37). Rather, "awfully remarkable" [HORSLEY]. God puts the "terror" of His people into the surrounding nations at the first (Exod. 23:27; Josh. 2:9); so it shall be again in the latter days (Zech. 12: 2, 3). **from . . . beginning hitherto**—so *English Version* rightly. But GESENIUS, "to the terrible nation (of upper Egypt) and further beyond" (to the Ethiopians, properly so called). **meted out**—*Hebrew,* "of line." The measuring line was used in *destroying* buildings (ch. 34:11; II Kings 21:13; Lam. 2:8). Hence, actively, it means here "a people *meting out,*" —an all-destroying people"; which suits the context better than "meted," passively [MAURER]. HORSLEY, understanding it of *the Jews,* translates it, "Expecting, expecting (in a continual attitude of expectation of Messiah) and trampled under foot"; a graphic picture of them. Most translate, *of strength, strength* (from a root, *to brace* the sinews), i.e., *a most powerful* people. **trodden down**—true of the Jews. But MAURER translates it actively, a people "treading under foot" all its enemies, i.e., *victorious* (ch. 14:25), viz., the Ethiopians. **spoiled**—"cut up." The Nile is formed by the junction of many streams in Abyssinia, the Atbara, the Astapus or Blue river (between which two rivers Meroe, the "Ethiopia" here meant, lies), and the Astaboras or White river; these streams *wash down* the soil along their banks in the "land" of Upper Egypt and deposit it on that of Lower Egypt. G. V. SMITH translates it, "Divide." HORSLEY takes it figuratively *of the conquering armies* which have often "spoiled" *Judea,* **3. see ye . . . hear ye**—rather, ye shall see—shall hear. Call to the whole earth to *be witnesses* of what *Jehovah* ("He") is about to do. He will "lift up an ensign," calling the Assyrian motley hosts together (ch. 5:26) on "the mountains" round Jerusalem, to their own destruction. This (ch. 18) declares the coming overthrow of those armies whose presence is announced in ch. 17:12, 13. The same motive, which led Hezekiah to seek aid from Egypt, led him to accept gladly the Ethiopian Tirhakah's aid (ch. 36: 6; 37:9). Ethiopia, Egypt, and Judea were probably leagued together against the common enemy, 713 B.C. See notes on ch. 22 where a difference of tone (as referring to a different period) as to Ethiopia is observable. HORSLEY takes the "ensign" to be the cross, and the "trumpet" the *Gospel trumpet,* which shall be sounded more loudly in the last days. **4. take . . . rest . . . consider**—I will *calmly look on* and not interpose, while all seems to promise success to the enemy; when fig., the sun's heat" and "the night dews" ripen their "harvest"; but "before" it reaches its maturity I will destroy it (vs. 5; Eccles. 8:11, 12). **like a clear heat**—rather, "at the time of the clear (serene) heat" [MAURER]. **upon herbs**—answering to "harvest" in the parallel clause. MAURER translates, "in the sunlight" (Job 31:26; 37:21; Hab. 3:4). **like . . . dew**—rather, "at the time of the dew-cloud." God's "silence" is mistaken by the ungodly for consent; His delay in taking vengeance for forgetfulness (Ps. 50:21); so it shall be before the vengeance which in the last day shall usher in the restoration of the Jews (ch. 34:1-8; 57:11, end of the verse; II Pet. 3:3-10). **5. For**—rather, "But." **perfect**—perfected. When the enemy's plans are on the verge of completion. **sour grape . . . flower**—rather, "when the flower shall become the ripening grape" [MAURER]. **sprigs**—the *shoots* with the grapes on them. God will not only disconcert their present plans, but pre-

ADAM CLARKE

2. *In vessels of bulrushes*—"In vessels of papyrus." This circumstance agrees perfectly well with Egypt. It is well-known that the Egyptians commonly used on the Nile a light sort of boats made of the reed papyrus. *Go, ye swift messengers.* To this nation before mentioned, who, by the Nile and by their numerous canals, have the means of spreading the report in the most expeditious manner through the whole country. *Go, ye swift messengers,* and carry this notice of God's designs in regard to them.

Scattered—"Stretched out in length." Egypt, that is, the fruitful part, exclusive of the deserts on each side, is one long vale, through the middle of which runs the Nile, bounded on each side to the east and west by a chain of mountains 750 miles in length. *Peeled*—"Smoothed." Made smooth, perfectly plain and level, by the overflowing of the Nile.

Meted out—"Meted out by line." It is generally referred to the frequent necessity of having recourse to mensuration in Egypt, in order to determine the boundaries after the inundations of the Nile, to which even the origin of the science of geometry is by some ascribed.

Trodden down. Supposed to allude to a peculiar method of tillage in use among the Egyptians. Both Herodotus (lib. ii) and Diodorus (lib. i) say that when the Nile had retired within its banks, and the ground became somewhat dry, they sowed their land, and then sent in their cattle to tread in the seed; and without any further care expected the harvest. *The rivers have spoiled*—"The rivers have nourished."

3. *When he lifteth up an ensign*—"When the standard is lifted up." I take God to be the Agent in this verse; and that by the standard and the trumpet are meant the meteors, the thunder, the lightning, the storm, earthquake, and tempest, by which Sennacherib's army shall be destroyed, or by which at least the destruction of it shall be accompanied; as it is described in chap. x. 16-17; xxix. 6; and xx. 30-31.

4. *For so the Lord said unto me.* The subject of the remaining part of this chapter is that God would comfort and support His own people, though threatened with immediate destruction by the Assyrians; that Sennacherib's great designs and mighty efforts against them should be frustrated; and that his vast expectations should be rendered abortive, when he thought them mature, and just ready to be crowned with success; that the chief part of his army should be made a prey for the beasts of the field and the fowls of the air; and that Egypt, being delivered from his oppression, and avenged by the hand of God of the wrongs which she had suffered, should return thanks for the wonderful deliverance, both of herself and of the Jews, from this most powerful adversary.

5. *The flower*—"The blossom."

MATTHEW HENRY

cut to pieces. *And they shall be left to the fowls of the earth*, to prey upon. *In that time*, when this shall be accomplished, *shall the present be brought unto the Lord of hosts.* Those that were *a people scattered and peeled, meted out, and trodden down* (*v.* 2), shall be a present to the Lord: and, though they seem useless and worthless, they shall be acceptable to him who judges men by the sincerity of their faith and love, not by the pomp and prosperity of their outward condition. It is prophesied (Ps. lxviii. 31) that *Ethiopia shall soon stretch out her hands unto God.* Others understand it of the spoil of Sennacherib's army, out of which, presents were brought to *the Lord of hosts.*

CHAPTER 19

Verses 1–17

Though the land of Egypt had of old been a house of bondage to the people of God, the unbelieving Jews trusted to Egypt for help (*ch.* xxx. 2), and thither they fled, in disobedience to God's express command, when things were brought to the last extremity in their own country, Jer. xliii. 7. Rabshakeh upbraided Hezekiah with this, *ch.* xxxvi. 6. While they kept up an alliance with Egypt they stood not in awe of the judgments of God; they depended upon Egypt to protect them. To prevent all this mischief, Egypt must be mortified.

I. The gods of Egypt shall appear utterly unable to help them, *v.* 1. "*The Lord rides upon a cloud, a swift cloud, and shall come into Egypt.* As a judge goes in state to try and condemn the malefactors, so shall God come into Egypt with his judgments." In all this burden of Egypt there is no mention of any foreign enemy invading them; but God himself will come against them, and raise up the causes of their destruction from among themselves. When he comes *the idols of Egypt shall be moved.* Isis, Osiris, and Apis, idols of Egypt, being found unable to relieve their worshippers, shall be disowned and rejected by them. The Egyptians *shall seek to the idols*, when they are at their wits' end, and consult *the charmers and wizards* (*v.* 3); but all in vain.

JAMIESON, FAUSSET, BROWN

vent them forming any future ones. HORSLEY takes the "harvest" and vintage here as referring to purifying judgments which cause the excision of the ungodly from the earth, and the placing of the faithful in a state of peace *on the earth:* not the last judgment (John 15:2; Rev. 14:15-20). **6. birds . . . beasts**—transition from the image "sprigs," "branches," to the thing meant: the Assyrian soldiers and leaders shall be the prey of birds and beasts, the whole year through, "winter" and "summer," so numerous shall be their carcasses. HORSLEY translates the Hebrew which is *singular:* "upon *it*," not "upon them"; the "it" refers to God's "dwelling-place" (vs. 4) in the Holy Land, which Antichrist ("the bird of prey" with the "beasts," his rebel hosts) is to possess himself of, and where he is to perish. **7. present . . . people scattered and peeled**—For the right rendering, see *Note* on vs. 2. The repetition of epithets enhances the honor paid to Jehovah by *so mighty a nation.* The Ethiopians, wonder-struck at such an interposition of Jehovah in behalf of His people, shall send gifts to Jerusalem in His honor (ch. 16:1; Ps. 68:31; 72:10). Thus translate: "a present—*from* a people." Or translate, as *English Version;* "the present" will mean "the people" of Ethiopia converted to God (Rom. 15:16). HORSLEY takes the people converted to Jehovah, as the Jews in the latter days. **place of the name**—where Jehovah peculiarly manifests His glory. Acts 2:10 and 8:27 show how worshippers came up to Jerusalem from Egypt" and "Ethiopia." Frumentius, an Egyptian, in the 4th century, converted Abyssinia to Christianity; and a Christian church, under an *abuna* or bishop, still flourishes there. The full accomplishment is probably still future.

CHAPTER 19

Vss. 1-25. Chaps. 19 and 20 are connected, but with an interval between. Egypt had been held by an Ethiopian dynasty, Sabacho, Sevechus, or Sabacho II, and Tirhakah, for forty or fifty years. Sevechus (called *So*, the ally of Hoshea, II Kings 17:4), retired from Lower Egypt on account of the resistance of the priests; and perhaps also, as the Assyrians threatened Lower Egypt. On his withdrawal, Sethos, one of the priestly caste, became supreme, having Tanis ("Zoan") or else Memphis as his capital, 718 B.C.; while the Ethiopians retained Upper Egypt, with Thebes as its capital, under Tirhakah. A third native dynasty was at Sais, in the west of Lower Egypt; to this at a later period belonged Psammetichus, the first who admitted Greeks into Egypt and its armies; he was one of the dodecarchy, a number of petty kings between whom Egypt was divided, and by aid of foreign auxiliaries overcame the rest, 670 B.C. To the divisions at this last time, GESENIUS refers vs. 2; and Psammetichus, vs. 4, "a cruel lord." The dissensions of the ruling castes are certainly referred to. But the time referred to is much earlier than that of Psammetichus. In vs. 1, the invasion of Egypt is represented as caused by "the LORD"; and in vs. 17, "Judah" is spoken of as "a terror to Egypt," which it could hardly have been *by itself*. Probably, therefore, the Assyrian invasion of Egypt under Sargon, when Judah was the ally of Assyria, and Hezekiah had not yet refused tribute as he did in the beginning of Sennacherib's reign, is meant. That Assyria was in Isaiah's mind appears from the way in which it is joined with Israel and Egypt in the worship of Jehovah (vss. 24, 25). Thus the dissensions referred to (vs. 2) allude to the time of the withdrawal of the Ethiopians from Lower Egypt, probably not without a struggle, espebetween 722-715 B.C., answering to 718 B.C., when Sethos usurped the throne and entered on the contest with the military caste, by the aid of the town populations: when the Saitic dynasty was another cause of division. Sargon's reign was between 722-715 B.C. answering to 718 B.C., when Sethos usurped his throne [G. V. SMITH]. **1. burden**—(*Note*, ch. 13:1.) **upon . . . cloud**—(Ps. 104: 3; 18:10.) **come into Egypt**—to inflict vengeance. "Egypt," in *Hebrew, Misraim, plural* form, to express the two regions of Egypt. BUNSEN observes, The title of their kings runs thus: "Lord of Upper and Lower Egypt." **idols**—the bull, crocodile, etc. The idols poetically are said to be "moved" with fear at the presence of one mightier than even they were *supposed* to be (Exod. 12:12; Jer. 43:12). **2. set**—stir up. GENESIUS translates, "arm." **Egyptians against the Egyptians**—Lower against Upper: and Saitic against both. (See ch. 3:10.) NEWTON refers it to the civil wars between Apries and Amasis at the time of Nebuchadnezzar's invasion; also between Tachos, Nectanebus, and the Mendesians, just be-

ADAM CLARKE

7. *The present*—"A gift." The Egyptians were in alliance with the kingdom of Judah, and were fellow sufferers with the Jews under the invasion of their common enemy Sennacherib, and so were very nearly interested in the great and miraculous deliverance of that kingdom by the destruction of the Assyrian army. Upon which wonderful event it is said, 2 Chron. xxxii. 23, that "many brought gifts unto the Lord to Jerusalem, and presents to Hezekiah king of Judah: so that he was magnified in the sight of all nations from thenceforth." It is not to be doubted that among these the Egyptians distinguished themselves in their acknowledgments on this occasion. *Of a people*—"From a people."

CHAPTER 19

Not many years after the destruction of Sennacherib's army before Jerusalem, by which the Egyptians were freed from the yoke with which they were threatened by so powerful an enemy, who had carried on a successful war of three years' continuance against them, the affairs of Egypt were again thrown into confusion by broils among themselves, which ended in a perfect anarchy, that lasted some few years. This was followed by an aristocracy, or rather tyranny, of twelve princes, who divided the country between them, and at last by the sole dominion of Psammitichus, which he held for fifty-four years. Not long after that followed the invasion and conquest of Egypt by Nebuchadnezzar, and then by the Persians under Cambyses, the son of Cyrus. The yoke of the Persians was so grievous that the conquest of the Persians by Alexander may well be considered as a deliverance to Egypt, especially as he and his successors greatly favored the people and improved the country. To all these events the prophet seems to have had a view in this chapter; and in particular, from v. 18, the prophecy of the propagation of the true religion in Egypt seems to point to the flourishing state of Judaism in that country, in consequence of the great favor shown to the Jews by the Ptolemies. Alexander himself settled a great many Jews in his new city Alexandria, granting them privileges equal to those of the Macedonians. The first Ptolemy, called Soter, carried great numbers of them thither, and gave them such encouragement that still more of them were collected there from different parts, so that Philo reckons that in his time there were a million of Jews in that country. These worshipped the God of their fathers, and their example and influence must have had a great effect in spreading the knowledge and worship of the true God through the whole country.

1. *The burden of Egypt.* That is, the prophet's declaration concerning Egypt.

MATTHEW HENRY

III. The Egyptians shall be embroiled in quarrels among themselves. There shall be no occasion to bring a foreign force upon them to destroy them; they shall destroy one another (*v.* 2): *I will set the Egyptians against the Egyptians; they shall fight everyone against his brother and neighbour, city against city, and kingdom against kingdom.* Egypt was then divided into twelve provinces, or dynasties; but Psammetichus, the governor of one of them, by setting them at variance with one another, at length made himself master of them all. A kingdom thus divided against itself would soon be brought to desolation.

II. The militia of Egypt, that had been famed for their valour, shall be disheartened. Their heroes, that used to be celebrated for courage, shall be posted for cowards: *The heart of Egypt shall melt in the midst of it,* like wax before the fire (*v.* 1); *the spirit of Egypt shall fail, v.* 3. They *shall be like women* (*v.* 16); they shall be frightened and put into confusion by the least alarm.

IV. Their politics shall be turned into foolishness. When God will destroy the nation he will *destroy the counsel thereof* (*v.* 3).

V. The rod of government shall be turned into the serpent of tyranny and oppression (*v.* 4): "*The Egyptians will I give over into the hand of a cruel lord,* not a foreigner, but one that shall rule over them by an hereditary right, but shall be a fierce king and rule them with rigour."

VI. Egypt was famous for its river Nile, which was its wealth, and strength, and is here threatened that *the waters shall fail from the sea* and the river shall be *wasted and dried up, v.* 5. The fruitfulness of the country depended wholly upon the overflowing of the river; if that be dried up, their fruitful land will soon be turned into barrenness and their harvests cease: *Everything sown by the brooks will wither* of course, will *be driven away, and be no more, v.* 7. If the paper-reeds at the very mouth wither, much more the corn, which lies at a greater distance. The drying up of their rivers is the destruction of their fortifications, for they are *brooks of defence* (*v.* 6). But these *shall be emptied and dried up,* not by an enemy, as Sennacherib with the *sole of his foot dried up mighty rivers* (*ch.* xxxvii. 25), but by the providence of God, which sometimes *turns water-springs into dry ground,* Ps. cvii. 33. The drying up of the rivers will *kill the fish* (Ps. cv. 29), and will thereby ruin those who make it their business to catch fish, whether by angling or nets (*v.* 8); they shall *lament* and *languish,* for their trade is at an end. There were those that *made sluices and ponds for fish* (*v.* 10), but *they shall be broken in the purposes thereof*; their business will fail for want of water to fill their ponds. The loss of these advantages by the river is their own doing (*v.* 6): *They shall turn the rivers far away.* Their kings and great men will drain water from the main river to their own houses, preferring their private convenience before the public good. Herodotus tells us that Pharaoh-Necho, projecting to cut a free passage by water from Nilus into the Red Sea, employed a vast number of men to make a channel for that purpose, impaired the river, lost 120,000 of his people, and yet left the work unaccomplished.

VII. Egypt was famous for the linen manufacture; but that trade shall be ruined. Solomon's merchants traded with Egypt for linen-yarn, 1 Kings x. 28. Their country produced the best flax and the best hands to work it; but *those that work in fine flax shall be confounded* (*v.* 9).

JAMIESON, FAUSSET, BROWN

fore Ochus subdued Egypt. **kingdom against kingdom**—The LXX has "nome against nome"; Egypt was divided into forty-two *nomes* or districts. **3. spirit**— *wisdom,* for which Egypt was famed (ch. 31:2; I Kings 4:30; Acts 7:22); answering to "counsel" in the parallel clause. **fail**—lit., "be poured out," i.e., be made void (Jer. 19:7). They shall "seek" help from sources that can afford none, "charmers," etc. (ch. 8:19). **charmers**—lit., "those making a faint sound"; the soothsayers imitated the faint sound which was attributed to the spirits of the dead (*Note,* ch. 8:19). **4. cruel lord**—Sargon, in *Hebrew* it is *lords*; but *plural* is often used to express *greatness,* where *one* alone is meant (Gen. 39:2). The parallel word "king" (singular) proves it. NEWTON makes the *general* reference to be to Nebuchadnezzar, and a *particular* reference to Cambyses, son of Cyrus (who killed the Egyptian god, Apis), and Ochus, Persian conquerors of Egypt, noted for their "fierce cruelty." GESENIUS refers it to Psammetichus, who had brought into Egypt Greek and other foreign mercenaries to subdue the other eleven princes of the dodecarchy. **5. the sea**—the Nile. Physical calamities, it is observed in history, often accompany political convulsions (Ezek. 30:12). The Nile shall "fail" to rise to its wonted height, the result of which will be barrenness and famine. Its "waters" at the time of the overflow resemble "a sea" (PLINY, *N.H.,* 85. 11); and it is still called *El-Bahr,* "the sea," by the Egyptians (ch. 18:2; Jer. 51:36). A public record is kept at Cairo of the daily rise of the water at the proper time of overflow, viz., August: if it rises to a less height than twelve cubits, it will not overflow the land, and famine must be the result. So, also, when it rises higher than sixteen; for the waters are not drained off in time sufficient to sow the seed. **6. they shall turn the rivers**—rather, "the streams shall become putrid"; i.e., the artificial streams made for irrigation shall become stagnant and offensive when the waters fail [MAURER]. HORSLEY, with LXX, translates, "And waters from the sea shall be drunk"; by the failure of the river-water they shall be reduced to sea-water. **brooks of defence**—rather, "canals of *Egypt*"; canals, lit., "Niles," *Nile canals,* the *plural* of the Egyptian term for the great river. The same *Hebrew* word, *Matzor,* whence comes *Mitzraim,* expresses *Egypt,* and a place of "defense." HORSLEY, as *English Version* translates it, "embanked canals," **reeds . . . flags**—the papyrus. "Reed and rush"; *utter* withering. **7. paper reeds**—rather, pastures, lit., "places naked" of wood, and famed for rich herbage, on the banks of the Nile [GESENIUS]. Cf. Gen. 13:10; Deut. 11:10. HORSLEY translates, "nakedness upon the river," descriptive of the appearance of a river when its bottom is bare and its banks stripped of verdure by long drought: so *Vulgate.* **the brooks**—the river. **mouth**—rather, "the source" [VULGATE]. "Even close to the river's *side* vegetation shall be so withered as to be scattered in the shape of powder by the wind" (*English Version,* "driven away") [HORSLEY]. **8. fishers**—The Nile was famed for fish (Num. 11:5); many would be thrown out of employment by the failure of fishes. **angle**—a hook. Used in the "brooks" or canals, as the "net" was in "the waters" of the river itself. **9. fine flax**—GESENIUS, for "fine," translates, "combed"; fine linen was worn by the rich only (Luke 16:19). Egypt was famous for it (Exod. 9:31; I Kings 10:28; Prov. 7:16; Ezek. 27:7). The processes of its manufacture are represented on the Egyptian tombs. Israel learned the art in Egypt (Exod. 26:36). The cloth now found on the mummies was *linen,* as is shown by the microscope. WILKINSON mentions linen from Egypt which has 540 (or 270 double) threads in one inch in the warp; whereas some modern cambric has but 160 [BARNES]. **networks**—rather, *white cloth* (Esther 1:6; 8:16). **10. in the purposes**—rather, the foundations, i.e., "the nobles shall be broken" or brought low: so ch. 3:1; Psalm 11:3; cf. vs. 13, "*Their weaving-frames*" [HORSLEY]. "Dykes" call a prince "a *pillar* of the people" [MAURER]. "*Their weaving-frames*" [HORSLEY]. "Dykes" [BARNES]. **all that make sluices,** etc.—"makers of *dams,*" made to confine the waters which overflow from the Nile in artificial fishponds [HORSLEY]. "Makers of gain," i.e., the common people who have to earn their livelihood, as opposed to the "nobles" previously [MAURER]. **11. Zoan**—The Greeks called it Tanis, a city of Lower Egypt, east of the Tanitic arms of the Nile, now *San*; it was one the Egyptian towns nearest to Palestine (Num. 13:22), the scene of Moses' miracles (Ps. 78:12, 43). It, or else Memphis, was the capital under Sethos. **I am . . . son of the wise . . . kings**—Ye have no advice to suggest to Pharaoh in the crisis, not-

ADAM CLARKE

4. *A cruel lord*—"Cruel lords." Nebuchadnezzar in the first place, and afterwards the whole succession of Persian kings, who in general where hard masters, and grievously oppressed the country.

5. *The river shall be wasted and dried up.* The Nile shall not overflow its banks; and if no inundation, the land must become barren. For, as there is little or no rain in Egypt, its fertility depends on the overflowing of the Nile.

6. *Shall turn the rivers far away*—"Shall become putrid."

8. *The fishers also.* There was great plenty of fish in Egypt; see Num. xi. 5.

9. *They that work in fine flax.* I.e., flax dressed on the comb used for that purpose.

MATTHEW HENRY

They make fools of one another, everyone betrays his own folly, and divine Providence makes fools of them all, *v.* 11. The nobles of Egypt boasted much of their antiquity, producing fabulous records of their succession for above 10,000 years. This humour prevailed much among them about this time, as appears by Herodotus, their common boast being that Egypt was some thousands of years more ancient than any other nation. "But *where are thy wise men? v.* 12. Let them with all their skill *know what the Lord of hosts has purposed upon Egypt*, and arm themselves accordingly. Nay, so far are they from doing this that they themselves are, in effect, contriving the ruin of Egypt, and, hastening it on, *v.* 13. *The princes of Noph* are not only deceived themselves, but they *have seduced Egypt*."

It is sad with a people when those that undertake for their safety are helping forward their destruction; so here (*v.* 14): *They have caused Egypt to err in every work thereof.*

The trade of Egypt must needs sink, for (*v.* 15) *there shall not be any work for Egypt*; and where there is nothing to be done there is nothing to be got. There shall be *no work which either head or tail, branch or rush, may do;* nothing for high or low, weak or strong, to do.

VIII. A general consternation shall seize the Egyptians; they *shall be afraid and fear* (*v.* 16), an evidence of decay and of ruin. When they hear of the desolations made in Judah by the army of Sennacherib (*v.* 17), they will conclude it must be their turn next to become a prey to that victorious army. They shall *fear* (*v.* 16) *because of the shaking of the hand of the Lord of hosts*, and (*v.* 17) *because of the counsel of the Lord of hosts*. From the shaking of his hand they shall conclude *he has determined* against Egypt as well as Judah. For, if judgment begin at the house of God, where will it end?

Verses 18–25

Out of the threatening clouds of the prophecy the sun here breaks forth, and it is the sun of righteousness. Still God has mercy in store for Egypt, and he will show it, by bringing the true religion among them, calling them to the worship of the one true God. The preaching (as is supposed) of Mark the Evangelist, led to the founding of Christian churches in Egypt. Many prophecies of this book point to the days of the Messiah; and why not this? It is no unusual thing to speak of gospel graces and ordinances in the language of the Old Testament institutions. And, in these prophecies, those words, *in that day*, perhaps have not always a reference to what goes immediately before, but have a peculiar significancy pointing at that day, when the day-spring from on high should visit this dark world. Yet it is not improbable that this prophecy was in part fulfilled when those Jews who fled from their own country to take shelter in Egypt, when Sennacherib invaded their land, brought their religion along with them. Josephus tells us that Onias the son of Onias the high priest, living an outlaw at Alexandria, obtained leave of Ptolemy Philometer, and Cleopatra his queen, to build a temple to the God of Israel, like that at Jerusalem, at Bubastis in Egypt, and pretended a warrant for doing it from this prophecy in Isaiah, that there shall be an *altar to the Lord in the land of Egypt*. The conversion of Egypt is here described.

I. They shall *speak the language of Canaan*, the holy language, the scripture language; they shall not only understand it, but use it (*v.* 18). *Five cities in Egypt* shall speak this language; so many Jews shall come to reside in Egypt, and shall soon replenish five cities, one of which shall be the city of Heliopolis, where the sun was worshipped, the most infamous of all the cities of Egypt for idolatry; even there shall be a wonderful reformation.

II. They shall swear to the Lord of hosts, not only swear by him, but shall by a solemn oath devote themselves to his honour and bind themselves to his service.

III. They shall set up the public worship of God in their land (*v.* 19): *There shall be an altar to the Lord* in the *midst of the land of Egypt*, an altar on which *they shall do sacrifice and oblation* (*v.* 21); this must be understood spiritually, for by the law of Moses there was to be no altar for sacrifice but that at Jerusalem. In Christ Jesus all distinction of nations is taken away; and a spiritual altar, a gospel church, in Egypt, is as acceptable to God as one in Israel.

JAMIESON, FAUSSET, BROWN

withstanding that ye boast of descent from wise and royal ancestors. The priests were the usual "counsellors" of the Egyptian king. He was generally chosen from the priestly caste, or, if from the warrior caste, he was admitted into the sacred order, and was called a priest. The priests are, therefore, meant by the expression, "son of the wise, and of ancient kings"; this was their favorite boast (Herodotus, 2. 141; cf. Amos 7:14; Acts 23:6; Phil. 3:5). "Pharaoh" was the common name of all the kings: Sethos, probably, is here meant. **12. let them know**—i.e., How is it that, with all their boast of knowing the future (Diodorus, 1. 81), they do not know what Jehovah of hosts. . . . **13. Noph**—called also *Moph; Greek, Memphis* (Hos. 9:6); on the western bank of the Nile, capital of Lower Egypt, second only to Thebes in all Egypt: residence of the kings, until the Ptolemies removed to Alexandria; the word means the "port of the good" (Plutarch). The *military* caste probably ruled in it: "*they also* are deceived," in fancying their country secure from Assyrian invasion. **stay of . . . tribes**—rather, "cornerstone of her castes" [MAURER], i.e., the princes, the two ruling castes, the priests and the warriors: image from a building which rests mainly on its cornerstones (vs. 10, *Note*: ch. 28:16; Ps. 118:22; Num. 24:17; *Margin:* Judg. 20:2; I Sam. 14:28, *Margin:* Zech. 10:4). **14. err in every work thereof**—referring to the anarchy arising from their internal feuds. HORSLEY translates, "with respect to all *His* (God's) work"; they misinterpreted God's dealings at every step. "Mingled" contains the same image as "drunken"; as one *mixes* spices with wine to make it intoxicating (ch. 5:22; Prov. 9:2,5), so Jehovah has poured among them a spirit of *giddiness,* so that they are as helpless as a "drunken man." **15. work for Egypt**—nothing which Egypt can do to extricate itself from the difficulty. **head or tail**—high or low (vss. 11-15, and 8-10). **branch or rush**—the lofty palm branch or the humble reed (ch. 9:14, 15; 10:33, 34). **16. like . . . women**—timid and helpless (Jer. 51:30; Nah. 3:13). **shaking of . . . hand**—His judgments by means of the invaders (ch. 10:5, 32; 11:15). **17. Judah . . . terror unto Egypt**—not by itself: but at this time Hezekiah was the active subordinate ally of Assyria in its invasion of Egypt under Sargon. Similarly to the alliance of Judah with Assyria here is II Kings 23:29, where Josiah takes the field against Pharaoh-necho of Egypt, probably as ally of Assyria against Egypt [G. V. SMITH]. VITRINGA explains it that Egypt in its calamities would remember that prophets of Judah had foretold them, and so Judah would be "a terror unto Egypt." **thereof**—of Judah. **it**—Egypt. **18-22.** Suffering shall lead to repentance. Struck with "terror" and "afraid" (vs. 17) because of Jehovah's judgments, Egypt shall be converted to Him: nay, even Assyria shall join in serving Him; so that Israel, Assyria, and Egypt, once mutual foes, shall be bound together by the tie of a common faith as one people. So a similar issue from other prophecies (ch. 18:7; 23:18). **five cities**—i.e., *several* cities, as in ch. 17:6; 30:17; Gen. 43:34; Lev. 26:8. Rather, *five* definite *cities* of Lower Egypt (vss. 11, 13; ch. 30:4), which had close intercourse with the neighboring Jewish cities [MAURER]; some say, Heliopolis, Leontopolis (else Diospolis), Migdol, Daphne (Tahpanes), and Memphis. **language of Canaan**—i.e., of the Hebrews in Canaan, the language of revelation. Fig. for, They shall embrace the Jewish *religion:* so "a pure *language*" and *conversion to God* are connected in Zephaniah 3:9; as also the first confounding and multiplication of languages was the punishment of the making of gods at Babel, other than the One God. Pentecost (Acts 2:4) was the counterpart of Babel: the separation of nations is not to hinder the unity of faith; the full realization of this is yet future (Zech. 14:9; John 17:21). The next clause, "swear to the LORD of Hosts," agrees with this view; i.e., bind themselves to Him by solemn covenant (ch. 45:23; 65:16; Deut. 6:13). **city of destruction**—Onias; "city of the *sun,*" i.e., On, or Heliopolis; he persuaded Ptolemy Philometer (149 B.C.) to let him build a temple in the prefecture (nome) of Heliopolis, on the ground that it would induce Jews to reside there, and that the very site was foretold by Isaiah 600 years before. The reading of the *Hebrew* text is, however, better supported, "city of *destruction*"; referring to Leontopolis, the site of Onias' temple: which casts a reproach on that city because *it* was about to contain a temple rivalling the only sanctioned temple, that at Jerusalem. MAURER, with some MSS., reads "city of *defense*" or "*deliverance*"; viz., Memphis, or some such city, to which God was about to send "a saviour" (vs. 20), to "deliver them." **19. altar**—not for *sacrifice*, but as the "pillar" for *memorial* and worship (Josh. 22:22-

ADAM CLARKE

JOSEPH PARKER:

Verse 14. When we read of a "perverse spirit" we may substitute for that expression *dizziness*. God turns a man dizzy, so that he is drunk, but not with wine. How many powers has the Almighty! We have seen by how many doors he may come in. How many are the actions of God in human history! He makes Egypt dizzy; he does not strike Egypt with a rod of iron, or confound her by some great phenomena that burn all over the face of heaven to affright her—he simply sends dizziness into the nation, so that the king feels all things going round, and the mean man is sure that he has lost his wit and sense and shrewdness; he fixes his eye upon stable pillars, and, behold, they move, they circulate, and he says, Is it I or is it the pillar moving? so that he cannot reason, he cannot put things together; when he begins to count he forgets his reckoning, when he commences a story he cuts it off at an inferior point, and cannot conduct it to a period; yet he says he is well, he is without a pain, he cannot account for this whirl, this movement, it is taking him on and on, and away and away; he says, What is it? How God can humble men!—*The People's Bible*

16. *Shall Egypt be*—"The Egyptians shall be."

17. *And the land of Judah.* The threatening hand of God will be held out and shaken over Egypt, from the side of Judea, through which the Assyrians will march to invade it. It signifies that kind of terror that drives one to his wit's end, that causes him to reel like a drunken man, to be giddy through astonishment.

18. *The city of destruction*—"The city of the sun." This passage is attended with much difficulty and obscurity. First, in regard to the true reading. It is well-known that Onias applied it to his own views, either to procure from the king of Egypt permission to build his temple in the Hieropolitan Nome or to gain credit and authority to it when built; from the notion which he industriously propagated that Isaiah had in this place prophesied of the building of such a temple. He pretended that the very place where it should be built was expressly named by the prophet, *ir hacheres,* "the city of the sun." This possibly may have been the original reading. The present text has *ir haheres,* "the city of destruction"; which some suppose to have been introduced into the text by the Jews of Palestine afterwards, to express their detestation of the place, being much offended with this schismatical temple in Egypt. Some think the latter to have been the true reading; and that the prophet himself gave this turn to the name out of contempt, and to intimate the demolition of this Hieropolitan temple; which in effect was destroyed by Vespasian's orders, after that of Jerusalem. I take the whole passage from the eighteenth verse to the end of the chapter to contain a general intimation of the future propagation of the knowledge of the true God in Egypt and Syria, under the successors of Alexander; and, in consequence of this propagation, of the early reception of the gospel in the same countries, when it should be published to the world.

MATTHEW HENRY

IV. There shall be a face of religion upon the nation. Not only in the heart of the country, but even in *the borders* of it, *there shall be a pillar,* inscribed, *To Jehovah,* to his honour. Even in the land of Egypt he had some faithful worshippers, who made his name their strong tower.

V. Being in distress, they shall seek to God, and he shall be found of them; and this *shall be a sign and a witness for the Lord of hosts* that he is a *prayer-hearing God* to *all flesh* that *come to him, v.* 20, 22.

VI. They shall have an interest in the great Redeemer. Repenting Egyptians shall find the same favour with God that repenting Ninevites did. But all these deliverances wrought for them, as those for Israel, were but figures of gospel salvation.

VII. The knowledge of God shall prevail among them, *v.* 21. Perhaps this may in part refer to the translation of the Old Testament out of Hebrew into Greek by the LXX, which was done at Alexandria in Egypt. By the help of this (the Greeks having introduced their language into that country) *the Lord was known to Egypt.* It is promised that *the Egyptians shall know the Lord.*

VIII. They shall come into the communion of saints. Being joined to the Lord, they shall be added to the church. Enmities shall be slain. Mortal feuds there had been between Egypt and Assyria; but now *there shall be a highway between Egypt and Assyria* (*v.* 23); they shall trade with one another, and everything that passes between them shall be friendly. *The Egyptians shall serve with the Assyrians.* Those who have communion with the same God, meeting at the same throne of grace, and serving with each other should put an end to all heats and animosities, and knit our hearts to each other in holy love. The Gentile nations shall not only unite with each other in the gospel fold under Christ the great shepherd, but they shall all be united with the Jews. When Egypt and Assyria become partners in serving God *Israel* shall *make a third with* them (*v.* 24); they shall become a *three-fold cord, not easily broken.* Thus united, they shall be *a blessing in the midst of the land, whom the Lord of hosts shall bless, v.* 24, 25. They shall all be a blessing to the world. Though Egypt was formerly a house of bondage, and Assyria an unjust invader, all this shall now be forgiven and forgotten, and they shall be as welcome to God as Israel. They are all alike his people whom he takes under his protection.

JAMIESON, FAUSSET, BROWN

26). Isaiah does not contemplate a *temple* in Egypt: for the only legal temple wat at Jerusalem; but, like the patriarchs, they shall have altars in various places. **pillar**—such as Jacob reared (Gen. 28:18; 35:14); it was a common practice in Egypt to raise obelisks commemorating divine and great events. **at the border**—of Egypt and Judah, to proclaim to both countries the common faith. This passage shows how the Holy Spirit raised Isaiah above a narrow-minded nationality to a charity anticipatory of gospel catholicity. **20. it**—the altar and pillar. **a sign**—(of the fulfilment of prophecy) to their contemporaries. **a witness**—to their descendants. **unto the Lord**—no longer, to their *idols,* but to *Jehovah.* **for they shall cry**—or, "a sign . . . *that they cried,* . . . and *He sent* to them a saviour"; probably, *Alexander the Great* (so "a great one"), whom the Egyptians welcomed as a deliverer (*Greek,* Soter, a title of the Ptolemies) out of the hands of the Persians, who under Cambyses had been their "oppressors." At Alexandria, called from him, the Old Testament was translated into Greek for the Greek-speaking Jews, who in large numbers dwelt in Egypt under the Ptolemies, his successors. Messiah is the antitype ultimately intended (cf. Acts 2:10, "Egypt"). **21. oblation**—unbloody. **22. return**—for heathen sin and idolatry are an *apostasy* from primitive truth. **heal**—as described (vss. 18-20). **23. highway**—free communication, resting on the highest basis, the common faith of both (vs. 18; ch. 11:16). Assyria and Egypt were joined under Alexander as parts of his empire: Jews and proselytes from both met at the feasts of Jerusalem. A type of gospel times to come. **serve with**—serve *Jehovah* with the Assyrians. So "serve" is used absolutely (Job 36:11). **24. third**—The three shall be joined as one nation. **blessing**—the source of blessings to other nations, and the object of their benedictions. **in the midst of the land**—rather, earth (Mic. 5:7). Judah is designed to be the grand center of the whole earth (Jer. 3:17). **25. Whom**—rather, "Which," viz., "the land," or "earth," i.e., the people of it [MAURER]. **my people**—the peculiar designation of Israel, the elect people, here applied to Egypt to express its entire admission to religious privileges (Rom. 9:24-26; I Pet. 2:9, 10). **work of my hands**—spiritually (Hos. 2:23; Eph. 2:10).

ADAM CLARKE

23. *Shall there be a highway.* Under the latter kings of Persia, and under Alexander, Egypt, Judea, and Assyria lived peaceably under the same government, and were on such friendly terms that there was a regular, uninterrupted intercourse between them, so that the Assyrian came into Egypt and the Egyptian into Assyria, and *Israel* became *the third, i.e.,* was in strict union with the other two; and was a *blessing* to both, as affording them some knowledge of the true God, v. 24.

25. *Blessed be Egypt . . . Assyria . . . and Israel.* All these countries shall be converted to the Lord. Concerning Egypt, it was said, chap. xviii. 7, that it should bring gifts to the Lord at Jerusalem. Here it is predicted, v. 19, that there shall be an altar to the Lord in Egypt itself; and that they, with the Assyrians, shall become the people of God with the Israelites. This remains partly to be fulfilled. These countries shall be all, and perhaps at no very distant time from this, converted to the faith of our Lord Jesus Christ.

CHAPTER 20

TODAY'S DICTIONARY OF THE BIBLE:

Sargon. (In the inscriptions, "Sarayukin" [*the god*] *has appointed the king;* also "Sarru kinu," *the legitimate king.*) On the death of Shalmaneser (722 B.C.), one of the Assyrian generals established himself on the vacant throne, taking the name of "Sargon," after that of the famous monarch, the Sargon of Accad, founder of one of the first Semetic empires. His dynasty was the last great flowering of Assyrian power. He later began a conquering career, and became one of the most powerful of the Assyrian monarchs. He is mentioned by name in the Bible only in connection with the siege of Ashdod (Isa. 20:1).

At the very beginning of his reign he claims to have besieged and taken the city of Samaria (2 Kings 17:6; 18:9–12). On an inscription found in the palace he built at Khorsabad, near Nineveh, he says, "The city of Samaria I besieged, I took; 27,280 of its inhabitants I carried away; fifty chariots that were among them I collected," etc. The northern kingdom he changed into an Assyrian satrapy. He afterward drove *Merodach-baladan,* who kept him at bay for twelve years, out of Babylon, which he entered in triumph. By a succession of victories he gradually enlarged and consolidated the empire, which now extended from the frontiers of Egypt in the west to the mountains of Elam in the east.

CHAPTER 20

VSS. 1-6. CONTINUATION OF THE SUBJECT OF CHAPTER 19, BUT AT A LATER DATE. CAPTIVITY OF EGYPT AND ETHIOPIA. In the reign of Sargon (722-715 B.C.), the successor of Shalmaneser, an Assyrian invasion of Egypt took place. Its success is here foretold, and hence a party among the Jews is warned of the folly of their "expectation" of aid from Egypt or Ethiopia. At a later period (ch. 18), when Tirhakah of Ethiopia was their ally, the Ethiopians are treated as *friends,* to whom God announces the overthrow of the common Assyrian foe, Sennacherib. Egypt and Ethiopia in this chapter (vss. 3, 4) are represented as *allied together,* the result no doubt of fear of the common foe; previously they had been at strife, and the Ethiopian king had, just before Sethos' usurpation, withdrawn from occupation of part of Lower Egypt. Hence, "Egypt" is mentioned *alone* in ch. 19, which refers to a somewhat earlier stage of the same event: a delicate mark of truth. Sargon seems to have been the king who finished the capture of Samaria which Shalmaneser began; the alliance of Hoshea with So or Sabacho II of Ethiopia, and his refusal to pay the usual tribute, provoked Shalmaneser to the invasion. On clay cylindrical seals found in Sennacherib's palace at Koyunjik, the name of Sabacho is deciphered; the two seals are thought, from the inscriptions, to have been attached to the treaty of peace between Egypt and Assyria, which resulted from the invasion of Egypt by Sargon, described in this chapter; II Kings 18:10 curiously confirms the view derived from Assyrian inscriptions, that though Shalmaneser began, Sargon finished the conquest of Samaria; "*they* took it" (cf. II Kings 17:4-6). In Sargon's palace at Khorsabad, inscriptions state that 27,280 Israelites were led captive by the founder of the palace. While Shalmaneser was engaged in the siege of Samaria, Sargon probably usurped the supreme power and destroyed him; the siege began in 723 B.C., and ended in 721 B.C., the first year of Sargon's reign. Hence arises the paucity of inscriptions of the two predecessors of Sargon. Tiglath-pileser and Shalmaneser; the usurper destroyed them, just as Tiglath-pileser de-

CHAPTER 20

Tartan besieged Ashdod or Azotus, which probably belonged at this time to Hezekiah's dominions; see 2 Kings xviii. 8. The people expected to be relieved by the Cushites of Arabia and by the Egyptians. Isaiah was ordered to go uncovered, that is, without his upper garment, the rough mantle commonly worn by the prophets (see Zech. xiii. 4), probably three days, to show that within three years the town should be taken, after the defeat of the Cushites and Egyptians by the king of Assyria, which event should make their case desperate and induce them to surrender. Azotus was a strong place; it afterwards held out twenty-nine years against Psammitichus, king of Egypt, Herod. ii. 157. Tartan was one of Sennacherib's generals, 2 Kings xviii. 17, and Tirhakah, king of the Cushites, was in alliance with the king of Egypt against Sennacherib. These circumstances make it probable that by Sargon is meant Sennacherib. It might be one of the seven names by which Jerome, on this place, says he was called. The taking of Azotus must have happened before Sennacherib's attempt on Jerusalem, when he boasted of his late conquests, chap. xxxvii. 25. And the warning of the prophet had a principal respect to the Jews also, who were too much inclined to depend upon the assistance of Egypt.

MATTHEW HENRY

Verses 1–6

God here, as King of nations, brings a sore calamity upon Egypt and Ethiopia, but, as King of saints, brings good to his people out of it.

I. The date of this prophecy. It was in the year that Ashdod, a strong city of the Philistines, was besieged and taken by an army of the Assyrians. It is uncertain what year of Hezekiah that was. He that was now king of Assyria is called *Sargon.* Tartan, who was general, or commander-in-chief, in this expedition, was one of Sennacherib's officers, sent by him to bid defiance to Hezekiah, in concurrence with Rabshakeh, 2 Kings xviii. 17.

II. The making of Isaiah a sign, by his unusual dress. He had been a sign to his own people of the melancholy times that had come and were coming upon them, by the sackcloth which he had worn. Sackcloth he wore as a prophet, to show himself mortified to the world. Elijah wore hair-cloth (2 Kings i. 8), and John Baptist (Matt. iii. 4), but Isaiah has orders to *loose his sackcloth from his loins,* not to exchange it for better clothing, but for none at all, and he must *put off his shoes,* and go barefoot. This was a great hardship upon the prophet and would expose him to contempt and ridicule, but God bade him do it, that he might give a proof of his obedience to God, and so shame the disobedience of his people. When we are in the way of our duty we may trust God both with our credit and with our safety.

III. The exposition of this sign, *v.* 3, 4. It was intended to signify that the Egyptians and the Ethiopians should be led away captive by the king of Assyria, thus stripped, as Isaiah was. God calls him his *servant Isaiah,* because in this matter he had approved himself God's willing, obedient servant; and for this very thing, God gloried in him. Isaiah is said to have *walked naked and barefoot three years,* whenever in that time he appeared as a prophet. Three campaigns successively shall the Assyrian army make, in spoiling the Egyptians and Ethiopians, and carrying them away captive, now stripped, and scarcely having rags to cover their nakedness. It is particularly said to be *to the shame of Egypt* (*v.* 4), because the Egyptians were a proud people.

IV. The use and application of this, *v.* 5, 6. Those countries that were in danger of being overrun by the Assyrians expected that Tirhakah, king of Ethiopia, would put a stop to the progress of their victorious arms, and be a barrier to his neighbours; and that Egypt, a kingdom so famous for policy and prowess, would oblige them to raise the siege of Ashdod and retire. But, instead of this, by attempting to oppose the king of Assyria they did but make their country a prey to him. They were more afraid now than ever of the growing greatness of the king of Assyria, before whom Egypt and Ethiopia proved but as briers and thorns put to stop a consuming fire. The Jews in particular should be convinced of their folly in resting upon such broken reeds (*v.* 6): *The inhabitants of this isle* (the land of Judah, situated upon the sea, though not surrounded by it), everyone shall now have his eyes opened, and shall say, "*Behold, such is our expectation!* We have fled to the Egyptians and Ethiopians, and have hoped by them to be delivered from the king of Assyria; but, now that they are broken, how shall we escape, that are not able to bring such armies into the field as they did?"

JAMIESON, FAUSSET, BROWN

stroyed those of Pul (Sardanapalus), the last of the old line of Ninus; the names of his father and grandfather, which have been deciphered in the palace of his son Sennacherib, do not appear in the list of Assyrian kings, which confirms the view that he was a satrap who usurped the throne. He was so able a general that Hezekiah made no attempt to shake off the tribute until the reign of Sennacherib; hence Judah was not invaded now as the lands of the Philistines and Egypt were. After conquering Israel he sent his general, Tartan, to attack the Philistine cities, "Ashdod," etc., preliminary to his invasion of Egypt and Ethiopia; for the line of march to Egypt lay along the southwest coast of Palestine. The inscriptions confirm the prophecy; they tell us he received tribute from a Pharaoh of "Egypt"; besides destroying in part the Ethiopian "No-ammon," or Thebes (Nah. 3:8); also that he warred with the kings of "Ashdod," Gaza, etc., in harmony with Isaiah here; a memorial tablet of him is found in Cyprus also, showing that he extended his arms to that island. His reign was six or seven years in duration—722-715 B.C. [G. V. SMITH]. **1. Tartan**—probably the same general as was sent by Sennacherib against Hezekiah (II Kings 18:17). GESENIUS takes "Tartan" as a title. **Ashdod**—called by the Greeks Azotus (Acts 8:40); on the Mediterranean, one of the "five" cities of the Philistines. The taking of it was a necessary preliminary to the invasion of Egypt, to which it was the key in that quarter, the Philistines being allies of Egypt. So strongly did the Assyrians fortify it that it stood a twenty-nine years' siege, when it was retaken by the Egyptian Psammetichus. **sent**—Sargon himself remained behind engaged with the Phœnician cities, or else led the main force more directly into Egypt out of Judah [G. V. SMITH]. **2. by**—lit., "by the hand of" (cf. Ezek. 3:14). **sackcloth**—the loose outer garment of coarse dark hair-cloth worn by mourners (II Sam. 3:31) and by prophets, fastened at the waist by a girdle (Matt. 3:4; II Kings 1:8; Zech. 13:4). **naked**—rather, uncovered; he merely put off the outer sackcloth, retaining still the tunic or inner vest(I Sam. 19:24; Amos 2:16; John 21:7); an emblem to show that Egypt should be stripped of its possessions; the very dress of Isaiah was a silent exhortation to repentance. **3. three years**—Isaiah's symbolical action did not continue all this time, but *at intervals,* to keep it before the people's mind during that period [ROSENMULLER]. Rather, join "three years" with "sign," *a three years' sign,* i.e., a sign that a three years' calamity would come on Egypt and Ethiopia [BARNES], (ch. 8:18). This is the only instance of a strictly symbolical act performed by Isaiah. With later prophets, as Jeremiah and Ezekiel, such acts were common. In some cases they were performed, not literally, but only in prophetic vision. **wonder**—rather, "omen"; conveying a threat as to the future [G. V. SMITH]. **upon**—in reference to, against. **4. buttocks uncovered**—BELZONI says that captives are found represented thus on Egyptian monuments (ch. 47:2, 3; Nah. 3:5, 8, 9), where as here, Egypt and Ethiopia are mentioned as in alliance. **5. they**—the Philistine allies of Egypt who trusted in it for help against Assyria. A warning to the party among the Jews, who, though Judah was then the subordinate ally of Assyria, were looking to Egypt as a preferable ally (ch. 30:7). Ethiopia was their "expectation"; for Palestine had not yet obtained, *but hoped* for alliance with it. Egypt was their "glory," i.e., boast (ch. 13:19); for the alliance with it was completed. **6. isle**—i.e., coast on the Mediterranean—Philistia, perhaps Phœnicia (cf. ch. 23:2; 11:11; 13:22, Ps. 72:10). **we**—emphatical; if Egypt, in which we trusted, was overcome, how shall *we,* a small weak state, escape?

ADAM CLARKE

KEIL-DELITZSCH:

Verse 2. We see from this that Isaiah was clothed in the same manner as Elijah, who wore a fur coat (2 Kings 1:8; cf. Zech. 8:4; Heb. 11:37), and John the Baptist, who had a garment of camel hair and a leather girdle round it (Matt. 3:4); for *sak* is a coarse linen or hairy overcoat of dark color (Rev. 6:12; cf. Isa. 50:3), such as was worn by mourners, either next to the skin (*'al-habbâsâr,* 1 Kings 21:27; 2 Kings 6:30; Job 16:15) or over the tunic, in either case being fastened by a girdle on account of its want of shape, for which reason the verb *châgar* is the word commonly used to signify the putting on of such a garment, instead of *lâbash.* The use of the word *'ârôm* does not prove that the former was the case in this instance (see, on the contrary, 2 Sam. 6:20, compared with v. 14 and John 21:7). With the great importance attached to the clothing in the East, where the feelings upon this are peculiarly sensitive and modest, a person was looked upon as stripped and naked if he had only taken off his upper garment. What Isaiah was directed to do, therefore, was simply opposed to common custom, and not to moral decency. He was to lay aside the dress of a mourner and preacher of repentance, and to have nothing on but his tunic (*cetoneth*); and in this, as well as barefooted, he was to show himself in public. This was the costume of a man who had been robbed and disgraced, or else of a beggar or prisoner.

—*Commentary on the Old Testament*

2. *Walking naked and barefoot.* It is not probable that the prophet walked uncovered and barefoot for three years; his appearing in that manner was a sign that within three years the Egyptians and Cushites should be in the same condition, being conquered and made captives by the king of Assyria. The time was denoted as well as the event; but his appearing in that manner for three whole years could give no premonition of the time at all. It is probable, therefore, that the prophet was ordered to walk so for three days to denote the accomplishment of the event in three years; a day for a year, according to the prophetical rule, Num. xiv. 34; Ezek. iv. 6.

MATTHEW HENRY

CHAPTER 21

Verses 1–10

We had one burden of Babylon before (*ch.* xiii); here we have another prediction of its fall. Babylon sometimes pretended to be a friend to them (as *ch.* xxxix. 1), and God would hereby warn them not to trust to that friendship, and not to be afraid of their enmity. Babylon is marked for ruin; and all that believe God's prophets can see it tottering. Babylon is here called the *desert* or *plain of the sea*; for it was a flat country, and full of lakes, and was abundantly watered with the many streams of the river Euphrates. It did but lately begin to be famous, Nineveh having outshone it while the monarchy was in the Assyrian hands; but it became the lady of kingdoms; and, before Nebuchadnezzar's time, God by this prophet plainly foretold its fall, again and again, that his people might not be terrified at its rise, nor despair

JAMIESON, FAUSSET, BROWN

CHAPTER 21

VSS. 1-10. REPETITION OF THE ASSURANCE GIVEN IN CHAPTERS 13 AND 14 TO THE JEWS ABOUT TO BE CAPTIVES IN BABYLON, THAT THEIR ENEMY SHOULD BE DESTROYED AND THEY BE DELIVERED. He does not narrate the event, but graphically supposes himself a watchman in Babylon, beholding the events as they pass. **1. desert**—the champaign between Babylon and Persia; it was once a *desert,* and it was to become so again. **of the sea**—The plain was covered with the water of the Euphrates like a "sea" (Jer. 51:13, 36; so ch. 11:15, the Nile), until Semiramis raised great dams against it. Cyrus removed these dykes, and so converted the whole country again into a vast desert-marsh. **whirlwinds in the south**—(Job 37:9; Zech. 9:14.) The south wind comes upon Babylon from the deserts of Arabia, and its violence is the greater from its course being un-

ADAM CLARKE

CHAPTER 21

The first ten verses of this chapter contain a prediction of the taking of Babylon by the Medes and Persians. It is a passage singular in its kind for its brevity and force, for the variety and rapidity of the movements, and for the strength and energy of coloring with which the action and event are painted. It opens with the prophet's seeing at a distance the dreadful storm that is gathering and ready to burst upon Babylon. The event is intimated in general terms, and God's orders are issued to the Persians and Medes to set forth upon the expedition which He has given them in charge. Upon this the prophet enters into the midst of the action; and in the person of Babylon expresses, in the strongest terms, the astonish-

MATTHEW HENRY

of relief when they were its prisoners, Job v. 3; Ps. xxxvii. 35, 36.

I. The powerful descent which the Medes and Persians should make upon Babylon (*v.* 1, 2): They will come *from the desert, from a terrible land.* The northern parts of Media and Persia were waste and mountainous, terrible to strangers. *Elam* (that is, Persia) is summoned to go up against Babylon, and, in conjunction with the forces of Media, to besiege it. These forces come *as whirlwinds from the south.* As is usual in such a case, some deserters will go over to them: *The treacherous dealers will deal treacherously.* Historians tell us of Gadatas and Gobryas, two great officers of the king of Babylon, that went over to Cyrus, and, being well acquainted with all the avenues of the city, led a party directly to the palace, where Belshazzar was slain. Thus with the help of the *treacherous dealers the spoilers spoiled.* The Persians shall pay the Babylonians in their own coin; those that by fraud, unrighteous wars and deceitful treaties, have made a prey of their neighbours, shall meet their match.

II. The different impressions made upon those in Babylon. To the poor captives it would be welcome news; for they had been told long ago that Babylon's destroyer would be their deliverer, and therefore, when they hear that Elam and Media are coming to besiege Babylon, *all their sighing will be made to cease.* To the proud oppressors it would be a grievous vision (*v.* 2), particularly to the king of Babylon, and it should seem that he it is who is here sadly lamenting his inevitable fate (*v.* 3, 4): *Therefore are my loins filled with pain; pangs have taken hold upon me, &c.*, which was literally fulfilled in Belshazzar, for that very night in which his city was taken, and himself slain, upon the sight of a hand writing mystic characters upon the wall *his countenance was changed and his thoughts troubled him, so that the joints of his loins were loosed and his knees smote one against another*, Dan. v. 6. He was slain on that night when he was in the height of his mirth and jollity, with his cups and concubines about him and a thousand of his lords revelling with him.

III. Babylon should be found all in festival gaiety (*v.* 5): "Prepare the table with all manner of dainties. Set the guards; let them watch in the watch-tower while we make merry; and, if any alarm should be given, the princes shall arise and anoint the shield, and be in readiness to give the enemy a warm reception."

IV. The alarm which should be given to Babylon upon its being forced by Cyrus and Darius. The Lord showed the prophet the watchman set in his watch-tower, and, according to the duty of a watchman, let *him declare what he sees, v.* 6.

This watchman here discovered a chariot with a couple of horsemen, in which the commander-in-chief rides. He saw another chariot drawn by mules, much in use among the Persians, and a chariot drawn by camels, much in use among the Medes; so that these two chariots signify the two nations combined against Babylon.

And (*v.* 8) *he cried, A lion;* this word, coming out of a watchman's mouth, no doubt everybody knew the meaning of it. Or *he cried as a lion*, very loud, the occasion being very urgent. "*I stand, my lord, continually upon the watch-tower*, and, till just now, all seemed safe and quiet."

He shouts again (*v.* 9): *Here comes a chariot of men with a couple of horsemen.*

JAMIESON, FAUSSET, BROWN

broken along the plain (Job 1:19). **desert**—the plain between Babylon and Persia. **terrible land**—Media; to guard against which was the object of Nitocris' great works (HERODOTUS, 1. 185). Cf. as to "terrible" applied to a wilderness, as being full of unknown dangers, Deuteronomy 1:29. **2. dealeth treacherously**—referring to the *military* stratagem employed by Cyrus in taking Babylon. It may be translated, "is repaid with treachery"; then the subject of the verb is *Babylon.* She is repaid in her own coin; ch. 33:1; Habakkuk 2:8, favor this. **Go up**—Isaiah abruptly recites the order which he hears God giving to the Persians, the instruments of His vengeance (ch. 13:3, 17). **Elam**—a province of Persia, the original place of their settlement (Gen. 10:22), east of the Euphrates. The name "Persia" was not in use until the captivity; it means a "horseman"; Cyrus first trained the Persians in horsemanship. It is a mark of authenticity that the name is not found before Daniel and Ezekiel [BOCHART]. **thereof**—the "sighing" *caused* by Babylon (ch. 14:7, 8). **3.** Isaiah imagines himself among the exiles in Babylon and cannot help feeling moved by the calamities which come on it. So for Moab (ch. 15:5; 16:11). **pain**—(Cf. ch. 13:8; Ezek. 30:4, 19; Nah. 2:10.) **at the hearing**—The *Hebrew* may mean, "I was so bowed down that *I could not hear;* I was so dismayed that *I could not see*" (Gen. 16:2; Ps. 69:23) [MAURER]. **4. panted**—"is bewildered" [BARNES]. **night of my pleasure**—The prophet supposes himself one of the banqueters at Belshazzar's feast, on the night that Babylon was about to be taken by surprise; hence his expression, "*my* pleasure" (ch. 14:11; Jer. 51:39; Dan. 5). **5. Prepare the table**—viz., the feast in Babylon; during which Cyrus opened the dykes made by Semiramis to confine the Euphrates to one channel and suffered them to overflow the country, so that he could enter Babylon by the channel of the river. Isaiah first represents the king ordering the feast to be got ready. The suddenness of the irruption of the foe is graphically expressed by the rapid turn in the language to an alarm addressed to the Babylonian princes, "Arise," etc. (cf. ch. 22:13). MAURER translates, "*They prepare* the table," etc. But see ch. 8:9. **watch in . . . watchtower**—rather, set the watch. This done, they thought they might feast in entire security. Babylon had many watchtowers on its walls. **anoint . . . shield**—This was done to prevent the leather of the shield becoming hard and liable to crack. "Make ready for *defense*"; the mention of the "shield" alone implies that it is the Babylonian revellers who are called on to prepare for instant *self-defense.* HORSLEY translates, "Gripe the oiled shield." **6.** God's direction to Isaiah to set a watchman to "declare" what he sees. But as in vs. 10, Isaiah himself is represented as the one who "declared." HORSLEY makes *him* the "watchman," and translates, "Come, let him who standeth on the watchtower report what he seeth." **7. chariot . . .**—rather, a body of riders, (namely), some riding in pairs on horses (lit., "pairs of horsemen," i.e., two abreast), others on asses, others on camels (cf. vs. 9; ch. 22:6). "Chariot" is not appropriate to be joined, as *English Version* translates, with "asses"; the *Hebrew* means plainly in vs. 7, as in vs. 9, "a body of men riding." The Persians used asses and camels for war [MAURER]. HORSLEY translates, "One drawn in a car, with a pair of riders, drawn by an ass, drawn by a camel"; Cyrus is the man; the car drawn by a camel and ass yoked together and driven by two postilions, one on each, is the joint army of Medes and Persians under their respective leaders. He thinks the more ancient military cars were driven by men riding on the beasts that drew them; vs. 9 favors this. **8. A lion**—rather, "(The watchman) cried, I am *as* a lion"; so *as* is understood (ch. 62:5; Ps. 11:1). The point of comparison to "a lion" is in Revelation 10:3, the *loudness* of the cry. But here it is rather his *vigilance.* The lion's eyelids are short, so that, even when asleep, he seems to be on the watch, awake; hence he was painted on doors of temples as the symbol of watchfulness, guarding the place (*Hor. Apollo*) [HORSLEY]. **9. chariot of men**—chariots with men in them; or rather, the same body of riders, horsemen two abreast, as in vs. 7 [MAURER]. But HORSLEY, "The man drawn in a car with a pair of riders." The first half of this verse describes what the watchman *sees;* the second half, what the watchman *says,* in consequence of what he sees. In the interval between vss. 7 and 9, the overthrow of Babylon by the horsemen, or man in the car, is accomplished. The overthrow needed to be announced to the prophet by the watchman, owing to the great extent of the city. HERODOTUS (1. 131) says that one part of the city was captured some time before the other received the tidings of it.

ADAM CLARKE

ment and horror that seize her on the sudden surprise of the city at the very season dedicated to pleasure and festivity, vv. 3-4. Then, in his own person, describes the situation of things there, the security of the Babylonians, and in the midst of their feasting the sudden alarm of war, v. 5. The event is then declared in a very singular manner. God orders the prophet to set a watchman to look out, and to report what he sees; he sees two companies marching onward, representing by their appearance the two nations that were to execute God's orders, who declare that Babylon is fallen, vv. 6-9.

1. *The desert of the sea.* This plainly means Babylon, which is the subject of the prophecy. The country about Babylon, and especially below it towards the sea, was a great flat morass, overflowed by the Euphrates and Tigris. It became habitable by being drained by the many canals that were made in it. *As whirlwinds in the south*—"Like the southern tempests." The most vehement storms to which Judea was subject came from the desert country to the south of it. "Out of the south cometh the whirlwind," Job xxxvii. 9. For the situation of Idumea, the country (as I suppose) of Job (see Lam. iv. 21 compared with Job i. 1), was the same in this respect with that of Judea.

2. *The treacherous dealer dealeth treacherously, and the spoiler spoileth*—"The plunderer is plundered, and the destroyer is destroyed." *All the sighing thereof have I made to cease*—"I have put an end to all her vexations." Hebrew, "Her sighing; that is, the sighing caused by her."

5. *Prepare the table*—"The table is prepared." In Hebrew the verbs are in the infinitive mood absolute, as in Ezek. i. 14: "And the living creatures ran and returned, as the appearance of a flash of lightning."

Arise, ye princes, and anoint the shield. Kimchi observes that several of the rabbins understood this of Belshazzar's impious feast and death.

7. *And he saw a chariot,* etc.—"And he saw a chariot with two riders: a rider on an ass, a rider on a camel." This passage is extremely obscure from the ambiguity of the term *recheb*, which is used three times, and which signifies a chariot, or any other vehicle, or the rider in it; or a rider on a horse, or any other animal; or a company of chariots, or riders. The prophet may possibly mean a cavalry in two parts, with two sorts of riders: riders on asses or mules, and riders on camels; or led on by two riders: one on an ass, and one on a camel. However, so far it is pretty clear that Darius and Cyrus, the Medes and the Persians, are intended to be distinguished by the two riders on the two sorts of cattle.

8. *And he cried, A lion*—"He that looked out on the watch." The present reading, *aryeh, a lion*, is so unintelligible, and the mistake so obvious, that I make no doubt that the true reading is *haroeh, the seer;* as the Syriac translator manifestly found it in his copy, who renders it by "a watchman."

9. *Here cometh a chariot of men*—"A man, one of the two riders." So the Syriac understands it.

MATTHEW HENRY

V. A certain account is at length given of the overthrow of Babylon. He in the chariot *answered and said* (when he heard the watchman speak), *Babylon has fallen, has fallen. All the graven images of her gods he has broken unto the ground.*

VI. Notice is given to the people of God, who were then captives in Babylon, that this prophecy of the downfall of Babylon was particularly intended for their encouragement, *v.* 10.

1. The title the prophet gives them in God's name: *O my threshing, and the corn of my floor!* The prophet calls them *his*, because they were his countrymen, but he speaks it as from God. The church is God's floor. True believers are the corn of God's floor. Hypocrites are but as the chaff and straw. The corn of God's floor must expect to be threshed by afflictions and persecutions. Even then God owns it for his threshing; it is his still.

2. The assurance he gives them which they might build their hopes upon: *That which I have heard of the Lord of hosts, the God of Israel, have I declared unto you.*

Verses 11–12

This prophecy concerning Dumah is very short, and hard to be understood. Some think that Dumah is a part of Arabia, and that the inhabitants descended from Dumah the sixth son of Ishmael. Others, because Mount Seir is here mentioned, by Dumah understand Idumea, the country of the Edomites. Some of Israel's neighbours are certainly meant, and their distress is foretold, not only for warning to them to prepare them for it, but for warning to Israel not to depend upon them. but upon God only. Someone *called out of Seir*, as the man of Macedonia, in a vision, desired Paul to come over and help them (Acts xvi. 9). The question is serious: *What of the night?* It is put to a proper person, the *watchman.* He repeats the question as one in earnest. God's prophets and ministers are appointed to be watchmen. They are as watchmen in the city in a time of peace, to see that all be safe, to knock at every door by personal enquiries ("Is it locked? Is the fire safe?"). They are as watchmen in the camp in time of war, Ezek. xxxiii. 7. They are to take notice of the enemy and give warning. It is our duty to ask again and again, *What of the night?* "Watchman, what o'clock is it? After a long dark night is there any hope of the day dawning?" *What from the night?* (so some); "what vision has the prophet had tonight? We are ready to receive it." Or, "What occurs tonight? What weather is it? What news?" The watchman was neither asleep nor dumb, though it was a man of Mount Seir that called to him. "The morning comes," he answers. "There comes first a morning of light and peace and opportunity; you will enjoy one day of comfort more; but afterwards comes a night of trouble and calamity." Improve the present morning in preparation for the night that is coming after it. "*Enquire, return, come.* Be inquisitive, be penitent, and obedient."

Verses 13–17

Arabia was a large country, eastward and southward of Canaan. The *Dedanim* (*v.* 13), were descended from Dedan, Abraham's son by Keturah; the inhabitants of Tema and Kedar descended from Ishmael, Gen. xxv. 3, 13, 15. The Arabians lived in tents, kept cattle, a hardy people, inured to labour; the Jews depended upon them as a wall between them and the more warlike eastern nations; and therefore, to alarm them, they shall hear *the burden of Arabia.*

I. A destroying army shall be brought upon them, with a sword, with *a drawn sword*, with *a bow* ready *bent*, and with all the *grievousness of war*, *v.* 15. It is probable that the king of Assyria took Arabia in his way, and made an easy prey of them.

II. The poor country people will be forced to flee for shelter; so that *the travelling companies of Dedanim* shall be obliged to *lodge in the forest in Arabia* (*v.* 13).

III. They shall need refreshment in their flight from the invading army: "*O you inhabitants of the land of Tema!*" (who probably were next neighbours to the companies of Dedanim) "*bring you water*" (so the margin reads it) "*to him that is thirsty*, and *prevent with your bread those that flee*, for they are objects of your compassion; *they flee from the sword.*" Let us learn to look with compassion upon those that are in distress, and with all cheerfulness to relieve them. It is here remembered to the praise of the land of Tema that they relieved even those that were on the falling side.

IV. All the glory of Kedar shall vanish and fail. Their numerous herds and flocks shall all be driven away by the enemy. Their archers, instead of foiling the enemy, shall fall themselves; and *the residue of their number shall be diminished* (*v.* 17); their able-

JAMIESON, FAUSSET, BROWN

answered—not to something *said* previously, but in reference to the subject in the mind of the writer, to be collected from the preceding discourse: *proclaimeth* (Job 3:2; *Margin,* Dan. 2:26; Acts 5:8). **fallen . . . fallen**—The repetition expresses emphasis and certainty (Ps. 92:9; 93:3; cf. Jer. 51:8; Rev. 18: 2). **images**—Bel, Merodach, etc. (Jer. 50:2; 51:44, 52). The Persians had no images, temples, or altars, and charged the makers of such with madness (HERODOTUS 1.131); therefore they dashed the Babylonian "images broken unto the ground." **10. my threshing**—i.e., my people (the Jews) trodden down by Babylon. **corn of my floor**—*Hebrew,* "my son of the floor," i.e., my people, treated as corn laid on the floor for threshing; implying, too, that by affliction, a remnant (grain) would be separated from the ungodly (chaff) [MAURER]. HORSLEY translates, "O thou object of my unremitting *prophetic pains.*" See ch. 28:27, 28. Some, from Jeremiah 51:33, make Babylon the object of the threshing; but Isaiah is plainly addressing his countrymen, as the next words show, not the Babylonians.

11, 12. A PROPHECY TO THE IDUMEANS WHO TAUNTED THE AFFLICTED JEWS IN THE BABYLONISH CAPTIVITY. One out of Seir asks, What of the night? Is there a hope of the dawn of deliverance? Isaiah replies, The morning is beginning to dawn (*to us*); but night is also coming (to you). Cf. Psalm 137:7. The Hebrew captives would be delivered, and taunting Edom punished. If the Idumean wish to ask again, he may do so; if he wishes an answer of peace for his country, then let him "return (repent), come" [BARNES]. **11. Dumah**—a tribe and region of Ishmael in Arabia (Gen. 25: 14; I Chron. 1:30); now called *Dumah the Stony,* situated on the confines of Arabia and the Syrian desert; a part put for the *whole* of Edom. VITRINGA thinks "Dumah," *Hebrew,* "silence," is here used for Idumea, to imply that it was soon to be reduced to *silence* or destruction. **Seir**—the principal mountain in Idumea, south of the Dead Sea, in Arabia Petrea. "He calleth" ought to be rather, "*There is a call* from Seir." **to me**—Isaiah. So the heathen Balak and Ahaziah received oracles from a Hebrew prophet. **Watchman**—the prophet (ch. 62:6; Jer. 6:17), so called, because, like a watchman on the lookout from a tower, he announces future events which he sees in prophetic vision (Hab. 2:1, 2). **what of the night**—What tidings have you to give as to the state of the night? Rather, "What *remains* of the night?" How much of it is past? [MAURER]. "Night" means calamity (Job 35:10; Mic. 3:6), which, then, in the wars between Egypt and Assyria, pressed sore on Edom; or on Judah (if, as BARNES thinks, the question is asked in mockery of the suffering Jews in Babylon). The *repetition* of the question marks, in the former view, the anxiety of the Idumeans. **12.** Reply of the prophet, The *morning* (prosperity) *cometh,* and (soon after follows) *the night* (adversity). Though you, Idumeans, may have a gleam of prosperity, it will soon be followed by adversity again. Otherwise, as BARNES, "Prosperity cometh (to the Jews) to be quickly followed by adversity (to you, Idumeans, who exult in the fall of Jerusalem, have seized on the southern part of their land in their absence during the captivity, and now deride them by your question") (ch. 34:5-7). This view is favored by Obadiah 10-21. **if ye will inquire, inquire**—If ye choose to consult me again, do so (similar phrases occur in Genesis 43: 14; II Kings 7:4; Esther 4:16). **return, come**—"Be converted to God (and then), come" [GESENIUS]; you will then receive a more favorable answer.

13-17. PROPHECY THAT ARABIA WOULD BE OVERRUN BY A FOREIGN FOE WITHIN A YEAR. Probably in the wars between Assyria and Egypt; Idumea and Arabia lay somewhat on the intermediate line of march. 13. **upon**—i.e., respecting. **forest**—not a grove of trees, but a region of thick underwood, rugged and inaccessible; for Arabia has no forest of trees. **travelling companies**—caravans: ye shall be driven through fear of the foe to unfrequented routes (ch. 33:8; Judg. 5:6; Jer. 49:8 is parallel to this passage). **Dedanim**—In North Arabia (Gen. 25:3; Jer. 25:23; Ezek. 25:13; 27:20; a different "Dedan" occurs Gen. 10:7). **14. Tema**—a kindred tribe: an oasis in that region (Jer. 25:23). The Temeans give water to the faint and thirsting Dedanites; the greatest act of hospitality in the burning lands of the East, where water is so scarce. **prevented**—i.e., anticipated the wants of the fugitive Dedanites by supplying bread (Gen. 14:18). **their bread**—rather, "*his* (the fugitive's) bread"; the bread *due to him,* necessary for his support; so "*thy* grave" (ch. 14:19), [MAURER]. **15. they**—the fugitive Dedanites and other Arabs.

ADAM CLARKE

10. *O my threshing.* The image of threshing is frequently used by the Hebrew poets, with great elegance and force, to express the punishment of the wicked and the trial of the good, or the utter dispersion and destruction of God's enemies.

11. *The burden of Dumah*—"The oracle concerning Dumah." This prophecy, from the uncertainty of the occasion on which it was uttered, and from the brevity of the expression, is extremely obscure. The Edomites as well as the Jews were subdued by the Babylonians. They inquire of the prophet how long their subjection is to last. He intimates that the Jews should be delivered from their captivity; not so the Edomites. Thus far the interpretation seems to carry with it some degree of probability. What the meaning of the last line may be, I cannot pretend to divine.

13. *The burden upon Arabia*—"The oracle concerning Arabia." This prophecy was to have been fulfilled within a year of the time of its delivery, see v. 16; and it was probably delivered about the same time with the rest in this part of the book, that is, soon before or after the fourteenth of Hezekiah, the year of Sennacherib's invasion. In his first march into Judea, or in his return from the Egyptian expedition, he might perhaps overrun these several clans of Arabians; their distress on some such occasion is the subject of this prophecy.

14. *The land of Tema*—"The southern country." To bring forth bread and water is an instance of common humanity in such cases of distress; especially in those desert countries in which the common necessaries of life, more particularly water, are not easily to be met with or procured.

MATTHEW HENRY

bodied men shall become very few; for they were most exposed, and fell first by the enemies' sword.

V. All this shall be done in a little time: "*Within one year according to the years of a hireling* (within one year precisely reckoned) this judgment shall come upon Kedar." This fixing of the time might be of great use to the Arabians, to awaken them to repentance, that, like the men of Nineveh, they might prevent the judgment when they were thus told it was just at the door.

VI. It is all ratified by the truth of God (*v.* 16): "*Thus hath the Lord said to me.*" And again (*v.* 17): *The Lord God of Israel hath spoken it.*

JAMIESON, FAUSSET, BROWN

16. years of . . . hireling–(*Note,* ch. 16:14.) **Kedar**–a wandering tribe (Ps. 120:5). North of Arabia Petrea, and south of Arabia Deserta; put for Arabia in general.

17. residue . . . diminished–The remnant of Arab warriors, famous in the bow, left after the invasion, shall be small.

ADAM CLARKE

17. *The archers, the mighty men of the children of Kedar*—"The mighty bowmen of the sons of Kedar."

MATTHEW HENRY

CHAPTER 22

Verses 1–7

The title of this prophecy is *the burden of the valley of vision*, of Judah and Jerusalem. Jerusalem is called a valley, for the mountains were round about it, and the land of Judah abounded with valleys. It is called a *valley of vision* because there God was known and there the prophets were made acquainted with his mind by visions. Babylon, being a stranger to God, though rich and great, was called *the desert of the sea*; but Jerusalem, being trusted with his oracles, is *a valley of vision*.

Now the *burden of the valley of vision* here is that which will not quite ruin it, but only frighten it; for it refers not to the destruction of Jerusalem by Nebuchadnezzar, but to the attempt made upon it by Sennacherib, *ch.* x, and *ch.* xxxvi.

I. The consternation that the city should be in upon the approach of Sennacherib's army. It used to be a city of great trade, populous and noisy, a joyous revelling city. "But what ails thee now, that the shops are quitted, and *thou hast wholly gone up to the house-tops* (*v.* 1), to secure thyself from the enemy." But why is Jerusalem in such a fright? *Her slain men are not slain with the sword* (*v.* 2), but with famine (so some), or with fear. They were so disheartened that they seemed as effectually stabbed with fear as if they had been run through with a sword.

II. The inglorious flight of the rulers of Judah, who fled from all parts of the country, to Jerusalem (*v.* 3), and were found in Jerusalem, having left their respective cities to be a prey to the Assyrian army, which, meeting with no opposition, when it *came up against all the defenced cities of Judah* easily *took them, ch.* xxxvi. 1. These rulers *were bound from the bow* (so the word is); they not only quitted like cowards, but, when they came to Jerusalem, trembled, so that they could not draw a bow.

III. The great grief which this should occasion to all serious people, the prophet laying the thing to heart himself, *v.* 4, 5. He is not willing to proclaim his sorrow, and therefore bids those about him to look away from him; he will weep secretly. But what is the occasion of his grief? A poor prophet had little to lose, and had been inured to hardship, but it is for *the spoiling of the daughter of his people*. Our enemies tread us down, and our friends know not what course to take to do us a kindness. The enemies with their battering rams are breaking down the walls, and we are in vain crying to the mountains (to keep off the enemy, or to fall on us and cover us), or appealing to the mountains to hear our controversy (Mic. vi. 1) and to judge between us and our neighbours.

IV. The great strength of the enemy, that should besiege their city, *v.* 6, 7. Elam (that is, the Persians) come with their quiver full of arrows, and with chariots. Kir (that is, the Medes) get everything ready for battle, for the besieging of Jerusalem. Then the choice valleys about Jerusalem, that used to be clothed with flocks, shall be full of chariots of war, and at the gate of the city *the horsemen shall set themselves in array*, to cut off all provisions from going in.

JAMIESON, FAUSSET, BROWN

CHAPTER 22

Vss. 1-14. Prophecy as to an Attack on Jerusalem: that by Sennacherib, in the 14th year of Hezekiah; vss. 8-11, the preparations for defense and securing of water exactly answer to those in II Chronicles 32:4, 5, 30. "Shebna," too (vs. 15), was scribe at this time (ch. 36:3) [Maurer]. The language of vss. 12, 13, and 14, as to the infidelity and consequent utter ruin of the Jews, seems rather to foreshadow the destruction by Nebuchadnezzar in Zedekiah's reign, and cannot be restricted to Hezekiah's time [Lowth]. **1. of . . . valley of vision**–rather, respecting the valley of visions; viz., Jerusalem, the seat of divine revelations and visions, "the nursery of prophets" [Jerome], (ch. 2:3; 29:1; Ezek. 23:4, *Margin:* Luke 13:33). It lay in a "valley" surrounded by hills higher than Zion and Moriah (Ps. 125:2; Jer. 21:13). **thee**–the people of Jerusalem personified. **housetops**–Panic-struck, they went up on the flat balustraded roofs to look forth and see whether the enemy was near, and partly to defend themselves from the roofs (Judg. 9:51, etc.). **2. art**–rather, wert; for it could not *now* be said to be "a joyous city" (ch. 32:13). The cause of their *joy* (vs. 13) may have been because Sennacherib had accepted Hezekiah's offer to renew the payment of tribute, and they were glad to have peace on any terms, however humiliating (II Kings 18:14-16), or on account of the alliance with Egypt. If the reference be to Zedekiah's time, the joy and feasting are not inapplicable, for this recklessness was a general characteristic of the unbelieving Jews (ch. 56:12). **not slain with the sword**–but with the famine and pestilence about to be caused by the coming siege (Lam. 4:9). Maurer refers this to the *plague* by which he thinks Sennacherib's army was destroyed, and Hezekiah was made sick (ch. 37:36; 38:1). But there is no authority for supposing that the Jews in the city suffered such extremities of plague at *this* time, when God destroyed their foes. Barnes refers it to those *slain in flight,* not in open honorable "battle"; vs. 3 favors this. **3. rulers**–rather, generals (Josh. 10:24; Judg. 11:6, 11). **bound**–rather, *"are taken."* **by the archers**–lit., "by the bow"; so ch. 21:17. Bowmen were the light troops, whose province it was to skirmish in front and (II Kings 6:22) pursue fugitives (II Kings 25:5); this verse applies better to the attack of Nebuchadnezzar than that of Sennacherib. **all . . . in thee**–all found in the city (ch. 13:15), not merely the "rulers" or generals. **fled from far**–those who had *fled from distant parts* to Jerusalem as a place of safety; rather, *fled afar.* **4. Look . . . from me**–Deep grief seeks to be alone; while others feast joyously, Isaiah mourns in prospect of the disaster coming on Jerusalem (Mic. 1:8, 9). **daughter . . .**–(*Note,* ch. 1:8; Lam. 2:11). **5. trouble . . . by the Lord**–i.e., sent by or from the Lord (*Note,* ch. 19:15; Luke 21:22-24). **valley of vision**– (*Note,* vs. 1). Some think a valley near Ophel is meant as about to be the scene of devastation (cf. ch. 32:13, 14, *Note*). **breaking . . . walls**–i.e., *"a day* of breaking the walls" of the city. **crying to the mountains**–the mournful cry of the townsmen *reaches* to (Maurer translates, *towards)* the mountains, and is echoed back by them. Josephus describes in the very same language the scene at the assault of Jerusalem under Titus. To this the prophecy, probably, refers ultimately. If, as some think, the "cry" is that of those *escaping* to the mountains, cf. Matthew 13:14; 24:16, with this. **6. Elam**–the country stretching east from the Lower Tigris, answering to what was afterwards called Persia (*Note,* ch. 21:2). Later, Elam was a province of Persia (Ezra 4:9). In Sennacherib's time, Elam was subject to Assyria (II Kings 18:11), and so furnished a contingent to its invading armies. Famed for the bow (ch. 13:18; Jer. 49:35), in which the Ethiopians alone excelled them. **with chariots of men and horsemen**–i.e., they used the bow both *in* chariots and on horseback. "Chariots of men," i.e., chariots in which men are

ADAM CLARKE

CHAPTER 22

This prophecy, ending with the fourteenth verse of this chapter, is entitled, "The oracle concerning the valley of vision," by which is meant Jerusalem. The prophecy foretells the invasion of Jerusalem by the Assyrians under Sennacherib, or by the Chaldeans under Nebuchadnezzar.

1. *Art . . . gone up to the house tops.* The houses in the East were in ancient times, as they are still, generally built in one and the same uniform manner. The roof or top of the house is always flat, covered with broad stones, or a strong plaster of terrace, and guarded on every side with a low parapet wall; see Deut. xxii. 8. The terrace is frequented as much as any part of the house. On this, as the season favors, they walk, they eat, they sleep, they transact business (1 Sam. ix. 25), they perform their devotions, Acts x. 9. The house is built with a court within, into which chiefly the windows open. Those that open to the street are so obstructed with latticework that no one either without or within can see through them. Whenever, therefore, anything is to be seen or heard in the streets, any public spectacle, any alarm of a public nature, everyone immediately goes up to the housetop to satisfy his curiosity. In the same manner, when anyone has occasion to make anything public, the readiest and most effectual way of doing it is to proclaim it from the housetops to the people in the streets. "What ye hear in the ear, that publish ye upon the house tops," saith our Saviour, Matt. x. 27. The people running all to the tops of their houses gives a lively image of a sudden general alarm.

MATTHEW HENRY

Verses 8–14

What is meant by *the covering of Judah*, which in the beginning of this paragraph is said to be *discovered*, is not agreed. The fenced cities of Judah were a covering to the country; but these, being taken by the army of the Assyrians, ceased to be a shelter. The weakness of Judah now appeared; thus the covering of Judah was discovered. Its stores were now laid open for the public use. Dr. Lightfoot gives another sense of it, that by this distress into which Judah should be brought God would discover their covering (that is, unlock their hypocrisy), 2 Chron. xxxii. 31. Now they discovered both their carnal confidence (*v.* 9) and their carnal security, *v.* 13.

They were in a great fright, and in this fright they manifested:

I. A great contempt of God's goodness, and his power to help them. They made use of all the means they could think of for their own preservation; but, in doing this, they did not acknowledge God. When Sennacherib had made himself master of all the defenced cities of Judah it was resolved to stand upon their defence, and not tamely to surrender. They inspected the magazines and stores, to see if they were well stocked with arms: *They looked to the armour of the house of the forest*, which Solomon built in Jerusalem for an armoury (1 Kings x. 17). They viewed the fortifications, the *breaches of the city of David*; they walked round the walls, and observed where they had gone to decay for want of repairs. These breaches were many. By public distresses, we should be awakened by them to *repair our breaches*, and amend what is amiss. They made sure of water for the city: *You gathered together the water of the lower pool*. They *numbered the houses of Jerusalem*, that every house might send in its quota of men for the public service, or contribute in money, so much a house. Because private property ought to give way to the public safety, those houses in their way, when the wall was to be fortified, were broken down. They made a ditch between the outer and inner wall, for the greater security of the city; and they contrived to draw the water of the old pool to it, that they might have plenty of water themselves and might deprive the besiegers of it; lest the Assyrian army *should come and find much water* (2 Chron. xxxii. 4). How regardless they were of God in all these preparations: *But you have not looked unto the Maker thereof* (that is, of Jerusalem, the city you are so solicitous for the defence of) and of all the advantages which nature has furnished it with for its defence. It is God that made his Jerusalem, and fashioned it long ago, in his counsels. It is here charged upon them that they did not look to God. They fortified Jerusalem because it was a rich city and their own houses were in it, not because it was the holy city and God's house was in it. They did not depend upon him for a blessing upon their endeavours, but thought their own powers sufficient for them. Of Hezekiah himself it is said that *he trusted in God* (2 Kings xviii. 5), and particularly upon this occasion (2 Chron. xxxii. 8); but there were those about him, it seems, who were great statesmen and soldiers, but had little religion in them.

II. A great contempt of God's wrath and justice, *v.* 12–14. God's design in bringing this calamity upon them was to humble them, bring them to repentance. In that day of trouble the Lord did thereby *call to weeping and mourning*, and all the expressions of sorrow, even to *baldness and girding with sackcloth*; and this to lament their sins, to enforce their prayers, and to dispose themselves to a reformation of their lives. To this God called them by his prophet's explaining his providences. How contrary they walked to this design of God (*v.* 13). They were as secure and cheerful as if they had had no enemy or were in no danger. When they had taken precautions for their security, they set dangers at defiance, and resolved to be merry: *Let us eat and drink, for tomorrow we shall die*. This was the language of the profane scoffers who *mocked the messengers of the Lord and misused his prophets*. They made a jest of dying. They ridiculed the doctrine of a future state on the other side death. A practical disbelief of another life after this is at the bottom of the carnal security and brutish sensuality which are the sin, and shame, and ruin of so great a part of mankind. God signified his resentment of it to the prophet, *revealed it in his ears*, to be by him proclaimed upon the house-top: *Surely this iniquity shall not be purged from you till you die*, *v.* 14. Those that walk contrary to God shall find that he will walk contrary to them; with the froward he will show himself froward.

Verses 15–25

We have here a prophecy concerning the displacing of Shebna, a great officer at court, and the preferring of Eliakim to the post of honour and trust. By the

JAMIESON, FAUSSET, BROWN

borne, war chariots (cf. *Note*, ch. 21:7, 9). **Kir**—another people subject to Assyria (II Kings 16:9); the region about the river Kur, between the Caspian and Black Seas. **uncovered**—took off for the battle the leather covering of the shield, intended to protect the embossed figures on it from dust or injury during the march. "The quiver" and "the shield" express two classes—light and heavy armed troops. **7. valleys**—east, north, and south of Jerusalem: Hinnom on the south side was the richest valley. **in array at the gate**—Rabshakeh stood at the upper pool close to the city (ch. 36:11-13). **8. he discovered the covering**—rather, "the veil of Judah shall be taken off" [HORSLEY]: fig. for, exposing to shame as a captive (ch. 47:3; Nah. 3:5). Sennacherib dismantled all "the defensed cities of Judah" (ch. 36:1). **thou didst look**—rather, "thou shalt look." **house of . . . forest**—The *house* of armory built of cedar from the *forest* of Lebanon by Solomon, on a slope of Zion called Ophel (I Kings 7:2; 10:17; Neh. 3:19). Isaiah says (vss. 8-13) his countrymen will look to their own strength *to defend* themselves, while others of them will drown their sorrows as to their country in *feasting*, but none will look to Jehovah. **9. Ye have seen**—rather, "Ye shall see." **city of David**—the upper city, on Zion, the south side of Jerusalem (II Sam. 5:7, 9; I Kings 8:1); surrounded by a wall of its own; but even in it there shall be "breaches." Hezekiah's preparations for defense accord with this (II Chron. 32:5). **ye gathered**—rather, "ye shall gather." **lower pool**—(*Note*, vs. 11.) Ye shall bring together into the city by subterranean passages cut in the rock of Zion, the fountain from which the lower pool (only mentioned here) is supplied. *Note*, ch. 7:3; II Kings 20: 20; II Chronicles 32:3-5, represent Hezekiah as having *stopped* the fountains to prevent the Assyrians getting water. But this is consistent with the passage here. The superflous waters of the lower pool usually flowed into Hinnom valley, and so through that of Jehoshaphat to the brook Kedron. Hezekiah built a wall round it, *stopped* the outflowing of its waters to debar the foe from the use of them, and turned them into the city. **10. numbered**— rather, "ye shall number," viz., in order to see which of them may be pulled down with the least loss to the city, and with most advantage for the repair of the walls and rearing of towers (II Chron. 32:5). **have ye broken down**—rather, "ye shall break down." **11. Ye made . . . a ditch**—rather, "Ye shall make a reservoir" for receiving the *water*. Hezekiah surrounded Siloah, from which the old (or king's, or upper) pool took its rise, with a wall joined to the wall of Zion on both sides; between these two walls he made a new pool, into which he directed the waters of the former, thus cutting off the foe from his supply of water also. The opening from which the upper pool received its water was nearer Zion than the other from which the lower pool took its rise, so that the water which flowed from the former could easily be shut in by a wall, whereas that which flowed from the latter could only be brought in by subterranean conduits (cf. *Note*, vs. 9; ch. 7:3; II Kings 20:20; II Chron. 32:3-5, 30; Eccles. 48:17). Both were southwest of Jerusalem. **have not looked . . . neither had respect**—answering by contrast to "*Thou didst look* to the armor, *ye have seen* (had respect, or regard to) the breaches" (vss. 8, 9). **maker thereof**—God, by whose command and aid these defenses were made, and who gave this fountain "long ago." G. V. SMITH translates, "Him who *doeth* it," i.e., has brought this danger on you—"Him who hath prepared it from afar," i.e., planned it even from a distant time. **12. did the Lord God call**—Usually the *priests* gave the summons to national mourning (Joel 1:14); now JEHOVAH Himself shall give it; the "call" shall consist in the presence of a terrible foe. Translate, "shall call." **baldness**—emblem of grief (Job 1:20; Mic. 1:16). **13.** Notwithstanding Jehovah's "call to mourning" (vs. 12), many shall make the desperate state of affairs a reason for reckless revelry (ch. 5:11, 12, 14; Jer. 18: 12; I Cor. 15:32).

15-25. PROPHECY THAT SHEBNA SHOULD BE DEPOSED FROM BEING PREFECT OF THE PALACE, AND

ADAM CLARKE

8. *The armour*—"The arsenal." Built by Solomon within the city, and called the house of the forest of Lebanon, probably from the great quantity of cedar from Lebanon which was employed in the building. See 1 Kings vii. 2-3.

9. *Ye gathered together the waters*—"And ye shall collect the waters." There were two pools in or near Jerusalem, supplied by springs: the upper pool, or the old pool, supplied by the spring called Gihon, 2 Chron. xxxii. 30, towards the higher part of the city, near Sion, or the city of David; and the lower pool, probably supplied by Siloam, towards the lower part. When Hezekiah was threatened with a siege by Sennacherib, he stopped up all the waters of the fountains without the city, and brought them into the city by a conduit, or subterranean passage cut through the rock; those of the old pool to the place where he had a double wall, so that the pool was between the two walls. This he did in order to distress the enemy, and to supply the city during the siege (2 Kings xx. 20; 2 Chron. xxxii. 2-3, 5, 30).

11. *Unto the maker thereof*—"To him that hath disposed this." That is, to God, the Author and Disposer of this visitation, the invasion with which He now threatens you.

13. *Let us eat and drink; for to morrow we shall die*. This has been the language of all those who have sought their portion in this life, since the foundation of the world. St. Paul quotes the same heathen sentiment, 1 Cor. xv. 32: "Let us eat and drink; for to morrow we die."

14. *It was revealed in mine ears*—"The voice of Jehovah."

MATTHEW HENRY

accomplishment of what was foretold concerning these particular persons God designed to confirm his word in the mouth of Isaiah concerning other and greater events. It is probable that this prophecy was delivered at the same time with that in the former part of the chapter, and began to be fulfilled before Sennacherib's invasion; for now Shebna was *over the house*, but then Eliakim was (*ch.* xxxvi. 3); and Shebna, coming down gradually, was only scribe.

I. The prophecy of Shebna's disgrace. He is called *this treasurer*, being entrusted with the management of the revenue; and he is likewise said to be *over the house*. The Jews say, "He kept up a traitorous correspondence with the king of Assyria, and was in treaty with him to deliver the city into his hands." His pride, vanity, and security (*v.* 16): "*What hast thou here, and whom hast thou here?* What a mighty noise and bustle dost thou make! Art thou not mean and obscure that comest we know not whence? What is the meaning of this then, that thou hast built thyself a fine house, *hast graved thyself a habitation?*" It seemed engraven in a rock, so firmly was it founded and so impregnable was it. "Nay, *thou hast hewed thee out a sepulchre*," as if he designed that his pomp should survive his funeral. A prophecy of his fall and the sullying of his glory (*v.* 19): *I will drive thee from thy station.* High places are slippery places; and those are justly deprived of their honour that are puffed up with it. To this *v.* 25 refers. "The nail that is *now fastened in the sure place* (that is, Shebna, who thinks himself immovably fixed in his office) *shall be removed, and cut down, and fall.*" After a while he should not only be driven from his station, but driven from his country: *The Lord will carry thee away with the captivity of a mighty man, v.* 17, 18. Some think the Assyrians seized him, and took him away, or perhaps Hezekiah, finding out his treachery, banished him. Grotius thinks he was striken with a leprosy, which was a disease commonly supposed to come from God's displeasure, particularly for the punishment of the proud, and by reason of this disease he was *tossed like a ball* out of Jerusalem. Shebna thought his place too strait for him. God will therefore send him *into a large country*, where he shall have room to wander, but never find the way back again; *there the chariots* which had been the chariots of his glory, should but serve to upbraid him with his former grandeur, *to the shame of his lord's house*, of the court of Ahaz, who had advanced him.

II. The prophecy of Eliakim's advancement, *v.* 20, &c. He is God's servant, has approved himself faithfully so in other employments, and therefore God will call him to this high station. It is here foretold Eliakim should be put into Shebna's place of lord-chamberlain of the household, lord-treasurer, and prime-minister of state. The prophet must tell Shebna this, *v.* 21. "He shall have *thy robe*, the badge of honour, and *thy girdle*, the badge of power; for he shall have *thy government.*" *I will clothe him;* and then it follows, *I will strengthen him.* Those that are called to places of trust and power should seek unto God for grace to enable them to do the duty of their places. Eliakim's advancement is further described by the laying of the *key of the house of David upon his shoulders, v.* 22. He had access to *the house of the precious things, the silver, and the gold, and the spices;* and to the *house of the armour* and the *treasures* (*ch.* xxxix. 2), and disposed of the stores there as he thought fit for the public service. He should be fixed and confirmed in that office. He shall have it for life (*v.* 23): *I will fasten him as a nail in a sure place*, not to be removed or cut down. He shall be a blessing to his country (*v.* 21): *He shall be a father to the inhabitants of Jerusalem and to the house of Judah.* He shall take care not only of the affairs of the king's household, but of all the public interests in Jerusalem and Judah. It is happy with a people when the court, the city, and the country, have no separate interests, but the courtiers are true patriots, and whom the court blesses the country has reason to bless too. He shall be a blessing to his family (*v.* 23, 24): *He shall be for a glorious throne to his father's house.* Eliakim is *a nail in a sure place*, and all his family are said to have a dependence upon him, as in a house the vessels that have handles to them are hung up upon nails and pins. It intimates likewise that he shall generously take care of them all, and bear the weight of that care: *All the vessels*, not only *the flagons*, but *the cups, the vessels of small quantity*, the meanest that belong to his family, shall be provided for by him. Our Lord Jesus, having the key of the house of David, is as a *nail in a sure place*, and all *the glory of his father's house hangs* upon him. That soul cannot perish, nor that concern fall to the ground, though ever so weighty, that is by faith hung upon Christ.

JAMIESON, FAUSSET, BROWN

Eliakim Promoted to the Office. In ch. 36:3, 22; 37:2, we find Shebna "a scribe," and no longer prefect of the palace ("over the household"), and Eliakim in that office, as is here foretold. Shebna is singled out as the subject of prophecy (the only instance of an *individual* being so in Isaiah), as being one of the irreligious faction that set at naught the prophet's warnings (ch. 28:33); perhaps it was he who advised the temporary ignominious submission of Hezekiah to Sennacherib. **15. Go, get thee unto**—rather, "Go in to" (i.e., into the house to). **treasurer**—"him who dwells in the tabernacle" [Jerome]; viz., in a room of the temple set apart for the treasurer. Rather, "the king's friend," or "*principal officer of the court*" (I Kings 4:5; 18:3; I Chron. 27:33, "the king's counsellor") [Maurer]. "This" is prefixed contemptuously (Exod. 32:1). **unto Shebna**—The *Hebrew* for "unto" indicates an accosting of Shebna *with an unwelcome message.* **16. What . . . whom**—The prophet accosts Shebna at the very place where he was building a grand sepulcher for himself and his family (cf. ch. 14:18; Gen. 23; 49:29; 50:13). "*What* (business) hast thou here, and *whom* hast thou (of thy family, who is likely to be buried) here, that thou *buildest*," etc., seeing that thou art soon to be deposed from office and carried into captivity? [Maurer]. **on high**—Sepulchers were made in the *highest* rocks (II Chron. 32:33, *Margin*). **habitation for himself**—cf. "his own house" (ch. 14:18). **17. carry . . . away with . . . captivity**—rather, "will cast thee away with a mighty throw" [Maurer]. "Mighty," lit., "of a man" (so Job 38:3). **surely cover**—viz., with shame, where thou art rearing a monument to perpetuate thy fame [Vitringa]. "Rolling will roll thee," i.e., will *continually* roll thee on, as a ball to be tossed away [Maurer]. Cf. vs. 18. **18. violently turn and toss**—lit., "whirling He will whirl thee," i.e., He will, *without intermission,* whirl thee [Maurer]. "He will whirl thee round and round, and (then) cast thee away," as a stone in a sling is first whirled round repeatedly, before the string is let go [Lowth]. **large country**—perhaps Assyria. **chariots . . . shall be the shame of thy lord's house**—rather, "thy splendid chariots shall be there, O thou disgrace of thy lord's house" [Noyes]; "chariots of thy glory" mean "thy magnificent chariots." It is not meant that he would have these in a distant land, as he had in Jerusalem, but that he would be borne thither in ignominy instead of in his magnificent chariots. The Jews say that he was tied to the tails of horses by the enemy, to whom he had designed to betray Jerusalem, as they thought he was mocking them; and so he died. **19. state**—office. **he**—God. A similar change of persons occurs in ch. 34:16. **20. son of Hilkiah**—supposed by Kimchi to be the same as Azariah, son of Hilkiah, who perhaps had two names, and who was "over the household" in Hezekiah's time (I Chron. 6:13). **21. thy robe**—of office. **girdle**—in which the purse was carried, and to it was attached the sword; often adorned with gold and jewels. **father**—i.e., a counsellor and friend. **22. key**—emblem of his office over the house; to "open" or "shut"; access rested with him. **upon . . . shoulder**—So keys are carried sometimes in the East, hanging from the kerchief on the shoulder. But the phrase is rather figurative for *sustaining the government on one's shoulders.* Eliakim, as his name implies, is here plainly a type of the God-man Christ, the son of "David," of whom Isaiah (ch. 9:6) uses the same language as the former clause of this verse. In Revelation 3:7, the same language as the latter clause is found (cf. Job 12:14). **23. nail . . . sure place**—Large nails or pegs stood in ancient houses on which were suspended the ornaments of the family. The sense is: all that is valuable to the nation shall rest securely on him. In Ezra 9:8 "nail" is used of the large spike driven into the ground to fasten the cords of the tent to. **throne**—resting-place to his family, as applied to Eliakim; but "throne," in the strict sense, as applied to Messiah, the antitype (Luke 1:32, 33). **24.** Same image as in vs. 23. It was customary to "hang" the valuables of a house on nails (I Kings 10:16, 17, 21; Song of Solomon 4:4). **offspring and the issue**—rather, "the offshoots of the family, high and low" [Vitringa]. Eliakim would reflect honor even on the latter. **vessels of cups**—of small capacity: answering to the *low* and humble *offshoots.* **vessels of flagons**—larger vessels: answering to the *high offshoots.* **25. nail . . . fastened**—Shebna, who was *supposed* to be firmly fixed in his post. **burden . . . upon it**—All that were dependent on Shebna, all his emoluments and rank will fail, as when a peg is suddenly "cut down," the ornaments on it fall with it. Sin reaches in its effects even to the family of the guilty (Exod. 20:5).

ADAM CLARKE

15. *Go . . . unto Shebna.* The following prophecy concerning Shebna seems to have very little relation to the foregoing, except that it might have been delivered about the same time; and Shebna might be a principal person among those whose luxury and profaneness are severely reprehended by the prophet in the conclusion of that prophecy, vv. 11-14. Shebna, the scribe, mentioned in the history of Hezekiah, chap. xxxvi, seems to have been a different person from this Shebna, the treasurer or steward of the household, to whom this prophecy relates. The Eliakim here mentioned was probably the person who, at the time of Sennacherib's invasion, was actually treasurer, the son of Hilkiah. If so, this prophecy was delivered, as the preceding plainly was, some time before the invasion of Sennacherib.

16. *A sepulchre on high . . . in a rock.* Persons of high rank in Judea, and in most parts of the East, were generally buried in large sepulchral vaults, hewn out in the rock for the use of themselves and their families. The vanity of Shebna is set forth by his being so studious and careful to have his sepulchre on high—in a lofty vault; and that probably in a high situation, that it might be more conspicuous. Hezekiah was buried "in the chiefest," says our translation—rather, in the highest part—"of the sepulchres of the sons of David," to do him the more honor, 2 Chron. xxxii. 33.

17. *Cover thee.* That is, thy face. This was the condition of mourners in general, and particularly of condemned persons. See Esther vi. 12; vii. 8.

22. *And the key of the house of David will I lay upon his shoulder.* As the robe and the baldric, mentioned in the preceding verse, were the ensigns of power and authority, so likewise was the key the mark of office, either sacred or civil. This mark of office was likewise among the Greeks, as here in Isaiah, borne on the shoulder. In allusion to the image of the key as the ensign of power, the unlimited extent of that power is expressed with great clearness as well as force by the sole and exclusive authority to open and shut. Our Saviour, therefore, has upon a similar occasion made use of a like manner of expression, Matt. xvi. 19; and in Rev. iii. 7 has applied to himself the very words of the prophet.

23. *A nail.* In ancient times and in the Eastern countries the houses were much more simple than ours at present. They had not that quantity and variety of furniture, nor those accommodations of all sorts, with which we abound. It was convenient and even necessary for them, and it made an essential part in the building of a house, to furnish the inside of the several apartments with sets of spikes, nails, or large pegs, upon which to dispose of and hang up the several movables and utensils in common use. These spikes they worked into the walls at the first erection of them, the walls being of such materials that they could not bear their being driven in afterwards; and they were contrived so as to strengthen the walls by binding the parts together, as well as to serve for convenience.

24. *All the glory.* One considerable part of the magnificence of the Eastern princes consisted in the great quantity of gold and silver vessels which they had for various uses. "Solomon's drinking vessels were of gold, and all the vessels of the house of the forest of Lebanon were of pure gold; none were of silver: it was nothing accounted of in the days of Solomon," 1 Kings x. 21. The vessels "in the house of the forest of Lebanon," the armory of Jerusalem so called, were "two hundred targets," and "three hundred shields of beaten gold," *ibid.* vv. 16-17. These were ranged in order upon the walls of the armory (see Cant. iv. 4), upon pins worked into the walls on purpose, as above mentioned. Eliakim is considered as a principal stake of this sort, immovably fastened in the wall for the support of all vessels destined for common or sacred uses; that is, as the principal support of the whole civil and ecclesiastical polity. And the consequence of his continued power will be the promotion and flourishing condition of his family and dependents, from the highest to the lowest.

MATTHEW HENRY

CHAPTER 23

Verses 1–14

Tyre being a sea-port town, this prophecy of its overthrow fitly begins and ends with, *Howl, you ships of Tarshish;* for all its business, wealth, and honour, depended upon its shipping; if that be ruined, they will be all undone.

I. Tyre flourishing. 1. *The merchants of Zidon,* who traded at sea, had at first *replenished her, v.* 2. Zidon was the more ancient city, situated upon the same sea-coast, a few leagues more to the north, and Tyre was at first only a colony of that; but the daughter had outgrown the mother. Egypt had helped very much to raise her, *v.* 3. Sihor was the river of Egypt: by that river, and the ocean into which it ran, the Egyptians traded with Tyre. Tyre became rich and great by industry, though she had no other ploughs going than those that plough the waters. She was a *joyous city,* noted for mirth and jollity, *v.* 7. This made them very loth to consider what warnings God gave them by his servants. Her *antiquity* likewise was *of ancient days,* and that helped to make her secure. She was *a crowning city* (*v.* 8), that crowned herself. *Her merchants are princes,* and *her traffickers,* whatever country they go to, *are the honourable of the earth,* respected by all.

II. Here is Tyre falling. It does not appear that she brought trouble upon herself by provoking her neighbours, but rather by tempting them with her wealth; but, if it was this that induced Nebuchadnezzar to fall upon Tyre, he was disappointed; for after it had stood out a siege of thirteen years, the inhabitants got away by sea, with their families and goods, and left Nebuchadnezzar nothing but the bare city. The destruction of Tyre is here foretold. The haven shall be spoiled, or at least neglected. There shall be no convenient harbour for the reception of the ships of Tarshish, but all *laid waste* (*v.* 1). Tyre is destroyed and laid waste; so that there is no more business there. The inhabitants are so overwhelmed with grief that they shall not be able to express it. The neighbours are amazed, and are in pain for them: *Zidon is ashamed* (*v.* 4), for the rolling waves of the sea brought to Zidon this news from Tyre; and there *the strength of the sea,* a high spring-tide, proclaimed saying, "*I travail not, nor bring forth children* now. I do not bring ship-loads of young people to Tyre, to be bred up there in trade and business," which was the thing that had made Tyre so rich and populous. Egypt indeed was a much larger and more considerable kingdom, and yet Tyre had so large a trade, that all the nations about shall be as much in pain, upon the report of the ruin of that one city, as they not long after were, upon the report of the ruin of all Egypt, *v.* 5. "*You* that have long been *inhabitants of this isle,* it is time to howl now, for you must pass over to Tarshish. The best course you can take is to make the best of your way to Tarshish, to the sea." Those that could not make their escape must expect no other than to be carried into captivity (*v.* 7): *Her own feet shall carry her afar off to sojourn;* they shall be hurried away on foot into captivity. Many of those that attempted to escape should fall into the hands of the enemy.

JAMIESON, FAUSSET, BROWN

CHAPTER 23

Vss. 1-18. PROPHECY RESPECTING TYRE. Menander, the historian, notices a siege of Tyre by Shalmaneser, about the time of the siege of Samaria. Sidon, Acco, and Old Tyre, on the mainland, were soon reduced; but New Tyre, on an island half a mile from the shore, held out for five years. Sargon probably finished the siege. Sennacherib does not, however, mention it among the cities which the Assyrian kings conquered (chs. 36, 37). The expression, "Chaldeans" (vs. 13), may imply reference to its siege under Nebuchadnezzar, which lasted thirteen years. Alexander the Great destroyed New Tyre after a seven months' siege. **1. Tyre**—*Hebrew, Tsur,* i.e., Rock. **ships of Tarshish**—ships of Tyre returning from their voyage to Tarshish, or Tartessus in Spain, with which the Phœnicians had much commerce (Ezek. 27:12-25). "Ships of Tarshish" is a phrase also used of large and distant-voyaging merchant vessels (ch. 2:16; I Kings 10:22; Ps. 48:7). **no house**—viz., left; such was the case as to Old Tyre, after Nebuchadnezzar's siege. **no entering**—There is *no* house to *enter* (ch. 24:10) [G. V. SMITH]. Or, Tyre is so laid waste, that there is no possibility of *entering the harbor* [BARNES]; which is appropriate to the previous "ships." **Chittim**—Cyprus, of which the cities, including *Citium* in the south (whence came "Chittim"), were mostly Phœnician (Ezek. 27:6). The ships from Tarshish on their way to Tyre learn the tidings ("it is revealed to them") of the downfall of Tyre. At a later period Chittim denoted the islands and coasts of the Mediterranean (Dan. 11:30). **2. Be still**—"struck dumb with awe." Addressed to those already in the country, eye-witnesses of its ruin (Lam. 2:10); or, in contrast to the *busy din* of commerce once heard in Tyre; now all is hushed and *still.* **isle**—strictly applicable to New Tyre: in the sense *coast,* to the mainland city, Old Tyre (cf. vs. 6; ch. 20:6). **Zidon**—of which Tyre was a colony, planted when Zidon was conquered by the Philistines of Ascalon. Zidon means a "fishing station"; this was its beginning. **replenished**—with wealth and an industrious population (Ezek. 27:3, 8, 23). Here "Zidon," as the oldest city of Phœnicia, includes all the Phœnician towns on the strip of "coast." Thus, Ethbaal, king of Tyre (Josephus, *Antiquities,* 8. 3, 2), is called king of the Sidonians (I Kings 16:31); and on coins Tyre is called the metropolis of the Sidonians. **3. great waters**—the wide waters of the sea. **seed**—"grain," or crop, as in I Samuel 8:15; Job 39:12. **Sihor**—lit., dark-colored; applied to the Nile, as the Egyptian *Jeor,* and the *Greek Melas,* to express the *dark, turbid* colors given to its waters by the fertilizing soil which it deposits at its yearly overflow (Jer. 2:18). **harvest of the river**—the growth of the Delta; the produce due to the overflow of the Nile: Egypt was the great granary of corn in the ancient world (Gen. 41; 42; 43). **her revenue**—Tyrian vessels carried Egyptian produce obtained in exchange for wine, oil, glass, etc., into various lands, and so made large profits. **mart**—(Ezek. 27:3.) No city was more favorably situated for commerce. **4. Zidon**—called on, as being the parent country of Tyre (vs. 12), and here equivalent to Phœnicia in general, to feel the shame (as it was esteemed in the East) of being now as childless as if she never had any. **"I** (no more now) travail, nor bring forth," etc. "Strength of the sea," i.e., stronghold, viz., New Tyre, on a rock (as "Tyre" means) surrounded by the sea (Ezek. 26:4; 15:17; so Venice was called "Bride of the sea"; Zech. 9:3). **5. As . . .**—rather, "*When* the report (shall reach) the people of Egypt, they shall be sorely pained at the report concerning Tyre" (viz., its overthrow). So JEROME, "When the Egyptians shall hear that so powerful a neighboring nation has been destroyed, they must know their own end is near" [LOWTH, etc.]. **6. Pass . . . over**—Escape from Tyre to your colonies as Tarshish (cf. vs. 12). The Tyrians fled to Carthage and elsewhere, both at the siege under Nebuchadnezzar and that under Alexander. **7.** *Is this* silent ruin all that is left of *your* once *joyous city* (vs. 12)? **antiquity**—The Tyrian priests boasted in Herodotus' time that their city had already existed 2300 years: an exaggeration, but still implying that it was *ancient* even then. **her own feet**—walking on foot as captives to an enemy's land. **8. Who**—answered in vs. 9, "The Lord of hosts." **crowning**—crown-giving; i.e., the city from which dependent kingdoms had arisen, as Tartessus in Spain, Citium in Cyprus, and Carthage in Africa (Ezek. 27:33). **traffickers**—lit., Canaanites, who were famed for commerce (cf. Hos. 12:7, *Margin*). **9.** Whoever be the instruments in overthrowing haughty sinners, God, who has all hosts at His command, is the First Cause (ch. 10:5-7). **stain**

ADAM CLARKE

CHAPTER 23

1. *The burden of Tyre.* There were two cities of this name: one on the continent, and the other on an island, about half a mile from the shore. The city on the island was about four miles in circumference. Old Tyre resisted Nebuchadnezzar for thirteen years; then the inhabitants carried, so to speak, the city to the forementioned island, v. 4. This new city held out against Alexander the Great for seven months; who, in order to take it, was obliged to fill up the channel which separated it from the mainland. In A.D 1289 it was totally destroyed by the sultan of Egypt, and now contains only a few huts. *Howl, ye ships of Tarshish.* This prophecy denounces the destruction of Tyre by Nebuchadnezzar. It opens with an address to the Tyrian negotiators and sailors at Tarshish (Tartessus, in Spain), a place which, in the course of their trade, they greatly frequented. The news of the destruction of Tyre by Nebuchadnezzar is said to be brought to them from Chittim, the islands and coasts of the Mediterranean. "For the Tyrians," says Jerome on v. 6, "when they saw they had no other means of escaping, fled in their ships, and took refuge in Carthage and in the islands of the Ionian and Aegean sea." From whence the news would spread and reach Tarshish.

2. *Be still*—"Be silent." Silence is a mark of grief and consternation. See chap. xlvii. 5.

3. *The seed of Sihor*—"The seed of the Nile." The Nile is called here Shichor, as it is in Jer. ii. 18 and 1 Chron. xiii. 5. It had this name from the blackness of its waters, charged with the mud which it brings down from Ethiopia when it overflows. Egypt by its extraordinary fertility, caused by the overflowing of the Nile, supplied the neighboring nations with corn, by which branch of trade the Tyrians gained great wealth.

4. *Be thou ashamed, O Zidon.* Tyre is called, v. 12, the daughter of Sidon. Sidon, as the mother city, is supposed to be deeply affected with the calamity of her daughter.

7. *Whose antiquity is of ancient days*—"Whose antiquity is of the earliest date." Tyre, though not so old as Sidon, was yet of very high antiquity; it was a strong city even in the time of Joshua. It is called "the city of the fortress of Sor," Josh. xix. 29. *Her own feet shall carry her afar off to sojourn.* This may belong to the new or insular Tyre; *her own feet,* that is, her own inhabitants, *shall carry her*—shall transport the city from the continent to the island. *Merachok* does not always signify a great distance, but distance or interval in general; for in Josh. iii. 4, *rachok* is used to express the space between the camp and the ark, which we know to have been only 2,000 cubits. Some refer the sojourning afar off to the extent of the commercial voyages undertaken by the Tyrians and their foreign connections.

MATTHEW HENRY

Tyre shall *pass through her land as a river* (*v.* 10), running down into the abyss of misery. *There is no more strength;* they fall an easy prey into the hands of the enemy.

And, as Tyre has no more strength, so her sister Zidon has no more comfort (*v.* 12): "*Thou shalt no more rejoice, O oppressed virgin, daughter of Zidon,* that art now ready to be overpowered by the victorious Chaldeans!" But whence shall all this trouble come? God will be the author of it; it is a *destruction from the Almighty.* It will be asked (*v.* 8): "*Who has taken this counsel against Tyre?*" God has designed it, who is infinitely wise and just. God did not bring those calamities upon Tyre to show an arbitrary power; but to punish the Tyrians for their pride. Many other sins, no doubt, reigned among them, but the sin of pride was the particular ground of God's controversy with Tyre. God tells the world what he meant. He designed to convince men of the vanity and uncertainty of all earthly glory, to show them what a withering thing it is even when it seems most substantial. Are men's learning and wealth, their pomp and power, their glory? Look upon the ruins of Tyre, and see all this glory stained, and sullied, and buried in the dust. *He stretched out his hand over the sea.* The Chaldeans shall be the instruments of it (*v.* 13): *Behold the land of the Chaldeans;* how easily they and their land were destroyed by the Assyrians. Though their own hands *founded it, set up the towers* of Babylon, and *raised up its palaces,* yet the Assyrians brought it to ruin, and so shall Tyre hereafter be brought to ruin by Nebuchadnezzar. If we looked more upon the falling of others, we should not be so confident as we commonly are of the continuance of our own standing.

Verses 15–18

I. The time fixed for the continuance of the desolations of Tyre, which were not to be perpetual desolations: *Tyre shall be forgotten seventy years, v.* 15. It was destroyed by Nebuchadnezzar about the time that Jerusalem was, and lay as long in its ruins. He trampled on the pride of Tyre, and therein served God's purpose; but with greater pride, for which God soon after humbled him.

II. A prophecy of the restoration of Tyre to its glory again: *After the end of seventy years, according to the years of one king,* or one dynasty, that of Nebuchadnezzar. And we may presume that Cyrus at the same time when he released the Jews, and encouraged them to rebuild Jerusalem, released the Tyrians also, and encouraged them to rebuild Tyre. *The Lord will visit Tyre* in mercy; for he will not contend for ever. She shall use her best endeavours to recover her trade again. She shall sing as a harlot, that has been some time under correction for her lewdness; but, when she is set at liberty, she will use her old arts of temptation. The Tyrians having returned from their captivity, shall contrive how to force a trade, procure the best choice of goods, and be obliging to all customers; as a harlot that has been forgotten, when she comes to be spoken of again, recommends herself to company by singing and playing, *takes a harp, goes about the city,* serenading. Tyre shall by degrees come to be the mart of nations again; she shall *return to her hire,* to her traffic, *and shall commit fornication* (that is, she shall have dealings in trade, for the prophet carries on the similitude of a harlot) *with all the kingdoms of the world* that she had formerly traded with in her prosperity. The love of worldly wealth is a spiritual whoredom, and therefore covetous people are called *adulterers and adulteresses* (James iv. 4). Having recovered her trade again, she shall make a better use of it than formerly (*v.* 18): *Her merchandise, and her hire, shall be holiness to the Lord.* The trade of Tyre, and all the gains of her trade, shall be devoted to God, and employed in his service. It shall not be hoarded, but it shall be laid out in acts of piety and charity. What they can spare from the maintenance of themselves and their families *shall be for those that dwell before the*

JAMIESON, FAUSSET, BROWN

—rather, "to profane"; as in Exodus 31:14, the *Sabbath,* and other objects of religious reverence; so here, "the pride of all glory" may refer to the Tyrian temple of Hercules, the oldest in the world, according to Arrian (ch. 2:16); the prophet of the true God would naturally single out for notice the idol of Tyre [G. V. SMITH]. It may, however, be a *general* proposition; the destruction of Tyre will exhibit to all how God mars the luster of whatever is haughty (ch. 2:11). **10. a river**—*Hebrew,* "the river," viz., Nile. **daughter of Tarshish**—Tyre and its inhabitants (ch. 1:8), about henceforth, owing to the ruin of Tyre, to become inhabitants of its colony, Tartessus: they would *pour forth* from Tyre, as waters flow on when the barriers are removed [LOWTH]. Rather, Tarshish, or Tartessus and its inhabitants, as the phrase usually means: they had been kept in hard bondage, working in silver and lead mines near Tarshish, by the parent city (Ezek. 26:17): but now "the bond of restraint" (for so "strength," *Margin,* girdle, i.e., bond, Ps. 2:3, ought to be translated) is removed, since Tyre is no more. **11. He**—Jehovah. **kingdoms**—the Phœnician cities and colonies. **the merchant city**—rather, *Canaan,* meaning the north of it, viz., Phœnicia. On their coins, they call their country *Canaan.* **12. he**—God. **rejoice**—riotously (vs. 7). **oppressed**—"deflowered"; laying aside the figure "taken by storm"; the Arabs compare a city never taken to an undefiled virgin (cf. Nah. 3:5, etc.). **daughter of Zidon**—Tyre: or else, sons of Zidon, i.e., the whole land and people of Phœnicia (*Note,* vs. 2) [MAURER]. **Chittim**—Citium in Cyprus (vs. 1). **there also . . . no rest**—Thy colonies, having been harshly treated by thee, will now repay thee in kind (*Note,* vs. 10). But VITRINGA refers it to the calamities which befell the Tyrians in their settlements subsequently, viz., Sicily, Corcyra, Carthage, and Spain, all flowing from the original curse of Noah against the posterity of Canaan (Gen. 9:25-27). **13. Behold**—Calling attention to the fact, so humiliating to Tyre, that a people of yesterday, like the Chaldees, should destroy the most ancient of cities, Tyre. **was not**—had no existence as a recognized nation; the Chaldees were previously but a rude, predatory people (Job 1:17). **Assyrian founded it**—The Chaldees ("them that dwell in the wilderness") lived a nomadic life in the mountains of Armenia originally (Arphaxad, in Gen. 10:22, refers to such a region of Assyria near Armenia), north and east of Assyria proper. Some may have settled in Mesopotamia and Babylonia very early and given origin to the astrologers called *Chaldees* in later times. But most of the people had been transferred only a little before the time of this prophecy from their original seats in the north to Mesopotamia, and soon afterwards to South Babylonia. "Founded it," means "assigned *it* (the land) to them who had (heretofore) dwelt in the wilderness" as a permanent settlement (so in Ps. 104:8) [MAURER]. It was the Assyrian policy to infuse into their own population of the plain the fresh blood of hardy mountaineers, for the sake of recruiting their armies. Ultimately the Chaldees, by their powerful priest-caste, gained the supremacy and established the later or Chaldean empire. HORSLEY refers it to Tyre, founded by an Assyrian race. **towers thereof**—viz., of Babylon, whose towers, HERODOTUS says, were "set up" by the Assyrians [BARNES]. Rather, "The *Chaldees* set up *their siege-towers*" against Tyre, made for the attack of high walls, from which the besiegers hurled missiles, as depicted in the Assyrian sculptures [G. V. SMITH]. **raised up**—rather, "They *lay bare,*" viz., the foundations of *her* (Tyre's) *palaces,* i.e., utterly overthrew them (Ps. 137:7). **14. strength**—stronghold (cf. Ezek. 26:15-18). **15. forgotten**—Having lost its former renown, Tyre shall be in obscurity. **seventy years**—(so Jer. 25:11, 12; 29:10). **days of one king**—i.e., a dynasty. The Babylonian monarchy lasted properly but seventy years. From the first year of Nebuchadnezzar to the taking of Babylon, by Cyrus, was seventy years; then the subjected nations would be restored to liberty. Tyre was taken in the middle of that period, but it is classed in common with the rest, some conquered sooner and others later, all, however, alike to be delivered at the end of the period. So "king" is used for dynasty (Dan. 7:17; 8:20): Nebuchadnezzar, his son Evil-merodach, and his grandson, Belshazzar, formed the whole dynasty (Jer. 25:11, 12; 27:7; 29:10). **shall Tyre sing as . . . harlot**—It shall be to Tyre as the song of the harlot, viz., a harlot that has been forgotten, but who attracts notice again by her song. Large marts of commerce are often compared to harlots seeking many lovers, i.e., they court merchants of all nations, and admit any one for the sake of gain (Nah. 3:4; Rev. 18:3). Covetousness is closely akin to

ADAM CLARKE

10. *O daughter of Tarshish.* Tyre is called the daughter of Tarshish; perhaps because, Tyre being ruined, Tarshish was become the superior city, and might be considered as the metropolis of the Tyrian people; or rather because of the close connection and perpetual intercourse between them, according to that latitude of signification in which the Hebrews use the words son and daughter to express any sort of conjunction and dependence whatever.

13. *Behold the land of the Chaldeans.* The Chaldeans, *Chasdim,* are supposed to have had their origin, and to have taken their name, from *Chesed,* the son of Nachor, the brother of Abraham. They were known by that name in the time of Moses, who calls Ur in Mesopotamia, from whence Abraham came, to distinguish it from other places of the same name, "Ur of the Chaldeans." And Jeremiah calls them an ancient nation. This is not inconsistent with what Isaiah here says of them: *This people was not,* that is, they were of no account (see Deut. xxxii. 21); they were not reckoned among the great and potent nations of the world till of later times; they were a rude, uncivilized, barbarous people, without laws, without settled habitations. Such they are represented to have been in the time of Job, chap. i. 17, and such they continued to be till Assur, some powerful king of Assyria, gathered them together, and settled them in Babylon in the neighboring country.

15. *According to the days of one king.* That is, of one "kingdom"; see Dan. vii. 17; viii. 20. Nebuchadnezzar began his conquests in the first year of his reign; from thence to the taking of Babylon by Cyrus are seventy years, at which time the nations subdued by Nebuchadnezzar were to be restored to liberty. These seventy years limit the duration of the Babylonish monarchy. Tyre was taken by him towards the middle of that period, so did not serve the king of Babylon during the whole period, but only for the remaining part of it. This seems to be the meaning of Isaiah. The days allotted to the one king or kingdom are seventy years; Tyre, with the rest of the conquered nations, shall continue in a state of subjection and desolation to the end of that period. Not from the beginning and through the whole of the period; for, by being one of the latest conquests, the duration of that state of subjection in

MATTHEW HENRY

Lord, for the priests, the Lord's ministers. They and theirs may *eat sufficiently*, and may have *durable clothing*, strong and lasting. This supposes that religion should be set up in New Tyre, that they should come to the knowledge of the true God and into communion with the Israel of God. We find men of Tyre then dwelling in the land of Judah, Neh. xiii. 16. Tyre and Sidon were better disposed to religion in Christ's time than the cities of Israel; for, if Christ had gone among them, *they would have repented*, Matt. xi. 21. And we meet with Christians at Tyre (Acts xxi. 3, 4). Both the merchandise of the tradesmen and the hire of the day-labourers shall be devoted to God, must *be holiness to the Lord*, alluding to the motto engraven on the frontlet of the high priest (Exod. xxxix. 30), and to the separation of the tithe under the law, Lev. xxvii. 30. We must first give up ourselves to be holiness to the Lord before what we do, or have, or get, can be so. When we are liberal in relieving the poor, and supporting the ministry, and encouraging the gospel—then our merchandise and our hire are holiness to the Lord, if we sincerely look at his glory in them.

CHAPTER 24

Verses 1–12

It is a very dark and melancholy scene that this prophecy presents to our view.

I. The earth is stripped; it is made *empty and waste* (*v.* 1), as if it were reduced to its first chaos, *Tohu* and *Bohu*, confusion and emptiness again (Gen. i. 2), *without form and void*. Earth sometimes signifies the *land*, and the same word *eretz* is here translated (*v.* 3): *The land shall be utterly emptied and utterly spoiled;* but it might be as *v.* 1, translated *the earth*. Many countries are empty of all solid comfort and satisfaction; a little thing makes them waste. We often see plentiful estates, utterly emptied and spoiled, by one judgment or other. Sin has turned the earth *upside down*; the earth has become quite a different thing to man from what it was when God made it to be his habitation. Sin has also *scattered abroad the inhabitants thereof*. The rebellion at Babel was the occasion of the dispersion there. To the same purport is *v.* 4: *The earth mourns, and fades away;* it disappoints those that placed their happiness in it. *The* whole *world languishes and fades away*. It is like a flower, which withers in the hands of those that please themselves too much with it. And, as the earth itself grows old, so those that dwell therein are desolate; men carry crazy sickly bodies along with them, are often solitary, and confined by affliction, *v.* 6. *The inhabitants of the earth are burned*, or consumed, some by one disease, others by another, and there are but *few men left*.

II. It is God that brings all these calamities upon the earth. *The Lord* that made the earth, and made it fruitful and beautiful, for the service and comfort of man, now *makes it empty and waste* (*v.* 1), for its Creator is and will be its Judge. It is *the Lord* that *has spoken this word*, and he will do the work (*v.* 3).

III. Persons of all ranks and conditions shall share in these calamities (*v.* 2): *It shall be as with the people, so with the priest*, &c. The dignity of magistrates and ministers shall not secure them. The priests had been as wicked as the people; and, if their character served not to restrain them from sin, how can they expect it should serve to secure them from judgments? *As with the servant, so with his master; as with the maid, so with her mistress*. Those that have money beforehand will fare no better than those that are impoverished.

IV. It is sin that brings these calamities upon the earth. The earth is made empty, and fades away, because it *is defiled under the inhabitants thereof* (*v.* 5); and therefore it is made desolate by the judgments of God. They have transgressed the laws of their creation, and their obligations to the God of nature. *They have changed the ordinances* of revealed religion, *neglected the ordinances* (so some read it), and made no conscience of observing them. They have passed over the laws, in the commission of sin, and have passed by the ordinance, in the omission of duty. Herein they have *broken the everlasting covenant*, which is a perpetual bond and will be to those that keep it a perpetual blessing.

V. These judgments shall humble men's pride (*v.* 4): *The haughty people of the earth do languish;* for they have lost that which supported their pride. It is a great damp to men's jollity. This is enlarged upon much (*v.* 7–9): *All the merry-hearted do sigh.* Such is the nature of carnal mirth, it is but *as the crackling of thorns under a pot*, Eccles. vii. 6. Carnal joy is a noisy thing; but the noise of it will soon be at an end, and the end of it is heaviness. Two things

JAMIESON, FAUSSET, BROWN

idolatry and licentiousness, as the connection (Eph. 5:5; Col. 3:5) proves (cf. ch. 2:6-8, 16). **16.** Same figure to express that Tyre would again prosper and attract commercial intercourse of nations to her, and be the same joyous, self-indulging city as before. **17. visit**—not in wrath, but mercy. **hire**—image from a harlot: her *gains* by commerce. After the Babylonian dynasty was ended, Tyre was rebuilt; also, again, after the destruction under Alexander. **18. merchandise . . . holiness**—Her traffic and gains shall at last (long after the restoration mentioned in vs. 17) be consecrated to Jehovah. Jesus Christ visited the neighborhood of Tyre (Matt. 15:21); Paul found disciples there (Acts 21:3-6); it early became a Christian bishopric, but the full evangelization of that whole race, as of the Ethiopians (ch. 18), of the Egyptians and Assyrians (ch. 19), is yet to come (ch. 60:5). **not treasured**—but freely expended in His service. **them that dwell before the Lord**—the ministers of religion. But HORSLEY translates, "them that *sit* before Jehovah" as *disciples*. **durable clothing**—Changes of raiment constituted much of the wealth of former days.

CHAPTER 24

THE LAST TIMES OF THE WORLD IN GENERAL, AND OF JUDAH AND THE CHURCH IN PARTICULAR. The four chaps. 24-27 form one continuous poetical prophecy: descriptive of the dispersion and successive calamities of the Jews (ch. 24:1-12); the preaching of the Gospel by the first Hebrew converts throughout the world (vss. 13-16); the judgments on the adversaries of the Church and its final triumph (vss. 16-23); thanksgiving for the overthrow of the apostate faction (ch. 25), and establishment of the righteous in lasting peace (ch. 26); judgment on leviathan and entire purgation of the Church (ch. 27). Having treated of the *several nations in particular*—Babylon, Philistia, Moab, Syria, Israel, Egypt, Edom, and Tyre (the miniature representative of all, as all kingdoms flocked into it)—he passes to the last times of *the world at large* and of Judah the representative and future head of the churches. **4. world**—the kingdom of Israel; as in ch. 13:11, Babylon. **haughty**—lit., "the height" of the people: abstract for concrete, i.e., the high people; even the nobles share the general distress. **6. earth**—the land. **burned**—viz., with the consuming wrath of heaven: either internally, as in Job 30:30 [ROSENMILLER]; or externally, the prophet has before his eyes the people being consumed with the withering dryness of their doomed land (so Joel 1: 10, 12), [MAURER].

Vss. 1-23. **1. the earth**—rather, *the land* of Judah (so in vss. 3, 5, 6; Joel 1:2). The desolation under Nebuchadnezzar prefigured that under Titus.

2. as with the people, so with the priest—All alike shall share the same calamity: no favored class shall escape (cf. Ezek. 7:12, 13; Hos. 4:9; Rev. 6:15).

5. earth—rather, the land. **defiled under . . . inhabitans**—viz., with innocent blood (Gen. 4:11; Num. 35:33; Ps. 106:38).

laws . . . ordinance . . . everlasting covenant—The *moral* laws, *positive* statutes, and *national* covenant designed to be for ever between God and them.

ADAM CLARKE

regard to her was not much more than half of it. All "these nations," saith Jeremiah, xxv. 11, "shall serve the king of Babylon seventy years." Some of them were conquered sooner, some later; but the end of this period was the common term for the deliverance of them all.

17. *After the end of seventy years.* Tyre, after its destruction by Nebuchadnezzar, recovered, as it is here foretold, its ancient trade, wealth, and grandeur, as it did likewise after a second destruction by Alexander. It became Christian early with the rest of the neighboring countries. St. Paul himself found many Christians there, Acts xxi. 4. It suffered much in the Diocletian persecution. It was an archbishopric under the patriarchate of Jerusalem, with fourteen bishoprics under its jurisdiction. It continued Christian till it was taken by the Saracens in 639; was recovered by the Christians in 1124; but in 1280 was conquered by the Mamelukes, and afterwards taken from them by the Turks in 1517. Since that time it has sunk into decay; is now a mere ruin.

CHAPTER 24

From the thirteenth chapter to the twenty-third inclusive, the fate of several cities and nations is denounced: of Babylon, of the Philistines, Moab, Damascus, Egypt, Tyre. After having foretold the destruction of the foreign nations, enemies of Judah, the prophet declares the judgments impending on the people of God themselves for their wickedness and apostasy, and the desolation that shall be brought on their whole country.

The twenty-fourth and the following three chapters seem to have been delivered about the same time: before the destruction of Moab by Shalmaneser; see chap. xxv. 10, consequently, before the destruction of Samaria; probably in the beginning of Hezekiah's reign. But concerning the particular subject of the twenty-fourth chapter interpreters are not at all agreed: some refer it to the desolation caused by the invasion of Shalmaneser; others, to the invasion of Nebuchadnezzar; and others, to the destruction of the city and nation by the Romans. Perhaps it may have a view to all of the three great desolations of the country, by Shalmaneser, by Nebuchadnezzar, and by the Romans; especially the last, to which some parts of it may seem more peculiarly applicable.

4. *The world languisheth.* The world is the same with the land; that is, the kingdoms of Judah and Israel.

6. *Are burned*—"Are destroyed."

5. *The laws*—"The law." *Torah*, singular: so read the Septuagint, Syriac, and Chaldee.

MATTHEW HENRY

excite and express vain mirth. (1) Drinking: *The new wine mourns;* it has grown sour for want of drinking. *The vine languishes*, and gives little hopes of a vintage, and therefore *the merry-hearted do sigh*; for if you *destroy their vines and their fig-trees, you make all their mirth to cease*, Hosea ii. 11, 12. (2) Music: *The mirth of tabrets ceases, and the joy of the harp*, which used to be at their feasts, *ch.* v. 12. In short, *All joy is darkened;* there is not a pleasant look to be seen, nor has anyone power to force a smile.

VI. The cities will feel these desolations (*v.* 10): *The city of confusion is broken, is broken down* (so we read it); it lies exposed to invading powers. *Every house is shut up*, perhaps by reason of the plague, so that there are *few men left*, *v.* 6. *In the city*, in Jerusalem itself, there shall be left nothing but *desolation*; grass shall grow in the streets, and *the gate is smitten with destruction* (*v.* 12); all that used to pass and repass through the gate are smitten.

Verses 13–15

Here is mercy remembered in the midst of wrath. In Judah and Jerusalem, and the neighbouring countries, when they are overrun by the enemy, Sennacherib or Nebuchadnezzar, there shall be a remnant preserved from the general ruin.

I. The small number of this remnant, *v.* 13. When all goes to ruin *there shall be as the shaking of an olive tree, and the gleaning grapes*, here and there one who shall escape the common calamity. These few are dispersed like the gleanings of the olive-tree; and they are hid under the leaves. The Lord knows those that are his; the world does not.

II. The great devotion of this remnant, having so narrowly escaped this great destruction (*v.* 14): *They shall lift up their voice; they shall sing*. Those that rejoice in the Lord can rejoice in tribulation. They shall sing not only for the mercy but *for the majesty of the Lord*. Their dispersion shall help to spread the knowledge of God, and they shall make even remote shores to ring with his praises.

III. Their holy zeal to excite others to the same devotion (*v.* 15), *in the fires*, in the furnace of affliction, those fires by which the *inhabitants of the earth are burned*, *v.* 6. Those who are *in the isles of the sea*, whither they are banished, or are forced to flee for shelter, went *through fire and water* (Ps. lxvi. 12); yet in both let them glorify the Lord.

Verses 16–23

I. Comfort to saints. They may be driven, by common calamities, into *the uttermost parts of the earth*, or perhaps they are forced thither for their religion; but there they are singing, not sighing. And this is their song, *even glory to the righteous*: the word is singular, and may refer to *the righteous God*, or the meaning may be, "These songs redound to the glory or beauty of the righteous that sing them."

II. Terror to sinners. The prophet returns to lament the miseries he saw breaking in upon the earth: "*But I said, My leanness! my leanness! woe unto me!* The very thought of it frets me, and makes me lean," *v.* 16. He foresees that iniquity should abound (*v.* 16): *The treacherous dealers have dealt treacherously*. Men are false to one another; there is universal dishonesty. Truth, that sacred bond of society, has departed, and there is nothing but treachery in men's dealings. They are all false to their God, all treacherous dealers, and have dealt very treacherously with their God, in departing from their allegiance to him. The inhabitants of the earth will be pursued from place to place, by one mischief or other (*v.* 17, 18): *Fear, and the pit, and the snare* (fear of the pit and the snare) are upon them wherever they are. It is a common instance of the calamitous state of human life that when we seek to avoid one mischief we fall into a worse. The earth itself will be shaken to pieces. It will be literally so at last, when all *the works therein shall be burnt up*; and it is often figuratively so before that period. This is expressed (*v.* 19, 20): *The earth is utterly broken down; it is clean dissolved; it is moved exceedingly*, moved out of its place. Those who lay up their treasure in the things of the earth place their confidence in that which will shortly be *utterly broken down and dissolved. The earth shall reel to and fro like a drunkard*. Worldly men dwell in it as in a castle, an impregnable tower; but *it shall be removed like a cottage*, so easily, so suddenly, and with so little loss to the great landlord. It *shall fall, and not rise again*; but there shall be new heavens and a new earth, in which shall dwell nothing but righteousness. But what is it that shakes the earth thus and sinks it? It is the transgression that shall be heavy upon it. Sin is a burden to the whole creation. Sin is the ruin of states, and kingdoms, and families. God will have a particular controversy with the kings and

JAMIESON, FAUSSET, BROWN

7. mourneth—because there are none to drink it [BARNES]. Rather, is become vapid [HORSLEY]. **languisheth**—because there are none to cultivate it now. **8.** (Rev. 18:22.) **9. with a song**—the usual accompaniment of feasts. **strong drink**—(*Note*, ch. 5:11.) "Date wine" [HORSLEY]. **bitter**—in consequence of the national calamities.

10. city of confusion—rather, desolation. What *Jerusalem* would be; by anticipation it is called so. HORSLEY translates, "The city is broken down; it is a ruin." **shut up**—through fear; or rather, choked up by ruins. **11. crying for wine**—to drown their sorrows in drink (ch. 16:9); Joel 1:5, written about the same time, resembles this. **12. with destruction**—rather "crash" [GESENIUS]. "With a great tumult the gate is battered down" [HORSLEY].

13. the land—Judea. Put the comma after "land," not after "people." "There shall be among the people (a remnant left), as the shaking (the after-picking) of an olive tree"; as in gathering olives, a few remain on the highest boughs (ch. 17:5, 6). **14. They**—those who are left: the remnant. **sing for the majesty of the Lord**—sing a thanksgiving for the goodness of the LORD, who has so mercifully preserved them. **from the sea**—from the distant lands beyond the sea, whither they have escaped. **15. in the fires**—VITRINGA translates, "in the *caves*." Could it mean *the fires of affliction* (I Peter 1:7)? They were exiles at the time. The fires only loose the carnal bonds off the soul, without injuring a hair, as in the case of Shadrach, Meshach, and Abed-nego. LOWTH reads, in the *islands* (Ezek. 26:18). Rather translate for "fires," "in the regions of morning light," i.e., the east, in antithesis to the "isles of the sea," i.e., the west [MAURER]. Wheresoever ye be scattered, east or west, still glorify the Lord (Mal. 1:11). **16.** Songs to God come in together to Palestine from distant lands, as a grand chorus. **glory to the righteous**—the burden of the songs (ch. 26:2, 7). Amidst exile, the loss of their temple, and all that is dear to man, their confidence in God is unshaken. These songs recall the joy of other times and draw from Jerusalem in her present calamities, the cry, "My leanness." HORSLEY translates, "glory to *the Just One*"; then My leanness expresses his sense of man's corruption, which led the Jews, "the treacherous dealers" (Jer. 5:11), to crucify the Just One; and his deficiency of righteousness which made him need to be clothed with the righteousness of the Just One (Ps. 106:15). **treacherous dealers**—the foreign nations that oppress Jerusalem, and overcome it by stratagem (so in ch. 21:2) [BARNES]. **17.** This verse explains the wretchedness spoken of in vs. 16. Jeremiah (48:43, 44) uses the same words. They are proverbial; vs. 18 expressing that the inhabitants were nowhere safe; if they escaped one danger, they fell into another, and worse, on the opposite side (Amos 5:19). "Fear" is the term applied to the cords with feathers of all colors which, when fluttered in the air, scare beasts into the pitfall, or birds into the snare. HORSLEY makes the connection. Indignant at the treatment which the Just One received, the prophet threatens the guilty land with instant vengeance. **18. noise of . . . fear**—the shout designed to rouse the game and drive it into the pitfall. **windows . . . open**—taken from the account of the deluge (Gen. 7:11); *the flood-gates*. So the final judgments of fire on the apostate world are compared to the deluge (II Pet. 3:5-7). **19. earth**—the land: image from an earthquake. **20. removed like a cottage**—(*Note*, ch. 1:8.) Here, *a hanging couch*, suspended from the trees by cords, such as Niebuhr describes the Arab keepers of lands as having, to enable them to keep watch, and at the same time to be secure from wild beasts. Translate, "Shall wave to and fro like a hammock" swung about by the wind. **heavy upon it**—like an overwhelming burden. **not rise again**—not meaning, that it *never* would rise (vs. 23), but *in those convulsions* it would not rise, it would surely fall.

ADAM CLARKE

8. *The mirth.* "The noise."

9. *Strong drink*—"Palm wine." All enjoyment shall cease; the sweetest wine shall become bitter to their taste.

11. *All joy is darkened*—"All gladness is passed away."

14. *They shall lift up their voice*—"But these shall lift up their voice." That is, they that escaped out of these calamities. The great distresses brought upon Israel and Judah drove the people away, and dispersed them all over the neighboring countries; they fled to Egypt, to Asia Minor, to the islands, and the coasts of Greece. They were to be found in great numbers in most of the principal cities of these countries. Alexandria was in a great measure peopled by them. They had synagogues for their worship in many places, and were greatly instrumental in propagating the knowledge of the true God among these heathen nations, and preparing them for the reception of Christianity. This is what the prophet seems to mean by the celebration of the name of Jehovah in the waters, in the distant coasts, and in the uttermost parts of the land.

16. *But I said.* The prophet speaks in the person of the inhabitants of the land still remaining there, who should be pursued by divine vengeance, and suffer repeated distresses from the inroads and depredations of their powerful enemies.

17. *Fear, and the pit*—"The terror, the pit." If they escape one calamity, another shall overtake them. The images are taken from the different methods of hunting and taking wild beasts, which were anciently in use. The *terror* was a line strung with feathers of all colors, which fluttering in the air scared and frightened the beasts into the toils, or into the pit which was prepared for them. The *pit* or pitfall, digged deep in the ground, and covered over with green boughs, turf, etc., in order to deceive them, that they might fall into it unawares. The *snare*, or toils; a series of nets, enclosing at first a great space of ground, in which the wild beasts were known to be, and then drawn in by degrees into a narrower compass, till they were at last closely shut up, and entangled in them.

19. *The earth*—"The land."

20. *Like a cottage*—"Like a lodge for a night."

MATTHEW HENRY

great men of the earth (*v.* 21): *He will punish the host of the high ones.* The high ones, that think themselves out of the reach of any danger, God will visit upon them all their pride and cruelty, and it shall return upon their own heads. Let those that are trampled upon by the high ones of the earth comfort themselves with this, that though they cannot resist them, yet there is a God that will call them to account. It is particularly foretold (*v.* 22) that they shall be *gathered together as prisoners,* convicted condemned prisoners, *gathered in the pit,* or dungeon, and there they shall *be shut up* under close confinement. Let not the free man glory in his freedom, any more than the strong man in his strength, for he knows not what restraints he is reserved for. But *after many days they shall be visited,* either in wrath, or shall be reserved to the day of execution, *to the judgment of the great day,* Jude 6. Or they shall be visited in mercy, and be discharged from their imprisonment, and shall again obtain, if not their dignity, yet their liberty. Nebuchadnezzar made many kings and princes his captives, and kept them in the dungeon in Babylon, and, among the rest, Jehoiachin king of Judah; but after many days, when Nebuchadnezzar's head was laid, his son visited them, and with particular kindness to Jehoiachin *set his throne above the throne of the rest of the kings that were with him,* Jer. lii. 32. When the proud enemies of God's church are humbled it shall appear, beyond contradiction, that the Lord reigns. When the kings of the earth are punished for their tyranny, then it is proved to all the world that God is King of kings, that he reigns as *Lord of hosts,* of all hosts, of their hosts—that he reigns *in Mount Zion, and in Jerusalem,* in his church—that he reigns *before his ancients.* God's ancients, the old disciples, the experienced Christians, that have often, when they have been perplexed, gone into the sanctuary of God in Zion and Jerusalem, shall see more than others of God's dominion and sovereignty. Then it shall appear that he reigns *gloriously,* in such brightness and lustre that *the moon shall be confounded and the sun ashamed,* as the smaller lights are eclipsed and extinguished by the greater. The glory of the Creator infinitely outshines the glory of the brightest creatures.

JAMIESON, FAUSSET, BROWN

21. host of . . . high ones—the heavenly host, i.e., either *the visible host of heaven* (the present economy of nature, affected by the sun, moon, and stars, the objects of idolatry, being abolished, ch. 65:17; 60:19, simultaneously with the corrupt polity of men); or rather, the *invisible* rulers of the darkness of this world, as the antithesis to "kings of the earth" shows. Angels, moreover, preside, as it were, over kingdoms of the world (Dan. 10:13, 20, 21). **22. in the pit**—rather, for the pit [HORSLEY]. **"In the** *dungeon***"** [MAURER]. Image from captives thrust together into a dungeon. **prison**—i.e., as in a prison. This sheds light on the disputed passage, I Peter 3:19, where also the *prison* is figurative: The "shutting up" of the Jews in Jerusalem under Nebuchadnezzar, and again under Titus, was to be followed by a *visitation* of mercy "after many days"—seventy years in the case of the former—the time is not yet elapsed in the case of the latter. HORSLEY takes "visited" in a bad sense, viz., in wrath, as in ch. 26:14; cf. ch. 29:6; the punishment being the heavier in the fact of the delay. Probably a double visitation is intended, deliverance to the elect, wrath to hardened unbelievers; as vs. 23 plainly contemplates judgments on proud sinners, symbolized by the "sun" and "moon."

23. (Jer. 3:17.) Still future: of which Jesus' triumphal entry into Jerusalem amidst hosannas was a pledge. **his ancients**—the elders of His people; or in general, His ancient people, the Jews. After the overthrow of the world-kingdoms, Jehovah's shall be set up with a splendor exceeding the light of the sun and moon under the previous order of things (ch. 60:19, 20).

ADAM CLARKE

21. *On high . . . upon the earth.* That is, the ecclesiastical and civil polity of the Jews, which shall be destroyed. The nation shall continue in a state of depression and dereliction for a long time. God shall at length revisit and restore His people in the last age.

E. H. PLUMPTRE:

Verse 21. "The Lord shall punish the host of the high ones that are on high." The prophet's utterance becomes more and more apocalyptic. He sees more than the condemnation of the kings of earth. Jehovah visits also the "principalities and powers in heavenly places" (Eph. 3:10) or "on high" (Eph. 6:12). Perhaps identifying these spiritual evil powers with the gods whom the nations worshiped, and these again with the stars in the firmament, Isaiah foresees a time when their long-protected rebellion shall come to an end, and all authority and power be put down under the might of Jehovah (1 Cor. 15:25). The antithetical parallelism of the two clauses is decisive against the interpretation which sees in the "high ones on high" *only* the representatives of earthly kingdoms, though we may admit that from the prophet's standpoint each rebel nation is thought of as swayed by a rebel spirit. (Cp. Dan 10:20 and the LXX. of Deut. 32:8: "He set the bounds of the nations according to the number of the angels of God.") The same thought is found in a Rabbinic proverb, "God never destroys a nation without having first of all destroyed its prince" (Delitzsch, but without a reference).

—*Ellicott's Commentary on the Whole Bible*

MATTHEW HENRY

CHAPTER 25

Verses 1–5

I. The prophet determines to praise God himself (*v.* 1): "*O Lord! thou art my God,* a God in covenant with me." When God is punishing *the kings of the earth upon the earth,* a poor prophet can go to him, and, with a humble boldness, say, *O Lord! thou art my God,* and therefore *I will exalt thee, I will praise thy name.*

II. He pleases himself with the thought that others also shall be brought to praise God, *v.* 3. "*Therefore,* because of the *desolations thou hast made in the earth,* and the just vengeance thou hast taken, *shall the strong people glorify thee* in concert, *and the city* (the metropolis) *of the terrible nations shall fear thee.*" This may be understood, 1. Of those that have been enemies to God's kingdom. They shall either be converted, and glorify God by joining with his people in his service, or at least convinced, so as to own themselves conquered. Or, 2. Of those that shall be now made strong and terrible for God and by him, though before they were weak. God shall so visibly appear for and with those that fear him and glorify him that all shall stand in awe of them.

III. He observes what ought to be, the matter of this praise. We must exalt God and praise him; for, 1. He has done wonders, according to the counsel of his own will, *v.* 1. These *wonderful things,* which are new and surprising to us, are according to his *counsels of old.* 2. He has in particular humbled the pride, and broken the power, of the mighty ones of the earth (*v.* 2): "*Thou hast made of a city a heap* of rubbish. Of many a defenced city, that thought itself well guarded by nature and art, thou hast made a ruin. Many a city so richly built that it might be called a *palace,* and so much visited by persons from all parts that it might be called a *palace of strangers,* is levelled with the ground, and shall never be built again." Cities that flourished once have gone to decay and are scarcely known (except by urns or coins digged up out of the earth). How many of the cities of Israel have long since been heaps and ruins! 3. He has relieved his necessitous people (*v.* 4): *Thou hast been a strength to the poor, a strength to the needy.* He strengthens the weak that are humble and stay themselves upon him. He not only makes them strong, but he is himself their strength. He is *a refuge from the storm* of rain or hail, and *a shadow*

JAMIESON, FAUSSET, BROWN

CHAPTER 25

VSS. 1-12. CONTINUATION OF CHAPTER 24. THANKSGIVING FOR THE OVERTHROW OF THE APOSTATE FACTION, AND THE SETTING UP OF JEHOVAH'S THRONE ON ZION. The restoration from Babylon and re-establishment of the theocracy was a type and pledge of this.

3. strong people—This cannot apply to the Jews; but other nations on which Babylon had exercised its cruelty (ch. 14:12) shall worship Jehovah, awed by the judgment inflicted on Babylon (ch. 23:18). **city**—not Babylon, which shall then be destroyed, but collectively for the *cities* of the surrounding nations.

1. wonderful—(Ch. 9:6). **counsels of old**—(Ch. 42:9; 46:10). Purposes planned long ago; here, as to the deliverance of His people. **truth**—*Hebrew, Amen;* covenant-keeping, faithful to promises; the peculiar characteristic of Jesus (Rev. 3:14). **2. a city . . . heap**—Babylon, type of the seat of Antichrist, to be destroyed in the last days (cf. Jer. 51:37, with Rev. 18, followed, as here, by the song of the saints' thanksgiving in Rev. 19). "Heaps" is a graphic picture of Babylon and Nineveh as they now are. **palace**—Babylon regarded, on account of its splendor, as a vast palace. But MAURER translates, "a citadel." **of strangers**—foreigners, whose capital pre-eminently Babylon was, the metropolis of the pagan world. "Aliens from the commonwealth of Israel, *strangers* from the covenants of promise" (ch. 29:5; Eph. 2:12; see in contrast, Joel 3:17). **never be built**—(Ch. 13:19, 20, etc.).

4. the poor . . . needy—the Jews, exiles from their country (ch. 26:6; 41:17).

ADAM CLARKE

CHAPTER 25

1. *Thy counsels of old are faithfulness and truth.* That is, All thy past declarations by the prophets shall be fulfilled in their proper time.

2. *A city*—"The city." Nineveh, Babylon, Ar, Moab, or any other strong fortress possessed by the enemies of the people of God.

A palace of strangers—"The palace of the proud ones."

MATTHEW HENRY

from the scorching *heat* of the sun in summer; *when the blast of the terrible ones is as a storm against the wall,* which makes a great noise, but cannot overthrow the wall. The enemies of God's poor are terrible ones. Their rage is like a blast of wind, loud, and blustering, and furious; but, like the wind, it is under a divine check; for God *holds the winds in his fist.* A storm beating on a ship tosses it, but that which beats on a wall never stirs it, Ps. lxxvi. 10; cxxxviii. 7. *Thou shalt,* or thou dost, *bring down the noise of strangers*; thou shalt abate and still it, as *the heat in a dry place* is abated and moderated *by the shadow of a cloud* interposing. The oppressors of God's people are called *strangers*; for they forget that those they oppress are of the same blood with them. They are called *terrible ones*; they would rather be feared than loved. The branches, even the top branches, of the terrible ones, will be broken off. **If the labourers in God's vineyard be called to *bear the burden and heat of the day,* he will refresh them, as with the shadow of a cloud.**

Verses 6–8

If we suppose (as many do) that this refers to the great joy which there should be in Zion and Jerusalem when the army of the Assyrians was routed by an angel, or when the Jews were released out of their captivity in Babylon, yet we cannot avoid making it to look further, to the grace of the gospel and the glory which is the crown and consummation of that grace. We have here a prophecy of the salvation and the grace brought unto us by Jesus Christ, into which *the prophets enquired and searched diligently,* 1 Pet. i. 10.

I. That the grace of the gospel should be a royal feast for all people; not like that of Ahasuerus, intended only to show the grandeur of the master of the feast (Esther i. 4); for this is intended to gratify the guests. 1. God himself is the Master of the feast. 2. The guests invited are *all people,* Gentiles as well as Jews. *Go preach the gospel to every creature.* 3. The place is *Mount Zion*; the preachers must begin at Jerusalem. The gospel church is the Jerusalem that is above. It is *a feast of fat things and full of marrow*; so nourishing are the comforts of the gospel to all those that feast upon them. It is a feast *of wines on the lees,* the strongest-bodied wines, that have been kept long upon the lees, and then are well refined.

II. That the world should be freed from that darkness of ignorance and mistake in the mists of which it had been so long lost and buried (*v.* 7): *He will destroy in this mountain the face of the covering* (the covering of the face). Their faces are covered as those of men condemned, or dead. There is *a veil spread over all nations,* for they all sit in darkness; the Jews themselves, among whom *God was known,* had a *veil upon their hearts,* 2 Cor. iii. 15. But this veil the Lord will destroy, by the light of his gospel shining in the world, and the power of his Spirit opening men's eyes to receive it.

III. That death should be conquered, the power of it broken: *He will swallow up death in victory, v.* 8. 1. Christ will himself, in his resurrection, triumph over death. The grave seemed to swallow him up, but really he swallowed it up. 2. The happiness of the saints shall be out of the reach of death. 3. Believers may triumph over death, as a conquered enemy: *O death! where is thy sting?* It is the last enemy.

IV. That grief shall be banished, and there shall be endless joy: *The Lord God will wipe away tears from off all faces.* In the covenant of grace there shall be that provided which is sufficient to counterbalance all the sorrows of this present time. God shall *wipe away all tears,* Rev. vii. 17; xxi. 4. And *there shall be no more sorrow,* because *there shall be no more death.* The hope of this should now wipe away all excessive tears, all the weeping that hinders sowing.

V. That all the reproach cast upon religion shall be for ever rolled away: *The rebuke of his people* the calumnies and misrepresentations by which they have been blackened, *shall be taken away.*

Verses 9–12

I. The welcome which the church shall give to these blessings (*v.* 9): *It shall be said in that day,* with humble exultation, *Lo, this is our God; we have waited for him!* With such a triumphant song as this will glorified saints *enter into the joy of their Lord.* It is an encouragement to hope for the perfection of this salvation: *We have waited for him, and he will save us,* will carry on what he has begun; for *as for God,* our God, *his work is perfect.*

II. A prospect of further blessings. *In this mountain shall the hand of the Lord rest, v.* 10. The church and people of God shall have continued proofs of God's presence among them. The power of their enemies

JAMIESON, FAUSSET, BROWN

heat–calamity (ch. 4:6; 32:2). **blast**–i.e., wrath. **storm**–*a tempest* of *rain,* a winter flood, rushing against and overthrowing the wall of a house. **5.** Translate, "As the heat in a dry land [is brought down by the shadow of a cloud, so] thou shalt bring down the tumult [the shout of triumph over their enemies] of strangers (foreigners); and as the heat by the shadow of the cloud [is brought low], so the branch [the offspring] of the terrible ones shall be brought low." PARKHURST translates the *Hebrew* for "branch," *the exulting song.* JEROME translates the last clause, "And as when the heat burns under a cloud, thou shalt make the branch of the terrible ones to wither"; the branch withering even under the friendly shade of a cloud typifies the wicked brought to ruin, not for want of natural means of prosperity, but by the immediate act of God.

6. in this mountain–Zion: Messiah's kingdom was to begin, and is to have its central seat hereafter, at Jerusalem, as the common country of "all nations" (ch. 2:2, etc.).

all people–(Ch. 56:7; Dan. 7:14; Luke 2:10). **feast**–image of felicity (Ps. 22:26, 27; Matt. 8:11; Luke 14. 15; Rev. 19:9; cf. Ps. 36:8; 87). **fat things**–delicacies; the rich mercies of God in Christ (ch. 55:2; Jer. 31:14; **Job 36:16). wines on the lees**–wine which has been long kept on the lees; i.e., the oldest and most generous wine (Jer. 48:11). **marrow**–the choicest dainties (Ps. 63:5). **well refined**–cleared of all dregs.

7. face of . . . covering–image from mourning, in which it was usual to *cover* the face with a veil (II Sam. 15:30). "Face of covering," i.e., the covering itself; as in Job 41:13, "the face of his garment," the garment itself. The covering or veil is the mist of ignorance as to a future state, and the way to eternal life, which enveloped the nations (Eph. 4:18) and the unbelieving Jew (II Cor. 3:15). The *Jew,* however, is *first* to be converted before the conversion of *"all nations";* for it is "in *this* mountain," viz., Zion, that the latter are to have the veil taken off (Ps. 102:13, 15, 16, 21, 22; Rom. 11: 12). **8.** Quoted in I Corinthians 15:54, in support of the resurrection. **swallow up . . . in victory**–completely and permanently "abolish" (II Tim. 1:10; Rev. 20:14; 21:4; cf. Gen. 2:17; 3:22).

rebuke–(Cf. Mark. 8:38; Heb. 11:26). **9.** "After death has been swallowed up for ever, the people of God, who had been delivered from the hand of death, shall say to the Lord, Lo, this is our *God,* whom unbelievers regarded as only a *man*" [JEROME]. "The words are so moulded as to point us specially to the person of the Son of God, who 'saves' us; as He vouchsafed to Israel temporal saving, so to His elect He appears for the purpose of conferring eternal salvation" [VITRINGA]. *The Jews,* however, have a special share in the words, This is *our* God (*Note,* vs. 6). "In day . . . glad . . . rejoice," cf. Psalm 118:24, which refers to the second coming of Jesus (cf. Ps. 118:26, with Luke 13:35). "Waited" is characteristic of God's people in all ages (Gen. 49:18; Titus 2:13). **10. rest**–as its *permanent protector;* on "hand" in this sense; cf. Ezra 7:6, 28. **Moab**–while Israel is being protected, the foe is destroyed; Moab is the representative of all the foes of God's people. **under him**–Rather, in his own place or country (Exod. 10:23; 16:29). **for the dunghill**–Rather, in the water of the dung-heap, in which straw was trodden to make it manure (Ps. 83:10). HORSLEY translates either, "in the waters of Madmenah," viz., for the making

ADAM CLARKE

4. *As a storm against the wall*—"Like a winter storm."

5. *Of strangers*—"Of the proud." *The heat with the shadow of a cloud*—"As the heat by a thick cloud."

6. *In this mountain.* Zion, at Jerusalem. In His Church.

Shall the Lord of hosts make unto all people a feast. Salvation by Jesus Christ. A feast is a proper and usual expression of joy in consequence of victory, or any other great success. The feast here spoken of is to be celebrated on Mount Sion; and all people, without distinction, are to be invited to it. This can be no other than the celebration of the establishment of Christ's kingdom, which is frequently represented in the gospel under the image of a feast; where "many shall come from the east and west, and shall sit down [at table] with Abraham, Isaac, and Jacob, in the kingdom of heaven," Matt. viii. 11. See also Luke xiv. 16; xxiv. 29-30. *Of wines on the lees*—"Of old wines"; that is, of wines kept long on the lees.

7. *The face of the covering cast over all people*—"The covering that covered the face of all the peoples." "The face of the covering"; He will unveil all the Mosaic ritual, and show by his apostles that it referred to, and was accomplished in, the sacrificial offering of Jesus Christ.

8. *He will swallow up death.* As in the Arabic countries a *covering* was put over the face of him who was condemned to suffer death, it is probable that the words in v. 7 may refer to this. The whole world was condemned to death, and about to be led out to execution, when the gracious Lord interposed, and, by a glorious sacrifice, procured a general pardon.

10. *Shall the hand of the Lord rest*—"The hand of Jehovah shall give rest." That is, "shall give peace and quiet to Sion, by destroying the enemy," as it follows. *As straw is trodden down*—"As the straw is threshed." *For the dunghill*—"Under the wheels of the car."

MATTHEW HENRY

shall be broken. *Moab* is here put for all the adversaries of God's people; they *shall* all *be trodden down* or threshed (for *then* they beat out the corn by treading it) and shall be thrown out as *straw to the dunghill,* being good for nothing else. God having *caused his hand to rest upon this mountain,* shall *spread forth his hands, in the midst* of his people, *like one that swims,* which intimates that he will employ and exert his power for them vigorously. On their behalf he will be continually active, for so the swimmer is. *He shall bring down the pride* of their enemies (and Moab was notoriously guilty of pride, *ch.* xvi. 6) by one humbling judgment after another. He shall bring down *the spoils of their hands,* shall take from them that which they have got by spoil and rapine. He shall ruin all their fortifications, *v.* 12. There is no fortress impregnable to Omnipotence. This destruction of Moab is typical of Christ's victory over death (spoken of *v.* 8), his spoiling principalities and powers in his cross (Col. ii. 15).

CHAPTER 26

Verses 1–4

To the prophecies of gospel grace very fitly is a song annexed: *In that day this song shall be sung;* it shall be sung *in the land of Judah,* which was a figure of the gospel church; for the gospel covenant is said to be made *with the house of Judah,* Heb. viii. 8.

I. The church of God is strongly fortified against those that are bad (*v.* 1): *We have a strong city.* It is a city incorporated by the charter of the everlasting covenant, fitted for the reception of all that are made free by that charter; it is a strong city, as Jerusalem was, while it was a city compact together, and had God himself a wall of fire round about it. The church is a strong city, for it has *walls and bulwarks* of God's own appointing; for he has, in his promise, appointed salvation itself to be its defence.

II. The inhabitants of Jerusalem, if they are such as they should be, are its strength, Zech. xii. 5. The gates are here ordered to be opened, *that the righteous nation, which keeps the truth, may enter in, v.* 2. They had been banished and driven out by the iniquity of the former times, but now they have liberty to enter in again.

III. All who belong to it are safe and easy, and have a security and serenity of mind in the assurance of God's favour. *Thou wilt keep him in peace,* in *perfect peace,* inward peace, outward peace, peace with God, peace of conscience, peace under all events. Those that trust in God must have their minds stayed upon him, and such as do so God will keep in perpetual peace, and that peace shall keep them (Ps. cxii. 7). Trust in him for ever, at all times, when you have nothing else to trust to. Whatever we trust to the world for is confined within the limits of time. But what we trust in God for will last as long as we shall last. For in the *Lord Jehovah—Jah, Jehovah,* in him who was, and is, and is to come, there is a rock of ages, a firm and lasting foundation for faith to build upon; and the house built on that rock will stand in a storm.

Verses 5–11

The prophet encourages us to trust in the word, for,

I. He will make humble souls that trust in him to triumph over their proud enemies, *v.* 5, 6. Even the lofty city Babylon itself, or Nineveh, he lays it low, *ch.* xxv. 12. He does not say, Great armies shall tread them down; but, When God will have it done, even the feet of the poor shall do it, Mal. iv. 3. See Ps. cxlvii. 6; Rom. xvi. 20.

II. He takes cognizance of the way of his people and has delight in it (*v.* 7): *The way of the just is evenness* (so it may be read): it is their endeavour to walk with God in steady obedience. *Thou, most upright, dost level* (or *make even) the path of the just,* by removing those things that would be stumbling-blocks. God *weighs* it (so we read it); he considers it, and will give them grace sufficient to help them over all difficulties.

III. It is our duty to wait for God in the darkest and most discouraging times, *v.* 8, 9. This has always been the practice of God's people: "*In the way of thy judgments we* have still *waited for thee;* when thou hast corrected us we have looked to no other hand than thine to relieve us." Our troubles must never turn us away from God; but still *the desire of our soul must be to his name and to the remembrance of him.* Our great concern must be for God's name: "*Father, glorify thy name,* and we are satisfied." The remembrance of God must be our great support and pleasure. Our desires towards God must be inward, fervent, and sincere (Ps. xlii. 1).

IV. It is God's design, in his judgments, to bring

JAMIESON, FAUSSET, BROWN

of bricks; or as LXX, "as the *threshing-floor* is trampled by the *corn-drag*" (see *Margin,* Mic. 4:11-13). **11. he**—*Jehovah* shall spread His hands to strike the foe on this side and on that, with as little effort as a swimmer spreads forth his arms to cleave a passage through the water [CALVIN]. (Zech. 5:3.) LOWTH takes "he" as Moab, who, in danger of sinking, shall strain every nerve to save himself; *but Jehovah* (and "he") shall cause him to sink ("bring down the pride" of Moab, ch. 16:6). **with the spoils of . . . hands**—lit., "the craftily acquired spoils" of his (Moab's) hands [BARNES]. Moab's pride, as well as the sudden gripe of his hands (viz., whereby he tries to save himself from drowning) [LOWTH]. "Together with *the joints* of his hands," i.e., though Moab struggle against Jehovah hand and foot [MAURER]. **12. fortress**—the strongholds of *Moab,* the representative of the foes of God's people [BARNES]. Babylon [MAURER]. The society of infidels represented as a city (Rev. 11:8).

CHAPTER 26

VSS. 1-21. CONNECTED WITH CHAPTERS 24, 25. SONG OF PRAISE OF ISRAEL AFTER BEING RESTORED TO THEIR OWN LAND. As the overthrow of the apostate faction is described in ch. 25, so the peace of the faithful is here described under the image of a well-fortified city. **1. strong city**—Jerusalem, strong in Jehovah's protection: type of the new Jerusalem (Ps. 48:1-3), contrasted with the overthrow of the ungodly foe (vss. 4-7, 12-14; Rev. 22:2, 10-12, etc.). **salvation . . . walls**—(Ch. 60:18; Jer. 3:23; Zech. 2:5). MAURER translates, "Jehovah makes His help serve as walls" (ch. 33:20, 21, etc.). **bulwarks**—the trench with the antemural earthworks exterior to the wall. **2.** Address of the returning people to the gates of Jerusalem (type of the heavenly city, Heb. 12:22); (Ps. 24:7, 9; 118:19). Antitypically (Rev. 22:14; 21: 25, 27). **righteous nation**—that had not apostatized during the captivity. HORSLEY translates, "The nation of the Just One," viz., the Jews.

3. mind . . . stayed—(Ps. 112:7, 8). Jesus can create "perfect peace" within thy mind, though storms of trial rage without (ch. 57:19; Mark 4:39); as a city kept securely by a strong garrison within, though besieged without (so Phil. 4:7). "Keep," lit., guard as with a garrison. HORSLEY translates, (God's) workmanship (the *Hebrew* does not probably mean "mind," but "a thing *formed,*" Eph. 2:10), so constantly "supported"; or else "formed and supported (by Thee) Thou shalt preserve (it, *viz.,* the righteous nation) in perpetual peace." **4. Lord JEHOVAH**—*Hebrew, Jah, Jehovah.* The union of the two names expresses in the highest degree God's unchanging love and power (cf. Ps. 68:4). This passage, and ch. 12:2; Exodus 6:3; Psalm 83:18, are the four in which the *English Version* retains the JEHOVAH of the original. MAURER translates, "For JAH (the eternal unchangeable One, Exodus 3: 14) is JEHOVAH, the rock of ages" (cf. ch. 45:17; Deut. 32:15; I Sam. 2:2). **5. lofty city**—Babylon; representative of the stronghold of the foes of God's people in all ages (ch. 25:2, 12; 13:14). **6. poor**—(ch. 25:4), the once afflicted Jewish captives. "Foot shall tread," is figurative for *exulting* in the fall of God's enemies (Rev. 18:20). **7. uprightness**—rather, "is direct," i.e., is directed by God to a *prosperous issue,* however many be their afflictions in the meantime (as in the case of the Jewish exiles); the context requires this sense (Ps. 34:19; Prov. 3:6; 11:5), [MAURER]: thus "way" means *God's dealings with the righteous* (Ps. 37:23). **most upright**—(Deut. 32: 4.) **dost weigh**—(I Sam. 2:3; Prov. 5:21.) Rather, thou dost make plain and level [MAURER], removing all obstacles (ch. 40:3, 4). **8. way of thy judgments**—We have waited for Thy proceeding to *punish* the enemy (vss. 9, 10) [MAURER]. HORSLEY translates vss. 7, 8, "The path of *the Just One* is perfectly even; an even road Thou wilt level for the Just One, *even the path of Thy laws,* O Jehovah. We have expected Thee." **name . . . remembrance**—the manifested *character* of God by which He would be *remembered* (ch. 64:5; Exod. 3:15). **9. With . . . soul . . . I**—lit., "I . . . my soul," in apposition; the faithful Jews here speak *individually.* The overthrow of the foe and the restoration of the Jews are to follow upon *prayer* on the part of the latter and of all God's people (ch. 62:1-4, 6, 7; Ps. 102:13-17). **in the night**—(Ps. 63:6; Song of Sol. 3:1.)

ADAM CLARKE

11. *As he that swimmeth spreadeth forth his hands to swim*—"As he that sinketh stretcheth out his hands to swim." There is great obscurity in this place. Some understand God as the Agent; others, Moab. I have chosen the latter sense, as I cannot conceive that the stretching out of the hands of a swimmer in swimming can be any illustration of the action of God stretching out His hands over Moab to destroy it.

CHAPTER 26

1. *We have a strong city.* In opposition to the city of the enemy, which God hath destroyed, chap. xxv. See the note there. *Salvation . . . for walls and bulwarks.* Or "the walls and the ditch." *Chel* properly signifies the *ditch* or *trench* without the wall; see Kimchi. The same rabbin says, This song refers to the time of salvation, i.e., the days of the Messiah.

2. *The righteous nation.* The converted Gentiles shall have the gates opened—a full entrance into all the glories and privileges of the gospel, being fellow heirs with the converted Jews. *The truth.* The gospel itself—as the fulfillment of all the ancient types, shadows, and ceremonies; and therefore termed *the truth,* in opposition to all those shadowy rites and ceremonies. "The law was given by Moses, but grace and truth came by Jesus Christ," John i. 17.

3. *In perfect peace. Shalom, shalom,* "peace, peace," i.e., peace upon peace—all kinds of prosperity—happiness in this world and in the world to come.

4. *Everlasting strength.* "The rock of ages"; or, according to Rab. Maimon, the "eternal Fountain, Source, or Spring." Does not this refer to the lasting streams from the rock in the desert? And that Rock was Christ.

8. *Have we waited for thee*—"We have placed our confidence in Thy name."

MATTHEW HENRY

men to seek him: *When thy judgments are upon the earth*, laying all waste, we have reason to expect that not only God's people, but even *the inhabitants of the world, will learn righteousness*, have their mistakes rectified and their lives reformed.

V. Those are wicked indeed that will not be wrought upon by the methods God takes to reform them; and it is necessary that God should deal with them in a severe way by his judgments. Sinners walk contrary to God, *v.* 10. *Favour is shown* to them. They receive many mercies from God, and the design of this is that they may be won to love and serve God; and yet it is all in vain: *they will not learn righteousness*. They live *in a land of uprightness*, in a land of *evenness*, where there are not so many stumbling-blocks as in other places —in a land of *correction*, where vice and profaneness are punished; yet there they will *deal unjustly*, and go on frowardly in their evil ways. Those that do wickedly deal unjustly and may expect the judgments of God upon them. They *will not behold the majesty of the Lord*. Even when we receive of the mercy of the Lord we must still behold the *majesty of the Lord and his goodness*. *They will not see*, and none so blind as those who will not see, who ascribe to chance, or common fate, a divine rebuke. *They will not see, but they shall see*, shall be made to see, whether they will or no, that God is angry with them. Atheists, scorners, and the secure, will shortly feel that *it is a fearful thing to fall into the hands of the living God*. They shall see that they have done God's people a great deal of wrong, and shall be ashamed of their enmity and ill usage of such as deserved better treatment. Their doom therefore is that, since they slighted the happiness of God's friends, *the fire of his enemies shall devour them*.

Verses 12–19

The prophet in these verses looks back and then looks forward.

I. His reviews and reflections are mixed. When he looks back upon the state of the church he finds God in many instances had done great things for them (*v.* 12): *Thou hast wrought all our works in us*, or *for* us. Whatever good work is done by us, it is owing to a good work wrought by the grace of God in us. In particular (*v.* 15): "*Thou hast increased the nation, O Lord!* so that a little one has become a thousand (in Egypt they multiplied exceedingly, and afterwards in Canaan, so that they filled the land); and in this *thou art glorified*, as faithful to the covenant with Abraham." The neighbouring nations had sometimes tyrannized over them (*v.* 13): "*O Lord our God!* thou who hast the sole right to rule us, whose subjects and servants we are, to thee we complain that *other lords besides thee have had dominion over us*." When they had been careless in the service of God, God suffered their enemies to have dominion over them, that they might know the difference between his service *and the service of the kingdoms of the countries*. It may be understood as a confession of sin, their serving other gods, by which other lords (for they called their idols *baals, lords*) had dominion over them, besides God. But now they promise that it shall be so no more: "Henceforth *by thee only will we make mention of thy name*; we will worship thee only, and in that way only which thou hast instituted and appointed." The same may be our penitent reflection: *Other lords, besides God, have had dominion over us;* every lust has been our lord, and we have thus wronged both God and ourselves. They had sometimes been carried into captivity before their enemies (*v.* 15): "The nation which at first thou didst increase, thou hast now diminished, and *removed to all the ends of the earth, driven out to the utmost parts of heaven*," as is threatened, Deut. xxx. 4; xxviii. 64. The prophet remembers that when they were thus oppressed and carried captive they cried unto God, which was evidence that they neither had quite forsaken him nor were quite forsaken of him, and that there were merciful intentions in the judgments they were under (*v.* 16): *Lord, in trouble have they visited thee*. Afflictions bring us to God, quicken us to our duty, and show us our dependence upon him. Afflictions bring us to secret prayer, in which we may be more free and particular in our addresses to him than we can be in public. He complains that their struggles for their liberty had been painful and perilous, but that they had not been successful, *v.* 17, 18. "We have been like a woman in labour, that cries out in her pangs; we have with a great deal of anxiety and toil endeavoured to help ourselves, and our troubles have been increased by those attempts." Whenever they came to *present themselves before the Lord* with their complaints and petitions they were in agonies like those of a woman in travail. "*We have been with child;* we have had great expectation of a happy deliverance. But, alas!

JAMIESON, FAUSSET, BROWN

world . . . learn . . . righteousness—the remnant left after judgments (Ps. 58:10, 11; Zech. 14:16).

10. uprightness—rather, as in vs. 7, "prosperity," answering to "favor" in the parallelism, and in antithesis to "judgments in the earth" (vs. 9); where prosperity attends the wicked as well as the just, "he will not learn righteousness," therefore *judgments* must be sent that he may "learn" it [MAURER].

11. lifted up—to punish the foes of God's people. They who *will* not see *shall* be made to "see" to their cost (ch. 5:12). **their envy at the** (i.e., Thy) **people**—LOWTH translates. "They shall see with confusion *Thy zeal for Thy* people."

fire of . . . enemies—i.e., the fire to which Thine enemies are doomed (ch. 9:18).

12. peace—God's favor, including all blessings, temporal and spiritual, opposed to their previous trials (Ps. 138:8).

13. other lords—temporal; heathen kings (II Chron. 12:8; 28:5, 6), Nebuchadnezzar, etc. Spiritual also, idols and lusts (Rom. 6:16-18).

by thee only—It is due to Thee alone, that we again worship Thee as our Lord [MAURER]. "(We are) Thine only, we will celebrate Thy name" [HORSLEY]. The sanctifying effect of affliction (Ps. 71:16; 119:67, 71). **14. They**—The "other lords" or tyrants (vs. 13). **shall not live**—viz., again. **deceased**—*Hebrew*, Rephaim; powerless, in the land of shades (ch. 14:9, 10). **therefore**—i.e., inasmuch as. Cf. "therefore" (Gen. 18:5; 19:8). **15. hast**—prophetical preterite (ch. 9:3). **hast removed . . . far . . . ends of . . . earth**—rather, "Thou hast extended far all the borders of the land" [VITRINGA].

16. visited—sought—**poured out** (Ps. 62:8), as a vessel emptying out all its contents. **prayer**—lit., a whispered prayer, *Margin*, a secret sighing to God for help (cf. Jer. 13:17; Deut. 8:16).

17. An image of anguish accompanied with expectation, to be followed by joy that will cause the anguish utterly to be forgotten. Zion, looking for deliverance, seemingly in vain, but really about to be gloriously saved (Mic. 4:9, 10-13; 5:1-3; John 16:21, 22).

ADAM CLARKE

9. *When thy judgments*. It would be better to read, When Thy judgments were in the earth, *the inhabitants of the world* have learned *righteousness*. Men seldom seek God in prosperity; they are apt to rest in an earthly portion. But God in mercy embitters this by adversity; then there is a general cry after himself as our chief, solid, and only permanent Good.

JOSEPH PARKER:

"Let favor be showed to the wicked, yet will he not learn righteousness: in the land of uprightness will he deal unjustly, and will not behold the majesty of the Lord" (v. 10).

All is lost upon him. Let the summer day rain all its gathered clouds upon the sand of the desert, and it will not make a garden of it; all the rich rain will be swallowed by the burning lips, and at eventide the desert shall thirst as with the thirst of fire: otherwise, the world would be converted today, and would have been converted at the very time of the revelation of the Son of Man. If Providence could have converted the world, the world would today have been in the attitude of prayer. But goodness is lost, as rain is lost. We ourselves have often wasted the sunshine. We had the whole broad, white, glistening day to work in, and instead of regarding it as an opportunity for service we complained of the heat, and sank under the burden as men oppressed. We say that some men never can be satisfied. There is a painful truth in that statement. The music does not satisfy them, nor does the appeal, nor the exposition, nor the prayer, nor the service of friendship, nor the sacrifice of love; they still ask for the impossible. Knowing what this is in common life we may know what it is in the higher ranges of experience. The spirit of discontentment is in some men, and do what you will for them you find no flowers in their conduct, no fruit upon their life-tree, nothing but leaves, and the leaves half-grown, as if ashamed to be seen upon the branches so unfruitful, so unblessed. Does not the goodness of God lead them to repentance? Think of it! health, and children, and love, and prosperity, and social honor, and all these a staircase leading them—no where! All these marble steps should conduct them to heaven. But as soon as the earthquake ceases men begin again to curse and swear, and as soon as the earth is felt to have recovered from her vibrations men go back to the tavern and drink themselves to death; when the heavy thunder ceases, and the vivid lightning withdraws itself, men come from the sanctuary of the cellar to repeat their brutalities in their higher chambers. "In the land of uprightness the wicked will deal unjustly." You cannot make him pious in the sanctuary. If he fold his hands in prayer as his mother bade him, his soul is not in any attitude of supplication. He could plot murder at the altar; he could plan the slaughter of an enemy during the singing of a hymn.—*The People's Bible*

MATTHEW HENRY

we have as it were brought forth wind; it has proved a false conception; our expectations have been frustrated. All our efforts have proved abortive: *We have not wrought any deliverance in the earth*, for ourselves or for our friends, *neither have the inhabitants of the world fallen* before us, but they are still as high and arrogant as ever."

II. His prospects and hopes are very pleasant. In general, "*Thou wilt ordain peace for us*" (*v.* 12). What trouble soever may for a time be appointed to the people of God, peace will at length be ordained for them; for the *end of those men is peace*. "Thou hast heard the desire of the humble, and therefore we will give the glory of it to thee only, will depend upon thy grace only to enable us to do so." *They are dead*, those *other lords* that *have had dominion over us;* their power is broken. He has *made all their memory to perish*. Though the church rejoices not in the birth of the man-child, of which she travailed in pain, *but has as it were brought forth wind* (*v.* 18), yet *Thy dead men shall live*. A spirit of life from God shall enter into the slain witnesses, Rev. xi. 11. The *dry bones shall live*, and become an *exceedingly great army*, Ezek. xxxvii. 10. *Together with my dead body shall they arise*. When God's time shall have come, Jerusalem, the city of God, now lying like a dead body, shall arise, shall be rebuilt, and flourish again. And therefore let the poor, desolate, melancholy inhabitants, that dwell as in dust, *awake and sing*. The dew of God's favour shall be to it as the evening dew to the herbs that were parched with the heat of the sun all day, shall revive and refresh them. And as the spring-dews, that water the earth, and make the herbs that lay buried in it to put forth and bud, so shall they flourish again. "The Gentiles shall live; with my body shall they arise; that is, they shall be called in after Christ's resurrection, shall rise with him, and sit with him in heavenly places; nay, they shall arise my body (says Dr. Lightfoot); they shall become the mystical body of Christ, and shall arise as part of him."

Verses 20–21

These two verses are supposed not to belong to the song which takes up the rest of the chapter, but to begin a new matter, and to be rather an introduction to the following chapter than the conclusion of this.

I. God invites the people (*v.* 20): "*Come, my people*, come to me, come with me, let the storm that disperses others bring you nearer together. Come, and *enter into thy chambers*; stay not abroad, lest you be caught in the storm." We must by faith find a way into these chambers, and there hide ourselves; with serenity of mind, we must put ourselves under the divine protection. Come, as Noah into the ark, for he *shut the doors about him*. When dangers are threatening it is good to retire, and lie hid, as Elijah did by the brook Cherith. *Enter into thy chamber*, to examine thyself, and commune with thy own heart, to pray, and humble thyself before God.

II. He assures them that the trouble would be over in a very short time: "*Hide thyself for a moment*, the smallest part of time we can conceive. When it is over it will seem as nothing to you." When Athanasius was banished from Alexandria by an edict of Julian, and his friends greatly lamented it, he bade them be of good cheer. *Nubecula est quæ cito pertransibit—It is a little cloud, that will soon blow over*.

III. He assures them that their enemies should be reckoned with for all the mischief they had done them by the sword, *v.* 21. *The Lord comes out of his place, to punish the inhabitants of the earth for their iniquity*. God *comes out of his place to punish*. Some observe that God's place is the mercy-seat; there he delights to be; when he punishes he comes out of his place, for he has no pleasure in the death of sinners. The criminals shall be convicted: *The earth shall disclose her blood;* the innocent blood of the saints and martyrs, which has been shed shall now be brought to light, Gen. iv. 10, 11; Job xx. 27.

JAMIESON, FAUSSET, BROWN

18. brought forth wind—MICHAELIS explains this of the disease *empneumatosis*. Rather, "wind" is a figure for that which proves an *abortive effort*. The "we" is in antithesis to "Thy," "my" (vs. 19), what *we* vainly attempt, *God* will accomplish. **not wrought . . . deliverance in . . . earth**—lit., the land (Judea) is *not made security*, i.e., is not become a place of security from our enemies. **neither . . . world fallen**—The "world" at large, is in antithesis to "the earth," i.e., Judea. The world at enmity with the city of God has not been subdued. But MAURER explains "fallen," according to *Arabic* idiom, of the *birth* of a child, which is said to *fall* when being born; "inhabitants of the world (*Israel*, ch. 24:4; not the world in general) are not yet born"; i.e., the country as yet lies desolate, and is not yet populated. **19.** In antithesis to vs. 14, "They (Israel's foes) shall not live"; "Thy (Jehovah's) dead men (the Jews) shall live," i.e., primarily, *be restored, spiritually* (ch. 54:1-3), *civilly and nationally* (vs. 15); whereas Thy foes shall not; ultimately, and in the fullest scope of the prophecy, *restored to life literally* (Ezek. 37:1-14; Dan. 12:2). **together with my dead body**—rather, *my dead body*, or *bodies* (the Jewish nation personified, which had been spiritually and civilly dead; or the nation, as a parent, speaking of the *bodies* of her children individually, *Note*, vs. 9, "I," "My"): Jehovah's "dead" and "my dead" are one and the same [HORSLEY]. However, as Jesus is the antitype to Israel (Matt. 2:15), *English Version* gives a true sense, and one ultimately contemplated in the prophecy: *Christ's* dead body being raised again is the source of Jehovah's people (*all*, and especially believers, the spiritual Israelites) also being raised (I Cor. 15:20-22). **Awake**—(Eph. 5: 14), spiritually. **in dust**—prostate and dead, spiritually and nationally; also literally (ch. 25:12; 47:1). **dew**—which falls copiously in the East and supplies somewhat the lack of rain (Hos. 14:5). **cast out . . . dead**—i.e., shall bring them forth to life again.

20. enter . . . chambers—When God is about to take vengeance on the ungodly, the saints shall be shut in by Him in a place of safety, as Noah and his family were in the days of the flood (Gen. 7:16), and as Israel was commanded not to go out of doors on the night of the slaying of the Egyptian first-born (Exod. 12:22, 23; Ps. 31:20; 83:3). The saints are calmly and confidently to await the issue (Exod. 14: 13, 14).

21. (Mic. 1:3; Jude 14.) **disclose . . . blood**—(Gen. 4:10, 11; Job 16:18; Ezek. 24:7, 8). All the innocent blood shed, and all other wrongs done, so long seemingly with impunity, shall then be avenged (Rev. 16:6).

ADAM CLARKE

19. *My dead body*—"My deceased." All the ancient versions render it in the plural. *The dew of herbs*—"The dew of the dawn." The deliverance of the people of God from a state of the lowest depression is explained by images plainly taken from the resurrection of the dead. In the same manner the Prophet Ezekiel represents the restoration of the Jewish nation from a state of utter dissolution by the restoring of the dry bones to life, exhibited to him in a vision, chap. xxxvii, which is directly thus applied and explained, vv. 11-13. And this deliverance is expressed with a manifest opposition to what is here said above, v. 14, of the great lords and tyrants, under whom they had groaned: "They are dead, they shall not live; they are deceased [tyrants], they shall not rise": that they should be destroyed utterly, and should never be restored to their former power and glory. It appears from hence that the doctrine of the resurrection of the dead was at that time a popular and common doctrine; for an image which is assumed in order to express or represent anything in the way of allegory or metaphor, whether poetical or prophetical, must be an image commonly known and understood; otherwise it will not answer the purpose for which it is assumed. Kimchi refers these words to the days of the Messiah, and says, "Then many of the saints shall rise from the dead," and quotes Dan. xii. 2. Do not these words speak of the resurrection of our blessed Lord; and of that resurrection of the bodies of men, which shall be the consequence of His body being raised from the dead? *Thy dead men shall live . . . with my dead body shall they arise*. This seems very express.

20. *Come, my people, enter thou into thy chambers*. An exhortation to patience and resignation under oppression, with a confident expectation of deliverance by the power of God manifestly to be exerted in the destruction of the oppressor. It seems to be an allusion to the command of Moses to the Israelites, when the destroying angel was to go through the land of Egypt, not to "go out at the door of his house until the morning," Exod. xii. 22.

21. *The earth also shall disclose her blood*. Crimes of cruelty and oppression, which have passed away from the eyes of men, God will bring into judgment, and exact punishment for them.

CHAPTER 27 (Matthew Henry)

Verses 1–6

The prophet is here singing of judgment and mercy,

I. Of judgment upon the enemies of God's church (*v.* 1). When the Lord *comes out of his place, to punish the inhabitants of the earth* (*ch.* xxvi. 21), he will be sure to punish *leviathan*, the *dragon that is in the sea*, every proud oppressing tyrant, that is the terror of the mighty, and, like the leviathan, is *so fierce that none dares stir him up*, Job xli. 10, 24, 25. So Sennacherib was in his day, and Nebuchadnezzar in his, and Antiochus in his; so Pharaoh had been

CHAPTER 27 (Jamieson, Fausset, Brown)

Vss. 1-13. CONTINUATION OF CHAPTERS 24, 25, 26. At the time when Israel shall be delivered, and the ungodly nations punished, God shall punish also the great enemy of the Church. **1. sore**—rather, hard, well-tempered. **leviathan**—lit., in *Arabic*, "the twisted animal," applicable to every great tenant of the waters, sea-serpents, crocodiles, etc. In Ezekiel 29:3; 32:2; Daniel 7:1, etc.; Revelation 12:3, etc., potentates hostile to Israel are similarly described; antitypically and ultimately Satan is intended (Rev. 20:10).

CHAPTER 27 (Adam Clarke)

MATTHEW HENRY

formerly, and is called *leviathan* and *the dragon, ch.* li. 9; Ps. lxxiv. 13, 14; Ezek. xxix. 3. The New Testament church has had its leviathans; we read of a great red dragon ready to devour it, Rev. xii. 3. Those malignant persecuting powers are here compared to the leviathan for bulk, and strength—to dragons for their rage and fury,—to serpents, *piercing serpents*, penetrating in their counsels,—to *crooked serpents*, subtle and insinuating, but perverse and mischievous. Great princes, if they oppose the people of God, are in God's account as dragons and serpents, the plagues of mankind. They are too big for men to deal with and call to an account, and therefore the great God will take the matter into his own hands. He has a *sore, and great, and strong sword*, when the *measure of their iniquity is full* and their *day has come to fall. In that day* he will punish, his day which is coming, Ps. xxxvii. 13. This is applicable to the spiritual victories obtained by our Lord Jesus over the powers of darkness. He not only disarmed the prince of this world, but with his strong sword, the virtue of his death and the preaching of his gospel, he does and will *destroy him that had the power of death, that is, the devil*, that great leviathan, that old serpent, the dragon (Rev. xx. 2, 3).

II. Of mercy to the church.

1. She is God's vineyard, and is under his particular care, *v.* 2, 3. She is, in God's eye, a *vineyard of red wine*. The world is as a worthless wilderness; but the church is enclosed as a vineyard, from which precious fruits are gathered, wherewith they honour God and man. It is a vineyard of *red wine*, yielding the best and choicest grapes, intimating the reformation of the church, whereas before it brought forth wild grapes, *ch.* v. 4. *I the Lord do keep it*. He has undertaken to be the keeper of Israel. Those that bring forth fruit to God are under his protection. God's vineyard in this world lies much exposed to injury; there are many that would hurt it (Ps. lxxx. 13); but God will suffer no real hurt to be done, but what he will bring good out of. God will keep it in the night of affliction and persecution, and in the day of peace and prosperity, the temptations of which are no less dangerous. This vineyard shall be well fenced. *I will water it every moment*, and yet it shall not be overwatered. The still and silent dews of God's grace and blessing shall continually descend upon it. God waters his vineyard by the ministry of the word by his servants the prophets. Paul plants, and Apollos waters, but God gives the increase.

2. Though sometimes he contends with his people, yet, upon their submission, he will be reconciled to them, *v.* 4, 5. *Fury is not in him* towards his vineyard. It is true if he find in it briers and thorns instead of vines, he will tread them down and burn them; but otherwise, "If I am angry with my people, let them humble themselves, and pray, and seek my face, and so *take hold of my strength* with a sincere desire to make their peace with me, and I will be reconciled to them, and all shall be well." Here is a quarrel supposed between God and man. It is an old quarrel, ever since sin first entered. Here is a gracious invitation given us to make up this quarrel. Pardoning mercy is called the power of our Lord; let him take hold of that. Christ is the *arm of the Lord, ch.* liii. 1. Christ *crucified is the power of God* (1 Cor. i. 24); let him by a lively faith take hold of him. God is willing to be reconciled to us if we be but willing to be reconciled to him.

3. The church of God in the world shall be a growing body (*v.* 6): *In times to come* (so some read it), *in after-times*, when these calamities are overpast, or in the days of the gospel, *he shall cause Jacob to take root*, deeper root than ever. Many shall be brought into the church, proselytes shall be numerous, some out of all the nations about, and the converts shall be fruitful in the fruits of righteousness. The preaching of the gospel *brought forth fruit in all the world* (Col. i. 6), fruit that remains, John xv. 16.

Verses 7–13

Here is the prophet singing of mercy and judgment to the church, and mercy mixed with that judgment.

I. Here is judgment threatened even to Jacob and Israel. *They shall blossom and bud* (*v.* 6), but some shall be *smitten* and *slain* (*v.* 7). Judgment shall begin at the house of God. Jerusalem, their *defenced city, shall be desolate*, *v.* 10, 11. "God having tried methods with them for their reformation, which as to many, have proved ineffectual, he will for a time lay their country waste," which was accomplished when Jerusalem was destroyed by the Chaldeans; then that *habitation* was for a long time *forsaken*. Jerusalem had been a defenced city, not so much by art or nature as by grace and the divine protection; but, when God was provoked to withdraw, she was left like a wilderness. "And in the pleasant gardens of Jerusalem

JAMIESON, FAUSSET, BROWN

piercing—rigid [LOWTH]. Flying [MAURER and LXX]. Long, extended, viz., as the crocodile which cannot readily bend back its body [HOUBIGANT]. **crooked**—winding. **dragon**—*Hebrew, tenin*; the crocodile. **sea**—the Euphrates, or the expansion of it near Babylon.

2. In that day when leviathan shall be destroyed, the vineyard (Ps. 80:8), the Church of God, purged of its blemishes, shall be *lovely* in God's eyes; to bring out this sense the better, LOWTH, by changing a *Hebrew* letter, reads "pleasant", "lovely," for "red wine." **sing**—a *responsive* song [LOWTH]. **unto her**—rather, concerning her (*Note*, ch. 5:1); viz., the Jewish state [MAURER].

3. lest any hurt it—attack it [MAURER]. "Lest aught be wanting in her" [HORSLEY].

4. Fury is not in me—i.e., I entertain no longer anger towards my vine. **who would set . . . in battle**—i.e., would that I had the briers, etc. (the wicked foe; ch. 9:18; 10:17; II Sam. 23:6), before me! "I would go through," or rather, "*against* them." **5. Or**—Else; the only alternative, if Israel's enemies wish to escape being "burnt together." **strength**—rather, the refuge which I afford [MAURER]. "Take hold," refers to the horns of the altar which fugitives often *laid hold* of as an asylum (I Kings 1:50; 2:28). Jesus is God's "strength", or "refuge" which sinners must repair to and take hold of, if they are to have "peace" with God (ch. 45:24; Rom. 5:1; Eph. 2:14; cf. Job 22:21).

6. He—Jehovah. Here the song of the Lord as to His vineyard (vss. 2-5) ends; and the prophet confirms the sentiment in the song, under the same image of a *vine* (cf. Ps. 92:13-15; Hos. 14:5, 6). **Israel . . . fill . . . world**—(Rom. 11:12.)

ADAM CLARKE

2. *A vineyard of red wine.* The redder the wine, the more it was valued, says Kimchi.

3. *Lest any hurt it, I will keep it night and day*—"I will take care of her by night; and by day I will keep guard over her."

4. *Fury is not in me*—"I have no wall." The vineyard wishes for a wall and a fence of thorns—human strength and protection (as the Jews were too apt to apply to their powerful neighbors for assistance, and to trust to the shadow of Egypt). Jehovah replies that this would not avail her, nor defend her against His wrath. He counsels her, therefore, to betake herself to His protection. On which she entreats Him to make peace with her. This song receives much light from being collated with that in chap. v. In v. 5 of that chapter, God threatens to take away the wall of His vineyard. This was done, and here the vineyard complains, "I have no wall," and wishes for any kind of defense rather than be thus naked. *Who would set the briers and thorns against me?*—"Oh, that I had a fence of the thorn and brier."

MATTHEW HENRY

cattle shall feed, shall lie down there, and there shall be none to drive them away; and they shall eat the tender branches of the fruit-trees," which perhaps further signifies that the people should become an easy prey to their enemies. "*When the boughs thereof are withered* as they grow upon the tree, blasted by winds and frosts and not pruned, *they shall be broken off* for fuel, and *the women* and children shall *come and set them on fire*. There shall be a total destruction, for the very trees shall be destroyed." And this is a figure of the deplorable state of the vineyards. Our Saviour seems to refer to this when he says of the branches of the vine which *abide not in him* that they are *cast forth and withered, and men gather them, and cast them into the fire, and they are burned* (John xv. 6). *It is a people of no understanding*, that have no relish or savour of divine things, like a withered branch that has no sap in it; and this is at the bottom of all sins. Wicked people in their greatest concerns are of no understanding. *He that formed them* into a people, to show forth his praise, seeing they do not answer the end of their formation, but hate to be reformed, to be new-formed, will reject them, and *show them no favour*. If he that made us by his power do not make us happy in his favour, we had better never have been made.

II. Here is great mercy mixed with this judgment; for there are good people mixed with those that are corrupt and degenerate, on whom God will have mercy. Though they shall be smitten and slain, yet not to that degree, and in that manner, in which their enemies shall be smitten and slain, *v.* 7. God's people and God's enemies are here represented struggling with each other. In this contest there are slain on both sides. God makes use of wicked men to slay his people; for they are his sword, Ps. xvii. 13. But, when the cup of trembling comes to be put into their hand, it will be much worse with them than ever it was with God's people in their greatest straits. The seed of the woman has only his heel bruised, but the serpent has his head crushed and broken. There is really a vast difference between the afflictions and deaths of good people and the afflictions and deaths of wicked people. The affliction shall be mitigated, moderated, and proportioned to their strength, not to their deserts, *v.* 8. Thus God orders the troubles of his people, not *suffering them to be tempted above what they are able*, 1 Cor. x. 13. He considers what we can bear when he begins to correct; and when it is the *day of his east-wind*, not only blustering and noisy, but blasting and noxious, he stays his rough wind, checks it, and sets bounds to it. When he is winnowing his corn, it is with a gentle gale, that shall only blow away the chaff, but not the good corn. Though God will afflict them, yet he will make their afflictions to work for the good of their souls, and correct them as the father does the child, to drive out the foolishness that is in their hearts (*v.* 9): *By this therefore shall the iniquity of Jacob be purged*. Therefore, because the affliction is moderated, and the rough wind stayed, we may conclude that he designs their reformation, not their destruction. The particular sin which the affliction was intended to cure was the sin of idolatry. But by the captivity in Babylon they were not only weaned from this sin, but set against it. *Ephraim shall say, What have I to do any more with idols?* Jacob has his sin taken away *when he makes all the stones of the altar*, of his idolatrous altar, the stones of which were precious and sacred to him, *as chalkstones that are beaten asunder*; he not only has them in contempt, and values them no more than chalkstones, but in a holy revenge, beats them asunder as easily as chalkstones are broken to pieces. *The groves and the images shall not* stand before this penitent, but they shall be thrown down too, never to be set up again. This was according to the law for the demolishing and destroying of all the monuments of idolatry (Deut. vii. 5); and since the captivity in Babylon, no people in the world have such a rooted aversion to idols and idolatry as the people of the Jews. Jerusalem shall be desolate and forsaken, for a time, yet there will come a day when its scattered friends shall resort to it again out of all the countries whither they were dispersed (*v.* 12, 13). These scattered Israelites shall be fetched: *The Lord shall beat them off* as fruit from the tree, or beat them out as corn out of the ear. He shall separate them from those among whom they dwelt, *from the channel of the river* Euphrates north-east, *unto* Nile, *the stream of Egypt*, which lay south-west—those that were driven into the land of Assyria, and were captives there in the land of their enemies, and those that were *outcasts in the land of Egypt*, whither many left behind, after the captivity in Babylon, went, contrary to God's express command (Jer. xliii. 6, 7), and there lived as outcasts: God has mercy in store for them all. Though they are cast out, they are not cast off. "*You shall be gathered one by*

JAMIESON, FAUSSET, BROWN

11. boughs . . . broken off—so the Jews are called (Rom. 11:17, 19, 20). **set . . . on fire**—burn them as fuel; "women" are specified, as probably it was their office to collect fuel and kindle the fire for cooking.

no understanding—as to the ways of God (Deut. 32:28, 29; Jer. 5:21; Hos. 4:6).

7. him . . . those—Israel—Israel's enemies. Has God punished His people as severely as He has those enemies whom He employed to chastise Israel? No! Far from it. Israel, after trials, He will restore; Israel's enemies He will utterly destroy at last. **the slaughter of them that are slain by him**—rather, "Is *Israel* slain according to the slaughter of *the enemy slain*?" the slaughter wherewith the enemy is slain [MAURER].

8. In measure—not beyond measure; in moderation (Job 23:6; Ps. 6:1; Jer. 10:24; 30:11; 46:28). **when it shooteth**—image from the vine; rather, passing from the image to the thing itself, "*when sending her away* (viz., Israel to exile; ch. 50:1, God only *putting* the adulteress *away* when He might justly have put her to death), Thou didst *punish* her" [GESENIUS]. **stayeth**—rather, as *Margin*, "*when He removeth it by* His rough wind in the day," etc. **east wind**—especially violent in the East (Job 27:21; Jer. 18:17).

9. By this—exile of Israel (the "sending away," vs. 8). **purged**—expiated [HORSLEY]. **all the fruit**—This is the whole *benefit* designed to be brought about by the chastisement; namely, the removal of his (Israel's) sin (viz., object of idolatry; Deut. 9:21; Hos. 10:8). **when he**—Jehovah; at the destruction of Jerusalem by Nebuchadnezzar, His instrument. The Jews ever since have abhorred idolatry (cf. ch. 17:8). **not stand up**—shall rise no more [HORSLEY]. **10. city**—Jerusalem; the beating asunder of whose altars and images was mentioned in vs. 9 (cf. ch. 24:10-12). **calf feed**—(ch. 17:2); it shall be a vast wild pasture. **branches**—resuming the image of the vine (vs. 6).

12. Restoration of the Jews from their dispersion, described under the image of fruits shaken from trees and collected. **beat off**—as fruit beaten off a tree with a stick (Deut. 24:20), and then gathered. **river**—Euphrates. **stream of Egypt**—on the confines of Palestine and Egypt (Num. 34:5; Josh. 15:4, 47), now *Wady el-Arish*, Jehovah's vineyard, Israel, extended according to His purpose from the Nile to the Euphrates (I Kings 4:21, 24; Ps. 72:8). **one by one**—gathered most carefully, not merely as a nation, but as *individuals*. **13. great trumpet**—image from the trumpets blown on the first day of the seventh month to summon the people to a holy convocation (Lev. 23:24). Antitypically, the gospel trumpet (Rev. 11:15; 14:6) which the Jews shall hearken to in the last days (Zech. 12:10; 13:1). As the passover in the first month answers to Christ's crucifixion, so the day of atonement and the idea of "sal-

ADAM CLARKE

11. *The boughs thereof*—"Her boughs." That is, the boughs of the vineyard.

JOSEPH PARKER:

Verse 8. The word "stayeth" is, in the first instance, a principal word. It is not a common term. We find it, however, in a strange place, even in the book of Proverbs. The fourth and fifth verses of the twenty-fifth chapter of that book will show what is meant—"Take away the dross from the silver, and there shall come forth a vessel for the finer. Take away the wicked from before the king, and his throne shall be established in righteousness." The word that is rendered "stayeth" is rendered in the passage now cited "take away." The literal meaning is that God's rough wind separates. It is a wind that blows away the chaff, but allows the weighty wheat to remain: Take away the dross—take away the wicked—take away the chaff. When God sends his rough wind it is to sift, it is that after it has done blowing there may be nothing left but the true wheat. God conducts evermore a great separating process in life. The process takes part in the individual life that longs to develop itself truly and wisely and divinely. Man is always losing something in the process of his education, as well as gaining something: God's wind blows through and through his character, shaking it, separating part from part—a great ventilating process goes on, and a wondrous economy of sifting, separation, purification, so that at the last when the wind has sobbed itself to rest there is a man left marked by pureness, health, reality; all that was mean, unworthy, dross-like, wicked, has been blown away and there now stands a man after God's own heart.
—*The People's Bible*

13. *The great trumpet shall be blown.* Does not this refer to the time spoken of by our Lord in Matt. xxiv. 31? "He shall send [forth] his angels"—the preachers of His gospel—"with a great sound of a trumpet"—the earnest invitation to be saved by Jesus Christ; "and they shall gather together his elect"—the Jews, His ancient chosen people—"from the four winds"—

MATTHEW HENRY

one, silently, and as it were by stealth, dropping in, first one, and then another." *The great trumpet shall be blown, and* then *they shall come.* Cyrus's proclamation of liberty to the captives is this great trumpet, which awakened the Jews that were asleep in their thraldom to bestir themselves. They shall be gathered together: *To worship the Lord in the holy mount at Jerusalem.* When the captives rallied again, and returned to their own land, the chief thing they applied themselves to, was the worship of God. The holy temple was in ruins, but they had the holy mount, *the place of the altar*, Gen. xiii. 4. Liberty to worship God is the most valuable and desirable liberty.

CHAPTER 28

Verses 1–8

I. The prophet warns the ten tribes of the judgments coming for their sins when the king of Assyria laid their country waste, and carried the people into captivity. Ephraim had his name from *fruitfulness*, and had a great many *fat valleys* (*v.* 1, 4), and Samaria, which was situated on a hill, was *on the head of the fat valleys.* Their country was the glory of Canaan, their valleys were covered over with corn and vines.

1. What an ill use they made of their plenty! The goodness with which God crowned their years was to them a *crown of pride.* Pride was a sin that prevailed among them, and therefore the prophet boldly proclaims a *woe to the crown of pride.* They indulged themselves in sensuality. Ephraim was notorious for drunkenness, and Samaria, the head of the fat valleys, was full of those that were *overcome with wine*, were *broken with it*, so the margin. Drunkards make fools and brutes of themselves; the sin overcomes them, and *brings them into bondage* (2 Pet. ii. 19). Their constitution is broken by it, and their health ruined. They are brought to ruin by it. Their peace with God is broken and all this for the gratification of a base lust. Woe to these *drunkards of Ephraim*! There is a particular woe to the drunkards of Ephraim, for they are of God's professing people. Some make the *crown of pride* to belong to the drunkards, and to mean the garlands with which those were crowned that got the victory in their wicked drinking matches and drank down the rest of the company.

2. The justice of God in taking away their plenty from them, which they thus abused. Their *glorious beauty*, the plenty they were proud of, *is but a fading flower.* God can easily *take away their corn in the season thereof* (Hosea ii. 9), and recover those goods of his which they prepared for Baal. God has an officer ready to make a seizure for him, *a mighty and strong one*, even the king of Assyria, who *shall cast down to the earth with the hand* all that of which they are proud, *v.* 2. Then *the crown of pride*, and *the drunkards of Ephraim, shall be trodden under foot* (*v.* 3). Drunkards, in their folly, are apt to talk proudly; but they thereby render themselves ridiculous. The beauty of their valleys will wither of itself, and has in itself the principles of its own corruption. *The hasty fruit*, as soon as it is discovered, is plucked and eaten up; so the wealth of this world, besides that it is apt to decay of itself, is subject to be devoured by others as greedily as the first-ripe fruit.

II. He next turns to the kingdom of Judah, whom he calls the *residue of his people* (*v.* 5), for they were but two tribes to the other ten.

1. He promises them God's favours, and that they shall be taken under his guidance and protection when the beauty of Ephraim shall be left exposed to be trodden down and eaten up, *v.* 5, 6. *In that day*, when the Assyrian army is laying Israel waste, God will be to the residue of his people all they need and can desire; not only to the kingdom of Judah, but to those of Israel who had kept their integrity. When the Assyrian is in Israel as *a tempest of hail*, noisy and battering, as *a destroying storm*, and as *a flood of mighty waters overflowing* the country (*v.* 2), then *in that day will the Lord of hosts* distinguish by peculiar favours his people who have distinguished themselves by a steady adherence to him. He will be to them *for a crown of glory and for a diadem of beauty.* He will so appear in them as to make it evident that they have his image renewed on them, and that shall be to them a diadem of beauty. He will give them all the wisdom and grace necessary. He will himself be *a spirit of judgment to those that sit in judgment*; the counsellors shall be guided by wisdom and discretion and the judges shall govern by justice and equity. He will give them all the courage requisite to carry them through difficulties. He will be *for*

JAMIESON, FAUSSET, BROWN

vation" connected with the feast of tabernacles in the same seventh month, answer to the *crowning* of "redemption" at His second coming; therefore *redemption* is put last in I Corinthians 1:30. **Assyria**—whither the ten tribes had been carried; Babylonia is mainly meant, to which Assyria at that time belonged; the two tribes were restored, and *some* of the ten accompanied them. However, "Assyria" is designedly used to point *ultimately* to the future restoration of the ten *fully*, never yet accomplished (Jer. 3:18). **Egypt**—whither many had fled at the Babylonish captivity (Jer. 41:17, 18). Cf. as to the future restoration, ch. 11:11, 12, 16; 51:9-16 ("Rahab" being Egypt).

CHAPTER 28

Vss. 1-29. CHAPS. 28-33 form almost one continuous prophecy concerning the destruction of Ephraim, the impiety and folly of Judah, the danger of their league with Egypt, the straits they would be reduced to by Assyria, from which Jehovah would deliver them on their turning to Him; ch. 28 refers to the time just before the sixth year of Hezekiah's reign, the rest not very long before his fourteenth year.

1. crown of pride—*Hebrew* for *"proud crown* of the drunkards," etc. [HORSLEY], viz., Samaria, the capital of Ephraim, or Israel. "Drunkards," lit. (vss. 7, 8; ch. 5:11, 22; Amos 4:1; 6:1-6) and metaphorically, *like drunkards,* rushing on to their own destruction.

beauty . . . flower—"whose glorious beauty or ornament is a fading flower." Carrying on the image of "drunkards"; it was the custom at feasts to wreathe the brow with *flowers;* so Samaria, "which is (not as English Version, 'which are') upon the head of the fertile valley," i.e., situated on a hill surrounded with the rich valleys as a garland (I Kings 16:24); but the garland is "fading," as garlands often do, because Ephraim is now close to ruin (cf. ch. 16:8); fulfilled 721 B.C. (II Kings 17:6, 24). **2. strong one**—the Assyrian (ch. 10:5). **cast down**—viz., Ephraim (vs. 1) and Samaria, its crown. **with . . . hand**—with violence (ch. 8:11). **3. crown . . . the drunkards**—rather, "the crown *of* the drunkards." **4.** Rather, "the fading flower, their glorious beauty (vs. 1), which is on the head of the fat (fertile) valley, shall be as the early fig" [G. V. SMITH]. Figs usually ripened in August; but earlier ones (*Hebrew bikkurah,* Spanish *bokkore*) in June, and were regarded as a delicacy (Jer. 24:2; Hos. 9:10; Mic. 7:1). **while it is yet**—i.e., *immediately,* without delay; describing the *eagerness* of the Assyrian Shalmaneser, not merely to conquer, but to *destroy utterly* Samaria; whereas other conquered cities were often spared. **5-13.** The prophet now turns to Judah; a gracious promise to the remnant ("residue"); a warning lest through like sins Judah should share the fate of Samaria.

crown—in antithesis to the "*fading* crown" of Ephraim (vss. 1, 3). **the residue**—primarily, *Judah,* in the prosperous reign of Hezekiah (II Kings 18:7), antitypically, *the elect of God*; as He here is called *their* "crown and diadem," so are they called *His* (ch. 62:3); a beautiful reciprocity.

ADAM CLARKE

from all parts of the habitable globe in which they have been dispersed.

CHAPTER 28

1. *Woe to the crown of pride.* By the crown of pride, etc., Samaria is primarily understood.

3. *The crown of pride, the drunkards of Ephraim*—"The proud crown of the drunkards of Ephraim."

4. *The hasty fruit before the summer*—"The early fruit before the summer." "No sooner doth the *boccore* (the early fig) draw near to perfection in the middle or latter end of June, than the *kermez* or summer fig begins to be formed, though it rarely ripens before August; about which time the same tree frequently throws out a third crop, or the winter fig, as we may call it. This is usually of a much longer shape and darker complexion than the kermez, hanging and ripening upon the tree even after the leaves are shed; and, provided the winter proves mild and temperate, is gathered as a delicious morsel in the spring" (Shaw, *Travels,* p. 370, fol.).

Which when he that looketh upon it seeth—"Which whoso seeth, he plucketh it immediately." The image expresses in the strongest manner the great ease with which the Assyrians shall take the city and the whole kingdom, and the avidity with which they shall seize the rich prey without resistance.

5. *In that day.* Thus far the prophecy relates to the Israelites, and manifestly denounces their approaching destruction by Shalmaneser. Here it turns to the two tribes of Judah and Benjamin, the remnant of God's people who were to continue a kingdom after the final captivity of the Israelites. It begins with a favorable prognostication of their affairs and threatenings for their intemperance, disobedience, and profaneness.

Jonathan's Targum on this verse is worthy of notice: "In that time Messiah, the Lord of hosts, shall be a crown of joy and a diadem of praise to the residue of his people." Kimchi says the rabbins in general are of this opinion. Here then the rabbins, and their most celebrated Targum, give the incommunicable name, *Yehovah tsebaoth,* "the Lord of hosts," to our ever blessed Redeemer, Jesus Christ.

MATTHEW HENRY

strength to those that turn the battle to the gate, to the gates of the cities they besiege, or to their own gates, when they sally out upon the enemies that besiege them. Where God gives these he is to that people a crown of glory. This may well be supposed to refer to Christ, and so the Chaldee understands it: *In that day shall the Messiah be a crown of glory.*

2. He complains of the many corrupt ones (*v.* 7): *But they also,* many of those of Judah, *have erred through wine.* There are drunkards of Jerusalem, as well as drunkards of Ephraim. Ephraim's sins are found in Judah, and yet not Ephraim's ruins. *They have erred through wine.* Their drinking to excess is itself a practical error; they ruin their judgment, and they think to preserve their health by it and help digestion, but they spoil their constitution and hasten diseases and deaths. Their understanding is clouded and their conscience debauched by it; and therefore they espouse corrupt notions, and form their minds in favour of their lusts. Three things are aggravations of this sin: (1) That those were guilty of it who ought to have set a better example: *The priest and the prophet are swallowed up of wine;* their office is drowned and lost in it. The priests, as sacrificers, were obliged by a particular law to be temperate (Lev. x. 9). The prophets were a kind of Nazarite (as appears by Amos ii. 11), and were concerned to keep at the utmost distance from the sins they reproved in others; yet there were many of them ensnared in this sin. (2) That the consequences of it were very pernicious, not only by the ill influence of their example, but the prophet, when he was drunk, *erred in vision.* The priest *stumbled in judgment and forgot the law* (Prov. xxxi. 5); he reeled and staggered as much in the operations of his mind as in the motions of his body. (3) That the disease was epidemic: *All tables are full of vomit, v.* 8. It is rude and ill-mannered enough to sicken the beholders, for the tables where they eat their meat are filthily stained.

Verses 9–13

The prophet here complains of the wretched stupidity of this people, that they were unteachable.

I. Their prophets and ministers designed to *teach knowledge,* the knowledge of God and his will, and to *make them understand doctrine, v.* 9. This is God's way of dealing with men, to enlighten men's minds first with the knowledge of his truth, and thus to gain their affections, and bring their wills into a compliance with his laws.

II. They left no means untried to do them good, but taught them as little children that are beginning to learn, that are taken from the breast to the book (*v.* 9), for among the Jews it was common for mothers to nurse their children till they were three years old, and almost ready for school. They teach them, as they are capable, the good knowledge of the Lord, and to instruct them even when they are but newly weaned from the milk. They have been taught, as children are taught to read, by *precept upon precept,* and taught to write by *line upon line, a little here* and *a little there,* a little of one thing and a little of another, that instructions might be pleasing—a little at one time and a little at another, that they might not have their memories overcharged—a little from one prophet and a little from another. It is requisite that we have precept upon precept and line upon line. The precept of justice must be upon the precept of piety, and the precept of charity upon that of justice. The same precept and the same line should be often repeated. Teachers should accommodate themselves to the capacity of the learners, give them what they most need, and a little at a time, Deut. vi. 6, 7. They courted and persuaded them to learn, *v.* 12. God, by his prophets, said to them, "*This* way that we are directing you, *is the rest, wherewith you may cause the weary to rest; and this will be the refreshing* of your own souls, and will bring rest to your country from the wars with which it has been long harassed."

III. They were as unapt to learn as young children (*v.* 9). They *would not hear* (*v.* 12) that which would be rest and refreshing to them. They kept up the old custom of attending upon the prophet's preaching and it was continually beating upon them, but it beat nothing into them.

IV. How severely God would reckon with them for this. He would deprive them of the privilege of plain preaching, and speak to them *with stammering lips and another tongue, v.* 11. Those that will not hear the comfortable voice of God's word shall be made to hear the dreadful voice of his rod. By their profane contempt of God and his word they are but hastening on their own ruin, and ripening themselves for it; it is *that they may go and fall back-*

JAMIESON, FAUSSET, BROWN

6. Jehovah will inspire their magistrates with justice, and their soldiers with strength of spirit. **turn . . . battle to . . . gate**—the defenders of their country who not only repel the foe from themselves, but drive him to the gates of his own cities (II Sam. 11:23; II Kings 18:8).

7. Though Judah is to survive the fall of Ephraim, yet "they also" (the men of Judah) have perpetrated like sins to those of Samaria (ch. 5:3, 11), which must be chastised by God. **erred . . . are out of the way**—"stagger" . . . "reel." Repeated, to express the *frequency* of the vice.

priest . . prophet—If the ministers of religion sin so grievously, how much more the other rulers (ch. 56-10, 12)! **vision**—even in that most sacred function of the prophet to declare God's will revealed to them.

judgment—The priests had the administration of the law committed to them (Deut. 17:9; 19:17). It was against the law for the priests to take wine before entering the tabernacle (Lev. 10:9; Ezek. 44:21).

9, 10. Here the drunkards are introduced as scoffingly commenting on Isaiah's warnings: "Whom *will* he (does *Isaiah* presume to) teach knowledge? And whom will He make to understand *instruction?*

Is it those (i.e., does he take us to be) just weaned, etc.? For (he is constantly repeating, as if to little children) precept upon precept," etc. **line**—a rule or law. [MAURER]. The repetition of sounds in *Hebrew. tzav latzav, tzav latzav, gav laqav, gav laquav,* expresses the scorn of the imitators of Isaiah's speaking; he spoke *stammering* (vs. 11). God's mode of teaching offends by its simplicity the pride of sinners (II Kings 5:11, 12; I Cor. 1:23). *Stammerers* as they were by drunkenness, and children in knowledge of God, they needed to be spoken to in the language of children, and "with stammering lips" (cf. Matt. 13:13). A just and merciful retribution. **11. For**—rather, "Truly." This is *Isaiah's reply to* the scoffers: Your drunken questions shall be answered by the severe lessons from God conveyed through the Assyrians and Babylonians; the dialect of these, though Semitic, like the Hebrew, was so far different as to sound to the Jews like the speech of *stammerers* (cf. ch. 33:19; 36:11). To them who will not understand God will speak still more unintelligibly. **12.** Rather, "He (Jehovah) who hath said to them." **this . . . the rest**—Reference may be primarily to "rest" from national warlike preparations, the Jews being at the time "weary" through various preceding calamities, as the Syro-Israelite invasion (ch. 7:8; cf. ch. 30:15; 22:8; 39:2; 36:1; II Kings, 18:8). But spiritually, the "rest" meant is that to be found in obeying those very "precepts" of God (vs. 10) which they jeered at (cf. Jer. 6:16; Matt. 11:29). **13. But**—rather, "Therefore," viz., because "they would not hear" (vs. 12). **that they might go**—the *designed result* to those who, from a defect of *the will,* so far from profiting by God's mode of instructing, "precept upon precept," etc., made it into a stumbling block (Hos. 6:5; 8:12; Matt. 13:14). **go, and fall**—image appropriately from "drunkards" (vs. 7, which they were) who in trying to "go" *forward* "fall *backward.*"

ADAM CLARKE

6. *The battle to the gate*—"The war to the gate *of the enemy.*" That is, who pursue the fleeing enemy even to the very gates of their own city. "We were upon them even unto the entering of the gate," 2 Sam. xi. 23; that is, we drove the enemy back to their own gates. The Targum says, The Messiah shall give the victory to those who go out to battle, that He may bring them back to their own houses in peace.

9. *Whom shall he teach knowledge?*—"Whom, say they, would He teach knowledge?" The scoffers mentioned below, v. 14, are here introduced as uttering their sententious speeches; they treat God's method of dealing with them, and warning them by His prophets, with contempt and derision. What, say they, doth He treat us as mere infants just weaned? Doth He teach us like little children, perpetually inculcating the same elementary lessons, the mere rudiments of knowledge; precept after precept, line after line, here and there, by little and little? imitating at the same time, and ridiculing, in v. 10, the concise prophetical manner. God, by His prophet, retorts upon them with great severity their own contemptuous mockery, turning it to a sense quite different from what they intended. Yes, saith He, it shall be in fact as you say. You shall be taught by a strange tongue and a stammering lip, in a strange country; you shall be carried into captivity by a people whose language shall be unintelligible to you, and which you shall be forced to learn like children. And My dealing with you shall be according to your own words. It shall be command upon command for your punishment; it shall be line upon line, stretched over you to mark your destruction (compare 2 Kings xxi. 13). It shall come upon you at different times, and by different degrees, till the judgments, with which from time to time I have threatened you, shall have their full accomplishment.

10. *For precept must be upon precept.* The original is remarkably abrupt: *latsav tsav latsav tsav ki; lakav kav lakav kav; sham zeeir sham zeeir.* "Command to command, command to command. Line to line, line to line. A little there, a little there." *Tsav* signifies a "little precept," such as is suited to the capacity of a child; see v. 9. *Kav* signifies the "line" that a mason stretches out to build a layer of stones by. After one layer or course is placed, he raises the line and builds another; thus the building is by degrees regularly completed. This is the method of teaching children, giving them such information as their narrow capacities can receive; and thus the prophet dealt with the Israelites.

12. *This is the rest*—"This is the true rest." The sense of this verse is: God had warned them by His prophets that their safety and security, their deliverance from their present calamities and from the apprehensions of still greater approaching, depended wholly on their trust in God, their faith and obedience; but they rejected this gracious warning with contempt and mockery.

MATTHEW HENRY

ward, and proceed from one sin to another, till they be quite *broken, and snared, and taken*, and ruined, *v.* 13.

Verses 14–22

The prophet, having reproved those that made a jest of the word of God, here goes on to reprove those that made a jest of the judgments of God. He addresses himself to *the scornful men who ruled in Jerusalem*, the magistrates of the city, *v.* 14.

I. These scornful men challenged God Almighty to do his worst (*v.* 15): *You have said, We have made a covenant with death and the grave.* They thought themselves sure of their lives, even when judgments were abroad, as if they had made a bargain with death not to take them away by violence but by old age. If we be at peace with God we have in effect made a covenant with death that, whenever it comes, it shall be no terror to us, nor do us any real damage (1 Cor. iii. 22, 23): but to think of making death our friend while by sin we are making God our enemy, is the greatest absurdity. It was a fond conceit which these scorners had, *When the overflowing scourge shall pass through* our country, and others shall fall under it, yet *it shall not come to us.* But what is the ground of their confidence? *We have made lies our refuge.* Those things which should be lies and falsehood to the enemy, who was *flagellum Dei—the scourge of God*, the overflowing scourge, would secure them by imposing upon the enemy their stratagems of war, or their feigned submissions in treaties of peace. The rulers of Jerusalem think themselves greater politicians than those of the country towns; they will compliment the king of Assyria with a promise to surrender their city, or to become tributaries to him, with a purpose to shake off his yoke as soon as the danger is over. Those that pursue their designs by trick and fraud may perhaps compass them, but cannot expect comfort in them.

II. God, by the prophet, shows them the folly of their security. He does not disturb their false confidences, till he has first shown them a firm bottom on which they may repose themselves (*v.* 16): *Behold, I lay in Zion for a foundation a stone.* The foundation is made up of (*a*) The promises of God in general—his covenant with Abraham is a foundation of stone, firm and lasting, for faith to build upon; it is *a tried stone*, for all the saints have stayed themselves upon it and it never failed them. (*b*) The promise of Christ in particular; for to him this is expressly applied in the New Testament, 1 Pet. ii. 6–8. He is that stone which has become *the head of the corner.* Jesus Christ is a foundation of God's laying. He is a tried stone, a corner-stone, in whom the sides of the building are united, the *head-stone of the corner.* And *he that believes* these promises, and rests upon them, *shall not make haste*, but with a fixed heart shall quietly wait the event, saying, *Welcome the will of God.* The grounds which they now built on could not be safe (*v.* 17): *Judgment will I lay to the line, and righteousness to the plummet.* This denotes,

1 The building up of his church; having laid the foundation (*v.* 16), he will raise the structure, as builders do, by line and plummet, Zech. iv. 10. Righteousness shall be the line and judgment the plummet. The church, being founded on Christ, shall be formed and reformed by the scripture. Or,

2 The punishing of the church's enemies, against whom he will proceed by an exact rule. These scornful men will be made ashamed of the vain hopes with which they had deluded themselves. Those that make lies their refuge build upon the sand, and the building will fall when the storm comes, and bury the builder in the ruins of it. They fancied that when the overflowing scourge should pass through the land it should not come near them; but the prophet tells them (*v.* 19), that they shall be the first that shall fall by it: "*From the time it goes forth it shall take you*, as if it came on purpose to seize you. *Morning by morning shall it pass over;* you shall never be safe; there shall be a pestilence walking in darkness and a destruction wasting at noonday." The very report of it at a distance will be a terror to you. Evil tidings are a terror to scorners, but he whose heart is fixed, *trusting in God, is not afraid of them*; whereas, when the *overflowing scourge* comes, then all the comforts and confidences of scorners fail them, *v.* 20. *The bed is shorter than that a man can stretch himself upon it*, so that he is forced to cramp and contract himself. That in which they thought to shelter themselves proves insufficient: *The covering is narrower than that a man can wrap himself in.* When God comes to contend with these scorners, *He will do his work, and bring to pass his act*, as the righteous Judge of the earth. He will do it now against his people, as formerly he did it against their enemies;

JAMIESON, FAUSSET, BROWN

14. scornful—(*Note*, vss. 9, 10.) **15. said**—virtually, in your conduct, if not in words. **covenant**—There may be a tacit reference to their confidence in their "covenant" with the Assyrians in the early part of Hezekiah's prosperous reign, before he ceased to pay tribute to them, as if it ensured Judah from evil, whatever might befall the neighboring Ephraim (vs. 1). The *full* meaning is shown by the language ("covenant with death—hell," or *sheol*) to apply to all lulled in false security spiritually (Ps. 12:4; Eccles. 8:8; Jer. 8:11); the godly alone are in covenant with death (Job 5:23; Hos. 2:18; I Cor. 3:22). **overflowing scourge**—two metaphors: the hostile Assyrian armies like an overwhelming flood. **pass through**—viz., through Judea on their way to Egypt, to punish it as the protector of Samaria (II Kings 17:4). **lies**—*They* did not use these *words*, but Isaiah designates their sentiments by their true name (Amos 2:4).

16. Lit., *Behold Me* as Him who *has laid;* viz., in My divine counsel (Rev. 13:8); none save I could lay it (ch. 63:5). **stone**—*Jesus Christ; Hezekiah* [MAURER], or *the temple* [EWALD], do not realize the full significancy of the language; but only in type point to Him, in whom the prophecy receives its exhaustive accomplishment; whether *Isaiah* understood its fulness or not (I Peter 1:11, 12), the Holy Ghost plainly contemplated its fulfilment in Christ alone; so in ch. 32:1; cf. Genesis 49:24; Psalm 118:22; Matthew 21:42; Romans 10:11; Ephesians 2:20 **tried**—both by the devil (Luke 4:1-13) and by men (Luke 20:1-38), and even by God (Matt. 27:46); a stone of tested solidity to bear the vast superstructure of man's redemption. The *tested righteousness* of Christ gives its peculiar merit to His vicarious sacrifice. The connection with the context is; though a "scourge" shall visit Judea (vs. 15), yet God's gracious purpose as to the elect remnant, and His kingdom of which "Zion" shall be the center, shall not fail, because its rests on Messiah (Matt. 7: 24, 25; II Tim. 2:19). **precious**—lit. "of preciousness," so in the *Greek*, (I Pet. 2:7). *He is preciousness.* **corner-stone**—(I Kings 5:17; 7:9; Job 38:6); the stone laid at the corner where two walls meet and connecting them; often costly. **make haste**—flee in hasty alarm; but LXX has "be ashamed"; so Romans 9:33, and I Peter 2:6, "be confounded," substantially the same idea; he who rests on Him shall not have the shame of disappointment, nor flee in sudden panic (see ch. 30:15; 32:17). **17. line**—the measuring-line of the plummet. HORSLEY translates, "I will appoint judgment for the rule, and justice for the plummet." As the cornerstone stands most perpendicular and exactly proportioned, so Jehovah, while holding out grace to believers in the Foundation-stone, will judge the scoffers (vs. 15) according to the exact *justice* of the law (cf. Jas. 2; 13). **hail**—divine judgment (ch. 30:30; 32:19). **18. disannulled**—obliterated, as letters traced on a waxen tablet are obliterated by passing the stylus over it. **trodden down**—passing from the metaphor in "scourge" to the thing meant, the *army* which *treads down* its enemies. **19. From the time . . .**—rather, "As often as it comes over (i.e., passes through), it shall overtake you" [HORSLEY]; like a flood returning *from time to time*, frequent hostile invasions shall assail Judah, after the deportation of the ten tribes. **vexation . . . understand . . . report**—rather, "It shall be a terror even to hear the mere report of it" [MAURER], (I Sam. 3:11). But G. V. SMITH, "Hard treatment (HORSLEY, dispersion) only shall make you to understand instruction"; they scorned at the simple way in which the prophet offered it (vs. 9); therefore, they must be taught by the severe teachings of adversity. **20.** Proverbial, for they shall find all their sources of confidence fail them; all shall be hopeless perplexity in their affairs.

ADAM CLARKE

15. *A covenant with death.* To be in covenant with is a kind of proverbial expression to denote perfect security from evil and mischief of any sort: "For thou shalt be in league with the stones of the field: and the beasts of the field shall be at peace with thee," Job v. 23. *We have made a covenant with death, and with hell are we at agreement.* We have made a "vision"; we have had an "interview," struck a bargain, and settled all preliminaries. So they had made a covenant with hell by diabolic sacrifice. "We have cut the covenant sacrifice"; they divided it for the contracting parties to pass between the separated victim. For the victim was split exactly down the middle; and being set opposite to each other, the contracting parties entered, one at the head part, the other at the feet; and, meeting in the center, took the covenant oath. Thus, it is intimated, these bad people made an agreement with *sheol*, with demons, with whom they had an interview; i.e., meeting them in the covenant sacrifice! To such a pitch had the Israelitish idolatry reached at that time!

18. *Your covenant with death shall be disannulled*—"Your covenant with death shall be broken."

20. *For the bed is shorter.* A *mashal* or proverbial saying, the meaning of which is that they will find all means of defense and protection insufficient to secure them, and cover them from the evils coming upon them.

MATTHEW HENRY

he will now *rise up against Jerusalem as,* in David's time, against the Philistines *in Mount Perazim* (2 Sam. v. 20), and as, in Joshua's time, against the Canaanites *in the valley of Gibeon.* If those that profess themselves members of God's church by their pride and scornfulness make themselves like Philistines and Canaanites, they must expect to be dealt with as such. This will be *his strange work, his strange act.* It is work that he is not used to as to his own people. It is a strange work indeed if he *turn to be their enemy and fight against them, ch.* lxiii. 10. The use and application of all this (*v.* 22): "*Therefore be you not mockers;* dare not to ridicule either the reproofs of God's word or his judgments. *Be you not mockers, lest your bands be made strong,* both the bands by which you are bound under the dominion of sin, and the bands by which you are bound over to the judgments of God." Let not these mockers make light of divine threatenings, for the prophet assures them that the Lord God of hosts has *determined a consumption upon the whole earth;* and can they think to escape?

Verses 23–29

This parable, which (like many of our Saviour's parables) is borrowed from the husbandman's calling, is ushered in with a solemn preface, *He that has ears to hear, let him hear, v.* 23.

I. The parable here is plain enough, that the husbandman applies himself to the business of his calling with pains and prudence, and observes a method and order in his work. 1. In his ploughing and sowing: *Does the ploughman plough all day to sow?* Yes, he *ploughs in hope* and *sows in hope,* 1 Cor. ix. 10. *Does he open and break the clods?* Yes, that the land may be fit to receive the seed. And *when he has thus made plain the face thereof* does he not sow seed suitable to the soil? For the husbandman knows what grain is fit for clay ground and what for sandy ground, and, accordingly, he sows each in its place—*wheat in the principal place* (so the margin reads it), for it was a staple commodity of Canaan (Ezek. xxvii. 17), *and barley in the appointed place.* 2. In his threshing, *v.* 27, 28. This also he proportions to the grain that is to be threshed out. *The fitches and the cummin,* being easily got out of their husk or ear, are only threshed with *a staff and a rod;* but *the bread-corn* requires more force, and therefore that must be bruised with *a threshing instrument,* a sledge shod with iron, that was drawn to and fro over it, to beat out the corn; and yet *he will not be ever threshing it,* nor any longer than is necessary to loosen the corn from the chaff; *he will not break it,* or crush it *with the wheel of his cart, nor bruise it* to pieces *with his horsemen;* the grinding of it is reserved for another operation. What pains are to be taken, not only for the earning, but for the preparing of our necessary food; and yet, after all, it is *meat that perishes!* Shall we then grudge to labour much more for the *meat which endures to everlasting life? Bread-corn is bruised.* Christ was so; *it pleased the Lord to bruise him,* that he might be the bread of life to us.

II. Most interpreters make the parable a further answer to those who set the judgments of God at defiance: "As the husbandman will not be always ploughing, but will at length sow his seed, so God will not be always threatening, but will at length bring upon sinners the judgments they have deserved; but in wisdom, that they may be reformed and brought to repentance." But we may give this parable a greater latitude. 1. It is God that *instructs the husbandman to discretion,* as *his God, v.* 26. Husbandmen have need of discretion wherewith to order their affairs. The advancing of the art of husbandry is a common service to mankind more than the cultivating of most other arts. The skill of the husbandman is from God. This takes off somewhat of the weight of the sentence passed on man for sin, that when God, in execution of it, sent man to till the ground, he taught him how to do it most to his advantage. It is he that gives men capacity for this business, an inclination to it, and a delight in it, and to him husbandmen must seek for direction for they, above other men, have an immediate dependence upon the divine Providence. As to the other instance of the husbandman's conduct in threshing his corn, it is said, *This also comes forth from the Lord of hosts, v.* 29. And, if it is from him that men do things wisely, we must needs acknowledge him to be *wise in counsel and excellent in working.* 2. God's church is his husbandry, 1 Cor. iii. 9. If Christ is the true vine, his Father is the husbandman (John xv. 1), and he is continually by his word and ordinances cultivating it. Does not God by his ministers break up the fallow ground? God sows his word by the hand of his ministers (Matt. xiii. 19). Whatever the soil of the heart is, there is some seed or other in the word proper for it. And, as the word

JAMIESON, FAUSSET, BROWN

21. **Perazim**—In the valley of Rephaim (II Sam. 5:18, 20; I Chron. 14:11), there Jehovah, by David, *broke forth* as waters do, and made a *breach* among the *Philistines,* David's enemies, as *Perazim* means, expressing a sudden and complete overthrow. **Gibeon**—(I Chron. 14:16; II Sam. 5:25; *Margin*); not Joshua's victory (Josh. 10:10). **strange**—as being against His own people; judgment is not what God delights in; it is, though necessary, yet strange to Him (Lam. 3:33). **work**—punishing the guilty (ch. 10:12). **22. mockers**—a sin which they had committed (vss. 9, 10).

bands—their Assyrian bondage (ch. 10:27); Judah was then tributary to Assyria; or, "lest your punishment be made still more severe" (ch. 24:22). **consumption**—destruction (ch. 10:22, 23; Dan. 9:27).

23. Calling attention to the following illustration from husbandry (Ps. 49:1, 2). As the husbandman does his different kinds of work, each in its *right time* and *due proportion,* so God adapts His measures to the varying exigencies of the several cases: now mercy, now judgments; now punishing sooner, now later (an answer to the scoff that His judgments, being put off so long, would never come at all, ch. 5:19); His object being not to *destroy* His people any more than the farmer's object in threshing is to destroy his crop; this vindicates God's "strange work" (vs. 21) in punishing His people. Cf. the same image, Jeremiah 24:6; Hosea 2:23; Matthew 3:12. **24. all day**—emphatic; he is not *always* ploughing: he also "sows," and that, too, in accordance with sure rules (vs. 25). **doth he open**—supply "always." Is he *always harrowing*? **25. face**—the "surface" of the ground: "made plain," or level, by harrowing. **fitches**—rather, dill, or fennel; *Nigella romana,* with black seed, easily beaten out, used as a condiment and medicine in the East. So the LXX, "cummin" was used in the same way. **cast in . . . principal wheat**—rather, *plant the wheat in rows* (for wheat was thought to yield the largest crop, by being planted sparingly; PLINY, H.N. 18. 21); [MAURER]; "sow the wheat regularly" [HORSLEY]. But GENESIUS, like *English Version,* "fat," or "principal," i.e., excellent wheat. **appointed barley**—rather, "barley in its appointed place [MAURER]. **in their place**—rather, "in its (the field's) border [MAURER]. **26. to discretion**—in the due rules of husbandry; God first taught it to man (Gen. 3:23). **27.** The husbandman uses the same discretion in threshing. The dill ("fitches") and cummin, leguminous and tender grains, are beaten out, not as wheat, etc., with the heavy corn drag ("threshing instrument"), but with "a staff"; heavy instruments would crush and injure the seed. **cart wheel**—two iron wheels armed with iron teeth, like a saw, joined together by a wooden axle. The "corndrag" was made of three or four wooden cylinders, armed with iron teeth or flint stones fixed underneath, and joined like a sledge. Both instruments cut the straw for fodder as well as separated the corn. **staff**—used also where they had but a small quantity of *corn;* the flail (Ruth 2:17). **28. Bread-corn**—corn of which bread is made. **bruised**—*threshed* with the corn-drag (as contrasted with dill and cummin, "beaten with the staff"), or, "trodden out" by the hoofs of cattle driven over it on the threshing-floor [G. V. SMITH], (Deut. 25:4; Mic. 4:13). **because**—rather, "but" [HORSLEY]; though the corn is threshed with the heavy instrument, *yet* he will not always be thus threshing it. **break it**—"drive over it (continually) the wheel" [MAURER]. **cart**—threshing-drag. **horsemen**—rather, "horses"; used to tread out corn.

29. **This also**—The skill wherewith the husbandman duly adjusts his modes of threshing is given by God, as well as the skill (vs. 26) wherewith he tills and sows (vss. 24, 25). Therefore He must also be able to adapt His modes of treatment to the several moral needs of His creatures. His object in sending *tribulation* (derived from the Latin *tribulum,* a "thresh ing instrument," Luke 22:31; Romans 5:3) is to sever the moral chaff from the wheat, not to crush utterly; "His judgments are usually in the line of our offenses; by the nature of the judgments we may usually ascertain the nature of the sin" [BARNES].

ADAM CLARKE

23. *Give ye ear, and hear my voice*—"Listen ye, and hear my voice." The foregoing discourse, consisting of severe reproofs, and threatenings of dreadful judgments impending on the Jews for their vices, and their profane contempt of God's warnings by His messengers, the prophet concludes with an explanation and defense of God's method of dealing with His people in an elegant parable or allegory; in which He employs a variety of images, all taken from the science of agriculture. As the *husbandman* uses various methods in preparing his land, and adapting it to the several kinds of seeds to be sown, with a due observation of times and seasons; and when he hath gathered in his harvest, employs methods as various in separating the corn from the straw and the chaff by different instruments, according to the nature of the different sorts of grain; so God, with unerring wisdom, and with strict justice, instructs, admonishes, and corrects His people; chastises and punishes them in various ways, as the exigence of the case requires, now more moderately, now more severely; always tempering justice with mercy, in order to reclaim the wicked, to improve the good, and, finally, to separate the one from the other.

27-28. Four methods of threshing are here mentioned, by different instruments; the "flail," the "drag," the "wain," and the "treading of the cattle." The staff or flail was used for, says Jerome, the grain that was too tender to be treated in the other methods. The drag consisted of a sort of strong planks, made rough at the bottom, with hard stones or iron; it was drawn by horses or oxen over the corn sheaves spread on the floor, the driver sitting upon it. The wain was much like the former; but had wheels with iron teeth, or edges like a saw.

28. *Bruise it with his horsemen*—"Bruise it with the hoofs of his cattle."

MATTHEW HENRY

of God, so the rod of God is thus wisely used. Afflictions are God's threshing-instruments, designed to loosen us from the world, to separate between us and our chaff, but he will proportion them to our strength. If the rod and the staff will answer the end, he will not make use of his cart-wheel and his horsemen.

CHAPTER 29

Verses 1–8

That it is Jerusalem which is here called *Ariel* is agreed, for that was the city where David dwelt; that part of it which was called *Zion* was in a particular manner the city of David, in which both the temple and the palace were. But why it is so called is uncertain. Cities, as well as persons, get surnames and nicknames. *Ariel* signifies *the lion of God*, or *the strong lion:* as the lion is king among beasts, so was Jerusalem among the cities. Jerusalem, while she was a righteous city, was bold as a lion. Some make *Ariel* to signify *the altar of burnt-offerings*, which devoured the beasts offered in sacrifice as the lion does his prey. I rather take it as a woe to Jerusalem, Jerusalem; it is repeated here, as it is Matt. xxiii. 37, that it might be the more awakening.

I. The distress of Jerusalem foretold. Though Jerusalem be a strong city, yet, if iniquity be found there, woe be to it. 1. Let Jerusalem know that her external performance of religious services will not serve as an exception from the judgments of God (*v.* 1): "*Add year to year;* go on in your annual feasts, let all your males appear there three times a year before the Lord, and none empty, and let them never miss any of these solemnities: *let them kill the sacrifices*, as they used to do; but, as long as their lives are unreformed and their hearts unhumbled, let them not think thus to pacify an offended God and to turn away his wrath." 2. Let her know that she shall be *visited of the Lord of hosts* (*v.* 6); her sins shall be punished with alarms like *thunder and earthquakes, storms and tempests, and devouring fire*. (1) Jerusalem shall be besieged. He does not say, *I will destroy Ariel*, but I will *distress Ariel*; and she is *therefore* brought into distress, that being awakened to repent, she may not be brought to destruction. *I will* (*v.* 3) *encamp against thee round about*. It was the enemy's army that encamped against it. When men fight against us we must, in them, see God contending with us. (2) She shall be in grief to see the country laid waste. "*There shall be heaviness and sorrow* (*v.* 2); they shall repent, and reform, and return to God, and then it shall be to me as Ariel. Jerusalem shall be like itself, shall become to me a Jerusalem again, a holy city," *ch.* i. 26. (3) She shall be humbled, and mortified (*v.* 4): "*Thou shalt be brought down* from the height of arrogancy, and now *thou shalt speak out of the ground, out of the dust, as one that has a familiar spirit, whispering out of the dust*. They should be faint and feeble, as those who are sick, their speech low and interrupted, being afraid lest their enemies should overhear them.

II. The destruction of Jerusalem's enemies is foretold (*v.* 5, 7): "*Thou shalt be brought down* (*v.* 4), *to speak out of the dust;* so low thou shalt be reduced. *But*" (so it may be rendered) "*the multitude of thy strangers and the terrible ones*, the numerous armies of the enemy, *shall* themselves *be like small dust*, not able to speak at all, or so much as whisper, but *as chaff that passes away*. Thou shalt be abased, but they shall be quite dispersed and slain (*ch.* xxvii. 7). *Yea, it shall be in an instant, suddenly:* the enemy shall be surprised with the destruction, and you with the salvation." The army of the Assyrians was by an angel laid dead upon the spot, in an instant, suddenly. *The multitude of the nations that fight against Zion shall be as a hungry man who dreams that he eats*, but still is hungry. Whereas they hoped to make a prey of Jerusalem, and to enrich themselves with plunder, their hopes shall prove vain dreams. They themselves, and all their pomp, and power, and prosperity, shall vanish like a dream.

Verses 9–16

I. The prophet stands amazed at the stupidity of the greatest part of the Jewish nation. They had Levites, who taught *the good knowledge of the Lord.* They had prophets, who brought them messages immediately from God. *Surely this great nation*, that has all the advantages of divine revelation, will be *a wise and understanding people*, Deut. iv. 6. But, alas! it was quite otherwise, *v.* 9. The prophet addresses himself to the sober thinking part of them. "The rest sport themselves with their own deceivings; they riot and revel; but do you *cry out*, lament their folly, cry to God by prayer for them." They were drunk with the love of pleasures, with prejudices against religion,

JAMIESON, FAUSSET, BROWN

CHAPTER 29

Vss. 1-24. Coming Invasion of Jerusalem: Its Failure: Unbelief of the Jews. This chapter opens the series of prophecies as to the invasion of Judea under Sennacherib, and its deliverance. **1. Ariel**—Jerusalem; Ariel means "Lion of God," i.e., city rendered by God invincible: the lion is emblem of a mighty hero (II Sam. 23:20). Otherwise "Hearth of God," i.e., place where the altar fire continually burns to God (ch. 31:9; Ezek. 43:15, 16).

add . . . year to year—ironically; suffer one year after another to glide on in the round of formal, heartless "sacrifices." Rather, "add yet another year" to the one just closed [Maurer]. Let a year elapse and a little more (ch. 32:10; *Margin*). **let . . . kill sacrifices**—rather, "let the beasts (of another year) go round" [Maurer]; i.e., after the completion of a year "I will distress Ariel." **2. Yet**—rather, "Then." **heaviness . . . sorrow**—rather, preserving the *Hebrew* paronomasia, "groaning" and "moaning." **as Ariel**—either, "the city shall be as *a lion* of *God,*" i.e., it shall emerge from its dangers unvanquished; or "it shall be as the *altar of burnt offering,*" consuming with fire the besiegers (vs. 6; ch. 30:30; 31:9; Lev. 10:2); or best, as the next verse continues the *threat,* and the promise of *deliverance* does not come till vs. 4, "it shall be like a hearth of burning," i.e., a scene of devastation by fire [G. V. Smith]. The prophecy, probably, contemplates *ultimately*, besides the affliction and deliverance in Sennacherib's time, the destruction of Jerusalem by Rome, the dispersion of the Jews, their restoration, the destruction of the enemies that besiege the city (Zech. 14:2), and the final glory of Israel (vss. 17-24). **3. I**—*Jehovah,* acting through the Assyrian, etc., His instruments (ch. 10:5). **mount**—an artificial *mound* formed to outtop high walls (ch. 37:33); else *a station,* viz., of warriors, for the siege. **round about**—not *fully* realized under Sennacherib, but in the Roman siege (Luke 19:43; 21:20). **forts**—siege-towers (Deut. 20: 20). **4.** Jerusalem shall be as a captive, humbled to the dust. Her voice shall come from the earth as that of the spirit-charmers or necromancers (ch. 8: 19), faint and shrill, as the voice of the dead was supposed to be. Ventriloquism was doubtless the trick caused to make the voice appear to come from the earth (ch. 19:3). An appropriate retribution that Jerusalem, which consulted necromancers, should be made like them! **5. Moreover**—rather, "Yet"; yet in this extremity help shall come, and the enemy be scattered. **strangers**—foreign enemies, invaders (ch. 25:2). **it shall be**—viz., the destruction of the enemy. **at an instant**—in a moment (ch. 30: 23). **6. Thou**—the Assyrian army. **thunder . . .**—not literally, in the case of the Assyrians (ch. 37: 36); but figuratively for an awful judgment (ch. 30: 30; 28:17). The ulterior fulfilment, in the case of the Jews' foes in the last days, may be more literal (see as to "earthquake," Zech. 14:4). **7. munition**—fortress. **8.** Their disappointment in the very height of their confident expectation of taking Jerusalem shall be as great as that of the hungry man who in a dream fancies he eats, but awakes to hunger still (Ps. 73:20); their dream shall be dissipated on the fatal morning (ch. 37:36). **soul**—simply *his appetite;* he is still thirsty. **9. Stay**—rather, "Be astounded"; expressing the stupid and amazed incredulity with which the Jews received Isaiah's announcement. **wonder**—The second imperative, as often (ch. 8:9), is a threat; the first is a simple declaration of a fact, "Be astounded, since you choose to be so, at the prophecy, soon *you will be amazed* at the sight of the actual event" [Maurer]. **cry . . . out . . . cry**—rather, "Be ye blinded (since you choose to be so, though the light shines all round you), and

ADAM CLARKE

CHAPTER 29

The subject of this and the following four chapters is the invasion of Sennacherib; the great distress of the Jews while it continued; their sudden and unexpected deliverance by God's immediate interposition in their favor; the subsequent prosperous state of the kingdom under Hezekiah; interspersed with severe reproofs, and threats of punishment, for their hypocrisy, stupidity, infidelity, their want of trust in God, and their vain reliance on the assistance of Egypt; and with promises of better times, both immediately to succeed, and to be expected in the future age.

1. *Ariel.* That Jerusalem is here called by this name is very certain; but the reason of this name, and the meaning of it as applied to Jerusalem, are very obscure and doubtful. From Ezek. xliii. 15, we learn that Ariel was the name of the altar of burnt offerings, put here for the city itself in which that altar was. In the second verse it is said, "I will distress Ariel . . . and it shall be unto me as Ariel." The first Ariel here seems to mean Jerusalem, which should be distressed by the Assyrians; the second Ariel seems to mean the altar of burnt offerings. But why is it said, "Ariel shall be unto me as Ariel"? As the altar of burnt offerings was surrounded daily by the victims which were offered, so the walls of Jerusalem shall be surrounded by the dead bodies of those who had rebelled against the Lord, and who should be victims to His justice. The translation of Bishop Lowth appears to embrace both meanings: "I will bring distress upon Ariel; and it shall be to me as the hearth of the great altar." *Add ye year to year.* Ironically. Go on year after year, keep your solemn feasts; yet know that God will punish you for your hypocritical worship, consisting of mere form destitute of true piety. Probably delivered at the time of some great feast, when they were thus employed.

2. *There shall be heaviness and sorrow*—"There shall be continual mourning and sorrow," instead of your present joy and festivity. *And it shall be unto me as Ariel*—"And it shall be unto me as the hearth of the great altar." That is, it shall be the seat of the fire of God, which shall issue from thence to consume His enemies. See note on v. 1. Or, perhaps, all on flame, as it was when taken by the Chaldeans; or covered with carcasses and blood, as when taken by the Romans—an intimation of which more distant events, though not immediate subjects of the prophecy, may perhaps be given in this obscure passage.

4. *And thy speech shall be low out of the dust*—"And from out of the dust thou shalt utter a feeble speech."

5. *The multitude of thy strangers*—"The multitude of the proud." The fifth, sixth, and seventh verses contain an admirable description of the destruction of Sennacherib's army, with a beautiful variety of the most expressive and sublime images; perhaps more adapted to show the greatness, the suddenness, and horror of the event than the means and manner by which it was effected. Compare chap. xxx. 30-33.

7. *As a dream.* This is the beginning of the comparison which is pursued and applied in the next verse. Sennacherib and his mighty army are not compared to a dream because of their sudden disappearance; but the disappointment of their eager hopes is compared to what happens to a hungry and thirsty man when he awakes from a dream in which fancy had presented to him meat and drink in abundance, and finds it nothing but a vain illusion.

8. Bishop Stock's translation of the prophet's text is both elegant and just: "As when a hungry man dreameth; and, lo! he is eating: and he awaketh; and his appetite is unsatisfied. And as a thirsty man dreameth; and, lo! he is

MATTHEW HENRY

and with the corrupt principles they had imbibed. Like drunken men, they are not sensible of the divine rebukes they are under. *They have beaten me, and I felt it not*, says the drunkard, Prov. xxiii. 35. There is such a thing as spiritual drunkenness. God himself *poured out upon them a spirit of deep sleep, and closed their eyes* (*v.* 10) in righteous judgment, to punish them for their *loving darkness rather than light*, their loving sleep. They said, *Yet a little sleep, a little slumber;* and therefore he gave them up to strong delusions, and said, *Sleep on now*. This is applied to the unbelieving Jews, who rejected the gospel of Christ, and were justly hardened in their infidelity, till wrath came upon them to the uttermost. Rom. xi. 8, *God has given them the spirit of slumber*. This was fulfilled when, in the latter days of the Jewish church, the chief priests, and the scribes, and the elders of the people, were the great opposers of Christ and his gospel, and brought themselves under a judicial infatuation. Every vision, particularly that this prophet had seen, and published, had become unintelligible; they had it among them, but were never the wiser for it, any more than a man (though a good scholar) is for a book delivered to him sealed up. He sees it is a book, and that is all. So they knew that what Isaiah said was a vision and prophecy, but the meaning of it was hidden from them. But the same vision which to you is a *savour of death unto death* to others is and shall be a *savour of life unto life*. Knowledge is easy to him that understands.

II. The prophet, in God's name, threatens those that were formal and hypocritical in their devotion, *v.* 13, 14.

1. Their sin is dissembling with God in their religious performances, *v.* 13. He that knows the heart cannot be imposed upon with shows and pretences. If the heart be full of his love and fear, out of the abundance of that the mouth will speak. But there are many whose religion is lip-labour only. It is only from the teeth outward. They do not apply their minds to the service. They do not make the word of God the rule of their worship, nor his will their reason: *Their fear towards me is taught by the precept of men*. The tradition of the elders was of more value than the laws which God commanded Moses. This our Saviour applies to the Jews in his time, who were formal in their devotions, Matt. xv. 8, 9.

2. It is a spiritual judgment with which God threatens to punish them for their spiritual wickedness (*v.* 14): *I will proceed to do a marvellous work*. They removed all sincerity from their hearts. Now God will remove all sagacity from their heads. *The wisdom of their wise men shall perish*. They played the hypocrite, and thought to put a cheat upon God, and now they are left to themselves to play the fool, to be easily cheated by all about them. This is a marvellous work; that wise men should of a sudden lose their wisdom and be given up to strong delusions.

III. He shows the folly of those that thought to act separately and secretly from God. Their politics described (*v.* 15): They *seek deep to hide their counsel from the Lord*, that he may not know either what they do or what they design. The absurdity of their politics demonstrated (*v.* 16): *Surely your turning of things upside down*—your inverting the order of things, and thinking to make God's providence give attendance to your projects, turning things upside down and beginning at the wrong end—*shall be esteemed as the potter's clay*. God will turn and manage you, and all your counsels, with as much ease as the potter fashions his clay.

Verses 17–24

God here tells them that he will turn things upside down. They disbelieve Providence: "Wait awhile," says God, "and you shall be convinced that there is a God who governs the world." The wonderful revolution here foretold may refer primarily to the happy settlement of the affairs of Judah and Jerusalem after the defeat of Sennacherib's attempt. But it may look further, to the rejection of the Jews at the first planting of the gospel.

I. A great change is here foretold, *v.* 17. *Lebanon*, that was a forest, *shall be turned into a fruitful field;* and Carmel, that was a fruitful field shall become a forest. It was a sign of the defeat of Sennacherib that the ground should be more than ordinarily fruitful (*ch.* xxxvii. 30): *You shall eat this year such as grows of itself;* food for man shall be (as food for beasts is) the spontaneous product of the soil. Then Lebanon became so fruitful that that which used to be reckoned a fruitful field in comparison with it was looked upon but as a forest. When a great harvest of souls was gathered in to Christ from among the Gentiles then the wilderness was turned into a fruitful field, *ch.* liv. 1.

JAMIESON, FAUSSET, BROWN

soon ye shall be blinded" in good earnest to your sorrow [MAURER], (ch. 6:9, 10). **not with wine**—but with spiritual paralysis (ch. 51:17, 21). **ye . . . they**—The change from speaking *to*, to speaking *of* them, intimates that the prophet turns away from them to a greater distance, because of their stupid unbelief. **10.** Jehovah gives them up judicially to their own hardness of heart (cf. Zech. 14:13). Quoted by Paul, with variations from the LXX, Romans 11:8. See ch. 6:10; Psalm 69:23. **eyes; the prophets . . .**—rather, "hath closed your eyes, the prophets; and your heads (*Margin*, see also ch. 3:2), the seers, He hath covered." The Orientals cover the head to sleep; thus "covered" is parallel to "closed your eyes" (Judg. 4:19). Covering the face was also preparatory to execution (Esther 7:8). This cannot apply to the time when Isaiah himself prophesied, but to subsequent times. **11. of all**—rather, "*the whole* vision." "Vision" is the same here as "revelation," or "law"; in ch. 28:15, the same *Hebrew* word is translated, "covenant" [MAURER]. **sealed**—(ch. 8:16), God seals up the truth so that even the learned, because they lack believing docility, cannot discern it (Matt. 13:10-17; 11:25). Prophecy remained comparatively a *sealed* volume (Dan. 12:4, 9), until Jesus, who "alone is worthy," "opened the seals" (Rev. 5:1-5, 9; 6:1). **12.** The unlearned succeed no better than the learned, not from want of human learning, as they fancy, but from not having the teaching of God (ch. 54:13; Jer. 31:34; John 6:45; I Cor. 2:7-10; I John 2:20).

13. precept of men—instead of the precepts of God, given by His prophets; also worship external, and by rule, not heartfelt as God requires (John 4:24). Cf. Christ's quotation of this verse from the LXX.

14. (Hab. 1:5; Acts 13:41.) The "*marvellous* work" is one of *unparalleled* vengeance on the hypocrites: cf. "*strange* work," ch. 28:21. The judgment, too, will visit the wise in that respect in which they most pride themselves; their *wisdom* shall be hid, i.e., shall no longer appear, so as to help the nation in its distress (cf. I Cor. 1:19).

15. seek deep to hide—rather, "That seek to hide deeply," etc. (cf. ch. 30:1, 2). The reference is to the *secret* plan which many of the Jewish nobles had of seeking Egyptian aid against Assyria, contrary to the advice of Isaiah. At the same time the hypocrite in general is described, who, under a plausible exterior, tries to hide his real character, not only from men, but even from God. **16.** Rather, "Ah! your perverseness! just as if the potter should be esteemed as the clay!" [MAURER]. Or, "Ye invert (turn upside down) the order of things, putting yourselves instead of God," and vice versa, just as if the potter should be esteemed as the clay [HORSLEY], (ch. 45:9; 64:8).

17. turned—as contrasted with *your* "turnings of things upside down" (vs. 16), there shall be other and better *turnings* or revolutions; the outpouring of the Spirit in the latter days (ch. 32:15); first on the Jews; which shall be followed by their national restoration (*Note*, vs. 2; Zech. 12:10); then on the Gentiles (Joel 2:28). **fruitful field**—lit., a Carmel (*Note*, ch. 10:18). The moral change in the Jewish nation shall be as great as if the wooded Lebanon were to become a fruitful field, and vice versa. Cf. Matthew 11:12, *Greek:* "the kingdom of heaven *forces itself*," as it were, on man's acceptance; instead of men having to seek Messiah, as they had John, in a *desert*, He presents Himself before them with loving invitations; thus men's hearts, once a moral desert, are reclaimed so as to bear fruits of righteousness: vice versa, the ungodly who seemed prosperous, both in the moral and literal sense, shall be exhibited in their real barrenness.

ADAM CLARKE

drinking: and he awaketh; and, lo! he is faint, and his appetite craveth."

9. *Stay yourselves, and wonder.* "Go on what-what-whatting," in a state of mental indetermination, till the overflowing scourge take you away.

13. *And their fear toward me is taught by the precept of men*—"And vain is their fear of Me, teaching the commandments of men."

17. *And Lebanon shall be turned into a fruitful field*—"Ere Lebanon become like Carmel." A *mashal*, or proverbial saying, expressing any great revolution of things; and, when respecting two subjects, an entire reciprocal change—explained here by some interpreters, I think with great probability, as having its principal view beyond the revolutions then near at hand, to the rejection of the Jews, and the calling of the Gentiles. Carmel stands here opposed to Lebanon, and therefore is to be taken as a proper name.

MATTHEW HENRY

II. Those that were ignorant shall become intelligent, *v.* 18. Those that understood not this prophecy shall, when it is accomplished, understand it, and shall acknowledge, not only the hand of God in the event, but the voice of God in the prediction of it: *The deaf shall then hear the words of the book.* The poor Gentiles shall then have divine revelation brought among them; and those that sat in darkness shall see a great light, for the gospel was sent to them to *open their eyes,* Acts xxvi. 18. Those that were erroneous shall become orthodox (*v.* 24): *Those that erred in spirit* shall come to a right understanding of things; the Spirit of truth shall lead them into all truth. Those that murmured at the truths of God as hard sayings, shall learn the true meaning and will be better reconciled to them. Those that erred concerning the providence of God and murmured shall see the issue of things and be aware of what God was designing in all, Hos. xiv. 9. Those that were melancholy shall become cheerful and pleasant (*v.* 19): *The meek also shall increase their joy in the Lord.* This intimates that even in their distress they kept up their joy in the Lord, but now they increased it. The grace of meekness will contribute very much to the increase of our holy joy. Sennacherib, that *terrible one,* and his great army, shall be *brought to nought* (*v.* 20). The power of Satan, that terrible one indeed, shall be broken by the prevalency of Christ's gospel, Heb. ii. 14. The persecutors shall be quieted. To complete the repose of God's people, the scorners at home shall be consumed and cut off by Hezekiah's reformation. They had been persecutors of God's people and prophets, probably of the prophet Isaiah. And this is very applicable to the chief priests and Pharisees, who persecuted Christ and his apostles, and for that sin were cut off and consumed. They lay in wait for an occasion against them. By their spies they *watch for iniquity,* to see if they can lay hold of anything that is said or done that may be called an iniquity. They *made a man,* though he were ever so wise and good, *an offender for a word,* a word mischosen or misplaced, when they could not but know that it was well meant, *v.* 21. Those that *reprove in the gates,* who were bound as prophets, as judges, and magistrates, to show people their transgressions, hated these and laid snares for them, as the Pharisees' emissaries, who were sent to watch our Saviour that they might *entangle him in his talk* (Matt. xxii. 15). *They turn aside the just for a thing of nought.* They run a man down, and misrepresent him, by all the little arts and tricks they can devise, as they did our Saviour.

Jacob made to blush by the reproaches of his enemies, shall now be relieved by the rolling away of those reproaches (*v.* 22): *Thus saith the Lord who redeemed Abraham* out of his troubles and will redeem all that are by faith his genuine seed out of theirs. He that began his care of his church in the redemption of Abraham will appear for the house of Jacob, and they shall not be ashamed, nor shall *their faces now wax pale*; but they shall gather courage. Jacob, who thought his family would be extinct, shall see his children, multitudes of believers and he *shall not be ashamed* (*v.* 22), but shall speak with his enemy in the gate, Ps. cxxvii. 5. It is some comfort to parents to think that their children are God's creatures, the work of the hands of his providence. But it will be much more a comfort to them to see their children his new creatures, the work of the hands of his grace.

JAMIESON, FAUSSET, BROWN

18. deaf . . . blind—(Cf. Matt. 11:5.) The spiritually blind, etc., are chiefly meant; "the book," as Revelation is called pre-eminently, shall be no longer "sealed," as is described (vs. 11), but the most unintelligent shall hear and see (ch. 35: 5). **24. They . . . that erred**—(Ch. 28:7.) **learn doctrine**—rather, shall receive discipline or instruction. "Murmuring" was the characteristic of Israel's rebellion against God (Exod. 16:8; Ps. 106:25). This shall be so no more. Chastisements, and, in HORSLEY'S view, the piety of the Gentiles provoking the Jews to holy jealousy (Rom. 11:11, 14), shall then produce the desired effect.

19. meek—rather, *the afflicted* godly: the idea is, *virtuous suffering* (ch. 61:1; Ps. 25:9; 37:11), [BARNES]. **poor among men**—i.e., the poorest of men, viz., the pious poor. **rejoice**—when they see their oppressors punished (vss. 20, 21), and Jehovah exhibited as their protector and rewarder (vss. 22-24; ch. 41:17; Jas. 2:5). **20. terrible**—viz., the persecutors among the Jewish nobles. **scorner**—(Ch. 28:14, 22.)

watch for—not only commit iniquity, but watch for opportunities of committing it, and make it their whole study (see Mic. 2:1; Matt. 26: 59; 27:1). **21.** Rather, "Who make a man guilty in his *cause*" [GESENIUS], i.e., unjustly condemn him. "A man" is in the *Hebrew a poor man,* upon whom such unjust condemnations might be practiced with more impunity than on the rich; cf. vs. 19, "the meek . . . the poor." **him that reproveth**—rather, pleadeth; one who has a suit at issue. **gate**—the place of concourse in a city, where courts of justice were held (Ruth 4:11; Prov. 31:23; Amos 5:10, 12). **just**—one who has a just cause; or, Jesus Christ, "the Just One" [HORSLEY]. **for a thing of naught**—rather, "through falsehood," "by a decision that is null in justice" [BARNES]. Cf. as to Christ, Proverbs 28:21; Matthew 26:15; Acts 3:13, 14; 8:33. **22.** Join "saith . . . concerning the house of Jacob." **redeemed**—out of Ur, a land of idolaters (Josh. 24:3). **not now**—After the moral revolution described (vs. 17), the children of Jacob shall no longer give cause to their forefathers to blush for them. **wax pale**—with shame and disappointment at the wicked degeneracy of his posterity, and fear as to their punishment. **23. But**—rather, "For." **he**—Jacob. **work of mine hands**—spiritually, as well as physically (ch. 19:25; 60:21; Eph. 2:10). By Jehovah's agency Israel shall be cleansed of its corruptions, and shall consist wholly of pious men (ch. 54:13, 14; 2:1; 60:21). **midst of him**—i.e., his land. Or else "His children" are the *Gentiles adopted among the Israelites. his lineal descendants* (Rom. 9:26; Eph. 3:6) [HORSLEY].

ADAM CLARKE

F. B. MEYER:

"The meek also shall increase their joy in the Lord" (v. 19). "Blessed are the meek," "Blessed are the poor in spirit," said the Lord. What is meekness, and why are meek and poor men so signally blessed with joy? Meekness is different from lowliness and humility. It is our attitude in the presence of our detractors and persecutors—not retaliating, nor opposing force to force, but bowing in silence and submission before high-handed wrong. It was in such a spirit of meekness that Jesus suffered Himself to be led as a lamb to the slaughter; and instead of calling for legions of angels, suffered Caiaphas' armed band to bind Him. This spirit is not natural to us. It is in our nature to retaliate and avenge ourselves. We want to call for fire, or legions of armored angels from the heaven of God. But this is not the way of peace and joy.

But the Holy Spirit waits to reproduce in us the meekness of Jesus. Then, when you meet all injury and unkindness with an unfailing Christian courtesy, bending like a rush before the storm, to rise when it has passed over, you will have joy.—*Great Verses Through the Bible*

21. *Him that reproveth in the gate*—"Him that pleaded in the gate."

22. *Who redeemed Abraham.* As God redeemed Abraham from among idolaters and workers of iniquity, so will He redeem those who hear the words of the Book, and are humbled before Him, vv. 18-19. *Concerning the house of Jacob*—"The God of the house of Jacob." I read *El* as a noun, not a preposition. The parallel line favors this sense, and there is no address to the house of Jacob to justify the other. *Neither shall his face now wax pale*—"His face shall no more be covered with confusion."

23. *But when he seeth his children, the work of mine hands*—"For when his children shall see the work of My hands."

MATTHEW HENRY — CHAPTER 30

Verses 1–7

It was often the fault and folly of the people of the Jews that, when they were insulted by their neighbours on one side, they sought for succour from their neighbours on the other side, instead of looking up to God and putting their confidence in him. Against the Israelites they sought to the Syrians, 2 Chron. xvi. 2, 3. Against the Syrians they sought to the Assyrians, 2 Kings xvi. 7. Against the Assyrians they here sought to the Egyptians, 2 Kings xviii. 21.

I. This sin of theirs is described. They would not consult God. "They *take counsel* among themselves, and one from another; but they do not ask counsel, much less will they take counsel, of me. They *cover with a covering but not of my Spirit,* and therefore it will prove too short a covering, and a refuge of lies." They *strengthened themselves in the strength of Pharaoh. The shadow of Egypt* (and it was but a shadow) was the covering in which they wrapped themselves.

II. The evil of this sin. They were, in profession, God's children; but, not trusting in him, they were justly stigmatized as rebellious. They added sin to sin. They took so much pains to secure the Egyptians

JAMIESON, FAUSSET, BROWN — CHAPTER 30

VSS. 1-32. CHAPTERS 30-32 REFER PROBABLY TO THE SUMMER OF 714 B.C., AS CHAPTER 29 TO THE PASSOVER OF THAT YEAR. Jewish ambassadors were now on their way to Egypt to seek aid against Assyria (ch. 30:2-6, 15; 31:1). Isaiah denounces this reliance on Egypt rather than on Jehovah. God had prohibited such alliances with heathen nations, and it was a leading part of Jewish polity that they should be a separate people (Exod. 23:32; Deut. 7:2). **1. take counsel**—rather, as vss. 4, 6 imply, "execute counsels." **cover . . . covering**—i.e., wrap themselves in reliances disloyal towards Jehovah. "Cover" thus answers to "seek to hide deeply their counsel from the Lord" (ch. 29:15). But the *Hebrew* is lit., "who pour out libations"; as it was by these that *leagues* were made (Exod. 24:8; Zech. 9: 11), translate, "who make a league." **not of**—not suggested by My Spirit" (Num. 27:21; Josh. 9:14). **that they may add**—The *consequence* is here spoken of as their *intention,* so reckless were they of sinning: one sin entails the commission of another (Deut. 29:19).

ADAM CLARKE — CHAPTER 30

1. *And that cover with a covering*—"Who ratify covenants." Hebrew, "Who pour out a libation." Sacrifice and libation were ceremonies constantly used in ancient times by most nations in the ratifying of covenants; a libation therefore is used for a covenant.

MATTHEW HENRY

for their allies: *They walk to go down to Egypt*, travel up and down to find an advantageous road thither; but they *have not asked at my mouth*, never considered whether God would approve of it. They were at a vast expense to do it, *v.* 6. They load *the beasts of the south* (horses fetched from Egypt, which lay south from Judæa) with their riches, fancying, as is common with people in a fright, that they were safer anywhere than where they were. Or they sent their riches thither as bribes to Pharaoh's courtiers. God would have helped them *gratis*; but, if they will have help from the Egyptians, they must pay dearly for it. They carried their effects to Egypt through a land (so it may be read) of trouble and anguish, that vast howling wilderness, which lay between Canaan and Egypt, *whence come the lion and fiery serpent*, Deut. viii. 15.

III. The consequence of it. The Egyptians would receive their ambassadors, and be willing to treat with them (*v.* 4): *His princes were at Zoan*, and the king encouraged them to depend upon the succours he would send them. But they would not answer their expectation: They *could not profit them*, *v.* 5. God says, *They shall not profit them* (*v.* 6). The forces they were to furnish them with could not be raised in time; or the Egyptians would secretly incline to the Assyrians. *The Egyptians shall help in vain, and to no purpose*, *v.* 7. *The strength of Pharaoh*, which was your pride, *shall be your shame*; and you will upbraid yourselves, with your folly in trusting to it. And the *shadow of Egypt*, that *land shadowing with wings* (*ch.* xviii. 1), which was your confidence, shall be your confusion. The princes of Israel, who were so forward to court an alliance *shall all be ashamed of a people that could not be a help or profit to them*, but a *shame and reproach*, *v.* 5. Those that put confidence in any creature will sooner or later find it a reproach to them. The Creator is a rock of ages, the creature a broken reed. We cannot expect too little from man nor too much from God. "*Therefore have I cried concerning this* matter. *Their strength is to sit still*, in a humble dependence upon God and not to wander about to seek help from this and the other creature."

Verses 8–17

I. The preface is very awful. The prophet must write it (*v.* 8), *write it in a table, in a book*, to be preserved for posterity, *for a standing testimony* against this wicked generation. Let it be written to shame the men of the present age: their children may profit by it, though they will not. People will be tempted to think God was too hard upon them unless they know how bad they were, and what fair means God tried with them before he brought it to this extremity. It is designed for admonition to those of the remotest place and age.

II. The character given of the profane and wicked Jews. *This is a rebellious people*, *v.* 9. "They are *lying children*, that will not stand to what they say, that promise fair, but perform nothing." They rebelled against the divine authority: "They are *children that will not hear the law of the Lord*, nor heed it."

III. The sentence passed upon them is dreadful. 1. They forbade the prophets to speak to them in God's name. They did in effect *say to the seers, See not*. The prophets told them of their faults, and warned them of their danger by reason of sin, and they could not bear that. They must speak to them smooth things. Let a thing be ever so right and true, if it be not smooth, they will not hear it. Those deserve to be deceived that desire to be so. The prophets stopped them in their sinful pursuits, and stood in their way like the angel in Balaam's road, with the sword of God's wrath drawn in their hand. When they went on frowardly in the way of their hearts they said to the prophets, "*Get you out of the way, turn aside out of the paths*." The prophets were continually telling them of the Holy One of Israel, and how severely he will reckon with sinners; and this they could not endure. If the prophets will speak to them, they will make it their bargain that they shall not call God *the Holy One of Israel*; for God's holiness is that attribute which wicked people most of all dread. The doom passed upon them for this, *v.* 12, 13. *Thus saith the Holy One of Israel.* We must tell men that God is the *Holy One of Israel.* The ground of the judgment is: *Because they despise this word*—either, in general, every word that the prophets said to them, or this word in particular, which declares God to be *the Holy One of Israel.* They *trust in oppression and perverseness*, in the wealth they have got by fraud and violence, or in the sinful methods they have taken for their own security. On these they lean, and therefore it is just that they should fall. Judgment is passed upon them: "*This*

JAMIESON, FAUSSET, BROWN

2. walk—are now setting out, viz, their ambassadors (vs. 4). **Egypt**—See *Note*, in the beginning of chs. 19 and 20. **Pharaoh**—the generic name of the kings of Egypt, as *Cæsar* was at Rome. The word in Egyptian means "king" (JOSEPHUS, *Antiquities*, 8.6, 2). *Phra*, "the sun," was the hieroglyphic symbol and title of the king. **shadow**—image from shelter against heat: *protection* (Ps. 121:5, 6). **3. shame**—disappointment. Egypt, weakened by its internal dissensions, can give no solid help. **4. his**—Judah's (cf. ch. 9:21). **at Zoan**—are already arrived there on their errand to Pharaoh (see ch. 19:11). **came to Hanes**—are come there. West of the Nile, in central Egypt: Egyptian *Hnes;* the *Greek Heracleopolis:* perhaps the Anysis of HERODOTUS (2.137); according to GROTIUS, *Tahpanhes* contracted (Jer. 43:7-9); the seat of a reigning prince at the time, as was Zoan, hence the Jewish ambassadors go to both. **5.** (Jer. 2:36) **6. burden**—the prophecy as to, etc. [MAURER]; so LXX, the fresh inscription here marks emphatically the prediction that follows. Or, rather, Isaiah sees in vision, the ambassador's beasts *burdened* with rich presents *travelling southwards* (viz., to Egypt, Dan. 11:5, 6), and exclaims, Oh, the *burden of treasure* on the beasts! etc. (Hos. 8:9; 12: 1). **land of trouble**—the desert between Palestine and Egypt, destitute of water and abounding in dangerous animals (Deut. 8:15; Jer. 2:6). **flying serpent**—(ch. 14:29), a species which springs like a dart from trees, on its prey. **will carry**—rather, present, "carry," viz., as presents to **Egypt** (I Kings 15:19) **young asses**—rather, full-grown asses [MAURER]. **7.** "Egypt is vanity, and to no purpose will they help" [G. V. SMITH]. **strength**—*Hebrew, Rabah*, a designation for Egypt (ch. 51:9; Ps. 87:4), implying her *haughty fierceness;* translate, "Therefore I call her Arrogance that sitteth still." She who boasted of the help she would give, when it came to the test, sat still (ch. 36:6). *English Version* agrees with vs. 15 and ch. 7:4.

8. table—a tablet (Hab. 2:2), which should be set in public, containing the prophecy in a briefer form, to be read by all. **a book**—viz., a parchment roll, containing the prophecy in full, for the use of distant posterity. Its truth will be seen hereafter when the event has come to pass. See ch. 8:1, 16, *Notes.* **for ever and ever**—rather read, "For a *testimony* for ever" [CHALDEE, JEROME, LOWTH]: "testimony is often joined to the notion of *perpetuity* (Deut. 31:19, 21, 26).

9. lying—unfaithful to Jehovah, whose covenant they had taken on them as His adopted *children* (ch. 59:13; Prov. 30:9).

10. (Mic. 2:6, 11; 3:5). **See not**—as you now do, foretelling misfortune. **Prophesy not . . . right things**—Not that they avowedly requested this, but their conduct *virtually* expressed it. No man, *professedly*, wished to be deceived; but many seek a kind of teaching which is deceit; and which, if they would examine, they might know to be such (I Kings 22:13). The Jews desired success to be foretold as the issue of their league with Egypt, though ill had been announced by God's prophet as the result; this constituted the "deceits." **11.** Depart from the true "way" (so in Acts 19:9, 23) of religion. **cause . . . to cease**—Let us hear no more of His name. God's *holiness* is what troubles sinners most.

12. Holy One—Isaiah so little yields to their wicked prejudices that he repeats the very name and truth which they disliked. **this word**—Isaiah's exhortation to reliance on Jehovah. **oppression**—whereby they levied the treasures to be sent to conciliate Egypt (vs. 6). **perverseness**—in relying on Egypt, rather than on Jehovah.

ADAM CLARKE

5. *But a shame*—"But proved even a shame."

6. *The burden. Massa* seems here to be taken in its proper sense; the "load," not the "oracle." The same subject is continued, and there seems to be no place here for a new title to a distinct prophecy. Does not *burden of the beasts of the south* in this place relate to the presents sent by Hoshea, king of Israel, to the south, to Egypt, to engage the Egyptians to succor him against the king of Assyria. *Into the land of trouble and anguish*—"Through a land of distress and difficulty." The same deserts are here spoken of which the Israelites passed through when they came out of Egypt, which Moses describes, Deut. viii. 15, as "that great and terrible wilderness, wherein were fiery serpents, and scorpions, and drought, where there was no water"; and which was designed to be a kind of barrier between them and Egypt, of which the Lord has said, "Ye shall henceforth return no more that way," Deut. xvii. 16.

7. *Their strength is to sit still*—"Rahab the Inactive."

8. *For ever and ever*—"For a testimony for-ever."

MATTHEW HENRY

iniquity shall be to you as a breach ready to fall. This confidence of yours will be like a house built upon the sand. Your contempt of that word of God which you might build upon will make everything else you trust to like a wall that bulges out, which, if any weight be laid upon it, often sinks with its own weight." *The breaking shall come suddenly, at an instant.* "You and all your confidences shall be not only weak as the potter's clay (*ch.* xxix. 16), but *broken to pieces as the potter's vessel.* But, when once it is broken so as to be unfit for use, let it be dashed, let it be crushed all to pieces, so that there may not remain one shred big enough to take up a little fire or water—two things we have daily need of, and which poor people commonly fetch in a piece of a broken pitcher.

2. They slighted the gracious directions God gave them; they would take their own way, *v.* 15–17. The God that knew them, and desired their welfare, gave them this prescription; and it is recommended to us all. Would we be saved from the evil of every calamity. It must be *in returning and rest*, in returning to God and reposing in him as our rest. Let us return from our evil ways, and settle in the way of God and duty, and that is the way to be saved. "Return from this project of going down to Egypt. *In returning* (in the thorough reformation of your hearts and lives) *and in rest* (in an entire submission of your souls to God) *you shall be saved.*" Would we be strengthened to do what is required of us? It must be *in quietness and in confidence.* We must rely upon God with a holy confidence that he can do what he will and will do what is best for his people. And this will be our strength. They would not take God's counsel, though it was so much for their own good. And justly will those die of their disease that will not take God for their physician. They would not so much as try the method prescribed: "*But you said, No* (*v.* 16), we will not compose ourselves, for *we will flee upon horses* and *we will ride upon the swift;* we will hurry hither and thither to fetch in foreign aids." When Sennacherib took all the fenced cities of Judah, those rebellious children would not be persuaded patiently to expect God's appearing for them, as he did wonderfully at last. Their sin shall be their punishment: "You will flee, and therefore *you shall flee*; you will be upon the full speed, and therefore so shall those be that pursue you." The dogs are most apt to run barking after him that rides fast. The conquerors protected those that sat still, but pursued those that made their escape. It is foretold, *v.* 17, that they should be easily cut off; one of the enemy should defeat a thousand of them, and five put an army to flight. Only here and there one should escape alone in a solitary place, and be left *as a beacon upon the top of a mountain*, a warning to others.

Verses 18–26

The closing words of the foregoing paragraph (*You shall be left as a beacon upon a mountain*) some understand as a promise that a remnant of them should be reserved as monuments of mercy. The first words in this paragraph may be read by way of antithesis, *Notwithstanding this, yet will the Lord wait that he may be gracious.*

I. God will be gracious to them and will have mercy on them. "He will *wait to be gracious* (*v.* 18); he will wait till you return to him and seek his face, and then he will be ready to meet you with mercy. He will stir up himself to deliver you, will be exalted, will be *raised up out of his holy habitation* (Zech. ii. 13), *and thus he will be exalted*, that is, he will glorify his name." "*He will be gracious to thee, at the voice of thy cry*, the cry of thy necessity, when that is most urgent—the cry of thy prayer, when that is most fervent. *When he shall hear it*, there needs no more; at the first word *he will answer thee*, and say, *Here I am.*" Those who were disturbed in the possession of their estates shall again enjoy them quietly. When the danger is over *the people shall dwell in Zion, at Jerusalem*, as they used to do; they shall dwell safely, free from the fear of evil. Those who dwell in Zion, the holy city, will find enough there to wipe away tears from their eyes. This is grounded upon two great truths: (1) That *the Lord is a God of judgment*; he is both wise and just in all the disposals of his providence, true to his word and tender of his people. (2) That therefore all those are blessed who *wait for him*, who not only wait on him with their prayers, but wait for him with their hopes.

II. They shall not again know the want of the means of grace, *v.* 20, 21. It was promised (*v.* 19), that they should *weep no more* and that God would be *gracious to them*; and yet here it is taken for granted that God may give them the *bread of adversity and the water of affliction.* It is promised that their eyes should *see their teachers*, that is, that they should

JAMIESON, FAUSSET, BROWN

13. Image from a curve swelling out in a wall (Ps. 62:3); when the former gives way, it causes the downfall of the whole wall; so their policy as to Egypt.

14. **he**—the enemy; or rather, God (Ps. 2: 9; Jer. 19:11). **it**—**the Jewish state. potter's vessel**—earthen and fragile. **sherd**—a fragment of the vessel large enough to take up a live coal, etc. **pit**—cistern or pool. The swell of the wall is at first imperceptible and gradual, but at last it comes to the crisis; so the decay of the Jewish state.

15. **returning and rest**—turning back from your embassy to Egypt, and ceasing from warlike preparations.

quietness—answering to "wait for Him" (God) (vs. 18).

16. **flee**—not as fugitives, but we will *speed* our course; viz., against the Assyrians, by the help of cavalry supplied by Egypt (ch. 31:1). This was expressly against the Mosaic law (Deut. 17:16; cf. *Note*, ch. 2:7; Hos. 14:3). **shall . . . flee**—lit., before your enemies; their sin and its punishment correspond. **17. One thousand**—A thousand *at once*, or, *As one man* [MAURER]. **rebuke**—the battle cry. **shall ye**—at the rebuke of five shall ye, viz., *all* (in contrast to the "one thousand") flee so utterly that even two shall not be left together, but each one shall be as solitary "as *a signal staff* [G. V. SMITH]. or a *banner on a hill*" (ch. 5:26; 11:12). The signal staff was erected to rally a nation in war. The remnant of Jews left would be beacons to warn all men of the justice of God, and the truth of His threatenings. GESENIUS (from Lev. 26:8; Deut. 32:30) arbitrarily inserts "ten thousand." "At the rebuke of five shall ten thousand of you flee."

18. **therefore**—on account of your wicked perverseness (vs. 1, 2, 9, 15, 16), Jehovah will *delay* to be gracious [HORSLEY]. Rather, *wait or delay* in punishing, to give you time for repentance (vss. 13, 14, 17) [MAURER]. Or, "Yet therefore" (viz., because of the distress spoken of in the previous verses; that distress will lead the Jews to repentance, and so Jehovah will pity them) [GESENIUS]. **be exalted**—Men will have more elevated views of God's mercy; or else, "He will rise up to pity you" [G. V. SMITH]. Or [taking the previous clause as MAURER, "*Therefore* Jehovah will delay" in punishing you, "*in order that He may be gracious to you,*" if ye repent], He will be *far removed* from you [so in Ps. 10:5, *far above out of sight*]; i.e., He will not immediately descend to punish, "in order that He may have mercy, etc. **judgment**—justice; faithfulness to His covenant. **wait**—cf. vs. 15, wait, viz., for His times of having mercy. **19.** (Ch. 65:9.) The restoration from Babylon only typifies the *full* accomplishment of the prophecy (vss. 18-33). **weep no more**—(ch. 25:8.) **thy cry**—(ch. 26:8, 9; Jer. 29:12-14). **20.** Rather, "The Lord will give"; the "though" is not in the original. **bread of adversity**—He will not deny you food enough to save you in your adversity (I Kings 22:27; Ps. 127:2). **be removed**—rather, "hide themselves"; they shall no more be forced to hide themselves from persecution, but shall be openly received with reverence [MAURER]. Contrast with this Psalm 74:9; Amos 8: 11.

ADAM CLARKE

13. *Swelling out in a high wall*—"A swelling in a high wall." It has been observed before that the buildings of Asia generally consist of little better than what we call mud walls.

14. *He shall not spare*—"And spareth it not."

17. *At the rebuke of five shall ye flee*—"At the rebuke of five, ten thousand of you shall flee." In the second line of this verse a word is manifestly omitted, which should answer to *one thousand* in the first. "How should one chase a thousand, and two put ten thousand to flight?" Deut. xxxii. 30 "And five of you shall chase an hundred, and an hundred of you shall put ten thousand to flight," Lev. xxvi. 8.

18. *And therefore will he be exalted*—"Even for this shall he expect in silence."

19. *For the people shall dwell in Zion*—"When a holy people shall dwell in Sion." The word *kadosh,* lost out of the text, but happily supplied by the Septuagint, clears up the sense, otherwise extremely obscure. When the rest of the cities of the land were taken by the king of Assyria, Zion was preserved, and all that were in it. *Thou shalt weep no more*—"Thou shalt implore him with weeping."

MATTHEW HENRY

have faithful teachers among them, and should have hearts to regard them and not slight them as they had done; and then they might the better be reconciled to the bread of adversity and the water of affliction. It was a common saying among the old Puritans, *Brown bread and the gospel are good fare.* It seems that their teachers had been removed into corners. But God will find a time to call the teachers out of their corners again, and to replace them in their solemn assemblies. It is promised that they shall have the benefit, not only of the public ministry, but of private admonition and advice (*v.* 21): "*Thy ears shall hear a word behind thee*, calling after thee as a man calls after a traveller that he sees going out of his road." This word shall come—from *behind thee*, from someone whom thou dost not see, but who sees thee. "Thy eyes see thy teachers; but this is a teacher out of sight, it is thy own conscience, which shall now by the grace of God be awakened to do its office." The word shall be: *This is the way, walk you in it.* This word shall come *when you turn to the right hand or to the left.* There are right-hand and left-hand errors, extremes on each side virtue; the tempter is busy courting us into the by-paths. It is happy then if by the particular counsels of a faithful minister or friend, or the checks of conscience and the strivings of God's Spirit, we be set right and prevented from going wrong. "It shall not only be spoken, but thy ears shall hear it; whereas God has formerly *spoken once, yea, twice*, and thou *hast not perceived it* (Job xxxiii. 14), now thou shalt listen attentively to these secret whispers, and hear them with an obedient ear."

III. They shall be cured of their idolatry, shall fall out with their idols, and never be reconciled to them again, *v.* 22. They shall break off from their best-beloved sin. How mad they had formerly been in the day of their apostasy. They had *graven images of silver*, and *molten images of gold*, and, though gold needs no painting, they had coverings and ornaments on these; they spared no cost in doing honour to their idols. What a holy indignation they conceived against them in the day of their repentance. They not only degraded their images, but defaced them, in a pious fury threw away the gold and silver they were made of. Probably this was fulfilled in many persons, who, by the deliverance of Jerusalem from Sennacherib's army, were convinced of the folly of their idolatry and forsook it. It was fulfilled in the Jewish nation at their return from captivity in Babylon, for they abhorred idols ever after; and it is accomplished daily in the conversion of souls, by the power of divine grace, from spiritual idolatry to the fear and love of God.

IV. God will then give them plenty of all good things. When he gives them their teachers, and they give him their hearts, *then all other things shall be added to them*, Matt. vi. 33. And when the people are brought to praise God *then shall the earth yield her increase, and with it God, even our own God, shall bless us*, Ps. lxvii. 5, 6. So it follows here: "When you shall have abandoned your idols, *then shall God give the rain of your seed*," *v.* 23. God will give you rain to water the seed you sow. *Thou shalt sow the ground*, that is thy part, and then *God will give the rain of thy seed*, that is his part. It is so in spiritual fruit. The increase of the earth shall be *fat and fat*, very fat and very good, *fat and plenteous* (so we read it), good and enough of it. *The cattle shall feed in large pastures, shall eat clean provender.* The corn shall not be given them in the chaff to make it go the further, but they shall have good clean corn, *winnowed with the fan.* Even the tops of the mountains shall be so well watered with the rain that there shall be *rivers and streams* running down to the valleys (*v.* 25), and this *in the day of the great slaughter* made by the angel in the camp of the Assyrians, *when the towers* they had erected for the siege of Jerusalem, *should fall.*

V. The effect of all this should be comfort and joy to the people of God, *v.* 26. Light shall increase; that is, knowledge shall increase (when the prophecies are accomplished they shall be fully understood). *The light of the moon shall become as* bright and as strong as *that of the sun, and that of the sun* shall increase proportionably and be *as the light of seven days—when the Lord binds up the breach of his people*, heals the wounds that have been given them by this invasion and makes up all their losses. The light which the gospel brought into the world to those that sat in darkness as far exceeded the Old Testament light as that of the sun does that of the moon.

Verses 27–33

This terrible prediction of the ruin of the Assyrian army, is part of the promise to the Israel of God, that God would deter them from doing the like again.

I. God Almighty is here introduced in all the power

JAMIESON, FAUSSET, BROWN

21. word—conscience, guided by the Holy Spirit (John 16:13).

22. covering of . . . images—rather, "images" (formed of wood or potter's clay, and) "covered with silver." Hezekiah, and afterwards Josiah, defiled them (II Kings 23:8, 10, 14, 16; II Chron. 31:1; cf. ch. 2:20; Deut. 7:25).

23. rain of—rather, "*for thy* seed." Physical prosperity accompanies national piety; especially under the Old Testament. The *early* rain fell soon after the seed was sown in October or November; the *latter* rain in the spring, before the ripening of the corn. Both were needed for a good harvest. **increase**—the produce. **fat**—bread made of the best wheat flour (cf. Gen. 49:20; Deut. 32:14). **24 ear**—i.e. till. Asses were employed in tillage, as well as oxen (Deut. 22:10). **clean**—rather, *salted* provender [GESENIUS]. The Arab proverb is. Sweet provender is as bread to camels—salted provender as confectionery. The very cattle shall share the coming felicity. Or else, *well-fermented maslin*, i.e., provender formed of a mixture of various substances: grain, beans, vetches, hay, and salt. **winnowed**—not as it is usually given to cattle before it is separated from the chaff; the grain shall be so abundant that it shall be given winnowed. **shovel**—by which the grain was thrown up in the wind to separate it from the chaff. **fan**—an instrument for winnowing. **25.** Even the otherwise barren hills shall then be well watered (ch. 44:3). **the day . . .**—when the disobedient among *the Jews* shall have been slain, as foretold in vs. 16: "towers," i.e., mighty men (ch. 2:15). Or else, the *towers of the Assyrian Sennacherib*, or of *Babylon*, types of all enemies of God's people. **26.** Image from the heavenly bodies to express the increase of spiritual light and felicity. "Sevenfold" implies the *perfection* of that felicity, seven being the sacred number. It shall also be literally fulfilled hereafter in the heavenly city (ch. 60:19, 20; Rev. 21:23, 24; 22:5). **breach**—the wound, or calamity, sent by God on account of their sins (ch. 1:5).

ADAM CLARKE

21. *When ye turn to the right hand, and when ye turn to the left*—"Turn not aside, to the right or to the left."

22. *Ye shall defile*—"Ye shall treat as defiled." The very prohibition of Moses, Deut. vii. 25, only thrown out of the prose into the poetical form.

25. *When the towers fall*—"When the mighty fall."

26. *Shall be sevenfold.* The text adds *as the light of seven days*, a manifest gloss, taken in from the margin; it is not in most of the copies of the Septuagint. It interrupts the rhythmical construction, and obscures the sense by a false, or at least an unnecessary, interpretation. By *moon, sun, light*, are to be understood the abundance of spiritual and temporal felicity, with which God should bless them in the days of the Messiah, which should be sevenfold, i.e., vastly exceed all that they had ever before possessed.

MATTHEW HENRY

and all the terror of his wrath, *v.* 27. *The name of Jehovah*, which the Assyrians disdain, *behold, it comes from far*. He is a messenger of wrath, *burning with his anger*. God's *lips are full of indignation* at the blasphemy of Rabshakeh, who compared the God of Israel with the gods of the heathen; *his tongue is as a devouring fire*. He does not stifle his resentments, but *shall cause his glorious voice to be heard*, *v.* 30. He shall display *the indignation of his anger* as *the flame of a devouring fire*, with *lightning* and with *tempest and hailstones*.

II. The execution done by this anger of the Lord. God will *show the lighting down of his arm*, *v.* 30. Those that *would not see the lifting up of his arm* (*ch.* xxvi. 11) shall feel the lighting down of it, and find to their cost, that the burden thereof is heavy (*v.* 27). Five things are here for the execution: 1. Here is *an overflowing stream*, that *shall reach to the midst of the neck*. The Assyrian army had been to Judah *as an overflowing stream, reaching even to the neck* (*ch.* viii. 7, 8), and now the breath of God's wrath will be so to it. 2. Here is *a sieve of vanity*, with which God would sift those nations of which the Assyrian army was composed, *v.* 28. He will sift them so as to shake them one against another, put them into great consternation, and shake them all away at last; for it is a sieve of vanity. 3. Here is *a bridle* to restrain them from doing mischief, and to force them to serve God's purposes against their own will, *ch.* x. 7. 4. Here is *a rod* and *a staff*, even *the voice of the Lord*, giving orders with which *the Assyrian shall be beaten down*, *v.* 31. There is no escaping it. In every place where an Assyrian is found, the Lord shall *lay it upon him*, and cause it to rest, *v.* 32. 5. Here is *Tophet ordained* and *prepared* for them, *v.* 33. The valley of the son of Hinnom, adjoining to Jerusalem, was called *Tophet*. In that valley, it is supposed, many of the Assyrian regiments lay encamped, and were there slain by the destroying angel.

III. The Assyrian's fall in Jerusalem's triumph (*v.* 29): *You shall have a song as in the night*, a psalm of praise such as those sing who *by night stand in the house of the Lord*, and sing to his glory who *gives songs in the night*.

JAMIESON, FAUSSET, BROWN

27. name of . . . Lord—i.e., Jehovah Himself (Ps. 44:5; 54:1); represented as a storm approaching and ready to burst over the Assyrians (vss. 30, 31). **burden . . . is heavy**—lit., "grievousness is the flame," i.e., the flame which darts from Him is grievous. Or else (as the Hebrew means an "uplifting") *the uprising cloud is grievous* [G. V. SMITH]; the gathering cloud gradually rising till it bursts. **28.** (Ch. 11:4; II Thess. 2:8.) **reach . . . neck**—the most extreme danger; yet as the *head*, or capital of Judah, was to be spared (ch. 8: 8), so the head, or sovereign of Assyria, Sennacherib, should escape. **sieve of vanity**—Rather, the winnowing fan of destruction [LOWTH] (ch. 41:16). **bridle in . . . jaws**—as prisoners are represented in the Assyrian inscriptions (ch. 37:29). **causing . . . to err**—(ch. 63:17.) "People," *Hebrew*, "peoples," viz., the various races composing the Assyrian armies (ch. 5:26). **29. the night . . . solemnity**—As in the passover night ye celebrate your deliverance from Egypt, so shall ye celebrate your rescue from Assyrian bondage. Translate, "*the* solemnity" (Exod. 12:42). **goeth with a pipe**—or flute. They used to go up to Jerusalem ("the mountain of the Lord," Zion) at the three feasts with music and gladness (Deut. 16:16; Ezra 2:65; Ps. 122:1-4). **30.** Jehovah's "glorious voice," raised against the enemy (vs. 27), is again mentioned here, in contrast to the music (vs. 29) with which His people shall come to worship Him. **lighting down of . . . arm**—(V. 32; Ps. 38:2.) The descent of His arm in striking. **scattering**—viz., a blast that scatters, or an "inundation" [MAURER]. **31.** The Assyrian rod which beat shall itself be beaten, and that by the mere *voice* of the Lord, i.e., an unseen divine agency (ch. 10:5, 24). **32. grounded**—rather, decreed, appointed [MAURER]. **staff**—the avenging rod. **him**—the Assyrian; type of all God's enemies in every age. *Margin* and MAURER construe, "Every passing through (infliction, ch. 28:15) of the appointed rod, which, (etc.), shall be with tabrets," i.e., accompanied with joy on the part of the rescued peoples. **battles of shaking**—i.e., shock of battles (ch. 19:16; cf. "sift . . . sieve," vs. 28). **with it**—viz., Assyria. **33. Tophet**—lit., "A place of abomination"; the valley of the sons of Hinnom, southeast of Jerusalem, where Israel offered human sacrifices to Moloch by fire; hence a place of burning (II Kings 23:10; Jer. 7:31). Latterly Ge-hinnom or Gehenna, i.e., valley of Hinnom, was the receptacle of the refuse of the city, to consume which fires were constantly burning. Hence it came to express hell, the place of torment. In the former sense it was a fit place to symbolize the funeral pyre of the Assyrian army (not that it actually perished there); the Hebrews did not burn, but buried their dead, but the heathen Assyrians are to be burnt as a mark of ignominy. In the latter sense Tophet is the receptacle "prepared for the devil (antitype to the king, ch. 14:12-15) and his angels," and unbelieving men (Matt. 5:22; 25:41; Mark 9:43, 44).

ADAM CLARKE

27. *And the burden thereof is heavy*—"And the flame raged violently."

28. *To sift the nations with a sieve of vanity*—"To toss the nations with the van of perdition." Kimchi's explanation is to the following effect: "*Naphah* is a van with which they winnow corn; and its use is to cleanse the corn from the chaff and straw: but the van with which God will winnow the nations will be the van of emptiness or perdition; for nothing useful shall remain behind, but all shall come to nothing, and perish. In like manner, a bridle is designed to guide the horse in the right way; but the bridle which God will put in the jaws of the people shall not direct them aright, but shall make them err, and lead them into destruction."

30. *The Lord shall cause his glorious voice to be heard.* Kimchi understands this of the great destruction of the Assyrian host by the angel of the Lord.

31. *Which smote with a rod*—"He that was ready to smite with his staff."

32. *The grounded staff*—"The rod of his correction." *With tabrets and harps.* With every demonstration of joy and thanksgiving for the destruction of the enemy in so wonderful a manner; with hymns of praise, accompanied with musical instruments. See v. 29.

33. *For Tophet is ordained.* Tophet is a valley very near to Jerusalem, to the southeast, called also the valley of Hinnom or Gehenna; where the Canaanites, and afterwards the Israelites, sacrificed their children, by making them pass through the fire, that is, by burning them in the fire, to Molech, as some suppose. It is therefore used for a place of punishment by fire; and by our blessed Saviour in the gospel for hellfire, as the Jews themselves had applied it. Here the place where the Assyrian army was destroyed is called Tophet by a metonymy.

MATTHEW HENRY — CHAPTER 31

Verses 1–5

I. The sin here reproved, *v.* 1. They *go down to Egypt for help* in every exigence, as if the worshippers of false gods were more likely to have success on earth than the servants of the living and true God. The Egyptians had many chariots and horses and horsemen, and, if they could get forces thence into their service, they would think themselves able to deal with the king of Assyria. Slighting the God of Israel: *They look not to the Holy One of Israel*.

II. The absurdity of this sin. They do not seek the Lord, *yet he also is wise*, *v.* 2. Would not infinite wisdom, engaged on their side, stand them in more stead than all the policies of Egypt? They are at the pains of going down to Egypt, a tedious journey, when they might have had better help by looking up to heaven. But, if they will not court God's wisdom he *will arise against the house of the evil-doers*, this cabal of them that go down to Egypt. They trusted to those who were unable to help them and would soon appear to be so, *v.* 3. Let them know that *the Egyptians*, whom they depend so much upon, *are men and not God*. Everyone knows this, that the Egyptians are not God and their horses are not spirit; but those that seek to them for help do not consider it, else they would not put such confidence in them. The Egyptians were shortly to be reckoned with, as appears by the *burden of Egypt* (*ch.* xix), and then those who fled to them for shelter and succour should fall with them. They took God's work out of his hands. They pretended a great deal of care to preserve Jerusalem, in advising to an alliance with

JAMIESON, FAUSSET, BROWN — CHAPTER 31

Vss. 1-9. THE CHIEF STRENGTH OF THE EGYPTIAN ARMIES LAY IN THEIR CAVALRY. In their level and fertile plains horses could easily be used and fed (Exod. 14:9; I Kings 10:28). In hilly Palestine horses were not so easily had or available. The Jews were therefore the more eager to get Egyptian chariots as allies against the Assyrian cavalry. In Assyrian sculptures chariots are represented drawn by three horses, and with three men in them (see ch. 36:9; Ps. 20:7; Dan. 9:13). **2. he also is wise**—as well as the Egyptian priests, so famed for wisdom (Acts 7:22), but who are "fools" before Him (ch. 19:11). He not only devises, but executes what He devises without "calling back His words" (Num. 23: 19).

house—the whole race. **help**—the Egyptian succor sought by the Jews. **3. not spirit**—not of divine power (Ps. 56:4; 146:3, 5; Zech. 4:6). **he that helpeth**—Egypt. **holpen**—Judah.

ADAM CLARKE — CHAPTER 31

1. *Woe to them that go down to Egypt.* This is a reproof to the Israelites for forming an alliance with the Egyptians, and not trusting in the Lord. *And stay on horses*—"Who trust in horses."

3. *He that helpeth* (the Egyptians) *shall fall, and he that is holpen* (the Israelites) *shall fall down . . . together.*

MATTHEW HENRY

Egypt. Now the prophet here tells them that Jerusalem should be preserved without aid from Egypt and that those who tarried there should be safe when those who fled to Egypt should be ruined. God would appear against Jerusalem's enemies with the boldness of a *lion over his prey, v.* 4. When the lion comes out to seize his prey *a multitude of shepherds come out against him.* These shepherds dare not come near the lion; all they can do is to make a *noise,* and with that they think to frighten him. But does he regard it? *No; he will not be afraid of their voice. Thus will the Lord of hosts come down to fight for Mount Zion,* will as easily and irresistibly destroy the Assyrian army as a lion tears a lamb in pieces. Whoever appear against God, they are but like a multitude of poor simple shepherds shouting at a lion. God would appear for Jerusalem's friends with the tenderness of a bird over her young, *v.* 5. *As birds flying* to their nests with all possible speed, when they see them attacked, hovering over their young ones to protect them drive away the assailants, with such compassion and affection *will the Lord of hosts defend Jerusalem. Defending, he will deliver it. Passing over he will preserve it;* the word for passing over is used in this sense only here and Exod. xii. 12, 13, 27, concerning the destroying angel's passing over the houses of the Israelites when he slew all the first-born of the Egyptians. The Assyrian army was to be routed by a destroying angel who should pass over Jerusalem. They shall be slain by the pestilence, but none of the besieged shall take the infection. Thus he will again pass over the houses of his people and secure them.

Verses 6–9

I. Jerusalem, reformed, shall be delivered from her enemies, *v.* 6, 7. This was the Lord's voice crying in the city, and the voice of the prophets interpreting the judgment: "*Turn you* from your evil ways, *unto God,* return to your allegiance to him from whom you, *O children of Israel!* have revolted." He reminds them of their birth and parentage. They have been backsliding children, yet children; therefore let them return, and their backslidings shall be healed. A gracious promise (*v.* 7): *In that day every man shall cast away his idols,* in obedience to Hezekiah's orders, which, till they were alarmed by the Assyrian invasion, many refused to do. That is a happy fright which frightens us from our sins. It shall be a general reformation: every man shall cast away his own idols. It shall be a reformation upon a principle of piety, not of politics. They shall cast away their idols, because they have been unto them *for a sin,* an occasion of sin.

II. Jerusalem's besiegers shall be routed. When they have cast away their idols, *then shall the Assyrian fall, v.* 8, 9. 1. The army of the Assyrians shall be laid dead upon the spot, by the sword of the Lord in the hand of an angel. The king of Assyria shall flee from that invisible sword to some stronghold of his own. *His princes* that accompany him *shall be afraid of the ensign,* of every ensign they see, suspecting it is a party of the Jews pursuing them. But who will do this? It is *the Lord, whose fire is in Zion and his furnace in Jerusalem.* God there keeps house, as a man does where his fire and his oven are. Let not the Assyrians think to turn him out of the possession of his own house. He is himself *a wall of fire round about Jerusalem,* so that whoever assaults her does so at his peril.

JAMIESON, FAUSSET, BROWN

4. (Ch. 42:13; Hos. 11:10.) **roaring on**—"growling over" his prey. **abase himself**—be disheartened or frightened.

5. As in the image of "the lion," the point of comparison is the fearless might of Jehovah; so in that of the birds, it is His solicitous affection (Deut. 32:11; Ps. 91:4; Matt. 23:37). **flying**—Rather, "which defend" their young with their wings; "to fly" is a secondary meaning of the Hebrew word [MAURER]. "Hovering over" to protect their young [G. V. SMITH]. **passing over**—as the destroying angel *passing over, so as to spare* the blood-marked houses of the Israelites on the first passover (Exod. 12:13, 23, 27). He passed, or *leaped forward* [LOWTH], to *destroy* the enemy and to spare His people.

6. The power and love of Jehovah, just mentioned, are the strongest incentives for returning to Him (Ezek. 16:62, 63; Hos. 6:1). **ye . . . Israel**—The change of person marks that when they return to the Lord, He will address them in more direct terms of communion in the second person; so long as they were *revolters,* God speaks *of* them, as more at a distance, in the third person, rather than *to* them. **7.** In the day of trial the idols will be found to render no help and will therefore be cast away. Cf. as to the future restoration and conversion of Israel simultaneously with the interposition of Jehovah in its defense, Zechariah 12:9-14; 13:1, 2. **for a sin**—i.e., whereby especially you contracted guilt (I Kings 12:30). **8. Assyrian**—Sennacherib, representative of some powerful head of the ungodly in the latter ages [HORSLEY]. **sword, not of . . . mighty . . . mean man**—but by the unseen sword of God. **flee**—Sennacherib alone *fled* homewards after his army had been destroyed (ch. 37:37). **young men**—the flower of his army. **discomfited**—rather, "shall be subject to slavery"; lit., shall be liable to tribute, i.e., personal service (Deut. 20:11; Josh. 9:21) [MAURER]. Or, not so well, "shall melt away" [ROSENMULLER]. **9.** Rather, *"shall pass beyond* his strongholds"; he shall not stop to take refuge in it through fear (Judg. 20:47; Jer. 48:28) [GESENIUS]. **ensign**—the banner of Jehovah protecting the Jews [MAURER]. **fire . . . furnace**—"light" and "fire," viz., of Jehovah's *altar* at Jerusalem (ch. 29:1). Perhaps "furnace," as distinguished from "fire," may mean that His *dwelling-place* (His hearth) was at Jerusalem (cf. ch. 4:5); or else the *fiery furnace* awaiting all the enemies who should attack Jerusalem.

ADAM CLARKE

5. *Passing over*—"Leaping forward." The generality of interpreters observe in this place an allusion to the deliverance which God vouchsafed to His people when He destroyed the firstborn of the Egyptians, and exempted those of the Israelites sojourning among them by a peculiar interposition. The same word is made use of here which is used upon that occasion, and which gave the name to the feast which was instituted in commemoration of that deliverance, *pesach.* But the difficulty is to reconcile the commonly received meaning of that word with the circumstances of the similitude here used to illustrate the deliverance represented as parallel to the deliverance in Egypt. The common meaning of the word *pasach* upon other occasions is "to halt, to be lame, to leap," as in a rude manner of dancing (as the prophets of Baal did, 1 Kings xviii. 26), all which agrees very well together; for the motion of a lame person is a perpetual springing forward, by throwing himself from the weaker upon the stronger leg. The common notion of God's passage over the houses of the Israelites is that in going through the land of Egypt to smite the firstborn, seeing the blood on the door of the houses of the Israelites, He passed over, or skipped, those houses, and forbore to smite them. But that this is not the true notion of the thing will be plain from considering the words of the sacred historian, where he describes very explicitly the action: "For Jehovah will pass through to smite the Egyptians; and when He seeth the blood on the lintels and on the two side posts, Jehovah will spring forward over (or before) the door, and will not suffer the destroyer to come into your houses to smite you" (see Exod. xii. 23). Here are manifestly two distinct agents, with which the notion of passing over is not consistent, for that supposes but one agent. The two agents are the destroying angel passing through to smite every house and Jehovah, the Protector, keeping pace with him; and who, seeing the door of the Israelite marked with the blood, *leaps forward,* throws himself with a sudden motion in the way, opposes the destroying angel, and covers and protects that house against the destroying angel, nor suffers him to smite it. In this way of considering the action, the beautiful similitude of the bird protecting her young answers exactly to the application by the allusion to the deliverance in Egypt.

6. *Have deeply revolted*—"Have so deeply engaged in revolt."

7. *Which your own hands have made unto you for a sin*—"The sin, which their own hands have made."

8. *Then shall the Assyrian fall.* Because he was to be discomfited by the angel of the Lord, destroying in his camp, in one night, upwards of one hundred and eighty thousand men; and Sennacherib himself fell by the hands of the princes, his own sons. Not mighty men, for they were not soldiers; not mean men, for they were princes.

MATTHEW HENRY — CHAPTER 32

Verses 1–8

The description of a flourishing kingdom. It may be taken as a directory both to magistrates and subjects, what both ought to do, or as a panegyric to Hezekiah.

I. That magistrates should do their duty in their places, and the powers answer the great ends for which they were ordained, *v.* 1, 2. The princes must have a king, a monarch over them as supreme, in whom they may unite; and the king must have princes under him as officers, by whom he may act, 1 Pet. ii. 13, 14. They shall use their power according to law, and not against it. They shall reign in righteousness with wisdom and equity. Christ himself reigns by rule. Thus they shall be great blessings to the people (*v.* 2): *A man,* that king that reigns in righteousness, *shall be as a hiding-place.* When princes are as they should be people are as they would be. This good magistrate is a covert to the subject from the tempest of injury and violence; he *defends the poor and fatherless.* He is *as rivers of water in a dry place,* cooling the earth and making it fruitful, and *as the shadow of a great rock,* under which a poor traveller

JAMIESON, FAUSSET, BROWN — CHAPTER 32

Vss. 1-20. MESSIAH'S KINGDOM; DESOLATIONS, TO BE SUCCEEDED BY LASTING PEACE, THE SPIRIT HAVING BEEN POURED OUT. The times of purity and happiness which shall follow the defeat of the enemies of Jehovah's people (vss. 1-8). The period of wrath before that happy state (vss. 9-14). The assurance of the final prosperity of the Church is repeated (vss. 15-20). **1. king**—not Hezekiah, who was already on the throne, whereas a *future* time is contemplated. If he be meant at all, it can only be as a type of Messiah the King, to whom alone the language is fully applicable (Hos. 3:5; Zech. 9:9; see ch. 11:3-5, *Notes*). The kingdom shall be transferred from the world kings, who have exercised their power *against* God, instead of *for* God, to the rightful King of kings (Ezek. 21:27; Dan. 7:13, 14). **princes**—subordinate; referring to all in authority under Christ in the coming kingdom on earth, e.g., the apostles, etc. (Luke 22:30; I Cor. 6:2; II Tim. 2:12; Rev. 2:26, 27; 3:21). **2. a man**—rather, *the man* Christ [LOWTH]; it is as "the Son of man" He is to reign, as it was as Son of man He suffered

ADAM CLARKE — CHAPTER 32

1. *Behold, a king shall reign in righteousness.* If King Hezekiah were a type of Christ, then this prophecy may refer to His time; but otherwise it seems to have Hezekiah primarily in view. It is evident, however, that in the fullest sense these words cannot be applied to any man; God alone can do all that is promised here.

MATTHEW HENRY

may shelter from the scorching heat. All this, and much more, the man Christ Jesus is to all the willing faithful subjects of his kingdom. In him we find rivers of water for those that hunger and thirst after righteousness, all the refreshment that a needy soul can desire, and the shadow of a rock, of a great rock, for the shelter of the traveller. As the covert, and the hiding-place, and the rock, do themselves receive the battering of the wind and storm, to save those that take shelter in them, so Christ bore the storm himself to keep it off from us.

II. That subjects should do their duty in their places. They shall be willing to be taught, and shall lay aside their prejudices against their rulers and teachers, and submit to the light and power of truth, *v.* 3. When this blessed work of reformation is set on foot, and men do their parts towards it, *the eyes of those that see*, of the prophets, the seers, *shall not be dim*; but God will bless them with visions, to be by them communicated to the people. Then *the ears of those that hear* the word preached *shall hearken.* There shall be a wonderful change wrought in them, *v.* 4. *The heart of those that were* hasty and *rash*, shall now be cured of their precipitation, and *shall understand knowledge*; for the Spirit of God will open their understanding. This blessed work Christ wrought in his disciples after his resurrection (Luke xxiv. 45, 1 John v. 20.) *The tongue of the stammerers*, that used to blunder whenever they spoke of the things of God, *shall* now *be ready to speak plainly*, as those that understand, believe, and therefore speak. The differences between good and evil shall be no more confounded by those who put darkness for light and light for darkness (*v.* 5): *The vile shall no more be called liberal. Vile* persons, when they are advanced, are called *liberal* and *bountiful benefactors* (Luke xxii. 25): but when the world grows wiser, men shall be preferred according to their merit. Bad men shall be no more had in reputation among the people. In short, it is well with a people when men are valued by their virtue, and usefulness, and beneficence to mankind, and not by their wealth or titles of honour. To enforce this rule, here is a description both of the vile person and of the liberal. A vile person and a churl will do mischief the more if he have power in his hand; his honours will make him worse, *v.* 6, 7. These base ill-conditioned men are always plotting some unjust thing. There appears not in them the least spark of generosity. The more there is of plot and management in a sin the more there is of Satan in it. They *speak villainy.* When they are in a passion you will see what they are by the base ill language they give to those about them. They *utter error against the Lord*, and therein they practise profaneness; for so the word which we translate *hypocrisy* signifies. Nothing can be more impudently done against God than to use his name to patronise wickedness. Instead of supplying the wants of the poor, they impoverish them, they *make empty the souls of the hungry*; either taking away the food they have or denying the supply which they have to give. And they *cause the drink of the thirsty to fail*; they cut off the relief they used to have, though they need it as much as ever. These churls and vile persons have always bad instruments about them, that are ready to serve their villainous purposes: *All their servants are wicked.* One that is truly liberal, and deserves the honour of being called so, makes it his business to do good to everybody according as his sphere is, *v.* 8. He *devises liberal things.* Charity must be directed by wisdom, that it may not be charity misplaced. *By liberal things he shall stand.* The providence of God will reward him with a settled prosperity and an established reputation. The grace of God will give him peace in his own bosom.

Verses 9–20

In these verses we have God rising up to judgment against the vile persons, but returning in mercy to the liberal, to reward them for their liberality.

I. When there was so great a corruption of manners bad times might well be expected. The alarm is sounded to the *women that were at ease* (*v.* 9) and the *careless daughters*, to feed whose pride and luxury, their husbands and fathers were tempted to starve the poor. "*Rise up, and hear* with reverence and attention."

1. God was about to bring wasting desolating judgments upon the land in which they *lived in pleasure and were wanton.* This seems to refer primarily to the desolations made by Sennacherib's army when he seized all the fenced cities of Judah: but those words, *many days and years*, must be rendered (as the margin reads them) *days above a year*, that is, something above a year shall this havoc be in the making: so long it was from the first entrance of that army into the land of Judah to the overthrow of it. *You shall*

JAMIESON, FAUSSET, BROWN

(Matt. 26:64; John 5:27; 19:5). Not as MAURER explains, "*every* one of the princes shall be," etc. **rivers**—as refreshing as water and the cool shade are to the heated traveller (ch. 35:6, 7; 41:18).

3. them that see—the seers or prophets. **them that hear**—the people under instruction (ch. 35:5, 6). **4. rash**—rather, the hasty; contrast "shall not make haste" (ch. 28:16); the reckless who will not take time to weigh religious truth aright. Or else, the well-instructed [HORSLEY].

stammers—those who speak confusedly on divine things (cf. Exod. 4:10-12; Jer. 1:6; Matt. 10:19, 20). Or, rather, those drunken *scorners* who in stammering style imitated Isaiah's warnings to mock them [MAURER] (ch. 28:7-11, 13, 14. 22; 29:20); in this view, translate, "speak *uprightly*" (agreeably to the divine law); not as *English Version*, referring to the distinctness of articulation, "plainly." **5. vile**—rather, "fool" [LOWTH]; i.e., ungodly (Ps. 14:1; 74:18). **liberal**—rather, "noble-minded." **churl**—rather, "fraudulent" [GESENIUS]. **bountiful**—religiously. The atheistic churl, who envies the believer his hope "full of immortality," shall no longer be held as a patriot struggling for the emancipation of mankind from superstition [HORSLEY].

6. vile . . . villainy—rather, "the (irreligious) fool—(his) folly." **will speak**—rather, present; for (so far is the "fool" from deserving the epithet "noble-minded") the fool "speaketh" folly and "worketh", etc. **hypocrisy**—rather, "profligacy" [HORSLEY]. **error**—impiety, perverse arguments. **hungry**—spiritually (Matt. 5:6).

7. churl—"the fraudulent"; this verse refers to the last clause of vs. 5; as vs. 6 referred to its first clause. **speaketh right**—pleadeth a just cause (ch. 29:21); spiritually, "the poor man's cause" is the divine doctrine, his rule of faith and practice. **8. liberal**—rather, "noble-minded." **stand**—shall be approved under the government of the righteous King.

9-20. Address to the women of Jerusalem who troubled themselves little about the political signs of the times, but lived a life of self-indulgence (ch. 3:16-23); the failure of food through the devastations of the enemy is here foretold, being what was most likely to affect them as mothers of families, heretofore accustomed to every luxury. VITRINGA understands "women—daughters" as the cities and villages of Judea (Ezek. 16). See Amos 6:1.

10. Many days and years—rather, "In little more than a year" [MAURER]; lit., days upon a year (so ch. 29).

ADAM CLARKE

2. *As the shadow of a great rock.* The shadow of a great projecting rock is the most refreshing that is possible in a hot country, not only as most perfectly excluding the rays of the sun, but also as having in itself a natural coolness, which it reflects and communicates to everything about it.

3. *And the eyes of them that see shall not be dim*—"And him the eyes of those that see shall regard."

5. *The vile person—nabal,* the pampered, fattened, brainless fellow, who eats to live, and lives to eat; who will scarcely part with anything, and that which he does give he gives with an evil eye and a grudging heart. *Liberal—nadib;* the generous, openhearted, princely man. *The churl—kilai,* the avaricious man; he who starves himself amidst his plenty, and will not take the necessaries of life for fear of lessening his stock. Thus he differs from *nabal,* who feeds himself to the full, and regards no one else; like the rich man in the Gospel. The avaricious man is called *kilai,* from *ki,* "for," and *li,* "myself"; or contracted from *col,* "all," and *li,* "to myself." All is mine; all I have is my own; and all I can get is for myself. *Bountiful—shoa,* he who is abundantly rich; who rejoices in his plenty, and deals out to the distressed with a liberal hand.

6. *The vile person will speak villany*—"The fool will still utter folly."

7. *The instruments also of the churl are evil*—"As for the niggard, his instruments are evil." His machinations, his designs. *To destroy the poor with lying words*—"To defeat the assertions of the poor in judgment."

8. *Liberal things*—"Generous purposes."

9. From this verse to the end of the fourteenth, the desolation of Judea by the Chaldeans appears to be foretold.

MATTHEW HENRY

be troubled, you careless women. The prophet here tells them the country whence they had their rents and dainties should shortly be laid waste: "*The vintage shall fail;* and then what will you do for wine to make merry with? *The gathering* of fruit *shall not come*, for there shall be none to be gathered, *v.* 10. You will want *the teats*, the good milk from the cows, *the pleasant fields* and their productions." The cities of Judah, where they lived at ease should be laid waste (*v.* 13, 14): *Briers and thorns*, the fruits of sin and the curse, *shall come up*, not only *upon the land of my people*, but upon *all the houses of joy in the joyous cities.* Then the stately houses *shall be for dens for ever*, which had been as forts and towers for strength and magnificence.

2. In the foresight of this let them *tremble* and *be troubled, strip themselves, and gird sackcloth upon their loins*, *v.* 11. This intimates not only that God's judgments would strip them, but that the best prevention of the trouble would be to repent and humble themselves before God in true remorse and godly sorrow. The best preparation for the trouble would be to deny themselves and to sit loose to all the delights of sense.

II. While there was still a remnant that kept their integrity they had reason to hope for good times at length. Such times they saw in the latter end of the reign of Hezekiah; but the prophecy may well be supposed to look further, to the days of the Messiah, who is *King of righteousness* and *King of peace.* Those blessed times shall be introduced—by the *pouring out of the Spirit from on high* (*v.* 15), which speaks not only of the good-will of God towards us, but the good work of God in us. God's *giving his Holy Spirit to those that ask him* is in effect his giving them all good things, as appears by comparing Luke xi. 13 with Matt. vii. 11. This is the great thing that God's people comfort themselves with the hopes of, that *the Spirit shall be poured out upon them.* When God designs favours for his church he pours out his Spirit to qualify those whom he designs to employ as instruments of his favour. (The kingdom of the Messiah was brought in, and set up, by the pouring out of the Spirit (Acts ii), and so it will be to the end.) That which was *a wilderness*, dry and barren, *shall become a fruitful field. Then shall the earth yield her increase.* It is promised that in the days of the Messiah the *fruit of the earth shall shake like Lebanon*, Ps. lxxii. 16. Some apply this to the admission of the Gentiles into the gospel church. When the Spirit is poured out upon a land, *then judgment shall dwell in the wilderness* and turn it into a fruitful field, and *righteousness shall remain in the fruitful field* and make it yet more fruitful. Ministers shall expound the law and magistrates execute it, so judiciously and faithfully that the bad shall be made good and the good made better. Among all sorts of people, the poor and low and unlearned, that are neglected as the wilderness, and the rich and great and learned, that are valued as the fruitful field, there shall be right thoughts of things. Inward peace, *v.* 17, follows upon the indwelling of righteousness, *v.* 16. It is itself peace, and the effect of it is *quietness and assurance for ever*, that is, a holy serenity and security of mind. Those are the quiet and peaceable lives that are spent *in all godliness and honesty*, 1 Tim. ii. 2. Even *the work of righteousness shall be peace.* In the doing of our duty we shall find true pleasure. Though the work of righteousness may be toilsome and expose us to contempt, yet it is peace. *The effect of righteousness shall be quietness and assurance*, to the endless ages of eternity. When the terror of Sennacherib's invasion was over, the people were more sensible than ever of the mercy of a quiet habitation, not disturbed with the alarms of war. Let every family keep itself quiet from strifes and jars within the house, and put itself under God's protection. Jerusalem shall be a peaceable habitation; compare *ch.* xxxiii. 20. Even *when it shall hail*, and there shall be a violent battering storm *coming down on the forest* that lies bleak, then shall Jerusalem be *a quiet resting-place, for the city shall be low in a low place*, under the wind, not exposed to the fury of the storm, but sheltered by the *mountains that are round about Jerusalem*, Ps. cxxv. 2. There shall be good crops gathered in everywhere, and every year. God will give the increase, but the husbandman must be industrious, and sow beside all waters; and, if he do this, the corn shall come up so thick that he shall turn in his cattle, even the ox and the ass, to eat the tops of it and keep it under. Some think it points at the ministry of the apostles, who, as husbandmen, went forth to sow their seed (Matt. xiii. 3) beside all waters. When God sends these happy times blessed are those that improve them in doing good with what they have, that sow beside all waters.

JAMIESON, FAUSSET, BROWN

vintage shall fail—through the arrival of the Assyrian invader. As the wheat harvest is omitted, Isaiah must look for the invasion in the summer or autumn of 714 B.C., when the wheat would have been secured already, and the later fruit "gathering," and vintage would be still in danger. **11. strip you**—of your gay clothing. (*Note*, ch. 2). **12. lament for . . . teats**—rather, shall smite on their breasts in lamentation "for thy pleasant fields" (Nah. 2:7) [MAURER]. "Teats" in *English Version* is used for fertile lands, which, like *breasts*, nourish life. The transition from "ye" to "they" (vss. 11, 12) is frequent. **13.** (Ch. 5:6; 7:23.) **houses of joy**—pleasure-houses outside of Jerusalem, not Jerusalem itself, but other cities destroyed by Sennacherib in his march (ch. 7:20-25). However, the prophecy, in its full accomplishment, refers to the *utter* desolation of Judea and its *capital* by Rome, and subsequently, previous to the second coming of the King (Ps. 118:26; Luke 13:35; 19:38); "the joyous city" is in this view, Jerusalem (ch. 22:2). **14. palaces**—most applicable to Jerusalem (*Note*, vs. 13). **multitude . . . left**—the noisy din of the city, i.e., the city with its noisy multitude shall lie forsaken [MAURER]. **forts**—rather, Ophel (i.e. the mound), the term applied specially to the declivity on the east of Zion, surrounded with its own wall (II Chron. 27:3; 33:14; II Kings 5:24), and furnished with "towers" (or watch-towers), perhaps referred to here (Neh. 3:26, 27). **for ever**—limited by thee, "until," etc., next verse, *for a long time*. **15.** This can only partially apply to the spiritual revival in Hezekiah's time; its full accomplishment belongs to the Christian dispensation, first at Pentecost (Joel 2:28; Acts 2:17), perfectly in coming times (Ps. 104:30; Ezek. 36:26; 39:29; Zech. 12:10), when the Spirit shall be poured on Israel, and through it on the Gentiles (Mic. 5:7).

wilderness . . . fruitful field . . . forest—when Judea, so long waste, shall be populous and fruitful, and the land of the enemies of God shall be desolate. Or, "the field, now fruitful, shall be but as a barren forest in comparison with what it shall be then" (ch. 29:17). The barren shall become fruitful by regeneration; those already regenerate shall bring forth fruits in such abundance that their former life shall seem but as a wilderness where no fruits were. **16. judgment**—justice. **wilderness**—then reclaimed. **fruitful field**—then become more fruitful (vs. 15); thus "wilderness" and "fruitful field" include the *whole* land of Judea.

17. work—the effect (Prov. 14:34; Jas. 3:18). **peace**—internal and external.

18. sure . . . quiet—free from fear of invasion. **19.** Lit., "But it shall hail with coming down of the forest, and in lowness shall the city (Nineveh) be brought low; i.e., humbled." The "hail" is Jehovah's wrathful visitation (ch. 30:30; 28:2, 17). The "forest" is the Assyrian host, dense as the trees of a forest (ch. 10:18, 19, 33, 34; Zech. 11:2). **20.** While the enemy shall be brought "low," the Jews shall cultivate their land in undisturbed prosperity. **all waters**—well-watered places (ch. 30:25). The *Hebrew* translation, "beside," ought rather to be translated, "upon" (Eccles. 11:1), where the meaning is, "Cast thy seed upon the waters when the river overflows its banks; the seed will sink into the mud and will spring up when the waters subside, and you will find it after many days in a rich harvest." Before sowing, they send oxen, etc., into the water to tread the ground for sowing. CASTALIO thinks there is an allusion to the Mosaic precept, not to plough with an ox and ass together, mystically implying that the Jew was to have no intercourse with Gentiles; the Gospel abolishes this distinction (Col. 3:11); thus the sense here is, Blessed are ye that sow the gospel seed without distinction of race in the teachers or the taught. But there is no need of supposing that the ox and ass here are *yoked together;* they are probably "sent forth" separately, as in ch. 30:24.

ADAM CLARKE

12. *They shall lament . . . for the pleasant fields*—"Mourn ye for the pleasant field."

13. *Shall come up thorns and briers*—"The thorn and the brier shall come up." The description of impending distress which begins at v. 13 belongs to other times than that of Sennacherib's invasion, from which they were so soon delivered. It must at least extend to the ruin of the country and city by the Chaldeans. And the promise of blessings which follows was not fulfilled under the Mosiac dispensation; they belong to the kingdom of Messiah. Compare v. 15 with chap. xxix. 17.

14. *The forts*—"Ophel." It was a part of Mount Zion, rising higher than the rest, at the eastern extremity, near to the Temple, a little to the south of it; called by Micah, chap. iv. 8, "Ophel of the daughter of Zion." It was naturally strong by its situation; and had a wall of its own, by which it was separated from the rest of Zion.

17. *The work of righteousness.* Righteousness works and produces peace.

19. *The city shall be low in a low place.*—"The city shall be laid level with the plain." *The city*—probably Nineveh or Babylon; but this verse is very obscure.

20. *That sow beside all waters*—"Who sow your seed in every well-watered place."

MATTHEW HENRY

CHAPTER 33

Verses 1–12

I. The proud and false Assyrian, for all his fraud and violence, laid under a woe, *v.* 1. He had spoiled the people of God, and broken his treaty of peace with them, and dealt treacherously. He spoiled those that had never done him any injury, and that he had no pretence to quarrel with, and dealt treacherously with those that had always dealt faithfully with him. He that spoiled the cities of Judah shall have his own army destroyed by an angel. The Chaldeans shall deal treacherously with the Assyrians and revolt from them. Two of Sennacherib's own sons shall deal treacherously with him and basely murder him at his devotions. When he shall have done his worst, when he shall have gone as far as God would permit him to go, then the cup of trembling shall be put into his hand.

II. The praying people of God, earnest at the throne of grace for mercy for the land now in its distress (*v.* 2): "*O Lord! be merciful to us.*" They prayed, 1. For those that were employed in military services for them: "*Be thou their arm every morning.* Hezekiah, and his princes, and all the men of war, need continual supplies of strength and courage from thee. Every morning, when they go forth and perhaps have new work to do and new difficulties to encounter, let them be invigorated, and, *as the day, so let the strength be.*" 2. For the body of the people: "*Be thou our salvation also in the time of trouble*, ours who sit still, and do not venture into the high places of the field." They depend upon God not only as their Saviour, to work deliverance for them, but as their salvation itself.

III. The Assyrian army ruined and their camp made a rich but easy prey to Judah and Jerusalem. No sooner is the prayer made (*v.* 2) than it is answered (*v.* 3), it is outdone. They prayed that God would save them from their enemies; but he did more than that; he gave them victory over their enemies. The strength of the Assyrian camp was broken (*v.* 3) when the destroying angel slew so many thousands of them: *At the noise of the tumult* the rest of *the people fled.* The spoil of the Assyrian camp is seized, by way of reprisal, for all the desolations of the defenced cities of Judah (*v.* 4): *Your spoil shall be gathered* by the inhabitants of Jerusalem, *like the gathering of the caterpillar*, and *as the running to and fro of locusts*, that is, the spoilers shall as easily and as quickly make themselves masters of the riches of the Assyrians as a host of caterpillars, or locusts make a field, or a tree, bare.

IV. The spoil of the enemy is thus gathered (*v.* 5): *The Lord is exalted.* His people will have the blessing of it. When God lifts up himself to scatter the nations in confederacy against Jerusalem (*v.* 3), *he has filled Zion with judgment and righteousness*, a sense of justice. It shall again be called, *The city of righteousness, ch.* i. 26. Hezekiah and his people are encouraged (*v.* 6) with an assurance that God would stand by them in their distress. *Wisdom and knowledge shall be the stability of thy times, and strength of salvation.* Here is a desirable end, that is *the stability of our times*, that things be not disturbed at home, and the *strength of salvation*, deliverance from enemies abroad. Here is also pious maxim of state for Hezekiah and his people to govern themselves by: *The fear of the Lord is his treasure.* True religion is the true treasure of any prince or people; it denominates them rich.

V. The great distress that Jerusalem was brought into described. It is here foretold, 1. That the enemy would be very insolent and there would be no dealing with him, either by treaties of peace (*for he has broken the covenant* as if it were below him to be a servant to his word), or by the preparations of war, for *he has despised the cities*; he scorns their petitions for mercy. He meets with so little resistance, that he despises them, and has no relentings when he puts all to the sword. He neither fears God nor regards man. 2. That therefore he would not be brought to any terms of reconciliation. *The ambassadors* sent by Hezekiah to treat *of peace*, finding him so unmanageable, *shall weep bitterly* for vexation like children, as despairing to find out any expedient to pacify him. 3. That the country should be made quite desolate for a time by his army. No man durst travel the roads; so that a stop was put to trade and commerce: *The highways lie waste. The traveller ceases.* No man had any profit from the grounds, *v.* 9. The desolation is universal. That part of the country which belonged to the ten tribes was already laid waste: "*Lebanon* famed for cedars, *Sharon* for roses, *Bashan* for cattle, *Carmel* for corn, all very fruitful, have now become like wildernesses, *are ashamed* to be called by their own names, they are so unlike what they were. They *shake off their fruits* before their time

JAMIESON, FAUSSET, BROWN

CHAPTER 33

Vss. 1-24. The Last of Isaiah's Prophecies as to Sennacherib's Overthrow (vs. 19). Vss. 1, 8, 9, describe the Assyrian spoiler; strong as he is, he shall fall before Jehovah who is stronger (vss. 2-6, 10-12). The time is the autumn of 713 B.C. **1. and thou**—i.e., though thou wast not spoiled—though thou wast not dealt treacherously with (*Note*, ch. 24:16), thy spoiling and treachery are therefore without excuse, being unprovoked. **cease**—When God has let thee do thy worst, in execution of His plans, thine own turn shall come (cf. ch. 10:12; 14:2; Hab. 2:8; Rev. 13:10).

2. us; we . . . their . . . our—He speaks interceding for His people, separating himself in thought for a moment from them, and immediately returns to his natural identification with them in the word "our." **every morning**—each day as it dawns, especially during our danger, as the parallel "time of trouble" shows.

3. the tumult—the approach of Jehovah is likened to an advancing thunderstorm (ch. 29:6; 30:27), which is His voice (Rev. 1:15), causing the people to "flee." **nation**—the Assyrian levies. **4.** The invaders' "spoil" shall be left behind by them in their flight, and the Jews shall gather it. **caterpillar**—rather, the wingless locust; as it gathers; the *Hebrew* word for "gathers" is properly used of the gathering of the fruits of harvest (ch. 32:10). **running to and fro**—viz., in gathering harvest fruits. **he**—rather, "they." **them**—rather, "it," i.e., the prey.

6. wisdom—sacred; i.e., piety. **thy**—Hezekiah's; or rather, Judea's. "His" refers to the same; such changes from the pronoun possessive of the second person to that of the third are common in Hebrew poetry. **treasure**—Not so much material wealth as piety shall constitute the riches of the nation (Prov. 10:22; 15:16).

7-9. From the vision of future glory Isaiah returns to the disastrous present; the grief of "the valiant ones" (parallel to, and identical with, "the ambassadors of peace"), men of rank, sent with presents to sue for peace, but standing "without" the enemy's camp, their suit being rejected (II Kings 18:14, 18, 37). The highways deserted through fear, the cities insulted, the lands devastated. **cry**—(ch. 15:4). **8. broken . . . covenant**—When Sennacherib invaded Judea, Hezekiah paid him a large sum to leave the land; Sennacherib received the money and yet sent his army against Jerusalem (II Kings 18:14, 17). **despised**—make slight of as unable to resist him (ch. 10:9; 36:19); easily captures them. **9.** (Ch. 24:4.) **Lebanon**—personified; the allusion may be to the Assyrian cutting down its choice trees (ch. 14:8; 37:24). **Sharon**—south of Carmel, along the Mediterranean, proverbial for fertility (ch. 35:2). **Bashan**—afterwards called Batanea (ch. 2:13). **fruits**—rather, understand "leaves"; they lie as desolate as in winter.

ADAM CLARKE

CHAPTER 33

The plan of the prophecy continued in this chapter, and which is manifestly distinct from the foregoing, is peculiarly elegant. To set it in a proper light, it will be necessary to mark the transitions from one part of it to another.

In v. 1 the prophet addresses himself to Sennacherib, expressing the injustice of his ambitious designs, and the sudden disappointments of them. In v. 2 the Jews are introduced offering up their earnest supplications to God in their present distressful condition.

In vv. 3 and 4 the prophet in the name of God, or rather God himself, is introduced addressing himself to Sennacherib, and threatening him that, notwithstanding the terror which he had occasioned in the invaded countries, yet he should fall. In vv. 5-6 a chorus of Jews is introduced, acknowledging the mercy and power of God, who had undertaken to protect them; extolling it with direct opposition to the boasted power of their enemies, and celebrating the wisdom and piety of their king, Hezekiah, who had placed his confidence in the favor of God.

Then follows, in vv. 7-9, a description of the distress and despair of the Jews, upon the king of Assyria's marching against Jerusalem, and sending his summons to them to surrender, after the treaty he had made with Hezekiah on the conditions of his paying, as he actually did pay to him, 300 talents of silver and 30 talents of gold, 2 Kings xviii. 14-16. In v. 10, God himself is again introduced, declaring that He will interpose in this critical situation of affairs, and disappoint the vain designs of the enemies of His people, by discomfiting and utterly consuming them.

Then follows, vv. 11-22, still in the person of God, which however falls at last into that of the prophet, a description of the dreadful apprehensions of the wicked in those times of distress and imminent danger; finely contrasted with the confidence and security of the righteous, and their trust in the promises of God that He will be their never-failing Strength and Protector. The whole concludes, in the person of the prophet, with a description of the security of the Jews under the protection of God, and of the wretched state of Sennacherib and his army, wholly discomfited, and exposed to be plundered even by the weakest of the enemy.

1. *And dealest treacherously*—"Thou plunderer." *When thou shalt make an end to deal treacherously*—"When thou art weary of plundering."

2. *Be thou their arm every morning*—"Be Thou our Strength every morning."

3. *At the noise of the tumult*—"From Thy terrible voice."

6. *His treasure*—"Thy treasure."

7. *Their valiant ones shall cry without*—"The mighty men raise a grievous cry."

9. *Bashan and Carmel shake off their fruits*—"Bashan and Carmel are stripped of their beauty."

MATTHEW HENRY

into the hand of the spoiler."

VI. God appearing, at length, against this proud invader, *v.* 10–12. He had seemed to sit by as an unconcerned spectator. He will not only demonstrate that there is a God that judges, but that he is God over all. When all other helpers fail, then is God's time to help. He will bring down the Assyrian. O Assyrians! *You shall conceive chaff, and bring forth stubble*, which is worthless and combustible, proper fuel for the fire, which it cannot escape, when *your* own *breath as fire shall devour you*. The threatenings and slaughter you breathe out against the people of God, this shall devour you. God would make their own breath to blow the fire that should consume them; and then no wonder that the people are *as the burnings of lime* in a lime-kiln, and *as thorns cut up*, which are withered, and therefore are soon burnt up. Such was the destruction of the Assyrian army.

Verses 13–24

What has God done in which we must acknowledge his might?

I. He has struck a terror upon the sinners in Zion (*v.* 14): *Fearfulness has surprised the hypocrites.* There are sinners that enjoy Zion's privileges and services, but their hearts are not right in the sight of God. Now those sinners in Zion, though always subject to secret rights and terrors, were struck with a more than ordinary consternation from the convictions of their own consciences. When they saw the Assyrian army besieging Jerusalem, and ready to set fire to it, they could not make their escape to Egypt, and distrusting the promises God had made by his prophets, they were at their wits' end, crying: "*Who among us shall dwell with devouring fire?* Let us therefore abandon the city, and shift for ourselves elsewhere." Or, it may mean that they saw the Assyrian army destroyed; for the destruction of that is the fire spoken of immediately before, *v.* 11, 12. When the sinners in Zion saw what dreadful execution the wrath of God made they were in a great fright, being conscious that they had provoked this God by secretly worshipping other gods.

II. He has graciously provided for the security of his people that trust in him: *Hear this, and acknowledge his* power in making those that *walk righteously*, and *speak uprightly*, to *dwell on high*, *v.* 15, 16. We have here,

1. The good man's character even in times of common iniquity: He walks righteously. He acts by rules of equity, rendering to all their due, to God his due, as well as to men theirs. He speaks uprightly, *uprightness* (so the word is); he speaks with an honest intention. He thinks it a mean and sordid thing to enrich himself by any hardship put upon his neighbour. If he have a bribe at any time thrust into his hand, to prevent justice, *he shakes his hands from holding it*, taking it as an affront to have it offered him. *He stops his ears from hearing* anything that tends to cruelty, or any suggestions stirring him up to revenge, Job xxxi. 31. He *shuts his eyes from seeing evil*. He has such an abhorrence of sin that he cannot bear to see others commit it. Those that would preserve the purity of their souls must stop their ears to temptations, and turn away their eyes from beholding vanity.

2. The good man's comfort, which he may preserve even in times of common calamity, *v.* 16. He shall be safe; shall have communion with that God who is a devouring fire, but shall be to him a rejoicing light. And, as to present troubles, *he shall dwell on high*; he shall not be really harmed by them. *The floods of great waters shall not come nigh him;* or, if they should attack him, *his place of defence shall be the munitions of rocks*, fortified by nature as well as art. God, the rock of ages, will be his high tower. He shall want nothing that is necessary for him: *Bread shall be given him*, even when the siege is straitest; and *his waters shall be sure*. Those that fear the Lord shall not want anything that is good for them.

III. He will protect Jerusalem, and deliver it out of the hands of the invaders. Hezekiah shall put off his sackcloth and shall appear publicly in his beauty, in his royal robes (*v.* 17), to the great joy of all his loving subjects. Those that walk uprightly shall with an eye of faith see the King of kings in his beauty, the beauty of holiness, and that beauty shall be upon them. The siege being raised, they shall now be at liberty to go abroad without danger of falling into the enemies' hand: *They shall behold the land that is very far off;* they shall visit the utmost corners of the nation. Thus believers behold the heavenly Canaan, that land that is very far off, and comfort themselves with the prospect of it in evil times. The remembrance of the fright they were in shall add to the pleasure of their deliverance (*v.* 18): *Thy heart shall meditate terror* with pleasure when it is over. Thou

JAMIESON, FAUSSET, BROWN

10. The sight of His people's misery arouses Jehovah; He has let the enemy go far enough. **I**—emphatic; God Himself will do what man could not. **11. Ye**—the enemy. **conceive chaff**—ch. 26:18; 59:4.) **your breath**—rather, *your own spirit* of anger and ambition [MAURER], (ch. 30:28).

12. (Ch. 9:19; Amos 2:1.) Perhaps alluding to their being about to be burnt on the funeral pyre (ch. 30: 33). **thorns**—the wicked (II Sam. 23:6, 7).

13. far off—distant nations. **near**—the Jews and adjoining peoples (ch. 49:1). **14. sinners in Zion**—false professors of religion among the elect people (Matt. 22: 12). **hypocrites**—rather, the profane; the abandoned [HORSLEY].

who, etc.—If Jehovah's wrath could thus consume such a host in one night, who could abide it, if continued for ever (Mark 9:46-48)? Fire is a common image for the divine judgments (ch. 29:6; 30:30). **among us**—If such awful judgments have fallen on those who knew not the true God, how infinitely worse shall fall on *us* who, amid religious privileges and profession, sin against God (Luke 12:47, 48; Jas 4:17)?

15. In contrast to the trembling "sinners in Zion" (vs. 14), the righteous shall be secure amid all judgments; they are described according to the Old Testament standpoint of righteousness (Ps. 15:2; 24:4). **stoppeth . . . ears . . . eyes**—"Rejoiceth not in iniquity" (I Cor. 13:6; contrast ch. 29:20; Ps. 10:3; Rom. 1:32). The senses are avenues for the entrance of sin (Ps. 119: 37).

16. on high—heights inaccessible to the foe (ch. 26:1).

bread . . . waters—image from the expected siege by Sennacherib; however besieged by trials without, the godly shall have literal and spiritual food, as God sees good for them (ch. 41:17; Ps. 37: 25; 34:10; 132:15). **17. Thine**—the saints'. **king in . . . beauty**—not as now, Hezekiah in sackcloth, oppressed by the enemy, but King Messiah (ch. 32: 1) "in His beauty" (Song of Sol. 5:10, 16; Rev. 4:3).

land . . . very far off—rather, the land in its remotest extent (no longer pent up as Hezekiah was with the siege); see *Margin*. For Jerusalem is made the scene of the king's glory (vs. 20, etc.), and it could not be said to be "very far off," unless the far-off land be *heaven*, the Jerusalem above, which is to follow the *earthly* reign of Messiah at literal Jerusalem (ch. 65:17-19; Jer. 3:17; Rev. 21:1, 2, 10). **18. meditate**—on the "terror" caused by the enemy, but now past. **where,** etc.—the language of the Jews exulting over their escape from danger. **scribe**—who

ADAM CLARKE

11. *Your breath*—"And my spirit."

14. *The sinners in Zion are afraid.* Zion has been generally considered as a type of the Church of God. Now all the members of God's Church should be holy, and given to good works; sinners in Zion, therefore, are portentous beings! but, alas! where are they not?

15. *That stoppeth his ears from hearing of blood*—"Who stoppeth his ears to the proposal of bloodshed."

MATTHEW HENRY

shalt think thou still hearest the alarm in thy ears, "Arm, arm, arm! every man to his post. *Where is the scribe* or secretary of war? Let him appear to draw up the muster-roll. *Where is the receiver* and pay-master of the army? Let him see what he has in bank, to defray the charge of a defence. *Where is he that counted the towers?* That care may be taken to put a competent number of men in each." They shall no more be terrified with the sight of the Assyrians, who were a fierce people, and were of a strange language, that could understand neither their petitions nor their complaints, and therefore had a pretence for being deaf to them, nor could themselves be understood: They are *of a deeper speech than thou canst perceive, v.* 19. "*Look upon Zion, the city of our solemnities*, the city where our solemn sacred feasts are kept, where we used to meet to worship God in religious assemblies." The good people were most in pain for Zion upon this account, that the conquerors would burn their temple. Two things are here promised to Jerusalem: 1. A well-grounded security. It shall be *a quiet habitation* for the people of God; they shall not be disturbed, as they have been, by the alarms of war or persecution, *ch.* xxix. 20. "*Thou shalt see the good of Jerusalem, and peace upon Israel;* thou shalt live to see it and share in it." 2. An unmoved stability. Jerusalem, the city of our solemnities, is indeed but *a tabernacle*, in comparison with the New Jerusalem. **The present manifestations of the divine glory and grace are nothing in comparison with those that are reserved for the future** state. But it is such a tabernacle as *shall not be taken down.* After this trouble is over Jerusalem shall long enjoy a confirmed peace; and her sacred privileges, which are the stakes and cords of her tabernacle, shall not be removed from her. God's church on earth is a tabernacle, which, though it may be shifted from one place to another, shall not be taken down while the world stands; for in every age Christ will have a seed to serve him. The promises of the covenant are its stakes, and the ordinances and institutions of the gospel are its cords, which shall never be broken. God himself will be their protector and Saviour, *v.* 21, 22. This is the principal ground of their confidence. God will be the Saviour of Jerusalem and her glorious Lord. He will be *a place of broad rivers and streams.* Jerusalem had no considerable river running by it, so wanted one of the best natural fortifications, as well as one of the greatest advantages for trade and commerce; but the presence and power of God are sufficient at any time to make up to us the deficiencies. If there be broad rivers and streams about Jerusalem, these are rivers and streams *in which shall go no galley with oars.* "*For the Lord is our Judge*, by whose judgment we abide. *He is our lawgiver;* and to him every thought is brought into obedience. *He is our King*, to whom we pay homage and therefore *he will save us.*" The enemies shall be broken, like a ship at sea that cannot ride out the storm, but having her tackle torn, her masts split, and nothing wherewith to repair them, is given up for a wreck, *v.* 23. They thought themselves sure of Jerusalem; but when they were just entering the port as it were, and thought all was their own, they *could not spread their sail.* The wealth of their camp shall be a rich booty for the Jews: *Then is the prey of a great spoil divided.* They *left their tents as they were*, so that all the treasure in them fell into the hands of the besieged; and even *the lame take the prey.* Thus God brought good out of evil, and not only delivered Jerusalem, but enriched it. Both sickness and sin shall be taken away. *The inhabitant shall not say, I am sick. As the lame shall take the prey*, so shall the sick. There shall be such a universal transport of joy that even the sick shall forget their sickness and join in rejoicings; the deliverance of their city shall be their cure. Or those that are sick shall bear their sickness without complaining as long as they see it goes well with Jerusalem. *The people that dwell therein shall be forgiven their iniquity.* Sin is the sickness of the soul. When God pardons the sin he heals the disease.

JAMIESON, FAUSSET, BROWN

enrolled the army [MAURER]; or, who prescribed the tribute to be paid [ROSENMULLER]; or, who kept an account of the spoil. "The principal scribe of the host" (II Kings 25:19; Jer. 52:25). The Assyrian records are free from the exaggerations of Egyptian records. Two scribes are seen in every Assyrian bas-relief, writing down the various objects brought to them, the heads of the slain, prisoners, cattle, sheep, etc. **receiver**—*Margin,* weigher. LAYARD mentions, among the Assyrian inscriptions, "a pair a scales for weighing the spoils." **counted . . . towers**—he whose duty it was to reconnoitre and report the strength of the city to be besieged. **19. fierce people**—The Assyrians shall not be allowed to enter Jerusalem (II Kings 19:32). Or, thou shalt not any longer see fierce enemies threatening thee as previously; such as the Assyrians, Romans, and the last Antichristian host that is yet to assail Jerusalem (Deut. 28:49, 50; Jer. 5:15; Zech. 14:2). **stammering**—barbarous; so "deeper," etc., i.e., unintelligible. The Assyrian tongue differed only in dialect from the Hebrew, but in the Assyrian levies were **many of non-Semitic race and language, as the Medes, Elamites, etc. (*Note*, ch. 28:11). 20. solemnities**—solemn assemblies at the great feasts (*Notes*, ch. 30:29; Ps. 42:4; 48:12). **not . . . taken down . . . removed**—image from captives "removed" from their land (ch. 36:17). There shall be no more "taking away" to an enemy's land. Or else, from nomads living in shifting tents. The saints, who sojourned once in tabernacles as pilgrims, shall have a "building of God—eternal in the heavens" (II Cor. 5:1; Heb. 11:9, 10; cf. ch. 54:2). **stakes**—driven into the ground; to these the "cords" were fastened. Christ's Church shall never fall (Matt. 16:18). So individual believers (Rev. 3:12). **21. there**—viz., in Jerusalem. **will be . . . rivers**—Jehovah will be as a broad river surrounding our city (cf. ch. 19:6; Nah. 3:8), and this, too, a river of such a kind as no ship of war can pass (cf. ch. 26:1). Jerusalem had not the advantage of a river; Jehovah will be as one to it, affording all the advantages, without any of the disadvantages of one. **galley with oars**—war-vessels of a long shape, and propelled by oars; merchant vessels were broader and carried sail. **gallant**—same *Hebrew* word as for "glorious," previously; "mighty" will suit both places; a ship of war is meant. No "mighty vessel" will dare to pass where the "mighty Lord" stands as our defense. **22. Lord**—thrice repeated, as often: the Trinity (Num. 6:24-26). **judge . . . lawgiver . . . king**—perfect ideal of the theocracy, to be realized under Messiah alone; the judicial, legislative, and administrative functions as king to be exercised by Him in person (ch. 11:4; 32:1; Jas. 4:12). **23. tacklings**—Continuing the allegory in vs. 21, he compares the enemies' host to a war-galley which is deprived of the tacklings or cords by which the mast is sustained and the sail is spread; and which therefore is sure to be wrecked on "the broad river" (vs. 21), and become the prey of Israel. **they**—the tacklings, "hold not firm the base of the mast." **then**—when the Assyrian host shall have been discomfited. Hezekiah had given Sennacherib three hundred talents of silver, and thirty of gold (II Kings 18:14-16), and had stripped the temple of its gold to give it to him; this treasure was probably part of the prey found in the foe's camp. After the invasion, Hezekiah had so much wealth that he made an improper display of it (II Kings 20:13-15); this wealth, probably, was in part got from the Assyrian. **the lame**—Even the most feeble shall spoil the Assyrian camp (cf. ch. 35:6; II Sam. 5:6). **24. sick**—SMITH thinks the allusion is to the beginning of the pestilence by which the Assyrians were destroyed, and which, while sparing the righteous, affected some within the city (**"sinners in Zion"**); it may have been the sickness that visited Hezekiah (ch. 38). In the Jerusalem to come there shall be no "sickness," because there will be no "iniquity," it being forgiven (Ps. 103:3). The latter clause of the verse contains the cause of the former (Mark 2:5-9).

ADAM CLARKE

18. *Where is the scribe?* The person appointed by the king of Assyria to estimate their number and property in reference to their being heavily taxed.

Where is the receiver? Or he who was to have collected this tribute. *Where is he that counted the towers?* That is, the commander of the enemy's forces, who surveyed the fortifications of the city, and took an account of the height, strength, and situation of the walls and towers, that he might know where to make the assault with the greatest advantage.

20. *Look upon Zion*—"Thou shalt see Zion."

21. *The glorious Lord*—"The glorious name of Jehovah."

23. *Thy tacklings are loosed.* Here the Assyrians are represented under the figure of a ship wrecked by a violent storm; and the people on the beach, young, old, feeble, and diseased, gathering the spoil without any to hinder them. *Their mast*—"Thy mast."

24. *And the inhabitant shall not say.* This verse is somewhat obscure. The meaning of it seems to be that the army of Sennacherib shall by the stroke of God be reduced to so shattered and so weak a condition that the Jews shall fall upon the remains of them, and plunder them without resistance; that the most infirm and disabled of the people of Jerusalem shall come in for their share of the spoil; the lame shall seize the prey; even the sick and the diseased shall throw aside their infirmities, and recover strength enough to hasten to the general plunder. The last line of the verse is parallel to the first, and expresses the same sense in other words. Sickness being considered as a visitation from God, a punishment of sin, the forgiveness of sin is equivalent to the removal of a disease. Thus the Psalmist: "Who forgiveth all thy sin; and healeth all thine infirmities" (see Ps. ciii. 3). That this prophecy was exactly fulfilled, I think we may gather from the history of this great event given by the prophet himself. It is plain that Hezekiah, by his treaty with Sennacherib, by which he agreed to pay him 300 talents of silver and 30 talents of gold, had stripped himself of his whole treasure. He not only gave him all the silver and gold that was in his own treasury and in that of the Temple, but was even forced to cut off the gold from the doors of the Temple and from the pillars, with which he had himself overlaid them, to satisfy the demands of the king of Assyria. But after the destruction of the Assyrian army, we find that he "had exceeding much riches," and that "he made himself treasuries for silver, and for gold, and for precious stones," 2 Chron. xxxii. 27. He was so rich that out of pride and vanity he displayed his wealth to the ambassadors from Babylon. This cannot be otherwise accounted for than by the prodigious spoil that was taken on the destruction of the Assyrian army. And thus, in the providence of God, he had the wealth which was exacted from him restored.

CHAPTER 34

CHAPTER 34

Vss. 1-17. JUDGMENT ON IDUMEA. Chapters 34 and 35 form one prophecy, the former part of which denounces God's judgment against His people's enemies, of whom Edom is the representative; the second part, of the flourishing state of the Church consequent on those judgments. **This forms the** termination of the prophecies of the **first** part of Isaiah (chs. 36-39 being historical) and is a kind of summary of what went before, setting forth the one main truth, ***Israel shall be delivered from all its foes, and happier times shall succeed under Messiah.* 1.**

CHAPTER 34

This and the following chapter make one distinct prophecy; an entire, regular, and beautiful poem, consisting of two parts: the first containing a denunciation of divine vengeance against the enemies of the people or Church of God, the second describing the flourishing state of the Church of God consequent upon the execution of those judgments. The event foretold is represented as of the highest importance, and of universal concern. All nations are called upon to attend to the declaration

MATTHEW HENRY

Verses 1–8

I. The war proclaimed, *v.* 1. All nations must hear and hearken because they are all concerned in it; God is angry with them; his indignation is upon all nations.

II. The manifesto published, setting forth,

1. Whom he makes war against (*v.* 2): *The indignation of the Lord is upon all nations;* they are all in confederacy against God and religion, all in the interests of the devil. As they have all had the benefit of his patience, so they must all expect now to feel his resentments. *His fury is* in a special manner *upon all their armies.* With them they have done mischief to the people of God. With them they hope to make their part good against the justice and power of God; and therefore on them, in the first place, God's fury will come.

2. Whom he makes war for, and what are the grounds and reasons of the war (*v.* 8): *It is the day of the Lord's vengeance.* As there is a day of the Lord's patience, so there will be a day of his vengeance; for, though he bear long, he will not bear always. It is *the year of recompences for the controversy of Zion.* Zion is the holy city, a type and figure of the church of God in the world. Zion has a just quarrel with her neighbours for the wrongs they have done her. She has left it to God to plead her cause, and he will do so when the time shall have come.

III. The operations of the war. The sword of the Lord is *bathed in heaven, v.* 5. It may allude to some custom they had of bathing their swords in some liquor or other, to harden them or brighten them, Ezek. xxi. 9–11. God's sword is bathed in heaven, in his counsel and decree, in his justice and power. *It shall come down upon Idumea, the people of God's curse,* the people that lie under his curse. God's sword of war is always a sword of justice. Pursuant to the sentence, a terrible slaughter shall be made among them (*v.* 6). When the day of God's abused mercy and patience is over the sword of his justice gives no quarter. Men have by sin lost the honour of the human nature and made themselves like the beasts that perish; they are therefore killed as beasts, and no more is made of slaying an army of men than of butchering a flock of lambs or goats and feeding on the fat of the kidneys of rams. Nay, the sword of the Lord shall not only dispatch the lambs and goats, the poor common soldiers, but (*v.* 7) *the unicorns* too *shall* be made to *come down with them, and the bullocks with the bulls—the great men, and the mighty men, and the chief captains,* make as easy a prey as the lambs and the goats. The greatest of men are nothing before the wrath of the great God. Even *the mountains,* which are hard and rocky, *shall be melted with their blood, v.* 3. These expressions are hyperbolical and are made use of because they sound very dreadful to sense. This great slaughter will be a great sacrifice to the justice of God (*v.* 6). Sacrifices were intended for the honour of God, to make it appear that he hates sin and demands satisfaction for it, and that nothing but blood will make atonement. And thus would the whole earth have been soaked with the blood of sinners if Jesus Christ, the great propitiation, had not shed his blood for us. These slain shall be detestable to mankind (*v.* 3). The effect shall be universal confusion and desolation, as if the whole frame of nature were dissolved and melted down (*v.* 4). *The heavens* themselves *shall be rolled together as a scroll* of parchment when we have done with it, and when it is shrivelled up by the heat of the fire. The stars shall fall as the leaves in autumn; all the beauty, joy, and comfort, of the vanquished nation shall be lost and done away, magistracy and government shall be abolished.

Verses 9–17

This prophecy describes the melancholy changes that are often made by the divine Providence, in countries, cities, palaces, and families. Places that have flourished go to decay. We know not where to find the places where many great towns, celebrated in history, once stood. It describes the judgments which are the just punishment which God will inflict when *the year of the redeemed has come,* and *the year of recompenses for the controversy of Zion.* Those that aim to ruin the church can never do that, but will infallibly ruin themselves.

I. The country shall become like the lake of Sodom, *v.* 9, 10. *The streams thereof,* that watered the land and refreshed the inhabitants, *shall* now *be turned into pitch,* shall be congealed. *The dust thereof shall be turned into brimstone;* so combustible has sin made their land that it shall take fire at the first spark of God's wrath. It shall burn continually, and *shall not be quenched night nor day.* The torment of those in hell, or that have a hell within them in their own consciences, is without interruption. As long as there are provoking sinners on earth, *from one*

JAMIESON, FAUSSET, BROWN

All creation is summoned to hear God's judgments (Ezek. 6:3; Deut. 32:1; Ps. 50:4; Mic. 6:1, 2), for they set forth His glory, which is the end of creation (Rev. 15:3; 4:11). **that come forth of it**—answering to "all that is therein"; or *Hebrew,* "all whatever fills it," *Margin.* **2. utterly destroyed**—rather, doomed them to an utter curse [HORSLEY]. **delivered**—rather, appointed. **3. cast out**—unburied (ch. 14:19). **melted**—washed away as with a descending torrent. **4.** (Ps. 102:26; Joel 2:31; 3:15; Matt. 24:29.) **dissolved**—(II Pet. 3:10-12.) Violent convulsions of nature are in Scripture made the *images* of great changes in the human world (ch. 24: 19-21), and shall *literally* accompany them at the winding up of the present dispensation. **scroll**—Books were in those days sheets of parchment rolled together (Rev. 6:14). **fall down**—The stars shall fall when the heavens in which they are fixed pass away. **fig tree**—(Rev. 6:13). **5. sword**—(Jer. 46:10.) Or else, *knife* for sacrifice for God does not here appear as a warrior with His sword, but as one about to sacrifice victims doomed to slaughter [VITRINGA], (Ezek. 39:17.) **bathed**—rather "intoxicated," viz., with anger (so Deut. 32:42). "In heaven" implies the place where God's *purpose* of wrath is formed in antithesis to its "coming down" in the next clause. **Idumea**—originally extending from the Dead Sea to the Red Sea; afterwards they obtained possession of the country east of Moab, of which Bozrah was capital. Petra or Selah, called Joktheel (II Kings 14:7), was capital of South Edom (*Note,* ch. 16:1). David subjugated Edom (II Sam. 8:13, 14). Under Jehoram they regained independence (II Chron. 21: 8). Under Amaziah they were again subdued, and Selah taken (II Kings 14:7). When Judah was captive in Babylon, Edom, in every way, insulted over her fallen mistress, killed many of those Jews whom the Chaldeans had left, and hence was held guilty of fratricide by God (Esau, their ancestor, having been brother to Jacob): this was the cause of the denunciations of the prophets against Edom (ch. 63:1, etc.; Jer. 49:7; Ezek. 25:12-14; 35:3-15; Joel 3:19; Amos 1:11, 12; Obadiah 8, 10, 12-18; Mal. 1:3, 4). Nebuchadnezzar humbled Idumea accordingly (Jer. 25: 15-21). **of my curse**—i.e., doomed to it. **to judgment**—i.e., to execute it. **6. filled**—glutted. The image of a sacrifice is continued. **blood . . . fat**—the parts especially devoted to God in a sacrifice (II Sam. 1:22). **famos . . . goats**—*sacrificial* animals: the Idumeans, of all classes, doomed to slaughter, are meant (Zeph. 1:7). **Bozrah**—called *Bostra* by the Romans, etc., assigned in Jeremiah 48:24 to Moab, so that it seems to have been at one time in the dominion of Edom, and at another in that of Moab (ch. 63:1; Jer. 49:13, 20, 22); it was strictly not in Edom, but the capital of Auranitis (the *Houran*). Edom seems to have extended its dominion so as to include it (cf. Lam. 4:21). **7. unicorns**—*Hebrew, reem:* conveying the idea of loftiness, power, and pre-eminence (see *Note,* Job 39:9), in the Bible. At one time the image in the term answers to a reality in nature; at another it symbolizes an abstraction. The rhinoceros was the original type. The Arab *rim* is two-horned: it was the oryx (the *leucoryx,* antelope, bold and pugnacious); but when accident or artifice deprived it of one horn, the notion of the unicorn arose. Here is meant the portion of the Edomites which was strong and warlike. **come down**—rather, "fall down," slain [LOWTH]. **with them**—with the "lambs and goats," the less powerful Edomites (vs. 6). **bullocks . . . bulls**—the young and old Edomites: *all* classes. **dust**—ground. **8. recompenses for the controversy of Zion**—i.e., the year when God will retaliate on those who have contended with Zion. Her controversy is *His.* Edom had thought to extend its borders by laying hold of its neighbor's lands and has instigated Babylon to cruelty towards fallen Judah (Ps. 137:7; Ezek. 36:5); therefore Edom shall suffer the same herself (Lam. 4:21, 22). The final winding up of the controversy between God and all enemies of Him and His people is also foreshadowed (ch. 61: 2; 63:4; 66:14-16; Mal. 4:1, 3; II Thess. 1:7, 8, 9; Rev. 11:18; 18:20; 19:2). **9.** Images from the overthrow of Sodom and Gomorrah (Gen. 19:24-28; so Deut. 29:23; Jer. 49:17, 18). **10. It**—The burning pitch, etc. (vs. 9). **smoke . . . for ever**—(Rev. 14:11; 18:18: 19:3). **generation to generation**—(Mal. 1:4). **none . . . pass through**—Edom's original offense was: they would not let Israel *pass through* their land in peace to Canaan: God *"recompenses"* them in kind, no traveller shall *pass through* Edom. VOLNEY, the infidel, was forced to confirm the truth of this prophecy: "From the reports of the Arabs, southeast of the Dead Sea, *within three days' journey* are upwards of thirty ruined towns, *absolutely deserted."* **11. cormorant**—The *Hebrew* is rendered, in Psalm

ADAM CLARKE

of it; and the wrath of God is denounced against all the nations, that is, all those that had provoked to anger the Defender of the cause of Zion. Among those, Edom is particularly specified. The principal provocation of Edom was their insulting the Jews in their distress, and joining against them with their enemies, the Chaldeans; see Amos i. 11; Ezek. xxv. 12; xxxv. 15; Ps. cxxxvii. 7. Accordingly the Edomites were, together with the rest of the neighboring nations, ravaged and laid waste by Nebuchadnezzar; see Jer. xxv. 15-26; Mal. i. 3-4. The general devastation spread through all these countries by Nebuchadnezzar may be the event which the prophet has primarily in view in the thirty-fourth chapter. But this event, as far as we have any account of it in history, seems by no means to come up to the terms of the prophecy, or to justify so highly wrought and terrible a description; and it is not easy to discover what connection the extremely flourishing state of the people of God described in the next chapter could have with those events, and how the former could be the consequence of the latter, as it is there represented to be. By a figure, very common in the prophetical writings, any city or people, remarkably distinguished as enemies of the people and kingdom of God, is put for those enemies in general. This seems here to be the case with Edom and Botsra. It seems, therefore, reasonable to suppose, with many learned expositors, that this prophecy has a further view to events still future; to some great revolutions to be effected in later times, antecedent to that more perfect state of the kingdom of God upon earth, and serving to introduce it, which the Holy Scriptures warrant us to expect.

That the thirty-fifth chapter has a view beyond anything that could be the immediate consequence of those events is plain from every part, especially from the middle of it, vv. 5-6, where the miraculous works wrought by our blessed Saviour are so clearly specified that we cannot avoid making the application; and our Saviour himself has moreover plainly referred to this very passage, as speaking of Him and His works, Matt. xi. 4-5. He bids the disciples of John to go and report to their master the things which they heard and saw, that the blind received their sight, the lame walked, and the deaf heard; and leaves it to him to draw the conclusion in answer to his inquiry, whether He who performed the very works which the prophets foretold should be performed by the Messiah was not indeed the Messiah himself. And where are these works so distinctly marked by any of the prophets as in this place? and how could they be marked more distinctly? To these the strictly literal interpretation of the prophet's words directs us. According to the allegorical interpretation, they may have a further view. This part of the prophecy may run parallel with the former, and relate to the future advent of Christ; to the conversion of the Jews, and their restitution to their land; to the extension and purification of the Christian faith; events predicted in the Holy Scriptures as preparatory to it.

1. *Hearken*—"Attend unto me."

5. *For my sword shall be bathed in heaven*—"For my sword is made bare in the heavens."

6. *The Lord hath a sacrifice*—"For Jehovah celebrateth a sacrifice." Ezekiel, chap. xxxix. 16-17, has manifestly imitated this place of Isaiah. He has set forth the great leaders and princes of the adverse powers under the same emblems of goats, bulls, rams, fatlings, and has added to the boldness of the imagery, by introducing God as summoning all the fowls of the air, and all the beasts of the field, and bidding them to the feast which He has prepared for them by the slaughter of the enemies of His people.

The sublime author of the Revelation, chap. xix. 17-18, has taken this image from Ezekiel, rather than from Isaiah.

7. *The unicorns shall come down. Reemim,* translated "wild goats" by Bishop Lowth.

8. *The year of recompences for the controversy of Zion*—"The year of recompense to the Defender of the cause of Zion."

MATTHEW HENRY

generation to another, it will be found, how light soever men make of it, that it is a *fearful thing to fall into the hands of the living God*.

II. The cities shall become like old decayed houses, deserted, being commonly possessed by beasts of prey or birds of ill omen. God shall mark them for ruin and destruction. *He shall stretch out upon Bozrah the line of confusion with the stones* or plummets *of emptiness, v.* 11. The confusion and emptiness that shall overspread the face of the whole country shall be like that of the whole earth when it was *Tohu and Bohu* (the very words here used)—*without form and void*. Gen. i. 2. Sin will soon turn a paradise into a chaos, and sully the beauty of the whole creation. When there is confusion there will soon be emptiness. Their great men shall be all cut off, and none of them shall dare to appear (*v.* 12): *They shall call the nobles of the kingdom* to take care of the arduous affairs which lie before them, but none shall be there.

III. Even the houses of state shall become as wildernesses (*v.* 13); *thorns shall come up, in her palaces, nettles and brambles in the fortresses thereof*.

IV. They shall become the residence and rendezvous of fearful beasts and birds. This desolation is much enlarged upon, *v.* 11. *The cormorant shall possess it*, or the pelican, which affects to be solitary (Ps. cii. 6); and *the bittern*, which makes a hideous noise, *the owl*, a melancholy bird, *the raven*, a bird of prey, invited by the dead carcases, shall dwell there, all the unclean birds, not for the service of man, *v.* 13. That which was a court for princes shall now be for owls or ostriches, *v.* 14. *The wild beasts of the desert* shall meet with the wild beasts of the island, the wet marshy country. *The satyr shall cry to his fellow* to go with him to this desert place. There shall *the screech-owl rest. The great owl shall there make her nest* (v. 15) *and lay and hatch. The vultures*, which feast on carcases, *shall be gathered there, every one with his mate*. What a dismal change sin makes; it turns a fruitful land into barrenness, a frequented city into a wilderness.

V. Here is an assurance given of the accomplishment of this prediction (*v.* 16, 17): *Seek you out of the book of the Lord and read*. What God's word has appointed his Spirit will effect and bring about, for no word of God shall fall to the ground. There is an exact order and proportion observed: *He has cast the lot* for these birds and beasts, so that each one shall know his place. *They shall not break their ranks, neither shall one thrust another*. Jerusalem of old recovered itself out of its ruins, till it gave place to the gospel Jerusalem, which may be brought low, but shall be rebuilt, and shall continue till it give place to the heavenly Jerusalem.

JAMIESON, FAUSSET, BROWN

102:6, "pelican," which is a seafowl, and cannot be meant here: some waterfowl (*katta*, according to BURCKHARDT) that tenants desert places is intended. **bittern**—rather, the hedgehog, or porcupine [GESENIUS] (ch. 14:23). **owl**—from its being enumerated among water birds in Leviticus 11:17; Deuteronomy 14:16. MAURER thinks rather the heron or crane is meant; from a *Hebrew* root, "to blow," as it utters a sound like the blowing of a horn (Rev. 18:2). **confusion**—devastation. **line . . . stones**—metaphor from an architect with line and *plummet-stone* (*Note*, ch. 18:2; 28:17); God will render to it the *exact measure of justice* without mercy (Jas. 2:13; II Kings 21:13; Lam. 2:8; Amos 7:7, 8). **emptiness**—desolation. Edom is now a waste of "stones." **12.** Rather, "As to her nobles, there shall be none there who shall declare a kingdom," i.e., a king [MAURER]; or else, "There shall be no one there whom they shall call to the kingdom" [ROSENMULLER] (ch. 3:6, etc.). Idumea was at first governed by dukes (Gen. 36:15); out of them the king was chosen when the constitution became a monarchy. **13. dragons**—(*Note*, ch. 13:21, 22.) **court for owls**—rather, "a dwelling for ostriches." **14. wild beasts of the desert . . . island**—rather, "wild cats" . . . "jackals" (ch. 13:21). **screech owl**—rather, "the night-specter"; in Jewish superstition a female, elegantly dressed, that carried off children by night. The text does not assert the *existence* of such objects of superstition, but describes the place as one which superstition would people with such beings. **15. great owl**—rather, the arrow-snake, so called from its darting on its prey [GESENIUS]. **lay**—viz., eggs. **gather under her shadow**—rather, "cherishes" her young under, etc. (Jer. 17:11). **16. book of the Lord**—the volume in which the various prophecies and other parts of Scripture began henceforward to be collected together (ch. 30:8; Dan. 9:2). **Seek**—(so ch. 8:16, 20; John 5:39; 7:52). **no one . . . fail**—of these prophecies (Matt. 5:18). **none shall want . . . mate**—image from *pairing* of animals mentioned, vs. 15 ("mate"); no prediction shall want a fulfilment as its companion. Or rather, "none of these wild animals (just spoken of) shall be wanting: none shall be without its mate" to pair and breed with, in desolate Idumea. **my . . . his**—Such changes of person are frequent in *Hebrew poetry*. **them**—the wild beasts. **17. cast . . . lot**—As conquerors apportion lands by lot, so Jehovah has appointed and marked out ("divided") Edom for the wild beasts (Num. 26: 55, 56; Josh. 18:4-6).

ADAM CLARKE

11. *The cormorant*. "The pelican." *The bittern*. The "hedgehog," or "porcupine." *The line of confusion, and the stones of emptiness*—"The plummet of emptiness over her scorched plains."

13. *A court for owls. Yaanah*, the "ostrich," from *anah*, "to cry," because of the noise it makes.

14. *The wild beasts of the desert*. The "mountain cats."—Bochart. *Wild beasts of the island*. The "jackals." *The satyr. Seir*, the "hairy one," probably the he-goat. *The screech owl. Lilith*, the "night-bird."

15. *The great owl. Kippoz*, the "darter," a serpent so called because of its suddenly leaping up or darting on its prey.

MATTHEW HENRY — CHAPTER 35

Verses 1–4

I. Here we have a wilderness turned into a good land. When the land of Judah was freed from the Assyrian army the country that had been made a wilderness began to recover and to blossom as the rose. When the Gentile nations, that had been long as a wilderness, bringing forth no fruit to God, received the gospel, joy came with it to them, Ps. lxvii. 3, 4; xcvi. 11, 12. When Christ was preached in Samaria there was *great joy in that city* (Acts viii. 8). Converting grace makes the soul that was *a wilderness to rejoice with joy and singing*, and to *blossom abundantly*. Whatever is valuable in any institution is brought into the gospel. All the beauty of the Jewish church was admitted into the Christian church as the apostle shows in his epistle to the Hebrews. Whatever was desirable in the Mosaic economy is translated into the evangelical institutes.

II. The glory of God shining forth: *They shall see the glory of the Lord*. God will manifest himself more than ever in his grace and love to mankind. This is that which will make the desert blossom. The more we see by faith of the glory of the Lord the more joyful and the more fruitful shall we be.

III. The feeble and faint-hearted encouraged, *v.* 3, 4. God's prophets and ministers are charged, by virtue of their office, to *strengthen the weak hands*, to comfort those who could not yet recover the fright they had been put into by the Assyrian army with an assurance that God would now return in mercy to them. This is the design of the gospel, 1. To strengthen those that are weak and to confirm them. Among true Christians there are many that have weak hands and feeble knees, that are yet but babes in Christ; but it is our duty (Luke xxii. 32), not only to bear with the weak, but to do what we can to confirm them, Rom. xv. 1; 1 Thess. v. 14. It is our duty also to strengthen ourselves (Heb. xii. 12), improving the strength God has given us. 2. To animate those that

JAMIESON, FAUSSET, BROWN — CHAPTER 35

Vss. 1-10. CONTINUATION OF THE PROPHECY IN CHAPTER 34. See *introduction* there. **1. solitary place**—lit., "a dry place," without springs of water. A *moral* wilderness is meant. **for them**—viz., on account of the punishment inflicted according to the preceding prophecy on the enemy; probably the blessings set forth in this chapter are included in the causes for joy (ch. 55:12).

rose—rather, the meadow saffron, an autumnal flower with bulbous roots; so *Syriac* translation.

2. glory of Lebanon—its ornament, viz., its cedars (ch. 10:34). **excellency of Carmel**—viz., its beauty. **Sharon**—famed for its fertility. **see . . . glory of the Lord . . . excellency**—(Ch. 40:5, 9.) While the wilderness which had neither "glory" nor "excellency" shall have both "given to it," the Lord shall have all the "glory" and "excellency" ascribed to *Him*, not to the transformed wilderness (Matt. 5:16). **3. Strengthen . . . hands . . . . confirm . . . . knees**—The Hebrew for "strengthen" refers to the strength residing in the *hand* for grasping and holding a thing manfully; "confirm," to the firmness with which one keeps his ground, so as not to be dislodged by any other [MAURER]. Encourage the Jews, now desponding, by the assurance of the blessings promised.

ADAM CLARKE — CHAPTER 35

The various miracles our Lord wrought are the best comment on this chapter, which predicts those wondrous works and the glorious state of the Christian Church.

1. *Shall be glad*. Probably the true reading is, "The wilderness and the dry place shall be glad." Not *for them*.

2. *Rejoice even with joy and singing*—"The well-watered plain of Jordan shall also rejoice."

MATTHEW HENRY

are timorous and discouraged: *Say to those that are of a fearful heart*, that are *hasty* (so the word is), that are for betaking themselves to flight upon the first alarm, that say, in their haste, "We are cut off and undone" (Ps. xxxi. 22), there is enough in the gospel to silence these fears. He that says to us *Be strong* has laid help for us upon one that is mighty.

IV. Assurance given of the approach of a Saviour: "*Your God will come with vengeance.* God will appear for you against your enemies, will recompense both their injuries and your losses." Those whose *hearts tremble for the ark of God*, and who are under a concern for his church in the world, may silence their fears with this, God will take the work into his own hands.

Verses 5–10

"*Then*, when your God shall come, even Christ, look for great things."

I. Wonders shall be wrought in the kingdoms both of nature and grace. 1. Wonders shall be wrought on men's bodies (*v.* 5, 6): *The eyes of the blind shall be opened;* this was often done by our Lord Jesus when he was here upon earth, Matt. ix. 27; xii. 22; xx. 30; John ix. 6. By his power the ears of the deaf also were unstopped, with one word, *Ephphatha—Be opened*, Mark vii. 34. Many that were lame had the use of their limbs restored, Acts iii. 8. The dumb also were enabled to speak, Matt. ix. 32, 33. These miracles Christ wrought to prove that he was sent of God (John iii. 2), nay, he was God, the same who at first made man's mouth, the hearing ear, and the seeing eye. 2. Wonders, greater wonders, shall be wrought on men's souls. By the word and Spirit of Christ those that were spiritually blind were enlightened (Acts xxvi. 18), those that were deaf to the calls of God were made to hear them readily, as Lydia, whose heart *the Lord opened*, so *that she attended*, Acts xvi. 14. Those also that were dumb, and knew not how to speak of God or to God, having their understandings opened to know him, shall thereby have their lips opened to show forth his praise.

II. The Spirit shall be poured out from on high. There shall be *waters and streams* (*v.* 6), *in the wilderness*, where one would least expect it, *shall waters break out*. This was fulfilled when the *Holy Ghost fell upon the Gentiles* that *heard the word* (Acts x. 44). These waters are said to *break out*, a surprise to the Gentiles, such as brought them, as it were, into a new world. The blessed effect of this shall be that the *parched ground shall become a pool*, *v.* 7. In *the thirsty land*, where no water was, no ordinances (Ps. lxiii. 1), there shall be *springs of water*, a gospel ministry, *the river that makes glad the city of our God*, Ps. xlvi. 4. *In the habitation of dragons*, who chose to dwell in the parched scorched ground (*ch.* xxxiv. 9, 13), these waters shall flow, and dispossess them, so that, *where each lay shall be grass with reeds and rushes.* Thus it was when Christian churches were planted, and flourished greatly, in the cities of the Gentiles, which, for many ages, had been habitations of dragons, or devils rather, when they were converted to Christianity, then the habitations of dragons became fruitful fields.

III. The way of religion and godliness is here called *the way of holiness* (*v.* 8). "When our God shall come to save us he shall chalk out to us this way by his gospel, so as it had never been described." It shall be an appointed way; *a highway*. It is the King's highway, the King of king's highway, in which, though we may be waylaid, we cannot be stopped. The *way of holiness* is the way of God's commandments; it is the *good old way*, Jer. vi. 16. *The unclean shall not pass over it*, either to defile it or to disturb those that walk in it. *It shall be for those* whom the Lord has *set apart for himself* (Ps. iv. 3), shall be reserved for them: *The redeemed shall walk there* out of the reach of molestation from an evil world. *The wayfaring men*, who choose to travel in it, *though fools*, of weak capacity in other things, shall have such plain directions from the word and Spirit of God in this way that they *shall not err therein*; they shall get well to their journey's end. Those that are in the narrow way, though some may fall into one path and others into another, not all equally right, yet all meet at last in the same end. The Spirit of truth shall lead them into all truth that is necessary for them. The way to heaven is a plain way, and easy to hit. It shall be a safe way: *No lion shall be there, nor any ravenous beast* (*v.* 9), none *to hurt or destroy.* Those that keep close to this way keep out of the reach of Satan the roaring lion. Those that walk in the way of holiness may proceed with serenity of mind, knowing that nothing can do them any real hurt. Those that walk in the *way of holiness* must separate themselves from the unclean and *save themselves from an untoward generation.* Let them walk *with*

JAMIESON, FAUSSET, BROWN

4. fearful—*Margin*, "hasty," i.e., with a heart fluttered with agitation.

with—the *Hebrew* is more forcible than the *English Version:* "God will come, vengeance! even God, a recompense!" The sense is the same.

5, 6. Language fig., descriptive of the joy felt at the deliverance from Assyria and Babylon; lit., true of the antitypical times of Messiah and His miracles (see *Margin references*). **6. leap**—lit., fulfilled (Acts 3:8; 14:10). **sing**—joyful thanksgiving.

in . . . wilderness . . . waters—(ch. 41:18.)

7. parched ground—rather, "the mirage (*Hebrew, Sharab*, the sun's heat) shall become a (real) lake." The sun's rays refracted on the glowing sands at midday give the appearance of a lake of water and often deceive the thirsty traveller (cf. Jer. 2:13; ch. 41:18). **dragons**—rather jackals. **each**—viz., jackal. **grass**—rather, "*a dwelling* or *receptacle* (answering to the previous habitation) for reeds." etc. (which only grow where there is water, Job 8:11). Where once there was no water, water shall abound.

8. highway—such a causeway (*raised way*, from a *Hebrew* root, *to cast up*) as was used for the march of armies; valleys being filled up, hills and other obstructions removed (ch. 62:10; cf. ch. 40:3, 4). **way of holiness**—Hebraism for "the holy way." HORSLEY translates, "the way of the Holy One;" but the words that follow, and vs. 10, show it is the way leading the redeemed back to Jerusalem, both the literal and the heavenly (ch. 52:1; Joel 3:17; Rev. 21:27); still Christ at His coming again shall be the Leader on the way, for which reason it is called, "The way *of the Lord*" (ch. 40:3; Mal. 3:1). **it shall be for those: the wayfaring men**—rather, "He (the Holy One) shall be with them, walking in the way" [HORSLEY]. **though fools**—rather, "And (even) fools," i.e., the simple shall not go astray, viz., because "He shall be with them" (Matt. 11:25; I Cor. 1:26-28).

9. No lion—such as might be feared on the way through the wilderness which abounded in wild beasts, back to Judea. Every danger shall be warded off the returning people (ch. 11:6-9; Ezek. 34:25; Hos. 2:18). Cf. spiritually, Proverbs 3:17.

ADAM CLARKE

CHARLES H. SPURGEON:

Verse 6. What a difference grace makes whenever it enters the heart! We find here the blind, but they are not blind in one sense; grace has touched their eyes, and the eyes of the blind are opened. Men are said to be deaf; but they are not deaf after grace has operated upon them: the ears of the deaf are unstopped. They have been lame before; but when once the omnipotent influence has come upon them, they leap like a hart. And the dumb, so far from being dumb, have a change that must be radical, for its effects are surprising. The tongue of the dumb not simply speaks, but it sings. Grace makes a great difference in man when it enters into him. How vain, then, are the boasts and professions of some persons who assert themselves to be the children of God, and yet live in sin! There is no perceivable difference in their conduct; they are just what they used to be before they pretended conversion; they are not changed in their acts, even in the least degree, and yet they do most positively affirm that they are the called and living children of God. Let such know that their professions are lies, that falsehood is the only groundwork that they have for their hopes; for, wherever the grace of God is, it makes a difference. A graceless man is not like a gracious man; and a gracious man is not like a graceless one; we are "new creatures in Christ Jesus." When God looks upon us with the eye of love, in conversion and regeneration, He makes us as opposite from what we were before as light is from darkness—as heaven itself is from hell. God works in man a change so great that no reformation can even so much as thoroughly imitate it. It is an entire change—a change of the will, of the being, of the desires, of the hates, of the dislikings, and of the likings. In every respect the man becomes new when divine grace enters into his heart.

—The Treasury of the Old Testament

7. *The parched ground*—"The glowing sand." The glowing sandy plain, which in the hot countries at a distance has the appearance of water.

8. *But it shall be for those*—"But He himself shall be with them, walking in the way." That is, God; see v. 4. "Who shall dwell among them, and set them an example that they should follow His steps."

9. *It shall not be found there*—"Neither shall he be found there." *The redeemed shall walk there. Geulim.* Those whose forfeited inheritances are brought back by the "kinsman," *goel.* This has been considered by all orthodox divines as referring to the incarnation of our Lord, and His sacrificial offering.

MATTHEW HENRY

the redeemed who *shall walk there.*

IV. The end of this way shall be everlasting joy, *v.* 10. Here is good news for the citizens of Zion. *The ransomed of the Lord shall return and come to Zion.* God will open to them a door of escape out of their captivity. They shall join themselves to the gospel church, that *Mount Zion* that *city of the living God*, Heb. xii. 22. Those that by faith are made citizens of the gospel Zion may *go on their way rejoicing* (Acts viii. 39). They rejoice in Christ Jesus, and they that mourn are blessed, for they shall be comforted. When God's people returned out of Babylon to Zion they came *weeping* (Jer. l. 4); but they shall come to heaven singing a new song, which no man can learn, Rev. xiv. 3. Their joy shall be visible, and no longer a secret thing, as it is here in this world; it shall be proclaimed, to the glory of God. Our joyful hopes and prospects of eternal life should swallow up both all the sorrows and all the joys of this present time.

JAMIESON, FAUSSET, BROWN

10. Language: lit., applying to the return from Babylon; fig. and more fully to the completed redemption of both literal and spiritual Israel. **joy upon . . . heads**—(Ps. 126:2.) Joy manifested in their countenances. Some fancy an allusion to the custom of pouring oil "upon the head," or wearing chaplets in times of public festivity (Eccles. 9:8).

ADAM CLARKE

10. *The ransomed. Peduyey*, from *padah*, "to redeem by paying a price." Those for whom a price was paid down to redeem them from bondage and death.

MATTHEW HENRY

CHAPTER 36

TODAY'S DICTIONARY OF THE BIBLE:

Sennacherib—*Sin* (the god) *sends many brothers*—son of Sargon, whom he succeeded on the throne of Assyria (705 B.C.), in the 23rd year of Hezekiah. He first set himself to break up the powerful combination of princes who were in league against him. Among these was Hezekiah, who had entered into an alliance with Egypt against Assyria. He accordingly led a very powerful army of at least 200,000 men into Judea, and devastated the land on every side, taking and destroying many cities (2 Kings 18:13–16; comp. Isa. 22, 24, 29, and 2 Chron. 32:1–8). His own account of this invasion, as given in the Assyrian annals, is in these words: "Because Hezekiah, king of Judah, would not submit to my yoke, I came up against him, and by force of arms and by the might of my power I took forty-six of his strong fenced cities; and of the smaller towns which were scattered about, I took and plundered a countless number. From these places I took and carried off 200,156 persons, old and young, male and female, together with horses and mules, asses and camels, oxen and sheep, a countless multitude; and Hezekiah himself I shut in Jerusalem, his capital city, like a bird in a cage, building towers round the city to hem him in, and raising banks of earth against the gates, so as to prevent escape. . . . Then upon Hezekiah there fell the fear of the power of my arms, and he sent out to me the chiefs and the elders of Jerusalem with 30 talents of gold and 800 talents of silver, and divers treasures, a rich and immense booty. . . . All these things were brought to me at Nineveh, the seat of my government." (Comp. Isa. 22:1–13 for description of the feelings of the inhabitants of Jerusalem at such a crisis.)

Verses 1–10

1. A people may be in the way of their duty and yet meet with trouble and distress. We must not wonder if, when we are doing well, God sends afflictions to quicken us to do better, to do our best, and to press forward towards perfection.

JAMIESON, FAUSSET, BROWN

CHAPTER 36

Vss. 1-22. SENNACHERIB'S INVASION; RABSHAKEH'S BLASPHEMOUS SOLICITATIONS; HEZEKIAH IS TOLD OF THEM. This and chaps. 37, 38, 39, form the historical appendix closing the first division of Isaiah's prophecies, and were added to make the parts of these referring to Assyria more intelligible. So ch. 52, in Jeremiah; cf. II Kings 25. The section occurs almost word for word in II Kings 18:13, 17-20; II Kings 18:14-16, however, is additional matter. Hezekiah's "writing" also is in Isaiah, not in Kings (ch. 38:9-20). We know from II Chronicles 32:32 that Isaiah wrote the acts of Hezekiah. It is, therefore, probable, that his record here (ch. 36-39) was incorporated into the Book of Kings by its compiler. Sennacherib lived, according to Assyrian inscriptions, more than twenty years after his invasion; but as Isaiah survived Hezekiah (II Chron. 32:32), who lived upwards of fifteen years after the invasion (ch. 38:5), the record of Sennacherib's death (ch. 37:38) is no objection to this section having come from Isaiah; II Chronicles 32 is probably an abstract drawn from Isaiah's account, as the chronicler himself implies (vs. 32). Pul was probably the last of the old dynasty, and Sargon, a powerful satrap, who contrived to possess himself of supreme power and found a new dynasty (see *Note*, ch. 20:1). No attempt was made by Judah to throw off the Assyrian yoke during his vigorous reign. The accession of his son Sennacherib was thought by Hezekiah the opportune time to refuse the long-paid tribute; Egypt and Ethiopia, to secure an ally against Assyria on their Asiatic frontier, promised help; Isaiah, while opposed to submission to Assyria, advised reliance on Jehovah, and not on Egypt, but his advice was disregarded, and so Sennacherib invaded Judea, 712 B.C. He was the builder of the largest of the excavated palaces, that of Koyunjik. HINCKS has deciphered his name in the inscriptions. In the third year of his reign, these state that he overran Syria, took Sidon and other Phœnician cities, and then passed to southwest Palestine, where he defeated the Egyptians and Ethiopians (cf. II Kings 18:21; 19:9). His subsequent retreat, after his host was destroyed by God, is of course suppressed in the inscriptions. But other particulars inscribed agree strikingly with the Bible; the capture of the "defensed cities of Judah," the devastation of the country and deportation of its inhabitants; the increased tribute imposed on Hezekiah—thirty talents of gold—this *exact number being given in both;* the silver is set down in the inscriptions at 800 talents, in the Bible 300; the latter may have been the actual amount carried off, the larger sum may include the silver from the temple doors, pillars, etc. (II Kings 18:16). **1. fourteenth**—the third of Sennacherib's reign. His ultimate object was Egypt, Hezekiah's ally. Hence he, with the great body of his army (II Chron. 32:9), advanced towards the Egyptian frontier, in southwest Palestine, and did not approach Jerusalem. **2. Rabshakeh**—In II Kings 18:17, Tartan and Rabsaris are joined with him. Rabshakeh was probably the chief leader; Rab is a title of authority. "chief—cup-bearer." **Lachish**—a frontier town southwest of Jerusalem, in Judah; represented as a great fortified city in a hilly and fruitful country in the Koyunjik bas-reliefs, now in the British Museum; also, its name is found on a slab over a figure of Sennacherib on his throne. **upper pool**—the side on which the Assyrians would approach Jerusalem coming from the southwest (*Note*, ch. 7:3). **3. Eliakim**—successor to Shebna, who had been "over the household," i.e., chief minister of the king; in ch. 22:15-20, this was foretold. **scribe**—secretary, recorder—lit., one who

ADAM CLARKE

CHAPTER 36

The history of the invasion of Sennacherib, and of the miraculous destruction of his army, which makes the subject of so many of Isaiah's prophecies, is very properly inserted here as affording the best light to many parts of those prophecies, and as almost necessary to introduce the prophecy in the thirty-seventh chapter, being the answer of God to Hezekiah's prayer, which could not be properly understood without it. We find the same narrative in the Second Book of Kings, chaps. xviii; xix; xx; and these chapters of Isaiah, xxxvi; xxxvii; xxxviii; xxix, for much the greater part (the account of the sickness of Hezekiah only excepted) are but a different copy of that narration.

JOHN GILL:

Verse 2. "And the king of Assyria sent Rabshakeh from Lachish to Jerusalem unto King Hezekiah with a great army." Notwithstanding he had taken Hezekiah's money to withdraw his army out of his country, yet sends it out to this very capital; along with this Rabshakeh he sent two other generals, Tartan and Rabsaris (2 Kings 18:17); though they are not mentioned, only Rabshakeh, because he was the principal person, however the chief speaker. Lachish was a city in the tribe of Judah (Josh. 15:39); which Sennacherib was now besieging (2 Chron. 32:9). This message was sent, Bishop Usher says, three years after the former expedition; "and he stood by the conduit of the upper pool, in the highway of the fullers' field"; where they spread their clothes, as the Targum, having washed them in the pool. Ben Melech thus describes the pool, conduit, and highway: the pool is a ditch, built with stone and lime, where rainwater was collected, or where they drew water from the fountain, and the waters were gathered into this pool; and there was in this pool a hole, which they stopped, until the time they pleased to fetch water out of the pool; and the conduit was a ditch near to the pool, and they brought water out of the pool into the conduit, when they chose to drink, or wash garments; the highway was a way paved with stones, so that they could walk upon it in rainy days; and here they stood and washed their garments in the waters of the conduit, and in the field they spread them to the sun. This pool lay without the city, yet just by the walls of it, which showed the daring insolence of Rabshakeh to come so very nigh, for he was in the hearing of the men upon the walls, v. 12; this Rabshakeh is by the Jewish writers thought to be an apostate Jew, because he spoke in the Jews' language.—*Gill's Commentary*

MATTHEW HENRY

The enemies of God's people endeavour to conquer them by frightening them, especially by frightening them from their confidence in God. Thus Rabshakeh here, with noise and banter, runs down Hezekiah as utterly unable to cope with his master. It concerns us therefore, that we may keep our ground against the enemies of our souls, to keep up our spirits by keeping up our hope in God. Those who forsake God's service forfeit his protection.

It is an easy thing, and very common, for those that persecute the church and people of God to pretend a commission from him for so doing. Rabshakeh could say, *Have I now come up without the Lord?* when really he had come up *against* the Lord, *ch.* xxxvii. 28.

Verses 11–22

While princes and counsellors have public matters under debate, it is not fair to appeal to the people. It is therefore an unfair practice to incense subjects against their rulers by base insinuations. Proud scorners, the fairer they are spoken to, speak the fouler. Nothing could be said more mildly and respectfully than that which Hezekiah's agents said to Rabshakeh. *Speak, we pray thee;* but this made him the more spiteful and imperious.

When Satan would tempt men from trusting in God, he does so by insinuating that in yielding to him they may better their condition. When the world and the flesh say to us, "*Make an agreement* with us *and come out to us,* submit to our dominion and come into our interests, and *you shall eat every one of his own vine,*" they do but deceive us, promising liberty when they would lead us into the basest captivity and slavery. Therefore, *when they speak fair, believe them not.* Nothing can be more absurd in itself, nor a greater affront to the true and living God, than to compare him with the gods of the heathen. They are nothing; he is the great *I AM*: they are the creatures of men's fancy and the works of men's hands; he is the Creator of all things. Presumptuous sinners are ready to think that, because they have been too hard for their fellow-creatures, they are therefore a match for their Creator. This and the other nation they have subdued, and therefore the Lord himself shall not deliver Jerusalem out of their hand. But, though the potsherds may strive with the potsherds of the earth, let them not strive with the potter.

JAMIESON, FAUSSET, BROWN

reminds; a remembrancer to keep the king informed on important facts, and to act as historiographer. In II Kings 18:18, the additional fact is given that the Assyrian envoys "called to the king," in consequence of which Eliakim, etc., "came out to them." **4. great king**—the usual title of the Persian and Assyrian kings, as they had many subordinate princes or kings under them over provinces (ch. 10:8). **5. counsel**—Egypt was famed for its wisdom. **6.** It was a similar alliance with So (i.e., Sabacho, or else Sevechus), the Ethiopian king of Egypt, which provoked the Assyrian to invade and destroy Israel, the northern kingdom, under Hoshea. **7.** The Assyrian mistakes Hezekiah's religious reforms whereby he took away the high places (II Kings 18:4) as directed *against Jehovah.* Some of the high places may have been dedicated to Jehovah, but worshipped under the form of an *image* in violation of the second commandment: the "brazen serpent," also (broken in pieces by Hezekiah, and called *Nehushtan,* "a piece of brass," because it was worshipped by Israel) was originally set up by *God's* command. Hence the Assyrian's allegation has a specious color: you cannot look for help from Jehovah, for your king has "taken away His altars." **to Jerusalem**—(Deut. 12:5, 11; John. 4:20.) **8. give pledges**—a taunting challenge. Only give the *guarantee* that you can supply as many as 2000 riders, and I will give thee 2000 horses. But seeing that you have not even this small number (*Note,* ch. 2:7), how can you stand against the hosts of Assyrian cavalry? The Jews tried to supply their weakness in this "arm" from Egypt (ch. 31:1). **9. captain**—a governor under a satrap; even *he* commands more horsemen than this. **10.** A boastful inference from the past successes of Assyria, designed to influence the Jews to surrender; their *own* principles bound them to yield to Jehovah's will. He may have heard from partisans in Judah what Isaiah had foretold (ch. 10:5, 6). **11. Syrian**—rather, *Aramean*: the language spoken north and east of Palestine, and understood by the Assyrians as belonging to the same family of languages as their own: nearly akin to *Hebrew* also, though not intelligible to the multitude (cf. II Kings 5:5-7). *Aram* means a "high land," and includes parts of Assyria as well as Syria. **Jews' language**—The men of Judah since the disruption of Israel, claimed the *Hebrew* as their own peculiarly, as if they were now the only true representatives of the whole Hebrew twelve tribes. **ears of . . . people on . . . wall**—The interview is within hearing distance of the city. The people crowd on the wall, curious to hear the Assyrian message. The Jewish rulers fear that it will terrify the people and therefore beg Rabshakeh to speak Aramean. **12.** Is it to *thy master* and *thee* that I am sent? Nay, it is to *the men on the wall,* to let them know (so far am I from wishing them *not* to hear, as *you* would wish), that unless they surrender, they shall be reduced to the direst extremities of famine in the siege (II Chron. 32:11, explains the word here), viz., to eat their own excrements: or, connecting, "that they may eat," etc., with "sit upon the wall"; who, as they hold the wall, are knowingly exposing themselves to the direst extremities [MAURER]. Isaiah, as a faithful historian, records the filthy and blasphemous language of the Assyrians to mark aright the true character of the attack on Jerusalem. **13.** Rabshakeh speaks louder and plainer than ever to the men on the wall. **15.** The foes of God's people cannot succeed against them, unless they can shake their trust in Him (cf. vs. 10). **16. agreement . . . by . . . present**—rather, "make *peace* with me"; lit., "blessing" so called from the mutual *congratulations* attending the ratification of peace. So CHALDEE. Or else, *"Do homage* to me" [HORSLEY]. **come out**—surrender to me; then you may remain in quiet possession of your lands till my return from Egypt, when I will lead you away to a land fruitful as your own. Rabshakeh tries to soften, in the eyes of the Jews, the well-known Assyrian policy of weakening the vanquished by deporting them to other lands (Gen. 47:21; II Kings 17:6). **19. Hamath . . . Arphad**—(*Note,* ch. 10:9.) **Sepharvaim**—lit., "the two scribes"; now Sipphara, on the east of Euphrates, above Babylon. It was a just retribution (Prov. 1:31; Jer. 2:19). Israel worshipped the gods of Sepharvaim, and so colonists of Sepharvaim were planted in the land of Israel (thenceforth called Samaria) by the Assyrian conqueror (II Kings 17:24; cf. Kings 18:34). **Samaria**—Shalmaneser began the siege against Hoshea, because of his conspiring with So of Egypt (II Kings 17:4). Sargon finished it; and, in his palace at Khorsabad, he has mentioned the number of Israelites carried captive—27, 280 [G. V. SMITH]. 20. (Cf. ch. 10:11; II Chron. 32:19.) Here he contradicts his own assertion (vs. 10), that

ADAM CLARKE

3. *Then came forth unto him.* Before these words the other copy, 2 Kings xviii. 18, adds, "And they demanded audience of the king."

5. *I say*—"Thou hast said." *But they are but vain words.* "A word of the lips." You talk about counsels, but you have none; about strength, but there is none with you.

6. *The staff of this broken reed.* A weakened, faithless ally. *It will go into his hand, and pierce it.* Will take subsidy after subsidy, and do nothing for it.

7. *But if thou say*—"But if ye say." *Ye shall worship before this altar*—"To worship only before this altar." See 2 Chron. xxxii. 12.

10. *Am I now come up without the Lord?* Probably some apostate Israelitish priest might have encouraged the king of Assyria by telling him that Jehovah had given him a commission against Jerusalem.

17. *And vineyards.* The other copy, 2 Kings xviii. 32, adds here: "A land of oil olive and of honey, that ye may live, and not die: and hearken not unto Hezekiah, when he persuadeth [seduceth] you."

MATTHEW HENRY

It is sometimes prudent not to *answer a fool according to his folly*. Hezekiah's command was, "*Answer him not;* leave it to God to stop his mouth, for you cannot." Though they *answered him not a word*, yet they rent their clothes, in zeal for the glory of God's name and indignation at the contempt put upon it.

CHAPTER 37

Verses 1–7

The best way to baffle the malicious designs of our enemies against us is to be driven by them to God and to our duty. Rabshakeh intended to frighten Hezekiah from the Lord, but it proves that he frightens him to the Lord. The wind, instead of forcing the traveller's coat from him, makes him wrap it the closer about him. The more Rabshakeh reproaches God the more Hezekiah studies to honour him. Hezekiah sent messengers to Isaiah, to desire his prayers, remembering how much his prophecies had looked towards the events of the present day. *This is a day of trouble*, therefore let it be a day of prayer. Now that the *children are brought to the birth*, but *there is not strength to bring forth*, now let prayer come. When pains are most strong let prayers be most lively. Prayer is the midwife of mercy, that helps to bring it forth. *It may be the Lord thy God will hear; who knows but he will return and repent?* Rabshakeh has blasphemed God, and therefore let not Hezekiah be afraid of him, *v.* 6. Judgment will certainly be given against him. Sinners' fears are but prefaces to their falls. He shall *hear the rumour* of the slaughter of his army, which shall oblige him to retire to his own land, and there he shall be slain, *v.* 7.

Verses 8–20

God, in his promise, may confirm us in our silently bearing reproaches. God answered Hezekiah, but it does not appear that he sent any answer to Rabshakeh; but quietly left the matter with him. *So Rabshakeh returned* to the king his master for fresh instructions.

Sennacherib, without provocation given to him or warning given by him, went to war against Judah; and now with as little ceremony the king of Ethiopia goes to war against him, *v.* 9. Those that are quarrelsome may expect to be quarrelled with. It is bad to talk proudly and profanely, but it is worse to write so, for this argues more deliberation and design, and what is written spreads further, lasts longer, and does the more mischief. Great successes often harden sinners' hearts and make them the more daring. The kings of Assyria doubt not but to destroy God's land, because the idolatrous kings of Hamath and Arphad became an easy prey to them therefore the religious reforming king of Judah must needs be so too.

Hezekiah took Sennacherib's letter, and spread it before the Lord, not designing to make any complaints against him but those grounded upon his own handwriting. Let the thing speak itself; here it is in black and white: *Open thy eyes, O Lord! and see.* He encouraged himself with this, that the God of Israel is *the Lord of hosts*, that he is God *alone*, the *God of all the kingdoms of the earth*, for he made heaven and earth, and therefore both can do anything and does everything. When we are afraid of men that are great destroyers we may with humble boldness appeal to God as the great Saviour.

JAMIESON, FAUSSET, BROWN

he had "come up against the land *with the Lord* Liars need good memories. He classes Jehovah with the idols of the other lands; nay, thinks Him inferior in proportion as Judah, under His tutelage, was less than the lands under the tutelage of the idols. **21. not a word**—so as not to enter into a war of words with the blasphemer (Exod. 14:14; Jude 9). **22. clothes rent**—in grief and horror at the blasphemy (Matt. 26:65).

CHAPTER 37

Vss. 1-38. CONTINUATION OF THE NARRATIVE IN CHAPTER 36. **1. sackcloth**—(*Note*, ch. 20:2.) **house of the Lord**—the sure resort of God's people in distress (Ps. 73:16, 17; 77:13). **2. unto Isaiah**—implying the importance of the prophet's position at the time; the chief officers of the court are deputed to wait on him (cf. II Kings 22:12-14). **3. rebuke**—i.e., the Lord's rebuke for His people's sins (Ps. 149:7; Hos. 5:9). **blasphemy**—blasphemous railing of Rabshakeh. **the children . . .**—a proverbial expression for, We are in the most extreme danger and have no power to avert it (cf. Hos. 13:13). **4. hear**—take cognizance of (II Sam. 16:12). **reprove**—will punish him for the words, etc. (Ps. 50:21). **remnant**—the two tribes of the kingdom of Judah, Israel being already captive. Isaiah is entreated to act as intercessor with God. **6. servants**—lit., "youths," mere lads, implying disparagement, not an embassy of venerable elders. The *Hebrew* is different from that for "servants" in vs. 5. **blasphemed me**—(ch. 36:20.) **7. blast**—rather, "I will put a *spirit* (ch. 28:6; I Kings 22:23) into him," i.e., so influence his judgment that when he hears the report (vs. 9, concerning Tirhakah), he shall return [GESENIUS]; the "report" also of the destruction of his army at Jerusalem, reaching Sennacherib, while he was in the southwest of Palestine on the borders of Egypt, led him to retreat. **by the sword**—(vs. 38.) **8. returned**—to the camp of his master. **Libnah**—meaning "*whiteness,*" the *Blanche-garde* of the Crusaders [STANLEY]. EUSEBIUS and JEROME place it more south, in the district of Eleutheropolis, ten miles northwest of Lachish, which Sennacherib had captured (*Note*, ch. 36:2). Libnah was in Judea and given to the priests (I Chron. 6:54, 57). **9. Tirhakah**—(see *Notes*, ch. 17:12; 18:6). Egypt was in part governed by three successive Ethiopian monarchs, for forty or fifty years: Sabacho, Sevechus, and Tirhakah. Sevechus retired from Lower Egypt owing to the resistance of the priests, whereupon Sethos, a prince-priest, obtained supreme power with Tanis (Zoan in Scripture), or Memphis, as his capital. The Ethiopians retained Upper Egypt under Tirhakah, with Thebes as the capital. Tirhakah's fame as a conqueror rivalled that of Sesostris; he, and one at least of the Pharaohs of Lower Egypt, were Hezekiah's allies against Assyria. The tidings of his approach made Sennacherib the more anxious to get possession of Jerusalem before his arrival. **sent**—II Kings 19:9 more fully expresses Sennacherib's eagerness by adding "again." **10.** He tries to influence *Hezekiah himself*, as Rabshakeh had addressed the people. **God . . . deceive**—(Cf. Num. 23:19). **11. all lands**—(ch. 14:17). He does not dare to enumerate *Egypt* in the list. **12. Gozan**—in Mesopotamia, on the Chabour (II Kings 17:6; 18:11). Gozan is the name of the *district*, Chabour of the *river*. **Haran**—more to the west. Abraham removed to it from Ur (Gen. 11:31); the *Carrœ* of the Romans. **Rezeph**—farther west, in Syria. **Eden**—There is an ancient village, *Adna*, north of Bagdad. Some think Eden to be the name of a *region* (of Mesopotamia or its vicinity) *in* which was Paradise; Paradise was not Eden itself (Gen. 2:8). "A garden in Eden." **Telassar**—now Tel-afer, west of Mosul [LAYARD]. *Tel* means a "hill" in *Arabic* and *Assyrian* names. **13. Hena . . . Ivah**—in Babylonia. From *Ava* colonists had been brought to Samaria (II Kings 17:24). **14. spread**—unrolled the scroll of writing. God "*knows* our necessities before we ask Him," but He delights in our unfolding them to Him with filial confidence (II Chron. 20:3, 11-13). **16. dwellest**—the Shekinah, or fiery symbol of God's presence, *dwelling* in the temple with His people, is from *shachan*, "to dwell" (Exod. 25:22; Ps. 80:1; 99:1). **cherubim**—derived by transposition from either a *Hebrew* root, *rachab*, to "ride"; or rather, *barach*, to "bless." They were formed out of the same mass of pure gold as the mercy seat itself (Exod. 25:19, *Margin*). The phrase, "dwellest between the cherubim," arose from their position at each end of the mercy seat, while the Shekinah, and the awful name, JEHOVAH, in written letters, were in the intervening space. They are so inseparably associated with

ADAM CLARKE

CHAPTER 37

6. *Thus shall ye say.* "Thus shall ye (explicitly, earnestly, and positively) say." The paragogic *nun* deepens and increases the sense.

7. *I will send a blast*—"I will infuse a spirit into him."

8. *Rabshakeh returned.* From chap. xxxvi. 2, we learn that the king of Assyria had sent Rabshakeh from Lachish to Jerusalem; now it is likely that Rabshakeh had besieged that place, and that the king of Assyria had taken his station before this city, and dispatched Rabshakeh against Jerusalem. But, as it is said he had "departed from Lachish," probably he had been obliged to raise the siege, and sat down before *Libnah*, which promised an easier conquest.

9. *He heard say concerning Tirhakah king of Ethiopia.* When he heard that Tirkah, king of Ethiopia, had come out against him, then he sent that blasphemous manifesto which is contained in vv. 10-13, to terrify Hezekiah into submission.

MATTHEW HENRY

ALEXANDER MACLAREN:

Hezekiah's address to God is no mere formal recapitulation of the divine names, but is the effort of faith to grasp firmly the truths which the enemy denies, and on which it builds. So considered, the accumulation of titles in verse 16 is very instructive, and shows how a trustful soul put forth energy of its faith in summoning to mind the great aspects of the divine name as bulwarks against suggested fears, and bases of supplication. Hezekiah appeals to "the God of Hosts," the Ruler of all the embattled forces of the universe, as well as of the armies of angels. What is Sennacherib's array compared with these? He appeals to the "God of Israel," as pleading the ancient relationship, which binds the unchangeable Guardian of the people to be still what He has been, and casts the responsibility of Israel's preservation upon Him. He appeals to Him "who sits between the cherubim," as thence defending and filling the threatened city. He grasps the thought that Jehovah is "God alone" with a vividness which is partly due no doubt to Isaiah's teaching, but is also the indignant recoil of faith from the assumption of the letter, that Jehovah was but as the beaten deities of Gozan and the rest. Faith clings the more tenaciously to truths denied, as a dog will hold on to the stick that one tries to pull from it.

Thus, having heartened himself and pled with God by all these names, Hezekiah comes to his petition. It is but translating into words the symbol of spreading the letter before God. He asks God to behold and to hear the defiant words. Prayer tells God what it knows that He knows already, for it relieves the burdened heart to tell Him. It asks Him to see and hear what it knows that He does see and hear. But the prayer is not for mere observance followed by no divine act, but for taking knowledge as the precursor of the appropriate help. Of such seeing and hearing by God, believing prayer is the appointed condition.

—*Expositions of Holy Scripture*

Verses 21–38

Those who receive messages of terror from men with patience, and send messages of faith to God by prayer, may expect messages of grace and peace from God for their comfort. Isaiah sent a long answer to Hezekiah's prayer in God's name by way of return to his prayer: "*Whereas thou hast prayed to me*, know, for thy comfort, that thy prayer is heard."

Those who abuse the people of God affront God himself. *Whom hast thou reproached?* Even *the Holy One of Israel.* And it aggravated the indignity Sennacherib did to God that he set his servants on to do the same: *By thy servants*, the abjects, *thou hast reproached me.*

Those who boast of their own achievements reflect upon God and his providence: "*Thou hast said, I have digged, and drunk water;* and wilt not own that *I have done it*," *v.* 24–26.

JAMIESON, FAUSSET, BROWN

the manifestation of God's glory, that whether the Lord is at rest or in motion, they always are mentioned with Him (Num. 7:89; Ps. 18:10). (1) They are first mentioned (Gen. 3:24) "on the edge of" (as "on the east" may be translated) Eden; the *Hebrew* for "placed" is properly to "place in a tabernacle," which implies that this was a local tabernacle in which the symbols of God's presence were manifested suitably to the altered circumstances in which man, after the fall, came before God. It was here that Cain and Abel, and the patriarchs down to the flood, presented their offerings: and it is called "the presence of the Lord" (Gen. 4:16). When those symbols were removed at the close of that early patriarchal dispensation, small models of them were made for domestic use, called, in *Chaldee*, "seraphim" or "teraphim." (2) The cherubim, in the Mosaic tabernacle and Solomon's temple, were the same in form as those at the outskirts of Eden: compound figures, combining the distinguishing properties of several creatures: the ox, chief among the tame and useful animals; the lion among the wild ones; the eagle among birds; and man, the head of all (the original headship of man over the animal kingdom, about to be restored in Jesus Christ, Ps. 8:4-8, is also implied in this combination). They are, throughout Scripture, represented as distinct from God; they could not be likenesses of Him which He forbade in any shape. (3) They are introduced in the third or gospel dispensation (Rev. 4:6) as *living creatures* (not so well translated "beasts" in English Version), not angels, but beings closely connected with the redeemed Church. So also in Ezekiel 1 and 10. Thus, throughout the three dispensations, they seem to be symbols of those who in every age should officially study and proclaim the manifold wisdom of God. **thou alone**—lit., *"Thou art He who alone* art God of all the kingdoms"; whereas Sennacherib had classed Jehovah with the heathen gods, he asserts the nothingness of the latter and the sole lordship of the former. **17. ear . . . eyes**—singular, plural. When we wish to hear a thing we lend one ear; when we wish to see a thing we open *both* eyes. **18. have laid waste**—conceding the truth of the Assyrian's allegation (ch. 36:18-20), but adding the reason, "For they were no gods." **19. cast . . . gods into . . . fire**—The policy of the Assyrians in order to alienate the conquered peoples from their own countries was, both to deport them elsewhere, and to destroy the tutelary idols of their nation, the strongest tie which bound them to their native land. The Roman policy was just the reverse. **20.** The strongest argument to plead before God in prayer, *the honor of God* (Exod. 32:12-14; Ps. 83:18; Dan. 9:18, 19). **21. Whereas thou hast prayed to me**—i.e., hast not relied on thy own strength but on Me (cf. II Kings 19:20.) "That which thou hast prayed to Me against Sennacherib, I have heard" (Ps. 65:2). **22.** Transition to poetry: in parallelism. **virgin . . . daughter**—honorable terms. "Virgin" implies that the city is, as yet, inviolate. "Daughter" is an abstract collective *feminine* personification of the *population*, the child of the place denoted (*Note*, ch. 23:10; 1-8). *Zion and her inhabitants.* **shaken . . . head**—in scorn (Ps. 22:7; 109:25; Matt. 27:39). With us to shake the head is a sign of denial or displeasure; but gestures have different meanings in different countries (ch. 58:9; Ezek. 25:6; Zeph. 2:15). **23. Whom**—not an idol. **24. said**—virtually. Hast thou within thyself? **height**—imagery from the Assyrian felling of trees in Lebanon (ch. 14:8; 33:9); fig. for, "I have carried my victorious army through the regions most difficult of access, to the most remote lands." **sides**—rather, "recesses" [G. V. SMITH]. **fir trees**—not cypresses, as some translate; pine foliage and cedars are still found on the northwest side of Lebanon [STANLEY]. **height of . . . border**—In II Kings 19:23, "the lodgings of his borders." Perhaps on the ascent to the top there was a place of repose or caravansary, which bounded the usual attempts of persons to ascend [BARNES]. Here, simply, "its extreme height." **forest of . . . Carmel**—rather, "its thickest forest." "Carmel" expresses thick luxuriance (*Note*, ch. 10:18; 29:17). **25. digged, and drunk water**—In II Kings 19:24, it is *"strange* waters." I have marched into foreign lands where I had to dig wells for the supply of my armies; even the natural destitution of water there did not impede my march. **rivers of . . . besieged places**—rather, "the streams (artificial canals from the Nile) of *Egypt*." "With the sole of my foot," expresses that as soon as his vast armies *marched* into a region, the streams were *drunk up* by them; or rather, that the rivers proved no *obstruction* to the onward *march* of his armies. So ch. 19:4-6, referring to *Egypt*, "the river—*brooks of defense*—shall be dried

ADAM CLARKE

JOSEPH PARKER:

In Psalm 80:1 we have an expression like that which Hezekiah uses when he says "that dwellest between the cherubims"—an expression which is supposed to refer to the dark thunder-clouds of heaven. In this case the reference is supposed to be the glory-cloud which was the symbol of the divine presence, and which rested when it manifested itself between the cherubim of the ark—figures which symbolize the elemental forces of the heavens. Rabshakeh had spoken of "the gods of the nations," but Hezekiah speaks another faith: "thou art the God, even thou alone." We must never forget that monotheism was the faith of Israel. Never was Israel allowed to suppose that God was many and not one. The majesty of the Lord lay in his unity, and not in his divisibleness. This may be called the majesty of simplicity, in contradistinction to the majesty of number, variety, and complication. Now Hezekiah cast the whole difficulty into the hands of the Lord, his plea being that if God would defend Judah, and deliver his chosen Israel, all the kingdoms of the earth would know that God was the Lord, and there was none beside him. It is curious to observe how, by a kind of necessity, we all endeavor to give motives to the Divine Being which may direct his action and account for it. God does not disallow this worship of what may be called suggestiveness.—*The People's Bible*

20. *That thou art the Lord, even thou only*—"That Thou Jehovah art the only God." The word *Elohim*, "God," is lost here in the Hebrew text, but preserved in the other copy, 2 Kings xix. 19.

25. *Water*—"Strange waters." The word *zarim*, "strange," lost out of the Hebrew text in this place, is supplied from the other copy. *With the sole of my feet.* With my *infantry. All the rivers of the besieged places*—"All the canals of fenced places." The principal cities of Egypt, the scene of his late exploits, were chiefly defended by deep moats, canals, or large lakes, made by labor and art, with which they were surrounded.

MATTHEW HENRY

The most active men are no more than God makes them: "*What I have formed of ancient times*, in an eternal counsel, *now have I brought to pass, that thou shouldst be to lay waste defenced cities;* it is therefore intolerable arrogance to make it thy own doing."

Sennacherib was active and quick, here, and there, and everywhere, but God knew his going out and coming in, *v.* 28.

And though he was very headstrong and unruly, he could and would *turn him back by the way which he came, v.* 29. *Hitherto he shall come and no further.*

God had signed Sennacherib's commission against Judah (*ch.* x. 6); here he supersedes it. Jerusalem shall be defended (*v.* 35), the siegers shall not come into it, but thall be routed before they begin the siege, *v.* 33. But this is not all: God will return in mercy to his people. Their land shall be more than ordinarily fruitful, so that their losses shall be abundantly repaired. And let them not think that the desolations of their country would excuse them from observing the sabbatical year, though they had not now their usual stock beforehand for that year, yet they must religiously observe it, and depend upon God to provide for them. There is no standing before the judgments of God when they come with commission.

JAMIESON, FAUSSET, BROWN

up." HORSLEY translates the *Hebrew* for "besieged places," rocks. **26.** Reply of God to Sennacherib. **long ago**—join, rather, with "I have done it." Thou dost boast that it is all by *thy* counsel and might: but it is *I who, long ago, have ordered* it so (ch. 22: 11); thou wert but the instrument in My hands (ch. 10:5, 15). This was the reason why "the inhabitants were of small power before thee" (vs. 27), viz., that I ordered it so; yet thou art in My hands, and I know thy ways (vs. 28), and I will check thee (vs. 29). Connect also, *"I from ancient times have arranged* ('formed') it." However, *English Version* is supported by ch. 33:13; 45:6, 21; 48:5. **27. Therefore**—not because of thy power, but because I made them unable to withstand thee. **grass**—which easily withers (ch. 40:6; Ps. 37:2). **on . . . housetops**—which having little earth to nourish it fades soonest (Ps. 129:6-8). **corn blasted before it be grown up**—SMITH translates, "The cornfield (frail and tender), before the corn is grown." **28. abode**—rather, "sitting down" (Ps. 139:2). The expressions here describe a man's whole course of life (Deut. 6:7; 28:6; I Kings 3:7; Ps. 121:8). There is also a special reference to Sennacherib's first being *at home,* then *going forth against* Judah and Egypt, and *raging* against Jehovah (vs. 4). **29. tumult**—insolence. **hook in . . . nose**—Like a wild beast led by a ring through the nose, he shall be forced back to his own country (cf. Job 41:1, 2; Ezek. 19:4; 29:4; 38:4). In a bas-relief of Khorsabad, captives are led before the king by a cord attached to a hook, or ring, passing through the under lip or the upper lip, and nose. **30.** Addressed to Hezekiah. **sign**—a token which, when fulfilled, would assure him of the truth of the whole prophecy as to the enemy's overthrow. The two years, in which they were sustained by the spontaneous growth of the earth, were the two in which Judea had been already ravaged by Sennacherib (ch. 32:10). Thus translate: "Ye *did eat* (the first year) such as groweth of itself, and in the second year that . . . , but *in this third year* sow ye," etc., for in this year the land shall be delivered from the foe. The fact that Sennacherib moved his camp away *immediately after* shows that the first two years refer to the past, not to the future [ROSENMULLER]. Others, referring the first two years to the future, get over the difficulty of Sennacherib's *speedy* departure, by supposing that year to have been the sabbatical year, and the second year the jubilee; no indication of this appears in the context. **31. remnant**—Judah *remained* after the ten tribes were carried away; also those of Judah who should survive Sennacherib's invasion are meant. **33. with shields**—He did come near it, but was not allowed to conduct a proper siege. **bank**—a mound to defend the assailants in attacking the walls. **34.** (See vss. 29, 37; ch. 29:5-8.) **35. I will defend**—Notwithstanding *Hezekiah's* measures of defense (II Chron. 32:3-5), *Jehovah* was its true defender. **mine own sake**—since Jehovah's name was blasphemed by Sennacherib (vs. 23). **David's sake**—on account of His promise to David (Ps. 132:17, 18), and to Messiah, the heir of David's throne (ch. 9:7; 11:1). **36.** Some attribute the destruction to the agency of the plague (*Note,* ch. 33:24), which may have caused Hezekiah's sickness, narrated immediately after; but ch. 33: 1, 4, proves that the Jews spoiled the corpses, which they would not have dared to do, had there been on them infection of a plague. The secondary agency seems, from ch. 29:6; 30:30, to have been a storm of hail, thunder, and lightning (cf. Exod. 9:22-25). The simoon belongs rather to Africa and Arabia than Palestine, and ordinarily could not produce such a destructive effect. Some few of the army, as II Chronicles 32:21 seems to imply, survived and accompanied Sennacherib home. HERODOTUS (2. 141) gives an account confirming Scripture in so far as the sudden discomfiture of the Assyrian army is concerned. The Egyptian priests told him that Sennacherib was forced to retreat from Pelusium owing to a multitude of field mice, sent by one of their gods, having gnawed the Assyrians' *bow-strings* and *shield-straps.* Cf. the language (vs. 33), "He shall not shoot an *arrow* there, nor come before it with *shields,"* which the Egyptians corrupted into their version of the story. Sennacherib was as the time with a part of his army, not at Jerusalem, but on the Egyptian frontier, southwest of Palestine. The sudden destruction of the host near Jerusalem, a considerable part of his whole army, as well as the advance of the Ethiopian Tirhakah, induced him to retreat, which the Egyptians accounted for in a way honoring to their own gods. The mouse was the Egyptian emblem of destruction. The *Greek* Apollo was called *Sminthian,* from a Cretan word for "a mouse," as a tutelary god of agriculture, he was represented with one foot upon a mouse, since field

ADAM CLARKE

26. *Lay waste defenced cities into ruinous heaps*—"Lay waste warlike nations, strong fenced cities."

JOSEPH PARKER:

"And this shall be a sign unto thee, Ye shall eat this year such as growth of itself; and the second year that which springeth of the same: and in the third year sow ye, and reap, and plant vineyards, and eat the fruit thereof" (v. 30).

In this verse the prophet turns to Hezekiah, and offers him pledges sufficiently near to assure him that all the prophecies of larger scope were perfectly literal in their intent. It is supposed that the time of the address was autumn, probably near the Equinox, which was the beginning of a new year. The best historians tell us that the Assyrian invasion had stopped all tillage in the previous spring, and the people had to rely upon the spontaneous products of the fields. "In the year that was about to open they would be still compelled to draw from the same source, but in twelve months' time the land would be clear of the invaders, and agriculture would resume its normal course, and the fulfillment of this prediction within the appointed limit of time would guarantee that wider promise that follows." Thus the providence of the Lord confirms itself. Sometimes we have a remote promise stretching far away beyond the ages, and which the living men can never hope to see fulfilled, but in order to assure their faith and brighten their hope, something is promised to them which they can immediately realize. Thus from point to point, and from day to day, we are drawn forward, we are drawn forward by the good hand of the living Spirit of God.

The prophet says, "The zeal of the Lord of hosts shall do this" (v. 32). It was not to be done by human energy, but wholly accomplished by divine wisdom and power. We may so look at prophecies of a large significance as to be overwhelmed by the range of time through which they had to pass, and thus we may blind ourselves and actually overpower our own faith; whereas we ought continually to look at the living God, and the eternity in which he dwells, and to feel that everything is in his hands, and that how great soever the time required it is as nothing compared with the eternity in which he lives.—*The People's Bible*

MATTHEW HENRY

One angel shall, in one night, lay a vast army of men dead upon the spot, when God commissions him so to do, *v.* 36. The greatest men cannot stand before them: *The great king, the king of Assyria*, looks very little when he is forced to return with terror and fear, lest the angel that had destroyed his army should destroy him; yet he is made to look less when his own sons, who should have guarded him, sacrificed him to his idol, whose protection he sought, *v.* 37, 38. He that has delivered does and will deliver.

JAMIESON, FAUSSET, BROWN

mice hurt corn. The Assyrian inscriptions, of course, suppress their own defeat, but nowhere boast of having taken Jerusalem; and the only reason to be given for Sennacherib not having, amidst his many subsequent expeditions recorded in the monuments, returned to Judah, is the terrible calamity he had sustained there, which convinced him that Hezekiah was under the divine protection. RAWLINSON says, In Sennacherib's account of his wars with Hezekiah, inscribed with cuneiform characters in the hall of the palace of Koyunjik, built by him (140 feet long by 120 broad), wherein even the Jewish physiognomy of the captives is portrayed, there occurs a remarkable passage; after his mentioning his taking two hundred thousand captive Jews, he adds, "Then I prayed unto God"; the only instance of an inscription wherein the name of GOD occurs without a heathen adjunct. The 46th Psalm probably commemorates Judah's deliverance. It occurred in one "night," according to II Kings 19:35, with which Isaiah's words, "when they arose *early in the morning*," etc., are in undesigned coincidence. **they . . . they**—"the Jews" . . . "the Assyrians." **37. dwelt at Nineveh**—for about twenty years after his disaster, according to the inscriptions. The word, "dwelt," is consistent with any indefinite length of time. "Nineveh," so called from Ninus, i.e., Nimrod, its founder; his name means "exceedingly impious rebel"; he subverted the existing patriarchal order of society, by setting up a system of chieftainship, founded on conquest; the hunting field was his training school for war; he was of the race of Ham, and transgressed the limits marked by God (Gen. 10:8-11, 25), encroaching on Shem's portion; he abandoned Babel for a time, after the miraculous confusion of tongues and went and founded Nineveh; he was, after death, worshipped as Orion, the constellation (*Note,* Job 9:9; 38:31). **38. Nisroch**—*Nisr,* in *Semitic,* means *"eagle"*; the termination *och,* means "great." The eagle-headed human figure in Assyrian sculptures is no doubt Nisroch, the same as Asshur, the chief Assyrian god; the corresponding goddess was Asheera, or Astarte; this means a "grove," or sacred tree, often found as the symbol of the heavenly hosts (*Saba*) in the sculptures, as Asshur the *Eponymus* hero of Assyria (Gen. 10:11) answered to the sun or Baal, Belus, the title of office, "Lord." This explains "image of the grove" (II Kings 21:7). The eagle was worshipped by the ancient Persians and Arabs. **Esar-haddon**—In Ezra 4: 2 he is mentioned as having brought colonists into Samaria. He is also thought to have been the king who carried Manasseh captive to Babylon (II Chron. 33:11). He built the palace on the mound Nebbiyunus, and that called the southwest palace of Nimroud. The latter was destroyed by fire, but his name and wars are recorded on the great bulls taken from the building. He obtained his building materials from the northwest palaces of the ancient dynasty, ending in Pul.

ADAM CLARKE

TODAY'S DICTIONARY OF THE BIBLE:

Esarhaddon—*Assur has given a brother*—successor of Sennacherib (2 Kings 19:37; Isa. 37:38). He ascended the throne about 681 B.C. Nothing further is recorded of him in Scripture, except that he settled certain colonists in Samaria (Ezra 4:2). But from the monuments it appears that he was one of the most powerful of all the Assyrian monarchs. He built many temples and palaces, the most magnificent of which was the southwest palace at Nimrud, which is said to have been in its general design almost the same as Solomon's palace, only much larger (1 Kings 7:1–12).

In December of 681 B.C. Sennacherib was murdered by two of his sons, who, after holding Nineveh for forty-two days, were compelled to flee to Erimenas of Ararat, or Armenia. Their brother Esar-haddon, who had been engaged in the campaign against Armenia, led his army against them. They were utterly overthrown in a battle fought April 680 B.C., near Malatiyeh, and in the following month Esar-haddon was crowned at Nineveh. He restored Babylon, conquered Egypt, and received tribute from Manasseh of Judah. He died in October 668 B.C., while on the march to suppress an Egyptian revolt, and was succeeded by his Assur-banipal, whose younger brother was made viceroy of Babylonia.

MATTHEW HENRY

CHAPTER 38

Verses 1–8

Neither men's greatness nor their goodness will exempt them from the arrests of sickness and death. Hezekiah, a potentate on earth and a favourite of Heaven, is struck with a disease, which, without a miracle, will certainly be mortal; and this in the midst of his days and usefulness. This sickness seized him in the midst of his triumphs over the ruined army of the Assyrians. Our being ready for death will make it come never the sooner, but much the easier; and those that are fit to die are most fit to live. Is any afflicted with sickness? *Let him pray*, James v. 13. Prayer is a salve for every sore, personal or public. Afflictions bring us to our Bibles and to our knees. When Hezekiah was in health he *went up to the house of the Lord* to pray. When he was sick in bed *he turned his face towards the wall*, probably towards the temple. The testimony of our consciences that by the grace of God we have walked closely and humbly with God, will be a great comfort to us when we come to look death in the face. And though we may not depend upon it as our righteousness, by which to be justified before God, yet we may humbly plead it as an evidence of our interest in the righteousness of the Mediator. Hezekiah does not demand a reward from God for his good services, but modestly begs that God would remember how he had approved himself to God with a single eye and an honest heart: *I have walked before thee in truth* and sincerity, *and with a perfect*, that is, an upright, *heart*; for uprightness is our gospel perfection. The same prophet that was sent to Hezekiah with warning to prepare for death is sent to him with a promise

JAMIESON, FAUSSET, BROWN

CHAPTER 38

Vss. 1-22. HEZEKIAH'S SICKNESS; PERHAPS CONNECTED WITH THE PLAGUE OR BLAST WHEREBY THE ASSYRIAN ARMY HAD BEEN DESTROYED. **1. Set . . . house in order**—Make arrangement as to the succession to the throne; for he had then no son; and as to thy other concerns. **thou shalt die**—speaking according to the ordinary course of the disease. His being spared fifteen years was not a change in God's mind, but an illustration of God's dealings being unchangeably regulated by the state of man in relation to Him. **2.** The couches in the East run along the walls of houses. He turned away from the spectators to hide his emotion and collect his thoughts for prayer. **3.** He mentions his past religious consistency, not as a boast or a ground for justification; but according to the Old Testament dispensation, wherein temporal rewards (as long life, etc., Exod. 20:12) followed legal obedience, he makes his religious conduct a plea for asking the prolongation of his life. **walked**—Life is a journey; the pious "walk with God" (Gen. 5:24; I Kings 9:4). **perfect**—sincere; not absolutely perfect, but *aiming* towards it (Matt. 5:45); single-minded in walking as in the presence of God (Gen. 17:1). The *letter* of the Old Testament legal righteousness was, however, a standard very much below the *spirit* of the law as unfolded by Christ (Matt. 5:20-48; II Cor. 3:6, 14, 17.) **wept sore**—JOSEPHUS says, the reason why he wept so sorely was that being childless, he was leaving the *kingdom* without a successor. How often our wishes, when gratified, prove curses! Hezekiah lived to have a son; that son was the idolater Manasseh, the chief cause of God's wrath against Judah,

ADAM CLARKE

CHAPTER 38

The narration of this chapter seems to be in some parts an abridgment of that of 2 Kings xx. The abridger, having finished his extract here with the eleventh verse, seems to have observed that the seventh and eighth verses of 2 Kings xx were wanted to complete the narration; he therefore added them at the end of the chapter, after he had inserted the song of Hezekiah.

MATTHEW HENRY	JAMIESON, FAUSSET, BROWN	ADAM CLARKE

that he shall not only recover, but be restored to a confirmed state of health and live fifteen years yet. When we pray in our sickness, though God send not to us such an answer, as he here sent to Hezekiah, yet, if by his Spirit he bids us be of good cheer, assures us that our sins are forgiven us, that his grace shall be sufficient for us, and that, whether we live or die, we shall be his, we have no reason to say that we pray in vain. God answers us if he *strengthens us with strength in our souls*, though not with bodily strength, Ps. cxxxviii. 3. God, knowing what lay near Hezekiah's heart, promised him not only that he should live, but that he should *see the good of Jerusalem all the days of his life* (Ps. cxxviii. 5). Jerusalem, now delivered, shall still be defended from the Assyrians. God had given Hezekiah repeated assurances of his favour; and yet, as if all were thought too little, a sign is given him.

The sign was the going back of the shadow upon the sundial. The sun is a faithful measurer of time, and he that set that clock going can set it back when he pleases, for the Father of all lights is the director of them.

Verses 9–22

Hezekiah's thanksgiving-song, which he penned, by divine direction, after his recovery. He might have taken some of the psalms of his father David, but the occasion was extraordinary, and, his heart being full of devout affections, he would offer up his affections in his own words. It is good to write a memorial of the affliction, and of the frame of our hearts under it,—to keep a record of the thoughts we had of things when we were sick, a thanksgiving to God. It is an excellent writing which Hezekiah here left, upon his recovery; and yet we find (2 Chron. xxxii. 25) that *he rendered not again according to the benefit done to him*. The impressions, one would think, should never have worn off, and yet, it seems, they did. Thanksgiving is good, but thanksliving is better. Now in this writing, when his disease prevailed, and his despair of recovery, *v.* 10–13:

I. **He tells us what his thoughts were of himself when he gave up himself for gone. We ought not** to make the worst of our case, nor to think that every sick man must needs be a dead man presently. He that brings low can raise up. Thus David sometimes, when he was delivered out of trouble, reflected upon the black and melancholy conclusions he had made upon his own case when he was in trouble, and what he had then *said in his haste*, as Ps. xxxi. 22; lxxvii. 7–9. Hezekiah was now about thirty-nine years of age, with a fair prospect of many years and happy ones. This distemper that suddenly seized him he concluded would be the *cutting off of his days*, that he should now be *deprived of the residue of his years*, and with them he should be deprived not only of the comforts of life, but of all the opportunities he had of serving God and his generation. To the same purport (*v.* 12), "*My age has departed* and gone, and

and of the overthrow of the kingdom (II Kings 23: 26, 27). **4.** In II Kings 20:4, the quickness of God's answer to the prayer is marked, "afore Isaiah had gone out into the middle court, the word of the LORD came to him"; i.e., before he had left Hezekiah, or at least when he had just left him, and Hezekiah was in the act of praying after having heard God's message by Isaiah (cf. ch. 65:24; Ps. 32:5; Dan. 9: 21). **5. God of David thy father**—God remembers the covenant with the father to the children (Exod. 20:5; Ps. 89:28, 29). **tears**—(Ps. 56:8). **days . . . years**—Man's *years,* however many, are but as so many *days* (Gen. 5:27). **6.** In II Kings 20:8, after this verse comes the statement which is put at the end, in order not to interrupt God's message (vss. 21, 22) by Isaiah (vss. 5-8). **will deliver**—The city was *already* delivered, but here assurance is given, that Hezekiah shall have *no more* to fear from the Assyrians. **7. sign**—a token that God would fulfil His promise that Hezekiah should "go up into the house of the LORD *the third day*" (II Kings 20:5, 8); the words in italics are not in Isaiah. **8. bring again**—cause to return (Josh. 10:12-14). In II Kings 20:9, 11, the choice is stated to have been given to Hezekiah, whether the shadow should go forward, or go back, ten degrees. Hezekiah replied, "It is a light thing (a less decisive miracle) for the shadow to go down (its usual direction) ten degrees: nay, but let it return backward ten degrees"; so Isaiah cried to Jehovah that it should be so, and it was so (cf. Josh. 10:12, 14). **sundial of Ahaz**—HERODOTUS (2.109) states that the sundial and the division of the day into twelve hours, were invented by the Babylonians; from them Ahaz borrowed the invention. He was one, from his connection with Tiglath-pileser, likely to have done so (II Kings 16:7, 10). "Shadow of the degrees" means the shadow made on the degrees. JOSEPHUS thinks these degrees were *steps ascending* to the palace of Ahaz; the time of day was indicated by the number of steps reached by the shadow. But probably a sundial, strictly so called, is meant; it was of such a size, and so placed, that Hezekiah, when convalescent, could witness the miracle from his chamber. Cf. vss. 21, 22 with II Kings 20:9, where translate, shall *this* shadow go forward, etc.; the dial was no doubt *in sight,* probably "in the middle court" (II Kings 20:4), the point where Isaiah turned back to announce God's gracious answers to Hezekiah. Hence this particular sign was given. The retrogression of the shadow may have been effected by refraction; a cloud denser than the air interposing between the gnomon and dial would cause the phenomenon, which does not take from the miracle, for God gave him the choice whether the shadow should go forward or back, and regulated the time and place. BOSANQUET makes the 14th year of Hezekiah to be 689 B.C., the known year of a solar eclipse, to which he ascribes the recession of the shadow. At all events, there is no need for supposing any revolution of the relative positions of the sun and earth, but merely an effect produced on the shadow (II Kings 20:9-11); that effect was only *local,* and designed for the satisfaction of Hezekiah, for the Babylonian astronomers and king "sent to inquire of the wonder that was done *in the land*" (II Chron. 32:31), implying that it had not extended to their country. No mention of any instrument for marking time occurs before this dial of Ahaz, 700 B.C. The first mention of the "hour" is made by Daniel at Babylon (Dan. 3:6). **9-20.** The prayer and thanksgiving song of Hezekiah is only given here, not in the parallel passages of II Kings and II Chron.; vs. 9 is the heading or inscription. **10. cutting off**—ROSENMULLER translates, "the meridian"; when the sun stands in the zenith: so "the perfect day" (Prov. 4:18). Rather, "in the *tranquillity* of my days," i.e., that period of life when I might now look forward to a tranquil reign [MAURER]. The *Hebrew* is so translated (ch. 62:6, 7). **go to**—rather, "go *into,*" as in ch. 46:2 [MAURER]. **residue of my years**—those which I had calculated on. God sends sickness to teach man not to calculate on the morrow, but to live more wholly to God, as if each day were the last. **11. Lord . . . Lord**—The repetition, as in vs. 19, expresses the excited feeling of the king's mind. **See the Lord** [Jehovah]—fig. for "to enjoy His good gifts." So, in a similar connection (Ps. 27:13). "I had fainted, unless I had believed *to see the goodness of the Lord* in the land of the living"; (Ps. 34:12), "What man is he that desireth life that he may *see good?*" **world**—rather, translate: "among the inhabitants of the land of *stillness,*" i.e., Hades [MAURER], in parallel antithesis to "the land of the living" in the first clause. The *Hebrew* comes from a root, to "rest" or "cease" (Job 14:6). **12. age**—rather, as the parallel "shepherd's tent" requires *habitation,* so the *Arabic* [GESE-

6. *I will defend this city.* The other copy, 2 Kings xx. 6, adds: "for mine own sake, and for my servant David's sake"; and the sentence seems somewhat abrupt without it.

8. *Which is gone down*—"By which the sun is gone down."

9. *The writing of Hezekiah.* Here the Book of Kings deserts us, the song of Hezekiah not being inserted in it.

12. *Mine age . . . is removed from me as a shepherd's tent.* I shall be removed from this

MATTHEW HENRY

is removed from me as a shepherd's tent, out of which I am forcibly dislodged by the pulling of it down in an instant." Our present residence is but like that of a shepherd in his tent, a poor, mean, and cold lodging, which will easily be taken down. But it is only the removal of it to another world, where the tents of Kedar that are taken down, coarse, black, and weather-beaten, shall be set up again in the New Jerusalem, *comely as the curtains of Solomon.* He adds another similitude: *I have cut off, like a weaver, my life.* Not that he did by any act of his own cut off the thread of his life; but, being told that he must needs die, he was forced to cut off all his projects, his *purposes were broken off,* even the *thoughts of his heart,* as Job's were, *ch.* xvii. 11. Our days are compared to the weaver's shuttle (Job. vii. 6), passing and repassing very swiftly, every throw leaving a thread behind it; and, when they are finished, the thread is cut off, and the piece taken out of the loom, and shown to our Master, to be judged of whether it be well woven or no, that we may *receive according to the things done in the body.* But as the weaver, when he has cut off his threads, has done his work, so a good man, when his life is cut off, his cares are cut off with it, and he rests from his labours. "But did I say, *I have cut off my life?* No, my times are not in my own hand; they are in God's hand, and it is he that *will cut me off from the thrum* (so the margin reads it); he has appointed what shall be the length of the piece, and, when it comes to that length, he will cut it off." He reckoned that he should go to the gates of the grave—the gates of which are always open; for it is still crying, *Give, give.* He reckoned that he was deprived of worshipping God and doing good in the world (*v.* 11): "*I said, I shall not see the Lord,* as he manifests himself in his temple, *even the Lord* here *in the land of the living.*" "*I shall see man no more.*" He shall see his subjects no more, whom he may relieve, shall see his friends no more. He reckoned that the agonies of death would be very sharp and severe: "*He will cut me off with pining sickness,* which will waste me, and wear me off, quickly." He concluded that God, whose servants all diseases are, would by them, *as a lion, break all his bones* with grinding pain, *v.* 13. He thought that next morning was the utmost he could expect to live in such pain and misery. *From day even to night wilt thou make an end of me.* When we are sick we are very apt to be thus calculating our time, but after all, we are still at uncertainty. It should be more our care how we shall get safely to another world than how long we are likely to live in this world.

II. The complaints he made in this condition (*v.* 14): "*Like a crane, or swallow, so did I chatter;* I made a noise as those birds do when they are frightened." What a change sickness makes in a little time. Some think he refers to his praying in his affliction; it was so interrupted with groanings that it was more like the chattering of a crane or a swallow. Such mean thoughts had he of his own prayers, which yet were acceptable to God. He *mourned like a dove,* sadly, but silently and patiently. He had found God so ready to answer his prayers at other times, but now his *eyes failed,* and therefore he prays, "*I am oppressed,* and ready to sink; *Lord, undertake for me.* Come between me and the gates of the grave, to which I am ready to be hurried." When we receive the sentence of death within ourselves, we are undone if the divine grace do not undertake to carry us through the valley of the shadow of death, to the heavenly kingdom on the other side of it—if Christ do not do all we need, and cannot do for ourselves.

III. The grateful acknowledgment he makes of God's goodness to him in his recovery. "*What shall I say? He has spoken unto me;* he has sent his prophet to tell me that I shall recover and live fifteen years yet; *and he himself has done it:* it is as sure to be done as if it were done already, for no word of his shall fall to the ground." God having spoken it, he is sure of it (*v.* 16): *Thou wilt restore me, and make me to live. I will go softly all my years in the bitterness of my soul,* as one in sorrow for my murmurings under my affliction. When God has delivered me I will walk cheerfully with him, as having tasted that he is gracious. He will encourage himself and others with the experiences he had had of the goodness of God (*v.* 16): "*By these things* which thou hast done for me *they live;* by the same power and goodness that have restored me all men have their souls held in life. *In all these things is the life of my spirit,* maintained by what God has done for the preservation of my natural life." He was raised up from great extremity (*v.* 17): *Behold, for peace I had great bitterness.* Upon the defeat of Sennacherib, he was suddenly seized with sickness, which embittered him, and it seemed to be the bitterness of death itself—*bitterness, bitterness,* nothing but gall and

JAMIESON, FAUSSET, BROWN

NIUS]. **departed**—is broken up, or shifted, as a tent to a different locality. The same image occurs (II Cor. 5:1; II Pet. 1:12, 13). He plainly expects to exist, and not cease to be in another state; as the shepherd still lives, after he has struck his tent and removed elsewhere.

I have cut off—He attributes to *himself* that which is *God's* will with respect to him; because he *declares* that will. So Jeremiah is said to "root out" kingdoms, because he *declares* God's purpose of doing so (Jer. 1:10). The weaver cuts off his web from the loom when completed. Job 7:6 has a like image. The Greeks represented the Fates as spinning and cutting off the threads of each man's life.

he—God. **with pining sickness**—rather, "from the thrum," or thread, which tied the loom to the weaver's beam. **from day . . . to night**—i.e., in the space of a single day between morning and night (Job 4:20). **13. I reckoned . . . that**—rather, *I composed* (my mind, during the night, expecting relief in the "morning," so Job 7:4): *for* (*that* is not, as in the *English Version,* to be supplied) as a lion He *was breaking* all my bones [VITRINGA] (Job 10:16; Lam. 3:10, 11). The *Hebrew,* in Psalm 131:2, is rendered, "I quieted." Or else, "I made myself like a lion (viz., in roaring, through pain), He was so breaking my bones!" Poets often compare great groaning to a lion's roaring, so, next verse, he compares his groans to the sounds of other animals (Ps. 22:1) [MAURER]. **14.** Rather, "Like a swallow, or a crane" (from a root; "to disturb the water," a bird frequenting the water) [MAURER], (Jer. 8:7). **chatter**—twitter: broken sounds expressive of pain. **dove**—called by the Arabs the daughter of mourning, from its plaintive note (ch. 59:11). **looking upward**—to God for relief. **undertake for**—lit., "be surety for" me; assure me that I shall be restored (Ps. 119:122). **15-20.** The second part of the song passes from prayer to thanksgiving at the prayer being heard. **What shall I say**—the language of one at a loss for words to express his sense of the unexpected deliverance. **both spoken . . . and . . . done it**—(Num. 23:19). Both promised and performed (I Thess. 5:24; Heb. 10:23). **himself**—No one else could have done it (Ps. 98:1). **go softly . . . in the bitterness**—rather, "*on account of* the bitterness"; I will behave myself humbly in remembrance of my past sorrow and sickness from which I have been delivered by God's mercy (see I Kings 21:27, 29). In Psalm 42:2, the same *Hebrew* verb expresses the slow and solemn gait of one going up to the house of God; it is found nowhere else, hence ROSENMULLER explains it, "I will reverently attend the sacred festivals in the temple"; but this ellipsis would be harsh; rather metaphorically the word is transferred to a *calm, solemn,* and *submissive* walk of life. **16. by these**—viz., *by God's benefits,* which are implied in the context (vs. 15, "He hath Himself done it" "unto me"). *All* "men live by these" benefits (Ps. 104:27-30), "and in all these is the life of my spirit," i.e., I also live by them (Deut. 8:3). **and** (wilt) **make me to live**—The *Hebrew is imperative,* "make me to live." In this view he adds a *prayer* to the confident hope founded on his comparative convalescence, which he expressed, "Thou *wilt* recover me" [MAURER]. **17. for peace**—instead of the prosperity which I had previously. **great bitterness**—lit., "bitterness to me, bitterness"; expressing intense emotion. **in love**—lit., "attachment," such as *joins* one to another tenderly; "Thou hast been lovingly attached to me from the pit"; pregnant phrase for, Thy love has gone down to the pit, and drawn me out from it. The "pit" is here simply *death,* in Hezekiah's sense; realized in its fulness only in reference to the *soul's* redemption from hell by Jesus Christ (ch. 61:1), who went down to the pit for that purpose Himself (Ps. 88:4-6; Zech. 9:11, 12; Heb. 13:20). "Sin" and sickness are connected (Ps. 103:3; cf. ch. 53:4, with Matt. 8:17; 9:5, 6), especially under the Old Testament dispensation of temporal sanctions; but even now, sickness, though not invariably arising from sin *in individuals,* is connected with it in the general moral view. **cast . . . behind back**—consigned my sins to oblivion. The same phrase occurs (I Kings 14:9; Neh. 9:26; Ps. 50:17). Contrast Psalm 90:8, "Thou hast set our iniquities *before* thee, our secret sins *in the light of thy countenance.*"

ADAM CLARKE

state to another, as a shepherd removes his tent from one place to another for the sake of his flock.

I have cut off like a weaver my life—"My life is cut off as by the weaver."

13. *I reckoned till morning,* etc.—"I roared until the morning like the lion."

14. *Undertake for me*—"Contend for me."

15. *I shall go softly all my years in the bitterness of my soul.*—"Through the rest of my years will I reflect on this bitterness of my soul."

16. *By these things men live*—"For this cause shall it be declared."

17. *For peace I had great bitterness*—"My anguish is changed into ease."

MATTHEW HENRY

wormwood. This was his condition when God sent him relief. It came from the love of God, from love to his soul. *He delivered me because he delighted in me* (Ps. xviii. 19); and the word here signifies a very affectionate love: *Thou hast loved my soul from the pit of corruption;* so it runs in the original. This is applicable to our redemption by Christ: *In his love and in his pity he redeemed us.* And the preservation of our bodies is doubly comfortable when it is in love to our souls—when God repairs the house because he has a kindness for the inhabitant. It was the effect of the pardon of sin: "*For thou hast cast all my sins behind thy back*, and thereby hast *delivered my soul from the pit of corruption*, in love to it." When we set them before our face in true repentance, as David did when his sin was ever before him, God casts them behind his back. If this sickness had been his death, it would have put a period to that course of service for the glory of God and the good of the church which he was now pursuing, *v.* 18. Having recovered from it, he resolves not only to proceed, but to abound, in praising and serving God (*v.* 19): *The living, the living, he shall praise thee.* We should not only praise him all the days of our life, but *the father to the children should make known his truth,* that the ages to come may give God the glory of his truth by trusting to it. Hezekiah, doubtless, did this himself, and yet Manasseh his son walked not in his steps. Parents may give their children many good things, good instructions, good examples, good books, but they cannot give them grace.

IV. In the last two verses of this chapter observe two lessons: 1. That God's promises are intended not to supersede, but to quicken and encourage, the use of means. Hezekiah is sure to recover, and yet he must *take a lump of figs and lay it on the boil, v.* 21. We must not put physicians, or physic, in the place of God, but make use of them in subordination to God and to his providence; help thyself and God will help thee. 2. That the chief end we should aim at, in desiring life and health, is that we may glorify God, and do good, and improve ourselves in knowledge and grace. Hezekiah, when he meant, *What is the sign that I shall recover?* asked, *What is the sign that I shall go up to the house of the Lord*, there to honour God? (*v.* 22).

JAMIESON, FAUSSET, BROWN

18. death—i.e., the dead; Hades and its inhabitants (Job 28:22; see *Note*, vs. 11), Plainly Hezekiah believed in a world of disembodied spirits; his language does not imply what skepticism has drawn from it, but simply that he regarded the disembodied state as one incapable of declaring the praises of God *before men*, for it is, *as regards this world*, an unseen land of stillness; "the living" alone can praise God *on earth*, in reference to which only he is speaking; ch. 57:1, 2 shows that at this time the true view of the blessedness of the righteous dead was held, though not with the full clearness of the Gospel, which "has brought life and immortality to light" (II Tim. 1:10). **hope for thy truth**—(Ps. 104:27). Their probation is at an end. They can no longer exercise faith and hope in regard to Thy faithfulness to Thy promises, which are limited to the present state. For "hope" ceases (even in the case of the godly) when sight begins (Rom. 8:24, 25); the ungodly have "no hope" (I Thess. 4:13). Hope in God's truth is one of the grounds of praise to God (Ps. 71:14; 119:49). Others translate, "cannot celebrate.". **19. living . . . living**—emphatic repetition, as in vss. 11, 17; his heart is so full of the main object of his prayer that, for want of adequate words, he repeats the same word. **father to the children**—one generation of the *living* to another. He probably, also, hints at his own desire to live until he should have a child, the successor to his throne, to whom he might make known and so perpetuate the memory of God's truth. **truth**—*faithfulness* to His promises; especially in Hezekiah's case, His promise of hearing prayer. **20. was ready**—not in the *Hebrew*; "Jehovah was for my salvation," i.e., saved me (cf. ch. 12:2). **we**—I and my people. **in the house of the Lord**—This song was designed, as many of the other Psalms, as a *form* to be used in public worship at stated times, perhaps on every anniversary of his recovery; hence "all the days of *our* life." **lump of figs**—a round cake of figs pressed into a mass (I Sam. 25:18). God works by means; the meanest of which He can make effectual. **boil**—inflamed ulcer, produced by the plague. **22. house of the Lord**—Hence he makes the praises to be sung there prominent in his song (vs. 20; Ps. 116:12-14, 17-19).

ADAM CLARKE

E. H. PLUMPTRE:

Verse 21. "For Isaiah had said." The direction implies some medical training on the part of Isaiah, such as entered naturally into the education of the prophet-priests. They were to Israel, especially in the case of leprosy and other kindred diseases, what the priests of Asclepios were to Greece. The Divine promise guaranteed success to the use of natural remedies, but did not dispense with them, and they, like the spittle laid on the eyes of the blind in the Gospel miracles (Mark 7:33; John 9:6), were also a help to the faith on which the miracle depended. Both this and the following verse seem, as has been said, to have been notes to verse 8, supplied from the narrative of 2 Kings 20, and placed at the end of the chapter instead of at the foot of the page, as in modern MSS. or print. The word for "boil" appears in connection with leprosy in Exod. 9:9; Lev. 13:18, but is used generically for any kind of abscess, carbuncle, and the like.
—*Ellicott's Commentary on the Whole Bible*

21. *Let them take a lump of figs.* God, in effecting this miraculous cure, was pleased to order the use of means not improper for that end.

MATTHEW HENRY

CHAPTER 39

Verses 1-4

Humanity and common civility teach us to rejoice with our friends and neighbours when they rejoice, particularly on their recoveries from sickness. The king of Babylon, having heard that Hezekiah had recovered, sent to compliment him. The sun was the Babylonians' god; and when they understood that it was with a respect to Hezekiah that the sun went back ten degrees, on such a day, they thought themselves obliged to do Hezekiah all the honour they could. The king of Babylon made his court to Hezekiah, not because he was pious, but because he was prosperous, as the Philistines coveted an alliance with Isaac, Gen. xxvi. 28. The king of Babylon was an enemy to the king of Assyria, and therefore was fond of Hezekiah, because the Assyrians were so weakened by the power of his God.

JAMIESON, FAUSSET, BROWN

CHAPTER 39

Vss. 1-8. Hezekiah's Error in the Display of His Riches to the Babylonian Ambassador. **1. Merodach-baladan**—For 150 years before the overthrow of Nineveh by Cyaxares the Mede, a succession of rulers, mostly viceroys of Assyria, ruled Babylon, from the time of Nabonassar, 747 B.C. That date is called "the Era of Nabonassar." Pul or Phallukha was then expelled, and a new dynasty set up at Nineveh, under Tiglath-pileser. Semiramis, Pul's wife, then retired to Babylon, with Nabonassar, her son, whose advent to the throne of Babylon, after the overthrow of the old line at Nineveh, marked a new era. Sometimes the viceroys of Babylon made themselves, for a time, independent of Assyria; thus Merodach-baladan at this time did so, encouraged by the Assyrian disaster in the Jewish campaign. He had done so before, and was defeated in the first year of Sennacherib's reign, as is recorded in cuneiform characters in that monarch's palace of Koyunjik. Nabopolassar was the first who established, *permanently*, his independence; his son, Nebuchadnezzar, raised Babylon to the position which Nineveh once occupied; but from the want of stone near the Lower Euphrates, the buildings of Babylon, formed of sun-dried brick, have not stood the wear of ages as Nineveh has. **Merodach**—an idol, the same as the god of war and planet Mars (Jer. 50:2). Often kings took their names from their gods, as if peculiarly under their tutelage. So Belshazzar from Bel. **Baladan**—means "Bel is his lord." The chronicle of Eusebius contains a fragment of Berosus, stating that Acises, an Assyrian viceroy, usurped the supreme command at Babylon. Merodach- (or Berodach) baladan murdered him and succeeded to the throne. Sennacherib conquered Merodach-baladan and left Esar-haddon, his son, as governor of Babylon. Merodach-baladan would naturally court the alliance of Hezekiah, who, like himself, had thrown off the yoke of the Assyrian king, and who would be equally glad of the Babylonian alliance against Assyria; hence arose the excessive attention which he paid to the usurper. **sick**—An additional reason is given (II Chron. 32:31). "The princes of Babylon sent to inquire of the wonder that was done in the land"; viz., the recession of the shadow on Ahaz' sundial; to the Chaldean astrono-

ADAM CLARKE

CHAPTER 39

TODAY'S DICTIONARY OF THE BIBLE:

Merodach—*Babylonian Marduk*—the name of the chief Babylonian god, later called Bel. The Babylonian creation story says he created heaven and earth from the body of the monster Tiamat. This name frequently occurs as a surname to the kings of Assyria and Babylon.

Merodachbaladan—*Merodach has given a son*—(Isa. 39:1), "the hereditary chief of the Chaldeans, a small tribe at the time settled in the marshes at the mouth of the Euphrates, but in consequence of his conquest of Babylon afterward, they became the dominant caste in Babylonia itself." One bearing this name sent ambassadors to Hezekiah (712 B.C.). He is also called Berodach-baladan (2 Kings 20:12).

MATTHEW HENRY

Hezekiah was a wise and good man, but, when one miracle after another was wrought in his favour, he found it hard to keep his heart from being lifted up into the snare of pride. What a poor thing it was for Hezekiah, whom God had so dignified, to be over proud of the respect paid him by a heathen prince as if that added anything to him! As far as we see cause to suspect that this sly and subtle sin of pride has insinuated itself into our breasts, let us be ashamed of it, as Hezekiah here.

Verses 5–8

If God love us, he will humble us. A mortifying message is sent to Hezekiah, that he might be humbled for the pride of his heart, and be convinced of the folly of it. When Hezekiah boasts of his treasures he is told that he acts like the foolish traveller who shows his money and gold to one that proves a thief and is thereby tempted to rob him. If Hezekiah had known that the successors of this king of Babylon would hereafter be the ruin of his family and kingdom, he would not have complimented his ambassadors as he did; and, when the prophet told him that it would be so, we may well imagine how he was vexed at himself for what he had done. Those that are fond of an alliance with irreligious men will have enough of it, and will have cause to repent it. Hezekiah thought himself very happy in the friendship of Babylon, though it was the mother of harlots and idolatries; but Babylon, who now courted Jerusalem, in process of time conquered her and carried her captive. Hezekiah reckoned *that* word of the Lord good which made him sensible that he had done amiss. When Hezekiah told of the punishment of his iniquity he said, *Good is the word of the Lord.*

JAMIESON, FAUSSET, BROWN

mers, such a fact would be especially interesting, the dial having been invented at Babylon. **2. glad**—It was not the mere act, but the spirit of it, which provoked God (II Chron. 32:25), "Hezekiah rendered not again according to the benefit done unto him, for *his heart was lifted up*"; also cf. vs. 31. God "tries" His people at different times by different ways, bringing out "all that is in their heart," to show them its varied corruptions. Cf. David in a similar case (I Chron. 21:1-8). **precious things**—rather, "the house of his (aromatic) spices"; from a *Hebrew* root, to "break to pieces," as is done to aromatics. **silver . . . gold**—partly obtained from the Assyrian camp (ch. 33:4); partly from presents (II Chron. 32:23, 27-29). **precious ointment**—used for anointing kings and priests. **armour**—or else vessels in general; the parallel passage (II Chron. 32:27), "treasuries . . . *for shields,*" favors *English Version.* His arsenal. **3. What . . . whence**—implying that any proposition coming from the idolatrous enemies of God, with whom Israel was forbidden to form alliance, should have been received with anything but *gladness.* Reliance on Babylon, rather than on God, was a similar sin to the previous reliance on Egypt (chs. 30 and 31). **far country**—implying that he had done nothing more than was proper in showing attention to strangers "from a far country. **4. All**—a frank confession of his *whole* fault; the king submits his conduct to the scrutiny of a subject, because that subject was accredited by God. Contrast Asa (II Chron. 16:7-10). **5. Lord of hosts**—who has all thy goods at His disposal. **6. days come**—120 years afterwards. This is the first intimation that the Jews would be carried to *Babylon*—the first designation of their *place* of punishment. The general prophecy of Moses (Lev. 26:33; Deut. 28:64); the more particular one of Ahijah in Jeroboam's time (I Kings 14:15), "beyond the river"; and of Amos 5:27, "captivity beyond Damascus"; are now concentrated in this specific one as to "Babylon" (Mic. 4:10). It was an exact retribution in kind, that as Babylon had been the instrument of Hezekiah and Judah's sin, so also it should be the instrument of their punishment. **7. sons . . . from thee**—The sons which Hezekiah (as Josephus tells us) wished to have (*Note,* ch. 28:3, on "wept sore") will be among the foremost in suffering. **eunuchs**—fulfilled (Dan. 1:2, 3, 7). **8. peace . . . in my days**—The punishment was not, as in David's case (II Sam. 24:13-15), sent in his time. True repentance acquiesces in all God's ways and finds cause of thanksgiving in any mitigation.

ADAM CLARKE

8. *Then said Hezekiah.* The nature of Hezekiah's crime, and his humiliation on the message of God to him by the prophet, is more expressly declared by the author of the Book of the Chronicles: "But Hezekiah rendered not again according to the benefit done unto him; for his heart was lifted up: therefore there was wrath upon him, and upon Judah and Jerusalem. Notwithstanding Hezekiah humbled himself for the pride of his heart, both he and the inhabitants of Jerusalem, so that the wrath of the Lord came not upon them in the days of Hezekiah. . . . And Hezekiah prospered in all his works. Howbeit in the business of the ambassadors of the princes of Babylon, who sent unto him to enquire of the wonder that was done in the land, God left him, to try him, that he might know all that was in his heart" (2 Chron. xxxii. 25-26, 30-31).

There shall be peace and truth in my days. I rather think these words should be understood as a humble inquiry of the king, addressed to the prophet. "Shall there be prosperity, *shalom,* and truth in my days?—Shall I escape the evil which you predict?" Understood otherwise, they manifest a pitiful unconcern both for his own family and for the nation. This is the view I have taken of the passage in 2 Kings xxi. 19.

MATTHEW HENRY

CHAPTER 40

Verses 1–2

The commission and instructions given, not to this prophet only, but to all the Lord's prophets, and to all Christ's ministers, to proclaim comfort to God's people. Let them be sure that, notwithstanding all this, God had mercy in store for them. It was especially a direction to the prophets that should live in the time of the captivity, when Jerusalem was in ruins; they must encourage the captives to hope. Gospel ministers, being employed by the blessed Spirit as comforters, and as helpers of the joy of Christians, are here put in mind of their business.

I. Comfortable words directed to God's people in general, *v.* 1. The prophets have instructions from their God to comfort the people of God. There are a people in the world that are God's people. It is the will of God that his people should be a comforted people, even in the worst of times. Words of conviction, such as we had in the former part of this book, must be followed with words of comfort, such as we have here; for he that has torn will heal us.

II. Comfortable words directed to Jerusalem in particular: "*Speak to the heart of Jerusalem* (*v.* 2). Do not whisper it, but *cry unto her*: show saints their comforts as well as sinners their transgressions; make her hear it." *Her warfare is accomplished,* the set time of her servitude; the campaign is now at an end. Human life is a warfare (Job vii. 1); the Christian life much more. But the struggle will not last always; the warfare will be accomplished, and then the good soldiers shall not only enter into rest, but be sure of their pay. The cause of her trouble is removed, and, when that is taken away, the effect will cease. Tell her that *her iniquity is pardoned,* God is reconciled to her. Nothing can be spoken more comfortably than this, *Son, be of good cheer; thy sins are forgiven thee.* Troubles are *then* removed in love when sin is pardoned. *She has received of the Lord double for* the cure of *all her sins,* more than sufficient to separate between her and her idols, the worship of which was the great sin from which God

JAMIESON, FAUSSET, BROWN

CHAPTER 40

Vss. 1-31. Second Part of the Prophecies of Isaiah. The former were local and temporary in their reference. These belong to the distant future, and are world-wide in their interest; the deliverance from Babylon under Cyrus, which he here foretells by prophetic suggestion, carries him on to the greater deliverance under Messiah, the Saviour of Jews and Gentiles in the present eclectic Church, and the restorer of Israel and Head of the world-wide kingdom, literal and spiritual, ultimately. As Assyria was the hostile world power in the former part, which refers to Isaiah's own time, so Babylon is so in the latter part, which refers to a period long subsequent. The connecting link, however, is furnished (ch. 39:6) at the close of the former part. The latter part was written in the old age of Isaiah, as appears from the greater mellowness of style and tone which pervades it; it is less fiery and more tender and gentle than the former part. **1. Comfort ye**—twice repeated to give double assurance. Having announced the coming captivity of the Jews in Babylon. God now desires His servants, the prophets (ch. 52:7), to comfort them. The scene is laid in Babylon; the time, near the close of the captivity; the ground of comfort is the speedy ending of the captivity, the Lord Himself being their leader. **my people . . . your God**—correlatives (Jer. 31:33; Hos. 1:9, 10). It is God's covenant relation with His people, and His "word" of promise (vs. 8) to their forefathers, which is the ground of His interposition in their behalf, after having for a time chastised them (ch. 54:8). **2. comfortably**—lit., "to the heart"; not merely to the intellect. **Jerusalem**—though then in ruins, regarded by God as about to be rebuilt; her *people* are chiefly meant, but the *city* is personified. **cry**—publicly and emphatically as a herald cries aloud (vs. 3). **warfare**—the *appointed time* of her misery (Job 7:1, *Margin:* 14:14; Dan. 10: 1). The ulterior and Messianic reference probably is *the definite time* when the legal economy of bur-

ADAM CLARKE

CHAPTER 40

The course of prophecies which follow, from hence to the end of the book, and which taken together constitute the most elegant part of the sacred writings of the Old Testament, interspersed also with many passages of the highest sublimity, was probably delivered in the latter part of the reign of Hezekiah. The prophet in the foregoing chapter had delivered a very explicit declaration of the impending dissolution of the kingdom, and of the captivity of the royal house of David, and of the people, under the kings of Babylon. As the subject of his subsequent prophecies was to be chiefly of the consolatory kind, he opens them with giving a promise of the restoration of the kingdom, and the return of the people from that captivity, by the merciful interposition of God in their favor. But the views of the prophet are not confined to this event. As the restoration of the royal family and of the tribe of Judah, which would otherwise have soon become undistinguished and have been irrecoverably lost, was necessary, in the design and order of Providence, for the fulfilling of God's promises of establishing a more glorious and an everlasting Kingdom, under the Messiah to be born of the tribe of Judah, and of the family of David, the prophet connects these two events together, and hardly ever treats of the former without throwing in some intimations of the latter; and sometimes is so fully possessed with the glories of the future and more remote Kingdom that he seems to leave the more immediate subject of his commission almost out of the question.

I have not the least doubt that the return of the Jews from the captivity of Babylon is the first, though not the principal, thing in the prophet's view. The redemption from Babylon is clearly foretold, and at the same time is em-

MATTHEW HENRY

designed to reclaim them by their captivity in Babylon. It begat in them a rooted antipathy to idolatry, and was physic doubly strong for the purging out of that iniquity. True penitents have indeed, in Christ and his sufferings, *received of the Lord's hand double for all their sins;* for the satisfaction Christ made by his death was of such an infinite value that it was more than double to the demerits of sin; *for God spared not his own Son.*

Verses 3–8

The time to favour Zion having come, the people of God must be prepared, by repentance and faith, for the favours designed them. We have here *the voice of one crying in the wilderness,* which *may* be applied to those prophets, with the captives who, when they saw the day of their deliverance dawn, called earnestly upon them to prepare for it. But it *must* be applied to John the Baptist; for, though God was the speaker, he was *the voice of one crying in the wilderness* to *prepare the way of the Lord,* to dispose men's minds for the reception of the gospel of Christ.

I. By repentance for sin; which John Baptist preached to all Judah and Jerusalem (Matt. iii. 2, 5), and thereby *made ready a people prepared for the Lord,* Luke i. 17. God is coming in a way of mercy, and we must prepare for him, *v.* 3–5. If we apply it to their captivity, it may be taken as a promise that, whatever difficulties lie in their way, when they return they shall be removed. This voice in the wilderness sets pioneers on work to level the roads. It is the same duty that we are called to, in preparation for Christ's entrance into our souls. We must get into such a frame of spirit as will dispose us to receive Christ and his gospel: "*Prepare you the way of the Lord;* and let all be suppressed which would be an obstruction to his entrance. Make room for Christ: *Make straight a highway for him.*" Those that are hindered from comfort in Christ by their dejections and despondencies are the valleys that must be exalted. Those that are hindered from comfort in Christ by a proud conceit are the mountains and hills that must be made low. Those that have entertained prejudices against the word and ways of God, that are untractable, are the crooked that must be made straight. When this is done *the glory of the Lord shall be revealed, v.* 5. When the captives are prepared for deliverance Cyrus shall proclaim it. When John Baptist has for some time preached repentance, and so made ready a people prepared for the Lord (Luke i. 17), then the Messiah himself shall be revealed in his glory, working miracles, and by his grace binding up and healing with consolations those whom John had wounded with convictions. And this revelation of divine glory shall be *a light to lighten the Gentiles. All flesh shall see it together,* and not the Jews only, as the return out of captivity was taken notice of by the neighbouring nations, Ps. cxxvi. 2.

II. By confidence in the word of the Lord, and not in any creature. By this accomplishment of the prophecies and promises of salvation, it appears that the word of the Lord is sure. The power of man, when it does appear against the deliverance, is not to be feared; for it shall be as grass before the word of the Lord: it shall wither and be trodden down. The insulting Babylonians are but as grass. The power of man, when it would appear for the deliverance, is not to be trusted, for it is but as grass. When God is about to work salvation for his people he will take them off from depending upon creatures, and looking for it from hills and mountains. The word of our God, that glory of the Lord which is now to be revealed, the gospel, and that grace which is brought with it to us and wrought by it in us, shall stand for ever. To prepare the way of the Lord we must be convinced that all flesh is grass, weak and withering. We ourselves therefore cannot save ourselves. All the beauty of the creature is but as the flower of grass. We must be convinced that the word of the Lord will furnish us with a happiness that will run parallel with the duration of our souls, which must live for ever.

Verses 9–11

It was promised (*v.* 5) *that the glory of the Lord shall be revealed.*

I. How it shall be revealed, *v.* 9. Notice shall be given of it to the remnant that are left in Zion and Jerusalem, the poor of the land, who were vine-dressers and husbandmen; it shall be told them that their brethren shall return to them. This shall be told also to the captives who belonged to Zion and Jerusalem. Zion is said to *dwell with the daughter of Babylon* (Zech ii. 7); and there she receives notice of Cyrus's gracious proclamation. It shall be published by Zion and Jerusalem (so the text reads it); those that remain there, or that have already returned, let them proclaim it as loudly as they can: let them

JAMIESON, FAUSSET, BROWN

densome rites is at an end (Gal. 4:3, 4). **pardoned**—The *Hebrew* expresses that her iniquity is so *expiated* that God now *delights* in restoring her. **double for all her sins**—This can only, in a very restricted sense, hold good of Judah's restoration after the first captivity. For how can it be said her "warfare was accomplished," when as yet the galling yoke of Antiochus and also of Rome was before them? The "double for her sins" must refer to the twofold captivity, the Assyrian and the Roman; at the coming close of this latter dispersion, and then only, can her "iniquity" be said to be "pardoned," or *fully* expiated [HOUBIGANT]. It does not mean double as much as she *deserved,* but *ample* punishment in her twofold captivity. Messiah is the antitypical Israel (cf. Matt. 2:15, with Hos. 11:1). He indeed has "received" of sufferings *amply* more than enough to expiate "for our sins" (Rom. 5:15, 17). Otherwise (cry unto her) "that she *shall* receive (*blessings*) of the Lord's hand double to the *punishment of all her sins*" (so "sin" is used, Zech. 14:19, *Margin*) [LOWTH]. *English Version* is simpler. **3. crieth in the wilderness**—So the LXX and Matt. 3:3 connect the words. The *Hebrew* accents, however, connect them thus: "In the wilderness prepare ye," etc., and the parallelism also requires this, "Prepare ye *in the wilderness,*" answering to "make straight *in the desert.*" Matthew was entitled, as under inspiration, to vary the connection, so as to bring out another sense, included in the Holy Spirit's intention; in Matthew 3:1, "John the Baptist, *preaching in the wilderness,*" answers thus to "The voice of one *crying in the wilderness.*" MAURER takes the participle as put for the finite verb (so in vs. 6), "A voice *crieth.*" The clause, "in the wilderness," alludes to Israel's passage through it from Egypt to Canaan (Ps. 68:7), Jehovah being their leader; so it shall be at the coming restoration of Israel, of which the restoration from Babylon was but a type (not the full realization; for their way from it was *not* through the "wilderness"). Where John preached (viz., in the wilderness; the type of this earth, a moral wilderness), *there* were the hearers who are ordered to prepare the way of the Lord, and *there* was to be the coming of the Lord [BENGEL]. John, though he was immediately followed by the suffering Messiah, is rather the herald of the coming *reigning* Messiah, as Malachi 4:5, 6 ("before *the great* and *dreadful day of the Lord*"), proves. Matthew 17:11 (cf. Acts 3:21) implies that John is not exclusively meant; and that though in one sense Elias has come, in another he is *yet to come.* John was the figurative Elias, coming "in the *spirit and power* of Elias" (Luke 1:17); John 1:21, where John the Baptist denies that he was the *actual* Elias, accords with this view. Malachi 4:5, 6 cannot have received its exhaustive fulfilment in John; the Jews always understood it of the literal Elijah. As there is another consummating advent of Messiah Himself, so perhaps there is to be of his forerunner Elias, who also was present at the transfiguration. **the Lord**—*Hebrew, Jehovah;* as this is applied to Jesus, He must be Jehovah (Matt. 3:3). **4.** Eastern monarchs send heralds before them in a journey to clear away obstacles, make causeways over valleys, and level hills. So John's duty was to bring back the people to obedience to the law and to remove all self-confidence, pride in national privileges, hypocrisy, and irreligion, so that they should be ready for His coming (Mal. 4:6; Luke 1:17). **crooked**—declivities. **5. see it**—The LXX for "it," has "the salvation of God." So Luke 3:6 (cf. Luke 2:30, i.e., Messiah); but the Evangelist probably took these words from ch. 52:10. **for**—rather, "All flesh shall see *that* the mouth of Jehovah hath spoken it" [BENGEL]. **6. The voice**—the same divine herald as in vs. 3. **he**—one of those ministers or prophets (*Note,* vs. 1) whose duty it was, by direction of "the voice," to "comfort the Lord's afflicted people with the promises of brighter days." **All flesh is grass**—The connection is, "All *human* things, however goodly, are transitory: *God's* promises alone are steadfast" (vs. 8, 15, 17, 23, 24); this contrast was already suggested in vs. 5, "*All flesh . . . the mouth of the Lord.*" I Peter 1:24, 25 applies this passage distinctly to the gospel word of Messiah (cf. John 12:24; Jas. 1:10). **7. spirit of the Lord**—rather, "wind of Jehovah" (Ps. 103:16). The withering east wind of those countries sent by Jehovah (Jonah 4:8). **the people**—rather, this people [LOWTH], which may refer to the Babylonians [ROSENMULLER]; but better, *mankind in general,* as in ch. 42:5, so vs. 6, "*all flesh*"; *this whole race,* i.e., man. **9. Rather,** "Oh, thou that bringest good things *to Zion;* thou that bringest good tidings *to Jerusalem.*" "Thou" is thus the collective personification of the *messengers* who announce God's gracious purpose to Zion

ADAM CLARKE

ployed as an image to shadow out a redemption of an infinitely higher and more important nature.

Yet obvious and plain as I think this literal sense is, we have nevertheless the irrefragable authority of John the Baptist, and of our blessed Saviour himself, as recorded by all the Evangelists, for explaining this exordium of the prophecy of the opening of the gospel by the preaching of John, and of the introduction of the kingdom of Messiah; who was to effect a much greater deliverance of the people of God, Gentiles as well as Jews, from the captivity of sin and the dominion of death. And this we shall find to be the case in many subsequent parts also of this prophecy, where passages manifestly relating to the deliverance of the Jewish nation, effected by Cyrus, are, with good reason, and upon undoubted authority, to be understood of the redemption wrought for mankind by Christ.

2. *Double for all her sins*—"Blessings double to the punishment." It does not seem reconcilable to our notions of the divine justice, which always punishes less than our iniquities deserve, to suppose that God had punished the sins of the Jews in double proportion; and it is more agreeable to the tenor of this consolatory message to understand it as a promise of ample recompense for the effects of past displeasure, on the reconciliation of God to His returning people.

3. *The voice of him that crieth in the wilderness.* The idea is taken from the practice of Eastern monarchs, who, whenever they entered upon an expedition or took a journey, especially through desert and unpracticed countries, sent harbingers before them to prepare all things for their passage, and pioneers to open the passes, to level the ways, and to remove all impediments. The Jewish church, to which John was sent to announce the coming of Messiah, was at that time in a barren and desert condition, unfit, without reformation, for the reception of her King. It was in this desert country, destitute at that time of all religious cultivation, in true piety and good works unfruitful, that John was sent to prepare the way of the Lord by preaching repentance.

6. *The voice said, Cry*—"A voice saith, Proclaim." To understand rightly this passage is a matter of importance; for it seems designed to give us the true key to the remaining part of Isaiah's prophecies, the general subject of which is the restoration of the people and Church of God. The prophet opens the subject with great clearness and elegance; he declares at once God's command to His messengers to comfort His people in captivity, to impart to them the joyful tidings, that their punishment has now satisfied the divine justice, and the time of reconciliation and favor is at hand. He then introduces a harbinger giving orders to prepare the way for God, leading His people from Babylon, as He did formerly from Egypt, through the wilderness; to remove all obstacles and to clear the way for their passage. Thus far nothing more appears to be intended than a return from the Babylonish captivity; but the next words seem to intimate something much greater: "And the glory of Jehovah shall be revealed; And all flesh shall see together the salvation of our God." He then introduces a voice commanding him to make a solemn proclamation. And what is the import of it? that the people—the *flesh*—is of a vain, temporary nature; that all its glory fadeth, and is soon gone; but that the word of God endureth for-ever.

7. *Because the spirit of the Lord*—"When the wind of Jehovah." *Ruach Yehovah,* a wind of Jehovah, is a Hebraism, meaning no more than a strong wind. It is well-known that a hot wind in the East destroys every green thing.

9. *O Zion, that bringest good tidings*—"O Daughter, that bringest glad tidings to Zion." The office of announcing and celebrating such glad tidings as are here spoken of belongs peculiarly to the women. On occasion of any

MATTHEW HENRY

lift up their voice with strength. Let them say to the cities of Judah, and all the inhabitants of the country, *Behold your God. This is our God, we have waited for him.* This may refer to the invitation which was sent forth from Jerusalem to the cities of Judah, as soon as they had set up an altar, immediately upon their return out of captivity, to come and join with them in their sacrifices, Ezra iii. 2–4. But this was to have its full accomplishment in the apostles' public and undaunted preaching of the gospel to all nations, beginning at Jerusalem.

II. What that glory is which shall be revealed. *He will come with strong hand,* too strong to be obstructed though it may be opposed. He shall recompense to all according to their works, as a righteous Judge: *His reward is with him. His work is before him. He himself knows what he will do.* God is the *Shepherd of Israel* (Ps. lxxx. 1); Christ is the good Shepherd, John x. 11. *He shall feed his flock like a shepherd.* His word is food for his flock to feed on; his ordinances are fields for them to feed in; his ministers are under-shepherds. He takes care of the lambs that are weak, and cannot help themselves and *those that are with young.* The good Shepherd has a tender care for children, for young converts, for weak believers, and those that are of a sorrowful spirit. These are the lambs of his flock. He will gather them in when they wander, gather them up when they fall, gather them together when they are dispersed, and gather them home to himself at last; and all this with his own arm, out of which none shall be able to pluck them, John x. 28. He will gently lead them.

Verses 12–17

These verses describe the greatness and glory of the Lord Jehovah, God of Israel, and were written to encourage his people that were captives in Babylon to hope, and depend upon him for deliverance, and to fill those who receive the glad tidings of redemption by Christ with a holy awe and reverence of God.

I. His power is unlimited, *v.* 12. 1. He has a vast reach. View the celestial globe, but the great God *metes the heavens with a span.* All the waters in the world he can *measure in the hollow of his hand,* and he *comprehends the dust of the earth in a measure,* or with his three fingers; it is no more to him that a *pugil,* or that which we take up between our thumb and two fingers. 2. He has a vast strength, and can as easily move mountains as the tradesman heaves his good into the scales; he poises them with his hand as exactly as if he weighed them in a pair of balances.

II. His wisdom is unsearchable, *v.* 13, 14. As none can do what God has done, so none can suggest anything to him which he thought not of. When the Lord made the world (Job xxvi. 13) there was none that gave him any advice. Nor does he need any counsellor to direct him in the government of the world.

III. The nations of the world are nothing in comparison, *v.* 15, 17. Take all the great and mighty nations, kings the most pompous, kingdoms the most populous; take the isles, the multitude of the isles of the Gentiles: *Before him* they are *as a drop of the bucket* compared with the vast ocean, or *the small dust of the balance* (which does not serve to turn it, and therefore is not regarded, it is so small) in comparison with all the dust of the earth. *He takes them up as a very little thing. They are counted by him,* **and are to be counted by us** *less than nothing, and vanity.* He can as easily bring them all into nothing as at first he brought them out of nothing. They are all *vanity;* the word used for the chaos (Gen. i. 2). This magnifies God's love to the world, that, though it is of such small account with him, yet, for the redemption of it, he *gave his only-begotten Son,* John iii. 16.

IV. The services of the church can make no addition to him (*v.* 16): *Lebanon is not sufficient to burn* for the fuel of the altar, nor the beasts of it for sacrifices, *v.* 16. He is exalted *far above all blessing and praise,* all burnt-offerings and sacrifices.

Verses 18–26

The prophet here reproves those, 1. Who made images and then said that they resembled God, and paid their homage to them. 2. Who put creatures in the place of God, who feared them more than God, or loved them more than God. Twice the challenge is here made, *To whom will you liken God? v.* 18, and again *v.* 25. *To whom will you liken me?* This shows the absurdity, (1) Of making visible images of him who is invisible, imagining the image to be animated by the deity. (2) Of making creatures equal with God in our affections. Proud people make themselves equal with God; covetous people make their money equal with God; and whatever we esteem or love,

JAMIESON, FAUSSET, BROWN

(*Note,* vs. 1); ch. 52:7 confirms this [VULGATE and GESENIUS]. If *English Version* be retained, the sense will be the glad message was first to be proclaimed to Jerusalem, and then from it as the center to all "Judea, Samaria, and the uttermost parts of the earth" (Luke 24:47, 49; Acts 1:8) [VITRINGA and HENGSTENBERG]. **mountain**—It was customary for those who were about to promulgate any great thing, to ascend a hill from which they could be seen and heard by all (Judg. 9:7; Matt. 5:1). **be not afraid**—to announce to the exiles that their coming return home is attended with danger in the midst of the Babylonians. The gospel minister must "open his mouth *boldly*" (Prov. 29:25; Eph. 6:19). **Behold**—especially at His second coming (Zech. 12:10; 14:5). **10. with strong hand**—rather, as a strong one [MAURER]. Or, against the strong one, viz., Satan (Matt. 12:29; Rev. 20:2, 3, 10) [VITRINGA]. **arm**—power (Ps. 89:13; 98:1). **for him**—i.e., He needs not to seek help for Himself from any external source, but by His own inherent power He gains rule for Himself (so vs. 14). **work**—rather, recompense which He gives for work (ch. 62:11; Rev. 22:12). **11. feed**—including all a shepherd's care—"tend" (Ezek. 34:23; Ps. 23:1; Heb. 13:20; I Pet. 2:25). **carry**—applicable to *Messiah's restoration of Israel,* as sheep scattered in all lands, and unable to move of themselves *to their own land* (Ps. 80:1; Jer. 23:3). As Israel was "carried from the womb" (i.e., in its earliest days) (ch. 63:9, 11, 12; Ps. 77:20), so it shall be in "old age" (its latter days) (ch. 46:3, 4). **gently lead**—as a thoughtful shepherd does the ewes "giving suck" (Margin) (Gen. 33:13, 14). **12.** Lest the Jews should suppose that He who was just before described as a "shepherd" is a mere man, He is now described as GOD. **Who**—Who else but GOD could do so? Therefore, though the redemption and restoration of His people, foretold here, was a work beyond man's power, they should not doubt its fulfilment since all things are possible to Him who can accurately *regulate the proportion of the waters* as if He had measured them with His hand (cf. vs. 15). But MAURER translates: "Who can measure . . . " i.e., How immeasurable are the works of God? The former is a better explanation (Job 28:25; Prov. 30: 4). **span**—the space from the end of the thumb to the end of the middle finger extended; God measures the vast heavens as one would measure a small object with his span. **dust of the earth**—All the *earth* is to Him but as a few grains of *dust contained in a small measure* (lit., the *third* part of a larger measure). **hills in a balance**—adjusted in their right proportions and places, **as exactly as if He had** *weighed* them out. **13.** Quoted in Romans 11: 34; I Corinthians 2:16. The *Hebrew* here for "directed" is the same as in vs. 12 for "meted out"; thus the sense is, "Jehovah measures out heaven with His span"; but who can measure Him? i.e., Who can *search out* His Spirit (*mind*) wherewith He searches out and accurately adjusts all things? MAURER rightly takes the *Hebrew* in the same sense as in vs. 12 (so Prov. 16:2; 21:2), "weigh," "ponder." "Direct," as in *English Version,* answers, however, better to "taught" in the parallel clause. **14. path of jugdment**—His wisdom, whereby He so beautifully adjusts the places and proportions of all created things. **15. of**—rather (hanging) *from* a bucket [MAURER]. **he taketh up . . . as a very little thing**—rather, "are as a mere grain of dust which is taken up," viz., by the wind; lit., "one taketh up," impersonally (Exod. 16:14) [MAURER]. **isles**—rather, *lands* in general, answering to "the nations" in the parallel clause; perhaps *lands,* like Mesopotamia, enclosed by rivers [JEROME] (so ch. 42:15). However, *English Version,* "isles" answers well to "mountains" (vs. 12), both alike being lifted up by the power of God; in fact, "isles" are mountains upheaved from the bed of the sea by volcanic agency; only that he seems here to have passed from unintelligent creatures (vs. 12) to intelligent, as *nations* and *lands,* i.e., their inhabitants. **16.** All Lebanon's forest would not supply fuel enough to burn sacrifices worthy of the glory of God (ch. 66:1; I Kings 8:27; Ps. 50:8-13). **beasts**—which abounded in Lebanon. **17.** (Ps. 62:9; Dan. 4:35). **less than nothing**—MAURER translates, as in ch. 41:24, "of nothing" (*partitively*; or expressive of the *nature* of a thing), a mere nothing. **vanity**—emptiness. **18.** Which of the heathen idols, then, is to be compared to this Almighty God? This passage, if not written (as BARNES thinks) so late as the idolatrous times of Manasseh, has at least a prospective warning reference to them and subsequent reigns; the result of the chastisement of Jewish idolatry in the Babylonish captivity was that thenceforth after the restoration the Jews never fell into it. Perhaps these prophecies here may have tended to

ADAM CLARKE

great public success, a signal victory, or any other joyful event, it was usual for the women to gather together, and with music, dances, and songs to publish and celebrate the happy news. So in this place, Jehovah having given the word by His prophet, the joyful tidings of the restoration of Zion, and of God's returning to Jerusalem (see chap. lii. 8), the women are exhorted by the prophet to publish the joyful news with a loud voice from eminences, whence they might best be heard all over the country; and the matter and burden of their song was to be, *Behold your God!*

10. *His reward is with him, and his work before him.*—"His reward is with Him, and the recompense of His work before him." That is, the reward and the recompense which He bestows, and which He will pay to His faithful servants; this He has ready at hand with Him, and holds it out before Him, to encourage those who trust in Him and wait for Him.

11. *Shall gently lead those that are with young*—"The nursing ewes shall he gently lead." A beautiful image, expressing, with the utmost propriety as well as elegance, the tender attention of the shepherd to his flock. That the greatest care in driving the cattle in regard to the dams and their young was necessary appears clearly from Jacob's apology to his brother, Esau, Gen. xxxiii. 13.

CHARLES H. SPURGEON:

Verse 11. Our Lord Jesus is very frequently described as the Shepherd of His people. The figure is inexhaustible, but it has been so often handled that I suppose it would be very difficult to say anything fresh upon it. We all know that the Lord Jesus Christ, as our Shepherd, exercises towards us all the kind and necessary offices which a shepherd performs towards his sheep. With gentle sway He *rules* us for our good: "Let us worship and bow down; let us kneel before the Lord our Maker; for he is our God, and we are the people of his pasture, and the sheep of his hand." He *guides* us: "And when he putteth forth his own sheep he goeth before them, and the sheep follow him, for they know his voice." He *provides* for us: "The Lord is my shepherd, I shall not want." He *protects* us from all forms of evil; therefore, "though we walk through the shadow of death, we will fear no evil, for he is with us: his rod and his staff, they comfort us." If we wander, he *seeks* us out and brings us back. "He restoreth my soul; he leadeth me in the paths of righteousness for his name's sake." If we be broken, He binds us up; if we be wounded, He heals according to His own word, "I will bind up that which was broken, and will strengthen that which was sick." The sheep is an animal of many diseases and many wants, and so the Christian is an individual of many sins and many infirmities; but as the shepherd endeavors to meet all the wants of His flock, so our Lord Jesus succours all the blood-bought company in all their needs.

—The Treasury of the Old Testament

16. *And Lebanon is not sufficient.* Does not the prophet mean here that all the burnt offerings and sacrifices that could be offered were insufficient to atone for sin? That the nations were as nothing before Him, not merely because of His immensity, but because of their insufficiency to make any atonement by their oblations for the iniquities which they had committed?

MATTHEW HENRY

fear or hope in, more than God, that creature we equal with God, which is the highest affront imaginable. Now, to show the absurdity of this,

I. The prophet describes idols as worthy of the greatest contempt (*v.* 19, 20): "Look upon the better sort of them, made of some base metal, cast into what shape the founder pleases, and gilded, or overlaid with plates of gold, that it may pass for a golden image. It is a creature; for the workman made it; *therefore it is not God,* Hos. viii. 6. It is a cheat; for it is gold on the outside, but within it is lead or copper, in this representing the deities, that they were not what they seemed to be. *He that is so impoverished* that he has scarcely a sacrifice to offer to his god when he has made him, though he cannot procure one of brass or stone, he will have a wooden one rather than none, and *chooses a tree that will not soon rot,* and of that he will have his graven image made. The better sort have silver chains to fix theirs with; and, though it be but a wooden image, care is taken that it *shall not be moved.*" How these idolaters shame their own reason, in dreaming that gods of their own making (*Nehushtans,* pieces of brass or logs of wood) should be able to do them any kindness! See how these idolaters shame us, who worship the only living and true God. They spared no cost upon their idols; we grudge that as waste which is spent in the service of our God.

II. He describes God as infinitely great, and worthy of the highest veneration. To prove the greatness of God he appeals,

1. To what they had *heard of him by the hearing of the ear* (*v.* 21): "*Have you not known* by the very light of nature? *Has it not been told you by your fathers* and teachers, according to the constant tradition received from their ancestors and predecessors, even from the beginning? *Have you not understood* it as always acknowledged *from the foundation of the earth,* that God is a great God, and a great King above all gods?" The invisible things of God are *clearly seen from the creation of the world,* Rom. i. 20. Thou mayest not only ask thy father, and thy elders (Deut. xxxii. 7); but *ask those that go by the way* (Job xxi. 29), ask the first man you meet. God has the command of all the creatures. The heaven and the earth themselves are under his management: *He sits upon the circle,* or globe, *of the earth, v.* 22. He is still stretching out the heavens, and will do so till the day comes that they shall be rolled together like a scroll. He spreads them out as easily as we draw a curtain, opening these curtains in the morning and drawing them close again at night. And the heaven is to this earth *as a tent to dwell in*; it is a canopy drawn over our heads. The numerous inhabitants of this earth are in his eye as grasshoppers in ours, so little and so easily crushed. If the spies thought themselves grasshoppers before the sons of Anak (Num. xiii. 33), what are we before the great God? Grasshoppers live but awhile, and live carelessly, not like the ant; so do the most of men. Those who act against him will certainly be brought down by the mighty hand of God, *v.* 23, 24. *They shall not be planted; they shall not be sown;* and those are the two ways of propagating plants, either by seed or slips. If they should so be planted or sown, yet *their stock shall not take root in the earth,* they shall not continue long in power.

2. He appeals to what *their eyes saw of him* (*v.* 26): "*Lift up your eyes on high;* be not always poring on this earth, but sometimes look up, behold the glorious lights of heaven, consider who has created them." What we see of the creature should lead us to the Creator. The idolaters, when they beheld the hosts of heaven, looked no further, but worshipped them, Deut. iv. 19. The Creator *brings out their host by number,* as a general draws out the squadrons and battalions of his army; *he calls them all by names* (Ps. cxlvii. 4); and *by the greatness of his might, not one of them fails,* but everyone does that to which he is appointed.

Verses 27–31

I. The prophet reproves the people of God, captives in Babylon for their unbelief and distrust of God (*v.* 27): "*Why sayest thou, O Jacob!* to thyself and to those about thee, *My way is hidden from the Lord?*" 1. The titles he here gives them were enough to shame them out of their distrusts: *O Jacob! O Israel!* They bore these names—as God's professing people, a people in covenant with him. 2. The way of reproving them is by reasoning with them. Many of our foolish fears would vanish before a strict enquiry into the causes of them. 3. They spoke of God, as if he had cast them off. 4. The ill word they said was a word of despair concerning their present condition. They were ready to conclude, (1) That God would not heed them: *My way is hidden from the Lord.* There are

JAMIESON, FAUSSET, BROWN

that result (see II Kings 23:26, 27).

19. graven—rather, *an image* in general; for it is incongruous to say "melteth" (i.e., casts out of metal) a *graven* image (i.e., one of carved wood); so Jeremiah 10:14, "molten image." **spreadeth it over**—(*Note,* ch. 30: 22). **chains**—an ornament lavishly worn by rich Orientals (ch. 3:18, 19), and so transferred to their idols. Egyptian relics show that idols were suspended in houses by chains. **20. impoverished**—lit., "sunk" in circumstances. **no oblation**—*he* who cannot afford to overlay his idol with gold and silver (vs. 19). **tree . . . not rot**—the cedar, cypress, oak, or ash (ch. 44:14). **graven**—of wood; not a *molten* one of metal. **not be moved**—that shall be durable.

21. ye—who worship idols. The question emphatically implies, they *had* known. **from the beginning**—(Ch. 41:4, 26; 48:16.) God is the beginning (Rev. 1:8). The tradition handed down *from the very first,* of the creation of all things by God at the beginning, ought to convince you of His omnipotence and of the folly of idolatry.

22. It is he—rather, connected with last verse, Have ye not known?—have ye not understood *Him* that sitteth . . .? (vs. 26) [MAURER]. **circle**—applicable to the globular form of the earth, above which, and the vault of sky around it, He sits. For "upon" translate "above." **as grasshoppers**—or locusts in His sight (Num. 13: 33), as He looks down from on high (Ps. 33:13, 14; 113:4-6). **curtain**—referring to the awning which the Orientals draw over the open court in the center of their houses as a shelter in rain or hot weather. **23.** (Ps. 107:4; Dan. 2:21.) **judges**—i.e., rulers; for these exercised judicial authority (Ps. 2:10). The *Hebrew, shophtee,* answers to the Carthaginian chief magistrates, *suffetes.* **24. they**—the "princes and judges" (vs. 23) who oppose God's purposes and God's people. Often compared to tall trees (Ps. 37:35; Dan. 4:10). **not . . . sown**—the seed, i.e., *race* shall become extinct (Nah. 1:14). **stock**—not even shall any shoots spring up from the stump when the tree has been cut down: no descendants whatever (Job 14:7; *Note,* ch. 11:1). **and . . . also**—so LXX. But MAURER translates, "They *are* hardly (lit., not yet, as in II Kings 20:4) planted [etc.] *when* He (God) blows upon them." **blow**—The image is from the hot east wind (simoon) that "withers" vegetation. **whirlwind . . . stubble**—(Ps. 83:13), refers to the rotatory action of the whirlwind on the stubble. **25.** (Cf. vs. 18.) **26. bringeth out . . . host**—image from a general reviewing his army: He is Lord of Sabaoth, the heavenly hosts (Job 38:32). **calleth . . . by names**—numerous as the stars are. God knows each in all its distinguishing *characteristics*—a sense which "name" often bears in Scripture; so in Genesis 2:19, 20, Adam, as *God's vicegerent,* called the beasts by *name* i.e., characterized them by their several *qualities,* which, indeed, He has imparted. **by the greatness . . . faileth**—rather, "by reason of abundance of (their inner essential) force *and firmness of strength,* not one of them *is driven astray*"; referring to the sufficiency of the physical forces with which He has endowed the heavenly bodies, to prevent all disorder in their motions [HORSLEY]. In *English Version* the sense is, "He has endowed them with their peculiar *attributes* ('names') by the greatness of His might," *and the power of His strength* (the better rendering, instead of, "for that He is strong"). **27.** Since these things are so, thou hast no reason to think that thine interest ("way," i.e., condition, Ps. 37:5; Jer. 12:1) is disregarded by God.

ADAM CLARKE

19. *And casteth silver chains*—"And forgeth for it chains of silver."

20. *Chooseth a tree that will not rot.* For what? To make a god out of it! The rich, we find, made theirs of gold and silver; the poor man was obliged to put up with a wooden god!

JOSEPH PARKER:

"Hast thou not known?"—this is not a new revelation. It is well to observe that, lest we find here an excuse for despondency, and a sufficient explanation of the plaintive and mournful tone to which life is often set. "Hast thou not known? hast thou not heard?"—it is an appeal to memory, and that is a strong point in all the divine pleading. We do not read here for the first time that God fainteth not, neither is weary. It is a mark of interrogation that is beautifully made a challenge of recollection. Our memory is to be as the prophet of the Lord in our life. Recollection is to be inspiration; the forty years gone are a pledge of the forty years to come. "Hast thou not known? hast thou not heard?" Let a man be faithful to his own recollections, and it is impossible he can long be despondent, weary, and slow of heart to lay hold of the great work and discipline of life. There is no heart that has not its own peculiar memories of the divine strength and of divine interposition, of divine interpretations of knotty questions in life, and of divine help in the hour of extremity, when sorrow was agony and when agony was despair. And it is the preacher's strength that he has to speak directly into people's hearts. He has not to argue something that is altogether outside of them, and that has no counterpart in their own life and spirit. He has to speak truths that are to be answered by the echoes of the heart, and every man is to say to him as he proceeds from point to point in his high argument and winning persuasion, "Master, thou hast said the truth." Let us gather ourselves around God's all-mightiness and God's all-knowingness, that we may be comforted, and stimulated, and enriched.

—*The People's Bible*

MATTHEW HENRY

such difficulties in our case that even divine wisdom and power will be nonplussed. (2) That God could not help them: "*My judgment is passed over from my God;* my case is past relief, so far past it that God himself cannot redress the grievances of it."

II. He reminds them of that which was sufficient to silence all those fears and distrusts. For the conviction of idolaters (*v.* 21), he appeals to what they had known. Jacob and Israel were a knowing people and their knowledge came by hearing. Among other things, they had heard that *God had spoken once, twice*, yea, many a time they had *heard it, That power belongs unto God* (Ps. lxii. 11).

1. He is himself an almighty God. He must needs be so, for he is *the everlasting God*, and therefore with him there is no decay. He is without beginning or end and therefore with him there is no change. He is also *the Creator of the ends of the earth* and therefore is the rightful ruler of all, and is able to save his church as he was at first to make the world. *There is no searching out of his understanding*, so as to defeat its intentions. None can say, "Thus far God's wisdom can go, and no further." *He faints not, nor is weary;* he upholds the whole creation, and governs all the creatures, and has power to relieve his church, when it is brought low.

2. He gives strength to his people, and helps them to help themselves. He that is the strong God is the strength of Israel. (1) He can help the weak, *v.* 29. (2) He will help the willing, will help those who, in a humble dependence upon him, help themselves, and will do well for those who do their best, *v.* 30, 31. *The youths* and *the young men* are strong, but are apt to think themselves stronger than they are. And they *shall faint and be weary, shall utterly fail* in their conflicts, and under their burdens; they shall soon be made to see the folly of trusting to themselves. *But those that wait on the Lord*, and by faith rely upon him and commit themselves to his guidance, shall find that God will not fail them. They shall have grace sufficient for them: They *shall renew their strength.* God will be their *arm every morning, ch.* xxxiii. 2. They shall use this grace for the best purposes. They shall soar upward, upward towards God. Devout affections are the eagles' wings on which gracious souls mount up, Ps. xxv. 1. They shall press forward, forward towards heaven. They shall walk, they shall run, the way of God's commandments, cheerfully and with alacrity.

CHAPTER 41

Verses 1–9

God's care for his people Israel in raising up Cryus to be their deliverer is a proof of his sovereignty above all idols and of his power to protect his people.

I. A general challenge to the worshippers of idols, *v.* 1. It is renewed (*v.* 21): *Produce your cause.* The court is set, summonses are sent to the islands. Silence (as usual) is proclaimed while the cause is in trying: "*Keep silence before me*, and judge nothing before the time." The defenders of idolatry are called to say what they can in defence of it: "*Let them renew their strength*, in opposition to God. *Let them come near;* in vindication and honour of their idols, let *them speak* freely: *Let us come near together to judgment.*"

II. He particularly challenges the idols to do that for their worshippers, which he had done and would do for his worshippers.

1. That which is to be proved is, (1) That *the Lord is God* alone, *the first and with the last* (*v.* 4), that he is infinite, eternal, and unchangeable, that he governed the world from the beginning, and will to the end of time. (2) That *Israel* is *his servant* (*v.* 8), whom he protects, and employs, and in whom he is and will be glorified.

2. To prove this he shows,

(1) That it was he who called Abraham, thef ather of this despised nation, out of an idolatrous country. He is *the righteous man whom God raised up from the east.* Of him the Chaldee paraphrast expressly understands it: *Who brought Abraham publicly from the east?* To maintain the honour of the people of Israel, it was very proper to point to this great ancestor of theirs; and (*v.* 8) God calls Israel the *seed of Abraham my friend.* Also to put contempt upon the Chaldean idolatry, it was proper to show how Abraham was called from serving other gods (Joshua. xxiv. 2, 3, &c.). Also, to encourage the captives in Babylon to hope that God would find a way for their return to their own land, it was proper to remind them how he brought their father Abraham out of the same country into this land, to give it to him for an inheritance, Gen. xv. 7. He was a *righteous man*, that *believed God, and it was counted to him for*

JAMIESON, FAUSSET, BROWN

judgment is passed over from—rather, My cause is neglected by my God; He *passes by my case* in my bondage and distress without noticing it. **my God**—who especially might be expected to care for me. **28. known**—by thine own observation and reading of Scripture. **heard**—from tradition of the fathers.

everlasting . . .—These attributes of Jehovah ought to inspire His afflicted people with confidence.

no searching of his understanding—therefore thy cause cannot, as thou sayest, escape His notice; though much in His ways is *unsearchable,* He cannot err (Job 11:7-9). He is never "faint" or "weary" with having the countless wants of His people ever before Him to attend to. **29.** Not only does He "not faint" (vs. 28) but He gives power to them who *do faint.* **no might . . . increaseth strength**—a seeming paradox. They "have no might" *in themselves;* but *in Him* they have strength, and He "*increases*" that strength (II Cor. 12:9). **30. young men**—lit., "those selected"; men picked out on account of their youthful vigor for an enterprise.

31. mount up—(II Sam. 1:23). Rather, "They shall put forth fresh feathers as eagles" are said to renovate themselves; the parallel clause, "renew their strength," confirms this. The eagle was thought to moult and renew his feathers, and with them his strength, in old age (so LXX, *Vulgate,* Ps. 103:5). However, *English Version* is favored by the descending climax, *mount up—run—walk;* in every attitude the praying, waiting child of God is "strong in the Lord" (Ps. 84:7; Mic. 4:5; Heb. 12:1).

CHAPTER 41

Vss. 1-29. ADDITIONAL REASONS WHY THE JEWS SHOULD PLACE CONFIDENCE IN GOD'S PROMISES OF DELIVERING THEM; HE WILL RAISE UP A PRINCE AS THEIR DELIVERER, WHEREAS THE IDOLS COULD NOT DELIVER THE HEATHEN NATIONS FROM THAT PRINCE. **1.** (Zech. 2:13.) God is about to argue the case; therefore let the nations listen in reverential silence. Cf. Genesis 28:16, 17, as to the spirit in which we ought to behave before God. **before me**—rather (turning), "towards me" [MAURER]. **islands**—including *all regions beyond sea* (Jer. 25:22), maritime regions, not merely isles in the strict sense. **renew . . . strength**—Let them gather their strength for the argument; let them *adduce their strongest arguments* (cf. ch. 1:18; Job 9:32). "Judgment" means here, to decide the point at issue between us.

2. Who—else but God? The fact that God "raiseth up" Cyrus and qualifies him for becoming the conqueror of the nations and deliverer of God's people, is a strong argument why they should trust in Him. The future is here prophetically represented as present or past.

the righteous man—Cyrus; as ch. 44:28; 45:1-4, 13; 46:11, "from the *East,*" prove. Called

ADAM CLARKE

28. *There is no searching of his understanding*—"And that His understanding is unsearchable."

31. *They shall mount up with wings as eagles*—"They shall put forth fresh feathers like the moulting eagle." It has been a common and popular opinion that the eagle lives and retains his vigor to a great age; and that, beyond the common lot of other birds, he molts in his old age, and renews his feathers, and with them his youth. "Thou shalt renew thy youth like the eagle," says the Psalmist, ciii. 5.

CHAPTER 41

1. *Keep silence before me, O islands*—"Let the distant nations repair to me with new force of mind."

2. *The righteous man.* Some explain it of Abraham, others of Cyrus. I rather think that

MATTHEW HENRY

righteousness; and so he became the father of all those who by faith in Christ are made the *righteousness of God through him*, Rom. iv. 3, 11; 2 Cor. v. 21; Gen. xviii. 19. God *raised him up from the east*, from Ur first and afterwards from Haran, which lay east from Canaan. He raised him out of iniquity and made him pious, out of obscurity and made him famous. He *called him to his foot*, to follow him with an implicit faith; for he *went out not knowing whither he went*, but whom he followed, Heb. xi. 8. We must all either come to his foot or be made his footstool. *He gave nations before him*, the nations of Canaan, and the Hittites acknowledged him a mighty prince, Gen. xxiii. 6. He *made him rule over* those *kings* whom he conquered for the rescue of his brother Lot, Gen. xiv. And when God *gave them as dust to his sword, and as driven stubble to his bow, he* then *pursued them, and passed safely*, or in peace, under the divine protection.

(2) That it is he who will, ere long, raise up Cyrus from the east. It is spoken of as a thing past, as if it were already done. *God will raise him up in righteousness* (so it may be read, *ch.* xlv. 13), *will call him to his foot*, make what use of him he pleases, and make him victorious over the nations that oppose his coming to the crown. He shall be a type of Christ, who is righteousness itself, whom God will, in the fulness of time, raise up and make victorious over the powers of darkness.

III. He exposes the folly of idolaters, who obstinately persisted in their idolatry (*v.* 5): *The isles of the Gentiles saw this*, not only what God did for Abraham himself, but what he did for his seed, how he brought them out of Egypt, and made them *rule over kings*, and *they feared*, Exod. xv. 14–16. They were afraid, *drew near, and came*; but, instead of helping to reason one another out of their sottish idolatries, they helped to confirm one another in them, *v.* 6, 7. They said one to another, *Be of good courage;* let us unanimously agree to keep up the reputation of our gods. One tradesman encourages another to come into a confederacy for the keeping up of the noble craft of god-making. They not only had recourse to their old gods for protection, but made *new ones*, Deut. xxxii. 17. *So the carpenter*, having done his part to the timber-work, *encouraged the goldsmith* to do his part in gilding or overlaying it; and, when it came into the goldsmith's hand, *he that smooths with the hammer*, that polishes it, or beats it thin, quickened *him that smote the anvil*, and told him it was *ready for the soldering*, which perhaps was the last operation about it, and then it is *fastened with nails*, and you have a god of it.

IV. He encourages his own people to trust in him (*v.* 8, 9): *But thou, Israel, art my servant.* "Idolaters put themselves under the protection of these impotent deities. *Those that make them are like unto them, and so is every one that trusts in them; but thou, O Israel!* art the servant of a better Master." They are God's servants. He has *chosen* them to be a peculiar people to himself. They were the seed of Abraham his friend. It was the honour of Abraham that he was *called the friend of God* (James ii. 23). And for the father's sake the people of Israel were beloved. He had not yet cast them away, though they had often provoked him, and therefore he would not now abandon them.

Verses 10–20

The scope of these verses is to silence the fears, and encourage the faith, of the servants of God in their distresses. Perhaps it is intended, in the first place, for the support of God's Israel, in captivity; but all that faithfully serve God *through patience and comfort of this scripture may have hope.* A word of caution, counsel, and comfort, which is so often repeated, *Fear thou not;* and again (v. 13), *Fear not;* and (*v.* 14). It is against the mind of God that his people should be a timorous people.

I. They may depend upon his presence with them as their God. "*I will hold thy right hand*, go hand in hand with thee" (so some); as their guide. When we are weak he will hold us up, will encourage us, and so *hold us by the right hand*, Ps. lxxiii. 23. He will silence fears: *Saying unto thee, Fear not.* He has said it again and again in his word, but he will go further; he will by his Spirit say it to their hearts.

II. Though their enemies be now very formidable, yet the day is coming when God will reckon with them. There are those that are incensed against God's people, that *strive with them* (*v.* 11), that war against them (*v.* 12), that hate them. But let God's people wait God's time. They shall be convinced of the folly of striving with God's people. *They shall be ashamed and confounded*, which might bring them to repentance, but will rather fill them with rage. They shall be ruined and undone (*v.* 11): *They shall be as*

JAMIESON, FAUSSET, BROWN

"righteous," not so much on account of his own equity (HERODOTUS, 3.89), as because he fulfilled *God's* righteous will in restoring the Jews from their unjust captivity. *Raised him up in righteousness.* The LXX takes the *Hebrew* as a noun "righteousness." MAURER translates, "Who raised up him whom salvation (national and temporal, the gift of God's 'righteousness' to the good, ch. 32:17; cf. ch. 45:8; 51:5) meets at his foot" (i.e., wherever he goes). Cyrus is said to come *from the East*, because Persia is east of Babylon; but in vs. 25, *from the north,* in reference to Media. At the same time the full sense of *righteousness,* or *righteous,* and of the whole passage, is realized only in Messiah, Cyrus' antitype (Cyrus *knew not* God, ch. 45:4). He goes forth as the Universal Conqueror of the "nations," in righteousness making war (Ps. 2:8, 9; Rev. 19:11-15; 6:2; 2:26, 27). "The idols He shall utterly abolish" (cf. vs. 7:23, with ch. 2:18). Righteousness was always raised up from the East. Paradise was east of Eden. The cherubim were at the east of the garden. Abraham was called from the East. Judea, the birthplace of Messiah, was in the East. **called . . . to . . . foot**—called him to attend His (God's) steps, i.e., follow His guidance. In Ezra 1:2, Cyrus acknowledges Jehovah as the Giver of his victories. He subdued the nations from the Euxine to the Red Sea, and even Egypt (says XENOPHON). **dust**—(Ch. 17:13; 29:5; Ps. 18:42). Persia, Cyrus' country, was famed for the use of the "bow" (ch. 22:6). "Before him" means "gave them *into his power"* (Josh. 10:12). MAURER translates, "Gave his (the enemy's) sword to be dust, and his (the enemy's) bow to be as stubble" (Job 41:26, 29). **3.** Cyrus had not visited the regions of the Euphrates and westward until he visited them for conquest. So the gospel conquests penetrated regions where the name of God was unknown before. **4. Who**—else but God? **calling . . . generations from . . . beginning**—The origin and position of all nations are from God (Deut. 32:8; Acts 17:26); what is true of Cyrus and his conquests is true of all the movements of history *from the first;* all are from God. **with the last**—i.e., the last (ch. 44:6; 48:12). **5. feared**—that they would be subdued. **drew near, and came**—together, for mutual defense. **6. Be of good courage**—Be not alarmed because of Cyrus, but make new images to secure the favor of the gods against him. **7.** One workman encourages the other to be quick in finishing the idol, so as to avert the impending danger. **nails**—to keep it steady in its place. Wisdom 13:15, 16, gives a similar picture of the folly of idolatry. **8.** Contrast between the idolatrous nations whom God will destroy by Cyrus, and Israel whom God will deliver by the same man for their forefathers' sake. **servant**—so termed as being chosen by God to worship Him themselves, and to lead other peoples to do the same (ch. 45:4). **Jacob . . . . chosen**—(Ps. 135:4.) **my friend**—lit., "loving me." **9.** Abraham, the father of the Jews, taken from the remote Ur of the Chaldees. Others take it of Israel, called out of Egypt (Deut. 4:37; Hos. 11:1). **from the chief men**—lit., "the elbows"; so *the joints;* hence *the root* which joins the tree to the earth; fig., those of ancient and *noble* stock. But the parallel clause "ends of the earth" favors GESENIUS, who translates, "the *extremities* of the earth"; so JEROME.

10. be not dismayed—lit., anxiously *to look at one another* in dismay.

right hand of my righteousness—i.e., My right hand prepared in accordance with My righteousness (faithfulness to My promises) to uphold thee.

11. ashamed—put to the shame of defeat (cf. ch. 54:17; Rom. 9:33). **12. seek . . . and . . . not find**—said of one so utterly put out of the way that not a trace of him can be found (Ps. 37:36). **thing of naught**—shall utterly perish. **13.** (Deut. 33: 26, 29.)

ADAM CLARKE

the former is meant; because the character of the righteous man, or righteousness, agrees better with Abraham than with Cyrus. Besides immediately after the description of the success given by God to Abraham and his posterity (who, I presume, are to be taken into the account), the idolaters are introduced as greatly alarmed at this event. Abraham was called out of the east; and his posterity were introduced into the land of Canaan, in order to destroy the idolaters of that country, and they were established there on purpose to stand as a barrier against the idolatry then prevailing, and threatening to overrun the whole face of the earth.

He gave them as the dust to his sword—"Hath made them like the dust before his sword."

4. *Who hath wrought and done it?*—"Who hath performed and made these things?"

5. *Were afraid*—"And they were terrified."

7. *That it should not be moved*—"That it shall not move."

9. *And called thee from the chief men thereof*—"And called from the extremities thereof."

MATTHEW HENRY

nothing before the justice and power of God. This is repeated (*v.* 12).

III. They themselves should become a terror to those who were now a terror to them, and victory should turn on their side, *v.* 14–16. Jacob and Israel are reduced and brought very low. It is the *worm Jacob*, so little, so weak, and so defenceless, trampled on by everybody, forced to creep even into the earth for safety. Jacob's King calls himself *a worm and no man*, Ps. xxii. 6. God's people are sometimes as worms, but not vipers, as their enemies are, not of the serpent's seed. God regards Jacob's low estate, and says, "*Fear not, thou worm Jacob;* fear not that thou shalt be crushed; and *you men of Israel*" (*you few men*, so some read it, *you dead men*, so others), "do not give up yourselves for gone." *By whom shall Jacob arise, for he is small?* We are here told: *I will help thee, saith the Lord;* and it is the honour of God to help the weak. The Lord will help them by enabling them to help themselves and making Jacob to become *a threshing instrument*. Observe, He is but an instrument, a tool in God's hand. But, if God make him a threshing instrument, he will make him fit for use, *new* and *sharp*, and *having teeth*, or sharp spikes; and then, by divine direction and strength, *thou shalt thresh the mountains*, the highest, and strongest, and most stubborn of thy enemies. He pursues the metaphor, *v.* 16. Having threshed them, *thou shalt winnow them, and the wind shall scatter them.* This had its accomplishment, in part, in the victories of the Jews in the times of the Maccabees; but it seems designed to read the final doom of all the implacable enemies of the church of God in the triumphs of the cross of Christ over the powers of darkness, and *he that overcomes shall have power over the nations*, Rev. ii. 26.

IV. They shall have abundance of comfort in God, and God shall have abundance of honour from them: *Thou shalt rejoice in the Lord*, *v.* 16. "Thou shalt also *glory in the Holy One of Israel*, in what he has done for thee."

V. If there be occasion, God will again do for them as he did for Israel in their march from Egypt to Canaan, *v.* 17–19. When the captives, either in Babylon or in their return thence, want water or shelter, God will take care of them. Their return out of Babylon was typical of our redemption by Christ; and so these promises, 1. Were provided by the gospel of Christ. That glorious discovery of his love has given full assurance that God has provided sufficient for the supply of all their wants, and the answering of all their prayers. 2. They are applied by the grace and Spirit of Christ to all believers, that they may have consolation in their way and a complete happiness in their end. It is here supposed that the people of God, in their passage through this world, are often in straits: *The poor and needy seek water, and there is none; the poor in spirit hunger and thirst after righteousness.* The soul of man seeks for satisfaction somewhere, but soon despairs of finding it in the world. It is here promised that their grievances shall be redressed: "*I the Lord will hear them*, will answer them, I will be with them as I have always been, in their distresses." While we are in the wilderness of this world this promise is to us what the pillar of cloud and fire was to Israel, an assurance of God's gracious presence. They shall have fresh water, as Israel had, even where one would least expect it (*v.* 18): *I will open rivers in high places*, rivers of grace, rivers of pleasure, *rivers of living water*, which he spoke of the Spirit (John vii. 38, 39). The preaching of the gospel to the world turned that wilderness into a pool of water. "*I will plant in the wilderness the cedar* (*v.* 19), so that they shall pass through with as much ease and delight as a man walks in his grove. These trees shall be to them what the pillar of cloud was to Israel, a shelter from the heat." Christ and his grace are so to believers. When God sets up his church in the Gentile wilderness there shall be as great a change in men's characters as if thorns and briers were turned into cedars. They shall see and acknowledge the hand of God in this, *v.* 20. *That they may see* this wonderful change is above the ordinary course of nature and therefore comes from a superior power.

Verses 21–29

The Lord, by the prophet, here repeats the challenge to idolaters: "*Produce your cause* (*v.* 21) and *bring forth the strongest reasons* you have to prove that your idols are gods, worthy of adoration."

I. The idols are here challenged to bring proofs of their knowledge and power. Understanding and active power are the accomplishments of a man. Whoever pretends to be a god must have these in perfection.

1. "They can tell us nothing that we did not know before, so ignorant are they. We challenge them to

JAMIESON, FAUSSET, BROWN

14. worm—in a state of contempt and affliction, whom all loathe and tread on, the very expression which Messiah, on the cross, applies to *Himself* (Ps. 22:6), so completely are the Lord and His people identified and assimilated. "God's people are as 'worms' in humble thoughts of themselves, and in their enemies' haughty thoughts of them; worms, but not vipers, or of the serpent's seed" [HENRY] **men**—The parallelism requires the word "men" here to have associated with it the idea of *fewness* or *feebleness*. LOWTH translates, "Ye *mortals* of Israel." The LXX, "altogether diminutive." MAURER supports *English Version*, which the *Hebrew* text best accord with. **the Lord**—in general. **and thy redeemer**—in particular; a still stronger reason why He should "help" them. **15.** God will make Israel to destroy their enemies as the Eastern corn-drag (ch. 28:27, 28) bruises out the grain with its teeth, and gives the chaff to the winds to scatter. **teeth**—serrated, so as to cut up the straw for fodder and separate the grain from the chaff. **mountains . . . hills**—kingdoms more or less powerful that were hostile to Israel (ch. 2:14). **16. fan**—winnowed (cf. Matt. 3:12). **whirlwind . . . scatter them**—(Job 27:21; 30:22).

17. poor and needy—primarily, the exiles in Babylon. **water**—fig., refreshment, prosperity after their affliction. The language is so constructed as only very partially to apply to the local and temporary event of the restoration from Babylon; but fully to be realized in the waters of life and of the Spirit, under the Gospel (ch. 30:25; 44:3; John 7:37-39; 4:14). God wrought no miracles that we read of, in any wilderness, during the return from Babylon. **faileth**—rather, "*is rigid*" or parched [HORSLEY]. **18.** Alluding to the waters with which Israel was miraculously supplied in the desert after having come out of Egypt. **high places**—bare of trees, barren, and unwatered (Jer. 4:11; 14:6). "High places . . . valleys" spiritually express that in *all* circumstances, whether *elevated* or *depressed*, God's people will have refreshment for their souls, however little to be expected it might seem. **19.** (Ch. 32:15; 55:13). **shittah**—rather, the acacia, or Egyptian thorn, from which the gum Arabic is obtained [LOWTH]. **oil tree**—the olive. **fir tree**—rather, the cypress: grateful by its shade. **pine**—GESENIUS translates, "the holm." **box tree**—not the shrub used for bordering flower-beds, but [GESENIUS] a kind of cedar, remarkable for the smallness of its cones, and the upward direction of its branches. **20. consider**—lit., "lay it (to heart)"; turn (their attention) to it. "They" refers to *all lands* (vs. 1; Ps. 64:9; 40:3). The effect on the Gentiles of God's open interposition hereafter in behalf of Israel shall be, they shall seek Israel's God (ch. 2:3; Zech. 8:21-23). **21.** A new challenge to the idolaters (see vss. 1, 7) to say, can their idols *predict future events* as Jehovah can (vss. 22-25, etc.)? **your strong reasons**—the reasons for idol-worship which you think especially strong.

ADAM CLARKE

15. *Thou shalt thresh the mountains.* Mountains and hills are here used metaphorically for the kings and princes of the Gentiles.—Kimchi.

19. *I will plant in the wilderness the cedar.* The preceding two verses express God's mercy to them in their passage through the dry deserts, in supplying them with abundant water, when distressed with thirst, in allusion to the Exodus. This verse expresses the relief afforded to them, fainting with heat in their journey through that hot country, destitute of shelter, by causing shady trees, and those of the tallest and most beautiful kinds, to spring up for their defense. *The oil tree.* This, Kimchi says, is not to be understood of the olive tree, for the olive is distinguished, Neh. viii. 15; but it means the pine or fir, from which pitch is extracted.

21. *Bring forth your strong reasons*—"Produce these your mighty powers." "Let your idols come forward which you consider to be so very strong" (*Hieron, in loc.*).

MATTHEW HENRY

inform us," (1) "What has been formerly: *Let them show the former things.* What did they ever do that was worth taking notice of?" (2) What shall happen; to declare to us *things to come* (*v.* 22), and again (*v.* 23). No creature can foretell things to come, otherwise than by divine information, with any certainty.

2. "They can do nothing that we cannot do ourselves, so impotent are they." That which is charged upon these idols is that *they are of nothing*, *v.* 24. Some read it: "*The work they do is of nought*, and so is the ado that is made about them. Therefore *he that chooses you*, and gives you your deity, *is an abomination* to God." A servant is at liberty to choose his master, but a man is not at liberty to choose his God.

II. God here produces proofs that he is the true God, and that there is none besides him.

1. He has an irresistible power. This he will shortly make to appear in the raising up of Cyrus, a type of Christ (*v.* 25): *He will raise him up from the north* and *from the rising of the sun.* Cyrus by his father was a Mede, by his mother a Persian; and his army consisted of Medes, whose country lay north, and Persians, whose country lay east, from Babylon. God will raise him up to great power, and he shall come against Babylon with ends of his own to serve. But, (1) *He shall proclaim God's name;* so it may be read. So he did when, in his proclamation for the release of the Jews, he acknowledged that the Lord God of Israel was *the God.* (2) All opposition shall fall before him: *He shall come upon the princes of Babylon* and trample upon them *as the potter treads clay.* Christ, as man, was raised up from the north, for Nazareth lay in the northern parts of Canaan; as the angel of the covenant, he ascends from the east. He maintained the honour of heaven (*he shall call upon my name*), and came upon the prince of darkness as mortar and trod him down.

2. He has an infallible foresight. Now the false gods not only could not do it, but they could not foresee it. (1) He challenges them to produce any of their pretended deities, or their diviners (*v.* 26). (2) He challenges to himself the sole honour of doing it and foretelling it (*v.* 27). I am he that *will give to Jerusalem one that brings good tidings.* This is applicable to the work of redemption, in which the Lord has given to us the glad tidings of reconciliation.

III. Judgment is here given upon this trial. 1. None of all the idols had foretold this work of wonder. Other nations besides the Jews were released out of captivity in Babylon by Cyrus, and yet none of them had any intelligence given them of it beforehand, by any of their gods or prophets. None of all the gods of the nations have shown their worshippers the way of salvation, which God will show by the Messiah. 2. None of those who pleaded for them could produce any instance of their knowledge or power that had in it any colour of proof that they were gods. Judgment must therefore be given against the defendant upon *Nihil dicit—He is mute.* 3. Sentence is therefore given according to the charge exhibited against them (*v.* 24).

JAMIESON, FAUSSET, BROWN

22. what shall happen—"Let them *bring near and declare future contingencies*" [HORSLEY]. **former things . . . the latter end of them**—show what former predictions the idols have given, that we may compare the event ("latter end") with them; or give new prophecies ("declare things to come") (ch. 42:9), [MAURER]. BARNES explains it more reconditely, "Let them foretell the *entire series* of events, showing, in their *order*, the things which shall *first* occur, as well as those which shall *finally* happen"; the false prophets tried to predict isolated events, having no mutual dependency; not a long *series* of events mutually and orderly connected, and stretching far into futurity. They did not even *try* to do this. None but God can do it (ch. 46:10; 44:7, 8). "Or . . . things to come" will, in this view, mean, Let them, if they cannot predict the *series*, even predict plainly *any detached* events. **23. do good . . . evil**—give any proof at all of your power, either to reward your friends or punish your enemies (Ps. 115:2-8). **that we may be dismayed, and behold it together**—MAURER translates, "That we (Jehovah and the idols) may look one another in the face (i.e., encounter one another, II Kings 14:8, 11), and see" our respective powers by a trial. HORSLEY translates, "Then the moment we behold, we shall be dismayed." "We" thus, and in *English Version*, refers to Jehovah and His worshippers. **24. of nothing**—(*Note*, ch. 40:17.) The *Hebrew* text is here corrupt; so *English Version* treats it. **abomination**—abstract for concrete: not merely *abominable*, but the *essence* of whatever is so (Deut. 18:12). **chooseth you**—as an object of worship. **25. raised up**—in purpose: not fulfilled till 150 years afterwards. **north**—In vs. 2, "from the East"; both are true: see the note there. **call . . . my name**—acknowledge Me as God, and attribute his success to Me; this he did in the proclamation (Ezra 1:2). This does not necessarily imply that Cyrus renounced idolatry, but hearing of Isaiah's prophecy given 150 years before, so fully realized in his own acts, he recognized God as the true God, but retained his idol (so Naaman, II Kings 5; cf. II Kings 17:33, 41; Dan. 3:28; 4:1-3, 34-37). **princes**—the Babylonian satraps or governors of provinces. **mortar**—"mire"; He shall tread them under foot as dirt (ch. 10:6). **26. Who**—of the idolatrous soothsayers? When this prophecy shall be fulfilled, all shall see that God foretold as to Cyrus, which none of the soothsayers have. **beforetime**—before the event occurred. **He is righteous**—rather, It is true; it was a true prophecy, as the event shows. "He is righteous," in *English Version*, must be interpreted, The fulfilment of the idol's words proves that *he is faithful*. **showeth . . .**—rather, "there was none (of the soothsayers) that showed . . . declared—no one has heard your words" foretelling the event. **27.** Rather, "I first will give to Zion and to Jerusalem the messenger of good tidings, Behold, behold them!" The clause, "Behold . . . them" (*the wished-for event is now present*) is inserted in the middle of the sentence as a detached exclamation, by an elegant transposition, the language being framed abruptly, as one would speak in putting vividly as it were, before the eyes of others, some joyous event which he had just learned [LUDOVICUS DE DIEU] (cf. ch. 40:9). None of the idols had foretold these events. Jehovah was the "first" to do so (see vs. 4). **28. no counsellor**—no one of the idolatrous soothsayers who could *inform* (Num. 24:14) *those who consulted* them what would take place. Cf. "*counsel* of His messenger" (ch. 44:26). **when I asked**—i.e., challenged them, in this chapter. **29. confusion**—"emptiness" [BARNES].

ADAM CLARKE

23. *That we may be dismayed, and behold it together*—"Then shall we be struck at once with admiration and terror."

24. *Your work of nought*—"Your operation is less than naught."

25. *I have raised up one from the north.* "That is," says Kimchi, "the Messiah." *He shall come upon princes*—"He shall trample on princes."

27. *The first shall say to Zion, Behold, behold them*—"I first to Zion gave the word, Behold, they are here." This verse is somewhat obscure by the transposition of the parts of the sentence, and the peculiar manner in which it is divided into two parallel lines. The following paraphrase will explain the form and the sense of it. "I first, by My prophets, give notice of these events, saying, Behold, they are at hand! and I give to Jerusalem a messenger of glad tidings."

28. *Among them*—"Among the idols."

MATTHEW HENRY — CHAPTER 42

Verses 1–4

We are sure that these verses are to be understood of Christ, for the evangelist tells us expressly that in him this prophecy was fulfilled, Matt. xii. 17–21.

I. The Father's confidence in him. 1. God owns him: He is *my servant.* Though he was a Son, yet, as a Mediator, he *took upon him the form of a servant.*

2. As chosen by him: He is *my elect.* Infinite Wisdom made the choice and then avowed it. 3. As one he

JAMIESON, FAUSSET, BROWN — CHAPTER 42

Vss. 1-25. MESSIAH THE ANTITYPE OF CYRUS.—God's description of His character (vss. 1-4). God addresses Him directly (vss. 5-7). Address to the people to attend to the subject (vss. 8, 9). Call to all, and especially the exile Jews to rejoice in the coming deliverance (vss. 10-25). **1. my servant**—The law of prophetic suggestion leads Isaiah from Cyrus to the far greater Deliverer, behind whom the former is lost sight of. The express quotation in Matthew 12:18-20, and the description can apply to *Messiah* alone (Ps. 40:6; with which cf. Exod. 21:6; John 6:38; Phil. 2:7). Israel, also, in its highest ideal, is called the "servant" of God (ch. 49:3). But this ideal is realized only in the antitypical Israel, its representative-man and Head, Messiah (cf. Matt. 2:15, with Hos. 11:1). "Servant" was the position assumed by the Son of God throughout His humiliation. **elect**—chosen by God before the foundation of the world for an atonement (I Pet. 1:20; Rev. 13:

ADAM CLARKE — CHAPTER 42

The prophet, having opened his subject with the preparation for the return from captivity at Babylon, and intimated that a much greater deliverance was covered under the veil of that event, proceeded to vindicate the power of God, as Creator and Disposer of all things; and His infinite knowledge, from His prediction of future events, and in particular of that deliverance. He went still further, and pointed out the instrument by which He should effect the redemption of His people, the Jews, from slavery; namely, a great conqueror, whom He would call forth from the north and the east to execute His orders. In this chapter he proceeds to the greater deliverance; and at once brings forth into full view, without throwing any veil of allegory over the subject, the Messiah. "Behold my servant, Messiah," says the Chaldee. Mat-

MATTHEW HENRY

put confidence in: He is *my servant on whom I lean*; so some read it. 4. As one he took care of: He is *my servant whom I uphold*; so we read it. The Father stood by him and strengthened him. His delight was in him from eternity.

II. The qualification for his office: *I have put my Spirit upon him*, to enable him to go through his undertaking, *ch.* lxi. 1.

III. The work to which he is appointed: it is to *bring forth judgment to the Gentiles*, that is, to set up a religion in the world under the bonds of which the Gentiles should come and the blessings of which they should enjoy.

IV. The mildness and tenderness with which he should pursue this undertaking, *v.* 2, 3. He shall carry it on without noise. He shall have no trumpet sounded before him, nor any noisy retinue to follow him. The opposition he meets with he shall not strive against, but patiently *endure the contradiction of sinners against himself*. His kingdom is spiritual and therefore its weapons are not carnal, nor is its appearance pompous. Those that are wicked he will be patient with; when he has begun to crush them, so that they are as bruised reeds, he will give them space to repent; though they are very offensive, as smoking flax (*ch.* lxv. 5), yet he will bear with them, as he did with Jerusalem. Those that are as a reed oppressed with doubts and fears, *as a bruised reed*, that are as *smoking flax*, as the wick of a candle newly lighted, which is ready to go out again, he will not despise. More is implied than is expressed. *He will not break the bruised reed*, but will strengthen it, that it may become as a cedar in the courts of our God. *He will not quench the smoking flax*, but blow it up into a flame.

V. The courage and constancy with which he should persevere (*v.* 4): Till he is able to say, *It is finished;* and he enables his apostles and ministers not to fail nor be discouraged, till they also have finished their testimony.

He *sets judgment in the earth*. He erects his government in the world, a church for himself among men, reforms the world by the power of his gospel and grace.

JAMIESON, FAUSSET, BROWN

8). Redemption was no afterthought to remedy an unforeseen evil (Rom. 16:25, 26; Eph. 3:9, 11; II Tim. 1:9, 10; Titus 1:2, 3). In Matthew 12:18 it is rendered "My beloved"; *the only beloved Son*, beloved in a sense distinct from all others. *Election* and the *love* of God are inseparably joined. **my soul**—a human phrase applied to God, because of the intended union of humanity with the Divinity: "I Myself." **delighteth**—is well pleased with, and accepts, *as a propitiation*. God could have "delighted" in no created being *as a mediator* (cf. vs. 21; ch. 63:5; Matt. 3:17). **spirit upon him**—(Ch. 11:2; 61:1; Luke 4:18; John 3:34.) **judgment**—the gospel dispensation, founded on *justice*, the canon of the divine rule and principle of judgment called "the law" (ch. 2:3; cf. vs. 4; 51:4; 49:6). The Gospel has a discriminating *judicial* effect: *saving* to penitents: *condemnatory* to Satan, the enemy (John 12:31; 16: 11), and the wilfully impenitent (John 9:39). Matthew 12:18 has, "He shall *show*," for "He shall bring forth," or "*cause to go forth*." Christ both *produced* and *announced* His "judgment." The *Hebrew* dwells most on His *producing* it; Matthew on His *announcement* of it: the two are joined in Him. **2.** Matthew marks the kind of "cry" as that of *altercation* by quoting it, "He shall not *strive*" (ch. 53:7). **street**—LXX translates "outside." An image from an altercation in a house, loud enough to be heard *in the street* outside: appropriate of Him who "withdrew Himself" from the public fame created by His miracles to privacy (Matt. 12:15; vs. 34, there, shows another and sterner aspect of His character, which is also implied in the term "judgment"). **3. bruised**—"It pleased the Lord to *bruise* Him" (ch. 53:5, 10; Gen. 3:15); so He can feel for *the bruised*. As vs. 2 described His unturbulent spirit towards His violent enemies (Matt. 12:14-16), and His utter freedom from love of notoriety, so vs. 3, His tenderness in cherishing the first spark of grace in the penitent (ch. 40:11). **reed**—fragile: easily "shaken with the wind" (Matt. 11:7). Those who are at best feeble, and who besides are oppressed by calamity or by the sense of sin. **break**—entirely crush or condemn. Cf. "bind up the broken-hearted" (ch. 50:4; 61:1; Matt. 11:28). **flax**—put for the lamp-*wick*, formed of flax. The believer is the *lamp* (so the *Greek*, Matt. 5:15; John 5:35): his conscience enlightened by the Holy Ghost is the *wick*. "Smoking" means dimly burning, smouldering, the flame not quite extinct. This expresses the positive side of the penitent's religion; as "bruised reed," the negative. Broken-hearted in himself, but not without some spark of flame: lit., from above. Christ will supply such a one with grace as with oil. Also, the light of nature smouldering in the Gentiles amidst the hurtful fumes of error. He not only did not quench, but cleared away the mists and superadded the light of revelation. See JEROME, ad Alg. Qu. 2. **truth**—Matthew 12:20 quotes it, "send forth judgment unto *victory*." Matthew, under the Spirit, gives the virtual sense, but varies the word, in order to bring out a fresh aspect of the same thing. Truth has in itself the elements of victory over all opposing forces. *Truth* is the *victory* of Him who is "the truth" (John 14:6). The *gospel judicial sifting* ("judgment") of believers and unbelievers, begun already in part (John 3:18, 19; 9:39), will be *consummated victoriously in truth* only at His second coming; vss. 13, 14, here, and Matthew 12:32, 36, 41, 42, show that there is reference to the *judicial* aspect of the Gospel, especially finally: besides the mild triumph of Jesus coming in mercy to the penitent *now* (vs. 2), there shall be *finally* the judgment on His enemies, when the "truth" shall be perfectly developed. Cf. ch. 61:1-3, where the two comings are similarly joined (Ps. 2:4-6, 8; Rev. 15:2, 4; 19:11-16). On "judgment," see *Note*, vs. 1. **4. fail**—faint; *man* in religion may become as the almost expiring flax-wick (vs. 3), but not so He in His purposes of grace. **discouraged**—lit., "broken," i.e., checked in zeal by discouragements (cf. ch. 49:4, 5). ROSENMULLER not so well translates, "He shall not be too slow on the one hand, nor *run too hastily* on the other." **judgment**—His true religion, the canon of His judgments and righteous reign. **isles . . . wait . . .**—The distant lands beyond sea shall put their *trust* in His gospel way of salvation. Matthew 12: 21 virtually gives the sense, with the inspired addition of another aspect of the same thing, "In his *name* shall the Gentiles *trust*" (as "wait for" here means, ch. 30:18). "His law" is not something distinct from Himself, but is indeed *Himself*, the manifestation of God's character ("name") in Christ, who is the *embodiment of the law* (ch. 42:21; Jer. 23:6; Rom. 10:4). "Isles" here, and in vs. 12, may refer to the fact that the populations of which the Church was primarily formed were Gentiles of

ADAM CLARKE

thew has applied it directly to Christ; nor can it with any justice or propriety be applied to any other person or character whatever.

1. *Behold my servant, whom I uphold.* "On whom I lean." Alluding to the custom of kings leaning on the arm of their most beloved and faithful servant. All, both Jews and Christians, agree, that the first seven verses of this chapter belong to Christ. Now, as they are evidently a continuation of the prophecy in the preceding chapter, that prophecy cannot belong to Cyrus, but to Christ. *He shall bring forth judgment to the Gentiles*—"He shall publish judgment to the nations." The word *mishpat*, "judgment," like *tsedakah*, "righteousness," is taken in a great latitude of signification. It means "rule, form, order, model, plan; rule of right, or of religion; an ordinance, institution; judicial process, cause, trial, sentence, condemnation, acquittal, deliverance, mercy." It certainly means in this place the law to be published by Messiah, the institution of the gospel.

ALEXANDER MACLAREN:

Verses 3, 4. The two metaphors which we have in the former part of these words are not altogether parallel. "A bruised reed" has suffered an injury which, however, is neither complete nor irreparable. "Smoking flax," on the other hand—by which, of course, is meant flax used as a wick in an old–fashioned oil lamp—is partially lit. In the one a process has been begun which, if continued, ends in destruction; in the other, a process has been begun which, if continued, ends in a bright flame. So the one metaphor may refer to the beginnings of evil which may still be averted, and the other the beginnings of incipient and incomplete good. If we keep this distinction in mind, the words of our text gain wonderfully in comprehensiveness.

Then again, it is to be noticed that in the last words of our text, which are separated from the former by a clause which we omit, we have an echo of these metaphors. The word translated "fail" is the same as that rendered in the previous verse "smoking," or "dimly burning"; and the word "discouraged" is the same as that rendered in the previous verse "bruised." So then, this "Servant of the Lord," who is not to break the bruised reed nor quench the smoking flax, is fitted for His works, because He Himself has no share in the evils which He would heal, and none in the weaknesses which He would heal, and none in the weaknesses which He would strengthen. His perfect manhood knows no flaws nor bruises; His complete goodness is capable of and needs no increase. Neither outward force nor inward weakness can hinder His power to heal and bless; therefore His work can never cease till it has attained its ultimate purpose. "He shall not fail nor be discouraged"; shall neither be broken by outward violence, nor shall the flame of His fading energy burn faint until He hath "set judgment in the earth," and crowned His purposes with complete success.

—Expositions of Holy Scripture

4. *He shall not fail nor be discouraged*—"His force shall not be abated nor broken."

MATTHEW HENRY

Verses 5–12

I. The covenant God made with and the commission he gave to the Messiah, *v.* 5–7.

1. The royal titles by which the great God here makes himself known (*v.* 5): He is the fountain of all being and therefore the fountain of all power. In the upper world *he created the heavens and stretched them out* (*ch.* xl. 22). In the lower world *he spread forth the earth,* and made it a habitation, *and that which comes out of it* is produced by his power. In the world of mankind: *He gives breath to the people upon it;* he gives *spirit,* the powers and faculties of a rational soul. Now this is prefixed to God's covenant with the Messiah, and the commission given him to show that the work of redemption was to restore man to the allegiance he owes to God as his Maker.

2. The assurances which he gives to the Messiah of his presence with him, *v.* 6. The Messiah was called of God. He was no intruder (Heb. v. 4). When an angel was sent from heaven to strengthen him in his agonies, the Father himself was with him, and this promise was fulfilled.

3. The great intentions of this commission speak comfort to the children of men. God, in giving us Christ, has with him freely given us all the blessings of the new covenant. Two glorious blessings Christ, in his gospel, brings with him to the Gentile word—light and liberty. He is given *for a light to the Gentiles.* By his Spirit in the word he presents the object; by his Spirit in the heart he prepares the organ. He is sent to proclaim liberty to the captives, as Cyrus did, *to bring out the prisoners;* not only to open the prison doors, and give them leave to go out, which was all that Cyrus could do, but to bring them out, to enable them to make use of their liberty. This Christ does by his grace.

II. The ratification and confirmation of this grant. 1. The authority of him that makes the promise (*v.* 8): *I am the Lord, Jehovah, that is my name.* If he is the Lord that gives being and birth to all things, he will give being and birth to this promise. 2. The accomplishment of the promises he had formerly made concerning his church, are proofs of the kindness he bears to his people (*v.* 9): "*Behold, the former things have come to pass. And* now *new things do I declare.* Now I will make new promises, now I will bestow new favours. Old Testament blessings you have had abundantly; now I declare New Testament blessings, not a fruitful country and dominion over your neighbours, but *spiritual blessings in heavenly things. Before they spring forth* in the preaching of the gospel *I tell you of them,* under the type and figure of the former things."

III. The song of joy and praise which should be sung hereupon to the glory of God (*v.* 10): *Sing unto the Lord a new song,* a New Testament song. The giving of Christ for *a light to the Gentiles* (*v.* 6) was a new thing. The praises of God's grace shall be sung with joy and thankfulness, 1. By those that live in *the end of the earth,* in countries that lie most remote from Jerusalem. 2. By mariners and merchants, and those that *go down to the sea.* The Jews traded little at sea; if therefore God's praises be sung by those that go down to the sea, it must be by Gentiles. 3. By *the islands and the inhabitants thereof, v.* 10, and again, *v.* 12. 4. *By the wilderness and the cities thereof, and the villages of Kedar.* These lay east from Jerusalem, as the islands lay west. 5. By *the inhabitants of the rock,* and those that dwell *on the tops of the mountains,* by the inhabitants of the rock, the inhabitants of that part of Arabia which is called *Petræa—the rocky.*

Verses 13–17

These verses may be the song itself that is to be sung by the Gentile world or a prophecy of what God will do to make way for the singing of that song.

I. He will appear in his power and glory more than ever. So he did in the preaching of his gospel, and in the wonderful success it had in the *pulling down of Satan's strongholds, v.* 13, 14. *He had long held his peace,* but now *he shall go forth* to attack the devil's kingdom and give it a fatal blow. Christ, in it, went forth conquering and to conquer. The ministry of the apostles is called their *warfare;* and they were the soldiers of Jesus Christ. *He shall stir up jealousy,* shall appear more jealous than ever for his own name and against idolatry. *He shall cry,* in the preaching of his word, *cry like a travailing woman;* for the ministers of Christ preached as men that travailed in birth again till they saw Christ formed in the souls of the people, Gal. iv. 19. He shall conquer by the power of his Spirit. As a type and figure of this, to make way for the redemption of the Jews out of Babylon, God will break the power of their oppressors, and *will at once destroy and devour* the Babylonian monarchy. In accomplishing this des-

JAMIESON, FAUSSET, BROWN

the countries bordering on the Mediterranean. **5.** Previously God had spoken *of* Messiah; now (vss. 5-7) He speaks *to* Him. To show to all that He is able to sustain the Messiah in His appointed work, and that all might accept Messiah as commissioned by such a mighty God, He commences by announcing Himself as the Almighty Creator and Preserver of all things. **spread . . . earth**—(Ps. 136:6). **6. in righteousness**—rather, "for a righteous purpose" [LOWTH]. (See vs. 21). God "set forth" His Son "to be a propitiation (so as) to declare His (God's) *righteousness,* that God might be just, and (yet) the justifier of him which believeth in Jesus" (Rom. 3: 25, 26; cf. *Note,* ch. 41:2; 45:13; 50:8, 9). **hold . . . hand**—cf. as to Israel, the type of Messiah, Hosea 11:3. **covenant**—the medium of the covenant, originally made between God and Abraham (ch. 49:8). "The mediator of a better covenant" (Heb. 8:6) than the law (see ch. 49:8; Jer. 31:33; 50:5). So the abstract "peace," for *peace-maker* (Mic. 5:5; Eph. 2:14). **the people**—Israel; as ch. 49:8, compared with vs. 6, proves (Luke 2:32). **7. blind**—spiritually (vss. 16, 18, 19; ch. 35:5; John 9:39). **prison**—(ch. 61:1, 2.) **darkness**—opposed to "light" (vs. 6; Eph. 5:8; I Pet. 2:9). **8.** God turns from addressing Messiah to the people. **Lord**—JEHOVAH: God's distinguishing and incommunicable name, indicating essential *being* and immutable faithfulness (cf. Exod. 6:3; Ps. 83:18; 96:5; Hos. 12:5). **my**—that is due to Me, and to Me alone. **9. former things**—Former predictions of God, which were now fulfilled, are here adduced as proof that they ought to trust in Him alone as God; viz., the predictions as to Israel's restoration from Babylon. **new**—viz., predictions as to Messiah, who is to bring all nations to the worship of Jehovah (vss. 1, 4, 6). **spring forth**—The same image from plants *just beginning to germinate* occurs in ch. 43:19; 58:8. Before there is *the slightest indication* to enable a sagacious observer to infer the coming event, God *foretells* it. **10. new song**—such as has never before been sung, called for by a new manifestation of God's grace, to express which no hymn for former mercies would be appropriate. The new song shall be sung when the Lord shall reign in Jerusalem, and all "nations shall flow unto it" (ch. 2:2; 26:1; Rev. 5:9; 14:3). **ye that go down to the sea**—whose conversion will be the means of diffusing the Gospel to distant lands. **all . . . therein**—all the living creatures *that fill* the sea (Ps. 96:11) [MAURER]. Or, *all sailors and voyagers* [GESENIUS]. But these were already mentioned in the previous clause: there he called on all who go *upon* the sea; in this clause all animals *in* the sea; so in vs. 11, he calls on the inanimate wilderness to lift up its voice. External nature shall be so renovated as to be in unison with the moral renovation. **11. cities**—in a region not wholly waste, but mainly so, with an oasis here and there. **Kedar**—in Arabia Deserta (ch. 21:16; Gen. 25:13). The Kedarenians led a nomadic, wandering life. So Kedar is here put in general for that class of men. **rock**—*Sela,* i.e. Petra, the metropolis of Idumea and the Nabathœan Ishmaelites. Or it may refer in general to those in Arabia Petræa, who had their dwellings cut out of the rock. **the mountains**—viz., of Paran, south of Sinai, in Arabic Petræa [VITRINGA]. **12. glory . . . islands**—(ch. 24:15).

13-16. Jehovah will no longer restrain His wrath: He will go forth as a mighty warrior (Exod. 15:3) to destroy His people's and His enemies, and to deliver Israel (cf. Ps. 45:3). **stir up jealousy**—rouse His indignation. **roar**—image from the battle cry of a warrior. **14. long time**—viz., during the desolation of Israel (ch. 32:14). **holden my peace**—(Cf. Ps. 50:21; Hab. 1:2.) **cry like a travailing woman . . .**—Like a woman in parturition, who, after having restrained her breathing for a time, at last, overcome with labor-pain, lets out her voice with a panting sigh; so Jehovah will give full vent to His long pent-up wrath. Translate, instead of "destroy . . . devour"; *I will at once breathe hard and pant,* viz., giving loose to My wrath. **15.** I will destroy all My foes. **mountains**—in Palestine usually planted with vines and olives in terraces, up to their tops. **islands—rather, "dry lands."** God

ADAM CLARKE

6. *A covenant of the people*—"A covenant to the people." But I think the word *berith,* here, should not be translated *covenant,* but "covenant sacrifice," which meaning it often has; and undoubtedly in this place. This gives a still stronger and clearer sense.

7. *To open the blind eyes.* In this verse the prophet seems to set forth the spiritual redemption, under images borrowed from the temporal deliverance.

8. *I am the Lord. Ani Yehovah.* This is the famous tetragrammation, or name of four letters, which we write *Jehovah, Yehovah,* etc. The letters are Y H U H. The Jews never pronounce it, and the true pronunciation is utterly unknown. *That is my name.* A name peculiar to myself.

11. *Let the wilderness.* The most uncultivated countries, and the most rude and uncivilized people, shall confess and celebrate with thanksgiving the blessing of the knowledge of God graciously imparted to them. *The villages that Kedar doth inhabit.* The Arabs, according to the Targum. *The inhabitants of the rock.* They who dwell in fortified places. The Vulgate has "the inhabitants of Arabia Petraea."

14. *I have been still*—"Shall I keep silence forever?"

MATTHEW HENRY

truction of Babylon by the Persian army under Cyrus, *he will make waste mountains and hills*, level the country, and *dry up all their herbs*. The army shall drain the fens and low grounds, to make way for the march of their army. Thus, when the gospel shall be preached, it shall have a free course.

II. He will manifest his favour and grace, and towards those who ask the way to Zion, he will show the way, and lead in it, *v*. 16. God will *lead by a way that they knew not*, will show them the way to life and happiness by Jesus Christ, who is the way. Thus, in the conversion of Paul, he was struck blind first, and then God revealed his Son, and made the scales to fall from his eyes. God will *make darkness light before them*. Insuperable difficulties are in the way of their obedience; but God will make *crooked things straight*; their way shall be plain. As a type of this, he will lead the Jews, when they return out of captivity, to their own land again.

III. He will put those to confusion who adhere to idols (*v*. 17). The Babylonians when they see how the Jews, who despise their images, are owned and delivered by the God they worship, shall be ashamed that ever they said to these molten images, *You are our gods*. In times of reformation sin becomes unfashionable.

Verses 18–25

The prophet, having spoken by way of encouragement to the believing Jews, here turns to those among them who were unbelieving. In them there was a type of the Jews who rejected Christ and were rejected by him.

I. The call that is given to this people (*v*. 18): "*Hear, you deaf*, and attend to the joyful sound, *and look you blind, that you may see* the joyful light." This call to the deaf to hear and the blind to see is like the command given to the man that had the withered hand to stretch it forth; though he could not do this, because it was withered, yet, if he had not attempted to do it, he would not have been healed.

II. The character that is given of them (*v*. 19, 20): *Who is blind, but my servant, or deaf as my messenger?* The people of the Jews were in profession God's servants, and their priests and elders his messengers (Mal. ii. 7); but they were deaf and blind. He complains of their sottishness—they are blind; and of their stubbornness—they are deaf. They were even worse than the Gentiles themselves. Blindness and deafness in spiritual things are worse in those that profess themselves to be God's servants and messengers than in others. The prophet goes on (*v*. 20) to describe the blindness and obstinacy of the Jewish nation, just as our Saviour describes it in his time (Matt. xiii. 14, 15).

III. The care God will take of the honour of his own name, notwithstanding their blindness and deafness. The scripture was fulfilled in the casting off of the Jews as well as in the calling in of the Gentiles. *He will magnify the law* (divine revelation in all the parts of it) *and will make it honourable*. The law is truly honourable, and, if men will not magnify it by their obedience to it, God will magnify it by punishing them for their disobedience.

IV. The calamities God will bring upon the Jewish nation for their wilful blindness and deafness, *v*. 22. They are *robbed and spoiled*. Those that were impenitent and unreformed in Babylon were sentenced to perpetual captivity. It was for their sins that they were spoiled of all their possessions. They were some of them *snared in holes*, and others *hidden in prison-houses*. There they lie, and there they are likely to lie. This had its full acomplishment in the final destruction of the Jewish nation by the Romans.

V. The counsel given them in order to their relief; for, though their case be sad, it is not desperate. The generality of them are deaf; they will not harken to the voice of God's word. He will therefore try his rod, and see *who among them will give ear to that*, *v*. 23. If one method do not take effect, another may. We may all of us, if we will, hear the voice of God. In hearing the word we must hear for hereafter; we must especially hear for eternity. Acknowledge the hand of God in afflictions, and, whoever were the instruments, have an eye to him as the principal agent (*v*. 24): "*Who gave Jacob and Israel*, that people that used to have such an interest in heaven and such a dominion on earth, who gave them *for a spoil to the robbers*, as they are now to the Babylonians and to the Romans? *Did not the Lord?*" It is he *against whom we have sinned*; the prophet puts himself into the number of the sinners, as Dan. ix. 7, 8. See the mischief that sin makes; it provokes God to anger against a people, and so kindles a universal conflagration, sets all on fire.

JAMIESON, FAUSSET, BROWN

will destroy His foes, the heathen, and their idols, and *"dry up"* the fountains of their oracles, their doctrines and institutions, the symbol of which is *water*, and their schools which promoted idolatry [VITRINGA]. **16. blind**—God's people, Israel, in captivity, needing a guide. In the ulterior sense the New Testament Church, which was about to be led and enlightened by the Son of God as its leader and shepherd in the wilderness of the Roman empire, until it should reach a city of habitation. "A way . . . they knew not," refers to the various means employed by Providence for the establishment of the Church in the world, such as would never have occurred to the mind of mere man. "Blind," they are called, as not having heretofore seen God's ways in ordering His Church. **make darkness light . . .**—implies that the glorious issue would only be known by the event itself [VITRINGA]. The same holds good of the *individual* believer (ch. 30:21; Ps. 107:7; cf. Hos. 2:6, 14; Eph. 5:8; Heb. 13:5). **17. turned back . . . ashamed**—disappointed in their trust; the same phrase occurs in Psalm 35:4. **18. deaf**—viz., to the voice of God. **blind**—to your duty and interest; wilfully so (vs. 20). In this they differ from "the blind" (vs. 16). The Jews are referred to. He had said, God would destroy the heathen idolatry; here he remembers that even Israel, His "servant" (vs. 19), from whom better things might have been expected, is tainted with this sin. **19. my servant**—viz., Israel. Who of the heathen is so blind? Considering Israel's high privileges, the heathen's blindness was as nothing compared with that of Israelite idolaters. **my messenger . . . sent**—Israel was designed by God to be the herald of His truth to other nations. **perfect**—furnished with institutions, civil and religious, suited to their *perfect* well-being. Cf. the title, "Jeshurun," the *perfect* one, applied to Israel (cf. ch. 44:2), as the type of Messiah [VITRINGA]. Or translate, the *friend* of God, which Israel was by virtue of descent from Abraham, who was so called (ch. 41:8), [GESENIUS]. The language, "my servant" (cf. vs. 1), "messenger" (Mal. 3:1), "perfect" (Rom. 10:4; Heb. 2:10; I Peter 2:22), can, in the full antitypical sense, only apply to Christ. So vs. 21 plainly refers to Him. "Blind" and "deaf" in His case refer to His endurance of suffering and reproach, as though He neither saw nor heard (Ps. 38:13, 14). Thus there is a transition by contrast from the moral *blindness* of Israel (vs. 18) to the patient blindness and deafness of Messiah [HORSLEY]. **20. observest**—Thou dost not *keep* them. The "many things" are the many proofs which all along from the first God had given Israel of His goodness and His power (Deut. 4:32-38; 29:2-4; Psalms 78; 105). **he**—transition from the second to the third person. "Opening . . . ears," i.e., though he (Israel) hath his ears open (*Note*, ch. 6:10). This language, too (*Note*, vs. 19), applies to Messiah as Jehovah's *servant* (ch. 50: 5; Ps. 40:6). **21. his righteousness**—not His people's, but His own; vs. 24 shows that they had no righteousness (ch. 45:24; 59:16). God is *well pleased* with His Son ("in whom My soul *delighteth*," vs. 1), "who fulfils all *righteousness*" (Matt. 3:15) for them, and with them for His sake (cf. vs. 6; Ps. 71:16, 19; Matt. 5:17; Rom. 10:3, 4; Phil. 3:9). Perhaps in God's "righteousness" here is included His *faithfulness to His promises* given to Israel's forefathers [ROSENMULLER]; because of this He is well pleased with Israel, even though displeased with their sin, which He here reproves; but that promise could only be based on the *righteousness of Messiah*, the promised seed, which is *God's* righteousness. **22. holes**—caught by their foes in the *caverns* where they had sought refuge [BARNES]. Or bound in subterranean dungeons [MAURER]. **prison houses**—either literal prisons, or their own houses, whence they dare not go forth for fear of the enemy. The connection is: Notwithstanding God's favor to His people for His righteousness' sake (vs. 21), they have fallen into misery (the Babylonish and Romish captivities and their present dispersion), owing to their disregard of the divine law: spiritual imprisonment is included (vs. 7). **none saith, Restore**—There is no deliverer (ch. 63:5). **23.** A call that they should be warned by the past judgments of God to obey Him for the time to come. **24. Who**—Their calamity was not the work of chance, but *God's* immediate act for their sins. **Jacob . . . Israel . . . we**—change from the third to the first person; Isaiah first speaking to them as a prophet, distinct from them; then identifying himself with them, and acknowledging His share in the nation's sins (cf. Josh. 5:1). **25. him**—Israel (vs. 24). **strength of battle**—violence of war. **it**—the *battle* or war (cf. ch. 10:16). **knew not**—knew not the lesson of repentance which the judgment was intended to teach (ch. 5:13; 9:13; Jer. 5:3).

ADAM CLARKE

19. *As my messenger that I sent*—"As he to whom I have sent My messengers." *As he that is perfect*—"As he who is perfectly instructed."

20. *Seeing many things*—"Thou hast seen indeed." *But he heareth not*—"Yet you will not hear."

21. *He will magnify the law*—"He hath exalted His own praise."

22. *They are all of them snared in holes*—"All their chosen youths are taken in the toils."

24. *We have sinned*—"They have sinned."

25. *The fury of his anger*—"The heat of His wrath."

MATTHEW HENRY

CHAPTER 43

Verses 1–7

This chapter has a plain connexion with the close of the foregoing chapter. It was there said that Jacob and Israel would not walk in God's ways, and now one would think it should have followed that God would abandon them; but no, the next words are, *But now, fear not, O Jacob! O Israel! I have redeemed thee, and thou art mine.* Though many among them were untractable, yet God would continue his love for his people, and the body of that nation should still be reserved for mercy. Now the sun, breaking out thus of a sudden from behind a thick and dark cloud, shines with a pleasing surprise. The expressions of God's goodwill to his people here speak abundance of comfort to all the spiritual seed of upright Jacob and praying Israel.

I. The grounds of God's care and concern for his people. Jacob and Israel, though in a sinful miserable condition, shall be looked after; for, 1. They are God's *workmanship, created by him unto good works*, Eph. ii. 10. He has created them, not only given them a being, but formed them into a people, constituted their government, and incorporated them by the charter of his covenant. 2. They are the people of his purchase: he has redeemed them. Out of the land of Egypt he first redeemed them, and out of many another bondage, *in his love, and in his pity* (*ch.* lxiii. 9); much more will he take care of those who are redeemed with the blood of his Son. 3. They are his peculiar people: he has called them by name. 4. He is their God in covenant (*v.* 3). Those that have God for them need not fear who or what can be against them.

II. The former instances of this care. 1. God had purchased them dearly: *I gave Egypt for thy ransom.* The Ethiopians had invaded them in Asa's time; but they shall be destroyed rather than Israel shall be disturbed. What are Ethiopia and Seba, all their lives and all their treasures, compared with the blood of Christ? 2. He had prized them accordingly, and they were very dear to him (*v.* 4).

III. The further instances God would yet give them of his care and kindness. 1. He would be present with them in their greatest difficulties and dangers (*v.* 2). 2. He would still, when there was occasion, make all the interests of the children of men give way to the interests of his own children. 3. Those of them that were scattered and dispersed in other nations should all be gathered in and share in the blessings of the public, *v.* 5–7. Some of the seed of Israel were dispersed into all countries, but those whose spirits God stirred up to go to Jerusalem should be fetched in from all parts. But who are the seed of Israel that shall be thus carefully gathered in? He tells us (*v.* 7) they are such as God has marked for mercy. They are called by his name. They are created for his glory. God is with the church, and therefore let her not fear; none that belong to her shall be lost.

Verses 8–13

God here challenges the worshippers of idols to produce proofs of the divinity of their false gods.

I. Their gods have *eyes and see not, ears and hear not*, and those that make them and trust in them are like unto them. They have the shape, capacities, and faculties, of men; but they are, in effect, destitute of reason and common sense, or they would never worship gods of their own making.

II. God's witnesses are summoned to appear, and give evidence for him (*v.* 10): "*You, O Israelites!* all you that are *called by my name*, you *are all my witnesses, and* so is *my servant whom I have chosen.*" It was Christ himself that was so described (*ch.* xlii. 1), *My servant and my elect*.

1. All the prophets that testified to Christ, and Christ himself, the great prophet, are here appealed to as God's witnesses. God's people are witnesses for him, and can attest, upon their own experience, concerning the power of his grace. But the Messiah especially is given to be a witness for him to the people; having lain in his bosom from eternity.

JAMIESON, FAUSSET, BROWN

CHAPTER 43

Vss. 1-28. A Succession of Arguments Wherein Israel May Be Assured that, notwithstanding Their Perversity towards God (ch. 42:25), He Will Deliver, and Restore Them. **1. But now**—notwithstanding God's past just judgments for Israel's sins. **created**—not only in the general sense, but specially *created* as a peculiar people unto Himself (vss. 7, 15, 21; ch. 44:2, 21, 24). So believers, "created in Christ Jesus" (Eph. 2:10), "a peculiar people" (I Pet. 2:9). **redeemed**—a second argument why they should trust Him besides *creation.* The *Hebrew* means *to ransom by a price paid in lieu of the captives* (cf. vs. 3). Babylon was to be the ransom in this case, i.e., was to be destroyed, in order that they might be delivered; so Christ became a curse, doomed to death, that we might be redeemed. **called . . . by . . . name**—not merely "called" in general, as in ch. 42:6; 48:12; 51:2, but *designated as His own* peculiar people (cf. ch. 45:3, 4; Exod. 32:1; 33:12; John 10:3). **2. rivers . . . not overflow thee**—so in passing Jordan, though at its "*overflow,*" when its "swellings" were especially dangerous (Josh. 3:15; Jer. 12:5). **waters . . . fire**—a proverbial phrase for the extremest perils (Ps. 66:12; also Ps. 138:7). Literally fulfilled at the Red Sea (Exod. 14), and in the case of the three youths cast into the fiery furnace for conscience' sake (Dan. 3:25, 27). **3. Egypt for thy ransom**—Either Egypt or Israel must perish; God chose that Egypt, though so much more mighty, should be destroyed, in order that His people might be delivered; thus Egypt stood, *instead* of Israel, as a kind of "ransom." The *Hebrew, kopher,* means properly "that with which anything is overlaid," as the pitch with which the ark was overlaid; hence that which *covers over* sins, an atonement. Nebuchadnezzar had subdued Egypt, Ethiopia (*Hebrew, Cush*), and Saba (descended from Cush, Genesis 10:7, probably Meroe of Ethiopia, a great island formed by the Astaboras and the Nile, conquered by Cambyses, successor of Cyrus). Cyrus received these from God with the rest of the Babylonian dominions, in consideration of his being about to deliver Israel. However, the reference may be to the three years' war in which Sargon overcame these countries, and so had his attention diverted **from Israel (see** *Notes,* **ch. 20) [Vitringa].** But the reference is probably more general, viz., to *all* the instances in which Jehovah sacrificed mighty heathen nations, when the safety of Israel required it. **4. Since**—All along from the beginning; for there was never a time when Israel was not Jehovah's people. The apodosis should be at, "I will give." "Since ever thou wast precious in My sight, honorable, and that I loved thee, I will give," etc. [Maurer]. Gesenius, as *English Version,* takes "Since" to mean, "Inasmuch as." If the apodosis be as in *English Version,* "Since thou wast precious" will refer to the time when God called His people out of Egypt, manifesting then first the love which He had from everlasting towards them (Jer. 31:3; Hos. 11:1); "honorable" and "loved," refer to *outward* marks of honor and love from God. **men . . . people**—*other* nations for thee (so. vs. 3). **thy life**—thy person. **5.** (Deut. 30:3). **seed**—descendants scattered in all lands. Vitringa understands it of the *spiritual* "seed" of the Church produced by mystical regeneration: for the expression is, "bring," not "bring back." This sense is perhaps included, but not to the exclusion of the literal Israel's restoration (Jer. 30:10, 11; Amos 9:9; Zech. 2:6-13). **6. Give up**—viz., My people. **sons . . . daughters**—The feminine joined to the masculine expresses the complete *totality* of anything (Zech. 9:17). **7. called by my name**—belong to Israel, whose people, as sons of God, bear the name of their Father (ch. 44:5; 48:1). **for my glory**—(vs. 21; ch. 29:23). **8.** Solemn challenge given by God to the nations to argue with Him the question of His superiority to their idols, and His power to deliver Israel (ch. 41:1). **blind people**—the Gentiles, who also, like Israel (ch. 42: 19), are blind (spiritually), though having eyes; i.e., natural faculties, whereby they might know God (Rom. 1:20, 21) [Lowth]. Or else, the Jews [Vitringa]. **9. who . . . can declare this**—who among the idolatrous soothsayers hath predicted *this;* i.e., as to Cyrus being the deliverer of Israel? **former**—predictions, as in ch. 42:9 [Maurer]. Or, things that shall first come to pass (*Note,* ch 41:21, 22) [Barnes]. **let them bring forth their witnesses**—as I do mine (vs. 10). **justified**—declared veracious in their pretended prophecies. **or**—rather, "and"; let men hear their prediction and say, from the event, It is verified (*Note,* ch. 41:26). **10. Ye**—the Jews, to whom I have given predictions, verified by the event;

ADAM CLARKE

CHAPTER 43

3. *I gave Egypt for thy ransom.* This is commonly supposed to refer to the time of Sennacherib's invasion; who, when he was just ready to fall upon Jerusalem, soon after his entering Judea, was providentially diverted from that design, and turned his arms against the Egyptians, and their allies the Cushean Arabians, with their neighbors the Sabeans, probably joined with them under Tirhakah. See chap. xx and chap xxxvii. 9. Or as there are some reasonable objections to this opinion, perhaps it may mean more generally that God has often saved His people at the expense of other nations whom He had, as it were in their stead, given up to destruction. Kimchi refers all this to the deliverance of Jerusalem from the invasion of Sennacherib. Tirhakah, king of Ethiopia, had come out to war against the king of Assyria, who was thereupon obliged to raise the siege of Jerusalem. Thus the Ethiopians, Egyptians, and Sabeans were delivered into the hands of the Assyrians as a ransom for Israel. I cannot help thinking this to be a very rational solution of the text.

7. *Every one that is called by my name.* All who worship the true God, and are obedient to His laws. *I have created him.* I have produced him out of nothing. *I have formed him. Yetsartiv.* I have given him that particular form and shape which are best suited to his station in life. *I have made him. Asithiv.* I have adapted him to the accomplishment of My counsels and designs.

8. *Bring forth the blind people that have eyes*—"Bring forth the people, blind, although they have eyes." I understand this of the Gentiles, as the verse following, not of the Jews. Their natural faculties, if they had made a proper use of them, must have led them to the knowledge of the being and attributes of the one true God; for "his eternal power and Godhead," if well attended to, are clearly seen in His works (Rom. i. 20), and would have preserved them from running into the folly and absurdity of worshipping idols. They are here challenged to produce the evidence of the power and foreknowledge of their idol gods; and the Jews are just afterwards, v. 10, appealed to as witnesses for God in this cause. Therefore these latter cannot here be meant by the people blind with eyes and deaf with ears.

MATTHEW HENRY

2. Let us see what the point is which these witnesses are called to prove (*v.* 12): *You are my witnesses, saith the Lord, that I am God.* I am a being self-existent and self-sufficient; I am he whom you are to fear, and worship, and trust in. Nay (*v.* 13), *before the day was* (before the first day of time, before the creation of the light, and, consequently, from eternity) *I am he.* The idols were gods formed (*dei facti—made gods*, or rather *fictitii—fictitious*); *by nature they were no gods*, Gal. iv. 8. But God had a being from eternity, before there were either idols or idolaters (truth is more ancient than error); and he will have a being to eternity. *I, even I, am the Lord*, the great Jehovah, who is, and was, and is to come; and *besides me there is no Saviour*, *v.* 11. God has an infinite and infallible knowledge, as is evident from *the predictions of his word* (*v.* 12): *I have declared and I have shown* that which has without fail come to pass. He has an infinite and irresistible power. He pleads not only, I have *shown*, but, I have *saved* (*v.* 13). The gods of the heathen cannot so much as inspire an historian, much less a prophet. They are challenged to join issue upon this: *Let them bring forth their witnesses*, to prove their omniscience and omnipotence.

Verses 14–21

I. God here takes to himself such titles as were very encouraging to his people. He is *the Lord their Redeemer*, the *Holy One of Israel* (*v.* 14), and again (*v.* 15), *their Holy One*, and therefore will make good every word he has spoken to them. He is *the Creator of Israel*, that made them a people out of nothing and he is their *King*.

II. He assures them he will break the power of their oppressors, *ch.* xiv. 17. God will take care to send a prince to Babylon, that shall *bring down all their nobles*, and all their people too, even *the Chaldeans, whose cry is in the ships*, or whose cry is *to the ships*, as their refuge when the city is taken, that they may escape by the river.

III. He reminds them of the great things he did for their fathers when he brought them out of the land of Egypt (*v.* 16, 17). He that did this can make a way for you in the sea when you return out of Babylon.

IV. He promises to do yet greater things for them than he had done in the days of old. They should see them repeated, nay, they should see them outdone (*v.* 18): "*Remember not the former things*, to undervalue the present things, as if *the former days were better than these. Behold, the Lord will do a new thing.*" The best exposition of this is, Jer. xvi. 14, 15; xxiii. 7, 8. Though former mercies must not be forgotten, fresh mercies must in a special manner be improved.

V. He promises not only to deliver them out of Babylon, but to conduct them safely and comfortably to their own land (*v.* 19, 20): *I will make a way in the wilderness and rivers in the desert.* The same power that made a *way in the sea* (*v.* 16) can make a *way in the wilderness.* And he can produce waters in the dryest land, in such abundance as not only to *give drink to his people, his chosen*, but to the *beasts of the field*, also *the dragons and the ostriches*, who are therefore said to honour God for it. This looks forward, not only to God's care of the Jewish church between their return from Babylon and the coming of Christ, but to the grace of the gospel, especially as it is manifested to the Gentile world. The sinners of the Gentiles, who had been as the beasts of the field, running wild, fierce as the dragons, stupid as the owls or ostriches, shall be brought to honour God for his grace.

VI. He traces up all these promised blessings to their great origin (*v.* 21): *This people have I formed for myself*, and therefore I do all this for them, that they may *show forth my praise.* The new heavens, the new earth, the new man, are the work of God's hand; they are fashioned according to his will. As he formed us, so he feeds us, and keeps us, and leads us.

Verses 22–28

This charge comes in here, 1. To clear God's justice in bringing them into captivity. They had neglected God and had cast him off, and therefore he justly rejected them and *gave them to the curse* (*v.* 28); and they must be brought to own this before they are prepared for deliverance.

I. The sins with which they are here charged.

1. Omissions of the good which God had commanded. Observe how it comes in with a *but*; compare *v.* 21, where God tells them what favours he had bestowed upon them and what his just expectations were from them. But they had made very ill returns to him for his favours. They had cast off prayer: *Thou hast not called upon me, O Jacob!* Jacob was a man famous for prayer (Hosea xii. 4). To boast of the name of Jacob, and yet live without

JAMIESON, FAUSSET, BROWN

and in delivering whom I have so often manifested My power (see vss. 3, 4; ch. 44:8). **and my servant**—i.e., the whole Jewish people (ch. 41:8). **believe**—trust in. **formed**—before I *existed* none of the false gods were *formed*. "Formed" applies to the idols, not to God. Revelation 1:11 uses the same language to prove the Godhead of *Jesus*, as Isaiah here to prove the Godhead of *Jehovah*. **11. Lord**—Jehovah. **saviour**—temporally, from Babylon: eternally, from sin and hell (Hos. 13:4; Acts 4:12). The same titles as are applied to God are applied to Jesus. **12. declared**—predicted the future (ch. 41:22, 23). **saved**—the nation, in past times of danger. **showed**—viz., that I was God. **when . . . no strange god . . .**—to whom the predictions uttered by Me could be assigned. "Strange" means *foreign*, introduced from abroad. **13. before**—lit., *from the time of* the first existence of day **let**—Old English for "hinder" (ch. 14:27). Rather, translate, "undo it" [HORSLEY]. **14. sent**—viz., the Medes and Persians (ch. 10:5, 6; 13:3). **brought down**—"made to go down" to the sea (ch. 42:10), in order to escape the impending destruction of Babylon. **nobles**—rather, "fugitives," viz., the foreigners who sojourned in populous Babylon (ch. 13:14), distinct from the Chaldeans [MAURER]. **whose cry is in the ships**—exulting in their ships with the joyous sailors—cry, boastingly; their joy heretofore in their ships contrasts sadly with their present panic in fleeing to them (ch. 22:2; Zeph. 2:15). Babylon was on the Euphrates, which was joined to the Tigris by a canal, and flowed into the Persian Gulf. Thus it was famed for ships and commerce until the Persian monarchs, to prevent revolt or invasion, obstructed navigation by dams across the Tigris and Euphrates. **15. creator of Israel**—(vs. 1.) **your**—proved to be specially *yours* by delivering you. **16, 17.** Allusion to the deliverance of Israel and overthrow of Pharaoh in the Red Sea, the standing illustration of God's unchanging character towards His people (Exod. 14). **the power**—the might of the enemies' host, every mighty warrior. **they shall lie down together**—as Pharaoh's army sank "together" in a watery grave. **18.** So wonderful shall be God's future interpositions in your behalf, that all past ones shall be forgotten in comparison. Plainly the future restoration of Israel is the event ultimately meant. Thus the "former things" are such events as the destruction of Sennacherib and the return from Babylon. "Things of old" are events still more ancient, the deliverance from Egypt and at the Red Sea, and entry into Canaan [VITRINGA]. **19. new**—unprecedented in its wonderful character (ch. 42:9). **spring forth**—as a germinating herb: a beautiful image of the *silent* but *certain gradual growth* of events in God's providence (Mark 4:26-28). **way in . . . wilderness**—just as Israel in the wilderness, between the Red Sea and Canaan, was guided, and supplied with water by Jehovah; but the "new" deliverance shall be attended with manifestations of God's power and love, eclipsing the old (cf. ch. 41:17-19). "I will open a way, not merely in the Red Sea, but in the wilderness of the whole world; and not merely one river shall gush out of the rock, but many, which shall refresh, not the bodies as formerly, but the souls of the thirsty, so that the prophecy shall be fulfilled: "With joy shall ye draw water out of the wells of salvation" [JEROME]. "A way" often stands for *the true religion* (Acts 9:2; 18:26). "Rivers" express the influences of the Holy Spirit (John 7:37-39). Israel's *literal* restoration hereafter is included, as appears by comparing ch. 11:15, 16. **20. beast**—image of idolaters, defiled with blood and pollutions, dwelling like dragons, etc., in the wastes of Gentile ignorance: even they shall be converted. Or else, lit., such copious floods of water shall be given by God in the desert, that the very beasts shall (in poetic language) praise the Lord (Ps. 148:10) [JEROME]. **dragons**—"serpents", or else jackals (*Note*, ch. 13: 22). **owls**—rather, ostriches. **21. This people**—viz., The same as "My people, My chosen" (see vss. 1, 7, Ps. 102:18). **my praise**—on account of the many and great benefits conferred on them, especially their restoration.

22. But—Israel, *however*, is not to think that these divine favors are due to their own piety towards God. So the believer (Titus 3:5). **but**—rather, "for."

ADAM CLARKE

10. *Ye* (the Israelites) *are my witnesses . . . and my servant* (the Prophet) *whom I have chosen*, that whatever has been said before concerning Sennacherib has been literally fulfilled. The prophet had predicted it; the Israelites saw it accomplished.

12. *I have declared, and have saved.* My prophets have always predicted your deliverances before they took place; and I have fulfilled their words to the uttermost.

14. *The Chaldeans, whose cry is in the ships*—"The Chaldeaans exulting in their ships." Babylon was very advantageously situated both in respect to commerce and as a naval power. It was open to the Persian Gulf by the Euphrates, which was navigable by large vessels; and being joined to the Tigris above Babylon by the canal called the Royal River, supplied the city with the produce of the whole country to the north of it, as far as the Euxine and Caspian seas (*Herod.* i. 194). Semiramis was the foundress of this part also of the Babylonian greatness. She improved the navigation of the Euphrates (*Herod.* i. 184; *Strabo*, lib. xvi), and is said to have had a fleet of 3,000 galleys. We are not to wonder that in later times we hear little of the commerce and naval power of Babylon; for, after the taking of the city by Cyrus, the Euphrates was not only rendered less fit for navigation by being on that occasion diverted from its course and left to spread over the whole country; but the Persian monarchs, residing in their own country, to prevent any invasion by sea on that part of their empire, purposely obstructed the navigation of both the rivers by making cataracts in them (*Strabo*, ib.), that is, by raising dams across the channel, and making artificial falls in them, that no vessel of any size or force could possibly come up. Alexander began to restore the navigation of the rivers by demolishing the cataracts upon the Tigris as far up as Seleucia (*Arrian*, lib. vii), but he did not live to finish his great designs; those upon the Euphrates still continued. The prophet therefore might very justly speak of the Chaldeans as glorying in their naval power in his time, though afterwards they had no foundation for making any such boast.

19. *Behold, I will do a new thing.* At v. 16 the prophet had referred to the deliverance from Egypt and the passage through the Red Sea; here he promises that the same power shall be employed in their redemption and return from the Babylonish captivity. This was to be a new prodigy.

20. *The beast of the field shall honour me*—"The wild beast of the field shall glorify Me." The image is elegant and highly poetical. God will give such an abundant miraculous supply of water to His people traversing the dry desert in their return to their country that even the wild beasts, the serpents, the ostriches, and other animals that haunt those arid regions, shall be sensible of the blessing, and shall break forth into thanksgiving and praises to Him for the unusual refreshment which they receive from His so plentifully watering the sandy wastes of Arabia Deserta, for the benefit of His people passing through them.

22. *But thou hast not called upon me.* The connection is: But you, Israel, whom I have chosen, whom I have formed for myself to be My witness against the false gods of the nations; even you have revolted from Me, have neglected My worship, and have been perpetually running after strange gods. The emphasis of this and the following parts of the sentence, on which the sense depends, is laid on the words *me, on my account.* The Jews were

MATTHEW HENRY

prayer, is to mock God and deceive ourselves. They had grown weary of their religion. They grudged the expense of their devotion. They were for a cheap religion; and in those acts of devotion that were costly they desired to be excused. They had *not brought*, no, not their *small cattle*, the lambs and kids, which God required for *burnt-offerings* (*v.* 23), much less did they bring their greater cattle. *Sweet cane*, or *calamus*, was used for the holy oil, incense, and perfume; but they were not willing to be at the charge of that, *v.* 24. They were, in effect, as no sacrifices (*v.* 23): *Neither hast thou honoured me with thy sacrifices.* As God had appointed it, it was no burdensome thing; it was not a service that they had any reason at all to complain of: "*I have not caused thee to serve with an offering;* I have not made it a drudgery to you. I have *not wearied thee with incense.*" They had many feasts and good days, but only one day in all the year in which they were to afflict their souls. The ordinances of the ceremonial law, though, in comparison with Christ's easy yoke, they are spoken of as heavy (Acts xv. 10), yet, in comparison with the service that idolaters did to their false gods, they were light. God did not require them to sacrifice their children, as Moloch did.

2. Commissions of the evil which God had forbidden. *Thou hast made me to serve with thy sins.* When we make God's gifts the food and fuel of our lusts, then we make God to serve with our sins. God had not made them to serve with their sacrifices, but they had made him to serve with their sins. The master had not tired the servants with his commands, but they had tired him with their disobedience.

II. What were the aggravations of their sin, *v.* 27. 1. That they were children of disobedience; for their *first father* (that is, their forefathers) *had sinned.* 2. That they were scholars of disobedience too; for *their teachers had transgressed against God*, were guilty of gross scandalous sins, and the people, no doubt, would learn to do as they did.

III. What were the tokens of God's displeasure against them for their sins, *v.* 28. *I have profaned the princes of the sanctuary*, that is, the priests and Levites who presided with great dignity in the temple-service; they profaned themselves, and made themselves vile, by their enormities, and then God profaned them and made them vile, by their calamities, Mal. ii. 9. The honour of their state was ruined likewise: "*I have given Jacob to the curse*, that is, to be cursed, and hated, and abused by all their neighbours, *and Israel to reproach*, to be insulted, ridiculed, and triumphed over by their enemies."

IV. What were the riches of God's mercy towards them notwithstanding (*v.* 25): *I, even I, am he who* notwithstanding all this *blotteth out thy transgressions.*

1. This gracious declaration of God's readiness to pardon sin comes in very strangely. The charge ran very high: *Thou hast wearied me with thy iniquities*, *v.* 24. Now one would think it should follow: "*I, even I, am he* that will destroy thee, and burden myself no longer with care about thee." No, *I, even I, am he that will forgive thee;* as if the great God would teach us that forgiving injuries is the best way to keep ourselves from being wearied with them. Of the sins of every believing penitent, the pardon is expressed; he will *blot them out*, as a cloud is blotted out by the beams of the sun (*ch.* xliv. 22), as a debt is blotted out not to appear against the debtor (the book is crossed as if the debt were paid, because it is pardoned upon the payment which the surety has made). He *will not remember* the sin, which shall be no diminution to his love for the future. When God forgives he forgets. It is not for the sake of anything in us, but for his own sake, for his mercies' sake, and especially for his Son's sake.

2. Those words (*v.* 26), *Put me in remembrance*, may be understood either (1) As a rebuke to a proud Pharisee, that expects to find favour for his merits and not to be beholden to free grace: "If you have anything to offer for the sake of which you should be pardoned, put me in remembrance of it." Or, (2) As a direction and encouragement to a penitent publican. Put him in remembrance of the promises he has made to penitents, and the satisfaction his Son has made for them. This is the only way, and it is a sure way, to peace. *Only acknowledge thy transgression.*

JAMIESON, FAUSSET, BROWN

weary of me—(Amos 8:5, 6; Mal. 1:13), though "*I* have not wearied thee" (vs. 23), yet "thou hast been weary of Me." **23. small cattle**—rather, the "lamb" or "kid," required by the law to be daily offered to God (Exod. 29:38; Num. 28:3). **sacrifices**—offered any way; whereas the *Hebrew* for holocaust, or "burnt offering," denotes that which *ascends* as an offering consumed by fire. **I have not caused thee to serve**—i.e., to render the service of a *slave* (Matt. 11:30; Rom. 8:15; I John 4:18; 5:3). **offering**—bloodless (Lev. 2:1, 2). **wearied**—antithetical to vs. 22, "*Thou* hast been weary of Me." Though God in the law required such offerings, yet not so as to "weary" the worshipper, or to exact them in cases where, as in the Babylonish captivity, they were physically unable to render them; God did not require them, save in subordination to the higher moral duties (Ps. 50:8-14; 51:16, 17; Mic. 6:3, 6-8). **24. bought**—for "sweet cane" (aromatic *calamus*) was not indigenous to Palestine, but had to be bought from foreign countries (Jer. 6:20). It was used among the Hebrews to make the sacred ointment (Exod. 30:23). It is often offered as a mark of hospitality. **filled**—satiated (Jer. 31:14). God deigns to use human language to adapt Himself to human modes of thought. **made me to serve**—though "I have not caused *thee* to serve" (vs. 23). Our sin made the Son of God to become "a *servant*." He *served* to save us from servile bondage (Phil. 2:7; Heb. 2:14, 15). **wearied me**—Though I have "not wearied thee" (vs. 23; see ch. 1: 14).

27. first father—collectively for "most ancient *ancestors*," as the parallelism ("teachers") proves [MAURER]. Or, *thy chief religious ministers* or *priests* [GESENIUS]. *Adam*, the common father of all nations, can hardly be meant here, as it would have been irrelevant to mention *his* sin in an address to *the Jews specially*. *Abraham* is equally out of place here, as he is everywhere cited as an example of faithfulness, not of *sin*. However, taking the passage in its ultimate application to the Church at large, Adam may be meant. **teachers**—lit., "interpreters" between God and man, the priests (Job 33:23; Mal. 2:7). **28. profaned the princes**—(Ps. 89:39; Lam. 2:2, 6, 7). I have esteemed, or treated, them as persons not sacred. I have left them to suffer the same treatment as the common people, stripped of their holy office and in captivity. **princes of the sanctuary**—"governors of" it (I Chron. 24:5); directing its holy services; priests. **curse**—*Hebrew, cherim,* a solemn anathema, or excommunication. **reproaches**—(Ps. 123:3, 4).

25. (Ch. 44:22.) **I, even I**—the God against whom your sin is committed, and who alone can and will pardon. **for mine own sake**—(ch. 48:9, 11). How abominable a thing sin is, since it is against such a God of grace!

"Blotted out" is an image from an account-book, in which, when a debt is paid, the charge is *cancelled* or *blotted out.* **not remember . . . sins**—(Jer. 31:34). When God forgives, He forgets; i.e., treats the sinner as if He had forgotten his sins.

26. Put me in remembrance—Remind Me of every plea which thou hast to urge before Me in thy defense. Image from a trial (ch. 1:18; 41:1). Our strongest plea is to remind God of His own promises. So Jacob did at Mahanaim and Peniel (Gen. 32:9, 12). God, then, instead of "pleading against us with His great power," "will put His strength" in us (Job 23:6); we thus become "the Lord's *remembrancers*" (ch. 62:6, *Margin*). "*Declare* God's righteousness" vindicated in Jesus Christ "that thou mayest be justified" (Rom. 3:26; cf. ch. 20, and Ps. 143:2).

ADAM CLARKE

diligent in performing the external services of religion; in offering prayers, incense, sacrifices, oblations; but their prayers were not offered with faith, and their oblations were made more frequently to their idols than to the God of their fathers. *But thou hast been weary of me, O Israel*—"Neither on My account have you labored, O Israel."

28. *I have profaned the princes of the sanctuary*— "Your princes have profaned My sanctuary."

25. *I, even I, am he.* The original is extremely abrupt: "I, I, he." *For mine own sake.* In the pardon of sin God can draw no reason but from His own infinite goodness.

MATTHEW HENRY — CHAPTER 44

Verses 1–8

Two great truths in these verses:

I. That the people of God are a happy people, especially upon account of the covenant that is between them and God. Three things complete their happiness:

JAMIESON, FAUSSET, BROWN — CHAPTER 44

ADAM CLARKE — CHAPTER 44

MATTHEW HENRY

1. The covenant-relations wherein they stand to God, *v.* 1, 2. Israel is here called *Jeshurun—the upright one*; for those only, like Nathanael, are Israelites indeed, in whom is no guile. Jacob and Israel had been represented as very provoking and obnoxious to God's wrath, but mercy steps in with a *notwithstanding*: "*Yet now hear, O Jacob my servant!* thou and I will be friends again for all this." So and so I will do for them, says God (Heb. viii. 12), *for I will be merciful to their unrighteousness.* Now the relations wherein they stand to him are very encouraging. (1) They are his *servants.* (2) They are his *chosen,* and he will abide by his choice; those whom he has chosen he takes under special protection. (3) They are his creatures. He *made them,* and therefore he will help them over their difficulties and help them in their services.

2. The covenant-blessings which he has secured to them and theirs, *v.* 3, 4. (1) Those that are sensible of their spiritual wants, and the insufficiency of the creature to supply them, shall have abundant satisfaction in God: *I will pour water upon him that is thirsty.* (2) Those that are barren as the dry ground shall be watered with the grace of God. (3) The water God will pour out is *his Spirit* (John vii. 39). This is the great New Testament promise, that God, having sent his servant Christ, and upheld him, will send his Spirit to uphold us. To all who are thus made to partake of the privileges of adoption God will give the spirit of adoption. Hereby there shall be a great increase of the church. Thus it shall be spread to distant places, *v.* 4.

3. The consent they cheerfully give to their part of the covenant, *v.* 5. Many of those that were without did at that time join themselves to them, invited by that glorious appearance of God for them, Zech. viii. 23. And doubtless it looks further yet, to the conversion of the Gentiles. These converts are *one and another*, very many, of different ranks and nations, and all welcome to God, Col. iii. 11. Everyone for himself shall say, "*I am the Lord's;* living and dying I will be his." They shall *call themselves by the name of Jacob.* They shall love all God's people, and be willing to take their lot with them in all conditions. They shall do this very solemnly. Some of them shall *subscribe with their hand unto the Lord,* as a man sets his hand to it, and delivers it as his act and deed. The more express we are in our covenanting with God the better, Exod. xxiv. 7.

II. That, as the Israel of God are a happy people, so the God of Israel is a great God, and he is God alone. This speaks abundant satisfaction to all that trust in him, *v.* 6–8. The God we trust in is a God of incontestable sovereignty and irresistible power. He is *the Lord*, Jehovah, self-existent and self-sufficient; and he is *the Lord of hosts*, of all the hosts of heaven and earth, of angels and men. He is *the King of Israel and his Redeemer*; and those that take God for their King shall have him for their Redeemer. He is God from everlasting, before the world was, and will be so to everlasting. If there were not a God to create nothing would ever have been; and, if there were not a God to uphold, all would soon come to nothing again. He is God alone (*v.* 6): *Besides me there is no God.* There is no God besides Jehovah. He is all-sufficient, and therefore there needs no other. His people needed not to hope in any other God. Those on whom the sun shines need neither moon nor stars, nor the light of their own fire. They needed not to fear any other god. None besides could foretell these things to come, which God now by his prophet gave notice of to the world, above 200 years before they came to pass (*v.* 7).

Verses 9–20

This discourse is intended, 1. To arm the people of Israel against the strong temptation to worship idols when they were captives in Babylon, and to humour those who were now their lords and masters. 2. To cure them of their inclination to idolatry, which was the sin that did most easily beset them and to reform them from which they were sent into Babylon. As the rod of God is of use to enforce the word, so the word of God is of use to explain the rod. 3. To furnish them with something to say to their Chaldean task-masters. When they insulted over them, when they asked, *Where is your God?* they might hence ask them, *What are your gods?*

For the conviction of idolaters, we have,

I. A challenge given to them to clear themselves from the imputation of the most shameful folly imaginable, *v.* 9–11. They set their wits to contrive, and their hands to frame, graven images, and they call them *their delectable things.* We tell them that they deceive themselves and one another. *Their delectable things shall not profit* them, neither supply

JAMIESON, FAUSSET, BROWN

Vss. 1-28. Continuation of the Previous Chapter (vss. 1-5). **1. Yet**—Though thou hast sinned, *yet* hear God's gracious promise as to thy deliverance. **chosen**—(ch. 41:8). **2.** (Ch. 43:1, 7.) **formed . . . from . . . womb**—(So vs. 24; ch. 49:1, 5). The sense is similar to that in ch. 1:2. "I have nourished and brought up children." **Jesurun**—A diminutive term of endearment applied to Israel. The full title of affection was *Israelun;* contracted it became Jeshurun, with an allusion to the *Hebrew* root, *jashar,* "upright," "perfect" (see *Note* on "He that is perfect," ch. 42:19) [Gesenius], (Deut. 32:15). **3.** (Ch. 41:18). **him . . . thirsty**—rather, "the land" (ch. 35: 6, 7), fig. for *man* thirsting after righteousness (Matt. 5:6). **floods**—the *abundant* influences of the Holy Spirit, stronger than "water." **spirit**—including all spiritual and temporal gifts, as the parallel, "blessing," proves (ch. 11:2; 32:15). **seed**—(ch. 59:21). **4. they**—thy "seed" and "offspring" (vs. 3). **as among**—needlessly inserted in *English Version.* Rather, "The seed shall spring up as willows among the grass beside canals of water" [Horsley]. Or, "They shall spring up among the grass (i.e., luxuriantly; for what grows in the midst of grass grows luxuriantly) as willows by the water-courses," which makes the parallel clauses better balanced [Maurer]. **5.** The third clause answers in parallelism to the first, the fourth to the second. **I am the Lord's**—(Jer. 50:5; I Cor. 6:19, 20; II Cor. 8:5). **call himself by the name of Jacob**—The Gentiles (as the result of the outpouring of the Holy Spirit on Israel, the Lord's "seed," first) shall join themselves to the children of Jacob, in order to worship their God (cf. ch. 43:7; Ps. **49:11). Or, "calls," i.e., invokes and celebrates** *the name of Jacob,* **attaches himself to his nation and religion [Maurer], (Ps. 24:6). subscribe . . . hand unto . . . Lord**—in solemn and public covenant, pledging himself to God's service (cf. Neh. 9:38), before "witnesses" (Heb. 12:1), after the manner of a civil contract (Jer. 32:10, 12, 44). So the Christian in the sacraments [Barnes]. Lit., "shall fill his hand with letters (Exod. 32:15; Ezek. 2:10) in honor of Jehovah"; or "shall write upon his hand, I am Jehovah's" (cf. ch. 49:16; Rev. 13:16); alluding to the puncture with ink on the hand, whereby a soldier marked himself as bound to his commander; and whereby the Christians used to mark themselves with the name of Christ [Lowth]. The former view is simpler. **surname himself . . . Israel**—**Maurer and Gesenius interpret this as the** *Hebrew* sanctions, answering to their rendering of the parallel second clause, "*calls blandly* (speaks in honorable terms of) the name of Israel." Retaining *English Version,* we must, from the *Hebrew* understand it thus, "Surname himself by the *honorable* name of Israel" (ch. 45:4). **6.** Here follows an argument for Jehovah, as the only God, and against the idols, as vanity (see *Notes,* ch. 41:4; 43:1, 10-12). **7.** Who but God can predict future events and declare also the *order* and time of each (*Note,* ch. 41:22, 23; 45:21)? **call**—"openly proclaim" (ch. 40:6) things to come [Maurer]. Or, "call forth" the event; command that it happen (ch. 46:11; 48:15), [Barnes]. **set . . . in order**—There is no chance or confusion; all events occur in the *order* best fitted to subserve God's plans. **for me**—It is for God that all things exist and take place (Rev. 4:11). But Maurer translates, "Let him *set it forth* (Job 37:19) *to me.*" **since . . . ancient people**—I have given the Jews predictions of the future ever since I appointed them as My people in ancient times; therefore they were qualified to be His witnesses (vs. 8). As to their being God's "ancient (everlasting) people," see Deuteronomy 32:7-9; Jeremiah 31:3; the type of the redeemed Church (Eph. 1:4). **8. be afraid**—lit., "be astounded," or "distracted with fear." **from that time**—viz., from the time that "I appointed the ancient people" (vs. 7). From the time of Abraham's call, his family were the depositories of the predictions of the Redeemer, whereas the promise of Cyrus was not heard of till Isaiah's time; therefore, the event to the prediction and accomplishment of which God appeals in proof of His sole Godhead, is the redemption of man by a descendant of Abraham, in whose person "the ancient people" was first formally "appointed." The deliverance of the Jews, by Cyrus, is mentioned afterwards only as an earnest of that greater mercy [Horsley]. **no God**—*Hebrew, tsur,* "rock" (Deut. 32:4); i.e., a stronghold to take refuge in, and a solid foundation to build on. **9.** (Ch. 40:18, 20; 41:29.) **delectable things**—the idols in which they take such pride and delight. **not profit**—(Hab. 2:18).

ADAM CLARKE

2. *Jesurun.* Jeshurun means Israel. This name was given to that people by Moses, Deut. xxxii. 15; xxxiii. 5, 26. The most probable account of it seems to be that in which the Jewish commentators agree; namely, that it is derived from *yashar,* and signifies "upright."

4. *They shall spring up as among the grass*—"They shall spring up as the grass among the waters."

5. *Shall call himself*—"Shall be called." *Another shall subscribe with his hand unto the Lord*—"This shall inscribe his hand to Jehovah."

7. *Let them shew unto them*—"Let them declare unto us."

MATTHEW HENRY

them with good nor protect them from evil. The *graven images* are *profitable for nothing* at all. *They are their own witnesses*, witnesses against themselves, if they would but give their own consciences leave to deal faithfully with them. *Who has formed a god?* Who but a madman, or one out of his wits, would think of forming a god, of making that which, if he make it a god, he must suppose to be his maker? *The workmen* that formed this god *are of men*, weak and impotent, and therefore cannot possibly make a being that shall be omnipotent.

II. A particular narrative of the whole proceeding in making a god.

1. The persons employed about it are handicraft tradesmen, the very same that you would employ in making the common utensils of your husbandry, a cart or a plough. You must have a *smith*, a blacksmith, who *with the tongs works in the coals*; and it is hard work. He cannot allow himself time to eat or drink, for *he drinks no water, and* therefore *is faint*, *v.* 12. The plates with which the smith was to cover the image, or whatever iron-work was to be done about it, *he fashioned with hammers*, and made it all very exact, according to the model given him. Then comes *the carpenter*, and he takes as much care and pains about the timber-work, *v.* 13. He brings his box of tools, for he has occasion for them all: *He stretches out his rule* upon the piece of wood, *marks it with a line*, where it must be sawed or cut off; *he fits it*, or polishes it, *with planes*, the greater first and then the less; *he marks out with the compasses* what must be the size and shape of it; and it is just what he pleases.

2. The form in which it is made is that of a man, a poor, weak, dying creature; but it is the noblest form and figure that he is acquainted with. He makes it *according to the beauty of a man*, but altogether unfit to represent the beauty of the Lord. God put a great honour upon man when, in respect of his soul, he made him after the image of God; but man does a great dishonour to God when he makes him, in respect of bodily parts, after the image of man. All the *beauty of the body of a man*, when pretended to be put upon him who is an infinite Spirit, is a deformity and diminution to him. And, when the goodly piece is finished, it must *remain in the house*, in the temple or shrine prepared for it.

3. The matter of which it is mostly made is sorry stuff to make a god of; it is the stock of a tree. (1) The tree itself was fetched out *of the forest*, where it grew among other trees, of no more virtue or value than its neighbours. It was a *cedar*, it may be, or a *cypress*, or an *oak*, *v.* 14. Perhaps he had an eye upon it some time before for this use, and *strengthened it for himself*, used some art or other to make it stronger and better-grown than other trees were. Or, it may be, it pleases his fancy better to take *an ash*, which is of a quicker growth, and which was of his own planting for this use, and which has been nourished with rain from heaven. What an affront he puts upon the God of heaven in setting up that as a rival which was nourished by his rain, that rain which falls upon the just and unjust.

(2) The boughs of this tree were good for nothing but for fuel; to that use were they put, and so were the chips that were cut off, *v.* 15, 16. To show that that tree has no innate virtue in it for its own protection, it is as capable of being burnt as any other tree; he who chose it had no more value for it than for any other tree, throwing part of it into the fire as common rubbish, asking no question for conscience' sake. It serves him for his parlour-fire: *He will take thereof and warm himself* (*v.* 15), and he finds the comfort of it, *Aha! I am warm; I have seen the fire;* and certainly that part of the tree which served him for fuel, the use for which God and nature designed it, does him a much greater kindness and yields him more satisfaction than ever that will of which he makes a god. It serves him for his kitchen-fire: he *roasteth roast, and is satisfied* that he has not done amiss to put it to this use. It serves him to heat the oven: *He kindles it and bakes bread* with the heat of it, and none charges him with doing wrong.

(3) The stock or body of the tree shall serve to make a god. It might as well have served to make a bench. When the besotted idolater has thus served the meanest purposes with part of his tree, and the rest has had time to season: He *makes it a graven image, and falls down thereto* (*v.* 15), that is (*v.* 17), *The residue thereof he makes a god, even his graven image;* he *falls down to it, and worships it*; *he prays to it*, as having a dependence upon it, and great expectations from it: *he saith, Deliver me, for thou art my god.*

III. Here is judgment given upon this whole matter, *v.* 18–20. Man has become worse than the beasts that perish; for they act according to the dictates of sense, but man acts not according to the

JAMIESON, FAUSSET, BROWN

they are their own witnesses—contrasted with, "*Ye* are *My* witnesses" (vs. 8). "They," i.e., both the makers and the idols, are witnesses against themselves, for the idols palpably see and know nothing (Ps. 115:4-8). **that they may be ashamed**—the consequence deducible from the whole previous argument, not merely from the words immediately preceding, as in ch. 28:13; 36:12. I say all this to show that they are doomed to *perish with shame,* which is their only fitting end. **10. Who . . . ?**—Sarcastic question: "How debased the man must be who *forms* a *god!*" It is a contradiction in terms. A *made god,* worshipped by its maker (I Cor. 8:4)! **11. his fellows**—the associates of him who makes an idol; or of the idol (see Deut. 7:26; Ps. 115:8; Hos. 4:17). **they are of men**—They are mortal men themselves; what better, then, can the idol be than its maker? **gathered together . . . stand up**—as in a court of justice, to try the issue between God and them (*Note,* ch. 41:1, 21). **yet**--wrongly inserted in *English Version.* The issue of the trial shall be, "they shall fear," etc. **12. tongs**—rather, "prepareth (to be supplied) *an axe,*" viz., with which to cut down the tree designed as the material of the idol. The "smith" (*Hebrew,* "workman in iron") here answers to the "carpenter" (*Hebrew,* "workman in wood"). "He worketh it (*the axe,* not the idol, which was wood, not metal) in the coals," etc. The axe was *wrought,* not cast. The smith makes the axe for the carpenter. **hungry . . . . drinketh no water**—so eager is he to expedite his work while the iron is hot. If the god were worth anything, it would not let him grow "faint" with hunger and thirst. WILLIAMS, the missionary, states that the South Sea islanders when they make an idol abstain from food and drink. **13.** After the smith's work in preparing the instruments comes the carpenter's work in forming the idol. **rule**—rather, "line" [BARNES]. **with a line**—rather, a "pencil," [HORSLEY]. Lit., "red ochre," which he uses to mark on the wood the outline of the figure [LOWTH]. Or best, the stylus or graver, with which the incision of the outline is made [GESENIUS]. **planes**—rather, chisels or carving tools, for a plane would not answer for carving. **compass**—from a *Hebrew* root, "to make a circle"; by it, symmetry of form is secured. **according to . . . beauty of a man**—irony. The highest idea the heathen could form of a god was one of a form like their own. Jerome says, "The more handsome the statue the more august the god was thought." The incarnation of the Son of God condescends to this anthropomorphic feeling so natural to man, but in such a way as to raise man's thoughts up to the infinite God who "is a spirit." **that it may remain in . . . house**—the only thing it was good for; it could not hear nor save (cf. Wisdom 13:15). **14.** Description of the material out of which the idol is formed. **cypress**—rather, from *Hebrew* root, "to be hard," the holm-oak," an evergreen abundant in Palestine [GESENIUS]. **strengtheneth**—lit., "and he getteth strength to himself in the trees of the forest;" i.e., he layeth in a *great store* of timber [LOWTH]. Or, "*chooseth,*" as "madest strong for thyself," i.e., hast chosen (Ps. 80: 15, 17) [GESENIUS]. But *English Version* gives a good sense: "strengtheneth"; i.e., rears to maturity; a meaning suitable also to the context of Psalm 80: 15, 17, where Israel is compared to a *vine* planted by Jehovah [MAURER]. **rain doth nourish it**—Though the man planted the tree, yet he could not make it grow. In preparing to make an idol, he has to depend on the true God for rain from heaven (Jer. 14:22). **15.** The same tree that furnishes the material for the god is in part used as fuel for a fire to cook his meals and warm himself! **thereto**—rather, "he falleth down before *them,*" i.e., such images [MAURER]. **16. part . . . part**—not distinct parts, but *the same part* of the wood (cf. vs. 17). **eateth**—i.e., cooks so as to eat (vs. 19). **I have seen**—I feel its power.

ADAM CLARKE

9-10. *That they may be ashamed. Who hath formed a god?*—"That everyone may be ashamed that he hath formed a god."

11. *And the workmen, they are of men*—"Even the workmen themselves shall blush."

12. *The smith with the tongs*—"The smith cutteth off a portion of iron." The sacred writers are generally large and eloquent upon the subject of idolatry; they treat it with great severity, and set forth the absurdity of it in the strongest light. But this passage of Isaiah, vv. 12-20, far exceeds anything that ever was written upon the subject, in force of argument, energy of expression, and elegence of composition. A heathen author, in the ludicrous way, has, in a line or two, given idolatry one of the severest strokes it ever received: "Formerly I was the stump of a fig tree, a useless log; when the carpenter, after hesitating whether to make me a *god* or a *stool,* at last determined to make me a *god.* Thus I became a god!" (Horat., *Satyr,* lib. 1. sat, viii.) From the tenth to the seventeenth verse, a most beautiful strain of irony is carried on against idolatry. And we may naturally think that every idolater who either read or heard it must have been forever ashamed of his own devices.

17. *He falleth down unto it.* There were four forms of adoration used among the Hebrews: (1) The prostration of the whole body, (2) The bowing of the head, (3) The bending of the upper part of the body down to the knees, (4) Bowing the knee, or kneeling.

MATTHEW HENRY

dictates of reason (*v.* 18). Men that act rationally in other things in this act most absurdly. They are rebels against the great law of consideration (*v.* 12) *None considers in his heart*, nor has so much application of mind as to reason thus with himself: "*I have burnt part of this tree in the fire*, for baking and roasting; *and* now *shall I make the residue thereof an abomination?* Shall I be such a fool as to fall down to the stock of a tree—a senseless, lifeless, helpless thing?" These idolaters put a cheat upon themselves (*v.* 20): *They feed on ashes;* they will be disappointed as much as a man that would expect nourishment by feeding on ashes. The apostasy of sinners from God is owing entirely to themselves and to the evil heart of unbelief that is in their own bosom. There is none of them that can be persuaded so far to suspect himself as to say, *Is there not a lie in my right hand?* and so to think of delivering his soul. Self-suspicion is the first step towards self-deliverance.

Verses 21–28

I. The duty which Jacob and Israel, now in captivity, were called to, that they might be qualified for deliverance. Our first care must be to get good by our afflictions, and then we may hope to get out of them. The duty is expressed in two words: *Remember* and *return.* 1. "*Remember these, O Jacob!* Remember the folly of idolatry, and that *thou art my servant*, and therefore must not serve other masters." 2. *Return unto me*, *v.* 22.

II. The favours of which Jacob and Israel, now in captivity, were assured; and what is here promised to them upon their remembering and returning to God is in a spiritual sense promised to all that in like manner return to God. When we begin to remember God he will begin to remember us; it is he that remembers us first.

1. The grounds upon which God's favourable intentions to his people were built. (1) They are his servants, and therefore he has a just quarrel with those that detain them. *Let my people go, that they may serve me.* (2) He formed them into a people, *v.* 24. From the first beginning of their increase into a nation they were under his particular care. (3) He has redeemed them formerly, and he is still the same. The *Lord has redeemed Jacob*; he is about to do it (*v.* 23); he has determined to do it; for he is the Lord their Redeemer, *v.* 24. (4) He has *glorified himself in them* (*v.* 23), and therefore will do so still, John xii. 28. (5) He has pardoned their sins, which were the only obstruction to their deliverance, *v.* 22. *Therefore* he will break the yoke of captivity because he has *blotted out, as a thick cloud, their transgressions.* Our transgressions and our sins as a cloud interpose between heaven and earth. When God pardons sin he blots out this cloud, this thick cloud, so that the intercourse with heaven is laid open again.

2. The universal joy which the deliverance of God's people should bring along with it (*v.* 23): *Sing, O you heavens!* The whole creation shall have cause for joy and rejoicing in the redemption of God's people; and it is assured that though now it groans, being burdened, it shall at last be delivered from the bondage of corruption. The greatest establishment of the world is the kingdom of God in it, Ps. xcvi. 11–13; xcviii. 7–9. The angels shall rejoice in it. The heavens shall sing, for the Lord has done it. And there is joy in heaven when God and man are reconciled (Luke xv. 7). Even the inhabitants of the Gentile world, should join in these praises, as sharing in these joys.

3. The encouragement we have to hope that though great difficulties lie in the way of the church's deliverance, yet, when the time for it shall come, they shall all be got over with ease; for *thus saith Israel's Redeemer, I am the Lord that maketh all things*, did make them at first and am still making them; for providence is a continued creation.

4. The confusion which this would put upon the oracles of Babylon, by the confutation it would give them, *v.* 25. God, by delivering his people out of Babylon, would *frustrate the tokens of the liars*, of all the lying prophets, that said the Babylonian monarchy had many ages yet to live. Nor would it only baffle their pretended prophets, but their celebrated politicians too: He *turns the wise men backward.* Those that are made acquainted with Christ see all the knowledge they had before to be foolishness, and themselves *taken in their own craftiness*, 1 Cor. iii. 19.

5. The confirmation which this would give to the oracles of God, which the Jews had distrusted and their enemies despised: God *confirms the word of his servant* (*v.* 26); and *performs the counsel of the messengers* whom he hath many a time sent to his people.

6. The particular favours God designed for his people, that were now in captivity, *v.* 26–28. It is

JAMIESON, FAUSSET, BROWN

18. he . . .—God hath given them over to judicial blindness; not His direct physical, but His providential agency in administering His moral government, is meant (ch. 6:9, 10). "Shut," lit., "daubed," plastered up; it is an Eastern custom in some cases to seal up the eyes of offenders. **19. considereth**—lit., "layeth it to heart," (ch. 42:25; Jer. 12:11). **abomination**—the scriptural term for an idol, not merely abominable, but the *essence* of what is so, in the eyes of a jealous God (I Kings 11:5, 7). **20. feedeth on ashes**—fig., for the idolater delights in what is vain (Prov. 15:14; Hos. 12:1). "Feedeth on wind." There is an allusion, perhaps, also, to the god being made of a tree, the half of which was *reduced to ashes by fire* (vss. 15, 16, 17); the idol, it is implied, was no better, and could, and ought, to have been reduced to ashes like the other half. **deceived heart**—The heart and will first go astray, then the intellect and life (Rom. 1:28; Eph. 4:18). **lie in . . . right hand**—Is not my handiwork (the idol) a self-deceit?

21. Remember—"Be not like the idolaters who consider not in their heart" (vs. 19). **these**—things just said as to the folly of idol worship. **my servant**—not like the idolaters, slaves to the stock of a tree (vs. 19). See vss. 1:2. **thou . . . not . . . forgotten of me**—Therefore *thou* oughtest to "remember" Me. **22. blotted out**—the debt of *thy* sin from the account book in which it was entered (Exod. 32: 32, 33; Rev. 20:12). **as a thick cloud**—scattered away by the wind (Ps. 103:12). **as a cloud**—a descending gradation. Not only the "thick cloud" of the heavier "transgressions," but the "cloud" ("vapor" [LOWTH], not so dense, but *covering* the sky as a mist) of the countless "sins." These latter, though not thought much of by man, need, as much as the former, to be cleared away by the Sun of righteousness; else they will be a *mist* separating us from heaven (Ps. 19:12, 13; I John 1:7-9). **return . . . for**—The antecedent redemption is the ground of, and motive to, repentance. We do not repent *in order that He may* redeem us, but *because He hath* redeemed us (Zech. 12:10; Luke 24:47; Acts 3:18, 19). He who believes in his being forgiven cannot but love (Luke 7:43, 47). **23.** Call to inanimate nature to praise God; for it also shall share in the coming deliverance from "the bondage of corruption" (Rom. 8:20, 21). **done it**—effected redemption for both the literal and spiritual Israel. **lower parts . . .**—antithetical to "heavens"; "mountains," "forest," and "tree," are the intermediate objects in a descending gradation (see Ps. 96:11, 12). **24-28.** Confirmation of His promises to the Church and Israel, by various instances of His omnipotence; among these the restoration of the Jews by Cyrus. **alone**—lit., "Who was with Me?" viz., when I did it; answering to "by Myself," in the parallel clause (cf. similar phrases, Hos. 8:4; John 5:30) [MAURER].

25. tokens—prognostics; the pretended miracles which they gave as *proofs* of their supernatural powers. **liars**—(Jer. 50:36). Conjurors; or, astrologers; men leading a retired contemplative life in order to study divination by the signs of the stars [VITRINGA]. **backward**—with shame at their predictions not being verified. "To turn away the face" is to *frustrate defeat* (ch. 36: 9; I Kings 2:15). The "wise men" are the diviners who, when Babylon was attacked by Cyrus, predicted his overthrow. **26. servant**—in a collective sense, for *the prophets* in general, who foretold the return from Babylon; answering to "His messengers" (*plural*, in the parallel clause) [MAURER]. Antitypically, and ultimately, *Messiah*, who is the consummating embodiment of all the prophets and messengers of God (Mal. 3:1; Matt. 21:34, 36, 37; John 10:36); hence the *singular*, "His servant." **counsel**—predictions; prophets' *counsels* concern the future (cf. "counsellor," ch. 41:28).

ADAM CLARKE

18. *He hath shut their eyes*—"Their eyes are closed up."

20. *He feedeth on ashes.* He feedeth on that which affordeth no nourishment; a proverbial expression for using ineffectual means, and bestowing labor to no purpose. In the same sense Hosea says, "Ephraim feedeth on wind," chap. xii. 1.

22. *I have blotted out, as a thick cloud, thy transgressions, and, as a cloud, thy sins*—"I have made your transgressions vanish away like a cloud, and your sins like a vapor."

F. B. MEYER:

The promise of redemption (vv. 21–28). What divine comfort there is in these gracious words! Notwithstanding all their wanderings and sins, the Chosen People were Jehovah's elect race. Nothing could make him forget them; he had redeemed them with the saving strength of his right hand. He could never forget *them*, but he would forget their sins. Their transgressions had melted into the blue azure of his love. If sought for, they could not be found. Nature was asked to be one great orchestra of praise. Notice that our redemption brings more glory to Jehovah than our undoing would.

In the following chapter, the people are assured that they would return from captivity to rebuild Jerusalem and reinhabit the cities of Judah. They probably expected that their return would be marked by miracles as marvelous as those through which their fathers emerged from Egyptian bondage. But God never repeats himself; his purposes would work out through a heathen monarch, Cyrus, whom God was preparing as the executor of his purpose (v. 28). "Deep in unfathomable mines of never-failing skill, he treaures up his bright designs, and works his sovereign will."—*Bible Commentary*

MATTHEW HENRY

here supposed that Jerusalem, and the cities of Judah, should for a time lie in ruins, dispeopled and uninhabited; but it is promised that they shall be rebuilt and repeopled. God has said to Jerusalem, *Thou shalt be inhabited;* for, while the world stands, God will have a church in it. The cities of Judah too shall again be built. The Assyrian army under Sennacherib only took them, and then, upon the defeat of that army, they returned undamaged to the right owners; but the Chaldean army demolished them, and by carrying away the inhabitants left them to go to decay of themselves. Yet these desolations shall not be perpetual. God will *raise up the* wastes and *decayed places.* It is here supposed that the temple too should be destroyed, and lie for a time razed to the foundations; but it is promised that the foundation of it shall again be laid, and no doubt built upon. As the desolation of the sanctuary was to all the pious Jews the most mournful part of the destruction, so the restoration and re-establishment of it would be the most joyful part of the deliverance. It is here supposed that very great difficulties would lie in the way of this deliverance, but it is promised that by a divine power they shall all be removed (*v.* 27): *God saith to the deep, Be dry;* so he did when he brought Israel out of Egypt, and so he will again when he brings them out of Babylon. *Who art thou, O great deep?* Dost thou retard their passage and think to block it up? Thou shalt be dry. When Cyrus took Babylon by draining the river Euphrates into many channels, and so making it passable for his army, this was fulfilled. *God saith of Cyrus, He is my shepherd* (*v.* 28). Israel is his people, and the sheep of his pasture. These sheep are now in the midst of wolves; they are impounded for trespass. Now Cyrus shall be his shepherd, employed by him to release these sheep. It was more the praise of Cyrus to be God's shepherd than to be emperor of Persia. God makes what use he pleases of men; in those very things wherein they are serving themselves, and look no further than that, God is serving his own purposes by them.

JAMIESON, FAUSSET, BROWN

Jerusalem—regarded prophetically, as lying in ruins.

27. Referring to the Euphrates, which was turned into a different channel, close to Babylon, by Cyrus, who thereby took the city. "The deep" is applied to Euphrates as "sea" (Jer. 51:32, 36). "Rivers" refers to the artificial canals from the Euphrates made to irrigate the country; when it was turned off into a different bed (viz., a lake, forty miles square, which was originally formed to receive the superfluous water in an inundation), the canals became dry. **28. my shepherd**—type of Messiah (ch. 40:11; Ps. 23:1; 77:20; Ezek. 34:23). **all my pleasure**—so Messiah (ch. 42:1; 53:10). This is the first time Cyrus is *named* expressly; and that, 150 years before the time when in 550 B.C. he began his reign. The name comes from the Persian *khorschid,* "the sun"; kings often taking their names from the gods; the sun was worshipped as a god in Persia. **saying**—rather, "and that saith"; construed with *God,* not with *Cyrus.* God's word is instantaneously efficient in accomplishing His will. **to . . . to**—or, *"of* Jerusalem . . . *of* the temple," as previously, the same *Hebrew* word is translated, *"of* Cyrus" [BARNES]. *English Version* is more graphic. Cyrus, according to JOSEPHUS, heard of this prophecy of Isaiah delivered so long before; hence he was induced to do that which was so contrary to Oriental policy, to aid in restoring the captive Jews and rebuilding their temple and city.

ADAM CLARKE

27. *That saith to the deep, Be dry*—"Who saith to the deep, Be thou wasted." Cyrus took Babylon by laying the bed of the Euphrates dry, and leading his army into the city by night through the empty channel of the river. The Euphrates, in the middle of the summer, from the melting of the snows on the mountains of Armenia, like the Nile, overflows the country. In order to diminish the inundation, and to carry off the waters, two canals were made by Nebuchadnezzar a hundred miles above the city; the first on the eastern side called Naharmalca, or the Royal River, by which the Euphrates was let into the Tigris; the other on the western side, called Pallacopas, or Naharaga, by which the redundant waters were carried into a vast lake, forty miles square, contrived, not only to lessen the inundation, but for a reservoir, with sluices, to water the barren country on the Arabian side. Cyrus, by turning the whole river into the lake by the Pallacopas, laid the channel, where it ran through the city, almost dry; so that his army entered it, both above and below, by the bed of the river, the water not reaching above the middle of the thigh (Herod. i, 185, 190; Xenophon, *Cyrop.* vii).

28. *That saith of Cyrus, He is my shepherd*—"Who saith to Cyrus, Thou art my shepherd." (1) Cyrus is called God's shepherd. Shepherd was an epithet which Cyrus took to himself; and what He gave to all good kings. (2) This Cyrus should say to the Temple: "Thy foundation shall be laid." Not—*Thou shalt be built.* The fact is, only the foundation was laid in the days of Cyrus; nor was it resumed till the second year of Darius, one of his successors. There is often a precision in the expressions of the prophets which is as honorable to truth as it is unnoticed by careless readers.

MATTHEW HENRY — CHAPTER 45

Verses 1–4

Cyrus was a Mede, descended (as some say) from Astyages, king of Media. The pagan writers are not agreed in their accounts of his origin. Some tell us that in his infancy, he was an outcast, left exposed, and was saved from perishing by a herdsman's wife. However, it is agreed that Croesus king of Lydia made a descent upon his country, which he repulsed, prosecuting the advantages he had gained against Croesus with such vigour that in a little time he took Sardis and made himself master of the rich kingdom of Lydia and the many provinces that then belonged to it. This made him very great (for Croesus was rich to a proverb); but it was nearly ten years afterwards that, in conjunction with his uncle Darius and with the forces of Persia, he made his famous attack upon Babylon. Babylon had now grown rich and strong. Some say the walls were so thick that six chariots might drive abreast upon them. Cyrus had a great ambition to make himself master of this place, and at last he performed it. Here, years before it came to pass, we are told,

I. What great things God would do for him, that he might put it into his power to release his people. In order to this he shall be a mighty conqueror and a wealthy monarch, and nations shall become tributaries to him and help him both with men and money. Cyrus is here called God's *anointed,* because he was designed for this great service by God, and was to be herein a type of the Messiah. God engages to hold his right hand, as Elisha put his hands upon the king's hands when he was to shoot his arrow against Syria, 2 Kings xiii. 16. Being under such direction,

1. He shall extend his conquests very far and shall make nothing of the opposition that will be given him. Populous kingdoms shall yield to him. God will *subdue nations before him*; the battle is his, and therefore his is the victory. Potent kings shall fall before him: *I will loose the loins of kings*, and it was literally fulfilled in Belshazzar, for, when he was terrified by the handwriting on the wall, *the joints of his loins were loosed*, Dan. v. 6. Great cities shall surrender themselves into his hands. God will incline the keepers of the city to *open before him the two-leaved gates*, from a full conviction that it is to no purpose to contend with him. The longest and most dangerous marches shall be made easy and ready to him: *I will go before thee*, to clear the way, and to conduct thee in it, and then the *crooked places* shall be made *straight*; or, as some read it, the hilly places

JAMIESON, FAUSSET, BROWN — CHAPTER 45

VSS. 1-25. THE SUBJECT OF THE DELIVERANCE BY CYRUS IS FOLLOWED UP (vss. 1-7). These seven verses should have been appended to previous chapter, and the new chapter should begin with vs. 8, "Drop down . . ." [HORSLEY]. Reference to the deliverance by Messiah often breaks out from amidst the local and temporary details of the deliverance from Babylon, as the great ultimate end of the prophecy.

1. his anointed—Cyrus is so called as being *set apart as king,* by God's providence, to fulfil His special purpose. Though kings were not *anointed* in Persia, the expression is applied to him in reference to the *Jewish* custom of setting apart kings to the regal office by anointing. **right hand . . . holden**—image from sustaining a feeble person by holding his right hand (ch. 42:6). **subdue nations**—viz., the Cilicians, Syrians, Babylonians, Lydians, Bactrians, etc.; his empire extended from Egypt and the Mediterranean to the Indian Ocean, and from Ethiopia to the Euxine Sea. **loose . . . loins**—i.e., the girdle off the loins; and so *enfeeble* them. The loose outer robe of the Orientals, when girt fast round the loins, was the emblem of strength and preparedness for action; ungirt, was indicative of *feebleness* (Job 38:3; 12:21); *"weakeneth the strength* of the mighty" (*Margin*), *"looseth the girdle* of the strong." *The joints of* Belshazzar's *loins,* we read in Daniel 5:6, *were loosed* during the siege by Cyrus, at the sight of the mysterious handwriting on the palace walls. His being taken by surprise, *unaccoutred,* is here foretold. **to open . . . gates**—In the revelry in Babylon on the night of its capture, the inner gates, leading from the streets to the river, were left open; for there were walls along each side of the Euphrates with gates, which, had they been kept shut, would have hemmed the invading hosts in the bed of the river, where the Babylonians could have easily destroyed them. Also, the gates of the palace were left open, so that there was access to every part of the city; and such was its extent, that they who lived in the extremities were taken prisoners before the alarm reached the center of the palace. [HERODOTUS, 1. sec. 191]. **2. crooked . . . straight**—(ch. 40:4), rather, "maketh mountains plain" [LOWTH], i.e., clear out of thy way all opposing persons and things. The KERI reads as in vs. 13, "make straight" (*Margin*).

ADAM CLARKE — CHAPTER 45

1. *Loose the loins of kings*—"Ungird the loins of kings."

To open before him the two leaved gates, etc.—"That I may open before him the valves; and the gates shall not be shut." The gates of Babylon within the city leading from the streets to the river were providentially left open, when Cyrus' forces entered the city in the night through the channel of the river, in the general disorder occasioned by the great feast which was then celebrated. Otherwise, says Herodotus, i. 191, the Persians would have been shut up in the bed of the river, and taken as in a net, and all destroyed. And the gates of the palace were opened imprudently by the king's orders, to inquire what was the cause of the tumult without; when the two parties under Gobrias and Gadatas rushed in, got possession of the palace, and slew the king (Xenoph., *Cyrop.* vii. p. 528).

2. *The crooked places*—"The mountains."

MATTHEW HENRY

shall be levelled and made even. No opposition shall stand before him. He that gives him his commission *will break in pieces the gates of brass* that are shut against him, *and cut asunder the bars of iron* wherewith they are fastened. This was fulfilled if that be true which Herodotus reports, that the city of Babylon had 100 gates all of brass, with posts and hooks of the same metal.

2. He shall replenish his coffers (*v.* 3): *I will give thee the treasures of darkness*, treasures of gold and silver, that had been buried under ground by the inhabitants. Cyrus owned God's goodness to him, and in consideration of that, released the captives. Ezra i. 2, *God has given me all the kingdoms of the earth* and thereby has obliged *me to build him a house at Jerusalem.*

II. We are here told what God designed in doing all this for Cyrus.

1. "*That thou mayest know* by all this *that I the Lord am the God of Israel*; for I have *called thee by thy name* long before thou wast born."

2. It was that the Israel of God might be released, *v.* 4. Though he knew not God, God bespoke him for his shepherd. He called him by his name, *Cyrus*, and called him his *anointed*. And why did God do all this for Cyrus? Not for his own sake, whether he was a man of virtue or no is questioned. Xenophon indeed, when he would describe the heroic virtues of an excellent prince, made use of Cyrus's name, but other historians represent him as haughty, cruel, and bloodthirsty. The reason why God preferred him was *for Jacob his servant's sake*. Cyrus was a type of Christ, victorious over principalities and powers, and entrusted with unsearchable riches, for the use and benefit of God's servants. *When he ascended on high he led captivity captive*, took those captives that had taken others captives, and *opened the prison to those that were bound.*

Verses 5–10

God here asserts his sole dominion, manifest to the world in all the great things he did for Cyrus and by him. Observe,

I. This doctrine is here laid down in two things: 1. That there is no God besides him. This is a fundamental truth, which would abolish idolatry out of the world. With what an awful, commanding, air of majesty and authority does the great God here proclaim it to the world: *I am the Lord, I the Lord, Jehovah*, and *there is none else, there is no God besides me*, no other self-existent, self-sufficient, infinite and eternal. *I am the Lord, and there is none else.* This is here said to Cyrus, not only to cure him of the sin of his ancestors, which was the worshipping of idols, but to prevent his falling into the sin of some of his predecessors in victory and universal monarchy, which was the setting up of themselves for gods and being idolized. Let Cyrus remember that still he is but a man, and there is no God but one. 2. That he is Lord of all, and there is nothing done without him (*v.* 7): *I form the light, I create darkness, I make peace* (put here for all good) and *I create evil*, not the evil of sin (God is not the author of that), but the evil of punishment. Light and darkness are opposite to each other. In the revolution of every day each takes its turn. The self-same cause of both is he that is the first Cause of all. He who formed the natural light (Gen. i. 3) still forms the providential light. He who at first made peace among the jarring principles of nature makes peace in the affairs of men. He who allowed the natural darkness, which was a mere privation, creates the providential darkness.

II. How this doctrine is here proved and published. 1. It is proved by that which God did for Cyrus: *There is no God besides me*, for (*v.* 5) *I girded thee, though thou hast not known me.* By *this* it appears that the God of Israel makes what use he pleases even of those that are strangers to him and pay their homage to other gods. 2. It is published to all the world by the word of God, by his providence, and by the testimony of the suffering Jews in Babylon. The wonderful deliverance of the Israel of God proclaimed to all the world that *there is none like unto the God of Jeshurun, that rides on the heavens for their help.*

III. How this doctrine is here improved and applied.

1. For the comfort of those that quietly waited, for the redemption of Israel (*v.* 8): *Drop down, you heavens, from above.* Some take this as the saints' prayer for the deliverance. I rather take it as God's precept concerning it; for he is said to *command deliverances*, Ps. xliv. 4. All the creatures shall be made to contribute to the carrying on of this great work. We must not expect salvation without righteousness, for they spring up together and together the Lord hath created them. Christ died to save us

JAMIESON, FAUSSET, BROWN

gates of brass—(Ps. 107:16.) HERODOTUS (1. sec. 179) says, Babylon had 100 massive gates, twenty-five on each of the four sides of the city, all, as well as their posts, of brass. **bars of iron**—with which the gates were fastened. **3. treasures of darkness**—i.e., hidden in subterranean places; a common Oriental practive. Sorcerers pretended to be able to show where such treasures were to be found; in opposition to their pretensions, God says, He will really give hidden treasures to Cyrus (Jer. 50:37; 51: 13). PLINY (*H. N.*, 33:3) says that Cyrus obtained from the conquest of Asia 34,000 pounds weight of gold, besides golden vases, and 500,000 talents of silver, and the goblet of Semiramis, weighing fifteen talents. **that thou mayest know**—viz., not merely that He was "the God of Israel," but that He was Jehovah, the true God. Ezra 1:1, 2 shows that the correspondence of the event with the prediction had the desired effect on Cyrus. **which call . . . thy name**—so long before designate thee by name (ch. 43:1). **4.** (*Note*, ch. 41:8; 43:14.) **surnamed**—i.e., designated to carry out My design of restoring Judah (see *Note*, ch. 44:5; 44:28; 45:1). MAURER here, as in ch. 44:5, translates, "I have *addressed thee by an honorable name.*" **hast not known me**—*previous* to My calling thee to this office; *after* God's call, Cyrus *did* know Him in some degree (Ezra 1:1-3).

5. (Ch. 42:8; 43:3, 11; 44:8; 46:9.) **girded thee**—whereas "I will loose (the girdle off) the loins of kings" (vs. 1), *strengthening* thee, but *enfeebling* them before thee. **though . . . not known me**—(vs. 4.) God *knows* His elect before they are made to know Him (Gal. 4:9; John 15:16). **6.** From the rising to the setting of the sun, i.e., from *east* to *west*, the whole *habitable* world. It is not said, "from *north* to *south*," for that would not imply the *habitable* world, as, "from *east* to *west*" does (Ezra 1:1, etc.). The conquest of Jerusalem by Babylon, the capital of the world, and the overthrow of Babylon and restoration of the Jews by Cyrus, who expressly acknowledged himself to be but the instrument in God's hands, were admirably suited to secure, throughout the world, the acknowledgment of Jehovah as the only true God. **7. form . . . create**—*yatzar*, to give "form" to previously existing matter. *Bara*, to "create" from nothing the chaotic dark material. **light . . . darkness**—**lit.** (**Gen. 1:1-3**), **emblematical** also, *prosperity* to Cyrus, *calamity* to Babylon and the nations to be vanquished [GROTIUS]. Isaiah refers also to the Oriental belief in two coexistent, eternal principles, ever struggling with each other, light or good, and darkness or evil, *Oromasden* and *Ahrimanen*. God, here, in opposition, asserts His sovereignty over both [VITRINGA]. **create evil**—not *moral* evil (Jas. 1:13), but in contrast to "peace" in the parallel clause, *war, disaster* (cf. Ps. 65:7; Amos 3:6).

8. Drop—viz., the fertilizing rain (Ps. 65:12). **skies**—clouds; lower than the "heavens." **righteousness**—i.e., the dews of the Holy Spirit, whereby "righteousness" shall "spring up." (See latter end of the verse.) **earth**—fig. for the *hearts of men* on it, *opened* for receiving the truth by the Holy Ghost (Acts 16:14). **them**—the earth and the heavens. HORSLEY prefers: "Let the earth open, and *let salvation and justice grow forth;* let *it bring them forth* together; I the Lord have created *him*" (vs. 13). MAURER translates, "Let all kinds of salvation (prosperity) be fruitful" (Ps. 72:3, 6, 7). The revival of religion after the return from Babylon suggests to the prophet the diffusion of *Messiah's Gospel*, especially in days still future; hence the elevation of the language to a pitch above what is applicable to the state of religion after the return.

ADAM CLARKE

The gates of brass—"The valves of brass." Herodotus, i. 179: "In the wall all round there are a hundred gates, all of brass; and so in like manner are the sides and the lintels." The gates likewise within the city, opening to the river from the several streets, were of brass; as were those also of the temple of Belus.—Herod. i., 180-81.

3. *I will give thee the treasures of darkness.* Sardes and Babylon, when taken by Cyrus, were the wealthiest cities in the world. Croesus, celebrated beyond all the kings of that age for his riches, gave up his treasures to Cyrus, with an exact account in writing of the whole, containing the particulars with which each wagon was loaded when they were carried away; and they were delivered to Cyrus at the palace of Babylon.—Xenoph. *Cyrop.* lib. vii, pp. 503, 515, 540. *Treasures of darkness* may refer to the custom of burying their jewels and money under the ground in their house floors, fearing robbers.

7. *I form the light, and create darkness.* It was the great principle of the Magian religion, which prevailed in Persia in the time of Cyrus, and in which probably he was educated, that there are two supreme, coeternal, and independent causes always acting in opposition one to the other; one the author of all good, the other of all evil. The good being they called light; the evil being, darkness. That when light had the ascendant, then good and happiness prevailed among men; when darkness had the superiority, then evil and misery abounded. With reference to this absurd opinion, held by the person to whom this prophecy is addressed, God, by His prophet, asserts His omnipotence and absolute supremacy:

I am Jehovah, and none else;
Forming light, and creating darkness,
Making peace, and creating evil;
I, Jehovah, am the Author of all these things.

Declaring that those powers whom the Persians held to be the original authors of good and evil to mankind, representing them by light and darkness, are no other than creatures of God, the instruments which He employs in His government of the world. *I make peace, and create evil. Evil* is here evidently put for war and its attendant miseries. I will procure *peace* for the Israelites, and destroy Babylon by war.

8. *Drop down, ye heavens.* The eighty-fifth psalm is a very elegant ode on the same subject with this part of Isaiah's prophecies, the restoration of Judah from captivity; and is in the most beautiful part of it (10-14) a manifest imitation of this passage of the prophet. *Let them bring forth salvation*—"Let salvation produce her fruit."

MATTHEW HENRY

from our sins, not in our sins, and is made redemption to us by being made to us righteousness and sanctification. This great deliverance is from heaven, and, if our hearts be open to receive it, the product will be the fruits of righteousness and the great salvation.

2. For reproof to those of the church's enemies that opposed this salvation, or those of her friends that despaired of it (*v.* 9): *Woe unto him that strives with his Maker!* Woe to the insulting Babylonians that set God at defiance, and will not let his people go! Let not the oppressed, in dejection quarrel with God for the prolonging of their captivity. *Shall the clay say to him that forms it, "What makest thou?* Why dost thou make me of this shape and not that?" Shall we impeach God's wisdom, or question his power, who are ourselves so wonderfully made? Shall we say, *He has no hands,* whose hands made us and in whose hands we are? It is as unnatural as for the child to find fault with the parents, to say to the father, *What begettest thou?* or to the mother, "*What hast thou brought forth;* Why was I not begotten and born an angel, exempt from the infirmities of human nature and the calamities of human life?"

Verses 11–19

The people in captivity, who reconciled themselves to the will of God and were content to wait his time for their deliverance, are assured they should not wait in vain.

I. They are invited to enquire concerning the issue of their troubles, *v.* 11. "*Ask of me things to come;* have recourse to the prophets and see what they say. Ask the watchmen, What of the night? Ask them, How long?" We may not strive with our Maker by passionate complaints, but we may wrestle with him by faithful and fervent prayer. See the power of prayer and its prevalency with God: *Thou shalt cry, and he shall say, Here I am; what would you that I should do unto you?*

II. They are encouraged to depend upon the power of God when they are brought very low and are utterly incapable of helping themselves, *v.* 12. Their *help stands in the name of the Lord, who made heaven and earth.*

III. They are particularly told what God would do for them, and this shall lead them to expect a more glorious Redeemer of whom Cyrus was a type.

1. Liberty shall be proclaimed to them, *v.* 13. Cyrus is the man that shall proclaim it: *I have raised him up in righteousness,* that is, in pursuance of my promises. *I will direct all his ways.* Two things Cyrus must do for God: (1) Jerusalem is God's city, now in ruins, and he must rebuild it. (2) Israel is God's people, but they are now captives, and he must release them, not demanding any ransom. And Christ is anointed to do that for poor captive souls which Cyrus was to do for the captive Jews, to proclaim the *opening of the prison to those that were bound* (*ch.* lxi. 1), in a worse bondage than that in Babylon.

2. Provision shall be made for them. They went out poor, and unable to bear the expenses of their re-establishment; and therefore it is promised that the labour of Egypt and other nations should *come over to them and be theirs, v.* 14. They did not go out empty from Babylon any more than from Egypt. Those that are redeemed by Christ shall be enriched. Those whose spirits God stirs up to go to the heavenly Zion may depend upon him to bear their charges. The world is theirs as far as is good for them.

3. Proselytes shall be brought over to them: *Men of stature shall come after thee in chains; they shall fall down to thee, saying, Surely God is in thee.* This was in part fulfilled when many of the people of the land became Jews (Esther viii. 17), *and said, We will go with you, for we have heard that God is with you,* Zech. viii. 23. But this was to have its full accomplishment in the gospel church,—when the Gentiles shall become obedient by word and deed to the faith of Christ (Rom. xv. 18).

IV. They are taught to trust God further than they can see him. The prophet puts this word into their mouths (*v.* 15): *Verily, thou art a God that hidest thyself.* He hid himself when he was bringing them out of the trouble. The salvation of the church is carried on in a mysterious way, by the Spirit of the Lord of hosts working on men's spirits (Zech. iv. 6), by weak and unlikely instruments, small and accidental occurrences, but this is our comfort, though God hide himself, we are sure he is *the God of Israel, the Saviour.* See Job xxxv. 14.

V. They are instructed to triumph over idolaters and all the worshippers of other gods (*v.* 16).

VI. They are assured that those who trust in God shall never be made ashamed of their confidence in him, *v.* 17. They shall be saved in him; for his name shall be their strong tower. Beyond this temporal deliverance they must think of that sal-

JAMIESON, FAUSSET, BROWN

9. Anticipating the objections which the Jews might raise as to why God permitted their captivity, and when He did restore them, why He did so by a foreign prince, Cyrus, not a Jew (ch. 40:27, etc.), but mainly and ultimately, the objections about to be raised by the Jews against *God's sovereign act in adopting the whole Gentile world as His spiritual Israel* (vs. 8, referring to this *catholic* diffusion of the Gospel), as if it were an infringement of their nation's privileges; so Paul expressly quotes it (Rom. 9:4-8, 11-21). **Let . . . strive**—Not in the *Hebrew;* rather, in apposition with "him," "A potsherd *among* the potsherds of the earth!" A creature fragile and worthless as the fragment of an earthen vessel, among others equally so, and yet presuming to strive with his Maker! *English Version* implies, it is appropriate for man to strive with man, in opposition to II Tim. 2:24 [GESENIUS]. **thy . . . He**—shall thy work *say of thee,* He . . . ? **10.** If it be wrong for a child, born in less favorable circumstances, to upbraid his parents with having given him birth, *a fortiori,* it is, to upbraid God for His dealings with us. Rather translate, "*a* father . . . *a* woman." The Jews considered themselves exclusively God's children and were angry that God should adopt the Gentiles besides. Woe to him who says to one already a father, Why dost thou beget other children? [HORSLEY]. **11. Ask . . . command**—Instead of striving with Me in regard to My purposes, your wisdom is in prayer to *ask,* and even *command* Me, in so far as it is for My glory, and for your real good (Mark 11:24; John 16:23, 13, latter part of the verse; I John 3:22). **sons**—(ch. 54:13; Gal. 3:26). **work of my hands**—spiritually (Eph. 2:10); also literal Israel (ch. 60:21). MAURER translates, instead of "command," *Leave it to Me,* in My dealings concerning My sons and concerning the work of My hands, to do what I will with My own. LOWTH reads it interrogatively, Do ye presume to question Me and dictate to Me (see vss. 9, 10)? The same sense is given, if the words be taken in irony. But *English Version* is best. **12.** The same argument for prayer, drawn from God's omnipotence and consequent power, to grant any request, occurs in ch. 40:26-31. **I, even my hands**—so *Hebrew* (Ps. 41:2), "Thou . . . thy hand" (both nominatives, in apposition). **13. him**—Cyrus, type of Messiah, who redeems the captives of Satan "without money and without price" (ch. 55:1), "freely" (gratuitously) (ch. 52:3; 61:1; Zech. 9:11; Rom. 3: 24). **in righteousness**—to fulfil My righteous purpose (*Note,* ch. 41:2; 42:6; Jer. 23:6).

14. The language but cursorily alludes to Egypt, Ethiopia, and Seba, being given to Cyrus as a ransom in lieu of Israel whom he restored (ch. 43:3), but mainly and fully describes *the gathering in of the Gentiles to Israel* (Acts 2:10, 11; 8:27-38), especially at Israel's future restoration (ch. 2:2; 14:1, 2; 19:18-22; 60:3-14; 49: 23; Ps. 68:31; 72:10, 11). **labour**—wealth acquired by labor (Jer. 3:24). **Sabeans . . . of stature**—the men of Meroe, in Upper Egypt. HERODOTUS (3.30) calls the Ethiopians "the tallest of men" (*Note,* ch. 18:2; I Chron. 11:23). **thee**—Jerusalem ("my city," vs. 13). **in chains**—(Ps. 149:8). "The saints shall judge the world" (I Cor. 6:2) and "rule the nations with a rod of iron" (Zech. 4:12-19; Rev. 2:26, 27). The "chains," in the case of the obedient, shall be the *easy yoke* of Messiah; as "the sword of the Spirit" also is saving to the believer, condemnatory to the unbeliever (John 12:48; Heb. 4:12; Rev. 19:15). **God is in thee**—(Jer. 3:19).

15. God that hidest thyself—HORSLEY, after JEROME, explains this as the confession of Egypt, etc., that *God is concealed in human form in the person of Jesus.* Rather, connected with vss. 9, 10, the prophet, contemplating the wonderful issue of the seemingly dark counsels of God, implies a censure on those who presume to question God's dealings (ch. 55:8, 9; Deut. 29:29). Faith still discerns, even under the veil, the covenant-keeping *God of Israel, the Saviour* (ch. 8:17). **16. ashamed**—*disappointed* in their expectation of help from their idols (*Note,* ch. 42:17; Ps. 97:7). **17. in the Lord**—(vss. 24, 25), contrasted with the idols which cannot give even temporary help (vs. 16); *in Jehovah* there is *everlasting* salvation (ch. 26: 4)

ADAM CLARKE

9. *Woe unto him that striveth with his Maker!*—"Woe unto him that contendeth with the Power that formed him." The prophet answers or prevents the objections and cavils of the unbelieving Jews, disposed to murmur against God, and to arraign the wisdom and justice of His dispensations in regard to them. *Or thy work, He hath no hands*—"And to the workman, Thou hast no hands."

11. *Ask me of things to come.* The learned bishop therefore reads the passage thus:

Thus saith Jehovah, the Holy One of Israel;
And he that formeth the things which are to come;
Do ye question me concerning my children?
And do ye give me directions concerning the work of my hands?

13. *I have raised him up.* This evidently refers to Cyrus, and to what he did for the Jews, and informs us by whom he was excited to do it.

14. *The labour of Egypt*—"The wealth of Egypt." This seems to relate to the future admission of the Gentiles into the Church of God. *The Sabeans, men of stature*—"The Sabeans, tall of stature." That the Sabeans were of a more majestic appearance than common is particularly remarked by Agatharchides, an ancient Greek historian quoted by Bochart. *They shall make supplication unto thee*—"They shall in suppliant guise address thee."

15. *Verily thou art a God that hidest thyself.* At present, from the nations of the world. *O God of Israel, the Saviour.* While Thou revealest thyself to the Israelites and savest them.

MATTHEW HENRY

vation by the Messiah which is the salvation of the soul, a restoration to everlasting bliss. "You shall not only be delivered from the *everlasting shame and contempt* which will be the portion of idolaters (Dan. xii. 2), but you shall have everlasting honour and glory." Those who are confounded as penitents for their own sin shall not be confounded as believers in God's promise and power.

VII. They are engaged for ever to cleave to God, and never to desert him. That the Lord we serve and trust is God alone appears by the two great lights, that of nature and that of revelation.

1. It appears by the light of nature; for he made the world, and therefore may justly demand its homage (*v.* 18): "*Thus saith the Lord, that created the heavens and formed the earth, I am the Lord,* the sovereign Lord of all, *and there is none else.*" When he had made it he established it, *founded it on the seas* (Ps. xxiv. 2), *hung it on nothing* (Job xxvi. 7) as at first he made it of nothing. He fitted it for the service of man, to whom he designed to give it. He made nothing in vain, but intended everything for some end. If any man prove to have been made in vain, it is his own fault.

2. It appears by the light of revelation. As the works of God abundantly prove that he is God alone, so does his word, and the discovery he has made of himself and of his mind and will by it. All that God has said is plain: *I have not spoken in secret, in a dark place of the earth.* The Pagan deities delivered their oracles out of dens and caverns, with a low and hollow voice, and in ambiguous expressions; those that had familiar spirits whispered and muttered (*ch.* viii. 19); but God delivered his law from the top of Mount Sinai, distinct, audible, and intelligible. The vision is written, and made plain, so that he who runs may read it. If it be obscure to any, they may thank themselves. Christ pleaded in his own defence what God says here, *In secret have I said nothing*, John xviii. 20. God has in his word invited men to seek him, so he never denied their believing prayers. If he did not think fit to give them the particular thing they prayed for, yet he gave them such grace, comfort and satisfaction of soul as were equivalent. What we say of winter is true of prayer, It never rots in the skies.

Verses 20–25

What is here said is intended,

I. For *idolaters*, to show them their folly in worshipping gods that cannot help them, and neglecting a God that can. Let all *that have escaped of the nations*, not only the Jews, but those of other nations that were by Cyrus released, hear what is to be said against the worshipping of idols. *They set up the wood of their graven image.* Though they overlay it with gold, deck it with ornaments, and make a god of it, yet still it is but wood. They *pray to a god that cannot save.* "Summon them all; tell them that the great cause shall again be tried between God and Baal. *There is no other God besides me.*" None besides is fit to rule. None besides is able to help. As he is a just god, so he is *the Saviour*.

II. For the comfort and encouragement of God's faithful worshippers, whoever they are, *v.* 22. God says it to all his people, though they seem to be lost and forgotten in their dispersion, "Let them but *look to me* by faith and prayer, look above second causes, look up to me, and they shall *be saved.*" When Christ is lifted up from the earth, as the brazen serpent upon the pole, he shall draw the eyes of all men to him. *I have sworn by myself* (and God can swear by no greater, Heb. vi. 13); *the word has gone out of my mouth*, that he who made all should be Lord of all, that, since all beings are derived from him, they should all be devoted to him. He has assured us that the kingdoms of the world shall become his kingdom. This is applied to the dominion of our Lord Jesus, Rom. xiv. 10, 11. *Unto him shall men of distant countries come*, to implore his favour. *All that are incensed against him shall be ashamed;* some shall be brought to a penitential shame for it, others to a remediless ruin. In the Lord the captive Jews had righteousness (that is, grace both to sanctify their afflictions and to qualify them for deliverance) and strength for their support and escape. In the Lord Jesus we have righteousness to recommend us to the goodwill of God towards us, and strength to begin and carry on the good work of God in us. The people of the Jews shall in the Lord be justified before men and openly glory in their God. All true Christians, that depend upon Christ for strength and righteousness, in him shall be justified and shall glory in that.

JAMIESON, FAUSSET, BROWN

not . . . ashamed–opposed to the doom of the idolaters, who, in the hour of need, shall be "ashamed" (*Note,* vs. 16).

18. (*Note,* vs. 12.) **not in vain** [but] **to be inhabited**–Therefore, Judah, lying waste during the Babylonish captivity, shall be peopled again by the exiles. The Jews, from this passage, infer that, after the resurrection, the earth shall be inhabited, for there can be no reason why the earth should *then* exist in vain any more than now (II Pet. 3:13). **19. not . . . secret**–not like the heathen oracles which gave their responses from dark caverns, with studied obscurity (ch. 48:16). Christ plainly quotes these words, thereby identifying Himself with Jehovah (John 18:20). **I said not . . . Seek . . . in vain**–When I commanded you to seek Me (Jehovah did so, vs. 11, "Ask Me," etc.), it was not in order that ye might be sent empty away (Deut. 32:47). Especially in Israel's time of trial, God's interposition, in behalf of Zion hereafter, is expressly stated as about to be the answer to prayer (ch. 62:6, 7-10; Ps. 102:13-17, 19-21). So in the case of all believers, the spiritual Israel. **righteousness**–that which is veracious: not in the equivocal terms of heathen responses, fitly symbolized by the *"dark places"* from which they were uttered. **right**–true (*Note,* ch. 41:26). **20. escaped of the nations**–those of the nations who shall have escaped the slaughter inflicted by Cyrus. Now, at last, ye shall see the folly of "praying to a god that cannot save" (vs. 16). Ultimately, those that shall be "left of all the nations which shall come against Jerusalem" are meant (Zech. 14:16). They shall then all be converted to the Lord (ch. 66:23, 24; Jer. 3:17; Zech. 8:20-23). **21.** Challenge the worshippers of idols (ch. 41:1). **take counsel together**–as to the best arguments wherewith to defend the cause of idolatry. **who . . . from that time**–(Ch. 41:22, 23; *Note,* ch. 44:8). Which of the idols has done what God hath, viz., foretold, primarily as to Cyrus; ultimately as to the final restoration of Israel hereafter? The idolatry of Israel before Cyrus' time will have its counterpart in the Antichrist and the apostasy, which shall precede Christ's manifestation. **just . . . and . . . Saviour**–*righteous* in keeping His promises, and therefore a *Saviour* to His people. Not only is it not inconsistent with, but it is the result of, His *righteousness,* or *justice,* that He should *save* His redeemed (ch. 42:6, 21; Ps. 85:10, 11; Rom. 3:26). **22. Look . . . and be ye saved**–The second imperative expresses the result which will follow obedience to the first (Gen. 42:18); *ye shall be saved* (John 3:14, 15). Numbers 21:9: "If a serpent had bitten any man, when he *beheld* the serpent of brass he lived." What so simple as a look? Not *do* something, but *look* to the Saviour (Acts 16:30, 31). Believers look by faith, the eye of the soul. The look is that of one *turning* (see *Margin*) to God, as at once "Just and the Saviour" (vs. 21), i.e., the look of *conversion* (Ps. 22:27). **23. sworn by myself**–equivalent to, "As I live," as Romans 14:11 quotes it. So Numbers 14:21. God could swear by no greater, therefore He swears by Himself (Heb. 6:13, 16). **word . . . in righteousness**–rather, "the truth (*Note,* vs. 19) is gone forth from My mouth, the word (of promise), and it shall not return (i.e., which shall not be revoked)" [LOWTH]. But the accents favor *English Version.* **tongue . . . swear**–viz., an oath of allegiance to God as their true King (*Note,* ch. 19:18; 65:16). Yet to be fulfilled (Zech. 14:9). **24.** Rather, "*Only* in Jehovah shall men say *of me* (this clause is parenthetical), is there righteousness" (which includes *salvation,* vs. 21, "a *just* God and a *Saviour,*" ch. 46:13), etc. [MAURER]. **strength**–viz., to save. **shall men come**–Those who have set themselves up against God shall come to Him in penitence for the past (ch. 19:22). **ashamed**–(vs. 16; ch. 54:17; 41:11.) **25. all . . . Israel**–the spiritual Israel (Rom. 2:29) and the literal Israel, i.e., the final remnant which shall *all be saved* (vs. 17; Rom. 11:26). **justified**–treated *as if* they were just, through Christ's righteousness and death (Jer. 23:5). **glory**–lit., "sing" in His praise (Jer. 9:24; I Cor. 1: 31).

ADAM CLARKE

16. *They shall be ashamed*—"They are ashamed." The reader cannot but observe the sudden transition from the solemn adoration of the secret and mysterious nature of God's counsels in regard to His people to the spirited denunciation of the confusion of idolaters, and the final destruction of idolatry; contrasted with the salvation of Israel, not from temporal captivity, but the eternal salvation by the Messiah, strongly marked by the repetition and augmentation of the phrase, "to the ages of eternity."

19. *I the Lord speak righteousness, I declare things that are right*—"I am Jehovah, who speak truth, who give direct answers." This also is said in opposition to the false and ambiguous answers given by the heathen oracles, of which there are many noted examples; none more so than that of the answer given to Croesus when he marched against Cyrus. "If Croesus march against Cyrus, he shall overthrow a great empire." He, supposing that this promised him success, fought, and lost his own, while he expected to destroy that of his enemy.

22. *Look unto me, and be ye saved.* This verse and the following contain a plain prediction of the universal spread of the knowledge of God through Christ; see Rom. xiv. 11; Phil. ii. 10.

24. *Surely, shall one say, In the Lord have I righteousness and strength*—"Saying, Only to Jehovah belongeth salvation and power."

MATTHEW HENRY

CHAPTER 46

Verses 1–4

I. The false gods will certainly fail their worshippers, *v.* 1, 2. Bel and Nebo were two celebrated idols of Babylon. As Bel was a deified prince, so (some think) Nebo was a deified prophet, for so Nebo signifies; so that Bel and Nebo were their Jupiter and their Mercury or Apollo. God here tells them what shall become of these idols. When Cyrus takes Babylon, down go the idols. Bel and Nebo, that were set up on high, shall *stoop and bow down* at the feet of the soldiers that plunder their temples. And because there is a great deal of gold and silver upon them they carry them away with the rest of the spoil. The mules are laden with them and their other idols, to be sent among other lumber (for so it seems they accounted them rather than treasure) into Persia. *They stoop, they bow down together.* They are all alike, tottering things, and their day has come to fall.

II. The true God will never fail his worshippers. He formed them into a people and gave them their constitution. Every good man is what God makes him. You have been *borne by me from the belly*, and *carried from the womb.* And as God began early to do them good he had constantly continued to do them good: he had carried them from the womb to this day. We have been carried in the arms of his power and in the bosom of his love and pity. Our spiritual life is sustained by his grace as necessarily and constantly as our natural life by his providence. "You have been *borne by me from the belly*, nursed when you were children; and *even to your old age I am he*, when, by reason of your infirmities, you will need help as much as in your infancy." Israel was now growing old. And they had hastened their old age, and the calamities of it, by their irregularities. But God is still their God, will still carry them in the same everlasting arms that were laid under them in Moses's time, Deut. xxxiii. 27. I will now bear them upon eagles' wings out of Babylon, as in their infancy I bore them out of Egypt. This promise to aged Israel is applicable to every aged Israelite. "*Even to your old age*, when you grow unfit for business, when you are compassed with infirmities, and perhaps your relations begin to grow weary of you, yet *I am he*, the very same by whom you have been borne from the belly and carried from the womb. You change, but I am the same. *I will carry you*, will bear you up and bear you out, and will carry you home at last."

Verses 5–13

The deliverance of Israel by the destruction of Babylon is again promised, for the conviction of idolaters and of oppressors.

I. For the conviction of those who made and worshipped idols, especially those of Israel who did so.

1. He challenges them either to frame an image that should be thought a resemblance of him (*v.* 5): *To whom will you liken me?* It is absurd to think of representing an infinite and eternal Spirit by the figure of any creature whatsoever. None ever saw any similitude of him, nor can see his face and live.

2. He exposes the folly of those who made idols and then prayed to them, *v.* 6, 7. *They lavish gold out of the bag*, though they pinch their families and weaken their estates by it. *They weigh silver in the balance*, either to be the matter of their idol, or to pay the workman's wages. They were in great care about their idols (*v.* 7): *They bear him upon their* own *shoulders*; they *carry him, and set him in his place*, more like a dead corpse than a living God. They set him on a pedestal, *and he stands.* They take pains to fasten him, and *from his place he shall not remove*, though they know he can neither move a hand nor stir a step to do them any kindness. When the goldsmith has made it that which they please to call a god *they fall down, yea, they worship it.* Now shall any that have some knowledge of the true and living God, thus make fools of themselves?

3. He puts it to their own reason, let that judge (*v.* 8): "*Remember this*, what senseless helpless things idols are, and *show yourselves men*—and not brutes, men and not babes. Act with reason and scorn to disparage your own judgment as you do when you worship idols."

4. He again produces incontestable proofs that he is God (*v.* 9): *I am God, and there is none like me.* "*Remember the former things of old*, what the God of Israel did for his people in their beginnings. Remember those things, and you will own that *I am God and there is none else.*" He is God alone, for it is he only that *declares the end from the beginning*, *v.* 10. Many scripture prophecies which are delivered long ago are not yet accomplished; but the accomplishment of some in the meantime is an earnest of

JAMIESON, FAUSSET, BROWN

CHAPTER 46

VSS. 1-13. BABYLON'S IDOLS COULD NOT SAVE THEMSELVES, MUCH LESS HER. BUT GOD CAN AND WILL SAVE ISRAEL: CYRUS IS HIS INSTRUMENT. **1. Bel**—**the same as the Phœnician Baal, i.e., lord, the chief god of Babylon; to it was dedicated the celebrated tower of Babylon, in the center of one of the two parts into which the city was divided, the palace being in the center of the other. Identical with the** *sun,* worshipped on turrets, housetops, and other high places, so as to be nearer the heavenly hosts *(Saba)* (Jer. 19:13; 32:29; Zeph. 1:5). GESENIUS identifies Bel with the planet Jupiter, which, with the **planet Venus (under the name Astarte or Astaroth), was worshipped in the East as the god of fortune, the most propitious star to be born under** (*Note*, **ch. 65:11). According to the Apocryphal book,** *Bel and the Dragon,* Bel was cast down by Cyrus. **boweth . . . stoopeth**—falleth prostrate (ch. 10:4; I Sam. 5:3, 4; Ps. 20:8). **Nebo**—**the planet Mercury or Hermes, in astrology. The scribe of heaven, answering to the Egyptian Anubis. The extensive worship of it is shown by the many proper names compounded of it: Neb-uchadnezzar. Neb-uzaradan, Nab-onassar, etc. were upon**—i.e., were *a burden* **(supplied from the following clause) upon. It was customary to transport the gods of the vanquished to the land of the conquerors, who thought thereby the more effectually to keep down the subject people** (I Sam. 5:1, etc.; Jer. 48:7; 49:3; Dan. 11:8). **carriages**—in the Old English sense of *the things carried, the images borne by you:* the lading (Acts 21:15), "carriages," not the vehicles, but the baggage. Or, the images *which used to be carried by you* formerly in your solemn processions [MAURER] **were heavy loaden**—rather, *are put as a load on* the beasts of burden [MAURER]. HORSLEY translates, "They who should have been your *carriers* (as Jehovah is to *His* people, vss. 3, 4) are become *burdens*" (see *Note,* vs. 4). **2. deliver**—from the enemies' hands. **burden**—their images laid on the beasts (vs. 1). **themselves**—the *gods,* here also distinguished from their images. **3.** in contrast to what precedes: Babylon's idols, so far from *bearing* its people safely are themselves *borne off, a burden* to the laden beast; but Jehovah *bears* His people in safety even from the womb to old age (ch. 63:9; Deut. 32:11; Ps. 71:6, 18). God compares Himself to a nurse tenderly carrying a child; contrast Moses' language (Num. 11:12). **4. old age**—As "your"–"you"–"you," are not in the *Hebrew,* the sentiment is more general than *English Version,* though of course it *includes* the Jews from the infancy to the more advanced age of their history (ch. 47:6). **I am he**—i.e. the same (Ps. 102:27; John 8:24; Heb. 13:8). **I will bear . . . carry**—Not only do I not need to be *borne* and *carried* Myself, as the idols (vs. 1). **5.** (Ch. 40: 18, 25.)

6. (Ch. 40:19, 20; 41:7.) They lavish gold out of their purses and spare no expense for their idol. Their profuseness shames the niggardliness of professors who worship God with what cost them nothing. Sin is always a costly service **7. cry . . . can . . . not . . . save**—(ch. 45:20, with which contrast vs. 19).

8. show yourselves men—Renounce the *childishness* of idolatry as shown in what precedes (I Cor. 14:20; 16:13; Eph. 4:14). In order to be *manly* we must be *godly;* for man was made "in the image of God," and only rises to his true dignity when joined to God; *virtue* is derived from the *Latin vir,* "a man." **bring . . . to mind**—rather, lay it to heart. **transgressors**—addressed to the idolaters among the Jews. **9. former**—viz., proofs of the sole Godship of Jehovah, from predictions fulfilled, and interpositions of God in behalf of Israel (ch. 45:5). **10.** (Ch. 45:21; 41:22, 23; 44: 26.) **yet**—not in the *Hebrew.* Translate, "What had not been done" [HORSLEY]. **do all my pleasure**—(Ch. 53:10; Rom. 9:19.)

ADAM CLARKE

CHAPTER 46

TODAY'S DICTIONARY OF THE BIBLE:

Bel, the Aramaic form of Baal, the national god of the Babylonians (Isa. 46:1; Jer. 50:2; 51:44). It signifies "lord."

Nebo—*proclaimer; prophet.* A Chaldean god identified in their astronomy with the planet Mercury. He was the son of Bel (Marduk), the god of writing and, by extension, of learning. The name Nebuchadnezzar contains the name of this deity, perhaps meaning "Nebo—protect the frontiers" (Isa. 46:1; Jer. 48:1).

1. *Their carriages were heavy loaden*—"Their burdens are heavy."

2. *They could not deliver the burden*—"They could not deliver their own charge." That is, their worshippers, who ought to have been borne by them. See the next two verses.

3. *Which are borne by me from the belly*—"Ye that have been borne by me from the birth." The prophet very ingeniously, and with great force, contrasts the power of God, and His tender goodness effectually exerted towards His people, with the inability of the false gods of the heathen. He like an indulgent father had carried His people in His arms, "as a man carrieth his son" (see Deut. i. 31). He had protected them, and delivered them from their distresses; whereas the idols of the heathen are forced to be carried about themselves, and removed from place to place, with great labor and fatigue, by their worshippers.

8. *Shew yourselves men. Hithoshashu.* This word is rather of doubtful derivation and signification. It occurs only in this place, and some of the ancient interpreters seem to have had something different in their copies. The Vulgate read *hithbosheshu,* "take shame to yourselves"; the Syriac, *hithbonenu,* "Consider with yourselves"; the Septuagint, perhaps *hithabbelu,* "Groan or mourn, within yourselves."

MATTHEW HENRY

the accomplishment of the rest in due time. The accomplishment of this particular prophecy, which relates to the elevation of Cyrus and his agency in the deliverance of God's people out of their captivity, is mentioned for the confirmation of this truth. God by his counsel *calls a ravenous bird from the east*, a bird of prey, *Cyrus*, who (they say) had a nose like the beak of a hawk or eagle, to which some think this alludes, or (as others say) to the eagle which was his standard, as it was afterwards that of the Romans, to which there is supposed to be a reference, Matt. xxiv. 28. Cyrus came from the east at God's call. "*I have spoken it* by my servants the prophets, and what I have spoken is what *I have purposed*." For, though God has many things in his purposes which are not in his prophecies, he had nothing in his prophecies but what are in his purposes.

II. For the conviction of those that opposed the counsels of God assurance is here given that they shall be accomplished very shortly, *v.* 12, 13.

1. This is addressed to the *stout-hearted*, that is, either, (1) The proud and obstinate Babylonians, *that are far from righteousness*, that say they will never let the oppressed go free, in spite of their petitions or God's predictions. Or, (2) The unhumbled Jews, that have been long in the furnace, but are not melted, that, like the unbelieving murmuring Israelites in the wilderness, keep good things from themselves, as their fathers, who could not enter into the land of promise because of unbelief. This is applicable to the Jewish nation when they rejected the gospel of Christ; though they *followed after the law of righteousness*, they *attained not to righteousness, because they sought it not by faith*, Rom. ix. 31, 32.

2. Now God says that, whatever they think, the one in presumption, the other in despair, (1) Salvation shall be certainly wrought for God's people. If men will not do them justice, God will. He *will place salvation in Zion*, that is, he will make Jerusalem a place of safety and defence to all those who will plant themselves there. (2) It shall be very shortly wrought.

JAMIESON, FAUSSET, BROWN

11. ravenous bird—Cyrus so called on account of the rapidity of his marches from the distant regions of Persia to pounce on his prey (see *Notes*, ch. 41:2, 25; Jer. 49:22; Ezek. 17:3). The standard of Cyrus, too, was a golden *eagle* on a spear (see the heathen historian, XENOPHON, 7, where almost the same word is used, *aetos*, as here, *ayit*). **executeth my counsel**—(ch. 44:28; 45:13). Babylon represents, mystically, the apostate faction: the destruction of its idols symbolizes the future general extirpation of all idolatry and unbelief. **purposed . . . also do it**—(ch. 43:13).

12. stout-hearted—stubborn in resisting God (Ps. 76:5; Acts 7:51). **far from righteousness**—(ch. 59:9; Hab. 2:4).

13. near—antithetical to "far" (vs. 12; ch. 51:5; 56:1; 61:10, 11; Rom. 10:6-8). **righteousness**—answering to "salvation" in the parallel clause; therefore it means here, "my righteous deliverance"; righteous, because proving the *truth* of God's promises, and so contrived as to not compromise, but vindicate, His righteousness (ch. 42:21; Rom. 3:26). **Zion . . . my glory**—rather, "I will give salvation in Zion; to Israel (I will give) my glory" [HORSLEY]. (Ch. 63:11; Ps. 14:7; Luke 2:32).

ADAM CLARKE

11. *Calling a ravenous bird from the east*—"Calling from the east the eagle." A very proper emblem for Cyrus, as in other respects, so particularly because the ensign of Cyrus was a golden eagle.

12. *Hearken unto me, ye stouthearted*—This is an address to the Babylonians, stubbornly bent on the practice of injustice towards the Israelites.

MATTHEW HENRY

CHAPTER 47

Verses 1–6

In these verses God by the prophet sends a messenger to Babylon, like that of Jonah to Nineveh: "The time is at hand when Babylon shall be destroyed." Fair warning is thus given her, that she may by repentance prevent the ruin and there may be a lengthening of her tranquillity.

I. God's controversy with Babylon. She has made God her enemy. Let her know that the righteous Judge, to whom vengeance belongs, has said (*v.* 3), *I will take vengeance*. He says, "*I will not meet thee as a man*, not with the strength of a man, which is easily resisted, but with the power of a God, which cannot be resisted. Not with the justice of a man, which may be bribed, but with the justice of a God, which can never be evaded."

II. The particular ground of this controversy. God will plead his people's cause against them. It is acknowledged.(*v.* 6) that God had delivered his people into the hands of the Babylonians, had made use of them for the correction of his children, and had by their means *polluted his inheritance*. But the Babylonians carried the matter too far, and, when they had them in their hands with a base and servile spirit they trampled upon them, *and showed them no mercy*. They *laid the yoke on very heavily*, adding affliction to the afflicted, *on the ancient*—the elders in years, who were past their labour, and must sink under a yoke—the elders in office.

III. The terror of this controversy. She has reason to tremble when she is told who it is that has this quarrel with her (*v.* 4). "He is *the Lord of hosts*, that has all the creatures at his command, and therefore has *all power both in heaven and in earth*. He is the *Holy One of Israel*, a God in covenant with us." This may fitly be applied to Christ, our great Redeemer He is both Lord of hosts and the Holy One of Israel.

IV. The consequences of it to Babylon. She was beautiful as a virgin, and courted by all about her; she had been called *tender and delicate* (*v.* 1), and *the lady of kingdoms* (*v.* 5); but now the case is altered. Her honour is gone, and she must bid farewell to all her dignity. Her power is gone, and she must bid farewell to all her dominion. *There is no throne*, none for thee, *O daughter of the Chaldeans!* Those that abuse their honour or power provoke God to deprive them of it, and to make them *come down and sit in the dust*. Her ease and pleasure are gone: "She shall *no more be called tender and delicate*, but shall be put to hard service and made to feel both want and pain. Her liberty is gone, and she is brought into a state of

JAMIESON, FAUSSET, BROWN

CHAPTER 47

VSS. 1-15. THE DESTRUCTION OF BABYLON IS REPRESENTED UNDER THE IMAGE OF A ROYAL VIRGIN BROUGHT DOWN IN A MOMENT FROM HER MAGNIFICENT THRONE TO THE EXTREME OF DEGRADATION. **1. in the dust**--(*Note*, ch. 3:26; Job 2:13; Lam. 2:10). **virgin**—i.e., heretofore *uncaptured* [HERODOTUS, 1. 191]. **daughter of Babylon**—Babylon and its inhabitants (*Notes*, ch. 1:8; 37:22). **no throne**—The seat of empire was transferred to Shushan. Alexander intended to have made Babylon his seat of empire, but Providence defeated his design. He soon died; and Seleucia, being built near, robbed it of its inhabitants, and even of its name, which was applied to Seleucia. **delicate**—alluding to the effeminate debauchery and prostitution of all classes at banquets and religious rites [CURTIUS, 5.1; HERODOTUS, 1.199; BARUCH, 6.43]. **2. millstones**—like the *querns* or hand-mills, found in this country, before the invention of water-mills and windmills: a convex stone, made by the hand to turn in a concave stone, fitted to receive it, the corn being ground between them: the office of a female slave in the East; most degrading (Job 31:10; Matt. 24:41). **uncover thy locks**—rather, "take off thy veil" [HORSLEY]: perhaps the removal of the *plaited hair* worn round the women's temples is included; it, too, is a *covering* (I Cor. 11:15); to remove it and the veil is the badge of the lowest female degradation; in the East the head is the seat of female modesty; the *face* of a woman is seldom, the whole *head* almost never, seen bare (*Note*, ch. 22:8). **make bare the leg**—rather "lift up (lit., "uncover"; as in lifting up the train the leg is uncovered) thy *flowing train*." In Mesopotamia, women of low rank, as occasion requires, wade across the rivers with stript legs, or else entirely put off their garments and swim across. "Exchange thy rich, loose, queenly robe, for the most abject condition, that of one going to and fro through rivers as a slave, to draw water," etc. **uncover . . . thigh**—gather up the robe, so as to wade across. **3. not meet . . . as a man**—rather, "I will not meet a man," i.e., suffer man to intercede with me—give man an audience [HORSLEY]. Or, "I will not *make peace with* any man," before all are destroyed. Lit., "strike a league with"; a phrase arising from the custom of *striking* hands together in making a compact [MAURER], (*Note*, Prov. 17:18; 22:26; 11:15, *Margin*). Or else from *striking* the victims sacrificed in making treaties. **4. As for**—rather supply, "*Thus saith* our Redeemer" [MAURER]. LOWTH

ADAM CLARKE

CHAPTER 47

2. *Take the millstones, and grind meal.* It was the work of slaves to grind the corn. They used hand mills. Water mills were not invented till a little before the time of Augustus; windmills, not until long after. It was not only the work of slaves, but the hardest work, and often inflicted upon them as a severe punishment. The words denote that state of captivity to which the Babylonians should be reduced.

Make bare the leg, uncover the thigh. This is repeatedly seen in Bengal, where there are few bridges, and both sexes, having neither shoes nor stockings, truss up their loose garments, and walk across, where the waters are not deep. In the deeper water they are obliged to truss very high, to which there seems a reference in the third verse: "Thy nakedness shall be uncovered."

3. *I will not meet thee as a man*—"Neither will I suffer man to intercede with me."

MATTHEW HENRY

servitude and sore bondage." Even the great men of Babylon must now receive the same law from the conquerors that they used to give to the conquered: "*Take the millstones and grind meal* (*v.* 2), set to work, to hard labour which will make thee sweat so that thou must throw off all thy head-dresses, and *uncover thy locks*." At the capricious humours of their masters, they must be forced to wade through the waters, to *make bare the leg* and *uncover the thigh*, that they might *pass over the rivers*, which would be a great mortification. All her glory, and all her glorying, are gone. Instead of glory, she has ignominy (*v.* 3). *Thy nakedness shall be uncovered and thy shame shall be seen*, according to the base and barbarous usage they commonly gave their captives. Instead of glorying she *sits silently, and gets into darkness* (*v.* 5), ashamed to show her face, for she *shall no more be called the lady of kingdoms*.

Verses 7–15

Babylon, now doomed to ruin, is here justly upbraided with her pride, in the day of her prosperity, and particularly in the prognostications and counsels of the astrologers.

I. The Babylonians are here upbraided with their pride and haughtiness; it was the language both of the government and of the body of the people: *Thou sayest in thy heart I am, and none else besides me*, *v.* 8 and 10. It is the very word that God has often said concerning himself, *I am, and none else besides me*, denoting his self-existence, his infinite and incomparable perfections, and his sole supremacy.

II. They are upbraided with their luxury and love of ease (*v.* 8): "*Thou that art given to pleasures* and *dwellest carelessly* and layest nothing to heart." Great wealth and plenty are great temptations to sensuality, and, where there is fulness of bread, there is commonly abundance of idleness.

III. They are upbraided with their carnal security and their vain confidence.

1. The cause of their security. They thought themselves safe. They lulled themselves asleep in ease and pleasure, and dreamt of nothing else but that *tomorrow should be as this day, and much more abundant*. They did not *remember the latter end of it*—the latter end of their prosperity, that it is a fading flower, and will wither—the latter end of their iniquity, that it will be bitterness. *She did not remember her latter end* (so some read it).

2. The ground of their security. They trusted in their wickedness and in their wisdom, *v.* 10. Their power and wealth, which they had gotten by fraud and oppression, were their confidence. They doubt not but they shall be too hard for all their enemies, because they dare lie, and kill, and forswear themselves, and do anything for their interest. Their policy and craft, which they called their *wisdom*, were their confidence. But their *wisdom and knowledge perverted them*.

3. The expressions of their security. Three things this proud and haughty monarchy said, in her security: (1) "*I shall be a lady for ever*," *v.* 7. Thus the New Testament Babylon says, *I sit as a queen, and shall see no sorrow*, Rev. xviii. 7. (2) "*I shall not sit as a widow*, in solitude and sorrow, shall never lose the power and wealth I am thus wedded to; the monarchy shall never want a monarch to espouse and protect it, and be a husband to the state; *nor shall I know the loss of children*," *v.* 8. (3) "*No one sees me* when I do amiss, and therefore there will be none to call me to an account," *v.* 10.

4. The punishment of their security. It shall be their ruin. "*These two things shall come upon thee* (the very two things that thou didst set at defiance), *loss of children and widowhood*, *v.* 9. Both thy princes and thy people shall be cut off, so that thou shalt be no more a government, no more a nation." It will be a sudden and surprising ruin. "*Evil shall come upon thee* (*v.* 11) and thou shalt have neither time nor way to prepare for it; for *thou shalt not know whence it rises*, and therefore shalt not know where to stand upon thy guard." Babylon pretended to great wisdom and knowledge (*v.* 10), but with all her knowledge she cannot foresee, nor with all her wisdom prevent, the ruin threatened. Fair warning was indeed given them, by Isaiah and other prophets of the Lord, of this desolation; but they slighted that notice, and would give no credit to it.

IV. They are upbraided with their divinations, their magical and astrological arts and sciences.

This is one of their provoking sins, *v.* 9. "These evils shall come upon thee to punish thee *for the multitude of thy sorceries, and the great abundance of thy enchantments*." Witchcraft is a sin in giving that honour to the devil which is due to God only, making God's enemy our guide. In Babylon it

JAMIESON, FAUSSET, BROWN

supposes this verse to be the exclamation of a chorus breaking in with praises, "Our Redeemer! Jehovah of hosts," etc. (Jer. 50:34). **5. Sit**–the posture of mourning (Ezra 9:4; Job 2:13; Lam. 2:10). **darkness**–mourning and misery (Lam. 3:2; Mic. 7:8). **lady of kingdoms**–mistress of the world (ch. 13:19). **6.** reason for God's vengeance on Babylon: in executing God's will against His people, she had done so with wanton cruelty (ch. 10:5, etc.; Jer. 50:17; 51:33; Zech. 1:15). **polluted my inheritance**–(ch. 43:28). **the ancient**–Even old age was disregarded by the Chaldeans, who treated all alike with cruelty (Lam. 4:16; 5:12) [ROSENMULLER]. Or, "the ancient" means Israel, worn out with calamities in the latter period of its history (ch. 46: 4), as its earlier stage of history is called its "youth" (ch. 54:6; Ezek. 16:60).

7. so that–Through thy vain expectation of being a queen for ever, thou didst advance to such a pitch of insolence as not to believe "these things" (viz., as to thy overthrow, vss. 1-5) possible. **end of it**–viz., of thy insolence, implied in her words, "I shall be a lady for ever." **8. given to pleasures**–(*Note*, vs. 1.) In no city were there so many incentives to licentiousness. **I am . . . none . . . beside me**–(vs. 10.) Language of arrogance in man's mouth; fitting for God alone (ch. 45:6). See ch. 5:8, latter part. **widow . . . loss of children**–A state, represented as a female, when it has fallen is called a *widow*, because its *king* is no more; and *childless*, because it has no inhabitants; they having been carried off as captives (ch. 23:4; 54:1, 4, 5; Rev. 18:7, 8). **9. in a moment**–It should not decay slowly, but be suddenly and unexpectedly destroyed; in a single night it was taken by Cyrus. The prophecy was again literally fulfilled when Babylon revolted against Darius; and, in order to hold out to the last, each man chose one *woman* of his family, and strangled the rest, to save provisions. Darius impaled 3000 of the revolters. **in . . . perfection**–i.e., "in full measure." **for . . . for**–rather, "notwithstanding the . . . notwithstanding"; "in spite of" [LOWTH]. So "for" (Num. 14:11). Babylon was famous for "expiations or sacrifices, and other incantations, whereby they tried to avert evil and obtain good" [DIODORUS SICULUS]. **10. wickedness**–as in ch. 13:11, the *cruelty* with which Babylon treated its subject states. **None seeth me**–(Ps. 10:11; 94:7). "There is none to exact punishment from me." Sinners are not safe, though seeming secret. **Thy wisdom**–astrological and *political* (ch. 19:11, etc., as to Egypt). **perverted**–turns thee aside from the right and safe path. **11. from whence it riseth**–*Hebrew*, "the dawn thereof," i.e., its first rising. Evil shall come on thee without the least previous intimation [ROSENMULLER]. But *dawn* is not applied to "evil," but to *prosperity* shining out after misery (ch. 21:12). Translate, "Thou shall not see any dawn" (of alleviation) [MAURER]. **put . . . off** rather, as *Margin*, "remove by *expiation*"; it shall be never ending. **not know**–unawares: which thou dost not apprehend. Proving the fallacy of thy divinations and astrology (Job 9:5; Ps. 35:8). **12. Stand**–forth: a scornful challenge to Babylon's magicians to show whether they can defend their city. **laboured**–The devil's service is a laborious yet fruitless one (ch. 55:2). **13. wearied**–(cf. 57:10; Ezek. 24:12). **astrologers**–lit., those who form *combinations* of the heavens;

ADAM CLARKE

4. *Our redeemer*—"Our Avenger." Here a chorus breaks in upon the midst of the subject, with a change of construction, as well as sentiment.

6. *I was wroth with my people*. God, in the course of His providence, makes use of great conquerors and tyrants as His instruments to execute His judgments in the earth; He employs one wicked nation to scourge another. The inflicter of the punishment may perhaps be as culpable as the sufferer, and may add to his guilt by indulging his cruelty in executing God's justice. When he has fulfilled the work to which the divine vengeance has ordained him, he will become himself the object of it; see chap. x. 5-12. God charges the Babylonians, though employed by himself to chastise His people, with cruelty in regard to them. They exceeded the bounds of justice and humanity in oppressing and destroying them; and though they were really executing the righteous decree of God, yet, as far as it regarded themselves, they were only indulging their own ambition and violence. The Prophet Zechariah sets this matter in the same light: "I was but a little displeased, and they helped forward the affliction," chap. i. 15.

9. *These two things shall come to thee in a moment*. That is, suddenly. Belshazzar was slain; thus the city became metaphorically a widow, the husband—the governor of it—being slain. In the time in which the king was slain, the Medes and Persians took the city, and slew many of its inhabitants; see Dan. v. 30-31. When Darius took the city, he is said to have crucified 3,000 of its principal inhabitants. *In their perfection*—"On a sudden." Instead of "in their perfection," as our translation renders it, the Septuagint and Syriac read, "suddenly"; parallel to *in a moment*, in the preceding alternate member of the sentence. *For the multitude*—"Notwithstanding the multitude."

MATTHEW HENRY

had the protection of the government. They are here upbraided with the mighty pains they had taken about their sorceries: Thou hast *laboured in them from thy youth, v.* 12. They had their *astrologers,* or viewers of the heavens, that under pretence of foretelling future events by them, viewed the heavens and forget him that made them. They had their *star-gazers,* who by the motions of the stars, their conjunctions and oppositions, read the doom of states and kingdoms. They are upbraided with the utter inability and insufficiency of all these pretenders in the day of their distress. This baffling of the diviners was literally fulfilled when, the night that Babylon was taken and Belshazzar slain, all his astrologers, soothsayers, and wise men, were quite nonplussed with the handwriting on the wall that pronounced the fatal sentence, Dan. v. 8. They are upbraided with the fall of the wise men themselves in the common ruin, *v.* 14. *They shall be as stubble* before a consuming fire. The Persians, to make room for their own wise men, will cut off those of Babylon; that *fire shall burn them,* and *they shall not deliver themselves from the power of the flame.* These astrologers, that dealt in the black art, were in effect their merchants; fortune-telling was one of the best trades in Babylon. Yet when some were devoured, others fled their country, *everyone to his quarter,* and there was none to save Babylon.

CHAPTER 48

Verses 1–8

I. The hypocritical profession which many of the Jews made of religion and relation to God.

1. How high their profession of religion soared, and what a good face they put upon a very bad heart. (1) They were the *house of Jacob;* they had a place and a name in the visible church. *Jacob have I loved.* (2) They were *called by the name of Israel,* an honourable name. *Israel* signifies *a prince with God;* and they prided themselves in being of that princely race. (3) *They came forth out of the waters of Judah,* and were of the royal tribe, the tribe that adhered to God when the rest revolted. (4) They *swore by the name of the Lord,* and thereby owned him to be the true God. (5) They *made mention of the God of Israel* in their prayers and praises. (6) They *called themselves of the holy city.* (7) They *stayed themselves upon the God of Israel,* and boasted of his promises and his covenant with them; they *leaned on the Lord,* Mic. iii. 11.

2. How low their profession of religion sunk, notwithstanding all this. It was all in vain. Their hearts were not true nor right in these professions.

II. The means God used to keep them close to himself, and to prevent their turning aside to idolatry. The many excellent laws he gave them would not serve to restrain them from sin, and therefore to those God added remarkable prophecies, and remarkable providences, which were all designed to convince them that it was their duty to adhere to him. 1. He favoured them with remarkable prophecies (*v.* 3): *I have declared the former things from the beginning.* Nothing material happened to their nation from its original which was not prophesied of before—their bondage in Egypt, their deliverance thence, the situation of their tribes in Canaan, &c. The very calamities they were now groaning under in Babylon God did from the beginning declare to them, Lev. xxvi. 31, &c.; Deut. xxviii. 26, &c.; xxix. 28. He also declared to them their return to God, and to their own land again, Deut. xxx. 4, &c.; Lev. xxvi. 44, 45. 2. He dignified them with remarkable providences (*v.* 6): *I have shown thee new things from this time.* He showed them new things by the prophets of their own day, and created them. They were *hidden things,* which they could not otherwise know, as the prophecy concerning Cyrus and the exact time of their release out of Babylon. These things God *created now, v.* 7. "Consider," says God, "how it was told you by the prophets, when it was the furthest thing from your thoughts, when you had not any reason to expect it (*v.* 7, 8), when the thing seemed utterly impossible." God had shown them hidden things, and done for them great things. "Now," says he (*v.* 6), "*thou hast heard; see all this.* Thou hast heard the prophecy; see the accomplishment of it. Will you not own that your God has been a good God to you? Declare this to his honour, and your own shame."

III. The reasons why God would take this method with them.

1. Because he would anticipate their boasting of themselves and their idols. "I spoke of it," says God, "*lest thou shouldst say, My idol has done it or has commanded it to be done,*" *v.* 5. Those that

JAMIESON, FAUSSET, BROWN

who watch conjunctions and oppositions of the stars. "Casters of the configurations of the sky" [HORSLEY]. GESENIUS explains it: the dividers of the heavens. In casting a nativity they observed four signs:—the *horoscope,* or sign which arose at the time one was born; the *mid-heaven; the sign opposite the horoscope* towards the west; and the *hypogee.* **monthly prognosticators**—those who at each new moon profess to tell thereby what is about to happen. Join, not as *English Version,* "save . . . *from those things,*" etc.; but, "They that at new moons make known from (by means of) *them* the things that shall come upon thee" [MAURER]. **14.** (Ch. 29:6; 30:30.) **not . . . a coal**—Like stubble, they shall burn to a dead ash, without leaving a live coal or cinder (cf. ch. 30:14), so utterly shall they be destroyed. **15. Thus . . .**—Such shall be the fate of those astrologers who cost thee such an amount of trouble and money. **thy merchants, from thy youth**—i.e., with whom thou hast trafficked from thy earliest history, the foreigners sojourning in Babylon for the sake of commerce (ch. 13:14; Jer. 51:6, 9; Nah. 3:16, 17) [BARNES]. Rather, the *astrologers,* with whom Babylon had so many dealings (vss. 12-14) [HORSLEY]. **to his quarter**—lit., "straight before him" (Ezek. 1:9, 12). The foreigners, whether soothsayers or merchants, shall flee home out of Babylon (Jer. 50:16).

CHAPTER 48

Vss. 1-22. THE THINGS THAT BEFALL BABYLON JEHOVAH PREDICTED LONG BEFORE, LEST ISRAEL SHOULD ATTRIBUTE THEM, IN ITS "OBSTINATE" PERVERSITY, TO STRANGE GODS (vss. 1-5). **1. the waters of Judah**—spring from the *fountain* of Judah (Num. 24:7; Deut. 33:28; Ps. 68:26; *Margin*). *Judah* has the "fountain" attributed to it, because it survived the ten tribes, and from it Messiah was to spring. **swear by . . . Lord**—(ch. 19:18; 45:23; 65: 16). **mention**—in prayers and praises. **not in truth**—(Jer. 5:2; John 4:24). **2. For**—Ye deserve these reproofs; "for" ye call yourselves citizens of "the holy city" (ch. 52:1), but not in truth (vs. 1; Neh. 11:1; Dan. 9:24); so the inscription on their coins of the time of the Maccabees. "Jerusalem the Holy." **3. former**—things which have happened in time past to Israel (ch. 42:9; 44:7, 8; 45:21; 46: 10). **suddenly**—They came to pass so unexpectedly that the prophecy could not have resulted from mere human sagacity.

5. (See *Notes,* vss., 1, 3.) **6. Thou . . .**—So "ye are my witnesses" (ch. 43:10). Thou canst testify the prediction was uttered long before the fulfilment: "see all this," viz., that the event answers to the prophecy. **declare**—make the fact known as a proof that Jehovah alone is God (ch. 44:8). **new things**—viz., the deliverance from Babylon by Cyrus, *new* in contradistinction from former predictions that had been fulfilled (ch. 42:9; 43:19). Antitypically, the prophecy has in view the "new things" of the gospel treasury (Song of Sol. 7:13; Matt. 13:52; II Cor. 5:17; Rev. 21:5). From this point forward, the prophecies as to Messiah's first and second advents and the restoration of Israel, have a *new* circumstantial distinctness, such as did not characterize the previous ones, even of Isaiah. Babylon. in this view, answers to the mystical Babylon of Revelation. **hidden**—which could not have been guessed by political sagacity (Dan. 2:22, 29; I Cor. 2:9, 10). **7.** Not like natural results from existing causes, the events when they took place were like acts of *creative* power, such as had never before been "from the beginning." **even before the day when**—rather [MAURER], "And before the day (of their occurrence) thou hast not heard of them"; i.e., by any human acuteness; they are only heard of by the present inspired announcement. **8. heardest not**—repeated, as also "knewest not," from last verse. **from that time** Mine anger *towards* thee. *first* thine ear did not open itself," viz., to *obey* them [ROSENMULLER]. "To open the ear" denotes obedient attention (ch. 50:5); or, "was not opened" to *receive* them; i.e., they were not *declared by Me to thee* previously, since, if thou hadst been informed of them, such is thy perversity, thou couldst not have been kept in check [MAURER]. In the former view, the sense of the words following is, "For I knew that, if I had not foretold the destruction of Babylon so plainly that there could be no perverting of it, thou wouldst have perversely ascribed it to idols, or something else than to Me" (vs. 5). Thus they would have relapsed into idolatry, to cure them of which the Babylonian captivity was sent: so they had done (Exod. 32:4). After the return, and ever since, they have utterly forsaken idols. **wast called**

ADAM CLARKE

15. *To his quarter.* "Everyone shall turn aside to his own business; none shall deliver thee."

CHAPTER 48

1. *Are come forth out of the waters of Judah* —"Ye that flow from the fountain of Judah."

6. *Thou hast heard, see all this*—"Thou didst hear it beforehand; behold, the whole is accomplished."

MATTHEW HENRY

were not so profane as to have ascribed the thing itself to an idol were yet so proud as to have pretended that by their own sagacity they foresaw it.

2. God took pains with them, because he knew they were obstinate, *v.* 4. *I knew that thou wast hard;* so the word is. "*Thy neck is an iron sinew*, unapt to submit to the yoke of God's commandments; not flexible to the will of God, nor manageable by his providence. *Thy brow is brass;* thou art impudent and canst not blush, but wilt thrust on in the way of thy heart." God sent his prophets to them, but they did not hear, they would not know. Thou *wast called* and not miscalled, *a transgressor from the womb*. They were prone to idolatry. They were murmurers as soon as ever they began their march to Canaan. Therefore *I knew that thou wouldst deal very treacherously*.

Verses 9–15

The deliverance of God's people out of their captivity in Babylon was so improbable that there was need of the encouragement of God's people concerning it. Two things were discouraging—their own unworthiness that God should do it for them and the many difficulties in the thing itself; now both these discouragements are removed,

I. A reason why God would do it for them, though they were unworthy, *v.* 9–11. 1. It is true they had been very provoking. Their captivity was the punishment of their iniquity. "But," says God, "*I will defer my anger*" (or, rather, *stifle and suppress it*). And why will God thus stay his hand? *For my name's sake;* because this people was called by his name, and, if they were cut off, the enemies would blaspheme his name. *It is for my praise;* because it would redound to the honour of his mercy. 2. It is true they were corrupt and ill-disposed, but God would make them fit for the mercy he intended for them: "*I have refined thee*, that thou mightest be made a vessel of honour." And this accounts for his bringing them into the trouble, and continuing them in it so long as he did. It was not to cut them off, but to do them good. He therefore takes them as they are, refined in part only, and not thoroughly. "*I have chosen thee in the furnace of affliction*, and then designed thee for great things." Many have been brought home to God as chosen vessels and a good work of grace has been begun in them in the furnace of affliction. God will do it, not because he owes them such a favour, but that they may not be polluted by the insolent triumphs of the heathen, who, in triumphing over Israel, thought they triumphed over the God of Israel. Moses pleaded this often with God: Lord, *what will the Egyptians say*?

II. Here is a proof that God could do it for them, though they were unable to help themselves and the thing seemed altogether impracticable. They are *called according to his purpose*, called by him out of Egypt. (Hos. xi. 1) and now out of Babylon. He will deliver them by his own strength. They need not fear then, for He is God alone, and the eternal God (*v.* 12): "*I am he* who can do what I will and will do what is best. *I am the first; I also am the last*." What room then is left to doubt of their deliverance when *he* undertakes it? He is the God that made the world, and he that did that can do anything, *v.* 13. *If the palm of his right hand* (so the margin reads it) has gone so far as to stretch out the heavens, what will he do with his outstretched arm? He has the command of all the hosts of earth and heaven. *They stand up together*, helping one another in the service of their Maker. If God therefore will deliver his people, he cannot be at a loss for instruments in effecting their deliverance. "*All you* of the house of Jacob, *assemble yourselves, and hear* this for your comfort, *Which among them*, among the gods of the heathen, or their wise men, *has declared these things*, or could declare them?" (*v.* 14). None could out-see him, and therefore we may be sure that none could outdo him. Cyrus is the man who must do it. *The Lord has loved him* (*v.* 14); he has done him this honour, to make him an instrument in the redemption of his people and therein a type of the great Redeemer, God's beloved Son, *in whom he was well pleased. I have called him*, and therefore will bear him out. "*I have brought him from a far* country, brought him step by step, beyond his own intentions." Cyrus will *do God's pleasure on Babylon. His arm* (Cyrus's army, and in it God's arm) *shall* come, and *be upon the Chaldeans*, to bring them down (*v.* 14); for, if God call him, he will certainly *make his way prosperous*, *v.* 15.

Verses 16–22

Jacob and Israel are summoned to hearken to God speaking in and by the prophet. Those that draw nigh to God may depend upon this, that his secret shall be with them.

I. God refers them to what he had said to them

JAMIESON, FAUSSET, BROWN

—as thine appropriate appellation (ch. 9:6). **from the womb**—from the beginning of Israel's national existence (ch. 44:2).

4. obstinate—*Hebrew*, "hard" (Deut. 9:27; Ezek. 3:7, *Margin*). **iron sinew**—inflexible (Acts 7:51). **brow brass**—shameless as a harlot (see Jer. 6:28; 3:3; Ezek. 3:7, *Margin*).

9. refrain—lit., "muzzle"; His wrath, after the return, was to be *restrained a while*, and then, because of their sins, let loose again (Ps. 78:38). **for thee**—i.e., *that*—omit *that:* "*From the* **10.** (*Note*, ch. 1:25.) **with silver**—rather, "*for* silver." I sought by affliction to purify thee, but thou wast not *as silver* obtained by melting, but as dross [GESENIUS]. Thy repentance is not complete: thou art not yet as refined silver. ROSENMULLER explains, "not as silver," not with *the intense heat* needed to melt silver (it being harder to melt than gold), i.e., not with the most extreme severity. The former view is better (ch. 1:25; 42:25; Ezek. 22:18-20, 22). **chosen**—or else [LOWTH], tried . . . proved: according to GESENIUS, lit., "to rub with the touchstone," or to cut in pieces so as to examine (Zech. 13:9; Mal. 3:3; I Peter 1:7). **11. how should my name**—MAURER, instead of "My name" from vs. 9, supplies "My glory" from the next clause; and translates, "How (shamefully) My glory has been profaned!" In *English Version* the sense is, "I will refrain (vs. 9, i.e., not utterly destroy thee), for why should I permit My name to be polluted, which it would be, if the Lord utterly destroyed His elect people" (Ezek. 20:9)? **not give my glory unto another**—If God forsook His people for ever, the heathen would attribute *their triumph over* Israel *to their idols;* so God's glory would be given *to another*. **12-15.** The Almighty, who has founded heaven and earth, can, and will, restore His people. **the first . . . last**—(ch. 41:4; 44:6).

13, spanned—measured out (ch. 40:12). **when I call . . . stand up together**—(ch. 40:26; Jer. 33:25). But it is not their creation so much which is meant, as that, like *ministers* of God, the heavens and the earth are prepared at His command to *execute His decrees* (Ps. 119:91) [ROSENMULLER]. **14. among them**—among the gods and astrologers of the Chaldees (ch. 41:22; 43:9; 44:7).

Lord . . . loved him; he will . . .—i.e., "He whom the Lord hath loved will do," etc. [LOWTH]; viz., Cyrus (ch. 44:28; 45:1, 13; 46:11). However, Jehovah's language of love is too strong to apply to Cyrus, except as type of *Messiah*, to whom alone it fully applies (Rev. 5:2-5). **his pleasure**—not Cyrus' own, but Jehovah's. **15. brought**—led him on his way. **he**—change from the first to the third person [BARNES]. *Jehovah* shall make his (Cyrus') way prosperous.

ADAM CLARKE

9. *And for my praise*—"And for the sake of My praise."

10. *I have chosen thee*—"I have tried thee." I cannot think *becheseph*, "with silver," is the true reading. *Kecheseph*, "like silver," as the Vulgate evidently read it, I suppose to have been the original reading, though no MS. yet found supports this word. The similarity of the two letters, *beth* and *caph*, might have easily led to the mistake in the first instance; and it has been but too faithfully copied ever since. *Cur*, which we translate *furnace*, should be rendered "crucible," the vessel in which the silver is melted. The meaning of the verse seems to be this: I have purified you, but not as silver is purified; for when it is purified, no dross of any kind is left behind. Had I done this with you, I should have consumed you altogether; but I have put you in the crucible of affliction, in captivity, that you may acknowledge your sins, and turn unto Me.

11. *For how should my name be polluted?*—"For how would My name be blasphemed?"

14. *Which among them hath declared these things?*—"Who among you hath predicted these things?"

The Lord hath loved him: he will do his pleasure on Babylon—"He whom Jehovah hath loved will execute His will on Babylon." That is, Cyrus.

MATTHEW HENRY

and done for them formerly. He had always spoken plainly to them *from the beginning*, by Moses and all the prophets: *I have not spoken in secret;* he did not deliver his oracles obscurely and ambiguously, but so that they might be understood, Hab. ii. 2. *"From the time* that they were first formed into a *people there am I* (he sent them prophets, raised them up judges, and frequently appeared for them), and therefore there I will be still."

II. The prophet himself asserts his own commission: *Now the Lord God has by his Spirit sent me, v.* 16. Whom God sends, the Spirit sends.

III. God by the prophet sends them a gracious message. The preface to this message is both awful and encouraging (*v.* 17): *Thus saith Jehovah*, the eternal God, *thy Redeemer*, for he is *the Holy One*, that cannot deceive. The same words that introduce the law, and give authority to that, introduce the promise, and give validity to that.

1. Here is the good work which God undertakes to fulfil in them. He that is their Redeemer will be their instructor: *"I am thy God that teaches thee to profit*, that is, teaches thee such things that belong to thy peace." Whom God redeems he teaches; whom he designs to deliver out of their afflictions he first teaches to profit by their afflictions. *He leads them* to the way and *in the way by which they should go.* He not only enlightens their eyes, but directs their steps. By his grace he leads them in the way of duty, by his providence he leads them in the way of deliverance.

2. Here is the goodwill which God declares he had for them, *v.* 18, 19. (1) As when he gave them his law, he earnestly wished they might be obedient, Deut. v. 29. *O that thou hadst hearkened to my commandments; v.* 18. This confirms what God had said and sworn that he has *no pleasure in the death of sinners.* (2) He assures them that, if they had been obedient, that would not only have prevented their captivity, but would have advanced and perpetuated their prosperity. *"Thy peace should have been as a river;* thou shouldst have enjoyed a series of mercies, one continually following another, as the waters of a river, which always last." Their honour, and the justice of their cause, should in all cases have borne down opposition by their own strength, *as the waves of the sea.* Such should their righteousness have been that nothing should have stood before it; whereas, now they had been disobedient, the current of their prosperity was interrupted, and their righteousness overpowered. The rising generation should have been numerous and prosperous; whereas they were now very few, as appears by the small number of the returning captives (Ezra ii. 64). The honour of Israel should still have been sustained, untouched: *His name should not have been cut off*, as now it is in the land of Israel, which is either desolate or inhabited by strangers; nor should it have *been destroyed from before God. This* should engage us (I might say, enrage us) against sin, that it has not only deprived us of the good things we have enjoyed, but prevented the good things God had in store for us. Nothing but a prerogative of mercy would have saved them.

3. Here is assurance given of the great work which God designed to work for them, even their salvation out of their captivity. God proclaimed, long before Cyrus did, that whoever would might return to his own land (*v.* 20). Send the tidings of it by word of mouth *to the ends of the earth.* This was a figure of the publishing of the gospel to all the world. Let them all know those whom God owns for his are such as he has dearly bought and paid for: *The Lord has redeemed his servant Jacob.* The bonds God had loosed tied them the faster to him. He that redeemed us has an unquestionable right to us. Those whom God designs to bring home to himself he will take care care of, that they want not for the necessary expenses of their journey. *Through the deserts*, they *thirsted not* (*v.* 21), for in all their removals the water out of the rock followed them. He can fetch in necessary supplies for his people in a way that they think the least likely. This refers to what he did for them when he brought them out of Egypt; when all this was literally true. But it should now be in effect done again, in their return out of Babylon. God does his work as effectually by marvellous providences as by miracles. This is applicable to those treasures of grace laid up for us in Jesus Christ, from which all good flows to us as the water did to Israel out of the rock, for that rock is Christ. But (*v.* 22), though God's thoughts were thoughts of peace, yet to those that were *wicked* and hated to be reformed *there is no peace*, no peace with God or their own consciences. What have those to do with peace who are enemies to God?

JAMIESON, FAUSSET, BROWN

16. not . . . in secret—(ch. 45:19). Jehovah foretold Cyrus' advent, not with the studied ambiguity of heathen oracles, but plainly. **from the time . . .**—From the moment that the purpose began to be accomplished in the raising up of Cyrus I was present. **sent me**—The prophet here speaks, claiming attention to his announcement as to Cyrus, on the ground of his mission from God and His Spirit. But he speaks not in his own person so much as in that of Messiah, to whom alone in the fullest sense the words apply (ch. 61:1; John 10:36). Plainly, ch. 49:1, which is the continuation of ch. 48 from vs. 16, where the change of speaker from God (vss. 1, 12-15) begins, is the language of Messiah. Luke 4:1, 14, 18, shows that the Spirit combined with the Father in sending the Son: therefore "His Spirit" is *nominative* to "sent," not *accusative*, following it.

17. teacheth . . . to profit—by affliction, such as the Babylonish captivity, and the present long-continued dispersion of Israel (Heb. 12:10).

18. peace—(Ps. 119:165). Cf. the desire expressed by the same Messiah (Matt. 23:37; Luke 19:42). **river**—(ch. 33:21; 41:18), a river flowing from God's throne is the symbol of *free, abundant, and ever flowing blessings from Him* (Ezek. 47:1; Zech. 14:8; Rev. 22:1). **righteousness**—*religious prosperity*; the parent of "peace" or *national prosperity;* therefroe "peace" corresponds to "righteousness" in the parallelism (ch. 32:17). **19. sand**—retaining the metaphor of "the sea" (vs. 18). **like the gravel thereof**—rather, as the *Hebrew*, "like that (the offspring) of its (the sea's) bowels"; referring to the countless living creatures, fishes, etc., of the sea, rather than the gravel [MAURER]. JEROME, *Chaldee*, and *Syriac* support *English Version.* **his name . . . cut off**—transition from the second person, "thy," to the third "his." Israel's name was cut off *as a nation* during the Babylonish captivity; also it is so now, to which the prophecy especially looks (Rom. 11: 20).

20. Go . . . forth . . . end of the earth—Primarily, a prophecy of their joyful deliverance from Babylon, and a direction that they should leave it when God opened the way. But the publication of it "to the ends of the earth" shows it has a more world-wide scope antitypically; Revelation 18:4 shows that the mystical Babylon is ultimately meant. **redeemed . . . Jacob**—(ch. 43:1; 44:22, 23). **21.** Ezra, in describing the return, makes no mention of God cleaving the rock for them in the desert [KIMCHI]. The circumstances, therefore, of the deliverance from Egypt (Exod. 17:6; Num. 20:11; Ps. 78:15; 105:41) and of that from Babylon, are blended together; the language, while more immediately referring to the latter deliverance, yet, as being blended with circumstances of the former not strictly applicable to the latter, cannot *wholly* refer to either, but to the mystic deliverance of man under Messiah, and literally to the final restoration of Israel. **22.** Repeated (ch. 57:21). All the blessings just mentioned (vs. 21) belong only to the godly, not to the wicked. Israel shall first cast away its wicked unbelief before it shall inherit *national prosperity* (Zech. 12:10-14; 13:1, 9; 14:3, 14, 20, 21). The sentiment holds good also as to *all* wicked men (Job 15:20-25, 31-34).

ADAM CLARKE

16. *From the time that it was*—"Before the time when it began to exist." From the time that the expedition of Cyrus was planned, there was God managing the whole by the economy of His providence. *There am I*—"I had decreed it." I take *sham* for a verb, not an adverb. *And now the Lord God, and his Spirit, hath sent me*—"And now the Lord Jehovah hath sent me, and His Spirit." "Who is it that saith in Isaiah, And now the Lord hath sent me and his Spirit? in which, as the expression is ambiguous, is it the Father and the Holy Spirit who have sent Jesus; or the Father, who hath sent both Christ and the Holy Spirit? The latter is the true interpretation."—Origen *cont. Cels.* lib. i. I have kept to the order of the words of the original on purpose that the ambiguity, which Origen remarks in the version of the Septuagint, and which is the same in the Hebrew, might still remain; and the sense which he gives to it be offered to the reader's judgment, which is wholly excluded in our translation.

18. *As a river*—"Like the river." That is, the Euphrates.

ALEXANDER MACLAREN:

Notice the wonderful thought of God here (v. 18). This is an exclamation of disappointment; of thwarted love. The good which He purposed has been missed by man's fault, and He regards the faulty Israel with sorrow and pity as a would-be benefactor balked of a kind intention might do. O Jerusalem! "how often would I have gathered thee." "If thou hadst known . . . the things that belong unto thy peace!"

Notice man's opposition to God's loving purpose for us. To have hearkened to His commandments would have enabled Him to let His kindness have its way.

It is not only our act contrary to God's Law, but the source of that act in our antagonistic will, which fatally bars out the possibility of God's intended good from us. It is "not hearkening" which is the root of not doing.

That possibility of lifting up our puny wills against the all-sovereign, Infinite Will is the mystery of mysteries.

The fact that the mysterious possibility becomes an actuality in us is still more mysterious. If we could solve those two mysteries, we should be far on the way to solve all the mysteries of man's relation to God, and God's to man.

A will absolutely submitted to Him is His great ideal of human nature. And that ideal we all can thwart, and alas, alas! we all do. It is the deepest mystery; it is the blackest sin; it is the intensest folly.

Sin is negative as well as positive. Not to hearken is as bad as to act in dead opposition to.

—Expositions of Holy Scripture

MATTHEW HENRY

CHAPTER 49

Verses 1–6

I. The foregoing chapter was directed to the house of Jacob and the people of Israel, *v.* 1, 12. But this is directed to the isles (that is, the Gentiles, for they are called *the isles of the Gentiles*, Gen. x. 5) and to *the people from far*, that were *strangers to the commonwealth of Israel*, and afar off. Let these listen. The tidings of a Redeemer are sent to the Gentiles, and they listened to the gospel when the Jews were deaf to it.

II. The great author of the redemption produces his authority from heaven. 1. God had appointed him; *The Lord has called me from the womb* to this office and *made mention of my name*, nominated me to be the Saviour. By an angel he called him *Jesus—a Saviour*, who *should save his people from their sins*, Matt. i. 21. This was said of some of the prophets, as types of him, Jer. i. 5. Paul was separated to the apostleship from his mother's womb, Gal. i. 15. 2. God had fitted him for the service. He *made his mouth like a sharp sword*, and *made him* like *a polished shaft*, or a bright arrow, to fight God's battles against the powers of darkness, to conquer Satan, and bring back God's revolted subjects to their allegiance, by his word: that is the *two-edged sword* (Heb. iv. 12). 3. God had preferred him to the service for which he had reserved him: *He has hidden me in the shadow of his hand*, which denotes, (1) Concealment. The gospel of Christ, and the calling in of the Gentiles by it, were long hidden in the shadow of the ceremonial law and the Old Testament types. (2) Protection. The house of David was the particular care of the divine Providence, because that blessing was in it. Christ in his infancy was sheltered from the rage of Herod. God had owned him, had said unto him, *Thou art my servant*, thou art Israel, in effect, *the prince with God*. Some read the words in two clauses: *Thou art my servant* (so Christ is, *ch.* xlii. 1); *it is Israel in whom I will be glorified by thee;* it is the spiritual Israel, the elect, in the salvation of whom by Jesus Christ, God will be glorified.

III. He is assured of the good success of his undertaking.

1. The discouragement he had met with at his first setting out (*v.* 4): "Then I said, with a sad heart, *I have laboured in vain*; those that were careless, and strangers to God, are so still: *I have called, and they have refused;* I have *stretched out my hands to a gainsaying people*." This was Isaiah's complaint. The same was a temptation to Jeremiah to resolve he would labour no more, Jer. xx. 9. It is the complaint of many a faithful minister, that has not loitered, but laboured, not spared, but spent, his strength, and himself with it, and yet, as to many, it is all in vain: they will not repent and believe. But here it seems to point at the obstinacy of the Jews, among whom Christ went in person preaching the gospel of the kingdom, laboured and spent his strength, and yet the rulers and the body of the nation rejected him and his doctrine. Let not the ministers think it strange that they are slighted when the Master himself was.

2. He comforts himself under this discouragement with this consideration, that it was the cause of God in which he was engaged: *Yet surely my judgment is with the Lord*, who is the Judge of all, *and my work with my God*, whose servant I am. His comfort may be the comfort of all faithful ministers, when they see little success of their labours. They are with God, and for God; they are on his side, and workers together with him. "*He knows the way that I take; my judgment is with the Lord*, to determine whether I have not delivered my soul and left the blood of those that perish on their own heads." Though the labour be in vain as to those that are laboured with, yet not as to the labourer himself, if he be faithful: the Lord will justify him and bear him out, though men condemn him. The work is with the Lord, to give them success, according to his purpose, in his own way and time.

3. He receives from God a further answer, *v.* 5, 6. Those whom God designs to employ as his servants he is fashioning and preparing when perhaps neither themselves nor others are aware of it. Christ was to be *his servant, to bring Jacob again to him*, that had treacherously departed from him. The seed of Jacob therefore, according to the flesh, must first be dealt with, and means used to bring them back. Christ, and the word of salvation by him, are sent first *to the lost sheep of the house of Israel.* But what if Jacob will not be brought back to God and Israel will not be gathered? In that case, (1) Christ will be glorious in the eyes of the Lord. Though few of the Jewish nation were converted by Christ's preaching and miracles, and many loaded him with ignominy, yet God made him glorious, at his baptism, and in his

JAMIESON, FAUSSET, BROWN

CHAPTER 49

Vss. 1-26. Similar to Chapter 42:1-7 (vss. 1-9). Messiah, as the ideal Israel (vs. 3), states the object of His mission, His want of success for a time, yet His certainty of ultimate success. **1. O isles**—Messiah is here regarded as having been rejected by the Jews (vss. 4, 5), and as now turning to the Gentiles, to whom the Father hath given Him "for a light and salvation." "Isles" mean all regions *beyond sea.*

from the womb—(ch. 44:2; Luke 1:31; John 10:36). **from . . . bowels . . . mention of my name**—His name "Jesus" (i.e., God-Saviour) was designated by God before His birth (Matt. 1:21). **2. my mouth . . . sword**—(ch. 11:4; Rev. 19: 15). The double office of the Word of God, saving and damnatory, is implied (ch. 50:4; John 12:48; Heb. 4:12). **shaft**—(Ps. 45:5). "Polished," i.e., free from all rust, implies His unsullied purity.

in . . . quiver . . . hid me—Like a sword in its scabbard, or a shaft in the quiver, Messiah, before His appearing, was *hid* with God, ready to be drawn forth at the moment God saw fit [Hengstenberg]; also always *protected* by God, as the arrow by the quiver (ch. 51:16). **3. Israel**—applied to Messiah, according to the true import of the name, *the Prince* who had power with *God* in wrestling in behalf of man, and who prevails (Gen. 32:28; Hos. 12:3, 4). He is also the ideal Israel, the representative man of the nation (cf. Matt. 2:15 with Hos. 11:1). **in whom . . . glorified**—John 14:13; 17:1-5).

4. I—Messiah. **in vain**—comparatively in the case of *the greater number* of His own countrymen. "He came unto His own, and His own received Him not" (ch. 53:1-3; Luke 19:14; John 1:11; 7:5). Only 120 disciples met after His personal ministry was ended (Acts 1:15).

yet . . . my judgment . . . with the Lord—Ultimately, God will do justice to My cause, and *reward* (*Margin* for *work*, cf. ch. 40:10; 62:11) My labors and sufferings. He was never "discouraged" (ch. 42:4; 50:7, 10). He calmly, in spite of seeming ill success for the time, left the result with God, confident of final triumph (ch. 53: 10-12; I Peter 2:23). So the ministers of Christ (I Cor. 4:1-5; I Pet. 4:19).

5. The reason why He was confident that His work would be accepted and rewarded, viz., because He is "glorious in the eyes of Jehovah," etc. **to bring Jacob again to him**—(Matt. 15:24; Acts 3:26). **Though Israel be not gathered**—metaphor from a scattered flock which the shepherd gathers together again; or a hen and her chickens (Matt. 23:37). Instead of the text "not," the *Keri* has the similar *Hebrew* word, "to Him," which the parallelism favors: "And that Israel may be gathered *to Him.*" **yet**—rather, parenthetically. "*For* I am glorious, etc., and My God is My strength." Then (vs. 6) resuming the words from the beginning of vs. 5, "He saith" (I repeat), etc. Horsley explains, "Notwithstanding the incredulity of the Jews, Messiah shall be glorified in

ADAM CLARKE

CHAPTER 49

1. *Listen, O isles, unto me*—"Hearken unto me, O ye distant lands." Hitherto the subject of the prophecy has been chiefly confined to the redemption from the captivity of Babylon; with strong intimations of a more important deliverance sometimes thrown in, to the refutation of idolatry, and the demonstration of the infinite power, wisdom, and foreknowledge of God. The character and office of the Messiah were exhibited in general terms at the beginning of chap. xlii; but here He is introduced in person, declaring the full extent of His commission, which is not only to restore the Israelites, and reconcile them to their Lord and Father, from whom they had so often revolted, but to be a Light to lighten the Gentiles, to call them to the knowledge and obedience of the true God, and to bring them to be one Church together with the Israelites, and to partake with them of the same common salvation procured for all by the great Redeemer and Reconciler of man to God.

2. *And he hath made my mouth like a sharp sword*—"And he hath made my mouth a sharp sword." The servant of God, who speaks in the former part of this chapter, must be the Messiah. If any part of this character can in any sense belong to the prophet, yet in some parts it must belong exclusively to Christ, who is represented as having "a sharp twoedged sword" going "out of his mouth," Rev. i. 16; who is himself the Word of God; which word is "quick, and powerful, and sharper than any twoedged sword, piercing even to the dividing asunder of soul and spirit, and of the joints and marrow, and is a discerner of the thoughts and intents of the heart," Heb. iv. 12.

This person, who is (v. 3) called *Israel*, cannot in any sense be Isaiah. That name, in its original design and full import, can only belong to him who contended powerfully with God in behalf of mankind, and prevailed, Gen. xxxii. 28. After all that Vitringa, Bp. Lowth, and others have said in proof of this chapter speaking of the Messiah, and of Him alone, I have my doubts whether sometimes Isaiah, sometimes Cyrus, and sometimes the Messiah be not intended; the former shadowing out the latter, of whom, in certain respects, they may be considered the types. The literal sense should be sought out first; this is of the utmost importance both in reading and interpreting the oracles of God.

5. *And now, saith the Lord*—"And now, thus saith Jehovah." *Though Israel be not gathered*—"And that Israel unto Him might be gathered."

MATTHEW HENRY

transfiguration, spoke to him from heaven, sent angels to minister to him, made even his shameful death glorious, much more his resurrection. In his sufferings God was his strength, so that though he met with all the discouragement imaginable, yet he *did not fail nor was discouraged.* An angel was sent from heaven to *strengthen* him, Luke xxii. 43. Faithful ministers, though they see not the fruit of their labours, shall yet be accepted of God, and in that they shall be truly glorious. (2) The gospel shall be glorious in the eyes of the world; it shall be entertained by the nations, *v.* 6. The Messiah seemed as if he had been primarily designed to *bring Jacob back, v.* 5. But it is comparatively but a small matter; a larger sphere of usefulness, is designed him: "And therefore *I will give thee for a light to the Gentiles, that thou mayest be my salvation to the end of the earth.*" Hence Simeon learned to call Christ *a light to lighten the Gentiles* (Luke ii. 32), and St. Paul's exposition serves for a key to the context, Acts xiii. 47. *Therefore,* says he, we turn to the Gentiles, to preach the gospel to them, *because so has the Lord commanded us, saying, I have set thee to be a light to the Gentiles.* In this the Redeemer was truly glorious, the setting up of his kingdom in the Gentile world was more his honour than if he had raised up all the tribes of Jacob. This promise is in part fulfilled already, and will have a further accomplishment.

Verses 7–12

I. The humiliation and exaltation of the Messiah (*v.* 7). He was one *whom man despised.* He is *despised and rejected of men, ch.* liii. 3. Man, whom he came to save and to put honour upon, yet despised him and put contempt upon him. They not only made him despicable, but odious. He was *one whom the nation abhorred*; they cried out, *Crucify him, crucify him.* He was *a servant of rulers,* trampled upon, abused, scourged, and crucified as a slave. Yet Herod the king stood in awe of him, saying, *It is John the Baptist;* noblemen, rulers, centurions came and kneeled to him. It is for the honour of his kingdom among men when the great ones of the earth appear for him and do homage to him. This shall be the accomplishment of God's promise, and he will give him the heathen for his inheritance.

II. The blessings he has in store for all those to whom he is made salvation. God will own and stand by him in his undertaking (*v.* 8). Violent attacks were made upon Lord Jesus by the powers of darkness, when it was their hour, to drive him off from his undertakings, but God promises to preserve him and would preserve his kingdom among men, though fought against on all sides.

1. He shall be guarantee of the treaty of peace between God and man: I will *give thee for a covenant of the people.* It was in him that God was *reconciling the world to himself*; and he that *spared not his own Son* will deny us nothing. He is given for a covenant, as he is the blessed *days-man who has laid his hand upon us both.*

2. He shall repair the decays of the church and build it upon a rock. He shall *cause the desolate heritages to be inherited*; so the cities of Judah were after the return out of captivity, and so the church, which in the last and degenerate ages of the Jewish nation had been as a country laid waste, was again replenished by the fruits of the preaching of the gospel.

3. He shall free the souls of men from the bondage of guilt and corruption and bring them into the glorious liberty of God's children. He shall *say to the prisoners* that were bound under the power of Satan, *Go forth, v.* 9. Pardoning mercy is a release from the curse of the law, and renewing grace is a release from the dominion of sin. Both are from Christ. It is he that says, *Go forth;* it is the Son that makes us free, and then we are free indeed. He saith *to those that are in darkness, Show yourselves;* "not only *see*, but *be seen*, to the glory of God and your own comfort."

4. He shall provide for the comfortable passage of those whom he sets at liberty to the place of their happy settlement, *v.* 9-11. These verses refer to the provision made for the Jews' return, but they are applicable to that guidance of divine grace which all God's spiritual Israel are under. The world leads its followers by broken cisterns, or brooks that fail in summer; but God leads those that are his by springs of water. And those whom God guides shall find a ready road (*v.* 11): *I will make all my mountains a way.*

5. He shall bring them all together from all parts, that they may return in a body, that they may encourage one another. They were dispersed as their enemies pleased, to prevent any combination among themselves. But, when God's time shall come to bring them home together, one spirit shall animate them all, *v* 12. Here shall a party *come from far,*

JAMIESON, FAUSSET, BROWN

the conversion of the Gentiles," reading as *English Version:* but if the *Keri* be read, "Israel shall at one time or other be gathered, notwithstanding their incredulity during Messiah's sojourn on earth." **6. It is a light thing**—"It is too little that Thou shouldest," [HENGSTENBERG], i.e., It is not enough honor to Thee to raise up *Jacob* and *Israel,* but I design for Thee more, viz., that Thou shouldest be the means of enlightening the *Gentiles* (ch. 42:6, 7; 60: 3). **the preserved** —viz., those remaining after the judgments of God on the nation—the elect remnant of Israel reserved for mercy. LOWTH, with a slight but needless change of the *Hebrew,* translates for "tribes" and "preserved," the "scions"—the "branches." **7. whom man despiseth**—*Hebrew,* "the despised of soul," i.e., by every soul, by all men (ch. 52:14, 15; 53:3; 50:6-9; Ps. 22:6). LOWTH translates, "whose *person* is despised." **abhorreth—lit.,** who is an abomination to the nation (Luke 23:18-23). The Jews contemptuously call Him always *Tolvi,* "the crucified." I prefer, on account of *Goi,* the *Hebrew* term for *nation* being usually applied to the *Gentiles,* and that for *people* to the Jews (Hos. 1:9; so the *Greek* terms respectively also *Laos* and *Ethne,* Rom. 9:25), to take "nation" here collectively for the *Gentile* world, which also spurned Him (Ps. 2:1-3; Acts 4:25-27). **servant of rulers**—(Matt. 17:27.) He who would not exert His power against the rulers (Matt. 26:52, 53). **shall see**—viz., the fulfilment of God's promises (vss. 3, 6), *when* He shall be *a light to the Gentiles.* **arise**—to reverence Thee (Ps. 72:10, 11; Phil. 2:10). **princes also**—rather, for the parallelism, supply the ellipsis, thus, "Princes *shall see* and shall worship." **faithful**—viz., to His promises. **choose thee**—as God's *elect* (ch. 42:1). **8.** Messiah is represented as having asked for the grace of God in behalf of sinners; this verse contains God the Father's favorable answer. **an acceptable time**—"In a time of grace" [HENGSTENBERG]. A limited time (ch. 61:2; II Cor. 6:2). The time judged by God to be the best fitted for effecting the purposes of His grace by Messiah. **heard thee**—(Ps. 2:8; Heb. 5:7). **day of salvation**—when "the fulness of time" (Gal. 4:4) shall have come. The day of salvation is "to-day" (Heb. 4:7). **helped**—given Thee the help needed to enable Thee, as man, to accomplish man's salvation. **preserve**—from the assaults and efforts of Satan, to divert Thee from Thy voluntary death to save man. **covenant of the people**—(*Note,* ch. 42:6). "The people," *in the singular,* is always applied exclusively to Israel. **establish the earth**—rather, "to restore the land," viz., Canaan to Israel. Spiritually, the restoration of *the Church* (the spiritual Israel) to the heavenly land forfeited by man's sin is also included. **cause to inherit . . . desolate heritages**—image from the desolate state of Judea during the Babylonish captivity. Spiritually, the Gentile world, a moral waste, shall become a garden of the Lord. Lit., Judea lying desolate for ages shall be possessed again by Israel (cf. ch. 61:7, "in their land"). *Jesus,* the antitype of, and bearing the same name as *Joshua* (Heb. 4:8), shall, like him, divide the land among its true heirs (ch. 54:3; 61:4). **9.** (Ch. 42:7; Zech. 9:12). **prisoners**—the Jews bound in legal bondage. **them . . . in darkness**—the Gentiles having no light as to the one true God [VITRINGA]. **Show yourselves**—not only see but be seen (Matt. 5:16; Mark 5:19). Come forth from the darkness of your prison into the light of the Sun of righteousness. **in the ways . . .**—In a desert there are no "ways," nor "high places," with "pastures"; thus the sense is: "They shall have their pastures, not in deserts, but in cultivated and inhabited places. Laying aside the figure, the churches of Christ at the first shall be gathered, not in obscure and unknown regions, but in the most populous parts of the Roman empire, Antioch, Alexandria, Rome, etc. [VITRINGA]. Another sense probably is the right one. Israel, on its way back to the Holy Land, shall not have to turn aside to devious paths in search of necessaries, but shall find them in *all places* wherever their route lies; so ROSENMULLER. God will supply them *as if* He should make the grass grow in the trodden *ways* and on the barren *high places* wherever their route lies; so ROSENMULLER. wants, both of literal Israel on their way to Palestine, and of the spiritual on their way to heaven, as their Shepherd (ch. 65:13; Matt. 5:6), also in heaven (Rev. 7:16, 17). **11. my**—All things are God's. **mountains a way**—I will remove all obstructions out of the way (ch. 40:4). **exalted**—i.e., cast up (ch. 57:14; 62:10); for instance, over valleys. VITRINGA explains **"mountains"** as *great kingdoms,* Egypt, Syria, etc., subjected to Rome, to facilitate the spreading of the Gospel; "highways," the *Christian doctrine* wherein those who join the

ADAM CLARKE

6. *And to restore the preserved of Israel*—"And to restore the branches of Israel."

7. *The Redeemer of Israel, and his Holy One*—"The Redeemer of Israel, His Holy One." *To him whom man despiseth*—"To Him whose person is despised."

CHARLES H. SPURGEON:

"I will give thee for a covenant of the people (v. 8). We all believe that our Savior has very much to do with the covenant of eternal salvation. We have been accustomed to regard Him as the Mediator of the covenant, as the Surety of the covenant, and as the scope or substance of the covenant. We have Him to be the *Mediator* of the covenant, for we were certain that God could make no covenant with man unless there were a mediator—a daysman, who should stand between them both. And we have hailed Him as the Mediator, who, with mercy in His hands, came down to tell to sinful man the news that grace was promised in the eternal counsel of the Most High. We have also loved our Savior as the *Surety* of the covenant, who, on our behalf, undertook to pay our debts; and on His Father's behalf undertook, also, to see that all our souls should be secure and safe, and ultimately presented unblemished and complete before Him. And I doubt not, we have also rejoiced in the thought that Christ is the *sum and substance* of the covenant; we believe that if we would sum up all spiritual blessings, we must say "Christ is all." He is the matter, He is the substance of it; and although much might be said concerning the glories of the covenant, yet nothing could be said which is not to be found in that one word "Christ." But I shall dwell on Christ, not as the Mediator, nor as the surety, nor as the scope of the covenant, but as one great and glorious article of the covenant which God has given to His children. It is our firm belief that Christ is ours, and is given to us of God; we know that "He delivered him up for us all," and we, therefore, believe that He will, "with him, freely give us all things." We can say, with the spouse, "My Beloved is mine." We feel that we have a personal property in our Lord and Savior Jesus Christ, and it is our delight in the simplest manner possible, without the garnishings of eloquence or the trappings of oratory, just to meditate upon this great thought, that Jesus Christ in the covenant is the property of every believer.

—The Treasury of the Old Testament

MATTHEW HENRY

some *from the north*, some *from the west*, some *from the land of Sinim*, a country belonging to one of the chief cities of Egypt, called *Sin*, of which we read, Ezek. xxx. 15, 16.

Verses 13–17

The return of the people of God, and the eternal redemption to be wrought out by Christ (of which that was a type), would be great occasions of joy and great proofs of the tender care God has of the church.

I. Nothing can furnish us with better matter for songs of praise and thanksgiving, *v.* 13. Let there be joy in heaven; let the earth and the mountains *be joyful*, and *break forth into singing* (Rom. viii. 19, 21), for *God has comforted his people* that were in sorrow.

II. Nothing can furnish us with more convincing arguments to prove the most tender concern God has for his church.

1. The troubles of the church have given some occasion to question God's care for it, *v.* 14. *Zion*, in distress, *said, The Lord has forsaken me*, and looks after me no more. Infidels, in their presumption, say *God has forsaken the earth* (Ezek. viii. 12). Weak believers, in their despondency, are ready to say, God has forsaken his church. But we have no more reason to question his promise and grace than we have to question his providence and justice.

2. The triumphs of the church, after her troubles, will put the matter out of question. What God will do for Zion we are told, *v.* 17. Her friends, who had deserted her, shall be gathered to her: *Thy children shall make haste*. Converts to the faith of Christ are the children of the church; they shall join themselves to her with great readiness. "*Thy builders shall make haste*" (so some read it), "who shall build up thy houses, thy walls, especially thy temple." Her enemies, who had threatened, shall be forced to withdraw from her. By Christ the prince of this world, the great destroyer, is cast out, and his attempts quite baffled. Zion's suggestions were altogether groundless. God had not forsaken her, nor forgotten her, nor ever will. "You think that I have forgotten you. *Can a woman forget her sucking child?*" A mother cannot but be concerned for her own child; for it is a piece of herself, and very lately one with her. It is possible that she may forget. But, says God, *I will not forget thee*. He has a constant care of his church and people (*v.* 16): *I have engraven thee upon the palms of my hands*. This alludes to the custom of those who tie a string upon their hands or fingers to put them in mind of things which they are afraid they shall forget, or to the wearing of signet or locket-rings in remembrance of some dear friend. His setting them thus as a seal upon his arm denotes his setting them as a seal upon his heart, and his being ever mindful of them and their interests. He adds, "*Thy walls shall be continually before me;* thy ruined walls, though no pleasing spectacle, shall be in my thoughts of compassion. The plan and model of thy walls, that are to be rebuilt, is before me, and they shall certainly be built according to it."

Verses 18–23

Two things are promised to be in part accomplished in the reviving of the Jewish church after its return, but more fully in the planting of the Christian church by the preaching of the gospel of Christ:

I. The church shall be replenished with great numbers added to it. It was promised (*v.* 17) that *her children should make haste*.

1. Multitudes shall flock to the church from all parts. *Look round, and see how they gather themselves to thee* (*v.* 18), by a local accession to the Jewish church. They come to Jerusalem for that was then the centre of their unity; but, under the gospel, it is by a spiritual accession to the mystical body of Christ in faith and love.

2. Such as are added to the church shall not be a burden and blemish to her, but her strength and ornament. *As I live, saith the Lord, thou shalt surely clothe thyself with them all.* When those that are added to the church are serious, and holy, and exemplary in their conversation, they are an ornament to it.

3. The country which was waste and desolate, and *without inhabitant* (*ch.* v. 9; vi. 11), shall be again peopled, nay, it shall be over-peopled (*v.* 19): "*Thy waste and thy desolate places*, that have long lain so, *and the land of thy destruction*, that land of thine which was destroyed with thee, shall now be so full of people that there shall be no room for the inhabitants." Thus the *kingdom of God among men*, which had been impoverished and almost depopulated, was again peopled and enriched by the setting up of the Christian church.

JAMIESON, FAUSSET, BROWN

Church walk, and which, at the time of Constantine, was to be raised into prominence before all, and publicly protected (ch. 35:8, 9). **12. Sinim**—The Arabians and other Asiatics called China *Sin*, or *Tchin;* the Chinese had no special name for themselves, but either adopted that of the reigning dynasty or some high-sounding titles. This view of "Sinim" suits the context which requires a people to be meant "from far," and distinct from those "from the north and from the west" [GESENIUS].

13. So Revelation 12:12. God will have mercy on *the* afflicted, because of His compassion; on *His* afflicted, because of His covenant.

14. Zion—the literal Israel's complaint, as if God had forsaken her in the Babylonian captivity; also in their dispersion previous to their future restoration; thereby God's mercy shall be called forth (ch. 63:15-19; Ps. 77:9, 10; 102:17). **15.** (Ch. 44:21; Ps. 103:13; Matt. 7:11).

17. Thy children—Israel (vss. 20, 21; ch. 43:6). JEROME reads, for "Thy children," "Thy builders"; they that destroyed thee shall hasten to build thee. **haste**—to rebuild thy desolate capital. **shall go forth**—Thy destroyers shall leave Judea to Israel in undisturbed possession.

16. Alluding to the Jews' custom (perhaps drawn from Exod. 13:9) of puncturing on their hands a representation of their city and temple, in token of zeal for them [LOWTH], (Song of Sol 8:6).

18. As Zion is often compared to a bride (ch. 54:5), so the accession of converts is like bridal ornaments ("jewels," ch. 62:3; Mal. 3:17). Her *literal* children are, however, more immediately meant, as the context refers to their restoration; and only secondarily to her *spiritual* children by conversion to Christ. Israel shall be the means of the final complete conversion of the nations (Micah 5:7; Rom. 11:12, 15). **as a bride**—viz., binds on her ornaments.

19. land of thy destruction—thy land once the scene of destruction. **too narrow**—(Ch. 54:1, 2; Zech. 10:10.)

ADAM CLARKE

17. *Thy children shall make haste*—"They that destroyed you shall soon become your builders." *Shall go forth of thee*—"Shall become your offspring." Shall "proceed, spring, issue, from thee," as your children. The phrase is frequently used in this sense: see chap. xi. 1; Mic. v. 2; Nah. i. 11. The accession of the Gentiles to the Church of God is considered as an addition made to the number of the family and children of Sion: see vv. 21-22 and chap. lx. 4.

18. *Bind them on thee, as a bride doeth*—"Bind them about you, as a bride her jewels." The end of the sentence is manifestly imperfect. Does a bride bind her children, or her new subjects, about her?

MATTHEW HENRY

4. The new converts shall strangely increase and multiply. Jerusalem, after she has lost abundance of her children by sword, famine, and captivity, shall have a new family growing up, children which she *shall have after she has lost the other* (*v.* 20), as Seth, who was *appointed another seed instead of Abel.* God will repair his church's losses and secure to himself a seed to serve him in it. The children shall complain for want of room: "Our numbers increase so fast that *the place is too strait for us*"; as the sons of the prophets complained, 2 Kings vi. 1. But, strait as the place is, still more shall desire to be admitted, even when the *poor and the maimed, the halt and the blind*, are brought in, *yet still there is room*, room enough for those that are in and room for more, Luke xiv. 21, 22. The mother shall stand amazed at the increase of her family, *v.* 21. She shall say, *Who has begotten me these?* and, *Who has brought up these?* They come to her with all the affection of children; and yet she never bore any pain for them, but has them ready reared to her hand. The church is not perpetually visible, but there are times when it is desolate, and made few in number. Yet on the other hand its desolations shall not be perpetual. God will out of stones raise up children unto Abraham. Sometimes this is done in a very surprising way, as when a nation is born at once, *ch.* lxvi. 8.

5. This shall be done with the help of the Gentiles, *v.* 22. The Jews were cast off, among whom it was expected that the church should be built up. The Gentiles shall be called in. God will *lift up his hand to them*, to invite or beckon them, having all the day stretched it out in vain to the Jews, *ch.* lxv. 2. And he will *set up his standard to them*, the preaching of the everlasting gospel. *They shall bring thy sons in their arms.* They shall assist the sons of Zion, which are found among them, in their return to their own country. God can raise up friends for returning Israelites even among Gentiles. "Dost thou ask, *Who has begotten and brought up these?* Know that they were begotten and brought up among the Gentiles, but they are now brought into thy family."

II. The church shall have a prevailing interest in the nations, *v.* 22, 23. *Kings shall be thy nursing fathers*, to carry thy sons in their arms (as Moses, Num. xi. 12); and *their queens shall be thy nursing mothers.* This promise was in part fulfilled to the Jews, after their return out of captivity. Several of the kings of Persia countenanced and encouraged them, as Cyrus, Darius, and Artaxerxes; Esther the queen was a nursing mother to the Jews that remained in their captivity, putting her life in her hand to snatch the child out of the flames. The Christian church, after a long captivity, was happy in some such kings and queens as Constantine and his mother Helena, and afterwards Theodosius, and others, who nursed the church with all possible care and tenderness. The church in this world is in an infant state, and it is in the power of princes and magistrates to do it great service. Others who stand out against the church's interests, will be forced to yield. *They shall bow down to thee and lick the dust.* The promise to the church of Philadelphia seems to be borrowed from this (Rev. iii. 9): *I will make those of the synagogue of Satan to come and worship before thy feet.*

Verses 24–26

I. An objection against the promise of the Jews' release suggesting that it was not to be expected; for (*v.* 24) they were a prey in the hand of the mighty, and therefore it was not likely they should be rescued by force. They were lawful captives; by the law of God, having offended, they were justly delivered into captivity; and by the law of nations, being taken in war, they were justly detained in captivity till they should be ransomed or exchanged. Now this is spoken either by the enemies, as justifying themselves in their refusal to let them go, or by their friends, either in a way of distrust, or in a way of thankfulness. "Who would have thought that ever the prey should be *taken from the mighty*? Yet it is done." This is applicable to our redemption by Christ.

II. This objection answered by express promises. "*Even the captives of the mighty*, though they are mighty, shall be taken away; *and the prey of the terrible*, though they are terrible, shall be delivered; they cannot with all their impudence outface, the deliverance and the counsels of God concerning it" (*v.* 25). Here is a further promise God will bring judgments upon the oppressors, and so will work salvation for the oppressed: "*I will contend with him that contends with thee*, and thus *I will save thy children.*" The captives shall be delivered by *leading captivity captive*, that is, sending those into captivity that had held God's people captive (*v.* 26): "*I will feed those that oppress thee with their own flesh*, and *they shall be drunken with their own blood.* The proud Baby-

JAMIESON, FAUSSET, BROWN

20. children . . . after . . . other–rather, "the children of thy widowhood," i.e., the children of whom thou hast been bereft during their dispersion in other lands (*Note*, ch. 47:8) [MAURER]. **again**–rather, "yet." **give place**–rather, "stand close to me," viz., in order that we may be the more able to *dwell* in in the *narrow* place [HORSLEY]. Cf. as to Israel's *spiritual* children, and the extension of the gospel sphere, Romans 15:19, 24; II Corinthians 10:14-16. But vs. 22 (cf. ch. 66:20) shows that her literal children are primarily meant. GESENIUS translates. "Make room." **21. Who . . .?**–Zion's joyful wonder at the unexpected restoration of *the ten tribes*. Secondarily, the accession of spiritual Israelites to the mother church of Jerusalem from the Gentiles is meant. This created surprise at first (Acts 10:45; 14:27; 15:3, 4). **lost . . . am desolate, a captive, and removing to and fro**–rather, "bereaved of . . . have been barren, an exile and outcast" [HORSLEY]. She had been "put away" by Jehovah, her husband (ch. 50:1); hence her wonder at the *children begotten to her.*

22. lift . . . hand–i.e., beckon to (*Note, ch.* 13:2). **standard**–(Ch. 11:12). **bring . . . sons in . . . arms**–The Gentiles shall aid in restoring Israel to its own land (ch. 60:4; 66:20). Children able to support themselves are carried on the shoulders in the East; but infants, in the arms, or astride on one haunch (ch. 60:12). "Thy sons" must be distinct from "the Gentiles," who *carry* them; and therefore cannot primarily refer to converts among the Gentiles.

23. lick . . . dust–i.e., kiss thy feet in token of humble submission. **for they . . . not . . . ashamed . . . wait for me**–The restoration of Israel shall be in answer to their prayerful waiting on the Lord (ch. 30:18, 19; Ps. 102:16, 17; Zech. 12:10; 14:3).

24. the prey–Israel, long a prey to mighty Gentile nations, whose oppression of her shall reach its highest point under Antichrist (Dan. 11:36, 37, 41, 45). **lawful captive**–the Jews justly consigned for their sins (ch. 50:1) as captives to the foe. Secondarily, Satan and Death are "the mighty" conquerors of man, upon whom his sin give them their "lawful" claim. Christ answers that claim for the sinners, and so the captive is set free (Job 19:25; 14:14; Matt. 12:29; Hos. 6:2, where vs. 4 shows the *primary* reference is to *Israel's restoration*, to which *the resurrection* corresponds; Isa. 26:19; Eph. 4:8; Heb. 2:14, 15). Others not so well translate, "the captives taken from among the *just* Israelites."

25. (Ch. 53:12; Ps. 68:18; Col. 2:15). **contend with him, . . .**–(Ch. 54:17).

26. feed . . . own flesh–a phrase for *internal strifes* (ch. 9:20). **own blood**–a just retribution for their having shed the blood of God's

ADAM CLARKE

KEIL–DELITZSCH:

The prophecy now takes a step backward in the domain of the future, and describes the manner in which the children of Zion get back to their home. Verse 22. "Thus saith the Lord Jehovah, Behold, I lift up my hand to nations, and set up my standard to peoples: and they bring thy sons in their bosom; and thy daughters, upon shoulders are they carried." The setting up of a standard (5:26; 11:12; 18:3) is a favorite figure with Isaiah, as well as swaying the hand. Jehovah gives a sign to the heathen nations with His hand, and points out to them the mark that they are to keep in view, with a signal pole which is set up. They understand it, and carry out His instructions, and bring Zion's sons and daughters thither, and that as a foster-father (*'ōmēn*) carries an infant in the bosom of his dress (*chōtsen,* as in Neh. 5:13; Arabic as in Ps. 129:7, *hidn,* from *hadana,* to embrace, to press tenderly to one's self); or upon his arms, so that it reclines upon his shoulder (60:4; 66:12).

Such affectionate treatment does the church receive, which is assembling once more upon its native soil, while kings and their consorts hasten to serve the re-assembled community.

—*Commentary on the Old Testament*

23. *With their face toward the earth*—"With their faces to the earth." It is well-known that expressions of submission, homage, and reverence always have been and are still carried to a great degree of extravagance in the Eastern countries. When Joseph's brethren were introduced to him, they "bowed down themselves before him with their faces to the earth," Gen. xlii. 6.

24. *Shall the prey be taken from the mighty?*—"Shall the prey seized by the terrible be rescued?" These last two verses contain a glorious promise of deliverance to the persecuted Church of Christ from the terrible one—Satan, and all his representatives and vicegerents, persecuting anichristian rulers.

MATTHEW HENRY

lonians shall become an easy prey to one another. Their ruin, which was begun by a foreign invasion, shall be completed by their intestine divisions. They shall *bite and devour one another*, till they are *consumed one of another*." See how cruel men sometimes are to themselves and to one another. They not only thirst after blood, but drink it with as much pleasure as if it were sweet wine.

III. The effect of Babylon's ruin: *All flesh shall know that I the Lord am thy Saviour*. God will make it to appear, to all the world, that, though Israel seem lost, they have a Redeemer.

CHAPTER 50

Verses 1–3

Those who have professed to be the people of God, and yet seem to be dealt severely with, are apt to complain of God. But, in answer to their murmurings, we have,

I. A challenge given them to prove that the quarrel began on God's side, *v.* 1. He had been a husband to them; and husbands were then allowed a power to put away their wives upon any little disgust, Deut. xxiv. 1; Matt. xix. 7. But they could not say that God had dealt so with them. It is true they were now separated from him, and had abode many days without ephod, altar, or sacrifice; but whose fault was that? He had been a father to them; and fathers had then a power to sell their children for slaves to their creditors, in satisfaction for debts. Now it is true the Jews were sold to the Babylonians then, and afterwards to the Romans; but did God sell them for payment of his debts? No, he was not indebted to any of those to whom they were sold.

II. A charge, showing that they were themselves the authors of their own ruin: "*Behold, for your iniquities*, for the pleasure of them and the gratification of your own base lusts, *you have sold yourselves, for your iniquities you are sold*. You sold yourselves to work wickedness, and therefore God justly sold you into the hands of your enemies," 2 Chron. xii. 5, 8. The Jews were sent into Babylon for their idolatry, and were at last rejected for crucifying the Lord of glory; these were the iniquities for which they were sold and put away.

III. The confirmation of this challenge and this charge. God came and offered them his favour, offered them his helping hand, either to prevent their trouble or to deliver them out of it, but they slighted him and his grace. "Do you lay it upon me?" (says God); "tell me, then, wherefore, *when I came, was there no man to* meet me, *when I called, was there none to answer me?*" *v.* 2. God came to them by his servants the prophets, but *there was* no man that had any regard to the warnings which the prophets gave them. Because they *mocked the messengers of the Lord*, therefore *God brought upon them the king of the Chaldeans*, 2 Chron. xxxvi. 16, 17. Last of all *he sent unto them his Son*. He *came to his own*, but *his own received him not*; they knew not, because they would not know, the things that belonged to their peace, and for that transgression it was that they were put away and their house was left desolate, Matt. xxi. 41; xxiii. 37, 38; Luke xix. 41, 42. It is plain that it was not owing to a want of power in God, for he is almighty, and could have recovered them from so great a death; nor was it owing to a want of power in Christ, for he is *able to save to the uttermost*. *Can this man save us?* For *himself he cannot save*. "But" (says God) "*is my hand shortened at all*, or is it weakened?" Can any limits be set to Omnipotence? Cannot he redeem who is the great Redeemer? The expression our Saviour sometimes used concerning the power of faith, that it will *remove mountains and plant sycamores in the sea*, is not unlike this; if their faith could do that, no doubt their faith would save them.

Verses 4–9

Our Lord Jesus, having proved himself able to save, here shows himself as willing as he is able. We suppose the prophet Isaiah to say something of himself in these verses, encouraging himself to go on in his work as a prophet, notwithstanding hardships, not doubting but that God would strengthen him; but, like David, he speaks of himself as a type of Christ.

I. As an acceptable preacher. Isaiah, as a prophet, was qualified for the work to which he was called, but Christ was anointed with the Spirit above his fellows. To make the man of God perfect, he has, 1. *The tongue of the learned*, to know how to give instruction, *how to speak a word in season to him that is weary*, *v.* 4. God gave to Christ the tongue of the learned, for the comfort of those that are weary and heavily laden under the burden of sin, Matt.

JAMIESON, FAUSSET, BROWN

servants (Rev. 16:6). **sweet wine**—i.e., must, or new wine, the pure juice which flows from the heap of grapes before they are pressed; the ancients could preserve it for a long time, so as to retain its flavor. It was so mild that it required a large quantity to intoxicate; thus the idea here is that *very much* blood would be shed (Rev. 14:10, 20).

all flesh shall . . .—the effect on the world of God's judgments (ch. 66:15, 16, 18, 19; Rev. 15:3, 4).

CHAPTER 50

Vss. 1-11. THE JUDGMENTS ON ISRAEL WERE PROVOKED BY THEIR CRIMES, YET THEY ARE NOT FINALLY CAST OFF BY GOD. **1. Where . . . mother's divorcement**—Zion is "the mother"; the Jews are the children; and God the Husband and Father (ch. 54: 5; 62:5; Jer. 3:14). GESENIUS thinks that God means by the question to *deny* that He had given "a bill of divorcement" to her, as was often done on slight pretexts by a husband (Deut. 24:1), or that He had "sold" His and her "children," as a poor parent sometimes did (Exod. 21:7; II Kings 4:1; Neh. 5:5) under pressure of his "creditors"; that it was they who sold themselves through their own sins. MAURER explains, *"Show* the bill of your mother's divorcement, whom . . . ; produce the creditors to whom ye have been sold; so it will be seen that it was not from any caprice of Mine, but through your own fault, your mother has been put away, and you sold" (ch. 52:3). HORSLEY best explains (as the antithesis between "I" and "yourselves" shows, though LOWTH translates, "Ye *are sold*") *I* have never given your mother a regular bill of divorcement; I have merely "put her away" for a time, and can, therefore, by right as her husband still take her back on her submission; I have not made you, the children, over to any "creditor" to satisfy a debt; I therefore still have the right of a father over you, and can take you back on repentance, though as rebellious children *you* have sold yourselves to sin and its penalty (I Kings 21:25). **bill . . . whom**—rather, "the bill *with which* I have put *her* away" [MAURER].

2. I—Messiah. **no man**—willing to believe in and obey Me (ch. 52:1, 3). The same Divine Person had "come" by His prophets in the Old Testament (appealing to them, but in vain, Jer. 7:25, 26), who was about to come under the New Testament. **hand shortened**—the Oriental emblem of weakness, as the long *streched-out hand* is of power (ch. 59:1). Notwithstanding your sins, I can still "redeem" you from your bondage and dispersion. **dry up . . . sea**—(Exod. 14:21.) The second exodus shall exceed, while it resembles in wonders, the first (ch. 11:11, 15; 51:15). **make . . . rivers . . . wilderness**—turn the prosperity of Israel's foes into adversity. **fish stinketh**—the very judgment inflicted on their Egyptian enemies at the first exodus (Exod. 7:18, 21). **3. heavens . . . blackness**—another of the judgments on Egypt to be repeated hereafter on the last enemy of God's people (Exod. 10:21). **sackcloth**—(Rev. 6:12).

4. Messiah, as "the servant of Jehovah" (ch. 42:1), declares that the office has been assigned to Him of encouraging the "weary" exiles of Israel by "words in season" suited to their case; and that, whatever suffering it is to cost Himself, He does not shrink from it (vss. 5, 6), for that He knows His cause will triumph at last (vss. 7, 8). **learned**—not in mere human learning, but in divinely taught modes of instruction and eloquence (ch. 49:

ADAM CLARKE

CHAPTER 50

1. *Thus saith the Lord*. This chapter has been understood of the prophet himself; but it certainly speaks more clearly about Jesus of Nazareth than of Isaiah, the son of Amoz. *Where is the bill?*—"Where is this bill?" Husbands, through moroseness or levity of temper, often sent bills of divorcement to their wives on slight occasions, as they were permitted to do by the law of Moses, Deut. xxiv. 1. And fathers, being oppressed with debt, often sold their children, which they might do for a time, till the year of release, Exod. xxi. 7. That this was frequently practiced appears from many passages of Scripture, and that the persons and the liberty of the children were answerable for the debts of the father. The widow, 2 Kings iv. 1, complains that "the creditor is come to take unto him my two sons to be bondmen." And in the parable, Matt. xviii. 25: The lord, forasmuch as his servant "had not to pay, . . . commanded him to be sold, and his wife, and children, and all that he had, and payment to be made." But this, saith God, cannot be My case; I am not governed by any such motives, neither am I urged by any such necessity. Your captivity therefore and your afflictions are to be imputed to yourselves, and to your own folly and wickedness.

2. *Their fish stinketh*—"Their fish is dried up."

MATTHEW HENRY

xi. 28. See what is the best learning of a minister, to know how to comfort troubled consciences, and to speak properly, and plainly, to the various cases of poor souls. An ability to do this is God's gift. 2. The ear of the learned, to receive instruction. Prophets have as much need of this as of the tongue of the learned; for they must hear the word from God's mouth attentively, that they may speak it exactly, Ezek. iii. 17. None must undertake to be teachers who have not first been learners. Christ's apostles were first disciples. Those that would hear as the learned must be awake, for we are naturally drowsy and hear by halves and do not heed. We need to be awakened *morning by morning*. The morning, when our spirits are most lively, is a proper time for communion with God. The people came *early in the morning* to hear Christ in the temple (Luke xxi. 38), for, it seems, his were morning lectures.

II. As a patient sufferer, *v.* 5, 6. One who is commissioned to speak comfort to the weary has hard work to do and hard usage to undergo. *My ear hast thou opened; then said I, Lo, I come; I was not rebellious, neither turned away back.* Though he foresaw difficulty and discouragement, though he was to give constant attendance as a servant, though he was to humble himself to that which was very mean, yet he did not fly off, did not fail, nor was discouraged. In submission he resigned himself. *I gave my back to the smiters; I gave my cheeks to those that* not only smote them, but *plucked off the hair* of the beard, which was a greater degree both of pain and of ignominy. *I hid not my face from shame and spitting.* All this Christ underwent for us, and voluntarily, to convince us of his willingness to save us.

III. As a courageous champion, *v.* 7–9. The Redeemer is as famous for his boldness as for his humility and patience, and, though he yields, yet he is more than a conqueror. What was the prophet Isaiah's support was the support of Christ himself (*v.* 7): *The Lord God will help me;* and again, *v.* 9. God, having laid help upon his Son for us, gave help to him, and his hand was all along *with the man of his right hand. He is near that justifieth me.* Isaiah, no doubt, was loaded with reproach and calumny, as other prophets were; but he despised the reproach, knowing that God would roll it away and bring forth his righteousness as the light, perhaps in this world (Ps. xxxvii. 6), at furthest in the great day, when there will be a resurrection of names as well as bodies, and the righteous shall shine forth as the morning sun. "If God will help me, if he will justify me, will stand by me and bear me out, *I shall not be confounded. I know that I shall not be ashamed.*" In this confidence he bids defiance to all opposers and opposition: God will help me, and *therefore have I set my face like a flint.* The prophet was bold in reproving sin, in warning sinners (Ezek. iii. 8, 9), and in asserting the truth of his predictions. Christ went on in his work, as Mediator, with unshaken constancy and undaunted resolution. *Who will contend with me,* either in law or by the sword? *Let us stand together,* as combatants, or as the plaintiff and defendant. Many offered to dispute with Christ, but he put them to silence. The prophet speaks this in the name of all faithful ministers; those who keep close to the pure word of God, in delivering their message, need not fear contradiction. *Great is the truth and will prevail.* Christ speaks this in the name of all believers, speaks it as their champion. *Who is he that shall condemn me?* The prophet perhaps was condemned to die; Christ we are sure was; and yet both could say, *Who is he that shall condemn?* For there is no condemnation to those whom God justifies. The righteous cause of Christ and his prophets shall outlive all opposition. The *moth shall eat them up* silently and insensibly; a little thing will serve to destroy them.

Verses 10–11

The prophet, having the tongue of the learned, here makes use of it. It is the summary of the gospel. *He that believes shall be saved,* though for a while he walk in darkness, but *he that believes not,* though for a while he walk in the light of his own fire, yet he shall lie down in sorrow.

I. Comfort is here spoken to disconsolate saints, and they are encouraged to trust in God's grace, *v.* 10. A child of God is one that fears the Lord with a filial fear, that stands in awe of his majesty and is afraid of incurring his displeasure. He is one that obeys the voice of God's servant, is willing to be ruled by the Lord Jesus in the great work of man's redemption. Those that truly fear God will obey the voice of Christ. It is no new thing for the children and heirs of light sometimes to walk in darkness, and for a time not to have any glimpse or gleam of light. He that is thus in the dark, *Let him trust in the name*

JAMIESON, FAUSSET, BROWN

2; Exod. 4:11; Matt. 7:28, 29; 13:54). **speak a word in season**–(Prov. 15:23; 25:11.) Lit., "to succor by words," viz., in their season of need, the "weary" dispersed ones of Israel (Deut. 28:65-67). Also, the spiritual "weary" (ch. 42:3; Matt. 11:28).

wakeneth [me] morning . . .–Cf. "daily rising up early" (Jer. 7:25; Mark 1:35). The image is drawn from a master *wakening* his pupils early for instruction. **wakeneth . . . ear**–prepares me for receiving His divine instructions. **as the learned**–as one taught by Him. He "learned obedience," experimentally, "by the things which He suffered"; thus gaining that practical learning which *adapted* Him for "speaking a word in season" to suffering men (Heb. 5:8). **5. opened . . . ear**–(see *Note,* ch. 42:20; 48:8); i.e., hath made me *obediently attentive* (but MAURER, "hath *informed me of my duty"),* as a *servant* to his master (cf. Ps. 40:6-8, with Phil. 2:7; ch. 42:1; 49:3, 6; 52:13; 53:11; Matt. 20:28; Luke 22:27). **not rebellious**–but, on the contrary, most willing to do the Father's will in proclaiming and procuring salvation for man, at the cost of His own sufferings (Heb. 10:5-10). **6. smiters**–with scourges and with the open hand (ch. 52:14; Mark 14:65). Literally fulfilled (Matt. 27:26; 26:27; Luke 18:33). To "pluck the hair" is the highest insult that can be offered an Oriental (II Samuel 10:4; Lam. 3:30). "I gave" implies the voluntary nature of His sufferings; His example corresponds to His precept (Matt. 5: 39). **spitting**–To spit in another's presence is an insult in the East, much more on one; most of all in the face (Job 30:10; Matt. 27:30; Luke 18:32). **7.** Sample of His not being "discouraged" (ch. 42:4; 49:5). **set . . . face like . . . flint**–set Myself resolutely, not to be daunted from My work of love by shame or suffering (Ezek. 3:8, 9). **8.** (Ch. 49:4.) The believer, by virtue of his oneness with Christ, uses the same language (Ps. 138:8; Rom. 8:32-34). But "justify" in *His* case, is God's judicial acceptance and vindication of Him on the ground of *His own* righteousness (Luke 23:44-47; Rom. 1:4; I Tim. 3:16, with which cf. I Pet. 3:18); in *their* case, on the ground of His righteousness and meritorious death *imputed* to them (Rom. 5:19). **stand together**–in judgment, to try the issue. **adversary**–lit., "master of my cause," i.e., who has real ground of accusation against me, so that he can demand judgment to be given in his favor (cf. Zech. 3:1, etc.; Rev. 12:10).

9. (Cf. ch. 52:13, *Margin;* ch. 53:10; Ps. 118:6; Jer. 23:5). **as a garment**–(Ch. 51:6, 8; Ps. 102:26.) A leading constituent of wealth in the East is change of raiment, which is always liable to the inroads of the moth; hence the frequency of the image in Scripture.

10. Messiah exhorts the godly after His example (ch. 49:4, 5; 42:4) when in circumstances of trial ("darkness," ch. 47:5), to trust in the arm of Jehovah alone. **Who is . . .**–i.e., Whosoever (Judg. 7:3). **obeyeth . . . servant**–viz., Messiah. The godly "honor the Son, even as they honor the Father" (John 5:23). **darkness**–(Mic. 7:8, 9.) God never had a son who was not sometimes in the dark. For even Christ, His only Son, cried out, "My God, My God, why hast Thou forsaken Me?" **light**–rather, splendor; bright sunshine; for the servant of God is never wholly without "light" [VITRINGA]. A godly man's way may be dark, but his end shall be peace and light. A wicked man's way may be bright, but his end shall be utter darkness (Ps. 112:4; 97:11; 37:24). **let him trust . . .**–as Messiah did (vss. 8, 9).

ADAM CLARKE

5. *Neither turned away back*—"Neither did I withdraw myself backward."

6. *And my cheeks to them that plucked off the hair.* The greatest indignity that could possibly be offered. *I hid not my face from shame and spitting.* Another instance of the utmost contempt and detestation. It was ordered by the law of Moses as a severe punishment, carrying with it a lasting disgrace, Deut. xxv. 9. Among the Medes it was highly offensive to spit in anyone's presence, Herod. i. 99; and so likewise among the Persians, Xenophon, *Cyrop.* lib. i., p. 18. But in this place it certainly means spitting in the face. So it is understood in St. Luke, where our Lord plainly refers to this prophecy: "All things that are written by the prophets concerning the Son of man shall be accomplished. For he shall be delivered unto the Gentiles, and shall be mocked, and spitefully entreated, and spitted on," xviii. 31-32, which was in fact fulfilled: "And some began to spit on him," Mark xiv. 65; xv. 19. If spitting in a person's presence was such an indignity, how much more spitting in His face?

7. *Therefore have I set my face like a flint.* The Prophet Ezekiel, chap. ii. 8-9, has expressed this with great force in his bold and vehement manner.

10. *Who is among you that feareth the Lord?* I believe this passage has been generally, if not dangerously, misunderstood. It has been quoted, and preached upon, to prove that "a man might conscientiously fear God, and be obedient to the words of the law and the prophets; obey the voice of His Servant—of Jesus Christ himself—that is, be sincerely and regularly obedient to the moral law and the commands of our blessed Lord, and yet walk in darkness and have no light, no sense of God's approbation, and no evidence of the safety of his state." This is utterly impossible; for Jesus hath said, "He that followeth me shall not walk in darkness, but shall have the light of life." Bishop Lowth's translation has set the whole in the clearest light. The text contains two questions, to each of which a particular answer is given: "Q. 1. Who is there among you that feareth Jehovah? Ans. Let him hearken unto the voice of his servant. Q. 2. Who that walketh in darkness and hath no light? Ans. Let him trust in the name of Jehovah; And lean himself (prop himself) upon his God."

That obeyeth the voice of his servant—"Let him hearken unto the voice of His servant."

MATTHEW HENRY

of the Lord, in the goodness of his nature, his wisdom, power, and goodness. *The name of the Lord is a strong tower.* If he walk before God, which a man may do though he walk in the dark, he shall find God all-sufficient to him. Let him keep hold of his covenant-relation to God, and call God *his God*, as Christ on the cross, *My God, My God.*

II. Presuming sinners are warned not to trust in themselves, *v.* 11. They *kindle a fire*, and *walk in the light of that fire*. They depend upon their own righteousness, and burn their incense, with that fire (as Nadab and Abihu) and not with the fire from heaven. They *compass themselves about with sparks of their own kindling*. As they trust in their own righteousness, and not in the righteousness of Christ, so they place their happiness in their worldly possessions and enjoyments, and not in the favour of God. Creature-comforts are as sparks, short-lived and soon gone. They are ironically told to *walk in the light of their own fire*. Those that make the world their comfort, and their own righteousness their confidence, will meet with bitterness in the end. A godly man's way may be melancholy, but his end shall be peace and everlasting light. A wicked man's way may be pleasant, but his end will be darkness.

JAMIESON, FAUSSET, BROWN

11. In contrast to the godly (vs. 10), the wicked, in times of darkness, instead of trusting in God, trust in themselves (*kindle a light* for themselves to walk by) (Eccles. 11:9). The image is continued from vs. 10, "darkness"; human devices for salvation (ch. 19:21; 16:9, 25) are like the spark that goes out in an instant in darkness (cf. Job 18:6; 21:17, with Ps. 18: 28). **sparks**—not a steady light, but blazing sparks extinguished in a moment. **walk**—not a command, but implying that *as surely as they would do so*, they should lie down in sorrow (Jer. 3:25). In exact proportion to mystic Babylon's previous "glorifying" of herself shall be her sorrow (Matt. 25:30; 8:12; Rev. 18:7).

ADAM CLARKE

11. *Ye that kindle a fire.* The fire of their own kindling, by the light of which they walk with security and satisfaction, is an image designed to express, in general, human devices and mere worldly policy, exclusive of faith, and trust in God. *That compass yourselves about with sparks*—"Who heap the fuel round about." Without faith, repentance, or a holy life, they are bold in their professed confidence in God—presumptuous in their trust in the mercy of God; and, while destitute of all preparation for and right to the kingdom of Heaven, would think it criminal to doubt their final salvation! Living in this way, what can they have at the hand of God but an endless bed of sorrow! *Ye shall lie down in sorrow.*

MATTHEW HENRY — CHAPTER 51

Verses 1–3

The people of God are such as *follow after righteousness*, those *that seek the Lord*, for it is only in the way of righteousness that we can seek him with any hope of finding him. They are here directed to look back to their original, and the smallness of their beginning: "*Look unto the rock whence you were hewn*" (the idolatrous family in Ur of the Chaldees, out of which Abraham was taken, the generation of slaves which the heads and fathers of their tribes were in Egypt); "look unto *the hole of the pit out of which you were digged*, as clay, when God formed you into a people." How hard was that rock out of which we were hewn, unapt to receive impressions, and how miserable *the hole of that pit out of which we were digged!* The consideration of this should fill us with low thoughts of ourselves and high thoughts of divine grace. "*Look unto Abraham your father*, the father of all the faithful, of all that follow after the righteousness of faith as he did (Rom. iv. 11), *and unto Sarah that bore you*, and whose daughters you all are as long as you do well. Think how Abraham was *called alone*, and yet was *blessed* and *multiplied*; and let that encourage you to depend upon the promise of God. "Look unto Abraham, and see what he got by trusting in the promise of God, and take example by him to follow God with an implicit faith." They are here assured that their present tears should at length end in joys, *v.* 3. God will find out a time and way to *comfort Zion*. It is the greatest comfort of the church to be made serviceable to the glory of God, and to be as his garden in which he delights. He will make them cheerful, and give them hearts to rejoice. With the *fruits of righteousness, joy and gladness shall be found therein;* for the more holiness men have, and the more good they do, the more gladness they have.

Verses 4–8

The perpetuity of God's righteousness and his salvation.

I. This comfort belongs to "*My people*, and *my nation*, that I have set apart for myself, that own me and are owned by me." They are a people who *know righteousness*, and are able to form a right judgment of truth and falsehood, good and evil. And, as they have good heads, so they have good hearts, for they have the law of God in them. Even those who know righteousness, and have the law of God in their hearts, may yet be in great distress and loaded with reproach and contempt; but their God will comfort them.

II. The comfort that belongs to God's people. 1. The gospel of Christ shall be preached to the world: *A law shall proceed from me*, an evangelical law, the law of Christ, the law of faith, *ch.* ii. 3. This is that law of liberty by which the world shall be governed. It shall take deep root in the world, not only for the benefit of the Jews, but *for a light of the people* of other nations. 2. This law shall open a ready way to the children of men, that they may be justified and saved, *v.* 5. There is no salvation without righteousness; and, wherever there is the *righteousness of God*, there shall be his salvation. 3. This righteousness and salvation shall shortly appear: *My righteousness is near*. It is near in time and in place, Rom. x. 8. 4. This evangelical righteousness and salvation shall not be confined to the Jewish nation, but shall be

JAMIESON, FAUSSET, BROWN — CHAPTER 51

Vss. 1-23. Encouragement to the Faithful Remnant of Israel to Trust in God for Deliverance, Both from Their Long Babylonian Exile, and from Their Present Dispersion. **1. me**—the God of your fathers. **ye . . . follow after righteousness**—the godly portion of the nation; vs. 7 shows this (Prov. 15:9; I Tim. 6:11). "Ye follow righteousness," seek it therefore from Me, who "bring it near," and that a righteousness "not about to be abolished" (vss. 6, 7); look to Abraham, your father (vs. 2), as a sample of how righteousness before Me is to be obtained; I, the same God who blessed him, will bless you at last (vs. 3); therefore trust in Me, and fear not man's opposition (vss. 7, 8, 12, 13). The mistake of the Jews, heretofore, has been, not in that they "followed after righteousness," but in that they followed it "by the works of the law," instead of "by faith," as Abraham did (Rom. 9:31, 32; 10:3, 4; 4:2-5). **hole of . . . pit**—The idea is not, as it is often quoted, the inculcation of humility, by reminding men of the fallen state from which they have been taken, but that as Abraham, the *quarry*, as it were (cf. ch. 48: 1), whence their nation was hewn, had been called out of a strange land to the inheritance of Canaan, and blessed by God, the same God is able to deliver and restore them also (cf. Matt. 3:9). **2. alone**—translate, "I called him when he was but one" (Ezek. 33:24). The argument is: the same God who had so blessed "one" individual, as to become a mighty nation (Gen. 12:1; 22:7), can also increase and bless the small remnant of Israel, both that left in the Babylonish captivity, and that left in the present and latter days (Zech. 14:2; "the residue" (ch. 13:8, 9). **3. For**—See for the argument, last *Note*. **the garden of the Lord**—restoration of the primeval paradise (Gen. 2:8; Ezek. 28:13; Rev. 2:7). **melody**—*Hebrew*, "psalm." God's praises shall again be heard.

4. my people—the Jews. This reading is better than that of Gesenius: "O peoples . . . nations," viz., the Gentiles. The Jews are called on to hear and rejoice in the extension of the true religion to the nations; for, at the first preaching of the Gospel, as in the final age to come, it was *from Jerusalem* that the gospel law was, and is, to go forth (ch. 2:3).

law . . . judgment—the gospel dispensation and institutions (ch. 42:1, "judgment"). **make . . . to rest**—establish firmly; found. **light . . .**—(Ch. 42:6).

5. righteousness . . . near—i.e., faithful fulfilment of the promised deliverance, answering to "salvation" in the parallel clause (ch. 46:13; 56:1; Rom. 10:8, 9). Ye follow after "righteousness"; seek it therefore, from Me, and you will not have far to go for it (vs. 1).

ADAM CLARKE — CHAPTER 51

1. *Ye that follow after righteousness.* The people who, feeling the want of salvation, seek the Lord in order to be justified.

The rock. Abraham. *The hole of the pit.* Sarah; as explained in v. 2.

2. *I called him alone.* As I have made out of one a great nation, so, although you are brought low, yet I can restore you to happiness, and greatly multiply your number.

4. *My people . . . O my nation*—"O ye peoples . . . O ye nations." The difference is very material; for in this case the address is made, not to the Jews, but to the Gentiles, as in all reason it ought to be; for this and the two following verses express the call of the Gentiles, the islands, or the distant lands on the coasts of the Mediterranean and other seas.

A law shall proceed from me. The new law, the gospel of our Lord Jesus.

5. *My righteousness is near.* The word *tsedek*, "righteousness," is used in such a great latitude of signification, for justice, truth, faithfulness, goodness, mercy, deliverance, salvation, that it is not easy sometimes to give the precise meaning of it without much circumlocution. It means

MATTHEW HENRY

extended to the Gentiles: *My arms shall judge the people.* Those that will not yield to the judgments of God's mouth shall be crushed by the judgments of his hand. Some shall thus be judged by the gospel, but others, and those of *the isles, shall wait upon him,* and bid his gospel, the commands as well as the comforts of it, welcome. It was a comfort to God's people, that multitudes should be added to them. It is added, *And on my arm shall they trust,* that *arm of the Lord* which is revealed in Christ, *ch.* liii. 1. 5. This righteousness and salvation *shall be for ever, v.* 8. As it shall spread through all the nations of the earth, so it shall last through all the ages of the world. The visible heavens above shall *vanish like smoke*; they shall be rolled like a scroll. The earth shall *wax old like a garment.* But when *heaven and earth pass away,* when all flesh and the glory of it wither as grass, the *word of the Lord endures for ever.* Those whose happiness is bound up in Christ's righteousness and salvation will have the comfort of it when time and days shall be no more.

III. If God's righteousness and salvation are near to them, then let them *not fear the reproach of men,* nor be *afraid of their revilings,* who bid you sing them the songs of Zion, or who ask you, in scorn, *Where is now your God?* Those can bear but little for Christ that cannot bear a hard word for him. Let us not fear the reproach of men. They will be quickly silenced (*v.* 8): *The moth shall eat them up like a garment, ch.* l. 9. *The worm shall eat them like wool,* or woollen cloth. The falsehood of their reproaches will be detected, but truth shall triumph. Clouds darken the sun, but give no obstruction to his progress.

Verses 9–16

I. A prayer that God would appear and act for the deliverance of his people. *Awake, awake! put on strength, O arm of the Lord! v.* 9. The arm of the Lord is Christ, or it is put for God himself, as Ps. xliv. 23. The arm of the Lord is said to awake when on his people's behalf it is stretched forth for action. God needs not to be reminded nor excited by us, but he gives us leave to be humbly earnest for such appearances of his power as will be for his own praise. The church sees her case bad, her enemies many and mighty, her friends few and feeble; and therefore she depends purely upon the strength of God's arm for her relief.

II. The pleas to enforce this prayer. 1. They plead precedents, their ancestors, and the great things God had done for them. "Let the arm of the Lord be made bare on our behalf. It did wonders against the Egyptians; it *cut Rahab* to pieces with one direful plague after another, *and wounded* Pharaoh, *the dragon.* It did wonders for Israel. *It dried up the sea,* to open *a way for the ransomed to pass over,*" *v.* 10. Past experiences are good pleas in prayer. *Thou hast; wilt thou not?* Ps. lxxxv. 1–6. 2. They plead promises (*v.* 11): *And the redeemed of the Lord shall return,* that is (as it may be supplied), *thou hast said, They shall,* referring to *ch.* xxxv. 10. Sinners, when they are brought out of the slavery of sin into the glorious liberty of God's children, may come singing, as a bird got loose out of the cage. The souls of believers, when they are delivered out of the prison of the body, come to the heavenly Zion with singing. He that designs such joy for us at last will he not work such deliverances for us in the meantime as our case requires?

III. The answer immediately given to this prayer (*v.* 12): *I, even I, am he that comforteth you.* They prayed for the operations of his power; he answers them with the consolations of his grace, which may well be accepted as an equivalent. If God do not answer immediately *with the saving strength of his right hand,* we must be thankful if he answer us, as an angel himself was answered (Zech. i. 13) *with good words and comfortable words.* See how God resolves to comfort his people: He takes the work into his own hands: *I, even I,* will do it.

1. He comforts the timorous by chiding them: *Why art thou cast down, and why disquieted? v.* 12, 13.

(1) The absurdity of those fears. It is a disparagement to us to give way to them: *Who art thou, that thou shouldst be afraid?* It is absurd to be in such dread of a dying man. What! *afraid of a man that shall die, who shall be made as grass,* shall wither and be trodden down or eaten up? We ought to look upon every man as a man that shall die. Those we fear we must look upon as frail and mortal, and consider what a foolish thing it is for the servants of the living God to be afraid of dying men, that are here today and gone tomorrow. It is absurd to *fear continually every day* (*v.* 13). Now and then a danger may be imminent and threatening, and it may be prudent to fear it; but to be always in a toss, and to tremble at the shaking of every leaf, is to make our-

JAMIESON, FAUSSET, BROWN

arms—put for Himself; *I by My might.* **judge**—(Ch. 2:3, 4; Ps. 98:9.) **isles . . .**—(Ch. 60:9.)

arm—(Rom. 1:16), "the power of God unto (the Gentiles as well as the Jews) salvation." **6.** (Ch. 40:6, 8; Ps. 102:26; Heb. 1:11, 12.) **vanish away**—lit., "shall be torn asunder," as a *garment* [MAURER]; which accords with the context. **in like manner**—But GESENIUS, "Like a gnat"; like the smallest and vilest insect. JEROME translates, as *English Version,* and infers that "in like manner" as man, the heavens (i.e., the sky) and earth are not to be annihilated, but changed for the better (ch. 65:17). **righteousness**—My faithfully fulfilled promise (*Note,* vs. 5). **7. know righteousness**—(*Note,* vs. 1).

8. (*Note,* ch. 50:9; Job 4:18-20.) Not that the *moth eats men up,* but they shall be destroyed by as insignificant instrumentality as the moth that eats a garment.

9. Impassioned prayer of the exiled Jews. **ancient days**—(Ps. 44:1). **Rahab**—poetical name for Egypt (*Note,* ch. 30:7). **dragon**—*Hebrew, tannin.* The crocodile, an emblem of Egypt, as represented on coins struck after the conquest of Egypt by Augustus; or rather here, its king, Pharaoh (*Note,* ch. 27:1; Ps. 74:13, 14; Ezek. 32:2, *Margin;* 29:3). **10. it**—the arm. Art not Thou the same Almighty power that . . . ? **dried the sea**—the Red Sea (ch. 43:16; Exod. 14:21). **11.** (Ch. 35:10.) **Therefore**—assurance of faith; or else the answer of Jehovah corresponding to their prayer. As surely as God redeemed Israel out of Egypt, He shall redeem them from Babylon, both the literal in the age following, and mystical in the last ages (Rev. 18:20, 21). There shall be a second exodus (ch. 11:11-16; 27:12, 13). **singing**—image from the custom of singing on a journey when a caravan is passing along the extended plains in the East. **everlasting joy**—(Jude 24.) **sorrow . . . flee away**—(Rev. 21:4.) **12. comforteth**—(vs. 3; ch. 40:1.)

thou—Zion. **son of man**—frail and dying as his *parent Adam.* **be made as grass**—wither as grass (ch. 40:6, 7).

13. (Ch. 40:12, 26, 28), the same argument of comfort drawn from the omnipotence of the Creator. **as if . . . ready . . .**—lit., "when he directs," viz., his arrow, to destroy (Ps. 21:12; 7:13; 11:2) [MAURER].

ADAM CLARKE

here the faithful completion of God's promises to deliver His people.

F. B. MEYER:

"I, even I, am he that comforteth you" (Isa. 51:12).

It is related that in the great Indian Mutiny, when some hundreds of English ladies with their children were shut up in the Residency at Lucknow, and threatened by an immense crowd of rebels, a leaf of the Bible, stained with blood, and used as a common piece of wrapping, was brought in to them, and proved to contain these words. It reminded them of God their Maker; and bade them fear no more the fury of the oppressor, or the failure of bread, because the Lord God was at hand to neutralize the tumult and fury of their foes.

In the Lord our Maker we have the only antidote for alarm and sorrow. At this time the cross had not been erected with its precious revelation of the love of God; and the prophet quotes two of the greatest proofs of God's might—the miracle of Creation, with its overarching heavens and deep-laid foundations of the earth; and that of the deliverance from Egypt.

Go out into nature, behold the might of God written on his glorious works, and then say to yourself, This God is my Father; and He would rather sacrifice worlds of matter, than forget or forsake his child. It were easier for Him to destroy all that He has made, and recreate it in a moment of time, than allow one of his weakest children that trusts in Him to be overwhelmed by trouble. Then go forth and stand at the cross, and remember that it was for you. Surely He who went to so great expenditure to purchase you from the power of hell, will not let you perish before the malice of man. Furious men are but the foam of the breaker which your Deliverer will put aside. The sea may roar, but it cannot overwhelm.

—*Great Verses Through the Bible*

MATTHEW HENRY

selves all our lifetime *subject to bondage* (Heb. ii. 15). It is absurd to fear beyond what there is cause: "Thou art *afraid of the fury of the oppressor. Where is the fury of the oppressor?* It is gone in an instant, and the danger is over ere thou art aware." *Pharaoh king of Egypt is but a noise*, and the king of Babylon no more. What has become of all the furious oppressors of God's Israel, that were a terror to them? they passed away, and, lo, they were not; and so shall these.

(2) The impiety of those fears: "Thou art *afraid of a man that shall die, and forgettest the Lord thy Maker*, who is also the Maker of all the world." Our inordinate fear of man is a tacit forgetfulness of God. When we disquiet ourselves with the fear of man we forget that there is a God above him. We forget the experiences we have had of his care, and his interposition for our relief many a time, when we thought the oppressor ready to destroy; we forget our Jehovah-jirehs, monuments of mercy in the mount of the Lord.

2. He comforts those that were in bonds, *v.* 14, 15. *The captive exile hastens that he may be loosed* and may return to his own country, from which he is banished; his care is *that he may not die in the pit* (not die a prisoner), and that *his bread should not fail.* Now some understand this as his fault. He is impatient of delays, cannot wait God's time, but thinks he must die in the pit if he be not released immediately. Others take it to be his praise, that when the doors are thrown open he does not linger. And then it follows, *But I am the Lord thy God*, which intimates God will do for them that which they cannot do for themselves. He will find out a way to still the threatening storm, and bring them safely into the harbour. *The Lord of hosts is his name*, the name by which his people have long known him.

3. He comforts all his people who depended upon what the prophets said to them in the name of the Lord. When the deliverances which the prophets spoke of either did not come soon or did not come up to their expectation they began to be cast down; but are encouraged (*v.* 16) by what God says to his messenger, as he does here, *I have put my words in thy mouth, that by* them *I may plant the heavens.* God undertook to comfort his people (*v.* 12); but he does it by his prophets, by his gospel. He owns what they have said to be what he had enjoined them to say: "*I have put my words in thy mouth*, and therefore he that receives thee and them receives me." God's Spirit revealed to them the words they should speak (2 Pet. i. 21; 1 Cor. ii. 13). I have *covered thee in the shadow of my hand* (as before, *ch.* xlix. 2) speaks the special protection not only of the prophets, but of their prophecies, not only of Christ, but of Christianity, of the gospel of Christ. "*I have put my words in thy mouth*, not that by the performance of them I may plant a nation, or found a city, but *that I may plant the heavens and lay the foundations of the earth*, which will be a new creation." This must look far forward to the great work done by the gospel of Christ and the setting up of his holy religion in the world. As God by Christ made the world at first (Heb. i. 2), so by him he will set up a new world, will again plant the heavens and found the earth. Sin having put the whole creation into disorder, Christ's taking away the sin of the world put all into order again.

Verses 17–23

A call to awake not so much out of the sleep of sin (though that also is necessary in order to their being ready for deliverance) as out of the stupor of despair. When the inhabitants of Jerusalem were in captivity they were so overwhelmed with the sense of their troubles that they had no heart to mind anything that tended to their comfort.

I. Jerusalem had long been in the depths of misery.

1. She had lain under the tokens of God's displeasure. He had put into her hand *the cup of his fury*. She had provoked him to anger and was made to taste the bitter fruits of it. The cup of God's fury is, and will be, a *cup of trembling* to all those that have it put into their hands. It is said (Ps. lxxv. 8) that *the dregs of the cup, all the wicked of the earth shall wring them out, and drink them.* Wherever there has been a cup of fornication, as there had been in Jerusalem's hand when she was idolatrous, sooner or later there will be a cup of fury.

2. Those that should have helped her in her distress failed her, *v.* 18. She staggers, and is very unsteady. She knows not what she says or does, much less what to say or do, and, in this unhappy condition, *of all the sons that she has brought forth* and brought up, *there is none to guide her*, none to lend either a hand to help her out of her trouble or a tongue to comfort her under it. *These two things have come unto thee*

JAMIESON, FAUSSET, BROWN

JOHN GILL:

Verse 13. "And forgettest the Lord thy Maker." That he is your maker, and therefore is able to protect and preserve you; when the fear of man prevails God is forgotten, his power, his providence, his promises, and past instances of divine favor and goodness; were these more frequently recollected, considered and thought of, they would prove an antidote against the fear of men; and especially when it is observed, that he that is our Maker is he "that hath stretched forth the heavens, and laid the foundations of the earth"; these are amazing works of his hands; and what is it that he cannot do that has made these? these he upholds and maintains in being, and does all things in them as he pleases, and overrules all for his own glory and his people's good, and therefore they have nothing to fear from men; and yet they are afraid of them, such is their distrust and unbelief.
—*Gill's Commentary*

14. captive exile—lit., one *bowed down* as a captive (ch. 10:4) [MAURER]. The scene is primarily Babylon, and the time near the close of the captivity. Secondarily, and antitypically, the mystical Babylon, the last enemy of Israel and the Church, in which they have long suffered, but from which they are to be gloriously delivered. **pit**—such as were many of the ancient dungeons (cf. Jer. 38:6, 11, 13; Gen. 37:20). **nor . . . bread . . . fail**—(Ch. 33:16; Jer. 37:21.) **15. divided . . . sea**—the Red Sea. The same *Hebrew* word as "make to rest" (vs. 4). Rather, "that terrify the sea," i.e., restrain it by My rebuke, "when its waves roar" [GESENIUS]. The *Hebrew* favors MAURER, "that terrify the sea so that the waves roar." The sense favors GESENIUS (Jer. 5:22; 31:35), or *English Version* (vss. 9, 10, which favors the special reference to the exodus from Egypt). **16.** Addressed to Israel, embodied in "the servant of Jehovah" (ch. 42:1), Messiah, its ideal and representative Head, through whom the elect remnant is to be restored.

put my words in thy mouth—true of Israel, the depository of true religion, but fully realized only in Israel's Head and antitype, Messiah (ch. 49:2; 50:4, 5; 59:21; Deut. 18:18; John 3:34). **covered . . . in . . . shadow of . . . hand**—protected thee (*Note*, ch. 49:2). **plant**—rather, "fix" as a tabernacle; so it ought to be rendered (Dan. 11:45). The "new creation," now going on in the spiritual world by the Gospel (Eph. 2:10), and hereafter to be extended to the visible world, is meant (ch. 65:17; 66:22; cf. ch. 13:13; II Pet. 3:10-13). **Zion**—Its restoration is a leading part in the new creation to come (ch. 65:17, 19).

17. (Ch. 52:1.) **drunk**—Jehovah's wrath is compared to an intoxicating draught because it confounds the sufferer under it, and makes him fall (Job 21:20; Ps. 60:3; 75:8; Jer. 25:15, 16; 49:12; Zech. 12:2; Rev. 14:10); ("poured out without mixture"; rather, the pure wine juice mixed with intoxicating drugs). **of trembling**—which produced trembling or intoxication. **wrung . . . out**—drained the last drop out; the dregs were the sediments from various substances, as honey, dates, and drugs, put into the wine to increase the strength and sweetness. **18.** Following up the image in vs. 17, intoxicated and confused by the cup of God's anger, she has none to guide her in her helpless state; she has not yet awakened out of the sleep caused by that draught. This cannot apply to the Babylonish captivity; for in it they had Ezekiel and Daniel, Ezra and Nehemiah, as "guides," and soon awoke out of that sleep; but it applies to the Jews now, and will be still more applicable in their coming oppression by Antichrist.

ADAM CLARKE

14. *The captive exile hasteneth that he may be loosed*—"He marcheth on with speed, who cometh to set free the captive." Cyrus, if understood of the temporal redemption from the captivity of Babylon; in the spiritual sense, the Messiah, who comes to open the prison to them that are bound.

16. *That I may plant the heavens*—"To stretch out the heavens."

17. *The cup of trembling.* "The cup of mortal poison." This may also allude to the ancient custom of taking off criminals by a cup of poison. Socrates is well known to have been sentenced by the Areopagus to drink a cup of the juice of hemlock, which occasioned his death.

MATTHEW HENRY

(*v.* 19), to complete thy desolation and destruction, even *the famine and the sword*, by which the city was wasted and by which the citizens perished. These two things that had come upon Jerusalem are the same with the two things that were afterwards to come upon Babylon (*ch.* xlvii. 9), *loss of children and widowhood*—piteous case that calls for comfort; and yet, when thou art froward under thy trouble, *by whom shall I comfort thee?* Those who should have been her comforters were their own tormenters (*v.* 20): *They have fainted*, driven to despair; they have no patience in which to keep possession of their own souls, nor any confidence in God's promise. They throw themselves upon the ground, in vexation at their troubles, and there *they lie at the head of all the streets*. There they lie like *a wild bull in a net*, fretting and raging, struggling to help themselves, but making their condition the worse by their own passions and discontents. Those that are of a froward peevish spirit never enquire wherefore he contends with them, and therefore nothing appears in them but anger at God.

II. It is promised that Jerusalem's troubles shall at length come to an end, and be transferred to her persecutors (*v.* 21): *Nevertheless hear this, thou afflicted: "Thus saith thy Lord, the Lord, and thy God*—the Lord, who is able to help thee—thy God, in covenant with thee, and who has undertaken to make thee happy—he is the God *who pleads the cause of his people*, who takes what is done against them as done against himself." It is his own cause; he has espoused it, and therefore will plead it. "*I will take out of thy hand the cup of trembling*, that bitter cup; it shall pass from thee." It is promised, "*Thou shalt no more drink it again.*" Their persecutors and oppressors should be made to drink of the same bitter cup of which they had drunk so deeply, *v.* 23. Herein the New Testament Babylon treads in the steps of that old oppressor, tyrannizing over men's consciences, putting them upon the rack, and compelling them to sinful compliances. Babylon's case shall be as bad as ever Jerusalem's was. Daniel's persecutors shall be thrown into Daniel's den.

JAMIESON, FAUSSET, BROWN

19. two—classes of evils, for he enumerates *four*, viz., *desolation* and *destruction* to the land and state; *famine* and *the sword* to the people.

who shall be sorry for thee—so as to give thee effectual relief: as the parallel clause, "By whom shall I comfort thee?" shows (Lam. 2:11-13).

20. head of all . . . streets—(Lam. 2:19; 4:1). **wild bull**—rather, *oryx* [JEROME], or gazelle [GESENIUS], or wild goat [BOCHART]; commonly in the East taken in a net, of a wide sweep, into which the beasts were hunted together. The streets of cities in the East often have gates, which are closed at night; a person wishing to escape would be stopped by them and caught, as a wild animal in a net. **21. drunken . . . not with wine**—(ch. 29:9; cf. vss. 17, 20, here; Lam. 3:15).

22. pleadeth . . . cause—(Ps. 35:1; Jer. 50:34; Mic. 7:9).

no more drink it—(ch. 54:7-9).This cannot apply to Israel after the return from Babylon, but only to them after their final restoration. **23.** (Ch. 49:26; Jer. 25:15-29; Zech. 12:2.) **Bow down that . . . go over**—Conquerors often literally trod on the necks of conquered kings, as Sapor of Persia did to the Roman emperor Valerian (Josh. 10:24; Ps. 18:40; 66: 11, 12).

ADAM CLARKE

19. *These two things . . . desolation, and destruction, and the famine, and the sword.* That is, desolation by famine, and destruction by the sword, taking the terms alternately.

By whom shall I comfort thee?—"Who shall comfort thee?"

MATTHEW HENRY

CHAPTER 52

Verses 1–6

I. God's people are stirred up to appear vigorous for their own deliverance, *v.* 1, 2. Let them awake from their despondency, and pluck up their spirits, encourage themselves and one another. Let them awake from their distrust, look above them, look about them, look into the promises, look into the providences of God that were working for them, and let them raise their expectations of great things from God. Let them awake from their dullness. God here gives them an assurance, 1. That they should be reformed by their captivity: *There shall no more come into thee the uncircumcised and the unclean* (*v.* 1); their idolatrous customs should be no more introduced, or at least not harboured. Thus the gospel Jerusalem is purified by the blood of Christ and the grace of God, and made indeed a holy city. 2. That they should be rescued out of their captivity, that they should not be any more invaded: *There shall no more come against thee* (so it may be read) *the uncircumcised and the unclean*. If they keep close to God, and keep in with him, God will keep off, will keep out the enemy; but, if they again corrupt themselves, Antiochus will profane their temple and the Romans will destroy it. However, for some time they shall have peace. Let them prepare for joy: "*Put on thy beautiful garments*, no longer appear in mourning weeds. Put on a new face, a smiling countenance, now that a new and pleasant scene begins to open." Let them prepare for liberty: "*Shake thyself from the dust* into which thy proud oppressors have trodden thee (*ch.* li. 23), or into which thou hast in thy sorrow rolled thyself." *Arise, and set up*; so it may be read. "O Jerusalem! get clear of all the marks of servitude: *Loose thyself from the bands of thy neck*; assert thy own liberty." The gospel proclaims liberty to those who were bound with fears and makes it their duty to take hold of their liberty. Let those who have been weary and heavily laden under the burden of sin, finding relief in Christ, loose themselves from those bands; for, *if the Son make them free, they shall be free indeed.*

II. God stirs up himself for the deliverance of his people.

1. The Chaldeans who oppressed them never acknowledged God any more than Sennacherib did, *ch.* x. 6, 7. "*You have sold yourselves for nought;* you got nothing by it, nor did I," *v.* 3. The Babylonians gave him no thanks for them, but rather reproached and blasphemed his name upon that account. "And therefore they, having so long had you for nothing,

JAMIESON, FAUSSET, BROWN

CHAPTER 52

Vss. 1-15. VERSES 1-13 CONNECTED WITH CHAPTER 51. Zion long in bondage (ch. 51:17-20) is called to put on beautiful garments appropriate to its future prosperity.

the holy city—(Neh. 11:1; Rev. 21:2.) **no more . . . unclean**—(ch. 35:8; 60:21; Joel 3:17; Rev. 21:27). A prophecy never yet fulfilled. **uncircumcised**—spiritually (Ezek. 44:9; Acts 7:51).

1. strength—as thy adornment; answering to "beautiful garments" in the parallel clause. Arouse thyself from dejection and assume confidence.
2. from the dust—the seat of mourners (Job 2:12, 13). **arise, and sit**—viz., in a more dignified place: on a divan or a throne [LOWTH], after having shaken off the dust gathered up by the flowing dress when seated on the ground; or simply, "Arise, and sit erect" [MAURER]. **bands of . . . neck**—the yoke of thy captivity.

3. As you became your foes' servants, without their paying any price for you (Jer. 15:13), so they shall release you without demanding any price or reward (ch. 45:13), (where Cyrus is represented as doing so: a type of their final restoration gratuitously in like manner). So the spiritual Israel, "sold under sin," gratuitously (Rom. 7:14), shall be redeemed also gratuitously (ch. 55:1).

ADAM CLARKE

CHAPTER 52

2. *Sit down, O Jerusalem*—"Ascend thy lofty seat, O Jerusalem."

MATTHEW HENRY

shall at last restore you for nothing: *You shall be redeemed without price*," as was promised, *ch.* xlv. 13.

2. They had been often before in similar distress, and it was a pity that they should now be left in the hand of these oppressors (*v.* 4): "*My people went down into Egypt*, in an amicable way to settle there; but they enslaved them, and ruled them with rigour." And then they were delivered. Why may we not think God will deliver his people now? At other times *the Assyrian oppressed* the people of God *without cause*, as when the ten tribes were carried away captive by the king of Assyria; soon afterwards Sennacherib, another Assyrian, made himself master of all the defenced cities of Judah. The Babylonians might be called *Assyrians*, their monarchy being a branch of the Assyrians; and they now oppressed them without cause.

3. God's glory suffered by the injuries that were done to his people (*v.* 5): *What have I here*, what do I get by it, *that my people are taken away for nought?* The captives are so dispirited that they cannot praise him: *Those that rule over them make them to howl*, as the Egyptians of old made them to sigh, Exod. ii. 23. However God heard them, and came down to deliver them, as he did out of Egypt, Exod. iii. 7, 8. The natives, blaspheming, boasted that they were too hard for God because they were too hard for his people, and set him at defiance, as unable to deliver them. "Now," says God, "I will go down to deliver them; for their oppressors will neither praise God themselves nor let them do it."

4. His glory would be manifested by their deliverance (*v.* 6): "*Therefore*, because my name is thus blasphemed, I will arise, and *my people shall know my name*, my name Jehovah."

Verses 7–12

The removal of the Jews from Babylon, and the application of *v.* 7 to the preaching of the gospel (by the apostle, Rom. x. 15) plainly intimates that that deliverance was a type and figure of the redemption of mankind by Jesus Christ.

I. It is here spoken of as a great blessing, which ought to be welcomed with joy. 1. Those that bring the tidings of their release shall be very acceptable (*v.* 7), as they come over the mountains round about Jerusalem. It is meant of some of the Jews themselves, who immediately went themselves, or sent their own messengers, to Jerusalem itself, to tell the few who remained there that their brethren would be with them shortly; for it is published as a proof that Zion's God reigns, for they say unto Zion, *Thy God reigns.* This must be applied to the preaching of the gospel, which is a proclamation of peace and salvation; it is gospel indeed, good news of victory over our spiritual enemies and liberty from our spiritual bondage. The good news is that the Lord Jesus reigns. Christ himself brought these tidings first (Luke iv. 18, Heb. ii. 3), and of him the text speaks: *How beautiful are his feet!* his feet that were nailed to the cross, how beautiful upon Mount Calvary! 2. Zion's watchmen shall rejoice, *v.* 8. The watchmen (*ch.* lxii. 6) were such as God set on the walls of Jerusalem, to make mention of his name, and to continue instant in prayer to him, till he again *made Jerusalem a praise in the earth.* They stand upon their watch-tower, waiting for an answer to their prayers (Hab. ii. 1); and therefore when the good news comes they have it first. They shall *lift up the voice, with the voice together shall they sing*, to invite others to join with them in their praises. They shall see an exact agreement between the prophecy and the event, the promise and the performance; they shall see how they look one upon another eye to eye, and be satisfied that the same God spoke the one and did the other. Applying this also, as the foregoing verse, to gospel times, it is a promise of the pouring out of the Spirit upon gospel ministers, as a spirit of wisdom and revelation, to lead them into all truth, so that they shall see eye to eye, and be unanimous in these great things concerning the common salvation. Zion's waste places shall then rejoice because they shall be surprisingly comforted (*v.* 9): *Break forth into joy, sing together, you waste places of Jerusalem.* The redemption of Jerusalem is the joy of all God's people, Luke ii. 38. God will have the glory of it, *v.* 10. He *has made bare his holy arm* (manifested and displayed his power) *in the eyes of all the nations.*

II. When the liberty is proclaimed, let the people of God hasten out of Babylon with all convenient speed: *Depart, depart* (*v.* 11), *go out from the midst of her;* be gone. Babylon is no place for Israelites, Ezra i. 5. And it is a call to all those who are yet in the bondage of sin and Satan to make use of the liberty which Christ has proclaimed to them. Let them take heed of carrying away with them any of the

JAMIESON, FAUSSET, BROWN

4. My people—Jacob and his sons. **went down**—Judea was an elevated country compared with Egypt. **sojourn**—They went there to stay only till the famine in Canaan should have ceased. **Assyrian**—Sennacherib. Remember how I delivered you from Egypt and the Assyrian; what, then, is to prevent Me from delivering you out of Babylon (and the mystical Babylon and the Antichrist in the last days)? **without cause**—answering to "for naught" in vs. 5; it was an act of *gratuitous* oppression in the present case, as in that case.

5. what have I here—i.e., what am I called on to do? The fact "that My people is taken away (into captivity; ch. 49:24, 25) for naught" (by *gratuitous* oppression, vs. 4; also vs. 3, where see *Note*) demands My interposition. **they that rule**—or "tyrannize", viz., Babylon, literal and mystical. **make ... to howl**—or, raise a cry of exultation over them [MAURER]. **blasphemed**—viz., in Babylon: God's reason for delivering His people, not their goodness, but for the sake of His holy name (Ezek. 20:9, 14).

6. shall know in that day—when Christ shall reveal Himself to Israel sensibly; the only means whereby their obstinate unbelief shall be overcome (Ps. 102:16; Zech. 12:10; 14:5).

7. beautiful ... feet—i.e., The *advent* of such a herald seen on the distant "mountains" (*Notes*, ch. 40:9; 41:27; 25:6, 7; Song of Sol. 2:17) *running in haste* with the long-expected good tidings, is most grateful to the desolated city (Nah. 1:15). **good tidings**—only partially applying to the return from Babylon. Fully, and antitypically, the Gospel (Luke 2:10, 11), "beginning at Jerusalem" (Luke 24:17), "the city of the great King" (Matt. 5:35), where Messiah shall, at the final restoration of Israel, "reign" as peculiarly Zion's God ("*Thy* God reigneth"; cf. Ps. 2:6). **8. watchmen**—set on towers separated by intervals to give the earliest notice of the approach of any messenger with tidings (cf. ch. 21:6-8). The *Hebrew* is more forcible than *English Version*, "The voice of thy watchmen" (exclamatory as in Song of Sol. 2:8). "They lift up their voice! together they sing." **eye to eye**—i.e., close at hand, and so clearly [GESENIUS]; Numbers 14:14, "face to face"; Numbers 12:8, "mouth to mouth." Cf. I Corinthians 13:12; Revelation 22:4, of which Simeon's sight of the Saviour was a prefiguration (Luke 2:30). The watchmen, spiritually, are ministers and others who pray for the peace of Jerusalem (ch. 62:6, 7), **bring again**—i.e., restore. Or else, "return to" [MAURER]. **9.** (Ch. 14:7, 8; 42:11.) **redeemed**—spiritually and nationally (ch. 48:20). **10. made bare ... arm**—metaphor from warriors who bare their arm for battle (Ezek. 4:7). **all ... earth ... see ... salvation of ... God**—The deliverance wrought by God for Israel will cause all nations to acknowledge the Lord (ch. 66:18-20). The partial fulfilment (Luke 3:6) is a forerunner of the future complete fulfilment. **11.** (Ch. 48:20; Zech. 2:6, 7.) Long residence in Babylon made many loath to leave it: so as to mystical Babylon (Rev. 18:4). **ye ... that bear ... vessels of the Lord**—the priests and Levites, whose office it was to carry the vessels of the temple (Jer. 27:18). Nebuchadnezzar had carried them to Babylon (II Chron. 36:18). Cyrus restored them (Ezra 1:7-11). **be ... clean**—by separating yourselves wholly from Babylonian idolaters, mystical and literal.

ADAM CLARKE

5. *They that rule over them*—"They that are lords over them." *Make them to howl*—"Make their boast of it."

6. *I am he that doth speak*—"I am he, Jehovah, that promised."

7. *How beautiful!* The watchmen discover afar off, on the mountains, the messenger bringing the expected and much-wished-for news of the deliverance from the Babylonish captivity. They immediately spread the joyful tidings, v. 8, and with a loud voice proclaim that Jehovah is returning to Zion, to resume His residence on His holy mountain, which for some time He seemed to have deserted. This is the literal sense of the place. "How beautiful on the mountains are the feet of the joyful messenger!" is an expression highly poetical. For how welcome is his arrival! how agreeable are the tidings which he brings! Nahum, chap. i. 15, who is generally supposed to have lived after Isaiah, has manifestly taken from him this very pleasing image. St. Paul has applied this passage to the preaching of the gospel, Rom. x. 15.

8. *Thy watchmen shall lift up the voice*—"All your watchmen lift up their voices." *They shall see eye to eye.* May not this be applied to the prophets and apostles; the one predicting, and the other discovering in the prediction the truth of the prophecy? The meaning of both Testaments is best understood by bringing them face-to-face. *When the Lord shall bring again Zion*—"When Jehovah returneth to Zion." God is considered as having deserted His people during the Captivity; and at the restoration, as returning himself with them to Zion, His former habitation.

9. *He hath redeemed Jerusalem*—"He hath redeemed Israel."

MATTHEW HENRY

pollutions of Babylon: *Touch no unclean thing.* Let them depend upon the presence of God with them and his protection in their removal (*v.* 12): *You shall not go out with haste.* They were to go with a diligent haste, but not with a diffident distrustful haste, as if they were afraid of being pursued. Cyrus shall give them an honourable discharge, and they shall have an honourable return, and not steal away; *for the Lord will go before them.* God will both lead their van and bring up their rear.

Verses 13–15

This prophecy, which begins here and is continued to the end of the next chapter, points as plainly as can be at Jesus Christ; the ancient Jews understood it of the Messiah, though some will have it understood of Jeremiah. But Philip has put it past dispute that *of him speaks the prophet this,* of him and of no other man, Acts viii. 34, 35.

CHARLES H. SPURGEON:

Too many who aspire to be leaders of the people study policy, craft, and diplomacy, and think it needful to use language as much for the concealment as for the declaration of their thoughts; such men watch their own words till their very soul seems withered within them. The Friend of sinners had not a fraction of that thing about Him; and yet He was wiser and more prudent than if diplomacy had been His study from His youth up. You see His wisdom when He baffles his adversaries; they think to entangle Him in His speech, but He breaks their snares asunder as with a wave of our hand we sweep cobwebs from our path. You see His wisdom when He deals with His friends: He has many things to say unto them, but He perceives that they cannot bear them; He, therefore, does not overload their intellects, lest undigested truth should breed mischief in their souls. Little by little, like the increasing brightness of the dawn, He lets light into their souls, lest their eyes should utterly fail before the brilliance thereof. He does not send them upon difficult errands at first; He reserves for their riper years and stronger days the sterner tasks and more heroic deeds of daring. As we see His career in the light of the four evangelists, it is distinguished for His prudence, and in that respect "never man spake like this Man." *—The Treasury of the Old Testament*

I. God owns Christ to be commissioned for his undertaking. He is appointed to it. "He is *my servant,* whom I employ and therefore will uphold." In his undertaking he does his Father's will, seeks his Father's honour, and serves the interests of his Father's kingdom. He *shall deal prudently,* for the *spirit of wisdom and understanding shall rest upon him, ch.* xi. 2.

II. He gives a short prospect both of his humiliation and his exaltation. *Many were astonished at him* by reason of his sorrows. *His visage was marred more than any man's* when he was buffeted, smitten on the cheek, and crowned with thorns, and *hid not his face from shame and spitting.* He was *a man of sorrows. Never was sorrow like unto his sorrow.* How highly God exalted him, and exalted him because he humbled himself! Three words are used for this (*v.* 13): *He shall be exalted and extolled and be very high.* God shall exalt him, men shall extol him, and with both he shall be higher than the highest, higher than the heavens. Many nations shall be the better for him, for *he shall sprinkle them;* the blood of sprinkling shall be applied to their consciences, to purify them, for in his death there was *a fountain opened,* Zech. xiii. 1. He shall do it by baptism. So that this promise had its accomplishment when Christ sent

JAMIESON, FAUSSET, BROWN

12. not . . . with haste— as when ye left Egypt (Exod. 12:33, 39; Deut. 16:3; cf. *Note,* ch. 28:16). Ye shall have time to cleanse yourselves and make deliberate preparation for departure. **Lord**—Jehovah, as your Leader in front (ch. 40:3; Exod. 23:20; Mic. 2:13). **rereward**—lit., "gather up," i.e., to bring up the rear of your host. The transition is frequent from the glory of Messiah in His advent to reign, to His humiliation in His advent to suffer. Indeed, so are both advents accounted one, that He is not said, in His second coming, to be about to *return,* but to *come.* **13.** Here ch. 53 ought to begin, and ch. 52 end with vs. 12. This section, from here to end of ch. 53 settles the controversy with the Jews, if Messiah be the person meant; and with infidels, if written by Isaiah, or at any time before Christ. The correspondence with the life and death of Jesus Christ is so minute, that it could not have resulted from conjecture or accident. An impostor could not have shaped *the course of events* so as to have made his character and life appear to be a fulfilment of it. The writing is, moreover, *declaredly prophetic.* The quotations of it in the New Testament show: (1) that it was, before the time of Jesus, a recognized part of the Old Testament; (2) that it refers to Messiah (Matt. 8:17; Mark 15:28; Luke 22:37; John 12:38; Acts 8:28-35; Rom. 10:16; I Peter 2:21-25). The indirect allusions to it still more clearly prove the Messianic interpretation; so universal was that interpretation, that it is simply *referred to* in connection with the atoning virtue of His death, without being formally quoted (Mark 9:12; Rom. 4:25; I Cor. 15:3; II Cor. 5:21; I Pet. 1:19; 2:21-25; I John 3:5). The genuineness of the passage is certain; for the Jews *would* not have forged it, since it is opposed to *their* notion of Messiah, as a triumphant temporal prince. The Christians *could* not have forged it; for the Jews, the enemies of Christianity, are "our librarians" [PALEY]. The Jews try to evade its force by the figment of two Messiahs, one a suffering Messiah (Ben Joseph), the other a triumphant Messiah (Ben David). **HILLEL** maintained that Messiah has already come in the person of Hezekiah. **BUXTORF** states that many of the modern Rabbins believe that He has been come a good while, but will not manifest Himself because of the sins of the Jews. But the ancient Jews, as the Chaldee paraphrast, Jonathan, refer it to Messiah; so the *Medrasch Tauchuma* (a commentary on the Pentateuch); also Rabbi Moses Haddarschan (see **HENGSTENBERG,** *Christol.*). Some explain it of *the Jewish people,* either in the Babylonish exile, or in their present sufferings and dispersion. Others, the *pious* portion of the nation taken collectively, whose sufferings made a vicarious satisfaction for the ungodly. Others, Isaiah, or Jeremiah [GESENIUS], the *prophets collectively.* But an *individual* is plainly described: he suffers *voluntarily, innocently,* patiently, and as the efficient cause of the righteousness of His people, which holds good of none other but Messiah (ch. 53:4-6, 9, 11; contrast Jeremiah 20:7; 15:10-21; Psalm 137:8, 9). Ch. 53:9 can hold good of none other. The objection that the sufferings (ch. 53:1-10) referred to are represented as *past,* the glorification alone as future (ch. 52:13-15; 53:11, 12) arises from not seeing that the prophet takes his stand *in the midst* of the scenes which he describes as future. The greater nearness of the first advent, and the interval between it and the second, are implied by the use of the *past tense* as to the first, the *future* as to the second. **Behold**—awakening attention to the striking picture of Messiah that follows (cf. John 19:5, 14). **my servant**—Messiah (ch. 42:1). **deal prudently**—rather, "prosper" [GESENIUS] as the parallel clause favors (ch. 53:10). Or, uniting both meanings, "shall reign well" [HENGSTENBERG]. This verse sets forth in the beginning the ultimate issue of His sufferings, the description of which follows: the conclusion (ch. 53:12) corresponds; the section (ch. 52:13; 53:12) begins as it ends with His final glory. **extolled**—elevated (Mark 16:19; Eph. 1:20-22; I Pet. 3:22). **14, 15.** Summary of Messiah's history, which is set forth more in detail in ch. 53. "Just as many were astonished (accompanied with *aversion,* Jer. 18:16; 19:8), etc.; his visage, etc.; so shall He sprinkle," etc.; Israel in this answers to its antitype Messiah, now "an *astonishment* and byword" (Deut. 28:37), hereafter about to be a blessing and means of salvation to many nations (ch. 2:2, 3; Mic. 5:7). **thee; his**—Such changes of persons are common in *Hebrew* poetry. **marred**—*Hebrew,* "disfigurement"; abstract for concrete; not only disfigured, but *disfigurement itself.* **more than man**--CASTELIO translates, "so that it was no longer that of a man" (cf. Ps. 22:6). The more perfect we may suppose the "body prepared" (Heb.

ADAM CLARKE

CHARLES H. SPURGEON:

The character of our Lord's dealings. He is called in the text, "My Servant," a title as honorable as it is condescending. The Lord Jesus has undertaken in infinite love to become the Servant of the Father for our sakes, and He is a servant like unto Moses, who was set over the Lord's house to manage the affairs of the dispensation. Jesus, though a Son and therefore Lord, has deigned to become the Great Servant of God under the present economy; He conducts the affairs of the household of God, and it is said in the text, and it is to that we have to draw attention, that "He deals prudently." He who took upon Him the form of a servant acts as a wise servant in everything; and indeed it could not be otherwise, for "in him are hid all the treasures of wisdom and knowledge." This prudence was manifest in the days of His flesh, from His childhood among the doctors in the temple on to His confession before Pontius Pilate. Our Lord was enthusiastic; there was a fire burning within Him which nothing could quench, He found His meat and drink in doing His Father's will; but that enthusiasm never carried Him into rashness, or forgetfulness of sound reason; He was as wise and prudent as the most cold-hearted calculator could have been. Our Savior was full of love, and that love made Him frank and open-hearted; no frigid reserve kept Him at a distance from the people, or shrouded Him in a cloud of mystery, He was a man among men, transparent, childlike, "the Holy Child Jesus"; but for all that He was ever prudent, and "committed himself unto no man, for he knew what was in man."

—The Treasury of the Old Testament

13. *My servant shall deal prudently. Yaskil,* "shall prosper" or "act prosperously." The subject of Isaiah's prophecy from the fortieth chapter inclusive, has hitherto been, in general, the deliverance of the people of God. This includes in it three distinct parts which, however, have a close connection with one another: (1) The deliverance of the Jews from the captivity of Babylon; (2) The deliverance of the Gentiles from their miserable state of ignorance and idolatry; and (3) The deliverance of mankind from the captivity of sin and death. Cyrus is expressly named as the immediate agent of God in effecting the first deliverance. A greater Person is spoken of as the Agent who is to effect the latter two deliverances, called the *servant,* the elect, of God, in whom His soul delighteth; Israel, in whom God will be glorified. Babylon has hitherto been kept pretty much in sight, at the same time that strong intimations of something much greater have frequently been thrown in. But here Babylon is at once dropped, and I think hardly ever comes in sight again, unless perhaps in chap. lv. 12 and lvii. 14. The prophet's views are almost wholly engrossed by the superior part of his subject. He introduces the Messiah as appearing at first in the lowest state of humiliation, which he had just touched upon before (chap. i. 5-6), and obviates the offense which would be occasioned by it by declaring the important and necessary cause of it, and foreshowing the glory which should follow it.

14. *As many were astonied at thee*—"As many were astonished at Him."

MATTHEW HENRY

his apostles to disciple all nations, by baptizing or sprinkling them. *Kings shall shut their mouths at him*, that is, they shall not open their mouths against him, as they have done. They shall with great humility and reverence receive his oracles and laws.

That which had not been told them shall they see; the gospel brings to light things which will awaken the reverence of kings and kingdoms. They shall see and consider the glory of God shining in the face of Christ, which before they had not been told of—*they had not heard*. Christ disappointed the expectations of those who looked for a Messiah according to their fancies, as the carnal Jews, but outdid theirs who looked for such a Messiah as was promised.

JAMIESON, FAUSSET, BROWN

10:5) for Him by God, the sadder by contrast was the "marring" of His visage and form. **15. sprinkle many**—GESENIUS, for the antithesis to "be astonished," translates, "shall cause . . . to exult." But the word universally in the Old Testament means either *to sprinkle with blood*, as the high priest makes an expiation (Lev. 4:6; 16:18, 19); or *with water*, to purify (Ezek. 36:25; cf. as to the Spirit, Acts 2:33), both appropriate to Messiah (John 13:8; Heb. 9:13, 14; 10:22; 12:24; I Pet. 1:2). The antithesis is sufficient without any forced rendering. *Many* were astonished; so *many* (not merely men, but) *nations* shall be sprinkled. They were amazed at such an *abject person claiming to be Messiah*; yet it is He who shall *justify and purify*. Men were *dumb with the amazement of scorn* at one marred more than the lowest of men, yet the *highest:* even *kings* (ch. 49:7, 23) shall be *dumb with awe and veneration* ("shut . . . mouths"; Job 29:9, 10; Mic. 7: 16). **that . . . not . . . told them**—the reason why kings shall so venerate them; the wonders of redemption, which had not been before told them, shall then be announced to them, wonders such as they had never heard or seen parallelled (ch. 55:1; Rom. 15: 21; 16:25, 26).

ADAM CLARKE

15. *For that which had not been told them.* The mystery of the gospel so long concealed. See Rom. xv. 21; xvi. 25. *Shall they see.* With the eyes of their faith. *And that which they had not heard.* The redemption of the world by Jesus Christ; the conversion of the Gentiles, and making them one flock with the converted Jews.

MATTHEW HENRY

CHAPTER 53

Verses 1–3

The prophet, in the close of the former chapter, had foreseen and foretold the kind reception which the gospel of Christ should find among the Gentiles. Now here he foretells, with wonder, the unbelief of the Jews, notwithstanding the previous notices they had of the coming of the Messiah.

I. The contempt they put upon the gospel of Christ, *v.* 1. And it is applied likewise to the little success which the apostles' preaching met with among Jews and Gentiles, Rom. x. 16. Few believed the prophets who spoke before of Christ; when he came himself none of the rulers nor of the Pharisees followed him, and but here and there one of the common people; and, when the apostles carried this report all the world over, some in every place believed, but comparatively very few. To this day, of the many that profess to believe this report, there are few that cordially embrace it and submit to the power of it. They do not discern that divine power which goes along with the word, that working of the Spirit which makes the word effectual. They believe not the gospel because, by rebelling against the light they had, they had forfeited the grace of God.

II. The contempt they put upon the person of Christ because of the meanness of his appearance, *v.* 2, 3.

1. The low condition he submitted to, and how he abased and emptied himself. The entry he made into the world, and the character he wore in it, were no way agreeable to the ideas which the Jews had formed of the Messiah. It was expected that his extraction would be very great and noble. He was to be the Son of David, but he sprang out of this royal and illustrious family when it was reduced and sunk, and Joseph was but a poor carpenter. This is here meant by his being *a root out of a dry ground*, his being born of a mean and despicable family, in the north, in Galilee, of a family out of which, like a dry and desert ground, nothing green, nothing great, was expected, in a country of such small repute that it was thought no good thing could come out of it. It was expected that he should make a public entry, and come in pomp and with observation; but, instead of that, he grew up before God, not before men. *He grew up as a tender plant*, silently and insensibly, as the corn grows up, *we know not how*, Mark iv. 27. It was expected that he should have some uncommon beauty in his face and person, which should charm the eye, attract the heart, and raise the expectations of all that saw him. But there was nothing of this kind in him; not that he was deformed or misshapen, but *he had no form nor comeliness*, nothing extraordinary, which one might have thought to meet in an incarnate deity. Moses, when he was born, was exceedingly fair, to such a degree that it was looked upon as a happy presage, Acts, vii. 20; Heb. xi. 23. David, when he was anointed, was *of a beautiful countenance, and goodly to look to*, 1 Sam. xvi. 12. But the appearing of our Lord Jesus in the world had nothing in it of sensible glory. His gospel is preached, *not with the enticing words of man's wisdom*, but with all plainness. It was expected that he should live a pleasant life, which would have invited all sorts to him; but, on the contrary, he was *a man of sorrows and acquainted with grief*. His condition was, upon many accounts, sorrowful. He was unsettled, had not where to lay his head, lived upon alms,

JAMIESON, FAUSSET, BROWN

CHAPTER 53

Vss. 1-12. MAN'S UNBELIEF: MESSIAH'S VICARIOUS SUFFERINGS, AND FINAL TRIUMPH FOR MAN. The speaker, according to HORSLEY, personates the repenting Jews in the latter ages of the world coming over to the faith of the Redeemer; the whole is their penitent confession. This view suits the context (ch. 52:7-9), which is not to be fully realized until Israel is restored. However, primarily, it is the abrupt exclamation of the prophet: "Who hath believed our report," that of Isaiah and the other prophets, as to Messiah? The infidel's objection from the unbelief of the Jews is anticipated and hereby answered: that unbelief and the cause of it (Messiah's humiliation, whereas *they* looked for One coming to reign) were foreseen and foretold. **1. report**—lit., "the thing heard," referring to which sense Paul says, "So, then, faith cometh by *hearing*" (Rom. 10:16, 17). **arm**—power (ch. 40:10; exercised in miracles and in saving men (Rom. 1:16; I Cor. 1:18). The prophet, as if present during Messiah's ministry on earth, is deeply moved to see *how few believed* on Him (ch. 49:4; Mark 6:6; 9:19; Acts 1:15). *Two* reasons are given why all *ought* to have believed: (1) The "report" of the "ancient prophets." (2) "The arm of Jehovah" exhibited in Messiah while on earth. In HORSLEY'S view, this will be the penitent confession of the Jews, "How few of our nation, in Messiah's days, believed in Him!"

2. tender plant—Messiah grew silently and insensibly, as a sucker from an ancient stock, seemingly dead (viz., the house of David, then in a decayed state) (*Note*, ch. 11:1). **shall grow . . . hath**—rather, "grew up . . . had." **before him**—before Jehovah. Though unknown to the world (John 1:11), Messiah was observed *by God*, who ordered the most minute circumstances attending His growth. **root**—i.e., sprout from a root. **form**—beautiful form: sorrow had marred His once beautiful form. **and when we shall see**—rather, joined with the previous words, "Nor comeliness (attractiveness) *that we should look* (with delight) on Him." **there is**—rather, "was." The studied reticence of the New Testament as to His form, stature, color, etc., was designed to prevent our dwelling on the bodily, rather than on His moral beauty, holiness, love, etc., also a providential protest against the making and veneration of images of Him. The letter of P. LENTULUS to the emperor Tiberius, describing His person, is spurious; so also the story of His sending His portrait to Abgar, king of Edessa; and the alleged impression of His countenance on the handkerchief of Veronica. The former part of this verse refers to His birth and childhood; the latter to His first public appearance [VITRINGA]. **3. rejected**—"*forsaken* of men" [GESENIUS]. "Most abject of men." Lit., "He who *ceases* from men," i.e., is no longer regarded as a man [HENGSTENBERG]. (*Note*, ch. 52:14; 49:7.) **man of sorrows**—i.e., whose distinguishing characteristic was sorrows. **acquainted with**—familiar by constant contact with. **grief**—lit., "disease"; fig. for all kinds of *calamity* (Jer. 6:14); *leprosy* especially represented this, being a direct judgment from God. It is remarkable Jesus is not mentioned as having ever suffered under sickness.

ADAM CLARKE

CHAPTER 53

That this chapter speaks of none but Jesus must be evident to every unprejudiced reader who has ever heard the history of His sufferings and death. The Jews have endeavored to apply it to their sufferings in captivity; but, alas for their cause! they can make nothing out in this way. Allowing that it belongs to our blessed Lord, then who can read verses 4, 5, 6, 8, 10, without being convinced that His death was a vicarious sacrifice for the sins of mankind?

2. *He hath no form nor comeliness.* "He hath no form, nor any beauty, that we should regard Him; nor is His countenance such that we should desire Him."—Symmachus; the only one of the ancients that has translated it rightly.

MATTHEW HENRY

was opposed and menaced, and *endured the contradiction of sinners against himself.* His spirit was tender, and he admitted the impressions of sorrow. Grief was his intimate acquaintance; for he acquainted himself with the griefs of others, and sympathized with them.

2. The low opinion that men had of him, upon this account. There was in him the beauty of holiness and the beauty of goodness, enough to render him *the desire of all nations*; but the greater part of those among whom he lived, saw none of this beauty, for it was spiritually discerned. He was rejected as a bad man. *We hid as it were our faces from him.* It may be read, *He hid as it were his face from us,* concealed the glory of his majesty, and drew a veil over it, and therefore *he was despised and we esteemed him not,* because we could not see through that veil.

Verses 4–9

I. A further account of the sufferings of Christ. More is said here of the condition to which he humbled himself, to which he became obedient even to the death of the cross. 1. He had griefs and sorrows. He bore them, and blamed not his lot; he did neither shrink from them, nor sink under them, but persevered to the end, till he said, *It is finished.* 2. He had blows and bruises; he was *stricken, smitten, and afflicted.* All along he was smitten with the tongue, when he was contradicted, put under the worst of characters, and had all manner of evil said against him. At last he was smitten with the hand, with blow after blow. 3. He was scourged, not under the merciful restriction of the Jewish law, which allowed not above forty stripes to be given to the worst of malefactors, but according to the usage of the Romans. Pilate intended it as an equivalent for his crucifixion, and yet it proved a preface to it. He was wounded in his hands, and feet, and side.

(2) Our sins are our sorrows and our griefs (*v.* 4), or, as it may be read, *our sicknesses and our wounds.*

(3) Our Lord Jesus was appointed and did undertake to make satisfaction for our sins. For *the Lord has laid on him the iniquity of us all.* The laying of our sins upon Christ implies the taking of them off from us; we shall not fall under the curse of the law if we submit to the grace of the gospel. They were laid upon Christ when he was *made sin* (that is, a sin-offering) *for us.* Thus he put himself into a capacity to make those easy that come to him heavily laden under the burden of sin. See Ps. xl. 6–12. None but God had power to lay our sins upon Christ, both because the sin was committed against him, and because Christ was his own Son, who himself knew no sin. It was *the iniquity of us all* that was laid on Christ; for in Christ there is a sufficiency of merit for the salvation of all, and a serious offer made of that salvation to all, which excludes none that do not exclude themselves. God laid upon him our iniquity; but did he consent to it? Yes, he did; for some think that the true reading of the next words (*v.* 7) is, *It was exacted, and he answered.*

(4) Having undertaken our debt, he underwent the penalty. *He bore our griefs and carried our sorrows, v.* 4. Christ bore our sins, and so *bore our griefs,* bore them off us, that we should never be pressed above measure. *He was wounded for our transgressions.* Our sins were the thorns in his head, the nails in his hands and feet, the spear in his side. *He was bruised,* or crushed, *for our iniquities;* they were the procuring cause of his death. To the same purport is *v.* 8, *for the transgression of my people was he smitten, the stroke* was *upon him* that should have been upon us.

(5) The consequence of this to us is our peace and healing, *v.* 5. *The chastisement of our peace was upon him. He is our peace,* Eph. ii. 14. Christ was in pain that we might be at ease, knowing that through him our sins are forgiven us. Hereby we have healing; for *by his stripes we are healed.* Sin is not only a crime, for which we were condemned to die, but it is a disease, which tends directly to the death of our souls and for which Christ provided the cure. By his stripes he purchased for us the Spirit and grace of God to mortify our corruptions, which are the distempers of our souls, and to put our souls in a good state of health, that they may be fit to serve God. The dominion of sin is broken in us and we are fortified against that which feeds the disease.

(6) The consequence of this to Christ was his resurrection, for, being *delivered for our offences,* he was *raised again for our justification.* He rose *to die no more; death had no more dominion over him.* He that *was dead is alive,* and *lives for evermore.*

3. It was for our good, and in our stead, that Jesus Christ suffered. This is asserted here plainly and fully.

(1) It is certain that we are all guilty before God.

JAMIESON, FAUSSET, BROWN

and we hid . . . faces—rather, *as one* who *causes* men *to hide* their faces from Him (in aversion) [MAURER]. Or, "He was as an hiding of the face before it," i.e., as a thing before which a man covers his face in disgust [HENGSTENBERG]. Or, "as one before whom is the covering of the face"; before whom one covers the face in disgust [GESENIUS]. **we**—the prophet identifying himself with the Jews. See HORSLEY'S view (*Note,* vs. 1). **esteemed . . . not**—*negative* contempt; the previous words express *positive.* **4. Surely . . . our griefs**—lit., *"But yet* He hath *taken* (or *borne*) our *sicknesses,"* i.e., they who despised Him because of His human infirmities ought rather to have esteemed Him on account of them; for thereby "Himself *took* OUR *infirmities"* (bodily diseases). So Matthew 8:17 quotes it. In the *Hebrew* for "borne," or *took,* there is probably the double notion, He *took on Himself* vicariously (so vss. 5, 6, 8, 12), and so He *took away;* His perfect humanity whereby He was bodily afflicted *for us,* and *in all our afflictions* (ch. 63:9; Heb. 4:15) was the ground on which He cured the sick; so that Matthew's quotation is not a mere *accommodation.* See *Note* 42 of Archbishop MAGEE, *Atonement.* The *Hebrew* there may mean to *overwhelm with darkness;* Messiah's time of darkness was temporary (Matt. 27:45), answering to the *bruising of His heel;* Satan's is to be eternal, answering to the *bruising of his head* (cf. ch. 50:10). **carried . . . sorrows**—The notion of *substitution* strictly. "Carried," viz., as a burden. "Sorrows," i.e., pains of the *mind;* as "griefs" refer to pains of the *body* (Ps. 32:10; 38:17). Matthew 8:17 might seem to oppose this: "And bare our *sicknesses."* But he uses "sicknesses" figuratively for *sins,* the cause of them. Christ took on Himself all man's "infirmities," so as to remove them; the bodily by direct miracle, grounded on His participation in human infirmities; those of the soul by His vicarious suffering, which did away with the *source* of both. Sin and sickness are ethically connected as cause and effect (ch. 33:24; Ps. 103:3; Matt. 9:2; John 5:14; Jas. 5:15). **we did esteem him stricken**—judicially [LOWTH], viz., for *His* sins; whereas it was for *ours.* "We thought Him to be a leper" [JEROME, VULGATE], leprosy being the direct divine judgment for guilt (Lev. 13; Num. 12:10, 15; II Chron. 26:18-21). **smitten**—by divine judgments. **afflicted**—for His sins; this was the point in which they so erred (Luke 23:34; Acts 3:17; I Cor. 2:8). He was, it is true, "afflicted," but not for *His* sins. **5. wounded**—a bodily wound; not mere mental sorrow; lit., "pierced"; minutely appropriate to Messiah, whose hands, feet, and side were pierced (Ps. 22:16). *Margin,* wrongly, from a *Hebrew* root, translates, "tormented." **for . . . for**—(Rom. 4:25; II Cor. 5:21; Heb. 9:28; I Pet. 2:24; 3:18)—*the cause for which* He suffered not His own, but *our* sins. **bruised**—crushing inward and outward suffering (*Note,* vs. 10). **chastisement**—lit., the correction inflicted by a *parent on children* for their good (Heb. 12:5-8, 10, 11). Not *punishment* strictly; for this can have place only where there is guilt, which He had not; but He took *on Himself the chastisement whereby the peace* (reconciliation with our Father; Rom. 5:1; Eph. 2:14, 15, 17) *of the children of God was to be effected* (Heb. 2:14). **upon him**—as a burden; parallel to "hath borne" and "carried." **stripes**—minutely prophetical of His being *scourged* (Matt. 27:26; I Pet. 2:24). **healed**—spiritually (Ps. 41:4; Jer. 8:22). **6.** Penitent confession of believers and of Israel in the last days (Zech. 12:10). **sheep . . . astray**—(Ps. 119:176; I Pet. 2:25). The antithesis is, "In ourselves we were scattered; in Christ we are collected together; by nature we wander, driven headlong to destruction; in Christ we find the way to the gate of life" [CALVIN]. True, also, literally of Israel before its coming restoration (Ezek. 34:5, 6; Zech. 10:2, 6; cf. with Ezek. 34:23, 24; Jer. 23:4, 5; also Matt. 9:36). **laid**—*"hath made to light* on Him" [LOWTH]. Rather, "hath made to rush upon Him" [MAURER]. **the iniquity**—i.e., its *penalty;* or rather, as in II Corinthians 5:21; He was not merely a *sin offering* (which would destroy the antithesis to "righteousness"), but, "sin for us"; sin itself vicariously; the representative of *the aggregate sin* of all mankind; not *sins* in the *plural,* for the "sin" of the world is *one* (Rom. 5:16, 17); thus we are made not merely *righteous,* but *righteousness,* even "the righteousness *of God."* The innocent was punished *as if* guilty, that the guilty might be rewarded *as if* innocent. This verse could be said of no mere *martyr.* **7. oppressed**—LOWTH translates, "It was *exacted,* and He was made answerable." The verb means, "to have payment of a debt sternly exacted" (Deut. 15:2, 3), and so *to be oppressed* in general; the *exaction* of the full penalty for our sins in His suffer-

ADAM CLARKE

3. *We hid as it were our faces from him*—"As one that hideth his face from us." Mourners covered up the lower part of their faces, and their heads, 2 Sam. xv. 30; Ezek. xxix. 17; and lepers were commanded by the law, Lev. xii. 45, to cover the upper lip.

4. *Surely he hath borne our griefs*—"Surely our infirmities He hath borne." *And carried our sorrows*—"And our sorrows, He hath carried them."

CHARLES H. SPURGEON:

"With His stripes"—that is, the stripes of the Lord Jesus—"we are healed." Through the sufferings of our Lord, sin is pardoned, and we are delivered from the power of evil: this is regarded as the healing of a deadly malady. The Lord in this present life treats sin as a disease. If He were to treat it at once as sin, and summon us to His bar to answer for it, we should at once sink beyond the reach of hope, for we could not answer His accusation, nor defend ourselves from His justice. In great mercy He looks upon us with pity, and for the while treats our ill manners as if they were diseases to be cured rather than rebellions to be punished. It is most gracious on His part to do so; for while sin is a disease, it is a great deal more. If our iniquities were the result of an unavoidable sickness, we might claim pity rather than censure; but we sin wilfully, we choose evil, we transgress in heart, and therefore we bear a moral responsibility, which makes sin an infinite evil. Our sin is our crime rather than our calamity: however, God looks at it in another way for a season. That He may be able to deal with us on hopeful grounds, He looks at the sickness of sin, and not, as yet, at the wickedness of sin. Nor is this without reason, for men who indulge in gross vices are often charitably judged by their fellows to be not only wholly wicked, but partly mad. Propensities to evil are usually associated with a greater or less degree of mental disease; perhaps, also, of physical disease. At any rate, sin is a spiritual malady of the worst kind.

—The Treasury of the Old Testament

5. *The chastisement of our peace*—"The chastisement by which our peace is effected," that by which we are brought into a state of peace and favor with God.

MATTHEW HENRY

We have all sinned, and have come short of the glory of God (*v.* 6): *All we like sheep have gone astray.* Every particular person stands charged with many actual transgressions. We have gone astray like sheep, which are apt to wander, and are unapt to find the way home again. That is our true character; we are bent to backslide from God, but altogether unable of ourselves to return to him. We turn aside everyone to his own way, and thereby set up our own will, in competition with God and his will, which is the malignity of sin.

2. Though he was *oppressed and afflicted*, yet he *opened not his mouth* (*v.* 7), no, not so much as to plead his own innocency, but freely offered himself to suffer and die for us. This takes away the scandal of the cross, that he voluntarily submitted to it, for great and holy ends. By his wisdom he could have evaded the sentence, and by his power have resisted the execution; but *thus it was written, and thus it behoved him to suffer. This commandment he received from his Father*, and therefore he was led *as a lamb to the slaughter.* As *a sheep is dumb before the shearers*, nay, before the butchers, so he *opened not his mouth*, which denotes his cheerful compliance with his Father's will. By this will we are sanctified, his making his own soul, his own life, an offering for our sin. 4. He was wronged and abused (*v.* 7): *He was oppressed*, but our Lord Jesus kept possession of his own soul. 5. He was *taken from prison and judgment*, *v.* 8. He was proceeded against as a malefactor; he was apprehended and taken into custody, and made a prisoner; he was judged, accused, tried, and condemned. 6. He was *cut off* by an untimely death *from the land of the living.*

He made his grave *with the wicked* (for he was crucified between two thieves, as if he had been the worst of the three) and yet *with the rich*, for he was buried in a sepulchre that belonged to Joseph, an honourable counsellor.

II. An account of the meaning of his sufferings. It is natural to ask with amazement, "How came it about? What evil had he done?" His enemies *esteemed him stricken, smitten of God, and afflicted*, *v.* 4. Because they hated him, and persecuted him, they thought that God did. It is true he was *smitten of God*, *v.* 10 (or, as some read it, *he was God's smitten and afflicted*, the Son of God, though smitten and afflicted), but not in the sense in which they meant it.

1. He never did anything in the least to deserve this hard usage. Whereas he was charged with perverting the nation, and sowing sedition, it was utterly false; he had *done no violence*, but went about doing good. And, whereas he was called *that deceiver, there was no deceit in his mouth* (*v.* 9), compare 1 Pet. ii. 22. He never offended either in word or deed. The judge that condemned him owned he found no fault in him, and the centurion that executed him professed that certainly he was a righteous man.

Verses 10–12

In the foregoing verses the prophet had testified of the sufferings of Christ; here he foretells the glory that should follow.

I. The services and sufferings of Christ's state of humiliation. Come, and see how he loved us, see what he did for us.

1. He submitted to the frowns of Heaven (*v.* 10): *Yet it pleased the Lord to bruise him, to put him to grief.* Men esteemed him smitten of God for some very great sin of his own (*v.* 4); now it was true that he was smitten of God, but it was for our sin.

JAMIESON, FAUSSET, BROWN

ings is probably alluded to. **and . . . afflicted**–or, *and yet He suffered*, or *bore Himself patiently*, etc. [HENGSTENBERG and MAURER]. LOWTH'S translation, "He was made answerable," is hardly admitted by the *Hebrew*. **opened not . . . mouth**–Jeremiah 11:19; and David in Psalms 38:13, 14; 39: 9, prefiguring Messiah (Matt. 26:63; 27:12, 14; I Pet. 2:23). **8.** Rather, "He was taken away (i.e., cut off) by oppression and by a judicial sentence"; a hendiadys for, "by an oppressive judicial sentence" [LOWTH and HENGSTENBERG]. GESENIUS not so well, "He was delivered from oppression and punishment" only by death. *English Version* also translates, "from . . . from," not "by . . . by." But "prison" is not true of Jesus, who was not *incarcerated;* restraint and *bonds* (John 18:24) more accord with the *Hebrew*. Acts 8:33; translate as LXX: "In His humiliation His judgment (legal trial) was taken away"; the virtual sense of the *Hebrew* as rendered by LOWTH and sanctioned by the inspired writer of Acts; He was treated as one so mean that a fair trial was denied Him (Matt. 26:59; Mark 14:55-59). HORSLEY translates, "After condemnation and judgment He was *accepted.*" **who . . . declare . . . generation**–who can set forth (the wickedness of) His generation? i.e., of His contemporaries [ALFORD on Acts 8:33], which suits best the parallelism, "the wickedness of His generation" corresponding to "oppressive judgment." But LUTHER, "His length of life," i.e., there shall be *no end of His future days* (vs. 10; Rom. 6:9). CALVIN includes *the days of His Church*, which is inseparable from Himself. HENGSTENBERG, "His posterity." He, indeed, shall be cut off, but His *race* shall be so numerous that none can fully declare it. CHRYSOSTOM, etc., "His eternal sonship and miraculous incarnation." **cut off**–implying a *violent death* (Dan. 9:26). **my people**–Isaiah, including himself among them by the word "my" [HENGSTENBERG]. Rather, JEHOVAH speaks in the person of His prophet, "*My* people," by the election of grace (Heb. 2:13). **was he stricken**–*Hebrew*, "the stroke (was laid) upon Him." GESENIUS says the *Hebrew* means "them"; the collective body, whether of the prophets or people, to which the Jews refer the whole prophecy. But JEROME, the SYRIAC, and ETHIOPIAC versions translate it "Him"; so it is *singular* in some passages; Psalm 11:7, *His*; Job 27:23, *Him;* Isaiah 44:15, *thereto.* The LXX, the *Hebrew, lamo,* "upon Him," read the similar words, *lamuth,* "unto death," which would at once set aside the Jewish interpretation, "upon *them.*" ORIGEN, who laboriously compared the *Hebrew* with the LXX, so read it, and urged it against the Jews of his day, who would have denied it to be the true reading if the word had not then really so stood in the *Hebrew* text [LOWTH]. If his sole authority be thought insufficient, perhaps *lamo* may imply that Messiah was the *representative of the collective body of all men;* hence the equivocal *plural-singular* form. **9.** Rather, "His grave was appointed," or "they appointed Him His grave" [HENGSTENBERG]; i.e., they *intended* (by crucifying Him with two thieves, Matt. 27:38) that He should have His grave "with the wicked." Cf. John 19:31, the denial of honorable burial being accounted a great ignominy (*Note*, ch. 14:19; Jer. 26:23). **and with . . . rich**–rather, "*but He was* with a rich man," etc. GESENIUS, for the parallelism to "the wicked," translates "ungodly" (the effect of *riches* being to make one ungodly); but the *Hebrew* everywhere means "rich," never by itself ungodly; the parallelism, too, is one of contrast; viz., between their *design* and the *fact*, as it was ordered by God (Matt. 27: 57; Mark 15:43-46; John 19:39, 40); two rich men honored Him at His death, Joseph of Arimathea, and Nicodemus. **in his death**–*Hebrew*, "deaths." LOWTH translates, "His tomb"; *bamoth*, from a different root, meaning "high places," and so mounds for sepulture (Ezek. 43:7). But all the versions oppose this, and the *Hebrew* hardly admits it. Rather translate, "*after* His death" [HENGSTENBERG]; as we say, "*at* His death." The *plural*, "deaths," intensifies the force; as Adam by sin "dying died" (Gen. 2:17, *Margin*); i.e., incurred death, physical and spiritual. So Messiah, His substitute, endured death in both senses; spiritual, during His temporary abandonment by the Father; physical, when He gave up the ghost. **because**–rather, as the sense demands (so in Job 16: 17), "*although* He had done no . . ." [HENGSTENBERG], (I Pet. 2:20-22; I John 8:5). **violence**–i.e., wrong. **10.** Transition from His humiliation to His exaltation. **pleased the Lord**–the secret of His sufferings. They were voluntarily borne by Messiah, in order that thereby He might "do *Jehovah's will*" (John 6:38; Heb. 10:7, 9), as to man's redemption; so at the end of the verse, "the *pleasure of the* LORD shall prosper in His hand." **bruise**–(see vs.

ADAM CLARKE

8. *And who shall declare his generation?*—"And His manner of life who would declare?" A learned friend has communicated to me the following passages from the Mishna, and the Gemara of Babylon, as leading to a satisfactory explication of this difficult place. It is said in the former that before anyone was punished for a capital crime proclamation was made before the prisoner by the public crier, in these words: "Whosoever knows anything of this man's innocence, let him come and declare it." Now it is plain from the history of the four Evangelists that in the trial and condemnation of Jesus no such rule was observed. And our Saviour seems to refer to such a custom, and to claim the benefit of it, by His answer to the high priest when he asked Him of His disciples and of His doctrine: "I spake openly to the world; I ever taught in the synagogue, and in the temple, whither the Jews always resort; and in secret have I said nothing. Why askest thou me? ask them which heard me, what I have said unto them: behold, they know what I said," John xviii. 20-21. This, therefore, was one remarkable instance of hardship and injustice, among others predicted by the prophet, which our Saviour underwent in His trial and sufferings. St. Paul likewise, in similar circumstances, standing before the judgment seat of Festus, seems to complain of the same unjust treatment: that no one was called, or would appear, to vindicate his character. "My manner of life [my generation] from my youth, which was at the first among mine own nation at Jerusalem, know all the Jews; which knew me from the beginning, if they would testify, that after the most straitest sect of our religion I lived a Pharisee," Acts xxvi. 4-5. *Dor* signifies age, duration, the time which one man or many together pass in this world, in this place; the course, tenor, or manner of life. *Was he stricken*—"He was smitten to death."

9. *With the rich in his death*—"With the rich man was His tomb." It may be necessary to introduce Bishop Lowth's translation: "And his grave was appointed with the wicked; but with the rich man was his tomb."

MATTHEW HENRY

2. He substituted himself in the room of sinners, as a sacrifice. He *made his soul an offering for sin*; he himself explains this (Matt. xx. 28), that *he came to give his life a ransom for many*. We could not put him in our stead, but he put himself.

3. He subjected himself to that which to us is the wages of sin (*v.* 12): *He has poured out his soul unto death*, poured it out as water, so little account did he make of it, when the laying of it down was the appointed means of our redemption and salvation.

4. He suffered himself to be ranked with sinners, and yet offered himself to be an intercessor for sinners, *v.* 12. He was *numbered with transgressors*, not only condemned as a malefactor, but executed in company with two notorious malefactors, and he in the midst, as if he had been the worst of the three. In his whole life he was numbered among the transgressors; for he was called and accounted a sabbath-breaker, a drunkard, and a friend to publicans and sinners. In his sufferings he *made intercession for the transgressors*, for those that reviled and crucified him; for he prayed, *Father, forgive them*, thereby showing, not only that he forgave them, but that he was now doing that upon which their forgiveness, and the forgiveness of all other transgressors, were to be founded. That prayer was the language of his blood, crying, not for vengeance, but for mercy.

II. The graces and glories of his state of exaltation. It is promised,

1. That the Redeemer shall have a seed to serve him and to bear up his name, Ps. xxii. 30. True believers are the seed of Christ; the Father gave them to him to be so, John xvii. 6.

2. That he shall live to see his seed, and because he lives they shall live also, for he is their life.

3. That he shall himself continue to take care of the affairs of this family: *He shall prolong his days*. Christ will not commit the care of his family to any other. *Of the increase of his government and peace there shall be no end*, for he ever lives.

4. That his great undertaking shall answer expectation: *The pleasure of the Lord shall prosper in his hand*. God's purposes shall take effect, and not one iota or tittle of them shall fail.

5. That he shall himself have abundant satisfaction in it (*v.* 11): *He shall see of the travail of his soul, and shall be satisfied*. He shall see it beforehand (so it may be understood); he shall with the prospect of his sufferings have a prospect of the fruit. He shall see it when it is accomplished in the conversion and salvation of poor sinners. Christ does and will see the blessed fruit of the travail of his soul in the founding and building up of his church and the eternal salvation of all that were given him.

Note, The great privilege that flows to us from the death of Christ is justification from sin, our being acquitted from that guilt which alone can ruin us, and accepted into God's favour, which alone can make us happy. Christ, who purchased our justification for us, applies it to us, by his intercession made for us, his gospel preached to us, and his Spirit witnessing in us. It is by faith that we are justified, by our consent to Christ and the covenant of grace; in this way we are saved. Faith is the knowledge of Christ, and without knowledge there can be no true faith. That knowledge of Christ, and that faith in him, by which we are justified, have reference to him both as a servant to God and as a surety for us. It is according to God's will that he does it. He is himself righteous, and of his righteousness have all we received. We must know him, and believe in him, as one that bore our iniquities —saved us from sinking under the load by taking it upon himself. The Father makes clear the victory of the Son. "I will set him among the great, highly exalt him, and give him a name above every name." Christ comes at his glory by conquest. He has vanquished principalities and powers, sin and Satan, death and hell, the world and the flesh; these are the strong that he has disarmed and taken the spoil of. The spoil which he has divided, consists in the vast multitudes of willing, faithful, loyal subjects, that shall be brought in to him; for so some read it: *I will give many to him, and he shall obtain many for a spoil*. God will *give him the heathen for his inheritance and the uttermost parts of the earth for his possession*, Ps. ii. 8. The spoil which God divided to Christ he divides (it is the same word), he distributes, among his followers; for, when he *led captivity captive*, he received gifts for men, that he might give gifts to men.

JAMIESON, FAUSSET, BROWN

5); Genesis 3:15, was hereby fulfilled, though the *Hebrew* word for "bruise," there, is not the one used here. The word "Himself," in Matthew, implies a personal *bearing on Himself* of our maladies, spiritual and physical, which *included as a consequence* His ministration to our bodily ailments: these latter are the reverse side of sin; His bearing on Him our spiritual malady involved with it His bearing sympathetically, and healing, the outward: which is its fruits and its type. HENGSTENBERG rightly objects to MAGEE's translation, "taken away," instead of "borne," that the parallelism to "carried" would be destroyed. Besides, the *Hebrew* word elsewhere, when connected with *sin*, means to bear it and its punishment (Ezek. 18:20). Matthew, elsewhere, also sets forth His vicarious atonement (Matt. 20: 28). **when thou . . .**—rather, as *Margin*, "when His soul (i.e., He) shall have made an offering . . . ." In *English Version* the change of person is harsh: from Jehovah, addressed in the second person (vs. 10), to Jehovah speaking in the first person in vs. 11. *Margin* rightly makes the prophet in the name of Jehovah Himself to speak in this verse. **offering for sin** —(Rom. 3:25; I John 2:2; 4:10.) **his seed**—His spiritual posterity shall be numerous (Ps. 22:30); nay, more, though He must die, He shall *see* them. A numerous posterity was accounted a high blessing among the Hebrews; still more so, for one to live to *see* them (Gen. 48:11; Ps. 128:6). **prolong . . . days** —also esteemed a special blessing among the Jews (Ps. 91:16). Messiah shall, after death, rise again to an endless life (Hos. 6:2; Rom. 6:9). **prosper**—(ch. 52:13, *Margin*). **11.** Jehovah is still speaking. **see of the travail**—He shall see such blessed fruits resulting from His sufferings as amply to repay Him for them (ch. 49:4, 5; 50:5, 9). The "satisfaction," in seeing the full fruit of His travail of soul in the conversion of Israel and the world, is to be realized in the last days (ch. 2:2-4). **his knowledge**—rather, *the knowledge* (experimentally) *of Him* (John 17:3; Phil. 3:10). **my . . . servant**—Messiah (ch. 42:1; 52: 13). **righteous**—the ground on which He justifies others, His own righteousness (I John 2:1). **justify** —treat *as if* righteous; forensically; on the ground of *His* meritorious righteousness, not *their* righteousness. **bear . . . iniquities**—(vss. 4, 5), as the sinner's substitute. **12. divide**—as a conqueror dividing the spoil after a victory (Ps. 2:8; Luke 11:22). **him**—**for Him. with . . . great**—HENGSTENBERG translates, "I will give Him the mighty for a portion"; so LXX. But the parallel clause, "with the strong," favors *English Version*. His triumphs shall be not merely among the few and weak, but among the many and mighty. **spoil . . . strong**—(Col. 2:15; cf. Prov. 16: 19). "With the great; with the mighty," may mean, as a great and mighty hero. **poured out . . . soul**— i.e., His life, which was considered as residing in the blood (Lev. 17:11; Rom. 3:25). **numbered with . . .**—not that He *was* a transgressor, but He was *treated as* such, when crucified with thieves (Mark 15:28; Luke 22:37). **made intercession . . .**—This office He began on the cross (Luke 23:34), and now continues in heaven (ch. 59:16; Heb. 9:24; I John 2:1). Understand *because* before "He was numbered . . . He bare . . . made intercession." His meritorious death and intercession are the cause of His ultimate triumph. MAURER, for the parallelism, translates, "He was put on the same footing with the transgressors." But *English Version* agrees better with the *Hebrew*, and with the sense and fact as to Christ. MAURER's translation would make a tautology after "He was numbered with the transgressors"; parallelism does not need so servile a repetition. "He *made intercession* for . . . ," answers to the parallel. "He *was numbered with* . . . ," as *effect* answers to *cause*, His intercession for sinners being the effect flowing from His having been numbered with them.

ADAM CLARKE

10. *To grief*—"With affliction." *When thou shalt make his soul*—"If His soul shall make." *When thou shalt make his soul an offering*. The word *nephesh*, "soul," is frequently used in Hebrew to signify "life." Throughout the New Testament the salvation of men is uniformly attributed to the death of Christ. *He shall see his seed*. True converts, genuine Christians. *He shall prolong his days*. Or this spiritual progeny shall prolong their days, i.e., Christianity shall endure to the end of time. *And the pleasure of the Lord*. To have all men saved and brought to the knowledge of the truth. *Shall prosper in his hand*. Shall go on in a state of progressive prosperity; and so completely has this been thus far accomplished that every succeeding century has witnessed more Christianity in the world than the preceding, or any former one.

11. *Shall be satisfied*—"And be satisfied." *Shall my righteous servant justify*—"Shall My Servant justify." Three MSS. (two of them ancient) omit the word *tsaddik*; it seems to be only an imperfect repetition, by mistake, of the preceding word. It makes a solecism in this place; for according to the constant usage of the Hebrew language the adjective, in a phrase of this kind, ought to follow the substantive; and *tsaddik abdi*, in Hebrew, would be as absurd as "shall my servant righteous justify" in English. Add to this that it makes the hemistich too long.

12. *He bare the sin of many*. The "multitudes," the many that were made sinners by the offenses of one; i.e., the whole human race; for all have sinned—all have fallen; and for all that have sinned, and for all that have fallen, Jesus Christ died. *He made intercession for the transgressors*.—This was literally fulfilled at His death, "Father, forgive them; for they know not what they do," Luke xxiii. 34. And to make intercession for transgressors is one part of His mediatorial office (Heb. vii. 25 and ix. 24).

MATTHEW HENRY

CHAPTER 54

Verses 1–5

If we apply this to the state of the Jews after their return out of captivity, it is a prophecy of the increase of their nation after they were settled in their own land. Jerusalem had been in the condition of a wife written childless, or a desolate solitary widow; but now it is promised that the city should be replenished and the country peopled again, that the ruins of Jerusalem should be repaired, and that those estates which had for many years been wrongfully held by the Babylonian Gentiles should now return to the right owners. God will again be a husband to them, and the reproach of their captivity, and the small number to which they were then reduced, shall be forgotten. But we must apply it to the church of God in general; I mean the kingdom of God among men, God's city in the world.

I. The low state of religion in the world long before Christianity was brought in. It was like one *barren, that did not bear*, or like one desolate, that had lost husband and children; the church lay in a little compass, and brought forth little fruit. The Gentiles had less religion among them than the Jews, and the children of God, like the children of a broken, reduced family, were *scattered abroad* (John xi. 52).

II. Its recovery from this low condition by the preaching of the gospel and the planting of the Christian church.

1. Multitudes were converted from idols to the living God. Those were the church's children that were born again, were partakers of a new and divine nature, by the word. There were more found in the Gentile church (when that was set up) than ever were found in the Jewish church. The increase of the church is the joy of all its friends and strengthens their hands. Even in heaven, among the angels of God, there is an uncommon joy for a sinner that repents, much more for a nation that does so.

2. The bounds of the church were extended much further than ever before, *v.* 2, 3. (1) It is here supposed that the present state of the church is a tabernacle state; it dwells in tents, like the heirs of promise of old (Heb. xi. 9). The city, the continuing city, is reserved for hereafter. A tent is soon taken down and shifted, and, when God pleases, it is as soon fixed elsewhere. (2) Though it be a tabernacle state, it is sometimes very remarkably a growing state, no matter though it be in a tent. Thus it was in the first preaching of the gospel; it was the business of the apostles to disciple all nations, and so to lengthen the cords of this tabernacle, that more might be enclosed, which would make it necessary to strengthen the stakes, that they might bear the weight of the enlarged curtains. The more numerous the church grows the more cautious she must be to fortify herself against errors and corruptions, and to support her seven pillars, Prov. ix. 1. (3) It was a proof of divine power that in all places it *grew and prevailed mightily*, Acts xix. 20. The gospel spread itself into all parts of the world; there were eastern and western churches.

3. This was the comfort and honour of the church (*v.* 4): *Fear not, for thou shalt not be ashamed*, as formerly, of the straitness of thy borders, and the fewness of thy children.

4. This was owing to the relation in which God stood to his church, as her husband (*v.* 5): *Thy Maker is thy husband.* Jesus Christ is the church's Maker, by whom she is formed into a people—her Redeemer, by whom she is brought out of captivity, the bondage of sin, the worst of slaveries. This is he that espoused her to himself: He is *the Lord of hosts, the Holy One of Israel*, the same that presided in the affairs of the Old Testament church and was the Mediator of the covenant made with it.

Verses 6–10

The succour and relief which God sent to his captives in Babylon are here foretold, as a type of all those consolations of God treasured up for all believers in the covenant of grace.

I. Look back to former troubles, and God's favours to his people, *v.* 6–8. 1. How sorrowful the church's condition had been. She had been as a woman forsaken, though she was *a wife of youth*, or she had been as one rejected, and full of discontent. Even those that are espoused to God may yet seem to be forsaken. The similitude is explained (*v.* 7, 8). When God continues his people long in trouble he seems to forsake them; so their enemies construe it (Ps. lxxi. 11). It was in wrath that he forsook them and hid his face from them (*ch.* lvii. 17); yet it was but in a little wrath in comparison with what they had deserved, and what others justly suffer. It was but *for a moment*, a *small* moment. As he is slow to anger, so he is swift to show mercy. 2. How sweet the

JAMIESON, FAUSSET, BROWN

CHAPTER 54

VSS. 1-17. THE FRUIT OF MESSIAH'S SUFFERINGS, AND OF ISRAEL'S FINAL PENITENCE AT HER PAST UNBELIEF (ch. 53:6): HER JOYFUL RESTORATION AND ENLARGEMENT BY JEHOVAH, WHOSE WRATH WAS MOMENTARY, BUT HIS KINDNESS EVERLASTING. Israel converted is compared to a wife (vs. 5; ch. 62:5) put away for unfaithfulness, but now forgiven and taken home again. The converted Gentiles are represented as a new progeny of the long-forsaken but now restored wife. The pre-eminence of the Hebrew Church as the mother Church of Christendom is the leading idea; the conversion of the Gentiles is mentioned only as part of her felicity [HORSLEY].

1. **Sing**—for joy (Zeph. 3:14). **barren**—the Jewish Church once forsaken by God, and therefore during that time destitute of spiritual children (vs. 6). **didst not bear**—during the Babylonian exile primarily. Secondarily, and chiefly, during Israel's present dispersion. **the children**—the Gentiles adopted by special grace into the original Church (vs. 3; ch. 49:20, 21). **than . . . married wife**—than were her spiritual children, when Israel was still a married wife (under the law, before the Babylonian exile), before God put her away [MAURER]. So Paul contrasts the universal Church of the New Testament with the Church of the Old Testament legal dispensation, quoting this very passage (Gal. 4:27). But the full accomplishment of it is yet future.

2. (Ch. 49:19, 20; Jer. 31:31-36, 38, 39.) Thy children shall be so many that thy borders must be extended to contain them. **curtains**—the cloth forming the covering of the tent. **spare not**—give abundantly the means for the enlargement of the Church (II Corinthians 9:5-7). **cords . . . stakes**—The more the tent is enlarged by lengthening the cords by which the cloth covering is fastened to the ground, the more the stakes supporting the tent need to be strengthened; the Church is not merely to seek new converts, but to strengthen those she has in the faith. The image is appropriate, as the tabernacle was the symbol of the old Israelitish Church (*Note*, ch. 33: 20). **3.** **break forth**—rather, burst forth with increase; thy offspring shall grow, answering to "thy seed" in the parallel clause. **thy seed**—Israel and her children, as distinguished from "the Gentiles." **desolate cities**—of Israel (ch. 44:26). **4.** (Ch. 41:10, 14.) **shame of thy youth**—Israel's *unfaithfulness* as wife of Jehovah, almost from her *earliest* history. **reproach of widowhood**—Israel's punishment in her consequent dismissal from God and barrenness of spiritual children in Babylon and her present dispersion (vs. 1; ch. 49:21; Jer. 3:24, 25; 31:19; Hos. 2:2-5). **5.** (Ch. 62:5; Jer. 3:14). That God was Israel's "Maker," both as individuals and as the theocratic kingdom, is the pledge of assurance that He will be her Redeemer (ch. 43:1-3). *Hebrew, "makers . . . husbands"; plural* for *singular,* to denote excellency. **of Israel . . . whole earth**—Not until He manifests Himself as God *of Israel* shall He appear as God *of the whole earth* (Ps. 102:13, 15, 16; Zech. 14:5, 9).

6. **called**—i.e., recalled: the prophetic past for the future. **forsaken**—that *had been* forsaken. **when thou**—or, "when *she* was rejected"; one who had been a wife of youth (Ezek. 16:8, 22, 60; Jer. 2:2) at the time when (*thou,* or) she was rejected for infidelity [MAURER]. "A wife of youth *but afterwards* rejected" [LOWTH].

7. **small moment**—as compared with Israel's coming *long* prosperity (ch. 26:20; 60:10). So the spiritual Israel (Ps. 30:5; II Cor. 4:17). **gather thee**—to Myself from thy dispersions.

ADAM CLARKE

CHAPTER 54

1. *Sing, O barren, thou that didst not bear*—"Shout for joy, O thou barren, that didst not bear." The Church of God under the Old Testament, confined within the narrow bounds of the Jewish nation, and still more so in respect of the very small number of true believers, and which sometimes seemed to be deserted of God, her Husband, is the barren woman, that did not bear, and was *desolate*. She is exhorted to rejoice, and to express her joy in the strongest manner, on the reconciliation of her Husband (see v. 6) and on the accession of the Gentiles to her family. The converted Gentiles are all along considered by the prophet as a new accession of adopted children, admitted into the original Church of God, and united with it. See chap. xlix. 20-21.

4. *For thou shalt forget the shame of thy youth.* That is, "The bondage of Egypt: widowhood, the captivity of Babylon."—Secker.

7. *For a small moment*—"In a little anger."

MATTHEW HENRY

returns of mercy would be to them when God should come and comfort them. God's gathering his people takes rise from his mercy, not any merit of theirs; and it is with *great mercies* (*v.* 7), *with everlasting kindness*, *v.* 8.

II. Look forward to future dangers, and in defiance of them God's favours appear constant, and his kindness everlasting; for it is formed into a *covenant of peace.*

1. This is as firm *as the waters of Noah*, that is, as that promise which was made concerning the deluge that there should never be the like again, *v.* 9; see Gen. viii. 21, 22; ix. 11. And God has kept his word, though the world has been very provoking. And thus inviolable is the covenant of grace: *I have sworn that I would not be wroth with thee*, as I have been, *and rebuke thee*, as I have done.

2. It is more firm than the strongest parts of the visible creation (*v.* 10): The *mountains shall depart*, and *the hills be removed*, Hab. iii. 6. Mountains have sometimes been shaken by earthquakes, and removed; but the promises of God were never broken by the shock of any event. When our friends fail us our God does not, nor does his kindness depart? Do the kings of the earth, and the rulers, set themselves against the Lord? They shall depart and be removed. God's kindness shall never depart from his people, for whom he loves he loves to the end. *Therefore* the covenant is immovable and inviolable, because it is built not on our merit, but on God's mercy, which is from everlasting to everlasting.

Verses 11–17

Very precious promises that God would not only continue his love to his people under their troubles, but that he would raise them to greater prosperity than any they had yet enjoyed. In the foregoing chapter we had the humiliation and exaltation of Christ; here we have the humiliation and exaltation of the church; for, if we suffer with him, we shall reign with him.

I. The distressed state of the church (*v.* 11): "*O thou afflicted*, poor, and indigent society, that art *tossed with tempests*, like a ship ready to be swallowed up by the waves, not comforted by any prospect of deliverance." This was the condition of the Jews in Babylon, and afterwards, for a time, under Antiochus. It is often the condition of Christian churches and of believers, like the disciples in a storm, ready to perish; and where is their faith?

II. The glorious state the church is advanced to by the promise of God. Let the people of God, when they are afflicted and tossed, think they hear God speaking comfortably to them by these words. In all their afflictions he is afflicted, and encourages her with the assurance of the great things he would do for her.

1. God promises that which would be her beauty and honour.

(1) This is promised by a similitude taken from a city, for the church is the city of the living God, the heavenly Jerusalem. Whereas now Jerusalem lay in ruins, a heap of rubbish, it shall be beautified, and appear more splendid than ever; the stones shall be laid not only firm, but fine. The foundations shall be garnished with *sapphires*, for Christ, and the foundation of the apostles and prophets, are precious above anything else. The windows of this house, city, or temple, shall be made of *agates*, the gates of *carbuncles*, and all the *borders* (the walls that enclose the courts) shall be *of pleasant stones*, *v.* 12. God, having graciously undertaken to build his church, the glory of the New Testament church shall far exceed that of the Jewish church, in those gifts and graces of the Spirit which are infinitely valuable.

(2) Those things that shall be the beauty and honour of the church are knowledge, holiness, and love, the very image of God, in which man was created, renewed, and restored. And these are the sapphires and carbuncles, the precious and pleasant stones, with which the gospel temple shall be beautified; *built upon the foundation*, 1 Cor. iii. 12. Then the church is all glorious, [1] When it is full of the knowledge of God (*v.* 13): *All thy children shall be taught of the Lord.* They shall be taught by those whom God shall appoint and whose labours shall be under his direction and blessing. It is a promise of the Spirit of illumination. Our Saviour quotes it with application to gospel grace (John vi. 45). [2] When the members of it live in love and unity among themselves: *Great shall be the peace of thy children.* All that are taught of God are taught to *love one another* (1 Thess. iv. 9). [3] When holiness reigns; for that above anything is the beauty of the church (*v.* 14): *In righteousness shalt thou be established.* The reformation of manners, the restoration of purity, the due administration of public justice, and the prevailing of honesty and fair dealing among men, are the strength and

JAMIESON, FAUSSET, BROWN

8. In a little wrath—rather, "In the overflowing of wrath"; as Proverbs 27:4, *Margin.* [GESENIUS]. The wrath, though but "for a moment," was overflowing while it lasted. **hid . . . face**—(ch. 8:17; Ps. 30:7). **everlasting**—in contrast to "for a moment." **9.** I am about to do the same in this instance as in Noah's flood. As I swore then that it should not return (Gen. 8:21; 9:11), and I kept that promise, so I swear now to My people, and will perform My promise, that there shall be no return of the deluge of My wrath upon them. LOWTH, on insufficient authority, reads (the same will I do now as), "in the days of Noah." **10.** (Ch. 51:6; Ps. 89: 33, 34; Rom. 11:29). **covenant of my peace**—(II Sam. 23:5). The covenant whereby I have made thee at peace with Me.

11. not comforted—by any-one; none gave her help or comfort.

lay . . . with fair colours—rather, "lay . . . in cement of *vermilion*" [LOWTH]. The *Hebrew* for "fair colors" means *stibium,* the paint with which Eastern women painted their eyelids and eyelashes (II Kings 9:30). The very cement shall be of the most beautiful color (Rev. 21:18-21). **12. windows**—rather, "battlements"; lit., "suns"; applied to battlements from their *radiated* appearance. **agates**—rather, rubies. **carbuncles**—lit., "sparkling gems"; the carbuncle when held to the sun becomes like a burning coal. **all thy borders**—rather, "thy whole circuit," consisting of *precious stones.* The glory of the Church on earth, when the Hebrew Church, according to the original design, shall be the metropolis of Christendom.

13. Quoted by the Saviour (John 6:45), to prove that in order to come to Him, men must be "drawn" by the Father. So Jeremiah 31:34; Micah 4:2; I Corinthians 2:10; Hebrews 8:10; 10:16; I John 2:20.

great . . . peace—generally (Ps. 119:165). Specially referring to the *peaceful prosperity* which shall prevail under Messiah in the latter days (ch. 2:4, 9:6). **14. righteousness**—the characteristic of the reign of Messiah (ch. 11:4, 5; Ps. 72:2, 4; Rev. 19:11).

ADAM CLARKE

9. *For this is as the waters of Noah unto me*—"The same will I do now, as in the days of Noah."

F. B. MEYER:

"O thou afflicted, tossed with tempest, and not comforted" (Isa. 54:11).

From his standpoint of vision on the hilltops of glory, He sees the tossings of your craft. Every billow, every lurch, every rebuff, is discerned and felt by Him. He, too, has sailed through stormy seas, and is acquainted with grief. Not comforted by man, you shall be consoled by the divine Comforter. Cast out by thy lovers, you shall be gathered to the bosom of God. When the man born blind was cast out of the synagogue, Jesus found him; and He will find you.

Deep down in the tossing waves, He will lay your foundations in fair colors, and will spare no stones, however precious, in the elaboration of your character. Sapphires, rubies, and carbuncles are very resplendent and beautiful, but they are all the children of fire. You cannot have them unless prepared to pay the cost in blood and tears. These jewels are produced of very ordinary ingredients, which have been subjected to tremendous pressure and terrific heat. When next your heart misgives you amid your fiery trials, remember that God is at work making the rubies and carbuncles of your eternal array. You will be well compensated.

There are destructive agencies around us on all hands—the smith with his coals; the waster with his scythe; the destroyer with his weapon—but they are all beneath the mighty hand of God. They cannot overstep the limits He assigns. When a man's ways please the Lord, He maketh even his enemies to be at peace with him. He restrains the wrath of his foes, and surrounds him with a munition of rocks.

The blessings of this chapter are not for the Jews only, but for all the servants of the Lord. It is expressly stated that this is their heritage (v. 17).—*Great Verses Through the Bible*

11. *Behold, I will lay thy stones*—"Behold, I lay your stones." These seem to be general images to express beauty, magnificence, purity, strength, and solidity, agreeably to the ideas of the Eastern nations.

MATTHEW HENRY

stability of any church or state.

2. Whereas now she lay in danger, God promises her protection and security. There shall be no fears within (*v.* 14): "*Thou shalt be far from oppression*, not only from evil, but from the fear of evil." There shall be no fightings without. Though attempts should be made upon them they should none of them succeed, *v.* 15. It is granted, "*They shall surely gather together against thee;* thou must expect it." As long as there is a devil in hell, and a persecutor out of it, God's people must expect frequent alarms; but God will not own them. Their attempt will end in their own ruin: "*Whosoever shall gather together against thee*, they *shall fall for thy sake*, or they shall fall before thee." We may with the greatest assurance depend upon God for the safety of his church. The smith that makes weapons is God's creature, and he gave him his skill to work in iron and brass (Exod. xxxi. 3, 4) and to make proper instruments for warlike purposes. *The smith blows the coals in the fire*, to make his iron malleable, that it may be hardened into steel, and so *he may bring forth an instrument proper for the work of those that seek to destroy*. It is the iron age that is the age of war. But *God has created the smith*, and therefore can tie his hands, so that the project of the enemy shall miscarry. They must have soldiers, and it is *God that created the waster to destroy*. Military men value themselves upon their splendid titles, but God calls them *wasters made to destroy*, for wasting and destruction are their business. They think their own ingenuity, labour, and experience, made them soldiers; but it was God that created them, and he will serve his own purposes and designs by them. The promise of God concerns the church's safety as *the heritage of the servants of the Lord* (*v.* 17). "*No weapon that is formed against thee shall prosper;* it shall not prove strong enough to do any harm to the people of God; it shall recoil in the face of him that uses it against thee." When the weapons of war do not prosper there are tongues that rise in judgment. They are such as misrepresent them, and falsely accuse them to make them odious to the people and obnoxious to the government. This the enemies of the Jews did, to incense the kings of Persia against them, Ezra iv. 12; Esther iii. 8. "But these insulting threatening tongues thou shalt put to silence *by well-doing* (1 Pet. ii. 15), by doing that which will make thee manifest in the consciences even of thy adversaries, that thou art not what thou art represented to be." *This is the heritage of the servants of the Lord*. God's servants are his sons. God's promises are their *heritage for ever* (Ps. cxix. 111).

JAMIESON, FAUSSET, BROWN

far from oppression . . .—far from *suffering oppression;* "for thou shalt have nothing to fear."

15. gather together . . .—i.e., If it should happen that enemies "gather together" against thee (Ps. 2:2), they will *not* have been sent *by Me* (cf. Hos. 8:4) as instruments of My wrath (nay, it *will* be with My disapproval); for "whosoever shall gather together," etc. (Ps. 59:3). **fall for thy sake**—rather, "shall come over to thy side" [LOWTH]. Lit., "*fall* to thee" (Jer. 21:9; 39:9). To be *fully* fulfilled to Jerusalem hereafter (Zech. 14:16).

16. The workman that forms "weapons against thee" (vs. 17) is wholly in My power, therefore thou needest not fear, having Me on thy side. **for his work**—rather, "by his labor [HORSLEY]. "According to the exigencies of his work" [MAURER]. **waster to destroy**—(ch. 10: 5-7; 37:26, 27; 45:1-6). Desolating conquerors who use the "instruments" framed by "the smith." The repetition of the "I" implies, however, something in the latter half of the verse contrasted with the former understand it, therefore, thus: "I have in My power both him who frames arms and him who destroys *them* (arms)" [ROSENMULLER].

17. tongue . . . condemn—image from a court of justice. Those who desire to "condemn" thee *thou* shalt "condemn" (Exod. 11:7; Josh. 10:21; Ps. 64:8; Rom. 8:1, 33). **righteousness . . . of me**—(ch. 45:24; 46:13). Rather (*this is*) *their justification from Me*. Their enemies would "condemn" them, but I justify and vindicate them, and so they condemn their enemies.

ADAM CLARKE

15. *Shall fall for thy sake*—"Shall come over to your side."

MATTHEW HENRY

CHAPTER 55

Verses 1–5

I. We are all invited to come and take that provision which the grace of God has made for poor souls in the new covenant.

1. Who are invited: *Ho, everyone*. Not the Jews only, but the Gentiles, the poor and the maimed, the halt and the blind, whoever can be picked up out of the highways and the hedges. Ministers are to make a general offer of life and in gospel times the invitation should be sent to the Gentiles. The gospel covenant excludes none that do not exclude themselves.

2. What is the qualification required—they must thirst. Those that are satisfied with the world and its enjoyments—those that depend upon the merit of their own works for a righteousness—these do not thirst; they have no sense of their need, are in no pain or uneasiness about their souls. But those that thirst are invited to the waters, as those that labour, and are heavy-laden, are invited to Christ for rest. Where God gives grace he first gives a thirsting after it; and, where he has given a thirsting after it, he will give it, Ps. lxxxi. 10.

3. Whither they are invited: *Come you to the waters*. Come to Christ; for he is the fountain opened; he is the rock smitten. Come to holy ordinances, to those streams that make glad the city of our God; to those who believe in Christ the things signified will be as wine and milk, abundantly refreshing. Come to the healing waters; come to the living waters. Our Saviour referred to it, John vii. 37. *If any man thirst, let him come to me and drink*.

4. What they are invited to do. (1) *Come and buy*. "Come and buy, stand not hesitating about the terms, nor deliberating whether you shall agree to them." (2) "*Come, and eat;* make it still more your own, as that which we eat is more our own than that which we only buy."

5. What is the provision they are invited to: "*Come, and buy wine and milk*, which will not only quench the thirst" (fair water would do that), "but nourish the body, and revive the spirits." Christ outdoes our

JAMIESON, FAUSSET, BROWN

CHAPTER 55

Vss. 1-13. THE CALL OF THE GENTILE WORLD TO FAITH THE RESULT OF GOD'S GRACE TO THE JEWS FIRST. **1. every one**—After the *special* privileges of Israel (ch. 54) there follow, as the consequence, the *universal* invitation to the Gentiles (Luke 24:47; Rom. 11:12, 15). **Ho**—calls the most earnest attention. **thirsteth**—has a keen sense of need (Matt. 5:6).

waters . . . wine and milk—a gradation. Not merely *water*, which is needed to maintain life at all, but *wine and milk* to strengthen, cheer, and nourish; the spiritual blessings of the Gospel are meant (ch. 25:6; Song of Sol. 5:1; John 7:37). "Waters," *plural*, to denote abundance (ch. 43:20; 44:3).

ADAM CLARKE

CHAPTER 55

JOSEPH PARKER:

The first promise that we have (v. 1) is the promise of "waters." A great appeal is addressed to those who are athirst. Thus the Lord accommodates his ministry to human necessity. When men are thirsting for water he does not offer them sublime visions of the future, or stately ideas concerning the economies and dominions of time. He would say to men, Let us, in the first place, supply your need; until your thirst is quenched your mind cannot be at rest; until your bodily necessities are supplied your imagination will be unable to exercise itself in high thoughts. The promises of God are addressed to our necessities for more than merely temporary reasons. There is a whole philosophy of government in such appeals. Only at certain points can we profess to understand God, and those points touch our need, our pain, our immediate desire; when we are quite sure that God gives us water for our bodily thirst we may begin at least to feel that there is a possibility that he may not neglect the more burning thirst of the soul. God approaches the spirit through the body.—*The People's Bible*

MATTHEW HENRY

expectations. We come to the waters, and would be glad of them, but we find there wine and milk, which were the staple commodities of the tribe of Judah. We must part with our puddle-water, nay, with our poison, that we may procure this wine and milk.

6. The free communication of this provision: *Buy it without money, and without price.* Our buying without money intimates, (1) That the gifts offered us are invaluable and such as no price can be set upon. (2) That he who offers them has no need of us, nor of any returns we can make him. (3) That the things offered are already bought and paid for. Christ purchased them not with money, but with *his own blood*, 1 Pet. i. 19. (4) That we shall be welcome to the benefits of the promise, and we must own it, that, if Christ and heaven be ours, we may see ourselves for ever indebted to free grace.

II. We are earnestly pressed to accept this invitation.

1. We are persuaded to hearken to God and to his proposals: "*Hearken diligently unto me, v.* 2. Not only give me the hearing, but apply it to yourselves (*v.* 3): *Incline your ear*, as you do to that which you find yourselves pleased with; come up to my terms."

2. The arguments used to persuade us,

(1) The unspeakable wrong we do to ourselves if we refuse this invitation: "*Wherefore do you spend money for that which is not bread*, when with me you may have wine and milk without money? *Wherefore do you spend your labour* and toil *for that which* will not be so much as dry bread to you, for it *satisfies not?*" The things of this world are not bread, not proper food for a soul. *They satisfy not.* The children of this world spend their money and labour for these uncertain unsatisfying things.

(2) The kindness we do to ourselves if we accept this invitation and comply with it. "If you hearken to Christ, you *eat that which is good*, which is both wholesome and pleasant, good in itself and good for you." God's good word and promise, a good conscience, and the comforts of God's good Spirit, are a continual feast to those that hearken obediently to Christ. Hereby we secure to ourselves lasting happiness: *Hear, and your soul shall live.* The great God graciously secures all this to us; "Come to me, *and I will make an everlasting covenant with you*, and thereby settle upon you *the sure mercies of David.*" The benefits of this covenant are the mercies of David, such mercies as God promised to David (Ps. lxxxix. 28, 29, &c.), which are called *the mercies of David his servant*, and are appealed to by Solomon, 2 Chron. vi. 42. By David here we are to understand the Messiah. Covenant-mercies are all *his* mercies; they are purchased by him; and out of his hands they are dispensed to us. He is the Mediator and trustee of the covenant. They are sure mercies for in Christ the promises are all yea and amen.

III. Jesus Christ is promised for the making good of all the other promises which we are here invited to accept, *v.* 4. He is that David whose sure mercies all the blessings and benefits of the covenant are. There was nothing in us to merit such a favour, but Christ is the gift of God. We know not how to find the way to the waters where we are to be supplied, but Christ is given to be *a leader.* We know not what to do, but he is given for *a commander*, to show us what to do and enable us to do it. Christ is a commander by his precept and a leader by his example; our business is to obey him and follow him.

IV. The Master of the feast being fixed, it is next to be furnished with guests. The Gentiles shall be called to this feast: *Thou shalt call a nation that thou knowest not*, that is, that was not formerly called and owned as thy nation. They shall come at the call: *Nations that knew not thee shall run unto thee.* There shall be a concourse of believing Gentiles to Christ, who, being lifted up from the earth, will draw all men to him. The Gentiles will thus flock to Christ because he is the Son of God. God will bring them to him because he is the Holy One of Israel, true to his promises, and he has promised to glorify him by giving him the heathen for his inheritance.

Verses 6–13

A further account of that covenant of grace which is made with us in Jesus Christ. This gracious discovery of God's goodwill is not to be confined either to the Jew or to the Gentile, to the Old Testament or to the New, much less to the captives in Babylon. The precepts and the promises are here given to all, to *everyone that thirsts after happiness, v.* 1.

I. A gracious offer made of pardon, and peace, and all happiness, to poor sinners, upon gospel terms, *v.* 6, 7.

1. Let them pray, and their prayers shall be heard and answered (*v.* 6): "*Seek the Lord while he may be found. Call upon him now while he is near*, and

JAMIESON, FAUSSET, BROWN

no money—Yet, in vs. 2, it is said, "ye spend money." A seeming paradox. Ye are really spiritual bankrupts: but thinking yourselves to have money, viz., a devotion of your own making, ye lavish it on that "which is not bread," i.e., on idols, whether literal or spiritual. **buy . . . without money**—another paradox. We are *bought*, but not with a *price* paid by ourselves (I Cor. 6:20; I Pet. 1:18, 19). In a different sense we are to "buy" salvation, viz., by parting with everything which comes between us and Christ who has bought it for us and by making it our own (Matt. 13:44, 46; Luke 12:33; Rev. 3:18).

2. not bread—(Hab. 2:13). "Bread of deceit" (Prov. 20:17). Contrast this with the "bread of life" (John. 6:32, 35; also Luke 14:16-20). **satisfieth not**—(Eccles. 1:8; 4:8).

hearken . . . and eat—When two *imperatives* are joined, the second expresses the *consequence* of obeying the command in the first (Gen. 42:18). *By hearkening ye shall eat.* So in vs. 1, "buy and eat." By buying, and so making it your own, ye shall eat, i.e., *experimentally enjoy* it (John 6:53). Cf. the invitation (Prov. 9:5, 6; Matt. 22:4). **fatness**—(Ps. 36:8; 63:5). **3. me . . . live**—by coming to *me* ye shall *live:* for **"*I* am the *life*"** (John 14:6). **everlasting covenant**—(Jer. 32:40; II Sam. 23:5). **with you . . . David**—God's covenant is with the antitypical David, Messiah (Ezek. 34:23), and so with us by our identification with Him. **sure**—answering to "everlasting," irrevocable, unfailing, to be relied on (Ps. 89:2-4, 28, 29, 34-36; Jer. 33:20, 21; II Sam. 7:15, 16; II Cor. 1:18-20). **mercies of David**—the mercies of grace (ch. 63:7; John 1:16) which I covenanted to give to David, and especially to Messiah, his antitype. Quoted in Acts 13:34. **4. him**—the mystical David (Ezek. 37:24, 25; Jer. 30:9; Hos. 3:5). Given by God (ch. 49:6). **witness**—He bore witness even unto death for God, to His law, claims, and plan of redeeming love (John 18:37; Rev. 1:5). Revelation is a "testimony"; because it is propounded to be received on the authority of the Giver, and not merely because it can be proved by arguments. **commander**—"preceptor" [HORSLEY]; "lawgiver" [BARNES]. **to the people**—rather, peoples.

5. thou—Jehovah addresses Messiah. **call . . . run**—God must *call*, before man can, or will, *run* (Song of Sol. 1:4; John 6:44). Not merely *come*, but *run* eagerly. **thou knowest not**—now as thy people (so in Matt. 7:23). **nation . . . nations**—gradation; from Israel, one *nation*, the Gospel spread to many *nations*, and will do so more fully on Israel's conversion. **knew not thee**—(ch. 52:15; Eph. 2:11, 12). **because of . . . thy God . . . glorified thee**—(ch. 60:5, 9; Zech. 8:23); where similar language is directed to *Israel*, because of the identification of Israel with Messiah, who is the ideal Israel (Matt. 2:15; cf. with Hos. 11:1; see Acts 3:13).

6. The condition and limit in the obtaining of the spiritual benefits (vss. 1-3): (1) Seek the Lord. (2) Seek Him while He is to be found (ch. 65:1; Ps. 32:6; Matt. 25:1-13; John 7-34; 8-21; II Cor. 6:2; Heb. 2:3; 3:13, 15). **call**—casting yourselves wholly on His mercy (Rom. 10:13). Stronger than "seek"; so "near" is more positive than "while He may be found" (Rom. 10:8, 9). **near**—propitious (Ps. 34:18; 145:18).

ADAM CLARKE

CHARLES H. SPURGEON:

According to the text, this provision for our souls is presented to us gratis. We are to buy it, that is to say, we are to have it with as good a right, and as full an assurance, as if we had purchased it; but the purchase is to be made "without money," and lest we should make mistakes and suppose that although money literally might not be brought, some other recompense must be offered to God, it is added, "without price." The double expression is most sweeping, clearing away once for all from the mercies of God all idea of their being purchasable by any method whatsoever. The gospel is not to be bought with gold. Vain are your treasures if you should lavish them at the feet of Christ. What cares He for gold and silver? Neither are they to be procured by knowledge and wisdom, which are the mind's wealth, the money of the soul. A man may know much, but his knowledge may only puff him up, or increase his condemnation. Neither are the gifts of God's grace to be obtained by human merit. Merit, indeed, connected with man is out of the question; call it demerit and you are right. If we had done all that we ought to have done, still we ought to have done it, and even in that case we should still be unprofitable servants. Away with the notion of merit as possible to fallen man. The day which saw Adam driven out of Paradise blotted the word "human merit" out of the dictionary of truth. Every sort of gift to God with the view of procuring His favor is excluded by the term, "without price."

—*The Treasury of the Old Testament*

3. *I will make an everlasting covenant.* Heb., "I will cut the old or everlasting covenant sacrifice with you." That covenant sacrifice which was pointed out of old from the very beginning, and which is to last to the consummation of ages; viz., the Lamb of God that was slain from the foundation of the world. *The sure mercies of David.* That is, says Kimchi, "The Messiah," called here *David.*

6. *Seek ye the Lord while he may be found.* Rab. David. Kimchi gives the true sense of this passage: "Seek ye the Lord, because He may be found: call upon Him, because he is near. Repent before ye die, for after death there is no conversion of the soul."

MATTHEW HENRY

within call. Pray to him, to be reconciled, and, being reconciled, pray to him for everything else you need." Now his patience is waiting on us, his word is calling to us, and his Spirit striving with us. Let us now improve our advantages and opportunities; for now is the accepted time.

2. Let them repent and reform, and their sins shall be pardoned, *v.* 7. Here is a call to the unconverted, to *the wicked and the unrighteous*—to the wicked, who live in known gross sins, to the unrighteous, who live in the neglect of plain duties: to them is the word of this salvation sent, and all possible assurance given that penitent sinners shall find God a pardoning God. There are two things involved in repentance: (1) It is to turn from sin; it is to forsake it. There must be a change of the mind; the unrighteous must *forsake his thoughts.* Repentance, if it be true, strikes at the root, and washes the heart from wickedness. We must alter our judgments concerning persons and things, dislodge the corrupt imaginations and quit the vain pretences under which an unsanctified heart shelters itself. (2) To repent is to *return to the Lord;* against whom we have rebelled; it is to return to the Lord as the fountain of life. If we do so God *will have mercy.* Misery is the object of mercy. With God there are tender mercies. *He will abundantly pardon. He will multiply to pardon* (so the word is), as we have multiplied to offend.

II. Encouragements given us to accept this offer and to venture our souls upon it.

1. If we look up to heaven, we find God's counsels there high and transcendent, his thoughts and ways infinitely above ours, *v.* 8, 9. The wicked are urged to forsake their evil ways and thoughts (*v.* 7) and to bring their ways and thoughts to comply with his; "for" (says he) "my thoughts and ways are not as yours. Yours are conversant only about things beneath; but mine are above, *as the heaven is high above the earth*; and, if you would approve yourselves true penitents, yours must be so too, and your affections must be set on things above." Sinners may be ready to fear that God will not be reconciled to them, because they could not find in their hearts to be reconciled to one who should have so basely and so frequently offended them. "But" (says God) "my thoughts in this matter are not as yours, but as far above them as heaven is above the earth." We think God apt to take offence and backward to forgive—that, if he forgives once, he will not forgive a second time. Peter thought it a great deal to *forgive seven times* (Matt. xviii. 21), but God meets returning sinners with pardoning mercy. We forgive and cannot forget; but, when God forgives sin, he remembers it no more.

2. If we look down to this earth, we find God's word there powerful and effectual, *v.* 10, 11. He saith to the snow, Be thou on the earth; he appoints when it shall come, to what degree, and how long it shall lie there; he saith so *to the small rain and the great rain of his strength,* Job. xxxvii. 6. It returns not *without having accomplished its end,* but waters the earth. And the watering of the earth is in order to its fruitfulness. Thus he makes it to *bring forth and bud*; and thus it gives not only *bread to the eater,* present maintenance to the owner and his family, but *seed* likewise *to the sower,* that he may have food for another year. The husbandman must be a sower as well as an eater, else he will soon see the end of what he has. "*So shall my word be,* as powerful in the mouth of prophets as it is in the hand of providence; *it shall not return unto me void, it shall accomplish that which I please, and it shall prosper in the thing for which I sent it.*" These promises of mercy and grace shall have as real an effect upon the souls of believers, for their sanctification and comfort, as ever the rain had upon the earth, to make it fruitful. Christ's coming into the world, as the dew from heaven (Hos. xiv. 5), will not be in vain.

3. If we take a special view of the church, we shall find what great things God has done, and will do, for it (*v.* 12, 13): *You shall go out with joy, and be led forth with peace.* This refers, (1) To the deliverance and return of the Jews out of Babylon. They shall go out of their captivity, and be led forth towards their own land again. They shall go out *with joy* and *peace.* They shall have the goodwill and good wishes of all the countries they pass through. *The hills* and their inhabitants *shall break forth into singing.* And, when they come to their own land, it shall be ready to bid them welcome. (2) Without doubt to something more. This shall be *for an everlasting sign,* that is, [1] The redemption of the Jews out of Babylon shall be a ratification of those promises that relate to gospel times. [2] It shall be a representation of the blessings promised and a figure of them. Gospel grace will set those at liberty that were in bondage to sin and Satan. They *shall go out and be led forth. Jacob shall rejoice, and Israel shall be glad.* It will make a great change

JAMIESON, FAUSSET, BROWN

7. unrighteous—*Hebrew,* "man of iniquity"; true of all men. The "wicked" sins more openly in "his way"; the "unrighteous" refers to the more subtle workings of sin in the "thoughts." All are guilty in the latter respect, thought many fancy themselves safe, because not openly "wicked in ways" (Ps. 94:11). The parallelism is that of gradation. The progress of the penitent is to be from negative reformation, "forsaking his way," and a farther step, "his thoughts," to positive repentance, "returning to the Lord" (the only true repentance, Zech. 12:10), and making God *his* God, along with the other children of God (the crowning-point; *appropriation* of God *to ourselves:* "to *our* God"). "Return" implies that man originally walked with God, but has apostatized. Isaiah saith, "*our* God," the God of the believing Israelites; those themselves redeemed desire others to come to *their* God (Ps. 34:8; Rev. 22:17). **abundantly pardon**—(lit., "multiply to pardon," still more than "have mercy"; God's graciousness is felt more and more the longer one knows Him (Ps. 130: 7). **8. For**—referring to vs. 7. You need not doubt His willingness "abundantly to pardon" (cf. vs. 12); *for,* though "the wicked" man's "*ways,*" and "the unrighteous man's *thoughts,*" are so aggravated as to seem unpardonable, God's "thoughts" and "ways" in pardoning are not regulated by the proportion of the former, as man's would be towards his fellow man who offended him; cf. the "for" (Ps. 25:11; Rom. 5:19). **9.** (Ps. 57:10; 89:2; 103:11.) "For" is repeated from vs. 8. But MAURER, after the negation, translates, "but."

10. The hearts of men, once barren of spirituality, shall be made, by the outpouring of the Spirit under Messiah, to bear fruits of righteousness (ch. 5:6; Deut. 32:2; II Sam. 23:4; Ps. 72:6). **snow**—which covers plants from frost in winter; and, when melted in spring, waters the earth. **returneth not**—void; as in vs. 11; it returns not in the same shape, or without "accomplishing" the desired end. **bud**—germinate.

11. (Matt. 24:35.) Rain may to us seem lost when it falls on a desert, but it fulfils some purpose of God. So the gospel word falling on the hard heart; it sometimes works a change at last; and even if not so, it leaves men without excuse. The full accomplishment of this verse, and vss. 12, 13, is, however, to be at the Jews' final restoration and conversion of the world (ch. 11:9-12; 60:1-5, 21).

12. go out—from the various countries in which ye (the Jews) are scattered, to your own land (Ezek. 11:17). **led**—by Messiah, your "Leader" (vs. 4; ch. 52:12; Mic. 2:12, 13). **mountains . . . trees . . .**—images justly used to express the seeming sympathy of nature with the joy of God's people. For, when sin is removed, the natural world shall be delivered from "vanity," and be renewed, so as to be in unison with the regenerated moral world (ch. 44:23; Ps. 98:8; Rom. 8:19-22). **13. thorn**—emblem of the wicked (II Sam. 23:6; Mic. 7:4). **fir tree**—the godly (ch. 60:13; Ps. 92:12). Cf. as to the change wrought Romans 6:19. **brier**—emblem of uncultivation (ch. 5:6). **myrtle**—*Hebrew, Hedes,* from which comes *Hedassah,* the original name of Esther. Type of the Christian Church; for it is a lowly, though beautiful, fragrant, and evergreen shrub (Ps. 92:13, 14). **for a name . . . everlasting sign**—a perpetual memorial to the glory of Jehovah (Jer. 13:11; 33:9).

ADAM CLARKE

CHARLES H. SPURGEON:

Verse 7. The pardon of God may well be abundant, for *it wells up from an infinite fountain*; "mercy, which endureth for ever," is the attribute from which that pardon springs. Pardon is the child of mercy, not of justice; and we may reckon that God will give abundant pardon because He delighteth in mercy. All the attributes of God are well balanced: like Himself, they are infinite, and no one of them entrenches upon or dims the lustre of another. He is infinitely just, yet infinitely good; infinitely powerful, yet infinitely tender. We are quite sure that whenever an attribute of God comes into action it will be sufficiently revealed to make its glory manifest. There could be no mercy exercised by God until there was sin. Where all was blameless, mercy had no sphere. As soon as the angels fell, the Lord might have exercised mercy had He pleased; but He did not choose to provide salvation for Satan and his rebellious hordes. As if to teach us that it is not inevitable that God should forgive, He suffered the fallen angels to fall irretrievably, and gave them up to everlasting fire as their due desert. Deceived by the old serpent, man also fell, and again there was space for mercy. Man was an inferior creature to the angels: should he be allowed to perish or should grace step in? In this case mercy bowed the heavens and came down, and the Lord of all, as if to show that He "will have mercy on whom he will have mercy, and will have compassion on whom he will have compassion," though He had passed the angels by, took up the race of men, and determined that His pardons should be bestowed upon them. Now, when He had resolved to let mercy come to the front and be seen—which I again say could not have been if there had been no sin—was it not wonderful that He allowed that blessed attribute to come forth in all the fulness of its might. In the creation you see power in its majesty, and wisdom in its grandeur; in providence you see goodness unbounded, and faithfulness unlimited; in the gulf to which the Lord has condemned the wicked you see justice in all its awful glory: and therefore when He determined to let mercy come forth from her ivory palaces it seemed but natural that He should give ample room and verge enough. It was not according to His mind that from the unfathomable depths of His love there should trickle forth a stinted stream of mercy, which might wash out a little sin, and water a scanty patch of the desert of our nature; but He poured floods upon the dry ground.

—*The Treasury of the Old Testament*

12. *The mountains and the hills.* These are highly poetical images to express a happy state attended with joy and exultation.

13. *Instead of the thorn*—"Instead of the thorny bushes." These likewise are general poetical images, expressing a great and happy change for the better. The wilderness turned into a paradise, Lebanon into Carmel; the desert of the Gentiles watered with the heavenly snow and rain, which fail not to have their due effect and becoming fruitful in piety and righteousness; or, as the Chaldee gives the moral sense of the emblem, "Instead of the wicked shall arise the just; and instead of sinners, such as fear to sin." Compare chap. xxxv. 1-2; xli. 19.

MATTHEW HENRY

in men's characters. Those that were as thorns and briers, good for nothing but the fire, shall become graceful and useful as the fir-tree and the myrtle-tree. The raising of pleasant trees in the room of them signifies the removal of the curse of the law and the introduction of gospel blessings. The covenant of grace is an everlasting covenant; for the present blessings of it are signs of everlasting ones.

CHAPTER 56

Verses 1–2

When God is coming towards us in mercy we must go to meet him in a way of duty.

I. God here tells us what are his intentions of mercy to us (*v.* 1): *My salvation is near to come*—the great salvation wrought out by Jesus Christ typified by the salvation of the Jews from Sennacherib or out of Babylon. 1. The gospel salvation is the salvation of the Lord. 2. In that salvation God's righteousness is revealed, which St. Paul makes the ground of his glorying in it (Rom. i. 17). The law revealed that righteousness of God by which all sinners stand condemned, but the gospel reveals that by which all believers stand acquitted. 3. The Old Testament saints saw this salvation coming long before it came; and they had notice by the prophets of its approach.

II. He tells us what are his expectations of duty from us. Say not, "We see the salvation near, and therefore we may live as we list, for there is no danger now of missing it or coming short of it"; that is turning the grace of God into wantonness. But, on the contrary, when the salvation is near double your guard against sin. That which is here required to qualify and prepare us for the approaching salvation is,

1. That we be honest and just in all our dealings: *Keep you judgment and do justice*. God is true to us; let us be so to one another.

2. That we religiously observe the sabbath day, *v.* 2. We are not just if we rob God of his time. Sabbath-sanctification is here put for all the duties of the first table, the fruits of our love to God, as justice and judgment are put for all those of the second table, the fruits of our love to our neighbour. They might distinguish themselves from the heathen by putting a difference between God's day and other days.

3. That we have nothing to do with sin: *Blessed is the man* that *keeps his hand from doing evil*, any wrong to his neighbour, in body, goods, or good name—or, more generally, anything that is displeasing to God and hurtful to his own soul. The best evidence of our having kept the sabbath well will be to keep a good conscience all the week. It will appear that we have been in the mount with God if our faces shine in a holy conversation before men.

Verses 3–8

The prophet is here, in God's name, encouraging those that were joining themselves to God, yet laboured under great discouragements. 1. Some were discouraged because they were not of the seed of Abraham. They had *joined themselves to the Lord*, but they questioned whether God would accept them, because they were of *the sons of the stranger*, *v.* 3. They were Gentiles, aliens from the covenants of promise, and therefore feared they had no part nor lot in the matter. They said, "*The Lord has utterly separated me from his people*, and will not own me as one of them, nor admit me to their privileges." 2. Others were discouraged because they were not fathers in Israel. The eunuch said, *Behold, I am a dry tree*. He was thought to be of no use because he had no children, nor was ever likely to have any. This was the more grievous because eunuchs were not admitted to be priests (Lev. xxi. 20), nor to *enter into the congregation* (Deut. xxiii. 1). Yet God would not have the eunuchs to think that they should be excluded from the gospel church, and from being spiritual priests. As the taking down of the partition wall, contained in ordinances, admitted the Gentiles, so it let in likewise those that had been kept out by ceremonial pollutions. Now encouragements are given

I. To those who have no children of their own, though they had the honour to be the children of the church and the covenant themselves.

1. What a good character they have! They *keep God's sabbaths* as he has appointed them to be kept. They *choose those things that please God*. They *take hold of his covenant*. The covenant of grace is proffered to us in the gospel; to take hold of it is to accept the offer deliberately and sincerely to take God to be to us a God and to give up ourselves to be to him a people. We take hold of it as a criminal took hold

JAMIESON, FAUSSET, BROWN

CHAPTER 56

VSS. 1-12. THE PREPARATION NEEDED ON THE PART OF THOSE WHO WISH TO BE ADMITTED TO THE KINGDOM OF GOD.

near to come—(Matt. 3:2; 4:17), also as to the second coming (ch. 62:10, 11; Luke 21:28, 31; Rom. 13:11, 12; Heb. 10:25). **righteousness**—answering to "salvation" in the parallel clause; therefore it means *righteousness which bringeth salvation* (ch. 46:13; Rom. 3:25, 26).

1. judgment—equity. John the Baptist preached similarly a return to righteousness, as needed to prepare men for Messiah's first coming (Luke 3:3, 8-14). So it shall be before the second coming (Mal. 4:4-6).

2. (Luke 12:43). **the man**—*Hebrew, enosh,* "a man in humble life," in contradistinction to *Hebrew, ish,*" "one of high rank." Even the humblest, as "the stranger" and "the eunuch" (vss. 4, 6), are admissible to these privileges. **this . . . it**—what follows: "keeping the Sabbath," etc. (ch. 58:13, 14; Ezek. 20:12). A proof that the Sabbath, in the *spirit* of its obligation, was to be binding under the Gospel (ch. 66:23). That gospel times are referred to is plain, from the blessing not being pronounced on the man who observed the *sacrificial* ritual of the Jewish law. **layeth hold**—image from one grasping firmly some precious object which he is afraid of having forcibly snatched from him. The "Sabbath" here includes all the ordinances of divine worship under the new gospel law. **keepeth . . . hand . . . from . . . evil**—The observance of the second table of the law; as the "Sabbath" referred to the first table. Together, they form the whole duty of man, the worship of God and a holy life. **3.** God welcomes all believers, without distinction of persons, under the new economy (Acts 10:34, 35). **joined . . . to . . . Lord**—(Num. 18:4, 7). "Proselytes." **separated**—Proselytes from the Gentiles were not admitted to the same privileges as native Israelites. This barrier between Jews and Gentiles was to be broken down (Eph. 2:14-16). **eunuch**—(Acts 8:27, etc.). Eunuchs were chamberlains over harems, or court ministers in general. **dry tree**—barren (cf. Luke 23:31); not admissible into the congregation of Israel (Deut. 23:1-3). Under the Gospel the eunuch and stranger should be released from religious and civil disabilities.

4. please me—sacrifice their own pleasure to mine. **take hold**—so "layeth hold" (*Note,* vs. 2).

ADAM CLARKE

CHAPTER 56

F. B. MEYER:

The blessedness of Sabbath-keeping. The bright array of Messianic promises which occupied the preceding chapters is now followed by a portion of lesser interest, seeing that our attention is not now fastened on Christ, but on Israel. Birk calls this sermon "The Middle Ages of Delay," and says: "This new section of advice and warning belongs to the whole period from Isaiah to Christ. The like message applies now to the Church of Christ and its prospect of the Second Advent."

Special emphasis is laid on Sabbath-keeping because it was the special sign of God's connection with Israel (Exod. 31:13–17; Ezek. 20:12). It was also a type and pledge of the redemption rest, soon to be brought in and perfected by Christ's finished work (Heb. 4:9, 10).

What an ideal is presented here for character and conduct! To keep God's rest in our heart—the rest of faith; to cease from ourselves; to be joined to the Lord by one Spirit; to minister to him; to love his name; to be his servants! What more could we imagine as characteristic of the Christain soul! Let us ask God to bring *us* to his "holy mountain" and to make *us* "joyful" in his "house of prayer."—*Bible Commentary*

2. *That keepeth the sabbath from polluting it.* Kimchi has an excellent note here. "The Sabbath is sanctified when it is distinguished in dignity; and separated from other days."

MATTHEW HENRY

of the horns of the altar to which he fled for refuge.

2. If they answer to this character, though they are not built up into families (*v.* 5): *Unto them will I give a better place and name.* There is a place and a name, which we have from sons and daughters, but there is a better place, and a better name, which those have that are in covenant with God, and it is sufficient to counterbalance the want of the former. A place and a name denote rest and reputation. Though they have not children to be the music of their house, yet they *shall* have a place and a name. God will give it to them by promise; he will himself be both their place and their name. He will give it to them in his house, and within his walls; there they shall have a place. Our relation to God, our interest in Christ, and our hopes of eternal life, are things that give us in God's house a blessed place and a blessed name. It shall be *an everlasting name, that shall never be cut off.*

II. To those that are themselves the children of strangers.

1. It is here promised that they shall now be welcome to the church, *v.* 6, 7. When God's Israel come out of Babylon, let them bring their neighbours along with them, and God will find room enough for them all in his house. Let them know that the sons of the strangers shall have a place and a name in God's house provided, [1] That they forsake other gods. [2] That they join themselves to him as subjects to their prince and soldiers to their general, by an oath of fidelity and obedience. [3] That they join themselves to him as friends to his honour, *to love the name of the Lord.* Serving him and loving him go together, and that obedience is most acceptable to him, which flows from a principle of love, for then *his commandments are not grievous,* 1 John v. 3. Three things are promised them, in their coming to God: Assistance: "*I will bring them to my holy mountain,* not only bid them welcome when they come, but incline them to come, will show them the way, and lead them in it." Acceptance: "*Their burnt-offerings and their sacrifices shall be accepted on my altar,* and be never the less acceptable for being theirs, though they are sons of the stranger." Comfort: They shall not only be accepted, but they themselves shall have the pleasure of it: *I will make them joyful in my house of prayer.* Many a sorrowful spirit has been made joyful in the house of prayer.

2. It is here promised that multitudes of the Gentiles shall come to the church. *My house shall be called a house of prayer for all people.* Now concerning this house it is promised, (1) That it shall not be a house of sacrifice, but a house of prayer. (2) That it shall be a house of prayer, not for the people of the Jews only, but for all people. This was fulfilled when Peter was made, not only to perceive it himself, but to tell it to the world, that *in every nation he that fears God and works righteousness is accepted of him,* Acts x. 35. It had been declared again and again that *the stranger that comes nigh shall be put to death,* but Gentiles shall now be looked upon no longer as strangers and foreigners, Eph. ii. 19. And it is intimated here (*v.* 8) that when the Gentiles are called in they shall be incorporated into one body with the Jews, that (as Christ says, John x. 16) there may be *one fold and one Shepherd.* There are still more and more to be brought in. The church is a growing body: we may still hope there shall be more, till the mystical body be completed. *Other sheep I have.*

Verses 9–12

From words of comfort the prophet here, by a very sudden change passes to words of reproof in the three following chapters; and therefore some here begin a new sermon. He had assured the people that in due time God would deliver them out of captivity. Now here he shows what their sins and provocations were.

I. Desolating judgments are here summoned, *v.* 9. The sheep of God's pasture are now to be made the sheep of his slaughter, to fall as victims to his justice, and therefore *the beasts of the field and the forest* are called to come and devour. If this refers primarily to the descent made upon them by the Babylonians, and their devouring them, yet it may look further, to the destruction of Jerusalem and the Jewish nation by the Romans. The Roman armies came upon them as beasts of the forest to devour them, and they quite *took away their place and nation.*

II. The reason of these judgments is here given. The shepherds, who should have been the watchmen of the flock, were treacherous and minded not the trust reposed in them, and so the sheep became an easy prey to the wild beasts. Now this may refer to the false prophets in Isaiah's, Jeremiah's, and Ezekiel's time, and to the priests that bore rule by their

JAMIESON, FAUSSET, BROWN

5. in mine house–the temple, the emblem of the Church (I Tim. 3:15). They shall no longer be confined as proselytes were, to the outer court, but shall be admitted "into the holiest" (Heb. 10:19, 20). **a place**–lit., "a hand." **than of sons**–Though the eunuch is barren of *children* (vs. 3), I will give him a more lasting name than that of being father of sons and daughters (regarded as a high honor among the Hebrews) (John 1:12; 10:3; I John 3:1; Rev. 2:17; 3:12).

6. join . . . Lord–(Jer. 50:6). Conditions of admission to the privileges of adoption.

7. Even them–(Eph. 2:11-13.) **to my holy mountain**–Jerusalem, the seat of the Lord's throne in His coming kingdom (ch. 2:2; Jer. 3:17). **joyful**–(Rom. 5:11). **burnt offerings . . . sacrifices**–spiritual, of which the literal were types (Rom. 12:1; Heb. 13:15; I Pet. 2:5). **accepted**–(Eph. 1:6.) **altar**–(Heb. 13:10), spiritually, the Cross of Christ, which sanctifies our sacrifices of prayer and praise.

house . . . for all people–or rather, "peoples." No longer restricted to *one* favored people (Mal. 1:11; John 4:21, 23; I Tim. 2:8). To be fully realized at the second coming (ch. 2:2-4). No longer literal, but spiritual sacrifice, viz., "prayer" shall be offered (Ps. 141:2; 52:17; Mal. 1:11; Matt. 21:13). **8. Jehovah will not only restore the scattered outcasts of Israel (ch. 11:12; Ps. 147:2) to their own land, but "will gather others ('strangers') to him (Israel), besides those gathered" (*Margin,* to his gathered; i.e., in addition to the Israelites collected from their dispersion), (John 10:16; Eph. 1:10; 2:19).**

9. beasts–Gentile **idolatrous nations hostile to the Jews, summoned by God to chastise them (Jer. 12:7-9; 50:17; Ezek. 34:5): the Chaldeans and subsequently the Romans. The mention of the "outcasts of Israel" (vs. 8) brings in view the outcasting, caused by the sins of their rulers (vss. 10-12).** **to devour**–viz., Israel.

10. His watchmen–Israel's spiritual leaders (ch. 62:16; Ezek. 3:17).

ADAM CLARKE

6. *The sons of the stranger.* The Gentiles. *That join themselves to the Lord.* Who shall enter into the Christian covenant by baptism and faith in Christ, as the Jews and proselytes did by circumcision. *To serve him.* To live according to the gospel, and ever do that which is right in the sight of the Lord. *To love the name of the Lord.* The name of Jesus, the Christ, the Saviour of sinners, the Anointed of God, and the Giver of the Holy Spirit to His followers. *To be his servants.* To worship no other God but Jehovah, and to trust in none for salvation but His Christ. *That keepeth the sabbath.* That observes it as a type of the rest that remains for the people of God. *And taketh hold of my covenant.* "Of My covenant sacrifice," as without this he can do nothing good; and without it nothing can be acceptable to the infinite majesty of the Most High.

9. *All ye beasts of the field.* Here manifestly begins a new section. The prophet in the foregoing chapters, having comforted the faithful Jews with many great promises of God's favor to be extended to them, in the restoration of their ruined state, and in the enlargement of His Church by the admission of the Gentiles, here on a sudden makes a transition to the more disagreeable part of the prospect, and to a sharp reproof of the wicked and unbelievers; and especially of the negligent and faithless governors and teachers, of the idolaters and hypocrites, who would still draw down His judgments upon the nation, probably having in view the destruction of their city and polity by the Chaldeans, and perhaps by the Romans. The same subject is continued in the next chapter, in which the charge of corruption and apostasy becomes more general against the whole Jewish church.

MATTHEW HENRY

means. Or it may refer to the wicked princes, the sons of Josiah, that *did evil in the sight of the Lord*, and wicked magistrates under them, who betrayed their trust, and augmented the fierce anger of the Lord instead of doing anything to turn it away. Or it may refer to those who were the nation's watchmen in our Saviour's time, the chief priests and the scribes, who should have given notice to the people of the approach of the Messiah, but who, instead of that, opposed him. *Woe unto thee, O land!* when thy guides are such. 1. They were ignorant of their work, and unfit to teach, being so ill-taught themselves: *His watchmen are blind*, and unfit to be watchmen. Christ describes the Pharisees to be *blind leaders of the blind*, Matt. xv. 14. The beasts of the field come to devour, and the watchmen are blind, and are not aware of them. *They are all ignorant* (*v.* 10), *shepherds that cannot understand* (*v.* 11), that know not what is to be done about the sheep. 2. As they were blind watchmen, that could not discern the danger, so they were *dumb dogs*, that would not give warning of it. They barked at God's prophets, bit them and worried the sheep, but made no opposition to the wolf or thief. 3. They were lazy, and loved their ease, *loving to slumber*. 4. They were covetous—*greedy dogs that can never have enough*. All their enquiry is what they shall get, not what they shall do. They are everyone looking to his *own way*, minding his own private interests, and have no regard at all to the public welfare. Everyone is for propagating his own opinion, advancing his own party, while the common concerns of the pubiic are wretchedly neglected and postponed. 5. They were never so much in their element as in their drunken revels (*v.* 12): *Come* (say they), *I will fetch wine and we will fill ourselves*, or be drunk, *with strong drink*. They courted the people to sit and drink with them, and so confirmed those in their wicked ways, whom they should have reproved. How could they think it any harm to be drunk when the watchmen themselves joined with them and led them to it! 6. They were confident of the continuance of their prosperity and ease; they said, "*To-morrow shall be as this day and much more abundant;* we shall have as much to spend upon our lusts tomorrow as we have today."

JAMIESON, FAUSSET, BROWN

dumb dogs—image from bad shepherds' watchdogs, which fail to give notice, by barking, of the approach of wild beasts. **blind**—(Matt. 23:16). **sleeping, lying down**—rather, "dreamers, sluggards" [LOWTH]. Not merely *sleeping* inactive, but under *visionary delusions*. **loving to slumber**—not merely slumbering involuntarily, but loving it.

11. greedy—lit., "strong" (i.e., insatiable) *in appetite* (Ezek. 34:2, 3; Mic. 3:11). **cannot understand**—unable to comprehend the wants of the people, spiritually: so vs. 10, "*cannot* bark." **look to . . . own way**—i.e., their own selfish interests; not to the spiritual welfare of the people (Jer. 6:13; Ezek. 22:27). **from his quarter**—rather, "from the highest to the lowest" [LOWTH]. "From his quarter"; i.e., from one end to the other of them, *one and all* (Gen. 19:4). **12. fetch wine**—language of the national teachers challenging one another to drink. BARNES translates, "I will take another cup" (ch. 5:11).

to-morrow . . .—Their self-indulgence was *habitual* and *intentional:* not merely they drink, but they mean to continue so.

ADAM CLARKE

11. *Greedy dogs.* Insatiably feeding themselves with the fat, and clothing themselves with the wool, while the flock is scattered, ravaged, and starved!

12. *I will fetch wine*—"Let us provide wine." The spirit of this epicurean sentiment is this: Let us indulge ourselves in the present time to the utmost, and instead of any gloomy forebodings of the future, let us expect nothing but increasing hilarity for every day we shall live.

MATTHEW HENRY

CHAPTER 57

Verses 1–2

The prophet had condemned the watchmen for their ignorance and sottishness; here he shows the general stupidity and senselessness of the people.

I. The providence of God removing good men out of this world. *The righteous*, as to this world, *perish;* Piety exempts none from death. Righteousness delivers from the sting of death, but not from the stroke of it. Those are often removed that could be worst spared; the fruitful trees are cut down by death and the barren left still to cumber the ground.

II. The careless world slighting these providences: *No man lays it to heart, none considers it.* There are very few that lament it as a public loss, very few that take notice of it as a public warning. Little children, when they are little, least lament the death of their parents, because they know not what a loss it is to them.

III. The happiness of the righteous in their removal. They *are taken away from the evil to come.* When the deluge is coming they are called into the ark. In wrath to the world those are taken away that stood in the gap to turn away the judgments of God. It is a sign that God intends war when he calls home his ambassadors. The righteous man, when he dies *enters into peace* and *rests in his bed.* Those that practised uprightness, and persevered in it to the end, shall find it well with them when they die. Their souls then enter into peace.

Verses 3–12

A high charge, but a just one, against that wicked generation out of which God's righteous ones were removed, because the world was not worthy of them.

I. The name and title by which they stand indicted, *v.* 3. They are arraigned as *sons of the sorceress*, or of a witch, *the seed of an adulterer and a whore.* Sin is sorcery and adultery, for it is departing from God and dealing with the devil. They were *children of disobedience.* "Come," says the prophet, "draw near hither, and I will read you your doom; you are *children of transgression, a seed of falsehood*" (*v.* 4).

II. The particular crimes laid to their charge.

1. Scoffing at God and his word. They were a generation of scorners (*v.* 4): "*Against whom do you sport yourselves?* You think it is only against the poor prophets, whom you trample upon, but really it is against God himself, whose message they deliver."

JAMIESON, FAUSSET, BROWN

CHAPTER 57

Vss. 1-21. THE PEACEFUL DEATH OF THE RIGHTEOUS FEW: THE UNGODLINESS OF THE MANY: A BELIEVING REMNANT SHALL SURVIVE THE GENERAL JUDGMENTS OF THE NATION, AND BE RESTORED BY HIM WHO CREATES PEACE. **In the midst of the excesses of the unfaithful watchmen (ch. 56:10, 11, 12), most of the few that are godly perish: partly by vexation at the prevailing ungodliness; partly by violent death in persecution: prophetical of the persecuting times of Manasseh, before God's judgments in causing the captivity in Babylon; and again those in the last age of the Church, before the final judgments on the apostasy (II Kings 21:16; Matt. 23:29-35, 37; Rev. 11:17).** The *Hebrew* for "perisheth," and "is taken away," expresses a *violent death* (Mic. 7:2). **1. no man layeth it to heart**—as a public calamity. **merciful men**—rather, *godly men;* the subjects of mercy. **none considering**—viz., what was the design of Providence in removing the godly. **from the evil**—*Hebrew,* from the face of the evil, i.e., both from the moral evil on every side (ch. 56:10-12), and from the evils about to come in punishment of the national sins, foreign invasions, etc. (ch. 56:9; 57:13). So Ahijah's death is represented as a blessing conferred on him by God for his piety (I Kings 14:10-13; see also II Kings 22:20). **2.** Or, "he *entereth* into peace"; in contrast to the *persecutions* which he suffered in this world (Job 3:13, 17). *Margin* not so well translates, "he shall go in peace" (Ps. 37:37; Luke 2:29). **rest**—the calm rest of their bodies in their graves (called "beds," II Chron. 16:14; cf. Isa. 14:18; because they "sleep" in them, with the certainty of awakening at the resurrection, I Thess. 4: 14) is the emblem of the eternal "rest" (Heb. 4:9; Rev. 14:13). **each one walking in . . . uprightness**—This clause defines the character of those who at death "rest in their beds," viz., all who walk uprightly. **3. But . . . ye**—In contrast to "the righteous" and their end, he announces to the unbelieving Jews their doom. **sons of the sorceress**—i.e., ye that are addicted to sorcery: this was connected with the worship of false gods (II Kings 21: 6). No insult is greater to an Oriental than any slur cast on his *mother* (I Sam. 20:30; Job 30:8). **seed of the adulterer**—*Spiritual* adultery is meant: idolatry and apostasy (Matt. 16:4). **4. sport yourselves**—make a mock (ch. 66:5). Are ye aware of

ADAM CLARKE

CHAPTER 57

I shall give Bishop Lowth's translation of the first two verses, and give the substance of his criticisms with additional evidence.

"Ver. 1. The righteous man perisheth, and
no one considereth;
And pious men are taken away, and
no one understandeth,
That the righteous man is taken away
because of the evil.

"2. He shall go in peace: he shall rest in
his bed;
Even the perfect man: he that walketh in the straight path."

1. *The righteous perisheth.* There is an emphasis here which seems intended to point out a particular person. *Perisheth*—As the root *abad* signifies the straying of cattle, their passing away from one pasture to another, I feel inclined to follow the grammatical meaning of the word "perish," *pereo.* So the Vulgate, *justus periit,* from *per,* "by" or "through," and *eo,* to "go." In his death the righteous man may be said to have passed "through" life, and to have passed by men, i.e., gone or passed before them into the eternal world. There are very few places in Isaiah where Jesus Christ is not intended; and I am inclined to think that He is intended here, that Just One; and perhaps Stephen had this place in view when he thus charged the Jews, "Ye denied the Holy One and the Just," Acts iii. 14. *Merciful men.* If the first refers to Christ, this may well refer to the apostles, and to others of the primitive Christians, who were *taken away,* some by death and martyrdom, and others by a providential escape from the city that they knew was devoted to destruction. *The evil to come.* That destruction which was to come upon this disobedient people by the Romans.

2. *He shall enter into peace*—"He shall go in peace." *Yabo shalom;* the expression is elliptical, such as the prophet frequently uses. The same sense is expressed at large and in full terms, Gen. xv. 15: "And thou shalt go to thy fathers in peace." *They shall rest in their beds, each one walking in his uprightness*—"He shall

MATTHEW HENRY

They made wry mouths at the prophets, and drew out the tongue, contrary to all the laws of good breeding: nor did they treat God's prophets with common civility.

2. Idolatry. This was that sin which the people of the Jews were most notoriously guilty of before the captivity; but that affliction cured them of it. In Isaiah's time it abounded, witness the abominable idolatries of Ahaz (which some think are particularly referred to here) and of Manasseh. (1) They were dotingly fond of their idols, inflamed themselves with them by their violent passions in the worship of them, 1 Kings xviii. 26, 28. They worshipped their idols *under every green tree*, in the open air, and in the shade; the beauty of the green trees made them the more fond of their idols which they worshipped there. (2) They were barbarous and unnaturally cruel in the worship of their idols. They slew their children, and offered them in sacrifice to their idols, in valleys, and *under the cliffs of the rock*, in dark and solitary places, the fittest for such works of darkness. (3) They were insatiable in their idolatries. [1] They had gods of the valleys, which they worshipped by the water side (*v.* 6): *Among the smooth stones of the valley*, or brook, *is thy portion.* If they saw a smooth carved stone, they were ready to worship it. "*To them hast thou poured a drink-offering, and offered a meat-offering*, as if they had given thee thy meat and drink." Have we taken the true God for our portion? Let us then serve him with our meat and drink, not by depriving ourselves of the use of them, but by eating and drinking to his glory. Here, in a parenthesis, comes in an expression of God's just resentment of this wickedness of theirs: *Should I receive comfort in these*—in such a people as this, who thus serve Baal? *Should I have compassion on these?* (so some), or *should I repent me concerning these?* so others. [2] They had gods of the hills too (*v.* 7): "*Upon a lofty and high mountain hast thou set thy bed*, thy idol, thy idol's temple and altar, the bed of thy uncleanness, where thou committest spiritual whoredom. *Thither wentest thou up* readily enough, though it was uphill, *to offer sacrifice*." [3] As if these were not enough, they had household-gods too, their *lares* and *penates. Behind the doors and the posts* (*v.* 8), where the law of God should be written, they set up the remembrance of their idols to show to others how mindful they were of them, and to put their children in mind of them. They were hardened in their wickedness; they went as publicly, and in as great crowds, to the idol-temples, as ever they had gone to God's house. This was like an impudent harlot, *discovering themselves to another than God.* They *enlarged their bed*, that is, their idol-temples, and (as the margin reads the following words) *thou hewedst it for thyself larger than theirs*, than theirs from whom thou copiedst it, 2 Kings xvi. 10. "*Thou hast made a covenant with them*, with the idols, with the idol-worshippers, to live and die together. *Thou lovedst their bed*, that is, the temple of an idol, wherever thou sawest it."

3. Another sin charged upon them is their trusting to foreign aids and contracting a communion with the Gentile powers (*v.* 9): *Thou wentest to the king* which some understand of *Moloch*, which signifies *a king.* Or it may be meant of the king of Assyria, whom Ahaz made his court to, or of the king of Babylon, whose ambassadors Hezekiah caressed, that they might strengthen themselves by an alliance with them. They went *with ointments and perfumes*, either to beautify their own faces and so make themselves worthy the friendship of the greatest king, or to be presented to those whose favour they desired. They hereby disparaged themselves and laid the honour of their crown and nation in the dust: *Thou didst debase thyself even unto hell.* They debased themselves by truckling to their heathen neighbours, and depending upon them, when they had a God to go to who is all-sufficient and in covenant with them.

III. The aggravations of their sin. 1. They had been tired with disappointments in their wicked courses, and yet they would not be convinced of the folly of them (*v.* 10): "*Thou art wearied in the greatness of thy way;* thou hast undertaken a mighty task, to find out true satisfaction and happiness in that which is vanity and a lie." *Thou art wearied in the multitude*, or *multiplicity, of thy ways* (so some read it): those that forsake the only right way wander endlessly in a thousand by-paths, and lose themselves in the many inventions which they have sought out. 2. Though they were convinced that the way they were in was a sinful way, yet, because they had found sensual pleasure and worldly profit by it, they could not persuade themselves to be sorry for it: "*Thou hast found the life of thy hand*" (or *the living of it*); thou art not grieved, any more than Ephraim when he said (Hos. xii. 8), "*I have become rich; I have found*

JAMIESON, FAUSSET, BROWN

the glory of Him whom you mock, by mocking His servants ("the righteous," vs. 1)? (II Chron. 36: 16.) **make . . . wide mouth**—(Ps. 22:7, 13; 35:21; Lam. 2:16). **children of transgression . . .**—not merely *children of transgressors*, and a *seed of false parents*, but of *transgression* and *falsehood* itself, utterly unfaithful to God.

5. Enflaming yourselves—burning with lust *towards idols* [GESENIUS]; or else (cf. *Margin*), *in the terebinth groves*, which the *Hebrew* and the parallelism favor (*Note*, ch. 1:29) [MAURER]. **under . . . tree**—(II Kings 17:10.) The tree, as in the Assyrian sculptures, was probably made an idolatrous symbol of *the heavenly hosts.* **slaying . . . children**—as a sacrifice to Molech, etc. (II Kings 17:31; II Chron. 28:3; 33:6). **in . . . valleys**—the valley of the son of Hinnom. Fire was put within a hollow brazen statue, and the child was put in his heated arms; kettle drums (*Hebrew, toph*) were beaten to drown the child's cries; whence the valley was called Tophet (II Chron. 33:6; Jer. 7:3). **under . . . clifts**—the gloom of caverns suiting their dark superstitions. **6.** The smooth stones, shaped as idols, are the gods chosen by thee as thy portion (Ps. 16:5). **meat offering**—not a bloody sacrifice, but one of meal and flour mingled with oil. "Meat" in Old English meant *food*, not *flesh*, as it means now (Lev. 14:10).

Should I receive comfort—rather, "Shall I bear these things with patience?" [HORSLEY].

7. Upon . . . high mountain . . . bed—image from adultery, *open and shameless* (Ezek. 23:7); the "bed" answers to the idolatrous *altar*, the scene of their spiritual unfaithfulness to their divine husband (Ezek. 16:16, 25; 23:41).

8. "Remembrance," i.e., memorials of thy idolatry: the objects which thou holdest in remembrance. *They hung up household tutelary gods* "behind the doors"; the very place where God has directed them to write His laws "on the posts and gates" (Deut. 6:9; 11:20); a curse, too, was pronounced on putting up an image "in a secret place" (Deut. 27:15). **discovered thyself**—image from an adulteress. **enlarged . . . bed**—so as to receive the more paramours. **made . . . covenant**—with idols: in open violation of thy "covenant" with *God* (Exod. 19:5; 23:32). Or, "hast made assignations with them for thyself" [HORSLEY]. **thy bed . . . their bed**—The Jews' sin was twofold; they resorted to places of idolatry ("*their* bed"), and they received idols into the temple of God ("*thy* bed"). **where**—rather, "ever since that" [HORSLEY]. The *Hebrew* for "*where*" means "*room*" (*Margin*), a place; therefore, translate, "thou hast provided a place for it" (for "their bed"), viz., by admitting idolatrous altars in thy land [BARNES]; or "thou choosest a (convenient) place for thyself" in their bed [MAURER] (ch. 56:5). **9. the king**—*the idol* which they came to worship, perfumed with oil, like harlots (Jer. 4:30; Ezek. 23:16, 40). So "king" means idol (Amos 5:26; Zeph. 1:5); (*malcham* meaning "king") [ROSENMULLER]. Rather, *the king of Assyria* or *Egypt*, and other foreign princes, on whom Israel relied, instead of on God; the "ointment" will thus refer to the presents (Hos. 12:1), and perhaps the compliances with foreigners' idolatries, whereby Israel sought to gain their favor [LOWTH] (ch. 30:6; Ezek. 16: 33; 23:16; Hos. 7:11). **send . . . messengers far off**—not merely to neighboring nations, but to those "far off," in search of new idols, or else alliances. **even unto hell**—the lowest possible degradation. **10. greatness of . . . way**—the *length* of thy journey in seeking strange gods, or else foreign aid (Jer. 2:23, 24). Notwithstanding thy deriving no good from these long journeys (so, "send . . . *far off*," vs. 9), thou dost not still give up hope (Jer. 2:25; 18:12).

hast found . . . life of . . . hand—for "thou still findest life (i.e., vigor) enough in thy hand" to make new idols [MAURER], or to seek new alliance ("hand" being then taken for *strength* in general).

ADAM CLARKE

rest in his bed; even the perfect man." To follow on my application of this to our Lord: *He*, the Just One, *shall enter into peace*—the peaceable, prosperous possession of the glorious mediatorial Kingdom. *They shall rest in their beds*—the hand of wrong and oppression can reach these persecuted followers of Christ no more. The perfect man *walking in his uprightness.* This may be considered as a general declaration. The separated spirit, though disunited from its body, walking in conscious existence in the paradise of God, reaping the fruit of righteousness.

6. *Among the smooth stones of the stream*—"Among the smooth stones of the valley." The Jews were extremly addicted to the practice of many superstitious and idolatrous rites, which the prophet here inveighs against with great vehemence. Of the worship of rude stones consecrated, there are many testimonials of the ancients. Kimchi says: "When they found a beautiful polished stone in a brook or river, they paid divine adoration to it."

8. *Behind the doors also and the posts hast thou set up thy remembrance*—"Behind the door, and the doorposts, have you set up your memorial." That is, the image of their tutelary gods, or something dedicated to them; in direct opposition to the law of God, which commanded them to write upon the doorposts of their house, and upon their gates, the words of God's law (Deut. vi. 9; xi. 20). If they chose for them such a situation as more private, it was in defiance of a particular curse denounced in the law against the man who should make a graven or a molten image, and put it in a secret place (Deut. xxvii. 15).

9. *And thou wentest to the king with ointment*—"And you have visited the king with a present of oil." That is, the king of Assyria, or Egypt. Hosea, chap. xii. 1, reproaches the Israelites for the same practice: "They do make a covenant with the Assyrians, and oil is carried into Egypt."

10. *Yet saidst thou not, There is no hope*—"You have said, There is hope." Now if we compare Jer. ii. 25 and xviii. 12, we shall find that the subject is in both places quite the same with this of Isaiah; and the sentiment expressed, that of a desperate resolution to continue at all hazards in their idolatrous practices—the very thing that in all reason we might expect here.

MATTHEW HENRY

out substance." Prosperity in sin is a great bar to conversion from sin. 3. They had dealt very unworthily with God by their sin; for, they pretended that the reason why they left God was because he was too terrible a majesty for them; they must have gods that they could be more familiar with. "But," says God, "*of whom hast thou been afraid or feared, that thou hast lied?* What did I ever do to frighten thee from me?" However, it is certain that they had no true reverence of God. "Thou *hast not remembered me,* neither what I have said nor what I have done, thou hast *not laid them to thy heart,* as thou wouldst have done if thou hadst feared me." They were hardened in their sin by the patience and forbearance of God.

IV. Here is God's resolution to call them to an account (*v.* 12): "*I will declare thy righteousness,* which thou makest thy boast of, and let the world see, and thyself too, to thy confusion, that it is all a sham. I will declare *thy works, they shall not profit thee,* nor turn to any account."

Verses 13–16

I. God shows how insufficient idols and creatures were to succour those that worshipped them (*v.* 13): "*When thou criest* in thy distress and callest for help, *let thy companies deliver thee,* thy idol-gods, the troops of the confederate forces which thou hast relied so much upon, let them deliver thee; expect no other relief than what they can give." *The wind shall carry them all away;* they have made themselves as chaff, and therefore the wind will of course hurry them away.

II. He shows that there was a sufficiency, an all-sufficiency, in him. "*He that puts his trust in me,* and in me only, he shall be happy, both for soul and body, for this world and the other." Those that trust in God's providence take the best course to secure their secular interests. They *shall possess the land,* as much of it as is good for them. Those that trust in God's grace take the best course to secure their sacred interests. They *shall inherit my holy mountain.* They shall enjoy the privileges of the church on earth, and be brought at length to the joys of heaven; and no wind shall carry them away. More particularly,

1. The captives, that trust in God, shall be released (*v.* 14): *They shall say* (that is, the messengers of his word, and all the ministers of his providence, in that great event shall say), *Cast you up, cast you up, prepare the way.* When God's time shall have come for their deliverance the way of bringing it about shall be made plain and obstacles shall be removed. This refers to the provision which the gospel, and the grace of it, have made for our ready passage through this world to a better. The way of religion is now cast up; it is a highway; ministers' business is to direct people in it.

2. The contrite, that trust in God, shall be *revived, v.* 15. God's glory appears here very bright, (1) In his greatness and majesty: He is *the high and lofty One that inhabits eternity. He is the high and lofty One,* and there is no creature like him, nor any to be compared with him. The language likewise intimates his sovereign dominion over all and the incontestable right he has to give both law and judgment to all. He is both immortal and immutable. There is an infinite rectitude in his nature. His name is *holy,* and all that desire to be acquainted with him must know him as a holy God. "*I dwell in the high and holy place,* and will have all the world to know it." Whoever have any business with God must direct to him as their Father in heaven, for there he dwells. Though he is thus high yet he has respect unto the lowly; he that rides on the heavens by his name JAH stoops to concern himself for poor *widows* and *fatherless,* Ps. lxviii. 4, 5. (2) In his grace and mercy. He has a tender pity for the humble and contrite. If they be his people, he will not overlook them though they are poor and despised and trampled upon by men; but he here refers to the temper of their mind; he will have a tender regard to those who, being in affliction, accommodate themselves to their affliction, and bring their mind to their condition. With these God will dwell. He will visit them graciously, will converse with them by his word and Spirit, as a man does with those of his own family. He that dwells in the highest heavens dwells in the lowest hearts and inhabits sincerity as surely as he inhabits eternity. In these he delights. He will revive their heart and spirit, will speak to them, and work in them by the word and Spirit of his grace.

3. Those with whom he contends, if they trust in him, shall be relieved, and received into favour, *v.* 16. He will *revive the heart of the contrite ones,* for he will not contend for ever. It is not promised that he will never be angry with his people, for their sins are displeasing to him, or that he will never contend with them, for they must expect the rod; but he *will not*

JAMIESON, FAUSSET, BROWN

grieved—rather, "therefore thou art not *weak*" [MAURER]; inasmuch as having "life in thy hand," thou art still strong in hope. **11.** Israel wished not to seem *altogether* to have denied God. Therefore they "lied" to Him. God asks, Why dost thou do so? "Whom dost thou fear? Certainly not *Me; for* thou hast not remembered Me." Translate, "*seeing that* thou hast not remembered Me." **laid it to . . . heart**—rather, "nor hast Me at heart"; hast no regard for Me; and that, because I have been long silent and have not punished thee. Lit., "Have I not held My peace, and that for long? and so thou fearest Me not" (Ps. 50:21; Eccles. 8:11). It would be better openly to renounce God, than to "flatter Him" with lies of false professions (Ps. 78:36) [LUDOVICUS DE DIEU]. However, ch. 51:12, 13 favors *English Version* of the whole verse; God's "silent" long-suffering, which was intended to lead them to repentance, caused them "not to fear Him" (Rom. 2:4, 5). **12. declare**—I will expose publicly thy (hypocritical) righteousness. I will show openly how vain thy works, in having recourse to idols, or foreign alliances, shall prove (vs. 3). **13. When thou criest**—In the time of thy trouble. **companies**—viz., of idols, collected by thee from every quarter; or else, of foreigners, summoned to thy aid. **wind . . . carry . . . away**—(Job 21:18; Matt. 7:27). **vanity**—rather, a breath [LOWTH].

possess . . . land . . . inherit—i.e., the literal land of Judea and Mount Zion; the believing remnant of Israel shall return and inherit the land. Secondarily, the heavenly inheritance, and the spiritual Zion (ch. 49:8; Ps. 37:9, 11; 69:35, 36; Matt. 5:5; Heb. 12:22). "He that putteth his trust in Me," of whatever extraction, shall succeed to the spiritual patrimony of the apostate Jew [HORSLEY]. **14. shall say**—The *nominative* is, "He that trusteth in Me" (vs. 13). The believing remnant shall have every obstacle to their return cleared out of the way, at the coming restoration of Israel, the antitype to the return from Babylon (ch. 35:8; 40:3, 4; 62:10, 11). **Cast . . . up**—a high road before the returning Jews. **stumbling block**—Jesus had been so to the Jews, but will not be so *then* any longer (I Cor. 1:23); their *prejudices* shall then be taken out of the way.

15. The pride and self-righteousness of the Jews were the stumbling block in the way of their acknowledging Christ. The *contrition* of Israel in the last days shall be attended with God's interposition in their behalf. So their self-humiliation, in ch. 66: 2, 5, 10, etc., precedes their final prosperity (Zech. 12:6, 10-14); there will, probably, be a previous period of unbelief even after their return (Zech. 12:8, 9).

16. For—referring to the promise in vss. 14, 15, of restoring Israel when "contrite" (Gen. 6:3; 8:21; Ps. 78:38, 39; 85:5; 103:9, 13, 14; Mic. 7:18). God "will not contend for ever" *with His*

ADAM CLARKE

11. *Nor laid it to thy heart*—"Nor revolved it in your hand." *Even of old*—"And winked." "As if not seeing," Vulgate. See Ps. x. 1. In one of my own MSS., "Is it not because I was silent, and winked?"

12. *Thy righteousness*—"My righteousness."

13. *Let thy companies deliver thee*—"Let your associates deliver you."

14. *And shall say*—"Then will I say." They are the words of God, as it is plain from the conclusion of the verse: *my people.*

16. *For I will not contend for ever.* The learned have taken a great deal of pains to little purpose on the latter part of this verse, which they suppose to be very obscure. I think

MATTHEW HENRY

contend for ever. As he is not soon angry, so he is not long angry. "If I should contend for ever, *the spirit would fail before me, even the souls which I have made.*" Though the Lord is for the body, yet he concerns himself chiefly for the souls of his people, that the spirit does not fail, nor its graces and comforts.

Verses 17–21

The body of the people of Israel, in this account of God's dealings with them, is spoken of as a particular person (*v.* 17, 18), but divided into two sorts, differently dealt with—some who were sons of peace, to whom peace is spoken (*v.* 19), and others who were not, who have nothing to do with peace, *v.* 20, 21.

I. The just rebukes which that people were brought under for their sin: *For the iniquity of his covetousness I was wroth, and smote him.* Covetousness was a sin that abounded. Those that did not worship images were yet carried away by this spiritual idolatry: for such is covetousness; it is making money the god, Col. iii. 5. Yet, covetous as they were, in the service of their idols they were prodigal, *v.* 6. And it is hard to say whether their profuseness in that or their covetousness in everything else was more provoking. Covetousness is an iniquity that is very displeasing to the God of heaven. He smote him, reproved him for it by his prophets, corrected him by his providence, punished him in those very things he so doted upon and was covetous of. God hid himself from him when he was under these rebukes. When we are under the rod, if God manifest himself to us, we may bear it the better; but if he hide himself from us, send us no prophets, speak to us no comfortable word, we are very miserable.

II. Their obstinacy and incorrigibleness under these rebukes: *He went on frowardly in the way of his heart,* in his evil way. See also how insufficient afflictions of themselves are to reform men, unless God's grace work with them.

III. God's wonderful return in mercy to them.

1. The greater part of them went on frowardly, but there were some among them that were mourners for the obstinacy of the rest; and God determines not to contend for ever with them. Such are the riches of divine mercy and grace, and so do they rejoice against judgment, that it follows, *I have seen his ways and will heal him.* Where sin has abounded grace much more abounds. God will first give him grace, and then, and not till then, give him peace: "I have seen his way, that he will never turn to me of himself, and therefore I will turn him." (1) God will heal him of his corrupt and vicious disposition. There is no spiritual disease so inveterate but almighty grace can conquer it. (2) God *will lead him also.* He goes on frowardly, as Saul, yet breathing out threatenings and slaughter, but God will lead him into a better mind, a better path. And then, (3) He will restore those comforts which he had forfeited, and for the return of which he had thus prepared him. There was a wonderful reformation wrought upon the captives in Babylon, and then a wonderful redemption wrought for them.

2. Now, as when that people went into captivity some of them were good figs, others of them bad figs, and accordingly their captivity was to them for their good or for *their hurt* (Jer. xxiv. 8, 9), so, when they came out of captivity, still some of them were good, others bad, and the deliverance was to them accordingly.

(1) To those among them that were good their return out of captivity was peace, a type of the peace which should be preached by Jesus Christ (*v.* 19): *I create the fruit of the lips, peace.* Creation is out of nothing, and this is surely out of worse than nothing, when God creates matter of praise for those that went on frowardly. In order to this, peace shall be published: *Peace, peace to him that is afar off* as well as *to him that is near.* Peace of conscience, a holy security and serenity of mind, after the many reproaches of conscience and agitations of spirit they had been under in their captivity. When he speaks peace to us, we must speak praises to him. This peace is itself of God's creating. It is the fruit of preaching lips and praying lips; it is the fruit of Christ's lips, Eph. ii. 17: *He came and preached peace to you who were afar off,* you Gentiles as well as to the Jews, who were nigh—to after-ages, who were afar off in time, as well as to those of the present age.

(2) To those among them that were wicked, though they might return with the rest, their return was no peace, *v.* 20. The wicked, wherever he is, in Babylon or in Jerusalem, carries about with him the principle of his own uneasiness. The wicked would not be healed by the grace of God and therefore shall not be healed by his comforts. They are always like the sea in a storm, for they carry about with them, [1] Unmortified corruptions. They are not cured and their

JAMIESON, FAUSSET, BROWN

people, for their human spirit would thereby be utterly crushed, whereas God's object is to chasten, not to destroy *them* (Lam. 3:33, 34; Mic. 7:8, 9). *With the ungodly* He is "angry *every day*" (Ps. 7:11; Rev. 14:11). **spirit . . . before me**—i.e., the human spirit which *went forth from Me* (Num. 16:22), answering to "which I have made" in the parallel clause.

17. covetousness—akin to idolatry; and, like it, having drawn off Israel's heart from God (ch. 2:7; 56:11; 58:3; Jer. 6:13; Col. 3:5). **hid me**—(ch. 8:17; 45:15).

went on frowardly—the result of God's hiding His face (Ps. 81:12; Rom. 1:24, 26).

18. Rather, "I have seen his ways (in sin), *yet* will I heal him," i.e., restore Israel spiritually and temporally (Jer. 33:6; 3:22; Hos. 14:4, 5 [HORSLEY]. However, the phrase, "his mourners," favors *English Version;* "his ways" will thus be his ways *of repentance;* and God's pardon on "seeing" them answers to the like promise (ch. 61:2, 3; Jer. 31:18, 20).

19. fruit of . . . lips—i.e., thanksgivings which flow from the lips. I make men to return thanks to Me (Hos. 14:2; Heb. 13:15). **Peace, peace**—"*perfect* peace" (see *Margin,* ch. 26:3; John 14:27). Primarily, the cessation of the troubles now afflicting the *Jews,* as formerly, under the Babylonian exile. More generally, the peace which the Gospel proclaims both to Israel "that is near," and to the Gentiles who are "far off" (Acts 2:39; Eph. 2:17).

20. when it cannot rest—rather, "*for* it can have no rest" (Job 15:20, etc.; Prov. 4:16, 17). *English Version* represents the sea as *occasionally* agitated; but the *Hebrew* expresses that it can *never* be at rest.

ADAM CLARKE

the best and easiest explication of it is given in the two following passages of the Psalms, which I presume are exactly parallel to it, and very clearly express the same sentiment: Ps. lxxviii. 38-39; ciii. 9, 13-14. *For the spirit. Ruach,* "the animal life." *And the souls. Neshamoth,* "the immortal spirits." The Targum understands this of the resurrection. "I will restore the souls of the dead," i.e., to their bodies.

17. *For the iniquity of his covetousness was I wroth*—"Because of his iniquity for a short time was I wroth."

18. *I have seen his ways.* Probably these verses refer to the restoration of the Jews from captivity.

19. *I create the fruit of the lips.* "The sacrifice of praise," saith St. Paul, Heb. xiii. 15, is "the fruit of our lips." God creates this fruit of the lips by giving new subject and cause of thanksgiving by His mercies conferred on those among His people who acknowledge and bewail their transgressions and return to Him. The great subject of thanksgiving is peace—reconciliation and pardon, offered to them that are nigh and to them that are afar off; not only to the Jew, but also to the Gentile, as St. Paul more than once applies those terms (Eph. ii. 13, 17). See also Acts ii. 39. *Peace to him that is far off*—"That is, to the penitent; *and to him that is near,* i.e., the righteous."—Kimchi.

21. *There is no peace, saith my God.* This verse has reference to the nineteenth. The per-

MATTHEW HENRY

ungoverned lusts and passions make them like the troubled sea. [2] Unpacified consciences. They are under a frightful apprehension of guilt and wrath, like Cain, who always dwelt in the land of shaking. It is a certain truth, what this prophet had said before (*ch.* xlviii. 22), and here repeats (*v.* 21), *There is no peace to the wicked*, no reconciliation to God, while they go on still in their trespasses.

JAMIESON, FAUSSET, BROWN

21. (Ch. 48:22; II Kings 9:22). **my God**—The prophet, having God as *his* God, speaks in the person of Israel, prophetically regarded as having now *appropriated* God and His "peace" (ch. 11:1-3), warning the impenitent that, while they continue so, they can have no peace.

ADAM CLARKE

severingly wicked and impenitent are excluded from all share in that peace above mentioned, that reconcilement and pardon which is promised to the penitent only. The forty-eighth chapter ends with the same declaration, to express the exclusion of the unbelievers and impenitent from the benefit of the foregoing promises.

MATTHEW HENRY — CHAPTER 58

Verses 1–2

When our Lord Jesus promised to send the Comforter he added, *When he shall come he shall convince* (John xvi. 7, 8); for conviction must prepare for comfort. God had appointed this prophet to comfort his people (*ch.* xl. 1); here he appoints him to convince them, and show them their sins.

I. He must tell them how bad they really were, *v.* 1. 1. He must deal faithfully and plainly with them. Though they are called *the people of God* and *the house of Jacob*, do not flatter them, but show them their transgressions, what sins are committed by them which they do not acknowledge to be sins; though in some things they are reformed, in other things they are still as bad as ever. 2. He must *cry aloud, and not spare*, not spare them, though he get their ill-will by it and get himself an ill name, yet he must not spare.

II. He must acknowledge how good they seemed to be, notwithstanding (*v.* 2): *Yet they seek me daily*. They pleaded that they could see no transgressions for they were diligent and constant in attending on God's worship—and what more would he have of them? Now,

1. He owns the fact to be true. As far as hypocrites do that which is good, they shall not be denied the praise of it. It is owned that they have a form of godliness. (1) They go to church, and observe their hours of prayer: *They seek me daily.* (2) They love to hear good preaching: *They delight to know my ways*, as Herod, who heard John gladly. (3) They seem to take pleasure in the exercises of religion. *They delight in approaching to God*, not for his sake to whom they approach, but for the sake of some pleasing circumstance, the company, or the festival. (4) They are inquisitive concerning their duty and seem desirous only to know it: *They ask of me the ordinances of justice*, the rules of piety in the worship of God, the rules of equity in their dealings with men, both which are ordinances of justice. (5) They appear to the eye of the world as if they made conscience of doing their duty: *They are as a nation that did righteousness and forsook not the ordinances of their God;* others took them for such, and they themselves pretended to be such. Men may go a great way towards heaven and yet come short; may go to hell with a good reputation. But,

2. He intimates that this was so far from being a cover for their sin that really it was an aggravation of it.

Verses 3–7

I. The pleasure which these hypocrites conceived against God (*v.* 3): *Wherefore have we fasted, say they, and thou seest not?* Thus they went in the way of Cain, who was angry at God, and resented it as a gross affront that his offering was not accepted. They magnify their own performances: "*We have fasted, and afflicted our souls;* we have not only sought God daily (*v.* 2), but have kept certain times of more solemn devotion." Some think this refers to the yearly fast (which was called *the day of atonement*), others to occasional fasts. The Pharisee (Luke xviii. 12) said *I fast twice in the week*. They thought God should take great notice of them, for their services. They charge God with injustice and partiality, and seem resolved to throw up their religion, and justify themselves in doing so with this, that they had found no *profit in praying* to God, Job xxi. 14, 15; Mal. iii. 14.

II. The true reason why God did not accept their fastings, nor answer the prayers they made on their fast-days; it was because they did not fast aright. They fasted indeed, but they did not, as the Ninevites, turn everyone from his evil way; but *in the day of their fast*, they went on to *find pleasure*, that is, to do whatsoever seemed right in their own eyes, *making their inclinations their law*. 1. They were as covetous and unmerciful as ever: "*You exact all your labours* from your servants, and will neither release them according to the law nor relax the rigour of their servitude. *You exact all your dues*, your *debts*" (so some read it); you are as rigorous and severe in extorting what you demand from those that are poor as ever you were, though it was at the close of the yearly fast that the release was proclaimed. 2. They were con-

JAMIESON, FAUSSET, BROWN — CHAPTER 58

Vss. 1-14. Reproof of the Jews for Their Dependence on Mere Outward Forms of Worship. **1. aloud**—*Hebrew*, with the throat, i.e., with full voice, not merely from the lips (I Sam. 1:13). Speak loud enough to arrest attention. **my people**—the Jews in Isaiah's time, and again in the time of our Lord, more zealous for externals than for inward holiness. Rosenmuller thinks the reference to be to the Jews in the captivity practising their rites to gain God's favor and a release; and that hence, *sacrifices* are not mentioned, but only *fasting* and *Sabbath observance*, which they could keep though far away from the temple in Jerusalem. The same also applies to their present dispersion, in which they cannot offer *sacrifices*, but can only show their zeal in *fastings*, etc. Cf. as to our Lord's time, Matthew 6:16; 23; Luke 18:12. **2.** Put the stop at "ways"; and connect "as a nation that . . ." with what follows; "As a nation that did righteousness," thus answers to, "they ask of Me *just judgments*" (i.e., as a matter of justice *due to them*, salvation to themselves, and destruction to their enemies); and "forsook not the ordinance of their God," answers to "they desire the drawing near of God" (that *God would draw near* to exercise those "just judgments" in behalf of them, and against their enemies) [Maurer]. So Jerome, "In the confidence, as it were, of a good conscience, they demand a just judgment, in the language of the saints: Judge me, O Lord, for I have walked in mine integrity." So in Malachi 2:17, they affect to be scandalized at the impunity of the wicked, and impugn God's *justice* [Horsley]. Thus, "seek Me daily, and desire (*English Version* not so well, 'delight') to know My ways," refers to their requiring to know why God delayed so long in helping them. *English Version* gives a good, though different sense; viz., dispelling the delusion that God would be satisfied with outward observances, while the *spirit* of the law was violated and the heart unchanged (vss. 3-14; Ezek. 33:31, 32; cf. John 18:28), scrupulosity side by side with murder. The prophets were the commentators on the law, as their *Magna Charta*, in its inward spirit and not the mere letter.

3. Wherefore—the words of the Jews: "Why is it that, when we fast, Thou dost not notice it" (by delivering us)? They think to lay God under *obligation* to their fasting (Ps. 73:13; Mal. 3:14). **afflicted . . . soul**—(Lev. 16:29).

Behold—God's reply. **pleasure**—in antithesis to their boast of having "*afflicted* their soul"; it was only in outward show they really *enjoyed* themselves. Gesenius not so well translates, "business." **exact . . . labours**—rather, "*oppressive* labors" [Maurer]. Horsley, with *Vulgate*, translates, "Exact the whole upon your *debtors*"; those who owe you labor (Neh. 5: 1-5, 8-10, etc.).

ADAM CLARKE — CHAPTER 58

1. *Cry aloud, spare not.* Never was a louder cry against the hypocrisy, nor a more cutting reproof of the wickedness, of a people professing a national established religion, having all the forms of godliness without a particle of its power.

3. *Have we afflicted our soul*—"Have we afflicted our souls."

In the day of your fast ye find pleasure. Fast days are generally called holidays, and holidays are days of idleness and pleasure. In numberless cases the fast is turned into a feast. *And exact all your labours.* Some disregard the most sacred fast, and will oblige their servant to work all day long; others use fast days for the purpose of settling their accounts, posting up their books, and drawing out their bills to be ready to collect their debts. These are sneaking hypocrites; the others are daringly irreligious.

MATTHEW HENRY

tentious and spiteful (*v.* 4): *Behold, you fast for strife and debate.* When they proclaimed a fast they pretended to search for those sins which provoked God, and under that pretence perhaps particular persons were falsely accused, as Naboth in the day of Jezebel's fast, 1 Kings xxi. 12. Thus, instead of judging themselves, which is the proper work of a fast-day, they condemned one another. They *fasted for strife,* with emulation which should make the most plausible appearance on a fast-day. Now while they thus *continued in sin,* God would not allow them the use of such solemnities: "*You shall not fast* at all if you fast *as you do this day, causing your voice to be heard on high. Bring me no more* of these empty, noisy, *vain oblations,*" *ch.* i. 13.

III. Plain instructions given concerning the true nature of a religious fast.

1. In general, a fast is intended, (1) For the honouring and pleasing of God. (2) For the humbling and abasing of ourselves. A fast is *a day to afflict the soul;* if it do not express a genuine sorrow for sin, and do not promote a real mortification of sin, it is not a fast.

2. It concerns us therefore to enquire, on a fast-day, what it is that will be acceptable to God, and afflictive to our corrupt nature.

(1) We are here told negatively what is not the fast that God has chosen. [1] It is not enough to put on a melancholy aspect, to bow down the head like a bulrush that is withered and broken: as the hypocrites, that were *of a sad countenance, and disfigured their faces, that they might appear unto men to fast,* Matt. vi. 16. The publican, whose heart was truly humbled, *would not so much as lift up his eyes to heaven* (Luke xviii. 13); but when it was only mimicked, as here, it was justly ridiculed: it is but *hanging down the head like a bulrush.* [2] It is not enough to do penance, to mortify the body a little, while the body of sin is untouched. *Wilt thou call this a fast?* No, it is but the shadow of a fast.

(2) We are here told positively what is the fast that God has chosen. It *is not afflicting the soul for a day* (as some read it, *v.* 5); it must be the business of our whole lives. It is here required, [1] That we be just to those with whom we have dealt hardly (*v.* 6): *To loose the bands of wickedness,* the bands which we have wickedly tied, and by which others are bound. "Let the prisoner for debt that has nothing to pay be discharged, let the vexatious action be quashed, let the servant that is forcibly detained beyond the time of his servitude be released, and thus *break every yoke;* not only let go those that are wrongfully kept under the yoke, but break the yoke of slavery itself." [2] That we be charitable to those that stand in need of charity, *v.* 7. Contribute to the rescue and ransom of those that are oppressed by others, to the release of captives and the payment of the debts of the poor. This then, is the fast that God has chosen. *First,* To provide food for those that want it. It is *to break thy bread to the hungry.* It must be *thy* bread, that which is honestly got, the bread of thy allowance. We must deny ourselves, that we may have to give to him that needeth. This is the true fast, to break thy bread to the hungry, to give them loaves and not to put them off with scraps. *Secondly,* To provide lodging for those that want it: It is *to take care of the poor that are cast out.* "If they suffer unjustly do not only pay for their lodging, but, which is a greater act of kindness, bring them to thy own house. Be not forgetful to entertain strangers: for thou mayest entertain Christ himself. *I was a stranger and you took me in.*" *Thirdly,* To provide clothing for those that want it: "*When thou seest the naked, that you cover him; hide not thyself from thy own flesh.*" Some understand it of a man's own relations. Others understand it more generally; all that partake of the human nature are to be looked upon as our own flesh, for have we not all one Father?

Verses 8–12

Precious promises for those to feast freely and cheerfully who keep the fast that God has chosen.

I. A further account of the duty to be done (*v.* 9, 10). 1. We must abstain from all acts of violence and fraud. "Those must be *taken away from the midst of thee,* from the midst of *thy person,* out of *thy heart*" (so some); "thou must not only refrain from the practice of injury, but mortify in thee all inclination towards it." Or *from the midst of thy people.* Those in authority must do all they can to prevent oppression in all within their jurisdiction. They must not only *break the yoke* (*v.* 6), but take away the yoke; they must likewise *forbear threatening* (Eph. vi. 9) and take away the *putting forth of the finger,* to point at those that are poor and in misery, and so to expose them to contempt. And let them not *speak vanity,* flattery to one another, but let all conversation be governed by sincerity. 2. We must abound in all acts of charity and beneficence. We must

JAMIESON, FAUSSET, BROWN

4. ye shall not fast—rather, "ye do not fast at this time, so as to make your voice to be heard on high," i.e., in heaven; your aim in fasting is strife, not to gain the ear of God [MAURER] (I Kings 21:9, 12, 13). In *English Version* the sense is, If you wish acceptance with God, ye must not fast as ye now do, to make your voice heard high *in strife.*

5. for a man to afflict his soul—The *pain* felt by abstinence is not the *end* to be sought, as if it were meritorious; it is of value only in so far as it leads us to amend our ways (vss. 6, 7).

bow . . . head . . . sackcloth—to affect the outward tokens, so as to "*appear* to men to fast' (Matt. 6: 17, 18; I Kings 21:27; Esther 4:3).

6. loose . . . bands of wickedness—i.e., to dissolve every tie wherewith one has unjustly bound his fellow men (Lev. 25:49, etc.). Servitude, a fraudulent contract, etc. **undo . . . heavy burdens**—*Hebrew,* loose the bands of the yoke. **oppressed**—lit., "the broken." The expression, "to let go free," implies that those "broken" with the yoke of *slavery* are meant (Neh. 5:10-12; Jer. 34:9-11, 14, 16). JEROME interprets it, broken with poverty; bankrupt.

7. deal—distribute (Job 31:16-21).

cast out—rather, reduced [HORSLEY]. **naked . . . cover him**—(Matt. 25:36). **flesh**—kindred (Gen. 29:14). Also brethren in common descent from Adam, and brethren in Christ (Jas. 2:15). "Hide . . . thyself," means to be strange towards them, and not to relieve them in their poverty (Matt. 15:5).

9. Then . . . call . . . answer—when sin is renounced (ch. 65:24). When the Lord's call is *not* hearkened to, He will not hear our "call" (Ps. 66:18; Prov. 1:24, 28; 15:29; 28:9). **putting forth of . . . finger**—the finger of scorn pointed at simple-minded godly men. The middle finger was so used by the Romans. **speaking vanity**—every *injurious* speech [LOWTH].

ADAM CLARKE

4. *To smite with the fist of wickedness: ye shall not fast as ye do this day*—"To smite with the fist the poor. Wherefore fast ye unto Me in this manner?"

JOHN GILL:

Verse 5. "Is it such a fast that I have chosen?" That is, can this be thought to be a fast approved of by me, and acceptable to me, before described, and is as follows: "a day for a man to afflict his soul?" only to appoint a certain day, and keep that, by abstaining from bodily food, and so for a short time afflict himself; or only after this manner to afflict himself, and not humble himself for his sin, and abstain from them, and do the duties of justice and charity incumbent on him: is it "to bow down his head as a bulrush"; when it is moved with the wind, or bruised, or withered; as if he was greatly depressed, and humbled, and very penitent and sorrowful. The Syriac version renders it, "as a hook"; like a fish-hook, which is very much bent; so Jarchi interprets the word: "and to spread sackcloth and ashes under him?" which were ceremonies used in times of mourning and fasting; sometimes sackcloth was put on their loins, and ashes on their heads; and sometimes these were strewed under them, and they laid down upon their sackcloth, which, being coarse, was uneasy to them, and rolled themselves in ashes, as expressive of their meanness and vileness: "wilt thou call this a fast, and an acceptable day to the Lord"; does this deserve the name of a fast; or can it be imagined that such a day, so spent, can be acceptable to God; that such persons and services will be accepted of by him: or that hereby sin is atoned for, and God is well pleased, and will show his favor and good will, and have respect to such worshipers of him? no, surely.

Verse 6. "Is not this the fast that I have chosen?" Which God has appointed, he approved of, and is well-pleasing in his sight; these are works and services more agreeable to him, which follow, without which the rest will be rejected; "to loose the bands of wickedness"; which some understand of combinations in courts of judicature to oppress and distress the poor: others of bonds and contracts unjustly made, or rigorously demanded and insisted on, when they cannot be answered; rather of those things with which the consciences of men are bound in religious matters; impositions upon conscience; binding to the use of stinted forms, and to habits in divine worship, which the word of God has not made necessary: "to undo the heavy burdens." The Septuagint render it, "dissolve the obligation of violent contracts": such as are obtained by violence; so the Arabic version; or by fraud.

—*Gill's Commentary*

MATTHEW HENRY

give freely and cheerfully, and from a principle of charity. We must *draw out our soul to the hungry* (*v.* 10), not only draw out the money, but do this from the heart with a tender affection to such as we see to be in misery. Let the heart go along with the gift; for God loves a cheerful giver, and so does a poor man too. When our Lord Jesus healed and fed the multitude it was as having compassion on them. We must give plentifully and largely, so as not to tantalize, but to *satisfy, the afflicted soul.*

II. A full account of the blessings and benefits which attend the performance of this duty. God will surprise them with the return of mercy after great affliction, which shall be as welcome as the light of the morning after a long and dark night (*v.* 8): *Then shall thy light break forth as the morning* and (*v.* 10) *thy light shall rise in obscurity.* Those that are cheerful in doing good God will make cheerful in enjoying good; and this also is a special *gift of God,* Eccles. ii. 24. Those that have helped others out of trouble will obtain help of God when it is their turn. Good works shall be recompensed with a good name; this is included in that *light which rises out of obscurity.* "*Thy righteousness shall go before* thee as thy vanguard, to secure thee from enemies that charge thee in the front, and *the glory of the Lord shall be thy rearward,* the gathering host, to bring up those of thee that are weary and are left behind, and to secure thee from the enemies, that, like Amalek, fall upon thy rear." Good people are safe on all sides. Their defence is their righteousness, and the glory of the Lord, that is, as some suppose, Christ. He it is that is our rearward, on whom alone we can depend for safety when our sins pursue us and are ready to take hold on us. "*Then shalt thou call,* on thy fast-days, which ought to be days of prayer, *and the Lord shall answer,* shall give thee the things thou callest to him for; *thou shalt cry* when thou art in any distress or sudden fright, *and he shall say, Here I am.*" Wherever they are praying, God says, "Here I am hearing: I am *in the midst of you.*" He is *nigh unto them in all things,* Deut. iv. 7. *The Lord shall guide thee continually.* While we are here, in the wilderness of this world, we have need of continual direction from heaven. To a good man God gives not only wisdom and knowledge, but joy; he is satisfied in himself with the testimony of his conscience and the assurances of God's favour. These will *satisfy thy soul,* will put gladness into thy heart, even *in the drought* of affliction; *these will make fat thy bones,* will give thee that pleasure which will be a support to thee as the bones to the body. "*Thou shalt be like a watered garden,* fruitful in graces *and like a spring of water, whose waters fail not* either in droughts or in frosts." As a spring of water, though it is continually sending forth its streams, is yet always full, so the charitable man abounds in good as he abounds in doing good, and is never the poorer for his liberality. "*Those that* hereafter *shall be of thee,* thy posterity, shall be serviceable to their generation, as thou art to thine." They *shall build the old waste places,* which had lain long desolate. This was fulfilled when the captives, after their return, repaired the cities of Judah, and many of those in Israel. They shall carry on and finish that good work which was begun long before. *They shall raise up* to the top that building *the foundation of* which was laid long since and has been for *many generations* in the rearing. This was fulfilled when the building of the temple was revived after it had stood still for many years, Ezra v. 2. They shall have the blessing and praise of all about them: "*Thou shalt be called the repairer of the breach.*" "Thou shalt be *the restorer of paths,* safe and quiet paths, not only to travel in, but *to dwell in,* so safe and quiet that people shall make no difficulty of building their houses by the roadside." The sum is that, if they keep such feasts as God has chosen, he will settle them again in their former peace and prosperity, and there shall be none to make them afraid.

Verses 13–14

Great stress was always laid upon the due observance of the sabbath day, and it was particularly required from the Jews when they were captives in Babylon, because by keeping that day, in honour of the Creator, they distinguished themselves from the worshippers of the gods that have not made the heavens and the earth. See *ch.* lvi. 1, 2.

I. How the sabbath is to be sanctified (*v.* 13); this law of the sabbath is still binding to us on our Lord's day.

1. Nothing must be done that puts contempt upon the sabbath day. We must *turn away our foot from the sabbath,* from trampling upon it; we must turn away our foot *from doing our pleasure on that holy day,* that is, from living at large, and taking a liberty

JAMIESON, FAUSSET, BROWN

10. draw out thy soul—"impart of thine own subsistence," or "sustenance" [HORSLEY]. "Soul" is figurative for "that wherewith thou sustainest thy soul," or "life."

8. light—emblem of prosperity (vs. 10; Job 11:17). **health**—lit., a long bandage, applied by surgeons to heal a wound (cf. ch. 1:6). Hence *restoration* from all past calamities. **go before thee**—Thy conformity to the divine covenant acts as a leader, conducting thee to peace and prosperity. **glory . . . reward**—like the pillar of cloud and fire, the symbol of God's "glory," which went *behind* Israel, separating them from their Egyptian pursuers (ch. 52:12; Exod. 14: 19, 20). **light . . . in obscurity**—Calamities shall be suddenly succeeded by prosperity (Ps. 112:4).

11. satisfy . . . in drought—(ch. 41:17, 18). Lit., "drought," i.e., parched places [MAURER]. **make fat**—rather, strengthen [NOYES]. "*Give thee the free use of* thy bones" [JEROME], *or, of thy strength* [HORSLEY]. **watered garden**—an Oriental picture of happiness. **fail not**—*Hebrew,* "deceive not"; as streams that disappoint the caravan which had expected to find water, as formerly, but find it dried up (Job 6:15-17).

12. they . . . of thee—thy people, the Israelites. **old waste places**—the old ruins of Jerusalem (ch. 61:4; Ezek. 36:33-36).

foundations of many generations—i.e., the buildings which had lain in ruins, even to their *foundations, for many ages;* called in the parallel passage (ch. 61:4), "the *former* desolations"; and in the preceding clause here, "the *old* waste places." The literal and spiritual restoration of Israel is meant, which shall produce like blessed results on the Gentile world (Amos 9:11, 12; Acts 15:16, 17). **be called**—appropriately: the name truly designating what thou shalt do. **breach**—the calamity wherewith God visited Israel for their sin (ch. 30:26; I Chron. 15:13). **paths to dwell in**—not that the *paths* were *to be dwelt in,* but *the paths leading to their dwellings* were to be restored; "paths, so as to dwell in *the land*" [MAURER].

13. (Ch. 56:2; Neh. 13:15-22.) The Sabbath, even under the new dispensation, was to be obligatory (ch. 66:23). **foot**—the instrument of motion (cf. Prov. 4:27); men are not to *travel* for mere pleasure on the Sabbath (Acts 1:12). The Jews were forbidden to travel on it farther than the tabernacle or temple. **If thou keep thy foot from going on thy own ways and "doing thy pleasure . . ."** (Exod. 20:10, 11). **my holy day**—**God claims it as *His***

ADAM CLARKE

8. *And thine health shall spring forth speedily*—"And your wounds shall speedily be healed over."

11. *And make fat thy bones*—"And he shall renew your strength."

12. *The restorer of paths to dwell in*—"The restorer of paths to be frequented by inhabitants."

13. *If thou turn away thy foot from the sabbath.* The meaning of this seems to be that they should be careful not to take their pleasure on the Sabbath day, by paying visits, and taking country jaunts; not going, as Kimchi interprets it, more than a Sabbath day's journey, which was only 2,000 cubits beyond the city's suburbs. How vilely is this rule transgressed by the inhabitants of this land! They seem to think that the Sabbath was made only for their recreation!

MATTHEW HENRY

to do what we please on sabbath days, without the control and restraint of conscience. On sabbath days we must not walk in *our own ways* (that is, not follow our callings), not *find our own pleasure* (that is, not follow our sports and recreations); nay, we must not *speak our own words*, for we must make religion the business of the day. We must speak of divine things as we sit in the house and walk by the way. In all we say and do we must put a difference between this day and other days.

2. We must call it *a delight*, not a *task and a burden*. We must not only count it a delight, but call it so. We must call it so to God, in thanksgiving for it. We must call it so to others, to invite them to come and share in the pleasure of it; and we must call it so to ourselves, that we may not entertain the least thought of wishing the sabbath gone that we may sell corn.

II. The reward of sabbath-sanctification, *v.* 14.

1. We shall have the comfort of it; the work will be its own wages. *If we call the sabbath a delight, then shall we delight ourselves in the Lord;* he will more and more manifest himself to us. If we go about duty with cheerfulness, we shall go from it with satisfaction.

2. We shall have the honour of it: *I will cause thee to ride upon the high places of the earth*, which denotes not only a great security, but great dignity. Those that honour God and his sabbath he will thus honour. If God by his grace enable us to live above the world, and so to manage it as not to be hindered by it, then he makes us *to ride on the high places of the earth*.

3. We shall have the profit of it: I will *feed thee with the heritage of Jacob thy father*, that is, with all the blessings of the covenant and all the precious products of Canaan (which was a type of heaven), for these were the heritage of Jacob.

JAMIESON, FAUSSET, BROWN

day; to take it for our pleasure is to rob Him of His own. This is the very way in which the Sabbath is mostly broken; it is made a day of carnal pleasure instead of spiritual "delight." **holy of the Lord**—not the predicate, but the subject; "if thou call the holy (day) of Jehovah honorable"; if thou treat it as a day to be honored. **him**—or else, *it*, **the Sabbath. not doing . . . own way**—answering to, "turn away thy foot from the Sabbath." **nor finding . . . pleasure**—answering to, "doing thy pleasure." "To keep the Sabbath in an idle manner is the sabbath of oxen and asses; to pass it in a jovial manner is the sabbath of the golden calf, when the people sat down to eat and drink, and rose again to play; to keep it in surfeiting and wantonness is the sabbath of Satan, the devil's holiday" [BISHOP ANDREWES]. **nor speaking . . . words**—answering to, "*call* Sabbath a delight . . . honorable." Man's "*own* words" would "call" it a "weariness"; it is the spiritual nature given from above which "calls it a delight" (Amos 8:5; Mal. 1:13). **14. delight . . . in . . . Lord**—God rewards in kind, as He punishes in kind. As we "delight" in keeping God's "Sabbath," so God will give us "delight" in Himself (Gen. 15:1; Job 22:21-26; Ps. 37:4). **ride upon . . . high places**—I will make thee *supreme lord* of the land; the phrase is taken from a conqueror riding in his chariot, and occupying the hills and fastnesses of a country [VITRINGA], (Deut. 32:13; Mic. 1:3; Hab. 3:19). Judea was a land of *hills;* the idea thus is, "I will restore thee to thine own land" [CALVIN]. The parallel words, "heritage of *Jacob*," confirm this (Gen. 27:28, 29; 28:13-15). **mouth of . . . Lord . . . spoken it**—a formula to assure men of the fulfilment of any solemn promise which God has made (ch. 40:5).

ADAM CLARKE

Nor speaking thine own words—"From speaking vain words."

CHAPTER 59 (MATTHEW HENRY)

Verses 1–8

The mistake of those who had been quarrelling with God because they had not the deliverances wrought for which they had been fasting and praying, *ch.* lviii. 3.

I. It was not owing to God. He was still as able to help as ever: *His hand is not shortened*, his power is not lessened. God can reach as far as ever and with as strong a hand as ever, that has not waxed weak nor is it at all shortened. *Has the Lord's hand waxed short?* (says God to Moses, Num. xi. 23). No, it has not; he will not have it thought so. Neither length of time nor strength of enemies, no, nor weakness of instruments, can shorten or straiten the power of God. He was still as ready and willing to help as ever in answer to prayer: *His ear is not heavy, that it cannot hear.* More is implied than is expressed; not only his ear is not heavy, but he is quick of hearing. *Even before they call he answers*, *ch.* lxv. 24. If your prayers be not answered it is not because God is weary of hearing prayer, but because we are weary of praying, not because his ear is heavy when we speak to him, but because our ears are heavy when he speaks to us.

II. They stood in their own light and put a bar in their own door. *Your iniquities have kept good things from you*, Jer. v. 25.

1. The mischief sin does. It hinders God's mercies; it is a partition wall between us and God. Sin *hides his face from us* (which denotes great displeasure, Deut. xxxi. 17). Sin in its consequences is exceedingly hurtful, separating us from God, and so separating us not only *from all good*, but *to all evil* (Deut. xxix. 21).

2. The prophet shows how many and great their iniquities were, according to the charge given him (*ch.* lviii. 1) *to show God's people their transgressions*. He must begin with their thoughts, for there all sin begins: *Their thoughts are thoughts of iniquity*, *v.* 7. Their imaginations are so (*v.* 4): *They conceive mischief* and then they *bring forth iniquity*. Though it is in pain perhaps that the iniquity is brought forth, through the oppositions of Providence and the checks of their own consciences, yet, when they have compassed their wicked purpose, they look upon it with as much pride as if it were a *man-child born into the world*; thus, *when lust has conceived, it bringeth forth sin*, James i. 15. This is called (*v.* 5) *hatching the cockatrice's egg and weaving the spider's web*. The spider's web is a weak insignificant thing, which the besom sweeps away in an instant: such are the thoughts which worldly men entertain, building castles in the air. They hatch the eggs of the cockatrice or adder, which are poisonous and produce venomous creatures; such are the thoughts of the wicked who delight in doing mischief. *He that eats of their eggs* (that is, has any dealings with them) *dies* (that is, he is in danger of having some mischief or other done him), *and*

CHAPTER 59 (JAMIESON, FAUSSET, BROWN)

VSS. 1-21. THE PEOPLE'S SIN THE CAUSE OF JUDGMENTS: THEY AT LAST OWN IT THEMSELVES: THE REDEEMER'S FUTURE INTERPOSITION IN THEIR EXTREMITY. The reason why Jehovah does not deliver His people, notwithstanding their religious services (ch. 58:3), is not want of power on His part, but because of their sins (vss. 1-8); vss. 9-15 contain their confession; vss. 16-21, the consequent promise of the Messiah. **1. hand . . . shortened**—(*Note*, **ch.** 50:2).

ear heavy—(**ch. 6:10**).

2. hid—*Hebrew*, caused Him to hide (Lam. 3:44).

7. feet—*All* their members are *active* in evil; in vs. 3, the "hands, fingers, lips, and tongue," are specified. **run . . . haste**—(Rom. 3:15). Contrast David's "running and hasting" in the ways of God (Ps. 119:32, 60). **thoughts**—not merely their acts, but their whole *thoughts*.

5. cockatrice—probably the basilisk serpent, *cerastes*. Instead of crushing evil in the egg, they foster it. **spider's web**—This refers not to the spider's web being made to *entrap*, but to its *thinness*, as contrasted with substantial "garments," as vs. 6 shows. Their works are vain and transitory (Job 8:14; Prov. 11:18).

eateth . . . their eggs—he who *partakes in their plans*, or *has anything to do with them*, finds them pestiferous.

CHAPTER 59 (ADAM CLARKE)

The foregoing elegant chapter contained a severe reproof of the Jews, in particular for their hypocrisy in pretending to make themselves accepted with God by fasting and outward humiliation without true repentance; while they still continued to oppress the poor, and indulge their own passions and vices; with great promises however of God's favor on condition of their reformation. This chapter contains a more general reproof of their wickedness, bloodshed, violence, falsehood, injustice. At v. 9 they are introduced as making an ample confession of their sins, and deploring their wretched state in consequence of their sins. On this act of humiliation a promise is given that God, in His mercy and zeal for His people, will rescue them from this miserable condition; that the Redeemer will come like a mighty Hero to deliver them; He will destroy His enemies, convert both Jews and Gentiles to himself, and give them a new covenant, and a law which shall never be abolished.

4. *They conceive mischief, and bring forth iniquity.* There is a curious propriety in this mode of expression. A thought or purpose is compared to conception; a word or act, which is the consequence of it, to the birth of a child. From the third to the fifteenth verse inclusive may be considered a true statement of the then moral state of the Jewish people; and that they were, in the most proper sense of the word, guilty of the iniquities with which they are charged.

MATTHEW HENRY

that which is crushed, or which begins to be hatched, *breaks out into a viper*, which you meddle with at your peril. Out of this abundance of wickedness in the heart their mouth speaks, and yet it does not always speak out, but for the more effectually compassing the mischievous design, it is covered *with much fair speech* (*v.* 3): *Your lips have spoken lies;* and again (*v.* 4), *They speak lies*, pretending kindness where they intend mischief. *Your tongue has muttered perverseness.* Backbiters are called *whisperers*. They were guilty of shedding innocent blood: *Your hands are defiled with blood* (*v.* 3); blood is defiling; it leaves an indelible stain of guilt upon the conscience, which nothing but the blood of Christ can cleanse. *Their feet ran to this evil. They made haste to shed innocent blood.* With other iniquities are their *fingers defiled* (*v.* 3); they make everything their own that they can lay their hands on. *They trust in vanity* (*v.* 4); they depend upon their arts to enrich themselves, and their deceiving others will but deceive themselves. *The act of violence is in their hands*, according to the arts of violence that are in their heads and the thoughts of violence in their hearts. No methods are taken to redress these grievances and reform these abuses (*v.* 4): *None calls for justice.* When justice is not done there is blame to be laid not only upon the magistrates, but upon the people. Private persons ought to contribute to the public good by discovering secret wickedness. Truth is opposed, and there is not any that *pleads for it*, not any that has the courage to confront a prosperous fraud. *The way of peace* is as little regarded as the way of truth; they *know it not*, that is, they never study the things that make for peace. *There is no judgment in their goings;* they have not any sense of justice in their dealings. Those that practise iniquity *trust in vanity*, *v.* 4. *Their webs*, which they weave with so much art and industry, *shall not become garments, neither shall they cover themselves*, either for shelter or for ornament, *with their works*, *v.* 6. There is nothing to be got by sin, and so it will appear when profit and loss come to be compared. Those paths of iniquity are *crooked paths* (*v.* 8), which will perplex them, but will never bring them to their journey's end.

Verses 9–15

Sin is the great mischief-maker. *Here* it seems to be spoken by the people to God, as an acknowledgment of their humble submission to the justice of God's proceedings.

I. They acknowledge that God had contended with them, *v.* 9–11. 1. They were in distress, oppressed by their enemies, and God did not appear for them, to plead their just and injured cause: "*Judgment is far from us, neither does justice overtake us*, *v.* 9. Though, as to our persecutors, we are sure that we have right on our side, and they are the wrong-doers, yet we have not done justice to one another, and therefore God suffers our enemies to deal thus unjustly with us." 2. Their expectations were sadly disappointed: *We wait for light* as those that wait for the morning, *but behold obscurity; we look for judgment, but there is none* (*v.* 11); we look for salvation, because God (we think) has promised it, and we have prayed for it with fasting; but still *we walk in darkness.* 3. They were at their wits' end (*v.* 10): *We grope for the wall like the blind.* Those that love darkness rather than light shall have their doom accordingly. 4. They sunk into despair. *We are in desolate places as dead men.* The state of the Jews in Babylon is represented by *dead and dry bones* (Ezek. xxxvii. 12) and the explanation of the comparison there (*v.* 11) explains this text: *Our hope is lost; we are cut off for our parts. We roar like bears;* the sorrow of others was silent, and preyed more upon their spirits: *We mourn sore like doves*, like doves of the valleys.

II. They acknowledge that they had provoked God, *v.* 12–15. 1. They owned that they had sinned. We are witnesses against ourselves: *As for our iniquities, we know them*, though we may have foolishly endeavoured to cover them. 2. They owned the evil of sin; it is *transgressing and lying against the Lord*, *v.* 13. The sins of God's people are upon *this* account worse than the sins of others, that in transgressing they *lie against the Lord*; they misrepresent him, perfidiously break covenant with him, which is *lying against him.* 3. They owned that there was a general decay of moral honesty; and those who were false to their God were unfaithful to one another. They *spoke oppression*, though it was a revolt from truth. They *conceived and uttered words of falsehood.* Many a word of falsehood is uttered in haste, for want of consideration; but these were conceived and uttered, were uttered deliberately and of malice prepense. They were words of falsehood, and yet they are said to be uttered *from the heart*, because they agreed with the malice and wickedness of the heart, and were the

JAMIESON, FAUSSET, BROWN

that which is crushed—The *egg, when it is broken*, breaketh out as a viper; their plans, however specious in their undeveloped form like the egg, when developed, are found pernicious. Though the viper is viviparous (from which "vi-per" is derived), yet during gestation, the young are included in eggs, which break at the birth [BOCHART]; however, metaphors often combine things without representing everything to the life.

3. (Ch. 1:15; Rom. 3:13-15.) **hands . . . fingers**—Not merely the "hands" perpetrate deeds of *grosser* enormity ("blood"), but the "fingers" commit more *minute* acts of "iniquity." **lips . . . tongue**—The *lips* "speak" *openly* "lies," the *tongue* "mutters" malicious *insinuations* ("perverseness"; perverse misrepresentations of others) (Jer. 6:28; 9:4). **4.** Rather, "No one calleth an adversary into court with justice," i.e., None bringeth a just suit: "No one pleadeth *with* truth." **they trust . . . iniquity**—(So Job 15:36; Ps. 7:14).

8. peace—whether in relation to God, to their own conscience, or to their fellow men (ch. 57:20, 21). **judgment**—justice. **crooked**—the opposite of "straightforward" (Prov. 2:15; 28:18).

6. not . . . garments—like the "fig leaves" wherewith Adam and Eve vainly tried to cover their shame, as contrasted with "the coats of skins" which the Lord God made to clothe them with (ch. 64:6; Rom. 13: 14; Gal. 3:27; Phil. 3:9). **The artificial self-deceiving sophisms of human philosophy (I Tim. 6:5; II Tim. 2:16, 23).**

9. judgment far—retribution in kind because *they* had shown "no *judgment* in their goings" (vs. 8). *"The vindication of our just rights* by God is withheld by Him from us." **us**—In vs. 8 and previous verses, it was "they," the third person; here, "us . . . we," the first person. The nation here speaks: God thus making *them* out of their own mouth condemn themselves; just as *He* by His prophet had condemned them before. Isaiah includes himself with his people and speaks in their name. **justice**—God's *justice* bringing salvation (ch. 46:13). **light**—the dawn of returning prosperity. **obscurity**—adversity (Jer. 8:15). **10. grope**—fulfilling Moses' threat (Deut. 28:29). **stumble at noon . . . as . . . night**—There is no relaxation of our evils; at the time when we might look for the noon of relief, there is still the night of our calamity. **in desolate places**—rather, to suit the parallel words "at noonday," in fertile (lit., fat; Gen. 27:28) fields [GESENIUS] (where all is promising) *we are like the dead* (who have no hope left them); or, where *others* are prosperous, *we* wander about as dead men; true of all unbelievers (ch. 26:10; Luke 15:17). **11. roar**—moan plaintively, like a hungry bear which growls for food. **doves**—(ch. 38:14; Ezek. 7:16). **salvation**—retribution in kind: because not salvation, but "destruction" was "in their paths" (vs. 7). **12.** (Dan. 9:5, etc.). **thee . . . us**—antithesis. **with us**—i.e., we are *conscious* of them (*Margin*, Job 12:3; 15:9). **know**—acknowledge they are *our* iniquities. **13.** The *particulars* of the sins *generally* confessed in the preceding verse (ch. 48:8; Jer. 2:19, 20). The act, the word, and the thought of apostasy, are all here marked: *transgression* and *departing*, etc.; *lying* (cf. vs. 4), and *speaking*, etc.; *conceiving* and uttering *from the heart.*

ADAM CLARKE

ALEXANDER MACLAREN:

"Their webs shall not become garments" (Isa. 59:6). "I counsel thee to buy of me . . . white raiment, that thou mayest be clothed, and that the shame of thy nakedness do not appear" (Rev. 3:18).

The force of these words of the prophet is very obvious. He has been pouring out swift, indignant denunciation on the evil doers in Israel; and, says he, "they hatch cockatrice's eggs and spin spiders' webs," pointing, as I suppose, to the patient perseverance, worthy of a better cause, which bad men will exercise in working out their plans. Then with a flash of bitter irony, led on by his imagination to say more than he had meant, he adds this scathing parenthesis, as if he said, "Yes, they spin spiders' webs, elaborate toil and creeping contrivance, and what comes of it all! The flimsy foul thing is swept away by God's broom sooner or later. A web indeed! but they will never make a garment out of it. It looks like cloth, but it is useless." That is the old lesson that all sin is profitless and comes to nothing.

I venture to connect with that strongly figurative declaration of the essential futility of godless living, our second text, in which Jesus uses a similar figure to express one aspect of His gifts to the believing soul. He is ready to clothe it, so that "being clothed, it will not be found naked."

—*Expositions of Holy Scripture*

10. *We stumble at noon day as in the night*—"We stumble at midday, as in the twilight."

MATTHEW HENRY

natural language of that; it was a *double heart*, Ps. xii. 2. 4. They owned that that was not done which might have been done to reform the land and to amend what was amiss, *v.* 14. "*Judgment*, that should run in its course like a river, like a mighty stream, *is turned away backward*, a contrary course. The administration of justice has become but a cover to the greatest injustice. *Justice stands afar off*, even from our courts of judicature. *Truth is fallen in the street, yea, truth fails* in common conversation, so that one knows not whom to believe nor whom to trust." 5. They owned that there was a prevailing enmity to those that were good: *He that does evil goes unpunished*, but *he that departs from evil makes himself a prey*. It is crime with them for a man not to do as they do, and they treat *him* as an enemy who will not partake with them in their wickedness. *He that departs from evil is accounted mad;* so the margin reads. 6. They owned that all this could not but be displeasing to the God of heaven. Though it was done secretly, and gilded over with specious pretences, yet it could not be concealed from his all-seeing eye. Though the sin displeased him, he would soon have been reconciled to the sinners upon their returning from their evil way.

Verses 16–21

Sin abounded in the former part of the chapter; grace does much more abound in these verses.

I. Why God wrought salvation, notwithstanding their provocations. It was purely for his own name's sake.

1. He took notice of their weakness and wickedness: *He saw that there was no man* that would do anything for the support of religion and virtue among them. Most were wicked, and those that were not so were weak. *There was no intercessor*, none to intercede with God (*v.* 16), no advocate to speak a good word for those who were made a prey because they kept their integrity, *v.* 15. They complained that God did not appear for them (*ch.* lviii. 3); but God with much more reason complains that they did nothing for themselves.

2. He engaged his own strength and righteousness for them. They shall be saved. The work of reformation (that is the first and principle article of the salvation) shall be wrought by the immediate influences of the divine grace on men's consciences. When God stirred up the spirit of Cyrus, and brought his people out of Babylon, *not by might, nor by power, but by the Spirit of the Lord of hosts*, then his own arm, which is never shortened, brought salvation. Divine justice, which by their sins they had armed against them, through grace appears for them. Though they can expect no favour as due to them, yet he will, in righteousness, punish the enemies of his people; see Deut. ix. 5. *Not for thy righteousness, but for the wickedness of these nations* they are driven out. In our redemption by Christ, since we had no righteousness of our own to produce, he brought in a righteousness by the merit and mediation of his own Son (it is called *the righteousness which is of God by faith*, Phil. iii. 9). *He put on righteousness as a breastplate*, securing his own honour, as a breastplate does the vitals, and put *a helmet of salvation upon his head.*

When righteousness is his coat of arms, salvation is his crest. In allusion to this, among the pieces of a Christian's armour we find *the breastplate of righteousness*, and for a helmet *the hope of salvation* (Eph. vi. 14–17; 1 Thess. v. 8), and it is called *the armour of God*, because he wore it first and so fitted it for us. Because they have no spirit or zeal to do anything for themselves, God will *put on the garments of vengeance for clothing, and clothe himself with zeal as a cloak*; he will make his justice upon the enemies of his church and people to appear evident.

II. The salvation that shall be wrought by the righteousness of God himself.

1. There shall be a present temporal salvation wrought for the Jews in Babylon, or elsewhere in distress and captivity. This is promised (*v.* 18, 19) as a type of something further. It is here promised, (1) That God will reckon with his enemies and will render to them according to their deeds, to the enemies of his people abroad, to the enemies of justice and truth at home, for they also are God's enemies; he will deal with both as they have deserved, *according to former retributions*; as he has rendered to his enemies formerly, *fury to his adversaries, recompense to his enemies*; his fury shall not exceed the rules of justice. Even *to the islands*, that lie most remote, if they have appeared against him, *he will repay recompense*; for *his hand shall find out all his enemies* (Ps. xxi. 8), and his arrows reach them. (2) That, whatever attempts the enemies of God's people may afterwards make to disturb their peace, they shall be brought to nought: *When the enemy shall come in like a flood,*

JAMIESON, FAUSSET, BROWN

14. Justice and righteousness are put away from our legal courts. **in the street**—in the forum, the place of judicature, usually at the gate of the city (Zech. 8:16). **cannot enter**—is shut out from the forum, or courts of justice. **15. faileth**—is not to be found. **he that departeth . . . prey**—He that will not fall in with the prevailing iniquity exposes himself as a prey to the wicked (Ps. 10:8, 9). **Lord saw it**—The iniquity of Israel, so desperate as to require nothing short of Jehovah's interposition to mend it, typifies the same necessity for a Divine Mediator existing in the deep corruption of man; Israel, the model nation, was chosen to illustrate his awful fact.

16. no man—viz., to atone by his righteousness for the unrighteousness of the people. "Man" is emphatic, as in I Kings 2:2; no representative man able to retrieve the cause of fallen men (ch. 41:28; 63:5, 6; Jer. 5:1; Ezek. 22:30). **no intercessor**—no one to interpose, "to help . . . uphold" (ch. 63:5).

his arm—(ch. 40:10; 51:5). Not *man's* arm, but *His* alone (Ps. 98:1; 44:3). **his righteousness**—the "arm" of Messiah. He won the victory for us, not by mere *might* as God, but by His invincible *righteousness*, as man having "the Spirit without measure" (ch. 11:5; 42:6, 21; 51:8; 53:11; I John 2:1). **17.** Messiah is represented as a warrior armed at all points, going forth to vindicate His people. Owing to the unity of Christ and His people, their armor is like His, except that they have no "garments of *vengeance*" (which is God's prerogative, Rom. 12:19), or "cloak of *zeal*" (in the sense of *judicial fury* punishing the wicked; this zeal belongs properly to God, II Kings 10:16; Rom. 10:2; Phil. 3:6; "zeal," in the sense of *anxiety for the Lord's honor*, they have, Num. 25:11, 13; Ps. 69:9; II Cor. 7:11; 9:2); and for "salvation," which is of God alone (Ps. 3:8), they have as their *helmet* "the *hope* of salvation" (I Thess. 5:8). The "helmet of salvation" is attributed to them (Eph. 6:14, 17) in a secondary sense; viz., derived from Him, and as yet only in *hope*, not fruition (Rom. 8:24). The *second* coming here, as often, is included in this representation of Messiah. His "zeal" (John 2:15-17) at His first coming was but a type of His zeal and vengeance against the foes of God at His second coming (II Thess. 1:8-10; Rev. 19:11-21).

18. deeds—*Hebrew*, "recompenses"; "according as their *deeds demand*" [MAURER]. This verse predicts the judgments at the Lord's second coming, which shall precede the final redemption of His people (ch. 66:18, 15, 16). **islands**—(*Note*, ch. 41:1). Distant countries.

19. (Ch. 45:6; Mal. 1:11). The result of God's judgments (ch. 26:9; 66:18-20). **like a flood**

ADAM CLARKE

16. *And wondered that there was no intercessor.* This and the following verses some of the most eminent rabbins understand as spoken of the Messiah.

F. B. MEYER:

The divine arm brings redemption. Israel's Savior. The almighty lover of souls is described as looking round to see if help were forthcoming from any other quarter; there being none, he girds himself for the conflict with the enemies of his people. He dons breastplate and helmet, clothing and cloak, and hastens to deliver (v. 17). This is surely a portrait of our Lord Jesus, who stands up to plead the cause and to achieve the redemption of the penitent and believing soul. When the enemy threatens to pour in like a pent-up stream, look to Jesus to raise the standard against him. Let him fight your battles! Let the blows that are meant for you be caught on his shield!—*Bible Commentary*

18. *According to their deeds, accordingly he will repay*—"He is mighty to recompense; He that is mighty to recompense will requite."

19. *When the enemy shall come in like a flood.* This all the rabbins refer to the coming

MATTHEW HENRY

then *the Spirit of the Lord shall lift up a standard against him*, and so (as the margin reads it) *put him to flight*. (3) That all this should redound to the glory of God and the advancement of religion in the world (*v.* 19). This had its full accomplishments in gospel times, when many came *from the east and west*, to fill up the places of *the children of the kingdom* that were *cast out*, when there were set up eastern and western churches, Matt. viii. 11.

2. There shall be a more glorious salvation wrought out by the Messiah in the fulness of time. The two great promises relating to that salvation:

(1) That the Son of God shall come to us to be our Redeemer (*v.* 20). The coming of Christ as the Redeemer is the summary of all the promises both of the Old and New Testament, and this was the redemption in Jerusalem which the believing Jews looked for, Luke ii. 38. Christ is our *Goël*, our next kinsman, that redeems both the person and the estate of the poor debtor. [1] The place where this Redeemer shall appear: He *shall come to Zion*, for there, on that holy hill, the Lord would set him up as his King, Ps. ii. 6. Zion was a type of the gospel church. [2] The persons that shall have the comfort of the Redeemer's coming, knowing that their redemption draws nigh. He shall come *to those that turn from ungodliness in Jacob*, but to those only that turn from transgression, that repent, and reform.

(2) That the Spirit of God shall come to us to be our sanctifier, *v.* 21. But the promise is made to a single person—*My Spirit that is upon thee*, being directed either, [1] To Christ as the head of the church, who received that he might give. Or, [2] To the church; and so it is a promise of the continuance and perpetuity of the church in the world to the end of time, parallel to those promises that the throne and seed of Christ shall endure for ever, Ps. lxxxix. 29, 36; xxii. 30. *Instead of the fathers shall be the children.* It shall be kept up—*henceforth and for ever*, even *unto the end of the world.* The Spirit that was upon Christ shall always continue in the hearts of the faithful; there shall be some in every age on whom he shall work, and in whom he shall dwell, and thus the Comforter shall abide with the church for ever, John xiv. 16. There shall be some in every age who, *believing with the heart* unto righteousness, shall *with the tongue make confession unto salvation.* On these foundations the church is built, stands firmly, and shall stand for ever, Christ himself being the chief corner-stone.

JAMIESON, FAUSSET, BROWN

—(Jer. 46:7, 8; Rev. 12:15). **lift up a standard—** rather, from a different *Hebrew* root, shall put him to flight, drive him away [MAURER]. LOWTH, giving a different sense to the *Hebrew* for "enemy" from that in vs. 18, and a forced meaning to the *Hebrew* for "Spirit of the Lord," translates, "When He shall come as a river *straitened* in its course, which a *mighty wind* drives along."

20. to Zion—Romans 11:26 quotes it, "*out of* Zion." Thus Paul, by inspiration, supplements the sense from Psalm 14:7: He was, and is come to *Zion*, first with redemption, being sprung as man *out of* Zion. LXX translates "*for the sake of* Zion." Paul applies this verse to the coming restoration of Israel spiritually. **them that turn from**—(Romans 11:26). "shall turn away ungodliness from Jacob"; so LXX, Paul herein gives the full sense under inspiration. *They* turn from transgression, because He first turns them from it, and it from them (Ps. 130:4; Lam. 5:21). **21. covenant with them . . . thee**—The covenant is with *Christ*, and with *them* only as united to Him (Heb. 2:13). Jehovah addresses Messiah the representative and ideal Israel. The literal and spiritual Israel are His seed, to whom the promise is to be fulfilled (Ps. 22:30). **spirit . . . not depart . . . for ever**—(Jer. 31:31-37; Matt. 28:20).

ADAM CLARKE

of the Messiah. If you see a generation which endures much tribulation, then (say they) expect Him, according to what is written: *When the enemy shall come in like a flood, the spirit of the Lord shall lift up a standard against him.*

20. *Unto them that turn from transgression in Jacob*—"And shall turn away iniquity from Jacob." So the Septuagint and St. Paul, Rom. xi. 26.

21. *My spirit that is upon thee.* This seems to be an address to the Messiah. *And my words which I have put in thy mouth.* Whatsoever Jesus spoke was the word and mind of God himself; and must, as such, be implicitly received. *Nor out of the mouth of thy seed.* The same doctrines which Jesus preached, all His faithful ministers preach; and His seed, genuine Christians who are all born of God, believe; and they shall continue, and the doctrines remain in the seed's seed through all generations, for ever and ever. This is God's covenant, ordered in all things and sure.

MATTHEW HENRY

CHAPTER 60

Verses 1–8

It is here promised that the gospel temple shall be very light and very large.

I. It shall be very light: *Thy light has come.* When the Jews returned out of captivity they had *light and gladness, and joy and honour*; they then were made to *know the Lord* and to *rejoice in his great goodness.* 1. What this light is, and whence it springs: *The Lord shall arise upon thee* (*v.* 2), *the glory of the Lord* (*v.* 1) *shall be seen upon thee.* When God appears to us, then *the glory of the Lord rises upon us* as the morning light; when he appears for us, then his glory is seen upon us. When Christ arose as the sun of righteousness, and in him *the day-spring from on high visited us*, then *the glory of the Lord was* seen upon us, the glory *as of the first-begotten of the Father.* 2. What a foil there shall be to this light: *Darkness shall cover the earth;* but, though it be gross darkness, that shall overspread the people, yet the church shall have light at the same time. 3. What is the duty which the rising of this light calls for: "*Arise, shine;* not only receive this light, and" (as the margin reads it) "*be enlightened by it*, but reflect this light: *arise and shine* with rays borrowed from it."

II. It shall be very large. When the Jews were settled in their own land, after their captivity, many of the people of the land joined themselves to them; but we must look further, to the bringing of the Gentiles into the gospel church, not their flocking to one particular place. There is no place now that is the centre of the church's unity; but the promise respects their flocking to Christ, and coming by faith, and hope, and holy love, into that family which is named from him, Eph. iii. 15. *You have come unto Mount Zion, to the city of the living God, the heavenly Jerusalem*, which serves for a key to this prophecy, Eph. ii. 19.

1. What shall invite such multitudes to the church: "They shall *come to thy light and to the brightness of thy rising*," *v.* 3. This light which discovers so much of God and his goodwill to man, by which life and immortality are brought to light, this shall invite all the serious well-affected part of mankind to come

JAMIESON, FAUSSET, BROWN

CHAPTER 60

Vss. 1-22. ISRAEL'S GLORY AFTER HER AFFLICTION. An ode of congratulation to Zion on her restoration at the Lord's second advent to her true position as the mother church from which the Gospel is to be diffused to the whole Gentile world; the first promulgation of the Gospel among the Gentiles, *beginning at Jerusalem*, is an earnest of this. The language is too glorious to apply to anything that as yet has happened **1. Arise**—from the dust in which thou hast been sitting as a mourning female captive (ch. 3:26; 52:1, 2). **shine**—impart to others the spiritual light now given thee (vs. 3). *Margin* and GESENIUS translate, "Be enlightened"; be resplendent with posterity; imperative for the future indicative, "Thou shalt be enlightened" (ch. 58:8, 10; Eph. 5:8, 14). **glory of the Lord**—not merely the Shekinah, or cloud of glory, such as rested above the ark in the old dispensation, but the glory of the Lord in person (Jer. 3:16, 17). **is risen**—as the sun (Mal. 4:2; Luke 1:78, *Margin*). **2. darkness . . . earth**—the *rest* of the earth: in contrast with "*light* . . . upon *thee*" (vs. 1). The earth will be afterwards enlightened through Israel (ch. 9:2). **be seen**—*conspicuously:* so the *Hebrew*. 3. (Ch. 2:3; 11:10; 43:6; 49:22; 66:12.) **kings**—(ch. 49:7, 23; 52:15).

thy rising—rather, "thy sun-rising," i.e., to the brightness that riseth upon thee.

ADAM CLARKE

CHAPTER 60

The subject of this chapter is the great increase and flourishing state of the Church of God by the conversion and accession of the heathen nations to it, which is set forth in such ample and exalted terms as plainly show that the full completion of this prophecy is reserved for future times. This subject is displayed in the most splendid colors under a great variety of images highly poetical, designed to give a general idea of the glories of that perfect state of the Church of God which we are taught to expect in the latter times; when the fullness of the Gentiles shall come in, and the Jews shall be converted and gathered from their dispersions, and the kingdoms of this world shall become the kingdoms of our Lord and of His Christ.

1. *Arise.* Call upon God through Christ, for His salvation; and *shine. Ori*, "be illuminated"; for till you arise and call upon God you will never receive true light. *For thy light is come.* "For your light cometh." The Messiah is at the door; who, while He is a Light to lighten the Gentiles, will be *the glory*—the effulgence—of His people Israel.

2. *Darkness shall cover the earth.* This is the state of the Gentile people.

MATTHEW HENRY

and join themselves to the church. The purity and love of the primitive Christians, their heavenly-mindedness, and patient sufferings, were the brightness of the church's rising, which drew many into it.

2. What multitudes shall come to the church. Great numbers *shall come, Gentiles* (or *nations*) *of those that are saved. Nations* shall be *discipled* (Matt. xxviii. 19). They come from all parts (*v.* 4): *Lift up thy eyes round about, and see* them coming, *devout men out of every nation under heaven,* Acts ii. 5. Sons and daughters shall come in the most dutiful manner, as thy sons and thy daughters, resolved to be of thy family. Those that would enjoy the dignities and privileges of Christ's family must submit to the discipline of it.

3. What they shall bring with them and what advantage shall accrue to the church by their accession to it. The merchants shall write *holiness to the Lord* upon their merchandise and their hire, as *ch.* xxiii. 18. "*The abundance of the sea* (the fish, the pearls) or that which is imported by sea, *shall* all *be converted to thee* and to thy use." The wealth of the rich merchants shall be laid out in works of piety and charity. The mighty men of the nations shall employ their might in the service of the church: "*The forces of the Gentiles shall come unto thee,* to guard thy coasts, and fight thy battles." *The camels and dromedaries that bring gold and incense, those of Midian and Sheba,* shall bring the richest commodities of their country, not to trade with, but to honour God with. This was in part fulfilled when the *wise men of the east came* to Christ, and presented to him treasures of *gold, frankincense, and myrrh,* Matt. ii. 11. Great numbers of sacrifices shall be brought to God's altar, and, though brought by Gentiles, shall find acceptance, *v.* 7. *Kedar* was famous for flocks, and probably the fattest rams were those of *Nebaioth*; these shall come up with acceptance on God's altar. This was fulfilled when by the decree of Darius the governors beyond the rivers were ordered to furnish the temple at Jerusalem *with bullocks, rams, and lambs, for the burnt-offering of the God of heaven,* Ezra vi. 9.

4. How God shall be honoured by the increase of the church! When they bring their gold and incense it shall be to *show forth the praises of the Lord, v.* 6. The church is the house of God's glory, where he manifests his glory to his people and receives that homage by which they do honour to him. And it is for the glory of this house that the Gentiles shall bring their offerings to it (*v.* 7).

5. How the church shall herself be affected with this increase of her numbers, *v.* 5. "*Thou shalt see* and *flow together*" (or flow to and fro). There shall be a mixture of fear with this joy: "*Thy heart shall fear,* doubting whether it be lawful to *go in to the uncircumcised* and *eat with them.*" Peter was so impressed with this fear that he needed a vision and voice from heaven to help him over it, Acts x. 28. "When this fear is conquered thy heart shall be so enlarged that thou shalt have room in it for all the Gentile converts." These converts flocking to the church shall be greatly admired (*v.* 8): *Who are these that fly as a cloud?* The conversion of souls is flying like a cloud in great multitudes, yet with great unanimity, as a cloud flying on the wings of the wind. They shall *fly as doves to their windows;* on the wings of the harmless dove, which flies low, denoting innocency and humility. They fly to Christ, to the church, as doves, by instinct, to their own windows, to their own home.

Verses 9–14

The promises made to the church are repeated for the encouragement of the Jews after their return out of captivity, but looking further, to the enlargement and advancement of the gospel church.

I. God will be very gracious and propitious to them. "All shall now make court to thee, *for in my wrath I smote thee,* while thou wast in captivity, but now *in my favour have I had mercy on thee,* and therefore have all this mercy in store for thee."

II. Many shall be brought into the church, even from far countries (*v.* 9): *Surely the isles shall wait for me,* shall welcome the gospel. *The ships of Tarshish,* transport-ships, shall carry the ministers of the church to remote parts, to preach the gospel. They live at such a distance that they cannot bring their flocks, so turned them into money to *bring their silver and gold with them.*

III. Those that come into the church shall be welcome. "*Therefore thy gates shall be open continually* (*v.* 11), not only because thou hast no reason to fear thy enemies, but because thou hast reason to expect thy friends." It is usual with us to leave our doors open, or leave someone ready to open them, all night, if we look for a child or a guest to come in late. The gate of mercy is always open, night and day, or shall soon be opened to those that knock.

JAMIESON, FAUSSET, BROWN

4. Lift up . . . eyes—Jerusalem is addressed as a female with *eyes cast down* from grief. **all they . . . they**—The Gentile peoples come together to bring back the dispersed Hebrews, restore their city, and worship Jehovah with offerings. **nursed at thy side**—rather carried . . . . It is the custom in the East to carry the children astride on the hip, with the arms around the body (ch. 66:12).

abundance of . . . sea—the *wealth* of the lands beyond *the sea,* as in Solomon's time, the type of the coming reign of the Prince of peace. **converted**—rather, *be turned,* instead of being turned to purposes of sin and idolatry. **forces**—rather, riches. **6. camels**—laden with merchandise; the camel is "the ship of the desert" (cf. ch. 30:6). **cover thee**—so many of them shall there be. **dromedaries**—They have one hunch on the back, whereas the *camel* has two: distinguished for swiftness (Jer. 2:23). **Midian**—east of the Elanitic branch of the Red Sea, and stretching northward along Mount Seir. Associated with the Ishmaelites in traffic (Gen. 37:25, 28). **Ephah**—part of Midian, east of the Dead Sea. It abounded in camels (Judg. 6:5). **Sheba**—in Arabia Felix, famed for frankincense and gold (Ps. 72:15; Jer. 6:20), which they traded in (ch. 45:14; Job 6:19; Ezek. 27: 22). **7. Kedar**—(ch. 21:16; Song of Sol. 1:5), in the south of Arabia Deserta, or north of Arabia Petræa; they traded in flocks (Ezek. 27:21). **Nebaioth**—son of Ishmael, as was Kedar. Father of the Nabatheans in Arabia Petræa. **minister**—by coming up as an acceptable sacrifice. **come up with acceptance**—i.e., acceptably. The rams *offering themselves* voluntarily (Ps. 68:30; Rom. 12:1; I Pet. 2:5), without waiting for any other priest, answer to believers strong in faith and lamblike meekness; and in the white fleecelike robe of sanctity [VITRINGA]. **house of my glory**—the temple (Ezek. 41; Hag. 2:7, 9; Mal. 3:1).

5. see—(vs. 4), viz., the bringing back of thy sons. **flow together**—rather, "overflow *with joy*" [LOWTH]; or, from a different *Hebrew* root, "*be bright with joy*" [GESENIUS] (Job 3:4). **fear**—rather, *beat with the agitation* of solemn joy at the marvellous sight [HORSLEY] (Jer. 33:9). **be enlarged**—*swell* with delight. Grief, on the contrary, *contracts* the heart.

8. The prophet, seeing in vision new hosts approaching quickly like a cloud of doves, asks who they are.

9. (*Note,* ch. 42:4.) **Tarshish first**—The ships of *Tartessus* (*Note,* ch. 2:16; 23:1, i.e., vessels that trade to the most distant regions) will be among the *foremost* to bring back the scattered Israelites (ch. 66:20). **their silver**—The nations among whom the Jews have been scattered shall help them with their money in returning (vss. 5-7, 11, 16), as was the case at the return from Babylon (Ezra 1:4; cf. Ps. 68:30, 31). **unto the name . . . to the Holy One**—rather, *because of* the name—*because of* the Holy One (cf. ch. 55:5) [LOWTH]. **11.** (Rev. 21:25.) The gates are ever open to receive new offerings and converts (ch. 26:2; Acts 14:27; Rev. 3:8). In time of *peace* the gates of a city are open: so, under the Prince of peace, there shall be no need of barring gates against invaders. **forces**—riches. **be brought**—as willing captives to the truth; or, *if not willingly,* be brought by *judgments to submit to Israel* (vss. 12, 14). GESENIUS explains it, "may come *escorted by a retinue.*"

ADAM CLARKE

3. *And the Gentiles shall come.* This has been in some sort already fulfilled. The Gentiles have received the light of the gospel from the land of Judea, and the Gentile kings have embraced that gospel, so that many nations of the earth are full of the doctrine of Christ.

4. *Shall be nursed at thy side*—"Shall be carried at the side."

5. *Then thou shalt see*—"Then shall you fear."

8. *And as the doves to their windows?*—"And like doves upon the wing?"

9. *The ships of Tarshish first*—"The ships of Tarshish among the first."

MATTHEW HENRY

IV. All that are about the church shall be made in some way or other serviceable to it. So here (*v.* 10), "Even *the sons of strangers*, that have neither knowledge of thee nor kindness for thee, *shall build up thy wall, and their kings shall* in that and other things *minister unto thee*." This was fulfilled when the king of Persia, and the governors of the provinces by his order, were aiding Nehemiah in building the wall about Jerusalem. Even those that do not belong to the church may be a protection to it, for (*v.* 12), *The nation and kingdom that will not serve thee shall perish.*

V. There shall be abundance of beauty added to the ordinances of divine worship (*v.* 13): *The glory of Lebanon*, the strong and stately cedars that grow there, *shall come unto thee*, as of old to Solomon, when he built the temple (2 Chron. ii. 16), and with them shall be brought other timber, proper for the carved work. The temple, the *place of God's sanctuary*, shall be not only rebuilt, but beautified. It was likewise *adorned with goodly stones and gifts* (Luke xxi. 5), yet so slightly did Christ speak of them there that we must suppose it to have its full accomplishment in the beauties of holiness.

VI. The church shall appear truly great and honourable, *v.* 14. The people of the Jews, after their return out of captivity, by degrees became more considerable. This prophecy is further fulfilled when those that have been enemies to the church are wrought upon by the grace of God to see their error: "*The sons of those that afflicted thee*, if not they themselves, yet their children, shall crouch to thee, shall beg pardon for their folly and beg an interest in thy favour and admission into thy family," 1 Sam. ii. 36. The poor oppressed ones of the church shall have an opportunity of doing good to those who have done evil to them and saving those alive who have afflicted and despised them. It is a pleasure to a good man, and he accounts it an honour, to show mercy to those with whom he has found no mercy.

Verses 15–22

The happy and glorious state of the church is further foretold, referring ultimately to the Christian church under the type of that little gleam of outward peace which the Jews sometimes enjoyed after their return out of captivity.

I. Compared with what it had been.

1. She had been despised, but now she should be honoured, *v.* 15, 16. Jerusalem had been forsaken and hated. But now it shall be *the joy* of good people for *many generations*. Yet considering how short Jerusalem's excellency was, and how short it came of the vast compass of this promise, we must look for the full accomplishment of it in the perpetual excellencies of the gospel church, and the glorious privileges and advantages of the Christian religion. She shall find herself countenanced by her neighbours. The nations, and their kings, that are brought to embrace Christianity, shall lay themselves out for the good of the church. "*Thou shalt suck the milk of the Gentiles*, not suck their blood (that is not the spirit of the gospel); thou *shalt suck the breast of kings*, who shall be to thee as nursing fathers." She shall find herself countenanced by her God: "*Thou shalt know that I the Lord am thy Saviour and thy Redeemer*, shalt know it by experience." They before knew the Lord to be their God; now they know him to be their Saviour, their Redeemer.

2. She had been impoverished, but now she shall be enriched, *v.* 17. Those, who were raised out of the dust, instead of brass money in their purses have gold, and instead of iron vessels in their houses have silver ones. So shall the spiritual glory of the New Testament church exceed the external pomp and splendour of the Jewish economy. When we had baptism in the room of circumcision, the Lord's supper in the room of the passover, and a gospel ministry in the room of a Levitical priesthood, we had gold instead of brass. Sin turned gold into brass when Rehoboam made brazen shields instead of the golden ones he had pawned; but God's favour, when that returns, will turn brass again into gold.

3. She had been oppressed by her own princes (*ch.* lix. 14); but now all the grievances of that kind shall be redressed (*v.* 17): "*I will make thy officers peace*. They shall *be peace*, that is, they shall sincerely seek thy welfare and by their means thou shalt enjoy good."

4. She had been insulted by her neighbours, invaded, and plundered; but now it shall be so no more (*v.* 18): "*Violence shall no more be heard in thy land;* but every man shall peaceably enjoy his own. There shall be no *wasting nor destruction*, but *thy walls shall be called salvation and thy gates shall be praise*."

II. Compared with what it would be.

In the close of this chapter we are directed to look further yet, as far forward as to the glory and

JAMIESON, FAUSSET, BROWN

10. kings . . . minister unto thee—(vs. 7 above, *Note;* ch. 49:23). **in my wrath I smote thee**—(ch. 54:7, 8; 57:17).

12. For—the reason which will lead Gentile kings and people to submit themselves; fear of the God in Israel (Zech. 14:17). **13. glory**—i.e., the *trees* which adorned Lebanon; emblem of men eminent in natural gifts, devoting all that is in them to the God of Israel (Hos. 14:5, 6). **fir . . . pine . . . box**—rather, "the cypress . . . ilex . . . cedar." **place of my sanctuary**—Jerusalem (Jer. 3:17). **place of my feet**—no longer the *ark* (Jer. 3:16), "the footstool" of Jehovah (Ps. 99:5; 132:7; I Chron. 28:2); but "the place of His throne, the place of the soles of His feet, where He will dwell in the midst of the children of Israel for ever," in the new temple (Ezek. 43:7).

14. The sons—Their *fathers* who "afflicted" Israel having been cut off by divine judgments (ch. 14:1, 2; 49:23). **The Zion of the Holy One**—The royal court of the Holy One. [MAURER] translates, "Zion, *the sanctuary* (*holy place*) of Israel" (ch. 57:15; Ps. 46:4).

15. forsaken—(Ps. 78:60, 61). **no man went through thee**—Thy land was so desolate that no traveller, or caravan, passed through thee; true only of Israel, not true of the Church (Lam. 1:4). **excellency**—glory, i.e., for ever honored.

16. suck—Thou shalt draw to thyself and enjoy all that is valuable of the possessions of the Gentiles, etc. (ch. 49:23; 61:6; 66:11, 12).

know—by the favors bestowed on thee, and through thee on the Gentiles.

17. Poetically, with figurative allusion to the furniture of the temple; all things in that happy age to come shall be changed for the better. **exactors**—viz., of tribute. **righteousness**—All rulers in restored Jerusalem shall not only be peaceable and righteous, but shall be, as it were, "peace" and "righteousness" itself in their administration. **18.** (Ch. 2:4.) Not only shall thy walls keep thee *safe* from foes, but "Salvation" shall serve as thy walls, converting thy foes into friends, and so ensuring thee perfect safety (ch. 26:1, 2). **gates**—once the scene of "destruction" when victorious foes burst through them (Neh. 1:3); henceforth to be not only the scene of praises, but "Praise" itself; the "gates," as the place of public concourse, were the scene of

ADAM CLARKE

13. *And I will make the place of my feet glorious*—"And that I may glorify the place whereon I rest my feet." The temple of Jerusalem was called the house of God, and the place of His rest or residence. The visible symbolical appearance of God, called by the Jews the Shekinah, was in the most holy place, between the wings of the cherubim, above the ark. This is considered as the throne of God, presiding as King over the Jewish state; and as a footstool is a necessary appendage to a throne, the ark is considered as the footstool of God, and is so called, Ps. xcix. 5; 1 Chron. xxviii. 2. *The glory of Lebanon.* That is, the cedar.

ALEXANDER MACLAREN:

"Thou shalt call thy walls Salvation, and thy gates Praise" (Isa. 60:18).

The prophet reaches the height of eloquence in his magnificent picture of the restored Jerusalem, "the city of the Lord, the Zion of the Holy One of Israel." To him the city stands for the embodiment of the nation, and his vision of the future is molded by his knowledge of the past. Israel and Jerusalem were to him the embodiments of the divine idea of God's dwelling with men, and of a society founded on the presence of God in its midst. We are not forcing meanings on his words which they will not bear, when we see in the society of men redeemed by Christ the perfect embodiment of his vision. Nor is the prophet of the New Testament doing so when he casts his vision of the future which is to follow Resurrection and Judgment into a like form, and shows us the new Jerusalem coming down out of heaven.

The end of the world's history is to be, not a garden but a city, a visible community, bound together because God dwells in it, and yet not having lost the blessed characteristics of the Garden from which man set out on his long and devious march.

The Christian form of the prophet's vision is the Christian Society, and in that society, each individual member possesses his own portion of the common blessings, so that the great words of this text have a personal as well as a general application. We shall best bring out their rich contents by simply taking them as they stand, and considering what is promised by the two eloquent metaphors, which liken salvation to the walls and praise to the gates of the City of God.—*Expositions of Holy Scripture*

MATTHEW HENRY

happiness of heaven, under the type and figure of the flourishing state of the church on earth. As the prophets sometimes insensibly pass from the blessings of the Jewish church to the spiritual blessings of the Christian church, which are eternal, so sometimes they rise from the church militant to the church triumphant, where, and where only, all the promised peace, and joy, and honour will be in perfection. 1. God shall be all in all in the happiness here promised (*v.* 19): *The sun and the moon shall be no more thy light.* "Idolaters worshipped the sun and moon (which some have thought the most ancient and plausible idolatry); but these *shall be no more thy light*, shall no more be idolized, but the Lord shall be to thee a constant light in the night of adversity as well as in the day of prosperity." 2. The happiness here promised shall know no change (*v.* 20): "*Thy sun shall no more go down*, but it shall be eternal sunshine with thee; that shall not be thy sun which is sometimes eclipsed, often clouded, and will certainly set and leave thee in the dark, in the cold, but *he* shall be a sun, who is himself the *Father of all lights*, with whom there is *no variableness*, nor *shadow of turning*," James i. 17. The comforts and joys that are in heaven, the glories provided for the soul, as the light of the sun, and those prepared for the glorified body too, as the light of the moon, shall never know the least cessation. *And the days of thy mourning shall be ended.* 3. Those that are entitled to this happiness shall never be put out of the possession of it (*v.* 21). And they shall be *all the righteous* together who shall replenish the New Jerusalem. And, because they are *all righteous*, therefore *they shall inherit the land for ever*, for nothing but sin can turn them out of it. 4. The glory of the church: "They shall appear to be the *branch of my planting, the work of my hands*, and I will own them as such." 5. They will appear the more glorious, and God will be the more glorified in them, if we compare what they are with what they were (*v.* 22): "*A little one shall become a thousand and a small one a strong nation.*" The captives that returned out of Babylon strangely multiplied, and became a strong nation. The Christian church was a little one, a very small one at first—the number of their names was once but 120; yet it became a thousand. When they come to heaven, and look back upon the smallness of their beginning, they will wonder how they got thither. It may seem to be delayed, but, as the Lord will do it, so he will *hasten it*; he will do it in the time appointed by his wisdom, though not in the time prescribed by our folly. And this is really hastening it; for, though it seem to tarry, it does not tarry if it come in God's time.

JAMIESON, FAUSSET, BROWN

thanksgivings (II Chron. 31:2; Ps. 9:14; 24:7; 100:4). "Judah," the favored tribe, means "praise."

19. The sun and moon, the brightest objects by day and night, shall be eclipsed by the surpassing glory of God manifesting Himself to thee (ch. 30:26; Zech. 2:5; Rev. 21:23; 22:5).

20. There shall be no national and spiritual obscuration again as formerly (Joel 2:10; Amos 8:9). **mourning . . . ended**—(ch. 25:8; Rev. 21:4).

21. all righteous—(ch. 4:3; 52:1; Rev. 21:27). **inherit . . . land**—(ch. 49:8; 54:3; 65:9; Ps. 37:11, 22; Matt. 5:5). **branch of my planting**—(ch. 61:3; Ps. 92:13; Matt. 15:13). **work of my hands**—the converted Israelites (ch. 29:23; 45:11). **that I may be glorified**—the final end of all God's gracious dealings (ch. 49:3; 61:3). **22. little one**—Even one, and that the smallest in number and rank, shall be multiplied a thousandfold in both respects (Mic. 5:2; Matt. 13:31, 32).

his time—not *our* time; *we* might wish to hasten it, but it will come in due time, as in the case of Jesus' first coming (Gal. 4:4); so in that of the restoration of Israel and the conversion of the world (ch. 66:8; Hab. 2:3; Acts 1:7; Heb. 10:37).

ADAM CLARKE

19. *Neither for brightness shall the moon give light unto thee*—"Nor by night shall the brightness of the moon enlighten you."

22. *I the Lord will hasten it in his time.* There is a time set for the fulfillment of this prophecy. That time must come before it begins to take place; but when it does begin, the whole will be performed in a short space.

MATTHEW HENRY

CHAPTER 61

Verses 1–3

He that is the best expositor of scripture has given us the best exposition of these verses, even our Lord Jesus himself, who read this in the synagogue at Nazareth (perhaps it was the lesson for the day) and applied it entirely to himself, saying, *This day is this scripture fulfilled in your ears* (Luke iv. 17, 18, 21). As Isaiah was directed to proclaim liberty to the Jews in Babylon, so was Christ, God's messenger, to publish a more joyful jubilee to a lost world.

I. How he was fitted and qualified for this work: *The Spirit of the Lord God is upon me, v.* 1. The prophets had the Spirit of God moving them at times, both instructing them what to say and exciting them to say it. Christ had the Spirit always resting on him without measure. When he entered upon the execution of his prophetical office the Spirit, as a dove, *descended upon him*, Matt. iii. 16. This Spirit he communicated to those whom he sent to proclaim the same glad tidings, saying to them, when he gave them their commission, *Receive you the Holy Ghost.*

II. How he was appointed and ordained to it: *The Spirit of God is upon me, because the Lord God has anointed me.* Hence the Redeemer was called the *Messiah*, the *Christ*, because he was *anointed with the oil of gladness above his fellows. He has sent me.*

III. What the work was to which he was appointed and ordained.

1. He was to be a preacher, was to execute the office of a prophet. He must preach *good tidings* (so *gospel* signifies) *to the meek*, to the penitent, and humble, and poor in spirit; to them the tidings of a Redeemer will be indeed good tidings.

2. He was to be a healer. He was sent to *bind up the broken-hearted.* Those whose hearts are broken for sin, who are truly humbled under the sense of guilt and dread of wrath, are furnished in the gospel of Christ with that which will make them easy and silence their fears.

JAMIESON, FAUSSET, BROWN

CHAPTER 61

Vss. 1-11. **Messiah's Offices: Restoration of Israel.** Messiah announces His twofold commission to bring gospel mercy at His first coming, and judgments on unbelievers and comfort to Zion at His second coming (vss. 1-9); the language can be applied to Isaiah, comforting by his prophecies the exiles in Babylon, only in a subordinate sense.

1. is upon me; because . . . hath anointed me—quoted by Jesus as His credentials in preaching (Luke 4:18-21). The Spirit *is* upon Me in preaching, because Jehovah *hath* anointed Me from the womb (Luke 1:35), and at baptism, with the Spirit "without measure," and permanently "abiding" on Me (ch. 11:2; John 1:32; 3:34; Ps. 45:7; with which cf. I Kings 1:39, 40; 19:16; Exod. 29:7). "Anointed" as *Messiah*, Prophet, Priest, and King. **good tidings**—as the word "gospel" means. **the meek**—rather, "the poor," as Luke 4:18 has it; i.e., those afflicted with calamity, poor in circumstances and in spirit (Matt. 11:5).

ADAM CLARKE

CHAPTER 61

1. *The Spirit of the Lord God is upon me*—"The Spirit of Jehovah is upon Me." The Septuagint, Vulgate, and St. Luke (chap. iv. 18) omit the word *Adonai*, "the Lord," which was probably added to the text through the superstition of the Jews, to prevent the pronunciation of the word *Yehovah* following. In most of Isaiah's prophecies there is a primary and secondary sense, or a remote subject illustrated by one that is near. The deliverance of the Jews from their captivity in Babylon is constantly used to shadow forth the salvation of men by Jesus Christ. Even the prophet himself is a typical person, and is sometimes intended to represent the great Saviour. It is evident from Luke iv. 18 that this is a prophecy of our blessed Lord and His preaching; and yet it is as evident that it primarily refers to Isaiah preaching the glad tidings of deliverance to the Jews.

MATTHEW HENRY

3. He was to be a deliverer. He was sent as a prophet to preach, as a priest to heal, and as a king to issue out proclamations: (1) Proclamations of peace to his friends: He shall *proclaim liberty to the captives* (as Cyrus did to the Jews in captivity) and the *opening of the prison to those that were bound.* Whereas, by the guilt of sin, we are bound over to the justice of God, sold for sin, Christ lets us know that he has made satisfaction to divine justice for that debt, that his satisfaction is accepted, and if we will plead that, and make over ourselves and all we have to him, we may by faith sue out our pardon; there is, and shall be, *no condemnation to us.* And whereas, by the dominion of sin in us, we are bound under the power of Satan, Christ lets us know that he has conquered Satan, and provided for us grace sufficient to enable us to shake off the yoke of sin and to loose ourselves from *those bands of our neck. The son* is ready by his Spirit to *make us free.* This is the gospel proclamation, and it is like the blowing of the jubilee-trumpet, which proclaimed the great year of release (Lev. xxv. 9, 40), in allusion to which it is here called *the acceptable year of the Lord,* because it publishes his free grace, and an *acceptable year* because it brings glad tidings to us, and what cannot but be very acceptable to those who know the capacities and necessities of their own souls. (2) Proclamations of war against his enemies. Christ proclaims *the day of vengeance of our God,* [1] On sin and Satan, death and hell, and all the powers of darkness, to be destroyed in order to our deliverance; these Christ triumphed over in his cross. [2] On those of the children of men that stand it out against those fair offers.

4. He was to be a comforter, and so he is a preacher, healer, and deliverer; he is sent to *comfort all who mourn,* and who, mourning, seek to him, and not to the world, for comfort. As *blessings out of Zion* are spiritual blessings, so *mourners in Zion* are holy mourners, such as carry their sorrows to the throne of grace. To such as these Christ has appointed by his gospel, and will give by his Spirit (*v.* 3), those consolations which will not only support them under their sorrows, but turn them into songs of praise. He will give them, (1) *Beauty for ashes.* Here is an elegant *paronomasia* in the original: He will give them *pheer—beauty,* for *epher*—ashes; he will turn their sorrow into joy as quickly and as easily as you can transpose a letter; for he speaks, and it is done. (2) *The oil of joy,* which *makes the face to shine,* instead of *mourning,* which *disfigures the countenance* and makes it unlovely. (3) *The garments of praise,* such beautiful garments as were worn on thanksgiving-days, instead of the *spirit of heaviness, dimness,* or *contraction*—open joys for secret mournings.

5. He was to be a planter; for the church is God's husbandry. All that Christ does for us is to make us God's people, and some way serviceable to him as living trees, *planted in the house of the Lord,* and *flourishing in the courts of our God*; that others also may take occasion from God's favour shining on his people, and his grace shining in them, to praise him, and that he may be for ever *glorified in his saints.*

Verses 4-9

Promises are here made to the Jews now returned out of captivity which are to be extended to the gospel church through grace delivered out of spiritual thraldom.

I. It is promised that their houses shall be rebuilt (*v.* 4), that their cities shall be raised out of the ruins. The setting up of Christianity in the world repaired the decays of natural religion and raised up those desolations both of piety and honesty which had been for many generations the reproach of mankind. An unsanctified soul is like a city that is broken down, but by the power of Christ's gospel and grace it is fitted to be a habitation of God through the Spirit.

II. Those that were servants, working for their oppressors, shall now have servants to do their work. *Strangers, and the sons of the alien,* shall *keep their sheep, till their ground,* and *dress their gardens. Strangers shall feed your flocks, v.* 5.

III. They shall be released and honourably employed (*v.* 6): "While the strangers are *keeping your flocks,* you shall be keeping *the charge of the sanctuary*; instead of being slaves to your task-masters, *you shall be named the priests of the Lord,* a high and holy calling." Those whom God sets at liberty he sets to work; he *delivers them out of the hands of their enemies* that they may *serve him,* Luke i. 74, 75; Ps. cxvi. 16. But his service is perfect freedom. And the gospel church is a *royal priesthood,* 1 Pet. ii. 9.

IV. The wealth and honour of the Gentile converts shall redound to the benefit and credit of the church, *v.* 6. Those that were strangers shall become *fellow-citizens with the saints.* 1. They shall *eat the riches*

JAMIESON, FAUSSET, BROWN

proclaim liberty—(John 8:31-36). Language drawn from the deliverance of the Babylonian captives, to describe the deliverance from sin and death (Heb. 2:15;) also from the "liberty proclaimed" to all bond-servants in the year of jubilee (vs. 2; Lev. 25:10; Jer. 34:8, 9). **opening of the prison**—The *Hebrew* rather is, "the *most complete* opening," viz., of the *eyes* to them that are bound, i.e., deliverance from *prison,* for captives are as it were *blind* in the darkness of prison (ch. 14:17; 35:5; 42:7) [EWALD]. So Luke 4:18 and LXX interpret it. Luke 4:18, under inspiration, adds to this, for the fuller explanation of the *single* clause in the *Hebrew,* "to set at liberty them that are bruised"; thus expressing the *double* "opening" implied; viz., that of the eyes (John 9:39), and that of the prison (Rom. 6:18; 7:24, 25; Heb. 2:15). His miracles were *acted parables.* **2. acceptable year**—the year of jubilee on which "liberty was proclaimed to the captives" (vs. 1; II Cor. 6:2).

day of vengeance—The "acceptable time of grace" is a "year"; the time of "vengeance" but "a day" (so ch. 34:8; 63:4; Mal. 4:1). Jesus (Luke 4:20, 21) "closed the book" before this clause; for the interval from His first to His second coming is "the acceptable year"; the day of vengeance" will not be till He comes again (II Thess. 1:7-9). **our God**—The saints call Him "*our* God"; for He cometh to "avenge" them (Rev. 6:10; 19:2). **all that mourn**—The "all" seems to include the *spiritual* Israelite mourners, as well as the *literal,* who are in vs. 3 called "them that mourn *in Zion,*" and to whom ch. 57:18 refers. **3. to appoint . . . to give**—The double verb, with the one and the same accusative, imparts glowing vehemence to the style.

beauty for ashes—There is a play on the sound and meaning of the *Hebrew* words, *peer, epher,* lit., "ornamental headdress" or *tiara* (Ezek. 24:17), worn in times of joy, instead of a headdress of "ashes," cast on the head in mourning (II Sam. 13:19). **oil of joy**—Perfumed ointment was poured on the guests at joyous feasts (Ps. 23:5; 45:7, 8; Amos 6:6). On occasions of grief its use was laid aside (II Sam. 14:2). **garment of praise**—bright-colored garments, indicative of thankfulness, instead of those that indicate despondency, as sackcloth (John 16:20). **trees of righteousness**—*Hebrew, terebinth* trees; symbolical of men *strong* in righteousness, instead of being, as heretofore, bowed down as a reed with sin and calamity (ch. 1:29, 30; 42:3; I Kings 14:15; Ps. 1:3; 92: 12-14; Jer. 17:8). **planting of . . . Lord**—(*Note,* ch. 60:21). **that he might be glorified**—(John 15:8).

4. old wastes—Jerusalem and the cities of Judah which long lay in ruins (*Note,* ch. 58:12).

5. stand—shall wait on you as servants (ch. 14:1, 2; 60:10).

6. But ye—as contrasted with the "strangers." *Ye* shall have no need to attend to your flocks and lands: *strangers* will do that for you; *your* exclusive business will be the service of Jehovah as His "priests" (Exod. 19:6, which remains yet to be realized; cf. as to the spiritual Israel, ch. 66:21; I Pet. 2:5, 9; Rev. 1:6; 5:10). **Ministers**—(Ezek. 44: 11).

ADAM CLARKE

The opening of the prison—"Perfect liberty." Not merely opening of prisons, but every kind of liberty—complete redemption. The proclaiming of perfect liberty to the bound, and the year of acceptance with Jehovah, is a manifest allusion to the proclaiming of the year of jubilee by sound of trumpet. See Lev. xxv. 9, etc. This was a year of general release of debts and obligations, of bondmen and bondwomen, of lands and possessions which had been sold from the families and tribes to which they belonged. Our Saviour, by applying this text to himself (Luke iv. 18-19), a text so manifestly relating to the institution above mentioned, plainly declares the typical design of that institution.

3. *To appoint unto them that mourn in Zion*—"To impart gladness to the mourners of Zion."

Beauty for ashes—"A beautiful crown instead of ashes." In times of mourning the Jews put on sackcloth, and spread dust and ashes on their heads; on the contrary, splendid clothing and ointment poured on the head were the signs of joy.

Trees of righteousness—"Trees approved." Hebrew, "oaks of righteousness or truth"; that is, such as by their flourishing condition should show that they were indeed of God's planting.

4. *The desolations of many generations.* It seems that these words cannot refer to the Jews in the Babylonish captivity, for they were not there many generations. But it may refer to their dispersions and state of ruin since the advent of our Lord, and consequently this may be a promise of the restoration of the Jewish people.

5. *Strangers shall . . . feed your flocks.* Gentiles shall first preach to you the salvation of Christ, and feed with divine knowledge the Jewish congregations.

MATTHEW HENRY

of the Gentiles honourably presented to them, as *gifts brought to the altar*. 2. They shall *boast themselves in their glory*. Whatever was the honour of the Gentile converts before their conversion, it shall turn to the reputation of the church to which they have joined themselves; and whatever is their glory after their conversion—their holy zeal, their patient suffering, and that blessed change which divine grace has made in them—shall be very much for the glory of God.

V. They shall have abundance of comfort, *v.* 7. The Jews were thus privileged after their return; they were in a new world, and now knew how to value their liberty. Much more do all those rejoice whom Christ has brought into the glorious liberty of God's children, especially when the privileges of their adoption shall be completed in the resurrection of the body. 1. *They shall rejoice in their portion.* Though the houses, as well as their temple, be much inferior, yet they shall be *in their land*, their own land, the holy land, Immanuel's land, and therefore they shall rejoice. 2. *Everlasting joy shall be unto them* which shall last much longer than the captivity had lasted. Yet we must look for the accomplishment of this promise in the spiritual joy which believers have in God and the eternal joy they hope for in heaven. 3. This shall be a double recompense to them, for all the reproach and vexation they have lain under in the land of their captivity: "*For your shame you shall have double* honour, and *in your land* you *shall possess double* wealth; the blessing of God upon it. You shall be owned not only as *God's sons*, but as his *first-born* (Exod. iv. 22), and therefore entitled to a double portion." As the miseries of their captivity were so great that in them they are said to have received *double for all their sins* (*ch.* xl. 2), so the joys of their return shall be so great that in them they shall receive *double for all their shame*. The former is applicable to the fulness of Christ's satisfaction, in which God received *double for all our sins*; the latter to the fulness of heaven's joys, in which we shall receive more than *double for all services* and sufferings. Job's case illustrates this: when God *turned again his captivity*, he gave him *twice as much as he had before*.

VI. God will be a God in covenant with them (*v.* 8): *I will direct their work in truth.* God by his providence will order their affairs for the best. As a reason both of this and of the foregoing promise, those words come in, in the former part of the verse, *I the Lord love judgment*. He loves that judgment should be done among men, both between magistrates and subjects and between neighbour and neighbour, and therefore he hates all injustice. If men do not do justice, he loves to do judgment himself in giving redress to those that suffer wrong and punishing those that do wrong. It is a truth that ritual services will never atone for the violation of moral precepts, nor will it justify any man's robbery to say, "It was for burnt-offerings," or *Corban—It is a gift*.

VII. God will entail a blessing upon their posterity (*v.* 9): *Their seed* (the children of those persons that are now the blessed of the Lord, or the church's seed) shall be *accounted to the Lord for a generation*, Ps. xxii. 30. 1. *They shall be known among the Gentiles*, shall distinguish themselves, especially by that brotherly love by which all men shall know them to be Christ's disciples. God shall dignify them, by making them the blessings of their age and instruments of his glory. 2. God shall have the glory of this, for all that see them shall see so much of the grace of God in them, that they shall *acknowledge them to be the seed which the Lord has blessed* and doth bless.

Verses 10–11

We are here taught to rejoice with holy joy, to God's honour, 1. In the beginning of this good work, the clothing of the church *with righteousness and salvation*, *v.* 10. Upon this account *I will greatly rejoice in the Lord*. The first gospel song begins like this, *My soul doth magnify the Lord, and my spirit hath rejoiced in God my Saviour*, Luke i. 46, 47. The salvation God wrought for the Jews, and that reformation which appeared among them, made them look as glorious as if they had been clothed in robes of state. Christ has clothed his church with an eternal salvation by clothing it with the righteousness both of justification and sanctification. Observe how these two are put together; those, and those only, shall be clothed with the garments of salvation hereafter that are covered with the robe of righteousness now. Such is the beauty of God's grace in those that are clothed with the robe of righteousness. 2. In the progress and continuance of this good work, *v.* 11. It is not like a day of triumph, which is glorious for the present, but is soon over. The church rejoices to think that these inestimable blessings shall both spring for future ages and spread to distant regions.

JAMIESON, FAUSSET, BROWN

eat . . . riches of . . . Gentiles—(ch. 60:5-11). **in their glory . . . boast yourselves**—rather, "in their splendor ye shall *be substituted* in their stead"; ye shall substitute yourselves [MAURER].

rejoice—They shall *celebrate with jubilation* their portion [MAURER]. Transition from the second to the third person. **in their land**—marking the reference to literal Israel, not to the Church at large. **everlasting joy**—(ch. 35:10).

7. double—Instead of your past share, ye shall have not merely as much, but "double" as much reward (ch. 40:2; Zech. 9:12; cf. the third clause in this verse). **confusion**—rather, humiliation, or contumely.

8. judgment—justice, which requires that I should restore My people, and give them double in compensation for their sufferings. **robbery for burnt offering**—rather, from a different *Hebrew* root, *the spoil of iniquity* [HORSLEY]. So in Job 5:6. Hating, as I do, the *rapine*, combined *with iniquity*, perpetrated on My people *by* their enemies, I will vindicate Israel. **direct . . . work in truth**—rather, "I will give them the *reward of their work*" (cf. *Margin*, ch. 40:10; 49:4; 62:11) in faithfulness.

9. known—honorably; shall be *illustrious* (Ps. 67:2). **people**—rather, "peoples." **seed . . . blessed**—(ch. 65:23).

10. Zion (vs. 3) gives thanks for God's returning favor (cf. Luke 1:46, 47; Hab. 3:18). **salvation . . . righteousness**—inseparably connected together. The "robe" is a loose mantle thrown over the other parts of the dress (Ps. 132:9, 16; 149:4; Rev. 21:2; 19:8). **decketh himself with ornaments**—rather "maketh himself a *priestly headdress*," i.e., a magnificent headdress, such as was worn by the high priest, viz., a miter and a plate, or crown of gold worn in front of it [AQUILA, etc.]; appropriate to the "kingdom of priests," dedicated to the offering of spiritual sacrifices to God continually (Exod. 19:6; Rev. 5:10; 20:6). **jewels**—rather, ornaments in general [BARNES].

ADAM CLARKE

7. *For your shame*—"Instead of your shame."

8. *I hate robbery for burnt offering*—"Who hate rapine and iniquity." The difference lies in the punctuation; *beolah*, "in a burnt offering"; *beavelah*, "in iniquity." The letters are the same in both words.

9. *Their seed shall be known among the Gentiles.* Both Jews and Gentiles are to make but one fold under one Shepherd, Christ Jesus. But still, notwithstanding this, they may retain their peculiarity and national distinction; so that though they are known to be Christians, yet they shall appear to be converted Jews.

10. *I will greatly rejoice in the Lord.* These may be the words of the Jews now converted, and brought into the Church of Christ, and with the Gentiles made fellow heirs of the blessings of the new covenant. *As a bridegroom decketh himself with ornaments*—"As the bridegroom decketh himself with a priestly crown." An allusion to the magnificent dress of the high priest, when performing his functions; and particularly to the mitre, and crown or plate of gold on the front of it, Exod. xxix. 6. The bonnet or mitre of the priests also was made, as Moses expresses it, "for glory and for beauty," Exod. xxviii. 40.

MATTHEW HENRY

They shall spring forth for ages to come, as the fruits of the earth which are produced every year. *As the garden* enclosed *causes the things that are sown in it to spring forth* in their season, so constantly *will the Lord God cause righteousness and praise to spring forth*, by virtue of the covenant of grace. Though it may sometimes be winter with the church, when those blessings seem to wither and do not appear, yet the root of them is fixed, a spring-time will come, when they shall flourish again. They shall spread far, and *spring forth before all the nations.*

CHAPTER 62

Verses 1–5

I. What he will do for the church. A prophet, as he is a seer, so he is a spokesman. He *will not hold his peace*; he *will not rest.* 1. What the prophet's resolution is: *He will not hold his peace.* He will continue instant in preaching. And he will continue instant in prayer. 2. What is the principle of this resolution—*for Zion's sake, and for Jerusalem's*, not for the sake of any private interest of his own, but for the church's sake, because he has an affection and concern for Zion, and it lies near his heart. It is God's Zion and his Jerusalem, and it is *therefore* dear to him, because it is so to God. 3. He resolves to continue this importunity—till the promise of the church's righteousness and salvation, given in the foregoing chapter, be accomplished. His prophecies will continue speaking of these things, and there shall in every age be a remnant that shall continue to pray for them. Then the church's *righteousness* and *salvation* will *go forth as brightness*, and *as a lamp that burns*, a light not only to the eyes but to the feet, and to *the paths* of those who before *sat in darkness and in the shadow of death.*

II. What God will do for the church. 1. The church shall be greatly admired. When that righteousness which is her salvation, her praise, and her glory, shall be *brought forth*, the *Gentiles shall see* it. "Even kings shall see and be in love with the *glory of thy righteousness*" (*v.* 2). 2. She shall be truly admirable. God is the fountain of honour and from him the church's honour comes: "*Thou shalt be called by a new name*, and those about thee shall have new thoughts of thee." Two names God shall give her: (1) He shall call her his crown (*v.* 3): *Thou shalt be a crown of glory in the hand of the Lord*, not on his head (as adding any real honour or power to him, as crowns do to those that are crowned with them), but in his hand, as a glory and beauty to him. "Thou shalt be a *crown o glory* and a *royal diadem*, through the hand, the good hand, of thy God upon thee. (2) He shall call her his spouse, *v.* 4, 5. This is a yet greater honour, considering what a forlorn condition she had been in. She was called *forsaken* and her land *desolate* during the captivity, like a woman reproachfully divorced or left a disconsolate widow. Such was the state of religion in the world before the preaching of the gospel. Instead of those two names of reproach, she shall be called by two honourable names. She shall be called *Hephzi-bah*, which signifies, *My delight is in her*, a proper name for a wife. God by his grace has wrought that in his church which makes her his delight, she being refined, and reformed, and brought home to him. She shall be called *Beulah*, which signifies *married*, whereas she had been desolate. *She shall be married.* Her sons shall heartily espouse the land of their nativity. *Thy sons shall marry thee*, that is, they shall live with thee and take delight in thee. When they were in Babylon, they seemed to have espoused that land, Jer. xxix. 5–7. But now they shall again marry their own land, *as a young man marries a virgin. Her God* will take pleasure in his church: *As the bridegroom rejoices over the bride, so shall thy God rejoice over thee.*

Verses 6–9

Two things are here promised to Jerusalem:

I. Plenty of the means of grace—abundance of good preaching and good praying (*v.* 6, 7). Provision is made,

1. That ministers may do their duty as watchmen. He would set *watchmen on their walls who should never hold their peace.* They must take all opportunities to give warning to sinners, in season, out of season, and must never betray the cause of Christ by a treacherous or cowardly silence. They must never hold their peace at the throne of grace; must *pray, and not faint.*

2. That people may do their duty. Let them not think it enough that their watchmen pray for them, but let them pray for themselves. God's professing people must be a praying people, must be public-

JAMIESON, FAUSSET, BROWN

11. (Ch. 45:8, 55: 10, 11; Ps. 72:3; 85:11.) **bud**—the tender shoots. **praise**—(ch. 60:18; 62:7).

CHAPTER 62

Vss. 1-12. Intercessory Prayers for Zion's Restoration, Accompanying God's Promises of It, as the Appointed Means of Accomplishing It. **1. I**—the prophet, as representative of all the praying people of God who love and intercede for Zion (cf. vss. 6, 7; Ps. 102:13-17), or else Messiah (cf. vs. 6). So Messiah is represented as unfainting in His efforts for His people (ch. 42:4; 50:7).

righteousness thereof—not its own inherently, but imputed to it, for its restoration to God's favor: hence "*salvation*" answers to it in the parallelism. "Judah" is to be "*saved*" through "the Lord *our* (Judah's and the Church's) *righteousness*" (Jer. 23:6). **as brightness**—properly the bright shining of the rising sun (ch. 60: 19; 4:5; II Sam. 23:4; Prov. 4:18). **lamp**—blazing torch.

2. (Ch. 11:10; 42:1-6; 49:7, 22, 23; 60:3, 5, 16.) **new name**—expression of thy new and improved condition (vs. 4), the more valuable and lasting as being conferred by Jehovah Himself (vs. 12; ch. 65:15; Rev. 2:17; 3:12). **3.** (Zech. 9:16) **in . . . hand of . . . Lord**—As a crown is worn on the *head* not "in the hand," *hand* must here be figurative for "under the Lord's *protection*" (cf. Deut. 33:3). "All His saints are in thy hand." His people are *in His hand* at the same time that they are "a crown of glory" to Him (Rev. 6:2; 19:12); reciprocally, *He* is "a crown of glory and a diadem of beauty" to them (ch. 28:5; cf. Mal. 3:17). **4. be termed**—*be* "forsaken," so as that that term could be applicable to thee. **Hephzi-bah**—(II Kings 21:1), the name of Hezekiah's wife, a type of Jerusalem, as Hezekiah was of Messiah (ch. 32:1): "my delight is in her." **Beulah**—"Thou art married." See the same contrast of Zion's past and future state under the same figure (ch. 54:4-6; Rev. 21.2, 4). **land . . . married**—to Jehovah as its *Lord and Husband:* implying not only ownership, but *protection* on the part of the Owner [Horsley]. **5. thy sons**—rather, changing the points, which are of no authority *in Hebrew*, "thy builder" or "restorer," i.e., God; for in the parallel clause, and in vs. 4, God is implied as being "married" to her; whereas her "sons" could hardly be said to marry their mother; and in ch. 49:18, they are said to be her *bridal ornaments*, not her husband. The *plural* form, *builders*, is used of God in reverence as "husbands" (*Note*, ch. 54:5). **over the bride**—in the possession of the bride (ch. 65:19; Jer. 32:41; Zeph. 3:17). **6. I**—Isaiah speaking in the person of the Messiah. **watchmen upon . . . walls**—image from the watches set upon a city's wall to look out for the approach of a messenger with good tidings (ch. 52:7, 8); the good tidings of the return of the Jewish exiles from Babylon, prefiguring the return from the present dispersion (cf. ch. 21:6-11; 56:10; Ezek. 3:17; 33:7). The watches in the East are announced by a loud cry to mark the vigilance of the watchmen. **ye that . . . mention . . . Lord**—*Hebrew*, "ye that are the Lord's remembrancers"; God's servants who by their prayers "put God in remembrance" of His promises (ch. 43:26); we are required to *remind* God, as if God could, which He cannot, *forget* His promises (Ps. 119:49; Jer. 14:21). **7. no rest**—*Hebrew*, "silence"; keep not silence *yourselves*, nor let *Him* rest in silence. Cf. as to Messiah Himself, "I will not hold . . . peace . . . not rest" (vs. 1); Messiah's watchmen (vss. 6, 7) imitate *Him* (vs. 1) in intercessory "prayer without ceasing" for Jerusalem (Ps. 122:6; 51:18); also for the spiritual Jerusalem, the Church (Luke 18:1, 7; Rom. 1:9). **a praise**—(*Note*, ch. 61:11; Zeph. 3:20).

ADAM CLARKE

CHAPTER 62

1. *For Zion's sake will I not hold my peace.* These are the words of Jehovah declaring His purpose relative to the events predicted in the preceding chapter.

4. *Thy land Beulah. Beulah,* "married." In the prophets, a desolate land is represented under the notion of a widow; an inhabited land, under that of a married woman, who has both a husband and children.

6. *Ye that make mention of the Lord, keep not silence.* The faithful, and in particular the priests and Levites, are exhorted by the prophet to beseech God with unremitted importunity to hasten the redemption of Sion. The image in this place is taken from the Temple service, in which there was appointed a constant watch, day and night, by the Levites; and among them this seems to have belonged particularly to the singers, see 1 Chron. ix. 33. Now the watches in the East, even to this day, are performed by a loud cry from time to time of the watchmen, to mark the time, and that very frequently, and in order to show that they themselves are constantly attentive to their duty. Hence the watchmen are said by the prophet, chap. lii. 8, to lift up their voice; and here they are commanded not to keep silence; and the greatest reproach to them is that they are "dumb dogs, they cannot bark"; dreamers; sluggards, "loving to slumber," chap. lvi. 10.

MATTHEW HENRY

spirited in prayer.

II. Plenty of all other good things, *v.* 8. Their corn had been meat for their enemies. Here was a double grievance, that they themselves wanted that which was necessary to the support of life, whilst their enemies were strengthened by it. God is said to give their corn to their enemies, as the just punishment of their abuse of plenty. The wine which they had laboured for, strangers drank to gratify their lusts. But see the great fulness and satisfaction they should now be restored to (*v.* 9): *Those that have gathered it shall eat it, and praise the Lord.* We must gather what God gives, with care and industry; we must eat it freely and cheerfully. We must serve him with our abundance, use it in works of piety and charity, eat it and *drink it in the courts of his holiness*, where the altar, the priest, and the poor must all have their share. *The Lord has sworn by his right hand, and by the arm of his strength*, that he will do this for his people. It is a great satisfaction to those who build their hopes on God's promise to be sure that *what he has promised he is able to perform*, Rom. iv. 21.

Verses 10–12

This, like passages before, refers to the deliverance of the Jews out of Babylon, and to the great redemption wrought out by Jesus Christ, and the proclaiming of gospel grace and liberty through him. 1. Way shall be made for this salvation, *v.* 10. The gates of Babylon shall be thrown open, the way from Babylon to the land of Israel shall be prepared; causeways shall be made and cast up through wet and miry places, and the stones gathered out from places rough and rocky. Thus John Baptist was sent to *prepare the way of the Lord*, Matt. iii. 3. 2. Notice shall be given of this salvation, *v.* 11, 12. It shall be proclaimed to the captives that they are set at liberty. Let it be said to Zion, for her comfort, *Behold, thy salvation comes* (that is, thy Saviour, who brings salvation). It follows, they shall be called, *The holy people*, and the *redeemed of the Lord*. *The work before him*, which shall be wrought in them and upon them, shall denominate them a holy people, cured of their inclination to idolatry and consecrated to God only; and the *reward with him*, the deliverance wrought for them, shall denominate them the *redeemed of the Lord*. Jerusalem shall then be called, *Sought out, a city not forsaken*. She shall be sought out, visited, as much as ever. When Jerusalem is called a *holy city*, then it is called *sought out*; for holiness draws respect. But this being proclaimed to the end of the world must have a reference to the gospel of Christ. It is published immediately to the church, but is echoed to every nation: *Behold, thy salvation cometh*. Christ is not only the Saviour, but the salvation itself. Christians shall be called *saints* (1 Cor. i. 2), *the holy people*, for they shall be called *the redeemed of the Lord*.

JAMIESON, FAUSSET, BROWN

8. sworn by . . . right hand—His mighty instrument of accomplishing His will (cf. ch. 45:23; Heb. 6:13). **sons of . . . stranger**—*Foreigners* shall no more rob thee of the fruit of thy labors (cf. ch. 65:21, 22).

9. eat . . . and praise—not consume it on their own lusts, and without thanksgiving.

drink it in . . . courts—They who have *gathered* the vintage shall drink it at the feasts held in the courts surrounding the temple (Deut. 12:17, 18; 14:23, etc.).

10. What Isaiah in the person of Messiah had engaged in (vs. 1) unrestingly to seek, and what the watchmen were unrestingly to pray for (vs. 7), and what Jehovah solemnly promised (vss. 8, 9), is now to be fulfilled; the Gentile nations are commanded to "go through the gates" (either of their own cities [ROSENMULLER] or of Jerusalem [MAURER]), in order to remove all obstacles out of "the way of *the* people" (Israel) (*Note*, 57:14; 40:3; 52:10-12). **standard**—for the dispersed Jews to rally round, with a view to their return (ch. 49: 22; 11:12).

11. salvation—embodied in the Saviour (see Zech. 9:9), **his work**—rather, *recompense* (ch. 40:10). **12. Sought out**—*Sought after and highly prized* by Jehovah; answering to "not forsaken" in the parallel clause; no longer abandoned, but loved; image from a wife (vs. 4; Jer. 30:14).

ADAM CLARKE

9. *But they that have gathered it shall eat it, and praise the Lord.* This and the following line have reference to the law of Moses: "Thou mayest not eat within thy gates the tithe of thy corn, or of thy wine, or of thy oil . . . but thou must eat them before the Lord thy God, in the place which the Lord thy God shall choose," Deut. xii. 17-18. "And when ye shall come into the land, and shall have planted all manner of trees for food, then ye shall count the fruit thereof as uncircumcised: three years it shall be as uncircumcised unto you; it shall not be eaten of. But . . . in the fifth year shall ye eat of the fruit thereof," Lev. xix. 23-25.

11. *Behold, thy salvation cometh*—"Lo, thy Saviour cometh." *Behold, his reward.* See note on chap. xl. 10-11. This reward He carries as it were in His hand. *His work* [*is*] *before him*—He perfectly knows what is to be done, and is perfectly able to do it.

MATTHEW HENRY — CHAPTER 63

Verses 1–6

A glorious victory is obtained by the providence of God over the enemies of Israel. The victory is obtained over the Edomites who had triumphed in the destruction of Jerusalem by the Chaldeans (Ps. cxxxvii. 7) who cut off those who, making their way as far as they could from the enemy, escaped to them (Obad. 12, 13), and who were therefore reckoned with when Babylon was. Yet this victory over Edom is put as an instance or specimen of the like victories obtained over other nations that had been enemies to Israel. But this is not all: It is a victory obtained by the grace of God in Christ over our spiritual enemies. We find the garments dipped in blood adorning him whose name is called *The Word of God*, Rev. xix. 13.

In this representation of the victory we have,

I. An admiring question put to the conqueror, *v.* 1, 2, by the church, or by the prophet in the name of the church. He sees a mighty hero returning in triumph from a bloody engagement, and makes bold to ask him two questions: 1. Who he is. He observes him to come from the country of Edom, in such apparel as was glorious to a soldier, besmeared with blood and dirt. He observes that he does not come as one either frightened or fatigued, but that he *travels in the greatness of his strength*. The question, *Who is this?* perhaps means: *Art thou for us or for our adversaries?* 2. The other question is, "*Wherefore art thou red in thy apparel?* What hard service hast thou been engaged in, that thou carriest with thee these marks of toil and danger?" Is it possible that one who has such majesty should be employed in the servile work of *treading the wine-press?*

II. An admirable answer returned by him.

JAMIESON, FAUSSET, BROWN — CHAPTER 63

VSS. 1-19. MESSIAH COMING AS THE AVENGER, IN ANSWER TO HIS PEOPLE'S PRAYERS. Messiah, approaching Jerusalem after having avenged His people on His and their enemies, is represented under imagery taken from the destruction of "Edom," the type of the last and most bitter foes of God and His people (see ch. 34:5, etc.).

1. Who—the question of the prophet in prophetic vision. **dyed**—scarlet with blood (vss. 2, 3; Rev. 19:13). **Bozrah**—(*Note*, ch. 34:6). **travelling**—rather, stately; lit., "throwing back the head" [GESENIUS]. **speak in righteousness**—answer of Messiah. I, who have in faithfulness given a promise of deliverance, am now about to fulfil it. Rather, speak *of* righteousness (ch. 45:19; 46:13); *salvation* being meant as the result of His "righteousness" [MAURER]. **save**—The same Messiah that destroys the unbeliever *saves* the believer. **2.** The prophet asks why His garments are "dyed" and "red." **winefat**—rather, the wine-press, wherein the grapes were trodden with the feet; the juice would stain the garment of him who trod them (Rev. 14:19, 20; 19:15). The image was appropriate, as the country round Bozrah abounded in grapes. This final blow inflicted by Messiah and His armies (Rev. 19:13-15) shall decide His claim to the kingdoms usurped by Satan, and by the "beast," to whom Satan delegates his power. It will be a day of judgment to the hostile Gentiles, as His first coming was a day of judgment to the unbelieving Jews.

ADAM CLARKE — CHAPTER 63

1. *Who is this that cometh from Edom?* Probably both *Edom* and *Bozrah* are only figurative expressions, to point out the place in which God should discomfit His enemies. Edom signifies "red," and Bozrah, "a vintage." *I that speak in righteousness*—"I who publish righteousness."

MATTHEW HENRY

1. He tells who he is: *I that speak in righteousness, mighty to save.* He is the Saviour. He speaks *in righteousness*, and will therefore make good every word that he has spoken. He is *mighty to save*, able to bring about the promised redemption.

2. He tells how he came to appear in this hue (*v.* 3): *I have trodden the wine-press alone.*

(1) He gains the victory purely by his own strength, *v.* 3. But his people, for whom the salvation was to be wrought, were weak and helpless, desponding and listless, and had no heart to do anything (*v.* 5): "*I looked, and there was none to help, none to uphold*, none that had the courage to join with Cyrus against their oppressors; *therefore my arm brought* about *the salvation*; *not by* created *might or power*, but *by the Spirit of the Lord of hosts*, my own arm." God can help when all other helpers fail; that is his time to help. But this is most fully applicable to Christ's victories over our spiritual enemies, which he obtained by a single combat. He trod the wine-press alone, and triumphed over principalities and powers *in himself*, Col. ii. 15. When he entered the lists with the powers of darkness, *all his disciples forsook him and fled.*

(2) He undertakes the war purely out of his own zeal. God wrought salvation for the oppressed Jews because he was very angry with the oppressing Babylonians, angry at their idolatries, their pride and cruelty, and the injuries they did to his people. Our Lord Jesus wrought out our redemption in a holy zeal for the honour of his Father and the happiness of mankind, and a holy indignation at the daring attempts Satan had made upon both. He had a zeal against his and his people's enemies: *The day of vengeance is in my heart* (*v.* 4). He had a zeal for his people, and for all that he designed to make sharers in the intended salvation: "*The year of my redeemed has come*, the year appointed for their redemption." With what pleasure he speaks of his people; they are his *redeemed*; they are his own, dear to him. Though their redemption is not yet wrought out, yet he calls them *his redeemed*, because it shall as surely be done as if it were done already.

(3) He will obtain a complete victory over them all. Much is already done; for he now appears *red in his apparel.* In the destruction of the antichristian powers we meet with abundance of bloodshed (Rev. xiv. 20; xix. 13), which yet, according to the dialect of prophecy, may be understood spiritually, and doubtless so may this here.

Verses 7–14

The prophet is here making a thankful recognition of God's dealings with his church all along, before he comes, in the latter end of this chapter and in the next, as a watchman upon the walls, earnestly to pray to God for his compassion towards her in her present deplorable state.

I. Here is a general acknowledgment of God's goodness to them all along, *v.* 7. He mentions the *kindness of God*, his loving-kindness; so plenteous are the springs of divine mercy, that he speaks of it in the plural number—*his loving-kindnesses.* He mentions his *praises*, that is, the thankful acknowledgements of his loving-kindness. He speaks of the goodness that is from God, *all that the Lord has bestowed* on us, relating to life and godliness, in our personal and family capacity. We must bless God for the mercies enjoyed by others as well as for those enjoyed by ourselves. God does good because he is good; what he bestowed upon us must be traced up to the original; it is *according to his mercies* (not according to our merits) and *according to the multitude of his loving-kindnesses.*

II. The steps of God's mercy to Israel ever since it was formed into a nation. When he brought them out of Egypt and took them into covenant he said, "*Surely they are my people, children that will not lie*," that will not *dissemble with God* in their covenantings. *So he was their Saviour* out of the bondage of Egypt, and many a time since he had been their Saviour. The principle that moved him to work salvation for them was *in his love and in his pity.* This is strangely expressed here: *In all their affliction he was afflicted;* thus far he sympathizes with them, that he takes what injury is done to them as done to himself. Their cries move him (Exod. iii. 7), as if he were pained in their pain. *Saul, Saul, why persecutest thou me?* God is so far from *afflicting willingly* (Lam. iii. 33) that, if they humble themselves he is *afflicted in their affliction*, as tender parents are in the case of a sick child. There is another reading of these words in the original: *In all their affliction there was no affliction;* though they were in great affliction, yet it was so altered by the grace of God for their good, and it was so allayed and balanced with mercies, they were so wonderfully supported and it ended so well, that it was in effect

JAMIESON, FAUSSET, BROWN

3. Reply of Messiah. For the image, see Lamentations 1: 15. He "treads the winepress" here not as a *sufferer*, but as an *inflicter* of vengeance. **will tread . . . shall be . . . will stain**— rather preterites," I trod . . . trampled . . . was sprinkled . . . I stained." **blood**—lit., "spirted juice" of the grape, pressed out by treading [GESENIUS].

5. The same words as in ch. 59:16, except that *there* it is His "righteousness," *here* it is His "fury," which is said to have upheld Him.

4. is—rather, "was." This assigns the reason why He has thus destroyed the foe (Zeph. 3:8). **my redeemed**—My people *to be redeemed.* **day . . . year**—here, as in ch. 34:8; 61:2, the time of "vengeance" is described as a "day"; that of grace and of "recompense" to the "redeemed," as a "year."

6. Rather, preterites, "I *trod* down . . . *made* them drunk." The same image occurs ch. 51:17, 21-23; Psalm 75: 8; Jeremiah 25:26, 27. **will bring down . . . strength to . . . earth**—rather, "I *spilled* their life-*blood* (the same *Hebrew* words as in vs. 3) on the earth" [LOWTH and LXX].

7. Israel's penitential confession and prayer for restoration (Ps. 102: 17, 20), extending from this verse to the end of ch. 64. **loving-kindnesses . . . praises . . . mercies . . . loving-kindnesses**—The *plurals* and the repetitions imply that language is inadequate to express the full extent of God's goodness. **us**—the dispersed Jews at the time just preceding their final restoration. **house of Israel**—of all ages; God was good not merely to the Jews now dispersed, but to Israel in every age of its history. **8. he**—Jehovah "said," i.e., thought, in choosing them as His covenant people; so "said" (Ps. 95:10). Not that God was ignorant that the Jews would not keep faith with Him; but God is here said, according to *human* modes of thought to *say within Himself* what He might *naturally* have expected, as the result of His goodness to the Jews; thus the enormity of their *unnatural* perversity is the more vividly set forth. **lie**—prove false to Me (cf. Ps. 44:17). **so**—in virtue of His having *chosen* them, He became their *Saviour.* So the "therefore" (Jer. 31:33). His eternal *choice* is the ground of His actually *saving* men (Eph. 1:3, 4). **9. he was afflicted**—*English Version* reads the *Hebrew* as the *Keri* (*Margin*) does, "There was affliction *to Him.*" But the *Chetib* (text) reads, "There was *no* affliction" (the change in *Hebrew* being only of one letter); i.e., "In all their affliction there was no (utterly overwhelming) affliction" [GESENIUS]; or, for "*Hardly* had an affliction befallen them, *when* the angel of His presence saved them" [MAURER]; or, as best suits the parallelism, "In all their straits there was no straitness in His goodness to them" [HOUBIGANT], (Judg. 10:16; Mic. 2:7; II Cor. 6:12).

ADAM CLARKE

3. *And of the people there was none with me.* I was wholly abandoned by them. But a good meaning is, No man has had any part in making the atonement; it is entirely the work of the Messiah alone. No created being could have any part in a sacrifice that was to be of infinite merit. *And I will stain*—"And I have stained."

5. *And my fury*—"And mine indignation."

6. *And make them drunk in my fury*—"And I crushed them in Mine indignation."

7. *I will mention the lovingkindnesses of the Lord.* The prophet connects the preceding mercies of God to the Jews with the present prospect he has of their redemption by the Messiah, thus making a circle in which eternal goodness revolves. The remaining part of this chapter, with the whole chapter following, contains a penitential confession and supplication of the Israelites in their present state of dispersion, in which they have so long marvellously subsisted, and still continue to subsist, as a people; cast out of their country; without any proper form of civil polity or religious worship; their Temple destroyed, their city desolated and lost to them, and their whole nation scattered over the face of the earth, apparently deserted and cast off by the God of their fathers, as no longer His peculiar people. They begin with acknowledging God's great mercies and favors to their nation, and the ungrateful returns made to them on their part, that by their disobedience they had forfeited the protection of God, and had caused Him to become their Adversary. And now the prophet represents them, enduced by the memory of the great things that God had done for them, as addressing their humble supplication for the renewal of His mercies. They beseech Him to regard them in consideration of his former loving-kindness; they acknowledge Him for their Father and Creator; they confess their wickedness and hardness of heart; they entreat His forgiveness, and deplore their present miserable condition under which they have so long suffered. It seems designed as a formulary of humiliation for the Israelites, in order to their conversion.

8-9. *So he was their Saviour. In all their affliction*—"And He became their Saviour in all their distress."

MATTHEW HENRY

no affliction. The troubles of the saints are not afflictions, but medicines; saints are enabled to call them *light*, and *but for a moment*, and, with an eye to heaven as all in all, to make nothing of them. The highest angel in heaven, even the angel of his presence, is not thought too great to be sent on this errand. Thus the little ones' angels are said to be those that *always behold the face of our Father*, Matt. xviii. 10. But this is rather to be understood of Jesus Christ, the eternal Word, that angel of whom God spoke to Moses (Exod. xxiii. 20, 21), whose *voice Israel was to obey*. He is the angel of the covenant, God's messenger to the world, Mal. iii. 1. He is the *angel of God's face*, for he is the *express image of his person*; and the glory of God shines in the face of Christ. He that was to work out the eternal salvation wrought out the temporal salvations. He not only redeemed them out of their bondage, but *he bore them and carried them all the days of old*; in the wars they made upon the nations he stood by them, and though they were peevish, he bore with them, Acts xiii. 18. *But they rebelled.* They revolted from their allegiance to God and took up arms against him: *They rebelled, and vexed his Holy Spirit* with their unbelief and murmuring. The ungrateful rebellions of God's children against him are a vexation to his Holy Spirit. Thereupon he justly withdrew his protection. He who had been so much their friend was *turned to be their enemy and fought against them*, by one judgment after another, both in the wilderness and after their settlement in Canaan. Sin makes God an enemy, and makes him angry who was all love and pity. Sinners wilfully lose him for a friend. This refers especially to those calamities that were brought upon them by their captivity in Babylon for their idolatries and other sins. *Then he remembered the days of old, v.* 11.

1. This may be understood either of the people or of God. (1) We may understand it of the people. Israel then (spoken of as a single person) *remembered the days of old*, and reasoned, *Where are all the wonders that our fathers told us of?* "*Where is he that brought them up* out of Egypt? Is he not as able to bring us up out of Babylon? *Where is the Lord God of Elijah? Where is the Lord God of our fathers?*" Their fathers were a provoking people and yet found him a pardoning God; and why may not they find him so if they return to him? They use it as a plea with God in prayer for the turning again of their captivity, like that *ch.* li. 9, 10. (2) We may understand it of God; he put himself in mind of the days of old, of his covenant with Abraham (Lev. xxvi. 42). "Why should not I appear for them now as I did for their fathers, who were as undeserving, as ill-deserving, as they are?" He might have said, "I have delivered them formerly, but they have again brought trouble upon themselves (Prov. xix. 19); therefore *I will deliver them no more*," Judges x. 13. But mercy turns the argument the other way: "I have formerly delivered them and therefore will now."

2. Which way soever we take it, whether the people plead it with God or God with himself, these verses call to mind what God did by Moses for his people, especially in bringing them through the Red Sea. God *led them by the right hand of Moses* (*v.* 12) and the wonder-working rod was in his hand. It was not Moses that led, any more than it was Moses that fed them (John vi. 32), but God by Moses. God was the owner of the flock, but Moses was a shepherd under him, inured to labour and patience, and so fitted for this pastoral care, by his being trained up to *keep the flock of his father Jethro*. Herein he was a type of Christ the good shepherd, that *lays down his life for his sheep*. *He put his holy Spirit within him; the Spirit of God was among them*, and not only his providence, but his grace, did work for them. He carried them safely through the Red Sea. *He divided the water before them* (*v.* 12), so that it gave them not only passage, but protection, a wall on either side. *He led them through the deep as a horse in the wilderness*, or *in the plain* (*v.* 13). If God make us a way, he will make it plain and level. He brought them safely to a place of rest: *As a beast goes down into the valley*, carefully and gradually, so *the Spirit of the Lord caused him to rest*. Many a time in their march through the wilderness they had resting-places provided for them, *v.* 14. And at length they were made to rest finally in Canaan, and the Spirit of the Lord gave them that rest according to the promise. God did it with his glorious arm, *the arm of his gallantry*, or *bravery*; so the word signifies.

Verses 15–19

This prayer, continued to the end of the next chapter, is an affectionate, importunate, pleading prayer. It is calculated for the time of the captivity. As they had promises, so they had prayers, prepared

JAMIESON, FAUSSET, BROWN

angel of his presence—lit., "of His face," i.e., who stands before Him continually; Messiah (Exod. 14:19; 23: 20, 21; Prov. 8:30), language applicable to no *creature* (Exod. 32:34; 33:2, 14; Num. 20:16; Mal. 3:1). **bare them**—(ch. 46:3, 4; 40:11; Exod. 19:4; Deut. 32:11, 12).

10. vexed—grieved (Ps. 78:40; 95:10; Acts 7:51; Eph. 4:30; Heb. 3:10, 17).

he fought—rather, "He it was that fought," viz., the angel of His presence [HORSLEY], (Lam. 2:5).

11. remembered—Notwithstanding *their* perversitiy, He forgot not *His* covenant of old; therefore He did not wholly forsake them (Lev. 26:40-42, 44, 45; Ps. 106: 45, 46); the Jews make this their plea with God, that He should not now forsake them. **saying**—God is represented, in human language, mentally speaking of Himself and His former acts of love to Israel, as His ground for pitying them notwithstanding their rebellion. **sea**—Red Sea. **shepherd**—Moses; or if the *Hebrew* be read *plural*, "shepherds," Moses, Aaron, and the other leaders (so Ps. 77:20). **put . . . Spirit . . . within him**—*Hebrew*, "in the inward parts of him," i.e., Moses; or it refers to the flock, "in the midst of his people" (Num. 11:17, 25; Neh. 9:20; Hag. 2:5).

12. The *right hand* of Moses was but the instrument; the *arm* of God was the real mover (Exod. 15:6; 14:21).

dividing the water—(Neh. 9: 11; Ps. 78:13). **13. deep**—lit., "the tossing and roaring sea." **wilderness**—rather, the open plain [HORSLEY], wherein there is no obstacle to cause a horse in its course the danger of stumbling. **14. As a beast . . . rest**—image from a herd led "down" from the hills to a fertile and well-watered "valley" (Ps. 23:2); so God's Spirit "caused Israel to rest" in the promised land after their weary wanderings. **to make . . . name**—(So. vs. 12; II Sam. 7:23).

ADAM CLARKE

An *angel of his presence* means an angel of superior order, in immediate attendance upon God. So the angel of the Lord says to Zacharias, "I am Gabriel, that stand in the presence of God," Luke i. 19.

11. *Moses, and his people*—"Moses his servant." *Where is he that brought them up out of the sea with the shepherd of his flock? where,* etc.?—"How he brought them up from the sea, with the shepherd of His flock; how," etc. *The shepherd of his flock.* That is, Moses.

13-14. *That led them through the deep . . . As a beast goeth down into the valley.* In both these verses there is an allusion to the Israelites going through the Red Sea, in the bottom of which they found no more inconvenience than a horse would in running in the desert, where there was neither stone nor mud; nor a beast in the valley, where all was plain and smooth. *The Spirit of the Lord caused him to rest*—"The Spirit of Jehovah conducted them."

MATTHEW HENRY

for them against that time of need. Some good interpreters think this prayer looks further, and that it expresses the complaints of the Jews under their last rejection from God and destruction by the Romans.

I. The petitions they put up to God. *Look down from heaven, and behold, v.* 15. *Look down from the habitation of thy holiness and of thy glory.* God's holiness is his glory. Heaven is his habitation, the throne of his glory (*v.* 17): "*Return;* change thy way towards us, return in mercy, and let us have thy gracious presence with us." God's people dread nothing more than his departures from them and desire nothing more than his returns to them.

II. The complaints they made to God. 1. That they were given up to themselves, and God's grace did not recover them, *v.* 17. It is a strange expostulation, *Why hast thou made us to err from thy ways; thou hast hardened our heart from thy fear.* Some make it to be the language of those that were impious and profane; when the prophets reproved them for the *error of their ways,* they with a daring impudence charged their sin upon God, made him the author of it. But I rather take it to be the language of those that lamented the unbelief and impenitence of their people, not accusing God of being the author of their wickedness, but complaining of it to him. They owned that they had *erred from God's ways,* that their *hearts* had been *hardened from his fear,* and this was the cause of all their errors from his ways; or *from his fear* may mean from the true worship of God. Now this they complain of, as their great misery and burden, that God had for their sins permitted them to *err from his ways* and had justly withheld his grace, so that their *hearts were hardened from his fear.* When they ask, *Why hast thou done this?* it is not as charging him with wrong, but lamenting it as a sore judgment. God had *caused them to err and hardened their hearts* (*v.* 10) by a judicial sentence. Their troubles had alienated many of them from God, and prejudiced them against his service; their afflictions were their temptations, and to many of them invincible ones. 2. That they were given up to their enemies (*v.* 18): *Our adversaries have trodden down thy sanctuary.* They complained not so much of the adversaries treading down their houses and cities as of their treading down God's sanctuary, because thereby God was immediately affronted, and they were robbed of the comforts they valued most.

III. The pleas for mercy and deliverance. 1. They pleaded the tender compassion God used to show to his people, *v.* 15. The most prevailing arguments in prayer are those that are taken *from God himself.* It cannot be that divine zeal, which is infinitely wise and just, should be cooled, that divine strength, which is infinite, should be weakened. Has God, who so often remembered to be gracious, now forgotten to be so? *Has he in anger shut up his tender mercies?* It can never be. 2. They pleaded God's relation to them as their Father (*v.* 16): Thy tender mercies are not restrained, for they are the tender mercies of a father. *However it be, yet God is good;* for he is our Father. When the father is dead *his sons come to honour and he knows it not,* Job xiv. 21. "But *thou, O Lord! art our Father still* (the fathers of our flesh may call themselves *ever-loving*; but they are not *ever-living*; it is God only that is the immortal Father, that always knows us, and is never at a distance from us), and therefore *our Redeemer from everlasting is thy name,* the name by which we will know and own thee. We are so degenerate and corrupt that Abraham and Israel would not own us for their children, yet we fly to thee as our Father. Abraham cast out his son Ishmael; Jacob disinherited his son Reuben and cursed Simeon and Levi; but our heavenly Father, in pardoning sin, is *God, and not man,*" Hos. xi. 9. 3. They pleaded that he was their Lord: "We are thy servants; what service we can do thou art entitled to, and therefore we ought not to serve strange kings and strange gods: *Return for thy servants' sake.*" We are the *tribes of thy inheritance,* not only thy servants, but thy tenants. Wilt thou suffer thy own servants and tenants to be thus abused? 4. They pleaded that they had had but a short enjoyment of the land of promise and the privileges of the sanctuary (*v.* 18): *The people of thy holiness have possessed it but a little while.* From Abraham to David were but fourteen generations, and from David to the captivity but fourteen more (Matt. i. 17), and that was but a little while in comparison with the promise of the *land of Canaan for an everlasting possession* (Gen. xvii. 8). 5. They pleaded that those who had their land were such as were strangers to God. "*Thou never didst bear rule over them,* nor did they ever yield thee any obedience. Will God suffer those that do not stand in any relation to him to trample upon those that do?"

JAMIESON, FAUSSET, BROWN

15. Here begins a fervent appeal to God to pity Israel now on the ground of His former benefits. **habitation of . . . holiness**–(ch. 57:15; Deut. 26:15; II Chron. 30:27; Ps. 33:14; 80:14). **zeal . . . strength**–evinced formerly for **Thy people. sounding of . . . bowels**–*Thine emotions of compassion* (ch. 16:11; Jer. 31:20; 48:36; Hos. 11:8).

17. made us to err–i.e., "suffer" us to err and to be hardened in our heart. They do not mean to deny their own blameworthiness, but confess that through their own fault God gave them over to a reprobate mind (ch. 6:9, 10; Ps. 119:10; Rom. 1:28). **Return**–(Num. 10:36; Ps. 90:13.)

ADAM CLARKE

15. *And thy strength*—"And Thy mighty power."

17. *Why hast thou made us to err?* A mere Hebraism for Why hast Thou permitted us to err?

KEIL-DELITZSCH:

The prayer for help, and the lamentation over its absence, are now justified in verse 16: "For Thou art our Father; for Abraham is ignorant of us, and Israel knoweth us not. Thou, O Jehovah, art our Father; our Redeemer is from olden time Thy name." Jehovah is Israel's Father (Deut. 32:6). His creative might, and the gracious counsels of His love, have called it into being: this has not yet the deep and unrestricted sense of the New Testament "Our Father." The second *kī* introduces the reason for this confession that Jehovah was Israel's Father, and could therefore look for paternal care and help from Him alone. Even the dearest and most honorable men, the forefathers of the nation, could not help it. Abraham and Jacob-Israel had been taken away from this world, and were unable to interfere on their own account in the history of their people. From the very earliest time the acts of Jehovah towards Israel had been such that Israel could call Him Redeemer.

But in the existing state of things there was a contrast which put their faith to a severe test. Verse 17. "O Jehovah, why leadest Thou us astray from Thy ways, hardenest our heart, so as not to fear Thee? Return for Thy servants' sake, the tribes of Thine inheritance." When men have scornfully and obstinately rejected the grace of God, God withdraws it from them judicially, gives them up to their wanderings, and makes their heart incapable of faith. The history of Israel from chapter 6 onwards has been the history of such a gradual judgment of hardening, and such a curse, eating deeper and deeper, and spreading its influence wider and wider round. The great mass are lost, but not without the possibility of deliverance for the better part of the nation, which now appeals to the mercy of God, and sighs deliverance from this ban. Two reasons are assigned for this petition for the return of the gracious presence of God: first, that there are still "servants of Jehovah" to be found, as this prayer itself actually proves; and secondly, that the divine election of grace cannot perish.—*Commentary on the Old Testament*

JAMIESON, FAUSSET, BROWN

16. thou . . . father–of Israel, by right not merely of creation, but also of electing adoption (ch. 64:8; Deut. 32:6; I Chron. 29:10). **though Abraham . . . Israel**–It had been the besetting temptation of the Jews to rest on the mere privilege of their descent from faithful Abraham and Jacob (Matt. 3:9; John 8:39; 4:12); now at last they renounce this, to trust in God alone as their Father, notwithstanding all appearances to the contrary. Even though Abraham, our earthly father, on whom we have prided ourselves, disown us, *Thou* wilt not (ch. 49:15; Ps. 27:10). Isaac is not mentioned, because not *all* his posterity was admitted to the covenant, whereas all Jacob's was; Abraham is specified because he was the first father of the Jewish race. **everlasting**–an argument why He should help them, viz., because of His *everlasting immutability.*

18. people of . . . holiness–Israel dedicated as holy unto God (ch. 62:12; Deut. 7:6). **possessed**–viz., the Holy Land, or Thy "sanctuary," taken from the following clause, which is parallel to this (cf. ch. 64:10, 11; Ps. 74:6-8). **thy**–an argument why God should help them; their cause is *His* cause. **19. thine . . . never**–rather, "We are Thine *from of old;* Thou barest not rule over them" [BARNES]. LOWTH translates, "We for long have been as those over whom Thou hast not ruled, who are not called by Thy name"; "for long" thus stands in contrast to "but a little while" (vs. 18). But the analogy of vs. 18 makes it likely that the first clause in this verse refers to the Jews, and the second to their foes, as *English Version* and BARNES translate it. The Jews' foes are aliens who have unjustly intruded into the Lord's heritage.

ADAM CLARKE

16. *Our redeemer; thy name is from everlasting*—"Oh, deliver us for the sake of Thy name."

18. *The people of thy holiness have possessed it but a little while*—"It is little that they have taken possession of Thy holy mountain."

MATTHEW HENRY

CHAPTER 64

Verses 1–5

Here, I. The petition is that God would appear wonderfully for them now, *v.* 1, 2. When God works some extraordinary deliverance for his people he is said to *shine forth*, to show himself strong; so, here, they pray that he would *rend the heavens and come down*. This is applicable to the second coming of Christ, when *the Lord himself shall descend from heaven with a shout*. They desire that *the mountains might flow down at thy presence*, that the fire of thy wrath may even dissolve the rockiest mountains and melt them as metal in the furnace, which is made liquid; so *the melting fire burns*, *v.* 2. Let things be put into a ferment, in order to a glorious revolution in favour of the church: *As the fire causes the waters to boil*. They desire that this may tend to the glory of God, *may make his name known*, not only to his friends, but to his adversaries, that they may know it and *tremble at his presence*. God's name, if it be not a stronghold for us, into which we may run and be safe, will be a stronghold against us, out of the reach of which we cannot run and be safe.

II. The plea is that God had appeared wonderfully for his people formerly.

1. They plead what he had done for his people Israel when he brought them out of Egypt, *v.* 3. He then *did terrible things* in the plagues of Egypt, *which they looked not for*. Then he came down upon Mount Sinai in such terror as made that and the adjacent mountains to *flow down at his presence*, to *skip like rams* (Ps. cxiv. 4). Some refer this to the defeat of Sennacherib's powerful army, which was as surprising an instance of the divine power as the melting down of rocks and mountains would be.

2. They plead the provision he has made for the safety and happiness of his people.

(1) It is very rich, *v.* 4. Men have not heard nor seen what God has *prepared for those that wait for him*. It is all that goodness which God has *laid up for those that fear him, and wrought for those that trust in him*, Ps. xxxi. 19. Much of it was concealed in former ages; they knew it not, because the *unsearchable riches of Christ* were *hidden in God*, were *hidden from the wise and prudent*; but in latter ages they were revealed by the gospel; so the apostle applies this (1 Cor. ii. 9), for it follows (*v.* 10), *But God has revealed them unto us by his Spirit*. That which men had not heard *since the beginning of the world* they should hear before the end of it. It cannot be fully comprehended by the human understanding; it is spiritual, and will far outdo our expectations. Even the present peace of believers, much more their future bliss, surpasses all expression, Phil. iv. 7. We must infer from God's works of wondrous grace, as well as from his works of wondrous power, from the kind things, as well as from the great things, he does, that there is *no god like him*.

(2) It is very ready (*v.* 5): "*Thou meetest him that rejoices and works righteousness*, meetest him with that good which thou hast prepared for him (*v.* 4), and dost not forget *those that remember thee in thy ways*." What communion there is between a gracious God and a gracious soul! We must be cheerful in doing our duty, we must *rejoice and work righteousness*, must delight ourselves in God and sing at our work. This intimates the friendship, fellowship, and familiarity to which God admits his people. He will *anticipate them with the blessings of his goodness*, will *rejoice to do good* to those that *rejoice in working righteousness*, and wait to be gracious to those that *wait for him*. He meets his penitent people with a pardon, as the father of the prodigal met his returning son, Luke xv. 20. He meets his praying people with an answer of peace, while they are yet speaking, *ch.* lxv. 24.

3. They plead the unchangeableness of God's favour and the stability of his promise: "*Behold, thou hast* many a time *been wroth with us because we have sinned*, and we have been under the tokens of thy wrath; *but in those*, those ways of thine, the ways of mercy in which we have *remembered thee*, *in those is continuance*," or *in those thou art ever*. And by this continuance of the covenant we hope to be saved, for its being an everlasting covenant is all our salvation.

Verses 6–12

The Lamentations of Isaiah—the destruction of Jerusalem by the Chaldeans and the sin of Israel that brought that destruction.

I. The people of God in their affliction confess and bewail their sins. Now that they were under divine rebukes for sin they had nothing to trust to but the mere mercy of God.

1. There was a general corruption of manners among them (*v.* 6): *We are all as an unclean thing*,

JAMIESON, FAUSSET, BROWN

CHAPTER 64

Vss. 1-12. Transition from Complaint to Prayer. **1. rend . . . heavens**—bursting forth to execute vengeance, suddenly descending on Thy people's foe (Ps. 18:9; 144:5; Hab. 3:5, 6). **flow down**—(Judg. 5:5; Mic. 1:4).

2. Oh, that Thy wrath would consume Thy foes *as the fire*. Rather, "as the fire burneth *the dry brushwood*" [Gesenius].

3. When—Supply from vs. 2, "As when." **terrible things**—(Ps. 65:5). **we looked not for**—far exceeding the expectation of any of our nation; unparalleled before (Exod. 34:10; Ps. 68:8). **camest down**—on Mount Sinai. **mountains flowed**—Repeated from vs. 1; they pray God to do the *very same things* for Israel now as in former ages. Gesenius, instead of "flowed" here, and "flow" in vs. 1, translates from a different Hebrew root, "quake . . . quaked"; but "fire" *melts* and *causes to flow*, rather than to *quake* (vs. 2). **4. perceived by the ear**—Paul (I Cor. 2:9) has for this, "nor have entered into the heart of man"; the virtual sense, sanctioned by his inspired authority; men might hear with the outward ear, but they could only by the Spirit "perceive" with the "heart" the spiritual significancy of God's acts, both those in relation to Israel, primarily referred to here, and those relating to the Gospel secondarily, which Paul refers to. **O God . . . what he . . . prepared**—rather, "nor hath eye seen *a god* beside thee *who doeth such things*." They refer to God's *past* marvellous acts in behalf of Israel as a plea for His now interposing for His people; but the Spirit, as Paul by inspiration shows, contemplated *further* God's revelation in the Gospel, which abounds in marvellous paradoxes never before heard of by carnal ear, not to be understood by mere human sagacity, and when foretold by the prophets not fully perceived or credited; and even after the manifestation of Christ not to be understood save through the inward teaching of the Holy Ghost. These are partly past and present, and partly future; therefore Paul substitutes "prepared" for "doeth," though his context shows he includes all three. For "waiteth" he has "love Him"; godly *waiting* on Him must flow from love, and not mere fear. **5. meetest**—i.e., Thou makest peace, or enterest into covenant with him (*Note*, ch. 47:3). **rejoiceth and worketh**—i.e., who *with joyful willingness* worketh [Gesenius] (Acts 10:35; John 7:17). **those**—Thou meetest "those," in apposition to "him" who represents a class whose characteristics "those that," etc., more fully describes. **remember thee in thy ways**—(ch. 26:8). **sinned**—lit., "tripped," carrying on the figure in "ways." **in those is continuance**—a plea to deprecate the *continuance* of God's *wrath;* it is not in Thy wrath that there is continuance (ch. 54:7, 8; Ps. 30:5; 103:9), but *in* Thy ways ("those"), viz., of covenant-mercy to Thy people (Mic. 7:18-20; Mal. 3:6); on the strength of the everlasting continuance of His covenant they infer by faith, "we shall be saved." God "remembered" for them His covenant (Ps. 106:45), though *they* often "remembered not" Him (Ps. 78:42). Castellio translates, "we have sinned for long in them ('thy ways'), and could we then be saved?' But they hardly would use such a plea when their very object was to be saved.

ADAM CLARKE

CHAPTER 64

1. *Oh, that thou wouldest rend the heavens*—This seems to allude to the wonderful manifestation of God upon Mount Sinai.

2. *As when the melting fire burneth*—"As the fire kindleth the dry fuel."

4. *For since the beginning of the world men have not heard.* I would read the whole verse thus: "Yea, from the time of old they have not heard, they have not hearkened to, an eye hath not seen a God besides Thee. He shall work for that one that waiteth for Him." This I really think on the whole to be the best translation of the original.

5. *Thou meetest him that rejoiceth and worketh righteousness*—"Thou meetest with joy those who work righteousness."

In those is continuance, and we shall be saved. "Thou art wroth, for we have sinned in them [Thy ways] of old; and can we be saved?"

MATTHEW HENRY

or as an unclean *person*, as one overspread with a leprosy, who was to be shut out of the camp. *Even all our righteousnesses are as filthy rags.* "The best of our persons are so; we are all corrupt and polluted. The best of our performances are so. There is not only a general corruption of manners, but a general defection in the exercises of devotion."

2. There was a general coldness of devotion among them, *v.* 7. Prayer was in a manner neglected: "*There is none that calls on thy name*, none that seeks to thee for grace to reform us, or for mercy to relieve us and take away the judgments which our sins have brought upon us." If there was here and there one that called on God's name, it was with a great deal of indifferency: *There is none that stirs up himself to take hold of God.* To pray is to *take hold of God*, by faith to take hold of the promises God has made of his goodwill to us—to take hold of him as he that wrestles takes hold of him he wrestles with. But when we *take hold of God* it is as the boatman with his hook takes hold on the shore, as if he would pull the shore to him, but really it is to pull himself to the shore; so we pray, not to bring God to our mind, but to bring ourselves to his. Those that would take hold of God in prayer must stir up themselves to do it; all that is within us must be employed in the duty (and all little enough), our thoughts fixed and our affections flaming.

II. They acknowledge their afflictions to be the fruit and product of their own sins and God's wrath. "*We are all as an unclean thing, and* therefore *we do all fade away as a leaf* (*v.* 6), we not only wither and lose our beauty, but we fall and drop off" (so the word signifies) "as leaves in autumn; our profession of religion withers, and we grow dry and sapless; and then *our iniquities like the wind have taken us away* and hurried us into captivity, as the winds in autumn blow off, and then blow away, the faded withered leaves," Ps. i. 3, 4.

III. They claim relation to God as their God, and humbly plead it with him (*v.* 8): "*But now, O Lord! thou art our Father.* Foolish and careless as we are, poor and despised by our enemies, yet still *thou art our Father*; to thee therefore we return in our repentance." God is their Father, he gave them their being, formed them into a people, shaped them as he pleased: "*We are the clay and thou our potter*, therefore we will hope that you who madest us wilt new-make us, new-form us, though we have unmade and deformed ourselves: *We are all as an unclean thing*, but *we are all the work of thy hands*, therefore *forsake us not*," Ps. cxxxviii. 8. *We are thy people;* and *should not a people seek unto their God? ch.* viii. 19. *We are thine;* save us, Ps. cxix. 94.

IV. They are importunate with God for the turning away of his anger and the pardoning of their sins (*v.* 9). They pray that God would be reconciled to them, and then they can be easy whether the affliction be continued or removed: "*Be not wroth to extremity*, but let thy anger be mitigated by the clemency and compassion of a father."

V. The lamentable condition they were in. 1. Their own houses were in ruins, *v.* 10.. The cities of Judah were destroyed by the Chaldeans and the inhabitants of them were carried away. *Thy holy cities are a wilderness.* The cities of Judah are called *holy cities*, for the people were unto God a kingdom of priests, therefore they lamented the ruins of them. Even "*Zion is a wilderness;* the city of David itself lies in ruins; *Jerusalem*, that was *beautiful*, has become the scorn and scandal of the whole earth; that noble city is a heap of rubbish." 2. God's house was in ruins, *v.* 11. This they lament most of all, that *the temple was burnt with fire.* It was *their holy and beautiful house*; the holiness of it was in their eye the greatest beauty of it, and consequently the profanation of it was the saddest part of its desolation. It was the place *where their fathers praised God* with their sacrifices and songs; what a pity is it that that should lie in ashes which had been for so many ages the glory of their nation! *All their pleasant things were laid waste*, all those things which were employed by them in the service of God; not only the furniture of the temple, the altars and table, but the sabbaths, and all their religious feasts, which they used to keep with gladness.

VI. They conclude by humbly arguing with God concerning their present desolations (*v.* 12): *Wilt thou refrain thyself for these things?* When we are abused we hold our peace, because vengeance does not belong to us. When God is injured in his honour it may justly be expected that he should speak in the vindication of it; his people prescribe not what he shall say, but their prayer is (as here) Ps. lxxxiii. 1, "*Keep not thou silence, O God!* Speak for the confusion of thy enemies, speak for the comfort and relief of thy people; for *wilt thou afflict us for ever?*"

JAMIESON, FAUSSET, BROWN

6. unclean thing—legally unclean, as a leper. True of Israel, everywhere now cut off by unbelief and by God's judgments from the congregation of the saints. **righteousness**—plural, "uncleanness" extended to *every particular act* of theirs, even to their prayers and praises. True of the best doings of the unregenerate (Phil. 3:6-8; Titus 1:15; Heb. 11:6). **filthy rags**—lit., a "menstruous rag" (Lev. 15:33; 20:18; Lam. —7). **fade . . . leaf**—(Ps. 90:5, 6).

7. stirreth—*rouseth* himself from spiritual drowsiness. **take hold**—(ch. 27:5).

8. father—(ch. 63:16). **clay . . . potter**—(ch. 29:16; 45:9). Unable to mould themselves aright, they beg the sovereign will of God to mould them unto salvation, even as He *made* them at the first, and is their "Father."

9. (Ps. 74:1, 2). **we are . . . thy people**—(Jer. 14:9, 21).

10. holy cities—No city but Jerusalem is called "the holy city" (ch. 48:2; 52:1); the *plural*, therefore, refers to *the upper and the lower parts* of the same city Jerusalem [VITRINGA]; or all Judea was holy to God, so its *cities* were deemed "holy" [MAURER]. But the parallelism favors VITRINGA. *Zion* and *Jerusalem* (the one city) answering to "holy cities." **11. house**—the temple. **beautiful**—includes the idea of *glorious* (Mark 13:1; Acts 3:2).

burned—(Ps. 74:7; Lam. 2:7; II Chron. 36:19). Its destruction under Nebuchadnezzar prefigured that under Titus. **pleasant things**—*Hebrew*, "objects of desire"; our homes, our city, and all its dear associations.

12. for these things—Wilt Thou, *notwithstanding* these calamities of Thy people, still refuse Thy aid (ch. 42:14)?

ADAM CLARKE

7. *And hast consumed us, because of our iniquities*—"And hast delivered us up into the hands of our iniquities."

CHARLES H. SPURGEON:

Verse 7. Notice carefully that according to our text the prophet traces much of the evil which he deplored to the lack of prayer. After he has compared their righteousnesses to filthy rags he adds, "there is none that calleth upon thy name, that stirreth up himself to take hold of thee." When there is a degeneracy of public manners, you may be sure that there has also occurred a serious decline of secret devotion. When the outward service of the Church begins to flag and her holiness declines, you may be sure that her communion with God has been sadly suspended. Devotion to God will be found to be the basis of holiness and the buttress of integrity. If you backslide in secret before God, you will soon err in public before men. You may judge yourselves as to your spiritual state by the condition of your hearts in the matter of prayer. How are you at the mercy seat? for that is what you really are. Are the consolations of God small with you? That is a minor matter: look deeper—Is there not a restraining of prayer before the living God? Do you find yourself weak in the presence of temptation? That is important; but search below the surface, and you will find that you have grown lax in supplication, and have failed to keep up continual communion with God.

The prophet also reveals the very essence and soul of prayer. It is a stirring up of oneself to take hold of God. If in prayer we do not take hold of God, we have prayed but feebly, if at all. The very soul of devotion lies in realizing the divine presence, in dealing with God as a real person, in firm confidence in His faithfulness—in a word, in "taking hold of Him." Men do not take hold of a shadow, they cannot grasp the unsubstantial fabric of a dream. Taking hold implies something real which we grasp; and there is wanted to make prayer truthful and acceptable with God the grip and grasp of a tenacious faith, which believes the fact that God is, and that He is the rewarder of them that diligently seek Him. Taking hold implies a reverent familiarity with the Lord, by which we use a holy force to win a blessing from His hand. It was because there was so little of this in Israel, that the nation had fallen into so forlorn a state; and if you trace up the evils of the church at the present day to their source it will come to this, that there are so few who stir up themselves to take hold upon the living God, so few who grapple with spiritual matters in downright earnest, and bring them before the Lord with resolute faith. We have few Elijahs now, and Jacobs are hard to find.

—*The Treasury of the Old Testament*

MATTHEW HENRY

God has said that he *will not contend for ever*, and therefore his people may depend upon it that their afflictions shall be neither to extremity nor to eternity, but *light* and *for a moment*.

CHAPTER 65

Verses 1–7

The apostle Paul has told us what was the event pointed at, namely, the calling in of the Gentiles and the rejection of the Jews, by the preaching of the gospel, Rom. x. 20, 21. And he observes that herein *Esaias is very bold* in foretelling it to the Jews, who would take it as a gross affront to their nation.

I. It is here foretold that the Gentiles, who had been afar off, should be made nigh, *v.* 1. Paul reads it thus: *I was found of those that sought me not; I was made manifest to those that asked not for me.* 1. Those who had long been without God in the world shall now be set seeking him; those who had not said, *Where is God my maker?* shall now begin to enquire after him. With what pleasure does the great God here speak of his being sought. For there is great joy in heaven over sinners who repent. 2. God shall anticipate their prayers with his blessings: *I am found of those that sought me not.* This happy acquaintance and correspondence between God and the Gentile world began on his side. Though in after-communion God is found of those that seek him (Prov. viii. 17), yet in the first conversion he is found of those that seek him not; for *therefore we love him because he first loved us.* 3. God gave the advantages of a divine revelation to those who had never made a profession of religion: *I said, Behold me, behold me* to those who *were not called by my name*, as the Jews for many ages had been. Christ said, *Behold me, behold me* with an eye of faith: *look unto me, and be you saved.*

II. It is here foretold that the Jews, who had long been a people near to God, should be cast off and set at a distance, *v.* 2. The apostle applies this to the Jews in his time, Rom. x. 21: *But to Israel he saith, All day long I have stretched forth my hands unto a disobedient and gainsaying people.*

1. How the Jews were courted by the divine grace. God himself, by his prophets, by his Son, by his apostles, *stretched forth his hands to them.* God *spread out his hands to them*, as one reasoning and expostulating with them. When Christ was crucified his hands were *spread out and stretched forth*, as if he were preparing to receive returning sinners. He waited to be gracious, and was not weary of waiting; even those that came in at the eleventh hour of the day were not rejected.

2. They contemned the invitation; they were invited to the wedding-supper, and would not come, but *rejected the counsel of God against themselves.* The world shall see that it was not for nothing that they were rejected of God. They were very wilful. Right or wrong they would do as they had a mind. God had told them his thoughts, what his mind and will were, but they would walk *after their own thoughts*, would do what they thought best. This was God's complaint of them all along—they grieved him, they *vexed his Holy Spirit*, as if they would contrive how to make him their enemy. The prophet speaks more particularly of *their iniquities and the iniquities of their fathers*, as the ground of God's casting them off, *v.* 7. The most provoking iniquity of their fathers was idolatry. This was the sin that brought them into captivity, and, though the captivity pretty well cured them of it, yet, when the final ruin of that nation came, that was again brought into the account against them. Perhaps there were many, long after the captivity, who, though they did not worship other gods, married strange wives. They forsook God's temple, and *sacrificed in gardens or groves*, doing it in their own way, for they liked not God's institutions. They forsook God's altar, and *burnt incense upon bricks*, altars of their own contriving in comparison with the golden altar which God appointed them. "They used necromancy, or consulting with the dead, and, in order to that, they *remained among the graves*, and *lodged in the monuments*." They violated the laws of God about their meat, and broke through the distinction between clean and unclean before it was taken away by the gospel. They *ate swine's flesh. And the broth*, or *pieces*, of other forbidden meats, called here *abominable things*, was *in their vessels*, and was made use of for food. The forbidden meat is called *an abomination*, and those that meddle with it are said to *make themselves abominable*, Lev. xi. 42, 43. Perhaps this is here put figuratively for all forbidden pleasures. But those who thus take a pride in venturing upon the borders of sin are in danger of falling into the depths of it. The iniquity of

JAMIESON, FAUSSET, BROWN

CHAPTER 65

Vss. 1-25. God's Reply in Justification of His Dealings with Israel. In ch. 64:9, their plea was, "we are all Thy people." In answer, God declares that *others* (Gentiles) would be taken into covenant with Him, while His ancient people would be rejected. The Jews were slow to believe this; hence Paul says (Rom. 10:20) that Isaiah was "very bold" in advancing so unpopular a sentiment; he implies what Paul states (Rom. 2:28; 9:6, 7; 11:1-31), that "they are not *all* (in opposition to the Jews' plea, ch. 64:9) Israel which are of Israel." God's reason for so severely dealing with Israel is not changeableness in Him, but sin in them (vss. 2-7). Yet the whole nation shall not be destroyed, but only the wicked; a remnant shall be saved (vss. 8-10, 11-16). There shall be, finally, universal blessedness to Israel, such as they had prayed for (vss. 17-25). **1. I am sought**–*Hebrew*, "I have *granted access* unto Me to them," etc. (so Ezek. 14:3, "Should I be *inquired of*"; Eph. 2:18). **found**–Romans 10:20 renders this, "I was made manifest." As an instance of the sentiment in the clause, "I am sought . . ." see John 12:21; of the sentiment in this clause, Acts 9:5. Cf. as to the Gentile converts, Ephesians 2:12, 13. **Behold me**–(ch. 45:22). **nation . . . not called by my name**–i.e., the Gentiles. God retorts in their own words (ch. 63:19) that their plea as being exclusively "called by His name" will not avail, for God's gospel invitation is not so exclusive (Rom. 9:25; 1:16). **2. spread out . . . hands**–inviting them earnestly (Prov. 1:24). **all . . . day**–continually, late and early (Jer. 7:13). **rebellious people**–Israel, whose rebellion was the occasion of God's turning to the Gentiles (Rom. 11:11, 12, 15). **way . . . not good**–i.e., the very reverse of good, very bad (Ezek. 36:31). **3. continually**–answering to "all the day" (vs. 2). God was continually inviting them, and they *continually* offending Him (Deut. 32:21). **to my face**–They made no attempt to hide their sin (ch. 3:9). Cf. "*before* Me" (Exod. 20:3). **in gardens**–(*Note*, ch. 1:29; 66:17; Lev. 17: 5). **altars of brick**–*Hebrew*, "bricks." God had commanded His altars to be of *unhewn stone* (Exod. 20:25). This was in order to separate them, even in *external respects*, from idolaters; also, as all chiselling was forbidden, they could not inscribe superstitious symbols on them as the heathen did. Bricks were more easily so inscribed than stone; hence their use for the cuneiform inscriptions at Babylon, and also for idolatrous altars. Some, not so well, have supposed that the "bricks" here mean the flat brick-paved *roofs* of houses on which they sacrificed to the sun, etc. (II Kings 23:12; Jer. 19: 13). **4. remain among . . . graves**–viz., for purposes of necromancy, as if to hold converse with the dead (ch. 8:19, 20; cf. Mark 5:3); or, for the sake of purifications, usually performed at night among sepulchers, to appease the manes [Maurer]. **monuments**–*Hebrew*, "pass the night in *hidden recesses*," either the idol's *inmost shrines* ("consecrated precincts") [Horsley], where they used to sleep, in order to have divine communications in dreams [Jerome]; or better, on account of the parallel "graves," *sepulchral caves* [Maurer]. **eat swine's flesh**–To eat it at all was contrary to God's law (Lev. 11:7), but it much increased their guilt that they ate it in idolatrous sacrifices (cf. ch. 66: 17). Varro (*Re Rust.*, 2.4) says that swine were first used in sacrifices; the Latins sacrificed a pig to Ceres; it was also offered on occasion of treaties and marriages. **broth**–so called from the "pieces" (*Margin*) or fragments of bread over which the broth was poured [Gesenius]; such broth, made of swine's flesh, offered in sacrifice, was thought to be especially acceptable to the idol and was used in magic rites. Or, "fragments (pieces) of abominable foods," etc. This fourth clause explains more fully the third, as the second does the first [Maurer]. **is in**–rather, lit., "is their vessels," i.e., constitute their vessels' contents. The Jews, in our Lord's days, and ever since the return from Babylon, have been free from idolatry; still the imagery from idolatrous abominations, as being the sin most loathsome in God's eyes and that most prevalent in Isaiah's time, is employed to describe the foul sin of Israel in all ages, culminating in their killing Messiah, and still rejecting Him.

ADAM CLARKE

CHAPTER 65

This chapter contains a defense of God's proceedings in regard to the Jews, with reference to their complaint in the chapter preceding. God is introduced, declaring that He had called the Gentiles, though they had not sought Him; and had rejected His own people for their refusal to attend to His repeated call; for their obstinate disobedience, their idolatrous practices, and detestable hypocrisy. That nevertheless He would not destroy them all, but would preserve a remnant, to whom He would make good His ancient promises. Severe punishments are threatened to the apostates, and great rewards are promised to the obedient in a future flourishing state of the Church.

1. *I am sought of them that asked not for me*—"I am made known to those that asked not for Me."

3. *That sacrificeth in gardens, and burneth incense upon altars of brick*—"Sacrificing in the gardens, and burning incense on the tiles." These are instances of heathenish superstition, and idolatrous practices, to which the Jews were immoderately addicted before the Babylonish captivity. The heathen worshipped their idols in groves; whereas God, in opposition to this species of idolatry, commanded His people, when they should come into the Promised Land, to destroy all the places wherein the Canaanites had served their gods, and in particular to burn their groves with fire, Deut. xii. 2-3. These apostate Jews sacrificed upon altars built of bricks, in opposition to the command of God in regard to His altar, which was to be of unhewn stone, Exod. xx. 25.

4. *In the monuments*—"In the caverns."

Which eat swine's flesh. This was expressly forbidden by the law, Lev. xi. 7, but among the heathen was in principal request in their sacrifices and feasts. Antiochus Epiphanes compelled the Jews to eat swine's flesh, as a full proof of their renouncing their religion, 2 Mac. vi. 18 and vii. 1.

MATTHEW HENRY

the Jews in our Saviour's time was their pride and hypocrisy, that sin of the scribes and Pharisees against which Christ denounced so many woes, *v.* 5. They say, "*Stand by thyself*, keep to thy own companions, but *come not near to me*, lest thou pollute me; *touch me not, for I am holier than thou.*" *These are a smoke in my nose*, such a smoke as comes not from a quick fire, which soon becomes glowing and pleasant, but from a fire of wet wood, which *burns all the day*, and is nothing but smoke. The proof against them is plain: *Behold, it is written before me*, *v.* 6. The *iniquity of their fathers* shall come against them; not but that their own sin deserved whatever judgments God brought upon them, and much heavier; and this they owned, Ezra ix. 13. *Your iniquities and the iniquities of your fathers* together, the one aggravating the other, shall be *measured into their bosom.*

Verses 8–10

This is expounded by St. *Paul*, Rom. xi. 1–5, where, when, upon occasion of the rejection of the Jews, it is asked, *Hath God then cast away his people?* he answers, No; for *at this time there is a remnant according to the election of grace*. This prophecy has reference to that distinguished remnant. Some of the Jews shall be brought to embrace the Christian faith, shall be added to the church, and so be saved. And our Saviour has told us that *for the sake of these elect* the days of the destruction of the Jews should be shortened, and a stop put to the desolation, Matt. xxiv. 22.

I. This is illustrated here by a comparison, *v.* 8. When a vine is so withered that there seems to be no sap nor life in it, and the dresser of the vineyard is inclined to cut it down, yet, if ever so little of the juice of the grape be found, though but in one cluster, a stander-by interposes, and says, *Destroy it not, for a blessing is in it;* there is life in the root. Sometimes God spares whole cities and nations for the sake of a few.

II. Those that shall make up this saving remnant. 1. They are such as serve God. It is *for my servants' sake* (*v.* 8), and they are *my servants* that *shall dwell there*, *v.* 9. God's faithful servants *serve their generation*. 2. They are such as seek God, make it the business of their lives to call upon him.

III. An account of the mercy God has in store for them. The remnant shall have a happy settlement again in their own land, as *a seed out of Jacob*; and these typify the remnant of Jacob that shall be incorporated into the gospel church by faith. They shall inherit *my mountains*, the holy mountains on which Jerusalem and the temple were built. They shall have a green pasture for their flocks, *v.* 10. *Sharon and the valley of Achor* shall again be well replenished with cattle. They shall recover possession of the whole land. Gospel-ordinances are the fields and valleys where the sheep of Christ *shall go in and out and find pasture* (John x. 9), and where they are *made to lie down* (Ps. xxiii. 2), as Israel's herds in *the valley of Achor*, Hos. ii. 15.

Verses 11–16

The different states of the godly and wicked, of the Jews that believed and of those that still persisted in unbelief.

I. The fearful doom of those that persisted in their idolatry after the deliverance out of Babylon, and in infidelity after the preaching of the gospel of Christ.

1. The doom is here threatened: "*I will number you to the sword* as sheep for the slaughter, and there shall be no escaping; *you shall all bow down to it,*" *v.* 12.

2. The sins that number them to the sword. (1) Idolatry was the ancient sin (*v.* 11): "*You are those* who, instead of serving me as my people, *forsake the Lord*, and cast him off to embrace other gods, who *forget my holy mountain* to burn incense upon the mountains of your idols (*v.* 7), and have deserted the one only living and true God." They *prepared a table for that troop of* deities which the heathen worship and *poured out drink-offerings to that* numberless number of them; for those that thought one God too little never thought scores and hundreds sufficient. (2) Infidelity was the sin of the later Jews (*v.* 12): *When I called, you did not answer*, which refers to the same that *v.* 2 did, and that is applied to those who rejected the gospel. Our Lord Jesus himself called (he *stood and cried*, John vii. 37), but they would not answer. It is not strange that those who will not be persuaded to choose that which is good persist in their choice of that which is evil.

II. The aggravation of this doom, from the consideration of the happy state of those that were brought to repentance and faith. The blessedness of those that serve God, and the woeful condition of those that rebel against him, are here set the *one over-against the other*, that they may serve as a foil

JAMIESON, FAUSSET, BROWN

5. (Matt. 9:11; Luke 5:30; 18:11; Jude 19). Applicable to the hypocritical self-justifiers of our Lord's time. **smoke**—alluding to the smoke of their self-righteous sacrifices; the fire of God's *wrath* was kindled at the sight, and exhibited itself in the *smoke* that breathed forth from His nostrils; in *Hebrew* the nose is the seat of anger; and the nostrils distended in wrath, as it were, breathe forth smoke [ROSENMULLER] (Ps. 18:8). **6. written before me**—"it is decreed by Me," viz., what follows (Job 13:26), [MAURER]; or, their guilt is recorded before Me (cf. Dan. 7:10; Rev. 20:12; Mal. 3:16). **into . . . bosom**—(Ps. 79:12; Jer. 32:18; Luke 6:38). The Orientals used the loose fold of the garment falling on "the bosom" or lap, as a receptacle for carrying things. The sense thus is: I will repay their sin so *abundantly* that the hand will not be able to receive it; it will need the spacious *fold on the bosom* to contain it [ROSENMULLER]. Rather it is, "I will repay it to *the very person from whom it has emanated.*" Cf. "God did render the evil of the men of Shechem upon their heads" (Judg. 9: 57; Ps. 7:16) [GESENIUS]. **7.** Their sin had been accumulating from age to age until God at last repaid it in full. **mountains**—(ch. 57:7; Ezek. 18:6; 20:27, 28; Hos. 4:13). **their**—"Your" had preceded. From speaking *to*, He speaks *of* them; this implies growing alienation from them and greater distance. **work**—the full *recompense* of their work (so ch. 49: 4).

8. new wine—*as if some grapes having good wine-producing juice in them*, be found in a cluster which the vinedresser was about to throw away as bad, and one saith, etc. **blessing**—i.e., good wine-producing juice (cf. Judg. 9:13; Joel 2:14). **so**—God will spare the godly "remnant," while the ungodly mass of the nation shall be destroyed (ch. 1: 9; 6:13; 10:21; 11:11, 12-16). **my servants**—the godly remnant. But HORSLEY, "for the sake of my *servant, Messiah.*"

9. seed—"the holy seed" (ch. 6:13), a posterity from Jacob, designed to repossess the Holy Land, forfeited by the sin of the former Jews. **my mountains**—Jerusalem and the rest of Judea, peculiarly God's (cf. ch. 2:2; 11:9; 14:32). **it**—the Holy Land. **elect**—(vss. 15, 22.) **10. Sharon**—(*Notes*, ch. 33:9; 35:2). **Achor**—meaning "trouble"; a valley near Jericho, so called from the trouble caused to Israel by Achan's sin (Josh. 7:24). "The valley of Achor," proverbial for whatever caused calamity, shall become proverbial joy and prosperity (Hos. 2:15).

11. holy mountain—Moriah, on which the temple was. **troop**—rather "Gad," the Babylonian god of fortune, the planet Jupiter, answering to Baal or Bel; the Arabs called it "the Greater Good Fortune"; and the planet Venus answering to Meni, "the Lesser Good Fortune" [GESENIUS, KIMCHI, etc.]. Tables were laid out for their idols with all kinds of viands, and a cup containing a mixture of wine and honey, in Egypt especially, on the last day of the year [JEROME]. **drink offering**—rather, mixed drink. **number**—rather, Meni; as goddess of fortune she was thought to *number* the fates of men. VITRINGA understands Gad to be the sun; Meni the moon, or Ashtaroth or Astarte (I Kings 11:33). **12. number**—"doom" you. Alluding to the "number," as Meni (vs. 11) means. Retribution in kind, the punishment answering to the sin (cf. II Chron. 36: 14-17). **I called, ye . . . not answer**—"I called," though "none had called" upon Me (ch. 64:7); yet even then none "answered" (Prov. 1:24). Contrast with this God and His people's mutual fellowship in prayer (vs. 24).

ADAM CLARKE

6. *Behold, it is written before me*. Their sin is registered in heaven, calling aloud for the punishment due to it.

7. *Your iniquities, and the iniquities of your fathers*—"Their iniquities, and the iniquities of their fathers."

8. *A blessing is in it*. The Hebrews call all things which serve for food *berachah*, "a blessing."

9. *An inheritor of my mountains*—"An inheritor of My mountain."

10. *Sharon . . . and the valley of Achor*. Two of the most fertile parts of Judea, famous for their rich pastures: the former to the west, not far from Joppa; the latter north of Jericho, near Gilgal.

11. *That prepare a table for that troop*—"Who set in order a table for Gad." The disquisitions and conjectures of the learned concerning Gad and Meni are infinite and uncertain; perhaps the most probable may be that Gad means good fortune, and Meni the moon.

12. *Therefore will I number you*. Referring to *Meni*, which signifies "number."

MATTHEW HENRY

to each other, *v.* 13–16. It will add to the grief of those that perish to see the happiness of God's servants and especially to think that they might have shared in their bliss if it had not been their own fault. The difference of their states lies in two things.

1. In point of comfort and satisfaction. God's servants shall want nothing that is good for them. But those who set their hearts upon the world, shall be hungry and thirsty, always empty, always craving; for it is not bread; it surfeits, but it satisfies not. God's servants *shall rejoice* and sing for joy of heart. Heaven will be a world of everlasting joy to all that are now sowing in tears. But, on the other hand, those that forsake the Lord shut themselves out from all true joy, for *they shall be ashamed* of their vain confidence, and their own righteousness, and the hopes they had built thereon.

2. In point of honour and reputation, *v.* 15, 16. *The memory of the just is*, and shall be, *blessed, but the name of the wicked shall rot.* The name of the idolaters shall be *for a curse to God's chosen*, that is, for a warning to them. The name of God's chosen shall become a blessing: *He shall call his servants by another name.* The children of the covenant shall be called *Christians*; and to them, under that name, all the promises and privileges of the new covenant shall be secured. This other name shall not be confined to one nation, but with it men shall *bless themselves in the earth*, all the world over. God shall have servants out of all nations. They shall bless themselves *in the God of truth*. They shall give honour to God both in their prayers and in their solemn oaths. This is a part of the homage we owe to God; we must bless ourselves in him, that is, we have enough to make us happy, and can desire no more, if we have him for our God. Worldly people bless themselves in the abundance they have of this world's goods (Ps. xlix. 18; Luke xii. 19); but God's servants bless themselves in him, as a God all-sufficient for them. They shall give honour to him as *the God of truth, the God of the Amen* (so the word is); some understand it of Christ, in whom all the promises are *yea and amen*, 2 Cor. i. 20. They shall give him honour as the author of this blessed change, who has made them to forget their former troubles, the remembrance of them being swallowed up in their present comforts.

Verses 17–25

If these promises were in part fulfilled when the Jews, after their return out of captivity, were settled in peace in their own land and brought as it were into a new world, yet they were to have their full accomplishment in the gospel church. In the graces and comforts which believers have in and from Christ we are to look for this new heaven and new earth. It is in the gospel that *old things have passed away and all things have become new*, and by it that those who are in Christ are *new creatures*, 2 Cor. v. 17. It was a mighty and happy change that was described *v.* 16, that *the former troubles were forgotten*; but here it rises much higher: even the *former world* shall be *forgotten* and *shall no more come into mind.* When God is reconciled to us, which gives us a new heaven, the creatures too are reconciled to us, which gives us a new earth.

I. There shall be new joys. All the church's friends, and all that belong to her, shall rejoice (*v.* 18): You shall *be glad and rejoice for ever in that which I create. I create Jerusalem a rejoicing and her people a joy.* The church shall not only rejoice but be rejoiced in. The prosperity of the church shall be a rejoicing to God himself, who has pleasure in the prosperity of his servants (*v.* 19): *I will rejoice in Jerusalem's* joy, and will *joy in my people;* for *in all their affliction he was afflicted.* There shall be no allay of this joy: *The voice of weeping shall be no more heard in her.* The former occasions of grief shall not return. But in heaven it shall have a full accomplishment; there *all tears shall be wiped away.*

II. There shall be new life, *v.* 20. Untimely deaths by the sword or sickness shall be no more known as they have been, *v.* 19. Believers through Christ shall be satisfied with life, though it be ever so short on earth. Even the child shall be reckoned to *die a hundred years old*, for he shall rise again at full age, shall rise to eternal life. And, as for old men, it is promised that *they shall fill their days* with the *fruits of righteousness*, which they shall *still bring forth in old age.* An old man who is wise, and good, and useful, may truly be said to have *filled his days.* Old men who have their hearts upon the world have never filled their days. Unbelievers shall be unsatisfied and unhappy in life, though it be ever so long. The sinner, though he live to be *a hundred years old, shall be accursed*, and his long life is but a long reprieve. So that the matter is not great whether our lives on earth be long or short, but whether we live the lives

JAMIESON, FAUSSET, BROWN

13. eat—enjoy all blessings from me (Song of Sol. 5:1). **hungry**—(Amos 4:6; 8:11). This may refer to the siege of Jerusalem under Titus, when 1,100,000 are said to have perished by famine; thus vs. 15 will refer to God's people without distinction of Jew and Gentile receiving "another name," viz., that of *Christians* [HOUBIGANT]. A farther fulfilment may still remain, just before the creation of the "new heavens and earth," as the context, vs. 17, implies. **14. howl**—(ch. 15:2; Matt. 8:12).

15. curse—The name of "Jew" has been for long a formula of execration (cf. Jer. 29: 22); if one wishes to curse another, he can utter nothing worse than this, "God make thee what the Jew is!" Contrast the formula (Gen. 48:20) [MAURER]. **my chosen**—the elect Church, gathered from Jews and Gentiles, called by "another name," *Christians* (Acts 11:26). However (*Note*, vs. 13), as "My chosen," or "elect," in vs. 3, refers to the "seed of Jacob," *the believing Jews*, hereafter about to possess their land (vss. 19, 22), are *ultimately* meant by "My chosen," as contrasted with the unbelieving Jews ("ye"). These elect Jews shall be called by "another," or a *new name*, i.e., shall no longer be "forsaken" of God for unbelief, but shall be His "delight" and "married" to Him (ch. 62:2, 4). **thee**—unbelieving Israel. *Isaiah* here speaks of God, whereas in the preceding sentences *God Himself* spake. This change of persons marks without design how completely the prophet realized God with him and in him, so that he passes, without formally announcing it, from God's words to his own, and vice versa, both alike being from God. **16. That he**—rather, "he who," etc. **blesseth . . .**—(Ps. 72:17; Jer. 4:2). **God of truth**—very God, as opposed to *false* gods; *Hebrew, Amen:* the very name of Messiah (II Cor. 1:20; Rev. 3:14), faithful to His promises (John 1:17; 6:32). Real, substantial, spiritual, eternal, as opposed to the shadowy types of the law. **sweareth . . .**—God alone shall be appealed to as God (ch. 19:18; Deut. 6:13; Ps. 63:11). **troubles**—i.e., sins, provocations [LOWTH]. Rather, *calamities* caused by your sins; so far from these visiting you again, the very *remembrance* of them is "hid from Mine eyes" by the magnitude of the blessings I will confer on you (vs. 17, etc.) [MAURER]. **17.** As Caleb inherited the same land which his feet trod on (Deut. 1:36; Josh. 14:9), so Messiah and His saints shall inherit the renovated earth which once they trod while defiled by the enemy (ch. 34:4; 51:16; 66:22; Ezek. 21:27; Ps. 2:8; 37:11; II Pet. 3:13; Heb. 12:26-28; Rev. 21: 1). **not be remembered**—See *Note* on "troubles," vs. 16; the words here answer to "the former . . . forgotten," etc. The former sorrows of the earth, under the fall, shall be so far from recurring, that their very remembrance shall be obliterated by the many mercies I will bestow on the new earth (Rev. 21:4-27). **18. rejoice for ever . . . Jerusalem**—(ch. 51:11). "Everlasting joy . . . Zion." Spiritually (I Thess. 5:16).

19. (Ch. 62:5.) **weeping . . . no more**—(ch. 25:7, 8; 35:10; Rev. 7:17; 21:4), primarily, foretold of *Jerusalem;* secondarily, of *all* the redeemed. **20.** The longevity of men in the first age of the world shall be enjoyed again. **thence**—from that time forward. **infant of days**—i.e., an infant who shall only complete a few days; short-lived. **filled . . . days**—None shall die without attaining a full old age. **child . . . die . . . hundred years**—i.e., "he that dieth an hundred years old shall die a mere child" [LOWTH]. **sinner . . . hundred . . . be accursed**—"The sinner that dieth at an hundred years shall be deemed accursed," i.e., his death at so early an age, which in those days the hundredth year will be regarded, just as if it were mere childhood, shall be deemed the effect of God's special visitation in wrath [ROSENMULLER]. This passage proves that the better age to come on earth, though much superior to the present will not be a perfect state; sin and death shall have place in it (cf. Rev. 20:7, 8), but much less frequently than now.

ADAM CLARKE

F. B. MEYER:

A new earth for God's servants. Notice the wide difference that religion makes to the soul. The children of God are secured against the evils which visit all others. *They* eat; *they* drink; *they* rejoice; *they* sing; *they* are called by another name (vv. 13–15).

Behold a new creation (vv. 17–25)! The present dispensation is ended. Jerusalem, restored to her former glory, sings for joy; and her rejoicing sends a thrill of joy through the nature of God. Long years of life and security of tenure are granted again to man. The red rapine of the forest is ended, for creation is emancipated from its bondage and participates in the glorious liberty of the sons of God. Peace shall reign in the forest glades, never again to abdicate her throne (v. 25). But, best of all, there shall be such unity between man and God that prayer will be anticipated, and the pleading soul shall be conscious of the listening ear of God. Hasten, O day of days, for which creation and the saints groan with inexpressible desire!—*Bible Commentary*

15. *Shall slay thee*—"Shall slay you."

17. *I create new heavens and a new earth.* This has been variously understood. Some Jews and some Christians understand it literally. God shall change the state of the atmosphere and render the earth more fruitful. Some refer it to what they call the millennium; others, to a glorious state of religion; others, to the re-creation of the earth after it shall have been destroyed by fire. I think it refers to the full conversion of the Jews ultimately, and primarily to the deliverance from the Babylonish captivity.

18. *Rejoice for ever in that which I create*—"Exult in the age to come which I create."

MATTHEW HENRY

of saints or the lives of sinners.

III. There shall be a new enjoyment of the comforts of life. Whereas before it was very uncertain and precarious, now it shall be otherwise; they shall *build houses and inhabit them*, shall *plant vineyards* and *eat the fruit of them*, *v.* 21, 22. Strangers shall not break in upon them, to expel them, as sometimes they have done: *My elect shall wear out*, or *long enjoy*, *the work of their hands;* it is honestly got, and it will wear well; it is *the work of their hands*, which they themselves have laboured for, and not the *bread of idleness*, or *bread of deceit*. If we live to enjoy it long, it is the gift of God's providence, for that is here promised: *As the days of a tree are the days of my people;* as the *days of an oak* (*ch.* vi. 13), *whose substance is in it, though it cast its leaves;* though it be stripped every winter, it lasts many years; as the days *of the tree of life;* so the LXX.

IV. There shall be a new generation rising up in their stead to inherit and enjoy these blessings (*v.* 23): *They shall not labour in vain*, for they shall not only enjoy the work of their hands themselves, but they shall leave it with satisfaction to those that shall come after them. God will make their children that rise up comforts to them; they shall have the joy of seeing them *walk in the truth*. He will make the times that come after comfortable to their children.

V. There shall be a good correspondence between them and their God (*v.* 24): *Even before they call, I will answer*. God will anticipate their prayers with the blessings of his goodness. The father of the prodigal met him in his return. God's readiness to hear prayer appears much more in the grace of the gospel than it did under the law.

VI. There shall be a good correspondence between them and their neighbours (*v.* 25): *The wolf and the lamb shall feed together*. God's people, though they are as sheep in the midst of wolves, shall be unhurt; for God will not so much break the power of their enemies as formerly, but he will turn their hearts, will alter their dispositions by his grace. When Paul, who had been a persecutor of the disciples (and who, being of the tribe of Benjamin, ravened *as a wolf*, Gen. xlix. 27) joined himself to them and became one of them, then *the wolf and the lamb fed together*. Men shall be changed: *The lion* shall no more be a beast of prey, but *shall eat straw like the bullock*, shall *know his owner*, and *his master's crib*, as *the ox* does. When those that lived by spoil and rapine to enrich themselves, right or wrong, are brought by the grace of God to live by honest labour—when those that stole steal no more, but work with their hands the thing that is good—then this is fulfilled, that *the lion shall eat straw like the bullock*. Satan shall be chained, the dragon bound; for *dust shall be the serpent's meat again*. That great enemy has glutted himself with the precious blood of saints, who by his instigation have been persecuted, and with the precious souls of sinners, who by his instigation have ruined themselves forever; but now he shall be confined to dust, according to the sentence, *On thy belly shalt thou go, and dust shalt thou eat*, Gen. iii. 14. Christ shall reign as Zion's King till all the enemies of his kingdom be made his footstool.

JAMIESON, FAUSSET, BROWN

21. (*Note*, ch. 62:8; Amos 9:14.) **22. They shall not** experience the curse pronounced (Lev. 26:16; Deut. 28:30).

tree—among the most *long-lived* of objects in nature. They shall live as long as the trees they "plant" (cf. ch. 61:3, end of verse; Ps. 92:12). **enjoy**—Hebrew, "consume," "wear out"; they shall live to enjoy the last of it (ch. 62:9). **23. bring forth for trouble**—lit., "for terror," i.e., "They shall not bring forth children for a *sudden death*" (Lev. 26:16; Jer. 15:8). **seed . . . blessed**—(ch. 61:9). **offspring with them**—(Hos. 9:12). "Their offspring shall be with themselves" [MAURER]; not "brought forth" only to be cut off by "sudden death" (see the parallel clause). **24.** Contrast ch. 64:7, "none . . . calleth," etc.; and *Note*, vs. 12, "*I* called, ye did not answer." MAURER translates, "They shall hardly (lit., "not yet") call, when (lit., "and") I will answer; they shall be still speaking, when I will hear" (Ps. 32:5; Dan 9:20, 21). **25.** (*Notes*, ch. 11:6-9). **and dust**—rather, "but dust," etc. The curse shall *remain* on the serpent [HORSLEY], (Gen. 3:14; Mic. 7:17). *To lick the dust* is figurative of the utter and perpetual *degradation* of Satan and his emissaries (ch. 49:23; Ps. 72:9). Satan fell *self-tempted;* therefore no atonement was contrived for him, as there was for man, who fell by *his* temptation (Jude 6; John 8:44). From his peculiar connection with the earth and man, it has been conjectured that the exciting cause of his rebellion was God's declaration that human nature was to be raised into union with the Godhead; this was "the truth" concerning the person of the Son of God which "he abode not in"; it galled his pride that a lower race was to be raised to that which he had aspired to (I Tim. 3:6). How exultingly he might say, when man fell through him, "*God* would raise manhood into union with Himself; *I* have brought it down below the beasts by sin!" At that very moment and spot he was told that the seed of the abhorred race, man, should bruise his head (I John 3:8). He was raised up for this, to show forth God's glory (Exod. 9:16; Rom. 9:17). In his unfallen state he may have been God's vicegerent over the earth and the animal kingdom before man: this will account for his assuming the form of a serpent (Gen. 3). Man succeeded to that office (Gen. 2:19, 20), but forfeited it by sin, whence Satan became "prince of this world"; Jesus Christ supplants the usurper, and as "Son of man" regains the lost inheritance (Ps. 8:4-8). The steps in Satan's overthrow are these: he is cast out, first, from heaven (Rev. 12:7-9) on earth; next, he is bound a thousand years (Rev. 20:2, 3); finally, he is cast into the lake of fire for ever (Rev. 20:10).

ADAM CLARKE

22. *They shall not build, and another inhabit.* The reverse of the curse denounced on the disobedient, Deut. xxviii. 30: "Thou shalt build an house, and thou shalt not dwell therein: thou shalt plant a vineyard, and shalt not gather the grapes thereof."

For as the days of a tree. It is commonly supposed that the oak, one of the most long-lived of the trees, lasts about a thousand years.

23. *They shall not labour in vain*—"My chosen shall not labor in vain." *Nor bring forth for trouble*—"Neither shall they generate a short-lived race."

E. H. PLUMPTRE:

Verse 25. "The wolf and the lamb." The words point to what have been called the discords in the harmony of Nature, the pain and death involved, of necessity, in the relation of one whole class of animals to another. In St. Paul's language, the "whole creation groaneth and travaileth together" (Rom. 8:22). In the new heaven and the new earth of the prophet's vision there would be no such discords. The flesh-eating beasts should change their nature; even the serpent, named, probably, with special reference to Gen. 3, as the starting point of the discords, shall find food in the dust in which he crawls, and shall be no longer a destroyer. The condition of the ideal Paradise should be restored. The picture finds a parallel, perhaps a *replica*, in Virgil, *Ecl.* iv. Do the poet and the prophet stand on the same footing? or may we look for a literal fulfilment of the words of the one, though not of the other? The answer must be given in words that are "wary and few." We dare not, on the one hand, fix times and seasons, or press the *letter* of prophetic visions as demanding a fulfilment. On the other, the permanence of Israel as a people suggests the possibility of a restored Jerusalem.

—*Ellicott's Commentary on the Whole Bible*

MATTHEW HENRY — CHAPTER 66

Verses 1–4

I. The temple is slighted in comparison with a gracious soul, *v.* 1, 2. The prophets and Christ foretold the ruin of the temple, that God would leave it and then it would soon be desolate. After it was destroyed by the Chaldeans it soon recovered itself and the ceremonial services were revived with it; but by the Romans it was made a perpetual desolation, and the ceremonial law was abolished with it. Heaven is the throne of God's glory and government. The earth is his footstool, on which he stands, overruling all the affairs of it according to his will. If God has so bright a throne, so large a footstool, *where then is the house they can build* unto God, that can be the residence of his glory, or *where is the place of his rest?* What satisfaction can the Eternal Mind take in a house made with men's hands? If he required a house for himself to dwell in, he would have made one himself when he made the world; he had no need of a temple made with hands. He would not heed it as he would a humble, penitent, gracious heart. He has a heaven and earth of his own making, and a temple of man's making; but he overlooks them all, that he may look with favour to him that is poor in spirit, humble and serious, self-abasing and self-denying, whose heart is truly contrite for sin, penitent for it, and in pain to get it pardoned. Such a heart is a living temple for God; he dwells there, and it is the place of his rest; it is like heaven and earth, his

JAMIESON, FAUSSET, BROWN — CHAPTER 66

Vss. 1-24. THE HUMBLE COMFORTED, THE UNGODLY CONDEMNED, AT THE LORD'S APPEARING: JERUSALEM MADE A JOY ON EARTH. This closing chapter is *the summary* of Isaiah's prophecies as to the last days, hence the similarity of its sentiments with what went before. **1. heaven . . . throne . . . where is . . . house . . . ye build**—The same sentiment is expressed, as a precautionary proviso for the majesty of God in deigning to own any earthly temple as His, as if He could be circumscribed by space (I Kings 8:27) in inaugurating the temple of stone; next, as to the temple of the Holy Ghost (Acts 7:48, 49); lastly here, as to "the tabernacle of God with men" (ch. 2:2, 3; Ezek. 43:4, 7; Rev. 21:3). **where**—rather, "what is this house that ye are building, etc.—what place is this for My rest?" [VITRINGA]. **2. have been**—viz., made by Me. Or, absolutely, *were* things *made;* and therefore belong to Me, the Creator [JEROME]. **look**—have regard. **poor**—humble (ch. 57:15). **trembleth at . . . word**—(II Kings 22:11, 19; Ezra 9:4). The spiritual temple of the heart, though not superseding the outward place of worship, is God's favorite dwelling (John 14:23). In the final state in heaven there shall be "no temple," but "the Lord God" Himself (Rev. 21:22).

ADAM CLARKE — CHAPTER 66

This chapter is a continuation of the subject of the foregoing. The Jews valued themselves much upon their Temple, and the pompous system of services performed in it, which they supposed were to be of perpetual duration; and they assumed great confidence and merit to themselves for their strict observance of all the externals of their religion. These two chapters manifestly relate to the calling of the Gentiles, the establishment of the Christian dispensation, and the reprobation of the apostate Jews, and their destruction executed by the Romans.

2. *And all those things have been*—"And all these things are Mine." A word absolutely necessary to the sense is here lost out of the text: "Mine." It is preserved by the Septuagint and Syriac.

MATTHEW HENRY

throne and his footstool.

II. Sacrifices are slighted when they come from ungracious hands. *The sacrifice of the wicked* is not only unacceptable, but it *is an abomination to the Lord* (Prov. xv. 8); this is largely shown here, *v.* 3, 4. The carnal Jews, after their return out of captivity, grew very loose in the service of God; they brought the *torn, and the lame, and the sick* for *sacrifice* (Mal. i. 8, 13), and this made their services abominable to God. *He that kills an ox* for his own table is welcome to do it; but he that now kills it for God's altar, *is as if he slew a man*; he that does it does in effect set aside Christ's sacrifice. *He that sacrifices a lamb*, if it be a corrupt thing, and not the best he has, affronts God, instead of pleasing him; it is *as if he cut off a dog's neck*, a creature in the eye of the law so vile that, whereas an ass might be redeemed, the price of a dog was never to be brought into the treasury, Deut. xxiii. 18. *He that offers an oblation*, a meat-offering or drink-offering, is as if he thought to make atonement with *swine's blood*, a creature that must not be eaten nor touched, the *broth of it* was abominable (*ch.* lxv. 4), much more the blood of it. *He that burns incense to God*, and so puts contempt upon the incense of Christ's intercession, is *as if he blessed an idol*. Their wickedness made their sacrifices detestable. *They had chosen their own ways*, the ways of their own wicked hearts, and *their souls delighted in their abominations*. They were vicious and immoral, chose the way of sin rather than the way of God's commandments, and this made their sacrifices offensive to God, *ch.* i. 11–15. They turned a deaf ear to all the warnings of divine justice and all the offers of divine grace. They *chose their own ways*, therefore, says God, I also will *choose their delusions*. *They have made their choice, and now I will make mine; they have taken what course they pleased with me, and I will take what course I please with them.* They shall be deceived by those vain confidences with which they have deceived themselves. God will make their sin their punishment; they shall be hurried into ruin by their own delusions.

Verses 5–14

The prophet, having denounced God's judgments against a hypocritical nation, that made a jest of God's word, here turns his speech to those that *trembled at his word*, to comfort and encourage them; they shall not be involved in the judgments that are coming upon their unbelieving nation. The word of God has comforts in store for those that by true humiliation for sin are prepared to receive them. There were those (*v.* 4) who, when *God spoke, would not hear*; but, if the heart *tremble at the word*, the ear will be open to it.

I. God will plead their just but injured cause against their persecutors (*v.* 5): *Your brethren that hated you said, Let the Lord be glorified. But he shall appear to your joy.* The apostles were Jews by birth, and yet even in the cities of the Gentiles the Jews they met were their most bitter and implacable enemies and *stirred up the Gentiles* against them. Their brethren, who should have loved them and encouraged them for their work's sake hated them, and cast them out of their synagogues. Our Saviour explains this, and seems to have reference to it, John xvi. 2. *They shall put you out of their synagogues*, and *whosoever kills you will think that he does God service*. They were encouraged under these persecutions: "Let your faith and patience hold out yet a little while; your enemies hate you and oppress you, your brethren hate you and cast you out, but your Father in heaven loves you, and will appear for you when no one else will or dare." This was fulfilled when, upon the signals given of Jerusalem's approaching ruin, the *Jews' hearts failed them for fear*; but the disciples of Christ, whom they had hated and persecuted, *lifted up their heads with joy, knowing that their redemption drew nigh*, Luke xxi. 26, 28.

II. God's appearances for them will be such as will make a great noise in the world (*v.* 6): There shall be *a voice of noise from the city, from the temple*. Some make it the joyful and triumphant voice of the church's friends, others the lamenting voice of her enemies, fleeing in vain to the temple for shelter. These voices do but echo to the *voice of the Lord*, who is now rendering a *recompence to his enemies*. A confused noise was in the city and temple when Jerusalem, after a long siege, was at last taken by the Romans. Some think this prophecy was fulfilled in the prodigies that went before that destruction of Jerusalem, related by Josephus in his History of the Wars of the Jews (*lib.* 7. *cap.* 31), that the temple-doors flew open suddenly of their own accord, and the priests heard a noise of motion or shifting in the most holy place, and presently a voice, saying, *Let us depart hence*. And, some time after, one Jesus

JAMIESON, FAUSSET, BROWN

3. God loathes even the sacrifices of the wicked (ch. 1:11; Prov. 15:8; 28:9). **is as if**—LOWTH not so well omits these words: "He that killeth an ox (presently after) murders a man (as in Ezek. 23:39). But the omission in the *Hebrew* of "is as if"—increases the force of the *comparison*. *Human* victims were often offered by the heathen.

dog's neck—an abomination according to the Jewish law (Deut. 23:18); perhaps made so, because dogs were venerated in Egypt.. He does not honor this abomination by using the word "sacrifice," but uses the degrading term, "cut off a dog's neck" (Exod. 13:13; 34:20). Dogs as unclean are associated with swine (Matt. 7:6; II Pet. 2:22). **oblation**—unbloody: in antithesis to "swine's *blood*" (ch. 65:4). **burneth**—*Hebrew*, "he who offereth as a memorial oblation" (Lev. 2:2). **they have chosen**—opposed to the two first clauses of vs. 4: "as *they* have chosen their own ways, etc., so *I* will choose their delusions." **4. delusions**—(II Thess. 2:11), answering to "their own ways" (vs. 3; so Prov. 1:31). However, the *Hebrew* means rather "vexations," "calamities," which also the parallelism to "fears" requires; "choose *their* calamities" means, "choose the calamities which they thought to escape by their own ways." **their fears**—the things they feared, to avert which their idolatrous "abominations" (vs. 3) were practised. **I called . . . none . . . answer**—(*Notes*, ch. 65:12, 24; Jer. 7:13). **did . . . chose**—not only *did* the evil deed, but did it deliberately as a matter of *choice* (Rom. 1:32). "*They* chose that in which *I* delighted not"; therefore, "*I* will choose" that in which *they* delight not, the "calamities" and "fears" which they were most anxious to avert. **before mine eyes**—(*Note*, ch. 65:3).

5. tremble at . . . word—the same persons as in vs. 2, the believing few among the Jews. **cast you out for my name's sake**—excommunicate, as if too polluted to worship with them (ch. 65:5). So in Christ's first sojourn on earth (Matt. 10:22; John 9:22, 34; 16:2; 15:21). So it shall be again in the last times, when the believing shall be few (Luke 18:8). **Let the Lord be glorified**—the mocking challenge of the persecutors, as if their violence towards you was from zeal for God. "Let the Lord show Himself glorious," viz., *by manifesting Himself in your behalf;* as the parallelism to, "He shall *appear to your joy*," requires (as in ch. 5:19; cf. ch. 28:15; 57:4). So again Christ on the cross (Matt. 27:42, 43). **appear to your joy**—giving you "joy" instead of your "rebuke" (ch. 25:8, 9).

6. God, from Jerusalem and His "temple," shall take vengeance on the enemy (Ezek. 43: 1-8; Zech. 12:2, 3; 14:3, 19-21). The abrupt language of this verse marks the suddenness with which God destroys the hostile *Gentile* host outside: as vs. 5 refers to the confounding of the unbelieving *Jews*. **voice of noise**—i.e., the *Lord's* loud-sounding voice (Ps. 68:33; 29:3-9; I Thess. 4:16).

ADAM CLARKE

3. *He that killeth an ox is as if he slew a man*—"He that slayeth an ox killeth a man." These are instances of wickedness joined with hypocrisy, of the most flagitious crimes committed by those who at the same time affected great strictness in the performance of all the external services of religion. God, by the prophet Ezekiel, upbraids the Jews with the same practices: "When they had slain their children to their idols, then they came the same day into my sanctuary to profane it," chap. xxiii. 39. Of the same kind was the hypocrisy of the Pharisees in our Saviour's time, who "devour widows' houses, and for a pretence make long prayers," Matt. xxiii. 14.

He that offereth an oblation, as if he offered swine's blood—"That maketh an oblation *offereth* swine's blood."

5. *Your brethren that hated you . . . said*—"Say to your brethren that hate you."

6. *A voice of noise from the city, a voice from the temple, a voice of the Lord.* It is very remarkable that similar words were spoken by Jesus, son of Ananias, previously to the destruction of Jerusalem. See his very affecting history related by Josephus *War*, B. vi, chap. v.

MATTHEW HENRY

Bar-Annas went up and down the city, at the feast of tabernacles, continually crying, *A voice from the east, a voice from the west, a voice from the four winds, a voice against Jerusalem and the temple, a voice against all this people.*

III. God will set up a church for himself in the world (*v.* 7): *Before she travailed she brought forth.* This is to be applied to the deliverance of the Jews out of their captivity in Babylon, which was brought about very easily and silently, without any pain or struggle. The man-child of the deliverance is rejoiced in, and yet the mother was never in labour for it; *before her pain came she was delivered.* This altogether without precedent, unless in the story which the Egyptian midwives told of the Hebrew women (Exod. i. 19), that *they were lively and were delivered ere the midwives came in unto them.* But *shall the earth be made to bring forth her fruits in one day?* No, it is the work of some weeks in the spring to *renew the face of the earth. Shall a land be brought forth in one day,* or *shall a nation be born at once? God does nothing abruptly.* Yet, in this case, *as soon as Zion travailed she brought forth.* Cyrus's proclamation was no sooner issued than the captives were ready to make the best of their way to their own land. And the reason is given (*v.* 9), because *it is the Lord's doing.* If he *bring to the birth* in preparing his people for deliverance, he will *cause to bring forth* in the accomplishment of the deliverance. When everything is ready, shall not I then *give strength to bring forth.* Does God cause mankind, and all the species of living creatures, to propagate, and *replenish the earth,* and *will he restrain Zion*? Will he not make her fruitful in a blessed offspring to replenish the church? But this was a figure of the setting up of the Christian church in the world, and the replenishing of that family with children to be named from Jesus Christ. When the Spirit was poured out, multitudes were converted in a little time and with little pains. The success of the gospel was astonishing. The same day that the Spirit was poured out there were 3,000 souls added to the church, *so mightily grew the word of God and prevailed.*

IV. Their present sorrows shall shortly be turned into abundant joys, *v.* 10, 11. The church's friends are such as *love her, and mourn* with her and *for her.* Those that have a sincere affection for the church have a cordial sympathy with her. They are encouraged: *Rejoice with her,* and again and again *I say, Rejoice.* Jerusalem shall have cause to rejoice; the days of her mourning shall be at an end. "You that mourned for her in her sorrows cannot but from the same principle rejoice with her in her joys." We must *suck and be satisfied with the breasts of her consolations.* The word of God, the covenant of grace (especially the promises of that covenant), the ordinances of God, and all the opportunities of conversing with him, are the breasts, which the church calls and counts the *breasts of her consolations.* We must take pleasure in our relation to God and communion with him. Whatever is the glory of the church must be *our glory and joy,* particularly her purity, unity, and increase.

V. He who gives them this call to rejoice will give them cause to do so and hearts to do so, *v.* 12–14. *I will extend peace to her* (that is, all good to her) *like a river* that runs in a constant stream. The gospel brings with it, wherever it is received in its power, such peace as this, which shall go on *like a river,* supplying souls with all good and making them fruitful, as a river does the lands it passes through. *The glory of the Gentiles* shall come to them *like a flowing stream.* God shall be glorified in all, and that ought to be more the matter of our joy than anything else (*v.* 14): *The hand of the Lord shall be known towards his servants,* he will at the same time make known *his indignation towards his enemies.* God's mercy and justice shall both be manifested. God will not only give them cause to rejoice, but will speak comfort *to their hearts.* Their country shall be their tender nurse: You shall be *carried on her sides,* under her arms, as little children are, and shall be *dandled upon her knees.* The great Shepherd *gathers the lambs in his arms and carries them in his bosom,* and so must the under-shepherds, that they may not be discouraged. God will himself be their powerful comforter: *As one whom his mother comforts,* when he is sick or in sorrow, *so will I comfort you*; not only with the rational arguments which a prudent father uses, but with the tender affections and compassions of a loving mother. They shall feel the blessed effects of this comfort in their own souls (*v.* 13). This was fulfilled in the wonderful satisfaction which Christ's disciples had in the success of their ministry. Christ tells them (John xvi. 22), *Your heart shall rejoice and your joy no man taketh from you.* Then *your bones,* that were dried and withered, shall recover a youthful

JAMIESON, FAUSSET, BROWN

7. she—Zion. **Before . . . travailed . . . brought forth**—The accession of numbers, and of prosperity to her, shall be *sudden beyond all expectation* and *unattended with painful effort* (ch. 54:1, 4, 5). Contrast with this case of the future Jewish Church the *travail-pains* of the *Christian* Church in bringing forth "a man-child" (Rev. 12:2, 5). A man-child's birth is in the East a matter of special joy, while that of a female is not so; therefore, it here means the *manly sons* of the restored Jewish Church, the *singular* being used collectively for the *plural:* or the many sons being regarded as *one* under Messiah, who shall then be manifested as their *one representative Head.* **8. earth**—rather, to suit the parallelism, "is a *country* (put for the *people* in it) *brought forth* in one day?" [LOWTH]. In *English Version* it means, The earth brings forth its productions gradually, not in one day (Mark 4:28). **at once**—In this case, contrary to the usual growth of the nations by degrees, Israel starts into maturity at once. **for**—rather, "is a nation born at once, *that* Zion has, so soon as she travailed, brought forth?" [MAURER]. **9. cause to bring forth, and shut**—rather, "Shall I who *beget,* restrain the birth?" [LOWTH], (ch. 37:3; Hos. 13:13); i.e., Shall I who have begun, not finish My work of restoring Israel? (I Sam. 3:12; Rom. 11:1; Phil. 1:6). **shut**—(cf. Rev. 3:7, 8).

10. love . . . mourn for her—(Ps. 102:14, 17, 20; 122:6).

11. suck—(ch. 60:5, 16; 61:6; 49:23). **abundance**—*Hebrew,* "the *raylike flow* of her opulence," i.e., with the milk spouting out from her full breasts (answering to the parallel, "breast of her consolations") in raylike streams [GESENIUS].

12. extend—I will *turn* peace (prosperity) upon her, like a river turned in its course [GESENIUS]. Or, "I will *spread* peace *over* her as an *overflowing* river" [BARNES], (ch. 48:18). **flowing stream**—as the Nile by its overflow fertilizes the whole of Egypt. **borne upon . . . sides**—(*Note,* ch. 60:4).

her . . . her—If "ye" refers to the Jews, translate, "ye shall be borne upon *their sides . . . their knees,*" viz., those of the *Gentiles,* as in ch. 49:22; and as "suck" (ch. 60:16) refers to the *Jews* sucking the *Gentile* wealth. However, *English Version* gives a good sense: The Jews, and all who love Jehovah (vs. 10), "shall suck, and be borne" by *her* as a mother. **13. mother**—(ch. 49:15). **comforteth**—(ch. 40:1, 2).

14. bones—which once were "dried up" by the "fire" of God's wrath (Lam. 1:13), shall live again (Prov. 3:8; 15:30; Ezek. 37:1, etc.). **flourish . . . herb**—Rom. 11:15-24). **known toward**—manifested in behalf of.

ADAM CLARKE

CHARLES H. SPURGEON:

"As soon as Zion travailed, she brought forth her children" (v. 8). Israel had fallen into the lowest condition, but an inward yearning of heart was felt in the midst of God's people for the return of the divine blessing; and no sooner had this anxious desire become intense than God heard the voice of its cry, and the blessing came. It was so at the time of the restoration of the captives from Babylon, and it was most evidently so in the days of our Lord. A faithful company had continued still to expect the coming of the Lord's anointed Messenger; they waited till He should suddenly come in His temple: the twelve tribes represented by an elect remnant cried day and night unto the Most High, and when at last their prayers reached the fulness of vehemence, and their anxiety wrought in them the deepest agony of spirit, then the Messiah came; the light of the Gentiles, and the glory of Israel. Then began that age of blessedness in which the barren woman did keep house and became the joyful mother of children. The Holy Spirit was given, and multitudes were born to the church of God, yea, we may say, a nation was born in a day. The wilderness and the solitary place were glad for them, and the desert rejoiced and blossomed as the rose. We are not, however, about to enter into the particular application of our text as Isaiah uttered it: the great declarations of revelation are applicable to all cases, and, once true, they stand fast forever and ever. Earnestly desiring that God may give a large spiritual blessing to His church, I shall first ask you to note that *in order to the obtaining of an increase to the church there must be travail*; and that, secondly, *this travail is frequently followed by surprising results.*

—*The Treasury of the Old Testament*

11. *With the abundance of her glory*—"From her abundant stores."

12. *Like a river, and . . . like a flowing stream*—"Like the great river, and like the overflowing stream." That is, the Euphrates.

MATTHEW HENRY

strength and vigour and *shall flourish like a herb.*

Verses 15–24

These verses have a dark side towards the enemies of God's kingdom, and a bright side towards his faithful loyal subjects. Probably they refer to the Jews in captivity in Babylon, of whom some hated to be reformed, and therefore should be ruined by the calamity (Jer. xxiv. 9); others were sent thither for their good, and should in due time get well through it. But doubtless the prophecy looks further, to the judgment for which Christ did come once, and will come again.

I. Christ will appear to the confusion of all those that stand out against him. Sometimes he will appear in temporal judgments. The Jews that persisted in infidelity were cut off *by fire* and *by his sword.* The *Lord* then *pleaded with all flesh*; and, it being his sword with which they are cut off, they are called *his slain.* Idolaters will especially be contended with in the day of wrath, *v.* 17. Perhaps some of those who returned out of Babylon had their *idols in their gardens*, and there *purified themselves* when they went about their idolatrous rites, *one after another*, or, as we read it, *behind one tree in the midst*, behind *Ahad* or *Ehad*, some idol in honour of which they *ate swine's flesh, and other abominations*, as *the mouse*, or some other like animal. But the prophecy may refer to all those judgments which God will bring upon sinners, who are devoted to the world and the flesh: They *shall be consumed together*. God knows both what men do and with what design they do it.

II. He will appear to the comfort and joy of all that are faithful to him in the setting up of the kingdom of grace, the first-fruits of the kingdom of glory. The time shall come that he will *gather all nations and tongues to himself*, that they may *come and see his glory* as it shines in the face of Jesus Christ, *v.* 18. This was fulfilled when all nations were to be discipled and the gift of tongues was bestowed in order thereunto. The church had hitherto been confined to one nation and in one tongue only God was worshipped.

1. Some of the Jewish nation should, by the grace of God, be distinguished from the rest, and marked for salvation: I will not only set up a *gathering ensign* among them, but there shall be those among them on whom *I will set a differencing sign.* Though they are a corrupt degenerate nation, yet God will set apart a remnant of them, that shall be devoted to him, and a mark shall be set upon them, with such certainty will God own them, Ezek. ix. 4. Christ's sheep are marked.

2. Those who are themselves distinguished thus shall be commissioned to be *sent to the nations* to carry the gospel among them, and preach it to every creature. They shall be sent to *the nations*, several of which are here named, Tarshish and Pul, and Lud, &c. It is uncertain what countries are here intended. *Tarshish* signifies in general *the sea*, yet some take it for Tarsus in Cilicia. *Pul* is the name of one of the kings of Assyria; perhaps some part of that country might likewise bear that name. *Lud* is supposed to be Lydia, a warlike nation, famed for archers, Jer. xlvi. 9. *Tubal*, some think, is Italy or Spain; and *Javan* Greece, the Iones; and the *isles of the Gentiles*, peopled by the posterity of Japhet (Gen. x. 5), probably are the *isles afar off*. In Judah only was God known, and other countries sat in darkness, heard not the joyful sound, saw not the joyful light. It is a pity that any of the children of men should be at such a distance from their Maker as not to hear his name and see his glory. Those that are sent to the nations shall go upon God's errand, to *declare his glory among the Gentiles.* The Jews that shall be dispersed among the nations shall declare the glory of God's providence concerning their nation all along. Some out of the nations shall *take hold of the skirt of him that is a Jew*, entreating him to take notice of them, "for *we will go with you, having heard that God is with you*," Zech. viii. 23.

3. Many converts shall hereby be made, *v.* 20. *They shall bring all your brethren* (for proselytes ought to be owned and embraced as brethren) *for an offering unto the Lord.* Some shall come *upon horses*, because they came from far. Some shall come in *chariots*, and the aged, and sickly, and little children, shall be brought *in litters* or covered waggons, and the young men *on mules and swift beasts.* They shall spare no trouble nor charge to get to Jerusalem. They shall come, not as formerly they used to come to Jerusalem, to be offerers, but to be themselves *an offering unto the Lord*, which must be understood spiritually, or their being presented to God as *living sacrifices*, Rom. xii. 1. They shall be brought *as the children of Israel bring an offering in a clean vessel*, with great care that they be holy, purified from sin,

JAMIESON, FAUSSET, BROWN

15. (Ch. 9:5; Ps. 50:3; Hab. 3:5; II Thess. 1:8; II Pet. 3:7.) **chariots . . . whirlwind**—Jer. 4:13). **render**—as the *Hebrew* elsewhere (Job 9:13; Ps. 78: 38) means to allay or stay wrath. MAURER translates it so here: *He stays His anger with* nothing but *fury*, etc.; nothing short of pouring out all His fiery fury will satisfy His wrath. **fury**—"burning heat" [LOWTH], to which the parallel, "flames of fire," answers. **16.** Rather, "With fire will Jehovah judge, and with His sword (He will judge) all flesh." The parallelism and collocation of the *Hebrew* words favor this (ch. 65:12). **all flesh**—i.e., *all* who are the objects of His wrath. The *godly* shall be hidden by the Lord in a place of safety away from the scene of judgment (ch. 26:20, 21; Ps. 31:20; I Thess. 4:16, 17). **17. in . . . gardens**—*Hebrew* and LXX rather require, "*for* (entering into) gardens," viz., to sacrifice there [MAURER]. **behind one tree**—rather, "following one," i.e., some idol or other, which, from contempt, he does not name [MAURER]. VITRINGA, etc., think the *Hebrew* for "one," *Ahhadh*, to be the name of the god; called *Adad* (meaning *One*) in Syria (cf. Acts 17:23). The idol's power was represented by inclined rays, as of the sun shining on the earth. GESENIUS translates, "following one," viz., *Hierophant* (priest), who led the rest in performing the sacred rites. **in . . . midst**—viz., of the garden (cf. *Notes*, ch. 65:3, 4). **mouse**—legally unclean (Lev. 11:29) because it was an idol to the heathen (see *Note*, ch. 37:36; I Sam. 6:4). Translate, "the fieldmouse," or "dormouse" [BOCHART]. The Pharisees with their self-righteous purifications, and all mere formalists, are included in the same condemnation, described in language taken from the idolatries prevalent in Isaiah's times. **18. know**—not in the *Hebrew*. Rather, understand the words by aposiopesis; it is usual in threats to leave the persons threatened to supply the hiatus from their own fears, owing to conscious guilt: "For I . . . their works and thoughts . . ." viz., will punish [MAURER]. **it shall come**—the time *is come* that I will, etc. [MAURER]. **gather . . . nations**—against Jerusalem, where the *ungodly* Jews shall perish; and then the Lord at last shall fight for Jerusalem against those nations: and the survivors (vs. 19) shall "see God's glory" (Zech. 12:8, 9; 14: 1-3, 9). **tongues**—which have been *many* owing to sin, being confounded at Babel, but which shall again be *one* in Christ (Dan. 7:14; Zeph. 3:9; Rev. 7:9, 10). **19. sign**—a *banner* on a high place, to indicate the place of meeting for the dispersed Jewish exiles, preparatory to their return to their land (ch. 5:26; 11:12; 62:10). **those that escape of them**—the Gentile survivors spared by God (*Note*, vs. 18; Zech. 14:16). Ch. 2:2, 3; Micah 5:7; and Zechariah 14:16-19 represent it, not that the Jews go as missionaries to the Gentiles, but that the Gentiles come up to Jerusalem to learn the Lord's ways there. **Tarshish**—Tartessus in Spain, in the west. **Pul**—east and north of Africa: probably the same as *Philæ*, an island in the Nile, called by the Egyptians *Pilak*, i.e., the border country, being between Egypt and Ethiopia [BOCHART]. **Lud**—the Libyans of Africa (Gen. 10:13), Ludim being son of Mizraim (Egypt): an Ethiopian people famous as bowmen (Jer. 46:9): employed as mercenaries by Tyre and Egypt (Ezek. 27:10; 30:5). **Tubal**—Tibarenians, in Asia Minor, south of the Caucasus, between the Black Sea and Araxes. Or, the Iberians [JOSEPHUS]. Italy [JEROME]. **Javan**—the Greeks; called Ionians, including all the descendants of Javan, both in Greece and in Asia Minor (Gen. 10:2-4). **my glory . . . Gentiles**—(Mal. 1:11). **20. they**—the Gentiles (vs. 19). **bring . . . your brethren**—the Jews, back to the Holy Land (ch. 49:22). It cannot mean the mere entrance of the Jews into the Christian Church; for such an entrance would be by *faith*, not upon "horses, litters, and mules" [HOUBIGANT]. "Offering" is metaphorical, as in Romans 15:16. **horses**—not much used by the Jews. The Gentiles are here represented as using *their* modes of conveyance to "bring" the Jews to Jerusalem. **chariots**—as these are not found in Oriental caravans, translate, "vehicles," viz., borne, not drawn on wheels. **litters**—covered sedans for the rich. **upon swift beasts**—dromedaries: from *Hebrew* root, "to dance," from their bounding motion, often accelerated by music [BOCHART]. Panniers were thrown across the dromedaries' back for poorer women [HORSLEY].

ADAM CLARKE

15. *The Lord will come with fire*—"Jehovah shall come as a fire." For *baesh*, "in fire," the Septuagint had in their copy *kaesh*, "as a fire." *To render his anger with fury*—"To breathe forth His anger in a burning heat." Instead of *lehashib*, as pointed by the Masoretes, "to render," I understand it as *lehashshib*, "to breathe."

17. *Behind one tree*—"After the rites of Achad." The Syrians worshipped a god called Adad, Plin. *Nat. Hist.* xxxvii. 11. They held him to be the highest and greatest of the gods, and to be the same with Jupiter and the sun.

18. *For I know their works.* The concluding verses of this chapter refer to the complete restoration of the Jews, and to the destruction of all the enemies of the gospel of Christ, so that the earth shall be filled with the knowledge and glory of the Lord. *It shall come*—"And I come."

19. *That draw the bow.* I much suspect that the words "that draw the bow" are a corruption of the word "Moschi," the name of a nation situated between the Euxine and Caspian seas. *That have not heard my fame*—"Who never heard My name." For *shimi*, "my fame," I read, with the Septuagint and Syriac, *shemi*, "My name."

MATTHEW HENRY

and sanctified to God. It is said of the converted Gentiles (Acts xv. 9) that *their hearts were purified by faith.* The apostle says of all true Christians that they *have come to Mount Zion, and the heavenly Jerusalem* (Heb. xii. 22), which explains this passage, and shows that the meaning of all this parade is only that they shall be brought into the church by the grace of God, as carefully as if they were carried in chariots and litters.

4. A gospel ministry shall be set up in the church (*v.* 21): *I will take of them* (the Gentile converts) *for priests and for Levites,* to minister in holy things. Hitherto the priests and Levites were all taken from among the Jews and all of one tribe; but in gospel times God will take of the converted Gentiles to minister, to teach the people, to be the stewards of the mysteries of God as the priests and Levites were under the law, to be pastors and teachers (or bishops), to *give themselves to the word and prayer,* and deacons to *serve tables,* and, as the Levites, to take care of the *outward business of the house of God,* Phil. i. 1; Acts vi. 2–4. The apostles were all Jews, and so were the seventy disciples; the great apostle of the Gentiles was himself *a Hebrew of the Hebrews*; but, when churches were planted among the Gentiles, they had ministers who were *of themselves, elders in every church* (Acts xiv. 23, Tit. i. 5). God says, *I will take of them,* some of them. It is God's work originally to choose ministers by qualifying them and inclining them to the service, as well as by giving them their commission.

5. The church and ministry, being thus settled, shall be kept up in a succession from one generation to another, *v.* 22. The kingdom of the Messiah shall be a new world, *ch.* lxv. 17. *Old things have passed away,* behold *all things have become new* (2 Cor. v. 17), the old covenant of peculiarity is set aside, and a new covenant, a covenant of grace, established, Heb. viii. 13. New commandments are given relating both to heaven and earth, and new promises relating to both, and both together make a New Testament. It will be an abiding change, a new world that will be always new. The gospel dispensation is to continue to the end of time. It will be maintained in a seed that shall serve Christ: *Your seed,* and in them *your name, shall remain*; as one generation passes away, another shall come. The gates of hell, though they fight against the church, shall not *prevail,* nor *wear out the saints of the Most High.*

6. The public worship of God in religious assemblies shall be attended by all that are thus brought *as an offering to the Lord, v.* 23. This is described in expressions suited to the Old Testament dispensation, to show that though the ceremonial law should be abolished, and the temple service should come to an end, yet God should be still as regularly worshipped as ever. Heretofore only Jews went up to appear before God, and they were bound to attend only three times a year, and the males only; but now all flesh, Gentiles as well as Jews, women as well as men, shall *come and worship before God,* in his presence, though not in his temple at Jerusalem, but in assemblies dispersed all the world over, which shall be to them as the tabernacle of meeting was to the Jews. God will in them record his name, and, though but two or three come together, he will be among them, and bless them. There is no necessity of one certain place, as the temple was of old. Christ is our temple, in whom by faith all believers meet. But it is fit that there should be a certain time appointed, that the service may be done frequently, and a token thereby given of the spiritual communion which all Christian assemblies have with each other by faith, hope, and holy love. Where the Lord's day is weekly sanctified, and the Lord's supper monthly celebrated, and both duly attended, there the Christian new moons and sabbaths are observed.

7. Their thankful sense of God's distinguishing favour to them should be increased by the consideration of the destruction of those that persist in their impiety, *v.* 24. The wicked are men that have *transgressed against God,* not only broken his laws, but broken covenant with him. It may be meant especially of the unbelieving Jews that rejected the gospel of Christ. Their misery is represented by the spectacle of a field of battle, covered with the *carcases* of the slain, so that they are an *abhorring to all flesh,* nobody cares to come near them. Now this is accomplished in the destruction of Jerusalem and the Jewish nation by the Romans. It may refer likewise to the spiritual judgments that came upon the unbelieving Jews, which St. Paul looks upon, and shows us, Rom. xi. 8, &c. It will illustrate the joys and glories of the blessed to see that they were themselves as brands plucked out of that burning.

JAMIESON, FAUSSET, BROWN

21. of them—the Gentiles. **priests . . . Levites**—for spiritual worship: enjoying the direct access to God which was formerly enjoyed by the ministers of the temple alone (I Pet. 2:9; Rev. 1:6).

22. (Ch. 65:17; II Pet. 3:13; Rev. 21:1.)

23. Lit., "As often as the new moon (shall be) in its own new moon," i.e., every month (Zech. 14:16). **sabbath**—which is therefore perpetually obligatory on earth. **all flesh**—(Ps. 65:2; 72: 11). **before me**—at Jerusalem (Jer. 3:16, 17).

24. go forth, and look—as the Israelites looked at the carcasses of the Egyptians destroyed at the Red Sea (Exod. 14:30; cf. ch. 26:14-19; Ps. 58:10; 49:14; Mal. 4:1-3). **carcasses . . .**—(vs. 16), those slain by the Lord in the last great battle near Jerusalem (Zech. 12:2-9; 14:2-4); type of the final destruction of *all* sinners. **worm . . . not die**—(Mark 9:44, 46, 48). Image of hell, from bodies left unburied in the valley of Hinnom (whence comes *Gehenna,* or hell), south of Jerusalem, where a *perpetual fire* was kept to consume the refuse thrown there (ch. 30:33). It shall not be inconsistent with true love for the godly to look with satisfaction on God's vengeance on the wicked (Rev. 14:10).

May God bless this Commentary, and especially its solemn close, to His glory, and to the edification of the writer and the readers of it, for Jesus' sake!

ADAM CLARKE

KEIL-DELITZSCH:

Verse 22. "For as the new heaven and the new earth, which I am about to make, continue before me, saith Jehovah, so will your family and your name continue." The great mass of the world of nations and of Israel also perish; but the seed and name of Israel, i.e. Israel as a people with the same ancestors and an independent name, continues for ever, like the new heaven and the new earth; and because the calling of Israel towards the world of nations is now fulfilled and everything has become new, the former fencing off of Israel from other nations comes to an end, and the qualification for priesthood and Levitical office in the temple of God is not longer merely natural descent, but inward nobility. The new heaven and the new earth, God's approaching creation, continue eternally before Him, for the old ones pass away because they do not please God; but these are pleasing to Him, and are eternally like His love, whose work and image they are. The prophet here thinks of the church of the future as being upon a new earth and under a new heaven. But he cannot conceive of the eternal in the form of eternity; all that he can do is to conceive of it as the endless continuance of the history of time.—*Commentary on the Old Testament*

24. *For their worm shall not die.* These words of the prophet are applied by our blessed Saviour, Mark ix. 44, to express the everlasting punishment of the wicked in Gehenna, or in hell. Gehenna, or the Valley of Hinnom, was very near to Jerusalem to the southeast. It was the place where the idolatrous Jews celebrated that horrible rite of making their children pass through the fire, that is, of burning them in sacrifice to Moloch. To put a stop to this abominable practice, Josiah defiled, or desecrated, the place, by filling it with human bones, 2 Kings xxiii. 10, 14; and probably it was the custom afterwards to throw out the carcasses of animals there, when it also became the common burying place for the poorer people of Jerusalem.

THE BOOK OF JEREMIAH

I. The prophet's call and commission (1:1-13:27)
A. The call (1:1-19)
1. Personal (1:1-10)
2. Official (1:11-19)

B. The commission (2:1-13:27)
1. First movement (2:1-6:30)
a. Impeachment (2:1-37)
b. Call to return (3:1-4:2)
c. Judgment (4:3-6:26)
d. The prophet strengthened (6:27-30)
2. Second movement (7:1-9:26)
a. The sins of worship (7:1-8:3)
b. Perpetual backsliding (8:4-17)
c. The prophet strengthened (8:18-9:26)
3. Third movement (10:1-13:27)
a. The sin of idolatry (10:1-25)
b. The broken covenant (11:1-17)
c. The prophet strengthened (11:18-13:27)

II. The prophet's ministry (14:1-51:64)
A. Prophecies before the fall of Jerusalem (14:1-39:18)
1. God's determination to punish (14:1-17:27)
2. God's absolute supremacy (18:1-20:18)
3. Message to Zedekiah (21:1-27:22)
4. Jeremiah and false prophets (28:1-29:32)
5. Prophecies of hope (30:1-33:26)
6. Prophecies of the siege (34:1-35:19)
7. The story of the roll (36:1-32)
8. History of the siege (37:1-39:18)

B. Prophecies after the fall of Jerusalem (40:1-45:5)
1. Against going into Egypt (40:1-42:22)
2. In Egypt (43:1-44:30)
3. The word to Baruch (45:1-5)

C. Prophecies concerning the nations (46:1-51:64)
1. Concerning Egypt (46:1-28)
2. Concerning the Philistines (47:1-7)
3. Concerning Moab (48:1-47)
4. Concerning Ammon (49:1-6)
5. Concerning Edom (49:7-22)
6. Concerning Damascus (49:23-27)
7. Concerning Dedar and Hazor (49:28-33)
8. Concerning Elam (49:34-39)
9. Concerning Babylon (50:1-51:64)

III. Historical appendix (52:1-34)

Concerning this prophet Jeremiah we may observe:

I. That he began young, and therefore could say, from his own experience, that it is good for a man to "bear the yoke in his youth," the yoke both of service and of affliction (Lam. 3:27). Jerome observes that Isaiah, who had more years, had his tongue touched with a coal of fire, to purge away his iniquity (Isa. 6:7), but that when God touched Jeremiah's mouth, nothing was said of the purging of his iniquity (1:9), because of his tender years.

II. That he continued long a prophet, some reckon fifty years, others above forty. He began in the thirteenth year of Josiah, that good king, but he continued through all the wicked reigns that followed.

III. That he was a reproving prophet, sent in God's name to tell Jacob of their sins and to warn them of the judgments of God; and the critics observe that therefore his style is more plain and rough, and less polite, than that of Isaiah and some others of the prophets. Plain-dealing is best when we are dealing with sinners to bring them to repentance.

IV. That he was a weeping prophet; so he is commonly called, not only because he penned the Lamentations, but because he was all along a mournful spectator of the sins of his people.

V. That he was a suffering prophet. He was persecuted by his own people more than any of them, as we shall find in the story of this book; for he lived and preached just before the Jews' destruction by the Chaldeans, when their character seems to have been the same as it was just before their destruction by the Romans, when they "killed the Lord Jesus, and persecuted his disciples, pleased not God, and were contrary to all men, for wrath had come upon them to the uttermost" (1 Thess. 2:15, 16). The last account we have of him is that the remaining Jews forced him to go down with them into Egypt; whereas the current tradition is, among Jews and Christians, that he suffered martyrdom. Hottinger, out of Elmakin, an Arabic historian, relates that, continuing to prophesy in Egypt against the Egyptians and other nations, he was stoned to death; and that long after, when Alexander entered Egypt, he took up the bones of Jeremiah where they were buried in obscurity and carried them to Alexandria and buried them there.

The prophecies of this book which we have in the first nineteen chapters seem to be the heads of the sermons he preached in a way of general reproof for sin; afterwards they are more particular, mixed with the history of his day, but not placed in due order of time. With the threatenings are intermixed many gracious promises of mercy to the penitent, of the deliverance of the Jews out of their captivity, and some that have a plain reference to the kingdom of the Messiah. Among the Apocryphal writings an epistle is extant said to be written by Jeremiah to the captives in Babylon, warning them against the worship of idols by exposing the vanity of idols and the folly of idolaters. It is in Baruch (ch. 6). But it is supposed not to be authentic; nor has it, I think, anything like the life and spirit of Jeremiah's writings. It is also related concerning Jeremiah (2 Mac. 2:4) that, when Jerusalem was destroyed by the Chaldeans, he, by direction from God, took the ark and the altar of incense, and, carrying them to Mount Nebo lodged them in a hollow cave there and stopped the door; but some that followed him, and thought that they had marked the place, could not find it. He blamed them for seeking it, telling them that the place should be unknown till the time that God should gather his people together again.

MATTHEW HENRY

CHAPTER 1

Verses 1–3

The genealogy of this prophet and the chronology of this prophecy. He was *the son of Hilkiah*, one *of the priests that were in Anathoth.* Jeremiah signifies one *raised up by the Lord.* He was *of the priests*, and, as a priest, was authorized and appointed to teach the people; but to that appointment God added the extraordinary commission of a prophet. Ezekiel also was a priest. Thus God would support the honour of the priesthood at a time when, by their sins and God's judgments upon them, it was sadly eclipsed. He was of the priests in Anathoth, a city of priests, which lay about three miles from Jerusalem. Abiathar had his country house there, 1 Kings ii. 26. He began to prophesy in the thirteenth year of Josiah's reign, *v.* 2. Josiah, in the twelfth year of his reign, began a work of reformation, applied himself with all sincerity to purge

JAMIESON, FAUSSET, BROWN

CHAPTER 1

Vss. 1-19. The General Title or Introduction (vss. 1-3); probably prefixed by Jeremiah, when he collected his prophecies and gave them to his countrymen to take with them to Babylon [Michaelis]. **1. Anathoth**—a town in Benjamin, twenty stadia, i.e., two or three miles north of Jerusalem; now Anata (cf. Isa. 10:30, and the context, 28-32). One of the four cities allotted to the Kohathites in Benjamin (Josh. 21:18). Cf. I Kings 2:26, 27; a stigma was cast thenceforth on the whole sacerdotal family resident there; this may be alluded to in the words here, "the priests . . . in Anathoth." God chooses "the weak, base, and despised things" "to confound the mighty." **2, 3. Jehoiakim . . . Josiah . . . Zedekiah**—Jehoahaz and Jehoiachin are omitted for they reigned only three months each. The first and last

ADAM CLARKE

CHAPTER 1

1-3. *The words of Jeremiah.* These three verses are the title of the book, and were probably added by Ezra when he collected and arranged the sacred books, and put them in that order in which they are found in Hebrew Bibles in general.

MATTHEW HENRY

Judah and Jerusalem from the *high places, and the groves, and the images,* 2 Chron. xxxiv. 3. And very seasonably was this young prophet raised up to assist the young king in that good work. Now, one would have expected when these two joined forces, such a prince, and such a prophet (as in a like case, Ezra v. 1, 2), and both young, such a complete reformation would be brought about as would prevent the ruin of the church and state; but it proved quite otherwise. In the eighteenth year of Josiah there were a great many of the relics of idolatry that were not purged out; for what can the best princes and prophets do to prevent the ruin of a people that hate to be reformed? And therefore Jeremiah continued to foretell the judgments that were coming upon them. Josiah and Jeremiah would have healed them, but they would not be healed. He continued to prophesy through the reigns of Jehoiakim and Zedekiah, each of whom reigned eleven years. He prophesied *to the carrying away of Jerusalem captive* (*v.* 3). He continued to prophesy after that, *ch.* xl. 1. From the thirteenth of Josiah to the captivity was just forty years. God, in this prophet, suffered their manners, their ill manners, forty years, and at length swore in his wrath that they should not continue in his rest.

Verses 4-10

I. Jeremiah's early designation to the office of a prophet (*v.* 4, 5): *The word of the Lord came to him,* and God told him, 1. That he had *ordained him a prophet to the nations,* the nation of the Jews in the first place, but to the neighbouring nations, to whom he was to *send yokes* (*ch.* xxvii. 2. 3) and whom he must make to *drink of the cup* of the Lord's anger, *ch.* xxv. 17. He is still, in his writings, a prophet to the nations (to our nation among the rest), to tell them what the national judgments are which may be expected for national sins. 2. That even in his eternal counsel, he had designed him to be so. This commission was given him in pursuance of the purpose God had purposed in himself concerning him, before he was born: "*I knew thee, and I sanctified thee,*" that is, "I determined that thou shouldst be a prophet and set thee apart for the office." What God has designed men for he will call them to. *Original endowment, not education, makes a prophet.*

II. His modestly declining this honourable employment, *v.* 6. "*Ah, Lord God! behold, I cannot speak* to great men and multitudes, as prophets must; I cannot speak fluently; I cannot speak with any authority, *for I am a child* and my youth will be despised." It becomes us, when we have any service to do for God, to be afraid lest we mismanage it, and lest it suffer through our weakness.

III. The assurance God graciously gave him that he would stand by him and carry him on in his work.

1. He is a child; he shall be a prophet for all that (*v.* 7): "Thou hast God's precept, and let not thy being young hinder thee from obeying it. Go to all *to whom I shall send thee and speak whatsoever I command thee.*" God was angry with Moses even for his modest excuses, Exod. iv. 14. Samuel delivered a message from God to Eli, when he was a little child. God can, when he pleases, make children prophets, and *ordain strength out of the mouth of babes and sucklings.*

2. Let him not object that he shall meet with much opposition; God will be his protector (*v.* 8): "*Be not afraid of their faces;* though they look big, and so think to outface thee. Thou speakest in the name of the King of kings, and by authority from him, and with that thou mayest *face them down.*" Those that have messages to deliver from God must not be *afraid of the face of man,* Ezek. iii. 9.

3. God will enable him to speak as one that had acquaintance with God, *v.* 9. He having now a vision of the divine glory, the Lord *put forth his hand, touched his mouth,* and with that touch *opened his lips.* God not only put knowledge into his head, but *words into his mouth;* for there are *words which the Holy Ghost teaches,* 1 Cor. ii. 13. He must speak as one that had authority from God, *v.* 10. *See, I have this day set thee over the nations and over the kingdoms.* This sounds very great, and yet Jeremiah is a poor priest still; he is not set over the kingdoms as a prince to rule them by the sword, but as a prophet by the power of the word of God. Jeremiah was *set over the nations,* not to demand tribute from them, but to *root out, and pull down,* and yet withal *to build and plant.* He must attempt to reform the nations, to *root out, and destroy* idolatry and other wickednesses among them, vicious habits and customs which had long taken root, to *throw down* the kingdom of sin, that religion and virtue might be *planted* and *built* among them. He must set before them *life and death, good and evil, ch.* xviii. 7-10. He must assure those who persisted in their wickedness that they should be

JAMIESON, FAUSSET, BROWN

of the kings under whom each prophet prophesied are often thus specified in the general title. See on these kings, and Jeremiah's life, my Introduction. **thirteenth . . . of his reign**—(ch. 25:3). **fifth month**—(II Kings 25:8).

4-10. *Jeremiah's call to the prophetical office.* **unto me**—other MSS. read "to him"; but *English Version* probably represents the true *Hebrew* text; this inscription was doubtless made by Jeremiah himself.

5. knew—approved of thee as My chosen instrument (Exod. 33:12, 17; cf. Isa. 49:1, 5; Rom. 8:29). **sanctified**—rather, separated. The primary meaning is, "to set apart" from a common to a special use; hence arose the secondary sense, "to sanctify," ceremonially and morally. It is not here meant that Jehovah cleansed Jeremiah from original sin or regenerated him by His Spirit; but separated him to his peculiar *prophetical office,* including in its range, not merely the Hebrews, but also the nations hostile to them (ch. 25:12-38; 27:46-51), [HENDERSON]. Not the effect, but the predestination in Jehovah's secret counsel, is meant by the sanctification here (cf. Luke 1:15, 41; Acts 15:18; Gal. 1:15; Eph. 1:11). **6.** From the long duration of his office (vss. 2, 3; ch. 40:1, etc.; 43:8, etc.), it is supposed that he was at the time of his call under twenty-five years of age. **child**—the same word is translated, "young man" (II Sam. 18:5). The reluctance often shown by inspired ministers of God (Exod. 4:10; 6:12, 30; Jonah 1:3) to accept the call, shows that they did not assume the office under the impulse of self-deceiving fanaticism, as false prophets often did. **7. to all that**—to all "to whom" [ROSENMULLER]. Rather, "to all *against* whom"; in a hostile sense (cf. vss. 8, 17, 18, 19) [MAURER]. Such was the perversity of the rulers and people of Judea at that time, that whoever would desire to be a faithful prophet needed to arm himself with an intrepid mind; Jeremiah was naturally timid and sensitive; yet the Spirit moulded him to the necessary degree of courage without taking away his peculiar individuality. **8.** (Ezek. 2:6; 3:9.) **I am with thee**—(Exod. 3:12; Josh. 1:5). **9. touched my mouth**—a symbolical act in supernatural vision, implying that God would give him *utterance,* notwithstanding *his* inability to speak (vs. 6). So Isaiah's lips were touched with a living coal (Isa. 6:7; cf. Ezek. 2:8, 9, 10; Dan. 10:16). **10. set thee over**—lit., "appointed thee to the oversight." He was to have his eye upon the nations, and to *predict* their destruction, or restoration, according as their conduct was bad or good. Prophets are said to *do* that which they *foretell* shall be done; for their word is God's word; and His word is His instrument whereby He doeth all things (Gen. 1:3; Ps. 33:6, 9). Word and deed are one thing with Him. What His prophet *saith* is as certain as if it were *done.* The prophet's own consciousness was absorbed into that of God; so closely united to God did he feel himself, that Jehovah's words and deeds are described as his. In ch. 31:28, God is said to do what Jeremiah here is represented as doing (cf. ch. 18:7; I Kings 19:17; Ezek. 43:3). **root out**—(Matt. 15:13). **pull down**—change of metaphor to architecture (II Cor. 10:4). There is a play on the similar sounds, *linthosh, linthotz,* in the *Hebrew* for "root out . . . pull down." **build . . . plant**—restore upon their repenting. His predictions were to be chiefly, and in the first instance, denunciatory; therefore the destruction of the nations is put first, and with a greater variety of terms than their restoration.

ADAM CLARKE

Eleventh year of Zedekiah. That is, the last year of his reign; for he was made prisoner by the Chaldeans in the fourth month of that year, and the carrying away of the inhabitants of Jerusalem was in the fifth month of the same year.

4. *The word of the Lord came unto me.* Then I first felt the inspiring influence of the Divine Spirit, not only revealing to me the subjects which He would have me to declare to the people, but also the words which I should use in these declarations.

5. *Before I formed thee.* I had destined you to the prophetic office before you were born. I had formed My plan, and appointed you to be My envoy to his people. St. Paul speaks of his own call to preach the gospel to the Gentiles in similar terms, Gal. i. 15-16.

6. *I cannot speak.* Being very young, and wholly inexperienced, I am utterly incapable of conceiving aright, or of clothing these divine subjects in suitable language. Those who are really called of God to the sacred ministry are such as have been brought to a deep acquaintance with themselves, feel their own ignorance, and know their own weakness. They know also the awful responsibility that attaches to the work, and nothing but the authority of God can induce such to undertake it.

7. *Whatsoever I command thee.* It is My words and message, not your own, that you shall deliver. I shall teach you; therefore your youth and inexperience can be no hindrance.

8. *Be not afraid of their faces.* That is, the Jews, whom he knew would persecute him because of the message which he brought. To be forewarned is to be half armed. He knew what he was to expect from the disobedient and the rebellious, and must now be prepared to meet it.

10. *I have . . . set thee over the nations.* God represents His messengers the prophets as doing what He commanded them to declare should be done. In this sense they rooted up, pulled down, and destroyed—declared God's judgments; they builded up and planted—declared the promises of His mercy. Thus God says to Isaiah, chap. vi. 10: "Make the heart of this people fat . . . and shut their eyes." Show them that they are stupid and blind; and that, because they have shut their eyes and hardened their hearts, God will in His judgments leave them to their hardness and darkness.

MATTHEW HENRY

rooted out and destroyed, and those who repented that they should be *built and planted.*

Verses 11–19

I. God gives Jeremiah, in vision, a view of the principal errand he was to go upon, which was to foretell the destruction of Judah and Jerusalem by the Chaldeans, for their sins, especially their idolatry.

1. He intimates to him that the people were ripening apace for ruin and that ruin was hastening apace towards him. He asks him, "*Jeremiah, what seest thou?* Look about thee, and observe now." "*I see a rod*, denoting affliction and chastisement, a correcting rod hanging over us; and it is a *rod of an almond-tree*, which is one of the forwardest trees in the spring, is in the bud and blossom quickly, when other trees are scarcely broken out." (In Hebrew it is called a *hasty* tree.) God explained it in the next words (*v.* 12): *Thou hast well seen.* God commended him that he was so observant as to be aware, though it was the first vision he ever saw, that it was *a rod of an almond-tree.* "Thou hast seen a *hasty tree*, which signifies that *I will hasten my word to perform it.*" Jeremiah shall prophesy that which he himself shall live to see accomplished.

2. He intimates to him whence the intended ruin should arise. Jeremiah is a second time asked: *What seest thou?* and he sees *a seething-pot* upon the fire (*v.* 13), representing Jerusalem and Judah in great commotion, like boiling water, by reason of the descent which the Chaldean army made upon them; as boiling water evaporating and growing less and less. Now the face of the furnace over which this pot boiled, was *towards the north*, for thence the fire and the fuel were to come that must *make the pot boil thus.* So the vision is explained (*v.* 14). It had been long designed by the justice of God, and long deserved by the sin of the people, and yet hitherto the divine patience had restrained it, the enemies had intended it, and God had checked them; but now all restraints shall be taken off, and the *evil shall break forth.* Look for this storm to arise *out of the north*, *whence fair weather usually comes*, Job. xxxvii. 22. Sometimes the fiercest tempests come whence we expected fair weather. This is further explained *v.* 15, *I will call all the families of the kingdoms of the north, saith the Lord.* All the northern crowns shall unite under Nebuchadnezzar, and join with him in this expedition. God's summons shall be obeyed; those whom he calls shall come. The commanders of the troops of the several nations shall take their post in carrying on the siege of Jerusalem and the other cities of Judah.

3. He tells him plainly what was the cause of all these judgments; it was the *sin of Jerusalem* and of the *cities of Judah* (*v.* 16): *I will pass sentence upon them* (so it may be read) *because of all their wickedness.* They *have forsaken God* and have *burnt incense to other gods*, new gods, strange gods, and all false gods. Jeremiah was young, and perhaps did not know what abominable idolatries the children of his people were guilty of; but God tells him that he might himself be satisfied in the equity of the sentence which in God's name he was to pass upon them.

II. God encourages Jeremiah. A great trust is committed to him. He is sent as a herald at arms; for God is pleased to give warning of his judgments beforehand, that sinners may be awakened to meet him by repentance, and so *turn away his wrath.* With this trust Jeremiah has a charge given him (*v.* 17). He must be quick: *Arise*, and lose no time. He must be busy: *Arise, and speak unto them* in season, out of season. He must be bold: *Be not dismayed at their faces*, as before, *v.* 8.

1. In two things he must be faithful: (1) He must speak all that he is charged with: *Speak all that I command thee.* He must conceal nothing for fear of offending; he must *declare the whole counsel of God.* (2) He must not whisper it in a corner to a few particular friends, but he must appear *against the kings of Judah*, if they be wicked kings. He must not spare *the priests thereof*; though he himself was a priest, and was concerned to maintain the dignity of his order. He must appear against the *people of the land*, though they were his own people, as far as they were against the Lord.

2. Two reasons are here given why he should do thus: (1) Because he had reason to fear the wrath of God if he should be false: "*Be not dismayed at their faces*, so as to desert thy office, or shrink from the duty of it, *lest I confound and dismay thee before them.*" The fear of God is the best antidote against the fear of man. It is better to have all the men in the world our enemies than God our enemy. (2) Because he had no reason to fear the wrath of men if he were faithful, *v.* 18. This young stripling of a prophet is made by the power of God as an impregnable city, fortified with iron pillars and surrounded with walls

JAMIESON, FAUSSET, BROWN

11. rod—shoot, or branch. **almond tree**—lit., "the wakeful tree," because it awakes from the sleep of winter earlier than the other trees, flowering in January, and bearing fruit in March; symbol of God's *early* execution of His purpose; vs. 12, "*hasten* My word" (cf. Amos 8:3).

12. hasten—rather, "I will *be wakeful* as to My word," etc.; alluding to vs. 11, *the wakeful tree* [MAURER]. **13.** Another vision, signifying what is the "word" about to be "performed," and by what instrumentality. **seething**—lit., "blown under"; so *boiling* by reason of the flame under it kept brisk by blowing. An Oriental symbol of a raging war.

toward—rather, "*from* the north." Lit., from the face of the region situated towards the north (cf. vss. 14, 15) [MAURER]. The pot in the north rested on one side, its mouth being about to pour forth its contents southwards, viz., on Judea. Babylon, though east of Judea, was regarded by the Hebrews as north, because they appropriated the term "east" to Arabia Deserta, stretching from Palestine to the Euphrates; or rather [BOCHART], the reference here is not to the site, but to the *route* of the Babylonians; not being able to cross the desert, they must enter the Holy Land by the northern frontier, through Riblah in Hamath (ch. 39:5; 52:9). **14. break forth**—"shall disclose itself." **Out of the north**—(ch. 4:6; 6:1, 22; 10:22; 25:9; Ezek. 26:7). The Chaldeans did not cast off the yoke of Assyria till several years after, under Nabopolassar, 625 B.C.; but long previously they had so increased as to threaten Assyria, which was now grown weak, and other neighboring peoples. **15. families**—the tribes or clans composing the various kingdoms of Babylon; the specification of these aggravates the picture of calamity (ch. 25:9). **throne at . . . gates**—the usual place of administering *justice*. The conquering princes will set up their tribunal there (ch. 39:3, 5; 52:9). Or the reference is to the military pavilion (ch. 43:10) [MAURER]. **16. utter**—pronounce. *The judicial sentences, pronounced* against the Jews by the invading princes, would be virtually the "judgments of God" (Isa. 10:5). **works**—idols. **17. gird . . . loins**—resolutely prepare for thy appointed task. Metaphor from the flowing robes worn in the East, which have to be *girt up* with a girdle, so as not to incommode one, when undertaking any active work (Job 38:3; Luke 12:35; I Pet. 1:13).

dismayed . . . confound—the same *Hebrew* word; lit., "to break." Be not *dismayed* at their faces (before them), lest I make thee *dismayed* before their faces (before them), i.e., "lest I should permit thee to be overcome by them" (cf. ch. 49:37). **18. defenced city . . .**—i.e., I will give thee strength which no power of thine enemies shall overcome (ch. 6:27; 15:20; Isa. 50:7; 54:17; Luke 21:15; Acts 6:10).

ADAM CLARKE

11. *A rod of an almond tree. Shaked*, from *shakad*, "to be ready," "to hasten," "to watch for an opportunity to do a thing," to awake; because the almond tree is the first to flower and bring forth fruit.

12. *I will hasten my word.* Here is a paronomasia. What do you see? I see *shaked*, "an almond," the hastening tree, that which first awakes. *Thou hast well seen, for* [*shoked*] *I will hasten my word.* I will awake, or watch over My word for the first opportunity to inflict the judgments which I threaten.

13. *A seething pot . . . toward the north.* We find, from Ezek. xxiv. 3, etc., that a boiling pot was an emblem of war, and the desolations it produces. Some have thought that by the seething pot Judea is intended, agitated by the invasion of the Chaldeans, whose land lay north of Judea. But Dr. Blayney contends that *mippeney tsaphonah* should be translated, "From the face of the north," as it is in the margin; for, from the next verse, it appears that the evil was to come from the north; and therefore the steam, which was designed as an emblem of that evil, must have arisen from that quarter also. The pot denotes the empire of the Babylonians and Chaldeans lying to the north of Judea, and pouring forth its multitudes like a thick vapor, to overspread the land. Either of these interpretations will suit the text.

14. *Shall break forth.* "Shall be opened." The door shall be thrown abroad, that these calamities may pass out freely.

15. *Shall set every one his throne at the entering of the gates.* As the gates of the cities were the ordinary places where justice was administered, so the enemies of Jerusalem are here represented as conquering the whole land, assuming the reins of government, and laying the whole country under their own laws; so that the Jews should no longer possess any political power. They should be wholly subjugated by their enemies.

16. *I will utter my judgments.* God denounced His judgments. The conquest of their cities and the destruction of the realm were the facts to which these judgments referred, and these facts prove that the threatening was fulfilled. *Worshipped the works of their own hands.* Idolatry was the source of all their wickedness, and was the cause of their desolations.

17. *Gird up thy loins.* Take courage and be ready, lest I confound you; take courage and be resolute, *pen*, lest by their opposition you be terrified and confounded. God is often represented as doing or causing to be done what He only permits or suffers to be done. Or, Do not fear them; I will not suffer you to be confounded.

18. *I have made thee this day a defenced city, and an iron pillar, and brazen walls.* Though you shall be exposed to persecutions and various indignities, they shall not prevail against you. To their attacks you shall be as an impregnable city, as unshaken as an iron pillar, and as imperishable as a wall of brass. The issue

MATTHEW HENRY

of brass; he sallies out upon the enemy in reproofs and threatenings, and *keeps them in awe*. They set upon him on every side; the kings and princes batter him with their power, the priests thunder against him with their church-censures, and *the people of the land* shoot their arrows at him, even slanderous and bitter words; but he shall keep his ground and shall still be a curb upon them (*v.* 19): *They shall fight against thee, but they shall not prevail to destroy thee, for I am with thee to deliver thee.*

JAMIESON, FAUSSET, BROWN

walls—*plural,* to express the *abundant* strength to be given him. DE ROSSI'S MSS. read *singular,* "wall." **people of the land**—the general masses, as distinguished from the princes and priests.

ADAM CLARKE

proved the truth of this promise; he outlived all their insults, and saw Jerusalem destroyed, and his enemies, and the enemies of his Lord, carried into captivity. Instead of *chomoth, walls,* many MSS. and editions read *chomath,* "a wall," which corresponds with the singular nouns preceding.

19. *They shall not prevail against thee.* Because I am determined to defend and support you against all your enemies.

MATTHEW HENRY — CHAPTER 2

Verses 1–8

I. A command given to Jeremiah to carry a message from God to the inhabitants of Jerusalem. Let a minister carefully compare what he has to deliver with the word of God, and see that it agrees with it, that he may be able to say, not only, *The Lord sent me*, but, He sent me to *speak this*. He must go from Anathoth, where he lived in a pleasant retirement, and in the study of the law, and make his appearance at Jerusalem, that noisy city, and *cry in their ears*: "Cry aloud, that all may hear. Go close to them, and *cry in the ears* of those that have stopped their ears."

II. The message he was commanded to deliver. He must upbraid them with their horrid ingratitude in forsaking a God who had been of old so kind to them.

1. God here puts them in mind of the favours he had of old bestowed upon them, when they were first formed into a people (*v.* 2): *"I remember for thy sake*, and I would have thee to remember it, and improve the remembrance of it for thy good; I cannot forget *the kindness of thy youth and the love of thy espousals.*" This may be understood of the kindness they had for God; it was not such indeed as they had any reason to boast of, yet God is pleased to mention it, for, though it was but little love that they showed him, he took it kindly. When *they believed the Lord and his servant Moses*, when they *sang God's praise at the Red Sea*, when at the foot of Mount Sinai they promised, *All that the Lord shall say unto us we will do and will be obedient*, then was the *kindness of their youth and the love of their espousals.* When they seemed so forward for God he said, *Surely they are my people*, and will be faithful to me, *children that will not lie.* In two things appeared the *kindness of their youth*: (1) That they followed the direction of the pillar of cloud and fire in the wilderness; and for forty years *went after God in the wilderness*, and trusted him to provide for them, though it was *a land that was not sown.* This God took kindly. Thus, though Christ often chid his disciples, yet he commended them, at parting, for continuing with him, Luke xxii. 28. (2) That they set up the tabernacle among them. Israel *was then holiness to the Lord.* Thus they began in the spirit, and God puts them in mind of it, that they might be ashamed of ending *in the flesh.*

Or it may be understood of God's kindness to them; of that he afterwards speaks largely. *When Israel was a child, then I loved him*, Hos. xi. 1. [1] God appropriated them to himself. They were the *first fruits of his increase*, the first constituted church he had in the world; but the full harvest was to be gathered from among the Gentiles. [2] Having espoused them, he espoused their cause, and became an *enemy to their enemies*, Exod. xxiii. 22. Whoever offered any injury to the people of God did so at their peril. He had in a special manner a controversy with those that attempted to debauch them and draw them off from being *holiness to the Lord*; witness his *quarrel with the Midianites about the matter of Peor*, Num. xxv. 17, 18. [3] He *brought them out of Egypt* with a high hand and great terror (Deut. iv. 34), and yet with a kind hand and great tenderness led them through a vast howling wilderness (*v.* 6). In that darksome valley they walked forty years; but *God was with them*; and even there God *prepared a table for them* (Ps. xxiii. 4, 5), gave them bread out of the clouds and drink out of the rocks. All God's spiritual Israel must own their obligations to him for a safe conduct through the wilderness of this world, no less dangerous to the soul than that was to the body. [4] At length he settled them in Canaan (*v.* 7): *I brought you into a plentiful country.* They did *eat the fruit thereof* and the *goodness thereof.* I brought you *into a land of Carmel* (so the word is); Carmel was a place of extraordinary fruitfulness, and Canaan was as one great fruitful field, Deut. viii. 7. [5] God gave them the means of knowledge and grace, and communion with him; this is implied, *v.* 8.

2. He upbraids them with their ingratitude (*v.* 4). (1) He challenges them to produce any instance of his being unjust and unkind to them. He puts it fairly to them to show cause for their deserting him

JAMIESON, FAUSSET, BROWN — CHAPTER 2

Vss. 1-37. EXPOSTULATION WITH THE JEWS, REMINDING THEM OF THEIR FORMER DEVOTEDNESS, AND GOD'S CONSEQUENT FAVOR, AND A DENUNCIATION OF GOD'S COMING JUDGMENTS FOR THEIR IDOLATRY. Probably in the thirteenth year of the reign of Josiah (ch. 1:2; cf. ch. 3:6, *"also . . . in . . . days of Josiah"*). The warning not to rely as they did on Egypt (vs. 18), was in accordance with Josiah's policy, who took part with Assyria and Babylon against Egypt (II Kings 23:29). Jeremiah, doubtless, supported the reformation begun by Josiah, in the previous year (the twelfth of his reign), and fully carried out in the eighteenth. **2. cry**—proclaim. **Jerusalem**—the headquarters and center of their idolatry; therefore addressed first.

thee—rather, "I remember *in regard to thee"* [HENDERSON]; *for thee* [MAURER]. **kindness of thy youth**—not so much Israel's kindness towards God, as *the kindness which Israel experienced from God* in their early history (cf. Ezek. 16:8, 22, 60; 23:3, 8, 19; Hos. 2:15). For Israel from the first showed perversity rather than *kindness* towards God (cf. Exod. 14:11, 12; 15:24; 32:1-7, etc.). The greater were God's favors to them from the first, the fouler was their ingratitude in forsaking Him (vss. 3, 5, etc.). **espousals**—the intervals between Israel's betrothal to God at the exodus from Egypt, and the formal execution of the marriage contract at Sinai. EWALD takes the "kindness" and "love" to be Israel's towards God at first (Exod. 19:8; 24:3; 35:20-29; 36:5; Josh. 24:16-17). But cf. Deuteronomy 32:16, 17; and Ezekiel 16:5, 6, 15, 22 ("days of thy *youth*") implies that the *love* here meant was on God's side, not Israel's. **thou wentest after me in . . . wilderness**—the next act of God's love, His leading them in the desert without needing any strange god, such as they since worshipped, to help Him (Deut. 2:7; 32:12). Verse 6 shows it is *God's* "leading" of them, not *their* following after God in the wilderness, which is implied. **3. holiness unto the Lord**—i.e., was *consecrated to* the service of *Jehovah* (Exod. 19:5, 6). They thus answered to the motto on their high priest's breastplate, "Holiness to the Lord" (Deut. 7:6; 14:2, 21).

first-fruits of his increase—i.e., of *Jehovah's* produce. As the *first-fruits* of the whole *produce* of the land were devoted to God (Exod. 23:19; Num. 18:12, 13), so Israel was devoted to Him as the first-fruit and representative nation among all nations. So the spiritual Israel (Jas. 1:18; Rev. 14:4). **devour**—carrying on the image of *first-fruits* which were *eaten* before the Lord by the priests as the Lord's representatives; all who *ate* (injured) Jehovah's first-fruits (Israel), contracted guilt: e.g., Amalek, the Amorites, etc., were extirpated for their guilt towards Israel. **shall come**—rather, "came."

4. Jacob . . . Israel—the whole nation. **families**—(*Note,* ch. 1:15). Hear God's word not only collectively, but individually (Zech. 12:12-14).

ADAM CLARKE — CHAPTER 2

2. *I remember thee.* The *youth* here refers to their infant political state when they came out of Egypt; they just then began to be a people.

Their *espousals* refer to their receiving the law at Mount Sinai, which they solemnly accepted, Exod. xxiv. 6-8, and which acceptance was compared to a betrothing or espousal.

Wentest after me. Received My law, and were obedient to it. The kindness was that which God showed them by taking them to be His people, not their kindness to Him.

3. *Israel was holiness unto the Lord.* Fully consecrated to His service.

The firstfruits of his increase. They were as wholly the Lord's as the firstfruits were the property of the priests according to the law, Num. xviii. 13.

All that devour him shall offend. As they were betrothed to the Lord, they were considered His especial property; they therefore who injured them were considered as laying violent hands on the property of God.

MATTHEW HENRY

(*v.* 5): "*What iniquity have your fathers found in me*, or you either? Have you found God a hard master? You that have forsaken the ordinances of God, can you say that it was because they were a wearisome service. The disappointments you have met with were owing to yourselves, not to God. The yoke of his commandments is easy, and in the *keeping of them there is great reward.*" Though he afflicts us, he does us no wrong; all the iniquity is in our ways. (2) He charges them with being unjust and unkind to him notwithstanding. "*They have gone from me*, nay, they have gone *far from me.*" *They have walked after vanity*, that is, idolatry. They had with idolatry introduced all manner of wickedness. When they entered into the good land which God gave them they defiled it (*v.* 7), by defiling themselves. It was God's land, a holy land, Immanuel's land; but they *made it an abomination.* Having forsaken God they had no thoughts of returning to him again. Neither the people nor the priests made any enquiry after him, nor expressed any desire to recover his favour. The *people* said not, *Where is the Lord?* (*v.* 6). The *priests* said not, *Where is the Lord?* (*v.* 8). Those who should have instructed the people in the knowledge of God took no care to get the knowledge of him themselves. The scribes, who *handled the law*, did not know God nor his will. The pastors, who should have kept the flock from transgressing, were themselves ring-leaders in transgression: *They have transgressed against me.* The pretenders to prophecy prophesied by Baal, to confront the Lord's prophets.

Verses 9–13

The prophet shows their unparalleled fickleness and folly (*v.* 9): *I will yet plead with you.* Before God punishes sinners he pleads with them, to bring them to repentance. Now he pleads with those who persisted in that *vain conversation received by tradition from their fathers*, and *with their children's children*, that is, with all that in every age tread in their steps.

I. He shows that they acted contrary to the usage of all nations. Their neighbours were more firm and faithful to their false gods than they were to the true God. Let them survey the present state of the isles of Chittim, Greece, and the European islands, the countries that were more polite and learned, and of Kedar; and they should not find an instance of a nation that had *changed their gods.* Such a veneration had they for their gods, that though they were gods of wood and stone they would not change them for gods of silver and gold, no, not for the living and true God. *We praise them not.* But it may well be urged, to the reproach of Israel, that they, who were the only people that had no cause to change their God, were yet the only people that had changed him. The zeal and constancy of idolaters should shame Christians out of their coldness and inconstancy.

II. He shows that they acted contrary to the dictates of common sense, but changed for the worse, and made a bad bargain for themselves. 1. They parted from a God who made them truly glorious, for his glory had often appeared on their tabernacle. 2. They closed with gods that could do them no good, gods that *do not profit* their worshippers. Heaven itself is here called upon to stand amazed at the sin and folly of these apostates from God (*v.* 12, 13): *Be astonished, O you heavens! at this.* The meaning is that the conduct of this people towards God was, (1) Such as we may well wonder at, that ever men, who pretend to reason, should do a thing so very absurd. (2) Such as we ought to have a holy indignation at as impious, and a high affront to our Maker. "*My people*, whom I have taught, *have committed two* great evils, ingratitude and folly; they have acted contrary both to their duty and to their interest. *They have forsaken me, the fountain of living waters*, in whom they have an abundant and constant supply." God is their *fountain of life*, Ps. xxxvi. 9. There is in him an all-sufficiency of grace and strength; all our springs are in him. He has been to us a *fountain of living-waters*, over-flowing, ever-flowing, in the gifts of his favour. They have cheated themselves. They forsook *their own mercies* for lying vanities. They took a great deal of pains to *hew themselves out cisterns*, but they proved *broken cisterns*, so that they could *hold no water.* When they came to quench their thirst there they found nothing but mud and mire, and the filthy sediments of a standing lake. Such idols were to their worshippers. If we make an idol of any creature—wealth, or pleasure, or honour—if we make it our joy and love, we shall find it a cistern, which we take a great deal of pains to hew out and fill, and at the best it will hold but a little water, and that dead and flat. It is a broken cistern, that cracks in hot weather, so that the water is lost when we have most need of it, Job vi. 15. Let us therefore cleave to the Lord, he has *the words of eternal life.*

JAMIESON, FAUSSET, BROWN

5. iniquity—*wrong* done to them (Isa. 5:4; Mic. 6:3; cf. Deut. 32:4). **walked after vanity**—contrasted with "*walkest after me* in the wilderness" (vs. 2): then *I* was their guide in the barren desert; now they take *idols* as their guides. **vanity . . . vain**—An idol is not only *vain* (impotent and empty), but *vanity* itself. Its worshippers acquire its character, becoming *vain* as it is (Deut. 7:26; Ps. 115:8). A people's character never rises above that of its gods, which are its "better nature" [BACON] (II Kings 17:15; Jonah 2:8). **6. Neither said they, Where . . .**—The very words which *God* uses (Isa. 63:9, 11, 13), when, as it were, reminding Himself of His former acts of love to Israel as a ground for interposing in their behalf again. When *they* would not say, Where is Jehovah, etc., *God Himself* at last said it for them (cf. *Note*, vs. 2, above). **deserts . . . pits**—The desert between Mount Sinai and Palestine abounds in chasms and pits, in which beasts of burden often sink down to the knees. "Shadow of death" refers to the *darkness* of the caverns amidst the rocky precipices (Deut. 8:15; 32:10). **7. plentiful**—lit., a land of Carmel, or well-cultivated land: a garden land, in contrast to the "land of deserts" (vs. 6). **defiled**—by idolatries (Judg. 2:10-17; Ps. 78:58, 59; 106:38). **you . . . ye**—change to the second person from the third, "they" (vs. 6), in order to bring home the guilt to the living generation. **8.** The three leading classes, whose very office under the theocracy was to lead the people to God, disowned Him in the same language as the nation at large, "Where is the Lord?" (See vs. 6). The **priests**—whose office it was to expound the law (Mal. 2:6, 7). **handle**—are occupied with the law as the subject of their profession. **pastors**—civil, not religious: princes (ch. 3:15), whose duty it was to tend their people. **prophets**—who should have reclaimed the people from their apostasy, encouraged them in it by pretended oracles from Baal, the Phœnician false god. **by Baal**—in his name and by his authority (cf. ch. 11:21). **walked after things . . . not profit**—answering to, "walked after *vanity*," i.e., idols (vs. 5; cf. vs. 11; Hab. 2:18). **9. yet plead**—viz., by inflicting still further judgments on you. **children's children**—Three MSS. and JEROME omit "children's"; they seem to have thought it unsuitable to read "children's children," when "children" had not preceded. But it is designedly so written, to intimate that the final judgment on the nation would be suspended *for* many generations [HORSLEY]. (Cf. Ezek. 20:35, 36; Mic. 6:2). **10. pass over the isles**—rather, "cross over to the isles." **Chittim . . . Kedar**—i.e., the heathen nations, *west* and *east*. Go where you will, you cannot find an instance of any heathen nation forsaking their own for other gods. Israel alone does this. Yet the heathen gods are false gods; whereas Israel, in forsaking Me for other gods, forsake their "glory" for unprofitable idols. **Chittim**—Cyprus, colonized by Phœnicians, who built in it the city of Citium, the modern *Chitti.* Then the term came to be applied to all maritime coasts of the Mediterranean, especially Greece (Num. 24:24; Isa. 23:1; Dan. 11:30). **Kedar**—descended from Ishmael; the Bedouins and Arabs, east of Palestine. **11. glory**—Jehovah, the glory of Israel (Ps. 106:20; Rom. 1:23). The Shekinah, or cloud resting on the sanctuary, was the symbol of "the glory of the Lord" (I Kings 8:11; cf. Rom. 9:4). The golden calf was intended as an image of the true God (cf. Exod. 32:4, 5), yet it is called an "idol" (Acts 7:41). It (like Roman Catholic images) was a violation of the *second* commandment, as the heathen multiplying of gods is a violation of the *first.* **not profit**—(vs. 8.) **12.** Impassioned personification (Isa. 1:2). **horribly afraid**—rather, "be horrified." **be . . . very desolate**—rather, "be exceedingly aghast" at the monstrous spectacle. Lit., "to be dried up," or "devastated," (places devastated have such an unsightly look) [MAURER]. **13. two evils**—not merely *one* evil, like the idolaters who know no better; besides *simple* idolatry, My people *add* the sin of forsaking the true God whom they have known; the heathen, though having the sin of idolatry, are free from the further sin of changing the true God for idols (vs. 11). **forsaken me**—The *Hebrew* collocation brings out the only living God into more prominent contrast with idol nonentities. "*Me* they have forsaken, the Fountain," etc. (ch. 17:13; Ps. 36:9; John 4:14). **broken cisterns**—tanks for rain water, common in the East, where wells are scarce. The tanks not only cannot give forth an ever-flowing fresh supply as fountains can, but cannot even retain the water poured into them; the stonework within being broken, the earth drinks up the collected water. So, in general, all earthly,

ADAM CLARKE

6. *Through the wilderness.* Egypt was the house of their bondage: the *desert* through which they passed after they came out of Egypt was a place where the means of life were not to be found, where no one family could subsist, much less a company of 600,000 men. God mentions these things to show that it was by the bounty of an especial providence that they were fed and preserved alive. Previously to this, it was a *land that no man passed through, and where no man dwelt.* And why? Because it did not produce the means of life; it was the *shadow of death* in its appearance, and the grave to those who committed themselves to it.

7. *And I brought you into a plentiful country.* The land of Canaan. *My land.* The particular property of God, which He gave to them as an inheritance.

8. *They that handle the law.* "They that draw out the law"; they whose office it is to explain it, draw out its spiritual meanings, and show to what its testimonies refer. *The pastors also.* Kings, political and civil rulers.

9. *I will yet plead with you.* I will maintain My "process," vindicate My own conduct, and prove the wickedness of yours.

10. *The isles of Chittim.* This is the island of Cyprus, according to Josephus. *Send unto Kedar.* The name of an Arabian tribe. See if nations either near or remote, cultivated or stupid, have acted with such fickleness and ingratitude as you have done! They have retained their gods to whom they had no obligation; you have abandoned your God, to whom you owe your life, breath, and all things!

12. *Be astonished, O ye heavens.* Or, "The heavens are astonished." The original will admit either sense. The conduct of this people was so altogether bad that, among all the iniquities of mankind, neither heaven nor earth had witnessed anything so excessively sinful and profligate.

13. *Two evils.* First, they forsook God, the Fountain of life, light, prosperity, and happiness. Secondly, they hewed out broken cisterns; they joined themselves to idols, from whom they could receive neither temporal nor spiritual good! Their conduct was the excess of folly and blindness. What we call here *broken cisterns* means more properly such vessels as were ill made, not staunch, ill put together, so that the water leaked through them.

MATTHEW HENRY

Verses 14–19

The folly of forsaking God had already cost them dear, for to this were owing all the calamities their country was now groaning under.

I. Their neighbours, who were their professed enemies, prevailed against them. 1. They were enslaved and lost their liberty (*v.* 14): *Is Israel a servant?* No; *Israel is my son, my first-born*, Exod. iv. 22. They are children; they are heirs, the seed of Abraham. They were designed for dominion, not for servitude. *Why then is he spoiled* of his liberty? Why is he used as a servant, as a *home-born slave*? Why does he *make himself a slave* to his lusts, to his idols, to that which does not profit? *v.* 11. What a thing is this, that such a birthright should be sold for a mess of pottage, such a crown profaned and laid in the dust! The princes made slaves of their subjects, and masters made slaves of their servants (*ch.* xxxiv. 11), and so made their country mean and miserable, which God had made happy and honourable. The neighbouring princes and powers broke in upon them, and made some of them slaves even in their own country, and perhaps sold others for slaves into foreign countries. For *their iniquities they sold themselves*, Isa. l. 1. We may apply this spiritually. Is the soul of man a *servant*? *Is it a home-born slave?* No, it is not. Why then is it spoiled? It is because it has sold its own liberty and enslaved itself to divers lusts and passions. 2. They were impoverished and had lost their wealth. God brought them into a plentiful country (*v.* 7), but all their neighbours made a prey of it (*v.* 15): *Young lions roar aloud over him and yell.* Sometimes one potent enemy, and sometimes another, and sometimes many in confederacy, fall upon him, and triumph over him. They carry off the fruits of his land, and make that *waste*, and *burn his cities*. 3. They were abused, and insulted over, and beaten by everybody (*v.* 16): "Even *the children of Noph and Tahapanes*, despicable people, not famed for military courage nor strength, *have broken the crown of thy head.*" How calamitous the condition of Judah had been of late in the reign of Manasseh we find, 2 Chron. xxxiii. 11. 4. All this was owing to their sin (*v.* 17): *Hast thou not procured this unto thyself?* By their sinful confederacies with the nations, and conformity to them in their idolatrous customs, they had made themselves contemptible. "*Thou hast forsaken thy God at the time that he was leading thee by the way*" (so it should be read).

II. Their neighbours, their pretended friends, helped them not, and this also was owing to their sin. 1. They did in vain seek to Egypt and Assyria for help (*v.* 18): "*What hast thou to do in the way of Egypt?* Thou art for *drinking the waters of Sihor*," that is, *Nilus*. "Thou reliest upon the fair promises they make thee. At other times thou art *in the way of Assyria*, going with all speed to fetch recruits thence, and thinkest to satisfy thyself with the *waters of the river Euphrates*; what *hast thou to do* there? What wilt thou get by applying to them? They shall *help in vain*, and what thou thoughtest a river will be but a broken cistern." 2. This also was because of their sin, *v.* 19. "*Thy own wickedness shall correct thee*, and then it is impossible for them to save thee; *know and see that it is an evil thing that thou hast forsaken God*, for it is that which makes thy enemies enemies indeed, and thy friends friends in vain." Sin is *forsaking the Lord* as our God; it is the soul's alienation from him. The cause of sin is because *his fear is not in us*. Sin is an evil that has no good in it. It is *bitter*; the wages of it is death, and death is bitter. As it is in itself evil and bitter, so it has a direct tendency to make us miserable: "*Thy own wickedness shall correct thee, and thy backslidings shall reprove thee;* the punishment will so inevitably follow the sin that the sin shall itself be said to punish thee. Thy own wickedness shall convince thee and stop thy mouth for ever and thou shalt be forced to own that *the Lord is righteous.*"

Verses 20–28

I. The sin itself—idolatry. 1. They frequented the places of idol-worship (*v.* 20): "*Upon every high hill and under every green tree*, in the high places and the groves, *thou wanderest*, unsettled, and unsatisfied; but in all *playing the harlot*," spiritual whoredom, and commonly accompanied with corporal whoredom. 2. They made images for themselves, and gave divine honour to them (*v.* 26, 27); not only the common people, but even the kings and princes, the priests and prophets, were themselves so stupid as to *say to a stock*, "*Thou art my father* (that is, Thou art my god, the author of my being, to whom I owe duty and on whom I have a dependence)," and *to a stone*, to an idol made of stone, "*Thou hast* begotten me, or *brought me forth*; therefore protect me." What greater affront could men put upon God our

JAMIESON, FAUSSET, BROWN

compared with heavenly, means of satisfying man's highest wants (Isa. 55:1, 2; cf. Luke 12:33). **14. is he a home-born slave**—No. "Israel is Jehovah's *son,* even His first-born" (Exod. 4:22). Verses 16, 18, and 36, and the absence of any *express* contrast of the two parts of the nation are against EICHORN'S view, that the prophet proposes to Judah, as yet spared, the case of Israel (the ten tribes) which had been carried away by Assyria as a warning of what they might expect if they should still put their trust in Egypt. "Were Israel's ten tribes of meaner birth than Judah? Certainly not. If, then, the former fell before Assyria, what can Judah hope from Egypt against Assyria?" "Israel" is rather here the whole of the remnant still left in their own land, i.e., Judah. "How comes it to pass that the nation which once was under God's special protection (vs. 3) is now left at the mercy of the foe as a worthless slave?" The prophet sees this event *as if* present, though it was still *future* to Judah (vs. 19). **15. lions**—the Babylonian princes (ch. 4:7; cf. Amos 3:4). The disaster from the Babylonians in the fourth year of Jehoiakim's reign, and again three years later when, relying on Egypt, he revolted from Nebuchadnezzar, is here referred to (ch. 46:2; II Kings 24:1, 2). **16. Noph ... Tahapanes**—*Memphis,* capital of Lower Egypt, on the west bank of the Nile, near the pyramids of Gizeh, opposite the site of modern Cairo. *Daphne,* on the Tanitic branch of the Nile, near Pelusium, on the frontier of Egypt towards Palestine. Isaiah 30:4 contracts it, *Hanes.* These two cities, one the capital, the other that with which the Jews came most in contact, stand for the whole of Egypt. *Tahapanes* takes its name from a goddess, Tphnet [CHAMPOLLION]. *Memphis* is from *Man-nofri,* "the abode of good men"; written in *Hebrew, Moph* (Hos. 9:6), or *Noph.* The reference is to the coming invasion of Judah by Pharaoh-necho of Egypt, on his return from the Euphrates, when he deposed Jehoahaz and levied a heavy tribute on the land (II Kings 23:33-35). Josiah's death in battle with the same Pharaoh is probably included (II Kings 23:29, 30). **have broken**—rather, *shall feed down* the crown, etc., i.e., affect with the greatest ignominy, such as *baldness* was regarded in the East (ch. 48:37; II Kings 2:23). Instead of "also," translate, "even" the Egyptians, in whom thou dost trust, shall miserably disappoint thy expectation [MAURER]. Jehoiakim was twice leagued with them (II Kings 23:34, 35): when he received the crown from them, and when he revolted from Nebuchadnezzar (II Kings 24:1, 2, 7). The Chaldeans, having become masters of Asia, threatened Egypt. Judea, situated between the contending powers, was thus exposed to the inroads of the one or other of the hostile armies; and unfortunately, except in Josiah's reign, took side with Egypt, contrary to God's warnings. **17.** Lit., "Has not thy forsaking the Lord . . . procured this (calamity) to thee?" So LXX: the Masoretic accents make "this" the *subject* of the verb, leaving the *object* to be understood. "Has not this procured (*it,* i.e., the impending calamity) unto thee, that hast forsaken?" etc. (ch. 4:18). **led**—(Deut. 32:10.) **the way**—The article expresses *the right* way, *the* way *of the Lord:* viz., the moral training which they enjoyed in the Mosaic covenant. **18. now**—used in a *reasoning* sense, not of *time.* **the way of Egypt**—What hast thou to do *with the way,* i.e., with going down *to Egypt; or what ... with* going to *Assyria*? **drink ... waters**—i.e., to seek *reinvigorating aid* from them; so vss. 13 and 36; cf. "waters," meaning *numerous forces* (Isa. 8:7). **Sihor**—i.e., the *black* river, in *Greek Melas* (black), the Nile: so called from the black deposit or soil it leaves after the inundation (Isa. 23:3). The LXX identifies it with Gihon, one of the rivers of Paradise. **the river**—*Euphrates,* called by pre-eminence, *the* river; figurative for the Assyrian power. In 625 B.C., the seventeenth year of Josiah, and the fourth of Jeremiah's office, the kingdom of Assyria fell before Babylon, therefore *Assyria* is here put for *Babylon* its successor: so in II Kings 23:29; Lamentations 5:6. There was doubtless a league between Judea and Assyria (i.e., Babylon), which caused Josiah to march against Pharaoh-necho of Egypt when that king went against Babylon: the evil consequences of this league are foretold in this verse and vs. 36. **19. correct ... reprove**—rather, in the severer sense, "chastise . . . punish" [MAURER]. **backslidings**—"apostasies"; *plural,* to express the number and variety of their defections. The very confederacies they entered into were the occasion of their overthrow (Prov. 1:31; Isa. 3:9; Hos. 5:5). **know ... see**—*imperative* for *futures: Thou shalt know and see* to thy cost. **my fear**—rather, "the fear *of Me.*"

ADAM CLARKE

14. *Is Israel a servant?* Is he a slave purchased with money, or a servant born in the family? He is a son himself. If so, then, *why is he spoiled?* Not because God has not shown him love and kindness, but because he forsook God, turned to and is joined with idols.

15. *The young lions roared upon him.* The Assyrians, who have sacked and destroyed the kingdom of Israel, with a fierceness like that of pouncing upon their prey.

16. *The children of Noph and Tahapanes.* Noph and Tahapanes were two cities of Egypt, otherwise called Memphis and Daphni. It is well-known that the good king was defeated by the Egyptians, and slain in battle. Thus was the crown of Judah's head broken.

18. *What hast thou to do in the way of Egypt?* Why do you make alliances with Egypt? *To drink the waters of Sihor?* This means the Nile. See Isa. xxiii. 3. *The way of Assyria.* Why make alliances with the Assyrians? All such connections will only expedite your ruin. *To drink the waters of the river?* The Euphrates, as *nahar* or *hannahar* always means Euphrates. The country between the Tigris and Euphrates is termed to this day "the country beyond the river," i.e., Mesopotamia. Instead of cleaving to the Lord, they joined affinity and made alliances with those two nations, who were ever jealous of them and sought their ruin. Egypt was to them a broken reed instead of a staff; Assyria was a leaky cistern, from which they could derive no help.

MATTHEW HENRY

Father that has made us? When these were first made the objects of worship they were supposed to be animated by some celestial power or spirit; but by degrees the thought of this was lost. *In their imagination* the very idol was supposed to be their father, and adored accordingly. 3. They multiplied these dunghill deities endlessly (*v.* 28): *According to the number of thy cities are thy gods, O Judah!* They could not agree in the same god. One city fancied one deity and another another.

II. The proof of this. They pretended that they would acquit themselves from this guilt, they *washed themselves with nitre*, and *took much soap*, *v.* 22. They pretended that they did not worship these as gods, but as demons, or that it was not divine honour that they gave them, but civil respect; thus they sought to evade the convictions of God's word. They said, *I am not polluted, I have not gone after Baalim*, *v.* 23. Because it was done secretly, and industriously concealed (Ezek. viii. 12), they thought it could never be proved upon them. "*How canst thou* deny the fact, and *say, I have not gone after Baalim?*" "It is *imprinted deeply* and *stained* before me"; so some read it. "Though thou endeavour to wash it out, as murderers to get the stain of the blood of the person slain out of their clothes, yet it will never be got out." *See thy way in the valley* (they had worshipped idols, not only on the high hills, but in the valleys, Isa. lvii. 5, 6), in the *valley over against Beth-peor* (so some), (Deut. xxiv. 6, Num. xxv. 3), but, if it mean any particular valley, surely it is the *valley of the son of Hinnom*, for that was the place where they sacrificed their children to Moloch and which therefore witnessed against them more than any other.

III. The aggravations of this sin with which they are charged.

1. God has done great things for them, and yet they revolted from him and rebelled against him (*v.* 20): *Of old time I have broken thy yoke and burst thy bonds.* These bonds of theirs which God had loosed should have bound them for ever to him.

2. They had promised fair, but had not made good their promise: "*Thou saidst, I will not transgress.*"

3. They had wretchedly degenerated from what they were when God first formed them into a people (*v.* 21): *I had planted thee a noble vine. Israel served the Lord*, and kept close to him *all the days of Joshua, and the elders that out-lived Joshua*, Joshua xxiv. 31. The very next generation *knew not the Lord, nor the works which he had done* (Judges ii. 10), and so they were worse and worse till they became *the degenerate plants of a strange vine.*

4. They were violent and eager in the pursuit of their idolatries, and they would not be restrained either by the word of God or by his providence. They are compared to a *swift dromedary traversing her ways*, a female hunting (*v.* 23), and, to the same purport, *a wild ass used to the wilderness* (*v.* 24), not tamed by labour, and therefore very wanton, *snuffing up the wind at her pleasure*, on such an *occasion who can turn her away*? Who can hinder her from that which she lusts after? *Those that seek her* then *will not weary themselves for her*, but will have patience till she is big with young, and then *they shall find her*, and she cannot out-run them. Eager lust is a brutish thing, and those that will not be turned away are to be reckoned as brute-beasts. Let them not be looked upon as rational creatures. Idolatry is strangely intoxicating. *Ephraim is joined to idols; let him alone.* The time will come when the most fierce will be tamed; when distress and anguish come upon them, then their ears will be open to discipline.

5. They were obstinate in their sin, and, as they could not be restrained, so they would not be reformed, *v.* 25. He would certainly bring them into a miserable captivity, when they should be forced to travel barefoot, and when they would be denied fair water, so that their throat should be dried with thirst. Those that affect strange gods, and strange ways of worship, will justly be made prisoners to a strange king in a strange land. They said to those that would have persuaded them to repent and reform, *There is no hope; no*, never expect us to cast away our idols, for *we have loved strangers, and after them we will go.* But, as we must not despair of the mercy of God, but believe that sufficient for the pardon of our sins, though ever so heinous, if we repent and sue for that mercy, so neither must we despair of the grace of God, but believe that able to subdue our corruptions, though ever so strong, if we pray for and improve that grace. A man must never say *There is no hope*, as long as he is on this side hell.

6. They had shamed themselves by putting him away that would have helped them, *v.* 26–28. *As the thief is ashamed* when he is found, and brought to

JAMIESON, FAUSSET, BROWN

22. nitre—not what is now so called, viz., saltpeter; but the *natron* of Egypt, a mineral alkali, an incrustation at the bottom of the lakes, after the summer heat has evaporated the water: used for washing (cf. Job 9:30; Prov. 25:20). **soap**—potash, the carbonate of which is obtained impure from burning different plants, especially the *kali* of Egypt and Arabia. Mixed with oil it was used for washing. **marked**—deeply ingrained, indelibly marked; the *Hebrew, catham*, being equivalent to *cathab*. Others translate, "is treasured up," from the *Arabic*. MAURER from a *Syriac* root, "is polluted." **23.** (Prov. 30:12). **Baalim**—plural, to express manifold excellency: cf. *Elohim*. **see**—consider. **the valley**—viz., of Hinnom, or Tophet, south and east of Jerusalem: rendered infamous by the human sacrifices to Moloch in it (cf. ch. 19:2, 6, 13, 14; 32:35; Isa. 30: 33, *Note*).

20. I—the *Hebrew* should be pointed as the second person *feminine*, a form common in Jeremiah: "*Thou* hast broken," etc. So LXX, and the sense requires it. **thy yoke . . . bands**—the yoke and bands which I laid *on thee*, My laws (ch. 5:5). **transgress**—so the *Keri* and many MSS. read. But LXX and most authorities read, "I will not serve," i.e., obey. The sense of *English Version* is, "I broke thy yoke (in Egypt), etc., and (at that time) thou saidst, I will not trangress; whereas thou hast (since then) wandered" (from Me) (Exod. 19:8). **hill . . . green tree**—the scene of idolatries (Deut. 12: 2; Isa. 57:5, 7). **wanderest**—rather, "thou hast *bowed down* thyself" (for the act of adultery: figurative of shameless idolatry Exod. 34:15, 16; cf. Job 31:10). **21.** The same image as in Deuteronomy 32:32; Psalm 80:8, 9; Isaiah 5:1, etc. **unto me**—with respect to Me.

thou art—omit. The substantive that follows in this verse (and also that in vs. 24) is in apposition with the preceding "thou." **dromedary**—rather, a young she-camel. **traversing**—lit., "enfolding"; making its ways *complicated* by wandering hither and thither, lusting after the male. Cf. as to the Jews' spiritual lust, Hosea 2:6, 7. **24.** (Ch. 14:6; Job 39:5). "A wild ass," agreeing with "thou" (vs. 23). **at her pleasure**—rather, "in her ardor," viz., in pursuit of a male, sniffing the wind to ascertain where one is to be found [MAURER]. **occasion**—either from a *Hebrew* root, "to meet"; "her meeting (with the male for sexual intercourse), who can avert it?" Or better from an *Arabic* root: "her *heat* (sexual impulse), who can allay it?" [MAURER]. **all they**—whichever of the males desire her company [HORSLEY]. **will not weary themselves**—have no need to weary themselves in searching for her. **her month**—in the *season of the year when her sexual impulse is strongest*, she puts herself in the way of the males, so that they have no difficulty in *finding* her. **25. Withhold . . .**—i.e., abstain from incontinence; fig. for idolatry [HOUBIGANT]. **unshod . . .**—do not run so violently in pursuing lovers, as to *wear out thy shoes:* do not "thirst" so incontinently after sexual intercourse. HITZIG thinks the reference is to penances performed *barefoot* to idols, and the *thirst* occasioned by loud and continued invocations to them. **no hope**—(ch. 18:12; Isa. 57:10). "It is hopeless," i.e., I am *desperately* resolved to go on in my own course. **strangers**—i.e., laying aside the metaphor, "strange gods" (ch. 3:13; Deut. 32:16).

26. is ashamed—is *put to shame.* **thief**—(John 10:1). **Israel**—i.e., Judah (vs. 28).

ADAM CLARKE

22. *For though thou wash thee with nitre.* It should be rendered *natar* or *natron*, a substance totally different from our *nitre*. It comes from the root *nathar*, "to dissolve, loosen," because a solution of it in water is abstersive, taking out spots from clothes. It is still used in the East for the purpose of washing. *Thine iniquity is marked before me.* No washing will take out your spots; the marks of your idolatry and corruption are too deeply rooted to be extracted by any human means.

23. *See thy way in the valley.* The Valley of Hinnom, where they offered their own children to Moloch, an idol of the Ammonites.

20. *Of old time I have broken thy yoke.* It is thought by able critics that the verbs should be read in the second person singular, "Thou hast broken thy yoke, thou hast burst thy bonds"; and thus the Septuagint, the Vulgate, and the Arabic. But the Chaldee gives it a meaning which removes the difficulty: "I have broken the yoke of the people from thy neck; I have cut your bonds asunder." And when this was done, they did promise fair; for *thou saidst, I will not transgress.* But still they played *the harlot*—committed idolatrous acts in the high places, where the heathen had built their altars.

21. *I had planted thee a noble vine.* I gave you the fullest instruction, the purest ordinances, the highest privileges; and reason would that I should expect you to live suitably to such advantages. But instead of this you have become degenerate; the tree is deteriorated, and the fruit is bad.

24. *Snuffeth up the wind.* In a high fever from the inward heat felt at such times, these animals open their mouths and nostrils as wide as possible, to take in large draughts of fresh air, in order to cool them.

26. *As the thief is ashamed.* As the pilferer is confounded when he is caught in the act, so shall you, your kings, princes, priests, and prophets, be confounded, when God shall arrest you in your idolatries, and deliver you into the hands of your enemies.

MATTHEW HENRY

punishment, *so are the house of Israel ashamed,* not with a penitent shame for the sin they had been guilty of, but with a penal shame for the disappointment they met with in that sin. In their prosperity they had turned the back to God, but in the time of their trouble they will find no satisfaction but in applying to him; then *they will say, Arise, and save us.* To bring them to this shame, if so they might be brought to repentance, they are sent *to the gods whom they served,* Judges x. 14. They cried to God, *Arise, and save us.* God says of the idols, "*Let them arise, and save thee,* for thou hast no reason to expect that I should."

Verses 29–37

I. The truth of the charge was evident beyond contradiction (*v.* 29): "*Wherefore will you plead with me?* You know *you have all transgressed,* one as well as another; why then do you *quarrel with me* for contending with you?"

II. He heightens it from the consideration both of their incorrigibleness and of their ingratitude. They had been under divine rebukes of many kinds. God therein designed to bring them to repentance; but it was *in vain.* Their consciences were not awakened, nor their hearts softened. *They received no instruction* by the *correction,* were not made the better by it. They *did not receive* the correction, and so they were *smitten in vain.* They had not been wrought upon by the word of God which he had sent them in the mouth of his servants the prophets; they had killed the messengers for the sake of the message: "*Your own sword has devoured your prophets like a destroying lion*" (*v.* 31): "*O generation!*" (he speaks gently, O you men of this generation!) "*see the word of the Lord,* do not only hear it." As we are bidden to *hear the rod* (Micah vi. 9), for that has its voice, so we are bidden to *see the word,* for that has its visions, its views. It is written as with a sunbeam, so that he that runs may read it: *Have I been a wilderness to Israel, a land of darkness?* The service of God has not been either an unpleasant or an unprofitable service. God sometimes has led his people *through a wilderness* and a *land of darkness,* but he himself was then to them all that which they needed; he so fed them with manna, and led them by a pillar of fire, that it was to them a fruitful field and a land of light. They had grown intolerably insolent and imperious. They say, *We are lords; we will come no more unto thee.* It is absurd for us who are beggars to say, *We are lords,* that is, We are rich, and we will come no more to God.

III. He lays the blame of all their wickedness upon their forgetting God (*v.* 32): *They have forgotten me;* they have avoided all those things that would put them in mind of God. They had neglected him, *days without number,* time out of mind. How many days of our lives have passed without suitable remembrance of God! Who can number those empty days? They had not had such a regard to him as young ladies have to their fine clothes: *Can a maid forget her ornaments or a bride her attire?* No; they are ever and anon thinking and speaking of them.

IV. He shows them what a bad influence their sins had had upon others (*v.* 33): *Why trimmest thou thy way to seek love?* There is an allusion here to lewd women who recommend themselves by their ogling looks and gay dress, as Jezebel, who *painted her face and tired her head.* Thus they courted their neighbours into sinful confederacies with them and *taught the wicked ones their ways* of mixing God's institutions with their idolatrous customs. Those have a great deal to answer for who, by their fellowship with the unfruitful works of darkness, made wicked ones more wicked than otherwise they would be.

V. He charges them with the guilt of murder (*v.* 34): *Also in thy skirts is found the blood of the souls,* the life-blood *of the poor innocents.* The reference is to the children that were offered in sacrifice to Moloch; or it may be taken more generally for all the *innocent blood* which Manasseh shed, and with which he had *filled Jerusalem* (2 Kings xxi. 16). This blood was found *not by secret search,* not *by digging* (so the word is), but *upon all these;* it was above ground. This intimates that the guilt was avowed and barefaced.

VI. He overrules their plea of *Not guilty* (*v.* 35). *I will plead with thee,* and will convince thee of thy mistake. They conclude that God will immediately let fall his action and *his anger shall be turned from them.* This is very provoking, and God will convince them that his anger is just, and he will never cease his controversy till they, instead of justifying themselves, judge and condemn themselves.

VII. He upbraids them with the shameful disappointments they met with, in making creatures their confidence, while they made God their enemy,

JAMIESON, FAUSSET, BROWN

27. Thou art my father—(Contrast ch. 3:4; Isa. 64:8). **in . . . trouble they will say**—viz., to God (Ps. 78:34; Isa. 26:16). Trouble often brings men to their senses (Luke 15: 16-18). **23. But**—God sends them to the gods for whom they forsook Him, to see if *they* can help them (Deut. 32:37, 38; Judg. 10:14). **according to the number of thy cities**—Besides national deities, each city had its tutelary god (ch. 11:13).

29. plead with me—i.e., contend with Me for afflicting you (vss. 23, 35).

30. (Ch. 5:3; 6:29; Isa. 1:5; 9:13.) **your children**—i.e., your people, you.

your . . . sword . . . devoured . . . prophets—(II Chron. 36:16; Neh. 9:26; Matt. 23:29, 31). **31.** The *Hebrew* collocation is, "O, the generation, ye," i.e., "O ye who now live." The generation needed only to be named, to call its degeneracy to view, so palpable was it.

wilderness—in which all the necessaries of life are wanting. On the contrary, Jehovah was a never-failing source of supply for all Israel's wants in the wilderness, and afterwards in Canaan. **darkness**—lit., "darkness of Jehovah," the strongest *Hebrew* term for "darkness; the densest darkness"; cf. "land of the shadow of death" (vs. 6).

We are lords—i.e., We are our own masters. We will worship what gods we like (Ps. 12:4; 82:6). But it is better to translate from a different *Hebrew* root: "We ramble at large," without restraint pursuing our idolatrous lusts. **32.** Oriental women greatly pride themselves on their ornaments (cf. Isa. 61:10).

attire—girdles for the breast. **forgotten me**—(ch. 12:25; Hos. 8:14).

33. Why trimmest—MAURER translates, "*How skilfully* thou dost prepare thy way . . . ." But see II Kings 9:30. "Trimmest" best suits the image of one *decking* herself as a harlot. **way**—course of life. **therefore**—accordingly. Or else, "*nay,* thou hast even . . . ." **also . . . wicked ones**—*even* the wicked harlots, i.e., (laying aside the metaphor) even the Gentiles who are wicked, thou teachest to be still more so [GROTIUS].

34. Also—not only art thou polluted with idolatry. but *also* with the guilt of shedding innocent blood [MAURER]. ROSENMULLER not so well translates, "even in thy skirts . . ."; i.e., there is no part of thee (*not even thy skirts*) that is not stained with innocent blood (ch. 19:4; II Kings 21:16; Ps. 106:38). See as to innocent blood shed, not as here in honor of idols, but of *prophets* for having reproved them (vs. 30; ch. 26:20-23). **souls**—i.e., persons. **search**—I did not need to "search deep" to find proof of thy guilt; for it was "upon all these" thy skirts. Not in deep caverns didst thou perpetrate these atrocities, but openly in the vale of Hinnom and within the precincts of the temple. **35.** (Vss. 23, 29.)

ADAM CLARKE

28. *According to the number of thy cities are thy gods.* Among heathen nations every city had its tutelary deity. Judah, far sunk in idolatry, had adopted this custom.

31. *Have I been a wilderness unto Israel?* Have I ever withheld from you any of the blessings necessary for your support? *A land of darkness.* Have you, since you passed through the wilderness, and came out of the darkness of Egypt, ever been brought into similar circumstances?

We are lords. We wish to be our own masters.

32. *Can a maid forget her ornaments?* This people has not so much attachment to Me as young females have to their dress and ornaments. *Days without number.* That is, for many years; during the whole reign of Manasses, which was fifty-five years, the land was deluged with idolatry, from which the reform by good King Josiah, his grandson, had not yet purified it.

33. *Why trimmest thou thy way?* You have used a multitude of artifices to gain alliances with the neighboring idolatrous nations. *Hast thou also taught the wicked ones thy ways?* You have made even these idolaters worse than they were before.

34. *The blood of the souls of the poor innocents.* We find from the sacred history that Manasseh had filled Jerusalem with innocent blood; see 2 Kings xxi. 16 and Ezek. xxxiv. 10.

I have not found it by secret search, but upon all these. Such deeds of darkness and profligacy are found only in Israel.

35. *Because I am innocent.* They continued to assert their innocence, and therefore expected that God's judgments would be speedily removed! *I will plead with thee.* I will maintain My process, follow it up to conviction, and inflict the deserved punishment.

MATTHEW HENRY

v. 36, 37. It was a piece of spiritual idolatry that they trusted in *an arm of flesh* and their hearts *departed from the Lord. Why gaddest thou about so much to change thy way?* Those that make God their hope, and walk in continual dependence upon him, need not *gad about to change their way*; for their souls may return to him, and repose in him, as their rest. They first trusted to Assyria, and, when that proved a broken reed, they depended upon Egypt, and that proved no better. *Thou shalt be ashamed of Egypt,* which thou now trustest in, as formerly *thou wast of Assyria, who distressed them and helped them not,* 2 Chron. xxviii. 20. Thy ambassadors or envoys shall return from Egypt *disappointed*, lamenting the desperate condition of their people. Or, *Thou shalt go forth hence,* that is, into captivity in a strange land, *with thy hands upon thy head.* "And Egypt, that thou reliest on, shall not be able to prevent it nor to rescue thee out of captivity." As *there is no counsel or wisdom* that can prevail against the Lord, so there is none that can prevail without him.

CHAPTER 3

Verses 1–5

These verses open a door of hope. God wounds that he may heal.

I. How basely this people had forsaken God and gone a-whoring from him. To have admitted one strange God among them would have been bad enough, but they were insatiable in their lustings after false worships: *Thou hast played the harlot with many lovers, v.* 1. They had sought opportunity for their idolatries and had sent about to enquire for new gods: *In the high-ways hast thou sat for them. As the Arabian in the wilderness*—the *Arabian huckster* (so some), that courts customers, or the *Arabian thief* (so others), that watches for his prey. They not only polluted themselves, but *their land, with their whoredoms and with their wickedness* (*v.* 2); for it became a national sin. And yet (*v.* 3), "*Thou hadst a whore's forehead*, a brazen face of thy own." *Thou refusedest to be ashamed.* Blushing is the colour of virtue, or at least a relic of it; but those that are past shame (we say) are past hope.

II. How gently God had corrected them for their sins. He only *withheld the showers from them,* and that only one part of the year.

III. How justly God might have refused ever to receive them again; this would have been but according to the known rule of divorces, *v.* 1. *They say* (Deut. xxiv. 4), that if a woman be once put away, and be joined to *another man*, her first husband shall never take her again to be his wife; such playing fast and loose with the marriage-bond would be a horrid profanation of that ordinance and would *greatly pollute that land.*

IV. How graciously he invites them to return to him. "Though thou hast been bad, *yet return again to me,*" *v.* 1. God has not tied himself by the laws which he made for us, nor has he the peevish resentment that men have; he will be more kind to Israel than ever any injured husband was to an adulterous wife. He kindly directs them what to say to him (*v.* 4): "*Wilt thou not from this time cry unto me?* Now that thou hast been made to see thy sins (*v.* 2) and to smart for them (*v.* 3), wilt thou not now forsake them and return to me, saying, *I will go and return to my first husband, for then it was better with me than now?*" (Hos. ii. 7). He expects that they will claim relation to God, as theirs: *Wilt thou not cry unto me, My father, thou art the guide of my youth?* They will surely come towards him as a father, to beg his pardon for their undutiful behaviour to him. Or it may be taken more generally: "As *my Father*, thou *art the guide of my youth.*" Youth needs a guide. In our return to God we must thankfully remember that he *was the guide of our youth* in the way of comfort; he shall be our guide henceforward in the way of duty.

Verses 6–11

The date of this sermon was *in the days of Josiah*, who set on foot a blessed work of reformation, in which he was hearty, but the people were not sincere. The case of the two kingdoms of Israel and Judah is here compared, the *ten tribes* that revolted from the throne of David and the temple of Jerusalem and the *two tribes* that adhered to both.

I. A short account of Israel, the ten tribes. She is called *backsliding Israel* because that kingdom was first founded in an apostasy from the divine institutions, both in church and state. They had *played the harlot upon every high mountain and under every green tree* (*v.* 6), that is, they had wor-

JAMIESON, FAUSSET, BROWN

36. gaddest—runnest to and fro, now seeking help from Assyria (II Chron. 28:16-21), now from Egypt (ch. 37; 7, 8; Isa. 30:3).

37. him—Egypt. **hands upon . . . head**—expressive of mourning (II Sam. 13:19). **in them**—in those stays in which thou trustest.

CHAPTER 3

VSS. 1-25. GOD'S MERCY NOTWITHSTANDING JUDAH'S VILENESS. Contrary to all precedent in the case of adultery, Jehovah offers a return to Judah, the spiritual adulteress (vss. 1-5). A new portion of the book, ending with ch. 6. Judah worse than Israel; yet both shall be restored in the last days (vss. 6-25). **1. They say**—rather, as *Hebrew*, "saying," in agreement with "the LORD"; vs. 37 of last chapter [MAURER]. Or, it is equivalent to, "Suppose this case." Some copyist may have omitted, "The word of the LORD came to me," *saying.* **shall he return unto her**—will he take her back? It was unlawful to do so (Deut. 24:1-4). **shall not**—Should not the land be polluted if this were done? **yet return**—(vs. 22; ch. 4:1; Zech. 1:3; cf. Ezek. 16:51, 58, 60.) "Nevertheless . . ." (Isa. 50:1, *Note*). **2. high places**—the scene of idolatries which were spiritual adulteries. **In . . . ways . . . sat for them**—watching for lovers like a prostitute (Gen. 38:14, 21; Prov. 7:12; 23:28; Ezek. 16:24, 25), and like an Arab who lies in wait for travellers. The Arabs of the desert, east and south of Palestine, are still notorious as robbers. **3. no latter rain**—essential to the crops in Palestine; withheld in judgment (Lev. 26:19; cf. Joel 2:23). **whore's forehead**—(ch. 8:12; Ezek. 3:8).

4. from this time—not referring, as MICHAELIS thinks, to the reformation begun the year before, i.e., the twelfth of Josiah; it means—now at once, now at last. **me**—contrasted with the "stock" whom they had heretofore called on as "father" (ch. 2:27; Luke 15:18). **thou art**—rather, "thou wast." **guide of . . . youth**—i.e., husband (ch. 2:2; Prov. 2:17; Hos. 2:7, 15). *Husband* and *father* are the two most endearing of ties. **5. he**—"thou," the second person, had preceded. The change to the third person implies a putting away of God to a *greater distance* from them; instead of repenting and forsaking their idols, they merely deprecate the continuance of their *punishment.* Verse 12 and Psalm 103:9, answer their question in the event of their penitence. **spoken and**—rather (God's reply to them), "Thou hast spoken (thus), *and yet* (all the while) thou hast done evil . . . ." **as thou couldest**—with all thy might; with incorrigible persistency [CALVIN]. **6.** From here to ch. 6:30, is a new discourse, delivered in Josiah's reign. It consists of two parts, the former extending to ch. 4:3, in which he warns Judah from the example of Israel's doom, and yet promises Israel final restoration; the latter a threat of Babylonian invasion; as Nabopolassar founded the Babylonian empire, 625 B.C., the seventeenth of Josiah, this prophecy is perhaps not earlier than that date (ch. 4:5, etc.; 5:14, etc.; 6:1, etc.; 22); and probably not later than the second thorough reformation in the eighteenth year of the same reign. **backsliding**—lit., apostasy; not merely *apostate*, but *apostasy itself*, the essence of it (vss. 14, 22).

ADAM CLARKE

36. *Why gaddest thou about?* When they had departed from the Lord, they sought foreign alliances for support. (1) The Assyrians, 2 Chron. xxviii. 13-21; but they injured instead of helping them. (2) The Egyptians; but in this they were utterly disappointed, and were ashamed of their confidence. See chap. xxxvii. 7-8, for the fulfilment of this prediction.

37. *Thou shalt go forth from him, and thine hands upon thine head.* The hand being placed on the head was the evidence of deep sorrow, occasioned by utter desolation. See the case of Tamar, when ruined and abandoned by her brother Amnon, 2 Sam. xiii. 19.

CHAPTER 3

1. *If a man put away his wife.* It was ever understood, by the law and practice of the country, that if a woman were divorced by her husband, and became the wife of another man, the first husband could never take her again. Now Israel had been married unto the Lord, joined in solemn covenant to Him to worship and serve Him only. Israel turned from following Him, and became idolatrous. On this ground, considering idolatry as a *spiritual whoredom*, and the precept and practice of the law to illustrate this case, Israel could never more be restored to the divine favor. But God, this first Husband, in the plenitude of His mercy, is willing to receive this adulterous spouse, if she will abandon her idolatries and return unto Him. And this and the following chapters are spent in affectionate remonstrances and loving exhortations addressed to these sinful people, to make them sensible of their own sin, and God's tender mercy in offering to receive them again into favor.

2. *As the Arabian in the wilderness.* They were as fully intent on the practice of their idolatry as the Arab in the desert is in lying in wait to plunder the caravans.

3. *There hath been no latter rain.* The former rain, which prepared the earth for tillage, fell in the beginning of November, or a little sooner; and the latter rain fell in the middle of April, after which there was scarcely any rain during the summer.

4. *Wilt thou not . . . cry unto me, My father?* Will you not allow Me to be your Creator and Preserver, and cease thus to acknowledge idols?

5. *Will he reserve his anger for ever?* Why should not wrath be continued against you, as you continue transgression against the Lord?

6. *The Lord said also unto me in the days of Josiah the king.* This is a new discourse, and is supposed to have been delivered after the eighteenth year of the reign of Josiah. Here the prophet shows the people of Judah the transgressions, idolatry, obstinacy, and punishment of their brethren, the ten tribes, whom he calls to return to the Lord, with the most gracious promises of restoration to their own country, their reunion with their brethren of Judah, and every degree of prosperity in consequence. He takes occasion also to show the Jews how much more culpable they were than the Israelites, because they practiced the same iniquities while they had the punishment and ruin of the others before their eyes. He therefore exhorts them to return to God with all their hearts, that they might not fall into the same condemnation.

MATTHEW HENRY

shipped other gods in their high places and groves. God by his prophets had invited and encouraged them to repent and reform (*v.* 7): "*After she had done all these things*, for which she might justly have been abandoned, yet *I said* unto her, *Turn thou unto me* and I will receive thee." God sent his prophets among them, to call them to *return to him*, to the worship of him only, not insisting so much upon their return to the house of David, but pressing their return to the house of Aaron. We read not that Elijah, that great reformer, ever mentioned their return to the house of David. Notwithstanding this, they had persisted in their idolatries: *But she returned not*, and God *saw it*, *v.* 7, 8. He had therefore given them into the hands of their enemies (*v.* 8): *When I saw* (so it may be read) *that for all the actions wherein she had committed adultery I must dismiss her, I gave her a bill of divorce*. He scattered all their synagogues and the schools of the prophets and excluded them from laying any further claim to the covenant made with their fathers.

II. The case of Judah, the kingdom of the two tribes. She is called *treacherous sister Judah*, a sister because descended from the same common stock, Abraham and Jacob; but, as Israel had the character of a *backslider*, so Judah is called *treacherous*, because, though she professed to keep close to God when Israel had backslidden (she adhered to the kings and priests that were of God's own appointing), yet she proved treacherous. Israel's captivity was intended for Judah's admonition; but it had not the designed effect. Judah thought herself safe because she had Levites to be her priests and sons of David to be her kings. She *defiled the land*, and made it an abomination to God; for she *committed adultery with stones and stocks*, with the basest idols, those made of *wood and stone*. In the reigns of Manasseh and Amon, all the country was corrupted. God tried whether they would be good in a good reign, but the evil disposition was still the same: *They returned not to me with their whole heart, but feignedly*, *v.* 10. Josiah went further in destroying idolatry than the best of his predecessors had done, and he *turned to the Lord with all his heart and with all his soul* (2 Kings xxiii. 25). The people were forced to an external compliance with him (2 Chron. xxxiv. 32, xxxv. 17); but they were not sincere in it, nor were their *hearts right with God*. For this reason God at that very time said, *I will remove Judah out of my sight, as I removed Israel* (2 Kings xxiii. 27). I know no religion without sincerity.

III. The case of these sister kingdoms is compared, and of the two Judah was the worse (*v.* 11). This comparative justification will stand Israel in little stead; what will it avail us to say, *We are not so bad as others*, when yet we are not really good ourselves? Judah was in two respects worse than Israel: 1. More was expected from Judah than from Israel; Judah vilified a more sacred profession, and falsified a more solemn promise, than Israel did. 2. Judah might have taken warning by the ruin of Israel and would not.

Verses 12–19

There is a great deal of gospel in these verses. The prophet is directed to *proclaim these words towards the north*, for they are a call to backsliding Israel, the ten tribes that were carried captive into Assyria, which lay north from Jerusalem. That way he must look to upbraid the men of Judah with their obstinacy in refusing to answer the calls given them. *Backsliding Israel* will sooner accept of mercy, and have the benefit of it, than *treacherous Judah*. And perhaps the proclaiming of these words towards the north looks as far forward as the *preaching of repentance and remission of sins unto all nations, beginning at Jerusalem*, Luke xxiv. 47.

I. Here is an invitation given to *backsliding Israel*, and in them to the backsliding Gentiles, to *return unto God*, the God from whom they had revolted (*v.* 12): *Return, thou backsliding Israel*. And again (*v.* 14): "*Turn, O backsliding children!* Come back to that good way, out of which you have turned aside." They are encouraged to return. "You have incurred God's displeasure, but return to me, and *I will not cause my anger to fall upon you*." They are directed how to return (*v.* 13): "*Only acknowledge thy iniquity*, own thyself in a fault and thereby take shame to thyself and give glory to God." This will aggravate the condemnation of sinners, that the terms of pardon and peace were brought so low, and yet they would not come up to them. *If the prophet had told thee to do some great thing wouldst thou not have done it? How much more when he says, Only acknowledge thy iniquity?* (2 Kings v. 13). We must own our actual sins: "*That thou hast transgressed against the Lord thy God*, hast affronted him and

JAMIESON, FAUSSET, BROWN

7. I said—(II Kings 17:13). **sister**—(Ezek. 16:46; 23:2, 4).

8. I saw that, though (whereas) it was for this very reason (namely), because backsliding (apostate) Israel had committed adultery I had put her away (II Kings 17:6, 18), and given her a bill of divorce, yet Judah, etc. (Ezek. 23: 11, etc.). **bill of divorce**—lit., "a writing of *cuttings* off." The *plural* implies the completeness of the severance. The use of this metaphor here, as in the former discourse (vs. 1), implies a close connection between the discourses. The epithets are characteristic; Israel "apostate" (as the *Hebrew* for "backsliding" is better rendered); Judah, not as yet utterly *apostate*, but *treacherous* or *faithless*. **also**—herself also, like Israel. **9. it**—Some take this verse of *Judah*, to whom the end of vs. 8 refers. But vs. 10 puts *Judah* in contrast to *Israel* in this verse. "Yet for all this," referring to the sad example of *Israel;* if vs. 9 referred to *Judah*, "she" would have been written in vs. 10, not "Judah." Translate, "It (the putting away of Israel) had come to pass through . . . whoredom; and (i.e., for) she (Israel) had defiled the land" etc. [MAURER]. *English Version*, however, *may* be explained to refer to *Israel*. **lightness**—"infamy." [EWALD.] MAURER not so well takes it from the *Hebrew* root, "voice," "fame." **10. yet**—notwithstanding the lesson given in Israel's case of the fatal results of apostasy. **not . . . whole heart**—The reformation in the eighteenth year of Josiah was not thorough on the part of the people, for at his death they relapsed into idolatry (II Chron. 34:33; Hos. 7:14).

11. justified herself—has been made to appear almost just (i.e., comparatively innocent) by the surpassing guilt of Judah, who adds hypocrisy and treachery to her sin; and who had the example of Israel to warn her, but in vain (cf. Ezek. 16:51; 23:11). **more than**—in comparison with. **12. Go**—not actually; but

12. Go—not actually; but turn and proclaim towards the north (Media and Assyria, where the ten tribes were located by Tiglath-pileser and Shalmaneser, II Kings 15:29; 17:6; 18:9, 11).

Return . . . backsliding—*Hebrew, Shubah, Meshubah*, a play on sounds. In order to excite Judah to godly jealousy (Rom. 11:14), Jehovah addresses the exiled ten tribes of Israel with a loving invitation.

cause . . . anger to fall—lit., I will not let fall My countenance (cf. Gen. 4:5, 6; Job 29:3), i.e., I will not *continue* to frown on you. **keep**—"anger" is to be supplied (*Note*, vs. 5). **13. Only acknowledge**—(Deut. 30:1, 3; Prov. 28:13.)

ADAM CLARKE

7. *And I said.* By the prophets Elijah, Elisha, Hosea, Amos; for all these prophesied to that rebellious people, and exhorted them to return to the Lord.

8. *I had put her away.* Given them up into the hands of the Assyrians.

9. *The lightness of her whoredom.* The grossness of her idolatry: worshipping objects the most degrading, with rites the most impure.

11. *Backsliding Israel hath justified herself more.* She was less offensive in My eyes, and more excusable, than treacherous Judah. So it is said, Luke xviii. 14, the humbled publican went down to his house justified rather than the boasting Pharisee.

12. *Proclaim these words toward the north.* The countries where the ten tribes were then in captivity, Mesopotamia, Assyria, Media, see 2 Kings xvii. 6; these lay north of Judea. How tender and compassionate are the exhortations in this and the following verses! Could these people believe that God had sent the prophet and yet prefer the land of their bondage to the blessings of freedom in their own country, and the approbation of their God?

MATTHEW HENRY

offended him." We must own the multitude of our transgressions: "That *thou hast scattered thy ways to the strangers*, run hither and thither in pursuit of thy idols, *under every green tree.* "You have not obeyed my voice; acknowledge that, and let that humble you more than anything else."

II. Here are precious promises made to these backsliding children, if they do return, which were in part fulfilled in the return of the Jews out of their captivity, but the prophecy is to have its full accomplishment in the gospel church, and the gathering together of *the children of God that were scattered abroad*: "Return, for, though you are backsliders, yet you are children; though a treacherous wife, yet a wife, for *I am married to you* (*v.* 14) and will not disown the relation." Thus God remembers his covenant with their fathers, Lev. xxvi. 42.

1. He promises to gather them together from all places whither they are dispersed and scattered abroad, John xi. 52, *I will take you, one of a city, and two of a family*, or clan; *and I will bring you to Zion, v.* 14. Of the many that have backslidden from God there are but few that return to him—*one of a city and two of a country.* Of those few, though dispersed, yet not one shall be lost. Though there be but *one in a city*, God will find out that one. God's chosen, scattered all the world over, shall be brought to *the gospel church*, that Mount Zion, the heavenly Jerusalem, that holy hill on which Christ reigns.

2. He promises to set those over them that shall be every way blessings to them (*v.* 15): *I will give you pastors after my heart.* (1) When a church is gathered it must be governed. "*I will bring them to Zion* to be under discipline, not as wild beasts, but as sheep, under the direction of a shepherd. *I will give them pastors*, that is, both magistrates and ministers." (2) It is well with a people when their pastors are *after God's own heart*, who shall make his will their rule in all their administrations, who rule for him, and, as they are capable, rule like him. (3) Those are pastors after God's own heart who feed the flock, not *fleece the flocks*, but who *feed them with wisdom and understanding.* Those who are not only pastors, but teachers, must feed them with the word of God, which is able to make us wise to salvation.

3. He promises that there shall be no more occasion for the *ark of the covenant*, which had been the token of God's presence with them; that shall be set aside (*v.* 16): *When you shall be multiplied and increased in the land*, when the kingdom of the Messiah shall be set up, then *they shall say no more, The ark of the covenant of the Lord*, because they shall have a pure spiritual way of worship set up, in which the whole ceremonial law shall be set aside, for Christ, the truth of all those types, exhibited to us in the word and sacraments of the New Testament, will be to us instead of all. But in the gospel temple Christ *is the ark*; he is the mercy-seat; and it is the spiritual presence of God in his ordinances that we are now to expect. Many expressions are here used concerning the setting aside of the ark, that it shall not *come to mind*, that they *shall not remember it*, that they shall *not visit it*, that none of these things shall be *any more done*; for the *true worshippers shall worship the Father in spirit and in truth*, John iv. 24.

4. He promises that the gospel church, here called *Jerusalem*, shall become eminent, *v.* 17. Two things shall make it famous: (1) God's special residence and dominion in it. It shall be called, *The throne of the Lord*—of his glory, of *his government, and his grace.* (2) The accession of the Gentiles to it. *All the nations shall* become subjects to that *throne of the Lord* which is there set up.

5. He promises that there shall be a wonderful reformation wrought in the church: *They shall not walk any more after the imagination of their evil hearts.* They shall not live as they list, but live by rules, according to the will of God. See what leads in sin—*the imagination of our own evil hearts*; sin is *walking after* that imagination, being governed by fancy and humour; converting grace takes us off from walking after *our own inventions* and brings us to be governed by religion and right reason.

6. That Judah and Israel shall be happily united in one body, *v.* 18. They were so in their return out of captivity and their settlement again in Canaan. This happy coalescence between Israel and Judah in Canaan was a type of the uniting of Jews and Gentiles in the gospel church, when, all enmities being slain, they should become one *sheepfold under one shepherd.*

III. Difficulty in the way of all this mercy.

1. God asks, *How shall I* do this for thee? Not as if God showed favour with reluctancy, but we are utterly unworthy of his favours, there is nothing in us to deserve them. How should we who are so mean and weak, so worthless and unworthy, and so provoking, ever be *put among the children*? To those

JAMIESON, FAUSSET, BROWN

scattered thy ways . . .—(ch. 2:25). **Not merely the** calves at Bethel, but the idols in every direction, were the objects of their worship (Ezek. 16:15, 24, 25).

14. I am married—lit., I am Lord, i.e., husband to you (so ch. 31:32; cf. Hos. 2:19, 20; Isa. 54: 5). GESENIUS, following the LXX version of ch. 31:32, and Paul's quotation of it (Heb. 8:9), translates, "I have *rejected* you"; so the corresponding *Arabic*, and the idea of *lordship*, may pass into that of *looking down upon*, and so *rejecting*. But LXX in *this* passage translates, "I will be Lord over you." And the "for" has much more force in *English Version* than in that of GESENIUS. The *Hebrew* hardly admits the rendering *though* HENGSTENBERG]. **take you one of a city**—Though but *one or two* Israelites were in a (foreign) city, they shall not be forgotten; *all* shall be restored (Amos 9:9). So, in the spiritual Israel, God gathers one convert here, another there, into His Church; not the least one is lost (Matt. 18:14; Rom. 11:5; cf. ch. 24:40, 41). **family**—a clan or tribe. **15. pastors**—not religious, but civil rulers, as Zerubbabel, Nehemiah (ch. 23:4; 2:8).

16. they shall say no more—The Jews shall no longer glory in the possession of the ark; it shall not be missed, so great shall be the blessings of the new dispensation. The throne of the Lord, *present Himself,* shall eclipse and put out of mind the ark of the covenant and the mercy seat between the cherubim, God's former throne. The ark, containing the two tables of the law, disappeared at the Babylonian captivity, and was not restored to the second temple, implying that the symbolical "glory" was to be superseded by a "greater glory" (Hag. 2:9). **neither . . . visit it**—rather, "neither shall *it be missed*" (so in ch. 23: 4). **done**—rather, "neither shall it (the ark) *be made* (i.e., be restored) any more" [MAURER]. **17. Jerusalem**—*the whole city,* not merely the temple. As it has been the center of the *Hebrew* theocracy, so it shall be the point of attraction to the whole earth (Isa. 2:2-4; Zech. 2:10, 11; 14:16-21). **throne of . . . Lord**—The Shekinah, the symbol of God's peculiar nearness to Israel (Deut. 4:7) shall be surpassed by the antitype, God's own throne in Jerusalem (Ps. 2:6, 8; Ezek. 34:23, 24; Zech. 2:5).

imagination—rather, as *Margin,* "the obstinacy" or stubbornness.

18. Judah . . . Israel . . . together—Two distinct apostasies, that of Israel and that of Judah, were foretold (vss. 8, 10). The two have never been united since the Babylonish captivity; therefore their joint restoration must be still future (Isa. 11:12, 13; Ezek. 37:16-22; Hos. 1:11). **north**—(*V.*, 12). **land . . . given . . . inheritance**—(Amos 9:15). **19.** The good land covenanted to Abraham is to be restored to his seed. But the question arises, How shall this be done? **put . . . among . . . children**—the *Greek* for *adoption* means, lit., "putting among the sons." **the children**—i.e., My

ADAM CLARKE

14. *I will take you one of a city, and two of a family.* If there should be but one of a city left, or one willing to return, and two only of a whole tribe, yet will I receive these, and bring them back from captivity into their own land.

15. *I will give you pastors according to mine heart.* The pastor means either the king or the prophet; and the pastors here promised may be either kings or prophets, or both. These shall be according to God's own heart; they shall be of His own choosing and shall be qualified by himself: and in consequence they shall *feed* the people with *knowledge, deah,* that divine truth concerning the true God and the best interests of man which was essentially necessary to their salvation; *and understanding, haskeil,* the full interpretation of every point, that in receiving the truth they might become wise, holy, and happy.

16. *The ark of the covenant of the Lord.* This symbol of the Divine Presence, given to the Jews as a token and pledge of God's dwelling among them, shall be no longer necessary, and shall no longer exist; for in the days of the Messiah, to which this promise seems to relate, God's worship shall not be confined either to one place or to one people. The temple of God shall be among men, and everywhere God be adored through Christ Jesus. *Neither shall that be done any more.* The ark shall be no more established, nor carried from place to place; nor shall men go to visit it. All its ceremonies and importance shall cease; and, if lost, shall never be rebuilt.

17. *They shall call Jerusalem the throne of the Lord.* The new Jerusalem, the universal Church of Christ, shall be God's throne; and wherever He is acknowledged as the Lamb of God who takes away the sin of the world, there God sits on His throne, and holds His court.

18. *The house of Judah shall walk with the house of Israel.* That is, in those days in which the Jews shall be brought in with the fullness of the Gentiles. *Out of the land of the north.* From Chaldea. This prophecy has two aspects: one refers to the return from the Babylonish captivity; the other, to the glorious days of Christianity. But the words may refer to that gathering together of the Jews, not only from Chaldea, but from the countries of their dispersion over the face of the whole earth, and uniting them in the Christian Church.

19. *How shall I put thee among the children?* As if He had said, How can you be accounted a holy seed, who are polluted? How can you

MATTHEW HENRY

whom God puts among the children he will *give the pleasant land*, the land of Canaan. It was a type of heaven, where there are *pleasures for evermore.* Who could expect a place in that *pleasant land* that has so often *despised it* (Ps. cvi. 24) and is so unfit for it?

2. He does himself return answer to this question: *But I said, Thou shalt call me, My Father.* God does himself answer all the objections. That he may put returning penitents *among the children*, he will give them the *Spirit of adoption*, teaching them *to cry, Abba, Father* (Gal. iv. 6). "*Thou shalt call me, My Father;* thou shalt return to me, and resign thyself to me as a father, and that shall recommend thee to my favour." He will *put his fear in their hearts*, that they may never *turn from him*, but may persevere to the end.

Verses 20–25

I. The charge against Israel for their treacherous departures, *v.* 20. They were joined to God by a marriage-covenant, but they broke that covenant, they *dealt treacherously* with God.

II. Their confession of the truth of this charge, *v.* 21. When God reproved them for their apostasy, there were some whose *voice was heard upon the high places weeping and praying*, humbling themselves before the God of their fathers, that *they have perverted their way and forgotten the Lord their God.* Sin is the turning aside to crooked ways. Forgetting the Lord our God is at the bottom of all sin. If men would remember God, they would not transgress.

III. The invitation God gives them to return to him (*v.* 22): *Return, you backsliding children.* He calls them *children* in tenderness and compassion to them, froward as children, yet *his sons*, whom though he corrects he will not disinherit. God bears with such children, and so must parents. When they are convinced of sin (*v.* 21), then they are *invited* to *return*, as Christ invites those to him that are *weary* and *heavy-laden.* The promise to those that return is, *I will heal your backslidings.* God will *heal our backslidings* by his pardoning mercy, his quieting peace, and his renewing grace.

IV. The ready consent they give to this invitation. This is an echo to God's call; as a voice returned from broken walls, so this from broken hearts. God says, *Return;* they answer, *Behold, we come.* It is an immediate answer. 1. They come devoting themselves to God as theirs: "*Thou art the Lord our God.* It is our sin and folly that we have gone from thee." 2. They come claiming succour from God only: "*In vain is salvation hoped for from the hills and from the multitude of the mountains.*" They worshipped their idols upon hills and mountains (*v.* 6), but now they will have no more to do with them. Therefore, 3. They come depending upon God only as their God: *In the Lord our God is the salvation of Israel.* It is applicable to the great salvation from sin, which Jesus Christ wrought for us; that is the *salvation of the Lord*, his *great salvation.* 4. They come justifying God in their troubles and judging themselves for their sins, *v.* 24, 25. They impute all the calamities they had been under to their idols. *Shame* (the idol, that shameful thing) *has devoured the labour of our fathers.* True penitents have learned to call sin *shame.* True penitents have learned to call sin death and ruin. "It has *devoured* all those good things which our fathers *laboured for* and left to us; we have found *from our youth* that our idolatry has been the destruction of our prosperity." Of the labour of their fathers, which their idols had devoured, they mention particularly *their flocks and their herds, their sons and their daughters.* They take to themselves the shame of their sin and folly (*v.* 25): "*We lie down in our shame*, being unable to bear up under it; *our confusion covers us*, that is, both our penal and our penitential shame. We are sinners by descent: *We and our fathers have sinned.* We have sinned *from our youth*; we have continued in sin, have sinned *even unto this day*, though often called to repent and forsake our sins. *We have not obeyed the voice of the Lord our God*, commanding us, when we have sinned, to repent." All this seems to be the language of the penitents of *the house of Israel* (*v.* 20), of the ten tribes, either of those that were in captivity or those of them that remained in their own land. And the prophet takes notice of their repentance to provoke the men of Judah to a holy emulation.

JAMIESON, FAUSSET, BROWN

children. "How shall I receive thee back into My family, after thou hast so long forsaken Me for idols?" The answer is, they would acknowledge Him as "Father," and no longer turn away from Him. God assumes the language of one wondering how so desperate apostates could be restored to His family and its privileges (cf. Ezek. 37:3; CALVIN makes it, How *the race of Abraham can be propagated again*, being as it were dead); yet as His purpose has decreed it so, He shows how it shall be effected, viz., they shall receive from Him the spirit of adoption to cry, "*My* Father" (John 1:12; Gal. 4:6). The elect are "children" already in God's purpose; this is the ground of the subsequent realization of this relationship (Eph. 1:5; Heb. 2:13). **pleasant land**—(ch. 11:5; Ezek. 20:6; Dan. 11:16, *Margin*. **heritage of . . . hosts**—a heritage the most goodly of all nations [MAURER]; or a "heritage possessed by powerful hosts" (Deut. 4:38; Amos 2:9). The rendering "splendors," instead of "hosts," is opposed by the fact that the *Hebrew* for "splendor" is not found in the *plural*. **20. Surely**—rather, But. **husband**—lit., "friend." **21.** In harmony with the preceding promises of God, the penitential confessions of Israel are heard. **high places**—The scene of their idolatries is the scene of their confessions. Cf. vs. 23, in which they cast aside their trust in these idolatrous high places. The publicity of their penitence is also implied (cf. ch. 7:29; 48:38).

22. Jehovah's renewed invitation (vss. 12, 14) and their immediate response. **heal**—forgive (II Chron. 30:18, 20; Hos. 14:4). **unto thee**—rather, "in obedience to thee"; lit., for thee [ROSENMULLER].

23. multitude of mountains—i.e., the multitude of *gods* worshipped on them (cf. Ps. 121:1, 2, Margin).

24. shame—i.e., the *idols*, whose worship only covers us with *shame* (ch. 11:13; Hos. 9:10). So far from bringing us "salvation," they have cost us our cattle and even our children, whom we have sacrificed to them.

25. (Ezra 9:7).

ADAM CLARKE

be united to the people of God, who walk in the path of sinners? How can you be taken to heaven, who are unholy within and unrighteous without? *And I said, Thou shalt call me, My Father.* This is the answer to the above question. They could not be put among the children unless they became legal members of the heavenly family; and they could not become members of this family unless they abandoned idolatry, and took the Lord for their Portion. Nor could they be continued in the privileges of the heavenly family unless they no more turned away from their Heavenly Father.

21. *A voice was heard upon the high places.* Here the Israelites are represented as assembled together to bewail their idolatry and to implore mercy. While thus engaged, they hear the gracious call of Jehovah—

22. *Return, ye backsliding children.* This they gladly receive, and with one voice make their confession to him: *"Behold, we come unto thee, for thou art* Jehovah *our God"*; and thence to the end of the chapter, show the reasons why they return unto God. (1) Because He is the true God. (2) Because the idols did not profit them; they could give no help in time of trouble. (3) Because it is the prerogative of God alone to give salvation. (4) Because they had no kind of prosperity since they had abandoned the worship of their Maker. And this was not only their case, but it was the case of their forefathers, who all suffered in consequence of their idolatry and disobedience. (5) These reasons are concluded with a hearty confession of sin, at the thought of which they are confounded; for the remembrance of their sin was grievous to them, and the burden was intolerable. This confession ended, God appears in the next chapter with gracious promises, and proper directions how they are to return, and how to conduct themselves in future.

24. *For shame hath devoured.* The word *shame*, here and in chap. xi. 13; Hos. ix. 10, is supposed to signify Baal, the idol which they worshipped.

MATTHEW HENRY

CHAPTER 4

Verses 1–2

When God called to backsliding Israel to return (*ch.* iii. 22) they immediately answered, *Lord, we return;* now God here takes notice of their answer.

I. "Dost thou say, *I will return?* Then thou must *return unto me*; make a thorough work of it. Return to the instituted worship of the God of Israel." Thou must utterly abandon all sin, and not retain any of the relics of idolatry: *Put away thy abominations out of my sight*. Their idolatries were not only obvious, but offensive, to the eye of God. They must be *put away out of his sight*, because they were a provocation to the pure eyes of God's glory. They must not return to sin again; so some understand that, *Thou shalt not remove*, reading it, *Thou shalt not*, or *must not wander*. They must give unto God the glory due unto his name (*v.* 2): "*Thou shalt swear, The Lord liveth*. His existence shall be with thee the most sacred fact."

II. He encourages them to keep their resolutions. "*If thou wilt return to me*, then *thou shalt return*, that is, thou shalt be brought back out of thy captivity into thy own land again, as was of old promised," Deut. iv. 29; xxx. 2. They shall be blessings to others; for their returning to God again will be a means of others turning to him who never knew him. See Isa. lxv. 16. They shall bless themselves *in the God of truth*, and not in false gods, and *in him shall they glory*; they shall make him their glory.

Verses 3–4

The prophet here turns his speech, in God's name, to the men of the place where he lived. We have heard what words he proclaimed *towards the north* (*ch.* iii. 12), for the comfort of those that were now in captivity; let us now see what he says to the *men of Judah and Jerusalem*, who were now in prosperity, for their conviction and awakening. In these two verses he exhorts them to repentance and reformation, to prevent the desolating judgments that were ready to break in upon them.

I. The duties required of them,

1. They must do by their hearts as they do by their ground that they expect any good of; they must plough it up (*v.* 3): "*Break up your fallow-ground. Plough to yourselves a ploughing* (or *plough up your plough land*), that you *sow not among thorns*, that you may not labour in vain as you have been doing a great while. Put yourselves into a frame fit to receive mercy from God, and put away all that which keeps it from you, and then you may expect to receive mercy and to prosper in your endeavours to help yourselves." An unconvinced unhumbled heart is like fallow-ground, untilled, unoccupied. It is ground capable of improvement; but it is unfenced, unfruitful, overgrown with thorns and weeds, which are the natural product of the corrupt heart; and, if it be not renewed with grace, rain and sunshine are lost upon it, Heb. vi. 7, 8. We are concerned to get this fallow-ground ploughed up. We must search into our own hearts, must pluck up by the roots those corruptions which, as thorns, choke our endeavours.

2. They must do that to their souls which was done to their bodies when they were taken into covenant with God (*v.* 4): "*Circumcise yourselves to the Lord, and take away the foreskins of your heart.* Mortify the flesh and the lusts of it. Boast not of the circumcision of the body, for that is but a sign, and will not serve without the thing signified. It is a dedicating sign. Do that in sincerity which was done in profession by your circumcision; devote and consecrate yourselves unto the Lord."

II. The danger threatened. Repent and reform, *lest my fury come forth like fire*. That which is to be dreaded by us more than anything else is the wrath of God. It is the *evil of our doings* that kindles the fire of God's wrath against us. The consideration of the imminent danger should awaken us to *sanctify ourselves to God's glory* and to see to it that we be *sanctified by his grace*.

Verses 5–18

God's usual method is to warn before he wounds. In these verses God gives notice to the Jews of the general desolation that would shortly be brought upon them by a foreign invasion. This must be declared in all the cities of Judah and streets of Jerusalem, that all might hear and be either brought to repentance or left inexcusable.

I. The war proclaimed, and notice given of the advance of the enemy. It is published now, some years before, by the prophet, *v.* 5, 6. The *trumpet* must be *blown*, the *standard* must be *set up*, a summons must be issued to the people, to *gather together* and to draw

JAMIESON, FAUSSET, BROWN

CHAPTER 4

Vss. 1-31. Continuation of Address to the Ten Tribes of Israel (vss. 1, 2). The Prophet Turns Again to Judah, to Whom He Had Originally Been Sent (vss. 3-31). **1. return . . . return**—play on words. "If thou wouldest *return to thy land* (thou must first), *return* (*by conversion* and repentance) *to Me.*"

not remove—no longer be an unsettled *wanderer* in a strange land. So Cain (Gen. 4:12, 14).

2. And thou—rather, "And *if* (carried on from vs. 1) thou shalt swear, 'Jehovah liveth,' in truth . . . ," i.e., if thou shalt *worship* Him (for we *swear* by the God whom we worship; cf. Deut. 6:13; 10:20; Isa. 19:18; Amos 8:14) in sincerity, etc. **and the nations**—Rather, this is apodosis to the "if"; *then* shall the nations bless themselves in (by) Him" (Isa. 65:16). The conversion of the nations will be the consequence of Israel's conversion (Ps. 102: 13, 15; Rom. 11:12, 15).

3. Transition to Judah. Supply mentally. All which (the foregoing declaration as to Israel) applies to Judah. **and Jerusalem**—i.e., and *especially* the men of Jerusalem, as being the most prominent in Judea.

Break . . . fallow ground—i.e., Repent of your idolatry, and so be prepared to serve the Lord in truth (Hos. 10:12, Matt. 13:7). The unhumbled heart is like ground which may be improved, being let out to us for that purpose, but which is as yet fallow, overgrown with weeds, its natural product.

4. Remove your natural corruption of heart (Deut. 10:16; 30:6; Rom. 2:29; Col. 2:11).

5. cry, gather together—rather, "cry fully" i.e., loudly. The Jews are warned to take measures against the impending Chaldean invasion (cf. ch. 8:14).

ADAM CLARKE

CHAPTER 4

1. *Shalt thou not remove.* This was spoken before the Babylonish captivity; and here is a promise that, if they will return from their idolatry, they shall not be led into captivity. So, even that positively threatened judgment would have been averted had they returned to the Lord.

2. *Thou shalt swear, The Lord liveth.* You shall not bind yourself by any false god; you shall acknowledge Me as the Supreme. Bind yourself by Me, and to Me; and do this *in truth, in judgment, and in righteousness. The nations shall bless themselves in him.* They shall be so fully convinced of the power and goodness of Jehovah in seeing the change wrought on you, and the mercies heaped upon you, that their usual mode of benediction shall be, "May the God of Israel bless thee!"

3. *Break up your fallow ground.* Fallow ground is either that which, having been once tilled, has lain long uncultivated; or, ground slightly ploughed, in order to be ploughed again previously to its being sown. You have been long uncultivated in righteousness; let true repentance break up your fruitless and hardened hearts; and when the seed of the word of life is sown in them, take heed that worldly cares and concerns do not arise, and, like thorns, choke the good seed.

4. *Circumcise yourselves.* Put away everything that has a tendency to grieve the Spirit of God, or to render your present holy resolutions unfruitful.

5. *Blow ye the trumpet.* Give full information to all parts of the land, that the people may assemble together and defend themselves against their invaders.

MATTHEW HENRY

towards Zion, either to guard it or expecting to be guarded by it. The militia must be raised and all the forces mustered. Those that are fit for service, must *go into the defenced cities*, to garrison them; those that are weak must *retire*, and *not stay*.

II. An express arrived with intelligence of the approach of the king of Babylon and his army. The enemy is here compared, 1. To *a lion* that *comes up from his thicket*, when he is hungry, to seek his prey, *v.* 7. The helpless beasts are terrified and so become an easy prey to him. Nebuchadnezzar is this roaring tearing lion, *the destroyer of the nations*, now *on his way* towards the land of Judah. The *destroyer of the Gentiles* shall be the *destroyer of the Jews* too, when they have by their idolatry made themselves like the Gentiles. He has *gone forth from his place*, from Babylon, against *this land*; the cities shall be *laid waste, without inhabitants*, shall be *overgrown with grass* as a field; so some read it. 2. To a *drying* blasting *wind* (*v.* 11), which spoils the fruits of the earth and withers them, such as comes *out of the north*, which *drives away rain* (Prov. xxv. 23). A *black* freezing wind. Wherever they go, it shall surround them. It is a *wind of the high places in the wilderness* that beats upon the tops of the hills or that carries all before it in the plain. It shall come in its full force *towards the daughters of my people*, that have been brought up so tenderly. Now this fierce wind shall come against them, *not to fan, nor cleanse* them, but a *full wind* (*v.* 12). This shall come *to me*, or rather *for me*; it shall come with commission from God and shall accomplish that for which he sends it. 3. To clouds and whirlwinds for swiftness, *v.* 13. The Chaldean army shall *come up as clouds* driven with the wind. The horses are *swifter than eagles* when they fly upon their prey. 4. To watchers and the keepers of a field, *v.* 15–17. *The voice declares from Dan*, furthest north of all the cities of Canaan. They received the news and transmitted it to Jerusalem. Now, what is the news? "*Tell the nations*, the cities of the ten tribes, that they may provide for their own safety; but publish it *against Jerusalem*, let them know that *watchers have come from a far country*, that is, soldiers, that will watch all opportunities to do mischief. They are coming in full career, and *give out their voice against the cities of Judah*. As *keepers of a field* surround it, to keep all out from it, so shall they surround the cities of Judah till they surrender. They are *against her round about, compassing her in on every side*." See Luke xix. 43.

III. The lamentable cause of this judgment. 1. They sinned against God; it was all owing to themselves. *She has been rebellious against me, saith the Lord*, *v.* 17. The Chaldeans were breaking in upon them, and it was sin that opened the gap at which they entered: *Thy way and thy doings have procured these things unto thee* (*v.* 18). Sin is the cause of all our troubles. 2. God was angry with them for their sin. It is the *fierce anger of the Lord* that makes the army of the Chaldeans thus fierce, *v.* 8. 3. In his just anger he condemned them to this punishment: *Now also will I give sentence against them*, *v.* 12.

IV. The lamentable effects of this judgment. The people that should fight shall despair and shall not have a heart to make the least stand against the enemy (*v.* 8): "*For this gird yourself with sackcloth, lament and howl.*" Instead of girding on the sword, they will gird on the sackcloth. While the enemy is yet at a distance they will give up and cry, *Woe unto us! for we are spoiled*, *v.* 13. Judah and Jerusalem had been famed for valiant men; but see the effect of sin: by depriving men of their confidence towards God, it deprives them of their courage towards men. *At that day the heart of the king shall perish*, both his wisdom and his courage. His princes and privy-counsellors shall be as much in despair as he. The business of the priests was to encourage the people; they were to say, *Fear not, and let not your hearts faint*, Deut. xx. 2, 3. But now *the priests* themselves *shall be astonished*, and shall have no heart to put spirit into the people. Our Saviour foretells that at the last destruction of Jerusalem *men's hearts* should *fail them for fear*, Luke xxi. 26.

V. The prophet's complaint of the people's being deceived, *v.* 10. It is expressed strangely: *Ah! Lord God, surely thou hast greatly deceived this people, saying, You shall have peace.* We are sure that God deceives none. But, 1. The people deceived themselves with the promises that God had made, building upon them, though they took no care to perform the conditions on which those promises did depend. Thus they cheated themselves and then wickedly complained that God had cheated them. 2. The false prophets deceived them with promises of peace, which they made them in God's name, *ch.* xxiii. 17; xxvii. 9. 3. God had permitted the false prophets to deceive,

JAMIESON, FAUSSET, BROWN

6. Zion—The standard *toward* Zion intimated that the people of the surrounding country were to fly *to* it, as being the strongest of their fortresses.

7. lion—Nebuchadnezzar and the Chaldeans (ch. 2:15; 5:6; Dan. 7:14). **his thicket**—lair; Babylon. **destroyer of the Gentiles**—rather, "the nations" (ch. 25:9). **8.** Nothing is left to the Jews but to bewail their desperate condition. **anger . . . not turned back**—(Isa. 9:12, 17, 21).

11. dry wind—the *simoom*, terrific and destructive, blowing from the southeast across the sandy deserts east of Palestine. Image of the invading Babylonian army (Hos. 13:15). Babylon in its turn shall be visited by a similar "destroying wind" (ch. 51:1). **of . . . high places**—i.e., that sweeps over the high places. **daughter**—i.e., the *children* of my people. **not to fan**—a very different wind from those ordinary winds employed for fanning the grain in the open air. **12. full . . . from those places**—rather, "a wind *fuller* (i.e., more impetuous) *than* those *winds*" (which fan the corn) (vs. 11) [ROSENMULLER]. **unto me**—*for Me*, as My instrument for executing My purpose. **sentence**—*judgments* against them (ch. 1:16). **13. clouds**—continuing the metaphor in vss. 11:12. Clouds of sand and dust accompany the simoom, and after rapid gyrations ascend like a pillar. **eagles**—(Deut. 28:49; Hab. 1:8). **Woe unto us**—The people are graphically presented before us, without it being formally so stated, bursting out in these exclamations. **14.** Only one means of deliverance is left to the Jews—a thorough repentance. GESENIUS translates, "How long *wilt thou harbor* vain thoughts?" **vain thoughts**—viz., projects for deliverance, such as enlisting the Egyptians on their side. **15. For . . . from Dan**—The connection is: There is danger in delay; *for* the voice of a messenger announces the approach of the Chaldean enemy from Dan, the northern frontier of Palestine (ch. 8:16; cf. vs. 6; ch. 1:14). **Mount Ephraim**—which borders closely on Judah; so that the foe is coming nearer and nearer. Dan and Bethel in *Ephraim* were the two places where Jeroboam set up the idolatrous calves (I Kings 12:29); just retribution. **16.** The neighboring foreign "nations" are summoned to witness Jehovah's judgments on His rebel people (ch. 6:18, 19). **watchers**—i.e., besiegers (cf. II Sam. 11:16); observed or watched, i.e., besieged. **their voice**—the war shout. **17. keepers of a field**—metaphor from those who watch a field, to frighten away the wild beasts.

9. heart—The *wisdom* of the most leading men will be utterly at a loss to devise means of relief.

10. thou hast . . . deceived—God, having even the false prophets in His hands, is here said to do that which for inscrutable purposes He *permits* them to do (Exod. 9:12; II Thess. 2:11; cf. ch. 8:15; which passage shows that the dupes of error were *self-prepared* for it, and that God's predestination did not destroy their moral freedom as voluntary agents). The false prophets foretold "peace," and the Jews believed them; God overruled this to His purposes (ch. 5:12; 14:13; Ezek. 14:9).

ADAM CLARKE

6. *I will bring evil from the north.* From the land of Chaldea.

7. *The lion is come up.* Nebuchadnezzar, king of Babylon. *The destroyer of the Gentiles.* Of the "nations," of all the people who resisted his authority.

11-13. *A dry wind . . . a full wind . . . as clouds . . . as a whirlwind.* All these expressions appear to refer to the pestilential winds. suffocating vapors, and clouds and pillars of sand collected by whirlwinds, which are so common and destructive in the East (see on Isa. xxi. 1); and these images are employed here to show the overwhelming effect of the invasion of the land by the Chaldeans.

13. *Woe unto us!* The people, deeply affected with these threatened judgments, interrupt the prophet with the lamentation—*Woe unto us! for we are spoiled.* The prophet then resumes:

14. *O Jerusalem, wash thine heart.* Why do you not put away your wickedness, that you may be saved from these tremendous judgments? *How long shall thy vain thoughts* of safety and prosperity *lodge within thee?* While you continue a rebel against God, and provoke Him daily by your abominations!

15. *For a voice declareth from Dan.* Dan was a city in the tribe of Dan, north of Jerusalem; the first city in Palestine, which occurs in the way from Babylon to Jerusalem. *Affliction from mount Ephraim.* Between Dan and Jerusalem are the mountains of Ephraim. These would be the first places attacked by the Chaldeans, and the rumor from thence would show that the land was invaded.

16. *Watchers come from a far country.* Persons to besiege fortified places.

17. *As keepers of a field.* In the Eastern countries grain is often sown in the open country; and, when nearly ripe, guards are placed at different distances round about it to preserve it from being plundered. Jerusalem was watched, like one of these fields, by guards all round about it; so that none could enter to give assistance, and none who wished to escape were permitted to go out.

8. *Lament and howl. Heililu.* The aboriginal Irish had a funeral song, still continued among their descendants, one part of which is termed the *ulaloo.* This is sung responsively or alternately, and is accompanied with a full chorus of sighs and groans. It has been thought that Ireland was originally peopled by the Phoenicians; if so, this will account for the similiarity of many words and customs among both these people.

9. *The heart of the king shall perish.* Shall lose all courage.

10. *Ah, Lord God! surely thou hast greatly deceived this people.* The prophet could not reconcile this devastation of the country with the promises already made; and he appears to ask the question, Hast Thou not then deceived this people in saying there shall be peace, i.e., prosperity?

MATTHEW HENRY

and the people to be deceived by them, giving both up to *strong delusions*, to punish them *for not receiving the truth in the love of it*. 4. It may be read with an interrogation, "*Hast thou indeed thus deceived this people?* It is plain that they are greatly deceived, for they expect *peace*, whereas *the sword reaches unto the soul*." Now, was it God that deceived them? No, he had often given them warning of judgments, but their own prophets deceive them, and cry peace to those to whom the God of heaven does not speak peace. It is a pitiable thing to see people flattered into their own ruin, and promising themselves peace when war is at the door.

VI. The prophet's endeavour to undeceive them. 1. He shows them their wound. They might discover their punishment in their sin (*v.* 18): "*This is thy wickedness, because it is bitter*. It produces bitter grief that *reaches unto the heart*; the sword *reaches to the soul*," *v.* 10. 2. He shows them the cure, *v.* 14. "*O Jerusalem! wash thy heart from wickedness, that thou mayest be saved*." By Jerusalem he means each one of the inhabitants of Jerusalem; for every man has a heart of his own, and it is personal reformation that must help the public. Every one must return from *his own evil way* and cleanse *his own evil heart*. Reformation is absolutely necessary to salvation. No reformation is saving but that which reaches the heart. There will be no effectual reformation of manners without a reformation of the mind. In the latter part of the verse he reasons with them: *How long shall thy vain thoughts lodge within thee? Thoughts of iniquity* or *mischief*, these are the evil thoughts that are the spawn of the evil *heart*, from which all other wickedness is produced, Matt. xv. 19. Some by vain thoughts here understand all those frivolous excuses with which they turned off the reproofs and calls of the word, and bolstered themselves up in their wickedness.

Verses 19–31

The prophet is here in an agony, and cries out like one upon the rack of pain. The expressions are pathetic enough to melt a heart of stone. *My bowels! my bowels! I am pained at my very heart*. A good man, in such a bad world as this is, cannot but be a *man of sorrows. My heart makes a noise in me*, through the tumult of my spirits, and *I cannot hold my peace*. It is not for himself, or any affliction in his family that he grieves thus; but it is purely upon the public account, it is his people's case that he lays to heart thus.

I. They are very sinful and will not be reformed, *v.* 22. These are the words of God himself. God calls them his people, though they are foolish. They have cast him off, but he has not cast them off, Rom. xi. 1. They are *foolish*, for *they have not known me*. They are *wise to do evil*, to plot mischief against the quiet in the land, wise to contrive the gratification of their lusts, and then to conceal and palliate them. But *to do good they have no knowledge*, no application of mind.

II. They are very miserable, and cannot be relieved. 1. He cries out, *Because thou hast heard, O my soul! the sound of the trumpet*, and *seen the standard*, both giving *the alarm of war*, *v.* 19, 21. He does not say, *Thou hast heard*, O my *ear!* but, O my *soul*! because it is by the spirit of prophecy that he sees it. His *soul* heard it from the words of God, as if he had heard it with his bodily ears. Though he foretold this calamity he was far from *desiring the woeful day*. He strove to awaken them to a holy fear, and so to prevent judgment by a true and timely repentance.

2. The destruction here foretold:

(1) It is swift and *sudden*. *Destruction upon destruction is cried* (*v.* 20), *breach upon breach*, one sad calamity treading upon the heels of another. The death of Josiah plucks up the floodgates; within three months after that his son and successor Jehoahaz is deposed by the king of Egypt; within two or three years after Nebuchadnezzar besieged Jerusalem and took it, and thenceforward he was continually making descents upon the land of Judah, till he completed the ruin in the destruction of Jerusalem: but *suddenly were their tents spoiled and their curtains in a moment*. The country was laid waste at first. The shepherds and all that lived in tents were plundered immediately; therefore we find the Rechabites, who dwelt in tents, upon the first coming of the army of the Chaldees into the land retiring to Jerusalem, Jer. xxxv. 11.

(2) This war continued, for the people were obstinate, and would not submit to the king of Babylon, but took all opportunities to rebel against him. This is complained of (*v.* 21): *How long shall I see the standard?* Shall the sword devour for ever?

(3) *The whole land is spoiled*, or plundered (*v.* 20); so it was at first, and at length it became a perfect chaos. The earth is *without form, and void* (*v.* 23), as it

JAMIESON, FAUSSET, BROWN

soul— rather, "reacheth to the *life*."

18. (Ch. 2:17, 19; Ps. 107:17.) **this is thy wickedness**—i.e., the fruit of thy wickedness.

19. The prophet suddenly assumes the language of the Jewish state personified, lamenting its affliction (ch. 10:19, 20; 9:1, 10; Isa. 15:5; cf. Luke 19:41). at my very heart—*Hebrew*, **"at the walls of my heart"; the muscles round the heart. There is a climax, the "bowels," the** *pericardium*, **the "heart" itself. maketh . . . noise**—moaneth [HENDERSON]. **alarm**—the battle shout.

22. Jehovah's reply; they cannot be otherwise than miserable, since they persevere in sin. The repetition of clauses gives greater force to the sentiment. **wise . . . evil . . . to do good . . . no knowledge**—reversing the rule (Rom. 16:19) "wise unto . . . good, simple concerning evil."

20. Destruction . . . cried—Breach upon breach is announced (Ps. 42:7; Ezek. 7:26). The war "trumpet" . . . the battle shout . . . the "destructions" . . . the havoc throughout "the whole land" . . . the spoiling of the shepherds' "tents" (ch. 10:20; or, "tents" means *cities*, which should be overthrown as easily as *tents* [CALVIN]), form a gradation.

21. Judah in perplexity asks, How long is this state of things to continue?

ADAM CLARKE

Whereas the sword reacheth unto the soul. That is, the life, the people being generally destroyed.

19. *My bowels*. From this to the twenty-ninth verse the prophet describes the ruin of Jerusalem and the desolation of Judea by the Chaldeans in the language and imagery scarcely paralleled in the whole Bible. At the sight of misery the bowels are first affected; pain is next felt by a sort of stricture in the pericardium; and then, the heart becoming strongly affected by irregular palpitations, a gush of tears, accompanied with wailings, is the issue.

20. *Destruction upon destruction*. Cities burnt, and their inhabitants destroyed. *My tents spoiled*. Even the solitary dwellings in the fields and open country do not escape.

MATTHEW HENRY

was Gen. i. 2. It is *Tohu* and *Bohu*, the words there used, as far as the land of Judæa goes. The *heavens* too are *without light*. This alludes to the *darkness* that was *upon the face of the deep* (Gen. i. 2). It was not only the earth that failed them, but heaven frowned upon them; and with their trouble they had darkness, for they could not see through their troubles. The smoke of their houses and cities which the enemy burnt, darkened the sun, so that *the heavens had no light*. Or it may be taken figuratively: *The earth* (that is, the common people) was impoverished and in confusion; and the *heavens* (that is, the princes and rulers) *had no light*, no wisdom in themselves, nor were any comfort to the people, nor a guide to them. The *mountains trembled, and the hills moved lightly*, *v.* 24. The *everlasting mountains* seemed to be *scattered*, Hab. iii. 6. The mountains on which they had worshipped their idols, the mountains trembled, as if they had been conscious of the people's guilt. The hills moved lightly, as being eased of the burden of a *sinful nation*, Isa. i. 24. *I beheld* the cities, *and, lo, there was no man* to be seen; even *the birds of the heavens*, that used to fly about and *sing among the branches*, were no more seen or heard. The *land of Judah* had now become like the *lake of Sodom*, see Deut. xxix. 23. *Lo, the fruitful place was a wilderness.* The *cities* also and their gates and walls are *broken down* and levelled. Those that look no further than second causes impute it to the policy and fury of the invaders; but the prophet, who looks to the first cause, says that it is *at the presence of the Lord*. The nation shall be entirely ruined, for *the whole land shall be desolate*, corn land and pasture land shall all be laid waste (*v.* 27). *The whole city shall flee for fear of the horsemen and bowmen.* Rather than lie exposed to their fury, they shall *go into the thickets*, and they shall *climb up upon the rocks*, for *every city shall be forsaken*. It is a dismal idea of the approaching desolation; but in the midst of all these threatenings comes one comfortable word (*v.* 27): *Yet will not I make a full end*—for God will reserve a remnant. Jerusalem shall again be built and the land inhabited. This comes for the comfort of those that *trembled at God's word*.

(4) Their case was helpless and without remedy. God would not help them; so he tells them plainly, *v.* 28. They would not repent and turn back from their sins (*ch.* ii. 25), and therefore God will not repent and turn back from his judgments. They could not help themselves, *v.* 30, 31. They flattered themselves with hopes that they should find some means. But the prophet tells them that, when it comes to the setting to, they will be quite at a loss: *When thou art spoiled, what wilt thou do?* They will be despised by their allies whom they depended upon. He compares Jerusalem to a harlot abandoned by all the lewd ones that used to make court to her. She does what she can to make herself appear considerable among the nations, and a valuable ally. She compliments them by her ambassadors. She *clothes herself with crimson*, as if she were rich, and *decks herself with ornaments of gold*, as if her treasuries were still full. She *rents her face with painting*, puts the best colours she can upon her present distresses. But this painting, though it beautifies the face for the present, really rends it; spoils the skin, cracks it, and makes it rough. "And, after all, *in vain shalt thou make thyself fair*; all thy neighbours are sensible how low thou art brought; the Chaldeans will strip thee of thy crimson and ornaments." Here seems to be an allusion to the story of Jezebel, who thought, by making herself look fair and fine, to outface her doom, but in vain, 2 Kings ix. 30, 33. They will find their troubles to be like the pains of a woman in travail, which she cannot escape: *I have heard the voices of the daughter of Zion*, her groans echoing to the triumphant shouts of the Chaldean army, *v.* 15. Zion, since her neighbours refuse to pity her, *bewails herself*, fetching *deep sighs* (so the word signifies), and she *spreads her hands*, reaching them forth for succour.

JAMIESON, FAUSSET, BROWN

23. Graphic picture of the utter desolation about to visit Palestine. "I beheld, and lo!" four times solemnly repeated, heightens the awful effect of the scene (cf. Isa. 24: 19; 34:11). **without form and void**—reduced to the primeval chaos (Gen. 1:2).

24. mountains—(Isa. 5:25). **moved lightly**—shook vehemently.

25. no man . . . birds—No vestige of the human, or of the feathered creation, is to be seen (Ezek. 38:20; Zeph. 1:3). **26. fruitful place**—*Hebrew, Carmel.* **a wilderness**—*Hebrew, "the* wilderness," in contrast to "*the* fruitful place"; the great desert, where *Carmel* was, there is now *the desert* of Arabia [MAURER]. **cities**—in contrast to *the fruitful place* or field.

27. full end—utter destruction: I will leave some hope of restoration (ch. 5:10, 18; 30:11; 46, 28; cf. Lev. 26:44).

28. For this—on account of the desolations just described (Isa. 5:30; Hos. 4:3). **not repent**—(Num. 23:19). **29. whole city**—Jerusalem: to it the inhabitants of the country had fled for refuge; but when it, too, is likely to fall, they flee out of it to hide in the "thickets." HENDERSON translates, *"every* city." **noise**—The mere noise of the hostile horsemen shall put you to flight. **30. when thou art spoiled**—rather, "thou, O *destroyed* one" [MAURER].

rentest . . . face with painting—Oriental women paint their eyes with stibium, or antimony, to make them look full and sparkling, the black margin causing the white of the eyes to appear the brighter by contrast (II Kings 9:30). He uses the term "distendest" in derision of their effort to make their eyes look large [MAURER]; or else, "rentest," i.e., dost lacerate by puncturing the eyelid in order to make the antimony adhere [ROSENMULLER]. So the Jews use every artifice to secure the aid of Egypt against Babylon. **face**—rather, thy *eyes* (Ezek. 23:40). **31. anguish**—viz., occasioned by the attack of the enemy. **daughter of Zion**—There is peculiar beauty in suppressing the name of the person in trouble, until that trouble had been fully described [HENDERSON]. **bewaileth herself**—rather, "draweth her breath short" [HORSLEY]. "panteth." **spreadeth . . . hands**—(Lam. 1: 17).

ADAM CLARKE

23. *I beheld the earth* (the land), *and, lo, it was without form, and void. Tohu vabohu;* the very words used in Genesis to denote the formless state of the chaotic mass before God had brought it into order.

24. *The mountains . . . hills.* Princes, rulers were astonished and fled.

25. *The birds of the heavens were fled.* The land was so desolated that even the fowls of heaven could not find meat, and therefore fled away to another region. How powerfully energetic is this description!

30. *Though thou rentest thy face with painting.* This probably refers to the custom of introducing *stibium*, a preparation of antimony, between the eye and the lids, in order to produce a fine lustre, which occasions a distension of the eyelid in the time of the operation. In order to heighten the effect from this, some may have introduced a more than ordinary quantity, so as nearly to rend the eyelid itself. Though you make use of every means of address, of cunning, and of solicitation, to get assistance from the neighboring states, it will be all in vain. Reference is here particularly made to the practice of harlots to allure men.

31. *Bringeth forth her first child.* In such a case the fear, danger, and pain were naturally the greatest. *Spreadeth her hands.* The gesture indicated by nature to signify distress and implore help. We have met with this figure in other parts, and among the classic writers it is frequent.

MATTHEW HENRY — CHAPTER 5

Verses 1–9

I. A challenge to produce any one right honest man in Jerusalem, *v.* 1. Jerusalem had become like the old world, in which *all flesh had corrupted their way*. "Look in *the streets*, and in *the broad places*, where they keep their markets; *see if you can find a man, a magistrate* (so some), *that executes judgment*, and administers justice impartially." *Truth has fallen in the street* (Isa. lix. 14). If there were but ten righteous men in Sodom, if but one of a thousand, of ten thousand, in Jerusalem, it should be spared. "What do you make of those in Jerusalem that continue to make profession of religion—men for

JAMIESON, FAUSSET, BROWN — CHAPTER 5

Vss. 1-31. THE CAUSE OF THE JUDGMENTS TO BE INFLICTED IS THE UNIVERSAL CORRUPTION OF THE PEOPLE. 1. a man—As the pious Josiah, Baruch, and Zephaniah lived in Jerusalem at that time, Jeremiah must here mean the mass of the people, the king, his counsellors, the false prophets, and the priests, as distinguished from the faithful few, whom God had openly separated from the reprobate people; **among the latter not even *one* just person was to be found** (Isa. 9:16) [CALVIN]; the godly, moreover, were forbidden to intercede for them (ch. 7:16; cf. Gen. 18:23, etc.; Ps. 12:1; Ezek.

ADAM CLARKE — CHAPTER 5

1. *Broad places.* Marketplaces, and those where there was most public resort. *If ye can find a man.* A certain philosopher went through the streets of Athens with a lighted lamp in his hand; and being asked what he sought, answered, "I am seeking to find a man." So in Jerusalem none was found, on the most diligent search, who acted worthy the character of a rational being. *I will pardon it.* I will spare the city for the sake of one righteous person. So at the intercession of Abraham, God would have spared Sodom if there had been ten righ-

MATTHEW HENRY

whose sakes Jerusalem may be spared?" No, they are not sincere in their profession (*v.* 2): *They say, The Lord liveth,* and will swear by his name only, but they *swear falsely.*

II. A complaint which the prophet makes to God of the wilfulness of these people. God had appealed to their eyes (*v.* 1); but here the prophet appeals to his eyes (*v.* 3): "*Are not thy eyes upon the truth?* Dost thou not see every man's true character? *They have made their faces harder than a rock. Thou hast consumed them,* hast corrected them severely; *but they have refused to receive correction.* They would not receive instruction by the correction."

III. The trial made both of rich and poor, and the bad character given of both.

1. The poor were ignorant. He found many that *refused to return,* for whom he was willing to make excuse (*v.* 4): "*Surely, these are poor, they are foolish.* They never had the advantage of a good education, nor have they wherewithal to help themselves now with the means of instruction." Prevailing ignorance is the lamentable cause of abounding impiety and iniquity. There are the devil's poor as well as God's, who, notwithstanding their poverty, might *know the way of the Lord,* so as to walk in it and do their duty, without being book-learned; but they are willingly ignorant.

2. The rich were insolent and haughty (*v.* 5): "*I will get me to the great men,* and see if I can find them more pliable to the word and providence of God. But though *they know the way of the Lord and the judgment of their God,* yet they are too stiff to stoop to his government: *These have altogether broken the yoke and burst the bonds.* They think themselves too big to be corrected even by the sovereign Lord of all himself. The poor are weak, the rich are wilful, and so neither do their duty."

IV. Some particular sins specified, which they were guilty of. *Their transgressions* indeed *were many* and they added to the number and grew more impudent in them, *v.* 6. Their spiritual whoredom gave that honour to idols which is due to God only. *They have sworn to them* (so it may be read), have joined themselves to them and covenanted with them. Their corporal whoredom: they had forsaken God and served idols, and those that dishonoured him were left to dishonour themselves and their own families. They *committed adultery* without sense of shame or fear of punishment, for they *assembled themselves by troops in the harlots' houses* and did not blush to be seen by one another. So impudent was their lust that they became beasts (*v.* 8); like high-fed horses, they *neighed everyone after his neighbour's wife, v.* 8.

V. God's wrath against them for the universal debauchery of their land. A foreign enemy shall break in and their country shall be as if it were overrun and perfectly mastered by *a lion of the forest,* or by *a wolf of the evening,* which comes out at night, when he is hungry, and is very fierce and ravenous, or by *a leopard,* which is very swift and cruel. The enemy shall *watch over their cities* to put the inhabitants to this sad dilemma—if they stay in, they are starved; if they stir out, they are stabbed: *Everyone that goeth out thence shall be torn in pieces.* And all this bloody work is owing to the *multitude of their transgressions.* It is sin that makes the slaughter. "*Shall I not visit for these things?* Can you think that a God of infinite purity will connive at such abominable uncleanness?" *Shall not my soul be avenged on such a nation as this?* (*v.* 9). Not but that those who have been guilty of these sins have found mercy with God (Manasseh himself did), but nations, *as such,* being punishable only in this life, it would not be for the glory of God to let a nation pass without some manifest tokens of his displeasure.

Verses 10–19

I. The sin of this people dooms them to destruction, *v.* 10. *The house of Israel and the house of Judah,* though at variance with one another, both agreed to *deal very treacherously against God.* They forsook the worship of him, and played the hypocrite. They defied the judgments of God and his threatenings in the mouth of his prophets, *v.* 12, 13. Multitudes are ruined by being made to believe that God will not be strict: *Neither shall we see sword nor famine.* The prophets gave them fair warning, but they turned it off with a jest: "They do but talk so, because it is their trade. It is not the word of the Lord, but only the language of their melancholy fancy." They threaten the prophets: "*They shall become wind,* and *thus shall it be done unto them.* Do they frighten us with famine? Let them be *fed with the bread of affliction.*" "Do they tell us of the sword? Let them perish by the sword," *ch.* ii. 30.

II. The punishment of this people for their sin. God turns to the prophet Jeremiah, who had been

JAMIESON, FAUSSET, BROWN

22:30). **see . . . know**—look . . . ascertain. **judgment**—justice, righteousness. **pardon it**—rather, *her.* **2.** (Titus 1:16.) **swear falsely**—not a judicial oath; but their profession of the worship of Jehovah is insincere (vs. 7; ch. 4:2). The reformation under Josiah was merely superficial in the case of the majority. **3. eyes upon the truth**—(Deut. 32:4; II Chron. 16:9). "Truth" is in contrast with "swear falsely" (vs. 2). The false-professing Jews could expect nothing but judgments from the God of truth. **stricken . . . not grieved**—(ch. 2:30; Isa. 1:5; 9:13). **refused . . . correction**—(ch. 7:28; Zeph. 3:2).

4. poor—rather, "*the* poor." He supposes for the moment that this utter depravity is confined to the uninstructed poor, and that he would find a different state of things in the higher ranks: but there he finds unbridled profligacy.

5. they have known—rather, "they must know." The prophet *supposes it as probable,* considering their position. **but these**—I found the very reverse to be the case. **burst . . . bonds**—set God's law at defiance (Ps. 2:3).

6. lion . . . wolf . . . leopard—the strongest, the most ravenous, and the swiftest, respectively, of beasts: illustrating the formidable character of the Babylonians. **of the evenings**—Others not so well translate, *of the deserts.* The *plural* means that it goes forth *every evening* to seek its prey (Ps. 104:20; Hab. 1:8; Zeph. 3:3). **leopard . . . watch . . . cities**—(Hos. 13:7). It shall lie in wait about their cities. **7.** It would not be consistent with God's holiness to let such wickedness pass unpunished. **sworn by**—(vs. 2; ch. 4:2); i.e., worshipped. **no gods**—(Deut. 32:21). **fed . . . to the full**—so the *Keri* (*Hebrew Margin*) reads, God's bountifulness is contrasted with their apostasy (Deut. 32:15). Prosperity, the gift of God, designed to lead men to Him, often produces the opposite effect. The *Hebrew Chetib* (text) reads: "I bound them (to Me) by oath," viz., in the *marriage covenant,* sealed at Sinai between God and Israel; in contrast to which stands their "adultery"; the antithesis favors this. **adultery . . . harlots' houses**—spiritually: idolatry in temples of idols; but literal prostitution is also included, being frequently part of idol worship: e.g., in the worship of the Babylonian *Mylitta.* **8. in the morning**—(Isa. 5:11). "Rising early in the morning" is a phrase for unceasing eagerness in any pursuit; such was the Jews' avidity after idol worship. MAURER translates from a different *Hebrew* root, "continually wander to and fro," inflamed with lust (ch. 2:23). But *English Version* is simpler (cf. ch. 13:27; Ezek. 22:11). **9.** (Vs. 29; ch. 9:9; 44:22.)

10. Abrupt apostrophe to the Babylonians, to take Jerusalem, but *not to destroy the nation utterly* (*Note,* ch. 4:27. **battlements**—rather, *tendrils* [MAURER]: the state being compared to a *vine* (ch. 12:-10), the stem of which was to be spared, while the tendrils (the chief men) were to be removed. **11.** (Ch. 3:20.) **12. belied**—denied. **It is not he**—rather, "(Jehovah) is not HE," i.e., the true and only God (ch. 14:22; Deut. 32:39; Isa. 43:10, 13). By their idolatry they virtually denied Him. Or, referring to what follows, and to vs. 9, "(Jehovah) is not," viz., about to be the punisher of our sins (ch. 14:13; Isa. 28:15). **13.** Continuation of the unbelieving language of the Jews. **the prophets**—who prophesy punishment coming on us. **the word**—the Holy Spirit, who speaks through true prophets, is not in them [MAURER]. Or else, "There is no word (divine communication) in them" (Hos. 1:2) [ROSENMULLER]. **thus . . .**—Their ill-omened prophecies shall fall on themselves.

ADAM CLARKE

teous persons found in it, Gen. xviii. 26.

2. *The Lord liveth.* Though they profess to bind themselves by Jehovah, as if they acknowledged Him their God and only Lord, yet they swore falsely. For not believing in Him, they took a false oath; one by which they did not believe themselves bound, not acknowledging Him as their Lord.

4. *These are poor.* They are ignorant; they have no education; they know no better.

5. *I will get me unto the great men.* Those whose circumstances and rank in life gave them opportunities of information which the others could not have, for the reasons already given. *These have altogether broken the yoke.* These have cast aside all restraint, have acted above law, and have trampled all moral obligations under their feet.

6. *Wherefore a lion.* Nebuchadnezzar, according to the general opinion; who is called here a *lion* for his courage and violence, a bear for his rapaciousness, and a *leopard* for his activity.

7. *In the harlots' houses.* In places consecrated to idolatry. In the language of the prophets, adultery generally signifies idolatry.

8. *After his neighbour's wife.* This may have been literally true, as the abominations of idolatry, in which they were so deeply practiced, would necessarily produce such a state of things as that here mentioned.

10. *Go ye up upon her walls.* This is the permission and authority given to the Chaldeans to pillage Jerusalem. *Take away her battlements.* Some translate "branches"; others, "vines." Destroy the branches, cut down the stem; but do not damage the root. Leave so many of the people that the state may be regenerated. The Septuagint, Syriac, and Arabic read, "Leave her foundations, for they are the Lord's"; and this agrees with "Destroy, but make not a full end."

12. *They have belied the Lord.* They have "denied" or disavowed the Lord. *It is not he. Lo hu,* "He is not"; there is no such being; therefore this evil shall not come upon us. On their premises, this conclusion was just. There is no Judge; therefore there shall be no judgment.

13. *And the prophets shall become wind.* What are the prophets? Empty persons. Their words are wind; we hear the sound of their threatenings, but of the matter of the threatenings we shall hear no more. *And the word is not in them.* There is no inspirer, but may their own predictions fall on their own heads!

MATTHEW HENRY

thus bantered: *Behold, I will make my words in thy mouth fire. The word shall be fire and the people wood.* Sinners by sin make themselves fuel. The enemy shall be brought upon them. God gives them their commission (*v.* 10): "*Go you up upon her walls,* mount them, trample upon them, tread them down. Walls of stone, before the divine commission, shall be but mud walls. You may *take away her battlements,* and leave the fenced fortified cities to lie open; for her battlements *are not the Lord's*; he will not protect and fortify them." What dreadful work these invaders should make is here described (*v.* 15): *Lo, I will bring a nation upon you, O house of Israel!* This nation of the Chaldeans is here said to be a remote nation; it is *brought upon them from afar,* and will make the longer stay, that the soldiers may pay themselves well for so long a march. It is a *mighty nation,* an *ancient nation,* that value themselves upon their antiquity and will therefore be the more imperious. It is *a nation whose language thou knowest not*; they spoke the Syriac tongue. The difference of language would make it the more difficult to treat with them of peace. "They shall not store up, but *eat up thy harvest* in the field *and thy bread* in the house, *which thy sons and thy daughters should eat.*" *They shall eat up thy flocks and herds,* out of which thou hast taken sacrifices for thy idols; they shall not leave thee the fruits of *thy vines and fig-trees.* They *shall impoverish thy fenced cities*—those cities *wherein thou trustedst* to be a protection to the country."

III. An intimation of the tender compassion God has yet for them. The enemy is commissioned to destroy and lay waste, but must not *make a full end, v.* 10. "Even *in those days,* dismal as they are, *I will not make a full end with you*"; and, if God will not, the enemy shall not.

IV. The justification of God in these proceedings. As he will appear to be gracious in not making a full end, so he will appear to be righteous in coming so near it, *v.* 19. The people *will say, Wherefore doth the Lord our God do all this unto us?* As if against such a sinful nation there did not appear cause enough of action. The prophet is instructed what answer to give them. He must tell them that God does this against them for what they have done against him, and that they may read their sin in their punishment. Have they forgotten how often they *served strange gods in their own land,* and therefore is it not just with God to make them *serve strangers* in a strange land, Deut. xxviii. 47, 48.

Verses 20–24

The prophet, having reproved them, is here sent to them again upon another errand, which he must *publish in Judah*; to persuade them to fear God.

I. He complains of the shameful stupidity of this people. They are a *foolish people and without understanding*; they apprehend not the mind of God, though ever so plainly declared to them by his prophets, and by his providence (*v.* 21): *They have eyes, but they see not, ears, but they hear not.* They had intellectual faculties, but they did not employ them as they ought. Their wills were stubborn and unapt to submit to the rules of the divine law (*v.* 23): *This people has a revolting and a rebellious heart.* It is the corrupt bias of the will that besots the understanding. The character of this people is the true character of all people till the grace of God has wrought a change. We are *foolish,* slow of understanding, and have *a revolting and a rebellious heart,* not only revolting from him by a rooted aversion to that which is good, but rebellious against him by a strong inclination to that which is evil.

II. He ascribed this to the want of the fear of God. When he observes them to be without understanding he asks, "*Fear you not me, saith the Lord, and will you not tremble at my presence?*" (*v.* 22). When he observes that *they have revolted and gone* he adds this, as the cause of their apostasy (*v.* 24), *Neither say they in their hearts, Let us now fear the Lord our God.* Therefore bad thoughts come into their mind, because they will not admit and entertain good thoughts.

III. He suggests some of those things to possess us with a holy fear of God.

1. We must fear the Lord and his greatness, *v.* 22. Here is one instance: he keeps the sea within compass. Though the tides flow with a mighty strength twice every day, and if they should flow on would drown the world, though in a storm the billows dash to the shore with incredible force, yet they return, and no harm is done. *This is the Lord's doing,* and if it were not common, it would be *marvellous in our eyes.* A wall of sand shall be as effectual as a wall of brass to check the flowing waves, to teach us that a *soft answer turns away wrath,* and quiets a foaming

JAMIESON, FAUSSET, BROWN

14. ye . . . thy . . . this people—He turns away from addressing the people to the prophet; implying that He puts them to a distance from Him, and only communicates with them through His prophet (vs. 19). **fire . . . wood**—Thy denunciations of judgments shall be fulfilled and shall consume them as fire does wood. In ch. 23:29 it is the *penetrating energy* of fire which is the point of comparison.

15. (Ch. 1:15; 6:22.) Alluding to Deuteronomy 28:49, etc. **Israel**—i.e., Judah. **mighty**—from an *Arabic* root, "enduring." The fourfold repetition of "nation" heightens the force. **ancient**—The Chaldeans came originally from the Carduchian and Armenian mountains north of Mesopotamia, whence they immigrated into Babylonia; like all mountaineers, they were brave and hardy (*Note,* Isa. 23:13). **language . . . knowest not**—Isaiah 36:11 shows that *Aramaic* was not understood by the *multitude,* but only by the educated classes [MAURER]. HENDERSON refers it to the *original language* of the Babylonians, which, he thinks, they brought with them from their native hills, akin to the Persic, not to the Aramaic, or any other Semitic tongue, the parent of the modern *Kurd.* **16. open sepulchre**—(Cf. Ps. 5:9). Their quiver is all-devouring, as the grave opened to receive the dead: as many as are the arrows, so many are the deaths. **17.** (Lev. 26:16.) **18.** (vs. 10; ch. 4:27.) **Nevertheless**—*Not even* in those days of judgments, will God utterly exterminate His people.

19. Retribution in kind. As ye have forsaken Me (ch. 2:13), so shall ye be forsaken by Me. As ye have served strange (foreign) gods in your land, so shall ye serve strangers (foreigners) in a land not yours.

21. eyes . . . ears, and—Translate, "and yet" (cf. Deut. 29:4; Isa. 6:9). Having powers of perception, they did not use them: still they were responsible for the exercise of them.

23. (Ch. 6:28.)

22. sand—Though made up of particles easily shifting about, I render it sufficient to curb the violence of the sea. Such is your monstrous perversity, that the raging, senseless sea sooner obeys Me, than ye do who profess to be intelligent [CALVIN], (Job 26:10; 38:10; 11; Prov. 8:29; Rev. 15:4).

ADAM CLARKE

14. *Because ye speak this word.* Because you thus treat My message, *I will make my words in thy mouth fire.* They have said, "They are but air"; but I will make them fire, and a fire too that shall devour them. And how this was to be done, and by whom, is mentioned in the next verse.

15. *I will bring a nation.* The Babylonians, whose antiquity was great, that empire being founded by Nimrod.

Whose language thou knowest not. The Chaldee, which, though a dialect of the Hebrew, is so very different in its words and construction that in hearing it spoken they could not possibly collect the meaning of what was said.

16. *Their quiver is an open sepulchre.* They are such exact archers as never to miss their mark; every arrow is sure to slay one man.

18. *I will not make a full end.* There are more evils in store for you. You shall not only be spoiled, and all your property destroyed, but you shall be carried into captivity; and you shall "serve strangers in a land that is not yours," v. 19.

23. *They are revolted and gone.* They have abandoned Me, and are gone farther and farther into transgression.

MATTHEW HENRY

rage, when *grievous words*, like hard rocks, do but exasperate. This bound is placed *by a perpetual decree*, and it sends us back to the creation of the world, when God divided between the sea and the dry land, Gen. i. 9, 10, Ps. civ. 6, &c., and Job xxxviii. 8, &c. It is a *perpetual decree*; it has had its effect to this day and shall still continue till day and night come to an end. Now this is a good reason why we should fear God; for we see that he is a God of universal sovereignty.

2. We must fear the Lord and his goodness, Hos. iii. 5. We must *fear the Lord our God*, that is, we must worship him, because he is continually doing us good: he gives us both *the former and the latter rain*, the former a little after seed-time, the latter a little before harvest, and by this means *he reserves to us the appointed weeks of harvest*. In harvest mercies therefore God is to be acknowledged, his power, and goodness, and faithfulness, for they all come from him. And it is a good reason why we should fear him, that we may keep ourselves in his love.

Verses 25–31

I. The prophet shows them what mischief their sins had done them: "It is *your sin* that *has withholden good from you*, when God was ready to bestow it upon you." It is that which makes the heavens as brass and the earth as iron.

II. He shows them how great their sins were. When they had forsaken the worship of the true God, even moral honesty was lost among them: *Among my people are found wicked men* (*v.* 26), and so much the worse they were for being found among God's people. They were *found* (that is, caught) in the very act of their wickedness. As hunters or fowlers lay snares for their game, so did they *lie in wait* to *catch men*, and made a sport of it. They contrived ways of doing mischief to good people (whom they hated for their goodness), especially to those that faithfully reproved them (Isa. xxix. 21), or to those whose estates they coveted; so Jezebel ensnared Naboth for his vineyard. They were false and treacherous (*v.* 27): *As a cage*, or *coop*, is *full of birds*, and of food for them to fatten them for the table, so are *their houses full of deceit*, of wealth obtained by fraudulent practices. Whoever deals with them, they will cheat him if they can. Herein *they overpass the deeds of the wicked*, *v.* 28. Those that act by deceit, with a colour of law and justice, do more mischief perhaps than those wicked men (*v.* 26) that carry all before them by open force and violence. They prosper in these wicked courses and therefore their hearts are hardened in them. *They have become great* in the world; *they have waxen rich*, and thrive upon it. They are sleek and smooth: *They shine;* they look fair and gay; everybody admires them. And they *pass by matters of evil* (so some read the following words); they *are not in trouble as other men*, much less as we might expect bad men. When they had got power in their hands they did not do good with it. *They judge not the cause, the cause of the fatherless, and the right of the needy* And *yet they prosper* still; *God layeth not folly to them.* Certainly then the things of this world are not the best things, for oftentimes the worst men have the most of them; yet we are not to think that God allows of their practices. No; *though sentence against* their *evil works be not executed speedily*, it will be executed. There was a general corruption (*v.* 30, 31): *A wonderful and horrible thing is committed in the land.* The degeneracy of such a people, so privileged and advanced, was a wonderful thing, a horrible thing, to be detested. The leaders misled the people: *The prophets prophesy falsely.* Religion is never more dangerously attacked than under colour and pretence of divine revelation. *The priests bear rule by their means;* in grandeur and wealth, laziness and luxury. The people were well enough pleased to be so misled: "They are *my people*," says God, "and should have borne their testimony against the wickedness of their priests and prophets; but they *love to have it so*." They love to be ridden with a loose rein, and like those rulers very well that will not restrain their lusts.

III. He shows them how fatal the consequences of this would be. *Shall not I visit for these things?* Here, judgment is reasoning against mercy: *Shall I not visit?* We are sure that Infinite Wisdom knows how to accommodate the matter between them. *Shall not my soul be avenged?* Yes, without doubt, if the sinner repent not. *What will you do in the end thereof?* Those that walk in bad ways would do well to consider the tendency of them both to greater sin and utter ruin.

JAMIESON, FAUSSET, BROWN

24. rain . . . former . . . latter—The "former" falls from the middle of October to the beginning of December. The "latter," or spring rain in Palestine, falls before harvest in March and April, and is essential for ripening the crops (Deut. 11:14; Joel 2:23). **weeks of . . . harvest**—the seven weeks between passover and pentecost, beginning on the 16th of Nisan (Deut. 16:9). By God's special providence no rain fell in Palestine during the harvest weeks, so that harvest work went on without interruption (see Gen. 8:22).

25. National guilt had caused the suspension of these national mercies mentioned in vs. 24 (cf. ch. 3:3).

26. (Prov. 1:11, 17, 18; Hab. 1:15.) **as he that setteth snares**—rather, "as fowlers crouch" [MAURER]. **trap**—lit., destruction: the instrument of destruction. **catch men**—not as Peter, to save (Luke 5:10), but to destroy men.

27. full of deceit—full of treasures got by deceit.

rich—(Ps. 73:12, 18-20). **28. shine**—the effect of fatness on the skin (Deut. 32:15). They live a life of self-indulgence. **overpass . . . the wicked**—exceed even the Gentiles in wickedness (ch. 2:33; Ezek. 5:6, 7). **judge not . . . fatherless**—(Isa. 1:23). **yet . . . prosper**—(ch. 12:1).

29. (Vs. 9; Mal. 3:5.) **30.** (Ch. 23:14; Hos. 6:10.)

31. bear rule by their means—lit., according to their hands, i.e., under their guidance (I Chron. 25:3). As a sample of the priests lending themselves to the deceits of the false prophets, to gain influence over the people, see ch. 29:24-32. **love to have it so**—(Mic. 2:11).

end thereof—the fatal issue of this sinful course when divine judgments shall come.

ADAM CLARKE

24. *Giveth rain, both the former and the latter.* See the note on chap. iii. 3. *The appointed weeks of the harvest.* As the early rains fell in the northern parts of Judea about the end of September, in the civil year of the Hebrews, so the latter rains fell before harvest, in the months of March and April. The appointed weeks of the harvest were those which fell between the Passover and Pentecost. In the southern parts the harvest was earlier than in the northern. If the word *weeks* be read with a *sin* instead of a *shin*, it will signify "fulness" or "sufficiency"; and thus the Septuagint and Vulgate have read it. I think the present reading is much to be preferred. God appoints a harvesttime, and in His good providence He generally gives harvest weather.

25. *Your iniquities have turned away these things.* When these appointed weeks of harvest do not come, should we not examine and see whether this be not in God's judgments? Have not our iniquities turned away these good things from us?

26. *They lay wait, as he that setteth snares.* A metaphor taken from fowlers, who, having fixed their nets, lie down and keep out of sight, that when birds come, they may be ready to draw and entangle them.

27. *As a cage is full of birds.* There is no doubt that the reference here is to a decoy or trap-cage; in these the fowlers put several tame birds, which when the wild ones see, they come and light on the cage, and fall into the snare.

28. *They judge not the cause . . . yet they prosper.* Perhaps we might be justified in translating, "And shall they prosper?"

31. *The prophets prophesy falsely.* The false prophets predict favorable things, that they may please both the princes and the people. *The priests bear rule by their means.* The false prophets affording them all that their influence and power can procure, to enable them to keep their places, and feed on the riches of the Lord's house. *And my people love to have it so.* Are perfectly satisfied with this state of things, because they are permitted to continue in their sins without reproof or restraint. The prophets and the priests united to deceive and ruin the people. The prophets gave out false predictions; by their means the priests got the government of the people into their own hands; and so infatuated were the people that they willingly abandoned themselves to those blind guides, and would not hearken to the voice of any reformer.

MATTHEW HENRY

CHAPTER 6

Verses 1–8

I. Judgment threatened against Judah and Jerusalem. The city saw no cloud gathering, but everything looked safe and serene: but the prophet tells them that they shall shortly be invaded by a foreign power *from the north,* which shall cause a general desolation. It is here foretold,

1. That the alarm should be loud and terrible. This is represented, *v.* 1. The children of Benjamin, in which tribe part of Jerusalem lay, are here called to shift for their own safety in the country; for the city (to which it was first thought advisible for them to flee, *ch.* iv. 5, 6) would soon be made too hot for them. They are told to send the alarm into the country, and to do what they can for their own safety: *Blow the trumpet in Tekoa,* a city which lay twelve miles north from Jerusalem. *Set up a sign of fire* (that is, kindle the beacons) *in Beth-haccerem,* the *house of the vineyard,* which lay on a hill between Jerusalem and Tekoa. This may be taken ironically: "When you have done your best, it will be a great destruction, for it is in vain to contend with God's judgments."

2. That the attempt upon them should be formidable. *The daughter of Zion,* on whom the assault is made, is compared *to a comely and delicate woman* (*v.* 2), and, not being accustomed to hardship, she will be the less able either to resist the enemy or to bear the destruction. The generals and their armies are compared to *shepherds* and *their flocks* (*v.* 3), in such numbers did they come, the soldiers following their leaders as sheep their shepherds. The shepherds easily make themselves masters of an open field, which lies common, owned by none, *pitch their tents* in it, and their flocks quickly eat it bare; so shall the Chaldean army easily break in upon the land of Judah, force for themselves a free quarter where they please, and in a little time devour all. God shall commission them to make this destruction. It is he that says (*v.* 4), *Prepare you war against her;* for he is the *Lord of hosts,* and he has said (*v.* 6), *Hew you down trees, and cast a mount against Jerusalem.* God has said, "*This is the city to be visited* by the divine justice, and this is the time of her visitation." They resolve to be very expeditious. *Arise, let us go up at noon,* though it be in the heat of the day; nay (*v.* 5), *Arise, let us go up by night,* though it be in the dark. "*Let us go up,* and let us destroy her palaces and make ourselves masters of the wealth that is in them."

II. The cause of this judgment is all for their wickedness; they have brought it upon themselves; they must bear the blame of it. They are thus oppressed because they have been oppressors; they have dealt hardly with one another, each in his turn, as they have had power and advantage, and now the enemy shall come and deal hardly with them all. Sin had become in a manner natural to them (*v.* 7): She *casts out wickedness,* in malice and mischievousness, *as a fountain casts out her waters,* plentifully and constantly. The cry of it had come up before God as that of Sodom: *Before me continually are grief and wounds*—the complaint of those that find themselves unjustly wounded in bodies or spirits, in estates or reputation. He that is the common Parent of mankind regards and resents, and sooner or later will revenge, the mischiefs and wrongs that men do to one another.

III. How to prevent this judgment. "*Be thou instructed, O Jerusalem! v.* 8. Receive the instruction given thee both by the law of God and by his prophets; be wise at length for thyself." *Lest my soul depart,* or *be disjoined, from thee.* This intimates what a tender affection and concern God had for them; his very soul had been joined to them, and nothing but sin could disjoin it. The God of mercy is loth to depart even from a provoking people, and is earnest with them by true repentance and reformation to prevent things coming to that extremity.

Verses 9–17

I. The ruin of Judah and Jerusalem is here threatened. We had before the haste which the Chaldean army made (*v.* 4, 5); now here we have the havoc. The enemy shall be insatiable in their thirst after treasure. *They shall thoroughly glean the remnant of Israel as a vine;* as the *grape-gatherer,* who is resolved to leave none behind, still *turns back his hand into the baskets,* to put more in. Perhaps the people, being *given to covetousness* (*v.* 13), had not observed that law of God which forbade them to *glean all their grapes* (Lev. xix. 10), and now they themselves shall be *thoroughly gleaned.* The children perish in the calamity which the fathers' sins have procured. The execution shall reach *the assembly of young men,* their merry meetings; they shall be *cut off together. Even the husband with the wife shall*

JAMIESON, FAUSSET, BROWN

CHAPTER 6

VSS. 1-30. ZION'S FOES PREPARE WAR AGAINST HER: HER SINS ARE THE CAUSE.

1. Benjamin—Jerusalem was situated in the tribe of Benjamin, which was here separated from that of Judah by the valley of Hinnom. Though it was inhabited partly by Benjamites, partly by men of Judah, he addresses the former as being his own countrymen. **blow . . . trumpet . . .Tekoa**—*Tikehu, Tekoa* form a play on sounds. The birthplace of Amos. **Beth-haccerem**—meaning in *Hebrew,* "vineyard-house." It and Tekoa were a few miles south of Jerusalem. As the enemy came from the north, the inhabitants of the surrounding country would naturally flee southwards. The fire-signal on the hills gave warning of danger approaching.

2. likened—rather, "I lay waste." Lit., "O comely and delicate one, I lay waste the daughter of Zion," i.e., thee. So Zechariah 3:9, "before *Joshua,*" i.e., before *thee* [MAURER]. **3. shepherds**—hostile leaders with their armies (ch. 1:15; 4:17; 49:20; 50:45). **feed**—They shall consume each one all that is near him; lit., "his *hand,*" i.e., the *place* which he occupies (Num. 2:17 *Note,* Isa. 56:5).

4, 5. The invading soldiers encourage one another to the attack on Jerusalem. **Prepare**—lit., "Sanctify" war, i.e., Proclaim it formally with solemn rites; the invasion was solemnly ordered by God (cf. Isa. 13:3). **at noon**—the hottest part of the day when attacks were rarely made (ch. 15:8; 20:16). Even at this time they wished to attack, such is their eagerness. **Woe unto us**—The words of the invaders, mourning the approach of night which would suspend their hostile operations; still, even in spite of the darkness, at *night* they renew the attack (vs. 5). **6. cast**—*Hebrew,* "pour out"; referring to the emptying of the baskets of earth to make the *mound,* formed of "trees" and earthwork, to overtop the city walls. The "trees" were also used to make warlike engines. **this**—pointing the invaders to Jerusalem. **visited**—i.e., punished. **wholly oppression**—or join "wholly" with "visited," i.e., she is altogether (in her whole extent) to be punished [MAURER]. **7. fountain**—rather, a *well* dug, from which water springs; distinct from a natural spring or fountain. **casteth out**—causeth to flow; lit., causeth to dig, the cause being put for the effect (II Kings 21:16, 24; Isa. 57:20). **me**—Jehovah.

8. Tender appeal in the midst of threats. **depart**—*Hebrew,* "be torn away"; Jehovah's affection making Him unwilling to depart; His attachment to Jerusalem was such that an effort was needed to tear Himself from it (Ezek. 23:18; Hos 9:12; 11:8).

9. The Jews are the grapes, their enemies the unsparing gleaners. **turn back . . . hand**—again and again bring freshly gathered handfuls to the baskets; referring to the repeated carrying away of captives to Babylon (ch. 52:28-30; II Kings 24:14; 25:11).

ADAM CLARKE

CHAPTER 6

1. *O ye children of Benjamin, gather yourselves to flee.* As the invading armies are fast approaching, the prophet calls on the inhabitants of Jerusalem to sound an alarm, and collect all the people to arm themselves and go against the invaders. They are called the children of Benjamin, because Jerusalem was in the tribe of Benjamin. *Tekoa.* Was a city about twelve miles to the south of Jerusalem. *Beth-haccerem.* Was the name of a small village situated on an eminence between Jerusalem and Tekoa. On this they were ordered to set up a beacon, or kindle a large *fire,* which might be seen at a distance, and give the people to understand that an enemy was entering the land. *Out of the north.* From Babylon.

3. *The shepherds with their flocks.* The chiefs and their battalions. The invading army is about to spoil and waste all the fertile fields round about the city, while engaged in the siege.

4. *Prepare ye war against her.* The words of the invaders exciting each other to the assault, and impatient lest any time should be lost; lest the besieged should have time to strengthen themselves, or get in supplies.

5. *Arise, and let us go by night.* Since we have lost the day, let us not lose the night; but, taking advantage of the darkness, let us make a powerful assault while they are under the impression of terror.

6. *Hew ye down trees.* To form machines. *And cast a mount.* That may overlook the city, on which to place our engines. *This is the city to be visited.* We are sure of success, for their God will deliver it into our hands; for it is full of oppression, and He has consigned it to destruction.

7. *As a fountain casteth out her waters.* The inhabitants are incessant in their acts of iniquity; they do nothing but sin.

8. *Be thou instructed.* Still there is respite. If they would even now return unto the Lord with all their heart, the advancing Chaldeans would be arrested on their march and turned back.

9. *They shall throughly glean the remnant of Israel as a vine: turn back thine hand.* The Chaldeans are here exhorted to *turn back* and glean up the remnant of the inhabitants that were left after the capture of Jerusalem; for even that remnant did not profit by the divine judgments that fell on the inhabitants at large.

MATTHEW HENRY

be taken and the old with the full of days, whose deaths can contribute no more to their safety than their lives to their service. *Their houses shall then be turned to others* (*v.* 12). The prophet justifies himself in preaching thus terribly (*v.* 11): *I am full of the fury of the Lord.* He took no delight in threatening, but he could not contain himself; he was *weary with holding in,* but he was so *full of power by the Spirit of the Lord of hosts* that he must speak. *The priest and the prophet* have *dealt falsely,* have not told the people their faults and the danger they were in; they should have been their physicians, but they murdered their patients by giving them everything they had a mind to, and flattering them that they were in no danger (*v.* 14): They have *healed the hurt of the daughter of my people slightly,* soothing people in their sins, and giving them opiates to make them easy, while the disease was preying upon the vitals. They said, "*Peace, peace*—all shall be well", when *there is no peace,* because they went on in their daring impieties. Those are to be reckoned our false friends (that is, our worst and most dangerous enemies) who flatter us in a sinful way.

II. The sin of Judah and Jerusalem which provoked God to bring this ruin. 1. They would by no means bear to be told of their danger. God bids the prophet give them warning of the judgment coming (*v.* 9); "but," says, he "*to whom shall I speak and give warning?* I cannot speak *that they may hear,* for *their ear is uncircumcised.* The *word of the Lord is unto them a reproach;* the reproofs and the threatenings are so." Those reproofs that are counted reproaches, will certainly be turned into woes. 2. They were set upon the world, and carried away by the love of it (*v.* 13): "*From the least of them even to the greatest, everyone is given to covetousness,* greedy of filthy lucre," and this made them oppressive and violent (*v.* 6, 7). This hardened their hearts against the word of God and his prophets. 3. They were past shame. Their hearts were so hardened that *they were not at all ashamed, neither could they blush,* they had so brazened their faces. They resolved to face it out against God himself. Those that will not submit to a penitential shame shall not escape utter ruin: *Therefore they shall fall among* those *that fall;* they shall be made to tremble, because they would not blush. Those that sin and cannot blush for it are in an evil case now, and it will be worse with them shortly. At first they hardened themselves and would not blush, afterwards they were so hardened that they could not. *They have lost the only good property which once blended itself with many bad ones, that is, shame for having done amiss.*

III. The good counsel often given them in vain. God used to say to them, *Stand in the ways and see.* He would have them do as travellers who are in care to find the right way which will bring them to their journey's end, and therefore enquire for it. O that men would be thus *wise for their souls.* "*Ask for the old paths, enquire of the former age* (Job viii. 8), *ask thy father, thy elders* (Deut. xxxii. 7), and thou wilt find that the way of godliness has always been the way which God has owned and blessed and in which men have prospered. Ask for the *old paths,* the paths that the patriarchs travelled, Abraham, and Isaac, and Jacob; and, as you hope to inherit the promises made to them, tread in their steps. *Ask for the old paths, Where is the good way?*" But there is an *old way which wicked men have trodden,* Job. xxii. 15. When we ask for the old paths, it is only to find out the *good way.* Note, The way of religion and godliness is a good old way, the way that all the saints in all ages have walked in. "When you have found out which is the good way, *walk therein,* and persevere in it." Some make this counsel to be given them with reference to the struggles between the true and false prophets. "*Stand in the way,*" says God, "and enquire, which agrees with the written word and the usual methods of God's providence, which of these directs you to the good way, and do accordingly. *Walk in the good old way* and you will enjoy God and yourselves, and the way will lead you to true rest. You will find an abundant recompence at your journey's end." *But they said,* "*We will not walk therein,* we will not deny ourselves and our humours so far as to *walk in it.*" Because they would not be ruled by fair reasoning, God, by less judgments threatens greater, and sends his prophets to frighten them with an apprehension of the danger they were in (*v.* 17): *Also I set watchmen over you.* This was the burden of their song; *Hearken to the sound of the trumpet.* God, in his providence, sounds the trumpet (Zech. ix. 14); the watchmen hear it (Jer. iv. 19), and they call upon others to hearken to it too. *But they said,* "*We will not hearken;* we will not heed, the prophets may as well save themselves and us the trouble."

JAMIESON, FAUSSET, BROWN

11. fury of . . . Lord—His denunciations against Judah communicated to the prophet. **weary with holding in**—(ch. 20:9). **I will pour**—or else imperative: the command of God (see vs. 12), "Pour it out" [MAURER]. **aged . . . full of days**—The former means *one becoming old;* the latter a *decrepit old man* [MAURER] (Job 5:26; Isa. 65:20). **12.** The very punishments threatened by Moses in the event of disobedience to God (Deut. 28:30). **turned**—transferred. **13.** (Ch. 8:10; Isa. 56:11; Mic. 3:11.) **14. hurt**—the spiritual *wound.* **slightly**—as if it were but a *slight* wound; or, *in a slight manner,* pronouncing all sound where there is no soundness. **saying**—viz., the prophets and priests (vs. 13). Whereas they ought to warn the people of impending judgments and the need of repentance, they say there is nothing to fear. **peace**—including soundness. All is *sound* in the nation's moral state, so all will be *peace* as to its political state (ch. 4:10; 8:11; 14:13; 23:17; Ezek. 13:5, 10; 22:28).

10. ear is uncircumcised—closed against the precepts of God by the foreskin of carnality (Lev. 26:41; Ezek. 44:7; Acts 7:51). **word . . . reproach**—(ch. 20:8).

15. ROSENMULLER translates, "They *ought to have been* ashamed, because . . . but," etc.; the *Hebrew* verb often expressing, not the action, but the *duty* to perform it, Gen. 20:9; Mal. 2:7). MAURER translates, "They shall be put to shame, for they commit abomination; nay (the prophet correcting himself), there is no shame in them" (ch. 3:3; 8:12; Ezek. 3:7; Zeph. 3:5). **them that fall**—They shall fall with the rest of their people who are doomed to fall, i.e., I will now cease from words; I will execute vengeance [CALVIN].

16. Image from travellers who have lost their road, stopping and inquiring which is the right way on which they once had been, but from which they have wandered. **old paths**—Idolatry and apostasy are the modern way; the worship of God the *old* way. Evil is not coeval with good, but a *modern degeneracy* from good. The forsaking of God is not, in a true sense, a "way cast up" at all (ch. 18:15; Ps. 139:24; Mal. 4:4). **rest**—(Isa. 28:12; Matt. 11:29).

17. watchmen—prophets, whose duty it was to announce impending calamities, so as to lead the people to repentance (Isa. 21:11; 58:1; Ezek. 3:17; Hab. 2:1).

ADAM CLARKE

11. *I am full of the fury of the Lord.* God has given me a dreadful revelation of the judgments He intends to inflict: my soul is burdened with this prophecy. I have endeavored to suppress it, but I must pour it forth.

14. *They have healed also the hurt of the daughter of my people slightly.* "Of the daughter" is not in the text, and is here improperly added.

10. *The word of the Lord is unto them a reproach.* It is an object of derision; they despise it.

16. *Thus saith the Lord, Stand ye in the ways, and see.* Let us observe the metaphor. A traveller is going to a particular city. He comes to a place where the road divides into several paths; he is afraid of going astray. He stops short—endeavors to find out the right path; he cannot fix his choice. At last he sees another traveller; he inquires of him, gets proper directions—proceeds on his journey—arrives at the desired place—and reposes after his fatigue. There is an excellent sermon on these words in the works of our first poet, Geoffrey Chaucer; it is among *The Canterbury Tales,* and is called "Chaucer's Tale."

17. *I set watchmen.* I have sent prophets to warn you.

MATTHEW HENRY

Verses 18–30

I. God appeals to the whole world concerning the equity of his proceedings against Judah and Jerusalem (*v.* 18, 19): "*Hear, you nations, and know* particularly, *O congregation* of the mighty, the great men of the nations. Observe now Judah and Jerusalem; you all wonder that *I* should *bring evil upon this people,* that are in covenant with me, *Wherefore has the Lord done thus to this land?* Know then the evil brought upon them is *the fruit of their thought.* They thought to strengthen themselves by their alliance with foreigners, and by that they weakened and exposed themselves. That is the just punishment of their disobedience and rebellion. It is because *they have not hearkened to my words nor to my law,* but rejected it all. Therefore you cannot say that they have any wrong done them."

II. God rejects their plea, by which they insisted upon their services as sufficient to atone for their sins. It is a frivolous plea (*v.* 20): "*To what purpose come there to me incense and sweet cane,* to be burnt for a perfume on the golden altar? What care I for *your burnt-offerings* and *your sacrifices?*" Sacrifice and incense were appointed to direct them to a Mediator, and assist their faith in him. Where this good use was made of them they were acceptable, God had respect to them and to those that offered them. But when they were offered with an opinion that they purchased a license to go on in sin, far from being pleasing to God, they were a provocation to him.

III. He foretells the desolation. God designs their ruin because they hate to be reformed (*v.* 21): *I will lay stumbling-blocks before this people,* occasions of falling not into sin, but into trouble. God retards all the methods they take for their own safety. The parties of the enemy, were stumbling-blocks to them. *The fathers and the sons together shall fall upon them;* neither the fathers with their wisdom, nor the sons with their strength shall escape them. He will make the Chaldeans instruments. Babylon a great way northward, and some of the countries that were subject to the king of Babylon, must be employed in this service, *v.* 22, 23. It is *a great nation,* a warlike people. *They lay hold on bow and spear,* know how to use them. *They ride upon horses,* and therefore move the more swiftly, and in battle press the harder. They *are cruel and have no mercy,* their voice *roars like the sea.* They are *set in array against thee, O daughter of Zion!*

IV. He describes the consternation which Judah and Jerusalem should be in upon the approach of this formidable enemy, *v.* 24–26. "When *we have but heard the fame thereof our hands wax feeble,* and we have no heart to make any resistance; *anguish has taken hold of us,* and we are like *a woman in travail.*" Sense of guilt dispirits men, upon the approach of trouble. They confine themselves to their houses; they would rather die tamely there than by fight or flight, to help themselves. They say one to another, "*Go not forth into the field, nor walk by the way;* it is at your peril if you do, for the *sword of the enemy,* and the fear of it, are *on every side.*" The prophet calls upon them to lament: "*O daughter of my people,* hear thy God calling thee to mourning: do not only put on sackcloth for a day; do not only put ashes on thy head, but *wallow thyself in ashes* as parents *mourn for an only son.*"

V. He constitutes the prophet a judge over this people that now stand upon their trial: *I have set thee for a tower,* or as a sentinel upon a tower, *among my people, that thou mayest know, and try their way,* *v.* 27. Thus God appeals to the prophet himself, and his own observation, that he might be fully satisfied in the equity of God's proceedings against them. God set him for a tower, but made him a *fortress, a strong tower,* gave him courage to bear the shock of their displeasure. He will find (*v.* 28): *They are all grievous revolters, revolters of revolters* (so the word is), the worst of revolters. They *walk with slanders,* backbiting one another. They are *brass and iron,* base metals. They were as silver and gold, but they have degenerated. As *they are all revolters,* so *they are all corrupters,* industrious to debauch others. It was in vain to think of reforming them, for various methods had been tried all to no purpose, *v.* 29, 30. He compares them to ore that was supposed to have some good metal in it, and was therefore put into the furnace by the refiner, but it proved all dross. God by his prophets and by his providences had used means to refine this people, but it was all in vain. By a series of afflictions, they had been kept in a constant fire, but all to no purpose. *The bellows* have been kept so near the fire, to blow it, that they *are burnt* with the heat of it. The *lead,* which was then used in refining silver, as quicksilver is now, *is consumed of the fire,* and has not done its work. *The founder melts in vain;* his labour is lost, *for the wicked are not*

JAMIESON, FAUSSET, BROWN

18. congregation—parallel to "nations"; it therefore means *the gathered peoples* who are invited to be witnesses as to how great is the perversity of the Israelites (vss. 16, 17), and that they deserve the severe punishment about to be inflicted on them (vs. 19). **what is among them**—what *deeds* are committed by the *Israelites* (vss. 16, 17) [MAURER]. Or, "what *punishments* are about to be inflicted on them" [CALVIN]. **19.** (Isa. 1:2.) **fruit of . . . thoughts**—(Prov. 1:31). **nor to my law, but rejected it**—lit., "and (as to) My law they have rejected it." The same construction occurs in Genesis 22:24. **20.** Lit., "To what purpose is this to Me, that incense cometh to Me?" **incense . . . cane**—(Isa. 43:24; 60: 6). No external services are accepted by God without obedience of the heart and life (ch. 7:21; Ps. 50:7-9; Isa. 1:11; Mic. 6:6, etc.). **sweet . . . sweet**—antithesis. Your *sweet* cane is not *sweet* to Me. The calamus.

21. stumbling-blocks—instruments of the Jews' ruin (cf. Matt. 21:44; Isa. 8:14; I Pet. 2:8). God Himself ("I") *lays* them before the reprobate (Ps. 69:22; Rom. 1:28; 11:9). **fathers . . . sons . . . neighbour . . . friend**—indiscriminate ruin. **22. north . . . sides of the earth**—The ancients were little acquainted with the *north;* therefore it is called *the remotest regions* (as the *Hebrew* for "sides" ought to be translated, see *Note,* Isa. 14:13) *of the earth.* The Chaldees are meant (ch. 1:15; 5:15). It is striking that the very same calamities which the Chaldeans had inflicted on Zion are threatened as the retribution to be dealt in turn to themselves by Jehovah (ch. 50:41-43). **23. like the sea**—(Isa. 5:30). **as men for war**—not that they were *like* warriors, for they *were* warriors; but "arrayed *most perfectly as warriors*" [MAURER]. **24. fame thereof**—the report of them. **25.** He addresses "the daughter of Zion" (vs. 23); caution to the citizens of Jerusalem not to expose themselves to the enemy by going outside of the city walls. **sword of the enemy**—lit., "there is a sword to the enemy"; the enemy hath a sword. **26. wallow . . . in ashes**—(ch. 25:34; Mic. 1:10). As they usually in mourning only "cast ashes on the head," *wallowing in them* means something more, viz., so entirely to cover one's self with ashes as to be like one who had rolled in them (Ezek. 27:30). **as for an only son**—(Amos 8:10; Zech. 12:10.) **lamentation**—lit., lamentation expressed by beating the breast. **27. tower . . . fortress**—(ch. 1:18), rather, "an assayer (and) explorer." By a metaphor from metallurgy in vss. 27-30, Jehovah, in conclusion, confirms the prophet in his office, and the latter sums up the description of the reprobate people on whom he had to work. The *Hebrew* for "assayer" (*English Version,* "tower") is from a root "to try" metals. "Explorer" (*English Version,* "fortress") is from an *Arabic* root, "keen-sighted"; or a *Hebrew* root, "cutting," i.e., separating the metal from the dross [EWALD]. GESENIUS translates as *English Version,* "fortress," which does not accord with the previous "assayer." **28. grievous revolters**—lit., "contumacious of the contumacious," i.e., most contumacious, the *Hebrew* mode of expressing a superlative. So "the strong among the mighty," i.e., the strongest (Ezek. 32:21). See ch. 5:23; Hosea 4:16. **walking with slanders**—(ch. 9:4). "Going about for the purpose of slandering" [MAURER]. **brass . . .**—i.e., copper. It and "iron" being the baser and harder metals express the debased and obdurate character of the Jews (Isa. 48:4; 60:17). **29. bellows . . . burned**—So intense a heat is made that the very bellows are almost set on fire. ROSENMULLER translates not so well from a *Hebrew* root, "pant" or "snort," referring to the sound of the bellows blown hard. **lead**—employed to separate the baser metal from the silver, as quicksilver is now used. In other words, the utmost pains have been used to purify Israel in the furnace of affliction, but in vain (ch. 5:3; I Pet. 1:7). **consumed of the fire**—In the *Chetib* or *Hebrew* text, the "consumed" is supplied out of the previous "burned." Translating as ROSENMULLER, "pant," this will be inadmissible; and the *Keri* (*Hebrew margin*) division of the *Hebrew* words will have to be read, to get "is consumed of the fire." This is an argument for the translation, "are burned." **founder**—the refiner.

ADAM CLARKE

20. *Incense from Sheba.* Sheba was in Arabia, famous for the best incense. It was situated towards the southern extremity of the peninsula of Arabia; and was, in respect of Judea, *a far country.*

23. *They shall lay hold on bow and spear.* Still pointing out the Chaldeans.

27. *I have set thee for a tower and a fortress.* The words refer to the office of an assayer of silver and gold. The people are here represented under the notion of "alloyed silver." They are full of impurities; and they are put into the hands of the prophet, the assayer, to be purified. The "bellows" are placed, the "fire" is lighted up, but all to no purpose; so intensely commixed is the alloy with the silver that it cannot be separated.

MATTHEW HENRY

plucked away, no care is taken to cast out of communion those who, being corrupt, are in danger of infecting others. Doom is passed upon them (*v.* 30): *Reprobate silver shall they be called*, useless and worthless; they glitter as if they had some silver in them, but there is nothing of real goodness to be found among them; and *the Lord has rejected them.* God has *no pleasure in the death* and ruin of sinners. He did not reject them till he had used all proper means to reform them; nor abandon them as dross till it appeared that they were *reprobate silver.*

CHAPTER 7

Verses 1-15

These verses begin another sermon, which is continued in the two following chapters, to reason them to repentance.

I. The orders given to the prophet: This was *a word* that *came to him from the Lord*, *v.* 1. 1. Where it must be preached—*in the gate of the Lord's house*, through which they entered into the outer court. It would affront the priests, and expose the prophets to their rage, but the prophet must not fear the face of man. 2. To whom it must be preached—to the men of *Judah, that enter in at these gates to worship the Lord;* probably it was at one of the three feasts, when all the males were to appear and not to *appear empty.*

II. The contents and scope of the sermon itself. It is delivered in the name of *the Lord of hosts, the God of Israel*, who commands the world, but covenants with his people. The prophet here tells them,

1. What were the true words of God. In short, if they would repent and return to God, he would restore their peace, redress their grievances, and return to them in mercy (*v.* 3): *Amend your ways and your doings.* God shows them where and how they must amend, and promises to accept them: "*I will cause you to dwell* quietly and peaceably *in this place*, and a stop shall be put to that which threatens your expulsion." They must *thoroughly amend*; it must be a universal, constant, persevering reformation, not wavering, but constant. They must be honest and just in all their dealings. Those that had power must *thoroughly execute judgment between a man and his neighbour*, without partiality. They must not *oppress the stranger, the fatherless, or the widow*, nor protect those that did oppress. They must *not shed innocent blood*, and with it defile *this place* and the land wherein they dwelt. They must keep closely to the worship of the true God only: *Neither walk after other gods;* do not hanker after them. "Set about such a work of reformation with all speed, *and I will cause you to dwell in this place*, this temple; it shall continue your refuge, the place of your meeting with God and one another; and you shall never be turned out either from God's house or from your own." They shall enjoy it by covenant not by providence, but by promise. They shall not be disturbed *for ever and ever*; nothing but sin could throw them out. An everlasting inheritance in the heavenly Canaan is hereby secured to all that live in godliness and honesty.

2. What were the lying words of their own hearts, which they must not trust. He cautions them (*v.* 4): "*Trust not in lying words.* You are told in what way you may be safe, and happy; do not flatter yourselves that you may be so in any other way." *Behold*, it is plain that *you* do *trust in lying words*, notwithstanding what is said to you; you trust in *words that cannot profit.* Now these lying words were, "*The temple of the Lord, the temple of the Lord, the temple of the Lord are these.* Here he resides, here he is worshipped, here we meet three times a year to pay our homage to him as our King in his palace." This they thought was security enough. When the prophets told them how sinful they were, still they appealed to the temple. It was the cant of the times; it was in their mouths upon all occasions. The privileges of a *form of godliness* are often the pride and confidence of those that are strangers and enemies to the power of it. It is common for those that are furthest from God to boast themselves most of their being near to the church (Zeph. iii. 11). If they knew anything either of the *temple of the Lord* or of the *Lord of the temple*, they must think that to plead that in excuse of their sin was most unreasonable. God is a holy God; but this plea made him the patron of sin, *v.* 9, 10. "When you have done the worst you can against God, will you brazen your faces so far as to *stand before him in this house which is called by his name*—stand before him as suppliants expecting his favour? It is as if you should say, *We are delivered*

JAMIESON, FAUSSET, BROWN

wicked . . . not plucked away—answering to the dross which has no good metal to be separated, the mass being all dross. **30. Reprobate**—silver so full of alloy as to be utterly worthless (Isa. 1:22). The Jews were fit only for rejection.

CHAPTER 7

Vss. 1-34. Chapters 7-9. Delivered in the Beginning of Jehoiakim's Reign, on the Occasion of Some Public Festival. The prophet stood at the gate of the temple in order that the multitudes from the country might hear him. His life was threatened, it appears from ch. 26:1-9, for this prophecy, denouncing the fate of Shiloh as about to befall the temple at Jerusalem. The prophecy given in detail here is summarily referred to there. After Josiah's death the nation relapsed into idolatry through Jehoiakim's bad influence; the worship of Jehovah was, however, combined with it (vss. 4, 10). **2. the gate**—i.e., the gate of the court of Israel within that of the women. Those whom Jeremiah addresses came through the gate leading into the court of the women, and the gate leading into the outer court, or court of the Gentiles ("these gates").

3. cause you to dwell—permit you still to dwell (ch. 18:11; 26:13).

5. For—"But" [Maurer]. **judgment**—justice (ch. 22:3).

6. this place—this city and land (vs. 7) **to your hurt**—so vs. 19; "to the confusion or their own faces" (ch. 13:10; Prov. 8:36). **7.** The apodosis to the "if . . . if" (vss. 5, 6). **to dwell**—to continue to dwell. **for ever and ever**—joined with "to dwell," not with the words "gave to your fathers" (cf ch. 3: 18; Deut. 4:40).

4. The Jews falsely thought that because their temple had been chosen by Jehovah as His peculiar dwelling, it could never be destroyed. Men think that ceremonial observances will supersede the need of holiness (Isa. 48:2; Mic. 3:11). The triple repetition of "the temple of Jehovah" expresses the intense confidence of the Jews (see ch. 22:29; Isa. 6:3). **these**—the temple buildings which the prophet points to with his finger (vs. 2).

8. that cannot profit—Maurer translates, "so that you profit nothing" (see vs. 4; ch. 5:31). **9, 10.** "Will ye steal . . . *and then* come and stand before Me?" **whom ye know not**—Ye have no grounds of "knowing" that *they* are gods; but I have manifested My Godhead by My law, by benefits conferred, and by miracles. This aggravates their crime [Calvin] (Judg. 5:8).

ADAM CLARKE

CHAPTER 7

1. *The word that came to Jeremiah.* This prophecy is supposed to have been delivered in the first year of the reign of Jehoiakim, son of Josiah, who, far from following the example of his pious father, restored idolatry, maintained bad priests and worse prophets, and filled Jerusalem with abominations of all kinds.

2. *Stand in the gate of the Lord's house.* There was a show of public worship kept up. The Temple was considered God's residence; the usual ceremonies of religion restored by Josiah were still observed; and the people were led to consider the Temple and its services as sacred things, which would be preservatives to them in case of the threatened invasion.

5. *If ye throughly amend your ways.* Literally, "If in making good you fully make good your ways." God will no longer admit of half-hearted work.

4. *The temple of the Lord.* They seem to express the conviction which the people had, that they should be safe while their Temple service continued; for they supposed that God would not give it up into profane hands. But sacred places and sacred symbols are nothing in the sight of God when the heart is not right with Him.

MATTHEW HENRY

to do all these abominations." Some take it thus: "You present yourselves before God with your sacrifices and sin-offerings, and then say, *We are delivered,* we are discharged from our guilt, when all this is but to blind the world, that you may the more easily *do all these abominations. Has this house, which is called by my name* and is a sign of God's kingdom, set up in opposition to the kingdom of sin and Satan—*has this become a den of robbers in your eyes?* Do you think it was built to be a refuge to malefactors?" Though the horns of the altar were a sanctuary to him that slew a man unawares, they were not so to a wilful murderer, Exod. xxi. 14; 1 Kings ii. 29. *Behold, I have seen it, saith the Lord,* have seen the real iniquity through the counterfeit piety. He shows them the insufficiency of this plea in the case of Shiloh. It is certain that Shiloh was ruined, though it had God's sanctuary in it, when by its wickedness it profaned that sanctuary (*v.* 12): *Go you now to my place which was in Shiloh.* There God *set his name at the first,* there the tabernacle was set up (Joshua xviii. 1), but those that attended the service of the tabernacle there corrupted both themselves and others, and from them arose the *wickedness of his people Israel,* and what came of it? Was it protected by its having the tabernacle in it? God *forsook* it (Ps. lxxviii. 60), sent his ark into captivity, cut off the house of Eli that presided there. *Remember Lot's wife;* remember Shiloh and the seven churches of Asia; and know that the ark and candlestick are movable things, Rev. ii. 5; Matt. xxi. 43. Jerusalem was now as sinful as ever Shiloh was (*v.* 13): "*You have done all these works,* you cannot deny it." God spoke, but they *heard not,* they never minded; he *called them,* but they *answered not;* they would not come at his call. Jerusalem shall shortly be as miserable as ever Shiloh was: *Therefore I will do unto this house as I did to Shiloh,* ruin it, and lay it waste, *v.* 14. "This house" (says God) "is *called by my name,* and therefore you may think that I should protect it; but the men of Shiloh thus flattered themselves and did but deceive themselves." He quotes another precedent (*v.* 15), the ruin of the kingdom of the ten tribes, who were the seed of Abraham, and yet their idolatries threw them out and extirpated them.

Verses 16–20

The temple and the service of it should not avail to prevent the judgment threatened. But there was the prophet's intercession for them; his prayers would do them more good than their own pleas: now that support is taken from those who have lost their interest in the prayers of God's ministers and people.

I. God here forbids the prophet to pray for them (*v.* 16): "The decree has gone forth, *pray not thou for this people,* that is, pray not for the preventing of this judgment threatened; they have *sinned unto death,* and therefore pray not for their life, but for the life of their souls," 1 John v. 16. God's prophets are praying men; Jeremiah foretold the destruction of Judah and Jerusalem, and yet prayed for their preservation. Even when we threaten sinners with damnation we must pray for their salvation, that they may *turn and live.* Jeremiah was persecuted, and reproached, by his people, and yet he prayed for them. God's praying prophets have a great interest in heaven. Those that will not regard good ministers' preaching cannot expect any benefit by their praying. If you will not hear us when we speak from God to you, God will not hear us when we speak to him for you.

II. He gives him a reason for this prohibition.

1. They are resolved to persist in their rebellion against God (*v.* 17): *Seest thou not what they do* openly and publicly, without either shame or fear, *in the cities of Judah and in the streets of Jerusalem?* This intimates that the sin was evident and that the sinners committed their wickedness even in the prophet's presence. He saw what they did, and yet they did it, which was an affront to him whose officer he was. Their idolatrous respects are paid to the *queen of heaven,* the moon, either in an image or in the original, or both. They worshipped it probably under the name of *Ashtaroth, ch.* xliv. 17, 19. They worshipped the creatures instead of him that made them, and the gifts instead of him that gave them. *With the queen of heaven* they worshipped *other gods,* for those that forsake the true God wander endlessly after false ones. To these deities of their own making they offer *cakes* for meat-offerings, and *pour out drink-offerings. The children* were sent to *gather wood; the fathers kindled the fire* to heat the oven, *the women kneaded the dough* with their own hands. Let us be instructed even by this bad example, in the service of our God. (1) Let us *honour him with our substance,* as those that have our subsistence from him, and eat and drink to the glory of him from whom

JAMIESON, FAUSSET, BROWN

10. And come—And yet come (Ezek. 23:39). **We are delivered**—viz., from all impending calamities. In spite of the prophet's threats, we have nothing to fear; we have offered our sacrifices, and therefore Jehovah will "deliver" us. **to do all these abominations**—viz., those enumerated (vs. 9). These words are not to be connected with "we are delivered," but thus: "Is it *with this design* that ye come and stand before Me in this house," in order that having offered your worthless sacrifices ye may be taken into My favor and so do all these abominations (vs. 9) with impunity? [MAURER]. **11. den of robbers**—Do you regard My temple as being what robbers make their den, viz., an asylum wherein ye may obtain impunity for your abominations (vs. 10)? **seen it**—viz., that ye treat My house as if it were a den of thieves. Jehovah implies more than is expressed, "I have seen *and will punish* it" (Isa. 56:7; Matt. 21:13). **12. my place . . . in Shiloh**—God caused His tabernacle to be set up in Shiloh in Joshua's days (Josh. 18:1; Judg. 18:31). In Eli's time God gave the ark, which had been at Shiloh, into the hands of the Philistines (ch. 26:6; I Sam. 4:10, 11; Ps. 78:56-61). Shiloh was situated between Bethel and Shechem in Ephraim. **at the first**—implying that *Shiloh* exceeded the Jewish temple in antiquity. But God's favor is not tied down to localities (Acts 7:44). **my people Israel**—Israel was *God's* people, yet He spared it not when rebellious: neither will He spare Judah, now that it rebels, though heretofore it has been His people. **13. rising . . . early**—implying unwearied earnestness in soliciting them (vs. 25; ch. 11:17; II Chron. 36:15). **14. I gave**—and I therefore can revoke the gift for it is still Mine (Lev. 25:23), now that ye fail in the only object for which it was given, the promotion of My glory. **Shiloh**—as I ceased to dwell there, transferring My temple to Jerusalem; so I will cease to dwell at Jerusalem. **15. your brethren**—children of Abraham, as much as you. **whole seed of Ephraim**—They were superior to you in numbers and power: they were *ten* tribes: ye but *two.* "Ephraim," as the leading tribe, stands for the whole ten tribes (II Kings 17:23; Ps. 78;67, 68).

16. When people are given up to judicial hardness of heart, intercessory prayer for them is unavailing (ch. 11:14; 14:11; 15:1; Exod. 32:10; I John 5:16).

17. Jehovah leaves it to Jeremiah himself to decide, is there not good reason that prayers should not be heard in behalf of such rebels? **18. children . . . fathers . . . women**—Not merely isolated individuals practised idolatry; young and old, men and women, and whole families, contributed their joint efforts to promote it. Oh, that there were the same zeal for the worship of God as there is for error (ch. 44:17, 19: 19:13)! **cakes . . . queen of heaven**—Cakes were made of honey, fine flour, etc., in a round flat shape to resemble the disc of *the moon,* to which they were offered. Others read as *Margin,* "the frame of heaven," i.e., the planets generally; so LXX here; but elsewhere LXX translates, "queen of heaven." The Phœnicians called the moon *Ashtoreth* or *Astarte:* the wife of Baal or Moloch, the *king* of heaven. The male and female pair of deities symbolized the generative powers of nature; hence arose the introduction of prostitution in the worship. The Babylonians worshipped Ashtoreth as Mylitta, i.e., generative. Our Monday, or *Moonday,* indicates the former prevalence of moon-worship (*Note,* Isa. 65:11).

ADAM CLARKE

12. *But go ye now unto my place which was in Shiloh.* See what I did to My tabernacle and ark formerly. After a long residence at Shiloh, for the iniquity of the priests and the people, I suffered it to fall into the hands of the Philistines, and to be carried captive into their land, and to be set up in the house of their idols. And because of *your* iniquities, I will deal with you and this Temple in the same way; for as I spared not Shiloh, though My ark was there, but made it a victim of My wrath, so will I do to Jerusalem and her Temple.

15. *The whole seed of Ephraim.* Taken here for all the ten tribes, that of Ephraim being the principal.

16. *Therefore pray not thou for this people.* They have filled up the measure of their iniquity, and they must become examples of My justice. How terrible must the state of that place be, where God refuses to pour out the spirit of supplication on His ministers and people in its behalf!

18. *The children gather wood.* Here is a description of a whole family gathered together, and acting unitedly in idolatrous worship. *The queen of heaven;* most probably the moon.

MATTHEW HENRY

we have our meat and drink. (2) Let us not decline the hardest services by which God may be honoured; for none shall *kindle a fire on God's altar for nought.* (3) Let our children be employed in doing something towards the keeping up of religious exercises. What is the direct tendency of this idolatry: "It is *that they may provoke me to anger;* they cannot design anything else in it. Is it because I am easily provoked? It is their own doing; and they alone shall bear it." *Is it against God that they provoke him to wrath?* It is malice against God, but it is impotent malice; it cannot hurt him: it will hurt themselves.

2. God is resolved to proceed in his judgments against them, and will not be turned back by the prophet's prayers (*v.* 20): *Thus saith the Lord God, Behold, my anger and my fury shall be poured out upon this place.* It shall reach both *man and beast,* like the plagues of Egypt, and shall destroy the *trees of the field and the fruit of the ground,* which they had *prepared for Baal,* and *cakes to the queen of heaven.* There is no extinguishing it: *It shall burn and shall not be quenched;* prayers and tears shall then avail nothing.

Verses 21–28

God, having shown the people that the temple would not protect them while they polluted it with their wickedness. here shows them that their sacrifices would not atone while they went on in disobedience. He speaks of their ceremonial service (*v.* 21): "*Put your burnt-offerings to your sacrifices;* add one sort of sacrifice to another; turn your *burnt-offerings* into *peace-offerings,* that you may *eat flesh,* but expect not any other benefit by them. *Keep your sacrifices to yourselves,* let them be served up at your own table, for they are no way acceptable at God's altars."

I. He shows them that obedience was the only thing he required of them, *v.* 22, 23. He appeals to the original contract, by which they were first formed into a people, when they were brought out of Egypt. God made them a *kingdom of priests* to himself, not that he might be regaled with their sacrifices, as the devils, whom the heathen worshipped, Deut. xxxii. 38. *I spoke not to your fathers concerning burnt-offerings or sacrifices, at first.* The precepts of the moral law were given before the ceremonial institutions; and those came afterwards, as trials of their obedience. The Levitical law begins thus: *If any man of you will bring an offering,* he must do so and so (Lev. i. 2, ii. 1), as if it were intended rather to regulate sacrifice than to require it. The condition of their being God's peculiar people was this (Exod. xix. 5), *If you will obey my voice indeed.* "Make conscience of the duties of natural religion, observe positive institutions from a principle of obedience, and then *I will be your God and you shall be my people.*" "Let your conversation be regular; *walk* within the bounds I have set, and *in all the ways that I have commanded you,* and then *it shall be well with you.*" The demand here is very reasonable, that we should be directed by Infinite Wisdom, that he that made us should command us, and that he should give us law who gives us our being.

II. He shows them that disobedience was the only thing for which he had a quarrel with them. 1. They set up their own will in competition with the will of God: *They hearkened not* to God and to his law; they *inclined not their ear* to attend to it, much less their hearts to comply with it. *Their own counsels* were their guide. *The imagination of their evil heart,* the appetites and passions of it, shall be a law to them. 2. They *went backward,* when they talked of making a captain, and returning to Egypt again, and would not go forward under God's conduct. They promised fair: *All that the Lord shall say unto us we will do;* but they drew back into the way of sin, and were worse than ever. 3. When God sent to them by the prophets, still they were disobedient. God had servants of his among them in every age, to tell them of their faults, whom he *rose up early to send* (as before, *v.* 13), but they were as deaf to the prophets as they were to the law (*v.* 26). Their practice and character were still the same. They are worse, and not better, *than their fathers.* Jeremiah can himself witness against them (*v.* 27): "*Thou shalt speak all these words to them. They will not hearken to thee,* nor heed thee. They will either give thee no answer at all or not an obedient answer; they will not come at thy call." The prophet must go to them and tell them (*v.* 28): "*Say unto them, This is a nation that obeys not the voice of the Lord their God.* They are notorious for their obstinacy; they sacrifice to the Lord, but they will not be ruled by him; they will not receive either the instruction of his word or the correction of his rod; they will not be reclaimed or reformed by either. They are false both to God and man."

Verses 29–34

I. A loud call to weeping and mourning. Jerusalem,

JAMIESON, FAUSSET, BROWN

that they may provoke me—implying *design:* in worshipping strange gods they seemed as if *purposely* to provoke Jehovah. **19.** Is it *I* that they provoke to anger? Is it not *themselves*? (Deut. 32:16, 21; Job 35:6, 8; Prov. 8:36).

20. beast . . . trees . . . ground—Why doth God vent His fury on these? On account of man, for whom these were created, that the sad spectacle may strike terror into him (Rom. 8:20-22).

21. Put . . . burnt offerings unto . . . sacrifices . . . eat flesh—*Add* the former (which the law required to be *wholly* burnt) to the latter (which were burnt only *in part*), and "eat flesh" even off the holocausts or burnt offerings. As far as I am concerned, saith Jehovah, you may do with one and the other alike. I will have neither (Isa. 1:11; Hos. 8:13; Amos 5:21, 22). **22.** Not contradicting the divine obligation of the legal sacrifices. But, "I did not require sacrifices, unless combined with moral obedience" (Ps. 50:8; 51:16, 17). The superior claim of the *moral* above the *positive* precepts of the law was marked by the ten commandments having been delivered first, and by the two tables of stone being deposited alone in the ark (Deut. 5:6). The negative in *Hebrew* often supplies the want of the comparative: not excluding the thing denied, but only implying the prior claim of the thing set in opposition to it (Hos. 6:6). "I will have mercy, and *not* sacrifice (I Sam. 15:22). Love to God is the supreme *end,* external observances only *means* towards that end. "The mere sacrifice was not *so much* what I commanded, as the sincere submission to My will gives to the sacrifice all its virtue" [MAGEE, *Atonement, Note* 57]. **23.** (Exod. 15:26; 19:5.)

24. hearkened not—They did not give even a partial hearing to Me (Ps. 81:11, 12). **imagination**—rather, as *Margin,* "the stubbornness." **backward . . .**—(ch. 2:27; 32:33; Hos. 4:16).

25. rising . . . early—(vs. 13). **26. hardened . . . neck**—(Deut. 31:27; Isa. 48:4; Acts 7:51). **worse than their fathers**—(ch. 16:12). In vs. 22 He had said, "*your* fathers"; here He says, "*their* fathers"; the change to the third person marks growing alienation from them. He no longer addresses *themselves,* as it would be a waste of words in the case of such hardened rebels. **27. Therefore**—rather, "*Though* thou speak . . . yet they will not hearken" [MAURER], (Ezek. 2:7), a trial to the prophet's faith; though he knew his warnings would be unheeded, still he was to give them in obedience to God. **28. unto them**—i.e., in reference to them. **a nation**—The word usually applied to the Gentile *nations* is here applied to the Jews, as being cast off and classed by God among the Gentiles. **nor receiveth correction**—(ch. 5:3). **truth . . . perished**—(ch. 9:3).

ADAM CLARKE

KEIL-DELITZSCH:

In the 18th verse the expression is generalized into "other gods," with reference to the fact that the service of the Queen of heaven was but one kind of idolatry along with others, since other strange gods were worshiped by sacrifices and libations. To provoke me (Deut 31:29; 32:16).

Verse 19. But instead of vexing Him (Jahveh) they rather vex themselves, inasmuch as God causes the consequences of their idolatry to fall on their own head. For the cause of the shame of their face, i.e. to prepare for themselves the shame of their face, to cover with shame.

—*Commentary on the Old Testament*

21. *Put your burnt offerings unto your sacrifices, and eat flesh.* I will receive neither sacrifice nor oblation from you; therefore you may take the beasts intended for sacrifice, and slay and eat them for your common nourishment.

23. *This thing commanded I them. . . . Obey my voice.* It was not sacrifices and oblations which I required of your fathers in the wilderness, but obedience.

MATTHEW HENRY

that had been a joyous city must now *take up a lamentation on high places* (*v.* 29), where they had served their idols. In token both of sorrow and slavery, Jerusalem must now *cut off her hair and cast it away*; the word is peculiar to the hair of the Nazarites, which was the badge and token of their dedication to God. Jerusalem had been a city which was a Nazarite to God, but now must *cut off her hair*, be degraded, and separated from God, as she had been separated to him. It is time for those that have lost their holiness to lay aside their joy.

II. Just cause given for this great lamentation.

1. The sin of Jerusalem appears here very heinous (*v.* 30): *The children of Judah have done evil in my sight;* they have affronted me to my face. Here are two things charged upon them: (1) That they were impudent towards God and set him at defiance: *They have set their abominations in the house that is called by my name*, in the very courts of the temple, *to pollute it*, as if they would reconcile heaven and hell, God and Baal. They have particularly *built the high places of Tophet*, where the image of Moloch was set up, *in the valley of the son of Hinnom*, adjoining Jerusalem; and there *they burnt their sons and their daughters in the fire*, burnt them alive, to honour or appease those idols that were devils and not gods. Surely it was righteous judgment, because they had changed the glory of God into the similitude of a beast, that God gave them up to such vile affections that changed them into worse than beasts. God says of this that it was *what he commanded them not*. It never came into his heart to have children offered to him, yet they had forsaken his service for the service of such gods as showed themselves to be indeed enemies to mankind.

2. The destruction of Jerusalem speaks misery in general (*v.* 29), *The Lord hath rejected and forsaken the generation of his wrath*. Sin makes those the generation of God's wrath that had been the generation of his love. And God will reject those who have by their impenitence made themselves *vessels of wrath fitted to destruction*. "Verily, I say unto you, I know you not." (1) Death shall triumph over them, *v.* 32, 33. *Tophet shall be called the valley of slaughter*, for there multitudes shall be slain, when, in their attempts to escape, they fall into the hands of the besiegers. This valley of Tophet was a place where they sacrificed some of their children, and dedicated others to Moloch, and there they should fall as victims to divine justice. Tophet had formerly been the burying place, or burning place, of the dead bodies of the besiegers, and God will now turn it into a burying place for the besieged. So great shall that slaughter be that even the spacious valley of Tophet shall not be able to contain the slain; and at length there shall not be enough left alive to bury the dead, so that *the carcases of the people shall be meat* for the birds and beasts of prey, that shall feed upon them like carrion. Joy shall depart from them (*v.* 34): *Then will I cause to cease the voice of mirth*. It is threatened here that there shall be nothing to rejoice in. There shall be none of the joy of weddings; no mirth, for there shall be no marriages. Nor shall there be any more of the joy of harvest, *for the land shall be desolate*, uncultivated and unimproved. Both *the cities of Judah and the streets of Jerusalem* shall look melancholy.

CHAPTER 8

Verses 1-3

These verses give a further description of the dreadful desolation which the army of the Chaldeans should make in the land.

I. Death shall not now be, as it always used to be—the repose of the dead. The ashes of the dead, even of *kings* and *princes*, shall be disturbed, and their *bones scattered at the grave's mouth*, Ps. cxli. 7. It was threatened in the close of the former chapter that the slain should be unburied, but here we find the graves of those that were buried maliciously opened by the enemy, who for covetousness, hoping to find treasure in the graves, *brought out the bones of the kings of Judah and the princes*. The dignity of their sepulchres could not secure them. The bones of the priests and prophets too were digged up and thrown about. The barbarous nations were sometimes guilty of these absurd and inhuman triumphs over those they had conquered. The bones, being dug out of the graves, were spread abroad upon the face of the earth in contempt. *They shall be spread before the sun* and before *the moon and stars*, even *all the host of heaven*, whom they have made idols of, *v.* 2. Before these lights of heaven, which they had courted, shall their dead bodies be cast, and left to putrefy.

II. Death shall now be what it never used to be—

JAMIESON, FAUSSET, BROWN

29. Jeremiah addresses Jerusalem under the figure of a woman, who, in grief for her lost children, deprives her head of its chief ornament and goes up to the hills to weep (Judg. 11:37, 38; Isa. 15:2). **hair**—flowing locks, like those of a Nazarite. **high places**—The scene of her idolatries is to be the scene of her mourning (ch. 3:21).

30. set their abominations in the house—(ch. 32:34; II Kings 21:4, 7; 23:4; Ezek. 8:5-14). **31. high places of Tophet**—the *altars* [Horsley] of Tophet; erected to Moloch, on the heights along the south of the valley facing Zion. **burn . . . sons**—(Ps. 106:38).

commanded . . . not—put for, "I forbade expressly" (Deut. 17:3; 12:31). See ch. 2:23; Isaiah 30:33; *Notes*.

generation of his wrath—the generation with which He is wroth. So Isa. 10:6; "the people of My wrath."

32. valley of slaughter—so named because of the great slaughter of the Jews about to take place at Jerusalem: a just retribution of their sin in slaying their children to Moloch in Tophet.

no place—no room, viz., to bury in, so many shall be those slain by the Chaldeans (ch. 19:11; Ezek. 6:5). **33. fray**—*scare* or *frighten* (Deut. 28:26). Typical of the last great battle between the Lord's host and the apostasy (Rev. 19:17, 18, 21). **34.** Referring to the joyous songs and music with which the bride and bridegroom were escorted in the procession to the home of the latter from that of the former; a custom still prevalent in the East (ch. 16:9; Isa. 24: 7, 8; Rev. 18:23).

CHAPTER 8

Vss. 1-22. The Jew's Coming Punishment; Their Universal and Incurable Impenitence. **1.** The victorious Babylonians were about to violate the sanctuaries of the dead in search of plunder; for ornaments, treasures, and insignia of royalty were usually buried with kings. Or rather, their purpose was to do the *greatest dishonor* to the dead (Isa. 14: 19).

2. spread . . . before the sun . . .—retribution in kind. The very objects which received their idolatries shall unconcernedly witness their dishonor. **lover . . . served . . . after . . . walked . . . sought . . . worshipped**—Words are accumulated, as if enough could not be said fully to express the mad fervor of their idolatry to the heavenly host (II Kings 23:5). **nor . . . buried**—(ch. 22:19). **dung**—(ch. 9:22; Ps. 83:10).

ADAM CLARKE

29. *Cut off thine hair*. "Shear thy Nazarite." The Nazarite was one who took upon him a particular vow, and separated himself from all worldly connections for a certain time, that he might devote himself without interruption to the service of God; and during all this time no razor was to pass on his head. After the vow was over, he shaved his head and beard, and returned to society. See Num. vi. 2, etc. Jerusalem is here considered under the notion of a Nazarite, by profession devoted to the service of God. But that profession was empty; it was not accompanied with any suitable practice. God tells them here to cut off their hair; to make no vain pretensions to holiness or religion; to throw off the mask, and attempt no longer to impose upon themselves and others by their hypocritical pretensions.

31. *Tophet . . . in the valley of the son of Hinnom*. Tophet was the place in that valley where the continual fires were kept up, in and through which they consecrated their children to Moloch.

32. *The valley of slaughter*. The place where the slaughtered thousands of this rebellious people shall be cast, in order to their being burnt, or becoming food for the beasts of the field and the fowls of the air, v. 33. These words are repeated, and their meaning more particularly explained, chap. xix. 6-15.

34. *Then will I cause to cease . . . the voice of mirth*. There shall no longer be in Jerusalem any cause of joy; they shall neither marry nor be given in marriage, for the land shall be totally desolated. Such horrible sins required such a horrible punishment.

CHAPTER 8

1-2. *They shall bring out the bones*. This and the following two verses are a continuation of the preceding prophecy, and should not have been separated from the foregoing chapter. In order to pour the utmost contempt upon the land, the victorious enemies dragged out of their graves, caves, and sepulchres, the bones of kings, princes, prophets, priests, and the principal inhabitants, and exposed them in the open air; so that they became, in the order of God's judgments, a reproach to them in the vain confidence they had in the *sun, moon*, and *the host of heaven*—all the planets and stars, whose worship they had set up in opposition to that of Jehovah. This custom of raising the bodies of the dead, and scattering their bones about, seems to have been general. It was the highest expression of hatred and contempt.

MATTHEW HENRY

the choice of the living, not because there appears in it anything delightsome; yet everything in this world shall become so irksome, and all the prospects so black that *death shall be chosen rather than life* (*v.* 3); not in a believing hope of happiness in the other life, but in an utter despair of any ease in this life. These *remain* alive (and that is all) in the many *places whither they were driven* by the judgments of God, some prisoners in the country of their enemies, others beggars in their neighbour's country, and others fugitives and vagabonds in their own country.

Verses 4–12

The prophet here is instructed to set before this people the folly of their impenitence. They are here represented as senseless people that would not be made wise by all the methods that Infinite Wisdom took to bring them to themselves.

I. They would not attend to the dictates of reason. They would not act in the affairs of their souls with the same common prudence with which they acted in other things. *Come, and let us reason together, saith the Lord* (*v.* 4, 5): *Shall men fall and not arise?* If men happen to fall to the ground, to fall into the dirt, will they not get up again as fast as they can? Shall *a man turn aside* out of the right way? The most careful traveller may miss his way; but then, as soon as he is aware of it, *will he not return*? Thus men do in other things. *Why then has this people of Jerusalem slidden back by a perpetual backsliding?* Why do not they, when they have fallen into sin, hasten to get up again by repentance? Why do not they, when they see they have missed their way, correct their error and reform? Sin is a *backsliding*, it is going back from the right way, not only into a by-path, but into a contrary path, back from the way that leads to life to that which leads to destruction. The sinner not only wanders endlessly, but proceeds end-ways towards ruin. The tempter brings men to sin, and holds them fast in it, and they contribute to their own captivity: *They hold fast deceit.* The excuses they make for their sins are deceits, yet they will not be undeceived, and therefore *they refuse to return.*

II. They would not attend to the dictates of conscience, which is our reason reflecting upon ourselves and our own actions, *v.* 6. The prophet listened to see what effect his preaching had upon them; God himself listened, as one that desires not the death of sinners, that would have been glad to hear anything that promised repentance. These expectations were disappointed: *They spoke not aright,* as I thought they would have done. God did not find any repenting of the national wickedness, which might have helped to empty the measure of public guilt. They did not so much as take the first step towards repentance; they did not say, *What have I done?* They went on resolutely in their sins: *Everyone turned to his course, as the horse rushes into the battle,* scorning to be curbed.

III. They would not attend to the dictates of providence, nor understand the voice of God in them, *v.* 7. They apprehend not the meaning either of a mercy or an affliction. They know not how to improve the grace that God affords them when he sends them his prophets, nor how to make use of the rebukes when *his voice cries in the city.* There is sagacity in the inferior creatures. *The stork in the heaven knows her appointed times;* so do other season-birds, *the turtle, the crane, and the swallow.* These by a natural instinct change their quarters, as the temper of the air alters; they come when the spring comes, and go when the winter approaches, probably into warmer climates.

IV. They would not attend to the dictates of the written word. They say, *We are wise;* but *how* can they say so? (*v.* 8). They think they are wise because *the law of the Lord is with them,* the book of the law and the interpreters of it, Deut. iv. 6. But their pretensions are groundless for all this. They might as well have been without the law, unless they had made a better use of it. *The pen of the scribes,* of those that first wrote the law and of those that now write expositions of it, *is in vain.* But it might be said, They have some wise men among them. To this it is answered (*v.* 9): *The wise men are ashamed* that they have not made a better use of their wisdom, and lived more up to it. *They are confounded and taken;* all their wisdom has not served to keep them from those courses that tend to their ruin. They talk of their wisdom, but, *Lo, they have rejected the word of the Lord.* The pretenders to wisdom, who said, "*We are wise and the law of the Lord is with us,*" were the priests and the false prophets; with them the prophet here deals plainly. Their families and estates shall be ruined (*v.* 10): *Their wives shall be given to others,* when they are taken captives, *and*

JAMIESON, FAUSSET, BROWN

3. The survivors shall be still worse off than the dead (Job 3:21, 22; Rev. 9:6). **which remain in all the places**—"in all places of them that remain, whither I . . . , i.e., in all places whither I have driven them that remain [MAURER].

4. "Is it not a natural instinct, that if one falls, he *rises again;* if one turns away (i.e., wanders from the way), he will *return* to the point from which he wandered? Why then does not Jerusalem do so?" He plays on the double sense of *return;* literal and metaphorical (ch. 3:12; 4:1). **5. slidden . . . backsliding**—rather, as the *Hebrew* is the same as in vs. 4, to which this verse refers, *"turned away* with a perpetual *turning away."* **perpetual**—in contrast to the "arise" (rise again," vs. 4).

refuse to return—in contrast to, "shall he . . . not return" (vs. 4; ch. 5:3).

6. spake not aright—i.e., not so as *penitently to confess* that they acted wrong. Cf. what follows.

every one . . . his course—The *Keri* reads **"course,"** but the *Chetib,* "courses." "They persevere in the *courses* whatever they have once entered on." Their wicked *ways* were *diversified.* **horse rusheth**—lit., "pours himself forth," as water that has burst its embankment. The *mad rapidity* of the war horse is the point of comparison (Job 39:19-25). **7.** The instinct of the migratory birds leads them with unfailing regularity to return every spring from their winter abodes in summer climes (Song of Sol. 2:12); but God's people will not return to Him even when the winter of His wrath is past, and He invites them back to the spring of His favor. **in the heaven**—emphatical. The birds whose very element is the *air,* in which they are never at rest, yet show a steady sagacity, which God's people do not. **times**—viz., of migrating, and of returning. **my people**—This honorable title aggravates the unnatural perversity of the Jews towards *their* God. **know not . . .**—(ch. 5:4, 5; Isa. 1:3). **8. law . . . with us**—(Rom. 2:17). Possessing the law, on which they prided themselves, the Jews might have become the wisest of nations; but by their neglecting its precepts, the law became given "in vain," as far as they were concerned. **scribes**—copyists. "In vain" copies were multiplied. MAURER translates, "The false pen of the scribes hath converted it [the law] into a lie." See *Margin,* which agrees with *Vulgate.* **9. dismayed**—confounded. **what wisdom**—lit., "the wisdom of what?" i.e., "wisdom in what respect?" the Word of the Lord being the only true source of wisdom (Ps. 119:98-100; Prov. 1:7; 9:10).

ADAM CLARKE

4. *Moreover thou shalt say.* Dr. Blayney very properly observes, "In that part of the prophecy which follows next, the difference of speakers requires to be attended to; the transition being quick and sudden, but full of life and energy. The prophet at first, in the name of God, reproves the people's incorrigibility; he charges their wise ones with folly, and threatens them with grievous calamities, vv. 4-13. In the three next verses he seems to apostrophize his countrymen in his own person, and as one of the people that dwelt in the open towns, advising those that were in the like situation to retire with him into some of the fortified cities, and there wait the event with patience, since there was nothing but terror abroad, and the noise of the enemy, who had already begun to ravage the country, vv. 14-16. God speaks, v. 17, and threatens to bring foes against them that should be irresistible. The prophet appears again in his own person, commiserating the daughter of his people, who is heard bewailing her forlorn case in a distant land; while the voice of God, like that of conscience, breaks in upon her complaints, and shows her that all this ruin is brought upon her by her own infidelities, vv. 18-20. The prophet once more resumes his discourse; he regrets that no remedy can be found to close up the wounds of his country, and pathetically weeps over the number of her slain, v. 21; chap. ix. 1."

Shall they fall, and not arise? shall he turn away, and not return? That is, It is as possible for sinners to return from their sin to God, for His grace is ever at hand to assist, as it is for God, who is pouring out His judgments, to return to them on their return to Him. But these held fast deceit, and refused to return; they would not be undeceived.

6. *As the horse rusheth into the battle.* This strongly marks the unthinking, careless desperation of their conduct.

7. *The stork in the heaven.* The birds of passage know the times of their going and return, and punctually observe them; they obey the dictates of nature, but My people do not obey My law.

8. *The pen of the scribes is in vain.* The "deceitful pen" of the scribes. They have written falsely, though they had the truth before them.

MATTHEW HENRY

their fields shall be taken from them by their victorious enemy and shall be given *to those that shall inherit them.* And (*v.* 12), notwithstanding all their pretensions to wisdom and sanctity, *they shall fall among those that fall. In the time of their visitation,* when the wickedness of the land comes to be enquired into, it will be found that they have contributed to it more than any. He gives a reason for these judgments (*v.* 10–12). They were greedy of the wealth of this world. The *priests teach for hire* and the *prophets divine for money,* Mic. iii. 11. *Everyone deals falsely,* looks one way and rows another. There is no such thing as sincerity among them. They flattered people in their sins, and pretended to be the physicians of the state, but knew not how to apply proper remedies; they *healed them slightly,* killed the patient with palliative cures, silencing their fears with, "*Peace, peace,* all is well, and there is no danger." *They could not blush,* so perfectly lost were they to all sense of virtue and honour.

Verses 13–22

I. God threatening the destruction of a sinful people. He has borne long with them, but they are still more and more provoking. They shall be stripped of all their comforts (*v.* 13): *There shall be no grapes on the vine,* nothing left them wherewith to *make glad their hearts.* It is expounded in the last clause: *The things that I have given them shall pass away from them.* Mercies abused are forfeited, and it is just with God to take the forfeiture. *I will send serpents among you,* the Chaldean army, fiery serpents. They *shall not be charmed* with music. These are serpents of another nature; they are as *the deaf adder, that stops her ear, and will not hear the voice of the charmer.*

II. The people sinking into despair under the pressure of those calamities. Those that were void of fear are void of hope now that it breaks in upon them, and have no heart either to make head against it or to bear up under it, *v.* 14. *Why do we sit still here?* Let us *assemble, and go* in a body *into the defenced cities.* Though they could expect no other than to be cut off there at last, yet not so soon as in the country, and therefore, "*Let us go, and be silent there;* let us attempt nothing, nor so much as make a complaint; for to what purpose?" It is a sullen silence.

1. They are sensible that God is angry with them: "*The Lord our God has put us to silence,* has struck us with astonishment, and *given us water of gall to drink. Thou hast made us to drink the wine of astonishment.* To what purpose is it to contend with our fate when God himself fights against us?" They seem to quarrel with God as if he had dealt hardly with them in not permitting them to speak for themselves. At length they begin to see the hand of God stretched out in the calamities, and to own that they have provoked him.

2. They are sensible that the enemy is likely to be too hard for them, *v.* 16. *The snorting of the horses was heard from Dan,* the report of the strength of their cavalry was soon carried all over and everybody *trembled at the sound of the neighing of his steeds. They have come,* and there is no opposing them; they *have devoured the land and all that is in the city.*

3. They are disappointed in their expectations of deliverance. *We looked for peace, but no good came,* no good news from abroad; we looked *for a time of health* and prosperity to our nation, but, *behold, trouble,* the alarms of war. Their false prophets had cried *Peace, peace,* to them. The deliverance did not come when they had long expected it (*v.* 20): *The harvest is past, the summer is ended;* that is, there is a great deal of time gone. Harvest and summer are parts of the year, so the meaning is, "One year passes after another, one campaign after another, and yet our affairs are as bad as ever; no relief comes. *We are not saved.*" The season of action is over the summer and harvest are gone, and a cold and melancholy winter succeeds. They stand in their own light, and put a bar in their own door, and are not saved because they are not ready for salvation.

4. They are deceived in those things which they thought would have secured their peace to them (*v.* 19): *The daughter of my people* cries, cries aloud, *because of those that dwell in a far country,* because of the foreign enemy that comes from a far country to take possession of ours. *Is not the Lord in Zion? Is not her king in her?* These were the two things that they had all along depended upon, (1) That they had among them the temple of God, and the tokens of his special presence with them. (2) That they had the throne of the house of David. *Is not Zion's king in her?* And will not Zion's God protect Zion's king and his kingdom? This outcry of theirs reflects upon

JAMIESON, FAUSSET, BROWN

10-12. Repeated from ch. 6:12-15. See a similar repetition, vs. 15; ch. 14:19. **inherit**—*succeed to the possession* of them. **11.** (Ezek. 13:10.)

13. surely consume—lit., "gathering I will gather," or "consuming I will consume." **no grapes . . . nor figs**—(Joel 1:7; Matt. 21:19). **things that I have given . . . shall pass away**—rather, "I will appoint to them those who shall overwhelm (pass over) them," i.e., I will send the enemy upon them [MAURER]. *English Version* accords well with the context; Though their grapes and figs ripen, they shall not be allowed to enjoy them. **17. I**—Jehovah. **cockatrices**—basilisks (Isa. 11:8), i.e., enemies whose destructive power no means, by persuasion or otherwise, can counteract. Serpent-charmers in the East entice serpents by music, and by a particular pressure on the neck render them incapable of darting (Ps. 58:4, 5).

14. assemble—for defense. **let us be silent**—not assault the enemy, but merely defend ourselves in quiet, until the storm blow over. **put us to silence**—brought us to that state that we can no longer resist the foe; implying silent despair.

water of gall—lit., "water of the poisonous plant," perhaps the poppy (ch. 9:15; 23:15).

16. his horses—the Chaldean's. **was heard**—the prophetical past for the future. **from Dan**—bordering on Phœnicia. This was to be Nebuchadnezzar's route in invading Israel; the *cavalry* in advance of the infantry would scour the country. **strong ones**—a poetical phrase for *steeds,* peculiar to Jeremiah (ch. 47:3; cf. ch. 4: 13, 29; 6:23). **15.** Repeated (ch. 14:19). **We looked for**—owing to the expectations held out by the false prophets. **health**—healing; i.e., restoration from adversity.

20. Proverbial. Meaning: One season of hope after another has passed, but the looked-for deliverance never came, and now all hope is gone.

19. The prophet in vision hears the cry of the exiled Jews, wondering that God should have delivered them up to the enemy, seeing that He is Zion's king, dwelling in her (Mic. 3:11). In the latter half of the verse God replies that their own idolatry, not want of faithfulness on His part, is the cause. **because of them that dwell in a far country**—rather, "from a land of distances," i.e., a distant land (Isa. 39:3). *English Version* understands the cry to be of the Jews *in their own land,* because of the enemy *coming from their far-off country.* **strange vanities**—foreign gods.

ADAM CLARKE

10. *Therefore will I give their wives.* From this to the end of v. 15 is repeated from chap. vi. 13-15.

17. *I will send serpents.* These were symbols of the enemies that were coming against them, a foe that would rather slay them and destroy the land than get booty and ransom.

16. *The snorting of his horses was.* From this to the end of v. 15 is repeated from Babylon to Jerusalem; and it was by this city, after the battle of Carchemish, that Nebuchadnezzar, in pursuing the Egyptians, entered Palestine. *The whole land trembled at the sound of the neighing of his strong ones.* Of his war horses. This is a fine image; so terrible was the united neighing of the cavalry of the Babylonians that the reverberation of the air caused the ground to tremble.

20. *The harvest is past.* The siege of Jerusalem lasted two years; for Nebuchadnezzar came against it in the ninth year of Zedekiah, and the city was taken in the eleventh; see 2 Kings xxv. 1-3.

MATTHEW HENRY

God, and therefore he returns an answer immediately: *Why have they provoked me to anger with their graven images?*

III. More of the lamentations of Jeremiah. He was an eye-witness of the desolations of his country: "*My heart is faint in me* (*v.* 18). *When I would comfort myself against my sorrow* every attempt to alleviate the grief does but aggravate it." Sometimes sorrow is such that the more it is repressed the more it recoils. This may be the case of very good men, as of the prophet here, whose soul refused to be comforted. He tells us (*v.* 21): "It is *for the hurt of the daughter of my people* that *I am* thus *hurt;* it is for their sin, and the miseries they have brought upon themselves that *I am black*, that I go in black as mourners do, and that *astonishment has taken hold on me*, so that I know not which way to turn." A gracious spirit will be a public spirit, a tender spirit, a mourning spirit. Jeremiah had prophesied the destruction of Jerusalem, and, though the truth of his prophecy was questioned, yet he did not rejoice in the proof of the truth of it, preferring the welfare of his country before his own reputation. How small his hopes were (*v.* 22): "*Is there no balm in Gilead*—no medicine proper for a sick and dying kingdom? *Is there no physician there*—no skilful faithful hand to apply the medicine?" This verse may be understood as laying all the blame of the incurableness of their disease upon themselves. The question must be answered affirmatively: *Is there no balm in Gilead—no physician there?* Yes, certainly there is; God is able to help and heal them. Gilead was a place in their own land, not far off. They had among themselves God's law and his prophets, with the help of which they might have been brought to repentance, and their ruin might have been prevented. They had princes and priests, whose business it was to reform the nation and redress their greivances. *Why then was not* their health restored? Certainly it was not for want of balm and a physician, but because they would not admit the application nor submit to the methods of cure. The physician and physic were both ready, but the patient was wilful and would not be tied to rules.

JAMIESON, FAUSSET, BROWN

18. (Isa. 22:4.) The lamentation of the prophet for the impending calamity of his country. **against sorrow**—or, *with respect to* sorrow. MAURER translates, "Oh, my exhilaration as to sorrow!" i.e., "Oh, that exhilaration (comfort, from an *Arabic* root, to *shine* as the rising sun) would shine upon me as to my sorrow!" **in me**—within me.

21. black—sad in visage with grief(Joel 2:6).

22. balm—*balsam;* to be applied to the wounds of my people. Brought into Judea first from Arabia Felix, by the queen of Sheba, in Solomon's time (JOSEPHUS, *Antiquities* 8.2). The *opobalsamum* of Pliny; or else [BOCHART] the resin drawn from the terebinth. It abounded in Gilead, east of Jordan, where, in consequence, many "physicians" established themselves (ch. 46:11; 51:8; Gen. 37:25; 43:11).

health . . . recovered–The *Hebrew* is lit., "lengthening out . . . gone up"; hence, *the long bandage applied* to bind up a wound. So the *Arabic* also [GESENIUS].

ADAM CLARKE

F. B. MEYER:

Verse 22. How many of God's children are discouraged! They have mourned, confessed, and resolved; but they do not expect to see any great alteration in themselves. They have lost hope. Now, it is evident that as long as this spirit prevails, there is very little prospect of improvement. Discouragement can only bring defeat. One of the first objects of a physician is always to awaken hope, for otherwise he knows that his medicines can profit but little. Now, bethink you, what is the cause of your failure? Is it in God? Is there not "balm in Gilead"? Is there not a physician there? Why, then, is not the health of the daughter of my people recovered?

—*Great Verses Through the Bible*

22. *Is there no balm in Gilead?* The Israelites are represented as a man dying through disease; and a disease for the cure of which the balm of Gilead was well-known to be a specific, when judiciously applied by a physician. But though there be balm and a physician, the people are not cured; neither their spiritual nor political evils are removed.

MATTHEW HENRY — CHAPTER 9

Verses 1–11

The prophet commissioned to foretell the destruction and to point out the sin. What he said of both came from the heart, and one would have thought it would reach to the heart.

I. He abandons himself to sorrow in consideration of the calamitous condition of his people.

1. He laments the bloodshed and the lives lost (*v.* 1): "*O that my head were waters*, that so *my eyes* might be *fountains of tears*, still sending forth floods of tears as there still occur fresh occasions for them!" The same word in Hebrew signifies both *the eye* and *a fountain*, as if in this land of sorrows our eyes were designed rather for weeping than seeing. While we find our hearts such fountains of sin, it is fit that our eyes should be fountains of tears. But Jeremiah's grief here is upon the public account: he would *weep day and night for the slain of the daughter of his people*, the multitudes of his countrymen that fell by the sword of war. When we hear of the numbers of slain in great battles we ought to be much affected, for whatever people they are of, they are of the same human nature with us, and there are so many precious lives lost, as dear to them as ours to us.

2. He laments the desolations of the country. "Not only for the towns and cities, but *for the mountains, will I take up a weeping and wailing*" (the fruitful hills with which Judea abounded), and for *the habitations of the wilderness*, or rather *the pastures of the plain*, that used to be *clothed with flocks* or *covered with corn*, but now *they are burnt up* by the Chaldean army. Everything looks so melancholy for they *hear not the voice of the cattle*. The havoc war makes in a country cannot but be for a lamentation to all tender spirits, for it is a tragedy which destroys the stage it is acted on.

II. He abandons himself to solitude. While all his neighbours are fleeing to the defenced cities (*ch.* iv. 5, 6), he is contriving to retire into some desert, in detestation of his people's sin (*v.* 2): "*O that I had in the wilderness a lodging-place of wayfaring men*, such as they have in the deserts of Arabia, for travellers, *that I might leave my people and go from them!*" We must not *go out of the world*, bad as it is, before our time. If he could not do good to many, yet he might to some. But it made him weary of his life to see them dishonouring God and destroying themselves. Jeremiah, in the courts of God's house,

JAMIESON, FAUSSET, BROWN — CHAPTER 9

VSS. 1-26. JEREMIAH'S LAMENTATION FOR THE JEWS' SINS AND CONSEQUENT PUNISHMENT.

1. This verse is more fitly joined to the last chapter, as vs. 23 in the *Hebrew* (cf. Isa. 22:4; Lam. 2:11; 3:48).

2. lodging place—a caravanserai for caravans, or companies travelling in the desert, remote from towns. It was a square building enclosing an open court. Though a lonely and often filthy dwelling, Jeremiah would prefer even it to the comforts of Jerusalem, so as to be removed from the pollutions of the capital (Ps. 55:7, 8).

ADAM CLARKE — CHAPTER 9

1. *Oh that my head were waters.* "Who will give to my head waters?" My mourning for the sins and desolations of my people has already exhausted the source of tears: I wish to have a fountain opened there, that I may *weep day and night for the slain . . . of my people.* This has been the sorrowful language of many a pastor who has preached long to a hardened, rebellious people, to little or no effect. This verse belongs to the preceding chapter.

2. *Oh that I had in the wilderness.* Several interpreters suppose this to be the speech of God. I cannot receive this. I believe this verse to be spoken by the prophet, and that God proceeds with the next verse, and so on to the ninth inclusive.

MATTHEW HENRY

wishes himself in a wilderness.

1. He would not think of leaving them because they were in distress, but because they were wicked. They were filthy: *They are all adulterers*, that is, the generality of them are, *ch.* v. 8. They were false. Those that had been unfaithful to their God were so to one another. Go to church, to court, or to the exchange—and they are *an assembly of treacherous men.* There they will cheat deliberately with a malicious design, for (*v.* 3) *they bend their tongues, like their bow, for lies*, with craft. Their tongue turns as naturally to a lie as the bow to the string. *But they are not valiant for the truth upon the earth.* They might do good service if they would use the art and resolution which they are so much masters of in the cause of truth; but they will not do so. Those that will be faithful to the truth must be valiant, and not daunted by opposition. We must answer, another day, not only for our enmity in opposing truth, but for our cowardice in defending it. They will cheat their own brethren (*every brother will utterly supplant*). Jacob had his name from *supplanting*; it is the word here used. Go into company and you will find there is nothing of sincerity or common honesty among them. No man thinks himself bound to be either grateful or sincere. *Every neighbour will walk with slander;* they care not what ill they say one of another, though ever so false; that way that the slander goes they will go; they will *walk with it. They have taught their tongue to speak lies. They weary themselves to commit iniquity.* They are wearied *with* their sinful pursuits and yet not weary *of* them. They grow worse and worse (*v.* 3): *They proceed from evil to evil*, from one degree of sin to another. *No one reaches the height of vice at once.* They began with equivocating, but at last came to downright lying.

2. The prophet shows what God had determined against them. God had marked their sin. He could tell the prophet what sort of people they were. So here (*v.* 6): "*Thy habitation is in the midst of deceit*, all about thee are addicted to it; therefore stand upon thy guard." This charge is enlarged upon, *v.* 8. Their tongue was a *bow bent* (*v.* 3), plotting and preparing mischief; here it is *an arrow shot out.* It is a *slaying arrow* (so some readings have it); their tongue has been to many an instrument of death. They *speak peaceably to their neighbours*, against whom they are at the same time *lying in wait*; as Joab kissed Abner when he was about to kill him. Fair words, when they are not attended with good intentions, are despicable, but, when they are intended as a cloak and cover for wicked intentions, they are abominable. Sinners might be taught the good knowledge of the Lord but they will not learn; and where no knowledge of God is, what good can be expected? Hos. iv. 1. God had marked them for ruin, *v.* 7, 9, 11. Those that will not know God as their lawgiver shall be made to know him as their judge. Some shall be refined (*v.* 7): "Because they are thus corrupt, *behold, I will melt them and try them*, and see whether the furnace of affliction will purify them from their dross, and whether, when they are melted, they will be new-cast in a better mould." They shall not be *rejected as reprobate silver* till *the founder has melted in vain*, *ch.* vi. 29, 30. He speaks as one that could not find in his heart to give them up to ruin till he had first tried all means likely to bring them to repentance. The rest shall be ruined (*v.* 9): *Shall I not visit for these things?* Fraud and falsehood are sins which God hates and which he will reckon for. The sentence is passed, the decree has gone forth (*v.* 11): *I will make Jerusalem heaps* of rubbish; it shall be fit for nothing but to be *a den of dragons*; and *the cities of Judah* shall be *a desolation.*

Verses 12–22

Two things the prophet designs, in these verses, with reference to the approaching destruction of Judah and Jerusalem: 1. To convince people of the justice of God in that they had by sin brought it upon themselves. 2. To affect people with the greatness of the desolation that by a terrible prospect of it they might be awakened to repentance and reformation.

I. He calls for the thinking men to show people the equity of God's proceedings, though they seemed harsh (*v.* 12): "*Who*, where, *is the wise men*, or the prophet, *to whom the mouth of the Lord hath spoken?* You boast of your wisdom, and of the prophets you have among you; produce one and he will soon understand that there is a just ground of God's controversy with this people." Do these wise men enquire, *For what does the land perish?* It used to be a land that God cared for, but it is now a land that he has forsaken. *Wherefore has the Lord done thus unto this land?* God here gives a full answer.

1. The indictment preferred against them, upon

JAMIESON, FAUSSET, BROWN

3. bend . . . tongues . . . for lies—i.e., with lies as their arrows; they direct lies on their tongue as their bow (Ps. 64:3, 4). **not valiant for . . . truth**—(ch. 7:28). MAURER translates, "They do not *prevail by* truth" or *faith* (Ps. 12:4). Their *tongue*, not *faith*, is their weapon. **upon . . . earth**—rather, "in the land." **know not me**—(Hos. 4:1).

4. supplant—lit., "trip up by the heel" (Hos. 12:3). **walk with slanders**—(ch. 6:28).

5. weary themselves—*are at laborious pains* to act perversely [MAURER]. Sin is a hard bondage (Hab. 2:13).

6. Thine—God addresses Jeremiah, who dwelt in the midst of deceitful men. **refuse to know me**—Their ignorance of God is wilful (vs. 3; ch, 5:4, 5). **8. tongue . . . arrow shot out**—rather, "a *murdering* arrow" [MAURER] (vs. 3). **speaketh peaceably . . . in heart . . . layeth . . . wait**—layeth his ambush [HENDERSON], (Ps. 55:21).

7. melt . . . try them—by sending calamities on them. **for how shall I do**—"What *else* can I do for the sake of the daughter of My people?" [MAURER], (Isa. 1:25; Mal. 3:3).

9. (Ch. 5:9, 29.) **10.** Jeremiah breaks in upon Jehovah's threats of wrath with lamentation for his desolated country. **mountains**—once cultivated and fruitful: the hillsides were cultivated in terraces between the rocks. **habitations of . . . wilderness**—rather, "the pleasant herbage (lit., "the choice parts" of any thing) of the pasture plain." The *Hebrew* for wilderness expresses not a barren desert, but an untilled plain, fit for pasture. **burned up**—because no one waters them, the inhabitants being all gone. **none can pass through them**—much less *inhabit* them. **fowl**—(ch. 4:25). **11. And**—omit "And." Jehovah here resumes His speech from vs. 9. **heaps**—(*Note*, Isa. 25:2). **dragons**—jackals.

12. Rather, "Who is a wise man? (i.e., *Whosoever* has inspired wisdom, II Peter 3:15); let him understand this (weigh well the evils impending, and the causes of their being sent); and he to whom the mouth of the Lord hath spoken (i.e., *whosoever is prophetically inspired*), let him declare it to his fellow countrymen," if haply they may be roused to repentance, the only hope of safety.

ADAM CLARKE

3. *They bend their tongues like their bow for lies.* And their lies are such that they as fully take away life as the keenest arrow shot from the best-strung bow. The false prophets told the people that there was no desolation at hand; the people believed them, made no preparation for their defense, did not return to the Lord; and the sword came and destroyed them.

7. *Behold, I will melt them.* I will put them in the furnace of affliction, and see if this will be a means of purging away their dross.

10. *Both the fowl of the heavens and the beast are fled.* The land shall be so utterly devastated that neither beast nor bird shall be able to live in it.

11. *A den of dragons.* "Jackals."

12. *Who is the wise man?* To whom has God revealed these things? He is the truly wise man.

MATTHEW HENRY

which they had been found guilty, *v.* 13, 14. (1) They have revolted from their allegiance to their rightful Sovereign. *Therefore* God has *forsaken their land*, because they have *forsaken his law*, and had not *obeyed his voice*, nor *walked in* the ways. (2) They have entered into the service of usurpers, have not only withdrawn themselves from their obedience to their prince, but have taken up arms against him. They have set up their own will, the wills of the flesh, and the carnal mind, in contradiction to the will of God: *They have walked after the imagination of their own hearts;* they would do as they pleased, whatever God and conscience said to the contrary. *They have walked after Baalim:* the word is plural; they had many Baals, Baal-peor and Baal-berith, the Baal of this place and the Baal of the other place; for they had *lords many*, which *their fathers taught them* to worship, but which the God of their fathers had again and again forbidden. This was why *the land perished.*

2. The sentence upon the convicted rebels must now be executed: *The Lord of hosts, the God of Israel, hath said it* (*v.* 15, 16), and who can reverse it? Their comforts at home shall be poisoned and embittered to them: *I will feed this people with wormwood* (or rather with *wolf's-bane*, some herb that is both nauseous and noxious), *and* I will *give them water of gall* (or *juice of hemlock* or some other herb that is poisonous) *to drink.* Everything about them shall be a terror to them. God will *curse their blessings*, Mal. ii. 2. Their dispersion abroad shall be their destruction (*v.* 16): *I will scatter them among the heathen.* They shall lose themselves, where they lost their virtue, *among the heathen*; they had violated that truth which is the bond and cement of society and commerce, and therefore are justly crumbled to dust and *scattered among the heathen.* And now we see for what the land perishes; all this desolation is the desert of their deeds.

II. He calls for the mourning women to lament these sad calamities that had come or were coming upon them, that the nation might prepare for them: *The Lord of hosts* himself *says, Call for the mourning women, that they may come*, *v.* 17. Here is work for the counterfeit mourners: *Send for the cunning women*, that are made use of at funerals to supply the want of true mourners. Let these *take up a wailing* for us, *v.* 18. Or, rather, it intimates the extreme stupidity of the people, that laid not to heart the judgments. God sent his mourning prophets to them, to call them to mourning, but his word in their mouths did not work upon their faith; rather therefore than they shall go laughing to their ruin, let the mourning women come. Here is work for the real mourners. The present scene is very tragical (*v.* 19): *A voice of wailing is heard out of Zion.* Some make this to be the song of the mourning women: it is rather an echo to it, returned by those whose affections were moved by their wailings. In Zion the voice of joy and praise used to be heard, while the people kept closely to God. But sin has altered the note; it is now the *voice of lamentation. We are confounded* because *we have forsaken the land* (forced so to do by the enemy), not because we *have* forsaken the Lord, being drawn aside of *our own lust and enticed—because our dwellings have cast us out*, not because our God has cast us off. Thus unhumbled hearts lament their calamity, but not their iniquity, the cause of it. Those whose land has *spewed them out* (as it did their predecessors the Canaanites, and justly, because they trod in their steps, Lev. xviii. 28) complain that they are driven into the city, but, after a while, those of the city, and they with them, shall be forced thence too: *Yet hear the word of the Lord* (*v.* 20); let *the women* hear it, for the men will not heed it, will not give it a patient hearing. The prophets will be glad to preach to a congregation of women that *tremble at God's word.* Let the women *teach their daughters wailing.* Let *everyone teach her neighbour lamentation*; this intimates that the trouble shall spread far, shall go from house to house. The judgment here threatened is made to look terrible. Multitudes shall be slain, *v.* 21. Death shall ride in triumph, and there shall be no escaping his arrest. Nor does it attack the cottages only, but it has *entered into our palaces.* Those that are slain shall be left unburied (*v.* 22).

Verses 23–26

The prophet had been endeavouring to possess this people with a holy fear of God and his judgments, but still they had recourse to some sorry subterfuge or other with which to excuse themselves in their obstinacy. He therefore sets himself here to drive them from these refuges of lies.

I. When they were told how inevitable the judgment would be they pleaded the defence of their

JAMIESON, FAUSSET, BROWN

13. Answer to the "for what the land perisheth" (vs. 12).

14. (Ch. 7:24.) **Baalim**—plural of Baal, to express his supposed manifold powers. **fathers taught them**—(Gal. 1:14; I Pet. 1:18). We are not to follow the errors of the fathers, but the authority of Scripture and of God [JEROME].

15. feed—(ch. 8:14; 23:15;Ps. 80:5).

16. nor their fathers have known—alluding to vs. 14, "Their fathers taught them" idolatry; therefore the children shall be scattered to a land which neither their fathers nor they have known. **send a sword after them**—Not even in flight shall they be safe.

17. mourning women—hired to heighten lamentation by plaintive cries baring the breast, beating the arms, and suffering the hair to flow dishevelled (II Chron. 35:25; Eccles. 12: 5; Matt. 9:23). **cunning**—skilled in wailing. **18.** (Ch. 14:17.)

19. The cry of "the mourning women." **spoiled**—laid waste. **dwellings . . . cast us out**—fulfilling Leviticus 18:28; 20:22. CALVIN translates, "*The enemy* have cast down our habitations." **20. Yet**—rather, "Only" [HENDERSON]. This particle calls attention to what follows. **teach . . . daughters wailing**—The deaths will be so many that there will be a lack of mourning women to bewail them. The mothers, therefore, must teach their daughters the science to supply the want. **21. death . . . windows**—The death-inflicting soldiery, finding the doors closed, burst in by the windows. **to cut off . . . children from . . . streets**—Death cannot be said to enter the *windows* to cut off the children *in* the streets, but to cut them off, so as no more to play in the streets without (Zech. 8:5). **22. saith the Lord**—continuing the thread of discourse from vs. 20. **dung**—(ch. 8:2). **handful . . . none . . . gather them**—implying that the handful has been so trodden as to be not worth even the poor *gleaner's* effort to gather it. Or the Eastern custom may be referred to: the reaper cuts the grain and is followed by another who *gathers it.* This grain shall not be worth gathering. How galling to the pride of the Jews to hear that so shall their carcasses be trodden contemptuously under foot!

ADAM CLARKE

15. *I will feed them . . . with wormwood.* They shall have the deepest sorrow and heaviest affliction. They shall have poison instead of meat and drink.

17. *Call for the mourning women.* Those whose office it was to make lamentations at funerals, and to bewail the dead, for which they received pay. This custom continues to the present in Asiatic countries.

20. *Teach your daughters.* This is not a common dirge that shall last only till the body is consigned to the earth; it must last longer. Teach it to your children, that it may be continued through every generation, till God turn again your captivity.

21. *For death is come up into our windows.* Here death is personified, and represented as scaling their wall; and after having slain the playful children without, and the vigorous youth employed in the labors of the field, he is now come into the private houses, to destroy the aged and infirm; and into the palaces, to destroy the king and the princes.

22. *And as the handful after the harvestman.* The reapers, after having cut enough to fill their hand, threw it down; and the binders, following after, collected those handfuls, and bound them in sheaves. Death is represented as having cut down the inhabitants of the land, as the reapers do the corn. But so general was the slaughter that there was none to bury the dead, to gather up these handfuls; so that they lay in a state of putrescence, *as dung upon the open field.*

MATTHEW HENRY

politics and powers, which, with their wealth and treasure, they thought made their city impregnable. In answer to this he shows them the folly of trusting to these stays, while they have not a God in covenant, *v.* 23, 24. *Let not the wise man glory in his wisdom* as if with the help of that he could find out some evasion or other. But, if a man's policies fail him, yet surely he may gain his point by might and dint of courage. No: *Let not the strong man glory in his strength,* for the battle is not always to the strong. David the stripling proves too hard for Goliath the giant. All human force is nothing without God, worse than nothing against him. But may not the *rich man's wealth* be *his strong city?* (money answers all things) No: *Let not the rich man glory in his riches,* as if they could make their part good against the Chaldeans because they have wise men to advise concerning the war, mighty men to fight their battles, and rich men to bear the charges of the war. Our only comfort in trouble will be that we have done our duty. Those that *refused to know God* (*v.* 6) will boast in vain of their wisdom and wealth; but those that *know God,* intelligently, that *understand* aright *that he is the Lord,* may *glory in this,* it will be their rejoicing in the day of evil. Our only confidence in trouble will be that, having through grace in some measure done our duty, we shall find God a God all-sufficient to us. We may *glory in this,* that, wherever we are, we have acquaintance with a God that *exercises lovingkindness, and judgment, and righteousness in the earth,* that is just to all his creatures, kind to all his children and will protect them and provide for them. The God they thus faithfully conform to they may cheerfully confide in, in their greatest straits. But the prophet intimates that the generality of this people took no care about this.

II. When they were told how provoking their sins were to God they vainly pleaded the covenant of their circumcision. They were undoubtedly the people of God; they had the mark of his children in their flesh. To this the prophet answers, God would punish all wicked people, without making any distinction between the circumcised and uncircumcised, *v.* 25, 26. They had lived in common with the uncircumcised nations, and so had forfeited the benefit of that peculiarity. The Judge of all the earth is impartial, and none shall fare the better at his bar for any external advantages. The condemnation of impenitent sinners that are baptized will be as sure as that of impenitent sinners that are unbaptized. Those *in the utmost corners, that dwell in the wilderness,* are supposed to be the Kedarenes and those of the kingdoms of Hazor, as appears by comparing *ch.* xlix. 28–32. Some think they are so called because they dwelt as it were in a corner of the world, others because they had *the hair of their head polled into corners.* However that was, they were uncircumcised in flesh, and the Jews are ranked with them; for *all the house of Israel are uncircumcised in the heart;* they have the sign, but not the thing signified, *ch.* iv. 4.

JAMIESON, FAUSSET, BROWN

23. wisdom—political sagacity; as if *it* could rescue from the impending calamities. **might**—military prowess.

24. Nothing but an experimental knowledge of God will save the nation. **understandeth**—*theoretically;* in the intellect. **knoweth**—*practically:* so as to walk in My ways (ch. 22:16; Job 22: 21: I Cor. 1:31). **loving-kindness**—God's mercy is put in the first and highest place, because without it we should flee from God in fear and despair. **judgment . . . righteousness**—*loving-kindness* towards the godly; *judgment* towards the ungodly; *righteousness* the most perfect fairness in all cases [GROTIUS]. *Faithfulness to His promises* to preserve the godly, as well as stern execution of judgment on the ungodly, is included in "righteousness." **in the earth**—contrary to the dogma of some philosophers, that God does not interfere in terrestrial concerns (Ps. 58:11). **in these . . . I delight**—as well in doing them as in seeing them done by others (Mic. 6:8; 7:18). **25. with the uncircumcised**—rather, "all that are circumcised *in uncircumcision*" [HENDERSON]. The *Hebrew* is an *abstract* term, not a *concrete*, as *English Version* translates, and as the pious "circumcised" is. The nations specified, Egypt, Judah, etc., were *outwardly* "circumcised," but *in heart* were "uncircumcised." The heathen nations were defiled, in spite of their literal circumcision, by idolatry. The Jews, with all their glorying in their spiritual privileges, were no better (ch. 4:4; Deut. 10:16; 30:6; Rom. 2:28, 29; Col. 2:11). However, Ezekiel 31:18; 32:19, *may* imply that the Egyptians were uncircumcised; and it is uncertain as to the other nations specified whether they were at that early time circumcised. HERODOTUS says the Egyptians were so; but others think this applies only to the priests and others having a sacred character, not to the mass of the nation; so *English Version* may be right (Rom. 2: 28, 29). **26. Egypt**—put first to degrade Judah, who, though in privileges above the Gentiles, by unfaithfulness sank below them. Egypt, too, was the power in which the Jews were so prone to trust, and by whose instigation they, as well as the other peoples specified, revolted from Babylon. **in the utmost corners**—rather, "having the hair shaven (or *clipped*) in angles," i.e., having the beard on the cheek narrowed or *cut:* a Canaanitish custom, forbidden to the Israelites (Lev. 19:27; 21:5). The Arabs are hereby referred to (cf. ch. 25:23; 49:32), as the words in apposition show, "that dwell in the wilderness." **uncircumcised . . . uncircumcised in the heart**—The addition of "in the heart" in *Israel's* case marks *its* greater guilt in proportion to its greater privileges, as compared with the rest.

ADAM CLARKE

23. *Let not the wise man glory in his wisdom.* Because God is the Fountain of all good, neither wisdom, nor might, nor riches, nor prosperity can come but from or through Him.

24. *But let him that glorieth.* To glory in a thing is to depend on it as the means or cause of procuring happiness.

25. *I will punish all them which are circumcised with the uncircumcised.* Do not imagine that you, because of your crimes, are the only objects of My displeasure; the circumcised and the uncircumcised, the Jew and the Gentile, shall equally feel the stroke of My justice. In like manner, other nations also were delivered into the hands of Nebuchadnezzar; these he immediately enumerates: Egypt and Edom, and the Moabites and the Ammonites, and the Arabians of the desert.

MATTHEW HENRY

CHAPTER 10

Verses 1–16

The prophet Jeremiah here arms people against the idolatrous usages of the heathen, that being convinced and reclaimed, by the word of God, the rod might be prevented; and it is *written for our learning.*

I. A solemn charge given to the people of God not to conform themselves to the ways of the heathen. Let Israel hear this word from the God of Israel: "*Learn not the way of the heathen,* do not approve of it, nor think indifferently concerning it. Let not any of their customs steal in among you nor mingle themselves with your religion." It was the way of the heathen to worship the host of heaven, the sun, moon, and stars; to them they gave divine honours, and from them they expected divine favours. Now God would not have his people to be *dismayed at the signs of heaven,* to reverence the stars as deities, nor to frighten themselves with any prognostications grounded upon them. Let them fear the God of heaven, and then they need not be *dismayed at the signs of heaven,* for the *stars in their courses* fight not against any that are at peace with God.

II. Good reasons given to enforce this charge.

1. The way of the heathen is absurd, and is condemned by the dictates of right reason, *v.* 3. The statutes and ordinances of the heathen are vanity. The Chaldeans valued themselves upon their wisdom, in which they thought that they excelled all their neighbours; but the prophet here shows that they, and all others that worshipped idols and expected

JAMIESON, FAUSSET, BROWN

CHAPTER 10

VSS. 1-25. CONTRAST BETWEEN THE IDOLS AND JEHOVAH. THE PROPHET'S LAMENTATION AND PRAYER. **1. Israel**—the Jews, the surviving representatives of the nation. 2. EICHORN thinks the reference here to be to some celestial portent which had appeared at that time, causing the Jews' dismay. Probably the reference is general, viz., to the Chaldeans, famed as astrologers, through contact with whom the Jews were likely to fall into the same superstition. **way**—the precepts or ordinances (Lev. 18:3; Acts 9:2).

signs of heaven—The Gentiles did not acknowledge a Great First Cause: many thought events depended on the power of the stars, which some, as PLATO, thought to be endued with spirit and reason. All heavenly phenomena, eclipses, comets, etc. are included.

ADAM CLARKE

CHAPTER 10

1. *Hear ye the word which the Lord speaketh unto you.* Dr. Dahler supposes this discourse to have been delivered in the fourth year of the reign of Jehoiakim. It contains an invective against idolatry, showing its absurdity, and that the Creator alone should be worshipped by all mankind.

2. *Learn not the way of the heathen.* These words are more particularly addressed to the ten tribes scattered among the heathen by the Assyrians, who carried them away captive; they may also regard those in the land of Israel, who still had the customs of the former heathen settlers before their eyes.

Be not dismayed at the signs of heaven; for the heathen are dismayed. The Chaldeans and Egyptians were notoriously addicted to astrology; and the Israelites here are cautioned against it.

3. *The customs of the people are vain.* The statutes and principles of the science are vain, empty, and illusory.

MATTHEW HENRY

help from them, had not common sense. Consider what the idol is that is worshipped. It was a *tree cut out of the forest* originally. It was fitted up by *the hands of the workmen*, squared, and sawed, and worked into shape; see Isa. xliv. 12, &c. But, after all, it was but the stock of a tree, fitter to make a gate-post of than anything else. But, to hide the wood, *they deck it with silver and gold. They fasten it* to its place *with nails and hammers*, that it fall not, nor is stolen, *v.* 4. The image is made straight enough; the workman did his part; it *is upright as the palm-tree* (*v.* 5); it looks stately, and stands up as if it were going to speak to you, but it *cannot speak*; nor can it take one step towards your relief. If there be any occasion for it to shift its place, it must be carried in procession, for it *cannot go*. Be not afraid of incurring their displeasure, for *they can do no evil*; be not afraid of forfeiting their favour, for *neither is it in them to do good*. Idols of gold and silver are as unworthy to be worshipped as wooden gods. *The stock is a doctrine of vanities*, *v.* 8. It teaches lies, teaches lies concerning God. It is *an instruction of vanities*; *it is wood*. A great deal of art is used, and pains taken, about it. They are not ordinary mechanics that are employed about these as about the wooden gods, *v.* 3. These are cunning men; it is *the work of the workman*; the graver must do his part when it has passed through *the hands of the founder*. And, that these gods might be reverenced as kings, *blue and purple are their clothing*, the colour of royal robes (*v.* 9). For what is the idol when it is made and when they have made the best they can of it? (*v.* 14): *They are falsehood;* they are not what they pretend to be. They are worshipped as the gods that give us breath and life and sense, whereas they are lifeless senseless things themselves, and *there is no breath in them*; there is *no spirit in them*, they are not animated, as they are supposed to be, by any *divine spirit* or *numen—divinity*. They have not so much as the *spirit of a beast that goes downward*. *They are vanity, and the work of errors*, *v.* 15. They are the creatures of a deluded fancy. The idolaters that worship these idols (*v.* 8), *are altogether brutish and foolish*. Though in the works of creation they cannot but see the eternal power and godhead of the Creator, yet they have become *vain in their imaginations, not liking to retain God in their knowledge*. See Rom. i. 21, 28.

2. The God of Israel is the one only living and true God; to set up any other in competition with him is the greatest affront that can be done him. The prophet turns from speaking with the utmost disdain of the idols of the heathen to speak with the most profound and awful reverence of the God of Israel (*v.* 6, 7). What is the glory of a man that invented a useful art or founded a flourishing kingdom (and these were grounds sufficient among the heathen to entitle a man to an apotheosis) compared with the glory of him that is the Creator of the world and that *forms the spirit of man within him*? What is the glory of the greatest prince or potentate, compared with the glory of him whose *kingdom rules over all*? He acknowledges (*v.* 6), *O Lord! thou art great*, infinite and immense, and *thy name is great in might*. It is not only the house of Israel that is bound to worship the great Jehovah as the *God of Israel*, but all the families of the earth are bound to worship him as *King of nations*. His verity is as evident as the idol's vanity, *v.* 10. They are the work of men's hands, and the God of truth is God in truth. He is *the living God*. He is life itself, has life in himself, and is the fountain of life to all the creatures. The gods of the heathen are dead things, but ours is a living God and hath immortality. He is *an everlasting king, a King of eternity*. Though the nations should join together they would be utterly unable to resist, or even to *abide his indignation*. He is the God of nature, the fountain of all being; and all the powers of nature are at his command, *v.* 12, 13. If we look back, we find that the whole world owed its origin to him as its first cause. It was a common saying even among the Greeks—*He that sets up to be another god ought first to make another world*. God made us and all things. *The earth* has valuable treasures in its bowels and more valuable fruit on its surface. It and them he has *made by his power*; and it is by no less than an infinite power that it *hangs upon nothing*. The habitable part of the earth is admirably fitted for the use and service of man, and *he hath established it* so *by his wisdom*. *The heavens* are wonderfully *stretched out by his discretion* and that the motions of the heavenly bodies are directed for the benefit of this lower world. These *declare his glory* (Ps. xix. 1), and oblige us to declare it, and not give that glory to the heavens which is due to him that made them. If we look up, we see his providence to be a continued creation (*v.*

JAMIESON, FAUSSET, BROWN

one **cutteth a tree . . .**—rather, "It (that which they busy themselves about: a sample of their 'customs') is a tree cut out of the forest" [MAURER]. **4. fasten . . . move not**—i.e., that it may stand upright without risk of falling, which the god (!) would do, if left to itself (Isa. 41:7). **5. upright**—or, "They are of turned work, resembling a palm tree" [MAURER]. The point of comparison between the idol and the palm is in the pillar-like uprightness of the latter, it having no branches except at the top. **speak not**—(Ps. 115:5). **cannot go**—i.e., walk (Ps. 115:7; Isa. 46:1, 7), **neither . . . do good**—(Isa. 41:23).

8. altogether—rather, all alike [MAURER]. Even the so-called "wise" men (vs. 7) of the Gentiles are on a level with the *brutes* and "foolish," viz., because they connive at the popular idolatry (cf. Rom. 1:21-28). Therefore, in Daniel and Revelation, the world power is represented under a bestial form. Man divests himself of his true humanity, and sinks to the level of the *brute*, when he severs his connection with God (Ps. 115:8; Jonah 2:8). **stock is a doctrine of vanities**—The stock (put for the worship of *all idols whatever*, made out of a stock) speaks for itself that the whole theory of idolatry is vanity (Isa. 44:9-11). CASTALIO translates, "the very wood itself confuting the vanity" (of the idol). **9.** Everything connected with idols is the result of human effort. **Silver spread**—(*Notes*, Isa. 30:22; 40:19). **Tarshish**—Tartessus, in Spain, famed for precious metals. **Uphaz**—(Dan. 10:5). As the *Septuagint* in the *Syrian Hexapla* in the *Margin*, Theodotus, the *Syrian* and *Chaldee versions* have "*Ophir*," GESENIUS thinks "Uphaz" a colloquial corruption (one letter only being changed) for "Ophir." Ophir, in Genesis 10:29, is mentioned among Arabian countries. Perhaps Malacca is the country meant, the natives of which still call their gold mines Ophirs. HEEREN thinks Ophir the general name for the rich countries of the south, on the Arabian, African, and Indian coasts; just as our term, East Indies. **cunning**—skilful.

14. in his knowledge—"is rendered brutish *by* his skill," viz., in idol-making (vss. 8, 9). Thus the parallel, "confounded *by* the graven image," corresponds (so ch. 51:17). Others not so well translate, "*without* knowledge," viz., of God (see Isa. 42:17; 45:16; Hos. 4:6). **15. errors**—deceptions; from a *Hebrew* root, "to stutter"; then meaning "to mock." **their visitation they**—When God shall punish the idol-worshippers (viz., by Cyrus), the idols themselves shall be destroyed [ROSENMULLER] (vs. 11).

6. none—lit., no particle of nothing: nothing whatever; the strongest possible denial (Exod. 15:11; Ps. 86:8, 10). **7.** (Rev. 15:4). **to thee doth it appertain**—to Thee it properly belongs, viz., that Thou shouldest be "feared" (taken out of the previous "fear Thee") (cf. Ezek. 21:27). He alone is the *becoming* object of worship. To worship any other is unseemly and an infringement of His inalienable prerogative. **none**—nothing whatever (*Note*, vs. 6; Ps. 89:6).

10. true God—lit., "God Jehovah is truth"; not merely *true*, i.e., veracious, but *truth* in the reality of His essence, as opposed to the "vanity" or emptiness which all idols are (vss. 3, 8, 15; II Chron. 15:3; Ps. 31:5; I John 5:20). **living God**—(John 5:26; I Tim. 6:17). He hath life *in Himself*, which no creature has. All else "live in Him" (Acts 17:28). In contrast to *dead* idols. **everlasting**—(Ps. 10:16). In contrast to the *temporary* existence of all other objects of worship.

12. Continuation of vs. 10, after the interruption of the thread of the discourse in vs. 11 (Ps. 136:5, 6).

ADAM CLARKE

One cutteth a tree out of the forest. See the notes on Isa. xl. 19 and xliv. 9, etc., which are all parallel places and where this conduct is strongly ridiculed.

5. *They are upright as the palm tree*. As straight and as stiff as the trees out of which they are hewn.

8. *The stock is a doctrine of vanities*. Dr. Blayney translates, "The wood itself is a rebuker of vanities." The very tree out of which the god is hewn demonstrates the vanity and folly of the idolaters.

9. *Brought from Tarshish*. Some suppose this to be Tartessus in Spain, from which the Phoenicians brought much silver. *Blue and purple is their clothing*. These were the most precious dyes; very rare, and of high price.

14. *Every man is brutish*. *Nibar*, is a boor, acts as a brute, who may suppose that a stock of a tree, formed like a man, may be an intellectual being; and therefore shuns the form as though it had life. See Isa. xliv. 10-11.

7. *Who would not fear thee?* Who would not worship Thee as the Author and Giver of all good? The fear of God is often taken for the whole of true religion.

10. *But the Lord*. The original word should be preserved; however we agree to pronounce it: "Yehovah is the true God." He is without beginning, and without end. This is true of no being else. *He is the living God*. His being is underived, and He gives life to all.

MATTHEW HENRY

13): *When he uttereth his voice there is a multitude of waters in the heavens*, which are poured out on the earth. *He causes the vapours to ascend from the ends of the earth.* All the earth pays the tribute of vapours, because all the earth receives the blessing of rain. And thus the moisture in the universe, like the money in a kingdom and the blood in the body, is continually circulating for the good of the whole. There is no sort of weather but what furnishes us with a proof and instance of the wisdom and power of the great Creator. This God is Israel's God in covenant. Therefore let the house of Israel cleave to him, and not forsake him to embrace idols; for (*v.* 16) *the portion of Jacob is not like them*; their rock is not as our rock (Deut. xxxii. 31), nor ours like their mole-hills. If we have satisfaction in God as our portion, he will have a gracious delight in us as his people, whom he owns as *the rod of his inheritance*, with whom he dwells and by whom he is served and honoured. It is the unspeakable comfort of all the Lord's people that he who is their God is *the former of all things*.

3. The prophet, having thus compared the gods of the heathen with the God of Israel, reads the doom of all those pretenders, and directs the Jews, in God's name, to read it to the worshippers of idols (*v.* 11): *Thus shall you say unto them, The gods which have not made the heavens and the earth shall perish.* The primitive Christians would say, when they were urged to worship such a god, *Let him make a world and he shall be my god.* When God comes to reckon with idolaters he will make them weary of their idols, and glad to be rid of them. They shall *cast them to the moles and to the bats*, Isa. ii. 20.

Verses 17–25

I. The prophet threatens, in God's name, the approaching ruin of Judah and Jerusalem, *v.* 17, 18. The Jews that continued in their own land, after some were carried into captivity, were very secure; they thought themselves *inhabitants of a fortress*; their country was their stronghold, impregnable; but they must prepare to go after their brethren, and pack up their effects in expectation: "*Gather up thy wares out of the land;* contract your affairs, and bring them into as small a compass as you can." Let not what you have lie scattered, for the Chaldeans will be upon you again, to be the executioners of the sentence God has passed upon you (*v.* 18): "*Behold, I will sling out the inhabitants of the land at this once;* they have hitherto dropped out, by a few at a time, but they shall be slung out as a stone out of a sling. They shall be thrown out with violence a great distance off, in a little time." He adds, *And I will distress them, that they may find it so.* Whithersoever they go, they shall be continually perplexed and straitened, that they may feel that which they would not believe. They were told that their sin would be their ruin, but now *they shall find it so*.

II. He brings in the people sadly lamenting their calamities (*v.* 19): *Woe is me for my hurt!* Some make this the prophet's own lamentation, not for himself, but for the calamities and desolations of his country. But it may be taken as the language of the people, considered as a body, and therefore speaking as a single person. The prophet puts into their mouths the words they *should* say; whether they would say them or no, they should have cause to say them. "*Woe is me for my hurt*, not for what I fear, but for what I feel." Nor is it a slight hurt, but a *wound* that is *grievous*. To what purpose is it to complain? *This is a grief, and I must bear it* as well as I can. This is patience per force, not a patience by principle. To say, "This is an evil, *and I must bear it*, because I cannot help it," argues a want of those good thoughts of God which we should always have, even under our afflictions, saying, not only, God can and will do what he pleases, but, *Let him do what he pleases.* The country was wasted (*v.* 20): *My tabernacle is spoiled.* Jerusalem, though a strong city, now proves weak: their government is dissolved, and their state has fallen to pieces. Their church is ruined, and all the supports of it fail. It was a general destruction of church and state, city and country, and there were none to repair these desolations. "*My children have gone forth of me;* some have fled, others are slain, others carried into captivity, so that *they are not*; for *there is none to stretch forth my tent any more*, none of my children to do me any service." The rulers took no proper measures for the re-establishing of their ruined state (*v.* 21): *The pastors have become brutish.* When the tents, the shepherds' tents, were spoiled (*v.* 20), it concerned the shepherds to look after them; but they were foolish shepherds. Their kings and princes had no regard at all for the public welfare. The priests, the pastors of God's tabernacle, did a great deal towards the ruin of re-

JAMIESON, FAUSSET, BROWN

13. Lit., "At the voice of His giving forth," i.e., when He thunders. (Job 38:34; Ps. 29:3-5). **waters**–(Gen. 1:7)–above the firmament; heavy rains accompany thunder. **vapours . . . ascend**–(Ps. 135:7). **treasures**–His stores.

16. portion–from a *Hebrew* root, "to divide." God is *the all-sufficient Good* of His people (Num. 18:20; Ps. 16:5; 73:26; Lam. 3:24). **not like them**–not like the idols, a vain object of trust (Deut. 32:31). **former of all things**–the Fashioner (as a potter, Isa. 64:8) of the universe. **rod of his inheritance**–The portion marked off as His inheritance by the measuring *rod* (Ezek. 48:21). As He is their portion, so are they His portion (Deut. 32:9). A reciprocal tie (cf. ch. 51:19; Ps. 74:2, *Margin*). Others make "rod" refer to the tribal rod or scepter.

11. This verse is in *Chaldee*, Jeremiah supplying his countrymen with a formula of reply to Chaldee idolaters in the tongue most intelligible to the latter. There may be also derision intended in imitating their barbarous dialect. ROSENMULLER objects to this view, that not merely the words put in the mouths of the Israelites, but *Jeremiah's* own introductory words, "Thus shall ye say to them," are in *Chaldee*, and thinks it to be a *marginal* gloss. But it is found in all the oldest versions. It was an old *Greek* saying. "Whoever thinks himself a god besides the one God, let him make another world" (Ps. 96:5). **shall perish**–(Isa. 2:18; Zech. 13:2). **these heavens**–the speaker pointing to them with his fingers. **17. wares**–thine effects or movable goods (Ezek. 12:3). Prepare for migrating as captives to Babylon. The address is to Jerusalem, as representative of the whole people. **inhabitant of the fortress**–rather, *inhabitress* of the fortress. Though thou now seemest to *inhabit* an impregnable *fortress*, thou shalt have to remove. "The land" is the champaign region opposed to the "fortified" cities. The "fortress" being taken, the whole "land" will share the disaster. HENDERSON translates, "Gather up thy *packages* from the ground." ROSENMULLER, for "fortress," translates, "siege," i.e., the besieged city. The various articles, in this view, are supposed to be lying about in confusion on the ground during the siege. **18. sling out**–expressing the violence and suddenness of the removal to Babylon. A similar image occurs in ch. 16:13; I Samuel 25:29; Isaiah 22:17, 18. **at this once**–at this time, now. **find it so**–find it by experience, i.e., feel it (Ezek. 6: 10). MICHAELIS translates, "I will bind them together (as in a sling) that they may reach the goal" (Babylon). *English Version* is best: "that they may find it so as I have said" (Num. 23:19; Ezek. 6:10). **19.** Judea bewails its calamity. **wound**–the stroke I suffer under.

I must bear–not humble submission to God's will (Mic. 7:9), but sullen impenitence. Or, rather, it is prophetical of their ultimate acknowledgment of their guilt as the cause of their calamity (Lam. 3:39).

20. tabernacle is spoiled–metaphor from the tents of nomadic life; as these are taken down in a few moments, so as not to leave a vestige of them, so Judea (ch. 4:20). **cords**–with which the coverings of the tent are extended. **curtains**–tent-curtains.

21. pastors–the rulers, civil and religious. This verse gives the cause of the impending calamity.

ADAM CLARKE

13. *When he uttereth his voice, there is a multitude of waters.* This is a plain allusion to a storm of thunder and lightning, and the abundance of rain which is the consequence.

This verse and the three following are the same in substance, and nearly in words, as chap. li. 16, and following.

16. *The portion of Jacob is not like them.* Every nation had its tutelary god; this was its "portion." *The portion,* i.e., the God, *of Jacob is not like them: for he is the former of all things,* and they are formed by their foolish worshippers.

11. *Thus shall ye say unto them.* This is the message you shall deliver to the Chaldean idolaters.

The gods that have not made the heavens and the earth, even they shall perish. Both they and their worshippers shall be destroyed, and idolatry shall finally be destroyed from the earth.

17. *Gather up thy wares.* Pack up your goods, or what necessaries of life your enemies will permit you to carry away; for,

18. *I will sling out the inhabitants of the land.* I will project you with violence from your country. I will send you all into captivity. This discourse, from v. 17, is supposed to have been delivered in the eleventh year of Jehoiakim.

19. *This is a grief, and I must bear it.* Oppressive as it is, I have deserved it, and worse.

20. *My tabernacle is spoiled.* The city is taken, and all our villages ruined and desolated.

21. *The pastors are become brutish.* The king and his counsellors, who, by refusing to pay the promised tribute to Nebuchadnezzar, had kindled a new war.

MATTHEW HENRY

ligion, but nothing towards the repair of it. They neither acknowledged the judgment, nor expected the deliverance, to come from his hand. *Therefore they shall not prosper;* none of their attempts for the public safety shall succeed. Those cannot expect to prosper who do not by faith and prayer take God along with them in all their ways. The report of the enemy's approach was dreadful (*v.* 22): *The noise of the bruit has come,* of the report which at first was but whispered abroad, as wanting confirmation. It now proves too true: *A great commotion* arises *out of the north country,* which threatens to make all *the cities of Judah desolate and a den of dragons;* for they must all expect to be sacrificed to the avarice and fury of the Chaldean army.

III. He turns to God, and addresses himself to him, finding it too little purpose to speak to the people.

1. The prophet here acknowledges the sovereignty and dominion of the divine Providence, *v.* 23. We are not at our own disposal, but under a divine direction; the event is often overruled so as to be quite contrary to our expectation. Some think that the way of the Chaldean army being not in themselves, they can do no more than God permits them; he can set bounds to these proud waves, and say, *Hitherto they shall come, and no further.*

2. He deprecates the divine wrath, that it might not fall upon God's Israel, *v.* 24. He speaks not for himself only, but on behalf of his people: *O Lord, correct me, but with judgment* (no more than is necessary for the driving out of the foolishness that is bound up in our hearts), *not in thy anger,* let it come from thy love, and be made to work for good, not to *bring us to nothing,* but to bring us home to thyself. Let it not be according to the desert of our sins, but according to the designs of thy grace. We cannot pray in faith that we may never be corrected, while we are conscious to ourselves that we need correction and deserve it, and know that as many as God loves he chastens.

3. He imprecates the divine wrath against the persecutors of Israel (*v.* 25): *Pour out thy fury upon the heathen that know thee not.* This prayer does not come from a spirit of malice or revenge. It is an appeal to his justice. As if he had said, "Lord, we are a provoking people; but are there not other nations that are more so? We are thy children, and may expect a fatherly correction; but they are thy enemies, and against them thy indignation should be, not against us." The heathen are strangers to God, and are content to be so. They *know him not,* nor desire to know him. They live without prayer, have nothing of religion among them; they *call not on God's name.* They are persecutors of the people of God. *They have eaten up Jacob* with as much greediness as those that are hungry eat their necessary food; they have *devoured him, and consumed him, and made his habitation desolate,* that is, the land in which he lives, or the temple of God, which is his habitation among them.

JAMIESON, FAUSSET, BROWN

22. bruit—rumor of invasion. The antithesis is between the *voice of God* in His prophets to whom they turned a deaf ear, and the *cry of the enemy,* a new teacher, whom they must hear [CALVIN]. **north country**—Babylon (ch. 1:15).

23. Despairing of influencing the people, he turns to God. **way of man not in himself**—(Prov. 16:1; 20:24; Jas. 4:13, 14). I know, O Jehovah, that the march of the Babylonian conqueror against me (Jeremiah identifying himself with his people) is not at his own discretion, but is overruled by Thee (Isa. 10:5-7; cf. vs. 19). **that walketh**—when he walketh, i.e., sets out in any undertaking. **direct . . . steps**—to give a prosperous issue to (Ps. 73: 23). **24, 25.** Since I (my nation) must be corrected (justice requiring it because of the deep guilt of the nation), I do not deprecate all chastisement, but pray only for moderation in it (ch. 30:11; Ps. 6:1; 38:1); and that the full tide of Thy fury may be poured out on the heathen invaders for their cruelty towards *Thy* people. Psalm 79:6, 7, a psalm to be referred to the time of the captivity, its composer probably repeated this from Jeremiah.

The imperative, "Pour out," is used instead of the future, expressing vividly the *certainty* of the prediction, and that the word of God itself effects its own declarations. Accordingly, the Jews were restored after *correction;* the Babylonians were utterly extinguished. **know thee . . . call . . . on thy name**—*Knowledge* of God is the beginning of piety; *calling* on Him the fruit. **heathen . . . Jacob**—He reminds God of the distinction He has made between His people whom *Jacob* represents, and the heathen aliens. *Correct* us as Thy adopted sons, the seed of Jacob; destroy them as outcasts (Zech. 1:14, 15, 21).

ADAM CLARKE

22. *The noise of the bruit is come.* How this silly French word *bruit,* which signifies "noise," got in here, I cannot imagine. The simple translation is this: "The voice of the report! behold, it is come; yea, great commotion from the land of the north [Chaldea], to make the cities of Judea a desolation, a habitation of wild beasts." That is, the report we had heard of the projected invasion of Judea by Nebuchadnezzar is confirmed. He has entered the land; the Chaldeans are at the doors, and the total desolation of Judea is their sole object.

25. *Pour out thy fury upon the heathen.* Even those who are now the executors of Thy justice upon us will, in their turn, feel its scourge. This was fulfilled in the Chaldeans. Nebuchadnezzar was punished with madness, his son was slain in his revels, and the city was taken and sacked by Cyrus; and the Babylonish empire was finally destroyed!

MATTHEW HENRY — CHAPTER 11

Verses 1–10

The prophet draws up an indictment against the Jews for wilful disobedience to the commands of their rightful Sovereign.

I. God commanded him to *speak it to the men of Judah, v.* 1, 2. In the original it is plural: *Speak you this.* For what he said to Jeremiah was the same that he gave in charge to all his servants the prophets. They none of them said any other than what Moses, in the law, had said; to that therefore they must direct the people: "*Hear the words of this covenant;* be judged by them." Jeremiah must now proclaim this in the cities *of Judah and the streets of Jerusalem,* that all may hear, for all are concerned. Then, by comparing yourselves with the covenant, you will soon be aware upon what terms you now stand with him.

II. He opens the charter upon which their state was founded and by which they held their privileges. They had forgotten the tenor of it, and lived as if they thought that they might do what they pleased and yet have what God had promised, or as if they thought that the keeping up of the ceremonial observances was all that God required of them. He therefore shows them that the thing God insisted upon was *obedience,* which was *better than sacrifice.* He said, *Obey my voice, v.* 4, and again *v.* 7. "Own God for your Master. *Do my commandments,* but *according to all which I command you;* make conscience of moral duties especially, and rest not in those that are merely ritual; hear the words of the covenant, and do them." This was the original contract between God and them, when he first formed them into

JAMIESON, FAUSSET, BROWN — CHAPTER 11

VSS. 1-23. EPITOME OF THE COVENANT FOUND IN THE TEMPLE IN JOSIAH'S REIGN. JUDAH'S REVOLT FROM IT, AND GOD'S CONSEQUENT WRATH.

2. this covenant—alluding to the book of the law (Deut. 27: 28) found in the temple by Hilkiah the high priest, five years after Jeremiah's call to the prophetic office (II Kings 22:8 to 23:25). **Hear ye**—Others besides Jeremiah were to promulgate God's will to the people; it was the duty of the priests to read the law to them (Mal. 2:7).

ADAM CLARKE — CHAPTER 11

1. *The word that came to Jeremiah.* This discourse is supposed to have been delivered in the first year of the reign of Zedekiah.

2. *Hear ye the words of this covenant.* It is possible that the prophet caused the words of the covenant made with their fathers in the desert (Exod. xxiv. 4-8) to be read to them on this occasion; or, at least, the blessings and the cursings which Moses caused to be pronounced to the people as soon as they had set foot in Canaan, Deuteronomy xxvii—xxviii.

MATTHEW HENRY

a people. It was what he *commanded their fathers* when he first *brought them forth out of the land of Egypt*, *v.* 4 and again *v.* 7. He redeemed them out of the service of the Egyptians, which was perfect slavery, that he might take them into his own service, which is perfect freedom, Luke i. 74, 75. This was made the condition of the relation between them and God: "*So shall you be my people and I will be your God;* I will own you for mine, and you may call upon me as yours." It was upon these terms that the land of Canaan was given them for a possession: *Obey my voice, that I may perform the oath sworn to your fathers, to give them a land flowing with milk and honey*, *v.* 5. *Cursed be the man*, though it were but a single person, *that obeys not the words of this covenant*, much more when it is the body of the nation that rebels. Lest this covenant should be forgotten God had from time to time called to them to remember it by his servants the prophets. This covenant was consented to (*v.* 5): *Then answered I, and said, So be it, O Lord!* These are the words of the prophet, expressing either, his own consent to the covenant for himself, and his desire to have the benefit of it. Or, his good will that his people might have the benefit of it. Or, his people's consent to the covenant: "*Then answered I*, in the name of the people, *So be it.*"

III. He charges them with breach of covenant, such a breach as amounted to a forfeiture of their charter, *v.* 8. "*Obey my voice*, do as you are bidden, and all shall be well"; *yet they obeyed not. They walked everyone in the imagination of their evil heart*; every man did as his fancy and humour led him, right or wrong, lawful or unlawful, both in their devotions and in their conversations; see *ch.* vii. 24. What then could they expect, but to fall under the curse of the covenant? That which aggravated their defection from God was that it was general, and as it were *by consent*, *v.* 9, 10. Jeremiah himself saw that many lived in open disobedience to God, but the Lord told him that the matter was worse than he thought: *A conspiracy is found among them.* There is a combination against God and religion, a dangerous design formed to overthrow God's government and bring in the counterfeit deities. They designed to overthrow divine revelation, and persuade people not to hear, not to heed, the words of God. Human reason shall be their god, a light within their god, an infallible judge their god, saints and angels their gods, the god of this or the other nation shall be theirs; thus, under several disguises, they are in the same confederacy *against the Lord and against his anointed. The inhabitants of Jerusalem* are in conspiracy with *the men of Judah.* Those of this generation seem to be in conspiracy with those of the foregoing generation, to carry on the war from age to age against religion. Judah and Israel, the kingdom of the ten tribes and that of the two, that were often at daggers-drawing one with another, were yet *in a conspiracy* to *break the covenant God had made with their fathers*, even with the heads of all the twelve tribes. The house of Israel began the revolt, but the house of Judah soon came into the conspiracy.

Verses 11–17

This paragraph contains much of God's wrath. *Therefore I will bring evil upon them* (*v.* 11), the evil of punishment for the evil of sin.

I. They cannot help themselves. It is *evil which they shall not be able to escape*, or to *go forth out of*, by any evasion whatsoever.

II. Their God will not help them; *Though they shall cry unto me, I will not hearken unto them.* For he has plainly told us that he that *turns away his ears from hearing the law*, as they did, for they *inclined not their ear* (*v.* 8), even his prayer shall be an abomination to him.

III. Their idols shall not help them, *v.* 12. They shall *go, and cry to the gods to whom they* now *offer incense. They shall not save them at all.* It is God only that is a friend at need, *a present* powerful *help in time of trouble.* If the idols could have done any real kindness to their worshippers, they would have done it for this people, who had multiplied them *according to the number of their cities* (*v.* 13), nay, in Jerusalem, *according to the number of their streets.*

IV. Jeremiah's prayers shall not help them, *v.* 14. God would give no encouragement to the prophets to pray for them, not for the body of the people, but for the remnant among them, to pray for their eternal salvation, not for their deliverance from the temporal judgments.

V. The profession they make of religion shall stand them in no stead, *v.* 15. Once they had a place *in God's house*; they partook of God's altar; they ate of the flesh of their peace-offerings, here called the *holy flesh.* What harm could come to those who were God's beloved, who were under the protection

JAMIESON, FAUSSET, BROWN

4. in the day–i.e., when. The Sinaitic covenant was made some time after the exodus, but the two events are so connected as to be viewed as one. **iron furnace**–(Deut. 4:20; I Kings 8:51). "Furnace" expresses the searching ordeal; "iron," the long duration of it. The furnace was *of earth*, not *of iron* (Ps. 12:6); a furnace, in heat and duration enough to melt even iron. God's deliverance of them from such an ordeal aggravates their present guilt. **do them**–viz., the words of the covenant (vs. 3). **so . . .**–(Lev. 26:3, 12). **5. oath**–(Ps. 105: 9, 10.)

3. (Deut. 27:26; Gal. 3:10.)

as it is this day–These are the concluding words of God to the Israelites when formerly brought out of Egypt, "Obey . . . , that I may *at this time* make good the promise I made to your fathers, to give . . ." [MAURER]. *English Version* makes the words apply to *Jeremiah's time*, "As ye know at this time, that God's promise has been fulfilled," viz., in Israel's acquisition of Canaan. **So be it**–*Hebrew, Amen.* Taken from Deuteronomy 27:15-26. Jeremiah hereby solemnly concurs in the justice of the curses pronounced there (see vs. 3). **6.** Jeremiah was to take a prophetic tour throughout Judah, to proclaim everywhere the denunciations in the book of the law found in the temple. **Hear . . . do**–(Rom. 2:13; Jas. 1:22.) **7. rising early**–(ch. 7:13). **8. imagination**–rather, stubbornness. **will bring**–The words, "even unto this day" (vs. 7), confirm *English Version* rather than the rendering of ROSENMULLER: "I *brought* upon them." **words**–threats (vs. 3; Deut. 27:15-26).

9. conspiracy–a *deliberate combination* against God and against Josiah's reformation. Their idolatry is not the result of a hasty impulse (Ps. 83:5; Ezek. 22:25).

11. cry unto me–contrasted with "cry unto the gods," (vs. 12). **not hearken**–(Ps. 18:41; Prov. 1:28; Isa. 1.15; Mic. 3:4).

12. cry unto the gods . . . not save–(Deut. 32:37, 38). Cf. this verse and beginning of vs. 13, ch. 2: 28. **in the time of their trouble**–i.e., calamity (ch. 2:27). **13. shameful thing**–*Hebrew*, "shame," viz., the idol, not merely shameful, but the *essence* of all that is shameful (ch. 3:24; Hos. 9:10), which will bring shame and confusion on yourselves [CALVIN]. **14.** There is a climax of guilt which admits of no further intercessory prayer (Exod. 32:10, in the *Chaldee version*, "leave off praying"; ch. 7:16; I. Sam. 16:1; 15:35; I John 5:16). Our mind should be at one with God in all that He is doing, even in the rejection of the reprobate. **for their trouble**–on account of their trouble. Other MSS. read, "*in the time* of their trouble" a gloss from vs. 12. **15. my beloved**–My elect people, Judea; this aggravates their ingratitude (ch. 12:7).

ADAM CLARKE

3. *Cursed be the man that obeyeth not.* After the reading, the prophet appears to sum up the things contained in what was read to them; as if he had said, "You hear what the Lord saith unto you: remember, the sum of it is this: The man is cursed who obeyeth not; and he is blessed who obeys."

5. *So be it, O Lord.* Let Thy promises be fulfilled; and let the incorrigible beware of Thy threatenings!

6. *Proclaim all these words.* Let the same covenant, with the blessings and cursings, be read in every city of Judah, and in all the streets of Jerusalem, that all the people may know their duty, their privileges, and their danger.

10. *They are turned back to the iniquities of their forefathers.* A great reformation had taken place under the reign of Josiah, and the public worship of idols had been abolished, and most of the high places destroyed. But under the reign of his son and his successors, they had turned back again to idolatry, and were become worse than ever. It required a captivity to cure them of this propensity, and God sent one; after that, there was no idolatry among the Jews.

14. *Therefore pray not thou for this people.* I am determined to give them up into the hands of their enemies; I will neither hear your intercession, nor regard their prayers. Their measure is full.

15. *What hath my beloved to do in mine house?* This is an endearing expression, which properly belonged to the Israelites. When God took them into covenant with himself, they were espoused to Him, and therefore His *beloved.*

MATTHEW HENRY

of his house? Even when they *did evil* yet *they rejoiced* and gloried in this, but their confidence would deceive them, they themselves having forfeited the privileges. They have *wrought lewdness with many*, have worshipped many idols; and therefore, God's temple will *yield them no protection.* God's altar will yield them no satisfaction: "*The holy flesh has passed from thee*, that is, an end will soon be put to thy sacrifices, when the temple shall be laid in ruins; and where then will the holy flesh be, that thou art so proud of?" A holy heart will be a comfort to us when the holy flesh has passed from us; an inward principle of grace will make up the want of the outward means of grace. But woe unto us if the departure of the holy flesh be accompanied with the departure of the Holy Spirit.

VI. God's former favours to them shall stand them in no stead, *v.* 16, 17. God had *called Israel's name a green olive-tree*, and had made them so, he had *planted* them (*v.* 17), had formed them into a people, with all the advantages they could have to make them a fruitful and flourishing people, so good was their law and so good was their land. He had planted them a green olive, a good olive, but they had degenerated into a *wild olive*, Rom. xi. 17. Both *the house of Israel* and the *house of Judah* had *done evil*, had *provoked God to anger in burning incense unto Baal*, setting up other mediators besides the promised Messiah. He that planted this green olive-tree, and expected fruit from it, finding it barren and grown wild, *has kindled fire upon it*, to burn it as it stands; for, being without fruit, it is *twice dead, plucked up by the roots* (Jude 12), it is *cut down and cast into the fire*. The *branches of it*, the *high and lofty boughs* (so the word signifies), are *broken down*, both princes and priests cut off. And thus it proves that the evil done against God is really done *against their own souls.*

Verses 18–23

The prophet Jeremiah has much in his writings concerning himself, the times he lived in being very troublesome. Here we have the beginning of his sorrows, which arose from the people of his own city, Anathoth, a priest's city.

I. Their plot against him, *v.* 19. They *devised devices against him*, laid their heads together to contrive how they might be the death of him. They said concerning Jeremiah, *Let us destroy the tree with the fruit thereof*—a proverbial expression, meaning, "Let us utterly destroy him root and branch." Or rather "both the prophet and the prophecy; let us kill the one and defeat the other. Let us sink his reputation, and so spoil the credit of his predictions." The persecutors of God's prophets *hunt for* no less than *the precious life.* They thought to put an end to his days, but he survived most of his enemies; they thought to blast his memory, but it lives to this day, and will while time lasts.

II. The information which God gave him of this conspiracy. He knew nothing of it himself, so artfully had they concealed it; he came to Anathoth fearing no harm, *like a lamb or an ox*, that thinks he is driven as usual to the field, *when he is brought to the slaughter*. There is but a step between Jeremiah and death; but then *the Lord gave him knowledge of it*, by dream or vision, or impression upon his spirit, that he might save himself, as the king of Israel did upon the notice Elisha gave him, 2 Kings vi. 10. Thus he came to *know it*. God *showed him their doings.* See what care God takes of his prophets: He *suffers no man to do them wrong*; all the rage of their enemies cannot prevail to take them off till they have finished their testimony.

III. His appeal to God hereupon, *v.* 20. When men deal unjustly with us we have a God to go to who will plead the cause of injured innocency and appear against the injurious. God's justice, which is a terror to the wicked, is a comfort to the godly. He knew the integrity that was in Jeremiah's heart, and knew the wickedness that was in their hearts, though ever so cunningly concealed. Now Jeremiah prays judgment against them: "*Let me see thy vengeance on them*, that is, do justice between me and them in such a way as thou pleasest." Some think there was something of human frailty in this prayer; at least Christ has taught us another lesson, both by precept and by pattern, which is to pray for our persecutors. He refers his cause entirely to the judgment of God: "*Unto thee have I revealed my cause;* not desiring nor expecting to interest any other in it." When we are wronged, we have a God to commit our cause to, with a resolution to acquiesce in his definitive sentence, to subscribe, and not prescribe, to him.

IV. Judgment given against his persecutors, *the men of Anathoth.* It was to no purpose for him to appeal to the courts at Jerusalem; the priests there

JAMIESON, FAUSSET, BROWN

lewdness with many—(Ezek. 16:25). Rather, "that great (or, manifold) enormity"; lit., the enormity, the manifold; viz., their idolatry, which made their worship of God in the temple a mockery (cf. ch. 7:10; Ezek. 23:39) [HENDERSON]. **holy flesh**—(Hag. 2:12-14; Titus 1:15), viz., the sacrifices, which, through the guilt of the Jews, were no longer *holy*, i.e., acceptable to God. The sacrifices on which they relied will, therefore, no longer protect them. Judah is represented as a priest's wife, who, by adultery, has forfeited her share in the flesh of the sacrifices, and yet boasts of her prerogative at the very same time [HORSLEY]. **when thou doest evil**—lit., "when thy evil" (is at hand). PISCATOR translates, "When thy *calamity* is at hand (according to God's threats). thou gloriest" (against God, instead of humbling thyself). *English Version* is best (cf. Prov. 2:14). **16. called thy name**—made thee. **olive**—(Ps. 52:8; Rom. 11:17). The "olive" is chosen to represent the adoption of Judah by the *free grace* of God, as its *oil* is the image of *richness* (cf. Ps. 23:5; 104:15). **with . . . noise of . . . tumult**—or, "*at* the noise . . . ," viz., at the tumult of the invading army (Isa. 13:4) [MAURER]. Or, rather, "with the sound of a mighty voice," viz., that of God, i.e., the thunder; thus there is no confusion of metaphors. The tree stricken with lightning has "*fire kindled* upon it, and the branches are *broken*," at one and the same time [HOUBIGANT]. **17. that planted thee**—(ch. 2:21; Isa. 5:2). **against themselves**—The sinner's sin is to his own hurt (*Note,* ch. 7:19).

devices—(ch. 18:18). **tree with . . . fruit**—lit., in its fruit or food, i.e., when it is in fruit. Proverbial, to express the destruction of cause and effect together. The man is the tree; his teaching, the fruit. Let us destroy the prophet and his prophecies; viz., those threatening destruction to the nation, which offended them. Cf. Matthew 7: 17, which also refers to *prophets* and their *doctrines*.

18, 19. Jeremiah here digresses to notice the attempt on his life plotted by his townsmen of Anathoth. He had no suspicion of it, until Jehovah revealed it to him (ch. 12:6). **the Lord . . . thou**—The change of person from the third to the second accords with the excited feelings of the prophet. **then**—when I was in peril of my life. **their doings**—those of the men of Anathoth. His thus alluding to them, before he has mentioned their name, is due to his excitement. **19. lamb**—lit., a pet lamb, such as the Jews often had in their houses, for their children to play with; and the Arabs still have (II Sam. 12:3). His own *familiar* friends had plotted against the prophet. The language is exactly the same as that applied to Messiah (Isa. 53:7). Each prophet and patriarch exemplified in his own person some one feature or more in the manifold attributes and sufferings of the Messiah to come; just as the saints have done since His coming (Gal. 2:20; Phil. 3:10; Col. 1:24). This adapted both the more experimentally to testify of Christ.

20. triest . . . heart—(Rev. 2:23). **revealed**—committed *my cause.* Jeremiah's wish for vengeance was not personal but ministerial, and accorded with God's purpose revealed to him against the enemies alike of God and of His servant (Ps. 37:34; 54:7; 112:8; 118:7).

ADAM CLARKE

But now that they have forsaken Him, and joined themselves to another, what have they to do with His house or its ordinances, which they wish now to frequent with vows and sacrifices, when they see the evil fast coming upon them?

16. *The Lord called thy name, A green olive tree.* That is, He made you like a green olive—fair, flourishing, and fruitful; but you are degenerated, and God has given the Chaldeans permission to burn you up.

Let us destroy the tree with the fruit. Let us slay the prophet, and his prophecies will come to an end.

18. *The Lord hath given me knowledge of it.* The men of Anathoth had conspired against his life, because he reproved them for their sins, and denounced the judgments of God against them. Of this God had given him a secret warning, that he might be on his guard.

19. *I was like a lamb or an ox.* "Like the familiar lamb"—the lamb bred up in the house, in a state of friendship with the family. The people of Anathoth were Jeremiah's townsmen; he was born and bred among them; they were his familiar friends; and now they lay wait for his life!

20. *Let me see thy vengeance on them.* Rather, "I shall see Thy punishment inflicted on them."

MATTHEW HENRY

would stand by the priests at Anathoth, but God will *therefore* take cognizance of the cause himself, and we are sure that *his judgment is according to truth.* They sought the prophet's life, for they forbad him to prophesy upon pain of death; they were resolved either to silence him or to slay him. The provocation he gave them was his prophesying *in the name of the Lord*, and not prophesying such smooth things as they always bespoke. It is as bad to God's faithful ministers to have their mouth stopped as to have their breath stopped. It used to be said that *a prophet could not perish but at Jerusalem*, for there the great council sat; but so bitter were the men of Anathoth against Jeremiah that they would undertake to be the death of him themselves. The sentence passed upon them for this crime, *v.* 22, 23: God says, *I will punish them; I will visit* this *upon them;* so the word is. *The sword* shall devour their *young men*, though they were young priests, and *famine* shall destroy the *sons and daughters*. They sought Jeremiah's life, they would destroy him *root and branch*, that *his name* might be *no more remembered*, and therefore *there shall be no remnant of them left*.

CHAPTER 12

Verses 1-6

The prophet doubts not but it would be of use to others to know what had passed between God and his soul, and therefore he here tells us,

I. What liberty he humbly took to reason with God concerning his judgments, *v.* 1. He is about to *plead* with God, not to find fault with his proceedings, but to enquire into the meaning of them. We may not *strive with our Maker*, but we may reason with him. When we are most in the dark concerning the meaning of God's dispensations we must still resolve to keep up right thoughts of God, that he never did, nor ever will do, the least wrong to any of his creatures. When we find it hard to understand particular providences we must have recourse to general truths as our first principles, and abide by them; however dark the providence may be, *the Lord is righteous*; see Ps. lxxiii. 1.

II. What it was in the dispensations of divine Providence that he stumbled at. The designs and projects of wicked people seem successful: *The way of the wicked prospers;* they compass their malicious designs. Hypocrites are chiefly meant (as appears, *v.* 2), who dissemble and depart from their good beginnings, deal treacherously, yet *they are happy*. The prophet shows (*v.* 2) God had been indulgent to them: "They are planted in a good land, a land flowing with milk and honey, and *thou hast planted them*! nay, thou didst cast out the heathen to plant them," Ps. xliv. 2; lxxx. 8. *They have taken root;* their prosperity seems to be confirmed and settled. God had favoured them, though they had dealt treacherously with him: *Thou art near in their mouth and far from their reins.* Though they cared not for thinking of God, nor had any sincere affection to him, yet they could easily persuade themselves to speak of him with an air of seriousness. Piety from the teeth outward is no difficult thing. Though they had the name of God ready in their mouth, and those forms of speech that savoured of piety, yet they could not keep the fear of God in their hearts.

III. What comfort he had in appealing to God concerning his own integrity (*v.* 3): *But thou, O Lord! knowest me.* God knew he was not a deceiver and false prophet; those that thus abused him did not know him, 1 Cor. ii. 8. We are as our hearts are, and our hearts are good or bad according as they are, or are not, towards God.

IV. He prays that God would turn his hand against these wicked people, and not suffer them to prosper always, though they had prospered long: "Let some judgment come to *pull them out* of this fat pasture *as sheep for the slaughter*, that it may appear their long prosperity was but like the feeding of lambs to *prepare them for the day of slaughter*," Hos. iv. 16. God suffered them to prosper that by their pride and luxury they might fill up the measure of their iniquity and so be ripened for destruction. "*How long shall the land mourn for the wickedness of those that dwell therein?* Lord, shall those prosper themselves that ruin all about them?" *The herbs of every field wither* (the grass is burnt up). The beasts are consumed. This was the effect of a long drought which happened at the latter end of Josiah's reign and the beginning of Jehoiakim's; *ch.* iii. 3, viii. 13, ix. 10, 12; *ch.* xiv. Now why was it that this *fruitful land* was *turned into barrenness for the wickedness of those that dwelt therein?* Therefore the prophet prays that these wicked people might *die for their own sin*, and that the whole nation might not suffer for it. *They said,*

JAMIESON, FAUSSET, BROWN

21. Prophesy not—(Isa. 30:10; Amos 2:12; Mic. 2:6). If Jeremiah had not uttered his denunciatory predictions, they would not have plotted against him. None were more bitter than his own fellow townsmen. Cf. the conduct of the Nazarites towards Jesus of Nazareth (Luke 4:24-29).

22. The retribution of their intended murder shall be in kind; just as in Messiah's case (Ps. 69:8-28). **23.** (Ch. 23:12.) **the year of . . . visitation**—LXX translates, "*in the* year of their . . ." i.e., at the time when I shall visit them in wrath. JEROME supports *English Version*. "Year" often means *a determined time.*

CHAPTER 12

VSS. 1-17. CONTINUATION OF THE SUBJECT AT THE CLOSE OF CHAPTER 11. He ventures to expostulate with Jehovah as to the prosperity of the wicked, who had plotted against his life (vss. 1-4); in reply he is told that he will have worse to endure, and that from his own relatives (vss. 5, 6). The heaviest judgments, however, would be inflicted on the faithless people (vss. 7-13); and then on the nations co-operating with the Chaldeans against Judah, with, however, a promise of mercy on repentance (vss. 14-17). **1.** (Ps. 51:4.) **let me talk . . .**—only let me reason the case with Thee: inquire of Thee the causes why such wicked men as these plotters against my life prosper (cf. Job 12:6; 21:7; Psalm 37:1, 35; 73:3; Mal. 3:15). It is right, when hard thoughts of God's providence suggest themselves, to fortify our minds by *justifying God beforehand* (as did Jeremiah), even before we hear the *reasons* of His dealings. **2. grow**—lit., go on, progress. Thou givest them sure dwellings and increasing prosperity.

near in . . . mouth . . . far from . . . reins—(Isa. 29:13; Matt. 15:8). Hypocrites.

3. knowest me—(Ps. 139:1). **tried . . . heart**—(ch. 11:20). **toward thee**—rather, with Thee, i.e., entirely devoted to Thee; contrasted with the hypocrites (vs. 2), "near in . . . mouth, and far from . . . reins." This being so, how is it that I fare so ill, they so well?

pull . . . out—containing the metaphor, from a "rooted tree" (vs. 2). **prepare**—lit., separate, or set apart as devoted. **day of slaughter**—(Jas. 5:5).

4. land mourn—personification (ch. 14: 2; 23:10). **for the wickedness**—(Ps. 107:34). **beasts**—(Hos. 4:3).

ADAM CLARKE

22. *Behold, I will punish them.* And the punishment is, *Their young men shall die by the sword* of the Chaldeans; and *their sons and their daughters shall die by famine* that shall come on the land through the desolations occasioned by the Chaldean army.

CHAPTER 12

1. *Righteous art thou, O Lord, when I plead with thee.* The prophet is grieved at the prosperity of the wicked; and he wonders how, consistently with God's righteousness, vice should often be in affluence, and piety in suffering and poverty. He knows that God is righteous, that everything is done well; but he wishes to inquire how these apparently unequal and undeserved lots take place. On this subject he wishes to reason with God, that he may receive instruction.

2. *Thou art near in their mouth.* They have no sincerity; they have something of the form of religion, but nothing of its power.

3. *But thou, O Lord, knowest me.* I know that the very secrets of my heart are known to Thee; and I am glad of it, for Thou knowest that my heart is towards Thee—is upright and sincere.

4. *How long shall the land mourn?* These hypocrites and open sinners are a curse to the country; pull them out, Lord, that the land may be delivered of that which is the cause of its desolation.

MATTHEW HENRY

He shall not see our last end, either, 1. God himself shall not. He knows not what way we take nor what it will end in. Or, 2. Jeremiah *shall not see our last end*. They look upon him as a false prophet.

V. He acquaints us with the answer God gave to those complaints of his, *v.* 5, 6. Ministers have lessons to learn as well as lessons to teach, and must themselves hear God's voice and preach to themselves. Jeremiah complained of the wickedness of the men of Anathoth, and that they prospered. Now this seems to be an answer to that complaint. 1. It is allowed that he had cause to complain (*v.* 6): "*Thy brethren*, the priests of Anathoth, of *the house of thy father, even they have dealt treacherously with thee*, and, under colour of friendship, have done thee all the mischief they could; they *have called a multitude after thee*, raised the mob upon thee, to whom they have endeavoured to render thee despicable. They are indeed such as thou canst *not believe, though they speak fair words to thee*. They seem to be thy friends, but are really thy enemies." 2. Yet he is told that he laid the unkindness of his countrymen too much to heart. *They wearied* him, because it was *in a land of peace wherein he trusted*, *v.* 5. It was very grievous to him to be thus hated and abused by his own kindred. He was disturbed in his mind by it. He was discouraged in his work by it, began to be weary of prophesying, and to think of giving it up. He did not see this was but the beginning of his sorrow, and that he had sorer trials yet before him; and, whereas he should, by a patient bearing of this trouble, prepare himself for greater, by his uneasiness he did but unfit himself for what lay before him: *If thou hast run with the footmen and they have wearied thee*, and run thee quite out of breath, *then how wilt thou contend with horses?* If the injuries done him by the men of Anathoth made such an impression upon him, what would he do when the princes and chief priests at Jerusalem should set upon him with their power, *ch.* xx. 2; xxxii. 2. If he was so soon tired *in a land of peace*, where there was little peril, *what would he do in the swellings of Jordan*, when that overflows all its banks and frightens even lions out of their thickets? (*ch.* xlix. 19). How shall we preserve our integrity and peace when we come to *the swellings of Jordan*? We must approve ourselves well in present smaller trials, keep up our spirits, keep hold of the promise, with our eye upon the prize, and so run that we may obtain it.

Verses 7–13

The people of the Jews are here marked for ruin.

I. It is a terrible word that God here says (*v.* 7): *I have forsaken my house*—the temple, his palace; they had polluted it, and so forced him out of it: *I have left my heritage*, and will look after it no more. If they would have conducted themselves with propriety, he would have made the best of them, for they were *the beloved of his soul*; but they had provoked him to *give them into the hand of their enemies*. They had degenerated, had become like *beasts of prey*, which nobody loves, but everybody avoids (*v.* 8): *My heritage is unto me as a lion in the forest*. They *cry out against God* in the threatenings they breathe against his prophets that speak to them in his name. They blaspheme his name, oppose his authority, and bid defiance to his justice, and so *cry out against him as a lion in the forest*. Those that were the *sheep of God's pasture* had become barbarous and ravenous, and as ungovernable as lions in the forest; *therefore he hated them;* for what delight could the God of love take in people that had become as roaring lions and raging beasts, a vexation to all about them? They had become like *birds of prey*, unworthy a place in God's house, where neither beasts nor birds of prey were admitted to be offered in sacrifice (*v.* 9): *My heritage is unto me as a bird with talons* (so some read it, and so the margin); they have by their unnatural contentions made their country a cock-pit. Or *as a speckled bird*, sprinkled, or bedewed with the blood of her prey. *The birds round about are against her*. Some made her a *speckled bird*, upon account of their mixing the superstitious usages of the heathen with divine institutions in the worship of God; they were fond of a party-coloured religion.

II. The enemies will fall upon them and lay them desolate. And some think it is upon this account that they are compared to a speckled bird, because fowls usually make a noise about a bird of an odd unusual colour. God's people are, among the children of this world, as *men wondered at*, as a *speckled bird*; but this people had by their own folly made themselves so. Let *all the birds round* be *against her*, for God has forsaken her. The utter desolation of the land by the Chaldean army is here

JAMIESON, FAUSSET, BROWN

He shall not see our last end—*Jehovah* knows not what is about to happen to us (ch. 5:12) ROSENMULLER]. So LXX. (Ps. 10:11; Ezek. 8:12; 9:9). Rather, "*The prophet* (Jeremiah, to whom the whole context refers) shall not see our last end." We need not trouble ourselves about his boding predictions. We shall not be destroyed as he says (ch. 5:12, 13). **5.** Jehovah's reply to Jeremiah's complaint. **horses**—i.e., horsemen: the argument a fortiori. A proverbial phrase. The injuries done thee by the men of Anathoth ("the footmen") are small compared with those which the men of Jerusalem ("the horsemen") are about to inflict on thee. If the former weary thee out, how wilt thou contend with the king, the court, and the priests at Jerusalem? ***wherein thou trustedst***, *they wearied thee*—*English Version* thus fills up the sentence with the italicized words, to answer to the parallel clause in the first sentence of the verse. The parallelism is, however, sufficiently retained with a less ellipsis: "If (it is only) in a land of peace thou art confident" [MAURER]. **swelling of Jordan**—In harvest time and earlier (April and May) it overflows its banks (Josh. 3:15), and fills the valley called the Ghor. Or, "the *pride* of Jordan," viz., its wooded banks abounding in lions and other wild beasts (ch. 49:19; 50:44; Zech. 11:3; cf. II Kings 6:2). MAUNDRELL says that between the Sea of Tiberias and Lake Merom the banks are so wooded that the traveller cannot see the river at all without first passing through the woods. If in the champaign country (alone) thou art secure, how wilt thou do when thou fallest into the wooded haunts of wild beasts? **6. even thy brethren**—as in Christ's case (Ps. 69:8; John 1:11; 7:5; cf. ch. 9:4; 11:19, 21; Matt. 10:36). Godly faithfulness is sure to provoke the ungodly, even of one's own family. **called a multitude after thee**—(Isa. 31:4). JEROME translates, "cry after thee with a loud (lit., full) voice." **believe . . . not . . . though . . . speak fair**—(Prov. 26:25).

7. I have forsaken—Jehovah will forsake His temple and the people peculiarly His. The mention of God's close tie to them, as heretofore *His*, aggravates their ingratitude, and shows that their past spiritual privileges will not prevent God from punishing them. **beloved of my soul**—image from a *wife* (ch. 11:15; Isa. 54:5).

8. is unto me—is become unto Me: behaves towards Me as a lion which roars against a man, so that he withdraws from the place where he hears it: so I withdrew from My people, once beloved, but now an object of abhorrence because of their rebellious cries against Me.

9. speckled bird—Many translate, "a ravenous beast, the hyena"; the corresponding *Arabic* word means *hyena*; so LXX. But the *Hebrew* always elsewhere means "a bird of prey." The *Hebrew* for "speckled" is from a root "to color"; answering to the Jewish *blending together* with paganism the altogether *diverse* Mosaic ritual. The neighboring nations, *birds of prey* like herself (for she had sinfully assimilated herself to them), were ready to pounce upon her. **assemble . . . beasts of . . . field**—The Chaldeans are told to gather the surrounding heathen peoples as allies against Judah (Isa. 56:9; Ezek. 34:5).

ADAM CLARKE

5. *If thou hast run with the footmen.* If the smallest evils to which you are exposed cause you to make so many bitter complaints, how will you feel when, in the course of your prophetic ministry, you shall be exposed to much greater, from enemies much more powerful?

And if in the land of peace, wherein thou trustedst. I believe the meaning is this, "If in a country now enjoying peace you scarcely think yourself in safety, what will you do *in the swelling of Jordan?* in the time when the enemy, like an overflowing torrent, shall deluge every part of the land?" The overflowing of Jordan, which generally happened in harvest, drove the lions and other beasts of prey from their coverts among the bushes that lined its banks; who, spreading themselves through the country, made terrible havoc, slaying men, and carrying off the cattle.

6. *For even thy brethren, and the house of thy father.* You have none to depend on but God; even your brethren will betray you when they have it in their power.

7. *I have forsaken mine house.* I have abandoned My temple. *I have given the dearly beloved of my soul.* The people once in covenant with Me, and inexpressibly dear to Me while faithful. *Into the hand of her enemies.* This was a condition in the covenant I made with them; if they forsook Me, they were to be abandoned to their enemies, and cast out of the good land I gave to their fathers.

8. *Mine heritage is unto me as a lion.* The people are enraged against Me; they roar like a furious lion against their God.

MATTHEW HENRY

spoken of as a thing done, so near was it. God speaks of it as a thing which he had no pleasure in, any more than in the death of other sinners.

1. See with what a tender affection he speaks of this land, notwithstanding the sinfulness of it, in remembrance of his covenant: It is *my vineyard, my portion, my pleasant portion, v.* 10. Note, God has a kindness and concern for his church, though there be much amiss in it.

2. See with what a tender compassion he speaks of the desolations of this land: *Many pastors* (the Chaldean generals that made themselves masters of the country and ate it up with their armies as easily as the Arabian shepherds with their flocks eat up the fruits of the ground that lies common) *have destroyed my vineyard.* That which was a pleasant land they have made *a desolate wilderness.* It is made so by the sword of war: *The spoilers,* the Chaldean soldiers, *have come through the plain upon all high places;* they have made themselves masters of all the fastnesses, *v.* 12. *The sword devours from one end of the land to the other;* the army of the invaders disperse into every corner, so that *no flesh shall have peace.*

3. See whence all this misery comes. It is *the sword of the Lord* that *devours, v.* 12. While God's people keep close to him the sword is the sword of the Lord, witness that of Gideon; but when they have forsaken him, then the sword of their destroyers becomes the *sword of the Lord;* witness this of the Chaldeans. It is *because of the fierce anger of the Lord* (*v.* 13). It is their sin that has made God their enemy (*v.* 11): The land *mourns unto me;* the country that lies desolate does, as it were, pour out its complaint, but the inhabitants are so senseless and stupid that *none of them lays it to heart;* they do not mourn to God while the very ground shames them.

4. "*They have sown wheat,* that is, they have taken pains for their own security, but it is all in vain; *they shall reap thorns,* that is, that which shall prove vexatious to them. *They shall be ashamed of your revenues,* ashamed that they have depended so much upon their preparations for war." Money constitutes the sinews of war; they thought they had enough of that, but shall be ashamed of it; for their silver and gold shall not profit them in the day of the Lord's anger.

Verses 14–17

Here is a message to all those who had in their turn been one way or other injurious to God's people.

I. What the quarrel was that God had with them. They were *his evil neighbours* (*v.* 14), evil neighbours to his church, and what they did against it he took as done against himself. These evil neighbours were the Moabites, Ammonites, Syrians, Edomites, Egyptians, that had been evil neighbours to Israel in helping to debauch them and draw them from God, and now they helped to make them desolate, and joined with the Chaldeans against them. That which God lays to their charge is: They have *meddled with the inheritance which I have caused my people Israel to inherit.* They sacrilegiously turned to their own use that which was given to God's peculiar people. He that said, *Touch not my anointed,* said also, "*Touch not their inheritance.*"

II. What course he would take with them. He would break the power they had got over his people. *I will pluck out the house of Judah from among them.* God's people had been taken captive by them, or, when they fled to them for shelter, had been made prisoners. God will pluck them out, will by his Spirit compel them to come out and compel their task-masters to let them go, as he plucked Israel out of Egypt. He would bring upon them the same calamities that they had been instrumental to bring upon his people: *I will pluck them out of their land.* Judgment began at the house of God, but it did not end there.

III. What mercy God had in store for such of them as would join themselves to him and become his people, *v.* 15, 16. They had drawn God's people to join with them in the service of idols. If now they would be drawn by a returning people to join with them in the service of the true and living God, they should be received to stand upon the same level with the Israel of God. This had its accomplishment in part when, after the return out of captivity, many of the people that had been evil neighbours to Israel became Jews; and it was to have its full accomplishment in the conversion of the Gentiles to the faith of Christ. *After that I have plucked them out,* in justice for their sins, *I will return and have compassion on them.*

1. God would show favour to them always provided *that they will diligently learn the ways of my people.* There are good ways that are peculiarly *the*

JAMIESON, FAUSSET, BROWN

my vineyard—(Isa. 5:1, 5). **trodden my portion**—(Isa. 63:18).

10. pastors—the Babylonian leaders (cf. vs. 12; ch. 6:3).

12. high places—Before, He had threatened the plains; now, the hills. **wilderness**—not an uninhabited desert, but high lands of pasturage, lying between Judea and Chaldea (ch. 4:11).

11. mourneth unto me—i.e., before Me. EICHORN translates, "by reason of Me," because I have given it to desolation (vs. 7). **because no man layeth it to heart**—because none by repentance and prayer seek to deprecate God's wrath. Or, "*yet* none lays it to heart"; as in ch. 5:3 [CALVIN].

13. Description in detail of the devastation of the land (Mic. 6:15). **they shall be ashamed of your**—The change of persons, in passing from indirect to direct address, is frequent in the prophets. Equivalent to, "Ye shall be put to the shame of disappointment at the smallness of your produce."

14-17. Prophecy as to the surrounding nations, the Syrians, Ammonites, etc., who helped forward Judah's calamity: they shall share her fall; and, on their conversion, they shall share with her in the future restoration. This is a brief anticipation of the predictions in chs. 47, 48, 49.

14. touch—(Zech. 2:8). **pluck them out . . . pluck out . . . Judah**—(Cf. end of vs. 16). During the thirteen years that the Babylonians besieged Tyre, Nebuchadnezzar, after subduing Cœlo-Syria, brought Ammon, Moab, etc., and finally Egypt, into subjection (JOSEPHUS, *Antiquities,* 10.9, sec. 7). On the restoration of these nations, they were to exchange places with the Jews. The latter were now in the midst of them, but on their restoration *they* were to be "in the midst of the Jews," i.e., as proselytes to the true God (cf. Mic. 5:7; Zech. 14:16). "Pluck *them,*" viz., the Gentile nations: in a bad sense. "Pluck Judah": in a good sense; used to express the force which was needed to snatch Judah from the tyranny of those nations by whom they had been made captives, or to whom they had fled; otherwise they never would have let Judah go. Previously he had been forbidden to pray for the mass of the Jewish people. But here he speaks consolation to the elect remnant among them. Whatever the Jews might be, God keeps *His* covenant.

ADAM CLARKE

10. *Many pastors have destroyed my vineyard.* My people have had many kinds of enemies which have fed upon their richest pastures: the Philistines, Moabites, Ammonites, Assyrians, Egyptians, and now the Chaldeans.

12. *The sword of the Lord shall devour.* It is the sword of the Lord that has devoured, and will devour; this is what no man layeth to heart. They think these things come in the course of events.

11. *No man layeth it to heart.* Notwithstanding all these desolations, from which the land everywhere mourns, and which are so plainly the consequences of the people's crimes, no man layeth it to heart, or considereth that these are God's judgments; and that the only way to have them removed is to repent of their sins, and turn to God with all their hearts.

14. *Against all mine evil neighbours.* All the neighboring nations who have united in desolating Judea shall be desolated in their turn; they also are wicked, and they shall be punished.

15. *I will return, and have compassion on them.* This is a promise of restoration from the Captivity, and an intimation also that some of their enemies would turn to the true God with them; learn the ways of His people; that is, would abjure idols, and take Jehovah for their God; and be built in the midst of His people, that is, Jew and Gentile forming one Church of the Most High.

MATTHEW HENRY | JAMIESON, FAUSSET, BROWN | ADAM CLARKE

ways of God's people. The ways of holiness and heavenly-mindedness, of love and peaceableness, the ways of prayer and sabbath-sanctification, and diligent attendance on ordinances—these, and the like, are *the ways of God's people*. They must learn to say, *The Lord liveth* (to own him, to adore him, and to abide by his judgment), *as they taught my people to swear by Baal*. We must not despair of the conversion of the worst; no, not of those who have been instrumental to pervert and debauch others; even they may be brought to repentance, and, if they be, shall find mercy. The conversion of the deceived may prove a happy occasion of the conversion even of the deceivers. Thus those who fall together into the ditch are sometimes plucked together out of it.

2. When they return to God and God to them (*v.* 15): *I will bring them again every man to his heritage*. They shall become entitled to the spiritual privileges of God's Israel: *Be built in the midst of my people*. They shall have a name and a place in the house of the Lord, where there was a court for the Gentiles, they shall be built among them. *If they will not obey*, if any continue to stand it out, *I will utterly pluck up and destroy that nation*, that family, that particular person, *saith the Lord*.

KEIL-DELITZSCH:

Verse 16. If then the heathen learn the ways of the people of God. What we are to understand by this is clear from the following infinitive clause: to swear in the name of Jahveh, viz. if they adopt the worship of Jahveh (for swearing is mentioned as one of the principal utterances of a religious confession). If they do so, then shall they be built in the midst of God's people, i.e. incorporated with it, and along with it favored and blessed.

Verse 17. But they who hearken not, namely, to the invitation to take Jahveh as the true God, these shall be utterly destroyed—so to pluck them out that they may perish. The promise is Messianic (16:19; Isa. 61:6f.; Mic. 4:1–4), inasmuch as it points to the end of God's way with all nations.

—Commentary on the Old Testament

15. A promise, applying to Judah, as well as to the nations specified (Amos 9:14). As to Moab, cf. ch. 48:47; as to Ammon, ch. 49:6. **16. swear by my name**—(ch. 4:2; Isa. 19:18; 65:16); i.e., confess solemnly the true God. **built**—be made spiritually and temporally prosperous: fixed in sure habitations (cf. ch. 24:6; 42:10; 45:4; Ps. 87:4, 5; Eph. 2:20, 21; I Pet. 2:5). **17.** (Isa. 60:12.)

17. *I will . . . destroy that nation*. Several of them did not obey, and are destroyed. Of the Moabites, Ammonites, and Chaldeans not one vestige remains. The sixteenth verse is supposed to be a promise of the conversion of the Gentiles. See Eph. ii. 13-22.

From the thirteenth verse to the end is a different discourse, and Dahler supposes it to have been delivered in the seventh or eighth year of the reign of Jehoiakim.

CHAPTER 13

Verses 1–11

I. A sign, the marring of a girdle, which the prophet had worn for some time, by hiding it in a hole of a rock near the river Euphrates. He was to wear a linen girdle for some time, *v.* 1, 2. Some think he wore it under his clothes, because it is said to *cleave to his loins*, *v.* 11. It should rather seem to be worn upon his clothes, and probably was a fine sash, such as officers wear. He must *not put it in water*, that it might be less likely to rot. The prophet, like John Baptist, was none of those that wore soft clothing, and therefore it would be the more strange to see him with a linen girdle. After he had worn this linen girdle for some time, he must go, and *hide it in a hole of a rock* (*v.* 4) by the water's side, where, when the water was high, it would be wet, and when it fell would grow dry again, and by that means would soon rot. After many days, he should find it spoiled, gone to rags and good for nothing, *v.* 7. It seems hard to imagine that the prophet should be sent on two such long journeys as to the river Euphrates. For this reason most incline to think the journey, at least, was only in vision, and the explanation of this sign given only to the prophet himself (*v.* 8), not to the people.

II. The thing signified by this sign, *v.* 9–11.

1. The people of Israel had been to God as this girdle in two respects: (1) He had taken them into covenant and communion with himself: *As the girdle cleaves* very closely *to the loins of a man* and surrounds him, *so have I caused to cleave to me the houses of Israel and Judah*. He *caused them to cleave* to him by the law he gave them, the prophets he sent among them, and the favours he showed them. (2) When he took them to be *to him for a people*, it was that they might be to him *for a name, and for a praise, and for a glory*, as a girdle is an ornament to a man, and particularly the *curious girdle of the ephod* was to the high-priest *for glory and for beauty*.

2. They had by their idolatries and other iniquities loosed themselves from him, buried themselves in the earth, and foreign earth too, mingled among the nations, and were so spoiled and corrupted that they were *good for nothing*. They would not *cleave to God*, but *walked after other gods, to serve them*, and *to worship them*; they doted upon the gods of the heathen nations that lay towards Euphrates, so that they were quite spoiled for the service of their own God, and were *as this girdle*, this rotten girdle.

3. God would by his judgments separate them from him, send them into captivity, deface all their beauty so that they should be like a fine girdle gone to rags, a worthless people. God will after this manner *mar the pride of Judah, and the great pride of Jerusalem*. He speaks of *the pride of Judah* (the country people were proud of their good land), but of *the great pride of Jerusalem*; there the temple was, and the royal palace, and therefore those citizens were more proud. Pride will have a fall, for God resists the proud. Even the temple, when it became Jerusalem's pride, was marred and laid in ashes.

Verses 12–21

I. A judgment threatened against this people (*v.* 12): *Thus saith the Lord God of Israel, every bottle shall be filled with wine;* that is, those that by their sins

CHAPTER 13

Vss. 1-27. SYMBOLICAL PROPHECY (vss. 1-7). Many of these figurative acts being either not possible, or not probable, or decorous, seem to have existed only in the mind of the prophet as part of his inward vision. [So CALVIN.] The world he moved in was not the sensible, but the spiritual, world. Inward acts were, however, when it was possible and proper, materialized by outward performance but not always, and necessarily so. The internal act made a naked statement more impressive and presented the subject when extending over long portions of space and time more concentrated. The interruption of Jeremiah's official duty by a journey of more than 200 miles twice is not likely to have *literally* taken place. **1. put it upon thy loins . . .**—expressing the close intimacy wherewith Jehovah had joined Israel and Judah to Him (vs. 11). **linen**—implying it was the inner garment next the skin, not the outer one. **put it not in water**—signifying the moral filth of His people, like the literal filth of a garment worn constantly next the skin, without being washed (vs. 10). GROTIUS understands a garment not bleached, but left in its native roughness, just as Judah had no beauty, but was adopted by the sole grace of God (Ezek. 16:4-6). "Neither wast thou washed in *water*," etc. **4. Euphrates**—In order to support the view that Jeremiah's act was outward, HENDERSON considers that the *Hebrew* Phrath here is *Ephratha*, the original name of Bethlehem, six miles south of Jerusalem, a journey easy to be made by Jeremiah. The non-addition of the word "river," which usually precedes *Phrath*, when meaning Euphrates, favors this view. But I prefer *English Version*. The Euphrates is specified as being near Babylon, the Jews' future place of exile. **hole**—typical of the prisons in which the Jews were to be confined. **the rock**—some well-known rock. A sterile region, such as was that to which the Jews were led away (cf. Isa. 7:19) [GROTIUS]. **6. after many days**—Time enough was given for the girdle to become unfit for use. So, in course of time, the Jews became corrupted by the heathen idolatries around, so as to cease to be witnesses of Jehovah; they must, therefore, be cast away as a "marred" or spoiled girdle. **9.** (Lev. 26:19.) **10. imagination**—rather, obstinacy. **11.** (Ch. 33:9; Exod. 19:5.) **glory**—an ornament to glory in.

12. A new image. **Do we not . . . know . . . wine**—The "bottles" are those used in the East, made of skins; our word "hogshead," original-

CHAPTER 13

1. *Thus saith the Lord unto me*. This discourse is supposed to have been delivered under the reign of Jeconiah, the son and successor of Jehoiakim, who came to the throne in the eighteenth year of his age; when the Chaldean generals had encamped near to Jerusalem, but did not besiege it in form till Nebuchadnezzar came up with the great body of the army. In these circumstances the prophet predicts the captivity; and, by a symbolical representation of a rotten girdle, shows the people their totally corrupt state; and by another of bottles filled with wine, shows the destruction and madness of their counsels, and the confusion that must ensue.

Go and get thee a linen girdle. This was either a vision or God simply describes the thing in order that the prophet might use it in the way of illustration. *Put it not in water*. After having worn it, let it not be washed, that it may more properly represent the uncleanness of the Israelites; for they were represented by the girdle. "For as the girdle cleaveth to the loins of a man, so have I caused to cleave unto me the whole house of Israel and the whole house of Judah."

4. *Go to Euphrates, and hide it there*. Intending to point out, by this distant place, the country into which they were to be carried away captive.

7. *And, behold, the girdle was marred, it was profitable for nothing*. This symbolically represented the state of the Jews. They were corrupt and abominable; and God, by sending them into captivity, marred "the pride of Judah, and the great pride of Jerusalem," v. 9.

MATTHEW HENRY

have made themselves *vessels of wrath fitted to destruction* shall be filled with the wrath of God as a bottle is with wine; and they shall be brittle as bottles; and, like old bottles into which new wine is put, they shall burst and be broken to pieces, Matt. ix. 17. Or, They shall have their heads as full of wine as bottles are; for so it is explained, *v.* 13, *They shall be filled with drunkenness;* compare Isa. li. 17. They, not being aware of the prophet's meaning in it, ridiculed him for it: "*Do we not certainly know* that *every bottle shall be filled with wine?*" Perhaps they were thus touchy with the prophet because they apprehended this to be a reflection upon them for their drunkenness, and probably it was in part so intended. They *loved flagons of wine,* Hos. iii. 1. "Well," says the prophet, "you shall have your *bottles full of wine,* but not such wine as you desire." What he meant was this,

1. That they should be as giddy as men in drink. A drunken man is fitly compared to a bottle or cask full of wine; for, when the wine is in, the wit, and wisdom, and virtue, and all that is good for anything, are out. Now God threatens (*v.* 13) that they shall all be *filled with drunkenness;* they shall be full of confusion in their counsels, shall falter and stagger. They shall expose themselves to the contempt of all about them. *All the inhabitants* both *of the land* and *of Jerusalem* were as far gone as they. Whom God will destroy he infatuates.

2. That being giddy, they shall do mischief to themselves and one another (*v.* 14): *I will dash a man against his brother.* Not only their drunken follies, but their drunken frays, shall help to ruin them. This decree against them having gone forth, God says, *I will not pity, nor spare, nor have mercy, but destroy them;* for they *will not pity, nor spare, nor have mercy,* but destroy one another; see Hab. ii. 15, 16.

II. Here is good counsel given, which, if taken, would prevent this desolation. It is, in short, to *humble themselves under the mighty hand of God.* This is that which God has to say to them, *Be not proud, v.* 15. This was one of the sins for which God had a controversy with them (*v.* 9). "*Be not proud;* when God speaks to you by his prophets do not think yourselves too good to be taught; be not scornful."

1. "*Give glory to the Lord your God,* and not to your idols. Give him glory by confessing your sins, and accepting the punishment of your iniquity, *v.* 16. Give him glory by a sincere repentance and reformation." Then, and not till then, we begin to live to some good purpose. "Do this quickly *before he cause darkness,* before he bring his judgments upon you, which you will see no way of escaping." Their attempts to escape shall hasten their ruin: *Their feet shall stumble* when they are making all the haste they can over *the dark mountains.* Note, Those that think to out-run the judgments of God will find their road impassable. Their hopes of a better state of things will be disappointed: *While you look for light,* for comfort and relief, he will *turn it into the shadow of death,* and make it *gross darkness,* like that of Egypt, when Pharaoh continued to harden his heart, which was darkness that might be felt.

2. They must abase themselves; the prerogative of the king and queen will not exempt them from this (*v.* 18): "*Say to the king and queen,* that, great as they are, they must *humble themselves* by true repentance, and so give both glory to God and a good example to their subjects." When you are led away captives, where will your principality and all the badges of it be then?

III. This counsel is enforced by some arguments.

1. It will be the prophet's unspeakable grief (*v.* 7): "*If you will not hear it,* will not submit to the word, but continue refractory, not only my eye, but *my soul shall weep in secret places.*" It would grieve him to see their sins unrepented of: "*My soul shall weep for your pride,* your haughtiness, and stubbornness, and vain confidence." The sins of others should be matter of sorrow to us. We must mourn for that which we cannot mend, and mourn the more for it because we cannot mend it.

2. It will be their own inevitable ruin, *v.* 19–21. *The cities of the south shall be shut up.* Some understand it of the cities of Egypt, which was south from Judah; the places there whence they expected succours shall fail them, and they shall find no access to them. *Judah shall be carried away captive.* So it was in the last captivity under Zedekiah, because they repented not. The enemy was now at hand that should do this (*v.* 20): "*Lift up your eyes. Behold, those that come from the north,* from the land of the Chaldeans; see how fast they advance, how fierce they appear." Upon this he addresses himself to the king, or rather (because the pronouns are feminine) to the city or state. "What will you do now with the people who are committed to your charge, and whom you ought

JAMIESON, FAUSSET, BROWN

ly "oxhide," alludes to the same custom. As they were used to hold water, milk, and other liquids, what the prophet said (viz., that they should be all filled with wine) was not, as the Jews' taunting reply implied, a truism even *literally.* The figurative sense which is what Jeremiah chiefly meant, they affected not to understand. As wine intoxicates, so God's wrath and judgments shall reduce them to that state of helpless distraction that they shall rush on to their own ruin (ch. 25:15; 49:12; Isa. 51: 17, 21, 22; 63:6).

13. upon David's throne—lit., who sit *for David on his throne;* implying the succession of the Davidic family (ch. 22:4). **all**—indiscriminately of every rank.

14. dash—(Ps. 2:9). As a potter's vessel (Rev. 2:27).

15. be not proud—Pride was the cause of their contumacy, as humility is the first step to obedience (vs. 17; Ps. 10:4).

16. Give glory . . .—Show by repentance and obedience to God, that you revere His majesty. So Joshua exhorted Achan to "give glory to God" by confessing his crime, thereby showing he revered the All-knowing God.

stumble—image from travellers stumbling into a fatal abyss when overtaken by nightfall (Isa. 5:30; 59:9, 10; Amos 8:9). **dark mountains**—lit., mountains of twilight or gloom, which cast such a gloomy shadow that the traveller stumbles against an opposing rock before he sees it (John 11:10; 12:35). **shadow of death**—the densest gloom; death-shade (Ps. 44:19). *Light* and *darkness* are images of prosperity and adversity.

18. king—Jehoiachin or Jeconiah. **queen**—the queen mother who, as the king was not more than eighteen years old, held the chief power. Nehushta, daughter of Elnathan, carried away captive with Jehoiachin by Nebuchadnezzar (II Kings 24:8-15). **Humble yourselves**—i.e., Ye shall be humbled, or brought low (ch. 22:26; 28:2). **your principalities**—rather, "your *head ornament.*"

17. hear it—my exhortation. **in secret**—as one mourning and humbling himself for their sin, not self-righteously condemning them (Phil. 3:18). **pride**—(*Note,* vs. 15; Job 33:17.) **flock**—(vs. 20), just as kings and leaders are called pastors.

19. cities of the south—viz., south of Judea; farthest off from the enemy, who advanced from the north. **shut up**—i.e., deserted (Isa. 24:10); so that none shall be left to open the gates to travellers and merchants again [HENDERSON]. Rather, *shut up so* closely by Nebuchadnezzar's forces, sent on before (II Kings 24: 10, 11), that none shall be allowed by the enemy to get out (cf. vs. 20). **wholly**—lit., "fully"; completely. **20. from . . . north**—Nebuchadnezzar and his hostile army (ch. 1:14; 6:22).

ADAM CLARKE

13. *Behold, I will fill all the inhabitants of this land . . . with drunkenness.* You, and your kings, and priests, and prophets are represented by these bottles. The wine is God's wrath against you, which shall first be shown by confounding your deliberations, filling you with foolish plans of defense, causing you from your divided counsels to fall out among yourselves, so that like so many drunken men you shall reel about and jostle each other; defend yourselves without plan, and fight without order, till you all fall an easy prey into the hands of your enemies. The ancient adage is here fulfilled: "Those whom God determines to destroy, He first renders foolish."

16. *Give glory to . . . God.* Confess your sins and turn to Him, that these sore evils may be averted. *While ye look for light.* While you expect prosperity, He turned *it into the shadow of death*—sent you adversity of the most distressing and ruinous kind.

Stumble upon the dark mountains. Before you meet with those great obstacles, which, having no light, no proper understanding in the matter, you shall be utterly unable to surmount.

18. *Say unto the king and to the queen.* Probably Jeconiah and his mother, under whose tutelage, being young when he began to reign, he was left, as is very likely.

19. *The cities of the south shall be shut up.* Not only the cities of the north, the quarter at which the Chaldeans entered, but the cities of the south also; for he shall proceed from one extremity of the land to the other, spreading devastation everywhere, and carrying off the inhabitants.

MATTHEW HENRY

to protect? *Where is the flock that was given thee, thy beautiful flock?* How can they escape these ravening wolves?" Masters of families, who neglect their children and suffer them to perish for want of a good education, and ministers who neglect their people, should think they hear God putting this question to them: *Where is the flock that was given thee* to feed, *that beauteous flock? What wilt thou say when he shall visit upon thee* the former days? (*v.* 21). Thou canst say nothing, but that *God is just in all that is brought upon thee.* "How will you bear the trouble that is at the door? *Shall not sorrows take thee as a woman in travail?* Sorrows will be more grievous in that there is no manchild to be born."

Verses 22–27

I. Ruin threatened as before, that the Jews shall go into captivity, and fall under all the miseries of beggary and bondage, shall be stripped of their clothes, *their skirts discovered* for want of upper garments to cover them, and their *heels made bare* for want of shoes, *v.* 22. Thus they used to deal with prisoners taken in war, when they drove them into captivity, *naked and barefoot,* Isa. xx. 4. Carried off into a strange country, they shall be scattered *as the stubble that is blown away by the wind of the wilderness, v.* 24. They shall be stripped of all their ornaments, and exposed to shame, as harlots, *v.* 26.

II. An enquiry made by the people into the cause of this ruin, *v.* 22. Thou wilt *say in thy heart: Wherefore came these things upon me?* They could not see that they had done anything which might justly provoke God to be thus angry with them.

III. God will be justified when he speaks and will oblige us to justify him, and therefore will set the sin of sinners in order before them.

1. It is for the greatness of their iniquities, *v.* 22. God does not take advantage against them for small faults; the sins for which he now punishes them are very heinous in their nature—for *the multitude of thy iniquity* (so it may be read), sins of every kind and often repeated. Some think we are more in danger from the multitude of our smaller sins than from the heinousness of our greater sins.

2. It is for their obstinacy in sin (*v.* 23): *Can the Ethiopian change his skin,* that is by nature black, or the *leopard his spots,* that are even woven into the skin? It is morally impossible to reclaim and reform these people. They were taught to do evil; they had served an apprenticeship to it. Their prophets despaired of ever bringing them to do good. Those that have been long accustomed to sin have shaken off the restraints of fear and shame; their consciences are seared; the habits of sin are confirmed. Sin is the blackness of the soul, the deformity of it. But there is an almighty grace that is able to change the Ethiopian's skin, and that grace shall not be wanting to those who in a sense of their need of it seek it earnestly.

3. It is for their treacherous departures from the God of truth (*v.* 25): "*This is thy lot,* to be driven away; this is *the portion of thy measures from me,* the punishment assigned thee as by measure; it is *because thou hast forgotten me,* the favours I have bestowed upon thee, thou hast no remembrance, of these." Forgetfulness of God is at the bottom of all sin, as the remembrance of our Creator betimes is the happy and hopeful beginning of a holy life.

4. It is for their idolatry, of all sins most provoking to the *jealous God.* They are exposed to a shameful calamity (*v.* 26) because they have been guilty of a shameful iniquity and yet are shameless in it (*v.* 27): "*I have seen thy adulteries* (thy inordinate fancy for strange gods), even the *lewdness of thy whoredoms,* thy eager worshipping of idols *on the hills in the fields,* upon the high places. This is that for which a *woe* is denounced against thee, *O Jerusalem!*"

IV. Here is an affectionate expostulation with them upon the whole matter. While there is life there is hope, and therefore still he reasons with them to bring them to repentance, *v.* 27. *Wilt thou not be made clean?* It is an instance of the wonderful grace of God that he desires the repentance and conversion of sinners, and thinks the time long till they are brought to relent; but it is an instance of the wonderful folly of sinners that they put that off from time to time which is of such absolute necessity. They do not say that they will never be cleansed, but not yet.

JAMIESON, FAUSSET, BROWN

flock . . . given thee—Jeremiah, amazed at the depopulation caused by Nebuchadnezzar's forces, addresses Jerusalem (a *noun of multitude,* which accounts for the blending of *plural* and *singular, Your* eyes . . . *thee* . . . *thy* flock), and asks where is the population (vs. 17, "flock") which God had given her? **21. captains, and as chief**—lit., "princes as to headship; or over thy head," viz., the Chaldeans. Rather, translate, "What wilt thou say when God will set them (the enemies, vs. 20) above thee, seeing that thou thyself hast accustomed them (to be) with thee as (thy) *lovers in the highest place* (lit., at thy head)? Thou canst not say God does thee wrong, seeing it was thou that gave occasion to His dealing so with thee, by so eagerly courting their intimacy." Cf. ch. 2: 18, 36; II Kings 23:29, as to the league of Judah with Babylon, which led Josiah to march against Pharaoh-necho, when the latter was about to attack Babylon [MAURER]. **sorrows**—pains, throes. **22. if thou say**—connecting this verse with "What wilt thou *say*" (vs. 21)? **skirts discovered**—i.e., are thrown up so as to expose the person (vs. 26; Isa. 3:17; Nah. 3:5). **heels made bare**—The sandal was fastened by a thong above the heel to the instep. The *Hebrew,* is, "are violently handled," or "torn off"; i.e., thou art exposed to ignominy. Image from an adulteress.

23. Ethiopian—the Cushite of Abyssinia. Habit is second nature; as therefore it is morally impossible that the Jews can alter their inveterate habits of sin, nothing remains but the infliction of the extremest punishment, their expatriation (vs. 24). **24.** (Ps. 1:4.) **by the wind**—*before* the wind. **of the wilderness**—where the wind has full sweep, not being broken by any obstacle.

25. portion of thy measures—the portion which I have measured out to thee (Job 20:29; Ps. 11:6). **falsehood**—(vs. 27), false gods and alliances with foreign idolaters.

26. discover . . . upon thy face—rather, "throw up thy skirts over thy face," or head; done by way of ignominy to captive women and to prostitutes (Nah. 3:5). The Jews' punishment should answer to their crime. As their sin had been perpetrated in the most public places, so God would expose them to the contempt of other nations most openly (Lam. 1:8). **27. neighings**—(ch. 5:8), image from the lust of horses; the lust after idols degrades to the level of the brute. **hills**—where, as being nearer heaven, sacrifices were thought most acceptable to the gods. **wilt thou not . . . ? when**—lit., "*thou wilt not be made clean after how long a time yet.*" (So vs. 23.) Jeremiah *denies* the moral possibility of one so long hardened in sin becoming *soon* cleansed. But see ch. 32:17; Luke 18:27.

ADAM CLARKE

20. *Where is the flock . . . thy beautiful flock?* Jerusalem is addressed. Where are the prosperous multitudes of men, women, and children? Alas! are they not driven before Babylonians, who have taken them captive?

21. *Thou hast taught them to be captains, and as chief over thee.* This is said of their enemies, whether Assyrians or Chaldeans; for ever since Ahaz submitted himself to the king of Assyria, the kings of Judah never regained their independence. Their enemies were thus taught to be their lords and masters.

22. *Are thy skirts discovered.* Your defenseless state is everywhere known; you are not only weak, but ignominiously so.

23. *Can the Ethiopian change his skin?* Can a *black,* at his own pleasure, change the color of his skin? Can the *leopard* at will change the variety of *his spots?* These things are natural to them, and they cannot be altered; so sin, and especially your attachment to idolatry, is become a second nature; and we may as well expect the Ethiopian to change his skin, and the leopard his spots, as you to do good, who have been accustomed to do evil.

24. *The wind of the wilderness.* Some strong, tempestuous wind, proverbially severe, coming from the desert to the south of Judea.

25. *Trusted in falsehood.* In idols, and in lying prophets.

27. *I have seen thine adulteries.* Your idolatries of different kinds, practiced in various ways; no doubt often accompanied with gross debauchery. *Woe unto thee, O Jerusalem! wilt thou not be made clean?* We see from this that, though the thing was difficult, yet it was not impossible, for these Ethiopians to change their skin, for these leopards to change their spots. It was only their obstinate refusal of the grace of God that rendered it impossible.

MATTHEW HENRY

CHAPTER 14

Verses 1–9

I. The language of nature lamenting the calamity. When the heavens were as brass, and distilled no dews, the earth was as iron, and produced no fruits; the grief and confusion were universal. The people of the land were all in tears. *Judah mourns* (*v.* 2), not for the sin, but for the withholding of the rain. *The gates thereof*, all that go in and out at their gates, *languish*, look pale, and grow feeble, for want of the necessary supports of life and for fear of further judgment. *The gates* now look melancholy; the inhabitants are departing through them to seek for bread in other countries. Even those that sit in the gates languish; *they are black unto the ground*, they go in black as mourners and sit on the ground, as beggars. They fall to the ground through weakness. *The cry of Jerusalem has gone up;* that is, of the citizens (for the city is *served by the field*), or of people from all parts of the country met at Jerusalem to pray for rain. But I fear it was rather the cry of their trouble, than the cry of their prayer. The great men of the land felt this judgment (*v.* 3): *The nobles sent their little ones to the water.* Or, *their meaner ones*, their servants, they sent to seek for water, but there was none to be found: They *returned with their vessels empty*; the springs were dried up when there was no rain to feed them; and then *they* (their masters) *were ashamed and confounded.* The husbandmen felt it most immediately (*v.* 4): *The ploughmen were ashamed*, for the ground was so parched and hard that it would not admit the plough. They were ashamed to be idle. See what an immediate dependence husbandmen have upon the divine Providence, for they cannot plough nor sow in hope unless God *water their furrows*, Ps. lxv. 10. The case even of the wild beasts was pitiable, *v.* 5, 6. Judah and Jerusalem have sinned, but the hinds and the wild asses, what have they done? The hinds are particularly tender of their young; and yet contrary to their nature, they leave their young, even when they most need them, to seek for grass elsewhere; and, if they can find none, they *abandon* them, because not able to suckle them. It grieved not the hind so much that she had no grass for herself as that she had none for her young, which will shame those who spend that upon their lusts which they should preserve for their families. One would be sorry even for the *wild asses*, for the *barren land* is now made too hot for them, so hot that they get to the *highest places* they can reach, where the air is coolest, and *snuff up the wind like dragons*, creatures which are continually panting for breath. *Their eyes fail*, and so does their strength, *because there is no grass.*

II. Here is the language of grace, lamenting the iniquity, and complaining to God of the calamity. The people are not forward to pray, but the prophet here prays for them, and so excites them to pray for themselves, *v.* 7–9. In this prayer, 1. Sin is humbly confessed. If we quarrel with God as dealing unjustly or unkindly with us in afflicting us, our iniquities testify that we do him wrong; "for *our backslidings are many* and too heinous to be excused, for they are against thee." 2. Mercy is earnestly begged: "*Though our iniquities testify against us*, yet *do thou it.*" As becomes penitents and beggars, they refer the matter to God: "Do with us as thou thinkest fit," Judges x. 15. We have nothing to plead in ourselves, but everything in thee. There is another petition in this prayer (*v.* 9): "*Leave us not*, withdraw not thy favour and presence." 3. Their relation to God and their expectations from him are most pathetically pleaded, *v.* 8, 9. They look upon him as one they have reason to think should deliver them. In him mercy has often rejoiced against judgment. God has encouraged his people to hope in him; in calling himself so often the *God of Israel*, the *rock of Israel*, and the *Holy One of Israel*, he has made himself the *hope of Israel.* They plead, "*Thou art in the midst of us;* we have the special tokens of thy presence with us, thy temple, thy ark, thy oracles, and *we are called by thy name*, the *Israel* of God; and therefore we hope thou wilt not leave us; *we are thine, save us.*" It grieves them to think that he does not appear for their deliverance. *What will the Egyptians say?* They will say, "Israel's hope and Saviour does not mind them; he has become *as a stranger in the land*, that does not interest himself in its interests; his temple, which he called *his rest for ever*, is no more so, but he is in it *as a wayfaring man, that turns aside to tarry but for a night* in an inn." The enemies once said, Because the Lord *was not able to bring* his people to Canaan, he let them *perish in the wilderness* (Num. xiv. 16); so now they will say, "Either his wisdom or his power fails him; either he is *as a man astonished*

JAMIESON, FAUSSET, BROWN

CHAPTER 14

Vss. 1-22. Prophecies on the Occasion of a Drought Sent in Judgment on Judea. **1.** Lit., "That which was the word of Jehovah to Jeremiah concerning. . . ." **drought**—lit., the "withholdings," viz., of rain (Deut. 11:17; II Chron. 7:13). This word should be used especially of the withholding of rain because *rain* is in those regions of all things the one chiefly needed (ch. 17:8, *Margin*). **2. gates** —*The place of public concourse* in each city looks sad, as being no longer frequented (Isa. 3:26; 24:4). **black**—i.e., they mourn (blackness being indicative of sorrow), (ch. 8:21). **unto the ground**—bowing towards it. **cry**—of distress (I Sam. 5:12; Isa. 24. 11).

3. little ones—rather, "their inferiors," i.e., domestics. **pits**—cisterns for collecting rain water, often met with in the *East* where there are no springs. **covered . . . heads**—(II Sam. 15:30). A sign of humiliation and mourning.

5. The brute creation is reduced to the utmost extremity for the want of food. The "hind," famed for her affection to her young, abandons them. **6. wild asses**—They repair to "the high places" most exposed to the winds, which they "snuff in" to relieve their thirst. **dragons**—jackals [Henderson]. **eyes**—which are usually most keen in detecting grass or water from the "heights," so much so that the traveller guesses from their presence that there must be herbage and water near; but now "their eyes fail." Rather the reference is to the great boas and python serpents which raise a large portion of their body up in a vertical column ten or twelve feet high, to survey the neighborhood above the surrounding bushes, while with open jaws they drink in the air. These giant serpents originated the widely spread notions which typified the deluge and all destructive agents under the form of a dragon or monster serpent; hence, the dragon temples always near water, in Asia, Africa, and Britain; e.g., at Abury, in Wiltshire; a symbol of the ark is often associated with the dragon as the preserver from the waters [Kitto's *Biblical Cyclopœdia*]. **7. do thou it**—what we beg of Thee; interpose to remove the drought. Jeremiah pleads in the name of his nation (Ps. 109:21). So "work for us," absolutely used (I Sam. 14:6). **for thy name's sake**—"for *our* backslidings are so many" that we cannot urge Thee for the sake of *our* doings, but for the glory of *Thy* name; lest, if Thou give us not aid, it should be said it was owing to Thy want of power (Josh. 7:9; Ps. 79:9; 106:8; Isa. 48: 9; Ezek. 20:44). The same appeal to God's mercy, "for *His* name's sake," as our only hope, since *our* sin precludes trust in ourselves, occurs in Psalm 25: 11.

8. (Ch. 17:13.) **hope of Israel**—The reference is, not to the faith of *Israel* which had almost ceased, but to the promise and everlasting covenant of *God.* None but the true Israel make God their "hope." **turneth aside to tarry**—The *traveller* cares little for the land he tarries but a night in; but Thou hast promised to *dwell* always in the midst of Thy people (II Chron. 33:7, 8). Maurer translates, "spreadeth," viz., his tent. **9. astonied**—like a "mighty man," at other times able to help (Isa. 59: 1). but now *stunned* by a sudden calamity so as to disappoint the hopes drawn from him. **art in the midst of us**—(Exod. 29:45, 46; Lev. 26:11, 12). **called by thy name**—(Dan. 9:18, 19) as Thine own peculiar people (Deut. 9:29).

ADAM CLARKE

CHAPTER 14

1. *The word . . . that came . . . concerning the dearth.* This discourse is supposed to have been delivered after the fourth year of Jehoiakim.

2. *The gates thereof languish.* The gates being the places of public resort, they are put here for the people. *They are black unto the ground.* Covered from head to foot with a black garment, the emblem of sorrow and calamity.

3. *Their nobles have sent their little ones.* So general was this calamity that the servants no longer attended to their lords, but everyone was interested alone for himself; and the nobles of the land were obliged to employ their own children to scour the land, to see if any water could be found in the tanks or the pits. In the dearth in the time of Elijah, Ahab, the king, and Obadiah, his counsellor, were obliged to traverse the land themselves in order to find out water to keep their cattle alive. This and the following three verses give a lively but distressing picture of this dearth and its effects.

4. *The ground is chapt.* The cracks in the earth before the descent of the rains are in some places a cubit wide, and deep enough to receive the greater part of a human body.

7. *O Lord, though our iniquities testify against us.* We deeply acknowledge that we have sinned, and deserve nothing but death. Yet act for Thy name's sake—work in our behalf, that we perish not.

8. *O the hope of Israel.* O Thou who art the only Object of the *hope* of this people. *The saviour thereof in time of trouble.* Who hast never yet abandoned them that seek Thee. *Why shouldest thou be as a stranger in the land?* As one who has no interest in the prosperity and safety of the country. *And as a wayfaring man.* A traveller on his journey. *That turneth aside to tarry for a night.* Who stays the shortest time he can; and takes up his lodging in a tent or caravanserai, for the dead of the night, that he may pursue his journey by break of day. Instead of dwelling among us, Thou hast scarcely paid the most transient visit to Thy land. Oh, come once more, and dwell among us.

MATTHEW HENRY

(who, though he has the reason of a man, yet is quite at his wits' end) or as a *mighty man*—a man, and therefore having his power limited." Either of these would be a most insufferable reproach to the divine perfections; and therefore, why has the God that we are sure *is in the midst of us* become *as a stranger*? Why does the almighty God seem as though he would, yet cannot save?

Verses 10–16

The dispute between God and his prophet, in this chapter, seems to be like that between the owner and the dresser of the vineyard concerning the barren fig-tree, Luke xiii. 7. The justice of the owner condemns it to be cut down; the clemency of the dresser intercedes for a reprieve.

I. God overrules the plea. Thus he says concerning *this people, v.* 10. He does not say, concerning *my people*, because they had broken covenant with him. It is true they were *called by his name*, but they had sinned, and provoked God to withdraw. God here tells him they were not qualified for a pardon. The prophet had owned that *their backslidings were many*; and yet there was hope for them if they returned. But *this people* show no disposition at all to return; *they have loved to wander;* their backslidings have been their pleasure, which should have been their shame. It is not through necessity that they wander: their wanderings forfeit God's favour. They have not taken warning and *refrained their feet*. This is that for which God is now reckoning with them. When he denies them rain from heaven he is *remembering their iniquity* and *visiting their sin*, for which their *fruitful land* is thus *turned into barrenness*. Though they betook themselves to fasting and prayer and burnt-offerings and sacrifice: *The Lord doth not accept them, v.* 10. *He takes no pleasure in them* (so the word is). "*When they fast* (*v.* 12), which is a proper expression of repentance and reformation,—*when they offer a burnt offering and an oblation*, which was designed to be an expression of faith in a Mediator,—though their prayers be offered up in those vehicles that used to be acceptable yet, because they do not proceed from humble, penitent, and renewed hearts, but still *love to wander*, therefore *I will not hear their cry, nor will I accept them*, neither their persons nor their performances." They had forfeited all benefit by the prophet's prayers for them because they had not regarded his preaching. This is the meaning of that repeated prohibition given to the prophet (*v.* 11): *Pray not thou for this people for their good*, as before, *ch.* vii. 16; xi. 14. This did not forbid him thus to express his *goodwill* to them, but it forbade them to expect any good effect from it as long as they *turned away their ear from hearing the law*. It therefore follows (*v.* 12), *I will consume them.*

II. The prophet offers another plea in excuse for the people's obstinacy. The prophets, who pretended a commission from heaven, imposed upon them, and flattered them with assurances of peace, *v.* 13. He speaks of it with lamentation: "*Ah! Lord God*, there are those who in thy name tell them that they *shall not see the sword nor famine*; and they say it as from thee: *I will* continue you *in this place*, and will *give you assured peace*. I tell them the contrary; but I am one against many; therefore, Lord, pity and spare them, for *their leaders cause them to err*." This excuse would have been of some weight if they had not had warning given them, before, of false prophets.

III. God not only overrules this plea, but condemns both the blind leaders and the blind followers to fall together into the ditch. He disowns the flatteries (*v.* 14): *They prophesy lies in my name.* They had no commission from God to prophesy at all: *I neither sent them, nor commanded them, nor spoke unto them.* Those that oppose their own thoughts to God's word (God indeed says so, but they think otherwise) walk in the *deceit of their heart*, and it will be their ruin. He passes sentence upon the flatterers, *v.* 15. As for the prophets, let them know that they shall have no peace themselves. They undertook to warrant people that *sword and famine* should *not be in the land*; but they themselves shall be cut off by sword and famine. The *people to whom they prophesy lies*, and who willingly suffer themselves to be thus imposed upon, *shall die by sword and famine, v.* 16. Their bodies shall be *cast out*, even *in the streets of Jerusalem*; there they shall lie unburied. Thus will God *pour their wickedness upon them*, that is, the punishment of their wickedness.

Verses 17–22

The present deplorable state of Judah and Jerusalem is here made the matter of the prophet's lamentation (*v.* 17, 18) and of his prayer for them (*v.* 19), and the latter, as well as the former, was by divine direction, and these words (*v.* 17), *Thus shalt thou say unto them,*

JAMIESON, FAUSSET, BROWN

F. B. MEYER:

"Why shouldest thou be as a man astonied, as a mighty man that cannot save?" (Jer. 14:9). A strong man may be rendered powerless by a reel of cotton being wound around him. Each thread so brittle, yet all together is irresistible. So a large number of inconsistencies and insincerities may make God powerless to help you, or to work mightily through you to the salvation of others. He may be in the midst of you, and you may be called by his name; great issues for his kingdom and glory may seem at stake; mighty possibilities within your reach; and yet He is as a mighty man that cannot save.

There is might enough in God to save the weakest and sinfullest of his children; and you are unsaved because of the limitations you have placed upon Him. First, you are not absolutely willing to be delivered from your sins. Secondly, you do not entirely believe in his power and will. Thirdly, you have not definitely handed the whole matter over to Him, and believed that He has accepted the charge.—*Great Verses Through the Bible*

10. Jehovah's reply to the prayer (vss. 7-9; ch. 2:23-25). **Thus**—*So greatly.* **loved**—(ch. 5:31.)

not refrained . . . feet—They did not obey God's command; "withhold thy foot" (ch. 2:25), viz., from following after idols. **remember . . . iniquity**—(Hos. 8:13; 9:9). Their sin is so great, God must punish them.

11. (Ch. 7: 16; Exod. 32:10.) **12. not hear**—because their prayers are hypocritical: their hearts are still idolatrous. God never refuses to hear *real* prayer (ch. 7: 21, 22; Prov. 1:28; Isa. 1:15; 58:3). **sword . . . famine . . . pestilence**—the three sorest judgments at once; any one of which would be enough for their ruin (II Sam. 24:12, 13).

13. Jeremiah urges that much of the guilt of the people is due to the false prophets' influence. assured peace—solid and lasting peace. Lit., "peace of truth" (Isa. 39:8).

14. (Ch. 23:21.)

15. (Ch. 5:12, 13.) **say, Sword and famine . . . consumed**—retribution in kind both to the false prophets and to their hearers (vs. 16). **16. none to bury**—(Ps. 79:3). **pour their wickedness**—i.e., the punishment incurred by their wickedness (ch. 2:19).

ADAM CLARKE

11. *Pray not for this people.* They are ripe for destruction; intercede not for them.

13. *Ah, Lord God! behold, the prophets say unto them.* True, Lord, they are exceedingly wicked; but the false prophets have deceived them; this is some mitigation of their offense. This plea God does not admit; and why? The people believed them, without having any proof of their divine mission.

14. *The prophets prophesy lies.* They say they have visions, but they have them by divination, and they are false. The people should know their character, and avoid them; but they love to have it so, and will not be undeceived.

15. *By sword and famine shall those prophets be consumed.* Jeremiah had told Jehoiakim that, if he rebelled against Nebuchadnezzar, he should be overthrown, and the land wasted by *sword* and *famine;* the false prophets said there should be neither sword nor famine, but peace and prosperity. The king believed *them*, and withheld the tribute. Nebuchadnezzar, being incensed, invaded and destroyed the land; and the false prophets fell in these calamities. See 2 Kings xxv. 3; Lam. ii. 11-19.

MATTHEW HENRY

refer to the intercession as well as to the lamentation, and then it amounts to a revocation of the directions given to the prophet not to pray for them, *v.* 11.

I. The prophet stands weeping over the ruins of his country. Jeremiah must say it not only to himself, but to them too: *Let my eyes run down with tears, v.* 17. Thus he must signify to them that he foresaw *the sword* coming, and another sort of famine, that would be in the city through the straitness of the siege. The prophet speaks as if he already saw the miseries attending the descent which the Chaldeans made upon them: *The virgin daughter of my people is broken with a great breach, with a very grievous blow,* more grievous than any she has yet sustained; for (*v.* 18) *in the field* multitudes lie dead that were *slain by the sword,* and in the city multitudes lie dying for want of food. "*The prophets and the priests,* the false prophets that flattered them with their lies and the wicked priests that persecuted the true prophets, are expelled, and *go about* either captives, or as fugitives and vagabonds, wherever they can find shelter *in a land that they know not.*" Some understand this of the true prophets, Ezekiel and Daniel, that were carried to Babylon with the rest. The prophet's eyes must run down *with tears day and night,* in prospect of this, that the people might be convinced, not only that this woeful day would infallibly come, but that he would gladly have brought them messages of peace, if he might have had warrant from heaven to do it.

II. He stands up to make intercession for them. There were some who would join with him in his devotions, and set the seal of their *Amen* to them.

1. He humbly expostulates with God concerning their case, *v.* 19. Their expectations from their God failed them; they thought he had avouched Judah to be his, but now, it seems, he has *utterly rejected* it. They thought Zion was beloved, but now *his soul* even *loathes Zion,* loathes even the services there performed. All their other expectations failed them: *They were smitten,* their wounds were multiplied, but there was *no healing* for them; they *looked for peace,* because after a storm there usually comes a calm. They looked for a *healing time,* but could not gain so much as a *breathing time.* "*Behold, trouble* at the door, by which we hoped peace would enter. But wilt thou not at length in wrath remember mercy?"

2. He makes a penitent confession of sin, which they all should have spoken, though but few did (*v.* 20): "*We acknowledge our wickedness,* the abounding wickedness of our land *and the iniquity of our fathers,* which we have imitated. *We know, we acknowledge,* that *we have sinned against thee,* and therefore thou art just in all that is brought upon us; but, because we confess our sins, we hope to find thee faithful and just in forgiving our sins."

3. He deprecates God's displeasure, and by faith appeals to his promise, *v.* 21. His petition is, "*Do not abhor us;* though thou afflict us, *do not abhor us*; though thy hand be turned *against* us, let not thy heart be so, nor let thy mind be alienated from us." They own God might justly abhor them, yet they pray: "*Do not abhor us, for thy name's sake,* that name of thine by which we are called and which we call upon." The honour of his sanctuary is pleaded: "Lord, do not abhor us, for that will *disgrace the throne of thy glory.*" We deserve to have disgrace put upon us, but let not the desolations of the temple give occasion to the heathen to reproach him that used to be worshipped there. We may be sure that God will not *disgrace the throne of his glory* on earth. They are humbly bold to put him in mind: *Remember thy covenant with us, and break not* that covenant.

4. He professes a dependence upon God for the mercy of rain, *v.* 22. They will never make application to the idols of the heathen. *Are there any among the vanities of the Gentiles that can cause rain?* In a time of great drought in Israel, Baal, though all Israel presented their prayers to him in the days of Ahab, could not relieve them; it was only that God who *answered by fire* that could answer *by water* too. *Can the heavens give showers?* Not without orders from the God of heaven; for it is he that has the key of the clouds, that *opens the bottles of heaven* and *waters the earth from his chambers.* All their expectation therefore is from him. *Art not thou he, O Lord our God!* from whom we may expect succour and to whom we must apply? Art thou not he that *causest rain* and *givest showers?* For *thou hast made all these things*; thou gavest them being, and therefore thou givest them law and hast them all at thy command. We will *ask of the Lord rain,* Zech. x. 1. We will trust in him to give it to us in due time.

JAMIESON, FAUSSET, BROWN

17. (Ch. 9:1; Lam. 1:16.) Jeremiah is desired to weep ceaselessly for the calamities coming on his nation (called a "virgin," as being heretofore never under foreign yoke), (Isa. 23:4).

18. go about—i.e., shall have to migrate into a land of exile. HORSLEY translates, "go *trafficking* about the land (see *Margin;* ch. 5:31; II Cor. 4:2; II Pet. 2:3), and take no knowledge" (i.e., pay no regard to the miseries before their eyes) (Isa. 1:3; 58:3). If the sense of the *Hebrew* verb be retained, I would with *English Version* understand the words as referring to the exile to Babylon; thus, "the prophet and the priest shall have to go to a strange land to *practise their religious traffic* (Isa. 56:11; Ezek. 34: 2, 3; Mic. 3:11).

19. The people plead with God, Jeremiah being forbidden to do so. **no healing**—ch. 15:18). **peace . . . no good**—(ch. 8:15).

20.(Dan. 9:8.)

21. us—"the throne of Thy glory" may be the object of "abhor not" ("reject not"); or "Zion" (vs. 19).

throne of thy glory—Jerusalem, or, *the temple,* called God's "footstool" and "habitation" (I Chron. 28:2; Ps. 132:5). **thy covenant**—(Ps. 106:45; Dan. 9:19).

22. vanities—idols (Deut. 32:21). **rain**—(Zech. 10:1, 2.)

heavens—viz., of themselves without God (Matt. 5:45; Acts 14:17); they are not the First Cause, and ought not to be deified, as they were by the heathen. The disjunctive "or" favors CALVIN's explanation: "Not even the heavens themselves can give rain, much less can the idol vanities." **art not thou he**—viz., who canst give rain?

ADAM CLARKE

17. *For the virgin daughter of my people is broken.* First, the land was sadly distressed by Pharaoh-necho, king of Egypt. Secondly, it was laid under a heavy tribute by Nebuchadnezzar. And, thirdly, it was nearly desolated by a famine afterwards. In a few years all these calamities fell upon them; these might be well called *a great breach . . . a very grievous blow.*

19. *We looked for peace.* We expected prosperity when Josiah purged the land of idolatry.

20. *We acknowledge, O Lord, our wickedness.* This the prophet did in behalf of the people; but, alas! they did not join him.

21. *Do not disgrace the throne of thy glory.* The Temple. Let not this sacred place be profaned by impious and sacrilegious hands. *Break not thy covenant.* See Exod. xxiv. 7-8; xix. 5. They had already broken the covenant, and they wish God to fulfil His part.

MATTHEW HENRY

CHAPTER 15

Verses 1–9

There are scarcely anywhere more pathetic expressions of divine wrath against a provoking people than in these verses. The prophet had prayed earnestly for them, and found some to join with him; and yet no reprieve was gained, nor the least mitigation of the judgment.

I. What the sin was upon which this severe sentence was grounded. It is because of Manasseh, for that which he did in Jerusalem, *v.* 4. What that was we are told, and that it was for it that Jerusalem was destroyed, 2 Kings xxiv. 3, 4. It was for his idolatry, and *the innocent blood which he shed, which the Lord would not pardon.* It is in consideration of their present impenitence. Their sin is described (*v.* 6): *Thou hast forsaken me,* my service and thy duty to me; *thou hast gone backward* and art become the reverse of what thou shouldst have been. The impenitence is described (*v.* 7): *They return not from their ways,* the ways of their own hearts, into the ways of God's commandments again. There is mercy for those who have turned aside if they will return; but what favour can those expect that persist in their apostasy?

II. What the sentence is. It is ruin.

1. God himself abandons them: *My mind cannot be towards them.* It is not in a passion, but with a just and holy indignation, that he says, "*Cast them out of my sight,* and let *them go forth,* for I will be troubled with them no more."

2. He will not admit any intercession to be made for them (*v.* 1): "*Though Moses and Samuel stood before me,* by prayer or sacrifice to reconcile me to them, yet I could not admit them into favour."

3. He condemns them all to one destroying judgment or other. When God casts them out of his presence, *whither shall they go forth?* (*v.* 2). *Such as are for death to death,* or *for the sword to the sword.* It is a choice like that which David was put to, and was thereby put into a *great strait,* 2 Sam. xxiv. 14. *Captivity* is mentioned last, some think, because the sorest judgment of all, it being a continuance of miseries. That of *the sword* is again repeated (*v.* 3), and is made the first of another four set of destroyers. As those that escape *the sword* shall be cut off by pestilence, famine, or captivity, so those that fall by the sword shall be cut off by divine vengeance. There shall be *dogs to tear* in the city and *fowls of the air* and *wild beasts* in the field to devour. And, if there be any that think to outrun justice: *They shall be removed into all kingdoms of the earth* (*v.* 4), like Cain, who became a *fugitive and a vagabond* in the earth.

4. They shall fall without being relieved. God appears against them: *I will stretch out my hand against thee,* a deliberate stroke, which will wound deeply. *I am weary with repenting* (*v.* 6); by their treacherous professions of repentance, they had put even infinite patience to the stretch. Now he will grant no more reprieves. Their own country expels them, and is ready to *spew them out. I will fan them with a fan in the gates of the land,* in their own gates, or *into the gates of the earth,* into the cities of all the nations about them, *v.* 7. *I will bereave them of children;* they shall have little hope that the next generation will retrieve their affairs, for *I will destroy my people.* Nebuchadnezzar is here called *a spoiler at noon-day,* not a thief in the night, afraid of being discovered, but one that without fear shall break through and destroy. *I have brought against the mother a young man, a spoiler* (so some read it); for Nebuchadnezzar, when he first invaded Judah, was but a *young man,* in the first year of his reign. We read it, *I have brought upon them,* even *against the mother of the young men, a spoiler,* that is, against Jerusalem, a mother city, that had a very numerous family of young men. God *caused him to fall upon it,* that is, upon the spoil delivered to him, *suddenly;* and then *terrors* came *upon the city. I will cause to fall suddenly upon her* (upon Jerusalem) *a watcher and terrors;* the word is used for a watcher (Dan. iv. 13, 23), and the Chaldean soldiers were called watchers, *ch.* iv. xvi. A dreadful slaughter is here described. The wives are deprived of their husbands: *Their widows are increased above the sand of the seas.* God says, *They are increased to me.* Though the husbands were cut off by the sword of his justice, their poor widows were gathered in the arms of his mercy, who has taken it among the titles of his honour to be *the God of the widows.* The parents are deprived of their children. When the children are slain the mother *gives up the ghost,* for her life was bound up in theirs: *Her sun has gone down while it was yet day.* Some understand, by this languishing mother, Jerusalem lamenting the death of her inhabitants as passionately as ever poor mother bewailed her children.

JAMIESON, FAUSSET, BROWN

CHAPTER 15

Vss. 1-21. GOD'S REPLY TO JEREMIAH'S INTERCESSORY PRAYER.

because of Manasseh—He was now dead, but the effects of his sins still remained. How much evil one bad man can cause! The evil fruits remain even after he himself has received repentance and forgiveness. The people had followed his wicked example ever since; and it is implied that it was only through the long-suffering of God that the penal consequences had been suspended up to the present time (cf. I Kings 14:16; II Kings 21:11, 23:26; 24:3, 4).

1. Moses . . . Samuel—eminent in intercessions (Exod. 32:11, 12; 1 Sam. 7:9; Ps. 99:6). **be toward**—could not be favorably inclined toward them. **out of my sight**—God speaks as if the people were present before Him, along with Jeremiah. **2. death**—deadly plague (ch. 18:21; 43:11; Ezek. 5:2, 12; Zech. 11:9). **3. appoint**—(Lev. 26:16). **kinds**—of punishments. **4. cause . . . to be removed**—(Deut. 28:25; Ezek. 23:46). Rather, "I will give them up to vexation," I will cause them to wander so as nowhere to have repose [CALVIN], (II Chron. 29:8, "trouble," *Margin,* "commotion"). **6. weary with repenting**—(Hos. 13:14; 11:8). I have so often *repented* of the evil that I threatened (ch. 26:19; Exod. 32:14; I Chron. 21:15), and have spared them, without My forbearance moving them to repentance, that I will not again change My purpose (God speaking in condescension to human modes of thought), but will take vengeance on them now. **7. fan**—tribulation—from *tribulum,* a threshing instrument, which separates the chaff from the wheat (Matt. 3:12). **gates of the land**—i.e., the extreme bounds of the land through which the entrance to and exit from it lie. MAURER translates, "I will fan," i.e., cast them forth "*to* the gates of the land" (Nah. 3:13). "In the gates"; *English Version* draws the image from a man cleaning corn with a fan; he stands at the gate of the threshing-floor in the open air, to remove the wheat from the chaff by means of the wind; so God threatens to remove Israel out of the bounds of the land [HOUBIGANT]. **8. Their widows**—My people's (vs. 7). **have brought**—prophetical past: I will bring. **mother of the young men**—"mother" is collective; after the "widows," He naturally mentions bereavement of their sons ("young men"), brought on the "mothers" by "the spoiler"; it was owing to the number of men slain that the "widows" were so many [CALVIN]. Others take "mother," as in II Samuel 20: 19, of Jerusalem, the metropolis; "I have brought on them, against the 'mother,' a young spoiler," viz., Nebuchadnezzar, sent by his father, Nabopolassar, to repulse the Egyptian invaders (II Kings 23:29; 24:1), and occupy Judea. But vs. 7 shows the future, not the past, is referred to; and "widows" being literal, "mother" is probably so, too. **at noonday**—the hottest part of the day, when military operations were usually suspended; thus it means *unexpectedly,* answering to the parallel, "suddenly"; *openly,* as others explain it, will not suit the parallelism (cf. Ps. 91:6). **it**—*English Version* seems to understand by "it" the mother city, and by "him" the "spoiler"; thus "it" will be parellel to "city." Rather, "I will cause to fall upon *them* (the 'mothers' about to be bereft of their sons) suddenly *anguish* and terrors." **the city**—rather, from a root "heat," *anguish,* or consternation. So LXX. **9. borne seven**—(I Sam. 2:5). Seven being the perfect number indicates full fruitfulness. **languisheth**—because not even one is left of all her sons (vs. 8). **sun is gone down while . . . yet day**—Fortune deserts her at the very height of her prosperity (Amos 8:9). **she . . . ashamed**—The mothers (*she* being collective) are put to the shame of disappointed hopes through the loss of all their children.

ADAM CLARKE

CHAPTER 15

1. *Though Moses and Samuel. Moses* had often supplicated for the people, and in consequence they were spared. See Exod. xxxii. 11 and following verses; Num. xiv. 13. *Samuel* also had prayed for the people, and God heard him, 1 Sam. vii. 9. But if these or the most holy men were now to supplicate for this people, He would not spare them.

2. *Whither shall we go forth? . . . Such as are for death, to death.* Some shall be destroyed by the pestilence, here termed *death.* See chap. xviii. 21. Others shall be slain by the *sword* in battle, and in the sackage of cities. Others shall perish by *famine,* shall be starved to death through the mere want of the necessaries of life; and the rest shall go into *captivity.*

3. *I will appoint over them four kinds.* There shall appear four instruments of My justice: (1) *The sword to slay.* (2) *The dogs to tear* what is slain. (3) *The fowls of the heaven* to feed on the dead carcasses. And (4) The wild *beasts* to *destroy* all that the fowls have left.

4. *I will cause them to be removed into all kingdoms of the earth.* This seems to have respect to the succeeding state of the Jews in their different generations; never was there a prophecy more literally fulfilled, and it is still a standing monument of divine truth.

6. *I am weary with repenting.* With repeatedly "changing My purpose."

7. *I will fan them with a fan.* There is no pure grain; all is chaff. *In the gates of the land.* The places of public justice; and there it shall be seen that the judgments that have fallen upon them have been highly merited. And from these places of fanning they shall go out into their captivity.

8. *The mother of the young men.* The metropolis or mother city, Jerusalem.

9. *She that hath borne seven.* She that hath had a numerous offspring; Jerusalem, the parent of so many cities, villages, and families in the land. *Seven* signifies a complete or full number.

MATTHEW HENRY

5. They shall fall without being pitied (*v.* 5): "*For who shall have pity on thee, O Jerusalem?* When thy God has *cast thee out of his sight*, neither thy enemies nor thy friends shall have any compassion for thee. *O Israel! thou hast destroyed thyself.*"

Verses 10–14

Jeremiah has now returned from his public work and retired into his closet; what passed between him and his God there we have an account of in these verses.

I. The complaint which the prophet makes to God of the many discouragements he met with in his work, *v.* 10.

1. He met with a great deal of contradiction and opposition. He was a *man of strife and contention.* Both city and country quarrelled with him, and did all they could to thwart him. He was a peaceable man, and yet *a man of strife*, not a man striving, but a man striven with; he was for peace, but, when he spoke, they were for war. The real cause of their quarrels with him was his faithfulness to God and to their souls. He showed them their sins that were working their ruin, and put them into a way to prevent that ruin, and yet they were incensed against him. The gospel of peace brings division, Matt. x. 34, 35; Luke xii. 49, 51. Now this made Jeremiah very uneasy. He cried out, *Woe is me, my mother, that thou hast borne me;* he is angry that she had *borne him a man of strife.* It was intended for a pathetic lamentation of his case. Even those who are most peaceable are often made men of strife. Yet, if we cannot live peaceably with our neighbours, we must not be so disturbed as to lose the repose of our own minds and put ourselves upon the fret.

2. He met with a great deal of contumely, and reproach. They branded him as a factious man and a sower of discord and sedition. They ought to have blessed him, and to have blessed God for him; but they cursed his messenger and did all they could to make him odious. But one would be apt to suspect that surely Jeremiah had given them some provocation! "*I have neither lent* money *nor borrowed* money." It is implied here that those who deal much in the business of this world are often involved in strife and contention. It was an instance of Jeremiah's prudence that, being called to be a prophet, he *entangled not himself in the affairs of this life*, that he might not give the least shadow of suspicion that he aimed at secular advantages in it. He *put out* no money, for he was no usurer; he *took up* no money, for he was no merchant. We find (*ch.* xvi. 2) that he had neither wife nor children to keep. And yet he lay under a general odium, through the iniquity of the times.

II. The answer which God gave to this complaint. 1. God assures him that he should weather the storm and be made easy at last, *v.* 11. "*If I* take not care of thee, let me never be counted faithful; *verily it shall go well with thy remnant*, with the remainder of thy life" (for so the word signifies); "the residue of thy days shall be more comfortable to thee than those hitherto have been." *Thy end shall be good;* so the Chaldee reads it. It should seem that Jeremiah was uneasy at the apprehension of sharing in the public judgments which he foresaw coming. "If my friends are thus abusive to me, and what will my enemies be?" But he quiets his mind with this promise: "*Verily I will cause the enemy to entreat thee well in the time of evil*, when all about thee shall be laid waste." This promise was accomplished when Nebuchadnezzar, having taken the city, charged the captain of the guard to be kind to Jeremiah, and let him have everything he had a mind to, *ch.* xxxix. 11, 12. The following words, *Shall iron break the northern iron, and the steel*, or *brass?* (*v.* 12), being compared with the promise of God made to Jeremiah (*ch.* i. 18), that he would make him an *iron pillar* and *brazen walls*, seem intended for his comfort. They were continually clashing with him, and were rough and hard as iron; but Jeremiah, being armed with power and courage from on high, is as northern iron, which is naturally stronger, and as steel, which is hardened by art; and therefore they shall not prevail against him; compare this with Ezek. ii. 6; iii. 8, 9. 2. God assures him that his enemies and persecutors should be lost in the storm, *v.* 13, 14. God here turns his speech from the prophet to the people. To them also *v.* 12 may be applied: *Shall iron break the northern iron, and the steel?* Shall their courage and strength, and the most hardy and vigorous of their efforts, be able to contest either with the counsel of God or with the army of the Chaldeans, which are as inflexible, as invincible, as the northern iron and steel. Let them therefore hear their doom: *Thy substance and thy treasure will I give to the spoil*, and that *without price.* The prophet was poor; he had nothing to lose, neither *substance* nor *treasure*, and therefore the

JAMIESON, FAUSSET, BROWN

5. go aside . . . how thou doest—Who will turn aside (in passing by) to *salute* thee (to wish thee "peace")?

10. (Ch. 20:14; Job 3:1, etc.). Jeremiah seems to have been of a peculiarly sensitive temperament; yet the Holy Spirit enabled him to deliver his message at the certain cost of having his sensitiveness wounded by the enmities of those whom his words offended. **man of strife**—exposed to strifes on the part of "the whole earth" (Ps. 80:6).

I have neither lent . . .—proverbial for, "I have given no cause for strife against me."

11. Verily—lit., Shall it not be? i.e., Surely it shall be. **thy remnant**—the *final issue* of thy life; thy life, which now seems to thee so sad, shall eventuate in prosperity [CALVIN]. They who think that they shall be the surviving remnant, whereas thou shalt perish, shall themselves fall, whereas *thou shalt remain* and be favored by the conquerors [JUNIUS], (ch. 40:4, 5; 39:11, 12). The *Keri* reads, "I will *set* thee *free* (or as [MAURER], 'I will establish thee') for good" (ch. 14:11; Ezra 8:22; Ps. 119:122). **to entreat thee well**—lit., "to meet thee"; so "to be placable, nay, of their own accord to *anticipate in meeting* thee with kindness" [CALVIN]. I prefer this translation as according with the event (ch. 39: 11, 12; 40:4, 5). GESENIUS, from ch. 7:16; 27:18: Job 21:15, translates (not only will I relieve thee from the enemy's vexations, but) "I will make thine enemy (that now vexeth thee) *apply to thee with prayers*" (ch. 38:14; 42:2-6). **12. steel**—rather, *brass* or *copper,* which mixed with "iron" (by the Chalybes near the Euxine Pontus, far north of Palestine), formed the hardest metal, like our *steel.* Can *the Jews,* hardy like common iron though they be, break the still hardier *Chaldees* of the north (ch. 1:14), who resemble the Chalybian iron hardened with copper? Certainly not [CALVIN]. HENDERSON translates. "Can *one* break iron, (even) the northern iron, and brass," on the ground that *English Version* makes ordinary *iron* not so hard as brass. But it is not brass, but a particular mixture of iron and *brass,* which is represented as harder than *common iron,* which was probably then of inferior texture, owing to ignorance of modern modes of preparation. **13. Thy substance . . . sins**—Judea's, not Jeremiah's. **without price**—God casts His people away as a thing *worth naught* (Ps. 44:12). So, on the contrary, Jehovah, when about to restore His people, says, He will give Egypt, etc., for their *"ransom"* (Isa. 43:3). **even in all thy borders**—joined with "Thy substance . . . treasures, as also with "all thy sins," their sin and punishment being commensurate (ch. 17:3).

ADAM CLARKE

10. *A man of contention to the whole earth!* To the whole "land," to all his countrymen, though he had done nothing to merit their displeasure.

11. *I will cause the enemy to entreat thee well in the time of evil.* This was literally fulfilled; see chap. xxxix. 11, etc. Nebuchadnezzar had given strict charge to Nebuzar-adan, commander in chief, to look well to Jeremiah, to do him no harm, and to grant him all the privileges he was pleased to ask.

12. *Shall iron break the northern iron and the steel?* Shall our weak forces be able to oppose and overcome the powers of the Chaldeans? *Nechasheth,* which we here translate *steel,* properly signifies brass or copper united with tin, which gives it much hardness, and enables it to bear a good edge.

13. *Thy substance . . . will I give to the spoil without price.* Invaluable property shall be given up to your adversaries. Or *without price*—you shall have nothing for it in return.

E. H. PLUMPTRE:

Verse 10. "Woe is me . . ."—The abruptness of the transition suggests the thought that we have a distinct fragment which has been merged in the artificial continuity of the chapter. Possibly, as some have thought, verses 10 and 11 have been misplaced in transcription, and should come after verse 14, where they fit in admirably with the context. The sequence of thought may, however, be that the picture of the sorrowing mother in the previous verses suggests the reflection that there may be other causes for a mother's sorrow than that of which he has spoken, and so he bursts out into the cry, "Woe is me, my mother!" The prophet feels more than ever the awfulness of his calling as a vessel of God's truth. He, too, found that he had come "not to send peace on earth, but a sword" (Matt. 10:34). His days were as full of strife as the life of the usurer, whose quarrels with his debtors had become the proverbial type of endless litigation. As examples of the working of the law of debt, see Exod. 22:25; 2 Kings 4:1; Prov. 6:1–5; Isa. 24:2; Ps. 15:5; 109:11.

We note, as characteristic of the pathetic tenderness of the prophet's character, the address to his mother. We may think of her probably as still living, and the thought of her suffering embitters her son's grief. The sword was piercing through her soul also (Luke 2:35).

—*Ellicott's Commentary on the Whole Bible*

MATTHEW HENRY

enemy will treat him well. But the people that had great estates in money and land would be slain for what they had. All parts of the country, even those which lay most remote, had contributed to the national guilt, and all shall now be brought to account. "*I will make thee to pass with thy enemies*, who shall lead thee in triumph *into a land that thou knowest not*, and therefore canst expect to find no comfort in it."

Verses 15–21

I. The prophet's humble address to God, "*O Lord! thou knowest;* thou knowest my sincerity, which men are resolved they will not acknowledge; thou knowest my distress, which men disdain to take notice of."

1. The prophet prays, *v.* 15. (1) That God would consider his case and be mindful of him: "*O Lord! remember me;* think upon me for good." (2) That God would communicate strength and comfort to him: "*Visit me.*" (3) That he would appear for him: *Revenge me of my persecutors*, or rather, *Vindicate me from my persecutors*. Further than this a good man will not desire that God should avenge him. Let something be done to convince the world that Jeremiah is a righteous man and the God whom he serves is a righteous God. (4) That he would yet spare him: "*Take me not away* by a sudden stroke, but *in thy long-suffering* lengthen out my days." Though in a passion he complained of his birth (*v.* 10), yet he desires here that his death might not be hastened; for life is sweet to nature, and the life of a useful man is so to grace.

2. He pleads with God for mercy and relief against his enemies, persecutors, and slanderers.

(1) That God's honour was interested in this case: *Know*, and make it known, *that for thy sake I have suffered rebuke*. If it is for doing well that we suffer ill, and for righteousness' sake that we have all manner of evil said against us, we may hope that God will vindicate our honour with his own. To the same purport (*v.* 16), *I am called by thy name, O Lord of hosts!*

(2) That the word of God, which he was employed to preach to others, he had experienced in his own soul, and therefore had the graces of the Spirit to qualify him for the divine favour, as well as his gifts. Jeremiah could say (*v.* 16): "*Thy words were found*, found *by me*, found *for me, and I did* not only taste them, but *did eat them*, received them entirely: they were welcome to me, as food to one that is hungry. The prophet was told to *eat the roll*, Ezek. ii. 8; Rev. x. 9. *I did eat it*—that is, as it follows, it *was to me the joy and rejoicing of my heart*, nothing could be more agreeable. Understand it, [1] Of the message itself which he was to deliver. Though he was to foretell the ruin of his country, which was dear to him, and in the ruin of which he could not but have a deep share, yet all natural affections were swallowed up in zeal for God's glory, and even these messages of wrath, being divine messages, were a satisfaction to him. He also rejoiced, at first, in hope that the people would take warning and prevent the judgment. Or, [2] Of the commission he received to deliver this message. Though the work he was called to was not attended with any secular advantages, but, on the contrary, exposed him to contempt and persecution, yet it was his *meat and drink to do the will of him that sent him*, John iv. 34. Or, [3] Of the promise God gave him that he would assist and own him in his work (*ch.* i. 8).

(3) That he had applied himself to the duty of his office with gravity and self-denial, though he had had of late but little satisfaction in it, *v.* 17. He *sat alone*, spent a great deal of time in his closet, *because of the hand* of the Lord that was strong upon him to carry him on in his work, Ezek. iii. 14. "*For thou hast filled me with indignation*, with such messages of wrath against this people as have made me always pensive." It is his complaint that he had had but little pleasure in his work. It was at first the rejoicing of his heart, but of late it had made him melancholy, so that he had no heart to *sit in the meeting of those that make merry*. He *sat alone*, fretting at the people's obstinacy and the little success of his labours among them.

(4) He throws himself upon God's pity and promise in a very passionate expostulation (*v.* 18): "*Why is my pain perpetual*, and nothing done to ease it? Will the God that has promised me his presence *be to me as a liar*, the God on whom I depend to be me *as waters that fail*?" No; I know thou wilt not. God is not a man that he should lie. The fountain of life will never be to his people as *waters that fail*.

II. God's gracious answer to this address, *v.* 19–21.

1. What God here requires of him. God will own him. But, (1) He must recover his temper, and be reconciled to his work. He must *return*, must shake off these distrustful discontented thoughts and passions, and not give way to them. (2) He must

JAMIESON, FAUSSET, BROWN

14. thee—MAURER supplies "them," viz., "thy treasures." EICHORN, needlessly, from *Syriac* and LXX, reads, "I will *make thee to serve* thine enemies"; a reading doubtless interpolated from ch. 17:4. **fire**—(Deut. 32:22).

15. thou knowest—viz., my case; what wrongs my adversaries have done me (ch. 12:3).

revenge me—(*Note*, ch. 11:20.) The prophet in this had regard to, not his own personal feelings of revenge, but the cause of God; he speaks by inspiration God's will against the ungodly. Contrast in this the law with the gospel (Luke 23:34; Acts 7:60). **take me not away in thy long-suffering**—By Thy long-suffering towards them, suffer them not meanwhile to take away my life.

for thy sake I have suffered rebuke—the very words of the antitype, Jesus Christ (Ps. 69:7, 22-28), which last cf. with Jeremiah's prayer in the beginning of this verse.

16. eat—(Ezek. 2:8; 3:1, 3; Rev. 10:9, 10). As soon as Thy words were found by me, I eagerly laid hold of and appropriated them. The *Keri* reads, "Thy *word*." **thy word . . . joy**—(Job 23:12; Ps. 119:72, 111; cf. Matt. 13:44). **called by thy name**—I am Thine, Thy minister. So the antitype, Jesus Christ (Exod. 23:21).

17. My "rejoicing" (vs. 16) was not that of the profane mockers (Ps. 1:1; 26:4, 5) at feasts. So far from having fellowship with these, he was expelled from society, and made to sit "alone," because of his faithful prophecies. **because of thy hand**—i.e., Thine inspiration (Isa. 8:11; Ezek. 1:3; 3:14). **filled me with indignation**—So ch. 6:11, "full of the fury of the Lord"; so full was he of the subject (God's "indignation" against the ungodly) with which God had inspired him, as not to be able to contain himself from expressing it. The same comparison by contrast between the effect of *inspiration*, and that of *wine*, both taking a man out of himself, occurs (Acts 2:13, 15, 18). **18.** (Ch. 30:15.) "Pain," viz., the perpetual persecution to which he was exposed, and his being left by God without consolation and "alone." Contrast his feeling here with that in vs. 16, when he enjoyed the full presence of God, and was inspired by His words. Therefore he utters words of his natural "infirmity" (so David, Ps. 77:10) here; as before he spoke under the higher spiritual nature given him. **as a liar, and as**—rather, "as a *deceiving* (river) . . . waters that are not sure" (lasting); opposed to "living (perennial) waters" (Job 6:15). Streams that the thirsty traveller had calculated on being full in winter, but which disappoint him in his sorest need, having run dry in the heat of summer. Jehovah had promised Jeremiah protection from his enemies (ch. 1:18, 19); his infirmity suggests that God had failed to do so. **19.** God's reply to Jeremiah. **return . . . bring . . . again**—Jeremiah, by his impatient language, had left his proper posture towards God; God saith, "If thou

ADAM CLARKE

15. *O Lord . . . remember me, and visit me.* Let me not be carried away into captivity; and it does not appear that he had ever been taken to Babylon. After the capture of the city he went into Egypt and either died there or was put to death by his countrymen.

16. *Thy word was . . . the joy and rejoicing of mine heart.* When I did receive the prophetic message, I did rejoice in the honor Thou hadst done me; and I faithfully testified Thy will to them. They have become mine enemies; not because there was any evil in me, but because I was faithful to Thee.

MATTHEW HENRY

resolve to be faithful in his work. Though there was no cause at all to charge Jeremiah with unfaithfulness, and God knew his heart to be sincere, yet God saw fit to give him this caution. Thou must *take forth the precious from the vile*. The righteous are the precious be they ever so mean and poor; the wicked are the vile be they ever so rich and great. In our congregations these are mixed, wheat and chaff in the same floor; we cannot distinguish them by name, but we must by character, and must give to each a portion, comfort to precious saints and terror to vile sinners: *Let them return to thee, but return not thou to them*, that is, he must do the utmost he can, in his preaching, to bring people up to the mind of God. Those that had flown off from him, "*Let them return to thee*, and, upon second thoughts, come up to the terms; but do not thou *return to them*, do not compliment them, nor think to make the matter easier to them than the word of God has made it."

2. What God here promises. If he approve himself well, (1) God will tranquillize his mind and pacify the present tumult of his spirits: *If thou return, I will bring thee again*, will *restore thy soul*, as Ps. xxiii. 3. (2) God will employ him in his service as a prophet. "*Thou shalt stand before me*, to receive instructions from me, as a servant from his master; and *thou shalt be as my mouth* to deliver my messages to the people, as an ambassador is the mouth of the prince that sends him." (3) He shall have strength and courage to face the many difficulties he meets in his work, and his spirit shall not fail as now it does (*v.* 20): "*I will make thee unto this people as a fenced brazen wall*, which the storm batters and beats violently upon, but cannot shake. *Return not thou to them* by any sinful compliances, and then trust thy God to arm thee by his grace with holy resolutions. Be not cowardly, and God will make thee daring." He had complained that he was made a *man of strife*. Expect to be so (says God); they will *fight against thee, but they shall not prevail against thee.* (4) He shall have God for his mighty deliverer: *I am with thee to save thee.* Those that have God with them have a Saviour with them who has wisdom and strength enough to deal with the most formidable enemy (*v.* 21). There are many things that appear very frightful that yet do not prove at all hurtful to a good man.

JAMIESON, FAUSSET, BROWN

wilt return (to thy former *patient* discharge of thy prophetic function) I will bring thee back" to thy former position: in the *Hebrew* there is a play of words, "*return . . . turn again*" (ch. 8:4; 4:1). **stand before me**—minister acceptably to Me (Deut. 10:8; I Kings 17:1; 18:15). **take . . . precious from . . . vile**—image from metals: "If thou wilt separate what is precious *in thee* (the divine graces imparted) from what is vile (thy natural corruptions, impatience, and hasty words), thou shalt be as My mouth": my mouthpiece (Exod. 4:16). **return not thou unto them**—Let not them lead you into their profane ways (as Jeremiah had spoken irreverently, vs. 18), but lead thou them to the ways of godliness (vss. 16, 17). Ezekiel 22:26 accords with the other interpretation, which, however, does not so well suit the context, "If thou wilt separate from the promiscuous mass the better ones, and lead them to conversion by faithful warnings . . . ."

20, 21. The promise of ch. 1:18, 19, in almost the same words, but with the addition, adapted to the present attacks of Jeremiah's formidable enemies, "I will deliver thee out of . . . wicked . . . redeem . . . terrible"; the repetition is in order to assure Jeremiah that God is *the same now* as when He first made the promise, in opposition to the prophet's irreverent accusation of unfaithfulness (vs. 18).

ADAM CLARKE

F. B. MEYER:

"If thou return, then will I bring thee again, and thou shalt stand before me" (Jer. 15:19). What a promise for backsliders is this! Here is a soul that had gone away from God's presence, and had ceased to be as his mouth. How long it had been in this castaway condition we need not inquire. It is enough to know that it had dipped beneath the horizon, and been permitted to know the bitter anguish of seeing others do its chosen work. Have you known this? Then these words were written for you; eat them, and let them be unto you the joy and rejoicing of your heart.

Will you return to God? Do you want it to be as in the old time? Tell Him so, and He will bring you again. It will not take Him a second's space to restore you to where you were to stand. Dare to believe that you are there again, forgiven, cleansed, sanctified. Live there. Go no more out for ever.—*Great Verses Through the Bible*

21. *I will deliver thee out of the hand of the wicked.* From the power of this evil people. *And I will redeem thee out of the hand of the terrible.* Out of the power of the Chaldean armies. Everything took place as God had promised, for no word of His can ever fall to the ground.

MATTHEW HENRY

CHAPTER 16

Verses 1–9

The prophet is here for a sign to the people. They would not regard what he said; let it be tried whether they will regard what he *does*. He must conduct himself as became one that expected to see his country in ruins very shortly. This he foretold, but he is to show that he is himself fully satisfied in the truth of it, he is forbidden marriage, mourning for the dead, and mirth.

I. Jeremiah must not marry, nor think of having a family (*v.* 2). The Jews valued early marriages and numerous offspring. But Jeremiah must live a bachelor. By this it appears that it was advisable only in calamitous times and times of *present distress*, 1 Cor. vii. 26. That it is so is a part of the calamity. When we see such times at hand it is wisdom for all, especially for prophets, to keep themselves from being encumbered with that which, the dearer it is to them, the more it will be their care, and fear, and grief. The reason here given is because the *fathers* and *mothers, the sons and the daughters, shall die of grievous deaths, v.* 3, 4. Those that have wives and children will have such a clog upon them that they cannot flee from those deaths. The death of every child, and the circumstances of it, will be a new death to the parent. Better have no children than have them brought forth and bred up *for the murderer* (Hos. ix. 13, 14), than see them live and die in misery. Bewailing the dead and burying them are denied: *They shall not be lamented*, but shall be carried off, as if all the world were weary of them; nay, they *shall not be buried*, but left exposed. *They shall be as dung upon the face of the earth*, not only despicable, but detestable. Being *consumed*, some *by the sword* and some *by famine, their carcases shall be meat for the fowls of heaven and the beasts of the earth.*

II. Jeremiah must not go to the house of mourning upon the death of any of his neighbours or relations (*v.* 5). It was usual to condole with those whose relations were dead, to *bemoan them*, to *cut themselves*, and *make themselves bald*, which was an expression of mourning, though forbidden by the law, Deut. xiv. 1. Sometimes, in a passion of grief, they did *tear themselves for them* (*v.* 6, 7). They used to mourn *to comfort them for the dead*, as the Jews with Martha and Mary; and it was a friendly office to *give them a cup of consolation to drink*, to provide cordials for

JAMIESON, FAUSSET, BROWN

CHAPTER 16

VSS. 1-21. CONTINUATION OF THE PREVIOUS PROPHECY.

2. in this place—in Judea. The direction to remain single was (whether literally obeyed, or only in prophetic vision) to symbolize the coming calamities of the Jews (Ezek. 24:15-27) as so severe that the single state would be then (contrary to the ordinary course of things) preferable to the married (cf. I Cor. 7:8; 26:29; Matt. 24:19; Luke 23:29).

4. grievous deaths—rather, deadly diseases (ch. 15: 2).

not . . . lamented—so many shall be the slain (ch. 22:18). **dung**—(Ps. 83:10).

6. cut themselves—indicating extravagant grief (ch. 41:5; 47:5), prohibited by the law (Lev. 19:28). **bald**—(ch. 7:29; Isa. 22:12). **7. tear themselves**—rather, "break bread," viz., that eaten at the funeral-feast (Deut. 26:14; Job 42:11; Ezek. 24:17; Hos. 9:4). "Bread" is to be supplied, as in Lamentations 4:4; cf. "take" (food) (Gen. 42:33). **give . . . cup of consolation . . . for . . . father**—It was the

ADAM CLARKE

CHAPTER 16

1. *The word of the Lord came also unto me.* This discourse Dahler supposes to have been delivered sometime in the reign of Jehoiakim.

2. *Thou shalt not take thee a wife.* As it would be very inconvenient to have a family when the threatened desolations should come on the place. The reason is given in the following verses.

4. *They shall die of grievous deaths.* All prematurely; see chap. xiv. 16.

As dung upon the face of the earth. See chap. viii. 2. *Be meat for the fowls.* See chap. vii. 33.

6. *Nor cut themselves.* A custom of the heathen forbidden to the Jews, Lev. xix. 28; Deut. xiv. 1, and which appears now to have prevailed among them; because, having become idolaters, they conformed to all the customs of the heathen.

MATTHEW HENRY

them for the support of their spirits. Though they have lost their parents, yet they have friends left that have a concern for them. It is a good work to *go to the house of mourning.* The prophet Jeremiah had been wont to abound in good offices of this kind. But now God bids him not lament the death of his friends. His sorrow for the destruction of his country in general must swallow up his sorrow for particular deaths. Men shall be in deaths so often that they shall have no time, no room, no heart, for the ceremonies that used to attend death. All shall be mourners then, and no comforters; everyone will find it enough to bear his own burden; for (*v.* 5), "*I have taken away my peace from this people,* put a full period to their prosperity, deprived them of health, and wealth, and quiet, and friends, and everything wherewith they might comfort themselves and one another." Whatever peace we enjoy, it is God's peace; it is his gift, and, *if he give quietness, who then can make trouble*? But, if we make not a good use of his peace, he can and will take it away. Then farewell all good. All is none when God takes away from us his lovingkindness and his mercies.

III. Jeremiah must not go to the house of mirth, any more than to the house of mourning, *v.* 8. God was coming against them in his judgments; and it was time for them to *humble themselves.* Ministers ought to be examples of self-denial. His friends wondered that he would not meet them, as he used to do, in the house of feasting. But he lets them know it was to intimate to them that all their feasting would be at an end shortly (*v.* 9): "*I will cause to cease the voice of mirth.* You shall have nothing to feast on, nothing to rejoice in, but be surrounded with calamities that shall mar your mirth and cast a damp upon it." God can find ways to tame the most jovial. "This shall be done *in this place,* in Jerusalem, that used to be the *joyous city* and thought her joys were all secure to her. It shall be done *in your eyes,* in your sight, to be a vexation to you, who now look so haughty and so merry." The voice of praise they had made to cease by their iniquities and idolatries, and therefore justly God made to cease among them *the voice of mirth and gladness.* The voice of God's prophets was not heard, was not heeded, among them, and therefore no longer shall *the voice of the bridegroom and of the bride,* of the songs that used to grace the nuptials, be heard among them. See *ch.* vii. 34.

Verses 10–13

1. The reasons why God would bring those judgments (*v.* 10). "*What is our iniquity? Or what is our sin?* What crime have we ever been guilty of, proportionable to such a sentence?" Instead of humbling and condemning themselves, they stand upon their own justification and insinuate that God did them wrong in pronouncing this evil against them. Do they ask the prophet why God is thus angry with them? The righteous God is never *angry without cause,* without good cause; but he must tell them particularly what is the cause, that they may be humbled, or at least that God may be justified. God visited upon them the iniquities of their fathers (*v.* 11): *Your fathers have forsaken me, and have not kept my law.* They shook off divine institutions, and *walked after other gods,* whose worship was more gay and pompous; and, being fond of variety and novelty, they *served them and worshipped them*; and this was the sin which God had said, in the second commandment, he would *visit upon their children,* who kept up these idolatrous usages. Also God reckoned with them for their own iniquities (*v.* 12): "You have made your father's sin your own, and have become obnoxious to the punishment which in their days was deferred, for *you have done worse than your fathers.*" If they had made a good use of their fathers' reprieve, and been led by the patience of God to repentance, the judgment would have been prevented, the reprieve turned into a national pardon. They were more impudent and obstinate in sin than their fathers. They suffered their own passions to be noisy, that they might drown the voice of their consciences. No wonder that God had taken this resolution (*v.* 13): "*I will cast you out of this land,* this land of light, this valley of vision—into a far country, *a land that you know not, neither you nor your fathers.*" Two things would make their case there very miserable, and both of them relate to the soul. (1) "It is the happiness of the soul to be employed in the service of God; but *there shall you serve other gods day and night*; perhaps compelled to do it by your cruel task-masters; and, when you are forced to worship idols, you will be as sick of such worship as ever you were fond of it when it was forbidden you by your godly kings." (2) "It is the happiness of the soul to have some tokens of the lovingkindness of God, but you shall

JAMIESON, FAUSSET, BROWN

Oriental custom for friends to send viands and wine (the "cup of consolation") to console relatives in mourning-feasts, e.g., to children upon the death of a "father" or "mother." **5.** (Ezek. 24:17, 22, 23.) **house of mourning**—(Mark 5:38). *Margin,* mourning-feast; such feasts were usual at funerals. The *Hebrew* means, in Amos 6:7, the *cry of joy* at a banquet; here, and Lamentations 2:19, the *cry of sorrow.*

8. house of feasting—joyous: as distinguished from mourning-feasts. Have no more to do with this people whether in mourning or joyous feasts.

9. (Ch. 7:34; 25:10; Ezek 26:13).

10. (Deut. 29:24; I Kings 9:8, 9).

11. (Ch. 5:19; 13:22; 22:8, 9).

12. ye—emphatic: so far from avoiding your fathers' bad example, ye have done worse (ch. 7:26; I Kings 14:9). **imagination**—rather, stubborn perversity. **that they may not hearken**—rather, connected with "ye"; "ye have walked . . . so as not to hearken to Me."

13. serve other gods—That which was their sin in their own land was their punishment in exile. Retribution in kind. They *voluntarily* forsook God for idols at home; they were *not allowed* to serve God, if they wished it, in captivity (Dan. 3 and 6). **day and night**—irony. You may there serve idols, which ye are so mad after, even to satiety, and without intermission.

ADAM CLARKE

5. *Enter not into the house of mourning.* The public calamities are too great to permit individual losses to come into consideration.

8. *Thou shalt not also go into the house of feasting.* Funeral banquets were made to commemorate the dead, and comfort the surviving relatives; and the cup of consolation, strong mingled wine, was given to those who were deepest in distress, to divert their minds and to soothe their sorrows.

JOHN GILL:

Verse 8. "Thou shalt not also go into the house of feasting." Which it was lawful to do, and which the prophet doubtless had done at other times; but now a time of calamity coming on, it was not proper he should; and the rather he was to abstain from such places, and from pleasant conversation with his friends, to assure them that such a time was coming, and this his conduct was a sign of it; for which reason he is forbidden to attend any entertainment of his friends, on account of marriage, or any other circumstances of life, for which feasts were used: "to sit with them to eat and to drink"; which not only expresses the position at table, but continuance there; for at feasts men not only eat and drink for necessity, or just to satisfy nature, but for pleasure, and unto and with cheerfulness; which may lawfully be done, provided that temperance and sobriety be preserved; but the prophet is not allowed to do that now, which at other times he might do, and did; and that on purpose that his friends might take notice of it, and inquire the reason of it, the distress that was coming upon them, as the words following show.—*Gill's Commentary*

12. *And ye have done worse than your fathers.* The sins of the fathers would not have been visited on the children, had they not followed their example, and become even worse than they.

13. *Will I cast you out of this land.* See chap. vii. 15 and ix. 15.

MATTHEW HENRY

go to a strange land, *where I will not show you favour*."

Verses 14–21

There is a mixture of mercy and judgment in these verses, and some seem to look as far forward as the times of the gospel.

I. God will certainly execute judgment upon them for their idolatries. The decree has gone forth. God sees all their sins (*v.* 17). As his omniscience convicts them, so his justice condemns them: *I will recompense their iniquity and their sin double*, not double to what it deserves, but double to what they expect. The sin for which God has a controversy with them is their having *defiled God's land* with their idolatries. Idols are *carcases of detestable things*. God hates them, and so should we. He will raise up instruments of his wrath, that shall *cast them out of their land*, according to the sentence passed (*v.* 16): *I will send for many fishers and many hunters*—the Chaldean army, that shall have ways of ensnaring them, by fraud as fishers, by force as hunters. They shall discover them wherever they are hid, in *hills* or *mountains*, or *holes of the rocks*. Their bondage in Babylon shall be more grievous than that in Egypt, their task-masters more cruel, and their lives more bitter. This is implied in the promise (*v.* 14, 15), that their deliverance out of Babylon shall be more welcome to them, than that out of Egypt. Their slavery in Egypt came upon them gradually; that in Babylon came upon them at once and with all the aggravating circumstances of terror. In Egypt they had a Goshen of their own, but none such in Babylon. In Egypt they were used as servants that were useful, in Babylon as captives that had been hateful. These judgments have a voice. When God chastens them he teaches them. By this rod God expostulates with them (*v.* 20): "*Shall a man make gods to himself?*" God will be known by the judgments which he executes. "For *this once*, and no more, *I will cause them to know my hand*, how far it can reach and how deeply it can wound."

II. Yet he has mercy in store for them. It was said, with an air of severity (*v.* 13), that God would banish them into a strange land; but there follow immediately words of comfort.

1. *The days will come*, the joyful days, when the same hand that dispersed them shall gather them again, *v.* 14, 15. They are cast out, but they are not cast off, they are not cast away. *I will bring them again into their own land*, and settle them there. And the following words (*v.* 16) may be understood as a promise; God will send for fishers and hunters, the Medes and Persians, that shall find them out in the countries where they are scattered, and send them back to their own land.

2. Their deliverance out of Babylon should be more memorable than their deliverance out of Egypt. The fresh mercy shall be so surprising, so welcome, that it shall even abolish the memory of the former. The bringing of Israel out of Egypt was done *by might and power*, this *by the Spirit of the Lord of hosts*, Zech. iv. 6. In this there was more of pardoning mercy for their captivity in Babylon had more in it of the punishment of sin than their bondage in Egypt.

3. Their deliverance out of captivity shall be accompanied with a blessed reformation, and they shall return cured of their inclination to idolatry. They had defiled their own land with their *detestable things*, *v.* 13. But, when they have smarted for so doing, they shall come and humble themselves before God, *v.* 19–21. They shall be quickened to return to him by the conversion of the Gentiles: *The Gentiles shall come to thee from the ends of the earth;* and therefore shall not we come? The prophet comforts himself with the hope of this: "*O Lord! my strength and my fortress*, I am now easy, since thou hast given me a prospect of multitudes that shall *come to thee from the ends of the earth*, both of Jewish converts and of Gentile proselytes." They were smarting for the sins of their ancestors: "*Surely our fathers have inherited lies, vanity, and things wherein there is no profit*. We are now sensible that they were cheated in their idolatrous worship; it did not prove what it promised, and therefore what have we to do any more with it?" They shall reason themselves out of their idolatry; and that reformation is likely to be durable which results from a rational conviction of the gross absurdity there is in sin, *v.* 20. They shall herein give honour to God, that they are brought to know his name by what they are made to know of his hand, *v.* 21. Nothing less than the mighty hand of divine grace, known experimentally, can make us know rightly the name of God as it is revealed to us.

4. Their deliverance out of captivity shall be a type and figure of the great salvation to be wrought out by the Messiah, who shall *gather together in one the children of God that were scattered abroad.*

JAMIESON, FAUSSET, BROWN

17. (Ch. 32: 19; Prov. 5:21; 15:3.) **their iniquity**—the cause of God's judgments on them. **18. first ... double**—Horsley translates, "I will recompense ... *once and again*"; lit., the first time repeated: alluding to the two captivities—the Babylonian and the Roman. Maurer, "I will recompense their *former* iniquities (those *long ago* committed by their fathers) and their (own) *repeated* sins" (vss. 11, 12). *English Version* gives a good sense, "*First* (before "I bring them again into their land"), I will doubly (i.e., *fully and amply*, ch. 17:18; Isa. 40:2) recompense." **carcasses**—not sweet-smelling *sacrifices* acceptable to God, but "carcasses" offered to idols, an offensive odor to God: human victims (ch. 19:5; Ezek. 16:20), and unclean animals (Isa. 65:4; 66:17). Maurer explains it, "the carcasses" *of the idols:* their images void of sense and life. Cf. vss. 19, 20. Leviticus 26:30 favors this.

16. send for—translate, "I will send many"; "I will give the commission to many" (II Chron. 17: 7). **fishers ... hunters**—successive invaders of Judea (Amos 4:2; Hab. 1:14, 15). So "net" (Ezek. 12:13). As to "hunters," see Genesis 10:9; Micah 7:2. The Chaldees were famous in hunting, as the Egyptians, the other enemy of Judea, were in fishing. "Fishers" expresses the *ease* of their victory over the Jews as that of the angler over fishes; "hunters," the keenness of their pursuit of them into every cave and nook. It is remarkable, the same image is used in a good sense of the Jews' restoration, implying that just as their enemies were employed by God to take them in hand for destruction, so the same shall be employed for their restoration (Ezek. 47:9, 10). So spiritually, those once enemies by nature (*fishermen* many of them literally) were employed by God to be heralds of salvation, "catching men" for life (Matt. 4:19; Luke 5: 10; Acts 2:41; 4:4); cf. here vs. 19, "the Gentiles shall come unto thee" (II Cor. 12:16).

14. Therefore—So severe shall be the Jews' bondage that their deliverance from it shall be a greater benefit than that out of Egypt. The consolation is incidental here; the prominent thought is the *severity* of their punishment, so great that their rescue from it will be greater than that from Egypt [Calvin]; so the context, vs.. 13, 17, 18, proves (ch. 23:7, 8; Isa. 43:18). **15. the north**—Chaldea. But while the return from Babylon is primarily meant, the return hereafter is the full and final accomplishment contemplated, as "from *all* the lands" proves. "*Israel*" was not, save in a very limited sense, "gathered from all the lands" at the return from Babylon (cf. ch. 24:6; 30:3; 32:15, *Notes*).

19, 20. The result of God's judgments on the Jews will be that both the Jews when restored, and the Gentiles who have witnessed those judgments, shall renounce idolatry for the worship of Jehovah. Fulfilled partly at the return from Babylon, after which the Jews entirely renounced idols, and many proselytes were gathered in from the Gentiles, but not to be realized in its fulness till the final restoration of Israel (Isa. 2). **20.** indignant protest of Jeremiah against idols. **and they are no gods**—(ch. 2:11; Isa. 37:19; Gal. 4: 8). "They" refers to the idols. A *man* (a creature himself) making *God* is a contradiction in terms. *Vulgate* takes "they" thus: "Shall man make gods, though *men* themselves are not gods?" **21. Therefore**—In order that all may be turned from idols to Jehovah, He will now give awful proof of His divine power in the judgments He will inflict. **this once**—If the punishments I have heretofore inflicted *have* not been severe enough to teach them. **my name ... Lord**—*Jehovah* (Ps. 83:18): God's incommunicable name, to apply which to idols would be blasphemy. Keeping His threats and promises (Exod. 6:3).

ADAM CLARKE

18. *The carcases of their detestable ... things.* Either meaning the idols themselves, which were only carcasses without life, or the sacrifices which were made to them.

16. *I will send for many fishers ... for many hunters.* I shall raise up enemies against them, some of whom shall destroy them by wiles, and others shall ruin them by violence. This seems to be the meaning of these symbolical *fishers* and *hunters*.

14. *The Lord liveth, that brought up.* See Isa. xliii. 18.

15. *The land of the north.* Chaldea; and their deliverance thence will be as remarkable as the deliverance of their fathers from the land of Egypt.

19. *The Gentiles shall come.* Even the days shall come when the Gentiles themselves, ashamed of their confidence, shall renounce their idols, and acknowledge that their fathers had believed lies and worshipped vanities. This may be a prediction of the calling of the Gentiles by the gospel of Christ.

21. *Therefore, behold, I will this once.* I will not now change My purpose. They shall be visited and carried into captivity; nothing shall prevent this. And they shall know that My name is Jehovah. Since they would not receive the abundance of My mercies, they shall know what the true God can do in the way of judgment.

MATTHEW HENRY

CHAPTER 17

Verses 1-4

The people had asked (*ch.* xvi. 10), *What is our iniquity, and what is our sin?*

I. The indictment is fully proved upon the prisoners, both the fact and the fault. They cannot plead *Not guilty*, for their sins are upon record in their own conscience; and they are obvious to the world, *v.* 1, 2. They are *written* before God in the most legible and indelible characters, Deut. xxxii. 34. They are written there with *a pen of iron and with the point of a diamond*; what is so written will not be worn out by time. The sin of sinners is never forgotten till it is forgiven. *It is graven upon the table of their heart.* What is *graven on the heart* cannot be erased. We need go no further, for proof of the charge, than *the horns of their altars*, on which the blood of their idolatrous sacrifices was sprinkled. Their neighbours will witness against them, and their own children shall *remember the altars and the groves* to which their parents took them when they were little, *v.* 2. The bias of their minds is still as strong as ever towards their idols, and they are not wrought upon either by the word or rod of God to abate their affection to them. It is written *upon the horns of their altars*, for they have given up their names to their idols and have bound themselves, as with cords.

II. The indictment being thus proved, the judgment is affirmed and the sentence ratified, *v.* 3, 4. Their treasures shall be given into the hands of strangers. Jerusalem is God's *mountain in the field*; it was built on a hill in the midst of a plain. *All the treasures* of that wealthy city will God *give to the spoil. My mountain* (so the whole land was, Ps. lxxviii. 54, Deut. xi. 11) you have turned into *your high places for sin*, have worshipped your idols upon *the high hills* (*v.* 2), and now they shall be *given for a spoil in all your borders.* They shall be made to part with their inheritance, and shall be carried captives into a strange land (*v.* 4). Sin works a discontinuance of our comforts and deprives us of the enjoyment of that which God has given us. But it is intimated that upon their repentance they shall recover possession again. For the present, *you have kindled a fire in my anger*, which burns so fiercely that it seems as if it would burn *for ever.*

Verses 5-11

The prophet's sermons were not all prophetical, but some of them practical.

I. Concerning the disappointment and vexation those will certainly meet with who depend upon creatures for success and relief when they are in trouble (*v.* 5, 6): *Cursed* (that is, miserable) *is the man* that does so, for he leans upon a broken reed. The sin here condemned is *making flesh the arm* we stay upon, the arm we work with and on which we depend for protection. God is his people's *arm*, Isa. xxxiii. 2. The great malignity there is in this sin; it is the *departure of the evil heart of unbelief from the living God.* Those that trust in man perhaps draw nigh to God with their mouth, but really *their heart departs from him.* Cleaving to the cistern is leaving the fountain, and is resented accordingly. He that puts a confidence in man puts a cheat upon himself; for (*v.* 6) *he shall be like the heath in the desert*, a sorry shrub, the product of barren ground, sapless, useless, and worthless; his comforts shall all fail him and he shall wither, be dejected and trampled on by all about him. *When good comes* he *shall not see* it, shall not share in it; when the times mend they shall not mend with him, but he shall *inhabit the parched places in the wilderness*; when others have a harvest he shall have none. Those that trust to their own righteousness and think they can do well enough without the grace of Christ, *make flesh their arm*, and their souls cannot prosper; they can neither produce the fruits of acceptable services to God nor reap the fruits of saving blessings from him; they *dwell in a dry land.*

II. Concerning the abundant satisfaction which those have who make God their confidence, who live by faith and repose themselves in him and his love in the most unquiet times, *v.* 7, 8. The duty required of us is to *make the Lord our hope*, his favour the good we hope for and his power the strength we hope in. He that does so shall be *as a tree planted by the waters*, a choice tree, about which great care has been taken to set it in the best soil. He shall be like a tree that *spreads out its roots*, and firmly fixed, spreads them out *by the rivers*, whence it draws abundance of sap. Those who make God their hope are easy, and enjoy a continual security and serenity of mind. A tree thus planted, thus watered, shall *not see when heat comes*, shall not sustain any damage from the most scorching heats of summer; it is so well moistened from its roots that it shall be sufficiently

JAMIESON, FAUSSET, BROWN

CHAPTER 17

VSS. 1-27. THE JEWS' INVETERATE LOVE OF IDOLATRY. The LXX omits the first four verses, but other *Greek* versions have them. **1.** The first of the four clauses relates to the third, the second to the fourth, by alternate parallelism. The sense is: They are as keen after idols as if their propensity was "graven with an iron pen (Job 19:24) on their hearts," or as if it were sanctioned by a law "inscribed with a diamond point" on their altars. The names of their gods used to be written on "the horns of the altars" (Acts 17:23). As the clause "on their hearts" refers to their *inward* propensity, so "on . . . altars," the *outward* exhibition of it. Others refer "on the horns of . . . altars" to their staining them with the blood of victims, in imitation of the Levitical precept (Exod. 29:12; Lev. 4:7, 18), but "written . . . graven," would thus be inappropriate. **table of . . . heart**—which God intended to be inscribed very differently, viz., with His truths (Prov. 3:3; II Cor. 3:3). **your**—Though "their" preceded, He directly addresses them to charge the guilt home to them in particular. **2. children remember**—Instead of forsaking the idolatries of their fathers, they keep them up (ch. 7:18). This is given as proof that their sin is "graven upon . . . altars" (vs. 1), i.e., is not merely temporary. They corrupt their posterity after them. CASTALIO less probably translates, "They remember their altars as (fondly as) they do their children." **groves**—rather, images of Astarte, the goddess of the heavenly hosts, represented as a sacred tree, such as is seen in the Assyrian sculptures (II Kings 21:7; II Chron. 24:18). "Image of the grove." The *Hebrew* for "grove" is Asherah, i.e., Assarak, Astarte, or Ashtaroth. **by the green trees**—i.e., near them: the sacred trees (idol symbols) of Astarte being placed in the midst of natural trees: "green trees" is thus distinguished from "groves," *artificial* trees. HENDERSON, to avoid taking the same *Hebrew* particle in the same sentence differently, "by . . . upon" translates "images of Astarte *on* the green trees." But it is not probable that images, in the form of a sacred tree, should be hung *on* trees, rather than *near* them. **3. mountain**—Jerusalem, and especially Zion and the temple. **in the field**—As Jerusalem was surrounded by *mountains* (Ps. 125:2), the sense probably is, Ye rely on your mountainous position (ch. 3:23), but I will make "My mountain" to become as if it were *in a plain* (field), so as to give thy substance an easy prey to the enemy [CALVIN]. "Field" may, however, mean *all Judea;* it and "My mountain" will thus express *the country and its capital.* (GESENIUS translates, "together with," instead of "in"; as the Hebrew is translated in ch. 11: 19; Hosea 5:6; but this is not absolutely needed), "the substance" of both of which God "will give to the spoil." **thy high places**—corresponding in parallelism to "My mountain" (cf. Isa. 11:9), as "all thy borders," to "the field" (which confirms the view that "field" means *all Judea*). **for sin**—connected with high places" in *English Version*, viz., frequented for sin, i.e., for idolatrous sacrifices. But ch. 15: 13 makes the rendering probable, "I will give thy substance . . . to . . . spoil . . . *on account of thy sin throughout all thy borders.*" **4. even thyself**—rather, "owing to thyself," i.e., by thy own fault (ch. 15:13). **discontinue from**—be dispossessed of. Not only thy substance, but thyself shall be carried off to a strange land (ch. 15:14). **5.** Referring to the Jews' proneness to rely on Egypt, in its fear of Assyria and Babylon (Isa. 31:1, 3). **trusteth**—This word is emphatic. We may expect help from men, so far as God enables them to help us, but we must rest our trust in God alone (Ps. 62:5). **6. heath**—In Psalm 102:17; Isaiah 32:11; Habakkuk 3:9, the *Hebrew* is translated, "bare," "naked," "destitute"; but as the parallel in vs. 8 is "tree," some plant must be meant of which this is the characteristic epithet (see ch. 48:6, *Margin*), "a naked tree." ROBINSON translates, "the juniper tree," found in the Arabah or Great Valley, here called "the desert," south of the Dead Sea. The "heath" was one of the plants, according to PLINY (13.21; 16.26), excluded from religious uses, because it has neither fruit nor seed, and is neither sown nor planted. **not see . . . good**—(Job 20:17.) **salt land**—(Deut. 29:23), barren ground. **7.** (Ps. 34: 8; Prov. 16:20; Isa. 30:18.) Jeremiah first removed the weeds (false trusts), so that there might be room for the good grain [CALVIN]. **8.** (Ps. 1:3.) **shall not see**—i.e., feel. Answering to vs. 6; whereas the unbelievers "shall not see (even) when *good* cometh," the believer "shall not see (so as to be overwhelmed by it even) when heat (fiery trial) cometh." Trials

ADAM CLARKE

CHAPTER 17

1. *The sin of Judah.* Idolatry. *Is written with a pen of iron.* It is deeply and indelibly written in their hearts, and shall be as indelibly written in their punishment.

2. *Whilst their children remember.* Even the rising generation have their imagination stocked with idol images, and their memories with the frantic rites and ceremonies which they saw their parents observe in this abominable worship.

3. *O my mountain in the field.* The prophet here addresses the land of Judea, which was a mountainous country, Deut. iii. 25; but Jerusalem itself may be meant, which is partly built upon hills which, like itself, are elevated above the rest of the country.

5. *Cursed be the man that trusteth in man.* This reprehends their vain confidence in trusting Egypt, which was too feeble itself to help, and, had it been otherwise, too ill disposed towards them to help them heartily. An arm of flesh is put here for a weak and ineffectual support.

6. *He shall be like the heath in the desert.* Or like a blasted tree, without moisture, parched and withered. *Shall not see when good cometh.* Shall not be sensible of it, the previous drought having rendered it incapable of absorbing any more vegetable juices. *A salt land.* Barren, and therefore unfit to be inhabited.

8. *As a tree planted by the waters.* Which is sufficiently supplied with moisture, though the heat be intense, and there be no rain; for the roots being spread out by the river, they absorb from it all the moisture requisite for the flourishing vegetation of the tree.

MATTHEW HENRY

guarded against drought. They shall flourish like a tree that is *always green*, whose leaf does not wither; they shall be cheerful to themselves and beautiful in the eyes of others. They shall be fixed in an inward peace and satisfaction: They *shall not be careful in a year of drought*, when there is want of rain; for, as the tree has *seed in itself*, so it has *its moisture*. We need not be solicitous about the breaking of a cistern as long as we have the fountain. Those who trust in God, and by faith derive strength and grace from him, *shall not cease from yielding fruit*.

III. Concerning the sinfulness of man's heart, and the divine inspection it is always under, *v.* 9, 10. It is folly to trust in man, for he is not only frail, but false and deceitful. We think that we trust in God when really we do not, as appears by this, that our hopes and fears rise or fall according as second causes smile or frown. There is wickedness in our hearts which we ourselves are not aware of and do not suspect to be there. *The heart*, the conscience of man, in his corrupt and fallen state, *is deceitful above all things*. It calls evil good and good evil, puts false colours upon things. When men say in their hearts that there is no God, or he does not see; in these, and a thousand similar suggestions, the heart is deceitful. The case is bad indeed, if the conscience which should rectify the errors of the other faculties is itself a mother of falsehood and a ring-leader in the delusion. We cannot know our own hearts, nor what they will do in an hour of temptation (Hezekiah did not, Peter did not). Much less can we know the hearts of others, or have any dependence upon them. Whatever wickedness there is in the heart, God sees it: *I the Lord search the heart*. And this judgment which he makes of the heart is *to give to every man according to his ways, and according to the fruit of his doings*.

IV. Concerning the curse that attends wealth unjustly gotten (*v.* 11): *He that gets riches and not by right*, though he may make them his hope, shall never have joy of them. He who has got *treasures* by *vanity* and a *lying tongue* may hug himself in his success, and say, *I am rich*, but they shall be taken from him, or he from them. Those that get grace will be wise *in the latter end*, will have the comfort of it in death and to eternity (Prov. xix. 20); but those that place their happiness in the wealth of the world will rue the folly of it when it is too late. This is like *the partridge that sits on eggs and hatches them not*, but they are broken (as Job xxxix. 15), or stolen (as Isa. x. 14), or they become addled. The rich man takes a great deal of pains to get an estate together, and sits brooding upon it, but never has any comfort nor satisfaction in it.

Verses 12–18

The prophet retired for private meditation, *alone with God*.

I. He acknowledges the great favour of God to his people in setting up a revealed religion among them, and dignifying them with divine institutions (*v.* 12): *A glorious high throne from the beginning is the place of our sanctuary*. The temple at Jerusalem, where God manifested his special presence, where the people paid their homage to their Sovereign, and whither they fled for refuge in distress, was the *place of their sanctuary*. It was a throne of holiness, God's throne. Jerusalem is called *the city of the great King*, not only Israel's King, but the King of the whole earth, so that it might justly be deemed the royal city, of the world. It was *from the beginning*, 2 Chron. ii. 9. Jeremiah here mentions this either as a plea with God for mercy to their land, or as an aggravation of the sin of his people in forsaking God though his throne was among them.

II. He acknowledges the righteousness of God in abandoning those to ruin that revolted from their allegiance to him, *v.* 13. He speaks to God, as subscribing to the equity of it: *O Lord! the hope of* those in Israel that adhere to thee, *all that forsake thee shall be ashamed. Let them be ashamed* (so some read it); and so it is a petition for his grace, to make them penitently ashamed. *"Those that depart from me*, from the word of God which I have preached, do in effect depart from God"; as those that return to God are said to return to the prophet, *ch.* xv. 19. *Those that depart from thee* (so some read it) shall be *written in the earth*. They shall soon be blotted out, as that is which is written in the dust. They have *forsaken the Lord, the fountain of living waters* (that is, spring waters), for broken cisterns.

III. He prays to God for healing saving mercy for himself. Lord, *heal me*, and *save me*, *v.* 14. He was wounded in spirit upon many accounts. He was continually exposed to the malice of unreasonable men. To enforce this petition he pleads: *Heal thou me, and then I shall be healed*. If God hold us up, we shall live; if he protect us, we shall be safe. *Thou shalt be*

JAMIESON, FAUSSET, BROWN

shall come upon him as on all, nay, upon him especially (Heb. 12:6); but he shall not sink under them, because the Lord is his secret strength, just as the "roots spread out by a river" (or, "water course") draw hidden support from it (II Cor. 4:8-11). **careful**—anxious, as one desponding (Luke 12:29; I Pet. 5:7). **drought**—lit., withholding, viz., of rain (ch. 14:1); he here probably alludes to the drought which had prevailed, but makes it the type of all kinds of distress.

9. deceitful—from a root, "supplanting," "tripping up insidiously by the heel," from which Jacob (Hos. 12:3) took his name. In speaking of the Jews' *deceit of heart*, he appropriately uses a term alluding to their forefather, whose deceit, but not whose faith, they followed. *His* "supplanting" was in order to obtain Jehovah's blessing. They plant Jehovah for "trust in man" (vs. 5), and then think to *deceive God*, as if it could escape His notice, that it is in *man*, not in Him, they trust. **desperately wicked**—"incurable" [HORSLEY], (Mic. 1:9). Trust in one's own heart is as foolish as in our fellow man (Prov. 28:26). **10.** Lest any should infer from vs. 9, "who can know it?" that even *the Lord* does not know, and therefore cannot punish, the hidden treachery of the heart, He says, "I the Lord search the heart," etc. (I Chron. 28:9; Ps. 7:9; Prov. 17:3; Rev. 2:23). **even to give**—*and that* in order that I may give (ch. 32:19). **11. partridge**—(I Sam. 26:20). *Hebrew* "korea," from a root, "to call," alluding to its cry; a name still applied to a bustard by the Arabs. Its nest is liable, being on the ground, to be trodden under foot, or robbed by carnivorous animals, notwithstanding all the beautiful manœuvres of the parent birds to save the brood. The translation, "sitteth on eggs *which it has not laid,"* alludes to the ancient notion that she stole the eggs of other birds and hatched them as her own; and that the young birds when grown left her for the true mother. It is not needful to make Scripture allude to an exploded notion, as if it were true. MAURER thinks the reference is to Jehoiakim's grasping cupidity (ch. 22:13-17). Probably the sense is more general; as previously He condemned trust in man (vs. 5), He now condemns another object of the deceitful hearts' trust, *unjustly gotten riches* (Ps. 39:6; 49:16, 17; 55:23). fool—(Prov. 23:5; Luke 12:20); "their folly" (Ps. 49:13). He himself, and all, shall at last perceive he was not the wise man he thought he was. **12. throne**—the temple of Jerusalem, the throne of Jehovah. Having condemned false objects of trust, "*high places* for sin" (vs. 3), and an "arm of flesh," he next sets forth Jehovah, and *His temple*, which was ever open to the Jews, as the true object of confidence, and sanctuary to flee to. HENDERSON makes Jehovah, in vs. 13, the subject, and this verse predicate, "A throne of glory, high from the beginning, the place of our sanctuary, the hope of Israel is Jehovah." "Throne" is thus used for Him who sits on it; cf. *thrones* (Col. 1:16). He is called a "sanctuary" to His people (Isa. 8:14; Ezek. 11:16). So *Syriac* and *Arabic*. **13. me**—"Jehovah." Though "Thee" precedes. This sudden transition is usual in the prophetic style, owing to the prophet's continual realization of Jehovah's presence. **all that forsake thee**—(Ps. 73:27; Isa. 1:28.) **written in the earth**—in the dust, i.e., shall be consigned to oblivion. So Jesus' significant writing "on the ground" (probably the accusers' names) (John 8:6). Names written in the dust are obliterated by a very slight wind. Their hopes and celebrity are wholly *in the earth*, not in the heavenly book of life (Rev. 13:8; 20:12, 15). The Jews, though boasting that they were the people of God, had no portion in heaven, no status before God and His angels. Contrast "written in heaven," i.e., in the muster-roll of its blessed citizens (Luke 10:20). Also, contrast "written in a book," and "in the rock *for ever*" (Job 19:23, 24). **living waters**—(ch. 2:13). **14-18.** Prayer of the prophet for deliverance from the enemies whom he excited by his faithful denunciations. **Heal . . . save**—not only *make me whole* (as to the evils of soul as well as body which I am exposed to by contact with ungodly foes, ch, 15:18), but *keep me so*.

ADAM CLARKE

9. *The heart is deceitful. Akob halleb*, "The heart is supplanting—tortuous—full of windings—insidious."

And desperately wicked. And is "wretched" or "feeble"; distressed beyond all things, in consequence of the wickedness that is in it. *Who can know it?* It even hides itself from itself, so that its owner does not know it. A corrupt heart is the worst enemy the fallen creature can have.

10. *I the Lord search the heart*. The Lord is called by His apostles, Acts i. 24, the Knower of the heart. To Him alone can this epithet be applied; and it is from Him alone that we can derive that instruction by which we can in any measure know ourselves.

11. *As the partridge. Kore*. It is very likely that this was a bird different from our partridge. The text Dr. Blayney translates thus: "(As) the koré that hatcheth what it doth not lay, (so is) he who getteth riches, and not according to right." *And at his end shall be a fool*. Shall be reputed as such. He was a fool all the way through; he lost his soul to get wealth, and this wealth he never enjoyed.

13. *Written in the earth*. They shall never come to true honor. Their names shall be written in the dust, and the first wind that blows over it shall render it illegible.

14. *Heal me . . . and I shall be healed*. That is, I shall be thoroughly healed, and effectually saved, if Thou undertake for me.

MATTHEW HENRY

my praise (so some read it); heal me, and save me, and thou shalt have the glory of it.

IV. He complains of the infidelity and daring impiety of the people to whom he preached. He had faithfully delivered God's message to them: and what answer has he to return to him that sent him? *Behold, they say unto me, Where is the word of the Lord? Let it come now, v.* 15; Isa. v. 19. They bantered the prophet. They denied the truth of what he said: "If that be the *word of the Lord* which thou speakest to us, *where is it*? Why is it not fulfilled?" They defied what he said. "Let God Almighty do his worst; let all he has said come to pass; we shall do well enough; the lion is not so fierce as he is painted," Amos v. 18.

V. He appeals to God concerning his faithful discharge of the duty to which he was called, *v.* 16. He continued constant to his work. His office, instead of being his protection, exposed him to contempt, and injury. "Yet," says he, "*I have not hastened from being a pastor after thee;* I have not left my work." Such a pastor Jeremiah was; and, though he met with as much difficulty and discouragement as ever any man did, yet he did not fly off as Jonah did, nor desire to be excused from going any more on God's errands. He kept up his affection to the people. Though they were very abusive to him, he was compassionate to them: *I have not desired the woeful day.* The day of the accomplishment of his prophecies would be a woeful day indeed to Jerusalem, and therefore he wished it might never come. God does not, and therefore ministers must not, desire the death of sinners, but rather that they may turn and live. He kept closely to his instructions. Though he might have curried favour with the people, if he had not been so sharp in his reproofs, yet he would deliver his message faithfully.

VI. He humbly begs God that he would own him, and protect him, and carry him on cheerfully in that work to which he had so plainly called him. Two things he here desires: 1. That he might have comfort in serving the God that sent him (*v.* 17): *Be not thou a terror to me.* He pleads, "*Thou art my hope;* and then nothing else is my fear. My dependence is upon thee; and therefore *be not a terror to me.*" 2. That he might have courage in dealing with the people to whom he was sent, *v.* 18. Those persecute him who should have entertained and encouraged him. "Lord," says he, "*let them be confounded* (let them be ashamed of their obstinacy, or else let the judgments threatened be at length executed upon them), *but let not me be confounded,* let not me be terrified by their menaces, so as to betray my trust." As to his persecutors, he prays, *Bring upon them the day of evil,* in hope that the bringing of it upon them might prevent the bringing of it upon the country.

Verses 19–27

These verses are a sermon concerning sabbath-sanctification. This message concerning the sabbath was probably sent in the days of Josiah, for the furtherance of that work of reformation which he set on foot. It must be proclaimed at the court-gate first, the gate *by which the kings of Judah come in and go out, v.* 19. Let them be told their duty first; for, if sabbaths be not sanctified *the rulers of Judah are to be contended with,* for they are certainly wanting in their duty. He must also preach it *in all the gates of Jerusalem.* It is a matter of great and general concern; therefore let all take notice of it.

I. How the sabbath is to be sanctified, and what is the law concerning it, *v.* 21, 22. They must rest from their worldly employment on the sabbath day. They must *bear no burden* into the city nor out of it; husbandmen's burdens of corn must not be carried in, nor manure carried out; nor tradesmen's burdens, nor merchandise. There must not a loaded horse, or cart, or waggon, be seen on the sabbath day in the streets or the roads; the porters must not ply on that day, nor must the servants be suffered to fetch in provisions or fuel. It is a day of rest, and must not be made a day of labour, unless in case of necessity. "*Hallow you the sabbath,* that is, consecrate it to the honour of God and spend it in his service and worship." Worldly business must be laid aside, that we may be intent upon that work which requires and deserves the whole man. "*Take heed to yourselves,* for it is at your peril if you rob God of that part of your time which he has reserved to himself." Let not the soul be burdened with the cares of this world on sabbath days. "This is no new imposition upon you, but is what *I commanded your fathers.*"

II. How the sabbath had been profaned (*v.* 23): "Your fathers were required to keep holy the sabbath day, *but they obeyed not*; they *hardened their necks* against this as well as other commands that were given them." Where sabbaths are neglected all religion sensibly goes to decay.

JAMIESON, FAUSSET, BROWN

my praise—He whom I have to praise for past favors, and therefore to whom alone I look for the time to come.

15. Where is the word?—(Isa. 5: 19; Amos 5:18). Where is the fulfilment of the threats which thou didst utter as from God? A characteristic of the last stage of apostasy (II Peter 3:4).

16. I have not refused Thy call of me to be a prophet (Jonah 1:3), however painful to me it was to utter what would be sure to irritate the hearers (ch. 1:4, etc.); therefore Thou shouldest not forsake me (ch. 15:15, etc.). **to follow thee**—lit., "after thee"; as an under-pastor following Thee, the Chief Shepherd (Eccles. 12:11; I Peter 5:4).

neither . . . desired—I have not *wished* for the day of calamity, though I foretell it as about to come on my countrymen; therefore they have no reason for persecuting me. **thou knowest**—I appeal to Thee for the truth of what I assert. **that which came out of my lips**—my words (Deut. 23:23). *right* **before thee**—rather, "was before Thee"; was *known to Thee*—(Prov. 5:21).

17. a terror—viz., by deserting me: all I fear is Thine abandoning me; if Thou art with me, I have no fear of evil from enemies. **18. destroy . . . destruction**—"break them with a double breach," *Hebrew* (ch. 14:17). On "double," see *Note,* ch. 16:18.

19-27. Delivered in the reign of Jehoiakim, who undid the good effected by Josiah's reformation, especially as to the observance of the Sabbath [EICHHORN]. **gate of . . . children of . . . people**—The gate next the king's palace, **called** *the gate of David,* **and** *the gate of the people,* **from its** being the principal thoroughfare: now the Jaffa gate. It is probably the same as "the gate of the fountain" at the foot of Zion, near which were the king's garden and pool (ch. 39:4; II Kings 25:4; Neh. 2:14; 3:15; 12:37). **20. kings**—He begins with the kings, as they ought to have repressed such a glaring profanation. **21. Take heed to yourselves**—lit., to your souls. MAURER explains, "as ye love your lives"; a phrase used here to give the greater weight to the command.

sabbath—The non-observance of it was a chief cause of the captivity, the number of years of the latter, seventy, being exactly made to agree with the number of Sabbaths which elapsed during the 490 years of their possession of Canaan from Saul to their removal (Lev. 26:34, 35; II Chron. 36:21). On the restoration, therefore, stress was especially laid on Sabbath observance (Neh. 13:19). **Jerusalem**—It would have been scandalous anywhere; but in the capital, *Jerusalem,* it was an open insult to God. Sabbath-hallowing is intended as a symbol of holiness in general (Ezek. 20:12); therefore much stress is laid on it; the Jews' gross impiety is manifested in their setting God's will at naught, in the case of such an easy and positive command. **23.** (Ch. 7:24, 26.)

ADAM CLARKE

15. *Where is the word of the Lord?* Where is the accomplishment of His threatenings? You have said that the city and the Temple should both be destroyed. No such events have yet taken place. But they did take place, and every tittle of the menace was strictly fulfilled.

16. *I have not hastened from being a pastor.* Dr. Blayney translates thus: "But I have not been in haste to outrun thy guidance." I was obliged to utter Thy prediction, but I have not hastened the evil day. For the credit of my prophecy I have not desired the calamity to come speedily; I have rather pleaded for respite.

17. *Be not a terror unto me.* Do not command me to predict miseries, and abandon me to them and to my enemies.

18. *Let them be confounded.* They shall be confounded. These words are to be understood as simple predictions, rather than prayers.

19. *The gate of the children of the people.* I suppose the most public gate is meant, that through which there was the greatest thoroughfare.

21. *Take heed to yourselves, and bear no burden.* From this and the following verses we find the ruin of the Jews attributed to the breach of the Sabbath; as this led to a neglect of sacrifice, the ordinances of religion, and all public worship, so it necessarily brought with it all immorality. This breach of the Sabbath was that which let in upon them all the waters of God's wrath.

MATTHEW HENRY

III. What blessings God had in store for them if they would make conscience of sabbath-sanctification, *v.* 24-26. The court shall flourish. *Kings* in succession, with the other *princes* that *sit upon the thrones* of judgment, shall ride in great pomp *through the gates of Jerusalem*. The city shall flourish. Jerusalem, *the holy city, shall remain for ever, shall for ever be inhabited*, shall not be destroyed and dispeopled, as is threatened. The country shall flourish: *The cities of Judah and the land of Benjamin* shall be replenished with vast numbers of inhabitants, abounding in plenty and living in peace. The church shall flourish: *Meat-offerings, and incense, and sacrifices of praise*, shall be brought *to the house of the Lord*. A people truly flourish when religion flourishes among them. And this is the effect of sabbath-sanctification; when that branch of religion is kept up other instances of it are kept up likewise; but, when that is lost, devotion is lost either in superstition or in profaneness. The streams of all religion run either deep or shallow according as the banks of the sabbath are kept up or neglected.

IV. What judgments they must expect would come upon them if they persisted in the profanation of the sabbath (*v.* 27): "*If you will not hearken to me* in this matter, to keep the gates shut on sabbath days, so that there may be no unnecessary *entering in*, or going out, on that day—if you will break through the enclosure of the divine law, and lay that day in common with other days—know that God will *kindle a fire in the gates* of your city." Justly shall those gates be fired that are not used as they ought to be to shut out sin and to keep people in to an attendance on their duty.

JAMIESON, FAUSSET, BROWN

24. A part put for the whole, "If ye keep the Sabbath and *My* other *laws*." **25. kings . . . in chariots**—The kingdom at this time had been brought so low that this promise here was a special favor. **remain**—*Hebrew*, be inhabited (vs. 6; Isa. 13:20). **26. plain . . . mountains . . . south**—(Josh. 15:1-4). The southern border had extended to the river of Egypt, but was now much curtailed by Egyptian invasions (II Chron. 35:20; 36:3, 4). The *Hebrew* for "south" means *dry;* the arid desert *south* of Judea is meant. The enumeration of all the parts of Judea, city, country, plain, hill, and desert, implies that no longer shall there be aught wanting of the integrity of the Jewish land (Zech. 7:7). **sacrifices**—As in vs. 22, one constituent of Judea's prosperity is mentioned, viz., its *kings* on David's throne, the pledge of God being its guardian; so in this verse another constituent, viz., its *priests*, a pledge of God being propitious to it (Ps. 107:22).

27. burden . . . in . . . gates . . . fire in the gates—retribution answering to the sin. The scene of their sin shall be the scene of their punishment (ch. 52:13; II Kings 25:9).

ADAM CLARKE

24. *If ye diligently hearken unto me.* So we find that, though their destruction was positively threatened, yet still there was an unexpressed proviso that, if they did return to the Lord, the calamities should be averted, and a succession of princes would have been continued on the throne of David, vv. 25-26.

MATTHEW HENRY

CHAPTER 18

Verses 1–10

The prophet is here sent to *the potter's house*, not to preach a sermon, but to prepare a sermon, or rather to receive it ready prepared. "*Go to the potter's house*, and observe how he manages his work, and there *I will cause thee*, by silent whispers, *to hear my words*. There thou shalt receive a message, to be delivered to the people." The prophet therefore went to the potter's house (*v.* 3) and took notice how he *wrought his work upon the wheels*. And (*v.* 4) when a lump of clay that he designed to form into one shape either proved too stiff, or had a stone in it, or came to be *marred in his hand*, he presently turned it into another shape; just *as seems good to the potter*. Ministers will make a good use of their converse with the business and affairs of this life if they learn thereby to speak more plainly and familiarly to people about the things of God, and to expound scripture comparisons. While Jeremiah looks carefully upon the potter's work, God darts into his mind these two great truths, which he must preach to *the house of Israel*:

I. That God has both an incontestable authority and an irresistible ability to form and fashion kingdoms and nations as he pleases to serve his own purposes. *Cannot I do with you as this potter, saith the Lord? v.* 6. God has a clearer title to a dominion over us than the potter has over the clay; for the potter only gives it its form, whereas we have both matter and form from God. This intimates that God has an incontestable sovereignty over us, and that it would be as absurd for us to dispute this as for the clay to quarrel with the potter. It is a very easy thing with God to make what use he pleases of us. One turn of the hand, one turn of the wheel, quite alters the shape of the clay, makes it a vessel, unmakes it, new-makes it. Thus are our times in God's hand. It is spoken here of nations. See this explained by Job (*ch.* xii. 23), Ps. cvii. 33, &c., and compare Job xxxiv. 29. If the potter's vessel be marred for one use, it shall serve for another; those that will not be monuments of mercy shall be monuments of justice. God formed us out of the clay (Job xxxiii. 6), and we are still as clay in his hands (Isa. lxiv. 8).

II. That, in the exercise of this authority and ability, he goes by fixed rules of equity and goodness. He dispenses favours indeed in a way of sovereignty, but never punishes by arbitrary power. In ways of judgment we may be sure that it is for our sins—national repentance will stop the progress of the judgments (*v.* 7, 8): *If God speak concerning a nation to pluck up* its fences that secure it, its fruit-trees that enrich it, pull down its fortifications, and so *destroy it* as either a vineyard or a city is destroyed—in this case, if *that nation* repent of their sins and reform their lives, turn every one from his evil way and return to God, God will return in mercy to them. It is an undoubted truth that a sincere conversion from the evil of sin will be an effectual prevention of

JAMIESON, FAUSSET, BROWN

CHAPTER 18

VSS. 1-23. GOD, AS THE SOLE SOVEREIGN, HAS AN ABSOLUTE RIGHT TO DEAL WITH NATIONS ACCORDING TO THEIR CONDUCT TOWARDS HIM; ILLUSTRATED IN A TANGIBLE FORM BY THE POTTER'S MOULDING OF VESSELS FROM CLAY. **2. go down**—viz., from the high ground on which the temple stood, near which Jeremiah exercised his prophetic office, to the low ground, where some well-known (this is the force of "the") potter had his workshop. **3. wheels**—lit., "on *both stones*." The potter's horizontal lathe consisted of two round plates, the lower one larger, the upper smaller; of stone originally, but afterwards of wood. On the upper the potter moulded the clay into what shapes he pleased. They are found represented in Egyptian remains. In Exodus 1:16 alone is the *Hebrew* word found elsewhere, but in a different sense. **4. marred**—spoiled. "*Of* clay" is the true reading, which was corrupted into "*as* clay" (*Margin*), through the similarity of the two *Hebrew* letters, and from vs. 6, "*as* the clay."

6. Refuting the Jews' reliance on their external privileges as God's elect people, as if God could never cast them off. But if the potter, a mere creature, has power to throw away a marred vessel and raise up other clay from the ground, a fortiori God, the Creator, can cast away the people who prove unfaithful to His election and can raise others in their stead (cf. Isa. 45:9; 64:8; Rom. 9:20, 21). It is curious that the *potter's field* should have been the purchase made with the price of Judas' treachery (Matt. 27:9, 10: a potter's vessel dashed to pieces, cf. Ps. 2:8, 9; Rev. 2:27), because of its failing to answer the maker's design, being the very image to depict God's sovereign power to give reprobates to destruction, not by caprice, but in the exercise of His righteous judgment. Matthew quotes Zechariah's words (Zech. 11:12, 13) *as Jeremiah's* because the latter (chs. 18, 19) was the source from which the former derived his summary in ch. 11:12, 13 [HENGSTENBERG]. **7. At what instant**—in a moment, when the nation least expects it. Hereby he reminds the Jews how marvellously God had delivered them from their original degradation, i.e., In one and the same day ye were the most wretched, and then the most favored of all people [CALVIN]. **8. their evil**—in antithesis to, "the evil that *I* thought to do." **repent**—God herein adapts Himself to human conceptions. The change is not in God, but in the circumstances which regulate God's dealings: just as we say the land recedes from us when we sail forth, whereas it is we who recede from the land (Ezek. 18:21; 33:11).

ADAM CLARKE

CHAPTER 18

1. *The word which came to Jeremiah.* This discourse is supposed to have been delivered sometime in the reign of Jehoiakim, probably within the first three years.

2. *Go down to the potter's house.* By this similitude God shows the absolute state of dependence on himself in which He has placed mankind. They are as clay in the hands of the potter; and in reference to everything here below, He can shape their destinies as He pleases. Again, though while under the providential care of God they may go morally astray and pervert themselves, yet they can be reclaimed by the almighty and all-wise Operator, and become such vessels as seemeth good for Him to make. In considering this parable we must take heed that in running parallels we do not destroy the free agency of man, nor disgrace the goodness and supremacy of God.

4. *The vessel . . . was marred in the hand of the potter.* It did not stand in the working; it got out of shape; or some gravel or small stone, having been incorporated with the mass of clay, made a breach in that part where it was found, so that the potter was obliged to knead up the clay afresh, place it on the wheel, and form it anew; and then it was such a vessel as seemed good to the potter to make it.

6. *Cannot I do with you as this potter?* Have I not a right to do with a people whom I have created as reason and justice may require? If they do not answer My intentions, may I not reject and destroy them; and act as this potter, make a new vessel out of that which at first did not succeed in his hands?

7-10. *At what instant I shall speak concerning a nation.* These verses contain what may be called God's decree by which the whole of His conduct towards man is regulated. If He purpose destruction against an offending person, if that person repent and turn to God, he shall live and not die.

MATTHEW HENRY

the evil of punishment; and God can as easily raise up a penitent people from their ruins as the potter can make anew the vessel of clay when it was *marred in his hand*. When God is coming towards us in ways of mercy, if any stop be given to the progress of that mercy, it is nothing but sin that gives it (*v.* 9, 10). Sin is the great mischief-maker between God and a people; it forfeits the benefit of his promises and spoils the success of their prayers. It defeats his kind intentions concerning them (Hos. vii. 1).

Verses 11–17

The application of the general truths laid down in the foregoing part of the chapter to the Jews.

I. "*Go, and tell* them" (saith God), "*Behold, I frame evil against you and devise a device against you.* Providence in all its operations is plainly working towards your ruin."

II. He invites them by repentance and reformation to meet him and so to prevent his further proceedings against them: "*Return you now everyone from his evil ways*, that so God may turn from the evil he had purposed to do unto you, and that providence which seemed to be framed like a vessel on the wheel against you shall immediately be thrown into a new shape, and the issue shall be in favour of you."

III. He foresees their obstinacy, and their perverse refusal (*v.* 12): *They said*, "*There is no hope*. We may even despair of ever being delivered, for we are resolved that *we will walk after our own devices*. It is to no purpose for the prophets to say any more to us; *we will do everyone the imagination of his* own *evil heart*, and will not be under the restraint of the divine law." They call it liberty to live at large; whereas for a man to be a slave to his lusts is the worst of slaveries.

IV. He upbraids them with the monstrous folly of their obstinacy, and their hating to be reformed (*v.* 13): *Ask you among the heathen*, even those that had not the benefit of divine revelation, no oracles, no prophets. *Who hath heard such a thing?* The Ninevites, when thus warned, turned from their evil ways. But *the virgin of Israel* bids defiance to repentance, whatever conscience and Providence say to the contrary, and thus *has done a horrible thing*. She should have preserved herself pure and chaste for God, who had espoused her to himself; but she has alienated herself from him, and refuses to return to him. Wilful impenitence is the grossest self-murder; and that is *a horrible thing*.

V. He shows their folly in two things:

1. In the nature of the sin itself: they forsook God for idols (*v.* 14, 15): *Will a* thirsty traveller *leave the snow*, which, being melted, runs down from the mountains *of Lebanon*, and, passing over *the rock of the field*, flows in clear, clean, crystal streams? Will he pass these by, and think to better himself with some dirty puddle-water? *Or shall the cold flowing waters that come from any other place be forsaken* in the heat of summer? When men are parched with heat and drought, and meet with cooling refreshing streams, they will make use of them. The margin reads it, "*Will a man* that is travelling the road *leave my fields*, which are plain and level, *for a rock*, which is rough and hard, *or for the snow of Lebanon*, which, lying in great drifts, makes the road impassable? *Or shall the running waters be forsaken for the strange cold waters?* But *my people have forgotten me* (*v.* 15), have quitted *a fountain of living waters for broken cisterns. They have burnt incense to* idols that are not what they pretend to be nor can perform what is expected from them." They left *the ancient paths*, appointed by the divine law, walked in by all the saints, therefore the right way to their journey's end, a safe way. But, when they were advised to keep to the good old way, they positively said that they would not, *ch.* vi. 16. They chose by-paths; they walked *in a way not cast up*, not in the highway, the King's highway. Such was the way of idolatry.

2. In the mischievous consequences of it. The direct tendency of it was *to make their land desolate, and*, consequently, themselves miserable. *Everyone that passes by* their land shall make his remarks upon it, and *shall be astonished, and wag his head*, some wondering, others commiserating, others triumphing in the desolations of a country that had been *the glory of all lands. Their land* being made *desolate*, in pursuance of their destruction, it is threatened (*v.* 17), *I will scatter them as with an east wind*, fierce and violent. That which completes their misery is, *I will show them the back, and not the face, in the day of their calamity*. Our calamities may be easily borne if God look towards us, and smile upon us, but if he turn *the back* upon us, if he show himself displeased, if he leave us to ourselves, we are quite undone.

JAMIESON, FAUSSET, BROWN

God's unchangeable principle is to do the best that can be done under all circumstances; if then He did not take into account the moral change in His people (their prayers, etc.), He would not be acting according to His own unchanging principle (vss. 9, 10). This is applied practically to the Jews' case (vs. 11; see ch. 26:3; Jonah 3:10).

11. frame evil—alluding to the preceding image of "the potter," i.e., I, Jehovah, am now as it were the potter *framing* evil against you; but in the event of your repenting, it is in My power to *frame anew* My course of dealing towards you. **return . . .**—(II Kings 17:13). **12. no hope**—Thy threats and exhortations are all thrown away (ch. 2:25). Our case is desperate; we are hopelessly abandoned to our sins and their penalty. In this and the following clauses, "We will walk after our own devices," Jeremiah makes them express the *real* state of the case, rather than the hypocritical subterfuges which *they* would have been inclined to put forth. So Isaiah 30:10, 11. **13.** (Ch. 2:10, 11.) Even among the heathen it was a thing unheard of, that a nation should lay aside its gods for foreign gods, though their gods are false gods. But Israel forsook the true God for foreign false gods. **virgin of Israel**—(II Kings 19:21). It enhances their guilt, that Israel was *the virgin* whom God had specially betrothed to Him. **horrible thing**—(ch. 5:30). **14.** Is there any man (living near it) who would leave the snow of Lebanon (i.e., the cool melted snow-water of Lebanon, as he presently explains), which cometh from the rock of the field (a poetical name for Lebanon, which towers aloft above the surrounding *field*, or comparatively plain country)? None. Yet Israel forsakes Jehovah, the living fountain close at hand, for foreign broken cisterns. Ch. 17:13; 2:13, accord with *English Version* here. MAURER translates, "Shall the snow of Lebanon *cease* from the rock *to water* (lit., forsake) My fields" (the whole land around being peculiarly *Jehovah's*)? *Lebanon* means the "white mountain"; so called from the perpetual snow which covers that part called Hermon, stretching northeast of Palestine. **that come from another place**—that come from far, viz., from the distant lofty rocks of Lebanon. HENDERSON translates, "the *compressed* waters," viz., contracted within a narrow channel while descending through the gorges of the rocks; "flowing" may in this view be rather "flowing down" (Song of Sol. 4:15). But the parallelism in *English Version* is better, "which cometh from the rock," "that cometh from another place." **be forsaken**—answering to the parallel, "Will a man leave . . . ." MAURER translates, "dry up," or "fail" (Isa. 19:5); the sense thus being, Will nature ever turn aside from its fixed course? The "cold waters" (cf. Prov. 25:25) refer to the perennial streams, fed from the partial melting of the snow in the hot weather. **15. Because**—rather, "And yet"; in defiance of the natural order of things. **forgotten me**—(ch. 2:32). This implies a previous knowledge of God, whereas He was unknown to the Gentiles; the Jews' forgetting of God, therefore, arose from determined perversity. **they have caused . . . to stumble**—viz., the false prophets and idolatrous priests have. **ancient paths**—(ch. 6:16): the paths which their pious ancestors trod. Not antiquity indiscriminately, but the example of the fathers who trod the right way, is here commended. **them**—the Jews. **not cast up**—not duly prepared: referring to the raised center of the road. CALVIN translates, "not trodden." They had no precedent of former saints to induce them to devise for themselves a new worship. **16. hissing**—(I Kings 9:8). In sign of contempt. That which was to be only the *event* is ascribed to the *purpose* of the people, although altogether different from what they would have been likely to hope for. Their *purpose* is represented as being the destruction of their country, because it was the *inevitable result* of their course of acting. **wag . . . head**—in mockery (II Kings 19:21; Matt. 27:39). As "wag . . . head" answers to "hissing," so "astonished" answers to "desolate," for which, therefore, MUNSTER and others rather translate, "an object of wonder" (ch. 19:8). **17. as with an east wind**—lit., "I will scatter them, *as an east wind*" (scatters all before it): a most violent wind (Job 27:21; Ps. 48:7; Isa. 27:8). Thirty-two MSS. read (without *as*), "*with* an east wind." **I will show them the back . . . not . . . face**—just retribution: as "they turned their back unto Me . . . not their face" (ch. 2:27).

ADAM CLARKE

12. *There is no hope.* See chap. ii. 25.

14. *Will a man leave the snow of Lebanon?* Lebanon was the highest mountain in Judea. Would any man in his senses abandon a farm that was always watered by the melted snows of Lebanon, and take a barren rock in its place? How stupid therefore and absurd are My people, who abandon the everlasting God for the worship of idols!

16. *A perpetual hissing.* A "shrieking, hissing"; an expression of contempt.

MATTHEW HENRY

Verses 18–23

The prophet here brings in his own affairs, for instruction to us.

I. The common methods of the persecutors, Jeremiah's enemies, *v.* 18.

1. They laid their heads together to consult what they should do against him, both to be revenged on him for what he had said and to stop his mouth for the future: *They said, Come and let us devise devices against Jeremiah,* not only against his person, but against the word he delivered to them.

2. Herein they pretended a mighty zeal for the church, which, they suggested, was in danger if Jeremiah was tolerated to preach as he did: "*Come,*" say they, "let us silence and crush him, *for the law shall not perish from the priest; the law of truth is in their mouths* (Mal. ii. 6) and there we will seek it; the administration of ordinances according to the law is in their hands, and neither the one nor the other shall be wrested from them." Two things they insinuated: (1) That Jeremiah could not be himself a true prophet, but was a pretender, because he neither was commissioned by the priests nor concurred with the other prophets. (2) That the matter of his prophecies could not be from God, because it reflected sometimes upon the prophets and priests (*ch.* v. 31), deceiving the people (*ch.* xiv. 14). He had foretold that their *heart should perish,* and *be astonished* (*ch.* iv. 9), that *the wise men should be dismayed* (*ch.* viii. 9, 10), that the priests and prophets should be intoxicated, *ch.* xiii. 13.

3. They agreed to do all they could to blast his reputation: *Come, let us smite him with the tongue.*

4. To set others an example, they resolved that they would not themselves regard anything he said. *Let us not give heed to any of his words;* for, right or wrong, they will look upon them to be *his words,* and not the words of God.

5. That they may effectually silence him, they resolve to be the death of him (*v.* 23): *All their counsel against me is to slay me.* They *hunt for the precious life.*

II. The common relief of the persecuted. This we may see in the course that Jeremiah took. He immediately applied to his God by prayer.

1. He referred himself and his cause to God's cognizance, *v.* 19. They would not regard a word he said, would not admit his complaints, nor take any notice of his grievances; but, *Lord* (says he), *do thou give heed to me.* Hear the voice of my contenders, how noisy and clamorous they are, how false and malicious all they say is, and let them be *judged out of their own mouth; cause their own tongues to fall upon them.*"

2. He complains of their base ingratitude to him (*v.* 20): "*Shall evil be recompensed for good,* and shall it go unpunished? Wilt not thou recompense me good for that evil?" *They have dug a pit for my soul;* they aimed to take away his life in a base, cowardly, clandestine way: *they dug pits for* him, which there was no fence against, Ps. cxix. 85. But how great the good he had done for them: *Remember that I stood before thee to speak good for them;* he had been an intercessor with God for them. But it was not strange that those who had forgotten their God did not know their best friends. It was very grievous to him, as the like was to David. Ps. xxxv. 13; cix. 4, *For my love they are my adversaries.* Thus do sinners deal with the great intercessor, crucifying him afresh, and speaking against him on earth, while his blood is speaking for them in heaven. It was a comfort to the prophet that, when they were so spiteful against him, he had the testimony of his conscience that he had done his duty to them.

3. He imprecates the judgments of God upon them, not from a revengeful disposition, but in indignation against their wickedness, *v.* 21–23. He prays, (1) That their families might be starved for want of bread. (2) That they might be cut off *by the sword* of war. (3) That the terrors and desolations of war might seize them suddenly and by surprise, that thus their punishment might answer to their sin (*v.* 22). (4) That they might be dealt with according to the desert of this sin, which was without excuse. (5) That God's wrath against them might be their ruin: *Let them be overthrown before thee.* Now this is not written for our imitation. Jeremiah was a prophet, and by the impulse of the spirit of prophecy, in the foresight of the ruin certainly coming upon his persecutors, might pray such prayers as we may not; our Master has taught us, by his precept and pattern, to *bless those that curse us and pray for those that despitefully use us.*

JAMIESON, FAUSSET, BROWN

18. (Ch. 11:19.) Let us bring a capital charge against him, as a false prophet; "for (whereas he foretells that this land shall be left without priests to teach the law, Malachi 2:7; without scribes to explain its difficulties; and without prophets to reveal God's will), the law shall not perish from the prophet . . ."; since God has made these a lasting institution in His church, and the law declares they shall never perish (Lev. 6:18; 10:11; cf. ch. 5:12) [GROTIUS].

the wise—scribes and elders joined to the priests. Perhaps they mean to say, we must have right on our side, in spite of Jeremiah's words against us and our prophets (ch. 28:15, 16; 29:25, 32; 5:31); "for the law shall not perish . . . ." I prefer GROTIUS' explanation. **with . . . tongue**—by a false accusation (Ps. 57:4; 64:3; 12:4; 50:19). "For the tongue" (*Margin*), i.e., for his speaking against us. "In the tongue," i.e., let us kill him, that he may speak no more against us [CASTALIO].

19. Give heed—contrasted with, "let us not give heed" (vs. 18). As *they* give no heed to me, do Thou, O Lord, give heed to me, and let my words at least have their weight with Thee.

20. In the particulars here specified, Jeremiah was a type of Jesus Christ (Ps. 109:4, 5; John 15:25). **my soul**—my life; me (Ps. 35:7). **I stood before thee . . . to turn away thy wrath**—so Moses (Ps. 106:23; cf. Ezek. 22:30). So Jesus Christ, the antitype of previous partial intercessors (Isa. 59:16).

21. pour out their blood by the force of the sword—lit., "by the hands of the sword." So Ezekiel 35:5. MAURER with JEROME translates, "*deliver them* over to the power of the sword." But cf. Psalm 63:10, *Margin;* Isaiah 53:12. In this prayer he does not indulge in personal revenge, as if it were his own cause that was at stake; but he speaks under the dictation of the Spirit, ceasing to intercede, and speaking prophetically, knowing they were doomed to destruction as reprobates; for those not so, he doubtless ceased not to intercede. *We* are not to draw an example from this, which is a special case. **put to death**—or, as in ch. 15:2, "perish by the *death-plague*" [MAURER]. **men . . . young men**—HORSLEY distinguishes the former as *married men* past middle age; the latter, the flower of *unmarried youth.* **22. cry**—by reason of the enemy bursting in: let their houses be no shelter to them in their calamities [CALVIN]. **digged . . . pit**—(V. 20; Ps. 57:6; 119:85). **23. forgive not**—(Ps. 109:9, 10, 14). **blot out**—image from an account book (Rev. 20:12). **before thee**—Hypocrites suppose God is not near, so long as they escape punishment; but when He punishes, they are said to stand before Him, because they can no longer flatter themselves they can escape His eye (cf. Ps. 90:8). **deal thus**—exert Thy power against them [MAURER]. **time of thine anger**—Though He seems to tarry, His time shall come at last (Eccles. 8:11, 12; II Peter 3:9, 10).

ADAM CLARKE

18. *Come, and let us devise devices.* Let us form a conspiracy against him, accuse him of being a false prophet, and a contradicter of the words of God; for God has promised us protection, and *he* says we shall be destroyed, and that God will forsake His people.

Let us smite him with the tongue. On the tongue; so it should be rendered. Lying and false testimony are punished in the Eastern countries, to the present day, by smiting the person on the mouth with a strong piece of leather like the sole of a shoe.

20. *They have digged a pit for my soul.* For my "life." *Stood before thee to speak good for them.* I was their continual intercessor.

21. *Therefore deliver up their children.* The execrations in these verses should be considered as simply prophetic declarations of the judgments which God was about to pour out on them.

MATTHEW HENRY

CHAPTER 19

Verses 1–9

The prophet is here sent with a message he had often delivered.

I. He must take of the elders and chief men, both in church and state, to be his auditors and witnesses to what he said—*the ancients of the people and the ancients of the priests.* Though the generality of the elders were disaffected to him, yet it is likely that there were some few who looked upon him as a prophet of the Lord, and would pay this respect to the heavenly vision.

II. He must *go to the valley of the son of Hinnom,* and deliver this message there; for *the word of the Lord* is not bound to any one place; as good a sermon may be preached in the valley of Tophet as in the gate of the temple. Christ preached on a mountain and out of a ship. This sermon must be preached in *the valley of the son of Hinnom,* 1. Because there they had been guilty of the vilest of their idolatries, the sacrificing of their children to Moloch. The sight of the place might serve to remind them. 2. Because there they should feel the sorest of their calamities; and, it being the common sink of the city, let them see what a miserable spectacle this magnificent city would be when it should be all like the valley of Tophet. God bids him *proclaim there the words that I shall tell thee,* when thou comest thither. God's messages were frequently not revealed to the prophets before they were to deliver them.

III. He must give general notice of a general ruin now shortly coming upon Judah and Jerusalem, *v.* 3. *Hear you the word of the Lord,* though it be a terrible word. Both rulers and ruled must attend to it; the *kings of Judah,* the king and his sons, the king and his privy-counsellors, must hear the word of the King of kings, for, high as they are, he is above them. The *inhabitants of Jerusalem* also must hear what God has to say to them. Both princes and people have contributed to the national guilt and must concur in the national repentance, or they will both share in the national ruin. The ruin of Eli's house is thus described (1 Sam. iii. 11), and of Jerusalem, 2 Kings xxi. 12.

IV. He must plainly tell them what their sins were, *v.* 4, 5. They are charged with apostasy from God (*They have forsaken me*) and abuse of the privileges of the visible church, with which they had been dignified—*They have estranged this place.* He charges them with an affection for and the adoration of false *gods,* such as *neither they nor their fathers have known.* They took them at a venture for their gods; being fond of change and novelty, they liked them the better and new fashions in religion were as grateful to their fancies as in other things. They also stand charged with murder, wilful murder, from malice prepense: *They have filled this place with the blood of innocents.* As if idolatry and murder, committed separately, were not bad enough, they have consolidated them into one complicated crime, that of burning their children in the fire to Baal (*v.* 5).

V. He must endeavour to affect them with the greatness of the desolation that was coming upon them. He must tell them that this *valley of the son of Hinnom* shall acquire a new name, *the valley of slaughter* (*v.* 6), for (*v.* 7) multitudes shall *fall* there *by the sword,* when either they sally out upon the besiegers and are repulsed or attempt to make their escape and are seized. And as for those that remain within the city, and will not capitulate with the besiegers, they shall perish for want of food, when first they have eaten *the flesh of their sons and daughters* and dearest *friends,* through the *straitness wherewith their enemies shall straiten them, v.* 9. And, *lastly,* the whole *city* shall be *desolate.* That place which holiness had made *the joy of the whole earth* sin had made the reproach and shame of the whole earth.

VI. He must assure them that all their attempts to prevent and avoid this ruin, so long as they continued impenitent and unreformed, would be fruitless and vain (*v.* 7): *I will make void the counsel of Judah and Jerusalem in this place.* There is no fleeing from God's justice but by fleeing to his mercy.

Verses 10–15

The message delivered in the foregoing verses is here enforced.

I. By a visible sign. The prophet was to take along with him an *earthen bottle* (*v.* 1), and, when he had delivered his message, he was to *break the bottle* to pieces (*v.* 10). He had compared this people, in the chapter before, to the potter's clay, which is easily marred in the making. But some might say, "It is past that with us; we have been made and hardened long since." "And what though you be," says he, "the potter's vessel is as soon broken in the hand of

JAMIESON, FAUSSET, BROWN

CHAPTER 19

Vss. 1-15. The Desolation of the Jews for Their Sins Foretold in the Valley of Hinnom; the Symbol of Breaking a Bottle. Referred by Maurer, etc., to the beginning of Zedekiah's reign. **1. bottle**—*Hebrew, bakuk,* so called from the gurgling sound which it makes when being emptied. **ancients**—elders. As witnesses of the symbolic action (vs. 10; Isa. 8:1, 2), that the Jews might not afterwards plead ignorance of the prophecy. The seventy-two elders, composing the Sanhedrim, or Great Council, were taken partly from "the priests," partly from the other tribes, i.e., "the people," the former presiding over spiritual matters, the latter over civil; the seventy-two represented the whole people. **2. valley of the son of Hinnom**—or Tophet, south of Jerusalem, where human victims were offered, and children made to pass through the fire, in honor of Molech. **east gate**—*Margin,* "sun gate," sunrise being in the *east.* Maurer translates, the "potter's gate." Through it lay the road to the valley of Hinnom (Josh. 15:8). The potters there formed vessels for the use of the temple, which was close by (cf. vss. 10, 14; ch. 18:2; Zech. 11:13). The same as "*the water gate* toward the east" (Neh. 3:26; 12:37); so called from the brook Kedron. Calvin translates, as *English Version* and *Margin.* "It was monstrous perversity to tread the law under foot in so conspicuous a place, over which the sun daily rising reminded them of the light of God's law." **3.** The scene of their guilt is chosen as the scene of the denunciation against them. **kings**—the king and queen (ch. 13:18); or including the king's counsellors and governors under him. **tingle**—as if struck by a thunder peal (I Sam. 3:11; II Kings 21:12).

4. (Isaiah 65:11.) **estranged this place**—devoted it to the worship of strange gods: alienating a portion of the sacred city from God, the rightful Lord of the temple, city, and whole land. **nor their fathers**—viz., the *godly* among them; their *ungodly* fathers God makes no account of. **blood of innocents**—slain in honor of Molech (ch. 7:31; Ps. 106: 37). **5. commanded not**—nay, more, I commanded the opposite (Lev. 18:21; see ch. 7:31, 32).

6. no more . . . Tophet—from *Hebrew, toph,* "drum"; for in sacrificing children to Molech drums were beaten to drown their cries. Thus the name indicated the *joy* of the people at the fancied propitiation of the god by this sacrifice; in antithesis to its joyless name subsequently. **valley of slaughter**—It should be the scene of slaughter, no longer of children, but of men; not of "innocents" (vs. 4), but of those who richly deserved their fate. The city could not be assailed without first occupying the valley of Hinnom, in which was the only fountain: hence arose the violent battle there. **7. make void the counsel**—defeat their plans for repelling the enemy (II Chron. 32:1-4; Isa. 19:3; 22:9, 11). Or their schemes of getting help by having recourse to idols [Calvin]. **in this place**—The valley of Hinnom was to be the place of the Chaldean encampment; the very place where they looked for help from idols was to be the scene of their own slaughter. **8.** (*Note,* ch. 18:16.) **9.** (Deut. 28:53; Lam. 4:10.)

10. break . . . bottle—a symbolical action, explained in vs. 11. **the men**—the elders of the people and of the priests (vs. 1; cf. ch. 51:63, 64).

ADAM CLARKE

CHAPTER 19

1. *Go and get a potter's earthen bottle.* This discourse was also delivered sometime in the reign of Jehoiakim. Under the type of breaking a potter's earthen bottle or jug, Jeremiah shows his enemies that the word of the Lord should stand, that Jerusalem should be taken and sacked, and they all carried into captivity.

TODAY'S DICTIONARY OF THE BIBLE:

Tophet = Topheth—from Heb. *tôph,* "a drum," because the cries of children here sacrificed by the priests of Moloch were drowned by the noise of such an instrument; the name of a particular part in the valley of Hinnom. An early writer describes it: "Fire being the most destructive of all elements is chosen by the sacred writers to symbolize the agency by which God punishes or destroys the wicked. We are not to assume from prophetical figures that material fire is the precise agent to be used. It was not the agency employed in the destruction of Sennacherib, mentioned in Isa. 30:33. . . . Tophet properly begins where the Vale of Hinnom bends round to the east, having the cliffs of Zion on the north, and the Hill of Evil Counsel on the south. It terminates at *Beer 'Ayub,* where it joins the Valley of Jehoshaphat. The cliffs on the southern side especially abound in ancient tombs. Here the dead carcasses of beasts and every offal and abomination were cast, and left to be either devoured by the worm that never died or consumed by that fire that was never quenched." Thus Tophet came to represent the place of punishment.

5. *Offerings unto Baal.* A general name for all the popular idols: Baal, Moloch, Ashtaroth, etc.

7. *I will make void the counsel of Judah.* Probably this refers to some determination made to proclaim themselves independent, and pay no more tribute to the Chaldeans.

9. *I will cause them to eat the flesh of their sons.* This was literally fulfilled when Jerusalem was besieged by the Romans.

MATTHEW HENRY

any man as the vessel while it is soft clay is marred in the potter's hand, and its case is, in this respect, much worse, that the vessel while it is soft clay, though it be marred, may be moulded again, but, after it is hardened, when it is broken it can never be pieced again." Sacramental signs, and teaching by symbols was anciently used. 1. As the bottle was easily and irrecoverably broken, so shall *Judah and Jerusalem* be broken by the Chaldean army, *v.* 11. They depended much upon the firmness of their constitution, and the fixedness of their courage, which they thought hardened them like a vessel of brass; but the prophet shows that all that did but harden them like a vessel of earth, which, though hard, is brittle and sooner broken than that which is not so hard. It is God himself, who made them, that resolves to unmake them: *I will break this people and this city,* dash them in pieces like *a potter's vessel;* the doom of the heathen (Ps. ii. 9, Rev. ii. 27), but now Jerusalem's doom, Isa. xxx. 14. *A potter's vessel,* when once broken, *cannot be made whole again, cannot be cured.* Jerusalem shall be an utter ruin; no hand can repair it but his that broke it; and if they return to him, though he has torn, he will heal. 2. This was done in Tophet, to signify two things: (1) *They shall bury in Tophet till there be no place to bury* any more there. (2) *I will make this city as Tophet.* As they had filled the valley of Tophet with the slain they sacrificed to their idols, so God will fill the whole city with the slain that shall fall as sacrifices to the justice of God. Dead carcases, and other filth of the city, were carried thither, and a fire was continually kept there for the burning of it. So execrable a place was it looked upon to be that, in the language of our Saviour's time, hell was called, in allusion to it, *Gehenna, the valley of Hinnom.* Even *the houses of Jerusalem, and* those *of the kings of Judah, shall be defiled as the place of Tophet* (*v.* 13), because of the idolatries that have been committed there. The flat roofs of their houses were sometimes used by devout people as convenient places for prayer (Acts x. 9), and by idolaters they were used as high places, on which they sacrificed to strange gods, especially to *the host of heaven,* the sun, moon, and stars. We read of those that *worshipped the host of heaven upon the house-tops* (Zeph. i. 5). This sin upon the house-tops brought a curse into the house.

II. By a solemn recognition and ratification of what he had said *in the court of the Lord's house, v.* 14, 15. The prophet returned from Tophet to the temple, which stood upon the hill over that valley, and there confirmed what he had said in the valley of Tophet. 1. The accomplishment of the prophecies is here the judgment threatened. The people flattered themselves that the threatening was but to frighten them, but the prophet tells them that they deceive themselves: *For thus saith the Lord of hosts,* who is able to make his words good, *I will bring upon this city, and upon all her towns, all the evil that I have pronounced against it.* God will appear as terrible against sin and sinners as the scripture makes him. 2. The contempt of the prophecies is here the sin charged upon them. It is *because they have hardened their necks,* and would *not hear my words.*

JAMIESON, FAUSSET, BROWN

11. as one breaketh a potter's vessel—expressing God's absolute sovereignty (ch. 18:6; Ps. 2:9; Isa. 30:14, *Margin;* Lam. 4:2; Rom. 9:20, 21).

cannot be made whole again—A broken potter's vessel cannot be restored, but a new one may be made of the same material. So God raised a new Jewish seed, not identical with the destroyed rebels, but by substituting another generation in their stead [GROTIUS]. **no place to bury**—(ch. 7:32). **12. make this city as Tophet**—i.e., as defiled with dead bodies as Tophet.

13. shall be defiled—with dead bodies (vs. 12; II Kings 23:10). **because of all the houses**—Rather, (explanatory of the previous "the houses . . . and . . . houses"), "*even* all the houses," etc. [CALVIN]. **roofs**—being flat, they were used as high places for sacrifices to the sun and planets (ch. 32:29; II Kings 23:11, 12; Zeph. 1:5). The Nabateans, south and east of the Dead Sea, a nation most friendly to the Jews, according to Strabo, had the same usage.

14. court of the Lord's house—near Tophet; the largest court, under the open air, where was the greatest crowd (II Chron. 20:5).

15. her towns—the suburban villages and towns near Jerusalem, such as Bethany.

ADAM CLARKE

11. *Even so will I break this people and this city.* The breaking of the bottle was the symbolical representation of the destruction of the city and of the state.

That cannot be made whole again. This seems to refer rather to the final destruction of Jerusalem by the Romans, than to what was done by the Chaldeans. Jerusalem was healed after seventy years: but nearly eighteen hundred years have elapsed since Jerusalem was taken and destroyed by the Romans; and it was then so broken that it could not be made whole again.

12. *And even make this city as Tophet.* A place of slaughter and destruction.

15. *Because they have hardened their necks.* A metaphor taken from unruly and unbroken oxen, who resist the yoke, break and run away with their gears. So this people had broken and destroyed the yoke of the law.

MATTHEW HENRY

CHAPTER 20

Verses 1–6

I. Pashur's unjust displeasure against Jeremiah, and the fruits of that displeasure, *v.* 1, 2. Pashur was a priest, and therefore should have protected Jeremiah, who was a priest too, and the more because he was a prophet of the Lord, whose interests the priests ought to consult. But this priest was a persecutor. He was *the son of Immer;* that is, he was of the sixteenth course of the priests, of which Immer, when these courses were first settled by David, was father (1 Chron. xxiv. 14). Thus this Pashur is distinguished from another of the same name mentioned *ch.* xxi. 1, who was of the fifth course. This Pashur was *chief governor in the temple;* perhaps he was only so *pro tempore—for a short period,* the course he was head of being now in waiting. This was Jeremiah's great enemy. We cannot suppose that Pashur was one of those that went with Jeremiah to the valley of Tophet to hear him prophesy; but, when he came into the courts of the Lord's house (*v.* 1): *He heard that Jeremiah prophesied these things,* and could not bear that he should dare to preach in the courts of the Lord's house, where he was *chief governor,* without his leave. Being incensed at Jeremiah, 1. He *smote* him, struck him with his hand or staff of authority. Perhaps it was a blow intended only to disgrace him. The method of proceeding here was illegal; the high priest, and the rest of the

JAMIESON, FAUSSET, BROWN

CHAPTER 20

VSS. 1-18. JEREMIAH'S INCARCERATION BY PASHUR, THE PRINCIPAL OFFICER OF THE TEMPLE, FOR PROPHESYING WITHIN ITS PRECINCTS; HIS RENEWED PREDICTIONS AGAINST THE CITY, *etc.*, ON HIS LIBERATION.

1. son—descendant. **of Immer**—one of the original "governors of the sanctuary and of the house of God," twenty-four in all, i.e., sixteen of the sons of Eleazar and eight of the sons of Ithamar (I Chron. 24:14). This Pashur is distinct from Pashur, *son of Melchiah* (ch. 21:1). The "captains" (Luke 22:4) seem to have been over the twenty-four guards of the temple, and had only the right of *apprehending* any who were guilty of delinquency within it; but the Sanhedrim had the *judicial power* over such delinquents [GROTIUS] (ch. 26:8, 10, 16).

2. The fact that Pashur was of the same order and of the same family as Jeremiah aggravates the indignity of the blow (I Kings 22:24; Matt. 26:67).

ADAM CLARKE

CHAPTER 20

MATTHEW HENRY

priests, ought to have been consulted, and Jeremiah's credentials examined. But these rules are set aside as mere formalities; right or wrong, Jeremiah must be run down. 2. He *put him in the stocks.* He continued in it all night, and in a public place too, *in the high gate of Benjamin, which was* in, or *by, the house of the Lord,* probably a gate through which they passed between the city and the temple. Pashur intended thus to chastise him, to expose him to contempt, that he might not be regarded if he did prophesy.

II. God's just displeasure against Pashur. *On the morrow Pashur* gave Jeremiah his discharge, *brought him out of the stocks* (*v.* 3). And now Jeremiah has a message from God to him. When he brought him out of the stocks, then God put a word into the prophet's mouth, which would awaken his conscience, if he had any.

1. Did he aim to establish himself by silencing one that told him of his faults and would be likely to lessen his reputation with the people? He shall not gain this point; for, (1) Though the prophet should be silent, his own conscience shall make him always uneasy. To confirm this he shall have a name given him, *Magor-missabib—Terror round about,* or *Fear on every side.* It seems to be a proverbial expression, bespeaking a man in despair, in fear on every side. *The wicked flee when no man pursues,* are in *great fear where no fear is.* This shall be Pashur's case (*v.* 4): "*Behold, I will make thee a terror to thyself;* and thy own imagination shall create thee a constant uneasiness." Those that will not hear of their faults from God's prophets, shall be made to hear of them from conscience, which is a reprover in their own bosoms. "*I will make thee a terror to all thy friends;* thou shalt express thyself with so much horror that all thy friends shall choose to stand aloof from thy torment." (2) His friends shall all fail him. God lets him live miserably, like Cain in the *land of shaking,* in such a continual consternation that wherever he goes it is asked, "What makes this man in such a continual terror?" It shall be answered, "It is God's hand upon him for putting Jeremiah in the stocks." His friends, who should encourage him, shall *fall by the sword of the enemy,* and *his eyes shall behold it.* (3) He shall find that divine vengeance is waiting for him (*v.* 6); he and his family shall *go into captivity,* even *to Babylon;* he shall die a captive, and shall be buried in his chains, he *and all his friends.* Thus far is the doom of Pashur.

2. Did he aim to keep the people easy, to prevent the destruction that Jeremiah prophesied, and by sinking his reputation make his words fall to the ground? It appears by *v.* 6 that he himself set up for a prophet, and told the people that they should have peace. He *prophesied lies to them;* and because Jeremiah's prophecy contradicted his, therefore he set himself against him. But could he gain his point? Jeremiah stands to what he has said against Judah and Jerusalem. (1) The country shall be ruined (*v.* 4): *I will give all Judah into the hand of the king of Babylon.* It had long been God's own land, but he will now transfer his title to it to Nebuchadnezzar, he shall be master of the country and dispose of the inhabitants as he pleases, but none shall escape him. (2) The city shall be ruined too, *v.* 5. The king of Babylon shall carry all that is valuable in it to Babylon. He shall seize their military stores (here called *the strength of the city*) and turn them against them. He shall carry off all their wares and merchandise, here called *their labours.* He shall plunder their fine houses, and take away their furniture, here called their *precious things.* He shall rifle the exchequer, and take away the jewels of the crown and *all the treasures of the kings of Judah.*

Verses 7–13

Jeremiah is here, through the infirmity of the flesh, strangely agitated within himself. In these verses it appears that, upon occasion of the great injury that Pashur did to Jeremiah, there was a struggle in his breast between his graces and his corruptions.

I. Here is a sad representation of the wrong that was done him. He complains,

1. That he was ridiculed and laughed at; they made a jest of everything he said and did (*v.* 7, 8): *I am in derision; I am mocked.* And what was it that thus exposed him to contempt and scorn? It was nothing but his faithful and zealous discharge of the duty of his office, *v.* 8. They could find nothing for which to deride him but his preaching; it was *the word of the Lord* that *was made a reproach.* Two things they derided him for: (1) The manner of his preaching: *Since he spoke, he cried out.* He had always been a lively affectionate preacher, and since he began to speak in God's name he always spoke as a man in earnest; he *cried aloud and did not spare.* Lively

JAMIESON, FAUSSET, BROWN

stocks—an instrument of torture with five holes, in which the neck, two hands, and two feet were thrust, the body being kept in a crooked posture (ch. 29: 26). From a *Hebrew* root, to "turn," or "rack." This marks Pashur's cruelty. **high**—i.e., *the upper* gate (II Kings 15:35). **gate of Benjamin**—a gate in the temple wall, corresponding to the gate of Benjamin, properly so called, in the city wall, in the direction of the territory of Benjamin (ch. 7:2; 37:13; 38:7). The temple gate of Benjamin, being on a lofty position, was called "the high gate," to distinguish it from the city wall gate of Benjamin. **3. Pashur**—compounded of two roots, meaning "largeness" (and so "security") "*on every side*"; in antithesis to *Magor-missabib,* "terror *round about*" (vs. 10; ch. 6:25; 46:5; 49:29; Ps. 31:13).

4. terror . . . to all thy friends—who have believed thy false promises (vs. 6). The sense must be in order to accord with "fear round about" (vs. 3). I will bring terror on thee and on all thy friends, that terror arising from thyself, viz., thy false prophecies. Thou and thy prophecies will be seen, to the dismay both of thee and thy dupes, to have caused their ruin and thine. MAURER's translation is therefore not needed, "I will give up thee and all thy friends *to* terror."

6. prophesied lies—viz., that God cannot possibly leave this land without prophets, priests, and teachers ("the wise") (ch. 18:18; cf. ch. 5:31).

5. strength—i.e., resources. **labours**—fruits of labor, gain, wealth.

7. Jeremiah's complaint, not unlike that of Job, breathing somewhat of human infirmity in consequence of his imprisonment. Thou didst promise never to give me up to the will of mine enemies, and yet Thou hast done so. But Jeremiah misunderstood God's promise, which was not that he should have nothing to suffer, but that God would deliver him out of sufferings (ch. 1:19).

8. Rather, "*Whenever* I speak, I cry out." *Concerning* violence and spoil, I (am compelled to) cry out," i.e., complain [MAURER]. *English Version* in the last clause is more graphic, "I cried violence and

ADAM CLARKE

3. *The Lord hath not called thy name Pashur.*—Security on all sides. *But Magor-missabib*—Fear on every side. This name has God given you because, in the course of His providence, you shall be placed in the circumstances signified by it; you shall be a terror to yourself.

6. *And thou, Pashur . . . shall go into captivity.* You shall suffer for the false prophecies which you have delivered, and for your insults to My prophet.

8. *I cried violence and spoil.* This was the burden of the message Thou didst give me.

MATTHEW HENRY

preachers are the scorn of careless unbelieving hearers. (2) The matter of his preaching: He *cried violence and spoil.* He reproved them for violence and spoil towards one another; and he prophesied violence and spoil should be brought upon them as punishment; for the former they ridiculed him as overprecise, for the latter as over-credulous. This was bad enough, yet he complains further.

2. That he was plotted against and his ruin contrived; he was not only ridiculed as a weak man, but reproached and misrepresented as a bad man and dangerous to the government, *v.* 10. But there were those that acted with more subtlety. (1) They spoke ill of him behind his back. *I heard,* at second hand, *the defaming of many, fear on every side* (*of many Magor-missabibs,* so some read it), of many such men as Pashur was. They represented Jeremiah as a man that instilled fears and jealousies on every side into the minds of the people, and so made them uneasy under the government, and disposed them to a rebellion. See how Jeremiah's enemies contrived the matter: *Report, say they, and we will report it.* "Let some very bad thing be said of him, which may render him obnoxious to the government, and, though it be false, we will second it, and spread it, and add to it." (2) They flattered him to his face, that they might get something from him on which to ground an accusation, as the spies that came to Christ, Luke xx. 20; xi. 53, 54. "If we accost him kindly we shall wheedle him to speak some treasonable words; and then *we shall prevail against him,* and *take our revenge on him* for telling us of our faults and threatening us with the judgment of God."

II. Here is an account of the temptation he was in under this affliction. 1. He was tempted to quarrel with God for making him a prophet. This he begins with (*v.* 7): *O Lord! thou hast deceived me, and I was deceived.* This is the language of Jeremiah's folly and corruption. He knew how the prophets before him had been persecuted, and had no reason to expect better treatment. God had expressly told him that all the *princes, priests, and people of the land would fight against him* (*ch.* i. 18, 19). Christ thus told his disciples what opposition they should meet with, *that they might not be offended,* John xvi. 1, 2. But the words may very well be read thus: *Thou hast persuaded me, and I was persuaded.* And this agrees best with what follows. Jeremiah was very backward to undertake the prophetic office; he pleaded that he was under age and unfit for the service; but God overruled his pleas, and told him that *he must go, ch.* i. 6, 7. "Now, Lord," says he, "since thou hast put this office upon me, why dost thou not stand by me in it? Had I thrust myself upon it, I might justly have been in derision; but why am I so when thou didst thrust me into it?" 2. He was tempted to quit his work partly because he himself met with so much hardship in it and partly because those to whom he was sent, instead of being edified and made better, were exasperated and made worse (*v.* 9).

III. An account of his faithful adherence to his work and cheerful dependence on his God notwithstanding.

1. He found the grace of God mighty in him to keep him to his business, "*I said,* in my haste, *I will speak no more in his name*; what I have in my heart to deliver I will stifle and suppress. But I soon found it was *in my heart as a burning fire shut up in my bones,* which glowed inwardly, and must have vent; it was impossible to smother it; while *I kept silence from good my heart was hot within me,* it was *pain and grief to me,* and I must speak, that I might be refreshed"; Ps. xxxix. 2, 3; Job xxxii. 20. Jeremiah was soon weary with forbearing to preach, and could not contain himself; nothing puts faithful ministers to pain so much as being silenced, nor to terror so much as silencing themselves. Their convictions will soon triumph, for *woe is unto me if I preach not the gospel,* whatever it cost me, 1 Cor. ix. 16.

2. He was assured of God's presence with him, which would be sufficient to baffle all the attempts of his enemies (*v.* 11): "They say, *We shall prevail against him.* But I am sure that *they shall not prevail, they shall not prosper.* I can set them at defiance, for *the Lord is with me,* to take my part against them (Rom. viii. 31). He is with me to bear me up under the burden. He is with me to make the word I preach answer the end he designs. He is with me to strike a terror upon them, and so to overcome them." The most formidable enemies that act against us appear despicable when we see the Lord for us as a *mighty terrible one,* Neh. iv. 14. Jeremiah speaks now with a good assurance: If *the Lord be with me, my persecutors shall stumble,* so that, when they pursue me, they shall not overtake me (Ps. xxvii. 2), and then *they shall be greatly ashamed* of their impotent malice and fruitless attempts.

JAMIESON, FAUSSET, BROWN

spoil" (ch. 6:7)! I could not speak in a calm tone; their desperate wickedness compelled me to "cry out." **because**—rather, "therefore," the apodosis of the previous sentence; *because* in discharging my prophetic functions, I not merely *spake,* but *cried;* and *cried, violence . . . ; therefore* the word of the Lord was made a reproach to me (vs. 7).

10. For—not referring to the words immediately preceding, but to "I will not make mention of Him." The "defaming" or *detraction* of the enemy on every side (see Ps. 31:13) tempted him to think of prophesying no more.

Report . . . we will report—The words of his adversaries one to the other; give any information against him (true or false) which will give color for accusing him; and "we will report it," viz., to the Sanhedrim, in order to crush him. **familiars**—lit., "men of my peace"; those who pretended to be on peaceable terms with me (Ps. 41:9). Jeremiah is a type of Messiah, referred to in that Psalm. (See ch. 38:22; Job 19:19; Ps. 55:13, 14; Luke 11:53, 54.) **watched for my halting**—(Ps. 35:15, *Margin,* "halting"; Ps. 38:17; 71:10, *Margin*). GESENIUS not so well translates, according to *Arabic* idiom, "those guarding my side" (i.e., my most intimate friends *always at my side*), in apposition to "familiars," and the subject of "say" (instead of "saying). The *Hebrew* means properly "side," then "halting," as the halt bend on one side. **enticed**—to commit some sin. **deceived**—Others translate as *Margin,* "Thou hast *enticed*" or "*persuaded* me," viz., to undertake the prophetic office, "and I was persuaded," i.e., suffered myself to be persuaded to undertake what I find too hard for me. So the *Hebrew* word is used in a good sense (Gen. 9:27, *Margin;* Prov. 25:15; Hos. 2:14). **stronger than I**—Thou whose strength I could not resist hast laid this burden on me, and hast prevailed (hast made me prophesy, in spite of my reluctance) (ch. 1:5-7); yet, when I exercise my office, I am treated with derision (Lam. 3:14).

9. *his* word was—or lit., "there was in my heart, as it were, a burning fire," i.e., the divine afflatus or impulse to speak was as . . . (Job 32:18, 19; Ps. 39:3).

weary with forbearing, and I could not—"I labored to contain myself, but I could not" (Acts 18:5; cf. ch. 23:9; I Cor. 9:16, 17).

11. not prevail—as they hoped to do (vs. 10; ch. 15:20). **prosper**—in their plot.

ADAM CLARKE

10. *Report . . . and we will report it.* Let us spread calumnies against him everywhere; or let us spread reports of dangers coming upon him, that we may intimidate him, and cause him to desist.

7. *O Lord, thou hast deceived me.* I think our translation of this passage is very exceptionable. The original word is *pittithani,* "Thou hast persuaded me," i.e., to go and prophesy to this people. I went, faithfully declared Thy message, and now I am likely to perish by their cruelty. As the root *pathah* signifies to "persuade" and "allure," as well as to "deceive," the above must be its meaning in this place. Taken as in our version, it is highly irreverent. It is used in the same sense here as in Gen. ix. 27; "God shall enlarge ['persuade,' margin] Japheth, and he shall dwell in the tents of Shem."

9. *I will not make mention of him.* I will renounce the prophetic office, and return to my house.

11. *But the Lord is with me as a mighty terrible one.* Thus was he, by his strong confidence in the strong God, delivered from all his fears, and enabled to go on comfortably with his work.

MATTHEW HENRY

3. He appeals to God against them as a righteous Judge, and prays judgment upon his cause, *v.* 12. He that tries the righteous tries the unrighteous too, for he *sees the reins and the heart*, and therefore can pass an unerring judgment on their words and actions. *Unto thee have I opened my cause.* Not but that God perfectly knew his cause, and all the merits of it, but the cause we commit to God we must spread before him. He knows it, but he will know it from us, and allows us to be particular in the opening of it, not to affect him, but to affect ourselves.

4. He greatly rejoices and praises God, in a full confidence that God would appear for his deliverance, *v.* 13. In a transport of joy he stirs up himself and others to give God the glory of it: *Sing unto the Lord, praise you the Lord.* Here appears a great change with him since he began this discourse; the clouds are blown over, his complaints all silenced and turned into thanksgiving. It was the lively exercise of faith that made this happy change, that turned his sighs into songs and his tremblings into triumphs. "He hath delivered me formerly when I was in distress, and now of late out of the hand of Pashur, and he will continue to deliver me, 2 Cor. i. 10. He will deliver my soul from the sin that I am in danger of falling into when I am thus persecuted."

Verses 14–18

What is the meaning of this? Does there *proceed out of the same mouth blessing and cursing?* Could he that said so cheerfully (*v.* 13), *Sing unto the Lord, praise you the Lord*, say so passionately (*v.* 14), *Cursed be the day wherein I was born?* It seems to be an account of the ferment he had been in while he was in the stocks, out of which by faith and hope he had recovered himself, rather than a new temptation. When grace has got the victory it is good to remember the struggles, that we may be ashamed of ourselves and our own folly, may admire the goodness of God in not taking us at our word.

I. The prophet's language in this temptation. 1. He fastened a brand of infamy upon his birthday, as Job did in a heat (*ch.* iii. 1). It is a wish that he had never been born. Judas in hell has reason to wish so (Matt. xxvi. 24), but no man on earth has reason to wish so, because he knows not but he may yet become a vessel of mercy, much less has any good man reason to wish so. 2. He wished ill to the messenger that brought his father the news of his birth, *v.* 15. He is very fierce in the curses he pronounces (*v.* 16): "*Let him be as the cities of Sodom and Gomorrah, which the Lord utterly overthrew, and repented not. Let him hear the cry* of the invading besieging enemy *in the morning*, as soon as he is stirring; and by noon let him hear their *shouting* for victory. And thus let him live in constant terror." 3. He is angry that he was not *slain from the womb*, that his first breath was not his last, and that he was not strangled as soon as he came into the world, *v.* 17. 4. He thinks his present calamities sufficient to justify these passionate wishes (*v.* 18): "*Wherefore came I forth out of the womb*, where I lay hid, was not hated, where I lay safely and knew no evil, to see all this *labour and sorrow*, to have my *days consumed with shame*, to be continually abused, to have my life wasted and worn away by trouble?"

II. What use we may make of this. It is not recorded for our imitation, and yet we may learn good lessons from it. 1. See the vanity of human life and the vexation of spirit that attends it. 2. See the folly and absurdity of sinful passion, how unreasonably it talks when it is suffered to ramble. What nonsense is it to curse a day—to curse a messenger for the sake of his message! When the heart is hot, let the tongue be bridled, Ps. xxxix. 1, 2.

JAMIESON, FAUSSET, BROWN

12. triest the righteous—in latent contrast to the hasty judgments of men (ch. 11:20; 17:10). **opened**—i.e., committed (cf. II Kings 19:14; Ps. 35:1).

13. delivered . . . soul—This deliverance took place when Zedekiah succeeded Jeconiah.

14-18. The contrast between the spirit of this passage and the preceding *thanksgiving* is to be explained thus: to show how great was the deliverance (vs. 13), he subjoins a picture of what his wounded spirit *had been* previous to his deliverance; I *had said* in the time of my imprisonment, "Cursed be the day"; my feeling was that of Job (Job 3:3, 10, 11, whose words Jeremiah therefore copies). Though Jeremiah's zeal had been stirred up, not so much for self as for God's honor trampled on by the rejection of the prophet's words, yet it was intemperate when he made his birth a subject for *cursing*, which was really a ground for thanksgiving. **15. A man child**—The birth of a son is in the *East* a special subject of joy; whereas that of a daughter is often not so.

16. the cities—Sodom and Gomorrah. **cry . . . morning . . . noontide**—i.e., Let him be kept in alarm the *whole day* (not merely at *night* when terrors ordinarily prevail, but in *daytime* when it is something extraordinary) with terrifying war shouts, as those in a besieged city (ch. 18:22). **17. he**—"that man" (vss. 15, 16). **from the womb**—i.e., at that time while I was still in the womb.

ADAM CLARKE

13. *Sing unto the Lord.* He was so completely delivered from all fear that, although he remained in the same circumstances, yet he exults in the divine protection, and does not fear the face of any adversary.

14. *Cursed be the day wherein I was born.* If we take these words literally, and suppose them to be in their proper place, they are utterly inconsistent with that state of confidence in which he exulted a few minutes before. If they are the language of Jeremiah, they must have been spoken on a prior occasion, when probably he had given way to a passionate hastiness. They might well comport with the state he was in in v. 9. I really believe these verses have got out of their proper place, which I conjecture to be between the eighth and ninth verses. There they will come in very properly, and might have been a part of his complaint in those moments when he had purposed to flee from God as did Jonah, and prophesy no more in His name. Transpositions in this prophet are frequent; therefore place these five verses after the eighth, and let the chapter end with the thirteenth, and the whole will form a piece of exquisite poetry. See Job iii. 3. The two passages are very similar.

MATTHEW HENRY

CHAPTER 21

Verses 1–7

I. A very humble message which king Zedekiah, when he was in distress, sent to Jeremiah the prophet. He humbled himself so far as to desire the prophet's assistance, but not so far as to take his advice, or to be ruled by him.

1. The distress which king Zedekiah was now in: *Nebuchadrezzar made war upon him*, invaded the land, besieged the city, and had now actually invested it.

2. The messengers he sent—*Pashur and Zephaniah.* It would have been better if he had desired a personal conference with the prophet, which he might have had if he would so far have humbled himself. These priests when they were commanded by the king, must carry a respectful message to the prophet, which was a mortification to them and an honour to Jeremiah.

JAMIESON, FAUSSET, BROWN

CHAPTER 21

Vss. 1-14. Zedekiah Consults Jeremiah What Is to Be the Event of the War: God's Answer. Written probably when, after having repulsed the Egyptians who brought succors to the Jews (ch. 37: 5-8; II Kings 24:7), the Chaldees were a second time advancing against Jerusalem, but were not yet closely besieging it (vss. 4, 13) [Rosenmuller]. This chapter probably ought to be placed between chs. 37 and 38; since what the "princes," in ch. 38:2, represent Jeremiah as having said, is exactly what we find in vs. 9 of this ch. 21. Moreover, the same persons as here (vs. 1) are mentioned in ch. 37:3; 38:1, viz., Pashur and Zephaniah. What is here more fully related is there simply referred to in the historical narrative. Cf. ch. 52:24; II Kings 25:18 [Maurer]. **Zedekiah**—a prince having some reverence for sacred things, for which reason he sends

ADAM CLARKE

CHAPTER 21

1. *The word which came unto Jeremiah.* The chapters in the remaining parts of this prophecy seem strangely interchanged. The discourse here was delivered about the ninth year of the reign of Zedekiah. This chapter, observes Dr. Blayney, contains the first of those prophecies which were delivered by Jeremiah subsequent to the revolt of Zedekiah and the breaking out of the war thereupon; and which are continued on to the taking of Jerusalem, related in chap. xxix, in the following order: ch. xxi; xxxiv; xxxvii; xxxii; xxxiii; xxxviii; xxxix. *Pashur the son of Melchiah.* There can be little doubt that this Pashur was a different person from him who was called the son of Immur in the preceding chapter.

MATTHEW HENRY

3. The message itself: *Enquire, I pray thee, of the Lord for us, v.* 2. Now that the Chaldean army had got into their borders, they were convinced that Jeremiah was a true prophet, though loth to own it. Under this conviction they desire him to stand their friend with God. "*Enquire of the Lord for us;* ask him what course we shall take in our present strait, for the measures we have hitherto taken are all broken." Those that will not take the direction of God's grace how to get clear of their sins would yet be glad of the directions of his providence how to get clear of their troubles. "*Entreat the Lord for us;* be an intercessor for us with God." *It may be the Lord will deal with us* now *according to the wondrous works he wrought for our fathers*, that the enemy may raise the siege and *go up from us.* All their care is to get rid of their trouble, not to make their peace with God and be reconciled to him—"That our enemy may *go up from us,*" not, "That our God may return to us." Thus Pharaoh (Exod. x. 17). All their hope is that God had done wondrous works in the deliverance of Jerusalem when Sennacherib besieged it, at the prayer of Isaiah (2 Chron. xxxii. 20, 21), and who can tell but he may destroy these besiegers at the prayer of Jeremiah? But they did not consider how different the character of Zedekiah and his people was from that of Hezekiah and his people: those were days of general reformation and piety, these of general corruption and apostasy.

II. A very startling cutting reply which God, by the prophet, sent to that message. God knows their hearts better than Jeremiah does, and sends them an answer which has scarcely one word of comfort in it. He sends it to them in the name of *the Lord God of Israel* (*v.* 3), to intimate to them that though God allowed himself to be called the *God of Israel*, and had done great things for Israel formerly, and had still great things in store for Israel, yet this should stand the present generation in no stead, who were Israelites in name only. It is here foretold,

1. That God will render all their endeavours for their own security fruitless and ineffectual (*v.* 4).

2. That the besiegers shall in a little time make themselves masters of Jerusalem, and of all its wealth and strength: *I will assemble* those *in the midst of this city* who are now surrounding it.

3. That God himself will be their enemy; and then I know not who can befriend them, no, not Jeremiah himself (*v.* 5). Those who rebel against God may justly expect that he will make war upon them.

4. That those who, for their own safety, decline sallying out upon the besiegers, and so avoid their sword, shall yet not escape the sword of God's justice (*v.* 6): *I will smite those that abide in the city, both man and beast; they shall die of a great pestilence.*

5. That the king himself, and all the people that escape the *sword, famine,* and *pestilence,* shall fall *into the hands* of the Chaldeans (*v.* 7): They *shall not spare them,* nor *have pity* on them.

Verses 8–14

By the civil message which the king sent to Jeremiah it appeared that both he and the people began to have a respect for him; but the reply which God obliges him to make is enough to crush the little respect they begin to have for him, and to exasperate them against him more than ever. Not only the predictions in the foregoing verses, but the prescriptions in these, were provoking.

I. He advises the people to surrender to the Chaldeans, as the only means left to save their lives, *v.* 8–10. This counsel was displeasing to those who were flattered by their false prophets into a desperate resolution to hold out to the last, trusting to the strength of their walls and the courage of their soldiery, or to their foreign aids to raise the siege. The prophet assures them, "*The city shall be given into the hand of the king of Babylon,* and he shall not only plunder it, but *burn it with fire,* for God himself hath *set his face against this city for evil and not for good*; and therefore, if you would make the best of bad, you must beg quarter of the Chaldeans, and surrender prisoners of war." It was the best course they could take now that God was against them. Both the law and the prophets had often set before them life and death in another sense—life if they obey the voice of God, death if they persist in disobedience, Deut. xxx. 19. The expression (*v.* 8): *Behold, I set before you the way of life and the way of death,* denotes not, as that, a fair proposal, but a melancholy dilemma, advising them of two evils to choose the less. *He that abides in the city* shall certainly die either by *the sword* without the walls or *famine* or *pestilence* within. But he that can quit his vain hopes, go out, and fall *to the Chaldeans, his life shall be given him for a prey*; he shall save his life, as a prey is taken from the mighty. They thought to

JAMIESON, FAUSSET, BROWN

an honorable embassy to Jeremiah; but not having moral courage to obey his better impulses. **Pashur**—son of Melchiah, of the fifth order of priests, distinct from Pashur, son of Immer (ch. 20:1), of the sixteenth order (I Chron. 24:9, 14). **Zephaniah**—of the twenty-fourth order. They are designated, not by their father, but by their family (I Chron. 24:18). **2. Nebuchadrezzar**—the more usual way of spelling the name in Jeremiah than Nebuchadnezzar. From *Persiac* roots, meaning either "Nebo, the chief of the gods," or, "Nebo, the god of fire." He was son of Nabopolassar, who committed the command of the army against Egypt, at Carchemish, and against Judea, to the crown prince. **according to all his wondrous works**—Zedekiah hopes for God's special interposition, such as was vouchsafed to Hezekiah against Sennacherib (II Kings 19:35, 36). **he**—Nebuchadnezzar. **go up from us**—*rise up* from the siege which he sat down to lay (ch. 37:5, 11, *Margin*; Num. 16: 24; 27; I Kings 15:19, *Margin*).

4. God of Israel—Those "wondrous works" (vs. 2) do not belong to you; *God* is faithful; it is *you* who forfeit the privileges of the covenant by unfaithfulness. "God will always remain *the God of Israel,* though He destroy thee and thy people" [CALVIN]. **turn back the weapons**—I will turn them to a very different use from what you intend them. With them you now fight against the Chaldees "without the walls" (the Jewish defenders being as yet able to sally forth more freely, and defend the fountains outside the walls in the valley under Mount Zion; see vs. 13; ch. 19:6, 7); but soon ye shall be driven back within the city [MAURER], and "in the midst" of it, I will cause all your arms to be gathered in one place ("I will assemble *them,*" viz., your arms) by the Chaldean conquerors [GROTIUS], who shall slay you with those very arms [MENOCHIUS]. **5.** The Jews shall have not merely the Chaldees, but Jehovah Himself in wrath at their provocations, fighting against them. Every word enhances the formidable character of God's opposition, "I myself . . . outstretched hand . . . strong arm (no longer as in Exod. 6:6, and in the case of Sennacherib, in your behalf, but) in anger . . . fury . . . great wrath." **7. the people, and such**—rather, explanatory, "the people, viz., such as are left." **seek their life**—content with nothing short of their death; not content with plundering and enslaving them. **smite with . . . sword**—This was the fate of Zedekiah's sons and many of the Jewish nobles. Zedekiah himself, though not put to a violent death, died of grief. Cf. as to the accurate fulfilment, ch. 34:4; Ezek. 12:13; II Kings 25:6, 7.

10. set . . . face against—determined to punish (Lev. 17:10).

8. "Life," if ye surrender; "death," if ye persist in opposing the Chaldees (cf. Deut. 30:19). The individuality of Jeremiah's mission from God is shown in that he urges to unconditional surrender; whereas all former prophets had urged the people to oppose their invaders (Isa. 7:16; 37:33, 35). **9.** (Ch. 38:2, 17, 18.) **falleth to**—deserts to. **life . . . a prey**—proverbial, to make one's escape with life, like a valuable spoil or prey that one carries off; the narrowness of the escape, and the joy felt at it, are included in the idea (ch. 39:18).

ADAM CLARKE

2. *Enquire, I pray thee.* See whether God intends to deliver us into or out of the hand of the Chaldeans.

4. *I will turn back the weapons.* Every attempt you make to repel the Chaldeans shall be unsuccessful. *I will assemble them into the midst of this city.* I will deliver the city into their hands.

6. *They shall die of a great pestilence.* The sword may appear to be that of man, though I have given the Chaldeans their commission; but the pestilence shall appear to be the immediate act of God.

7. *Nebuchadrezzar.* This name is spelt as above in twenty-six places of this book; and in ten places it is spelt Nebuchadnezzar, which is the common orthography.

10. *He shall burn it with fire.* What a heavy message to all; and especially to them who had any fear of God, or reverence for the Temple and its sacred services!

8. *Behold, I set before you the way of life, and the way of death.* Meaning escape or destruction in the present instance. This is explained in the next verse.

MATTHEW HENRY

make a prey of the camp of the Chaldeans, as their ancestors did that of the Assyrians (Isa. xxxiii. 23), but if by yielding at discretion they can but save their lives, that is all the prey they must promise themselves.

II. He advises the king and princes to reform. In the reply there was a particular word for *the house of the king* to give them wholesome counsel (*v.* 11, 12): "*Execute judgment in the morning;* do it carefully and diligently. Do it quickly, and do not delay to do justice upon appeals made to you. You would be delivered out of the hand of those that distress you, and expect that God should do you justice; see then that you do justice to those that apply to you, and *deliver them out of the hand of their oppressors, lest my fury go out like fire*, and you fare worst who think to escape best, *because of the evil of your doings.*" It was the *evil of their doings* that kindled the fire of God's wrath. Thus plainly does he deal even with the *house of the king*; for those that would have the benefit of a prophet's prayers must thankfully take a prophet's reproofs. The princes must begin, and set a good example, and then the people will be invited to reform. They must use their power for the punishment of wrong, and then the people will be obliged to reform. He reminds them that they are *the house of David*, and therefore should tread in his steps, who executed judgment and justice to his people.

III. He shows them the vanity of all their hopes so long as they continued unreformed, *v.* 13, 14. Jerusalem is an *inhabitant of the valley*, guarded with mountains on all sides, which were their natural fortifications, making it difficult for an army to approach them. It is a *rock of the plain*, which made it difficult for an enemy to undermine them. These advantages they trusted to more than to the power and promise of God; and, thinking their city impregnable, they set the judgments of God at defiance, saying, "*Who shall come down against us?*" God soon shows the vanity of that challenge, *Who shall come down against us?* when he says (*v.* 13), *Behold, I am against thee.* He comes against them as a judge that cannot be resisted; for he says (*v.* 14), *I will punish you*, by due course of law, *according to the fruit of your doings.*

CHAPTER 22

Verses 1–9

I. Orders given to Jeremiah to go and preach before the king (*v.* 2): *Hear the word of the Lord, O king of Judah!* The *king of Judah* is here spoken to *as sitting upon the throne of David*, who was a man after God's own heart, as holding his dignity and power by the covenant made with David; let him therefore conform to his example, that he may have the benefit of the promises made to him.

II. Instructions given him what to preach.

1. He must tell them what the Lord their God required of them, *v.* 3. They must take care, (1) That they do all the good they can with the power they have. They must do justice in defence of those that were injured. (2) That they do no hurt with it. They must *do no wrong to the stranger, fatherless, and widow;* for these God does in a particular manner take under his tuition, Exod. xxii. 21, 22.

2. He must assure them that the faithful discharge of their duty would advance their prosperity, *v.* 4. There shall then be an uninterrupted succession, *upon the throne of David*, enjoying tranquillity, and living in dignity. The most effectual way to preserve the dignity of the government is to do the duty of it.

3. He must likewise assure them that the iniquity, if they persisted in it, would be the ruin of their family (*v.* 5). Sin has often been the ruin of royal palaces, though ever so stately, ever so strong. Sin will be the ruin of the houses of princes as well as of mean men.

JAMIESON, FAUSSET, BROWN

12. house of David—the royal family and all in office about the king. He calls them so, because it was the greater disgrace that they had so degenerated from the piety of their forefather, *David;* and to repress their glorying in their descent from him, as if they were therefore inviolable; but God will not spare them as apostates. **in the morning**—alluding to *the time* of dispensing justice (Job 24:17; Ps. 101:8); but the sense is mainly proverbial, for "with promptness" (Ps. 90:14; 143:8). MAURER translates, "every morning." **lest my fury . . . like fire**—Already it was kindled, and the decree of God gone forth against the city (vss. 4, 5), but the king and his house may yet be preserved by repentance and reformation. God urges to righteousness, not as if they can thereby escape punishment wholly, but as the condition of a *mitigation* of it.

13. inhabitant of the valley, and rock of the plain—Jerusalem personified; situated for the most part on hills, with valleys at the bottom of them, as the valley of Hinnom, etc.; and beyond the valleys and mountains again, a position most fortified by nature, whence the inhabitants fancied themselves beyond the reach of enemies; but since God is "against" them, their position will avail nothing for them. The "valley" between Mount Zion and Moriah is called Tyropœon. ROBINSON takes, "rock of the plain" as Mount Zion, *on which* is a *level tract* of some extent. It is appropriately here referred to, being the site of the royal residence of the "house of David," addressed (vs. 12). **14. fruit of your doings**—(Prov. 1:31; Isa. 3:10, 11).. **forest thereof**—viz., of your city, taken from vs. 13. "Forest" refers to the dense mass of houses built of cedar, etc. brought from Lebanon (ch. 22:7; 52:13; II Kings 25:9).

CHAPTER 22

Vss. 1-30. EXHORTATION TO REPENTANCE; JUDGMENT ON SHALLUM, JEHOIAKIM, AND CONIAH. Belonging to an earlier period than ch. 21, viz., the reigns of Shallum or Jehoahaz, Jehoiakim, and Jeconiah (vss. 10, 13, 20). Jeremiah often groups his prophecies, not by chronological order, but by *similarity of subjects;* thus vs. 3 in this chapter corresponds to ch. 21:12. GROTIUS thinks that Jeremiah here *repeats* to Zedekiah what he had announced to that king's predecessors *formerly* (viz., his brother and brother's son), of a similar bearing, and which had since come to pass; a warning to Zedekiah. Probably, in *arranging* his prophecies they were grouped for the first time in the present order, designed by the Holy Spirit to set forth the series of kings of Judah, all four alike, failing in "righteousness," followed at last by the "King," *a righteous Branch raised unto David*, in the house of Judah, "the Lord our righteousness" (ch. 23:6). The unrighteousness of Zedekiah suggested the review of his predecessors' failure in the same respects, and consequent punishment, which ought to have warned him, but did not. **1. Go down**—The temple (where Jeremiah had been prophesying) was higher than the king's palace on Mount Zion (ch. 36:10, 12; II Chron. 23:20). Hence the phrase, "Go down." **the king of Judah**—perhaps including *each* of *the four successive kings,* to whom it was consecutively addressed, here brought together in one picture: Shallum, vs. 11; Jehoiakim, vss. 13-18; Jeconiah, vs. 24; Zedekiah, the address to whom (ch. 21:1, 11, 12) suggests notice of the rest. **2. these gates**—of the king's palace. **3. *Jehoiakim*** is meant here especially: he, by oppression, levied the tribute imposed on him by Pharaoh-necho, king of Egypt (II Chron. 36:3), and taxed his people, and took their labor without pay, to build gorgeous palaces for himself (vss. 13-17), and shed innocent blood, e.g., that of Urijah the prophet (ch. 26:20-24: II Kings 23:35; 24:4). **4. upon the throne of David**—lit., "or David on his throne" (see *Note*, ch. 13; 13). This verse is repeated substantially from ch. 17:25. **his servants**—so the *Keri*. But *Chetib, singular,* "his servant;" i.e., distributively, "*each* with his servants;" ch. 17:25, "their princes." **5. I swear by myself**—(Heb. 6:13, 17). God swears because it seemed to them incredible that the family

ADAM CLARKE

12. *Execute judgment in the morning.* Probably the time for dispensing the judgment was the morning, when the people were going to their work; but the words may mean, Do justice promptly, do not delay.

13. *O inhabitant of the valley, and rock of the plain.* Jerusalem itself, though partly on two hills, was also extended in the valley; and Zion, the city of David, was properly a rock, strongly fortified by both nature and art; and by its ancient possessors, the Jebusites, was deemed impregnable. *Who shall come down against us?* Probably the words of those courtiers who had persuaded Zedekiah to rebel against the king of Babylon.

14. *I will kindle a fire in the forest thereof.* I will send destruction into its center, that shall spread to every part of the circumference, and so consume the whole.

CHAPTER 22

1. *Go down to the house of the king of Judah, and speak there this word.* This is supposed by Dahler to have been published in the first year of the reign of Zedekiah.

2. *O king of Judah . . . thou, and thy servants.* His ministers are here addressed, as chiefly governing the nation, and who had counselled Zedekiah to rebel.

MATTHEW HENRY

4. He must show how fatal their wickedness would be to their kingdom as well as to themselves, to Jerusalem especially, the royal city, *v.* 6-9. Judah and Jerusalem had been valuable in God's eyes: *Thou art Gilead unto me and the head of Lebanon.* Their lot was cast in a place that was rich and pleasant as Gilead; Zion was a stronghold, as stately as Lebanon: this they trusted as their security. But the country that is now fruitful as Gilead shall be made *a wilderness.* The cities that are now strong as Lebanon shall be cities *not inhabited.* There shall be those that shall do it effectually (*v.* 7): "*I will prepare destroyers against thee;* I will *sanctify* them" (so the word is). And who can contend with destroyers of God's preparing? There shall be those who shall be ready to justify God in the doing of it (*v.* 8, 9); persons of *many nations,* when they *pass by* the ruins of *this city* in their travels, will ask, "*Wherefore hath the Lord done thus unto this city?*" Ask the next man you meet, and he will tell you it was because they changed their gods. God never casts any off until they first cast him off.

Verses 10–19

I. Here is the doom of Shallum, who doubtless is the same with Jehoahaz, for he is that son of Josiah king of Judah who reigned *in the stead of Josiah his father* (*v.* 11), which Jehoahaz did by the act of the people, who made him king though he was not the eldest son, 2 Kings xxiii. 30; 2 Chron. xxxvi. 1. Perhaps the people preferred him before his elder brother because they thought him a more active young man, and fitter to rule; but God soon showed them the folly of their injustice, for within three months the king of Egypt came upon him, deposed him, and carried him away prisoner into Egypt, as God had threatened, Deut. xxviii. 68. It does not appear that any of the people were taken into captivity with him. We have the story 2 Kings xxiii. 34; 2 Chron. xxxvi. 4. Now here, 1. The people are directed to lament him rather than his father Josiah: "*Weep not for the dead,* weep not any more for Josiah." Jeremiah had been himself a true mourner for him (2 Chron. xxxv. 25): yet now he will have them to turn their tears into another channel. They must weep sorely for Jehoahaz, who had gone into Egypt. Josiah went to the grave in peace and honour. *Weep not for him,* but for his unhappy son, who is likely to live and die in disgrace and misery, a wretched captive. Dying saints may be justly envied, while living sinners are justly pitied. He shall never return out of captivity, as he and his people expected, but shall die there. They were loth to believe this, therefore it is repeated here again and again. This came of his forsaking the good example of his father, and usurping the right of his elder brother.

II. The doom of Jehoiakim, who succeeded him. He ruled no better, and fared no better at last.

1. His sins reproved. Jehoiakim is not here charged with idolatry, but the crimes for which he is here reproved are pride, and affection and splendour; as if all the business of a king were to look great, and to do good were to be the least of his care. He must build himself a stately palace, a *wide house,* and *large chambers, v.* 14. He must have *windows cut out* after the newest fashion. The rooms must be *ceiled with cedar,* the richest sort of wood, painted with *minium,* or *vermilion,* or as some read it, with *indigo.* Those therefore that are enlarging their houses, and making them more sumptuous, have need to look well to the frame of their own spirits in the doing of it, and carefully to watch against vain-glory. He reigned his first three years by the permission of the king of Egypt, and all the rest by the permission of the king of Babylon; and yet he that was no better than a viceroy will covet to vie with the greatest monarchs. He thought he must reign without any disturbance or interruption because he had *enclosed himself in cedar* (*v.* 15). Some think he is here charged with sacrilege, and robbing the house of God to beautify and adorn his own house. He *cuts him out* my *windows* (so it is in the margin), which some understand as if he had taken windows out of the temple to put into his own palace and then *painted them with vermilion,* that it might not be discovered. He is here charged with extortion and oppression, violence and injustice. He *built his house by unrighteousness,* with money unjustly got and materials not honestly come by. God takes notice of the wrong done by the greatest of men to their poor servants and labourers, and will repay those, in justice, that will not in justice pay those whom they employ. That which was at the bottom of all was covetousness, that love of *money which is the root of all evil. Thy eyes and thy heart are not but for covetousness;* for that, and nothing else. In covetousness the heart walks after the eyes: it is therefore called *the lust of the eye,* 1 John ii. 16;

JAMIESON, FAUSSET, BROWN

of David should be cast off. **this house**—the king's, where Jeremiah spake (vs. 4). **6.** Though thou art as beautiful as Gilead, and as majestic in Mine eyes (before Me) as the summit of Lebanon, *yet* surely (the *Hebrew* is a formula of swearing to express *certainly: If I do not* make thee. . . ., believe Me not ever hereafter: so "as truly as I live," Num. 14:28; "surely," Num. 14:35). The mention of Gilead may allude not only to its past beauty, but covertly also to its desolation by the judgment on Israel; a warning now to Judah and the house of David. "Lebanon" is appropriately mentioned, as the king's house was built of its noble cedars. **cities**—not other *cities,* but the different *parts* of the *city* of Jerusalem (II Sam. 12:27; II Kings 10:25) [MAURER]. **7.** prepare—lit., "sanctify," or solemnly set apart for a particular work (cf. Isa. 13:3). **thy choice cedars**—(Isa. 37:24). Thy palaces built of choice cedars (Song of Sol. 1:17). **8.** (Deut. 29:24, 25.) The Gentile nations, more intelligent than you, shall understand that which ye do not, viz., that this city is a spectacle of God's vengeance [CALVIN]. **9.** (II Kings 22:17.) **10, 11. Weep . . . not for**—i.e., not so much for Josiah, who was taken away by death from the evil to come (II Kings 22:20; Isa. 57:1); as for Shallum or Jehoahaz, his son (II Kings 23:30), who, after a three months' reign, was carried off by Pharaoh-necho into Egypt, never to see his native land again (II Kings 23:31-34). Dying saints are justly to be envied, while living sinners are to be pitied. The allusion is to the great weeping of the people at the death of Josiah, and on each anniversary of it, in which Jeremiah himself took a prominent part (II Chron. 35:24, 25). The name "Shallum" is here given in irony to Jehoahaz, who reigned but three months; as if he were a second Shallum, son of Jabesh, who reigned only *one month* in Samaria (II Kings 15:13; II Chron. 36:1-4). Shallum means "retribution," a name of no good omen to him [GROTIUS]; originally the people called him *Shallom,* indicative of *peace* and prosperity. But Jeremiah applies it in irony. I Chronicles 3:15, calls Shallum the *fourth* son of Josiah. The people raised him to the throne before his brother Eliakim or Jehoiakim, though the latter was the older (II Kings 23:31, 36; II Chron. 36:1); perhaps on account of Jehoiakim's extravagance (vss. 13, 15). Jehoiakim was put in Shallum's (Jehoahaz') stead by Pharaoh-necho. Jeconiah, his son, succeeded. Zedekiah (Mattaniah), uncle of Jeconiah, and brother of Jehoiakim and Jehoahaz, was last of all raised to the throne by Nebuchadnezzar. **He shall not return**—The people perhaps entertained hopes of Shallum's return from Egypt, in which case they would replace him on the throne, and thereby free themselves from the oppressive taxes imposed by Jehoiakim. **13.** Not only did Jehoiakim tax the people (II Kings 23:35) for Pharaoh's tribute, but also took their forced labor, without pay, for building a splendid palace; in violation of Leviticus 19: 13; Deuteronomy 24:14, 15. Cf. Micah 3:10; Habakkuk 2:9; James 5:4. God will repay in justice those who will not in justice pay those whom they employ. **14. wide**—lit., a house of dimensions ("measures"). Cf. Numbers 13:32, *Margin,* "men of statures." **large**—rather, as *Margin,* "airy," from Hebrew root, "to breathe freely." Upper rooms in the East are the principal apartments. **cutteth him out windows**—The Hebrew, if a noun, is rather, "my windows"; then the translation ought to be, "and let my windows (Jehoiakim speaking) be cut out for it," i.e., in the house; or, "and let (the workman) cut out my windows for it." But the word is rather an adjective; "he cutteth it (the house) out for himself, so as to be *full of windows.*" The following words accord with this construction, "and (he makes it) ceiled with cedar," etc. [MAURER]. Retaining *English Version,* there must be understood something remarkable about the windows, since they are deemed worthy of notice. GESENIUS thinks the word *dual,* "double windows." the *blinds* being *two-leaved.* **vermilion**—*Hebrew, shashar,* called so from a people of India beyond the Ganges, by whom it is exported (PLINY, 6.19). The old vermilion was composed of sulphur and quicksilver; not of red lead, as our vermilion. **15. closest thyself**—rather, thou viest, i.e., art emulous to surpass thy forefathers in the magnificence of thy palaces.

ADAM CLARKE

6. *Thou art Gilead unto me, and the head of Lebanon. Lebanon* was the highest mountain in Israel, and *Gilead* the richest and most fertile part of the country; and were, therefore, proper emblems of the reigning family. Though you are the richest and most powerful, I, who raised you up, can bring you down and make you a *wilderness.*

7. *They shall cut down thy choice cedars.* The destruction of the country is expressed under the symbol of the destruction of a fine forest.

8. *Many nations shall pass.* These words seem borrowed from Deut. xxix. 22, etc.

10. *Weep ye not for the dead.* Josiah, dead in consequence of the wound he had received at Megiddo, in a battle with Pharaoh-necho, king of Egypt; but he died in peace with God.

But weep sore for him that goeth away. Namely, Jehoahaz, the son of Josiah, called below Shallum, whom Pharaoh-necho had carried captive into Egypt, from which it was prophesied he should never return, 2 Kings xxiii. 30-34. He was called Shallum before he ascended the throne, and Jehoahaz afterwards; so his brother Eliakim changed his name to Jehoiakim, and Mattaniah to Zedekiah.

13. *Woe unto him that buildeth his house.* These evils, charged against Jehoiakim, are nowhere else circumstantially related. We learn from 2 Kings xxiii. 35-37 that he taxed his subjects heavily, to give to Pharaoh-necho, king of Egypt: "He exacted the silver and gold of the people of the land," and "did that which was evil in the sight of the Lord." The mode of taxation is here intimated; he took the wages of the hirelings, and caused the people to work without wages in his own buildings.

15. *Shalt thou reign?* Do you think you are a great king, because you dwell in a splendid palace?

MATTHEW HENRY

Job xxxi. 7. That which aggravated all his sins was that he was the son of a good father, who had left him a good example, if he would but have followed it (*v.* 15, 16). Jeremiah tells him he was directed to do his duty by his father's practice: He *did judgment and justice*. He not only did not abuse his power for the support of wrong, but he used it for the maintaining of right. He *judged the cause of the poor and needy*. He was encouraged to do his duty by his father's prosperity. God accepted him: "*Was not this to know me, saith the Lord?*" He had the comfort of it *Did he not eat and drink* soberly and cheerfully, so as to fit himself for his business, *for strength and not for drunkenness?* Eccles. x. 17. God blessed him with plenty, and he had the comfortable enjoyment of it himself and was hospitable and very charitable. It was Jehoiakim's pride that he had built a fine house, but Josiah's true praise that he kept a good house. It is better to live with Josiah in an old-fashioned house, and do good, than live with Jehoiakim in a stately house, and leave debts unpaid.

2. Jehoiakim's doom faithfully read, *v.* 18, 19. We may suppose that it was in peril of his own life that Jeremiah here foretold the shameful death of Jehoiakim; but *thus saith the Lord concerning* him and therefore thus saith he. He shall die unlamented; he shall make himself so odious by his oppression and cruelty that none shall do him the honour of dropping one tear for him. His relations shall not *lament him*. His subjects shall not lament him, as they used to do at the graves of their princes.

Jehoiakim shall be *buried with the burial of an ass*, that is, he shall have no burial at all, but his dead body shall be cast into a ditch or upon a dunghill; it shall be *drawn*, or dragged, ignominiously, and *cast forth beyond the gates of Jerusalem*. Josephus says that Nebuchadnezzar slew him at Jerusalem, and left his body thus exposed, somewhere at a great distance from the *gates of Jerusalem*.

Verses 20–30

This prophecy seems to have been calculated for the inglorious reign of Jeconiah, or Jehoiachin, the son of Jehoiakim, who reigned but three months, and was then carried captive to Babylon, where he lived many years, *ch.* lii. 31.

I. The desolations of the kingdom were now hastening on apace, *v.* 20–23. Jerusalem and Judah are here spoken to as a single person, "*I spoke unto thee in thy prosperity*, spoke by my servants the prophets, reproofs, admonitions, counsels, *but thou saidest, I will not hear*." It is common for those that live at ease to live in contempt of the word of God. *This has been thy manner from thy youth.* "When thou seest *all thy lovers destroyed*, when thou findest thy idols unable to help thee and thy foreign alliances failing thee, thou wilt cry, *Help, help, or we are lost;* thou wilt *lift up thy voice* in fearful shrieks upon *Lebanon* and *Bashan*. Thou wilt *cry from the passages*, from the roads. Thou wilt cry to all about thee; but in vain, for (*v.* 22) *the wind shall eat up all thy pastors*, that should provide for thy safety; they shall be blasted, and withered, as buds and blossoms are by a bleak or freezing wind. *Thy lovers*, that thou hast an affection for, shall *go into captivity*, and shall not be able to save themselves. When there appears no relief from any of thy confederates, *then shalt thou be ashamed and confounded for all thy wickedness*," *v.* 22. The Jewish state is here called *an inhabitant of Lebanon*, because that famous forest was within their border (*v.* 23), and all their country was well-guarded as with Lebanon's natural fastnesses; but so proud were they that they are said to *make their nest in the cedars*, out of the reach of all danger, whence they looked with contempt upon all about them. "But, *how gracious wilt thou be when pangs come upon thee!* Then thou wilt humble thyself before God and promise amendment." Some give another sense of it: "What will all thy pomp and wealth avail thee? No more than *a woman in travail*, full of pains and fears, can take comfort in her ornaments while she is in that condition."

JAMIESON, FAUSSET, BROWN

eat and drink—Did not Josiah, thy father, enjoy all that man *really needs* for his bodily wants? Did he need to build costly palaces to secure his throne? Nay, he *did secure* it by "judgment and justice"; whereas thou, with all thy luxurious building, sittest on a *tottering* throne. **then**—on that account, therefore. **16. was not this to know me**—viz., to show by *deeds* that one knows God's will, as was the case with Josiah (cf. John 13:17; contrast Titus 1:16). **17. thine**—as opposed to thy father, Josiah. **18. Ah my brother! . . . sister!**—addressing him with such titles of affection as one would address to a deceased friend beloved as a *brother* or *sister* (cf. I Kings 13:30). This expresses, They shall not lament him with the lamentation of *private individuals* [VATABLUS], or of *blood relatives* [GROTIUS]: as "Ah! lord," expresses *public* lamentation *in the case of a king* [VATABLUS], or that of *subjects* [GROTIUS]. HENDERSON thinks, "Ah! sister," refers to Jehoiakim's queen, who, though taken to Babylon and not left unburied on the way, as Jehoiakim, yet was not honored at her death with royal lamentations, such as would have been poured forth over her at Jerusalem. He notices the beauty of Jeremiah's manner in his prophecy against Jehoiakim. In vss. 13, 14 he describes him in general terms; then, in vss. 15-17, he directly addresses him without naming him; at last, in vs. 18, he names him, but in the third person, to imply that God puts him to a distance from Him. The boldness of the Hebrew prophets proves their divine mission; were it not so, their reproofs to the Hebrew kings, who held the throne by divine authority, would have been treason. **Ah his glory!**—"Alas! his majesty." **19. burial of an ass**—i.e., he shall have the same burial as an ass would get, viz., he shall be left a prey for beasts and birds [JEROME]. This is not formally narrated. But II Chronicles 36:6 states that "Nebuchadnezzar bound him in fetters to carry him to Babylon"; his treatment there is nowhere mentioned. The prophecy here, and in ch. 36:30, harmonizes these two facts. He was slain by Nebuchadnezzar, who changed his purpose of taking him to Babylon, on the way thither, and left him unburied outside Jerusalem. II Kings 24:6, "Jehoiakim slept with his fathers," does not contradict this; it simply expresses his being gathered to his fathers by *death*, not his being *buried* with his fathers (Ps. 49:19). The two phrases are found together, as expressing two distinct ideas (II Kings 15:38; 16:20). **20.** Delivered in the reign of Jehoiachin (Jeconiah or Coniah), son of Jehoiakim; appended to the previous prophecy respecting Jehoiakim, on account of the similiarity of the two prophecies. He calls on Jerusalem, personified as a mourning female, to go up to the highest points visible from Jerusalem, and lament there (ch. 3:21, *Note*) the calamity of herself, bereft of allies and of her princes, who are one after the other being cast down. **Bashan**—north of the region beyond Jordan; the mountains of Anti-libanus are referred to (Ps. 68:15). **from the passages**—viz., of the rivers (Judg. 12:6); or else the borders of the country (I Sam. 13:23; Isa. 10:29). The passes (I Sam. 14. 4). MAURER translates, "Abarim," a mountainous tract beyond Jordan, opposite Jericho, and south of Bashan; this accords with the mention of the mountains Lebanon and Bashan (Num. 27:12; 33: 47). **lovers**—the allies of Judea, especially Egypt, now unable to help the Jews, being crippled by Babylon (II Kings 24:7). **21.** I admonished thee in time. Thy sin has not been a sin of ignorance or thoughtlessness, but wilful. **prosperity**—given thee by Me; yet thou wouldest not hearken to the gracious Giver. The *Hebrew* is *plural*, to express, "**In** *the height of* thy prosperity"; so "droughts" (Isa. 58:11). **thou saidst**—not in words, but in thy conduct, virtually. **thy youth**—from the time that I brought thee out of Egypt, and formed thee into a people (ch. 7:25; 2:2; Isa. 47:12). **22. wind**—the Chaldees, as a parching wind that sweeps over rapidly and withers vegetation (ch. 4:11, 12; Ps. 103: 16; Isa. 40:7). **eat up . . . pastors**—i.e., thy kings (ch. 2:8). There is a happy play on words. The *pastors*, whose office it is to feed the sheep, shall themselves be *fed on*. They who should *drive* the flock from place to place for pasture shall be *driven* into exile by the Chaldees. **23. inhabitant of Lebanon**—viz., Jerusalem, whose temple, palaces, and principal habitations were built of cedars of Lebanon. **how gracious**—irony. How graciously thou wilt be treated by the Chaldees, when they come on thee suddenly, as pangs on a woman in travail (ch. 6:24)! Nay, all thy fine buildings will win no favor for thee from them. MAURER translates, "How shalt thou be *to be pitied*!" **24. As I live**—God's most solemn formula of oath (ch. 46:

ADAM CLARKE

JOSEPH PARKER:

Verses 18, 19. The description of Jehoiakim really begins in the thirteenth verse. Johoiakim had revived forced labor, such as was known in the days of Solomon—a labor which pressed not only on strangers, but on the Israelites themselves. Jehoiakim went on building palaces when his kingdom was threatened with ruin, and when his subjects were overborne by burdens which it was impossible to sustain. In the thirteenth verse the prophet begins a description of a man without naming him; a man who builds his house by unrighteousness, and his chambers by ruin; a man who uses his neighbor's services without wages, and gives him not for his work; a man who yields to the impulses of a foolish ambition, saying, I will build me a wide house and large chambers, and who gratifies himself by cutting out windows, and ceiling his chambers with cedars, and painting his retreats with vermilion. It is not until we come to the eighteenth verse that the prophet specially indicates the man against whom this accusation is levelled. Jehoiakim was king, and yet not one word of thanks do we find, nor one word of love, nor one word of regret expressed concerning his fate. We should learn from this how possible it is to pass through the world without leaving behind us one sacred or loving memory. He that seeketh his life shall lose it.

—*The People's Bible*

19. *With the burial of an ass.* Cast out, and left unburied, or buried without any funeral solemnities, and without such lamentations as the above.

20. *Go up to Lebanon.* Probably Anti-Libanus, which, together with Bashan and Abarim, which we here translate "passages," were on the way by which the captives should be led out of their own country.

21. *I spake unto thee in thy prosperity.* In all states and circumstances I warned you by My prophets; and you will be ashamed of your conduct only when you shall be stripped of all your excellencies, and reduced to poverty and disgrace, v. 22.

22. *The wind shall eat up all thy pastors.* A blast from God's mouth shall carry off your kings, princes, prophets, and priests.

23. *How gracious shalt thou be!* A strong irony.

MATTHEW HENRY

II. Here is a prophecy of the disgrace of the king; his name was *Jeconiah*, but he is here once and again called *Coniah*, in contempt. He shall be carried away *into captivity* and shall spend and end his days in bondage. God will abandon him, *v.* 24. "*Though he were the signet upon my right hand I will pluck him thence.*" The godly kings of Judah had been as signets on God's right hand, near and dear to him; he had gloried in them. The king of Babylon shall seize him. *Those* know not what mischiefs they lie exposed to who have thrown themselves out of God's protection, *v.* 25. The Chaldeans had a spite to *Coniah*; they *sought his life* (they are those *whose face thou fearest*). He and his family shall be carried to Babylon, where they shall wear out many tedious years in a miserable captivity—*he and his mother* (*v.* 26), *he and his seed* (*v.* 28), that is, he and all the royal family—shall all be cast out to another country, *a country where they were not born, a land which they know not*, in which they have no acquaintance from whom to expect any kindness. *To the land whereunto they desire to return, thither shall they not return*, *v.* 27. Jehoahaz was carried to Egypt, the land of the south, Jeconiah to Babylon, the land of the north, never to meet again, nor to breathe their native air. There is something very emphatic in that part of this threatening (*v.* 26), *In the country where you were not born, there shall you die.* This shall render him despicable in the eyes of all his neighbours. They shall be ready to say (*v.* 28), "*Is this Coniah a despised broken idol?*" Time was when he was dignified, nay, when he was almost deified. The people who had seen his father lately deposed were ready to adore him when they saw him upon the throne, but now *he is a despised broken idol.* He shall leave no posterity to inherit his honour. Let all the world notice these judgments of God upon a nation and a family that had been near and dear to him, and thence infer that God is impartial in the administration of justice. Now that which is here to be taken notice of is that Jeconiah is *written childless* (*v.* 30), that is, as it follows, *No man of his seed shall prosper, sitting upon the throne of David.* Some think that he had children born in Babylon (*v.* 28) and that they died before him. We read in the genealogy (1 Chron. iii. 17) of seven sons of Jeconiah Assir (that is, Jeconiah the captive) of whom Salathiel is the first. Some think that they were only his adopted sons, and that when it is said (Matt. i. 12), *Jeconiah begat Salathiel*, no more is meant than that he bequeathed to him what claims he had to the government, because Salathiel is called the *son of Neri* of *the house of Nathan*, Luke iii. 27, 31. Whether he had children begotten, or only adopted, none of his seed ruled as kings in Judah.

JAMIESON, FAUSSET, BROWN

18; 4:2; Deut. 32:40; I Sam. 25:34). **Coniah**—Jeconiah or Jehoiachin. The contraction of the name is meant in contempt. **signet**—Such ring-seals were often of the greatest value (Song of Sol. 8:6; Hag. 2:23). Jehoiachin's popularity is probably here referred to. **right hand**—the hand most valued. **I would pluck thee thence**—(Cf. Obad. 4); on account of thy father's sins, as well as thine own (II Chron. 36:9). There is a change here, as often in *Hebrew* poetry, from the third to the second person, to bring the threat more directly home to him. After a three months' and ten days' reign, the Chaldees deposed him. In Babylon, however, by God's favor he was ultimately treated more kindly than other royal captives (ch. 52:31-34). But none of his direct posterity ever came to the throne. **25. give . . . into . . . hand**—"I will pluck thee" from "*my right hand*," and "will give thee *into the hand of them that seek thy life.*" **26. thy mother**—Nehushta, the queen dowager (II Kings 24:6, 8, 15; see ch. 13: 18). **27. they**—Coniah and his mother. He passes from the second person (vs. 26) to the third person here, to express alienation. The king is as it were put out of sight, as if unworthy of being spoken with directly. **desire**—lit., "lift up their soul" (ch. 44:14; Ps. 24:4; 25:1). Judea was the land which they in Babylon should pine after in vain. **28. broken idol**—Coniah was idolized once by the Jews; Jeremiah, therefore, in their person, expresses their astonishment at one from whom so much had been expected being now so utterly cast aside. **vessel . . . no pleasure**—(Ps. 31:12; Hos. 8:8). The answer to this is given (Rom. 9:20-23; contrast II Tim. 2:21). **his seed**—(See *Note*, vs. 29). **29, 30. O earth! earth! earth!**—Jeconiah was not actually without offspring (cf. vs. 28, "his seed"; I Chron. 3:17, 18; Matt. 1:12), but he was to be "written childless," as a warning to posterity, i.e., without a lineal heir to his throne. It is with a reference to the *three* kings, Shallum, Jehoiakim, and Jeconiah, that the earth is *thrice* invoked [Bengel]. Or, the *triple* invocation is to give intensity to the call for attention to the announcement of the end of the royal line, so far as Jehoiachin's seed is concerned. Though Messiah (Matt. 1), the heir of David's throne, was lineally descended from Jeconiah, it was only through Joseph, who, though His legal, was not His real father. Matthew gives the legal pedigree through *Solomon* down to Joseph; Luke the real pedigree, from Mary, the real parent, through *Nathan*, brother of Solomon, upwards (Luke 3:31). **no man of his seed . . . upon the throne**—This explains the sense in which "childless" is used. Though the succession to the throne failed in his line, still the promise to David (Ps. 89:30-37) was revived in Zerubbabel and consummated in Christ.

ADAM CLARKE

24. *Though Coniah.* Called Jeconiah, probably on ascending the throne. See on v. 10. *The signet upon my right hand.* The most precious seal, ring, or armlet. Though dearer to Me than the most splendid gem to its possessor.

26. *I will cast thee out, and thy mother.* See all this fulfilled, 2 Kings xxiv. 12-13. All were carried by Nebuchadnezzar into captivity together.

28. *Is this man Coniah a despised broken idol?* These are probably the exclamations of the people, when they heard those solemn denunciations against their king and their country.

29. *O earth.* These are the words of the prophet in reply: O land! unhappy land! desolate land! Hear the judgment of the Lord!

30. *Write ye this man childless.* Though he had seven sons, 1 Chron. iii. 17, yet, having no successor, he is to be entered on the genealogical tables as one without children, for none of his posterity ever sat on the throne of David.

MATTHEW HENRY — CHAPTER 23

Verses 1–8

I. A word of terror to the negligent shepherds. *Woe be to the pastors* (to the *rulers*, both in church and state) who should be pastors to lead them, feed them, protect them, and take care of them. They are not owners of the sheep. God here calls them *the sheep of my pasture*, whom I have provided good pasture for. Woe be to those therefore who are commanded to feed God's people, and pretend to do it, but who, instead of that, *scatter the flock* by their violence and oppression. In not visiting them they did in effect drive them away. The beasts of prey scattered them, and the shepherds are in the fault, who should have kept them together.

II. A word of comfort to the neglected sheep. Though the under-shepherds take no care of them, the chief Shepherd will look after them. God will perform his promise, though those he employs do not perform their duty.

1. The dispersed Jews shall at length return to their own land, and be happily settled there under a good government, *v.* 3, 4. Though there be but a remnant of God's flock left, he will gather that remnant wherever they are and bring them back out of all countries *whither he had driven them. They shall be brought* to their former habitations, as sheep to their folds, and there *they shall be fruitful, and increase* in numbers. Formerly they were continually disturbed, but now *they shall fear no more, nor be dismayed.* Such pastors as Zerubbabel and Nehemiah, though they lived not in the pomp that Jehoiakim and Jeconiah did, were as great blessings to the people as the others were plagues to them.

2. Messiah the Prince, that great and good Shepherd of the sheep, shall in the latter days be raised up to bless his church, and to be *the glory of his people Israel*, *v.* 5, 6. The house of David seemed to

JAMIESON, FAUSSET, BROWN — CHAPTER 23

Vss. 1-40. The Wicked Rulers to Be Superseded by the King, Who Should Reign over the Again United Peoples, Israel and Judah. This forms the *epilogue* to the denunciations of the four kings, in ch. 21:22. **1. pastors**—Shallum, Jehoiakim, Jeconiah, and Zedekiah (Ezek. 34:2). **2. Ye have not . . . visited them . . . I will visit upon you**—just retribution. Play upon the double sense of "visit." "Visit upon," viz., in wrath (Exod. 32:34).

3, 4. Restoration of Judah from Babylon foretold in language which in its fulness can only apply to the final restoration of *both* "Judah" and "*Israel*" (cf. vs. 6); also "out of *all* countries," in this verse and vs. 8; also, "neither shall they be lacking," i.e., none shall be missing or detached from the rest: a prophecy never yet fully accomplished. It holds good also of the spiritual Israel, the elect of both Jews and Gentiles (Mal. 3:16, 17; John 10:28; 17:12). As to the literal Israel also, see ch. 32:37; Isa. 54:13; 60:21; Ezek. 34:11-16). **shepherds . . . shall feed them**—(ch. 3:15; Ezek. 34:23-31). Zerubbabel, Ezra, Nehemiah, and the Maccabees were but typical of the consummating fulfilment of these prophecies under Messiah. **5.** As Messianic prophecy extended over many years in which many political changes took place in harmony with these, it displayed its riches by a variety more effective than if it had been manifested all at once. As the moral condition of the Jews required in each instance, so Messiah was exhibited in a corresponding phase, thus becoming more and more the soul of the nation's life: so that He is represented as the

ADAM CLARKE — CHAPTER 23

1. *Woe be unto the pastors!* There shall a curse fall on the kings, princes, priests, and prophets; who, by their vicious conduct and example, have brought desolation upon the people.

2. *Ye have scattered my flock.* The bad government in both church and state was a principal cause of the people's profligacy.

MATTHEW HENRY

be ruined by that threatening against Jeconiah (*ch.* xxii. 30). But here is a promise which effectually secures the honour of the covenant made with David; for by it the house will be raised out of its ruins to a greater lustre than ever. We have not so many prophecies of Christ in this book as we had in that of the prophet Isaiah; but here we have a very illustrious one. The first words intimate that it would be long ere this promise should have its accomplishment: *The days come*, but they are not yet. *I shall see him, but not now.* Christ is here spoken of as a *branch from David*, his appearance mean, his beginnings small, like those of a bud, and his rise seemingly out of the earth, but growing to be loaded with fruits. A branch from David's family, when it seemed to be a *root in a dry ground*, buried, and not likely to revive. In him doth the *horn of David bud*, Ps. cxxxii. 17, 18. He is *a righteous branch*, for he is righteous himself, and through him many, even all that are his, are made righteous. As an advocate, he is *Jesus Christ the righteous.* He is here spoken of as his church's King. He shall set up a kingdom in the world that shall be victorious over all opposition. In the chariot of the everlasting gospel he shall go forth, he shall go on *conquering and to conquer*. Christ shall, by his gospel, break the usurped power of Satan, institute a perfect rule of holy living, and, as far as it prevails, make all the world righteous. The effect of this shall be a holy security and serenity of mind in all his faithful loyal subjects. *In his days*, under his dominion, *Judah shall be saved and Israel shall dwell safely*. See Luke i. 74, 75. In the days of Christ's government in the soul, when he is uppermost there, the soul *dwells at ease*. He is *the Lord of our righteousness.* As God, he is *Jehovah*, the incommunicable name of God, denoting his eternity and self-existence. As Mediator, he is *our righteousness.* By making satisfaction to the justice of God for the sin of man, he has brought in an everlasting righteousness, and so made it over to us in the covenant of grace that, upon our consent to that covenant, it becomes ours. He is a sovereign, all-sufficient, eternal righteousness. All our righteousness has its being from him, and by him it subsists. *This is the name whereby he shall be called*, not only he shall be so, but he shall be known to be so. That is our righteousness by which we are justified before God, acquitted from guilt, and accepted into favour; and nothing else have we to plead but this, "Christ has died, yea, rather has risen again"; and we have taken him for our Lord.

3. This great salvation, which will come to the Jews in the latter days, after their return out of Babylon, shall far outshine the deliverance of Israel out of Egypt (*v.* 7, 8): *They shall no more say, The Lord liveth that brought up Israel out of Egypt; but, The Lord liveth that brought them up out of the north.* After they came out of Babylon Messiah the Prince set up the gospel temple, the greatest glory of that nation that was so wonderfully brought out of Babylon.

Verses 9–32

A long lesson for the false prophets. The prophet had complained to God of those false prophets (*ch.* xiv. 13), and had often foretold that they should be involved in the common ruin; but here they have woes of their own.

I. He expresses what a trouble it was to him to see men who pretended to a divine commission and inspiration ruining themselves, and the people among whom they dwelt, by their falsehood and treachery (*v.* 9): *My heart within me is broken; I am like a drunken man.* Jeremiah was a man that laid things much to heart, and what was any way threatening to his country made a deep impression upon his spirits. He is here in trouble, 1. *Because of the prophets* and their sin, the false doctrine they preached, the wicked lives they lived, pretending to have their instructions from him. 2. "*Because of the Lord*, and his judgments, which by this means are brought in upon us like a deluge." He trembled to think of the ruin and desolation which were coming *from the face of the Lord* (so the word is) *and from the face of the word of his holiness.*

II. He laments the abounding abominable wickedness of the land and the present tokens of God's displeasure they were under for it (*v.* 10): *The land is full of adulterers;* it is full both of spiritual and corporal whoredom. Their land mourned now under the judgment of famine; the *pleasant places*, or rather *the pastures*, are dried up for want of rain, and yet we see no signs of repentance. They have a great deal of resolution, but it is turned the wrong way; they are *zealously affected*, but not *in a good thing*, though they see God thus contending with them.

JAMIESON, FAUSSET, BROWN

antitypical Israel (Isa. 49:3). **unto David**—HENGSTENBERG observes that Isaiah dwells more on His *prophetical* and *priestly* office, which had already been partly set forth (Deut. 18:18; Ps. 110:4). Other prophets dwell more on His *kingly* office. Therefore here He is associated with "David" *the king:* but in Isaiah 11:1 with the then poor and unknown "Jesse." **righteous Branch**—"the Branch of righteousness" (ch. 33:15); "The Branch" simply (Zech. 3:8; 6:12); "The Branch of the Lord" (Isa. 4:2). **prosper**—the very term applied to Messiah's undertaking (Isa. 52:13; *Margin*; 53:10). *Righteousness* or *justice* is the characteristic of Messiah elsewhere, too, in connection with our *salvation* or *justification* (Isa. 53:11; Dan. 9:24; Zech. 9:9). So in the New Testament He is not merely "righteous" Himself, but "righteousness to us" (I Cor. 1:30), so that we become "the righteousness of God in Him" (Rom. 10:3, 4; II Cor. 5:19-21; Phil. 3:9). **execute judgment and justice in the earth**—(Ps. 72:2; Isa. 9:7; 32:1, 18). Not merely a spiritual reign in the sense in which He is "our righteousness," but a righteous reign "in the earth" (ch. 3:17, 18). In some passages He is said to come to *judge*, in others to *reign*. In Matthew 25:34, He is called "the King." Psalm 9:7 unites them. Cf. Daniel 7:22, 26, 27. **6. Judah . . . Israel . . . dwell safely**—Cf. ch. 33:16, where "Jerusalem" is substituted for "Israel" here. Only *Judah*, and that only in part, has as yet returned. So far are the Jews from having enjoyed, as yet, the temporal blessings here foretold as the result of Messiah's reign, that their lot has been, for eighteen centuries, worse than ever before. The accomplishment must, therefore, be still future, when both Judah and Israel in their own land shall dwell safely under a Christocracy, far more privileged than even the old theocracy (ch. 32:37; Deut. 33:28; Isa. 54:60; 65:17-25; Zech. 14: 11). **shall be called, the Lord**—i.e., shall *be* (Isa. 9:6) "Jehovah," God's incommunicable name. Though when applied to created things, it expresses only some peculiar *connection* they have with Jehovah (Gen. 22:14; Exod. 17:15), yet when applied to Messiah it must express His *Godhead* manifested in justifying power *towards us* (I Tim. 3:16). **our**—marks His *manhood*, which is also implied in His being a *Branch raised unto David*, whence His human title, "Son of David" (cf. Matt. 22:42-45). **Righteousness**—marks His *Godhead*, for God alone can justify the ungodly (cf. Rom. 4:5; Isa. 45:17, 24, 25). **7, 8.** Repeated from ch. 16:14, 15. —The prophet said the same things often, in order that his sayings might make the more impression. The same promise as in vss. 3, 4. The wide dispersion of the Jews at the Babylonish captivity prefigures their present wider dispersion (Isa. 11:11; Joel 3:6). Their second deliverance is to exceed far the former one from Egypt. But the deliverance from Babylon was inferior to that from Egypt in respect to the miracles performed and the numbers delivered. The final deliverance under Messiah must, therefore, be meant, of which that from Babylon was the earnest. **9. because of the prophets**—so the Masorites and Targum. But *Vulgate*, LXX, etc., make this the inscription of the prophecy, CONCERNING THE PROPHETS: as in ch. 46:2; 48:1; 49: 1. Jeremiah expresses his horror at the so-called "prophets" not warning the people, though iniquity so fearfully abounded, soon to be followed by awful judgments. **bones shake**—(Hab. 3:16). **drunken**—God's judgments are represented as stupefying like wine. The effects of the Holy Spirit also are compared to those of wine (Acts 2:17). In both cases ecstasy was produced. This accounts for the denial of wine to those likely to be inspired, Nazarites, etc. (Luke 1:15). It was necessary to put it out of men's power to ascribe inspired ecstasy to the effects of wine. **because of . . . words of . . . holiness**—because of Jehovah's holy words, wherewith He threatened severe penalties, soon to be inflicted, against the breakers of His law. **10. adulterers**—spiritual, i.e., forsakers of God, Israel's true Husband (Isa. 54:5) for idols, at the instigation of the false "prophets" (vss. 9, 15). *Literal* "adultery" and fornication, the usual concomitants of idolatry, are also meant. **swearing**—MAURER, etc., translate, "Because of the curse (of God on it), the land mourneth" (Deut. 27:15–26; 28:15-68; Isa. 24: 6). More than usual notoriety had been given to the curses of the law, by the finding and reading of it in Josiah's time (II Kings 22:11, etc.). But Hosea 4:2, 3, favors *English Version* (cf. ch. 12:4). A drought was sent by God on the pastures ("pleasant places," oases) in the desert, on account of the "profaneness" of the priests, prophets, and people (vs. 11). **course . . . evil**—They (both prophets and people) rush into wickedness (vs. 21; Isa. 59:7).

ADAM CLARKE

5. *I will raise unto David a righteous Branch.* As there has been no age, from the Babylonish captivity to the destruction of Jerusalem by the Romans, in which such a state of prosperity existed, and no king or governor who could answer at all to the character here given, the passage has been understood to refer to our blessed Lord, Jesus Christ, who was a Branch out of the stem of Jesse; a righteous King; by the power of His Spirit and influence of His religion reigning, prospering, and executing judgment and justice in the earth.

6. *In his days Judah shall be saved.* The real Jew is not one who has his circumcision in the flesh, but in the spirit. The real Israel are true believers in Christ Jesus; and the genuine Jerusalem is the Church of the Firstborn, made free, with all her children, from the bondage of sin, Satan, death, and hell.

And this is his name whereby he shall be called, THE LORD OUR RIGHTEOUSNESS. Dr. Blayney seems to follow the Septuagint; he translates thus, "And this is the name by which Jehovah shall call him, Our Righteousness." I prefer the translation of Blayney to all others.

9. *Mine heart within me is broken because of the prophets.* The first word of this clause is *lannebiim*, which we incorporate with the whole clause, and translate, *because of the prophets.* But as a new prophecy begins here, it is evident that the word is the title to this prophecy; and is thus distinguished by both Blayney and Dahler, "Concerning the Prophets." This discourse was delivered probably in the reign of Jehoiakim. *All my bones shake.* He was terrified even by his own message, and shocked at the profanity of the false prophets.

10. *The land is full of adulterers.* Of idolaters. Of persons who break their faith to Me, as an impure wife does to her husband.

The pleasant places of the wilderness are dried up. He speaks here, most probably, in reference to dearth. Profane oaths, false swearing, evil courses, violence, etc., had provoked God to send this among other judgments; see v. 19.

MATTHEW HENRY

III. He charges it all upon the prophets and priests, especially the prophets. They are *both profane* (*v.* 11); the priests profane the ordinances of God they pretend to administer; the prophets profane the word of God they pretend to deliver. They both *play the hypocrite* (so some read it); under sacred pretensions they carry on the vilest designs; *in my house have I found their wickedness;* in the temple, where the priests ministered, where the prophets prophesied, there were they guilty both of idolatry and immorality. Two things are charged upon them: 1. That they taught people to sin by their examples. He compares them with the prophets of Samaria, the head city of the kingdom of the ten tribes, which had been long since laid waste. It was the folly of the prophets of Samaria that *they prophesied in Baal,* in Baal's name; and so *they caused my people Israel to err,* to forsake the service of the true God and to worship Baal, *v.* 13. Now the prophets of Jerusalem did not do so; they prophesied in the name of the true God, and valued themselves upon that, that they were not like the prophets of Samaria, who prophesied in Baal; but they debauched the nation as much by their immoralities as the other had done by their idolatries! They make use of the name and the holy God, and yet wallow in all manner of impurity. They make use of the name of the God of truth, and yet *walk in lies.* Thus they encourage sinners for everyone will say, "Surely we may do as the prophets do; who can expect that we should be better than our teachers?" By this means Judah and Jerusalem have become *as Sodom and Gormorrah,* and God looked upon them accordingly as fit for nothing but to be destroyed. 2. That they encouraged people in sin by their false prophecies. They made themselves believe that there was no harm, no danger in sin, and practised accordingly (*v.* 16): *They speak a vision of their own heart;* it is *not out of the mouth of the Lord.* They tell sinners that it shall be well with them though they persist in their sins, *v.* 17. Those that are devoted to their pleasures put contempt upon their God. These prophets flattered them: they should have been still saying, There is no peace to those that go on in their evil ways, but they still said, *You shall have peace; no evil shall come upon you;* and, which was worst of all, they told them, *God has said so.*

IV. God disowns all that these false prophets said to sooth people in their sins (*v.* 21): *I have not sent these prophets;* they never had any mission from God. Yet they were very forward—*they ran;* they were very bold—*they prophesied* without any of that difficulty with which the true prophets sometimes struggled. They said to sinners, *You shall have peace.* But (*v.* 18): "*Who hath stood in the counsel of the Lord?* You deliver this message with a great deal of assurance; but have you consulted God about it? You have not *perceived and heard his word,* you have not compared this with the scripture; if you had taken notice of the constant tenor of it, you would never have delivered such a message." That they did not *stand in God's counsel* nor *hear his word* is proved afterwards, *v.* 22. *If they had stood in my counsel,* as they pretended, 1. They would have made the scriptures their standard: *They would have caused my people to hear my words.* 2. They would have made the conversion of souls their business, and would have aimed at that in all their preaching. 3. They would have had some seals of their ministry. *If they had stood in my counsel,* and the words they had preached had been *my words,* then they should *have turned from their evil way.*

V. God threatens to punish these prophets for their wickedness. They promised the people *peace;* and to show them the folly of that God tells them that they should have no peace themselves. Evil is coming upon themselves and they are not aware of it, *v.* 12. Because the prophets and priests are profane, *therefore their ways shall be unto them as slippery ways in the darkness.* They pretend to show others the way, but they shall themselves be in the dark, or in a mist. They pretend to give assurances to others, but they themselves shall find no firm footing. They pretend to make the people easy with their flatteries, but they shall themselves be uneasy: *They shall be driven,* making their escape, *they shall fall in the way.* They pretend to prevent the evil that threatens others, but God will *bring evil upon them, even the year of their visitation. The year of visitation* is the year of recompenses. It is further threatened (*v.* 15), *I will feed them with wormwood,* which is not only nauseous, but noxious, and *make them drink waters of gall,* or (as some read it) *juice of hemlock*; see *ch.* ix. 15.

VI. The people are here warned not to give any credit to these false prophets (*v.* 16): "Take notice of what God says, and *hearken not to the words of*

JAMIESON, FAUSSET, BROWN

force . . . not right—Their *powers* are used not on the side of *rectitude,* but on that of falsehood. **11. profane**—(Ezek. 23:39; Zeph. 3:4).

in my house—(ch. 7:30). They built altars to idols in the very temple (II Kings 23:12; Ezek. 8:3-16). Cf. as to covetousness under the roof of the sanctuary, Matthew 21:13; John 2:16.

13. folly—lit., insipidity, unsavouriness (Job 6:6), not having the salt of godliness (Col. 4:6). **in Baal**—in the name of Baal; in connection with his worship (see ch. 2:8). **caused . . . to err**—(Isa. 9:16).

14. "Jerusalem" and Judah were even worse than "Samaria" and the ten tribes; the greater were the privileges of the former, the greater was their guilt. They had the temple in their midst, which the ten tribes had not; yet in the temple itself they practised idolatry. **strengthen . . . hands of evildoers**—(Ezek. 13:22). **as Sodom**—(Deut. 32:32; Isa. 1:10).

16. make you vain—They seduce you to vanity, i.e., idolatry, which will prove a vain trust to you (ch. 2:5; II Kings 17:15; Jonah 2:8), [GESENIUS]. Rather, "they delude you with vain promises of security" (vs. 17; cf. Ps. 62:10) [MAURER]. **of . . . own heart**—of their own invention (vs. 21; ch. 14:14). **17. say still**—*Hebrew,* "say in saying," i.e., say *incessantly.* **peace**—(ch. 6:14; Ezek. 13:10; Zech. 10:2). **imagination**—*Hebrew,* obstinacy. **no evil**—(Mic. 3:11).

21. sent . . . spoken—"sent" refers to the primary *call*: "spoken" to the subsequent *charges* given to be executed. A call is required, not only external, on the part of men, but also internal from God, that one should undertake a pastor's office [CALVIN].

18. A reason is given why the false prophets should not be heeded: *They have not stood in the counsels of Jehovah* (an image from ministers present in a *standing* posture at councils of Eastern kings) (cf. vs. 22; Job 15:8). The spiritual man alone has the privilege (Gen. 18:17; Ps. 25:14; Amos 3:7; John 15:15; I Cor. 2:16).

22. stood in . . . counsel—(vs. 18). **they should have turned them from their evil way**—They would have given such counsels to the people as would have turned them from their sins (ch. 25:5; Isa. 55:11), and so would have averted punishment. Their not teaching the law in which God's counsel is set forth proves they are not His prophets, though they boast of being so (Matt. 7:15-20).

12. slippery ways in . . . darkness—Their "way" is their false doctrine which proves fatal to them (ch. 13:16; Ps. 35:6; Prov. 4:19).

I will bring evil . . . visitation—still more calamities than those already inflicted. See *Note,* ch. 11:23; "visitation," viz., in wrath.

15. gall—poison (*Note,* ch. 8:14; 9:15).

ADAM CLARKE

11. *In my house.* They had even introduced idolatry into the temple of God!

13. *I have seen folly in the prophets of Samaria.* This was not to be wondered at, for their religion was a system of corruption.

14. *I have seen also in the prophets of Jerusalem.* That is, the prophets of Jerusalem, while professing a pure faith, have followed the ways of, and become as corrupt as, the prophets of Samaria. *They are all of them unto me as Sodom.* Incorrigible, brutish sinners, who will as surely be destroyed as Sodom and Gomorrah were.

16. *Harken not unto the words of the prophets.* That is, of those who promise you safety, without requiring you to forsake your sins and turn unto the Lord; see v. 17.

18. *Who hath stood in the counsel of the Lord?* Who of them has ever received a word of prophecy from Me?

MATTHEW HENRY

these prophets; for you will find that God's word shall stand, and not theirs. They tell you, *No evil shall come upon you;* but hear what God says (*v.* 19), *Behold, a whirlwind of the Lord has gone forth in fury.* They tell you, All shall be calm and serene; but God tells you, There is a storm coming, a *whirlwind of the Lord,* there is no standing before it." This sentence is irreversible (*v.* 20): *The anger of the Lord shall not return.* God will not alter his mind, nor suffer his anger to be turned away, *till he have executed* the sentence and *performed the thoughts of his heart.* This they will not consider now; but *in the latter days you shall consider it perfectly,* consider it *with understanding* (so the word is) or *with consideration.*

VII. Several things are here offered to the consideration of these false prophets that they might be brought to recant their error.

1. Let them consider that though they may impose upon men God is too wise to be imposed upon.

(1) God asserts his own omnipresence and omniscience in general, *v.* 23, 24. Though God's throne is prepared in the heavens, and this earth seems to be at a distance from him, yet he is a God here in this lower world, *v.* 23. The eye of God is the same on earth that it is in heaven. The power of God is the same on earth among its inhabitants that it is in heaven. With us nearness and distance make a great difference both in our observations and in our operations, but it is not so with God; to him darkness and light, at hand and afar off, are both alike. Men's characters and counsels cannot possibly be concealed from God's all-seeing eye (*v.* 24): "*Can any hide himself in the secret places?* Can any hide his projects and intentions in the secret places of the heart, that I shall not see them?" He is everywhere present; he does not only rule heaven and earth, but he *fills heaven and earth* by his essential presence, Ps. cxxxix. 7, 8, &c. No place can either include him or exclude him.

(2) He applies this to these prophets, who had a notable art of disguising themselves (*v.* 25, 26). God will make them know that he knows all the shame they have put upon the world, under colour of divine revelation. God discovered the fraud. *Is it in the hearts of those prophets* (so some read it) *to be ever prophesying lies and prophesying the deceits of their own hearts?*

2. Let them consider that their palming upon people counterfeit revelations, and fathering their own fancies upon divine inspiration, was the ready way to bring all religion into contempt and make men turn atheists and infidels. *Thus saith the Lord, They think to cause my people to forget my name by their dreams.* The great thing Satan aims at is to make people forget God, and all that whereby he has made himself known. Sometimes he does it by setting up false gods (bring men in love with Baal, and they soon forget the name of God), sometimes by misrepresenting the true God.

3. Let them consider what a vast difference there was between their prophecies and those that were delivered by the true prophets of the Lord (*v.* 28): *The prophet that has a dream, let him tell it as a dream.* "Let him lay no more stress upon it than men do upon their dreams, nor expect any more regard to be had to it. But let the true prophet, that *has my word, speak my word faithfully,* speak it *as a truth*" (so some read it): "let him keep closely to his instructions, and you will soon perceive a vast difference between the dreams that the false prophets tell and the divine dictates which the true prophets deliver. Those that have spiritual senses exercised will be able to distinguish; for *what is the chaff to the wheat?*" Men's fancies are light and worthless, as the chaff *which the wind drives away.* But the word of God has substance in it; it is of value, is food for the soul, the bread of life. *Is not my word like a fire, saith the Lord?* Is their word so? Has it the power and efficacy that the word of God has? Fire has different effects, according as the matter is on which it works; it hardens clay, but softens wax; it consumes the dross, but purifies the gold. So the word of God is to some *a savour of life unto life, to others of death unto death.* It is compared likewise to a *hammer breaking the rock in pieces.* The unhumbled heart of man is like a rock; if it will not be melted by the word of God as the fire, it will be broken to pieces by it as the hammer.

4. Let them consider that while they went on in this course God was against them. Three times they are told this, *v.* 30, 31, 32. They stand indicted here. *They steal my word everyone from his neighbour.* Those that were strangers to the spirit of the true prophets mimicked their language, picked up some good sayings of theirs, and delivered them to the people as if they had been their own, but with an ill grace. Others understand it of the word of God as it was received by some of the people; they stole it

JAMIESON, FAUSSET, BROWN

19. So far from all prosperity awaiting the people as the false prophets say (vs. 17), wrath is in store for them. **grievous**—lit., eddying, whirling itself about, a tornado. In ch. 30: 23, "continuing" is substituted for "grievous." **fall grievously**—it shall be hurled on. **20. in . . . latter days**—i.e., "the year of their visitation" (vs. 12). *Primarily* the meaning is: the Jews will not "consider" now God's warnings (Deut. 32:29); but when the prophecies shall be fulfilled in their Babylonish exile, they will consider and see, by bitter experience, their sinful folly. The *ultimate* scope of the prophecy is: the Jews, in their final dispersion, shall at last "consider" their sin and turn to Messiah "perfectly" (Hos. 3:5; Zech. 12:5, 10-14; Luke 13:35).

23. Let not the false prophets fancy that their devices (vs. 25) are unknown to Me. Are ye so ignorant as to suppose that I can only see things near Me, viz., things in heaven, and not earthly things as being too remote?

24. (Ps. 139:7, etc.; Amos 9:2, 3.) **fill heaven and earth**—with My omniscience providence, power, and essential being (I Kings 8:27).

26. prophets—a different *Hebrew* form from the usual one, "prophesiers." "How long," cries Jeremiah, impatient of their impious audacity, "shall these *prophecy-mongers* go on prophesying lies?" The answer is given in vss. 29-34.

25. dreamed—I have received a prophetic communication by dream (Num. 12:6; Deut. 13:1, etc.; Joel 2:28). **27.** They "think" to make My people utterly to forget Me. But I will oppose to those dreamers my true prophets. **fathers . . . for Baal**—(Judg. 3:7; 8:33, 34).

28. God answers the objection which might be stated, "What, then, must we do, when lies are spoken as truths, and prophets oppose prophets?" Do the same as when wheat is mixed with chaff: do not reject the wheat because of the chaff mixed with it, but discriminate between the false and the true revelations. The test is adherence to, or *forgetfulness* of, Me and My law (vs. 27). **that hath a dream**—that pretends to have a divine communication by dream, let him tell it "faithfully," that it may be compared with "my word" (II Cor. 4:2). The result will be the former (both the prophets and their fictions) will soon be seen to be *chaff;* the latter (the true prophets and the word of God in their mouth) *wheat* (Ps. 1:4; Hos 13:3). **29.** As the "fire" consumes the "chaff," so "My word" will consume the false prophets (Matt. 3:12; Heb. 4:12). "My word" which is "wheat," i.e., food to the true prophet and his hearers, is a consuming "fire," and a crushing "hammer" (Matt. 21:44) to false prophets and their followers (II Cor. 2:16). The word of the false prophets may be known by its promising men *peace* in sin. "My word," on the contrary, burns and *breaks* the hard-hearted (ch. 20:9). The "hammer" symbolizes destructive power (ch. 50:23; Nah. 2:1, *Margin*).

30 steal my words—a twofold plagiarism; one steals from the other, and all steal words from Jehovah's true prophets, but misapply them (see ch. 28:2; John 10:1; Rev. 22:19).

ADAM CLARKE

23. *Am I a God at hand, . . . and not a God afar off?* You act as if you thought I could not see you! Am I not omnipresent? "Do not I fill heaven and earth?" (v. 24)

27. *By their dreams.* Dreams were anciently reputed as a species of inspiration; see Num. xii. 6; 1 Sam. xxviii. 6; Joel iii. 1; Dan. vii. 1.

28. *What is the chaff to the wheat? saith the Lord.* Do not mingle these equivocal matters with positive revelations.

29. *Is not my word like as a fire?* It enlightens, warms, and penetrates every part. When it is communicated to the true prophet, it is like a fire shut up in his bones. He cannot retain it; he must publish it. And when published, it is *like a hammer that breaketh the rock in pieces.* It is ever accompanied by a divine power that causes both sinner and saint to feel its weight and importance.

MATTHEW HENRY

out of their hearts, as the wicked one in the parable is said to steal the good seed of the word, Matt. xiii. 19. By their insinuations they diminished the authority, and so weakened the efficacy, of the word of God upon the minds of those that seemed to be under convictions by it. God is against them (*v.* 31), because they *use their tongues* at their pleasure in their discourses to the people, and then father it upon God, and say, He saith it. Some read it, *They smooth their tongues;* they are very complaisant to the people, and say nothing but what is pleasing and plausible. They stand indicted as common cheats (*v.* 32): *I am against them*, for they *prophesy false dreams*, pretending that to be a divine inspiration which is but an invention of their own. It is the people's fault that they err, that they take things upon trust, but it is much more the prophets' fault that they cause God's people to *err by their lies and by their lightness.* God disowns their having any commission from him: *I sent them not, nor commanded them;* they are not God's messengers. *Therefore they shall not profit this people at all.*

Verses 33–40

The profaneness of the people, of the priests and prophets, is here reproved in a particular instance, which may seem of small moment, but profaneness in common discourse, and the debauching of the language of a nation, is a notorious evidence of the prevalency of wickedness in it.

I. The sin here charged upon them is bantering God's prophets and the dialect they used. They asked, *What is the burden of the Lord?* (*v.* 33 and *v.* 34). This was the word that gave great offence to God, that, whenever they spoke of *the word of the Lord*, they called it, in scorn and derision, *the burden of the Lord.* This was a word that the prophets much used, and used it seriously, to show what a weight the word of God was upon their spirits. Now the profane scoffers took this word, and made a jest of it. The mocking of God's messengers was the baffling of his messages. Some think that when the *word of the Lord* is called a *burden* it signifies some word of reproof and threatening. In using this word *the burden of the Lord* in a canting way they reflected upon God as always bearing hard upon them, always frightening them, and so making the word of God a perpetual uneasiness to them. Those that were guilty of this sin were some of the false prophets, some of the priests and some of the people, who had learned of the profane priests and prophets to play with the things of God.

II. When they are reproved for this profane way of speaking they are directed how to express themselves decently. We find it used long after this (Zech. ix. 1; Mal. i. 1; Nah. i. 1; Hab. i. 1). But here God will have the prophet keep to his rule (*ch.* xv. 19). Do not thou leave off using this word, but let them leave off abusing it. You *shall not mention the burden of the Lord any more* in this profane careless manner (*v.* 36). How then must they express themselves? He tells them (*v.* 37): *Thus shalt thou say to the prophet*, when thou art enquiring of him, *What hath the Lord answered thee? And what hath the Lord spoken?* And they must say thus when they enquire of *their neighbours*, *v.* 35.

III. They would still say, *The burden of the Lord*, though God had sent to them to forbid them, *v.* 38. Those shall be severely reckoned with that thus *pervert the words of God*, that put a wrong construction on them. It is a great provocation to God to mock his messengers *v.* 34. *Every man's word shall be his own burden;* that is, the guilt of this sin shall be heavy upon him. God will give them enough of their jest, so that it will be too heavy to make a jest of. Do they ask, *What is the burden of the Lord?* Let the prophet ask them, *What burden* do you mean? Is it this: *I will even forsake you? v.* 33. This is the burden that shall be laid and bound upon them (*v.* 39, 40): "*Behold I, even I, will utterly forget you, and I will forsake you.*" God's word will be magnified and made honourable when those that mock at it shall be vilified and made contemptible.

JAMIESON, FAUSSET, BROWN

31. use—rather, "take" their tongue: a second class (cf. vs. 30) require, in order to bring forth a revelation, nothing more than their *tongues,* wherewith they say, He (Jehovah) saith: they bungle in the very formula instead of the usual "*Jehovah* saith," being only able to say "(He) saith."

32. Third class: inventors of lies: the climax, and worst of the three **lightness**—wanton inventions (Zeph. 3:4). **not profit**—i.e., greatly injure.

33. What is the burden—play on the double sense of the *Hebrew*: an *oracle* and a *burden.* They scoffingly ask, Has he got any new burden (*burdensome oracle*: for all his prophecies are *disasters*) to announce (Mal. 1:1)? Jeremiah indignantly repeats their own question, Do you ask, What burden? This, then, it is, "I will forsake you." My word is burdensome in your eyes, and you long to be rid if it. You shall get your wish. There will be no more prophecy: *I will forsake you,* and that will be a far worse "burden" to you. **34. The burden**—Whoever shall in mockery call the Lord's word "a burden," shall be *visited (Margin)* in wrath. **35. The result of My judgments shall be,** ye shall address the prophet more reverentially hereafter, no longer calling his message a *burden,* but a divine *response* or *word.* "What hath the LORD *answered?*"

36. every man's word . . . his burden—As they mockingly *call* all prophecies *burdens,* as if calamities were the sole subject of prophecy, so it shall prove to them. *God will take them at their own word.* **living God**—not lifeless as their dumb idols, ever living so as to be able to punish.

39. I will . . . forget you—just retribution for their *forgetting* Him (Hos. 4:6). But God cannot possibly *forget* His children (Isa. 49:15). Rather for "forget" translate, "I will altogether lift you up (like a 'burden,' alluding to their mocking term for God's messages) and cast you off." God makes their wicked language fall on their own head [CALVIN]. Cf. vs. 36: "every man's word shall be his burden." **40. not be forgotten**—If we translate vs. 39 as *English Version,* the antithesis is, though *I forget you,* your *shame shall not be forgotten.*

ADAM CLARKE

E. H. PLUMPTRE:

"The burden of the Lord" (v. 33). The English expresses the literal meaning of the word, "something lifted up, or borne." It passed, however, as the English equivalent has done, through many shades of meaning, and became, in the language of the prophets, one of the received terms for a solemn, emphatic utterance. In 1 Chron. 15:22, 27 it is applied to the chanted music of the Temple. Isaiah had brought it into use and employs it twelve times as the title of special prophecies. Jeremiah never uses it of his own messages, probably, as this verse indicates, because it had become a favorite formula with the false prophets. This seems a more rational view than that which assumes that the false prophets applied the words in mockery to his utterances as being "burdens" in the ordinary sense of the word, oppressive and intolerable.

—*Ellicott's Commentary on the Whole Bible*

33. *What is the burden of the Lord?* The word *massa,* here used, signifies "burden, oracle, prophetic discourse," and is used by almost every prophet. But the persons in the text appear to have been mockers. "Where is this burden of the Lord?"—"What is the burden now?" To this insolent question the prophet answers in the following verses. *I will even forsake you.* I will punish the prophet, the priest, and the people, that speak thus, v. 34. Here are burdens.

36. *Every man's word shall be his burden.* You say that all God's messages are burdens, and to you they shall be such; whereas, had you used them as you ought, they would have been blessings to you. *For ye have perverted the words of the living God.* And thus have sinned against your own souls.

39. *I will utterly forget you, and I will forsake you, and the city.* Dr. Blayney translates: "I will both take you up altogether, and will cast you off together with the city." You are a burden to Me; but I will take you up, and then cast you off. I will do with you as a man weary with his burden will do: cast it off his shoulders, and bear it no more.

40. *I will bring an everlasting reproach upon you.* And this reproach of having rebelled against so good a God, and rejected so powerful a Saviour, follows them to this day through all their dispersions, in every part of the habitable earth. The word of the Lord cannot fail.

MATTHEW HENRY

CHAPTER 24

Verses 1–10

This short chapter helps us to put a comfortable construction upon many long ones, by showing us that the same providence which to some is a *savour of death unto death* may by the grace of God be made to others a *savour of life unto life*; and that, though God's people share with others in the same calamity, yet it is designed for their good; it is a correcting rod in the hand of a tender Father.

JAMIESON, FAUSSET, BROWN

CHAPTER 24

VS. 1-10. THE RESTORATION OF THE CAPTIVES IN BABYLON AND THE DESTRUCTION OF THE REFRACTORY PARTY IN JUDEA AND IN EGYPT, REPRESENTED UNDER THE TYPE OF A BASKET OF GOOD, AND ONE OF BAD, FIGS.

ADAM CLARKE

CHAPTER 24

MATTHEW HENRY

I. The date of this sermon. It was a little after Jeconiah's captivity, *v.* 1. Jeconiah was himself a *despised broken vessel*, but with him were carried away some very valuable persons, Ezekiel for one (Ezek. i. 12); many of the *princes of Judah* went into captivity; of the people only *the carpenters and the smiths* were forced away, because the Chaldeans needed men of those trades (they had plenty of astrologers and stargazers, but a great scarcity of smiths and carpenters). There were many good people carried away in that captivity, which the prophet laid to heart, while there were those that triumphed in it, and insulted over those to whose lot it fell to go into captivity.

II. The vision by which this distinction of the captives was represented to the prophet's mind. He saw *two baskets of figs, set before the temple*, ready to be offered as first-fruits to the honour of God. The figs in one basket were extraordinarily good, those in the other basket extremely bad. The children of men are all as the fruits of the fig-tree, capable of being made serviceable to God and man (Judges ix. 11); but some are as good figs, than which nothing is more pleasant, others as damaged rotten figs, than which nothing is more nauseous. The good figs were like those that are first ripe, which are most acceptable (Mic. vii. 1) and most prized. The bad figs are such as could *not be eaten, they were so evil*; were neither pleasant nor good for food. If God has no honour from men, nor their generation any service, they are like the bad figs, that cannot be eaten, that will not answer any good purpose. Of the persons that are presented to the Lord at the door of his tabernacle, some are sincere, and they are very good; others dissemble with God, and they are very bad.

III. The exposition and application of this vision. God intended by it to raise the dejected spirit of those that had gone into captivity, by assuring them of a happy return, and to humble and awaken the proud spirits of those who continued yet in Jerusalem, by assuring them of a miserable captivity.

1. The moral of the good figs, the first ripe. These represented the pious captives, that seemed first ripe for ruin, for they went first into captivity, but should prove first ripe for mercy, and their captivity should help to ripen them; these are pleasing to God and shall be carefully preserved. When God's judgments are abroad those are not always the worst that are first seized by them. Early suffering sometimes proves for the best. The sooner the child is corrected the better effect the correction is likely to have. Those that went first into captivity were as the son whom the *father loves, and chastens betimes*, chastens while there is hope. But those that stayed behind were like a child long *left to himself*, who, when afterwards corrected, is stubborn, and made worse, Lam. iii. 27. God owns their captivity to be his doing (*v.* 5): *I have sent them out of this place into the land of the Chaldeans.* It is God that puts his gold into the furnace, to be tried; his hand is, in a special manner, in the afflictions of good people. The judge orders the malefactor into the hand of an executioner, but the father corrects the child with his own hand. It seemed to be every way for their hurt, not only as it was the ruin of their estates and liberties, but as it sunk their spirits, discouraged their faith, deprived them of the benefit of God's oracles and ordinances, and exposed them to temptations; and yet it was designed for their good, and proved so. By their afflictions they were convinced of sin, humbled under the hand of God, weaned from the world, taught to pray, and turned from their iniquity. The scornful relations they left behind will scarcely own them, but God says, *I will acknowledge them.* Being sent into captivity *for their good*, they shall not be lost there; but it shall be with them as it is with gold which the refiner puts into the furnace. He has his eye upon it while it is there, and it is a careful eye, to see that it sustain no damage: "*I will set my eyes upon them for good.*" He will take it out of the furnace again as soon as the work designed is done: *I will bring them again to this land.* They were sent abroad for improvement under a severe discipline; but they shall be fetched back to their Father's house. He will fashion his gold when he has refined it, will make it a vessel of honour fit for his use; so, when God has brought them back from their trial, he *will build them* and make them a habitation for himself, will *plant them* and make them a vineyard for himself. Their captivity was to square the rough stones and make them fit for his building, to prune up the young trees and make them fit for his planting. He engages to prepare them for these temporal mercies which he designed for them by bestowing spiritual mercies upon them, *v.* 7. They should learn more of God by his providences in Babylon than they had learned by all his oracles and ordinances in Jerusalem. It is

JAMIESON, FAUSSET, BROWN

1. Lord showed me—Amos 7:1, 4, 7; 8:1, contains the same formula, with the addition of "thus" prefixed. **carried . . . captive Jeconiah**—(ch 22:24; II Kings 24:12, etc.; II Chron. 36:10). **carpenters . . .**—One thousand artisans were carried to Babylon, both to work for the king there, and to deprive Jerusalem of their services in the event of a future siege (II Kings 24:16).

2. figs . . . first ripe—the boccora, or early fig (*Note*, Isa. 28:4). Baskets of figs used to be offered as first-fruits in the temple.

The *good figs* represent Jeconiah and the exiles in Babylon; *the bad*, Zedekiah and the obstinate Jews in Judea. They are called *good* and *bad* respectively, not in an absolute, but a comparative sense, and in reference to the punishment of the latter. This prophecy was designed to encourage the despairing exiles, and to reprove the people at home, who prided themselves as superior to those in Babylon and abused the forbearance of God (cf. ch. 52:31-34).

5. acknowledge—*regard with favor*, like as thou lookest on the good figs favorably. **for their good**—Their removal to Babylon saved them from the calamities which befell the rest of the nation and led them to repentance there: so God bettered their condition (II Kings 25:27-30). Daniel and Ezekiel were among these captives. **6.** (Ch. 12:15.) **not pull . . . down . . . not pluck . . . up**—only partially fulfilled in the restoration from Babylon; antitypically and fully to be fulfilled hereafter (ch. 32:41; 33:7).

7. (Ch. 30:22; 31:33; 32:38.) Their conversion from idolatry to the one true God, through the chastening effect of the Babylonish captivity, is here expressed in language which, in its fulness, applies to the more complete conversion hereafter of the Jews, "with their whole

ADAM CLARKE

1. *The Lord shewed me, and, behold, two baskets of figs.* Besides the transposition of whole chapters in this book, there is not infrequently a transposition of verses, and parts of verses. Of this we have an instance in the verse before us, the first clause of which should be the last. Thus: "After that Nebuchadrezzar king of Babylon had carried away captive Jeconiah the son of Jehoiakim king of Judah . . . with the carpenters and smiths. from Jerusalem, and had brought them to Babylon, the Lord shewed me, and, behold, two baskets of figs were set before the temple of the Lord." This prophecy was undoubtedly delivered in the first year of the reign of Zedekiah.

2. Under the type of good and bad figs, God represents the state of the persons who had already been carried captives into Babylon, with their king, Jeconiah, compared with the state of those who should be carried away with Zedekiah. Those already carried away, being the choice of the people, are represented by the bad figs, that were good for nothing. The state also of the former in their captivity was vastly preferable to the state of those who were now about to be delivered into the hand of the king of Babylon. The latter would be treated as double rebels; the former, being the most respectable of the inhabitants, were treated well; and even in captivity, a marked distinction would be made between them, God ordering it so. But the prophet sufficiently explains his own meaning. "Set before the temple"—as an offering of the firstfruits of that kind. *Very good figs.* Or figs of the early sort. The fig trees in Palestine, says Dr. Shaw, produce fruit thrice each year. The first sort, called *boccore*, those here mentioned, come to perfection about the middle or end of June. The second sort, called *kermez*, or summer fig, is seldom ripe before August. And the third, which is called the winter fig, which is larger and of a darker complexion than the preceding, hangs all the winter on the tree, ripening even when the leaves are shed, and is fit for gathering in the beginning of spring. *Could not be eaten,* The "winter fig"—then in its crude or unripe state, the spring not being yet come.

5. *Like these good figs, so will I acknowledge.* Those already carried away into captivity, I esteem as far more excellent than those who still remain in the land. They have not sinned so deeply, and they are now penitent; and, therefore, "I will set mine eyes upon them for good," v. 6. I will watch over them by an especial providence, and they shall be restored to their own land.

MATTHEW HENRY

here promised, *I will give them,* not so much a head to know me, but *a heart to know me. They shall return to me with their whole heart.* God himself undertakes for them that they shall; and, if he turn us, we shall be turned. Thus they should be again taken into covenant with God: *They shall be my people, and I will be their God.* Those that have backslidden from God, if they do in sincerity return to him, are admitted as freely as any to all the privileges and comforts of the everlasting covenant.

2. The moral of the bad figs. *Zedekiah and his princes* and partisans *yet remain in the land,* proud and secure enough, Ezek. xi. 3. Many had fled into Egypt, for shelter, and their own safety, and boasted that though therein they had gone contrary to the command of God yet they had acted prudently for themselves. Now as to these, that looked so scornfully upon those that had gone into captivity, it is here threatened, (1) That, whereas those who were already carried away were settled in one country, where they had the comfort of one another's society, these should be dispersed *and removed into all the kingdoms of the earth.* (2) That, whereas those were carried captives for their good, these should be removed into all countries *for their hurt.* Their afflictions should harden them; not bring them nearer to God, but set them at a greater distance from him. (3) That, whereas those should have the honour of being owned of God in their troubles, these should have the shame of being abandoned by all mankind: *In all places whither I shall drive them they shall be a reproach and a proverb.* (4) That, whereas those should *return to their own land,* these should be *consumed from that land,* never to see it more. (5) That, whereas those were reserved for better times, these were reserved for worse; wherever they are removed *the sword, and famine, and pestilence,* shall be sent after them. It is probable that this has a typical reference to the last destruction of the Jews by the Romans, in which those that believed were taken care of, but those that continued obstinate in unbelief were driven into all countries for *a taunt and a curse.*

CHAPTER 25

Verses 1–7

A message from God concerning all the people of Judah (*v.* 1), which Jeremiah delivered unto all the people of Judah, *v.* 2. Jeremiah is sent to *all the people,* probably when they had all come up to Jerusalem to worship at one of the solemn feasts.

This prophecy is dated in the fourth year of Jehoiakim and the first of Nebuchadrezzar. Now that that martial prince began to set up for the world's master, God, by his prophet, gives notice that he is his servant. Nebuchadrezzar should not bid so fair for universal monarchy (universal tyranny) but that God had purposes of his own to serve by them.

In this message observe the great pains that had been taken with the people to bring them to repentance, which they are here put in mind of, as a justification of God in his proceedings against them.

I. Jeremiah, for his part, had been a constant preacher among them twenty-three years. *These three years* (these three and twenty years) *have I come seeking fruit on this fig-tree.* All this while God had been constant in sending messages to them, as there was occasion: "From that time *to this very day the word of the Lord has come unto me,* for your use." Thus God's Spirit was striving with them, as with the old world, Gen. vi. 3. Jeremiah had been faithful and industrious in delivering those messages. *I have spoken to you, rising early and speaking.* He had declared to them *the whole counsel of God.*

II. Besides him, God had sent them other prophets, on the same errand, *v.* 4. There were many other of God's *servants the prophets* who preached awakening sermons, which were never published.

III. They all told them of their faults, *their evil way,* and the *evil of their doings.* Those were not of God's sending who flattered them as if there were nothing amiss. They all reproved them for their idolatry, their *going after other gods, to serve them and to worship them,* gods that were *the work of their own hands.* They all called on them to repent of their sins and to reform their lives. This was the burden of every song. Personal reformation must be insisted on as necessary to a national deliverance: *every one* must *turn from his* own *evil way.* The street will not be clean unless everyone sweep before his own door. The mercies they enjoyed should be continued to them: "*You shall dwell in the land,* dwell at ease, dwell in peace, in this good land, *which the Lord has given you and your fathers.* Nothing but sin will turn you out of it, and that shall not if you turn from it."

JAMIESON, FAUSSET, BROWN

heart" (ch. 29:13), through the painful discipline of their present dispersion. The source of their conversion is here stated to be *God's prevenient grace.* **for they shall return**—Repentance, though not the cause of pardon, is its invariable accompaniment: it is the effect of God's *giving a heart to know Him.*

8. in . . . Egypt—Many Jews had fled for refuge to Egypt, which was leagued with Judea against Babylon.

9. removed . . .—(ch. 15:4). CALVIN translates, "I will give them up to *agitation,* in all . . . ." This verse quotes the curse (Deut. 28:25, 37). Cf. ch. 29:18, 22; Psalm 44:13, 14.

CHAPTER 25

VSS. 1-38. PROPHECY OF THE SEVENTY YEARS' CAPTIVITY; AND AFTER THAT THE DESTRUCTION OF BABYLON, AND OF ALL THE NATIONS THAT OPPRESSED THE JEWS. **1. fourth year of Jehoiakim**—called the *third* year in Daniel 1:1. But probably Jehoiakim was set on the throne by Pharaoh-necho on his return from Carchemish about *July,* whereas Nebuchadnezzar mounted the throne January 21, 604 B.C.; so that Nebuchadnezzar's first year was partly the *third,* partly the *fourth,* of Jehoiakim's. Here first Jeremiah gives specific dates. Nebuchadnezzar had previously entered Judea in the reign of his father Nabopolassar.

3. From the thirteenth year of Josiah, in which Jeremiah began to prophesy (ch. 1:1), to the end of Josiah's reign, was nineteen years (II Kings 22:1); the three months (II Kings 23:31) of Jehoahaz' reign, with the not quite complete four years of Jehoiakim (vs. 1), added to the nineteen years, make up twenty-three years in all. **4. rising early**—(Ch. 7:13, *Note*). "The prophets" refer to Urijah, Zephaniah, Habakkuk, etc. It aggravates their sin, that God sent not merely one but many messengers, and those messengers, prophets; and, that during all those years specified, Jeremiah and his fellow prophets *spared no effort, late and early.* **5. Turn . . . dwell**—In *Hebrew* there is expressed by sameness of sounds the correspondence between their *turning* to God and God's turning to them to permit them to *dwell* in their land: *Shubu . . . shebu,* "*Return*" . . . so shall ye "remain." **every one from . . . evil**—*Each must* separately repent and turn from *his* own sin. None is excepted, lest they should think their guilt extenuated because the evil is general. **6.** He instances one sin, idolatry, as representative of all their sins; as nothing is dearer to God than a pure worship of Himself. **7.** Though ye provoke *Me* to anger (Deut. 32:21), yet it is not I, but *yourselves,* whom ye thereby hurt (Prov. 8:36; 20:2).

ADAM CLARKE

7. *They shall be my people.* I will renew My covenant with them, *for they shall return unto me with their whole heart.*

8. *So will I give Zedekiah.* I will treat these as they deserve. They shall be carried into captivity, and scattered through all nations. Multitudes of those never returned to Judea; the others returned at the end of seventy years.

10. *I will send the sword.* Many of them fell by sword and famine in the war with the Chaldeans, and many more by such means afterwards. The first received their captivity as a correction, and turned to God; the latter still hardened their hearts more and more, and probably very many of them never returned—perhaps they are now amalgamated with heathen nations.

CHAPTER 25

1. *The word that came to Jeremiah . . . in the fourth year.* This prophecy, we see, was delivered in the fourth year of Jehoiakim, and the chapter that contains it is utterly out of its place. It should be between chapters xxxv and xxxvi. The defeat of the Egyptians by Nebuchadnezzar at Carchemish, and the subsequent taking of Jerusalem, occurred in this year.

The first year of Nebuchadrezzar. This king was associated with his father two years before the death of the latter. The Jews reckon his reign from this time, and this was the first of those two years; but the Chaldeans date the commencement of his reign two years later, viz., at the death of his father.

7. *That ye might provoke.* You would not hearken, but chose to provoke Me with anger.

MATTHEW HENRY

IV. Yet all was to no purpose. They were not wrought upon to take the right and only method to turn away the wrath of God. Jeremiah was a very lively affectionate preacher, yet *they hearkened not* to him, *v.* 3. The other prophets dealt faithfully with them, but neither did they *hearken to them,* nor *incline their ear, v.* 4.

Verses 8–14

Here is the sentence grounded upon the foregoing charge: "*Because you have not heard my words,* I must take another course with you," *v.* 8. The sinner must either be parted from his sin or perish in it.

I. The ruin of the land of Judah by the king of Babylon's armies is here decreed, *v.* 9. God sent to them *his servants the prophets,* and they were not heeded, and therefore God will send for *his servant the king of Babylon.* The messengers of God's wrath will be sent against those that would not receive the messengers of his mercy. Nebuchadrezzar, though a stranger to the true God, was yet, in the descent he made upon this country, *God's servant,* an instrument in his hand for the correction of his people. He was really serving God's designs when he thought he was serving his own ends. The most potent and absolute monarchs are his servants. Nebuchadrezzar, who is an instrument of his wrath, is as truly his servant as Cyrus, who is an instrument of his mercy. The utter destruction of this and all the neighbouring lands is here described, *v.* 9–11. This desolation shall be the ruin of their credit among their neighbours; it shall *make them an astonishment and a hissing. I will take from them the voice of mirth;* they shall neither have cause for it nor hearts for it. *The sound of the millstones shall not be heard;* for, when the enemy has seized their stores, the sound of the grinding must needs be low. An end shall be put to all business; there shall not be seen *the light of a candle,* for there shall be no work to be done worth candle-light. And, *lastly,* they shall be deprived of their liberty: *Those nations shall serve the king of Babylon seventy years.* The fixing of the time during which the captivity should last would be of great use, not only for the confirmation of the prophecy, but for the comfort of the people of God in their calamity and the encouragement of faith and prayer. *Known unto God are all his works from the beginning of the world,* which appears by this, that, when he has thought fit, some of them have been made known to his servants the prophets and by them to his church.

II. The ruin of Babylon, at last, is here foretold, as it had been, long before, by Isaiah, *v.* 12–14. The destroyers must themselves be destroyed. This shall be done when *seventy years are accomplished.* It is doubtful when these *seventy years* commence; some date them from the captivity in the fourth year of Jehoiakim and first of Nebuchadrezzar, others from the captivity of Jehoiachin eight years after. When the set time to favour Zion has come, the king of Babylon must be visited, and all his tyranny reckoned for; then that nation shall be punished *for their iniquity.* That land must then be a *perpetual desolation,* such as they had made other lands. This destruction of Babylon was to be brought about by the Medes and Persians. God had said: *I will bring upon that land all my words.* The same Jeremiah that prophesied the destruction of other nations by the Chaldeans foretold also the destruction of the Chaldeans themselves, *v.* 13. *I will recompense them according to their deeds,* by which they transgressed the law of God, even then when they were made to serve his purposes. *Many nations and great kings,* in alliance with Cyrus king of Persia, shall *serve themselves of them* also, shall make themselves masters of their country, and make them the footstool by which to mount the throne of universal monarchy.

Verses 15–29

Under the similitude of a cup going round, is here represented the universal desolation that was now coming. The cup in the vision is to be a sword in the accomplishment of it: so it is explained, *v.* 16.

I. The circumstances of this judgment,

1. This destroying sword should come—*from the hand of God.* Wicked men are made use of as his sword, Ps. xvii. 13. It is *the wine-cup of his fury.* It is the just anger of God that sends this judgment. These are compared to some intoxicating liquor, which they shall be forced to drink of, as, formerly, condemned malefactors were sometimes executed by being compelled to drink poison. The wicked are said to *drink the wrath of the Almighty,* Job xxi. 20; Rev. xiv. 10.

2. It should be sent to them—by the hand of Jeremiah as the judge *set over the nations* (*ch.* i. 10), to pass sentence upon them, and by the hand of Nebuchadrezzar as the executioner. Jeremiah must

JAMIESON, FAUSSET, BROWN

9. the north—(*Note,* ch. 1:14, 15). The Medes and other northern peoples, confederate with Babylon, are included with the Chaldeans. **my servant**—My agent for punishing (ch. 27:6; 43:10; cf. ch. 40:2). Cf. Isaiah 44:28; Cyrus, "My shepherd." God makes even unbelievers unconsciously to fulfil His designs. A reproof to the Jews, who boasted that they were the *servants of God;* yet a heathen king is to be more the servant of God than they, and that as the agent of their punishment.

10. (Ch. 7:34; Rev. 18:23.) The land shall be so desolated that even in the houses left standing there shall be no inhabitant; a terrible stillness shall prevail; no sound of the *hand-mill* (two circular stones, one above the other, for grinding corn, worked by two women, Exod. 11:5; Matt. 24:41; in daily use in every house, and therefore forbidden to be taken in pledge, Deut. 24:6); no *night-light,* so universal in the East that the poorest house has it, burning all night. **candle**—lamp (Job 21:17; 18:6). **11. seventy years**—(Ch. 27:7). The exact number of years of Sabbaths in 490 years, the period from Saul to the Babylonian captivity; righteous retribution for their violation of the Sabbath (Lev. 26:34, 35; II Chron. 36:21). The seventy years probably begin from the fourth year of Jehoiakim, when Jerusalem was first captured, and many captives, as well as the treasures of the temple, were carried away; they end with the first year of Cyrus, who, on taking Babylon, issued an edict for the restoration of the Jews (Ezra 1:1). Daniel's *seventy prophetic weeks* are based on the seventy years of the captivity (cf. Dan. 9:2, 24). **13. all . . . written in this book, which Jeremiah . . . prophesied against all . . . nations**—It follows from this, that the prophecies against foreign nations (chs. 46-51) must have been already written. Hence LXX inserts here those prophecies. But if they had followed immediately (vs. 13), there would have been no propriety in the observation in the verse. The very wording of the reference shows that they existed in some other part of the book, and not in the immediate context. **It was in this very year, the** fourth of Jehoiakim (ch. 36:1, 2), that Jeremiah was directed to write in a regular *book* for the first time all that he had prophesied against Judah and *foreign "nations"* from the beginning of his ministry. Probably, at a subsequent time, when he completed the whole work, including chs. 46-51, Jeremiah himself inserted the clause, "all that is written in this book, which Jeremiah hath prophesied against all the nations." **The prophecies in question may have** been repeated, as others in Jeremiah, more than once; so in the original smaller collection they may have stood in an earlier position; and, in the fuller subsequent collection, in their later and present position. **14. serve themselves**—(ch. 27:7; 30:8; 34:10). Avail themselves of their services as slaves. **them also**—the Chaldees, who heretofore have made other nations their slaves, shall *themselves also* in their turn be slaves to them. MAURER translates, "shall impose servitude *on them, even them."* **recompense them**—viz., the Chaldees and other nations against whom Jeremiah had prophesied (vs. 13), as having oppressed the Jews. **their deeds**—rather, "deed," viz., their bad treatment of the Jews (ch. 50:29; 51:6, 24; cf. II Chron. 36:17). **15. wine cup**—Cf. ch. 13:12, 13, as to this image, to express *stupefying judgments;* also ch. 49:12; 51:7. Jeremiah often embodies the imagery of Isaiah in his prophecies (Lam. 4:21; Isa. 51:17-22; Rev. 16:19; 18:6).

ADAM CLARKE

9. *Behold, I will send.* At this time Nebuchadrezzar had not invaded the land, according to this version. But the Hebrew may be translated, "Behold, I am sending, and have taken all the families"; that is, all the allies of the king of Babylon.

10. *I will take from them.* See chap. vii. 34 and xvi. 9. *The sound of the millstones, and the light of the candle.* These two are conjoined, because they generally ground the corn before day, by the light of the candle. Sir J. Chardin has remarked that everywhere in the morning may be heard the noise of the mills, for they generally grind every day just as much as is necessary for the day's consumption. Where then the noise of the mill is not heard, nor the light of the candle seen, there must be desolation.

11. *Shall serve the king of Babylon seventy years.* As this prophecy was delivered in the fourth year of Jehoiakim, and in the first of Nebuchadnezzar, and began to be accomplished in the same year (for then Nebuchadnezzar invaded Judea and took Jerusalem), seventy years from this time will reach down to the first year of Cyrus, when he made his proclamation for the restoration of the Jews, and the rebuilding of Jerusalem.

14. *Many nations and great kings.* The Medes and the Persians, under Cyrus; and several princes, his vassals or allies.

15. *Take the wine cup of this fury.* For an ample illustration of this passage and simile, see Isa. li. 21.

MATTHEW HENRY

take the cup at God's hand, and compel the nations to *drink it*.

3. It should be sent on all the nations within the lines of Israel's communication. Jeremiah took the cup, and *made all the nations to drink of it*, that is, he prophesied concerning each of the nations here mentioned that they should share in this great desolation. *Jerusalem and the cities of Judah* are put first (*v.* 18); for *judgment begins at the house of God* (1 Pet. iv. 17), at the sanctuary, Ezek. ix. 6. And this part of the prophecy was already begun to be accomplished; this is denoted by that parenthesis (*as it is this day*), for in the fourth year of Jehoiakim things had come into a very bad posture. *Pharaoh king of Egypt* comes next, because the Jews trusted to that broken reed (*v.* 19); the remains of them fled to Egypt, and there Jeremiah particularly foretold the destruction of that country, *ch.* xliii. 10, 11. All the other nations that bordered upon Canaan must pledge Jerusalem in this bitter cup. The *mingled people*, the Arabians, rovers of divers nations that lived by rapine; *the kings of the land of Uz*, joined to the country of the Edomites. The Philistines had been vexatious to Israel, but now their cities become a prey. Edom, Moab, Ammon, Tyre, and Zidon, are places well known to border upon Israel; the *Isles beyond*, or *beside, the sea*, are supposed to be those parts of Phoenicia and Syria that lay upon the coast of the Mediterranean Sea. Dedan and the other countries mentioned (*v.* 23, 24) seem to have lain upon the confines of Idumea and Arabia the desert. Those of Elam are the Persians. with whom the Medes are joined. The *kings of the north*, that lay nearer to Babylon will be seized by the victorious sword of Nebuchadrezzar. He shall push on his victories with such incredible fury that all the kingdoms of the world should become sacrifices to his ambition. Thus Alexander is said to have conquered *the world*, and the Roman empire is called *the world*, Luke ii. 1. Or it may be taken as reading the doom of *all the kingdoms* of the earth; one time or other, they shall feel the dreadful effects of war. The world has been, and will be, a great cockpit, while men's lusts war as they do *in their members*, Jas. iv. 1. *The king of Sheshach shall drink after them*, that is, the king of Babylon himself, who has given his neighbours all this trouble, shall at length have it return upon his own head. That by Sheshach is meant Babylon is plain from *ch.* li. 41. Babylon's ruin was foretold, *v.* 12, 13.

4. The desolations in all these kingdoms are represented by the consequences of excessive drinking (*v.* 16): *They shall drink, and be moved, and be mad. They shall be drunken, and spew, and fall and rise no more*, *v.* 27. Men in drink often *fall and rise no more*; it is a sin that is its own punishment. When God sends the sword upon a nation, with warrant to make it desolate, it soon becomes like a drunken man, filled with confusion; its counsellors *mad*, and at their wits' end, sick at heart with continual vexation, *falling* down before the enemy, and unable to do anything to help themselves.

5. They will *refuse to take the cup at thy hand*; they will not give credit to the prediction of so despicable a man as Jeremiah. But he must tell them that it is *the word of the Lord of hosts*, and it is vain for them to struggle with Omnipotence: *You shall certainly drink*. And he must give them this reason, It is a time of visitation, it is a reckoning day, and Jerusalem has been called to account already: *I begin to bring evil on the city that is called by my name;* and *should you be utterly unpunished?* If Jerusalem be punished for learning idolatry of the nations. shall not the nations be punished, of whom they learned it? *I will call for a sword upon all the inhabitants of the earth*, for they have helped to debauch the inhabitants of Jerusalem.

II. There is a God that judges in the earth, to whom all the nations of the earth are accountable, and by whose judgment they must abide. Those who have been vexatious and mischievous to the people of God will be reckoned with for it at last. The year of the redeemer will come, even the *year of recompenses.* The *burden of the word of the Lord* will at last become the burden of his judgments. Isaiah had prophesied long since against most of these nations (*ch.* xiii. &c) and now all his prophecies will have their fulfilling. Nebuchadrezzar was so proud of his might that he had no sense of right. These are the men that turn the world upside down, and yet expect to be admired and adored. Alexander thought himself a great prince when others thought him no better than a great pirate.

Verses 30–38

A further description of those terrible desolations which the king of Babylon with his armies should make in all the countries round about Jerusalem.

They will soon be aware of Nebuchadrezzar's

JAMIESON, FAUSSET, BROWN

The wine cup was not literally given by Jeremiah to the representatives of the different nations; but only in symbolical vision. **16. be moved**—reel (Nah. 3:11). **18. Jerusalem**—put first: for "judgment begins at the house of God"; they being most guilty whose religious privileges are greatest (I Pet. 4:17). **kings**—Jehoiakim, Jeconiah, and Zedekiah. **as it is this day**—The accomplishment of the curse had already begun under Jehoiakim. This clause, however, may have been inserted by Jeremiah at his final revision of his prophecies in Egypt. **19. Pharaoh**—put next after Jerusalem, because the Jews had relied most on him, and Egypt and Judea stood on a common footing (ch. 46:2, 25). **20. mingled people**—mercenary foreign troops serving under Pharaoh-hophra in the time of Jeremiah. The employment of these foreigners provoked the native Egyptians to overthrow him. Psammetichus, father of Pharaoh-necho, also had given a settlement in Egypt to Ionian and Carian adventurers (HERODOTUS, 2.152, 154). Cf. ch. 50:37; *Note*, Isaiah 19:2, 3; 20:1; Ezekiel 30:5. The term is first found in Exodus 12:38. **Uz**—in the geographical order here, between Egypt and the states along the Mediterranean; therefore not the "Uz" of Job 1:1 (north of Arabia Deserta), but the northern part of Arabia Petræa, between the sea and Idumea (Lam. 4:21; see Gen. 36:20, 28). **remnant of Ashdod**—called a "remnant," because Ashdod had lost most of its inhabitants in the twenty-nine years' siege by Psammetichus. Cf. also Isaiah 20:1, *Note*. Gath is not mentioned because it was overthrown in the same war. **21. Edom . . . Moab . . . Ammon**—joined together, as being related to Israel (see ch. 48:49). **22. all the kings of Tyrus**—the petty kings of the various dependencies of Tyre. **isles**—a term including all *maritime regions* (Ps. 72:10). **23. Dedan**—north of Arabia (Gen. 25:3, 4). **Tema . . . Buz**—neighboring tribes north of Arabia (Job 32:2). **all . . . in . . . utmost corners**—rather, "having the hair cut in angles," a heathenish custom (see *Note*, ch. 9:26). **24. mingled people**—not in the same sense as in vs. 20; the "motley crowd," so called in contempt (cf. ch. 49:28, 31; 50:37). By a different pointing it may be translated the "Arabs"; but the repetition of the name is not likely. BLANEY thinks there were two divisions of what we call Arabia, the west (*Araba*) and the east. The west included Arabia Petræa and the parts on the sea bordering on Egypt, the land of Cush; the east, Arabia Felix and Deserta. The latter are "the mixed race" inhabiting the desert. **25. Zimri**—perhaps the *Zabra* mentioned by PTOLEMY between Mecca and Medina. *Zimran* also, as Dedan, was one of Abraham's sons by Keturah (Gen. 25:2). **Elam**—properly, west of Persia; but used for Persia in general. **26. Sheshach**—Babylon; as the parallelism in ch. 51:41 proves. In the Cabalistic system (called *Athbash*, the first *Hebrew* letter in the alphabet being expressed by the last) *Sheshach* would exactly answer to *Babel*. Jeremiah *may* have used this system (as perhaps in ch. 51:41) for concealment at the time of this prediction, in the fourth year of Jehoiakim, while Nebuchadnezzar was before Jerusalem. In ch. 51:41 there can be no concealment, as Babylon is expressly mentioned. MICHAELIS more simply explains the term "brazen-gated" (cf. Isa. 45:2); others, "the house of a prince." Rather, it comes from the Babylonian goddess, *Shach*, by reduplication of the first letter; from her *Misael* was named *Meshach* by the Babylonians. The term *Shace* was applied to a festival at Babylon, alluded to in ch. 51:39, 57; Isaiah 21:5. It was during this feast that Cyrus took Babylon (HERODOTUS, 1). Thus Jeremiah mystically denotes the time of its capture by this term [GLASSIUS]. **27. rise no more**—The heathen nations in question should fall to rise no more. The Jews should fall but for a time, and then rise again. Therefore, the epithet is given, "the God *of Israel*." **28. if they refuse to take the cup**—No effort of theirs to escape destruction will avail. **29. If I spared not Mine elect people on account of sin, much less will I spare you** (Ezek. 9:6; Obad. 16; Luke 23:31; I Pet. 4:17). **be unpunished**—"be treated as innocent."

ADAM CLARKE

17. *Then took I the cup . . . and made all the nations to drink*. This cup of God's wrath is merely symbolical, and simply means that the prophet should declare to all these people that they shall fall under the Chaldean yoke, and that this is a punishment inflicted on them by God for their iniquities. *Then took I the cup;* I declared publicly the tribulation that God was about to bring on Jerusalem, the cities of Judah, and all the nations.

19. *Pharaoh king of Egypt*. This was Pharaoh-necho, who was the principal cause of instigating the neighboring nations to form a league against the Chaldeans.

20. *All the mingled people*. The strangers and foreigners; Abyssinians and others who had settled in Egypt.

Land of Uz. A part of Arabia near to Idumea. See Job i. 1.

22. *Tyrus, and . . . Zidon*. The most ancient of all the cities of the Phoenicians. *Kings of the isles which are beyond the sea*. As the Mediterranean Sea is most probably meant, and the Phoenicians had numerous colonies on its coasts, I prefer the marginal reading, "the kings of the region by the sea side."

23. *Dedan* was the son of Abraham by Keturah, Gen. xxv. 3. *Tema* was one of the sons of Ishmael, in the north of Arabia, Gen. xxxvi. 15. *Buz*. Brother of *Uz*, descendants of Nahor, brother of Abraham, settled in Arabia Deserta, Gen. xxii. 21.

25. *Zimri*. Descendants of Abraham, by Keturah, Gen. xxv. 2, 6. *Elam*. On the south frontier of Media, not far from Babylon.

26. *The kings of the north, far and near*. The first may mean Syria; the latter, the Hyrcanians and Bactrians. *And the king of Sheshach shall drink after them*. Sheshach was an ancient king of Babylon, who was deified after his death. Here it means either Babylon, or Nebuchadnezzar, the king of it. After it has been the occasion of ruin to so many other nations, Babylon itself shall be destroyed by the Medo-Persians.

27. *Be drunken, and spue*. Why did we not use the word vomit, less offensive than the other, and yet of the same signification?

29. *The city which is called by my name*. Jerusalem, which should be first given up to the destruction.

MATTHEW HENRY

making war upon them; but the prophet is directed to tell them that it is God himself that makes war upon them (*v.* 30): *The Lord shall roar from on high. He shall mightily roar upon his habitation* on earth from that above. He *roars as a lion* that has *forsaken his covert* (*v.* 38), and is going abroad to seek his prey. *The Lord has a controversy with the nations.* His quarrel with them is for their wickedness, their contempt of his authority and kindness to them. *He will give those that are wicked to the sword.* They have provoked God to anger, and thence comes all this destruction. *A noise will come even to the ends of the earth. v.* 31. The alarm is not given by trumpet, or beat of drum, but by a *whirlwind*, *a great whirlwind, storm,* or *tempest*, which shall be *raised up from the coasts*, the remote coasts *of the earth, v.* 32. The Chaldean army shall be like a hurricane raised in the north, but thence carried on with swiftness, bearing down all before it. Now the shepherds shall *howl and cry*, the kings, and princes, and the great ones of the earth, the *principal of the flock*. They used to be the most courageous but now their hearts shall fail them; *they shall wallow themselves in the ashes, v.* 34. There shall be *a voice of the cry of the shepherds*, and a *howling of the principal of the flock shall be heard, v.* 36. Perhaps, carrying on the metaphor of a lion roaring, it alludes to the great fright that shepherds are in when they hear a roaring lion coming towards their flocks, and find they have *no way to flee* (*v.* 35) for their own safety, neither can the *principal of their flock escape.* When our neighbour's house is on fire it is time to be concerned for our own. When one nation is a seat of war every neighbouring nation should hear, and fear, and make its peace with God. Multitudes shall fall by the sword of the merciless Chaldeans so that *the slain of the Lord* shall be everywhere found. The slain for sin are the *slain of the Lord.* They shall have no friends left to bury them, and the enemies shall not have so much humanity in them as to do it. The effect of this war will be the *desolation of the whole land* that is the seat of it (*v.* 38), one land after another. But here are two expressions more that make the case piteous. (1) *You shall fall like a pleasant vessel, v.* 34. The most desirable persons among them, who were looked upon as *vessels of honour*, shall fall by the sword. You shall fall as a Venice glass or a China dish, which is soon broken all to pieces. (2) Even *the peaceable habitations are cut down.* Those who used to be quiet, and not molesting any of their neighbours, those who lived in peace, and gave no provocation to any, even those shall not escape. This is one of the direful effects of war. Blessed be God, there is a *peaceable habitation* above for all the sons of peace, which is out of the reach of fire and sword.

JAMIESON, FAUSSET, BROWN

30. roar—image from a destructive lion (Isa. 42:13; Joel 3:16). **upon his habitation**—rather, "His pasturage"; keeping up the image of a lion roaring against the flock in the pasture. The roar was first to go forth over Judea wherein were "the sheep of His pasture" (Ps. 100:3), and thence into heathen lands. **shout . . . tread . . . grapes**—(ch. 48:33; Isa. 16:9, 10). **31. controversy**—cause at issue (Mic. 6:2). **plead with all flesh**—(Isa. 66:16). God shows the whole world that He does what is altogether just in punishing. **32. from the coasts**—rather, "from the uttermost regions." Like a storm which arises in one region and then diffuses itself far and wide, so God's judgments shall pass "from nation to nation," till all has been fulfilled; no distance shall prevent the fulfilment. **33. not be lamented**—(ch. 16:4, 6). **neither gathered**—to their fathers, in their ancestral tombs (ch. 8:2). **dung**—(Ps. 83:10). **34. shepherds**—princes (ch. 22:22). Here he returns to *the Jews* and their rulers, using the same image as in vs. 30, "pasture" (see *Note*). **wallow yourselves**—Cover yourselves as thickly with ashes, in token of sorrow, as one who rolls in them (ch. 6:26; Ezek. 27:30) [MAURER]. **principal**—leaders. LXX translates "rams," carrying out the image (cf. Isa. 14:9, *Margin;* Zech. 10:3). **days of your slaughter . . . of . . . dispersions**—rather, "your days *for* slaughter (i.e., the time of your being slain), and your dispersions (not '*of* your dispersions'), are accomplished" (are come). **pleasant vessel**—Ye were once a *precious vessel*, but ye shall *fall*, and so be a *broken vessel* (cf. ch. 22:28, *Note*). "Your past excellency shall not render you safe now. I will turn to your ignominy whatever glory I conferred on you" [CALVIN]. **35.** Lit., "Flight shall fail the shepherds . . . , escaping (shall fail) the principal . . ." (Amos 2:14). The leaders will be the first objects for slaughter; escape by flight will be out of their power. **37. habitations**—rather, carrying out the image "pastures" (vs. 30, *Note*). The pasturages where, *peaceably* and without incursion of wild beasts, the flocks have fed, shall be destroyed; i.e., the regions where, heretofore, there was *peace* and security (alluding to the name *Salem*, or Jerusalem, "possessing *peace*"). **38. his covert**—the temple, where heretofore, like a lion, as its defender, by the mere terror of His voice He warded off the foe; but now He leaves it a prey to the Gentiles [CALVIN]. **fierceness of . . . oppressor**—rather, as the *Hebrew*, for "oppressor" is an adjective *feminine*, the word *sword* is understood, which, in ch. 46:16; 50:16, is expressed (indeed, some MSS. and LXX read "sword" instead of "fierceness" here; probably interpolated from ch. 46:16), "*the oppressing* sword." The *Hebrew* for "oppressing" means also a "dove": there may be, therefore, a covert allusion to the Chaldean standard bearing a dove on it, in honor of Semiramis, the first queen, said in popular superstition to have been nourished by doves when exposed at birth, and at death to have been transformed into a dove. Her name may come from a root referring to the *cooing* of a dove. That bird was held sacred to the goddess Venus. *Vulgate* so translates "the anger of *the dove.*" **his . . . anger**—If the anger of Nebuchadnezzar cannot be evaded, how much less that of God (cf. vs. 37)!

ADAM CLARKE

32. *Evil shall go forth from nation to nation.* One nation after another shall fall before the Chaldeans.

33. *From one end of the earth.* From one end of the "land" to the other. All Palestine shall be desolated by it.

34. *Howl, ye shepherds.* You kings and chiefs of the people.

Ye shall fall like a pleasant vessel. As a fall will break and utterly ruin a precious vessel of crystal, agate, etc., so your overthrow will be to you irreparable ruin.

38. *As the lion.* Leaving the banks of Jordan when overflowed, and coming with ravening fierceness to the champaign country.

MATTHEW HENRY

CHAPTER 26

Verses 1–6

The sermon that Jeremiah preached, which gave such offence that he was in danger of losing his life for it. It is left upon record, by way of appeal to the judgment of impartial men in all ages.

I. God directed him where to preach this sermon, and when, and to what auditory, *v.* 2. God gave him orders to preach *in the court of the Lord's house*, which was within the peculiar jurisdiction of his sworn enemies the priests. He must preach this, at the time of one of the most solemn festivals, when persons had come from all the *cities of Judah* to *worship in the Lord's house.* These worshippers had a great veneration for their priests, and would strengthen their hands against Jeremiah. But none of these things must daunt him; he must preach this sermon, which, if it were not convincing, would be provoking. God charges him particularly *not to diminish a word*, but to speak *all the words*, that he had commanded him.

II. God directed him what to preach. He must assure them that if they would *repent of their sins*, and turn from them, though judgments were just at the door, yet a stop should be put to them, and God would proceed no further in his controversy with them, *v.* 3. This was the main thing God intended in sending him to them. God *waits to be gracious*,

JAMIESON, FAUSSET, BROWN

CHAPTER 26

Vss. 1-24. JEREMIAH DECLARED WORTHY OF DEATH, BUT BY THE INTERPOSITION OF AHIKAM SAVED; THE SIMILAR CASES OF MICAH AND URIJAH BEING ADDUCED IN THE PROPHET'S FAVOR. The prophecies which gave the offense were those given in detail in chs. 7, 8, 9 (cf. vs. 6 here with ch. 7:12, 14); and summarily referred to here [MAURER], probably pronounced at one of the great feasts (that of tabernacles, according to USSHER; for the inhabitants of "all the cities of Judah" are represented as present, vs. 2). See *Note*, ch. 7:1. **2. in the court**—the largest court, from which he could be heard by the whole people **come to worship**—*Worship* is vain without *obedience* (I Sam. 15:21, 22). **all the words**—(Ezek. 3:10). **diminish not a word**—(Deut. 4:2; 12:32; Prov. 30:6; Acts 20:27; II Cor. 2:17; 4:2; Rev. 22:19). Not suppressing or softening aught for fear of giving offense; nor setting forth coldly and indirectly what can only by forcible statement do good. **3. If so be**—expressed according to human conceptions; not as if God did not foreknow all contingencies, but to mark the obstinacy of the people and the difficulty of healing them; and to show His own goodness in making the offer which left them without excuse [CALVIN].

ADAM CLARKE

CHAPTER 26

1. *In the beginning of the reign of Jehoiakim.* As this prophecy must have been delivered in the first or second year of the reign of Jehoiakim, it is totally out of its place here.

MATTHEW HENRY

waits till we are duly qualified, till we are fit, and in the meantime tries a variety of methods. He must, on the other hand, assure them that if they continued obstinate to all the calls God gave them, it would certainly end in the ruin of their city and temple, *v.* 4–6. That which God required of them was that they should *walk in all his law which he set before them,* the law of Moses and the ordinances and commandments of it, and should *hearken to the words of his servants the prophets.* The law was what God himself set before them. The prophets were his own servants, and were sent by him to them. They had hitherto been deaf both to the law and to the prophets: *You have not hearkened.* All he expects now is that at length they should heed what he said, and make his word their rule. In case of refusal this city, and the temple in it, shall fare as their predecessors did, Shiloh and the tabernacle there, for a like refusal to hearken. This was not the first time he had given them warning to this effect; see *ch.* vii. 12–14.

Verses 7–15

The sermon instead of awakening their convictions, did but exasperate their corruptions.

I. Jeremiah is charged with a crime that he had preached such a sermon, and is apprehended for it as a criminal. The *priests,* and *false prophets,* and *people, heard him speak these words, v.* 7. This shall suffice to ground an indictment upon: He hath said, *This house shall be like Shiloh, v.* 9. See how unfair they are in representing his words. He had said, in God's name, *If you will not hearken to me, then will I make this house like Shiloh;* but they leave out God's hand and their own hand in not hearkening to the voice of God, and charge it upon him that he *blasphemed this holy place,* the crime charged both on our Lord Jesus and on Stephen: He said, *This house shall be like Shiloh.* When the accusation was so weakly grounded, no marvel that the sentence was unjust: *Thou shalt surely die.* What he had said agreed with what God had said (1 Kings ix. 6–8), *If you shall at all turn from following after me, then this house shall be* abandoned; and yet he is condemned to die for saying it. This outcry of the priests and prophets raised the mob, and *all the people were gathered together against Jeremiah* in a popular tumult, ready to pull him to pieces.

II. He is arraigned and indicted for it. The *princes of Judah* were his judges, *v.* 10. The elders of Israel, hearing of this tumult in the temple, *came up from the king's house of the Lord,* to enquire into this matter. They *sat down in the entry of the new gate of the Lord's house,* and held a court. The *priests and prophets* were his prosecutors and accusers, and were violently set against him. They appealed to *the princes,* and *to all the people,* whether *this man* were not *worthy to die, v.* 11. When Jeremiah prophesied in the house of the king concerning the fall of the royal family (*ch.* xxii. 1, &c.), the court, though very corrupt, bore it patiently, and we do not find that they persecuted him for it; but when he comes into the *house of the Lord,* and touches the copyhold of the priests, and contradicts the lies and flatteries of the false prophets, then he is adjudged *worthy to die, ch.* v. 31.

III. Jeremiah makes his defence before the princes and the people. He does not deny the words. What he has said he will stand to, though it cost him his life; he had prophesied against *this house* and *this city,* but, 1. He asserts that he did this by good authority, not maliciously nor seditiously, but, *The Lord sent me* to prophesy thus: so he begins his apology (*v.* 12), and so he concludes it (*v.* 15): *Of a truth the Lord hath sent me unto you, to speak all these words.* As long as ministers keep closely to the instructions they have from heaven they need not fear the opposition they may meet with from hell or earth. He is under the divine protection, and whatever affront they offer to the ambassador will be resented by the Prince that sent him. It was said, not by way of fatal sentence, but of fair warning, *v.* 13. "*As for me,* the matter is not great what becomes of me; *behold, I am in your hand;* I neither have any power, to oppose you, nor is it so much my concern to save my own life: *do with me as seems meet unto you.*" But, for themselves, he tells them that it is at their peril if they put him to death: *You shall surely bring innocent blood upon yourselves, v.* 15.

Verses 16–24

I. The acquitting of Jeremiah. He had indeed spoken the words laid in the indictment, but they are not looked upon to be seditious or treasonable, and the court find him not guilty. The priests and prophets continued to demand judgment against him; but the princes, and all the people, are clear that *this man is not worthy to die* (*v.* 16); for (say they)

JAMIESON, FAUSSET, BROWN

5. prophets—the inspired interpreters of the *law* (vs. 4), who adapted it to the use of the people. **6. like Shiloh**—(*Note,* ch. 7:12, 14; 1 Sam. 4:10-12; Ps. 78:60). **curse**—(ch. 24:9; Isa. 65:15).

8. priests—The captain (or prefect) of the temple had the power of apprehending offenders in the temple with the sanction of the priests. **prophets**—the false prophets. The charge against Jeremiah was that of uttering falsehood in Jehovah's name, an act punishable with death (Deut. 18:20). His prophecy against the temple and city (vs. 11) might speciously be represented as contradicting God's own words (Ps. 132:14). Cf. the similar charge against Stephen (Acts 6:13, 14).

10. princes—members of the Council of State or Great Council, which took cognizance of such offenses. **heard**—the clamor of the popular tumult. **came up**—from the king's house to the temple, which stood higher than the palace. **sat**—as judges, in the gate, the usual place of trying such cases. **new gate**—originally built by Jotham (II Kings 15:35, "the higher gate") and now recently restored.

12. Lord sent me—a valid justification against any laws alleged against him. **against . . . against**—rather, "concerning." Jeremiah purposely avoids saying, "against," which would needlessly irritate. They had used the same *Hebrew* word (vs. 11), which ought to be translated "concerning," though they meant it in the unfavorable sense. Jeremiah takes up their word in a better sense, implying that there is still room for repentance: that his prophecies aim at the real good of the city; *for* or *concerning* this house . . . city [GROTIUS].

13. (Vss. 3, 19.) **14.** Jeremiah's humility is herein shown, and submission to the powers that be (Rom. 13:1). **15. bring . . . upon yourselves**—So far will you be from escaping the predicted evils by shedding my blood, that you will, by that very act, only incur heavier penalties (Matt. 23:35).

16. princes . . . all the people—The fickle people, as they were previously influenced by the priests to clamor for his death

ADAM CLARKE

4. *If ye will not hearken.* This and several of the following verses are nearly the same with those in chap. vii. 13, etc.

8. *And all the people.* That were in company with the priests and the prophets.

10. *The princes of Judah.* The king's court; his cabinet counsellors.

12. *The Lord sent me to prophesy.* My commission is from Him, and my words are His own. I sought not this painful office. I did not run before I was sent.

13. *Therefore now amend your ways.* If you wish to escape the judgment which I have predicted, turn to God, and iniquity shall not be your ruin.

14. *As for me, behold, I am in your hand.* I am the messenger of God; you may do with me what you please. But if you slay me, you will bring innocent blood upon yourselves.

16. *This man is not worthy to die.* The whole court acquitted him.

MATTHEW HENRY

he hath spoken to us, not of himself, but *in the name of the Lord our God.* And are they willing to own that he did indeed speak to them *in the name of the Lord* and that that Lord is their God? Why then did they not amend their ways and doings?

II. A precedent quoted to justify them in acquitting Jeremiah. Some of the *elders of the land*, or the more intelligent men of the people, stood up, and put the assembly in mind of a former case. The case referred to is that of Micah. 1. Was it thought strange that Jeremiah prophesied against this city and the temple? Micah did so before him, even in the reign of Hezekiah, that reign of reformation, *v.* 18. Micah said it as publicly as Jeremiah had now spoken, *Zion shall be ploughed like a field*, the building shall be all destroyed, so that nothing shall hinder but it may be ploughed; *Jerusalem shall become heaps* of ruins, and *the mountain of the house* on which the temple is built shall be *as the high places of the forest*, overrun with briers and thorns, Mic. iii. 12. By this it appears that a man may be, as Micah was, a true prophet of the Lord, and yet may prophesy the destruction of Zion and Jerusalem. 2. Was it thought fit by the princes to justify Jeremiah in what he had done? It was what Hezekiah did before them in a like case. Did Hezekiah, and the people of Judah put Micah to death? On the contrary, they took the warning he gave them. Hezekiah set a good example before his successors, for he *feared the Lord* (*v.* 19). Micah's preaching drove him to his knees; he *besought the Lord* to turn away the judgment threatened and to be reconciled to them, and he found it was not in vain for *the Lord repented him of the evil* and returned in mercy to them; he sent an angel, who routed the army of the Assyrians, that threatened to plough *Zion like a field.*

III. An instance of another prophet that was put to death by Jehoiakim for prophesying as Jeremiah had done, *v.* 12, &c. Some make this to be urged by the prosecutors, as a case that favoured the prosecution, a modern case, in which speaking such words as Jeremiah had spoken was adjudged treason. Others think that the elders, who were advocates for Jeremiah, alleged this to show that thus they might *procure great evil against their souls*, for it would be adding sin to sin. Jehoiakim, the present king, had slain one prophet already; let them not fill up the measure by slaying another. But some good interpreters take this narrative from the historian that penned the book, Jeremiah himself, or Baruch. Urijah's prophecy was *against this city, and this land, according to all the words of Jeremiah.* The prophets of the Lord agreed in their testimony, and one would have thought that out of the mouth of so many witnesses the word would be regarded. Jehoiakim and his courtiers were exasperated against him, and *sought to put him to death. When he heard* that the king sought his life, *he was afraid, and fled, and went into Egypt.* This was certainly an effect of the weakness of his faith, and it sped accordingly. He distrusted God, and his power to protect him and bear him out. It was especially unbecoming to flee *into Egypt.* There are many that have much grace, but they have little courage, that are very honest, but withal very timorous. Jehoiakim's malice, one would think, might have contented itself with his banishment. So implacable is his revenge that he sends soldiers into Egypt, and they bring him back by force of arms. They *brought him to Jehoiakim*, and he *slew him with the sword.* He loads the dead body with infamy, cast it into *the graves of the common people*, as if he had not been a prophet of the Lord. Thus Jehoiakim hoped both to ruin his reputation with the people, that no heed might be given to his predictions, and to deter others from prophesying in like manner; but in vain. Herod thought he had gained his point when he had cut off John Baptist's head, but found himself deceived when, soon after, he heard of Jesus Christ, and said, in a fright, *This is John the Baptist.*

IV. Jeremiah's deliverance. Urijah was lately put to death, yet God wonderfully preserved Jeremiah, though he did not flee, but stood his ground. He that had an extraordinary mission might expect an extraordinary protection. God raised up a friend for Jeremiah; he took him by the hand in a friendly way, and assisted him. It was *Ahikam the son of Shaphan*, one that was a minister of state in Josiah's time; we read of him, 2 Kings xxii. 12. He had great influence among the princes, and he used it in favour of Jeremiah.

JAMIESON, FAUSSET, BROWN

(vs. 8), so now under the princes' influence require that he shall not be put to death. Cf. as to Jesus, Jeremiah's antitype, the hosannas of the multitude a few days before the same people, persuaded by the priests as in this case, cried, Away with Him, crucify Him (Matt. 21 and 27:20-25). The priests, through envy of his holy zeal, were more his enemies than the princes, whose office was more secular than religious. A prophet could not legally be put to death unless he prophesied *in the name of other gods* (therefore, they say, "in the name of the Lord"), or after his prophecy had failed in its accomplishment. Meanwhile, if he foretold calamity, he might be imprisoned. Cf. Micaiah's case (I Kings 22:1-28). **17.** Cf. Gamaliel's interposition (Acts 5:34, etc.). **elders**–some of the "princes" mentioned (vs. 16) those whose age, as well as dignity, would give weight to the precedents of past times which they adduce. **18.** (Mic. 3:12.) **Morasthite**–called so from a village of the tribe Judah. **Hezekiah**–The precedent in the reign of such a good king proved that Jeremiah was not the only prophet, or the first, who threatened the city and the temple without incurring death. **mountain of the house**–Moriah, on which stood the temple (peculiarly called "*the* house") shall be covered with woods instead of buildings. Jeremiah, in quoting previous prophecies, never does so without alteration; he adapts the language to his own style, showing thereby his authority in his treatment of Scripture, as being himself inspired. **19.** Hezekiah, so far from killing him, was led "to fear the Lord," and pray for remission of the sentence against Judah (II Chron. 32:26). **Lord repented**–(Exod. 32:14; II Sam. 24:16). **Thus**–if we kill Jeremiah. **20.** As the flight and capture of Urijah must have occupied some time, "the beginning of the reign of Jehoiakim" (vs. 1) must not mean the *very* beginning, but the second or third year of his eleven years' reign. **And . . . also**–perhaps connected with vs. 24, as the comment of the writer, not the continuation of the speech of the elders: "And although *also* a man that prophesied . . . Urijah . . . (proving how great was the danger in which Jeremiah stood, and how wonderful the providence of God in preserving him), *nevertheless* the hand of Ahikam . . ." [GLASSIUS]. The context, however, implies rather that the words are the continuation of the previous speech of the elders. They adduce another instance besides that of Micah, though of a different kind, viz., that of Urijah: he suffered for his prophecies, but they *imply*, though they do not venture to *express* it, that thereby sin has been added to sin, and that it has done no good to Jehoiakim, for that the notorious condition of the state at this time shows that a heavier vengeance is impending if they persevere in such acts of violence [CALVIN]. **22. Jehoiakim sent . . . into Egypt**–He had been put on the throne by Pharaoh of Egypt (II Kings 23:34). This explains the readiness with which he got the Egyptians to give up Urijah to him, when that prophet had sought an asylum in Egypt. Urijah was faithful in delivering his message, but faulty in leaving his work, so God permitted him to lose his life, while Jeremiah was protected in danger. The path of duty is often the path of safety. **23. graves of the common people**–lit., "sons of the people" (cf. II Kings 23:6). The prophets seem to have had a separate cemetery (Matt. 23:29). Urijah's corpse was denied this honor, in order that he should not be regarded as a true prophet. **24. Ahikan**–son of Shaphan the scribe, or royal secretary. He was one of those whom King Josiah, when struck by the words of the book of the law, sent to inquire of the Lord (II Kings 22:12, 14). Hence his interference here in behalf of Jeremiah is what we should expect from his past association with that good king. His son, Gedaliah, followed in his father's steps, so that he was chosen by the Babylonians as the one to whom they committed Jeremiah for safety after taking Jerusalem, and on whose loyalty they could depend in setting him over the remnant of the people in Judea (ch. 39:14; II Kings 25:22). **people to put him to death**–Princes often, when they want to destroy a good man, prefer it to be done by a popular tumult rather than by their own order, so as to reap the fruit of the crime without odium to themselves (Matt. 27:20).

ADAM CLARKE

17. *Certain of the elders.* This is really a fine defense, and the argument was perfectly conclusive. Some think that it was **Ahikam** who undertook the prophet's defense.

18. *Micah the Morasthite.* The same as stands among the prophets. Now all these prophesied as hard things against the land as Jeremiah has done; yet they were not put to death, for the people saw that they were sent of God.

20. *Urijah . . . who prophesied.* The process against Jeremiah is finished at the nineteenth verse; and the case of Urijah is next brought on, for he was also to be tried for his life; but hearing of it, he fled to Egypt. He was however condemned in his absence; and the king sent to Egypt, and brought him thence and slew him, and caused him to have an ignominious burial, vv. 21-23.

24. *The hand of Ahikam . . . was with Jeremiah.* And it was probably by his influence that Jeremiah did not share the same fate with Urijah. The Ahikam mentioned here was probably the father of Gedaliah, who, after the capture of Jerusalem, was appointed governor of the country by Nebuchadnezzar, chap. xl. 5. Of the Prophet Urijah we know nothing but what we learn from this place. *That they should not give him into the hand of the people.* Though acquitted in the supreme court, he was not out of danger; there was a popular prejudice against him, and it is likely that Ahikam was obliged to conceal him, that they might not put him to death.

MATTHEW HENRY

CHAPTER 27

Verses 1-11

Some difficulty occurs in the date of this prophecy. Dr. Lightfoot solves it thus: In the beginning of Jehoiakim's reign Jeremiah is to make these bonds and yokes, and to put them upon his own neck, in token of Judah's subjection to the king of Babylon, which began at that time; but he is to send them to the neighbouring kings afterwards in the reign of Zedekiah, of whose succession to Jehoiakim, and the ambassadors sent to him, mention is made by way of prediction.

I. Jeremiah is to prepare a sign of the general reduction of all these countries into subjection to the king of Babylon (*v.* 2): *Make thee bonds and yokes*, yokes with bonds to fasten them, that the beast may not slip his neck out of the yoke. Into these the prophet must put his own neck for everyone would enquire, What is the meaning of Jeremiah's yokes? We find him with one on, *ch.* xxviii. 10. Hereby he intimated that he advised them to nothing but what he was resolved to do himself.

II. He is to send this, with a sermon annexed to it, to all the neighbouring princes; those are mentioned (*v.* 3) that lay next to the land of Canaan. It should seem, there was a treaty of alliance on foot between the king of Judah and all those other kings. Jerusalem was the place appointed for the treaty. Thither they all sent their plenipotentiaries; and it was agreed that they should bind themselves in a league offensive and defensive, in opposition to the threatening greatness of the king of Babylon. They had great confidence in their strength thus united; but, when the envoys were returning to their respective masters with the ratification of this treaty, Jeremiah gives each of them a yoke to carry to his master, to signify to him that he must become a servant to the king of Babylon, In the sermon, 1. God asserts his own indisputable right to dispose of kingdoms as he pleases, *v.* 5. He is the Creator of all things; he *made the earth* at first, established it, and it abides: it is still the same, though *one generation passes away and another comes.* He still by a continued creation produces *man and beast upon the ground*, and it is by his *great power* and *outstretched arm.* As he hath graciously *given the earth to the children of men* in general (Ps. cxv. 16), so he gives to each his share of it, be it more or less. 2. He publishes a grant of all these countries to Nebuchadnezzar. "This is to certify to all whom it may concern that I have *given all these lands*, with all the wealth of them, into *the hands of the king of Babylon*; even the beasts *of the field*, whether tame or wild, *have I given to him*, parks and pastures; they are all his own." Nebuchadnezzar was a proud wicked man, an idolater; and yet God, in his providence, gives him this large dominion, these vast possessions. Note, The things of this world are not the best things, for God often gives the largest share of them to bad men, that are rebels against him. Dominion is not founded in grace. Nebuchadnezzar is a bad man, and yet God calls him his servant, because he employed him as an instrument of his providence for the chastising of the nations. 3. He assures them that they should all be unavoidably brought under the dominion of the king of Babylon for a time (*v.* 7): *All nations*, all these nations and many others, shall serve *him, and his son, and his son's son.* His son was Evil-merodach, and his son's son Belshazzar, in whom his kingdom ceased: then the time of reckoning came, and *many nations and great kings*, incorporated into the empire of the Medes and Persians, *served themselves of him*, as before, *ch.* xxv. 14. 4. He threatens those that stood out and would not submit to the king of Babylon (*v.* 8): That nation that will not *put their neck under his yoke* I will *punish with sword and famine*, with one judgment after another, till it is *consumed by his hand.* 5. He shows them the vanity of all the hopes they fed themselves with, that they should preserve their liberties, *v.* 9, 10. These nations had their prophets too, that pretended to foretell future events by the stars, or by dreams, or enchantments; and they, to please their patrons, assured them that they *should not serve the king of Babylon.* Thus they designed to animate them to a vigorous resistance. But he tells them that it would prove to their destruction. Particular prophesies against these nations that bordered on Israel we shall meet with, *ch.* xlviii and xlix, and Ezek. xxv. 6. He puts them in a fair way to prevent their destruction by a quiet and easy submission, *v.* 11. The nations that will be content to *serve the king of Babylon*, and pay him tribute for seventy years (ten apprenticeships), *those will I let remain still in their own land. Serve the king of Babylon and you shall till the land* and *dwell therein.* Some would condemn this as the evidence of a mean spirit, but the prophet recommends

JAMIESON, FAUSSET, BROWN

CHAPTER 27

Vss. 1-22. The Futility of Resisting Nebuchadnezzar Illustrated to the Ambassadors of the King, Desiring to Have the King of Judah Confederate with Them, under the Type of Yokes. Jeremiah Exhorts Them and Zedekiah to Yield. **1. Jehoiakim**—The prophecy that follows was according to this reading given in the fourth year of Jehoiakim, fifteen years before it was published in the reign of Zedekiah to whom it refers; it was thus long deposited in the prophet's bosom, in order that by it he might be supported under trials in his prophetic career in the interim [Calvin]. But "Zedekiah" *may be* the true reading. So the *Syriac* and *Arabic Versions.* Vss. 3, 12; ch. 28:1, confirm this; also, one of Kennicott's MSS. The *English Version* reading *may* have originated from the first verse of ch. 26. "Son of Josiah" applies to Zedekiah as truly as to "Jehoiakim" or "Eliakim." The *fourth year* may, in a general sense here, as in ch. 28:1, be called "the beginning of his reign," as it lasted eleven years (II Kings 24:18). It was not long after the fourth year of his reign that he rebelled against Nebuchadnezzar (ch. 51:59; 52:3; II Kings 24:20), in violation of an oath before God (II Chron. 36:13). **2. bonds**—by which the yoke is made fast to the neck (ch. 5:5). **yokes**—lit., the carved piece of wood attached at both ends to the two yokes on the necks of a pair of oxen, so as to connect them. Here the *yoke* itself. The *plural* is used, as he was to wear one himself, and give the others to the ambassadors; (vs. 3; ch. 28:10, 12) proves that the symbolical act was in this instance (though not in others, ch. 25:15) actually done (cf. Isa. 20:2, etc.; Ezek. 12:3, 11, 18). **3.** Appropriate symbol, as these ambassadors had come to Jerusalem to consult as to shaking off the yoke of Nebuchadnezzar. According to Pherecydes in Clemens Alexandrinus, *Stromateis*, 567, Idanthura, king of the Scythians, intimated to Darius, who had crossed the Danube, that he would lead an army against him, by sending him, instead of a letter, *a mouse, a frog, a bird, an arrow*, and *a plough.* The task assigned to Jeremiah required great faith, as it was sure to provoke alike his own countrymen and the foreign ambassadors and their kings, by a seeming insult, at the very time that all were full of confident hopes grounded on the confederacy. **5.** God here, as elsewhere, connects with the symbol doctrine, which is as it were its soul, without which it would be not only cold and frivolous, but even dead [Calvin]. God's mention of His supreme power is in order to refute the pride of those who rely on their own power (Isa. 45:12). **given it unto whom it seemed meet unto me**—(Ps. 115:15, 16; Dan. 4:17, 25, 32). Not for his merits, but of My own sole good pleasure [Estius]. **6. beasts of the field**—not merely the horses to carry his Chaldean soldiers, and oxen to draw his provisions [Grotius]; not merely the deserts, mountains, and woods, the haunts of wild beasts, implying his unlimited extent of empire [Estius]; but the beasts themselves by a mysterious instinct of nature. A reproof to men that they did not recognize God's will, which the very beasts acknowledged (cf. Isa. 1:3). As the beasts are to submit to Christ, the Restorer of the dominion over nature, lost by the first Adam (cf. Gen. 1:28; 2:19, 20; Ps. 8:6-8), so they were appointed to submit to Nebuchadnezzar, the representative of the world power and prefigurer of Antichrist; this universal power was suffered to be held by him to show the unfitness of any to wield it "until He come whose right it is" (Ezek. 21:27). **7. son . . . son's son**—(II Chron. 36:20). Nebuchadnezzar had *four* successors—Evil-merodach, his *son;* Neriglissar, husband of Nebuchadnezzar's daughter; his son, Labosodarchod; and Naboned (with whom his son, Belshazzar, was joint king), *son* of Evil-merodach. But Neriglissar and Labosodarchod were not in the *direct male line;* so that the prophecy held good to "his son and his son's son," and the intermediate two are omitted. **time of his land**—i.e., of its subjugation or its being "visited" in wrath (vs. 22; ch. 25:12; 29:10; 50:27; Dan. 5:26). **serve themselves of him**—make him their servant (ch. 25:14; Isa. 13:22). So "his day" for the destined day of his calamity (Job 18:20). **8. until I have consumed them by his hand**—until by these consuming visitations I have brought them under his power. **9. ye**—the Jews especially, for whom the address to the rest was intended. **enchanters**—augurs [Calvin], from a root, the "eyes," i.e., lookers at the stars and other means of taking omens of futurity; or another root, a "fixed time," observers of times: forbidden in the law (Lev. 19:26; Deut. 18:10, 11, 14). **10. to remove you**—expressing the *event* which would result.

ADAM CLARKE

CHAPTER 27

1. *In the beginning of the reign of Jehoiakim.* It is most evident that his prophecy was delivered about the fourth year of Zedekiah, and not *Jehoiakim*, as in the text. See chap. xxviii. 1. And it is clear from the third and twelfth verses, where Zedekiah is expressly mentioned, that this is the true reading.

2. *Make thee bonds and yokes.* Probably yokes with straps, by which they were attached to the neck. This was a symbolical action, to show that the several kings mentioned below should be brought under the dominion of the Chaldeans.

5. *I have made the earth.* I am the Creator and Governor of all things, and I dispose of the several kingdoms of the world as seemeth best to Me.

6. *And now have I given.* These kingdoms are at My sovereign disposal; and at present, for the punishment of their rulers and people, I shall give them into the hands of Nebuchadnezzar, king of Babylon.

7. *And all nations shall serve him* (Nebuchadnezzar), *and his son* (Evil-merodach, chap. lii. 31), *and his son's son* (Belshazzar, Dan. v. 11)—all which was literally fulfilled.

9. *Therefore hearken not ye to your prophets.* Who pretend to have a revelation from heaven. *Nor to your diviners.* Persons who guessed at futurity by certain signs in the animate or inanimate creation.

MATTHEW HENRY

it as that of a meek spirit, which yields to necessity, and by a quiet submission to the hardest turns of Providence makes the best of bad. Many might have prevented destroying providences by humbling themselves under humbling providences. It is better to take up a lighter cross in our way than to pull a heavier on our own head.

What was said to all the nations is here with a particular tenderness applied to the Jews, for whom Jeremiah was concerned. The case at present stood thus: Judah and Jerusalem had contested with the king of Babylon, and were worsted; many both of their valuable persons and goods were carried to Babylon already, and some of the *vessels of the Lord's house.* Now how this struggle would issue was the question. They had those at Jerusalem who pretended to be prophets, who bade them hold out and recover all that they had lost. Now Jeremiah is sent to bid them yield, for instead of recovering what they had lost, they would otherwise lose all that remained.

I. Jeremiah humbly addresses the king of Judah, to persuade him to surrender to the king of Babylon. His act would be the people's and therefore he speaks to him as to them all (*v.* 12): *Bring your necks under the yoke of the king of Babylon and live.* Is it their wisdom to submit to the heavy iron yoke of a cruel tyrant, that they may secure the lives of their bodies? And is it not much more our wisdom to submit to the sweet and easy yoke of our rightful Lord and Master Jesus Christ, that we may secure the lives of our souls? Bring down your spirits to repentance and faith, and that is the way to bring up your spirits to heaven and glory.

II. He addresses himself likewise to the priests and the people (*v.* 16), to persuade them to *serve the king of Babylon,* that they might *live,* and might prevent the desolation of the city (*v.* 17): "*Wherefore should it be laid waste,* as certainly it will be if you stand out?"

III. In both these addresses he warns them against giving credit to the false prophets that rocked them asleep in their security: "*Hearken not to the word of the prophets* (*v.* 14), *your prophets, v.* 16. They are not God's prophets; he never sent them; they are yours, for they say what you would have them say, and aim at nothing but to please you." Two things their prophets said: 1. That the power which the king of Babylon had gained over them should now shortly be broken. They said (*v.* 14), "*You shall not serve the king of Babylon;* you need not submit voluntarily, for you shall not be compelled to submit." This they prophesied *in the name of the Lord* (*v.* 15), as if God had sent them. But it was a lie: *I have not sent them, saith the Lord.* 2. They prophesied that the vessels of the temple, which the king of Babylon had already carried away, should now shortly be brought back (*v.* 16); knowing how acceptable it would be to the priests who loved the *gold of the temple* better than the *temple that sanctified the gold.* These vessels were taken away when Jeconiah was carried captive into Babylon, *v.* 20. We have the story, and it is a melancholy one, 2 Kings xxiv. 13, 15; 2 Chron. xxxvi. 10. The temple was their pride, and the stripping of that was too plain an indication of that which the true prophet told them, that their *God had departed from them.* Their false prophets therefore had no other way to make them easy than by telling them that the king of Babylon should be forced to restore them in a little while. Now here Jeremiah bids them think of preserving the vessels that remained by their prayers, rather than of bringing back those that were gone by their prophecies (*v.* 18): *If they be prophets,* as they pretend, and if *the word of the Lord be with them*—if they have any intercourse with heaven, let them stand *between the living and the dead,* between that which is carried away and that which remains, that *the plague may be stayed; let them make intercession with the Lord of hosts,* that the vessels which are left go not after the rest. Instead of prophesying, let them pray. He assures them that the brazen vessels should go after the golden ones, *v.* 19, 20. Nebuchadnezzar would be sure to come again and take all he could find, not only in *the house of the Lord,* but in the *king's house.* But he concludes with a gracious promise that the time should come when they should all be returned: *Until the day that I visit them in mercy,* and *then I will bring* those vessels *up again, and restore them to this place.* Surely they were under the protection of a special Providence, else they would have been melted down, but there was to be a second temple, for which they were to be reserved. We read particularly of the return of them, Ezra i. 8. Though the return of the church's prosperity do not come in our time, we must not therefore despair of it, for it will come in God's time.

JAMIESON, FAUSSET, BROWN

The very thing they profess by their enchantments to avert, they are by them bringing on you. Better to submit to Nebuchadnezzar, and remain in your land, than to rebel, and be removed from it. **11. serve . . . till it**—The same *Hebrew* root expresses "serve" and "till," or "cultivate." *Serve* ye the king of Babylon, and the land will *serve* you [CALVIN].

12. I spake also—translate, "And I spake. . . ." Special application of the subject to Zedekiah. **13. Why . . . die**—by running on your own ruin in resisting Nebuchadnezzar after this warning (Ezek. 18: 31).

14. lie—(Ch. 14:14.) **15. in my name**—The devil often makes *God's name* the plea for lies (Matt. 4:6; 7:22, 23; vss. 15-20, the test whereby to know false prophets). **16.** The "vessels" had been carried away to Babylon in the reign of Jeconiah (II Kings 24:13); also previously in that of Jehoiakim (II Chron. 36:5-7).

18. at Jerusalem—i.e., in other houses containing such vessels, besides the house of God and the king's palace. Nebuzaradan, captain of the guard under Nebuchadnezzar, carried all away (II Kings 25:13-17; II Chron. 36:18). The more costly vessels had been previously removed in the reigns of Jehoiakim and Jeconiah. **19.** (Ch. 52: 17, 20, 21.)

22. until . . . I visit them—in wrath by Cyrus (ch. 32:5). In seventy years from the first carrying away of captives in Jehoiachin's reign (ch. 29:10; II Chron. 36:21). **restore them**—by the hand of Cyrus (Ezra 1:7). By Artaxerxes (Ezra 7:19).

ADAM CLARKE

13. *Why will ye die?* If you resist the king of Babylon, to whom I have given a commission against you, you shall be destroyed by the sword and by famine; but if you submit, you shall escape all these evils.

16. *The vessels of the Lord's house.* Which had been carried away by Nebuchadnezzar under the reigns of Jehoiakim and Jeconiah, 2 Chron. xxxvi. 7-10. *Shall now shortly be brought again.* This is a lie. They shall not be restored till I bring them up, v. 22, which was after the Captivity, when they were sent back by Cyrus, the Lord inclining his heart to do it, Ezra i. 7 and vii. 19.

19. *Concerning the pillars.* Two brazen columns placed by Solomon in the portico of the Temple, eighteen cubits high, and twelve in circumference, 1 Kings vii. 15-22; Jer. lii. 11. *The sea.* The brazen sea, ten cubits in diameter. It contained water for different washings in the divine worship, and was supported on twelve brazen oxen. Perhaps these are what are called the bases here.

22. *They shall be carried to Babylon.* Far from those already taken being brought back, those which now remain shall be carried thither, unless ye submit to the Chaldeans. They did not submit, and the prophecy was literally fulfilled; see chap. lii. 17-23; 2 Kings xxv. 13.

MATTHEW HENRY

CHAPTER 28

Verses 1–9

This struggle between a true prophet and a false one is said to have happened *in the beginning of the reign of Zedekiah*, and yet *in the fourth year*, for the the first four years of his reign might well be called *the beginning*, because during those years he reigned under the dominion of the king of Babylon and as a tributary to him; whereas the rest of his reign, which might well be called the *latter part* of it, in distinction from that *former part*, he reigned in rebellion against the king of Babylon. In this fourth year of his reign he went in person to Babylon (as we find, *ch.* li. 59). This gave the people some hope that in person he would put a good end to the war, in which hope the false prophets encouraged them, Hananiah particularly.

I. The prediction which Hananiah delivered solemnly, *in the house of the Lord*, and in the name of the Lord, *in the presence of the priests and of all the people*. In delivering this prophecy, he faced Jeremiah, he spoke it to him (*v.* 1), designing to contradict him, as much as to say, "Jeremiah, thou liest." Now this prediction is that the king of Babylon's power over Judah and Jerusalem should be speedily broken, that *within two full years* the vessels of the temple should be brought back, and Jeremiah, and all the captives carried away with him, should return; whereas Jeremiah had foretold that the yoke of the king of Babylon should be bound on yet faster, and that the vessels and captives should not return for 70 years, *v.* 2–4. Upon the reading of this sham prophecy, and comparing it with the messages that God sent by the true prophets, what a vast difference there is between them. Here is nothing of the spirit and life, the sublimity of expression, that appear in the discourses of God's prophets. But that which is especially wanting here is an air of piety; he speaks of the return of their prosperity, but not a word of good counsel given them to repent, and return to God, to pray, and seek his face. He promises them temporal mercies, in God's name, but makes no mention of those spiritual mercies which God always promised, *ch.* xxiv. 7: *I will give them a heart to know me.*

II. Jeremiah's reply to this pretended prophecy. 1. He heartily wishes it might prove true. Such an affection has he for his country, and so truly desirous is he that their ruin might be prevented. He said, *Amen; the Lord do so; the Lord perform thy words*, *v.* 5, 6. This was not the first time that Jeremiah had prayed for his people, though he had prophesied against them, as Christ prayed, *Father, if it be possible, let this cup pass from me*, when yet he knew it must not pass from him. God himself, though he has determined, does not desire, the death of sinners, but would *have all men to be saved*. 2. He appeals to the event, to prove it false, *v.* 7–9. The false prophets reflected upon Jeremiah, as Ahab upon Micaiah, because he never *prophesied good concerning them, but evil*. Prophets of old prophesied against *many countries and great kingdoms*, so bold were they in delivering the messages which God sent by them, and so far from fearing men, or seeking to please them, as Hananiah did. They made no difficulty, any more than Jeremiah did, of threatening war, famine, and pestilence, and what they said was regarded as coming from God; why then should Jeremiah be run down as *a pestilent fellow, and a sower of sedition*, when he preached no otherwise than God's prophets had always done before him? But the prophet that *prophesied of peace* and prosperity especially as Hananiah did, absolutely and unconditionally, without adding that necessary proviso, that they do not by wilful sin put a bar in their own door and stop the current of God's favours, will be proved a true prophet only by the accomplishment of his prediction; if it come to pass, then it shall be known that *the Lord has sent him*, but, if not, he will appear to be a cheat and an impostor.

Verses 10–17

I. The insolence of the false prophet. To complete the affront he designed Jeremiah, *he took the yoke from off his neck* which he carried as a memorial of what he had prophesied concerning the enslaving of the nations of Nebuchadnezzar, and he broke it, that he might give a sign of the accomplishment of his prophecy, as Jeremiah had given of his, and might seem to have defeated the intention of his prophecy. The lying spirit, in the mouth of this false prophet, mimics the language of the Spirit of truth: *Thus saith the Lord, So will I break the yoke of the king of Babylon*, not only from the neck of this nation, but *from the neck of all nations, within two full years.*

II. The patience of the true prophet. Jeremiah quietly *went his way*, not because he had nothing to

JAMIESON, FAUSSET, BROWN

CHAPTER 28

Vss. 1-17. Prophecies Immediately Following Those in Chapter 27. Hananiah Breaks the Yokes to Signify that Nebuchadnezzar's Yoke Shall Be Broken. Jeremiah Foretells that Yokes of Iron Are to Succeed Those of Wood, and that Hananiah Shall Die. **1. in the beginning of the reign of Zedekiah**—The Jews often divided any period into two halves, *the beginning* and *the end*. As Zedekiah reigned eleven years, the fourth year would be called the *beginning* of his reign, especially as during the first three years affairs were in such a disturbed state that he had little power or dignity, being a tributary; but in the fourth year he became strong in power. **Hananiah**—Another of this name was one of the three godly youths who braved Nebuchadnezzar's wrath in the fear of God (Dan. 1:6, 7; 3:12). Probably a near relation, for *Azariah* is associated with him; as *Azur* with the Hananiah here. The godly and ungodly are often in the same family (Ezek. 18:14-20). **Gibeon**—one of the cities of the priests, to which order he must have belonged. **2. broken the yoke**—*I have determined to break:* referring to Jeremiah's prophecy (ch. 27:12). **3. two full years**—lit., "years of days." So "a month of days," i.e., all its days complete (Gen. 29:14, *Margin;* 41:1). It was marvellous presumption to speak so definitely without having any divine revelation. **4. bring again—Jeconiah**—not *necessarily* implying that Hananiah wished Zedekiah to be superseded by Jeconiah. The main point intended was that the restoration from Babylon should be complete. But, doubtless, the false prophet foretold Jeconiah's return (II Kings 24:12-15), to ingratiate himself with the populace, with whom Jeconiah was a favorite (ch. 22:24, *Note*). **5. the prophet Jeremiah**—the epithet, "the prophet," is prefixed to "Jeremiah" throughout this chapter, to correspond to the same epithet before "Hananiah"; except in vs. 12, where "*the prophet*" has been inserted in *English Version*. The rival claims of the true and the false prophet are thus put in the more prominent contrast. **6. Amen**—Jeremiah prays *for* the people, though constrained to prophesy against them (I Kings 1:36). The *event* was the appointed test between contradictory predictions (Deut. 18:21, 22). "Would that what you say were true!" I prefer the safety of my country even to my own estimation. The prophets had no pleasure in announcing God's judgment, but did so as a matter of stern duty, not thereby divesting themselves of their natural feelings of sorrow for their country's woe. Cf. Exodus 32:32; Romans 9:3, as instances of how God's servants, intent only on the glory of God and the salvation of the country, forgot self and uttered wishes in a state of feeling transported out of themselves. So Jeremiah wished not to diminish aught from the word of God, though as a Jew he uttered the wish for his people [Calvin]. **8. prophets . . . before me**—Hosea, Joel, Amos, and others. **evil**—a few MSS, read *famine*, which is more usually associated with the specification of *war* and *pestilence* (ch. 15:2; 18:21; 27:8, 13). But *evil* here includes *all* the calamities flowing from *war*, not merely *famine*, but also *desolation*, etc. *Evil*, being the more difficult reading, is less likely to be the interpolated one than *famine*, which probably originated in copying the parallel passages. **9. peace**—Hananiah had given no warning as to the need of conversion, but had foretold *prosperity* unconditionally. Jeremiah does not say that all are true prophets who foretell truths in any instance (which Deut. 13:1, 2, disproves); but asserts only the converse, viz., that whoever, as Hananiah, predicts what the event does not confirm, is a false prophet. There are two tests of prophets: (1) The event, Deuteronomy 18:22. (2) The word of God, Isaiah 8:20.

10. the yoke—(ch. 27:2). Impious audacity to break what God had appointed as a solemn pledge of the fulfilment of His word. Hence Jeremiah deigns no reply (vs. 11; Matt. 7:6).

11. neck of all nations—opposed to ch. 27:7.

ADAM CLARKE

CHAPTER 28

1. *And it came to pass the same year . . . the fifth month.* Which commenced with the first new moon of August, according to our calendar. This verse gives the precise date of the prophecy in the preceding chapter; and proves that Zedekiah, not Jehoiakim, is the name that should be read in the first verse of that chapter. *Hananiah the son of Azur the prophet.* One who called himself a prophet; who pretended to be in commerce with the Lord, and to receive revelations from Him. He was probably a priest; for he was of Gibeon, a sacerdotal city in the tribe of Benjamin.

2. *Thus speaketh the Lord.* What awful impudence, when he knew in his conscience that God had given him no such commission!

3. *Within two full years.* Time sufficient for the Chaldeans to destroy the city, and carry away the rest of the sacred vessels; but he did not live to see the end of this short period.

6. *Amen: the Lord do so.* Oh, that it might be according to your word! May the people find this to be true!

8. *The prophets that have been before me.* Namely, Joel, Amos, Hosea, Micah, Zephaniah, Nahum, Habakkuk, and others—all of whom denounced similar evils against a corrupt people.

9. *When the word of the prophet shall come to pass.* Here is the criterion. He is a true prophet who specifies things that he says shall happen, and also fixes the time of the event; and the things do happen, and in that time. You say that Nebuchadnezzar shall not overthrow this city; and that in two years from this time, not only the sacred vessels already taken away shall be restored, but also that Jeconiah and all the Jewish captives shall be restored, and the Babylonish yoke broken (see vv. 2-4). Now I say that Nebuchadnezzar will come this year, and destroy this city, and lead away the rest of the people into captivity, and the rest of the sacred vessels; and that there will be no restoration of any kind till seventy years from this time.

10. *Then Hananiah . . . took the yoke . . . and brake it.* He endeavored by this symbolical act to persuade them of the truth of his prediction.

MATTHEW HENRY

answer, but because he was willing to stay till God was pleased to furnish him with a direct answer, which as yet he had not received. He expected that God would send a special message to Hananiah. *I, as a deaf man, heard not, for thou wilt hear*, and *thou shalt answer, Lord, for me*.

III. The justice of God in giving judgment between Jeremiah and his adversary. Jeremiah went his way, as a man *in whose mouth there was no rebuke*, but God soon put a word into his mouth. Let not Jeremiah himself distrust the truth of what he had delivered in God's name because it met with such contradiction. If what we have spoken be the truth of God, we must not unsay it because men gainsay it; for *great is the truth and will prevail*. Hananiah has broken the *yokes of wood*, but Jeremiah must make for them *yokes of iron*, which cannot be broken (*v.* 13), for (says God), "*I have put a yoke of iron upon the neck of all these nations*, which shall lie heavier, and bind harder, upon them (*v.* 14), *that they may serve the king of Babylon*." What was said before is repeated again: *I have given him the beasts of the field also*, as if there were something significant in that. Men had by their wickedness made themselves *like the beasts that perish*, and therefore deserved to be ruled as beasts are ruled, and such a power Nebuchadnezzar ruled with; for *whom he would he slew and whom he would he kept alive*. Hananiah is sentenced to die for contradicting it, and Jeremiah, when he has received commission from God, boldly tells him so to his face. The crimes of which Hananiah stands convicted are cheating the people and affronting God: *Thou makest this people to trust in a lie; thou hast taught rebellion against the Lord*. The judgment given against him is, "*I will cast thee off from the face of the earth. This year thou shalt die*, and die as a rebel against the Lord." This sentence was executed, *v.* 17. Hananiah died the same year, within two months.

JAMIESON, FAUSSET, BROWN

13. **Thou hast broken . . . wood . . . thou shalt make . . . iron**—Not here, "*Thou* hast broken . . . wood," and "*I* will make . . . iron" (cf. vs. 16). The same false prophets who, by urging the Jews to rebel, had caused them to throw off the then comparatively *easy* yoke of Babylon, thereby brought on them a *more severe* yoke imposed by that city. "Yokes of iron," alluding to Deuteronomy 28:48. It is better to take up a light cross in our way, than to pull a heavier on our own heads. We may escape destroying providences by submitting to humbling providences. So, spiritually, contrast the "easy yoke" of Christ with the "yoke of bondage" of the law (Acts 15:10; Gal. 5:1). **14. I have put**—Though Hananiah and those like him were secondary instruments in bringing the iron yoke on Judea, *God* was the great First Cause (ch. 27:4-7). **15. makest . . . trust in a lie**—(ch. 29:31; Ezek. 13:22.) **16. this year . . . die**—The prediction was uttered in the *fifth* month (vs. 1); Hananiah's death took place in the *seventh* month, i.e., within *two months* after the prediction, answering with awful significance to the *two years* in which Hananiah had foretold that the yoke imposed by Babylon would end. **rebellion**—opposition to God's plain direction, that all should submit to Babylon (ch. 29:32).

ADAM CLARKE

13. *Yokes of iron*. Instead of Nebuchadnezzar's yoke being broken, this captivity shall be more severe than the preceding. All these nations shall have a yoke of iron on their neck. He shall subdue them, and take all their property, even the beasts of the field.

15. *Hear now, Hananiah; the Lord hath not sent thee*. This was a bold speech in the presence of those priests and people who were prejudiced in favor of this false prophet, who prophesied to them smooth things.

16. *This year thou shalt die*. By this shall the people know who is the true prophet. You have taught rebellion against the Lord, and God will cut you off; and this shall take place, not within seventy years, or two years, but in this very year, and within two months from this time.

17. *So Hananiah . . . died the same year in the seventh month*. The prophecy was delivered in the fifth month (v. 1), and Hananiah died in the seventh month. And thus God, in mercy, gave him about two months in which he might prepare to meet his Judge.

MATTHEW HENRY — CHAPTER 29

Verses 1–7

I. Jeremiah wrote to the captives in Babylon, in the name of the Lord. Jeconiah had surrendered himself a prisoner, with the queen his mother, the chamberlains of his household, called there the *eunuchs*, and many of *the princes of Judah and Jerusalem. The carpenters and smiths* likewise were yielded up, that those who remained might not have any proper hands to fortify their city. By this tame submission it was hoped that Nebuchadnezzar would be pacified, but the imperious conqueror grows upon their concessions. And, not content with this, when these had *departed from Jerusalem* he comes again, and fetches away many more of *the elders, the priests, the prophets, and the people* (*v.* 1). The case of these captives was very melancholy, the rather because they looked as if they were greater sinners than all men who dwelt at Jerusalem. Jeremiah therefore writes a letter to them, to comfort them. This letter of Jeremiah's was sent to the captives in Babylon by the hands of the ambassadors whom king Zedekiah sent to Nebuchadnezzar, probably to pay him his tribute and renew his submission to him. By such messengers Jeremiah chose to send this message, because it was a message from God.

II. A copy of the letter at large follows here to *v.* 24.

1. He assures them that he wrote in the name of the *Lord of hosts, the God of Israel*; Jeremiah was but the scribe or amanuensis. It would be comfortable to them, in their captivity, to hear that God is *the Lord of hosts*, able to help and deliver them; and that he is the *God of Israel* still, in covenant with his people. This would be an admonition to stand upon their guard against all temptations to the idolatry of Babylon. God's sending to them in this letter might be an encouragement, as it was evidence that he had not cast them off, had not disinherited them, though he was displeased with them and corrected them.

2. God by him owns the hand he had in their captivity: *I have caused you to be carried away*, *v.* 4 and again, *v.* 7. If God caused them to be carried captives, they might be sure that he neither did them any wrong nor meant them any hurt.

3. He bids them think of nothing but settling there; and therefore let them resolve to make the best of it (*v.* 5, 6): *Build yourselves houses and dwell in them*, &c. They must not feed themselves with hopes of a speedy return out of their captivity. Let them therefore accommodate themselves to it as well as they can. Let them *build*, and *plant*, and *marry*, and dispose of their children there as if they were at home in their own land. If they live in the fear of God, what should hinder them but they may live comfortably in Babylon? They cannot but *weep* sometimes *when they remember Zion*. But let not weeping hinder

JAMIESON, FAUSSET, BROWN — CHAPTER 29

Vss. 1-32. Letter of Jeremiah to the Captives in Babylon, to Counteract the Assurances Given by the False Prophets of a Speedy Restoration. **1. residue of the elders**—those still surviving from the time when they were carried to Babylon with Jeconiah; the other elders of the captives had died by either a natural or a violent death. **2. queen**—Nehushta, the queen mother, daughter of Elnathan (II Kings 24:8, 15). (Elnathan, her father, is perhaps the same as the one mentioned in ch. 26:22.) She reigned jointly with her son. **princes**—All the men of authority were taken away lest they should organize a rebellion. Jeremiah wrote his letter while the calamity was still recent, to console the captives under it. **3. Zedekiah . . . sent unto Babylon**—In ch. 51:59, Zedekiah himself goes to Babylon; *here* he *sends* ambassadors. Whatever was the object of the embassy, it shows that Zedekiah only reigned at the pleasure of the king of Babylon, who might have restored Jeconiah, had he pleased. Hence, Zedekiah permitted Jeremiah's letter to be sent, not only as being led by Hananiah's death to attach greater credit to the prophet's words, but also as the letter accorded with his own wish that the Jews should remain in Chaldea till Jeconiah's death. **Hilkiah**—the high priest who found the book of the law in the house of the Lord, and showed it to "Shaphan" the scribe (the same Shaphan probably as here), who showed it to King Josiah (II Kings 22: 8, etc.). The sons of Hilkiah and Shaphan inherited from their fathers some respect for sacred things. So in ch. 36: 25, "Gemariah" interceded with King Jehoiakim that the prophet's roll should not be burned.

5. Build . . . houses—In opposition to the false prophets' suggestions, who told the captives that their captivity would soon cease, Jeremiah tells them that it will be of long duration, and that therefore they should build houses, as Babylon is to be for long their home. **6. that ye . . . be . . . not diminished**—It was God's will that the seed of Abraham should not fail; thus consolation is given them, and the hope, though not of an immediate, yet of an ultimate, return.

ADAM CLARKE — CHAPTER 29

1. *Now these are the words of the letter*. This transaction took place in the first or second year of Zedekiah. It appears that the prophet had been informed that the Jews who had already been carried into captivity had, through the instigations of false prophets, been led to believe that they were to be brought out of their captivity speedily. Jeremiah, fearing that this delusion might induce them to take some hasty steps, ill comporting with their present state, wrote a letter to them, which he entrusted to an embassy which Zedekiah had sent on some political concerns to Nebuchadnezzar. The letter was directed to the elders, priests, prophets, and people who had been carried away captives to Babylon.

4. *Thus saith the Lord of hosts*. This was the commencement of the letter.

5. *Build ye houses*. Prepare for a long continuance in your present captivity. Provide yourselves with the necessaries of life, and multiply in the land, that you may become a powerful people.

MATTHEW HENRY

sowing. In all conditions of life it is our wisdom and duty to make the best of that which is, and not to throw away the comfort of what we may have because we have not all we would have. We have a natural affection for our native country; if Providence remove us to some other country, we must resolve to live easy there. If the *earth be the Lord's*, then, wherever a child of God goes, he does not go off his Father's ground. They must not disquiet themselves with fears of intolerable hardships in their captivity.

4. He directs them to seek the good of the country where they were captives (*v.* 7), to pray for it, to endeavour to promote it. This forbids them to attempt anything against the public peace while they were subjects to the king of Babylon. They must live *quiet and peaceable lives* under him, *in all godliness and honesty*, not plotting to shake off his yoke, but patiently leaving it to God in due time to work deliverance for them. *For in the peace thereof you shall have peace.* Thus the primitive Christians, according to the temper of their holy religion, prayed for the powers that were, though they were persecuting powers. Every passenger is concerned in the safety of the ship.

Verses 8–14

I. God takes them from building upon the false foundation which their pretended prophets laid, *v.* 8, 9. They told them that their captivity should be short, and therefore that they must not think of taking root in Babylon. "Now herein *they deceive you*," says God; "they *prophesy a lie to you*, though they prophesy *in my name*. But *let them not deceive you*, suffer not yourselves to be deluded by them." *Hearken not to your dreams, which you cause to be dreamed.* He means either the dreams or fancies which the people pleased themselves with, or the dreams which the prophets dreamed and grounded their prophecies upon. They *caused them to be dreamed*; for they encouraged the prophets to put such deceits upon them, desiring them to prophesy nothing but *smooth things*, Isa. xxx. 10. They were dreams of their own bespeaking.

II. He gives them a good foundation to build their hopes upon. God here promises them that, though they should not return quickly, they should return at length, *after seventy years be accomplished.* He will put an end to *their captivity*. Though they are dispersed, some in one country and some in another, he will *gather them from all the places whither they are driven*, and incorporate them again in one body. They shall be brought again to their own land, *to the place whence* they were *carried captive*, *v.* 14. This shall be the performance of God's promise to them (*v.* 10): *I will perform my good word towards you.* This will make their return out of captivity very comfortable, that it will be the performance of God's good word to them, the product of a gracious promise. This shall be in pursuance of God's purposes concerning them (*v.* 11): *I know the thoughts that I think towards you.* His thoughts are all working towards the expected end, which he will give in due time. Let them have patience till the fruit is ripe, and then they shall have it. He will give them *an end, and expectation*, so it is in the original. When things are at the worst they will begin to mend; and he will give them to see the glorious perfection of their deliverance. He that in the beginning finished the *heavens and the earth*, and all the *hosts* of both, will finish all the blessings of both to his people. God does nothing by halves. He will give them to see the *expectation*, that *end* which they desire. He will give them not the expectations of their fears, nor the expectations of their fancies, but the expectations of their faith. This shall be in answer to their prayers (*v.* 12–14). *Then shall you call upon me*, and *you shall go, and pray unto me.* When deliverance is coming we must by prayer go forth to meet it. *I will hearken unto you*, and *I will be found of you.* God has said it, and we may depend upon it, *Seek and you shall find.* We have a general rule laid down (*v.* 13): *You shall find me when you shall search for me with all your heart.*

Verses 15–23

Jeremiah here turns to those who slighted the counsels and comforts that Jeremiah ministered and depended upon the false prophets. When this letter came from Jeremiah they would be ready to say, "Why should he make himself so busy, and take upon him to advise us? *The Lord has raised us up prophets in Babylon*, *v.* 15. We are satisfied with those prophets, and can depend upon them, and have no occasion to hear from any prophets in Jerusalem." These prophets of their own told them that no more should be carried captive, but that those who were in captivity should shortly return. In answer to this the prophet here foretells the utter destruction

JAMIESON, FAUSSET, BROWN

7. (Ezra 6:10; Rom. 13:1; I. Tim. 2:2.) Not only bear the Babylonian yoke patiently, but *pray for* your masters, i.e., while the captivity lasts. God's good time was to come when they were to pray for Babylon's downfall (ch. 51:35; Ps. 137:8). They were not to forestall that time. True religion teaches patient submission, not sedition, even though the prince be an unbeliever. In all states of life let us not throw away the comfort we *may* have, because we have not all we *would* have. There is here a foretaste of gospel love towards enemies (Matt. 5:44).

8. your dreams which ye caused to be dreamed—The Latin adage says, "The people wish to be deceived, so let them be deceived." Not mere credulity misleads men, but their own perverse "love of darkness rather than light." It was not priests who originated priestcraft, but the people's own morbid appetite to be deceived; e.g., Aaron and the golden calf (Exod. 32: 1-4). So the Jews *caused* or *made* the prophets to tell them encouraging dreams (ch. 23:25, 26; Eccles. 5:7; Zech. 10:2; John 3:19-21).

10. (*Note*, ch. 25: 11, 12; Dan. 9:2.) This proves that the seventy years date from Jeconiah's captivity, not from the last captivity. The specification of time was to curb the impatience of the Jews lest they should hasten before God's time. **good word**—promise of a return. **11. I know**—*I* alone; not the false prophets who *know* nothing of My purposes, though they pretend to know. **thoughts . . . I think**—(Isa. 55:9.) Glancing at the Jews who had no "thoughts of peace," but only of "evil" (misfortune), because *they* could not conceive how deliverance could come to them. The moral malady of man is twofold—at one time *vain confidence;* then, when that is disappointed, *despair.* So the Jews first laughed at God's threats, confident that they should speedily return; then, when cast down from that confidence, they sank in inconsolable despondency. **expected end**—lit., "end and expectation," i.e., an end, and that such an end as you wish for. Two nouns joined by "and," standing for a noun and adjective. So in ch. 36:27, "the roll and the words," i.e., the roll of words; Genesis 3:16, "sorrow and conception," i.e., sorrow in conception. Cf. Proverbs 23: 18, where, as here "end" means "a happy issue." **12. Fulfilled (Daniel 9:3, etc.). When God designs mercy, He puts it into the hearts of His people to pray for the mercy designed. When such a spirit of prayer is poured out, it is a sure sign of coming mercy. go**—to the temple and other places of prayer: contrasted with their previous sloth as to going to seek God. **13.** (Lev. 26:40-42, 44, 45.) **14. to be found**—(Ps. 32:6; Isa. 55:6). **turn . . . captivity**—play upon sounds, *shabti . . . shebith.*

15. Because—referring not to the preceding words, but to vss. 10, 11, "Jehovah saith this to you" (i.e., the prophecy of the continuance of the captivity seventy years), "because ye have said, The Lord hath raised us up prophets in Babylon," viz., foretelling our *speedy* deliverance (this their prophecy is *supposed*, not *expressed;* accordingly, vss. 16-19 contradict this false hope again, vss. 8, 9, 21). He, in this 15th verse, turns his address from the godly (vss. 12-14) to the ungodly listeners, to false prophets.

ADAM CLARKE

7. *Seek the peace of the city.* Endeavor to promote, as far as you can, the "prosperity" of the places in which you sojourn.

8. *Neither hearken to your dreams.* Rather, "dreamers"; for it appears there was a class of such persons, who not only had acquired a facility of dreaming themselves, but who undertook to interpret the dreams of others.

10. *For thus saith the Lord.* It has been supposed that a very serious transposition of verses has taken place here; and it has been proposed to read after v. 9 the sixteenth to the nineteenth inclusive; then the tenth, and on to the fourteenth inclusive; then the twentieth, the fifteenth, the twenty-first, and the rest regularly to the end.

14. *I will gather you from all the nations.* A quotation from Deut. xxx. 8, and see also Deut. iv. 7.

15. *Because ye have said.* The Septuagint very properly insert this verse between the twentieth and the twenty-first, and thus the connection here is not disturbed, and the connection below is completed.

MATTHEW HENRY

of those who remained still at Jerusalem: "As for the *king* and *people* that *dwell in the city*, who, you think, will be ready to bid you welcome when you return, you are deceived; they shall be followed with one judgment after another, *sword, famine*, and *pestilence*, which shall cut off multitudes; and the poor and miserable remains shall be *removed into all kingdoms of the earth*," *v.* 16, 18. And thus God *will make them*, or rather deal with them, *like vile figs*. This refers to the vision and the prophecy which we had *ch.* xxiv. And the reason given is the same (*v.* 19): *Because they have not hearkened to my words. I called, but they refused.* He calls upon all the children of the captivity, who boasted of them as prophets of God's raising up (*v.* 20): "Stand still, and hear the doom of the prophets you are so fond of." The two prophets are named here, *Ahab* and *Zedekiah*, *v.* 21. The crimes charged upon them—impiety and immorality: They *prophesied lies in God's name* (*v.* 21), and again (*v.* 23), They have *spoken lying words in my name*. Fathering their lies upon the God of truth was worst of all. Here it appears why they flattered others in their sins—because they could not reprove them without condemning themselves. *The king of Babylon shall slay them before your eyes;* nay, he shall put them to a miserable death, *roast them in the fire*, *v.* 22. We may suppose that it was not for their impiety and immorality that Nebuchadnezzar punished them thus severely, but for sedition, and some attempts of their turbulent spirits upon the public peace, and stirring up the people to revolt and rebel. Their names shall be a curse among the captives in Babylon, *v.* 22. When men would imprecate the greatest evil upon one they hated they could not load them with a heavier curse, in fewer words, than to say, *The Lord make thee like Zedekiah and like Ahab.*

Verses 24–32

The false prophets were enraged at the contents of Jeremiah's letter. One of them, Shemaiah, showed his malice against the prophet.

I. This busy fellow is called *Shemaiah the Nehelamite*, the *dreamer* (so the margin reads it), because all his prophecies he pretended to have received from God in a dream. He had got a copy of Jeremiah's letter to the captives, or information was given to him concerning it, and it nettled him exceedingly; he will answer it, yea, that he will. But how? He does not write to Jeremiah in justification of his own mission, but he writes to the priests, and instigates them to persecute Jeremiah. He writes in his own name as if he must be dictator to all mankind. But it is chiefly directed to Zephaniah, who was either the immediate son of Maaseiah, or of the 24th course of the priests, of which Maaseiah was the father and head. He was not the high priest, but suffragan to the high priest, or in some considerable post of command in the temple, as Pashur, *ch.* xx. 1. 1. He puts him and the other priests in mind of the duty of their place (*v.* 26): *The Lord hath made thee priest instead of Jehoiada the priest.* Some think that he refers to the famous Jehoiada, that great reformer in the days of Joash. Or, rather, it was some other Jehoiada, his immediate predecessor in this office, who perhaps was carried to Babylon among the priests, *v.* 1. Zephaniah is advanced, sooner than he expected, to this place of trust and power, and Shemaiah would have him think that Providence had preferred him that he might persecute God's prophets, that he had come to this government for such a time as this. These priests' business was to examine *every man that is mad and makes himself a prophet*. God's faithful prophets are here represented as prophets of their own making, usurpers of the office, and lay-intruders, as men that were mad, actuated by some demon, distracted men and men in a frenzy. 2. He informs them of the letter which Jeremiah had written to the captives (*v.* 28). The false prophets had formerly said that the captivity would never come, *ch.* xiv. 13. Jeremiah had said that it would come, and the event had already proved him in the right. 3. He demands judgment against him, taking it for granted that he is *mad*, and *makes himself a prophet*. He expects that they will order him to be put *in prison* and *in the stocks* (*v.* 26), hoping that the captives in Babylon would not be influenced by him. He takes upon him to chide Zephaniah for his neglect (*v.* 27): *Why hast thou not rebuked and restrained Jeremiah of Anathoth?* God had confirmed his word in the mouth of Jeremiah; it had *taken hold* of them (Zech. i. 6); and yet, because he does not prophesy to them the smooth things they desired, they are resolved to look upon him as not duly called to the office of a prophet. They were now sent into a miserable thraldom for *mocking the messengers of the Lord* and *misusing his prophets*. Afflictions will not of themselves cure

JAMIESON, FAUSSET, BROWN

16. people . . . in this city . . . not gone forth—So far from your returning to Jerusalem soon, even *your brethren* still left dwelling there shall themselves also be cast into exile. He mentions "the throne of *David*," lest they should think that, because David's kingdom was to be perpetual, no severe, though temporary, chastisements could interpose (Ps. 89:29-36). **17. vile figs**—*Hebrew*, "horrible," or nauseous, from a root, "to regard with loathing" (see ch. 24:8, 10). **18. removed to all . . . kingdoms**—(ch. 15:4; Deut. 28:25). **curse . . .**—(ch. 29:6; 18:16; 19:8).

21. Zedekiah—brother of Zephaniah (vs. 25), both being sons of Maaseiah; probably of the same family as the false prophet under Ahab in Israel (I Kings 22: 11, 24). **22. shall be taken . . . a curse**—i.e., a formula of imprecation. **Lord make thee like Zedekiah**—(Cf. Gen. 48:20; Isa. 65:15). **roasted in the fire**—a Chaldean punishment (Dan. 3:6). **23. villainy**—lit., "sinful folly" (Isa. 32:6).

24-32. A second communication which Jeremiah sent to Babylon, after the messenger who carried his first letter had brought a letter from the false prophet Shemaiah to Zephaniah, etc., condemning Jeremiah and reproving the authorities for not having apprehended him. **Nehelamite**—a name derived either from his father or from a place: alluding at the same time to the *Hebrew* meaning, "a dreamer" (cf. vs. 8). **25. in thy name**—without sanction of "the Lord of hosts, the God of Israel," which words stand in antithesis to "thy name" (John 5:43). **Zephaniah**—the second priest, or substitute (*Sagan*) of the high priest. He was one of those sent to consult Jeremiah by Zedekiah (ch. 21:1). Slain by Nebuchadnezzar at the capture of Jerusalem (II Kings 25:18-21). Zephaniah was in particular addressed, as being likely to take up against Jeremiah the prophet's prediction against his brother Zedekiah at Babylon (vs. 21). Zephaniah was to read it to the *priests*, and in the presence of *all the people*, in the temple. **26. thee . . . in the stead of Jehoiada**—Zephaniah's promotion as second priest, owing to Jehoiada's being then in exile, was unexpected. Shemaiah thus accuses him of ingratitude towards God, who had so highly exalted him before his regular time. **ye should be officers . . . for every man**—Ye should, as bearing rule in the temple (ch. 20:1, *Note*), apprehend every false prophet like Jeremiah.

mad—Inspired prophets were often so called by the ungodly (II Kings 9:11; Acts 26:24; 2:13, 15, 17, 18). Jeremiah is in this a type of Christ, against whom the same charge was brought (John 10:20).

28. Referring to Jeremiah's first letter to Babylon (vs. 5).

prison—rather, "the stocks" (ch. 20:2, *Note*). **stocks**—from a root, "to confine"; hence rather, a narrow dungeon. According to Deuteronomy 17:8, 9, the priest was judge in such cases, but had no right to put into the stocks; this right he had assumed to himself in the troubled state of the times. **27. of Anathoth**—said contemptuously, as "Jesus *of Nazareth*." **maketh himself**—as if *God* had not made him one, but he *himself* had done so.

ADAM CLARKE

17. *Behold, I will send upon them the sword.* Do not envy the state of Zedekiah, who sits on the throne of David, nor that of the people who are now in the land whence ye have been carried captive (v. 16). For I will send the *sword*, the *pestilence*, and the *famine* upon them; and afterwards shall cause them to be carried into a miserable captivity in all nations (v. 18). But you see the worst of your own case, and you have God's promise of enlargement when the proper time is come. The reader will not forget that the prophet is addressing the captives in Babylon.

21. *He shall slay them before your eyes.* Nebuchadnezzar would be led by political reasons to punish these pretended prophets, as their predictions tended to make his Israelitish subjects uneasy and disaffected, and might excite them to rebellion. He therefore slew them; two of them, it appears, he burnt alive, viz., Ahab and Zedekiah.

24. *Speak to Shemaiah.* Zephaniah was the second priest, *sagan*, or chief priest's deputy, and Seraiah, high priest, when Jerusalem was taken. See chap. lii. 24. Shemaiah directs his letter to the former, and tells him that God had appointed him to supply the place of the high priest, who was probably then absent. His name was either Azariah or Seraiah, his son, but called Jehoiada from the remarkable zeal and courage of that pontiff. After the taking of Jerusalem, Zephaniah was put to death by Nebuchadnezzar at Riblah; see chap. xxxvii. 3. The history of Jehoiada may be seen in 2 Kings xi. 3, etc.

26. *For every man that is mad, and maketh himself a prophet. Mad,* "in ecstatic rapture"; such as appeared in the prophets, whether true or false, when under the influence, the one of God, the other of a demon. See 2 Kings ix. 11; Hos. ix. 7.

MATTHEW HENRY

men of their sins, unless the grace of God work with them, but will rather exasperate the corruptions they are intended to mortify (Prov. xxvii. 22), *Though thou shouldst bray a fool in a mortar, yet will not his foolishness depart from him.*

II. *Zephaniah read this letter in the ears of Jeremiah.* He had a respect for Jeremiah (for we find him employed in messages to him as a *prophet, ch.* xxi. 1, xxxvii. 3), and therefore protected him. He made Jeremiah acquainted with the contents of the letter, that he might see what enemies he had even among the captives.

III. The sentence passed upon Shemaiah for writing this letter. God sent him an answer: it was ordered to be sent *to those of the captivity*, who encouraged and countenanced him as if he had been a prophet of God's raising up, *v.* 31, 32. Shemaiah had made fools of them. He promised them peace in God's name, but God did not send him; he forced a commission, and made the people *to trust in a lie*, and by preaching false comfort to them deprived them of true comfort. He had made traitors of them; he had *taught rebellion against the Lord*, as Hananiah had done, *ch.* xxviii. 16. At his end *he shall also be a fool* (as the expression is, *ch.* xvii. 11); his name and family shall be buried in oblivion: *He shall not have a man to dwell among this people;* and neither he nor any that come from him shall *behold the good that I will do for my people.*

JAMIESON, FAUSSET, BROWN

29. Zephaniah . . . read . . . in the ears of Jeremiah—He seems to have been less prejudiced against Jeremiah than the others; hence he reads the charge to the prophet, that he should not be condemned without a hearing. This accords with Shemaiah's imputation against Zephaniah for want of zeal against Jeremiah (vss. 26, 27). Hence the latter was chosen by King Zedekiah as one of the deputation to Jeremiah (ch. 21:1; 37:3). **30.** This resumes the thread of the sentence which began at vs. 25, but was left there not completed. Here, in vs. 30, it is completed, not however in continuity, but by a new period. The same construction occurs in Romans 5:12-15.

32. not . . . a man to dwell—(Deut. 28:18). **not . . . behold the good**—As he despised the lawful time and wished to return before the time God had expressly announced, in just retribution he should not share in the restoration from Babylon at all. **rebellion**—going against God's revealed will as to the time (ch. 28:16).

ADAM CLARKE

TODAY'S DICTIONARY OF THE BIBLE:

Zephaniah—*Jehovah has concealed,* or *Jehovah has treasured.* The son of Maaseiah, the "second priest" in the reign of Zedekiah, often mentioned in Jeremiah as having been sent from the king to inquire (Jer. 21:1) regarding the coming woes which he had denounced, and to entreat the prophet's intercession that the judgment threatened might be averted (Jer. 29:25, 26, 29; 37:3; 52:24). He, along with some other captive Jews, was put to death by the king of Babylon "at Riblah in the land of Hamath" (2 Kings 25:21).

MATTHEW HENRY

CHAPTER 30

Verses 1-9

I. Jeremiah is directed to *write* what God had spoken to him in hopes that those might take more notice of it when in reading it they had leisure for a more considerate review. He must collect them and put them together, and God will now add unto them many like words. He must write them for the generations to come, who should see them accomplished. He must write them not *in a letter*, but *in a book*, to be preserved in the archives. And this prophecy must be written, that it may be read so it may appear how exactly the accomplishment answers the prediction. It is intimated that they shall be *beloved for their fathers' sake* (Rom. xi. 28); for *therefore* God will bring them again to Canaan, because it was *the land that he gave to their fathers*, which therefore *they shall possess.*

II. He is directed what to write. The very words are such as the Holy Ghost teaches, *v.* 4. 1. He must write a description of the consternation which the people were now in, and were likely to be in upon every attack that the Chaldeans made upon them (*v.* 5): *We have heard a voice of trembling*—terror echoing to the alarms of danger. The false prophets told them that they should have *peace*, but *there is fear and not peace*, so the margin reads. Even the men of war shall be overwhelmed with the calamities of their nation, and shall look like *women in labour*, whose pains come upon them in great extremity and they know that they cannot escape them, *v.* 6. *Alas! for that day is great*, a day of judgment, which is called the *great day*, the *great and terrible day of the Lord* (Joel ii. 31, Jude 6), great, so that *there has been none like it*. The last destruction of Jerusalem is thus spoken of by our Saviour as unparalleled, Matt. xxiv. 21. *It is even the time of Jacob's trouble*, a sad time, when God's professing people shall be in distress above other people. The whole time of the captivity was a time of Jacob's trouble. 2. He must write the assurances which God had given that a happy end should at length be put to these calamities. (1) Jacob's troubles shall cease: *He shall be saved out of them.* (2) Jacob's troublers shall be disabled from doing him any further mischief, *v.* 8. "*I will break his yoke from off thy neck*, which has long lain so heavy, and has so sorely galled thee. *I will burst thy bonds* and restore thee to liberty and ease, they shall no more enrich themselves either by thy possessions or by thy labours." (3) That which crowns and completes the mercy is that they shall be restored to the free exercise of their religion again, *v.* 9. When the time shall come that they should be *saved out of their trouble*, God will prepare and qualify them for it by giving them a *heart to serve him*, and by giving them opportunity to serve him. *Therefore* we are *delivered out of the hands of our enemies*, that we may *serve God*, Luke i. 74, 75. They shall serve their own God, and neither be inclined, nor compelled, as they had been in the day of their captivity, to serve other gods. They shall serve *David their king*, such governors as God should from time to time set over them, of the line of David (as Zerubbabel). But this has a further meaning. The Chaldee

JAMIESON, FAUSSET, BROWN

CHAPTER 30

Vss. 1-24. Restoration of the Jews from Babylon after Its Capture, and Raising Up of Messiah. **2. Write . . . in a book**—After the destruction of Jerusalem Jeremiah is not ordered as heretofore to *speak*, but to *write* the succeeding prophecy (vs. 4, etc.), so as thereby it might be read by his countrymen wheresoever they might be in their dispersion. **3. bring again . . . captivity of . . . Israel and Judah**—the restoration not merely of the *Jews* (treated of in this ch. 30), but also of the ten tribes ("Israel"; treated in ch. 31), together forming the whole nation (vs. 18; ch. 32:44; Ezek. 39:25; Amos 9:14, 15). "Israel" is mentioned first because its exile was longer than that of Judah. *Some* captives of the Israelite ten tribes returned with those of Judah (Luke 2:36; "Aser" is mentioned). But these are only a pledge of the *full* restoration hereafter (Rom. 11:26, "*All* Israel"). Cf. ch. 16:15. This third verse is a brief statement of the subject before the prophecy itself is given. **5. We have heard . . . trembling**—God introduces the Jews speaking that which they will be reduced to at last in spite of their stubbornness. Threat and promise are combined: the former briefly; viz., the misery of the Jews in the Babylonian captivity down to their "trembling" and "fear" arising from the approach of the Medo-Persian army of Cyrus against Babylon; the promise is more fully dwelt on; viz., their "trembling" will issue in a deliverance as speedy as is the transition from a woman's labor-pangs to her joy at giving birth to a child (vs. 6). **6. Ask**—Consult all the authorities, men or books, you can, you will not find an instance. Yet in that coming day men will be seen with their hands pressed on their loins, as women do to repress their pangs. God will drive men through pain to gestures more fitting a woman than a man (ch. 4:31; 6:24). The metaphor is often used to express the previous pain followed by the sudden deliverance of Israel, as in the case of a woman in childbirth (Isa. 66:7-9). **paleness**—properly the color of herbs blasted and fading: the *green paleness* of one in jaundice: the *sickly paleness* of terror. **7. great**—marked by great calamities (Joel 2:11, 31; Amos 5:18; Zeph. 1:14). **none like it . . . but he shall be saved**—(Dan. 12:1). The partial deliverance at Babylon's downfall prefigures the final, complete deliverance of Israel, literal and spiritual, at the downfall of the mystical Babylon (Rev. 18, 19). **8. his yoke . . . thy neck**—his, i.e., Jacob's (vs. 7), the yoke imposed *on him*. The transition to the second person is frequent, God speaking *of* Jacob or Israel, at the same time addressing him directly. So "him" rightly follows; "foreigners shall no more make him their servant" (ch. 25:14). After the deliverance by Cyrus, Persia, Alexander, Antiochus, and Rome made Judah their servant. The full of deliverance meant must, therefore, be still future. **9.** Instead of *serving strangers* (vs. 8), they shall serve the Lord, their rightful King in the theocracy (Ezek. 21:27).

ADAM CLARKE

CHAPTER 30

1. *The word that came to Jeremiah from the Lord.* This prophecy was delivered about a year after the taking of Jerusalem; so Dahler.

2. *Write thee all the words that I have spoken unto thee in a book.* The *book* here recommended I believe to be the thirtieth and thirty-first chapters; for among the Hebrews any portion of writing, in which the subject was finished, however small, was termed *sepher,* a "book," a treatise or discourse.

3. *The days come.* First, after the conclusion of the seventy years. Secondly, under the Messiah. *That I will bring again the captivity of . . . Israel.* The ten tribes, led captive by the king of Assyria, and dispersed among the nations. *And Judah.* The people carried into Babylon at two different times: first, under Jeconiah; and, secondly, under Zedekiah, by Nebuchadnezzar.

5. *We have heard a voice of trembling.* This may refer to the state and feelings of the people during the war which Cyrus carried on against the Babylonians. Trembling and terror would no doubt affect them, and put an end to peace and all prosperity; as they could not tell what would be the issue of the struggle, and whether their state would be better or worse should their present masters fall in the conflict. This is well described in the next verse, where men are represented as being, through pain and anguish, like women in travail. See the same comparison in Isa. xiii. 6-8.

7. *Alas! for that day is great.* When the Medes and Persians with all their forces shall come on the Chaldeans, it will be the day *of Jacob's trouble*—trial, dismay, and uncertainty; but he shall be delivered out of it—the Chaldean empire shall fall, but the Jews shall be delivered by Cyrus.

8. *I will break his yoke.* That is, the yoke of Nebuchadnezzar. *Of him.* Of Jacob (v. 7), viz., the then captive Jews.

MATTHEW HENRY

paraphrase reads it, *They shall obey* (or *hearken to*) *the Messiah* (or *Christ*), the *Son of David, their king.* To him the Jewish interpreters apply it. That dispensation which commenced at their return out of captivity brought them to the Messiah. He is called *David their king* because he was the *Son of David* (Matt. xxii. 42) and he answered to the name, Matt. xx, 31, 32. God is often in the New Testament said to have *raised up Jesus*, raised him up as a King, Acts iii. 26; xiii. 23, 33. Those that serve the Lord as their God must give up themselves to Jesus Christ, to be ruled by him. For all men must *honour the Son as they honour the Father*, and come into the service and worship of God by him as Mediator. Those to whom he gives rest must take his yoke upon them.

Verses 10–17

The deplorable case of the Jews in captivity is set forth, but many precious promises are given them.

I. God himself appeared against them: he *scattered* them (*v.* 11); he did *all these things unto them*, *v.* 15. This was intended by him as a fatherly chastisement, and no other (*v.* 11): "*I will correct thee in measure*, or *according to judgment*, no more than thou deservest, no more than thou canst well bear." God hates sin most in those that are nearest to him. God here corrects his people *for the multitude of their iniquity*, and *because their sins were increased*, *v.* 14, 15. What God intended as a fatherly chastisement they and others interpreted as an act of hostility; they looked upon him as having *wounded them with the wound of an enemy* and *with the chastisement of a cruel one* (*v.* 14). It did indeed seem as if God had dealt thus severely with them, as if he had fought against them, Isa. lxiii. 10. Job complains that God had become cruel to him and *multiplied his wounds*.

II. Their friends forsook them, *v.* 13. If we be reproached, we expect that our friends should appear in vindication of us. If we be sick, or sore, or wounded, we expect our friends should sympathise with us, and, if occasion be, lend a hand for the healing. Here there is none to do that, none to bind up thy wounds. *All thy lovers have forgotten thee.* When God is against a people who will be for them? Their case seemed desperate and past relief (*v.* 12): *Thy bruise is incurable, thy wound grievous*, and (*v.* 15) *thy sorrow is incurable*. Their sorrow would not admit of any alleviation, but they seemed to be hardened in it. In this deplorable condition they are looked upon with disdain (*v.* 17): *They called thee an outcast*, abandoned to ruin; they said, *This is Zion, whom no man seeks after*. Now all was in ruins. When they looked on the people that formerly dwelt in Zion, but were now in captivity, they called them outcasts; these are those who belong to Zion, but *no man seeks after* them, or enquires concerning them.

III. For all this God will work deliverance and salvation for them in due time. 1. Though he seemed to stand at a distance from them, yet he assures them of his presence with them, *I will save thee*, *v.* 10 *I am with thee, to save thee*, *v.* 11. 2. Though they were remote from their own land, *afar* off *in the land of their captivity*, yet there shall salvation find them out, thence shall it fetch them, and their *seed*, *v.* 10. 3. Though they were now full of fears, yet the time shall come when they *shall be in rest and quiet*, safe and easy, *and none shall make them afraid*, *v.* 10. 4. Though the nations into which they were dispersed should be brought to ruin, yet they should be preserved (*v.* 11): *Though I make a full end of the nations whither I have scattered thee, yet I will not make a full end of thee.* God's church may sometimes be brought very low, but he *will not make a full end of it*, *ch.* v. 10, 18. 5. Though God correct them, and justly, yet he will return in mercy to them, and even their sin shall not prevent their deliverance when God's time shall come. 6. Though their adversaries were mighty, God will break their power (*v.* 16): *All that devour thee shall be devoured.* "They *shall everyone of them*, without exception, *go into captivity*, and the day will come when *those that* now *spoil thee shall be a spoil*." 7. Though the wound seem incurable, God will make a cure of it (*v.* 17): *I will restore health unto thee.*

IV. They are cautioned against inordinate fear and grief, for in these precious promises there is enough to silence both. *Fear thou not, O my servant Jacob! neither be dismayed.* They must not sorrow as those that have no hope, *v.* 15. "*Why criest thou for thy affliction?* It is *for thy sin* (*v.* 14, 15), and therefore, instead of repining, thou shouldst be repenting."

Verses 18–24

Further intimations of the favour God had in reserve for them after the days of their calamity were over.

JAMIESON, FAUSSET, BROWN

David, their king—No *king* of David's seed has held the scepter since the captivity; for Zerubbabel, though of David's line, never claimed the title of "king." The *Son of David*, Messiah, must therefore be meant; so the *Targum* (cf. Isa. 55:3, 4; Ezek. 34:23, 24; 37:24; Hos. 3:5; Rom. 11:25-32). He was appointed to the throne of David (Isa. 9:7; Luke 1:32). He is here joined with Jehovah as claiming equal allegiance. God is our "King," only when we are subject to Christ; God rules us not immediately, but through His Son (John 5:22, 23, 27). **raise up**—applied to the judges whom God *raised up* as *deliverers* of Israel out of the hand of its oppressors (Judg. 2:16; 3:9). So Christ was *raised up* as the antitypical Deliverer (Ps. 2:6; Luke 1:69; Acts 2:30; 13:23).

in measure—lit., "with judgment," i.e., moderation, not in the full rigor of justice (ch. 10:24; 46:28; Ps. 6:1; Isa. 27:8). **not . . . altogether unpunished**—(Exod. 34:7).

14. lovers—the peoples formerly allied to thee, Assyria and Egypt (cf. Lam. 1:2). **seek thee not**—have cast away all concern for thee in thy distress. **wound of an enemy**—a wound such as an enemy would inflict. God condescends to employ language adapted to human conceptions. He is incapable of "enmity" or "cruelty"; it was their grievous sin which righteously demanded a grievous punishment, *as though* He were an "enemy" (ch. 5:6; Job 13:24; 30:21).

13. none to plead—a new image from a court of justice. **bound up**—viz., with the *bandages* applied to tie up a wound. **no healing medicines**—lit., "medicines of healing," or else applications, (lit., ascensions) of medicaments.

12. The desperate circumstances of the Jews are here represented as an incurable wound. Their sin is so grievous that their hope of the punishment (their exile) soon coming to an end is vain (ch. 8:22; 15:18; II Chron. 36:16).

17. (Ch. 8:22; 33:6.) **Outcast**—as a wife put away by her husband (Isa. 62:4, contrasted with vs. 12). **Zion**—alluding to its *Hebrew* meaning, "dryness"; "sought after" by none, as would be the case with an *arid* region (Isa. 62:12). The extremity of the people, so far from being an obstacle to, will be the chosen opportunity of, God's grace.

10. from afar—Be not afraid as if the distance of the places whither ye are to be dispersed precludes the possibility of return. **seed**—Though through the many years of captivity intervening, you yourselves may not see the restoration, the promise shall be fulfilled to your *seed*, primarily at the return from Babylon, fully at the final restoration. **quiet . . . none . . . make . . . afraid**—(ch. 23:6; Zech. 14:11).

11. though . . . full end of all nations . . . yet . . . not . . . of thee—(Amos 9:8). The punishment of reprobates is final and fatal; that of God's people temporary and corrective. Babylon was utterly destroyed: Israel after chastisement was delivered.

16. Therefore—connected with vs. 13, because "There is none to plead thy cause . . . *therefore*" *I* will plead thy cause, and heal thy wound, by overwhelming thy foes. Verse 15 is inserted to amplify what was said at the close of vs. 14. When the false ways of peace, suggested by the so-called prophets, had only ended in the people's irremediable ruin, the true prophet comes forward to announce the grace of God as bestowing repentance and healing. **devour thee . . . be devoured . . . spoil . . . be a spoil . . . prey upon . . . give for a prey**—retribution in kind (cf. *Note*, ch. 2:3; Exod. 23:22; Isa. 33:1).

15. Why criest thou—as if God's severity was excessive. Thou hast no reason to complain, for thine affliction is just. Thy cry is too late, for the time of repentance and mercy is past [CALVIN].

ADAM CLARKE

9. *But they shall serve the Lord their God, and David their king.* This must refer to the times of the Messiah; and hence the Chaldee has, "They shall obey the Lord their God, and they shall obey the Messiah, the Son of David." This is a very remarkable version; and shows that it was a version, not according to the letter, but according to their doctrine and their expectation.

Christ is promised under the name of His progenitor, David, Isa. lv. 3-4; Ezek. xxxiv. 23-24; xxxvii. 24-25; Hos. iii. 5.

13. *There is none to plead thy cause.* All your friends and allies have forsaken you.

12. *Thy bruise is incurable. Anush*, "desperate," not *incurable;* for the cure is promised in v. 17, "I will restore health unto thee, and I will heal thee of thy wounds."

15. *Thy sorrow is incurable.* "Desperate." See v. 12.

11. *Though I make a full end of all nations.* Though the Persians destroy the nations whom they vanquish, yet they shall not destroy *thee.*

16. *They that devour thee*, the Chaldeans. *Shall be devoured*, by the Medes and Persians. *All that prey upon thee will I give for a prey.* The Assyrians were destroyed by the Babylonians; the Babylonians, by the Medes and Persians; the Egyptians and Persians were destroyed by the Greeks, under Alexander.

MATTHEW HENRY

I. The city and temple should be rebuilt, *v.* 18. *Jacob's tents*, and *his dwelling-places*, felt the effects of *the captivity*, for they lay in ruins, but the habitations shall be repaired, and therein God will *have mercy upon their dwelling-places*, that had been monuments of his justice. Then *the city* of Jerusalem *shall be built upon her own heap*, her own hill, though now it be no better than a ruinous heap. He that can *make of a city a heap* (Isa. xxv. 2) can when he pleases *make of a heap a city* again. *The palace* (the temple, God's palace) *shall remain after the manner thereof;* it shall be built after the old model.

II. The sacred feasts should again be solemnized (*v.* 19): *Out of* the city, and the temple, and all the dwelling-places of Jacob, *shall proceed thanksgiving and the voice of those that make merry.*

III. The people should be multiplied, and increased: *They shall not be few, they shall not be small*, but shall make a figure among the nations: for *I will multiply them* and *I will glorify them.* It is for the honour of the church to have many added to it that shall be saved. There shall be a constant succession of faithful magistrates in the congregation of the elders, and of faithful worshippers in the congregation of the saints.

IV. They shall be blessed with a good government (*v.* 21): *Their nobles* and judges *shall be of themselves*, of their own nation, and they shall no longer be ruled by strangers and enemies; *their governor shall proceed from the midst of them*, shall be one that has been a sharer with them in the afflictions of their captive state; and this has reference to Christ our *governor, David our king* (*v.* 9); he is of ourselves, *in all things made like unto his brethren. And I will cause him to draw near;* this may be understood either, 1. Of the people, Jacob and Israel: "*I will cause* them *to draw near* to me in the temple service, as formerly, to come into covenant with me, as *my people*" (*v.* 22). 2. It may be understood of the governor; for it is a single person that is spoken of: *Their governor shall* be duly called to his office, shall *draw near* to God to consult him upon all occasions. But it looks further, to Christ, to him as Mediator. The proper work and office of Christ, as Mediator, is *to draw near and approach unto* God, for us, and in our name and stead, as the high priest of our profession. God the Father did *cause* Jesus Christ thus *to draw near and approach to* him as Mediator. He anointed him for this purpose, and declared himself well pleased in him. His own voluntary undertaking, in compliance with his Father's will and in compassion to fallen man, engaged him.

V. They shall be taken again into covenant with God, according to the covenant made with their fathers (*v.* 22): *You shall be my people;* and it is God's good work in us that makes us *to him a people, a people for his name*, Acts. xv. 14.

VI. Their enemies shall be reckoned with and brought down (*v.* 20): *I will punish all* those *that oppress them*, so that it shall appear to all a dangerous thing to *touch God's anointed*, Ps. cv. 15. These two verses (23–24) we had before (*ch.* xxiii. 19, 20); *there* they were a denunciation of God's wrath against the wicked hypocrites in Israel; *here* against the wicked oppressors of Israel. The wrath of God against the wicked is here represented to be like a whirlwind, irresistible. Whirlwinds are usually short, but this shall be *a continuing whirlwind.* It shall accomplish that for which it is sent: *The anger of the Lord shall not return till he have done it.* The purposes of his wrath, as well as the purposes of his love, will all be fulfilled; he will *perform the intents of his heart.*

CHAPTER 31

Verses 1–9

God assures his people,

I. That he will again take them into a covenant relation to himself. His own people shall be owned by him as the children of his love: *I will be the God* (that is, I will show myself to be the God) *of all the families of Israel* (*v.* 1)—not of the two tribes only, but of all the tribes; not only their state in general, but their particular families, and the interests of them, shall have a special relation to God. If we and our houses serve the Lord, we and our houses shall be protected and blessed by him, Prov. iii. 33.

II. That he will do for them, in bringing them out of Babylon, as he had done for their fathers when he delivered them out of Egypt. 1. He puts them in mind of what he did for their fathers when he brought them out of Egypt, *v.* 2. They were then, as these were, *a people left of the sword*, that sword of Pharaoh with which he cut off all the male children as soon as they were born. They were then *in the wilderness*,

JAMIESON, FAUSSET, BROWN

18. bring again . . . captivity—(Ch. 33:7, 11). **tents**—used to intimate that their present dwellings in Chaldea were but temporary as *tents.* **have mercy on . . . dwelling-places**—(Ps. 102:13). **own heap**—on the same hill, i.e., site, a hill being the usual site chosen for a city (cf. Josh. 11:13, *Margin*). This better answers the parallel clause, "after the manner thereof" (i.e., in the same becoming ways as formerly), than the rendering, "its own heap of *ruins,*" as in ch. 49:2. **palace**—the king's, on Mount Zion. **remain**—rather, "shall be inhabited" (*Note*, ch. 17: 6, 25). This confirms *English Version*, "palace," not as others translate, "the temple" (see I Kings 16:18; II Kings 15:25). **19. thanksgiving**—The *Hebrew* word includes *confession* as well as *praise;* for, in the case of God, the highest *praises* we can bestow are only *confessing* what God really is [BENGEL], (ch. 17:26; 31:12, 13; 33:11; Isa. 35:10; 51:11). **multiply them**—(Zech. 10:8). **20. as aforetime**—as flourishing as in the time of David.

21. their nobles—rather, "their Glorious One," or "Leader" (cf. Acts 3:15; Heb. 2:10), answering to "their Governor" in the parallel clause. **of themselves**—of their own nation, a Jew, not a foreigner; applicable to Zerubbabel, or J. Hyrcanus (hereditary high priest and governor), only as types of Christ (Gen. 49:10; Mic. 5:2; Rom. 9:5), the antitypical "David" (vs. 9). **cause him to draw near**—as the great Priest (Exod. 19:22; Lev. 21:17), through whom believers also have access to God (Heb. 10:19-22). His priestly and kingly characters are similarly combined (Ps. 110:4; Zech. 6:13). **who . . . engaged . . . heart to approach**—lit., "pledged his heart," i.e., his life; a thing unique; Messiah alone has made His life responsible as the surety (Heb. 7:22; 9:11-15), in order to gain access not only for Himself, but for us to God. *Heart* is here used for *life,* to express the *courage* which it needed to undertake such a tremendous suretyship. The question implies admiration at one being found competent by His twofold nature, as God and man, for the task. Cf. the interrogation (Isa. 63:1-3).

22. ye shall be my people . . .—The covenant shall be renewed between God and His people through Messiah's mediation (vs. 21; ch. 31:1, 33; 32:38; Ezek. 11:20; 36:28).

23, 24. (Ch. 23:19.) Vengeance upon God's foes always accompanies manifestations of His grace to His people. **continuing**—lit., "sojourning," abiding constantly; appropriately here in the case of Babylon, which was to be *permanently* destroyed, substituted for "whirling itself about" ("grievous" in *English Version*) (ch. 23:19, 20, see *Notes* there), where the *temporary* downfall of Judea is spoken of.

CHAPTER 31

Vss. 1-40. CONTINUATION OF THE PROPHECY IN CHAPTER 30. As in that chapter the restoration of Judah, so in this the restoration of Israel's ten tribes is foretold. **1. At the same time**—"In the latter days" (ch. 30:24). **the God of**—manifesting My *grace* to (Gen. 17:7; Matt. 22:32; Rev. 21:3). **all . . . Israel**—not the exiles of the *south* kingdom of Judah only, but also the *north* kingdom of the ten tribes; and not merely Israel in general, but "*all* the families of Israel." Never yet fulfilled (Rom. 11: 26).

2. Upon the grace manifested to Israel "in the wilderness" God grounds His argument for renewing His favors to them *now* in their exile; because His covenant is "everlasting" (vs. 3), and changes not. The same argument occurs in Hosea 13:5, 9, 10; 14:4, 5, 8. Babylon is fitly compared to

ADAM CLARKE

18. *The city shall be builded upon her own heap.* See the Book of Nehemiah. *And the palace shall remain.* Meaning, the king's house shall be restored; or, more probably, the Temple shall be rebuilt; which was true, for after the Babylonish captivity it was rebuilt by Nehemiah, etc. By the *tents,* distinguished from the *dwellingplaces* of Jacob, we may understand all the minor dispersions of the Jews, as well as those numerous synagogues found in large cities.

21. *Their nobles shall be of themselves.* Strangers shall not rule over them; *and their governor shall proceed from the midst of them.* Both Nehemiah and Zerubbabel, their nobles and governors after the return from Babylon, were Jews.

22. *Ye shall be my people.* The old covenant shall be renewed.

23. *The whirlwind of the Lord.* A grievous tempest of desolation *shall fall with pain upon the head of the wicked,* on Nebuchadnezzar and the Chaldeans.

24. *In the latter days ye shall consider it.* By the *latter days* the gospel dispensation is generally meant; and that restoration which is the principal topic in this and the succeeding chapter refers to this time.

CHAPTER 31

1. *At the same time.* This discourse was delivered at the same time with the former; and, with that, constitutes the book which God ordered the prophet to write. *Will I be the God of all the families of Israel.* I shall bring back the ten tribes, as well as their brethren the Jews. The restoration of the Israelites is the principal subject of this chapter.

2. *The people which were left of the sword.* Those of the ten tribes that had escaped death by the sword of the Assyrians. *Found grace in the wilderness.* The place of their exile; a wilderness, compared to their own land. See Isa. xl. 3.

MATTHEW HENRY

where they seemed to be lost and forgotten, as these were now in a strange land, and yet they found grace in God's sight, were owned and highly honoured by him, and he was at this time going *to cause them to rest* in Canaan. God is still the same. 2. They put him in mind of what God had done for their fathers, intimating that they now saw not such signs, and were ready to ask, as Gideon did, *Where are all the wonders that our fathers told us of?* The years of ancient times were glorious years; but now it is otherwise; what good will it do us that he *appeared of old* to us when now he is *a God that hides himself* from us? Isa. xlv. 15. 3. To this he answers with an assurance of the constancy of his love: *Yea, I have loved thee*, not only with an ancient love, but *with an everlasting love*, a love that shall never fail, however the comforts of it may for a time be suspended. Nothing can separate them from that love. Those whom God loves with this love he will draw into covenant and communion with himself, by the influences of his Spirit upon their souls.

III. That he will again form them into a people, and give them a very joyful settlement in their own land, *v.* 4, 5. They shall resume their harps which had been hung upon the willow-trees, shall tune them, and shall themselves be in tune to make use of them. Is the joy of the city maintained by the products of the country? It is so; and therefore it is promised (*v.* 5), *Thou shalt yet plant vines upon the mountains of Samaria*, which had been the head city of the kingdom of Israel, in opposition to that of Judah; but they shall now be united (Ezek. xxxvii. 22), and there shall be such perfect peace and security that men shall apply themselves wholly to the improvement of their ground: *The planters shall plant*, not fearing the soldiers' coming to eat the fruits of what they had planted, or to pluck it up; but they themselves *shall eat them* freely, as *common things*, not forbidden fruits.

IV. That they shall have liberty and opportunity to worship God in the ordinances of his own appointment (*v.* 6): *There shall be a day*, and a glorious day it will be, when *the watchmen upon Mount Ephraim*, that are set to stand sentinel there, to give notice of the approach of the enemy, finding that all is very quiet and that there is no appearance of danger, shall desire for a time to be discharged from their post, that they may *go up to Zion*, to praise God for the public peace. But that which is most observable here is *that the watchmen of Ephraim* are forward to promote the worship of God at Jerusalem, whereas formerly *the watchman of Ephraim was hatred against the house of his God* (Hos. ix. 8), and, instead of inviting people to Zion, laid snares for those that set their faces thitherward, Hos. v. 1.

V. That God shall have the glory and the church, the honour and comfort of this blessed change (*v.* 7): *Sing with gladness for Jacob*, that is, let all her friends and wellwishers rejoice with her, Deut. xxxii. 43. *Rejoice, you Gentiles with his people*, Rom. xv. 10. *Publish you, praise you.* In publishing these tidings, praise the God of Israel, praise the Israel of God, speak honourably of both.

VI. That, in order to a happy settlement in their own land, they shall have a joyful return out of the land of their captivity (*v.* 8, 9). 1. Though they are scattered to places far remote, yet they shall be brought together *from the north country, and from the coasts of the earth.* 2. Though many of them are very unfit for travel, yet that shall be no hindrance to them: *The blind and the lame* shall come; such a goodwill shall they have to their journey, and such a good heart upon it, that they shall not make their blindness and lameness an excuse for staying where they are. Their companions will be ready to help them, will be *eyes to the blind and legs to the lame*, as good Christians ought to be to one another in their travels heavenward, Job. xxix. 15. But, above all, their God will help them; and let none plead that he is blind who has God for his guide, or lame who has God for his strength. *The women with child* are heavy, and it is not fit that they should undertake such a journey, much less those *that travail with child*; and yet, when it is to return to Zion, neither the one nor the other shall make any difficulty of it. When God calls we must not plead any inability to come; for he that calls us will help us, will strengthen us. They shall weep with more bitterness and more tenderness for sin, when they are delivered out of their captivity, than ever they did when they were groaning under it. Prayers help to wipe away tears. *With favours will I lead them* (so the margin reads it). Is the country they pass through dry and thirsty? *I will cause them to walk by the rivers of waters*, not the waters of a land-flood, which fail in summer. Is it a wilderness where there is no road, no track? *I will cause them to walk in a straight way*, which they shall not miss. Is it a

JAMIESON, FAUSSET, BROWN

the "wilderness," as in both alike Israel was as a stranger far from his appointed "rest" or home, and Babylon is in Isaiah 40:3 called a "desert" (cf. ch. 50:12). **I went to cause him to rest**—viz., in the pillar of cloud and fire, the symbol of God's presence, which *went* before Israel to *search a resting-place* (Num. 10:33; Isa. 63:14) for the people, both a temporary one at each halt in the wilderness, and a permanent one in Canaan (Exod. 33:14; Deut. 3:20; Josh. 21:44; Ps. 95:11; Heb. 3:11). **3.** Israel gratefully acknowledges in reply God's *past* grace; but at the same time tacitly implies by the expression "of old," that God does not appear to her *now*. "God appeared to me *of old*, but now I am forsaken!" God replies, Nay, I love thee with the same love now as of old. My love was not a momentary impulse, but *from* "everlasting" in My counsels, and *to* "everlasting" in its continuance; hence originated the covenant whereby I gratuitously adopted thee (Mal. 1:2; Rom. 11:28, 29). *Margin* translates, "from afar," which does not answer so well as "of old," to "in the wilderness" (vs. 2), which refers to the *olden* times of Israel's history. **with loving-kindness . . . drawn**—(Hos. 11:4). Rather, "I have *drawn out continually* My loving-kindness toward thee." So Psalm 36:10, "Continue (*Margin*, Draw out at length) Thy loving-kindness." By virtue of My *everlasting* love I will *still extend* My loving-kindness to thee. So Isaiah 44:21, "O Israel, thou shalt not be forgotten of Me." **4. I will build . . . thou shalt be built**—The combination of the *active* and *passive* to express the same fact implies the infallible certainty of its accomplishment. "Build," i.e., establish in prosperity (ch. 33:7). **adorned with . . . tabrets**—(I Sam. 18:6). Or, *"adorn thyself* with thy *timbrels"*; used by damsels on occasions of public rejoicings (Exod. 15:20; Judg. 11:34). Israel had cast away all instruments of joy in her exile (Ps. 137:4). **dances**—holy joy, not carnal mirth. **5. Samaria**—the metropolis of the ten tribes; here equivalent to *Israel.* The *mountainous* nature of their country suited the growth of the *vine.* **eat . . . as common**—lit., "shall profane," i.e., shall put to common use. For the first three years after planting, the vine was "not to be eaten of"; on the fourth year the fruit was to be "holy to praise the Lord withal"; on the fifth year the fruit was to be *eaten as common*, no longer restricted to *holy* use (Lev. 19:23-25; cf. Deut. 20:6, 28:30, *Margin*). Thus the idea here is, "The same persons who plant shall reap the fruits"; it shall no longer be that one shall plant and another reap the fruit. **6.** The watchmen, stationed on eminences (types of the preachers of the gospel), shall summon the ten tribes to go up to the annual feasts at Jerusalem ("Zion"), as they used to do before the revolt and the setting up of the idol calves at Dan and Beer-sheba (Ezek. 37:21, 22). **Mount Ephraim**—not one single mountain, but the whole mountainous region of the ten tribes. **our God**—from whom we formerly revolted, but who is now *our God.* An earnest of that good time to come is given in the partial success of the gospel in its first preaching in Samaria (John 4; Acts 8:5-25). **7.** The people are urged with praises and prayers to supplicate for their universal restoration. Jehovah is represented in the context (vss. 1, 8), as promising immediately to restore Israel. They therefore praise God for the restoration, being as certain of it as if it were actually accomplished; and at the same time *pray for* it, as prayer was a means to the desired end. Prayer does not move God to grant our wishes, but when God has determined to grant our wishes, He puts it into our hearts to pray for the thing desired. Cf. Psalm 102:13-17, as to the connection of Israel's restoration with the prayers of His people (Isa. 62:1-6). **for Jacob**—on account of Jacob; on account of his approaching deliverance by Jehovah. **among**—"for," i.e., on account of, would more exactly suit the parallelism to *"for* Jacob." **chief of the nations**—Israel: as the parallelism to "Jacob" proves (cf. Exod. 19:5; Ps. 135:4; Amos 6:1). God estimates the greatness of nations not by man's standard of material resources, but by His electing favor. **8. north**—Assyria, Media, etc. (*Note*, ch. 3:12, 18, 23:8). **gather from . . . coasts of . . . earth**—(Ezek. 20:34, 41, 34:13). **blind . . . lame . . .**—Not even the most infirm and unfit persons for a journey shall be left behind, so universal shall be the restoration. **a great company**—or, they shall return *"in a great company"* [MAURER]. **9. weeping**—for their past sins which caused their exile (Ps. 126:5, 6). Although they come with weeping, they shall return with joy (ch. 50:4, 5). **supplications**—(Cf. vss. 18, 19; ch. 3:21-25; Zech. 12:10). *Margin* translates "favors," as in Joshua 11:20; Ezra 9:8; thus God's *favors* or *compassions* are put in opposition to the

ADAM CLARKE

3. *I have loved thee with an everlasting love.* I still bear to the Jewish people that love which I showed to their fathers in Egypt, in the wilderness, and in the Promised Land.

Therefore with lovingkindness have I drawn thee. The exiles, who had not for a long time received any proofs of the divine protection, are represented as deploring their state. But God answers that, though this may seem to be the case, He has always loved them; and this continued love He will show by bringing them out of their captivity.

4. *O virgin of Israel.* Israelites in general; now called virgin, because restored to their ancient purity. *With thy tabrets.* Women in general played on these; they were used in times of rejoicing, and accompanied with dancing.

5. *Thou shalt yet plant vines upon the mountains of Samaria.* This was the regal city of the Israelites, as Jerusalem was of the Jews. *Shall eat them as common things.* By the law of Moses no man was permitted to eat of the fruit of his vineyard till the fifth year after planting. For the first three years it was considered uncircumcised, unclean, not fit to be eaten. In the fourth year it was holy to the Lord; the fruit belonged to Him. In the fifth year he might use it for himself, Lev. xix. 23-25. But in the time here mentioned the fruit should be considered *common*—lawful at all times to be eaten.

6. *For there shall be a day.* Literally, "for this is the day," or "the day is come." The *watchmen*—the prophets. *Arise ye, and let us go up to Zion.* Let both Israelites and Jews join together in the worship of the Lord.

8. *I will bring them from the north country.* From Babylon. *From the coasts of the earth.* The ten tribes were carried away partly into Assyria by Tiglath-pileser, and partly into Mesopotamia and Media by Shalmaneser, 2 Kings xv. 29; xvii. 6. Assyria and Media, being very distant from Palestine, might have been called, in prophetic language, *the coasts of the earth. The blind and the lame.* I will so effectually remove all difficulties out of the way, so provide for them on the journey, so supernaturally support their bodies and minds, that the veriest invalids shall safely proceed to, and happily arrive at, the end of their journey.

9. *They shall come with weeping.* Duly penetrated with a sense of their sins, they shall deeply deplore them; and, while weeping for them, earnestly supplicate God to have mercy upon them.

MATTHEW HENRY

rough and rocky country? Yet *they shall not stumble.* Whithersoever God gives his people a clear call he will either find them or make them a ready way. A reason given why God will take all this care of his people: *For I am a Father to Israel*, and therefore will maintain him (Ps. ciii. 13): *and Ephraim is my first-born;* even *Ephraim*, who, having gone astray from God, was *no more worthy to be called a son*, shall yet be owned as a *first-born*, particularly dear, and heir of a double portion of blessings. The same reason that was given for their release out of Egypt is given for their release out of Babylon; they are free-born and therefore must not be enslaved, are born to God and therefore must not be the servants of men. Exod iv. 22, 23, *Israel is my son, even my first-born; let my son go that he may serve me.*

Verses 10–17

The purposes of God's love concerning his people. This is a *word of the Lord* which the *nations* must *hear*, for it is a prophecy of a work of the Lord. It will be a piece of news that will spread all the world over.

It is foretold, 1. That those who are dispersed shall be brought together again from their dispersions: *He that scattereth Israel will gather him, v.* 10, and when he has gathered him into one body, one fold, he will *keep him, as a shepherd does his flock*, from being scattered again. 2. That those who are sold and alienated shall be redeemed and brought back, *v.* 11. Though the enemy that had got possession of him was *stronger than he*, yet *the Lord*, who is stronger than all, *has redeemed and ransomed him*, not by price, but by power. 3. That with their liberty they shall have plenty and joy, and God shall be honoured, *v.* 12, 13. When they shall have returned to their own land *they shall come and sing in the high place of Zion*; on the top of that holy mountain they shall sing to the praise and glory of God. We read that they did so when the foundation of the temple was laid there, Ezra iii. 11. They *shall flow together to the goodness of the Lord;* that is, they shall flock in great numbers and with great cheerfulness, as streams of water, *to the goodness of the Lord*, to the temple where he causes his goodness to pass before his people. They shall come together in solemn assemblies, to *praise him for his goodness*, and to pray for the continuance of it; they shall come to bless him for his goodness, in giving them *wheat, and wine, and oil, and the young of the flock and of the herd.* Therefore they honour God with the first-fruits out of which they bring offerings to his altar. Our souls are as gardens when they are watered with the dews of God's Spirit and grace. It is a precious promise that *they shall not sorrow any more at all;* it is only in that new Jerusalem *that all tears shall be wiped away*, Rev. xxi. 4. However, the returned captives had not any more those causes for sorrow which they had formerly had; and therefore (*v.* 13) *young men and old shall rejoice together.* 4. That both the ministers and those they minister to shall have abundant satisfaction in what God gives them (*v.* 14): *I will satiate the soul of the priests with fatness;* there shall be such a plenty of sacrifices brought to the altar that those who *live upon the altar* shall live comfortably, and they and their families shall be *satiated with fatness, and my people shall be satisfied with my goodness.* This is applicable to the spiritual blessings which the redeemed of the Lord enjoy by Jesus Christ, infinitely more valuable than corn, and wine, and oil. 5. That those particularly who had been in sorrow for the loss of their children who were carried into captivity should have that sorrow turned into joy upon their return, *v.* 15–17. *In Ramah was there a voice heard*, at the time when the general captivity was nothing but *lamentation, and bitter weeping*, more there than in other places, because there Nebuzaradan had the general rendezvous of his captives, as appears, *ch.* xl. 1, where we find him sending Jeremiah back from Ramah. *Rachel* is here said to *weep for her children.* The sepulchre of Rachel was between Ramah and Bethlehem. Benjamin, one of the two tribes, and Ephraim, head of the ten tribes, were both descendants from Rachel. She had but two sons, the elder of whom was one for whom his father grieved and *refused to be comforted* (Gen. xxxvii. 35); the other she herself called *Benoni—the son of my sorrow.* Now the inhabitants of Ramah did in like manner *grieve for their sons and their daughters* that were carried away (as 1 Sam. xxx. 6). The tender parents even *refused to be comforted for their children, because they were not*, were not with them, but were in the hands of their enemies; they were never likely to see them any more. This is applied by the evangelists to the great mourning that was at Bethlehem for the murder of the infants there by Herod (Matt. ii. 17–18), and this scripture is said to be then fulfilled. Though we mourn, we must not murmur. In order

JAMIESON, FAUSSET, BROWN

people's *weeping;* their tears shall be turned into joy. But *English Version* suits the parellelism best. **I will cause . . . to walk by . . . waters . . . straight way**—(Isa. 35:6-8; 43:19; 49:10, 11). God will give them waters to satisfy their thirst as in the wilderness journey from Egypt. So spiritually (Matt. 5:6; John 7:37). **Ephraim**—the ten tribes no longer severed from Judah, but forming one people with it. **my firstborn**—(Exod. 4:22; Hos. 11:1; Rom. 9:4). So the elect Church (II Cor. 6:18; Jas. 1:18).

10. The tidings of God's interposition in behalf of Israel will arrest the attention of even the uttermost Gentile nations. **He that scattered will gather**—He who scattered knows where to find Israel; He who smote can also heal. **keep**—not only will *gather*, but *keep safely* to the end (John 13:1; 17:11). **shepherd**—(Isa. 40:11; Ezek. 34:12-14). **11. ransomed . . . from . . . hand of . . . stronger**—No strength of the foe can prevent the Lord from delivering Jacob (Isa. 49:24, 25).

12. height of Zion—(Ezek. 17:23). **flow**—There shall be a *conflux* of worshippers to the temple on Zion (Isa. 2:2; Mic. 4:1). **to the goodness of . . . Lord**—(See vs. 14). *Beneficence*, i.e., to the Lord as the *source of all good* things (Hos. 3:5), to pray to Him and praise Him for these blessings of which He is the Fountainhead. **watered garden**—(Isa. 58:11.) Not merely for a time, but continually full of holy comfort. **not sorrow any more**—referring to the Church triumphant, as well as to literal Israel (Isa. 35:10; 65:19; Rev. 21:4). **13. young . . . old**—(Zech. 8:4, 5). **14. my goodness**—(vs. 12). **15. Ramah**—In Benjamin, east of the great northern road, two hours' journey from Jerusalem. Rachel, who all her life had pined for children (Gen. 30:1), and who died with "sorrow" in giving birth to Benjamin (Gen. 35:18, 19, *Margin;* I Sam. 10:2), and was buried at Ramah, near Bethlehem, is represented as raising her head from the tomb, and as breaking forth into "weeping" at seeing the whole land depopulated of her sons, the Ephraimites. Ramah was the place where Nebuzaradan collected all the Jews in chains, previous to their removal to Babylon (ch. 40:1). God therefore consoles her with the promise of their restoration. Matthew 2:17, 18 quotes this as fulfilled in the massacre of the innocents under Herod. "A lesser and a greater event, of different times, may answer to the single sense of one passage of Scripture, until the prophecy is *exhausted*" [BENGEL]. Besides the temporary reference to the exiles in Babylon, the Holy Spirit foreshadowed ultimately Messiah's exile in Egypt, and the desolation caused in the neighborhood of Rachel's tomb by Herod's massacre of the children, whose mothers had "sons of sorrow" (Benoni), just as Rachel had. The return of Messiah (the representative of Israel) from Egypt, and the future restoration of Israel, both the literal and the spiritual (including the innocents), at the Lord's second advent, are antitypical of the restoration of Israel from Babylon, which is the ground of consolation held out here by Jeremiah. The clause, "They were not," i.e., were dead (Gen. 42:13), does not apply so strictly to the exiles in Babylon as it does to the history of Messiah and His people—past, present, and future. So the words, "There is hope in thine end," are to be fulfilled ultimately, when Rachel shall meet her murdered children at the resurrection, at the same time that literal Israel is to be restored. "They were not," in *Hebrew*, is *singular; each was not*: each mother at the Bethlehem massacre had but *one* child to lament, as the limitation of age in Herod's order, "two years and under," implies; this use of the *singular* distributively (the mothers weeping severally, *each for her own* child), is a coincidence between the prophecy of the Bethlehem massacre and the event, the more remarkable as not being obvious: the *singular*, too, is appropriate as to *Messiah* in His Egyptian exile, who was to be a leading object of Rachel's lamentation.

ADAM CLARKE

By the rivers of waters. I will so guide and provide for them in the arid deserts that they shall find streams of water whenever necessary. *Ephraim is my firstborn.* Ephraim, being the most considerable, is often put for the whole of the ten tribes.

12. *And shall flow together.* Perhaps this may refer to their assembling at the three great national feasts: the Passover, Pentecost, and Tabernacles.

14. *And I will satiate the soul of the priests.* The worship of God being restored, they shall have their proper share of the victims brought to the Temple.

15. *A voice was heard in Ramah.* The Ramah mentioned here (for there were several towns of this name) was situated in the tribe of Benjamin, about six or seven miles from Jerusalem. Near this place Rachel was buried; who is here, in a beautiful figure of poetry, represented as coming out of her grave, and lamenting bitterly for the loss of her children, none of whom presented themselves to her view, all being slain or gone into exile. St. Matthew, who is ever fond of accommodation, applies these words, chap. ii. 17-18, to the massacre of the children at Bethlehem. That is, they were suitable to that occasion, and therefore he so applied them, but they are not a prediction of that event.

MATTHEW HENRY

to repress inordinate grief, we must consider that *there is hope in our end,* hope that the trouble will not last always, that it will be a happy end—the end will be peace. Though one generation falls in the wilderness, the next shall enter Canaan. *Thy* suffering *work shall be rewarded.* God makes his people *glad according to the days wherein he has afflicted them,* and so there is a proportion between the joys and the sorrows, as between the reward and the work, Rom. viii. 18. There is hope concerning children removed by death that they shall *return to their own border,* to the happy lot assigned them in the resurrection, a lot in the heavenly Canaan, that border of his sanctuary.

Verses 18–26

I. Ephraim's repentance, and return to God. *Ephraim shall say, What have I to do any more with idols?* Ephraim, the people, shall be as one man in their repentance. Ephraim is here weeping for sin, perhaps because Ephraim, the person from whom that tribe had its denomination, was a man of a tender spirit, *mourned for his children many days* (1 Chron. vii. 21, 22), and sorrow for sin is compared to that *for an only son.* He charges upon himself, in the first place, impatience under correction: "*Thou hast chastised me;* I have been under the rod, and I needed it, I deserved it; I was justly chastised, chastised *as a bullock,* who would never have felt the goad if he had not first rebelled against the yoke." This is the sin he finds himself guilty of now; but (*v.* 19) he reflects upon his sins in the days of his youth; now he remembers *the reproach of his youth.* He is here angry, having a holy indignation at himself for his sin and folly: He *smote upon his thigh,* as the publican upon his breast. He was amazed at his own stupidity and frowardness: He *was ashamed, yea even confounded.* He finds he cannot by any power of his own keep himself close with God, much less, when he has revolted, bring himself back to God, and therefore he prays, *Turn thou me and I shall be turned.* See *ch.* xvii. 14, *Heal me and I shall be healed.* He is here rejoicing in the experience he had of the blessed effect of divine grace: *Surely after that I was turned I repented.* All the pious workings of our heart towards God are the consequence of the working of his grace in us. When sinners come to a right knowledge they will come to a right way. Ephraim was chastised, and that did not produce the desired effect, it went no further: *I was chastised,* and that was all. But, when the instructions of God's Spirit accompanied the corrections of his providence, then the work was done.

II. God's compassion on Ephraim and the kind reception he finds with God, *v.* 20. 1. God owns him for a child, though he has been an undutiful child and a prodigal: *Is Ephraim my dear son? Is he a pleasant child?* Or, as it is sometimes supplied, *Is not Ephraim my dear son? Is he not a pleasant child?* Yes, now he repents and returns. *I do earnestly remember him still,* my thoughts towards him are thoughts of peace. When God afflicts his people, he does not forget them; when he casts them out of their land, he does not cast them out of sight, nor out of mind. It was God's compassion that mitigated Ephraim's punishment. *My heart is turned within me* (Hos. xi. 8, 9); and now the same compassion accepted Ephraim's repentance. He resolves to do him good: *I will surely have mercy upon him, saith the Lord.*

III. Gracious encouragements given to the people of God in Babylon to prepare for their return to their own land. Let them not tremble and lose their spirits; let them not trifle and lose their time; but with a firm resolution and a close application address themselves to their journey, *v.* 21, 22. "*Turn again, O virgin of Israel!* a virgin to be again espoused to thy God; *turn again to these thy cities;* though they are laid waste and in ruins, they are *thy cities,* which thy God gave thee, and therefore *turn again* to them." They must return the same way that they went, that the remembrance of the sorrows which attended them, or which their fathers had told them of, might make them the more thankful for their deliverance. Those that departed into the bondage of sin must return to the duties they neglected, must *do their first works. Set thy heart towards the highway.* The way from Babylon to Zion, from the bondage of sin to the glorious liberty of God's children, is a highway; yet none are likely to walk in it, unless they *set their hearts towards it. Set thee up way-marks,* and *make thee high heaps* or *pillars;* send before to have such set up in all places where there is any danger of missing the road. Let those that go first, and are best acquainted with the way, set up such directions for those that follow. *How long wilt thou go about, O backsliding daughter?* Let not their minds fluctuate, or be uncertain. Let them not distract themselves with care and fear, but let them cast themselves upon God, and then let their minds

JAMIESON, FAUSSET, BROWN

16. thy work—thy parental weeping for thy children [ROSENMULLER]. Thine affliction in the loss of thy children, murdered for Christ's sake, shall not be fruitless to thee, as was the case in thy giving birth to the "child of thy sorrow," Benjamin. Primarily, also, thy grief shall not be perpetual: the exiles shall return, and the land be inhabited again [CALVIN]. **come again**—(Hos. 1:11). **17. hope in ... end**—All thy calamities shall have a prosperous issue. **18. Ephraim**—representing the ten tribes. **bemoaning himself**—The spirit of penitent supplication shall at last be poured on Israel as the necessary forerunner of their restoration (Zech. 12:10-14). **Thou hast chastised me, and I was chastised**—In the first clause the chastisement itself is meant; in the second the *beneficial effect* of it in teaching the penitent true wisdom. **bullock unaccustomed to ... yoke**—A similar image occurs in Deuteronomy 32:15. Cf. "stiff-necked," Acts 7:51; Exodus 32:9, an image from *refractory* oxen. Before my chastisement I needed the severe correction I received, as much as an untamed bullock needs the goad. Cf. Acts 9:5, where the same figure is used of Saul while unconverted. Israel has had a longer chastisement than Judah, not having been restored even at the Jews' return from Babylon. Hereafter, at its restoration, it shall confess the sore discipline was all needed to "accustom" it to God's "easy yoke" (Matt. 11:29, 30). **turn thou me**—by Thy converting Spirit (Lam. 5:21). But why does Ephraim pray for conversion, seeing that he is already converted? Because we are converted by progressive steps, and need the same power of God to carry forward, as to originate, our conversion (John 6: 44, 65; cf. with Isa. 27:3; I Pet. 1:5; Phil. 1:6). **19. after that I was turned, I repented**—Repentance in the full sense follows, not precedes, our being turned *to God by* God (Zech. 12:10). The Jews' "*looking to* Him whom they pierced" shall result in their "*mourning for* Him." Repentance is the tear that flows from the eye of faith turned to Jesus. He Himself gives it: we give it not of ourselves, but must come to Him for it (Acts 5:31). **instructed**—made to learn by chastisement. God's Spirit often works through the corrections of His providence. **smote upon ... thigh**—(Ezek. 21:12). A token of indignant remorse, shame, and grief, because of his past sin. **bear ... reproach of ... youth**—"because the calamities which I *bore* were the just punishment of my *scandalous wantonness* against God in *my youth*"; alluding to the idols set up at Dan and Bethel immediately after the ten tribes revolted from Judah. His sense of *shame* shows that he no longer delights in his sin. **20. Is Ephraim my dear son?** etc.—The question implies that a negative answer was to be expected. Who would have thought that one so undutiful to His heavenly Father as Ephraim had been should still be regarded by God as a "pleasant child?" Certainly he was *not* so in respect to his sin. But by virtue of God's "everlasting love" (vs. 3) on Ephraim's being "turned" to God, he was immediately welcomed as God's "dear son." This 20th verse sets forth God's readiness to welcome the penitent (vss. 18, 19), anticipating his return with prevenient grace and love. Cf. Luke 15:20: "When he was *yet a great way off,* his father saw him and had compassion ...." **spake against**—threatened him for his idolatry. **remember**—with favor and concern, as in Genesis 8:1; 30:22. **bowels ... troubled for him**—(Deut. 32:36; Isa. 63:15; Hos. 11:8)—viz., with the yearnings of compassionate love. The "bowels" include the region of the heart, the seat of the affections. **21. waymarks**—*pillars* to mark the road for the returning exiles. Caravans set up *pillars,* or pointed *heaps* of stones, to mark the way through the desert against their return. So Israel is told by God to mark the way by which they went in leaving their country for exile; for by the same way they shall return. **highway**—(Isa. 35:8, 10). **22. go about**—viz., after human helps (ch. 2:18, 23, 36). Why not return immediately to me? MAURER translates, as in Song of Solomon 5:6, "How long wilt thou *withdraw thyself*?" Let thy past backslidings suffice thee now that a *new* era approaches. What God finds fault with in them is, that they looked *hither and thither,* leaning on contingencies, instead of at once trusting the word of God, which promised their restoration. To assure them of this, God promises to *create a new thing in their land, A woman shall compass a man.* CALVIN explains this: Israel, who is feeble as a woman, shall be superior to the warlike Chaldeans; the captives shall reduce their captors to captivity. HENGSTENBERG makes the "woman" the Jewish Church, and the "man" Jehovah, her husband, whose love she will

ADAM CLARKE

16. *They shall come again from the land of the enemy.* This could not be said of the murdered innocents at Bethlehem; they never came again. But the Jews, who had gone into captivity, did come again from the land of their enemy to their own border.

18. *I have surely heard Ephraim bemoaning himself.* The exiled Israelites are in a state of deep repentance.

Thou hast chastised me, and I was chastised. I was at first like an unbroken steer; the more I was chastised, the more I rebelled. But now I have benefited by Thy correction.

Turn thou me. I am now willing to take Thy yoke upon me, but I have no power.

19. *After that I was turned.* Converted from my sin, folly, and idolatry. *I repented.* To conviction of sin, I now added contrition for sin. Conviction, in this sense of the word, must precede contrition or repentance.

I smote upon my thigh. My sorrow grew deeper and deeper; I smote upon my thigh through the extremity of my distress. This was a usual sign of deep affliction. See Ezek. xxi. 12.

20. *Is Ephraim my dear son?* It is impossible to conceive anything more tenderly affectionate than this.

21. *Set thee up waymarks.* Alluding to stones, or heaps of stones, which travellers in the desert set up to ascertain the way, that they may know how to return. Mark the way to Babylon: thither you shall certainly go; but from it you shall as certainly return.

22. *A woman shall compass a man.* "A weak woman shall compass or circumvent a strong man." I think it likely that the Jews in their present distressed circumstances are represented under the similitude of a weak, defenseless female; and the Chaldeans under that of a

MATTHEW HENRY

be fixed. They are encouraged to do this by an assurance God gives them that he would *create a new thing in the earth, a woman shall compass a man.* The church of God, that is weak and feeble as a woman, altogether unapt for military employments (Isa. liv. 6), shall besiege, and prevail against a mighty man. The church is compared to a woman, Rev. xii. 1. And, whereas we find *armies compassing the camp of the saints* (Rev. xx. 9), now the camp of the saints shall compass them. Many good interpreters understand this *new thing* to be the incarnation of Christ, which had sometimes been given them for a sign, Isa. vii. 14; ix. 6. *A woman*, the virgin Mary, enclosed in her womb *the Mighty One*; for so *Geber*, the word here used, signifies; and God is called *Gibbor, the Mighty God* (*ch.* xxxii. 18), as also is Christ in Isa. ix. 6. He is *El-Gibbor*, the *mighty God.*

IV. A prospect given them of a happy settlement in their own land again. All their neighbours will give them a good word and put up a good prayer for them (*v.* 23): *As yet*, or rather *yet again* (though Judah and Jerusalem have long been a hissing), *this speech shall be used*, as it was formerly, *concerning the land of Judah and the cities thereof, The Lord bless you, O habitation of justice and mountain of holiness!* This intimates that they shall return much reformed; and this reformation shall be so conspicuous that all about them shall take notice of it. The *cities*, that used to be nests of pirates, shall be *habitations of justice*; the *mountain of Israel*, and especially Mount Zion, shall be a *mountain of holiness*. There shall be great plenty among them (*v.* 24, 25): *There shall dwell in Judah itself*, though it has now long lain waste, both husbandmen and shepherds, the two ancient and honourable employments of Cain and Abel, Gen. iv. 2. "I have *satiated the weary and sorrowful soul*"; those that have been long sorrowful in their captivity, shall now enjoy great plenty. This is applicable to the spiritual blessings God has in store for all true penitents.

V. The prophet tells us what pleasure the discovery of this brought, *v.* 26. "*Upon this I awaked*, overcome with joy, which burst the fetters of sleep; and I reflected upon my dream, and it was such as had made *my sleep sweet to me;* I was refreshed, as men are with quiet sleep."

Verses 27–34

It is here further promised,

I. The people of God shall become both numerous and prosperous. Israel and Judah shall be replenished both with men and cattle, *v.* 27. This should be a type of the wonderful increase of the gospel-church. God will build them, and plant them, *v.* 28. He *will watch over them* to do them good. Everything for a long time had turned so much against them, that it seemed as if God had *watched over them to pluck up and to throw down*; but now everything shall happily strengthen and advance their interests.

II. They shall be reckoned with no further for the sins of their fathers (*v.* 29, 30). Our Saviour tells the wicked Jews in his days that they should smart for their fathers' sins, because they persisted in them, Matt. xxiii. 35, 36. But it is here promised that God would proceed no further for their fathers' sins, but remember his covenant with their fathers and do them good according to that covenant: *They shall no more* complain, as they have done, that *the fathers have eaten sour grapes and the children's teeth are set on edge*, but *everyone shall die for his own iniquity* still; he will reckon with particular persons that provoke him.

III. God will renew his covenant with them, so that all these blessings they shall have, not by providence only, but by promise. But this covenant refers to gospel times, the latter days that *shall come*; for of gospel grace the apostle understands it (Heb. viii. 8, 9, &c.), where this whole passage is quoted as a summary of the covenant of grace made with believers in Jesus Christ. This covenant is made—*with the house of Israel and Judah*, with the gospel church, *the Israel of God* on whicn *peace shall be* (Gal. vi. 16), with the spiritual seed of believing Abraham and praying Jacob. Judah and Israel had been two separate kingdoms, but were united after their return, in the joint favours God bestowed upon them; so Jews and Gentiles were in the gospel church and covenant. It is a *new covenant* and *not according to the covenant made with them when they came out of Egypt*. The ordinances and promises are more spiritual and heavenly, and the discoveries much more clear. That covenant God made with them when he *took them by the hand*, as if they had been blind, or lame, or weak, *to lead them out of the land of Egypt, which covenant they broke.* It was God that made this covenant, but it was the people that broke it; for our salvation is of God, but our sin and ruin are of our-

JAMIESON, FAUSSET, BROWN

again seek (Hos. 2:6, 7). MAURER, A woman shall protect (Deut. 32:10, *Margin*; Ps. 32:10) a man, i.e., You need fear no foes in returning, for all things shall be so peaceful that *a woman* would be able to take man's part, and act as his *protector*. But the Christian fathers (Augustine, etc.) almost unanimously interpreted it of *the Virgin Mary compassing Christ in her womb*. This view is favored:—(1) By the connection; it gives a reason why the exiles should desire a return to their country, viz., because Christ was conceived there. (2) The word "created" implies a divine power put forth in the creation of a body in the Virgin's womb by the Holy Ghost for the second Adam, such as was exerted in creating the first Adam (Luke 1:35; Heb. 10:5). (3) The phrase, "a *new* thing," something unprecedented; a man whose like had never existed before, at once God and man; a mother out of the ordinary course of nature, at once mother and virgin. An extraordinary mode of generation; one conceived by the Holy Ghost without man. (4) The specification "in the land" (not "earth," as *English Version*), viz., of *Judah*, where probably Christ was *conceived*, in *Hebron* (cf. Luke 1:39, 41, 42, 44, with Josh. 21:11) or else in *Nazareth*, "in the territory" of *Israel*, to whom vss. 5, 6, 15, 18, 21 refer; His *birth* was at Bethlehem (Mic. 5:2; Matt. 2:5, 6). As the place of His nativity, and of His being reared (Matt. 2:23), and of His preaching (Hag. 2:7; Mal. 3:1), are specified, so it is likely the Holy Spirit designated the place of His being conceived. (5) The *Hebrew* for "woman" implies an *individual*, as the Virgin Mary, rather than a *collection of persons*. (6) The restoration of Israel is grounded on God's covenant in *Christ*, to whom, therefore, allusion is naturally made as the foundation of Israel's hope (cf. Isa. 7:14). The *Virgin* Mary's conception of Messiah in the womb answers to the "Virgin of Israel" (therefore so called, vs. 21), i.e., Israel and her sons at their final restoration, receiving Jesus as Messiah (Zech. 12:10). (7) The reference to the conception of the *child* Messiah accords with the mention of the massacre of "children" referred to in vs. 15 (cf. Matt. 2:17). (8) The *Hebrew* for "man" is properly "mighty man," a term applied to *God* (Deut. 10:17); and to Christ (Zech. 13:7; cf. Ps. 45:3; Isa. 9:6) [CALOVIUS]. **23.** Jerusalem again shall be the metropolis of the whole nation, the seat of "justice" (Ps. 122:5-8; Isa. 1:26), and of sacred worship ("holiness," Zech. 8:3) on "Mount" Moriah. **24. Judah . . . cities . . . husbandmen . . . they with flocks**—Two classes, citizens and countrymen, the latter divided into agriculturists and shepherds, all alike in security, though the latter were to be outside the protection of city walls. "Judah" here stands for the *country*, as distinguished from its *cities*. **25.** The "weary, sorrowful," and indigent state of Israel will prove no obstacle in the way of My helping them. **26.** The words of Jeremiah: *Upon this* (or, *By reason of this*) announcement of a happy restoration, "I awaked" from the prophetic *dream* vouchsafed to me (ch. 23:25) with the "sweet" impression thereof remaining on my mind. "Sleep" here means *dream*, as in Psalm 90:5. **27.** He shows how a land so depopulated shall again be peopled. God will cause both *men* and *beasts* in it to increase to a multitude (Ezek. 36:9-11; Hos. 2:23). **28.** (Ch. 44:27.) The same God who, as it were (in human language), was *on the watch* for all means to destroy, shall be as much on the watch for the means of their restoration. **29. In those days**—after their punishment has been completed, and mercy again visits them. **fathers . . . eaten . . . sour grape . . . children's teeth . . . on edge**—the proverb among the exiles' children born in Babylon, to express that they suffered the evil consequences of their fathers' sins rather than of their own (Lam. 5:7; Ezek. 18:2, 3). **30.** (Gal. 6:5, 7.) **31. the days . . . new covenant with . . . Israel . . . Judah**—The new covenant is made with literal *Israel* and *Judah*, not with the *spiritual* Israel, i.e., believers, except secondarily, and as grafted on the stock of Israel (Rom. 11:16-27). For the whole subject of chs. 30 and 31 is the restoration of the Hebrews (ch. 30:4, 7, 10, 18; 31:7, 10, 11, 23, 24, 27, 36). With the "remnant according to the election of grace" in Israel, the new covenant has already taken effect. But with regard to the *whole* nation, its realization is reserved for the last days, to which Paul refers this prophecy in an abridged form (Rom. 11:27). **32. Not . . . the covenant that I made with . . . fathers**—the Old Testament covenant, as contrasted with our gospel covenant (Heb. 8:8-12; 10:16, 17, where this prophecy is quoted to prove the abrogation of the law by the gospel), of which the distinguishing features are its securing by an adequate atonement the forgiveness of sins, and by

ADAM CLARKE

fierce, strong man, who had prevailed over and oppressed this weak woman. But, notwithstanding the disparity between them, God would cause the *woman*—the weak, defenseless Jews, to *compass*—to overcome, the strong *man*—the powerful Babylonians.

23. *The Lord bless thee, O habitation of of justice.* After their return they shall be remarkably prosperous.

26. *Upon this I awaked.* It appears that the prophecy, commencing with chap. xxx. 2 and ending with v. 25 of this chapter, was delivered to the prophet in a dream.

27. *I will sow . . . with the seed of man, and with the seed of beast.* I will multiply both men and cattle.

29. *The fathers have eaten a sour grape.* A proverbial expression for "The children suffer for the offenses of their parents." This is explained in the next verse: "Every one shall die for his own iniquity." No child shall suffer divine punition for the sin of his father; only so far as he acts in the same way can he be said to bear the sins of his parents.

31. *A new covenant.* The Christian dispensation.

MATTHEW HENRY

selves. The particular articles of his covenant all contain spiritual blessings; not, "I will give them the land of Canaan and a numerous issue," but, "I will give them pardon, and peace, and grace, good heads and good hearts." He promises he will incline them to their duty: *I will put my law in their inward part and write it in their heart.* He will take them into relation to himself: *I will be their God*, a God all-sufficient to them, *and they shall be my people*, a loyal obedient people to me. Those that rightly know God's name will seek him, and serve him, and put their trust in him (*v.* 34): *All shall know me;* all shall be welcome to the knowledge of God and shall have the means of that knowledge; *his ways shall be known upon earth*, whereas, for many ages, *in Judah only was God known.* The priests preached but now and then, and in the temple, and to a few in comparison; but now all shall or may know God by frequenting the assemblies of Christians, wherein, through all parts of the church, the good knowledge of God shall be taught. In short, the things of God shall by the gospel of Christ be brought to a clearer light than ever (2. Tim. i. 10), and the people of God shall by the grace of Christ be brought to a clearer sight of those things than ever, Eph. i. 17, 18. Sin shall be pardoned. This is made the reason of all the rest: *For I will forgive their iniquity, will forgive* and forget: *I will remember their sin no more.*

Verses 35–40

The great thing here secured to us is that while the world stands God will have a church in it, which, though sometimes it may be brought very low, shall yet be raised again, and its interests re-established; it is *built upon a rock, and the gates of hell shall not prevail against it.*

I. The building of the world, and the firmness of that building, are evidences of the power and faithfulness of God who has undertaken the establishment of his church. *He that built all things* at first *is God* (Heb. iii. 4). The constancy of the kingdom of nature may encourage us to depend upon the divine promise for the continuance of the glories of the kingdom of grace.

1. The glories of the kingdom of nature. *He gives the sun for a light by day* (*v.* 35), not only made it at first to be so, but still gives it to be so; for the light and heat, and all the influences of the sun, continually depend upon its great Creator. He gives *the ordinances of the moon and stars for a light by night*; their motions are called *ordinances* because they are regular and under rule. See Job xxxviii. 31–33. Notice the government of the sea, and the check that is given to its proud billows: *The Lord of hosts divides the sea*, or (as some read it) *settles the sea, when the waves thereof roar.* Notice the vastness of the heavens and the unmeasurable extent of the firmament; the *heavens above cannot be measured* (*v.* 37), and yet God fills them. Notice the mysteriousness even of that part of the creation in which our lot is cast. Notice the immovable steadfastness of all these (*v.* 36): *These ordinances cannot depart from before God; for all are his servants*, Ps. cxix. 90, 91. The heavens are often clouded, and the sun and moon often eclipsed, the earth may quake and the sea be tossed, but they all keep their place, are moved, but not removed.

2. The securities of the kingdom of grace inferred hence: *the seed of Israel shall not cease from being a nation*, 1 Pet. ii. 9. When Israel according to the flesh is no longer a nation the *children of the promise are counted for the seed* (Rom. ix. 8) and God *will not cast off all the seed of Israel*, though they have done very wickedly, *v.* 37. The God that has undertaken the preservation of the church is a God of almighty power, who *upholds all things by his* almighty *word. Our help stands in his name who made heaven and earth*, and therefore can do anything. God would not take all this care of the world but that he designs glory; and how shall he have it but by securing to himself a church in it, a people that *shall be to him for a name and a praise?* If the order of the creation therefore continues firm because it was well-fixed at first, and is not altered because it needs no alteration, the method of grace shall for the same reason continue invariable, as it was at first well settled. He who has promised to preserve a church for himself has approved himself faithful to the word which he has spoken concerning the stability of the world.

II. The rebuilding of Jerusalem, now in ruins, shall be an earnest of these great things that God will do for the gospel church, the *heavenly Jerusalem*, *v.* 38–40. *The days will come*, though they may be long in coming, when Jerusalem shall be entirely built again, as large as ever it was. The wall which Nehemiah built, and which, the more punctually to fulfil the prophecy, began about the *tower of Hananeel*, here mentioned (Neh. iii. 1), enclosed as much ground

JAMIESON, FAUSSET, BROWN

the inworking of effectual grace ensuring permanent obedience. An earnest of this is given partially in the present eclectic or elect Church gathered out of Jews and Gentiles. But the promise here to Israel in the last days is national and universal, and effected by an extraordinary outpouring of the Spirit (vss. 33, 34; Ezek. 11:17-20), independent of any merit on their part (Ezek. 36:25-32; 37:1-28; 39:29; Joel 2:23-28; Zech. 12:10; II Cor. 3:16). **took . . . by . . . hand**–(Deut. 1:31; Hos. 11:3). **although I was an husband**–(cf. ch. 3:14; Hos. 2:7, 8). But LXX, *Syriac*, and St. Paul (Heb. 8:9) translate, "I *regarded* them not"; and GESENIUS, etc., justify this rendering of the *Hebrew* from the *Arabic*. The Hebrews *regarded not* God, so God *regarded* them *not*. **33. will be their God**–(ch. 32:38). **34.** True, specially of Israel (Isa. 54:13); secondarily, true of believers (John 6:45; I Cor. 2:10; I John 2:20).

forgive . . . iniquity . . . remember . . . no more–(ch. 33:8; 50:20; Mic. 7:18); applying peculiarly to Israel (Rom. 11:27). Secondarily, all believers (Acts 10:43).

35. divideth . . . sea when . . . waves . . . roar . . . Lord of hosts . . . name–quoted from Isaiah 51:15, the genuineness of which passage is thus established on Jeremiah's authority.

36. a nation
–Israel's *national* polity has been broken up by the Romans. But their preservation as a *distinct people* amidst violent persecutions, though scattered among all nations for eighteen centuries, *unamalgamated*, whereas all other peoples under such circumstances have become incorporated with the nations in which they have been dispersed, is a perpetual standing miracle (cf. ch. 33:20; Ps. 148:6; Isa. 54:9, 10). **37.** (Cf. 33:22.) **for all that they have done**–viz., all the sins. God will regard His own covenant promise, rather than their merits.

38. tower of Hananeel–The city shall extend beyond its former bounds (Neh. 3:1; 12:39; Zech. 14:10).

ADAM CLARKE

33. *After those days.* When vision and prophecy shall be sealed up, and Jesus have assumed that body which was prepared for Him, and have laid down His life for the redemption of a lost world, and, having ascended on high, shall have obtained the gift of the Holy Spirit to purify the heart, then God's *law* shall, by it, be put *in their inward parts*, and written on their *hearts*, so that all within and all without shall be holiness to the Lord. Then God will be truly *their God*, received and acknowledged as their Portion, and the sole Object of their devotion; and they shall be His people, filled with holiness, and made partakers of the divine nature, so that they shall perfectly love Him and worthily magnify His name.

34. *And they shall teach no more.* It shall be a time of universal light and knowledge; all shall know God in Christ, from the least to the greatest. The children shall be taught to read the new covenant, and to understand the terms of their salvation.

36. *If those ordinances.* As sure as the sun shall give light to the day, and the moon to the night, so surely shall the Jews continue to be a distinct people.

38. *The city shall be built to the Lord.* This cannot mean the city built after the return from Babylon, for two reasons: (1) This is to be much greater in extent; (2) It is to be permanent, never to be thrown down, v. 40. It must therefore mean, if taken literally at all, the city that is to be built by them when they are brought in with the fullness of the Gentiles. *The tower of Hananeel.* This stood in the northeast part of the city; from thence the wall proceeded to the corner gate.

E. H. PLUMPTRE:

"Which giveth the sun for a light by day" (vv. 35, 36). The leading thought in the lofty language of this passage is that the reign of law which we recognize in God's creative work has its counterpart in His spiritual kingdom. The stability and permanence of natural order is a pledge and earnest of the fulfillment of His promises to Israel as a people. The new Covenant of pardon and illumination is to be what the first Covenant was not, eternal in its duration. We have learnt, through the teaching of St. Paul, while not excluding Israel according to the flesh from its share in that fulfillment, to extend its range to the children of the faith of Abraham, the true Israel of God (Rom. 2:28, 29; 4:11, 12).—*Ellicott's Commentary on the Whole Bible*

MATTHEW HENRY

as is here intended, though we cannot certainly determine the places here called *the gate of the corner, the hill Gareb*, &c. When built it shall be consecrated to God and to his service (*v.* 38), and even the suburbs and fields adjacent *shall be holy unto the Lord.* The whole city shall be as it were one temple, one holy place, as the new Jerusalem is, which *therefore* has no temple, because it is all temple. It shall continue very long, the time of the new city from the return to its last destruction being as long as that of the old from David to the captivity. But this promise was to have its full accomplishment in the gospel church, which is the spiritual Israel, and therefore God will not cast it off. It is the holy city, and therefore all the powers of men *shall not pluck it up, nor throw it down.*

CHAPTER 32

Verses 1-15

The desolations of Judah and Jerusalem by the Chaldeans came gradually upon them, but, they not meeting him by repentance in the way of his judgments, he proceeded till all was laid waste, which was in the eleventh year of Zedekiah; now what is here recorded happened in the tenth. The king of Babylon's army had now invested Jerusalem and was carrying on the siege with vigour.

I. Jeremiah prophesies that both the city and the court shall fall into the hands of the king of Babylon. He tells them that God, whose city it was, will give it into their hands and put it out of his protection (*v.* 3)—that, though Zedekiah attempt to make his escape, he shall be overtaken, and shall be delivered a prisoner into the hands of Nebuchadnezzar. He shall hear the king of Babylon pronounce his doom, and see with what fury and indignation he will look upon him (*His eyes shall behold his eyes*, *v.* 4)—that Zedekiah shall be carried to Babylon, and continue a miserable captive there, *until God visit him*, that is, till God put an end to his life by a natural death, as Nebuchadnezzar had long before put an end to his days by putting out his eyes.

II. For prophesying thus he is imprisoned, not in the common gaol, but *in the king of Judah's house*, and there not closely confined, but would be sheltered from the abuses of the mob. However, it was a prison, and Zedekiah shut him up in it for prophesying as he did, *v.* 2, 3. So far was he from *humbling himself before Jeremiah* (2 Chron. xxxvi. 12), that he *hardened himself* against him. Though he had formerly so far owned him a prophet as to desire him to *enquire of the Lord for them* (*ch.* xxi. 2), yet now he chides him for prophesying (*v.* 3), and shuts him up in prison, perhaps to restrain him from prophesying any further.

III. Being in prison, he purchases from a near relation of his a piece of ground that lay in Anathoth, *v.* 6, 7, &c. It was most strange that he should buy a *piece of land* when he himself knew that the whole land was now to be laid waste and fall into the hands of the Chaldeans. But it was the will of God that he should buy it, and he submitted, though the money seemed to be thrown away.

His kinsman came to offer it to him; it was not of his own seeking; besides, the *right of redemption* belonged to him (*v.* 8), and if he refused he would not do the kinsman's part. It was land that lay within the suburbs of a priests' city, and, if he should refuse it, there was danger lest, in these times of disorder, it might be sold to one of another tribe, which was contrary to the law. It would likewise be a kindness to his kinsman, who probably was at this time in great want of money. When Jeremiah knew by Hanameel's coming to him, as God had foretold he would, that *it was the word of the Lord*, that it was his mind that he should make this purchase, he made no more difficulty of it, but *bought the field.* He was very honest and exact in paying. He *weighed him the money*, did not press him to take it upon his report. It was *seventeen shekels of silver.* We shall not wonder at the smallness of the price if we consider what scarcity there was of money at this time and how little lands were counted upon.

JAMIESON, FAUSSET, BROWN

gate of . . . corner—(II Kings 14:13; II Chron. 26:9). **39. measuring-line**—(Ezek. 40:8; Zech. 2:1). **Gareb**—from a *Hebrew* root, "to scrape"; *Syriac,* "leprosy"; the locality outside of the city, to which *lepers* were removed. **Goath**—from a root, "to toil," referring to the *toilsome* ascent there: outside of the city of David, towards the southwest, as Gareb was northwest [JUNIUS]. **40. valley of . . . dead**—Tophet, where the bodies of malefactors were cast (Isa. 30:33), south of the city. **fields . . . Kidron**—so II Kings 23:4. Fields in the suburbs reaching as far as Kidron, east of the city. **horse gate**—Through it the king's horses were led forth for watering to the brook Kidron (II Kings 11:16; Neh. 3:28). **for ever**—The city shall not only be spacious, but both "holy to the Lord," i.e., freed from all pollutions, and *everlasting* (Joel 3:17, 20; Rev. 21:2, 10, 27).

CHAPTER 32

Vss. 1-14. JEREMIAH, IMPRISONED FOR HIS PROPHECY AGAINST JERUSALEM, BUYS A PATRIMONIAL PROPERTY (HIS RELATIVE HANAMEEL'S), IN ORDER TO CERTIFY TO THE JEWS THEIR FUTURE RETURN FROM BABYLON. **1. tenth year**—The siege of Jerusalem had already begun, in the tenth month of the ninth year of Zedekiah (ch. 39:1; II Kings 25:1). **2. in . . . court of . . . prison**—i.e., in the open space occupied by the guard, from which he was not allowed to depart, but where any of his friends might visit him (vs. 12; ch. 38:13, 28). Marvellous obstinacy, that at the time when they were experiencing the truth of Jeremiah's words in the pressure of the siege, they should still keep the prophet in confinement [CALVIN]. The circumstances narrated (vss. 3-5) occurred at the beginning of the siege, when Jeremiah foretold the capture of the city (vs. 1; ch. 34:1-7; 39:1). He was at that time put into free custody in the court of the prison. At the raising of the siege by Pharaoh-hophra, Jeremiah was on the point of repairing to Benjamin, when he was cast into "the dungeon," but obtained leave to be removed again to the court of the prison (ch. 37:12-21). When there he urged the Jews, on the second advance of the Chaldeans to the siege, to save themselves by submission to Nebuchadnezzar (ch. 38:2, 3); in consequence of this the king, at the instigation of the princes, had him cast into a miry dungeon (ch. 38:4-6); again he was removed to the prison court at the intercession of a courtier (vss. 7-13), where he remained till the capture of the city (vs. 28), when he was liberated (ch. 39:11, etc.; 40:1, etc.). **4. his eyes shall behold his eyes**—i.e., only *before* reaching Babylon, which he was *not to see.* Ch. 39:6, 7 harmonizes this prophecy (ch. 32:4) with the seemingly opposite prophecy, Ezekiel 12:13, "He shall *not see.*" **5. visit him**—in a good sense (ch. 27:22); referring to the honor paid Zedekiah at his death and burial (ch. 34:4, 5). Perhaps, too, before his death he was treated by Nebuchadnezzar with some favor. **though ye fight . . . shall not prosper**—(ch. 21:4). **6. Jeremiah said**—resuming the thread of vs. 1, which was interrupted by the parenthesis (vss. 2-5). **7. son of Shallum thine uncle**—therefore, Jeremiah's first cousin. **field . . . in Anathoth**—a sacerdotal city: and so having 1000 cubits of suburban fields outside the wall attached to it (Num. 35:4, 5). The prohibition to sell these suburban fields (Lev. 25:34) applied merely to their alienating them from Levites to another tribe; so that this chapter does not contravene that prohibition. Besides, what is here meant is only the purchase of the use of the field till the year of jubilee. On the failure of the owner, the next of kin had the right of redeeming it (Lev. 25:25, etc.; Ruth 4: 3-6). **8. Then I knew**—Not that Jeremiah previously doubted the reality of the divine communication, but, the effect following it, and the prophet's experimentally knowing it, confirmed his faith and was the seal to the vision. The Roman historian, FLORUS (2.6), records a similar instance: During the days that Rome was being besieged by Hannibal, the very ground on which he was encamped was put up for sale at Rome, and found a purchaser; implying the calm confidence of the ultimate issue entertained by the Roman people. **9. seventeen shekels of silver**—As the shekel was only about 50 cents, the whole would be under $10.00, a rather small sum, even taking into account the fact of the Chaldean occupation of the land, and the uncertainty of the time when it might come to Jeremiah or his heirs. Perhaps the "seven shekels," which in the *Hebrew* (see *Margin*) are distinguished from the "ten pieces of silver," were shekels *of gold* [MAURER]. **10. sub-**

ADAM CLARKE

39. *Upon the hill Gareb.* Gareb and Goath are out of the limits of this city. The latter is supposed to be Golgotha; that is, the heap of Gotha, which, being the place where our Lord was crucified, was without the city. These hills were a little to the northwest of the old city walls, but are destined to be within the new city.

40. *The whole valley of the dead bodies.* The valley of the son of Hinnom. *And all the fields unto the brook of Kidron, unto the corner of the horse gate toward the east.* All these places, the fuller's field, etc., shall be consecrated to the Lord, and become a part of this new city; so that this will appear to be a city much more extensive than the city of Jerusalem ever was.

CHAPTER 32

1. *The word that came.* This prophecy bears its own date: it was delivered in the tenth year of Zedekiah, which answered to the eighteenth of Nebuchadnezzar.

2. *Then the king of Babylon's army besieged Jerusalem.* The siege had commenced the year before, and continued a year after, ending in the fifth month of the following year; consequently the siege must have lasted about eighteen months and twenty-seven days. See 2 Kings xxv. 18.

7. *The right of redemption is thine.* The law had established that the estates of a family should never be alienated. If, therefore, a man through poverty was obliged to sell his patrimony, the nearest relative had a right to purchase it before all others, and even to redeem it, if it had been sold to another. This is what is called the right of *goel*, or "kinsman," Lev. xxv. 25. And in the year of jubilee the whole reverted to its ancient master, Lev. xxv. 13.

8. *This was the word of the Lord.* It was by His appointment that I was to make this purchase. The whole was designed as a symbolical act, to show the people that there would be a return from Babylon, that each family should reenter on its former possessions, and that a man might safely purchase on the certainty of this event.

9. *Weighed him the money.* It does not appear that there was any coined or stamped money among the Jews before the Captivity; the Scripture, therefore, never speaks of counting money, but of weighing it.

MATTHEW HENRY

He was very prudent in preserving the writings. They were subscribed *before witnesses*. One copy was *sealed up*, the other was *open*. The deeds of purchase were lodged in the hands of Baruch, before witnesses, and he was ordered to lay them up in an *earthen vessel* that they might *continue many days*, for the use of Jeremiah's heirs. The design of having this bargain made was to signify that though Jerusalem was now besieged, and the whole country was likely to be laid waste, yet the time should come when *houses, and fields, and vineyards should be again possessed in this land, v.* 15. As God appointed Jeremiah to confirm his predictions of the approaching destruction of Jerusalem by his own practice in living unmarried, so he now appointed him to confirm his predictions of the future restoration of Jerusalem by his own practice in purchasing this field. Lucius Florus relates it as a great instance of the bravery of the Roman citizens that in the time of the second Punic War, when Hannibal besieged Rome and was very near making himself master of it, a field on which part of his army lay, being offered to sale at that time, was immediately purchased, in a firm belief that the Roman valour would raise the siege, *lib.* ii. *cap.* 6. And have not we much more reason to venture our all upon the word of God.

Verses 16–25

Jeremiah's prayer to God upon occasion of the discoveries God had made to him of his purposes concerning this nation, to pull it down, and in time to build it up again, which puzzled the prophet, who, though he delivered his messages faithfully, yet, in reflecting upon them, was greatly at a loss how to reconcile them; in that perplexity he poured out his soul before God in prayer. Jeremiah was in prison, in distress, in the dark about the meaning of God's providences, and then he prays.

I. Jeremiah adores God and gives him the glory due to his name as the Creator, *v.* 17–19. When at any time we are perplexed about the particular dispensations of Providence it is good for us to satisfy ourselves with the general doctrines of God's wisdom, power, and goodness. Let us consider, as Jeremiah does here, 1. That God is the fountain of all being, power, life, motion, and perfection: He *made the heaven and the earth with his outstretched arm.* 2. That with him nothing is impossible: *Nothing is too hard for thee.* 3. That he is a God of boundless mercy: "Thou not only art kind, but thou *showest loving-kindness*, not to a few, to here and there one, but *to thousands*, thousands of persons, thousands of generations." 4. That he is a God of impartial and inflexible justice. 5. That he is a God of universal dominion and command: He is *the great* God, for he is *the mighty God.* He is *the Lord of hosts*, of all hosts, that *is his name.* 6. That he contrives everything for the best: He is *great in counsel*, so deep are the designs of his wisdom.

II. He acknowledges the universal cognizance God takes of all the actions of the children of men (*v.* 19): *Thy eyes are open upon all the sons of men*, wherever they are, beholding the evil and the good, and upon all *their ways*, not as an unconcerned spectator, but as an observing judge; for men shall find God as they are found of him.

III. He recounts the great things God had done for his people Israel formerly. 1. He brought them out of Egypt, that house of bondage, with *signs and wonders. Israel* were reminded of it every year by the ordinance of the passover. All the neighbouring nations spoke of it, as that which redounded exceedingly to the glory of the God of Israel, and made him *a name as at this day.* 2. He brought them into Canaan, that *land flowing with milk and honey.* He *swore to their fathers to give it them*, and he did give it to the children (*v.* 22) *and they came in and possessed it.* It is good for us often to reflect upon the great things God did for his church formerly, especially in the first erecting of it, that work of wonder.

IV. He bewails the rebellions they had been guilty of against God, and the judgments God had brought upon them for these rebellions. It is a sad account he here gives of the ungrateful conduct of that people towards God. He had done everything that he had promised to do, but they had *done nothing of all that he commanded them to do* (*v.* 23). 1. He compares the present state of Jerusalem with the divine predictions, and finds that what God *has spoken* has *come to pass.* God had given them fair warning of it before; and, if they had regarded this, the ruin would have been prevented. 2. He commits the present state of Jerusalem to the divine compassion (*v.* 24): *Behold the mounts*, or *ramparts*, or the *engines* which they make use of to batter the city. "*Behold thou seest it.* Is this the city that thou hast chosen to put thy name there? And shall it be thus abandoned?" He neither

JAMIESON, FAUSSET, BROWN

scribed–*I wrote* in the deed, "book of purchase" (vs. 12). **weighed**–coined money was not in early use; hence money was "weighed" (Gen. 23:16). **11. evidence . . . sealed . . . open**–Two deeds were drawn up in a contract of sale; the one, the original copy, witnessed and sealed with the public seal; the other not so, but open, and therefore less authoritative, being but a *copy.* GATAKER **thinks that the** purchaser sealed the one with *his own* seal; the other he showed to witnesses that they might write their names on the back of it and know the contents; and that some details, e.g., the conditions and time of redemption were in the *sealed* copy, which the parties might not choose to be known to the witnesses, and which were therefore not in the *open* copy. The sealed copy, when opened after the seventy years' captivity, would greatly confirm the faith of those living at that time. The "law and custom" refer, probably, not merely to the sealing up of the conditions and details of purchase, but also to the law of redemption, according to which, at the return to Judea, the deed would show that Jeremiah had bought the field by his right as next of kin (Lev. 25: 13-16), [LUDOVICUS DE DIEU]. **12. Baruch**–Jeremiah's amanuensis and agent (ch. 36:4, etc.). **before all**–In sales everything clandestine was avoided; publicity was required. So here, in the court of prison, where Jeremiah was confined, there were soldiers and others, who had free access to him, present (ch. 38:1). **14. in an earthen vessel**–that the documents might not be injured by the moisture of the surrounding earth; at the same time, being buried, they could not be stolen, but would remain as a pledge of the Jews' deliverance until God's time should come. **15.** (Cf. vss. 24, 25, 37, 43, 44.) **16.** Jeremiah, not comprehending how God's threat of destroying Judah could be reconciled with God's commanding him to purchase land in it as if in a free country, has recourse to his grand remedy against perplexities, prayer.

17. hast made . . . heaven–Jeremiah extols God's creative power, as a ground of humility on his part as man: It is not my part to call Thee, the mighty God, to account for Thy ways (cf. ch. 12:1). **too hard**–In vs. 27 God's reply exactly accords with Jeremiah's prayer (Gen. 18:14; Zech. 8:6; Luke 1:37). **18.** Exod. 34:7; Isa. 65:6.) This is taken from the decalogue (Exod. 20: 5, 6). This is a second consideration to check hasty judgments as to God's ways: Thou art the gracious and righteous Judge of the world.

19. counsel . . . work–devising . . . executing (Isa. 28: 29). **eyes . . . open upon all**–(Job 34:21; Prov. 5: 21). **to give . . . according to . . . ways**–(ch. 17:10).

20. even unto this day–Thou hast given "signs" of Thy power from the day when Thou didst deliver Israel out of Egypt by mighty miracles, down to the present time [MAURER]. CALVIN explains it, "memorable even unto this day." **among other men**–not in Israel only, but among foreign peoples also. Cf. for "other" understood, Psalm 73:5. **made thee a name**–(Exod. 9:16; I Chron. 17:21; Isa. 63:12). **as at this day**–*a name* of power, such as Thou hast at this day. **21.** (Ps. 136:11, 12.) **22. given . . . didst swear**–God gave it by a gratuitous covenant, not for their deserts.

23. all . . . thou commandedst . . . all this evil–Their punishment was thus exactly commensurate with their sin. It was not fortuitous. **24. mounts**–mounds of earth raised as breastworks by the besieging army, behind which they employed their engines, and which they gradually pushed forward to the walls of the city. **behold, thou seest it**–connected with vs. 25. Thou seest all this with Thine own eyes, and yet (what seems inconsistent with it) Thou commandest me to buy a field.

ADAM CLARKE

10. *I subscribed the evidence.* We have here all the circumstances of this legal act: (1) An offer is made of the reversion of the ground, till the jubilee, to him who would then of right come into possession. (2) The price is agreed on, and the silver weighed in the balances. (3) A contract or deed of sale is drawn up, to which both parties agreeing, (4) Witnesses are brought forward to see it signed and sealed, for the contract was both subscribed and sealed. (5) A *duplicate* of the deed was drawn, which was not to be sealed, but to lie open for the inspection of those concerned, in some public place where it might be safe, and always to be seen. (6) The original, which was sealed up, was put in an earthen pitcher, in order to be preserved from accidents. (7) This was delivered by the purchaser into the hands of a third party, to be preserved for the use of the purchaser, and witnesses were called to attest this delivery. (8) They subscribed the book of the purchase, perhaps a town book, or register, where such purchases were entered. Baruch was a scribe by profession; and the deeds were delivered into his hands, before witnesses, to be preserved as above. Perhaps the law, in this case, required that the instrument should be thus lodged. But, in the present case, both the deeds, the original and the duplicate, were put into the earthen pitcher, because the city was about to be burnt; and, if lodged as usual, they would be destroyed in the general conflagration.

15. *Houses and fields . . . shall be possessed again.* That is, this is an evidence that the Captivity shall not last long; houses, etc., shall here be possessed again, either by their present owners or by immediate descendants.

24. *Behold the mounts.* The huge terraces raised up to plant their engines on, that they might throw darts, stones, etc., into the city. *Because of the sword, and of the famine, and of the pestilence.* The city was now reduced to extreme necessity; and from the siege continuing nearly a year longer, we may conclude that the besieged made a noble defense.

CHARLES H. SPURGEON:

Verse 17. He bought the piece of land, and it was secured to him; he did as he was commanded, and returned to his dungeon. When he came into his chamber alone, it is possible that he began to question himself as to what he had been doing, and troubled thoughts rolled over his mind. "I have been purchasing a useless possession," said he. See how he refuses to indulge the thought. He gets as far as saying, "Ah, Lord God!" as if he were about to utter some unbelieving or rebellious sentence, but he stops himself, "Thou canst make this plot of ground of use to me; Thou canst rid this land of these oppressors; Thou canst make me sit under my vine and my fig tree in the heritage which I have bought; for Thou didst make the heavens and the earth, and there is nothing too hard for Thee." Beloved, this gave a majesty to the early saints, that they dared to do at God's command, things which were unaccountable to sense, and which reason would condemn.

—*The Treasury of the Old Testament*

MATTHEW HENRY

complains of God for what he had done nor prescribes to God what he should do, but desires he would behold their case. Whatever trouble we are in we may comfort ourselves with this, that God sees it and sees how to remedy it.

V. He seems desirous to be let further into the meaning of the order God had now given him to purchase his kinsman's field (*v.* 25): "*Though the city is given into the hands of the Chaldeans*, and no man is likely to enjoy what he has, yet *thou hast said unto me, Buy thou the field.*" As soon as he understood that it was the mind of God he did it; but, when he had done it, he desired better to understand why God had ordered him to do it. Though we are bound to follow God with an implicit obedience, yet we should endeavour that it may be more and more an intelligent obedience. We must never dispute God's statutes and judgments, but we may and must enquire, *What mean these statutes and judgments?* Deut. vi. 20.

Verses 26–44

God's answer to Jeremiah's prayer to quiet his mind. It is a full discovery of the purposes of God's wrath against the present generation and the purposes of his grace concerning the future generations. Jeremiah knew not how to *sing both of mercy and judgment*, but God here teaches to sing unto him of both. When Jeremiah was ordered to buy the field in Anathoth he hoped that God was about to order the Chaldeans to raise the siege. "No," says God, "the execution of the sentence shall go on; Jerusalem shall be laid in ruins." But, lest Jeremiah should think that his being ordered to buy this field intimated that all the mercy God had in store for his people, after their return, was only that they should have the possession of their own land again, he informs him that that was but a type of those spiritual blessings which should then be abundantly bestowed upon them, unspeakably more valuable than fields and vineyards; in this *word of the Lord* to Jeremiah, we have first as dreadful threatenings and then as precious promises as perhaps any we have in the Old Testament.

I. The ruin of Judah and Jerusalem is here pronounced. 1. God here asserts his own sovereignty and power (*v.* 27): *Behold, I am Jehovah*, a self-existent self-sufficient being; *I am that I am; I am the God of all flesh*, that is, of all mankind. 2. He abides by what he had often said of the destruction of Jerusalem by the king of Babylon (*v.* 28): *I will give this city into his hand, and he shall take it*, *v.* 29. *The Chaldeans shall come and set fire to it*, shall burn it and all the *houses in it*, God's house not excepted, nor the king's either. 3. The reason for these severe proceedings against the city. It is sin that ruins it. They were impudent and daring in sin. They *offered incense to Baal*, not in corners, as men ashamed, but upon the *tops of their houses* (*v.* 29). They did it *to provoke me to anger*, *v.* 29. *They have only provoked me to anger with the works of their hands*, *v.* 30. And again (*v.* 32), *All the evil which they have done was to provoke me to anger.* They resolved to try his jealousy and dare him to his face. "Jerusalem has been *to me a provocation of my anger and fury*," *v.* 31. They had continued provoking God: "They have *done evil before me from their youth*, ever since they were first formed into a people (*v.* 30), witness their murmurings and rebellions in the wilderness." And as for Jerusalem, though it was the *holy city*, it has been *a provocation from the day that they built it, even to this day*, *v.* 31. All contributed to the common guilt, and therefore were justly involved in the common ruin. Not only the *children of Israel*, that had revolted from the temple, but the *children of Judah* too, that still adhered to it. God had again and again called them to repentance, but they rudely turned their back on him. "*I taught them* better manners, *rising up early, in teaching them*, studying to adapt the teaching to their capacities, but all in vain." There was in their idolatries an impious contempt of God; for (*v.* 34) *they set their abominations* (their idols) *in the house which is called by my name, to defile it.* They were guilty of the most unnatural cruelty to their own children; for they *sacrificed them to Moloch*, *v.* 35. They *caused Judah to sin*, *v.* 35. The whole country was infected with the contagious idolatries and iniquities of Jerusalem.

II. The restoration of Judah and Jerusalem is here promised, *v.* 36, &c. God will in judgment remember mercy, and there will a time come, a set time, to favour Zion. This people were now at length brought to despair. When the judgment was threatened at a distance they had no fear; when it attacked them they had no hope. They said concerning the city (*v.* 36), *It shall be delivered into the hand of the king of Babylon*, by *the sword, famine, and pestilence.* Concerning the country they said, with vexation (*v.* 43),

JAMIESON, FAUSSET, BROWN

25. for the city . . .—rather, "though . . . ."

27. Jehovah retorts Jeremiah's own words: I am indeed, as thou sayest (vs. 17), the God and Creator of "all flesh," and "nothing is too hard for Me"; thine own words ought to have taught thee that, though Judea and Jerusalem are given up to the Chaldeans now for the sins of the Jews, yet it will not be *hard* to Me, when I please, to restore the state so that houses and lands therein shall be possessed in safety (vss. 36-44). **29. burn . . . houses upon whose roofs . . . incense unto Baal**—retribution in kind. They *burnt incense to Baal, on the houses,* so the *houses* shall be *burnt* (ch. 19:13). The god of fire was the object of their worship; so fire shall be the instrument of their punishment. **to provoke me**—indicating the *design,* not merely the *event.* They seemed to court God's "anger," and *purposely* to "provoke" Him. **30. have . . . done**—lit., "have been doing"; implying *continuous* action. **only . . . evil . . . only provoked me**—They have been doing *nothing else but* evil; their *sole* aim seems to have been to provoke Me. **their youth**—the time when they were in the wilderness, having just before come into national existence. **31. provocation of mine anger**—lit., *"for* mine anger." CALVIN, therefore, connects these words with those at the end of the verse, "this city has been to me an *object for mine anger* (viz., by reason of the provocations mentioned, vs. 30), etc., that I should remove it . . . ." Thus, there will not be the repetition of the sentiment, vs. 30, as in *English Version;* the *Hebrew* also favors this rendering. However, Jeremiah delights in repetitions. In *English Version* the words, "that I should remove it . . ." stand independently, as the result of what precedes. The time is ripe for taking vengeance on them (II Kings 23:27). **from the day that they built it**—Solomon completed the building of the city; and it was he who, first of the Jewish kings, turned to idolatry. It was originally built by the idolatrous Canaanites. **32. priests . . . prophets**—(Neh. 9:32, 34). Hence, learn, though ministers of God apostatize, we must remain faithful. **33.** (Ch. 2:27; 7:13.) **34.** (Ch. 7:30; 31; Ezek. 8:5-17.) **35. cause . . . pass through . . . fire**—By way of purification, they passed through with bare feet (Lev. 18:21). **Molech**—meaning "king"; the same as *Milcom* (I Kings 11:33). **I commanded . . . not**—This cuts off from the superstitious the plea of a good intention. All "will-worship" exposes to God's wrath (Col. 2:18, 23). **36. And now therefore**—rather, "But now, nevertheless." Notwithstanding that their guilt deserves lasting vengeance, God, for the elect's sake and for His covenant's sake, will, contrary to all that might have been expected, restore them. **ye say, It shall be delivered into . . . king of Babylon**—The reprobate pass from the extreme of self-confidence to that of despair of God's fulfilling His promise of restoring them.

ADAM CLARKE

JOHN GILL:

Verse 25. "And thou hast said to me, O Lord God." Or, "O Lord God, yet thou hast said to me"; notwithstanding this is the case, the country all around is in the hand of the enemy, and the city is as good as delivered up to them, yet thou hast given me such orders, as follows; "buy thee a field for money, and take witnesses"; for though these words were not expressly said to him by the Lord; yet inasmuch as he told him that his uncle's son would come to him, and propose the selling of his field to him; and accordingly did come, agreeably to the word of the Lord; Jeremiah understood it as the will of the Lord, that he should buy it before witnesses; which he did, as before related; "for the city is given into the hand of the Chaldeans"; or rather, "though the city is given"; yet thou hast said so: now by this the prophet suggests, that though he had obeyed the divine order, as he ought to have done, yet there was some difficulty upon his mind: or there were some objections started, by the Jews that were with him, how these things could be reconciled; that he should be ordered to buy a field at such a time as this, and thereby signify that fields and vineyards should be bought and possessed in the land, and yet the city was just going to be surrendered into the hands of the Chaldeans.

Verse 26. "Then came the word of the Lord unto Jeremiah." This is an answer to the prophet's prayer, and particularly to the latter part of it; showing the consistency of the destruction of the city with his purchase of a field, and with God's promise of fields and vineyards being purchased and possessed again.

—*Gill's Commentary*

29. *With the houses, upon whose roofs.* As it is most probable that Baal was the sun, they might have chosen the tops of the houses, which were always flat, with battlements around, to offer incense and sacrifice to him at his rising, and while he was in sight above the horizon.

30. *For the children of Israel and the children of Judah have only done evil.* They have all been transgressors from their earliest history. *For the children of Israel.* The ten tribes. *Have only provoked me to anger with the work of their hands.* They have been sinners beyond all others, being excessive idolaters. Their hands have formed the objects of their worship.

MATTHEW HENRY

It is desolate, without man or beast; there is no relief, there is no remedy. *It is given into the hand of the Chaldeans.* The hope that God gives them of mercy: Though their carcases must fall in captivity, yet their children shall again see this good land and the goodness of God in it. They shall be brought up from their captivity and shall come and settle again in this land, *v.* 37. He had dispersed them, and *driven them into all countries.* Those that fled dispersed themselves; those that fell into the enemies' hands were dispersed by them, in policy, to prevent combinations among them. God's hand was in both. But now God will *gather them out of all the countries whither they were driven,* as he promised in the law (Deut. xxx. 3, 4). Being reformed, and having returned to God, neither their own consciences within nor their enemies without shall be a terror to them. He promises (*v.* 41): *I will plant them in this land assuredly;* they shall here enjoy a holy security and repose, and they shall take root here, shall be *planted in stability.* God will renew his covenant with them, a covenant of grace, the blessings of which are spiritual. It is called an *everlasting covenant* (*v.* 40), not only because God will be for ever faithful to it, but because the consequences of it will be everlasting. For, doubtless, here the promises look further than to Israel according to the flesh, and are sure to all believers. Good Christians may apply them to themselves and plead them with God. *They shall be my people.* He will make them his by working in them all the characters and dispositions of his people. "And, to make them truly, completely, and eternally happy, *I will be their God.*" God will give them a heart to fear him, *v.* 39. That which he requires of those whom he takes into covenant with him as his people is that they reverence his majesty, dread his wrath, stand in awe of his authority, pay homage to him, and give him the glory due unto his name. It is repeated (*v.* 40): *I will put my fear in their hearts,* that is, work in them gracious principles and dispositions, that shall influence and govern their whole conversation. Teachers may put good things into our heads, but it is God only that can put them into our hearts, that can work in us *both to will and to do.* He will effectually provide for their perseverance in grace and the perpetuating of the covenant between himself and them. God will never leave nor forsake them: *I will not turn away from them to do them good.* Earthly princes are fickle, but God's *mercy endures for ever.* God may seem to turn from this people (Isa. liv. 8), but even then he does not turn from doing and designing them good. We have no reason to distrust God's fidelity and constancy, but our own; and therefore it is here promised that God will *give them a heart to fear him for ever* (Prov. xxiii. 17). He will entail a blessing upon their seed, will give them grace to fear him, *for the good of them and of their children after them.* As their departures from God had been to the prejudice of their children, so their adherence to God should be to the advantage of their children. We cannot better consult the good of posterity than by setting up the fear and worship of God in our families. When he punishes them it is with reluctance. *How shall I give thee up, Ephraim?* But, when he restores them he rejoices in doing them good. He is himself a cheerful giver, and therefore loves a cheerful servant. All things shall appear at last so to have been working for the good of the church that it will be said, The governor of the world is entirely taken up with the care of his church. These promises shall as surely be performed as the foregoing threatenings were. *As I have brought all this great evil upon them,* pursuant to divine justice, *so I will bring upon them all this good,* pursuant to the promise, and for the glory of divine mercy. As an earnest of all this, houses and lands shall again fetch a good price in Judah and Jerusalem (*v.* 43, 44): *Fields shall be bought in this land;* here rather than anywhere else. In *the places about Jerusalem, in the cities of Judah* and of Israel, in all parts of the country, *men shall buy fields, and subscribe evidences.* Trade shall revive. Husbandry shall revive. Laws shall again have their due course, for they shall *subscribe evidences and seal them.* This is mentioned to reconcile Jeremiah to his new purchase. Though he had bought a piece of ground and could not go to see it, this was the pledge of many a purchase, and those but faint resemblances of the purchased possessions in the heavenly Canaan, reserved for all those who have God's fear in their hearts.

JAMIESON, FAUSSET, BROWN

37. (*Note,* ch. 16:15.) The "all" countries implies a future restoration of Israel more universal than that from Babylon. **38.** (Ch. 30:22; 24:7.)

39. one heart–all seeking the Lord *with one accord,* in contrast to their state when only scattered individuals sought Him (Ezek. 11:19, 20; Zeph. 3:9). **for . . . good of them**–(Ps. 34:12-15). **40.** (Ch. 31: 31, 33; Isa. 55:3.) **not depart from me**–never yet fully realized as to the Israelites. **I will not turn away from them . . . good**–(Isa. 30:21). Jehovah compares Himself to a sedulous preceptor following his pupils everywhere to direct their words, gestures. **put my fear in . . . hearts . . . not depart from me**–Both the conversion and perseverance of the saints are the work of God alone, by the operation of the Holy Spirit.

41. rejoice over them–(Deut. 30:9; Isa. 62:5; 65:19; Zeph. 3:17). **plant . . . assuredly**–rather, in stability, i.e., permanently, for ever (ch. 24:6; Amos 9:15). **42.** (Ch. 31:28.) The restoration from Babylon was only a slight foretaste of the grace to be expected by Israel at last through Christ.

43. (Vs. 15.) **whereof ye say, It is desolate**–(ch. 33:10). **44.** Referring to the forms of contract (vss. 10-12). **Benjamin**–specified as Anathoth; Jeremiah's place of residence where the field lay (vs. 8), was in it.

ADAM CLARKE

37. *Behold, I will gather them out of all countries.* A promise often repeated. See chap. xxix. 14 and chap. xxxi. 8, etc.

44. *Men shall buy fields for money.* This is a reference to the symbolical purchase mentioned at the beginning of the chapter; *that* may be considered by them as a sure sign of their restoration, not only to the same land, but to their respective inheritances in that land. **This the power of God could alone perform.**

E. H. PLUMPTRE:

Verse 39. "I will give them one heart, and one way." The previous verse has described the restoration of Israel in the old familiar all-inclusive terms—"They shall be my people, and I will be their God" (Exod. 6:7; Deut. 14:2; Hos. 2:23). Here a new feature is added. The prophet, in his vision of the future, in place of the discords of the present—some serving Jehovah, and some Baal and Molech; some urging submission to Babylon, and some intriguing with Egypt—sees a unity in faith showing itself in unity of action. The hope of Jeremiah has never yet been realized, but it has appeared as with a transfigured glory in the prayer of the Christ for His people that they "all may be one," even as He and the Father are one (John 17:21–23), in the prayer of the Apostle, that all might be joined together "in the unity of the faith" (Eph. 4:13). And that prayer also waits for its fulfillment, and receives only partial and (to use Bacon's phrase) "germinant" accomplishments. "For ever" represents the Hebrew *all the days.*

Verse 40. "I will make an everlasting covenant." The "covenant" thus promised is, it must be remembered, identical with that of 31:31—the "new covenant," which shall never wax old and decay, but shall abide forever. "My fear" is identified with "the fear of the Lord," which is "the beginning of wisdom." The curse of Israel had been that they had been without that fear to restrain them from evil, and that the mere dread of punishment had proved powerless to supply its place.

Verse 41. "I will plant them in this land assuredly." Literally, *in truth,* as in 1 Sam. 12:24, and elsewhere. By some interpreters the words have been referred to the stability of possession implied in the promise, but it is better to see in them an attestation of the faithfulness of the Promiser. In meaning, as in form, the word corresponds closely with the frequent "Amen," "Verily, verily," in our Lord's teaching.

—*Ellicott's Commentary on the Whole Bible*

MATTHEW HENRY

CHAPTER 33

Verses 1–9

I. The date of this comfortable prophecy was after that in the foregoing chapter, when things were still growing worse and worse; it was *the second time. God speaketh once, yea, twice*, for the encouragement of his people. We are not only so disobedient that we have need of *precept upon precept* to bring us to our duty, but so distrustful that we have need of promise upon promise to bring us to our comfort. This word, as the former, *came to Jeremiah* when *he was in prison*.

II. The prophecy itself.

1. Who it is that secures this comfort to them (*v.* 2): It is *the Lord, the maker thereof, the Lord that framed it*. He is the maker and former of heaven and earth. He is the maker and former of Jerusalem, of Zion, built them at first, and therefore can rebuild them—built them for his own praise, and therefore *will*. He is the maker and former of this promise; he has laid the scheme for Jerusalem's restoration, and he that has made the promise will make it good; for Jehovah *is his name*, a God giving being to his promises by the performance of them, known by that name (Exod. vi. 3), a perfecting God. When the heavens and the earth were finished, then, and not till then, the Creator is called *Jehovah*, Gen. ii. 4.

2. How this comfort must be obtained—by prayer (*v.* 3): *Call upon me, and I will answer thee.* Christ himself must *ask, and it shall be given him*, Ps. ii. 8. *I will show thee great and mighty things, hidden things, which*, though in part discovered already, yet *thou knowest not*. Promises are given, not to supersede, but to quicken and encourage prayer. See Ezek. xxxvi. 37.

3. The condition of Jerusalem made it necessary that such comforts as these should be provided for it (*v.* 4, 5): *The houses of this city*, not excepting those *of the kings of Judah, are thrown down by the mounts*, or engines of battery, *and by the sword*, or axes, or hammers. The strongest stateliest houses were levelled with the ground. Those that *came to fight with the Chaldeans* did more hurt than good, provoked the enemy to be more fierce and furious in their assaults, so that the houses in Jerusalem were filled *with the dead bodies of men*. God says that they were such as he had *slain in his anger*, for the enemies' sword was his sword. But, it seems, the men that were slain had distinguished themselves by their wickedness, the very men *for whose wickedness* God did now *hide himself from this city*.

4. The blessings which God has in store for Judah and Jerusalem, such as will redress all their grievances. God will provide for the healing, though the disease was thought mortal and incurable, *ch.* viii. 22. "*The whole head is sick, and the whole heart faint* (Isa. i. 5); but (*v.* 6) *I will bring it health and cure;* I will prevent the death, remove the sickness, and set all to rights again," *ch.* xxx. 17. The sin of Jerusalem was the sickness of it (Isa. i. 6); its reformation therefore will be its recovery. "*I will reveal unto them the abundance of peace and truth.*" *Peace* stands here for all good; peace and the true religion, peace and the true worship of God, in opposition to the many falsehoods and deceits by which they had been led away from God. We may apply it more generally. Peace and truth are the great subject-matter of divine revelation. These promises here lead us to the gospel of Christ, and in that God has revealed to us *peace and truth*—truth to direct us, peace to make us easy. *Grace and truth*, and abundance of both, *come by Jesus Christ*. Peace and truth are the life of the soul, and Christ *came that we might have* that *life, and might have it more abundantly*. Christ rules by the power of truth (John xviii. 37) and by it he gives *abundance of peace*, Ps. lxxii. 7; lxxxv. 10. The divine revelation of peace and truth brings health and cure to all those that by faith receive it. Are they scattered and enslaved, and is their nation laid in ruins? "*I will cause their captivity to return* (*v.* 7), both that of Israel and that of Judah." Is sin the procuring cause of all their troubles? That shall be pardoned and subdued, and so the root of the judgments shall be killed, *v.* 8. As those that were ceremonially unclean, and were therefore shut out from the tabernacle, when they were sprinkled with the *water of purification* had liberty of access to it again, so had they to their own land, and the privileges of it, when God had *cleansed them from their iniquities*. Have both their sins and their sufferings turned to the dishonour of God? Their reformation and restoration shall redound as much to his praise, *v.* 9. The neighbouring nations shall look upon the growing greatness of the Jewish nation as really formidable, and shall be afraid of making them their enemies. When the church is *fair as the moon*, and *clear as the sun*, she is *terrible as an army with banners*.

JAMIESON, FAUSSET, BROWN

CHAPTER 33

Vss. 1-26. PROPHECY OF THE RESTORATION FROM BABYLON, AND OF MESSIAH AS KING AND PRIEST. **1. shut up**–(ch. 32: 2, 3; II Tim. 2:9). Though Jeremiah was shut up in bondage, the word of God was "not bound."

2. maker thereof–rather, the doer of it, viz., that which Jeremiah is about to prophesy, the restoration of Israel, an act which is thought now impossible, but which the Almighty will effect. **formed it**–viz., Jerusalem (ch. 32:44) [CALVIN]. Rather, that formed, i.e., moulds *His purpose* into due shape for execution (Isa. 37:26). **Lord . . . his name**–(Exod. 3:14, 15).

3. Call . . . I will answer–(ch. 29:12; Ps. 91:15). Jeremiah, as the representative of the people of God, is urged by God to pray for that which God has determined to grant; viz., the restoration. God's promises are not to slacken, but to quicken the prayers of His people (Ps. 132: 13, 17; Isa. 62:6, 7). **mighty things**–*Hebrew*, "inaccessible things," i.e., incredible, hard to man's understanding [MAURER], viz., the restoration of the Jews, an event despaired of. "Hidden," or "recondite" [PISCATOR]. **thou knowest not**–Yet God had revealed those things to Jeremiah, but the unbelief of the people in rejecting the grace of God had caused him to forget God's promise, as though the case of the people admitted of no remedy. **4. houses . . . thrown down by the mounts**–viz., by the missiles cast from the besiegers' *mounds* (ch. 32:24); "and by the sword" follows properly, as, after missiles had prepared the way, the foe next advanced to close quarters "with the sword." **5. They**–the Jews; the defenders of the "houses" (vs. 4), "come forward to fight with the Chaldeans," who burst into the city through the "thrown-down houses," but all the effect that they produce "is, to fill them (the houses) with their own "dead bodies."

6. (Ch. 30:17.) The answer to Jeremiah's mournful question (ch. 8:22). **cure**–lit., the long linen bandage employed in dressing wounds.

truth–i.e., stability; I will bring forth for them abundant and *permanent* peace, i.e., prosperity.

7. cause . . . to return–i.e., reverse (vs. 11; ch. 32:44). The specification, both of "Judah" and "Israel," can only apply fully to the future restoration. **as at the first**–(Isa. 1:26). **8. cleanse**–(Ezek. 36:25; Zech. 13:1; Heb. 9:13, 14). Alluding to the legal rites of purification. **all their iniquity . . . all their iniquities**–both the *principle* of sin within, and its outward manifestations in *acts*. The repetition is in order that the Jews may consider how great is the grace of God in not merely *pardoning* (as to the punishment), but also *cleansing* them (as to the pollution of guilt); not merely one iniquity, but *all* (Mic. 7:18). **9. it**–the city. **a name . . . a praise**–(ch. 13:11; Isa. 62:7). **them**–the inhabitants of Jerusalem. **they shall fear . . . for all the goodness**–(Ps. 130:4). The Gentiles shall be led to "fear" God by the proofs of His power displayed in behalf of the Jews; the ungodly among them shall "tremble" for fear of God's judgments on them; the penitent shall reverentially fear and be converted to Him (Ps. 102:15; Isa. 60:3).

ADAM CLARKE

CHAPTER 33

1. *Moreover the word of the Lord.* This was in the eleventh year of the reign of Zedekiah, Jeremiah being still shut up in prison. But he was now *in the court of the prison*, where the elders and the king's officers, etc., might consult him with the greater ease. For they continued to inquire, foolishly thinking that if he would but prophesy good things these must come; or that he had sufficient power with God to induce Him to alter His mind—destroy the Chaldeans, and deliver the city.

2. *Thus saith the Lord the maker thereof.* The Doer of it. That is, He who is to perform that which He is now about to promise.

3. *Call unto me, and I will answer thee.* To Me alone it belongs to reveal what is future, and the stupendous things which are now coming are known only to myself.

4. *Thus saith the Lord.* This is a new confirmation of what has already been said, viz., The city shall fall, a number of the inhabitants shall perish, the rest shall be carried into captivity; but the nation shall be preserved, and the people return from their captivity.

7. *The captivity of Judah and the captivity of Israel.* This must respect the latter times, for the ten tribes did not return with the Jews at the termination of the seventy years.

8. *I will cleanse them.* These promises of pardon and holiness must be referred to their state under the gospel, when they shall have received Jesus as the promised Messiah.

MATTHEW HENRY

Verses 10–16

A further prediction of the happy state of Judah and Jerusalem after their glorious return out of captivity, issuing gloriously at length in the kingdom of the Messiah.

I. It is promised that the people who were long in sorrow shall again be filled with joy. Everyone concluded now that the country would lie for ever desolate, that *no beasts* would be found in the land of Judah, no inhabitant *in the streets of Jerusalem* (*v.* 10); but, though weeping may endure for a time, joy will return. There shall be common joy there, *the voice of the bridegroom and the voice of the bride;* marriages shall again be celebrated, as formerly, with songs. There shall be religious joy there; temple-songs shall be revived, *the Lord's songs,* which they could not *sing in a strange land.* They shall praise him both as *the Lord of hosts* and as the God who *is good* and whose *mercy endures for ever.* This, though a song of old, yet, being sung upon this fresh occasion, will be a new song. We find this literally fulfilled at their return out of Babylon, Ezra iii. 11. All the sacrifices were intended for the praise of God, but this seems to be meant of the spiritual sacrifices of humble adorations and joyful thanksgivings, *the calves of our lips* (Hos. xiv. 2), which *shall please the Lord better than an ox or bullock.*

II. It is promised that the country, which had lain long depopulated, shall be replenished and stocked again. *In all the cities of Judah and Benjamin there shall be a habitation of shepherds, v.* 12, 13. The country, after their return, shall not be a habitation of beggars, who have nothing, but of shepherds and husbandmen. The seed of Jacob, in their beginning, gloried in this, that they were shepherds (Gen. xlvii. 3), and so they shall now be again, giving themselves wholly to that innocent employment, *causing their flocks to lie down* (*v.* 12) and to *pass under the hands of him that telleth them* (*v.* 13); flocks to number them, that they may know if any be missing. Now because it seemed incredible that a people, reduced as now they were, should ever recover such a degree of peace and plenty as this, here is subjoined a general ratification of these promises (*v.* 14): *I will perform that good thing which I have promised.*

III. To crown all these blessings which God has in store for them, here is a promise of the Messiah, and of that everlasting righteousness which he should bring in (*v.* 15, 16), and probably this is *that good thing,* that great good thing, which in the latter days, days that were yet to come, God would perform, as he had promised to Judah and Israel, and to which their return out of captivity and their settlement again in their own land was preparatory. *From the captivity to Christ* is one of the famous periods, Matt. i. 17. This promise of the Messiah we had before (*ch.* xxiii. 5, 6), and there it came in as a confirmation of the promise of the shepherds whom God would set over them, which would make one think that the promise here concerning the shepherds and their flocks, which introduces it, is to be understood figuratively. Christ is here prophesied, 1. As a rightful King. He is a *branch of righteousness,* not a usurper, for he *grows up unto David.* 2. As a righteous king, righteous in enacting laws, waging wars, and giving judgment, righteous in vindicating those that suffer wrong and punishing those that do wrong: *He shall execute judgment and righteousness in the land.* 3. As a king that shall protect his subjects from all injury. By him *Judah shall be saved* from wrath and the curse, and, being so saved, *Jerusalem shall dwell safely,* quiet from the fear of evil, and enjoying serenity of mind, in dependence upon this prince of their peace. 4. As a king that shall be praised by his subjects: "*This is the name whereby they shall call him*" (so the Chaldee reads it, the Syriac, and vulgar Latin); "this name of his they shall celebrate and triumph in, and by this name they shall call upon him." The city is called *The Lord our righteousness,* because they glory in Jehovah as their righteousness. That which was before said to be the name of Christ is here made the name of Jerusalem, the city of the Messiah, the church of Christ. He it is that imparts righteousness to her, for he is *made of God to us righteousness,* and she, by bearing that name, professes to have her whole righteousness, not from herself, but from him.

Verses 17–26

Three of God's covenants, that of royalty with David and his seed, that of the priesthood with Aaron and his seed, and that with Abraham and his seed, seemed to be all broken and lost while the captivity lasted; but it is here promised that the true intents and meaning of them shall be abundantly answered in the New Testament blessings, typified by those conferred on the Jews after their return out of cap-

JAMIESON, FAUSSET, BROWN

10. ye say . . . desolate–(ch. 32:43).

11. (Ch. 7:34; 16:9.) **Praise the Lord . . .**–the words of Psalm 136:1, which were actually used by the Jews at their restoration (Ezra 3:11). **sacrifice of praise**–(Ps. 107:22; 116: 17). This shall continue when all other sacrifices shall be at an end.

12. habitation of shepherds . . . flocks–in contrast to vs. 10, "without man . . . *inhabitant* . . . without *beast*" (ch. 32:43; cf. ch. 31: 24; 50:19; Isa. 65:10). **13. pass . . . under . . . hands of him that telleth them**–Shepherds, in sending forth and bringing back their sheep to the folds, *count* them by striking each as it passes with a rod, implying the shepherd's provident care that not one should be lost (Lev. 27:32; Mic. 7:14; cf. John 10: 28, 29; 17:12). **14. perform**–"I will make to *rise*"; God's promise having for a time seemed to *lie* dead and abortive [CALVIN].

15. Repeated from ch. 23: 5. **the land**–the Holy Land: Israel and Judah (ch. 23:6).

16. Jerusalem–In ch. 23:6, instead of this, it is "Israel." *"The name"* in the *Hebrew* has here to be supplied from that passage; and for "he" (Messiah, the antitypical "Israel"), the antecedent there (Isa. 49:3), we have "she" here, i.e., Jerusalem. She is called by the same name as Messiah, "The LORD our Righteousness," by virtue of the mystical oneness between her (as the literal representative of the spiritual Church) and her Lord and Husband. Thus, whatever belongs to the Head belongs also to the members (Eph. 5:30, 32). Hence, the Church is called "Christ" (Rom. 16:7; I Cor. 12:12). The Church hereby professes to draw all her righteousness from Christ (Isa. 45:24, 25). It is for the sake of Jerusalem, literal and spiritual, that God the Father gives this name (*Jehovah, Tsidkenu,* "The Lord our Righteousness") to Christ.

ADAM CLARKE

11. *The voice of them that shall say, Praise the Lord of hosts.* That is, the voice of the Levites in the sacred service, intimating that the Temple should be rebuilt and the public service restored.

12. *An habitation of shepherds.* See chap. xxxi. 12.

14. *Behold, the days come.* See chap. xxiii. 5 and xxxi. 31. *That good thing which I have promised.* By My prophets; for those who have predicted the Captivity have also foretold its conclusion, though not in such express terms as Jeremiah did. See Hos. i. 10, etc.; ii. 15, etc.; vi. 11, etc.; Amos ix. 14, etc.; and Jer. iii. 12. etc. The end of the Captivity has been foretold by Micah, chap. vii. 9, etc.; Zephaniah, iii. 10, etc.; and by Jeremiah, chap. xvi. 15; xxiii. 3; xxix. 10; xxxii. 37.

16. *And this is the name wherewith she shall be called, The Lord our righteousness.* See what has been said on chap. xxiii. 6, which is generally supposed to be a strictly parallel passage; but they are very different, and I doubt whether they mean exactly the same thing. As to our translation here, it is ignorant, and almost impious; it says that Jerusalem, for that is the antecedent, shall be called "The Lord our righteousness." I will give the original, "And this One who shall call to her is the Lord our Justification"; that is, the salvation of the Jews shall take place when Jesus Christ is proclaimed to them as their Justifier, and they receive Him as such.

MATTHEW HENRY

tivity.

I. The covenant of royalty shall have full accomplishment in the kingdom of Christ, the Son of David, *v.* 17. The throne of Israel was overturned in the captivity; there was not *a man to sit on the throne of Israel.* After their return the house of David made a figure again; but it is in the Messiah that this promise is performed that *David shall never want a man to sit on the throne of Israel.* For as long as Christ Jesus sits on the right hand of the throne of God, glorified head over all things, as long as he is *King upon the holy hill of Zion,* David does not want a successor, nor is the covenant with him broken. *The Lord God shall give him the throne of his father David and he shall reign over the house of Jacob for ever,* Luke i. 32, 33. It is promised that the covenant with David shall be as firm as the ordinances of heaven. There is a covenant of nature here called *a covenant of the day and the night* (*v.* 20, 25), because this is one of the articles of it, That there shall be *day and night in their season.* God divided between the light and the darkness, and established a government to each, that *the sun* should *rule by day* and *the moon and stars by night* (Gen. i. 4, 5, 16). The *morning and* the *evening* have both of them their regular *outgoings* (Ps. lxv. 8); the *day-spring knows its place, knows its time,* and keeps both, so do *the shadows of the evening*; and, while the world stands, this course shall not be altered, this covenant shall not be broken. Thus firm shall the covenant of redemption be with the Redeemer—God's servant, but David our King, *v.* 21. Christ shall have a church on earth to the world's end; till time and day shall be no more. Christ's *kingdom is an everlasting kingdom*; and when *the end cometh,* and not till then, it *shall be delivered up to God,* even *the Father.* But the condition of it in this world shall be intermixed, prosperity and adversity succeeding each other, as day and night. Though the sun will set to-night, it will rise again tomorrow morning, whether we live to see it or no, so sure we may be that, though the kingdom of the Redeemer in the world may for a time be clouded by corruptions and persecutions, yet it will shine forth again in the time appointed. *The seed of David* shall be as numerous *as the host of heaven,* that is, the spiritual seed of the Messiah, born to him by the efficacy of his gospel and his Spirit working with it. Christ's seed are not, as David's were, his successors, but his subjects; yet the day is coming when they also shall reign with him (*v.* 22).

II. The covenant of priesthood shall be secured, and the promises of that also shall have their full accomplishment. During the captivity there was no altar, no temple service, for the priests to attend upon; but this also shall revive. Immediately upon their coming back to Jerusalem there were priests and Levites ready *to offer burnt-offerings* and to *do sacrifice continually* (Ezra iii. 2, 3), as is here promised, *v.* 18. But that priesthood soon grew corrupt; *the covenant of Levi was profaned* (as appears Mal. ii. 8), and in the destruction of Jerusalem by the Romans it came to a final period. The priesthood of Christ supersedes that of Aaron, and is the substance of that shadow. While that great *high priest of our profession* is always appearing *in the presence of God for us,* it may truly be said that *the Levites do not want a man before God to offer continually,* Heb. vii. 3, 17. He is a priest for ever. While there are faithful ministers to preside in religious assemblies, and to offer up the spiritual sacrifices of prayer and praise, *the priests, the Levites,* do not want successors, and such as *have obtained a more excellent ministry.* The apostle makes those that preach the gospel to come in the room of those that served at the altar, 1 Cor. ix. 13, 14. All true believers are *a holy priesthood, a royal priesthood* (1 Pet. ii. 5, 9), who are *made to our God kings and priests* (Rev. i. 6); they *offer up spiritual sacrifices, acceptable to God,* and themselves, in the first place, *living sacrifices.* Of these Levites this promise must be understood (*v.* 22), that they shall be as numerous *as the sand of the sea,* for all God's spiritual Israel are spiritual priests, Rev. v. 9, 10; vii. 9, 15.

III. The covenant of peculiarity likewise shall be secured and the promises of that covenant shall have their full accomplishment in the gospel Israel. This covenant was looked upon as broken during the captivity, *v.* 24. Either the enemies of Israel, or the unbelieving Israelites themselves, have broken covenant with God, as if he had not dealt faithfully with them. "*Thus have they despised my people,* that is, despised the privilege of being my people as if it were a privilege of no value at all." The covenant stands notwithstanding, as firm as that with day and night; sooner will God suffer day and night to cease than he will *cast away the seed of Jacob.* This cannot refer to the seed of Jacob according to the flesh, for they are cast away, but to the Christian church, in which

JAMIESON, FAUSSET, BROWN

17. The promises of perpetuity of the throne of David fulfilled in Messiah, the son of David (II Sam. 7:16; I Kings 2:4; Ps. 89:4, 29, 36; cf. Luke 1: 32, 33).

20. covenant of the day—i.e., covenant *with* the day: answering to "covenant *with* David" (vs. 21, also vs. 25, "*with* day"; cf. ch. 31:35, 36; Lev. 26:42; Ps. 89:34, 37).

18. Messiah's literal priesthood (Heb. 7:17, 21, 24-28), and His followers' spiritual priesthood and sacrifices (vs. 11; Rom. 12:1; 15:16; I Pet. 2:5, 9; Rev. 1:6), shall never cease, according to the *covenant* with Levi, broken by the priests, but fulfilled by Messiah (Num. 25:12, 13; Mal. 2:4, 5, 8).

22. (Gen. 15:5; 22:17.) The blessing there promised belonged to *all* the tribes; here it is restricted to the family of David and the tribe of Levi, because it was on these that the welfare of the whole people rested. When the kingdom and priesthood flourish in the person of Messiah, the whole nation shall temporally and spiritually prosper.

24. this people—certain of the Jews, especially those who spoke with Jeremiah in the court of the prison (ch. 32:12; 38:1). **the two families**—Judah and Israel. **before them**—in their judgment. They suppose that I have utterly cast off Israel so as to be no more a nation. The expression, "*My* people," of itself, shows God has not cast off Israel for ever.

ADAM CLARKE

KEIL-DELITZSCH :

Verse 20f. "If ye shall break my covenant with the day . . . then also will my covenant with David . . . be broken." This *if* betokens the impossible; man cannot alter the arrangement in nature for the regular alternation of day and night. These are in apposition, "my covenant the day—the night," for "my covenant with regard to the day and the night, which is this, that day and night shall return at their appointed times." These divine arrangements in nature are called a *covenant*; because God, after the flood, gave a pledge that they should uninterruptedly continue, in a covenant made with the human race (cf. Gen. 9:9 with 8:22). As this covenant of nature cannot be broken by men, so also the covenant of grace of the Lord with David and the Levites cannot be broken, i.e. annulled. The covenant with David consisted in the promise that his kingdom should endure for ever (see v. 17); that with the Levites, in the eternal possession of the right to the priesthood. The institution of the priesthood is certainly not represented in the law as a covenant; it consisted merely in the choice of Aaron and his sons as priests by God (Ex. 28:1). But, inasmuch as they were thereby brought into a peculiar relation to the Lord, and thus had vouchsafed to them not merely privileges and promises, but also had laid on them duties, the fulfillment of which was a condition of receiving the privileges, this relation might be called a covenant; and indeed, in Num. 25:11ff., the promise given to Phinehas, that he should have the priesthood as an eternal possession, is called a covenant of peace and an eternal covenant of priesthood.

—*Commentary on the Old Testament*

18. *Neither shall the priests the Levites want a man.* This is a repetition of the promise made to Phinehas, Num. xxv. 13.

22. *So will I multiply the seed of David.* This must be understood of the spiritual David, Jesus Christ, and His progeny, genuine Christians. The two families which God chose for the priesthood, that of Aaron and Phinehas, or, on its being taken away from him, that of Ithamar, 1 Sam. ii. 35, are both extinct. Nor has the office of high priest, or priest of any kind offering sacrifice, been exercised among the Jews for nearly eighteen hundred years. Therefore what is said here of the priesthood must refer to the spiritual priesthood, at the head of which is Jesus Christ.

MATTHEW HENRY

all these promises were to be lodged, as appears by the apostle's discourse, Rom. xi. 1, &c. Christianity shall continue in the dominion of Christ, and the subjection of Christians to him, till day and night come to an end. *I will cause their captivity to return;* and, having brought them back, *I will have mercy on them.* To whom this promise refers appears Gal. vi. 16, where all that *walk according to the gospel rule* are made to be the *Israel of God*, on whom *peace and mercy* shall be.

JAMIESON, FAUSSET, BROWN

25. (Ch. 31:35, 36; Gen. 8:22; Ps. 74:16, 17.) I who have established the laws of nature am the same God who has made a covenant with the Church. **26. Isaac**—(Ps. 105: 9; Amos 7:9, 16).

ADAM CLARKE

MATTHEW HENRY — CHAPTER 34

Verses 1–7

This prophecy concerning Zedekiah was delivered to Jeremiah, and by him to the parties concerned, before he was shut up in the prison, *ch.* xxxii. 4.

I. This message was sent to Zedekiah *when the king of Babylon*, with all his forces, *fought against Jerusalem and the cities thereof* (*v.* 1), designing to destroy them. The cities that now remained, and yet held out, are named (*v.* 7), *Lachish and Azekah.* This intimates that things were now brought to the last extremity, and yet Zedekiah obstinately stood it out.

II. The message was sent to him. He is told that which he had been often told before, that the city shall be taken by the Chaldeans *and burnt with fire* (*v.* 2), that he shall be made a prisoner, brought before Nebuchadnezzar, and be carried away captive into Babylon (*v.* 3); yet Ezekiel prophesied that he *should not see Babylon*; nor did he, for his eyes were put out, Ezek. xii. 13. He shall die a captive, but *not by the sword*; he *shall die in peace*, *v.* 5. What evil he had *done in the sight of the Lord* he repented of in his captivity, and, God being reconciled to him, he might truly be said to *die in peace*. A man may die in a prison and yet *die in peace*. His afflictions wrought such a change in him that his death was looked upon as a great loss. It is better to live and die penitent in a prison than to live and die impenitent in a palace. *They will lament thee, saying, Ah lord!* an honour which his brother Jehoiakim had not, *ch.* xxii. 18.

III. Jeremiah's faithfulness in delivering this message. Though he knew it might prove, as indeed it did, dangerous to himself (for he was imprisoned for it), yet he *spoke all these words to Zedekiah*, *v.* 6.

Verses 8–22

Another prophecy upon a particular occasion.

I. When Jerusalem was closely besieged by the Chaldean army the princes and people agreed upon a reformation concerning their servants. The law of God was very express, that those of their own nation should not be held in servitude above seven years, but, after they had served one apprenticeship, they should have their liberty; though they had sold themselves for the payment of their debts, or though they were *sold by the judges* for the punishment of their crimes. Those of other nations taken in war, or bought with money, might be held in perpetual slavery, but their brethren must serve but for seven years. This God calls the covenant that he had made with them when he *brought them out of the land of Egypt*, *v.* 13, 14. This was the first of the judicial laws which God gave them (Exod. xxi. 2). God had brought them out of slavery in Egypt, and he would have them thus to express their grateful sense of that favour, by letting those go to whom their houses were *houses of bondage*, as Egypt had been to their forefathers. God's compassions towards us should engage our compassions towards our brethren; we must release as we are released. This law they and their fathers had broken. Their worldly profit swayed more with them than God's covenant. When their servants had lived seven years with them they understood their business better than they did, and therefore they would by no means part with them. *Your fathers hearkened not to me* in this matter (*v.* 14), and they thought they might do it because their fathers did it. For this sin of theirs, and their fathers, God now brought them into servitude, and justly. When they were besieged by the Chaldeans, they, being told of their fault in this matter, immediately reformed, and let go all their servants that were entitled to their freedom, as Pharaoh, when the plague was upon him, consented to *let the people go*. The prophets admonished them concerning their sin. From them they heard that they should let their Hebrew servants *go free*, *v.* 10. The *king*, and the *princes*, and *all the people*, agreed to *let go their servants*. The people could not for shame but follow. They bound themselves by a solemn oath and covenant that they would do this, whereby they engaged themselves to God and one another. This covenant was made in a sacred place, *made before me, in the house which is called by my name* (*v.* 15), in the presence of God. It was ratified

JAMIESON, FAUSSET, BROWN — CHAPTER 34

Vss. 1-22. Captivity of Zedekiah and the People Foretold for Their Disobedience and Perfidy. The prophecy (vss. 1-7) as to Zedekiah is an amplification of that in ch. 32:1-5, in consequence of which Jeremiah was then shut up in the court of the prison. The prophecy (vss. 8-22) refers to the Jews, who, afraid of the capture of the city, had, in obedience to the law, granted freedom to their servants at the end of seven years, but on the intermission of the siege forced them back into bondage. **1. Jerusalem and . . . all the cities thereof**—(*Note,* ch. 19:15). It was amazing blindness in the king, that, in such a desperate position, he should reject admonition. **3.** (Ch. 32:4.) **4, 5.** Mitigation of Zedekiah's punishment. **the burnings of thy fathers**—Thy funeral shall be honored with the same burning of aromatic spices as there was at the funerals of thy fathers (II Chron. 16:14; 21:19). The honors here mentioned were denied to Jehoiakim (ch. 22:18). **Ah, lord!**—The Hebrews in their chronology (Sederolam) mention the wailing used over him, "Alas! King Zedekiah is dead, drinking the dregs (i.e., paying the penalty for the sins) of former ages." **7. these . . . retained**—alone (cf. II Chron. 11:5,9).

8. By the law a Hebrew, after having been a bond-servant for six years, on the seventh was to be let go free (Exod. 21:22; Deut. 15:12). **Zedekiah made a covenant**—with solemn ceremonial in the temple (vss. 15, 18, 19). **them**—bond-servants (vs. 9). **9. none . . . serve himself of a Jew**—(Lev. 25:39-46). **11.** During the interruption of the siege by Pharaoh-hophra (cf. vss. 21, 22, with ch. 37:5-10), the Jews reduced their servants to bondage again. **13.** The last year of Zedekiah was the sabbatical year. How just the retribution, that they who, against God's law and their own covenant, enslaved their brethren, should be doomed to bondage themselves: and that the bond-servants should enjoy the sabbatical freedom at the hands of the foe (ch. 52:16) which their own countrymen denied them!

14. At the end of seven years—i.e., not on the *eighth* year, but within the limit of the seventh year, not later than the end of the seventh year (Exod. 21:2; 23:10; Deut. 15:12). So "at the end of three years" (Deut. 14:28; II Kings 18:10), and "*after three days,* I will rise again" (Matt. 27:63), i.e., on the *third day* (cf. Matt. 27:64).

15. in the house . . . called by my name—the usual place of making such covenants (II Kings 23:3; cf. I Kings 8:31; Neh. 10:29).

ADAM CLARKE — CHAPTER 34

1. *The word which came unto Jeremiah.* This discourse was delivered in the tenth year of the reign of Zedekiah. The chapter contains two discourses; one, vv. 1-7, which concerns the taking of the city, and Zedekiah's captivity and death; the other, vv. 8-22, which is an invective against the inhabitants of Jerusalem for having Hebrew male and female slaves. These, having been manumitted at the instance of the prophet, were afterwards brought back by their old masters, and put in the same thraldom; for which God threatens them with severe judgments.

2. *He shall burn it with fire.* This was a newly added circumstance.

3. *Thou shalt not escape.* This, however, he had attempted, but was taken in his flight. See chap. xxxix. 4 and lii. 7, etc.

5. *Thou shalt die in peace.* You shall not die a violent death; and at your death you shall have all those funereal solemnities which were usual at the demise of kings. See 2 Chron. xvi. 14.

6. *Spake all these words unto Zedekiah.* He delivered this message at the hazard of his life. Jeremiah feared God, and had no other fear.

7. *Against Lachish, and against Azekah.* These were two cities of Judah of considerable importance; they had been strongly fortified by Rehoboam, 2 Chron. xi. 9-11; xxxii. 9.

8. *The word that came unto Jeremiah.* Here the second discourse begins, which was delivered probably a short time, even a few days, after the former. *Zedekiah had made a covenant.* We find no account elsewhere of this covenant: "Every man should let his manservant, and . . . his maidservant . . . go free"; i.e., as we learn from v. 14, on the sabbatical year, for the seventh year was the year of release. See Deut. xv. 12.

11. *But afterward they turned.* They had agreed to manumit them at the end of the seventh year; but when the seventh year was ended, they recalled their engagement, and detained their servants.

MATTHEW HENRY

by a significant sign; they *cut a calf in two, and passed between the parts thereof* (*v.* 18, 19) with this dreadful imprecation, "Let us be in like manner cut asunder if we do not perform what we now promise." They conformed themselves herein to the command of God and *let their servants go*, though the city was besieged and they could very ill spare them. Thus they did *right in God's sight*, *v.* 15.

II. When there was some hope that the siege was raised and the danger over they undid the good they had done, and forced the servants they had released into their services again. The *king of Babylon's army* had now *gone up from them*, *v.* 21. Pharaoh was bringing an army of Egyptians to oppose the progress of the king of Babylon's victories, and the Chaldeans raised the siege for a time, *ch.* xxxvii. 5. It was especially an affront to God; in doing this they *polluted his name*, *v.* 16.

III. For this treacherous dealing with God they are here severely threatened. *Be not deceived; God is not mocked.* Those that think to put a cheat upon God by a partial temporary reformation, will put the greatest cheat upon their own souls. Since they had not given liberty to their servants to go where they pleased, God would give all his judgments liberty to take their course (*v.* 17): *You have not proclaimed liberty to your servants. "Therefore I will proclaim a liberty for you;* I will discharge you from my service, and put you out of my protection, which those forfeit that withdraw from their allegiance. You shall have liberty to choose which of these judgments you will be cut off by, *sword, famine, or pestilence.*" Since they had brought their servants back into confinement in their houses, God would *make them to be removed into all the kingdoms of the earth*, where they should live in servitude. "*I will make the men which have transgressed my covenant as the calf which they cut in twain;* I will divide them asunder as they divided it asunder." They had all dealt treacherously with God, and therefore shall all be involved in the common ruin without exception, *v.* 19. Since they had emboldened themselves in returning to their sin, contrary to their covenant, by the retreat of the Chaldean army from them, God would therefore bring it upon them again: "They have now *gone up from you*, and your fright is over for the present, but I *will command them* to face about as they were; they shall *return to this city, and take it and burn it*," *v.* 22. If we repent of the good we had purposed, God will repent of the good he had purposed. *With the froward thou wilt show thyself froward.*

JAMIESON, FAUSSET, BROWN

18. passed between the parts thereof—The contracting parties in the "covenant" (not here the *law* in general, but their *covenant* made before God in His house to emancipate their slaves, vss. 8, 9) passed through the parts of the animal cut in two, implying that they prayed so to be cut in sunder (Matt. 24:51; *Greek*, "cut in two") if they should break the covenant (Gen. 15:10, 17).

21. gone up—i.e., raised the siege in order to meet Pharaoh-hophra (ch. 37:7-10). The departure of the Chaldeans was a kind of manumission of the Jews; but as their manumission of their bond-servants was recalled, so God revoked His manumission of them from the Chaldeans.

16. polluted my name—by violating your oath (Exod. 20:7). **17. not . . . proclaiming liberty**—Though the Jews had ostensibly emancipated their bond-servants, they *virtually* did not do so by revoking the liberty which they had granted. God looks not to outward appearances, but to the sincere intention. **I proclaim a liberty**—retribution answering to the offense (Matt. 7:2; 18:32, 33; Gal. 6:7; Jas. 2:13). The Jews who would not give liberty to their brethren shall themselves receive "a liberty" calamitous to them. God will manumit them from His happy and safe service (Ps. 121:3), which is real "liberty" (Ps. 119:45; John 8:36; II Cor. 3:17), only to pass under the terrible bondage of other taskmasters, the "sword," etc. **to be removed**—The *Hebrew* expresses *agitation* (*Note*, ch. 15:4). Cf. Deuteronomy 28:25, 48, 64, 65, as to the *restless agitation* of the Jews in their ceaseless removals from place to place in their dispersion. **20. I will even give**—resuming the sentence begun, but not completed (vs. 18), "I will give," etc. **seek their life**—implacably: satisfied with nothing short of their blood; not content with booty. **dead bodies**—The breakers of the covenant shall be cut in pieces, as the calf between whose parts they passed.

22. I will command—Nebuchadnezzar, impelled unconsciously by a divine instigation, returned on the withdrawal of the Egyptians.

ADAM CLARKE

18. *When they cut the calf in twain, and passed between the parts thereof.* This was the ancient and most solemn way of making a covenant. (1) A calf as sacrifice was offered to God to secure His approbation and support. (2) The victim was then exactly divided from the nose to the rump. (3) These divided parts were laid opposite to each other, a passage being left between them. (4) The contracting parties entered this passage at each end, met in the middle, and there took the covenant oath, adjudging themselves to death should they break this covenant. (5) Then they both feasted on the victim. In reference to this last circumstance, God says He will give their "bodies . . . for meat unto the fowls of heaven, and to the beasts." This is a further conformity between the crime and the punishment.

21. *The king of Babylon's army, which are gone up from you.* Nebuchadnezzar, hearing that there was an Egyptian army coming to the relief of Jerusalem, raised the siege, went out, and met and defeated the Egyptians. It was in the interim this prophecy was delivered.

17. *I proclaim a liberty for you.* You proclaimed liberty to your slaves, and afterward resumed your authority over them; and I had in consequence restrained the sword from cutting you off. But now I give liberty *to the sword, to the pestilence, and to the famine,* and to the captivity, to destroy and consume you, and enslave you; for you shall *be removed into all the kingdoms of the earth.* The prophet loves to express the conformity between the crime and its punishment.

22. *I will . . . cause them to return.* They did return; reinvested the city; and, after an obstinate defense, took it, plundered it, and burned it to the ground, taking Zedekiah and his princes captive.

MATTHEW HENRY — CHAPTER 35

Verses 1–11

What is contained in this chapter was said and done *in the days of Jehoiakim* (*v.* 1); in the latter part of his reign, for it was after the king of Babylon with his army *came up into the land* (*v.* 11), which seems to refer to the invasion mentioned 2 Kings xxiv. 2, upon occasion of Jehoiakim's rebelling against Nebuchadnezzar. Jeremiah sets before the rebellious people the example of the Rechabites, a family that kept distinct by themselves. They were originally Kenites, as appears 1 Chron. ii. 55, *These are the Kenites that came out of Hemath, the father of the house of Rechab.* The Kenites, at least those of them that gained a settlement in the land of Israel, were of the posterity of Hobab, Moses's father-in-law, Judges i. 16; 1 Sam. xv. 6; Judges iv. 17. One family of these Kenites had their name from Rechab. His son, or a lineal descendant from him, was Jonadab, a man famous in his time for wisdom and piety. He flourished in the days of Jehu, king of Israel, nearly 300 years before this (2 Kings x. 15, 16).

I. The rules of living which Jonadab charged his children, and his posterity religiously to observe; they were such as he himself had all his days observed.

1. They were comprised in two remarkable precepts: (1) He forbade them to *drink wine*, according to the law of the Nazarites. We are so apt to abuse it and get hurt by it that it is a commendable piece of self-denial either not to use it at all or very sparingly and medicinally, as Timothy used it, 1 Tim. v. 23. (2) He appointed them to *dwell in tents*, and not to build houses, nor purchase lands, nor rent or occupy either, *v.* 7. This was an instance of strictness and mortification. Tents were mean dwellings, so that this would teach them to be humble; they were cold dwellings, so that this would teach them to be hardy and not to indulge the body; they were movable dwellings, so that this would teach them not to think of settling or taking root anywhere in this world. They must dwell in tents *all their days.* They must thus accustom themselves to endure hardness.

2. Why did Jonadab prescribe these rules of living

JAMIESON, FAUSSET, BROWN — CHAPTER 35

VSS. 1-19. PROPHECY IN THE REIGN OF JEHOIAKIM, WHEN THE CHALDEANS, IN CONJUNCTION WITH THE SYRIANS AND MOABITES, INVADED JUDEA. By the obedience of the Rechabites to their father, Jeremiah condemns the disobedience of the Jews to God their Father. The Holy Spirit has arranged Jeremiah's prophecies by the *moral* rather than the chronological connection. From the history of an event fifteen years before, the Jews, who had brought back their manumitted servants into bondage, are taught how much God loves and rewards obedience, and hates and punishes disobedience. **2. Rechabites**—a nomadic tribe belonging to the Kenites of Hemath (I Chron. 2:55), of the family of Jethro, or Hobab, Moses' father-in-law (Exod. 18:9, etc.; Num. 10:29-32; Judg. 1:16). They came into Canaan with the Israelites, but, in order to preserve their independence, chose a life in tents without a fixed habitation (I Sam. 15:6). Besides the branch of them associated with Judah and extending to Amalek, there was another section at Kadesh, in Naphtali (Judg. 4:11, 17). They seem to have been proselytes of the gate. Jonadab, son of Rechab, whose charge not to drink wine they so strictly obeyed, was zealous for God (II Kings 10:15-23). The Nabatheans of Arabia observed the same rules (Diodorus Siculus, 19.94). **bring . . . into . . . house of . . . Lord**—because there were suitable witnesses at hand there from among the priests and chief men, as also because he had the power immediately to address the people assembled there (vs. 13). It may have been also as a reproof of the priests, who drank wine freely, though commanded to refrain from it when in the discharge of their duties [CALVIN]. **chambers**—which were round about the temple, applied to various uses, e.g., to contain the vestments, sacred vessels, etc. **3. Jaazaniah**—the elder and chief of the clan. **4. man of God**—a prophet (Deut. 33:1; I Sam. 2:27; I Kings 12:22; II Kings 4:7), also "a servant of God" in general (I Tim. 6:11), one not his own, but God's;

ADAM CLARKE — CHAPTER 35

1. *The word which came . . . in the days of Jehoiakim.* What strange confusion in the placing of these chapters! Who could have expected to hear of Jehoiakim again, whom we have long ago buried? And we have now arrived in the history at the very last year of the last Jewish king. This discourse was probably delivered in the fourth or fifth year of Jehoiakim's reign.

2. *The house of the Rechabites.* The Rechabites were not descendants of Jacob; they were Kenites, 1 Chron. ii. 55, a people originally settled in the land of Midian; and most probably the descendants of Jethro, the father-in-law of Moses. Compare Num. x. 29-32 with Judg. i. 16; iv. 11. Those mentioned here seem to have been a tribe who fed their flocks in the deserts of Judea; they preserved the simple manners of their ancestors, considering the life of the inhabitants of cities and large towns as the death of liberty; believing that they would dishonor themselves by using that sort of food that would oblige them to live a sedentary life. Jonadab, one of their ancestors, had required his children and descendants to abide faithful to the customs of their forefathers; to continue to live in tents, and to nourish themselves on the produce of their flocks; to abstain from the cultivation of the ground, and from that particularly of the vine and its produce. His descendants religiously observed this rule, till the time when the armies of the Chaldeans had entered Judea; when, to preserve their lives, they retired within the walls of Jerusalem. But even there we find, from the account in this chapter, they did not quit their frugal manner of life, but most scrupulously observed the law of Jonadab, their ancestor, and probably of this family.

3. *The whole house of the Rechabites.* That is, the family—the chiefs of which are here

MATTHEW HENRY

to his posterity? It was to show his wisdom, and the real concern he had for their welfare, not tying them by any oath or vow, but only advising them to conform to this discipline as far as they found it for edification, *v.* 11. His ancestors had addicted themselves to a pastoral life (Exod ii. 16), and he would have his posterity keep to it. Moses had put them in hopes that they should be naturalized (Num. x. 32); but they were still *strangers in the land* (*v.* 7), had no inheritance in it, and therefore must live by their employment and accustom themselves to hard fare and hard lodging. Humility and contentment in obscurity are often the best policy and men's surest protection. Jonadab saw a general corruption of manners; the drunkards of Ephraim abounded, and he was afraid lest his children should be debauched by them; and therefore he obliged them to live by themselves, retired in the country; and, that they might not run into any unlawful pleasures, to deny themselves the use even of lawful delights. Jonadab might foresee the destruction of a people so wretchedly degenerated, and he would have his family provide, that, even in the midst of the troubles, *they might have peace.* Let them sit loose to what they had, and then they might with less pain be stripped of it. They must learn to live by rule and under discipline. It is good for us all to do so, and to teach our children to do so.

II. How strictly his posterity observed these rules, *v.* 8–10. They had in their respective generations all of them *obeyed the voice of Jonadab their father,* had *done according to all that he commanded them.* They *drank no wine,* though they dwelt in a country where there was plenty of it. They built no houses, tilled no ground, but lived upon the products of their cattle. As to one of the particulars, in a case of necessity they dispensed with it (*v.* 11): *When the king of Babylon came into the land* with his army, though they had hitherto dwelt in tents, they now quitted their tents, and came and dwelt in Jerusalem, and in houses there. The rules of a strict discipline must not be made too strict, but so as to admit of a dispensation when the necessity of a case calls for it. These Rechabites would have tempted God, and not trusted him, if they had not used proper means for their own safety, notwithstanding the law and custom of their family. Jeremiah took them into the temple (*v.* 2), into a *prophet's chamber,* because he had a message from God. There he not only asked the Rechabites whether they would drink any wine, but he set *pots full of wine before them,* made the temptation as strong as possible, and said, "*Drink you wine,* you shall have it free. You have broken one of the rules of your order, in coming to live at Jerusalem; why may you not break this too, and when you are in the city do as they there do?" But they peremptorily refused. They all agreed in the refusal. "No, *we will drink no wine*; for with us it is against the law." The prophet saw they were steadfastly resolved.

Verses 12–19

The trial of the Rechabites' constancy was intended but for a sign; here we have the application of it.

I. The Rechabites' observance of their father's charge to them and the disobedience of the Jews to God. Let them see it and be ashamed. The prophet asks them, in God's name, "*Will you not* at length *receive instruction? v.* 13. Will nothing prevail to discover sin and duty to you? You see how obedient the Rechabites are to their father's commandment (*v.* 14); but *you have not inclined your ear to me*" (*v.* 15). The Rechabites were obedient to one who was but a man like themselves, but the Jews were disobedient to an infinite and eternal God, who had an absolute authority over them, as the Father of their spirits. The Rechabites were never put in mind of their obligations to their father; but God often sent his prophets to his people (*v.* 14). God had given his people a *good land,* and promised them that, if they would be obedient, they should still dwell in it, so that they were bound both in gratitude and interest to be obedient, and yet they would not *hearken.*

II. Judgments are threatened, as often before, against Judah and Jerusalem. The Rechabites shall rise up in judgment against them, for they *performed the commandment of their father,* and continued in their obedience to it (*v.* 16); but *this people,* this rebellious and gainsaying people, *have not hearkened unto me.* "*I will bring upon them,* by the Chaldean army, *all the evil pronounced against them* both in the law, and in the prophets, for *I have spoken to them, I have called to them*—spoken by my word, called by my providence, and yet they have not *heard* nor *answered.*"

III. Mercy is here promised to the family of the

JAMIESON, FAUSSET, BROWN

one who has parted with all right in himself to give himself wholly to God (II Tim. 3:17). He was so reverenced that none would call in question what was transacted in his chamber. **keeper of the door**—*Hebrew,* "of the vessel." Probably the office meant is that of the priest who kept in charge the capitation money paid for the use of the temple and the votive offerings, such as silver vessels, etc. There were seven such keepers [GROTIUS]. Cf. II Kings 12:9; 25:18; I Chron. 9:18, 19, which support *English Version.* **I said . . . Drink**—Jeremiah does not say, *The Lord* saith, Drink: for then they would have been bound to obey. Contrast the case in I Kings 13:7-26. **6. Jonadab . . . our father**—i.e., forefather and director, 300 years before (II Kings 10:15). They were called Rechabites, not Jonadabites, having received their name from Rechab *the father,* previously to their adopting the injunctions of Jonadab his *son.* This case affords no justification for slavish deference to the religious opinions of the Christian fathers: for Jonadab's injunction only affected matters of the present life; moreover, it was not binding on their consciences, for they deemed it not unlawful to go to Jerusalem in the invasion (vs. 11). What is praised here is not the father's injunction, but the obedience of the sons [CALVIN]. **7. tents** (Judg. 4:17). **live many days**—according to the promise connected with the fifth commandment (Exod. 20:12; Eph. 6:2, 3). **strangers**—They were not of the stock of Jacob, but sojourners in Israel. Types of the children of God, pilgrims on earth, looking for heaven as their home: having little to lose, so that losing times cost them little alarm; sitting loose to what they have (Heb. 10:34; 11:9, 10, 13-16). **8. all that he . . . charged us . . . all our days, we . . . wives . . . sons . . . daughters**—unreserved obedience in all particulars, at all times, and on the part of all, without exception: in these respects Israel's obedience to God was wanting. Contrast I Samuel 15:20, 21; Psalm 78:34-37, 41, 56, 57. **11. Chaldeans . . . Syrians**—when Jehoiakim revolted from Nebuchadnezzar (II Kings 24:1, 2). Necessity sets aside all other laws. This is the Rechabites' excuse for their seeming disobedience to Jonadab in temporarily settling in a city. Herein was seen the prescient wisdom of Jonadab's commands; they could at a moment's notice migrate, having no land possessions to tie them.

14. obey . . . father's commandment: notwithstanding I—(Mal. 1:6). **rising early and speaking**—*God Himself speaking* late and early by His various ways of providence and grace. **15.** In vs. 15 and in II Chronicles 36:15, a distinct mode of address is alluded to, viz., *God sending His servants.* (Ch. 18:11; 25:5, 6.) I enjoined nothing unreasonable, but simply to serve Me, and I attached to the command a gracious promise, but in vain. If Jonadab's commands, which were arbitrary and not moral obligations in themselves, were obeyed, much more ought Mine, which are in themselves right.

17. because I have spoken . . . not heard . . . I . . . called . . . not answered—(Prov. 1:24; Isa. 65:12.)

ADAM CLARKE

specified.

4. *Igdaliah, a man of God.* A prophet or holy man, having some office in the Temple.

6-7. *We will drink no wine.* The reason is given above. Their whole religious and political institution consisted in obedience to three simple precepts, each of which has an appropriate spiritual meaning: (1) *Ye shall drink no wine.* You shall preserve your bodies in temperance. (2) *Neither shall ye build house.* You shall not become residents in any place; you shall not court earthly possessions.

(3) *But . . . ye shall dwell in tents.* You shall imitate your forefathers, Abraham, Isaac, and Jacob, and the rest of the patriarchs, who dwelt in tents, being strangers and pilgrims upon earth, looking for a heavenly country, and being determined to have nothing here that would indispose their minds towards that place of endless rest.

11. *But . . . when Nebuchadrezzar . . . came up.* If at present we appear to be acting contrary in any respect to our institutions, in being found in the city, necessity alone has induced us to take this temporary step. We have sought the shelter of the city for the preservation of our lives; *so* [*now*] *we dwell at Jerusalem.*

14. *The words of Jonadab . . . are performed . . . but ye hearkened not unto me.* The Lord, knowing the fidelity of this people, chose to try them in this way, that He might, by their conscientious obedience to the precepts of their forefathers, show the Jews, to their confusion, their ingratitude to Him, and their neglect of His precepts, which if a man do, he shall live by them.

MATTHEW HENRY

Rechabites for their steady adherence to the laws of their house. Though it was only for the shaming of Israel that their constancy was tried, yet, being unshaken, it was *found unto praise, and honour, and glory* (*v.* 18, 19). The family shall *never want a man* to inherit what they had, though they had no inheritance to leave. Though they are neither priests nor Levites, nor appear to have had any post in the temple service, yet in a constant course of regular devotion, they stand before God, to minister to him.

CHAPTER 36

Verses 1–8

In the beginning of Ezekiel's prophecy we meet with *a roll* written *in vision*, Ezek. ii. 9, 10; iii. 1. Here, in the latter end of Jeremiah's prophecy, we meet with *a roll* written *in fact*, for discovery of the things contained therein to the people.

I. The command which God gave to Jeremiah to write a summary of his sermons, ever since he first began to be a preacher, in the thirteenth year of Josiah, *to this day*, which was in the fourth year of Jehoiakim, *v.* 2, 3. What they had heard once must be recapitulated, and rehearsed to them again, that what was forgotten might be called to mind again and what made no impression upon them at the first hearing might take hold of them when they heard it the second time. The reason here given for the writing of this roll (*v.* 3): *It may be the house of Judah will hear.* What it is hoped they will thus hear: *All that evil which I purpose to do unto them.* What it is hoped will be produced thereby: *They will hear, that they may return every man from his evil way.* The conversion of sinners is that which ministers should aim at in preaching; and people hear the word in vain if that point be not gained with them. *That I may forgive their iniquity.* This plainly implies God's justice. It is not consistent that he should forgive the sin unless the sinner repent of it. It plainly expresses his mercy, that he is very ready to forgive sin and only waits till the sinner be qualified to receive forgiveness, and therefore uses various means to bring us to repentance, *that he may forgive.*

II. The instructions which Jeremiah gave to Baruch his scribe, pursuant to the command he had received from God, *v.* 4. God bade Jeremiah write, but, it should seem, he had not the *pen of a ready writer*, he could not write fast, or fair, as Baruch could, and therefore he made use of him as his amanuensis. St. Paul wrote but few of his epistles with his own hand, Gal. vi. 11; Rom. xvi. 22. God dispenses his gifts variously; some have a good faculty at speaking, others at writing, and neither can say to the other, We have *no need of you*, 1 Cor. xii. 21. The Spirit of God dictated to Jeremiah, and he to Baruch. If we may credit the apocryphal book that bears his name, he was afterwards himself a prophet to the captives in Babylon. Baruch wrote in a *roll of a book*, on pieces of parchment, or vellum, which were joined together, so making one long scroll, which was rolled perhaps upon a staff.

III. The orders which Jeremiah gave to Baruch to read what he had written to the people. Jeremiah, it seems, was *shut up*, and *could not go to the house of the Lord* himself, *v.* 5. Though he was not a close prisoner, for then there would have been no occasion to send officers to seize him (*v.* 26), yet he was forbidden by the king to appear in the temple. Thus St. Paul wrote epistles to the churches which he could not visit in person. When God ordered the reading of the roll he said, *It may be they will hear and return from their evil ways, v.* 3. When Jeremiah orders it, he says, *It may be they will pray* and will *return from their evil way.* Prayer to God for grace to turn us is necessary in order to our turning. According to these orders, Baruch did read *out of the book the words of the Lord*, whenever there was a *holy convocation, v.* 8.

Verses 9–19

It would seem that Baruch had been frequently reading the book, to all that would give him hearing, before the most solemn reading of it altogether; for the directions were given about it in the *fourth year of Jehoiakim*, whereas this was done *in the fifth year, v.* 9. But some think that the writing of the book took up so much time that it was another year ere it was perfected. 1. The government appointed a public fast to be religiously observed (*v.* 9), on account either of the distress brought by the army of the Chaldeans or of the want of rain (*ch.* xiv. 1): *They proclaimed a fast to the people.* Great shows of piety and devotion may be found even among those who, though they keep up these *forms of godliness*, are strangers and enemies to *the power* of it. But what will such

JAMIESON, FAUSSET, BROWN

19. not want a man to stand before me—There shall always be left representatives of the clan *to worship Me* (ch. 15:1, 19); or, "before Me" means simple *existence*, for all things in existence are *in God's sight* (Ps. 89:36). The Rechabites returned from the captivity. WOLFF found traces of them in Arabia.

CHAPTER 36

VSS. 1-32. BARUCH WRITES, AND READS PUBLICLY JEREMIAH'S PROPHECIES COLLECTED IN A VOLUME. THE ROLL IS BURNT BY JEHOIAKIM, AND WRITTEN AGAIN BY BARUCH AT JEREMIAH'S DICTATION. **1. fourth year**—The command to write the roll was given in the fourth year, but it was not read publicly till the fifth year. As Isaiah subjoined to his predictions a history of events confirming his prophecies (Isa. 36, 37, 38, 39), so Jeremiah also in chs. 37, 38, 39, 40, 41, 42, 43; but he prefaces his history with the narrative of an incident that occurred some time ago, showing that he, not only by word, but in writing, and that twice, had testified all that he is about to state as having subsequently come to pass [GROTIUS]. At the end of Jehoiakim's third year, Nebuchadnezzar enrolled an army against Jerusalem and took it in the end of the fifth or beginning of the sixth year, carrying away captive Jehoiakim, Daniel, etc. Jehoiakim returned the same year, and for three years was tributary: then he withheld tribute. Nebuchadnezzar returned and took Jerusalem, and carried off Jehoiakim, who died on the road. This harmonizes this chapter with II Kings 24: and Daniel 1. See *Note,* ch. 22:19. **2. roll of a book**—a book formed of prepared skins made into a roll. Cf. "volume of the book," i.e., the Pentateuch (Ps. 40:7). It does not follow that his prophecies were not before committed to writing; what is implied is, they were now written together in *one* volume, so as to be read continuously to the Jews in the temple. **against . . . nations**—(ch. 25:15, etc.). **from . . . days of Josiah**—(ch. 25:3). From Josiah's thirteenth year (ch. 1:2). **3. hear**—consider seriously. **return . . . from . . . evil way**—(Jonah 3:8.) **4. all . . . words of . . . Lord**—God specially suggesting what might otherwise have escaped his memory, and directing the choice of words, as well as the substance (John 14:26; 16:13).

5. I am shut up—not in prison, for there is no account of his imprisonment under Jehoiakim, and vss. 19, 26 are inconsistent with it: but, *"I am prevented,"* viz., by some hindrance; or, through fear of the king, to whose anger Baruch was less exposed, as not being the author of the prophecy. **6. go**—on the following year (vs. 9). **fasting day**—(See vs. 9.) An extraordinary fast, in the *ninth* month (whereas the fast on the great day of atonement was on the tenth day of the *seventh* month, Lev. 16:29; 23:27-32), appointed to avert the impending calamity, when it was feared Nebuchadnezzar, having in the year before (i.e., the fourth of Jehoiakim), smitten Pharaoh-necho at Carchemish, would attack Judea, as the ally of Egypt (II Kings 23:34, 35). The fast was likely to be an occasion on which Jeremiah would find the Jews more softened, as well as a larger number of them met together. **7. present . . . supplication**—lit., "supplication shall fall"; alluding to the *prostrate attitude* of the supplicants (Deut. 9:25; Matt. 26:39), as petitioners fall at the feet of a king in the East. So *Hebrew*, ch. 38:26; Daniel 9:18, *Margin.*

9. they proclaimed . . . to all the people . . . to all . . .—rather, "all the people . . . all the people proclaimed a fast" [MICHAELIS]. The chiefs appointed the fast by the wish of the people. In either version the ungodly king had no share in appointing the fast.

ADAM CLARKE

CHAPTER 36

1. *And it came to pass in the fourth year.* About the end of this year; see v. 9. This discourse also bears its own date, and was probably delivered at a time when the people enjoyed peace, and were about to celebrate one of their annual fasts.

2. *Take thee a roll of a book.* Take a sufficient quantity of parchment; cut and stitch it together, that it may make a roll on which to write the words that I have already spoken, that they may serve for a testimony to future generations. The Jewish rolls were made of vellum, or of sheepskins dressed in the half-tanned manner. These were cut into certain lengths, and those parts were all stitched together, and rolled upon a roller. The matter was written on these skins in columns. Sometimes two rollers are used, that as the matter is read from the roll in the left hand, the reader may coil it on the roller in his right. In this form the Pentateuch is written which is read in the synagogues.

3. *It may be that the house of Judah will hear.* It was yet possible to avert the judgments which had been so often denounced against them.

4. *Then Jeremiah called Baruch.* This man, so useful to the prophet, and so faithfully attached to him, was by office a scribe; which signifies, not only a writer, but also a man in office; a chancellor, secretary, etc., a learned man; one acquainted with laws and customs.

6. *Upon the fasting day.* A day when multitudes of people would be gathered together from all parts to implore the mercy of God. This was a favorable time to read these tremendous prophecies.

9. *In the ninth month.* Answering to a part of our December.

MATTHEW HENRY

hypocritical services avail? Fasting, without reforming and turning away from sin, will never turn away the judgments of God, Jonah iii. 10. 2. Baruch repeated Jeremiah's sermons publicly in the house of the Lord, on the fast-day. He stood in a chamber that belonged to Gemariah, and out of a window, or balcony, read to the people that were in the court, *v.* 10. 3. An account was brought to the princes that were now together in the secretary's office, here called *the scribe's chamber*, *v.* 12. It should seem, though the princes had called the people to meet in the house of God, to fast, and pray, and hear the word, they did not think fit to attend there themselves. Michaiah informed the princes of what Baruch had read; for his father Gemariah so far countenanced Baruch as to lend him his chamber. 4. Baruch is sent for, and is ordered to sit down among them and read it all over again to them (*v.* 14, 15), which he readily did. 5. The princes were for the present much affected with the word that was read to them, *v.* 16. And, *when they had heard all, they were afraid*, were all afraid, *one* as well as *another*; like Felix, who trembled at Paul's reasonings. The reproofs were just, and the predictions now in a fair way to be fulfilled; so that they were in a great consternation. We are not told what impressions this reading of the roll made upon the people (*v.* 10), but the princes were put into a fright by it, and (as some read it) *looked one upon another*, not knowing what to say. They agreed to *tell the king of all these words*; and, if he think fit to give credit to them, they will. At the same time they knew the king's mind so far that they advised Baruch and Jeremiah to hide themselves (*v.* 19) and to shift for their own safety, expecting that the king, instead of being convinced would be exasperated. 6. They asked Baruch a trifling question, *How he wrote all these words* (*v.* 17), as if they suspected there was something extraordinary in it; but Baruch gives them a plain answer—Jeremiah dictated, and he wrote, *v.* 18.

Verses 20–32

The roll and the king.

I. Upon notice given him concerning it, he sent for it, and ordered it to be read to him, *v.* 20, 21. He did not desire that Baruch would read it himself, who could read it more intelligently and with more authority and affection than anyone else; but Jehudi, one of his pages now in waiting, who was sent to fetch it, is bidden to read it. Those who thus despise the word of God will soon make it to appear, as this king did, that they hate it, and have not only low, but ill thoughts of it.

II. He had not patience to hear it read through as the princes had, but, when he had heard *three or four leaves* read, in a rage he *cut it with his penknife*, and threw it piece by piece *into the fire*, that he might be sure to see it *all consumed*, *v.* 22, 23. This was a most impudent affront to the God of heaven, whose message this was. Thus he showed his impatience of reproof. 2. Thus he showed his indignation at Baruch and Jeremiah; he would have cut them in pieces, and burnt them, if he had had them in his reach, when he was in this passion. 3. Thus he expressed an obstinate resolution never to comply with the intentions of the warnings given him. 4. Thus he foolishly hoped to defeat the threatenings denounced against him. He thought he had effectually provided that the things contained in this roll should spread no further.

III. Neither the king himself nor any of his princes were at all affected with the word: *They were not afraid* (*v.* 24), no, not those princes that *trembled at the word* when they heard it the first time, *v.* 16. They showed some concern till they saw how light the king made of it, and then they shook off all that concern.

IV. There were three of the princes who had so much sense and grace left as to interpose for the preventing of the burning of the roll, but in vain. *v.* 25.

V. Jehoiakim, when he had thus in effect burnt God's warrant by which he was arrested, in a way of revenge, now signed a warrant for the apprehending of Jeremiah and Baruch, God's ministers (*v.* 26): *But the Lord hid them.*

VI. Jeremiah had orders and instructions to write in another roll the same words that were written in the roll which Jehoiakim had burnt, *v.* 27, 28. Enemies may prevail to burn many a Bible, but they cannot abolish the word of God, nor defeat the accomplishment of it. Though the tables of the law were broken, they were renewed again; and so out of the ashes of the roll that was burnt arose another Phoenix. *The word of the Lord endures for ever.*

VII. The king of Judah, though a king, was severely reckoned with by the King of kings for this indignity done to the written word. Jehoiakim was angry because it was *written therein, saying,* Surely *the king of Babylon shall come and destroy this land*, *v.* 29.

JAMIESON, FAUSSET, BROWN

10. chamber—Baruch read from the window or balcony of the chamber looking into the court where the people were assembled. However, some of the chambers were large enough to contain a considerable number (Neh. 13:5). **Gemariah**—distinct from the Gemariah, son of Hilkiah, in ch. 29:3. **Shaphan**—the same person as in II Kings 22:3. **scribe**—secretary of state, or he who presided over the public records. **higher court**—that of the priests, the court of the people being lower (II Chron. 4:9). **new gate**—(ch. 26:10). The east gate. **12. scribe's chamber**—an apartment in the palace occupied by the secretary of state. **princes**—holding a counsel of state at the time. **Elnathan**—who had already been an instrument of evil in Jehoiakim's hand (ch. 26:22, 23). **Hananiah**—the false prophet (ch. 28: 10-17). **14. Jehudi**—of a good family, as appears from his pedigree being given so fully, but in a subordinate position. **come**—Instead of requiring Baruch to *come* to them, they ought to have *gone* to the temple, and there professed their penitence. But pride forbade it [CALVIN]. **16. afraid, both one and other**—*Hebrew*, fear-stricken, they turned to one another (cf. Gen. 42:28). This showed, on their part, hesitancy, and some degree of fear of God, but not enough to make them willing to sacrifice the favor of an earthly king. **We will surely tell the king**—not the language of threatening, but implying that the matter is of such moment that the king ought to be made acquainted with it, so as to seek some remedy against the divine anger. **17.** What they wished to know was, whether what Baruch had read to them was written by him from memory after hearing Jeremiah repeating his prophecies continuously, or accurately from the prophet's own dictation. **18. his mouth**—Baruch replies it was by the *oral* dictation of the prophet; vs. 2 accords with this view, rather than with the notion that Jeremiah repeated his prophecies from MSS. **ink**—his specification of the "ink" implies: I added nothing save the hand, pen, and ink. **19.** Showing that they were not altogether without better feelings (cf. vss. 16, 25). **20. chamber**—There were chambers in the king's palace round the court or great hall, as in the temple (vs. 10). The roll was "laid up" there for safekeeping, with other public records. **21. sent Jehudi**—Note how unbelievers flee from God, and yet seek Him through some kind of involuntary impulse [CALVIN]. Jehudi seems to have been the king's ready tool for evil.

22. winter-house—(Amos 3: 15.) **ninth month**—viz., of the religious year, i.e., November or December. **fire on . . . hearth**—rather, *the stove* was burning before him. In the East neither chimneys nor ovens are used, but, in cold weather, a brazen vessel containing burning charcoal; when the wood has burned to embers, a cover is placed over the pot to make it retain the heat. **23. three or four leaves**—not distinct leaves as in a book, but the consecutive spaces on the long roll in the shape of *doors* (whence the *Hebrew* name is derived), into which the writing is divided: as the books of Moses in the synagogue in the present day are written in a long parchment rolled round a stick, the writing divided into columns, like pages. **penknife**—the writer's knife with which the reed, used as a pen, was mended. "He" refers to the king (vs. 22). As often as Jehudi read three or four columns, the king cut asunder the part of the roll read; and so he treated the whole, until all the parts read consecutively were cut and burnt; vs. 24, "*all* these words," implies that the *whole* volume was read through, not merely the first three or four columns (I Kings 22:8). **24.** The king and his "servants" were more hardened than the "princes" and councillors (vss. 12-16, *Notes*). Contrast the humble fear exhibited by Josiah at the reading of the law (II Kings 22:11). **25.** (*Note*, vs. 16.) The "nevertheless" aggravates the king's sin; though God would have drawn him back through their intercession, he persisted: judicial blindness and reprobation! **26. Hammelech**—not as *Margin*, "of the king." Jehoiakim at this time (the fifth year of his reign) had no grown-up son: Jeconiah, his successor, was then a boy of eleven (cf. II Kings 23:36, with 24:8). **hid them**—(Ps. 31:20; 83:3; Isa. 26:20). **27. roll, and . . . words**—i.e., the roll of words. **28. all the former words**—It is in vain that the ungodly resist the power of Jehovah: not one of His words shall fall to the ground (Matt. 5:18; Acts 9:5; 5:39). **29. say to Jehoiakim**—not in person, as Jeremiah was "hidden" (vs. 26), but by the written word of prophecy.

ADAM CLARKE

10. *In the chamber of Gemariah.* He was one of the princes of Judah. See v. 12.

17. *How didst thou write all these words? At his mouth?* So the text should be pointed. They wished to know whether he had not copied them, or whether he wrote as Jeremiah prophesied.

19. *Go, hide thee, thou and Jeremiah.* They saw that the king would be displeased, and most probably seek their lives; and as they believed the prophecy was from God, they wished to save both the prophet and his scribe; but they were obliged to inform the king of what they had heard.

22. *Winterhouse.* A warm apartment suited to the season of the year (December) when in Palestine there is often snow upon the ground, though it does not last long. *A fire on the hearth*—a pan or brazier of burning coals.

23. *When Jehudi had read three or four leaves.* Rather columns; for the law, and the sacred Hebrew books, are written in columns of a certain breadth. *He cut it with the penknife.* "The knife of the scribe." *And cast it into the fire.* To show his contempt for God's words.

25. *Elnathan and Delaiah and Gemariah.* Three of the princes wished to save the roll, and entreated the king that it might not be burnt. They would have saved it out of the fire, but the king would not permit it to be done.

26. *But the Lord hid them.* They had, at the counsel of some of the princes, hidden themselves, v. 19. And now, though a diligent search was made, the Lord did not permit them to be found.

28. *Take thee again another roll.* There was no duplicate of the former preserved; and now God inspired the prophet with the same matter that He had given him before; and there is to be added the heavy judgment that is to fall on Jehoiakim and his courtiers.

MATTHEW HENRY

God and his prophets had *therefore become his enemies because they told him the truth*, told him of the desolation that was coming, but at the same time putting him in a fair way to prevent it. The wrath of God shall come upon him and his family, in the first place, by the hand of Nebuchadnezzar. He shall be cut off, and in a few weeks his son shall be dethroned, and exchange his royal robes for prison-garments, so that *he shall have none to sit upon the throne of David; his dead body* shall lie unburied, or *he shall be buried with the burial of an ass*, that is, thrown into the ditch. Even *his seed and his servants* shall fare the worse for their relation to him (*v.* 31), for they shall be punished, not for his iniquity, but so much the sooner for their own. All the evil pronounced against Judah and Jerusalem in that roll shall be brought upon them.

VIII. When the roll was written anew, *there were added* to the former *many like words* (*v.* 32), many more threatenings, for, since they will yet *walk contrary to God*, he will *heat the furnace seven times hotter*.

JAMIESON, FAUSSET, BROWN

saying, Why—This is what the king had desired to be said to Jeremiah if he should be found; kings often dislike the truth to be told them.

30. He shall have none to sit upon the throne—fulfilled (II Kings 24:8, etc.; 25). He had *successors,* but not directly of his posterity, *except his son Jeconiah,* whose three months' reign is counted as nothing. Zedekiah was not the son, but the uncle of Jeconiah, and was raised to the throne in contempt of him and his father Jehoiakim (ch. 22:30). **dead body . . . cast out**—(ch. 22:18, 19). **day . . . heat . . . night . . . frost**—There are often these variations of temperature in the East between night and day (Gen. 31:40). **32. added besides . . . many like words**—Sinners gain nothing but additional punishment by setting aside the word of Jehovah. The law was similarly rewritten after the first tables had been broken owing to Israel's idolatry (Exod. 32, 34).

ADAM CLARKE

30. *He shall have none to sit upon the throne of David.* He shall have no successor, and himself shall have an untimely end, and shall not even be buried, but his body be exposed to the open air, both night and day.

MATTHEW HENRY

CHAPTER 37

Verses 1–10

1. Jeremiah's preaching slighted, *v.* 1, 2. Zedekiah succeeded Coniah, or Jeconiah, and, though he saw in his predecessor the fatal consequences of condemning the word of God, yet he did not take warning. *Neither he, nor his* courtiers, *nor the people of the land, hearkened unto the words of the Lord,* though they already began to be fulfilled. 2. Jeremiah's prayers desired. Zedekiah sent messengers to him, saying, *Pray now unto the Lord our God for us.* He did so before (*ch.* xxi. 1, 2), and one of the messengers, Zephaniah, is the same there and here. Zedekiah is to be commended for this, and it shows that he had some good in him, some sense of his need of God's favour. When we are in distress we ought to desire the prayers of our ministers and Christian friends, for thereby we put an honour upon prayer, and an esteem upon our brethren. Kings themselves should look upon their praying people as the strength of the nation, Zech. xii. 5, 10. And yet this does but help to condemn Zedekiah out of his own mouth. If indeed he looked upon Jeremiah as a prophet, whose prayers might avail, why did he not *hearken to the words of the Lord* which he spoke by him? How can we expect that God should hear others speaking to him for us if we will not hear them speaking to us from him and for him? When Zedekiah sent to the prophet to pray for him, he had better have sent for the prophet to pray with him. 3. Jerusalem flattered by the retreat of the Chaldean army from it. Jeremiah was now at liberty (*v.* 4); Jerusalem also, for the present, was at liberty, *v.* 5. Zedekiah, though a tributary to the king of Babylon, had entered into a private league with Pharaoh king of Egypt (Ezek. xvii. 15), pursuant to which, when the king of Babylon came to chastise him for his treachery, the king of Egypt sent forces to relieve Jerusalem when it was besieged. The Chaldeans raised the siege, probably not for fear of them, but in policy, to fight them at a distance, before any of the Jewish forces could join them. From this they encouraged themselves to hope that Jerusalem was delivered for good. 4. Jerusalem threatened with the return of the Chaldean army. Zedekiah sent to Jeremiah to desire him to pray that the Chaldean army might not return; but Jeremiah sends him word back that the decree had gone forth, and that it was but a folly for them to expect peace. *Thus saith the Lord, Deceive not yourselves, v.* 9. Satan himself though he is the great deceiver, could not deceive us if we did not deceive ourselves. Jeremiah uses no dark metaphors, but tells them plainly, (1) That the Egyptians shall retreat into *their own land, v.* 7. (2) That the Chaldeans shall return, and shall renew the siege: *They shall not depart* for good and all (*v.* 9); *they shall come again* (*v.* 8); they shall *fight against the city.* (3) That Jerusalem shall certainly be delivered into the hand of the Chaldeans: *They shall take it, and burn it with fire, v* 8. "*Though you had smitten* their army, so that many were slain and all the rest wounded, yet those *wounded men should rise up and burn this city,*" *v.* 10.

Verses 11–21

A further account concerning Jeremiah, who relates more passages concerning himself than any other of the prophets.

I. Jeremiah, when he had opportunity, attempted to retire out of Jerusalem into the country (*v.* 11, 12): *When the Chaldeans* had *broken up from Jerusalem* because *of Pharaoh's army,* Jeremiah determined *to go into the* country, and (as the margin reads it)

JAMIESON, FAUSSET, BROWN

CHAPTER 37

Vss. 1-21. Historical Sections, Chapters 37-44. The Chaldeans Raise the Siege to Go and Meet Pharaoh-hophra. Zedekiah Sends to Jeremiah to Pray to God in Behalf of the Jews: in Vain, Jeremiah Tries to Escape to His Native Place, but Is Arrested. Zedekiah Abates the Rigor of His Imprisonment. **1. Coniah**—curtailed from Jeconiah by way of reproach. **whom**—referring to Zedekiah, not to Coniah (II Kings 24:17). **2.** Amazing stupidity, that they were not admonished by the punishment of Jeconiah [Calvin], (II Chron. 36:12, 14)! **3. Zedekiah . . . sent**—fearing lest, in the event of the Chaldeans overcoming Pharaoh-hophra, they should return to besiege Jerusalem. See *Note* in beginning of ch. 21; that chapter chronologically comes in between chs. 37 and 38. The message of the king to Jeremiah here in ch. 37 is, however, somewhat earlier than that in ch. 21; here it is while the issue between the Chaldeans and Pharaoh was undecided; there it is when, after the repulse of Pharaoh, the Chaldeans were again advancing against Jerusalem; hence, while Zephaniah is named in both embassies, *Jehucal* accompanies him here, *Pashur* there. But, as Pashur and Jehucal are both mentioned in ch. 38:1, 2, as hearing Jeremiah's reply, which is identical with that in ch. 21:9, it is probable the two messages followed one another at a short interval; that in this ch. 37:3, and the answer, vss. 7-10, being the earlier of the two. **Zephaniah**—an abettor of rebellion against God (ch. 29:25), though less virulent than many (vs. 29; ch. 29), punished accordingly (ch. 52:24-27). **4. Jeremiah . . . not put . . . into prison**—He was no longer in the prison court, as he had been (ch. 32:2; 33:1), which passages refer to the beginning of the siege, not to the time when the Chaldeans renewed the siege, after having withdrawn for a time to meet Pharaoh. **5.** After this temporary diversion, caused by Pharaoh in favor of Jerusalem, the Egyptians returned no more to its help (II Kings 24:7). Judea had the misfortune to lie between the two great contending powers, Babylon and Egypt, and so was exposed to the alternate inroads of the one or the other. Josiah, taking side with Assyria, fell in battle with Pharaoh-necho at Megiddo (II Kings 23: 29). Zedekiah, seeking the Egyptian alliance in violation of his oath, was now about to be taken by Nebuchadnezzar (II Chron. 36:13; Ezek. 17:15, 17).

7. shall return—without accomplishing any deliverance for you. **8.** (Ch. 34:22.) **9. yourselves**—*Hebrew,* "souls."

10. yet . . . they—Even a few wounded men would suffice for your destruction.

11. broken up—"gone up."

ADAM CLARKE

CHAPTER 37

1. *And king Zedekiah the son of Josiah.* Of the siege and taking of Jerusalem referred to here, and the making of Zedekiah king instead of Jeconiah, see 2 Kings xxiv. 1, etc.

3. *Zedekiah . . . to the prophet Jeremiah.* He was willing to hear a message from the Lord, provided it were according to his own mind. He did not fully trust in his own prophets.

4. *Now Jeremiah came in and went out.* After the siege was raised, he had a measure of liberty; he was not closely confined, as he afterwards was. See v. 16.

5. *Then Pharaoh's army.* This was Pharaoh-hophra, who then reigned in Egypt in place of his father, Necho. See Ezek. xxix. 6, etc. Nebuchadnezzar, hearing that the Egyptian army, on which the Jews so much depended, were on their march to relieve the city, suddenly raised the siege, and went to meet them. In the interim Zedekiah sent to Jeremiah to inquire of the Lord to know whether they might consider themselves in safety.

7. *Pharaoh's army . . . shall return to Egypt.* They were defeated by the Chaldeans; and, not being hearty in the cause, returned immediately to Egypt, leaving Nebuchadnezzar unmolested to recommence the siege.

10. *For though ye had smitten the whole army.* Strong words; but they show how fully God was determined to give up this city to fire and sword, and how fully He had instructed His prophet on this point.

MATTHEW HENRY

to slip away from Jerusalem in the midst of the people, who, in that interval of the siege, went out into the country to look after their affairs. He endeavoured to steal away in the crowd; for, though he was a man of great eminence, he was content to be lost in the multitude and buried alive in a cottage. Jeremiah found he could do no good in Jerusalem; he laboured in vain among them, and therefore determined to leave them.

II. In this attempt he was seized as a deserter and committed to prison (*v.* 13–15): *He was in the gate of Benjamin*, when *a captain of the ward*, who probably had the charge of that gate, discovered him and *took him* into custody. He was the grandson of Hananiah, who, the Jews say, was Hananiah the false prophet, who contested with Jeremiah (*ch.* xxviii. 10), and they add that this young captain had a spite to Jeremiah upon that account. That which he charges upon him is, *Thou fallest away to the Chaldeans*—an unlikely story, for the Chaldeans had now gone. Jeremiah therefore with good reason, and with both the confidence and the mildness of an innocent man, denies the charge: "*It is false; I fall not away to the Chaldeans;* I am going upon my own lawful occasions." Jeremiah's protestation of his integrity, though he is a prophet, and is ready to say it *on the word of a priest*, is not regarded; but is brought before the privy-council, who without examining him, but upon the base insinuation of the captain, fell into a passion with him: they *were wroth.* They beat him and then *put him in prison*, in the worst prison they had, that *in the house of Jonathan the scribe.* Into this prison Jeremiah was thrust, *into the dungeon*, which was dark and cold, damp and dirty. In the cells or *cabins*, there he must lodge. *There Jeremiah remained many days.*

III. Zedekiah at length sent for him, and showed him some favour; but probably not till the Chaldean army had returned and had laid fresh siege to the city. When their vain hopes had all vanished, then they were in a greater confusion and consternation than ever. "O then" (says Zedekiah), "send in all haste for the prophet; let me have some talk with him." 1. The king sent for him to give him private audience as an ambassador from God. He *asked him secretly in his house*, being ashamed to be seen in his company, "*Is there any word from the Lord? (v.* 17)—any word of comfort? Canst thou give us any hopes that the Chaldeans shall again retire?" Jeremiah's life and comfort are in Zedekiah's hand, and he has now a petition to present to him for his favour, and yet, having this opportunity, he tells him plainly that *there is a word from the Lord*, but no word of comfort for him or his people: *Thou shalt be delivered into the hand of the king of Babylon.* If Jeremiah had consulted with flesh and blood, he would have given him a plausible answer; he might have chosen whether he would tell him the worst at this time. But Jeremiah was one that had *obtained mercy of the Lord to be faithful*, and would not, to obtain mercy of man, be unfaithful either to God or to his prince; he therefore tells him the truth, the whole truth. Jeremiah takes this occasion to upbraid him and his people with the credit they gave to the false prophets, who told them that *the king of Babylon* should *not come* at all, or, when he had withdrawn, should *not come* again *against* them, *v.* 19. "*Where are now your prophets*, who told you that you should have peace?" 2. He improved this opportunity for the presenting of a private petition, as a poor prisoner, *v.* 18, 20. He humbly expostulates with the king: "*What have I offended against thee, or thy servants, or this people*, what law have I broken, *that you have put me in prison?*" He likewise earnestly begs, and very pathetically (*v.* 20), *Cause me not to return* to yonder noisome gaol, *to the house of Jonathan the scribe, lest I die there. Hear me, I pray thee, O my Lord the king! let my supplication, I pray thee, be accepted before thee.* Here is not a word of complaint of the princes that unjustly committed him, but a modest supplication to the king. A lion in God's cause must be a lamb in his own. (1) The king gave him his request, took care that he should not die in the dungeon, but ordered that he should have the liberty of the *court of the prison*, where he might breathe a free air. (2) He ordered him his *daily bread out of the* public stock, *till all the bread was spent.* Zedekiah ought to have released him, but he had not courage to do that; it was well he did as he did. God can make even confinement turn to advantage and the court of a prison to become as green pastures.

JAMIESON, FAUSSET, BROWN

12. Benjamin—to his own town, Anathoth. **to separate himself**—*Margin* translates, "to slip away," from a *Hebrew* root, "to be smooth," so, to slip away as a slippery thing that cannot be held. But it is not likely the prophet of God would flee in a dishonorable way; and "in the midst of the people" rather implies open departure along with others, than clandestine slipping away by mixing with the crowd of departing people. Rather, it means, *to separate himself*, or to *divide his place of residence*, so as to live partly here, partly there, without fixed habitation, going to and fro among the people [Ludovicus de Dieu]. Maurer translates, "to take his portion thence," to realize the produce of his property in Anathoth [Henderson], or to take possession of the land which he bought from Hanameel [Maurer]. **13. ward**—i.e., the "guard," or "watch." **Hananiah**—whose death Jeremiah predicted (ch. 28:16). The grandson in revenge takes Jeremiah into custody on the charge of *deserting* ("thou fallest away," ch. 38:19; 52:15; I Sam. 29:3) to the enemy. His prophecies gave color to the charge (ch. 21:9; 38:4).

15. scribe—one of the court secretaries; often in the East part of the private house of a public officer serves as a prison. **16. dungeon . . . cabins**—The prison consisted of a *pit* (the "dungeon") with *vaulted cells* round the sides of it. The "cabins," from a root, "to bend one's self."

17. secretly—Zedekiah was ashamed to be seen by his courtiers consulting Jeremiah (John 12:43; 5:44; 19:38).

thou shalt be delivered—Had Jeremiah consulted his earthly interests, he would have answered very differently. Contrast ch. 6:14; Isaiah 30:10; Ezekiel 13:10.

18. What—In what respect have I offended? **19. Where are now your prophets**—The event has showed them to be liars; and, as surely as the king of Babylon has come already, notwithstanding their prophecy, so surely shall he return.

20. be accepted—rather, "Let my supplication *be humbly presented*" (ch. 36:7, *Note*), [Henderson]. **lest I die there**—in the subterranean dungeon (vs. 16), from want of proper sustenance (vs. 21.) The prophet *naturally* shrank from death, which makes his *spiritual* firmness the more remarkable; he was ready to die rather than swerve from his duty [Calvin]. **21. court of the prison**—(ch. 32:2; 38:13, 28). **bakers' street**—Persons in the same business in cities in the East commonly reside in the same street. **all the bread . . . spent**—Jeremiah had bread supplied to him until he was thrown into the dungeon of Malchiah, at which time the bread in the city was spent. Cf. this verse with ch. 38:9; that time must have been very shortly before the capture of the city (ch. 52:6). God saith of His children, "In the days of famine they shall be satisfied" (Ps. 37:19; Isa. 33:16). Honest reproof (vs. 17), in the end often gains more favor than flattery (Prov. 28:23).

ADAM CLARKE

12. *Jeremiah went forth.* At the time that Nebuchadnezzar had raised the siege, and gone to meet the Egyptian army. *Go into the land of Benjamin.* To Anathoth, his native city. *To separate himself thence.* The Chaldee: "He went that he might divide the inheritance which he had there among the people."

13. *Thou fallest away to the Chaldeans.* You are a deserter, and a traitor to your country. As he had always declared that the Chaldeans should take the city, etc., his enemies took occasion from this to say he was in the interest of the Chaldeans, and that he wished now to go to them, and betray the place.

15. *And smote him.* Without any proof of the alleged treachery, without any form of justice. *In prison in the house of Jonathan.* In Asiatic countries there is an apartment in the houses of the officers of the law, to confine all the accused that are brought before them. Jonathan was a scribe or secretary, and had a prison of this kind in his house.

16. *Entered into the dungeon, and into the cabins.* The dungeon was probably a deep pit; and *the cabins* or cells, niches in the sides, where different malefactors were confined.

17. *Is there any word from the Lord?* Is there any further revelation?

There is: . . . thou shalt be delivered. What bold faithfulness! And to a king, in whose hands his life now lay.

19. *Where are now your prophets?* They told you that the Chaldeans should not come; I told you they would. According to my word the Chaldeans are come, and are departed only for a short time.

20. *Cause me not to return to the house of Jonathan.* He had been ill used in this man's custody, so as to endanger his life, the place being cold, and probably unhealthy.

21. *Then Zedekiah . . . the court of the prison.* Was contiguous to the king's house, where the prisoners could readily see their friends. *Give him daily a piece of bread out of the bakers' street.* From the public stores, which he received till all the provisions were spent.

MATTHEW HENRY

CHAPTER 38

Verses 1–13

1. Jeremiah persists in his plain preaching (*v.* 3): *This city shall be given into the hand of the king of Babylon;* though it hold out long, it will be taken at last. Nor would he have so often repeated this unwelcome message but that he could put them in a certain way, though not to save the city, yet to save themselves, *v.* 2. Let him *go forth to the Chaldeans,* and throw himself upon their mercy, before things come to extremity, and then he *shall live;* they will give him quarter, and he shall escape *the famine and pestilence,* which will be the death of multitudes within the city. 2. The princes persist in their malice against Jeremiah. He was faithful to his country and to his trust as a prophet, and, though at this time he ate the king's bread, yet that did not stop his mouth. But his persecutors complained that he abused the liberty he had of walking in the court of the prison; for, though he could not go to the temple to preach, yet he said the same things in private conversation to those that came to visit him, and therefore (*v.* 4) they represented him to the king as a dangerous man, disaffected to the government he lived under: *He seeks not the welfare of this people, but the hurt*—yet no man had done more for the good of Jerusalem than he. They represent his preaching *as weakening their hands* and discouraging them. It is common for wicked people to look upon God's faithful ministers as their enemies, only because they show them what enemies they are to themselves while they continue impenitent. 3. Jeremiah hereupon, by the king's permission, is put into a dungeon, with a view to his destruction there. Zedekiah, though he felt a conviction that Jeremiah was a prophet, sent of God, had not courage to own it. *He is in your hand.* Those will have a great deal to answer for who, though they have a secret kindness for good people, dare not own it in a time of need. The princes, having this general warrant from the king, immediately put poor *Jeremiah into the dungeon of Malchiah, that was in the court of the prison* (*v.* 6), a deep dungeon, for they *let* him *down* into it *with cords,* and a dirty one, for *there was no water* in it, *but mire;* and he *sunk in the mire, up to his neck,* says Josephus. Those that put him here doubtless designed that he should die of hunger and cold, and so die obscurely, fearing, if they should put him to death openly, the people might be incensed against them. Many of God's faithful witnesses have thus been privately made away, and starved to death, in prisons, whose blood will be brought to account in the day of discovery. What Jeremiah did in this distress, he tells us himself (Lam. iii. 55, 57), *I called upon thy name, O Lord! out of the low dungeon, and thou drewest near, saying, Fear not.* 4. Application is made to the king by *Ebed-melech,* one of the gentlemen of the bed-chamber, in behalf of the poor sufferer. *Ebed-melech* was an Ethiopian a *stranger to the commonwealth of Israel,* and yet had in him more humanity and more divinity too, than Israelites had. Christ found more faith among Gentiles than among Jews. Ebed-melech lived in a wicked court and in a corrupt degenerate age, and yet had a great sense both of equity and piety. God has his remnant in all places. There were *saints* even *in Cæsar's household.* The king was now *sitting in the gate of Benjamin* to receive appeals and petitions. Thither Ebed-melech went immediately, for the case would not admit delay. He boldly asserts that Jeremiah had a deal of wrong done him, and is not afraid to tell the king so. He does not mince the matter; he tells the king faithfully, let him take it as he will, *These men have done ill in all that they have done to Jeremiah.* God can raise up friends for his people in distress where they little thought of them. 5. Orders are immediately given for his release, and Ebed-melech takes care to see them executed. The king had his heart wonderfully changed on a sudden, and will now have Jeremiah released in defiance of the princes, for he orders no less than thirty men to be employed in fetching him out of the dungeon, lest the princes should raise a party to oppose it, *v.* 10. Ebed-melech gained his point, and soon brought Jeremiah the good news. Special notice is taken of his great tenderness in providing old soft rags for Jeremiah to put under his arm-holes, to keep the cords wherewith he was to be drawn up from hurting him, his arm-holes being probably galled by the cords wherewith he was let down. Nor did he throw the rags down to him, lest they should be lost in the mire, but carefully let them down, *v.* 11, 12. Jeremiah is brought up out of the dungeon, and is now where he was, *in the court of the prison, v.* 13.

Verses 14–28

The king in close conference with Jeremiah, though

JAMIESON, FAUSSET, BROWN

CHAPTER 38

Vss. 1-28. JEREMIAH PREDICTS THE CAPTURE OF JERUSALEM, FOR WHICH HE IS CAST INTO A DUNGEON, BUT IS TRANSFERRED TO THE PRISON COURT ON THE INTERCESSION OF EBED-MELECH, AND HAS A SECRET INTERVIEW WITH ZEDEKIAH. All this was subsequent to his imprisonment in Jonathan's house, and his release on his interview with Zedekiah. The latter occurred *before* the return of the Chaldeans to the siege; the similar events in this chapter occurred *after* it. **1. Jucal**—Jehucal (ch. 37:3). **Pashur**—(ch. 21: 1; cf. vs. 9 of ch. 21 with vs. 2 of this ch. 38). The deputation in ch. 21:1, to whom Jeremiah gave this reply, if not identical with the hearers of Jeremiah (ch. 38:1), must have been sent just before the latter "heard" him speaking the same words. *Zephaniah* is not mentioned here as in ch. 21:1, but is so in ch. 37:3. *Jucal* is mentioned here and in the previous deputation (ch. 37:3), but not in ch. 21:1. *Shephatiah* and *Gedaliah* here do not occur either in ch. 21:1 or ch. 37:3. The identity of his words in both cases is natural, when uttered, at a very short interval, and one of the hearers (Pashur) being present on both occasions. **unto all the people**—They had free access to him in the court of the prison (ch. 32: 12). **2. life . . . a prey**—He shall escape with his life; though losing all else in a shipwreck, he shall carry off his life as his gain, saved by his going over to the Chaldeans. (*Note,* ch. 21:9.) **4.** Had Jeremiah not had a divine commission, he might justly have been accused of treason; but having one, which made the result of the siege certain, he acted humanely as interpreter of God's will under the theocracy, in advising surrender (cf. ch. 26:11). **5. the king is not he**—Zedekiah was a weak prince, and now in his straits afraid to oppose his princes. He hides his dislike of their overweening power, which prevented him shielding Jeremiah as he would have wished, under complimentary speeches. "It is not right that the king should deny aught to such faithful and wise statesmen"; the king is not such a one as to deny you your wishes [JEROME]. **6. dungeon**—lit., the "cistern." It was not a subterranean prison as that in Jonathan's house (ch. 37:15), but a pit or cistern, which had been full of water, but was emptied of it during the siege, so that only "mire" remained. Such empty cisterns were often used as prisons (Zech. 9:11); the depth forbade hope of escape. **Hammelech**—(ch. 36:26). His son followed in the father's steps, a ready tool for evil. **sunk in the mire**—Jeremiah herein was a type of Messiah (Ps. 69:2, 14). "I sink in deep mire . . . ." **7. Ebed-melech**—The *Hebrew* designation given this Ethiopian, meaning "king's servant." Already, even at this early time, God wished to show what good reason there was for calling the Gentiles to salvation. An Ethiopian stranger saves the prophet whom his own countrymen, the Jews, tried to destroy. So the Gentiles believed in Christ whom the Jews crucified, and Ethiopians were among the earliest converts (Acts 2:10, 41; 8:27-39). Ebed-melech probably was keeper of the royal harem, and so had private access to the king. The eunuchs over harems in the present day are mostly from Nubia or Abyssinia. **8. went forth . . . and spake**—not privately, but in public; a proof of fearless magnanimity. **9. die for hunger in the place where he is; for . . . no . . . bread in . . . . city**—(Cf. ch. 37: 21). He had heretofore got a piece of bread supplied to him. "Seeing that there is the *utmost want of bread* in the city, so that even if he were at large, there could *no more* be regularly supplied to him, much less now in a place where none remember or pity him, so that he is likely to die for hunger." "No more bread," i.e., no more left of the *public store* in the city (ch. 37:21); or, *all but* no bread left anywhere [MAURER]. **10. with thee**—*Hebrew,* "in thine hand," i.e., at "thy disposal" (I Sam. 16:2). "From hence," i.e., from the gate of Benjamin where the king was sitting (vs. 7). **thirty men**—not merely to draw up Jeremiah, but to guard Ebed-melech against any opposition on the part of the princes (vss. 1-4), in executing the king's command. Ebed-melech was rewarded for his faith, love, and courage, exhibited at a time when he might well fear the wrath of the princes, to which even the king had to yield (ch. 39:16-18). **11. cast clouts**—"torn clothes" [HENDERSON]. **rotten rags**—"worn-out garments." God can make the meanest things His instruments of goodness to His people (I Cor. 1:27-29). **under . . . armholes**—"under the joints of thine hands," i.e., where the fingers join the hand, the clothes being in order that the hands should not be cut by the cords [MAURER]. **13. court of . . . prison**—Ebed-melech prudently put him there to be out of the way of his enemies.

ADAM CLARKE

CHAPTER 38

1. *Then Shephatiah.* This was the faction who were enemies to Jeremiah, and sought his life.

3. *This city shall surely be given.* This was a testimony that he constantly bore; he had the authority of God for it. He knew it was true, and he never wavered nor equivocated.

4. *Let this man be put to death.* And they gave their reasons plain enough, but the proof was wanting.

6. *So Jeremiah sunk in the mire.* Their obvious design was that he might be stifled in that place.

7. *Ebed-melech.* "The servant of the king," one of the eunuchs who belonged to the palace. Perhaps it should be read, "Now, a servant of the king, a Cushite, one of the eunuchs." *The king then sitting in the gate of Benjamin.* To give audience, and to administer justice.

9. *My lord the king, these men have done evil.* He must have been much in the king's confidence, and a humane and noble-spirited man, thus to have raised his voice against the powerful cabal already mentioned.

10. *Take from hence thirty men.* The king was determined that he should be rescued by force, if the princes opposed.

MATTHEW HENRY

(*v.* 5) he had before given him up into the hands of his enemies.

I. The honour that Zedekiah did to the prophet. When he was newly fetched out of the dungeon he sent for him to advise with him privately. He met him in *the third entry*, or (as the margin reads it) *the principal entry*, that *is in*, or leads towards, *the house of the Lord*, *v.* 14. Perhaps he intended to show a respect for *the house of God*, now that he was desiring to hear *the word of God*. Zedekiah would ask *Jeremiah a thing*; it should rather be rendered, *a word.* "I am here asking thee for *a word of prediction*, of counsel, of comfort, *a word from the Lord*, *ch.* xxxvii. 17. Whatever word thou hast *hide it not from me*; let me know the worst." He hopes to get a more pleasing answer, as if God, who is *in one mind*, were such a one as himself, who was in many minds.

II. The bargain that Jeremiah made with him before he would give him his advice, *v.* 15. "And if I do," says Jeremiah, "*wilt thou not put me to death?* I am afraid *thou wilt*" (so some take it); "what else can I expect when thou art led blindfold by the princes?" Not that Jeremiah was backward to seal the doctrine he preached with his blood, but, in doing our duty, we ought to use all lawful means for our own preservation; even the apostles of Christ did so. He is willing to give him wholesome advice, and does not upbraid him with his unkindness in suffering him to be put into the dungeon. "*Wilt thou not hearken unto me?* Surely thou wilt; I am in hopes to find thee pliable at last, and now *in this thy day willing to know the things that belong to thy peace*." Some read it as spoken despairingly: "*If I give thee counsel, thou wilt not hearken unto me;* I have reason to fear thou wilt not, and then I might as well keep my counsel to myself." Zedekiah makes him no answer, will not promise to hearken to his advice. As to the prophet's safety, he promises him, upon the word of a king, *I will neither put thee to death nor deliver thee into the hands of those that will*, *v.* 16. Zedekiah's oath on this occasion is solemn: "*As the Lord liveth, who made us this soul*, who gave me my life and thee thine, I dare not take away thy life unjustly, knowing that then I should forfeit my own to him that is the Lord of life."

III. The good advice that Jeremiah gave him, with good reason why he should take it, not from any prudence or politics of his own, but in the *name of the Lord, the God of hosts* and *God of Israel*. Not as a statesman, but as a prophet, he advises him by all means to surrender himself and his city *to the king of Babylon's princes*: "*Go forth to them*, and make the best terms thou canst with them," *v.* 17. This was the advice he had given to the people (*v.* 2, and before, *ch.* xxi. 9), to submit to divine judgments. To persuade him to take this counsel, he sets before him good and evil, life and death. If he will yield he shall save his children from the sword and Jerusalem from the flames. If he will but acknowledge God's justice, he shall experience his mercy: *The city shall not be burnt*, and *thou shalt live and thy house*. But, if he will obstinately stand out, it will be the ruin both of his house and Jerusalem (*v.* 18). This is the case of sinners with God; let them humbly submit to his grace and government and they shall live.

IV. The objection which Zedekiah made against the prophet's advice, *v.* 19. If he had had a due regard to the divine authority, wisdom, and goodness, as soon as he understood what the mind of God was he would immediately have acquiesced, but he advances against it some prudential considerations of his own. All he suggests is, "*I am afraid*, not of the Chaldeans; their princes are men of honour, but of the Jews, that have already gone over to the Chaldeans; when they see *me* follow them, who had so much opposed their going, they will laugh at me, and say, *Hast thou also become weak as water?*" Isa. xiv. 10. Though it had been really the greatest personal mischief that he could imagine it to be, yet he ought to have ventured it, in obedience to God, and for the preservation of his family and city.

V. The pressing importunity with which Jeremiah followed the advice he had given the king. He assures him that, if he would comply with the will of God herein, the thing he feared should not come upon him (*v.* 20): *They shall not deliver thee up*, but treat thee as becomes thy character. *Obey, I beseech thee, the voice of the Lord*, because it is his voice, so it *shall be well unto thee*. But he tells him what would be the consequence if he would not obey. He himself would *fall into the hands of the Chaldeans*. "*Thou shalt not escape*, as thou hopest to do," *v.* 23. He would himself be chargeable with the destruction of Jerusalem: "*Thou shalt cause this city to be burnt with fire*, for by a little submission and self-denial thou mightest have prevented it." He should certainly fall under a just reproach for standing out, and that from women

JAMIESON, FAUSSET, BROWN

14. third entry—The Hebrews in determining the position of places faced the *east*, which they termed "that which is in front"; the *south* was thus called "that which is on the right hand"; the *north*, "that which is on the left hand"; the *west*, "that which is behind." So beginning with the *east* they might term it the *first* or principal entry; the *south* the *second* entry; the *north* the "*third* entry" of the outer or inner court [MAURER]. The third gate of the temple facing the palace; for through it the entrance lay from the palace into the temple (I Kings 10:5, 12). It was westward (I Chron. 26:16, 18; II Chron. 9:11) [GROTIUS]. But in the future temple it is eastward (Ezek. 46:1, 2, 8).

15. wilt thou not hearken unto me—Zedekiah does not answer this last query; the former one he replies to in vs. 16. Rather translate, "Thou wilt not hearken to me." Jeremiah judges so from the past conduct of the king. Cf. vs. 17 with vs. 19.

16. Lord . . . made us this soul—(Isa. 57:16). Implying, "may my life (soul) be forfeited if I deceive thee" [CALVIN].

17. princes—(ch. 39:3). He does not say "to the king himself," for he was at Riblah, in Hamath (ch. 39:5; II Kings 25:6). "*If* thou go forth" (viz., to surrender; II Kings 24:12; Isa. 36:16), God foreknows future conditional contingencies, and ordains not only the end, but also the *means* to the end.

19. afraid of the Jews—more than of God (Prov. 29:25; John 9:22; 12:43). **mock me**—treat me injuriously (I Sam. 31:4).

22. women—The very evil which Zedekiah wished to escape by disobeying the command to go forth shall befall him in its worst form thereby. Not merely the Jewish deserters shall "mock" him (vs. 19), but the very "women" of his own palace and harem, to gratify their new lords, will taunt him. A noble king in sooth, to suffer thyself to be so imposed on! **Thy friends**—*Hebrew*, men of thy peace (see ch. 20:10; Ps. 41:9, *Margin*). The king's ministers and the false prophets who misled him. **sunk in . . . mire**—proverbial for, Thou art involved by "thy friends'" counsels in inextricable difficulties. The phrase perhaps alludes to vs. 6; a just retribution for the treatment of Jeremiah, who literally "sank in the mire." **they are turned . . . back**—Having involved thee in the calamity, they themselves shall provide for their own safety by deserting to the Chaldeans (vs. 19).

ADAM CLARKE

F. B. MEYER:

"Obey . . . . So it shall be well unto thee, and thy soul shall live" (Jer. 38:20). Of many Christians it can hardly be said that their souls live; they exist, but do not thrive. The food of the soul is in part the Word of God; but in part it is obedience. As we obey we are fed; for our Master said, "My meat is to do the will of him that sent me, and to finish his work" (John 4:34). The same truth is suggested here; if we obey the voice of the Lord, it is well with us, and our soul thrives.

The voice of God speaks from the page of his Word. Let us not accept that to be his voice which does not come to us through Scripture, or is not corroborated by Scripture. But let us be very careful to obey God's Word, so far as we know it, even when, as in Zedekiah's case, it seems to contradict all the suggestions of prudence and common sense. Better be with God in a minority of one, than have the plaudits of an immense host of godless men.

How well I remember, years ago now, entering the bed-chamber of an eminent saint, one autumn morning, whose diminishing candles told how long he had been feeding on the Word of God. I asked him what had been the subject of his study. He said he had been engaged since four o'clock in discovering all the Lord's positive commandments, that he might be sure that he was not wittingly neglecting any one of them. It is very sad to find how many in the present day are neglecting to observe to do the Lord's precepts—concerning his ordinances, the laying-up of money, the evangelization of the world, and the manifestation of perfect love. They know the Lord's will, and do it not. They appear to think that they are absolved from the "observing to do," which was so characteristic of Deuteronomy. As though Love were not more inexorable than Law!

—*Great Verses Through the Bible*

22. *All the women . . . brought forth.* I think this place speaks of a kind of defection among the women of the harem; many of whom had already gone forth privately to the principal officers of the Chaldean army, and made the report mentioned in the end of this verse. These were the concubines or women of the second rank.

MATTHEW HENRY

too, *v.* 22. Thus will Zedekiah be bantered by the women, when all his wives and children shall be made a prey to the conquerors, *v.* 23.

VI. The care which Zedekiah took to keep this conference private (*v.* 24): *Let no man know of these words.* He has nothing to object against Jeremiah's advice, and yet he will not follow it. Zedekiah is concerned to keep it private, not so much for Jeremiah's safety, but for his own reputation. He is instructed what to say to the princes if they should examine him about it. He must tell them that he was petitioning the king not to remand him back to *the house of Jonathan the scribe* (*v.* 25, 26), and he did tell them so (*v.* 27), and no doubt it was true.

JAMIESON, FAUSSET, BROWN

23. children—(ch. 39:6; 41:10). "wives . . . children . . . thou"; an ascending climax. **24. Let no man know**—If thou wilt not tell this to the people, I will engage thy safety. **25.** Kings are often such only in title; they are really under the power of their subjects. **26. presented**—lit., "made my supplication to fall"; implying supplication with humble prostration (*Note,* ch. 36:7). **Jonathan's house**—(ch. 37:15), different from Malchiah's dungeon (vs. 6). This statement was true, though not the whole truth; the princes had no right to the information; no sanction is given by Scripture here to Jeremiah's representation of this being the cause of his having come to the king. Fear drove him to it. Cf. Genesis 20:2, 12; on the other hand, I Samuel 16:2, 5. **left off speaking with**—*Hebrew,* "were silent from him," i.e., withdrawing from him they left him quiet (I Sam. 7:8, *Margin*). **28. he was [*there*] when Jerusalem was taken**—These words are made the beginning of ch. 39 by many; but the accents and sense support *English Version.*

ADAM CLARKE

23. *They shall bring out all thy wives and thy children.* These were the women of the first rank, by whom the king had children. These had no temptation to go out to the Chaldeans, nor would they have been made welcome; but the others being young, and without children, would be well received by the Chaldean princes.

26. *I presented my supplication.* This was telling the truth, and nothing but the truth, but not the whole truth. The king did not wish him to defile his conscience, nor did he propose anything that was not consistent with the truth.

MATTHEW HENRY — CHAPTER 39

Verses 1–10

Jeremiah abode patiently in the court of the prison, until the day that Jerusalem was taken. He gave the princes no further disturbance by his prophesying, nor they him by their persecutions.

I. The city is at length taken by storm. Nebuchadnezzar's army sat down before it in the *ninth* year of Zedekiah, *in the tenth month* (*v.* 1). Nebuchadnezzar left his generals to carry on the siege: they renewed it with redoubled vigour. At length, *in the eleventh year, in the fourth month,* they entered the city, the soldiers being so weakened by famine, that they were not able to make any resistance, *v.* 2. Sin had provoked God to withdraw his protection, and then, like Samson when his hair was cut, it was weak as other cities.

II. The princes of the king of Babylon take possession of the *middle gate, v.* 3. Some think that this was the *second gate* (Zeph. i. 10), in the middle wall that divided one part of the city from the other. Here they cautiously made a halt, and durst not go forward among men that perhaps would sell their lives as dearly as they could, until they searched all places, that they might not be surprised by any ambush. There, where *Eliakim* and *Hilkiah,* who bore the name of the God of Israel, used to sit, now sit *Nergal-sharezer,* and *Samgar-nebo,* &c., who bore the names of the heathen gods. *Sarsechim* was *Rab-saris,* that is, *captain of the guard*; and *Nergal-sharezer, camp-master,* or quarter-master. And now was fulfilled what Jeremiah prophesied (*ch.* i. 15), that the families of the kingdoms of the north should set everyone his throne at the entering of the gates of Jerusalem.

III. Zedekiah thought it high time to shift for his own safety, and, loaded with guilt and fear, he *went out of the city,* under protection of *the night* (*v.* 4). He was discovered, pursued, and overtaken *in the plains of Jericho, v.* 5. Thence he was brought prisoner to Riblah, where the king of Babylon passed sentence. He *slew his sons before his eyes.* Zedekiah himself was now but thirty-two years of age, and the death of these babes must needs be so many deaths to himself, especially when he considered that his own obstinacy was the cause of it. *They shall bring forth thy wives and children to the Chaldeans, ch.* xxxviii. 23. He *slew all the nobles of Judah* (*v.* 6). He ordered *Zedekiah to have his eyes put out* (*v.* 7), so condemning *him* to darkness for life who had shut his eyes against the clear light of God's word. He *bound him with two brazen chains or fetters* (so the margin reads it), to carry him away to Babylon, there to spend the rest of his days in misery.

IV. Some time afterwards the city was burnt, temple and palace, and the wall of it broken down, *v.* 8.

V. The people that were left were all *carried away captives to Babylon, v.* 9. They must be driven hundreds of miles, like beasts, before the conquerors, that were now their cruel masters; must lie at their mercy in a strange land.

JAMIESON, FAUSSET, BROWN — CHAPTER 39

Vss. 1-18. Jerusalem Taken. Zedekiah's Fate. Jeremiah Cared for. Ebed-melech Assured. This chapter consists of two parts: the first describes the capture of Jerusalem, the removal of the people to Babylon, and the fate of Zedekiah, and that of Jeremiah. The second tells of the assurance of safety to Ebed-melech. **1. ninth year . . . tenth month**—and on the tenth day of it (ch. 52:4; II Kings 25:1-4). From vs. 2, "eleventh year . . . fourth month . . . ninth day," we know the siege lasted one and a half years, excepting the suspension of it caused by Pharaoh. Nebuchadnezzar was present in the beginning of the siege, but was at Riblah at its close (vss. 3, 6; cf. ch. 38:17). **3. sat**—expressing military occupation or encampment. **middle gate**—the gate from the upper city (comprehending Mount Zion) to the lower city (*north* of the former and much lower); it was into the latter (the *north* side) that the Chaldeans forced an entry and took up their position opposite the gate of the "middle" wall, between the lower and upper city. Zedekiah fled in the opposite, i.e., the south direction (vs. 4). **Nergalsharezer, Samgarnebo**—proper names formed from those of the idols, Nergal and Nebo (II Kings 17:30; Isa. 46:1). **Rab-saris**—meaning "chief of the eunuchs." **Rab-mag**—chief of the magi; brought with the expedition in order that its issue might be foreknown through his astrological skill. *Mag* is a Persian word, meaning "great," "powerful." The magi were a sacerdotal caste among the Medes, and supported the Zoroastrian religion. **4. the king's garden**—The "gate" to it from the upper city above was appropriated to the kings alone; "stairs" led down from Mount Zion and the palace to the king's garden below (Neh. 3:15). **two walls**—Zedekiah might have held the upper city longer, but want of provisions drove him to flee by the double wall south of Zion, towards the plains of Jericho (vs. 5), in order to escape beyond Jordan to Arabia Deserta. He broke an opening in the wall to get out (Ezek. 12:12). **5. Riblah**—north of Palestine (see ch. 1:14; Num. 34:11). Hamath is identified by commentators with Antioch, in Syria, on the Orontes, called Epiphania, from Antiochus Epiphanes. **gave judgment upon him**—lit., "spake judgments with him," i.e., brought him to trial as a common criminal, not as a king. He had violated his oath (Ezek. 17:13-19; II Chron. 36: 13). **6. slew . . . sons . . . before his eyes**—previous to his eyes being "put out" (vs. 7); lit., "dug out." The Assyrian sculptures depict the delight with which the kings struck out, often with their own hands, the eyes of captive princes. This passage reconciles ch. 32:4, "his eyes shall behold his eyes"; with Ezekiel 12:13, "he shall not see Babylon, though he shall die there." **slew all . . . nobles**—(ch. 27:20). **8. burned . . . the houses**—(ch. 52:12, 13). Not immediately after the taking of the city, but in the month after, viz., the fifth month (cf. vs. 2). The delay was probably caused by the princes having to send to Riblah to know the king's pleasure as to the city. **9. remnant**—excepting the poorest (vs. 10), who caused Nebuchadnezzar no apprehensions. **those . . . that fell to him**—the *deserters* were distrusted; or they may have been removed at their own request, lest the people should vent their rage on them as traitors, after the departure of the Chaldeans. **rest . . . that remained**—distinct from the previous "remnant"; *there* he means the remnant of those besieged in the city, whom Nebuchadnezzar spared; here, those scattered through various

ADAM CLARKE — CHAPTER 39

1. *In the ninth year of Zedekiah . . . in the tenth month.* This month is called Tebeth in Esther ii. 16. It began with the first new moon of our January, and it was on the tenth day of this month that Nebuchadnezzar invested the city.

2. *The eleventh year . . . in the fourth month.* This month in the Hebrew calendar is called Thammuz, and commences with the first new moon of our July. The siege had lasted just eighteen months. *The city was broken up.* A breach was made in the wall by which the Chaldeans entered.

3. *Sat in the middle gate.* The city of Jerusalem stood upon two hills, Sion to the south, and Acra to the north, with a deep valley between them. The "gate of the center," as the term seems plainly to import, was a gate of communication in the middle of the valley, between the two parts of the city, sometimes called the higher and the lower city. The Chaldeans entered the city on the north side by a breach in the walls, and rushing forward and posting themselves in this gate, in the very heart or center of the city, became thereby masters at will of the whole. Zedekiah with his troop, perceiving this, fled out of the opposite gate on the south side. *Nergal-sharezer.* These were the principal commanders; but Dr. Blayney thinks that instead of six persons, we have in reality but three, as the name that follows each is a title of office.

4. *Went forth out of the city by night.* Probably there was a private passage underground, leading without the walls, by which Zedekiah and his followers might escape unperceived, till they had got some way from the city. *The way of the plain.* There were two roads from Jerusalem to Jericho. One passed over the mount of Olives; but, as this might have retarded his flight, he chose the way of the plain, and was overtaken near Jericho, perhaps about sixteen or eighteen miles from Jerusalem. He had probably intended to pass the Jordan, in order to escape to Egypt, as the Egyptians were then his professed allies.

5. *To Riblah.* This city was situated on the northern frontier of Palestine, and Hamath was a large city belonging also to Syria. See Gen. x. 18.

9. *Those that fell away.* That deserted to the Chaldeans during the siege.

MATTHEW HENRY

Some few, *the poor of the people*, never made any resistance, and were left to tarry at home. The *captain of the guard gave them vineyards and fields at the same time*, such as they were never masters of before, *v.* 10. The rich had been proud oppressors, and now they were justly punished for their injustice; the poor had been patient sufferers, and now they were graciously rewarded for their patience.

Verses 11–18

I. A gracious providence concerning Jeremiah. Nebuchadnezzar had given orders that care should be taken of him, and that he should be in all respects well used, *v.* 11, 12. Nebuzar-adan and the rest of the king of Babylon's princes discharged him out of prison, and did everything to make him easy, *v.* 13, 14. 1. A very generous act of Nebuchadnezzar, who took cognizance of this poor prophet. It was honourably done of the king to give this charge even before the city was taken, and of the captains to observe it even in the heat of action, and it is recorded for imitation. 2. A reproach to Zedekiah and the princes of Israel. They put him in prison, and the king of Babylon and his princes took him out. 3. The performance of God's promise to Jeremiah, in recompence for his services. *I will cause the enemy to treat thee well in the day of evil, ch.* xv. 11. Jeremiah had been fathful to his trust as a prophet, and now God approves himself faithful to him and the promise he had made him. The same that were the instruments of punishing the persecutors were the instruments of relieving the persecuted; and Jeremiah thought never the worse of his deliverance for its coming by the hand of the king of Babylon, but saw the more of the hand of God in it.

II. A gracious message to Ebed-melech, to assure him of a recompence for his kindness to Jeremiah. He relieved *a prophet in the name of a prophet*, and thus he had *a prophet's reward*. Jeremiah tells him that God would certainly bring upon Jerusalem the ruin that had been long threatened; and, for his further satisfaction in having been kind to Jeremiah he should see him abundantly proved a true prophet, *v.* 16. He shall be delivered from having a share in the common calamity: *I will deliver thee; I will surely deliver thee.* He had been instrumental to deliver God's prophet out of the dungeon, and now God promises to deliver him, *because thou hast put thy trust in me, saith the Lord.* Ebed-melech trusted in God that he would own him, and stand by him, and then he was not afraid of the face of man. And those who trust God, as this good man did, in the way of duty, will find that their hope shall not make them ashamed in times of the greatest danger.

JAMIESON, FAUSSET, BROWN

districts of the country which had not been besieged [CALVIN]. **10. left . . . the poor . . . which had nothing**—The poor have least to lose; one of the providential compensations of their lot. They who before had been stripped of their possessions by the wealthier Jews obtain, not only their own, but those of others.

11. Jeremiah's prophecies were known to Nebuchadnezzar through deserters (vs. 9; ch. 38:19), also through the Jews carried to Babylon with Jeconiah (cf. ch. 40:2). Hence the king's kindness to him. **12. look well to him**—*Hebrew*, set thine eyes upon him; provide for his well-being. **13. Nebuzaradan . . . sent**—He was then at Ramah (ch. 40:1). **14. Gedaliah**—son of Ahikam, the former supporter of Jeremiah (ch. 26:24). Gedaliah was the chief of the deserters to the Chaldeans, and was set over the remnant in Judea as one likely to remain faithful to Nebuchadnezzar. His residence was at Mizpah (ch. 40:5). **home**—the house of Gedaliah, wherein Jeremiah might remain as in a safe asylum. As in ch. 40:1 Jeremiah is represented as "bound in chains" when he came to Ramah among the captives to be carried to Babylon, this release of Jeremiah is thought by MAURER to be distinct from that in ch. 40:5, 6. But he seems first to have been released from the court of the prison and to have been taken to Ramah, still in chains, and then committed in freedom to Gedaliah. **dwelt among the people**—i.e., was made free. **15-18.** Belonging to the time when the city was not yet taken, and when Jeremiah was still in the court of the prison (ch. 38:13). This passage is inserted here because it was now that Ebed-melech's good act (ch. 38:7-12; Matt. 25:43) was to be rewarded in his deliverance. **16. Go**—not literally, for he was in confinement, but figuratively. **16. before thee**—in thy sight. **17. the men of whom thou art afraid**—(ch. 38:1, 4-6). The courtiers and princes hostile to thee for having delivered Jeremiah shall have no power to hurt. Heretofore intrepid, he was now afraid; this prophecy was therefore the more welcome to him. **18. life . . . for a prey**—(*Notes*, ch. 21:9; 38:2; 45:5). **put . . . trust in me**—(ch. 38:7-9). Trust in God was the root of his fearlessness of the wrath of men, in his humanity to the prophet (I Chron. 5:20; Ps. 37:40). The "life" he thus risked was to be his reward, being spared beyond all hope, when the lives of his enemies should be forfeited ("for a prey").

ADAM CLARKE

10. *Left of the poor of the people.* The very refuse of the inhabitants, who were not worthy of being carried away; and among them he divided the fields and vineyards of those whom he took away.

12. *Take him . . . look well to him.* Nebuchadnezzar had heard that this prophet had foretold his capture of the city, and had frequently used all his influence to induce Zedekiah to pay the tribute, and not rebel against him; and on this account would be inclined to show the prophet especial favor.

MATTHEW HENRY

CHAPTER 40

Verses 1–6

In these verses we have Jeremiah's adhering, by the advice of Nebuzar-adan, to Gedaliah. Jeremiah was very honourably fetched out of the court of the prison by the king of Babylon's princes (*ch.* xxxix. 13, 14), but afterwards being found among the people in the city, when orders were given to the inferior officers to bind all they found in order to their being carried captives to Babylon, he, through ignorance and mistake, was bound among the rest and hurried away. But when the captives were brought manacled to Ramah, Jeremiah was soon distinguished from the rest, and discharged. 1. The captain of the guard solemnly owns him to be a true prophet (*v.* 2, 3): "*The Lord thy God has* by thee *pronounced this evil upon this place*; they had fair warning given, but they would not take the warning, and *now the Lord hath brought it*, and, as by thy mouth he said it, so by my hand *he hath done what he said.*" He tells all the people that were now in chains before him, *It is because you have sinned against the Lord that this thing has come upon you.* The princes of Israel would never be brought to acknowledge this, but this heathen prince plainly sees it. 2. He gives the prophet leave to dispose of himself as he thought fit. He *loosed him from his chains* a second time (*v.* 4), invited him to come to Babylon as a friend, as a companion; and *I will set my eye upon thee* (so the word is), "I will show thee respect, and will see that thou be well provided for." If he was not disposed to go to Babylon, he might dwell where he pleased in his own country. 3. He advises him to go to Gedaliah and settle with him. This Gedaliah, *made governor of the* land under *the king of Babylon,* was an honest Jew who (it is probable) went over to the Chaldeans, and approved himself so well that he had this great trust put into his hands, *v.* 5. *While* Jeremiah had *not yet gone back*, but stood considering what he should do,

JAMIESON, FAUSSET, BROWN

CHAPTER 40

VSS. 1-16. JEREMIAH IS SET FREE AT RAMAH, AND GOES TO GEDALIAH, TO WHOM THE REMNANT OF JEWS REPAIR. JOHANAN WARNS GEDALIAH OF ISHMAEL'S CONSPIRACY IN VAIN. **1. word that came**—the heading of a new part of the book (chs. 41-44) viz., the prophecies to the Jews in Judea and Egypt after the *taking* of the city, blended with history. The prophecy does not begin till ch. 42:7, and the previous history is introductory to it. **bound in chains**—Though released from the court of the prison (*Note*, ch. 39:14), in the confusion at the burning of the city he seems to have been led away in chains with the other captives, and not till he reached Ramah to have gained full liberty. Nebuzaradan had his quarters at Ramah, in Benjamin; and there he collected the captives previous to their removal to Babylon (ch. 31:15). He in releasing Jeremiah obeyed the king's commands (ch. 39:11). Jeremiah's "chains" for a time were due to the negligence of those to whom he had been committed; or else to Nebuzaradan's wish to upbraid the people with their perverse ingratitude in imprisoning Jeremiah [CALVIN]; hence he addresses the people (*ye . . . you*) as much as Jeremiah (vss. 2, 3). **2.** The Babylonians were in some measure aware, through Jeremiah's prophecies (ch. 39:11), that they were the instruments of God's wrath on His people. **3. ye**—(*Note*, vs. 1). His address is directed to the Jews as well as to Jeremiah. God makes the very heathen testify for Him against them (Deut. 29:24, 25). **4. look well unto thee**—the very words of Nebuchadnezzar's charge (ch. 39:12). **all the land is before thee . . . seemeth good**—(Gen. 20:15, *Margin*). Jeremiah alone had the option given him of staying where he pleased, when all the rest were either carried off or forced to remain there. **5. while he was not yet gone back**—parenthetical. When Jeremiah hesitated whether it would be best

ADAM CLARKE

CHAPTER 40

1. *The word that came to Jeremiah.* This and the following four chapters contain a particular account of what passed in the land of Judea from the taking of the city to the retreat of the people into Egypt, and the prophecies of Jeremiah concerning them there.

2. *The Lord thy God hath pronounced.* I know that you are a true prophet, for what you have predicted from your God is come to pass.

4. *Come; and I will look well unto thee.* You are now at full liberty to do as you please, either to come to Babylon or to stay in your own land.

MATTHEW HENRY

Nebuzar-adan bade him by all means *go to Gedaliah.* Nor does he only give him his liberty, and an approbation of the measures he shall take, but provides for his support: He *gave him victuals and a present,* either in clothes or money, *and* so *let him go.* Jeremiah accepted his kindness, took his advice, and went to Gedaliah, to Mizpah, *and dwelt with him, v.* 6. It did not prove at all to his comfort. However, we may commend his pious affection to the land of Israel, that he would not forsake it, but chose rather to dwell with the poor in the holy land than with princes in an unholy one.

Verses 7–16

I. A bright sky opening upon the remnant of the Jews that were left in their own land, and a prospect given them of peace and quietness after the many years of trouble and terror. Providence seemed to raise and encourage such an expectation, and it would be to that miserable people as life from the dead.

1. Gedaliah, one of themselves, is made *governor in the land,* by *the king of Babylon, v.* 7. He was *the son of Ahikam, the son of Shaphan,* one of the princes. His father (*ch.* xxvi. 24) took Jeremiah's part against the people. He seems to have been a man of great wisdom and a mild temper, and under whose government the few that were left might have been very happy.

2. All those that were now the Jews of the dispersion came and put themselves under his government and protection. The great men that had escaped the Chaldeans came and quietly submitted to Gedaliah. Several are here named, *v.* 8. *They came* with *their men,* their servants, their soldiers, and the king of Babylon had such a good opinion of Gedaliah that he was not jealous of the increase of their numbers, but rather pleased with it. The poor men that had escaped by flight into the neighbouring countries of Moab, Ammon, and Edom, were induced by the love they bore to their own land to return as soon as they heard that Gedaliah was in authority there, *v.* 11, 12. God remembered mercy, and admitted some of them upon a further trial of their obedience.

3. The model of this new government is drawn up and settled by an original contract (*v.* 9): "Come" (says Gedaliah), "*fear not to serve the Chaldeans.*" Though the divine law had forbidden them to make leagues with the heathen, yet the divine sentence had obliged them to yield to the king of Babylon. It is no disgrace to any to comply with him. Fear not the consequences of it. If you will but live peaceably, peaceably, you shall live; disturb not the government, and it will not disturb you. *Serve the king of Babylon and it shall be well with you.* Gedaliah, probably by instruction from the king of Babylon, undertakes upon all occasions to act for them (*v.* 10): "*As for me, behold, I will dwell at Mizpah, to serve the Chaldeans,* to do homage to them in the name of the whole body if there be occasion, to receive orders, and to pay them their tribute when they *come to us.*" Gedaliah gives them the assurance of an oath that he will protect them, but, being charitable, he did not require an oath from them that they would be faithful to him, else the following mischief might have been prevented. Though they own their lands to belong to the Chaldeans, yet, upon that condition, they shall have the free enjoyment of them and all the profits of them (*v.* 10): "*Gather you wine and summer fruits,* and take them for your own use; *put them in your vessels,* to be laid up for winter-store, as those do that live in a land of peace and hope to *eat the labour of your hand.*" And accordingly they *gathered wine and summer fruits very much,* for their corn-harvest was over some time before Jerusalem was taken. Gedaliah left them to enjoy the advantages of the public plenty, and, for aught that appears, demanded no tribute from them; for he sought not his own profit.

II. Here is a dark cloud gathering over this infant state, and threatening a dreadful storm. *Baalis the king of the Ammonites* hated Gedaliah, and was contriving to kill him, either out of malice to the Jews, or personal pique against Gedaliah, *v.* 14. Some make Baalis to signify the queen-mother of the king of the Ammonites, or queen-dowager. One would have thought this little remnant might be safe when the great king of Babylon protected it; and yet it is ruined by the artifices of this petty prince or princess. Happy are those that have the King of kings on their side, for the greatest earthly king cannot with all his power secure us against treachery. He employed *Ishmael, the son of Nethaniah,* as the instrument of his malice, instigated him to murder Gedaliah, and, that he might have a fair opportunity, directed him to enrol himself among his subjects and promise him fealty. Ishmael was of the seed royal, and would therefore be easily

JAMIESON, FAUSSET, BROWN

for him to go, Nebuzaradan proceeded to say, "Go, *then,* to Gedaliah," (not as *English Version,* "Go back, *also*"), if thou preferrest (as Nebuzaradan inferred from Jeremiah's hesitancy) to stop here rather than go with me. **victuals**—(Isa. 33:16). **reward—rather, a present.** This must have been a seasonable relief to the prophet, who probably lost his all in the siege. **6. Mizpah**—in Benjamin, northwest of Jerusalem (ch. 41:5, 6, 9). Not the Mizpah in Gilead, beyond Jordan (Judg. 10:17). Jeremiah showed his patriotism and piety in remaining in his country amidst afflictions and notwithstanding the ingratitude of the Jews, rather than go to enjoy honors and pleasures in a heathen court (Heb. 11:24-26). This vindicates his purity of motive in his withdrawal (ch. 37:12-14).

7. captains . . . in the fields—The leaders of the Jewish army had been "scattered" throughout the country on the capture of Zedekiah (ch. 52:8), in order to escape the notice of the Chaldeans.

8. Netophathite—from Netophah, a town in Judah (II Sam. 23:28). **Maachathite**—from Maachathi, at the foot of Mount Hermon (Deut. 3:14).

11. Jews . . . in Moab—who had fled thither at the approach of the Chaldeans. God thus tempered the severity of His vengeance that a remnant might be left.

9. Fear not—They were afraid that they should not obtain pardon from the Chaldeans for their acts. He therefore assured them of safety by an oath. **serve**—lit., to stand before (vs. 10; ch. 52:12), i.e., to be at hand ready to execute the commands of the king of Babylon.

10. Mizpah—lying on the way between Babylon and Judah, and so convenient for transacting business between the two countries.

As for me . . . but ye—He artfully, in order to conciliate them, represents the burden of the service to the Chaldeans as falling on *him,* while *they* may freely gather their wine, fruits, and oil. He does not now add that these very fruits were to constitute the chief part of the tribute to be paid to Babylon: which, though fruitful in corn, was less productive of grapes, figs, and olives [HERODOTUS, 1.193]. The grant of "vineyards" to the "poor" (ch. 39:10) would give hope to the discontended of enjoying the best fruits (vs. 12).

13. in the fields—not in the city, but scattered in the country (vs. 7). **14. Baalis**—named from the idol Baal, as was often the case in heathen names.

Ammonites—So it was to them that Ishmael went after murdering Gedaliah (ch. 41:10). **slay**—lit., "strike thee in the soul," i.e., a deadly stroke.

Ishmael—Being of the royal seed of David (ch. 41:1), he envied Gedaliah the presidency to which he thought himself entitled; therefore he leagued himself with the ancient heathen enemy of Judah. **believed . . . not**—generous, but unwise unsuspiciousness (Eccles. 9:16).

ADAM CLARKE

5. *Go back also to Gedaliah.* If you will stay in your own land, you had best put yourself under the protection of your countryman Gedaliah, whom the king of Babylon has made governor of the land.

8. *Ishmael the son of Nethaniah.* This is he who afterwards murdered Gedaliah. He had been employed to do this by Baalis, king of the Ammonites, with whom he appears to have taken refuge during the siege. See v. 14.

14. *But Gedaliah the son of Ahikam believed them not.* The account given of this man proves him to have been a person of uncommon greatness of soul. Conscious of his own integrity and benevolence, he took the portrait of others from his own mind; and therefore believed evil of no man, because he felt none towards any in his own breast. He may be reproached for being too credulous and confident, but anything of this kind that may be justly charged against him serves only to show the greatness of his mind.

MATTHEW HENRY

tempted to envy one that set up for a governor in Judah, who was not of David's line. Johanan, a brisk and active man, having got scent of this plot, informed Gedaliah of it: *Dost thou certainly know?* surely thou dost, *v.* 14. He gave him private intelligence of it (*v.* 15). He proffered his service to prevent it: *I will slay* him. *Wherefore should he slay thee?* Gedaliah, being a man of sincerity himself, would by no means give credit to Ishmael's treachery. He said, *Thou speakest falsely of Ishmael.* Many have been ruined by being over-confident of the fidelity of those about them.

JAMIESON, FAUSSET, BROWN

16. thou speakest falsely—a mystery of providence that God should permit the righteous, in spite of warning, thus to rush into the trap laid for them! Isaiah 57:1 suggests a solution.

ADAM CLARKE

MATTHEW HENRY — CHAPTER 41

Verses 1–10

Such base, barbarous, bloody work is here done by men who by their birth should have been men of honour, by their religion just men, and this done upon those of their own nation, their own religion, and their brethren in affliction, upon no provocation—all done in cold blood.

I. Ishmael and his party treacherously killed Gedaliah himself in the first place. The king of Babylon had made him a great man, *governor of the land.* God had made him a good man and a great blessing to his country, and his agency for its welfare was as life from the dead. Ishmael was of *the seed royal* (*v.* 1) and therefore jealous of Gedaliah's growing greatness. He had *ten men* with him that were *princes of the king* too, guided by the same peevish resentments. These had put themselves under his protection (*ch.* xl. 8), and now came again, *and they did eat bread together in Mizpah.* He entertained them generously. They pretended friendship and gave him no warning to stand on his guard. But those that did *eat bread* with him *lifted up the heel* against him. They watched an opportunity, when they had him alone, and assassinated him, *v.* 2.

II. They likewise put all to the sword, both Jews and Chaldeans, all that were employed under Gedaliah, *v.* 3. The vine-dressers and the husbandmen were busy in the fields, and knew nothing of this bloody massacre; so artfully concealed.

III. Some good honest men, that were going to lament the desolations of Jerusalem, were murdered with the rest. They came (*v.* 5)—*from Shechem, Samaria,* and *Shiloh,* places that had been famous, but were now reduced. They were going—*to the house of the Lord,* the temple at Jerusalem, to pay their respects to its ashes. They took *offerings and incense in their hand,* that they might not be without something to offer. They showed their goodwill, though the altar was gone. These went with *their clothes rent* and *their heads shaven.* They were decoyed into a fatal snare by Ishmael's malice. These pilgrims towards Jerusalem he hated for the sake of their errand. Ishmael went out to meet them with crocodiles' tears, pretending to bewail the desolations of Jerusalem as much as they; and, to try how they stood to Gedaliah and his government, he courted them and found them to have a respect for him, which confirmed him in his resolution to murder them. *He said, Come to Gedaliah,* pretending he would have them come and live with him, when really he intended that they should come and die with him, *v.* 6. Ishmael, when he had them *in the midst of the* town, fell upon them and *slew them* (*v.* 7). The dead bodies of these and the rest that he had slain he tumbled into a great *pit* (*v.* 7), the same pit that Asa king of Judah had digged long before, to be a frontier-garrison against *Baasha king of Israel* and *for fear of* him, *v.* 9. Among these last that were doomed to the slaughter there were ten that obtained a pardon, by working on the covetousness of those that had them at their mercy, *v.* 8. They *said to Ishmael, Slay us not, for we have treasures in the field,* country treasures, large stocks upon the ground, *wheat and barley, and oil and honey.* This bait prevailed. Ishmael saved them, not for the love of mercy, but for the love of money.

IV. He carried off the people prisoners. *The king's daughters* and the poor of the land, the vine-dressers and husbandmen, that were committed to Gedaliah's charge, were all led away prisoners towards the country of *the Ammonites* (*v.* 10). These prisoners thought, *Surely the bitterness of death,* and of captivity, *is past;* and yet some died by the sword and others went into captivity. There is many a ship wrecked in the harbour. We can never be sure of peace on this side heaven.

Verses 11–18

It would have been well if Johanan, when he gave information to Gedaliah of Ishmael's treasonable design, had stayed with Gedaliah; for he, and his

JAMIESON, FAUSSET, BROWN — CHAPTER 41

Vss. 1-18. Ishmael Murders Gedaliah and Others, Then Flees to the Ammonites. Johanan Pursues Him, Recovers the Captives, and Purposes to Flee to Egypt for Fear of the Chaldeans. **1. seventh month**—the second month after the burning of the city (ch. 52:12, 13). **and the princes**—not the nominative. And the princes *came,* for the "princes" are not mentioned either in the next verse or in II Kings 25:25: but, "Ishmael being of the seed royal and of the princes of the king" [Maurer]. But the *ten men* were the "princes of the king"; thus Maurer's objection has no weight: so *English Version.* **eat bread together**—Ishmael murdered Gedaliah, by whom he was hospitably received, in violation of the sacred right of hospitality (Ps. 41:9). **2. slew him whom the king of Babylon had made governor**—This assigns a reason for their slaying him, as well as showing the magnitude of their crime (Dan. 2:21; Rom. 13:1). **3. slew all the Jews**—namely, the attendants and ministers of Gedaliah; or, the military alone, about his person; translate, "*even* (not 'and,' as *English Version*) the men of war." The main portion of the people with Gedaliah, including Jeremiah, Ishmael carried away captive (vss. 10, 16). **4. no man knew it**—i.e., outside Mizpah. Before tidings of the murder had gone abroad. **5. beards shaven . . .**—indicating their deep sorrow at the destruction of the temple and city. **cut themselves**—a heathen custom, forbidden (Lev. 19:27, 28; Deut. 14:1). These men were mostly from Samaria, where the ten tribes, previous to their deportation, had fallen into heathen practices. **offerings**—unbloody. They do not bring sacrificial victims, but "incense," etc., to testify their piety. **house of . . . Lord**—i.e., the place where the house of the Lord had stood (II Kings 25:9). The place in which a temple had stood, even when it had been destroyed, was held sacred [Papinian]. Those "from Shiloh" would naturally seek the house of the Lord, since it was at Shiloh it originally was set up (Josh. 18:1). **6. weeping**—pretending to weep, as they did, for the ruin of the temple. **Come to Gedaliah**—as if he was one of Gedaliah's retinue. *7. and cast them* **into . . . pit**—He had not killed them in the pit (cf. vs. 9); these words are therefore rightly supplied in *English Version.* **the pit**—the pit or cistern made by Asa to guard against a want of water when Baasha was about to besiege the city (I Kings 15:22). The trench or fosse round the city [Grotius]. Ishmael's motive for the murder seems to have been a suspicion that they were coming to live under Gedaliah. **8. treasures**—It was customary to hide grain in cavities underground in troubled times. "We have treasures," which we will give, if our lives be spared. **slew . . . not**—(Prov. 13:8). Ishmael's avarice and needs overcame his cruelty. **9. because of Gedaliah**—rather, "*near* Gedaliah," viz., those intercepted by Ishmael on their way from Samaria to Jerusalem and killed *at Mizpah,* where Gedaliah had lived. So II Chronicles 17:15, "next"; Nehemiah 3:2, *Margin,* lit., as here, "at his hand." "In the reign of Gedaliah" [Calvin]. However, *English Version* gives a good sense: Ishmael's reason for killing them was *because* of his supposing them to be connected with Gedaliah. **10. the king's daughters**—(ch. 43:6). Zedekiah's. Ishmael must have got additional followers (whom the hope of gain attracted), besides those who originally set out with him (vs. 1), so as to have been able to carry off all the residue of the people. He probably meant to sell them as slaves to the Ammonites (ch. 40:14, *Note*).

11. Johanan—the friend of Gedaliah who had warned him of Ishmael's treachery, but in vain (ch. 40:8, 13).

ADAM CLARKE — CHAPTER 41

1. *Now . . . in the seventh month.* Answering to the first new moon in our month of October.

There they did eat bread together. This was the same as making a solemn covenant, for he who ate bread with another was ever reputed a friend.

2. *Smote Gedaliah.* See the preceding chapter, v. 14.

5. *Having their beards shaven.* All these were signs of deep mourning, probably on account of the destruction of the city.

6. *Weeping all along as he went.* This felonious hypocrite pretended that he also was deeply afflicted, and wished to bear them company in their sorrow. *Come to Gedaliah.* He will appoint you vineyards and fields.

7. *Slew them.* He kept the murder of Gedaliah secret, and no doubt had a band of his assassins lodged in Mizpah; and he decoyed these fourscore men thither that he might have strength to slay them. He kept ten alive because they told him they had treasures hidden in a field, which they would show him. Whether he kept his word with them is not recorded. He could do nothing good or great; and it is likely that, when he had possessed himself of those treasures, he served them as he had served their companions.

9. *Now the pit . . . was it which Asa the king had made for fear of Baasha.* See 1 Kings xv. 22. Asa made this cistern as a reservoir for water for the supply of the place; for he built and fortified Mizpah at the time that he was at war with Baasha, king of Israel.

10. *Carried them away captive.* He took all these that he might sell them for slaves among the Ammonites.

MATTHEW HENRY

captains and their forces, might have been a life-guard to Gedaliah, but it seems they were out upon some expedition when they should have been upon the best service. Those that affect to ramble are many times out of their place when they are most needed. However, at length they *hear of all the evil that Ishmael had done* (*v.* 11). Johanan prevailed only to rescue the captives. Johanan gathered what forces he could *and went to fight with Ishmael* (*v.* 12). He pursued him, and overtook him by the great *pool of Gibeon*, which we read of, 2 Sam. ii. 13. And, upon his appearing with such a force, Ishmael's heart failed him, and he durst not stand his ground. The poor captives *were glad when they saw Johanan* and *the captains that were with him*, looking upon them as their deliverers (*v.* 13), and they found a way to wheel about and come over to them (*v.* 14), Ishmael not offering to detain them. Ishmael quitted his prey to save his life, and *escaped with eight men*, *v.* 15. It seems, two of his ten men, that were his banditti or assassins (spoken of *v.* 1), deserted him. He made his way to the Ammonites, and we hear no more of him. The resolution of Johanan and the captains was very rash; nothing would serve them but they would *go to enter into Egypt* (*v.* 17), and, in order to that, they encamped for a time *in the habitation of Chimham, by Bethlehem*, David's city. Here Johanan made his headquarters, steering his course towards Egypt, either from a personal affection to that country or an ancient confidence in the Egyptians. Some of the *mighty men of war*, it seems, had escaped; those he took with him, *and the women and children, whom he had recovered from Ishmael.*

JAMIESON, FAUSSET, BROWN

12. the . . . waters . . . in Gibeon—(II Sam. 2:13); a large reservoir or lake. **Gibeon**—on the road from Mizpah to Ammon: one of the sacerdotal cities of Benjamin, four miles northwest of Jerusalem, now *El-jib*. **13. glad**—at the prospect of having a deliverer from their captivity. **14. cast about**—came round. **16. men of war**—"The men of war," stated in vs. 3 to have been slain by Ishmael, must refer to the military about Gedaliah's person; "the men of war" here to those not so. **eunuchs**—The kings of Judah had adopted the bad practice of having harems and eunuchs from the surrounding heathen kingdoms. **17. dwelt**—for a time, until they were ready for their journey to Egypt (ch. 42). **habitation to Chimham**—his caravanserai close by Bethlehem. David, in reward for Barzillai's loyalty, took Chimham his son under his patronage, and made over to him his own patrimony in the land of Bethlehem. It was thence called the habitation of Chimham (Geruth-Chimham), though it reverted to David's heirs in the year of jubilee. Caravanserais (a compound *Persian* word, meaning "the house of a company of travellers") differ from our inns, in that there is no host to supply food, but each traveller must carry with him his own. **18. afraid**—lest the Chaldeans should suspect all the Jews of being implicated in Ishmael's treason, as though the Jews sought to have a prince of the house of David (vs. 1). Their better way towards gaining God's favor would have been to have laid the blame on the real culprit, and to have cleared themselves. A tortuous policy is the parent of fear. Righteousness inspires with boldness (Ps. 53:5; Prov. 28:1).

ADAM CLARKE

14. *Went unto Johanan.* They were weary of the tyranny of Ishmael, and were glad of an opportunity to abandon him.

16. *The women . . . children, and the eunuchs.* These were all, most probably, persons who belonged to the palace and harem of Zedekiah: some of them his own concubines, and their children.

17. *Dwelt in the habitation of Chimham.* The estate that David gave Chimham, the son of Barzillai. See 2 Sam. xix. 37, etc. He took this merely as a resting place; as he designed to carry all into Egypt, fearing the Chaldeans, who would endeavor to revenge the death of Gedaliah.

CHAPTER 42

MATTHEW HENRY

Verses 1–6

Jeremiah the prophet escaped the sword of Ishmael; and it was not the first time that the Lord hid him. At length, to serve a turn, Jeremiah is sought out, and *all the captains, Johanan* himself not excepted, with *all the people from the least to the greatest*, make him a visit; they *came near* (*v.* 1). Hitherto they had kept at a distance from the prophet and had been shy of him.

I. They desire him by prayer to ask direction from God what they should do in the present critical juncture, *v.* 2, 3. They express themselves with great respect to the prophet. Though he was poor and low, yet they apply to him with humility as petitioners for his assistance: *Let, we beseech thee, our supplication be accepted before thee.* They compliment him thus to persuade him to say as they would have him say. "*Pray for us*, who know not how to pray for ourselves. *Pray to the Lord thy God*, for we are unworthy to call him ours, nor have we reason to expect any favour from him." They speak of themselves as objects of compassion: "*We are but a remnant, but a few of many;* how easily will such a remnant be swallowed up. *Thy eyes* see what distress we are in; if thou canst do anything, help us. Let *the Lord thy God* take this ruin into his thoughts, and *show us the way wherein we may walk* and may expect to have his presence with us, *and the thing that we may do*, the course we may take for our own safety."

II. Jeremiah faithfully promises to pray for direction for them, and, whatever message God should send to them by him, he would deliver it to them just as he received it, *v.* 4. Though they had slighted him, yet, like Samuel when he was slighted, he will not *sin against the Lord in ceasing to pray for* them, 1 Sam. xii. 23. He will *declare to them the whole counsel of God*, that they may approve themselves true to their trust.

III. They promise that they will be governed by the will of God, as soon as they know what it is (*v.* 5, 6). They now call God *their* God, for Jeremiah had encouraged them to call him so (*v.* 4): *I will pray to the Lord your God.* They promise to *obey his voice* because they sent the prophet to him to consult him. They will do what God appoints them to do, *whether it be good or whether it be evil*; "Though it may seem evil to us, yet we will believe that if God command it it is certainly good, and we must not dispute it, but do it. Whatever God commands, whether it be easy or difficult, if it be our duty, we will do it."

Verses 7–22

The answer which Jeremiah was sent to deliver to those who employed him to ask counsel of God.

I. It did not come till *ten days after*, *v.* 7. They were thus long held in suspense, perhaps, to punish them for their hypocrisy or to show that Jeremiah did not

JAMIESON, FAUSSET, BROWN

VSS. 1-22. THE JEWS AND JOHANAN INQUIRE OF GOD, THROUGH JEREMIAH, AS TO GOING TO EGYPT, PROMISING OBEDIENCE TO HIS WILL. THEIR SAFETY ON CONDITION OF STAYING IN JUDEA, AND THEIR DESTRUCTION IN THE EVENT OF GOING TO EGYPT, ARE FORETOLD. THEIR HYPOCRISY IN ASKING FOR COUNSEL WHICH THEY MEANT NOT TO FOLLOW, IF CONTRARY TO THEIR OWN DETERMINATION, IS REPROVED. **2. Jeremiah**—He probably was one of the number carried off from Mizpah, and dwelt with Johanan (ch. 41:16). Hence the expression is, "came near" (vs. 1), not "sent." **Let . . . supplication be accepted**—lit., "fall" (*Note*, ch. 36:7; 37:20). **pray for us**—(Gen. 20:7; Isa. 37:4; Jas. 5:16). **thy God**—(vs. 5). The Jews use this form to express their belief in the peculiar relation in which *Jeremiah* stood to God as His accredited prophet. Jeremiah in his reply reminds them that God is *their* God ("*your* God") as well as his as being the covenant people (vs. 4). They in turn acknowledge this in vs. 6, "the Lord *our* God." **few of many**—as had been foretold (Lev. 26:22). **3.** They consulted God, like many, not so much to know what was right, as wishing Him to authorize what they had already determined on, whether agreeable to His will or not. So Ahab in consulting Micaiah (I Kings 22:13). Cf. Jeremiah's answer (vs. 4) with Micaiah's (I Kings 22:14).

4. I have heard—i.e., I accede to your request. **your God**—Being His by adoption, ye are not your own, and are bound to whatever He wills (Exod. 19:5, 6; I Cor 6:19, 20). **answer you**—i.e., through me. **keep nothing back**—(I Sam. 3:18; Acts 20:20.) **5. Lord be a true . . . witness**—(Gen. 31:50; Ps. 89:37; Rev. 1:5; 3:14; 19: 11). **6. evil**—not moral evil, which God cannot command (Jas. 1:13), but what may be *disagreeable* and *hard* to us. Piety obeys God, without questioning, at all costs. See the instance defective in this, that it obeyed only so far as was agreeable to itself (I Sam. 15:3, 9, 13-15, 20-23).

7. ten days—Jeremiah did not speak of himself, but waited God's time and revelation, showing the reality of his in-

ADAM CLARKE

1. *The captains of the forces.* The different leaders of the small bands or companies, collected from different parts of the land. The principal are those here named.

3. *That the Lord thy God may shew us.* They all thought there was no safety in Jerusalem or in Judea, and therefore determined to leave the land. But they did not know which might be the safest direction to take; for though they inclined to Egypt, yet they wished to know the mind of God on that point.

5. *The Lord be a true and faithful witness.* The Lord is such; and as you have bound yourselves to obey His voice, He will register the covenant, and bless or curse according as you shall conduct yourselves in this matter.

7. *After ten days.* All this time he was waiting upon God; for it is evident the prophets could not prophesy when they pleased, any

MATTHEW HENRY

speak of himself, but must wait for instructions. *The vision is for an appointed time, and at the end it shall speak.*

II. When it did come he delivered it publicly, both to the *captains* and to all the *people*, fully and faithfully as he received it. What he has to advise is what *the Lord the God of Israel saith*, to whom they had sent him.

1. It is the will of God that they should stay where they are, and his promise that, if they do so, it shall be *well with them, v.* 10. Their brethren were forced out of it into captivity; let those therefore count it a mercy that they may stay in it and a duty to stay in it. He expresses a very tender concern for them in their calamitous condition: *It repenteth me of the evil that I have done unto you.* Not that he changed his mind, but he was very ready to change his way and to return in mercy to them. He answers the argument they had against abiding in this land. *They feared the king of Babylon* (*ch.* xli. 18), lest he should come and avenge the death of Gedaliah upon them, though they were no way accessory to it. "*Be not afraid of the king of Babylon*, for that fear will bring a snare: fear not for *I am with you*; and, if God be for you to save you, who can be against you to hurt you?" He assures them that if they will still abide in this land they shall not only be safe from the king of Babylon, but be made happy by the King of kings: "*I will build you and plant you;* you shall take root again, and be the new foundation of another state, a phoenix-kingdom, rising out of the ashes of the last." God will show them mercy in this, that not only the king of Babylon shall not destroy them, but he shall *have mercy upon them* and help to settle them. God has made that our duty which is really our privilege, and our obedience will be its own recompence.

2. They must by no means think of going into Egypt of all places, not to that land out of which God had delivered their fathers and with which he had so often warned them not to make alliance. "You begin to say, *We will not dwell in this land* (*v.* 13); no, not though God himself undertake our protection. We will *go into the land of Egypt*, and *there will we dwell*, whether God give us leave and go along with us or no," *v.* 14. It is supposed that their hearts were upon it: "*If you wholly set your faces to enter into Egypt*, then take what follows." Now the reason for their resolution is that "*in Egypt we shall see no war, nor have hunger of bread*, as we have had for a long time in this land," *v.* 14. The sentence passed upon them for this sin, if they will persist in it is pronounced in God's name (*v.* 15): "*Hear the word of the Lord, you remnant of Judah*, who think that because you are a remnant you must be spared" (*v.* 2). Did the sword and famine frighten them? Those very judgments shall pursue them into Egypt and overcome them there (*v.* 16, 17): "You think, because war and famine have long been raging in this land, that they are entailed upon it; whereas, if you trust in God, he can make even this land a land of peace to you." The men that go to Egypt in contradiction to God's will, to escape *the sword and famine*, shall *die in Egypt by sword and famine*. Did the desolations of Jerusalem frighten them? Were they willing to get as far as they could from them? They shall meet with the second part of them too in Egypt (*v.* 18). When God's professing people mingle with infidels, and make their court to them, they lose their dignity and make themselves a reproach.

3. God knew their hypocrisy in their enquiries of him, and that when they asked what he would have them to do they were resolved to take their own way; and therefore the sentence. The prophet solemnly protests that he had faithfully delivered his message, *v.* 19. The conclusion of the whole matter is, "*Go not down into Egypt;* you disobey the command of God if you do. I have plainly *admonished you*; you cannot now plead ignorance of the mind of God." He charges them with base dissimulation in the application they made to him for divine direction (*v.* 20) "*You dissembled in your hearts;* you professed one thing and intended another, promising what you never meant to perform." *You have used deceit against your souls* (so the margin reads it). *Know certainly that you shall die by the sword, v.* 22. God's threatenings may be vilified, but cannot be nullified, by the unbelief of man.

JAMIESON, FAUSSET, BROWN

spiration. Man left to himself would have given an immediate response to the people, who were impatient of delay. The delay was designed to test the sincerity of their professed willingness to obey, and that they should have full time to deliberate (Deut. 8:2). True obedience bows to God's time, as well as His way and will.

10. If ye . . . abide—viz., under the Babylonian authority, to which God hath appointed that all should be subject (Dan. 2: 37, 38). To resist was to resist God. **build . . . plant**—metaphor for, *I will firmly establish* you (ch. 24:6). **I repent . . . of the evil**—(ch. 18:8; Deut. 32:36). *I am satisfied with the punishment I have inflicted on you*, if only you add not a new offense [GROTIUS]. God is said to "repent," when He alters His outward ways of dealing.

12. show mercies—rather, I *will excite* (in him) *feelings of mercy* towards you [CALVIN]. **cause you to return**—permit you to return to the peaceable enjoyment of the possessions from which you are wishing to withdraw through fear of the Chaldeans. By departing in disobedience they should incur the very evils they wished thereby to escape; and by staying they should gain the blessings which they feared to lose by doing so. **13. if ye say . . .**—avowed rebellion against God, who had often (Deut. 17:16), as now, forbidden their going to Egypt, lest they should be entangled in its idolatry. **14. where we shall see no war**—Here they betray their impiety in not believing God's promise (vss. 10, 11), as if He were a liar (I John 5:10). **15. wholly set your faces**—*firmly resolve* (Luke 9:51) in spite of all warnings (ch. 44: 12). **16. sword, which ye feared, shall overtake you**—The very evils we think to escape by sin, we bring on ourselves thereby. What our hearts are most set on often proves fatal to us. Those who think to escape troubles by changing their place will find them wherever they go (Ezek. 11:8). The "sword" here is that of Nebuchadnezzar, who fulfilled the prediction in his expedition to Africa (according to MEGASTHENES, a heathen writer), 300 B.C. **17. all the men**—excepting the "small number" mentioned (ch. 44:14, 28); viz., those who were forced into Egypt against their will, Jeremiah, Baruch, etc., and those who took Jeremiah's advice and fled from Egypt before the arrival of the Chaldeans. **18. As mine anger . . .**—As ye have already, to your sorrow, found Me true to My word, so shall ye again (ch. 7:20; 18:16). **shall see this place no more**—Ye shall not return to Judea, as those shall who have been removed to Babylon. **19. I have admonished**—lit., "testified," i.e., solemnly admonished, having yourselves as My *witnesses;* so that if ye perish, ye yourselves will have to confess that it was through your own fault, not through ignorance, ye perished. **20. dissembled in your hearts**—rather, "ye have used deceit against your (own) souls." It is not God, but yourselves, whom ye deceive, to your own ruin, by your own dissimulation (Gal. 6:7) [CALVIN]. But the words following accord best with *English Version, ye have dissembled in your hearts* (vs. 3, *Note*) towards me, *when ye sent me* to consult God for you. **21. declared it**—viz., the divine will. **I . . . but ye**—antithesis. *I* have done my part; *but ye* do not yours. It is no fault of mine that ye act not rightly. **22. sojourn**—*for a time*, until they could return to their country. They expected, therefore, to be restored, in spite of God's prediction to the contrary.

ADAM CLARKE

more than the disciples of our Lord could work miracles when they wished. The gift of prophecy and the gift of miracles were both dependent on the will of the Most High, and each of them was given only for the moment; and when the necessity was over, the influence ceased.

10. *For I repent me of the evil.* The meaning is, As I have punished you only because you continued to be rebellious, I will arrest this punishment as soon as you become obedient to My word. You need not fear the king of Babylon if you have Me for your Helper; and I will so show mercy to you that he shall see it, and cease from afflicting you, as he shall see that I am on your side.

15. *If ye . . . set your faces to enter into Egypt*, etc. Every evil that you dreaded by staying in your own land shall come upon you in Egypt.

16. *The sword . . . and the famine . . . shall follow close after you.* Shall be at your heels, shall overtake and destroy you; for *there ye shall die.*

19. *Go ye not into Egypt.* Why? Because God knew, such was their miserable propensity to idolatry, that they would there adopt the worship of the country, and serve idols.

MATTHEW HENRY

CHAPTER 43

Verses 1–7

What God said to the builders of Babel may be truly said of this people: *Now nothing will be restrained from them which they have imagined to do*, Gen. xi. 6. They have a fancy for Egypt, and to Egypt they will go, whatever God himself says. Jeremiah made them

JAMIESON, FAUSSET, BROWN

CHAPTER 43

VSS. 1-13. THE JEWS CARRY JEREMIAH AND BARUCH INTO EGYPT. JEREMIAH FORETELLS BY A TYPE THE CONQUEST OF EGYPT BY NEBUCHADNEZZAR, AND THE FATE OF THE FUGITIVES.

ADAM CLARKE

CHAPTER 43

MATTHEW HENRY

hear all he had to say; it was what the Lord their God had sent him to speak to them, and they shall have it all.

I. They deny it to be a message from God: *Johanan, and all the proud men, said to Jeremiah, Thou speakest falsely, v.* 2. The cause of their disobedience was pride. They were *proud men* that gave the lie to the prophet. They could not bear the control of their designs, no, not by the divine wisdom, by the divine will itself. Either they were not convinced that what was said came from God or though they were convinced of it they would not own it. Had they not consulted Jeremiah as a prophet? Had he not waited to receive instructions from God what to say to them? And had not God proved him a prophet indeed? They had some good thoughts of Jeremiah, but they suggest (*v.* 3), *Baruch sets thee on against us.* If Jeremiah and he had been so well affected to the Chaldeans they would have gone away with Nebuzaradan to Babylon, and not have stayed to take their lot with this despised ungrateful remnant. If Baruch had been so ill disposed, could they think Jeremiah would be so influenced by him as to make God's name an authority to patronise so villainous a purpose?

II. They determine to go to Egypt notwithstanding. They resolve not to *dwell in the land of Judah*, as God had ordered them (*v.* 4), but to go with one consent to Egypt. Those that came *from all the nations whither they had been driven, to dwell in the land of Judah*, out of a sincere affection to that land, they would not leave to their liberty, but forced them to go with them into Egypt (*v.* 5), *men, women, and children* (*v.* 6). These proud men compelled even Jeremiah the prophet and Baruch his scribe to go along with them to Egypt. They *came to Tahpanhes*, a famous city of Egypt (so called from a queen of that name, 1 Kings xi. 19). Pharaoh's house was there, *v.* 9. If they had had the spirit of Israelites, they would have chosen rather to dwell in the wilderness of Judah than in the most pompous populous cities of Egypt.

Verses 8–13

Here, as also in the next chapter, Jeremiah is prophesying in Egypt. Jeremiah was now in Tahpanhes, among idolatrous Egyptians and treacherous Israelites; but there he received *the word of the Lord*; it *came to him.* God can find his people, with the visits of his grace, wherever they are. The spirit of prophecy was not confined to the land of Israel. When Jeremiah went into Egypt by constraint, God withdrew not his wonted favour from him. What he received of the Lord he delivered to the people. These two messages Jeremiah was appointed and entrusted to deliver when he was in Egypt—one in this chapter, relating to Egypt, and foretelling its destruction, the other in the next chapter, relating to the Jews in Egypt. God had told them that if they went into Egypt the sword should follow them; here he tells them further that the sword of Nebuchadrezzar should follow them.

I. This is foretold by a sign. Jeremiah must take *great stones* and *lay them in the clay of the* furnace, or *brick-kiln*, which is *in the open way*, or *beside the way* that leads *to Pharaoh's house* (*v.* 9). Egypt was famous for brick-kilns (Exod. v. 7). The foundation of Egypt's desolation was laid in those brick-kilns, in *that clay.* This he must do *in the sight of the men of Judah* to whom he was sent, that, since he could not prevent their going into Egypt, he might bring them to repent of their going.

II. It is foretold, 1. That the present king of Babylon, Nebuchadrezzar, should come in person against the land of Egypt, and should *set his throne* in that very place where *these stones* were laid, *v.* 10. This circumstance is particularly foretold, that, when it was accomplished, they might be confirmed in their belief of the certainty of the divine prescience, to which the smallest events are evident. God calls Nebuchadnezzar his servant, because herein he executed God's will. 2. That he should destroy many of the Egyptians, and have them all at his mercy (*v.* 11): *He shall smite the land of Egypt;* whom he will he shall slay. And whom he will he shall save alive and carry into *captivity*. 3. That he shall destroy the idols of Egypt, the temples and the images of their gods (*v.* 12): *He shall burn the houses of the Gods of Egypt. Beth-shemesh*, or *the house of the sun*, was so called from a temple there built to the sun. The statues he shall *break in pieces* (*v.* 13) The king of Babylon was himself a great idolater and had his temples and images in honour of the sun. Yet he is employed to destroy the idols of Egypt. 4. That he shall make himself master of the land. *He shall array himself with the rich spoils of the land of Egypt.* He shall array himself with them as ornaments and as armour; and this, though it shall be a heavy booty, he shall slip on with as much ease *as a shepherd slips on his garment*, when he goes to turn out his sheep in

JAMIESON, FAUSSET, BROWN

2. Azariah—the author of the project of going into Egypt; a very different man from the Azariah in Babylon (Dan. 1:7; 3:12-18). **proud**—Pride is the parent of disobedience and contempt of God.

3. Baruch—He being the younger spake out the revelations which he received from Jeremiah more vehemently. From this cause, and from their knowing that he was in favor with the Chaldeans, arose their suspicion of him. Their perverse fickleness was astonishing. In ch. 42 they acknowledged the trustworthiness of Jeremiah, of which they had for so long so many proofs; yet here they accuse him of a lie. The mind of the unregenerate man is full of deceits.

5. remnant . . . returned from all nations—(ch. 40:11, 12). **6. the king's daughters**—Zedekiah's (ch. 41:10). **7. Tahpanhes**—(ch. 2:16, *Note*); Daphne on the Tanitic branch of the Nile, near Pelusium. They naturally came to it first, being on the frontier of Egypt, towards Palestine.

9. stones—to be laid as the foundation beneath Nebuchadnezzar's throne (vs. 10). **clay**—mortar. **brick-kiln**—Bricks in that hot country are generally dried in the sun, not burned. The palace of Pharaoh was being built or repaired at this time; hence arose the mortar and brick-kiln at the entry. Of the same materials as that of which Pharaoh's house was built, the substructure of Nebuchadnezzar's throne should be constructed. By a visible symbol implying that the throne of the latter shall be raised on the downfall of the former. Egypt at that time contended with Babylon for the empire of the East. **10. my servant**—God often makes one wicked man or nation a scourge to another (Ezek. 29:18, 19, 20). **royal pavilion**—the rich tapestry (lit., ornament) which hung round the throne from above. **11. such as are for death to death**—i.e., the deadly plague. Some he shall cause to die by the plague arising from insufficient or bad food; others, by the sword; others he shall lead captive, according as God shall order it (ch. 15:2, *Note*). **12. houses of . . . gods**—He shall not spare even the temple, such will be His fury. A reproof to the Jews that they betook themselves to Egypt, a land whose own safety depended on helpless idols. **burn . . . carry . . . captives**—*burn* the Egyptian idols of wood, *carry* to Babylon those of gold and other metals. **array himself with the land . . .**—Isaiah 49:18 has the same metaphor. **as a shepherd . . .**—He shall become master of Egypt as speedily and easily as a shepherd, about to pass on with his flock to another place, puts on his garment. **13. images**—statues or obelisks. **Beth-shemesh**—i.e., "the house of the sun," in *Hebrew;* called by the Greeks Heliopolis; by the Egyptians, On (Gen. 41:45); east of the Nile, and a few miles north of Memphis. Ephraim Syrus says, the statue rose to the height of sixty cubits; the base was ten cubits. Above there was a miter of 1000 pounds weight. Hieroglyphics are traced around the only obelisk remaining in the present day, sixty or seventy feet high. On the fifth year after the overthrow of Jerusalem, Nebuchadnezzar, leaving the siege of Tyre, undertook his expedition to Egypt (JOSEPHUS, *Antiquities*, 10.9, 7). The Egyptians, according to the Arabs, have a tradition that their land was devastated by Nebuchadnezzar in consequence of their king having received the Jews under his protection, and that it lay desolate forty years. But see *Note*, Ezekiel 29:2, 13. **shall he burn**—Here the act is attributed to *Nebuchadnezzar*, the instrument, which in vs. 12 is attributed to God. If even the temples be not spared, much less private houses.

ADAM CLARKE

2. *Thou speakest falsely.* They had no other color for their rebellion than flatly to deny that God had spoken what the prophet related.

6. *Men, and women, and children, and the king's daughters.* See chap. xli. 10. It is truly surprising that the Chaldeans should have left behind any of the royal family of Judah! But (1) Perhaps they knew not there were any. (2) If they did know, they might think, being children of concubines, they could not inherit. Or, (3) That, being females, they were not eligible. And they had taken care to seize all Zedekiah's sons, and slay them before his eyes.

7. *Came they even to Tahpanhes.* This city was called Daphne by the Greeks, and was situated at the extremity of Lower Egypt, near to Heliopolis. It was called Daphne Pelusiaca. They halted at this place, most probably for the purpose of obtaining the king's permission to penetrate farther into Egypt. It was at this place that, according to St. Jerome, tradition says the faithful Jeremiah was stoned to death by these rebellious wretches; for whose welfare he had watched, prayed, gone through many indignities, and suffered every kind of hardship. And now he sealed the truth of his divine mission with his blood.

9. *Take great stones.* This discourse seems to have been delivered about a year after the destruction of Jerusalem. They pretended that they dared not stay in Judea for fear of the Chaldeans. The prophet here assures them that Nebuchadnezzar shall come to Egypt, extend his conquests in that kingdom, and place his tent over the very place where these stones were laid up, and destroy them. How these prophecies were fulfilled, see at the end of chap. xliv.

11. *Such as are for death to death.* See chap. xv. 2.

12. *He shall burn them, and carry them away captives.* Some of these gods, such as were of wood, he will burn; those of metal he will carry away. Some of them were of gold. *Shall array himself with the land of Egypt.* Shall take all its wealth and all its grandeur, shall take all its spoils. *As a shepherd putteth on his garment.* With as much ease, and with as little opposition, and with as full a confidence that it is now his own. *He shall go forth from thence in peace.* He shall suffer no interruption, nor endure any disaster in his return from his Egyptian expedition.

13. *He shall break also the images of Beth-shemesh. Beith shemesh* is, literally, "the house or temple of the sun"; which was worshipped here, and whose images are said to have been of solid gold. These Nebuchadnezzar was to break and carry away; *and the houses of the gods*—all the temples of Egypt, he was to burn with fire. Beth-shemesh is the same as Heliopolis.

MATTHEW HENRY

JAMIESON, FAUSSET, BROWN

ADAM CLARKE

a morning. He shall make no more of the spoils of the land of Egypt than of a shepherd's coat. He shall *go forth in peace*, without any molestation so effectually reduced shall the land of Egypt be. This destruction of Egypt by the king of Babylon is foretold, Ezek. xxix. 19 and xxx. 10.

CHAPTER 44

Verses 1–14

The Jews in Egypt were now dispersed into various parts of the country, into *Migdol, and Noph*, and other places, and Jeremiah was sent on an errand from God to them (*v.* 15).

I. God puts them in mind of the desolations of Judah and Jerusalem, which the fugitives in the cities of Egypt seem to have forgotten (*v.* 2): *You have seen* what a deplorable condition Judah and Jerusalem are brought into; now will you consider whence those desolations came? From the wrath of God; it was his anger which made Jerusalem and *the cities of Judah waste and desolate* (*v.* 6).

II. He puts them in mind of the sins that brought those desolations upon Judah and Jerusalem. It was for *their wickedness* (*v.* 3), giving honour to counterfeit deities, which should have been given to the true God only. They forsook the God who was known among them. "*Neither they nor you, nor your fathers*, could give any rational account why *the God of Israel* was exchanged for such impostors."

III. He puts them in mind of the frequent and fair warnings he had given them by his word not to serve other gods, *v.* 4. *The prophets* were sent with a great deal of care to call to them, saying, *Oh! do not this abominable thing that I hate.* It becomes us to give warning of the danger of sin: "*Oh! do not* do it. If you love God, do not, for it is provoking to him; if you love your own souls do not, for it is destructive to them." If God hates it, thou shouldst hate it. But "*They hearkened not, nor inclined their ear* (*v.* 5). Now this was intended for warning to you, who have not only heard the judgments of God's mouth, as they did, but have likewise seen the judgments of his hand."

IV. He reproves them for their continued idolatries (*v.* 8): You *burn incense to other gods in the land of Egypt.* They went against God's mind into Egypt, and when we thrust ourselves into places of temptation, it is just with God to leave us to ourselves. They did a great deal of injury to themselves and their families: "*You commit this great evil against your souls*" (*v.* 7). "It is the ready way to *cut yourselves off* from all comfort and hope (*v.* 8), to cut off your name and honour; so that you will by your sin and by your misery, become *a curse and a reproach among all nations.*" They filled up the iniquity of their fathers, and added to it (*v.* 9): "*Have you forgotten the wickedness* of those who are gone before you?" *Have you forgotten the punishments of your fathers?* so some read it. He reminds them of the sins and punishments *of the kings of Judah*, and *the wickedness of their wives*, who had seduced them to idolatry. In the original it is, *And of his wives*, which, Dr. Lightfoot thinks, tacitly reflects upon Solomon's wives, particularly his Egyptian wives. *Have you forgotten your own wickedness and the wickedness of your wives*, when you lived in prosperity in Jerusalem, and what ruin it brought upon you?

V. He threatens their utter ruin for their persisting in their idolatry now that they were in Egypt. They shall perish in Egypt. Those that think not only to affront, but to confront, God Almighty, will find themselves outfaced. They shall not be wasted by natural deaths, as Israel in the wilderness, but by sore judgments. None (except a very few that will narrowly escape) shall ever *return to the land of Judah* again, *v.* 14. Those that are fretful and discontented will be uneasy and fond of change wherever they are. The Israelites, when they were in the land of Judah, desired to go into Egypt (*ch.* xlii. 22), but when they were in Egypt they desired to *return to the land of Judah* again; they *lifted up their soul* to it (so it is in the margin), which denotes an earnest desire.

Verses 15–19

The people's obstinate refusal to submit to the power of the word of God in the mouth of Jeremiah.

I. The persons who thus set God and his judgments at defiance were such as knew either themselves or their wives to be guilty of the idolatry Jeremiah had reproved, *v.* 15. The women had been more guilty of idolatry and superstition than the men, not because the men stuck closer to the true God, but because they were generally atheists, and were for no God and no religion at all, and therefore could easily allow their wives to be of a false religion. It was consciousness

CHAPTER 44

VSS. 1-30. JEREMIAH REPROVES THE JEWS FOR THEIR IDOLATRY IN EGYPT, AND DENOUNCES GOD'S JUDGMENTS ON THEM AND EGYPT ALIKE. **1. Migdol**—meaning a "tower." A city east of Egypt, towards the Red Sea (Exod. 14:2; Num. 33:7). **Noph**—Memphis, now Cairo (ch. 2:16). **Pathros**—Upper Egypt (Isa. 11:11). **2. evil . . . upon Jerusalem**—If I spared not My own sacred city, much less shall ye be safe in Egypt, which I loathe.

3. they went—implying perverse assiduity: they *went out of their way* to burn incense (one species of idolatry put for all kinds), etc.

4. (II Chron. 36:15.)

7. now—after so many warnings. **commit . . . this . . . evil against your souls**—(ch. 7:19; Num. 16:38; Prov. 8:36). It is not God whom you injure, but yourselves. **8. in . . . Egypt**—where they polluted themselves to ingratiate themselves with the Egyptians. **ye be gone**—not compelled by fear, but of your own accord, when I forbade you, and when it was free to you to stay in Judea. **that ye might cut yourselves off**—They, as it were, *purposely* courted their own ruin. **9.** Have you forgotten how the *wickednesses* of your fathers were the source of the greatest calamities to you? **their wives**—The Jews' worldly queens were great promoters of idolatry (I Kings 11:1-8; 15:13; 16:31). **the land of Judah**—They defiled the land which was holy unto God. **10. They . . . you**—The third person puts them to a distance from God on account of their alienating themselves from Him. The second person implies that God formerly had directly addressed them. **humbled**—lit., "contrite" (Ps. 51:17). **neither . . . feared**—(Prov. 28:14). **11. cut off all Judah**—i.e., all the idolaters; vs. 28 shows that some returned to Judea (cf. ch. 42:17). **14. none . . . shall escape . . . that they should return, . . .**—The Jews had gone to Egypt *with the idea* that a return to Judea, which they thought hopeless to their brethren in Babylon, would be an easy matter to themselves in Egypt: the exact reverse should happen in the case of each respectively. The Jews whom God sent to Babylon were there weaned from idolatry, and were restored; those who went to Egypt by their perverse will were hardened in idolatry, and perished there. **have a desire**—lit., *lift up* their *soul*, i.e., their hopes (cf. ch. 22:27, *Margin;* Deut. 24:15). **none shall return but such as shall escape**—viz., the "small number" (vs. 28) who were brought by force into Egypt, as Jeremiah and Baruch, and those who, in accordance with Jeremiah's advice, should flee from Egypt before the arrival of the Chaldeans (*Note,* ch. 42:17). CALVIN less probably refers the words to the return of the exiles in Babylon, which the Jews in Egypt regarded as hopeless.

CHAPTER 44

1. *The word that came to Jeremiah concerning all the Jews.* Dahler supposes this discourse to have been delivered in the seventeenth or eighteenth year after the taking of Jerusalem. *Which dwell at Migdol.* A city of Lower Egypt, not far from Pelusium. *Noph.* Memphis, a celebrated city of Middle Egypt, and the capital of its district. *The country of Pathros.* A district of Upper Egypt, known by the name of the Thebais. Thus we find that the Jews were scattered over the principal parts of Egypt.

2. *No man dwelleth therein.* The desolation of the land of Judea must have been exceedingly great when this, in almost any sense, could be spoken of it.

4. *Oh, do not this abominable thing.* A strong specimen of affectionate entreaty. One of the finest figures of poetry, when judiciously managed, the anthropopathia, the ascribing human passions to God, is often used by this prophet; so God is said to grieve, to mourn, to repent, to be angry, etc. Here He is represented as tenderly expostulating: "Oh, do not"; or, "I entreat you, do not that abominable thing which I hate."

7. *This great evil against your souls.* Will not self-interest weigh with you? See what ruin your conduct has brought upon your country. Your fathers sinned as you are doing; and where are they now? Either destroyed, or in captivity. And you are now taking the same way to your own destruction.

9. *Have ye forgotten the wickedness of your fathers?* It seems that the women were principal agents in idolatrous practices; for the queens—the wives, of rulers and of common people, burnt incense to the queen of heaven (the moon), v. 17, and poured out drink offerings to her.

MATTHEW HENRY

of guilt that made them impatient of reproof: *They knew that their wives had burnt incense to other gods*, and that they had countenanced them in it, *and the women that stood by* knew that they had joined with them in idolatrous usages; so that what Jeremiah said touched them in a sore place.

II. The reply which these persons made to Jeremiah, and in him to God himself.

1. They declare their resolution not to do as God commanded them, but what they themselves had a mind to do; that is, they would worship the moon, here called *the queen of heaven*; some understand it of the sun, which was much worshipped in Egypt (*ch.* xliii. 13) and had been so at Jerusalem (2 Kings xxiii. 11). And others understand it of all *the host of heaven*, or *the frame of heaven*, the whole machine, *ch.* vii. 18. These daring sinners do not now go about to make excuses for their refusal, nor suggest that Jeremiah spoke from himself and not from God (as before, *ch.* xliii. 2), but they tell him flatly, "*We will not hearken unto thee;* we will do that which is forbidden and run the hazard of that which is threatened." Those that live in disobedience to God commonly grow worse and worse, and the heart is more and more hardened by *the deceitfulness of sin*. What they said many think. It is that which the young man would be at *in the days of his youth*; he would have and do everything he has a mind to, Eccles. xi. 9.

2. They give some sort of reasons for their resolution. They plead antiquity: We are resolved *to burn incense to the queen of heaven*, for *our fathers* did so. They plead authority. Those that had power practised it themselves and prescribed it to others: *Our kings and our princes* did it, whom God set over us, and who were of the seed of David. They plead unity. We all with one consent, we that are a *great multitude* (*v.* 15), we did it. They plead universality. It was done *in the cities of Judah*. They plead visibility. It was not done in dark and shady groves only, but *in the streets*, openly. They plead that it was the practice of the mother-church; it had been done in *Jerusalem*. They plead prosperity: *Then had we plenty of* bread, *and* of all good things: we *were well and saw no evil*. But, supposing all to be true, yet this does not excuse them from idolatry; it is the law of God that we must be judged by, not the practice of men. They suggest that the judgments they had been under were brought upon them for *leaving off to burn incense to the queen of heaven*, *v.* 18. Thus, in the first ages of Christianity, when God chastised the nations by any public calamities for opposing the Christians and persecuting them, they put a contrary sense upon the calamities, as if they were sent to punish them for conniving at the Christians and tolerating them, and cried, *Christianos ad leones—Throw the Christians to the lions.* They plead that, though the women were most active in their idolatries, yet they did it with the approbation of their husbands; the women were busy to *make cakes* for meat-offerings *to the queen of heaven* and to prepare *and pour out the drink-offerings*, *v.* 19. Some understand this as spoken by the husbands (*v.* 15), who plead that they did not do it *without their men*, that is, without their elders and rulers, but, because the making of the *cakes* and the pouring out of *the drink-offerings* are expressly spoke of as the women's work (*ch.* vii. 18), it seems rather to be understood as their plea.

Verses 20–30

I. Jeremiah has something to say to them from himself. They said that these miseries came upon them because they had now *left off burning incense to the queen of heaven*. "No," says he, "it was because you had formerly done it, not because you had now left it off." The incense which they and their fathers had burnt to other gods did indeed go unpunished a great while, for God was long-suffering, and during the day of his patience it was perhaps, as they said, *well with them, and* they *saw no evil*; but at length they grew so provoking *that the Lord could no longer bear* (*v.* 22), whereupon some of them did a little reform. But their old corrupt inclinations being still the same, God remembered against them the idolatries of *their fathers, their kings, and their princes, in the streets of Jerusalem*, which they gloried in (*v.* 21). All the *abominations which they had committed* were brought to account; and *therefore is their land a desolation and a curse, as at this day* (*v.* 22); *therefore* for their old transgressions, has all *this evil happened to them, as at this day*, *v.* 23.

II. Jeremiah has something to say to them, *to the women* particularly, from *the Lord of hosts, the God of Israel*. They have given their answer; now let them hear God's reply, *v.* 24.

1. Since they were fully determined to persist in their idolatry, he would go on to punish them. God repeats what they had said (*v.* 25): "*You and your*

JAMIESON, FAUSSET, BROWN

15. their wives—The idolatry began with them (I Kings 11:4; I Tim. 2:14). Their husbands' connivance implicated them in the guilt.

16. we will not—(ch. 6:16). **17. whatsoever . . . goeth . . . out of our . . . mouth**—whatever *vow* we have uttered to our gods (vs. 25; Deut. 23:23; Judg. 11:36). The source of all superstitions is that men oppose their own will and fancies to God's commands. **queen of heaven**—(*Note*, ch. 7:18); Ashtaroth or Astarte.

we . . . fathers . . . king . . . .—The evil was restricted to no one class: all from the highest to the lowest shared the guilt.

then had we plenty—Fools attribute their seeming prosperity to God's connivance at their sin: but see Proverbs 1: 32; Ecclesiastes 8:11-13. In fact, God had often chastised them for their idolatry (see Judg. 2:14); but it is the curse of impiety not to perceive the hand of God in calamities. **victuals**—Men cast away the bread of the soul for the bread that perisheth (Deut. 8:3; John 6:27). So Esau (Heb. 12:16). **18.** They impute their calamities to their service of God, but these are often marks of His favor, not of wrath, to do His people good at their latter end (Deut. 8:16).

19. make . . . cakes to worship her—MAURER translates, "to form her image." *Crescent-shaped cakes* were offered to the moon. *Vulgate* supports *English Version*. **without our men**—The women mentioned (vs. 15); "a great multitude" here speak: we have not engaged in secret night-orgies which might justly be regarded unfavorably by *our husbands:* our sacred rites have been open, and with their privity. They wish to show how unreasonable it is that Jeremiah should oppose himself alone to the act of all, not merely women, but *men* also. The guilty, like these women, desire to shield themselves under the complicity of others. Instead of helping one another towards heaven, husband and wife often ripen one another for hell. **21. The incense . . . did not the Lord remember**—Jeremiah owns that they did as they said, but in retort asks, did not God repay their own evil-doing? Their very land in its present desolation attests this (vs. 22), as was foretold (ch. 25:11, 18, 38).

23. law—the moral precepts. **statutes**—the ceremonial. **testimonies**—the judicial (Dan. 9:11, 12).

ADAM CLARKE

15. *Then all the men . . . and all the women.* We have not seen the women in determined rebellion before. Here they make a common cause with their idolatrous husbands.

19. *And when we burned incense to the queen of heaven.* The moon seems to have been called *melecheth,* as the sun was called *molech.*

22. *Therefore is your land a desolation.* I grant that you and your husbands have joined together in these abominations; and what is the consequence? *The Lord could no longer bear, because of your evil doings; and therefore is your land a desolation, and an astonishment, and a curse, without an inhabitant, . . . this day.*

TODAY'S DICTIONARY OF THE BIBLE:

Ashtoreth, the moon goddess of the Phoenicians, representing the passive principle in nature, their principal female deity; frequently associated with the name of Baal, the storm god, their chief male deity (Judg. 10:6; 1 Sam. 7:4; 12:10). These names often occur in the plural (Ashtaroth, Baalim), probably as indicating either different statues or different modifications of the deities. This deity is spoken of as Ashtoreth of the Sidonians. She was the Ishtar of the Assyrians and the Astarte of the Greeks (1 Kings 11:5, 33; 2 Kings 23:13; Jer. 44:17). There was a temple of this goddess among the Philistines in the time of Saul (1 Kings 31:10). Under the name of Ishtar, she was one of the great deities of the Assyrians. The Phoenicians called her Astarte. Solomon introduced the worship of this idol (1 Kings 11:33). Jezebel's 400 priests were probably employed in its service (1 Kings 18:19). It was called the "queen of heaven" (Jer. 44:25).

MATTHEW HENRY

wives are agreed in this obstinacy; *you have spoken with your mouths and fulfilled with your hands;* you have said, *We will surely perform our vows that we have vowed, to burn incense to the queen of heaven,*" as if, though it were a sin, yet their having vowed to do it were sufficient to justify them in the doing of it; whereas no man can by his vow make that lawful to himself, much less duty, which God has already made sin.

He had sworn that what little remains of religion there were among them, should be lost, *v.* 26. Though they joined with the Egyptians in their idolatries, yet they continued to make mention of the name of Jehovah, particularly in their solemn oaths; they said, *Jehovah liveth,* he is *the living God,* so they owned him to be, though they worshipped dead idols; they swear, *The Lord liveth* (*ch.* v. 2). But God declares that his *name shall no more be* thus *named* by *any man of Judah in all the land of Egypt.* Those are very miserable whom God has so far left to themselves that they have quite forgotten their religion. To those whom God finds impenitent sinners he will be found an implacable Judge. They said that they should recover themselves when they returned to worship *the queen of heaven;* God said they should ruin themselves.

2. He tells them that few of them should *escape the sword,* and *return into the land of Judah, a small number* (*v.* 28), in comparison with the great numbers that should return out of the land of the Chaldeans.

3. He gives them a sign that all these threatenings shall be accomplished in Egypt. *Pharaoh-hophra,* the present *king of Egypt,* shall be delivered *into the hand of his enemies that seek his life—of his own rebellious subjects* (so some) under Amasis, who usurped his throne—*of Nebuchadnezzar king of Babylon* (so others), who invaded his kingdom; the former is related by Herodotus, the latter by Josephus. They expected more from him than from Zedekiah king of Judah; he was a more potent prince. "But," says God, "*I will give him into the hand of his enemies,* as I gave Zedekiah."

JAMIESON, FAUSSET, BROWN

25. Ye . . . have both spoken with . . . mouths, and fulfilled with . . . hand—ironical praise. They had pleaded their obligation to fulfil their vows, in excuse for their idolatry. He answers, no one can accuse you of unsteadiness as to your idolatrous vows; but steadfastness towards God ought to have prevented you from making, or, when made, from keeping such vows. **ye will surely accomplish . . . vows**—Jeremiah hereby gives them up to their own fatal obstinacy. **26. I have sworn**—*I,* too have made **a** *vow* which I will fulfil. Since ye will not hear **Me** speaking and warning, hear Me *swearing.* **by my great name**—i.e., by Myself (Gen. 22:16), the greatest by whom God can swear (Heb. 6:13, 14). **my name shall no more be named**—The Jews, heretofore, amidst all their idolatry, had retained the form of appeal to the name of God and the law, the distinctive glory of their nation; God will allow this no more (Ezek. 20:39): there shall be none left there to profane His name thus any more. **27. watch over . . . for evil**—(ch. 1:10; Ezek. 7:6). The God, whose providence is ever solicitously watching over His people for good, shall solicitously, as it were, watch for their hurt. Contrast ch. 31:28; 32:41. **28. small number**—(*Notes,* vss. **14,** 28; and ch. **42:** 17; Isa. 27:13); cf. "all-consumed" (vs. 27). *A band easily counted,* whereas they were expecting to return triumphantly in large numbers. **shall know**—most of them experimentally, and to their cost. **whose words . . . mine, or theirs**—*Hebrew,* "that from Me and them." Jehovah's words are His threats of destruction to the Jews; theirs, the assertion that they expected all goods from their gods (vs. 17), etc. "Mine"; by which I predict ruin to them. "Theirs"; by which they give themselves free scope in iniquity. **shall stand** (Ps. 33:11). **29. this . . . sign unto you**—The calamity of Pharaoh-hophra (*Note,* vs. 30) shall be a sign to you that as he shall fall before his enemy, so you shall subsequently fall before Nebuchadnezzar (Matt. 24:8) [Grotius]. Calvin makes the "sign" to be simultaneous with the event signified, not antecedent to it, as in Exodus 3:12. The Jews believed Egypt impregnable, so shut in was it by natural barriers. The Jews being "punished *in this place*" will be a sign that their view is false, and God's threat true. He calls it "a sign *unto you,*" because God's prediction is equivalent to the event, so that they may even now take it as a sign. When fulfilled it would cease to be a sign *to them:* for they would be dead. **30. Hophra**—in Herodotus called Apries. He succeeded Psammis, the successor of Pharaoh-necho, who was beaten by Nebuchadnezzar at Carchemish, on the Euphrates. Amasis rebelled against, and overcame him, in the city Sais. **them that seek his life**—Herodotus, in curious accordance with this, records that Amasis, after treating Hophra well at first, was instigated, by persons who thought they could not be safe unless he were put to death, to strangle him. "His enemies" refer to Amasis, etc.; the words are accurately chosen, so as not to refer to Nebuchadnezzar, who is not mentioned till the end of the verse, and in connection with Zedekiah (Ezek. 20:3; 30:21). Amasis' civil war with Hophra pioneered the way for Nebuchadnezzar's invasion in the twenty-third year of his reign (Josephus, *Antiquities,* 10.11).

ADAM CLARKE

E. H. PLUMPTRE:

"Hear the word of the Lord." The appeal to the experience of the past is followed by a prediction of the future, addressed to the wives as well as to the husbands. The new sin would lead to a new punishment. A tone of irony is perceptible in the words, "Ye will surely accomplish your vows." That, at all events, was a promise they were likely to keep, however faithless they might have shown themselves in keeping their vows to the God of their fathers. But the Lord of Israel meets that vow by another. By that "great name" (Gen. 22:16) of the Lord God (*Jehovah Adonai*), which they had slighted and profaned, He declares that it shall be profaned no more by the Egyptian exiles, not because they, of their own accord, would cease to use it, but because none of them should be left there. The small remnant that survived the sword and the famine should return to Judah as a witness of the judgment that had fallen on them, and of the truth of the prophet's warning. The words of Jehovah should stand, while those of men should fail.

—Ellicott's Commentary on the Whole Bible

30. *Behold, I will give Pharoah-hophra.* That is, Pharaoh Apries. How this and the prophecies in the preceding chapter were fulfilled, we learn from ancient historians. The sum of such information is this: The subjects of Pharaoh Apries rebelling, he sent Amasis, one of his generals, to reduce them to their duty. But no sooner had Amasis begun to make his speech than they fixed a helmet on his head, and proclaimed him king. Amasis accepted the title, and confirmed the Egyptians in their revolt; and the greater part of the nation declaring for him, Apries was obliged to retire into Upper Egypt; and the country being thus weakened by intestine war, was attacked and easily overcome by Nebuchadnezzar, who on quitting it left Amasis his viceroy. After Nebuchadnezzar's departure, Apries marched against Amasis; but, being defeated at Memphis, was taken prisoner, carried to Sais, and was strangled in his own palace, thus verifying this prophecy.

Thus Nebuchadnezzar made an easy conquest of the land. He conquered it as easily as "a shepherd puts on his cloak: he went thence in peace," having clothed himself with its spoils; and left all quiet under a viceroy of his own choosing. The rebellion of Pharaoh's subjects was the fire that God kindled in Egypt, chap. xliii. 12. And thus was he delivered into the hands of his enemies, his revolted people; and into the hand of him who sought his life, i.e., Amasis, his general. And thus the whole prophecy was literally fulfilled.

CHAPTER 45

MATTHEW HENRY

Verses 1–5

Baruch was employed in writing Jeremiah's prophecies, and reading them, *ch.* xxxvi, and was threatened for it by the king. He escaped under a divine protection to which story this chapter is a sequel.

I. The consternation that poor Baruch was in when he was sought for by the king's messengers, and the notice which God took of it. He was a young man willing to serve God and his prophet. But when he found it exposed him to contempt, he cried out, "I am undone; I shall fall into the pursuers' hands, and be imprisoned, and put to death, or banished: *The Lord has added grief to my sorrow.* After the grief of writing and reading the prophecies of my country's ruin, I have the sorrow of being treated as a criminal for so doing; it is a burden too heavy for me. *I fainted in my sighing and I find no rest.*" Young beginners in religion are apt to be discouraged with the little difficulties which they meet at first in the service of God. They do but *run with the footmen,*

JAMIESON, FAUSSET, BROWN

Vss. 1-5. Jeremiah Comforts Baruch. After the completion of the prophecies and histories appertaining to the Jewish people and kings, Jeremiah subjoins one referring to an individual, Baruch; even as there are subjoined to the epistles of Paul addressed to churches, epistles to individuals, some of which were prior in date to the former. Afterwards follow the prophecies referring to other nations, closing the book [Grotius]. The date of the events here told is eighteen years before the taking of the city; this chapter in point of time follows ch. 36. Baruch seems to have been regularly employed by Jeremiah to commit his prophecies to writing (ch. 36:1, 4, 32). **1. these words**—his prophecies from the thirteenth year of Josiah to the fourth of Jehoiakim. **3. Thou didst say . . .**—Jeremiah does not spare his disciple, but unveils his fault, viz., fear for his life by reason of the suspicions which he incurred in the eyes of his countrymen (cf. ch. 36: 17), as if he was in sympathy with the Chaldeans (ch. 43:3), and instigator of Jeremiah; also ingratitude in speaking of his "grief," etc., whereas he ought to deem himself highly blessed in being employed by God to record Jeremiah's prophecies. **added**—rescued from the peril of my first writing

ADAM CLARKE

1. *The word that Jeremiah . . . spake unto Baruch.* This is another instance of shameless transposition. This discourse was delivered in the fourth year of Jehoiakim, several years before Jerusalem was taken by the Chaldeans. It is a simple appendage to chap. xxxvi, and there it should have been inserted.

3. *Thou didst say, Woe is me now!* All that were the enemies of Jeremiah became his enemies too, and he needed these promises of support. *The Lord hath added grief to my sorrow.* He had mourned for the desolations that were coming on his country, and now he

MATTHEW HENRY

and it *wearies them*; they *faint* upon the very dawning of *the day of adversity*, and it is an evidence that *their strength is small* (Prov. xxiv. 10), their faith weak. Baruch should have rejoiced that he was counted worthy to suffer in such a good cause and with such good company, but, instead of that, he reflects upon his god, as if he had dealt hardly with him.

II. Jeremiah was troubled to see him in such agitation, and knew not what to say to him. He was loth to chide him, and willing to comfort him, but God tells him what he *shall say to him, v.* 4. It is our over-fondness for the good things of this present time that makes us impatient under its evil things. Now God shows him that it was his fault and folly to desire an abundance of the wealth and honour of this world. The ship was sinking. Ruin was coming upon the Jewish nation: "*That which I have built*, to be a house for myself, *I am breaking down, and that which I have planted*, to be a vineyard for myself, *I am plucking up, even this whole land*, the Jewish church and state; and dost thou now *seek great things for thyself?* Dost thou expect to be rich and honourable and to make a figure now? Canst thou expect to be high when all are brought low?"

III. God gave him hope that though he should not be great, yet he should be safe: "*I will bring evil upon all flesh*, all nations, *but thy life will I give to thee for a prey*" (*thy soul*, so the word is) "*in all places whither thou goest.* Thou must be hurried from place to place, and in danger, but thou shalt escape, though often very narrowly, shalt have thy life, but it shall be as a prey, got with much difficulty and danger; thou shalt be saved as by fire."

CHAPTER 46

Verses 1–11

The first verse is the title of that part of this book which relates to the neighbouring nations. It is *the word of the Lord which came to Jeremiah against the Gentiles*. In the Old Testament we have *the word of the Lord* against *the Gentiles*; in the New Testament we have *the word of the Lord* for *the Gentiles*, that those who were *afar off are made nigh*.

He begins with Egypt, because they were of old Israel's oppressors and of late their deceivers. In these verses he foretells the overthrow of *the army of Pharaoh-necho*, by Nebuchadnezzar, *in the fourth year of Jehoakim*. This defeat (as we find, 2 Kings xxiv. 7), made him pay dearly for his expedition against the king of Assyria four years before, in which he slew Josiah, 2 Kings xxiii. 29. This event is here foretold in lofty expressions of triumph over Egypt thus foiled, which Jeremiah would speak of with pleasure, because the death of Josiah was now avenged on Pharaoh-necho.

I. The Egyptians are upbraided with the mighty preparations they made for this expedition, in which the prophet challenges them to do their utmost: "Come then, *order the buckler*, let the weapons of war be got ready," *v.* 3. Egypt was famous for *horses*—let them be *harnessed* and the cavalry well mounted: *Get up, you horsemen, and stand forth*, &c., *v.* 4. He compares this expedition to the rising of their river Nile (*v.* 7, 8): *Egypt* now *rises up like a flood*, threatening to overflow all the neighbouring lands. It is a very formidable army. The prophet summons them (*v.* 9): *Come up, you horses; rage, you chariots.* He challenges them to bring all their confederate troops together, *the Ethiopians*, who descended from the same stock as the Egyptians (Gen. x. 6), and were their neighbours and allies, *the Libyans and Lydians*, both in Africa, to the west of Egypt, from whom the Egyptians fetched their auxiliary forces. It shall be all in vain; they shall be shamefully defeated, for God will fight against them, Prov. xxi. 30, 31.

III. They are upbraided with their cowardice (*v.* 5, 6): "*Wherefore have I seen them*, notwithstanding all these mighty and vast preparations, when the Chaldean army faces them, *dismayed, turned back*, and no spirit left in them." Even *their mighty ones*, who, one would think, should have stood their ground, *flee a flight*, flee by consent, in confusion; they have neither time nor heart to *look back*, but *fear is rouna about* them. They cannot make their escape. *They shall stumble* in their flight, *and fall towards the north*, towards their enemies' country; for such confusion were they in that instead of making homeward, they made forward.

JAMIESON, FAUSSET, BROWN

(ch. 36:26). I am again involved in a similar peril. He upbraids God as dealing harshly with him. **1 fainted**—rather, I am weary. **no rest**—no quiet resting-place. **4. that which I have built . . . planted I will pluck up**—(Isa. 5:5). This whole nation (the Jews) which I founded and planted with such extraordinary care and favor, I will overthrow. **5. seekest thou great things for thyself**—Thou art overfastidious and self-seeking. When My own peculiar people, a "whole" nation (vs. 4), and the temple, are being given to ruin, dost *thou* expect to be exempt from all hardship? Baruch had raised his expectations too high in this world, and this made his distresses harder to be borne. The frowns of the world would not disquiet us if we did not so eagerly covet its smiles. What folly to seek great things for ourselves here, where everything is little, and nothing certain! **all flesh**—the whole Jewish nation and even foreign peoples (ch. 25:26). **but thy life . . . for a prey**—Esteem it enough at such a general crisis that thy life shall be granted thee. Be content with this boon of life which I will rescue from imminent death, even as when all things are given up to plunder, if one escape with aught, he has a something saved as his "prey" (ch. 21:9). It is striking how Jeremiah, who once used such complaining language himself, is enabled now to minister the counsel requisite for Baruch when falling into the same sin (ch. 12:1-5; 15:10-18). This is part of God's design in suffering His servants to be tempted, that their temptations may adapt them for ministering to their fellow servants when tempted.

CHAPTER 46

Vss. 1-28. The Prophecies, Chapters 46-52, Refer to Foreign Peoples. He begins with Egypt, being the country to which he had been removed. Chapter 46 contains two prophecies concerning it: the discomfiture of Pharaoh-necho at Carchemish by Nebuchadnezzar, and the long subsequent conquest of Egypt by the same king; also the preservation of the Jews (vss. 27, 28). **1.** General heading of the next six chapters of prophecies concerning the Gentiles; the prophecies are arranged according to nations, not by the dates. **2.** Inscription of the first prophecy. **Pharaoh-necho**—He, when going against Carchemish (Cercusium, near the Euphrates), encountered Josiah, king of Judah (the ally of Assyria), at Megiddo, and slew him there (II Kings 23:29; II Chron. 35:20-24); but he was four years subsequently overcome at Carchemish, by Nebuchadnezzar, as is foretold here; and lost all the territory which had been subject to the Pharaohs west of the Euphrates, and between it and the Nile. The prediction would mitigate the Jews' grief for Josiah, and show his death was not to be unavenged (II Kings 24:7). He is famed as having fitted out a fleet of discovery from the Red Sea, which doubled the Cape of Good Hope and returned to Egypt by the Mediterranean. **3.** Derisive summons to battle. With all your mighty preparation for the invasion of Nebuchadnezzar, when ye come to the encounter, ye shall be "dismayed" (vs. 5). Your mighty threats shall end in nothing. **buckler**—smaller, and carried by the light-armed cavalry. **shield**—of larger size, and carried by the heavily armed infantry. **4. Harness the horses**—viz., to the war-chariots, for which Egypt was famed (Exod. 14:7; 15:4). **get up, ye horsemen**—*get up* into the chariots. Maurer, because of the parallel "horses," translates, "Mount the *steeds*." But it is rather describing the successive steps in equipping the war-chariots; first *harness* the horses to them, then let the horsemen *mount* them. **brigandines**—cuirasses, or coats of mail. **5.** (*Note*, vs. 3.) The language of astonishment, that an army so well equipped should be driven back in "dismay." The prophet sees this in prophetic vision. **fled apace**—lit., "fled a flight," i.e., flee precipitately. **look not back**—They do not even dare to look back at their pursuers. **6. Let not**—equivalent to the strongest *negation*. *Let not* any of the Egyptian warriors think to *escape by swiftness or by might.* **toward the north**—i.e., in respect to Egypt or Judea. In the northward region, by the Euphrates (see vs. 2). **7. as a flood**—(ch. 47:2; Isa. 8:7, 8; Dan. 11:22). The figure is appropriate in addressing Egyptians, as the Nile, their great river, yearly overspreads their lands with a turbid, muddy flood. So their army, swelling with arrogance, shall overspread the region south of Euphrates; but it, like the Nile, shall retreat as fast as it advanced. **8.** Answer to the question in vs. 7. **waters . . . moved like the rivers**

ADAM CLARKE

mourns for the dangers to which he feels his own life exposed; for we find, from chap. xxxvi. 26, that the king had given commandment to take both Baruch and Jeremiah, in order that they might be put to death at the instance of his nobles.

4. *Behold, that which I have built.* I most certainly will fulfil all those threatenings contained in the roll you have written, for I will destroy this whole land.

5. *And seekest thou great things for thyself?* Nothing better can be expected of this people; your hopes in reference to them are vain. Expect no national amendment, till national judgments have taken place.

But thy life will I give unto thee for a prey. This is a proverbial expression. We have met with it before, chap. xxi. 9, xxxviii. 2, xxxix. 18; and it appears to have this meaning. As a prey or spoil is that which is gained from a vanquished enemy, so it is preserved with pleasure as the proof and reward of a man's own valor. So Baruch's life should be doubly precious unto him, not only on account of the dangers through which God had caused him to pass safely, but also on account of those services he had been enabled to render, the consolations he had received, and the continual and very evident interposition of God in his behalf. All these would be dearer to him than the spoils of a vanquished foe to the hero who had overcome in battle.

CHAPTER 46

1. *The word of the Lord . . . against the Gentiles.* This is a general title to the following collection of prophecies, written concerning different nations, which had less or more connection with the Jews, either as enemies, neighbors, or allies. They were not written at the same time; and though some of them bear dates, yet it would be difficult to give them any chronological arrangement.

2. *Pharaoh-necho.* This was the person who defeated the army of Josiah, in which engagement Josiah received a mortal wound, of which he died, greatly regretted, soon after at Megiddo. After this victory he defeated the Babylonians, and took Carchemish; and, having fortified it, returned to his own country. Nabo-polassar sent his son, Nebuchadnezzar, with an army against him, defeated him with immense slaughter near the river Euphrates, retook Carchemish, and subdued all the revolted provinces, according to the following prophecies.

3. *Order ye the buckler.* This is the call to the general armament of the people against the Chaldeans.

6. *Let not the swift flee away.* Even the swiftest shall not be able to escape. *They shall . . . fall toward the north.* By the Euphrates, which was northward of Judea. Here the Egyptian army was routed with great slaughter.

7. *Who is this that cometh up as a flood?* The vast concourse of people is here represented as a river; for instance, the Jordan, suddenly swollen with the rains in harvest, rolling its waters along, and overflowing the whole country. A fine image to represent the incursions of vast armies carrying all before them. Such was the army of Pharaoh-necho in its march to Carchemish.

MATTHEW HENRY

II. They are upbraided with the great expectations they had from this expedition. They knew their own thoughts, and God knew them, *but they knew not the thoughts of the Lord, for he gathers them as sheaves into the floor*, Mic. iv. 11, 12. Egypt saith (*v.* 8): *I will go up; I will cover the earth*, and none *shall hinder me*; *I will destroy the city*, whatever city it is that stands in my way. Like Pharaoh of old, *I will pursue, I will overtake*.

But God saith that it shall be his day: *This is the day of the Lord God of hosts* (*v.* 10), in which he will be exalted in the overthrow of the Egyptians.

IV. They are upbraided with their inability ever to recover this blow, *v.* 11, 12. The damsel, *the daughter of Egypt*, that lived in great pomp and state, is sorely wounded by this defeat. Let her now seek for *balm in Gilead*; let her use all the medicines her wise men can prescribe for the repairing of the loss sustained by this defeat; but all in vain; *no cure shall be* to them; they shall never be able to bring such a powerful army into the field again. "*The nations* that rang of thy glory and strength *have* now *heard of thy shame*, how shamefully thou wast routed and how thou art weakened by it." *Thy cry hath filled the* country about; such confusion were they in.

Verses 12–28

I. Confusion and terror spoken to Egypt. The accomplishment of the prediction in the former part of the chapter disabled the Egyptians from making any attempts upon other nations. But still they remained strong at home, and none of their neighbours durst make any attempts upon them. The scope of the prophecy here is to show *how the king of Babylon should* shortly *come and smite the land of Egypt*, *v.* 13. This was fulfilled by the same hand with the former, even Nebuchadnezzar's, but many years after.

1. The alarm of war sounded in Egypt (*v.* 14). The enemy is approaching, *the sword is devouring round about* in the neighbouring countries, and it is time for the Egyptians to prepare to give the enemy a warm reception. This must be proclaimed in all parts of Egypt, particularly in Migdol, Noph, and Tahpanhes, because in these places the Jewish refugees had planted themselves, in contempt of God's command (*ch.* xliv. 1). Let them hear what a sorry shelter Egypt is likely to be to them.

2. The retreat of the forces of other nations which the Egyptians had in their pay is here foretold. Some were posted upon the frontiers to guard them, where they were beaten off by the invaders and put to flight. Then were the *valiant men swept away* (*v.* 15) as with *a sweeping rain* (it is the word that is used Prov. xxviii. 3); they can none of them stand their ground, *because the Lord drives them* from their posts; he drives them by enabling the Chaldeans to drive them. If God please, they shall be made to *fall upon one another, every man's sword against his fellow. Her hired men*, the troops Egypt has in her service, are indeed *in the midst of her like fatted bullocks*, lusty men, able bodied, who were likely to make good against the enemy: but *they are turned back*; and, instead of fighting, they have *fled away together*. They all made homeward towards their own country (*v.* 16): *They said, "Arise, and let us go again to our own people*, safe *from the oppressing sword* of the Chaldeans, that bears down all before it." In times of exigence little confidence is to be put in mercenary troops, that fight purely for pay. They exclaimed vehemently against Pharaoh, to whose bad management their defeat was owing. When he posted them there upon the borders of his country it is probable that he told them he would come himself with a gallant army to support them, but he failed them. No marvel that they deserted crying out, *Pharaoh king of Egypt is but a noise* (*v.* 17). *He has passed the time appointed;* he did not keep his word.

3. The formidable power of the Chaldean army is described as bearing down all before it. *The King* of kings, *whose name is the Lord of hosts*, hath said it, *As I live, saith* this *King*, *as Tabor* overtops *the mountains and Carmel* overlooks *the sea, so shall* the king of Babylon overpower all the force of Egypt, *v.* 18. He and his *army shall come against* Egypt *with axes, as hewers of wood* (*v.* 22), and the Egyptians shall be no more able to resist them than the tree is to resist the man that comes with an axe to *cut it down*.

JAMIESON, FAUSSET, BROWN

–The rise of the Nile is gentle; but at the mouth it, unlike most rivers, is much agitated, owing to the sandbanks impeding its course, and so it rushes into the sea like a cataract. **9.** Ironical exhortation, as in vs. 3. The Egyptians, owing to the heat of their climate and abstinence from animal food, were physically weak, and therefore employed mercenary soldiers. **Ethiopians**–*Hebrew, Cush:* Abyssinia and Nubia. **Libyans**–*Phut*, Mauritania, west of Egypt (cf. Gen. 10:6). **shield**–The Libyans borrowed from Egypt the use of the long shield extending to the feet [XENOPHON, *Cyr.*, 6 and 7). **Lydians**–not the Lydians west of Asia Minor (Gen. 10:22; Ezek. 30:5), but the *Ludim*, an African nation descended from Egypt (Mizraim) (Gen. 10:13; Ezek. 30:5; Nah. 3:9). **handle and bend the bow**–The employment of *two* verbs expresses the manner of bending the bow, viz., the foot being pressed on the center, and the hands holding the ends of it. **10. vengeance**–for the slaughter of Josiah (II Kings 23:29). **sword shall devour . . . be . . . drunk**–poetical personification (Deut. 32:42). **a sacrifice**–(Isa. 34:6; Ezek. 39:17). The slaughter of the Egyptians is represented as a sacrifice to satiate His righteous vengeance. **11. Gilead . . . balm**–(*Note*, ch. 8:22); viz., for curing the wounds; but no medicine will avail, so desperate shall be the slaughter. **virgin**–Egypt is so called on account of her effeminate luxury, and as having never yet been brought under foreign yoke. **thou shalt not be cured**–lit., "there shall be no cure for thee" (ch. 30:13; Ezek. 30:21). Not that the kingdom of Egypt should cease to exist, but it should not recover its former strength; the blow should be irretrievable. **12. mighty . . . stumbled against . . . mighty . . . fallen both together**–Their very multitude shall prove an impediment in their confused flight, one treading on the other. **13-26.** Prophecy of the invasion of Egypt by Nebuchadnezzar, which took place sixteen years after the taking of Jerusalem. Having spent thirteen years in the siege of Tyre, and having obtained nothing for his pains, he is promised by God Egypt for his reward in humbling Tyre (Ezek. 29: 17-20; 30:31). The intestine commotions between Amasis and Pharaoh-hophra prepared his way (cf. Isaiah 19:1, etc., *Notes*). **14. Declare . . . publish**–as if giving sentence from a tribunal. **Migdol . . . Noph . . . Tahpanhes**–east, south, and north. He mentions the three other quarters, but omits the west, because the Chaldeans did not advance thither. These cities, too, were the best known to the Jews, as being in their direction. **sword shall devour round about thee**–viz., the Syrians, Jews, Moabites, and Ammonites (*Note*, ch. 48:1). The exhortation is ironical, as in vss. 4, 10. **15. thy valiant men**–MSS., the LXX, and *Vulgate* read, "thy valiant one," Apis, the bull-shaped Egyptian idol worshipped at Noph or Memphis. The contrast thus is between the palpable impotence of the idol and the *might* attributed to it by the worshippers. The *Hebrew* term, "strong," or "valiant," is applied to bulls (Ps. 22:12). Cambyses in his invasion of Egypt destroyed the sacred bull. **drive them**–(Cf. vs. 5). The *Hebrew* word is used of a sweeping rain (Prov. 28:3). **16. He**–Jehovah. **made many to fall**–lit., "multiplied the faller," i.e., fallers. **one fell upon another**–(V. 6, 12): even before the enemy strikes them (Lev. 26:37). **let us go again to our own people**–the language of the confederates and mercenaries, exhorting one another to desert the Egyptian standard, and return to their respective homes (vss. 9, 21). **from the oppressing sword**–from the cruel sword, viz., of the Chaldeans (cf. ch. 25:38). **17. there**–in their own country severally, the foreign soldiers (vs. 16) cry, "Pharaoh is . . . ." **but a noise**–He threatens great things, but when the need arises, he does nothing. His threats are mere "noise" (ch. I Cor. 13:1). MAURER translates, "is *ruined*," lit. (in appropriate abruptness of language), "Pharaoh, king . . . *ruin*." The context favors English Version. His vauntings of what he would do when the time of battle should come have proved to be *empty sounds; he hath passed the time appointed* (viz., for battle with the Chaldeans). **18.** As the mountains Tabor and Carmel tower high above the other hills of Palestine, *so* Nebuchadnezzar (vs. 26) when he comes shall prove himself superior to all his foes. Carmel forms a bold promontory jutting out into the Mediterranean. Tabor is the higher of the two; therefore it is said to be "among the *mountains*"; and Carmel "by the *sea*." **the King . . . Lord of hosts**–(ch. 48:15); in contrast to "Pharaoh *king* of Egypt . . . but a noise" (vs. 17). God the true "*King* . . . the Lord *of hosts*," shall cause Nebuchadnezzar to *come*. Whereas Pharaoh shall not come to battle at *the time appointed*, notwithstanding his

ADAM CLARKE

9. *The Ethiopians.* Hebrew, *Cush*, *Phut*, and the *Ludim*. This army was composed of many nations. *Cush*, which we translate "Ethiopians," almost invariably means the Arabians; and here, those Arabs that bordered on Egypt near the Red Sea. *Phut* probably means the "Libyans"; for Phut settled in Libya, according to Josephus. Phut and Cush were two of the sons of Ham, and brothers to Mitsraim, the father of the Egyptians, Gen. x. 6; and the Ludim were descended from Mitsraim; see Gen. x. 13.

10. *For this is the day of the Lord God of hosts.* The prophet represents this as a mighty sacrifice, where innumerable victims were slain.

11. *Go up into Gilead, and take balm.* An irony. Egypt is so completely enfeebled by this overthrow that her political wound is utterly incurable. This figure is used with the more propriety here, as the Egyptians have been celebrated from the remotest antiquity for their knowledge of medicine.

12. *The nations have heard of thy shame.* Of your disgrace, by this prodigious slaughter of your troops.

13. *How Nebuchadrezzar . . . should come and smite the land of Egypt.* See on chap. xliv. This was after Amasis had driven Pharaoh-necho into Upper Egypt. See chap. xliv. 30.

15. *They stood not, because the Lord did drive them.* The Lord panic-struck them, and drove them back.

16. *One fell upon another.* In their terror and confusion ranks fell on ranks, and overturned each other. *Let us go again to our own people.* Let us flee to our own country with all possible speed. These were the auxiliaries.

17. *They did cry there.* These allies sent their excuse to Pharaoh that the disasters they had met with had prevented them from joining him as they had intended.

18. *As Tabor is among the mountains.* This mountain is situated in the plain of Esdraelon in Galilee, on the confines of the tribes of Zebulun and Issachar, Josh. xix. 22. It stood by itself, separated from all the other mountains by deep valleys, and is the highest of the whole. *And as Carmel by the sea.* Carmel is a mountain on the coast of the Mediterranean Sea, on the southern frontier of the tribe of Asher. Were the Egyptians as distinguished for valor and strength as the mountains Tabor and Carmel are for height among the other mountains in their vicinity, they should not be able to stand the shock of the Chaldean army.

MATTHEW HENRY

4. The desolation of Egypt is foretold, and the waste that should be made of that rich country. *Egypt* is now *like a very fair heifer*, or calf (*v.* 20), fat and shining, and not *accustomed to the yoke* of subjection, wanton as a heifer that is well fed. Some think here is an allusion to Apis, the bull or calf which the Egyptians worshipped, from whom the children of Israel learned to worship the golden calf. Egypt is as fair as a goddess, *but destruction comes*; *cutting up comes* (so some read it); *it comes out of the north*; thence the Chaldean soldiers shall come to kill and cut up this *fair heifer. The daughters of Egypt shall be confounded* (*v.* 24), shall be filled with astonishment. *Their voice shall go like a serpent*, that is, it shall be very low and submissive. They shall not dare to make loud complaints of the cruelty of the conquerors, but vent their griefs in silent murmurs. They shall not now answer roughly, but, with *the poor, use entreaties* and beg for their lives. They shall be carried away prisoners into their enemy's land (*v.* 19): "*O thou daughter! dwelling* securely and delicately *in Egypt, furnish thyself to go into captivity;* instead of rich clothes, which will but tempt the enemy to strip thee, get plain and warm clothes; and inure thyself to hardship, that thou mayest bear it the better." The Egyptians must prepare to flee; for their cities shall be evacuated. Noph particularly *shall be desolate, without an inhabitant. The multitude of No shall be punished:* it is called *populous No*, Nah. iii. 8. *Though hand join in hand*, they shall not escape; nor think to go off in the crowd. Pharaoh shall be brought down, and *all those that trust in him* (*v.* 25), particularly the Jews that came to sojourn in his country, trusting in him rather than in God. All these shall be *delivered into the hands of the northern nations* (*v.* 24).

5. An intimation is given that in process of time Egypt shall recover itself again (*v.* 26): *Afterwards it shall be inhabited.*

II. Comfort and peace are here spoken to the Israel of God, *v.* 27, 28. It may refer to the captives in Babylon, whom God had mercy in store for, or, more generally, to all the people of God, designed for their encouragement in the most difficult times, when the judgments of God are abroad among the nations. Let the wicked of the earth tremble, *but fear not thou, O my servant Jacob! and be not dismayed, O Israel!* and again, *Fear thou not, O Jacob!* God would not have his people to be a timorous people. God's people shall be found out and gathered though they be far off. The wicked *is like the troubled sea when it cannot rest;* they *flee when none pursues*. But Jacob, being at home in God, *shall be at rest and at ease, and none shall make him afraid;* for *what time he is afraid* he has a *God to trust to*. Nations have their periods, but the gospel church, God's spiritual Israel, still continues, and will to the end of time.

CHAPTER 47

Verses 1–7

As the Egyptians had often proved false friends, so the Philistines had always been sworn enemies, to the Israel of God, and the more dangerous, for their being such near neighbours to them. They were humbled in David's time, but, it seems, they had got head again till Nebuchadnezzar cut them off with their neighbours, which is the event here foretold. The date of this prophecy was *before Pharaoh* smote Gaza. When this blow was given to Gaza by the king of Egypt is not certain, but this word of the Lord came to Jeremiah against the Philistines when they were in no peril from any adversary, yet then Jeremiah foretold their ruin. It is here foretold, 1. That a foreign enemy shall be brought upon them: *Waters rise up out of the north*, *v.* 2. Now a terrible storm comes out of that cold climate. The Chaldean army shall overflow the land like a deluge. 2. That they shall all be in a consternation upon it. The men shall have no heart to fight: *All the inhabitants of the land shall howl*, so that nothing but lamentation shall be heard in all places. Before it comes to killing and slaying, the very

JAMIESON, FAUSSET, BROWN

boasts, Nebuchadnezzar *shall come* according to the prediction of the *King*, who has all *hosts* in His power, however ye Egyptians may despise the prediction. **19. furnish thyself**—lit., "make for thyself vessels" (viz., to contain food and other necessaries for the journey) for captivity. **daughter**—so in vs. 11. **dwelling in Egypt**—i.e., the *inhabitants* of Egypt, the Egyptians, represented as *the daughter of Egypt* (ch. 48:18; II Kings 19:21). "Dwelling" implies that they thought themselves to be securely fixed in their habitations beyond the reach of invasion. **20. heifer**—wanton, like a fat, untamed heifer (Hos. 10:11). Appropriate to Egypt, where Apis was worshipped under the form of a fair bull marked with spots. **destruction**—i.e., a destroyer: Nebuchadnezzar. *Vulgate* translates, "a goader," answering to the metaphor, "one who will *goad* the *heifer*" and tame her. The *Arabic* idiom favors this [ROSENMULLER]. **cometh . . . cometh**—The repetition implies, it cometh surely and quickly (Ps. 96:13). **out of the north**—(*Note,* ch. 1:14; 47:2). **21.** Translate, "Also her hired men (mercenary soldiers, vss 9, 16), who are in the midst of her like fatted bullocks, even they also are turned back," i.e., shall turn their backs to flee. The same image, "heifer . . . bullocks" (vss. 20, 21), is applied to Egypt's foreign mercenaries, as to *herself*. Pampered with the luxuries of Egypt, they become as enervated for battle as the natives themselves. **22.** The cry of Egypt when invaded shall be like the hissing of a serpent roused by the woodcutters from its lair. No longer shall she loudly roar like a heifer, but with a low murmur of fear, as a serpent hissing. **with axes**—the Scythian mode of armor. The Chaldeans shall come with such confidence as if not about to have to fight with soldiers, but merely to cut down trees offering no resistance. **23. her forest**—(Isa. 10:34). **though it cannot be searched**—They cut down her forest, dense and unsearchable (Job 5:9; 9:10; 36:26) as it may seem: referring to the thickly set cities of Egypt, which were at that time a thousand and twenty. The *Hebrew* particle is properly, "for," "because." **because**—the reason why the Chaldeans shall be able to cut down so dense a forest of cities as Egypt: they themselves are countless in numbers. **grasshoppers**—locusts (Judg. 6:5). **25. multitude**—*Hebrew*, "Amon" (Nah. 3:8, *Margin*, "No-Ammon"), the same as Thebes or Diospolis in Upper Egypt, where Jupiter Ammon had his famous temple. In *English Version*, "multitude" answers to "*populous* No" (Nah. 3:8; and Ezekiel 30:15). The reference to "their *gods*" which follows, makes the translation more likely, "*Ammon* of No," i.e., No and her idol Ammon; so the *Chaldee Version*. So called either from Ham, the son of Noah; or, the "nourisher," as the word means. **their kings**—the kings of the nations in league with Egypt. **26. afterward . . . inhabited**—Under Cyrus forty years after the conquest of Egypt by Nebuchadnezzar, it threw off the Babylonian yoke but has never regained its former prowess (vs. 11; Ezek. 29:11-15). **27, 28.** Repeated from ch. 30:10, 11. When the Church [and literal Israel] might seem utterly consumed, there still remains hidden hope, because God, as it were, raises His people from the dead (Rom. 11:15). Whereas the godless "nations" are consumed even though they survive, as are the Egyptians after their overthrow; because they are radically accursed and doomed [CALVIN].

CHAPTER 47

Vss. 1-7. PROPHECY AGAINST THE PHILISTINES. **1.** *Pharaoh-necho* probably smote Gaza on his return after defeating Josiah at Megiddo (II Chron. 35:20) [GROTIUS]. Or, *Pharaoh-hophra* (ch. 37:5, 7) is intended: probably on his return from his fruitless attempt to save Jerusalem from the Chaldeans, he smote Gaza in order that his expedition might not be thought altogether in vain [CALVIN], (Amos 1:6, 7). **2. waters**—(Isa. 8:7). The Chaldeans from the north are compared to the overwhelming waters of their own Euphrates. The smiting of Gaza was to be only the prelude of a greater disaster to the Philistines. Nebuzaradan was left by Nebuchadnezzar, after he had taken Jerusalem, to subdue the rest of the adjoining cities and country. **3.** (Cf. ch. 4:29.) **fathers . . . not look back to . . . children**—Each shall think only of his own safety, not even the fathers regarding their own children. So desperate shall be the calamity that men shall divest themselves of the natural affections. **for feebleness of hands**—The hands, the principal instruments of action, shall have lost all power; their whole hope shall be in their feet. **4.**

ADAM CLARKE

19. *Furnish thyself to go into captivity.* The thing is unavoidable; prepare for this calamity.

20. *Egypt is like a very fair heifer.* Fruitful and useful; but destruction cometh out of the north, from Chaldea. It may be that there is an allusion here to Isis, worshipped in Egypt under the form of a beautiful cow.

22. *The voice . . . shall go like a serpent.* See Isa. xxix. 4.

23. *They shall cut down her forest.* Supposed to mean her cities, of which Egypt had no fewer than 1,020.

24. *The hand of the people of the north.* The Chaldeans.

25. *The multitude of No. Amon minno,* the Amon of No, called by the Greeks "Jupiter's city." It was the famous Thebes, celebrated anciently for its hundred gates. *Amon* was the name by which the Egyptians called Jupiter, who had a famous temple at Thebes.

26. *Afterward it shall be inhabited.* That is, within forty years, as Ezekiel had predicted, chap. xxix. 13.

27. *Fear not . . . my servant Jacob.* In the midst of wrath God remembers mercy. Though Judah shall be destroyed, Jerusalem taken, the Temple burnt to the ground, and the people carried into captivity, yet the nation shall not be destroyed. A seed shall be preserved, out of which the nation shall revive.

CHAPTER 47

1. *The word of the Lord . . . against the Philistines.* The date of this prophecy cannot be easily ascertained. *Before that Pharaoh smote Gaza.* We have no historical relation of any Egyptian king smiting Gaza. It was no doubt smitten by some of them; but when, and by whom, does not appear from either sacred or profane history.

2. *Waters rise up out of the north. Waters* is a common prophetic image for a multitude of people. The *north* here, as in other places of this prophecy, means Chaldea.

3. *The stamping of the hoofs.* At the "galloping sound." *The fathers shall not look back.* Though their children are left behind, they have neither strength nor courage to go back to bring them off.

MATTHEW HENRY

stamping of the horses and *rattling of the chariots*, shall strike terror to such a degree that parents in their fright shall seem void of natural affection, *for they shall not look back to their children*, to provide for their safety. 3. That the country of the Philistines shall be spoiled and laid waste, *v.* 4. Tyre and Zidon were strong and wealthy cities, and they used to help the Philistines in a strait, but now they shall themselves be involved in the common ruin, and God will cut off from them every *helper that remains*. Who the *remnant of the country of Caphtor* were is uncertain, but the Caphtorim were near akin to the Philistines (Gen. x. 14), and probably when their own country was destroyed such as remained settled with their kinsmen the Philistines.

Some particular places are here named, *Gaza, and Ashkelon, v.* 5. *Baldness has come upon them;* the invaders have stripped them of all their ornaments, and they are *cut off*. The prophet, with his usual tenderness, asks them first (*v.* 5), *How long will you cut yourselves*, as men in extreme sorrow and anguish do?

But he turns from the effect to the cause: *They cut themselves*, for the sword of the Lord cuts them. *O thou sword of the Lord! how long will it be ere thou be quiet?* He begs it would *put up itself into the scabbard*. This expresses the prophet's earnest desire to see an end of the war, looking with compassion, even upon the Philistines themselves. Yet he stops the mouth of his own complaint (*v.* 7): *How can it be quiet, seeing the Lord hath given it a charge* against such and such places. When the sword is drawn we cannot expect it should be sheathed till it has fulfilled its charge. As the word of God, so his rod and his sword, shall accomplish that for which he sends them.

JAMIESON, FAUSSET, BROWN

every helper—The Philistines, being neighbors to the Phœnicians of Tyre and Sidon, would naturally make common cause with them in the case of invasion. These cities would have no *helper* left when the Philistines should be destroyed. **Caphtor**—the Caphtorim and Philistines both came from Mizraim (Gen. 10:13, 14). The Philistines are said to have been delivered by God from Caphtor (Amos 9:7). Perhaps before the time of Moses they dwelt near and were subjugated by the Caphtorim (Deut. 2:23) and subsequently delivered. "The remnant" means here those still left after the Egyptians had attacked Gaza and Palestine; or rather, those left of the Caphtorim after the Chaldeans had attacked them previous to their attack on the Philistines. Some identify Caphtor with Cappadocia; GESENIUS, with Crete (Ezek. 25:16, Cherethims); KITTO, Cyprus. Between Palestine and Idumea there was a city Caparorsa; and their close connection with Palestine on the one hand, and Egypt (Mizraim, Gen. 10:13, 14) on the other hand, makes this locality the most likely. **5. Baldness ... cut thyself**—Palestine is represented as a female who has torn off her hair and cut her flesh, the heathenish (Lev. 19:28) token of mourning (ch. 48:37). **their valley**—the long strip of low plain occupied by the Philistines along the Mediterranean, west of the mountains of Judea. LXX reads *Anakim*, the remains of whom were settled in those regions (Num. 13:28). Joshua dislodged them so that none were left but in Gaza, Gath, and Ashdod (Josh. 11:21, 22). But the parallel (vs. 7), "Ashkelon ... the *seashore*," established *English Version* here, **"Ashkelon ... their** *valley*." **6. Jeremiah, in the person** of the Philistines afflicting themselves (vs. 5), apostrophizes the "sword of the Lord," entreating mercy (cf. Deut. 32:41; Ezek. 21:3-5, 9, 10). **put up thyself**—*Hebrew*, "Gather thyself," i.e., retire or return. **7.** Jeremiah, from addressing the sword in the second person, turns to his hearers and speaks of it in the third person. **Lord ... given it a charge**—(Ezek. 14:17). **the seashore**—the strip of land between the mountains and Mediterranean, held by the Philistines: "their valley" (*Note*, vs. 5). **there hath he appointed it**—(Mic. 6:9). There hath He ordered it to rage.

ADAM CLARKE

4. *To spoil all the Philistines.* These people, of whom there were five seignories, occupied the coast of the Mediterranean Sea, to the south of the Phoenicians. *Tyrus and Zidon.* Places sufficiently remarkable in both the Old and New Testament, and in profane history. They belonged to the Phoenicians; and at this time were depending on the succor of their allies, the Philistines. But their expectation was cut off. *The remnant of the country of Caphtor.* Crete, or Cyprus. Some think it was a district along the coast of the Mediterranean, belonging to the Philistines.

5. *Baldness is come upon Gaza.* They have cut off their hair in token of deep sorrow and distress. *Ashkelon is cut off.* Or "put to silence," another mark of the deepest sorrow. Askelon was one of the five seignories of the Philistines; Gaza was another. *The remnant of their valley.* Or "plain"; for the whole land of the Philistines was a vast plain, which extended along the coast of the Mediterranean Sea from Phoenicia to the frontiers of Egypt. The whole of this plain, the territory of the Philistines, shall be desolated.

6. *O thou sword of the Lord.* This is a most grand prosopopoeia—a dialogue between the sword of the Lord and the prophet. Nothing can be imagined more sublime. *Put up thyself into thy scabbard, rest, and be still.* Shed no more blood, destroy no more lives, erase no more cities, desolate no more countries.

7. *How can it be quiet?* This is the answer of the sword. I am the officer of God's judgments, and He has given me a commission against Ashkelon, and against the seashore, all the coast where the Philistines have their territories. The measure of their iniquities is full, and these God hath appointed this sword to ravage. The Philistines were ever the implacable enemies of the Jews, and the basest and worst of all idolaters. On these accounts the sword of the Lord had its commission against them, and it did its office most fearfully and effectually by the hand of the Chaldeans.

MATTHEW HENRY

CHAPTER 48

Verses 1–13

I. The author of Moab's destruction is *the Lord of hosts*, and *the God of Israel* (*v.* 1), who will herein plead the cause of his Israel against a people that have always been vexatious to them, and will punish them now for the injuries done to Israel of old.

II. The instruments of it: *Spoilers shall come* (*v.* 8), shall come with a sword, a sword that shall *pursue them, v.* 2. "*I will send unto him wanderers*, such as come from afar, as if they had missed their way, but they shall *cause him to wander*."

These destroyers *have devised evil against Heshbon*, one of the principal cities of Moab, and they aim at the ruin of the kingdom: *Come, and let us cut it off from being a nation* (*v.* 2). The prophet, in God's name, engages them to make thorough work of it (*v.* 10): *Cursed be he that does the work of the Lord deceitfully*. To this work is applied that general rule given to all that are employed in any service for God, *Cursed be he that does the work of the Lord deceitfully* or negligently.

JAMIESON, FAUSSET, BROWN

CHAPTER 48

Vss. 1-47. PROPHECY AGAINST MOAB. **It had** taken part with the Chaldeans against Judea (II Kings 24:2). Fulfilled by Nebuchadnezzar five years after the destruction of Jerusalem, when also he attacked Egypt (ch. 43:8-13) and Ammon (ch. 49:1-6). [JOSEPHUS, *Antiquities*, 10.9, 7]. Jeremiah in this prophecy uses that of Isaiah 15:16, amplifying and adapting it to his purpose under inspiration, at the same time confirming its divine authority. Isaiah, however, in his prophecy refers to the devastation of Moab by the Assyrian king, *Shalmaneser;* Jeremiah refers to that by *Nebuchadnezzar.* **1. Nebo**—a mountain and town of Moab; its meaning is "that which fructifies." **Kiriathaim**—a city of Moab, *consisting of two cities*, as the word signifies; originally held by the Emim (Gen. 14:5). **Misgab**—meaning "elevation." It lay on an elevation. **2. no more praise**—(Isa. 16:14). **in Heshbon**—The foe having taken Heshbon, the chief city of Moab (vs. 45), in it *devise* evil against *Moab* ("it") saying, Come .... Heshbon was midway between the rivers Arnon and Jabbok; it was the residence of Sihon, king of the Amorites, and afterwards a Levitical city in Gad (Num. 21:26). There is a play on words in the *Hebrew*, "*Heshbon, Hashbu.*" *Heshbon* means a place of *devising* or *counsel.* The city, heretofore called the ***seat of counsel*, shall find other *counsellors* viz.**, those who devise its destruction. **thou shalt be cut down ... Madmen**—rather, by a play on words on the meaning of *madmen* (silence), *Thou shalt be brought to silence*, so as well to deserve thy name (Isa. 15:1). Thou shalt not dare to utter a sound. **3. Horonaim**—the same as the city Avara, mentioned by Ptolemy. The word means "double caves" (Neh. 2:10; Isa. 15:5). **4. little ones ... cry**—heightening the distress of the scene. The foe does not spare even infants. **5. going up of Luhith ... going down of Horonaim**—Horonaim lay in a plain, Luhith on a height. To the latter, therefore, the Moabites would flee with "continual *weeping*," as a place of safety from the Chaldeans. Lit., "Weeping shall go up upon weeping." **6.** They exhort one another to flee. **heath**—or the juniper (see *Note*, ch. 17:6). MAURER translates, "Be like one *naked* in the wil-

ADAM CLARKE

CHAPTER 48

1. *Against Moab.* This was delivered some time after the destruction of Jerusalem. The Moabites were in the neighborhood of the Ammonites, and whatever evils fell on the one would naturally involve the other. See Isa. xv and xvi on this same subject. *Woe unto Nebo! for it is spoiled.* This was a city in the tribe of Reuben, afterwards possessed by the Moabites. It probably had its name from Nebo, one of the principal idols of the Moabites. *Kiriathaim.* Another city of the Moabites. *Misgab is confounded.* There is no place of this name known; and therefore several learned men translate *hammisgab*, literally, "the high tower," or "fortress," which may apply to Kiriathaim, or any other high and well-fortified place.

2. *No more praise of Moab.* Dr. Blayney translates: "Moab shall have no more glorying in Heshbon; they have devised evil against her (saying.)" And this most certainly is the best translation of the original.

3. *Horonaim.* Another city of Moab, near to Luhith. At this latter place the hill country of Moab commenced.

6. *Flee, save your lives.* The enemy is in full pursuit of you. *Be like the heath. Caaroer,* "like Aroer," which some take for a city, others

MATTHEW HENRY

IV. God will now reckon with Moab because they have been secure, and have trusted in their wealth and strength, *in their works* and *in their treasures, v.* 7. They trusted *in the abundance of their riches and strengthened themselves in their wickedness*, Ps. lii. 7. They had been long undisturbed: *Moab has been at ease from his youth.* It was an ancient kingdom before Israel was, and had enjoyed great tranquillity, though a small country. He has not been unsettled, nor *gone into captivity*, and yet Moab is a wicked idolatrous nation, and one of the confederates against *God's hidden ones*, Ps. lxxxiii. 3, 6. They had been long corrupt and unreformed: He *has settled on his lees*; he has been secure and sensual in his prosperity. *His taste remained in him, and his scent is not changed;* he is still the same, as bad as ever he was.

III. The effects of this destruction. The cities shall be laid in ruins; they shall be *spoiled* (*v.* 1) and cut down (*v.* 2); they shall be *desolate* (*v.* 9), *without any to dwell therein.* The *country* also shall be wasted, the *valley shall perish*, and the *plain be destroyed, v.* 8. The corn and the flocks, which used to cover the plains and make the valleys rejoice, shall all be destroyed, eaten up, trodden down, or carried off. The *priests and princes shall go together into captivity.* Chemosh, the god they worship, shall share with them in the ruin; his temples shall be laid in ashes and his image carried away with the rest of the spoil. The consequence will be shame and confusion: *Kirjathaim is confounded*, and Misgah is so. *There shall be no more vaunting in Moab concerning Heshbon* (so it might be read, *v.* 2). Nor shall they any more boast of their gods (*v.* 13); they *shall be ashamed of Chemosh, as Israel was ashamed of Beth-el*, of the golden calf they had at Beth-el, for it was not able to save them from the Assyrians; nor shall Chemosh be able to save the Moabites from the Chaldeans. Go up to the hills, go down to the valleys, and you meet with *continual weeping* (*weeping with weeping*); all are in tears; you meet none with dry eyes. They will cry to one another: "Away, away! *flee, save your lives* (*v.* 6); shift for your own safety, though you escape as naked as the *heath*, or grig, or dry shrub, *in the wilderness.* Take shelter, though it be in a barren wilderness. The danger will come suddenly and swiftly; and therefore *give wings unto Moab* (*v.* 9)."

Verses 14–47

The destruction is here further prophesied in moving language, designed not only to awaken them by a national repentance to prevent the trouble, or by a personal repentance to prepare for it, but to affect us with the calamitous state of human life, and with the power of God's anger with a provoking people.

I. It is a surprising destruction, and very sudden, that is here threatened. They thought themselves *strong for war* and able to deal with the most powerful enemy (*v.* 14), and yet the calamity is near, and he is not able to keep it off. As an eagle flies upon his prey, *he shall spread his wings*, the wings of his army, *over Moab*; that none may escape. *The strongholds* of Moab are taken by *surprise* (*v.* 41), so that all their strength stood them in no stead. It requires more than ordinary courage not to be *afraid of sudden fear.*

II. It lays Moab all in ruins: *Moab is spoiled* (*v.* 15), quite spoiled, is *confounded and broken down* (*v.* 20).

Moabites themselves shall lament. Those that sat in *glory*, in the midst of wealth, and mirth, shall *sit in thirst*, in a dry land, where no water, no comfort is, *v.* 18. The Moabites in the remote corners of the country, will ask everyone *that escapes, What is done? v.* 19. And when they are told that all is gone, they will *howl and cry*, in anguish of spirit (*v.* 20).

JAMIESON, FAUSSET, BROWN

derness." But the sense is, Live *in the wilderness like the heath*, or juniper; do not "*trust in*" *walls* (vs. 7) [GROTIUS]. (Cf. Matt. 24:16-18). **7. thy works**—viz., fortifications built by thy work. Moab was famous for its fortresses (vs. 18). The antithesis is to vs. 6, "Be . . . in the wilderness," where there are no fortified cities. **thou . . . also**—like the rest of the surrounding peoples, Judah, etc. **Chemosh**—the tutelary god of Moab (Num. 21:29; Judg. 11:24; I Kings 11:7; II Kings 23:13). When a people were vanquished, their gods also were taken away by the victors (ch. 43:12). **8. the valley . . . shall perish**—i.e., those dwelling in the valley. **9. Give wings . . .**—(Ps. 55:6). Unless it get wings, it cannot escape the foe. "Wings," the *Hebrew* root meaning is a "flower" (Job 14:2); so the flower-like *plumage* of a bird. **10. work of . . . Lord**—the divinely appointed utter devastation of Moab. To represent how entirely this is God's will, a curse is pronounced on the Chaldeans, the instrument, if they do it *negligently* (*Margin*) or by halves (Judg. 5:23); cf. Saul's sin as to Amalek (I Sam. 15:3, 9), and Ahab's as to Syria (I Kings 20:42). **11. settled on . . . lees**— (*Note*, Isa. 25:6; Zeph. 1:12). As wine left to settle on its own lees retains its flavor and strength (which it would lose by being poured from one vessel into another), so Moab, owing to its never having been dislodged from its settlements, retains its pride of strength unimpaired. **emptied from vessel . . .**—To make it fit for use, it used to be filtered from vessel to vessel. **scent**—retaining the image: the bouquet or perfume of the wine. **12. wanderers**—rather, "pourers out," retaining the image of vs. 11, i.e., the Chaldeans who shall remove Moab from his settlements, as men pour wine from off the lees into other vessels. "His vessels" are the cities of Moab; the broken "bottles" the men slain [GROTIUS]. The *Hebrew* and the kindred *Arabic* word means, "to turn on one side," so as to empty a vessel [MAURER]. **13. ashamed**—have the shame of disappointment as to the hopes they entertained of aid from Chemosh, their idol. **Beth-el**—(I Kings 12:27, 29)—i.e., *the golden calf* set up there by Jeroboam. **15. gone up . . . gone down**—in antithesis. **out of her cities**—Rather, "Moab . . . and her cities are gone up," viz., pass away in the ascending smoke of their conflagration (Josh. 8:20, 21; Judg. 20:40). When this took place, the young warriors would *go down* from the burning citadels only to meet their own *slaughter* [GROTIUS]. *English Version* is somewhat favored by the fact that "gone out" is *singular*, and "cities" *plural*. The antithesis favors GROTIUS. **16. near**—to the prophet's eye, though probably twenty-three years elapsed between the utterance of the prophecy in the fourth year of Jehoiakim (II Kings 24:2) and its fulfilment in the fifth year of Nebuchadnezzar. **17. bemoan**—Not that Moab deserves pity, but this mode of expression pictures more vividly the grievousness of Moab's calamities. **all ye that know his name**—those at a greater distance whom the fame of Moab's "name" had reached, as distinguished from those "about him," i.e., near. **strong staff . . . rod**—Moab is so called as striking terror into and oppressing other peoples (Isa. 9:4; 14:4, 5); also because of its dignity and power (Ps. 110:2; Zech. 11:7). **18.** (Isa. 47:1). **dost inhabit**—now so securely settled as if in a lasting habitation. **thirst**—Dibon, being situated on the Arnon, abounded in water (Isa. 15:9). In sad contrast with this, and with her "glory" in general, she shall be reduced not only to shame, but to the want of the commonest necessaries "(thirst") in the arid wilderness (vs. 6). **19. Aroer**—on the north bank of the Arnon, a city of Ammon (Deut. 2:36; 3:12). As it was on "*the way*" of the Moabites who fled into the desert, its inhabitants "ask" what is the occasion of Moab's flight, and so learn the lot that awaits themselves (cf. I Sam. 4:13, 16). **20.** Answer of the fleeing Moabites to the Ammonite inquirers (vs. 19; Isa. 16:2). He enumerates the Moabite cities at length, as it seemed so incredible that all should be so utterly ruined. Many of them were assigned to the Levites, while Israel stood. **in Arnon**—the north boundary between Moab and Ammon (vs. 19; Num. 21:13). **21. plain**—(vs. 8). Not only the mountainous regions, but also the plain, shall be wasted. **Holon**—(Cf. Joshua 15:51). **Jahazah**—(Num. 21: 23; Isa. 15:4). **Mephaath**—(Josh. 13:18; 21:37). **22. Beth-diblathaim**—"the house of Diblathaim": Almon-diblathaim (Num. 33:46); "Diblath" (Ezek. 6:13); not far from Mount Nebo (Num. 33:46, 47). **23. Beth-gamul**—meaning "the city of camels." **Beth-meon**—"the house of habitation": Beth-baal-meon (Josh. 13:17). Now its ruins are called Miun. **24. Kerioth**—(Josh. 15:25; Amos 2:2). **Bozrah**—(See *Note*, Isaiah 34:6); at one time under

ADAM CLARKE

for a blasted or withered tree. It is supposed that a place of this name lay towards the north, in the land of the Ammonites, on a branch of the river Jabbok, surrounded by deserts. Save yourselves by getting into the wilderness, where the pursuing foe will scarcely think it worth his while to follow you, as the wilderness itself must soon destroy you.

7. *Chemosh shall go forth into captivity.* The grand national idol of the Moabites, Num. xxi. 29; Judg. xi. 24. Ancient idolaters used to take their gods with them to the field of battle.

9. *Give wings unto Moab.* There is no hope in resistance, and to escape requires the speediest flight.

10. *Cursed be he that doeth the work of the Lord deceitfully.* Moab is doomed to destruction, and the Lord pronounces a curse on their enemies if they do not proceed to utter extirpation. God is the Author of life, and has a sovereign right to dispose of it as He pleases, and these had forfeited theirs long ago by their idolatry and other crimes.

11. *Moab hath been at ease.* The metaphor here is taken from the mode of preserving wines. They let them rest upon their lees for a considerable time, as this improves them in both strength and flavor; and when this is sufficiently done, they pour them off into other vessels. Moab had been very little molested by war since he was a nation; he had never gone out of his own land. Though some had been carried away by Shalmaneser forty years before this, he has had neither wars nor captivity. *Therefore his taste remained in him.* Still carrying on the allusion to the curing of wines; by resting long upon the lees, the taste and smell are both improved.

13. *Beth-el their confidence.* Alluding to the golden calves which Jeroboam had there set up, and commanded all the Israelites to worship.

17. *How is the strong staff broken!* The sceptre. The sovereignty of Moab is destroyed.

18. *That dost inhabit Dibon.* This was anciently a city of the Reubenites, afterwards inhabited by the Moabites, about two leagues north of the river Arnon, and about six to the east of the Dead Sea.

19. *O inhabitant of Aroer.* See the note on v. 6. This place, being at a greater distance, is counselled to watch for its own safety, and inquire of every passenger, *What is done?* that it may know when to pack up and be gone.

20. *Tell ye it in Arnon.* Apprise the inhabitants there that the territories of Moab are invaded, and the country about to be destroyed, that they may provide for their own safety.

21. *Upon Holon*, etc. All these were cities of the Moabites, but several of them are mentioned in no other place.

MATTHEW HENRY

The kingdom is deprived of its dignity and authority: *The horn of Moab is cut off*, the horn of its strength and power, both offensive and defensive; *his arm is broken*, that he can neither give a blow nor prevent a blow, *v.* 25. The youth of the kingdom went down to the battle promising themselves that they should return victorious; but God told them that they went *down to the slaughter*. Those that are enemies to God's people will soon be made no people.

IV. It is a shameful destruction and such as shall expose them to contempt: *Moab is made drunk* (*v.* 26).

They will *leave the cities and dwell in the rock*, where they may have their fill of melancholy; they shall no more be singing birds, but mourning birds, *like the dove* (*v.* 28), *the doves of the valley*, Ezek. vii. 16. That which Moab used to rejoice in was their pleasant fruits and the abundance of their rich wines. The delights of sense were all the matter of their joy. Take away these, destroy their gardens and vineyards, and you make *all their mirth to cease*, Hos. ii. 11, 12.

VI. It is a just destruction which they have deserved and brought upon themselves by sin.

1. The sin which they had been most notoriously guilty of, was pride. It is mentioned six times, *v.* 29. *We have* all *heard of the pride of Moab*. It was charged upon them, Isa. xvi. 6, but here it is expressed more largely than there. Two instances are here given of the pride of Moab: (1) He had conducted himself insolently towards God. He must be brought down with shame (*v.* 26), for *he* has *magnified himself against the Lord*. The Moabites preferred Chemosh before Jehovah, and thought themselves a match for the God of Israel. (2) He had conducted himself scornfully towards Israel, in their late troubles; therefore Moab shall fall into the same troubles, and be a derision, for Israel was *a derision to him*, *v.* 26, 27. But the Moabites industriously proclaimed their joy, triumphing over every Israelite they met with in distress and laughing at him.

2. Besides this they had been guilty of malice against God's people, and treachery in their dealings with them, *v.* 30. The nation, whose fall they triumph in, shall recover itself.

III. It is a lamentable destruction and will turn joy into heaviness. The prophet does himself lament it. His very *heart shall mourn for* them (*v.* 31); he will *weep for the vine of Sibmah* (*v.* 32); his heart *shall sound like pipes for Moab*, *v.* 36. The ruin of sinners is no pleasure to God, and therefore should be a pain to us. These passages, and many others in this chapter, are much the same as Isaiah's in his prophecies against Moab (Isa. xv. 1); for, though there was a long distance of time between that prophecy and this, yet they were both dictated by one and the same Spirit.

Take joy and gladness from the plentiful field, and you take it *from the land of Moab*, *v.* 33. Those who make the delights of sense their chief joy, since these are things they may easily be deprived of in a little time, subject themselves to the tyranny of the greatest grief; whereas those who rejoice in God may do that even when *the fig-tree does not blossom and there is no fruit in the vine*. All their neighbours are called to mourn with them, and to condole with them on their ruin (*v.* 17): *All you that are about him bemoan him*. Let none be puffed up with or put confidence in their strength or beauty, for neither will be a security against the judgments of God.

JAMIESON, FAUSSET, BROWN

the dominion of Edom, though belonging originally to Moab (Gen. 36:33; Isa. 63:1). Others think the Bozrah in Edom distinct from that of Moab. "Bezer" (Josh. 21:36). **25. horn**—the emblem of strength and sovereignty: it is the horned animal's means of offense and defense (Ps. 75:5, 10; Lam. 2: 3). **26. drunken**—(*Note*, ch. 13:12; 25:17). Intoxicated with the cup of divine wrath, so as to be in helpless distraction. **magnified . . . against . . . Lord**—boasted arrogantly against *God's people*, that whereas Israel was fallen, Moab remained flourishing. **wallow in . . . vomit**—following up the image of a drunken man, i.e., shall be so afflicted by God's wrath as to *disgorge* all his past pride, riches, and vainglory, and *fall* in his shameful abasement. **he also . . . derision**—He in his disaster shall be an object of derision to us, as we in ours have been to him (vs. 27). Retribution in kind. **27.** (Zeph. 2:8.) **a derision**—The *Hebrew* has the article: referring to vs. 26, "Was not Israel (*the whole* nation) *the* object of derision to thee?" Therefore, Moab is to suffer as formerly for its exultation over the calamity (II Kings 17:6) of the ten tribes under the Assyrian Shalmaneser (Isa. 15:16), so now for its exultation over the fall of Judah, under the Chaldean Nebuchadnezzar. God takes up His people's cause as His own (Obad. 13-18). **was he . . . among thieves**—(Ch. 2:26). Proverbial. What did Israel do to deserve such derision? *Was he detected in theft*, that thou didst so *exult* over him *in speaking of him*? Though guilty before God, Israel was guiltless towards thee. **since**—"since ever" thou didst begin speaking of him. **skippedst for joy**—at Israel's calamity [CALVIN]; or, "thou didst *shake thy head*" in "derision" [MAURER]. **28.** Doves often have their nests in the "sides" of caverns. No longer shalt thou have cities to shelter thee: thou shalt have to flee for shelter to caves and deserts (Ps. 55:6, 8; Song of Sol. 2:14). **29. pride**—(Isa. 16:6, 7). Moab was the trumpeter of his own fame. Jeremiah adds "loftiness and arrogancy' 'to Isaiah's picture, so that Moab had not only not been bettered by the chastisement previously endured as foretold by Isaiah, but had even become worse; so that his guilt, and therefore his sentence of punishment, are increased now. Six times Moab's pride (or the synonyms) are mentioned, to show the exceeding hatefulness of his sin. **30. I know**—Moab's "proud arrogancy" (vs. 29) or "wrath," against My people, is not unknown to Me. **it shall not be so**—The result shall *not* be so as he thinks: *his lies shall not so effect* what he aims at by them. CALVIN translates, "his lies are not right (i.e., his vauntings are vain because God will not give them effect); they shall not do so" as they project in their minds, for God will set at naught their plans. **31. I will cry . . . for . . . Moab**—Not that it deserves pity, but the prophet's "crying" for it vividly represents the greatness of the calamity. **Kir-heres**—Kir-hareseth, in Isaiah 16:7; see *Note* there. It means "the city of potters," or else "the city of the sun" [GROTIUS]. Here "the *men* of Kir-heres" are substituted for "the *foundations* of Kir-hareseth," in Isaiah 16:7. The change answers probably to the different bearing of the disaster under Nebuchadnezzar, as compared with that former one under Shalmaneser. **32. with the weeping**—with the same weeping as Jazer, now vanquished, wept with for the destruction of its vines. The same calamity shall befall thee, Sibmah, as befell Jazer. The *Hebrew* preposition here is different from that in Isaiah 16:9, for which reason MAURER translates, "with *more than* the weeping of Jazer." *English Version* understands it of the *continuation* of the weeping; after they have wept for Jazer, fresh subject of lamentation will present itself for the wasting of the vine-abounding Sibmah. **plants . . . gone over . . . sea of Jazer**—As LXX reads "*cities* of Jazer," and as no traces of a lake near Jazer are found, the reading of *English Version* is doubtful. Retaining the present reading, we avoid the difficulty by translating [GROTIUS], "Thy plants (i.e., *citizens:* alluding to the 'vine') are gone over the sea (i.e., shall be transported beyond the sea to Cyprus, and such distant lands subject to Babylon; and this, too, in summertime), whereas Jazer (i.e., the men of Jazer) reached the sea" (shore only, but are not transported beyond the sea); so that worse shall befall thee than befalls Jazer. **spoiler**—Nebuzaradan. **33. the plentiful field**—rather, "Carmel": as the parallel "land of Moab" requires, though in Isaiah 16:10, it is "the plentiful field." Joy is taken away as from the nearer regions (Canaan and Palestine), so from the farther "land of Moab"; what has happened to Judah shall befall Moab, too (vss. 26, 27) [MAURER]. However, Moab alone seems to be spoken of here; nor does the parallelism forbid "plentiful field" answering to "Moab." *Eng-*

ADAM CLARKE

25. *The horn of Moab is cut off, and his arm is broken.* His political and physical powers are no more.

27. *Was not Israel a derision unto thee?* Did you not mock My people, and say their God was no better than the gods of other nations? See Ezek. xxv. 8. *Was he found among thieves?* Did the Israelites come to rob and plunder you? Why then mock them, and rejoice at their desolation, when their enemies prevailed over them? This the Lord particularly resents.

28. *Dwell in the rock.* Go to the most inaccessible places in the mountains. *The hole's mouth.* And into the most secret caves and holes of the earth.

29. *The pride of Moab.* See Isa. xvi. 1.

32. *O vine of Sibmah.* See Isa. xvi. 8.

MATTHEW HENRY

V. It is the destruction of that which is dear to them, not only of their summer fruits and their vintage, but of their wealth (*v.* 36): *The riches that he has gotten have perished.* Riches, like dust, slip through our fingers even when we hold them fast. Yet this is not the worst; even those whose religion was false were fond of it above anything, and therefore, though it was really a promise, yet to them it was a threatening (*v.* 35), that God *will cause to cease him that offers in the high places*, for the high places shall be destroyed, and the fields of offerings shall be laid waste, and the priests themselves, *who burnt incense to their gods*, shall be slain or carried into captivity, *v.* 7.

What was said of sinners in general (Isa. xxiv. 17, 18), that those who *flee from the fear shall fall into the pit* and those who come *up out of the pit shall be taken in the snare*, is here particularly foretold concerning the sinners of Moab (*v.* 44). The figurative expressions used *v.* 44 are explained in one instance (*v.* 45): *Those that fled* out of the villages for fear of the enemy's forces put themselves *under the shadow of Heshbon*, stood there, and supposed they stood safely, as now armies sometimes retire under the cannon of a fortified city, but here they should be disappointed, for, when *they flee out of the pit, they fall into the snare;* Heshbon, which they thought would shelter them, devours them as Moses had foretold long since (Num. xxi. 28).

The chapter concludes with a short promise of their return out of *captivity in the latter days.* God, who brings them into captivity, *will bring again* their *captivity*, *v.* 47. Thus tenderly does God deal with Moabites, much more with his own people! Even with Moabites he *will not contend for ever, nor be always wrath.* This prophecy concerning Moab is long, but here it ends; it ends comfortably: *Thus far is the judgment of Moab.*

JAMIESON, FAUSSET, BROWN

lish Version is therefore better. **shouting**—repeated; as at the conclusion of the vintage, men sing over and over again the same cry of joy. **their shouting . . . no shouting**—A shouting shall be heard, but not the joyous shouting of laborers treading the grapes, but the terrible battle cry of the foe. **34. From the cry of Heshbon . . .**—Those who fly from Heshbon on its capture shall continue the cry even as far as Elealeh. . . . There will be continued cries in all quarters, from one end to the other, everywhere slaughter and wasting. **as an heifer of three years old**—Moab heretofore not having known foreign yoke, and in its full strength, is compared to an heifer of three years old, never yet yoked, nor as yet worn out with many birth-givings (cf. *Note,* Isa. 15: 5). **waters . . . of Nimrim**—i.e., the *well-watered* and therefore luxuriant *pastures* of Nimrim. **desolate**—The *Hebrew* is stronger: not merely shall be "desolate," but *desolation* itself multiplied: *plural,* "desolations." The most fertile tracts shall be dried up. **35. him that offereth**—viz., *whole burnt offerings* as the *Hebrew* requires [GROTIUS]. Cf. the awful burnt offering of the king of Moab (II Kings 3:27) **high places**—(Isa. 16:12). **36.** (*Notes,* Isa. 15:7; 16:11). **like pipes**—a plaintive instrument, therefore used at funerals and in general mourning. **riches . . . gotten**—lit., *the abundance . . . that which is over and above* the necessaries of life. GROTIUS translates, "They who have been left remaining shall perish"; they who have not been slain by the enemy shall perish by disease and famine. **37.** (*Note,* ch. 47:5; Isa. 15:2, 3.) **upon all . . . hands**—i.e, arms, in which such cuttings used to be made in token of grief (cf. Zech. 13:6). **38. vessel . . . no pleasure**—(*Note,* ch. 22:28); a vessel cast aside by the potter as refuse, not answering his design. **39. it**—Moab. **How . . . how**—prodigious, yet sure to happen. **turned the back**—not daring to show her face. **derision . . . dismaying to all**—a derision to some; a dismaying to others in beholding such a judgment of God, fearing a like fate for themselves. **40. he**—Nebuzaradan, the captain of Nebuchadnezzar. **as . . . eagle**—not to bear them "on eagles' wings" (Exod. 19:4; Deut. 32:11, 12), as God does His people, but to pounce on them as a prey (ch. 49:22; Deut. 28:49; Hab. 1:8). **41. as . . . woman in . . . pangs**—(Isa. 13:8). **42.** (*Note,* vs. 26.) **43, 44.** (*Note,* Isaiah 24:17, 18.) **44.** When thou thinkest thou hast escaped one kind of danger, a fresh one will start up. **45. under . . . shadow of Heshbon**—They thought that they would be safe in Heshbon. **because of the force**—i.e., "they that fled because of the force" of *the enemy*: they that fled *from* it. GLASSIUS translates, "through want of strength." So the *Hebrew* particle is translated (Ps. 109:24), "faileth of fatness," i.e., "faileth through *want* of fatness"; also Lamentations 4:9. **but a fire . . .**—copied in part from Sihon's hymn of victory (Num. 21:27, 28). The old "proverb" shall hold good again. As in ancient times Sihon, king of the Amorites, issued forth from his city, Heshbon, as a devouring "flame" and consumed Moab, so now the Chaldeans, making Heshbon their starting-point, shall advance to the destruction of Moab. **midst of Sihon**—i.e., the city of Sihon. **corner of Moab**—i.e., Moab from one corner to the other. **crown of . . . head**—the most *elevated* points of Moab. Making some alterations, he here copies Balaam's prophecy (Num. 24:17). *Margin* there translates "princes" for corners; if so, "crown of . . . head" here refers to the nobles. **tumultuous ones**—*sons of tumult;* those who have tumultuously revolted from Babylon. Heshbon passed from the Amorite to the Israelite sway. Moab had wrested it from Israel and helped the Chaldeans against the Jews; but revolting from Babylon, they brought ruin on themselves in turn. **46.** Copied from Numbers 21:29. **47.** Restoration promised to Moab, for the sake of righteous Lot, their progenitor (Gen. 19:37; Exod. 20:6; Ps. 89:30-33). Cf. as to Egypt, ch. 46: 26; Ammon, ch. 49:6; Elam, ch. 49:39. Gospel blessings, temporal and spiritual, to the Gentiles in the last days, are intended.

ADAM CLARKE

34. *As an heifer of three years old.* Which runs lowing from place to place in search of her calf, which is lost or taken from her.

37. *For every head shall be bald.* These, as we have seen before, were signs of the deepest distress and desolation.

40. *He shall fly as an eagle.* The enemy will pounce upon him, carry him off, and tear him to pieces.

42. *Moab shall be destroyed from being a people.* They shall not have a king or civil governor, and I doubt whether there be any evidence that they were ever reinstated in their national character.

45. *They that fled stood under the shadow of Heshbon.* Heshbon being a fortified place, they who were worsted in the fight fled to it, and rallied under its walls; but, instead of safety, they found themselves disappointed, betrayed, and ruined. See v. 2. *But a fire shall come forth out of Heshbon.* Jeremiah has borrowed this part of his discourse from an ancient poet quoted by Moses, Num. xxi. 28. *The crown of the head.* The choicest persons of the whole nation.

46. *The people of Chemosh* The Moabites, who worshipped Chemosh as their supreme god.

47. *Will I bring again the captivity of Moab in the latter days.* That many of them returned on the edict of Cyrus, by virtue of which the Jews were restored, I doubt not; but neither the Ammonites, Moabites, Philistines, nor even the Jews themselves, were ever restored to their national consequence. Perhaps the restoration spoken of here, which was to take place in the latter days, may mean the conversion of these people, in their existing remnants, to the faith of the gospel.

MATTHEW HENRY — CHAPTER 49

Verses 1–6

The Ammonites were next, both in kindred and neighbourhood, to the Moabites. 1. An action is here brought, in God's name, against the Ammonites, for an illegal encroachment upon the rightful possessions of the tribe of Gad, that lay next them, *v.* 1. Those territories upon the carrying away of the Gileadites, by the king of Assyria (2 Kings xv. 29, 1 Chron. v. 26), were left almost dispeopled, and an

JAMIESON, FAUSSET, BROWN — CHAPTER 49

VSS. 1-39. PREDICTIONS AS TO AMMON, IDUMEA, DAMASCUS, KEDAR, HAZOR, AND ELAM. The event of the prophecy as to Ammon preceded that as to Moab (*Note,* vs. 3); and in Ezekiel 21:26-28, the destruction of Ammon is subjoined to the deposition of Zedekiah. **Hath Israel . . . no heir?**—viz., to occupy the land of Gad, after it itself has been carried away captive by Shalmaneser. Ammon, like Moab, descended from Lot, lay north of Moab, from

ADAM CLARKE — CHAPTER 49

1. *Concerning the Ammonites.* This prophetic discourse was also delivered after the capture of Jerusalem. *Hath Israel no sons? . . . no heir?* The Ammonites, it appears, took advantage of the depressed state of Israel, and invaded their territories in the tribe of Gad, hoping to make them their own forever. But the prophet intimates that God will preserve the descendants of Israel, and will bring them back to their

MATTHEW HENRY

easy prey to the next invader. "Are there no Gadites left, to whom the right of inheritance belongs? Or, if there were not, are there no Israelites, none left of Judah, that are nearer akin to them than you are?" *Why then does their king,* as if he were entitled to the forfeited estates, or Milcom, their idol, as if he had the right to dispose of it to his worshippers, *inherit Gad, and his people dwell in the cities* which fell by lot to that tribe of God's people? *They magnified themselves against their border* and boasted it was their own, Zeph. ii. 8. Those will find themselves mistaken who think everything their own which they can lay their hands on. As there is justice owing to owners, so also to their heirs, whom it is a great sin to defraud, though they either know not their right or know not how to come at it. 2. Judgment is here given against them for this violence. God *will cause an alarm of war to be heard,* even *in Rabbah,* their capital city and a very strong one, *v.* 2. Their cities shall be laid in ruins. Their country, which they were so proud of, shall be wasted (*v.* 4). They are charged with backsliding, for they were the posterity of righteous Lot. *They were untoward and refractory* (so some read it); and, when they had forsaken their God, *they gloried in their valleys.* These they had violently taken away from Israel. They gloried in the strength of their valleys, so surrounded with mountains that they were inaccessible, gloried in the products of them. They flattered themselves that they should never be disturbed in the enjoyment of them: *To-morrow shall be as this day;* therefore they set God and his judgments at defiance. *Their king and his princes,* and Milcom, their god, *and his priests, shall go into captivity* (*v.* 3), *and every man shall be driven out right forth,* shall make the best of it in his flight (*v.* 5). And, to complete their misery, *none shall gather up him that wanders,* none shall open their doors to them. Then the country of the Ammonites shall fall into the hands of the remaining Israelites (*v.* 2).

3. Yet there is a prospect given them of mercy hereafter (*v.* 6), as before to Moab.

Verses 7–22

The Edomites come next to receive their doom from God, by the mouth of Jeremiah: they also were old enemies to the Israel of God. Many of the expressions used in this prophecy *concerning Edom* are borrowed from the prophecy of Obadiah, which is *concerning Edom*; for, all the prophets are inspired by one and the same Spirit.

III. That the Edomites' confidences should all fail them in the day of their distress. 1. They trusted to their wisdom, but that shall stand them in no stead. This is the first thing fastened upon in this prophecy against Edom, *v.* 7. That nation used to be famous for wisdom, and their statesmen were thought to excel in politics; and yet now they shall take such wrong measures, and be so baffled in all their designs, that people shall ask, with wonder, What is the matter with the Edomites? *Is wisdom no more in Teman?* It is so, when God is designing the ruin of a people; for whom he will destroy he infatuates. See Job xii. 20. *Has their wisdom vanished? Is it tired?* (so some); *is it worn out?* (so others); *has it become useless?* (so others).

I. That the country of Edom should be all wasted and made desolate, that *the calamity of Esau* should be *brought upon him,* the calamity he has deserved, for his old sins, *v.* 8. The time is at hand when God *will visit him,* and call him to an account, and then they shall *flee* from the sword, *turn back* from the battle, and *dwell deep* in caverns, where they shall hide. All they have shall be carried off by the conqueror; those that destroy them shall never be satiated (*v.* 9, 10); they shall make *Esau* quite *bare,* shall strip the Edomites of all they have. *His brethren* the Moabites, *and his neighbours* the Philistines, whom he might have expected succours from, or at least shelter, are spoiled as well as he. The Chaldee makes these to be the words of God to his people, distinguishing them from the Edomites in this calamity; and they read it, "*But you, O house of Israel! you shall not leave your orphans; I will secure them, and let your widows rest on my word.* Whatever becomes of the widows and fatherless of the Edomites, I will take care of yours." They had made a mighty figure, but God will make *them small among the heathen*; and those that despised God's people shall themselves be *despised among men* (*v.* 15, Obad. 2).

JAMIESON, FAUSSET, BROWN

which it was separated by the river Arnon, and east of Reuben and Gad (Josh. 13:24, 25) on the same side of Jordan. It seized on Gad when Israel was carried captive. Judah was by the right of kindred the heir, not Ammon; but Ammon joined with Nebuchadnezzar against Judah and Jerusalem (II Kings 24:2) and exulted over its fall (Ps. 83:4-7, 8; Zeph. 2:8, 9). It had already, in the days of Jeroboam, in Israel's affliction, tried to "enlarge its border" (II Kings 14:26; Amos 1:1, 13). **their king**–(Amos 1: 15); referring to Melchom, their tutelary idol (Zeph. 1:5); and so the LXX reads it here as a proper name (I Kings 11:5, 33; II Kings 23:13). The Ammonite god is said to do what *they* do, viz., occupy the Israelite land of Gad. To Jehovah, the theocratic "King" of Israel, the land belonged of right; so **that their Molech** or Melchom was a usurper-*king.* **his people**–the people of Melchom, "their king." Cf. "people of Chemosh," ch. 48:46. **2. Rabbah**–"the great," metropolis of Ammon (II Sam. 12:26-30). Its destruction is foretold also in Ezekiel 25: 5; Amos 1:14, 15. **her daughters**–the towns and villages, dependencies of the metropolis (Josh. 15: 45). **shall . . . be heir**–shall *possess* those who possessed him. The full accomplishment of this is still future; partially fulfilled under the Maccabees (I Maccabees 5:6). **3. Heshbon . . . Ai**–Nebuchadnezzar, coming from the north, first attacked Ammon, then its brother and neighbor, Moab. As Ai of Ammon had already suffered destruction, Heshbon of Moab being near it might well fear the same fate. **hedges**–Their cities being destroyed, the outcasts have no place of shelter save behind the "hedges" of vineyards and gardens; or else the *enclosures* of their villages. **their king**–Melchom, the idol, as the mention of "his priests" shows (cf. ch. 48:7). **4. thy flowing valley**–rather, "thy valley shall flow," viz., with the blood of the slain; in sad contrast to their "valleys" in which they had heretofore "gloried," as *flowing* with milk and honey [GROTIUS]. Or else, as *Margin,* "shall flow *away.*" **backsliding**–apostate from Jehovah, the God of their father Lot, to Molech. **treasures**–her resources for resisting the foe. **Who shall . . .**–Who *can* come . . . (ch. 21:13). **5. every man right forth**–whithersoever chance may lead him (ch. 46:5; Gen. 19:17); straight *before him,* onwards at random (Amos 4:3). **none . . . gather up him . . .**–There shall be none to *gather* together the *wandering* fugitives, so as to care for them and restore them to their own homes. **6.** (Cf. ch. 48:47.) For the sake of "righteous" Lot their progenitor. Partially fulfilled under Cyrus; in gospel times more fully. **7. Concerning Edom**–a distinct prophecy, copied in part from Obadiah, but with the freedom of one himself inspired and foretelling a later calamity. Obadiah's was fulfilled probably in Sennacherib's time (cf. Isa. 34:5; Amos 1:11); Jeremiah's about the same time as his preceding prophecies (vs. 12; Ezek. 25:12). **wisdom**–for which the Arabs and the people of Teman (a city of Edom) in particular, were famed (Gen. 36:15; I Kings 4:30; see Job, everywhere; Obadiah 8). **vanished**–lit., "poured out," i.e., exhausted (cf. Isa. 19:3, *Margin*) [MAURER]. Or, as the kindred Ethiopic word means, "worn out" [LUDOVICUS DE DIEU]. **8. turn**–viz., your backs in flight. **dwell deep**–in deep defiles and caves [GROTIUS], which abound in Idumea. Others refer it to the Arab custom of retiring into the depth of the desert when avoiding an offended foe (vs. 30). **Dedan**–a tribe bordering on and made subject by Idumea; descended from Jokshan, son of Abraham and Keturah (Gen. 25:1-3). **Esau**–The naming of Edom's progenitor, reprobated by God, recalls the remembrance of the old curse on him for his profanity, both his sin and its punishment being perpetuated in his descendants (Heb. 12:16, 17). **9.** (Obadiah 5.) *Grape-gatherers,* yea even *thieves,* leave something behind them; but the Chaldeans will sweep Idumea clean of everything. **10.** Edom became politically extinct after the time of the Romans. **uncovered his secret places**–where he hid himself (vs. 8) and his treasures (Isa. 45:3). I have caused that nothing should be so hidden as that the conqueror should not find it. **brethren**–Ammon. **neighbours**–the Philistines. **11.** Thy fatherless and widows must rest their hope in God alone, as none of the adult males shall be left alive, so desperate will be the affairs of Edom. The verse also, besides this threat, implies a promise of mercy to Esau in God's good time, as there was to Moab and Ammon (vs. 6; ch. 48:47); the extinction of the adult males is the prominent idea (cf. vs. 12). **12.** (Cf. 25:15, 16, 29.) **they whose judgment was not to drink of the cup**–the Jews to whom, by virtue of the covenant relation, it did not belong to drink the cup. It might have been expected that they

ADAM CLARKE

forfeited inheritances.

Why then doth their king? Malcom or *Milcom,* the chief idol of the Ammonites. That the idol Milcom is here meant is sufficiently evident from v. 3.

3. *Run to and fro by the hedges.* It is supposed that this may refer to the women making lamentations for the dead, that were in general buried by the walls of their gardens. But others think that it refers to the smaller cities or villages, called here the daughters of *Rabbah,* the metropolis, the inhabitants of which are exhorted to seek safety somewhere else, as none can be expected from them, now that the enemy is at hand.

6. *Afterward I will bring again.* The Ammonites are supposed to have returned with the Moabites and Israelites, on permission given by the edict of Cyrus.

7. *Concerning Edom.* This is a new and separate discourse. *Teman.* A part of Idumea, put here for the whole country.

8. *Dwell deep.* An allusion to the custom of the Arabs, who, when about to be attacked by a powerful foe, strike their tents, pack up their utensils, lade their camels, and set off to the great desert, and so bury themselves in it that no enemy either will or can pursue. *Dedan.* Was a city of Idumea, not far from Teman.

9. *If grapegatherers.* Both in vintage and in harvest every grape and every stalk are not gathered; hence the gleaners get something for their pains. But your enemies shall not leave one of you behind; all shall be carried into captivity.

10. *I have made Esau bare.* I have stripped him of all defense, and have discovered his hiding places to his enemies.

11. *Leave thy fatherless children.* The connection of this with the context is not easy to be discerned; but, as a general maxim, it is of great importance. Widows and orphans are the peculiar care of God. He is as the best of fathers to the one, and the most loving of husbands to the other. Even the widows and orphans of Esau, who escape the general destruction, shall be taken by the Lord.

MATTHEW HENRY

IV. That their destruction should be inevitable. 1. God hath determined it (*v.* 12); (*v.* 13), he hath *sworn it*, that they shall *drink the cup of trembling*, which is put into the hands of all their neighbours.

2. They trusted to their strength, but neither shall that avail them, *v.* 16. They had been a terror to all their neighbours, because no neighbouring nation durst meddle with them, they thought no nation in the world durst. Their country was mountainous, having many passes, which they thought themselves able to make good against any invader. See Obad. 3, 4, 8.
Edom shall be such *a desolation* that none shall care for coming near the ruins of it, *no man shall abide there* (*v.* 18).

II. That the instruments of this destruction should be very resolute and formidable. God has determined that Edom shall be laid waste, and then he that is to be employed in wasting it shall come swiftly and strongly. Nebuchadnezzar is he of whom it is here foretold. He *shall come up like a lion*, with fierceness and fury, like a lion enraged by *the swelling of Jordan* overflowing his banks, which forces him out of his covert by the water-side into the higher grounds, *v.* 19.

Even the least of the flock shall draw them out (*v.* 20); the meanest servant in Nebuchadnezzar's retinue shall *draw them out* for the slaughter, shall force them to surrender. Nebuchadnezzar shall come, not only like a lion, the king of beasts, but like an eagle, the king of birds (*v.* 22): *He shall fly as the eagle* upon his prey, so swiftly, so strongly, and immediately *the hearts of the mighty men* shall fail them, for they shall see he is an enemy that it is in vain to struggle with.
2. All the world shall take notice of it (*v.* 21): *The earth is moved*, and all the nations are put into a concern, *at the noise of their fall. The noise of the outcry is heard to the Red Sea*, which flowed upon the coasts of Edom. It shall be heard among the ships that lie in the Red Sea to take in lading (1 Kings ix. 26).

Verses 23–27

The kingdom of Syria, north of Canaan, had been often vexatious to the Israel of God. Damascus was the metropolis of that kingdom. Hamath and Arpad, two other considerable cities, are named (*v.* 23), and *the palaces of Ben-hadad*, which he built, are particularly marked for ruin, *v.* 27; see also Amos i. 4. The judgment of Damascus begins with fright and faint-heartedness. They *hear evil tidings*, that the king of Babylon, with all his force, is coming against them, and *they are confounded*; their souls are melted, *they are faint-hearted*, they are like *the troubled sea, that cannot be quiet* (Isa. lvii. 20), or like men *in a storm* at sea (Ps. cvii. 26); or the sorrow that begins in the city shall go to the sea-coast, *v.* 23. *Damascus* now *waxes feeble* (*v.* 24), and owns it is to no more purpose to think of contending with her fate than for *a woman in* labour to contend with her pains, which she cannot escape. It was a *city of praise* (*v.* 25), not praise to God, but to herself, a city much admired by all strangers that visited it. It was a *city of joy*. But now it is all overwhelmed with fear and grief. It ends with a terrible fall and fire. The inhabitants are slain (*v.* 26): The *young men*, who should defend the city, *shall fall* by the sword *in her streets*; *and all the men of war shall be cut off*. The city is laid in ashes (*v.* 27): The *fire* is *kindled* by the besiegers *in the wall*, but it shall devour *the palaces of Ben-hadad* particularly, where so much mischief had formerly been hatched against God's Israel.

JAMIESON, FAUSSET, BROWN

would be spared. He regards not the merits of the Jews, for they were as bad or worse than others: but the grace and adoption of God; it is just and natural ("judgment") that God should pardon His sons sooner than aliens [CALVIN]. **13. Bozrah**—(*Note*, ch. 48:24.) **14.** (Obadiah 1-3.) **ambassador . . . unto the heathen**—a messenger from God to stir up the Chaldeans against Edom. **15.** David and Joab had already humbled Edom (II Sam. 8:14). **16. terribleness**—the terror which thou didst inspire into others. **deceived thee**—rendered thee proudly confident, as if none would dare to assail thee. **dwellest in . . . rock**—Petra, the chief of Idumea, was cut in the rocks; its ruins are very remarkable. The whole south of Idumea abounds in cave-dwellings and rocks. **though . . . nest . . . eagle**—(Job 39:27; Obadiah 3, 4). The eagle builds its nest in the highest craggy eyry. **17.** (Cf. I Kings 9:8.) **18.** (Ch. 50:40; Deut. 29:23; Amos 4:11.) **no man shall abide there**—i.e., of the Idumeans. The Romans had a garrison there. **19. he**—Nebuchadnezzar, or Nebuzaradan; the name would at once suggest itself to the minds of the hearers (ch. 48:40; 46:18). **swelling**—as a lion which the overflow of the Jordan forced out of his lair on the banks, to ascend the neighboring heights [CALVIN]. See as to the translation, "pride of the Jordan," *Note*, ch. 12:5. **habitation of . . . strong**—the fastnesses of Idumea (cf. Num. 24:21). MAURER translates, "An ever verdant (lit., perennial) pasturage," i.e., Idumea heretofore having enjoyed uninterrupted tranquillity; so in vs. 20 the image is retained, the Idumeans being compared to "a flock," and their king to "a shepherd," in this verse, and the enemy to "a lion" (cf. ch. 50:17-19). *English Version* accords more with the *Hebrew*. **suddenly**—"in the twinkling of an eye," as the *Hebrew* implies. **him . . . her**—I will make *Nebuzaradan* enter *Idumea*, and then, having in the twinkling of an eye effected the conquest, go *away speedily* elsewhere. Instead of "but," translate, "for." GROTIUS translates, "run *upon* her, or "to her," instead of "run away from her." MAURER understands it, "I will make him (the Idumean) run away from her" (i.e., from his own land); the similar change of reference of the pronouns (ch. 50:44) favors this. **who is a chosen man . . .**—God calls the *choicest* warriors to Him, to set "*over*" the work of devastating Idumea. God will surely execute His purpose, for He can call forth from all sides the agents He chooses. **who is like me?**—(Exod. 15:11). **who will appoint me the time?**—viz., for entering into a trial in judgment with Me (see *Margin*). Image from law courts (Job 9:19). **shepherd**—leader of the Idumeans; following up the previous image, "a lion"; no Idumean shepherd shall withstand the lion sent by Jehovah (Job 41:10), or save the Idumean flock. **20. least of the flock**—the weakest and humblest of the Chaldean host. Cf. ch. 6:3, where the hostile leaders and their hosts are called "shepherds and their flocks." **draw . . . out**—"shall drag them away captive" [GROTIUS]; *shall drag them to and fro*, as a lion (vs. 19) does feeble sheep [MAURER]. *with them*—i.e., the habitation which they possess. **21. was heard in**—i.e., shall be heard *at*. **Red Sea**—a considerable distance from Idumea; though the district at the Elantic bay of the Red Sea originally belonged to Idumea, and the sea itself was called from Edom, i.e., "red" (Gen. 25:30, *Margin*). Others translate, "the weedy sea" (*Margin*), and derive the name, "Red Sea," from its red weeds; the former view is preferable. **22.** (Cf. ch. 48:40, 41.) **Bozrah**—(*Note*, ch. 48:24). **23.** Prophecy as to Damascus, etc. (Isa 17:1; 10:9). The *kingdom* of Damascus was destroyed by Assyria, but the *city* revived, and it is as to the latter Jeremiah now prophesies. The fulfil ment was probably about five years after the destruction of Jerusalem by Nebuchadnezzar (JOSEPHUS, 10.9, 7). **Hamath is confounded**—at the tidings of the overthrow of the neighboring Damascus. **on the sea**—i.e., at the sea; the dwellers there are alarmed. Other MSS. read, "like the sea." "There is anxiety (restless) as is the sea: they cannot quiet it," i.e., it cannot be quieted (Isa. 57:20). **it**—Whatever dwellers are there "cannot be quiet." **25. city of praise**—The prophet, in the person of a citizen of Damascus deploring its calamity, calls it "the city of praise," i.e., celebrated with praises everywhere for its beauty (ch. 33:9; 51:41). "How is it possible that such a city *has not been left* whole—has not been spared by the foe?" Cf. "left," Luke 17:35, 36. So Israel *left* standing some of the Canaanite cities (Josh. 11:13). **of my joy**—i.e., in which I delighted. **26. Therefore**—i.e., Since Damascus is doomed to fall, *therefore. . . .* **27. palaces of Ben-hadad**—that palace from which so many evils and such cruelty to Israel emanated;

ADAM CLARKE

12. *Art thou he that shall altogether go unpunished?* A similar form of speech appears in chap. xxv. 29. Others, less wicked than you, have been punished; and can you expect to escape? You shall not escape.

13. *Bozrah shall become a desolation.* Bozrah, a city of Idumea, is here put for the whole country.

14. *I have heard a rumour.* The Lord has revealed to me what He is about to do to the Edomites. *An ambassador is sent.* I believe this means only that God has given permission, and has stirred up the hearts of these nations to go against those whom He has doomed to destruction.

16. *O thou that dwellest.* All Idumea is full of mountains and rocks, and these rocks and mountains full of caves, where, in time of great heats, and in time of war, the people take shelter.

18. *As in the overthrow of Sodom.* The destruction of Sodom and Gomorrah and the neighboring cities was so terrible that, when God denounces judgments against incorrigible sinners, He tells them they shall be like Sodom and Gomorrah. *No man shall abide there.* It shall be so desolate as not to be habitable. Travellers may lodge on the ground for a night, but it cannot become a permanent dwelling.

19. *Behold, he shall come up like a lion.* See chap. xii. 5. The similitude used here is well illustrated by Dr. Blayney: "When I shall occasion a like commotion in her (Idumea) as a fierce and strong lion may be supposed to do in the sheep-folds, then I will cause him (the man of whom it is said in the preceding verse that he should not dwell in it) to run away from her as the affrighted shepherds and their flocks run from the lion." *A chosen man.* Nebuchadnezzar. That is, God has chosen this man, and given him a commission against Idumea.

20. *The inhabitants of Teman.* Taken here for the whole of Idumea. These are a kind of synonyms which prevent monotony, and give variety to the poet's versification. *Surely the least of the flock shall draw them out.* They shall be like timid sheep; the weakest foe shall overcome them.

21. *The earth is moved.* The whole state is represented here as a vast building suddenly thrown down, so as to cause the earth to tremble, and the noise to be heard at a great distance.

22. *He shall come up and fly as the eagle.* Nebuchadnezzar. See chap. xlviii. 40.

23. *Concerning Damascus.* This is the head or title of another prophecy. Damascus was one of the principal cities of Syria. It was taken by David, 2 Sam. viii. 6, was retaken in the reign of Solomon, 1 Kings xi. 24, etc., and regained its independence. Its kings were often at war with the ten tribes, and once it joined with them for the destruction of Judah. To defend himself against these powerful enemies Ahaz made a league with the king of Assyria, who besieged Damascus, took, and demolished it. From that time we hear nothing of Damascus till we meet with it in this prophecy. It appears to have been rebuilt and restored to some consequence. It made an obstinate resistance to Nebuchadnezzar, but was at last taken and sacked by him. At present it is both a large and populous city, with considerable commerce. *Hamath is confounded.* This is a city of Syria, on the Orontes. *Arpad.* Not far from Damascus. *Sorrow on the sea.* They are like the troubled sea, that cannot rest.

25. *How is the city of praise not left!* Damascus is so ruined that she can no more be called a praiseworthy or happy city.

27. *The palaces of Ben-hadad.* Damascus was a seat of the Syrian kings, and Ben-hadad was a name common to several of its kings.

MATTHEW HENRY

Verses 28–33

These verses foretell the desolation that Nebuchadnezzar and his forces should make among the people of Kedar (who descended from Kedar the son of Ishmael, and inhabited a part of Arabia the Stony), and of Hazor, who perhaps were originally Canaanites, of the kingdom of Hazor, in the north of Canaan, which had Jabin for its king, but, being driven thence, settled in the deserts of Arabia. They dwelt in *tents* and had no walls, but *curtains* (*v.* 29), no fortified cities; they had *neither gates nor bars*, *v.* 31. They were shepherds, and had no treasures, no money, but flocks and camels. They had no soldiers among them, for they were in no fear of invaders for they *dwelt alone*, *v.* 31. Though they had no trade, no treasures, yet they are here said to be a *wealthy nation* (*v.* 31). Those are truly rich who have enough to supply their necessities, and know when they have enough. We need not go to the treasures of kings and provinces, or to the cash of merchants, to look for wealthy people; they may be found among shepherds *that dwell in tents.* The king of Babylon resolves it shall never be said that he, who had conquered so many strong cities, will leave those unconquered *that dwell in tents.* It was strange that that eagle should stoop to catch these flies. These people had lived inoffensively among their neighbours. God said (*v.* 28): *Arise, go up to Kedar, and spoil the men of the east.* God orders it for the correcting of an unthankful people. The amazement that this put them into, and the desolation hereby made among them: *They shall cry unto them;* those on the borders shall send the alarm into all parts of the country, which shall be put into the utmost confusion by it; they shall cry, "*Fear is on every side*—We are surrounded by the enemy." They shall none of them have any heart to make resistance. The enemy need not strike a stroke; they shall shout them out of their tents, *v.* 29. There are *fears on every side* when there are foes on every side. The Chaldeans shall *take to themselves their curtains and vessels*; though they are but plain and coarse, yet they shall spoil for spoiling sake. *They shall carry away their tents and their flocks*, *v.* 29. *Their camels* shall be a booty to those that came for nothing else, *v.* 32. It is not said that any of them shall be slain, for they attempt not to make any resistance and their tents and flocks are accepted as a ransom for their lives; but they shall be dislodged and dispersed. Their country shall lie uninhabited; remote and having neither cities nor lands inviting to strangers, none shall care to succeed them, so that *Hazor shall be a desolation for ever*, *v.* 33.

Verses 34–39

This prophecy is dated in the beginning of Zedekiah's reign. The Elamites were the Persians, descended from Elam the son of Shem (Gen. x. 22); yet some think it was only that part of Persia which lay nearest to the Jews which, say they, had acted against God's Israel, *bore the quiver* in an expedition against them (Isa. xxii. 6), and therefore must be reckoned with among the rest. It is here foretold, in general, that God will *bring evil upon them, even* his *fierce anger*, *v.* 37. Their forces shall be disabled. The Elamites were famous archers, but, *Behold, I will break the bow of Elam* (*v.* 35), will ruin their artillery, and then *the chief of their might* is gone. God often orders it so that that which we most trust to first fails us, and that which was *the chief of our might* proves the least of our help. Their people shall be dispersed. There shall come enemies against them from all parts and they shall all carry some of them away captive into their respective countries, *v.* 36. *The four winds* shall be brought upon them; the storm shall come sometimes from one point and sometimes from another. Their princes shall be destroyed and the government quite changed (*v.* 38): *I will set my throne in Elam.* The throne of Nebuchadnezzar shall be set there, or the throne of Cyrus, who began his conquests with Elymais. Or it may be meant of the throne on which God sits for judgment. The king of Elam was famous of old, Gen. xiv. 1. Chedorlaomer was king of Elam, and a mighty man he was in his day; his successors, we may suppose, made a great figure; but the king of Elam is no more to God than another man. Yet the destruction of Elam shall not be perpetual (*v.* 39): *In the latter days I will bring again the captivity of Elam.* When Cyrus had destroyed Babylon, brought the empire into the hands of the Persians, the Elamites no doubt returned in triumph, and settled again in their own country. But this promise was to have its full accomplishment in the days of the Messiah, when we find Elamites among those who, when the Holy Ghost was given, heard spoken *in their own tongues the wonderful works of God* (Acts ii. 9, 11), and that is the most desirable return of the captivity.

JAMIESON, FAUSSET, BROWN

thus implying the *cause* of Damascus' overthrow. Not the Ben-hadad of II Kings 13:3; Amos 1:4; it was a common name of the Syrian kings (cf. I Kings 15:18; meaning "son of Hadad," the idol). **28. Kedar**—son of Ishmael (Gen. 25:13). The Kedarenes led a wandering predatory life in Arabia Petræa, as the Bedouin Arabs (II Chron. 21:16, 17; Ps. 120: 5). Kedar means "blackness" (Song of Sol. 1:5). **Hazor**—not the city in Palestine, but a district in Arabia Petræa. "Kingdoms" refer to the several combinations of clans, each under its own sheik. **men of the east**—Kedar and Hazor were east of Judea (Judg. 6:3; Job 1:3). **29. tents**—in which they dwelt, from which they are called Scenites, i.e., tent-dwellers. **curtains**—viz., with which the tents were covered (ch. 4:20; 10:20; Ps. 104:2). **they shall cry unto them, Fear . . .**—*The foe*, on crying, Fear . . ., shall discomfit them (the Kedarenes) by their mere cry. **30.** (*Note,* vs. 8.) No conqueror would venture to follow them into the desert. **31. wealthy**—rather, "tranquil" (I Chron. 4:40). **neither gates nor bars**—The Arabs, lying out of the track of the contending powers of Asia and Africa, took no measures of defense and had neither walled cities nor gates (Ezek. 38:11). They thought their scanty resources and wilderness position would tempt no foe. **alone**—separated from other nations, without allies; and from one another scattered asunder. So as to Israel's isolation (Num. 23:9; Deut. 33:28; Mic. 7:14).

32. camels—their chief possessions; not fields or vineyards. **in utmost . . . corners**—who seemed least likely to be dispersed. Or else, "having the hair shaven (or clipped) in angles" (ch. 9:26, 25:23) [GROTIUS]. **calamity from all sides**—which will force even those in "corners" to "scatter" themselves. **33.** (Mal. 1:3.)

34. Elam—part of Susiana, west of Persia proper, but used to designate Persia in general. Elam proper, or Elymais, nearer Judea than Persia, is probably here meant; it had helped Nebuchadnezzar against Judea; hence its punishment. It may have been idolatrous, whereas Persia proper was mainly monotheistic.

35. bow—Elam was famed for its bowmen (Isa. 22:6). **chief of their might**—in opposition to "bow," i.e., bowmen, who constituted their main strength.

36. four winds . . .—Nebuchadnezzar's army containing soldiers from the four quarters. **37. consumed**—as a distinct nation (Dan. 8:2-27). Fulfilled under Alexander and his successors. **38. I will show** Myself King by My judgments there, as though My tribunal were erected there. The throne of Cyrus, God's instrument, set up over Media, of which Elam was a part, may be meant [GROTIUS]; or rather, that of Nebuchadnezzar (ch. 43:10). Then the restoration of Elam (vs. 39) will refer *partly* to that which took place on the reduction of Babylon by Cyrus, prince of Persia and Media.

39. latter days—The *full* restoration belongs to gospel times. Elamites were among the first who heard and accepted it (Acts 2.9).

ADAM CLARKE

28. *Concerning Kedar, and concerning the kingdoms of Hazor.* This is the title of another new prophecy. *Kedar* was the name of one of the sons of Ishmael (Gen. xxv. 13) who settled in Arabia, and who gave name to a powerful tribe of Arabs who used to traffic with the Tyrians in cattle. It appears from this prophecy that Nebuchadnezzar got a commission to go against and reduce them to great misery.

30. *Dwell deep.* Retire into the depths of the desert. See on v. 8.

31. *The wealthy nation.* "The peaceable nation." *Have neither gates nor bars.* The Arabs, who had nothing but their tents; no cities, nor even permanent villages.

32. *The utmost corners.* Even in these utmost, inaccessible recesses the sword and pillage shall reach them.

33. *Hazor shall be a dwelling for dragons.* Shall be turned into a wilderness. *A desolation for ever.* Never to be repeopled.

34. *The word . . . against Elam.* Another new head of prophecy. As this was delivered in the beginning of the reign of Zedekiah, it can have no natural nor historical connection with the other prophecies in this various chapter. Some think that, by Elam, Persia is always meant; but this is not at all likely. It was a part of the Babylonian empire in the time of Daniel (chap. viii. 2) and is most probably what is called Elymais by the Greeks.

35. *I will break the bow of Elam.* They were eminent archers, and had acquired their power and eminence by their dexterity in the use of the bow. See Isa. xxii. 6. Strabo, Livy, and others speak of their eminence in archery.

36. *Will I bring the four winds.* Nebuchadnezzar and his armies, gathered out of different provinces, and attacking this people at all points in the same time.

38. *I will set my throne in Elam.* This is spoken of either Nebuchadnezzar or Cyrus. It is certain that Cyrus did render himself master of Elymais and Media, which are in the land of Elam.

39. *I will bring again the captivity of Elam.* As this is to be in *the latter days*, probably it may mean the spiritual freedom which these people would receive under the gospel dispensation. Under Cyrus, the Elamites, collected out of all quarters, were united with the Persians, their neighbors, and became, with them, masters of the East.

MATTHEW HENRY

CHAPTER 50

Verses 1–8

I. Here is a word spoken against Babylon. The king of Babylon had been very kind to Jeremiah, and yet he must foretell the ruin of that kingdom; for God's prophets must not be governed by favour or affection. Whoever are our friends, if, notwithstanding, they are God's enemies, we dare not speak peace to them. 1. The destruction of Babylon is here spoken of as a thing done, *v.* 2. 2. It is spoken of as a thing done thoroughly. The very idols of Babylon, which the people would protect with all possible care, shall be destroyed. Bel and Merodach their two principal deities shall be *confounded*, and the images of them *broken to pieces*. The country shall be laid waste (*v.* 3) out *of the north*, from Media, which lay north of Babylon, and from Assyria, through which Cyrus made his descent upon Babylon; thence the nation shall come that shall make *her land desolate*.

II. Here is a word spoken for the people of God for their comfort, both *the children of Israel* and *of Judah*.

1. It is promised that they shall return to their God first and then to their own land; and the promise of their conversion and reformation is that which makes way for all the other promises, *v.* 4, 5. They shall *lament after the Lord* as the whole house of Israel did in Samuel's time (1 Sam. vii. 2); they shall *go weeping*. These tears flow from godly sorrow; they are tears of repentance for sin, tears of joy for the goodness of God, in the dawning of the day of their deliverance. That prevails to *lead them to repentance* when captivity did not prevail to drive them to it. They shall *enquire after the Lord*; they shall not sink under their sorrows, but *shall go weeping to seek the Lord their God*. They shall *seek the Lord as their God*, and shall now have no more to do with idols. They shall think of returning to their own country again; they shall think of it not only as a mercy, but as a duty (*v.* 5): *They shall ask the way to Zion with their faces thitherward*. The journey is long and they know not the road, but they will *ask the way*. This represents the return of poor souls to God. In all true converts there are both a sincere desire to attain the end and a constant care to keep in the way. They shall renew their covenant to walk with God more closely for the future: *Come, and let us join ourselves to the Lord in a perpetual covenant*.

2. Their present case is lamented as very sad, and as having been long so: "*My people have been lost sheep* (*v.* 6); they have *gone from mountain to hill*, and could find no pasture; *they have forgotten their resting-place* in their own country and cannot find their way to it." They were *led astray by their own shepherds*, their own princes and priests; they turned them from their duty, and so provoked God to turn them out of their own land. It is with them as with wandering sheep, *all that found them have devoured them* and made a prey of them; they laughed at them, telling them it was what their own prophets had many a time told them they deserved. They had put a contempt upon the temple and upon the tradition of their ancestors, and therefore deserved to suffer these hard things.

3. They are called upon to hasten away, as soon as ever the door of liberty was opened to them (*v.* 8): "*Remove*, not only out of the borders, but *out of the midst of Babylon;* hasten to Zion, and *be as the he-goats before the flocks*; strive which shall be foremost, which shall lead in so good a work."

JAMIESON, FAUSSET, BROWN

CHAPTER 50

VSS. 1-46. BABYLON'S COMING DOWNFALL; ISRAEL'S REDEMPTION. After the predictions of judgment to be inflicted on other nations by Babylon, follows this one against Babylon itself, the longest prophecy, consisting of 100 verses. The date of its utterance was the fourth year of Zedekiah, when Seraiah, to whom it was committed, was sent to Babylon (ch. 51:59, 60). The repetitions in it make it likely that it consists of prophecies uttered at different times, now collected by Jeremiah to console the Jews in exile and to vindicate God's ways by exhibiting the final doom of Babylon, the enemy of the people of God, after her long prosperity. The style, imagery, and dialogues prove its genuineness in opposition to those who deny this. It shows his faithfulness; though under obligation to the king of Babylon, he owed a higher one to God, who directed him to prophesy against Babylon. **1.** Cf. Isaiah 45; 46; 47. But as the time of fulfilment drew nearer, the prophecies are now proportionally more distinct than then. **2. Declare . . . among . . . nations**—who would rejoice at the fall of Babylon their oppressor. **standard**—to indicate the place of meeting to the nations where they were to hear the good news of Babylon's fall [ROSENMULLER]; or, the signal to summon the nations together against Babylon (ch. 51: 12, 27), [MAURER]. **Bel**—the tutelary god of Baby lon; the same idol as the Phœnician Baal, i.e., lord, the sun (Isa. 46:1). **confounded**—because unable to defend the city under their protection. **Merodach**—another Babylonian idol; meaning in Syria "little lord"; from which Merodach-baladan took his name. **3. a nation**—the Medes, north of Babylon (ch. 51:48). The devastation of Babylon here foretold includes not only that by Cyrus, but also that more utter one by Darius, who took Babylon by artifice when it had revolted from Persia, and mercilessly slaughtered the inhabitants, hanging 4000 of the nobles; also the final desertion of Babylon, owing to Seleucia having been built close by under Seleucus Nicanor. **4.** Fulfilled only in part when some few of the ten tribes of "Israel" joined Judah in a "covenant" with God, at the restoration of Judah to its land (Neh. 9:38; 10:29). The full event is yet to come (ch. 31:9; Hos. 1:11; Zech. 12: 10). **weeping**—with joy at their restoration beyond all hope; and with sorrow at the remembrance of their sins and sufferings (Ezra 3:12, 13; Ps. 126:5, 6). **seek . . . Lord**—(Hos. 3:5). **5. thitherward**—rather, "hitherward," Jeremiah's prophetical standpoint being at Zion. "Faces hitherward" implies their steadfastness of purpose not to be turned aside by any difficulties on the way. **perpetual covenant**—in contrast to the old covenant "which they brake" (ch. 31:31, etc.; 32:40). They shall return to their God first, then to their own land. **6.** (Isa. 53:6.) **on the mountains**—whereon they sacrificed to idols (ch. 2:20; 3:6, 23). **resting-place**—for the "sheep," continuing the image; *Jehovah* is the resting-place of His sheep (Matt. 11:28). They rest in His "bosom" (Isa. 40:11). Also *His temple* at Zion, their "rest," because it is His (Ps. 132:8, 14). **7. devoured**—(Ps. 79:7). "Found them" implies that they were exposed to the attacks of those whoever happened to meet them. **adversaries said**—for instance, Nebuzaradan (ch. 40:2, 3; cf. Zech. 11:5). The Gentiles acknowledged some supreme divinity. The Jews' guilt was so palpable that they were condemned even in the judgment of heathens. Some knowledge of God's peculiar relation to Judea reached its heathen invaders from the prophets (ch. 2:3; Dan. 9:16); hence the strong language they use of Jehovah here, not as worshippers of Him themselves, but as believing Him to be the tutelary God *of Judah* ("the hope of *their* fathers," Ps. 22:4; they do not say *our* hope), as each country was thought to have its *local god*, whose power extended no farther. **habitation**—(Ps. 90:1; 91:1). Alluding to the tabernacle, or, as in Ezekiel 34:14, "fold," which carries out the image in vs. 6, "resting-place" of the "sheep." But it can only mean "habitation" (ch. 31:23), which confirms *English Version* here. **hope of their fathers**—This especially condemned the Jews that their apostasy was from that God whose faithfulness their fathers had experienced. At the same time these "adversaries" unconsciously use language which corrects their own notions. The covenant with the Jews' "fathers" is not utterly set aside by their sin, as their adversaries thought; there is still "a habitation" or refuge for them with the God *of their fathers*. **8.** (Ch. 51:6, 45; Isa. 48:20; Zech. 2:6, 7; Rev. 18:4). Immediately avail yourselves of the opportunity of escape. **be as . . . he-goats before . . . flocks**—Let each try to be foremost in returning, animating the weak, as he-goats lead

ADAM CLARKE

CHAPTER 50

1. *The word that the Lord spake against Babylon.* This is also a new head of discourse. The prophecies contained in this and the following chapter were sent to the captives in Babylon in the fourth year of the reign of Zedekiah. They are very important; they predict the total destruction of the Babylonish empire, and the return of the Jews from their captivity. These chapters were probably composed, with several additions, out of the book that was then sent by Jeremiah to the captives by the hand of Seraiah. See chap. li. 59-64.

2. *Declare ye among the nations.* God's determination relative to this empire. *Set up a standard.* Show the people where they are to assemble. *Say, Babylon is taken.* It is a thing so firmly determined that it is as good as already done. *Bel,* the tutelar deity of Babylon, *is confounded,* because it cannot save its own city. *Merodach,* another of their idols, *is broken in pieces;* it was not able to save itself, much less the whole empire.

3. *Out of the north there cometh up a nation.* The Medes, who formed the chief part of the army of Cyrus, lay to the north or northeast of Babylon. *Shall make her land desolate.* This war, and the consequent taking of the city, began those disasters that brought Babylon in process of time to complete desolation; so that now it is not known where it stood, the whole country being a total solitude.

4. *In those days, and in that time.* In the times in which Babylon shall be opposed by the Medes and Persians, both Israel and Judah, seeing the commencement of the fulfilling of the prophecies, shall begin to seek the Lord with much prayer, and broken and contrite hearts. When the decree of Cyrus comes, they shall be ready to set off for their own country, deploring their offenses, yet rejoicing in the mercy of God which has given them this reviving in their bondage.

5. *Let us join ourselves to the Lord in a perpetual covenant.* All our former covenants have been broken; let us now make one that shall last forever. He shall be the Lord our God, and we will no more worship idols. This covenant they have kept to the present day; whatever their present moral and spiritual state may be, they are no idolaters, in the gross sense of the term.

6. *My people hath been lost sheep.* He pities them; for their pastors, kings, and prophets have caused them to err. *They have gone from mountain to hill.* In all high places they have practiced idolatry.

7. *Their adversaries said, We offend not.* God has abandoned them; we are only fulfilling His designs in plaguing them.

8. *Remove out of the midst of Babylon.* The sentence of destruction is gone out against it; prepare for your flight, that you be not overwhelmed in its ruin. *Be as the he goats before the flocks.* Who always run to the head of

MATTHEW HENRY

Verses 9–20

God is here by his prophet proceeding in his controversy with Babylon.

I. The commission and charge given to the instruments that were to be employed in destroying Babylon. The army that is to do it is called *an assembly of great nations* (*v.* 9), the Medes and Persians, and all their allies and auxiliaries. God will *raise them up* to do it, and fit them for this service, and then he will *cause them to come up*, to *put themselves in array against Babylon* (*v.* 14). God shall bid them *shoot at her and spare no arrows* (*v.* 14). When God gives commission he will give success. They are bidden not only to *shoot at her* (*v.* 14), but to *shout against her* (*v.* 15) with a triumphant shout, as those that are already sure of victory.

II. The desolation and destruction that shall be brought upon Babylon is set forth in a great variety of expressions. 1. The wealth of Babylon shall be a rich and easy prey to the conquerors (*v.* 10). 2. The country of Babylon shall be depopulated and lie uninhabited (*v.* 13). 3. Their ancestors shall be ashamed of their cowardice, in fleeing from the first onset (*v.* 12), or, *Your mother*, Babylon itself, the mother-city, *shall be confounded*, when she sees herself deserted. 4. The great admirers of Babylon shall see it rendered despicable: the very tail of the nations, *shall it be, a wilderness, a dry land, a desert*, *v.* 12. 5. The great city, the head of it, shall be quite ruined. It is the vengeance of the Lord, which nothing can contend with either in law or battle. 6. There shall not be left in Babylon so much as *the poor of the land, for vine-dressers and husbandmen* (*v.* 16). Harvest shall come, and there shall be no reapers; seed-time shall come, but there shall be no sower.

III. The cause of this destruction. It comes from God's displeasure; it is *because of the wrath of the Lord* that Babylon *shall be wholly desolate* (*v.* 13), and his wrath is righteous, for (*v.* 14) *she hath sinned against the Lord*, therefore *spare no arrows*. What they did against Jerusalem they did with pleasure (*v.* 11): *You were glad, you rejoiced*. When Titus Vespasian destroyed Jerusalem he wept over it, but these Chaldeans triumphed over it. The spoils of Jerusalem they made use of to feed their own luxury. Those that have thus swallowed riches must vomit them up again. Therefore they have *given their hand* (*v.* 15). They aimed at nothing less than the utter ruin of God's Israel: *Israel is a scattered sheep*, as before (*v.* 6), that is not only barked at and worried by dogs, but even lions have roared and *driven him away*, *v.* 17. One king of Assyria carried the ten tribes away and devoured them; another invaded Judah, and impoverished it, tore the fleece and flesh of this poor sheep; and now at last this Nebuchadnezzar has fallen upon him and *broken his bones*, and therefore the king of Babylon must be punished as the king of Assyria was, *v.* 18.

IV. The mercy promised to the Israel of God. They shall be released out of their bondage, and *brought again to their own habitation* as sheep that were scattered to their own fold, *v.* 19. He will restore their prosperity; they shall not only live, but live comfortably, in their own land again; they shall *feed upon Carmel and Bashan*, the richest and most fruitful parts of the country. They *enquired the way to Zion* (*v.* 5), where God was to be served and worshipped. This was what they chiefly aimed at in their return; but God will bring them to Carmel and Bashan, where they shall abundantly feed themselves. God will pardon their iniquity; this is the root of all the rest (*v.* 20): *In these days the iniquity of Israel shall be sought for, and there shall be none*. Not only the punishments of their iniquity shall be taken off, but the offence which it gave to God shall be forgotten, and he will be reconciled to them. This denotes how fully God forgives sin; he *remembers it no more*. This may include also a thorough reformation of hearts and lives, as well as a full remission of sins. Those whose sins God pardons he reserves for something very great; for *whom he justifies, them he glorifies*.

Verses 21–32

1. The forces are mustered and commissioned to destroy Babylon. The forces of Cyrus are called to go up against Babylon (*v.* 21), to *come against her from the utmost border*. Let all come together, for there will be both work and pay enough for them all, *v.* 26. *The archers* particularly must be *called together against Babylon*, *v.* 29. Thus *the Lord hath opened his armoury* (*v.* 25), *his treasury* (so the word is), *and hath brought forth the weapons of his indignation*. Media and Persia are now God's armoury; thence he fetches the weapons of his wrath, Cyrus and his officers and armies. 2. Instructions are given them what to do, *v.* 21. They must *open her store-houses*

JAMIESON, FAUSSET, BROWN

the flock; such were the companions of Ezra (Ezra 1:5, 6). **9. from thence**—i.e., from the north country. **expert**—lit., prosperous. Besides "might," "expertness" is needed, that an arrow may do execution. The *Margin* has a different *Hebrew* reading; "destroying," lit., bereaving, childless-making (ch. 15:7). LXX and *Syriac* support *English Version*. **in vain**—without killing him at whom it was aimed (II Sam. 1:22). **11.** (Isa. 47:6.) **grown fat**—and so, skip wantonly. **at grass**—fat and frisky. But there is a disagreement of gender in *Hebrew* reading thus. The *Keri* reading is better: "a heifer *threshing*"; the strongest were used for threshing, and as the law did not allow their mouth to be muzzled in threshing (Deut. 25:4), they waxed wanton with eating. **bellow as bulls**—rather, "neigh as *steeds*," lit., "strong ones," a poetical expression for *steeds* (*Note*, ch. 8:16) [MAURER]. **12. Your mother**—Babylon, the metropolis of the empire. **hindermost**—marvellous change, that Babylon, once the queen of the world, should be now the hindermost of nations, and at last, becoming "a desert," cease to be a nation! **13.** (Isa. 13. 20.) **14.** Summons to the Median army to attack Babylon. **against . . . Lord**—By oppressing His people, their cause is His cause. Also by profaning His sacred vessels (Dan. 5:2). **15. Shout**—Inspirit one another to the onset with the battle cry. **given . . . hand**—an idiom for, "submitted to" the conquerors (I Chron. 29:24, *Margin;* Lam. 5:6). **as she hath done, do unto her**—just retribution in kind. She had destroyed many, so must she be destroyed (Ps. 137:8). So as to spiritual Babylon (Rev. 18:6). This is right because "it is the vengeance *of the Lord*"; but this will not justify *private* revenge in kind (Matt. 5:44; Rom. 12:19-21); even the Old Testament law forbade this, though breathing a sterner spirit than the New Testament (Exod. 23:4, 5; Prov. 25:21, 22). **16.** Babylon had the extent rather of a nation than of a city. Therefore grain was grown within the city wall sufficient to last for a long siege (ARISTOTLE, *Pol.* 3.2; PLINY, 18.17). Conquerors usually spare agriculturists, but in this case *all* alike were to be "cut off." **for fear of . . . oppressing sword**—because of the sword of the oppressor. **every one to his people**—from which they had been removed to Babylon from all quarters by the Chaldean conquerors (ch. 51:9; Isa. 13:14). **17. lions**—hostile kings (ch. 4:7; 49:19). **Assyria**—(II Kings 17:6, Shalmaneser; Ezra 4:2, Esar-haddon). **Nebuchadnezzar**—(II Kings 24:10, 14). **18. punish . . . king of Babylon**—Nabonidus, or Labynitus. **as . . . punished . . . Assyrian**—Sennacherib and other kings [GROTIUS] (II Kings 19:37). **19.** (Isa. 65: 10; Ezek. 34:13, 14.) **20.** The specification of "Israel," as well as Judah, shows the reference is to times yet to come. **iniquity . . . none**—not merely idolatry, which ceased among the Jews ever since the Babylonian captivity, but chiefly their rejection of Messiah. As in a cancelled debt, it shall be as if it had never been; God, for Christ's sake, shall treat them as innocent (ch. 31:34). Without cleansing away of sin, remission of punishment would be neither to the honor of God nor to the highest interests of the elect. **whom I reserve**—the elect "remnant" (Isa. 1:9). The "residue" (Zech. 14:2; 13:8, 9). **21. Merathaim**—a symbolical name for Babylon, the doubly rebellious, viz., against God. Cf. vs. 24, "thou hast striven against the Lord"; and vs. 29, "proud against the Lord." The "doubly" refers to: first, the *Assyrian's* oppression of Israel; next, the kindred *Chaldean's* oppression of Judah (cf. vss. 17-20, 33; especially vs. 18). **Pekod**—(Ezek. 23:23); a chief province of Assyria, in which Nineveh, now overthrown, once lay. But, as in Merathraim, the allusion is to the meaning of *Pekod*, viz., "visitation"; the inhabitants whose time of deserved visitation in punishment is come; not, however, without reference to the now Babylonian province, Pekod. The visitation on Babylon was a following up of that on Assyria. **after them**—even *their posterity*, and all that is still left of Babylon, until the very name is extinct [GROTIUS]. Devastate the city, *after* its inhabitants have deserted it. **all . . . I . . . commanded**—by Isaiah (Isa. 13:1, etc.). **23. hammer**—i.e., Babylon, so called because of its ponderous destructive power; just as "Martel," i.e., "a little hammer," was the surname of a king of the Franks (Isa. 14:6). **24. I**—Thou hast to do with God, not merely with men. **taken . . . not aware**—HERODOTUS relates that one half of the city was taken before those in the other half were "aware" of it. Cyrus turned the waters of the Euphrates where it was defended into a different channel, and so entered the city by the dried-up channel at night, by the upper and lower gates (Dan. 5:30, 31). **25. weapons of his indignation**—the Medes and Persians

ADAM CLARKE

the flock, giving the example for others to follow. This may be addressed to the elders and persons of authority among the people.

9. *An assembly of great nations.* The army of Cyrus was composed of Medes, Persians, Armenians, Caducians, etc. Though all these did not come *from the north,* yet they were arranged under the Medes, who did come from the north, in reference to Babylon. *Their arrows.* They are such expert archers that they shall never miss their mark.

10. *Chaldea shall be a spoil.* She has been a spoiler, and she shall be spoiled. They had destroyed Judea, God's heritage; and now God shall cause her to be destroyed.

11. *As the heifer at grass.* You were wanton in the desolations you brought upon Judea.

12. *Your mother.* Speaking to the Chaldeans; Babylon, the metropolis, or mother city, shall be a wilderness, a dry land, a desert, fit for neither man nor beast.

15. *Shout against her round about.* Encompass her with lines and with troops; let none go in with relief, none come out to escape from her ruin.

16. *Cut off the sower.* Destroy the gardens and the fields, that there may be neither fruits nor tillage.

17. *Israel.* All the descendants of Jacob have been harassed and spoiled, first by the Assyrians, and afterwards by the Chaldeans. They acted towards them as a lion to a sheep which he has caught; first he devours all the flesh, next he breaks all the bones to extract the marrow.

18. *As I have punished the king of Assyria.* The Assyrians were overthrown by the Medes and the Chaldeans. The king is here taken for all their kings, generals, etc.: Tiglath-pileser, Shalmaneser, Sennacherib, Esar-haddon, etc. To them succeeded the Chaldean or Babylonish kings. Nebuchadnezzar came against Judea several times, and at last took the city and burnt it, profaned and demolished the Temple, wasted the land, and carried the princes and people into captivity.

19. *I will bring Israel again.* This seems to refer wholly to the ten tribes; for Carmel, Bashan, Mount Ephraim, and Gilead were in their territories.

20. *In those days, and in that time.* This phrase appears to take in the whole of an epoch, from its commencement to its end. See v. 4. *I will pardon them.* So as to deliver them from their captivity, and exact no more punishment from them whom I reserve, namely, the remnant left in the Babylonish captivity.

21. *Go up against the land of Merathaim . . . and against the inhabitants of Pekod.* No such places as these are to be found anywhere else, and it is not likely that places are at all meant. The ancient versions agree in rendering the first as an appellative, and the last as a verb, except the Chaldee, which has *Pekod* as a proper name. Dr. Dahler renders thus: "March against the country doubly rebellious, and against its inhabitants worthy of punishment." The words are addressed to the Medes and Persians; and the country is Chaldea, doubly rebellious by its idolatry and its insufferable pride. In these two it was exceeded by no other land.

23. *The hammer of the whole earth.* Nebuchadnezzar dashed to pieces the nations against whom he warred. He was the scourge of the Lord.

24. *I have laid a snare for thee.* It was not by storm that Cyrus took the city. The Euphrates ran through it; he dug a channel for the river in another direction, to divert its stream. He waited for that time in which the inhabitants had delivered themselves up to dabauchery; in the dead of the night he turned off the stream, and he and his army entered by the old channel, now void of its waters. This was the snare of which the prophet here speaks. See Herodotus, lib. i., c. 191.

MATTHEW HENRY

(*v.* 26), rifle her treasures, *cast her up as heaps.* Their princes and great men shall fall by the sword, not as men of war in the field of battle, but as beasts (*v.* 27). 3. Assurances are given them of success. Let them do what God commands, and they shall accomplish what he threatens. Cyrus shall no doubt prevail, for he fights under God. 4. Reasons are given for these severe dealings with Babylon. (1) Babylon has been very troublesome, vexatious, and injurious, to all its neighbours; it has been *the hammer of the whole earth* (*v.* 23). He that is the God of nations will sooner or later assert the injured rights of nations against those that unjustly and violently invade them. (2) Babylon has bidden defiance to God himself: *Thou hast striven against the Lord* (*v.* 24), *hast joined issue with him* (so the word signifies) as in law or battle, hast openly opposed him, therefore *thou art* now *found, and caught,* as in a snare. (3) Babylon ruined Jerusalem, the holy city, and the holy house there, *v.* 28. The burning of the temple, and the carrying away of its vessels, were articles in the charge against Babylon on which greater stress was laid than upon its being *the hammer of the whole earth*; for Zion was *the joy* and glory *of the whole earth.* (4) Babylon has been haughty and insolent, and therefore must have a fall, Job. xl. 12. They shall fall not so much by others thrusting them down as by their own stumbling; for they hold their heads so high that they never look under their feet.

Verses 33–46

I. Israel's sufferings, and their deliverance out of those sufferings. *Israel and Judah were oppressed together, v.* 33. Those that remained of the captives of the ten tribes, upon the uniting of the kingdoms of Assyria and Chaldea, seem to have come and mingled with those of the two tribes, so that they were *oppressed together.* This is their comfort in distress, that, though they are weak, *their Redeemer is strong* (*v.* 34), *their Avenger* (so the word signifies). *The Lord of hosts is his name,* and he will answer to his name, and will be that to them for which they depend upon him. *He shall thoroughly plead their cause that he may give rest to the land,* to his people's land, rest from all their enemies round about. This is applicable to all believers, who complain of the dominion of sin and corruption, and of their own weakness. Let them know that *their Redeemer is strong*; he is able to keep what they commit to him. Sin shall not have dominion over them; he will *make them free,* and they shall be *free indeed*; he will give them *rest,* that *rest which remains for the people of God.*

II. Babylon's sin, and their punishment for that sin.

1. The sins they are charged with are idolatry and persecution. (1) They oppressed the people of God; they *held them fast,* and would not let *them go.* They *opened not the house of his prisoners,* Isa. xiv. 17. (2) They wronged God himself, and robbed him, giving that glory to others which is due to him alone; for (*v.* 38) *it is the land of graven images.* The word here used for idols properly signifies *terrors—Enim,* the name given to giants that were formidable, because they made the images of their gods to look frightful, to strike terror upon fools and children. Babylon was *the mother of harlots* (Rev. xvii. 5), the source of idolatry.

2. The judgments of God upon them for these sins are such as will ruin them.

(1) All that should be their defence and support shall be cut off by the sword. The Chaldeans had long been God's sword, wherewith he had done execution upon the sinful nations round about: but now, they being as bad as any of them, or worse, *a sword* is brought upon them (*v.* 35), a sword of war; and in God's hand a sword of justice. It shall be *Upon their princes* and *their wise men.* Their philosophers, their statesmen, and privy-counsellors; their learning and policy shall neither secure them nor stand the public in any stead. Their soothsayers and astrologers, here called *the liars* (*v.* 36), for they cheated with their prognostications of peace and prosperity, shall talk like fools, and be as men that have lost all their wits. *Their mighty men shall be dismayed,* and shall be no longer *mighty men. The sword shall be upon their horses and chariots;* the invaders shall seize their horses and chariots. The troops of other nations that were in their service shall be disheartened: *The mingled people shall become as* weak and timorous as *women.* The *sword* shall be *upon her treasures,* which are the sinews of war, *and they shall be robbed,* and made use of by the enemy against them.

(2) The country shall be made desolate (*v.* 38): *The waters shall be dried up,* the water that secures the city. Cyrus drew the river Euphrates into so many channels as made it passable for his army, so that

JAMIESON, FAUSSET, BROWN

(Isa. 13:5). **26. from the utmost border**—viz., of the earth. Or, from all sides LUDOVICUS DE DIEU]. **storehouses**—or, "her houses filled with men and goods" [MICHAELIS]. When Cyrus took it, the provisions found there were enough to have lasted for many years. **as heaps**—make of the once glorious city *heaps* of ruins. Vast mounds of rubbish now mark the site of ancient Babylon. "Tread her as heaps of corn which are wont to be trodden down in the threshing-floor" [GROTIUS]. **27. bullocks**—i.e., princes and strong warriors (ch. 46:21; Ps. 22: 12; Isa. 34:7). **go down to . . . slaughter**—The slaughterhouses lay low beside the river; therefore it is said, "go down"; appropriate to Babylon on the Euphrates, the avenue through which the slaughterers entered the city. **28. declare in Zion . . . temple**—Some Jews "fleeing" from Babylon at its fall shall tell in Judea how God avenged the cause of Zion and her temple that had been profaned (ch. 52:13; Dan. 1:2; 5:2). **29. archers**—lit., very many and powerful; hence the *Hebrew* word is used of *archers* (Job 16:13) from the multitude and force of their arrows. **according to all that she hath done**—(*Note,* vs. 15). **proud against the Lord**—not merely cruel towards men (Isa. 47:10). **30.** (*Note,* ch. 49:26.) **in the streets**—The Babylonians were so discouraged by having lost some battles that they retired within their walls and would not again meet Cyrus in the field. **31. most proud**—lit., "pride"; i.e., man of pride; the king of Babylon. **visit**—punish (vs. 27).

33. Israel and . . . Judah were oppressed—He anticipates an objection, in order to answer it: Ye have been, no doubt, "oppressed," therefore ye despair of deliverance; but, remember your "Redeemer is strong," and therefore can and will deliver you. **34. strong**—as opposed to the power of Israel's oppressor (Rev. 18:8). **plead . . . cause**—as their advocate. Image from a court of justice; appropriate as God delivers His people not by mere might, but by *righteousness.* His plea against Satan and all their enemies is His own everlasting love, reconciling mercy and justice in the Redeemer's work and person (Mic. 7:9; Zech. 3:1-5; I John 2:1). **give rest . . . disquiet**—There is a play on the similarity of sounds in the two *Hebrew* verbs to express more vividly the contrast: "that He may give quiet to the land of Judah (heretofore disquieted by Babylon); but disquiet to the inhabitants of Babylon (heretofore quietly secure)" (Isa. 14:6-8). **35-37.** The repetition of "A sword" in the beginning of each verse, by the figure *anaphora,* heightens the effect; the reiterated judgment is universal; the same sad stroke of the sword is upon each and all connected with guilty Babylon. **wise men**—(Isa. 47:13). Babylon boasted that it was the peculiar seat of wisdom and wise men, especially in astronomy and astrology. **36. liars**—Those whom he before termed "wise men," he here calls "liars" (impostors), viz., the astrologers (cf. Isa. 44:25; Rom. 1:21-25; I Cor. 1: 20). **37. as women**—divested of all manliness (Nah. 3:13). **38. drought**—Altering the pointing, this verse will begin as the three previous verses, "A sword." However, all the pointed MSS. read, "A drought," as *English Version.* Cyrus turned off the waters of the Euphrates into a new channel and so marched through the dried-up bed into the city (ch. 51:32). Babylonia once was famed for its corn, which often yielded from one to two hundredfold [HERODOTUS]. This was due to its network of watercourses from the Euphrates for irrigation, traces of which [LAYARD] are seen still on all sides, but dry and barren (Isa. 44:27). **their idols**—lit., "terrors." They are mad after idols that are more calculated to *frighten* than to attract (ch. 51:44, 47, 52; Dan. 3:1). Mere bugbears with which to frighten children. **39. wild beasts of the desert**—wild cats, remarkable for their howl [BOCHART]. **wild beasts of the islands**—jackals (*Note,* Isa. 13:21). **owls**—rather female ostriches; they delight in solitary places. Lit., "daughters of crying." Cf. as to spiritual Babylon, Revelation 18:2. **no more inhabited for ever**—The accumulation of phrases is to express the final and utter extinction of Babylon; fulfilled not immediately, but by degrees; Cyrus took away its supremacy. Darius Hystaspes deprived it, when it had rebelled, of its fortifications. Seleucus Nicanor removed its citizens and wealth to Seleucia, which he founded in the neighborhood; and the Parthians removed all that was left to Ctesiphon. Nothing but its walls was left under the Roman emperor Adrian. **40.** (Isa. 13:19.) Repeated from ch. 49:18. **41-43.** (Cf. ch. 6:22-24.)

ADAM CLARKE

26. *Open her storehouses.* At the time that Cyrus took the city, it was full of provisions and treasures of all kinds; the walls had suffered no injury; and when the inhabitants heard that the enemy was within, they thought they must have arisen out of the earth in the center of the city!

27. *Slay all her bullocks.* Princes, magistrates.

28. *Declare in Zion the vengeance of the Lord.* Zion was desolated by Babylon; tell Zion that God hath desolated the desolator. *The vengeance of his temple.* Which Nebuchadnezzar had pillaged, profaned, and demolished, transporting its sacred vessels to Babylon, and putting them in the temple of his god Bel.

29. *Call together the archers.* The preceding verses are the prediction; here God calls the Medes and Persians to fulfil it.

31. *O thou most proud.* "Pride" in the abstract; proudest of all people.

32. *And the most proud.* Here "pride" is personified and addressed, as if possessing a being and rational powers.

34. *Their Redeemer is strong.* And it was not that He wanted power, and that Nebuchadnezzar had much, that Jerusalem was taken; but because the people had sinned, and would not return; and therefore national sins called for national punishments. These have taken place, and now the Lord of Hosts shows them that the power of the Chaldeans is mere weakness against His might.

35. *A sword.* War and its calamities, or any grievous plague; and so in the following verses.

38. *A drought is upon her waters.* May not this refer to the draining of the channel of the Euphrates, by which the army of Cyrus entered the city. See on v. 24. The original is, however, *chereb,* "a sword," as in the preceding verses, which signifies war, or any calamity by which the thing on which it falls is ruined.

MATTHEW HENRY

they got with ease to the walls of Babylon, which, it was thought, that river had rendered inaccessible. The water likewise that made the country fruitful shall *be dried up*, *v.* 39. This was foretold concerning Babylon, Isa. xiii. 19–22.

(3) The king and kingdom shall be put into the utmost confusion and consternation by the enemies' invading them, *v.* 41–43. Those who have dealt cruelly, and have shown no mercy, may expect to be cruelly dealt with, and to find no mercy.

(4) They shall be as much hurt as frightened, for the invader shall *come up like a lion* to tear and destroy (*v.* 44) and shall make them and their *habitation desolate* (*v.* 45), and the desolation shall be so astonishing that all the nations about shall be terrified by it, *v.* 46. These three verses we had before (*ch.* xlix. 19–21) in the prophecy of the destruction of Edom, which was accomplished by the Chaldeans, and they are here repeated in the prophecy of the destruction of Babylon, which was to be accomplished upon the Chaldeans.

JAMIESON, FAUSSET, BROWN

The very language used to describe the calamities which Babylon inflicted on Zion is that here employed to describe Babylon's own calamity inflicted by the Medes. Retribution in kind. **kinds**—the allies and satraps of the various provinces of the Medo-Persian empire: Armenia, Hyrcania, Lydia, etc. **coasts**—the remote parts. **42. cruel**—the character of the Persians, and even of Cyrus, notwithstanding his wish to be thought magnanimous (Isa. 13:18). **like a man**—So orderly and united is their "array," that the whole army moves to battle as *one man* [GROTIUS]. **43. hands waxed feeble**—attempted no resistance; immediately was overcome, as HERODOTUS tells us. **44-46.** Repeated mainly from ch. 49:19-21. The identity of God's principle in His dealing with Edom, and in that with Babylon, is implied by the similarity of language as to both. **46. cry . . . among the nations**—In Edom's case it is, "at the cry the noise thereof was heard *in the Red Sea*." The change implies the wider extent to which the crash of Babylon's downfall shall be heard.

ADAM CLARKE

40. *As God overthrew Sodom.* As the very ground on which these cities stood, with all the plain, now lies under the Dead Sea, so Babylon and the adjacent country shall be rendered totally barren and unfruitful, and utterly incapable of being inhabited. And this is the fact concerning both countries.

41. *Behold, a people shall come from the north.* This and the two following verses are nearly the same with chap. vi. 22-24. But here, destroyers against Babylon are intended; there, destroyers against Jerusalem.

44. *Behold, he shall come up like a lion.* The same words as in chap. xlix. 19, etc.

46. *At the noise of the taking of Babylon.* See the parallel place, chap. xlix. 21. In the forty-ninth chapter, these words are spoken of Nebuchadnezzar; here, of Cyrus. The taking of Babylon was a wonder to all the surrounding nations. It was thought to be impregnable.

MATTHEW HENRY

CHAPTER 51

V. A description of the instruments that are to be employed in this service. God has *raised up the spirit of the kings of the Medes* (*v.* 11), Darius and Cyrus, who come against Babylon by a divine instinct; for *God's device is against Babylon to destroy it*. Those whom God employs against Babylon are compared (*v.* 1) to a *destroying wind*, which either by its coldness blasts the fruits of the earth or by its fierceness blows down all before it. This wind is *brought out of God's treasuries* (*v.* 16), *raised up against those that dwell in the midst of the Chaldeans*, those of other nations that are incorporated with them. These enemies are compared to fanners (*v.* 2), who shall *drive them away as chaff* is driven away by the fan. The Chaldeans had been fanners to winnow God's people (*ch.* xv. 7).

VI. An ample commission given them to lay all waste. Let them *bend their bow* against the archers of the Chaldeans (*v.* 3).

IX. Here is a call to God's people to go out of Babylon. It is their wisdom, when the ruin is approaching, to quit the city (*v.* 6): "*Flee out of the midst of Babylon*, that you may not be cut off in her iniquity."

I. An acknowledgment of the great pomp and power that Babylon had been in and the use that God in his providence had made of it (*v.* 7): *Babylon hath been a golden cup*, a rich and glorious empire, *a golden city* (Isa. xiv. 4), *a head of gold* (Dan. ii. 38), *a golden cup in the Lord's hand;* he had made the earth *drunk with this cup*; some were intoxicated with her pleasures, others intoxicated with her terrors and destroyed by her. In both senses the New Testament Babylon is said to have made the kings of the earth drunk, Rev. xvii. 2; xviii. 3.

VIII. It is a certain destruction; a divine power is engaged against it, which cannot be resisted (*v.* 8), though when Jeremiah prophesied this, and many a year after, it was in the height of its power and greatness. It is a righteous destruction. Babylon has made herself meet for it, and therefore cannot fail to meet with it.

II. A charge drawn up against her by the Israel of God. 1. She is complained of for her incorrigible wickedness (*v.* 9). The people of God that were captives among the Babylonians endeavoured (Jer. x. 11), to convince them of the folly of their idolatry, but they could not do it. Yet some understand this as spoken by the forces they had hired for their assistance, declaring that they had done their best to save her from ruin, but that it was all to no purpose, and therefore they might as well go home to their respective countries; "for *her judgment reaches unto heaven*, and it is in vain to withstand it or think to avert it."

JAMIESON, FAUSSET, BROWN

CHAPTER 51

Vss. 1-65. CONTINUATION OF THE PROPHECY AGAINST BABYLON BEGUN IN CHAPTER 50. **1. in the midst of them that rise . . . against me**—lit., in the heart of them . . . . Cf. Psalm 46:2, "the midst of the sea," *Margin*, "the *heart* of the seas"; Ezekiel 27:4, *Margin;* Matthew 12:40. In the center of the Chaldeans. "Against Me," because they persecute My people. The cabalistic mode of interpreting *Hebrew* words (by taking the letters in the inverse order of the alphabet, the last letter representing the first, and so on, ch. 25:26) would give the very word *Chaldeans* here; but the *mystical* method cannot be intended, as "Babylon" is plainly so called in the immediately preceding parallel clause. **wind**—God needs not warlike weapons to "destroy" His foes; a *wind* or blast is sufficient; though, no doubt, the "wind" here is the invading host of Medes and Persians (ch. 4:11; II Kings 19:7). **2. fanners**—(*Note*, ch. 15:7). The fanners separate the wheat from the chaff; so God's judgments shall sweep away guilty Babylon as chaff (Ps. 1:4). **3. Against him that bendeth**—viz., the bow; i.e., the Babylonian archer. **let the archer bend**—i.e., the Persian archer (ch. 50:4). The *Chaldean version* and JEROME, by changing the vowel points, read, "Let not him (the Babylonian) who bendeth his bow bend it." But the close of the verse is addressed to the Median invaders; therefore it is more likely that the first part of the verse is addressed to them, as in *English Version*, not to the *Babylonians*, to warn them against resistance as vain, as in the *Chaldean version*. The word "bend" is thrice repeated: "Against him that bendeth let him that bendeth bend," to imply the utmost straining of the bow. **4.** (*Notes*, ch. 49:26; 50:30, 37). **5. forsaken**—as a widow (*Hebrew*). Israel is not severed from her husband, Jehovah (Isa. 54:5-7), by a perpetual divorce. **though . . . sin**—though the land *of Israel* has been filled with sin, i.e., with *the punishment of their sin*, devastation. But, as the *Hebrew* means "for," or "and therefore," not "though," translate, "and therefore their (the Chaldeans') land has been filled with (the penal consequences of) their sin" [GROTIUS]. **6.** Warning to the Israelite captives to flee from Babylon, lest they should be involved in the punishment of her "iniquity." So as to spiritual Babylon and her captives (Rev. 18:4). **7.** Babylon is compared to a *cup*, because she was the vessel in the hand of God, to make drunken with His vengeance the other peoples (ch. 13:12; 25:15, 16). Cf. as to spiritual Babylon, Revelation 14:8; 17:4. The cup is termed "golden," to express the splendor and opulence of Babylon; whence also in the image seen by Nebuchadnezzar (Dan. 2:38) the *head* representing Babylon is of *gold* (cf. Isa. 14:4). **8, 9.** Her friends and confederates, who behold her fall, are invited to her aid. They reply, her case is incurable, and that they must leave her to her fate. **8.** (Isa. 21:9; Rev. 14:8; 18:2, 9.) **balm**—(Ch. 8:22; 46:11.) **9. We would have healed**—We attempted to heal. **her judgment**—*her crimes* provoking God's "judgments" [GROTIUS]. **reacheth unto heaven**—(Gen. 18:21; Jonah 1:2; Rev. 18:5). Even the heathen nations perceive that her awful fall must be God's judgment for her crying sins (Ps. 9:16; 64:9). **10.** Next after the speech of the confederates of Babylon, comes that of the Jews celebrating with thanksgivings the promise-keeping faithfulness of their covenant God. **brought forth . . .**—(Ps. 37:6). **our righteousness**—not the Jews' merits, but God's faithfulness to Himself and to His covenant, which constituted the

ADAM CLARKE

CHAPTER 51

1. *Thus saith the Lord.* This chapter is a continuation of the preceding prophecy.

A destroying wind. Such as the pestilential winds in the East; and here the emblem of a destroying army, carrying all before them, and wasting with fire and sword.

2. *And will send . . . fanners.* When the corn is trodden out with the feet of cattle, or crushed out with a heavy wheel armed with iron, with a shovel they throw it up against the wind, that the chaff and broken straw may be separated from it. This is the image used by the Prophet; these people shall be trodden, crushed, and fanned by their enemies.

5. *For Israel hath not been forsaken.* God still continued His prophets among them; He had never cast them wholly off. Even in the midst of wrath—highly deserved and inflicted punishment—He has remembered mercy; and is now about to crown what He has done by restoring them to their own land. I conceive *asham*, which we translate *sin*, as rather signifying "punishment," which meaning it often has.

7. *Made all the earth drunken.* The cup of God's wrath is the plenitude of punishment that He inflicts on transgressors. It is represented as intoxicating and making them mad.

8. *Babylon is suddenly fallen and destroyed.* These appear to be the words of some of the spectators of Babylon's misery.

9. *We would have healed Babylon.* Had it been in our power, we would have saved her, but we could not turn away the judgment of God.

10. *The Lord hath brought forth our righteousness.* This is the answer of the Jews. God has vindicated our cause.

MATTHEW HENRY

Zion's children shall triumph (*v.* 10): *The Lord has brought forth our righteousness;* he has appeared in our behalf against those that dealt unjustly with us, and has given us redress. Let it therefore be spoken of to his praise: *Come and let us declare in Zion the work of the Lord our God,* that others may be invited to join with us in praising him.

VII. The weakness of the Chaldeans, and their inability to make head against this threatening force. They are called upon here to prepare for action, but it is ironical (*v.* 11): *Make bright the arrows,* which have grown rusty through disuse; *gather the shields,* which in a long time of peace and security have been scattered and thrown out of the way (*v.* 12); *set up the standard upon the walls of Babylon.*

Babylon seems to be well-fenced and fortified against it: *She dwells upon many waters* (*v.* 13); the march of an enemy into it is so embarrassed by rivers. *Babylon* is *abundant in treasures;* and yet "*thy end has come,* and neither thy waters nor thy wealth shall secure thee.

IV. A declaration of the sovereignty of God who espouses Zion's cause and undertakes to reckon with this proud and potent enemy, *v.* 14. He will fill Babylon with vast numbers of the enemy's forces, will *fill it with men as with caterpillars,* that shall overpower it. But who is he that can break so powerful a kingdom as Babylon? The prophet gives an account of him from the description he had formerly given (Jer. x. 12–16), and it is here repeated to show that God will convince those by his judgments who would not be convinced by his word that he is *God over all.* 1. He is the God that made the world (*v.* 15). 2. He has the command of all the creatures that he has made (*v.* 16); his providence is a continued creation. 3. The idols that oppose the accomplishment of his word are a mere sham and their worshippers brutish people, *v.* 17, 18. But between the God of Israel and these gods of the heathen there is no comparison (*v.* 19): *The portion of Jacob is not like them;* the God who speaks this and will do it is the *former of all things* and *the Lord of all hosts,* and there is a near relation between him and his people, for he is *their portion* and they are his.

Babylon had also been God's *battle-axe;* it was so at this time, when Jeremiah prophesied, *v.* 20. The forces of Babylon were God's *weapons of war,* tools in his hand, with which he broke in pieces *nations* and *kingdoms,—horses* and *chariots,* which are so much the strength of kingdoms (*v.* 21),—*man and woman, young and old,* with which kingdoms are replenished (*v.* 22),—*the shepherd and his flock, the husbandman and his oxen,* with which kingdoms are maintained and supplied, *v.* 23. Such havoc as this the Chaldeans had made when God employed them as instruments of his wrath for the chastising of the nations; and yet now Babylon itself must fall.

The Lord God of recompences, the *God to whom vengeance belongs, will surely requite* (*v.* 56), will pay them home; he will *render unto Babylon all the evil they have done in Zion* (*v.* 24). Cyrus shall measure to the Chaldeans the same that they measured to the Jews.

For (*v.* 25) *Babylon* has been a *destroying mountain, destroying all the earth,* as the stones that are tumbled from high mountains spoil the grounds about them; but now it shall itself be *rolled down from its rocks. Babylon* shall *become heaps* (*v.* 37), no use shall be made even of the ruins (*v.* 26): *They shall not take of thee a stone for a corner, nor a stone for foundations.*

Let all necessary preparations be made. This they are called to, *v.* 27, 28. Let *a standard be set up,* under which to enlist soldiers, *let a trumpet be blown* to call men together to it, let the nations, out of which Cyrus's army is to be raised, prepare their recruits. Let the kingdoms of *Ararat,* and *Minni, and Ashkenaz,* of Armenia, both the higher and the lower, and of Ascania, about Phrygia and Bithynia, send in their quota of men for his service; let them lay the country waste, as *caterpillars* do (Joel i. 4).

JAMIESON, FAUSSET, BROWN

"righteousness" of His people, i.e., their *justification* in their controversy with Babylon, the cruel enemy of God and His people. Cf. ch. 23:6, "The Lord *our righteousness*"; Mic. 7:9. *Their* righteousness is *His* righteousness. **declare in Zion**—(Ps. 102:13-21). **11. Make bright**—lit., "pure." Polish and sharpen. **gather**—lit., "fill"; i.e., gather in full number, so that none be wanting. So, "gave in *full* tale" (I Sam. 18:27). GESENIUS, not so well, translates, "Fill *with your bodies* the shields" (cf. Song of Sol. 4:4). He means to tell the Babylonians, Make what preparations you will, all will be in vain (cf. ch. 46:3-6). **kings of . . . Medes**—He names the Medes rather than the Persians, because Darius, or Cyaxares, was above Cyrus in power and the greatness of his kingdom. **temple**—(ch. 50:28). **12.** With all your efforts, your city shall be taken. **standard**—to summon the defenders together to any point threatened by the besiegers. **13. waters**—(V. 32, 36; *Note,* Isa. 21:1.) The Euphrates surrounded the city and, being divided into many channels, formed islands. Cf. as to spiritual Babylon "waters," i.e., "many peoples," Revelation 17:1, 15. A large lake also was near Babylon. **measure**—lit., "cubit," which was the most common measure, and therefore is used for a *measure* in general. The time for putting a *limit* to thy covetousness [GESENIUS]. There is no "*and*" in the Hebrew: translate, "thine end, the *retribution* for thy covetousness" [GROTIUS]. MAURER takes the image to be from weaving: "the cubit where thou art to be cut off"; for the web is cut off, when the required number of cubits is completed (Isa. 38:12). **14. by himself**—lit., "by His soul" (II Sam. 15:21; Heb. 6:13). **fill . . . with caterpillars**—locusts (Nah. 3:15). Numerous as are the citizens of Babylon, the invaders shall be more numerous. **15-19.** Repeated from ch. 10: 12-16; except that "Israel" is not in the *Hebrew* of vs. 19, which ought, therefore, to be translated, "He is the Former of all things, and (therefore) of the rod of His inheritance" (i.e., of the nation peculiarly His own). In ch. 10 the contrast is between the *idols* and God; here it is between the power of populous *Babylon* and that of God: *"Thou* dwellest upon many waters" (vs. 13); but God can, by merely "uttering His voice," create "many waters" (vs. 16). The "earth" (in its *material* aspect) is the result of His "power"; the "world" (viewed in its *orderly system*) is the result of His "wisdom . . ." (vs. 15). Such an Almighty Being can be at no loss for resources to effect His purpose against Babylon. **20.** (*Note,* ch. 50:23.) "Break in pieces" refers to the "hammer" there (cf. Nah. 2:1, *Margin*). The *club* also was often used by ancient warriors. **22. old and young**—(II Chron. 36:17). **24.** The detail of particulars (vss. 20-23) is in order to express the indiscriminate slaughters perpetrated by Babylon on Zion, which, in just retribution, are all to befall her in turn (ch. 50:15, 29). **in your sight**—addressed to the Jews. **25. destroying mountain**—called so, not from its position, for it lay low (vs. 13; Gen. 11:2, 9), but from its eminence above other nations, many of which it had "destroyed"; also, because of its lofty palaces, towers, hanging gardens resting on arches, and walls, fifty royal cubits broad and two hundred high. **roll thee down from the rocks**—i.e., from thy rocklike fortifications and walls. **burnt mountain**—(Rev. 8:8.) A volcano, which, after having spent itself in pouring its "destroying" lava on all the country around, falls into the vacuum and becomes extinct, the surrounding "rocks" alone marking where the crater had been. Such was the appearance of Babylon after its destruction, and as the pumice stones of the volcano are left in their place, being unfit for building, so Babylon should never rise from its ruins. **26. corner . . . stone . . . foundations**—The *corner-stone* was the most important one in the building, the *foundation-stones* came next in importance (Eph. 2:20). So the sense is, even as there shall be no stones useful for building left of thee, so no leading *prince,* or *governors,* shall come forth from thy inhabitants. **27.** (Ch. 50:29.) As in vs. 12 the Babylonians were told to "set up the standard," so here her foes are told to do so: the latter, to good purpose; the former, in vain. **Ararat**—Upper or Major Armenia, the regions about Mount Ararat. **Minni**—Lower or Lesser Armenia. RAWLINSON says that Van was the capital of Minni. It was conquered by Tettarrassa, the general of Tetembar II, the Assyrian king whose wars are recorded on the black obelisk now in the British Museum. **Aschenaz**—a descendant of Japhet (Gen. 10: 3), who gave his name to the sea now called the Black Sea; the region bordering on it is probably here meant, viz., Asia Minor, including places named Ascania in Phrygia and Bithynia. Cyrus had subdued Asia Minor and the neighboring re-

ADAM CLARKE

11. *Make bright the arrows.* This is the prophet's address to Babylon.

12. *Set up the standard.* A call to the enemies of Babylon to invest the city and press the siege.

13. *O thou that dwellest upon many waters.* You who have an abundant supply of waters. It was built on the confluence of the Tigris and Euphrates, the latter running through the city. But the *many waters* may mean the many nations which belonged to the Babylonish empire; nations and people are frequently so called in Scripture,

14. *I will fill thee with men.* By means of these very waters through the channel of your boasted river, you shall be filled with men, suddenly appearing as an army of "locusts"; and, without being expected, shall lift up a terrific cry, as soon as they have risen from the channel of the river.

15. *He hath made the earth by his power.* The omnipotence of God is particularly manifested in the works of creation. *He hath established the world by his wisdom.* The omniscience of God is particularly seen in the government of *tebel,* the inhabited surface of the globe. What a profusion of wisdom and skill is apparent in that wondrous system of providence by which He governs and provides for every living thing!

16. *When he uttereth his voice.* Sends thunder.

17. *Every man is brutish by his knowledge.* He is brutish for want of real knowledge, and he is brutish when he acknowledges that an idol is anything in the world. These verses, from fifteen to nineteen, are transcribed from chap. x. 12-16.

20. *Thou art my battle ax.* I believe Nebuchadnezzar is meant, who is called, chap. l. 23, "the hammer of the whole earth." Others think the words are spoken of Cyrus. All the verbs are in the past tense: "With thee have I broken in pieces," etc., etc.

25. *O destroying mountain.* An epithet which He applies to the Babylonish government; it is like a burning mountain, which, by vomiting continual streams of burning lava, inundates and destroys all towns, villages, fields in its vicinity. *And roll thee down from the rocks.* I will tumble you from the rocky base on which you rest. The combustible matter in your bowels being exhausted, you shall appear as an extinguished crater; and the stony matter which you cast out shall not be of sufficient substance to make a foundation stone for solidity, or a cornerstone for beauty, v. 26. Under this beautiful and most expressive metaphor, the prophet shows the nature of the Babylonish government; setting the nations on fire, deluging and destroying them by its troops, till at last, exhausted, it tumbles down, is extinguished, and leaves nothing as a basis to erect a new form of government on; but is altogether useless, like the cooled lava, which is, properly speaking, fit for no human purpose.

27. *Set ye up a standard.* Another summons to the Medes and Persians to attack Babylon. *Ararat, Minni.* The Greater and Lesser Armenia. *And Ashchenaz.* A part of Phrygia, near the Hellespont.

MATTHEW HENRY

But they shall have no heart to come at the call, *v.* 29. *The mighty men of Babylon have forborne to fight, v.* 30. God having taken away their strength and spirit, they have *remained in their holds*, so that the enemy has, without any resistance, *burnt her dwelling-places* and *broken her bars.*

A rumour will come one year that Cyrus is making vast preparations for war, *and after that, in another year, shall come a rumour* that his design is upon Babylon"; when he was a great way off they might have sent and desired conditions of peace; but they were too proud, and their hearts were hardened to their destruction. The king of Babylon was himself at such a distance from the place where the attack was made that it was a great while ere he had notice that the city was taken; so that those posted near the place sent one messenger after another, *v.* 31. They are to tell him that the enemy has *seized the passes* (*v.* 32), the forts or blockades upon the river, and that, having got over the river, he has set fire to the reeds on the river side, to alarm and terrify the city, so that all the men surrendered. The messengers come with these tidings, which are immediately confirmed by the enemies' being in the palace and slaying the king himself, Dan. v. 30.

Again (*v.* 33), "*Babylon is like a threshing-floor*, in which the people of God have been long threshed; but now the time has come that she shall herself be threshed.

2. She is complained of for her inveterate malice against Israel. Other nations had been hardly used by the Chaldeans, but Israel only complains to God of it, and with confidence appeals to him (*v.* 34, 35). *Zion and Jerusalem shall say,* "Let *the violence done to me and* my children, that are *my* own *flesh*, and pieces of myself, and all the blood of my people, which they have shed like water, *be upon* them; let the guilt of it lie upon them, and let it be required at their hands."

III. Judgment given upon this appeal by the righteous Judge of heaven and earth, on behalf of Israel against Babylon. He answers (*v.* 36): "*I will plead thy cause.* Leave it with me; I will in due time plead it effectually *and take vengeance for thee*, and every drop of Jerusalem's blood shall be accounted for with interest." God deals better with Israel than they deserve, and, notwithstanding their iniquities and his severities, *Israel is not forsaken.* God is his God still, and will act for him as the Lord of hosts, a God of power.

That profane feast which they were celebrating at the very time when the city was taken seems here to be referred to (*v.* 38, 39): *They shall roar together like lions*, as men in their revels do, when the wine has got into their heads. They have passed their cup round; now *the cup of the Lord's right hand shall be turned unto them* (Hab. ii. 15, 16); let them be as merry as they can with that bitter cup, for *on that night*, in the midst of the jollity, was *Belshazzar slain.*

JAMIESON, FAUSSET, BROWN

gions, and from these he drew levies in proceeding against Babylon. **rough caterpillars**–The horsemen in multitude, and in appearance bristling with javelins and with crests, resemble "rough caterpillars," or locusts of the hairy-crested kind (Nah. 3: 15). **28. kings of . . . Medes**–(vs. 11). The satraps and tributary kings under Darius, or Cyaxares. **his dominion**–the king of Media's dominion. **29. land shall tremble . . . every purpose of . . . Lord shall be performed**–elegant antithesis between the *trembling* of the *land* or earth, and the stability of "every purpose of the Lord" (cf. Ps. 46:1-3). **30. forborne to fight**–for the city was not taken by force of arms, but by stratagem, according to the counsel given to Cyrus by two eunuchs of Belshazzar who deserted. **remained in . . . holds**–not daring to go forth to fight; many, with Nabonidus, withdrew to the fortified city Borsippa. **31.** (*Note*, ch. 50:24.) **One post**–*One courier* after another shall announce the capture of the city. The couriers despatched from the walls, where Cyrus enters, shall *"meet"* those sent by the king. Their confused running to and fro would result from the sudden panic at the entrance of Cyrus into the city, which he had so long besieged ineffectually; the Babylonians had laughed at his attempts and were feasting at the time without fear. **taken at one end**–which was not known for a long time to the king and his courtiers feasting in the middle of the city; so great was its extent that, when the city was already three days in the enemy's hands, the fact was not known in some parts of the city [ARISTOTLE, *Pol.* 3.2]. **32. passages are stopped**–The guarded fords of the Euphrates are occupied by the enemy (*Note*, ch. 50:38). **reeds . . . burned**–lit., "the marsh." After draining off the river, Cyrus "burned" the stockade of dense tree-like *"reeds"* on its banks, forming the outworks of the city's fortifications. The burning of these would give the appearance of the *marsh* or river itself being on "fire." **33. like a threshing-floor, it is time to thresh her**–rather, "like a threshing-floor at the time of threshing," or "at the time when it is trodden." The *treading*, or *threshing*, is here put before the *harvest*, out of the natural order, because the prominent thought is the *treading down* or destruction of Babylon. In the East the treading out of the corn took place only at harvest-time. Babylon is like a threshing-floor not trodden for a long time; but the time of harvest, when her citizens shall be trodden under foot, shall come [CALVIN]. "Like a threshing-floor full of corn, so is Babylon now full of riches, but the time of harvest shall come, when all her prosperity shall be cut off" [LUDOVICUS DE DIEU]. GROTIUS distinguishes the "harvest" from the "threshing"; the former is the slaying of her citizens, the latter the pillaging and destruction of the city (cf. Joel 3:13; Rev. 14:15, 18). **34. me**–Zion speaks. Her groans are what bring down retribution in kind on Babylon (ch. 50:17; Ps. 102:13, 17, 20). **empty vessel**–He has drained me out. **dragon**–The serpent often "swallows" its prey whole; or a sea monster [GROTIUS]. **filled his belly . . . cast me out**–like a beast, which, having "filled" himself to satiety, "casts out" the rest [CALVIN]. After filling all his storehouses with my goods, he has *cast me out of this land* [GROTIUS]. **35. my flesh**–which Nebuchadnezzar hath "devoured" (vs. 34). Zion thus calls her *kinsmen* (Rom. 11:14) slain throughout the country or carried captives to Babylon [GROTIUS]. Or, as "my blood" follows, it and "my flesh" constitute the *whole man:* Zion, in its totality, its citizens and all its substance, have been a prey to Babylon's violence (Ps. 137:8). **36. plead . . . cause**–(ch. 50:34). **sea**–the Euphrates (vs. 13; ch. 50:38). Cf. Isaiah 19:5, "sea," i.e., the Nile (Isa. 21:1). **37.** (Ch. 50:26, 39; Rev. 18:2). 38, 39. The capture of Babylon was effected on the night of a festival in honor of its idols. **roar . . . yell**–The Babylonians were *shouting* in drunken revelry (cf. Dan. 5:4). **39. In their heat I will make their feasts**–In the midst of their being heated with wine, I will give them "their" potions,–a very different cup to drink, but one which is *their due*, the wine-cup of My stupefying wrath (ch. 25:15; 49:12; Isa. 51:17; Lam. 4:21). **rejoice, and sleep . . . perpetual . . .**–that they may *exult*, and in the midst of their jubilant exultation sleep the sleep of death (**vs.** 57; Isa. 21:4, 5). **41. Sheshach**–Babylon (cf. *Note*, ch. 25:26); called so from the goddess Shach, to whom a five days' festival was kept, during which, as in the Roman Saturnalia, the most unbridled licentiousness was permitted; slaves ruled their masters, and in every house one called Zogan, arrayed in a royal garment, was chosen to rule all the rest. He calls Babylon "Sheshach," to imply that it was during this feast the city was taken [SCALIGER]. **42. The sea**–the host of Median invaders.

ADAM CLARKE

29. *And the land shall tremble.* It is represented here as trembling under the numerous armies that are passing over it, and the prancing of their horses.

30. *The mighty men . . . have forborn to fight.* They were panic-struck when they found the Medes and Persians within their walls, and at once saw that resistance was useless.

31. *One post shall run to meet another.* As the city was taken by surprise, in the manner already related, so now messengers, one after another, were dispatched to give the king information of what was done; viz., that the city was taken at one end. Herodotus tells us that the extreme parts of the city were taken before those of the center knew anything of the invasion. Herodot., lib. i, c. 191.

32. *That the passages are stopped.* Either the bridges or slips for boats, by which the inhabitants passed from one side to the other, and may mean the principal gates or passes in the city, which the victorious army would immediately seize, that they might prevent all communication between the inhabitants.

33. *The daughter of Babylon is like a threshingfloor.* The threshing wheel is gone over her; she is trodden underfoot.

34. *Nebuchadrezzar . . . hath devoured me.* These are the words of Judea; he has taken away all my riches. *He hath cast me out.* He shall vomit all up; i.e., they shall be regained.

35. *The violence done to me . . . be upon Babylon, . . . and my blood upon the inhabitants of Chaldea.* Zion begins to speak, v. 34, and ends with this verse. The answer of Jehovah begins with the next verse. Though the Chaldeans have been the instrument of God to punish the Jews, yet in return they, being themselves exceedingly wicked, shall suffer for all the carnage they have made, and for all the blood they have shed.

36. *I will dry up her sea.* Exhaust all her treasures.

37. *Without an inhabitant.* See chap. i. 39.

39. *In their heat I will make their feasts.* It was on the night of a feast day, while their hearts were heated with wine and revelry, that Babylon was taken; see Dan. v. 1-3. This feast was held in honor of the goddess Sheshach (or perhaps of Bel), who is mentioned, v. 41, as being taken with her worshippers. As it was in the night the city was taken, many had retired to rest, and never awoke; slain in their beds, they slept a perpetual sleep.

41. *How is Sheshach taken!* Perhaps the city is here called by the name of its idol. *The praise of the whole earth.* One of the seven wonders of the world; superexcellent for the height, breadth, and compass of its walls, its hanging gardens, the temple of Belus.

42. *The sea is come up.* A multitude of foes have inundated the city.

MATTHEW HENRY

The strength of the enemy is here compared to an inundation of waters (*v.* 42): *The sea has come up upon Babylon,* which, when it has once broken through its bounds, there is no fence against, so that she is *covered with the multitude of its waves,* overpowered by a numerous army; *her cities* then become *a desolation,* an uninhabited uncultivated desert, *v.* 43.

Bel was the principal idol that the Babylonians worshipped, and therefore that is by name here marked for destruction (*v.* 44): *I will punish Bel,* that image to which such abundance of sacrifices are offered. His altars shall be forsaken, none shall regard him any more, and so that idol shall fail them.

It is their wisdom to *get out of the midst of Babylon,* lest they be involved, if not in her ruins, yet in her fears (*v.* 45, 46). Those who have not grace enough to keep their temper in temptation should have wisdom enough to keep out of the way of temptation.

It is a destruction that shall reach the gods of Babylon, the idols and images. "In token that *the whole land shall be confounded* and all *her slain shall fall,* and that throughout all the country *the wounded shall groan, I will do judgment upon her graven images,*" *v.* 47 and again *v.* 53. Though the invaders are themselves idolaters, yet they shall destroy the images and temples of the gods of Babylon.

2. Yet some shall rejoice in Babylon's fall, not as the misery of their fellow-creatures, but as the manifestation of the righteous judgment of God and as it opens the way for the release of God's captives (*v.* 48).

They are told, *v.* 50, 51: "*You* Israelites, *who have escaped the sword of the Chaldeans* your oppressors, and of the Persians their destroyers, *go away, stand not still*; hasten to your own country, for this is not your rest, but Canaan is."

The returning captives (*v.* 51), being reminded of Jerusalem, cry out, "*We are confounded;* we cannot bear the thought of it; *shame covers our faces* at the mention of it, for *we have heard of the reproach of the sanctuary,* that is profaned and ruined by strangers; how can we think of it with any pleasure?"

To this he answers (*v.* 52) that the God of Israel will now triumph over the gods of Babylon, and so that reproach will be for ever rolled away.

X. The diversified feeling excited by Babylon's fall. 1. Some shall lament the destruction of Babylon. There *is the sound of a cry* from Babylon (*v.* 54), lamenting this great destruction, *v.* 55. They shall say in their lamentations (*v.* 41): "*How is Sheshach taken,* and how are we mistaken concerning her! How is that city become an *astonishment among the nations* that was the glory, and admiration of the whole earth!"

JAMIESON, FAUSSET, BROWN

The image (cf. ch. 47:2; Isa. 8:7, 8) is appropriately taken from the Euphrates, which, overflowing in spring, is like a "sea" near Babylon (vss. 13:32, 36). **43. Her cities**–the cities, her dependencies. So, "Jerusalem and the cities thereof" (ch. 34:1). Or, the "cities" are the inner and outer cities, the two parts into which Babylon was divided by the Euphrates [GROTIUS]. **44. Bel . . . swallowed**–in allusion to the many sacrifices to the idol which its priests pretended it swallowed at night; or rather, the precious gifts taken from other nations and offered to it (which it is said to have "swallowed"; cf. "devoured," "swallowed," vs. 34; ch. 50:17), which it should have to disgorge (cf. vs. 13; ch. 50:37). Of these gifts were the vessels of Jehovah's temple in Jerusalem (II Chron. 36:7; Dan. 1:2). The restoration of these, as foretold here, is recorded in Ezra 1:7-11. **flow**–as a river; fitly depicting the *influx* of pilgrims of all "nations" to the idol. **45, 46.** (*Note,* vs. 6.) **46. And lest**–Cf., for the same ellipsis, Genesis 3:22; Exodus 13:17; Deuteronomy 8:12. "And in order that your heart may not faint at the (first) rumor" (of war), I will give you some intimation of the time. In the first "year" there shall "come a rumor" that Cyrus is preparing for war against Babylon. "After that, in another year, shall come a rumor," viz., that Cyrus is approaching, and has already entered Assyria. Then is your time to "go out" (vs. 45). Babylon was taken the following or third year of Belshazzar's reign [GROTIUS]. **violence in the land**–of Babylon (Ps. 7:16). **ruler against ruler**–or, "ruler upon ruler," a continual change of rulers in a short space. Belshazzar and Nabonidus, supplanted by Darius or Cyaxares, who is succeeded by Cyrus. **47.** GROTIUS translates, "Because then (viz., on the third year) the time shall have come that," etc. **confounded**–at seeing their gods powerless to help them. **her slain**–in retribution for "*Israel's* slain" (vs. 49) who fell by her hand. GROTIUS translates, "her dancers," as in Judges 21:21, 23; I Samuel 18:6, the same *Hebrew* word is translated, alluding to the dancing revelry of the festival during which Cyrus took Babylon. **48. heaven . . . earth . . . sing for Babylon**–(Isa. 14:7-13; 44:23; Rev. 18:20). **49. caused . . . to fall**–lit., "has been for the falling," i.e., as Babylon made this its one aim to fill all places with the slain of Israel, so at Babylon shall all the slain *of that whole land* (not as *English Version,* "of all the *earth*") [MAURER]. HENDERSON translates, "Babylon also shall fall, ye slain of Israel. Those also of Babylon shall fall, O ye slain of all the earth." But, "in the midst of her," vs. 47, plainly answers to "at Babylon," vs. 49, *English Version.* **50. escaped . . . sword**–viz., of the Medes. So great will be the slaughter that even some of God's people shall be involved in it, as they had deserved. **afar off**–though ye are banished far off from where ye used formerly to worship God. **let Jerusalem come into your mind**–While in exile remember your temple and city, so as to prefer them to all the rest of the world wherever ye may be (Isa. 62:6). **51.** The prophet anticipates the Jews' reply; I know you will say in despair, "We are confounded . . . ." "Wherefore (God saith to you) behold, I will . . ." (vs. 52) [CALVIN]. I prefer taking vs. 51 as the *prayer* which the Jews are directed to offer in exile (vs. 50), "let Jerusalem come into your mind" (and say in prayer to God), "We are confounded." This view is confirmed by Psalm 44:15, 16; 79:4; 102:17-20; Isa. 62:6, 7. **for strangers**–The "reproach," which especially has stung us, came when they taunted us with the fact that they had burned the temple, our peculiar glory, as though our religion was a thing of naught. **52. Wherefore**–because of these sighs of the Jews directed to God (vs. 21). **I . . . judgment upon . . . images**–in opposition to the Babylonian taunt that Jehovah's religion was a thing of naught, since they had burned His temple (vs. 51): I will show that, though I have thus visited the Jews' neglect of Me, yet those gods of Babylon cannot save themselves, much less their votaries, who shall "through all her land" lie and "groan" with wounds. **53.** Cf. Obadiah 4 as to Edom (Amos 9:2). **Though . . . yet from me**–We are not to measure God's power by what seems to our perceptions natural or probable. **55. great voice**–Where once was the *great din* of a mighty city, there shall be the silence of death [VATABLUS]. Or, the "great voice" of the revellers (vss. 38, 39; Isa. 22:2). Or, the voice of *mighty boasting* [CALVIN], (cf. vs. 53). **her waves**–"when" her calamities shall cause her to give forth a widely different "voice," even such a one as the waves give that lash the shores (vs. 42) [GROTIUS]. Or, "when" is connected thus: "the great voice" in her, when her "waves . . ." (cf. vs. 13). CALVIN translates, "*their* waves," i.e., the Medes bursting

ADAM CLARKE

44. *I will punish Bel in Babylon.* Bel was their supreme deity. *That which he hath swallowed up.* The sacred vessels of the Temple of Jerusalem, which were taken thence by Nebuchadnezzar, and dedicated to him in his temple at Babylon. *The wall of Babylon shall fall.* It shall cease to be a defense, and shall molder away until, in process of time, it shall not be discernible.

45. *My people, go ye out.* A warning to all the Jews in Babylon to leave the city, and escape for their lives.

46. *A rumour shall . . . come one year.* A year before the capture of the city there shall be a rumor of war—and in that year Belshazzar was defeated by Cyrus. In the following year the city was taken.

48. *The heaven and the earth . . . shall sing for Babylon.* Its fall shall be a subject of universal rejoicing.

50. *Ye that have escaped the sword.* The Jews. *Let Jerusalem come into your mind.* Pray for its restoration, and embrace the first opportunity offered of returning thither.

51. *Strangers are come into the sanctuaries.* The lamentation of the pious Jews for the profanation of the Temple by the Chaldeans.

53. *Though Babylon should mount up to heaven.* Though it were fortified even to the skies, it shall fall by the enemies that I will send against it.

55. *The great voice.* Its pride and insufferable boasting.

MATTHEW HENRY

It is to the same purport with *v.* 56–58. When the spoiler comes upon Babylon her mighty men are immediately taken, *everyone of their bows is broken.* Their politics fail them. Their princes and captains, who sit in council as men intoxicated through stupidity or despair. The *walls of their city* fail them, *v.* 58. When the enemy had found ways to ford Euphrates, which was thought impassable, yet surely, think they, the walls are impregnable, they are *the broad walls of Babylon.* Some say that there was a threefold wall about the inner city and the like about the outer, and yet these shall be *utterly broken,* and *the high gates and towers shall be burnt.*

Verses 59–64

1. A copy is taken of this prophecy, it should seem by Jeremiah himself, for Baruch his scribe is not mentioned here (*v.* 60): *Jeremiah wrote in a book all these words that are here written against Babylon.* 2. It is sent to Babylon, to the captives there, by the hand of Seraiah, who went there attendant on king Zedekiah, *in the fourth year of his reign, v.* 59. He *went with Zedekiah,* or (as the margin reads it) *on the behalf of Zedekiah, into Babylon.* The character given of him is that *Seraiah was a quiet prince,* a prince of rest. He was in honour, but not hot and heady, heading factions. He was of a calm temper, and studied the things that made for peace. Jeremiah might safely entrust such a man with his errand. It is the real honour of great men to be quiet men. 3. Seraiah is desired to read it to his countrymen that had already gone into captivity: "*When thou shalt come to Babylon, and shalt see* what a magnificent place it is, how large a city, how rich, and how well fortified, and shalt be tempted to think, Surely, it will stand for ever, *then thou shalt read all these words* to thyself and thy friends, for their encouragement in captivity: let them with an eye of faith see the end of these threatening powers." 4. He is directed to make a solemn protestation of the divine authority and certainty of that which he had read (*v.* 63). Though Seraiah sees Babylon flourishing, having read this prophecy he must foresee Babylon falling. When we see what this world is, how glittering its shows are and how flattering its proposals, let us read in the book of the Lord that its *fashion passes away,* and we shall learn to look upon it with a holy contempt. 5. He must then tie a stone to the book and throw it into the midst of the river Euphrates, as a confirming sign of the things contained in it, saying, "*Thus shall Babylon sink, and not rise,*" *v.* 53, 64. In the sign it was the stone that sunk the book. But in *the thing signified* it was rather the book that sunk the stone; it was the divine sentence passed upon Babylon in this prophecy that sunk that city, which seemed *as firm as a stone.* The last words of the chapter seal up the vision and prophecy of this book: *Thus far are the words of Jeremiah.* This prophecy was dated in the *fourth year* of Zedekiah (*v.* 59), long before he finished his testimony; but it was to be last accomplished of all his prophecies against the Gentiles, *ch.* xlvi. 1. And the chapter which remains is purely historical, and, as some think, was added by some other hand.

CHAPTER 52

Verses 1–11

This narrative begins in the beginning of the reign of Zedekiah, though there were two captivities before, one in the fourth year of Jehoiakim, the other in the first of Jeconiah. 1. God's just displeasure against Judah and Jerusalem for their sin, *v.* 3. He determined to *cast them out from his presence.* He expelled them from that good land that had such tokens of his presence in providential bounty and that holy city and temple that had such tokens of his presence in covenant-grace and love. 2. Zedekiah's bad conduct and management for which God punished him. Zedekiah had arrived at years of discretion when he came to the throne; he *was twenty-one years old* (*v.* 1); he was not the worst of the kings (we never read of his idolatries), yet he *did evil in the eyes of the Lord,* for he did not do the good he should have done. But that evil deed of his which did hasten this destruction was his *rebelling against the king of Babylon,* which was both his sin and his folly, and

JAMIESON, FAUSSET, BROWN

on her as impetuous waves; so vs. 42. But the parallel, "a great voice," belongs to *her,* therefore the wave-like "roar" of "their voice" ought also belong to *her* (cf. vs. 54). The "great voice" of commercial din, boasting, and feasting, is "destroyed"; but in its stead there is the wave-like roar of *her voice* in her "destruction" (vs. 54). **56. taken**—when they were least expecting it, and in such a way that resistance was impossible. **57.** (Vs. 39; Dan. 5:1, etc.). **58. broad walls**—eighty-seven feet broad [ROSENMULLER]; fifty cubits [GROTIUS]. A chariot of four horses abreast could meet another on it without collision. The walls were two hundred cubits high, and four hundred and eighty-five stadia, or sixty miles in extent. **gates**—one hundred in number, of brass; twenty-five on each of the four sides, the city being square; between the gates were two hundred and fifty towers. BEROSUS says triple walls encompassed the outer, and the same number the inner city. Cyrus caused the outer walls to be demolished. Taking the extent of the walls to be three hundred and sixty-five stadia, as DIODORUS states, it is said two hundred thousand men completed a stadium each day, so that the whole was completed in one year. **labour . . . in the fire**—The event will show that the builders of the walls have "labored" only for the "fire" in which they shall be consumed. "In the fire" answers to the parallel, "burned with fire." Translate, "*shall have labored* in vain . . . ." Cf. Job 3:14, " built desolate places for themselves," i.e., grand places, soon about to be desolate ruins. Jeremiah has in view here Habbakkuk 2:13. **59-64.** A special copy of the prophecy prepared by Jeremiah was delivered to Seraiah, to console the Jews in their Babylonian exile. Though he was to throw it into the Euphrates, a symbol of Babylon's fate, no doubt he retained the substance in memory, so as to be able orally to communicate it to his countrymen. **went with Zedekiah**—rather, "in behalf of Zedekiah"; sent by Zedekiah to appease Nebuchadnezzar's anger at his revolt [CALVIN]. **fourth year**—so that Jeremiah's prediction of Babylon's downfall was thus solemnly written and sealed by a symbolical action, six whole years before the capture of Jerusalem by the Babylonians. **quiet prince**—Cf. I Chron. 22:9, "a man of rest." Seraiah was not one of the courtiers hostile to God's prophets, but "quiet" and docile; ready to execute Jeremiah's commission, notwithstanding the risk attending it. GLASSIUS translates, "prince of Menuchah" (cf. I Chron. 2:52, *Margin*). MAURER translates, "commander of the caravan," on whom it devolved to appoint the resting-place for the night. *English Version* suits the context best. **61. read**—not in public, for the Chaldeans would not have understood *Hebrew;* but in private, as is to be inferred from his addressing himself altogether to God (vs. 62) [CALVIN]. **62. O Lord, thou**—and not merely Jeremiah or any man is the author of this prophecy; I therefore here in Thy presence embrace as true all that I read. **63. bind a stone . . .**—(Rev. 18:21). So the Phoceans in leaving their country, when about to found Marseilles, threw lead into the sea, binding themselves not to return till the lead should swim. **64. they shall be weary**—The Babylonians shall be worn out, so as not to be able to recover their strength. **Thus far . . . Jeremiah**—Hence it is to be inferred that the last chapter is not included in Jeremiah's writings but was added by some inspired man, mainly from II Kings 24:18 to ch. 25, to explain and confirm what precedes [CALVIN].

CHAPTER 52

Vss. 1-34. WRITTEN BY SOME OTHER THAN JEREMIAH (PROBABLY EZRA) AS AN HISTORICAL SUPPLEMENT TO THE PREVIOUS PROPHECIES (*Note,* ch. 51: 64). Jeremiah, having already (chs. 39, 40) given the history in the proper place, was not likely to repeat it here. Its canonical authority as inspired is shown by its being in the LXX *version.* It contains the capture and burning of Jerusalem, etc., Zedekiah's punishment, and the better treatment of Jehoiachin under Evil-merodach, down to his death. These last events were probably subsequent to Jeremiah's time. **3. through . . . anger of . . . Lord . . . Zedekiah rebelled**—His "anger" against Jerusalem, determining Him to "cast out" His people "from His presence" heretofore manifested there, led Him to permit Zedekiah to rebel (II Kings 23:26, 27; cf. Exod. 9:12; 10:1; Rom. 9:18). That rebellion, being in violation of his oath "by God," was sure to bring down God's vengeance (II Chron. 36:13; Ezek. 17:15, 16, 18).

ADAM CLARKE

56. *The Lord God of recompences.* The fall of Babylon is an act of divine justice; whatever it suffers, it is in consequence of its crimes.

57. *I will make drunk her princes.* See. v. 39.

58. *The broad walls of Babylon.* Herodotus, who saw these walls, says, "The city was a regular square, each side of which was one hundred and twenty stadia, the circumference four hundred and eighty stadia. It was surrounded by a wall fifty cubits broad, and two hundred cubits high; and each side had twenty-five brazen gates."—Herod., lib. i, c. 178. Had not Cyrus resorted to stratagem, humanly speaking, he could not have taken this city. For the destruction of this wall and its very vestiges, see Isa. xiii. 19.

59. *The word which Jeremiah.* On account of the message sent by Jeremiah to the Jewish captives in Babylon.

60. *Wrote in a book.* Whether this book contained any more than is recorded in this place we do not know; probably it contained no more than what is found in vv. 62-64. A *book, sepher,* signifies, in Hebrew, any writing, great or small.

64. *Thus shall Babylon sink.* This is the emblem of its overthrow and irretrievable ruin. See Rev. xviii. 21, where we find that this is an emblem of the total ruin of mystical Babylon.

Thus far are the words of Jeremiah. It appears that the following chapter is not the work of this prophet; it is not his style. The author of it writes "Jehoachin"; Jeremiah writes him always "Jeconiah" or "Coniah." It is merely historical, and is very similar to 2 Kings xxiv. 18—xxv. 30. The author, whoever he was, relates the capture of Jerusalem, the fate of Zedekiah, the pillage and burning of the city and the Temple. He mentions also certain persons of distinction who were slain by the Chaldeans. He mentions the number of the captives that were carried to Babylon at three different times, and concludes with the deliverance of King Jehoiachin from prison in Babylon, in which he had been for thirty-seven years.

CHAPTER 52

1. *Zedekiah was one and twenty years old.* See 2 Kings xxiv. 18.

2. *And he did . . . evil.* This and the following verse are the same as 2 Kings xxiv. 19.

3. *Through the anger of the Lord.* Here is a king given to a people in God's anger, and taken away in His displeasure.

MATTHEW HENRY

brought ruin upon his people. God was greatly displeased with him for his perfidious dealing with the king of Babylon (Ezek. xvii. 15, &c.). 3. The Chaldeans gained Jerusalem, after eighteen months' siege. In remembrance of two steps towards their ruin, while they were in captivity, they kept a *fast in the fourth month, and a fast in the tenth* (Zech. viii. 19): that in the *fifth month* was in remembrance of the burning of the temple, and that in the *seventh* of the murder of Gedaliah. For a year and a half the city was besieged. Supplies of food were cut off. In spite of constant attacks, the garrison refused to surrender, but soon there was *famine in the city* (*v.* 6); *no bread for the people of the land*, and then no wonder that *the city was broken up*, *v.* 7. Walls, in such a case, will not hold out long without men, any more than men without walls; nor will both together stand people in any stead without God and his protection. 4. The king and his mighty men got out of the city *by night* (*v.* 7); but the king was overtaken by pursuers *in the plains of Jericho*, his guards were dispersed, and all his army was *scattered from him*, *v.* 8. 5. The doom passed upon Zedekiah by the king of Babylon. He treated him as a rebel, *gave judgment upon him*, *v.* 9. *His sons were slain before his eyes*, and all *the princes of Judah* (*v.* 10); then *his eyes were put out*, and he was *bound in chains*, carried in triumph to Babylon. He was condemned to perpetual imprisonment, wearing out the remainder of his life (I cannot say his days, for he saw day no more) in darkness and misery. Jeremiah had often told him what it would come to, but he would not take warning when he might have prevented it.

Verses 12–23

An account of the woeful havoc that was made by the Chaldean army, a month after the city was taken, under the command of Nebuzaradan, who was *captain of the guard.* 1. He laid the temple in ashes, having first plundered it of every thing that was valuable: He *burnt the house of the Lord*, that holy and beautiful house, where their *fathers praised him*, Isa. lxiv. 11. 2. He burnt the royal palace, probably that which Solomon built after he had built the temple, which was, ever since, *the king's house.* 3. He burnt *all the houses of Jerusalem.* 4. He *broke down all the walls of Jerusalem*, to be revenged upon them for standing in the way of his army so long. Thus, of a defenced city, it was made a ruin, Isa. xxv. 2. 5. He *carried away many into captivity* (*v.* 15); he took away *certain of the poor of the people*, that is, of the people in the city, for *the poor of the land* (the poor of the country) he left for *vine-dressers and husbandmen.* He also carried off *the residue of the people that remained in the city*, that had escaped the sword and famine, and the deserters. 6. The vessels which were still in the temple were looted. All that were of great value had been carried away before, *the vessels of silver and gold*, yet some remained, *v.* 19. But most of the temple-prey that was now seized was of brass, which being of less value, was carried off last. When the walls of the city were demolished, the pillars of the temple were pulled down, too, and both in token that God, who was the strength and stay both of their civil and their ecclesiastical government, had departed from them. No walls can protect those, nor pillars sustain those, from whom God withdraws. These pillars of the temple were for ornament. They were called *Jachin—He will establish;* and *Boaz—In him is strength*; so that the breaking of these signified that God would no longer establish his house nor be the strength of it. These pillars are here described (*v.* 21–23, from 1 Kings vii. 15). All the vessels that belonged to the brazen altar were carried away; for the iniquity of Jerusalem, like that of Eli's house, was not to be purged by sacrifice or offering, 1 Sam. iii. 14. It is said (*v.* 20), *The brass of all these vessels was without weight;* so it was in the making of them (1 Kings vii. 47), *the weight of the brass was not* then *found out* (2 Chron. iv. 18). Those that made spoil of them did not stand to weigh them, as purchasers do.

Verses 24–30

A very melancholy account, 1. Of the slaughter of some great men, in cold blood, at Riblah, seventy-two in number (according to the number of the elders of Israel, Num. xi. 24, 25), so they are computed, 2 Kings xxv. 18, 19. The account here agrees except that there it is said that there were five, here there were seven *near the king*. Dr. Lightfoot thinks that he took away seven of those near the king, but two of them were Jeremiah and Ebed-melech, who were both discharged, so that there were only five of them put to death. *Seraiah the chief priest* is put first. Seraiah the prince was *a quiet prince* (*ch.* li. 59), but

JAMIESON, FAUSSET, BROWN

4. forts—rather, *towers* of wood [KIMCHI], for watching the movements of the besieged from the height and annoying them with missiles. **7.** (*Note*, ch. 39:4.) **9. gave judgment upon him**—as guilty of rebellion and perjury (vs. 3; cf. Ezek. 23:24). **11.** Ezekiel 12:13: "I will bring him to Babylon, yet shall he not *see it.*" **prison**—lit., the house of visitations, or punishments, i.e., where there was penal work enforced on the prisoners, such as grinding. Hence LXX renders it "the house of the mill." So Samson, after his eyes were put out, "ground" in the Philistine prison-house (Judg. 16:21). **12. tenth day**—But in II Kings 25:8, it is said "the *seventh* day." Nebuzaradan *started* from Riblah on the "seventh" day and *arrived* in Jerusalem on the "tenth" day. Seeming discrepancies, when cleared up, confirm the genuineness of Scripture; for they show there was no collusion between the writers; as in all God's works there is latent harmony under outward varieties. **13. all the houses . . . and all the houses of the great**—the "and" defines what houses especially are meant, viz., the houses of the great men. **15. poor of . . . people**—added to the account in II Kings 25:11. "The poor of the people" are *of the city*, as distinguished from "the poor of the land," i.e., *of the country*. **17. brake**—that they might be more portable. Fulfilling the prophecy (ch. 27:19). See I Kings 7:15, 23, 27, 50. Nothing is so particularly related here as the carrying away of the articles in the temple. The remembrance of their beauty and preciousness heightens the bitterness of their loss and the evil of sin which caused it. **brass . . . brazen**—rather "copper . . . of copper." **18.** (Exod. 27:3.) **19. of gold in gold**—implying that the articles were of solid gold and silver respectively, not of a different metal inside, or alloyed [GROTIUS]. *Whole:* not breaking them as was done to the *brass* (vs. 17). **20. bulls . . . under the bases**—But the bulls were not "*under* the *bases*," but under the *sea* (I Kings 7:25, 27, 38); the ten bases were not under the sea, but under the ten lavers. In *English Version*, "bases," therefore, must mean the *lower parts of the sea* under which the bulls were. Rather, translate, "the bulls were *in the place of* (i.e., by way of; so the *Hebrew*, I Sam. 14:9), bases," or supports to the sea [BUXTORF]. So LXX. II Kings 25:16 omits the "bulls," and has "*and* the bases"; so GROTIUS here reads "the bulls (which were) under (the sea) *and* the bases." **21. eighteen cubits**—but in II Chronicles 3:15, it is "thirty-five cubits." The discrepancy is thus removed. *Each* pillar was eighteen common cubits. The two together, deducting the base, were thirty-five, as stated in II Chronicles 3:15 [GROTIUS]. Other ways (e.g., by reference to the difference between the common and the sacred cubit) are proposed: though we are not able positively to decide now which is the true way, at least those proposed do show that *the discrepancies are not irreconcilable.* **22. five cubits**—so I Kings 7:16. But II Kings 25:17 has "three cubits." There were two parts in the chapiter: the one lower and plain, of two cubits; the other, higher and curiously carved, of three cubits. The former is omitted in II Kings 25:17, as belonging to the shaft of the pillar; the latter alone is there mentioned. Here the *whole* chapiter of five cubits is referred to. **23. on a side**—lit., (on the side) *towards the air* or *wind*, i.e., the outside of the capitals of the pillars conspicuous to the eye, opposed to the four remaining pomegranates which were not seen from the outside. The pomegranates here are ninety-six; but in I Kings 7:20 they are 200 on each chapiter, and 400 on the two (II Chron. 4:13). It seems there were *two* rows of them, one above the other, and in each row 100. They are here said to be ninety-six, but immediately following 100, and so in I Kings 7:20. *Four* seem to have been unseen to one looking from one point; and the ninety-six are only those that could be seen [VATABLUS]; or, the *four* omitted here are those separating the four sides, one pomegranate at each point of separation (or at the four corners) between the four sides [GROTIUS]. **24. Seraiah**—different from the Seraiah (ch. 51:59), son of Neriah; probably son of Azariah (I Chron. 6:14). **Zephaniah**—son of Maaseiah (*Notes*, ch. 21:1; 29:25). **25. seven men**—but in II Kings 25:19 it is "*five.*" Perhaps two were less illustrious persons and are therefore omitted. **principal scribe of the host**—(Isa. 33:18). His office was to preside over the levy and enroll recruits. RAW-

ADAM CLARKE

4. *Ninth year . . . tenth month.* Answering nearly to our January.

5. *So the city was besieged.* It held out one year and six months.

6. *And in the fourth month.* See chap. xxxix. 1, etc. The fourth month answers nearly to our July.

8. *The army of the Chaldeans pursued.* See 2 Kings xxv. 5.

9. *King of Babylon to Riblah.* See chap. xxxix. 5.

11. *He put out the eyes of Zedekiah.* See chap. xxxix. 7.

12. *Now in the fifth month.* Answering nearly to our August.

13. *And burned the house of the Lord.* Thus perished this magnificent structure, after it had stood 424 years, 3 months, and 8 days.

15. *Those that fell away.* The deserters to the Chaldeans during the siege.

16. *The poor of the land.* See chap. xxxix. 1.

17. *Also the pillars.* See chap. xxvii. 19.

KEIL-DELITZSCH:

Verses 17–23. The carrying away of the vessels of the temple is more fully stated than in 2 Kings 25:13–17. The large brazen articles, the two pillars at the porch (1 Kings 7:15ff.), the bases (1 Kings 7:27ff.), and the brazen sea (1 Kings 7:23ff.), which were too vast in their proportions to be easily carried away to Babylon, were broken to pieces by the Chaldeans, who carried off the brass of which they were made.

"All their brass" is more precise than simply "their brass" (Kings). In the enumeration of the smaller brazen vessels used for the temple service, verse 18, there is omitted, in 2 Kings, "and the bowls" (used in sacrifice); this omission is perhaps due merely to an error in transcription. The enumeration of the gold and silver vessels in verse 19 has been much more abbreviated in 2 Kings 25:15, where only "the fire-pans and the bowls" are mentioned, while in the text here, besides these there are named "the basins," then "the pots (Eng. vers. *caldrons*), and the candlesticks, and the pans (Eng. vers. *spoons*), and the cups." For particulars regarding these different vessels, see on 1 Kings 7:40, 45, 50.

—*Commentary on the Old Testament*

24. *The second priest.* See 2 Kings xxv. 18. *The three keepers.* The priests who stood at the door to receive the offerings of the people; see 2 Kings xx. 9 and xxiii. 4.

25. *Seven men . . . that were near the king's person.* These were privy counsellors.

MATTHEW HENRY

perhaps Seraiah the priest was turbulent and had made himself obnoxious to the king of Babylon. The leaders of this people had caused them to err, and now they are objects of divine justice. 2. Of the captivity of the rest. *Judah was carried away captive out of his own land* (*v.* 27), Lev. xviii. 28. An account, (1) Of two captivities, one in the seventh year of Nebuchadnezzar (the same with that which is said to be in his eighth year, 2 Kings xxiv. 12), another in his eighteenth year, the same with that which is said (*v.* 12) to be in his nineteenth year. But the numbers here are small, in comparison with what we find expressed concerning the former (2 Kings xxiv. 14, 16), when there were 18,000 carried captive, whereas here they are said to be 3,023. When all the residue of the people were carried away (*v.* 15), one would think there should be more than 832 souls; therefore Dr. Lightfoot conjectures that, these accounts being joined to the story of the putting to death of the great men at Riblah, all that are here said to be carried away were *put to death* as rebels. (2) Of a third captivity, not mentioned before, which was in the twenty-third year of Nebuchadnezzar, four years after the destruction of Jerusalem (*v.* 30): Then *Nebuzaradan* came, and *carried away* 745 Jews; it is probable that this was done in revenge of the murder of Gedaliah, which was another rebellion against the king of Babylon, and that those who were now taken were put to death. If this be the sum total of the captives (*all the persons were* 4,600, *v.* 30), they were reduced from what they had been, but the Lord made them fruitful in the land of their affliction, and the more they were oppressed the more they multiplied.

Verses 31–34

This story concerning the reviving which king Jehoiachin had in his bondage we had before (2 Kings xxv. 27–30), only there it is said to be done on *the twenty-seventh day of the twelfth month*, here *on the twenty-fifth*. It is probable that the orders were given for his release on the twenty-fifth day, but that he was not presented to the king till the twenty-seventh. Nebuchadnezzar had long kept this unhappy prince in prison; and his son, though well-affected to the prisoner, could not procure him any favour; but, when the old man was dead, his son countenanced Jehoiachin and made him a favourite. Jehoiachin fell from a throne into a prison, but here he is advanced again to a throne of state (*v.* 32), though not to a throne of power. As, before, the robes were changed into prison-garments, so now they were converted into robes again. Though the night of affliction be very long, yet we must not despair. The day may dawn at last. Jehoiachin was thirty-seven years a prisoner, in confinement, in contempt, since he was eighteen years old. Let those whose afflictions have been lengthened out encourage themselves with this instance; the vision will at the end speak comfortably, and therefore wait for it. God can make his people find favour in the eyes of their oppressors, and turn their hearts to pity them (Ps. cvi. 46), *He made them to be pitied of all those that carried them captives.* It is not in vain to hope and quietly to *wait for the salvation of the Lord.* And now, comparing the prophecy and the history of this book, we may learn, (1) That it is no new thing for churches and persons highly dignified to degenerate, and become corrupt. (2) That iniquity tends to the ruin of those that harbour it; and, if it be not repented of and forsaken, will certainly end in ruin.

JAMIESON, FAUSSET, BROWN

LINSON observes that the Assyrian records are free from the exaggerated expressions found in the Egyptian. A minute account was taken of the spoil. Two "scribes of the host" are seen in every bas-relief, writing down the various objects brought to them: the heads of the slain, the prisoners, cattle, sheep, etc. **28. seventh year**—in II Kings 24:12, 14, 16, it is said "the *eighth year*" of Nebuchadnezzar. No doubt it was in part about the end of the seventh year, in part about the beginning of the eighth. Also in II Kings 24, 10000 (vs. 14), and 7000 men of might, and 1000 craftsmen (vs. 16), are said to have been carried away, But here 3023. Probably the latter 3023 were of the tribe of Judah, the remaining 7000 out of the 10,000 were of the other tribes, out of which many Israelites still had been left in the land. The 1000 "craftsmen" were exclusive of the 10,000, as appears, by comparing II Kings 24:14 with vs. 16. Probably the 3023 of Judah were first removed in the end of "the seventh year"; the 7000 and 1000 craftsmen in the "eighth year." This was at the first captivity under Jehoiachin. **29. eighteenth year**—when Jerusalem was taken. But in vs. 15, and II Kings 25:8, "the nineteenth year." Probably it was at the end of the eighteenth and the beginning of the nineteenth [LYRA]. **eight hundred and thirty and two**—The most illustrious persons are meant, who no doubt were carried away first, at the end of the eighteenth year. **30.** Not recorded in Kings or Chronicles. Probably it took place during the commotions that followed the death of Gedaliah (ch. 41:18; II Kings 25:26). **four thousand and six hundred**—The exact sum-total of the numbers specified here, viz., 3023, 832, 745, not including the general multitude and the women and children (vs. 15; ch. 39:9; II Kings 25:11). **31.** (II Kings 25:27-30.) **five and twentieth day**— but in II Kings 25:27, it is "the twenty-seventh day." Probably on the twenty-fifth the decree for his elevation was given, and the preparations for it made by releasing him from prison; and on the twenty-seventh day it was carried into effect. **Evil-merodach**—son and successor of Nebuchadnezzar [LYRA]; and the *Hebrew* writers say that during Nebuchadnezzar's exclusion from men among beasts, Evil-merodach administered the government. When Nebuchadnezzar at the end of seven years was restored, hearing of his son's misconduct and that he had exulted in his father's calamity, he threw him into prison, where the latter met Jeconiah and contracted a friendship with him, whence arose the favor which subsequently he showed him. God, in his elevation, rewarded his having surrendered to Nebuchadnezzar (cf. ch. 38:17 with II Kings 24:12). **lifted up . . . head**—(Cf. Gen. 40:13, 20; Ps. 3:3; 27:6). **32. set his throne above**—a mark of respect. **the kings**—The *Hebrew* text reads (the other) "kings." "*The* kings" is a Masoretic correction. **33. changed . . . garments**—gave him garments suitable to a king. **did . . . eat bread before him**—(II Sam. 9:13). **34. every day a portion**—rather, "*its* portion," *Margin* (cf. *Margin*, I Kings 8:59).

ADAM CLARKE

28-30. On these verses Dr. Blayney has some sensible remarks; I will extract the substance. These verses are not inserted in 2 Kings xxv.

Here then we have three deportations, and those the most considerable ones, in the first, in the eighth, and nineteenth years of Nebuchadnezzar, sufficiently distinguished from those in the seventh, eighteenth, and twenty-third years. So that it seems most reasonable to conclude that by the latter three the historian meant to point out deportations of a minor kind, not elsewhere noticed in direct terms in Scripture.

The first of these, said to have been in the seventh year of Nebuchadnezzar, was one of those that had been picked up in several parts of Judah by the band of Chaldeans, Syrians, and others, whom the king of Babylon sent against the land previously to his own coming, 2 Kings xxiv. 2.

That in the eighteenth year corresponds with the time when the Chaldean army broke off the siege before Jerusalem, and marched to meet the Egyptian army, at which time they might think it proper to send off the prisoners that were in camp, under a guard to Babylon.

And the last, in the twenty-third year of Nebuchadnezzar, was when that monarch, being engaged in the siege of Tyre, sent off Nebuzaradan against the Moabites, Ammonites, and other neighboring nations, who at the same time carried away the gleanings of Jews that remained in their own land, amounting in all to no more than 745.

31. *Lifted up the head of Jehoiachin.* This phrase is taken from Gen. xl. 13. It is founded on the observation that those who are in sorrow hold down their heads, and when they are comforted, or the cause of their sorrow removed, they lift up their heads. The Hebrew phrase "lift up the head" signifies to "comfort, cheer, make happy."

32. *Spake kindly.* Conversed freely with him. *Set his throne.* Gave him a more respectable *seat* than any of the captive princes, or better than even his own princes had, probably near his person.

33. *And changed his prison garments.* That is, Jehoiachin changed his own garments, that he might be suited in that respect to the state of his elevation. Kings also, in token of favor, gave caftans or robes to those whom they wish to honor. *And he did continually eat bread before him.* Was a constant guest at the king's table.

34. *And . . . there was a continual diet given him.* This was probably a ration allowed by the king for the support of Jehoiachin's household. For other particulars, see 2 Kings xxv. 30.

THE BOOK OF LAMENTATIONS

I. The solitary city (1:1-22)
A. The desolation (1:1-11)
B. The confession (1:12-22)

II. The sources of her sorrow (2:1-22)
A. The act of the Lord (2:1-10)
B. The affliction of iniquity (2:11-17)
C. The appeal of penitence (2:18-22)

III. The prophet's identification (3:1-66)
A. In affliction (3:1-21)
B. In assurance (3:22-33)
C. In appeal (3:34-54)
D. In assurance (3:55-66)

IV. The desolation (4:1-22)
A. The description (4:1-12)
B. The cause (4:13-16)
C. Vain help (4:17-20)
D. Hope (4:21-22)

V. The appeal out of sorrow (5:1-22)
A. "Remember, O Lord" (5:1-18)
B. "Turn Thou us unto Thee" (5:19-22)

I. The title of this book; in the Hebrew it has none, but is called (as the books of Moses are) from the first word *Ecah—How;* but the Jewish commentators call it, as the Greeks do, and we from them, *Kinoth—Lamentations.* As we have sacred odes or songs of joy, so have we sacred elegies or songs of lamentations.

II. The penman of this book is here Jeremiah the poet, therefore this book is fitly joined to the book of his prophecy, and is as an appendix to it. We have there the predictions of the desolations of Judah and Jerusalem, and then the history of them, to show how the predictions were accomplished, and here we have the expressions of his sorrow upon occasion of them. When he saw these calamities at a distance, he wished that his head "were waters and his eyes fountains of tears": and, when they came, he wept and was far from being disaffected to his country. Though his country had been unkind to him, and though the ruin of it was a proof that he was a true prophet, yet he sadly lamented it.

III. The occasion of these Lamentations was the destruction of Judah and Jerusalem by the Chaldean army and the dissolution of the Jewish state both civil and ecclesiastical. Some will have these to be the Lamentations which Jeremiah penned upon occasion of the death of Josiah (2 Chron. 35:25). But, they seem to be penned of those calamities when they had already come, and there is nothing of Josiah in them. No, it is Jerusalem's funeral that this is an elegy upon.

IV. The composition of it is not only poetical, but alphabetical, all except the 5th chapter. Each verse begins with a letter in the order of the Hebrew alphabet, the first *aleph,* the second, *beth,* etc., but the 3rd chapter is a triple alphabet, the first three beginning with *aleph,* the next three with *beth,* etc., which was a help to memory and an elegance in writing. In the 2nd, 3rd, and 4th chapters the letter *pe* is put before *ajin,* which in all the Hebrew alphabets follows it. Dr. Lightfoot offers this conjecture, that the letter *ajin,* which is the numeral letter for LXX, by being displaced, put them in mind of the seventy years at the end of which God would turn again their captivity.

V. The use of it to the pious Jews in their sufferings, furnishing them with spiritual language to express their natural grief, helping to preserve the remembrance of Zion among them, when they were in Babylon. They are here taught to mourn for sin and mourn to God.

MATTHEW HENRY

CHAPTER 1

Verses 1–11

I. The miseries of Jerusalem.

1. As to their civil state. (1) A city that was populous is now depopulated, *v.* 1. She was full of her own people that replenished her, and full of the people of other nations that resorted to her, with whom she had profitable commerce, but now her own people are carried into captivity, and she *sits solitary.* The *chief places of the city* are not now, as they used to be, *places of concourse. How has she become as a widow!* Her king that was as a husband to her is gone; her God has departed from her; she is emptied of her children, is solitary and sorrowful as a widow. (2) A city that had dominion is now in subjection. She had been *great among the nations,* greatly loved by some and greatly feared by others. Some made her presents, and others paid her taxes; so that she was really *princess among the provinces.* But now she has not only lost her friends and *sits solitary,* but has lost her freedom and sits *tributary;* she paid tribute to Egypt first and then to Babylon. Sin brings a people not only into solitude, but into slavery. (3) A city that used to be full of mirth has now become full of grief. Jerusalem had been a joyous city, whither the tribes went to rejoice before the Lord: she was *the joy of the whole earth,* but now *she weeps sorely,* she weeps *in the night,* in silence and solitude; *in the night,* when others rest, her thoughts are intent upon her troubles. Her head is—*as waters, and her eyes fountains of tears,* so that she *weeps day and night* (Jer. ix. 1); *her tears are* continually *on her cheeks.* (4) Those that were separated from the heathen now *dwell among the heathen;* those that were a peculiar people are now a mingled people (*v.* 3): *Judah has gone into captivity,* out of her own land into the land of her enemies, among those that are aliens to God and the covenants of promise, with whom *she finds no rest.* "*Her children have gone into captivity before the enemy;* those that were to have been the seed of the next generation are carried off; so that the land is likely to be still desolate for want of heirs." Those that dwell among their own people, a free people, and in their own land, would be more thankful for

JAMIESON, FAUSSET, BROWN

CHAPTER 1

Vss. 1-22. *Aleph,* א. **1. how is she . . . widow! she that was great . . .**—*English Version* is according to the accents. But the members of each sentence are better balanced in antithesis, thus, "how is she that was great among the nations become as a widow! (how) she who was princess among the provinces (i.e., she who ruled over the surrounding provinces from the Nile to the Euphrates, Gen. 15: 18; I Kings 4:21; II Chron. 9:26; Ezra 4:20) become tributary!" [MAURER]. **sit**—on the ground; the posture of mourners (ch. 2:10; Ezra 9:3). The coin struck on the taking of Jerusalem by Titus, representing Judea as a female sitting solitary under a palm tree, with the inscription, *Judæa Capta,* singularly corresponds to the image here; the language therefore must be prophetical of her state subsequent to Titus, as well as referring retrospectively to her Babylonian captivity. *Beth,* ב. **2. in the night**—even in the night, the period of rest and oblivion of griefs (Job 7:3). **lovers . . . friends**—the heathen states allied to Judah, and their idols. The idols whom she "loved" (Jer. 2:20-25) *could* not comfort her. Her former allies *would* not: nay, some "treacherously" joined her enemies against her (II Kings 24:2, 7; Ps. 137:7). *Gimel,* ג. **3.** (Jer. 52: 27.) **because of great servitude**—i.e., in a state "of great servitude," endured from the Chaldeans. "Because" is made by VATABLUS indicative of the *cause* of her captivity; viz., her having "afflicted" and unjustly brought into "servitude" the manumitted bond-servants (Jer. 34:8-22). MAURER explains it, "Judah has *left her land* (not literally "gone into captivity") because of the yoke imposed on it by Nebuchadnezzar." **no rest**—(Deut. 28:64, 65).

ADAM CLARKE

CHAPTER 1

In all copies of the Septuagint the following words are found as a part of the text: "And it came to pass after Israel had been carried away captive, and Jerusalem was become desolate, that Jeremiah sat weeping: and he lamented with this lamentation over Jerusalem; and he said." I subjoin another taken from the first printed edition of the English Bible, that by Coverdale, 1535. "And it came to passe, (after Israel was brought into captyvitie, and Jerusalem destroyed;) that Jeremy the prophet sat weeping, mournynge, and makinge his mone in Jerusalem; so that with an hevy herte he sighed and sobbed, sayenge."

1. *How doth the city sit solitary!* Sitting down, with the elbow on the knee, and the head supported by the hand, without any company, unless an oppressor near—all these were signs of mourning and distress. The coin struck by Vespasian on the capture of Jerusalem, on the obverse of which there is a palm tree, the emblem of Judea, and under it a woman, the emblem of Jerusalem, sitting, leaning as before described, with the legend *Judea capta,* illustrates this expression as well as that in Isa. xlvii. 1. *Become as a widow.* Having lost her king. Cities are commonly described as the mothers of their inhabitants, the kings as husbands, and the princes as children. When therefore they are bereaved of these, they are represented as widows, and childless.

2. *Among all her lovers.* Her allies; her friends, instead of helping her, have helped her enemies. Several who sought her friendship when she was in prosperity, in the time of David and Solomon, are now among her enemies.

MATTHEW HENRY

mercies if they would but consider the miseries of those forced into strange countries. (5) Those that used to conquer are now conquered. *All her persecutors overlook her between the straits* (*v.* 3); so that her people unavoidably *fell into the hand of the enemy*, for there was no way to escape (*v.* 7). Everywhere *her adversaries are the chief and her enemies prosper* (*v.* 5). (6) Those that had been a dignified people, on whom God had put honour, and to whom their neighbours had paid respect, are now brought into contempt (*v.* 8): *All that honoured her* before *despise her*. They have vilified themselves by their sins: *The enemies magnify themselves* against them (*v.* 9). *Sin is the reproach of any people*. (7) Those that lived in a fruitful land were ready to perish for want of necessary food (*v.* 11): *All her people sigh* in despondency and despair. There was *no bread for the people of the land* (Jer. lii. 6), and in their captivity they had much ado to get bread, *ch.* v. 6. *They have given their pleasant things for meat to relieve the soul*, or (as the margin is) *to make the soul come again*, when they were ready to faint away.

2. An account of their miseries in their ecclesiastical state. (1) Their religious feasts were no more observed (*v.* 4): *The ways of Zion do mourn;* overgrown with weeds. *The solemn feasts* had been neglected and profaned (Isa. i. 11, 12), and therefore justly is an end now put to them. And, as *the ways of Zion mourned*, so *the gates of Zion*, in which the faithful worshippers used to meet, *are desolate*. (2) *Her priests sigh* for the desolations of the temple; their songs are turned into sighs. In the day of Zion's prosperity, Ps. lxviii. 25, *Among them were the damsels playing with timbrels*, and notice is taken of the failing now. *Her virgins are afflicted*, and therefore *she is in bitterness*; that is, all the inhabitants of Zion are *sorrowful for the solemn assembly*, and to them *the reproach of it is a burden*, Zeph. iii. 18. (3) Their religious places were profaned (*v.* 10): *The heathen entered into her sanctuary*, into the temple itself, into which no Israelite was permitted to enter, though ever so reverently and devoutly, but the priests only. The heathen now crowd rudely in, not to worship, but to plunder. (4) All the rich things with which the temple was adorned, and which were made use of in the worship of God, were a prey to the enemy (*v.* 10): *The adversary has spread out his hand upon all her pleasant things*. What these pleasant things are we may learn from Isa. lxiv. 11, where, to the complaint of the burning of the temple, it is added, *All our pleasant things are laid waste;* the ark and the altar, and all the other tokens of God's presence with them, pleasant above any other things, were now broken to pieces and carried away. Thus from *the daughter of Zion all her beauty has departed*, *v.* 6. *The beauty of holiness* was the *beauty of the daughter of Zion;* when the temple, that holy and beautiful house, was destroyed, her beauty was gone. (5) Their religious days were made a jest of (*v.* 7): *The adversaries saw her, and did mock at her sabbaths*. They laughed at them for observing one day in seven as a day of rest. Juvenal ridicules the Jews for losing a seventh part of their time:

——cui septima quæque fuit lux
Ignava et vitæ partem non attigit ullam—
They keep their sabbaths to their cost,
For thus one day in sev'n is lost;

whereas sabbaths, if they be sanctified as they ought to be, will turn to a better account than all the days of the week besides. And whereas the Jews professed that they did it in obedience to their God, their adversaries asked them, "What profit have you in keeping the ordinances of your God, who now deserts you in your distress?" (6) Her state at present was just the reverse of what it had been formerly, *v.* 7. Now, *in the days of affliction and misery*, when everything was dismal and black, *she remembers all her pleasant things that she had in the days of old*. God often makes us know the worth of mercies by the want of them.

II. The sins of Jerusalem are the cause of all these calamities. It is *the Lord* that *has afflicted her* (*v.* 5) and he had done it as a righteous Judge, for *she has sinned*. Are her troubles many? Her sins are many more. See Jer. xxx. 14. They are heinous (*v.* 8): *Jerusalem has grievously sinned*, has *sinned sin* (so the word is), sinned wilfully, deliberately. Jerusalem, that makes such a profession and enjoys such privileges, *sinned grievously* (*v.* 8), and therefore (*v.* 9) she *came down wonderfully*. They have been oppressive and therefore are justly oppressed (*v.* 3): *Judah has gone into captivity*, and it is *because of affliction and great servitude*, because the rich among them afflicted the poor, and particularly (as the Chaldee paraphrases it) because they had oppressed their Hebrew servants,

JAMIESON, FAUSSET, BROWN

overtook her between . . . straits—image from robbers, who in the East intercept travellers at the narrow passes in hilly regions.

He, ה. **5. the chief**—rule her (Deut. 28:43, 44). **adversaries . . . prosper; for the Lord**—All the foes' attempts would have failed, had not God delivered His people into their hands (Jer. 30:15).

Daleth, ד. **4. feasts**—the passover, pentecost (or the feast of weeks), and the feast of tabernacles. **gates**—once the place of concourse.

Jod, י. **10. for**–*surely* she hath seen . . . . **heathen . . . command . . . not enter . . . congregation**—for instance, the Ammonites and Moabites (Deut. 23:3; Neh. 13:1, 2). If the heathen, as such, were not allowed to enter the sanctuary for worship, much less were they allowed to enter in order to rob and destroy.

Vau, ו. **6. beauty . . . departed**—her temple, throne, and priesthood. **harts that find no pasture**—an animal timid and fleet, especially when seeking and not able to "find pasture."

mock at her sabbaths—The heathen used to mock at the Jews' Sabbath, as showing their idleness, and term them *Sabbatarians* (MARTIAL, 4.4). Now, said they ironically, ye may keep a continuous Sabbath. So God appointed the length of the captivity (seventy years) to be exactly that of the sum of the Sabbaths in the 490 years in which the land was denied its Sabbaths (Lev. 26:33-35). MAURER translates it "ruin." But *English Version* better expresses the point of their "mocking," viz., their involuntary "Sabbaths," i.e., the *cessation* of all national movements. A fourth line is added in this stanza, whereas in all the others there are but three. So in Elegy 2:19.

Zain, ז. **7. remembered**—rather, "remembers," now, in her afflicted state. In the days of her prosperity she did not appreciate, as she ought, the favors of God to her. Now, awakening out of her past lethargy, she feels from what high privileges she has fallen. **when her people fell . . .**—i.e., after which days of prosperity "her people fell."

ADAM CLARKE

3. *Between the straits*. She has been brought into such difficulties that it was impossible for her to escape. Has this any reference to the circumstances in which Zedekiah and the princes of Judah endeavored to escape from Jerusalem, "by the way of the gate between the two walls" Jer. lii. 7?

4. *The ways of Zion do mourn*. The ways in which the people trod coming to the sacred solemnities, being now no longer frequented, are represented as shedding tears; and the gates themselves partake of the general distress.

7. *Did mock at her sabbaths. Mishbatteha*. Some contend that *sabbaths* are not intended here. The Septuagint has "her habitation."

MATTHEW HENRY

which is charged upon them, Jer. xxxiv. 11. They all *despise her* (*v.* 8), for *her filthiness is in her skirts*; she has rolled them in the mire of sin.

III. Jerusalem's friends are here complained of as false and unkind: They *have all dealt treacherously with her* (*v.* 2), so that, in effect, *they have become her enemies. Her princes are like harts*, that, upon the first alarm, betake themselves to flight. They *are like harts*, famished for want of *pasture*, and therefore *are gone without strength before the pursuer*. Her neighbours are unneighbourly. There is none *to help her* (*v.* 7). *She has no comforter*, none to sympathize, or alleviate her griefs, *v.* 7, 9.

IV. Jerusalem's God is here besought, and all is referred to his compassionate consideration (*v.* 9): "*O Lord! behold my affliction*," and (*v.* 11), "*See, O Lord! and consider*." The only way to make ourselves easy under our burdens is to cast them upon God first, and leave it to him to do with us as seemeth him good.

Verses 12–22

In these verses the prophet, in the name of the lamenting church, does more particularly acknowledge the hand of God in these calamities, and the righteousness of his hand.

I. The church in distress here magnifies her affliction. She appeals to all spectators: *See if there be any sorrow like unto my sorrow*, *v.* 12. This might perhaps be truly said of Jerusalem's griefs; but we are apt to apply it too sensibly to ourselves when we are in trouble. If our troubles were to be thrown into a common stock with those of others, and then an equal dividend made, share and share alike, we should each of us say, "Pray, give me my own again."

II. She here looks beyond the instruments to the author of her troubles: "It is *the Lord* that *has afflicted me*, and he has *afflicted me* because he is angry with me; it is *in the day of his fierce anger*," *v.* 12. She is as one in a fever: "*He has sent fire into my bones*" (*v.* 13). She is as one in a net, which the more he struggles to get out the more he is entangled. She is as one in a wilderness, whose way is solitary: "*He has turned me back*, that I cannot go on, *has made me desolate*, that I have nothing to support me with, but am *faint all the day*." She is as one in a yoke, not yoked for service, but for penance (*v.* 14): *The yoke of my transgressions is bound by his hand.* The yoke of Christ's commands is an *easy yoke* (Matt. xi. 30), but that of our own transgressions is a heavy one. When conscience, as his deputy, binds us over to his judgment, then *the yoke is bound* and *wreathed by the hand* of his justice, and nothing but the hand of his pardoning mercy will unbind it. He it is that has *trodden under foot all her mighty men*, *v.* 15. She is as one in a wine-press, and it is God that has thus *trodden the virgin, the daughter of Judah*. She is in the hand of her enemies, and it is the Lord that has delivered her *into their hands* (*v.* 14). He that has many a time *commanded deliverances for Jacob* (Ps. xliv. 4) now commands an invasion against Jacob, because Jacob has disobeyed the commands of his law.

III. She justly demands a share in the compassion of those that were the spectators of her misery (*v.* 12): "*Is it nothing to you, all you that pass by?* Can you look upon me without concern? Is it nothing to you that your neighbour's house is on fire?"

IV. She justifies her own grief (*v.* 16): "*For these things I weep*, I weep in the night (*v.* 2), when none sees; *my eye, my eye, runs down with water*." *Zion spreads forth her hands* (*v.* 17), which is here an expression rather of despair than of desire. Her God has withdrawn from her. It is no marvel that the souls of the saints faint away, when God, who is the only Comforter that can relieve them, keeps at a distance. Her children are removed from her, and are in no capacity to help her: they cannot help themselves, and how should they help her? Both the damsels and the youths, that were her joy and hope; *have gone into captivity*, *v.* 18. Her friends failed her, some would not and others could not give her any relief. She *spread forth her hands*, as begging relief, but *there is none to comfort her* (*v.* 17). Her idols were her lovers. Egypt and Assyria were her confidants. But they deceived her. The *priests* and the *elders*, that should have appeared at the head of affairs, died for hunger (*v.* 19); or went begging for bread to keep them alive. *Abroad the sword bereaves* and slays all that comes in its way, and *at home* all provisions are cut off by the besiegers, so that *there is as death*, that is, famine. The enemies, that were the instruments of the calamity, were barbarous, so were those that were the standers by, the Edomites and Ammonites, that bore ill will to Israel: They have *heard of my trouble, and are glad that thou hast done it* (*v.* 21). It pleases them to find that God and his Israel have fallen out.

JAMIESON, FAUSSET, BROWN

Cheth, ח. **8.** (I Kings 8:46.) **is removed**—as a woman separated from the congregation of God for legal impurity, which is a type of moral impurity. So vs. 17; Lev. 12:2; 15:19, etc. **her nakedness**—They have treated her as contumeliously as courtesans from whom their clothes are stripped. **turneth backward**—as modest women do from shame, i.e., she is cast down from all hope of restoration [CALVIN]. *Teth*, ט. **9.** Continuation of the image in vs. 8. Her ignominy and misery cannot be concealed but are apparent to all, as if a woman were suffering under such a flow as to reach the end of her skirts. **remembereth not . . . last end**—(Deut. 32:29; Isa. 47:7). She forgot how fatal must be the end of her iniquity. Or, as the words following imply: She, in despair, cannot lift herself up to lay hold of God's promises as to her "latter end" [CALVIN]. **wonderfully**—*Hebrew*, "wonders," i.e., with amazing dejection. **O Lord, behold**—Judah here breaks in, speaking for herself. **for the enemy hath magnified himself**—What might seem ground for despair, the elated insulting of the enemy, is rather ground for good hope. *Caph*, כ. **11.** (Jer. 37:21; 38:9; 52:6.) **given . . . pleasant things for meat**—(II Kings 6:25; Job 2:4). **relieve . . . soul**—lit., to cause the soul or life to return. **for I am become vile**—Her sins and consequent sorrows are made the plea in craving God's mercy. Cf. the like plea in Psalm 25:11. *Lamed*, ל. **12.** The pathetic appeal of Jerusalem, not only to her neighbors, but even to the strangers "passing by," as her sorrow is such as should excite the compassion even of those unconnected with her. She here prefigures Christ, whom the language is prophetically made to suit, more than Jerusalem. Cf. Israel, i.e., Messiah, Isaiah 49:3. Cf. with "pass by," Matthew 27:39; Mark 15:29. As to Jerusalem, Daniel 9:12. MAURER, from the *Arabic* idiom, translates, "do not go off on your way," i.e., stop, whoever ye are that pass by. *English Version* is simpler. *Mem*, מ. **13. bones**—a fire which not only consumes the skin and flesh, but penetrates even to my "bones" (i.e., my vital powers). **prevaileth against**—not as ROSENMULLER, "He (Jehovah) hath *broken* them"; a sense not in the *Hebrew*. **net**—(Ezek. 12:13); image from hunting wild beasts. He has so entangled me in His judgments that I cannot escape. **turned me back**—so that I cannot go forward and get free from His meshes. *Nun*, נ. **14. yoke . . . is bound by his hand**—(Deut. 28:48). Metaphor from husbandmen, who, after they have bound the yoke to the neck of oxen, hold the rein firmly twisted *round the hand*. Thus the translation will be, "*in* His hand." Or else, "the yoke of my transgressions" (i.e., of punishment for my transgressions) is held so fast fixed on me "*by*" God, that there is no loosening of it; thus *English Version*, "*by* His hand." **wreathed**—My sins are like the withes *entwined* about the neck to fasten the yoke to. **into their hands, from whom**—into the hands of those, from whom . . . . MAURER translates, "*before* whom I am not able to stand." *Samech*, ס **15. trodden . . .**—MAURER, from *Syriac* root, translates, "cast away"; so II Kings 23:27. But Psalm 119:118, supports *English Version*. **in . . . midst of me**—They fell not on the battlefield, but in the heart of the city; a sign of the divine wrath. **assembly**—the collected forces of Babylon; a very different "assembly" from the solemn ones which once met at Jerusalem on the great feasts. **The *Hebrew* means**, lit., such a solemn **"assembly" or feast** (cf. ch. 2:22). **trodden . . . virgin . . . in a wine-press**—hath forced her blood to burst forth, as the red wine from the grapes trodden in the press (Isa. 63:3; Rev. 14:19, 20; 19:15). *Ain*, ע. **16.** (Jer. 13:17; 14:17.) Jerusalem is the speaker. **mine eye, mine eye**—so ch. 4:18, "our end . . . our end"; repetition for emphasis. *Pe*, פ. **17.** Like a woman in labor-throes (Jer. 4:31). **menstruous woman**—held unclean, and shunned by all; separated from her husband and **from** the temple (cf. vs. 8; Lev. 14:19, etc.).

ADAM CLARKE

11. *They have given their pleasant things.* Jerusalem is compared to a woman brought into great straits, who parts with her jewels and trinkets in order to purchase by them the necessaries of life.

12. *Is it nothing to you, all ye that pass by?* The desolations and distress brought upon this city and its inhabitants had scarcely any parallel. Excessive abuse of God's accumulated mercies calls for singular and exemplary punishment.

14. *The yoke of my transgressions.* I am now tied and bound by the chain of my sins; and it is so wreathed, so doubled and twisted around me, that I cannot free myself. A fine representation of the miseries of a penitent soul, which feels that nothing but the pitifulness of God's mercy can loose it.

15. *Called an assembly.* The Chaldean army, composed of various nations, which God commissioned to destroy Jerusalem.

17. *Zion spreadeth forth her hands.* Extending the hands is the form in supplication. *Jerusalem is as a menstruous woman.* To whom none dared to approach, either to help or comfort, because of the law, Lev. xv. 19-27.

MATTHEW HENRY

V. She justifies God, acknowledging that her sins had deserved these chastenings. The yoke that lies so heavily, and binds so hard, is *the yoke of her transgressions, v.* 14. It is with our own rod that we are beaten. She owns the equity of God's actions, by owning the iniquity of her own: *I have rebelled against his commandments* (*v.* 18); and again (*v.* 20), *I have grievously rebelled.* We cannot speak ill enough of sin, and we must always speak worst of our own sin, must call it *rebellion, grievous rebellion.* Sorrow for sin must be great sorrow and must affect the soul.

VI. She appeals both to the mercy and to the justice of God in her present case. *Behold, O Lord! for I am in distress.* She appeals to the justice of God concerning the injuries that her enemies did her (*v.* 21, 22): "*Thou wilt bring the day that thou hast called,* the day that is fixed in the counsels of God and published in the prophecies, when my enemies *shall be like unto me,* when the cup of trembling, now put into my hands, shall be put into theirs." It may be read as a prayer, "Let the day appointed come," and so it goes on, "*Let their wickedness come before thee;* hasten the time when thou wilt *do to them* for their transgressions *as thou hast done to me* for mine." This prayer amounts to a protestation against all thoughts of a coalition with them. Our prayers must agree with God's word; and though we are bound in charity to forgive our enemies, and to pray for them, yet we may in faith pray for the accomplishment of that which God has spoken against his and his church's enemies.

JAMIESON, FAUSSET, BROWN

Tzaddi, צ.
18. The sure sign of repentance; justifying God, condemning herself (Neh. 9:33; Ps. 51:4; Dan. 9:7-14). **his commandment**—lit., "mouth"; His word in the mouth of the prophets. *Koph,* ק. **19. lovers**—(vs. 2; Jer. 30:14). **elders**—in dignity, not merely age. **sought . . . meat**—Their dignity did not exempt them from having to go and seek bread (vs. 11). *Resh,* ר. **20. bowels . . . troubled**—(Job 30:27; Isa 16:11; Jer. 4:19; 31:20). Extreme mental distress affects the bowels and the whole internal frame. **heart . . . turned**—(Hos. 11:8); is agitated or fluttered. **abroad . . . sword . . . at home . . . as death**—(Deut. 32:25; Ezek. 7:15). The "as" does not modify, but intensifies. "Abroad the sword bereaveth, at home *as it were death itself*" (personified), in the form of famine and pestilence (II Kings 25:3; Jer. 14:18; 52:6). So Habakkuk 2:5, "as death" (MICHAELIS]. *Schin,* ש. **21. they are glad that thou hast done it**—because they thought that therefore Judah is irretrievably ruined (Jer. 40:3). **the day . . . called**—(but) thou wilt bring on them the day of calamity which thou hast *announced,* viz., by the prophets (Jer. 50; 48:27). **like . . . me**—in calamities (Ps. 137:8, 9; Jer. 51:25, etc.). *Tau,* ת. **22.** Such prayers against foes are lawful, if the foe be an enemy of God, and if our concern be not for our own personal feeling, but for the glory of God and the welfare of His people. **come before thee**—so Revelation 16:19, "Babylon *came* in remembrance *before God*" (cf. Ps. 109:15).

ADAM CLARKE

19. *I called for my lovers.* My allies; the Egyptians and others.

20. *Abroad the sword bereaveth.* War is through the country, *and at home . . . death;* the pestilence and famine rage in the city; calamity in every shape is fallen upon me.

21. *They have heard that I sigh.* My affliction is public enough, but no one comes to comfort me. *They are glad that thou hast done it.* On the contrary, they exult in my misery; and they see that Thou hast done what they were incapable of performing. *Thou wilt bring the day that thou hast called, and they shall be like unto me.* Babylon shall be visited in her turn, and Thy judgments poured out upon her shall equal her state with my own. See the last six chapters of the preceding prophecy for the accomplishment of this prediction.

22. *Let all their wickedness come before thee.* That is, Thou wilt call their crimes also into remembrance; and Thou wilt do unto them by siege, sword, famine, and captivity what Thou hast done to me. Though Thy judgments, because of Thy long-suffering, are slow, yet because of thy righteousness they are sure. Imprecations in the sacred writings are generally to be understood as declarative of the evils they indicate, or that such evils will take place. No prophet of God ever wished desolation on those against whom he was directed to prophesy.

MATTHEW HENRY

CHAPTER 2

Verses 1–9

A very sad representation is here made of the state of God's church, of Jacob and Israel, of Zion and Jerusalem; but the emphasis in these verses seems to be laid all along upon the hand of God. The grief is that God appears angry with them; it is he that chastens them, and chastens them *in his displeasure.*

I. Time was when God's delight was in his church, and he appeared to her as a friend. But now he is angry with her, and appears against her as an enemy. To those who know how to value God's favour nothing appears more dreadful than his finger; corrections in love are easily borne, but rebukes in love wound deeply. It is God's wrath that *burns against Jacob like a flaming fire* (*v.* 3), but it was their sin that kindled this fire. God is such a tender Father to his children that we may be sure he is never angry with them but when they give him cause to be angry. Now he is an enemy to them; at least he is *as an enemy, v.* 5. He has *bent his bow like an enemy, v.* 4. He stood *with his right hand* stretched out against them, and a sword drawn in it *as an adversary.* God is not really an enemy to his people, no, not when he is angry with them and corrects them in anger. But sometimes he is *as an enemy* to them, when all his providences concerning them seem in outward appearance to have a tendency to their ruin. But, blessed be God, Christ is *our peace,* our peacemaker, who has slain the enmity.

II. Time was when God's church appeared very bright, and considerable among the nations; but now *the Lord has covered the daughter of Zion with a cloud* (*v.* 1), a dark cloud, through which she cannot see his face; *a thick cloud* (so the word signifies), a *black cloud,* not such as that under which God conducted them through the wilderness, or that in which God took possession of the temple and filled it with his glory: no, that side of the cloud is now turned towards them which was turned towards the Egyptians in the Red Sea. He *turned back their right hand,* so that they were not able to ward off the blow which was given them. What can their right hand do against the enemy when God draws it back, and withers it, as he did Jeroboam's?

III. Time was when Jerusalem and the cities of Judah were strong and well fortified. But now the Lord has in anger *swallowed them up.* They are so totally ruined that they seem to have been *swallowed up.* He has *swallowed up all her palaces* (*v.* 5), though those were stately, and strong, rich and well guarded. He has destroyed not only their dwelling-places, but their *strongholds.* Thus has he *increased in the daughter of Judah mourning and lamentation,* when they saw all their defence departed from them. This is again insisted on, *v.* 7–9. He has *given up into the hand of the enemy the walls of her palaces.* The walls of palaces cannot protect them, unless God himself be a wall of fire round about them. Whatever desolations God makes in his church, they are all according to his

JAMIESON, FAUSSET, BROWN

CHAPTER 2

Vss. 1-22. *Aleph,* א. **1. How**—The title of the collection repeated here, and in Elegy 4:1.

Gimel, ג. **3. horn**—worn in the East as an ornament on the forehead, and an emblem of power and majesty (I Sam. 2:10; Ps. 132:17; Jer. 48:25, *Note*). **drawn back . . . right hand**—(Ps. 74:11). God has withdrawn the help which He before gave them. Not as HENDERSON, "He has turned back his (*Israel's*) right hand" (Ps. 89:43). *Daleth,* ד. **4.** (Isa. 63:10.) **stood with . . . right hand**—He took His stand so as to use His right hand as an adversary. HENDERSON makes the image to be that of an archer *steadying* his right hand to take aim. Not only did He *withdraw* His help, but also took arms against Israel.

covered . . . with a cloud—i.e., with the darkness of ignominy. **cast down from heaven unto . . . earth**—(Matt. 11:23); dashed down from the highest prosperity to the lowest misery.

He, ה
5. an enemy—(Jer. 30:14). **mourning and lamentation**—There is a play of similar sounds in the original, "sorrow and sadness," to heighten the effect (Job 30:3, *Hebrew;* Ezek. 35:3, *Margin*).

ADAM CLARKE

CHAPTER 2

3. *The horn of Israel.* His power and strength. It is a metaphor taken from cattle, whose principal strength lies in their horns. *Hath drawn back his right hand.* He did not support us when our enemies came against us.

4. *He hath bent his bow . . . he stood with his right hand.* This is the attitude of the archer. He first bends his bow; then sets his arrow upon the string; and, lastly, placing his right hand on the lower end of the arrow, in connection with the string, takes his aim, and prepares to let fly.

1. *How hath the Lord covered the daughter of Zion with a cloud!* The women in the Eastern countries wear veils, and often very costly ones. Here Zion is represented as being veiled by the hand of God's judgment. And what is the veil? A dark cloud, by which she is entirely obscured.

2. *The Lord hath swallowed up.* It is a strange figure when thus applied, but Jehovah is here represented as having swallowed down Jerusalem and all the cities and fortifications in the land; that is, He has permitted them to be destroyed. See v. 5.

MATTHEW HENRY

counsels. But, when it is done, he has *stretched out a line*, a measuring line, to do it exactly and by measure: hitherto the destruction shall go, and no further.

IV. Time was when their government flourished, and the balance of power was on their side; but now it is otherwise: *He has polluted the kingdom and the princes thereof*, *v.* 2. They had first polluted themselves with their idolatries, and then God dealt with them as with polluted things. No marvel that the king and the priest, whose characters were always deemed venerable and inviolable, are despised by everybody, when God has, *in the indignation of his anger, despised the king and the priest*, *v.* 6. The crown has fallen from their heads, for *her king and her princes are among the Gentiles*, prisoners among them (*v.* 9), and treated as the basest, without any regard to their character. It is just with God to debase those by his judgments who have by sin debased themselves.

V. Time was when the ordinances of God were administered in their purity, and they had those tokens of God's presence with them; but now that part of the *beauty of Israel* was gone which was indeed their greatest beauty. The ark was God's footstool, under the mercy-seat, between the cherubim; this was of all others the most sacred symbol of God's presence (it is called his *footstool*, 1 Chron. xxviii. 2; Ps. xcix. 5; cxxxii. 7); there the Shechinah rested, but now he *remembered not his footstool*. The ark itself was suffered, as it should seem, to fall into the hands of the Chaldeans. Of what little value are the tokens of his presence when his presence is gone! God and his kingdom can stand without that footstool. Those that ministered in holy things had been *pleasant to the eye in the tabernacle of the daughter of Zion* (*v.* 4); they had been *purer than snow, whiter than milk* (*ch.* iv. 7). But now these are slain, and their *blood is mingled with their sacrifices*. The temple was God's tabernacle (as the tabernacle, while that was in being, was called *his temple*, Ps. xxvii. 4) and this *he has violently taken away* (*v.* 6); he has plucked up the stakes of it and cut the cords; it shall be no more a tabernacle, much less his. When men profane God's tabernacle it is just with him to take it from them. He has now *abhorred his sanctuary* (*v.* 7); it has been defiled with sin, that only thing which he hates, and for the sake of that he abhors even his sanctuary, which he had delighted in and called *his rest for ever*, Ps. cxxxii. 14. Some, by the *places of the assembly* (*v.* 6), understand not only the temple, but the synagogues, and the schools of the prophets, which the enemy had *burnt up*, Ps. lxxiv. 8. The solemn feasts and the sabbaths had been carefully remembered, but now the Lord has *caused those to be forgotten* even in Zion itself. Now that Zion was in ruins no difference was made between sabbath time and other times; every day was a day of mourning, so that all the *solemn feasts were forgotten*. The altar that had sanctified their gifts is now cast off, for God will no more accept their gifts, nor be honoured by their sacrifices, *v.* 7. The altar was *the table of the Lord*, but God will no longer keep house among them; he will neither feast them nor feast with them. They had been blest with prophets and teachers of the law; but now *the law is no more* (*v.* 9); it is no more read by the people, no more expounded by the scribes; the tables of the law are gone with the ark; the book of the law is taken from them. *Her prophets also find no vision from the Lord*. They had persecuted God's prophets, and despised the visions they had from the Lord, and therefore it is just with God to say that they shall have no more prophets, no more visions.

Verses 10–22

Justly are these called *Lamentations*, the expressions of grief in perfection, like the contents of Ezekiel's roll, Ezek. ii. 10.

I. Copies of lamentations are here presented and they are painted to the life. 1. The judges and magistrates, who used to appear in robes of state, are stripped of them, and put on the habit of mourners (*v.* 10); the elders now sit no longer in the judgment-seats, the *thrones of the house of David*, but they *sit upon the ground*. They *keep silence*, overwhelmed with grief, and not knowing what to say. They have *cast dust upon their heads, and girded themselves with sackcloth*. 2. *The virgins of Jerusalem hang down their heads to the ground;* those know sorrow who were always disposed to be merry. 3. The prophet himself is a pattern to the mourners, *v.* 11. His *eyes do fail with tears;* he has wept till he can weep no more; wept himself blind. Jeremiah himself had better treatment than his neighbours, better than he had had before from his own countrymen; their destruction was his deliverance, and yet his private interests are swallowed up in a concern for the public,

JAMIESON, FAUSSET, BROWN

Cheth, ח. **8. stretched . . . a line**—The Easterns used a measuring-line not merely in building, but in destroying edifices (II Kings 21:13; Isa. 34:11); implying here the unsparing rigidness with which He would exact punishment.

Beth, ב. **2. polluted**—by delivering it into the hands of the profane foe. Cf. Psalm 89: 39, "*profaned . . . crown*."

Teth, ט. **9.** Her gates cannot oppose the entrance of the foe into the city, for they are sunk under a mass of rubbish and earth. **broken . . . bars**—(Jer. 51:30). **her king . . . among . . . Gentiles**—(Deut. 28:36).

Aleph, א. **1. beauty of Israel**—the beautiful temple (Ps. 29:2; 74:7; 96:9, *Margin;* Isa. 60:7; 64: 11). **his footstool**—the ark (cf. I Chron. 28:2, with Ps. 99:5; 132:7). They once had gloried more in the ark than in the God whose symbol it was; they now feel it was but His "footstool," yet that it had been a great glory to them that God deigned to use it as such.

Daleth, ד. **4. all . . . pleasant to . . . eye**—(Ezek. 24:25). All that were conspicuous for youth, beauty, and rank. **in . . . tabernacle**—the dwellings of Jerusalem.

Vau, ו. **6. tabernacle**—rather, "He hath violently taken away His *hedge* (the hedge of the place sacred to Him, Ps. 80:12; 89:40; Isa. 5:5), as that of a garden" [MAURER]. CALVIN supports *English Version*, "His tabernacle (i.e., temple) as (one would take away the temporary cottage or booth) of a garden." Isaiah 1:8 accords with this (Job 27:18). **places of . . . assembly**—the temple and synagogues (Ps. 74:7, 8). **solemn feasts**—(ch. 1:4).

Zain, ז. **7. they . . . made a noise in . . . house of . . . Lord, as in . . . feast**—The foe's shout of triumph in the captured temple bore a resemblance (but oh, how sad a contrast as to the *occasion* of it!) to the joyous thanksgivings we used to offer in the same place at our "solemn feasts" (cf. vs. 22).

Teth, ט. **9. law . . . no more**—(II Chron. 15:3). The civil and religious laws were one under the theocracy. "All the legal ordinances (prophetical as well as priestly) of the theocracy, are no more" (Ps. 74:9; Ezek. 7:26).

Jod, י. **10.** (Job 2:12, 13.) The "elders," by their example, would draw the others to violent grief. **the virgins**—who usually are so anxious to set off their personal appearances to advantage. *Caph*, כ. **11. liver is poured . . .**—i.e., as the liver was thought to be the seat of the passions, *all my feelings are poured out and prostrated for . . . .* The "liver," is here put for the *bile* (see Job 16:13, "gall"; Ps. 22:14) in a bladder on the surface of the liver, copiously discharged when the passions are agitated.

ADAM CLARKE

8. *He hath stretched out a line*. The line of devastation, marking what was to be pulled down and demolished.

9. *Her gates are sunk into the ground*. The consequence of their being long thrown down and neglected. From this it appears that the Captivity had already lasted a considerable time. *Her king and her princes are among the Gentiles*. Zedekiah and many of the princes were then prisoners in Babylon, another proof that the Captivity had endured some time, unless all this be spoken prophetically of what should be done.

The beauty of Israel. His temple. *His footstool*. The ark of the covenant, often so called.

7. *They have made a noise in the house of the Lord*. Instead of the silver trumpets of the sanctuary, nothing but the sounds of warlike instruments are to be heard.

10. *Sit upon the ground*. See the note on chap. i. 1. *Keep silence*. No words can express their sorrows; small griefs are eloquent, great ones dumb.

MATTHEW HENRY

and he bewails the *destruction of the daughter of his people* as if he himself had been the greatest sufferer in that common calamity.

II. *The heart of the people cried unto the Lord, v.* 18. Some fear it was a cry of bitter complaint, but many of them did in sincerity cry unto God for mercy in their distress; and the prophet bids them go on to do so: "*O wall of the daughter of Zion!* either you that stand upon the wall, you *watchmen on the walls* (Isa. lxii. 6), or *because* of the *breaking down of the wall* (which was not done till about a month after the city was taken), let *the daughter of Zion lament* still." This was a thing which Nehemiah lamented long after, Neh. i. 3, 4. "*Let tears run down like a river day and night,* weep without intermission, give thyself no rest from weeping, *let not the apple of thy eye cease.*" The calamities would be continuing, and the causes of grief would recur, and fresh occasion be given them every day and every night to bemoan themselves. They would be apt, by degrees, to grow insensible, and would need to afflict their souls, till their proud and hard hearts were thoroughly humbled and softened.

III. Causes for lamentation are here assigned,

1. Multitudes perish by famine. God had corrected them by scarcity of provisions through want of rain some time before (Jer. xiv. 1), and now by the straitness of the siege God brought it upon them in extremity; for, The children died for hunger in their mothers' arms (*v.* 11). This is mentioned again (*v.* 19): *They faint for hunger in the top of every street.* There were little children that were slain by their mothers' hands and eaten, *v.* 20. The like was done in the siege of Samaria, 2 Kings vi. 29.

2. Multitudes fall by the sword, which devours one as well as another, especially when it is in the hand of such cruel enemies as the Chaldeans were. They spared no age, not those who, by reason of their tender or their decrepit age, were exempted from taking up the sword; for even they *perished by the sword.* They spared no sex: *My virgins and my young men have fallen by the sword.* This was the *Lord's doing.* But that which follows is very harsh: *Thou hast killed, and not pitied;* for his soul is *grieved for the misery of Israel.*

3. Their false prophets cheated them, *v.* 14. This was a thing which Jeremiah had lamented long before, and had observed with a great concern (Jer. xiv. 13): *Ah! Lord God, the prophets say unto them, You shall not see the sword;* and here he inserts it among his lamentations. Their visions were all their own fancies, and it is most likely that they themselves knew that the visions they pretended were counterfeit. The people set them up, told them what they should say, so that they were *prophets after their hearts.* Prophets should tell people of their faults, should show them their sins, that they may bring them to repentance, and so prevent their ruin; but these prophets knew that would lose them the people's affections and contributions. Therefore *they have not discovered thy iniquity*; though that might have been a means, by taking away their iniquity, to turn away their captivity.

4. Their neighbours laughed at them (*v.* 15): *All that pass by thee clap their hands at thee. Is this the city* (said they) *that men called the perfection of beauty?* (Ps. l. 2). How is it now the perfection of deformity! Where is all its beauty now?

5. Their enemies triumphed over them, *v.* 16. Those that wished ill to Jerusalem now *open their mouths,* nay, they widen them; they *hiss and gnash their teeth* in scorn and indignation. "*We have swallowed her up;* it is our doing, and it is our gain; it is all our own now. *Certainly this is the day that we have* long *looked for; we have found it; we have seen it; aha! so would we have it.*"

6. Their God, in all this, appeared against them (*v.* 17): *The Lord has done that which he had devised.* What God devises against his people is designed for them, and so it will be found in the issue. When he gave them his law by Moses he told them what judgments he would certainly inflict upon them if they transgressed that law; and now that they had been guilty of the transgression of this law he had executed the sentence of it, according to Lev. xxvi. 16, &c., Deut. xxviii. 15.

IV. Comforts for the cure of these lamentations are here sought for and prescribed. They are sought for, *v.* 13. The prophet seeks to find out some suitable acceptable words to say to her in this case: *Wherewith shall I comfort thee, O virgin! daughter of Zion?* We endeavour to comfort our friends by telling them their case is not singular; there are many whose trouble is greater than theirs; but Jerusalem's case will not admit this argument: "*What thing shall I liken to thee,* or *what shall I equal to thee, that I may comfort thee?* What city, what country, is there,

JAMIESON, FAUSSET, BROWN

Tzaddi, צ. **18. wall**–(vs. 8). Personified. "*Their* heart, i.e., the Jews'; while their heart is lifted up to the Lord in prayer, their speech is addressed to the "wall" (the part being put for *the whole city*). **let tears . . .**–(Jer. 14:17). The wall is called on to weep for its own ruin and that of the city. Cf. the similar personification (ch. 1:4). **apple**–the pupil of the eye (Ps. 17:8).

swoon–through faintness from the effects of hunger.

Lamed, ל. **12. as the wounded**–famine being as deadly as the sword (Jer. 52:6). **soul . . . poured . . . into . . . mother's bosom**–Instinctively turning to their mother's bosom, but finding no milk there, they *breathe out their life* as it were "into her bosom."

Nun, נ. **14. Thy prophets**–not God's (Jer. 23:26). **vain . . . for thee**–to gratify thy appetite, not for truth, but for false things. **not discovered thine iniquity**–in opposition to God's command to the true prophets (Isa. 58:1). Lit., *They have not taken off* the veil *which was on thine iniquity,* so as to set it before thee. **burdens**–Their prophecies were soothing and flattering; but the result of them was *heavy* calamities to the people, worse than even what the prophecies of Jeremiah, which they in derision called "burdens," threatened. Hence he terms their pretended prophecies "false burdens," which proved to the Jews "causes of their banishment" [CALVIN].

Samech, ס. **15. clap . . . hands**–in derision (Job 27:23; 34:37). **wag . . . head**–(II Kings 19:21; Ps. 44:14). **perfection of beauty . . . joy of . . . earth**–(Ps. 48:2; 50:2). The Jews' enemies quote their very words in scorn. *Pe,* פ. **16, 17.** For the transposition of *Hebrew* letters (*Pe* and *Ain*) in the order of verses, see *Introduction.* **opened . . . mouth**–as ravening, roaring wild beasts (Job 16:9, 10; Ps. 22:13). Herein Jerusalem was a type of Messiah. **gnash . . . teeth**–in vindictive malice. **we have seen it**–(Ps. 35:21).

Ain, ע. **17. Lord**–Let not the foe exult as if it was *their* doing. It was "the Lord" who thus fulfilled the threats uttered by His prophets for the guilt of Judea (Lev. 26:16-25; Deut. 28:36-48, 53; Jer. 19:9).

Mem מ. **13. What thing shall I take to witness**–What can I bring forward as a witness, or instance, to prove that others have sustained as grievous ills as thou? I cannot console thee as mourners are often consoled by showing that thy lot is only what others, too, suffer.

ADAM CLARKE

18. *O wall of the daughter of* Zion. These words are probably those of the passengers, who appear to be affected by the desolations of the land; and they address the people, and urge them to plead with God day and night for their restoration. *Let not the apple of thine eye cease. Bath ayin* means either the pupil of the eye or the tears. Tears are the produce of the eye, and are here elegantly termed "the daughter of the eye." Let not your tears cease.

11. *Swoon in the streets of the city.* Through the excess of the famine.

12. *When their soul was poured out into their mothers' bosom.* When, in endeavoring to draw nourishment from the breasts of their exhausted mothers, they breathed their last in their bosoms! How dreadfully afflicting was this!

14. *They have not discovered thine iniquity.* They did not reprove for sin; they flattered you in your transgressions; and instead of turning away your captivity, by turning you from your sins, they have pretended visions of good in your favor, and false burdens for your enemies.

15. *The perfection of beauty.* This probably applied only to the Temple. Jerusalem never was a fine or splendid city, but the Temple was most assuredly the most splendid building in the world.

16. *This is the day that we looked for.* Jerusalem was the envy of the surrounding nations; they longed for its destruction, and rejoiced when it took place.

17. *The Lord hath done that.* This and the sixteenth verse should be interchanged, to follow the order of the letters in the Hebrew alphabet; as the sixteenth has *phe* for its acrostic letter, and the seventeenth has *ain,* which should precede the other in the order of the alphabet.

13. *What thing shall I take?* Or, rather, as Dr. Blayney, "What shall I urge to thee?" How shall I comfort you?

MATTHEW HENRY

whose case is parallel to thine?" Alas! there is none, no sorrow like thine, because there is none whose honour was like thine. We tell them that their case is not desperate, but that it may easily be remedied; but neither will that be admitted here, upon a view of human probabilities; for *thy breach is great, like the sea*, like the breach which the sea sometimes makes upon the land, which cannot be repaired, but grows wider and wider. Thou art wounded, and *who shall heal thee?* No wisdom nor power of man can repair such a broken shattered state. It is to no purpose therefore to administer any of these common cordials. The method of cure prescribed is to address themselves to God, and by a penitent prayer to commit their case to him, and to be instant and constant in such prayers (*v.* 19): "*Arise* out of thy dust, out of thy despondency, *cry out in the night*, when others are asleep, be thou upon thy knees, importunate with God for mercy; *in the beginning of the watches*, of each of the four watches of the night, then *pour out thy heart like water before the Lord*, be free and full in prayer, be sincere and serious in prayer, open thy mind, spread thy case before the Lord; *lift up thy hands towards him* in holy desire and expectation; beg for *the life of thy young children*. These poor lambs, what have they done? Take with you words, take with you these words (*v.* 20), *Behold, O Lord! and consider to whom thou hast done this*. Are they not thy own, the seed of Abraham thy friend and of Jacob thy chosen? Lord, take their case into thy compassionate consideration!"

JAMIESON, FAUSSET, BROWN

The "sea" affords the only suitable emblem of thy woes, by its boundless extent and depth (ch. 1:12; Dan. 9:12). *Koph,* ק. **19. cry . . . in . . . night**—(Ps. 119:147.) **beginning of . . . watches**—i.e., the *first* of the three equal divisions (four hours each) into which the ancient Jews divided the night; viz., from sunset to ten o'clock. The second was called "the middle watch" (Judg. 7:19), from ten till two o'clock. The third, "the morning watch," from two to sunrise (Exod. 14:24; I Sam. 11:11). Afterwards, under the Romans, they had *four* watches (Matt. 14:25; Luke 12: 38). **for . . . thy . . . children**—that God, if He will not spare thee, may *at least* preserve "thy young children." **top of . . . street**—(Isa. 51:20; Nah. 3: 10). *Resh.* ר. **20. women eat . . . fruit**—as threatened (Lev. 26:29; Deut. 28:53, 56, 57; Jer. 19:9). **children . . . span long**—or else, "children whom they carry in their arms" [MAURER].

Schin, ש. **21.** (II Chron. 36:17.) **22. Thou hast called as in . . . solemn day . . . terrors**—Thou hast summoned my enemies against me from all quarters, just as multitudes used to be convened to Jerusalem, on the solemn feast-days. The objects, for which the enemies and the festal multitude respectively met, formed a sad contrast. Cf. ch. 1:15: "called an assembly against me."

ADAM CLARKE

Thy breach is great like the sea. You have a flood of afflictions, a sea of troubles, an ocean of miseries.

19. *Arise, cry out in the night.* This seems to refer to Jerusalem besieged. You who keep the night watches, pour out your hearts before the Lord, instead of calling the time of night, etc.; or, when you call it, send up a fervent prayer to God for the safety and relief of the place.

20. *Consider to whom thou hast done this.* Perhaps the best sense of this difficult verse is this: "Thou art our Father, we are Thy children. Wilt Thou destroy Thy own offspring? Was it ever heard that a mother devoured her own child, a helpless infant of a span long?" That it was foretold that there should be such distress in the siege that mothers should be obliged to eat their own children is evident enough from Lev. xxvi. 29; Deut. xxviii. 53, 56-57; but the former view of the subject seems the most natural, and is best supported by the context. *The priest and the prophet* are *slain;* "the young and old lie on the ground in the streets"; the "virgins and . . . young men are fallen by the sword; thou hast slain them in the day of thine anger; thou hast killed, and not pitied." See chap. iv. 10.

22. *Thou hast called as in a solemn day.* It is by Thy influence alone that so many enemies are called together at one time; and they have so hemmed us in that none could escape, and none remained unslain or uncaptivated. Perhaps the figure is the collecting of the people in Jerusalem on one of the solemn annual festivals.

MATTHEW HENRY — CHAPTER 3

Verses 1–20

The title of the 102nd Psalm might very fitly be prefixed to this chapter—*The prayer of the afflicted, when he is overwhelmed, and pours out his complaint before the Lord.* The prophet complains, 1. That God is angry. This gives both birth and bitterness to the affliction (*v.* 1): *I am the man that has seen affliction*, and has felt it sensibly, *by the rod of his wrath.* God is sometimes angry with his own people; yet it is not as a sword to cut off, but only as a rod to correct; it is to them *the rod of his wrath*, though grievous for the present, in the issue advantageous. By this rod we must expect to *see affliction*, and if we be made to see more than ordinary affliction, we must not quarrel, for we are sure that the anger is just and the affliction mixed with mercy. 2. That he is in the dark. Darkness is put for trouble and perplexity; this was the case of the complainant (*v.* 2): "*He has led me* by an unaccountable chain of events, *into darkness and not into light*, the darkness I feared and not into the light I hoped for." And (*v.* 6), *He has set me in dark places*, dark as the grave, *like those that are dead of old*, that are quite forgotten. 3. That God appears against him as an enemy. "*Surely against me is he turned* (*v.* 3), as far as I can discern; for *his hand is turned against me all the day. I am chastened every morning*," Ps. lxxiii. 14. When God's hand is turned against us, we are tempted to think that his heart is turned against us too. "*He was unto me as a bear lying in wait*, surprising me with his judgments, *and as a lion in secret places*; so that which way soever I went I could never think myself safe." *He has bent his bow*, v. 12. *He has set me as a mark for his sorrow*, and *the arrows of his quiver enter into my veins*, give me an inward wound, *v.* 13. 4. That the Jewish state may be fitly compared to a man wrinkled with age (*v.* 4): "*My flesh and my skin has he made old;* they are wasted and withered, and *he has broken my bones*, v. 15. *He has filled me with bitterness*, a bitter sense of these calamities." *He has* mingled *gravel* with my bread, so that *my teeth* are *broken* with it (*v.* 16). *He has covered me with ashes*, as mourners used to be, or (as some read it) *he has fed me with ashes.* 5. That he is not able to discern any way of escape (*v.* 5): "*He has built against me*, as forts and batteries are built against a besieged city. Where there was a way open it is now quite made up: *He has compassed me* on every side *with gall and travail*; I vex and fret, and tire myself, to find a way of escape, but can find none, *v.* 7. *He has hedged me about, that I cannot get out.* I am chained; and as notorious malefactors are double-fettered, so he *has made my chain heavy. He has* also (*v.* 9) *enclosed my ways with hewn stone*, with a stone wall, which cannot be broken through, so that *my paths are made crooked*; I traverse to and

JAMIESON, FAUSSET, BROWN — CHAPTER 3

Vss. 1-66. Jeremiah proposes his own experience under afflictions, as an example as to how the Jews should behave under theirs, so as to have hope of a restoration; hence the change from *singular* to *plural* (vss. 22, 40-47). The stanzas consist of three lines, each of which begins with the same Hebrew letter. *Aleph,* א. **1-3. seen affliction**—his own in the dungeon of Malchiah (Jer. 38:6); that of his countrymen also in the siege. Both were types of that of Christ.

2. darkness—calamity. **light**—prosperity.

6. set me—HENDERSON refers this to the custom of placing the dead in a sitting posture. **dark places**—sepulchers. As those "dead long since"; so Jeremiah and his people are consigned to oblivion (Ps. 88:5, 6; 143:3; Ezek. 37: 13).
3. turneth . . . hand—to inflict again and again new strokes. "His hand," which once used to protect me. "Turned . . . turneth" implies *repeated* inflictions. *Beth,* ב. **4-6.** (Job 16:8.)

12. (Job 7:20.) *He,* ה. **13-15. 13. arrows**—lit., *sons* of His quiver (cf. Job 6:4).

15. wormwood—(Jer. 9:15). There it is regarded as *food*, viz., the leaves: here as *drink*, viz., the juice. *Vau,* ו. **16-18. gravel**—referring to the *grit* that often mixes with bread baked in ashes, as is the custom of baking in the East (Prov. 20:17). We fare as hardly as those who eat such bread. The same allusion is in "Covered me with ashes," viz., as bread. **5. builded**—mounds, as against a besieged city, so as to allow none to escape (so vss. 7, 9).

Gimel, ג. **7-9. hedged**—(Job 3:23; Hos. 2:6). **chain**—lit., chain of *brass.* **9. hewn stone**—which coheres so closely as not to admit of being broken through. **paths crooked**—thwarted our plans and efforts so that none went right.

ADAM CLARKE — CHAPTER 3

1. *I am the man that hath seen affliction.* Either the prophet speaks here of himself or he is personating his miserable countrymen. This and other passages in this poem have been applied to Jesus Christ's passion but, in my opinion, without any foundation.

2. *He hath . . . brought me into darkness.* In the sacred writings, *darkness* is often taken for calamity; *light*, for prosperity.

13. *The arrows of his quiver.* "The sons of his quiver." *Arrows* that issue from a *quiver* are here termed "the sons of the quiver."

16. *He hath also broken my teeth with gravel stones.* What a figure to express disgust, pain, and the consequent incapacity of taking food for the support of life; a man, instead of bread, being obliged to eat small pebbles, till all his teeth are broken to pieces by endeavoring to grind them! *He hath covered me with ashes. Hichphishani beepher*, "He hath plunged me into the dust." To be thrown into a mass or bed of perfect dust, where the eyes are blinded by it, the ears stopped, and the mouth and lungs filled at the very first attempt to respire after having been thrown into it—what a horrible idea of suffocation!

5. *He hath builded against me.* Perhaps there is a reference here to the mounds and ramparts raised by the Chaldeans in order to take the city.

7. *He hath hedged me about.* This also may refer to the lines drawn round the city during the siege. But these and similar expressions in the following verses may be merely metaphorical, to point out their straitened, oppressed, and distressed state.

9. *He hath inclosed my ways with hewn stone.* He has put insuperable obstacles in my way, and confounded all my projects of deliverance and all my expectations of prosperity.

MATTHEW HENRY

fro, but am still turned back." So (*v.* 11), "*He has turned aside my ways;* ruined my projects. He has *pulled me in pieces*; and *made me desolate*, has deprived me of all comfort in my own soul." 6. That God turns a deaf ear to his prayers (*v.* 8): "*When I cry and shout*, as one in earnest, that would make him hear, yet he *shuts out my prayer.* Sometimes God seems to be angry even against *the prayers of his people* (Ps. lxxx. 4), and their case is deplorable indeed when they are denied the comfort of acceptance. 7. That his neighbours make a laughing matter of his troubles (*v.* 14): *I was a derision to all my people*, to all the wicked among them, who made one another merry with the public judgments, and particularly the prophet Jeremiah's griefs. 8. That he was ready to despair of deliverance: "Thou hast not only taken peace from me, but hast *removed my soul far off from peace* (*v.* 17). *I forget prosperity;* it is so long since I had it that I have lost the idea of it. I have been so inured to sorrow and servitude that I know not what joy and liberty mean. *My strength and my hope have perished from the Lord* (*v.* 18); I can no longer stay myself upon God as my support, even my God inexorable." 9. That grief returned upon every remembrance of his troubles, and his reflections were as melancholy as his prospects, *v.* 19, 20. *My affliction and my transgression* (so some read it), my trouble and my sin that brought it upon me; this was *the wormwood and the gall* in *the affliction and the misery.* It is sin that makes the cup of affliction a bitter cup. The captives in Babylon had all the miseries of the siege in their mind continually, and *wept when* they *remembered Zion*; nay, they could *never forget Jerusalem*, Ps. cxxxvii. 1, 5.

Verses 21–36

Here the clouds begin to disperse and the sky to clear up. Here the tune is altered and the mourners in Zion begin to look a little pleasant. But for hope, the heart would break. To save the heart from being quite broken, here is something *called to mind*, which gives ground for *hope* (*v.* 21). *I make to return to my heart* (so the margin words it): what we have had in our hearts is sometimes as if it were forgotten, till God by his grace make it return to our hearts. "*I recall* it *to mind; therefore have I hope*, and am kept from downright despair."

I. Bad as things are, it is owing to the mercy of God that they are not worse. We are *afflicted by the rod of his wrath*, but *it is of the Lord's mercies that we are not consumed*, *v.* 22. 1. The streams of mercy acknowledged: *We are not consumed.* The church of God is like Moses's bush, burning, yet *not consumed.* It is *persecuted* of men, *but not forsaken* of God, and therefore, though it is *cast down*, it is *not destroyed* (2 Cor. iv. 9), corrected, yet *not consumed*, refined in the furnace as silver, but *not consumed* as dross. 2. These streams followed up to the fountain: *It is of the Lord's mercies.* God is an inexhaustible *fountain of mercy, the Father of mercies.* Had we been dealt with *according to our sins*, we should have been consumed long ago; but we have been dealt with *according to God's mercies.*

II. Even in the depth of their affliction they still have experience of the tenderness of the divine pity and the truth of the divine promise. They had several times complained that God had not pitied (*ch.* ii. 17, 21), but here they correct themselves, and own, 1. That *God's compassions fail not*; they do not really fail, no, not even when in anger he seems to have *shut up his tender mercies.* These rivers of mercy run fully and constantly, but never run dry. *They are new every morning;* every morning we have fresh instances of God's compassion towards us; *every morning does he bring his judgment to light*, Zeph. iii. 5. When our comforts fail, yet God's compassions do not. 2. That *great is his faithfulness.* Though Jerusalem be in ruins, *the truth of the Lord endures for ever.*

III. God is, and ever will be, the all-sufficient happiness of his people, and they depend upon him to be such (*v.* 24): *The Lord is my portion, saith my soul;* that is, 1. "When I have lost all I have in the world, liberty, and livelihood, and almost life itself, yet I have not lost my interest in God." 2. "While I have an interest in God, therein I have enough; I have that which is sufficient to counterbalance all my troubles and make up all my losses." 3. "This is that which I depend upon: *Therefore will I hope in him.* I will stay myself upon him, when all other supports fail me."

IV. Those who deal with God will find it is not in vain to trust in him, *v.* 25. While we *wait for him* by faith, we must *seek him* by prayer. Our seeking will help to keep up our waiting. *It is good* (it is our duty and will be our unspeakable comfort and satisfaction) *to hope and quietly to wait for the salvation of the*

JAMIESON, FAUSSET, BROWN

Daleth, ד. **10-13.** (Job 10:16; Hos. 13:7, 8). **11. turned aside**–made me wander out of the right way, so as to become a prey to wild beasts. **pulled . . . in pieces**–(Hos. 6:1), as a "bear" or a "lion" (vs. 10). **8. shutteth out**–image from a door *shutting out* any entrance (Job 30:20). So the antitype, Christ (Ps. 22:2).

14. (Jer. 20:7.) **their song**–(Ps. 69:12). Jeremiah herein was a type of Messiah. "All my people" (John 1:11).

17. Not only present, but all hope of future prosperity is removed; so much so, that I am as one who never was prosperous ("I forgat prosperity"). **18. from the Lord**–i.e., my hope derived from Him (Ps. 31:22).

Zain, ז. **19-21.** (Jer. 9:15). **Remembering . . .**–This gives the reason why he gave way to the temptation to despair. The *Margin*, "Remember" does not suit the sense so well. **20.** As often as *my soul calls them to remembrance, it is humbled* or bowed down in me.

21. This–viz., what follows; the view of the divine character (vss. 22, 23). CALVIN makes "this" refer to Jeremiah's infirmity. His very weakness (vss. 19, 20) gives him hope of God interposing His strength for him (cf. Ps. 25:11, 17; 42:5, 8; II Cor. 12:9, 10).

Cheth, ח. **22-24.** (Mal. 3:6).

23. (Isa. 33:2.)

24. (Num. 18:20; Ps. 16:5; 73:26; 119:57; Jer. 10:16.) To have God for our portion is the one only foundation of hope.

Teth, ט. **25-27.** The repetition of "good" at the beginning of each of the three verses heightens the effect. **wait**–(Isa. 30:18). **26. quietly wait**–lit., "be in silence." Cf. vs. 28 and Psalm 39: 2, 9, i.e., to be patiently quiet under afflictions, resting in the will of God (Ps. 37:7). So Aaron (Lev. 10:2, 3); and Job (40:4, 5).

ADAM CLARKE

17. *Thou hast removed my soul.* Prosperity is at such an utter distance from me that it is impossible I should ever reach it; and as to happiness, I have forgotten whether I have ever tasted of it.

20. *My soul . . . is humbled in me.* It is evident that in the preceding verses there is a bitterness of complaint against the bitterness of adversity that is not becoming to man when under the chastising hand of God; and, while indulging this feeling, all hope fled. Here we find a different feeling; he humbles himself under the mighty hand of God, and then his hope revives, v. 21.

22. *It is of the Lord's mercy that we are not consumed.* Being thus humbled, and seeing himself and his sinfulness in a proper point of view, he finds that God, instead of dealing with him in judgment, has dealt with him in mercy; and that though the affliction was excessive, yet it was less than his iniquity deserved. If, indeed, any sinner be kept out of hell, it is because God's compassion faileth not.

23. *They are new every morning.* Day and night proclaim the mercy and compassion of God. Who could exist throughout the day if there were not a continual superintending Providence? Who could be preserved in the night if the Watchman of Israel ever slumbered or slept?

26. *It is good that a man should both hope.* Hope is essentially necessary to faith. He that hopes not cannot believe; if there be no expectation, there can be no confidence.

MATTHEW HENRY

Lord, to hope that it will come, to wait till it does come, and while we wait to be quiet and silent, not quarrelling with God but acquiescing in the divine disposals. *Father, thy will be done*.

V. Afflictions are really good for us, and, if we bear them aright, will work for our good. It is not only good to wait for the salvation, but it is good to be under the trouble in the meantime (*v.* 27): *It is good for a man that he bear the yoke in his youth*. Many of the young men were carried into captivity. He tells them that it was good for them to *bear the yoke* of that captivity, and they would find it so if they would labour to answer God's ends in laying that heavy yoke upon them. Here it seems to be meant of the yoke of affliction. Many have found it good to bear this in youth; it has made those humble who otherwise would have been proud and unruly, and *as a bullock unaccustomed to the yoke*. But when do we *bear the yoke* so that it is really *good for us to bear it in our youth?* 1. When we are quiet under our afflictions, when we *sit alone and keep silence*, that we may converse with God and *commune with our own hearts*, silencing all discontented distrustful thoughts. 2. When we are humble and patient under our affliction. *He* gets good by the yoke who *puts his mouth in the dust*, not only *lays his hand upon his mouth*, in token of submission to the will of God, but *puts it in the dust*, in token of sorrow at the remembrance of sin. Those who are truly humbled for sin will be glad to obtain a good hope, through grace, though they *put their mouth in the dust* for it. 3. When we are meek towards those who are the instruments of our trouble, and are of a forgiving spirit, *v.* 30. Our Lord Jesus has left us an example of this, for he *gave his back to the smiter*, Isa. l. 6. He who can bear contempt and reproach, and not *render railing for railing* and bitterness for bitterness, shall find that *it is good to bear the yoke*, that it shall turn to his spiritual advantage.

VI. God will graciously return to his people with comforts *according to the time that he has afflicted them*, *v.* 31, 32. We may bear ourselves up with this, 1. That, when we are cast down, yet we are not cast off; the father's correcting his son is not a disinheriting of him. 2. That though we may seem to be cast off for a time, yet we are not really cast off. 3. That, whatever sorrow we are in, his hand is in it, and therefore we may be assured it is but *for a season*, 1. Pet. i. 6. 4. That God has compassions and comforts in store even for those whom he has himself grieved. He has torn, and he will heal us, Hos. vi. 1. 5. That, when God returns to deal graciously with us, it will not be according to our merits, but according to his mercies.

VII. When God does cause grief, it is for wise and holy ends, and he takes not delight in our calamities, *v.* 33. He does not do it *willingly*, not *from the heart*; so the word is. 1. He never afflicts us but when we give him cause to do it. If he show us kindness, it is because *so it seems good* unto him; but, if he write bitter things against us, it is because we both deserve them and need them. 2. He delights not in the death of sinners, or the disquiet of saints, but punishes with reluctance. He delights not in the misery of any of his creatures, he is so far from it that in all their afflictions he is afflicted and his soul is grieved for the misery of Israel. 3. He retains his kindness for his people even when he afflicts them. If he does not *willingly grieve the children of men*, much less his own children. They may by faith see love in his heart even when they see frowns in his face and a rod in his hand.

VIII. Though he makes use of men as his hand, or rather instruments in his hand, for the correcting of his people, yet he is far from being pleased with the injustice and the wrong they do them, *v.* 34–36. Two ways the people of God are oppressed by their enemies, and the prophet here assures us that God does not approve of either of them: 1. If men injure them by force of arms, God does not approve of that. He does not himself *crush under his feet the prisoners of the earth*, but he regards the cry of the prisoners; nor does he approve of men's doing it. It is barbarous to trample on those that are down. 2. If men injure them in the pretended administration of justice,—if they *turn aside the right of a man*, so that he cannot discover what his rights are,—if they *subvert a man in his cause*, and bring in a wrong verdict, or give a false judgment, let them know God sees them. It is *before the face of the Most High* (*v.* 35). God does not approve of them. More is implied than is expressed. The perverting of justice, and the subverting of the just, are a great affront to God; he will sooner or later severely reckon with those that do thus.

Verses 37–41

I. We must not quarrel with God for any affliction that he lays upon us at any time (*v.* 39): *Wherefore*

JAMIESON, FAUSSET, BROWN

27. yoke—of the Lord's *disciplinary* teaching (Ps. 90:12; 119:71). CALVIN interprets it, The Lord's *doctrine* (Matt. 11:29, 30), which is to be received in a docile spirit. The earlier the better; for the old are full of prejudices (Prov. 8:17; Eccles. 12:1). Jeremiah himself received the yoke, both of doctrine and chastisement in his youth (Jer. 1:6, 7).

Jod, י. **28-30.** The fruit of true docility and patience. He does not fight against the yoke (Jer. 31:18; Acts 9:5), but accommodates himself to it. **alone**—The heathen applauded magnanimity, but they looked to display and the praise of men. The child of God, in the absence of any witness, "alone," silently submits to the will of God. **borne it upon him**—i.e., because he is used to bearing it on him. Rather, "because He (the Lord, vs. 26) *hath laid it on* him" [VATABLUS]. **29.** (Job 42:6.) The mouth in the dust is the attitude of suppliant and humble submission to God's dealings as righteous and loving in design (cf. Ezra 9:6; I Cor. 14:25). **if so be there may be hope**—This does not express doubt as to whether GOD be willing to receive the penitent, but the *penitent's* doubt as to himself; he whispers to himself this consolation, "Perhaps there may be hope for me." **30.** Messiah, the Antitype, fulfilled this; His practice agreeing with His precept (Isa. 50:6; Matt. 5:39). Many take patiently afflictions from God, but when man wrongs them, they take it impatiently. The godly bear resignedly the latter, like the former, as sent by God (Ps. 17:13). *Caph*, כ. **31-33. 31.** True repentance is never without hope (Ps. 94:14). **32.** The punishments of the godly are but for a time.

33. He does not afflict any willingly (lit., "from His heart." i.e., as if He had any pleasure in it, Ezek. 33:11), much less the godly (Heb. 12:10).

Lamed, ל. **34-36.** This triplet has an infinitive in the beginning of each verse, the governing finite verb being in the end of vs. 36, "the Lord approveth not," which is to be repeated in each verse. Jeremiah here anticipates and answers the objections which the Jews might start, that it was by His connivance they were "crushed under the feet" of those who "turned aside the right of a man." God approves (lit., "seeth," Hab. 1:13; so "behold," "look on," i.e., look on *with approval*) not of such unrighteous acts; and so the Jews may look for deliverance and the punishment of their foes. **35. before . . . face of . . . most High**—Any "turning aside" of justice in court is done *before the face of God*, who is present, and "regardeth," though unseen (Eccles. 5:8). **36. subvert**—to wrong.

ADAM CLARKE

27. *That he bear the yoke in his youth*. He who has not got under wholesome restraint in youth will never make a useful man, a good man, nor a happy man.

CHARLES H. SPURGEON:

Yoke-bearing is not pleasant, but it is good. It is not every pleasant thing that is good, nor every good thing that is pleasant. Sometimes the goodness may be just in proportion to the unpleasantness. Now, it is childish to be always craving for sweets; those who by reason of use have had their senses exercised, should prefer the wholesome to the palatable. It ought to reconcile us to that which is unsavory when we are informed that it is good! A little child is not easily reconciled that way, because as yet, he cannot think and judge; but the man of God ought to find it very easy to quiet every murmur and complaint as soon as he perceives that, though unpleasant, the thing is good. Since, my dear friends, we are not very good judges ourselves of that which is good for us, any more than our children are, and since we expect our little ones to leave the choice of their diet with us, will it not be wise of us to leave everything with our heavenly Father? We can judge what is pleasant, but we cannot discern that which is good for us, but He can judge, and therefore it will be always well for us to leave all our affairs in His hands, and say, "Nevertheless, not as I will, but as thou wilt." Since we are quite certain upon Scriptural authority that whatever the Lord sends to His people will work out their benefit, we ought to be perfectly resigned to the Lord's will; nay, much more, we ought to be thankful for all His appointments even when they displease the flesh, being quite certain that His will is the best that can be, and that if we could see the end from the beginning it is exactly what we should choose, if we were as wise and good as our heavenly Father is. Our shoulders bow themselves with gladness to the burden which Jesus declares to be profitable unto us: this assurance from His lips makes His yoke easy to bear.

Our text tells us of something which, though not very comfortable, is good—"It is good for a man that he bear the yoke in his youth." The illustration is drawn from cattle. The bullocks have to bear the yoke. They go in pairs, and the yoke is borne upon their shoulders. The yoke is somewhat burdensome. If the bullock is not broken-in when it is young it will never make a good ploughing ox. It will be fretted and troubled with the labor it will have to do; it will be very hard work to drive it, and the husbandman will accomplish but little ploughing. It is good for the bullock to be brought into subjection while it is young, and so it is with all sorts of animals: the horse must be broken-in while he is a colt; and if a certain period of the horse's life be allowed to pass over without its being under the trainer's hand, it will never make a thoroughly useful horse. If you want to train a dog you must take him while he is young, and teach him his work. That is the metaphor. It is just so with men. It is good for us that we be broken-in while we are yet young, and learn to bear the yoke in our youth.

—*The Treasury of the Old Testament*

MATTHEW HENRY

does a living man complain? From the doctrine of God's sovereign and universal providence he draws this inference, *Wherefore does a living man complain?* The sufferers in the captivity must submit to the will of God in all their sufferings. Shall *a living man complain, a man for the punishment of his sins?* We are sinful men, and that which we complain of is the just *punishment of our sins*; it is far less than our iniquities have deserved. Then let us not complain; instead of repining, we must be repenting; and, as an evidence that God is reconciled to us, we must be endeavouring to reconcile ourselves to his holy will.

II. We must set ourselves to answer God's intention in afflicting us, which is to bring sin to our remembrance, and to bring us home to himself, *v.* 40. *Let us search and try our ways.* Let conscience be employed both to search and to try. *Let us try our ways,* that by them we may try ourselves, for we are to judge of our state not by our faint wishes, but by our step, not by one particular step, but by our ways, the ends we aim at, the rules we go by, and the tenor of our lives to those ends and those rules. When we are in affliction it is seasonable to *consider our ways* (Hag. i. 5), that what is amiss may be repented of and amended for the future, and so we may answer the intention of the affliction. We are apt, in times of public calamity, to reflect upon other people's ways, and lay blame upon them; whereas our business is to *search and try our* own *ways.* "Let us *turn again to the Lord.* We have been with him, and it has never been well with us since we forsook him; let us therefore now turn again to him." Our hearts must go along with our prayers. We must *lift up our hearts with our hands,* as we must pour out our souls with our words. Praying is lifting up the soul to God (Ps. xxv. 1) as to *our Father in heaven*; and the soul that hopes to be with God in heaven for ever will, by frequent acts of devotion, be still learning the way thither and pressing forward in that way.

Verses 42–54

The prophet had owned that a living man should not complain, yet here the clouds return.

I. They confess the righteousness of God in afflicting them (*v.* 42): *We have transgressed and have rebelled.* Call sin a transgression, call it a rebellion, and you do not miscall it.

II. They complain of the afflictions they are under, not without some reflections upon God.

1. They complain of the tokens of his displeasure (*v.* 42), *Thou hast not pardoned. Thou hast not pitied, v.* 43. They complain that there was a wall of partition between them and God. *"Thou hast covered us* up as men that are buried are covered up and forgotten." It hindered their prayers from coming up unto God (*v.* 44): *Thou hast covered thyself with a cloud* so thick *that our prayers* seem as if they were lost in it."

2. They complain of the contempt of their neighbours (*v.* 45): *"Thou hast made us as the off-scouring."* If they had not made themselves vile, their enemies could not have made them so.

3. They complain of the destruction that their enemies made of them (*v.* 37): *The destruction of the daughter of my people* (*v.* 48), *of all the daughters of my city, v.* 51. Their enemies chased them till they had quite prevailed over them (*v.* 53): *They have cut off my life in the dungeon.* They are as it were thrown into the dungeon or grave and a *stone cast upon them,* such as used to be *rolled to the door of the sepulchres.* They look upon the Jewish nation as dead and buried. Their destruction is compared to the sinking of a living man into the water, *v.* 54.

4. They complain of their own excessive grief and fear (*v.* 48, 49). It is added (*v.* 51), *"My eye affects my heart.* The more I look upon the desolations of the city and country the more I am grieved."

5. In the midst of these sad complaints here is one word of comfort, *v.* 50. We continue weeping *till the Lord look down and behold from heaven.* Bad as the case is, one favourable look from heaven will set all to rights. While they continued weeping they continued waiting; nothing shall wipe tears from their eyes *till he look down.*

Verses 55–65

A struggle in the prophet's breast between faith, fear and hope. But faith gets the last word and comes off conqueror. In three things the prophet and his friends had found God good: 1. He had *heard their prayers*; though they had been ready to fear that the cloud of wrath was such as their *prayers could not pass through* (*v.* 44). When they were *in the low dungeon,* as *free among the dead,* they *called upon God's name* (*v.* 55). *Thou didst not hide thy ear at my breathing, at my cry.* Observe how he calls prayer

JAMIESON, FAUSSET, BROWN

Mem, מ. **37-39.** Who is it that can (as God, Ps. 33:9) effect by a word anything, without the will of God? **38. evil . . . good**—*Calamity* and prosperity alike proceed from God (Job 2:10; Isa. 45:7; Amos 3:6). **39. living**—and so having a time yet given him by God for repentance. If sin were punished as it deserves, *life* itself would be forfeited by the sinner. "Complaining" (murmuring) ill becomes him who enjoys such a favor as life (Prov. 19:3). **for the punishment of his sins**—Instead of blaming God for his sufferings, he ought to recognize in them God's righteousness and the just rewards of his own sin.

Nun, נ. **40-42. us**—Jeremiah and his fellow countrymen in their calamity. **search**—as opposed to the torpor wherewith men rest only on their outward sufferings, without attending to the cause of them (Ps. 139:23, 24).

41. heart with . . . hands—the antidote to hypocrisy (Ps. 86:4; I Tim. 2:8).

42. not pardoned—The Babylonian captivity had not yet ended. *Samech,* ס. **43-45. covered**—viz., thyself (so vs. 44), so as not to see and pity our calamities, for even the most cruel in seeing a sad spectacle are moved to pity. Cf. as to God "hiding His face," Psalm 10:11; 22:25. **44.** (Vs. 8.) The "cloud" is our sins, and God's wrath because of them (Isa. 44: 22; 59:2). **45.** So the apostles were treated; but, instead of murmuring, they rejoiced at it (I Cor. 4: 13). *Pe,* פ. **46-48.** *Pe* is put before *Ain,* as in Elegy 2:16, 17; 4:16, 17. **46.** (Ch. 2:16.) **47.** Like animals fleeing in fear, we fall into the snare laid for us. **48.** (Jer. 4:19.) *Ain,* ע. **49-51. without . . . intermission**—or else, "because there is no intermission" [PISCATOR], viz., of my miseries. **50. Till**—His prayer is not without hope, wherein it differs from the blind grief of unbelievers. **look down . . .**—(Isa. 63:15). **51. eye affecteth mine heart**—i.e., causeth me grief with continual tears; or, "affecteth my *life*" (lit., "soul," *Margin*), i.e., my health [GROTIUS]. **daughters of . . . city**—the towns around, dependencies of Jerusalem, taken by the foe. *Tzaddi,* צ. **52-54. a bird**—which is destitute of counsel and strength. The allusion seems to be to Proverbs 1:17 [CALVIN]. **without cause**—(Ps. 69:4; 109:3, 4). Type of Messiah (John 15:25). **53. in . . . dungeon**—(Jer. 37:16). **stone**—usually put at the mouth of a dungeon to secure the prisoners (Josh. 10:18; Dan. 6:17; Matt. 27:60). **54. Waters**—not literally, for there was "no water" (Jer. 38:6) in the place of Jeremiah's confinement, but emblematical of overwhelming calamities (Ps. 69:2; 124:4, 5). **cut off**—(Isa. 38:10, 11). I am abandoned by God. He speaks according to carnal sense. *Koph,* ק. **55-57. I called . . . out of . . . dungeon**—Thus the spirit resists the flesh, and faith spurns the temptation [CALVIN], (Ps. 130:1; Jonah 2:2). **56. Thou hast heard**—viz., formerly (so in vss. 57, 58).

breathing . . . cry—two kinds of prayer; the sigh of a prayer silently *breathed* forth, and the loud, earnest cry (cf. Isa. 26:16, "Prayer," *Margin,* "*secret speech,*" with Ps. 55:17, "cry aloud").

ADAM CLARKE

E. H. PLUMPTRE:

Verse 39. Since happiness and misfortune are both equally willed of God, both must be good, and nothing belonging to either of them should cause us to murmur. As a man who has brought upon himself wholesome sickness by means of bitter medicine, ought not to complain of that medicine, but should blame himself for having caused the necessity of using it, so a man should not complain of the evils which befall him, for these are only the necessary means of curing the sickness of sin, of which he himself is guilty. If he will lament, let him lament for his sin (Jer. 30:15). "Wherefore doth a living man complain" (mar. *murmur*). "For what sighs the man who lives?" The verb is *respirare, gemere, to sigh* with the kindred idea of *murmuring,* (Num. 11:1), which is the only place except this, where the word occurs. The expression *a living man,* is difficult. It cannot be taken as synonymous with *a man,* in which case *living* would be, properly speaking, superfluous. Neither can it be taken for *vita, life,* in which case the sense would be "why complains man of life," i.e., because it is calamitous? As little can it be called *as long as he lives*; or, *although he lives,* since he yet lives and could do something better than sigh. The only sense corresponding to the context is, *what does the man as a living one sigh for? As a living one,* i.e., as one who still finds himself in this life's school of discipline. How should we in the time appointed for affliction mourn over our afflictions? A living man should not allow himself to be surprised by "the fiery trial" as if thereby some strange thing happened unto him (1 Peter 4:12): only that happens to him which is natural and inevitable. "A man for the punishment of his sins?" *Every one, on account of his sins.* This can only be the answer to the question proposed in this first member of the verse, designed to rectify the evil in view,—not sufferings, but sins should be lamented.

—Ellicott's Commentary on the Whole Bible

51. *Mine eye affecteth mine heart.* What I see I feel. I see nothing but misery; and I feel, in consequence, nothing but pain. *The daughters of my city.* The villages about Jerusalem.

52. *Mine enemies chased me.* From this to the end of the chapter the prophet speaks of his own personal sufferings, and especially of those which he endured in the dungeon. See Jer. xxxviii. 6, etc.

MATTHEW HENRY

his breathing; for in prayer we breathe towards God, we breathe after him. Prayer is the breath of the new man, sucking in the air of mercy in petitions and returning it in praises; it is both the evidence and the maintenance of the spiritual life. 2. He had silenced their fears (*v.* 57): "*Thou drewest near in the day that I called upon thee.*" When we draw nigh to God in a way of duty we may by faith see him drawing nigh to us in a way of mercy. *Thou saidst, Fear not.* 3. He had already begun to appear for them (*v.* 58): "*O Lord! thou hast pleaded the causes of my soul*" (that is, as it follows), "*thou hast redeemed my life.*" He comforts himself with an appeal to God's justice, and to his omniscience. "*O Lord! thou hast seen my wrong*, that I have done no wrong at all, but suffer a great deal." *Thou hast seen all their imaginations against me* (*v.* 60). They make themselves and one another merry with my miseries, as the Philistines made sport with Samson. Let them be dealt with as they have dealt with us; let thy hand be against them as their hand has been against us.

JAMIESON, FAUSSET, BROWN

57. **Thou drewest near**—with Thy help (Jas. 4:8). *Resh,* ר. **58-60.** Jeremiah cites God's gracious answers to his prayers as an encouragement to his fellow countrymen, to trust in Him. **pleaded**—(Ps. 35:1; Mic. 7:9). **59.** God's past deliverances and His knowledge of Judah's wrongs are made the grounds of prayer for relief. **60. imaginations**—devices (Jer. 11:19). **Their vengeance**—means *their malice.* Jeremiah gives his conduct, when plotted against by his foes, as an example how the Jews should bring their wrongs at the hands of the Chaldeans before God. *Schin,* ש. **61-63. their reproach**—their reproachful language against me. **62. lips**—speeches. **63. sitting down . . . rising up**—whether they sit or rise, i.e., whether they be actively engaged or sedentary, and at rest "all the day" (vs. 62), I am the subject of their derisive songs (vs. 14). *Tau,* ת. **64-66.** (Jer. 11:20; II Tim. 4:14). **65. sorrow**—rather, *blindness* or *hardness;* lit., "a veil" covering their heart, so that they may rush on to their own ruin (Isa. 6:10; II Cor. 3:14, 15). **66. from under . . . heavens of . . . Lord**—*destroy* them so that it may be seen everywhere *under heaven* that thou sittest above as Judge of the world.

ADAM CLARKE

66. *Persecute and destroy them.* Thou wilt pursue them with destruction. These are all declaratory, not imprecatory. *From under the heavens of the Lord.* This verse seems to allude to the Chaldaic prediction in Jer. x. 11. By their conduct they will bring on themselves the curse denounced against their enemies.

MATTHEW HENRY

CHAPTER 4

Verses 1–12

The elegy in this chapter begins with a lamentation of the sad change in Jerusalem. The city that was formerly as *the most fine gold* has lost its lustre; it has become dross.

I. The temple was laid waste, which was the glory of Jerusalem and its protection. And some understand the gold (*v.* 1) to be the *gold of the temple*, the find gold with which it was overlaid (1 Kings vi. 22); when the temple was burned the gold was sullied. *The stones of the sanctuary* were brought down by the fire, and thrown about *in the top of every street*; they lay mingled among the common ruins.

II. The princes and priests, who were in a special manner the *sons of Zion*, were abused, *v.* 2. Israel was more rich in them than in treasures of gold and silver. But now they are broken as *earthen pitchers.* They have grown poor, are brought into captivity, and rendered mean and despicable.

III. Little children were starved for want of bread and water, *v.* 3, 4.

IV. Persons of rank were reduced to poverty, *v.* 5. Those who were well-born and well bred, being stripped of all by the war, are *desolate in the streets*, have not a bed to lie on. As sometimes the *needy* are *raised out of the dunghill* (Ps. cxiii. 7), so there are instances of the *wealthy* being brought *to the dunghill.*

V. Persons who were eminent for dignity, perhaps for sanctity, shared with others in the common calamity, *v.* 7, 8. *Her Nazarites* are changed. These *Nazarites*, by reason of their temperate diet, especially the pleasure they had in devoting themselves to God, which made their faces to shine as *Moses's*, were *purer than snow* and *whiter than milk*; drinking no wine nor strong drink, they had a healthful complexion and cheerful countenance.

But now *their visage is marred* (as is said of Christ, Isa. lii. 14); it is *blacker than a coal*; they look miserably, partly through hunger and partly through grief and perplexity. *They are not known in the streets;* those who respected them now take no notice of them.

VI. Jerusalem died a lingering death; for the famine contributed more to her destruction than any other judgment. Jerusalem dies by inches, dies so as to feel herself die. The iniquity of Jerusalem is more aggravated than that of Sodom, no wonder that the punishment of it is so. Sodom never had the means of grace that Jerusalem had. *The hands of the pitiful women have* slain and then *sodden their own children.* The case was sad enough that they had not wherewithal to feed their children and make meat for them (*v.* 4), but much worse that they could find in their hearts to feed upon their children and make meat of them. The destruction of Jerusalem is a complete destruction (*v.* 11), an amazing destruction, *v.* 12. It was a surprise to the kings of the earth, and to

JAMIESON, FAUSSET, BROWN

CHAPTER 4

VSS. 1-22. THE SAD CAPTURE OF JERUSALEM, THE HOPE OF RESTORATION, AND THE RETRIBUTION AWAITING IDUMEA FOR JOINING BABYLON AGAINST JUDEA. *Aleph,* א. **1. gold**—the splendid adornment of the temple [CALVIN] (ch. 1:10; I Kings 6:22; Jer. 52:19); or, *the principal men* of Judea [GROTIUS] (vs. 2). **stones of . . . sanctuary**—the gems on the breastplate of the high priest; or, metaphorically, the priests and Levites. *Beth,* ב. **2. comparable to . . . gold**—(Job 28:16, 19). **earthen pitchers**—(Isa. 30:14; Jer. 19:11). *Gimel,* ג. **3. sea monsters . . . breast**—Whales and other cetaceous monsters are mammalian. Even they suckle their young; but the Jewish women in the siege, so desperate was their misery, ate theirs (vs. 10; ch. 2:20). Others translate, "jackals." **ostriches**—see *Note,* Job 39:14-16, on their forsaking their young. *Daleth,* ד. **4. thirst**—The mothers have no milk to give through the famine. *He,* ה. **5. delicately**—on dainties. **are desolate**—or, *perish.* **in scarlet embrace dunghills**—Instead of the *scarlet* couches on which the grandees were nursed, they must lie on *dunghills.* **embrace**—They who once shrank sensitively from any soil, gladly *cling close* to heaps of filth as their only resting-place. Cf. "embrace the rock" (Job 24:8). *Vau,* ו. **6. greater than . . . Sodom**—(Matt. 11:23). No prophets had been sent to Sodom, as there had been to Judea; therefore the punishment of the latter was heavier than that of the former. **overthrown . . . in a moment**—whereas the Jews had to endure the protracted and manifold hardships of a siege. **no hands stayed on her**—No *hostile force,* as the Chaldeans in the case of Jerusalem, *continually pressed on her* before her overthrow. Jeremiah thus shows the greater severity of Jerusalem's punishment than that of Sodom. *Zain,* ז. **7. Nazarites**—lit., "separated ones" (Num. 6). They were held once in the highest estimation, but now they are degraded. God's blessing formerly caused their body not to be the less fair and ruddy for their abstinence from strong drink. Cf. the similar case of Daniel, etc. (Dan. 1:8-15). Also David (I Sam. 16:12; 17:42). Type of Messiah (Song of Sol. 5: 10). **rubies**—GESENIUS translates, "corals," from a *Hebrew* root, "to divide into branches," from the branching form of corals. **polishing**—They were like exquisitely cut and *polished sapphires.* The "sapphires" may represent the *blue* veins of a healthy person. *Cheth,* ח. **8. blacker than . . . coal**—or, "than blackness" itself (Joel 2:6; Nah. 2: 10). **like a stick**—as withered as a dry stick. *Teth,* ט. **9.** The speedy death by the sword is better than the lingering death by famine. **pine away**—lit., "flow out"; referring to the flow of blood. This expression, and "stricken through," are drawn from death by "the sword." *want of . . .* **fruits**—The words in italics have to be supplied in the original (Gen. 18:28; Ps. 109:24). *Jod,* י. **10.** (Ch. 2:20; Deut. 28:56, 57.) **pitiful**—naturally at other times compassionate (Isa. 49:15). JOSEPHUS describes the unnatural act as it took place in the siege under Titus. **sodden**—boiled. *Caph,* כ. **11. fire . . . devoured . . . foundations**—(Deut. 32:22; Jer. 21:14). A most rare event. Fire usually consumes only the surface; but this reached even to the *foundation,* cutting off all hope of restoration. *Lamed,* ל. **12.** Jerusalem was so fortified that all thought it im-

ADAM CLARKE

CHAPTER 4

1. *How is the gold become dim!* The prophet contrasts, in various affecting instances, the wretched circumstances of the Jewish nation with the flourishing state of their affairs in former times. Here they are compared to *gold, zahab,* native gold from the mine, which, contrary to its nature, is *become dim,* is tarnished; and even the *fine,* the "sterling," *gold, kethem,* that which was stamped to make it current, is *changed* or "adulterated," so as to be no longer passable. *The stones of the sanctuary.* "The holy stones."

2. *The precious sons of Zion.* The Jewish priests and Jewish believers. *Comparable to fine gold.* Who were of the pure standard of holiness; holy, because God who called them is holy; but now esteemed no better than *earthen pitchers*—vessels of dishonor in comparison of what they once were.

3. *Even the sea monsters draw out the breast.* The whales give suck to their young ones. *Like the ostriches in the wilderness.* For her carelessness about her eggs, and her inattention to her young, the ostrich is proverbial.

4. *The tongue of the sucking child.* See chap. ii. 12.

5. *Embrace dunghills.* Lie on straw or rubbish, instead of the costly carpets and sofas on which they formerly stretched themselves.

6. *For the punishment.* He thinks the punishment of Jerusalem far greater than that of Sodom. That was destroyed in a moment, while all her inhabitants were in health and strength. Jerusalem fell by the most lingering calamities, her men partly destroyed by the sword, and partly by the famine.

7. *Her Nazarites were purer than snow. Nazir* does not always signify a person separated under a religious vow; it sometimes denotes what is chief or eminent.

10. *The hands of the pitiful women have sodden their own children.* See chap. ii. 20. But here there is a reference to mothers eating their own children; and this was done, not by mothers cruel and brutal, but by the "compassionate," the "tenderhearted" mothers.

MATTHEW HENRY

all the inhabitants of the world who knew Jerusalem. They knew that it was the *city of the great King*, and therefore they thought that it was so much under the divine protection that it would be in vain for any of its enemies to make an attack upon it.

Verses 13–20

I. The sins for which God brought this destruction upon them served to justify God in it (*v.* 13, 14): It is *for the sins of her prophets*, and the *iniquities of her priests*. The particular sin charged upon them is persecution; the false prophets and corrupt priests joined to *shed the blood of the just in the midst of her*. They not only shed the blood of their innocent children, whom they sacrificed to Moloch, but the blood of the righteous men among them, whom they sacrificed to that more cruel idol of enmity to the truth and true religion. There is nothing that will make prophets and priests to be abhorred so much as a spirit of persecution.

II. The testimony of their neighbours to convict them of sin and to show the equity of God's proceedings against them. They upbraided them with their pretended purity, while they lived in iniquity. *They cried to them, Depart you; it is unclean.* They all cried out shame on them, and could easily foresee that God would not long suffer so provoking a people to continue in so good a land. The land would spew them out, as it had done their predecessors, and, when they saw the dispersed of *Jacob fleeing and wandering*, they told them of it. They said, Now *the anger of the Lord has divided them*. They said, when they saw them expelled, *God will no more regard them*, and how then can they help themselves? Herein they were mistaken. God has not cast them off, for all this.

III. Their despair under their calamities. "*As for us*, we look upon our case to be in a manner helpless. *Our end is near* (*v.* 18), the end both of our church and of our state." The refuges they fled to disappointed them. They looked for help from this and the other powerful ally, but to no purpose. Looking for that which never came (*v.* 17); they *watched in watching*; *for a nation* that frustrated their expectations. The persecutors overcame them (*v.* 18): *They hunt our steps, that we cannot go in our streets.* When the Chaldeans besieged the city they raised their batteries so high above the walls that they could shoot at people as they went along the streets. They *hunted them* with the arrows from place to place. Their *persecutors were swifter than the eagles of heaven*, *v.* 19.

Verses 21–22

David's psalms of lamentation commonly conclude with some word of comfort, which is as life from the dead and light shining out of darkness; so does this lamentation in this chapter. It is here foretold, for the encouragement of God's people,

I. That an end shall be put to Zion's troubles (*v.* 22). The troubles of God's people shall be continued no longer than till they have done their work for which they were sent.

II. That an end shall be put to Edom's triumphs. It is spoken ironically (*v.* 21): *Rejoice and be glad, O daughter of Edom! The cup* of trembling, which it is now Jerusalem's turn to drink deeply of, *shall pass through unto thee.* The destruction of the Edomites was foretold by this prophet (Jer. xlix. 7, &c.). "*The cup* that *shall pass unto thee* shall intoxicate thee. *Thou shalt be drunken*, and at thy wits' end, shalt stagger and stumble, and then, as Noah when he was drunk, *thou shalt make thyself naked* and expose thyself to contempt."

JAMIESON, FAUSSET, BROWN

pregnable. It therefore could only have been the hand of God, not the force of man, which overthrew it. *Mem*, מ. **13. prophets**—the false prophets (Jer. 23:11, 21). Supply the sense thus: "For the sins . . . *these calamities have befallen her.*" **shed the blood of the just**—(Matt. 23:31, 37). This received its full fulfilment in the slaying of Messiah and the Jews' consequent dispersion (Jas. 5:6). *Nun*, נ. **14. blind**—with mental aberration. **polluted . . . with blood**—both with blood of one another mutually shed (e.g., Jer. 2:34), and with their blood shed by the enemy [GLASSIUS]. **not touch . . . garments**—as being defiled with blood (Num. 19:16). *Samech*, ס. **15. They . . . them**—"They," i.e., "men" (vs. 14). Even the very *Gentiles*, regarded as unclean by *the Jews*, who were ordered most religiously to avoid all defilements, cried unto the *latter*, "depart," as being unclean: so universal was the defilement of the city by blood. **wandered**—As the false prophets and their followers had "wandered" blind with infatuated and idolatrous crime in the city (vs. 14), so they must now "wander" among the heathen in blind consternation with calamity. **they said**—i.e., the Gentiles said: *it was said* among the heathen, "The Jews shall no more sojourn in their own land" [GROTIUS]; or, wheresoever they go in their wandering exile, "they shall not stay long" [LUDOVICUS DE DIEU], (Deut. 28: 65). *Pe*, פ. *Ain* and *Pe* are here transposed, as in ch. 2:16, 17; 3:46-51. **16. anger**—lit., "face"; it is the countenance which, by its expression, manifests anger (Ps. 34:16). GESENIUS translates, "the *person* of Jehovah"; Jehovah present; Jehovah Himself (Exod. 33:14; II Sam. 17:11). **divided**—dispersed the Jews. **they respected not . . . priests**—This is the language of the *Gentiles*. "The Jews have no hope of a return: for *they respected not* even good *priests*" (II Chron. 24:19-22) [GROTIUS]. MAURER explains it, "They (the victorious foe) regard not the (Jewish) priests when imploring their pity" (ch. 5:12). The evident antithesis to "As for *us*" (vs. 17) and the language of "the heathen" at the close of vs. 15, of which vs. 16 is the continuation, favor the former view. *Ain*, ע. **17. As for us**—This translation forms the best antithesis to the language of *the heathen* (vss. 15, 16). CALVIN translates, "While as *yet* we stood as a state, our eyes failed," etc. **watched for a nation that could not save us**—Egypt (II Kings 24:7; Isa. 30:7; Jer. 37:5-11). *Tzaddi*, צ. **18. They**—the Chaldeans. **cannot go**—without danger. *Koph*, ק. The last times just before the taking of the city. There was no place of escape; the foe intercepted those wishing to escape from the famine-stricken city, "on the mountains and in the wilderness." **swifter . . . than . . . eagles**—the Chaldean cavalry (Jer. 4:13). **pursued**—lit., "to be hot"; then, "to pursue hotly" (Gen. 31:36). Thus they pursued and overtook Zedekiah (Jer. 52:8, 9). *Resh*, ר. **20. breath . . . anointed of . . . Lord**—our king, with whose life ours was bound up. The original reference seems to have been to Josiah (II Chron. 35:25), killed in battle with Pharaoh-necho; but the language is here applied to Zedekiah, who, though worthless, was still lineal representative of David, and type of Messiah, the "Anointed." Viewed *personally* the language is too favorable to apply to him. **live among the heathen**—Under him we hoped to live securely, even in spite of the surrounding heathen nations [GROTIUS]. *Schin*, ש. **21. Rejoice**—at our calamities (Ps. 137:7). This is a *prophecy* that Edom should exult over the fall of Jerusalem. At the same time it is implied, Edom's joy shall be short-lived. *Ironically* she is told, Rejoice while thou mayest (*Eccles.* 11:9). **cup**—for this image of the confounding effects of God's wrath, see Jeremiah 13:12; 25:15, 16, 21; as to Edom, Jeremiah 49:7-22. *Tau*, ת. **22.** (Isa. 40:2.) Thou hast been punished enough: the end of thy punishment is at hand. **no more carry thee . . . into captivity**—i.e., by the Chaldeans. The Romans carried them away subsequently. The *full* accomplishment of this prophecy must therefore refer to the Jews' final restoration. **discover**—By the severity of His punishments on thee, God shall let men see how great was thy sin (Jer. 49:10). God "covers" sin when He forgives it (Ps. 32:1, 5). He "discovers," or "reveals," it, when He punishes it (Job 20:27). Jeremiah 49:10 shows that *Margin* is wrong, "carry captive" (this rendering is as in Nah. 2:7; cf. *Margin*).

ADAM CLARKE

12. *The kings of the earth.* Jerusalem was so well fortified, by both nature and art, that it appeared as a miracle that it should be taken at all.

13. *For the sins of her prophets, and the iniquities of her priests.* These most wretched beings, under the pretense of zeal for the true religion, persecuted the genuine prophets, priests, and people of God, and caused their blood to be shed in the midst of the city, in the most open and public manner.

14. *They have wandered as blind men in the streets.* Rather, "They ran frantic through the streets; they were stained with blood." This was in their pretended zeal for their cause.

15. *When they fled away.* These priests and prophets were so bad that the very heathen did not like to permit them to sojourn among them. The prophet now resumes the history of the siege.

17. *We have watched for a nation.* Viz., the Egyptians, who were their pretended allies, but were neither able nor willing to help them against the Chaldeans.

18. *We cannot go in our streets.* Supposed to refer to the darts and other missiles cast from the mounds which they had raised on the outside of the walls, by which those who walked in the streets could not shield themselves.

19. *They pursued us upon the mountains.* They hunted down the poor Jews like wild beasts in every part of the country by their marauding parties, whilst the great army besieged Jerusalem. But this may apply to the pursuit of Zedekiah. See what follows.

20. *The breath of our nostrils, the anointed of the Lord.* That is, Zedekiah, the king, who was as the life of the city, was taken in his flight by the Chaldeans, and his eyes were put out; so that he was wholly unfit to perform any function of government; though they had fondly hoped that, if they surrendered and should be led captives, yet they should be permitted to live under their own laws and king in the land of their bondage.

21. *Rejoice and be glad, O daughter of Edom.* A strong irony. *The cup also shall pass through unto thee.* You who have triumphed in our disasters shall shortly have enough of your own. They had joined themselves to the Chaldeans (see Ps. cxxxvii. 7) and therefore they should share in the desolations of Babylon.

MATTHEW HENRY

CHAPTER 5

Verses 1–16

The people of God, overwhelmed with grief, give vent to their sorrows at the throne of grace. *Remember what is* past, *consider and behold* what is present, and *let not all the trouble* we are in *seem little to thee*, and not worth taking notice of," Neh. ix. 32. The one word in which all their grievances are summed up is *reproach*: *Consider, and behold, our reproach.* As it was a reproach, it reflected upon the name and honour of that God who had owned them for his people.

I. They acknowledge the reproach of sin, *the reproach of their youth*, of the early days of their nation. It is a penitent confession of the sins of their ancestors, which they themselves had persisted in, for which they now justly suffered.

II. They represent the reproach they bear, in divers particulars, which tend to their disgrace.

1. They are robbed of that good land which God gave them, *v.* 2. "It is turned to strangers; they dwell in the houses that we built, and this is our reproach."

2. Their state and nation are like widows and orphans (*v.* 3): "*We are fatherless* (that is, helpless). Our king, who is the father of the country, is cut off; nay, God our Father seems to have forsaken us; *our mothers*, our cities, *are* now *as widows*, exposed to wrong and injury, and this is our reproach."

3. They are put hard to it to provide necessaries. Water used to be free but now (*v.* 4), *We have drunk our water for money.* Formerly they had fuel for the fetching; but now, "*Our wood is sold to us*, and we pay dearly for every faggot." But what must they do for bread? Some of them sold their liberty for it (*v.* 6): "*We have given the hand to the Egyptians and to the Assyrians*, have made the best bargain we could, that we might *be satisfied with bread. We got our bread with the peril of our lives.*" They stole out of the city to fetch in some supply; they were in danger of being put to the sword, *the sword of the wilderness* it is called.

4. They are brought into slavery, and this is as much as anything their reproach (*v.* 5): *Our necks are under* the grievous yoke of *persecution*. The poor captives in Babylon *laboured and had no rest*, no night's rest, no sabbath-rest. They would not be ruled by their God, and by his servants the prophets, whose rule was gentle and gracious, and therefore justly are they ruled with rigour by their enemies and their servants.

5. Those who used to be feasted are now famished (*v.* 10): *Our skin was black like an oven*, dried and parched too, *because of the terrible famine*, the *storms of famine* (so the word is).

6. All sorts of people were abused and dishonoured. The *women* were *ravished*, even *the women in Zion*, that holy mountain, *v.* 11.

7. An end was put to all their gladness (*v.* 14): *The young men*, who used to be disposed to mirth, have ceased *from their music.* It was so with the body of the people (*v.* 15): *The joy of their heart ceased. Our dance is turned into mourning.* This may refer to the joy of their solemn feasts, and the dancing used in them (Judges xxi. 21), which was not only modest, but sacred dancing.

8. An end was put to all their glory. The public administration of justice was their glory, but that was gone (*v.* 14). The royal dignity was their glory, but that also was gone: *The crown has fallen from our head*, not only the *king* himself fallen into disgrace, but *the crown*; he has no successor. Earthly crowns are fading falling things; but, blessed be God, there is *a crown of glory that fades not away*, that never falls, *a kingdom that cannot be moved.*

Verses 17–22

I. The people of God express the deep concern they had for the ruins of the temple, more than for any other of their calamities (*v.* 17, 18). "The people have polluted the *mountain of Zion* with their sins, and God has justly made it *desolate*; *the foxes walk upon it* as freely and commonly as they do in the woods."

JAMIESON, FAUSSET, BROWN

CHAPTER 5

VSS. 1-22. EPIPHONEMA, OR A CLOSING RECAPITULATION OF THE CALAMITIES TREATED IN THE PREVIOUS ELEGIES. **1.** (Ps. 89:50, 51.)

2. Our inheritance—"Thine inheritance" (Ps. 79:1). The land given of old to us by Thy gift. **3. fatherless**—Our whole land is full of orphans [CALVIN]. Or, "we are fatherless," being abandoned by Thee our "Father" (Jer. 3:19), [GROTIUS]. **4. water for money**—The Jews were compelled to pay the enemy for the water of their own cisterns after the overthrow of Jerusalem; or rather, it refers to their sojourn in Babylon; they had to pay tax for access to the rivers and fountains. Thus, "our" means the water which we need, the commonest necessary of life. **our wood**—In Judea each one could get wood without pay; in Babylon, "our wood," the wood we need, must be paid for. **5.** Lit., "On our necks we are persecuted"; i.e., Men tread on our necks (Ps. 66:12; Isa. 51:23; cf. Josh. 10:24). The extremest oppression. The foe not merely galled the Jews' face, back, and sides, but their neck. A just retribution, as they had been stiff in neck against the yoke of God (II Chron. 30:8, *Margin;* Neh. 9:29; Isa. 48:4). **6. given . . . hand to**—in token of submission (*Note*, Jer. 50:15). **to . . . Egyptians**—at the death of Josiah (II Chron. 36:3, 4). **Assyrians**—i.e., the Chaldeans who occupied the empire which Assyria had held. So Jeremiah 2:18. **to be satisfied with bread**—(Deut. 28:48). **7.** (Jer. 31:29.) **borne their iniquities**—i.e., the punishment of them. The accumulated sins of our fathers from age to age, as well as our own, are visited on us. They say this as a plea why God should pity them (cf. Ezek. 18:2, etc.). **8. Servants . . . ruled . . . us**—Servants under the Chaldean governors ruled the Jews (Neh. 5:15). Israel, once a "kingdom of priests" (Exod. 19:6), is become like Canaan, "a servant of servants," according to the curse (Gen. 9:25). The Chaldeans were designed to be "servants" of Shem, being descended from Ham (Gen. 9:26). Now through the Jews' sin, their positions are reversed. **9. We gat our bread with . . . peril**—i.e., those of us left in the city after its capture by the Chaldeans. **because of . . . sword of . . . wilderness**—because of the liability to attack by the robber Arabs of the wilderness, through which the Jews had to pass to get "bread" from Egypt (cf. vs. 6). **10.** As an oven is scorched with too much fire, so our skin with the hot blast of famine (*Margin*, rightly, "storms," like the hot simoom). Hunger dries up the pores so that the skin becomes like as if it were scorched by the sun (Job 30:30; Ps. 119:83). **11.** So in just retribution Babylon itself should fare in the end. Jerusalem shall for the last time suffer these woes before her final restoration (Zech. 14:2). **12. hanged . . . by their hand**—a piece of wanton cruelty invented by the Chaldeans. GROTIUS translates, "Princes were hung by the hand *of the enemy*"; hanging was a usual mode of execution (Gen. 40: 19). **elders**—officials (ch. 4:16).

13. young men . . . grind—The work of the lowest *female* slave was laid on young men (Judg. 16:21; Job 31:10). **children fell under . . . wood**—Mere children had to bear burdens of wood so heavy that they sank beneath them. **14.** Aged men in the East meet in the open space round the gate to decide judicial trials and to hold social converse (Job 29:7, 8). **16. The crown**—all our glory, the kingdom and the priesthood (Job 19:9; Ps. 89:39, 44).

17. (Ch. 1:22; 2:11.) **18. foxes**—They frequent desolate places where they can freely and fearlessly roam.

ADAM CLARKE

CHAPTER 5

1. *Remember, O Lord.* In the Vulgate, Syriac, and Arabic, this is headed, "The prayer of Jeremiah." Though this chapter consists of exactly twenty-two verses, the number of letters in the Hebrew alphabet, yet the acrostic form is no longer observed. Perhaps anything so technical was not thought proper when in agony and distress (under a sense of God's displeasure on account of sin) they prostrated themselves before Him to ask for mercy. Be this as it may, no attempt appears to have been made to throw these verses into the form of the preceding chapters. It is properly a solemn prayer of all the people, stating their past and present sufferings, and praying for God's mercy.

2. *Our inheritance is turned to strangers.* The greater part of the Jews were either slain or carried away captive; and even those who were left under Gedaliah were not free, for they were vassals to the Chaldeans.

4. *We have drunken our water for money.* I suppose the meaning of this is that everything was taxed by the Chaldeans, and that they kept the management in their own hands, so that wood and water were both sold, the people not being permitted to help themselves. They were now so lowly reduced by servitude that they were obliged to pay dearly for those things which formerly were common and of no price.

5. *Our necks are under persecution.* We feel the yoke of our bondage; we are driven to our work like the bullock, which has a yoke upon his neck.

6. *We have given the hand to the Egyptians.* We have sought alliances with both the Egyptians and the Assyrians, and made covenants with them in order to get the necessaries of life.

7. *Our fathers have sinned, and are not.* Nations, as such, cannot be punished in the other world; therefore national judgments are to be looked for only in this life. The punishment which the Jewish nation had been meriting for a series of years came now upon them, because they copied and increased the sins of their fathers, and the cup of their iniquity was full.

8. *Servants have ruled over us.* Perhaps he here alludes to the Chaldean soldiers, whose will the wretched Jews were obliged to obey.

9. *We gat our bread with the peril of our lives.* They could not go into the wilderness to feed their cattle, or to get the necessaries of life, without being harassed and plundered by marauding parties, and by these were often exposed to the peril of their lives. This was predicted by Moses, Deut. xxviii. 31.

10. *Our skin was black . . . because of the terrible famine.* Because of the searching winds that burnt up every green thing, destroying vegetation, and in consequence producing a famine.

11. *They ravished the women in Zion, and the maids in the cities of Judah.* The evil mentioned here was predicted by Moses, Deut. xxviii. 30, 32, and by Jeremiah, chap. vi. 12.

12. *Princes are hanged up by their hand.* It is very probable that this was a species of punishment. They were suspended from hooks in the wall by their hands till they died through torture and exhaustion. The body of Saul was fastened to the wall of Beth-shan, probably in the same way; but his head had already been taken off. They were hung in this way that they might be devoured by the fowls of the air.

13. *They took the young men to grind.* This was the work of female slaves. See Isa. xlvii. 2.

14. *The elders have ceased from the gate.* There is now no more justice administered to the people; they are under military law, or disposed of in every sense according to the caprice of their masters.

16. *The crown is fallen from our head.* At feasts, marriages, etc., they used to crown themselves with garlands of flowers; all festivity of this kind was now at an end. Or it may refer to their having lost all sovereignty, being made slaves.

18. *The foxes walk upon it.* Foxes are very numerous in Palestine; see Judg. xv. 4. It was usual among the Hebrews to consider all desolated land to be the resort of wild beasts;

MATTHEW HENRY

II. They comfort themselves with the doctrine of God's eternity (*v.* 19): But *thou, O Lord! remainest for ever*. What shakes the world gives no disturbance to him who made it; whatever revolutions there are on earth there is no change in the Eternal Mind; God is still the same, and *remains for ever* infinitely wise and holy, just and good.

III. They humbly expostulate with God concerning the frowns of heaven they were now under (*v.* 20): "*Wherefore dost thou forget us for ever*, as if we were quite cast out of mind? Thou art the same, and, though the throne of thy sanctuary is demolished, wilt thou not be the same to us?" Though we may not quarrel with God, yet we may plead with him (Jer. xii. 1).

IV. They earnestly pray to God for mercy and grace; "Lord, do not reject *us for ever*, but *turn thou us unto thee*; *renew our days*," *v.* 21. Though these words are not put last, yet the Rabbin, because they would not have the book to conclude with those melancholy words (*v.* 22), repeat this prayer again, and so make these the last words both in writing and reading this chapter. This agrees with that repeated prayer (Ps. lxxx. 3, 7, 19), *Turn us again, and then cause thy face to shine. Turn us* from our idols to thyself, by a sincere repentance and reformation, *and* then *we shall be turned*. If God by his grace renew our hearts, he will by his favour *renew our days*.

JAMIESON, FAUSSET, BROWN

19. (Ps. 102:12.) The perpetuity of God's rule over human affairs, however He may seem to let His people be oppressed for a time, is their ground of hope of restoration.

20. for ever—i.e., for "so long a time." **21.** (Ps. 80:3; Jer. 31:18.) "Restore us to favor with Thee, and so we shall be restored to our old position" [GROTIUS]. Jeremiah is not speaking of spiritual conversion, but of that outward turning whereby God receives men into His fatherly favor, manifested in bestowing prosperity [CALVIN]. Still, as Israel is a type of the Church, temporal goods typify spiritual blessings; and so the sinner may use this prayer for God to convert him. **22.** Rather, "Unless haply Thou hast utterly rejected us, and art beyond measure wroth against us," i.e., Unless Thou art implacable, which is impossible, hear our prayer [CALVIN]. Or, as *Margin*, "For wouldest Thou utterly reject us?" etc.—No; that cannot be. The Jews, in this book, and in Isaiah and Malachi, to avoid the ill-omen of a mournful closing sentence, repeat the verse immediately preceding the last [CALVIN].

ADAM CLARKE

which is, in fact, the case everywhere when the inhabitants are removed from a country.

19. *Thou, O Lord, remainest for ever.* Thou sufferest no change. Thou didst once love us; oh, let that love be renewed towards us!

21. *Renew our days as of old.* Restore us to our former state. Let us regain our country, our Temple, and all the divine offices of our religion; but, more especially, Thy favor.

22. *But thou hast utterly rejected us.* It appears as if Thou hadst sealed our final reprobation, because Thou showest against us exceeding great wrath. But "convert us, O Lord, unto thee, and we shall be converted." He heard the prayer, and at the end of seventy years they were restored to their own land.

THE BOOK OF EZEKIEL

I. The prophet's preparation (1:1-3:27)
A. The visions (1:1-28)
1. Fire (1:1-4)
2. Living ones (1:5-14)
3. Wheels (1:15-21)
4. The likeness (1:22-28)

B. The voice (2:1-3:27)
1. The message (2:1-3:3)
2. The equipment (3:4-15)
3. The responsibility (3:16-21)
4. The commission (3:22-27)

II. Reprobation (4:1-24:27)
A. Results of reprobation (4:1-14:23)
1. The four signs (4:1-5:23)
2. The denunciations (6:1-7:27)
3. The judgment (8:1-14:23)

B. Reason of reprobation (15:1-19:14)
1. The two general figures (15:1-16:63)
2. The riddle (17:1-24)
3. The false excuse (18:1-32)
4. The lament (19:1-14)

C. Righteousness of reprobation (20:1-24:27)
1. Vindicated to elders (20:1-44)
2. The song of the sword (20:45-21:32)
3. The utter evil of the city (22:1-49)
4. Oholah and Oholibah (23:1-49)
5. The destruction of the city (24:1-27)

III. Restoration (25:1-48:35)
A. The nations (25:1-32:32)
1. The doom of four—Ammon, Moab, Edom, Philistia (25:1-17)
2. The doom of two—Tyre and Sidon (26:1-28:24)
3. Parenthesis—restoration of Israel (28:25, 26)
4. The doom of one—Egypt (29:1-32:32)

B. The nation (33:1-39:29)
1. The watchman (33:1-33)
2. The shepherds, false and true (34:1-31)
3. The new order (35:1-36:38)
4. The vision of the bones (37:1-28)
5. The last enemy (38:1-39:29)

C. The restored order (40:1-48:35)
1. The Temple (40:1-42:20)
2. Jehovah (43:1-27)
3. The service of the Temple (44:1-46:24)
4. The river (47:1-12)
5. The land (47:13-23)
6. The people (48:1-29)
7. The city (48:30-35)

The writings of the prophets, which speak of the "things that should be hereafter," seem to utter the same call that St. John had (Rev. 4:1), "Come up hither"; but the prophecy of this book is as if the voice said, "Come up higher"; as we go forward in time (for Ezekiel prophesied in the captivity, as Jeremiah prophesied just before it), so we soar upward in discoveries yet more sublime of the divine glory. These waters of the sanctuary still grow deeper; so far are they from being fordable that in some places they are scarcely fathomable; yet, deep as they are, out of them flow streams which "make glad the city of our God."

I. The writer was Ezekiel; his name signifies, "The strength of God," or one "girt or strengthened of God." He girded up the loins of his mind to the service, and God put strength into him. "I have made thy face strong against their faces." If we give credit to the tradition of the Jews, he was put to death by the captives in Babylon for his boldness in reproving them; it is stated that his brains were dashed out. An Arabic historian says that he was put to death and was buried in the sepulchre of Shem the son of Noah.

II. Concerning the date, the place, and the time. The scene is laid in Babylon, when it was a "house" of bondage to the "Israel of God"; there the prophecies of this book were written, when the prophet himself, and the people to whom he prophesied, were captives there. Ezekiel prophesied in the beginning of the captivity. It was an indication of God's goodwill and his gracious designs in their affliction, that he raised up prophets to convince them when, in the beginning of their troubles they were unhumbled, which was Ezekiel's business, and to comfort them when they were dejected and discouraged.

III. Concerning the matter and scope of it:

A. There is much that is mysterious, dark, and hard to be understood, especially in the beginning and the latter end of it; therefore the Jews forbade the reading of it to their young men, till they came to be thirty years of age, lest by the difficulties they met they should be prejudiced against the Scriptures; but if we read these difficult parts with humility and reverence and search them diligently, though we may not be able to untie all the knots, any more than we can solve all the phenomena in the book of nature, yet we may from them gather a great deal for the confirming of our faith and the encouraging of our hope in God.

B. Though the visions here be intricate, such as an elephant may swim in, yet the sermons are mostly plain, such as a lamb may wade in; and the chief design is to "show God's people their transgressions," that in their captivity they might be repenting and not complaining. As it was of great use to the oppressed captives themselves to have a prophet with them, so it was a testimony to their religion against their oppressors who ridiculed it and them.

C. Though the reproofs and the threatenings here are sharp and bold, yet towards the close of the book very comfortable assurances are given of great mercy God had in store for them; and there one finds some reference to gospel times and its accomplishment in the kingdom of the Messiah. By opening the "terrors of the Lord" he prepares Christ's way. The visions were the prophet's credentials. In chapters 1—3, the reproofs and threatenings; chapters 4—24, the comforts in the latter part of the book, and in between are messages sent to the nations that bordered upon the land of Israel, whose destruction is foretold (ch. 25—35), to make way for the restoration of God's Israel and the re-establishment of their city and temple (ch. 36 to the end).

MATTHEW HENRY

CHAPTER 1

Verses 1–3

The circumstances of the vision which Ezekiel saw, and in which he received his commission, are here particularly set down, that the narrative may appear to be authentic. It may be of use to keep an account when and where God has been pleased to manifest himself to our souls in a peculiar manner.

JAMIESON, FAUSSET, BROWN

CHAPTER 1

VSS. 1-28. EZEKIEL'S VISION BY THE CHEBAR. FOUR CHERUBIM AND WHEELS. **1. Now it came to pass**—rather, *And* it came. . . . As this formula in Joshua 1:1 has reference to the *written* history of previous times, so here (and in Ruth 1:1, and Esther 1:1), it refers to the *unwritten* history which was before the mind of the writer. The prophet by it, as it were, continues the history of the preceding times. In the fourth year of Zedekiah's reign (Jer. 51:59), Jeremiah sent by Seraiah a message to the

ADAM CLARKE

CHAPTER 1

MATTHEW HENRY

I. The time when Ezekiel had this vision was *in the thirtieth year, v.* 1. Some make it the thirtieth year of the prophet's age; being a priest, he was at that age to enter upon the full execution of the priestly office. Others make it to be the thirtieth year from the beginning of the reign of Nabopolassar, the father of Nebuchadnezzar. But the Chaldee paraphrase fixes upon another era, and says that this was the thirtieth year after *Hilkiah the priest found the book of the law in the house of the sanctuary, at midnight, after the setting of the moon, in the days of Josiah the king.* It was in the *fourth month,* answering to our June, and in the *fifth day of the month,* that Ezekiel had this vision, *v.* 2. It is probable that it was on the sabbath day, because we read (*ch.* iii. 16) that *at the end of seven days,* the next sabbath, the word of the Lord came to him again.

II. The melancholy circumstances he was in when God honoured him. He was *among the captives, by the river of Chebar, and it was in the fifth year of king Jehoiachin's captivity.*

1. The people of God were now, some of them, *captives in the land of the Chaldeans.* The body of the Jewish nation yet remained in their own land, but these were the first-fruits of the captivity, and they were some of the best. The word of instruction and the rod of correction may be of great service to us, in concert and concurrence with each other, the word to explain the rod and the rod to enforce the word: both together give wisdom. In their captivity they were destitute of ordinary helps for their souls, and therefore God raised them up these extraordinary ones; for God's children, if they be hindered in their education one way, shall have it made up another way. The Jews that remained in their own land had Jeremiah with them, those that had gone into captivity had Ezekiel with them; for wherever the children of God are scattered abroad he will find out tutors for them.

2. The prophet was himself among the captives by *the river Chebar.* Interpreters agree not what river this of Chebar was. The best men, and those that are dearest to God, often share in the public and national judgments that are inflicted for sin; those feel the smart who contributed nothing to the guilt. The captives will be best instructed by one who is a captive among them and experimentally knows their sorrows. Wherever we are we may keep up our communion with God. When St. Paul was a prisoner the gospel had a free course. When St. John was banished into the Isle of Patmos Christ visited him there.

III. The discovery which God was pleased to make of himself to the prophet. He here tells us what he saw, what he heard, and what he felt. 1. He *saw visions of God, v.* 1. No man can *see God and live;* but many have seen visions of God, displays of the divine glory as have instructed them. Ezekiel was employed in turning the hearts of the people to the Lord their God, and therefore he must himself see the visions of God. It concerns those to be well acquainted with God themselves, and much affected with what they know of him, whose business it is to bring others to the knowledge and love of him. That he might see the *visions of God the heavens were opened;* the darkness and distance which hindered his visions were conquered. 2. He heard the voice of God (*v.* 3): *The word of the Lord came expressly* to him, and what he saw was designed to prepare him for what he was to hear. *The essential Word* (so we may take it), *the Word who is, who is what he is, came to Ezekiel,* to send him on his errand. 3. He felt the power of God opening his eyes to see the visions, opening his ear to hear the voice, and opening his heart to receive both.

Verses 4–14

I. The introduction to this vision of the angels is magnificent and awakening, *v.* 4. The prophet, observing the heavens to open, *looked,* looked up. To clear the way, *behold, a whirlwind came out of the north,* which would drive away the interposing mists. God can by a whirlwind clear the sky and air, and produce that serenity of mind which is necessary to our communion with Heaven. This whirlwind came to Ezekiel (as that to Elijah, 1 Kings xix. 11), to *prepare the way of the Lord.*

II. The vision itself. God's pavilion in which he rests, his chariot in which he rides, is *darkness and thick clouds,* Ps. xviii. 11; civ. 3. The cloud is accompanied with *a fire,* as upon Mount Sinai, where God resided in a *thick cloud;* but *the sight of his glory was like devouring fire* (Exod. xxiv. 16, 17), and his first appearance to Moses was *in a flame of fire in the bush;* for *our God is a consuming fire.* The fire is surrounded with a glory: *A brightness was about it.* Though we cannot see into the fire, cannot by searching find out God to perfection, yet we see the bright-

JAMIESON, FAUSSET, BROWN

captives (Jer. 29) to submit themselves to God and lay aside their flattering hopes of a speedy restoration. This communication was in the next year, the fifth, and the fourth month of the same king (for Jehoiachin's captivity and Zedekiah's accession coincide in time), *followed up* by a prophet raised up among the captives themselves, the energetic Ezekiel. **thirtieth year**—i.e., counting from the beginning of the reign of Nabopolassar, father of Nebuchadnezzar, the era of the Babylonian empire, 625 B.C., which epoch coincides with the eighteenth year of Josiah, that in which the book of the law was found, and the consequent reformation began [SCALIGER]; or the thirtieth year of Ezekiel's life. As the Lord was about to be a "little sanctuary" (ch. 11:16) to the exiles on the Chebar, so Ezekiel was to be the ministering priest; therefore he marks his priestly relation to God and the people at the outset; the close, which describes the future temple, thus answering to the beginning. By designating himself expressly as "the priest" (vs. 3), and as having reached his thirtieth year (the regular year of priests commencing their office), he marks his office as the priest among the prophets. Thus the opening vision follows naturally as the formal institution of that spiritual temple in which he was to minister [FAIRBAIRN]. **Chebar**—the same as Chabor or Habor, whither the ten tribes had been transported by Tiglath-pileser and Shalmaneser (II Kings 17:6; I Chron. 5:26). It flows into the Euphrates near Carchemish or Circesium, 200 miles north of Babylon. **visions of God**—Four expressions are used as to the revelation granted to Ezekiel, the three first having respect to what was presented from without, to assure him of its *reality,* the fourth to his being internally made fit to receive the revelation; "the heavens were opened" (so Matt. 3:16; Acts 7:56; 10:11; Rev. 19:11); "he saw visions of God"; "the word of Jehovah came *verily* (as the meaning is rather than 'expressly,' *English Version,* vs. 3) unto him" (it was no unreal hallucination); and "the hand of Jehovah was upon him" (Isa. 8:11; Dan. 10:10, 18; Rev. 1:17; the Lord by His touch strengthening him for his high and arduous ministry, that he might be able to witness and report aright the revelations made to him). **2. Jehoiachin's captivity**—In the third or fourth year of Jehoiakim, father of Jehoiachin, the *first* carrying away of Jewish captives to Babylon took place, and among them was Daniel. The *second* was under Jehoiachin, when Ezekiel was carried away. The *third* and final one was at the taking of Jerusalem under Zedekiah. **4. whirlwind**—emblematic of God's judgments (Jer. 23:19; 25:32). **out of the north**—i.e., from Chaldea, whose hostile forces would invade Judea from a *northerly* direction. The prophet conceives himself in the temple. **fire infolding itself**—laying hold on whatever surrounds it, drawing it to itself, and devouring it. Lit., "catching itself," i.e., kindling itself [FAIRBAIRN]. The same *Hebrew* occurs in Exodus 9:24, as to the "fire *mingled with* the hail." **brightness . . . about it**—i.e., about the "cloud." **out of the midst thereof**—i.e., out of the midst of the "fire." **colour of amber**—rather, "the glancing brightness (lit., the eye, and so *the glancing appearance*) of polished brass." The *Hebrew, chasmal,* is from two roots, "smooth" and "brass" (cf. vs. 7 and Rev. 1:15) [GESENIUS]. LXX and *Vulgate* translate it, "electrum"; a brilliant metal compounded of gold and silver. **5.** Ezekiel was himself of a "gigantic nature, and thereby suited to counteract the Babylonish spirit of the times, which loved to manifest itself in gigantic, grotesque forms" [HENGSTENBERG]. **living creatures**—So the Greek ought to have been translated in the parallel passage, Revelation 4:6, not as *English Version,* "beasts"; for one of the "four" is *a man,* and man cannot be termed "beast." Ch. 10:20 shows that it is the cherubim that are meant. **likeness of a man**—Man, the noblest of the four, is the ideal model after which they are fashioned (vs. 10; ch. 10:14). The point of comparison between him and them is the erect posture of their bodies, though doubtless including also the general mien. Also the *hands* (ch. 10:21). **6.** Not only were there four distinct living creatures, but each of the four had four faces, making sixteen in all. The four living creatures of the cherubim answer by contrast to the four world monarchies represented by four *beasts,* Assyria, Persia, Greece, and Rome (Dan. 7). The Fathers identified them with the four Gospels: Matthew the lion, Mark the ox, Luke the man, John the eagle. Two cherubim only stood over the ark in the temple; two more are now added, to imply that, while the law is retained as the basis, a new form is needed to be added to impart new life to it. The

ADAM CLARKE

1. *In the thirtieth year.* We know not what this date refers to. Some think it was the age of the prophet; others think the date is taken from the time that Josiah renewed the covenant with the people, 2 Kings xxii. 3. *Fourth month.* Thammuz, answering nearly to our July.

I saw visions of God. Emblems and symbols of the Divine Majesty. He particularly refers to those in this chapter.

2. *Jehoiachin's captivity.* Called also Jeconiah and Coniah; see 2 Kings xxiv. 12. He was carried away by Nebuchadnezzar; see 2 Kings xxiv. 14.

3. *The hand of the Lord.* I was filled with His power, and with the influence of the prophetic spirit.

4. *A whirlwind came out of the north.* Nebuchadnezzar, whose land, Babylonia, lay north of Judea. Chaldea is thus frequently denominated by Jeremiah. *A great cloud, and a fire infolding itself.* A mass of fire concentrated in a vast cloud, that the flames might be more distinctly observable, the fire never escaping from the cloud, but issuing, and then returning in upon itself. It was in a state of powerful agitation; but always involving itself, or returning back to the center whence it appeared to issue. *A brightness was about it.* A fine tinge of light surrounded the cloud, in order to make its limits the more discernible, beyond which verge the turmoiling fire did not proceed. *The colour of amber.* This was in the center of the cloud, and this amber-color substance was the center of the laboring flame. The word which we translate *amber* was used to signify a compound metal, very bright, made of gold and brass.

5. *Also out of the midst thereof came . . . four living creatures.* As the amber-colored body was the center of the fire, and this fire was in the center of the cloud; so out of this amber-colored igneous center came the living creatures just mentioned.

6. *Every one had four faces.* There were four several figures of these living creatures, and each of these figures had four distinct faces. But as the face of the man was that which was presented to the prophet's view, so that he saw it more plainly than any of the others, hence it is said, v. 5, that each of these figures had the likeness of a man; and the whole of this compound image bore a general resemblance to the human figure.

MATTHEW HENRY

ness that is round about it. Moses might see God's back parts, but not his face. Nothing is more easy than to determine that God is, nothing more difficult than to describe what he is. The *living creatures* which he saw coming *out of the midst of the fire* were *seraphim—burners*—not the *living creatures* themselves (angels are spirits, and cannot be seen), but *the likeness* of them, such as God saw fit to use for the leading of the prophet. *The likeness of these living creatures came out of the midst of the fire.* The prophet himself explains this vision (*ch.* x. 20): *I knew that the living creatures were the cherubim.* They are living creatures; the creatures of God, the work of his hands. The sun (say some) is a flame of *fire enfolding itself*, but it is not a living creature. The prophet sees four of these living creatures to intimate that they are sent towards the four winds of heaven, Matt. xxiv. 31. Zechariah saw them as four chariots going forth east, west, north and south, Zech. vi. 1. God has messengers to send every way. *They had the likeness of a man;* they are reasonable, intelligent beings, who have that *spirit of a man* which is the *candle of the Lord.* The angels of God appear in *the likeness of man* because in *the fulness of time* the Son of God was not only to appear in that likeness, but to assume that nature. They *all four had the face of a man, v.* 5, but, besides that, they had *the face of a lion, an ox*, and *an eagle*, each masterly in its kind, *the lion* among *wild* beasts, *the ox* among *tame* ones, and *the eagle* among fowls, *v.* 10. The scattered perfections of the living creatures on earth meet in the angels of heaven. They have *the understanding of a man*, and such as far exceeds it; they also resemble man in tenderness and humanity. But a *lion* excels man in strength, and boldness, therefore the angels, who in this resemble them, put on the *face of a lion. An ox* excels man in diligence, and patience, in the work he has to do; therefore the angels, employed in the service of God and the church, put on *the face of an ox. An eagle* excels man in quickness and piercing sight, and in soaring high; and therefore the angels, who seek things above, and see far into divine mysteries, put on *the face of a flying eagle. Every one had four wings, v.* 6.

The scope and intention of these visions, 1. To possess the prophet's mind with high, and honourable thoughts of God by whom he was commissioned. It is *the likeness of the glory of the Lord* that he sees (*v.* 28). So great a God as this must be served *with reverence and godly fear.* 2. To strike a terror upon the sinners who remained in Zion, and those who had already come to Babylon, who bade defiance to the threatenings of Jerusalem's ruin. That this vision had a reference to the destruction of Jerusalem seems plain from *ch.* xliii. 3. 3. To speak comfort to those that feared God, and humbled themselves under his mighty hand. "Let them know that, though they are captives in Babylon, yet they have God nigh unto them; though they have not *the place of the sanctuary* they have the God of the sanctuary. Now that the church is to be planted for a long time in another country, the Lord shows a glory in the midst of them, as he had done at their first constituting into a church in the wilderness." The first part of the vision represents God as attended and served by an innumerable company of angels, who are all his ministers, *doing his commandments* and *hearkening to the voice of his word.*

Faith and hope are the soul's wings, upon which it soars upward; pious and devout affections are its wings on which it is carried forward. Their wings were joined (*v.* 9–11) in token of their perfect unity and unanimity. Two of their wings were made use of in covering their bodies, the spiritual bodies they assumed. Their feet were *straight feet* (*v.* 7); they stood straight, and firm, and steady.

Their feet were winged (so the LXX); they went so swiftly that it was as if they flew. They had not only wings for motion, but hands for action (*v.* 8). They are *the hands of a man*, which are wonderfully made and fitted for service, guided by reason and understanding. Calves' feet denote the swiftness of their motion. The living creatures are active beings.

JAMIESON, FAUSSET, BROWN

number four may have respect to the four quarters of the world, to imply that God's angels execute His commands everywhere. Each head in front had the face of a man as the primary and prominent one: on the right the face of a lion, on the left the face of an ox, above from behind the face of an eagle. The Mosaic cherubim were similar, only that the human faces were put looking towards each other, and towards the mercy seat between, being formed out of the same mass of pure gold as the latter (Exod. 25:19, 20). In Isaiah 6:2 two wings are added to cover their countenances; because there they stand by the throne, here under the throne; there God deigns to consult them, and His condescension calls forth their humility, so that they veil their faces before Him; here they execute His commands. The face expresses their intelligence; the wings, their rapidity in fulfilling God's will. The Shekinah or flame, that signified God's presence, and the written name, JEHOVAH, occupied the intervening space between the cherubim. Genesis 4:14, 16 and 3:24 ("placed"; properly, "to place in *a tabernacle*"), imply that the cherubim were appointed at the fall as symbols of God's presence in a consecrated place, and that man was to worship there. In the patriarchal dispensation when the flood had caused the removal of the cherubim from Eden, *seraphim* or *teraphim* (*Chaldean* dialect) were made as models of them for domestic use (Gen. 31:19, *Margin* 30). The silence of Exodus 25 and 26 as to their configuration, whereas everything else is minutely described, is because their form was so well known already to Bezaleel and all Israel by tradition as to need no detailed description. Hence Ezekiel (ch. 10:20) at once knows them, for he had seen them repeatedly in the carved work of the outer sanctuary of Solomon's temple (I Kings 6:23-29). He therefore consoles the exiles with the hope of having the same cherubim in the renovated temple which should be reared; and he assures them that the same God who dwelt between the cherubim of the temple would be still with His people by the Chebar. But they were not in Zerubbabel's temple; therefore Ezekiel's foretold temple, if literal, is yet future. The ox is selected as chief of the tame animals, the lion among the wild, the eagle among birds, and man the head of all, in his ideal, realized by the Lord Jesus, combining all the excellencies of the animal kingdom. The cherubim probably represent the ruling powers by which God acts in the natural and moral world. Hence they sometimes answer to the ministering angels; elsewhere, to the redeemed saints (the elect Church) through whom, as by the angels, God shall hereafter rule the world and proclaim the manifold wisdom of God (Matt. 19:28; I Cor. 6:2; Eph. 3:10; Rev. 3:21; 4:6-8). The "lions" and "oxen," amidst "palms" and "open flowers" carved in the temple, were the four-faced cherubim which, being traced on a flat surface, presented only one aspect of the four. The human-headed winged bulls and eagle-headed gods found in Nineveh, sculptured amidst palms and tulip-shaped flowers, were borrowed by corrupted tradition from the cherubim placed in Eden near its fruits and flowers. So the Aaronic calf (Exod. 32:4, 5) and Jeroboam's calves at Dan and Bethel, a schismatic imitation of the sacred symbols in the temple at Jerusalem. So the ox figures of Apis on the sacred arks of Egypt. **7. straight feet**–i.e., straight *legs*. Not protruding in any part as the legs of an ox, but straight like a man's [GROTIUS]. Or, like solid pillars; *not bending*, as man's, at the knee. They glided along, rather than walked. Their movements were all sure, right, and without effort [KITTO, *Cyclopedia*]. **sole . . . calf's foot**–HENDERSON hence supposes that "*straight feet*" implies that they did not project horizontally like men's feet, but vertically as calves' feet. The *solid firmness* of the round foot of a calf seems to be the point of comparison. **colour**–*the glittering appearance*, indicating God's purity. **8.** The hands of each were the hands of a man. The hand is the symbol of *active power, guided by "skifulness"* (Ps. 78:72). **under their wings**–signifying their operations are hidden from our too curious prying; and as the "wings" signify something more than human, viz., the secret prompting of God, it is also implied that they are moved by it and not by their own power, so that they do nothing at random, but all with divine wisdom. **they four had . . . faces and . . . wings**–He returns to what he had stated already in vs. 6; this gives a reason why they had hands on their four sides, viz., because they had faces and wings on the four sides. They moved whithersoever they would, not by active energy merely, but also by knowledge (expressed by their *faces*) and divine guidance (expressed by their "wings"). **9. they**–had no occasion

ADAM CLARKE

F. B. MEYER:

A vision of God's majesty (1:1–21). A dark storm cloud approached the prophet, from which an incessant blaze of lightning scintillated. As it drew near, the forms of four living creatures became visible, combining, under various figures, intelligence, strength, patience, and soaring aspiration. The wheels were evidently symbolical of the cycles of divine providence, which cooperate with the ministers of the divine will. The slab of blue expanse supported a human semblance, suggestive of that great later event—God manifest in the flesh. The whole conception impresses us with the reality, order and majesty of the Eternal God. Those holy beings surely represent the intelligent company of innumerable angels and servants, while the wheels represent the material creation. All these are sent forth to minister to us if we are in union with God. All things serve the servants of the Most High.—*Bible Commentary*

7. *Their feet were straight feet.* There did not seem to be any flexure at the knee, nor were the legs separated in that way as to indicate progression by walking. *Like the sole of a calf's foot.* Before it is stated to be a straight foot, one that did not lay down a flat horizontal sole, like that of the human foot. *And they sparkled like the colour of burnished brass.* I suppose this refers rather to the hoof of the calf's foot than to the whole appearance of the leg. There is scarcely anything that gives a higher lustre than highly polished or burnished brass. Our blessed Lord is represented with legs like burnished brass, Rev. i. 15.

MATTHEW HENRY

Whatever service they went about *they went everyone straight forward* (*v.* 9, 12). If thus *our eye be single*, our *whole body will be full of light*. The singleness of the eye is the sincerity of the heart. *They went straight forward*, everyone about his own work; they did not thwart one another. *They turned not when they went*, *v.* 9, 12. They minded no diversions; as they turned not back, so they turned not aside.

They went whither the Spirit was to go (*v.* 12). Whithersoever *the Spirit* of God would have them *go*, thither *they went*. The prophet saw these living creatures (*v.* 13), by their own light, for *their appearance was like burning coals of fire*.

He saw them by the light of *lamps*, which *went up and down among* them, the shining whereof *was* very *bright*. The angels of light are in the light, but we see them and their works only by candle-light, by the dim light *of lamps* that go *up and down among* them; when *the day breaks, and the shadows flee away*, we shall see them clearly.

Verses 15–25

I. The vision of the *wheels*, *v.* 15–21. The glory of God appears not only in the splendour of the upper world, but in the steadiness of his government here in this lower world. *As he beheld the living creatures*, and was contemplating the glory this other vision presented itself to his view. 1. The dispensations of Providence are compared to *wheels*, the wheels of a chariot. *Wheels*, though they move not of themselves, as *the living creatures* do, are yet made movable. The wheel is said to have four *faces*, looking four several ways (*v.* 15), denoting that the providence of God exerts itself east, west, north, and south, and extends itself to the remotest corners. At first Ezekiel saw it as *one wheel* (*v.* 15), one sphere; but afterwards he saw it was four, but *they* four *had one likeness* (*v.* 16). Various events answer the same intention. *Their appearance and their work* are said to be *like the colour of a beryl* (*v.* 16), *the colour of Tarshish* (so the word is), that is, of the sea. The nature of things in this world is like that of the sea, in continual flux and yet there is a constant coherence. The sea ebbs and flows, so does Providence in its disposals. The sea looks blue, as the air does, because of the shortness of our sight, which can see but a little way of either. We cannot find out that which God does *from the beginning to the end*, Eccles. iii. 11. We see but *parts of his ways* (Job. xxvi. 14), and all beyond looks blue. It is *far above out of our sight. Their appearance and their work* are *as it were a wheel in the middle of a wheel.* We pretend not to give a mathematical description of it. The disposals of Providence seem to us intricate, perplexed, and unaccountable, and yet they will appear in the issue to have been all wisely ordered. The motion of these wheels was steady and constant: *They returned not when they went* (*v.* 17), because they never went amiss. God takes his work before him, and he will have it forward; and it is going on even when it seems to us to be going backward. *They went* as the Spirit directed them, and therefore *returned not.* We should not have occasion to return back as we have, and to undo that by repentance which we have done amiss, and to do it over again, if we were but *led by the Spirit*

JAMIESON, FAUSSET, BROWN

to turn themselves round when changing their direction, for they had a face (vs. 6) looking to each of the four quarters of heaven. They made no mistakes; and their work needed not be gone over again. Their wings were joined above in pairs (see vs. 11). **10. they . . . had the face of a man**–viz., in front. The human face was the primary and prominent one and the fundamental part of the composite whole. On its right was the lion's face; on the left, the ox's (called "cherub," ch. 10:14); at the back from above was the eagle's. **11.** The tips of the two outstretched wings reached to one another, while the other two, in token of humble awe, formed a veil for the lower parts of the body. **stretched upward**–rather, "were parted from above" (cf. *Margin*, Isa. 6:2, *Note*). The joining together of their wings above implies that, though the movements of Providence on earth may seem conflicting and confused, yet if one lift up his eyes to heaven, he will see that they admirably conspire towards the one end at last. **12.** The same idea as in vs. 9. The repetition is because we men are so hard to be brought to acknowledge the wisdom of God's doings; they seem tortuous and confused to us, but they are all tending steadily to one aim. **the spirit**–the secret impulse whereby God moves His angels to the end designed. They do not turn back or aside till they have fulfilled the office assigned them. **13. likeness . . . appearance**–not tautology. "Likeness" expresses the general form; "appearance," the particular aspect. **coals of fire**–denoting the intensely pure and burning justice wherewith God punishes by His angels those who, like Israel, have hardened themselves against His long-suffering. So in Isaiah 6, instead of cherubim, the name "seraphim," ***the** burning ones*, is applied, indicating God's consuming righteousness; whence their cry to Him is, "Holy! holy! holy!" and the burning coal is applied to his lips, for the message through his mouth was to be one of judicial severance of the godly from the ungodly, to the ruin of the latter. **lamps**–torches. The fire emitted sparks and flashes of light, as torches do. **went up and down**–expressing the marvellous vigor of God's Spirit, in all His movements never resting, never wearied. **fire . . . bright**–indicating the glory of God. **out of the fire . . . lightning**–God's righteousness will at last cause the bolt of His wrath to fall on the guilty; as now, on Jerusalem. **14. ran and returned**–Incessant, restless motion indicates the plenitude of life in these cherubim; so in Revelation 4:8, "they rest not day or night" (Zech. 4:10). **flash of lightning**–rather, as distinct from "lightning" (vs. 13), "the meteor-flash," or sheet lightning [FAIRBAIRN]. **15. one wheel**–The "dreadful height" of the wheel (vs. 18) indicates the gigantic, terrible energy of the complicated revolutions of God's providence, bringing about His purposes with unerring certainty. One wheel appeared traversely within another, so that the movement might be without turning, whithersoever the living creatures might advance (vs. 17). Thus each wheel was composed of two circles cutting one another at right angles, "one" only of which appeared to touch the ground ("upon the earth)," according to the direction the cherubim desired to move in. **with his four faces**–rather, '*according* to its four faces" or sides; as there was a side or direction to each of the four creatures, so there was a wheel for each of the sides [FAIRBAIRN]. The four sides or semicircles of each composite wheel pointed, as the four faces of each of the living creatures, to the four quarters of heaven. HAVERNICK refers "his" or "its" to *the wheels.* The cherubim and their wings and wheels stood in contrast to the symbolical figures, somewhat similar, then existing in Chaldea, and found in the remains of Assyria. The latter, though derived from the original revelation by tradition, came by corruption to symbolize the astronomical zodiac, or the sun and celestial sphere, by a circle with wings or irradiations. But Ezekiel's cherubim rise above natural objects, the gods of the heathen, to the representation of the one true God, who made and continually upholds them. **16. appearance . . . work**–their *form* and the *material* of their work. **beryl**–rather, "the glancing appearance of the Tarshish-stone"; the chrysolite or topaz, brought fron Tarshish or Tartessus in Spain. It was one of the gems in the breastplate of the high priest (Exod. 28:20; Song of Sol. 5:14; Dan. 10:6). **four had one likeness**–The similarity of the wheels to one another implies that there is no inequality in all God's works, that all have a beautiful analogy and proportion. **17. went upon their four sides**–Those faces or sides of the four wheels moved which answered to the direction in which the cherubim desired to move; while the transverse circles in each of the four com-

ADAM CLARKE

9. *Their wings were joined one to another.* When their wings were extended, they formed a sort of canopy level with their own heads or shoulders; and on this canopy was the throne, and the "likeness of the man" upon it, v. 26. *They turned not when they went.* The wings did not flap in flying; as they glided in reference to their feet, so they soared in reference to their wings.

10. *As for the likeness of their faces.* There was but one body to each of those compound animals, but each body had four faces: the faces of a man and of a lion on the right side; the faces of an ox and an eagle on the left side.

12. *They went every one straight forward.* Not by progressive stepping, but by gliding. *Whither the spirit was to go.* Whither that whirlwind blew, they went, being borne on by the wind; see v. 4.

13. *Like burning coals of fire.* The whole substance appeared to be of flame; and among them frequent coruscations of fire, like vibrating lamps, often emitting lightning, or rather sparks of fire, as we have seen struck out of strongly ignited iron in a forge.

14. *The living creatures ran and returned.* They had a circular movement; they were in rapid motion, but did not increase their distance from the spectator.

15. *One wheel upon the earth.* Most probably the wheel within means merely the nave in which the spokes are inserted, in reference to the ring, rim, or periphery, where these spokes terminate from the center or nave.

MATTHEW HENRY

and followed his direction. *The Spirit of life* (so some read it) *was in the wheels*, which carried them on with ease and evenness. They were *full of eyes round about*, plainly denoting that the motions of Providence are all directed by infinite wisdom. The issues of things are not determined by a blind fortune, but by those *eyes of the Lord* which *run to and fro through the earth*, and *are in every place, beholding the evil and the good*. The wheel is said to be *by the living creatures*. Such a close connexion is there between *the living creatures* and the *wheels* that they moved and rested together. *When the living creatures went, the wheels went by them;* when God has work to do by the ministry of angels second causes are all found, or made, ready to concur in it. If *the living creatures were lifted up from the earth*, were elevated to any service above the common course of nature, the wheels move in concert with them, and *are lifted up over against them*, *v.* 19–21. The reason is because *the spirit of the living creatures was in the wheels*; the same wisdom, power, and holiness of God, that guides and governs the angels, orders all the motions of the ceatures in this lower world. God is the soul of the world, and animates the whole, both that above and that beneath, so that they move in perfect harmony, as the upper and lower parts of the natural body do, so that *whithersoever the Spirit is to go* (whatever God wills and purposes to be done) *thither their spirit is to go*.

II. The notice he took of *the firmament* above *over the heads of the living creatures*. What is done on earth is done under the heaven, under its inspection and influence. He saw: *The firmament was as the colour of the terrible crystal;* the vastness and brightness of it struck him with an awful reverence. God is on high, *above the firmament*; the angels are *under the firmament*, which denotes their subjection to God's dominion. He heard the *noise of the angels' wings*, *v.* 24—to awaken the attention of the prophet to that which God was about to say to him from *the firmament*, *v.* 25. He heard a *voice from the firmament*, from him that sits upon the throne, *v.* 25. When the angels had roused a careless world, they stood still, and *let down their wings*, that there might be a profound silence, and so God's voice might be the better heard. The voice of Providence is designed to open men's ears to the voice of the word.

Verses 26–28

The other parts of this vision were but a preface. God in them had made himself known as Lord of angels and supreme director of all the affairs of this lower world. But now that a divine revelation is to be given to a prophet, we must look higher than the living creatures or the wheels, and must expect that from the eternal Word. Ezekiel, hearing a voice from the firmament, looked up, as John did, to *see the voice that spoke with him*, and he *saw one like unto the Son of man*, Rev. i. 12, 13. This glory of Christ that the prophet saw *was above the firmament* that was *over the heads* of the living creatures, *v.* 26. This dignity and dominion of the Redeemer before his incarnation magnify his condescension in his incarnation. The first thing he observed was a *throne*; for divine revelation comes backed with a royal authority. We must have an eye of faith to God and Christ as upon a throne. The first thing that John discovered in his visions was *a throne set in heaven* (Rev. iv. 2). It is a throne of glory, a throne of grace, a throne of triumph, a throne of government, a throne of judgment. On the throne he saw *the appearance of a man*. This is good news to the children of men, that the throne above the firmament is filled with one that is not ashamed to appear, even there, in the likeness of man. He saw him as a prince and judge upon this throne, in more than human glory, *v.* 27, for God dwells in light, and *covers himself with light as with a garment*. There was the *appearance of fire, round about within the amber;* it was inward and involved. That below was outward. Some make the former to signify Christ's divine nature, hidden within the *colour of amber*; it is what no man has seen nor can see. The latter they suppose to be his human nature, the glory of which there were those who saw; the glory as of *the only begotten of the Father, full of grace and truth*, John i. 14. The throne is surrounded with a rainbow, *v.* 28. It is so in St. John's vision, Rev. iv. 3. As it is a display of majesty, so it is a pledge of mercy, for it is a confirmation of the gracious promise God has made. Now that the fire of God's wrath was breaking out against Jerusalem, he would *look upon the bow and remember the covenant*, as he promised in such a case, Lev. xxvi. 42. The conclusion of this vision. *This was the appearance of the likeness of the glory of the Lord*. Here, as all along, the prophet is careful to guard against all gross corporeal thoughts

JAMIESON, FAUSSET, BROWN

posite wheels remained suspended from the ground, so as not to impede the movements of the others. **18. rings**—i.e., felloes or circumferences of the wheels. **eyes**—The multiplicity of eyes here in the wheels, and ch. 10:12, in the cherubim themselves, symbolizes the *plenitude of intelligent life*, the eye being the window through which "the spirit of the living creatures" in the wheels (vs. 20) looks forth (cf. Zech. 4:10). As the wheels signify the providence of God, so the eyes imply that He sees all the circumstances of each case, and does nothing by blind impulse. **19. went by them**—went *beside* them. **20. the spirit was to go**—i.e., their will was for going whithersoever the Spirit was for going. **over against them**—rather, *beside* or *in conjunction with them.*

spirit of the living creature—put collectively for "the living *creatures*"; the cherubim. Having first viewed them separately, he next views them in the aggregate as the composite living *creature* in which the Spirit resided. The life intended is that connected with God, holy, spiritual life, in the plenitude of its active power. **21. over against**—rather, "along with" [HENDERSON]; or, "beside" [FAIRBAIRN].

22. upon the heads—rather, "above the heads" [FAIRBAIRN]. **colour**—glitter. **terrible crystal**—dazzling the spectator by its brightness. **23. straight**—erect [FAIRBAIRN]. expanded upright. **two . . . two . . . covered . . . bodies**—not, as it might seem, contradicting vs. 11. The two wings expanded upwards, though chiefly used for flying, yet up to the summit of the figure where they were parted from each other, covered the upper part of the body, while the other two wings covered the lower parts. **24. voice of . . . Almighty**—the thunder (Ps. 29:3, 4). **voice of speech**—rather, "the voice" or "sound of *tumult*," as in Jeremiah 11:16. From an *Arabic* root, meaning the "impetuous rush of heavy rain." **noise of . . . host**—(Isa. 13:4; Dan. 10:6). **25. let down . . . wings**—While the Almighty gave forth His voice, they reverently let their wings fall, to listen stilly to His communication.

26. The Godhead appears in the likeness of enthroned humanity, as in Exodus 24:10. Besides the "paved work of a sapphire stone, as it were the body of heaven in clearness," there, we have here the "throne," and God "as a man," with the "appearance of fire round about." This last was a prelude of the incarnation of Messiah, but in His character as Saviour and as Judge (Rev. 19:11-16). The azure sapphire answers to the color of the sky. As others are called "sons of God," but He "the Son of God," so others are called "sons of man" (ch. 2:1, 3), but He "the Son of man" (Matt. 16:13), being the embodied representative of humanity and the whole human race; as, on the other hand, He is the representative of "the fulness of the Godhead" (Col. 2:9). While the cherubim are movable, the throne above, and Jehovah who moves them, are firmly fixed. It is good news to man, that the throne above is filled by One who even there appears as "a man."

27. colour of amber—"the glitter of chasmal" [FAIRBAIRN]. See *Note*, vs. 4; rather, "polished brass" [HENDERSON]. Messiah is described here as in Daniel 10:5, 6; Revelation 1:14, 15.

28. the bow . . . in . . . rain—the symbol of the sure covenant of mercy to God's children remembered amidst judgments on the wicked; as in the flood in Noah's days (Rev. 4:3). "Like hanging out from the throne of the Eternal a flag of peace, assuring all that the

ADAM CLARKE

18. *As for their rings.* The rim or periphery. *They were dreadful.* They were exceedingly great in their diameter, so that it was tremendous to look from the part that touched the ground to that which was opposite above. *Were full of eyes.* Does not this refer to the appearance of nails keeping the spokes upon the rim?

19. *When the living creatures went, the wheels went.* The wheels were attached to the living creatures, so that, in progress, they had the same motion.

20. *The spirit of the living creature was in the wheels.* That is, the wheels were instinct with a vital spirit. Here then is the chariot of Jehovah. There are four wheels, on each of which one of the compound animals stands. The four compound animals form the body of the chariot, their wings spread horizontally above, forming the canopy or covering of this chariot; on the top of which, or upon the extended wings of the four living creatures, was the throne, on which was the appearance of a man, v. 26.

22. *The colour of the terrible crystal.* Like a crystal, well-cut and well-polished, with various faces, by which rays of light were refracted, assuming either a variety of prismatic colors or an insufferably brilliant splendor.

23. *Every one had two, which covered on this side.* While they employed two of their wings to form a foundation for the firmament to rest on, two other wings were let down to cover the lower part of their bodies; but this they did only when they stood, v. 24.

24. *The noise of their wings.* When the whirlwind drove the wheels, the wind rustling among the wings was like the noise of many waters. *As the voice of the Almighty.* Like distant thunder; for this is termed the voice of God, Ps. xviii. 13; Exod. ix. 23, 28-29; xx. 18.

26. *A sapphire.* The pure Oriental sapphire—a large, well-cut specimen of which is now before me—is one of the most beautiful and resplendent blues that can be conceived. I have sometimes seen the heavens assume this illustrious hue. The human form above this canopy is supposed to represent Him who, in the fullness of time, was manifested in the flesh.

27. *The colour of amber.* There are specimens of amber which are very pure and beautifully transparent. One which I now hold up to the light gives a most beautiful bright yellow color. Such a splendid appearance had the august Being who sat upon this throne from the reins upward; but from thence downward He had the appearance of fire, burning with a clear and brilliant flame.

28. *As the appearance of the bow.* Over the canopy on which this glorious personage sat there was a fine rainbow, which, from the description here, had all its colors vivid, distinct, and in perfection—red, orange, yellow, green, blue, indigo, and violet. And *this*, as above

MATTHEW HENRY

of God. He does not say, *This was the Lord* (for he is invisible), but, *This was the glory of the Lord*, in which he was pleased to manifest himself a glorious being; yet it is not *the glory of the Lord*, but *the likeness of that glory*, some faint resemblance of it; nor is it any adequate likeness of that glory, but only *the appearance of that likeness*, a shadow of it, and not the very *image of the thing*, Heb. x. 1. *When I saw it, I fell upon my face*. He was overpowered by it. He fell upon his face in token of that holy awe and reverence with which his mind was possessed and filled. All he saw was only to prepare him for that which he was to hear; for *faith comes by hearing*. God delights to teach the humble.

CHAPTER 2

Verses 1–5

God calls him, *Son of man* (*v.* 1, 3), *Son of Adam, Son of the earth*. We may take it, 1. As a humble diminishing title. Lest Ezekiel should be lifted up with the abundance of the revelations, he is put in mind of this, that still he is a *son of man*. Or, 2. We may take it as an honourable title; for it is one of the titles of the Messiah in the Old Testament (Dan. vii. 13, *I saw one like the Son of man come with the clouds of heaven*).

I. Ezekiel is made to stand, that he might receive his commission, *v.* 1, 2.

1. By a divine command: *Son of man, stand upon thy feet*. His lying prostrate was a posture of greater reverence, but his standing up would be a posture of greater readiness.

2. By a divine power going along with that command, *v.* 2. God made him *stand up*; but, because he had not strength of his own to recover his feet nor courage to face the vision, *the Spirit entered into him* and *set him upon his feet*. The *Spirit set him upon his feet*, made him willing to do as he was bidden, and then he *heard him that spoke* to him.

II. Ezekiel is sent with a message to the children of Israel (*v.* 3): *I send thee to the children of Israel*. They were now sent into captivity, for abusing God's messengers, and yet even there God sends this prophet among them.

1. The rebellion of the people to whom this ambassador is sent. They are called *children of Israel*; they retain the name of their pious ancestors, but they have degenerated, they have become *Goim—nations*, the word commonly used for the Gentiles. They had been all along a rebellious generation and had persisted in their rebellion: *They and their fathers have transgressed against me*. They were now hardened, *impudent children*, brazen-faced, self-willed.

2. "*I do send thee unto them*, and therefore *thou shalt say* thus and thus unto them," *v.* 4. All he said to them must be spoken in God's name, enforced by his authority, and delivered as from him. The writings of the prophets are the word of God, and so are to be regarded. When men's hearts are made to burn under the word, and their wills to bow to it, then they know and bear the witness in themselves that it is not the *word of men, but of God*. If they turn a deaf ear to the word they shall be made to know that he whom they slighted was indeed a prophet, by the reproaches of their own consciences and the just judgments of God upon them for refusing him.

Verses 6–10

The prophet, having received his commission, here receives a charge. It is here required of him,

I. That he be bold. *Son of man, be not afraid of them, v.* 6. Those to whom he sent him are *briers and thorns*, vexing a man, which way soever he turns. Wicked men are as briers and thorns, which hinder God's husbandry. They are *scorpions*, venomous and malignant. The sting of a scorpion is a thousand times more hurtful than the scratch of a brier. Ezekiel had been in vision, conversing with angels, but when he comes down from this mount he finds he *dwells with scorpions*. They would hector him and threaten him, that they might drive him off from being a prophet, or at least from threatening them with the judgments of God.

II. It is required that he be faithful, *v.* 7. 1. He must be faithful to Christ who sent him. 2. He must be faithful to the souls of those to whom he was sent. "It is true they are *most rebellious*; but, *speak my words* to them, whether they are pleasing or unpleasing."

III. It is required that he be observant of,

1. The instructions that were given him in the book which was *spread before him, v.* 10. The roll was *written within and without*, on the inside and on the outside. One side contained their sins; the other side contained the judgments of God coming upon

JAMIESON, FAUSSET, BROWN

purpose of Heaven was to preserve rather than to destroy. Even if the divine work should require a deluge of wrath, still the faithfulness of God would only shine forth the more brightly at last to the children of promise, in consequence of the *tribulations* needed to prepare for the ultimate good" [FAIRBAIRN]. (Isa. 54:8-10). **I fell upon . . . face**—the right attitude, spiritually, before we enter on any active work for God (ch. 2:2; 3:23, 24; Rev. 1:17). In this first chapter God gathered into one vision the substance of all that was to occupy the prophetic agency of Ezekiel; as was done afterwards in the opening vision of the Revelation of Saint John.

CHAPTER 2

Vss. 1-10. EZEKIEL'S COMMISSION. **1. Son of man**—often applied to Ezekiel; once only to Daniel (Dan. 8:17), and not to any other prophet. The phrase was no doubt taken from Chaldean usage during the sojourn of Daniel and Ezekiel in Chaldea. But the spirit who sanctioned the words of the prophet implied by it the *lowliness and frailty* of the prophet as man "lower than the angels," though now admitted to the vision of angels and of God Himself, "lest he should be exalted through the abundance of the revelations" (II Cor. 12:7). He is appropriately so called as being type of the divine "Son of man" here revealed as "man" (*Note*, ch. 1:26). That title, as applied to Messiah, implies at once His *lowliness* and His *exaltation*, in His manifestations as *the Representative man*, at His first and second comings respectively (Ps. 8:4-8; Matt. 16:13; 20:18; and on the other hand, Dan. 7:13, 14; Matt. 26:64; John 5:27). **2. spirit entered . . . when he spake**—The divine word is ever accompanied by the Spirit (Gen. 1:2, 3). **set . . . upon . . . feet**—He had been "upon his face" (ch. 1:28). Humiliation on our part is followed by exaltation on God's part (ch. 3:23, 24; Job 22:29; Jas. 4:6; I Pet. 5:5). "On the feet" was the fitting attitude when he was called on to walk and work for God (Eph. 5:8; 6:15). **that I heard**—rather, "*then* I heard."

3. nation—rather, "nations"; the word usually applied to the *heathen* or *Gentiles;* here to the Jews, as being altogether *heathenized* with idolatries. So in Isaiah 1:10, they are named "Sodom" and "Gomorrah." They were now become "Lo-ammi," not the *people* of God (Hos. 1:9). **4. impudent**—lit., "hard-faced" (ch. 3:7, 9). **children**—resumptive of "they" (vs. 3); the "children" walk in their "fathers' " steps. **I . . . send thee**—God opposes His command to all obstacles. Duties are ours; events are God's. **Thus saith the Lord God**—God opposes His name to the obstinacy of the people.

5. forbear—viz., to hear. **yet shall know**—Even if they will not hear, at least they will not have ignorance to plead as the cause of their perversity (ch. 33:33).

6. briers—not as *Margin* and GESENIUS, "rebels," which would not correspond so well to "thorns." The *Hebrew* is from a root meaning "to sting" as *nettles* do. The wicked are often so called (II Sam. 23:6; Song of Sol. 2:2; Isa. 9:18). **scorpions**—a reptile about six inches long with a deadly sting at the end of the tail. **be not afraid**—(Luke 12:4; I Peter 3:14).

7. most rebellious—lit., "rebellion" itself: its very essence.

9. roll—the form in which ancient books were made. **10. within and without**—on the face and the back. Usually the parchment was written only on its *inside* when rolled up; but so full was God's message of impending woes that it was written also on the back.

ADAM CLARKE

described, *was the appearance of the likeness of the glory of the Lord*. Splendid and glorious as it was, it was only *the appearance of the likeness*, a faint representation of the real thing.

CHAPTER 2

1. *And he said unto me*. In the last verse of the preceding chapter we find that the prophet was so penetrated with awe at the sight of the glory of God in the mystical chariot that he fell upon his face; and, while he was in this posture of adoration, he heard the voice mentioned here.

2. *And the spirit entered into me*. This spirit was different to that mentioned above, by which the wheels, etc., were moved. The spirit of prophecy is here intended, whose office was not merely to enable him to foresee and foretell future events, but to purify and refine his heart, and qualify him to be a successful preacher of the word of life. *And set me upon my feet*. That he might stand as a servant before his master, to receive his orders.

3. *Son of man*. This appellative, so often mentioned in this book, seems to have been given first to this prophet, afterwards to Daniel, and after that to the Man Christ Jesus. Perhaps it was given to the two former to remind them of their frailty, and that they should not be exalted in their own minds by the extraordinary revelations granted to them, and that they should feel themselves of the same nature with those to whom they were sent. To the latter it might have been appropriated merely to show that, though all His actions demonstrated Him to be God, yet that He was also really man; and that in the Man Christ Jesus dwelt "all the fulness of the Godhead bodily." *I send thee to the children of Israel*. To those who were now in captivity, in Chaldea particularly; and to the Jews in general, both far and near.

4. *Thou shalt say unto them, Thus saith the Lord*. Let them know that what you have to declare is the message of the Lord, that they may receive it with reverence.

5. *Yet shall know that there hath been a prophet among them*. By this time they shall be assured of *two* things: (1) That God in His mercy had given them due warning. (2) That themselves were inexcusable for not taking it.

6. *Be not afraid of them*. They will maltreat you for your message, but let not the apprehension of this induce you to suppress it. Though they be rebels, fear them not; I will sustain and preserve you.

7. *Whether they will hear*. Whether they receive the message or persecute you for it, declare it to them, that they may be without excuse.

9. *A roll of a book. Megillath sepher*. All ancient books were written so as to be rolled up; hence *volumen*, a "volume," from *volve*, "I roll."

10. *It was written within and without*. Contrary to the state of rolls in general, which are written on the inside only.

MATTHEW HENRY

them for those sins. He was sent on a sad errand; the matter contained in the book was, *lamentations, and mourning, and woe.* What could be more lamentable, more mournful, more woeful, than to see a holy happy people sunk into such sin and misery!

2. An express charge is given to the prophet both in receiving his message and delivering it. He is to attend diligently to it: *Son of man, hear what I say unto thee, v.* 8. If ministers connive at sin and indulge sinners for fear of displeasing them, they hereby make themselves partakers of their guilt. "Do not only *hear what I say unto thee,* but *open thy mouth, and eat that which I give thee.* Eat it willingly and with an appetite." He that brought it to the prophet *spread it before him,* that he might fully understand the contents of it, and then receive it and make it his own.

JAMIESON, FAUSSET, BROWN

8. eat–(Jer. 15:16, *Note;* Rev. 10:9, 10). The idea is to possess himself fully of the message and digest it in the mind; not literal *eating,* but such an *appropriation* of its unsavory contents that they should become, as it were, part of himself, so as to impart them the more vividly to his hearers.

ADAM CLARKE

There was written therein lamentations, and mourning, and woe. What an awful assemblage! "Lamentations, and a groan, and alas!"

CHAPTER 3

Verses 1–15

These verses are fitly joined by some translators to the foregoing chapter, as being a continuation of the same vision.

I. How he must receive divine revelation himself, *v.* 1. "*Son of man, eat this roll,* imprint it in thy mind, let thy soul be nourished and strengthened by it; be full of it, as thou art of the meat thou hast eaten." Whatever we find to be the word of God, whatever is brought to us by him who is the Word of God, we must receive it without disputing. If he that *opens the roll,* and by his Spirit, spreads it before us, did not also *open our understanding,* and by his Spirit, give us the knowledge of it and *cause us to eat* it, we should be for ever strangers to it. Though *the roll was filled with lamentations, and mourning, and woe,* yet it was to the prophet *as honey for sweetness.*

II. He must deliver that divine revelation to others which he himself had received (*v.* 1): *Eat this roll, and* then *go, speak to the house of Israel.* He is not sent to the Chaldeans to reprove them for their sins, but *to the house of Israel* to reprove them for theirs; for the father corrects his own child if he do amiss, not the child of a stranger. He must remember that they are *the house of Israel* whom he is sent to speak to, God's house and his own. They were such as he had an intimate acquaintance with, being not only their countryman, but their *companion in tribulation.* He must remember what God had already told him of the character of those to whom he was sent, that, if he met with discouragement and disappointment he might not be offended. They *are impudent and hard-hearted* (*v.* 7), no convictions of sin would make them blush, no denunciations would make them tremble. They were obstinate against God himself: "They *will not hearken unto thee,* and no marvel, *for they will not hearken unto me.*" They are prejudiced against the law of God, and for that reason turn a deaf ear to his prophets, whose business it is to enforce his law. God will enable him to put a good face on it: "*I have made thy face strong against their faces,* endued thee with all firmness and boldness." The more impudent wicked people are in their opposition to religion the more openly and resolutely should God's people appear in the practice and defence of it. When vice is daring let not virtue be sneaking. He is therefore commanded to have a good heart and to go on in his work, not valuing either the censures or the threats of his enemies. Let not the angry countenance that drives away a backbiting tongue give any check to a reproving tongue. He must *tell them:* not only what the Lord said, but that the Lord said it: *Thus saith the Lord God; tell them* so, *whether they will hear or whether they will forbear.* Not that it may be indifferent to us what success our ministry has, but, whatever it be, we must go on with our work and leave the issue to God. He *heard a voice of a great rushing* (*v.* 12), as if the angels thronged and crowded to see the inauguration of a prophet. He *heard the noise of their wings that touched,* and *the noise of the wheels* of Providence moving *over against* the angels and in concert with them. But all this noise ended in the voice of praise. He heard them saying, *Blessed be the glory of the Lord from his place.* With reluctance of his own spirit, and yet with a mighty efficacy of *the Spirit of God,* the prophet was brought to the execution of his office. The Spirit led him with a strong hand. God bade him go, but he stirred not till *the Spirit took him up* (*v.* 14), *lifted him up, and took him away* to his work. Ezekiel would willingly have kept all he heard and saw to himself, but he was carried on by the prophetical impulse, so that he could not *but speak the things which he had heard and seen,* as the apostles, Acts iv. 20. He followed with a sad heart: *The Spirit*

CHAPTER 3

VSS. 1-27. EZEKIEL EATS THE ROLL. IS COMMISSIONED TO GO TO THEM OF THE CAPTIVITY AND GOES TO TEL-ABIB BY THE CHEBAR: AGAIN BEHOLDS THE SHEKINAH GLORY: IS TOLD TO RETIRE TO HIS HOUSE, AND ONLY SPEAK WHEN GOD OPENS HIS MOUTH. **1. eat . . . and . . . speak**–God's messenger must first inwardly appropriate God's truth himself, before he "speaks" it to others (*Note,* ch. 2:8). Symbolic actions were, when possible and proper, performed outwardly; otherwise, internally and in spiritual vision, the action so narrated making the naked statement more intuitive and impressive by presenting the subject in a concentrated, embodied form. **3. honey for sweetness**–Cf. Psalm 19:10; 119:103; Revelation 10:9, where, as here in vs. 14, the "sweetness" is followed by "bitterness." The former being due to the painful nature of the message; the latter because it was the Lord's service which he was engaged in; and his eating the roll and finding it sweet, implied that, divesting himself of carnal feeling, he made God's will his will, however painful the message that God might require him to announce. The fact that God would be glorified was his greatest pleasure. **5.** See *Margin, Hebrew,* "deep of lip and heavy of tongue," i.e., men speaking an obscure and unintelligible tongue. Even they would have listened to the prophet; but the Jews, though addressed in their own tongue, will not hear him. **6. many people**–It would have increased the difficulty had he been sent, not merely to one, but to "many people" differing in tongues, so that the missionary would have needed to acquire a new tongue for addressing each. The after mission of the apostles to many peoples, and the gift of tongues for that end, are foreshadowed (cf. I Cor. 14:21 with Isa. 28:11). **had I sent thee to them, they would have hearkened**–(Matt. 11:21, 23). **7. will not hearken unto thee: for . . . not . . . me**–(John 15:20). Take patiently their rejection of thee, for I thy Lord bear it along with thee. **8.** Ezekiel means one "strengthened by God." Such he was in godly firmness, in spite of his people's opposition, according to the divine command to the priest tribe to which he belonged (Deut. 33:9). **9. As . . . flint**–so Messiah the antitype (Isa. 50:7; cf. Jer. 1:8, 17). **10. receive in . . . heart . . . ears**–The transposition from the natural order, viz., first receiving with the *ears,* then in the *heart,* is designed. The preparation of the heart for God's message should precede the reception of it with the ears (cf. Prov. 16:1; Ps. 10:17). **11. thy people**–who ought to be better disposed to hearken to thee, their fellow countryman, than hadst thou been a foreigner (vss. 5, 6). **12.** (Acts 8:39.) Ezekiel's abode heretofore had not been the most suitable for his work. He, therefore, is guided by the Spirit to Tel-abib, the chief town of the Jewish colony of captives: there he sat on the ground, "the throne of the miserable" (Ezra 9:3; Lam. 1:1-3), seven days, the usual period for manifesting deep grief (Job 2:13; see Ps. 137:1), thus winning their confidence by sympathy in their sorrow. He is accompanied by the cherubim which had been manifested at Chebar (ch. 1:3, 4), after their departure from Jerusalem. They now are heard moving with the "*voice of a great rushing* (cf. Acts 2:2), *saying,* Blessed be the glory of the Lord from His place," i.e., moving *from the place* in which it had been at Chebar, to accompany Ezekiel to his new destination (ch. 9:3); or, "from His place" may rather mean, *in His place and manifested "from" it.* Though God may seem to have forsaken His temple, He is still in it and will restore His people to it. His glory is "blessed," in opposition to those Jews who spoke evil of Him, as if He had been unjustly rigorous towards their nation [CALVIN]. **13. touched**–

CHAPTER 3

1. *Eat this roll, and go speak.* This must have passed in vision, but the meaning is plain. Receive My word—let it enter into your soul; digest it—let it be your nourishment.

3. *It was in my mouth as honey.* It was joyous to me to receive the divine message, to be thus let into the secrets of the divine counsel, and I promised myself much comfort in that intimate acquaintance with which I was favored by the Supreme Being. In Rev. x. 10 we find St. John receiving a little book, which he ate, and found it sweet as honey in his mouth; but after he had eaten it, it made his belly bitter, signifying that a deep consideration of the awful matter contained in God's word against sinners, which multitudes of them will turn to their endless confusion, must deeply afflict those who know anything of the worth of an immortal spirit.

7. *Impudent and hardhearted.* "Stiff of forehead, and hard of heart" (margin).

MATTHEW HENRY

took me away, says he, *and* then *I went*, but it was *in bitterness, in the heat of my spirit*. He had perhaps seen what a hard task Jeremiah had at Jerusalem, what ill treatment he met with, and all to no purpose. "*I went*, not *disobedient to the heavenly vision*, or shrinking from the work, as Jonah, but *I went in bitterness*, not at all pleased with it." He *went in the heat of his spirit*, because of the discouragements he foresaw, *but the hand of the Lord was strong upon* him, to fit him and animate him against the difficulties he would meet and, when he found it so, he was reconciled to his business and applied himself to it: *Then he came to those of the captivity* (*v.* 15), *and sat where they sat*, and continued *among them seven days* to hear what they said and observe what they did; and all that time he was waiting for *the word of the Lord* to come to him. He was *there astonished*, overwhelmed with grief for the sins and miseries of his people and overpowered by the vision he had seen.

Verses 16–21

These further instructions God gave to the prophet *at the end of seven days*, that is, on the seventh day after the vision he had; and it is probable that both that and this were on the sabbath day. *The word of the Lord* then and there *came to* him. He that had been musing and meditating on the things of God all the week, was fit to speak to the people in God's name on the sabbath day, and to hear God speak to him. He is plainly, and by a similitude, told his duty, which he is to communicate to the people.

I. The office to which the prophet is called: *Son of man, I have made thee a watchman to the house of Israel*, *v.* 17. He is *a watchman*, appointed to be as *a watchman* in the city, as *a watchman* over the flock, as *a watchman* in the camp, in an invaded country or a besieged town, to watch the motions of the enemy, and to sound an alarm upon the approach of danger. This supposes *the house of Israel* to be in a military state, and exposed to enemies, who are subtle. Watchmen are in peril of death from the enemy, who gain their point if they kill the sentinel; and yet they dare not quit their post upon pain of death from their general. Such a dilemma are the church's watchmen in; men will curse them if they be faithful, and God will curse them if they be false.

II. The work of a watchman is to take notice and to give notice.

1. The prophet, as a watchman, must take notice of what God said concerning this people. He must not, as other watchmen, look round to spy danger and gain intelligence, but he must look up to God, and further he need not look: *Hear the word at my mouth*, *v.* 17.

2. He must give notice of what he heard, not in his own name, or as from himself, but in God's name, and from him. God has said, and does say, to every wicked man, that if he go on still in his trespasses he *shall surely die*. *His iniquity* shall undoubtedly be his ruin. If *a wicked man turn from his wickedness*, and *from his wicked way, he shall live*, and the ruin he is threatened with shall be prevented; and, that he may do so, he is warned of the danger he is in. It is the duty of ministers both to warn sinners of the danger of sin and to assure them of the benefit of repentance. Those that are faithful shall have their reward, though they be not successful. Some of those Ezekiel had to deal with were *righteous*, and he must warn them not to *turn away from their righteousness*, *v.* 20, 21. One good means to keep us from falling is to keep up a holy fear of falling, Heb. iv. 1. When men *turn from their righteousness* they soon learn to commit iniquity. When they grow careless and remiss in the duties of God's worship, they become an easy prey to the tempter. The righteousness which men relinquish will stand them in no stead because not continued. We must not only not flatter the wicked, but not flatter even the righteous as if they were perfectly safe anywhere on this side heaven. Nothing is more beautiful than *a wise reprover upon an obedient ear*; the one *shall live because he is warned* and the other *has delivered his soul*.

Verses 22–27

After all this discovery which God had made of himself to the prophet, and the full instructions he had given him, his work, at first, seems not in proportion to his call. To encourage him against the difficulties he foresaw, God favours him with another vision of his glory. God calls him out *to the plain* (*v.* 22) to *talk with him*. See the condescension of God in conversing thus familiarly with a poor captive, nay, with a sinful man, who *went in bitterness of spirit*, and was at this time out of humour with his work. It is very comfortable to be alone with God, withdrawn from the world for converse with him,

JAMIESON, FAUSSET, BROWN

lit., "kissed," i.e., closely embraced. **noise of a great rushing**—typical of great disasters impending over the Jews. **14. bitterness**—sadness on account of the impending calamities of which I was required to be the unwelcome messenger. But the "hand," or powerful impulse of Jehovah, urged me forward. **15. Tel-abib**—*Tel* means an "elevation." It is identified by MICHAELIS with *Thallaba* on the Chabor. Perhaps the name expressed the Jew's hopes of restoration, or else the fertility of the region. *Abib* means the *green ears* of corn which appeared in the month Nisan, the pledge of the harvest. **I sat . . .** —This is the *Hebrew Margin* reading. The *text* is rather, "I *beheld* them sitting there" [GESENIUS]; or, "And those that were settled there," viz., the older settlers, as distinguished from the more recent ones alluded to in the previous clause. The ten tribes had been long since settled on the Chabor or Habor (II Kings 17:6) [HAVERNICK].

17. watchman—Ezekiel alone, among the prophets, is called a "watchman," not merely to sympathize, but to give timely warning of danger to his people where none was suspected. Habakkuk (2:1) speaks of standing upon his "watch," but it was only in order to be on the lookout for the manifestation of God's power (so Isa. 52:8; 62:6); not as Ezekiel, to act as a watchman to others. **18. warning . . . speakest to warn**—The repetition implies that it is not enough to warn once in passing, but that the warning is to be inculcated continually (II Tim. 4:2, "in season, out of season"; Acts 20:31, "night and day with tears"). **save**—Ch. 2:5 had seemingly taken away all hope of salvation; but the reference there was to the mass of the people whose case was hopeless; a few individuals, however, were reclaimable. **die in . . . iniquity**—(John 8:21, 24). Men are not to flatter themselves that their ignorance, owing to the negligence of their teachers, will save them (Rom. 2:12, "As many as have sinned without law, shall also *perish* without law"). **19. wickedness . . . wicked way**—*internal* wickedness of *heart*, and *external* of the *life*, respectively. **delivered thy soul**—(Isa. 49:4, 5; Acts 20:26). **20. righteous . . . turn from . . . righteousness**—not one "righteous" as to the *root* and *spirit of regeneration* (Ps. 89:33; 138:8; Isa. 26:12; 27:3; John 10:28; Phil. 1:6), but as to its *outward appearance* and performances. So the "righteous" (Prov. 18:17; Matt. 9:13). As in vs. 19 the minister is required to lead the wicked to good, so in vs. 20 he is to confirm the well-disposed in their duty. **commit iniquity**—i.e., give himself up *wholly* to it (I John 3:8, 9), for even the best often fall, but not *wilfully* and *habitually*. **I lay a stumbling-block**—not that God tempts to sin (Jas. 1:13, 14), but God gives men over to judicial blindness, and to *their own* corruptions (Ps. 9:16, 17; 94:23) when they "like not to retain God in their knowledge" (Rom. 1:24, 26); just as, on the contrary, God makes "the way of the righteous plain" (Prov. 4:11, 12; 15:19), so that they do "not stumble." CALVIN refers "stumbling-block" not to the *guilt*, but to its *punishment;* "I bring *ruin* on him." The former is best. Ahab, after a kind of righteousness (I Kings 21:27-29), relapsed and consulted lying spirits in false prophets; so God permitted one of these to be his "stumbling-block," both to sin and its corresponding punishment (I Kings 22:21-23). **his blood will I require**—(Heb. 13:17).

ADAM CLARKE

14. *I went in bitterness.* Being filled with indignation at the wickedness and obstinacy of my people, I went, determining to speak the word of God without disguise, and to reprove them sharply for their rebellion; and yet I was greatly distressed because of the heavy message which I was commanded to deliver.

15. *Tel-abib.* "A heap of corn."

CHARLES H. SPURGEON:

There are, and always will be, in the Christian Church, special watchmen; chosen men are set apart by God for the warning of the people, whose one business it is to cry aloud and spare not, whether men will hear or whether they will forbear. Let us be thankful that the Lord gives us such men, and let us beseech Him to multiply their number. We prayerfully expect still to have our Ezekiels, to whom the Lord shall say, "Son of man, I have made thee a watchman"; but still, beloved, when the camp is in imminent danger every man should turn watchman; and though the special sentinels must keep their posts, and walk their beats, and must with double vigilance act as if everything depended upon them, yet all the rest of the host must mount guard also, and aid in keeping the watches both by day and night. It seems to me, brother, that if the Lord has opened your eyes you have become a seer, and when you have become a seer, and can see, you should also become a watchman, and watch for the good of the Church of God, and for the salvation of souls. If this country were invaded, which may God grant it never be, we could not confine the defense to our professional soldiers. No, every man would grasp such weapon as he could reach, and use it vigorously to drive the intruder over our white cliffs, I might even venture to say every woman would do the same, and matrons would become Amazons. Dear are our homes, and none of us would ask to be excused the defense of our loved isle. Even so in the work of the salvation of souls, every saved one longs to have a share. Can we let sinners perish? Can we permit our own kinsmen to go down into the pit? No, not if our prayers, and tears, and earnest teachings can rescue them.

—*The Treasury of the Old Testament*

20. *When a righteous man doth turn from his righteousness.* From these passages we see that a righteous man may fall from grace, and perish everlastingly.

And I lay a stumblingblock before him. That is, I permit him to be tried, and he fall in the trial. God is repeatedly represented as doing things which He only permits to be done. He lays a stumbling block, i.e., he permits one to be laid.

MATTHEW HENRY

to speak to him; and a good man will say that he is never less alone than when thus alone. Ezekiel *went forth into the plain* more willingly than he went *among those of the captivity* (*v.* 15). He *went out into the plain*, and there saw the same vision that he had seen *by the river of Chebar*. God called him out to *talk with him*, but did more than that: he showed him his *glory*, *v.* 23. We are not now to expect such visions, but we must own that we have a favour done us if we so by faith *behold the glory of the Lord* as to be *changed into the same image, by the Spirit of the Lord*. One would have expected now that God would send him directly to the chief place of concourse, and make him and his message acceptable, that he would have a wider door of opportunity opened to him, but what is here said to him is the reverse of all this. Instead of sending him to a public assembly, he orders him to confine himself to his own lodgings: *Go, shut thyself within thy house*, *v.* 24. He was not willing to appear in public, and, when he did, the people did not regard him, and as a just rebuke both to him and them, to him for his shyness and to them for their coldness, God forbids him to appear in public. He must *shut himself within his house*, that he might receive further discoveries of the mind of God. *The elders of Judah* visited him and *sat before* him *in his house* (*ch.* viii. 1), to be witnesses of his ecstasies; but it was not till *ch.* xi. 25 that he *spoke to those of the captivity all the things that the Lord had shown him*. Instead of securing him the esteem and affections of those to whom he sent him God tells him that *they shall put bands upon him* and bind him (*v.* 25) in order to further punish him as a disturber of the peace. Though they were themselves sent into bondage in Babylon for persecuting the prophets, yet there they continue to persecute them. They would bind him, under pretence of his being mad. Instead of opening his lips that his mouth might show forth God's praise, God silenced him, so that he was dumb for a considerable time, *v.* 26. He that can speak best is forbidden to speak at all; and the reason given is because *they are a rebellious house* to whom he is sent, and they are not worthy to have him for *a reprover*. *But when* God *speaks with* him, and designs to speak by him, he *will open* his *mouth*, *v.* 27. Instead of giving him assurance of success when he should at any time speak to the people, he here leaves the matter doubtful, and Ezekiel must not perplex and disquiet himself about it, but let it be as it will.

JAMIESON, FAUSSET, BROWN

22. hand of the Lord—(ch. 1:3). **go . . . into the plain**—in order that he might there, in a fresh place secluded from unbelieving men, receive a fresh manifestation of the divine glory, to inspirit him for his trying work. **23. glory of the Lord**—(ch. 1:28).

24. set me upon my feet—having been previously prostrate and unable to rise until raised by the divine power. **shut thyself within . . . house**—implying that in the work he had to do, he must look for no sympathy from man but must be often alone with God and draw his strength from Him [FAIRBAIRN]. "Do not go out of thy house till I reveal the future to thee by signs and words," which God does in the following chapters, down to the eleventh. Thus a representation was given of the city shut up by siege [GROTIUS]. Thereby God proved the obedience of His servant, and Ezekiel showed the reality of His call by proceeding, not through rash impulse, but by the directions of God [CALVIN]. **25. put bands upon thee**—not literally, but spritually, the binding, depressing influence which their rebellious conduct would exert on his spirit. Their perversity, like bands, would repress his freedom in preaching; as in II Corinthians 6:12, Paul calls himself "straitened" because his teaching did not find easy access to them. Or else, it is said to console the prophet for being shut up; if thou wert now at once to announce God's message, they *would* rush on thee and *bind* thee with "bands" [CALVIN]. **26. I will make my tongue . . . dumb**—Israel had rejected the prophets; therefore God deprives Israel of the prophets and of His word—God's sorest judgment (I Sam. 7:2; Amos 8:11, 12). **27. when I speak . . . I will open thy mouth**—opposed to the silence imposed on the prophet, to punish the people (vs. 26). After the interval of silence has awakened their attention to the cause of it, viz., their sins, they may then hearken to the prophecies which they would not do before. **He that heareth, let him hear . . . forbear**—i.e., thou hast done thy part, whether they hear or forbear. He who shall forbear to hear, it shall be at his own peril; he who hears, it shall be to his own eternal good (cf. Rev. 22:11).

ADAM CLARKE

22. *Arise, go forth into the plain.* Into a place remote from observation and noise; a place where the glory of God might have sufficient room to manifest itself, that the prophet might see all its movements distinctly.

24. *The spirit . . . said unto me, Go, shut thyself within thine house.* Hide yourself for the present. The reason is immediately subjoined.

25. *They shall put bands upon thee.* Your countrymen will rise up against you and, to prevent your prophesying, will confine you.

26. *I will make thy tongue cleave to the roof of thy mouth.* I will not give you any message to deliver to them. They are so rebellious, it is useless to give them further warning.

MATTHEW HENRY — CHAPTER 4

Verses 1–8

The prophet is here ordered to represent by signs *the siege of Jerusalem*; and this amounted to a prediction.

I. He was ordered to engrave a draught of Jerusalem upon a tile, *v.* 1. It was Jerusalem's honour that God had *graven her upon the palms of his hands* (Isa. xlix. 16), and the names of the tribes were engraven in precious stones on the breastplate of the high priest; but, now that *the faithful city has become a harlot*, a worthless brittle tile or brick is thought good enough to *portray it upon*.

II. He was ordered to build little forts against this portraiture of the city, resembling the batteries raised by the besiegers, *v.* 2. Between the city and the besieger he was to set up an *iron pan*, as an *iron wall*, *v.* 3. This represented the inflexible resolution of both sides; the Chaldeans resolved they would never quit till they had conquered; the Jews resolved never to capitulate.

III. He was ordered to lie upon his side before it, as it were to surround it, representing the Chaldean army lying before it to block it up. He was to lie on his left side 390 *days* (*v.* 5); the siege of Jerusalem is to last eighteen months (Jer. lii. 4–6), but if we deduct from that five months' interval, when the besiegers withdrew upon the approach of Pharaoh's army (Jer. xxxvii. 5–8), the number of the days of the close siege will be 390. Yet that also had another signification. The 390 days signified 390 years; and, when the prophet lies so many days on his side, he bears the guilt of that iniquity which *the house of Israel*, the ten tribes, had borne 390 years, reckoning from their first apostasy under Jeroboam to the destruction of Jerusalem, which completed the ruin of those small remains of them that had incorporated with Judah. He is then to lie forty days *upon his right side*, and so long to bear *the iniquity of the house of Judah*, the kingdom of the two tribes, because their sins were those which they were guilty of during the last forty years before their captivity. Judah, that had Josiah and Jeremiah, fills the measure

JAMIESON, FAUSSET, BROWN — CHAPTER 4

Vss. 1-17. SYMBOLICAL VISION OF THE SIEGE AND THE INIQUITY-BEARING. **1. tile**—a sun-dried brick, such as are found in Babylon, covered with cuneiform inscriptions, often two feet long and one foot broad. **2. forth**—rather, watch-tower (Jer. 52:4) wherein the besiegers could watch the movements of the besieged [GESENIUS]. A wall of circumvallation [LXX and ROSENMULLER]. A kind of battering-ram [MAURER]. The first view is best. **a mount**—wherewith the Chaldeans could be defended from missiles. **batterings-rams**—lit., "through-borers." In ch. 21:22 the same *Hebrew* is translated, "captains." **3. iron pan**—the divine decree as to the Chaldean army investing the city. **set it for a wall of iron between thee and the city**—Ezekiel, in the person of God, represents the wall of separation between him and the people as one of iron: and the Chaldean investing army, His instrument of separating them from him, as one impossible to burst through. **set . . . face against it**—inexorably (Ps. 34:16). The exiles envied their brethren remaining in Jerusalem, but exile is better than the straitness of a siege. **4.** Another symbolical act performed at the same time as the former, in vision, not in external action, wherein it would have been only puerile: narrated as a thing ideally done, it would make a vivid impression. The second action is supplementary to the first, to bring out more fully the same prophetic idea. **left side**—referring to the *position* of the ten tribes, the *northern* kingdom, as Judah, the *southern*, answers to "the right side" (vs. 6). The Orientals, **facing the east in their mode, had the north on their** *left,* and the south on their *right* (ch. 16:46). Also the right was more honorable than the left: so Judah, as being the seat of the temple, was more so than Israel. **bear their iniquity**—iniquity being regarded as a *burden*; so it means, "bear the *punishment* of their iniquity" (Num. 14:34). A type of Him who was the great *sin-bearer*, not in mimic show as Ezekiel, but in reality (Isa. 53:4, 6, 12). **5. three hundred and ninety days**—The 390 years of punishment appointed for Israel, and 40 for Judah, cannot refer

ADAM CLARKE — CHAPTER 4

1. *Take thee a tile.* A "brick" is most undoubtedly meant; yet even the larger dimensions here will not help us through the difficulty, unless we have recourse to the ancients, who have spoken of the dimensions of the bricks commonly used in building. Palladius is very particular on this subject: "Let the bricks be two feet long, one foot broad, and four inches thick." On such a surface as this the whole siege might be easily portrayed. But the tempered clay out of which the bricks were made might be meant here; of this substance he might spread out a sufficient quantity to receive all his figures.

2. *Battering rams.* This is the earliest account we have of this military engine. It was a long beam with a head of brass, like the head and horns of a ram, whence its name. It was hung by chains or ropes, between two beams, or three legs, so that it could admit of being drawn backward and forward some yards. Several stout men, by means of ropes, pulled it as far back as it could go; and then, suddenly letting it loose, it struck with great force against the wall which it was intended to batter and bring down. This machine was not known in the time of Homer, as in the siege of Troy there is not the slightest mention of such. And the first notice we have of it is here, where we see that it was employed by Nebuchadnezzar in the siege of Jerusalem.

3. *Take thou unto thee an iron pan.* A "flat plate" or slice, as the margin properly renders it; such as are used in some countries to bake bread on, called a *griddle*, being suspended above the fire, and kept in a proper degree of heat for the purpose. The Chaldeans threw such a wall round Jerusalem, to prevent the besieged from receiving any succors, and from escaping from the city. *This shall be a sign to the house of Israel.* This shall be an emblematical repre-

MATTHEW HENRY

of its iniquity in less time than Israel does. The prophet lay every day at a certain time of the day. When he received visits he was found lying 390 *days on his left side* and *forty days on his right side* before his portraiture of Jerusalem, which all might understand to mean the besieging of that city.

IV. He was ordered to prosecute the siege with vigour (*v.* 7): *Thou shalt set thy face towards the siege of Jerusalem*, as wholly intent upon it; so the Chaldeans would be. Nebuchadnezzar's indignation at Zedekiah's treachery in breaking his league with him made him very furious in pushing on this siege, that he might chastise that faithless prince and people. They exerted themselves to the utmost in all the operations of the siege, which the prophet was to represent by the *uncovering of his arm*, the *stretching out* of his arm, as it were to deal blows. He is said to *make bare his arm*, Isa. lii. 10. In short, The Chaldeans will go about their business, and go on in it, as men in earnest, who resolve to go through with it. Now, 1. This is intended to be a *sign to the house of Israel* (*v.* 3), to those in Babylon, and to those who remained in their own land. The prophet was *dumb* and *could not speak* (*ch.* iii. 26); but God *left not himself without witness*, but ordered him to make signs, to *make known his mind* (that is, the mind of God) to the people, who through their stupidity and dullness must be taught as children are, by pictures. Or the prophet made use of signs for the same reason that Christ made use of parables. Thus the prophet *prophesies against Jerusalem* (*v.* 7); and there were those who were the more affected with it by its being so represented, for images to the eye make deeper impressions upon the mind than words can, and for this reason sacraments are instituted to represent divine things. The power of imagination, if it be rightly used, and kept under the direction and correction of reason and faith, may be of good use to kindle devout affections. Fancy is like fire, a *good servant, but a bad master*. This whole transaction seemed childish and tiresome, but our ease must be sacrificed to our duty, and we must never call God's service a hard service. It could not but be against the grain to appear thus against Jerusalem, the city of God; but he is a prophet, and must follow his instructions, not his affections, and must plainly preach the ruin of a sinful place, though its welfare is what he passionately desires. All this that the prophet sets before the children of his people concerning the destruction of Jerusalem is designed to bring them to repentance. But observe, It is a day of punishment for a year of sin: *I have appointed thee each day for a year*. The siege is a calamity of 390 days.

Verses 9–17

The best exposition of this part of Ezekiel's prediction of Jerusalem's desolation is Jeremiah's lamentation of it, Lam. iv. 3, 4, &c., and v. 10.

I. The prophet here, to affect the people with the foresight of it, must confine himself for 390 days to coarse fare and short commons, ill-dressed, for they should want both food and fuel.

1. His food was to be of the worst bread, made of but little wheat and barley, and the rest of beans, and lentiles, and millet, and fitches, such as we feed horses or hogs, mixed as that in the beggar's bag, that has a dish full of one sort of corn at one house and of another at another house, *v.* 9. The prophet must eat but twenty *shekels'* weight of bread a day (*v.* 10), that was about ten ounces; and he must drink but the *sixth part of a bin of water*, that was half a pint, about eight ounces, *v.* 11. The prophet in Babylon had bread enough and to spare, yet, that he might confirm his prediction and be a sign to the children of Israel, God obliges him to live thus sparingly. Nature is content with a little, grace with less, but lust with nothing. It is good to stint ourselves of choice, that we may the better bear it if ever we should come to be stinted by necessity. He must *bake it with man's dung* (*v.* 12); that must serve for fuel to heat his oven. The coarse bread, thus baked, he must *eat as barley-cakes*. This nauseous piece of cookery he must exercise publicly *in their sight*, that they might be the more affected with the calamity approaching. In the extremity of the famine they should not only have nothing that was dainty, but nothing that was cleanly, about them. This circumstance of the sign, the baking of his bread with man's dung, the prophet humbly desired might be dispensed with (*v.* 14); it seemed a ceremonial pollution, for there was a law that man's dung should *be covered with earth*, that God might *see no unclean thing in their camp*, Deut. xxiii. 13, 14. And must he go and gather a thing so offensive, and use it in the dressing of his meat in the sight of the people? "*Ah! Lord God*," says he, "*behold, my soul has not been polluted*, and I am

JAMIESON, FAUSSET, BROWN

to the siege of Jerusalem. That siege is referred to in vss. 1-3, not in a sense restricted to the literal siege, but comprehending the *whole* train of punishment to be inflicted for their sin; therefore we read here merely of its sore pressure, not of its result. The sum of 390 and 40 years is 430, a period famous in the history of the covenant people, being that of their sojourn in Egypt (Exod. 12:40, 41; Gal. 3:17). The forty alludes to the forty years in the wilderness. Elsewhere (Deut. 28:68; Hos. 9:3), God threatened to bring them back to Egypt, which must mean, not Egypt literally, but a bondage as bad as that one in Egypt. So now God will reduce them to a kind of new Egyptian bondage to the world: Israel, the greater transgressor, for a longer period than Judah (cf. ch. 20:35-38). Not the whole of the 430 years of the Egypt state is appointed to Israel; but this shortened by the forty years of the wilderness sojourn, to imply, that a way is open to their return to life by their having the Egypt state merged into that of the wilderness; i.e., by ceasing from idolatry and seeking in their sifting and sore troubles, through God's covenant, a restoration to righteousness and peace [FAIRBAIRN]. The 390, in reference to the *sin* of Israel, was also literally true, being the years from the setting up of the calves by Jeroboam (I Kings 12:20-33), i.e., from 975 to 585 B.C.: *about* the year of the Babylonian captivity; and perhaps the 40 of Judah refers to that part of Manasseh's fifty-five year's reign in which he had not repented, and which, we are expressly told, was the cause of God's removal of Judah, notwithstanding Josiah's reformation (I Kings 21:10-16; 23:26, 27). **6. each day for a year**—lit., "a day for a year, a day for a year." Twice repeated, to mark more distinctly the reference to Numbers 14:34. The picturing of the future under the image of the past, wherein the meaning was far from lying on the surface, was intended to arouse to a less superficial mode of thinking, just as the partial veiling of truth in Jesus' parables was designed to stimulate inquiry; also to remind men that God's dealings in the past are a key to the future, for He moves on the same everlasting *principles*, the *forms* alone being transitory. **7. arm . . . uncovered**—to be ready for action, which the long Oriental garment usually covering it would prevent (Isa. 52:10). **thou shalt prophesy against it**—This gesture of thine will be a tacit prophecy against it. **8. bands**—(Ch. 3:25.) **not turn from . . . side**—to imply the impossibility of their being able to shake off their punishment. **9. wheat . . . barley . . .**—Instead of simple flour used for delicate cakes (Gen. 18:6), the Jews should have a coarse mixture of six different kinds of grain, such as the poorest alone would eat. **fitches**—spelt or *dhourra*. **three hundred and ninety**—The forty days are omitted, since these latter typify the *wilderness period* when Israel stood *separate from the Gentiles and their pollutions,* though partially chastened by stint of bread and water (vs. 16), whereas the eating of the polluted bread in the 390 days implies a forced residence *"among the Gentiles"* who were polluted with idolatry (vs. 13). This last is said of "Israel" primarily, as being the most debased (vss. 9-15); they had *spiritually* sunk to a level with the heathen, therefore God will make their condition *outwardly* to correspond. Judah and Jerusalem fare less severely, being less guilty: they are to "eat bread by weight and with care," i.e., have a stinted supply and be chastened with the milder discipline of the wilderness period. But Judah also is secondarily referred to in the 390 days, as having fallen, like Israel, into Gentile defilements; if, then, the Jews are to escape from the exile *among Gentiles,* which is their just punishment, they must submit again to the wilderness probation (vs. 16). **10. twenty shekels**—i.e., little more than ten ounces; a scant measure to sustain life (Jer. 52:6). But it applies not only to the siege, but to their whole subsequent state. **11. sixth . . . of . . . hin**—about a pint and a half. **12. dung**—as fuel; so the Arabs use beasts' dung, wood-fuel being scarce. But to use human dung so implies the most cruel necessity. It was in violation of the law (Deut. 14:3; 23:12-14); it must therefore have been done only *in vision.*

14. Ezekiel, as a priest, had been accustomed to the strictest abstinence from everything legally impure. Peter felt the same scruple at a similar command (Acts 10:14; cf. Isa. 65:4). *Positive precepts,* being dependent on a particular command can be set aside at the will of the divine ruler; but *moral precepts* are everlasting in their obligation because God can-

ADAM CLARKE

sentation of what shall actually take place.

4. *Lie thou also upon thy left side.* It appears that all that is mentioned here and in the following verses was done, not in idea, but in fact. The prophet lay down on his left side upon a couch to which he was chained, v. 5, for 390 days; and afterwards he lay in the same manner, upon his right side, for 40 days. And thus was signified the state of the Jews, and the punishment that was coming upon them. The days signify years, a day for a year; during which they were to bear their iniquity, or the temporal punishment due to their sins. The "three hundred and ninety days," during which he was to lie on his left side, and bear the iniquity of the house of Israel, point out two things: first, the duration of the siege of Jerusalem; second, the duration of the Captivity of the ten tribes, and that of Judah.

6. *Forty days.* Reckon, says Archbishop Newcome, near fifteen years and six months in the reign of Manasseh, two years in that of Amon, three months in that of Jehoahaz, eleven years in that of Jehoiakim, three months and ten days in that of Jehoiachin, and eleven years in that of Zedekiah; and there arises a period of forty years during which gross idolatry was practiced in the kingdom of Judah. *Forty days* may have been employed in spoiling and desolating the city and the Temple.

9. *Take thou also unto thee wheat.* In times of scarcity, it is customary in all countries to mix several kinds of coarser grain with the finer, to make it last the longer. This which the prophet is commanded to take, of wheat, barley, beans, lentils, millet, and fitches, was intended to show how scarce the necessaries of life should be during the siege.

10. *Twenty shekels a day.* The whole of the above grain, being ground, was to be formed into one mass, out of which he was to make 390 loaves, one loaf for each day; and this loaf was to be of 20 shekels in weight. Now a shekel, being in weight about half an ounce, this would be 10 ounces of bread for each day; and with this water to the amount of one-sixth part of a hin, which is about a pint and a half of our measure. All this shows that so reduced should provisions be during the siege that they should be obliged to eat the meanest sort of aliment, and that by weight, and their water by measure.

12. *Thou shalt bake it with dung.* Dried ox and cow dung is a common fuel in the East; and with this, for want of wood and coals, they are obliged to prepare their food. Here the prophet is to prepare his bread with dry human excrement. And when we know that this did not come in contact with the bread, and was only used to warm the plate on which the bread was laid over the fire, it removes all the horror and much of the disgust. This was required to show the extreme degree of wretchedness to which they should be exposed; for, not being able to leave the city to collect the dried excrements of beasts, the inhabitants during the siege would be obliged, literally, to use dried human ordure for fuel. However, we find that the prophet was relieved from using this kind of fuel, for cows' dung was substituted at his request. See v. 15.

MATTHEW HENRY

afraid lest by this it be polluted." The pollution of the soul by sin is what good people dread, and yet sometimes tender consciences fear it without cause, with scruples about lawful things, as the prophet here, who had not yet learned that it is not that which *goes into the mouth that defiles the man*, Matt. xv. 11. Now, because Ezekiel with a manifest tenderness of conscience made this scruple, God dispensed with him in this matter. God allowed Ezekiel to use *cow's dung* instead of *man's dung*, *v.* 15.

II. This sign signified,

1. That those who remained in Jerusalem should be brought to extreme misery for want of necessary food. All supplies being cut off by the besiegers, *the staff of bread* would be *broken in Jerusalem*, *v.* 16. Multitudes of them shall die of famine, they shall die so as to *feel themselves die.* And it is sin that brings all this misery upon them: *They shall consume away in their iniquity* (so it may be read). It is a righteous thing with God to deprive us of those enjoyments which we have made the food and fuel of our lusts.

2. It signified that those who were carried into captivity should be forced to *eat their defiled bread among the Gentiles* (*v.* 13), to eat meat made up by Gentile hands otherwise than according to the law of the Jewish church, which they were always taught to call *defiled.* Or they should be forced to eat putrid meat, such as their oppressors would allow them in their slavery, and such as formerly they would have scorned to touch.

JAMIESON, FAUSSET, BROWN

not be inconsistent with His unchanging moral nature. **abominable flesh**—lit., flesh that stank from putridity. Flesh of animals three days killed was prohibited (Lev. 7:17, 18; 19:6, 7).

15. cow's dung—a mitigation of the former order (vs. 12); no longer "the dung of man"; still the bread so baked is "defiled," to imply that, whatever partial abatement there might be for the prophet's sake, the main decree of God, as to the pollution of Israel by exile among Gentiles, is unalterable. **16. staff of bread**—bread by which life is supported, as a man's weight is by the staff he leans on (Lev. 26:26; Ps. 105:16; Isa. 3:1). **by weight, and with care**—in scant measure (vs. 10). **17. astonied one with another**—mutually regard one another with astonishment: the stupefied look of despairing want.

13. Implying that Israel's peculiar distinction was to be abolished and that they were to be outwardly blended with the idolatrous heathen (Deut. 28:68; Hos. 9:3).

ADAM CLARKE

16. *I will break the staff of bread.* They shall be besieged till all the bread is consumed; see 2 Kings xxv. 3: "And on the ninth day of the fourth month, the famine prevailed in the city, and there was no bread for the people of the land." All this was accurately foretold, and as accurately fulfilled.

MATTHEW HENRY — CHAPTER 5

Verses 1–4

The sign by which the utter destruction of Jerusalem is set forth; as before, the prophet is himself the sign, that the people might see how much he affected himself with the case of Jerusalem, and how near it lay to his heart.

I. He must *shave off the hair of his head and beard* (*v.* 1), which signified God's utter rejecting that people, as a worthless generation, such as could well be spared. Jerusalem had been the head, but, having degenerated, had become as the *hair*, which, when it grows thick and long, is but a burden. Ezekiel must not cut off that hair only which was superfluous but *cut it all off*, denoting the end that God would make of Jerusalem.

II. He must *weigh the hair* and *divide it into three parts.* Some make the shaving of the hair to denote the loss of their liberty and of their honour: it was looked upon as a mark of ignominy, as in the disgrace of Hanun put on David's ambassadors. It denotes also the loss of their joy, for they shaved their heads upon occasion of great mourning.

III. He must dispose of the hair so that it might all be destroyed, *v.* 2. 1. One *third part* must *be burnt in the midst of the city*, denoting the multitudes that should perish by famine and pestilence, and perhaps in the conflagration of the city, *when the days of the siege were fulfilled.* 2. Another third part was to be *cut in pieces with a knife*, representing the many who, during the siege, were slain by the sword. 3. Another third part was to be *scattered in the wind*, denoting the carrying away of some into the land of the conqueror and the flight of others into the neighbouring countries for shelter.

IV. He must preserve a small quantity of the third sort that were to be *scattered in the wind*, and *bind them in his skirts*, *v.* 3. This signified perhaps that little handful of people which were left under the government of Gedaliah, who, it was hoped, would keep possession of the land when the body of the people was carried into captivity. Thus God would have done well for them if they would have done well for themselves.

Verses 5–17

The explanation of the foregoing similitude: *This is Jerusalem.* The prophet's head, which was to be shaved, signified Jerusalem, which by the judgments of God was now to be stripped of its ornaments, to be emptied of its inhabitants, and to be set *naked and bare*, to be *shaved with a razor that is hired*, Isa. vii. 20. The head of one that was a priest, a prophet, a holy person, was fittest to represent Jerusalem, the holy city.

I. The privileges Jerusalem was honoured with (*v.* 5): *I have set it in the midst of the nations and countries that are round about her.* Jerusalem was situated in the midst of kingdoms that were populous, civilized, famed for learning, arts, and sciences. It was *set in the midst of* them as excelling them all—set in the midst of them as a candle upon a candlestick to spread the light of divine revelation to all the dark corners of the neighbouring nations, even to the ends

JAMIESON, FAUSSET, BROWN — CHAPTER 5

Vss. 1-17. Vision of Cutting the Hairs, and the Calamities Foreshadowed Thereby. **1. knife . . . razor**—the sword of the foe (cf. Isa. 7:20). This vision implies even severer judgments than the Egyptian afflictions foreshadowed in the former, for their guilt was greater than that of their forefathers. **thine head**—as representative of the Jews. The whole hair being shaven off was significant of severe and humiliating (II Sam. 10:4, 5) treatment. Especially in the case of a priest; for priests (Lev. 21: 5) were forbidden "to make baldness on their head," their hair being the token of consecration; hereby it was intimated that the ceremonial must give place to the moral. **balances**—implying the *just discrimination* with which Jehovah weighs out the portion of punishment "divided," i.e., allotted to each: the "hairs" are the Jews: the divine scales do not allow even one hair to escape accurate weighing (cf. Matt. 10:30). **2.** Three classes are described. The sword was to destroy one third of the people; famine and plague another third ("fire" in vs. 2 being explained in vs. 12 to mean pestilence and famine); that which remained was to be scattered among the nations. A few only of the last portion were to escape, symbolized by the hairs bound in Ezekiel's skirts (vs. 3; Jer. 40:6; 52: 16). Even of these some were to be thrown into the fiery ordeal again (vs. 4; Jer. 41:1, 2, etc.; 44: 14, etc.). The "skirts" being able to contain but few express that extreme limit to which God's goodness can reach. **5, 6.** Explanation of the symbols: **Jerusalem**—not the mere city, but the people of Israel generally, of which it was the center and representative. **in . . . midst**—Jerusalem is regarded in God's point of view as center of the whole earth, designed *to radiate the true light over the nations in all directions.* Cf. *Margin* ("navel"), ch. 38:12; Psalm 48:2; Jeremiah 3:17. No center in the ancient heathen world could have been selected more fitted than Canaan to be a vantage-ground, whence the people of God might have acted with success upon the heathenism of the world. It lay midway between the oldest and most civilized states, Egypt and Ethiopia on one side, and Babylon, Nineveh, and India on the other, and afterwards Persia, Greece, and Rome. The Phœnician mariners were close by, through whom they might have transmitted the true religion to the remotest lands; and all around the Ishmaelites, the great *inland* traders in South Asia and North Africa. Israel was thus placed, not for its own selfish good, but to be the spiritual benefactor of the whole world. Cf. Psalm 67 throughout. Failing in this, and falling into idolatry, its guilt was far worse than that of the heathen; not that Israel *literally* went beyond the heathen in abominable idolatries. But *"corruptio optimi pessima";* the perversion of that which in itself is the best is worse than the perversion of that which is less perfect: is in fact the worst of all kinds of perversion. Therefore their punishment was the severest. So the position of the Christian professing Church now, if it be not a light to the

ADAM CLARKE — CHAPTER 5

1-4. *Take thee a sharp knife.* It is likely that only one kind of instrument is here intended, a *knife* to be employed as a *razor.* Here is a new emblem produced, in order to mark out the coming evils. The prophet represents the Jewish nation; his hair, the people; the razor, the Chaldeans; the cutting the beard and hair, the calamities, sorrows, and disgrace coming upon the people. Cutting off the hair was a sign of mourning; see on Jer. xlv. 5; xlviii. 37; and also a sign of great disgrace; see 2 Sam. x. 4. He is ordered to divide the hair, v. 2, into three equal parts, to intimate the different degrees and kinds of punishment which should fall upon the people. The *balances,* v. 1, were to represent the divine justice, and the exactness with which God's judgments should be distributed among the offenders. This hair, divided into three parts, is to be disposed of thus: (1) A third part is to be burnt in the midst of the city, to show that so many should perish by famine and pestilence during the siege. (2) Another third part he was to cut in small portions about the city (that figure which he had portrayed upon the brick) to signify those who should perish in different sorties, and in defending the walls. (3) And the remaining third part he was to scatter in the wind, to point out those who should be driven into captivity. The sword following them was intended to show that their lives should be at the will of their captors, and that many of them should perish by the *sword* in their dispersions. The few hairs which he was to take in his skirts, v. 3, were intended to represent those few Jews that should be left in the land under Gedaliah, after the taking of the city. The throwing a part of these last into the fire, v. 4, was intended to show the miseries that these suffered in Judea, in Egypt, and finally in their being also carried away into Babylon on the conquest of Egypt by Nebuchadnezzar.

MATTHEW HENRY

of the earth. Jerusalem was to be as the heart in the body, to invigorate this dead world with a divine life. Had they preserved this reputation (1 Kings iv. 34), what a blessing would Jerusalem have been to all the nations about! But, failing to be so, the accomplishment of this intention was reserved for its latter days, *when out of Zion went forth the* gospel *law and the word of the Lord* Jesus *from Jerusalem.*

II. Jerusalem was guilty. A charge is here drawn up and proved beyond contradiction. 1. She had *not walked in God's statutes*, nor *kept his judgments* (*v.* 7); nay, the inhabitants of Jerusalem had *refused his judgments and his statutes* (*v.* 6). The people had not only broken God's laws, but had so perverted and abused them that they had made them the excuse and colour of their wickedness. They introduced the abominable customs and usages of the heathen, instead of God's institutions. *She has changed my judgments*, by idolatries and false worship, *more than the nations* (*v.* 6), and she has *multiplied* idols and altars, gods and temples, *more than the nations that were round about.* Israel's God is one, his name one, his altar one; but they multiplied their gods. They corrupted revealed religion more than the Gentiles had corrupted natural religion. Jerusalem profaned the holy things, which she had been both entrusted and honoured with (*v.* 11).

III. The punishments that Jerusalem should fall under.

1. God will take this work of punishing Jerusalem into his own hands. "You think it is only the Chaldean army that is against you, but they are God's hand, or rather the staff in his hand; it is *I, even I*, that *am against thee*, to speak against thee by prophets, to act against thee by providence." Those who will not observe the judgments of God's mouth shall not escape the judgments of his hand.

2. These punishments shall come from his displeasure. As to the body of the people, it shall not be a correction in love, but *in furious rebukes* (*v.* 15), strange expressions to come from a God who has said, *Fury is not in me*, and who has declared himself *gracious, and merciful*, and *slow to anger*. But they are designed to show the malignity of sin. As, when God is dishonoured by the sins of men, he is said to be *grieved* (Ps. xcv. 10), so when he is honoured by their destruction he is said to *be comforted*.

3. Punishments shall be public and open: *I will execute* these *judgments in the sight of the nations* (*v.* 8). Public sins call for public reproofs, so, if those prevail not, they call for public judgments. The nations will fear before the God of Israel, when they see how severely he punishes sin even in those that are nearest to him. *It shall be an instruction to the nations*, *v.* 15. Jerusalem should have taught her neighbours the fear of God by her piety and virtue, but, she not doing that, God will teach it to them by her ruin.

4. These punishments shall be such as have no precedent (*v.* 9): "*I will do in thee that which I have not done* in thee before, though thou hast long since deserved it." This is a rhetorical expression of the most grievous judgments, like that character of Hezekiah, that there was *none like him, before or after him.* The strongest bonds of natural affection will be broken which will be a just punishment for their wilfully breaking the bonds of duty to God (*v.* 10): *The fathers shall eat the sons, and the sons shall eat the fathers*, through the famine, or shall be compelled to do it by their barbarous conquerors. Some shall be taken away by the plague (*v.* 12); the *pestilence shall pass through thee* (*v.* 17), others *shall be consumed with famine* (*v.* 12).

And, *lastly*, those who escape shall be *scattered into* all parts of the world, *into all the winds* (so it is expressed, *v.* 10, 12).

5. These punishments will prove their ruin by degrees. They shall be *diminished* (*v.* 11); *bereaved* (*v.* 17), emptied of all that which was their joy and confidence. We may well suppose that it looks further, to the final destruction of that great city by the Romans.

6. All this is ratified by the divine authority and veracity, *v.* 17. *And they shall know that I the Lord have spoken it*, *v.* 13. There were those who thought it was only the prophet that spoke it in his delirium; but God's word will prove itself.

JAMIESON, FAUSSET, BROWN

heathen world, its condemnation will be sorer than theirs (Matt. 5:13; 11:21-24; Heb. 10:28, 29). **6. changed . . . into**—rather, "hath *resisted* My judgments wickedly"; "hath *rebelled* against My ordinances for wickedness" [BUXTORF]. But see end of *Note* on vs. 7. **7. multiplied**—rather, "have been more abundantly outrageous"; lit., "to tumultuate"; to have an extravagant rage for idols. **neither have done according to the judgments of the nations**—have not been as tenacious of the true religion as the nations have been of the false. The heathen "changed" not their gods, but the Jews changed Jehovah for idols (see vs. 6, "changed My judgments into wickedness," i.e., idolatry, Jer. 2:11). The *Chaldean version* and the *Masora* support the negative. Others omit it (as it is omitted in ch. 11: 12), and translate, *"but* have done according to the judgments . . . . However, both ch. 11:12 and also this verse are true. They in one sense "did according to the heathen," viz., in all that was bad; in another, viz., in that which was good, zeal for religion, they did *not*. Verse 9 also proves the negative to be genuine; because in changing their religion, they have *not* done as the nations which have not changed theirs, "*I* (also) will do in thee that which I have not done." **8. I, even I**—awfully emphatic. I, even I, whom thou thinkest to be asleep, but who am ever reigning as the Omnipotent Avenger of sin, will vindicate My righteous government before the nations by judgments on thee. **9.** See *Note*, vs. 7. **that which I have not done**—worse than any former judgments (Lam. 4:6; Dan. 9:12). The prophecy includes the destruction of Jerusalem by the Romans, and the final one by Antichrist (Zech. 13:8, 9; 14:2), as well as that by Nebuchadnezzar. Their doom of evil was not exhausted by the Chaldean conquest. There was to be a germinating evil in their destiny, because there would be, as the Lord foresaw, a germinating evil in their character. As God connected Himself peculiarly with Israel, so there was to be a peculiar manifestation of God's wrath against sin in their case [FAIRBAIRN]. The higher the privileges the greater the punishment in the case of abuse of them. When God's greatest favor, the gospel, was given, and was abused by them, then "the wrath was to come on them to the uttermost" (I Thess. 2:16). **10. fathers . . . eat . . . sons**—alluding to Moses' words (Lev. 26:29; Deut. 28:53), with the additional sad feature, that "the sons should eat their fathers" (see II Kings 6:28; Jer. 19:9; Lam. 2:20; 4:10). **11. as I live**—the most solemn of oaths, pledging the self-existence of God for the certainty of the event. **defiled my sanctuary**—the climax of Jewish guilt: their defiling Jehovah's temple by introducing idols. **diminish**—lit., "withdraw," viz., Mine "eye" (which presently follows), i.e., My favors; Job 36:7 uses the *Hebrew* verb in the same way. As the Jews had *withdrawn* from God's sanctuary its sacredness by "defiling" it, so God *withdraws* His countenance from them. The significance of the expression lies in the allusion to Deuteronomy 4:2, "Ye shall not *diminish* aught from the word which I command you"; they had done so, therefore God *diminishes* them. The reading found in six MSS., "I will cut thee off," is not so good. **12.** Statement in plain terms of what was intended by the symbols (vs. 2; see ch. 6:12; Jer. 15:2; 21:9). **draw out . . . sword after them**—(Lev. 26:33). Skeptics object; no such thing happened under Zedekiah, as is here foretold; viz., that a third part of the nation should die by pestilence, a third part by the sword, and a third be scattered unto all winds, and a sword sent after them. But the prophecy is not restricted to Zedekiah's time. It includes all that Israel suffered, or was still to suffer, for their sins, especially those committed at that period (ch. 17:21). It only received its primary fulfilment under Zedekiah: numbers then died by the pestilence and by the sword; and numbers were scattered in all quarters and not carried to Babylonia alone, as the objectors assert (cf. Ezra 1:4; Esther 3:8; Obadiah 14). **pestilence . . . and famine**—signified by the symbol "fire" (vs. 2). Cf. Isaiah 13:8; Lamentations 5:10; plague and famine burning and withering the countenance, as fire does. **13. cause my fury to rest upon them**—as on its proper and permanent *resting-place* (Isa. 30: 32, *Margin*). **I will be comforted**—expressed in condescension to man's conceptions; signifying His *satisfaction* in the vindication of His justice by His righteous judgments (Deut. 28:63; Prov. 1:26; Isa. 1:24). **they shall know**—by bitter experience. **14. reproach among the nations**—They whose idolatries Israel had adopted, instead of comforting, would only exult in their calamities brought on by those idolatries (cf. Luke 15:15). **15. instruction**—lit., "a corrective chastisement," i.e., a striking *example* to warn all of the fatal consequences of sin. For

ADAM CLARKE

6. *She hath changed my judgments.* God shows the reason why He deals with Jerusalem in greater severity than with the surrounding nations, because she was more wicked than they.

9. *I will do in thee that which I have not done.* The destruction of Jerusalem by Nebuchadnezzar was one of the greatest calamities that ever fell on any nation or place before, and that by the Romans under Titus exceeded all that has taken place since.

JOSEPH PARKER:

Verses 11, 12. And so the judgment passes on from thunder to thunder, and the last grand note of that judgment-thunder is, "I the Lord have spoken it." It was impossible for Ezekiel to invent all these moral judgments. We feel that they must have come up from eternity, because they express what never entered into the heart of man to conceive concerning the proper desert and issue of sin. Hell itself is a revelation. Make of that part of the invisible state what we may, it surely never entered into the heart of man to invent it. We may have perverted the idea; by our foolish exaggerations we may have distorted the divine revelation; but the great central fact of judgment, of burning indignation, of unquenchable anger against sin, we must always recognize as one of the unchangeable realities of true religion. It is clear that all judgment was not future in the Old Testament. There was an immediate degradation, and an immediate infliction of tremendous penalty. "I will make thee waste, and a reproach . . . I shall send upon them the evil arrows of famine . . . and will break your staff of bread . . . pestilence and blood shall pass through thee; and I will bring the sword upon thee." These were immediate visitations. In the New Testament we are supposed to come upon a prediction rather than a realized judgment. What we have to suffer for our sins is supposed to be in the future, while here we may enjoy ourselves in the very act of drinking goblets of iniquity. All this is an error on our part. Under the New Testament dispensation, as under the Old, judgment is immediate, penalty is now impending, our very next step may be into a burning pit. They allegorize who postpone judgment, not they who immediately feel it and respond to it penitentially. Every serpent that bites the hedge-breaker is but a hint of the still greater punishment that awaits us when all life is looked at by a judicial eye and pronounced upon by a judicial voice—*The People's Bible*

MATTHEW HENRY

Others *shall fall by the sword round about* Jerusalem, *v.* 17. Others are devoured by *evil beasts,* which will make a prey of those that fly for shelter to the deserts and mountains.

CHAPTER 6

Verses 1–7

I. The prophecy is directed to *the mountains of Israel* (*v.* 1, 2); the prophet must *set his face towards* them. If he could see so far as the land of Israel, *the mountains* would be first seen; towards them therefore he must look, steadfastly, as the judge looks at the prisoner, when he passes sentence upon him. Though *the mountains of Israel* be ever so strong, he must *set his face against* them, as having judgments to denounce that should shake their foundation. *The mountains of Israel* had been *holy mountains,* but now that they had polluted them with their high places God set his face against them and therefore the prophet must. But from *the mountains the word of the Lord* echoes *to the hills, to the rivers, and to the valleys*; for to them also *the Lord God* speaks.

II. That which is threatened is the utter destruction of the idols and the idolaters. God himself says, *Behold, I, even I, will bring a sword upon you* (*v.* 3); the sword of the Chaldeans is at God's command. The *high places,* which were on the tops of mountains (*v.* 3), shall be levelled *and made desolate* (*v.* 6). The *altars,* on which they offered sacrifice to strange gods, *shall be broken* to pieces and *laid waste*; the *images* and *idols* shall be defaced, *shall be broken and cease, v.* 4, 6. As *all their high places shall be laid waste,* so shall all *their dwelling-places* too, even *all their cities, v.* 6. It is added as a remarkable circumstance that they shall fall *before their idols* (*v.* 4), that their *dead carcases* should be *laid,* and their *bones scattered, about their altars, v.* 5. Thus the idols were upbraided with their inability to help their worshippers, and idolaters were upbraided with the folly of trusting in them.

Verses 8–10

Judgment had hitherto triumphed, but in these verses mercy rejoices against judgment. The ruin seems to be universal, and *yet will I leave a remnant,* a little remnant, and it is God that leaves them.

I. It is a preserved remnant, saved from the ruin (*v.* 8). None of those who were to *fall by the sword about* Jerusalem *shall escape*; for they trust to Jerusalem's walls for security. But some of them *shall escape the sword among the nations,* where, being deprived of all other steps, they stay themselves upon God only. They shall be the seed of another generation, out of which Jerusalem shall flourish again.

II. It is a penitent remnant (*v.* 9): *Those who escape of you shall remember me.* Where God designs grace to repent he allows space to repent; yet many who have the space want the grace, many who *escape the sword* do not forsake the sin.

1. The occasion of their repentance is a mixture of judgment and mercy—they were *carried captives,* but they *escaped the sword* in the land of their captivity. True repentance shall be accepted of God, though we are brought to it by our troubles; nay, sanctified afflictions often prove means of conversion.

2. The root and principle of their repentance: *They shall remember me among the nations.* The prodigal son never bethought himself of his father's house till he was ready to perish for hunger in the far country. Their remembering God was the first step they took in returning to him. They *departed from* God, from his word, which they should have made their rule, from his work, which they should have made their business. *Their hearts departed from* him. *Their eyes* also *go after their idols.* The malignity of this sin is that it is spiritual whoredom; it is a *whorish heart* that *departs from* God. They remember what a grief this was to him and how he resented it. In the day of their repentance it shall humble them more than anything, not so much that their peace was broken, and their country broken, as *that God was broken* by their sin.

3. The evidence of their repentance: *They shall loathe themselves for the evils which they have committed in all their abominations.* True penitents see

JAMIESON, FAUSSET, BROWN

"*it* shall be"; all ancient versions have "*thou,*" which the connection favors. **16. arrows of famine**—hail, rain, mice, locusts, mildew (see Deut. 32:23, 24). **increase the famine**—lit., "congregate" or "collect." When ye think your harvest safe because ye have escaped drought, mildew, etc., I will find other means [CALVIN], which I will *congregate* as the *forces of an invading army,* to bring famine on you. **17. beasts**—perhaps meaning destructive conquerors (Dan. 7:4). Rather, literal "beasts," which infest *desolated* regions such as Judea was to become (cf. ch. 34:28; Exod. 23:29; Deut. 32:24; II Kings 17:25). The same threat is repeated in manifold forms to awaken the careless. **sword**—civil war.

CHAPTER 6

VSS. 1-14. CONTINUATION OF THE SAME SUBJECT. **2. mountains of Israel**—i.e., of Palestine in general. The *mountains* are addressed by personification; implying that the Israelites themselves are incurable and unworthy of any more appeals; so the prophet sent to Jeroboam did not deign to address the king, but addressed the altar (I Kings 13:2). The mountains are specified as being the scene of Jewish idolatries on "the high places" (vs. 3; Lev. 26:30).

3. rivers—lit., the "channels" of torrents. Rivers were often the scene and objects of idolatrous worship.

4. images—called so from a *Hebrew* root, "to wax hot," implying the mad *ardor* of Israel after idolatry [CALVIN]. Others translate it, "sun-images"; and so in vs. 6 (see II Kings 23:11; II Chron. 34:4; Isa. 17:8, *Margin*). **cast your slain men before your idols**—The foolish objects of their trust in the day of evil should witness their ruin. **5. carcasses . . . before . . . idols**—polluting thus with the dead bones of you, the worshippers, the idols which seemed to you so sacrosanct. **6. your works**—not gods, as you supposed, but the mere work of men's hands (Isa. 40:18-20). **7. ye shall know that I am the Lord**—and not your idols, lords. Ye shall know Me as the all-powerful Punisher of sin.

8. Mitigation of the extreme severity of their punishment; still their life shall be a wretched one, and linked with exile (ch. 5:2, 12; 12:16; 14:22; Jer. 44:28).

9. they that escape of you shall remember me—The object of God's chastisements shall at last be effected by working in them true contrition. This partially took place in the complete eradication of idolatry from the Jews ever since the Babylonian captivity. But they have yet to repent of their crowning sin, the crucifixion of Messiah; their full repentance is therefore future, after the ordeal of trials for many centuries, ending with that foretold in Zechariah 10:9; 13:8, 9; 14:1-4, 11. "They shall *remember* me in far countries" (ch. 7:16; Deut. 30:1-8).

I am broken with their whorish heart—FAIRBAIRN translates, actively, "I will break" their whorish heart; *English Version* is better. In their exile they shall remember how long I bore with them, but was at last compelled to punish, after I was "broken" (My long-suffering wearied out) by their desperate (Num. 15:39) spiritual whorishness [CALVIN], (Ps. 78:40; Isa. 7:13; 43:24; 63:10). **loathe themselves**—(Lev. 26:39-45; Job 42:6). They

ADAM CLARKE

CHAPTER 6

2. *Set thy face toward the mountains of Israel.* This is a new prophecy, and was most probably given after the 430 days of his lying on his left and right sides were accomplished. By *Israel* here, Judea is simply meant; not the ten tribes, who had long before been carried into captivity. Ezekiel uses this term in reference to the Jews only. *The mountains* may be addressed here particularly because it was on them the chief scenes of idolatry were exhibited.

5. *Will scatter your bones round about your altars.* This was literally fulfilled by the Chaldeans. According to Baruch, chap. ii. 24-25, they opened the sepulchres of the principal people, and threw the bones about on every side.

9. *They that escape of you shall remember me.* Those that escape the sword, the pestilence, and the famine, and shall be led into captivity, shall plainly see that it is God who has done this; and shall humble themselves on account of their abominations, leave their idolatry, and worship Me alone. And this they have done from the Babylonish captivity to the present day.

MATTHEW HENRY

sin to be an abominable thing, that *abominable thing which the Lord hates* and which makes sinners, and even their services, odious to him, Jer. xliv. 4; Isa. i. 11. It defiles the sinner's own conscience, and makes him, unless he be past feeling, an abomination to himself.

4. The glory that will redound to God by their repentance (*v.* 10): "*They shall know that I am the Lord;* finding that what I have said is made good, and made to work for good, and to answer a good intention."

Verses 11–14

The same threatenings are repeated, with a direction to the prophet to lament them.

I. He must by his gestures in preaching express the sense he had of the iniquities and the calamities of the house of Israel (*v.* 11): *Smite with thy hand and stamp with thy foot.* Two things the prophet must thus lament: 1. National sins. *Alas! for all the evil abominations of the house of Israel.* The sins of sinners are the sorrows of God's faithful servants. 2. National judgments. It is our duty to be affected not only with our own sins and sufferings, but with the sins and sufferings of others; and to look with compassion upon the miseries that wicked people bring upon themselves; as Christ *beheld Jerusalem and wept over it.*

II. He must inculcate what he had said before concerning the destruction that was coming upon them. 1. They shall be run down and ruined by a variety of judgments which shall find them out and follow them wherever they are (*v.* 12). 2. They shall read their sin in their punishment, *v.* 5–7. Where they had prostrated themselves in honour of their idols, God will lay them dead, to their own reproach and the reproach of their idols. 3. The country shall be all laid waste, as, before, *the cities* (*v.* 6): *I will make the land desolate.*

JAMIESON, FAUSSET, BROWN

shall not wait for men to condemn them but shall condemn themselves (ch. 20:43; 36:31; Job 42:6; I Cor. 11:31).

11. Gesticulations vividly setting before the hearers the greatness of the calamity about to be inflicted. In indignation at the abominations of Israel extend thine hand towards Judea, as if about to "strike," and "stamp," shaking off the dust with thy foot, in token of how God shall "stretch out His hand upon them," and *tread* them down (vs. 14; ch. 21:14). **12. He that is far off**—viz., from the foe; those who in a distant exile fear no evil. **he that remaineth**—*he that is left* in the city; not carried away into captivity, nor having escaped into the country. Distinct from "he that is near," viz., those outside the city who are within reach of "the sword" of the foe, and so fall by it; not by "famine," as those left in the city. **14. Diblath**—another form of Diblathaim, a city in Moab (Num. 33:46; Jer. 48:22), near which, east and south of the Dead Sea, was the wilderness of Arabia Deserta.

ADAM CLARKE

11. *Smite with thine hand, and stamp with thy foot.* Show the utmost marks of your astonishment and indignation, and dread of the evils that are coming upon them.

14. *And make the land . . . more desolate than the wilderness toward Diblath.* Diblath is situated in the land of Moab. It is mentioned in Num. xxxiii. 46 and in Jer. xlviii. 22. It was a part of that horrible wilderness mentioned by Moses, Deut. viii. 15, "wherein were fiery serpents, and scorpions, and drought."

MATTHEW HENRY

CHAPTER 7

Verses 1–15

The prophet here proclaims, *An end! an end! it has come, it has come. He that hath ears to hear let him hear.*

I. The end which all the foregoing judgments had been working towards, as means to bring it about, was long in coming, but *now it has come.* This perhaps looks further, to the last destruction of that nation by the Romans. *The end of all things is at hand;* and Jerusalem's last end was a type of *the end of the world,* Matt. xxiv. 3.

II. *An evil, an only evil, behold, has come, v.* 5. Sin is *an evil, an only evil, an evil* that has no good in it; it is the worst of evils. But this is spoken of the evil of trouble. It is *an evil* without precedent or parallel, *an evil* that stands alone; you cannot produce such another instance. The wicked have *the dregs of that cup* to drink which to the righteous is full of *mixtures of mercy,* Ps. lxxv. 8.

III. *The time has come,* the set time, for to all God's purposes *there is a time,* a proper time. Though threatened judgments may be long deferred, yet they shall not be dropped. Though God's patience may put them off, nothing but man's sincere repentance and reformation will put them by.

IV. The whole body of the nation has become a *vessel of wrath, fitted for destruction.* Those shall *have judgment without mercy* who made light of mercy when it was offered them.

V. All this is the just punishment of their sins, and it is what they have by their own folly brought upon themselves. Two sins are particularly specified as provoking God to bring these judgments upon them—pride and oppression. 1. God will humble them by his judgments, for they have magnified themselves. *The rod* of affliction *has blossomed,* but it was *pride* that *budded, v.* 10.

JAMIESON, FAUSSET, BROWN

CHAPTER 7

Vss. 1-27. LAMENTATION OVER THE COMING RUIN OF ISRAEL; THE PENITENT REFORMATION OF A REMNANT; THE CHAIN SYMBOLIZING THE CAPTIVITY. **2. An end, the end**—The indefinite "an" expresses the general fact of God bringing His long-suffering towards the whole of Judea to an end; "the," following, marks it as more definitely fixed (Amos 8:2). **4. thine abominations**—the punishment of thine abominations. **shall be in the midst of thee**—shall be manifest to all. They and thou shall recognize the fact of thine abominations by thy punishment which shall everywhere befall thee, and that manifestly. **5. An evil, an only evil**—a peculiar calamity such as was never before; unparalleled. The abruptness of the style and the repetitions express the agitation of the prophet's mind in foreseeing these calamities. **6. watcheth for thee**—rather, "waketh for thee." It awakes up from its past slumber against thee (Ps. 78:65, 66). **7. The morning**—so *Chaldean* and *Syriac versions* (cf. Joel 2:2). Ezekiel wishes to awaken them from their lethargy, whereby they were promising to themselves an uninterrupted *night* (I Thess. 5:5-7), as if they were never to be called to account [CALVIN]. The expression, "morning," refers to the fact that this was the usual time for magistrates giving sentence against offenders (cf. vs. 10, below; Ps. 101:8; Jer. 21:12). GESENIUS, less probably, translates, "the *order* of fate"; thy turn to be punished. **not the sounding again**—not an empty *echo,* such as is produced by the reverberation of *sounds* in "the mountains," but a real cry of tumult is coming [CALVIN]. Perhaps it alludes to the joyous cries of the grape-gatherers at vintage on the hills [GROTIUS], or of the idolaters in their dances on their festivals in honor of their false gods [TIRINUS]. HAVERNICK translates, "no *brightness.*" **8, 9.** Repetition of vss. 3, 4; sadly expressive of accumulated woes by the monotonous sameness. **10. rod . . . blossomed, pride . . . budded**—The "rod" is the Chaldean Nebuchadnezzar, the instrument of God's vengeance (Isa. 10:5; Jer. 51:20). The rod *sprouting* (as the word ought to be translated), etc., implies that God does not move precipitately, but in successive steps. He as it were has planted the ministers of His vengeance, and leaves them to grow till all is ripe for executing His purpose. "Pride" refers to the insolence of the Babylonian conqueror (Jer. 50:31, 32). The parallelism ("pride" answering to "rod") opposes JEROME's view, that "pride" refers to the *Jews* who despised God's threats; (also CALVIN's, "though the *rod* grew in Chaldea, the *root* was with the Jews"). The "rod" cannot refer, as GROTIUS thought, to the *tribe* of Judah, for it evidently refers to the "smiteth"

ADAM CLARKE

CHAPTER 7

2. *The end is come upon the four corners of the land.* This is not a partial calamity; it shall cover and sweep the whole land. This whole chapter is poetical.

5. *An evil, an only evil.* The great, the sovereign, the last exterminating evil, is come: the sword, the pestilence, the famine, and the captivity.

6. *An end is come, the end is come: it watcheth for thee.* This is similar to the second verse; but there is a paronomasia, or play upon letters and words, which is worthy of note. *Kets ba, ba hakkets, hekits elayich. Katsah* signifies to make an end or extremity, by cutting off something, and *yakats* signifies to awake from sleep. The *end* or final destruction is here personified; and represented as an executioner who has arisen early from his sleep, and is waiting for his orders to execute judgment upon these offenders. Hence it is said—

7. *The morning is come unto thee.* Every note of time is used in order to show the certainty of the thing. *And not the sounding again of the mountains.* The hostile troops are advancing! You hear a sound, a tumultuous noise; do not suppose that this proceeds from festivals upon the mountains; from the joy of harvestmen or the treaders of the winepress. It is the noise of those by whom you and your country are to fall. "Now will I shortly pour out," v. 8. Here they come!

10. *Behold the day.* The same words are repeated, sometimes varied, and pressed on the attention with new figures and new circumstances, in order to alarm this infatuated people. Look at the day! It is come! *The morning is gone forth.* It will wait no longer. The *rod* that is to chastise you *hath blossomed;* it is quite ready. *Pride hath budded.* Your insolence, obstinacy, and daring opposition to God have brought forth their proper fruits.

MATTHEW HENRY

2. Their enemies shall deal hardly with them, for they have dealt hardly with one another (*v.* 11).

VI. There is no escape from these judgments. Men shall be safe nowhere; for *he that is in the field shall die by the sword* (every field shall be to them a field of battle) *and he that is in the city*, though it be a holy city, yet it shall not be his *protection*, but *famine and pestilence shall devour him.* Sin had abounded both in city and country. Those that fall shall not be lamented (*v.* 11): *There shall be no wailing for them*, for there shall be none left to bewail them. *None ever hardened his heart against God and prospered.* Those that strengthen themselves in their wickedness will be found not only to weaken, but to ruin, themselves, Ps. lii. 7. *The multitude* cannot resist the torrent of these judgments, nor make head against them (*v.* 14): *They have blown the trumpet*, to call their soldiers, but all in vain. "*Let not the buyer rejoice that he is increasing his estate and has become a purchaser*; nor let *the seller mourn* that he is lessening his estate and has become a bankrupt," *v.* 12. See the vanity of the things of this world, and how worthless they are—in a time of trouble.

It is added (*v.* 13), "*The seller shall not return*, at the year of jubilee, *to that which is sold*, according to the law, though he should escape the sword, and live till that year comes; for no inheritances shall be enjoyed here till the seventy years be accomplished, and then men shall return to their possessions, shall claim and have their own again."

Verses 16–22

Some of them *shall escape* (*v.* 16), but what the better? As good die once as, in a miserable life, die a thousand deaths, and escape only like Cain to be *fugitives and vagabonds*, and afraid of being slain by everyone they meet; so shall these be.

I. They shall have no comforter or satisfaction in their own minds, for, wherever they go, they carry about with them guilty consciences, which make them a burden to themselves. They shall be always solitary, alone *upon the mountains*, ashamed of the low circumstances to which they are reduced. They shall be always sorrowful. Those that once thought themselves as lions, now become as the *doves of the valleys*, so timid, and so dispirited, ready to *flee when none pursues* and to tremble at the shaking of a leaf. Sooner or later sin will have sorrow of one kind or other; and those that will not repent of their iniquity may justly be left to pine away in it. They shall be deprived of all their strength of body and mind (*v.* 17). They shall be deprived of all their hopes (*v.* 18).

II. They shall have no benefit from their wealth and riches, *v.* 19. They thought their wealth would be *their strong city*, that with it they could bribe enemies and buy friends, that it would be the ransom of their lives. It was no relief to them now in the day of their adversity; for *gold and silver* could not protect them from the judgments of God. Their *gold and silver* could not satisfy their hunger, nor serve to make one meal's meat for them. We could better be without mines of gold than fields of corn. Much less could they satisfy their souls, or yield them any inward comfort. Their *gold and silver shall be thrown into the streets*, because it would be an incumbrance to them and retard their flight, or because it would expose them and be a temptation to the enemy to cut their throats for their money.

III. God's temple shall stand them in no stead, *v.* 20–22. But here is the great dishonour they had done to God in profaning his sanctuary; they *made the images of their* counterfeit deities, and these they set up in God's temple, than which a greater affront could not be put upon him.

JAMIESON, FAUSSET, BROWN

(vs. 9) as the instrument of smiting. **11.** *Violence* (i.e., the violent foe) *is risen up as a rod of* (i.e., to punish the Jews') *wickedness* (Zech. 5:8). **theirs**—their possessions, or all that belongs to them, whether children or goods. GROTIUS translates from a different *Hebrew* root, "their nobles," lit., their *tumultuous* trains (*Margin*) which usually escorted the nobles. Thus "nobles" will form a contrast to the general "multitude." **neither . . . wailing**—(Jer. 16:4-7; 25:33). GESENIUS translates, "nor shall there be left any *beauty* among them." *English Version* is supported by the old Jewish interpreters. So general shall be the slaughter, none shall be left to mourn the dead. **12. let not . . . buyer rejoice**—because he has bought an estate at a bargain price. **nor . . . seller mourn**—because he has had to sell his land at a sacrifice through poverty. The Chaldeans will be masters of the land, so that neither shall the buyer have any good of his purchase, nor the seller any loss; nor shall the latter (vs. 13) return to his inheritance at the jubilee year (see Lev. 25:13). Spiritually this holds good now, seeing that "the time is short"; "they that rejoice should be as though they rejoiced not, and they that buy as though they possessed not": Paul (I Cor. 7: 30) seems to allude to Ezekiel here. Jeremiah 32: 15, 37, 43, seems to contradict Ezekiel here. But Ezekiel is speaking of the parents, and of the present; Jeremiah, of the children, and of the future. Jeremiah is addressing believers, that they should hope for a restoration; Ezekiel, the reprobate, who were excluded from hope of deliverance. **13. although they were yet alive**—although they should live to the year of jubilee. **multitude thereof**—viz., of the Jews. **which shall not return**—answering to "the seller shall not return"; not only he, but *the whole multitude*, shall not return. CALVIN omits "is" and "which": "the vision touching the whole multitude shall not return" void (Isa. 55:11). **neither shall any strengthen himself in the iniquity of his life**—No hardening of one's self in iniquity will avail against God's threat of punishment. FAIRBAIRN translates, "no one by his iniquity shall invigorate his life"; referring to the jubilee, which was regarded as a revivification of the whole commonwealth, when, its disorders being rectified, the body politic sprang up again into renewed life. That for which God thus provided by the institution of the jubilee and which is now to cease through the nation's iniquity, let none think to bring about by his iniquity. **14. They have blown the trumpet**—rather, "Blow the trumpet," or, "Let them blow the trumpet" to collect soldiers as they will, "to make all ready" for encountering the foe, it will be of no avail; none will have the courage to go to the battle (cf. Jer. 6:1), [CALVIN]. **15.** No security should anywhere be found (Deut. 32:25). Fulfilled (Lam. 1:20); also at the Roman invasion (Matt. 24:16-18). **16.** (Ch. 6:6.) **like doves**—which, though usually frequenting the valleys, mount up to the mountains when fearing the bird-catcher (Ps. 11:1). So Israel, once dwelling in its peaceful valleys, shall flee from the foe to the mountains, which, as being the scene of its idolatries, were justly to be made the scene of its flight and shame. The plaintive note of the dove (Isa. 59:11) represents the mournful repentance of Israel hereafter (Zech. 12:10-12). **17. shall be weak as water**—lit., "shall go (as) waters"; incapable of resistance (Josh. 7:5; Ps. 22:14; Isa. 13:7). **18. cover them**—as a garment. **baldness**—a sign of mourning (Isa. 3:24; Jer. 48:37; Mic. 1:16). **19. cast . . . silver in . . . streets**—just retribution; they had abused their silver and gold by converting them into idols, "the stumbling-block of their iniquity" (ch. 14:3, 4, i.e., an occasion of sinning); so these silver and gold idols, so far from "being able to deliver them in the day of the Lord's wrath" (see Prov. 11:4), shall, in despair, be cast by them into the streets as a prey to the foe, by whom they shall be "removed" (GROTIUS translates as *Margin*, "shall be despised as an *unclean* thing"); or rather, as suits the parallelism, "shall be put away from them" *by the Jews* [CALVIN]. "They (the silver and gold) shall not satisfy their souls," i.e., their cravings of appetite and other needs. **20. beauty of his ornament**—the temple of Jehovah, the especial glory of the Jews, as a bride glories in her ornaments (the very imagery used by God as to the temple, ch. 16: 10, 11). Cf. ch. 24:21: "My sanctuary, the excellency of your strength, the desire of your eyes." **images . . . therein**—viz., in the temple (ch. 8:3-17). **set it far from them**—God had "set" the temple (their "beauty of ornament") "for His majesty"; but they had set up "abominations therein"; therefore God, in just retribution, "set it far from them," (i.e., removed them far from it, or took it away from them [VATABLUS]. *Margin* translates, "Made it

ADAM CLARKE

11. *Violence is risen up into a rod of wickedness.* The prophet continues his metaphor: "Pride has budded."—And what has it brought forth? Violence and iniquity. To meet these, the rod of God cometh.

12. *Let not the buyer rejoice, nor the seller mourn.* Such is now the state of public affairs that he who through want has been obliged to sell his inheritance need not mourn on the account, as of this the enemy would soon have deprived him. And he who has bought it need not rejoice in his bargain, as he shall soon be stripped of his purchase, and either fall by the sword or be glad to flee for his life.

13. *For the seller shall not return.* In the sale of all heritages among the Jews, it was always understood that the heritage must return to the family on the year of jubilee, which was every fiftieth year; but in this case the seller should not return to possess it, as it was not likely that he should be alive when the next jubilee should come; and if he were even to live till that time, he could not possess it, as he would then be in captivity.

14. *They have blown the trumpet.* Vain are all the efforts you make to collect and arm the people, and stand on your own defense; for all shall be dispirited, and none go to the battle.

15. *The sword is without.* War through all the country, and *pestilence* and *famine* within the city, shall destroy the whole, except a small remnant. He who endeavors to flee from the one shall fall by the other.

16. *They . . . shall be on the mountains like doves of the valleys.* Rather, "like mourning doves" chased from their dovecotes, and separated from their mates.

19. *They shall cast their silver in the streets.* Their riches can be of no use, as in a time of famine there is no necessary of life to be purchased, and gold and silver cannot fill their bowels. *It is the stumblingblock of their iniquity.* They loved riches, and placed in the possession of them their supreme happiness. Now they find a pound of gold not worth an ounce of bread.

20. *As for the beauty of his ornament.* Their beautiful Temple was their highest ornament, and God made it majestic by His presence. But they have even taken its riches to make their idols, which they have brought into the very courts of the Lord's house; and therefore God hath *set it*, the Temple, *from them*, given it up to pillage.

MATTHEW HENRY

And therefore, they shall be deprived of the temple, and it shall be no succour to them. Let the soldiers do as they will; let them *enter into the secret place*, into the holy of holies; its defence has departed.

Verses 23-27

I. The prisoner arraigned: *Make a chain*, in which to drag the criminal to the bar. The chain signified the siege of Jerusalem, or the slavery of those that were carried into captivity, or that they were all bound by the righteous judgment of God.

II. The indictment drawn up against the prisoner: *The land is full of bloody crimes*, full of *the judgments of blood* (so the word is). It is full of such crimes as by the law were to be punished with death, *the judgment of blood*. Idolatry, blasphemy, witchcraft, sodomy, and the like, were *bloody crimes*.

III. Judgment given upon this indictment. God will reckon with them not only for the profaning of his sanctuary, but for the perverting of justice between man and man. Since they had walked in the way of the heathen, and done worse than they, God would *bring the worst of the heathen upon them* to destroy them. Since they had filled their house with goods unjustly gotten, and used their power for oppressing the weak, God would give their houses to be possessed by strangers, and *make the pomp of the strong to cease*. Since they had set up the images of other gods in the temple, God would remove thence the tokens of the presence of their own God.

Since they had followed one sin with another, God would pursue them with one judgment upon another—*mischief upon mischief*, and *rumour upon rumour* to frighten you, like the waves in a storm. They shall not have the direction in the trouble that they expect (*v.* 26): *They shall seek a vision of the prophet* to be assured of a happy issue. They did not desire a vision to reprove them for sin, nor to warn them of danger, but to promise them deliverance. They would not hear what God had to say to them by way of conviction, and therefore he has nothing to say to them by way of encouragement. *Counsel shall perish from the ancients;* the elders of the people, that should advise them what to do in this difficult juncture, shall be at their wits' end. None of the men of might shall *find their hands*.

JAMIESON, FAUSSET, BROWN

unto them an *unclean thing*" (cf. *Margin* on vs. 19, "removed"); what I designed for their glory they turned to their shame, therefore I will make it turn to their ignominy and ruin. **21. strangers**—barbarous and savage nations. **22. pollute my secret place**—just retribution for the Jews' pollution of the temple. "*Robbers* shall enter and defile" the holy of holies, the place of God's manifested presence, entrance into which was denied even to the Levites and priests and was permitted to the high priest only once a year on the great day of atonement. **23. chain**—symbol of the captivity (cf. Jer. 27:2). As they enchained the land with violence, so shall they be chained themselves. It was customary to lead away captives in a row with a chain passed from the neck of one to the other. Therefore translate as the *Hebrew* requires, "*the* chain," viz., that usually employed on such occasions. CALVIN explains it, that the Jews should be dragged, whether they would or no, before God's tribunal to be tried as culprits in chains. The next words favor this: "bloody crimes," rather, "*judgment* of bloods," i.e., with blood-sheddings deserving the extreme judicial penalty. Cf. Jeremiah 51:9: "Her *judgment* reacheth unto heaven." **24. worst of the heathen**—lit., "wicked of the nations"; the giving up of Israel to their power will convince the Jews that this is a final overthrow. **pomp of . . . strong**—the *pride* wherewith men "stiff of forehead" despise the prophet. **holy places**—the sacred compartments of the temple (Ps. 68:35; Jer. 51:51) [CALVIN]. God calls it "*their* holy places," because they had so defiled it that He regarded it no longer as *His*. However, as the defilement of the temple has already been mentioned (vss. 20, 22), and "their sacred places" are introduced as a new subject, it seems better to understand this of *the places dedicated to their idols*. As they defiled God's sanctuary, He will defile their self-constituted "sacred places." **25. peace, and . . . none**—(I Thess. 5:3.) **26. Mischief . . . upon . . . mischief**—(Deut. 32:23; Jer. 4:20). This is said because the Jews were apt to fancy, at every abatement of suffering, that their calamities were about to cease; but God will accumulate woe on woe. **rumour**—of the advance of the foe, and of his cruelty (Matt. 24:6). **seek a vision**—to find some way of escape from their difficulties (Isa. 26:9). So Zedekiah consulted Jeremiah (Jer. 37:17; 38:14). **law shall perish**—fulfilled (ch. 20:1, 3; Ps. 74:9; Lam. 2:9; cf. Amos 8:11); God will thus set aside the idle boast, "The law shall not perish from the priest" (Jer. 18:18). **ancients**—the ecclesiastical rulers of the people. **27. people of the land**—the general multitude, as distinguished from the "king" and the "prince." The consternation shall pervade all ranks. The king, whose duty it was to animate others and find a remedy for existing evils, shall himself be in the utmost anxiety; a mark of the desperate state of affairs. **clothed with desolation**—Clothing is designed to keep off shame; but in this case shame shall be the clothing. **after their way**—because of their wicked ways. **deserts**—lit., "judgments," i.e., what just judgment awards to them; used to imply the exact correspondence of God's judgment with the judicial penalties they had incurred: they oppressed the poor and deprived them of liberty; therefore they shall be oppressed and lose their own liberty.

ADAM CLARKE

22. *The robbers shall enter into it.* The Chaldeans shall not only destroy the city, but they shall enter the Temple, deface it, plunder it, and burn it to the ground.

23. *Make a chain.* Point out the Captivity; show them that it shall come, and show them the reason: Because *the land is full of bloody crimes*, etc.

24. *The worst of the heathen.* The Chaldeans, the most cruel and idolatrous of all nations.

25. *They shall seek peace.* They see now that their ceasing to pay the tribute to the king of Babylon has brought the Chaldeans against them, and now they sue for peace in vain. He will not hear; he is resolved on their destruction.

MATTHEW HENRY

CHAPTER 8

Verses 1-6

Ezekiel was now in Babylon; but the messages of wrath he had delivered in the foregoing chapters related to Jerusalem. Here he has a vision of what was done at Jerusalem, and this vision is continued to the close of the 11th chapter.

I. The date of this vision. The first vision he had was in *the fifth year of the captivity, in the fourth month* and *the fifth day of the month, ch.* i. 1, 2. This was just fourteen months after. Perhaps it was after he had lain 390 days on his left side, to bear the iniquity of Israel, and before he began the forty days on his right side, to bear the iniquity of Judah; for now he was sitting in the house, not lying.

II. The prophet was himself *sitting in his house* deep perhaps in contemplation. *The elders of Judah*, that were now in captivity with him, *sat before him*. Some think it was on some extraordinary occasion that they attended him, to enquire of the Lord, and *sat down* at his feet to *hear his word*. Now that the elders of Judah were in captivity they paid more respect to God's prophets, and his word in their mouth. A minister's house should be a church for all his neighbours. Paul preached in his own hired

JAMIESON, FAUSSET, BROWN

CHAPTER 8

Vss. 1-18. This eighth chapter begins a new stage of Ezekiel's prophecies and continues to the end of the eleventh chapter. The connected visions from ch. 3:12 to the end of ch. 7 comprehended Judah and Israel; but the visions (ch. 8-11) refer immediately to Jerusalem and the remnant of Judah under Zedekiah, as distinguished from the Babylonian exiles. **1. sixth year**—viz., of the captivity of Jehoiachin, as in ch. 1:2, the "fifth year" is specified. The lying on his sides 390 and 40 days (ch. 4:5, 6) had by this time been completed, at least *in vision*. That event was naturally a memorable epoch to the exiles; and the computation of years from it was to humble the Jews, as well as to show their perversity in not having repented, though so long and severely chastised. **elders**—viz., those carried away with Jehoiachin, and now at the Chebar. **sat before me**—to hear the word of God from me, in the absence of the temple and other public places of Sabbath worship, during the exile (ch. 33:30, 31). It was so ordered that they were present at the giving of the prophecy, and so left without excuse. **hand of . . . Lord God fell . . . upon me**—God's mighty operation *fell*, like a thunderbolt, *upon me*

ADAM CLARKE

CHAPTER 8

1. *In the sixth year, in the sixth month, in the fifth day of the month.* This, according to Archbishop Ussher, was the sixth year of Ezekiel's captivity. The sixth day of the fifth month of the ecclesiastical year, which answers to August. This chapter and the three following contain but one vision, of which I judge it necessary to give a general idea, that the attention of the reader may not be too much divided. The prophet, in the visions of God, is carried to Jerusalem, to the northern gate of the Temple, which leads by the north side to the Court of the Priests. There he sees the glory of the Lord in the same manner as he did by the river Chebar. At one side he sees the "image of jealousy." Going thence to the Court of the People, he sees through an opening in the wall seventy elders of the people, who were worshipping all sorts of beasts and reptiles, which were painted on the wall. Being brought thence to the gate of the door of the house, he saw women weeping for "Tammuz" or Adonis. As he returned to the court of the priests, between the porch and the altar, he saw

MATTHEW HENRY

house at Rome, and God owned him there, and *no man forbad him.*

III. The divine influence that the prophet was now under: *The hand of the Lord fell there upon me.*

IV. The vision that the prophet saw, *v.* 2. He *beheld a likeness*, all *brightness* above and all *fire* below, fire and flame. This agreed with the description we had before, *ch.* i. 27.

V. The prophet's vision of Jerusalem. He was *lifted up between heaven and earth*, and then perhaps in a trance or ecstasy, he had the following visions, *whether in the body or out of the body*, we may suppose, he *could not tell*, any more than Paul in a like case, much less can we. Those are best prepared for communion with God and the communications of divine light that by divine grace are raised up above the earth and the things of it. He was carried in vision to Jerusalem, and to God's sanctuary there.

VI. The discoveries made to him.

2. There he saw the reproach of Israel—*the image of jealousy*, set *northward, at the gate of the altar*, *v.* 3, 5. This was probably an image of Baal, which Manasseh made and set in the temple (2 Kings xxi. 7, 2 Chron. xxxiii. 3), which Josiah removed, but his successors, it seems, replaced there, as probably they did the *chariots of the sun* which he found *at the entering in of the house of the Lord* (2 Kings xxiii. 11), here said to be *in the entry*. But the prophet tells us that it was *the image of jealousy*, to convince our consciences that, whatever image it was, it was in the highest degree offensive to God and *provoked him to jealousy*. And now God appeals to him whether this was not sufficient ground for God to cast off this people. He will no more dignify and protect his sanctuary, but will give it up to reproach. *But turn thyself yet again.* Where there is one abomination it will be found that there are many more. Sins do not go alone.

1. He saw the glory of God (*v.* 4), the same appearance that he had seen, *ch.* i. Ezekiel has this repeated vision of the glory of God. But it seems to have a further intention here. The more glorious we see God to be, the more odious we shall see sin to be, especially idolatry.

Verses 7–12

A further discovery of the abominations committed at Jerusalem within the confines of the temple.

I. How this discovery is made. God, in vision, brought Ezekiel to the *door of the court*, the outer court, along the sides of which the priests' lodgings were. But, *behold, a hole in the wall* (*v.* 7), a spy-hole. This *hole in the wall* Ezekiel made wider, and *behold a door*, *v.* 8. This door he goes in by into *the treasury*, or some of the apartments of the priests, and sees *the wicked abominations that they do there*, *v.* 9.

II. What the discovery is. He sees a chamber set round with idolatrous pictures (*v.* 10). This was a sort of pantheon, a collection of all the idols together. Though the second commandment, in the letter of it, forbids any graven images, yet painted ones are as bad and as dangerous. He sees this chamber filled with idolatrous worshippers (*v.* 11): There were *seventy men of the elders of Israel* offering incense to these painted idols.

JAMIESON, FAUSSET, BROWN

(in ch. 1:3, it is less forcible, "was upon him"); whatever, therefore, he is to utter is not his own, for he has put off the mere man, while the power of God reigns in him [CALVIN]. **2. likeness**—understand, "of a man," i.e., of Messiah, the Angel of the covenant, in the person of whom alone God manifests Himself (ch. 1:26; John 1:18). **The "fire,"** from "His loins downward," betokens the vengeance of God kindled against the wicked Jews, while searching and purifying the remnant to be spared. The "brightness" "upward" betokens His unapproachable majesty (I Tim. 6:16). For *Hebrew*, *eesh*, "fire," LXX, etc., read *ish*, "a man." **colour of amber**—the glitter of chasmal [FAIRBAIRN], (*Note*, ch. 1:4, "polished brass"). **3.** Instead of prompting him to address directly the elders before him, the Spirit carried him away *in vision* (not in person bodily) to the temple at Jerusalem; he proceeds to report to them what he witnessed: his message thus falls into two parts: (1) The abominations reported in ch. 8. (2) The dealings of judgment and mercy to be adopted towards the impenitent and penitent Israelites respectively (ch. 9-11). The exiles looked hopefully towards Jerusalem and, so far from believing things there to be on the verge of ruin, expected a return in peace; while those left in Jerusalem eyed the exiles with contempt, as if cast away from the Lord, whereas they themselves were near God and ensured in the possessions of the land (ch. 11:15). Hence the vision here of what affected those in Jerusalem immediately was a seasonable communication to the exiles away from it. **door of the inner gate**—facing the north, the direction in which he came from Chebar, called the "altar-gate" (vs. 5); it opened into the inner court, wherein stood the altar of burnt offering; the inner court (I Kings 6: 36) was that of the priests; the outer court (ch. 10:5), that of the people, where they assembled. **seat**—the *pedestal* of the image. **image of jealousy**—Astarte, or Asheera (as the *Hebrew* for "grove" ought to be translated, II Kings 21:3, 7; 23: 4, 7), set up by Manasseh as a rival to Jehovah in His temple, and arresting the attention of all worshippers as they entered; it was the Syrian Venus, worshipped with licentious rites; the "queen of heaven," wife of Phœnician Baal. HAVERNICK thinks all the scenes of idolatry in the chapter are successive portions of the festival held in honor of Tammuz or Adonis (vs. 14). Probably, however, the scenes are separate proofs of Jewish idolatry, rather than restricted to one idol. **provoketh to jealousy**—calleth for a visitation in wrath of the "jealous God," who will not give His honor to another (cf. the second commandment, Exod. 20:5). JEROME refers this verse to a statue of Baal, which Josiah had overthrown and his successors had replaced. **4.** The Shekinah cloud of Jehovah's glory, notwithstanding the provocation of the idol, still remains in the temple, like that which Ezekiel saw "in the plain" (ch. 3:22, 23); not till ch. 10:4, 18 did it leave the temple at Jerusalem, showing the long-suffering of God, which ought to move the Jews to repentance. **5. gate of ... altar**—the principal avenue to the altar of burnt offering; as to the *northern* position, see II Kings 16:14. Ahaz had removed the brazen altar from the front of the Lord's house to the north of the altar which he had himself erected. The locality of the idol before God's own altar enhances the heinousness of the sin. **6. that I should** [be compelled by their sin to] **go far off from my sanctuary**—(ch. 10:18); the sure precursor of its destruction. **7. door of the court**—i.e., of the inner court (vs. 3); the court of the priests and Levites, into which now others were admitted in violation of the law [GROTIUS]. **hole in ... wall**—i.e., an aperture or window in the wall of the priests' chambers, through which he could see into the various apartments, wherein was the idolatrous shrine. **8. dig**—for it had been blocked up during Josiah's reformation. Or rather, the vision is not of an actual scene, but an ideal pictorial representation of the Egyptian idolatries into which the covenant-people had relapsed, practising them in secret places where they shrank from the light of day [FAIRBAIRN], (John 3:20). But cf, as to the *literal* introduction of idolatries into the temple, ch. 5:11; Jer. 7:30; 32:34. **10. creeping things ... beasts**—worshipped in Egypt; still found portrayed on their chamber walls; so among the troglodytæ. **round about**—On every side they surrounded themselves with incentives to superstition. **11. seventy men**—the seventy members composing the Sanhedrim, or great council of the nation, the origination of which we find in the seventy elders, representatives of the congregation, who went up with Moses to the mount to behold the glory of Jehovah, and to witness the secret trans-

ADAM CLARKE

twenty-five men with their backs to the sanctuary and their faces towards the east, worshipping the rising sun. This is the substance of the vision contained in the *eighth* chapter. About the same time he saw six men come from the higher gate with swords in their hands, and among them, one with an inkhorn. Then the Divine Presence left the cherubim, and took post at the entrance of the Temple, and gave orders to the man with the inkhorn to put a mark on the foreheads of those who sighed and prayed because of the abominations of the land; and then commanded the men with the swords to go forward, and slay every person who had not this mark. The prophet, being left alone among the dead, fell on his face, and made intercession for the people. The Lord gives him the reason of his conduct; and the man with the inkhorn returns, and reports to the Lord what was done. These are the general contents of the *ninth* chapter. The Lord commands the same person to go in between the wheels of the cherubim, and take his hand full of live coals, and scatter them over the city. He went as commanded, and one of the cherubim gave him the coals; at the same time the glory of the Lord, that had removed to the threshold of the house, now returned, and stood over the cherubim. The cherubim, wheels, wings, etc., are here described as in the first chapter. This is the substance of the *tenth* chapter. The prophet then finds himself transported to the east gate of the Temple, where he saw twenty-five men, and among them "Jaazaniah the son of Azur, and Pelatiah the son of Benaiah, princes of the people," against whom the Lord commands him to prophesy, and to threaten them with the utmost calamities because of their crimes. Afterwards God himself speaks, and shows that the Jews who should be left in the land should be driven out because of their iniquities, and that those who had been led captive, and who acknowledged their sins and repented of them, should be restored to their own land. Then the glory of the Lord arose out of the city, and rested for a time on one of the mountains on the east of Jerusalem, and the prophet being carried in vision by the Spirit to Chaldea, lost sight of the chariot of the divine glory, and began to show to the captivity what the Lord had shown to him. This is the substance of the *eleventh* chapter.

3. *The image of jealousy.* We do not know certainly of what form this image was, nor what god it represented. Some say it was the image of Baal, which was placed in the Temple by Manasses; others, that it was the image of Tammuz. The prophet being returned towards the northern gate, where he had seen the image of jealousy, v. 14, there saw the women lamenting for Tammuz.

4. *The vision that I saw in the plain.* See the note on chap. iii. 23; see also chap. i. 3.

10. *And saw . . . every form of creeping things.* It is very likely that these images portrayed on the wall were the objects of Egyptian adoration.

MATTHEW HENRY

They had *every man his censer in his hand.* They would all be their own priests. They think themselves out of God's sight: *They say, The Lord seeth us not.*

Verses 13–18

I. More abominations discovered to the prophet, *v.* 13–15. *Women weeping for Tammuz, v.* 14. Some think it was for Adonis, an idol among the Greeks, others for Osiris, an idol of the Egyptians, that they shed these tears. The image, they say, was made to weep, and then the worshippers wept with it. They bewailed the death of this Tammuz, and anon rejoiced in its returning to life again. These mourning women *sat at the door of the gate of the Lord's house,* and there shed their idolatrous tears, and some think, prostrating themselves also to corporeal whoredom.

Men worshipping the sun, v. 16. And this was practised *in the inner court of the Lord's house at the door of the temple of the Lord, between the porch and the altar.* They turned *their backs towards the temple of the Lord,* and turned *their faces towards the east, and worshipped the sun,* the rising sun.

II. The inference drawn from these discoveries (*v.* 17): "*Hast thou seen this, O son of man!* and couldst thou have thought ever to see such things done in the temple of the Lord?" He appeals to the prophet himself. Is it an excusable thing in those that have God's oracles and ordinances *that they commit the abominations which they commit here?* Do not those deserve to suffer that thus sin? "They *return to provoke me* (they repeat the provocation, do it, and do it again), *and lo, they put the branch to their nose*"—a proverbial expression denoting per-

JAMIESON, FAUSSET, BROWN

actions relating to the establishment of the covenant; also, in the seventy elders appointed to share the burden of the people with Moses. How awfully it aggravates the national sin, that the seventy, once admitted to the Lord's secret council (Ps. 25:14), should now, "in the dark," enter "the secret" of the wicked (Gen. 49:6), those judicially bound to suppress idolatry being the ringleaders of it! **Jaazaniah**—perhaps chief of the seventy: son of Shaphan, the scribe who read to Josiah the book of the law; the spiritual privileges of the son (II Kings 22:10-14) increased his guilt. The very name means, "Jehovah hears," giving the lie to the unbelief which virtually said (ch. 9:9), "The Lord seeth us not," etc. (cf. Ps. 10:11, 14; 50:21; 94:7, 9). The offering of incense belonged not to the elders, but to the priests; this usurpation added to the guilt of the former. **cloud of incense**—They spared no expense for their idols. Oh, that there were the same liberality toward the cause of God! **12. every man in . . . chambers of . . . imagery**—The elders ("ancients") are here the representatives of the people, rather than to be regarded literally. Mostly, the *leaders* of heathen superstitions laughed at them secretly, while publicly professing them in order to keep the people in subjection. Here what is meant is that the *people* generally addicted themselves to secret idolatry, led on by their elders; there is no doubt, also, allusion to *the mysteries,* as in the worship of Isis in Egypt, the Eleusinian in Greece, etc., to which the initiated alone were admitted. "The chambers of imagery" are their own *perverse imaginations,* answering to the *priests' chambers* in the vision, whereon the pictures were portrayed (vs. 10). **Lord . . . forsaken . . . earth**—They infer this because God has left them to their miseries, without succoring them, so that they seek help from other gods. Instead of repenting, as they ought, they bite the curb [CALVIN]. **14.** From the *secret* abominations of the chambers of imagery, the prophet's eye is turned to the *outer* court at the *north door; within* the outer court women were not admitted, but only to the *door.* **sat**—the attitude of mourners (Job 2:13; Isa. 3:26). **Tammuz**—from a *Hebrew* root, "to melt down." Instead of weeping for the national sins, they wept for the idol. Tammuz (the *Syrian* for Adonis), the paramour of Venus, and of the same name as the river flowing from Lebanon; killed by a wild boar, and, according to the fable, permitted to spend half the year on earth, and obliged to spend the other half in the lower world. An annual feast was celebrated to him in June (hence called Tammuz in the Jewish calendar) at Byblos, when the Syrian women, in wild grief, tore off their hair and yielded their persons to prostitution, consecrating the hire of their infamy to Venus; next followed days of rejoicing for his return to the earth; the former feast being called "the disappearance of Adonis," the latter, "the finding of Adonis." This Phœnician feast answered to the similar Egyptian one in honor of Osiris. The idea thus fabled was that of the waters of the river and the beauties of spring destroyed by the summer during the half year when the sun is in the upper heat. Or else, the earth being clothed with beauty, hemisphere, and losing it when he departs to the lower. The name *Adonis* is not here used, as *Adon* is the appropriated title of Jehovah. **15, 16.** The next are *"greater* abominations," not in respect to the idolatry, but in respect to the place and persons committing it. In "the inner court," immediately before the door of the temple of Jehovah, between the porch and the altar, where the priests advanced only on extraordinary occasions (Joel 2:17), twenty-five men (the leaders of the twenty-four courses or orders of the priests, I Chron. 24:18, 19, with the high priest, "the princes of the sanctuary," Isa. 43:28), representing the whole priesthood, as the seventy elders represented the people, stood with their backs turned on the temple, and their faces towards the east, making obeisance to the rising sun (contrast I Kings 8:44). Sun-worship came from the Persians, who made the sun the eye of their god Ormuzd. It existed as early as Job (Job 31:26; cf. Deut. 4:19). Josiah could only suspend it for the time of his reign (II Kings 23:5, 11); it revived under his successors. **16. worshipped**—In the *Hebrew* a corrupt form is used to express Ezekiel's sense of the foul corruption of such worship. **17. put . . . branch to . . . nose**—proverbial, for "they turn up the nose in scorn," expressing their insolent security [LXX]. Not content with outraging "with their violence" the second table of the law, viz., that of duty towards one's neighbor, "they have returned" (i.e., they turn back afresh) to provoke Me by violations of the first table [CALVIN]. Rather, they held up a branch or bundle of tamarisk (called *barsom*)

ADAM CLARKE

11. *Jaazaniah the son of Shaphan.* Shaphan was a scribe, or what some call comptroller of the Temple, in the days of Josiah; and Jaazaniah, his son, probably succeeded him in this office. He was at the head of this band of idolaters.

14. *There sat women weeping for Tammuz.* This was Adonis, and so the Vulgate here translates. He is fabled to have been a beautiful youth beloved by Venus, and killed by a wild boar in Mount Lebanon. The women of Phoenicia, Assyria, and Judea worshipped him as dead with deep lamentation. *Tammuz* signifies "hidden" or "obscure," and hence the worship of his image was in some secret place.

16. *Five and twenty men.* These most probably represented the twenty-four courses of the priests, with the high priest for the twenty-fifth. This was the Persian worship, as their turning their faces to the east plainly shows they were worshipping the rising sun.

17. *They put the branch to their nose.* This is supposed to mean some branch or branches, which they carried in succession in honor of the idol, and with which they covered their faces, or from which they inhaled a pleasant smell, the branches being odoriferous.

MATTHEW HENRY

haps their scoffing at God. Dr. Lightfoot says, *They put the branch to their wrath*, or *to his wrath*, as the Masorites read it; that is, they are still bringing more fuel to the fire of divine wrath, which they have already kindled. *Though they cry in my ears with a loud voice, yet will I not hear them;* for still their sins cry more loudly for vengeance than their prayers cry for mercy.

CHAPTER 9

Verses 1-4

I. The summons given to Jerusalem's destroyers. God's angels have received a charge now to lay that city waste, which they had long had a charge to protect and watch over. They are at hand, as destroying angels, as ministers of wrath, for *every man has his destroying weapon in his hand*, as the angel that kept the way of the tree of life with a flaming sword.

II. Their appearance, upon this summons, is recorded. Immediately *six men came* (*v.* 2), one for each of the principal gates of Jerusalem. The nations of which the king of Babylon's army was composed, which some reckon to be six, and the commanders of his army (of whom *six* are named as principal, Jer. xxxix. 3), may be called *the slaughter-weapons* in the hands of the angels. They came—*from the way of the higher gate, which lies towards the north* (*v.* 2), either because the Chaldeans came from the north (Jer. i. 14), or because the image of jealousy was set up *at the door of the inner gate that looks towards the north, ch.* viii. 3, 5.

III. The notice taken of one among the destroying angels. It should seem he was not one of the six, but *among them*, to see that mercy was mixed with judgment, *v.* 2. This *man was clothed with linen*, as the priests were, and he had *a writer's inkhorn* hanging at *his side*, as anciently attorneys had, which he was to make use of, as the other six were to make use of their *destroying weapons*. Here the honours of the pen exceeded those of the sword, for it is generally agreed that he represented Christ as Mediator saving those that are his from the flaming sword of divine justice. As high priest he wears fine *linen*, Rev. xix. 8. As a prophet he wears the *writer's inkhorn*. The book of life is the Lamb's book. The great things of the law and gospel which God has written to us are of his writing, and the Bible is *the revelation of Jesus* Christ. In the midst of the destroyers and the destructions that are abroad, there is a Mediator, a great high priest.

IV. The removal of the appearance of the divine glory from over the cherubim. Some think it was that display of the divine glory which the prophet now saw over the cherubim in vision. Ezekiel immediately observed that *the glory of the God of Israel had gone up from the cherub*: and what is a vision of angels if God be gone?

V. The charge given *to the man clothed in linen* to secure the pious remnant from the general desolation. We do not read that this Saviour was summoned and sent for, as the destroyers were; for he is always ready, *appearing in the presence of God for us*. This remnant that is to be saved are such as *sigh and cry*, sigh in themselves, as men in distress, cry to God in prayer. These pious few had witnessed against those abominations and had done what they could to suppress them. Orders are given to find those

JAMIESON, FAUSSET, BROWN

to their nose at daybreak, while singing hymns to the rising sun [STRABO, 1.15, p. 733]. Sacred trees were frequent symbols in idol-worship. CALVIN translates, "to their own ruin," lit., "to their nose," i.e., with the effect of rousing *My anger* (of which *the Hebrew* is "nose") to their ruin. **18. though they cry . . . yet will I not hear**—(Prov. 1:28; Isa. 1:15.)

CHAPTER 9

Vss. 1-11. CONTINUATION OF THE PRECEDING VISION: THE SEALING OF THE FAITHFUL. **1. cried**—contrasted with their "cry" for mercy (ch. 8:18) is the "cry" here for vengeance, showing how vain was the former. **them that have charge**—lit., "officers"; so *officers* (Isa. 60:17), having the city in charge, not to guard, but to punish it. The angels who as "watchers" fulfil God's judgments (Dan. 4:13, 17, 23; 10:20, 21); the "princes" (Jer. 39:3) of Nebuchadnezzar's army were under their guidance. **draw near**—in the *Hebrew* intensive, "to draw near quickly." **2. clothed with linen**—(Dan. 10:5; 12:6, 7). His clothing marked his office as distinct from that of the six officers of vengeance; "linen" characterized the high priest (Lev. 16:4); emblematic of purity. The same garment is assigned to the angel of the Lord (for whom Michael is but another name) by the contemporary prophet Daniel (Dan. 10:5; 12:6, 7). Therefore the intercessory High Priest in heaven must be meant (Zech. 1:12). The six with Him are His subordinates; therefore He is said to be "among them," lit., "in the midst of them," *as their recognized Lord* (Heb. 1:6). He appears as a "man," implying His incarnation; as "one" (cf. I Tim. 2:5). Salvation is peculiarly assigned to Him, and so He bears the "inkhorn" in order to "mark" His elect (vs. 4; cf. Exod. 12:7; Rev. 7:3; 9:4; 13:16, 17; 20:4), and to write their names in His book of life (Rev. 13:8). As Oriental scribes suspend their inkhorn at their side in the present day, and as a "scribe of the host is found in Assyrian inscriptions accompanying the host" to number the heads of the slain, so He stands ready for the work before Him. "The higher gate" was probably where now the gate of Damascus is. The six with Him make up the sacred and perfect number, *seven* (Zech. 3:9; Rev. 5:6). The executors of judgment on the wicked, in Scripture teaching, are good, not bad, angels; the bad have permitted to them the trial of the pious (Job 1:12; II Cor. 12:7). The judgment is executed by Him (ch. 10:2, 7; John 5:22, 27) through the six (Matt. 13:41; 25:31); so beautifully does the Old Testament harmonize with the New Testament. The seven come "from the way of the north"; for it was there the idolatries were seen, and from the same quarter must proceed the judgment (Babylon lying northeast of Judea). So Matthew 24:28. **stood**—the attitude of waiting reverently for Jehovah's commands. **brazen altar**—the altar of burnt offerings, not the altar of incense, which was *of gold*. They "stood" there to imply reverent obedience; for there God gave His answers to prayer [CALVIN]; also as being about to slay victims to God's justice, they stand where sacrifices are usually slain [GROTIUS], (ch. 39:17; Isa. 34:6; Jer. 12:3; 46: 10). **3. glory of . . . God**—which had heretofore, as a bright cloud, rested on the mercy seat between the cherubim in the holy of holies (II Sam. 6:2; Ps. 80: 1); its departure was the presage of the temple being given up to ruin; its going from the inner sanctuary to the threshold without, towards the officers standing at the altar outside, was in order to give them the commission of vengeance. **4. midst of . . . city . . . midst of Jerusalem**—This twofold designation marks more emphatically the scene of the divine judgments. **a mark**—lit., the Hebrew letter *Tau*, the last in the alphabet, used as a *mark* (Job 31:35, *Margin*, "my sign"); lit., *Tau;* originally written in the form of a *cross*, which TERTULLIAN explains as referring to the badge and only means of salvation, the cross of Christ. But nowhere in Scripture are the words which are now employed as names of letters used to denote the letters themselves or their figures [VITRINGA]. The noun here is cognate to the verb, "*mark a mark.*" So in Revelation 7:3 no particular mark is specified. We *seal* what we wish to guard securely. When all things else on earth are confounded, God will secure His people from the common ruin. God gives the *first* charge as to their safety before He orders the punishment of the rest (Ps. 31:20; Isa. 26:20, 21). So in the case of Lot and Sodom (Gen. 19:22); also the Egyptian first-born were not slain till Israel had time to sprinkle the blood-mark, ensuring their safety (cf. Rev. 7:3; Amos 9:9). So the early Christians had Pella

ADAM CLARKE

CHAPTER 9

1. *Cause them that have charge over the city.* By those six men with destroying weapons the Chaldeans are represented, who had received commission to destroy the city; and when the north is mentioned in such cases, Chaldea and the Chaldean armies are generally intended. There appear to have been six men with a sort of slaughter-bills, and one man with an inkhorn. These may represent the seven counsellors of the Eastern monarchs, who always saw the king's face, and knew all the secrets of the government. This person with the inkhorn might be termed, in our phrase, the recorder.

2. *Stood beside the brasen altar.* To signify that the people against whom they had their commission were, for their crimes, to be sacrificed to the demands of divine justice.

3. *And he called to the man.* The person here who called was that who sat on the chariot of the divine glory. See chap. i. 26.

MATTHEW HENRY

all out that are of such a pious public spirit: "*Go through the midst of the city* in quest of them, discover them, *and set a mark upon* their *foreheads*." A work of grace in the soul is to God *a mark upon the forehead*, which he will acknowledge as his mark, and by which *he knows those that are his*. God will set a mark upon his mourners, will book their sighs and bottle their tears.

Verses 5–11

I. A command given to the destroyers to do execution according to their commission.

1. They are ordered to destroy all. This was fulfilled in the death of multitudes by famine and pestilence, especially by the sword of the Chaldeans, as far as the military execution went. But what an evil thing is sin, then, which provokes the God of infinite mercy to such severity! *Let not your eye spare, neither have you pity* (*v.* 5). Those that live in sin, and hate to be reformed, will perish in sin; they might easily have prevented the ruin, and would not.

2. They are warned not to do the least hurt to those that were marked for salvation: "*Come not near any man upon whom is the mark;* do not so much as threaten or frighten any of them." God had promised that *it should go well with his remnant* and they *should be well treated* (Jer. xv. 11); and we have reason to think that none of the mourning praying remnant fell by the sword of the Chaldeans. In the last destruction of Jerusalem by the Romans the Christians were all secured in a city called *Pella*, and none of them perished.

3. They are directed to *begin at the sanctuary* (*v.* 6). They must begin there because there the wickedness began which provoked God to send these judgments. God's temple is a sanctuary, a refuge and protection for penitent sinners, but not for any that *go on still in their trespasses*.

4. They are appointed to *go forth into the city*, *v.* 6, 7. Though *judgment begins at the house of God*, yet it shall not end there.

II. They observed their orders. *They began at the* elders, *the ancient men that were before the house*, either those seventy ancients who worshipped idols in their chambers (*ch.* viii. 12) or those twenty-five who *worshipped the sun between the porch and the altar*. They proceeded to the common people.

III. Here is the prophet's intercession for a mitigation of the judgment (*v.* 8): *While they were slaying them, and I was left, I fell upon my face.* He speaks as one that narrowly escaped the destruction, attributing it to God's goodness, not his own deserts. We must look upon it that we are spared, that we may do good in our places, may do good by our prayers.

IV. Here is God's denial of the prophet's request for a mitigation of the judgment, *v.* 9, 10. God was as willing to show mercy as the prophet could desire; he always is so. But here the case will not admit of it; it is such that mercy cannot be granted without wrong to justice. The sinners justify themselves with the same atheistical profane principle with which they flattered themselves in their idolatry, *ch.* viii. 12. "*The Lord has forsaken the earth*, and left it to us to do what we will in it; he will not intermeddle in the affairs of it; and, whatever wrong we do, he *sees not*." Now how can those expect benefit by the mercy of God who thus bid defiance to his justice?

V. The writ of protection for the securing of those that mourned in Zion (*v.* 11): *The man clothed with linen reported the matter*, gave an account of what he had done: He had found out all that mourned in secret for the sins of the land, and cried out against them, and had marked them all in the forehead. Lord, *I have done as thou hast commanded me.*

JAMIESON, FAUSSET, BROWN

provided as a refuge for them, before the destruction of Jerusalem. **upon the foreheads**—the most conspicuous part of the person, to imply how their safety would be manifested to all (cf. Jer. 15:11; 39: 11-18). It was customary thus to mark worshippers (Rev. 13:16; 14:1, 9) and servants. So the Church of England marks the forehead with the sign of the cross in baptizing. At the exodus the mark was on the *houses,* for then it was families; here, it is on the *foreheads,* for it is individuals whose safety is guaranteed. **sigh and . . . cry**—similarly sounding verbs in *Hebrew*, as in *English Version*, expressing the prolonged sound of their grief. "Sigh" implies their *inward grief* ("groanings which cannot be uttered," Rom. 8:26); "cry," the outward expression of it. So Lot (II Pet. 2:7, 8). Tenderness should characterize the man of God, not harsh sternness in opposing the ungodly (Ps. 119:53, 136; Jer. 13:17; II Cor. 12:21); at the same time zeal for the honor of God (Ps. 69:9, 10; I John 5:19). **5. the others**—the six officers of judgment (vs. 2). **6. come not near any . . . upon whom . . . mark**—(Rev. 9:4). It may be objected that Daniel, Jeremiah, and others were carried away, whereas many of the vilest were left in the land. But God does not promise believers exemption from all suffering, but only from what will prove really and lastingly hurtful to them. His sparing the ungodly turns to their destruction and leaves them without excuse [CALVIN]. However, the prophecy waits a fuller and final fulfilment, for Revelation 7:3-8, in ages long after Babylon, foretells, as still future, the same sealing of a remnant (144,000) of Israel previous to the final outpouring of wrath on the rest of the nation; the correspondence is exact; the same pouring of fire from the altar follows the marking of the remnant in both (cf. Rev. 8:5, with ch. 10:2). So Zechariah 13:9 and 14:2, distinguish the remnant from the rest of Israel. **begin at . . . sanctuary**—For in it the greatest abominations had been committed; it had lost the reality of consecration by the blood of victims sacrificed to idols; it must, therefore, lose its semblance by the dead bodies of the slain idolaters (vs. 7). God's heaviest wrath falls on those who have sinned against the highest privileges; these are made to feel it first (I Pet. 4:17, 18). He hates sin most in those nearest to Him; e.g., the priests, etc. **ancient men**—the seventy elders. **8. I was left**—lit., "there was left I." So universal seemed the slaughter that Ezekiel thought himself the only one left [CALVIN]. He was the only one left *of the priests* "in the sanctuary." **fell upon my face**—to intercede for his countrymen (so Num. 16:22). **all the residue**—a plea drawn from God's covenant promise to save the elect *remnant.* **9. exceeding**—lit., "very, very"; doubled. **perverseness**—"apostasy" [GROTIUS]; or, "wresting aside of justice." **Lord . . . forsaken . . . earth . . . seeth not**—The order is reversed from ch. 8:12. There they speak of His neglect of His people in their misery; here they go farther and deny His providence (Ps. 10:11), so that they may sin fearlessly. God, in answer to Ezekiel's question (vs. 8), leaves the difficulty unsolved; He merely vindicates His justice by showing it did not exceed their sin: He would have us humbly acquiesce in His judgments, and wait and trust. **10. mine eye**—to show them their mistake in saying, "The Lord *seeth* not." **recompense their way upon their head**—(Prov. 1:31). Retribution in kind. **11. I have done as thou hast commanded**—The characteristic of Messiah (John 17:4). So the angels (Ps. 103:21); and the apostles report their fulfilment of their orders (Mark 6:30).

ADAM CLARKE

4. *Set a mark upon the foreheads of the men that sigh.* This is in allusion to the ancient, everywhere-used custom of setting marks on servants and slaves, to distinguish them from others. It was also common for the worshippers of particular idols to have their idol's mark upon their foreheads, arms, etc.

6. *Begin at my sanctuary.* Let those who have sinned against most mercy, and most privileges, be the first victims of justice. Those who know their Lord's will, and do it not, shall be beaten with many stripes. The unfaithful members of Christ's Church will be first visited and most punished.

9. *For they say, The Lord hath forsaken the earth. Eth haarets,* "this land." He has no more place in Israel; He has quite abandoned it; He neither sees nor cares, and He can be no longer the Object of worship to any man in Israel. This seems to be the meaning; and God highly resents it, because it was bringing Him on a level with idols and provincial deities, who had, according to supposition, regency only in some one place.

10. *Mine eye shall not spare.* They say, "The Lord seeth not." This is false; I have seen all their iniquities, and do see all their abominations; and I will bring deserved judgment upon them, and then that eye which now sees will neither *pity* nor *spare.*

MATTHEW HENRY — CHAPTER 10

Verses 1–7

I. The glorious appearance of divine majesty. Something of the invisible world is here made visible, faint representations of its brightness and beauty, shadows, but such as are no more to be compared with the truth and substance than a picture with the life. He is here *in the firmament above the head of the cherubim, v.* 1. It is *the firmament of his power* and of his prospect too; for thence *he beholds* all *the children of men.*

JAMIESON, FAUSSET, BROWN — CHAPTER 10

VSS. 1-22. VISION OF COALS OF FIRE SCATTERED OVER THE CITY: REPETITION OF THE VISION OF THE CHERUBIM. **1.** The throne of Jehovah appearing in the midst of the judgments implies that whatever intermediate agencies be employed, He controls them, and that the whole flows as a necessary consequence from His essential holiness (ch. 1:22, 26). **cherubim**—in ch. 1:5, called "living creatures." The repetition of the vision implies that the judgments are approaching nearer and nearer. These two visions of Deity were granted in the beginning of Ezekiel's career, to qualify him for witnessing to God's glory amidst his God-forgetting people and to stamp truth on his announcements; also to signify the removal of God's manifestation from the visible temple (vs. 18) for a long period (ch. 43:2). The feature (vs. 12) mentioned as to the cherubim that they were "full of eyes," though omitted in the former vision, is not a difference, but a more specific detail observed by Ezekiel now on closer inspec-

ADAM CLARKE — CHAPTER 10

1. *As it were a sapphire stone.* See the note on chap. i. 22, 26. The chariot, here mentioned by the prophet, was precisely the same as that which he saw at the river Chebar, as himself tells us, v. 15, of which see the description in chap. i.

MATTHEW HENRY

He is here upon the throne. God's glory and government infinitely transcend all the brightest ideas our minds can either form or receive.

II. Further orders are to be given for the destruction of Jerusalem. Here we have a command to lay the city in ashes, by *scattering coals of fire* upon it, which in the vision were fetched *from between the cherubim. The glory of the Lord* was lifted *up from the cherub and stood* upon *the threshold of the house*, in imitation of the courts of judgment, which they kept in the gates of their cities. He that sits on the throne calls *to the man clothed in linen* to *go in between the wheels, and fill his hand with coals of fire from between the cherubim, and scatter them over the city.* This intimates the burning of the city and temple by the Chaldeans. The fire on God's altar, where atonement was made, had been slighted.

The appearance of his glory is veiled with a cloud, and yet out of that cloud darts forth a dazzling lustre; in *the house* and *inner court* there was *a cloud* and darkness, which filled them, and yet the outer court *was full of the brightness of the Lord's glory, v.* 3, 4. Thus (Hab. iii. 4) *he had rays coming out of his hand, and yet there was the hiding of his power.* Nothing is more clear than that God *is,* nothing more dark than *what* he is. God *covers himself with light,* and yet *makes darkness his pavilion.* (See also, comments on Ezekiel *ch.* i.)

The prophet, when he first saw this vision, observed that there were *burning coals of fire,* and *lamps,* that *went up and down among the living creatures* (*ch.* i. 13); thence this fire was taken, *v.* 7. The *spirit of burning, the refiner's fire,* by which Christ purifies his church, is of a divine original.

Verses 8–22

A further account of the vision of God's glory which Ezekiel saw, here intended to introduce the departure of that glory from them.

I. Ezekiel sees the glory of God shining in the sanctuary, as he had seen it *by the river of Chebar.* Ezekiel here sees the operations of divine Providence in the government of the lower world. The agency of the angels in directing the affairs of this world is represented by the close communication that was between the *living creatures* and the *wheels,* the wheels being guided by them in all their motions, as the chariot is by him that drives it. But the same Spirit being both in the *living creatures* and in the *wheels* denotes that infinite wisdom which serves its own purposes by the ministration of angels and all the occurrences of this lower world. The prophet observes that this was *the same vision* with that he saw by the river of Chebar (*v.* 15, 22). This world is subject to changes and revolutions. The course of affairs in it is represented by *wheels* (*v.* 9). Their appearance is as if there were a *wheel in the midst of a wheel* (*v.* 10), which intimates the references of providences to each other, their dependence on each other, and the tendency of all to one common end, while their motions are intricate and seemingly contrary.

JAMIESON, FAUSSET, BROWN

tion. Also, here, there is no rainbow (the symbol of *mercy* after the flood of wrath) as in the former; for here *judgment* is the prominent thought, though the *marking* of the remnant in ch. 9:4, 6 shows that there was mercy in the background. The cherubim, perhaps, represent redeemed humanity combining in and with itself the highest forms of subordinate creaturely life (cf. Rom. 8:20). Therefore they are associated with the twenty-four elders and are distinguished from the angels (Rev. 5). They stand on the mercy seat of the ark, and *on that ground* become the habitation of God from which His glory is to shine upon the world. The different forms symbolize the different phases of the Church. So the quadriform Gospel, in which the incarnate Saviour has lodged the revelation of Himself in a fourfold aspect, and from which His glory shines on the Christian world, answers to the emblematic throne from which He shone on the Jewish Church. **2. he**—Jehovah; He who sat on the "throne." **the man**—the Messenger of mercy becoming the Messenger of judgment (*Note*, ch. 9:2). *Human* agents of destruction shall fulfil the will of "the Man," who is Lord of men. **wheels**—*Hebrew, galgal,* implying *quick* revolution; so *the impetuous onset of the foe* (cf. ch. 23:24; 26:10); whereas "*ophan,*" in ch. 1:15, 16 implies mere revolution. **coals of fire**—the wrath of God about to *burn the city,* as His sword had previously *slain* its guilty inhabitants. This "fire," how different from *the fire on the altar never going out* (Lev. 6:12, 13), whereby, in type, peace was made with God! Cf. Isaiah 33:12, 14. It is therefore not taken from the altar of reconciliation, but from between the wheels of the cherubim, representing the providence of God, whereby, and not by chance, judgment is to fall. **3. right . . . of . . . house**—The scene of the locality whence judgment emanates is the temple, to mark God's vindication of His holiness injured there. The cherubim here are not those in the holy of holies, for the latter had not "wheels." They stood on "the right of the house," i.e., the south, for the Chaldean power, guided by them, had already advanced from the north (the direction of Babylon), and had destroyed *the men in the temple,* and was now proceeding to destroy the *city,* which lay south and west. **the cherubim . . . the man**—There was perfect concert of action between the cherubic representative of the angels and "the Man," to minister to whom they "stood" there (vs. 7). **cloud**—emblem of God's displeasure; as the "glory" or "brightness" (vs. 4) typifies His majesty and clearness in judgment. **4.** The court outside was full of the Lord's *brightness,* while it was only the *cloud* that filled the *house inside,* the scene of idolatries, and therefore of God's displeasure. God's throne was *on the threshold.* The temple, once filled with brightness, is now darkened with cloud. **5. sound of . . . wings**—prognostic of great and awful changes. **voice of . . . God**—the thunder (Ps. 29:3, etc.). **6. went in**—not into the temple, but between the cherubim. Ezekiel sets aside the Jews' boast of the presence of God with them. The cherubim, once the ministers of grace, are now the ministers of vengeance. When "commanded," He without delay obeys (Ps. 40:8; Heb. 10:7). **7.** See vs. 3, *Note.* **one cherub**—one of the four cherubim. **his hand**—(ch. 1:8). **went out**—to burn the city. **8.** "wings" denote alacrity, the "hands" efficacy and aptness, in executing the functions assigned to them. **9. wheels**—(*Note,* ch. 1:15, 16). The things which, from vs. 8 to the end of the chapter, are repeated from ch. 1 are expressed more decidedly, now that he gets a nearer view: the words "as it were," and "as if," so often occurring in ch. 1, are therefore mostly omitted. The "wheels" express the manifold changes and revolutions in the world; also that in the chariot of His providence God transports the Church from one place to another and everywhere can preserve it; a truth calculated to alarm the people in Jerusalem and to console the exiles [POLANUS]. **10. four had one likeness**—In the wonderful variety of God's works there is the greatest harmony:—

"In human works, though labored on with pain,
One thousand movements scarce one purpose gain;
In God's one single doth its end produce,
Yet serves to second, too, some other use."

(*See note,* ch. 1:16.) **wheel . . . in . . . a wheel**—cutting one another at right angles, so that the whole might move in any of the four directions or quarters of the world. God's doings, however involved they seem to us, cohere, so that lower causes subserve the higher. **11.** (*Note,* ch. 1:17). **turned not**—without accomplishing their course (Isa. 55:11) [GROTIUS]. Rather, "they moved *straight on* without turning" (so ch. 1:9). Having a face towards

ADAM CLARKE

2. *Coals of fire.* These were to signify the burning of the city by the Chaldeans. It seems that the space between the four wheels, which was all on fire, was that from which those coals were taken.

3. *On the right side of the house.* The right hand always marked the south among the Hebrews.

4. *The glory of the Lord went up.* This is repeated from chap. ix. 3. *The house was filled with the cloud.* This is a fact similar to what occurred frequently at the Tabernacle in the wilderness, and in the dedication of the Temple by Solomon. What is mentioned here was the divine Shekinah, the symbolical representation of the majesty of God.

5. *As the voice of the Almighty God.* That is, as thunder; for this was called the voice of God.

9. *The colour of a beryl stone. Eben Tarshish,* "the stone of Tarshish." The Vulgate translates it "chrysolith"; Symmachus, the "jacinct"; the Septuagint, the "carbuncle." The *beryl* is a gem of a green color, passing from one side into blue, on the other side into yellow.

MATTHEW HENRY

There is an admirable harmony and uniformity in the various occurrences of providence (*v.* 13): *As for the wheels*, though they moved several ways, yet *it was cried to them, O wheel!* they were all as one, being guided by one Spirit to one end. The motions of Providence are steady and regular, and whatever the Lord pleases that he does.

II. Ezekiel sees the glory of God removing out of the sanctuary, the place where God's honour had long dwelt, and this sight is sad. The *glory of the Lord stood over the threshold*, *v.* 4. But now it *departed from off the threshold*, and it *stood over the cherubim*, those that Ezekiel now saw in vision, *v.* 18. And immediately *the cherubim lifted up their wings* (*v.* 19), *mounted up from the earth*, and, *when they went out*, the wheels of this chariot were not drawn, but went *beside them*, by which it appeared that *the Spirit of the living creatures was in the wheels*. In the courts of the temple the people of Israel had dishonoured their God. The *cherubim, and the glory of God above them, stood at the door of the east gate of the Lord's house*, ready to depart and leave the house, *v.* 19. But with many stops and pauses God departs, as loth to go as if to see if there be any that will intercede with him to return. God removes by degrees from a provoking people; and, when he is ready to depart in displeasure, would return to them in mercy if they were but a repenting praying people.

The wheels turned not as they went (*v.* 11), and the *living creatures went everyone straight forward*, *v.* 22. The Spirit of God directs all the creatures, both upper and lower, so as to make them serve the divine purpose. Events are not determined by the *wheel of fortune*, which is blind, but by the *wheels of Providence*, which are full of eyes.

JAMIESON, FAUSSET, BROWN

each of the four quarters, they needed not to turn around when changing their direction. **whither . . . head looked**—i.e., "whither the head" of the animal cherub-form, belonging to and directing each wheel, "looked," thither the wheel "followed." The wheels were not guided by some external adventitious impetus, but by some secret divine impulse of the cherubim themselves. **12. body**—lit., flesh, because a body consists of flesh. **wheels . . . full of eyes**—The description (ch. 1:18) attributes eyes to the "*wheels*" alone; here there is added, on closer observation, that the *cherubim* themselves had them. The "eyes" imply that God, by His wisdom, beautifully reconciles seeming contrarieties (cf. II Chron. 16:9; Prov. 15:3; Zech. 4:10). **13. O wheel**—rather, "they were called, whirling," i.e., they were *most rapid in their revolutions* [MAURER]; or, better, "It was cried unto them, The whirling" [FAIRBAIRN]. *Galgal* here used for "wheel," is different from *ophan*, the simple word for "wheel." *Galgal* is the whole *wheelwork* machinery with its *whirlwind-like rotation*. Their being so addressed is in order to call them immediately to put themselves in rapid motion. **14. cherub**—but in ch. 1:10 it is *an ox*. The chief of the four cherubic forms was not the *ox, but man*. Therefore "cherub" cannot be synonymous with "ox." Probably Ezekiel, standing in front of one of the cherubim (viz., that which handed the coals to the man in linen), saw of him, not merely the ox-form, but the *whole fourfold* form, and therefore calls him simply "cherub"; whereas of the other three, having only a side view, he specifies the form of each which met his eye [FAIRBAIRN]. As to the likelihood of the lower animals sharing in "the restoration of all things," see Isaiah 11:6; 65:25; Romans 8:20, 21; this accords with the animal forms combined with the human to typify redeemed man. **15.** The repeated declaration of the identity of the vision with that at the Chebar is to arouse attention to it (vs. 22; ch. 3:23). **the living creature**—used collectively, as in vss. 17, 20; ch. 1:20. **16.** (*Note*, vs. 11; ch. 1:19.) **lifted up . . . wings**—to depart, following "the glory of the Lord" which was on the point of departing (vs. 18). **17.** (Ch. 1:12, 20, 21). **stood**—God never *stands* still (John 5:17), therefore neither do the angels; but to human perceptions He seems to do so. **18.** The departure of the symbol of God's presence from the temple preparatory to the destruction of the city. Foretold in Deuteronomy 31:17. Woe be to those from whom God departs (Hos. 9:12)! Cf. I Sam. 28:15, 16; 4:21: "I-chabod, Thy glory is departed." Successive steps are marked in His departure; so slowly and reluctantly does the merciful God leave His house. First He leaves the sanctuary (ch. 9:3); He elevates His throne above the threshold of the house (vs. 1); leaving the cherubim He sits on the throne (vs. 4); He and the cherubim, after *standing* for a time *at the door of the east gate* (where was the exit to the lower court of the people), leave the house altogether (vss. 18, 19), not to return till ch. 43:2. **20. I knew . . . cherubim**—By the second sight of the cherubim, he learned to identify them with the angelic forms situated above the ark of the covenant in the temple, which as a priest, he "knew" about from the high priest. **21.** The repetition is in order that the people about to live without the temple might have, instead, the knowledge of the temple mysteries, thus preparing them for a future restoration of the covenant. So perverse were they that they would say, "Ezekiel fancies he saw what has no existence." He, therefore, repeats it over and over again. **22. straight forward**—intent upon the object they aimed at, not deviating from the way nor losing sight of the end (Luke 9:52).

ADAM CLARKE

13. *As for the wheels, it was cried unto them . . . O wheel.* Never was there a more unfortunate and unmeaning translation. The word *haggalgal* may signify, simply, "the roller, or a chariot, or roll on, or the swift roller." Any of these will do: "And as to the wheels, they were called in my hearing the chariot."

20. *And I knew that they were the cherubims.* This formation of the plural is quite improper. In general, Hebrew nouns of the masculine gender end in *im* in the plural; the *s*, therefore should never be added to such. *Cherub* is singular; *cherubim* is plural.

MATTHEW HENRY

CHAPTER 11

Verses 1–13

I. The security of the princes of Jerusalem. The prophet was brought, in vision, to the gate of the temple where these princes sat in council. *The Spirit lifted me up, and brought me to the east gate of the Lord's house, and behold twenty-five men were there.*

JAMIESON, FAUSSET, BROWN

CHAPTER 11

VSS. 1-25. PROPHECY OF THE DESTRUCTION OF THE CORRUPT "PRINCES OF THE PEOPLE;" PELATIAH DIES; PROMISE OF GRACE TO THE BELIEVING REMNANT; DEPARTURE OF THE GLORY OF GOD FROM THE CITY; EZEKIEL'S RETURN TO THE CAPTIVES. **1. east gate**—to which the glory of God had moved itself (ch. 10:19), the chief entrance of the sanctuary; the portico or porch of Solomon. The Spirit moves the prophet thither, to witness, in the presence of the divine glory, a new scene of destruction. **five and twenty men**—The same as the twenty-five (i.e., twenty-four heads of courses, and the high priest) sun-worshippers seen in ch. 8:16. The leading *priests* were usually called "princes of the sanctuary" (Isa. 43:28) and "chiefs of the priests" (II Chron. 36:14); but here two of them are called "princes of the people," with irony, as using their priestly influence to

ADAM CLARKE

CHAPTER 11

1. *At the door of the gate five and twenty men.* The same persons, no doubt, who appear, chap. viii. 16, worshipping the sun.

MATTHEW HENRY

They are charged, not with corruptions in worship, but with mal-administration in the government; two of them are named, *Pelatiah* and *Jaazaniah*, the *son of Azur*. Some tell us that Jerusalem was divided into twenty-four wards, and that these were the aldermen of those wards, with their mayor or president. "*These are the men that devise mischief;* under pretence of public safety they harden people in their sins, and take off their fear of God's judgments threatened by the prophets; they *give wicked counsel in this city*, counselling them to silence the prophets, to rebel against the king of Babylon, and to resolve upon holding out to the last extremity." They are indicted for words spoken at their council-board (*v.* 3); they said to this effect, "*It is not near;* the destruction of our city, so often threatened by the prophets." Where Satan cannot persuade men to look upon the judgment to come as a thing doubtful and uncertain, yet he gains his point by persuading them to look upon it as a thing at a distance. If the destruction is not near, they conclude, *Let us build houses;* let us count upon a continuance, for *this city is the cauldron and we are the flesh*. This seems to be a proverbial expression, signifying, "We are as safe in this city as flesh in a boiling pot; the walls of the city shall be to us as *walls of brass*, and shall receive no more damage from the besiegers about it than the *cauldron* does from *the fire under it*." Perhaps it has reference to *the flesh of the peace-offerings*, which it was so great an offence for the priests themselves to take out of the *cauldron* while it was in seething (as we find 1 Sam. ii. 13, 14), and then it intimates that they were the more secure because Jerusalem was the holy city, and they thought themselves a holy people in it, not to be meddled with.

II. The method taken to awaken them out of their security. To help them to understand, the word of God is sent to them to give them warning (*v.* 4): *Therefore prophesy against them*, and try to undeceive them; *prophesy, O son of man!* upon these dead and dry bones. *The Spirit of the Lord fell upon him*, to make him full of power and courage, and *said unto him, Speak*. Let them know that God takes notice (*v.* 5): "*I know the things which come into your minds every one of them*, what secret reasons you have for these resolutions, putting so good a face upon a matter you know to be bad." God knows not only the things that come out of our mouths, but the things that come into our minds, not only all we say, but all we think. Thus you, with your stubborn humour, have *filled the streets of Jerusalem with the slain*, *v.* 6. Now these slain are the only flesh that shall be left in this *cauldron*, *v.* 7. They had provoked God to forsake the city, and thought they should do well enough by their own policy and strength when he was gone; but God will make them know that there is no peace to those that have left their God. Let them know that all this is the due punishment of their sin, and *the revelation of the righteous judgment of God* against them: *You shall know that I am the Lord*, *v.* 10 and again *v.* 12.

III. This awakening word is here immediately followed by an awakening providence, *v.* 13. *It came to pass, when I prophesied, that Pelatiah the son of Benaiah died.* It should seem, this was done in vision now, but it was an assurance that when this prophecy should be published it should be done in fact. The death of Pelatiah was an earnest of the complete accomplishment of this prophecy. Though the sudden death of Pelatiah was a confirmation of Ezekiel's prophecy, he was in deep concern about it, and laid it to heart as if he had been his relation or friend: *He fell on his face and cried with a loud voice*, "*Ah! Lord God, wilt thou make a full end of the remnant of Israel?* Shall the remnant which have escaped the sword die thus by the immediate hand of heaven?"

Verses 14–21

The prophet Ezekiel, having received instructions for the awakening of those that were *at ease in Zion*, is in these verses furnished with comfortable words for those that mourned in Babylon when they *remembered Zion*.

I. The pious captives were trampled upon and insulted by those who continued in Jerusalem, *v.* 15. They are *thy brethren* (says God to the prophet),

JAMIESON, FAUSSET, BROWN

be ringleaders of the people in sin (vs. 2). Already the wrath of God had visited the *people* represented by the *elders* (ch. 9:6); also the glory of the Lord had left its place in the holy of holies, and, like the cherubim and flaming sword in Eden, had occupied the gate into the deserted sanctuary. The judgment on the representatives of the *priesthood* naturally follows here, just as the *sin* of the priests had followed in the description (ch. 8:12, 16) after the sin of the elders. **Jaazaniah**—signifying "God hears." **son of Azur**—different from Jaazaniah the son of Shaphan (ch. 8:11). Azur means "help." He and Pelatiah ("God delivers"), son of Benaiah ("God builds"), are singled out as Jaazaniah, son of Shaphan, in the case of the seventy elders (ch. 8:11, 12), because their names ought to have reminded them that "God" would have "heard" had they sought His "help" to "deliver" and "build" them up. But, neglecting this, they incurred the heavier judgment by the very relation in which they stood to God [FAIRBAIRN]. **2. he**—the Lord sitting on the cherubim (ch. 10:2). **wicked counsel**—in opposition to the prophets of God (vs. 3). **3. It is not near**—viz., the destruction of the city; therefore "let us build houses," as if there was no fear. But the *Hebrew* opposes *English Version*, which would require the infinitive absolute. Rather, "Not at hand is the building of houses." They sneer at Jeremiah's letter to the captives, among whom Ezekiel lived (Jer. 29:5). "*Build* ye *houses*, and dwell in them," i.e., do not fancy, as many persuade you, that your sojourn in Babylon is to be short; it will be for seventy years (Jer. 25:11, 12; 29:10); therefore build houses and settle quietly there. The scorners in Jerusalem reply, Those far off in exile may build if they please, but it is *too remote* a concern for us to trouble ourselves about [FAIRBAIRN], (cf. ch. 12:22, 27; II Pet. 3:4). **this city . . . caldron . . . we . . . flesh**—sneering at Jer. 1:13, when he compared the city to a caldron with its mouth towards the north. "Let Jerusalem be so if you will, and we the flesh, exposed to the raging foe from the north, still its fortifications will secure us from the flame of war outside; the city must stand for our sakes, just as the pot exists for the safety of the flesh in it." In opposition to this God says (vs. 11), "This city shall not be your caldron, to defend you *in* it from the foe *outside*: nay, ye shall be driven out of your imaginary sanctuary and slain *in the border of the land*." "But," says God, in vs. 7, "your slain are the flesh, and this city the caldron; but (not as you fancy shall ye be kept safe *inside*) I will bring you forth *out of the midst of it*"; and again, in ch. 24:3, "Though not a caldron in *your* sense, Jerusalem shall be so in the sense of its being exposed to a consuming foe, and you yourselves in it and with it." **4. prophesy . . . prophesy**—The repetition marks emphatic earnestness. **5. Spirit . . . fell upon me**—stronger than "entered into me" (ch. 2:2; 3:24), implying the zeal of the Spirit of God roused to immediate indignation at the contempt of God shown by the scorners. **I know**—(Ps. 139:1-4). Your scornful jests at My word escape not My notice. **6. your slain**—those on whom you have brought ruin by your wicked counsels. Bloody crimes within the city brought on it a bloody foe from without (ch. 7:23, 24). They had made it a caldron in which to boil the flesh of God's people (Mic. 3:1-3), and eat it by unrighteous oppression; therefore God will make it a caldron in a different sense, one not wherein they may be safe in their guilt, but "out of the midst of" which they shall be "brought forth" (Jer. 34:4, 5). **7.** The city is a caldron to them, but it shall not be so to you. Ye shall meet your doom on the frontier. **8.** The Chaldean sword, to escape which ye abandoned your God, shall be brought on you by God because of that very abandonment of Him. **9. out of the midst thereof**—i.e., of the city, as captives led into the open plain for judgment. **10. in the border of Israel**—on the frontier: at Riblah, in the land of Hamath (cf. II Kings 25:19-21, with I Kings 8:65). **ye shall know that I am the Lord**—by the judgments I inflict (Ps. 9:16). **11.** (*Note*, vs. 3). **12.** (Deut. 12:30, 31). **13. Pelatiah**—probably the ringleader of the scorners (vs. 1). His being stricken dead (like Ananias, Acts 5:5) was an earnest of the destruction of the rest of the twenty-five, as Ezekiel had foretold, as also of the general ruin. **fell . . . upon . . . face**—(*Note*, ch. 9:8). **wilt thou make a full end of the remnant**—Is Pelatiah's destruction to be the token of the destruction of all, even of the remnant? The people regarded Pelatiah as a mainstay of the city. His name (derived from a *Hebrew* root, "a remnant," or else "God delivers") suggested hope. Is that hope, asks Ezekiel, to be disappointed? **15. thy brethren . . . brethren**—The repetition implies, "Thy real brethren" are no longer the priests at Jerusalem

ADAM CLARKE

Jaazaniah the son of Azur. In chap. viii. 11, we find a "Jaazaniah the son of Shaphan." If Shaphan was also called Azur, they may be the same person. But it is most likely that there were two of this name, and both chiefs among the people.

3. *It is not near.* That is, the threatened invasion.

This city is the caldron, and we be the flesh. See the vision of the seething pot, Jer. i. 13. These infidels seem to say: "We will run all risks, we will abide in the city. Though it be the caldron, and we the flesh, yet we will share its fate: if it perish, we will perish with it."

7. *Your slain . . . they are the flesh.* Jerusalem is the caldron, and those who have been slain in it, they are the flesh; and though you purpose to stay and share its fate, you shall not be permitted to do so; you shall be carried into captivity.

9. *And deliver you into the hands of strangers.* This seems to refer chiefly to Zedekiah and his family.

11. *I will judge you in the border of Israel.* Though Riblah was in Syria, yet it was on the very frontiers of Israel; and it was here that Zedekiah's sons were slain, and his own eyes put out.

13. *Pelatiah the son of Benaiah died.* Most probably he was struck dead the very hour in which Ezekiel prophesied against him. His death appears to have resembled that of Ananias and Sapphira, Acts v. 1, etc.

MATTHEW HENRY

they are *the men of thy kindred*. They are *the whole house of Israel*; God so accounts of them because they only have retained their integrity. They were not only of the same family and nation with Ezekiel, but of the same spirit. Those that were at ease scorned their brethren that were humbled. They cut them off from being members of their church.

Because they had in compliance with the will of God surrendered themselves to the king of Babylon, they excommunicated them, and said, "*Get you far from the Lord;* we will have nothing to do with you. *Unto us is this land given in possession*, and you have forfeited your estates by surrendering to the king of Babylon, and we have thereby become entitled to them."

II. The gracious promises which God made to them. Those that hated them and cast them out said, *Let the Lord be glorified;* but *he shall appear to their joy*, Isa. lxvi. 5. God owns that his hand had gone out against them (*v.* 16): "It is true *I have cast them far off among the heathen* and *scattered them among the countries*; they look as if they were an abandoned people, but I have mercy in store for them."

He will make up to them the want of the temple (*v.* 16): *I will be to them as a little sanctuary, in the countries where they shall come*. Those at Jerusalem have the temple, but without God; those in Babylon have God, though without the temple. God would in due time put an end to their afflictions, bring them out of the land of their captivity, and settle them again, them or their children, in their own land (*v.* 17). "*You* shall have the title as the patriarchs had, and *those* that come after shall have the possession." Their captivity shall effectually cure them of their idolatry.

God will plant good principles in them; he will make the tree good, *v.* 19. This is a gospel promise, and is made good to all those whom God designs for the heavenly Canaan.

All that are sanctified have *a new spirit*; they act from new principles, walk by new rules, and aim at new ends. A new name, or a new face, will not serve without a new spirit. This is God's work, his gift by promise. Their practices shall be consonant to those principles: *That they may walk in my statutes* in their whole conversation *and keep my ordinances* in all acts of religious worship, *v.* 20. *But, as for those* that have no grace, what have they *to do with peace?* Their *heart walks after the heart of their detestable things*. They have a *heart after the heart of their idols*.

Verses 22–25

The departure of God's presence from the city and temple. When the message was committed to the prophet, and he was fully apprized of it, *then the*

JAMIESON, FAUSSET, BROWN

with whom thou art connected by the *natural* ties of blood and common temple service, but thy fellow exiles on the Chebar, and the house of Israel whosoever of them belong to the remnant to be spared. **men of thy kindred**—lit., "of thy redemption," i.e., the nearest relatives, whose duty it was to do the part of Goel, or vindicator and redeemer of a forfeited inheritance (Lev. 25:25). Ezekiel, seeing the priesthood doomed to destruction, as a priest, felt anxious to vindicate their cause, as if they were his nearest kinsmen and he their Goel. But he is told to look for his true kinsmen in those, his fellow exiles, whom his natural kinsmen at Jerusalem despised, and he is to be their vindicator. Spiritual ties, as in the case of Levi (Deut. 33:9), the type of Messiah (Matt. 12:47-50) are to supersede natural ones where the two clash. The hope of better days was to rise from the despised exiles. The gospel principle is shadowed forth here, that the despised of men are often the chosen of God and the highly esteemed among men are often an abomination before Him (Luke 16:15; I Cor. 1:26-28). "No door of hope but in the valley of Achor" ("trouble," Hos. 2:15), [FAIRBAIRN]. **Get you far . . . unto us is this land**—the contemptuous words of those left still in the city at the carrying away of Jeconiah to the exiles, "However far ye be outcasts from the Lord and His temple, *we* are secure in our possession of the land." **16. Although**—anticipating the objection of the priests at Jerusalem, that the exiles were "cast far off." Though this be so, and they are far from the outer temple at Jerusalem, I will be their asylum or sanctuary instead (Ps. 90:1; 91:9; Isa. 8:14). My shrine is the humble heart: a preparation for gospel catholicity when the local and material temple should give place to the spiritual (Isa. 57:15; 66:1; Mal. 1:11; John 4:21-24; Acts 7:48, 49). The trying discipline of the exile was to chasten the outcasts so as to be meet recipients of God's grace, for which the carnal confidence of the priests disqualified them. The dispersion served the end of spiritualizing and enlarging the views even of the better Jews, so as to be able to worship God *everywhere* without a material temple; and, at the same time, it diffused some knowledge of God among the greatest Gentile nations, thus providing materials for the gathering in of the Christian Church among the Gentiles; so marvellously did God overrule a present evil for an ultimate good. Still more does all this hold good in the present much longer dispersion which is preparing for a more perfect and universal restoration (Isa. 2:2-4; Jer. 3:16-18). Their long privation of the temple will prepare them for appreciating the more, but without Jewish narrowness, the temple that is to be (chs. 40-44). **a little**—rather, "for a little season"; No matter how long the captivity may be, the seventy years will be but as a little season, compared with their long subsequent settlement in their land. This holds true only partially in the case of the first restoration; but as in a few centuries they were dispersed again, the full and permanent restoration is yet future (Jer. 24:6). **17.** (Ch. 28:25; 34:13; 36:24.) **18.** They have eschewed every vestige of idolatry ever since their return from Babylon. But still the Shekinah glory had departed, the ark was not restored, nor was the second temple strictly inhabited by God until He came who made it more glorious than the first temple (Hag. 2:9); even then His stay was short, and ended in His being rejected; so that the full realization of the promise must still be future. **19. I will give them**—lest they should claim to *themselves* the praise given them in vs. 18, God declares it is to be *the free gift of His Spirit*. **one heart**—not *singleness*, i.e., uprightness, but *oneness* of heart in all, *unanimously* seeking Him in contrast to their state at that time, when only single scattered individuals sought God (Jer. 32:39; Zeph. 3:9) [HENGSTENBERG]. Or, "content with *one God*," not distracted with "the many detestable things" (vs. 18; I Kings 18:21; Hos. 10:2) [CALVIN]. **new spirit**—(Ps. 51:10; Jer. 31:33). Realized fully in the "new creature" of the New Testament (II Cor. 5:17); having new motives, new rules, new aims. **stony heart**—like "adamant" (Zech. 7:12); the natural heart of every man. **heart of flesh**—impressible to what is good, tender. **20. walk in my statutes**—Regeneration shows itself by its fruits (Gal. 5:22, 25). **they . . . my people, . . . I . . . their God**—(Ch. 14:11; 36:28; 37:27; Jer. 24:7). In its fullest sense still future (Zech. 13:9). **21. whose heart . . . after . . . heart of . . . detestable things**—The repetition of "heart" is emphatic, signifying that the heart of those who so obstinately clung to idols, impelled itself to fresh superstitions in one continuous tenor [CALVIN]. Perhaps it is implied that they and their idols are much alike in character (Ps. 115:8). The *heart* walks

ADAM CLARKE

15. *Get you far from the Lord*. These are the words of the inhabitants of Jerusalem, against those of Israel who had been carried away to Babylon with Jeconiah. Go ye far from the Lord; but as for us, the land of Israel is given to us for a possession. We shall never be removed from it, and they shall never return to it.

16. *Yet will I be to them as a little sanctuary.* Though thus exiled from their own land, yet not forgotten by their God. While in their captivity, I will dispense many blessings to them; and I will restore them to their own land, v. 17, from which they shall put away all idolatry, v. 18.

MATTHEW HENRY

cherubim lifted up their wings and the wheels beside them (*v.* 22) as before, *ch.* x. 19. The glory of the Lord removed to *the mountain which is on the east side of the city* (*v.* 23); that was the *mount of Olives.* On this mountain they had set up their idols, to confront God in his temple (1 Kings xi. 7). From that mountain there was a full prospect of the city; thither God removed, to make good what he had said (Deut. xxxii. 20), *I will hide my face from them, I will see what their end shall be.* It was from this mountain that Christ *beheld the city and wept over it,* in the foresight of its last destruction by the Romans. *The glory of the Lord* removed thither, to be as it were yet within call, if *in this their day,* they would have *understood the things that belonged to their peace.* The departure of this vision from the prophet: it *went up from him* (*v.* 24); he saw it mount upwards, till it went out of sight, a confirmation to his faith that it was a heavenly vision. The same spirit that had carried him in a trance or ecstasy to Jerusalem brought him back to Chaldea; for that is the place of his service. He delivered his message very honestly: he *spoke all that,* and that only, which God *had shown* him. It is better to be in Babylon under the favour of God than in Jerusalem under his wrath and curse.

JAMIESON, FAUSSET, BROWN

astray first, the feet follow. **recompense . . . way upon . . . heads**—They have abandoned Me, so will I abandon them; they profaned My temple, so will I profane it by the Chaldeans (ch. 9:10). **23.** The Shekinah glory now moves from the east gate (ch. 10:4, 19) to the Mount of Olives, altogether abandoning the temple. The mount was chosen as being the height whence the missiles of the foe were about to descend on the city. So it was from it that Jesus ascended to heaven when about to send His judgments on the Jews; and from it He predicted its overthrow before His crucifixion (Matt. 24:3). It is also to be the scene of His return in person to deliver His people (Zech. 14:4), when He shall come by the same way as He went, "the way of the east" (ch. 43:2). **24. brought me in a vision**—not in actual fact, but in ecstatic vision. He had been as to the outward world all the time before the elders (ch. 8:3) in Chaldea; he now reports what he had witnessed with the inner eye. **25. things . . . showed me**—lit., "words"; an appropriate expression; for the word communicated to him was not simply a word, but one clothed with outward symbols "shown" to him as in the sacrament, which Augustine terms "the visible word" [CALVIN].

ADAM CLARKE

23. *The glory of the Lord went up from the midst of the city.* This vision is no mean proof of the long-suffering of God. He did not abandon this people all at once; He departed by little and little. First, He left the Temple. Secondly, He stopped a little at the gate of the city. Thirdly, He departed entirely from the city and went to the Mount of Olives, which lay on the east side of the city. Having tarried there for some time to see if they would repent and turn to Him—fourthly, He departed to heaven. The vision being now concluded, the prophet is taken away by the Spirit of God into Chaldea, and there announces to the captive Israelites what God had showed him in the preceding visions, and the good that He had spoken concerning them; who at first did not seem to profit much by them, which the prophet severely reproves.

MATTHEW HENRY — CHAPTER 12

Verses 1-16

Perhaps Ezekiel reflected upon the vision he had had of the glory of God, that often he was wishing it might come down to him again, but we do not find that he ever saw it any more, and yet *the word of the Lord comes to* him. We may keep up our communion with God without raptures and ecstasies. In these verses the prophet is directed,

I. By what signs and actions to express the approaching captivity of Zedekiah king of Judah; that was the thing to be foretold, and it is foretold to those that are already in captivity, because as long as Zedekiah was upon the throne they flattered themselves with hopes that he would rescue them shortly. It was therefore necessary to convince them that Zedekiah, instead of being their deliverer, should very shortly be their fellow-sufferer. To prepare them he must first give them a sign, must speak to their eyes first and then to their ears. He must speak to them by signs, as deaf people are taught. He must furnish himself with all necessaries *for removing* (*v.* 3), provide for a journey clothes and money; he must *remove from one place to another,* as one unsettled and forced to shift; this he must do *by day, in the sight* of the people; he must bring out all his household goods, to be packed up and sent away (*v.* 4); and, because all the doors and gates were either locked up or guarded he must *dig through the wall,* and convey his goods away clandestinely through that breach in the wall, *v.* 5. He must carry his goods away himself upon his own shoulders, *in the twilight,* that he might not be discovered; must himself steal away *at evening in their sight,* with fear and trembling, and must go *as those that go forth into captivity* (*v.* 4); he must *cover* his *face* (*v.* 6) in token of very great sorrow and must go away as a poor broken man, who quits his country. Thus Ezekiel must be himself a sign to them. God says (*v.* 3) "*It may be they will consider,* and will by it be taken off from their vain confidences, *though they be a rebellious house.*" Ezekiel's ready obedience to the orders God gave him (*v.* 7): *I did so as I was commanded.*

II. He is directed by what words to explain those signs and actions. The prophet must do a strange uncouth thing, that they might enquire what it meant. The prophet is to tell them (*v.* 10), *This burden concerns the prince in Jerusalem.* "But tell them," says God, "that in what thou hast done they may read the doom of their friends at Jerusalem.

Say, I am your sign," *v.* 11. The people shall be led away into

JAMIESON, FAUSSET, BROWN — CHAPTER 12

VSS. 1-28. EZEKIEL'S TYPICAL MOVING TO EXILE: PROPHECY OF ZEDEKIAH'S CAPTIVITY AND PRIVATION OF SIGHT: THE JEWS' UNBELIEVING SURMISE AS TO THE DISTANCE OF THE EVENT REPROVED. **1, 2. eyes to see, and see not, . . . ears to hear, and hear not**—fulfilling the prophecy of Deuteronomy 29:4, here quoted by Ezekiel (cf. Isa. 6:9; Jer. 5:21). Ezekiel needed often to be reminded of the people's perversity, lest he should be discouraged by the little effect produced by his prophecies. Their "not seeing" is the result of perversity, not incapacity. They are wilfully blind. The persons most interested in this prophecy were those dwelling at Jerusalem; and it is among them that Ezekiel was transported in spirit, and performed in vision, not outwardly, the typical acts. At the same time, the symbolical prophecy was designed to warn the exiles at Chebar against cherishing hopes, as many did in opposition to God's revealed word, of returning to Jerusalem, as if that city was to stand; externally living afar off, their hearts dwelt in that corrupt and doomed capital. **3. stuff for removing**—rather, "an exile's outfit," the articles proper to a person going as an exile, a staff and knapsack, with a supply of food and clothing; so in Jeremiah 46:19, *Margin,* "instruments of captivity," i.e., the needful equipments for it. His simple announcements having failed, he is symbolically to give them an ocular demonstration conveyed by a word-painting of actions performed in vision. **consider**—(Deut. 32:29). **4. by day**—in broad daylight, when all can see thee. **at even**—not contradicting the words "by day." The baggage was to be sent before *by day,* and Ezekiel was to follow *at nightfall* [GROTIUS]; or, the preparations were to be made by day, the actual departure was to be effected at night [HENDERSON]. **as they that go forth into captivity**—lit., as the goings forth of the captivity, i.e., of the captive band of exiles, viz., amid the silent darkness: typifying Zedekiah's flight by night on the taking of the city (Jer. 39:4; 52:7). **5. Dig**—as Zedekiah was to escape like one digging through a wall, furtively to effect an escape (vs. 12). **carry out**—viz., "thy stuff" (vs. 4). **thereby**—by the opening in the wall. Zedekiah escaped "by the gate betwixt the two walls" (Jer. 39:4). **6. in . . . twilight**—rather, "in the dark." So in Genesis 15:17, "it" refers to "thy stuff." **cover thy face**—as one who muffles his face, afraid of being recognized by anyone meeting him. So the Jews and Zedekiah should make their exit stealthily and afraid to look around, so hurried should be their flight [CALVIN]. **sign**—rather, a portent, viz., for evil. **9. What doest thou?**—They ask not in a docile spirit, but making a jest of his proceedings. **10. burden**—i.e., weighty oracle. **the prince**—The very man Zedekiah, in whom they trust for safety, is to be the chief sufferer. JOSEPHUS (*Antiquities,* 10.7) reports that Ezekiel sent a copy of this prophecy to Zedekiah. As Jeremiah had sent a letter to the captives at the Chebar, which was the means of calling forth at first the agency of Ezekiel, so it was natural for Ezekiel to send a message to Jerusalem confirming the warnings of Jeremiah. The prince, however, fancying a contradiction between ch. 12:13; "he shall not see Babylon," and Jeremiah 24:8, 9, declaring he should be carried to Babylon, believed neither. Seeming discrepancies in Scripture on deeper search prove to be hidden harmonies. **11. sign**—*portent of evil* to come (ch.

ADAM CLARKE — CHAPTER 12

2. *Which have eyes to see, and see not.* It is not want of grace that brings them to destruction. They have eyes to see, but they will not use them. No man is lost because he had not sufficient grace to save him, but because he abused that grace.

3. *Prepare thee stuff for removing.* Get carriages to transport your goods to another place, signifying by this the captivity that was at hand.

5. *Dig thou through the wall.* This refers to the manner in which Zedekiah and his family would escape from the city. They escaped by night through a breach in the wall. See Jer. xxxix. 2-4 and 2 Kings xxv. 4.

6. *Thou shalt cover thy face, that thou see not the ground.* Referring to the blinding of Zedekiah. Even the covering of the face might be intended to signify that in this way Zedekiah should be carried to Babylon on men's shoulders in some sort of palanquin, with a cloth tied over his eyes, because of the recent wounds made by extracting them. All the prophecies from this to the twentieth chapter are supposed to have been delivered in the sixth year of Zedekiah, five years before the taking of Jerusalem.

10. *This burden.* By this I point out the capture, misery, and ruin of Zedekiah.

MATTHEW HENRY

captivity (*v.* 11): *As I have done, so shall it be done unto them;* they shall be forced away from their own houses, no more to return to them. The prince shall in vain attempt to make his escape; for he also shall go into captivity. Ezekiel here foretells it to those who promised themselves relief through him. He shall himself carry away his own goods. God can turn a prince into a porter. He that was wont to have the regalia carried before him, shall now himself carry his goods on his back and steal away out of the city in the twilight. All the avenues to the palace being carefully watched by the enemy, *they shall dig through the wall to carry out thereby.* He shall attempt to escape in a disguise, with a mask which *shall cover his face,* so that he shall *not see the ground with his eyes.* He shall be made a prisoner and carried captive into Babylon (*v.* 13). Jeremiah had said that king Zedekiah should *see the king of Babylon* and that he should *go to Babylon*; Ezekiel says, He shall be *brought to Babylon,* yet he *shall not see it,* though *he shall die there.* One said, He shall *see the king of Babylon,* the other said, He shall *not see Babylon*; and yet both proved true: he did *see the king of Babylon* at Riblah, where he passed sentence upon him for his rebellion, but there he had his eyes put out, so that he did *not see Babylon* when he was brought thither. Little joy could they have in seeing him when he could not see them. All his guards should be dispersed (*v.* 14): *I will scatter all that are about him to help him,* so that he shall be left helpless; *and disperse them in the countries* (*v.* 15). Yet of Zedekiah's scattered troops some shall escape (*v.* 16): *That they may declare all their abominations among the heathen whither they come;* and then they will acknowledge the justice of God and will make confession of their sins; and by this it shall appear that they were spared in mercy.

Verses 17–20

Here again the prophet is made a sign to them of the desolations that were coming on Judah and Jerusalem. He must himself eat and drink in care and fear, especially when he was in company, *v.* 17, 18, that he might express the calamitous condition of those that should be in Jerusalem during the siege. He must tell them that *the inhabitants of Jerusalem* should in like manner eat and drink with care and fear, *v.* 19, 20, either because they are afraid it will not hold out, or because they are continually expecting the alarms of the enemy. The decay of virtue in a nation brings on a decay of everything else; and when neighbours devour one another it is just with God to bring enemies upon them to devour them all.

Verses 21–28

Various methods had been used to awaken this secure and careless people, that they might be stirred up, by repentance and reformation. The prophecies of their ruin were confirmed by visions, and illustrated by signs, but here we are told how they evaded the conviction, by telling themselves, and one another, that though these judgments threatened should come at last yet they would not come for a long time.

I. One saying they had, which had become proverbial *in the land of Israel, v.* 22. They said, "*The days are prolonged;* because the destruction has not come yet it will never come; we will never trust a prophet again, for we have been more frightened than hurt." And another saying was, "*The vision* is *for* a great while *to come*; it refers to events at a vast distance, so that we need not trouble our heads about them" (*v.* 27). That forbearance of God which should have led them to repentance hardened them in sin.

II. They are assured that they do but deceive themselves: *Tell them, therefore, The days are at hand* (*v.* 23), and again, *There shall none of my words be prolonged any more, v.* 28. God will certainly silence the lying proverbs, and the lying prophecies, with which they buoyed up their vain hopes: *There shall be no more any vain vision, v.* 24. God will certainly, and very shortly, accomplish every word that he has spoken. With what majesty does he say it (*v.* 25): I *am the* LORD! *I am Jehovah!* Those that *see the visions of the Almighty* do not see *vain visions*; God *confirms the word of his servants* by performing it. *The days are at hand* when you shall see *the effect of every vision, v.* 23.

JAMIESON, FAUSSET, BROWN

24:27; Zech. 3:8, *Margin*). Fulfilled (II Kings 25: 1-7; Jer. 52:1-11). **12. prince . . . among them**—lit., that is in the midst of them, i.e., on whom the eyes of all are cast, and "under whose shadow" they hope to live (Lam. 4:20). **shall bear**—viz., his "stuff for removing"; his equipments for his journey. **cover his face, that he see not the ground**—*Note,* vs. 6; the symbol in vs. 6 is explained in this verse. He shall muffle his face so as not to be recognized: a humiliation for a king! **13. My net**—the Chaldean army. He shall be inextricably entangled in it, as in the meshes of a net. It is *God's* net (Job 19:6). Babylon was God's instrument (Isa. 10:5). Called "a net" (Hab. 1:14-16). **bring him to Babylon . . .; yet shall he not see it**—because he should be deprived of sight before he arrived there (Jer. 52:11). **14. all . . . about him**—his satellites: his bodyguard. **bands**—lit., the wings of an army (Isa. 8:8). **draw out . . . sword after them**—(*Note,* ch. 5:2, 12). **16. I will leave a few . . . that they may declare . . . abominations**—God's purpose in scattering a remnant of Jews among the Gentiles; viz., not only that they themselves should be weaned from idolatry (see vs. 15), but that by their own *word,* as also *by their whole state as exiles,* they should make God's righteousness manifest among the Gentiles, as vindicated in their punishment for their sins (cf. Isa. 43:10; Zech. 8:13). **18.** Symbolical representation of the famine and fear with which they should eat their scanty morsel, in their exile, and especially at the siege. **19. people of the land**—the Jews "in the land" of Chaldea who thought themselves miserable as being exiles and envied the Jews left in Jerusalem as fortunate. **land of Israel**—contrasted with "the people in the land" of Chaldea. So far from being fortunate as the exiles in Chaldea regarded them, the Jews in Jerusalem are truly miserable, for the worst is before them, whereas the exiles have escaped the miseries of the coming siege. **land . . . desolate from all that is therein**—lit., "that the land (viz., Judea) may be despoiled of the fulness thereof"; emptied of the inhabitants and abundance of flocks and corn with which it was filled. **because of . . . violence**—(Ps. 107:34). **20. the cities**—left in Judea after the destruction of Jerusalem. **22. proverb**—The infidel scoff, that the threatened judgment was so long in coming, it would not come at all, had by frequent repetition come to be a "proverb" with them. This skeptical habit contemporary prophets testify to (Jer. 17:15; 20:7; Zeph. 1:12). Ezekiel, at the Chebar, thus sympathizes with Jeremiah and strengthens his testimony at Jerusalem. The *tendency* to the same scoff showed itself in earlier times, but had not then developed into a settled "proverb" (Isa. 5:19; Amos 5:18). It shall again be the characteristic of the last times, when "faith" shall be regarded as an antiquated thing (Luke 18:8), seeing that it remains stationary, whereas worldly arts and sciences progress, and when the "continuance of all things from creation" will be the argument against the possibility of their being suddenly brought to a standstill by the coming of the Lord (Isa. 66:5; II Pet. 3:3, 4). The very long-suffering of God, which ought to lead men to repentance, is made an argument against His word (Eccles. 8:11; Amos 6:3). **days . . . prolonged . . . vision faileth**—their twofold argument: (1) The predictions shall not come to pass till long after our time. (2) They shall fail and prove vain shadows. God answers both in vss. 23, 25. **23. effect**—lit., "the word," viz., fulfilled; i.e., the effective fulfilment of whatever the prophets have spoken is at hand. **24. no more . . . vain vision . . . flattering divination**—All those false prophets (Lam. 2:14), who "flattered" the people with promises of peace and safety, shall be detected and confounded by the event itself. **25. word . . . shall come to pass**—in opposition to their scoff "the vision faileth" (vs. 22). The repetition, "I will speak . . . speak . . ." (or as FAIRBAIRN, "For I, Jehovah, will speak whatever word I shall speak, and it shall be done") implies that whenever God speaks, the effect must follow; for God, who speaks, is not divided in Himself (vs. 28; Isa. 55:11; Dan. 9:12; Luke 21:33). **no more prolonged**—in opposition to the scoff (vs. 22), "The days are prolonged." **in your days**—while you are living (cf. Matt. 24:34). **27.** Not a mere repetition of the scoff (vs. 22); there the *scoffers* asserted that the evil was so often threatened and postponed, it must have no reality; here *formalists* do not go so far as to deny that a day of evil is coming, but assert it is still far off (Amos 6:3). The transition is easy from this carnal security to the gross infidelity of the former class.

ADAM CLARKE

13. *I will bring him to Babylon . . . yet shall he not see it.* Because Nebuchadnezzar caused him to have his eyes put out at Riblah. To Babylon he was carried in his blind state, and there he died.

18. *Eat thy bread with quaking.* Assume the manner of a person who is every moment afraid of his life, who has nothing but a morsel of bread to eat and a little water to drink, thus signifying the siege, and the straits to which they should be reduced.

22. *The days are prolonged, and every vision faileth.* These are the words of the infidels and scoffers, who, because vengeance was not speedily executed on an evil work, set their heart to do iniquity. "These predictions either will not come in our days, or will wholly fail; why then should we disquiet ourselves about them?" Strange that the very means used by the most gracious God to bring sinners to repentance, should be made by them the very instruments of their own destruction! See 2 Pet. iii. 4.

23. *The days are at hand.* Far from failing or being prolonged, time is posting on, and the destruction threatened is at the door.

25. *In your days . . . will I say the word, and will perform it.* Even these mockers shall live to see and feel this desolation. This is more particularly intimated in the following verses.

MATTHEW HENRY

CHAPTER 13

Verses 1–9

The false prophets were some of them at Jerusalem (Jer. xxiii. 14): *I have seen in the prophets at Jerusalem a horrible thing;* some of them among the captives in Babylon, for to them Jeremiah writes (Jer. xxix. 8), *Let not your diviners, that be in the midst of you, deceive you.* Ezekiel must prophesy against them, in hopes that the people might be cautioned not to hearken unto them.

Ezekiel had express orders to *prophesy against the prophets of Israel;* so they called themselves, as if none but they had been worthy of the name of Israel's prophets, who were indeed Israel's deceivers.

Ezekiel is directed

I. To discover their sin to them. They are here called *foolish prophets* (*v.* 3). They thrust themselves into the prophetic office, without warrant from him who is *the Lord God* of the holy prophets, which was a foolish thing; for how could they expect that God should own them in a work to which he never called them? They are *prophets out of their own hearts* (so the margin reads it, *v.* 2), prophets of their own making, *v.* 6. They put a reproach upon divine revelation, lessen its credit, and weaken its credibility. When these pretenders are found to be deceivers, atheists and infidels will thence infer, They are all so. *The Lord has not sent them. They followed their own spirit* (*v.* 3); they delivered that as a message from God which was the product either of their subtle invention, or of their own crazed and heated imagination. For *they have seen nothing*, they have not really had any heavenly vision. *You have spoken vanity and seen lies;* what they saw and what they said was all alike, a mere sham. Again (*v.* 9), They *see vanity and divine lies*; they pretended to have had visions, as the true prophets had, but either it was the creature of their own fancy that was *seeing vanity*, or it was a fiction of their own politics, and they knew they had none, and then they *saw lies, and divined lies.*

They are like *the foxes in the deserts*, seeming to be in a great hurry, but it was to get away and shift for their own safety, not to do any good.

They should have made intercession to turn away the wrath of God; but they were not praying prophets. They should have made it their business by preaching and advice to bring people to repentance and reformation, and so have *made up the hedge*, but they contrived how to please people, not how to profit them.

JAMIESON, FAUSSET, BROWN

CHAPTER 13

VSS. 1-23. DENUNCIATION OF FALSE PROPHETS AND PROPHETESSES; THEIR FALSE TEACHINGS, AND GOD'S CONSEQUENT JUDGMENTS. **1.** As ch. 12 denounced the false expectations of the people, so this denounces the false leaders who fed those expectations. As an independent witness, Ezekiel confirms at the Chebar the testimony of Jeremiah (ch. 29:21, 31) in his letter from Jerusalem to the captive exiles, against the false prophets; of these some were conscious knaves, others fanatical dupes of their own frauds; e.g., Ahab, Zedekiah, and Shemaiah. Hananiah must have believed his own lie, else he would not have specified so *circumstantial* details (Jer. 28:2-4). The conscious knaves gave only *general* assurances of peace (Jer. 5:31; 6:14; 14:13). The language of Ezekiel has plain references to the similar language of Jeremiah (e.g., Jeremiah 23:9-38); the bane of false prophecy, which had its stronghold in Jerusalem, having in some degree extended to the Chebar; this chapter, therefore, is primarily intended as a message to those still in the Jewish metropolis; and, secondarily, for the good of the exiles at the Chebar. **2. that prophesy**—viz., a speedy return to Jerusalem. **out of . . . own hearts**—alluding to the words of Jeremiah (Jer. 23:16, 26); i.e., what they prophesied was what they and the people *wished*; the wish was father to the thought. The people *wished* to be deceived, and so were deceived. They were inexcusable, for they had among them true prophets (who spoke not *their own* thoughts, but as they were moved by the Holy Ghost, II Peter 1:21), whom they might have known to be such, but they did not wish to know (John 3: 19). **3. foolish**—though vaunting as though exclusively possessing "wisdom" (I Cor. 1:19-21); the fear of God being the only beginning of wisdom (Ps. 111:10). **their own spirit**—instead of the Spirit of God. A threefold distinction lay between the false and the true prophets: (1) The source of their messages respectively; of the false, "their own hearts"; of the true, an object presented to the spiritual sense (named from the noblest of the senses, a *seeing*) by the Spirit of God as from without, not produced by their own natural powers of reflection. The word, the body of the thought, presented itself not audibly to the natural sense, but directly to the spirit of the prophet; and so the perception of it is properly called a *seeing,* he perceiving that which thereafter forms itself in his soul as the cover of the external word [DELITZSCH]; hence the peculiar expression, *seeing the word of God* (Isa. 2:1; 13:1; Amos 1:1; Mic. 1:1). (2) The point aimed at; the false "walking after their own spirit"; the true, after the Spirit of God. (3) The result; the false saw nothing, but spake as if they had seen; the true had a vision, not subjective, but objectively real [FAIRBAIRN]. A refutation of those who set the *inward* word above the *objective,* and represent the Bible as flowing subjectively from the inner light of its writers, not from the revelation of the Holy Ghost from without. "They are impatient to get possession of the kernel without its fostering shell—they would have Christ without the Bible" [BENGEL]. **4. foxes**—which cunningly "spoil the vines" (Song of Sol. 2:15), Israel being the vineyard (Ps. 80:8-15; Isa. 5:1-7; 27:2; Jer. 2:21); their duty was to have guarded it from being spoiled, whereas they themselves spoiled it by corruptions. **in . . . deserts**—where there is nothing to eat; whence the foxes become so ravenous and crafty in their devices to get food. So the prophets wander in Israel, a moral desert, unrestrained, greedy of gain which they get by craft. **5. not gone up into . . . gaps**—metaphor from *breaches* made in a wall, to which the defenders ought to betake themselves in order to repel the entrance of the foe. The breach is that made in the theocracy through the nation's sin; and, unless it be made up, the vengeance of God will break in through it. Those who would advise the people to repentance are the restorers of the breach (ch. 22: 30; Ps. 106:23, 30). **hedge**—the law of God (Ps. 80: 12; Isa. 5:2, 5); by violating it, the people stripped themselves of the *fence* of God's protection and lay exposed to the foe. The false prophets did not try to repair the evil by bringing back the people to the law with good counsels, or by checking the bad with reproofs. These two duties answer to the double office of defenders in case of a breach made in a wall: (1) To repair the breach from within; (2) To oppose the foe from without. **to stand**—i.e., that the city may "stand." **in . . . day of . . . Lord**—In the day of the battle which God wages against Israel for their sins, ye do not try to stay God's vengeance by prayers, and by leading the nation to repentance. **6. made others to hope . . .**—rather,

ADAM CLARKE

CHAPTER 13

F. B. MEYER:

"Prophesy against the prophets of Israel . . . that prophesy out of their own hearts" (Ezek. 13:2). It is a great temptation of those of us who are often called to speak for God, to prophesy out of our own heart, to follow our own spirit, and to profess to see what we have not seen. We are apt to say, "The Lord saith," when the Lord has not sent us. These words of ours always tend towards soothing and pacifying guilty consciences with assurances of peace, peace. You may always tell when a man is speaking from the vanity of his own heart. He glosses over sin, and speaks with bated breath of its consequences.

This is what the Word of God describes as daubing a slight wall with untempered mortar, and sewing pillows on elbows for handfuls of barley and pieces of bread. The daubing makes the wall look as strong as possible, but it cannot save it from collapsing before the overflowing shower of God's judgment and the great hailstones of his wrath. The pillows may save the flesh from chafing, but cannot avert the blows of a broken law. Oh, take care, lest you give men licence to sin, by the slight views you circulate of its nature or penalty. Are not these lying divinations? Do they not grieve the heart of the righteous, and strengthen the hands of the wicked? Take care lest the fate of the daubing be the fate also of the false prophets: "The wall is no more; neither they that daubed it."

It is not an easy thing to speak to the prophets. But how necessary that there should be a Prophet to prophets: for these get into the way of supposing that they must be right, whose least word is so reverenced by their people. "You are very fond of preaching," said Dr. Andrew Bonar to one to whom he had been listening. "Yes, doctor; very." "But are you as fond of lost souls?"—*Great Verses Through the Bible*

4. *Thy prophets are like the foxes in the deserts.* These false prophets are represented as the foxes who, having got their prey by great subtlety, run to the desert to hide both themselves and it. So the false prophets, when the event did not answer to their prediction, got out of the way, that they might not be overwhelmed with the reproaches and indignation of the people.

5. *Ye have not gone up into the gaps.* Far from opposing sinners, who are bringing down the wrath of God upon the place, you prevent their repentance by your flattering promises and false predictions.

MATTHEW HENRY

II. He is directed to declare the judgments of God against them for these sins, from which their pretending to the character of prophets would not exempt them. They are sentenced to be excluded from all the privileges of the commonwealth of Israel, for they are adjudged to have forfeited them all (*v.* 9). *They shall not be in the secret of my people;* their folly shall be so clearly manifested that they shall never be consulted, nor their advice asked; they shall not be in the assembly of God's people for religious worship. They shall die in their captivity, and shall die childless.

Verses 10–16

I. How the people are deceived by the false prophets. Those flatterers seduce them, saying, *Peace, and there was no peace, v.* 10. They told the idolaters and other sinners that there was neither harm nor danger in the way they were in. Thus they *seduced God's people.* Now this is compared to the building of a slight rotten wall, or, according to our Saviour's similitude (Matt. vii. 26), the *building of a house upon the sand,* which seems to be a shelter and protection for a while, but will fall when a storm comes. One false prophet built the wall, set up the notion that God was not at all displeased with Jerusalem, but that the city should be victorious over the powers that now threatened it. This notion was very pleasing, and he that started it made himself very acceptable by it. They made the matter look yet more plausible and promising; they *daubed the wall,* which the first had built, but it was with *untempered mortar.* And the wall thus built, when it comes to any stress, much more to any distress, will bulge and totter, and come down by degrees.

II. How they will be soon undeceived by the judgment of God, which, we are sure, is according to truth. The descent which the Chaldean army shall make upon Judah, and the siege which they shall lay to Jerusalem, will be as *an overflowing shower.* The fury of Nebuchadnezzar and his princes, who highly resented Zedekiah's treachery, made the invasion very formidable, but that was nothing in comparison with God's displeasure. This storm shall overturn the wall: *it shall fall,* and the wind shall *rend it* (*v.* 11), the *hailstones shall consume it* (*v.* 13); I will *break it down* (*v.* 14) and *bring it to the ground,* so that the *foundation thereof shall be discovered*; it will appear how false, how rotten it was, to the prophetical reproach of the builders. Men's anger cannot shake that which God has built, but God's anger will overthrow that which men have built in opposition to him. The builders of the wall, and those that daubed it, will themselves be buried in the ruins of it: *It shall fall, and you shall* be *consumed in the midst thereof, v.* 14. Both the deceivers and the deceived, when they thus perish together, will justly be ridiculed (*v.* 12): *When the wall has fallen shall it not be said unto you,* by those that gave credit to the true prophets, and feared the word of the Lord, "Now *where is the daubing wherewith you have daubed the wall?* What has become of all the fair promises wherewith you flattered and all the assurances you gave that the troubles of the nation should soon be at an end?" They will say unto you (*v.* 15), "*The wall is no more, neither he that daubed it;* your hopes have vanished, and those that supported them, even *the prophets of Israel,*" *v.* 16.

Verses 17–23

As God has promised that when he pours out his Spirit upon his people both *their sons and their daughters shall prophesy,* so the devil, when he acts as a spirit of lies and falsehood, is so in the mouth not only of false prophets, but of false prophetesses too. *Son of man, set thy face against the daughters of thy people, v.* 17. The women pretend to a spirit of prophecy, and are in the same song with the men. They *prophesy out of their own heart* too; they say what comes uppermost. The prophet must *set his face against them.*

JAMIESON, FAUSSET, BROWN

"they *hoped*" to confirm (i.e., make good) their word, by the event corresponding to their prophecy. The *Hebrew* requires this [HAVERNICK]. Also the parallel clause, "they have *seen* vanity," implies that they believed their own lie (II Thess. 2:11). Subjective revelation is false unless it rests on the objective. **8. I am against you**—rather understand, "I *come* against you," to punish your wicked profanation of My name (cf. Rev. 2:5, 16). **9. mine hand**—My power in vengeance. **not ... in ... assembly**—rather, the "council"; "They shall not occupy the honorable office of *councillors* in the senate of elders after the return from Babylon" (Ezra 2:1, 2). **neither ... written in ... Israel**—They shall not even have a place in the *register* kept of all *citizens'* names; they shall be erased from it, just as the names of those who died in the year, or had been deprived of citizenship for their crimes, were at the annual revisal erased. Cf. Jeremiah 17:13; Luke 10:20; Revelation 3:5, as to those *spiritually* Israelites; John 1:47, and those not so. Literally fulfilled (Ezra 2:59, 62; cf. Neh. 7:5; Ps. 69:28). **neither ... enter ... land**—They shall not so much as be allowed to come back at all to their country. **10. Because, even because**—The repetition heightens the emphasis. **Peace**—*safety* to the nation. Ezekiel confirms Jeremiah 6:14; 8:11. **one**—lit., "this one"; said contemptuously, as in II Chronicles 28:22. **a wall**—rather, a loose wall. Ezekiel had said that the false prophets did not "go up into the gaps, or make up the breaches" (vs. 5), as good architects do; now he adds that they make a bustling show of anxiety about repairing the wall; but it is without right mortar, and therefore of no use. **one ... others**—besides *individual* effort, they *jointly co-operated* to delude the people. **daubed ... with untempered mortar**—as sand without lime, mud without straw [GROTIUS]. FAIRBAIRN translates, "plaster it with whitewash." But besides the hypocrisy of merely *outwardly* "daubing" to make the wall look fair (Matt. 23:27, 29; Acts 23:3), there is implied the unsoundness of the wall from the absence of *true uniting cement;* the "untempered cement" answering to *the lie* of the prophets, who say, *in support of their prophecies,* "Thus saith the Lord, when the Lord hath not spoken" (ch. 22:28). **11. overflowing**—*inundating;* such as will at once wash away the mere clay mortar. The three most destructive agents shall co-operate against the wall—wind, rain, and hailstones. These last in the East are more out of the regular course of nature and are therefore often particularly specified as the instruments of God's displeasure against His foes (Exod. 9:18; Josh. 10:11; Job 38:22; Ps. 18:12, 13; Isa. 28:2; 30:30; Rev. 16:21). The *Hebrew* here is, lit., "stones of ice." They fall in Palestine at times an inch thick with a destructive velocity. The personification heightens the vivid effect, "O ye hailstones." The Chaldeans will be the violent agency whereby God will unmask and refute them, overthrowing their edifice of lies. **12. shall it not be said**—Your vanity and folly shall be so manifested that it shall pass into a proverb, "Where is the daubing?" **13.** God repeats, *in His own name,* as the Source of the coming calamity, what had been expressed generally in vs. 11. **14.** The repetition of the same threat is to awaken the people out of their dream of safety by the *certainty* of the event. **foundation**—As the "wall" represents the security of the nation, so the "foundation" is *Jerusalem,* on the fortifications of which they rested their confidence. GROTIUS makes the "foundation" refer to *the false principles* on which they rested; vs. 16 supports the former view. **16. prophesy concerning Jerusalem**—With all their "seeing visions of peace for her," they cannot ensure peace or safety to themselves. **17. set thy face**—put on a bold countenance, fearlessly to denounce them (ch. 3:8, 9; Isa. 50:7). **daughters**—the false prophetesses; alluded to only here; elsewhere the guilt specified in the women is the active share they took in maintaining idolatry (ch. 8:14). It was only in extraordinary emergencies that God bestowed prophecy on women, e.g. on Miriam, Deborah, Huldah (Exod. 15:20; Judg. 4:4; II Kings 22:14); so in the last days to come (Joel 2:28). The rareness of such instances enhanced their guilt in pretending inspiration. **18. sew pillows to ... armholes**—rather, *elbows and wrists,* for which the false prophetesses made cushions to lean on, as a symbolical act, typifying the perfect tranquility which they foretold to those consulting them. Perhaps they made their dupes rest on these cushions in a fancied state of ecstasy after they had made them at first *stand* (whence the expression, "every *stature,*" is used for "men of every *age*"). As the men are said to have built a wall (vs. 10), so the women are said to sew pillows, etc., both alike

ADAM CLARKE

9. *They shall not be in the assembly of my people.* They shall not be reputed members of My Church. They shall not be reckoned in the genealogy of true Israelites that return from captivity, and they shall never have a possession in the land; they shall be exhereditated and expatriated. They shall all perish in the siege, by the sword, the famine, and the pestilence.

10. *One built up a wall.* A true prophet is as a wall of defense to the people. These false prophets pretend to be a wall of defense; but their wall is bad, and their mortar is worse. One gives a lying vision; another pledges himself that it is true; and the people believe what they say, and trust not in God, nor turn from their sins.

11. *There shall be an overflowing shower* that shall wash off this bad mortar, sweep away the ground on which the wall stands, and level it with the earth. In the Eastern countries, where the walls are built with unbaked bricks, desolations of this kind are often occasioned by tempestuous rains.

17. *Set thy face against the daughters of thy people, which prophesy.* From this it appears that there were prophetesses in the land of Israel that were really inspired by the Lord; for false prophetesses necessarily imply true ones, whom they endeavored to imitate.

18. *That sew pillows to all armholes.* I believe this refers to those cushions which are so copiously provided in the Eastern countries for the apartments of women, on which they sit, lean, rest their heads, and prop up their arms. I have several drawings of Eastern ladies who are represented on sofas, and often with their arm thrown over a pillow, which is thereby pressed close to their side, and against which they thus recline. The prophet's discourse seems to point out that state of softness and

MATTHEW HENRY

I. The sin of these false prophetesses is described. They told deliberate lies to those who consulted them, and came to them to be advised, and to be told their fortune: You do mischief *by your lying to my people that hear your lies* (*v.* 19). *You pollute my name among my people*, and make use of that for the patronising of your lies. Yet this they did *for handfuls of barley and pieces of bread.* They would sell you a false prophecy that should please you for the beggar's dole, a *piece of bread* or *a handful of barley*; and yet that was more than it was worth. They kept people in awe, and terrified them with their pretensions: *You hunt the souls of my people* (*v.* 18), *hunt them to make them flee* (*v.* 20). Thus they beguiled unstable souls that had a concern about salvation. They discouraged those that were honest and good, and encouraged those that were wicked and profane, *v.* 19. "You have promised sinners life in their sinful ways, have told them that they shall have peace though they go on, by which their *hands have been strengthened* and their hearts hardened." They mimicked the true prophets, by giving signs illustrating their false predictions (as Hananiah did, Jer. xxviii. 10), signs agreeable to their sex; they *sewed little pillows to the people's arm-holes*, to signify that they might repose themselves, and not be disquieted with apprehensions of trouble. And they *made kerchiefs upon the head of every stature*, of persons of every age, young and old, distinguishable by their stature, *v.* 18. These kerchiefs were badges of liberty or triumph, intimating that they should be delivered from the Chaldeans. Some think these were superstitious rites which they used with those to whom they delivered their divinations, preparing them by putting enchanted pillows under their arms and handkerchiefs on their heads.

II. God declares himself against the methods they took to delude and deceive, *v.* 20. They shall be confounded in their attempts (*v.* 23). God's people shall be delivered out of their hands. The *pillows shall be torn from their arms*, and the *kerchiefs from their heads*; the fallacies shall be discovered, their frauds detected, and the people of God shall no more be in their hand, to be hunted as they had been.

CHAPTER 14

Verses 1–11

I. The address which some of the elders of Israel made to the prophet, as an oracle, to enquire of the Lord by him. They *came, and sat before him*, *v.* 1. By the severe answer given them one would suspect they had a design to ensnare the prophet.

II. God gives him their real character (*v.* 3); they were idolaters, and did only consult Ezekiel as they would any oracle of a pretended deity, to gratify their curiosity, and therefore God says: "*Should I be enquired of at all by them?* They *have set up their idols in their heart.*" It may be understood of spiritual idolatry; those whose affections are placed upon the wealth of the world and the pleasures of sense, whose god is their money, *whose god is their belly*, they *set up their idols in their heart.* It intimates that they are resolved to go on in sin, whatever comes of it. *I have loved strangers, and after them I will go;* that is the language of their hearts. Can those expect an answer of peace from God who thus continue their acts of hostility against him?

JAMIESON, FAUSSET, BROWN

typifying the "peace" they promised the impenitent. **make kerchiefs**—magical *veils*, which they put over the heads of those consulting them, as if to fit them for receiving a response, that they might be rapt in spiritual trance above the world. **head of every stature**—"men of every age," old and young, great and small, if only these had pay to offer them. **hunt souls**—eagerly trying to allure them to the love of yourselves (Prov. 6:26; II Pet. 2:14), so as unwarily to become your prey. **will ye save . . . souls . . . that come unto you**—Will ye haul after souls, and when they are yours ("come unto you"), will ye *promise them life?* "Save" is explained (vs. 22), "*promising* life" [GROTIUS]. CALVIN explains, "Will ye hunt My people's souls and yet will ye save *your own* souls"; I, the Lord God, will not allow it. But "save" is used (vs. 19) of the false prophetesses *promising life* to the impenitent, so that *English Version* and GROTIUS explain it best. **19. handfuls**—expressing the paltry gain for which they bartered immortal souls (cf. Mic. 3:5, 11; Heb. 12: 16). **They "polluted" God by making His name the cloak under which they uttered falsehoods. among my people**—an aggravation of their sin, that they committed it "among the people" whom God had chosen as peculiarly *His own,* and among whom He had His temple. It would have been a sin to have done so even among the Gentiles, who knew not God; much more so among the people of God (cf. Prov. 28:21). **slay . . . souls that should not die, . . .**—to *predict* the slaying or perdition of the godly whom I will save. As true ministers are said to save and slay their hearers, according to the spirit respectively in which these receive their message (II Cor. 2:15, 16), so false ministers imitate them; but they promise safety to those on the broad way to ruin and predict ruin to those on the narrow way of God. **my people that hear your lies**—who are therefore *wilfully* deceived, so that their guilt lies at their own door (John 3:19). **20. I am against your pillows**—i.e., against your lying ceremonial tricks by which ye cheat the people. **to make them fly**—viz., into their snares, as fowlers disturb birds so as to be suddenly caught in the net spread for them. "Fly" is peculiarly appropriate as to those lofty spiritual *flights* to which they pretended to raise their dupes when they veiled their heads with kerchiefs and made them rest on luxurious arm-cushions (vs. 18). **let . . . souls go**—"Ye make them fly" in order to destroy them; "I will let them go" in order to save them (Ps. 91:3; Prov. 6:5; Hos. 9:8). **21. in your hand**—in your power. "My people" are the elect remnant of Israel to be saved. **ye shall know**—by the judgments which ye shall suffer. **22. ye have made . . . the righteous sad**—by *lying* predictions of calamities impending over the godly. **strengthened . . . wicked**—(Jer. 23:14). **heart of . . . righteous . . . hands of . . . wicked**—*Heart* is applied to the righteous because the terrors foretold penetrated to their inmost feelings; *hands,* to the wicked because they were so hardened as not only to despise God in their minds, but also to manifest it in their whole *acts,* as if avowedly waging war with Him. **23. ye shall see no more vanity**—The event shall confute your lies, involving yourselves in destruction (vs. 9; ch. 14:8; 15:7; Mic. 3:6).

CHAPTER 14

Vss. 1-23. HYPOCRITICAL INQUIRERS ARE ANSWERED ACCORDING TO THEIR HYPOCRISY. THE CALAMITIES COMING ON THE PEOPLE; BUT A REMNANT IS TO ESCAPE. **1. elders**—persons holding that dignity among the exiles at the Chebar. GROTIUS refers this to Seraiah and those sent with him *from Judea* (Jer. 51:59). The prophet's reply, first, reflecting on the character of the inquirers, and, secondly, foretelling the calamities coming on Judea, may furnish an idea of the subject of their inquiry. **sat before me**—not at once able to find a beginning of their speech; indicative of anxiety and despondency. **3. heart . . . face**—The *heart* is first corrupted, and then the *outward manifestation* of idol-worship follows; they set their idols *before their eyes.* With all their pretense of consulting God now, they have not even put away their idols *outwardly;* implying gross contempt of God. **"Set up," lit., "raised** aloft"; implying that their idols had gained the supreme *ascendancy* over them. **stumbling block of . . . iniquity**—See Proverbs 3:21, 23, "Let not them (God's laws) depart *from thine eyes,* then . . . thy foot shall not *stumble.*" Instead of God's law, which (by being kept before their eyes) would have saved them from stumbling, they set up their idols before their eyes, which proved a stumbling block, causing them to stumble (ch. 7:19). **inquired of at**

ADAM CLARKE

effeminacy to which the predictions of those false prophetesses allured the inhabitants of Jerusalem. A careless, voluptuous life is that which is here particularly reprehended. *And make kerchiefs.* Probably some kind of ornamental dress which rendered women more enticing, so that they could the more successfully hunt or inveigle souls (men) into the worship of their false gods.

20. *The souls that ye hunt to make them fly.* These false prophetesses decoyed men into gardens, where probably some impure rites of worship were performed, as in that of Asherah or Venus.

22. *With lies ye have made the heart of the righteous sad.* Here is the ministry of these false prophetesses, and its effects. They told lies: they would speak, and they had no truth to tell, and therefore spoke falsities. They "saddened the souls of the righteous, and strengthened the hands of the wicked." They promised them life, and prevented them from repenting and turning from their sins.

23. *Ye shall see no more vanity.* They pretended visions, but they were empty of reality. *Nor divine divinations.* As God would not speak to them, they employed demons.

CHAPTER 14

1. *Then came certain of the elders of Israel unto me.* These probably came to tempt him, or get him to say something that would embroil him with the government. They were bad men, as we shall see in the third verse.

3. *These men have set up their idols in their heart.* Not only in their houses, in the streets, but they had them in their hearts. These were stumbling blocks of iniquity; they fell over them, and broke the neck of their souls.

MATTHEW HENRY

III. The answer which God orders Ezekiel to give them, *v.* 4. Let them know that it is a rule for *every man of the house of Israel*, that if he continue in love and league with his idols, and come to enquire of God, God will answer him according to his real iniquity, not according to his pretended piety. *I the Lord*, who *speak and it is done*, *I will answer him that cometh, according to the multitude of his idols.* He will give them up *to their own hearts' lust*, and leave them to themselves to be as bad as they have a mind to be, till they *have filled up the measure of their iniquity*. If God discover them, if he bind them over to his judgment, it is all by *their own hearts. O Israel!* thou hast destroyed thyself.

VI. The counsel that is given them for the preventing of this fearful doom (*v.* 6): *"Therefore repent, and turn yourselves from your idols.* Turn from them as from abominations that you are sick of; and then you will be welcome to enquire of the Lord."

IV. This answer was for all *the house of Israel*, *v.* 7, 8. It concerns not only everyone of the house of Israel (as before, *v.* 4), but *the stranger that sojourns in Israel*. Even proselytes shall not be countenanced if they be not sincere. Hypocrites *separate themselves from* God by their fellowship with idols; they cut themselves off from their relation to God. He shall have his answer, not by the words of the prophet, but by the judgments of God. *And I will set my face against that man.* God will make him an example; for *thus shall it be done to the man that separates himself from* God, and yet pretends to *enquire concerning him.* The hypocrite thought to pass for one of God's people, but God *will cut him off from the midst of his people.*

V. The doom of those pretenders to prophecy who give countenance to these pretenders to piety, *v.* 9, 10. These hypocritical enquirers, though Ezekiel will not give them a comfortable answer, yet hope to meet with some other prophets that will; and if they do, as perhaps they may, let them know that God permits those lying prophets to deceive them in punishment. *I will stretch out my hand upon him and will destroy him.*

VII. The pretending prophets, and the pretending saints, shall perish together, that, some being made examples, the body of the people may be reformed, *that the house of Israel may go no more astray from me*, *v.* 11.

Verses 12–23

I. National sins bring national judgments. *When the land sins against me*, when vice and wickedness become epidemical, when gross impieties and immoralities universally prevail, *then I will stretch forth my hand upon it*, for the punishment of it.

JAMIESON, FAUSSET, BROWN

all—lit., "should I with inquiry be inquired of" by such hypocrites as they are? (Ps. 66:18; Prov. 15:29; 28:9). **4. and cometh**—*and yet* cometh, feigning himself to be a true worshipper of Jehovah. **him that cometh**—so the *Margin Hebrew* reads. But the *text Hebrew* reading is, *"according to it,* according to the multitude of his idols"; the anticipative clause with the pronoun not being pleonastic, but increasing the emphasis of the following clause with the noun. "I will answer," lit., reflexively, "I will Myself (or *for Myself*) answer him." **according to . . . idols**—thus, "answering a fool according to his folly"; making the sinner's sin his punishment; retributive justice (Prov. 1:31; 26:5). **5. That I may take**—i.e., unveil and *overtake with punishment* the dissimulation and impiety of Israel hid *in their own heart*. Or, rather, "That I may punish them by answering them *after their own hearts*"; corresponding to "according to the multitude of his idols" (*Note*, vs. 4); an instance is given in vs. 9; Rom. 1:28; II Thess. 2:11, God giving them up in wrath to their own lie. **idols**—though pretending to "inquire" of Me, "in their hearts" they are "estranged from Me," and love "idols." **6.** Though God so threatened the people for their idolatry (vs. 5), yet He would rather they should avert the calamity by "repentance." **turn** *yourselves*—CALVIN translates, "turn *others*" (viz., the stranger proselytes in the land). As ye have been the advisers of others (see vs. 7, "the stranger that sojourneth in Israel") to idolatry, so bestow at least as much pains in turning them to the truth; the surest proof of repentance. But the parallelism to vss. 3, 4 favors ***English Version.*** Their sin was twofold: (1) "In their *heart*" or *inner* man; (2) "Put before their *face*," i.e., exhibited *outwardly*. So their repentance is generally expressed by "repent," and is then divided into: (1) "Turn *yourselves* (inwardly) from your idols"; (2) "Turn away your *faces* (outwardly) from all your abominations." It is not likely that an exhortation to convert others should come *between* the two affecting themselves. **7. stranger**—the proselyte, tolerated in Israel only on condition of worshipping no God but Jehovah (Lev. 17:8, 9). **inquire of him concerning me**—i.e., concerning My will. **by myself**—not by word, but by deed, i.e., by *judgments, marking My hand and direct agency;* instead of answering him through the prophet he consults. FAIRBAIRN translates, as it is the same *Hebrew* as in the previous clause, "concerning Me," it is natural that God should use *the same expression* in His reply as was used in the consultation of Him. But the *sense*, I think, is the same. The hypocrite inquires of the prophet *concerning God;* and God, instead of replying through the prophet, replies for Himself *concerning Himself*. **8. make him a sign**—lit., "I will destroy him so as to become a sign"; it will be no ordinary destruction, but such as will make him be an object pointed at with wonder by all, as Korah, etc. (Num. 26:10; Deut. 28:37). **9. I the Lord have deceived that prophet**—not directly, but through Satan and his ministers; not merely permissively, but by overruling their evil to serve the purposes of *His righteous judgment,* to be a touchstone to separate the precious from the vile, and to "prove" His people (Deut. 13:3; I Kings 22:23; Jer. 4:10; II Thess. 2:11, 12). Evil comes not from God, though God overrules it to serve His will (Job 12:16; Jas. 1:3). This declaration of God is intended to answer their objection, "Jeremiah and Ezekiel are but two opposed to the many prophets who announce 'peace' to us." "Nay, deceive not yourselves, those prophets of yours are deluding you, and I permit them to do so as a righteous judgment on your wilful blindness." **10.** As they dealt deceitfully with God by seeking answers of peace without repentance, so God would let them be dealt with deceitfully by the prophets whom they consulted. God would chastise their sin with a corresponding sin; as they rejected the safe directions of the true light, He would send the pernicious delusions of a false one; prophets would be given them who should re-echo the deceitfulness that already wrought in their own bosom, to their ruin [FAIRBAIRN]. The people had themselves alone to blame, for they were long ago forewarned how to discern and to treat a false prophet (Deut. 13:3); the very existence of such deceivers among them was a sign of God's judicial displeasure (cf. in Saul's case, I Sam. 16:14; 28:6, 7). They and the prophet, being dupes of a common delusion, should be involved in a common ruin. **11.** Love was the spring of God's very judgments on His people, who were incurable by any other process (ch. 11:20; 37:27). **12.** The second part of the chapter: the effect which the presence of a few righteous persons was to have on the purposes

ADAM CLARKE

4. *According to the multitude of his idols.* I will treat him as an idolater, as a flagrant idolater.

7. *And cometh to a prophet.* Generally supposed to mean a false prophet. *I the Lord will answer him by myself.* I shall discover to him, by My own true prophet, what shall be the fruit of his ways. So, while their false prophets were assuring them of peace and prosperity, God's prophets were predicting the calamities that afterwards fell upon them. Yet they believed the false prophets in preference to the true.

9. *I the Lord have deceived that prophet.* That is, he ran before he was sent; he willingly became the servant of Satan's illusions; and I suffered this to take place, because he and his followers refused to consult and serve Me. I have often had occasion to remark that it is common in the Hebrew language to state a thing as done by the Lord which He only suffers or permits to be done, for so absolute and universal is the government of God that the smallest occurrence cannot take place without His will or permission.

10. *The punishment of the prophet.* They are both equally guilty; both have left the Lord, and both shall be equally punished.

MATTHEW HENRY

II. God has a variety of judgments wherewith to punish sinful nations. *Four sore judgments* are here specified: 1. *Famine*, *v.* 13. The denying and withholding of common mercies is itself judgment enough; he *cuts off man and beast* by cutting off the provisions which nature makes for both in the annual products of the earth. 2. Hurtful *beasts, noisome* and noxious. God can make these *to pass through the land* (*v.* 15), so *that no man may pass through because of the beasts*. When men revolt from their allegiance to God it is just that the inferior creatures should rise up in arms against man, Lev. xxvi. 22. 3. War. God often chastises sinful nations by bringing a sword upon them (*v.* 17): He says, *Sword, go through the land*. 4. *Pestilence* (*v.* 19), a dreadful disease, which has sometimes depopulated cities.

III. When God's professing people rebel against him, they may justly expect a complication of judgments to fall upon them.

IV. There commonly are some few very good men, even in those places that by sin are ripened for ruin. Even in a land that has *trespassed grievously*, there may be *three* such *men* as *Noah, Daniel, and Job*. Daniel was carried away into captivity, Dan. i. 6. Some of the better sort of people in Jerusalem might perhaps think that, if Daniel (of whose fame in the king of Babylon's court they had heard much) had but continued in Jerusalem, it would have been spared for his sake. "No," says God, "though you had him, who was as eminently good in bad times and places as Noah in the old world and Job in the land of Uz, yet a reprieve snould not be obtained."

V. God often spares very wicked places for the sake of a few godly people in them. This is implied here as the expectation of Jerusalem's friends: "Surely God will stay his controversy with us; for are there not some among us that are emptying the measure of national guilt by their prayers, as others are filling it by their sins? And, rather than God will *destroy the righteous with the wicked*, he will preserve *the wicked with the righteous*."

VI. Such men as Noah, Daniel, and Job, will prevail, if any can, to turn away the wrath of God from a sinful people. Noah kept his integrity, and, for his sake, his family, though one of them was wicked (Ham), was saved in the ark. Job was mighty in prayer for his children, for his friends; and God turned his captivity when he prayed. Daniel, their neighbour, and *companion in tribulation*, being a man of great humility, instant and constant in prayer, had as good an interest in heaven as Noah or Job. Why may not God raise up as great and good men now as he did formerly, and do as much for them?

VII. When the sin of a people has come to its height, and the decree has gone forth for their ruin, the piety and prayers of the best men shall not prevail to finish the controversy. *Though these three men were in* Jerusalem at this time, yet they should *deliver neither son nor daughter*.

VIII. Though pious praying men may not prevail to deliver others, yet *they shall deliver their own souls by their righteousness*, so that, though they may suffer in the common calamity, yet it is not to them what it is to the wicked; it is sanctified, and does them good. If their bodies be not *delivered*, yet *their souls* are.

IX. Even when God makes the greatest desolations by his judgments, he reserves some to be monuments of his mercy, *v.* 22, 23. In Jerusalem itself, though marked for utter ruin, yet *there shall be left a remnant*, who shall be carried into captivity, both *sons and daughters*, the seed of a new generation. The young ones *shall be brought forth* by the victorious enemy, and *behold they shall come forth to you* that are in captivity, and shall come the more willingly to Babylon because so many of their friends have gone thither before them. And, when they come, *you shall see their ways and their doings*; you shall hear them make a free confession of sins and a humble profession of repentance with promises of reformation; and you shall see instances of their reformation, shall see what good their affliction has done them. *They shall comfort you when you see their ways. "You shall be comforted concerning all the evil that I have brought upon Jerusalem* when you better understand. *You shall know that I have not done without cause*, not without a just provocation, and yet not without a gracious design, *all that I have done in it*."

JAMIESON, FAUSSET, BROWN

of God (cf. Gen. 18:24-32). God had told Jeremiah that the guilt of Judah was too great to be pardoned even for the intercession of Moses and Samuel (Ps. 99:6; Jer. 14:2; 15:1), which had prevailed formerly (Exod. 32:11-14; Num. 14:13-20; I Sam. 7:8-12), implying the extraordinary heinousness of their guilt, since in *ordinary* cases "the effectual fervent prayer of a righteous man [for others] availeth much" (Jas. 5:16). Ezekiel supplements Jeremiah by adding that not only those two once successful *intercessors,* but not even the three preeminently *righteous* men, Noah, Daniel, and Job, could stay God's judgments by their righteousness. **13. staff of . . . bread**—on which man's existence is supported as on a staff (ch. 4:16; 5:16; Lev. 26:26; Ps. 104:15; Isa. 3:1). I will send a famine. **14. Noah, Daniel . . . Job**—specified in particular as having been saved from overwhelming calamities for their personal righteousness. Noah had the members of his family alone given to him, amidst the general wreck. Daniel saved from the fury of the king of Babylon the three youths (Dan. 2:17, 18, 48, 49). Though his *prophecies* mostly were later than those of Ezekiel, his *fame for piety and wisdom* was already established, and the events recorded in Daniel 1, 2 had transpired. The Jews would naturally, in their fallen condition, pride themselves on one who reflected such glory on his nation at the heathen capital, and would build vain hopes (here set aside) on his influence in averting ruin from them. Thus the objection to the authenticity of Daniel from this passage vanishes. "Job" forms the climax (and is therefore put out of chronological order), having not even been left a son or a daughter, and having had himself to pass through an ordeal of suffering before his final deliverance, and therefore forming the most simple instance of the righteousness of God, which would save the righteous themselves alone in the nation, and that after an ordeal of suffering, but not spare even a son or daughter for their sake (vss. 16, 18, 20; cf. Jer. 7:16; 11:14; 14:11). **deliver . . . souls by . . . righteousness**—(Prov. 11:4); not the righteousness of works, but that of grace, a truth less clearly understood under the law (Rom. 4:3). **15-21.** The argument is cumulative. He first puts the case of the land sinning so as to fall under the judgment of a famine (vs. 13); then (vs. 15) "noisome beasts" (Lev. 26:22); then "the sword"; then, worst of all, "pestilence." The three most righteous of men should deliver only themselves in these several four cases. In vs. 21 he concentrates the whole in one mass of condemnation. If Noah, Daniel, Job, could not deliver the land, when deserving only *one* judgment, "how much more" when all *four* judgments combined are justly to visit the land for sin, shall these three righteous men not deliver it. **19. in blood**—not literally. In *Hebrew*, "blood" expresses every premature kind of death. **21. How much more**—lit., "Surely shall it be so now, when I send . . . ." If none could avert *the one only* judgment incurred, *surely now*, when all four are incurred by sin, *much more* impossible it will be to deliver the land.

22. Yet . . . a remnant—not of righteous persons, but some of the guilty who should "come forth" from the destruction of Jerusalem to Babylon, to lead a life of hopeless exile there. The reference here is to judgment, not mercy, as vs. 23 shows. **ye shall see their . . . doings; and . . . be comforted**—Ye, the exiles at the Chebar, who now murmur at God's judgment about to be inflicted on Jerusalem as harsh, when ye shall see the wicked "ways" and character of the escaped remnant, shall acknowledge that both Jerusalem and its inhabitants deserved their fate; his recognition of the righteousness of the judgment will reconcile you to it, and so ye shall be "comforted" under it [CALVIN]. Then would follow mercy to the elect remnant, though *that* is not referred to here, but in ch. 20:43. **23. they shall comfort you**—not in words, but by your recognizing in their manifest guilt, that God had not been unjustly severe to them and the city.

ADAM CLARKE

13. *By trespassing grievously*. Having been frequently warned, and having refused to leave their sin, and so filled up the measure of their iniquity.

14. *Though . . . Noah, Daniel, and Job*. The intercession even the holiest of men shall not avert My judgments. Noah, though a righteous man, could not by his intercession preserve the old world from being drowned. Job, though a righteous man, could not preserve his children from being killed by the fall of their house. Daniel, though a righteous man, could not prevent the captivity of his country. Daniel must have been contemporary with Ezekiel. He was taken captive in the third year of Jehoiakim, Dan. i. 1. After this Jehoiakim reigned eight years, 2 Kings xxiii. 36. And this prophecy, as appears from chap. viii. 1, was uttered in the sixth year of Jehoiachin's captivity, who succeeded Jehoiakim, and reigned only three months, 2 Kings xxiv. 6, 8. Therefore at this time Daniel had been fourteen years in captivity. Even at this time he had gained much public celebrity. From this account we may infer that Job was as real a person as Noah or Daniel, and of their identity no man has pretended to doubt. When God, as above, has determined to punish a nation, no intercession shall avail.

21. *My four sore judgments. Sword,* war. *Famine,* occasioned by drought. *Pestilence* epidemic diseases which sweep off a great part of the inhabitants of a land. The *noisome beast*, the multiplication of wild beasts in consequence of the general destruction of the inhabitants.

22. *Behold, they shall come forth unto you*. Though there shall be great desolations in the land of Judea, yet a remnant shall be left that shall come here also as captives, and their account of the abominations of the people shall prove to you with what propriety I have acted in abandoning them to such general destruction. This speech is addressed to those who were already in captivity; i.e., those who had been led to Babylon with their king Jeconiah.

MATTHEW HENRY

CHAPTER 15

Verses 1-8

The prophet, we may suppose, was thinking what a glorious city Jerusalem was, and therefore what a pity it was that it should be destroyed. God here returns an answer to them by comparing Jerusalem to a vine. It is true, if a vine be fruitful, it is a most valuable tree. So Jerusalem was *planted a choice and noble vine, wholly a right seed* (Jer. ii. 21); and, if it had brought forth fruit suitable to its character as a holy city, it would have been the glory both of God and Israel. But, if it be not fruitful, it is as worthless as thorns and briers are. *What is the vine more than any tree if the branch of it be as the trees of the forest;* that is, if it bear no fruit, as forest-trees seldom do, being designed for timber-trees, not fruit-trees? Now there are some fruit-trees which, if they do not bear, are nevertheless of good use, as the wood of them may be made to turn to a good account; but the vine is not of this sort: if that do not answer its end as a fruit-tree, it is worth nothing as a timber-tree.

I. How this similitude is expressed here. The wild vine or the empty vine (which Israel is compared to, Hos. x. 1), is good for nothing. The *wood* of it is not *taken to do any work*; one cannot so much as make *a pin of it to hang a vessel upon, v.* 3. Among the plants, the roots of some, the seed or fruits of others, the leaves of others, and of some the stalks, are most serviceable to us; so, among trees, some are strong and not fruitful, as the oaks and cedars; others are weak but very fruitful, as the vine. The unfruitful tree *is not meet for any work, it is cast into the fire, v.* 4. When it is good for nothing else it is useful this way.

II. This similitude is applied to Jerusalem. 1. That holy city had become unprofitable and good for nothing. It had been as *the vine-tree among the trees of the* vineyard, abounding in the fruits of righteousness to the glory of God. When the pure worship of God was kept up, many a joyful vintage was gathered from it; and, while it continued so, God made a hedge about it, it was his *pleasant plant* (Isa. v. 7); he *watered it every moment* and *kept it night and day* (Isa. xxvii. 3); but it had now become *the degenerate plant of a strange vine, a vine-tree among the trees of the forest*, which, being wild, *brings forth wild grapes* (Isa. v. 4), nauseous and noxious (Deut. xxxii. 32), *their grapes are grapes of gall, and their clusters are bitter*. It is explained (*v.* 8): "*They have trespassed a trespass*, treacherously prevaricated with God." The Jewish nation, being famous as a holy people, when they became wicked, were thenceforth *good for nothing*; they lost all their usefulness, and became the most base and despicable people under the sun, *trodden under foot of the Gentiles*. Those who are not fruitful to the glory of God's grace will be fuel to the fire of his wrath (*v.* 6). *The inhabitants of Jerusalem* were like a vinebranch, rotten and awkward; and therefore (*v.* 7), *I will set my face against them*, as they set their faces against God, to defeat all his designs. *I will make the land* quite *desolate*, and therefore, when they *go out from one fire, another fire shall devour them* (*v.* 7); they shall go from misery in their own country to misery in Babylon.

JAMIESON, FAUSSET, BROWN

CHAPTER 15

Vss. 1-8. The Worthlessness of the Vine as Wood Especially when Burnt, Is the Image of the Worthlessness and Guilt of the Jews, Who Shall Pass from One Fire to Another. This chapter represents, in the way of a brief introduction, what ch. 16 details minutely. **2, 3. What has** the vine-*wood* to make it pre-eminent above other forest-*wood*? Nothing. Nay, the reverse. Other trees yield useful timber, but vine-wood is soft, brittle, crooked, and seldom large; not so much as a "pin" (the large wooden peg used inside houses in the East to hang household articles on, Isa. 22:23-25) can be made of it. Its sole excellency is that it should bear fruit; when it does not bear fruit, it is not only not better, but inferior to other trees: so if God's people lose their distinctive excellency by not bearing fruits of righteousness, they are more unprofitable than the worldly (Deut. 32:32), for they are the vine; the sole end of their being is to bear fruit to His glory (Ps. 80:8, 9; Isa. 5:1, etc.; Jer. 2:21; Hos. 10:1; Matt. 21:33). In all respects, except in their being planted by God, the Jews were inferior to other nations, as Egypt, Babylon, etc., e.g., in antiquity, extent of territory, resources, military power, attainments in arts and sciences. **2.** *or than* **a branch** –rather, in apposition with "the vine tree." Omit "*or than.*" What superiority has the vine *if it be but a branch among the trees of the forest*, i.e., if, as having no fruit, it lies cut down among other woods of trees? **4. cast into . . . fire**–(John 15:6). **both the ends**–the north kingdom having been already overturned by Assyria under Tiglath-pileser; the south being pressed on by Egypt (II Kings 23:29-35). **midst of it is burned**–rather, "is on flame"; viz., Jerusalem, which had now caught the flame by the attack of Nebuchadnezzar. **Is it meet for any work**–"it," i.e., the scorched part still remaining. **5.** If useless before, much more so when almost wholly burnt.

8. trespass–rather, "they have perversely fallen into perverse rebellion." The Jews were not merely *sinners* as the other nations, but *revolters* and *apostates*. It is one thing to neglect what we know not, but quite another thing to despise what we profess to worship [Jerome], as the Jews did towards God and the law.

6. So will I give the inhabitants of Jerusalem, as being utterly unprofitable (Matt. 21:33-41; 25:30; Mark 11:12-14; Luke 13:6-9) in answering God's design that they should be witnesses for Jehovah before the heathen (Matt. 3:10; 5:13). **7. from one fire . . . another**–(Cf. Isa. 24:18). "Fire" means here every kind of calamity (Ps. 66:12). The Jewish fugitives shall escape from the ruin of Jerusalem, only to fall into some other calamity.

ADAM CLARKE

CHAPTER 15

2. *What is the vine tree more than any tree?* It is certain that the vine is esteemed only on account of its fruit. In some countries, it is true, it grows to a considerable size and thickness; but, even then, it is not of a sufficient density to work into furniture. But whatever may be said of the stock of the vine, it is the branch that the prophet speaks of here; and I scarcely know the branch of any tree in the forest more useless than is the branch of the vine. Out of it who can even make "a pin" to drive into a mud wall, or hang any vessel on? A vine would never be cultivated for the sake of its wood; it is really worthless but as it bears fruit. What is Israel? Good for nothing, but as God influenced them to bring forth fruit to His glory. But now that they have ceased to be fruitful, they are good for nothing, but, like a withered branch of the vine, to be burnt.

4. *The fire devoureth both the ends of it, and the midst of it is burned.* Judea is like a vine branch thrown into the fire, which seizes on both the ends, and scorches the middle. So both the extremities of the land are wasted; and the middle, Jerusalem, is now threatened with a siege, and by and by will be totally destroyed.

6. *Therefore thus saith the Lord.* As surely as I have allotted such a vine branch, or vine branches, for fuel, so surely have I appointed the inhabitants of Jerusalem to be consumed.

7. *They shall go out from one fire, and another fire shall devour them.* If they escape the sword, they shall perish by the famine; if they escape the famine, they shall be led away captives. To escape will be impossible.

MATTHEW HENRY

CHAPTER 16

Verses 1-5

Ezekiel is now among the captives in Babylon; but, as Jeremiah at Jerusalem wrote for the use of the captives (*ch.* xxix), so Ezekiel wrote for the use of Jerusalem. Jeremiah wrote to the captives for their consolation, Ezekiel is directed to write to the inhabitants of Jerusalem for their conviction and humiliation.

I. This is his commission (*v.* 2): "*Cause Jerusalem to know her abominations* (that is, her sins); set them in order before her." We should know our sins, that we may confess them.

II. That Jerusalem may be made *to know her abominations*, it was requisite that she should be put in mind of the great things God had done for her. She is in these verses made to know from what poor beginnings God raised her, and how unworthy she was of his favour. Jerusalem is here put for the Jewish church and nation, which is here compared to an outcast child, base-born and abandoned. 1. The extraction of the Jewish nation was mean: "*Thy birth is of the land of Canaan* (*v.* 3); thou hadst from the very first the spirit and disposition of a Canaanite." The patriarchs dwelt in Canaan, and they were there but *strangers and sojourners*, had not one foot of ground of their own but a burying-

JAMIESON, FAUSSET, BROWN

CHAPTER 16

Vss. 1-63. Detailed Application of the Parabolical Delineation of Chapter 15 to Jerusalem Personified as a Daughter. 1. Taken up by God's gratuitous favor from infancy (vss. 1-7); 2. and, when grown up, joined to Him in spiritual marriage (vss. 8-14); 3. her unfaithfulness, her sin (vss. 15-34); 4. the judgment (vss. 35-52); 5. her unlooked-for restoration (vss. 53 to the close). **2. cause Jerusalem to know**–Men often are so blind as not to perceive their guilt which is patent to all. "Jerusalem" represents the whole kingdom of Judah. **3. birth . . . nativity**–thy origin and birth; lit., "thy diggings" (cf. Isa. 51:1) "and thy bringings forth." **of . . . Canaan**–in which Abraham, Isaac, and Jacob sojourned before going to Egypt, and from which thou didst derive far more of thy innate characteristics than from the virtues of those thy progenitors (ch. 21:30). **an Amorite . . . an Hittite** –These, being the most powerful tribes, stand for the whole of the Canaanite nations (cf. Josh. 1:4; Amos 2:9), which were so abominably corrupt as to have been doomed to utter extermination by God (Lev. 18:24, 25, 28; Deut. 18:12). Translate rather, "*the* Amorite . . . *the* Canaanite," i.e., these two tribes personified; their wicked characteristics, respectively, were concentrated in the parentage of

ADAM CLARKE

CHAPTER 16

2. *Cause Jerusalem to know her abominations.* This chapter contains God's manifesto against this most abominable people; and although there are many metaphors here, yet all is not metaphorical. Where there was so much idolatry, there must have been adulteries, fornications, prostitutions, and lewdness of every description. For its key, see on the thirteenth and sixty-third verses.

3. *Thy birth and thy nativity is of the land of Canaan.* It would dishonor Abraham to say that you sprang from him; you are rather Canaanites than Israelites. The Canaanites were accursed; so are you. *Thy father was an Amorite, and thy mother an Hittite.* These tribes were the most famous, and probably the most corrupt, of all the Canaanites. So Isaiah calls the princes of Judah "rulers of Sodom," chap. i. 10; and John the Baptist calls the

MATTHEW HENRY

place. Abraham and Sarah were indeed their *father and mother*, but they were only inmates with the Amorites and Hittites, who, having the dominion, seemed to be as parents to the seed of Abraham (Gen. xxiii. 4, 8); the dependence they had upon their neighbours the Canaanites, and the fear they were in of them, Gen. xiii. 7; xxxiv. 30. The patriarchs, at their first coming to Canaan, *went from one nation to another* (Ps. cv. 13), as tenants from one farm to another. Their fathers had *served other gods in Ur of the Chaldees* (Joshua xxiv. 2); even in Jacob's family there were *strange gods*, Gen. xxxv. 2. The children of Israel, when they began to increase into a people were thrown out from the country intended for them; a famine drove them thence. Egypt was *the open field* into which they were cast; there they were ruled with rigour, and their lives embittered. The nation of Israel was doomed to destruction, like an infant newborn, not clothed, *not swaddled*, because not *pitied*, *v.* 4, 5. This infant is said to be *cast out, to the loathing of her person. The Israelites were an abomination to the Egyptians*, as we find Gen. xliii. 32; xlvi. 34. Moses tells them (*v.* 24), *You have been rebellious against the Lord from the day that I knew you.* They were not *suppled*, nor *washed*, nor *swaddled*; they were not at all tractable or manageable, nor cast into any good shape. God took them to be his people, not because he saw anything in them inviting or promising, but *so it seemed good in his sight.*

Verses 6–14

An account of the great things which God did for the Jewish nation in raising them up by degrees to be very considerable. 1. God saved them from the ruin they were upon the brink of in Egypt (*v.* 6). Those shall live to whom God commands life. God looked upon the world of mankind, designing it *life, and that more abundantly.* By converting grace, he says to the soul, *Live.* 2. He looked upon them with kindness and a tender affection, *set his love upon them*, though there was nothing lovely in them; but *I looked upon thee*, and, *behold, thy time was the time of love*, *v.* 8. It was *the kindness and love of God our Saviour* that sent Christ to redeem us, that sends the Spirit to sanctify us, that brought us out of a state of nature into a state of grace. 3. He took them under his protection. God took them into his care, as an *eagle bears her young ones upon her wings*, Deut. xxxii. 11, 12. When God sent Moses to Egypt to deliver them, then he *spread his skirt over them.* 4. He cleared them from the reproachful character which their bondage in Egypt laid them under (*v.* 9). All the disgrace of their slavery was rolled away when they were brought, *with a high hand and a stretched-out arm, into the glorious liberty of the children of God.* 5. He multiplied them and built them up into a people. This is here mentioned (*v.* 7) before his *spreading his skirt over them*, because *their numbers increased exceedingly* while they were yet bond-slaves in Egypt. 6. He admitted them into covenant with himself. This was done at Mount Sinai; "when the covenant between God and Israel was sealed and ratified then *thou becamest mine.*" God called them his people, and himself the God of Israel.

7. He beautified and adorned them. This maid cannot forget her ornaments, and she is gratified with abundance of them, *v.* 10–13. We need not be particular in the application of these. Her wardrobe was well furnished with rich apparel. It may be taken figuratively for all those blessings of heaven which adorned both their church and state. In a little time they came to *excellent ornaments*, *v.* 7. The laws and ordinances which God gave them were to them as *ornaments of grace to the head and chains about the neck*, Prov. i. 9. God's sanctuary, which he set up among them, was *a beautiful crown upon their head*; it was the *beauty of holiness.*

8. He fed them with abundance, with plenty, with dainty. In Canaan they did eat bread to the full, the finest of the wheat, Deut. xxxii. 13, 14. 9. He gave them great reputation among their neighbours, and made them considerable. *Thou didst prosper into a kingdom* (*v.* 13), and, *Thy renown went forth among the heathen for thy beauty*, *v.* 14. Solomon's wisdom, and Solomon's temple, were very much *the renown* of that nation; and, if we put all the privileges of the Jewish church and kingdom together, we must own that it was the most accomplished beauty of all the nations of the earth.

JAMIESON, FAUSSET, BROWN

Israel (Gen. 15:16). "The Hittite" is made their "mother"; alluding to Esau's wives, daughters of *Heth*, whose ways vexed Rebekah (Gen. 26:34, 35; 27:46), but pleased the degenerate descendants of Jacob, so that these are called, in respect of morals, children of the Hittite (cf. vs. 45). **4.** Israel's helplessness in her first struggling into national existence, under the image of an infant (Hos. 2:3) cast forth without receiving the commonest acts of parental regard. Its very life was a miracle (Exod. 1:15-22). **navel ... not cut**—Without proper attention to the navel cord, the infant just born is liable to die. **neither ... washed in water to supple thee**—i.e., to make the skin soft. Rather, "for purification"; from an *Arabic* root [MAURER]. GESENIUS translates as *Margin*, "that thou mightest (be presented to thy parents to) be *looked* upon," as is customary on the birth of a child. **salted**—Anciently they rubbed infants with salt to make the skin firm. **5. cast ... in ... open field**—The exposure of infants was common in ancient times. **to the loathing of thy person**—referring to the unsightly aspect of the exposed infant. FAIRBAIRN translates, "With contempt (or disdainful indifference) of thy *life.*" **6. when I passed by**—as if a traveller. **polluted in ... blood**—but PISCATOR, "ready to be trodden on." **I said**—In contrast to Israel's helplessness stands God's omnipotent word of grace which bids the outcast little one "live." **in thy blood**—Though thou wast foul with blood, I said, "Live" [GROTIUS]. "Live in thy blood," i.e., Live, but live a life exposed to many deaths, as was the case in the beginnings of Israel's national existence, in order to magnify the grace of God [CALVIN]. The former view is preferable. Spiritually, till the sinner is made sensible of his abject helplessness, he will not appreciate the provisions of God's grace. **7. caused ... to multiply**—lit., "I ... made thee a myriad." **bud of ... field**—the produce of the field. In 250 years they increased from seventy-five persons to eight hundred thousand (Acts 7:14) [CALVIN]. But see Exodus 12: 37, 38. **excellent ornaments**—lit., "ornament of ornaments." **naked ... bare**—(Hos. 2:3). Lit., "nakedness ... bareness" itself; more emphatic. **8. thy time of love**—lit., "loves" (cf. Song of Sol. 2:10-13). Thou wast of marriageable age, but none was willing to marry thee, naked as thou wast. I then regarded thee with a look of grace when the full time of thy deliverance was come (Gen. 15:13, 14; Acts 7:6, 7). It is not she that makes the advance to God, but God to her; she has nothing to entitle her to such notice, yet He regards her not with mere benevolence, but with *love*, such as one cherishes to the person of his wife (Song of Sol. 1:3-6; Jer. 31:3; Mal. 1:2). **spread my skirt over thee**—the mode of espousals (Ruth 3:9). I betrothed thee (Deut. 4: 37; 10:15; Hos. 11:1). The cloak is often used as a bed coverlet in the East. God explains what He means, "I entered into ... covenant with thee," i.e., at Sinai. So Israel became "the wife of God's covenant" (Isa. 54:5; Jer. 3:14; Hos. 2:19, 20); Mal. 2:14). **thou ... mine**—(Exod. 19:5; Jer. 2:2). **9. washed I thee**—as brides used to pass through a preparatory purification (Esther 2:12). So Israel, before the giving of the law at Sinai (Exod. 19:14); "Moses sanctified the people, and they washed their clothes." So believers (I Cor. 6:11). **oil**—emblem of the Levitical priesthood, the type of Messiah (Ps. 45:7). **10.** Psalm 45:13, 14, similarly describes the Church (Israel, the appointed mother of Christendom) adorned as a bride (so Isa. 61:10). It is Messiah who provides the wedding garment (Rev. 3:18; 19:8). **badgers' skin**—*tahash;* others translate, "seal skins." They formed the over-covering of the tabernacle, which was, as it were, the nuptial tent of God and Israel (Exod. 26:14), and the material of the shoes worn by the Hebrews on festival days. **fine linen**—used by the priests (Lev. 6:10); emblem of purity. **11.** The marriage gifts to Rebekah (Gen. 24:22, 47). **12. jewel on thy forehead**—rather, "a ring in thy nose" (Isa. 3:21). **a crown**—at once the badge of a bride, and of her being made a queen, as being consort of the King; the very name *Israel* meaning "a prince of God." So they are called "a *kingdom* of priests" (Exod. 19:6; cf. Rev. 1:6). Though the external blessings bestowed on Israel were great, yet not these, but the internal and spiritual, form the main reference in the kingly marriage to which Israel was advanced. **13. flour ... honey ... oil**—These three mixed form the sweetest cakes; not dry bread and leeks as in Egypt. From raiment He passes to food (Deut. 32:13, 14). **exceeding beautiful**—Psalm 48:2, the city; also, Psalm 29:2, the temple. **prosper into a kingdom**—exercising empire over surrounding nations. **14. thy renown ... among ... heathen**—The theocracy reached its highest point under Solomon, when distant poten-

ADAM CLARKE

Pharisees a "generation [or brood] of vipers," Matt. iii. 7.

4. *As for thy nativity.* This verse refers to what is ordinarily done for every infant on its birth. The umbilical cord, by which it received all its nourishment while in the womb, being no longer necessary, is cut at a certain distance from the abdomen; on this part a knot is tied, which firmly uniting the sides of the tubes, they coalesce, and incarnate together. The extra part of the cord on the outside of the ligature, being cut off from the circulation by which it was originally fed, soon drops off, and the part where the ligature was is called the navel. In many places, when this was done, the infant was plunged into cold water; in all cases washed, and sometimes with a mixture of salt and water, in order to give a greater firmness to the skin, and constringe the pores. The last process was swathing the body, to support mechanically the tender muscles till they should acquire sufficient strength to support the body.

5. *Thou wast cast out in the open field.* This is an allusion to the custom of some heathen and barbarous nations, who exposed those children in the open fields to be devoured by wild beasts who had any kind of deformity, or whom they could not support.

6. *I said . . . Live.* I received the exposed child from the death that awaited it, while in such a state as rendered it at once an object of horror and also of compassion.

8. *Was the time of love.* You were marriageable.

I spread my skirt over thee. I espoused you. This was one of their initiatory marriage ceremonies. See Ruth iii. 9. *I . . . entered into a covenant with thee.* Married you. Espousing preceded marriage.

10. *I clothed thee also with broidered work.* Cloth on which various figures, in various colors, were wrought by the needle.

12. *I put a jewel on thy forehead.* "Upon your nose." This is one of the most common ornaments among ladies in the East. European translators, not knowing what to make of a ring in the nose, have rendered it, *a jewel on thy forehead* or mouth.

13. *Thou didst prosper into a kingdom.* Here the figure explains itself: By this wretched infant, the low estate of the Jewish nation in its origin is pointed out; by the growing up of this child into woman's estate, the increase and multiplication of the people; by her being decked out and ornamented, her Tabernacle service and religious ordinances; by her betrothing and consequent marriage, the covenant which God made with the Jews; by her fornica-

MATTHEW HENRY

We may apply this spiritually. Sanctified souls are truly beautiful; they are so in God's sight and they themselves may take the comfort of it.

Verses 15–34

An account of the great wickedness of the people of Israel, notwithstanding the great favours that God had conferred upon them. This wickedness of theirs is here represented by the lewd and scandalous conversation of that beautiful maid which was rescued from ruin. Their idolatry was the great provoking sin that they were guilty of; it began in the latter end of Solomon's time, and thenceforward continued till the captivity; and, though it now and then met with some check from the reforming kings, yet it was never totally suppressed.

This is that which is here represented under the similitude of whoredom and adultery, 1. Because it is the violation of a marriage-covenant with God. 2. Because it is the corrupting and defiling of the mind, and the enslaving of the spiritual part of the man. 3. Because it debauches the conscience.

I. The causes of this sin. 1. They grew proud (*v.* 15): "*Thou trustedst to thy beauty*, and didst expect that that should make thee an interest, and didst *play the harlot because of thy renown*." Solomon admitted idolatry, to gratify his wives and their relations. 2. They forgot their beginning (*v.* 22). 3. They were weak in understanding and in resolution (*v.* 30). The strength of men's lusts is an evidence of the weakness of their hearts.

II. The particulars of it. 1. They worshipped all the idols that came in their way, all that they were ever courted to the worship of; they were at the beck of all their neighbours (*v.* 15). 2. They adorned their idol-temples, and groves, and high places, with the fine rich clothing that God had given them (*v.* 16, 18). 3. They made images for worship of the jewels which God had given them (*v.* 17): *The jewels of my gold and my silver which I had given thee.* It is God that gives us our gold and silver. It is his still, so that we ought to serve and honour him with it, and are accountable to him for the disposal of it. Every penny has God's image upon it as well as Cæsar's. 4. They served their idols with the good things which God gave them (*v.* 18): "*Thou hast set my oil and my incense before them*, upon their altars; *my meat, and fine flour, and oil*, and that honey which Canaan flowed with, and *wherewith I fed thee*, thou hast regaled their hungry priests with, hast made an offering of it to them for *a sweet savour*. He that knows all things knows it." 5. They had sacrificed their children to their idols. *Thou hast taken thy sons and thy daughters*, and not only made them to pass through the fire, in token of their being dedicated to Moloch, but thou hast *sacrificed them to be devoured*, *v.* 20. It was an irreparable wrong to God himself. They are *my children* (*v.* 21), the *sons and daughters which thou hast borne unto me*, *v.* 20. He is the *Father of spirits*, and rational souls are in a particular manner his; and therefore the taking away of life, human life, unjustly, is a high affront to the *God of life*. How absurd was this, that the children which were born to God should be *sacrificed to devils*! The children of parents that are members of the visible church are to be looked upon as born unto God, and his children; as such, we are to love them, and pray for them, bring them up for him, and, if he calls for them, cheerfully part with them to him; for *may he not do what he will with his own*?

6. They built temples in honour of their idols. "*After all thy wickedness* of this kind committed in private, thou hast at length arrived at such a pitch of impudence as to proclaim it; now thou canst not blush," *v.* 23–25. *Thou hast built there an eminent place*, a *brothel-house* (so the margin reads it), and such their idol temples were.

Thou hast made thy beauty to be abhorred. The Jewish nation, by leaving their own God, and doting on the gods of the nations round about them, had made themselves despicable in the eyes even of their heathen neighbours.

JAMIESON, FAUSSET, BROWN

tates heard of his "fame" (I Kings 10:1, etc), e.g., the queen of Sheba, Hiram, etc. (Lam. 2:15). **my comeliness**—It was not thine own, but imparted by Me. **15.** Instead of attributing the glory of her privileges and gifts to God, Israel prided herself on them as her own (Deut. 32:15; Jer. 7:4; Mic. 3:11), and then wantonly devoted them to her idols (Hos. 2:8; cf. Luke 15:12, 13). **playedst . . . harlot because of thy renown**—"didst play the wanton upon thy name" [FAIRBAIRN], viz., by allowing thy renown to lead thee into idolatry and leagues with idolaters (Isa. 1:21; 57:8; Jer. 3:2, 6). *English Version* is better, "because of thy renown," i.e., relying on it; answering to "thou didst *trust in* thine own beauty." **his it was**—Thy beauty was yielded up to every passer-by. Israel's zest for the worship of foul idols was but an anxiety to have the approbation of heaven for their carnal lusts, of which the idols were the personification; hence, too, their tendency to wander from Jehovah, who was a restraint on corrupt nature. **16. deckedst . . . with divers colours**—or, "didst make . . . of divers colors" [FAIRBAIRN]; the metaphor and the literal are here mixed. The high places whereon they sacrificed to Astarte are here compared to *tents of divers colors,* which an impudent harlot would spread to show her house was open to all [CALVIN]. Cf. as to "woven hangings for Astarte" (the right translation for "grove") II Kings 23:7. **the like . . . shall not come, neither shall . . . be**—rather, "have not come, nor shall be." These thy doings are unparalleled in the past, and shall be so in the future. **17. my gold . . . my silver**—(Hag. 2:8). **images of men**—rather, "of the *phallus,"* the Hindoo *lingam,* or membrum virile [HAVERNICK], deified as the emblem of fecundity; man making his lust his god. *English Version,* however, is appropriate; Israel being represented as a *woman* playing the harlot with *"male* images," i.e., images of male gods, as distinguished from female deities. **18. tookest thy . . . garments . . . coveredst them**—i.e., the idols, as if an adulteress were to cover her paramours with garments which she had received from the liberality of her husband. **my oil**—the holy anointing oil sacred to God (Exod. 30:22-25). Also that used in sacrifices (Lev. 2:1, 2). **19. My meat . . . I gave**—(Hos. 2:83). **set it before them**—as a *minchah* or "meat offering" (Lev. 2:1). **a sweet savour**—lit., "a savor of rest," i.e., whereby they might be propitiated, and be at peace ("rest") with you; how ridiculous to seek to propitiate gods of wood! **thus it was**—The fact cannot be denied, for I saw it, and say it was so, saith Jehovah. **20, 21. sons and . . . daughters borne unto me**—Though "thy children," yet they belong "unto Me," rather than to thee, for they were born under the immutable covenant with Israel, which even Israel's sin could not set aside, and they have received the sign of adoption as Mine, viz., circumcision. This aggravates the guilt of sacrificing them to Molech. **to be devoured**—not merely to *pass through* the fire, as sometimes children were made to do (Lev. 18:21) *without hurt,* but to pass through so as to be made *the food* of the flame in honor of idols (Isa. 57:5; Jer. 7:31; 19:5; 32:35, *Notes*). **Is this of thy whoredoms a small matter, that thou hast slain my children**—rather, "Were thy whoredoms a small matter (i.e., not enough, but) that thou hast slain (i.e., must also slay)," etc. As if thy unchastity was not enough, thou hast added this unnatural and sacrilegious cruelty (Mic. 6:7). **22. not remembered . . . youth**—Forgetfulness of God's love is the source of all sins. Israel forgot her deliverance by God in the infancy of her national life. See vs. 43, to which vs. 60 forms a lovely contrast (Jer. 2:2, Hos. 11:1). **23. woe, woe unto thee . . .**—This parenthetical exclamation has an awful effect coming like a lightning flash of judgment amidst the black clouds of Israel's guilt. **24. eminent place**—rather, "a fornication-chamber," often connected with the impure rites of idolatry; spiritual fornication, on "an eminent place," answering to "fornication-chamber," is mainly meant, with an allusion also to the literal fornication associated with it (Jer. 2:20; 3:2). **25. at every head of the way**—in the most frequented places (Prov. 9:14). **thy beauty . . . abhorred, . . . opened . . . feet to every one**—The wanton advances were all on Israel's part; the idolatrous nations yielded to her nothing in return. She had yielded so much that, like a worn-out prostitute, her tempters became weary of her. When the Church lowers her testimony for God to the carnal tastes of the world, with a view to conciliation, she loses everything and gains nothing. **26. fornication with . . . Egyptians**—alliances with Egypt, cemented by sharing their idolatries. **great of flesh**—of powerful virile parts; fig. for the gross and lustful religion of Egypt (e.g., Isis, etc.), which alone could satisfy the

ADAM CLARKE

tion and adulteries, their apostasy from God, and the establishment of idolatrous worship, with all its abominable rites; by her fornication and whoredoms with the Egyptians and Assyrians, the sinful alliances which the Jews made with those nations, and the incorporation of their idolatrous worship with that of Jehovah; by her lovers being brought against her, and stripping her naked, the delivery of the Jews into the hands of the Egyptians, Assyrians, and Chaldeans, who stripped them of all their excellencies, and at last carried them into captivity. This is the key to the whole of this long chapter of metaphors, and the reader will do well to forget the figures and look at the facts. The language and figures may in many places appear to us exceptionable, but these are quite in conformity to those times and places, and to every reader and hearer would appear perfectly appropriate, nor would engender either a thought or passion of an irregular or improper kind. Among naked savages irregular passions and propensities are not known to predominate above those in civilized life. And why? Because such sights are customary, and therefore in themselves innocent. And the same may be said of the language by which such states and circumstances of life are described. Had Ezekiel spoken in such language as would have been called chaste and unexceptionable among us, it would have appeared to his auditors as a strange dialect, and would have lost at least one-half of its power and effect. Let this be the prophet's apology for the apparent indelicacy of his metaphors; and mine, for not entering into any particular discussion concerning them.

24. *Thou hast also built unto thee an eminent place. Gab,* "a brothel."

26. *Great of flesh.* The most extensive idolaters.

MATTHEW HENRY

III. The aggravations of this sin.

1. They were fond of the idols of those nations which had been their oppressors and persecutors. As, (1) The Egyptians, (2) The Assyrians.

2. They had been under the rebukes of Providence, and yet persisted (*v.* 27): *I have stretched out my hand over thee*, to threaten and frighten thee. So God did before he *laid his hand upon them* to destroy them; and that is his method, to try to bring men to repentance first by less judgments.

3. They were insatiable in their spiritual whoredom: Thou *couldst not be satisfied*, *v.* 28 and again *v.* 29.

4. They were at great expense with their idolatry, and laid out a great deal of wealth in images and altars, and hiring priests to attend upon them from other countries. This is much insisted on, *v.* 31-34.

And now is not Jerusalem in all this made to know her abominations? Here we see with wonder and horror what the corrupt nature of men is when God leaves them to themselves, yea, though they have the greatest advantages to be better and do better.

Verses 35–43

This notorious adulteress, being found guilty, has sentence passed upon her. It is ushered in with solemnity, *v.* 53. An apostate church is a harlot. Jerusalem is so if she become idolatrous. *How has the faithful city become a harlot!*

I. The crime is stated and the articles of the charge are summed up (*v.* 36 and 43). 1. The violation of the first two commandments of the first table by idolatry, her *whoredoms with her lovers*, that is, with *all the idols of her abominations*. 2. The violation of the first two commandments of the second table by the murder of their own innocent infants: *The blood of thy children which thou didst give unto them.* Their base ingratitude is another aggravation of their sins: "*Thou hast not remembered the days of thy youth*, and the kindness that was done thee then, when otherwise thou wouldst have perished," *v.* 43. "*Thou hast fretted me in all these things*, not only angered me, but grieved me."

II. The sentence is passed in general: *I will judge thee as women that break wedlock and shed blood are judged* (*v.* 38), and those two crimes were punished with an ignominious death. This criminal must be exposed to public shame, *v.* 37. The calamities of Jerusalem will be the grief of her friends and the joy of her foes. Those whom they have suffered to strip them of their virtue shall see them stripped. And *they shall stone thee with stones*, and *thrust thee through with their swords*. When the walls of Jerusalem were battered down with stones shot against them, and the inhabitants of Jerusalem were put to the sword, then this sentence was executed in the letter of it.

They shall throw down thy eminent place, and (*v.* 41) they *shall burn thy houses*, as the habitations of bad women are destroyed. It was the complaint, in the best reigns of the kings of Judah, that *the high places were not taken away*; but now the army of the Chaldeans shall break them down.

JAMIESON, FAUSSET, BROWN

abominable lust of Israel (ch. 20:7, 8; 23:19, 20, 21). **to provoke me**—wantonly and purposely. **27.** The consequent judgments, which, however, proved of no avail in reforming the people (Isa. 9:13; Jer. 5: 3). **delivered thee unto . . . Philistines**—(II Kings 16:6; II Chron. 28:18, 19). **ashamed of thy lewd way**—The Philistines were less wanton in idolatry, in that they did not, like Israel, adopt the idols of every foreign country but were content with their own (vs. 57; Jer. 2:11). **28. unsatiable**—Not satisfied with whoredoms with neighbors, thou hast gone off to the distant Assyrians, i.e., hast sought a league with them, and with it adopted their idolatries. **29. multiplied . . . fornication in . . . Canaan unto Chaldea**—Thou hast multiplied thy idolatries "in Canaan" by sending "unto Chaldea" to borrow from thence the Chaldean rites, to add to the abominations already practised "in Canaan," before the carrying away of Jehoiachin to Chaldea. The name "Canaan" is used to imply that they had made Judea as much the scene of abominations as it was in the days of the corrupt Canaanites. The land had become utterly Canaanitish (ch. 23:14, etc.). **30. weak . . . heart**—Sin weakens the *intellect* ("heart") as, on the contrary, "the way of the Lord is strength to the upright" (Prov. 10:29). **31.** Repetition of vs. 24. **not . . . as . . . harlot . . . thou scornest hire**—Unlike an ordinary harlot thou dost prostitute thy person gratis, merely to satisfy thy lust. JEROME translates, "Thou hast not been as a harlot in scorning (i.e., who ordinarily scorns) a hire offered," *in order to get a larger one:* nay, thou hast offered hire thyself to thy lovers (vss. 33, 34). But these verses show *English Version* to be preferable, for they state that Israel prostituted herself, not merely for *any small reward without demanding more*, but for "no reward." **32. instead of her husband**—referring to Numbers 5:19, 20, 29. FAIRBAIRN translates, "whilst under her husband." **33, 34.** Israel hired her paramours, instead of being, like other harlots, hired by them; she also followed them without their following her. **35.** Here begins the threat of wrath to be poured out on her. **36. filthiness**—lit., brass; metaphor for *the lowest part of the person* [CALVIN]. *English Version* is better: thy filthy lewdness is poured out without restraint (cf. Jer. 13:27). As silver is an emblem of purity, *brass* typifies "filthiness," because it easily contracts rust. HENDERSON explains it, "Because thy *money* was lavished on thy lovers (vss. 31, 33, 34). **blood of thy children**—(vs. 20; Jer. 2:34). **37. thy lovers**—the Chaldeans and the Assyrians. The law of retribution is the more signally exemplified by God employing, as His instruments of judgment on Israel, those very nations whose alliance and idols Israel had so eagerly sought, besides giving her up to those who had been always her enemies. "God will make him, who leaves God for the world, disgraced even in the eyes of the world, and indeed the more so the nearer he formerly stood to Himself" [HENGSTENBERG], (Isa. 47:3; Jer. 13:26; Hos. 2:12; Nah. 3:5). **all . . . thou hast hated**—the Edomites and Philistines; also Moab and Ammon especially (Deut. 23:3). **I . . . will discover thy nakedness**—punishment in kind, as she had "discovered her nakedness through whoredoms" (vs. 36); the sin and its penalty corresponded. I will expose thee to public infamy. **38-40. judge thee, as women that break wedlock**—(Lev. 20:10; cf. vs. 2). In the case of *individual* adulteresses, *stoning* was the penalty (John 8:4, 5). In the case of *communities*, the *sword*. Also apostasy (Deut. 13:10) and sacrificing children to Molech (Lev. 20:1-5) incurred stoning. Thus the penalty was doubly due to Israel; so the other which was decreed against an apostate city (Deut. 13:15, 16) is added, "they shall stone thee with stones and thrust thee through with . . . swords." The Chaldeans hurled *stones* on Jerusalem at the siege and slew with the *sword* on its capture. **shed blood . . . judged**—(Gen. 9:6). **jealousy**—image taken from the fury of a husband in jealousy shedding the blood of an unfaithful wife, such as Israel had been towards God, her husband spiritually. Lit., "I will *make thee* (to become) *blood* of fury and jealousy." **39. thine eminent place**—lit., "fornication-chamber" (*Note*, vs. 24), the temple which Israel had converted into a place of spiritual fornication with idols, to please the Chaldeans (ch. 23:14-17). **strip thee of . . . clothes**—(Ch 23:26; Hos. 2:3). They shall *dismantle* thy city of its walls. **fair jewels**—lit., "vessels of thy fairness" or beauty; the vessels of the temple [GROTIUS]. All the gifts wherewith God hath adorned thee [CALVIN]. **40.** (Ch. 23:10, 47.) Cf. as to the destruction under Titus, Luke 19:43, 44. **41.** The result of the awful judgment shall be, when divine vengeance has run its course, it shall cease. **burn**—(Deut. 13:16; II Kings 25:9). **women**—the surrounding Gentile

ADAM CLARKE

27. ***Have diminished thine ordinary.*** ***Chukkech*** **means here the household provision made for a wife—food, clothing, and money.**

F. GARDINER:

Verse 27. "Diminished thine ordinary food." This cutting short of the power and prosperity of Israel was a discipline of correction designed to bring her to a consciousness of her sin.

"The daughters of the Philistines," i.e., their cities, according to the figurative language of the chapter, and indeed the common figurative language of Scripture. Philistia was but a small power in the southwest corner of Palestine, yet from the time of the Judges down through the whole period of the monarchy, they were the persistent foes of Israel. During the time immediately before Samuel, they held nearly the entire land in subjection, and although subdued by David, they became troublesome again in the times of the later kings (2 Chron. 26:7; 28:18), and are often spoken of not only by the earlier prophets, Isaiah and Amos, but also by Jeremiah (25:20; 47:1, 4), Ezekiel (25:15, 16), and Zechariah (9:6).

"Ashamed of thy lewd way." The Philistines, true to their own false gods, despised the Israelites for unfaithfulness to Jehovah. It is the old but ever new story of the heathen repelled from the truth by the unworthiness of its professed followers.

Verse 28. "With the Assyrians." The Assyrians and Egyptians were for many centuries in deadly hostility against each other, and it would seem that Israel could hardly have formed alliances with and adopted the idolatries of both. Nevertheless they had done so, and in addition to their Egyptian idolatries, had gone to the extent, in the time of Ahaz, of displacing the altar in the court of the Temple, and putting in its stead an altar of the gods of Assyria (2 Kings 16:10–16).

Verse 29. "In the land of Canaan unto Chaldea." Canaan was originally the name of only that strip of land between the hills and the sea occupied by the Phoenicians, in other words, the lowlands. Thence it became extended over the whole land. It is thought by some writers to revert here to its original meaning, and be equivalent to the low, flat land. The word, however, bears also the meaning of traffic, commerce (Isa. 23:8; Hos. 12:7; Zeph. 1:11), and in this sense is applied to Babylon in chapter 17:4, and this is the better meaning here. The idea will then be that Israel, beginning its idolatries in the actual Canaan, had extended them along with her commercial intercourse on every side, until at last she had carried them even to Chaldea, the great commercial emporium of the time.

—*Ellicott's Commentary on the Whole Bible*

39. ***They shall strip thee also of thy clothes . . . thy fair jewels.*** **Alluding to a lot common enough to prostitutes, their maintainers in the end stripping them of all they had given them.**

MATTHEW HENRY

The captivity in Babylon made the people of Israel to cease for ever *from playing the harlot*; it effectually cured them of their inclination to idolatry. Then (*v.* 42) *my jealousy shall depart. I will be quiet, and no more angry.*

Verses 44–59

Now God by the prophet shows Jerusalem,

I. That she was as bad as *her mother*, that is, as the accursed Canaanites that were the possessors of this land before her. *As is the mother, so is her daughter*, *v.* 44. The character of the mother was that she *loathed her husband and her children*, she had all the marks of an adulteress; and that is the character of the daughter. When God brought Israel into Canaan he particularly warned them not to do according to the abominations of *the men of that land, who went before them* (for which *it had spewed them out*, Lev. xviii. 27, 28), but they learned their way, and trod in their steps. It might truly be said that *their mother* was a *Hittite* and their *father* an *Amorite* (*v.* 45), for they resembled them more than Abraham and Sarah.

II. That she was worse than her sisters Sodom and Samaria, that were adulteresses too, that were weary of the gods of their fathers, and were for introducing new gods, and new fashions in religion.

1. Jerusalem's sisters, *v.* 45. Samaria is called the *elder* sister, or rather the *greater*, because it was much larger, and more nearly allied to Israel. This city of Samaria, and its villages, had been *lately* destroyed for their *spiritual whoredom*. Sodom, and the adjacent towns and villages was her *less sister*, less than Jerusalem, less than Samaria, and these were of old destroyed for their corporeal whoredom, Jude 7.

2. Jerusalem's sins resembled her sisters', particularly Sodom's (*v.* 49): *This was the iniquity of Sodom, pride, fulness of bread, and abundance of idleness.* Their *going after strange flesh*, which was Sodom's most flagrant wickedness, is not mentioned, but those sins which opened the door to these more enormous crimes by their unnatural filthiness. Pride was the first sin that turned angels into devils, and the *garden of the Lord* into a *hell upon earth.* Gluttony is here called *fulness of bread.* Idleness, *abundance of idleness* was a dread of labour and a love of ease. Idleness is an inlet to much sin. The standing waters gather filth, and the sitting bird is the fowler's mark. Neither did she *strengthen the hands of the poor and needy*; probably it is implied that she weakened their hands and *broke* their arms.

3. The sins of Jerusalem exceeded those of Sodom and Samaria. The wickedness of the holy city, that was so dear to God, was more provoking to him than the wickedness of Sodom and Samaria, that had not Jerusalem's privileges and means of grace, *v.* 48. *Samaria has not committed half thy sins* (*v.* 51), has not worshipped half so many idols, nor slain half so many prophets. By this they *justified Sodom and Samaria*, *v.* 51.

JAMIESON, FAUSSET, BROWN

nations to whom thou shalt be an object of mocking (Ps. 137:7). **I will cause thee to cease . . . harlot**—(Ch. 23:27). Thou shalt *no longer be able* to play the harlot *through My judgments.* **thou . . . shalt give . . . no hire . . . any more**—Thou shalt have none to give. **42. my fury . . . rest**—when My justice has exacted the full penalty commensurate with thy awful guilt (*Note,* ch. 5:13). It is not a mitigation of the penalty that is here foretold, but such an utter destruction of *all* the guilty that there shall be no need of further punishment [CALVIN]. **43.** (Vs. 22; Ps. 78:42.) In gratitude for God's favors to her in her early history. **fretted me**—(Isa. 63:10; Eph. 4:30). **thou shalt not commit this lewdness above all thine abominations**—i.e., this the wickedness (cf. Zech. 5:8), peculiarly hateful to God, viz., spiritual unchastity or idolatry, over and "above" (i.e., besides) all thine other abominations. I will put it out of thy power to commit it by cutting thee off. FAIRBAIRN translates, "I will not do what is scandalous (viz., encouraging thee in thy sin by letting it pass with impunity) upon all thine abominations"; referring to Leviticus 19:29, the conduct of a father who encouraged his daughter in harlotry. *English Version* is much better. **44. As . . . mother . . . her daughter**—"*Is,*" and "*so is,*" are not in the original; the ellipsis gives the proverb (but two words in the *Hebrew*) epigrammatic brevity. Jerusalem proved herself a true daughter of the Hittite mother in sin (vs. 3). **45. mother's . . . that loatheth her husband**—i.e., God (haters of God," Rom. 1:30); therefore the knowledge of the true God had originally been in Canaan, handed down from Noah (hence we find Melchizedek, king of Salem, in Canaan, "priest of the most high God," Gen. 14:18), but Canaan apostatized from it; this was what constituted the blackness of the Canaanites' guilt. **loathed . . . children**—whom she put to death in honor of Saturn; a practice common among the Phœnicians. **sister of thy sisters**—Thou art akin in guilt to Samaria and Sodom, to which thou art akin by birth. Moab and Ammon, the incestuous children of Lot, nephew of Abraham, Israel's progenitor, had their origin from Sodom; so Sodom might be called Judah's sister. Samaria, answering to the ten tribes of Israel, is, of course, sister to Judah. **46. elder sister . . . Samaria . . .** *older* than Sodom, to whom Judah was *less nearly related by kindred* than she was to Samaria. Sodom is therefore called her *younger* sister; Samaria, her "elder sister" [GROTIUS]. Samaria is called the "elder," because *in a moral respect more nearly related* to Judah [FAIRBAIRN]. Samaria had made the calves at Dan and Bethel in imitation of the cherubim. **her daughters**—the inferior towns subject to Samaria (cf. Num. 21:25, *Margin*). **left**—The Orientals faced the east in marking the directions of the sky; thus the north was "left," the south "right." **Sodom . . . daughters**—Ammon and Moab, offshoots from Sodom; also the towns subject to it. **47. their abominations**—Milcom and Chemosh, the "abominations of Ammon and Moab" (I Kings 11:5, 7). **corrupted more than they**—So it is expressly recorded of Manasseh (II Kings 21:9). **48. Sodom**—(Matt. 11:24). Judah's guilt was not positively, but *relatively*, greater than Sodom's; because it was in the midst of such higher privileges, and such solemn warnings; *a fortiori,* the guilt of unbelievers in the midst of the highest of all lights, viz., the Gospel, is the greatest. **49. pride**—inherited by Moab, her offspring (Isa. 16:6; Jer. 48:26), and by Ammon (Jer. 49:4). God, the heart-searcher, here specifies as Sodom's sin, not merely her notorious lusts, but the secret spring of them, "pride" flowing from "fullness of bread," caused by the fertility of the soil (Gen. 13:10), and producing "idleness." **abundance of idleness**—lit., "the secure carelessness of ease" or idleness. **neither did she strengthen . . . the poor**—Pride is always cruel; it arrogates to itself all things, and despises brethren, for whose needs it therefore has no feeling; as Moab had not for the outcast Jews (Isa. 16:3, 4; Jer. 48:27; Luke 16:19-21; Jas. 5:1-5). **50. haughty**—puffed up with prosperity. **abomination before me**—"sinners *before the Lord*" (Gen. 13:13); said of those whose sin is so heinous as to cry out to God for immediate judgments; presumptuous sins, daring God *to the face* (Gen. 18:20; 19:5). **I took them away**—(Gen. 19:24). **as I saw good**—rather, "according to what I saw"; referring to Genesis 18:21, where God says, "I will go down, and *see* whether they have done altogether *according* to the cry of it which is come unto Me." **51. Samaria**—the kingdom of the ten tribes of Israel less guilty than Judah; for Judah betrayed greater ingratitude, having greater privileges, viz., the temple, the priesthood, and the regular order of kings. **justified thy sisters**—made them appear almost innocent by com-

ADAM CLARKE

42. *I will be quiet, and will be no more angry.* I will completely abandon you, have nothing more to do with you, think no more of you. When God in judgment ceases to reprehend, this is the severest judgment.

46. *Thine elder sister is Samaria, she and her daughters that dwell at thy left.* It is supposed that the prophet by Sodom in this place means the Israelites that dwelt beyond Jordan, in the land of the Moabites and Ammonites, or rather of the Moabites and Ammonites themselves. Literally, Sodom could not be called the younger sister of Jerusalem, as it existed before Jerusalem had a name. In looking east from Jerusalem, Samaria was on the left, and Sodom on the right hand; that is, the first was on the north, the second on the south of Jerusalem.

MATTHEW HENRY

They pretended, in their haughtiness to *judge them*, and in the days of old, when they retained their integrity, they did judge them, *v.* 52. It will look like some extenuation of their sins that, bad as they were, Jerusalem was worse. For this they ought themselves to be greatly ashamed: "Thou who hast *judged thy sisters*, and cried out shame on them, now *bear thy own shame, for thy sins which thou hast committed* are *more abominable than theirs*," *v.* 52. There is nothing in sin which we have more reason to be ashamed of than that by our sin we have encouraged others in sin.

They had looked with so much disdain upon their neighbours: *Thy sister Sodom was not mentioned by thee in the day of thy pride*, *v.* 56. If the Jews had but talked more frequently and seriously to one another, and to their children, concerning *the wrath of God revealed from heaven* against *Sodom's ungodliness and unrighteousness*, it might have prevented their treading in their steps.

4. What desolations God had brought and was bringing upon Jerusalem for these wickednesses, wherein they had exceeded Sodom and Samaria. (1) She has already long ago been disgraced, and has fallen into contempt, among her neighbours (*v.* 57). (2) She is now *in captivity*, or hastening into captivity, not only for her lewdness (*v.* 58), but for her perfidiousness and covenant-breaking (*v.* 59). Those that will not adhere to God as their God have no reason to expect that he should continue to own them as his people. (3) The captivity of the wicked Jews, and their ruin, shall be as irrevocable as that of Sodom and Samaria. In this sense, as a threatening, most interpreters take *v.* 53, 55. Sodom and Samaria were never brought back, nor ever returned to their former estate, and therefore let not Jerusalem expect it, that is, those who now remained there, whom God would *deliver to be removed into all the kingdoms of the earth for their hurt*, Jer. xxiv. 9, 10.

Verses 60–63

In the close of the chapter, after a most shameful conviction of sin and most dreadful judgments, mercy is remembered, for those who shall come after. As was when God swore in his wrath concerning those who came out of Egypt that they should not enter Canaan, "Yet" (says God) "your little ones shall"; so here. And some think that what is said of the return of Sodom and Samaria (*v.* 53, 55), and of Jerusalem with them, is a promise; it may be understood so, if by Sodom we understand the Moabites and Ammonites, the posterity of Lot, who once dwelt in Sodom (Jer. xlviii. 47; xlix. 6). But these closing verses are, without doubt, a precious promise, which was in part fulfilled at the return of the penitent and reformed Jews out of Babylon, but was to have its full accomplishment in gospel-times, and in that *repentance and* that *remission of sins preached to all nations, beginning at Jerusalem.*

I. This mercy should take rise—from *God himself*, and his *remembering his covenant* with them (*v.* 60): "*Nevertheless, I will remember my covenant with thee*, that covenant which I made with thee *in the days of thy youth*, and will revive it again. Though thou hast *broken the covenant* (*v.* 59), I will remember it, and it shall flourish again."

II. They should be prepared and qualified for this mercy (*v.* 61): "*Thou shalt remember thy ways*, thy evil ways; God will put thee in mind of them, will set them in order before thee, that thou mayest be *ashamed of them*."

JAMIESON, FAUSSET, BROWN

parison with thy guilt (Jer. 3:11; Matt. 12:41, 42). **52. Thou . . . which hast judged . . . bear thine own**—(Matt. 7:1, 2; Rom. 2:1, 17-23). Judah had judged Sodom (representing the heathen nations) and Samaria (Israel), saying they were justly punished, as if she herself was innocent (Luke 13:2). **thy shame**—ignominious punishment. **53.** Here follows a promise of restoration. Even the sore chastisements coming on Judah would fail to reform its people; God's returning goodness alone would effect this, to show how entirely of grace was to be their restoration. The restoration of her erring sisters is mentioned before hers, even as their punishment preceded her punishment; so all self-boasting is excluded [Fairbairn]. "Ye shall, indeed, at some time or other return, but Moab and Ammon shall return with you, and some of the ten tribes" [Grotius]. **bring again . . . captivity**—i.e., change the affliction into prosperity (so Job 42:10). Sodom itself was not so restored (Jer. 20:16), but Ammon and Moab (her representatives, as sprung from Lot who dwelt in Sodom) were (Jer. 48:47; 49:6); probably most of the ten tribes and the adjoining nations, Ammon and Moab, etc., were in part restored under Cyrus; but the full realization of the restoration is yet future; *the heathen nations* to be brought to Christ being typified by "Sodom," whose sins they now reproduce (Deut. 32:32). **captivity of thy captives**—lit., "of thy captivities." However, the gracious promise rather begins with the "nevertheless" (vs. 60), not here; for vs. 59 is a threat, not a promise. The sense here thus is, Thou shalt be restored when Sodom and Samaria are, but not till then (vs. 55), i.e., *never*. This applies to the guilty who should be utterly destroyed (vss. 41, 42); but it does not contradict the subsequent promise of restoration to their posterity (Num. 14:29-33), and to the elect remnant of grace [Calvin]. **54. bear thine own shame**—by being put on a level with those whom thou hast so much despised. **thou art a comfort unto them**—since they see thee as miserable as themselves. It is a kind of melancholy "comfort" to those chastised to see others as sorely punished as themselves (ch. 14:22, 23). **55.** (*Note*, vs. 53.) **56. Sodom was not mentioned**—lit., "was not for a report." Thou didst not deign to mention her name as if her case could possibly apply as a warning to thee, but it did apply (II Pet. 2:6). **57. Before thy wickedness was discovered**—manifested to all, viz., by the punishment inflicted on thee. **thy reproach of . . . Syria and . . . Philistines**—the indignity and injuries done thee by Syria and the Philistines (II Kings 16:5; II Chron. 28:18; Isa. 9:11, 12). **58. borne thy lewdness**—i.e., the punishment of it (ch. 23:49). I do not treat thee with excessive rigor. Thy sin and punishment are exactly commensurate. **59. the oath**—the covenant between God and Israel (Deut. 29:12, 14). As thou hast despised it, so will I despise thee. No covenant is one-sided; where Israel broke faith, God's promise of favor ceased. **60.** The promise here bursts forth unexpectedly like the sun from the dark clouds. With all her forgetfulness of God, God still remembers her; showing that her redemption is altogether of grace. Contrast "I will remember," with "thou hast not remembered" (vss. 22, 43); also "*My* covenant," with "*Thy* covenant" (vs. 61; Ps. 106:45); then the effect produced on her is (vs. 63) "that thou mayest remember." God's promise was one of *promise* and of *grace*. The law, *in its letter*, was *Israel's* ("thy") *covenant*, and in this restricted view was long subsequent (Gal. 3:17). Israel interpreted it as a covenant of works, which she while boasting of, failed to fulfil, and so fell under its condemnation (II Cor. 3:3, 6). The law, *in its spirit*, contains the germ of the Gospel; the New Testament is the full development of the Old, the husk of the outer form being laid aside when the inner spirit was fulfilled in Messiah. God's covenant with Israel, in the person of Abraham, was the reason why, notwithstanding all her guilt, mercy was, and is, in store for her. Therefore the heathen or Gentile nations must come to her for blessings, not she to them. **everlasting covenant**—(ch. 37:26; II Sam. 23:5; Isa. 55:3). The temporary forms of the law were to be laid aside, that in its permanent and "everlasting" spirit it might be established (Jer. 31:31-37; 32:40; 50:4, 5; Heb. 8:8-13). **61. thou shalt remember**—It is God who first remembers her before she remembers Him and her own ways before Him (vs. 60; ch. 20:43; 36:31). **ashamed**—the fruit of repentance (II Cor. 7:10, 11). None please God unless those who displease themselves; a foretaste of the Gospel (Luke 18:9-14). **I will give them unto thee for daughters**—(Isa. 54:1; 60:3, 4; Gal. 4:26, etc.). All the heathen nations, not merely Sodom and Samaria, are meant by "thy

ADAM CLARKE

52. *They are more righteous than thou.* "They shall be justified more than you." They are less guilty in the sight of God, for their crimes were not accompanied with so many aggravations.

60. *I will remember my covenant.* That is, the covenant I made with Abraham in the day of your youth, when in him you began to be a nation.

KEIL-DELITZSCH:

Samaria and Sodom are called sisters of Jerusalem, not because both cities belonged to the same mother-land of Canaan, for the origin of the cities does not come into consideration here at all, and cities represent the kingdoms, as the additional words "her daughters," that is to say, the cities of a land or kingdom dependent upon the capital, clearly prove. Samaria and Sodom, with the daughter cities belonging to them, are sisters of Jerusalem in a spiritual sense, as animated by the same spirit of idolatry. Samaria is called the great (greater) sister of Jerusalem, and Sodom the smaller sister. This is not equivalent to the older and the younger, for Samaria was not more deeply sunk in idolatry than Sodom, nor was her idolatry more ancient than that of Sodom (Theodoret and Grotius); and Hävernick's explanation, that "the finer form of idolatry, the mixture of the worship of Jehovah with that of nature, as represented by Samaria, was the first to find an entrance into Judah, and this was afterwards followed by the coarser abominations of heathenism," is unsatisfactory, for the simple reason that, according to the historical books of the Old Testament, the coarser forms of idolatry forced their way into Judah at quite as early a period as the more refined. The idolatry of the time of Rehoboam and Abijam was not merely a mixture of Jehovah-worship with the worship of nature, but the introduction of heathen idols into Judah, along with which there is no doubt that the syncretistic worship of the high places was also practiced.

—*Commentary on the Old Testament*

MATTHEW HENRY

III. The mercy that God has in reserve for them. 1. He will take them into covenant with himself (*v.* 60): *I will establish unto thee an everlasting covenant;* and again (*v.* 62), *I will establish*, re-establish, and establish more firmly than ever, *my covenant with thee.* 2. He will bring the Gentiles into church-communion with them (*v.* 61): "*Thou shalt receive thy sisters*, the Gentile nations that are round about thee, *thy elder and thy younger*, ancient nations and modern, and *I will give them unto thee for daughters*; they shall be nursed and educated, by that gospel which shall *go forth from* Zion and from *Jerusalem*; so that all the neighbours shall call Jerusalem *mother*. They shall be thy *daughters*, but *not by thy covenant*, not as being proselytes to the Jewish religion, but as being converts with thee to the Christian religion." Or *not by thy covenant* may mean, "not upon such terms as thou shalt think fit to impose upon them as conquered nations, to whom thou mayest give law at pleasure; they shall be thy *daughters by my covenant*, the covenant of grace made with thee and them. I will be a Father both to Jews and Gentiles, and so they shall become sisters to one another."

IV. What the fruit and effect of this will be. 1. God will hereby be glorified (*v.* 62): "*Thou shalt know that I am the Lord.* It shall hereby be known that the God of Israel is a God of power, faithful to his covenant." You shall know it to your comfort. 2. They shall hereby be more humbled for sin (*v.* 63): "*That thou mayest be* the more *confounded* at the *remembrance of all that thou hast done* amiss, and mayest never *open thy mouth any more* in contradiction to God, but mayest be for ever submissive *because of thy shame.*"

JAMIESON, FAUSSET, BROWN

sisters, elder and younger." In Jerusalem first, *individual* believers were gathered into the elect Church. From Jerusalem the Gospel went forth to gather in *individuals* of the Gentiles; and Judah with Jerusalem shall also be the first *nation* which, as such, shall be converted to Christ; and to her the other *nations* shall attach themselves as believers in Messiah, Jerusalem's King (Ps. 110:2; Isa. 2:2, 3). "The king's daughter" in Psalm 45:12-14 is Judah; her "companions," as "the daughter of Tyre," are the nations given to her as converts, here called "daughters." **not by thy covenant**—This does not set aside the Old Testament in its spirit, but in its mere letter on which the Jews had rested, while they broke it: the latter ("thy covenant") was to give place to *God's* covenant of grace and promise in Christ who "fulfilled" the law. God means, "not that thou on thy part hast stood to the covenant, but that 'I am the Lord, I change not' (Mal. 3:6) from My original love to thee in thy youth" (see Rom. 3:3). **62.** (Hos. 2:19, 20.) **thou shalt know that I am the Lord**—not, as elsewhere, by the judgments falling on thee, but by My so marvellously restoring thee through grace. **63. never open thy mouth**—in vindication, or even palliation, of thyself, or expostulation with God for His dealings (Rom. 3:19), when thou seest thine own exceeding unworthiness, and My superabounding grace which has so wonderfully overcome with love thy sin (Rom. 5:20). "If we would judge ourselves, we should not be judged" (I Cor. 11:31). **all that thou hast done**—enhancing the grace of God which has pardoned so many and so great sins. Nothing so melts into love and humility as the sense of the riches of God's pardoning grace (Luke 7:47).

ADAM CLARKE

61. *Thy sisters, thine elder and thy younger.* The Gentiles, who were before the Jews were called, and after the Jews were cast off, are here termed the elder and younger sister. These were to be given to Jerusalem for daughters; the latter should be converted to God by the ministry of men who should spring out of the Jewish church.

63. *When I am pacified toward thee.* This intimates that the Jews shall certainly share in the blessings of the gospel covenant, and that they shall be restored to the favor and image of God. And when shall this be? Whenever they please.

MATTHEW HENRY

CHAPTER 17

Verses 1–21

1. The prophet is appointed to *put forth a riddle* to the *house of Israel* (*v.* 2), not to puzzle them for he is immediately to tell them the meaning of it. But he must deliver this message in a riddle or parable that they might the better remember it and tell it to others. Ministers should try various methods to do good; and should both bring that which is familiar into their preaching and their preaching too into their familiar discourse. 2. He is appointed to expound this riddle to *the rebellious house*, *v.* 12.

I. Nebuchadnezzar had some time ago carried off Jehoiachin, the same that was called *Jeconiah*, when he was but eighteen years of age and had reigned in Jerusalem but *three months*, him and his great men, and had brought them captives to Babylon, 2 Kings xxiv. 12. This in the parable is represented by an eagle's cropping the top and tender branch of *a cedar*, and carrying it into *a land of traffic*, a *city of merchants* (*v.* 3, 4), which is explained, *v.* 12. The *king of Babylon* took the *king of Jerusalem*, who was no more able to resist him than a young twig of a tree is to contend with the strongest bird of prey, that easily crops it off, perhaps towards the making of *her nest*. Nebuchadnezzar, in this parable, is the king of birds, a *great eagle*, that lives upon spoil. His dominion extends itself far and wide, like the great and long wings of an eagle; the people are numerous, for it is *full of feathers*; the court is splendid, for it has *divers colours*, which look like *embroidering*, as the word is. Jerusalem is Lebanon, a forest of houses.

The royal family is *the cedar*; Jehoiachin is the *top branch*, the *top of the young twigs*. Babylon is the *land of traffic* and *city of merchants* where it is set.

II. When he carried him to Babylon he made his uncle Zedekiah king in his room, *v.* 5, 6. His name was *Mattaniah—the gift of the Lord*, which Nebuchadnezzar changed into *Zedekiah—the justice of the Lord*, to remind him to be just like the God he called his. This was *one of the seed of the land*, a native, not one

JAMIESON, FAUSSET, BROWN

CHAPTER 17

Vss. 1-24. Parable of the Two Great Eagles, and the Cropping of the Cedar of Lebanon. Judah Is to Be Judged for Revolting from Babylon, Which Had Set Up Zedekiah instead of Jehoiachin, to Egypt; God Himself, as the Rival of the Babylonian King, Is to Plant the Gospel Cedar of Messiah. The date of the prophecy is between the sixth month of Zedekiah's sixth year of reign and the fifth month of the seventh year after the carrying away of Jehoiachin, i.e., five years before the destruction of Jerusalem [Henderson]. **2. riddle**—a continued allegory, expressed enigmatically, requiring more than common acumen and serious thought. The *Hebrew* is derived from a root, "sharp," i.e., calculated to stimulate attention and whet the intellect. Distinct from "fable," in that it teaches not fiction, but fact. Not like the ordinary riddle, designed to puzzle, but to instruct. The "riddle" is here identical with the "parable," only that the former refers to the obscurity, the latter to the likeness of the figure to the thing compared. **3. eagle**—the king of birds. The literal *Hebrew* is, "*the* great eagle." The symbol of the Assyrian supreme god, *Nisroch;* so applied to "the great king" of Babylon, his vicegerent on earth (Jer. 48:40; 49:22). His "wings" are his great forces. Such symbols were familiar to the Jews, who saw them portrayed on the great buildings of Babylon; such as are now seen in the Assyrian remains. **long-winged**—implying the wide extent of his empire. **full of feathers**—when they have been renewed after moulting; and so in the full freshness of renovated youth (Ps. 103:5; Isa. 40:31). Answering to the many peoples which, as tributaries, constituted the strength of Babylon: **divers colours**—the golden eagle, marked with starlike spots, supposed to be the largest of eagles [Bochart]. Answering to the variety of languages, habits, and costumes of the peoples subject to Babylon. **came unto Lebanon**—continuing the methaphor: as the eagle frequents mountains, not cities. The temple at Jerusalem was called "Lebanon" by the Jews [Eusebius], because its woodwork was wholly of cedars of Lebanon. "The mountain of the Lord's house" (Isa. 2:2). *Jerusalem*, however, is chiefly meant, the chief seat of civil honor, as Lebanon was of external elevation. **took the highest branch**—King Jeconiah, then but eighteen years old, and many of the chiefs and people with him (II Kings 24:8, 12-16). The *Hebrew* for "highest branch" is, properly, the *fleecelike tuft* at the top of the tree. (So in ch. 31:3-14.) The cedar, as a tall tree, is the symbol of kingly elevation (cf. Dan. 4:10-12). **4. land of traffic . . . merchants**—Babylon (II Kings 24:15, 16), famous for its transport traffic on the Tigris and Euphrates. Also, by its connection with the Persian Gulf, it carried on much commerce with India. **5. seed of the land**—not a foreign production, but one native in the region; a son of the

ADAM CLARKE

CHAPTER 17

2. *Son of man, put forth a riddle.* An instrument formerly used for divination. This is not far removed from the Hebrew *chidah,* from *chad,* "to penetrate"; not that which penetrates the mind, but which we must penetrate to find out the sense.

3. *A great eagle.* Nebuchadnezzar. See Jer. xlviii. 40; xlix. 22; Dan. vii. 4. And see here, v. 12, where it is so applied. *Great wings.* Extensive empire.

Long-winged. Rapid in his conquests. *Full of feathers.* Having multitudes of subjects.

Divers colours. People of various nations. *Came unto Lebanon.* Came against Judea.

The highest branch. King Jehoiachin he took captive to Babylon. *The cedar.* The Jewish state and king.

4. *The top of his young twigs.* The princes of Judah. *A land of traffic.* Chaldea. *A city of merchants.* Babylon, for which this city was the most celebrated of all the cities of the East. Its situation procured it innumerable advantages; its two rivers, the Tigris and Euphrates, and the Persian Gulf, gave it communication with the richest and the most distant nations.

5. *The seed of the land.* Zedekiah, brother

MATTHEW HENRY

of his Babylonian princes; he was *planted in a fruitful field*, for so Jerusalem as yet was; he *placed it by great waters*, like *a willow-tree*, which grows quickly, and grows best in moist ground, but is never expected to be a stately tree. He *set it with* care and *circumspection* (so some read it); that it might grow, but that it might not grow too big. *He took of the king's seed* (so it is explained, *v.* 13) and *made a covenant with him* that he should have the kingdom, and enjoy regal power, provided he held it as his vassal. He *took an oath of him*, made him swear allegiance by his own God, the God of Israel, that he would be a faithful tributary to him, 2 Chron. xxxvi. 13. He also *took away the mighty of the land*, the chief of the men of war, as hostages for the performance of the covenant, and that the king might be the less in temptation, to break his league. What he designed we are told (*v.* 14): *That the kingdom might be base*, might neither be a rival with its powerful neighbours, nor a terror to its feeble ones, that *it might not lift up itself* to vie with the kingdom of Babylon. But yet he designed that by *the keeping of this covenant it might stand*, and continue a kingdom. How sad a change sin made with the royal family of Judah. Time was when all the nations about were tributaries.

III. Zedekiah, while he continued faithful to the king of Babylon, did very well, and, if he would but have reformed his kingdom, and returned to God and his duty, he might soon have recovered his former dignity, *v.* 6. This plant grew, and though it was *set as a willow-tree*, and little account was made of it, yet it became *a spreading vine of low stature*, a blessing to his own country, and his fruits *made glad their hearts*; and it is better to be a spreading vine of low stature than a lofty cedar of no use. Nebuchadnezzar was pleased, for *the branches turned towards him*, and rested on him as the vine on the wall, and he had his share of the fruits of this vine; *the roots thereof* too were *under him*, and at his disposal. The Jews had reason to be pleased, for they sat under their own vine, which *brought forth branches, and shot forth sprigs*. See how gradually the judgments of God came upon this provoking people, and so gave them space to repent. He made *their kingdom base*, to try if that would humble them.

IV. Zedekiah knew not when he was well off, but grew impatient of being a tributary to the king of Babylon, and entered into a private league with the king of Egypt. If he had dealt faithfully, he might have been *a goodly vine*. But there was *another great eagle* that he had an affection for, and put a confidence in, and that was the *king of Egypt*, *v.* 7. Those two great potentates, the kings of Babylon and Egypt, were two great eagles, *birds of prey*. This great eagle of Egypt is said to have *great wings*, but not to be *long-winged* as the king of Babylon, because it was not of such a vast extent as that of Babylon was. The great eagle is said to have *many feathers*, much wealth and many soldiers, but which really were no more than so *many feathers*. Zedekiah, promising himself liberty, made himself a vassal to the king of Egypt. Now *this vine* did secretly and under-hand *bend her roots towards* the king of Egypt, and after awhile did openly *shoot forth her branches towards him*, give him an intimation how much she coveted an alliance with him, *that he might water it by the furrows of her plantation*, whereas it was *planted by great waters*, and did not need any assistance from him. This is expounded, *v.* 15. Zedekiah rebelled against the king of Babylon in *sending his ambassadors into Egypt*, that they might *give him horses and much people*, to enable him to contend with the king of Babylon.

V. God here threatens Zedekiah with the utter destruction of him and his kingdom, for his treacherous revolt from the king of Babylon. This is represented in the parable (*v.* 9, 19) by the *plucking up of this vine by the roots, the cutting off of the fruit*, and *the withering of the leaves*. The project shall be blasted; it shall *utterly wither*. Shall he *break the covenant, and be delivered* from that vengeance which is the just punishment of his treachery?

1. His doom is ratified by the oath of God (*v.* 16): *As I live, saith the Lord God, he shall die* for it.

2. It is justified by the heinousness of the crime he had been guilty of. He had been very ungrateful to his benefactor, who had *made him king*, and had made him a prince when he might as easily have made him a prisoner. He had been very false. He *despised the oath* and *broke it*, *v.* 15, 16, 18, 19. The oath by which he had bound himself to the king of Babylon was a solemn oath.

JAMIESON, FAUSSET, BROWN

soil, not a foreigner: Zedekiah, uncle of Jehoiachin, of David's family. **in a fruitful field**—lit., a "field of seed"; i.e., fit for propagating and continuing the seed of the royal family. **as a willow**—derived from a *Hebrew* root, "to overflow," from its fondness for water (Isa. 44:4). Judea was "a land of brooks of *water* and fountains" (Deut. 8:7-9; cf. John 3:23). **6. vine of low stature**—not now, as before, a stately "cedar"; the kingdom of Judah was to be prosperous, but not elevated. **branches turned toward him**—expressing the fealty of Zedekiah as a vassal looking up to Nebuchadnezzar, to whom Judah owed its peace and very existence as a separate state. The "branches" mean his sons and the other princes and nobles. **The roots . . . under him**—The stability of Judah depended on Babylon. The repetition "branches" and "springs" is in order to mark the ingratitude of Zedekiah, who, not content with moderate prosperity, revolted from him to whom he had sworn allegiance. **7. another . . . eagle**—the king of Egypt (vs. 15). The "long-winged" of vs. 3 is omitted, as Egypt had not such a wide empire and large armies as Babylon. **vine . . . bend . . . roots towards him**—lit., "thirsted after him with its roots"; expressing the longings after Egypt in the Jewish heart. Zedekiah sought the alliance of Egypt, as though by it he could throw off his dependence on Babylon (II Kings 24:7, 20; II Chron. 36:13; Jer. 37:5, 7). **water it by . . . furrows of . . . plantation**—i.e., *in* the garden beds (Judea) wherein (the vine) it was planted. Rather, "*by*" or "*out of* the furrows." It refers to the waters of Egypt, the Nile being made to water the fields by means of small canals or "furrows"; these waters are the figure of the auxiliary forces wherewith Egypt tried to help Judah. See the same figure, Isaiah 8:7. But see *Note*, vs. 10, "furrows *where it grew*." **8. It was planted in a good soil**—It was not want of the necessaries of life, nor oppression on the part of Nebuchadnezzar, which caused Zedekiah to revolt: it was gratuitous ambition, pride, and ingratitude. **9. Shall it prosper?**—Could it be that gratuitous treason should prosper? God will not allow it. "It," i.e., the vine. **he . . . pull up**—i.e., the first eagle, or Nebuchadnezzar. **in all . . . leaves of her spring**—i.e., all its springing (sprouting) leaves. **without great power or many**—It shall not need all the forces of Babylon to destroy it; a small division of the army will suffice because God will deliver it into Nebuchadnezzar's hand (Jer. 37:10). **10 being planted**—i.e., *though* planted, **east wind**—The east wind was noxious to vegetation in Palestine; a fit emblem of Babylon, which came from the northeast. **wither in . . . furrows where it grew**—Zedekiah was taken at Jericho, on Jewish soil (Jer. 52:8). "It shall wither, although it has furrows from which it expects continual waterings" [CALVIN], (ch. 19:12; Hos. 13:15). **12. Know ye not**—He upbraided them with moral, leading to intellectual, stupidity. **hath taken the king**—Jeconiah or Jehoiachin (II Kings 24:11, 12-16). **13. the king's seed**—Zedekiah, Jeconiah's uncle. **taken . . . oath of him**—swearing fealty as a vassal to Nebuchadnezzar (II Chron. 36:13). **also taken the mighty**—as hostages for the fulfilment of the covenant; whom, therefore, Zedekiah exposed to death by his treason. **14. That the kingdom might be base**—i.e., low as to national elevation by being Nebuchadnezzar's dependent; but, at the same time, safe and prosperous, if faithful to the "oath." Nebuchadnezzar dealt sincerely and openly in proposing conditions, and these moderate ones; therefore Zedekiah's treachery was the baser and was a counterpart to their treachery towards God. **15. he rebelled**—God permitted this because of His wrath against Jerusalem (II Kings 24: 20). **horses**—in which Egypt abounded and which were forbidden to Israel to seek from Egypt, or indeed to "multiply" at all (Deut. 17:16; Isa. 31:1, 3; cf. Isa. 36:9). DIODORUS SICULUS (1.45) says that the whole region from Thebes to Memphis was filled with royal stalls, so that 20,000 chariots with two horses in each could be furnished for war. **Shall he prosper?**—The third time this question is asked, with an indignant denial understood (vss. 9, 10). Even the heathen believed that breakers of an oath would not "escape" punishment. **16. in the place where the king dwelleth**—righteous retribution. He brought on himself in the worst form the evil which, in a mild form, he had sought to deliver himself from by perjured treachery, viz., vassalage (ch. 12: 13; Jer. 32:5; 34:3; 52:11). **17. Pharaoh**—Pharaoh-hophra (Jer. 37:7; 44:30), the successor of Necho (II Kings 23:29). **Neither . . . make for him**—lit., "*effect* (anything) *with* him," i.e., be of any avail to Zedekiah. Pharaoh did not *act in concert with* him, for he was himself compelled to retire to Egypt. **by casting up mounts . . .**—So far from Pharaoh doing so *for* Jerusalem, this was what Nebuchadnezzar did

ADAM CLARKE

of Jehoiachin. *Planted it in a fruitful field.* Made him king of Judea in place of his brother. *Placed it by great waters.* Put him under the protection of Babylon, situated on the confluence of the Tigris and Euphrates. *And set it as a willow tree.* Made him dependent on this city of great waters, as the willow is on humidity.

6. *A spreading vine of low stature.* The Jewish state having then no height of dominion, it must abide under the wings or branches of the Chaldean king. *Whose branches turned toward him, and the roots . . . under him.* Zedekiah was wholly dependent on Nebuchadnezzar, for both his elevation to the throne and his support on it.

7. *Another great eagle.* Pharaoh-hophra, or Apries, king of Egypt. *With great wings.* Extensive dominion. *And many feathers.* Numerous subjects. *Did bend her roots.* Looked to him for support in her intended rebellion against Nebuchadnezzar.

8. *It was planted in a good soil.* Though he depended on Babylon, he lived and reigned as Nebuchadnezzar's vicegerent in the land of Judea.

9 *Shall it prosper?* Shall Zedekiah succeed in casting off the yoke of the king of Babylon, to whom he had sworn fealty? *Shall he not pull up the roots?* Nebuchadnezzar will come and dethrone him. *And cut off the fruit.* The children of Zedekiah. *The leaves.* All the nobles; all shall perish with Zedekiah.

10. *Shall . . . utterly wither.* The regal govermnent shall be no more restored. Zedekiah shall be the last king, and the monarchy shall finally terminate with him.

12. *Know ye not what these things mean?* They are explained in this and the following verses.

15. *Sending his ambassadors into Egypt.* Zedekiah must have sent his ambassadors into Egypt between the sixth month of his sixth year and the fifth month of his seventh year. Compare chap. viii. 1 with chap. xx. 1.

16. *In the midst of Babylon he shall die.* His eyes were put out; he was carried to Babylon, and never returned.

MATTHEW HENRY

An emphasis is laid upon this (*v.* 18): *When, lo, he had given his hand*, as a confederate with the king of Babylon, as his friend, the joining of hands being a token of the joining of hearts. God says (*v.* 19): It is *my oath* that he has despised and *my covenant that he has broken.* The oath of allegiance to a prince is particularly called *the oath of God* (Eccles. viii. 2). Now Zedekiah's breaking this oath is the sin which God will *recompense upon his own head* (*v.* 19), the *trespass which he has trespassed against God, v.* 20. Though Nebuchadnezzar was a worshipper of false gods, yet the true God will avenge this quarrel when one of his worshippers breaks his league with him; for truth is a debt due to all men. Having *despised the oath*, and *broken the covenant*, he *shall not escape.*

3. The punishment is made to answer the sin. He had rebelled against the king of Babylon, and the king of Babylon should be his effectual conqueror, *v.* 16. God himself will now take part with the king of Babylon against him: *I will spread my net upon him, v.* 20. He had *relied upon the king of Egypt*, and the king of Egypt should be his ineffectual helper: *Pharaoh with his mighty army shall not make for him in the war* (*v.* 17). On the approach of the Egyptian army, the Chaldeans withdrew from the siege of Jerusalem, upon their retreat they returned to it again and took it. Yet Zedekiah had bands but those bands, though we may suppose they were the best soldiers his kingdom afforded, shall become *fugitives*, shall *fall by the sword* of the enemy, *v.* 21. This was fulfilled *when the city was broken up and all the men of war fled*, Jer. lii. 7.

Verses 22–24

The unbelief of man shall not invalidate the promise of God. He will find out another *seed of David* in which it shall be accomplished.

I. The house of David shall again be magnified, and out of its ashes another phœnix shall arise. The metaphor of a tree, which was made use of in the threatening, is here presented in the promise, *v.* 22, 23. This promise had its accomplishment in part when Zerubbabel, a branch of the house of David, was raised up to head the Jews in their return out of captivity, and to rebuild the city and temple and re-establish their church and state; but it was to have its full accomplishment in the kingdom of the Messiah, Luke i. 32. 1. God himself undertakes the restoring of the house of David. Nebuchadnezzar had attempted the re-establishing of the house of David in dependence upon him, *v.* 5. But his plantation withered and was plucked up. "Well," says God, "the next shall be of my planting: *I will also take of the highest branch of the high cedar and I will set it.*" 2. The house of David is revived in a *tender one cropped from the top of his young twigs.* Zerubbabel was so; that which was hopeful in him was but the *day of small things* (Zech. iv. 10), yet before him *great mountains* were *made plain.* Our Lord Jesus was *the highest branch of the high cedar*, the furthest of all from *the root*, but the nearest of all to heaven, for his kingdom was not of this world. He was *taken from the top of the young twigs, a tender* plant, and a *root out of a dry ground* (Isa. liii. 2), but a *branch of righteousness, the planting of the Lord.* 3. This branch is planted *in a high mountain* (*v.* 22), in the *mountain of the height of Israel, v.* 23. Thither he brought Zerubbabel in triumph; there he raised up Jesus, to gather the *lost sheep of the house of Israel* that were *scattered upon the mountains*, set him *his king* upon *his holy hill of Zion*, sent forth the gospel from *Mount Zion, the word of the Lord from Jerusalem*; there was the Christian church first planted. The churches of Judæa were the most primitive churches. 4. Thence it spreads far and wide. The Jewish state, though it began very low in Zerubbabel's time, was set as a tender branch, which might easily be plucked up, yet took root, spread and after some time those of other nations, *fowl of every wing*, put themselves under the protection of it. When the Gentiles flocked into the church then did the *fowl of every wing* come and *dwell under the shadow of this goodly cedar.* See Dan. iv. 21.

II. God himself will herein be glorified, *v.* 24. Never was there a more full conviction given of this truth, that all things are governed by an infinitely wise and mighty Providence, than that which was given by the exaltation of Christ and the establishment of his kingdom among men. *All the trees of the field shall know*, 1. That the tree which God will have to be *brought down*, and *dried up*, shall be so. 2. That the trees which God will have to be exalted, and to flourish, shall so be, though ever so low, and ever so dry. The house of Nebuchadnezzar, that now makes so great a figure, shall be extirpated, and the house of

JAMIESON, FAUSSET, BROWN

against it (Jer. 52:4). CALVIN, MAURER, etc., refer it to *Nebuchadnezzar*, "when Nebuchadnezzar shall cast up mounts." **18. given his hand**—in ratification of the oath (II Kings 10:15; Ezra 10:19), and also in token of subjection to Nebuchadnezzar (I Chron. 29: 24, *Margin;* II Chron. 30:8, *Margin;* Lam. 5:6). **19. mine oath**—The "covenant" being sworn in God's name was really *His* covenant; a new instance in relation to man of the treacherous spirit which had been so often betrayed in relation to God. God Himself must therefore avenge the violation of *His covenant* "on the head" of the perjurer (cf. Ps. 7:16).

20. my net—(ch. 12:13; 32:3). God entraps him as he had tried to entrap others (Ps. 7:15). This was spoken at least upwards of three years before the fall of Jerusalem (cf. ch. 8:1, with ch. 20:1).

21. all his fugitives—the soldiers that accompany him in his flight.

22. When the state of Israel shall seem past recovery, Messiah, Jehovah Himself, will unexpectedly appear on the scene as Redeemer of His people (Isa. 63:5).

I . . . also—God opposes Himself to Nebuchadnezzar: "*He* took of the seed of the land and planted it (vss. 3, 5), so will *I*, but with better success than he had. The branch he plucked (Zedekiah) and planted, flourished but for a time, to perish at last; *I* will plant a scion of the same tree, the house of David, to whom the kingdom belongs by an everlasting covenant, and it shall be the shelter of the whole world, and shall be for ever." **branch**—the peculiar title of Messiah (Zech. 3:8; 6:12; Isa. 11:1; 4:2; Jer. 23:5; 33:15). **a tender one**—Zerubbabel never reigned as a universal (vs. 23) king, nor could the great things mentioned here be said of him, except as a type of Messiah. Messiah alone can be meant: originally "a *tender* plant and root out of a dry ground" (Isa. 53:2); the beginning of His kingdom being humble, His reputed parents of lowly rank, though King David's lineal representatives; yet, even then, God here calls Him, in respect to His everlasting purpose, "the highest . . . of the high" (Ps. 89:27). **I . . . will plant it upon an high mountain**—Zion; destined to be the *moral* center and eminence of grace and glory shining forth to the world, outtopping all mundane elevation. The kingdom, typically begun at the return from Babylon, and the rebuilding of the temple, fully began with Christ's appearing, and shall have its highest manifestation at His reappearing to reign on Zion, and thence over the whole earth (Ps. 2:6, 8; Isa. 2:2, 3; Jer. 3:17). **23. under it . . . all fowl**—the Gospel "mustard tree," small at first, but at length receiving all under its covert (Matt. 13:32); the antithesis to Antichrist, symbolized by Assyria, of which the same is said (ch. 31:6), and Babylon (Dan. 4:12). Antichrist assumes in mimicry the universal power really belonging to Christ. **24. I . . . brought down the high**—the very attribute given to God by the virgin mother of Him, under whom this was to be accomplished. **high . . . low tree**—i.e., princes elevated . . . lowered. All the empires of the world, represented by Babylon, once flourishing ("green"), shall be brought low before the once depressed ("dry"), but then exalted, kingdom of Messiah and His people, the head of whom shall be Israel (Dan. 2:44).

ADAM CLARKE

18. *Seeing he despised the oath.* This God particularly resents. He had bound himself by oath, in the presence of Jehovah, to be faithful to the covenant that he made with Nebuchadnezzar, and he took the first opportunity to break it; therefore he shall not escape.

21. *All his fugitives.* All who attempted to escape with him, and all that ran to Egypt shall fall by the sword.

22. *I will also take of the highest branch of the high cedar.* I will raise up another monarchy, which shall come in the line of David, namely, the Messiah; who shall appear as a tender plant, as to His incarnation; but He shall be high and eminent; His Church, the royal city, the highest and purest ever seen on the face of the earth.

23. *In the mountain of the height of Israel.* He shall make His appearance at the Temple, and found His Church at Jerusalem. *Shall bring forth boughs.* Apostles, evangelists, and their successors in the gospel ministry. *And bear fruit.* Multitudes of souls shall be converted by their preaching. *And under it shall dwell all fowl of every wing.* All the nations of the earth shall receive His gospel. *In the shadow of the branches thereof shall they dwell.* Trust in Him alone for salvation, and be saved in their trusting.

24. *All the trees of the field shall know.* All the people of Israel and of Chaldea. *I the Lord have brought down the high tree.* Have dethroned Jehoiachin. *Have exalted the low tree.* Put Zedekiah, brother of Jehoiachin, in his place. *Have dried up the green tree.* Zedekiah, who had numerous children, but who were all slain before his eyes at Riblah. *And have made the dry tree to flourish.* Have raised up a rod out of the stem of Jesse, the family of David being then apparently dried up and extinct. This was the promised Messiah, of the increase and government of whose Kingdom

MATTHEW HENRY

David that now makes so mean a figure, shall become famous again; and the Jewish nation, that is now despicable, shall be considerable. The kingdom of Satan, that has borne so long a sway, shall be broken, and the kingdom of Christ, that was looked upon with contempt, shall be established.

CHAPTER 18

Verses 1–9

Sometimes evil proverbs beget good prophecies.

I. An evil proverb commonly used by the Jews in their captivity. *This* charges God with injustice: "You use this proverb *concerning the land of Israel*, now that it is laid waste by the judgments of God, saying, *The fathers have eaten sour grapes and the children's teeth are set on edge;* we are punished for the sins of our ancestors, which is as absurd as if the children should have their teeth set on edge by the fathers' eating sour grapes, whereas, if men eat or drink anything amiss, they only themselves suffer by it." Now God had often said that he would *visit the iniquity of the fathers upon the children*, especially the sin of idolatry, intending thereby to express the evil of sin. He had often declared by his prophets that in bringing the present ruin upon Judah and Jerusalem he had an eye to the sins of Manasseh and other preceding kings. They intended it as a reflection upon God. It is true that those who are guilty of wilful sin *eat sour grapes*; they will set the sinner's teeth on edge. When conscience is awake it will spoil the relish. But they suggest it as unreasonable that the children should smart for the fathers' folly and feel the pain of that which they never tasted.

II. A just reply to this proverb: "Your own consciences shall tell you that you yourselves have eaten the same sour grapes that your fathers ate before you, or else your teeth would not have been set on edge." God does not punish the children for the fathers' sins unless they tread in their fathers' steps and *fill up the measure of their iniquity* (Matt. xxiii. 32). It is only in temporal calamities that children fare the worse for their parents' wickedness, and God can make them work for good to those that are visited with them; but as to spiritual and eternal misery (and that is the death here spoken of) the children shall by no means smart for the parents' sins. He asserts his own absolute sovereignty: *Behold, all souls are mine, v.* 4. He that is the Maker of *all things* is in a particular manner the *Father of spirits*, for his image is stamped on the souls of men; it was so in their creation; it is so in their renovation. He *forms the spirit of man within him.* God bears a goodwill both to father and son, and will put no hardship upon either. He has such a kindness for all souls that none die but through their own default.

Sin is the act of the *soul* therefore the punishment of sin is the *tribulation and the anguish of the soul,* Rom. ii. 9.

JAMIESON, FAUSSET, BROWN

CHAPTER 18

Vss. 1-32. The Parable of the Sour Grapes Reproved. Vindication of God's moral government as to His retributive righteousness from the Jewish imputation of injustice, as if they were suffering, not for their own sin, but for that of their fathers. As in ch. 17 he foretold Messiah's happy reign in Jerusalem, so now he warns them that its blessings can be theirs only upon their individually turning to righteousness. **2. fathers . . . eaten sour grapes, . . . children's teeth . . . set on edge**—Their unbelieving calumnies on God's justice had become so common as to have assumed a proverbial form. The sin of Adam in eating the forbidden fruit, visited on his posterity, seems to have suggested the peculiar form; noticed also by Jeremiah (31:29); and explained in Lamentations 5:7, "Our fathers have sinned, and are not; and we have borne their iniquities." They mean by "the children" *themselves,* as though they were innocent, whereas they were far from being so. The partial reformation effected since Manasseh's wicked reign, especially among the exiles at Chebar, was their ground for thinking so; but the improvement was only superficial and only fostered their self-righteous spirit, which sought anywhere but in themselves the cause of their calamities; just as the modern Jews attribute their present dispersion, not to their own sins, but to those of their forefathers. It is a universal mark of corrupt nature to lay the blame, which belongs to ourselves, on others and to arraign the justice of God. Cf. Genesis 3:12, where Adam transfers the blame of his sin to Eve, and even to God, "The *woman* whom *thou* gavest to be with me, she gave me of the tree, and I did eat." **3. ye shall not have occasion any more to use this proverb**—because I will let it be seen by the whole world in the very fact that you are not righteous, as ye fancy yourselves, but wicked, and that you suffer only the just penalty of your guilt; while the elect righteous remnant alone escapes. **4. all souls are mine**—Therefore I can deal with all, being My own creation, as I please (Jer. 18:6). As the Creator of all alike I can have no reason, but the principle of equity, according to men's works, to make any difference, so as to punish some, and to save others (Gen. 18:25). "The soul that sinneth it shall die." The curse descending from father to son assumes guilt shared in by the son; there is a natural tendency in the child to follow the sin of his father, and so he shares in the father's punishment: hence the principles of God's government, involved in Exodus 20:5 and Jeremiah 15.4, are justified. The sons, therefore (as the Jews here), cannot complain of being unjustly afflicted by God (Lam. 5:7); for they filled up the guilt of their fathers (Matt. 23:32, 34-36). The same God who "recompenses the iniquity of the fathers into the bosom of their children," is immediately after set forth as "giving to every man according to his ways" (Jer. 32:18, 19). In the same law (Exod. 20:5) which "visited the iniquities of the fathers upon the children unto the third and fourth generation" (where the explanation is added, "of them that *hate me,*" i.e., the *children hating God,* as well as their fathers: the former being too likely to follow their parents, sin going down with cumulative force from parent to child), we find (Deut. 24:16), "the fathers shall not be put to death for the children, neither the children for the fathers: every man shall be put to death for his own sin." The inherited guilt of sin in infants (Rom. 5:14) is an awful *fact,* but one met by the atonement of Christ; but it is of adults that he speaks here. Whatever penalties fall on *communities* for connection with sins of their fathers, *individual* adults who repent shall escape (II Kings 23:25, 26). This was no new thing, as some misinterpret the passage here; it had been *always* God's principle to punish only the guilty, and not also the innocent, for the sins of their fathers. God does not here change the principle of His administration, but is merely about to *manifest it* so personally to each that the Jews should no longer throw on God and on their fathers the blame which was their own. **soul that sinneth, it shall die**—and it *alone* (Rom. 6:23); not also the innocent. **5.** Here begins the illustration of God's impartiality in a series of supposed cases. The first case is given in vss. 5-9, the just man. The excellencies are selected in ref-

ADAM CLARKE

and "peace there shall be no end, upon the throne of David, and upon his kingdom, to order it and to establish it with judgment and justice from henceforth even for ever."

CHAPTER 18

2. *The fathers have eaten sour grapes, and the children's teeth are set on edge.* We have seen this proverb already, Jer. xxxi. 29, etc., and have considered its general meaning. But the subject is here proposed in greater detail, with a variety of circumstances, to adapt it to all those cases to which it should apply. It refers simply to these questions: How far can the moral evil of the parent be extended to his offspring? And, Are the faults and evil propensities of the parents, not only transferred to the children, but punished in them? Do parents transfer their evil nature, and are their children punished for their offenses?

3. *As I live, saith the Lord, God, ye shall not have occasion any more to use this proverb in Israel.* I will now, by this present declaration, settle this question forever.

4. *All souls are mine.* Equally so; I am the Father of the spirits of all flesh, and shall deal impartially with the whole.

The soul that sinneth, it shall die. None shall die for another's crimes; none shall be saved by another's righteousness.

MATTHEW HENRY

If a man be just, do judgment and justice (*v.* 5), *he shall surely live, saith the Lord God, v.* 9. A just man is careful to keep himself: 1. From sins against the second commandment. In the matters of God's worship he has not so much as *eaten upon the mountains*, that is, not had any communion with idolaters by *eating things sacrificed to idols*, 1 Cor. x. 20.

2. From sins against the seventh commandment. He will keep the appetites of the body always in subjection to reason and virtue. 3. From sins against the eighth commandment. He is a *just man*, who has not, by fraud, *oppressed any, spoiled any by violence, v.* 7.

A just man will not take advantage of his neighbour's necessity, but is willing to share in loss as well as profit.

This is his character towards his neighbours; to complete his character he must be so to his God likewise (*v.* 9). This is a just man, and *living he shall live.*

Verses 10–20

God, by the prophet, having laid down the general rule of judgment, comes, in these verses, to show that men's parentage shall not alter the case.

I. It often happens that godly parents have wicked children and wicked parents have godly children.

1. A wicked man shall perish in his iniquity, though he be the son of a pious father. He is here supposed to allow himself in all those enormities which his good father dreaded. This wicked man shall perish, notwithstanding his being the son of a good father.

2. A righteous man shall be happy, though he be the son of a wicked father. Though the father did eat the sour grapes, if the children do not meddle with them, they shall fare never the worse for that. The graceless father alone shall die in his iniquity, but his gracious son shall fare never the worse for it.

JAMIESON, FAUSSET, BROWN

erence to the prevailing sins of the age, from which such a one stood aloof; hence arises the omission of some features of righteousness, which, under different circumstances, would have been desirable to be enumerated. Each age has *its own* besetting temptations, and the just man will be distinguished by his guarding against the peculiar defilements, inward and outward, of his age. **just . . . lawful . . . right**—the duties of the second table of the law, which flow from the fear of God. Piety is the root of all charity; to render to each his own, as well to our neighbor, as to God. **6. not eaten upon . . . . mountains**—the high places, where altars were reared. A double sin: sacrificing elsewhere than at the temple, where only God sanctioned sacrifice (Deut. 12:13, 14); and this to idols instead of to Jehovah. "Eaten" refers to the feasts which were connected with the sacrifices (see Exod. 32:6; Deut. 32:38; Judg. 9:27; I Cor. 8:4, 10; 10:7). **lifted . . . eyes to**—viz., in adoration (Ps. 121:1). The superstitious are compared to harlots; their eyes go eagerly after spiritual lusts. The righteous man not merely refrains from the act, but from the *glance* of spiritual lust (Job 31:1; Matt. 5:28). **idols of . . . Israel**—not merely those of the Gentiles, but even those of Israel. The fashions of his countrymen could not lead him astray. **defiled . . . neighbour's wife**—Not only does he shrink from spiritual, but also from carnal, adultery (cf. I Cor. 6:18). **neither . . . menstruous woman**—Leprosy and elephantiasis were said to be the fruit of such a connection [JEROME]. Chastity is to be observed even towards one's own wife (Lev. 18:19; 20:18). **7. restored . . . pledge**—that which the poor debtor absolutely needed; as his raiment, which the creditor was bound to restore before sunset (Exod. 22:26, 27), and his millstone, which was needed for preparing his food (Deut. 24:6, 10-13). **bread to . . . hungry . . . covered . . . naked**—(Isa. 58:7; Matt. 25:35, 36). After duties of justice come those of benevolence. It is not enough to refrain from doing a wrong to our neighbor, we must also do him good. The bread owned by a man, though "his," is given to him, not to keep to himself, but to impart to the needy. **8. usury**—lit., "biting." The law forbade the Jew to take interest from brethren but permitted him to do so from a foreigner (Exod. 22:25; Deut. 23:19, 20; Neh. 5:7; Ps. 15:5). The letter of the law was restricted to the Jewish polity, and is not binding now; and indeed the principle of taking interest was even then sanctioned, by its being allowed in the case of a foreigner. The *spirit* of the law still binds us, that we are not to take advantage of our neighbor's necessities to enrich ourselves, but be satisfied with moderate, or even no, interest, in the case of the needy. **increase**—in the case of *other* kinds of wealth; as "usury" refers to *money* (Lev. 25:36). **withdrawn . . . hand . . .**—Where he has the opportunity and might find a plausible plea for promoting his own gain at the cost of a wrong to his neighbor, he keeps back his hand from what selfishness prompts. **judgment**—justice. **9. truly**—with integrity. **surely live**—lit., "live in life." Prosper in this life, but still more in the life to come (Prov. 3:1, 2; Amos 5:4). **10-13.** The second case is that of an impious son of a pious father. His pious parentage, so far from excusing, aggravates his guilt. **robber**—or lit., "a breaker," viz., through all constraints of right. **doeth the like to any one**—The *Hebrew* and the parallel (vs. 18) require us to translate rather, "doeth to his *brother* any of these things," viz., the things which follow in vs. 11, etc. [MAURER]. **11. those duties**—which his father did (vss. 5, 9). **12. oppressed the poor**—an aggravation to his oppressions, that they were practised against *the poor;* whereas in vs. 7 the expression is simply "oppressed *any.*" **abomination**—singular number referring to the particular one mentioned at the end of vs. 6. **13. shall he . . . live?**—because of the merits of his father; answering, by contrast, to "die for the iniquity of his father" (vs. 17). **his blood shall be upon him**—The cause of his bloody death shall rest with himself; God is not to blame, but is vindicated as just in punishing him. **14-18.** The third case: a son who walks not in the steps of an unrighteous father, but in the ways of God; e.g., Josiah, the pious son of guilty Amon; Hezekiah, of Ahaz (II Kings 16:18, 21, 22). **seeth . . . and considereth**—The same *Hebrew* stands for both verbs, "seeth . . . yea, seeth." The repetition implies the attentive observation needed, in order that the son may not be led astray by his father's bad example; as sons generally are blind to parents' sins, and even imitate them as if they were virtues. **17. taken off his hand from the poor**—i.e., *abstained* from oppressing the poor, when he had the opportunity of doing so with impunity.The different sense of the phrase in ch. 16:49, in reference to *re-*

ADAM CLARKE

5. *If a man be just, and do that which is lawful and right.* What is meant by this is immediately specified.

6. (1) *Hath not eaten upon the mountains.* Idolatrous worship was generally performed on mountains and hills; and those who offered sacrifices feasted on the sacrifice, and thus held communion with the idol.

(2) *Neither hath lifted up his eyes to the idols.* Has paid them no religious adoration; has trusted in them for nothing, and has not made prayer nor supplication before them. (3) *Neither hath defiled his neighbour's wife.* Has had no adulterous connection with any woman, to which idolatrous feasts and worship particularly led. (4) *Neither hath come near to a menstruous woman.* Has abstained from the use of the marriage-bed during the periodical indisposition of his wife, Lev. xx. 18.

7. (5) *Hath not oppressed any.* Has not used his power or influence to oppress, pain, or injure another. (6) *Hath restored to the debtor his pledge.* Has carefully surrendered the pawn or pledge when its owner came to redeem it. As the pledge is generally of more worth than that for which it is pledged, an unprincipled man will make some pretense to keep it, which is highly abominable in the sight of God. (7) *Hath spoiled none by violence.* Either by robbery or personal insult, for a man may be spoiled both ways. (8) *Hath given his bread to the hungry.* Has been kindhearted and charitable, especially to them that are in the deepest want. (9) *Hath covered the naked with a garment.* Has divided both his bread and his clothing with the necessitous.

8. (10) *Hath not given forth upon usury. Nasach* signifies "to bite"; *usury* is properly so termed, because it bites into and devours the principal. (11) *Neither hath taken any increase.* In lending has not required more than was lent. (12) *That hath withdrawn his hand from iniquity.* Never associates with those who act contrary to justice and equity. (13) *Hath executed true judgment between man and man.* Being swayed by neither prejudice, fear, nor favor. These thirteen points concern his social and civil relations.

10. *If he beget a son.* Who is the reverse of the above righteous character, according to the thirteen articles already specified and explained.

MATTHEW HENRY

II. He appeals to themselves then whether they did not wrong God with their proverb. "Thus plain the case is, and *yet you say, Does not the son bear the iniquity of the father?* No, he does not; he shall not if he will himself *do that which is lawful and right,*" *v.* 19. But this people that bore the iniquity of their fathers had not done that which is lawful and right, and therefore justly suffered for their own sin and had no reason to complain of God's proceedings against them as at all unjust, though they had reason to complain of the bad example their fathers had left them as very unkind. *Our fathers have sinned and are not, and we have borne their iniquity*, Lam. v. 7. It is true that there is a curse entailed upon wicked families, but it is as true that the entail may be cut off by repentance and reformation; let the impenitent and unreformed therefore thank themselves if they fall under it. The settled rule of judgment is therefore repeated (*v.* 20): *The soul that sins shall die*, and not another for it. What direction God has given to earthly judges (Deut. xxiv. 16) he will himself pursue: *The son shall not die*, not die eternally, *for the iniquity of the father*, if he do not tread in the steps of it, nor the father *for the iniquity of the son*, if he endeavour to do his duty for the preventing of it. In *the day of the revelation of the righteous judgment of God*, which is now clouded and eclipsed, *the righteousness of the righteous shall* appear before all the world to be *upon him*, to his everlasting comfort and honour, upon him as a robe, upon him as a crown; and *the wickedness of the wicked* shall be *upon him*, to his everlasting confusion, upon him as a chain, upon him as a load, as a mountain of lead to sink him to the bottomless pit.

Verses 21–29

Another rule of judgment by which is demonstrated the equity of God's government. Here he shows that he will reward or punish according to the change made in the person himself. While we are in this world we are in a state of probation; the time of trial lasts as long as the time of life.

I. The case fairly stated, much as it had been before (*ch.* iii. 18, &c.), and here it is laid down once (*v.* 21–24) and again (*v.* 26–28), because it is a matter of life and death.

1. A fair invitation given to wicked people, to turn from their wickedness. Assurance is given that, *if the wicked will turn*, he shall *surely live*, *v.* 21, 27.

A repenting returning sinner is conscious that his obedience for the future can never be compensation for his former disobedience; but God's nature and delight, is to have mercy and to forgive (*v.* 23).

2. A fair warning given to righteous people not to turn from their righteousness, *v.* 24–26.

JAMIESON, FAUSSET, BROWN

lieving the poor, seems to have suggested the reading followed by FAIRBAIRN, but not sanctioned by the *Hebrew*, "hath *not* turned his hand from . . . ." But ch. 20:22 uses the phrase in a somewhat similar sense to *English Version* here, *abstained from hurting*. **19.** Here the Jews object to the prophet's word and in their objection seem to seek a continuance of that very thing which they had originally made a matter of complaint. Therefore translate, "Wherefore doth not the son bear the iniquity of his father?" It now would seem a consolation to them to think the son might suffer for his father's misdeeds; for it would soothe their self-love to regard themselves as innocent sufferers for the guilt of others and would justify them in their present course of life, which they did not choose to abandon for a better. In reply, Ezekiel reiterates the truth of each being dealt with according to his own merits [FAIRBAIRN]. But GROTIUS supports *English Version*, wherein the Jews contradict the prophet, "Why (sayest thou so) doth not the son (often, as in our case, though innocent) bear (i.e., suffer for) the iniquity of their father?" Ezekiel replies, It is not as you say, but as I in the name of God say: "When the son hath done . . . ." *English Version* is simpler than that of FAIRBAIRN. **20. son shall not bear . . . iniquity of . . . father**—(Deut. 24:16; II Kings 14:6). **righteousness . . . wickedness**—i.e., the reward for righteousness . . . the punishment of wickedness. "Righteousness" is not used as if any were *absolutely* righteous; but, of such as have it *imputed* to them for Christ's sake, though not under the Old Testament themselves understanding the ground on which they were regarded as righteous, but sincerely seeking after it in the way of God's appointment, so far as they then understood this way. **21-24.** Two last cases, showing the equity of God: (1) The penitent sinner is dealt with according to his new obedience, not according to his former sins. (2) The righteous man who turns from righteousness to sin shall be punished for the latter, and his former righteousness will be of no avail to him **21. he shall surely live**—Despair drives men into hardened recklessness; God therefore allures men to repentance by holding out hope [CALVIN].

> To threats the stubborn sinner oft is hard,
> Wrapt in his crimes, against the storm prepared,
> But when the milder beams of mercy play,
> He melts, and throws the cumbrous cloak away.

Hitherto the cases had been of a change from bad to good, or vice versa, in one generation compared with another. Here it is such a change in one and the same individual. This, as practically affecting the persons here addressed, is properly put last. So far from God laying on men the penalty of others' sins, He will not even punish them for their own, if they turn from sin to righteousness; but if they turn from righteousness to sin, they must expect in justice that their former goodness will not atone for subsequent sin (Heb. 10:38, 39; II Pet. 2: 20-22). The exile in Babylon gave a season for repentance of those sins which would have brought death on the perpetrator in Judea while the law could be enforced; so it prepared the way for the Gospel [GROTIUS]. **22. in his righteousness . . . he shall live**—*in* it, not *for* it, as if that atoned for his former sins; but "*in* his righteousness" he shall live, as the *evidence* of his being already in favor with God through the merit of Messiah, who was to come. The Gospel clears up for us many such passages (I Pet. 1:12), which were dimly understood at the time, while men, however, had light enough for salvation. **23.** (I Tim. 2:4; II Pet. 3:9). If men perish, it is because they *will not* come to the Lord for salvation; not that the Lord is not willing to save them (John 5:40). They trample on not merely justice, but mercy; what farther hope can there be for them, when even mercy is against them? (Heb. 10:26-29). **24. righteous**—one *apparently* such; as in Matt. 9:13, "I came not to call the righteous . . . ," i.e., those who fancy themselves righteous. Those alone are true saints who by the grace of God persevere (Matt. 24:13; I Cor. 10:12; John 10:28, 29). **turneth away from . . . righteousness**—an utter apostasy; not like the exceptional offenses of the godly through infirmity or heedlessness, which they afterwards mourn over and repent of. **not be mentioned**—not be taken into account so as to save them. **his trespass**—utter apostasy. **25.** Their plea for saying, "The way of the Lord is not equal," was that God treated different classes in a different way. But it was really their way that was unequal, since living in sin they expected to be dealt with as if they were righteous. God's way was invariably to deal with different men according to their deserts. **26-**

ADAM CLARKE

17. *He shall not die for the iniquity of his father.* He shall no more be affected by his father's crimes than his father was benefited by his grandfather's righteousness.

CHARLES H. SPURGEON:

Sin having a thorough possession of the human heart, entrenches itself within the soul, as one who has taken a stronghold speedily attends to the repairing of the breaches, and the strengthening of the walls, lest haply he should be dislodged. Among the most subtle devices of sin to keep the soul under its power, and prevent the man's turning to God, is the slandering of the Most High by misrepresenting His character. As dusts blinds the eye, so does sin prevent the sinner from seeing God aright. "Blessed are the pure in heart: for they shall see God"; but the wicked only see what they think to be God, and that, alas, is an image as unlike to God as possible! They say, for instance, that God is unmerciful, whereas He delights in mercy. The unfaithful servant in the parable was quite sure about it, and said most positively, "I knew that thou wast an asture man": whereas the nature of God is as opposite to overbearing and exaction as light is from darkness.

When men once get this false idea of God into their minds they become hardened in heart: believing that it is useless to turn to God, they go on in their sins with greater determination. Either they conceive that God is implacable, or that He is indifferent to human prayers, or that if He should hear them yet He is not in the least likely to grant a favorable answer. Thus they belie the Most High: they make Him who is the best of Kings to be a tyrant; Him who is the dearest of friends they regard as an enemy; and Him whose very name is love they look upon as the embodiment of hate.

This is one of Satan's most mischievous devices to prevent repentance. As in the old times of plague they fastened up the house-door, and marked a red cross upon it, and thus the inhabitants of that dwelling were sealed unto death, even so the devil writes upon the man's door the words, "*no hope,*" and then the sick soul determines to die, and refuses admission to the Physician. No man sins more unreservedly than he who sins in desperation, believing that there is no pardon for him from God. When a man believes that there is no hope for him in the right way, he determines that he will get what he can out of the wrong way; and if he cannot please God, he will, at least, please himself. If he must go to hell, he will be as merry as he can on the road, and, as he puts it, he will "die game." All this comes of a mistaken view of God. Do you not see the likeness between sin and falsehood? They are twin brothers. Holiness is truth, but sin is a lie, and the mother of lies. Sin brings forth falsehood, and then falsehood nourishes sin. Especially in this fashion does falsehood maintain sin, by calumniating the God of love. He is a God ready to pardon, and by no means hard to be moved to forgiveness; why do men stand off from confessing their wrong, and finding mercy? He is not a God who takes pleasure in the miseries of men; why do they think so ill of Him?

—*The Treasury of the Old Testament*

MATTHEW HENRY

The first step towards conversion is consideration (*v.* 28): *Because he considers and turns.* This consideration must produce an aversion to sin. He must turn from *all* his sins without a reserve for any Delilah, any house of Rimmon. This must be accompanied with a conversion to God and duty. Those that do thus turn from sin to God shall *save their souls alive*, *v.* 27.

II. An appeal to the consciences even of the house of Israel, though very corrupt, concerning God's equity in all these proceedings. The charge they drew up against God is blasphemous, *v.* 25, 29. God's reasonings with them are very gracious, for even these blasphemers God would rather have convinced and saved than condemned.

Verses 30–32

Behold, a miracle of mercy; the day of grace and divine patience is yet lengthened out; and therefore, though God will at last judge *everyone according to his ways*, yet he waits to be gracious, and closes with a call to repentance and a promise of pardon upon repentance.

JAMIESON, FAUSSET, BROWN

28. The two last instances repeated in inverse order. God's emphatic statement of His principle of government needs no further proof than the simple statement of it. **26. in them**—in the actual *sins*, which are the manifestations of the principle of "iniquity," mentioned just before. **27. he shall save his soul**—i.e., he shall have it saved upon his repentance. **28. considereth**—the first step to repentance; for the ungodly do not consider either God or themselves (Deut. 32:29; Ps. 119:59, 60; Luke 15:17, 18). **29.** Though God's justice is so plainly manifested, sinners still object to it because they do not wish to see it (Mic. 2:7; Matt. 11:18, 19). **30-32.** As God is to judge them "according to their ways" (Prov. 1:31), their only hope is to "repent"; and this is a sure hope, for God takes no delight in judging them in wrath, but graciously desires their salvation on repentance. **30. I will judge you**—Though ye cavil, it is a sufficient answer that I, your Judge, declare it so, and will judge you according to My will; and then your cavils must end. **Repent**—*inward* conversion (Rev. 2:5). In the *Hebrew* there is a play of like sounds, "*Turn* ye and *return*." **turn** *yourselves* . . .—the *outward* fruits of repentance. Not as *Margin*, "turn *others*"; for the parallel clause (vs. 31) is, "cast away from *you* all *your* transgressions." Perhaps, however, the omission of the object after the verb in the *Hebrew* implies that *both* are included: Turn alike *yourselves* and *all whom you can influence.* **from all . . . transgressions**—not as if believers are perfect; but they sincerely *aim* at perfection, so as to be habitually and wilfully on terms with no sin (I John 3:6-9). **your ruin**—lit., "your snare," entangling you in ruin. **31. Cast away from you**—for the cause of your evil rests with yourselves; your sole way of escape is to be reconciled to God (Eph. 4:22, 23). **make you a new heart**—This shows, not what men *can* do, but what they *ought* to do: what God requires of us. God alone can make us a new heart (ch. 11:19; 36: 26, 27). The command to do what men cannot themselves do is designed to drive them (instead of laying the blame, as the Jews did, elsewhere rather than on themselves) to feel their own helplessness, and to seek God's Holy Spirit (Ps. 51:11, 12). Thus the outward exhortation is, as it were, the organ or instrument which God uses for conferring grace. So we may say with AUGUSTINE, "Give what thou requirest, and (then) require what thou wilt." Our strength (which is weakness in itself) shall suffice for whatever He exacts, if only He gives the supply [CALVIN]. **spirit**—the *understanding:* as the "heart" means *the will and affections.* The root must be changed before the fruit can be good. **why will ye die**—bring on your own selves your ruin. God's decrees are secret to us; it is enough for us that He invites all, and will reject none that seek Him. **32.** (Lam. 3:33; II Pet. 3:9). God is "slow to anger"; punishment is "His strange work" (Isa. 28:21).

ADAM CLARKE

JOSEPH PARKER:

Verses 30—32. Now the Lord God becomes preacher, apostle, missionary, and he says: "Repent, and turn yourselves from all your transgressions; so iniquity shall not be your ruin. Cast away from you all your transgressions, whereby ye have transgressed; and make you a new heart and a new spirit: for why will ye die, O house of Israel? For I have no pleasure in the death of him that dieth, saith the Lord God: wherefore turn yourselves, and live ye." That is preaching. It is so righteous, so stern in law, so noble in reason, so tender to tears of the heart in mercy and grace. The old preachers used to wrestle with their hearers. The great men of the pulpit that made the pulpit what it was in its best days wrestled with their hearers, seized them, arrested them, in the name of the Cross, in the name of God the Father, God the Son, and God the Holy Ghost, and would not let them go until there was a clear understanding as to the responsibility of the preacher and the hearer. Such preaching has its vindication in God's own voice and in God's own method. Here is the exhortation, here is the appeal, here is the application. What is forgotten in the modern sermon is the application, the last tug, the final wrestle, that concluding importunity. A sermon should have reason, doctrine, philosophy, Scripture, experience: but it should never be without emotion, exhortation, appeal, tenderness. The preacher stands up to call men to repentance, to forgiveness, to heaven.—*The People's Bible*

MATTHEW HENRY

CHAPTER 19

Verses 1–9

I. Orders given to the prophet to bewail the fall of the royal family. The kings of Judah are here called *princes of Israel*; for their glory was diminished.

II. The prophet must compare the kingdom of Judah to a *lioness*, *v.* 2. The royal family is as a mother to the kingdom, a *lioness*, fierce, and cruel, and ravenous.

She *nourished her whelps among young lions*, taught the young princes the way of tyrants. If they had adhered to the divine law and promise, God would have preserved to them the might and majesty of a lion, and does it in Christ, the *Lion of the tribe of Judah*. But these *lions' whelps* were cruel and oppressive. Jehoahaz, one of the whelps *became a young lion* (*v.* 3); he was made king, and thought he was made so that he might do what he pleased. He did not prosper long in his tyranny: *The nations heard of him* (*v.* 4), *he was taken*, as a beast of prey, *in their pit*, and *brought in chains to the land of Egypt*.

JAMIESON, FAUSSET, BROWN

CHAPTER 19

VSS. 1-14. ELEGY OVER THE FALL OF DAVID'S HOUSE. There is a tacit antithesis between this lamentation and that of the Jews for their own miseries, into the causes of which, however, they did not inquire. **1. princes of Israel**—i.e., Judah, whose "princes" alone were recognized by prophecy; those of the ten tribes were, in respect to the theocracy, usurpers. **2. thy mother**—the mother of Jehoiachin, the representative of David's line in exile with Ezekiel. The "mother" is Judea: "a lioness," as being fierce in catching prey (vs. 3), referring to her heathenish practices. Jerusalem was called Ariel (the lion of God) in a good sense (Isa. 29:1); and Judah "a lion's whelp . . . a lion . . . an old lion" (Gen. 49: 9), to which, as also to Numbers 23:24; 24:9, this passage alludes. **nourished . . . among young lions**—She herself had "lain" among lions, i.e., had intercourse with the corruptions of the surrounding heathen and had brought up the royal young ones similarly: utterly degenerate from the stock of Abraham. **Lay down**—or "couched," is appropriate to the lion, the Arab name of which means "the coucher." **3. young lion**—Jehoahaz, son of Josiah, carried captive from Riblah to Egypt by Pharaoh-necho (II Kings 23:33). **4. The nations**—Egypt, in the case of Jehoahaz, who probably provoked Pharaoh by trying to avenge the death of his father by assailing the bordering cities of Egypt (II Kings 23:29, 30). **in their pit**—image from the *pitfalls* used for catching wild beasts (Jer. 22:11, 12). **chains**—or hooks, which were fastened in the noses of wild beasts (see *Note*, vs. 9). **5. saw that she had waited, and her hope was lost**—i.e., that her long-waited-for hope was disappointed, Jehoahaz not being restored to

ADAM CLARKE

CHAPTER 19

1. *Moreover take thou up a lamentation.* Declare what is the great subject of sorrow in Israel. Compose a funeral dirge. Show the melancholy fate of the kings who proceeded from Josiah. The prophet deplores the misfortune of Jehoahaz and Jehoiakim, under the figure of two lion whelps, which were taken by hunters, and confined in cages. Next he shows the desolation of Jerusalem under Zedekiah, which he compares to a beautiful vine pulled up by the roots, withered, and at last burned.

2. *What is thy mother? A lioness.* Judea may here be the mother; the lioness, Jerusalem. *She lay down among lions*, having confederacy with the neighboring kings; for *lion* here means king.

3. *She brought up one of her whelps.* Jehoahaz, son of Josiah, whose father was conquered and slain by Pharaoh-necho, king of Egypt. It learned to catch the prey. His reign was a reign of oppression and cruelty. He made his subjects his prey, and devoured their substance.

4. *The nations also heard of him.* The king of Egypt, whose subjects were of divers nations, marched against Jerusalem, took Jehoahaz prisoner, and brought him to Egypt.

5. *When she saw that she had waited.* Being very weak, the Jews found that they could not resist with any hope of success; so the king of

MATTHEW HENRY

Jehoiakim, instead of taking warning by his brother's fate, trod in his brother's steps: *He went up and down among the lions, v.* 6. And he soon learned to *catch the prey,* and he *devoured men* (*v.* 6); he seized his subjects' estates, and swallowed up all that stood in his way. He had the art of discovering where the treasures were which they had hoarded up: he *knew their desolate places* (*v.* 7).

By his oppression he *laid waste their cities.* It did but hasten his own ruin (*v.* 8). God brought against Jehoiakim bands of the Syrians, Moabites and Ammonites, with the Chaldees (2 Kings xxiv. 2), and he was *taken in their pit. Nebuchadnezzar bound him in fetters to carry him to Babylon,* 2 Chron. xxxvi. 6. There was an end of his tyranny: he was *buried with the burial of an ass* (Jer. xxii. 19).

Verses 10–14

Jerusalem, the mother-city, is here represented by another similitude; she is a vine, and the princes are her branches. This comparison we had before, *ch.* xv. Jerusalem is as *a vine*; the Jewish nation is so: *Like a vine in thy blood* (*v.* 10). Places of great wickedness may prosper for a while; and a vine set in blood may be full of branches.

Jerusalem was full of able magistrates, that were *strong rods,* branches of uncommon strength, or poles for the support of this vine, for such magistrates are. The boughs had grown to such maturity that they were fit to make white staves for *the sceptres of those that bore rule, v.* 11. When the royal family of Judah was numerous, and the courts of justice were filled with men of sense and probity, then *Jerusalem's stature was exalted among thick branches.* When Zedekiah was quiet and easy under the king of Babylon's yoke his kingdom flourished thus. This vine is now destroyed.

Nebuchadnezzar, provoked by Zedekiah's treachery, *plucked it up in fury* (*v.* 12), ruined the city, and cut off all the branches of the royal family. *The vine itself is planted in the wilderness, v.* 13. Babylon was as a wilderness to those of the people that were carried captives thither; the land of Judah was as a wilderness to Jerusalem. Those strong rods had been instruments of oppression, and now they are destroyed with him.

Tyranny is the inlet to anarchy; and, when the rod of government is turned into the serpent of oppression, it is just with God to say, "There shall be no strong rod to be a sceptre to rule; but let men be as *are the fishes of the sea,* where the greater devour the less."

JAMIESON, FAUSSET, BROWN

her from Egypt. **she took another of her whelps**—Jehoiakim, brother of Jehoahaz, who was placed on the throne by Pharaoh (II Kings 23:34), according to the wish of Judah. **6. went up and down among the lions**—imitated the recklessness and tyranny of the surrounding kings (Jer. 22:13-17). **catch . . . prey**—to do evil, gratifying his lusts by oppression (II Kings 23:37). **7. knew . . . desolate palaces**—i.e., *claimed as his own* their palaces, which he then proceeded to "desolate." The *Hebrew,* literally "widows"; hence *widowed palaces* (Isa. 13:22). VATABLUS (whom FAIRBAIRN follows) explains it, "He knew (carnally) the widows of those whom he devoured" (vs. 6). But thus the metaphor and the literal reality would be blended: the *lion* being represented as *knowing widows.* The reality, however, often elsewhere thus breaks through the veil. **fulness thereof**—all that it contained; its inhabitants. **8. the nations**—the Chaldeans, Syrians, Moab, and Ammon (II Kings 24:2). **9. in chains**—(II Chron. 36:6; Jer. 22:18). *Margin,* "hooks"; perhaps referring to the hook often passed through the nose of beasts; so, too, through that of captives, as seen in the Assyrian sculptures (see *Note,* vs. 4). **voice**—i.e., his roaring. **no more be heard upon the mountains**—carrying on the metaphor of the lion, whose roaring on the mountains frightens all the other beasts. The insolence of the prince, not at all abated though his kingdom was impaired, was now to cease. **10.** A new metaphor taken from the *vine,* the chief of the fruit-bearing trees, as the *lion* is of the beasts of prey (see ch. 17:6). **in thy blood**—"planted when thou wast in thy blood," i.e., in thy very infancy; as in ch. 16:6, when thou hadst just come from the womb, and hadst not yet the blood washed from thee. The Jews from the first were planted in Canaan to take root there [CALVIN]. GROTIUS translates as *Margin,* "in thy quietness," i.e., in the period when Judah had not yet fallen into her present troubles. *English Version* is better. GLASSIUS explains it well, retaining the metaphor, which CALVIN's explanation breaks, "in the blood of thy grapes," i.e., in her full strength, as the red wine is the strength of the grape. Genesis 49:11 is evidently alluded to. **many waters**—the well-watered land of Canaan (Deut. 8:7-9). **11. strong rods**—princes of the royal house of David. The vine shot forth her branches like so many scepters, not creeping lowly on the ground like many vines, but trained aloft on a tree or wall. The mention of their former royal dignity, contrasting sadly with her present sunken state, would remind the Jews of their sins whereby they had incurred such judgments. **stature**—(Dan. 4:11). **among the thick branches**—i.e., the central stock or trunk of the tree shot up highest "among its own branches" or offshoots, surrounding it. Emblematic of the numbers and resources of the people. HENGSTENBERG translates, "among the clouds." But ch. 31:3, 10, 14, supports *English Version.* **12. plucked up**—not *gradually* withered. The *sudden* upturning of the state was designed to awaken the Jews out of their torpor to see the hand of God in the national judgment. **east wind**—(*Note,* ch. 17: 10). **13. planted**—i.e., transplanted. Though already "dried up" in regard to the nation generally, the vine is said to be "transplanted" as regards God's mercy to the remnant in Babylon. **dry . . . ground**—Chaldea was well watered and fertile; but it is the condition of the captive people, not that of the land, which is referred to. **14. fire . . . out of a rod of her branches**—The Jews' disaster was to be ascribed, not so much to the Chaldeans as to *themselves;* the "fire out of the rod" is *God's wrath* kindled by the perjury of Zedekiah (ch. 17:18). "The anger of the Lord" against Judah is specified as the cause why Zedekiah was permitted to rebel against Babylon (II Kings 24:20; cf. Judg. 9:15), thus bringing Nebuchadnezzar against Jerusalem. **no strong rod . . . sceptre to rule**—No more kings of David's stock are now to rule the nation. Not at least until "the Lord shall send the rod of His strength (Messiah, Ps. 110:2; Isa. 11:1) out of Zion," to reign first as a spiritual, then hereafter as a literal king. **is . . . and shall be for a lamentation**—Part of the lamentation (that as to Jehoahaz and Jehoiakim) was matter of history as already accomplished; part (as to Zedekiah) was yet to be fulfilled; or, this prophecy both is a subject for lamentation, and shall be so to distant posterity.

ADAM CLARKE

Egypt was permitted to do as he pleased. *She took another of her whelps.* Jehoiakim. *And made him a young lion.* King of Judea.

6. *And he went up and down among the lions.* He became a perfect heathen, and made Judea as idolatrous as any of the surrounding nations. He reigned eleven years, a monster of iniquity, 2 Kings xxiii. 30, etc.

8. *The nations set against him.* The Chaldeans, Syrians, Moabites, and Ammonites, and the king of Babylon—king of many nations. *He was taken.* The city was taken by Nebuchadnezzar; and Jehoiakim was taken prisoner, and sent in chains to Babylon.

9. *That his voice should no more be heard.* He continued in prison many years, till the reign of Evil-merodach, who set him at liberty, but never suffered him to return to the mountains of Israel.

10. *Thy mother* (Jerusalem) *is like a vine in thy blood.* Of this expression I know not what to make. Some think the meaning is, "A vine planted by the waters to produce the blood of the grape." See Deut. xxxii. 14. Calmet reads *carmecha,* "thy vineyard," instead of *bedamecha,* "in thy blood." Here is no change but a *resh* for a *daleth.* This reading is supported by one of Kennicott's and one of De Rossi's MSS.: "Thy mother is like a vine in thy vineyard, planted by the waters." Of the textual reading no sense can be made. There is a corruption somewhere. *Full of branches.* Many princes. See next verse.

11. *She had strong rods.* Zedekiah and his many sons.

Her stature was exalted. Zedekiah grew proud of his numerous offspring and prosperity; and although he copied the example of Jehoiakim, yet he thought he might safely rebel against the king of Babylon.

12. *But she was plucked up in fury.* Jerusalem, taken after a violent and most destructive siege, Nebuchadnezzar being violently enraged against Zedekiah for breaking his oath to him. *She was cast down to the ground.* Jerusalem was totally ruined by being burned to the ground. *Her strong rods were broken.* The children of Zedekiah were slain before his eyes, and after that his own eyes pulled out; and he was laden with chains, and carried into Babylon.

13. *And now she is planted in the wilderness.* In the land of Chaldea, whither the people have been carried captives; and which, compared with their own land, was to them a dreary wilderness.

14. *Fire is gone out.* A vindictive and murderous disposition has taken hold—*of a rod of her branches.* Ishmael, son of Nethaniah, who was of the blood-royal of Judah—*hath devoured her fruit.* Hath assassinated Gedaliah, slain many people, and carried off others into the country of the Ammonites. But he was pursued by Jonathan, the son of Kareah, who slew many of his adherents, and delivered much of the people. *She hath no strong rod.* None of the blood-royal of Judah left. And from that time not one of her own royal race ever sat upon the throne of Israel. *This is a lamentation.* This is a most lamentable business. *And shall be* so punctually fulfilled, and the catastrophe shall be so complete, that it shall ever remain as a lamentation, as this state of Jerusalem shall never be restored.

MATTHEW HENRY — CHAPTER 20

JAMIESON, FAUSSET, BROWN — CHAPTER 20

VSS. 1-49. REJECTION OF THE ELDERS' APPLICATION TO THE PROPHET: EXPOSURE OF ISRAEL'S PROTRACTED REBELLIONS, NOTWITHSTANDING GOD'S LONG-SUFFERING GOODNESS: YET WILL GOD RE-

ADAM CLARKE — CHAPTER 20

MATTHEW HENRY

Verses 1–4
Certain of the elders of Israel came to enquire of the Lord. Their enquiry was whether now that they were captives in Babylon, where they had no temple, no synagogue, for the worship of God, it was not lawful for them, to join in worship and do *as the families of these countries* do, that *serve wood and stone.*

They must be made to know that God is justly angry with them (*v.* 4): "*Wilt thou judge them, son of man, wilt thou judge them? See, I have set thee over the nation;* wilt thou not declare to them the judgment of the Lord? Cause them therefore *to know the abominations of their fathers.*"

Verses 5–9
I. The gracious purposes of God's law concerning Israel in Egypt, where they were bond-slaves to Pharaoh. 1. He chose Israel to be a peculiar people to himself, though their condition was bad and their character worse, that he might have the honour of mending both. 2. He *made himself known to them* by his name *Jehovah* (a new name, Exod. vi. 3), when by reason of their servitude they had almost lost the knowledge of that name by which he was known to their fathers, *God Almighty.* 3. He made over himself to them as their God in covenant: *I lifted up my hand unto them,* saying it, and confirming it with an oath, *I am the Lord your God.* 4. He promised to bring them out of Egypt; and made good what he promised. 5. He assured them that he would put them in possession of the land of Canaan. He *therefore* brought them out of Egypt, *that he might bring them into a land that he had spied* out *for them,* a second garden of Eden.

II. The reasonable commands he gave them: "*Cast you away every man* his images that he uses for worship, that should be the *abominations, of his eyes. Defile not yourselves with the idols of Egypt.*"

III. Their unreasonable disobedience to these commands, for which God might justly have cut them off as soon as ever they were formed into a people (*v.* 8). It was strange that all the plagues of Egypt would not prevail to cure them of their affection to the *idols of Egypt.* Justly might he have said, "Let them die with the Egyptians."

IV. The wonderful deliverance which God wrought for them, notwithstanding. Though they forfeited the favour while it was in the bestowing, yet *mercy rejoiced against judgment,* and God did what he designed purely *for his own name's sake, v.* 9. When nothing in us will furnish him with a reason for his favours he furnishes himself with one.

Verses 10–26
The history of the struggle between the sins of Israel, by which they endeavoured to ruin themselves, and the mercies of God, by which he endeavoured to save them and make them happy, is here continued. The story of Israel in the wilderness is referred to in the New Testament (1 Cor. x and Heb. iii), as well as often in the Old, for warning to us Christians.

I. The great things God did for them, which he puts them in mind of, not as grudging them his favours, but to show how ungrateful they had been. God *brought them forth out of Egypt* (*v.* 10), though, as it follows, he *brought them into the wilderness* and not into Canaan immediately. It is better to be at liberty in a wilderness than bond-slaves in a land of plenty. But, when they met with the difficulties of a desert, some wished themselves in Egypt again. God *made them to know his judgments,* not only enacted laws for them, but showed them the reasonableness and equity of those laws. He revived the ancient institution of the sabbath day, which was lost and forgotten while they were bond-slaves in Egypt. Sabbaths are signs; it is a sign that men have a sense of religion. Sabbaths, if duly sanctified are the means of our sanctification.

JAMIESON, FAUSSET, BROWN

STORE HIS PEOPLE AT LAST. **1. seventh year . . .**—viz., from the carrying away of Jeconiah (ch. 1:2; 8: 1). This computation was calculated to make them cherish the more ardently the hope of the restoration promised them in seventy years; for, when prospects are hopeless, years are not computed [CALVIN]. **elders . . . came to inquire**—The object of their inquiry, as in ch. 14:1, is not stated; probably it was to ascertain the cause of the national calamities and the time of their termination, as their false prophets assured them of a speedy restoration. **3.** The chapter falls into two great parts: vss. 1-32, the recital of the people's rebellions during five distinct periods: in Egypt, the wilderness, on the borders of Canaan when a new generation arose, in Canaan, and in the time of the prophet. **I will not be inquired of by you**—because their moral state precluded them from capability of knowing the will of God (Ps. 66:18; Prov. 28:9; John 7:17). **4. Wilt thou judge? . . . judge**—The emphatical repetition expresses, "Wilt thou *not* judge? yes, judge them. There is a loud call for immediate judgment." The *Hebrew* interrogative here is a *command,* not a prohibition]MAURER[. Instead of spending time in *teaching* them, tell them of the abomination of their fathers, of which their own are the complement and counterpart, and which call for *judgment.* **5, 6.** The thrice lifting up of God's hand (the sign of His *oath,* Rev. 10:5, 6; Exod. 6:8, *Margin*; Num. 14:30; to which passages the form of words here alludes) implies the solemn earnestness of God's purpose of grace to them. **made myself known unto them**—proving Myself faithful and true by the actual fulfilment of My promises (Exod. 4:31; 6:3); revealing Myself as "Jehovah," i.e., not that the *name* was unknown before, but that then first the *force* of that name was manifested in the promises of God then being realized in performances. **6. espied for them**—as though God had spied out all other lands, and chose Canaan as the best of all lands (Deut. 8:7, 8). See Daniel 8:9; 11:16, 41, "the glorious land"; see *Margin,* "land of delight or *ornament*"; Zechariah 7: 14, "the pleasant land," or land of desire. **glory of all lands**—i.e., *Canaan* was "the beauty of all lands"; the most lovely and delightful land; "milk and honey" are not the antecedents to "which." **7.** Moses gives no formal statement of idolatries practised by Israel in Egypt. But it is implied in their readiness to worship the golden calf (resembling the Egyptian ox, Apis) (Exod. 32), which makes it likely they had worshipped such idols in Egypt. Also, in Leviticus 17:7, "They shall *no more* offer their sacrifices unto devils (lit., *seirim,* 'he-goats,' the symbol of the false god, Pan), after whom they have gone a-whoring." The call of God by Moses was as much to them to separate from idols and follow Jehovah, as it was to Pharaoh to let them go forth. Exodus 6:6, 7 and Joshua 24:14, expressly mention their idolatry "in Egypt." Hence the need of their being removed out of the contagion of Egyptian idolatries by the exodus. **every man**—so universal was the evil. **of his eyes**—It was not fear of their Egyptian masters, but their own *lust of the eye* that drew them to idols (ch. 6:9; 18:6). **8, 9. then I said, I will . . . But . . .**—i.e., (God speaking in condescension to human modes of conception) their spiritual degradation *deserved* I should destroy them, "but I wrought (viz., the deliverance 'out of . . . Egypt') for My name's sake"; not for their merits (a rebuke to their national pride). God's "name" means the sum-total of His perfections. To manifest these, His gratuitous mercy abounding above their sins, yet without wrong to His justice, and so to set forth His glory, was and is the ultimate end of His dealings (vss. 14, 22; II Sam. 7:23; Isa. 63:12; Rom. 9: 17). **11. which if a man do, he shall . . . live in them**—not *"by* them," as though they could justify a man, seeing that man cannot render the faultless obedience required (Lev. 18:5; Gal. 3:12). "By them" is the expression indeed in Romans 10:5; but there the design is to show that, *if man could* obey all God's laws, he would be justified "by them" (Gal. 3:21); but he cannot; he therefore needs to have justification by "the Lord our righteousness" (Jer. 23;6); then, having thus received life, he "lives," i.e., maintains, enjoys, and exercises this life only in so far as he walks *"in"* the laws of God. So Deuteronomy 30:15, 16. The Israelites, *as a nation,* had life already freely given to them by God's covenant of promise; the laws of God were designed to be the means of the outward expression of their spiritual life. As the natural life has its healthy manifestation in the full exercise of its powers, so their spiritual being as a nation was to be developed in vigor, or else decay, according as they did, or did not, walk in God's laws. **12. sabbaths, . . . a sign between me and them**—a kind of sacramental pledge

ADAM CLARKE

1. *In the seventh year.* Of the captivity of Jeconiah, and the seventh of the reign of Zedekiah.

Certain of the elders of Israel. What these came to inquire about is not known. They were doubtless hypocrites and deceivers, from the manner in which God commands the prophet to treat them. It seems to have been such a deputation of elders as those mentioned chap. viii. 1 and xiv. 1.

3. *I will not be enquired of by you.* I will not hear you. I will have nothing to do with you.

4. *Wilt thou judge them?* The whole chapter is a counsecutive history of the unfaithfulness, ingratitude, rebellion, and idolatry of the Jews, from the earliest times to that day; and vindicates the sentence which God had pronounced against them, and which He was about to execute more fully in delivering them and the city into the hands of the Chaldeans.

5. *I chose Israel.* They did not choose Me for their God till I had chosen them to be My people. *I lifted up mine hand.* I bound myself in a covenant to them to continue to be their God, if they should be faithful, and continue to be My people. Among the Jews the juror lifted up his right hand to heaven; which explains Ps. cxliv. 8: "Their right hand is a right hand of falsehood."

6. *To bring them forth of the land of Egypt.* When they had been long in a very disgraceful and oppressive bondage.

7. *Cast ye away . . . the abominations.* Put away all your idols, these incentives to idolatry that you have looked on with delight.

8. *They did not . . . cast away.* They continued attached to the idolatry of Egypt; so that, had I consulted My justice only, I should have consumed them even in Egypt itself. This is a circumstance that Moses has not mentioned, namely, their provoking God by their idolatry, after He had sent Moses and Aaron to them in Egypt.

9. *But I wrought for my name's sake.* I bare with them and did not punish them, lest the heathen, who had known My promises made to them, might suppose that I had either broken them through some caprice or was not able to fulfill them.

10. *I caused them to go forth.* Though greatly oppressed and degraded, they were not willing to leave their house of bondage. I was obliged to force them away.

11. *I gave them my statutes.* I showed them what they should do in order to be safe, comfortable, wise, and happy and what they should avoid in order to be uninjured in body, mind, and possessions. Had they attended to these things, they should have lived by them. They would have been holy, healthy, and happy.

12. *I gave them my sabbaths.* The religious observance of the Sabbath was the first statute

MATTHEW HENRY

II. Their disobedient undutiful conduct towards God, for which he might justly have thrown them out of covenant (*v.* 13): *They rebelled in the wilderness.* There where they received so much mercy from God, and were in their way to Canaan, they broke out in open rebellions against the God that led them and fed them.

III. God's determination to cut off that generation of them in the wilderness. That which was at the bottom of their disobedience to God, and their neglect of his institutions, was a secret affection to the gods of Egypt: *Their heart went after their idols.*

IV. When he looked upon them he had compassion on them, and did not *make an end of them*, but reprieved them till a new generation was reared.

V. The revolt of the next generation from God, by which they also made themselves obnoxious to the wrath of God (*v.* 21): *The children rebelled against me* too. They *polluted God's sabbaths*, as their fathers.

It is said of the children (*v.* 24) that *their eyes went after their fathers' idols.* If they must have gods, they would have such as they could see.

VI. The judgments of God upon them for their rebellion. God *gave them statutes and judgments* which *were not good*, and *by which they should not live*, *v.* 25. By this we may understand the several ways by which God punished them while they were in the wilderness—the plague that broke in upon them, the fiery serpent, and the like—which are called *judgments*, because inflicted by the justice of God, and *statutes*, because he commanded desolations as sometimes he had commanded deliverances. Spiritual judgments are the most dreadful. He made their sin to be their punishment, gave them up to a *reprobate mind*, as he did the Gentile idolaters (Rom. i. 24, 26). God sometimes makes sin to be its own punishment, and there needs no more to make men miserable than to give them up to their own vile appetites and passions.

JAMIESON, FAUSSET, BROWN

of the covenant of adoption between God and His people. The Sabbath is specified as a sample of the whole law, to show that the law is not merely precepts, but privileges, of which the Sabbath is one of the highest. Not that the Sabbath was first instituted at Sinai, as if it were an exclusively Jewish ordinance (Gen. 2:2, 3), but it was then more formally enacted, when, owing to the apostasy of the world from the original revelation, one people was called out (Deut. 5:15) to be the covenant people of God. **sanctify them**—The observance of the Sabbath contemplated by God was not a mere *outward* rest, but a *spiritual* dedication of the day to the glory of God and the good of man. Otherwise it would not be, as it is made, the pledge of universal *sanctification* (Exod. 31:13-17; Isa. 58:13, 14). Virtually it is said, all sanctity will flourish or decay, according as this ordinance is observed in its full spirituality or not. **13. in the wilderness**—They "rebelled" in the very place where death and terror were on every side and where they depended on My miraculous bounty every moment! **15.** I swore against them (Ps. 95:11; 106:26) that I would not permit the generation that came out of Egypt to enter Canaan. **16.** The *special* reason is stated by Moses (Num. 13, 14) to be that they, through fear arising from the false report of the spies, wished to return to Egypt; the *general* reasons are stated here which lay at the root of their rejection of God's grace; viz., contempt of God and His laws, and love of idols. **their heart**—The fault lay in it (Ps. 78:37). **17. Nevertheless**—How marvellous that God should spare such sinners! His everlasting covenant explains it, His long-suffering standing out in striking contrast to their rebellions (Ps. 78:38; Jer. 30:11). **18. I said unto their children**—being unwilling to speak any more to the fathers as being incorrigible. **Walk ye not in ... statutes of ... fathers**—The traditions of the fathers are to be carefully weighed, not indiscriminately followed. He forbids the imitation of not only their gross sins, but even their plausible statutes [CALVIN]. **19.** It is an indirect denial of God, and a robbing Him of His due, to add man's inventions to His precepts. **20.** (Jer. 17:22). **21.** Though warned by the judgment on their fathers, the next generation also rebelled against God. The "kindness of Israel's youth and love of her espousals in the wilderness" (Jer. 2:2, 3) were only comparative (the corruption in later times being more general), and confined to the minority; as a whole, Israel at no time fully served God. The "children" it was that fell into the fearful apostasy on the plains of Moab at the close of the wilderness sojourn (Num. 25:1, 2; Deut. 31:27). **23.** It was to that generation the threat of dispersion was proclaimed (Deut. 28:64; cf. ch. 29:4). **25. I gave them ... statutes ... not good**—Since they would not follow My statutes that were good, "I gave them" their own (vs. 18) and their fathers' "which were not good"; statutes spiritually corrupting, and, finally, as the consequence, destroying them. Righteous retribution (Ps. 81:12; Hos. 8:11; Rom. 1:24; II Thess. 2:11). Verse 39 proves this view to be correct (cf. Isa. 63:17). Thus on the plains of Moab (Num. 25), in chastisement for the secret unfaithfulness to God in their hearts, He permitted Baal's worshippers to tempt them to idolatry (the ready success of the tempters, moreover, proving the inward unsoundness of the tempted); and this again ended necessarily in punitive judgments. **26. I polluted them**—not directly; "but I judicially *gave them up* to pollute themselves." A just retribution for their "polluting My sabbaths" (vs. 24). This vs. 26 is explanatory of vs. 25. Their own sin I made their punishment. **caused to pass through** *the fire*—FAIRBAIRN translates, "In their *presenting* (lit., the causing to pass over) all their first-born," viz., *to the Lord;* referring to the command (Exod. 13:12, *Margin,* where the very same expression is used). The lustration of children by passing through the fire was *a later abomination* (vs. 31). The evil here spoken of was the admixture of heathenish practices with Jehovah's worship, which made Him regard all as "polluted." Here, "to the Lord" is omitted purposely, to imply, "They kept up the outward service indeed, but I did not own it as done unto Me, since it was mingled with such *pollutions.*" But *English Version* is supported by the similar phraseology in vs. 31, where see *Note.* They made *all* their children pass through the fire; but he names the *first-born,* in aggravation of their guilt; i.e., "I had willed that the first-born should be redeemed as being Mine, but they imposed on themselves the cruel rites of offering them to Molech" (Deut. 18:10). **might know ... the Lord**—that they may be compelled to know Me as a powerful Judge, since they were unwilling to know Me as a gracious Father.

ADAM CLARKE

or command of God to men. This institution was a sign between God and them, to keep them in remembrance of the creation of the world, of the rest that he designed them in Canaan, and of the eternal inheritance among the saints in light.

13. *But the house of Israel rebelled.* They acted in the wilderness just as they had done in Egypt, and He spared them there for the same reason. See v. 9.

15. *I lifted up my hand.* Their provocations in the wilderness were so great that I vowed never to bring them into the Promised Land. I did not consume them, but I disinherited them.

18. *But I said unto their children.* These I chose in their fathers' stead, and to them I purposed to give the inheritance which their fathers by disobedience lost.

22. *I withdrew mine hand.* I had just lifted it up to crush them as in a moment; for they also were idolatrous, and walked in the steps of their fathers.

25. *I gave them also statutes that were not good.* The simple meaning of this place and all such places is that, when they had rebelled against the Lord, despised His statutes, and polluted His Sabbaths—in effect cast Him off, and given themselves wholly to their idols—then He abandoned them, and they abandoned themselves to the customs and ordinances of the heathen.

26. *I polluted them in their own gifts.* I permitted them to pollute themselves by the offerings which they made to their idols.

MATTHEW HENRY

Verses 27-32

The prophet goes on with the story of their rebellions.

I. They had persisted in them after they were settled in the land of Canaan, *v.* 27. They were often very near being cut off in the wilderness, and yet they came to Canaan at last. Even God's Israel get to heaven by hell-gates; so many are their transgressions, and so strong their corruptions, that it is a miracle of mercy they are happy at last; as hypocrites go to hell by heaven-gates.

They obstinately persisted notwithstanding all the admonitions that were given them (*v.* 29).

II. They are persisting still. The prophet must *say to* the present *house of Israel,* some of whose elders were now sitting before him, *"Are you polluted after the manner of your fathers?"*

These elders seem to have been projecting a coalition with the heathen. Now the prophet is here ordered to tell those who were for compounding between God and Baal, that they should have no comfort or benefit from either. There is nothing got by sinful compliances; and the carnal projects of hypocrites will stand them in no stead.

Verses 33-44

The design on foot among the elders was that the people of Israel should conform to those among whom they lived; but God had told them that the design should not take effect, *v.* 32. In these verses, he shows how it should be frustrated.

I. Babylon shall not protect them, nor any of the countries of the heathen; for God will cast them out of his protection and then what prince, what place, can be a sanctuary to them? They shall be brought *into the wilderness of the people* (*v.* 35), either into Babylon, which is called a *wilderness* (*ch.* xix. 13),

JAMIESON, FAUSSET, BROWN

27-29. The next period, viz., that which followed the settlement in Canaan: the fathers of the generation existing in Ezekiel's time walked in the same steps of apostasy as the generation in the wilderness. **Yet in this**—Not content with past rebellions, and not moved with gratitude for God's goodness, "yet in this" *still further* they rebelled. **blasphemed**—"have insulted me" [CALVIN]. Even those who did not sacrifice to heathen gods have offered "their sacrifices" (vs. 28) in forbidden places. **28. provocation of their offering**—an offering as it were purposely made to provoke God. **sweet savour**—What ought to have been *sweet* became offensive by their corruptions. He specifies the various kinds of offerings, to show that in *all* alike they violated the law. **29. What is the high place whereunto ye go?**—What is the meaning of this name? For My *altar* is not so called. What excellence do ye see in it, that ye go there, rather than to My temple, the only lawful place of sacrificing? The very name, "high place," convicts you of sinning, not from ignorance but perverse rebellion. **is called . . . unto this day**—whereas this name ought to have been long since laid aside, along with the custom of sacrificing on high places which it represents, being borrowed from the heathen, who so called their places of sacrifice (the Greeks, for instance, called them by a cognate term, *Bomoi*), whereas I call mine *Mizbeaach,* "altar." The very name implies the place is not that sanctioned by Me, and therefore your sacrifices even to ME there (much more those you offer to idols) are only a "provocation" to Me (vs. 28; Deut. 12:1-5). David and others, it is true, sacrificed to God on high places, but it was under exceptional circumstances, and before the altar was set up on Mount Moriah. **30.** The interrogation implies a strong affirmation, as in vs. 4, "Are ye *not* polluted . . . ? Do ye *not* commit . . .?" Or, connecting this verse with vs. 31, "Are ye thus polluted . . . , and yet (do ye expect that) I shall be inquired of by you?" **31. through the fire**—As "the fire" is omitted in vs. 26, FAIRBAIRN represents the generation here referred to (viz., that of Ezekiel's day) as attaining the climax of guilt (see *Note,* vs. 26), in making their children pass through the fire, which that former generation did not. The reason, however, for the omission of "the fire" in vs. 26 is, perhaps, that there it is implied the children only *"passed through* the fire" for purification, whereas here they are actually *burnt to death* before the idol; and therefore "the fire" is specified in the latter, not in the former case (cf. II Kings 3:27). **32. We will be as the heathen**—and so escape the odium to which we are exposed, of having a peculiar God and law of our own. "We shall live on better terms with them by having a similar worship. Besides, we get from God nothing but threats and calamities, whereas the heathen, Chaldeans, etc., get riches and power from their idols." How literally God's words here ("that . . . shall not be at all") are fulfilled in the modern Jews! Though the Jews seemed so likely (had Ezekiel spoken as an uninspired man) to have blended with the rest of mankind and laid aside their distinctive peculiarities, as was their wish at that time, yet they have remained for eighteen centuries dispersed among all nations and without a home, but still distinct: a standing witness for the truth of the prophecy given so long ago. **33.** Here begins the second division of the prophecy. Lest the covenant people should abandon their distinctive hopes and amalgamate with the surrounding heathen, He tells them that, as the wilderness journey from Egypt was made subservient to discipline and also to the taking from among them the rebellious, so a severe discipline (such as the Jews are now for long actually undergoing) should be administered to them during the next exodus for the same purpose (vs. 38), and so to prepare them for the restored possession of their land (Hos. 2:14, 15). This was only partially fulfilled before, and at the return from Babylon: its full and final accomplishment is future. **with a mighty hand, . . . will I rule over you**—I will assert My right over you in spite of your resistance (vs. 32), as a master would in the case of his slave, and I will not let you be wrested from Me, because of My regard to My covenant. **34.** The Jews in exile might think themselves set free from the "rule" of God (vs. 33); therefore, He intimates, He will reassert His right over them by chastening judgments, and these, with an ultimate view, not to destroy, but to restore them. **people**—rather, "peoples." **35. wilderness of the people**—rather, "peoples," the various *peoples* among whom they were to be scattered, and about whom God saith (vs. 34), "I will bring you out." In contrast to the literal "wilderness of Egypt" (vs. 36), "the wilderness of the peoples" is their *spiritual*

ADAM CLARKE

29. *What is the high place?* What is it good for? Its being a place shows it to be a place of idolatry.

31. *Ye pollute yourselves.* This shows the sense in which God says, v. 26, "I polluted them in their own gifts." They chose to pollute themselves, and I permitted them to do so.

32. *And that which cometh into your mind.* You wish to be naturalized among idolaters. But this shall not be at all; you shall be preserved as a distinct people. You shall not be permitted to mingle yourselves with the people of those countries; even they, idolaters as they are, will despise and reject you.

35. *I will bring you into the wilderness of the people.* I will bring you out of your captivity, and bring you into your own land, which you will find to be a wilderness, the consequence of your crimes.

MATTHEW HENRY

or into some place which, though full of people, shall be a place where God will *plead with them face to face*, as he *pleaded with their fathers in the wilderness of Egypt* (*v.* 36)—where he will avenge the breach of his law with as much terror as that with which he gave it in the wilderness of Sinai.

II. Israel shall be no more able to protect them than Babylon could. There will come a distinguishing day, when God will separate between the precious and the vile; he will *cause them*, as the shepherd causes his sheep, to *pass under the rod*, when he tithes them (Lev. xxvii. 32), that he may mark which is for God. Or it may refer to those among them that repented and reformed; he will cause them to pass under the rod of affliction, and will bring them again *into the bond of the covenant*. The judgments of God shall find them out, and their naming the name of Israel shall be no shelter to them.

It is promised that those who preserved their integrity, and would not serve idols, in other lands, shall return to their prosperity and shall serve the true God in their own land: *All of them in the land shall serve me.*

He will give them true repentance for their sins, *v.* 43. He will give them the knowledge of himself: *They shall know* by experience that *he is the Lord*, kind to his people and faithful to his covenant with them.

JAMIESON, FAUSSET, BROWN

wilderness period of trial, discipline, and purification while exiled among the nations. As the state when they are "brought into the wilderness of the peoples" and that when they were among the peoples "from" which God was to "bring them out" (vs. 34) are distinguished, the wilderness state probably answers partially to the transition period of discipline from the first decree for their restoration by Cyrus to the time of their complete settlement in their land, and the rebuilding of Jerusalem and the temple. But the full and final fulfilment is future; the wilderness state will comprise not only the transition period of their restoration, but the beginning of their occupancy of Palestine, a time in which they shall endure the sorest of all their chastisements, to "purge out the rebels" (vs. 38; Dan. 12:1); and then the remnant (Zech. 13:8, 9; 14:2, 3) shall "all serve God in the land" (vs. 40). Thus the wilderness period does not denote *locality*, but their *state* intervening between their rejection and future restoration. **plead**—bring the matter in debate between us to an issue. Image is from a plaintiff in a law court meeting the defendant "face to face." Appropriate, as God in His dealings acts not arbitrarily, but in most *righteous justice* (Jer. 2:9; Mic. 6:2). **36.** (Num. 14:21-29.) Though God saved them out of Egypt, He afterwards destroyed in the wilderness them that believed not (Jude 5); so, though He brought the exiles out of Babylon, yet their wilderness state of chastening discipline continued even after they were again in Canaan. **37. pass under the rod**—metaphor from a shepherd who makes his sheep *pass under his rod* in counting them (Lev. 27: 32; Jer. 33:13). Whether you will or not, ye shall be counted as Mine, and so shall be subjected to My chastening discipline (Mic. 7:14), with a view to My ultimate saving of the chosen remnant (cf. John 10: 27-29). **bond of . . . covenant**—I will constrain you by sore chastisements to submit yourselves to the *covenant* to which ye are lastingly *bound*, though now you have cast away God's bond from you. Fulfilled in part, Nehemiah 9:8, 26, 32-38; 10:1-39; fully hereafter (Isa. 54:10-13; 52:1, 2). **38.** (Zech. 13:9; 14:2.) **purge out**—or, "separate." *Hebrew, barothi*, forming a designed alliteration with *"berith," the covenant;* not a promise of grace, but a threat against those Jews who thought they could in exile escape the observation and "rule" of God. **land of Israel**—Though brought out of the country of their sojourn or exile (Babylon formerly, and the various lands of their exile hereafter) into the literal land of *Palestine*, even it shall be to them an exile state, "they shall not enter into the land of *Israel,*" i.e., the spiritual state of restored favor of God to His covenant people, which shall only be given to the remnant to be saved (Zech. 13:8, 9). **39.** Equivalent to, "I would rather have you open idolaters than hypocrites, fancying you can worship Me and yet at the same time serve idols" (Amos 5:21, 22, 25, 26; cf. I Kings 18:21; II Kings 17:41; Matt. 6:24; Rev. 3:15, 16). **Go ye, serve**—This is not a *command* to serve idols, but a judicial declaration of God's giving up of the half-idol, half-Jehovah worshippers to utter idolatry, if they will not serve Jehovah alone (Ps. 81:12; Rev. 22:11). **hereafter also**—God anticipates the same apostasy *afterwards*, as *now*. **40. For**—Though ye, the rebellious portion, withdraw from My worship, others, even the believing remnant, will succeed after you perish, and will serve Me purely. **in mine holy mountain**—(Isa. 2:2, 3). Zion, or Moriah, "the height of Israel" (pre-eminent above all mountains because of the manifested presence of God there with *Israel*), as opposed to their "high places," the worship on which was an abomination to God. **all**—not merely individuals, such as constitute the elect Church now; but the whole *nation*, to be followed by the conversion of the Gentile *nations* (Isa. 2:2, "*all* nations"; Rom. 11:26; Rev. 11:15). **with**—rather, "*in* all your holy things" [MAURER]. **41. with**—i.e., in respect to your sweet savor (lit., "savor of rest," *Note*, ch. 16: 19). Or, I will accept you (your worship) "*as* a sweet savor" [MAURER], (Eph. 5:2; Phil. 4:18). God first accepts the *person* in Messiah, then the *offering* (vs. 40; Gen. 4:4). **bring . . . out from . . . . people . . .**—the same words as in vs. 34; but there applied to the bringing forth of the hypocrites, as well as the elect; here restricted to the saved remnant, who alone shall be at last restored literally and spiritually in the fullest sense. **sanctified in you before . . . heathen**—(Jer. 33:9). All the nations will acknowledge My power displayed in restoring you, and so shall be led to seek Me (Isa. 66:18; Zech. 14:16-19). **43. there**—not merely in exile when suffering punishment which makes even reprobates sorry for sin, but when received into favor *in your own land*. **remember**—(ch. 16:61, 63). The humiliation of Judah

ADAM CLARKE

There will I plead with you. There I will be your King, and rule you with a sovereign rule; and the dispensations of My justice and mercy shall either end you or mend you.

37. *I will cause you to pass under the rod.* This alludes to the custom of tithing the sheep. I take it from the rabbins. The sheep were all penned; and the shepherd stood at the door of the fold, where only one sheep could come out at once. He had in his hand a rod dipped in vermillion; and as they came out, he counted one, two, three, four, five, six, seven, eight, nine; and as the tenth came out, he marked it with the rod, and said, "This is the tenth"; and that was set apart for the Lord. *I will bring you into the bond of the covenant.* You shall be placed under the same obligations as before, and acknowledge yourselves bound; you shall feel your obligation, and live according to its nature.

38. *I will purge out from among you the rebels.* The incorrigibly wicked I will destroy, those who will not receive Him whom I have appointed for this purpose as the Saviour of Israel.

39. *Go ye, serve ye every one his idols.* Thus God gave them statutes that were not good, and judgments whereby they could not live, by thus permitting them to take their own way, serve their gods, and follow the maxims and rites of that abominable worship.

40. *For in mine holy mountain.* The days shall come in which all true Israelites shall receive Him whom I have sent to be the true Sacrifice for the life of the world; and shall bring to Jerusalem, the pure Christian Church, their offerings, which I will there accept, for they will give Me thanks for My unspeakable Gift.

42. *And ye shall know.* "Shall acknowledge" *that I am* Jehovah.

43. *And there shall ye remember your ways.* You shall be ashamed of your past conduct, and of your long opposition to the gospel of your salvation. These promises may, in a certain

MATTHEW HENRY

Verses 45–48

A prophecy of wrath against Judah and Jerusalem, which would more fitly have begun the next chapter than conclude this. The beginning of the next chapter is the explication of it, when the people complained that this was a parable which they understood not. In this parable, 1. It is a forest that is prophesied against, *the forest of the south field*, Judah and Jerusalem. These lay south from Babylon, and therefore he is directed to *set his face towards the south* (*v.* 46), to intimate that God had set his face against them. But, though it be a message of wrath, he must deliver it with tenderness; he must *drop his word towards the south*; his doctrine must *distil as the rain* (Deut. xxxii. 2), that people's hearts might be softened by it. Judah and Jerusalem are called *forests* because they had been empty of fruit, for fruit-trees grow not in a forest. Those that should have been as the garden of the Lord had become like a forest, overgrown with *briers and thorns.* It is a fire kindled in his forest that is prophesied, *v.* 47. *I will kindle a fire in thee.* He that had been himself a protecting fire about Jerusalem is now a consuming fire in it. *All faces* (that is, all that covers the face of the earth) *from the south* of Canaan to the north, from Beersheba to Dan, shall be *burnt therein.* The people, on occasion of this discourse, said, *Does he not speak parables?*

JAMIESON, FAUSSET, BROWN

(Neh. 9) is a type of the future penitence of the whole nation (Hos. 5:15; 6:1; Zech. 12:10-14). God's goodness realized by the sinner is the only thing that leads to true repentance (Hos. 3:5; Luke 7:37, 38). **44.** The *English Version* chapter ought to have ended here, and ch. 21 begun with "Moreover . . . ," as in the *Hebrew* Bible. **for my name's sake**—(ch. 36:22). Gratuitously; according to My compassion, not your merits. After having commented on this verse, CALVIN was laid on his death-bed, and his commentary ended. **45-49.** An introductory brief description in enigma of the destruction by fire and sword, detailed more explicitly in ch. 21. **46. south . . . south . . . south**—three different *Hebrew* words, to express the certainty of the divine displeasure resting on the region specified. The third term is from a root meaning "dry," referring to the sun's heat in the south; representing the burning judgments of God on the southern parts of Judea, of which Jerusalem was the capital. **set thy face**—determinately. The prophets used to turn themselves towards those who were to be the subjects of their prophecies. **drop**—as the rain, which *flows* in a continuous stream, sometimes gently (Deut. 32:2), sometimes violently (Amos 7:16; Mic. 2:6, *Margin*), as here. **forest**—the densely populated country of Judea; trees representing people. **47. fire**—every kind of judgment (ch. 19:12; 21:3, "my sword"; Jer. 21:14). **green tree . . . dry**—fit and unfit materials for fuel alike; "the righteous and the wicked," as explained in ch. 21:3, 4; Luke 23: 31. Unsparing universality of the judgment! **flaming flame**—one continued and unextinguished flame. "The glowing flame" [FAIRBAIRN]. **faces**—persons; here the metaphor is merged in the reality. **49.** Ezekiel complains that by this parabolic form of prophecy he only makes himself and it a jest to his countrymen. God therefore in ch. 21 permits him to express the same prophecy more plainly.

ADAM CLARKE

limited sense, be applied to the restoration from the Babylonish captivity; but they must have their proper fulfilment when the Jews shall accept Jesus as their Saviour, and in consequence be brought back from all their dispersions to their own land.

46. *Set thy face toward the south.* Towards Judea, which lay south from Babylon, or Mesopotamia, where the prophet then dwelt. *The forest of the south field.* The city of Jerusalem, as full of inhabitants as the forest is of trees.

47. *I will kindle a fire.* I will send war, *and it shall devour every green tree,* the most eminent and substantial of the inhabitants; *and every dry tree,* the lowest and meanest also. *The flaming flame shall not be quenched.* The fierce ravages of Nebuchadnezzar and the Chaldeans shall not be stopped till the whole land is ruined. *All faces from the south to the north shall be burned.* From the one end of the land to the other there shall be nothing but fear, dismay, terror, and confusion, occasioned by the wide-wasting violence of the Chaldeans. Judea lay in length from north to south.

48. *All flesh.* All the people shall see that this war is a judgment of the Lord. *It shall not be quenched.* Till the whole land shall be utterly ruined.

MATTHEW HENRY

CHAPTER 21

Verses 1–7

The prophet faithfully delivered the message in the terms wherein he received it, but the word of the Lord came to him again, and gave him a key to that figurative discourse. 1. The prophet is here directed against whom to level the arrow of this prophecy. He must *drop his word towards the holy places* (*v.* 2), towards Canaan the holy land, Jerusalem, the holy city, the temple, the holy house. 2. The meaning of the fire that was to consume the forest of the south: it signified the sword of war which should make the land desolate (*v.* 3). Did the fire devour *every green tree* and *every dry tree*? The sword in like manner shall *cut off the righteous and the wicked.* The righteous were *cut off from the land of Israel* when they were sent captives in Babylon. In the beginning such excellent men as Daniel and his fellows, and Ezekiel, were cut off from it and conveyed to Babylon. But far be it from us to think that *the righteous are as the wicked.* God's graces and comforts make a great difference. The *good figs* are sent into Babylon *for their good*, Jer. xxiv. 5, 6. 3. The prophet is ordered, by expressions of his own grief and concern for these calamities that were coming on, to try to make impressions of the like upon the people. He must sigh as if his heart would burst, *sigh with bitterness.*

Verses 8–17

Another prophecy of the sword. The sword was unsheathed in the foregoing verses; here it is fitted up to do execution, which the prophet is commanded to lament.

I. The sword is *sharpened.* It is *furbished*, that *it may glitter*, to the terror of those against whom it is drawn. This sword is *that rod of iron* which *contemns every tree* and will bear it down. Or, This sword is *the rod of my son*, a correcting rod, for the chastening of the transgression of God's people (2 Sam. vii. 14), not to cut them off from being a people. It is a sword to others, a rod to my son.

II. How the sword is here put into the hand of the executioners. *It is given into the hand*, not of the fencer to be played with, but *of the slayer* to do execution.

III. Against whom it is sent (*v.* 12): *It shall be upon my people;* they shall fall by this sword. *The sword* of the heathen shall be upon God's own people. But, if the sword be at any time upon God's people, have they not comfort within sufficient to arm them against everything that is frightful? They have, while they conduct themselves as becomes his people; but these had not done so, and therefore *terrors, by reason of the sword*, shall be upon those that call themselves

JAMIESON, FAUSSET, BROWN

CHAPTER 21

Vss. 1-32. PROPHECY AGAINST ISRAEL AND JERUSALEM, AND AGAINST AMMON. **2. the holy places**—the three parts of the temple: the courts, the holy place, and the holiest. If "synagogues" existed before the Babylonian captivity, as Psalm 74:8 seems to imply, they and the *proseuchæ*, or oratories, may be included in the "holy places" here. **3. righteous . . . wicked**—not contradictory of ch. 18:4, 9 and Genesis 18:23. Ezekiel here views the mere *outward* aspect of the indiscriminate universality of the national calamity. But *really* the same captivity to the "righteous" would prove a blessing as a wholesome discipline, which to the "wicked" would be an unmitigated punishment. The godly were sealed with a mark (ch. 9:4), not for outward exemption from the common calamity, but as marked for the secret interpositions of Providence, overruling even evil to their good. The godly were by comparison so few, that not their salvation but the universality of the judgment is brought into view here. **4.** The "sword" did not, literally, *slay* all; but the *judgments* of God by the foe swept through the land "from the south to the north." **6. with the breaking of thy loins**—as one afflicted with pleurisy; or as a woman, in labor-throes, clasps her loins in pain, and heaves and sighs till *the girdle of the loins is broken* by the violent action of the body (Jer. 30:6). **7.** The abrupt sentences and mournful repetitions imply violent emotions. **9. sword**—viz., of God (Deut. 32:41). The Chaldeans are His instrument. **10. to make a sore slaughter**—lit., "that killing it may kill." **glitter**—lit., "glitter as the lightning-flash": flashing terror into the foe. **should we . . . make mirth**—It is no time for levity when such a calamity is impending (Isa. 22:12, 13). **it contemneth the rod of my son . . .**—The sword has no more respect to the trivial "rod" or scepter of Judah (Gen. 49:10) than if it were any common "tree." "Tree" is the image retained from ch. 20:47; explained in ch. 21:2, 3. God calls Judah "My son" (cf. Exod. 4:22; Hos. 11:1). FAIRBAIRN arbitrarily translates, "Perchance the scepter of My son rejoiceth; it (the sword) despiseth every tree." **11. the slayer**—the Babylonian king in this case; in general, *all* the instruments of God's wrath (Rev. 19:15). **12. terrors by reason of the sword . . .**—rather, "they (the princes of Israel) are *delivered up to* the sword together with My people" [GLASSIUS]. **smite . . . upon . . . thigh**—a mark of grief (Jer. 31: 19). **13. it is a trial**—rather, "There is a trial" being made: the sword of the Lord will subject all to the ordeal. "What, then, if it contemn even the rod" (scepter of Judah)? Cf. as to a similar scourge of unsparing trial, Job 9:23. **it shall be no more**—the

ADAM CLARKE

CHAPTER 21

2. *Set thy face toward Jerusalem.* This is a continuation of the preceding prophecy; and in this chapter the prophet sets before them, in the plainest language, what the foregoing metaphors meant, so that they could not complain of his parables.

3. *Behold, I am against thee.* Dismal news! When God is against us, who can be for us? *And will draw forth my sword.* War. *And will cut off from thee.* The land of Judea.

4. *From the south to the north.* The whole land shall be ravaged from one end to the other.

5. *It shall not return any more.* That is, till all the work that I have designed for it is done. Nor did it; for Nebuchadnezzar never rested till he had subdued all the lands from the south to the north, from the Euphrates to the Nile.

6. *Sigh . . . with the breaking of thy loins.* Let your mourning for this sore calamity be like that of a woman in the pains of travail.

7. *Wherefore sighest thou?* The prophet was a sign unto them. His sighing and mourning showed them how they should act.

10. *It contemneth the rod of my son. It,* the sword of Nebuchadnezzar, *contemneth the rod,* despises the power of influence, *of my son*—Israel, the Jewish people.

13. *Because it is a trial.* This will be a trial of strength and skill between the Chaldeans and the Jews, and a trial of faith and patience to the righteous. *And what if the sword* (Nebuchadnezzar) *contemn even the rod?* Overthrow

MATTHEW HENRY

my people. This sword is directed particularly *against the great men*, for they had been the greatest sinners among them.

IV. The nature of this sword, and the limitations of it as to the people of God, *v.* 13. It is a correction; it is designed to be so; the sword to others is a rod to them. This is a comfortable word which comes in in the midst of these terrible ones. Fears are silenced with an assurance that the sword shall not forget the errand on which it is sent: *It is a trial*, and it is *no more than a trial.* It is matter of comfort to the people of God, when his judgments are abroad that *when they are tried, they shall come forth as gold*, and the proving of their faith shall be the improving of it.

V. Here the prophet and the people must show themselves affected with these judgments threatened. The prophet must not study for fine words, *A sword! a sword!* and (*v.* 14), *Let the sword be doubled* the *third time* in thy preaching. Again (*v.* 14), *Prophesy, and smite thy hands together*, wring *thy hands*, as lamenting the desolation.

The sword, the *point of this sword*, is directed against *all their gates* (*v.* 15), against all those things with which they thought to keep it out.

This sword is sent with a running warrant (*v.* 16): "*Go thee, one way or other*, which way thou wilt, turn *to the right hand or to the left*, thou wilt find those that are obnoxious, for there are none free from guilt."

Verses 18–27

The prophet, in the verses before, had shown them the sword coming.

I. He must show the Chaldean army coming against Jerusalem. The prophet must *appoint him two ways*, two roads (*v.* 19), and must bring the king of Babylon's army to the place where the roads part, for there they will make a stand.

One road leads to Rabbath, the head city of the Ammonites, and the other to Jerusalem. He is resolved to be the ruin of both, yet he is not determined which to attack first. Many of the inhabitants of Judah had now taken shelter in Jerusalem, and therefore it is called *Judah in Jerusalem the defenced.*

The prophet must describe this dilemma (*v.* 21); for *the king of Babylon stood at the head of the two ways.* It seems, he knew neither his own interest nor his own mind. To come to a resolution he *used divination.*

He *made his arrows bright*, to be drawn for the lots. Perhaps *Jerusalem* was written on one arrow and *Rabbath* on the other, and that which was first drawn out of the quiver he determined to attack first.

JAMIESON, FAUSSET, BROWN

scepter, i.e., *the state,* must necessarily then come to an end. Fulfilled in part at the overthrow of Judah by Nebuchadnezzar, but fully at the time of "Shiloh's" (Messiah's) coming (Gen. 49:10), when Judea became a Roman province. **14. smite . . . , hands together**—(Num. 24:10), indicative of the indignant fury with which God will "smite" the people. **sword . . . doubled the third time**—referring to the threefold calamity:—1. The taking of Zedekiah (to whom the "rod," or scepter, may refer); 2. the taking of the city; 3. the removal of all those who remained with Gedaliah. "Doubled" means "multiplied" or "repeated." The stroke shall be doubled and even trebled. **of the slain**—i.e., by which many are slain. As the *Hebrew* is *singular*, FAIRBAIRN makes it refer to the king, "the sword of the great one that is slain," or "pierced through." **entereth . . . privy chambers**—(Jer. 9:21). The sword shall overtake them, not merely in the open battlefield, but in the chambers whither they flee to hide themselves (I Kings 20:30; 22:25). MAURER translates, "which *besieged* them"; FAIRBAIRN, "which penetrates to them." *English Version* is more literal. **15. point**—"the *whirling glance* of the sword" [FAIRBAIRN]. "The *naked* (bared) sword" [HENDERSON]. **ruins**—lit., "stumbling blocks." Their own houses and walls shall be stumbling blocks in their way, whether they wish to fight or flee. **made bright**—made to glitter. **wrapped . . .**—viz., in the hand of him who holds the hilt, or in its scabbard, that the edge may not be blunt when it is presently drawn forth to strike. GESENIUS, translates, "sharpened . . . ." **16.** Apostrophe to the sword. **Go . . . one way**—or, "*Concentrate* thyself"; "*Unite* thy forces on the right hand" [GROTIUS]. The sword is commanded to take the nearest route for Jerusalem, "whither their face was set,' whether south or north ("right hand or left"), according to where the several parts of the Chaldean host may be. **or other, . . . on the left**—rather "*set thyself* on the left." The verbs are well chosen. The main "*concentration*" of forces was to be on "the right hand," or *south*, the part of Judea in which Jerusalem was, and which lay south in marching from Babylon, whereas the Chaldean forces advancing on Jerusalem from Egypt, of which Jerusalem was north, were fewer, and therefore "set thyself" is the verb used. **17.** Jehovah Himself smites His hands together, doing what He had commanded Ezekiel to do (*Note*, vs. 14), in token of His smiting Jerusalem; cf. the similar symbolical action (II Kings 13:18, 19). **cause . . . fury to rest**—give it full vent, and so satisfy it (ch. 5:13). **19. two ways**—The king coming from Babylon is represented in the graphic style of Ezekiel as reaching the point where the road branched off in two ways, one leading by the south, by Tadmor or Palmyra, to Rabbath of Ammon, east of Jordan; the other by the north, by Riblah in Syria, to Jerusalem—and hesitating which way to take. Ezekiel is told to "appoint the two ways" (as in ch. 4:1); for Nebuchadnezzar, though knowing no other control but his own will and superstition, had really this path "appointed" for him by the all-ruling God. **out of one land**—viz., Babylon. **choose . . . a place**—lit., "a hand." So it is translated by FAIRBAIRN, "make a *finger-post*," viz., at the head of the two ways, the hand-post pointing Nebuchadnezzar to the way to Jerusalem as the way he should select. But MAURER rightly supports *English Version.* Ezekiel is told to "choose the place" where Nebuchadnezzar should do as is described in vss. 20, 21; so entirely does God order by the prophet every particular of place and time in the movements of the invader. **20. Rabbath of the Ammonites**—distinct from Rabbah in Judah (II Sam. 12:26). Rabbath is put first, as it was from her that Jerusalem, that doomed city, had borrowed many of her idols. **to Judah in Jerusalem**—instead of simply putting "Jerusalem," to imply the sword was to come not merely to Judah, but to its people *within* Jerusalem, defended though it was; its defenses on which the Jews relied so much would not keep the foe out. **21. parting**—lit., "mother of the way." As "head of the two ways" follows, which seems tautology after "parting of the way," HAVERNICK translates, according to *Arabic* idiom, "the highway," or principal road. *English Version* is not tautology, "head of the two ways" defining more accurately "parting of the way." **made . . . bright**—rather, "shook," from an *Arabic* root. **arrows**—Divination by arrows is here referred to: they were put into a quiver marked with the names of particular places to be attacked, and then *shaken* together; whichever came forth first intimated the one selected as the first to be attacked [JEROME]. The same usage existed among the Arabs, and is mentioned in the Koran. In the

ADAM CLARKE

Zedekiah? It will do so, for the regal government of Judea shall be no more. Or, "it is tried"; that is, the sword. Nebuchadnezzar has already shown himself strong and skillful.

14. *Let the sword be doubled the third time.* The sword has been doubled, and it shall come the third time. Nebuchadnezzar came against Judea thrice: (1) against Jehoiakim, (2) against Jeconiah, (3) against Zedekiah. The sword had already been doubled; it is to come now the third time, i.e., against Zedekiah. *The sword of the slain.* "The sword of the soldiers" of the Chaldeans. So in the next clause, "It is the sword of that great soldier," that eminent king and conqueror.

15. *Wrapped up.* It is not a blunt sword; it is carefully sharpened and preserved for the slaughter.

16. *Go thee one way or other.* You shall prosper, O sword, whithersoever you turn—against Ammon, or Judea, or Egypt.

19. *Appoint thee two ways.* Set off from Babylon, and lay down two ways, either of which you may take: that to the right, which leads to Jerusalem; or that to the left, which leads to Rabbath of the Ammonites, v. 20. But why against the Ammonites? Because both they and the Moabites were united with Zedekiah against the Chaldeans (see Jer. xxvii. 3), though they afterwards fought against Judea, chap. xii. 6.

21. *For the king of Babylon stood at the parting of the way.* He was in doubt which way he should first take, whether to humble the Ammonites by taking their metropolis, Riblath, or to go at once against Jerusalem. In this case of uncertainty he made use of divination. And this was of three kinds: (1) by *arrows,* (2) by *images* or talismans, (3) by inspecting the entrails of a sacrifice offered on the occasion.

MATTHEW HENRY

Or he heard the observations which the augurs made upon the entrails of the sacrifices: *he looked in the liver*. Jerusalem being the mark set up (*v.* 22), the campaign is opened.

II. He must show the people and the prince that they bring this destruction upon themselves by their own sin.

1. The people do so, *v.* 23, 24. They slight the notices that are given them of the judgment coming. Ezekiel's prophecy is to them a *false divination.*

2. The prince likewise brings his ruin upon himself. Zedekiah was wicked, as he promoted sin among his people; he sinned, and *made Israel to sin.*

He has forfeited his crown, and he shall no longer wear it; he has by his profaneness profaned his crown, and it shall be *cast to the ground* (*v.* 26): *Remove the diadem.* Crowns and diadems are losable things; it is only in the other world that there is a crown of glory that fades not away.

Attempts to re-establish the government shall come to nothing. This monarchy shall never be restored till it is fixed for perpetuity in the hands of the Messiah.

JAMIESON, FAUSSET, BROWN

Nineveh sculptures the king is represented with a cup in his right hand, his left resting on a bow; also with two arrows in the right, and the bow in the left, probably practising divination. **images**–*Hebrew,* "teraphim"; household gods, worshipped as family talismans, to obtain direction as to the future and other blessings. First mentioned in Mesopotamia, whence Rachel brought them (Gen. 31:19, 34); put away by Jacob (Gen. 35:4); set up by Micah as his household gods (Judg. 17:5); stigmatized as idolatry (I Sam. 15:23, *Hebrew;* cf. Zech. 10:2, *Margin*). **liver**–They judged of the success, or failure, of an undertaking by the healthy, or unhealthy, state of the liver and entrails of a sacrifice. **22.** Rather, "*In* his right hand was [is] the divination," i.e., he holds up in his right hand the arrow marked with "Jerusalem," to encourage his army to march for it. **captains**–The *Margin,* "battering-rams," adopted by FAIRBAIRN, is less appropriate, for "battering-rams" follow presently after [GROTIUS]. **open the mouth in . . . slaughter**–i.e., commanding slaughter: raising the war cry of death. Not as GESENIUS, "to open the mouth *with the war shout.*" **23.** Unto *the Jews,* though credulous of divinations when in their favor, Nebuchadnezzar's divination "shall be [seen] as false." **unto them . . .**–This gives the reason which makes the Jews fancy themselves safe from the Chaldeans, viz., that they "have sworn" to the latter "oaths" of allegiance, forgetting that they had violated them (ch. 17:13, 15, 16, 18). **but he . . .**–*Nebuchadnezzar* will remember in consulting his idols that he swore to Zedekiah by them, but that Zedekiah broke the league [GROTIUS]. Rather, *God* will remember against them (Rev. 16:19) their violating their oath sworn by the true God, whereas Nebuchadnezzar kept his oath sworn by a false god; vs. 24 confirms this. **24.** Their unfaithfulness to Nebuchadnezzar was a type of their general unfaithfulness to their covenant God. **with the hand**–viz., of the king of Babylon. **25. profane**–as having desecrated by idolatry and perjury his office as the Lord's anointed. HAVERNICK translates, as in vs. 14, "slain," i.e., not literally, but virtually; to Ezekiel's idealizing view Zedekiah was the grand victim "pierced through" by God's sword of judgment, as his sons were slain before his eyes, which were then put out, and he was led a captive in chains to Babylon. *English Version* is better: so GESENIUS (II Chron. 36:13; Jer. 52:2). **25. when iniquity shall have an end**–(vs. 29). When thine iniquity, having reached its last stage of guilt, shall be put an end to by judgment (ch. 35:5). **26. diadem**–rather, "the miter" of the holy priest (Exod. 28:4; Zech. 3:5). His priestly emblem as representative of the priestly people. Both this and "the crown," the emblem of the kingdom, were to be removed, until they should be restored and united in the Mediator, Messiah (Ps. 110:2, 4; Zech. 6:13), [FAIRBAIRN]. As, however, King Zedekiah alone, not the high priest also, is referred to in the context, *English Version* is supported by GENESIUS. **this shall not be the same**–The diadem shall not be as it was [ROSENMULLER]. Nothing shall remain what it was [FAIRBAIRN]. **exalt . . . low, . . . abase . . . high**–not the general truth expressed (Prov. 3:34; Luke 1:52; Jas. 4:6; I Pet. 5:5); but specially referring to Messiah and Zedekiah contrasted together. The "tender plant . . . out of the dry ground" (Isa. 53:2) is to be "exalted" in the end (vs. 27); the now "high" representative on David's throne, Zedekiah, is to be "abased." The *outward* relations of things shall be made to change places in just retaliation on the people for having so perverted the *moral* relations of things [HENGSTENBERG]. **27.** Lit., "An overturning, overturning, overturning, will I make it." The threefold repetition denotes the awful *certainty* of the event; not as ROSENMULLER explains, the overthrow of the *three,* Jehoiakim, Jeconiah, and Zedekiah; for Zedekiah alone is referred to. **it shall be no more, until he come whose right it is**–strikingly parallel to Genesis 49:10. Nowhere shall there be rest or permanence; all things shall be in fluctuation until He comes who, as the rightful Heir, shall restore the throne of David that fell with Zedekiah. The *Hebrew* for "right" is "judgment"; it perhaps includes, besides the *right* to rule, the idea of His rule being one in *righteousness* (Ps. 72:2; Isa. 9:6, 7; 11:4; Rev. 19:11). Others (Nebuchadnezzar, etc.), who held the rule of the earth delegated to them by God, abused it by unrighteousness, and so forfeited the "right." He both has the truest "right" to the rule, and exercises it in "right." It is true the *tribal* "scepter" continued with Judah "till Shiloh came" (Gen. 49:10); but there was no *kingly* scepter till Messiah came, as the *spiritual* King then (John 18:36, 37); this spiritual kingdom being about to pass into the *literal, personal* kingdom over Israel

ADAM CLARKE

22. *At his right hand was the divination for Jerusalem.* He had probably written on two arrows: one, Jerusalem; the other, Riblath; the third, left blank. He drew, and that on which Jerusalem was written came to his hand, in consequence of which he marched immediately against that city. It was ripe for destruction, and had he marched before or after, it would have fallen; but he never considered himself as sure of the conquest till now.

23. *To them that have sworn oaths.* To Zedekiah and his ministers, who had bound themselves by the oath of the Lord to be faithful to the Chaldeans, and to pay them the promised tribute. The oaths may refer, further, to the alliances formed with the Egyptians, Ammonites, and others. They will not believe that Nebuchadnezzar shall succeed against them, while they expect the powerful assistance of the Egyptians.

25. *And thou, profane wicked prince of Israel.* Zedekiah, called here *profane,* because he had broken his oath; and *wicked,* because of his opposition to God and His prophet.

26. *Exalt him that is low.* Give Gedaliah the government of Judea. *Abase him that is high.* Depose Zedekiah—remove his diadem, and take off his crown.

27. *I will overturn.* I will utterly destroy the Jewish government.

Until he come whose . . . is. I.e., till the coming of the Son of David, the Lord Jesus, who, in a mystic and spiritual sense, shall have the throne of Israel, and *whose right it is.* See the famous prophecy, Gen. xlix. 10, and Luke i. 32. The *overturn* is thrice repeated here to point out, say the rabbins, the three conquests of Jerusalem, in which Jehoiakim, Jeconiah, and Zedekiah were overthrown.

MATTHEW HENRY

Verses 28–32

The prediction of the destruction of the Ammonites, was effected by Nebuchadnezzar about five years after the destruction of Jerusalem.

I. The sin of the Ammonites is here intimated, *v.* 28. The reproach they put upon the Israel of God, when they triumphed in their afflictions, was inhuman. A conceit that they were a better people than Israel, being spared when they were cut off, made them so haughty that they did even *tread on the necks of the Israelites that were slain.*

II. The utter destruction of the Ammonites is threatened. God resents the indignities and injuries done to his people as done to himself (*v.* 31). "*I will judge thee where thou wast created,* where thou wast first formed into a people, and where thou hast been settled ever since, and therefore where thou seemest to have taken root; *the land of thy nativity* shall be the land of thy destruction."

JAMIESON, FAUSSET, BROWN

at His second coming, when, and not before, this prophecy shall have its exhaustive fulfilment (Luke 1:32, 33; Jer. 3:17; 10:7; "To thee doth it appertain"). **28.** Lest Ammon should think to escape because Nebuchadnezzar had taken the route to Jerusalem, Ezekiel denounces judgment against Ammon, without the prospect of a restoration such as awaited Israel. Jeremiah 49:6, it is true, speaks of a "bringing again of its captivity," but this probably refers to its *spiritual* restoration under Messiah; or, if referring to it *politically,* must refer to but a partial restoration at the downfall of Babylon under Cyrus. **their reproach**—This constituted a leading feature in their guilt; they treated with proud contumely the covenant people after the taking of Jerusalem by Nebuchadnezzar (ch. 25:3, 6; Zeph. 2:9, 10), and appropriated Israel's territory (Jer. 49:1; Amos 1:13-15). **furbished, to consume**—MAURER punctuates thus, "Drawn for the slaughter, it is furbished to devour ('consume'), to glitter." *English Version,* "to consume because of the glittering," means, "to consume *by reason of the lightning, flash-like rapidity* with which it falls." Five years after the fall of Jerusalem, Ammon was destroyed for aiding Ishmael in usurping the government of Judea against the will of the king of Babylon (II Kings 25: 25; Jer. 41:15) [GROTIUS]. **29. see vanity . . . divine a lie**—Ammon, too, had false diviners who flattered them with assurances of safety; the only result of which will be to "bring Ammon upon the necks . . . ," i.e., to add the Ammonites to the *headless trunks* of the slain of Judah, whose bad example Ammon followed, and "whose day" of visitation for their guilt "is come." **when their iniquity shall have an end**—See *Note,* vs. 25. **30. Shall I cause it to return into his sheath**—viz., without first destroying Ammon. Certainly not (Jer. 47:6, 7). Others, as *Margin,* less suitably read it imperatively, "Cause it to return," i.e., after it has done the work appointed to it. **in the land of thy nativity**—Ammon was not to be carried away captive as Judah, but to perish in his own land. **31. blow against thee in . . .**—rather, "blow upon thee with the fire . . . ." Image from smelting metals (ch. 22: 20, 21). **brutish**—ferocious. **skilful to destroy**—lit., "artificers of destruction"; alluding to Isaiah 54:16. **32. thy blood shall be**—i.e., shall flow. **be no more remembered**—be consigned as a nation to oblivion.

ADAM CLARKE

28. *Concerning the Ammonites.* They had reproached and insulted Judea in its low estate; see chap. xxv. This prophecy against them was fulfilled about five years after the taking of Jerusalem. See Joseph. *Ant.*, lib. x; c. 11; and Jeremiah xxvii; xlviii; **xlix; Ezekiel xxv.**

30. *I will judge thee.* This seems to refer to Nebuchadnezzar, who, after his return from Jerusalem, became insane, and lived like a beast for seven years; but was afterwards restored, and acknowledged the Lord.

MATTHEW HENRY

CHAPTER 22

Verses 1–16

The prophet is authorized to *judge the bloody city,* the *city of bloods.* Jerusalem is so called because her crimes in general were bloody crimes (*ch.* vii. 23), such as polluted her in her blood.

I. He is to find Jerusalem guilty of many heinous crimes. *The city sheds blood in the midst of it,* where the magistrates would, if anywhere, be vigilant. *She makes idols against herself to destroy herself, v.* 3. *In thee have* the children *set light by their father and mother,* mocked them, and despised them, *v.* 7. To enrich themselves they wronged the poor (*v.* 7). *Thou hast despised my holy things,* holy oracles, holy ordinances, *v.* 8. Jerusalem had been famous for its purity, but now *in the midst of thee they commit lewdness* (*v.* 9). Unmindfulness of God was at the bottom of all this wickedness (*v.* 12): "*Thou hast forgotten me,* else thou wouldst not have done thus."

II. He is to pass sentence upon Jerusalem for these crimes. Let her know that she has filled up the measure of her iniquity, and that her sins call for speedy vengeance. She has made *her time to come* (*v.* 3), *her days to draw near* for punishment (*v.* 4). God has justly exposed her to the contempt and scorn of all her neighbours (*v.* 4). Since she has walked in the way of the heathen, and learned their works, she shall have enough of them (*v.* 15): "*I will* not only send thee *among the heathen,* out of thy own land, but *I will scatter thee* among them and *disperse thee in the countries.*"

JAMIESON, FAUSSET, BROWN

CHAPTER 22

VSS. 1-31. GOD'S JUDGMENT ON THE SINFULNESS OF JERUSALEM. Repetition of the charges in ch. 20; only that there they were stated in an historical review of the *past* and present; here the *present* sins of the nation exclusively are brought forward. **2.** See ch. 20:4; i.e., "Wilt thou *not* judge . . . ?" (cf. ch. 23:36). **the bloody city**—lit., "the city of bloods"; so called on account of murders perpetrated in her, and sacrifices of children to Molech (vss. 3, 4, 6, 9; ch. 24:6, 9). **3. sheddeth blood . . . that her time may come**—Instead of deriving advantage from her bloody sacrifices to idols, she only thereby brought on herself "the time" of her punishment. **against herself**—(Prov. 8:36). **4. thy days**—the shorter period, viz., that of the *siege.* **thy years**—the longer period of the *captivity.* The "days" and "years" express that she is ripe for punishment. **5. infamous**—They mockingly call thee, "Thou polluted one in name (*Margin*), and full of confusion" [FAIRBAIRN], (referring to the tumultuous violence prevalent in it). Thus the nations "far and near" mocked her as at once sullied in character and in actual fact lawless. What a sad contrast to the Jerusalem once designated "the holy city!" **6.** Rather, "The princes . . . each according to his power, were in thee, to shed blood" (as if this was the only object of their existence). "Power," lit., "arm"; they, who ought to have been patterns of justice, made their own arm of might their only law. **7. set light by**—Children have made light of, disrespected, father . . . (Deut. 27:16). From vs. 7 to vs. 12 are enumerated the sins committed in violation of Moses' law. **9. men that carry tales**—*informers,* who by misrepresentations cause innocent blood to be shed (Lev. 19:16). Lit., "one who goes to and fro as a *merchant.*" **10. set apart for pollution**—i.e., set apart *as unclean* (Lev. 18:19). **12. forgotten me**—(Deut. 32:18; Jer. 2:32; 3:21). **13. smitten mine hand**—in token of the indignant vengeance which I will execute on thee (*Note,* ch. 21:17). **14.** (Ch. 21:7.) **15. consume thy filthiness out of thee**—the object of God in scattering the Jews. **16. take thine inheritance in thyself**—Formerly thou wast Mine inheritance; but now, full of guilt, thou

ADAM CLARKE

CHAPTER 22

2. *Wilt thou judge the bloody city?* Pronounce the sentence of death against the murderers. *Shew her all her abominations.* And a most revolting and dreadful catalogue of these is in consequence exhibited.

3. *Her time may come.* Till now, it was My long-suffering; she has fulfilled her days—completed the time of her probation; has not mended, but is daily worse; therefore her judgment can linger no longer.

5. *Those that be near.* Both distant as well as neighboring provinces consider you the most abandoned of characters, and through you many have been involved in distress and ruin.

6. *Behold, the princes.* You are a vile and murderous people, and your princes have been of the same character.

7. *In thee have they set light.* The children do not reverence their parents. The stranger is not only not succored, but he is oppressed. The widows and fatherless are vexed by wrongs and exactions.

8. *Thou hast despised.* All My ordinances are not only neglected, but treated with contempt, and My Sabbaths profaned. There is not only no power of godliness among you, but there is no form.

9. *In thee are men that carry tales.* Witnesses that will swear anything, even where life is concerned. *They eat upon the mountains.* Sacrifice to idols, and celebrate their festivals.

10. *In thee have they discovered.* They are guilty of the most abominable incest and unnatural lust. *In thee have they humbled.* In their unholy and unnatural connections, they have not abstained from those set apart because of their infirmities. The catalogue of crimes that follow is too plain to require comment.

MATTHEW HENRY

Verses 17–22

I. The wretched degeneracy of the house of Israel is described. In David's and Solomon's time it had been *a head of gold*; when the kingdoms were divided it was as the *arms of silver*. It has degenerated into baser metal. *They are all brass, and tin, and iron, and lead*, which some make to signify divers sorts of sinners among them. The *house of Israel has become dross to me*. So she is in God's account. They were silver, but now they are *even the dross of silver*; the word signifies all the dirt, and rubbish, and worthless stuff, that are separated from the silver in the washing, melting, and refining of it.

II. The woeful destruction of this degenerate house of Israel is foretold. They are all gathered together in Jerusalem; thither people fled from all parts of the country as to a city of refuge. Now God tells them that their flocking into Jerusalem should be as the gathering of various sorts of metal into the furnace or crucible, to be melted down, and to have the dross separated from them.

Verses 23–31

I. A general idea given of the land of Israel, how well it deserved the judgments coming to destroy it and how much it needed these judgments to refine it. Let the prophet tell her plainly, "*Thou art the land that is not cleansed*, not refined as metal is, and therefore needest to be again put into the furnace."

II. They had all helped to fill the measure of the nation's guilt, but none had done anything towards the emptying of it. The *prophets*, who pretended to make known the mind of God to them, were not only *deceivers*, but *devourers* (*v.* 25). They devoured souls by flattering sinners into a false peace. The priests, who were teachers by office, violated the law of God, which they should have observed and taught others to observe. They did not *put a difference between the holy and profane*, *the clean and the unclean*, according to the directions of the law. They *hid their eyes from God's sabbaths* and looked another way when they should have inspected the behaviour of the people on sabbath days. The princes were as daring transgressors of the law as any (*v.* 27): *They are like wolves ravening the prey;* for such is power without justice and goodness to direct it. The prophets *daubed them with untempered mortar*, told them in God's name that there was no harm in what they did. Daubing prophets are the great supporters of ravening princes. The people that had any power in their hands learned of their princes to abuse it, *v.* 29.

There is none that appears as an intercessor for them (*v.* 30): *I sought for a man among them that should stand in the gap, but I found none.* Sin makes a gap in the hedge of protection that is about a people at which good things run out from them and evil things pour in upon them. There is a way of standing in the gap, by repentance, and prayer, and reformation. Moses stood in the gap when he made intercession for Israel to *turn away the wrath of God*, Ps. cvi. 23.

JAMIESON, FAUSSET, BROWN

art no longer Mine, but *thine own inheritance to thyself;* "in the sight of the heathen," i.e., even they shall see that, now that thou hast become a captive, thou art no longer owned as Mine [VATABLUS]. FAIRBAIRN and others needlessly take the *Hebrew* from a different root, "thou shalt be *polluted by* ('in' [HENDERSON]) *thyself . . .*"; the heathen shall regard thee as a polluted thing, who hast brought thine own reproach on thyself. **18. dross . . . brass**—Israel has become a worthless compound of the dross of silver (implying not merely corruption, but *degeneracy* from good to bad, Isa. 1:22, especially offensive) and of the baser metals. Hence the people must be thrown into the furnace of judgment, that the bad may be consumed, and the good separated (Jer. 6:29, 30). **23.** From this verse to the end he shows the general corruption of all ranks. **24. land . . . not cleansed**—not cleared or cultivated; all a scene of desolation; a fit emblem of the moral wilderness state of the people. **nor rained upon**—a mark of divine "indignation"; as the early and latter rain, on which the productiveness of the land depended, was one of the great covenant blessings. Joel (2:23) promises the return of the former and latter rain, with the restoration of God's favor. **25. conspiracy**—The false prophets have conspired both to propagate error and to oppose the messages of God's servants. *They* are mentioned first, as their bad influence extended the widest. **prey**—Their aim was greed of gain, "treasure, and precious things" (Hos. 6:9; Zeph. 3:3, 4; Matt. 23:14). **made . . . many widows**—by occasioning, through false prophecies, the war with the Chaldeans in which the husbands fell. **26. Her priests**—whose "lips should have kept knowledge" (Mal. 2:7). **violated**—not simply *transgressed;* but, *have done violence to* the law, by wresting it to wrong ends, and putting wrong constructions on it. **put no difference between the holy and profane . . .**—made no distinction between the clean and unclean (Lev. 10:10), the Sabbath and other days, sanctioning violations of that holy day. "Holy" means, *what is dedicated to God;* "profane," *what is in common use;* "unclean," *what is forbidden to be eaten;* "clean," *what is lawful to be eaten.* **I am profaned among them**—They abuse My name to false or unjust purposes. **27. princes**—who should have employed the influence of their position for the people's welfare, made "gain" their sole aim. **wolves**—notorious for fierce and ravening cruelty (Mic. 3:2, 3, 9-11; John 10:12). **28.** Referring to the false assurances of peace with which the prophets flattered the people, that they should not submit to the king of Babylon (*Note*, ch. 13:10; 21:29; Jer. 6:14; 23:16, 17; 27:9, 10). **29. The people**—put last, after the mention of those in office. Corruption had spread downwards through the whole community. **wrongfully**—i.e., "without cause," gratuitously, without the stranger proselyte giving any just provocation; nay, he of all others being one who ought to have been won to the worship of Jehovah by kindness, instead of being alienated by oppression; especially as the Israelites were commanded to remember that they themselves had been "strangers in Egypt" (Exod. 22:21; 23:9). **30. the hedge**—the wall (*Note*, ch. 13:5); image for *leading the people to repentance.* **the gap**—the breach (Ps. 106:23); image for *interceding between the people and God* (Gen. 20:7; Exod. 32:11; Num. 16:48). **I found none**—(Jer. 5:1)—not that literally there was not a righteous man in the city. For Jeremiah, Baruch, etc., were still there; but Jeremiah had been forbidden to pray for the people (Jer. 11:14), as being doomed to wrath. None now, of the godly, knowing the desperate state of the people, and God's purpose as to them, was *willing* longer to interpose between God's wrath and them. And none "among them," i.e., among those just enumerated as guilty of such sins (vss. 25-29), was morally *able* for such an office. **31. their own way . . . recompensed upon their heads**—(ch. 9:10; 11:21; 16:43; Prov. 1:31; Isa. 3:11; Jer. 6:19).

ADAM CLARKE

18. *The house of Israel is to me become dross.* You must be put in the furnace, and subjected to the most intense fire, till your impurities are consumed away.

19. *I will gather you.* Jerusalem is represented here as the fining pot; all the people are to be gathered together in it, and the Chaldean fire is to melt the whole. And God will increase your sufferings; as the refiner blows the fire with his bellows, so God will blow upon you with the fire of His wrath, v. 21.

25. *There is a conspiracy.* The false prophets have united together to say and support the same things; and have been the cause of the destruction of souls, and the death of many, so that widows, through their means, are multiplied in you.

26. *Her priests.* Even they whose lips should preserve knowledge have not instructed the people; they have violated My law, not only in their private conduct, but in their careless and corrupt manner of serving in My temple.

27. *Her princes.* Are as bad as her priests; they are rapacious, and grievously oppress the people by unjust impositions in order to increase their revenues.

28. *Her prophets.* Even those who profess themselves to be My prophets have been unfaithful in the discharge of their office; have soothed the people in their sins, and pretended to have oracles of peace and safety when I had not spoken to them.

30. *I sought for a man.* I saw that there was a grievous breach made in the moral state of the people, and I sought for a man that would *stand in the gap;* that would faithfully exhort, reprove, and counsel, with all long-suffering and doctrine. But none was to be found!

MATTHEW HENRY

CHAPTER 23

Verses 1–10

The sinners that are here to be exposed are *two women*, two kingdoms, sister-kingdoms, Israel and

JAMIESON, FAUSSET, BROWN

CHAPTER 23

Vss. 1-49. ISRAEL'S AND JUDAH'S SIN AND PUNISHMENT ARE PARABOLICALLY PORTRAYED UNDER THE NAMES AHOLAH AND AHOLIBAH. The imagery is similar to that in ch. 16; but here the reference is not as there so much to the breach of the spiritual marriage covenant with God by the people's *idolatries*, as by their *worldly spirit*, and their trusting to alliances with the heathen for safety, rather than to God. **2. two . . . of one mother**—Israel and Judah, one nation by birth from the same ancestress, Sarah.

ADAM CLARKE

CHAPTER 23

2. *Son of man, there were two women.* All the Hebrews were derived from one source,

MATTHEW HENRY

Judah, *daughters of one mother*, having been for a long time but *one people*. 1. When they were one (*v.* 3): *They committed whoredoms in Egypt*, for there they were guilty of idolatry, as we read before, *ch.* xx. 8. 2. Their names when they became two, *v.* 4. The kingdom of Israel is called the *elder sister*, because that first made the breach—the *greater sister* (so the word is), for ten tribes belonged to that kingdom and only two to the other. In this parable Samaria and the kingdom of Israel shall bear the name of *Aholah—her own tabernacle*, because the places of worship which that kingdom had were of their own devising, and the worship itself was their own invention. Jerusalem and the kingdom of Judah bear the name of *Aholibah—my tabernacle is in her*, because *their* temple was the place which God himself had *chosen* to *put his name there*.

3. The treacherous departure of the kingdom of Israel from God (*v.* 5). Though the ten tribes had deserted the house of David, yet God owned them for *his* still; as long as they worshipped the God of Israel only, though by images, he did not quite cast them off. But Aholah played the harlot, brought in the worship of Baal (1 Kings xvi. 31), in competition with Jehovah (1 Kings xviii. 21), as a vile adulteress *dotes on her lovers*, so she doted upon her neighbours, particularly the Assyrians. She admired their idols and worshipped them.

The destruction of the kingdom of Israel for their apostasy from God (*v.* 9, 10): *I have delivered her into the hand of her lovers*. God first justly gave her up to her lust, and then gave her up *to her lovers*. We have the story at large 2 Kings xvii. 6, &c.

Verses 11–21

The prophet Hosea, in his time, observed that the two tribes retained their integrity, in a great measure, when the ten tribes had apostatized (Hos. xi. 12). By some unhappy matches made between the house of David and the house of Ahab the worship of Baal had been brought into the kingdom of Judah, but had been by the reforming kings worked out again. In the reign of Manasseh, soon after the kingdom of Judah had seen the destruction of the kingdom of Israel, they became more corrupt than Israel had been in their inordinate love of idols, *v.* 11.

I. Jerusalem, that had been a *faithful city, became a harlot*, Isa. i. 21. She also *doted upon the Assyrians* (*v.* 12), joined in league with them, joined in worship with them. And thus they grew to affect everything that was foreign and to despise their own nation; and even the religion of it was mean and homely. She doted upon the Babylonian captains (*v.* 15, 16), joined in alliance with that kingdom, and sent for patterns of their images, altars, and temples, and made use of them in their worship.

II. God justly gives a bill of divorce to this now faithless city. Sin alienates God's mind from the sinner, and justly, for it is the alienation of the sinner's mind from God.

JAMIESON, FAUSSET, BROWN

3. Even so early in their history as their Egyptian sojourn, they committed idolatries (*Notes*, ch. 20: 6-8; Josh. 24:14). **in their youth**—an aggravation of their sin. It was at the very time of their receiving extraordinary favors from God (ch. 16:6, 22). **they bruised**—viz., the Egyptians. **4. Aholah**—i.e., "*Her* tent" (put for *worship*, as the first worship of God in Israel was in a *tent* or tabernacle), as contrasted with Aholibah, i.e., "*My* tent in her." The Bethel worship of Samaria was of *her own* devising, not of God's appointment; the temple-worship of Jerusalem was expressly *appointed by Jehovah*, who "dwelt" there, "setting up His tabernacle among the people as His" (Exod. 25:8; Lev. 26:11, 12; Josh. 22: 19; Ps. 76:2). **the elder**—Samaria is called "the elder" because she preceded Judah in her apostasy and its punishment. **they were mine**—Previous to apostasy under Jeroboam, Samaria (Israel, or the ten tribes), equally with Judah, worshipped the true God. God therefore never renounced the right over Israel, but sent prophets, as Elijah and Elisha, to declare His will to them. **5. when . . . mine**—lit., "under Me," i.e., subject to Me as her lawful husband. **neighbours**—On the northeast the kingdom of Israel bordered on that of Assyria; for the latter had occupied much of Syria. Their neighborhood in locality was emblematical of their being near in corruption of morals and worship. The *alliances* of Israel with Assyria, which are the chief subject of reprobation here, tended to this (II Kings 15:19; 16:7, 9; 17:3; Hos. 8:9). **6. blue**—rather, "purple" [FAIRBAIRN]. As a lustful woman's passions are fired by showy dress and youthful appearance in men, so Israel was seduced by the pomp and power of Assyria (cf. Isa. 10:8). **horsemen**—cavaliers. **7. all their idols**—There was nothing that she refused to her lovers. **8. whoredoms brought from Egypt**—the calves set up in Dan and Bethel by Jeroboam, answering to the Egyptian bull-formed idol Apis. Her *alliances* with Egypt *politically* are also meant (Isa. 30:2, 3; 31:1). The ten tribes probably resumed the Egyptian rites, in order to enlist the Egyptians against Judah (II Chron. 12:2-4). **9.** God, in righteous retribution, turned their objects of trust into the instruments of their punishment: Pul, Tiglath-pileser, Esar-haddon, and Shalmaneser (II Kings 15:19, 29; 17:3, 6, 24; Ezra 4:2, 10). "It was their sin to have sought after such lovers, and it was to be their punishment that these lovers should become their destroyers" [FAIRBAIRN]. **10. became famous**—lit., "she became a name," i.e., as notorious by her punishment as she had been by her sins, so as to be quoted as a *warning* to others. **women**—i.e., neighboring peoples. **11.** Judah, the southern kingdom, though having the "warning" (*Note*, vs. 10) of the northern kingdom before her eyes, instead of profiting by it, went to even greater lengths in corruption than Israel. Her greater spiritual privileges made her guilt the greater (ch. 16:47, 51; Jer. 3:11). **12.** (Vss. 6, 23.) **most gorgeously**—lit., "to perfection." GROTIUS translates, "wearing a crown," or "chaplet," such as lovers wore in visiting their mistresses. **13. one way**—both alike forsaking God for heathen confidences. **14. vermilion**—the peculiar color of the Chaldeans, as purple was of the Assyrians. In striking agreement with this verse is the fact that the Assyrian sculptures lately discovered have painted and colored bas-reliefs in red, blue, and black. The Jews (for instance Jehoiakim, Jer. 22:14) copied these (cf. ch. 8:10). **15. exceeding in dyed attire**—rather, "in ample dyed *turbans*"; lit., "redundant with dyed turbans." The Assyrians delighted in ample, flowing, and richly colored tunics, scarfs, girdles, and head-dresses or turbans, varying in ornaments according to the rank. **Chaldea, . . . land of their nativity**—between the Black and Caspian Seas (*Note*, Isa. 23:13). **princes**—lit., a first-rate military class that fought by threes in the chariots, one guiding the horses, the other two fighting. **16. sent messengers . . . into Chaldea**—(ch. 16: 29). It was she that solicited the Chaldeans, not they her. Probably the occasion was when Judah sought to strengthen herself by a Chaldean alliance against a menaced attack by Egypt (cf. II Kings 23: 29-35; 24:1-7). God made the object of their sinful desire the instrument of their punishment. Jehoiakim, probably by a stipulation of tribute, enlisted Nebuchadnezzar against Pharaoh, whose tributary he previously had been; failing to keep his stipulation, he brought on himself Nebuchadnezzar's vengeance. **17. alienated from them**—viz., from the Chaldeans: turning again to the Egyptians (vs. 19), trying by their help to throw off her solemn engagements to Babylon (cf. Jer. 37:5, 7; II Kings 24:7). **18. my mind was alienated from her**—lit., "was broken off from her." Just retribution for "her mind being alienated (broken off) from the

ADAM CLARKE

Abraham and Sarah; and, till the schism under Rehoboam, formed but one people. But as these ten tribes and a half separated from Judah and Benjamin, they became two distinct people under different kings, called the kingdom of Judah, and the kingdom of Israel. They are called here, because of their consanguinity, two sisters. The elder, Samaria, was called *Aholah*, "a tent." The younger, Judah, was called *Aholibah*, "my tent is in her," because the temple of God was in Jerusalem, the seat of the government of the kingdom of Judah.

5. *And Aholah played the harlot.* Without entering into detail here, or following the figures, they both became idolatrous, and received the impure rites of the Egyptians, Assyrians, and Chaldeans, of which connection the prophet speaks here as he did in chap. xvi.

In this chapter there are many of what we would call indelicate expressions, because a parallel is run between idolatry and prostitution, and the circumstances of the latter illustrate the peculiarities of the former. In such cases, perhaps, the matter alone was given to the prophet, and he was left to use his own language and amplify as he saw good. Ezekiel was among the Jews what Juvenal was among the Romans—a rough reprover of the most abominable vices. They both spoke of things as they found them; stripped vice naked, and scourged it publicly.

6. *Clothed with blue.* The "purple" dye was highly valued among the ancients, and at first was used only by kings; at last it was used among the military, particularly by officers of high rank in the country.

14. *Men portrayed upon the wall.* See chap. viii. 10.

MATTHEW HENRY

And when she had had enough of the Chaldeans, she courted the *Egyptians* (*v.* 20), would come into an alliance with them, and would join with them in their idolatries. Thus *she multiplied her whoredoms*, repeated her former whoredoms, and encouraged herself by calling *to remembrance the days of her youth*. Those who, instead of reflecting upon their former sins with sorrow and shame, reflect upon them with pleasure and pride, bid defiance to repentance. They called it *God's remembrance*, and provoked him to remember it against them.

Verses 22–35

Jerusalem indicted by the name of *Aholibah*, as a false traitor to her sovereign Lord the God of heaven, not having his fear before her eyes, but moved by the instigation of the devil, had revolted from her allegiance to him.

I. Her old confederates must be her executioners (*v.* 22): "*I will raise up thy lovers against thee*, the Chaldeans, whom formerly thou didst admire and with whom thou hast perfidiously broken covenant."

II. The execution to be done upon her. Her enemies shall come against her *on every side* (*v.* 22). They shall come with military force (*v.* 24), a vast army, and well armed. They shall have justice on their side: "*I will set judgment before them.*" It being a war of revenge, *they shall deal with thee hatefully*, *v.* 29. The *clothes* and the *fair jewels*, with which she had endeavoured to recommend herself to her lovers, these she shall be stripped of, *v.* 26. Both city and country shall be impoverished and her children shall go into captivity. She shall be stigmatized and deformed: "They shall *take away thy nose and thy ears*, shall mark thee for a harlot, and render thee for ever odious," *v.* 25. Some will have this to be understood figuratively; and by the nose they think is meant the kingly dignity, and by the ears that of the priesthood. Because she had trod in the steps of Samaria's sins, she must expect no other than Samaria's fate, *v.* 31. They have been bad, very bad, and that justifies God in all that is brought upon them (*v.* 30): *I will do these things unto thee because thou hast gone a-whoring after the heathen*, and (*v.* 35) *because thou hast forgotten me and cast me behind thy back*. Forgetfulness of God is at the bottom of all our treacherous departures from him. This fire, though consuming to many, shall be refining to a remnant (*v.* 27). Before the captivity, no nation (all things considered) was more impetuously bent upon idols and idolatry than they were, after that captivity no nation was more vehemently set against idols and idolatry.

Verses 36–49

After the ten tribes were carried into captivity, the remains of it by degrees incorporated with the kingdom of Judah, and gained a settlement in Jerusalem; so that the *two sisters* had in effect become *one* again; and therefore, "Thou shalt now be employed, in God's name, to *judge them, ch.* xx. 4. The matter is rather worse than better since the union."

I. *Declare unto them* openly and boldly *their abominations*. They have been guilty of gross idolatry, here called *adultery* (*v.* 37), have broken their marriage-covenant with God. They have committed the most barbarous murders, in sacrificing their children to Moloch. They have profaned the sacred things with which God had dignified and distinguished them, *v.* 38. They *defiled the sanctuary* on *the same day* that they *profaned the sabbath*. They have courted foreign alliances. This also is represented by the sin of adultery, for it was a departure from God, *in* whom alone they ought to put their trust. Great preparation was made for the reception of these foreign ministers, for their public entry and public audience, which is compared to the pains that an adulteress takes to make herself look handsome, *v.* 40–42. The *men of the common sort* were there to increase the crowd; and *with them were brought Sabeans from the wilderness*. The margin reads it *drunkards from the wilderness*, that would drink healths to the prosperity of this grand alliance. But an alliance between the nation of the Jews and a heathen nation can never be for the advantage of either. They are *iron and clay*, that will not mix, nor will God bless such an alliance.

JAMIESON, FAUSSET, BROWN

Chaldeans" (vs. 17), to whom she had sworn fealty (ch. 17:12-19). "Discovered" implies the open shamelessness of her apostasy. **19.** Israel first "called" her lusts, practised when in Egypt, "to her (fond) *remembrance*," and then actually returned to them. Mark the danger of suffering the memory to dwell on the pleasure felt in past sins. **20. their paramours**—i.e., her paramours *among them* (the Egyptians); she doted upon their persons as her paramours (vss. 5, 12, 16). **flesh**—the membrum virile (very large in the ass). Cf. Leviticus 15:2, *Margin;* Ezekiel 16:26. **issue of horses**—the seminal issue. The horse was made by the Egyptians the hieroglyphic for a lustful person. **21. calledst to remembrance**—"didst repeat" [MAURER]. **in bruising**—in suffering . . . to be bruised. **22. lovers . . . alienated**—(vs. 17). Illicit love, soon or late, ends in open hatred (II Sam. 13:15). The Babylonians, the objects formerly of their God-forgetting love, but now, with characteristic fickleness, objects of their hatred, shall be made by God the instruments of their punishment. **23. Pekod . . .**—(Jer. 50:21). Not a geographical name, but descriptive of Babylon. "Visitation," peculiarly the *land of "judgment";* in a double sense: *actively*, the inflicter of judgment on Judah; *passively*, as about to be afterwards herself the object of judgment. **Shoa . . . Koa**—"rich . . . noble"; descriptive of Babylon in her prosperity, having all the world's wealth and dignity at her disposal. MAURER suggests that, as descriptive appellatives are subjoined to the proper name, "all the Assyrians" in the second hemistich of the verse (as the verse ought to be divided at "Koa"), so Pekod, Shoa, and Koa must be appellatives descriptive of "The Babylonians and . . . Chaldeans" in the first hemistich; "Pekod" meaning "prefects"; Shoa . . . Koa, "rich . . . princely." **desirable young men**—strong irony. Alluding to vs. 12, these "desirable young men" whom thou didst so "dote upon" for their manly vigor of appearance, shall by that very vigor be the better able to chastise thee. **24. with chariots**—or, "with armaments"; so LXX; "axes" [MAURER]; or, joining it with "wagons," translate, "with *scythe-armed* wagons," or "chariots" [GROTIUS]. **weels**—The unusual height of these increased their formidable appearance (ch. 1:16-20). **their judgments**—which awarded barbarously severe punishments (Jer. 52:9; 29:22). **25. take away thy nose . . . ears**—Adulteresses were punished so among the Egyptians and Chaldeans. Oriental beauties wore ornaments in the ear and nose. How just the retribution, that the features most bejewelled should be mutilated! So, allegorically as to Judah, the spiritual adulteress. **26. strip . . . of . . . clothes**—whereby she attracted her paramours (ch. 16:39). **27. Thus . . . make . . . lewdness to cease**—The captivity has made the Jews ever since abhor idolatry, not only on their return from Babylon, but for the last nineteen centuries of their dispersion, as foretold (Hos. 3:4). **28.** (Vss. 17, 18; ch. 16:37.) **29. take away . . . thy labour**—i.e., the fruits of thy labor. **leave thee naked**—as captive females are treated. **31. her cup**—of punishment (Ps. 11:6; 75:8; Jer. 25:15, etc.). Thy guilt and that of Israel being alike, your punishment shall be alike. **34. break . . . sherds**—So greedily shalt thou suck out every drop like one drinking to madness (the effect invariably ascribed to drinking God's cup of wrath, Jer. 51:7; Hab. 2: 16) that thou shalt crunch the very shreds of it; i.e., there shall be no evil left which thou shalt not taste. **pluck off thine own breasts**—enraged against them as the ministers to thine adultery. **35. forgotten me**—(Jer. 2:32; 13:25). **cast me behind thy back**—(I Kings 14:9; Neh. 9:26). **bear . . . thy lewdness**—i.e., its penal consequences (Prov. 1:31). **36-44.** A summing up of the sins of the two sisters, especially those of Judah. **36. Wilt thou** (not) judge (*Note*, ch. 20:4)? **38. the same day**—On the very day that they had burned their children to Molech in the valley of Gehenna, they shamelessly and hypocritically presented themselves as worshippers in Jehovah's temple (Jer. 7:9, 10). **40. messenger was sent**—viz., by Judah (vs. 16; Isa. 57:9). **paintedst . . . eyes**—(II Kings 9:30, *Margin;* Jer. 4:30). Black paint was spread on the eyelids of beauties to make the white of the eye more attractive by the contrast, so Judah left no seductive art untried. **41. bed**—divan. While men reclined at table, women sat, as it seemed indelicate for them to lie down (Amos 6:4), [GROTIUS]. **table**—i.e., the idolatrous altar. **mine incense**—which I had given thee, and which thou oughtest to have offered to Me (ch. 16: 18, 19; Hos. 2:8; cf. Prov. 7:17). **42. Sabeans**—Not content with the princely, handsome Assyrians, the sisters brought to themselves the rude robber hordes of *Sabeans* (Job 1:15). The *Keri*, or *Margin*, reads

ADAM CLARKE

23. *Pekod, and Shoa, and Koa*. These names have been thought to designate certain people bordering on the Chaldeans, but no geographer has ever been able to find them out. In our old translations these names were considered appellatives—"rulers, mighty men, and tyrants." Others, following the literal import of the words, have translated, "visiting, shouting, and retreating."

25. *Shall take away thy nose*. A punishment frequent among the Persians and Chaldeans, as ancient authors tell.

32. *Thou shalt drink of thy sisters' cup*. You shall be ruined and desolated as Samaria was.

38. *They have defiled my sanctuary*. By placing idols there.

41. *And satest upon a stately bed*. Hast raised a stately altar to your idols, probably alluding to that which Ahaz ordered to be made, after the similitude of that which he saw at Damascus. The *bed* here is in allusion to the sofas on which the ancients were accustomed to recline at their meals, or to the couches on which they place Asiatic brides, with incense pots and sweetmeats on a table before them.

42. *And a voice of a multitude*. This seems to be an account of an idolatrous festival, where a riotous multitude was assembled, and fellows of the baser sort, with bracelets on their arms and chaplets on their heads, performed the religious rites.

MATTHEW HENRY

II. Let them be made to foresee the judgments that are coming upon them for these sins (*v.* 45). The prophets, whose office it was, in God's name, judge them and pass sentence upon them. This judgment being given by the righteous men, the righteous God will award execution, *v.* 46, 47. The same as before, *v.* 23, &c. The destruction of God's city, like the death of God's saints, shall do that for them which ordinances and providences before could not do; so that Jerusalem shall rise out of its ashes a new lump, as gold comes out of the furnace purified from its dross.

CHAPTER 24

Verses 1–14

I. The notice God gives to Ezekiel in Babylon of Nebuchadnezzar's laying siege to Jerusalem (*v.* 2): "*Son of man*, take notice, *the king of Babylon*, who is now abroad with his army, thou knowest not where, *set himself against Jerusalem this same day*." He tells the prophet, that the prophet might tell the people, that so when it proved to be punctually true, it might be a confirmation of the prophet's mission.

II. The notice which he orders him to take of it. He must enter it in his book, *memorandum*, that *in the ninth year* of Jehoiachin's captivity, in the tenth month, on the tenth day of the month, the king of Babylon laid siege to Jerusalem; and the date here agrees with the date in the history, 2 Kings xxv. 1.

III. The notice which he orders him to give to the people. A rebellious house will soon be a ruinous house.

1. He must show them this by a sign; that of a *boiling pot*. This agrees with Jeremiah's vision many years before (Jer. i. 13, *I see a seething pot, with the face towards the north;* and the explanation of it (*v.* 15) makes it to signify the besieging of Jerusalem by the *northern* nations); to confront the vain confidence of the princes of Jerusalem, who had said (*ch.* xi. 3), *This city is the cauldron and we are the flesh*, meaning, "We are as safe here as if we were surrounded with walls of brass." "Well," says God, "it shall be so; you shall be boiled in Jerusalem, as the *flesh in the cauldron*." Those that from all parts of the country fled into Jerusalem for safety would be sadly disappointed; and yet there was no getting out of it, but they must be forced to abide by it, as the flesh in a boiling pot.

2. He must give them a comment upon this sign. It is to be construed as a *woe to the bloody city*, *v.* 6. Jerusalem, during the siege, is like a pot boiling over the fire. Care is taken to keep a good fire under the pot, which signifies the closeness of the siege. Commission is given to the Chaldeans (*v.* 10) to *heap on wood, and kindle the fire*. Here is no line, no lot of mercy, made use of; all goes to destruction. God would not take these severe methods with Jerusalem but that he is provoked to it (*v.* 7, 8).

Jerusalem was to be made an example and therefore was made a spectacle, to the world.

JAMIESON, FAUSSET, BROWN

"drunkards." **upon their hands**—upon the hands of the sisters, i.e., they allured Samaria and Judah to worship their gods. **43. Will they . . .**—Is it possible that paramours will desire any longer to commit whoredoms with so worn-out an old adulteress? **45. the righteous men**—the Chaldeans; the executioners of God's righteous vengeance (ch. 16:38), not that they were "righteous" in themselves (Hab. 1:3, 12, 13). **46. a company**—properly, "a council of judges" passing sentence on a criminal [GROTIUS]. The "removal" and "spoiling" by the Chaldean army is the execution of the judicial sentence of God. **47. stones**—the legal penalty of the adulteress (ch. 16:40, 41; John 8:5). Answering to the *stones* hurled by the Babylonians from engines in besieging Jerusalem. **houses . . . fire**—fulfilled (II Chron. 36: 17, 19). **48. (Vs. 27.) that all . . . may be taught not to do . . .**—(Deut. 13:11). **49. bear the sins of your idols**—i.e., the punishment of your idolatry. **know that I am the Lord God**—i.e., know it to your cost . . . by bitter suffering.

CHAPTER 24

Vss. 1-27. VISION OF THE BOILING CALDRON, AND OF THE DEATH OF EZEKIEL'S WIFE. **1, 2.** Ezekiel proves his divine mission by announcing the very day ("this same day") of the beginning of the investment of the city by Nebuchadnezzar; "the ninth year," viz., of Jehoiachin's captivity, "the tenth day of the tenth month"; though he was 300 miles away from Jerusalem among the captives at the Chebar (II Kings 25:1; Jer. 39:1). **set himself**—*laid siege;* "lay against." **3. pot**—caldron. Alluding to the self-confident proverb used among the people, ch. 11:3 (see my *Note*), "This city is the caldron and we be the flesh"; your proverb shall prove awfully true, but in a different sense from what you intend. So far from the city proving an iron, caldron-like defense from the fire, it shall be as a caldron set on the fire, and the people as so many pieces of meat subjected to boiling heat. See Jeremiah 1:13. **4. pieces thereof**—those which properly *belong to it, as its own.* **every good piece . . . choice bones**—i.e., the most distinguished of the people. The "choice bones" *in* the pot have flesh adhering to them. The "bones" *under* the pot (vs. 5) are those having no flesh and used as fuel, answering to the poorest who suffer first, and are put out of pain sooner than the rich who endure what answers to the slower process of boiling. **5. burn . . . bones**—rather, "*pile* the bones." Lit., "Let there be a *round* pile of the bones." **therein**—lit., "in the midst of it." **6. scum**—not ordinary, but *poisonous scum,* i.e., the people's all-pervading wickedness. **bring it out piece by piece**—"it," the contents of the pot; its flesh, i.e., "I will destroy the people of the city, not all at the same time, but by a series of successive attacks." Not as FAIRBAIRN, "on its every piece let it (the poisonous scum) go forth." **let no lot fall upon it**—i.e., no lot, such as is sometimes cast, to decide who are to be destroyed and who saved (II Sam. 8:2; Joel 3:3; Obadiah 11; Nah. 3:10). In former carryings away of captives, lots were cast to settle who were to go, and who to stay, but now all alike are to be cast out without distinction of rank, age, or sex. **7. upon the top of a rock**—or, "the dry, bare, exposed rock," so as to be conspicuous to all. Blood poured on a rock is not so soon absorbed as blood poured on the earth. The law ordered the blood even of a beast or fowl to be "covered with the dust" (Lev. 17:13); but Jerusalem was so shameless as to be at no pains to cover up the blood of innocent men slain in her. *Blood,* as the consummation of all sin, presupposes every other form of guilt. **8. That it might cause**—God *purposely* let her so shamelessly pour the blood on the bare rock, "*that it might*" the more loudly and openly cry for vengeance from on high; and that the connection between the guilt and the punishment might be the more palpable. The blood of Abel, though the ground received it, still cries to heaven for vengeance (Gen. 4:10, 11); much more blood shamelessly exposed on the bare rock. **set her blood**—She *shall* be paid back in kind (Matt. 7:2). She openly shed blood, and her blood shall openly be shed. **9. the pile for fire**—the hostile materials for the city's destruction. **10. spice it well**—that the meat may be the more palatable, i.e., I will make the foe delight in its destruction as much as one delights in well-seasoned, savory meat. GROTIUS, needlessly departing from the obvious sense, translates, "Let it be boiled down to a compound." **11. set it empty . . . that . . . brass . . . may burn, . . . that . . . scum . . . may be consumed**—Even the consumption of the contents is not enough; the caldron itself which is infected by

ADAM CLARKE

45. *And the righteous men.* The Chaldeans, thus called because they are appointed by God to execute judgment on these criminals.

47. *Shall stone them with stones.* As they did adulteresses under the law. See Lev. xx. 10; Deut. xxii. 22, compared with John viii. 3.

48. *Thus will I cause lewdness to cease.* Idolatry; and from that time to the present day the Jews never relapsed into idolatry.

49. *Ye shall bear the sins of your idols.* The punishment due to your adultery; your apostasy from God, and setting up idolatry in the land.

CHAPTER 24

1. *The ninth year.* This prophecy was given in the ninth year of Zedekiah, the very day in which the king of Babylon commenced the siege of Jerusalem.

3. *Set on a pot.* The pot was Jerusalem; the flesh, the inhabitants in general; "every good piece, the thigh, and the shoulder," King Zedekiah and his family; the "bones," the soldiers; and the setting on the pot, the commencement of the siege. The prophet was then in Mesopotamia; and he was told particularly to mark the day, that it might be seen how precisely the spirit of prophecy had shown the very day in which the siege took place. Under the same image of a boiling pot, Jeremiah had represented the siege of Jerusalem, chap. i. 13. Ezekiel was a priest; the action of boiling pots was familiar to him, as these things were much in use in the Temple service.

5. *Make it boil well.* Let it boil over, that its own scum may augment the fire, that the *bones*—the soldiers—may be seethed therein. Let its contentions, divided counsels, and disunion be the means of increasing its miseries.

6. *Let no lot fall upon it.* Pull out the flesh indiscriminately; let no piece be chosen for king or priest, thus showing that all should be involved in one indiscriminate ruin.

7. *For her blood is in the midst of her.* She gloried in her idol sacrifices; she offered them upon a rock, where the blood should remain evident; and she poured none upon the ground to cover it with dust, in horror of that moral evil that required the blood of an innocent creature to be shed, in order to the atonement of the offender's guilt. To cover the blood of the victim, was a command of the law, Lev. xvii. 13; Deut. xii. 24.

8. *That it might cause fury.* This very blood shall be against them, as the blood of Abel was against Cain.

10. *Heap on wood.* Let the siege be severe, the carnage great, and the ruin and catastrophe complete.

MATTHEW HENRY

Because she is incurably wicked she is abandoned to ruin, without remedy. Methods and means of reformation had been tried in vain (*v.* 13). It is therefore resolved that no more such methods shall be used: *Thou shalt not be purged from thy filthiness any more.* The fire shall no longer be a refining fire, but a consuming fire.

Verses 15–27

These verses conclude Ezekiel's prophecies of the destruction of Jerusalem; for after this, though he prophesied much concerning other nations, he said no more concerning Jerusalem, till he heard of the destruction of it, almost three years after, *ch.* xxxiii. 21.

I. The sign by which this was represented to them.

1. He must lose a good wife, that should suddenly be taken from him by death. God gave him notice of it before (*v.* 16). A beloved wife is the *desire of the eyes.* When the desire of our eyes is taken away with a stroke we must see and own the hand of God in it: *I take away the desire of thy eyes.*

2. He must deny himself the satisfaction of mourning for his wife, which would have been both an honour to her and an ease to the oppression of his own spirit. But Ezekiel is not allowed to do this, though he would perhaps be ill thought of by the people if he did it not.

He must not *eat the bread of men,* nor expect that his neighbours and friends should send him in provisions, as usually they did in such cases, presuming the mourners had no heart to provide meat for themselves; but, if it were sent, he must not eat of it. It could not but be greatly against the grain to flesh and blood not to lament the death of one he loved so dearly, but so God commands; and *I did in the morning as I was commanded.* He appeared in public without any signs of mourning. Here Ezekiel, to make himself a sign to the people, must exercise an extraordinary piece of self-denial.

II. The application of this sign. The people enquired the meaning of it (*v.* 19): *Wilt thou not tell us what these things are to us that thou doest so?* They knew that the death of his wife was a great affliction to him, and that he would not appear so unconcerned at it but for some good reason.

1. Let them know that if a faithful servant of God was thus afflicted only for his trial, shall such a generation of rebels against God go unpunished? That which was their public pride, the temple: "*I will profane my sanctuary,* by giving that into the enemy's hand, to be plundered and burnt." That which was their family-pleasure, which they looked upon with delight: "*Your sons and your daughters* (which are the dearer to you because they are but a few left of many, the rest having perished by famine and pestilence) shall *fall by the sword* of the Chaldeans." This was the punishment of sin.

2. Let them know that as Ezekiel wept not for his affliction so neither should they weep for theirs. He must say, *You shall do as I have done, v.* 22. *You shall not mourn nor weep, v.* 23. Their grief shall be so great that they shall be overwhelmed. Their calamities shall come so fast upon them, that by long custom they shall be *hardened in their sorrows* (Job. vi. 10) and stupefied. There shall be none of that sense of sorrow which would help to bring them to repentance, but that only which shall drive them to despair: "*You shall pine away for your iniquities,* with seared consciences and reprobate minds, and *you shall mourn,* not to God in prayer and confession of sin, but *one towards another,*" complaining of God.

JAMIESON, FAUSSET, BROWN

the poisonous scum must be destroyed, i.e., the city itself must be destroyed, not merely the inhabitants, just as the very house infected with leprosy was to be destroyed (Lev. 14:34-45). **12.** *herself*—rather, "she hath wearied *Me* out with lies"; or rather "with vain labors" on My part to purify her without being obliged to have recourse to judgments (cf. Isa. 43:24; Mal. 2:17) [MAURER]. However, *English Version* gives a good sense (cf. Isa. 47:13; 57:10). **13. lewdness**—determined, deliberate wickedness; from a *Hebrew* root, "to purpose." **I have purged thee**—i.e., I have left nothing untried which would tend towards purging thee, by sending prophets to invite thee to repentance, by giving thee the law with all its promises, privileges, and threats. **thou shalt not be purged . . . any more**—i.e., by My gracious interpositions; thou shalt be left to thine own course to take its fatal consequences. **14. go back**—desist; relax [FAIRBAIRN]. **15.** Second part of the vision; announcement of the death of Ezekiel's wife, and prohibition of the usual signs of mourning. **16. desire of . . . eyes**—his wife: representing the sanctuary (vs. 21) in which the Jews so much gloried. The energy and subordination of Ezekiel's whole life to his prophetic office is strikingly displayed in this narrative of his wife's death. It is the only memorable event of his personal history which he records, and this only in reference to his soul-absorbing work. His natural tenderness is shown by that graphic touch, "the desire of thine eyes." What amazing subjection, then, of his individual feeling to his prophetic duty is manifested in the simple statement (vs. 18), "So I spake . . . in the morning; and at even my wife died; and I did in the morning as I was commanded." **stroke**—a sudden visitation. The suddenness of it enhances the self-control of Ezekiel in so entirely merging individual feeling, which must have been especially acute under such trying circumstances, in the higher claims of duty to God. **17. Forbear to cry**—or, "Lament in silence"; not forbidding sorrow, but the *loud expression* of it [GROTIUS]. **no mourning**—typical of the universality of the ruin of Jerusalem, which would preclude mourning, such as is usual where calamity is but partial. "The dead" are purposely put in the *plural,* as referring ultimately to the *dead* who should perish at the taking of Jerusalem; though the *singular* might have been expected, as Ezekiel's wife was the immediate subject referred to: "make no mourning" *such as is usual* "for *the dead,* and such as shall be hereafter in Jerusalem" (Jer. 16:5-7). **tire of thine head**—thy headdress [FAIRBAIRN]. JEROME explains, "Thou shalt retain the hair which is usually cut in mourning." The fillet, binding the hair about the temples like a chaplet, was laid aside at such times. Uncovering the head was an ordinary sign of mourning in priests; whereas others covered their heads in mourning (II Sam. 15:30). The reason was, the priests had their headdress of fine twined linen given them for ornament, and as a badge of office. The high priest, as having on his head the holy anointing oil, was forbidden in *any* case to lay aside his headdress. But the priests might do so in the case of the death of the nearest relatives (Lev. 21:2, 3, 10). They then put on inferior attire, sprinkling also on their heads dust and ashes (cf. Lev. 10:6, 7). **shoes upon thy feet**—whereas mourners went "barefoot" (II Sam. 15:30). **cover not . . . lips**—rather, the "upper lip," with the moustache (Lev. 13:45; Mic. 3:7). **bread of men**—the bread usually brought to mourners by friends in token of sympathy. So the "cup of consolation" brought (Jer. 16:7). "Of men" means such as is usually furnished *by men.* So Isaiah 8:1, "a *man's* pen"; Revelation 21:17, "the measure *of a man.*" **19. what these things are to us**—The people perceive that Ezekiel's strange conduct has a symbolical meaning as to themselves; they ask, "What is that meaning?" **21. excellency of your strength**—(cf. Amos 6:8). The object of your pride and confidence (Jer. 7:4, 10, 14). **desire of . . . eyes**—(Ps. 27:4). The antitype to Ezekiel's wife (vs. 16). **pitieth**—loveth, as pity is akin to love: "yearned over." **Profane**—an appropriate word. They had profaned the temple with idolatry; God, in just retribution, will profane it with the Chaldean sword, i.e., lay it in the dust, as Ezekiel's wife. **sons . . . daughters . . . left**—the children *left* behind in Judea, when the parents were carried away. **22.** (Jer. 16:6, 7.) So general shall be the calamity, that all ordinary usages of mourning shall be suspended. **23. ye shall not mourn . . . but . . . pine away for your iniquities**—The Jews' not mourning was to be not the result of insensibility, any more than Ezekiel's not mourning for his wife was not from want of feeling. They could not in their exile manifest publicly their lamentation, but they would

ADAM CLARKE

13. *In thy filthiness is lewdness. Zimmah,* a word that denominates the worst kinds of impurity; adultery, incest, and the purpose, wish, design, and ardent desire to do these things.

16. *Behold, I take away from thee the desire of thine eyes.* Here is an intimation that the stroke he was to suffer was to be above all grief, that it would be so great as to prevent the relief of tears.

17. *Make no mourning.* As a priest, he could make no public mourning, Lev. xxi. 1, etc.

Bind the tire of thine head. This seems to refer to the high priest's bonnet, or perhaps one worn by the ordinary priests. It might have been a black veil to cover the head.

Put on thy shoes upon thy feet. Walking barefoot was a sign of grief. *Cover not thy lips.* Mourners covered the under part of the face, from the nose to the bottom of the chin. *Eat not the bread of men.* "the bread of miserable men," i.e., mourners; probably, the funeral banquet.

18. *At even my wife died.* The prophet's wife was a type of the city, which was to him exceedingly dear. The death of his wife represented the destruction of the city by the Chaldeans; see v. 21, where the Temple is represented to be the desire of his eyes, as his wife was, v. 16.

19. *Wilt thou not tell us?* In the following verses he explains and applies the whole of what he had done and said.

MATTHEW HENRY

III. "*When this comes,* as it is foretold, when Jerusalem, which is this day besieged, is quite destroyed, which now you cannot believe will ever be, *then you shall know that I am the Lord God,* who have given you this fair warning of it. Then you will remember that Ezekiel was to you a sign." "*He that escapes in that day* shall, by a special direction of Providence, *come to thee,* to bring thee intelligence of it," which we find was done, *ch.* xxxiii. 21. Whereas, from this time to that, Ezekiel was thus far dumb that he prophesied no more against the land of Israel, but against the neighbouring nations, as we shall find in the following chapters, then he shall have orders given him to *speak again to the children of his people* (*ch.* xxxiii. 2, 22). When God was speaking so loudly by the rod, there was the less need of speaking by the word.

JAMIESON, FAUSSET, BROWN

privately "mourn *one to another.*" Their "iniquities" would then be their chief sorrow ("pining away"), as feeling that these were the cause of their sufferings (cf. Lev. 26:39; Lam. 3:39). The fullest fulfilment is still future (Zech. 12:10-14). **24. sign**—a typical representative in his own person of what was to befall them (Isa. 20:3). **when this cometh**—alluding probably to their taunt, as if God's word spoken by His prophets would never come to pass. "Where is the word of the Lord? Let it *come* now" (Jer. 17:15). When the prophecy is fulfilled, "ye shall know (to your cost) that I am the Lord," who thereby show My power and fulfil My word spoken by My prophet (John 13:19; 14:29). **25, 26.** "The day" referred to in these verses is the day of the overthrow of the temple, when the fugitive "escapes." But "that day," in vs. 27, is the day on which the fugitive brings the sad news to Ezekiel, at the Chebar. In the interval the prophet suspended his prophecies *as to the Jews,* as was foretold. Afterwards his mouth was "opened," and no more "dumb" (ch. 3:26, 27; cf. vs. 27 here in ch. 24; and ch. 33:21, 22).

ADAM CLARKE

27. *In that day shall thy mouth be opened.* That is, When someone who shall have escaped from Jerusalem, having arrived among the captives, shall inform them of the destruction of the city, the Temple, the royal family, and the people at large, till then he might suppress his tears and lamentations. And we find from chap. xxxiii. 21 that one did actually escape from the city, and informed the prophet and his brethren in captivity that the city was smitten. Thus he was not only a prophet to foretell such things, but he was also a sign or portent, shadowing them out by circumstances in his own person and family; and thus the prediction, agreeing so perfectly with the event, proved that the previous information was from the Lord.

MATTHEW HENRY — CHAPTER 25

Verses 1–7

I. The prophet is ordered to address himself to the Ammonites, in the name of *the Lord Jehovah* the *God of Israel,* who is also the God of the whole earth. He is bidden to *set his face against the Ammonites,* for he is God's representative and thus he must signify that God *set his face against them,* for *the face of the Lord is against those that do evil,* Ps. xxxiv. 16. He must show that, though he had prophesied so long *against Israel,* yet still he was for Israel, and, while he witnessed against their corruptions, he gloried in God's covenant with them.

II. He is directed what to say to them. Ezekiel is now a captive in Babylon, and knows little of the nations that were about it; but God tells him what they were doing and what he was about to do with them.

1. He must upbraid the Ammonites with their insolent and barbarous triumphs over the people of Israel in their calamities, *v.* 3. The Ammonites, of all people, should not have rejoiced in Jerusalem's ruin, but should rather have trembled, because they themselves had such a narrow escape, *ch.* xxi. 20. And they had reason to think that the king of Babylon would set upon them next. It is a wicked thing to be glad at the calamities of any.

2. He must threaten the Ammonites with utter ruin for this insolence. He had before predicted the destruction of the Ammonites, *ch.* xxi. 28. Had they repented, that would have been revoked; but now it is ratified. The Chaldeans came from the north-east, and their army, under the command of Nebuchadnezzar, destroyed the country of the Ammonites, about five years after the destruction of Jerusalem, and then the Arabians, who were properly the *children of the east,* when the Chaldeans had made the country desolate, came and took possession of it for themselves.

They made use even of the royal city for their cattle (*v.* 5): *I will make Rabbath,* that was a nice and splendid city, to be *a stable for camels.* Thus God will maintain his own honour, and will make it appear that he is the God of Israel, though he suffers them for a time to be captives in Babylon. Thus he will bring those that were strangers to him into an acquaintance with him.

Verses 8–17

Three more of Israel's ill-natured neighbours are here condemned to destruction, for contributing to and triumphing in Jerusalem's fall.

I. The Moabites. Seir, which was the seat of the Edomites, is joined with them (*v.* 8).

1. The Moabites said, *Behold, the house of Judah is like unto all the heathen.* They were pleased to see them forsake their God and worship idols. Let

JAMIESON, FAUSSET, BROWN — CHAPTER 25

Vss. 1-17. Appropriately in the Interval of Silence as to the Jews in the Eight Chapters, 25-32, Ezekiel Denounces Judgments on the Heathen World Kingdoms. If Israel was not spared, much less the heathen utterly corrupt, and having no mixture of truth, such as Israel in its worst state possessed (I Pet. 4:17, 18). Their ruin was to be utter: Israel's but temporary (Jer. 46:28). The nations denounced are *seven,* the perfect number; implying that God's judgments would visit, not merely these, but *the whole round* of the heathen foes of God. Babylon is excepted, because she is now for the present viewed as the rod of God's retributive justice, a view too much then lost sight of by those who fretted against her universal supremacy. **3.** (Jer. 49:1). **when . . . profaned; . . . when . . . desolate; . . . when . . . captivity**—rather, "for . . . for . . . for": the *cause* of the insolent exultation of Ammon over Jerusalem. They triumphed especially over the fall of the "sanctuary," as the triumph of heathenism over the rival claims of Jehovah. In Jehoshaphat's time, when Psalm 83 was written (Ps. 83:4, 7, 8, 12, "Ammon . . . *holpen the children of Lot,*" who were, therefore, the *leaders* of the unholy conspiracy, "Let us take to ourselves the *houses of God* in possession"), we see the same profane spirit. Now at last their wicked wish seems accomplished in the fall of Jerusalem. Ammon, descended from Lot, held the region east of Jordan, separated from the Amorites on the north by the river Jabbok, and from Moab on the south by the Arnon. They were auxiliaries to Babylon in the destruction of Jerusalem (II Kings 24:2). **4. men of . . . east**—lit., "children of the East," the nomad tribes of Arabia Deserta, east of the Jordan and the Dead Sea. **palaces**—their nomadic encampments or folds, surrounded with mud walls, are so called in irony. Where thy "palaces" once stood, there shall their very different "palaces" stand. Fulfilled after the ravaging of their region by Nebuchadnezzar, shortly after the destruction of Jerusalem (cf. ch. 21:22; Jer. 49:1-28). **5. Rabbah**—meaning "the Great," Ammon's metropolis. Under the Ptolemies it was rebuilt under the name Philadelphia; the ruins are called *Amman* now, but there is no dwelling inhabited. **Ammonites**—i.e., the Ammonite *region* is to be a "couching-place for flocks," viz., of the Arabs. The "camels," being the chief beast of burden of the Chaldeans, are put first, as their invasion was to prepare the Ammonite land for the Arab "flocks." Instead of busy men, there shall be "still and couching flocks." **6, 7.** "Because *thou* hast clapped *thine* hands," exulting over the downfall of Jerusalem, "*I* also will stretch out *Mine* hand upon thee" (to which ch. 21:17 also may refer, "I will smite Mine hands together"). **hands . . . feet . . . heart**—with the whole inward feeling, and with every outward indication. *Stamping with the foot* means *dancing for joy.* **7. a spoil**—so *Hebrew Margin* or *Keri,* for the text or *Chetib,* "meat" (so ch. 26:5; 34:28). Their *goods* were to be a "spoil to the foe"; their *state* was to be "cut off," so as to be no more a "people"; and they were as *individuals,* for the most part, to be "destroyed." **8.** Moab, Seir, and Ammon were contiguous countries, stretching in one line from Gilead on the north to the Red Sea. They therefore naturally acted in concert, and in joint hostility to Judea. **Judah is like . . . all . . . heathen**—The Jews fare no better than others: it is of no use to them to serve Jehovah, who, they say, is the only

ADAM CLARKE — CHAPTER 25

1. *The word of the Lord.* The chronological order of this chapter is after chap. xxxiii. 21, etc.

2. *Set thy face against the Ammonites.* We have already seen, chap. xxi. 19, etc., that when Nebuchadnezzar left Babylon, he was in doubt whether he should besiege Riblath, the capital of the Ammonites, or Jerusalem, the capital of the Jews, first; and having used his divination, he was determined, by the result, to attack Jerusalem the first. He did so; and the Ammonites, seeing the success of his arms, made friends with him, and exulted in the ruin of the Jews. God resents this, and predicts their downfall with that of Edom, Moab, and the Philistines. The fulfillment of this prediction is not noted in Scripture, but Josephus tells us that, about five years after the taking of Jerusalem, Nebuchadnezzar turned his arms against the Ammonites and Moabites, and afterwards against Egypt; and having subdued those nations, he returned to Babylon (Joseph. *Antiq.* l. x., c. ii).

7. *I will cause thee to perish.* Except in history, the name of the Ammonites does not now exist.

8. *Moab and Seir do say. Seir* means the Idumeans. It appears that both these, with the Ammonites, had made a league with Zedekiah, Jer. xxvii. 3, which they did not keep; and it is supposed that they even joined with the Chaldeans.

MATTHEW HENRY

the Moabites know that, though there are those of the house of Judah who have made themselves *like the heathen*, yet there is a remnant that retain their integrity, the religion of the house of Judah shall recover itself. Their God is no more able to deliver them from this *overflowing scourge* of these parts of the world than the gods of the heathen are to deliver them. Those who judge only by outward appearance are ready to conclude that the people of God have lost all their privileges when they have lost their worldly prosperity.

2. The punishment of Moab for this sin; their country shall be in like manner overthrown with that of the Ammonites, who were guilty of the same sin (*v.* 9, 10). The frontier-towns, that were its strength, shall be demolished by the Chaldean forces, and laid open. *The men of the east*, when they come to take possession of the country of the Ammonites, shall seize that of the Moabites too. The Arabians, who are shepherds, and live quietly, plain men dwelling in tents, shall by an overruling Providence be put in possession of the land of the Moabites, who are soldiers, that live turbulently. The Chaldeans shall get it by war, and the Arabians shall enjoy it in peace.

II. The Edomites were the posterity of Esau, between whom and Jacob there had been an old enmity. They not only triumphed in the ruin of Judah and Jerusalem, as the Moabites and Ammonites had done, but they took advantage from the present distressed state to which the Jews were reduced to do them some real mischiefs, probably made inroads upon their frontiers and plundered their country, *v.* 12.

Amaziah severely chastised them (2 Kings xiv. 7), and for this they *took vengeance*. Now they would pay off all the old scores. God will take them to task for it (*v.* 13): *I will stretch out my hand upon Edom.* Their country shall be desolate *from Teman* in the south, and *they shall fall by the sword unto Dedan*, which lay north. They suffered much by the Chaldeans, which seems to be referred to, Jer. xlix. 8. *Judas Maccabeus fought against the children of Esau in Idumea, gave them a great overthrow, abated their courage, and took their spoil* (1 Mac. v. 3), and Josephus says (*Antiq. lib.* 13, *cap.* 17), that Hircanus made the Edomites tributaries to Israel.

III. The Philistines. Their sin is much the same with that of the Edomites: They have *dealt by revenge* with the people of Israel, and have *taken vengeance with a despiteful heart*, to *destroy them*, for *the old hatred* (*v.* 15), the old grudge they bore them.

Their punishment likewise is much the same, *v.* 16. Their country was wasted by the Chaldean army, not long after the destruction of Jerusalem, which is foretold, Jer. xlvii.

JAMIESON, FAUSSET, BROWN

true God. **9, 10. open . . . from the cities**—*I will open up the side,* or border *of Moab* (metaphor from a man whose side is open to blows), *from the* direction of *the cities* on his northwest border beyond the Arnon, once assigned to Reuben (Josh. 13:15-21), but now in the hands of their original owners; and the "men of the east," the wandering Bedouin hordes, shall enter through these cities into Moab and waste it. Moab accordingly was so wasted by them, that long before the time of Christ it had melted away among the hordes of the desert. For "cities," GROTIUS translates the *Hebrew* as proper names, the *Ar* and *Aroer,* on the Arnon. Hence the *Hebrew* for "cities," "Ar" is repeated twice (Num. 21:28; Deut. 2:36; Isa. 15:1). **glory of the country**—The region of Moab was richer than that of Ammon; it answers to the modern Belka, the richest district in South Syria, and the scene in consequence of many a contest among the Bedouins. Hence it is called here a "glorious land" (lit., "a glory," or "ornament of a land") [FAIRBAIRN]. Rather, "the glory of the country" is in apposition with "cities" which immediately precedes, and the names of which presently follow. **Beth-jeshimoth**—meaning "the city of desolations"; perhaps so named from some siege it sustained; it was towards the west. **Baal-meon**—called also "Beth-meon" (Jer. 48:23), and "Beth-baal-meon" (Josh. 13:17, called so from the worship of Baal), and "Bajith," simply (Isa. 15:2). **Kiriathaim**—"the double city." The strength of these cities engendered "the pride" of Moab (Isa. 16:6). **10. with the Ammonites**—FAIRBAIRN explains and translates, *"upon* the children of Ammon" (elliptically for, "I will open Moab to the men of the east, who, having overrun the children of Ammon, shall then fall on Moab"). MAURER, as *English Version, "with* the Ammonites," i.e., Moab, *"together with* the land of Ammon," is to be thrown "open to the men of the east," to enter and take possession (Jer. 49). **12. taking vengeance**—lit., "revenging with revengement," i.e., the most unrelenting vengeance. It was not simple hatred, but deep-brooding, implacable revenge. The grudge of Edom or Esau was originally for Jacob's robbing him of Isaac's blessing (Gen. 25:23; 27:27-41). This purpose of revenge yielded to the extraordinary kindness of Jacob, through the blessing of Him with whom Jacob wrestled in prayer; but it was revived as an hereditary grudge in the posterity of Esau when they saw the younger branch rising to the pre-eminence which they thought of right belonged to themselves. More recently, for David's subjugation of Edom to Israel (II Sam. 8:14). They therefore gave vent to their spite by joining the Chaldeans in destroying Jerusalem (Ps. 137:7; Lam. 4:22; Obadiah 10-14), and then intercepting and killing the fugitive Jews (Amos 1:11) and occupying part of the Jewish land as far as Hebron. **13. Teman . . . they of Dedan**—rather, "I will make it desolate from Teman (in the south) *even to* Dedan" (in the northwest) [GROTIUS], (Jer. 49:8), i.e., the whole country from north to south, stretching from the south of the Dead Sea to the Elanitic gulf of the Red Sea. **14. by . . . my people Israel**—viz., by Judas Maccabeus. The Idumeans were finally, by compulsory circumcision, incorporated with the Jewish state by John Hyrcanus (see Isa. 34:5; 63:1, etc.; I Maccabees 5:3). So complete was the amalgamation in Christ's time, that the Herods of Idumean origin, as Jews, ruled over the two races as one people. Thus the ancient prophecy was fulfilled (Gen. 25:23), "The elder shall serve the younger." **15.** (I Sam. 13, 14; II Chron. 28:18.) The "old hatred" refers to their continual enmity to the covenant people. They lay along Judea on the seacoast at the opposite side from Ammon and Moab. They were overthrown by Uzziah (II Chron. 26:6), and by Hezekiah (II Kings 18:8). Nebuchadnezzar overran the cities on the seacoast on his way to Egypt after besieging Tyre (Jer. 47). God will take vengeance on those who take the avenging of themselves out of His hands into their own (Rom. 12:19-21; Jas. 2:13). **16. cut off the Cherethims**—There is a play on similar sounds in the *Hebrew, hichratti cherethim,* "I will slay the slayers." The name may have been given to a section of the Philistines from their warlike disposition (I Sam. 30:14; 31:3). They excelled in archery, whence David enrolled a bodyguard from them (II Sam. 8:18; 15:18; 20:7). They sprang from Caphtor, identified by many with Crete. which was famed for archery, and to which the name *Cherethim* seems akin. Though in emigration, which mostly tended westwards, Crete seems more likely to be colonized from Philistia than Philistia from Crete, a *section* of Cretans may have settled at Cherethim in South Philistia, while the Philistines, *as a*

ADAM CLARKE

9. *I will open the side. Ketheph,* the shoulder, the strongest frontier place.

Beth-jeshimoth, Baal-meon, and Kiriathaim were strong frontier towns of Moab.

12. *Because that Edom hath dealt.* The Edomites were the most inveterate enemies of the Jews from the very earliest times, and ever did all that they could to annoy them.

13. *I will make it desolate from Teman.* Teman and Dedan were both cities of the Moabites, and apparently at each extremity of the land.

14. *I will lay my vengeance upon Edom.* God will not allow men to insult those whom He has cast down. His judgment is sufficient; to add more is an insult to God. *By the hand of my people Israel.* This was fulfilled by the Maccabees, who not only defeated them and brought them under complete subjection, but obliged them to receive circumcision (Joseph. *Antiq.* l. xiii., c. 17; 1 Macc. v. 65).

15. *Because the Philistines.* They were as inimical to the Jews as the Ammonites were. Nebuchadnezzar punished them because they had assisted the Tyrians during the time he was besieging their city.

16. *I will cut off the Cherethims.* See 2 Sam. viii. 18.

MATTHEW HENRY | JAMIESON, FAUSSET, BROWN | ADAM CLARKE

nation, may have come originally from the east (cf. Deut. 2:23; Jer. 47:4; Amos 9:7; Zeph. 2:5). In Genesis 10:14 the Philistines are made *distinct from the Caphtorim,* and are said to come from the Casluhim; so that the Cherethim were but *a part* of the Philistines, which I Samuel 30:14 confirms. **remnant of**—i.e., "on the seacoast" of the Mediterranean: those left *remaining* after the former overthrows inflicted by Samuel, David, Hezekiah, and Psammetichus of Egypt, father of Pharaoh-necho (Jer. 25:20). **17. know . . . vengeance**—They shall know Me, not in mercy, but by My vengeance on them (Ps. 9:16).

The remnant of the sea coast. The different seignories of the Philistines inhabited the coast of the Mediterranean Sea, from Judea to Egypt. For other matters relative to these prophecies, see the passages in the margin.

MATTHEW HENRY — CHAPTER 26

Verses 1–14

This prophecy is dated in the eleventh year, which was the year that Jerusalem was taken, and *in the first day of the month,* but it is not said what month.

I. The pleasure with which the Tyrians looked upon the ruins of Jerusalem (*v.* 2): "*Aha! she is broken,* broken to pieces, that was *the gates of the people!* all the wealth, power, and interest, which Jerusalem had, shall be turned to Tyre, and so *now* that *she is laid waste I shall be replenished.*" They were men of business, and therefore were not of a persecuting spirit. All their care was to get estates and enlarge their trade, and they looked upon Jerusalem not as an enemy, but as a rival. Tyre promised herself that the fall of Jerusalem would be an advantage to her in respect of trade and commerce, that now she shall have Jerusalem's customers, and thus the prosperity of Tyre will rise out of the ruins of Jerusalem. It is just with God to blast the designs and projects ot those who thus contrive to raise themselves upon the ruins of others.

II. Tyrus was a pleasant and wealthy city, and might have continued so if she had sympathized with Jerusalem in her calamities. *Many nations shall come against thee,* an army made up of many nations, or one nation that shall be as strong as many.

JAMIESON, FAUSSET, BROWN — CHAPTER 26

Vss. 1-21. The Judgment on Tyre through Nebuchadnezzar (Chs. 26-28). In ch. 26, Ezekiel sets forth:—1. Tyre's sin; 2. its doom; 3. the instruments executing it; 4. the effects produced on other nations by her downfall. In ch. 27, a lamentation over the fall of such earthly splendor. In ch. 28, an elegy addressed to the king, on the humiliation of his sacrilegious pride. Ezekiel, in his prophecies as to the heathen, exhibits *the dark side only;* because he views them simply in their hostility to the people of God, who shall outlive them all. Isaiah (Isa. 23), on the other hand, at the close of judgments, holds out the prospect of blessing, when Tyre should turn to the Lord. **1.** The specification of the date, which had been omitted in the case of the four preceding objects of judgment, marks the greater weight attached to the fall of Tyre. **eleventh year**—viz., after the carrying away of Jehoiachin, the year of the fall of Jerusalem. The number of the month is, however, omitted, and the day only given. As the month of the *taking* of Jerusalem was regarded as one of particular note, viz., *the fourth month,* also *the fifth,* on which it was actually *destroyed* (Jer. 52:6, 12, 13), Rabbi-David reasonably supposes that Tyre uttered her taunt at the close of the fourth month, as her nearness to Jerusalem enabled her to hear of its fall very soon, and that Ezekiel met it with his threat against herself on "the first day" *of the fifth month.* **2. Tyre**—(Josh. 19:29; II Sam. 24:7), lit., meaning "the rock-city," *Zor;* a name applying to the *island Tyre,* called New Tyre, rather than *Old Tyre* on the *mainland.* They were half a mile apart. New Tyre, a century and a half before the fall of Jerusalem, had successfully resisted Shalmaneser of Assyria, for five years besieging it (Menander, from the Tyrian archives, quoted by Josephus, *Antiquities,* 9. 14. 2). It was the stronger and more important of the two cities, and is the one chiefly, though not exclusively, here meant. Tyre was originally a colony of Zidon. Nebuchadnezzar's siege of it lasted thirteen years (ch. 29:18; Isa. 23). Though no profane author mentions his having succeeded in the siege, Jerome states he read the fact in Assyrian histories. **Aha!**—exultation over a fallen rival (Ps. 35:21, 25). **she . . . that was the gates**—i.e., the single gate composed of two folding doors. Hence the verb is *singular.* "Gates" were the place of resort for traffic and public business: so here it expresses *a mart of commerce* frequented by merchants. Tyre regards Jerusalem not as an open enemy, for her territory being the narrow, long strip of land north of Philistia, between Mount Lebanon and the sea, her interest was to cultivate friendly relations with the Jews, on whom she was dependent for corn (ch. 27:17; I Kings 5:9; Acts 12:20). But Jerusalem had intercepted some of the inland traffic which she wished to monopolize to herself; so, in her intensely selfish wordly-mindedness, she exulted heartlessly over the fall of Jerusalem as her own gain. Hence she incurred the wrath of God as pre-eminently the world's representative in its ambition, selfishness, and pride, in defiance of the will of God (Isa. 23:9). **she is turned unto me**—i.e., the mart of corn, wine, oil, balsam, etc. which she once was, is transferred to me. The caravans from Palmyra, Petra, and the East will no longer be intercepted by the market ("the gates") of Jerusalem, but will come to me. **3, 4. nations . . . as the sea . . . waves**—In striking contrast to the boasting of Tyre, God threatens to bring against her Babylon's army levied from "many nations," even as the Mediterranean waves that dashed against her rock-founded city on all sides. **scrape her dust . . . make her . . . top of . . . rock**—or, "a bare rock" [Grotius]. The soil which the Tyrians had brought together upon the rock on which they built their city, I will scrape so clean away as to leave no dust, but only the bare rock as it was. An awful contrast to her expectation of filling herself with *all* the wealth of the East now that Jerusalem has fallen. **5. in the**

ADAM CLARKE — CHAPTER 26

1. *The eleventh year.* This was the year in which Jerusalem was taken; the eleventh of the captivity of Jeconiah, and the eleventh of the reign of Zedekiah.

2. *Tyrus hath said.* From this it would appear that Jerusalem had been taken, which was on the fourth month of this year; but it is possible that the prophet speaks of the event beforehand.

She is broken that was the gates of the people. Jerusalem, a general emporium.

I shall be replenished. The merchandise that went to Jerusalem will come to me (to Tyre).

3. *Will cause many nations to come up against thee.* We have already seen that the empire of the Chaldeans was composed of many different provinces, and that Nebuchadnezzar's army was composed of soldiers from different nations. These may be the people meant, but I doubt whether this may not refer to the different nations which in successive ages fought against Tyre. It was at last finally destroyed in the sixteenth century of the Christian era.

4. *I will also scrape her dust from her.* I will totally destroy her fortifications, and leave her nothing but a barren rock, as she was before. This cannot refer to the capture of Tyre by Nebuchadnezzar. It flourished long after his time.

MATTHEW HENRY

The person is named that shall bring this army upon them—*Nebuchadnezzar king of Babylon, a king of kings*, that had many kings tributaries to him, besides those that were his captives, Dan. ii. 37, 38.

He shall come with a vast army, *horses and chariots*, &c. He shall (*v.* 8), *make a fort, and cast a mount*, and (*v.* 9) shall set *engines of war against the walls.*

His troops shall raise a dust that shall cover the city, *v.* 10.

The city held out a long siege, but it was taken at last. Not only the soldiers that are found in arms, but the burghers, shall be *put to the sword*, the king of Babylon being highly incensed against them for holding out so long. The wealth of the city shall all become a spoil to the conqueror (*v.* 12). All the *pleasant houses* shall be *destroyed* (*v.* 12).

When Jerusalem was destroyed it was *ploughed like a field*, Mic. iii. 12. But the destruction of Tyre is carried further; the very soil of it shall be scraped away, and it shall be made *like the top of a rock* (*v.* 4, 14), that has no earth to cover it; it shall only be a place *for the spreading of nets* (*v.* 5, 14); it shall serve fishermen to dry their nets upon.

3. What a distress the inhabitants of Tyre are in (*v.* 15): *There is a great slaughter made in the midst of thee.*

4. What a consternation all the neighbours are in upon the fall of Tyre. The *islands* shall *shake at the sound of thy fall* (*v.* 15).

The *princes of the sea* shall be affected, who ruled in those islands. The rich merchants, who live like princes (Isa. xxiii. 8), and the

JAMIESON, FAUSSET, BROWN

midst of the sea—plainly referring to New Tyre (ch. 27:32). **6. her daughters ... in the field**—The surrounding villages, dependent on her in the open country, shall share the fate of the mother city. **7. from the north**—the original locality of the Chaldeans; also, the direction by which they entered Palestine, taking the route of Riblah and Hamath on the Orontes, in preference to that across the desert between Babylon and Judea. **king of kings**—so called because of the many kings who owned allegiance to him II Kings 18:28). God had delegated to him the universal earth-empire which is His (Dan. 2:47). The Son of God alone has the right and title inherently, and shall assume it when the world-kings shall have been fully proved as abusers of the trust (I Tim. 6:15; Rev. 17:12-14; 19:15, 16). Ezekiel's prophecy was not based on conjecture from the past, for Shalmaneser, with all the might of the Assyrian empire, had failed in his siege of Tyre. Yet Nebuchadnezzar was to succeed. JOSEPHUS tells us that Nebuchadnezzar began the siege in the seventh year of Ithobal's reign, king of Tyre. **9. engines of war**—lit., "an apparatus for *striking*." "He shall apply *the stroke* of the battering-ram *against* thy walls." HAVERNICK translates, "His enginery of *destruction*;" lit., the "*destruction* (not merely *the stroke*) of his enginery." **axes**—lit., "swords." **10. dust**—So thick shall be the "dust" stirred up by the immense numbers of "horses," that it shall "cover" the whole city as a cloud. **horses ... chariots**—As in vss. 3-5, *New Tyre* on the insular rock in the sea (cf. Isa. 23:2, 4, 6) is referred to; so here, in vss. 9-11, *Old Tyre* on the mainland. *Both* are included in the prophecies under one name. **wheels**—FAIRBAIRN thinks that here, and in ch. 23:24, as "the wheels" are distinct from the "chariots," some wheelwork for riding on, or for the operations of the siege, are meant. **11. thy strong garrisons**—lit., "the statutes of thy strength"; so *the forts* which are "monuments of thy strength." MAURER understands, in stricter agreement with the literal meaning, "the statues" or "obelisks erected in honor of the idols, the tutelary gods of Tyre," as Melecarte, answering to the Grecian Hercules, whose temple stood in Old Tyre (cf. Jer. 43:13, *Margin*). **12. lay thy stones ... timber ... in ... midst of ... water**—referring to the insular New Tyre (vss. 3, 5; ch. 27: 4, 25, 26). When its lofty buildings and towers fall, surrounded as it was with the sea which entered its double harbor and washed its ramparts, the "stones ... timbers ... and dust" appropriately are described as thrown down "in the midst of the water." Though Ezekiel attributes the capture of Tyre to Nebuchadnezzar (*Note*, ch. 29:18), yet it does not follow that the *final* destruction of it described is attributed by him to the same monarch. The overthrow of Tyre by Nebuchadnezzar was the first link in the long chain of evil—the first deadly blow which prepared for, and was the earnest of, the final doom. The change in this verse from the individual conqueror "he," to the general "they," marks that what he did was not the whole, but only paved the way for others to complete the work begun by him. It was to be a progressive work until she was utterly destroyed. Thus the words here answer exactly to what Alexander did. With the "stones, timber," and rubbish of Old Tyre, he built a causeway in seven months to New Tyre on the island and so took it [QUINT. CURT., 4, 2], 322 B.C. **13.** Instead of the joyousness of thy prosperity, a deathlike silence shall reign (Isa. 24:8; Jer. 7:34). **14.** He concludes in nearly the same words as he began (vss. 4, 5). **built no more**—fulfilled as to the mainland Tyre, under Nebuchadnezzar. The insular Tyre recovered partly, after seventy years (Isa. 23:17, 18), but again suffered under Alexander, then under Antigonus, then under the Saracens at the beginning of the fourteenth century. Now its harbors are choked with sand, precluding all hope of future restoration, "not one entire house is left, and only a few fishermen take shelter in the vaults" [MAUNDRELL]. So accurately has God's word come to pass. **15-21.** The impression which the overthrow of Tyre produced on other maritime nations and upon her own colonies, e.g., Utica, Carthage, and Tartessus or Tarshish in Spain. **15. isles**—maritime lands. Even mighty Carthage used to send a yearly offering to the temple of Hercules at Tyre: and the mother city gave high priests to her colonies. Hence the consternation at her fall felt in the widely scattered dependencies with which she was so closely connected by the ties of religion, as well as commercial intercourse. **shake**—metaphorically: "be agitated" (Jer. 49:21). **16. come down from their thrones...upon the ground**—"the throne of the mourners" (Job 2:13; Jonah 3:6). **princes of the sea**—are the merchant rulers of Carthage and other colonies of Tyre, who had made themselves

ADAM CLARKE

5. *A place for the spreading of nets.* A place for the habitation of some poor fishermen, who spent the fishing season there, and were accustomed to dry their nets upon the rocks. See v. 11.

6. *And her daughters.* The places dependent on Tyre. As there were two places called Tyre, one on the mainland, and the other on a rock in the sea, opposite to that on the mainland, sometimes the one seems to be spoken of, and sometimes the other. That on the land was soon taken; but that in the sea cost Nebuchadnezzar thirteen years of siege and blockade. The two formed only one city, and one state.

7. *Nebuchadrezzar . . . king of kings.* An ancient title among those proud Asiatic despots.

8. *Thy daughters in the field.* This seems to be spoken of Tyre on the mainland.

12. *And they shall lay thy stones and thy timber and thy dust in the midst of the water.* This answers to the taking of Tyre by Alexander; he actually took the timbers, stones, rubbish, etc., of old Tyre, and filled up the space between it and new Tyre, and thus connected the latter with the mainland; and this he was obliged to do before he could take it.

14. *Thou shalt be built no more.* If this refer to Nebuchadnezzar's capture of the city, old Tyre must be intended; that was destroyed by him, and never rebuilt. But I doubt whether the whole of this prophecy do not refer to the taking of Tyre by Alexander, 300 years after its capture by Nebuchadnezzar.

15. *The isles shake at the sound of thy fall.* All those which had traded with this city, which was the grand mart, and on which they all depended. Her ruin involved them all, and caused general wailing.

MATTHEW HENRY

masters of ships, who command like princes, these shall condole the fall of Tyre. When Jerusalem, the holy city, was destroyed, there were no such lamentations for it; it was *nothing* to *those that passed by* (Lam. i. 12); but when Tyre, the trading city, fell, it was universally bemoaned.

1. How high, how great, Tyre had been, how little likely ever to come to this! She was *inhabited of seas*, that is, of those that trade at sea, of those who from all parts came thither by sea. Everybody stood in awe of the Tyrians and was afraid of disobliging them.

2. How low, how little, Tyre is made, *v.* 19, 20. This *renowned city* is made a *desolate city*, a city overflowed by an inundation of waters, which *cover* it, and upon which the *deep* is *brought up*. The Tyrians shall be lost among the nations, so that people will look in vain for Tyre in Tyre: *Thou shalt be sought for, and never found again.*

5. The irreparable ruin of Tyre is aggravated by the prospect of the restoration of Israel. Thus shall Tyre sink *when I shall set glory in the land of the living*, *v.* 20. None but holy souls are properly living souls.

JAMIESON, FAUSSET, BROWN

rich and powerful by trading on the sea (Isa. 23:8). **clothe . . . with trembling**—*Heb.* "tremblings." Cf. ch. 7:27, "clothed with desolation"; Psalm 132:18. In a public calamity the garment was changed for a mourning garb. **17. inhabited of seafaring men**—i.e., which was frequented by merchants of various sea-bordering lands [GROTIUS]. FAIRBAIRN translates with Peschito, "Thou inhabitant of the seas" (the *Hebrew* literal meaning). Tyre rose as it were *out of* the seas as if she got thence her inhabitants, being peopled so closely down to the waters. So Venice was called "the bride of the sea." **strong in the sea**—through her insular position. **cause their terror to be on all that haunt it**—viz., the sea. The *Hebrew* is rather, "they put their terror upon all *her* (the city's) inhabitants," i.e., they make the name of every Tyrian to be feared [FAIRBAIRN]. **18. thy departure**—Isaiah 23:6, 12 predicts that the Tyrians, in consequence of the siege, should pass over the Mediterranean to the lands bordering on it ("Chittim," "Tarshish," etc.). So Ezekiel here. Accordingly JEROME says that he read in Assyrian histories that, "when the Tyrians saw no hope of escaping, they *fled* to Carthage or some islands of the Ionian and Ægean Seas" [BISHOP NEWTON]. (See my *Note* on ch. 29:18.) GROTIUS explains "departure," i.e., "in the day when hostages shall be *carried away* from thee to Babylon." The parallelism to "thy *fall*" makes me think "departure" must mean "thy end" in general, but with an *included* allusion to the "departure" of most of her people to her colonies at *the fall* of the city. **19. great waters**—appropriate metaphor of the Babylonian hosts, which literally, by breaking down insular Tyre's ramparts, caused the sea to "cover" part of her. **20. the pit**—Tyre's disappearance is compared to that of *the dead placed in their sepulchers* and no more seen among the living (cf. ch. 32:18, 23; Isa. 14:11, 15, 19). **I shall set glory in the land**—In contrast to Tyre consigned to the "pit" of *death*, I shall set glory (i.e., My presence symbolized by the Shekinah cloud, the antitype to which shall be Messiah, "the *glory* as of the only-begotten of the Father," John 1:14; Isa. 4:2, 5; Zech. 6:13) in Judah. **of the living**—as opposed to Tyre consigned to the "pit" of death. Judea is to be the land of national and spiritual *life*, being restored after its captivity (ch. 47:9). FAIRBAIRN loses the antithesis by applying the negative to both clauses, "and that thou be *not* set as a glory in the land of the living." **21. terror**—an example of judgment calculated to terrify all evildoers. **thou shalt be no more**—Not that there was to be no more *a* Tyre, but she was no more to be *the* Tyre that once was: her glory and name were to be no more. As to Old Tyre, the prophecy was literally fulfilled, not a vestige of it being left.

ADAM CLARKE

17. *Wast strong in the sea.* The strength of Tyre was so great that Alexander despaired of being able to reduce it unless he could fill up that arm of the sea that ran between it and the mainland. And this work cost his army seven months of labor.

20. *And I shall set glory in the land of the living.* Judea so called, the land of the living God.

MATTHEW HENRY

CHAPTER 27

Verses 1–25

I. The prophet is ordered to take up a lamentation for Tyrus, *v.* 2. It was yet in the height of its prosperity, and there appeared not the least symptom of its decay; yet the prophet must lament it, because its prosperity is its snare, which will make its fall the more grievous.

II. He is directed what to say, and to say it in the name of *the Lord Jehovah.*

1. He must upbraid Tyre with her pride: *O Tyrus! thou hast said, I am of perfect beauty* (*v.* 3), of *universal beauty* (so the word is), well-built and well-filled with money and trade.

2. He must upbraid Tyre with her prosperity, which was the matter of her pride. The city of Tyre stood at the east end of the Mediterranean, convenient for trade by land into all the Levant, so that she became a *merchant of the people for many isles.* Lying between Greece and Asia, it became the rendezvous of merchants from all parts: *Thy borders are in the heart of the seas*, *v.* 4.

JAMIESON, FAUSSET, BROWN

CHAPTER 27

Vss. 1-36. TYRE'S FORMER GREATNESS, SUGGESTING A LAMENTATION OVER HER SAD DOWNFALL. **2. lamentation**—a funeral dirge, eulogizing her great attributes, to make the contrast the greater between her former and her latter state. **3. situate at the entry of the sea**—lit., plural, "entrances," i.e., ports or havens; referring to the double port of Tyre, at which vessels entered round the north and south ends of the island, so that ships could find a ready entrance from whatever point the wind might blow (cf. ch. 28:2). **merchant of . . . people for many isles**—i.e., a mercantile emporium of the peoples of many seacoasts, both from the east and from the west (Isa. 23:3), "a mart of nations." **of perfect beauty**—(ch. 28:12). **4.** Tyre, in consonance with her seagirt position, separated by a strait of half a mile from the mainland, is described as a ship built of the best material, and manned with the best mariners and skilful pilots, but at last wrecked in tempestuous seas (vs. 26). **5. Senir**—the Amorite name of Hermon, or the southern height of Anti-libanus (Deut. 3:9); the Sidonian name was *Sirion.* "All thy . . . boards"; dual in *Hebrew*, "*double*-boards," viz., placed in a double order on the two sides of which the ship consisted [VATABLUS]. Or, referring to the two sides or the two ends, the prow and the stern, which every ship has [MUNSTER]. **cedars**—most suited for "masts," from their height and durability. **6. Bashan**—celebrated for its oaks, as Lebanon was for its cedars. **the company of . . . Ashurites**—the most skilful workmen summoned from Assyria. Rather, as the *Hebrew* orthography requires, "They have made thy (rowing) benches of ivory inlaid *in the daughter of cedars*" [MAURER], or, *the best boxwood.* FAIRBAIRN, with BOCHART, reads the *Hebrew* two words as *one:* "Thy plankwork (*deck:* instead of 'benches,' as the *Hebrew* is *singular*)

ADAM CLARKE

CHAPTER 27

2. *Take up a lamentation for Tyrus.* This is a singular and curious chapter. It gives a very circumstantial account of the trade of Tyre with different parts of the world, and the different sorts of merchandise in which she trafficked. The places and the imports are as regularly entered here as they could have been in a European customhouse.

3. *The entry of the sea.* Tyre was a small island, or rather rock, in the sea, at a short distance from the mainland. We have already seen that there was another Tyre on the mainland, but they are both considered as one city.

4. *Thy builders have perfected thy beauty.* Under the allegory of a beautiful ship, the prophet, here and in the following verses, paints the glory of this ancient city.

5. *Fir trees of Senir.* *Senir* is a mountain which the Sidonians called Sirion, and the Hebrews "Hermon," Deut. iii. 9. It was beyond Jordan, and extended from Libanus to the mountains of Gilead.

6. *Of the oaks of Bashan.* Some translate "alder," others the "pine." *The company of the Ashurites.* The word *asherim* is by several translated "boxwood." The "seats" or *benches* being made of this wood inlaid with *ivory.*

MATTHEW HENRY

It has its haven replenished with abundance of *gallant ships*, Isa. xxxiii. 21. They made their *sails* of *fine linen* fetched from Egypt, and that *embroidered* too, *v.* 7. The word signifies a *banner* as well as a *sail.* They hung rooms on ship-board with *blue and purple*, the richest cloths and richest colours they could get. Tyre was itself famous for purple, which is therefore called the *Tyrian dye.* These gallant ships were well-manned. The pilots and masters of the ships were of their own city (*v.* 8): *Thy wise men, O Tyrus! that were in thee, were thy pilots. The inhabitants of Arvad and Zidon were thy mariners.*

They sent to Gebal in Syria for *calkers*, or *strengtheners of the clefts* or *chinks*, to stop them when the ships come home, after long voyages, to be repaired. Their city was guarded by a military force that was considerable, *v.* 10, 11. The land of Israel (though it lay next them), furnished them with timber, but we do not find that it furnished them with men; that would have trenched upon the liberty and dignity of the Jewish nation, 2 Chron. ii. 17, 18. They had a vast trade and a correspondence with all parts of the known world. Ezekiel knew little, of his own knowledge, concerning the trade of Tyre. He was a priest, carried away captive far from Tyre, and there he had been eleven years. Yet he speaks of the particular merchandise of Tyre as nicely as if he had been comptroller of the custom-house there. The wisdom of God, and his goodness, as the common Father of mankind is seen in making one country to abound in one commodity and another in another, and all more or less serviceable. *One land does not supply all the varieties of produce.* Providence dispenses its gifts variously, some to each, and all to none, that there may be a mutual commerce among those whom God has *made of one blood*, though they are made *to dwell on all the face of the earth*, Acts xvii. 26. Let every nation therefore thank God for the productions of its country; though they be not so rich as those of others, yet there is use for them in the public service of the world.

Judah and the *land of Israel* were merchants in Tyre. They traded mostly *in wheat*, a substantial commodity. Tyre was maintained by corn fetched from the land of Israel. Though Tyre got abundance by buying and selling, importing commodities from one place and exporting them, the *wares of their own making*, and a *multitude of such wares*, are here spoken of, *v.* 16, 18. It is the wisdom of a nation to encourage art and industry, for it contributes much to the wealth and honour of a nation to send abroad *wares of their own making.*

JAMIESON, FAUSSET, BROWN

they made ivory *with boxes." English Version*, with MAURER's correction, is simpler. **Chittim**—Cyprus and Macedonia, from which, PLINY tells us, the best boxwood came [GROTIUS]. **7. broidered . . . sail**—The ancients embroidered their sails often at great expense, especially the Egyptians, whose linen, still preserved in mummies, is of the finest texture. **Elishah**—Greece; so called from Elis, a large and ancient division of Peloponnesus. Pausanias says that the best of linen was produced in it, and in no other part of Greece; called by Homer, *Alisium.* **that which covered thee**—thy awning. **8. Arvad**—a small island and city near Phœnicia, now *Ruad:* its inhabitants are still noted for seafaring habits. **thy wise men, O Tyrus . . . thy pilots**—While the men of Arvad, once thy equals (Gen. 10:18), and the Sidonians, once thy superiors, were employed by thee in subordinate positions as "mariners," thou madest thine own skilled men alone to be commanders and pilots. Implying the political and mercantile superiority of Tyre. **9. Gebal**—a Phœnician city and region between Beirut and Tripolis, famed for skilled workmen (*Margin*, I Kings 5:18; Ps. 83:7). **calkers**—*stoppers of chinks* in a vessel: carrying on the metaphor as to Tyre. **occupy thy merchandise**—i.e., to exchange merchandise with thee. **10. Persia . . . Phut**—warriors from the extreme east and west. **Lud**—the Lydians of Asia Minor, near the Meander, famed for archery (Isa. 66:19); rather than those of Ethiopia, as the Lydians of Asia Minor form a kind of intermediate step between Persia and Phut (the Libyans about Cyrene, shielded warriors, Jer. 46:9, descended from Phut, son of Ham). **hanged . . . shield . . . comeliness**—Warriors hanged their accoutrements on the walls for ornament. Divested of the metaphor, it means that it was an honor to thee to have so many nations supplying thee with hired soldiers. **11. Gammadims**—rather, as the Tyrians were Syro-Phœnicians, from a *Syriac* root, meaning *daring*, "men of daring" [LUDOVICUS DE DIEU]. It is not likely the keeping of watch "in the towers" would have been entrusted to foreigners. Others take it from a *Hebrew* root, "a dagger," or short sword (Judg. 3:16), "short-swordsmen." **12. Tarshish**—Tartessus in Spain, a country famed for various metals, which were exported to Tyre. Much of the "tin" probably was conveyed by the Phœnicians from Cornwall to Tarshish. **traded in thy fairs**—"did barter with thee" [FAIRBAIRN]; from a root, "to leave," something *left* in barter for something else. **13. Javan**—the Ionians or *Greeks:* for the *Ionians* of Asia Minor were the first Greeks with whom the Asiatics came in contact. **Tubal . . . Meshech**—the Tibareni and Moschi, in the mountain region between the Black and Caspian Seas. **persons of men**—i.e., as slaves. So the Turkish harems are supplied with female slaves from Circassia and Georgia. **vessels**—all kinds of *articles.* Superior weapons are still manufactured in the Caucasus region. **14. Togarmah**—Armenia: descended from Gomer (Gen. 10:3). Their mountainous region south of the Caucasus was celebrated for horses. **horsemen**—rather, "riding-horses," as distinct from "horses" for chariots [FAIRBAIRN]. **15. Dedan**—near the Persian Sea: thus an avenue to the commerce of India. Not the Dedan in Arabia (vs. 20), as the names in the context here prove, but the Dedan sprung from Cush [BOCHART], (Gen. 10:7). **merchandise of thine hand**—i.e., were dependent on thee for trade [FAIRBAIRN]; came to buy *the produce of thy hands* [GROTIUS]. **a present**—lit., "a reward in return"; a price paid for merchandise. **horns of ivory**—Ivory is so termed from its resemblance to *horns.* The *Hebrew* word for "ivory" means "tooth"; so that they cannot have mistaken ivory as if *coming from the horns* of certain animals, instead of from the tusks of the elephant. **16.** "Syria was thy mart for the multitude . . . ." For "Syria" the LXX reads "Edom." But the Syrians were famed as merchants. **occupied**—old English for "traded"; so in Luke 19:13. **agate**—Others translate, "ruby," "chalcedony," or "pearls." **17. Minnith . . . Pannag**—names of places in Israel famed for good wheat, wherewith Tyre was supplied (I Kings 5:9, 11; Ezra 3:7; Acts 12:20); Minnith was formerly an Ammonite city (Judg. 11:33). "Pannag" is identified by GROTIUS with "Phenice," the Greek name for "Canaan". "They traded . . . wheat," i.e., they supplied thy market with wheat. **balm**—or, "balsam." **18. Helbon**—or Chalybon, in Syria, now Aleppo; famed for its wines; the Persian monarchs would drink no other. **19. Dan also**—None of the other places enumerated commence with the copula ("also"; *Hebrew, ve*). Moreover, the products specified, "cassia, calamus," apply rather to places in Arabia. Therefore, FAIRBAIRN translates, "Vedan"; perhaps the modern Aden, near the straits of Bab-el-man-

ADAM CLARKE

Isles of Chittim. The Italian islands; the islands of Greece; Cyprus.

8. *Zidon and Arvad.* Two powerful cities on the Phoenician coast, in the neighborhood of Tyre, from which Tyre had her sailors; and the best instructed of her own inhabitants were her pilots or steersmen.

9. *The ancients of Gebal.* This was a city of Phoenicia, near Mount Libanus, Josh. xiii. 5. It was called Biblos by the Greeks. *Thy calkers.* Those who repaired their vessels.

10. *They of Persia. Lud,* the Lydians; *Phut,* a people of Africa—see Gen. x. 6. From these places they had auxiliary troops; for as they traded with the then known world, were rich, and could afford to give good pay, they no doubt had soldiers and sailors from every part.

11. *The Gammadims were in thy towers.* Some think these were a people of Phoenicia; others, that tutelar images are meant; others, that the word expresses strong men, who acted as guards.

12. *Tarshish was thy merchant.* After having given an account of the naval and military equipment of this city, he now speaks of the various places and peoples with whom the Tyrians traded, and the different kinds of merchandise imported from those places.

13. *Javan, Tubal, and Meshech.* The Ionians, the Tybarenians, and the Cappadocians, or Muscovites. *They traded the persons of men.* That is, they trafficked in slaves. The bodies and souls of men were bought and sold in those days, as in our degenerate age. With these also they traded in brazen vessels.

15. *The men of Dedan.* Dedan was one of the descendants of Abraham by Keturah, and dwelt in Arabia, Gen. xxv. 3.

Ivory and ebony might come from that quarter. By way of distinction ivory is called both in Hebrew *shen*, and in Arabic *shen*, the "tooth," as that beautiful substance is the tooth of the elephant.

16. *Syria.* These were always a mercantile people. For the precious stones mentioned here see Exod. xxviii. 17.

17. *Judah, and the land of Israel . . . traded in thy market wheat.* The words have been understood as articles of merchandise, not names of places. So the Jews traded with the Tyrians in wheat, stacte, balsam, honey, oil, and resin.

18. *Damascus . . . wine of Helbon.* Now called by the Turks Haleb, and by us Aleppo. *White wool.* Very fine wool, wool of a fine quality.

MATTHEW HENRY

JAMIESON, FAUSSET, BROWN

deb. GROTIUS refers it to Dana, mentioned by Ptolemy. **Javan**—not the Greeks of *Europe* or *Asia Minor,* but of a Greek settlement in *Arabia.* **going to and fro**—rather, as *Hebrew* admits, "from *Uzal.*" This is added to "Javan," to mark *which* Javan is meant" (Gen. 10:27). The metropolis of Arabia Felix, or Yemen; called also Sanaa [BOCHART]. *English Version* gives a good sense, thus: All peoples, whether near as the Israelite "Dan," or far as the Greeks or "Javan," who were wont to "go to and fro" from their love of traffic, frequented thy marts, bringing bright iron, etc., these products not being necessarily represented as those of Dan or Javan. **bright iron**—Yemen is still famed for its sword blades. **calamus**—aromatic cane. **20. Dedan**—in Arabia; distinct from the Dedan in vs. 15 (see *note*). Descended from Abraham and Keturah (Gen. 25:3) [BOCHART]. **precious clothes**—splendid coverlets. **21. Arabia**—the nomadic tribes of Arabia, among which Kedar was pre-eminent. **occupied with thee**—lit., "of thy hand," i.e., they *traded* with thee for wares, the product *of thy hand* (see *Notes,* vss. 15, 16). **22. Sheba . . . Raamah**—in Arabia. **spices . . .**—obtained from India and conveyed in caravans to Tyre. **chief of . . . spices**—i.e., *best* spices (Deut. 33:15). **23. Haran**—the dwelling-place of Abraham in Mesopotamia, after he moved from Ur (Gen. 11:31). **Canneh**—Calneh, an Assyrian city on the Tigris; the Ctesiphon of the Greeks (Gen. 10:10). **Eden**—probably a region in Babylonia (see Gen. 2:8). **Chilmad**—a compound; the place designated by Ptolemy "Gaala of Media." The *Chaldee version* interprets it of Media. HENDERSON refers it to Carmanda, which Xenophon describes as a large city beyond the Euphrates. **24. all sorts of things**—*Hebrew,* "perfections"; exquisite articles of finery [GROTIUS]. **clothes**—rather, "mantles" or "cloaks"; lit., "wrappings." For "blue," HENDERSON translates, purple." **chests of rich apparel, bound with cords**—treasures or repositories of damask stuffs, consisting of variegated threads woven together in figures [HENDERSON]. **cedar**—The "chests" were made of *cedar,* in order to last the longer; and it also keeps off decay and has a sweet odor. **25. sing of thee**—personification; thy great merchant ships were palpable proofs of thy greatness. Others translate from a different *Hebrew* root, "were thy (mercantile) travellers." FAIRBAIRN translates, "Were thy walls." But the parallelism to "thou wast glorious" favors *English Version,* "sing of thee." **26.** In contrast to her previous greatness, her downfall is here, by a sudden transition, depicted under the image of a vessel foundering at sea. **east wind**—blowing from Lebanon, the most violent wind in the Mediterranean (Ps. 48:7). A Levanter, as it is called. Nebuchadnezzar is meant. The "sea" is the war with him which the "rowers," or rulers of the state vessel, had "brought" it into, to its ruin. **27.** The detailed enumeration implies the *utter completeness* of the ruin. **and in all thy company**—"even with all thy collected multitude" [HENDERSON]. **28. The suburbs**—the buildings of Tyre on the adjoining continent. **29.** So on the downfall of spiritual Babylon (Rev. 18:17, etc.). **shall stand upon . . . land**—being cast out of their ships in which heretofore they prided themselves. **30. against thee**—rather, "concerning thee." **31. utterly bald**—lit., "bald with baldness." The Phœnician custom in mourning; which, as being connected with heathenish superstitions, was forbidden to Israel (Deut. 14:1). **32. take up**—lift up. **the destroyed**—a destroyed one. Lit., (as opposed to its previous bustle of thronging merchants and mariners, vs. 27), "one brought to death's stillness." **in . . . midst of . . . sea**—insular Tyre. **33. out of the seas**—brought on shore *out of* the ships. **filledst**—didst supply plentifully with wares. **enrich . . . kings**—with the custom dues levied on the *wares.* **34. In the time when . . . shalt . . . shall**—*Now* that thou *art* broken (wrecked) . . ., thy merchandise . . . are fallen [MAURER]. **35. isles**—seacoasts. **36. hiss**—with astonishment; as in I Kings 9:8.

ADAM CLARKE

19. *Dan also and Javan.* It is probable that both these words mean some of the Grecian islands. *Going to and fro.* They both imported and exported; but *meuzal* may be a proper name.

20. *Dedan.* Possibly the descendants of Dedan, son of Raamah; see Gen. x. 7. *In precious clothes for chariots.* Either fine carpets, or rich housings for horses, camels, etc., used for riding.

22. *Sheba and Raamah.* Inhabitants of Arabia Felix, at the entrance of the Persian Gulf, who were famous for their riches and spices.

23. *Haran.* In Mesopotamia; well-known in Scripture. *Canneh.* It is supposed to be a cape or port of Arabia Felix, on the Indian Sea. *Eden.* Equally famous; supposed to have been situated near the confluence of the Tigris and Euphrates. *Sheba.* Different from that in v. 22. This was probably near the country of the Edomites. *Asshur.* Perhaps the Assyrians.

24. *These were thy merchants in all sorts of things.* The above people traded with the Tyrians in a great variety of the most valuable merchandise.

TODAY'S DICTIONARY OF THE BIBLE:

Kedar—*dark-skinned*—the second son of Ishmael (Gen. 25:13).

It is the name for the nomadic tribes of Arabs, the Bedouins generally (Isa. 21:16; 42:11; 60:7; Jer. 2:10; Ezek. 27:21), who dwelt in the north-west of Arabia. They lived in black hair-tents (Song of Sol. 1:5). To "dwell in the tents of Kedar" was to be cut off from the worship of the true God (Ps. 120:5). The Kedarites suffered at the hands of Nebuchadnezzar (Jer. 49:28, 29).

Dedan—*low ground.* A son of Raamah (Gen. 10:7). His descendants are mentioned in Isa. 21:13 and Ezek. 27:15. They probably settled among the sons of Cush, on the northwest coast of the Persian Gulf.

Verses 26–36

The destruction of Tyre was sudden. Her *sun went down at noon.* And all her wealth and grandeur, pomp and power, did but aggravate her ruin. She is as a great ship richly laden, that is sunk by the indiscretion of her steersmen: *Thy rowers have* themselves *brought thee into great* and dangerous *waters;* the governors of the city involved them in war with the Chaldeans which was the ruin of their state. By their insolence they provoked Nebuchadnezzar to make a descent upon them, and, by their obstinacy enraged him to such a degree that he determined on the ruin of their state, and, *like an east wind, broke them in the midst of the seas.* All her wealth shall be buried with her, *her riches, her fairs, and her merchandise* (*v.* 27); all shall *fall with her into the midst of the seas, in the day of her ruin.* The pilots, her princes and governors, when they see how wretchedly they have mismanaged and how they have contributed to their own ruin, shall *cry out* so loud as to make even the *suburbs shake* (*v.* 28). Tyre should be upbraided with her former prosperity (*v.* 32, 33); she that was Tyrus the *renowned* shall now be called *Tyrus the destroyed* in the *midst of the sea.*

Some shall be *sorely afraid,* and shall *be troubled* (*v.* 35). Others shall *hiss at her* (*v.* 36), shall ridicule her pride, and bad management, and think her ruin just.

26. *Thy rowers have brought thee into great waters.* Tyre is still considered under the allegory of a ship; and all the vessels of different nations trading with her are represented as towing her into deep waters—bringing her into great affluence. But while in this state, a stormy *east wind,* or a destructive wind, meaning the Chaldeans, arises, and dashes her to pieces!

27. *Thy riches.* This vast ship, laden with all kinds of valuable wares, and manned in the best manner, being wrecked, all her valuables, sailors, officers, went to the bottom.

28. *The cry of thy pilots.* When the ship was dashed against the rocks by the violence of the winds and the waves, and all hope of life was taken away, then a universal cry was set up by all on board.

CHAPTER 28

Verses 1–10

The prince of Tyrus is singled out from the rest. Here is a *message to him from God,* which the prophet must send him.

CHAPTER 28

VSS. 1-26. PROPHETICAL DIRGE ON THE KING OF TYRE, AS THE CULMINATION AND EMBODIMENT OF THE SPIRIT OF CARNAL PRIDE AND SELF-SUFFICIENCY OF THE WHOLE STATE. THE FALL OF ZIDON, THE MOTHER CITY. THE RESTORATION OF ISRAEL IN CONTRAST WITH TYRE AND ZIDON. **2. Because . . .**—repeated resumptively in vs. 6. The apodosis begins at vs. 7. "The prince of Tyrus" at the time was Ithobal, or Ithbaal II; the name implying his close connection with Baal, the Phœnician supreme god, whose representative he was. **I am a god, I sit in**

CHAPTER 28

2. *Say unto the prince of Tyrus.* But who was this prince of Tyrus? Some think Hiram; some, Sin; some, the devil.

MATTHEW HENRY

I. He must tell him of his pride. *His heart was lifted up*, *v.* 2. Out of the pride of his heart he said, *I am a god.* He thought that the city of Tyre had as necessary a dependence upon him as the world has upon the God that made it. "*I am the strong God*, and therefore will not be contradicted, because I cannot be controlled. *I sit in the seat of God;* I sit as safely as God, as safely *in the heart of the seas*, and as far out of the reach of danger, as he in the *height of heaven*." He shall be told, *Thou art a man, and not God*, a depending creature, a dying creature; thou art *flesh, and not spirit*, Isa. xxxi. 3. The king of Tyre, though he has such a mighty influence and though he is flattered by his courtiers and made a god of by his poets, yet he is *but a man*; he knows it; he fears it. He was proud of his wisdom. When the king of Tyre dreams himself to be a god he says, I am *wiser than Daniel. There is no secret that they can hide from thee.* He that was *wiser than Daniel* was prouder than Lucifer. As some of the kings of Judah *loved husbandry* (2 Chron. xxvi. 10), so the king of Tyre loved merchandise, and by it he *got riches, increased his riches, and filled his treasures with gold and silver*, *v.* 4, 5. He attributed the increase of his wealth, to himself and not to the providence of God, forgetting him who *gave him power to get wealth*, Deut. viii. 17, 18. He thought himself a wise man because he was a rich man; whereas a fool may have an estate (Eccles. ii. 19).

II. Since *pride goes before destruction, and a haughty spirit before a fall*, he must tell him of that destruction, of that fall. "Because thou hast pretended to be a god (*v.* 6), therefore thou shalt not be long a man," *v.* 7. *I will bring strangers upon thee*—the Chaldeans. They are people of a *strange language*. They are the *terrible of the nations*; it was an army made up of many nations, formidable both for strength and fury. *They shall draw their swords against the beauty of thy wisdom* (*v.* 7), against all those things which thou gloriest in as thy beauty and the product of thy wisdom. The king of Tyre's palace, his treasury, his city, his navy, his army, these he glories in as his brightness, these the victorious enemy shall defile, shall deface, shall deform. He shall be so vilified in his death that he may despair of being deified after his death. The sentence of death here passed upon the king of Tyre is ratified by a divine authority: *I have spoken it, saith the Lord God.* When the conqueror sets his sword to thy breast, and thou seest no way of escape, *wilt thou then say, I am God*? The fear of it will force thee to own that thou art not a god, but a weak, timorous, trembling, dying man.

Verses 11–19

After the ruin of the king of Tyre is foretold it is bewailed.

I. This is commonly understood of the prince who then reigned over Tyre, spoken to, *v.* 2. His name was *Ethbaal*, or *Ithobalus*, as Diodorus Siculus calls him that was king of Tyre when Nebuchadnezzar destroyed it. He was an accomplished man, but his iniquity was his ruin.

II. Some think that by *the king of Tyre* is meant the whole royal family. He is here spoken of as having lived in great splendour, *v.* 12–15. He was looked upon to be as wise as the reason of men could make him, and as happy as the wealth of this world and the enjoyment of it could make him. He seemed to be as wise and happy as Adam in innocency (*v.* 13): "*Thou hast been in Eden*, even *in the garden of God*; thou hast lived as it were in paradise all thy days, hast had dominion over all about thee, as Adam had." His rooms were set round with jewels, so that he walked in the midst of them, and fancied himself as glorious as if, like God, he had been surrounded by so many angels, who are compared to a *flame of fire*. *Gold* is mentioned last, as far inferior in value to those precious stones; and he used to speak of it accordingly. Another thing that made him think his palace a paradise was the curious music he had, the *tabrets and pipes*, hand-instruments and wind-instruments.

JAMIESON, FAUSSET, BROWN

. . . seat of God . . . the seas—As God sits enthroned in His heavenly citadel exempt from all injury, so I sit secure in my impregnable stronghold amidst the stormiest elements, able to control them at will, and make them subserve my interests. The language, though primarily here applied to the king of Tyre, as similar language is to the king of Babylon (Isa. 14:13, 14), yet has an ulterior and fuller accomplishment in Satan and his embodiment in Antichrist (Dan. 7:25; 11:36, 37; II Thess. 2:4; Rev. 13:6). This feeling of superhuman elevation in the king of Tyre was fostered by the fact that the island on which Tyre stood was called "the holy island" [SANCONIATHON], being sacred to Hercules, so much so that the colonies looked up to Tyre as the mother city of their religion, as well as of their political existence. The *Hebrew* for "God" is *El*, i.e., "the Mighty One." **yet . . .**—keen irony. **set thine heart as . . . heart of God**—Thou thinkest of thyself as if thou wert God. **3.** **Ezekiel ironically alludes to Ithbaal's overweening opinion of the wisdom of himself and the Tyrians, as though superior to that of** Daniel, whose fame had reached even Tyre as eclipsing the Chaldean sages. "Thou art wiser," viz., in thine own opinion (Zech. 9:2). **no secret**—viz., forgetting riches (vs. 4). **that they can hide**—i.e., that can be hidden. **5.** (Ps. 62:10.) **6. Because . . .**—resumptive of vs. 2. **7. therefore**—apodosis. **strangers . . . terrible of the nations**—the Chaldean foreigners noted for their ferocity (ch. 30:11; 31:12). **against the beauty of thy wisdom**—i.e., against thy beautiful possessions acquired by thy wisdom on which thou pridest thyself (vss. 3-5). **defile thy brightness**—obscure the brightness of thy kingdom. **8. the pit** i.e., the bottom of the sea; the image being that of one conquered in a sea-fight. **the deaths**—*plural*, as various kinds of deaths are meant (Jer. 16:4). **of them . . . slain**—lit., "pierced through." Such deaths as those pierced with many wounds die. **9. yet say**—i.e., still say; referring to vs. 2. **but . . .**—But thy blasphemous boastings shall be falsified, and thou shalt be shown to be but man, and not God, in the hand (at the mercy) of Him. **10. deaths of . . . uncircumcised**—i.e., such a death as the uncircumcised or godless heathen *deserve;* and perhaps, also, such as the uncircumcised *inflict*, a great ignominy in the eyes of a Jew (I Sam. 31:4); a fit retribution on him who had scoffed at the circumcised Jews. **12. sealest up the sum**—lit., "Thou art the one sealing the sum of perfection." A thing is *sealed* when *completed* (Dan. 9:24). "The sum" implies *the full measure of beauty*, from a *Hebrew* root, "to measure." The normal man—one formed after accurate rule. **13. in Eden**—The king of Tyre is represented in his former high state (contrasted with his subsequent downfall), under images drawn from the primeval man in Eden, the type of humanity in its most Godlike form. **garden of God**—the model of ideal loveliness (ch. 31:8, 9; 36:35). In the person of the king of Tyre a new trial was made of humanity with the greatest earthly advantages. But as in the case of Adam, the good gifts of God were only turned into ministers to pride and self. **every precious stone**—so in Eden (Gen. 2:12), "gold, bdellium, and the onyx stone." So the king of Tyre was arrayed in jewel-bespangled robes after the fashion of Oriental monarchs. The nine precious stones here mentioned answer to nine of the twelve (representing the twelve tribes) in the high priest's breastplate (Exod. 39:10-13; Rev. 21:14, 19-21). Of the four rows of three in each, the third is omitted in the *Hebrew*, but is supplied in the LXX. In this, too, there is an ulterior reference to Antichrist, who is blasphemously to arrogate the office of our divine High Priest (Zech. 6:13). **tabrets**—tambourines. **pipes**—lit., "holes" in musical pipes or flutes. **created**—i.e., in *the day of thine accession to the throne.* Tambourines and all the marks of joy were ready prepared for thee ("in thee," i.e., with and for thee). Thou hadst not, like others, to work thy way to the throne through arduous struggles. No sooner created than, like Adam, thou wast surrounded with the gratifications of Eden. FAIRBAIRN, for "pipes," translates, "females" (having reference to Gen. 1:27), i.e., musician-women. MAURER explains the *Hebrew* not as to music, but as to the *setting* and *mounting* of the gems previously mentioned. **14. anointed cherub**—GESENIUS translates from an *Aramaic* root, "extended cherub." *English Version*, from a *Hebrew* root, is better. "The cherub consecrated to the Lord by the anointing oil" [FAIRBAIRN]. **covereth**—The imagery employed by Ezekiel as a priest is from the Jewish temple, wherein the cherubim overshadowed the mercy seat, as the king of Tyre, a demi-god in his own esteem, extended his protection over the inter-

ADAM CLARKE

I am a god. That is, I am absolute, independent, and accountable to none. He was a man of great pride and arrogance.

3. *Thou art wiser than Daniel.* Daniel was at this time living, and was reputable for his great wisdom. This is said ironically. See chap. xiv. 14; xxvi. 1.

5. *By thy great wisdom.* He attributed everything to himself; he did not acknowledge a divine providence. As he got all by himself, so he believed he could keep all by himself, and had no need of any foreign help.

7. *I will bring strangers upon thee.* The Chaldeans.

9. *Wilt thou yet say before him that slayeth thee?* Will you continue your pride and arrogance when the sword is sheathed in you, and still imagine that you are self-sufficient and independent?

12. *Thou sealest up.* This has been translated, "Thou drawest thy own likeness." "Thou formest a portrait of thyself; and hast represented thyself the perfection of wisdom and beauty." I believe this to be the meaning of the place.

13. *Thou hast been in Eden.* This also is a strong irony. Thou art like Adam, when in his innocence and excellence he was in the Garden of Eden!

14. *Thou art the anointed cherub that covereth.* The irony is continued; and here he is likened to the cherub that guarded the gates of paradise, and kept the way of the tree of life; or to one of the cherubs whose wings, spread out, covered the mercy seat.

MATTHEW HENRY

He appeared in as much splendour as the high priest when he was clothed with his garments for glory and beauty. *Thou wast perfect in thy ways;* thou didst prosper in all thy affairs and everything went well with thee; *from the day thou wast created, till iniquity was found in thee;* and that spoiled all (*v.* 15). And when iniquity was once *found in him* it increased; he grew worse and worse (*v.* 18). The king had so much to do with his merchandise, and was so wholly intent upon the gains of that, that he took no care to do justice, to give redress, to those that suffered wrong and to protect them from violence (*v.* 16). "*Thy heart was lifted up because of thy beauty;* thou wast in love with thyself, *v.* 17." He disgraces the crown he wears, and so has forfeited it, and shall be destroyed *from the midst of the stones of fire*, the precious stones with which his palace was garnished.

Verses 20–26

The destruction of Zidon, a city that lay near to Tyre, was more ancient, but not so considerable, had a dependence upon it and stood and fell with it. The Zidonians were more addicted to idolatry than the Tyrians, who, being men of business, were less under the power of bigotry and superstition. The Zidonians were noted for the worship of Ashtaroth. Jezebel was daughter to the king of Zidon, who brought the worship of Baal into Israel (1 Kings xvi. 31); so that God had been much dishonoured by the Zidonians. The judgments that shall be executed upon Zidon are war and pestilence, *v.* 23. Nor is it Tyre and Zidon only on which God would execute judgments, but on all those that despised his people Israel, and triumphed in their calamities; for this was now God's controversy with the nations that were *round about them*, *v.* 26. God will be glorified in the restoration of his people to their former prosperity. He had been dishonoured by the sins of his people, and their sufferings too had given occasion to the enemy to blaspheme (Isa. lii. 5); but God will now both cure them of their sins and ease them of their troubles, and so *will be sanctified in them in the sight of the heathen*, *v.* 25. They shall enjoy great tranquillity there. When those that have been vexatious to them are taken off they shall live in quietness; there shall be no more *a pricking brier nor a grieving thorn*, *v.* 24. They shall have a happy settlement, for they shall *build houses*, and *plant vineyards*, and there shall be none to disquiet them or make them afraid, *v.* 26. But the full accomplishment of this promise is reserved for the heavenly Canaan, everything that offends shall be removed, and all griefs and fears for ever banished.

JAMIESON, FAUSSET, BROWN

ests of Tyre. The cherub—an ideal compound of the highest kinds of aimal existence and the type of redeemed man in his ultimate state of perfection—is made the image of the king of Tyre, as if the beau ideal of humanity. The pretensions of Antichrist are the ulterior reference, of whom the king of Tyre is a type. Cf. "As God . . . in the *temple* of God" (II Thess. 2:4). **I have set thee**—not *thou* set thyself (Prov. 8:16; Rom. 13:1). **upon the holy mountain of God**—Zion, following up the image. **in . . . midst of . . . stones of fire**—In ambitious imagination he stood in the place of God, "under whose feet was, as it were, a pavement of sapphire," while His glory was like "devouring fire" (Exod. 24:10, 17). **15. perfect**—prosperous [GROTIUS], and having no defect. So Hiram was a sample of the Tyrian monarch in his early days of wisdom and prosperity (I Kings 5:7, etc.). **till iniquity . . . in thee**—Like the primeval man thou hast fallen by abusing God's gifts, and so hast provoked God's wrath. **16. filled the midst of thee**—i.e., they have filled *the midst of the city;* he as the head of the state being involved in the guilt of the state, which he did not check, but fostered. **cast thee as profane**—no longer treated as sacred, but driven out of the place of sanctity (see vs. 14) which thou hast occupied (cf. Ps. 89:39). **17. brightness**—thy splendor. **lay thee before kings**—as an example of God's wrath against presumptuous pride. **18. thy sanctuaries**—i.e., the holy places, attributed to the king of Tyre in vs. 14, as his ideal position. As he "profaned" it, so God will "profane" him (vs. 16). **fire . . . devour**—As he abused his supposed elevation amidst "the stones of fire" (vs. 16), so God will make His "fire" to "devour" him. **21. Zidon**—famous for its fishery (from a root, *Zud*, "to fish"); and afterwards for its wide extended commerce; its artistic elegance was proverbial. Founded by Canaan's first-born (Gen. 10:15). Tyre was an offshoot from it, so that it was involved in the same overthrow by the Chaldeans as Tyre. It is mentioned separately, because its idolatry (Ashtaroth, Tammuz, or Adonis) infected Israel more than that of Tyre did (ch. 8; Judg. 10:6; I Kings 11:33). The notorious Jezebel was a daughter of the Zidonian king. **22. shall be sanctified in her**—when all nations shall see that I am the Holy Judge in the vengeance that I will inflict on her for sin. **24. no more . . . brier . . . unto . . . Israel**—as the idolatrous nations left in Canaan (among which Zidon is expressly specified in the limits of Asher, Judg. 1:31) had been (Num. 33:55; Josh. 23:13). "A brier," first ensnaring the Israelites in sin, and then being made the instrument of punishing them. **pricking**—lit., "causing *bitterness*." The same *Hebrew* is translated "fretting" (Lev. 13:51, 52). The wicked are often called "thorns" (II Sam. 23:6). **25, 26.** Fulfilled in part at the restoration from Babylon, when Judaism, so far from being merged in heathenism, made inroads by conversions on the idolatry of surrounding nations. The full accomplishment is yet future, when Israel, under Christ, shall be the center of Christendom; of which an earnest was given in the woman from the coasts of Tyre and Sidon who sought the Saviour (Matt. 15:21, 24, 26-28; cf. Isa. 11:12). **dwell safely**—(Jer. 23:6).

ADAM CLARKE

Thou wast upon the holy mountain of God. The irony is still continued; and now he is compared to Moses, and afterwards to one of the chief angels, who has walked up and down among the stones of fire; that is, your floors have been paved with precious stones, that shone and sparkled like fire.

15. *Thou wast perfect in thy ways.* The irony seems still to be kept up. You have been like the angels, like Moses, like the cherubs, like Adam, like God, till your iniquity was found out.

16. *I will cast thee as profane.* You shall be cast down from your eminence. *From the midst of the stones of fire.* Some, supposing that *stones of fire* means the stars, have thought that the whole refers to the fall of Satan.

18. *Thou hast defiled thy sanctuaries.* Irony continued. As God, as the angels, as the cherubim, you must have had your sanctuaries, but you have defiled them; and as Adam, you have polluted your Eden, and have been expelled from paradise.

19. *Thou shalt be a terror.* Instead of being an object of adoration you shall be a subject of horror, and at last be destroyed with your city, so that nothing but your name shall remain. It was entirely burnt by Alexander the Great, as it had been before by Nebuchadnezzar.

22. *I am against thee, O Zidon.* Sidon for a long time had possessed the empire of the sea and of all Phoenicia, and Tyre was one of its colonies; but in process of time the daughter became greater than the mother. It seems to have been an independent place at the time in which Tyre was taken, but it is likely that it was taken by the Chaldeans soon after the former.

23. *And the wounded.* Chalal, "the soldiery." All its supports shall be taken away, and its defenders destroyed.

24. *There shall be no more a pricking brier.* Nothing to excite Israel to idolatry when restored from their captivity. Sidon being destroyed, there would come no encourager of idolatry from that quarter.

MATTHEW HENRY — CHAPTER 29

Verses 1–7

I. The date of this prophecy against Egypt. It was in the *tenth year of the captivity*. The first prophecy against Egypt was just at the time when the king of Egypt was coming to relieve Jerusalem and raise the siege (Jer. xxxvii. 5), but did not answer the expectations of the Jews.

II. This prophecy is directed against *Pharaoh king of Egypt, and against all Egypt*, *v.* 2. This begins with the prince, because it began to have its accomplishment in the rebellions of the people against the prince, not long after this.

JAMIESON, FAUSSET, BROWN — CHAPTER 29

VSS. 1-21. THE JUDGMENT ON EGYPT BY NEBUCHADNEZZAR; THOUGH ABOUT TO BE RESTORED AFTER FORTY YEARS, IT WAS STILL TO BE IN A STATE OF DEGRADATION. This is the last of the world kingdoms against which Ezekiel's prophecies are directed, and occupies the largest space in them, viz., the next four chapters. Though farther off than Tyre, it exercised a more powerful influence on Israel. **2. Pharaoh**—a common name of all the kings of Egypt, meaning "the sun"; or, as others say, a "crocodile," which was worshipped in parts of Egypt (cf. vs. 3). Hophra or Apries was on the throne at this time. His reign began prosperously. He took Gaza (Jer. 47:1) and Zidon and made himself master of Phœnicia and Palestine, recovering much that was lost to Egypt by the victory of Nebuchadnezzar at Carchemish (II Kings 24:7; Jer. 46:2), in the fourth year of Jehoiakim [WILKINSON'S *Ancient Egypt,* 1. 169]. So proudly secure because of his successes for twenty-five years did he feel, that he said not even a god could deprive him of his kingdom [HERODOTUS, 2. 169]. Hence the appropriateness of the description of him in vs. 3. No mere human sagacity could have enabled Ezekiel to foresee Egypt's downfall in the height of its prosperity. There are four divisions of these prophecies; the first in the tenth year of Ezekiel's cap-

ADAM CLARKE — CHAPTER 29

1. *In the tenth year.* Of Zedekiah; and tenth of the captivity of Jeconiah.

2. *Set thy face against Pharaoh king of Egypt.* This was Pharaoh-hophra or Pharaoh-apries, whom we have so frequently met with in the prophecies of Jeremiah, and much of whose history has been given in the notes.

MATTHEW HENRY

III. The prophecy itself. Pharaoh Hophrah (for so was the reigning Pharaoh surnamed) is here represented by a *great dragon*, or crocodile, that *lies in the midst of his rivers* to *play therein*, *v.* 3. Nilus, the river of Egypt, was famed for crocodiles.

1. The pride and security of Pharaoh. He boasts that he is an absolute prince, a sole prince, and has neither partner in the government nor competitor. Pharaoh's reason for his pretensions is absurd: *My river is my own*, for *I have made it for myself*. Here he usurps two of the divine prerogatives, to be the author and the end of his own being and felicity. Self is the great idol that all the world worships, in contempt of God and his sovereignty.

2. The course God will take with this proud man, to humble him. He is a great dragon in the waters, and God will accordingly deal with him, *v.* 4, 5. Herodotus relates of this Pharaoh, who was now king of Egypt, that he had reigned in great prosperity for twenty-five years, and was so elevated with his successes that he said that *God himself could not cast him out of his kingdom. All his fish* shall be drawn out with him, his servants, his soldiers, and all that had a dependence on him. These shall *stick to his scales*, adhere to their king, resolving to live and die with him. But king and army, the dragon and all the fish that stick to his scales, shall perish together, as fish cast upon dry ground, *v.* 5. Now this is supposed to have had its accomplishment soon after, when this Pharaoh, in defence of Aricius king of Libya, who had been expelled his kingdom by the Cyrenians, levied a great army, and went out against the Cyrenians, to re-establish his friend, but was defeated in battle, which gave such disgust to his kingdom that they rose in rebellion against him. Thus was he left *thrown into the wilderness, he and all the fish of the river* with him.

3. The ground of the controversy God has with the Egyptians; it is because they have cheated his people. They failed them (*v.* 6, 7). When any stress was laid upon them, they either could not or would not do that for them which was expected. The king of Egypt, it is probable, had encouraged Zedekiah to break his league with the king of Babylon, with a promise that he would stand by him, which he failed to do. God had told them, long since, that the Egyptians were broken reeds, Isa. xxx. 6, 7. And now they found it so.

Verses 8–16

I. A prophecy of the ruin of Egypt. The threatening is particular; and the sin is their pride, *v.* 9. God is against the king and against the people, *against thee and against thy rivers*. Waters signify *people and multitudes*, Rev. xvii. 15. Multitudes shall be cut off by war, the sword of civil war. The country shall be depopulated. The *land of Egypt shall be utterly waste* (*wastes of waste*, so the margin reads it), *and desolate* (*v.* 10); *neither men nor beasts shall pass through it, nor shall it be inhabited* (*v.* 11); it shall be *desolate in the midst of the countries that are so*, *v.* 12.

JAMIESON, FAUSSET, BROWN

tivity; the last in the twelfth. Between the first and second comes one of much later date, not having been given till the twenty-seventh year (ch. 29:17; 30:19), but placed there as appropriate to the subject matter. Pharaoh-hophra, or Apries, was dethroned and strangled, and Amasis substituted as king, by Nebuchadnezzar (cf. Jer. 44:30). The Egyptian priests, from national vanity, made no mention to HERODOTUS of the Egyptian loss of territory in Syria through Nebuchadnezzar, of which JOSEPHUS tells us, but attributed the change in the succession from Apries to Amasis solely to the Egyptian soldiery. The civil war between the two rivals no doubt lasted several years, affording an opportunity to Nebuchadnezzar of interfering and of elevating the usurper Amasis, on condition of his becoming tributary to Babylon [WILKINSON]. Cf. Jeremiah 43:10-12, and my *Note*, vs. 13, for another view of the grounds of interference of Nebuchadnezzar. **3. dragon**—*Hebrew, tanim*, any large aquatic animal, here the crocodile, which on Roman coins is the emblem of Egypt. **lieth**—restest proudly secure. **his rivers**—the mouths, branches, and canals of the Nile, to which Egypt owed its fertility. **4. hooks in thy jaws**—(Isa. 37:29; cf. Job 41:1, 2). Amasis was the "hook." In the Assyrian sculptures prisoners are represented with a hook in the underlip, and a cord from it held by the king. **cause . . . fish . . . stick unto . . . scales**—Pharaoh, presuming on his power as if he were God (vs. 3, "I have made it"), wished to stand in the stead of God as defender of the covenant people, his motive being, not love to them, but rivalry with Babylon. He raised the siege of Jerusalem, but it was only for a time (cf. vs. 6; Jer. 37:5, 7-10); ruin overtook not only them, but himself. As the fish that clung to the horny scales of the crocodile, the lord of the Nile, when he was caught, shared his fate, so the adherents of Pharaoh, lord of Egypt, when he was overthrown by Amasis, should share his fate. **5. wilderness**—captivity beyond thy kingdom. The expression is used perhaps to imply retribution in kind. As Egypt pursued after Israel, saying, "The *wilderness* hath shut them in" (Exod. 14:3), so she herself shall be brought into a *wilderness state*. **open fields**—lit., "face of the field." **not be brought together**—As the crocodile is not, when caught, restored to the river, so no remnant of thy routed army shall be brought together, and rallied, after its defeat in the wilderness. Pharaoh led an army against Cyrene in Africa, in support of Aricranes, who had been stripped of his kingdom by the Cyrenians. The army perished and Egypt rebelled against him [JUNIUS]. But the reference is mainly to the defeat by Nebuchadnezzar. **beasts . . . fowls**—hostile and savage men. **6. staff of reed to . . . Israel**—alluding to the reeds on the banks of the Nile, which broke if one leaned upon them (*Note*, vs. 4; Isa. 36:6). All Israel's dependence on Egypt proved hurtful instead of beneficial (Isa. 30:1-5). **7. hand**—or handle of the reed. **rend . . . shoulder**—by the splinters on which the shoulder or arm would fall, on the support failing the hand. **madest . . . loins . . . at a stand**—i.e., made them to be disabled. MAURER somewhat similarly (referring to a kindred *Arabic* form), "Thou hast stricken both their loins." FAIRBAIRN, not so well, "Thou lettest all their loins stand," i.e., by themselves, bereft of the support which they looked for from thee. **8. a sword**—Nebuchadnezzar's army (vs. 19). Also Amasis and the Egyptian revolters who after Pharaoh-hophra's discomfiture in Cyrene dethroned and strangled him, having defeated him in a battle fought at Memphis [JUNIUS]. **9. I am the Lord**—in antithesis to the blasphemous boast repeated here from vs. 3, "The river is mine, and I have made it." **10. from the tower of Syene**—GROTIUS translates, "from Migdol (a fortress near Pelusium on the north of Suez) to Syene" (in the farthest south); i.e., from one end of Egypt to the other. So in ch. 30:6, *Margin*. However, *English Version* rightly refers Syene to Seveneh, i.e., Sebennytus, in the eastern delta of the Nile, the capital of the Lower Egyptian kings. The Sebennyte Pharaohs, with the help of the Canaanites, who, as shepherds or merchants, ranged the desert of Suez, extended their borders beyond the narrow province east of the delta, to which they had been confined by the Pharaohs of Upper Egypt. The defeated party, in derision, named the Sebennyte or Lower Egyptians *foreigners* and *shepherd kings* (a shepherd being an abomination in Egypt, Genesis 46:34). They were really a *native* dynasty. Thus, in *English Version*, "Ethiopia" in the extreme south is rightly contrasted with Sebennytus or Syene in the north. **11. forty years**—answering to the forty years in which the Israelites, their former bondsmen, wandered in "the wilder-

ADAM CLARKE

3. *The great dragon*. The original signifies any large animal. *The midst of his rivers*. This refers to the several branches of the Nile by which this river empties itself into Mediterranean. The crocodile was the emblem of Egypt.

4. *I will put hooks in thy jaws*. Amasis, one of this king's generals, being proclaimed king by an insurrection of the people, dethroned Apries, and seized upon the kingdom; and Apries was obliged to flee to Upper Egypt for safety.

5. *I will leave thee thrown into the wilderness*. Referring to his being obliged to take refuge in Upper Egypt. But he was afterwards taken prisoner, and strangled by Amasis. Herod., lib. ii. x. 169.

6. *They have been a staff of reed*. An inefficient and faithless ally. The Israelites expected assistance from them when Nebuchadnezzar came against Jerusalem; and they made a feint to help them, but retired when Nebuchadnezzar went against them. Thus were the Jews deceived and ultimately ruined; see v. 7.

10. *From the tower of Syene*. *Mimmigdol seveneh*, "from Migdol to Syene." Syene was the last city in Egypt, going towards Ethiopia. It was famous for a well into which the rays of the sun fell perpendicularly at midday.

MATTHEW HENRY

This was the effect of the war which the king of Babylon made upon them. The people shall be dispersed and scattered among the nations (*v.* 12), so that those who thought the balance of power was in their hand should now become a contemptible people.

II. Of the restoration of Egypt after awhile, *v.* 13. Egypt shall lie *desolate forty years* (*v.* 12) and then *I will bring again the captivity of Egypt*, *v.* 14. The forty years end about the first year of Cyrus, when the seventy years' captivity of Judah ended, or soon after. God will gather the Egyptians, and make them to *return to the land of their habitation*, *v.* 14. They shall not make a figure as they have done. Egypt shall be *a kingdom* again, but it shall be the *basest of the kingdoms* (*v.* 15). For two reasons it shall be thus mortified: (1) That it may not domineer over its neighbours, but that it may know what it is to be low and despised. (2) That it may not deceive the people of God (*v.* 16): *It shall no more be the confidence of the house of Israel;* they shall no more trust in it as they have done.

Verses 17–21

The date of this prophecy is in the twenty-seventh year of Ezekiel's captivity, sixteen years after the prophecy in the former part of the chapter. After the destruction of Jerusalem Nebuchadnezzar spent two or three campaigns in the conquest of the Ammonites and Moabites. Then he spent thirteen years in the siege of Tyre. During all that time the Egyptians were embroiled in war with the Cyrenians, by which they were much weakened and impoverished; and at the end of the siege of Tyre God delivers this prophecy to Ezekiel, to signify to him that that utter destruction of Egypt which he had foretold fifteen or sixteen years before, should now be completed by Nebuchadnezzar. The prophecy which begins here, it should seem, is continued to the twentieth verse of the next chapter. It is the last prophecy we have of this prophet, but is laid here, that all the prophecies against Egypt might come together.

I. The success God would give to Nebuchadnezzar against Egypt, *v.* 19, 20. It was a cheap and easy prey. Jeremiah foretold that Nebuchadnezzar should *array himself with the land of Egypt as a shepherd puts on his coat*, which intimates what a rich and cheap prey it should be.

II. This success was a recompense for the hard service with which he had caused his army to serve against Tyre, *v.* 18, 20. 1. The taking of Tyre cost Nebuchadnezzar abundance of blood and treasure. In this siege *every head was made bald, and every shoulder peeled*, with carrying burdens and labouring in the water when they had a strong tide to contend with. 2. In this service God owns that they *wrought for him*, *v.* 20. He set them at work, for the humbling of a proud city and its king, though *they meant not so, neither did their heart think so*. 3. For this service he had *no wages*. He was at vast expense to take Tyre; and he promised himself good plunder, but the Tyrians sent away by ship their best effects, and threw the rest into the sea, so that they had nothing but bare walls. 4. He shall have the spoil of Egypt to recompense him for his service against Tyre.

III. The mercy God had in store for the house of Israel. When the tide is at the highest it will turn, and so it will when it is at the lowest. Nebuchadnezzar was in the zenith of his glory when he had conquered Egypt, but within a year after he ran mad (Dan. iv). When he was at the highest Israel was at the lowest; but *in that day the horn of the house of Israel shall bud forth*, *v.* 21. Their princes are the *horns of the house of Israel*, the seat of their glory and power. These began to bud forth when Daniel and his fellows were highly preferred in Babylon (Dan. ii. 49). Within a year after the conquest of Egypt they were thus preferred; and, soon after, three of them were made famous by the honour God put upon them in bringing them alive out of the burning fiery furnace. And this promise had a further accomplishment in the elevation of Jehoiachin king of Judah, Jer. lii. 31, 32. God will honour their prophets: And *I will give thee the opening of the mouth.* Though none of Ezekiel's prophecies, after this, are recorded, yet we think he went on prophesying, and with more liberty, when Daniel and his fellows were in power, ready to protect him.

JAMIESON, FAUSSET, BROWN

ness" (cf. *Note,* vs. 5). JEROME remarks the number *forty* is one often connected with affliction and judgment. The rains of the flood in forty days brought destruction on the world. Moses, Elias, and the Saviour fasted forty days. The interval between Egypt's overthrow by Nebuchadnezzar and the deliverance by Cyrus, was about forty years. The *ideal* forty years' wilderness state of social and political degradation, rather than a *literal* non passing of man or beast for that term, is mainly intended (so ch. 4:6; Isa. 19:2, 11). **12.** As Israel passed through a term of wilderness discipline (cf. ch. 20: 35, etc.), which was in its essential features to be repeated again, so it was to be with Egypt [FAIRBAIRN]. Some Egyptians were to be carried to Babylon, also many "scattered" in Arabia and Ethiopia through fear; but mainly the "scattering" was to be the *dissipation of their power,* even though the people still remained in their own land. **13.** (Jer. 46:26). **14. Pathros**—the Thebaid, or Upper Egypt, which had been especially harassed by Nebuchadnezzar (Nah. 3:8, 10). The oldest part of Egypt as to civilization and art. The Thebaid was anciently called "Egypt" [ARISTOTLE]. Therefore it is called the "land of the Egyptians' *birth*" (*Margin,* for "habitation"). **base kingdom**—Under Amasis it was made dependent on Babylon; humbled still more under Cambyses; and though somewhat raised under the Ptolemies, never has it regained its ancient pre-eminence. **16.** Egypt, when restored, shall be so circumscribed in power that it shall be no longer an object of confidence to Israel, as formerly; e.g., as when, relying on it, Israel broke faith with Nebuchadnezzar (ch. 17:13, 15, 16). **which bringeth their iniquity to remembrance, when they shall look after them**—rather, "while they (the Israelites) look to (or, *turn after*) them" [HENDERSON]. Israel's looking to Egypt, rather than to God, causes their iniquity (unfaithfulness to the covenant) to be remembered by God. **17.** The departure from the chronological order occurs here only, among the prophecies as to foreign nations, in order to secure greater unity of subject. **18. every head . . . bald, . . . shoulder . . . peeled**—with carrying baskets of earth and stones for the siege-works. **no wages . . . for the service**—i.e., *in proportion to* it and the time and labor which he expended on the siege of Tyre. Not that he actually failed in the siege (JEROME expressly states, from Assyrian histories, that Nebuchadnezzar succeeded); but, so much of the Tyrian resources had been exhausted, or transported to her colonies in ships, that little was left to compensate Nebuchadnezzar for his thirteen year's siege. **19. multitude**—not as FAIRBAIRN, "store"; but, he shall take away a *multitude of captives* out of Egypt. The success of Nebuchadnezzar is implied in Tyre's receiving a king from Babylon, probably one of her captives there, Merbal. **take her spoil . . . prey**—lit., "spoil her spoil, prey her prey," i.e., as she spoiled other nations, so shall she herself be a spoil to Babylon. **20. because they wrought for me**—the Chaldeans, fulfilling My will as to Tyre (cf. Jer. 25:9).

21. In the evil only, not in the good, was Egypt to be parallel to Israel. The very downfall of Egypt will be the signal for the rise of Israel, because of God's covenant with the latter. **I cause the horn of . . . Israel to bud**—(Ps. 132:17). I will cause its ancient glory to revive: an earnest of Israel's full glory under Messiah, the son of David (Luke 1:69). Even in Babylon an earnest was given of this in Daniel (Dan. 6:2) and Jeconiah (Jer. 52:31).

I will give thee . . . opening of . . . mouth—When thy predictions shall have come to pass, thy words henceforth shall be more heeded (cf. ch. 24:27).

ADAM CLARKE

12. *Shall be desolate forty years.* The country from Migdol, which was on the isthmus between the Mediterranean and the Red Sea, was so completely ruined that it might well be called desert; and it is probable that this desolation continued during the whole of the reign of Amasis, which was just forty years. See Herod., lib. iii, c. 10.

13. *Will I gather the Egyptians.* It is probable that Cyrus gave permission to the Egyptians brought to Babylon by Nebuchadnezzar to return to their own country. And if we reckon from the commencement of the war against Pharaoh-hophra by Nebuchadnezzar to the third or fourth year of Cyrus, the term will be about forty years.

14. *Into the land of Pathros.* Supposed to mean the Delta, a country included between the branches of the Nile. It may mean the *Pathrusim,* in Upper Egypt, near to the Thebaid. This is most likely.

17. *The seven and twentieth year.* That is, of the captivity of Jeconiah, fifteen years after the taking of Jerusalem. The preceding prophecy was delivered one year before the taking of Jerusalem; this, sixteen years after; and it is supposed to be the last which this prophet wrote.

18. *Caused his army to serve a great service against Tyrus.* He was thirteen years employed in the siege. See Joseph. *Antiq.,* lib. x, c. 11. In this siege his soldiers endured great hardships. Being continually on duty, their heads became bald by wearing their helmets; and their shoulders bruised and peeled by carrying baskets of earth to the fortifications, and wood, to build towers. *Yet had he no wages, nor his army.* The Tyrians, finding it at last impossible to defend their city, put all their wealth aboard their vessels, sailed out of the port, and escaped for Carthage; and thus Nebuchadnezzar lost all the spoil of one of the richest cities in the world.

20. *I have given him the land of Egypt for his labour.* Because he fulfilled the designs of God against Tyre, God promises to reward him with the spoil of Egypt.

21. *Will I cause the horn of the house of Israel to bud.* This may refer generally to the restoration; but particularly to Zerubbabel, who became one of the leaders of the people from Babylon.

MATTHEW HENRY — CHAPTER 30

Verses 1–19

The prophecy of the destruction of Egypt is here very full.

JAMIESON, FAUSSET, BROWN — CHAPTER 30

Vss. 1-26. CONTINUATION OF THE PROPHECIES AGAINST EGYPT. Two distinct messages: (1) From vs. 1 to vs. 9, a repetition of ch. 29:1-16, with fuller details of lifelike distinctness. The date is probably not long after that mentioned in ch. 29:17, on the

ADAM CLARKE — CHAPTER 30

MATTHEW HENRY

I. It shall be a lamentable destruction, and such as shall occasion great sorrow (*v.* 2, 3). You have your day now, when you carry all before you, and trample on all about you, but God will have his day shortly. It will be *a cloudy day*, that is, dark and dismal, and it shall threaten a storm. *It shall be the time of the heathen*, of reckoning with the heathen for all their heathenish practices.

II. It shall be the destruction of Egypt, and of all the countries in confederacy with her. 1. Egypt herself shall fall (*v.* 4). 2. Her neighbours shall fall with her. When the slain fall so thickly in Egypt *great pain shall be in Ethiopia*, both in Africa, and in Asia. There were those of other countries who upon some account or other resided in Egypt, as did also *the men of the land that is in league*, some of the remains of the people of Israel and Judah, the *children of the covenant*, or league, as they are called (Acts iii. 25). These sojourned in Egypt contrary to God's command, and these shall *fall with them.*

III. All that pretend to support the sinking interests of Egypt shall come down with her (*v.* 6).

Even *the multitude of Egypt shall be made to cease*, *v.* 10. That populous country shall be depopulated. Is the river Nile her support and are the several channels of it a defence to her? *I will make the rivers dry* (*v.* 12). Are her idols a support to her? They shall be destroyed.

Is her royal family her support? *There shall be no more a prince in the land of Egypt;* the royal family shall be extirpated. Is her courage her support: *I will put a fear in the land of Egypt.* Is the rising generation her support?

Alas! *the young men shall fall by the sword* (*v.* 17) and *the daughters shall go into captivity* (*v.* 18), and so she shall be robbed of all her hopes.

IV. God shall inflict these desolating judgments on Egypt (*v.* 8).

V. The king of Babylon and his army shall be employed as instruments of this destruction, *v.* 10. Those that undertook to protect Israel from the king of Babylon shall not be able to protect themselves.

VI. No place in the land of Egypt shall be exempted from the fury of the Chaldean army, not the strongest, not the remotest: *The sword shall go through the land.* Various places are here named: *Pathros, Zoan, and No* (*v.* 14), *Sin and Noph* (*v.* 15, 16), *Aven and Pi-beseth* (*v.* 17), and *Tehaphnehes*, *v.* 18. These shall be made desolate. The *pomp of their strength shall cease*, and *a cloud shall cover them.* And, *lastly*, the Ethiopians, who are at a distance from them, as well as those who are mingled with them, shall share in their pain and terror. The close of this prediction leaves, 1. The land of Egypt mortified: *Thus will I execute judgments on Egypt*, *v.* 19. 2. The God of Israel herein glorified: *They shall know that I am the Lord.*

Verses 20–26

This short prophecy of the weakening of the power of Egypt was delivered about the time that the army of the Egyptians, which attempted to raise the siege of Jerusalem, was frustrated and returned *without accomplishing their purpose.*

I. It is here foretold that the king of Egypt shall grow weaker and weaker. 1. This was in part done already (*v.* 21): *I have broken the arm of Pharaoh.* One arm of that kingdom might well be reckoned broken when the king of Babylon routed the forces of Pharaoh-Necho at Carchemish (Jer. xlvi. 2), and made himself master of *all that pertained to Egypt from the river of Egypt to Euphrates*, 2 Kings xxiv. 7. Before Egypt's heart and neck were broken its arm was.

JAMIESON, FAUSSET, BROWN

eve of Nebuchadnezzar's march against Egypt after subjugating Tyre. (2) A vision relating directly to Pharaoh and the overthrow of his kingdom; communicated at an earlier date, the seventh of the first month of the eleventh year. Not a year after the date in ch. 29:1, and three months before the taking of Jerusalem by Nebuchadnezzar. **2. Woe worth the day!**—i.e., Alas for the day! **3. the time of the heathen**—viz., for taking vengeance on them. The judgment on Egypt is the beginning of a world-wide judgment on all the heathen enemies of God (Joel 1: 15; 2:1, 2; 3; Obadiah 15). **4. pain**—lit., "pangs with trembling as of a woman in childbirth." **5. the mingled people**—the mercenary troops of Egypt from various lands, mostly from the interior of Africa (cf. ch. 27:10; Jer. 25:20, 24; 46:9, 21). **Chub**-the people named *Kufa* on the monuments [HAVERNICK], a people considerably north of Palestine [WILKINSON]; *Coba* or *Chobat*, a city of Mauritania [MAURER]. **men of the land that is in league**—too definite an expression to mean merely, "men in league" with Egypt; rather, "*sons* of the land *of the covenant,*" i.e., the *Jews* who migrated to Egypt and carried Jeremiah with them (Jer. 42-44). Even they shall not escape (Jer. 42:22; 44:14). **6. from the tower of Syene**—(see *Note*, ch. 29:10). **7. in the midst of . . . countries . . . desolate**—Egypt shall fare no better than they (ch. 29:10). **9. messengers . . . in ships to . . . Ethiopians** (Isa. 18:1, 2). The cataracts interposing between them and Egypt should not save them. Egyptians "fleeing from before Me" in My execution of judgment, as "messengers" in "skiffs" ("vessels of bulrushes," Isa. 18:2) shall go up the Nile as far as navigable, to announce the advance of the Chaldeans. **as in the day of Egypt**—The day of Ethiopia's "pain" shall come shortly, as Egypt's day came. **10. the multitude**—the large population. **12. rivers**—the artificial canals made from the Nile for irrigation. The drying up of these would cause scarcity of grain, and so prepare the way for the invaders (Isa. 19:5-10). **13. Noph**—Memphis, the capital of Middle Egypt, and the stronghold of "idols." Though no record exists of Nebuchadnezzar's "destroying" these, we know from HERODOTUS and others, that Cambyses took Pelusium, the key of Egypt, by placing before his army dogs, cats, etc., all held sacred in Egypt, so that no Egyptian would use any weapon against them. He slew Apis, the sacred ox, and burnt other idols of Egypt. **no more a prince**—referring to the anarchy that prevailed in the civil wars between Apries and Amasis at the time of Nebuchadnezzar's invasion. There shall no more be a prince of the land of Egypt, ruling the whole country; or, no *independent* prince. **14. Pathros**—Upper Egypt, with "No" or Thebes its capital (famed for its stupendous buildings, of which grand ruins remain), in antithesis to Zoan or Tanis, a chief city in Lower Egypt, within the Delta. **15. Sin**—i.e., Pelusium, the frontier fortress on the north-east, therefore called "the strength (i.e., the key) of Egypt." It stands in antithesis to No or Thebes at the opposite end of Egypt; i.e., I will afflict Egypt from one end to the other. **16. distresses daily**—MAURER translates, "enemies during the day," i.e., open enemies who do not wait for the covert of night to make their attacks (cf. Jer. 6:4; 15:8). However, the *Hebrew*, though rarely, is sometimes rendered (see Ps. 13:2) as in *English Version.* **17. Aven**—meaning "vanity" or "iniquity": applied by a slight change of the *Hebrew* name, to On or Heliopolis, in allusion to its idolatry. Here stood the temple of the sun, whence it was called in *Hebrew, Beth-shemesh* (Jer. 43:13). The Egyptian hieroglyphics call it, *Re Athom*, the sun, the father of the gods, being impersonate in *Athom* or *Adam*, the father of mankind. **Pi-beseth**—i.e., Bubastis, in Lower Egypt, near the Pelusiac branch of the Nile: notorious for the worship of the goddess of the same name (*Coptic, Pasht*), the granite stones of whose temple still attest its former magnificence. **these** ***cities***—rather, as LXX, "the women," viz., of Aven and Pi-beseth, in antithesis to "the young men." So in vs. 18, "*daughters* shall go into captivity" [MAURER]. **18. Tehaphnehes**—called from the queen of Egypt mentioned in I Kings 11:19. The same as Daphne, near Pelusium, a royal residence of the Pharaohs (Jer. 43:7, 9). Called Hanes (Isa. 30:4). **break . . . the yokes of Egypt**—**i.e., the tyrannical supremacy which she exercised over other nations. Cf. "bands of their yoke" (ch. 34:7). a cloud**—**viz., of calamity. 20. Here begins the earlier vision, not long after that in ch. 29, about three months before the taking of Jerusalem, as to Pharaoh and his kingdom. 21. broken . . . arm of Pharaoh**—**(Ps. 37:17; Jer. 48:25). Referring to the defeat which Pharaoh-hophra sustained from the Chaldeans, when trying to raise the siege of Je-**

ADAM CLARKE

2. *Howl ye, Woe worth the day! Heylilu, hah laiyom!* "Howl ye, Alas for the day!" The expressions signify that a most dreadful calamity was about to fall on Egypt and the neighboring countries, called here the "time of the heathen," or of the "nations," the day of calamity to them. They are afterwards specified: Ethiopia, Libya, Lydia, and Chub, and the "mingled people," probably persons from different nations, who had followed the ill fortune of Pharaoh-hophra or Pharaoh-apries, when he fled from Amasis, and settled in Upper Egypt.

5. *Lydia.* This place is not well-known. The Ludim were contiguous to Egypt, Gen. xi. 13. *Chub.* Probably instead of *vechub*, "and Chub," we should read *vechol*, "and all the men of the land," etc.

7. *Shall be desolate.* All these countries shall be desolated, and the places named shall be chief in these desolations.

9. *Messengers go forth from me in ships.* Ships can ascend the Nile up to Syene or Essuan, by the cataracts; and when Nebuchadnezzar's vessel went up, they struck terror into the Ethiopians. They are represented here as the "messengers of God."

12. *I will make the rivers dry.* As the overflowing of the Nile was the grand cause of fertility to Egypt, the drying it up, or preventing that annual inundation, must be the cause of dearth, famine, etc. By *rivers* we may understand the various canals cut from the Nile to carry water into the different parts of the land. When the Nile did not rise to its usual height; these canals were quite dry.

13. *Their images to cease out of Noph.* Afterwards Memphis, and now Cairo. This was the seat of Egyptian idolatry, the place where Apis was particularly worshipped.

14. *I will make Pathros desolate.* See the preceding chapter, v. 14. *Zoan.* Tanis, the ancient capital of Egypt. *No.* Thebes, the city of Jupiter.

15. *My fury upon Sin.* Pelusium, a strong city of Egypt, on the coast of the Mediterranean Sea.

16. *Noph.* Cairo; see v. 13.

17. *Aven.* Or On, the famous Heliopolis, or city of the sun.

18. *Tehaphnehes.* Called also Tahapanes, Jer. ii. 16. *Break there the yokes.* The sceptres. Nebuchadnezzar broke the sceptre of Egypt when he confirmed the kingdom to Amasis, who had rebelled against Apries.

20. *In the eleventh year, in the first month, in the seventh day.* This was the eleventh year of the captivity of Jeconiah; a prophecy anterior by several years to that already delivered. In collecting the writings of Ezekiel, more care was taken to put all that related to one subject together than to attend to chronological arrangement.

21. *I have broken the arm of Pharaoh.* Perhaps this may refer to his defeat by Nebuchadnezzar when he was coming with the Egyptian army to succor Jerusalem.

MATTHEW HENRY

2. This was to be done again. Now (*v.* 22), *I am against Pharaoh, and will break both his arms.* The king of Egypt shall be dispirited when he finds himself in danger of the king of Babylon's forces: he *shall groan before him with the groaning of a deadly wounded man.* The people of Egypt shall be dispersed (*v.* 23 and again *v.* 26): *I will scatter them among the nations.*

II. It is here foretold that the king of Babylon shall grow stronger and stronger, *v.* 24, 25.

CHAPTER 31

Verses 1–9

This prophecy bears date the month before Jerusalem was taken, as that in the close of the foregoing chapter about four months before. When God's people were in the depth of their distress, it would be some comfort to them to be told from heaven that the cup was going round, even the cup of trembling, that it would shortly be taken out of the hands of God's people and put into the hands of those that hated them, Isa. li. 22, 23.

I. The prophet is directed to put Pharaoh searching for a case parallel to his own (*v.* 2). The falls of others, both into sin and ruin, are intended as admonitions to us not to be secure or *high-minded*, nor to think we stand out of danger.

II. He is directed to show him an instance of one whom he resembled in greatness (*v.* 3). Sennacherib was one of the mighty princes of that monarchy; but it sunk down soon after him, and the monarchy of Nebuchadnezzar was built upon its ruins. The king of Assyria is here compared to a stately cedar, *v.* 3. 1. The Assyrian monarch was a tall cedar, of a *high stature*, and *his top among the thick boughs.* He surpassed all the princes in his neighbourhood; they were all shrubs to him (*v.* 5): *His height was exalted above all the trees of the field;* he overtopped them all, *v.* 8. 2. He was a spreading cedar, denoting that his territories were large, and he extended his conquests far and his influences much further. His large dominions were well managed. His government was admirable in the eyes of all men. In all the surrounding nations there was no prince so much admired, so much courted, as the king of Assyria. 3. He was serviceable by his shadow (*v.* 6). The meaning is, *Under his shadow dwelt all great nations;* they all fled to him for safety, and were willing to swear allegiance to him if he would undertake to protect them. But the utmost security that any creature, even the king of Assyria himself, can give, is but like the shadow of a tree, which is but a scanty protection. God will take us *under the shadow of his wings*, where we shall be warmer and safer than under the shadow of the strongest and stateliest cedar, Ps. xvii. 8; xci. 4. 4. He seemed to be settled and established in his greatness and power. This cedar was not like the *heath in the desert, made to inhabit the parched places* (Jer. xvii. 6); it was not a *root in a dry ground*, Isa. liii. 2. He had abundance of wealth to support his power and grandeur (*v.* 4): *The waters made him great;* he had vast treasures, which were as *the deep that set him up on high, as rivers running round about his plants;* these enabled him to strengthen and secure his interests everywhere, for he *sent out his little rivers to all the trees of the field*, to water them; *their country was nourished by the king's country* (Acts xii. 20), and they would be serviceable and faithful to him.

Verses 10–18

The king of Egypt resembled the king of Assyria in pomp, and power, and prosperity.

I. He does likewise resemble him in his pride, *v.* 10. For the same temptation of a prosperous state by which some are overcome are fatal to many others too. "*Thou*, O king of Egypt! *hast lifted up thyself in height*, has been proud of thy wealth and power, *ch.* xxix. 3. And the king of Assyria *shot up his top among the thick boughs*, and grew insolent and imperious, set God himself at defiance, and trampled upon his people"; Isa. xxxvi. 4. How haughtily does he speak of his achievements!

II. How he shall therefore resemble him in his fall. 1. The fall of the king of Assyria. Cyaxares, king of the Medes, in conjunction with Nebuchadnezzar king of Babylon, destroyed Nineveh, and with it the Assyrian empire. Respecting the Assyrian three things are affirmed: (1) It is God himself that orders his ruin: *I have delivered him into the hand* of the executioner; *I have driven him out.* (2) It is his own sin that procures his ruin: *I have driven him out for his wickedness.* (3) It is a *mighty one of the heathen* that

JAMIESON, FAUSSET, BROWN

rusalem (Jer. 37:5, 7); and previous to the deprivation of Pharaoh-necho of all his conquests from the river of Egypt to the Euphrates (II Kings 24:7; Jer. 46:2); also to the Egyptian disaster in Cyrene. **22. arms**—Not only the "one arm" broken already (vs. 21) was not to be healed, but the other two should be broken. Not a corporal wound, but a *breaking of the power* of Pharaoh is intended. **cause . . . sword to fall out of . . . hand**—deprive him of the resources of making war.

CHAPTER 31

Vss. 1-18. The Overthrow of Egypt Illustrated by That of Assyria. Not that Egypt was, like Assyria, utterly to cease to be, but it was, like Assyria, to lose its prominence in the empire of the world. **1. third month**—two months later than the prophecy delivered in ch. 30:20. **2. Whom art thou like**—The answer is, Thou art like the haughty king of Assyria; as he was overthrown by the Chaldeans, so shalt thou be by the same. **3.** He illustrates the pride and the consequent overthrow of the Assyrian, that Egypt may the better know what she must expect. **cedar in Lebanon**—often eighty feet high, and the diameter of the space covered by its boughs still greater: the symmetry perfect. Cf. the similar image (ch. 17:3; Dan. 4:20-22). **with a shadowing shroud**—with an overshadowing thicket. **top . . . among . . . thick boughs**—rather [Hengstenberg], "among the clouds." But *English Version* agrees better with the *Hebrew*. The *top*, or *topmost shoot*, represents the king; the *thick boughs*, the large resources of the empire. **4. waters . . . little rivers**—the Tigris with its branches and "rivulets," or "conduits" for irrigation, the source of Assyria's fertility. "The deep" is the ever flowing water, never dry. Metaphorically, for Assyria's resources, as the "conduits" are her colonies. **5. when he shot forth**—because of the abundant moisture which nourished him in shooting forth. But see *Margin*. **6. fowls . . . made . . . nests in . . . boughs**—so ch. 17:23; Daniel 4:12. The gospel kingdom shall gather all under its covert, for their good and for the glory of God, which the world kingdoms did for evil and for self-aggrandizement (Matt. 13:32). **8. cedars . . . could not hide him**—could not outtop him. No other king eclipsed him. **were not like**—were not comparable to. **garden of God**—As in the case of Tyre (ch. 28:13), the imagery, that is applied to the Assyrian king, is taken from Eden; peculiarly appropriate, as Eden was watered by rivers that afterwards watered Assyria (Gen. 2:10-14). This cedar seemed to revive in itself all the glories of paradise, so that no tree there outtopped it. **9. I . . . made him**—It was all due to *My* free grace. **10. thou . . . he**—The change of persons is because the language refers partly to the cedar, partly to the person signified by the cedar. **11.** Here the literal supersedes the figurative. **shall surely deal with him**—according to his own pleasure, and according to the Assyrian's (Sardanapalus) desert. Nebuchadnezzar is called "the mighty one" (*El*, a name of God), because he was God's representative and instrument of judgment (Dan. 2:37, 38). **12. from his shadow**—*under* which they had formerly *dwelt* as their covert (vs. 6). **13.** Birds and beasts shall insult over his fallen trunk. **14. trees by the waters**—i.e., that are plentifully supplied by the waters: nations abounding in resources. **stand up in their height**—i.e., trust in their height: *stand upon* it as their ground of confidence. Fairbairn points the *Hebrew* differently, so as for "their trees," to translate, "(And that none that drink water may stand) *on themselves*, (because of their greatness)." But the usual reading is better, as Assyria and the confederate states throughout are compared to strong trees. The clause, "All that drink water," marks the ground of the trees' confidence "in their height," viz., that they have ample sources of supply. Maurer, retaining the same *Hebrew*, translates, "that neither their *terebinth trees* may stand up in their height, nor all (the other trees) that drink water." **to . . . nether . . . earth . . . pit**—(ch. 32:18; Ps. 82:7). **15. covered the deep**—as mourners cover their heads in token of mourning, "I made the deep that watered the cedar" to wrap itself in mourning for him. The waters of the deep are the tributary peoples of Assyria (Rev. 17:15). **fainted**—lit., were "faintness" (itself); more forcible than the verb. **16. hell**—Sheol or Hades, the unseen world: equivalent to, "I cast him into oblivion" (cf. Isa. 14:9-11). **shall be**

ADAM CLARKE

22. *I will cause the sword to fall out of his hand.* When the arm is broken, the sword will naturally fall. But these expressions show that the Egyptians would be rendered wholly useless to Zedekiah, and should never more recover their political strength. This was the case from the time of the rebellion of Amasis.

26. *I will scatter the Egyptians.* Several fled with Apries to Upper Egypt; and when Nebuchadnezzar wasted the country, he carried many of them to Babylon. See chap. xxix. 12.

CHAPTER 31

1. *In the eleventh year.* A month before Jerusalem was taken by the Chaldeans.

3. *Behold, the Assyrian was a cedar.* Why is the *Assyrian* introduced here, when the whole chapter concerns Egypt? Bishop Lowth has shown that *ashshur erez* should be translated "the tall cedar," "the very stately cedar." Hence there is reference to his lofty top; and all the following description belongs to Egypt, not to Assyria. But see on v. 11.

4. *The waters made him great.* Alluding to the fertility of Egypt by the overflowing of the Nile. But *waters* often mean peoples. By means of the different nations under the Egyptians, that government became very opulent. These nations are represented as fowls and beasts, taking shelter under the protection of this great, political Egyptian tree, v. 6.

8. *The cedars in the garden of God.* Egypt was one of the most eminent and affluent of all the neighboring nations.

11. *The mighty one of the heathen.* Nebuchadnezzar. It is worthy of notice that Nebuchadnezzar, in the first year of his reign, rendered himself master of Nineveh, the capital of the Assyrian empire. This happened about twenty years before Ezekiel delivered this prophecy; on this account, *Ashshur*, v. 3, may relate to the Assyrians, to whom it is possible the prophet here compares the Egyptians. But see on v. 3.

13. *Upon his ruin shall all the fowls.* The fall of Egypt is likened to the fall of a great tree; and as the fowls and beasts sheltered under its branches before, v. 6, so they now feed upon its ruins.

14. *To the end that none of all the trees.* Let this ruin, fallen upon Egypt, teach all the nations that shall hear of it to be humble, because, however elevated, God can soon bring them down; and pride and arrogance, in either states or individuals, have the peculiar abhorrence of God.

15. *I caused Lebanon to mourn for him.* All the confederates of Pharaoh are represented as deploring his fall, vv. 16-17.

MATTHEW HENRY

shall be the instrument of his ruin. In this history of the fall of the Assyrian there is still the similitude of the cedar. He grew very high, and extended his boughs very far; but his day comes to fall. This stately cedar was dropped: *The terrible of the nations cut him off.* They have lopped off his branches first, cities or countries broken off from the Assyrian monarchy. It was deserted: *All the people of the earth,* that had fled to him for shelter, have *gone down from his shadow and have left him. Upon his ruin shall all the fowls of the heaven remain,* to tread upon the broken branches of this cedar. *All the trees of Eden,* that had fallen before him, *all that drank water* of the rain of heaven, as the stump of the tree that is left in the *south* (Dan. iv. 23), *shall be comforted in the nether parts of the earth* when they see this proud cedar brought as low as themselves. But the trees of Lebanon, that are yet standing, *mourned for him,* because they could read their own destiny in his fall. By the cutting down of this cedar is signified the slaughter of this mighty monarch and all his supporters. God designed thereby, *First,* To give an alarm to the nations about (*v.* 16): *I made the nations to shake at the sound of his fall. Secondly,* To give an admonition to their kings (*v.* 14). It would have been well for Nebuchadnezzar, who was himself active in bringing down the Assyrian, if he had taken the admonition.

2. A prophecy of the fall of the king of Egypt in like manner, *v.* 18.

JAMIESON, FAUSSET, BROWN

comforted—because so great a king as the Assyrian is brought down to a level with them. It is a kind of consolation to the wretched to have companions in misery. **17. his arm, that dwelt under his shadow**—those who were the helpers or tool of his tyranny, and therefore enjoyed his protection (e.g., Syria and her neighbors). These were sure to share her fate. Cf. the same phrase as to the Jews living under the protection of their king (Lam. 4:20); both alike "making flesh their arm, and in heart departing from the Lord" (Jer. 17:5). **18.** Application of the parabolic description of Assyria to the parallel case of Egypt. "All that has been said of the Assyrian consider as said to thyself. To whom art thou so like, as thou art to the Assyrian? To none." The lesson on a gigantic scale of Eden-like privileges abused to pride and sin by the Assyrian, as in the case of the first man in Eden, ending in ruin, was to be repeated in Egypt's case. For the unchangeable God governs the world on the same unchangeable principles. **thou shalt lie in . . . uncircumcised**—As circumcision was an object of mocking to thee, thou shalt lie in the midst of the uncircumcised, slain by their sword [GROTIUS]. Retribution in kind (ch. 28: 10). **This is Pharaoh**—Pharaoh's end shall be the same humiliating one as I have depicted the Assyrian's to have been. "This" is demonstrative, as if he were pointing with the finger to Pharaoh lying prostrate, a spectacle to all, as on the shore of the Red Sea (Exod. 14:30, 31).

ADAM CLARKE

17. *They also went down into hell with him.* Into remediless destruction.

18. *This is Pharaoh.* All that I have spoken in this allegory of the lofty cedar refers to Pharaoh, king of Egypt, his princes, confederates, and people.

MATTHEW HENRY — CHAPTER 32

Verses 1–16

I. The prophet is ordered to *take up a lamentation for Pharaoh king of Egypt, v.* 2.

II. He is ordered to show cause for that lamentation.

1. Pharaoh has been a troubler of the nations, even of his own nation. He is *like a young lion of the nations* (*v.* 2), threatening as a lion when he roars. He is like *a whale,* like a crocodile (so some) *in the seas,* vexatious, as the *leviathan* that *makes the deep to boil like a pot,* Job. xli. 31. When Pharaoh engaged in an unnecessary war with the Cyrenians he *came forth with his rivers,* with his armies, *troubled the waters,* disturbed his own kingdom and the neighbouring nations.

2. He that has troubled others must expect to be himself troubled; for the Lord is righteous, Joshua vii. 25. This is set forth by a comparison. Is Pharaoh like a *great whale?* God has a net strong enough to secure him (*v.* 3): *I will spread my net over thee,* even the army of the Chaldeans, a *company of many people. The flesh* of this great whale shall be *laid upon the mountains* (*v.* 5) and the *valleys* shall be *filled with his height.*

Such members of Pharaoh's soldiers shall be slain that the dead bodies shall be scattered upon the hills and piled up in the valleys. It is set forth by a prophecy of the deep impression which the destruction of Egypt should make upon the neighbouring nations. When Pharaoh, who had been like a blazing burning torch, is *put out* and *extinguished* it shall make all about him look black, *v.* 7. The *hearts of many people* will be *vexed* to see the word of the God of Israel fulfilled in the destruction of Egypt, and that all the *gods of Egypt* were not able to relieve it. It shall fill them with admiration (*v.* 10): They shall be *amazed at thee,* shall wonder to see such *great riches* and power *come to nothing,* Rev. xviii. 17. It shall fill them with fear. When others are ruined by sin we have reason to quake for fear, as knowing ourselves guilty and obnoxious. It is the *sword of the king of Babylon* that shall *come upon thee* (*v.* 11), the *swords of the mighty,* even the *terrible of the nations, all of them* (*v.* 12). The multitude of Egypt shall be destroyed. The pomp of Egypt shall be spoiled. The cattle of Egypt, that used to feed by the rivers, shall be destroyed (*v.* 13), either by the sword or carried off for a prey.

JAMIESON, FAUSSET, BROWN — CHAPTER 32

VSS. 1-32. TWO ELEGIES OVER PHARAOH, ONE DELIVERED ON THE FIRST DAY (VS. 1), THE OTHER ON THE FIFTEENTH DAY OF THE SAME MONTH, THE TWELFTH OF THE TWELFTH YEAR. **1.** The twelfth year from the carrying away of Jehoiachin; Jerusalem was by this time overthrown, and Amasis was beginning his revolt against Pharaoh-hophra. **2. Pharaoh**—"Phra" in Burmah, signifies the king, high priest, and idol. **whale**—rather, any monster of the waters; here, the crocodile of the Nile. Pharaoh is as a lion on dry land, a crocodile in the waters; i.e., an object of terror everywhere. **camest forth with thy rivers** "breakest forth" [FAIRBAIRN]. The antithesis of "seas" and "rivers" favors GROTIUS' rendering, "Thou camest forth from the sea *into* the rivers"; i.e., from thy own empire into other states. However, *English Version* is favored by the "thy": thou camest forth with *thy* rivers (i.e., with thy forces) and with thy feet didst fall irrecoverably; so Israel, once desolate, troubles the waters (i.e., neighboring states). **3. with a company of many people**—viz., the Chaldeans (ch. 29:3, 4; Hos. 7:12). **my net**—for they are My instrument. **4. leave thee upon the land**—as a fish drawn out of the water loses all its strength, so Pharaoh (in vs. 3, compared to a water monster) shall be (ch. 29:5). **5. thy height**—thy hugeness [FAIRBAIRN]. The great heap of corpses of thy forces, on which thou pridest thyself. "Height" may refer to *mental elevation,* as well as bodily [VATABLUS]. **6. land wherein thou swimmest**—Egypt: the land watered by the Nile, the the source of its fertility, wherein thou swimmest (carrying on the image of the crocodile, i.e., wherein thou dost exercise thy wanton power at will). Irony. The land shall still afford seas to swim in, but they shall be seas of blood. Alluding to the plague (Exod. 7:19; Rev. 8:8). HAVERNICK translates, "I will water the land with *what flows from thee,* even thy blood, reaching to the mountains": "with thy blood *overflowing* even to the mountains." Perhaps this is better. **7. put thee out**—extinguish thy light (Job 18:5). Pharaoh is represented as a bright star, at the extinguishing of whose light in the political sky the whole heavenly host is shrouded in sympathetic darkness. Here, too, as in vs. 6, there is an allusion to the supernatural darkness sent formerly (Exod. 10:21-23). The heavenly bodies are often made images of earthly dynasties (Isa. 13:10; Matt. 24:29). **9. thy destruction**—i.e., tidings of thy destruction (lit., "thy breakage") carried by captive and dispersed Egyptians "among the nations" [GROTIUS]; or, *thy broken people,* resembling one great *fracture,* the ruins of what they had been [FAIRBAIRN]. **10. brandish my sword before them**—lit., "in their faces," or sight. **13.** (See *Note* on ch. 29:11.) The picture is ideally true, not to be interpreted by the letter. The political ascendency of Egypt was to cease with the Chaldean conquest [FAIRBAIRN]. Henceforth Pharaoh must figuratively no longer *trouble the waters by man or beast,* i.e., no longer was he to flood other peoples with his overwhelming forces. **14. make their waters deep**—rather, "make . . . *to subside*";

ADAM CLARKE — CHAPTER 32

1. *In the twelfth year, in the twelfth month, in the first day of the month.* The *twelfth year* of the captivity of Jeconiah.

2. *Thou art like a young lion . . . and thou art as a whale in the seas.* You may be likened to two of the fiercest animals in the creation: to a lion, the fiercest on the land; to a "crocodile," *tannim,* the fiercest in the waters. It may, however, point out the hippopotamus, as there seems to be a reference to his mode of feeding. He walks deliberately into the water over head, and pursues his way in the same manner; still keeping on his feet, and feeding on the plants, etc., that grow at the bottom. Thus he fouls the water with his feet.

6. *The land wherein thou swimmest.* Egypt; so called because intersected with canals, and overflowed annually by the Nile.

7. *I will cover the heaven.* Destroy the empire. *Make the stars thereof dark.* Overwhelm all the dependent states. *I will cover the sun.* The king himself. *And the moon shall not give her light.* The queen may be meant, or some state less than the kingdom.

8. *And set darkness upon thy land.* As I did when a former king refused to let My people go to the wilderness to worship Me. I will involve you, and your house, and your people, and the whole land, in desolation and woe.

9. *I will also vex the hearts.* Even the remote nations, who had no connection with you, shall be amazed at the judgments which have fallen upon you.

MATTHEW HENRY

The *waters of Egypt*, that used to flow briskly, shall now grow slow, and heavy, and shall *run like oil* (*v.* 14), a figurative expression signifying that there should be such universal sadness and heaviness upon the whole nation that even the rivers should go softly and silently like mourners. The whole country of Egypt shall be stripped of its wealth (*v.* 15). *Then shall they know that I am the Lord.*

Verses 17–32

This prophecy completes the burden of Egypt.

I. The funeral of that once flourishing kingdom.

1. This dead kingdom is here brought to the grave. The prophet is ordered (*v.* 18), to foretell their destruction. Yet he must foretell it as one that had an affectionate concern for them; he must *wail for the multitude of Egypt*, even when he *casts them down.* When Egypt is slain, let her have an honourable funeral; let her be buried *with the daughters of the famous nations.*

2. This corpse of a kingdom is bid welcome to the grave, and Pharaoh is made free of the congregation of the dead, not without some pomp and ceremony. There lie the Assyrian empire, and all the princes and mighty men of that monarchy (*v.* 22).

There lies the kingdom of Persia, which perhaps within the memory of man at that time had been wasted and brought down: *There is Elam and all her multitude*, the king of Elam and his numerous armies, *v.* 24, 25.

There lies the Scythian power. *Meshech* and *Tubal*, those barbarous northern nations, had lately made a descent upon the Medes, and lived among them upon free quarter for some years, but at length Cyaxares, king of the Medes, obliged them to quit his country, *v.* 26. These Scythians are not buried with marks of honour.

There lies the kingdom of Edom, which had flourished long, but before the destruction of Egypt, was made desolate, as was foretold, *ch.* xxv. 13. Among the sepulchres of the nations *there is Edom*, *v.* 29. There lie the *princes of the north*, *and all the Zidonians.* These were as well acquainted with maritime affairs as the Egyptians were, who relied much upon that part of their strength, but they have *gone down with the slain* (*v.* 30). All this is applied to Pharaoh and the Egyptians, who have no reason to flatter themselves with hopes of tranquillity when they see how the wisest, and wealthiest, and strongest of their neighbours have been laid waste (*v.* 28).

II. The view which this prophecy gives us of ruined states may show us something of this present world, and the empire of death in it. Men are ingenious at finding out ways to destroy one another. It is not only a great pit, but a great cockpit.

JAMIESON, FAUSSET, BROWN

lit., "sink" [FAIRBAIRN]. **like oil**—emblem of *quietness.* No longer shall they descend violently on other countries as the overflowing Nile, but shall be still and sluggish in political action. **16.** As in ch. 19:14. This is a prophetical lamentation; yet so it shall come to pass [GROTIUS]. **17.** The second lamentation for Pharaoh. This funeral dirge in imagination accompanies him to the unseen world. Egypt personified in its political head is ideally represented as undergoing the change by death to which man is liable. Expressing that Egypt's supremacy is no more, a thing of the past, never to be again. **the month**—the twelfth month (vs. 1); fourteen days after the former vision. **18. cast them down**—i.e., predict that they shall be *cast down* (so Jer. 1:10). The prophet's word was God's, and carried with it its own fulfilment. **daughters of . . . nations**—i.e., the nations with their peoples. Egypt is to share the fate of other ancient nations once famous, now consigned to oblivion: Elam (vs. 24), Meshech, etc. (vs. 26), Edom (vs. 29), Zidon (vs. 30). **19. Whom dost thou pass in beauty?**—Beautiful as thou art, thou art not more so than other nations, which nevertheless have perished. **go down . . .**—to the nether world, where all "beauty" is speedily marred. **20. she is delivered to the sword**—viz., by God. **draw her**—as if addressing her executioners: drag her forth to death. **21.** (Ch. 31:16.) Ezekiel has before his eyes Isaiah 14:9, etc. **shall speak to him**—with "him" join "with them that help him"; *shall speak to him and his helpers* with a taunting welcome, as now one of themselves. **22. her . . . his**—The abrupt change of gender is, because Ezekiel has in view at one time the *kingdom* (feminine), at another the *monarch.* "Asshur," or Assyria, is placed first in punishment, as being first in guilt. **23. in the sides of the pit**—Sepulchers in the East were caves hollowed out of the rock, and the bodies were laid in niches formed at the sides. MAURER needlessly departs from the ordinary meaning, and translates, "extremities" (cf. Isa. 14:13, 15). **which caused terror**—They, who alive were a terror to others, are now, in the nether world, themselves a terrible object to behold. **24. Elam**—placed next, as having been an auxiliary to Assyria. Its territory lay in Persia. In Abraham's time an independent kingdom (Gen. 14:1). Famous for its bowmen (Isa. 22:6). **borne their shame**—the just retribution of their lawless *pride.* Destroyed by Nebuchadnezzar (Jer. 49:34-38). **25. a bed**—a sepulchral niche. **all . . . slain by . . . sword, . . .**—(vss. 21, 23, 24). The very monotony of the phraseology gives to the dirge an awe-inspiring effect. **26. Meshech, Tubal**—northern nations: the Moschi and Tibareni, between the Black and Caspian Seas. HERODOTUS, 3. 94, mentions them as a subjugated people, tributaries to Darius Hystaspes (see ch. 27:13). **27. they shall not lie with the mighty**—i.e., they shall not have separate tombs such as mighty conquerors have: but shall all be heaped together in one pit, as is the case with the vanquished [GROTIUS]. HAVERNICK reads it interrogatively, "Shall they not lie with the mighty that are fallen?" But *English Version* is supported by the parallel (Isa. 14:18, 19), to which Ezekiel refers, and which represents them as *not* lying as mighty kings lie in a grave, but cast out of one, as a carcass trodden under foot. **with . . . weapons of war**—alluding to the custom of burying warriors with their arms (I Maccabees 13:29). Though honored by the laying of "their swords under their heads," yet the punishment of "their iniquities shall be upon their bones." Their swords shall thus attest their shame, not their glory (Matt. 26:52), being the instruments of their violence, the penalty of which they are paying. **28. Yea, thou**—Thou, too, Egypt, like them, shalt lie as one vanquished. **29. princes**—Edom was not only governed by kings, but by subordinate "princes" or "dukes" (Gen. 36:40). **with their might**—notwithstanding their might, they shall be brought down (Isa. 34:5, 10-17; Jer. 49:7, 13-18). **lie with the uncircumcised**—Though Edom was circumcised, being descended from Isaac, he shall lie with the uncircumcised; much more shall Egypt, who had no hereditary right to circumcision. **30. princes of the north**—Syria, which is still called by the Arabs the north; or the Tyrians, north of Palestine, conquered by Nebuchadnezzar (chs. 26, 27, 28), [GROTIUS]. **Zidonians**—who shared the fate of Tyre (ch. 28:21). **with their terror they are ashamed of their might**—i.e., notwithstanding the terror which they inspired in their contemporaries. "Might" is connected by MAURER thus, "Notwithstanding the terror *which resulted from* their might." **31. comforted**—with the melancholy satisfaction of not being alone, but of having other kingdoms companions in his downfall. This shall be his only comfort—a very poor

ADAM CLARKE

14. *Cause their rivers to run like oil.* Bring the whole state into quietness, there being no longer a political hippopotamus to foul the waters—to disturb the peace of the country.

17. *In the twelfth year.* This prophecy concerns the people of Egypt.

18. *Cast them down.* Show them that they shall be cast down.

21. *Out of the midst of hell. Sheol*, the place of burial. There is something here similar to Isa. xiv. 9, where the descent of the king of Babylon to the state of the dead is described.

22. *Asshur is there.* The mightiest conquerors of the earth have gone down to the grave before you; there they and their soldiers lie together, all slain by the sword.

23. *Whose graves are set in the sides of the pit.* Alluding to the niches in the sides of the subterranean caves or burying places, where the bodies are laid. These are numerous in Egypt.

24. *There is Elam.* The Elamites, not far from the Assyrians; others think that Persia is meant. It was invaded by the joint forces of Cyaxares and Nebuchadnezzar.

26. *There is Meshech, Tubal.* See chap. xxvii. 13.

27. *Gone down to hell with their weapons of war.* Are buried in their armor, and with their weapons lying by their sides. It was a very ancient practice, in different nations, to bury a warrior's weapons in the same grave with himself.

29. *There is Edom.* All the glory and pomp of the Idumean kings, who also helped to oppress the Israelites, are gone down into the grave. Their kings, princes, and all their mighty men lie mingled with the *uncircumcised*, not distinguished from the common dead.

30. *There be the princes of the north.* The kings of Media and Assyria, *and all the Zidonians*—the kings of Tyre, Sidon, and Damascus.

31. *Pharaoh shall see them.* Pharaoh also, who said he was a god, shall be found among the vulgar dead. *And shall be comforted.* Shall console himself, on finding that all other proud boasters are in the same circumstances with himself. Here is a reference to a consciousness after death.

MATTHEW HENRY | JAMIESON, FAUSSET, BROWN | ADAM CLARKE

one! **32. my terror**—the reading of the *Margin* or *Keri*. The *Hebrew* text or *Chetib* is "*his* terror," which gives good sense (vss. 25, 30). "*My* terror" implies that God puts *His* terror on Pharaoh's multitude, as they put "their terror" on others, e.g., under Pharaoh-necho on Judea. As "the land of the living" was the scene of "their terror," so it shall be God's; especially in Judea, He will display His glory to the terror of Israel's foes (ch. 26:20). In Israel's case the judgment is temporary, ending in their future restoration under Messiah. In the case of the world kingdoms which flourished for a time, they fall to rise no more.

CHAPTER 33

Verses 1–9

The prophet, now that Jerusalem is taken, is appointed again to direct his speech to them; and here his commission is renewed.

I. The office of a watchman laid down, the trust reposed in him, the charge given him, *v.* 2, 6. 1. It is supposed to be a public danger that gives occasion for the appointing of a watchman, *v.* 2. When a country is in fear of a foreign invasion, that they may not be surprised, but may have early notice of it, in order to give the invader a warm reception, they *set a man of their coast*, some likely person, that lives upon the borders of their country, and make him *their watchman.* One man may be of public service to a whole country. 2. It is supposed to be a public trust that is lodged in the watchman and that he is accountable to the public for the discharge of it. If he do his part, if he betimes give warning, he has discharged his trust, and not only *delivered his soul*, but earned his wages. If the people do not take warning it is their own fault; the blame is not to be laid upon the watchman. If the watchman did not do his duty, and *blew not the trumpet* to *warn the people*, so that some are surprised and cut off *in their iniquity* (*v.* 6), he shall be found guilty because he did not *give warning*. But if the watchman do his part, and the people do theirs, all is well.

II. The application of this to the prophet, *v.* 7, 9.

1. He is a *watchman to the house of Israel.* He had occasionally given warning to the nations about, but to the house of Israel he was a watchman by office. They did not *set him for a watchman*, but God did it for them; he appointed them a watchman.

2. His business as a watchman is to give warning to sinners of their danger by reason of sin. This is the word he must *hear from God's mouth* and *speak to them.* God has said, *The wicked man shall surely die.* Unless he repent, he shall be cut off from God. The wrath of God is revealed from heaven, not only against wicked nations, but against wicked persons. It is the will of God that the wicked man should be warned of this: *Warn them from me.* This intimates that there is a possibility of preventing it, else it were a jest to give warning of it; and that God is desirous it should be prevented. It is the work of ministers to say to the wicked, *It shall be ill with thee*, Isa. iii. 11. And he must say this, not in passion, to provoke the sinner, but in compassion, to *warn the wicked from his way*, warn him to *turn from it*, that he may live.

3. If souls perish through his neglect of his duty, he brings guilt upon himself.

4. If he do his duty, he may take the comfort of it, though he do not see the success of it (*v.* 9).

Verses 10–20

I. The cavils of the people against God's proceedings with them. God had *set life before them*, but they plead that he had set it out of their reach. The prophet had said (*ch.* xxiv. 23), *You shall pine away for your iniquities;* and this they now upbraided him with, as if it had been spoken to drive them to despair; whereas it was spoken conditionally, to bring them to repentance. They said, *The way of the Lord is not equal* (*ch.* xviii. 25), suggesting that God was partial in his proceedings, and that he was more severe against sin and sinners than there was cause.

II. A satisfactory answer given to both these cavils.

1. When they spoke of *pining away in their iniquity* God sent the prophet to them, with all speed, to tell them that there was yet *hope in Israel* (*v.* 11). God has no delight in the ruin of sinners, nor does he desire it. They questioned whether they should *live*, though they did repent and reform; yea, says God, as sure *as I live*, true penitents shall live also; for *their life is hid with Christ in God.* It is certain that, if sinners perish in their impenitency, it is owing to themselves; they die because they will die.

2. The most plausible professors, if they apostatize, shall certainly perish for ever in their apostasy from

CHAPTER 33

VSS. 1-33. RENEWAL OF EZEKIEL'S COMMISSION, NOW THAT HE IS AGAIN TO ADDRESS HIS COUNTRYMEN, AND IN A NEW TONE. Heretofore his functions had been chiefly threatening; from this point, after the evil had got to its worst in the overthrow of Jerusalem, the consolatory element preponderates. **2. to the children of thy people**—whom he had been forbidden to address from ch. 24:26, 27, till Jerusalem was overthrown, and the "escaped" came with tidings of the judgment being completed. So now, in vs. 21, the tidings of the fact having arrived, he opens his heretofore closed lips to the Jews. In the interval he had prophesied as to foreign nations. The former part of the chapter, from vs. 2 to vs. 20, seems to have been imparted to Ezekiel on the evening previous (vs. 22), being a preparation for the latter part (vss. 23-33) imparted after the tidings had come. This accounts for the first part standing without intimation of the date, which was properly reserved for the latter part, to which the former was the anticipatory introduction [FAIRBAIRN]. **watchman**—The first nine verses exhibit Ezekiel's office as a spiritual watchman; so in ch. 3:16-21; only here the duties of the earthly watchman (cf. II Sam. 18:24, 25; II Kings 9:17) are detailed first, and then the application is made to the spiritual watchman's duty (cf. Isa. 21:6-10; Hos. 9:8; Hab. 2:1). "A man of their coasts" is a man specially chosen for the office *out of their whole number.* So Judges 18:2, "five men *from their coasts*"; also the *Hebrew* of Genesis 47:2; implying the care needed in the choice of the watchman, the spiritual as well as the temporal (Acts 1:21, 22, 24-26; I Tim. 5:22). **3. the sword**—invaders. An appropriate illustration at the time of the invasion of Judea by Nebuchadnezzar. **4. blood . . . upon his own head**—metaphor from sacrificial victims, on the heads of which they used to lay their hands, praying that their guilt should be upon the victims. **6. his iniquity**—his negligence in not maintaining constant watchfulness, as they who are in warfare ought to do. The thing signified here appears from under the image. **7. I have set thee a watchman**—application of the image. Ezekiel's appointment to be a watchman spiritually is far more solemn, as it is derived from God, not from the people. **8. thou shalt surely die**—by a violent death, the earnest of everlasting death; the qualification being supposed, "if thou dost not repent."

9. Blood had by this time been shed (vs. 21), but Ezekiel was clear.

10. be upon us—i.e., their guilt remain on us. **pine away in them**—if we suffer the penalty threatened for them in ch. 24:23, according to the law (Lev. 26:39). **how should we . . . live?**—as Thou dost promise in vs. 5 (cf. ch. 37:11; Isa. 49:14).

11. To meet the Jews' cry of despair in vs. 10, Ezekiel here cheers them by the assurance that God has no pleasure in their death, but that they should repent and live (II Pet. 3:9). A yearning tenderness manifests itself here, notwithstanding all their past sins; yet with it a holiness that abates nothing of its demands for the honor of God's authority. God's righteousness is vindicated as in ch. 3:18-21 and ch. 18, by the statement that each should be treated with the closest adaptation of God's justice to his particular case.

CHAPTER 33

2. *Son of man . . . if the people of the land take a man.* The first ten verses of this chapter are the same with chap. iii. 17-22; and to what is said there on this most important and awful subject I must refer the reader. Here the people choose the watchman; there the Lord appoints him. When God chooses, the people should approve.

11. *As I live, saith the Lord God, I have no pleasure in the death of the wicked.* From this to the twentieth verse inclusive is nearly the same with chap. xviii, on which I wish the reader to consult the notes.

MATTHEW HENRY

God; and the most notorious sinners, if they repent, shall certainly be happy for ever in their return to God. These rules of judgment are so plainly just that they need no other confirmation of them than the repetition of them. If those that have made a great profession of religion throw off their profession, the profession they made shall stand them in no stead, *v.* 12, 13, 18. He that lives regularly shall live. Surely such a man as this cannot but be happy. Righteous men, who have very good hopes of themselves, are yet in danger of turning to iniquity by trusting to their righteousness. Or, he trusts to the strength of his own righteousness, and so by presuming on his own sufficiency he is brought to commit iniquity. If those that have lived a wicked life repent and reform, their sins shall be pardoned, and they shall be justified and saved. Thus even the threatenings of the word are to some, by the grace of God, a savour of life unto life, while even the promises of the word become to others, by their own corruption, a savour of death unto death. There is many a wicked man hastening to destruction who yet is wrought upon by the grace of God to return and repent. He *turns from his sin* (*v.* 14), and *restores the pledge* (*v.* 15) which he had taken uncharitably from the poor, *he gives again that which he had robbed* and taken unjustly from the rich. Nor does he only *cease to do evil*, but he *learns to do well.* And in this good way he perseveres *without committing iniquity*, though not free from infirmity, yet under the dominion of no iniquity. He *shall surely live; he shall not die*, *v.* 15. Again (*v.* 16), *He shall surely live.* Again (*v.* 19), *He has done that which is lawful and right*, and *he shall live thereby.* Now that there is a settled separation between him and sin there shall be no longer a separation between him and God. *None of the sins that he has committed shall be mentioned unto him* (*v.* 16), either as a clog to his pardon or as any diminution to the glory that is prepared for him. The conclusion of the whole matter is (*v.* 20): "*O you house of Israel*, though you are all involved now in the common calamity, yet there shall be a distinction of persons made in the spiritual and eternal state, and *I will judge you every one after his ways.*"

Verses 21–29

I. The tidings brought to Ezekiel of the burning of Jerusalem by the Chaldeans. The city was burnt in the eleventh year of the captivity and the fifth month, Jer. lii. 12, 13. Tidings were brought to the prophet by one that was an eye-witness of the destruction (*v.* 21), a year and almost five months after the thing was done. This was the first time he had an account of it from a refuge, from one who escaped.

II. The divine influences he was under, to prepare him for those heavy tidings (*v.* 22): *The hand of the Lord was upon me before he came, and had opened my mouth* to speak to the house of Israel. He prophesied now with more freedom and boldness. Now *the hand of the Lord came upon him*, renewed his commission, gave him fresh instructions, and *opened his mouth*, furnished him with power to speak to the people *as he ought to speak.*

III. The particular message he was entrusted with, relating to these Jews that yet remained in the *land of Israel*, and *inhabited the wastes* of that land, *v.* 24. Some few that had escaped the sword and captivity still continued there and began to think of re-settling. Though the providence of God concerning them had been very humbling, and still was very threatening, yet they were intolerably haughty. *They say*, "*The land is given us for inheritance*, *v.* 24. Our partners being gone, it is now all our own; we shall have it all to ourselves." They think they can make out as good a title from God to this land as Abraham could: "If God *gave this land* to him, who was but one worshipper of him, as a reward of his service, much more will he give it to us, who are many worshippers of him, as the reward of our service." Since God's providences did neither humble them nor terrify them, he sends them a message sufficient to do both. He tells them of the wickedness they still persisted in, which rendered them utterly unworthy to possess this land. "You make no conscience of forbidden fruit, forbidden food: *You eat with the blood*," Gen. ix. 4. "Idolatry is still the sin that most easily besets you. You are as fierce, and cruel, and barbarous as ever: *You shed blood*, innocent blood. You confide in your own strength, *You stand upon your sword* (*v.* 26); you think to carry all before you by force of arms. You are guilty of all manner of abominations, and, particularly, *you defile everyone his neighbour's wife, and shall you possess the land?*" To terrify them, he tells them of the further judgments God had in store for them. These that are in the cities, here called the *wastes*, shall

JAMIESON, FAUSSET, BROWN

12. not fall . . . in the day that he turneth—(II Chron. 7:14; see ch. 3:20; 18:24).

15. give again that he had robbed—(Luke 19:8). **statutes of life**—in the obeying of which life is promised (Lev. 18:5). If the law has failed to give life to man, it has not been the fault of the law, but of man's sinful inability to keep it (Rom. 7:10, 12; Gal. 3:21). It becomes life-giving through Christ's righteous obedience to it (II Cor. 3:6). **17. The way of the Lord**—The Lord's way of dealing in His moral government.

21. twelfth year . . . tenth month—a year and a half after the capture of the city (Jer. 39:2; 52:5, 6), in the eleventh year and fourth month. The one who escaped (as foretold, ch. 24:26) may have been so long on the road through fear of entering the enemy's country [HENDERSON]; or, the *singular* is used for the *plural* in a collective sense, "the escaped remnant." Cf. similar phrases, "the escaped of Moab," Isaiah 15:9; "He that escapeth of them," Amos 9:1. Naturally the reopening of the prophet's mouth for consolation would be deferred till the number of the escaped remnant was complete: the removal of such a large number would easily have occupied seventeen or eighteen months. **22. in the evening**—(see *Note*, vs. 2). Thus the capture of Jerusalem was known to Ezekiel by revelation before the messenger came. **my mouth . . . no more dumb**—i.e., to my countrymen; as foretold (ch. 24:27), He spake (vss. 2-20) in the evening before the tidings came. **24. they that inhabit . . . wastes of . . . Israel**—marking the blindness of the fraction of Jews under Gedaliah who, though dwelling amidst regions laid waste by the foe, still cherished hopes of deliverance, and this without repentance. **Abraham was one . . . but we are many**—If God gave the land for an inheritance to Abraham, who was but one (Isa. 51:2), much more it is given to us, who, though reduced, are still many. If he, with 318 servants, was able to defend himself amid so many foes, much more shall we, so much more numerous, retain our own. The grant of the land was not for his sole use, but for his numerous posterity. **inherited the land**—not actually possessed it (Acts 7:5), but had the right of dwelling and pasturing his flocks in it [GROTIUS]. The Jews boasted similarly of their Abrahamic descent in Matthew 3:9 and John 8:39.

25. eat with the blood—in opposition to the law (Lev. 19:26; cf. Gen. 9:4). They did so as an idolatrous rite.

26. Ye stand upon your sword—Your dependence is, not on right and equity, but on force and arms. **every one**—Scarcely anyone refrains from adultery.

ADAM CLARKE

F. B. MEYER:

"Why will ye die?" (33:1–16). The prophet depicts the peasantry of a fertile valley as engaged in pastoral pursuits. It is a peaceful, happy scene; but creeping through the mountain passes are their deadliest foes. How necessary that there should be a watchman, trumpet in hand, to give notice; and how unspeakable his guilt if he forbear to sound a warning! We are not responsible for those who refuse to take warning from our announcements, faithfully given; but if we perceive a soul in mortal danger and forbear to warn it, we are not only responsible for its ruin, but we bring awful retribution upon ourselves. Well might many lie awake at night beneath an awful sense of responsibility for the souls of men. God desires our salvation. If only the sinner will confess his sins to the faithful and merciful High Priest, not one of his sins shall be remembered against him.

—Bible Commentary

19. *He shall live thereby.* "The wages of sin is death"; "the gift of God is eternal life." It is a miserable trade by which a man *cannot live;* such a trade is *sin.*

21. *One that had escaped out of Jerusalem.* After it had been taken by the Chaldeans. *Came unto me, saying, The city is smitten.* This very message God had promised to the prophet, chap. xxiv. 26.

22. *My mouth was opened.* They had now the fullest evidence that I had spoken from the Lord. I therefore spoke freely and fully what God delivered to me, chap. xxiv. 27.

24. *Abraham was one.* If he was called to inherit the land when he was alone, and had the whole to himself, why may we not expect to be established here, who are his posterity, and are many? They wished to remain in the land and be happy after the Chaldeans had carried the rest away captives.

25. *Ye eat with the blood.* Abraham was *righteous;* ye are *unrighteous.* Eating of blood, in any way dressed, or of flesh from which the blood had not been extracted, was and is in the sight of God abominable. All such practices He has absolutely and forever forbidden.

26. *Ye stand upon your sword.* You live by plunder, rapine, and murder.

MATTHEW HENRY

fall by the sword, either by the sword of the Chaldeans, or by one another's swords. Those that are in the open field shall be *devoured by* wild *beasts.* Those that are *in the forts and in the caves,* that think themselves safe in artificial or natural fastnesses, shall *die of the pestilence.*

Verses 30–33

Those are reproved who were now in captivity in Babylon, under divine rebukes, and yet were not reformed by them. They made some show of religion and devotion; but their hearts were not right with God. The thing they are here accused of is *mocking the messengers of the Lord.* Two ways they mocked the prophet Ezekiel:

I. By invidious ill-natured reflections upon him, privately among themselves. The prophet did not know it. But God comes and tells him, *The children of thy people are still talking against thee* (*v.* 30). Those have arrived at a great pitch of profaneness who can make the preaching and hearing of the word of God a matter of sport and ridicule, though it be done in private conversation among themselves.

II. By dissembling with him in their attendance upon his ministry. Hypocrites mock God and mock his prophets.

1. The plausible profession which these people made. They are like those (Matt. xv. 8) who *draw nigh to God with their mouths and honour him with their lips, but their hearts are far from him.* They were diligent and constant in their attendance upon the means of grace: *They come unto thee as the people come.* In Babylon they had no temple or synagogue, but they went to the prophet's house (*ch.* viii. 1). Now these hypocrites came, *according to the coming of the people,* as duly and as early as any of the prophet's hearers. They behaved themselves very decently and reverently in the public assembly. They were very attentive to the word preached. They pretended to have a great kindness and respect for the prophet. Though, behind his back, they could not give him a good word, yet, to his face, *they showed much love* to him and his doctrine. They took a great deal of pleasure in the word. Ezekiel was to them as one *that had a pleasant voice* and could sing well, *or play well on an instrument.* Men may have their fancies pleased by the word, and yet not have their consciences touched nor their hearts changed, the itching ear gratified and yet not the corrupt nature sanctified.

2. The hypocrisy of these professions and pretensions. While they *show much love* it is only *with the mouth,* from the teeth outward, but *their heart goes after their covetousness;* they are as much set upon the world as ever. They *hear thy words,* but it is only a hearing that they *give thee,* for they *will not do them, v.* 31.

3. The end hereof: *Shall their unbelief* and carelessness *make the word of God of no effect?* God will confirm the prophet's word, though they make light of it, *v.* 33. When it comes to pass *they shall know,* shall know to their cost, that *a prophet has been among them,* though they made no more of him than as one that *had a pleasant voice.*

CHAPTER 34

Verses 1–6

The prophecy of this chapter is not dated, nor any of those that follow it, till chap. xl.

I. The prophet is ordered to *prophesy against the shepherds of Israel*—the princes and magistrates, the priests and Levites, the kings especially, for there were two now captives in Babylon, who, as well as the people, must have their transgressions shown them, that they might repent. *Woe to the shepherds of Israel!* Though they are shepherds, and shepherds of Israel, yet he must not spare them.

II. Two things they are charged with: 1. That all their care was to advance and enrich themselves and to make themselves great. *Should not the shepherds feed the flocks?* They betray their trust if they do not. But *these* shepherds *fed themselves,* contrived everything to gratify and indulge their own appetite. They made sure of the fleece, and *clothed themselves with the wool.*

JAMIESON, FAUSSET, BROWN

27. shall fall by the sword—The very object of their confidence would be the instrument of their destruction. Thinking to "stand" by it, by it they shall "fall." Just retribution! Some fell by the sword of Ishmael; others by the Chaldeans in revenge for the murder of Gedaliah (Jer. 40:44). **caves**—(Judg. 6:2; I Sam. 13:6). In the hilly parts of Judea there were caves almost inaccessible, as having only crooked and extremely narrow paths of ascent, with rock in front stretching down into the valleys beneath perpendicularly (JOSEPHUS, *Jew. War,* 1. 16. 4). **28. most desolate**—(Jer. 4:27; 12:11). **none . . . pass through**—from fear of wild beasts and pestilence [GROTIUS]. **30.** Not only the remnant in Judea, but those at the Chebar, though less flagrantly, betrayed the same unbelieving spirit. **talking against thee**—Though going to the prophet to hear the word of the Lord, they criticised, *in an unfriendly spirit,* his peculiarities of manner and his enigmatical style (ch. 20:49); making these the excuse for their impenitence. Their talking was not directly "*against*" Ezekiel, for they professed to like his ministrations; but God's word speaks of things as they really are, not as they appear. **by the walls**—in the public haunts. In the East groups assemble under the walls of their houses in winter for conversation. **in the doors**—privately. **what is the word**—Their motive was curiosity, seeking pastime and gratification of the ear (II Tim. 4:3); not reformation of the heart. Cf. Johanan's consultation of Jeremiah, to hear the word of the Lord without desiring to *do* it (Jer. 42:43). **31. as the people cometh**—i.e., in crowds, as disciples flock to their teacher. **sit before thee**—on lower seats at thy feet, according to the Jewish custom of pupils (Deut. 33:3; II Kings 4:38; Luke 10:39; Acts 22:3). **as my people**—though they are not. **hear . . . not do**—(Matt. 13:20, 21; Jas. 1:23, 24).

they show much love—lit., "make love," i.e., act the part of lovers. Profess love to the Lord (Matt. 7:21). GESENIUS translates, according to *Arabic* idiom, "They do the delights of God," i.e., all that is agreeable to God. *Vulgate* translates, "They turn thy words into a song of their mouths." **heart goeth after . . . covetousness**—the grand rival to the love of God; therefore called "idolatry," and therefore associated with impure carnal love, as both alike transfer the heart's affection from the Creator to the creature (Matt. 13:22; Eph. 5:5, I Tim. 6:10). **32. very lovely song**—lit., a "song of loves": a lover's song. They praise thy eloquence, but care not for the subject of it as a real and personal thing; just as many do in the modern church [JEROME]. **play well on an instrument**—Hebrew singers accompanied the "voice" with the harp. **33. when this cometh to pass**—when My predictions are verified. **lo, it will come**—rather, "lo it *is* come" (see vs. 22). **know**—experimentally, and to their cost.

CHAPTER 34

Vss. 1-31. REPROOF OF THE FALSE SHEPHERDS; PROMISE OF THE TRUE AND GOOD SHEPHERD. Having in chapter 33 laid down repentance as the necessary preliminary to happier times for the people, He now promises the removal of the false shepherds as preparatory to the raising up of the Good Shepherd. **2.** Jeremiah 23:1 and Zechariah 11:17 similarly make the removal of the false shepherds the preliminary to the interposition of Messiah the Good Shepherd in behalf of His people Israel. The "shepherds" are not prophets or priests, but *rulers* who sought in their government their own selfish ends, not the good of the people ruled. The term was appropriate, as David, the first king and the type of the true David (vss. 23, 24), was taken from being a shepherd (II Sam. 5:2; Ps. 78:70, 71); and the office, like that of a shepherd for his flock, is to guard and provide for his people. The choice of a *shepherd* for the first king was therefore designed to suggest this thought, just as Jesus' selection of *fishermen* for apostles was designed to remind them of their spiritual office of catching men (cf. Isa. 44:28; Jer. 2:8; 3:15; 10:21; 23:1, 2). **3. fat**—or, by differently pointing the *Hebrew,* "milk" [LXX]. Thus the repetition "fat" and "fed" is avoided: also the eating of "fat" would not probably be put before the "killing" of the sheep. The eating of sheep's or goats' milk as food (Deut. 32:14; Prov. 27:27) was unobjectionable, had not these shepherds milked them too often, and that without duly "feeding"

ADAM CLARKE

27. *They that are in the wastes.* He seems to speak of those Jews who had fled to rocks, caves, and fortresses in the mountains; whose death he predicts, partly by the sword, partly by wild beasts, and partly by famine.

30. *Thy people still are talking against thee. Bach* should be rather translated, "concerning thee," than "against thee"; for the following verses show that the prophet was much respected.

32. *As a very lovely song.* They admired the fine voice and correct delivery of the prophet; this was their religion, and this is the whole of the religion of thousands to the present day.

CHAPTER 34

2. *Prophesy against the shepherds of Israel.* The *shepherds* include, first, the priests and Levites; secondly, the kings, princes, and magistrates. The *flocks* mean the whole of the people; the "fat" and the "wool," the tithes and offerings, the taxes and imposts.

MATTHEW HENRY

2. That they took no care for the benefit and welfare of those that were committed to their charge: *You feed not the flock*. The princes and judges took no care to right those that suffered wrong. They took no care of the poor. The priests took no care to instruct the ignorant. The ministers of state took no care to check the growing distempers of the kingdom. They did not do their duty to those of the flock that were driven away by enemies and forced to seek for shelter where they could find a place, or that *wandered* of choice upon *the mountains and hills* (*v.* 6). Thus were *they scattered because there was no shepherd*, *v.* 5. Christ complains that his flock were *as sheep having no shepherd*, when yet the scribes and Pharisees *sat in Moses' seat*, Matt. ix. 36.

Verses 7–16

I. How much displeased God is at the shepherds. Their crimes are repeated, *v.* 8. God's flock became a prey to the deceivers that drew them to idolatry, and to the destroyers that carried them into captivity; and these shepherds took no care to prevent either the one or the other. God is *against them*, and they shall know it. They shall be made to account for the manner in which they have discharged their trust: "*I will require my flock at their hands*, and charge it upon them that so many of them are missing." *They shall cease from feeding the flock*, that is, from pretending to feed it. "*Neither shall the shepherds feed themselves any more*."

II. How much concerned God is for the flock; for *with him the fatherless finds mercy*. Precious promises, made here, were to have their accomplishment in the return of the Jews out of their captivity and their re-establishment in their own land. Let the shepherds *hear this word of the Lord*, and know that they have no part nor lot in the matter.

1. God will gather his sheep together that were scattered, and bring those back to the fold that had wandered from it. "*I will both search my sheep and find them out* (*v.* 11) as a *shepherd* does (*v.* 12), and bring them back as he does the stray-sheep, upon his shoulders, *from all the places where they have been scattered in the cloudy and dark day*." God will both incline their hearts to come by his grace and will by his providence open a door for them and remove every difficulty that lies in the way. *I will seek that which was lost and bring again that which was driven away*, *v.* 16. This was done when so many thousand Jews returned triumphantly out of Babylon, under the conduct of Zerubbabel, Ezra, and others.

2. God will bring the returning captives safely to their own land (*v.* 13), *will feed them upon the mountains of Israel*, and that is a *good pasture*, and a *fat pasture* (*v.* 14); there shall their *feeding* be, and there shall be *their fold*; and it is a *good fold*. There God will *cause them to lie down* (*v.* 15), which denotes rest after their wanderings, and a continuing residence.

3. He will succour those that are hurt, will *bind up that which was broken and strengthen that which was sick*, will comfort those that *mourn in Zion* and with Zion.

Verses 17–31

The prophet has now a message to deliver to the flock. God had ordered him to speak tenderly to them, and to assure them of the mercy he had in store for them. But here he is ordered to make a difference between the precious and the vile and then to give them a promise of the Messiah.

I. Conviction spoken to those of the flock that were fat and strong, the *rams and the he-goats* (*v.* 17), those that, though they had not power, as shepherds and rulers, yet, being rich and wealthy, made use of the opportunity which this gave them to bear hard upon their poor neighbours. The *rams* and the *he-goats* not only kept all the good pasture to themselves, but they would not let the poor of the flock have any enjoyment of the little that was left them; they *trod down the residue of the pastures and fouled the residue of the waters*, *v.* 18, 19.

They not only robbed the poor, to make them poorer, but were troublesome to the sick and weak of the flock (*v.* 21).

II. Comfort spoken to those of the flock that are poor and feeble, and that wait for the consolation of Israel (*v.* 22): "*I will save my flock*, and they shall no more be spoiled by the beasts of prey, by their own shepherds or by the rams and he-goats among themselves." Upon this occasion, as is usual in the prophets, comes in a prediction of the coming of the Messiah, and the setting up of his kingdom.

JAMIESON, FAUSSET, BROWN

them [Bochart], (Isa. 56:11). The rulers levied exorbitant tributes. **kill . . . fed**—kill the rich by false accusation so as to get possession of their property. **feed not . . . flock**—take no care of the people (John 10:12). **4. The diseased**—rather, those *weak* from the effects of "disease," as "strengthened" (i.e., with due nourishment) requires [Grotius]. **broken**—i.e., fractures from wounds inflicted by the wolf. **brought again . . . driven away**—(Exod. 23:4). Those "driven away" by the enemy into foreign lands through God's judgments are meant (Jer. 23:3). A spiritual reformation of the state by the rulers would have turned away God's wrath, and "brought again" the exiles. The rulers are censured as *chiefly* guilty (though the people, too, were guilty), because they, who ought to have been foremost in checking the evil, promoted it. **neither . . . sought . . . lost**—Contrast the Good Shepherd's love (Luke 15:4). **with force . . . ruled**—(Exod. 1:13, 14). With an Egyptian bondage. The very thing forbidden by the law they did (Lev. 25:43; cf. I Pet. 5:3). **5. scattered, because . . . no shepherd**—i.e., none worthy of the name, though there were some *called* shepherds (I Kings 22:17; Matt. 9:36). Cf. Matt. 26:31, where the sheep were scattered when the true Shepherd was smitten. God calls them "*My sheep*"; for they were not, as the shepherds treated them, *their* patrimony whereby to "feed themselves." **meat to all . . . beasts**—They became a prey to the Syrians, Ammon, Moab, and Assyria. **6. every high hill**—the scene of their idolatries sanctioned by the rulers. **search . . . seek**—rather, "seek" . . . "search." The former is the part of the superior rulers *to inquire after: to search out* is the duty of the subordinate rulers [Junius]. **10. I will require my flock**—(Heb. 13:17), rather, "*I require* . . . ," for God already had begun to do so, punishing Zedekiah and the other princes severely (Jer. 52:10). **11. . . . will . . . search**—doing that which the so-called shepherds had failed to do, I being the rightful owner of the flock. **12. in the day that he is among**—*in the midst of* (*Hebrew*) His sheep that had been scattered. Referring to Messiah's second advent, when He shall be "the glory *in the midst of* Israel" (Zech. 2:5). **in the cloudy . . . day**—the day of the nation's calamity (Joel 2:2). **13.** (Ch. 28:25; 36:24; 37:21, 22; Isa. 65:9, 10; Jer. 23:3.) **14. good pasture**—(Ps. 23:2). **high mountains of Israel**—In chs. 17:23 and 20:40, the phrase is "the mountain of the height of Israel" in the *singular* number. The reason for the difference is: *there* Ezekiel spoke of the central seat of the kingdom, Mount Zion, where the people met for the worship of Jehovah; *here* he speaks of the kingdom of Israel at large, all the parts of which are regarded as possessing a moral elevation. **16.** In contrast to the unfaithful shepherds (vs. 4). The several duties neglected by *them I* will faithfully discharge. **fat . . . strong**—i.e., those rendered wanton by prosperity (Deut. 32:15; Jer. 5:28), who use their strength to oppress the weak. Cf. vs. 20, "the fat cattle" (Isa. 10:16). The image is from fat cattle that wax refractory. **with judgment**—i.e., justice and equity, as contrasted with the "force" and "cruelty" with which the unfaithful shepherds ruled the flock (vs. 4). **17. you, . . . my flock**—passing from the rulers to the people. **cattle and cattle**—rather, "sheep and sheep"; *Margin*, "small cattle," or "flocks of lambs and kids," i.e., I judge between one class of citizens and another, so as to award what is right to each. He then defines the class about to be punitively "judged," viz., "the rams and he goats," or great he goats (cf. Isa. 14:9, *Margin;* Zech. 10:3; Matt. 25:32, 33). They answer to "the fat and strong," as opposed to the "sick" (vs. 16). The rich and ungodly of the people are meant, who imitated the bad rulers in oppressing their poorer brethren, as if it enhanced their own joys to trample on others' rights (vs. 18). **18, 19.** Not content with appropriating to their own use the goods of others, they from mere wantonness spoiled what they did not use, so as to be of no use to the owners. **deep waters**—i.e., "limpid," as deep waters are generally *clear*. Grotius explains the image as referring to the usuries with which the rich ground the poor (ch. 22:12; Isa. 24:2). **they eat**—scantily. **they drink**—sorrowfully. **20. fat . . . lean**—the rich oppressors . . . the humble poor. **21. scattered them abroad**—down to the time of the carrying away to Babylon [Grotius]. **22.** After the restoration from Babylon, the Jews were delivered in some degree from the oppression, not only of foreigners, but also of their own great people (Neh. 5:1-19). The full and final fulfilment of this prophecy is future. **23. set up**—i.e., raise up by divine appointment; alluding to the declaration of God to David, "I will *set up* thy seed after thee" (II Sam. 7:12); and, "Yet have I *set* My king on My

ADAM CLARKE

5. *And they were scattered.* There was no discipline kept up; and the flock, the Church, became disorganized, and separated from each other, in both affection and fellowship. And the consequence was, the grievous wolves, false and worldly interested teachers, seized on and made a prey of them.

6. *My sheep wandered through all the mountains.* They all became idolaters, and lost the knowledge of the true God.

16. *I will destroy the fat and the strong.* I will destroy those cruel and imperious shepherds who abuse their authority, and tyrannize over the flock.

17. *And as for you, O my flock.* After having spoken to the shepherds, he now addresses the flock. *I judge between cattle and cattle.* Between false and true professors.

18. *Have eaten up the good pasture.* Arrogate to yourselves all the promises of God, and will hardly permit the simple believer to claim or possess any token of God's favor.

20. *I will judge between the fat cattle and between the lean cattle.* Between the rich and the poor, those who fare sumptuously every day and those who have not the necessaries of life.

MATTHEW HENRY

1. Concerning the Messiah himself. He shall have his commission from God: I will *set him up* (*v.* 23); *I will raise him up*, *v.* 29. He shall be the great *Shepherd* of the sheep, who shall do that for his flock which no one else could do. He is the *one Shepherd*, under whom Jews and Gentiles should be *one fold.* He is *God's servant* to re-establish his kingdom among men. He is David, one after God's own heart, set as his King upon the holy hill of Zion, made the head of the corner, with whom the covenant of royalty is made, and to whom God would *give the throne of his father David.* He is the *plant of renown*, because a *righteous branch* (Jer. xxiii. 5), *beautiful* and *glorious*, Isa. iv. 2. Some understand it of the church, the *planting of the Lord*, Isa. lxi. 3.

2. Concerning the great charter by which the kingdom of the Messiah should be founded (*v.* 25): *I will make with them a covenant of peace.* The covenant of grace is a covenant of peace. The tenor of this covenant is: "*I the Lord will be their God*, a God all-sufficient to them (*v.* 24)." Those, and those only, that have the Lord Jesus for *their prince* have the Lord Jehovah for *their God.*

3. Concerning the privileges of those that are the faithful subjects of this kingdom of the Messiah. These are here set forth figuratively, as the blessings of the flock. But we have a key to it, *v.* 31. Those that belong to this flock, though they are spoken of as *sheep*, are really men.

(1) They shall enjoy a holy security under the divine protection. Christ, our good Shepherd, has *caused the evil beasts to cease out of the land* (*v.* 25), having vanquished all our spiritual enemies. Sin and Satan, death and hell, are conquered. And then *they shall dwell safely*, not only in the folds, but in the fields, *in the wilderness, in the woods.* Through Christ, God delivers his people not only from the things they have reason to fear, but from their fear even of death itself.

(2) They shall enjoy a spiritual plenty of all good things. *They shall no more be consumed with hunger in the land*, *v.* 29. *Showers of blessings* shall come upon them, *v.* 26, 27. The heavens shall yield their dews; the *trees of the field* also shall *yield their fruit.* All that are in the neighbourhood of Zion shall fare the better for it; and the nearer the church the nearer its God. The *effect of this plenty* is, *I will make them a blessing.* They shall be blessings to all about them. Those that are the *blessed of the Lord* must study to make themselves blessings to the world. He that is good, let him do *good*; he that has received the gift, the grace, let him minister the same.

CHAPTER 35

Verses 1–9

Mount Seir was mentioned as partner with Moab in one of the threatenings we had before (*ch.* xxv. 8); but here it has woes of its own.

II. What should be the effect and issue of that controversy. If God stretch out his hand against the country of Edom, he will *make it most desolate*, *v.* 3.

JAMIESON, FAUSSET, BROWN

holy hill of Zion" (Ps. 2:6; cf. Acts 2:30; 13:23). **one shepherd**—lit., "a Shepherd, one": singularly and pre-eminently *one:* the only one of His kind, to whom none is comparable (Song of Sol. 5:10). The Lord Jesus refers to this prophecy (John 10:14), "I am THE Good Shepherd." Also "one" as uniting in one the heretofore divided kingdoms of Israel and Judah, and also "gathering together in one all things in Christ, both which are in heaven and on earth" (Eph. 1:10); thus healing worse breaches than that between Israel and Judah (Col. 1:20). "God by Him reconciling all things unto Himself, whether things in earth or in heaven." **David**—the antitypical David, Messiah, of the seed of David, which no other king after the captivity was: who was *fully*, what David was only in a degree, "the man after God's own heart." Also, David means *beloved:* Messiah was truly God's *beloved* Son (Isa. 42:1; Matt. 3:17). Shepherd means *King*, rather than religious instructor; in this pre-eminently He was the true David, who was the *Shepherd King* (Luke 1:32, 33). Messiah is called "David" in Isaiah 55:3, 4; Jeremiah 30:9; Hosea 3:5. **24. my servant**—implying fitness for ruling in the name of God, not pursuing a self-chosen course, as other kings, but acting as the faithful administrator of the will of God; Messiah realized fully this character (Ps. 40:7, 8; Isa. 42:1; 49:3, 6; 53:11; Phil. 2:7), which David typically and partially represented (Acts 13:36); so He is the fittest person to wield the world scepter, abused by all the world kings (Dan. 2:34, 35, 44, 45). **25. covenant of peace . . . evil beasts . . . to cease . . . dwell safely**—The original promise of the law (Lev. 26:6) shall be realized for the first time fully under Messiah (Isa. 11:6-9; 35:9; Hos. 2:18). **26. them and the places round about my hill**—The Jews, and Zion, God's hill (Ps. 2:6), are to be sources of blessing, not merely to themselves, but to the surrounding heathen (Isa. 19:24; 56:6, 7; 60:3; Mic. 5: 7; Zech. 8:13). The literal fulfilment is, however, the primary one, though the spiritual also is designed. In correspondence with the settled reign of righteousness internally, all is to be prosperity externally, fertilizing showers (according to the promise of the ancient covenant, Lev. 26:4; Ps. 68: 9; Mal. 3:10), and productive trees and lands (vs. 27). Thus shall they realize the image of vs. 14; viz., a flock richly pastured by God Himself. **27. served themselves of them**—availed themselves of their services, as if the Jews were their slaves (Jer. 22:13; 25:14; cf. Gen. 15:13; Exod. 1:14). **28. dwell safely**—(Jer. 23:6). **29. plant of renown**—Messiah, the "Rod" and "Branch" (Isa. 11:1), the "righteous Branch" (Jer. 23:5), who shall obtain for them "renown." FAIRBAIRN less probably translates, "A plantation for a name," i.e., a flourishing condition, represented as a garden (alluding to Eden, Gen. 2:8-11, with its various trees, good for food and pleasant to the sight), the planting of the Lord (Isa. 60:21; 61:3), and an object of "renown" among the heathen. **31. ye my flock . . . are men**—not merely an explanation of the image, as JEROME represents. But as God had promised many things which mere "men" could not expect to realize, He shows that it is not from *man's* might their realization is to be looked for, but from GOD, who would perform them for His covenant people, "*His* flock" [ROSENMULLER]. When we realize most our weakness and God's power and faithfulness to HIS covenant, we are in the fittest state for receiving His blessings.

CHAPTER 35

Vss. 1-15. JUDGMENT ON EDOM. Another feature of Israel's prosperity; those who exulted over Israel's humiliation, shall themselves be a "prey." Already stated in ch. 25:12-14; properly repeated here in full detail, as a commentary on vs. 28 of last chapter. The Israelites "shall be no more a prey"; but Edom, the type of their most bitter foes, shall be destroyed irrecoverably. **2. Mount Seir**—i.e., Idumea (Gen. 36:9). Singled out as badly preeminent in its bitterness against God's people, to represent all their enemies everywhere and in all ages. So in Isaiah 34:5, and 63:1-4, Edom, the region of the greatest enmity towards God's people, is the ideal scene of the final judgments of all God's foes. "Seir" means "shaggy," alluding to its rugged hills and forests. **3. most desolate**—lit., "desolation and desolateness" (Jer. 49:17, etc.). It is only in their national character of foes to God's people, that the Edomites are to be utterly destroyed. A *remnant* of Edom, as of the other heathen, is to be "called by the name of God" (Amos 9:12). **5. perpetual hatred**—(Ps. 137:7; Amos 1:11; Obad. 10-

ADAM CLARKE

23. *I will set up one Shepherd . . . my servant David.* From the texts marked in the margin we understand that Jesus Christ alone is meant, as both Old and New Testaments agree in this. And from this one Shepherd all Christian ministers must derive their authority to teach, and their grace to teach effectually.

25. *I will make with them a covenant of peace.* The original is emphatic: "And I will cut with them the peace covenant"; that is, a covenant sacrifice, procuring and establishing peace between God and man, and between man and his fellows. I need not tell the reader that the cutting refers to the ancient mode of making covenants. The blood was poured out; the animal was divided from mouth to tail, exactly in two; the divisions placed opposite to each other; the contracting parties entered into the space, going in at each end, and met in the middle, and there took the covenant oath. *And will cause the evil beasts to cease.* These false and ravenous pastors. Christ purges them out of His Church, and destroys that power by which they lorded it over God's heritage.

26. *The shower to come down.* The Holy Spirit's influence. *There shall be showers of blessing.* Light, life, joy, peace, and power shall be manifest in all the assemblies of Christ's people.

29. *I will raise up . . . a plant of renown.* "A plantation to the name"; to the name of Christ. A Christian Church composed of men who are Christians, who have the spirit of Christ in them, and do not bear His name in vain.

CHAPTER 35

2. *Set thy face against mount Seir.* That is, against the Edomites. This prophecy was probably delivered about the time of the preceding, and before the destruction of Idumea by Nebuchadnezzar, which took place about five years after. Calmet supposes that two destructions of Idumea are here foretold: one by Nebuchadnezzar, and the other by the Jews after their return from their captivity.

3. *Most desolate.* Literally, "A desolation and a wilderness."

MATTHEW HENRY

I. God espouses his people's cause, and takes what is done against them as done against himself; and it is upon their account that God now contends with the Edomites. 1. Because of the enmity they had against the people of God. "Thou hast had a *perpetual hatred* to them, to the very name of an Israelite." The Edomites kept up an *hereditary* malice against Israel, the same that Esau bore to Jacob. The posterity of Esau would never be reconciled to the seed of Jacob. It is strange how deeply-rooted national antipathies sometimes are, and how long they last. 2. Because of the injuries they had done to the people of God. They did not attack them as fair and open enemies, but laid wait for them, to *cut off* those of them that had escaped (Obad. 14).

Thou hast not hated blood; it implies, "Thou hast delighted in it and thirsted after it." Some read it, "*Unless thou hatest blood*" (that is, unless thou dost repent, and put off this bloody disposition) *blood shall pursue thee.*"

Those that help forward the desolations of Israel may expect to be themselves made desolate. And that which completes the judgment is that Edom shall be made *perpetual desolations* (*v.* 9).

Verses 10–15

I. A further account of the sin of the Edomites, and their bad conduct towards the people of God. We find the church complaining of them for setting on the Babylonians, and irritating them against Jerusalem, saying, *Rase it, rase it* (Ps. cxxxvii. 7), inflaming a rage that needed no spur. They were glad when the Chaldeans did them a mischief. They pleased themselves with hopes that when the people of Israel were destroyed they should be let into the possession of their country. Those have the spirit of Edomites who desire the death of others, because they hope to get by it, or are pleased with their failing because they expect to come into their business. But in this case of the Edomites' coveting the land of Israel, and gaping for it, there was a particular affront to God. They expected possession upon a vacancy, because Israel was driven out, *whereas the Lord was* still *there*, *v.* 10. That was Immanuel's land (Isa. viii. 8); in that land he was to be born.

II. The notice God took of the barbarous insolence of the Edomites, and the doom passed upon them for it: *I have heard all thy blasphemies*, *v.* 12. And again (*v.* 13), *You have multiplied your words against me*, and *I have heard them.* God has heard the Edomites' blasphemy; let them therefore hear their doom, *v.* 14, 15. It was a national sin and therefore shall be punished with a national desolation. The punishment shall answer to the sin: "*As thou didst rejoice in the desolation of the house of Israel*, God will give thee enough of desolation; since thou art so fond of it, *thou shalt be desolate*; *I will make thee so.*" Some read *v.* 14 so as to complete the resemblance between the sin and the punishment: *The whole earth shall rejoice when I make thee desolate, as thou didst rejoice when Israel* was made desolate.

CHAPTER 36

Verses 1–15

Now God is returning in mercy the prophet must speak good words and comfortable words, *v.* 1 and again *v.* 4. *You mountains of Israel, hear the word of*

JAMIESON, FAUSSET, BROWN

16). Edom perpetuated the hereditary hatred derived from Esau against Jacob. **shed** *the blood of* . . .—The lit., translation is better. "Thou hast *poured* out the children of Israel"; viz., like water. So Psalm 22:14; 63:10, *Margin;* Jeremiah 18:21. Cf. II Samuel 14:14. **by the force of the sword**—lit., "by" or "upon the hands of the sword"; the sword being personified as a devourer whose "hands" were the instruments of destruction. **in the time that their iniquity had an end**—i.e., had its consummation (ch. 21:25, 29). Edom consummated his guilt when he exulted over Jerusalem's downfall, and helped the foe to destroy it (Ps. 137: 7; Obad. 11). **6. I will prepare thee unto blood**—I will expose thee to slaughter. **sith**—old English for "seeing that" or "since." **thou hast not hated blood**—The *Hebrew* order is, "thou hast hated not-blood"; i.e., thou couldst not bear to live without bloodshed [GROTIUS]. There is a play on similar sounds in the *Hebrew; Edom* resembling *dam,* the *Hebrew* for "blood"; as Edom means "red," the transition to "blood" is easy. Edom, akin to blood in name, so also in nature and acts; "blood therefore shall pursue thee." The measure which Edom meted to others should be meted to himself (Ps. 109: 17; Matt. 7:2; 26:52). **7. cut off . . . him that passeth**—i.e., every passer to and fro; "the highways shall be unoccupied" (ch. 29:11; Judg. 5:6). **9. shall not return**—to their former state (ch. 16:55); shall not be restored. The *Hebrew* text (*Chetib*) reads, "shall not *be inhabited*" (cf. ch. 26:20; Mal. 1:3, 4). **10.** So far from being allowed to enter on Israel's vacated inheritance, as Edom hoped (ch. 36:5; Ps. 83:4, 12; Obad. 13), it shall be that he shall be deprived of his own; and whereas Israel's humiliation was temporary, Edom's shall be perpetual. **Lord was there**—(ch. 48:35; Ps. 48:1, 3; 132:13, 14). Jehovah claimed Judea as His own, even when the Chaldeans had overthrown the state; they could not remove Him, as they did the idols of heathen lands. The broken sentences express the excited feelings of the prophet at Edom's wicked presumption. The transition from the "two nations and two countries" to "it" marks that the two are regarded as one whole. The last clause, "and Jehovah was there," bursts in, like a flash of lightning, reproving the wicked presumption of Edom's thought. **11. according to thine anger**—(Jas. 2:13). As thou in anger and envy hast injured them, so I will injure thee. **I will make myself known among them**—viz., the Israelites. I will manifest My favor to them, after I have punished thee. **12, 13. blasphemies . . . against . . . Israel . . . against me**—God regards what is done against His people as done against Himself (Matt. 25:45; Acts 9:2, 4, 5). Edom *implied*, if he did not express it, in his taunts against Israel, that God had not sufficient power to protect His people. A type of the spirit of all the foes of God and His people (I Sam. 2:3; Rev. 13:6). **14.** (Isa. 65:13, 14.) "The whole earth" refers to *Judea and the nations that submit themselves to Judea's God;* when these rejoice, the foes of God and His people, represented by Edom *as a nation,* shall be desolate. Things shall be completely reversed; Israel, that now for a time mourns, shall then rejoice and for ever. Edom, that now rejoices over fallen Israel, shall then, when elsewhere all is joy, mourn, and for ever (Isa. 65:17-19; Matt. 5:4; Luke 6:25). HAVERNICK loses this striking antithesis by translating, "According to the joy of the whole land (of Edom), so I will make thee desolate"; which would make the next verse a mere repetition of this. **15.** (Obadiah 12, 15.)

CHAPTER 36

VSS. 1-38. ISRAEL AVENGED OF HER FOES, AND RESTORED, FIRST TO INWARD HOLINESS, THEN TO OUTWARD PROSPERITY. The distinction between Israel and the heathen (as Edom) is: Israel has a covenant relation to God ensuring restoration after chastisement, so that the heathen's hope of getting possession of the elect people's inheritance must fail, and they themselves be made desolate (vss. 1-15). The reason for the chastisement of Israel was Israel's sin and profanation of God's name (vss. 16-21). God has good in store for Israel, for His own name's sake, to revive His people; first, by a spiritual renewal of their hearts, and, next, by an external restoration to prosperity (vss. 22-33). The result is that the heathen shall be impressed with the power and goodness of God manifested so palpably towards the restored people (vss. 34-38). **1, 2. mountains of Israel**—in contrast to *"Mount* Seir" of the previous prophecy. They are here

ADAM CLARKE

5. *A perpetual hatred.* The Edomites were the descendants of Esau; the Israelites, the descendants of Jacob. Both these were brothers; and between them there was contention even in the womb, and they lived generally in a state of enmity. Their descendants kept up the ancient feud. But the Edomites were implacable; they had not only a rooted but perpetual enmity to the Israelites, harassing and distressing them by all possible means; and they seized the opportunity, when the Israelites were most harassed by other enemies, to make inroads upon them, and cut them off wherever they found them.

9. *Perpetual desolations.* You shall have perpetual desolation for your perpetual hatred.

10. *These two nations.* Israel and Judah. The Idumeans thought of conquering and possessing both; and they would have succeeded, but only the Lord was there; and this spoiled their projects, and blasted their hopes.

12. *They are laid desolate, they are given us to consume.* They exulted in seeing Judea overrun; and they rejoiced in the prospect of completing the ruin, when the Chaldeans had withdrawn from the land.

13. *Thus with your mouth ye have boasted against me.* You have said you would enter into those lands, and take them for your inheritance, though you knew that God had promised them to the Israelites, and that you should never have them for your portion.

14. *When the whole earth rejoiceth.* When the whole land shall rejoice in the restoration of the Jews, I will make you desolate.

15. *So will I do unto thee.* Others shall rejoice in your downfall as you have rejoiced at their downfall.

CHAPTER 36

1. *Prophesy unto the mountains of Israel.* This is a part of the preceding prophecy, though

MATTHEW HENRY

the Lord; and what he says to them he says *to the hills, to the rivers, to the valleys, to the desolate wastes* in the country, and to the cities *that are forsaken, v.* 4. and again *v.* 6. The people were gone, but the places, the mountains and valleys; these the Chaldeans could not carry away with them. Now, to show the mercy God had in reserve for the people, he is to speak of him as having a dormant kindness for the place.

I. The compassionate notice God takes of the present deplorable condition of the land of Israel. It has become both a *prey* and a *derision to the heathen that are round about, v.* 4. 1. They are all enriched with the blunder of it. No one thought it any crime to strip an Israelite. It is the common cry, when a man is down, *Down with him.* 2. It has become a derision to them. *The enemy said, "Aha! even the ancient high places are ours in possession," v.* 2. God takes notice of it here as an aggravation of the present calamity of Israel: *You are taken up in the lips of talkers and are an infamy of the people, v.* 3.

II. The expressions of God's just displeasure against those who triumphed in the desolations of the land of Israel, and Idumea particularly. 1. They carved out large possessions to themselves out of God's land; for so indeed it was: *"They have appointed my land into their possession* (*v.*5), and so not only invaded their neighbour's property, but intrenched upon God's prerogative." Those that had not an opportunity of making a prey of God's people made a reproach of them; so that they were *the shame of the heathen, v.* 6. 2. God has determined to reckon with them for it, and this *in the fire of his jealousy,* both for his own honour and for the honour of his people, *v.* 5. They spoke in their malice against God's people, and God will speak *in his jealousy and in his fury, v.* 6. *Surely the heathen that are about you, they shall bear their shame, v.* 7.

III. The promises of God's favour to his Israel and assurances given of great mercy in store for them. The prophet must say to the *mountains of Israel,* now *desolate and despised,* that God is *for them* and will *turn to them, v.* 9. Their rightful owners should return to the possession of them: *My people Israel are at hand to come, v.* 8. Though they are dispersed in many countries, yet they shall *come again to their own border,* Jer. xxxi. 17. The time is at hand for their return. The mountains of Israel are now desolate; but God will *cause men to walk upon them* again, *even his people Israel,* not as travellers, but as inhabitants. It was a type of the heavenly Canaan, to which all God's children are heirs. When the land had *enjoyed her sabbaths* for so many years, it should be so much the more fruitful. *You shall be tilled and sown* (*v.* 9) and shall *yield your fruit to my people Israel, v.* 8. The people of Israel should have a comfortable settlement, in their own land: The *cities shall be inhabited; the wastes shall be builded, v.* 10. And *I will settle you after your old estates, v.* 11. *I will do better unto you* now *than at your beginnings.* God will bring back to it *all the house of Israel, even all of it* (observe what an emphasis is laid upon that, *v.* 10), all *whose spirits God stirred up* to return. God's kingdom in the world is a growing kingdom; and his church, though for a time it may be diminished, shall recover itself and be again replenished. The reproach long since cast upon the land of Israel by the evil spies, and of late revived, that *it was a land that ate up the inhabitants* of it by famine, sickness, and the sword, should be quite rolled away. *Thou shalt no more bereave them of men* (*v.* 12), shalt *devour men no more, v.* 14. When the nation is made to flourish in peace (*v.* 15), especially when it is reformed; when sin is taken away, then they *hear no more the reproach of the people.*

Verses 16–24

I. How God's name had suffered both by the sins and by the miseries of Israel. 1. God's glory had been injured by the sin of Israel when they were in their own land, *v.* 17. It was a good land, a land that had the eye of God upon it. *But they defiled it by their own way.* What was unclean might not be made use of. By the abuse of the gifts of God's bounty to us we forfeit the use of them; and, the mind and conscience being defiled with guilt, no comfort is allowed us, *nothing is pure* to us. They *shed blood and worshipped idols* (*v.* 18) and with those sins *defiled the land.* God was righteous for he *judged them according to their way and according to their doings, v.* 19. 2. When they *entered into the land of the heathen* God had no glory by them there; but, on the contrary, his holy name was profaned, *v.* 20. The enemies of God took occasion to reproach God, as unable to protect his own worshippers and to make good his own grants.

JAMIESON, FAUSSET, BROWN

personified; Israel's elevation is moral, not merely physical, as Edom's. Her hills are "the everlasting hills" of Jacob's prophecy (Gen. 49:26). "The enemy" (Edom, the singled-out representative of all God's foes), with a shout of exultation, "Aha!" had claimed, as the nearest kinsman of Israel (the brother of their father Esau), his vacated inheritance; as much as to say, the so-called "everlasting" inheritance of Israel and of the "hills," which typified the unmoved perpetuity of it (Ps. 125:1, 2), has come to an end, in spite of the promise of God, and has become "ours" (cf. Deut. 32:13; 33:15). **3.** Lit., "Because, even because." **swallowed you up**—lit., "panted after" you, as a beast after its prey; implying the greedy cupidity of Edom as to Israel's inheritance (Ps. 56:1, 2). **lips of talkers**—lit., "lips of *the tongue,*" i.e., of the slanderer, the man of tongue. Edom slandered Israel because of the connection of the latter with Jehovah, as though He were unable to save them. Deuteronomy 28:37, and Jeremiah 24:9 had foretold Israel's reproach among the heathen (Dan. 9:16). **4.** Inanimate creatures are addressed, to imply that the creature also, as it were, groans for deliverance from the bondage of corruption into the glorious liberty of the children of God (Rom. 8:19-21) [POLANUS]. The completeness of the renewed blessedness of all parts of the land is implied. **derision**—(Ps. 79:4). **5. to cast it out for a prey**—i.e., to take the land for a prey, its inhabitants being cast out. Or the land is compared to a prey cast forth to wild beasts. FAIRBAIRN needlessly alters the *Hebrew* pointing and translates, "that they may plunder its pasturage." **6. the shame of the heathen**—viz., the shame with which the heathen cover you (Ps. 123:3, 4). **7. lifted . . . mine hand**—in token of an oath (ch. 20:5; Gen. 14:22). **they shall bear their shame**—a *perpetual* shame; whereas the "shame" which Israel bore from these heathen was only for a time. **8. they are at hand to come** —i.e., the Israelites are soon about to return to their land. This proves that the primary reference of the prophecy is to the return from Babylon, which was "at hand," or comparatively near. But this only in part fulfilled the prediction, the full and final blessing in future, and the restoration from Babylon was an earnest of it. **10. wastes . . . builded**—Isaiah 58:12; 61:4; Amos 9:11, 12, 14, where, as here (ch. 34:23, 24), the names of David, Messiah's type, and Edom, Israel's foe, are introduced in connection with the coming restoration. **11. do better . . . than at your beginnings**— as in the case of Job (Job 42:12). Whereas the heathen nations fall irrevocably, Israel shall be more than restored; its last estate shall exceed even its first. **12. to walk upon you**—O mountains of Israel (vs. 8)! **thee . . . thou**—change from *plural* to *singular:* O hill of Zion, singled out from the other mountains of Israel (ch. 34:26); or land. **thou shalt no more . . . bereave them** *of men*—Thou shalt no more provoke God to bereave them *of children* (so the ellipsis ought to be supplied, as Ezekiel probably alludes to Jer. 15:7, "I will bereave them *of children*"). **13. Thou land devourest up men**—alluding to the words of the spies (Num. 13:32). The land personified is represented as doing that which was done in it. Like an unnatural mother it devoured, i.e., it was the grave of its people; of the Canaanites, its former possessors, through mutual wars, and finally by the sword of Israel; and now, of the Jews, through internal and external ills; e.g., wars, famine (to which vs. 30, "reproach of *famine* among the heathen," implies the allusion here is). **14. bereave**—so the *Keri* or *Hebrew Margin* reads, to correspond to "bereave" in vs. 13; but "cause to fall" or "stumble," in the *Hebrew* text or *Chetib,* being the more difficult reading, is the one least likely to come from a corrector; also, it forms a good transition to the next subject, viz., the moral *cause* of the people's calamities, viz., their *falls,* or *stumblings* through sin. The latter ceasing, the former also cease. So the same expression follows in vs. 15, "Neither shalt thou cause thy nations to *fall* any more." **17. removed woman**—(Lev. 15:19, etc.). **18, 19.** The reason for their removal was their sin, which God's holiness could not let pass unpunished; just as a woman's legal uncleanness was the reason for her being *separated* from the congregation. **20. profaned my holy name, when they**—the heathen—**said to them**—the Israelites. **These . . .** —The Israelites gave a handle of reproach to the heathen against God, who would naturally say, These who take usury, oppress, commit adultery, etc., and who, in such an abject plight, are "gone forth" as exiles "out of His land," are specimens of what Jehovah can or will effect, for His people,

ADAM CLARKE

it chiefly concerns the Jews. In it they are encouraged to expect a glorious restoration, and that none of the evil wishes of their adversaries should take place against them.

2. *Because the enemy hath said.* The Idumeans thought they would shortly be put in possession of all the strong places of Israel.

4. *Therefore . . . thus saith the Lord God to the mountains.* They shall possess neither mountain nor valley, hill nor dale, fountain nor river; for though in My justice I made you desolate, yet they shall not profit by your disasters. See vv. 5-7.

8. *For they are at hand to come.* The restoration of the Jews is so absolutely determined that you may rest assured it will take place, and be as confident relative to it as if you saw the different families entering into the Israelitish borders. It was near at hand in God's determination, though there were about fifty-eight of the seventy years unelapsed.

9. *Ye shall be tilled and sown.* The land shall be cultivated as it formerly was, when best peopled and at peace.

JOSEPH PARKER:

Verse 11. At the last he invariably says something that opens up a distant and ever-receding because ever-enlarging horizon. He says in this instance, "I will do better unto you than at your beginnings." He is able, let us say again with rising thankfulness, to do exceeding abundantly above all that we ask or think. The Church constantly exclaims, "Thou hast kept the good wine until now!" We never can get in advance of God. When we have reaped our most abundant harvest, he says, "This is only an earnest of the harvest you shall one day possess; I will do more for you and better unto you than at your beginnings." When does God move backwards? When does God give less and less to the children that love him and obey him?—*The People's Bible*

MATTHEW HENRY

Not for your sake, for you are most unworthy, but *for my holy name's sake* (*v.* 22), that *I may sanctify my great name*," *v.* 23.

II. How God would retrieve his honour by working a great reformation upon them and then working a great salvation for them. "I *will gather you out of all countries and bring you into your own land, v.* 24.

Verses 25–38

The people of God might be discouraged in their hopes of a restoration by the sense of their unfitness, and that is answered in these verses, with a promise that God would by his grace prepare them for the mercy and then bestow it. And this was in part fulfilled in that wonderful effect which the captivity in Babylon had upon the Jews there, that it effectually cured them of their inclination to idolatry.

I. God here promises that he will work a good work in them, *v.* 25–27. 1. That God would cleanse them from the pollutions of sin (*v.* 25): *I will sprinkle clean water upon you*, which signifies both the blood of Christ sprinkled upon the conscience to purify that and to take away the sense of guilt, and the grace of the Spirit sprinkled on the whole soul to purify it from all corrupt inclinations, as Naaman was cleansed from his leprosy by dipping in Jordan. And (*v.* 29) *I will save you from all your uncleannesses.* 2. That God would give them a *new heart*, a disposition of mind vastly different from what it was before. 3. That, instead of a *heart of stone*, insensible and unapt to receive divine impressions and to return devout affections, God would give a *heart of flesh*, a soft and tender heart, that has spiritual senses exercised, complying in everything with the will of God. 4. That since, besides our inclination to sin, we complain of an inability to do our duty, God will *cause them to walk in his statutes* and thoroughly furnish them with wisdom and will, and active powers, for every good work.

II. God here promises that he will take them into covenant with himself. The sum of the covenant of grace we have, *v.* 28.

III. When they are thus prepared for mercy they shall return to their possessions and be settled again in them (*v.* 28): *You shall dwell in the land that I gave to your fathers.* This shall follow upon the blessed reformation God would work among them (*v.* 33): "*In the day that I shall have cleansed you from all your iniquities*, and so shall have made you meet for the inheritance, *I will cause you to dwell in the cities*, and so put you in possession of the inheritance." This is God's method of mercy indeed, first to part men from their sins, and then to restore them to their comforts. Then they shall enjoy a plenty of all good things. *I will call for the corn and will increase it, v.* 29. The land that had long *lain desolate in the sight of all that passed by*, who looked upon it, some with contempt and some with compassion, shall again *be tilled* (*v.* 34). And such a blessing will God command on the *hand of the diligent* that all who pass by shall take notice of it, with wonder, *v.* 35. Crowds are a lovely sight in God's temple.

IV. He shows what shall be *the happy effects of this blessed change.* It shall bring them to an ingenuous repentance for their sins (*v.* 31): *Then shall you remember your own evil ways and shall loathe yourselves.* It shall have a happy effect upon their neighbours, for it shall bring them to a more clear knowledge of God (*v.* 36).

JAMIESON, FAUSSET, BROWN

and show what kind of a God this so-called holy, omnipotent, covenant-keeping God must be! (Isa. 52:5; Rom. 2:24). **21. I had pity for mine holy name**—i.e., I felt pity for it; God's own name, so dishonored, was the primary object of His pitying concern; then His people, secondarily, through His concern for it [FAIRBAIRN]. **22. not . . . for your sakes**—i.e., not for any merit in you; for, on the contrary, on your part, there is everything to call down continued severity (cf. Deut. 9:5, 6). The sole and sure ground of hope was God's regard to "His own name," as the God of covenant grace (Ps. 106:45), which He must vindicate from the dishonor brought on it by the Jews, before the heathen. **23. sanctify**—vindicate and manifest as holy, in opposition to the heathen reproaches of it brought on by the Jews' sins and their punishment (*Note,* vs. 20). **sanctified in you**—i.e., in respect of you; I shall be regarded in their eyes as the Holy One, and righteous in My dealings towards you (ch. 20:41; 28:22). **24.** Fulfilled primarily in the restoration from Babylon; ultimately to be so in the restoration "from all countries." **25.** The *external* restoration must be preceded by an *internal* one. The change in their condition must not be superficial, but must be based on a radical renewal of the heart. Then the heathen, understanding from the regenerated lives of God's people how holy God is, would perceive Israel's past troubles to have been only the necessary vindications of His righteousness. Thus God's name would be "sanctified" before the heathen, and God's people be prepared for outward blessings. **sprinkle . . . water**—phraseology taken from the law; viz., the water mixed with the ashes of a heifer sprinkled with a hyssop on the unclean (Num. 19:9-18); the thing signified being the cleansing blood of Christ sprinkled on the conscience and heart (Heb. 9:13, 14; 10:22; cf. Jer. 33:8; Eph. 5:26). **from all your idols**—Literal idolatry has ceased among the Jews ever since the captivity; so far, the prophecy has been already fulfilled; but "cleansing from *all* their idols," e.g., covetousness, prejudices against Jesus of Nazareth, is yet future. **26. new heart**—mind and will. **spirit**—motive and principle of action. **stony heart**—unimpressible in serious things; like the "stony ground" (Matt. 13), unfit for receiving the good seed so as to bring forth fruit. **heart of flesh**—not "carnal" in opposition to "spiritual"; but impressible and docile, fit for receiving the good seed. In ch. 18:31 they are commanded, "*Make you* a new heart, and a new spirit." Here God says, "A new heart will *I give* you, and a new spirit will *I put* within you." Thus the responsibility of man, and the sovereign grace of God, are shown to be coexistent. Man cannot make himself a new heart unless God gives it (Phil. 2:12, 13). **27. my spirit**—(ch. 11:19; Jer. 32:39). The partial reformation at the return from Babylon (Ezra 10:6, etc.; Neh. 8, 9) was an earnest of the full renewal hereafter under Messiah. **28. ye . . . my people, . . . I . . . your God**—(ch. 11:20; Jer. 30:22). **29. save . . . from all . . . uncleannesses**—the province of Jesus, according to the signification of His name (Matt. 1:21). To be specially exercised in behalf of the Jews in the latter days (Rom. 11:26). **call for . . . corn**—as a master "calls for" a servant; all the powers and productions of nature are the servants of Jehovah (Ps. 105:16; Matt. 8:8, 9). Cf. as to the subordination of all the intermediate agents to the Great First Cause, who will give "corn" and all good things to His people, Hos. 2: 21, 22; Zech. 8:12. **30. no more reproach of famine among the heathen**—to which their taunt (vs. 13), "Thou land devourest up men," in part referred. **31. remember your . . . evil ways**—with shame and loathing. The unexpected grace and love of God, manifested in Christ to Israel, shall melt the people into true repentance, which mere legal fear could not (ch. 16:61, 63; Ps. 130:4; Zech. 12:10; cf. Jer. 33:8, 9). **35. they shall say**—The heathen, who once made Israel's desolation a ground of reproach against the name of Jehovah Himself (vss. 20, 21); but now He so vindicates its sanctity (vss. 22, 23) that these same heathen are constrained to acknowledge Israel's more than renewed blessedness to be God's own work, and a ground for glorifying His name (vs. 36). **Eden**—as Tyre (the type of the world powers in general: so Assyria, a cedar "in the garden of God, Eden," ch. 31:8, 9), in original advantages, had been compared to "Eden, the garden of God" (ch. 28:13), from which she had fallen irrecoverably; so Israel, once desolate, is to be as "the garden of Eden" (Isa. 51:3), and is to be so unchangeably. **36. Lord . . . spoken . . . do it**—(Num. 23:19). **37. I will yet for this be inquired of**—so as to grant it. On

ADAM CLARKE

F. GARDINER:

"Not . . . for your sakes . . . but for mine holy name's sake" (v. 22). Compare Ex. 32; Num. 14; Deut. 6. This is the constant burden of God's teaching to His people throughout their history. Hence it is an idle objection to the Scripture narrative that it represents Israel as the favorite of heaven, and is thus just like the human legends of every other ancient nation. In fact, this narrative is unlike any other. It speaks of God as having chosen one nation as the means of accomplishing His purpose for the salvation of the whole world, but continually chastising them for their sins, again and again setting aside the mass of them, and restoring and purifying and blessing a remnant, not for their own sake, but for the accomplishment of His own holy purpose and promise, thus sanctifying His name.

—*Ellicott's Commentary on the Whole Bible*

25. *Then* (at the time of this great restoration) *will I sprinkle clean water upon you*—the truly cleansing water; the influences of the Holy Spirit typified by *water*, whose property it is to cleanse, whiten, purify, refresh, render healthy and fruitful. *And from all your idols.* False gods, false worship, false opinions, and false hopes.

26. *A new heart also will I give you.* I will change the whole of your infected nature; and give you new appetites, new passions; or, at least, the old ones purified and refined. The *heart* is generally understood to mean all the affections and passions.

29. *I will also save you from all your uncleannesses.* I repeat it, "I will save you from all your sins."

MATTHEW HENRY

V. He proposes these things to them, not as the *recompence* of their merits, but as the return of their prayers. They must own that the mercies they receive from God are not only not merited, but that they are a thousand times forfeited; they must be so far from boasting of their good works that they must be ashamed of their evil ways, and then they are best prepared for mercy. He requires that his people should *seek unto him*, when he is coming towards them in ways of mercy. They must pray for it, for by prayer God is sought.

JAMIESON, FAUSSET, BROWN

former occasions He had refused to be inquired of by Israel because the inquirers were not in a fit condition of mind to receive a blessing (ch. 14:3; 20:3). But hereafter, as in the restoration from Babylon (Neh. 8, 9; Dan. 9:3-20, 21, 23), God will prepare His people's hearts (vs. 26) to pray aright for the blessings which He is about to give (Ps. 102:13-17, 20; Zech. 12:10-14; 13:1). **like a flock**—resuming the image (ch. 34:23, 31). **38. As the holy flock**—the great flock of choice animals for sacrifice, brought up to Jerusalem at the three great yearly festivals, the passover, pentecost, and feast of the tabernacles.

ADAM CLARKE

MATTHEW HENRY — CHAPTER 37

Verses 1-14

I. The vision of a resurrection from death to life.

1. It is without doubt a most lively representation of a threefold resurrection. (1) The resurrection of souls from the death of sin to the life of righteousness, to a holy, heavenly, spiritual, and divine life, by the power of divine grace going along with the word of Christ, John v. 24, 25. (2) The resurrection of the gospel church, from an afflicted persecuted state, to liberty and peace. (3) The resurrection of the body at the great day, especially the bodies of believers that shall rise to life eternal.

2. The particulars of this vision.

(1) The deplorable condition of these dead bones. The prophet was in vision, carried out and set *in the midst of a valley*, probably that plain spoken of *ch.* iii. 22, where God then *talked with him*; and it was *full of bones*, of dead men's bones, scattered upon the face of the ground, as if some bloody battle had been fought there, and the slain left unburied, and nothing left but the bones, and those disjointed from one another and dispersed. *Lo, they were very dry*, having been long exposed to the sun and wind. The Jews in Babylon were like those dead and dry bones, unlikely ever to come together, less likely to be formed into a body, and least of all to be a living body. He was made to own their case deplorable, and not to be helped by any power less than that of God himself (*v.* 3): "Son of man, *can these bones live?* Can thy philosophy reach to put life into dry bones, or thy politics to restore a captive nation?" "Lord, thou knowest whether they can and whether they shall; if thou dost not put life into them, it is certain that they cannot live."

(2) The means used for the bringing of these dispersed bones together and these dead and dry bones to life. Ezekiel is ordered to *prophesy upon these bones* (*v.* 4 and again *v.* 9) to *prophesy to the wind.* So he *prophesied as he was commanded*, *v.* 7, 10. He must preach, and he did so; and the dead bones lived by a power that went along with the word of God which he preached. He must pray, and he did so; and the dead bones were made to live in answer to prayer; for *a spirit of life* entered into them. See the efficacy of the word and prayer, and the necessity of both, for the raising of dead souls. But we call in vain, still they are dead: still they are very dry; we must therefore be earnest with God in prayer for the working of the Spirit with the word: *Come, O breath!* and breathe upon them. God's grace can save souls without our preaching, but our preaching cannot save them without God's grace, and that grace must be sought by prayer.

(3) The wonderful effect of these means. Those that do as they are commanded, in the face of the greatest discouragements, need not doubt of success. Ezekiel looked down and prophesied upon the bones in the valley, and they became human bodies. *First*, That which he had to *say to them* was that God would infallibly raise them to life, *v.* 5 and again *v.* 6. *Secondly*, That which was immediately done for them was that they were moulded anew into shape. Even dead and dry bones begin to move when they are called to hear the word of the Lord. This was fulfilled, when, upon Cyrus's proclamation of liberty, those whose spirits God had stirred up began to think of making use of that liberty, and getting ready to be gone. But this was not all: *The bones came together bone to his bone*, under a divine direction; and, though there is in man a multitude of bones, yet of all the bones of those numerous slain not one was missing, not one missed its way, not one missed its place, but each knew and found its fellow. The dispersed bones came together and the displaced bones were knit together. Thus it was in the return of the Jews; those that were scattered in several parts of the province of Babylon came to their respective families. By degrees *sinews* and *flesh* came upon these bones, and the *skin covered them*, *v.* 8. This was fulfilled

JAMIESON, FAUSSET, BROWN — CHAPTER 37

Vss. 1-28. THE VISION OF DRY BONES REVIVIFIED, SYMBOLIZING ISRAEL'S DEATH AND RESURRECTION. Three stages in Israel's revival present themselves to the prophet's eye. 1. The new awakening of the people, the resurrection of the dead (ch. 37:1-14). 2. The reunion of the formerly hostile members of the community, whose contentions had affected the whole (ch. 37:15-28). 3. The community thus restored is strong enough to withstand the assault of Gog, etc. (chs. 38, 29) [EWALD]. **1. carried . . . in the spirit**—The matters transacted, therefore, were not literal, but in vision. **the valley**—probably that by the Chebar (ch. 3:22). The valley represents Mesopotamia, the scene of Israel's sojourn in her state of national deadness. **2. dry**—bleached by long exposure to the atmosphere. **3. can these bones live? . . . thou knowest**—implying that, humanly speaking, they could not; but faith leaves the question of possibility to rest with God, with whom nothing is impossible (Deut. 32: 39). An image of Christian faith which believes in the coming general resurrection of the dead, in spite of all appearances against it, because God has said it (John 5:21; Rom. 4:17; II Cor. 1:9). **4. Prophesy**—Proclaim God's quickening word to them. On account of this innate power of the divine word to effect its end, prophets are said to *do* that which they *prophesy as about to be done* (Jer. 1:10). **5. I . . . cause breath to enter into you**—So Isaiah 26:19, containing the same vision, refers *primarily* to Israel's restoration. Cf. as to God's renovation of the earth and all its creatures hereafter by His breath, Psalm 104:30. **ye shall live**—come to life *again.* **6. ye shall know that I am the Lord**—by the actual proof of My divinity which I will give in reviving Israel. **7. noise**—of the bones when coming in mutual collision. Perhaps referring to the decree of Cyrus, or the noise of the Jews' exultation at their deliverance and return. **bones came together**—lit., "*ye* bones came together"; as in Jeremiah 49:11 (*Hebrew*), "*ye* widows of thine shall trust in Me." The second person puts the scene vividly before one's eyes, for the whole resurrection scene is a *prophecy in action* to render more palpably to the people the prophecy in word (vs. 21). **8.** So far, they were only cohering in order as unsightly skeletons. The next step, that of covering them successively with sinews, skin, and flesh, gives them beauty; but still "no breath" of life in them. This may imply that Israel hereafter, as at the restoration from Babylon was the case in part, shall return to Judea unconverted at first (Zech. 13:8, 9). Spiritually: a man may assume all the semblances of spiritual life, yet have none, and so be dead before God. **9. wind**—rather, *the spirit* of life or *life-breath* (*Margin*). For it is distinct from "the four *winds*" from which it is summoned. **from the four winds**—implying that Israel is to be gathered from the four quarters of the earth (Isa. 43:5, 6; Jer. 31:8), even as they were "scattered into all the winds" (ch. 5:10; 12:14; 17:21; cf. Rev. 7:1, 4). **10.** Such honor God gives to the divine word, even in the mouth of a man. How much more when in the mouth of the Son of God! (John 5:25-29). Though this chapter does not *directly* prove the resurrection of the dead, it does so *indirectly;* for it takes for granted the future fact as one recognized by believing Jews, and so made the image of their national restoration (so Isa. 25:8; 26:19; Dan. 12:2; Hos. 6:2; 13:14; cf. *Note*, vs. 12). **11. Our bones are dried**—(Ps. 141: 7), explained by "our hope is lost" (Isa. 49:14); our national state is as hopeless of resuscitation, as marrowless bones are of reanimation. **cut off for our parts**—i.e., so far as we are concerned. There is nothing in us to give hope, like a withered branch "cut off" from a tree, or a limb from the body. **12. my people**—in antithesis to "for our parts" (vs. 11). The hope that is utterly gone, if looking at *them-*

ADAM CLARKE — CHAPTER 37

1. *The hand of the Lord was upon me.* The prophetic influence was communicated. *And carried me out in the spirit.* Or, And the Lord brought me out in the spirit; that is, a spiritual vision, in which all these things were doubtless transacted. *The valley which was full of bones.* This vision of the dry bones was designed, first, as an emblem of the then wretched state of the Jews; secondly, of the general resurrection of the body.

3. *Can these bones live?* Is it possible that the persons whose bones these are can return to life?

4. *Prophesy upon these bones.* Declare to your miserable countrymen the gracious designs of the Lord; show them that their state, however deplorable, is not hopeless.

5. *Behold, I will cause breath. Ruach* signifies both "soul, breath, and wind," and sometimes the "Spirit of God." "Soul" is its proper meaning in this vision, where it refers to the bones: "I will cause the soul to enter into you."

9. *Prophesy unto the wind. Ruach.* Address yourself to the "soul," and command it to enter into these well-organized bodies, that they may live. *Come from the four winds.* Souls, come from all parts where you are scattered, and reanimate these bodies from which you have been so long separated. *The four winds* signify all parts—in every direction. Literally it is, "Souls, come from the four souls"; "Breath, come from the four breaths"; or, "Wind, come from the four winds." But here *ruach* has both of its most general meanings, "wind" or "breath," and "soul."

11. *These bones are the whole house of Israel.* That is, their state is represented by these bones, and their restoration to their own land is represented by the revivification of these bones.

MATTHEW HENRY

when the captives got their effects about them, and the *men of their place helped them* with *silver*, and *gold*, and whatever they needed for their remove, Ezra i. 4. But still there was *no breath in them*; they wanted spirit and courage for such a difficult and hazardous enterprise as this was of returning to their own land. Ezekiel then looked up and prophesied to the *wind*, or *breath*, or *spirit*, and said, *Come, O breath! and breathe upon these slain*. In answer to this request, *the breath* immediately came *into them*, *v.* 10. The spirit of life is from God; he at first in the creation breathed into man the breath of life, and so he will at last in the resurrection. The dispirited captives were animated with resolution to break through all the discouragements that lay in the way of their return. And then they *stood upon their feet, an exceedingly great army*; not only living men, but effective men, fit for service and formidable.

II. The application of this vision to the present calamitous condition of the Jews in captivity: *These bones are the whole house of Israel*, both the ten tribes and the two.

1. The depth of despair to which they are now reduced, *v.* 11. When troubles continue long, hopes have been often frustrated, nothing but an active faith in the power, promise, and providence of God will keep them from quite dying away. "*Therefore*, because things have come thus to the last extremity, *prophesy to them*, and tell them, now is God's time to appear for them. *Jehovah-jireh—in the mount of the Lord it shall be seen*," *v.* 12–14.

Verses 15–28

Precious promises made of the happy state of the Jews after their return to their own land; but they have a further reference to the kingdom of the Messiah and the glories of gospel-times.

I. It is here promised that Ephraim and Judah shall be happily united. Ever since the desertion of the ten tribes from the house of David under Jeroboam, there had been continual feuds and animosities between the two kingdoms of Israel and Judah, even in the land of their captivity. Now there should be a coalition between them. This is here illustrated by a sign. The prophet was to take *two sticks*, and write upon one, *For Judah* (including Benjamin, those of the *children of Israel* that were *his companions*), upon the other, *For Joseph*, including the rest of the tribes, *v.* 16. These two sticks must be so framed as to fall into *one in his hand*, *v.* 17. The meaning was that Judah and Israel should become *one in the hand of God*, *v.* 19. 1. They shall be one, one nation, *v.* 22. They shall have no separate interests, and, consequently, no divided affections. They had been two sticks crossing and thwarting one another, beating and bruising one another; but now they shall become one, supporting and strengthening one another. 2. They shall be one in *God's hand*; by his power they shall be united. They shall be one in his hand, for his glory shall be the centre of their unity and his grace the cement of it. 3. They shall be one in their return out of captivity (*v.* 21). Their having been joint-sufferers will contribute to this blessed comprehension. Put many pieces of metal together into the furnace, and, when they are melted, they will run all together. God's loving them all was a good reason why they should love one another. 4. They shall all be the subjects of one king, and so they shall become one. The Jews, after their return, were under one government, and not divided as formerly. But this certainly looks further, to the kingdom of Christ; he is that one King in allegiance to whom all God's spiritual Israel shall cheerfully unite.

II. It is here promised that the Jews shall by their captivity be cured of their inclination to idolatry (*v.* 23). Two ways God will take to cure them of their idolatry: 1. By bringing them out of the way of temptation to it. 2. By changing the disposition of their mind: *I will cleanse them* (*v.* 23).

III. It is here promised that they shall be the people of God, and the subjects and sheep of Christ their King and Shepherd. These promises are here repeated (*v.* 23, 24) for the encouragement of the faith of Israel. *David, my servant, shall be king over them.* Christ is this David, Israel's King of old.

IV. It is here promised that they shall dwell comfortably, *v.* 25, 26. They shall dwell in the land of Israel. They shall have it by covenant; they shall come in again upon their old title, by virtue of the grant made unto *Jacob*, God's *servant*. They shall come to it by prescription. It was the inheritance of their ancestors, and therefore shall be theirs. They are *beloved for their fathers' sakes. They shall dwell therein* all their time, and shall leave it for an inheritance *to their children and their children's children for ever*. They shall live under a good government.

JAMIESON, FAUSSET, BROWN

selves, is sure for them in *God*, because He regards them as *His* people. Their covenant relation to God ensures His not letting death permanently reign over them. Christ makes the same principle the ground on which the literal resurrection rests. God had said, "I am the God of Abraham," etc.; God, by taking the patriarchs as *His*, undertook to do for them all that Omnipotence can perform: He, being the ever living God, is necessarily the God of, not dead, but living persons, i.e., of those whose bodies His covenant love binds Him to raise again. He can—and because He can—He will—He must [FAIRBAIRN]. He calls them "*My* people" when receiving them into favor; but "*thy* people," in addressing His servant, as if He would put them away from Him (ch. 13:17; 33:2; Exod. 32:7). **out of your graves**—out of your politically dead state, primarily in Babylon, finally hereafter in all lands (cf. ch. 6:8; Hos. 13:14). The Jews regarded the lands of their captivity and dispersion as their "graves"; their restoration was to be as "life from the dead" (Rom. 11:15). Before, the bones were in the open plain (vss. 1, 2); now, in the graves, i.e., some of the Jews were in the graves of actual captivity, others at large but dispersed. Both alike were nationally dead. **16. stick**—alluding to Numbers 17:2, the tribal rod. The union of the two rods was a prophecy in action of the brotherly union which is to reunite the ten tribes and Judah. As their severance under Jeroboam was fraught with the greatest evil to the covenant people, so the first result of both being joined by the spirit of life to God is that they become joined to one another under the one covenant King, Messiah-David. **Judah, and ... children of Israel his companions**—i.e., Judah and, besides Benjamin and Levi, those who had joined themselves to him of Ephraim, Manasseh, Simeon, Asher, Zebulun, Issachar, as having the temple and lawful priesthood in his borders (II Chron. 11:12, 13, 16; 15:9; 30:11, 18). The latter became identified with Judah after the carrying away of the ten tribes, and returned with Judah from Babylon, and so shall be associated with that tribe at the future restoration. **For Joseph, the stick of Ephraim**—Ephraim's posterity took the lead, not only of the other descendants of Joseph (cf. vs. 19), but of the ten tribes of Israel. For 400 years, during the period of the judges, with Manasseh and Benjamin, its dependent tribes, it had formerly taken the lead: Shiloh was its religious capital; Shechem, its civil capital. God had transferred the birthright from Reuben (for dishonoring his father's bed) to Joseph, whose representative, Ephraim, though the younger, was made (Gen. 48:19; I Chron. 5:1). From its pre-eminence "Israel" is attached to it as "companions." The "all" in this case, not in that of Judah, which has only attached as "companions" the children of Israel" (i.e., some of them, viz., those who followed the fortunes of Judah), implies that the *bulk* of the ten tribes did not return at the restoration from Babylon, but are distinct from Judah, until the coming union with it at the restoration. **18.** God does not explain the symbolical prophecy until the Jews have been stimulated by the type to consult the prophet. **19.** The union effected at the restoration from Babylon embraced but comparatively few of Israel; a future complete fulfilment must therefore be looked for. **stick of Joseph ... in the hand of Ephraim**—Ephraim, of the descendants of Joseph, had exercised the rule among the ten tribes: that rule, symbolized by the "stick," was now to be withdrawn from him, and to be made one with the other, Judah's rule, in God's hand. **them**—the "*stick* of Joseph," would strictly require "it"; but Ezekiel expresses the sense, viz., the ten tribes who were subject to it. **with him**—i.e., Judah; or "it," i.e., the stick of Judah. **22. one nation**—(Isa. 11: 13; Jer. 3:18; Hos. 1:11). **one king**—not Zerubbabel, who was not a king either in fact or name, and who ruled over but a few Jews, and that only for a few years; whereas the King here reigns for ever. MESSIAH is meant (ch. 34:23, 24). The union of Judah and Israel under King Messiah symbolizes the union of Jews and Gentiles under Him, partly now, perfectly hereafter (vs. 24; John 10:16). **23.** (Ch. 36:25.) **out of ... their dwelling-places**—(Ch. 36:28, 33). I will remove them from the scene of their idolatries to dwell in their own land, and to serve idols no more. **24. David**—Messiah (*Notes*, ch. 34:23, 24). **25. for ever**—(Isa. 60:21; Joel 3:20; Amos 9:15).

ADAM CLARKE

12. *I will open your graves.* Here is a pointed allusion to the general resurrection; a doctrine properly credited and understood by the Jews, and to which our Lord refers, John v. 25, 28-29: "The hour is coming, in the which all that are in the graves shall hear his voice, and shall come forth." *And cause you to come up out of your graves.* I am determined that you shall be restored; so that were you even in your graves, as mankind at the general resurrection, yet My all-powerful voice shall call you forth.

13. *When I have opened your graves.* When I shall have done for you what was beyond your hope, and deemed impossible, then you shall know that I am Jehovah.

14. *And shall put my spirit. Ruchi.* Here *ruach* is taken for the Holy Ghost.

Three degrees or processes have been remarked in this mystic vision. When the prophet was commanded to prophesy—to foretell, on the authority of God, that there should be a restoration to their own land—(1) There was a noise, which was followed by a general shaking, during which the bones became arranged and united. (2) The flesh and skin came upon them, so that the dry bones were no longer seen. (3) The spirit or soul came into them, and they stood up perfectly vivified.

Perhaps these might be illustrated by three periods of time, which marked the regeneration of the Jewish polity. (1) The publication of the edict of Cyrus in behalf of the Jews, which caused a general shaking or stir among the people, so that the several families began to approach each other, and prepare for their return to Judea, Ezra i. 2-3. (2) The edict published by Darius in the second year of his reign, Ezra iv. 23-24, which removed the impediments thrown in the way of the Jews, Ezra vi. 6-7, etc. (3) The mission of Nehemiah, with orders from Artaxerxes to complete the building of the Temple and the city, Neh. ii. 7, etc. Then the Jews became a great army, and found themselves in sufficient force to defend themselves and city against all their enemies.

16. *Son of man, take thee one stick.* The two sticks mentioned in this symbolical transaction represented, as the text declares, the two kingdoms of Israel and Judah, which were formed in the days of Rehoboam, and continued distinct till the time of the Captivity. The kingdom of Judah was composed of the tribes of Judah and Benjamin, with the Levites; all the rest went off in the schism with Jeroboam, and formed the kingdom of Israel. Though some out of those tribes did rejoin themselves to Judah, yet no whole tribe ever returned to that kingdom.

19. *The stick of Joseph, which is in the hand of Ephraim.* Jeroboam, the first king of the ten tribes, was an Ephraimite. Joseph represents the ten tribes in general; they were *in the hand of Ephraim*, that is, under the government of Jeroboam.

22. *I will make them one nation.* There was no distinction after the return from Babylon.

24. *And David my servant shall be king.* That this refers to Jesus Christ, see proved, chap. xxxiv. 23.

25. *The land that I have given unto Jacob my servant.* Jacob means here the twelve tribes; and the land given to them was the whole land of Palestine; consequently the promise states that, when they return, they are to possess the whole of the Promised Land.

MATTHEW HENRY

V. It is here promised that God will dwell among them: *I will set my sanctuary in the midst of them for evermore; my tabernacle also shall be with them, v.* 26, 27. They shall have opportunity of keeping up communion with him, which will be the comfort of their lives. They shall have the means of grace. By the oracles of God in his tabernacle they shall be made wiser and better, and all their children shall be taught of the Lord. Thus their covenant relation to God shall be improved and the bond of it strengthened.

VI. Both God and Israel shall have the honour of this among the heathen, *v.* 26. "The very heathen shall be made to know that *the Lord sanctifies* Israel, because his sanctuary is, and shall be, in the midst of them."

JAMIESON, FAUSSET, BROWN

26. covenant of peace—better than the old legal covenant, because an unchangeable covenant of grace (ch. 34: 25; Isa. 55:3; Jer. 32:40). **I will place them**—set them in an established position; no longer unsettled as heretofore. **my sanctuary**—the temple of God; spiritual in the heart of all true followers of Messiah (II Cor. 6:16); and, in some literal sense, in the restored Israel (chs. 40-44). **27. My tabernacle . . . with them**—as foretold (Gen. 9:27); John 1:14, "The Word . . . *dwelt* among us" (lit., "tabernacled"); first, in humiliation; hereafter, in manifested glory (Rev. 21:3). **28.** (Ch. 36:23.) **sanctify Israel**—set it apart as holy unto Myself and inviolable (Exod. 19:5, 6).

ADAM CLARKE

26. *Covenant of peace.* See this explained, chap. xxxiv. 25.

27. *My tabernacle.* Jesus Christ, the true Tabernacle, in whom dwelt all the fullness of the Godhead bodily.

CHAPTER 38

TODAY'S DICTIONARY OF THE BIBLE:

Gog. The name of the leader of the hostile party described in Ezek. 38, 39, as coming from the "north country" and assailing the people of Israel to their own destruction. This prophecy has been regarded as fulfilled in the conflicts of the Maccabees with Antiochus, the invasion and overthrow of the Chaldeans, and the temporary successes and destined overthrow of the Turks. But "all these interpretations are unsatisfactory and inadequate. The vision respecting God and Magog in the Apocalypse (Rev. 20:8) is in substance a reannouncment of this prophecy of Ezekiel. But while Ezekiel contemplates the great conflict in a more general light as what was certainly to be connected with the times of the Messiah, and should come then to its last decisive issues, John, on the other hand, writing from the commencement of Messiah's times, describes there the last struggles and victories of the cause of Christ. In both cases alike the vision describes the final workings of the world's evil and its results in connection with the kingdom of God, only the starting point is placed further in advance in the one case than in the other."

The only reasonable historical identification would equate Gog with Gyges, king of Lydia. The popular equation with Russia is impossible to maintain on etymological grounds, and any specific modern identification would be speculative.

Magog—*region of Gog*—the second of the "sons" of Japheth (Gen. 10:2; 1 Chron. 1:5). In Ezekiel (38:2; 39:6) it is the name of a nation, probably some Scythian or Tartar tribe descended from Japheth. They are described as skilled horsemen, and expert in the use of the bow. The Latin father Jerome says that this word denotes "Scythian nations, fierce and innumerable, who live beyond the Caucasus and the Lake Maeotis, and near the Caspian Sea, and spread out even onward to India." Perhaps the name "represents the Assyrian *Mat Gugi*, or 'country of Gugu,' the Gyges of the Greeks" (Sayce's *Races*, etc.).

Verses 1–13

The critical expositors have enough to do here to enquire about Gog and Magog. Some think they find them afar off, in Scythia, Tartary, and Russia. Others think they find them nearer the land of Israel, in Syria, and Asia the Less. Ezekiel is appointed to prophesy against Gog, and to tell him that *God is against him, v.* 2, 3.

CHAPTER 38

Vss. 1-23. The Assault of Gog, and God's Judgment on Him. The objections to a *literal* interpretation of the prophecy are—1. The ideal nature of the name Gog, which is the root of Magog, the only kindred name found in Scripture or history. 2. The nations congregated are selected from places most distant from Israel, and from one another, and therefore most unlikely to act in concert (Persians and Libyans, etc.). 3. The whole spoil of Israel could not have given a handful to a tithe of their number, or maintained the myriads of invaders a single day (ch. 38:12, 13). 4. The wood of their invaders' weapons was to serve for fuel to Israel for seven years! And *all* Israel were to take seven months in burying the dead! Supposing a million of Israelites to bury each two corpses a day, the aggregate buried in the 180 working days of the seven months would be 360 millions of corpses! Then the pestilential vapors from such masses of victims before they were all buried! What Israelite could live in such an atmosphere? 5. The scene of the Lord's controversy here is different from that in Isaiah 34:6, Edom, which creates a discrepancy. (But probably a different judgment is alluded to.) 6. The gross carnality of the representation of God's dealings with His adversaries is inconsistent with Messianic times. It therefore requires a non-literal interpretation. The prophetical delineations of the divine principles of government are thrown into the familiar forms of Old Testament relations. The final triumph of Messiah's truth over the most distant and barbarous nations is represented as a literal conflict on a gigantic scale, Israel being the battlefield, ending in the complete triumph of Israel's anointed King, the Saviour of the world. It is a *prophetical* parable [Fairbairn]. However, though the *details* are not literal, the distinctiveness in this picture, characterizing also parallel descriptions in writers less idealy picturesque than Ezekiel, gives probability to a more definite and *generally* literal interpretation. The awful desolations caused in Judea by Antiochus Epiphanes, of Syria (I Maccabees; and Porphyry, quoted by Jerome on Ezekiel), his defilement of Jehovah's temple by sacrificing swine and sprinkling the altar with the broth, and setting up the altar of Jupiter Olympius, seem to be an earnst of the final desolations to be caused by Antichrist in Israel, previous to His overthrow by the Lord Himself, coming to reign (cf. Dan. 8:10-26; 11:21-45; 12:1; Zech. 13:9; 14:2, 3). Grotius explains Gog as a name taken from Gyges, king of Lydia; and Magog as Syria, in which was a city called Magag (Pliny 5. 28). What Ezekiel stated more generally, Revelation 20:7-9 states more definitely as to the anti-Christian confederacy which is to assail the beloved city. **2. Gog**—the prince of the land of Magog. The title was probably a common one of the kings of the country, as "Pharaoh" in Egypt. Chakan was the name given by the Northern Asiatics to their king, and is still a title of the Turkish sultan: "Gog" may be a contraction of this. In Ezekiel's time a horde of northern Asiatics, termed by the Greeks "Scythians," and probably including the Moschi and Tibareni, near the Caucasus, here ("Meshech . . . Tubal") undertook an expedition against Egypt (Herodotus, 1. 103-106). These names might be adopted by Ezekiel from the historical fact familiar to men at the time, as ideal titles for the great last anti-Christian confederacy. **1. Magog**—(Gen. 10:2; I Chron. 1:5). The name of a land belonging to Japheth's posterity. *Maha*, in Sanscrit, means "land." Gog is the ideal political head of the region. In Revelation 20:8, Gog and Magog are two peoples. **the chief prince**—rather, "prince of *Rosh*," or "*Rhos*" [LXX]. The Scythian Tauri in the Crimea were so called. The Araxes also was called "Rhos." The modern Rus-

CHAPTER 38

JOSEPH PARKER:

Gog, in the land of Magog, prince of Rosh, Meshech, and Tubal, will invade the restored land of Israel from the far distant northern land by the appointment of God in the last times, and with a powerful army of numerous nations (ch. 38:1–9), with the intention of plundering Israel, now dwelling in security, that the Lord may sanctify Himself upon him before the world (vv. 10–16). But when Gog, of whom earlier prophets have already prophesied, shall fall upon Israel, he is to be destroyed by a wrathful judgment from the Lord, that the nations may know that God is the Lord (vv. 17–23). On the mountains of Israel will Gog with all his hosts and nations succumb to the judgment of God (ch. 39:1–8). The inhabitants of the cities of Israel will spend seven years in burning the weapons of the fallen foe, and seven months burying the corpses in a valley, which will receive its name from this, so as to purify the land (vv. 9–16); while in the meantime all the birds and wild beasts will satiate themselves with the flesh and blood of the fallen (vv. 17–20). By this judgment will all the nations as well as Israel know that it was on account of its sins that the Lord formerly gave up Israel into the power of the heathen, but that now He will no more forsake His redeemed people, because He has poured out His Spirit upon it (vv. 21–29).—*The People's Bible*

2. *Son of man, set thy face against Gog, the land of Magog.* This is allowed to be the most difficult prophecy in the Old Testament. It is difficult to us, because we know not the king nor people intended by it; but I am satisfied they were well-known by these names in the time that the prophet wrote. Rev. David Martin, pastor of the Waloon Church at Utrecht, concludes, after examining all previous opinions, that Antiochus Epiphanes, the great enemy of the Israelites, is alone intended here; and that *Gog*, which signifies "covered," is an allusion to the well-known character of Antiochus, whom historians describe as an artful, cunning, and dissembling man. See Dan. viii. 23, 25; xi. 23, 27, 32. *Magog* he supposes to mean the country of Syria. Of this opinion the following quotation from Pliny, *Hist. Nat.*, lib. v, c. 23, seems a proof; who, speaking of Coele-Syria, says: "Coele-Syria has Apamia separated from the tetrarchy of the Nazarenes by the river Marsyia; and Bambyce, otherwise called Hierapolis; but by the Syrians, Magog." I shall at present examine the text by this latter opinion. *Chief prince of Meshech and Tubal.* These probably mean the auxiliary forces, over whom Antiochus was supreme; they were the Muscovites and Cappadocians.

MATTHEW HENRY

I. The confusion which God designed to put this enemy to. It is remarkable that this is put first in the prophecy; before it is foretold that God will *bring him forth* against Israel it is foretold that God will *put hooks into his jaws* and *turn him back* (*v.* 4).

II. The undertaking which he designed to engage him in, in order to this defeat. 1. The nations that shall be confederate in this enterprise against Israel are many, and great, and mighty (*v.* 5, 6), *Persia, Ethiopia,* &c. Antiochus had an army made up of all the nations here named. 2. They are well furnished with arms—*horses and horsemen* (*v.* 4) bravely equipped *with all sorts of armour, bucklers and shields* for defence, *and all handling swords* for offence. "*Be thou prepared, and do thou prepare*" (*v.* 7). This call to prepare seems to be ironical—*Do thy worst,* but I will *turn thee back;* like that Isa. viii. 9. 3. Their design is against *the mountains of Israel* (*v.* 8), against *the land that is brought back from the sword.* It is not long since it was harassed with the sword of war, and it has scarcely recovered any strength since it was brought down by war. It is a people that *dwell safely, all of them, in unwalled villages,* very secure, and *having neither bars nor gates, v.* 11. They intend no mischief to their neighbours, for they fear no mischief from them. 4. That which the enemy has in view, in forming this project, is to enrich himself and to make himself master, not of the country, but of the wealth of it. It came into Antiochus's mind what a singular people these religious Jews were, and how their worship condemned the idolatries of their neighbours, and therefore, in enmity to their religion, he would plague them. It came into his mind what a wealthy people they were, that they had *gotten cattle and goods in the midst of the land* (*v.* 12). He came to this resolve (*v.* 11, 12): "*I will go up to the land of unwalled villages;* yea, that I will; it will cost me nothing to make them all my own." These were the thoughts that came into the mind of this wicked prince, and God knew them. 5. According to the project thus formed he pours in all his forces upon the land of Israel, and finds those that are ready to come in to his assistance with the same prospects (*v.* 9).

Verses 14–23

This latter part of the chapter is a repetition of the former.

I. It is again foretold that this spiteful enemy should make a formidable descent upon the land of Israel (*v.* 15). Thou shalt soon find that there is *no enchantment against Jacob,* that *no weapon formed against them shall prosper;* thou shalt know to thy cost, shalt know to thy shame, that though they have no walls, nor bars, nor gates, they have God himself, a *wall of fire, round about them,* and that he who *touches them touches the apple of his eye;* whosoever meddles with them meddles to his own hurt. But God said: *I will bring thee against my land.* This is strange news, that God will not only permit his enemies to come against his own children, but will himself bring them. It is "*that the heathen may know me* to be the only living and true God *when I shall be sanctified in thee,* O Gog! that is, in thy defeat and destruction *before their eyes,* that all the nations may see, and say, *There is none like unto the God of Jeshurun, that rides on the heavens for the help of his people.*"

II. Reference is herein had to the predictions of the former prophets (*v.* 17). Moses spoke in his prophecy of the latter days, Deut. xxxii. 43, and David, Ps. ix. 15, and often elsewhere in the Psalms. This is the leviathan of whom Isaiah spoke (Isa. xxvii. 1), that congress of the nations of which Joel spoke, Joel iii. 1.

III. It is here foretold that this furious formidable enemy should be utterly cut off in this attempt upon Israel. This is supposed by many to have its accomplishment in the many defeats given by the Maccabees to the forces of Antiochus. *When he comes up* in pride and anger *against the land of Israel,* then *God's fury shall come up in his face,* which is an allusion to men, whose colour rises in their faces when some high affront is offered them, *v.* 18. His forces shall be put into the greatest confusion and consternation imaginable (*v.* 19): *There shall be a great shaking of* them *in the land of Israel* (*v.* 20), such as shall affect the *fishes* and *fowls,* the *beasts* and *creeping things,* and

JAMIESON, FAUSSET, BROWN

sians may have hence *assumed* their name, as Moscow and Tobolsk from Meshech and Tubal, though their *proper* ancient name was *Slavi,* or *Wends.* HENGSTENBERG supports *English Version,* as "Rosh" is not found in the Bible. "Magog was Gog's original kingdom, though he acquired also Meshech and Tubal, so as to be called their *chief prince.*" 3. His high sounding titles are repeated to imply the haughty selfconfidence of the invader as if invincible. **4. turn thee back**—as a refractory wild beast, which thinks to take its own way, but is bent by a superior power to turn on a course which must end in its destruction. Satan shall be, by overruling Providence, permitted to deceive them to their ruin (Rev. 20:7, 8). **hooks into thy jaws**—(ch. 29:4; II Kings 19:28). **5. Persia . . . Libya**—expressly specified by APPIAN as supplying the ranks of Antiochus' army. **6. Gomer**—the Celtic Cimmerians of Crim-Tartary. **Togarmah**—the Armenians of the Caucasus, south of Iberia. **7.** Irony. **Prepare thee** and all thine with all needful accoutrements for war —that ye may perish together. **be . . a guard unto them**—i.e., *if thou canst.* **8. thou shalt be visited** —in wrath, by God (Isa. 29:6). Probably there is allusion to Isaiah 24:21, 22, "The host of the high ones . . . shall be gathered . . . as prisoners . . . in the pit, . . . and *after many days shall they be visited.*" I therefore prefer *English Version* to GROTIUS' rendering, "Thou shalt get *the command*" of the expedition. The "after many days" is defined by "in the latter years," i.e., in the times just before the coming of Messiah, viz., under Antiochus, before His first coming; under Antichrist, before His second coming. **the mountains of Israel . . . always waste**—i.e., waste during the long period of the captivity, the earnest of the much longer period of Judea's present desolation (to which the language "always waste" more fully applies). This marks the impious atrocity of the act, to assail God's people, who had only begun to recover from their protracted calamities. **but it is brought . . . and they shall dwell**—rather, "And they (the Israelites) were brought . . . dwelt safely" [FAIRBAIRN]. *English Version* means, "Against Israel, which has been waste, but which (i.e., whose people) is now (at the time of the invasion) brought forth out of the nations where they were dispersed, and shall be found by the invader dwelling securely, so as to seem an easy prey to him." **9. cloud to cover the land**—with the multitude of thy forces. **10. an evil thought**—as to attacking God's people in their defenseless state. **11. dwell safely**—i.e., securely, without fear of danger (cf. Esther 9:19). Antiochus, the type of Antichrist, took Jerusalem without a blow. **12. midst of the land**—lit., "the navel" of the land (Judg. 9:37, *Margin*). So, in ch. 5:5, Israel is said to be set "in the midst of the nations"; not physically, but morally, a central position for being a blessing to the world: so (as the favored or "beloved city," Rev. 20:9) an object of envy. GROTIUS translates, "In the *height* of the land" (so vs. 8), "the mountains of Israel," Israel being morally elevated above the rest of the world. **13. Sheba . . .** —These mercantile peoples, though not taking an active part against the cause of God, are well pleased to see others do it. Worldliness makes them ready to deal in the ill-gotten spoil of the invaders of God's people. Gain is before godliness with them (I Maccabees 3:41). **young lions**—daring princes and leaders. **14. shalt thou not know it?**—to thy cost, being visited with punishment, while Israel dwells safely. **16. I will bring thee against my land, that the heathen may know me**— So in Exodus 9:16, God tells Pharaoh, "For this cause have I raised thee up, for to show in thee My power; and that My name may be declared throughout all the earth." **17. thou he of whom I have spoken in old time**—Gog, etc. are here identified with the enemies spoken of in other prophecies (Num. 24:17-24; Isa. 27:1; cf. Isa. 26:20, 21; Jer. 30:23, 24; Joel 3:1; Mic. 5:5, 6; Isa. 14:12-14; 59: 19). God is represented as addressing Gog at the time of his assault; therefore, the "old time" is the time long prior, when Ezekiel uttered these prophecies; so, he also, as well as Daniel (11) and Zechariah (14) are included among "the prophets of Israel" here. **many years**—ago. **18. fury shall come up in my face**—lit., "nose"; in *Hebrew,* the idiomatic expression for *anger,* as men in anger breathe strongly through the nostrils. Anthropopathy: God stooping to human modes of thought (Ps. 18: 8). **19. great shaking**—an earthquake: physical agitations after accompanying social and moral revolutions. Foretold also in Joel 3:16; (cf. Hag. 2: 6, 7; Matt. 24:7, 29; Rev. 16:18). **20. fishes**—disturbed by the fleets which I will bring. **fowls . . .** frightened at the sight of so many men: an ideal

ADAM CLARKE

4. *I will turn thee back.* Your enterprise shall fail.

5. *Persia.* That a part of this country was tributary to Antiochus, see 1 Macc. iii. 31. *Ethiopia, and Libya.* That these were auxiliaries of Antiochus is evident from Dan. xi. 43: "The Libyans and Ethiopians shall be at his steps."

9. *Thou shalt ascend and come like a storm.* It is observable that Antiochus is thus spoken of by Daniel, chap. xi. 40: "The king of the north"—Antiochus, "shall come against him" ("the king of the south" is the king of Egypt) "like a whirlwind."

10. *Shall things come into thy mind, and thou shalt think an evil thought.* Antiochus purposed to invade and destroy Egypt, as well as Judea; see Dan. xi. 31-32, 36.

12. *To take a spoil . . . and a prey.* When Antiochus took Jerusalem he gave the pillage of it to his soldiers, and spoiled the Temple of its riches, which were immense. See Joseph. *War,* lib. 1, c. 1.

13. *Sheba, and Dedan.* The Arabians, anciently great plunderers; and Tarshish, the inhabitants of the famous isle of Tartessus, the most noted merchants of the time. They are here represented as coming to Antiochus before he undertook the expedition, and bargaining for the spoils of the Jews. *Art thou come to take a spoil . . . to carry away silver and gold . . . cattle and goods?*

16. *When I shall be sanctified in thee, O Gog.* By the defeat of his troops under Lysias, his general, 1 Mac. iii. 32-33, etc., and chap. vi. 6.

MATTHEW HENRY

much more *the men that are upon the face of the earth.* He shall be routed and utterly ruined; both earth and heaven shall be armed against him. The great men of Syria shall undermine and overthrow one another.

The artillery of heaven shall also be drawn out against them: *I will rain upon him an overflowing rain, v.* 22. He comes like a storm upon Israel, *v.* 9. But God will come like a storm upon him.

JAMIESON, FAUSSET, BROWN

picture. **mountains**—i.e., the fortresses on the mountains. **steep places**—lit., "stairs" (Song of Sol. 2:14); steep terraces for vines on the sides of hills, to prevent the earth being washed down by the rains. **every wall**—of towns. **21. every man's sword . . . against his brother**—I will destroy them partly by My people's sword, partly by their swords being turned against one another (cf. II Chron. 20: 23). **22. plead**—a forensic term; because God in His inflictions acts on the principles of His own immutable *justice,* not by arbitrary impulse (Isa. 66: 16; Jer. 25:31). **blood . . . hailstones, fire**—(Rev. 8: 7; 16:21). The imagery is taken from the destruction of Sodom and the plagues of Egypt (cf. Ps. 11: 6). Antiochus died by "pestilence" (II Maccabees 9:5).

ADAM CLARKE

21. *I will call for a sword against him.* Meaning Judas Maccabeus, who defeated his army under Lysias, making a horrible carnage.

22. *Great hailstones, fire, and brimstone.* These are probably figurative expressions, to signify that the whole tide of the war should be against him, and that his defeat and slaughter should be great.

MATTHEW HENRY — CHAPTER 39

Verses 1–7

This prophecy begins as that before (*ch.* xxxviii. 3, 4, *I am against thee, and I will turn thee back*). 1. His soldiers shall be disarmed and so disabled to carry on their enterprise, *v.* 3. 2. He and the greatest part of his army shall be slain in the field of battle (*v.* 4). Thou shalt *fall upon the open field* (*v.* 5). Even upon the mountains he shall not find a pass that he shall be able to maintain, and upon the open field he shall not find a road for his escape. Never was army so totally routed as this. And, for its greater infamy and reproach, their bodies shall be a feast to the birds of prey, *v.* 4. 3. His country also shall be made desolate: *I will send a fire on Magog* (*v.* 6) and *among those that dwell carelessly,* or confidently, *in the isles,* that is, the nations of the Gentiles. His people Israel shall hereby know more of God's name, of his power and goodness, his care of them, his faithfulness to them. And this is God's method of dealing with men, first to enlighten their understandings, and by that means to influence the whole man; he first makes us to know his holy name, and so keeps us from polluting it and engages us to honour it. The heathen those that never knew it, or would not own it, shall *know that I am the Lord, the Holy One in Israel.*

Verses 8–22

Though this prophecy was to have its accomplishment in the latter days, yet it is here spoken of as if it were already accomplished, because it is certain (*v.* 8). To represent the routing of the army of Gog as very great, here are three things specified as the consequences of it. It was God himself that gave the defeat; we do not find that the people of Israel drew a sword or struck a stroke: but,

I. They shall *burn their weapons,* their *bows and arrows,* which *fell out of their hands* (*v.* 3), everything that is combustible. They should have no occasion to *take wood out of the field or forests* for *seven years* together (*v.* 10), such vast quantities of weapons shall there be left upon the open field where the enemy fell.

II. They shall bury their dead. The slain lie dispersed on the mountains of Israel, and it is left to the house of Israel to bury them. A place shall be appointed for the burying of them, *the valley of the passengers, on the east of the sea,* either the salt sea or the sea of Tiberias. And it shall be called, *The valley of Hamon-gog,* that is, *of the multitude of Gog.* Acts of humanity add much to the renown of God's Israel; and a good work it is to bury the dead, though they be strangers and enemies to the commonwealth of Israel.

JAMIESON, FAUSSET, BROWN — CHAPTER 39

Vss. 1-29. Continuation of the Prophecy against Gog. **1.** Repeated from ch. 38:3, to impress the prophecy more on the mind. **2. leave but the sixth part of thee**—*Margin,* "strike thee with six plagues" (viz., pestilence, blood, overflowing rain, hailstones, fire, brimstone, ch. 38:22); or, "draw thee back with an hook of six teeth" (ch. 38:4), the six teeth being those six plagues. Rather, "lead thee about" [Ludovicus de Dieu and LXX]. As Antiochus was led (to his ruin) to leave Egypt for an expedition against Palestine, so shall the last great enemy of God be. **north parts**—from the extreme north [Fairbairn]. **3. bow**—in which the Scythians were most expert. **4, 5.** (Cf. vss. 17-20.) **upon the mountains of Israel**—The scene of Israel's preservation shall be that of the ungodly foe's destruction. **6. carelessly**—in self-confident security. **the isles**—Those dwelling in maritime regions, who had helped Gog with fleets and troops, shall be visited with the fire of God's wrath in their own lands. **7. not let them pollute my holy name**—by their sins bringing down judgments which made the heathen think that I was unable or unwilling to save My people. **8. it is come . . . it is done**—The prediction of the salvation of My people, and the ruin of their enemy, is come to pass—is done: expressing that the event foretold is as certain as if it were already accomplished. **9, 10.** The burning of the foe's weapons implies that nothing belonging to them should be left to pollute the land. The *seven* years (*seven* being the sacred number) spent on this work, implies the completeness of the cleansing, and the people's zeal for purity. How different from the ancient Israelites, who left not merely the arms, but the heathen themselves, to remain among them [Fairbairn], (Judg. 1:27, 28; 2:2, 3; Ps. 106:34-36). The desolation by Antiochus began in the one hundred and forty-first year of the Seleucidæ. From this date to 148, a period of six years and four months ("2300 days," Dan. 8:14), when the temple worship was restored (I Maccabees 4:52), God vouchsafed many triumphs to His people; from this time to the death of Antiochus, early in 149, a period of seven months, the Jews had rest from Antiochus, and purified their land, and on the twenty-fifth day of the ninth month celebrated the Encænia, or feast of dedication (John 10:22) and purification of the temple. The whole period, in round numbers, was seven years. Mattathias was the patriotic Jewish leader, and his third son, Judas, the military commander under whom the Syrian generals were defeated. He retook Jerusalem and purified the temple. Simon and Jonathan, his brothers, succeeded him: the independence of the Jews was secured, and the crown vested in the Asmonean family, in which it continued till Herod the Great. **11. place . . . of graves**—Gog found only a grave where he had expected the spoils of conquest. **valley**—So vast were to be the masses that nothing but a deep valley would suffice for their corpses. **the passengers on the east of the sea**—those travelling on the high road, east of the Dead Sea, from Syria to Petra and Egypt. The publicity of the road would cause many to observe God's judgments, as the stench (as *English Version* translates) or the multitude of graves (as Henderson translates, "it shall *stop the passengers*") would arrest the attention of passersby. Their grave would be close to that of their ancient prototypes, Sodom and Gomorrah in the Dead Sea, both alike being signal instances of God's judgments. **13. I . . . glorified**—in destroying the foe (ch. 28:22). **14. with the passengers**—The men employed continually in the burying were to be helped by those happening to pass by; all were to combine. **after the end of seven months shall they search**—to see if the work was complete [Munster]. **15.** First *"all* the people of the land" en-

ADAM CLARKE — CHAPTER 39

2. *And leave but the sixth part of thee.* The margin has, "strike thee with six plagues; or, draw thee back with an hook of six teeth."

3. *I will smite thy bow out of thy left hand.* The Persians whom Antiochus had in his army, chap. xxxviii. 5, were famous as archers, and they may be intended here.

6. *I will send a fire on Magog.* On Syria. I will destroy the Syrian troops. *And among them that dwell carelessly in the isles.* The auxiliary troops that came to Antiochus from the borders of the Euxine Sea.

7. *In the midst of my people Israel.* This defeat of Gog is to be in Israel; and it was there, according to this prophecy, that the immense army of Antiochus was so completely defeated. *And I will not let them pollute my holy name any more.* See on 1 Macc. i. 11, etc., how Antiochus had profaned the Temple, insulted Jehovah and His worship, etc. God permitted that as a scourge to His disobedient people; but now the scourger shall be scourged, and he shall pollute the sanctuary no more.

9. *And shall set on fire . . . the weapons.* The Israelites shall make bonfires and fuel of the weapons, tents, etc., which the defeated Syrians shall leave behind them, as expressive of the joy which they shall feel for the destruction of their enemies. *They shall burn them with fire seven years.* These may be figurative expressions, after the manner of the Asiatics, whose language abounds with such descriptions. But as the slaughter was great, and the bows, arrows, quivers, shields, bucklers, hand staves, and spears were in vast multitudes, it must have taken a long time to gather them up in the different parts of the fields of battle, and the roads in which the Syrians had retreated, throwing away their arms as they proceeded; so there might have been a long time employed in collecting and burning them. Mariana, in his *History of Spain,* lib. xi, c. 24, says that after the Spaniards had given that signal overthrow to the Saracens, A.D. 1212, they found such a vast quantity of lances, javelins, and suchlike that they served them for four years for fuel.

11. *The valley of the passengers on the east of the sea.* That is, of Gennesareth, according to the Targum. *There shall they bury Gog and all his multitude.* Some read, "There shall they bury Gog, that is, all his multitude." Not Gog, or Antiochus himself, for he was not in this battle; but his generals, captains, and soldiers, by whom he was represented. As to *Hamon-gog,* we know no valley of this name but here. But we may understand the words thus: The place where this great slaughter was, and where the multitudes of the slain were buried, might be better called *Hamon-gog,* the "valley of the multitude of Gog," than the "valley of passengers."

12. *And seven months.* It shall require a long time to bury the dead. This is another figurative expression; which, however, may admit of a good deal of literal meaning. Many of the Syrian soldiers had secreted themselves in different places during the pursuit after the battle, where they died of their wounds, of hunger, and of fatigue, so that they were not all found and buried till seven months after the defeat of the Syrian army. This slow process of burying is distinctly related in the

MATTHEW HENRY

Verses 23–29

This has reference not only to the predictions concerning Gog and Magog, but to all the prophecies of this book concerning the captivity of the house of Israel, and their restoration and return out of their captivity.

I. God will let the heathen know the meaning of his people's troubles. Upon their reformation and return to him, he turned again their captivity, and brought them back to their own land, and wrought great salvations for them. Then it would be made to appear, even to the heathen, that there was no ground at all for their reflection, that Israel went into captivity because God could not protect them, but because they had by sin forfeited his favour and thrown themselves out of his protection (*v.* 23, 24). That was the true reason why God *hid his face from them* and *gave them into the hand of their enemies*. 1. God punishes sin even in his own people, because he hates it most in those that are nearest and dearest to him, Amos iii. 2. 2. When God gives up his people for a prey, it is to correct them and reform them, not to gratify their enemies, Isa. x. 7; xlii. 24. 3. No sooner do God's people humble themselves under the rod than he returns in mercy to them.

II. God will give his own people to know what favour he has in store for them (*v.* 25, 26).

1. Now God will *have mercy upon the whole house of Israel*, because they repent of their sins. God has justly brought them into a land of trouble, where everyone makes them afraid, because they had trespassed against him in a land of peace, where none made them afraid. And, when they thus humble themselves under humbling providences, God will bring again their captivity.

2. As God was reproached in the reproach they were under during their captivity, so he will be sanctified in their reformation and the making of them a holy people again, and will be glorified in their restoration and the making of them a happy glorious people again, *v.* 27. Then they shall have the benefit of it (*v.* 28): *They shall know that I am the Lord their God.*

JAMIESON, FAUSSET, BROWN

gaged in the burying for seven months; then special men were employed, at the end of the seven months, to search for any still left unburied. The passers-by helped them by setting up a mark near any such bones, in order to keep others from being defiled by casually touching them, and that the buriers might come and remove them. Denoting the minute care to put away every relic of heathen pollution from the Holy Land. **16.** A city in the neighborhood was to receive the name Hamonah, "multitude," to commemorate the overthrow of the multitudes of the foe [HENDERSON]. The multitude of the slain shall give a name to the city of Jerusalem after the land shall have been cleansed [GROTIUS]. Jerusalem shall be famed as the conqueror of multitudes. **17.** (Rev. 19:17.) **sacrifice**—Anciently worshippers feasted on the sacrifices. The birds and beasts of prey are invited to the sacrificial feast provided by God (cf. Isa. 18:6; 34:6; Zeph. 1:7; Mark 9:49). Here this sacrifice holds only a subordinate place in the picture, and so is put last. Not only shall their bones lie long unburied, but they shall be stripped of the flesh by beasts and birds of prey. **18. rams . . . lambs . . . goats**—By these various animal victims used in sacrifices are meant various ranks of men, princes, generals, and soldiers (cf. Isa. 34:6). **fatlings of Bashan**—ungodly men of might (Ps. 22:12). Bashan, beyond Jordan, was famed for its fat cattle. Fat implies prosperity which often makes men refractory towards God (Deut. 32:14, 15). **20. my table**—the field of battle on the mountains of Israel (ch. 38:8, 20). **chariots**—i.e., charioteers. **22. So the house of Israel shall know . . . Lord**—by My interposition for them. So, too, the heathen shall be led to fear the name of the Lord (Ps. 102:15). **23. hid I my face**—(Deut. 31:17; Isa. 59:2). **25. bring again the captivity**—restore **from calamity to prosperity. the whole house of Israel**—so "*all* Israel" (Rom. 11:26). The restorations of Israel heretofore have been partial; there must be one yet future that is to be *universal* (Hos. 1:11). **26. After that they have borne their shame**—the punishment of their sin: after they have become sensible of their guilt, and ashamed of it (ch. 20:43; 36:31). **27. sanctified in them**—vindicated as holy in My dealings with them. **28.** The Jews, having no dominion, settled country, or fixed property to detain them, may return at any time without difficulty (cf. Hos. 3:4, 5). **29. poured out my Spirit upon . . . Israel**—the sure forerunner of their conversion (Joel 2:28; Zech. 12:10). The pouring out of His Spirit is a pledge that He will hide His face no more (II Cor. 1:22; Eph. 1:14; Phil. 1:6).

ADAM CLARKE

following three verses, and extended even to a bone, v. 15; which, when it was found by a passenger, the place was marked, that the buriers might see and inter it. Seven months was little time enough for all this work; and in that country putrescency does not easily take place, the scorching winds serving to desiccate the flesh and preserve it from decomposition.

17. *Gather yourselves . . . to my sacrifice.* This is an allusion to a custom common in the East: when a sacrifice is made, the friends and neighbors of the party sacrificing are invited to come and feast on the sacrifice.

19. *And ye shall eat fat . . . and drink blood.* Who shall eat and drink, etc.? Not the Jews. It is the fowls and the beasts that God invites, v. 17: "Speak unto every feathered fowl, and to every beast of the field, Assemble yourselves . . . that ye may eat flesh, and drink blood"; nor are the persons altered in all these verses, 17-20.

25. *Now will I bring again the captivity of Jacob.* Both they and the heathen shall know that it was for their iniquity that I gave them into the hands of their enemies; and now I will redeem them from those hands in such a way as to prove that I am a merciful God, as well as a just God.

26. *After that they have borne their shame.* After they shall have borne the punishment due to a line of conduct which is their shame and reproach, viz., idolatry.

27. *When I have . . . gathered them.* Antiochus had before captured many of the Jews, and sold them for slaves; see Dan. xi. 33.

28. *And have left none of them any more there.* All that chose had liberty to return, but many remained behind. This promise may therefore refer to a greater restoration, when not a Jew shall be left behind. This, the next verse intimates, will be in the gospel dispensation.

29. *For I have poured out my spirit.* That is, I will pour out My Spirit; see the notes on chap. xxxvi. 25-29, where this subject is largely considered. This Spirit is to enlighten, quicken, purify, and cleanse their hearts; so that, being completely changed, they shall become God's people, and be a praise in the earth.

CHAPTER 40: INTRODUCTION BY JFB

Vss. 1-49. THE REMAINING CHAPTERS, 40-48. GIVE AN IDEAL PICTURE OF THE RESTORED JEWISH TEMPLE. The arrangements as to the land and the temple are, in many particulars, different from those subsisting before the captivity. There are things in it so improbable physically as to preclude a *purely* literal interpretation. The general truth seems to hold good that, as Israel served the nations for his rejection of Messiah, so shall they serve him in the person of Messiah, when he shall acknowledge Messiah (Isa. 60:12; Zech. 14:17-19; cf. Ps. 72:11). The ideal temple exhibits, under Old Testament forms (used as being those then familiar to the men whom Ezekiel, a priest himself, and one who delighted in sacrificial images, addresses), not the precise literal outline, but *the essential character* of the worship of Messiah as it shall be when He shall exercise sway in Jerusalem among His own people, the Jews, and thence to the ends of the earth. The very fact that the whole is a vision (vs. 2), not an oral face-to-face communication such as that granted to Moses (Num. 12:6-8), implies that the directions are not to be understood so precisely literally as those given to the Jewish lawgiver. The description involves things which, taken literally, almost involve natural impossibilities. The square of the temple, in ch. 42:20, is six times as large as the circuit of the wall enclosing the old temple, and larger than all the earthly Jerusalem. Ezekiel gives three and a half miles and 140 yards to his temple square. The boundaries of the ancient city were about two and a half miles. Again, the city in Ezekiel has an area between three or four thousand square miles, including the holy ground set apart for the prince, priests, and Levites. This is nearly as large as the whole of Judea west of the Jordan. As Zion lay in the center of the ideal city, the onehalf of the sacred portion extended to nearly thirty miles south of Jerusalem, i.e., covered nearly the whole southern territory, which reached only to the Dead Sea (ch. 47:19), and yet five tribes were to have their inheritance on that side of Jerusalem, *beyond* the sacred portion (ch. 48:23-28). Where was land to be found for them there? A breadth of but four or five miles apiece would be left. As the boundaries of the land are given the same as under Moses, these incongruities cannot be explained away by supposing physical changes about to be effected in the land such as will meet the difficulties of the purely literal interpretation. The distribution of the land is in equal portions among the twelve tribes, without respect to their relative numbers, and the parallel sections running from east to west. There is a difficulty also in the supposed separate existence of the twelve tribes, such separate tribeships no longer existing, and it being hard to imagine how they could be restored as distinct tribes, mingled as they now are. So the stream that issued from the east threshold of the temple and flowed into the Dead Sea, in the rapidity of its increase and the quality of its waters, is unlike anything ever known in Judea or elsewhere in the world. Lastly, the catholicity of the Christian dispensation, and the spirituality of its worship, seem incompatible with a return to the local narrowness and "beggarly elements" of the Jewish ritual and carnal ordinances, disannulled "because of the unprofitableness thereof" [FAIRBAIRN], (Gal. 4:3, 9; 5:1; Heb. 9:10; 10:18). "A temple with sacrifices now would be a denial of the all-sufficiency of the sacrifice of Christ. He who sacrificed before confessed the Messiah. He who should sacrifice now would solemnly deny Him" [DOUGLAS]. These difficulties, however, may be all *seeming*, not real. Faith accepts God's Word as it is, waits for the event, sure that it will clear up all such difficulties. Perhaps, as some think, the beau ideal of a sacred commonwealth is given according to the then existing pattern of temple services, which would be the imagery most familiar to the prophet and his hearers at the time. The minute particularizing of details is in accordance with Ezekiel's style, even in describing purely ideal scenes. The old temple embodied in visible forms and rites spiritual truths affecting the people even when absent from it. So this ideal temple is made in the absence of the outward temple to serve by description the same purpose of symbolical instruction as the old literal temple did by forms and acts. As in the beginning God promised to be a "sanctuary" (ch. 11:16) to the captives at the Chebar, so now at the close is promised a complete restoration and realization of the theocratic worship and polity under Messiah in its noblest ideal (cf. Jer. 31:38-40). In Revelation 21:22 "no temple" is seen, as in the perfection of the new dispensation the accidents of place and form are no longer needed to realize to Christians what Ezekiel imparts to Jewish minds by the imagery familiar to them. In Ezekiel's temple holiness stretches over the entire temple, so that in this there is no longer a distinction between the different parts, as in the old temple: parts left undeterminate in the latter obtain now a divine sanction, so that all arbitrariness is excluded. So that it is be a perfect manifestation of the love of God to His covenant people (chs. 40-43:12); and from it, as from a new center of religious life, there gushes forth the fulness of blessings to them, and so to all people (ch. 47) [FAIRBAIRN and HAVERNICK]. The temple built at the return from Babylon can only very partially have realized the model here given. The law is seemingly opposed to the gospel (Matt. 5:21, 22, 27, 28, 33, 34). It is not really so (cf. Matt. 5:17, 18; Rom. 3:31; Gal. 3:21, 22). It is true Christ's sacrifice superseded the law sacrifices (Heb. 10:12-18). Israel's province may hereafter be to show the essential identity, even in the minute details of the temple sacrifices, between the law and gospel (Rom. 10:8). The ideal of the theocratic temple will then first be realized.

MATTHEW HENRY

Verses 1–4

1. The date of this vision. It was in the twenty-fifth year of Ezekiel's captivity (*v.* 1), which some compute to be the thirty-third year of the first captivity, and is here said to be the *fourteenth year after the city was smitten.* "Then *the hand of the Lord was upon me* and *brought me thither* to Jerusalem, now that it was in ruins, desolate and deserted"—a pitiable sight to the prophet. 2. The prophet was brought, *in the visions of God, to the land of Israel, v.* 2. Here he is carried thither to have a pleasing prospect of it in its glory. He was set *upon a very high mountain,* as Moses upon the top of Pisgah, to view this land, which was now a second time a *land of promise.* From the top of this mountain he saw this city was a temple as large as a city. It is a city for men to dwell in; it is a temple for God to dwell in; for in the church on earth God dwells with men, in that in heaven men dwell with God. 3. The particular discoveries of this city were made to him by *a man whose appearance was like the appearance of brass* (*v.* 3), Jesus Christ. It is through Christ that we have both acquaintance with and access to the benefits and privileges of God's house. His appearing like brass intimates both his brightness and his strength. 4. The dimensions of this city or temple were taken with a *line of flax* and a *measuring reed,* or *rod* (*v.* 3). 5. Directions are here given to the prophet to receive this revelation from the Lord and transmit it pure and entire to the church, *v.* 4.

Verses 5–26

The measuring-reed which was in the hand of the surveyor-general was mentioned before, *v.* 3. Here we are told (*v.* 5) what was the exact length of it. It was *six cubits long,* not the common cubit, but the *cubit of the sanctuary,* and that was a hand-breadth (that is, four inches) longer than the common cubit: the common cubit was eighteen inches, this twenty-two, see *ch.* xliii. 13. Some critics contend that this *measuring-reed* was but six common cubits in length, and one hand-breadth added to the whole. The former seems more probable. Here is an account,

I. Of the outer wall of the house, which encompassed it round, which denotes the separation between the church and the world.

II. Of the several gates with the chambers adjoining to them.

1. He begins with the *east gate,* because that was the usual way of entering into the lower end of the temple, the holy of holies being at the west end. Now, in the account of this gate, observe, (1) That he went up to it by *stairs* (*v.* 6), for when we go to worship God we must ascend; so is the call, Rev. iv. 1. (2) That the chambers adjoining to the gates were but *little chambers,* about ten feet square, *v.* 7. These were for those to lodge in who attended the service of the house. (3) The chambers, as they were each of them four-square, so they were all of *one measure,* that there might be an equality among the attendants. (4) The chambers were very many; for in our Father's house there are *many mansions* (John xiv. 2), in his house above, and in that here on earth. Some make these chambers to represent the particular congregations of believers, which are parts of the great temple, the universal church. (5) It is said (*v.* 14), *He made also the posts.* (6) Here are posts of sixty cubits, which, some think, was literally fulfilled when Cyrus, in his edict for rebuilding the temple at Jerusalem, ordered that the height thereof should be sixty cubits, that is, thirty yards and more, Ezra vi. 3. (7) Here were windows to the little chambers, and windows to *the posts and arches* (that is, to the cloisters below), and *windows round about* (*v.* 16), to signify the light from heaven with which the church is illuminated. There were lights to the little chambers; even the least. But they are *narrow windows.* The discoveries made to the church on earth are but narrow compared with what shall be in the future state. (8) Divers courts are here spoken of, an outermost of all, then an outer court, then an inner, and then the innermost of all, into which the priests only entered. These courts had porches, or piazzas, round them, for the shelter of those that attended in them from wind and weather. (9) On the posts were palm-trees engraven (*v.* 16), to signify that *the righteous shall flourish like the palm-tree* in the courts of God's house, Ps. xcii. 12. The more they are depressed with the burden of affliction the more strongly do they grow, as they say of the palm-trees. (10) Notice is taken of the pavement of the court, *v.* 17, 18. The word intimates that the pavement was made of *porphyry-stone,* which was of the colour of *burning coals;* for the brightest glories of this world should be put under our feet when we draw near to God.

2. The gates that looked towards the north (*v.* 20) and towards the south (*v.* 24), are much the same with

JAMIESON, FAUSSET, BROWN

1. beginning of the year—the ecclesiastical year, the first month of which was Nisan.

the city . . . thither—Jerusalem, the center to which all the prophet's thoughts tended. **2. visions of God**—divinely sent visions. **very high mountain**—Moriah, very high, as compared with the plains of Babylon, still more so as to its *moral* elevation (ch. 17:22; 20:40). **by which**—Ezekiel coming from the north is set down *at* (as the *Hebrew* for "upon" may be translated) Mount Moriah, and sees the city-like frame of the temple stretching *southward.* In vs. 3, "God brings him thither," i.e., close up to it, so as to inspect it minutely (cf. Rev. 21:10). In this closing vision, as in the opening one of the book, the divine hand is laid on the prophet, and he is borne away in the visions of God. But the scene there was by the Chebar, Jehovah having forsaken Jerusalem; now it is the mountain of God, Jehovah having returned thither; there, the vision was calculated to inspire terror; here, hope and assurance. **3. man**—The Old Testament manifestations of heavenly beings as *men* prepared men's minds for the coming incarnation. **brass**—resplendent. **line**—used for longer measurements (Zech. 2:1). **reed**—used in measuring houses (Rev. 21:15). It marked the straightness of the walls.

5. Measures were mostly taken from the human body. The *greater cubit,* the length from the elbow to the end of the middle finger, a little more than two feet: exceeding the ordinary *cubit* (from the elbow to the wrist) by an hand-breadth, i.e., twenty-one inches in all. Cf. ch. 43:13, with ch. 40:5. The *palm* was the full breadth of the hand, three and a half inches. **breadth of the building**—i.e., the boundary wall. The imperfections in the old temple's boundary wall were to have no place here. The buildings attached to it had been sometimes turned to common uses; e.g., Jeremiah was imprisoned in one (Jer. 20:2; 29:26). But now all these were to be holy to the Lord. The gates and doorways to the city of God were to be imprinted in their architecture with the idea of the exclusion of everything defiled (Rev. 21:27). The east gate was to be especially sacred, as it was through it the glory of God had departed (ch. 11:23), and through it the glory was to return (ch. 43:1, 2; 44:2, 3). **6. the stairs**—seven in number (vs. 26). **threshold**—the sill [FAIRBAIRN]. **other threshold**—FAIRBAIRN considers there is but one threshold, and translates, "even the one threshold, one rod broad." But there is another threshold mentioned in vs. 7. The two thresholds here seem to be the upper and the lower. **7. chamber**—These chambers were for the use of the Levites who watched at the temple gates; *guard-chambers* (II Kings 22:4; I Chron. 9:26, 27); also used for storing utensils and musical instruments. **9. posts**—projecting column-faced fronts of the sides of the doorway, opposite to one another. **12. space**—rather, "the boundary." the straightness of the walls.

16. narrow—latticed [HENDERSON]. The ancients had no glass, so they had them latticed, narrow in the interior of the walls, and widening at the exterior. "Made fast," or "firmly fixed in the chambers" [MAURER]. **arches**—rather, "porches." **17. pavement**—tesselated mosaic (Esther 1:6). **chambers**—serving as lodgings for the priests on duty in the temple, and as receptacles of the tithes of salt, wine, and oil. **18.** The higher pavement was level with the entrance of the gates, the lower was on either side of the raised pavement thus formed. Whereas Solomon's temple had an outer court open to alterations and even idolatrous innovations (II Kings 23:11, 12; I Chron. 20:5), in this there was to be no room for human corruptions. Its compass was exactly defined, 100 cubits; and the fine pavement implied it was to be trodden only by clean feet (cf. Isa. 35:8). **20-27.** The different approaches corresponded in plan. In the case of these two other gates, however, no mention is made of a building with thirty chambers such as was found on the east side. Only one was needed, and it was assigned to the east as being the sacred quarter, and that most conveniently situated for the officiating priests.

ADAM CLARKE

1. *In the five and twentieth year of our captivity.* In the twenty-fifth year of the captivity of Jeconiah, and fourteen years after the taking of Jerusalem.

The Temple here described by Ezekiel is, in all probability, the same which he saw before his captivity, and which had been burned by the Chaldeans fourteen years before this vision. On comparing the Books of Kings and Chronicles with this prophet, we shall find the same dimensions in the parts described by both; for instance, the Temple, or place which comprehended the sanctuary, the holy place, and the vestibule or porch before the Temple, is found to measure equally the same in both Ezekiel and the Kings. Compare 1 Kings vi. 3-16 with chap. xli. 2, etc. The inside ornaments of the Temple are entirely the same; in both we see two courts; an inner one for the priests, and an outer one for the people. Compare 1 Kings vi. 29-36; 2 Chron. iv. 9; and Ezek. xli. 16-17 and xlviii. 7-10. So that there is room to suppose that, in all the rest, the Temple of Ezekiel resembled the old one; and that God's design in retracing these ideas in the prophet's memory was to preserve the remembrance of the plan, the dimensions, the ornaments, and whole structure of this divine edifice; and that at the return from captivity the people might more easily repair it, agreeably to this model. The prophet's applying himself to describe this edifice was a motive of hope to the Jews of seeing themselves one day delivered from captivity, the Temple rebuilt, and their nation restored to its ancient inheritance. Ezekiel touches very slightly upon the description of the Temple or house of the Lord, which comprehended the holy place or sanctuary, and which are so exactly described in the Books of Kings. He dwells more largely upon the gates, the galleries, and apartments of the Temple, concerning which the history of the kings had not spoken, or only just taken notice of by the way.

As the prophet knew that the Chaldeans had utterly destroyed the Temple, he thought it necessary to preserve an exact description of it, that on their restoration the people might build one on the same model.

2. *Set me upon a very high mountain.* Mount Moriah, the mount on which Solomon's Temple was built, 2 Chron. iii. 1.

3. *A man, whose appearance was like . . . brass.* Like bright polished brass, which strongly reflected the rays of light.

4. *Declare all that thou seest to the house of Israel.* That they may know how to build the second Temple, when they shall be restored from their captivity.

MATTHEW HENRY

that towards the east, *after the measure of the first gate, v.* 21. This temple had not only a gate towards the east, to let into it the *children of the east,* that were famous for their wealth and wisdom, but it had a gate to the north, and another to the south, for the admission of the poorer and less civilised nations. The new Jerusalem has *twelve gates,* three towards each quarter of the world (Rev. xxi. 13); for many shall come from all parts to sit down there, Matt. viii. 11.

Verses 27–38

A delineation of the inner court. The survey of the inner court begins with the south side (*v.* 27), proceeds to the east (*v.* 32), and so to the north (*v.* 35). 1. These gates into the inner court were exactly uniform with those into the outer court. The work of grace is the same, for substance, in grown Christians that they are in young beginners. 2. The ascent into the outer court at each gate was by *seven steps,* but the ascent into the inner court at each gate was by *eight steps.* This is expressly taken notice of (*v.* 31, 34, 37), to signify that the nearer we approach to God the more we should rise above this world and the things of it. The people, who worshipped in the outer court, must rise seven steps above other people, but the priests, who attended in the inner court, must rise eight steps above them.

Verses 39–49

An account,

I. Of the tables that were in the porch of the gates of the inner court. Here were eight tables provided, whereon to *slay the sacrifices, v.* 41. They are to intimate the multitude of spiritual sacrifices that should be brought to God's house in gospel-times. Here were the shambles for the altar (*v.* 43), and there also they washed the burnt-offerings (*v.* 38), to intimate that before we draw near to God's altar we must wash our hands, our hearts, those spiritual sacrifices.

II. Of the use of the chambers. 1. Some were for the *singers, v.* 44. The singing of psalms should still continue a gospel-ordinance. Christians should be singers. 2. Others of them were for *the priests,* both those that kept *the charge of the house,* to cleanse it, and to keep it in good repair (*v.* 45), and those that *kept the charge of the altar* (*v.* 46).

III. Of the inner court, the court of the priests, which was fifty yards square, *v.* 47. The altar that *was before the house* was placed in the midst of this court. Christ is both our altar and our sacrifice, to whom we must look with faith in all our approaches to God.

IV. Of the porch of the house. There was a porch, to teach us not to rush hastily and inconsiderately into the presence of God, but gravely, and with solemnity, passing first through the outer court, then the inner, then the porch, ere we enter into the house.

JAMIESON, FAUSSET, BROWN

23. and toward the east—an elliptical expression for "The gate of the inner court was over against the (outer) gate toward the north (just as the inner gate was over against the outer gate) toward the east." **28-37.** The inner court and its gates. **28. according to these measures**—viz., the measures of the outer gate. The figure and proportions of the inner answered to the outer. **30.** This verse is omitted in the LXX, the Vatican MS., and others. The dimensions here of the inner gate do not correspond to the outer, though vs. 28 asserts that they do. HAVERNICK, retaining the verse, understands it of another porch looking inwards toward the temple. **arches**—the porch [FAIRBAIRN]; the columns on which the arches rest [HENDERSON]. **31. eight steps**—The outer porch had only *seven* (vs. 26). **37. posts**—LXX and *Vulgate* read, "the porch," which answers better to vss. 31-34. "The arches" or "porch" [MAURER]. **38. chambers . . . entries**—lit., "a chamber and its door." **by the posts**—i.e., *at* or *close by* the posts or *columns.* **where they washed the burnt offering**—This does not apply to all the gates but only to the north gate. For Leviticus 1:11 directs the sacrifices to be killed north of the altar; and ch. 8:5 calls the north gate, "the gate of the altar." And vs. 40 particularly mentions the *north gate.* **43. hooks**—cooking apparatus for cooking the flesh of the sacrifices that fell to the priests. The hooks were "fastened" in the walls within the apartment, to hang the meat from, so as to roast it. The *Hebrew* comes from a root "fixed" or "placed." **44. the chambers of the singers**—two in number, as proved by what follows: "and their prospect (i.e., the prospect of *one*) was toward the south, (and) one toward the north." So LXX. **46. Zadok**—lineally descended from Aaron. He had the high priesthood conferred on him by Solomon, who had set aside the family of Ithamar because of the part which Abiathar had taken in the rebellion of Adonijah (I Kings 1:7; 2:26, 27). **47. court, an hundred cubits . . . foursquare**—not to be confounded with the inner court, or court of Israel, which was open to all who had sacrifices to bring, and went round the three sides of the sacred territory, 100 cubits broad. This court was 100 cubits square, and had the altar in it, in front of the temple. It was the court of the priests, and hence is connected with those who had charge of the altar and the music. The description here is brief, as the things connected with this portion were from the first divinely regulated. **48, 49.** These two verses belong to ch. 41, which treats of the temple itself. **twenty . . . eleven cubits**—in Solomon's temple (I Kings 6:3) "twenty . . . *ten* cubits." The breadth perhaps was ten *and a half;* I Kings 6:3 designates the number by the *lesser* next round number, "ten"; Ezekiel here, by the *larger* number, "eleven" [MENOCHIUS]. LXX reads "twelve." **he brought me by the steps**—They were *ten* in number [LXX].

ADAM CLARKE

F. GARDINER:

"The sons of Zadok" (v. 46). By the law all sons of Aaron were entitled to become priests, but in Ezekiel the offering of sacrifice appears to be confined to the sons of Zadok (43:19; 44:15; 48:11). The reason for this is obscure. According to 1 Sam. 2:30–36 the high priesthood was to be transferred from the house of Eli, and this was accomplished by Solomon in deposing Abiathar and putting Zadok into his place (1 Kings 2:26, 27); but there must have been many other priests descended from Ithamar and Eleazar besides the families of Eli and Zadok, and it is hardly possible that all these could have perished in the slaughter of the eighty-five priests by Saul at Nob (1 Sam. 22:17–19). But the body of the priests must have been thereby much reduced, and it is very possible that in the subsequent disorders of the times so few were left who, outside of the family of Zadok, had not fallen into idolatry, that all who were allowed to officiate at the altar came to be called by his name.

"The porch of the house." Verses 48, 49 describe the porch of the Temple itself and may be considered as belonging more properly to the next chapter; still, as this porch projected into the inner court, they are not inappropriate here.

—Ellicott's Commentary on the Whole Bible

MATTHEW HENRY — CHAPTER 41

Verses 1–11

1. After the prophet had observed the courts he was at length *brought to the temple, v.* 1. If we diligently attend to the instructions given us in the plainer parts of religion, and profit by them, we shall be led further into an acquaintance with the mysteries of the kingdom of heaven. Those that are willing to dwell in God's courts shall at length be brought into his temple. 2. When our Lord Jesus spoke of the destroying of *this temple,* which his hearers understood of this second temple of Jerusalem, he spoke of the temple of his body (John ii. 19, 21); Ezekiel's vision had respect to them both, including also his mystical body the church, called the *house of God* (1 Tim. iii. 15), and all the members of that body, *living temples,* in which the Spirit dwells. 3. The very posts of this temple, the door-posts, were far one from the other, and consequently the door was wide. In comparison with what had been under the law we may say, *Wide is the gate* which leads into the church, the ceremonial law, that wall of partition which had so much straitened the gate, being taken down. 4. The most holy place was an exact square, *v.* 4. The new Jerusalem is exactly square (Rev. xxi. 16), denoting its stability.

JAMIESON, FAUSSET, BROWN — CHAPTER 41

Vss. 1-26. THE CHAMBERS AND ORNAMENTS OF THE TEMPLE. **1. tabernacle**—As in the measurement of the outer porch he had pointed to Solomon's *temple,* so here in the edifice itself, he points to the old *tabernacle,* which being eight boards in breadth (each one and a half cubits broad) would make in all twelve cubits, as here. On the interior it was only ten cubits. **2. length thereof**—viz., of the holy place [FAIRBAIRN]. **3. inward**—towards the most holy place. **4. thereof**—of the holy of holies. **before the temple**—i.e., before, or in front of the most holy place (so "temple" is used in I Kings 6:3). The angel went in and measured it, while Ezekiel stood in front, in the only part of the temple accessible to him. The dimensions of the two apartments are the same as in Solomon's temple, since being fixed originally by God, they are regarded as finally determined. **5. side chamber**—the singular used collectively for the plural. These chambers were appendages attached to the outside of the temple, on the west, north, and south; for on the east side, the principal entrance, there were no chambers. The narrowness of the chambers was in order that the beams could be supported without needing pillars. **6. might . . . hold, but . . . not hold in . . . wall of the house**—I Kings 6:6 tells us there were rests made in the walls of the temple for supports to the side chambers; but the temple walls did not thereby become part of this side building; they stood separate from it. "They entered," viz., the beams of the chambers, which were three-storied and thirty in consecutive order, entered into the wall, i.e., were made to lean on rests projecting from the wall. **7.**

ADAM CLARKE — CHAPTER 41

1. *To the temple.* He had first described the courts and the porch. See chap. xl.

2. *The breadth of the door.* This was the door, or gate, of the sanctuary and this doorway was filled up with folding gates. The measurements are exactly the same as those of Solomon's Temple. See 1 Kings vi. 2, 17.

4. *The length thereof, twenty cubits.* This is the measurement of the sanctuary, or holy of holies. This also was the exact measurement of Solomon's Temple; see 1 Kings vi. 20. This and the other resemblances here sufficiently prove that Ezekiel's Temple and that of Solomon were on the same plan, and that the latter Temple was intended to be an exact resemblance of the former.

6. *The side chambers were three.* We find, by Joseph. *Antiq.* viii. 3. 2, that around Solomon's Temple were chambers three stories high, each story consisting of thirty chambers. *Entered into the wall.* The beams were admitted into the outer wall, but they rested on projections of the inner wall.

MATTHEW HENRY

5. The upper stories were larger than the lower, *v.* 7. Care was taken that the timber might have *fast hold* (though God builds high, he builds firmly). The higher we build up ourselves in our most holy faith the more should our hearts, those living temples, be enlarged.

Verses 12–26

1. An account of a building that was *before the separate place* (that is, before the temple), *at the end towards the west* (*v.* 12). This stood in a court by itself. Perhaps, in this vision, it signified the setting up of a church among the Gentiles not inferior to the Jewish temple, but of quite another nature. 2. A description of the ornaments of the temple, and the other building. The walls on the inside from top to bottom were adorned with *cherubim and palm-trees*, placed alternately. Each cherub is said to have two *faces*, the *face of a man* and the *face of a young lion*, *v.* 19. These seem to represent the angels, who have more than the wisdom of a man and the courage of a lion; the palms of victory are set before them. 3. A description of the posts of the doors both of the temple and of the sanctuary; they were *squared* (*v.* 21). In the tabernacle, and in Solomon's temple, the door of the sanctuary was narrower than that of the temple, but here it was as broad; for in gospel-times *the way into the holiest of all is made* more *manifest* than it was under the Old Testament (Heb. ix. 8). These doors are described, *v.* 23, 24. 4. The altar of incense, here said to be an *altar of wood*, *v.* 22. It would not bear the fire with which the incense was to be burned, unless it intimates that the incense to be offered in the gospel-temple shall be purely spiritual, and the fire spiritual. This altar is called a table. The great sacrifice being now offered, that which we have to do is to feast upon the sacrifice at the Lord's table.

CHAPTER 42

Verses 1–14

The prophet has taken a very exact view of the temple and is now brought again into the outer court.

I. A description of chambers which seems to us very intricate. We shall only observe, in general, 1. That about the temple, which was the place of public worship, there were private chambers. We must not only worship in the courts of God's house, but must, both before and after our attendance there, enter into our chambers, and read and meditate, and *pray to our Father in secret*. 2. That these chambers were many; there were *three stories* of them, *v.* 5, 6. There were many for such devout people as Anna the prophetess, who *departed not from the temple night or day*, Luke ii. 37. 3. That these chambers, though they were private, yet were near the temple, to prepare us for the exercises of devotion in public. 4. That before these chambers there were *walks of five yards broad* (*v.* 4), in which those that had lodgings in these chambers might meet and talk together, and share their experiences. Man is made for society, and Christians for the communion of saints.

II. The use of these chambers appointed, *v.* 13, 14. 1. They were *for the priests* that approach unto the Lord. *Therefore* they are called *holy chambers*, because they were for use of those that ministered in holy things during their ministration. 2. There the priests were to deposit *the most holy things*, those parts of the offerings which fell to their share. 3. There they were to lay their vestments, which God had appointed them to wear when they ministered at the altar. We read of the providing of priests garments

JAMIESON, FAUSSET, BROWN

the breadth . . . so increased from the lowest . . . to the highest—i.e., the breadth of the interior space above was greater than that below. **8. foundations . . . six . . . cubits**—the substructure, on which the foundations rested, was a full reed of six cubits. **great**—lit., "to the extremity" or root, viz., of the hand [HENDERSON]. "To the joining," or point, where the foundation of one chamber ceased and another began [FAIRBAIRN]. **9. that which was left**—There was an unoccupied place within chambers that belonged to the house. The buildings in this unoccupied place, west of the temple, and so much resembling it in size, imply that no place was to be left which was to be held, as of old, not sacred. Manasseh (II Kings 23:11) had abused these "suburbs of the temple" to keeping horses sacred to the sun. All excuse for such abominations was henceforth to be taken away, the Lord claiming every space, and filling up this also with sacred erections [FAIRBAIRN]. **10. the chambers**—i.e., of the priests in the court: between these and the side chambers was the wideness, etc. While long details are given as to the chambers, etc., no mention is made of the ark of the covenant. FAIRBAIRN thus interprets this: In future there was to be a perfect conformity to the divine idea, such as there had not been before. The dwellings of His people should all become true sanctuaries of piety. Jehovah Himself, in the full display of the divine Shekinah, shall come in the room of the ark of the covenant (Jer. 3:16, 17). The interior of the temple stands empty, waiting for His entrance to fill it with His glory (ch. 43:1-12). It is the same temple, but the courts of it have become different to accommodate a more numerous people. The entire compass of the temple mount has become a holy of holies (ch. 43:12). **12-15.** Sum of the measures of the temple, and of the buildings behind and on the side of it. **15. galleries**—terrace buildings. On the west or back of the temple, there was a separate place occupied by buildings of the same external dimensions as the temple, i.e., one hundred cubits square in the entire compass [FAIRBAIRN]. **16. covered**—being the highest windows they were "covered" from the view below. Or else "covered" *with lattice-work.* **17. by measure**—Measurements were taken [FAIRBAIRN]. **21. appearance of the one as the appearance of the other**—The appearance of the sanctuary or holy of holies was similar to that of the temple. They differed only in magnitude. **22. table . . . before the Lord**—the altar of incense (ch. 44:16). At it, not at the table of shewbread, the priests daily ministered. It stood in front of the veil, and is therefore said to be "before the Lord." It is called a table, as being that at which the Lord will take delight in His people, as at a feast. Hence its dimensions are larger than that of old—three cubits high, two broad, instead of two and one. **25. thick planks**—a thick-plank work at the threshold.

CHAPTER 42

Vss. 1-20. CHAMBERS OF THE PRIESTS: MEASUREMENTS OF THE TEMPLE. **2. Before the length of an hundred cubits**—i.e., before "the separate place," which was that length (ch. 41:13). He had before spoken of chambers for the officiating priests on the north and south gates of the inner court (ch. 40:44-46). He now returns to take a more exact view of them.

5. shorter—i.e., the building became *narrower* as it rose in height. The chambers were many: so "in My Father's house are many mansions" (John 14:2); and besides these there was much "room" still left (cf. Luke 14:22). The chambers, though private, were near the temple. Prayer in our chambers is to prepare us for public devotions, and to help us in improving them.

ADAM CLARKE

7. *An enlarging, and a winding about.* Perhaps a winding staircase that widened upward as the inner wall decreased in thickness, this wall being six cubits thick as high as the first story, five from the floor of the second story to that of the third, and four from the floor to the ceiling of the third story; and thus there was a rest of one cubit in breadth to support the stories.

18. *A palm tree was between a cherub and a cherub.* That is, the palm trees and the cherubs were alternated, and each cherub had two faces, one of a lion and the other of a man; one of which was turned to the palm tree on the right, and the other to the palm tree on the left.

22. *The altar of wood.* This was the altar of incense, and was covered with plates of gold.

CHAPTER 42

1. *He brought me forth into the utter court.* He brought him out of the Temple into the court of the priests. This, in reference to the Temple, was called the outer court; but the court of the people was beyond this.

4. *A walk of ten cubits breadth inward.* This seems to have been a sort of parapet.

MATTHEW HENRY

after their return out of captivity, Neh. vii. 70, 72. When they had ended their service at the altar they must lay by those garments, but they must *put on other garments*, such as other people wear, when they *approached to those things which were for the people*, that is, to teach them the law and to answer their enquiries.

Verses 15–20

The measuring of this mystical temple to see how far the holy ground on which we tread extends. 1. It extended each way 500 reeds (*v.* 16–19), each reed above three yards and a half, so that it reached every way about an English measured mile. Thus large were the suburbs of this mystical temple, signifying the great extent of the church in gospel-times. Room should be made in God's courts for the numerous Gentiles, Isa. xlix. 18; lx. 4. 2. The dimensions were thus large to *make a separation*, by putting a distance *between the sanctuary* and *the profane place*. A difference is to be put between common and sacred things, between God's name and other names, between his day and other days, his book and other books.

JAMIESON, FAUSSET, BROWN

16. five hundred reeds—LXX substitutes "cubits" for "reeds," to escape the immense compass assigned to the whole, viz., a square of 500 rods or 3000 cubits (two feet each; ch. 40:5), i.e., in all a square of one and one-seventh miles, i.e., more than all ancient Jerusalem; also, there is much space thus left unappropriated. FAIRBAIRN rightly supports *English Version*, which agrees with the *Hebrew*. The vast extent is another feature marking the ideal character of the temple. It symbolizes the great enlargement of the kingdom of God, when Jehovah-Messiah shall reign at Jerusalem, and from thence to the ends of the earth (Isa. 2:2-4; Jer. 3:17; Rom. 11:12, 15). **20. wall . . . separation between . . . sanctuary and . . . profane**—No longer shall the wall of partition be to separate the Jew and the Gentile (Eph. 2:14), but to separate the sacred from the profane. The lowness of it renders it unfit for the purpose of defense (the object of the wall, Rev. 21:12). But its square form (as in the city, Rev. 21:16) is the emblem of the kingdom that cannot be shaken (Heb. 12:28), resting on prophets and apostles, Jesus Christ being the chief cornerstone.

ADAM CLARKE

14. *They shall lay their garments wherein they minister*. The priests were not permitted to wear their robes in the outer court. These vestments were to be used only when they ministered; and when they had done, they were to deposit them in one of the chambers mentioned in the thirteenth verse.

20. *It had a wall round about . . . to make a separation between the sanctuary and the profane place*. The holy place was that which was consecrated to the Lord, into which no heathen, nor stranger, nor any in a state of impurity might enter. *The profane place* was that in which men, women, Gentiles, pure or impure, might be admitted. Josephus says (*War*, lib. vi, c. 14) that in his time there was a wall built before the entrance three cubits high, on which there were posts fixed at certain distances, with inscriptions on them in Latin and Greek, containing the laws which enjoined purity on those that entered, and forbidding all strangers to enter, on pain of death.

MATTHEW HENRY

CHAPTER 43

Verses 1–6

After Ezekiel has patiently surveyed the temple of God, the greatest glory of this earth, he is honoured with a sight of the glories of the upper world; *Come up hither*. He has seen the temple, spacious and splendid; but, till the glory of God comes into it, it is but like the dead bodies he had seen in vision (*ch.* xxxvii), that had *no breath* till the Spirit of life entered into them. Here therefore he sees the house filled with God's glory.

I. A vision of *the glory of God* (*v.* 2), *the glory of the God of Israel*, who is in covenant with Israel. The idols of the heathen have no glory but what they owe to the goldsmith or the painter. This glory *came from the way of the east*. Christ's *star was seen in the east*. For he is the morning star, he is the sun of righteousness. Two things in this appearance of the glory of God: 1. The power of his word which he heard: *His voice was like a noise of many waters*. Christ's gospel, in the glory of which he shines, was to be proclaimed aloud, the report of it to be heard far. 2. The brightness of his appearance which he saw: *The earth shone with his glory;* for God is light, and none can bear the lustre of his light, none *has seen* nor *can see it*. That glory of God which shines in the church shines on the world.

II. A vision of the entrance of this glory into the temple. When he saw this glory he *fell upon his face* (*v.* 3), in humble and reverent adoration. But the Spirit *took him up* (*v.* 5) when the *glory of the Lord* had *come into the house* (*v.* 4), that he might see how the house was filled with it. This was to have its accomplishment in that glory of the divine grace which shines so brightly in the gospel church, and fills it. Here is no mention of a cloud filling the house as formerly, for we now *with open face behold the glory of the Lord*, in the face of Christ, and not as of old through the cloud of types.

III. He receives instructions more immediately from the glory of the Lord, as Moses did when God had taken possession of the tabernacle (Lev. i. 1): *I heard him speaking to me out of the house*, *v.* 6.

Verses 7–12

God does here, in effect, renew his covenant with his people Israel, upon his retaking possession of the house.

I. God, by the prophet, puts them in mind of their former provocations. This is spoken to make way for the comforts designed them. They had formerly *defiled God's holy name*, *v.* 7. *They and their kings* had brought contempt on the religion they professed by setting up altars to their idols even in the courts of the temple, than which a more impudent affront could not be put upon the divine Majesty. Thus they set up a separation *wall between him and them*, which stopped the current of his favours to them. If often proves too true, *The nearer the church the further from God*.

II. He calls upon them to repent (*v.* 9): "*Now let them put away their whoredom;* and now that God is returning in mercy to them and setting up his sanctuary again in the midst of them, let them cast away their idols, those loathsome *carcases of their kings*." The prophet had the model or pattern of the temple to set before them. 1. If *they see that pattern*, they will surely be ashamed of their sins (*v.* 10). The goodness of God to us should lead us to repentance. Let *them measure the pattern* themselves, and see how much it exceeds the former pattern, and guess by that

JAMIESON, FAUSSET, BROWN

CHAPTER 43

VSS. 1-27. JEHOVAH'S RETURN TO THE TEMPLE. Everything was now ready for His reception. As the Shekinah glory was the peculiar distinction of the old temple, so it was to be in the new in a degree as much more transcendent as the proportions of the new exceeded those of the old. The fact that the Shekinah glory was not in the second temple proves that it cannot be that temple which is meant in the prophecy.

2. the way of the east—the way whereby the glory had departed (ch. 11:22, 23), and rested on Mount Olivet (cf. Zech. 14:4). **his voice . . . like . . . many waters**—So *English Version* rightly, as in ch. 1:24, "voice of the Almighty"; Revelation 1:15; 14:2, prove this. Not as FAIRBAIRN translates, "its noise." **earth his glory**—(Rev. 18:1).

3. when I came to destroy the city—i.e., to pronounce God's word for its destruction. So completely did the prophets identify themselves with Him in whose name they spake.

6. the man—who had been measuring the buildings (ch. 40:3). **7. the place**—i.e., *behold* the place of My throne . . . —the place on which your thoughts have so much dwelt (Isa. 2:1-3; Jer. 3:17; Zech. 14:16-20; Mal. 3:1). God from the first claimed to be their King politically as well as religiously: and He had resisted their wish to have a human king, as implying a rejection of Him as the proper Head of the state. Even when He yielded to their wish, it was with a protest against their king ruling except as His vicegerent. When Messiah shall reign at Jerusalem, He shall then first realize the original idea of the theocracy, with its at once divine and human king reigning in righteousness over a people all righteous (vs. 12; Isa. 52:1; 54:13: 60:21). **9. carcasses of their kings**—It is supposed that some of their idolatrous kings were buried within the bounds of Solomon's temple [HENDERSON]. Rather, "the carcasses of their *idols*," here called "kings," as having had lordship over them in past times (Isa. 26:13); but henceforth Jehovah, alone their rightful lord, shall be their king, and the idols that had been their "king" would appear but as "carcasses." Hence these defunct kings are associated with the "high places" in vs. 7 [FAIRBAIRN]. Leviticus 26:30 and Jeremiah 16:18, confirm this. Manasseh had built altars in the courts of the temple to the host of heaven (II Kings 21:5; 23:6).

ADAM CLARKE

CHAPTER 43

2. *The glory of the God of Israel came from the way of the east*. This was the chariot of cherubim, wheels, etc., which he saw at the river Chebar. And this glory, coming from the east, is going to enter into the eastern gate of the Temple, and thence to shine out upon the whole earth.

7. *Son of man, the place of my throne*. The throne refers to His majesty; the soles of His feet, to His condescension in dwelling among men. *Where I will dwell in the midst of the children of Israel*. The Tabernacle and Temple were types of the incarnation of Jesus Christ.

8. *In their setting of their threshold*. They had even gone so far as to set up their idol altars by those of Jehovah, so that their abominable idols were found in the very house of God! Therefore, He *consumed them in His anger*.

9. *Now let them put away their whoredom*. Their idolatry. *And the carcases of their kings*. It appears that God was displeased with their bringing their kings so near His temple. David was buried in the city of David, which was on Mount Zion, near to the Temple; and so were almost all the kings of Judah. But God requires that the place of His temple and its vicinity shall be kept unpolluted; and when they put away all kinds of defilement, then will He dwell among them.

10. *Shew the house to the house of Israel*. Show them this holy house where the holy God dwells, that they may be ashamed of their iniquities. Their name, their profession, their Temple, their religious services, all bound them to a holy life; all within them, all without them, should have been holiness unto the Lord. But alas! they have been bound by no ties, and they have sinned against all their obligations. Nevertheless, *let them measure the pattern*, let them see the rule by which they should have walked, and let them measure themselves by this standard, and walk accordingly.

MATTHEW HENRY

what great things God has in store for them. 2. If *they be ashamed* of their sins, they shall surely see more of the pattern, *v.* 11. "*Show them the form of the house;* and show them the ordinances and laws of it." With the privileges of God's house we must acquaint ourselves with the rules of it. *Show them* these ordinances, that they may *keep them* and *do them.*

III. He promises that they should be such as they should be, and then he will be to them such as they would have him to be, *v.* 7. Then *I will dwell in the midst of them for ever*; again *v.* 9.

IV. The general law of God's house is laid down (*v.* 12), That, whereas formerly only the chancel, or sanctuary, was *most holy*, now the whole *mountain of the house* shall be so. In gospel-times, 1. The whole church shall have the privilege of the *holy of holies*, that of a near access to God. All believers have now, under the gospel, *boldness to enter into the holiest* (Heb. x. 19), whereas the high priest entered in the virtue of the blood of bulls and goats, we enter in the virtue of the blood of Jesus, and, wherever we are, we have through him *access to the Father*.

Verses 13–27

This relates to the altar in this mystical temple, and that is mystical too; for Christ is our altar. The Jews, after their return out of captivity, had an altar long before they had a temple, Ezra iii. 3. But this was an altar in the temple.

I. The measures of the altar, *v.* 13. It was six yards square at the top and seven yards square at the bottom; it was four yards and a half high; it had a lower bench or shelf, here called a *settle*, a yard from the ground, on which some of the priests stood to minister, and another two yards above that, on which others of them stood. What was to be burnt on the altar was given up to those on the lower bench, and handed by them to those on the higher, and they laid it on the altar.

II. The ordinances of the altar. 1. *Seven days* were to be spent in the dedication of it, and every day sacrifices were to be offered (*v.* 25). Neither our persons nor our performances can be acceptable to God unless sin be taken away, and that cannot be taken away but by the blood of Christ, which both sanctifies the altar, and the gift upon the altar. The dedication of the altar is here called the *cleansing* and *purging* of it, *v.* 20, 26. All the sacrifices must be seasoned with salt (*v.* 24). *Grace* is the *salt* with which all our religious performances must be seasoned, Col. iv. 6. 2. Concerning the constant use that should be made of the temple when it was dedicated (*v.* 27). It was *sanctified*, that it might *sanctify the gift* that was offered upon it. (1) Who were to serve at the altar: The *priests of the seed of Zadok*, *v.* 19. His name signifies *righteous*, for they are the righteous seed that are priests to God, through Christ *the Lord our righteousness*. (2) How they should prepare for this service (*v.* 26). Before we minister to the Lord in holy things we must consecrate ourselves.

JAMIESON, FAUSSET, BROWN

I will dwell in the midst . . . for ever—(Rev. 21:3). **10. show the house . . . that they may be ashamed of their iniquities**—When the spirituality of the Christian scheme is *shown* to men by the Holy Ghost, it makes them "ashamed of their iniquities."

12. whole . . . most holy—This superlative, which had been used exclusively of the holy of holies (Exod. 26:34), was now to characterize the entire building. This all-pervading sanctity was to be "*the* law of the (whole) house," as distinguished from the Levitical law, which confined the peculiar sanctity to a single apartment of it. **13-27.** As to the altar of burnt offering, which was the appointed means of access to God. **15. altar**—*Hebrew, Harel,* i.e., "mount of God"; denoting the high security to be imparted by it to the restored Israel. It was a high place, but a high place *of God,* not of idols. **from the altar**—lit., "the lion of God," *Ariel* (in Isa. 29:1, "Ariel" is applied to Jerusalem). MENOCHIUS supposes that on it four animals were carved; the lion perhaps was the uppermost, whence the horns were made to issue. GESENIUS regards the two words as expressing the "hearth" or fireplace of the altar. **16. square in the four squares**—square on the four sides of its squares [FAIRBAIRN]. **17. settle**—ledge [FAIRBAIRN]. **stairs**—rather, "the ascent," as "steps" up to God's altar were forbidden in Exodus 20:26. **18-27.** The sacrifices here are not mere commemorative, but propitiatory ones. The expressions, "blood" (vs. 18), and "for a sin offering (vss. 19, 21, 22), prove this. In the *literal* sense they can only apply to the second temple. Under the Christian dispensation they would directly oppose the doctrine taught in Hebrews 10:1-18, viz., that Christ has by one offering for ever atoned for sin. However, it is *possible* that they might exist with a *retrospective* reference to Christ's sufferings, as the Levitical sacrifices had a *prospective* reference to them; not propitiatory in themselves, but memorials to keep up the remembrance of His propitiatory sufferings, which form the foundation of His kingdom, lest they should be lost sight of in the glory of that kingdom [DE BURGH]. The particularity of the directions make it unlikely that they are to be understood in a merely vague spiritual sense. **20. cleanse**—lit., "make expiation for." **21. burn it . . . without the sanctuary**—(Heb. 13:11). **26. consecrate themselves**—lit., "fill their hands," viz., with offerings; referring to the mode of consecrating a priest (Exod. 29: 24, 35). **26. Seven days**—referring to the original directions of Moses for seven days' purification services of the altar (Exod. 29:37). **27. I will accept you**—(Ch. 20:40, 41; Rom. 12:1; I Pet. 2:5).

ADAM CLARKE

11. *And if they be ashamed.* If, in a spirit of true repentance, they acknowledge their past transgressions, and purpose in His help never more to offend their God, then teach them everything that concerns My worship, and their profiting by it.

12. *This is the law of the house.* From the top of the mountain on which it stands, to the bottom, all round about, all shall be holy. No buildings shall be erected in any part, nor place nor spot be appropriated to a common use; all shall be considered as being most holy.

15. *So the altar. Haharel,* "the mount of God." *And from the altar.* "And from the lion of God." Perhaps the first was a name given to the altar when elevated to the honor of God, and on which the victims were offered to Him; and the second, the "lion of God," may mean the hearth, which might have been thus called because it devoured and consumed the burnt offerings, as a lion does his prey. See Isa. xxix. 1.

17. *And the settle.* The "ledge" on which the priests walked round the altar; see v. 14. By these settles or ledges the altar was narrowed towards the top.

19. *The priests . . . that be of the seed of Zadok.* It was this Zadok that was put in the place of Abiathar by Solomon, 1 Kings ii. 35, in whose family the priesthood had continued ever since.

MATTHEW HENRY — CHAPTER 44

Verses 1–3

The prophet is brought a third time to the east gate, and finds it shut, which intimates that the rest of the gates were open at all times to the worshippers. But such an account is given of this gate's being shut as puts honour, 1. Upon the God of Israel. It is for the honour of him that the gate of the inner court, at which his glory entered when he took possession of the house, was ever after kept shut, *v.* 2. 2. Upon the prince of Israel, *v.* 3. (1) He shall *sit in this gate* to *eat* his share of the peace-offerings *before the Lord.* (2) He shall *enter by the way of the porch of that gate*, by some little door or wicket. Some by the prince here understand the high priest, and that he only was allowed to enter by this gate, for he was God's representative. Christ is the high priest of our profession, who entered himself into the holy place, and *opened the kingdom of heaven to all believers.*

Verses 4–9

The prophet must look again upon what he had before seen, and must be told again what he had before heard. Here, as before, he sees the house *filled with the glory of the Lord*, which strikes an awe upon him: *I fell upon my face*, *v.* 4.

I. God charges the prophet to take notice of all he saw, and all that was said to him (*v.* 5). 1. "*Behold with thy eyes* what is *shown* thee, particularly the *entering in of the house* and *every going forth* of it, all the inlets and all the outlets of the sanctuary." 2. *Hear with thy ears all that I say unto thee* about *the laws* and *ordinances* of the *house*, to instruct the

JAMIESON, FAUSSET, BROWN — CHAPTER 44

VSS. 1-31. ORDINANCES FOR THE PRINCE AND THE PRIESTS. **2. shut . . . not be opened**—(Job 12:14; Isa. 22:22; Rev. 3:7). "Shut" to the people (Exod. 19:21, 22), but open to "the prince" (vs. 3), he holding the place of God in political concerns, as the priests do in spiritual. As a mark of respect to an Eastern monarch, the gate by which he enters is thenceforth shut to all other persons (cf. Exod. 19: 24). **3. the prince**—not King Messiah, as He never would offer a burnt offering for Himself, as the prince is to do (ch. 46:4). The prince must mean the civil ruler under Messiah. His connection with the east gate (by which the Lord had returned to His temple) implies, that, as ruling under God, he is to stand in a place of peculiar nearness to God. He represents Messiah, who entered heaven, the true sanctuary, by a way that none other could, viz., by His own holiness; all others must enter as sinners by faith in His blood, through grace. **eat bread before the Lord**—a custom connected with sacrifices (Gen. 31:54; Exod. 18:12; 24:11; I Cor. 10:18). **4-6.** Directions as to the priests.

ADAM CLARKE — CHAPTER 44

1. *The outward sanctuary.* In opposition to the Temple itself, which was the inner sanctuary.

2. *This gate shall be shut.* It was not to be opened on ordinary occasions, nor at all on the weekdays, but only on the Sabbaths and the new moons.

5. *Mark well, and behold.* Take notice of everything; register all so fully that you shall be able to give the most minute information to the children of Israel.

MATTHEW HENRY

people.

II. He sends him upon an errand to the people, *to the rebellious, even to the house of Israel, v.* 6.

1. He must show the house of Jacob their sins. They had admitted those to the privileges of the sanctuary that were not entitled to them (*v.* 7). Yet if these strangers had been devout, though they were not circumcised, the crime would not have been so great; but they were *uncircumcised in heart* too, strangers indeed to God and all goodness. They had employed those in the service of the sanctuary who were not fit for it. "*You have set keepers of my charge in my sanctuary for yourselves,* such as you had some favour or affection for; *thus you have not kept the charge of my holy things.*"

2. He must tell them their duty (*v.* 9): "*No stranger shall enter into my sanctuary* till he has first submitted to the laws of it."

Verses 10–16

The Master of the house, being about to set up house again, takes account of his servants the priests, and sees who are fit to be kept.

I. Those who have been treacherous are degraded and put lower. Those Levites—or priests who were carried down the stream of the apostasy of Israel formerly (*v.* 10), who had complied with the idolatrous kings of Israel or Judah, who *ministered to them before their idols* (*v.* 12)—were justly put under the mark of God's displeasure. They are sentenced to be deprived in part, of their office, and from the dignity of priests are put down into the condition of ordinary Levites. Yet there is a mixture of mercy in this sentence. God mitigates the sentence, *v.* 11, 14. They shall help to *slay the sacrifice,* not at the altar, but *at the tables, ch.* xl. 39. They shall be porters *at the gates of the house.*

II. Those who have been faithful are honoured and established, *v.* 15, 16. "*But the sons of Zadok,* who kept their integrity in a time of general apostasy, who *went not astray* when others did, *they shall come near to me, shall come near to my table.*"

Verses 17–31

God's priests must be *regulars,* not *seculars;* and therefore here are rules laid down for them.

I. Concerning their clothes; they must wear *linen garments* when they *went in to minister,* and nothing that was *woollen,* because it would *cause sweat, v.* 17, 18. When they had finished their service they must change their clothes again, and lay up their linen garments in the chambers appointed for that purpose, *v.* 19, as before, *ch.* xlii. 14.

II. Concerning their hair; in that they must avoid extremes on both hands (*v.* 20); *They must not shave their heads,* in imitation of the Gentile priests; nor, on the other hand, must they *suffer their locks to grow long,* that they might be thought Nazarites, when really they were not; but they must be grave and modest, must *poll their heads* and keep their hair short.

III. Concerning their diet; they must be sure to *drink no wine* when they went in to minister, lest they should drink to excess, should drink and forget the law, *v.* 21.

IV. Concerning their marriages, *v.* 22. Here they must consult the credit of their office, and not marry one that had been *divorced,* that was under the suspicion of immodesty, nor a *widow,* unless she were a priest's widow, accustomed to the usages of the priests' families.

V. Concerning their preaching and church-government. It was part of their business to teach the people; and herein they must approve themselves both skilful and faithful (*v.* 23). It was part of their business to judge upon appeals made to them (Deut. xvii. 8, 9), and *in controversy they shall stand in judgment, v.* 24. They shall have the honesty to stand up for what is right, and, when they have passed a right judgment, shall have the courage to stand by it. Another part of their work, as church governors, is to *hallow God's sabbaths,* and to see that God's people also sanctify that day and do nothing to pollute it.

VI. Concerning their mourning for dead relations; the rule here agrees with the law of Moses, Lev. xxi. 1, 11. A priest shall not come near any *dead body* (for they must be purified *from dead works*) except of his next relations, *v.* 25.

VII. Concerning their maintenance; they must live upon the altar at which they served (*v.* 28). Some land was allowed them (*ch.* xlviii. 10), but their principal subsistence was by their office.

1. What the priests were to have from the people, for their maintenance and encouragement. They must have the flesh of many of the offerings. They must have every dedicated thing in Israel, which was

JAMIESON, FAUSSET, BROWN

Their acts of desecration are attributed to "the house of Israel" (vss. 6, 7), as the sins of the priesthood and of the people acted and reacted on one another; "like people, like priest" (Jer. 5:31; Hos. 4:9). **7. uncircumcised in heart**—Israelites circumcised outwardly, but wanting the true circumcision of the heart (Deut. 10:16; Acts 7:51). **uncircumcised in flesh**—not having even the outward badge of the covenant people. **8. keepers . . . for yourselves**—such as you yourselves thought fit, not such as I approve of. Or else, "Ye have not *yourselves* kept the charge of My holy things, but have set *others as* keepers of My charge in My sanctuary for yourselves" [MAURER].

10, 11. Levites . . . shall . . . bear—viz., the punishment of—**their iniquity . . . Yet they shall be ministers**—So Mark, a *Levite,* nephew of Barnabas (Acts 4:36), was punished by Paul for losing an opportunity of bearing the cross of Christ, and yet was afterwards admitted into his friendship again, and showed his zeal (Acts 13:13; 15:37; Col. 4:10; II Tim. 4:11). One may be a believer, and that too in a distinguished place, and yet lose some special honor—be acknowledged as pious, yet be excluded from some dignity [BENGEL]. **charge at the gates**—Better to be "a doorkeeper in the house of God, than to dwell in the tents of wickedness" (Ps. 84:10). Though standing as a mere doorkeeper, it is in the *house* of God, which hath foundations: whereas he who *dwells* with the wicked, **dwells** in but shifting *tents.* **15. Zadok**—The priests of the line of Ithamar were to be discharged from ministrations in the temple, because of their corruptions, following in the steps of Eli's sons, against whom the same denunciation was uttered (I Sam. 2:32, 35). Zadok, according to his name (which means "righteous") and his line, were to succeed (I Kings 2:35; I Chron. 24:3), as they did not take part in the general apostasy to the same degree, and perhaps [FAIRBAIRN] the prophet, referring to their original state, speaks of them as they appeared when first chosen to the office. **17. linen**—symbolical of purity. Wool soon induces perspiration in the sultry East and so becomes uncleanly. **18. bonnets**—turbans. **19. not sanctify the people with their garments**—viz., those peculiarly priestly vestments in which they ministered in the sanctuary. **20. Neither . . . shave . . . heads**—as mourners do (Lev. 21:1-5). The worshippers of the Egyptian idols Serapis and Isis shaved their heads; another reason why Jehovah's priests are not to do so. **nor suffer . . . locks to grow long**—as the luxurious, barbarians, and soldiers in warfare did [JEROME]. **21. Neither . . . wine**—lest the holy enthusiasm of their devotion should be mistaken for inebriation, as in Peter's case (Acts 2:13, 15, 18).

28. I am their inheritance—(Num. 18:20; Deut. 10:9; 18:1; Josh. 13:14, 32).

ADAM CLARKE

7. *The fat and the blood.* These never went into common use; they were wholly offered to God. The *blood* was poured out; the *fat* consumed.

10. *And the Levites that are gone away far from me.* This refers to the schism of Jeroboam, who, when he set up a new worship, got as many of the priests and Levites to join him in his idolatry as he could. These, on the return from the Captivity, should not be permitted to perform the functions of priests in the new Temple; but they might be continued as keepers of all the charge of the house—be treasurers, guards of the Temple, porters, etc.; see vv. 11-15. The whole of these passages refer to the period of time when the second Temple was built.

16. *Come near to my table.* To place the shewbread there, and to burn incense on the golden altar in the holy of holies.

17. *No wool shall come upon them.* The reason is plain. Wool is more apt than linen to contract dirt and breed insects; linen breeds none; besides, this is a vegetable and the other an animal substance. It was an ancient maxim that whatever was taken from a dead body was impure in matters of religion, and should not be permitted to enter into the Temple. The Egyptian priests always wore linen on their bodies, and shoes of matting or rushes on their feet.

22. *Neither shall they take for their wives a widow.* This was prohibited to the high priest only, by Moses, Lev. xxi. 13-14.

MATTHEW HENRY

in many cases to be turned into money and given to the priest. This is explained, *v.* 30. They were to have *the first of the dough* when it was going to the oven, as well as the first of their fruits when they were going to the barn. The priests being so well provided for, it would be inexcusable in them if they should *eat that which is torn or which died of itself, v.* 31.

2. What the people might expect from the priest for their recompence. Those that are kind to a prophet, to a priest, shall have a prophet's, a priest's reward (*v.* 30). It was part of the priest's work to *bless the people in the name of the Lord*, not only their congregations, but their families.

JAMIESON, FAUSSET, BROWN

30. give . . . priest the first . . . that he may cause the blessing to rest—(Prov. 3:9, 10; Mal. 3:10).

ADAM CLARKE

MATTHEW HENRY — CHAPTER 45

Verses 1–8

Directions are here given for the dividing of the land after their return to it. 1. Here is the portion of land assigned to *the sanctuary*, in the midst of which the temple was to be built (*v.* 1), *an oblation to the Lord;* for what is given for the maintenance of the worship of God and the advancement of religion, God accepts as given to him. This *holy portion of the land* was to be measured, and the borders of it fixed. The priests and Levites that were to come near to minister were to have their dwellings in this *portion of the land* that was round about the sanctuary. 2. Next to the lands of the sanctuary the city-lands are assigned, in which the holy city was to be built, and with the issues and profits of which the citizens were to be maintained (*v.* 6). 3. The next allotment after the church-lands and the city-lands is of the crown-lands, *v.* 7, 8. They are said to lie *on the one side and on the other side* of the church-lands and city-lands, to intimate that the prince with his wealth and power was to be a protection to both. *My princes shall no more oppress my people;* for God will make the *officers peace* and the *exactors righteousness*. Nehemiah was one that did not do as the *former governors*, Neh. v. 15, 18. 4. The rest of the lands were to be distributed to the people *according to their tribes.*

Verses 9–12

Some general rules of justice laid down both for prince and people. 1. That *princes do not oppress their subjects*, but duly and faithfully administer justice among them (*v.* 9). Let them *take away their exactions*, ease their subjects of those taxes which they find lie heavily upon them, and let them *execute judgment and justice* according to law. 2. That one neighbour do not cheat another in commerce (*v.* 10): *You shall have just balances.* It concerns God's Israel to be honest and just in all their dealings, punctual and exact in rendering to all their due, because otherwise they spoil the acceptableness of their profession with God and the reputation of it before men.

Verses 13–25

Having laid down the rules of righteousness towards men, he comes next to give some directions for their religion towards God.

I. It is required that they offer an oblation to the Lord (*v.* 13): *All the people of the land* must give an oblation, *v.* 16. They had offered an oblation out of their real estates (*v.* 1), a *holy portion of their land*; now they are directed to offer an oblation out of their **goods and chattels.**

II. The proportion of this oblation is here determined, which was not done by the law of Moses. 1. Out of their corn they were to offer a sixtieth part, *v.* 13. 2. Out of their oil they were to offer a hundredth part, *v.* 14. 3. Out of their flocks they were to give *one lamb* out of 200, *v.* 15. But it must be *out of the fat pastures of Israel.* They must offer to God the fattest and best they had, for *burnt-offerings* and *peace-offerings*. These sacrifices were to *make reconciliations* for them. Christ is our sacrifice of atonement, by whom reconciliation is made.

III. This oblation must be given *for the prince in Israel, v.* 16. Some read it *to* the prince, and understand it of Christ, to whom we must offer our oblations, to be presented to the Father. Or, They shall give it *with* the prince (*v.* 17). The people were to bring their oblations to him, and he was to bring them to the sanctuary, and to make up what fell short out of his own.

IV. Some particular solemnities are here appointed.

1. In the beginning of the year is the annual solemnity of cleansing the sanctuary. (1) *On the first day of the first month* they were to offer a sacrifice for the *cleansing of the sanctuary* (*v.* 18), and to implore grace for the better performance of the service of the sanctuary the ensuing year. By it atonement was

JAMIESON, FAUSSET, BROWN — CHAPTER 45

Vss. 1-25. Allotment of the Land for the Sanctuary, the City, and the Prince. **1. offer an oblation**—from a *Hebrew* root to "heave" or "raise"; when anything was offered to God, the offerer raised the hand. The special territorial division for the tribes is given in chapters 47, 48. Only Jehovah's portion is here subdivided into its three parts: (1) that for the sanctuary (vss. 2, 3); (2) that for the priests (vs. 4); (3) that for the Levites (vs. 5). Cf. ch. 48:8-13. **five and twenty thousand** *reeds* . . .—So *English Version* rightly fills the ellipsis (cf. *Note*, ch. 42:16). Hence "cubits" are mentioned in vs. 2, not here, implying that *there alone* cubits are meant. Taking each reed at twelve feet, the area of the whole would be a square of sixty miles on each side. The whole forming a square betokens the settled stability of the community and the harmony of all classes. "An holy portion of the land" (vs. 1) comprised the whole length, and only two-fifths of the breadth. The outer territory in its distribution harmonizes with the inner and more sacred arrangements of the sanctuary. No room is to be given for *oppression* (see vs. 8), all having ample provision made for their wants and comforts. All will mutually co-operate without constraint or contention. **7.** The prince's possession is to consist of two halves, one on the west, the other on the east, of the sacred territory. The prince, as head of the holy community, stands in closest connection with the sanctuary; his possession, therefore, on both sides must adjoin that which was peculiarly the Lord's [Fairbairn]. **12.** The standard weights were lost when the Chaldeans destroyed the temple. The threefold enumeration of shekels (twenty, twenty-five, fifteen) probably refers to coins of different value, representing respectively so many shekels, the three collectively making up a *maneh*. By weighing these together against the *maneh*, a test was afforded whether they severally had their proper weight: sixty shekels in all, containing one coin a fourth of the whole (fifteen shekels), another a third (twenty shekels), another a third and a twelfth (twenty-five shekels) [Menochius]. LXX reads, "*fifty* shekels shall be your *maneh*." **13-15.** In these oblations there is a progression as to the relation between the kind and the quantity: of the corn, the sixth of a tenth, i.e., a sixtieth part of the quantity specified; of the oil, the tenth of a tenth, i.e., an hundredth part; and of the flock, one from every 200.

18. The year is to begin with a consecration service, not mentioned under the Levitical law; but an earnest of it is given in the feast of dedication of the second temple, which celebrated its purification by Judas Maccabeus, after its defilement by Antiochus.

ADAM CLARKE — CHAPTER 45

1. *When ye shall divide by lot.* That is, when on your repossessing your land every family settles according to the allotment which it formerly had, for it is certain that the land was not divided afresh by lot after the Babylonish captivity. The allotment mentioned and described here was merely for the service of the Temple, the use of the priests, and the prince or governor of the people. A division of the whole land is not intended.

7. *A portion shall be for the prince. Nasi*, he who had the authority of chief magistrate; for there was neither king nor prince among the Jews after the Babylonish captivity.

8. *My princes shall no more oppress my people.* By exorbitant taxes to maintain profligate courts, or subsidize other powers to help to keep up a system of tyranny in the earth. The former princes even robbed the temple of God to give subsidies to other states.

16. *All . . . this oblation for the prince.* A present or offering to the prince.

18. *Thou shalt take a young bullock . . . and cleanse the sanctuary.* There is nothing of this in the Mosaic law; it seems to have been a new ceremony. An annual purification of the sanctuary may be intended.

MATTHEW HENRY

intended to be made for the sins of all the servants that attended that house, priests, Levites, and people, even the sins that were found in all their services. They were here appointed to *cleanse the sanctuary* upon the first day of the month, because on the fourteenth day of the month they were to eat the *passover*, an ordinance which, of all Old Testament institutions, had most in it of Christ and gospel grace. (2) This sacrifice was to be repeated on *the seventh day of the first month, v.* 20. And then it was intended to make atonement *for everyone that errs, and for him that is simple.* It is spoken of those sins which are committed through ignorance, mistake, or inadvertency.

2. The passover was to be religiously observed at the time appointed, *v.* 21. Christ is *our passover*, that is *sacrificed for us.* We celebrate the memorial of that sacrifice in the Lord's supper, which is our passover-feast.

3. The feast of tabernacles; that is spoken of next (*v.* 25), and there is no mention of the feast of pentecost, which came between that of the passover and that of tabernacles. See the deficiency of the legal sacrifices for sin; they were therefore often repeated, not only every year, but every feast, every day of the feast. See the necessity of our frequently repeating the same religious exercises. Though the sacrifice of atonement is offered *once for all*, yet the sacrifices of acknowledgment, that of a broken heart, that of a thankful heart, those spiritual sacrifices which are acceptable to God through Christ Jesus, must be every day offered.

CHAPTER 46

Verses 1–15

We do not find in the history of that latter part of the Jewish church that they governed themselves by these ordinances, but only by the law of Moses, looking upon this *then* in the next age after as mystical, and not literal.

I. The place of worship was fixed, and rules given to prince and people.

1. The east gate, kept shut at other times, was to be opened on the sabbath days, on the new moons (*v.* 1), and whenever the prince offered a voluntary offering, *v.* 12. Some think he went in with the priests and Levites into the *inner court*, and they observe that magistrates and ministers should go hand in hand, in promoting the service of God. But it should rather seem that he went *by the way of the porch of the gate*, stood *at the post of the gate*, and *worshipped at the threshold of the gate* (*v.* 2), where he had a full view of the priests' performances at the altar, and the people stood behind him *at the door of that gate, v.* 3.

2. As to the north gate and south gate, by which they entered into the *court of the people*—whoever came in at the *north gate* should go out at the *south gate*, and whoever came in at the *south gate* should go out at the *north gate, v.* 9. Some think this was to prevent jostling.

3. *The people shall worship at the door of the east gate*, where the prince does, both *on the sabbath and on the new moons* (*v.* 3).

II. The ordinances of worship were fixed. 1. Every morning they must offer *a lamb* for a *burnt-offering, v.* 13. 2. On the sabbath days, whereas by the law of Moses two lambs were to be offered (Num. xxviii. 9) there shall be six lambs offered. 3. On the new moons, in the beginning of their months, there was the additional offering of a young bullock, *v.* 6. 4. All the sacrifices were to be *without blemish*; so Christ, the great sacrifice, was (1 Pet. i. 19), and so Christians, who present themselves to God as living sacrifices, should be—*blameless, and harmless, and without rebuke.* 5. All the sacrifices were to have their meat-offerings annexed to them, to show that we ought to honour him with the fruit of our ground as well as with the fruit of our cattle, Deut. xxviii. 4. The meat-offerings here are much larger in proportion than they were by the law of Moses, which intimates that under the gospel, the great atoning sacrifice having been offered, these unbloody sacrifices shall be more.

Verses 16–18

A law for the limiting of the power of the prince in disposing of the crown-lands. 1. If he have a *son* that has merited well, he may, in recompence for his services, settle some parts of his lands upon him (*v.* 16). 2. Yet, if he have a servant that is a favourite, he may not settle lands upon him, *v.* 17. But he may give him lands to the year of jubilee, and then they must return to the family again, *v.* 17. 3. What estates he gives his children must be of his own (*v.* 18): He

JAMIESON, FAUSSET, BROWN

20. for him that is simple—for sins of ignorance (Lev. 4:2, 13, 27). **21.** As a new solemnity, the feast of consecration is to prepare for the passover; so the passover itself is to have different sacrifices from those of the Mosaic law. Instead of one ram and seven lambs for the daily burnt offering, there are to be seven bullocks and seven rams. So also whereas the feast of tabernacles had its own offerings, which diminished as the days of the feast advanced, here the same are appointed as on the passover. Thus it is implied that the letter of the law is to give place to its spirit, those outward rites of Judaism having no intrinsic efficacy, but symbolizing the spiritual truths of Messiah's kingdom, as for instance the perfect holiness which is to characterize it. Cf. I Corinthians 5:7, 8, as to our spiritual "passover," wherein, at the Lord's supper, we feed on Christ by faith, accompanied with "the unleavened bread of sincerity and truth." Literal ordinances, though not slavishly bound to the letter of the law, will set forth the catholic and eternal verities of Messiah's kingdom.

CHAPTER 46

VSS. 1-24. CONTINUATION OF THE ORDINANCES FOR THE PRINCE AND FOR THE PEOPLE IN THEIR WORSHIP. **2.** The prince is to go through the east gate without (open on the Sabbath only, to mark its peculiar sanctity) to the entrance of the gate of the inner court; he is to go no further, but "stand by the post" (cf. I Kings 8:14, 22, Solomon standing before the altar of the Lord in the presence of the congregation; also II Kings 11:14; 23:3, "by a pillar": the customary place), the court within belonging exclusively to the priests. There, as representative of the people, in a peculiarly near relation to God, he is to present his offerings to Jehovah, while at a greater distance, the people are to stand worshipping at the outer gate of the same entrance. The offerings on Sabbaths are larger than those of the Mosaic law, to imply that the worship of God is to be conducted by the prince and people in a more munificent spirit of self-sacrificing liberality than formerly. **9.** The worshippers were on the great feasts to pass from one side to the other, through the temple courts, in order that, in such a throng as should attend the festivals, the ingress and egress should be the more unimpeded, those going out not being in the way of those coming in. **10. prince in the midst**—not isolated as at other times, but joining the great throng of worshippers, at their head, after the example of David (Ps. 42:4, "I had gone with the multitude . . . to the house of God, with the voice of joy and praise, with a multitude that kept holy day"); the highest in rank animating the devotions of the rest by his presence and example. **12-15.** Not only is he to perform *official* acts of worship on holy days and feasts, but in "voluntary" offerings daily he is to show his individual zeal, surpassing all his people in liberality, and so setting them a princely example.

16-18. The prince's possession is to be inalienable, and any portion given to a servant is to revert to his sons at the year of jubilee, that he may have no temptation to spoil his people of their inheritance, as formerly (cf. Ahab and Naboth, I Kings 21). The mention of the year of jubilee implies that there is something literal meant, besides the spiritual sense. The jubilee year was restored after the captivity [JOSEPHUS, *Antiquities*, 14. 10, 6; I Maccabees 6:49]. Perhaps it will be restored under Messiah's coming reign. Cf. Isaiah 61:2, 3, where "the acceptable year of the Lord" is closely connected with the comforting of the mourners in Zion, and "the day of vengeance" on Zion's foes. The mention of the prince's *sons* is another argument against Messiah being meant by "the prince."

ADAM CLARKE

20. *For him that is simple.* That wants understanding to conduct himself properly.

CHAPTER 46

4. *The burnt offering that the prince shall offer.* The chief magistrate was always obliged to attend the public worship of God, as well as the priest, to show that the civil and ecclesiastical states were both under the same government of the Lord; and that no one was capable of being prince or priest who did not acknowledge God in all his ways.

9. *He that entereth in by the way of the north.* As the north and the south gates were opposite to each other, he that came in at the north must go out at the south; he that came in at the south must go out at the north. No person was to come in at the east gate, because there was no gate at the west; and the people were not permitted to turn round and go out at the same place by which they came in, for this was like turning their backs on God, and the decorum and reverence with which public worship was to be conducted would not admit of this. Besides, returning by the same way must have occasioned a great deal of confusion, where so many people must have jostled each other in their meetings in different parts of this space.

10. *And the prince in the midst of them.* Even he shall act in the same way; he must also go straight forward, and never turn his back to go out at the same gate by which he entered. The prince and the people were to begin and end their worship at the same time.

13. *Thou shalt prepare it every morning.* The evening offering is entirely omitted, which makes an important difference between this and the old laws. See Exod. xxix. 31-46.

17. *To the year of liberty.* That is, to the year of jubilee, called the "year of liberty" because there was then a general release. All servants had their liberty, and all alienated estates returned to their former owners.

MATTHEW HENRY

shall not take of the people's inheritance. It is the interest of princes to rule in the hearts of their subjects. It is better to gain their affections by protecting their rights than to gain their estates by invading them.

Verses 19–24

Places in which to boil the flesh of the offerings, *v.* 20. There were some at the entry into the inner court (*v.* 19) and others in the four corners of the outer court, *v.* 21–23. In those places they were to *boil the trespass-offering and the sin-offering,* those parts of them which were allotted to the priests. There also they were to *bake the meat-offering, v.* 20.

CHAPTER 47

Verses 1–12

This part of Ezekiel's vision must necessarily have a mystical and spiritual meaning. The prophecy, Zech. xiv. 8, may explain it, of *living waters* that shall *go out* from Jerusalem, *half of them towards the former sea and half of them towards the hinder sea.* And there is plainly a reference to this in St. John's vision of *a pure river of water of life,* Rev. xxii. 1. That seems to represent the glory and joy which are grace perfected. This seems to represent the grace and joy which are glory begun. Most interpreters agree that these waters signify the gospel of Christ, which went forth from Jerusalem, and spread itself into the countries about, and the gifts and powers of the Holy Ghost which accompanied it, by virtue of which it spread far and produced blessed effects.

I. The rise of these waters (*v.* 1). *Waters issued out from the threshold of the house eastward,* and from *under the right side of the house,* that is, the south side of *the altar.* And again (*v.* 2), *There ran out waters on the right side,* signifying that *from Zion should go forth the law and the word of the Lord from Jerusalem,* Isa. ii. 3. There it was that the Spirit was poured out upon the apostles, and endued them with the gift of tongues, that they might carry these waters to all nations. In the temple first they were to stand and *preach the words of this life,* Acts v. 20. They must preach the gospel to all nations, but must *begin at Jerusalem,* Luke xxiv. 47. Christ is the temple; he is the door; from him those living waters flow, out of his pierced side. It is by believing in him that we receive from him *rivers of living water;* and *this spoke he of the Spirit,* John vii. 38, 39. The original of these waters was not above-ground, but they sprang up from under the threshold; for the fountain of a believer's life is a mystery; it is *hid with Christ in God,* Col. iii. 3.

II. The progress and increase of these waters: They *went forth eastward* (*v.* 3), *towards the east country* (*v.* 8). The prophet and his guide followed the stream as it ran down from the holy mountains, and when they had followed it about *a thousand cubits* they went across, to try the depth, and it was *to the ankles, v.* 3. Then they walked along on the bank of the river on the other side, a thousand cubits more, and then, to try the depth, they waded through it the second time, and it was up to *their knees, v.* 4. They walked along by it a thousand cubits more, and then forded it the third time, and then it was up to their middle—*the waters were to the loins.* They then walked a thousand cubits further, and attempted to repass it the fourth time, but found it impracticable: *The waters had risen,* so that they were *waters to swim in, a river that could not be passed over, v.* 5. Note, 1. The waters of the sanctuary are running waters, as those of a river, not standing waters, as those of a pond. Grace in the soul is still pressing forward; *onward still,* till it comes to perfection. 2. They are increasing waters. This river runs constantly, the further it goes the fuller it grows. The gospel-church was very small in its beginnings, like a little purling brook; but by degrees it came *to the ankles, to the knees:* many were added to it daily. The gifts of the Spirit increase by being exercised, and grace is growing, like the light of the morning, which *shines more and more to the perfect day.* 3. It is good for us to follow these waters. Observe the progress of the gospel in the world; observe the process of the work of grace in the heart; attend the motions of the blessed

JAMIESON, FAUSSET, BROWN

19-24. Due regard is to be had for the sanctity of the officiating priests' food, by cooking-courts being provided close to their chambers. One set of apartments for cooking was to be at the corners of the *inner* court, reserved for the flesh of the sin offerings, to be eaten only by the priests whose perquisite it was (Lev. 6:25; 7:7), before coming forth to mingle again with the people; another set at the corners of the *outer* court, for cooking the flesh of the peace offerings, of which the people partook along with the priests. All this implies that no longer are the common and unclean to be confounded with the sacred and divine, but that in even the least things, as eating and drinking, the glory of God is to be the aim (I Cor. 10:31). **22. courts joined**—FAIRBAIRN translates, "roofed" or "vaulted." But these cooking apartments seem to have been uncovered, to let the smoke and smell of the meat the more easily pass away. They were "joined" or "attached" to the walls of the courts at the corners of the latter [MENOCHIUS]. **23. boiling-places**—boilers. **under the rows**—At the foot of the rows, i.e., in the lowest part of the *walls,* were the places for boiling made.

CHAPTER 47

Vss. 1-23. VISION OF THE TEMPLE WATERS. BORDERS AND DIVISION OF THE LAND. The happy fruit to the earth at large of God's dwelling with Israel in holy fellowship is that the blessing is no longer restricted to the one people and locality, but is to be diffused with comprehensive catholicity through the whole world. So the plant from the cedar of Lebanon is represented as gathering under its shelter "all fowl of every wing" (ch. 17:23). Even the desert places of the earth shall be made fruitful by the healing waters of the Gospel (cf. Isa. 35:1).

1. waters—So Revelation 22:1, represents "the water of life as proceeding out of the throne of God and of the Lamb." His throne was set up in the temple at Jerusalem (ch. 43:7). Thence it is to flow over the earth (Joel 3:18; Zech. 13:1; 14:8). Messiah is the temple and the door; from His pierced side flow the living waters, ever increasing, both in the individual believer and in the heart. The fountains in the vicinity of Moriah suggested the image here.

The waters flow eastward, i.e., towards the Kedron, and thence towards the Jordan, and so along the Ghor into the Dead Sea. The main point in the picture is the rapid augmentation from a petty stream into a mighty river, not by the influx of side streams, but by its own self-supply from the sacred miraculous source in the temple [HENDERSON]. (Cf. Ps. 36:8, 9; 46:4; Isa. 11:9; Hab. 2:14).

Searching into the things of God, we find some easy to understand, as the water up to the ankles; others more difficult, which require a deeper search, as the waters up to the knees or loins; others beyond our reach, of which we can only adore the depth (Rom. 11:33). The *healing* of the waters of the Dead Sea here answers to "there shall be no more curse" (Rev. 22:3; cf. Zech. 14:11).

ADAM CLARKE

20. *The trespass offering.* Part of this, and of the sin offering, and the flour offering, was the portion of the priests, See Num. xviii. 9-10.

CHAPTER 47

1. *Behold, waters issued out from under the threshold.* Ezekiel, after having made the whole compass of the court of the people, is brought back by the north gate into the courts of the priests; and, having reached the gate of the Temple, he saw waters which had their spring under the threshold of that gate, that looked towards the east; and which, passing to the south of the altar of burnt offerings on the right of the Temple, ran from the west to the east, that they might fall into the brook Kidron, and thence be carried into the Dead Sea. Literally, no such waters were ever in the Temple; and because there were none, Solomon had what is called the brazen sea made, which held water for the use of the Temple. It is true that the water which supplied this sea might have been brought by pipes to the place; but a fountain producing abundance of water was not there, and could not be there, on the top of such a hill; and consequently these waters, as well as those spoken of in Joel iii. 18 and in Zech. xiv. 8, are to be understood spiritually or typically; and indeed the whole complexion of the place here shows that they are thus to be understood. Taken in this view, I shall proceed to apply the whole of this vision to the effusion of light and salvation by the outpouring of the Spirit of God under the gospel dispensation, by which the knowledge of the true God was multiplied in the earth; and have only one previous remark to make, that the farther the waters flowed from the Temple, the deeper they grew. With respect to the phraseology of this chapter, it may be said that St. John had it particularly in view while he wrote his celebrated description of the paradise of God, Revelation xxii. The prophet may therefore be referring to the same thing which the apostle describes, viz., the grace of the gospel, and its effects in the world.

2. *There ran out waters.* The waters seem to have been at first in small quantity, for the words imply that they *oozed* or "dropped out."

3-5. *He measured a thousand cubits, . . . the waters were to the ancles; a thousand* more . . . *the waters were to the knees . . . a thousand* more . . . they became *a river* that could not be forded. *the waters were risen,* and they were *waters to swim in.*

A. This may be applied to the gradual discoveries of the plan of salvation—(1) in the patriarchal ages, (2) in the giving of the law, (3) in the ministry of John the Baptist, and, (4) in the full manifestation of Christ by the communication of the Holy Ghost.

B. This vision may be applied also to the growth of a believer in the grace and knowledge of God. There is—(1) the seed of the Kingdom, (2) the blade from that seed, (3) the ear out of that blade, and (4) the full corn in that ear.

C. It may be applied to the discoveries a penitent believer receives of the mercy of God in his salvation. (1) He is a little child, born of God, born from above, and begins to taste the bread of life, and live on the heavenly food. (2) He grows up and increases in stature and

MATTHEW HENRY

Spirit, as Ezekiel here did. If we search into the things of God, we shall find some very plain and easy to be understood, as the waters that were but to the ankles, others more difficult, as the water to the knees, and some quite beyond our reach, which we cannot penetrate, but, despairing to find the bottom, must, as St. Paul, sit down at the brink, and adore the *depth*, Rom. xi. 33.

III. The extent of this river: *It issues towards the east country*, but *goes down into the desert*, and so *goes into the sea*, either into the *dead sea*, which lay *south-east*, or the sea of Tiberias, which lay *north-east*, or the great sea, which lay *west*, *v.* 8. This was accomplished when the gospel was preached throughout all the regions of Judæa and Samaria (Acts viii. 1), and afterwards the nations about, and even in the isles of the sea, were enlightened.

IV. The healing virtue of this river. Being *brought forth into the sea*, the sulphurous lake of Sodom, even those *waters shall be healed* (*v.* 8), shall become sweet, and healthful. This intimates the blessed change that the gospel would make, as great a change, as the turning of the dead sea into a fountain of gardens. The gospel was as that salt which Elisha cast, 2 Kings ii. 20, 21. Christ, coming into the world to be its physician, sent his gospel as the great medicine. Wherever these rivers come, they *make things to live* (*v.* 9); they are *the water of life*, Rev. xxii. 1, 17. Christ came, *that we might have life*, and for that end he sends his gospel. The grace of God makes dead sinners alive and living saints lively; everything is made fruitful and flourishing by it. But its effect is according as it is received, and as the mind is prepared and disposed to receive it.

V. The great plenty of fish that should be in this river. Every living moving thing shall be found here, shall *live here* (*v.* 9).

VI. The trees that were on the banks of this river—*many trees on the one side and on the other* (*v.* 7); they *are trees for meat*, and the *fruit* of them *shall not be consumed*, for it shall produce fresh fruit *every month* (*v.* 12). The *leaf* shall be *for medicine*, and it *shall not fade*. This part of the vision compares with St. John's vision (Rev. xxii. 2), where, on either side of the river, is said to grow the *tree of life*, which *yielded her fruit every month*, and *the leaves* were *for the healing of the nations*. The very leaves of these trees *are for medicine*, for *bruises* and sores, *margin*. Good Christians do good to those about them; they *strengthen the weak*, and bind up the broken-hearted. Their cheerfulness *does good like a medicine*. Their *leaf shall not fade*, having not only life in their root, but sap in all their branches. Each one of them shall bring forth fruit monthly, which denotes an abundant disposition to fruit-bearing (they shall never be weary of well-doing). And the reason of this extraordinary fruitfulness is *because their waters issued out of the sanctuary*; it is to be ascribed to the continual supplies of divine grace.

Verses 13–22

The affairs of the state. The land of Canaan is here secured to them for an inheritance (*v.* 14): *I lifted up my hand to give it unto your fathers*. God had not forgotten his oath which he swore to their fathers. *I lifted up my hand to give it*, and therefore it shall without fail *fall to you for an inheritance*. The bounds are fixed. It is God that *appoints the bounds of our habitation*. It is here ordered to be divided among the tribes of Israel, reckoning Joseph for two tribes, to make up the number of twelve, when Levi was taken out to attend the sanctuary, and had his lot adjoining to that (*v.* 13, 21): *You shall inherit it, one as well as another*, *v.* 14.

JAMIESON, FAUSSET, BROWN

7. trees—not merely *one* tree of life as in Paradise (Gen. 2), but many: to supply immortal food and medicine to the people of God, who themselves also become "trees of righteousness" (Isa. 61:3) planted by the waters and (Ps. 1:3) bearing fruit unto holiness. **8. the desert**—or "plain," *Hebrew, Arabah* (Deut. 3:17; 4:49; Josh. 3:16), which is the name still given to the valley of the Jordan and the plain south of the Dead Sea, and extending to the Elanitic gulf of the Red Sea. **the sea**—the Dead Sea. *"The sea"* noted as covering with its waters the guilty cities of the plain, Sodom and Gomorrah. In its bituminous waters no vegetable or animal life is said to be found. But now death is to give place to life in Judea, and throughout the world, as symbolized by the healing of these death-pervaded waters covering the doomed cities. Cf. as to "the sea" in general, regarded as a symbol of the troubled powers of nature, disordered by the fall, henceforth to rage no more, Revelation 21:1. **9. rivers**—in *Hebrew*, *"two* rivers." Hence *Hebrew* expositors think that the waters from the temple were divided into two branches, the one emptying itself into the eastern or Dead Sea, the other into the western or Mediterranean. So Zechariah 14:8. However, though this probably is covertly implied in the *Hebrew dual*, the flowing of the waters into the *Dead Sea only* is expressed. Cf. vs. 8, "waters . . . healed," which can apply only to it, not to the Mediterranean: also vs. 10, "fish as the fish of the great sea"; the Dead Sea, when healed, containing fish, as the Mediterranean does. **10. En-gedi . . . En-eglaim**—En-gedi (meaning "fountain of the kid"), anciently, Hazazon-Tamar, now Ain-Jidy; west of the Dead Sea; David's place of refuge from Saul. En-eglaim means "fountain of two calves," on the confines of Moab, over against En-gedi, and near where Jordan enters the Dead Sea (Isa. 15:8). These two limits are fixed on, to comprise between them the whole Dead Sea. **fish . . . according to their kinds**—JEROME quotes an ancient theory that "there are 153 kinds of fishes," all of which were taken by the apostles (John 21:11), and not one remained uncaptured; signifying that both the noble and baseborn, the rich and the poor, and every class, are being drawn out of the sea of the world to salvation. Cf. Matthew 14:47, the gospel net; the apostles being fishermen, at first literally, afterwards spiritually (Matt. 4:19). **11. marshes**—marshy places. The region is known to have such pits and marshes. The Arabs take the salt collected by evaporation in these pits for their own use, and that of their flocks. **not be healed**—Those not reached by the healing waters of the Gospel, through their sloth and earthly-mindedness, are given over (Rev. 22:11) to their own bitterness and barrenness (as "saltness" is often employed to express, Deut. 29:23; Ps. 107:34; Zeph. 2:9); and awful example to others in the punishment they suffer (II Peter 2:6). **12.** Instead of the "vine of Sodom and grapes of Gomorrah" (Deut. 32:32), nauseous and unwholesome, trees of life-giving and life-restoring virtue shall bloom similar in properties to, and exceeding in number, the tree of life in Eden (Rev. 2:7; 22:2, 14). **leaf . . . not fade**—expressing not only the unfailing character of the heavenly medicine of the tree of life, but also that the graces of the believer (as a tree of righteousness), which are the *leaves*, and his deeds, which are the fruits that flow from those graces, are immortal (Ps. 1:3; Jer. 17:8; Matt. 10:42; I Cor. 15:58). **new fruit**—lit., "firstlings," or first fruit. They are still, each month afresh, as it were, yielding their first fruit [FAIRBAIRN]. The *first-born* of a thing, in *Hebrew* idiom, means *the chiefest*. As Job 18:13, "the first-born of death," i.e., *the most fatal* death. **13.** *The redivision of the land: the boundaries.* The latter are substantially the same as those given by Moses in Numbers 34; they here begin with the north, but in Numbers 34 they begin with the south. It is only Canaan proper, exclusive of the possession of the two and a half tribes beyond Jordan, that is here divided. **Joseph . . . two portions**—according to the original promise of Jacob (Gen. 48:5, 22). Joseph's sons were given the birthright forfeited by Reuben, the first-born (I Chron. 5:1). Therefore the former is here put first. His *two* sons having distinct portions make up the whole number *twelve* portions, as he had just before specified "*twelve* tribes of Israel"; for Levi had no separate inheritance, so that he is not reckoned in the twelve. **15. Zedad**—on the north boundary of Canaan. **16. Hamath**—As Israel was a separate people, so their land was a separate land. On no scene could the sacred history have been so well transacted as on it. On the east was the sandy desert. On the north and south, mountains. On

ADAM CLARKE

strength, and becomes a young man. (3) He becomes matured in the divine life, and has his spiritual senses exercised so as to become a father in Christ. (4) In thus following on to know the Lord he finds a continual increase of light and life, till at last he is carried by the streams of grace to the ocean of eternal mercy.

D. These waters may be considered as a type of the progress which Christianity shall make in the world. (1) There were only a few poor fishermen. (2) Afterwards many Jews. (3) Then the Gentiles of Asia Minor and Greece. (4) The continent and isles of Europe. And, (5) now spreading through Africa, Asia, and America, at present these waters are no longer a river, but an immense sea; and the gospel fishers are daily bringing multitudes of souls to Christ.

9. *Every thing . . . whithersoever the rivers shall come, shall live.* Life and salvation shall continually accompany the preaching of the gospel; the death of sin being removed, the life of righteousness shall be brought in. *There shall be a very great multitude of fish.* On the above plan this must refer to genuine converts to the Christian faith; true believers, who have got life and salvation by the streams of God's grace. The apostles were fishers of men; converts were the fish caught.

10. *The fishers shall stand upon it.* On the above plan of interpretation these must mean—(1) the apostles of our Lord Jesus, (2) the preachers of the everlasting gospel. *From En-gedi.* At the southern extremity of the Dead Sea. *Unto En-eglaim.* At the northern extremity of the same.

12. *The leaf thereof for medicine.* See Rev. xxii. 1-5.

13. *Joseph shall have two portions.* That is, in Ephraim and Manasseh, his two sons, who each had a separate inheritance.

MATTHEW HENRY

The strangers who sojourn among them, *who shall beget children* and be built up into families, and so help to people their country, *shall have inheritance among* the tribes, as if they had been native Israelites (*v.* 22, 23). It certainly looks at gospel-times, when the partition-wall between Jew and Gentile was taken down, and both were put upon a level before God, both made one in Christ, in whom *there is no difference*, Rom. x. 12.

JAMIESON, FAUSSET, BROWN

the west, an inhospitable seashore. But it was not always to be a separate land. Between the parallel ranges of Lebanon is the long valley of El-Bekaa, leading to "the entering in of Hamath" on the Orontes, in the Syrian frontier. Roman roads, and the harbor made at Cæsarea, opened out doors through which the Gospel should go from it to all lands. So in the last days, when all shall flock to Jerusalem as the religious center of the world. **Berothah**—a city in Syria conquered by David (II Sam. 8:8); meaning "wells." **Hazar-hatticon**—meaning "the middle village." **Hauran**—a tract in Syria, south of Damascus; Auranitis. **17. Hazar-enan**—a town in the north of Canaan, meaning "village of fountains." **18. east sea**—the Dead Sea. The border is to go down straight to it by the valley of the Jordan. So Numbers 34:11, 12. **19. Tamar**—not Tadmor in the desert, but Tamar, the last town of Judea, by the Dead Sea. Meaning "palm tree"; so called from palm trees abounding near it. **22. to the strangers**—It is altogether unprecedented under the old covenant, that "strangers" should have "inheritance" among the tribes. There would not be room locally within Canaan for more than the tribes. The literal sense must therefore be modified, as expressing that Gentiles are not to be excluded from settling among the covenant people, and that spiritually their privileges are not to be less than those of Israel (Rom. 10:12; Gal. 3:28; Eph. 3:6; Col. 3:11; Rev. 7:9, 10). Still, "sojourneth," in vs. 23, implies that in Canaan, the covenant people are regarded as *at home*, the strangers as *settlers*.

ADAM CLARKE

17. *The border from the sea.* The north border eastward is ascertained, vv. 15-16; here it is shown how far it extends itself northward.

18. *The east sea.* The same as the Dead Sea.

19. *Tamar.* Called Hazazon-tamar, or En-gedi, 2 Chron. xx. 2. *The river.* Besor, which runs into the sea near Gaza.

20. *The great sea.* The Mediterranean. *From the border.* The southern border, mentioned in v. 19.

CHAPTER 48

Verses 1–30

A short way taken for the dividing of the land among the twelve tribes. In this distribution of the land we may observe, 1. That it differs very much from the division of it in Joshua's time. It is not so much to be understood literally as spiritually, though the mystery of it is very much hidden from us. The Israel of God is cast into a new method. 2. That the tribe of Dan, which was last provided for in the first division of Canaan (Joshua xix. 40), is first provided for here, *v.* 1. God, in the dispensation of his grace, does not follow the same method that he does in the disposals of his providence. 3. That all the ten tribes that were carried away by the king of Assyria, as well as the two tribes that were long afterwards carried to Babylon, have their allotment in this visionary land. We believe it has its designed accomplishment in the establishment and enlargement of the gospel church, and in the sure and sweet enjoyment of the privileges of the new covenant, in which there is enough for all and enough for each. 4. That every tribe in this visionary distribution had its particular lot assigned it by a divine appointment. We must not only acknowledge, but acquiesce, in the hand of God appointing us our lot, and be well pleased with it, believing it fittest for us. *He shall choose our inheritance for us*, Ps. xlvii. 4. 5. That the tribes lay contiguous. By *the border* of one tribe was *the portion* of another. It was a figure of the communion of churches and saints under the gospel-government; thus, though they are many, yet they are one, and should hold together in holy love and mutual assistance. 6. That the lot of Reuben, which before lay at a distance beyond Jordan, now lies next to Judah, and next but one to the sanctuary; for the scandal he lay under, for which he was told *he should not excel*, began by this time to wear off. 7. That the sanctuary was *in the midst* of them. There were seven tribes to the north of it, and the Levites, the princes, and the city's portion, with that of five tribes more, to the south of it; so that it was, as it ought to be, *in the heart of the kingdom*. 8. That where the sanctuary was the priests were: *For them, even for the priests, shall this holy oblation be*, *v.* 10. 9. Those priests had the priests' share of these lands that had approved themselves faithful to God in times of trial (*v.* 11): *It shall be for the sons of Zadok*, who, it seems, had signalized themselves in some critical juncture, and *went not astray* when the *children of Israel*, and the other *Levites, went astray*. 10. The land which was appropriated to the ministers of the sanctuary might by no means be alienated. They might not *sell it nor exchange it*, *v.* 14. It is sacrilege to convert that to other uses which is dedicated to God. 11. The land allotted for the city and its suburbs is called a *profane place* (*v.* 15), or *common*. In comparison with the sanctuary, it was a profane place. 12. The city is made to be exactly square, and the suburbs extending themselves equally on all sides, as the Levites' cities did in the first division of the

CHAPTER 48

Vss. 1-35. Allotment of the Land to the Several Tribes. **1. Dan**—The lands are divided into portions of ideal exactness, running alongside of each other, the whole breadth from west to east, standing in a common relation to the temple in the center: seven tribes' portions on the north, five in the smaller division in the south. The portions of the city, the temple, the prince, and the priesthood, are in the middle, not within the boundaries of any tribe, all alike having a common interest in them. Judah has the place of honor next the center on the north, Benjamin the corresponding place of honor next the center on the south; because of the adherence of these two to the temple ordinances and to the house of David for so long, when the others deserted them. Dan, on the contrary, so long locally and morally semi-heathen (Judg. 18), is to have the least honorable place, at the extreme north. For the same reason, St. John (Rev. 7:5-8) omits Dan altogether. **3. Asher**—a tribe of which no one of note is mentioned in the Old Testament. In the New Testament one is singled out of it, the prophetess Anna. **4. Manasseh**—The intercourse and unity between the two and a half tribes east of the Jordan, and the nine and a half west of it, had been much kept up by the splitting of Manasseh, causing the visits of kinsmen one to the other from both sides of the Jordan. There shall be no need for this in the new order of things. **5. Ephraim**—This tribe, within its two dependent tribes, Manasseh and Benjamin, for upwards of 400 years under the judges held the pre-eminence. **6. Reuben**—doomed formerly for incest and instability "not to excel" (Gen. 49:4). So no distinguished prophet, priest, or king had come from it. Of it were the notorious Dathan and Abiram, the mutineers. A pastoral and Bedouin character marked it and Gad (Judg. 5:16).

15-17. The 5000 rods, apportioned to the city out of the 25,000 square, are to be laid off in a square of 4500, with the 250 all around for suburbs. **profane**—i.e., not strictly sacred as the sacerdotal portions, but applied to secular uses.

CHAPTER 48

1. *Now these are the names of the tribes.* See the division mentioned Num. xxxiv. 7-12, which casts much light upon this.

9. *The oblation.* This was a portion of land 25,000 cubits in length, by 10,000 broad; in the center of which was the Temple, which must be destined for the use of the priests, the Levites, and the prince.

15. *And the five thousand, that are left.* The territory of the Levites was 25,000 square cubits, v. 20. But their city was only 4,500 square cubits; see vv. 13 and 16. There remained, therefore, 10,000 cubits square to be

MATTHEW HENRY

land (*v.* 16, 17), which, never being literally fulfilled in any city, intimates that it is to be understood spiritually of the beauty and stability of the gospel church, that *city of the living God.* 13. Whereas, before, the inhabitants of Jerusalem were principally of Judah and Benjamin, in whose tribe it lay, now *those that serve the city*, and bear office in it, *shall serve it out of all the tribes of Israel*, *v.* 19. 14. Those who applied themselves to public business in the city, as well as in the sanctuary, should have an honourable comfortable maintenance; lands are appointed, *the increase* whereof *shall be food unto those that serve the city*, *v.* 18. 15. The prince had a lot for himself, suited to the dignity of his high station (*v.* 21). 16. As Judah had his lot next the sanctuary on one side, so Benjamin had, of all the tribes, his lot nearest to it on the other side, which honour was reserved for those who adhered to the house of David and the temple at Jerusalem when the other ten tribes went astray from both.

Verses 31–35

A further account of the city that should be built for those who should come to worship in the sanctuary adjoining. It is nowhere called Jerusalem, nor is the land called Canaan; *old things are done away, behold all things have become new.* Concerning this city, 1. The measures of its out-lets and the grounds, *v.* 35. But what these measures were is uncertain. These things are to be understood spiritually. 2. The number of its gates. It had twelve gates in all, three on each side, inscribed to the twelve tribes. In St. John's vision, the new Jerusalem has *twelve gates*, three on a side, and on them are written *the names of the twelve tribes of the children of Israel*, Rev. xxi. 12, 13. Into the church of Christ, there is a free access by faith for all that come of every tribe, from every quarter. Christ has *opened the kingdom of heaven for all believers.* 3. The name given to this city: it shall be, not, as before, *Jerusalem—The vision of peace*, but, which is the original of that, *Jehovah Shammah—The Lord is there*, *v.* 35. This intimated, (1) That the captives, after their return, should have manifest tokens of God's presence with them and his residence among them. (2) That the gospel-church should likewise have the presence of God in it, though not in the *Shechinah*, as of old, yet in a token of it no less sure, that of his Spirit. *Lo, I am with you always even unto the end of the world.* Whatever soul has in it a living principle of grace, it may be truly said, *The Lord is there.* (3) That the glory and happiness of heaven should consist chiefly in this, that *the Lord is there.*

JAMIESON, FAUSSET, BROWN

24. Benjamin—Cf. Jacob's prophecy (Gen. 49:27; Deut. 33:12). It alone with Judah had been throughout loyal to the house of David, so its prowess at the "night" of the national history was celebrated as well as in the "morning." **25. Simeon**—omitted in the blessing of Moses in Deuteronomy 33 perhaps because of the Simeonite "prince," who at Baal-peor led the Israelites in their idolatrous whoredoms with Midian (Num. 25:14). **26. Issachar**—Its ancient portion had been on the plain of Esdraelon. Compared (Gen. 49:14) to "a strong ass crouching between two burdens," i.e., tribute and tillage; never meddling with wars except in self-defense. **31. gates**—(Rev. 21:12, etc.). The twelve gates bear the names of the twelve tribes to imply that all are regarded as having an interest in it.

35. Lord is there—*Jehovah-Shammah.* Not that the city will be called so in mere name, but that the reality will be best expressed by this descriptive title (Jer. 3:17; 33:16; Zech. 2:10; Rev. 21:3; 22:3).

ADAM CLARKE

divided, of which 5,000 cubits in breadth by 25,000 in length, on the east and west sides, were reserved for a sort of second city; or for suburbs where laymen might dwell who were employed by those priests and Levites who lodged in the Temple and in the city, v. 18. And another space of 1,000 cubits in breadth by 25,000 in length, which extended only from north to south, was for fields and gardens appointed for the support of those lay servants. On which we may remark, there was no cultivated land between the portion of the Levites and that of the prince, but only on the east and west sides.

21. *And the residue . . . for the prince.* His portion was alongside that of the Levites, from west to east; these were on each side 25,000 cubits in length, from the east to the west, by 12,500 cubits in breadth from north to south. The space both above and below was equal, between the tribe of Judah and that of Benjamin to north and south, and the portion of the Levites, which had Judah and Benjamin to the north and south, and the portion of the prince to the east and to the west.

28. *From Tamar . . . in Kadesh.* The former was on the south of the Dead Sea; and the latter, or Kadesh-barnea, was still farther south, and at the extremity of the portion of Gad, which was the most southern tribe, as Dan was the most northern.

30. *These are the goings out.* Each of the four sides of the city was 4,500 cubits long. There were three gates on each side, as mentioned below; and the whole circumference of the city was 18,000 cubits.

THE BOOK OF DANIEL

I. The historic night (1:1-6:28)
A. The reign of Nebuchadnezzar (1:1-4:37)
1. Daniel's history (1:1-21)
2. Nebuchadnezzar's dream (2:1-49)
3. Nebuchadnezzar's pride (3:1-30)
4. Nebuchadnezzar's manifesto (4:1-37)

B. The reign of Belshazzar (5:1-31)
1. The carousal (5:1-4)
2. The writing (5:5-12)
3. Daniel (5:13-29)
4. The fulfillment (5:30-31)

C. The reign of Darius (6:1-28)
1. The appointment of Daniel (6:1-3)
2. The plot (6:4-15)
3. The deliverance (6:16-24)
4. The proclamation (6:25-28)

II. The prophetic light (7:1-12:13)
A. Belshazzar's reign (7:1-8:27)
1. Daniel's first vision, in first year (7:1-28)
   a. The vision (7:1-14)
   b. The explanation (7:15-28)
2. Daniel's second vision, in third year (8:1-27)
   a. The vision (8:1-14)
   b. The explanation (8:15-27)

B. Darius' reign (9:1-27)
1. Daniel and the prophecy of Jeremiah (9:1, 2)
2. Daniel's confession and prayer (9:3-19)
3. The coming of Gabriel (9:20-23)
4. The revelation (9:24-27)

C. Cyrus' reign (10:1-12:13)
1. The introductory apocalypse (10:1-21)
2. Prophetic history (11:1-45)
3. The last things foretold (12:1-3)
4. The closing of the book (12:4-13)

The book of Ezekiel left Jerusalem all in ruins, but with a joyful prospect of all in glory again. This of Daniel properly follows. Ezekiel told us what was foreseen by him in the former years of the captivity: Daniel tells us what was seen, and foreseen, in the latter years of the captivity. And it was a comfort to the captives that they had first one prophet and then another, to show them that God had not quite cast them off.

I. Concerning this prophet. His Hebrew name was *Daniel*, which signifies the *judgment of God*; his Chaldean name was *Belteshazzar*. He was of the tribe of Judah and of the royal family, eminent for wisdom and piety. Ezekiel, his senior, speaks of him as an oracle when he upbraids the king of Tyre with his conceit: "Thou art wiser than Daniel" (Ezek. 28:3). Noah, Daniel, and Job are reckoned as three men that had the greatest interest in heaven (Ezek. 14:14). Some of the Jewish rabbis rank his book among the *Hagiographa,* not among the prophecies. One reason is because he did not live such a mortified life as Jeremiah and other prophets, but lived like a prince and was a prime minister; whereas we find him persecuted as other prophets (ch. 6), and mortifying himself as other prophets did, when he "ate no pleasant bread" (10:3), and fainting and sick when he was under the power of the Spirit of prophecy (8:27). Another reason they suggest is because he wrote his book in a heathen country, and there had his visions, and not in the land of Israel; but, for the same reason, Ezekiel also would be expunged out of the roll of prophets. But the true reason is that he speaks so plainly of the time of the Messiah's coming that the Jews do not care to hear of it. Josephus calls him one of the "greatest" prophets. He lived an active life in the courts and councils of some of the greatest monarchs: Nebuchadnezzar, Cyrus, Darius. The Spirit, as the wind, blows where it lists. And, if those that have much to do in the world plead that as an excuse for slightness of their converse with God, Daniel will condemn them.

II. Concerning this book. The first six chapters of it are historical, and are plain and easy; the last six are prophetical, and in them are many things hard to be understood, which would be more intelligible if we had a more complete history of the Jewish nation, from Daniel's time to the coming of the Messiah. The first chapter, and the first three verses of the second chapter, are in Hebrew; thence to the eighth chapter is in the Chaldee dialect; and thence to the end is Hebrew. Mr. Broughton observes that, as the Chaldeans were kind to Daniel, and gave cups of cold water to him when he requested it, rather than the king's wine, God would not have them lose their reward, but made that language to have honor in his writings. Daniel, according to his computation, continues the holy story from the first surprising of Jerusalem by the Chaldean Babel, when he himself was carried away captive, until the last destruction of it by Rome, the mystical Babel (9:27). The fables of Susannah, and of Bel and the Dragon are apocryphal stories being found only in the Greek, nor ever admitted by the Jewish church. There are some of the histories and prophecies of this book that bear date in the latter end of the Chaldean monarchy, and others that are dated in the beginning of the Persian monarchy. But both Nebuchadnezzar's dream, which Daniel interpreted, and his own visions, point at the Grecian and Roman monarchies, and particularly at the Jews' troubles under Antiochus.

MATTHEW HENRY

CHAPTER 1

Verses 1–7

I. The first descent which Nebuchadnezzar, king of Babylon, in the first year of his reign, made upon Judah and Jerusalem, in the third year of the reign of Jehoiakim (*v.* 1, 2): He *besieged Jerusalem*, made himself master of it, seized the king, took whom he pleased and what he pleased, and then left Jehoiakim to reign as tributary to him.

JAMIESON, FAUSSET, BROWN

CHAPTER 1

Vss. 1-21. The Babylonian Captivity Begins; Daniel's Education at Babylon, etc. **1. third year** —cf. Jeremiah 25:1, "the *fourth* year; Jehoiakim came to the throne at the *end* of the year, which Jeremiah reckons as the *first* year, but which Daniel leaves out of count, being an incomplete year: thus, in Jeremiah, it is "the *fourth* year"; in Daniel, "the *third*" [Jahn]. However, Jeremiah (25:1; 46:2) merely says, the fourth year of Jehoiakim concided with the first of Nebuchadnezzar, when the latter *conquered the Egyptians at Carchemish*; not that the *deportation of captives from Jerusalem* was in the fourth year of Jehoiakim: this probably took place in the end of the third year of Jehoiakim, shortly *before* the battle of Carchemish [Fairbairn]. Nebuchadnezzar took away the captives as hostages for the submission of the Hebrews. *Historical* Scripture gives no positive account of this first deportation, with which the Babylonian captivity, i.e., Judah's subjection to Babylon for seventy years (Jer. 29:10), begins. But II Chronicles 36:6, 7, states that Nebuchadnezzar had intended "to carry Jehoiakim to Babylon," and that he "carried off the vessels of the house of the Lord" thither. But Jehoiakim died at Jerusalem, before the conqueror's intention as to him was carried into effect (Jer. 22:

ADAM CLARKE

CHAPTER 1

1. *In the third year of the reign of Jehoiakim.* This king was raised to the throne of Judea in the place of his brother Jehoahaz, by Pharaoh-necho, king of Egypt, 2 Kings xxiii. 34-36, and continued tributary to him during the first three years of his reign. But in the fourth, which was the first of Nebuchadnezzar, Jer. xxv. 1, Nebuchadnezzar completely defeated the Egyptian army near the Euphrates, Jer. xlvi. 2; and this victory put the neighboring countries of Syria, among which Judea was the chief, under the Chaldean government. Thus Jehoiakim, who had first been tributary to Egypt, became now the vassal of the king of Babylon, 2 Kings xxiv. 1. At the end of three years Jehoiakim rebelled against Nebuchadnezzar, who, then occupied with others wars, did not proceed against Jerusalem till three years after, which was the eleventh and last of Jehoiakim, 2 Kings xxiii. 36. There are some difficulties in the chronology of this place. Calmet takes rather a different view of these transactions. He connects the history thus: Nabopolassar, king of Babylon, finding that one of his lords whom he had made governor of Coelesyria and Phoenicia had revolted

MATTHEW HENRY

II. He did not destroy the city or kingdom, but accomplished the first threatening of mischief by Babylon made when Hezekiah showed his treasures to the king of Babylon's ambassadors (Isa. xxxix. 6, 7). The vessels of the sanctuary were carried away, *v.* 2. Many of the holy vessels were taken away by the king of Babylon and brought to the *house of his god*, to whom, with a blind devotion, he gave the praise of his success. See the righteousness of God; his people had brought the images of other gods into his temple, and now he suffers the vessels of the temple to be carried into the treasuries of those other gods. It was only *part of them* that went now; some were left, to see if they would take the right course to prevent the carrying away of the remainder. See Jer. xxvii. 18. The children and young men, especially such as were of noble or royal extraction, sightly and promising, were carried away. These were taken away by Nebuchadnezzar as hostages for the fidelity of their parents in their own land. He took them away to train them up for employment and preferment. The directions which the king of Babylon gave for the choice of these youths, *v.* 4. They must not choose such as were deformed in body, but comely and well-favoured, *skilful in all wisdom*, and *cunning*, or *well-seen in knowledge*, and *understanding science*. He chose such as were young, because they would be tractable, would forget their own people and become Chaldeans. They must be such as had ability to *stand in the king's palace*, and to preside in his affairs. The care which he took concerning their education. They should be taught *the learning and tongue of the Chaldeans*. They must be trained in such learning as might qualify them to serve their generation. They had *daily provision of the king's meat, and of the wine which he drank*, *v.* 5. This was an instance of his generosity and humanity. With a liberal education there should be a liberal maintenance.

III. Daniel and his fellows were of the *children of Judah*, the royal tribe, and probably of the house of David. The *prince of the eunuchs* changed the names of Daniel and his fellows, in token of their being naturalized and made Chaldeans. Their Hebrew names, which they received at their circumcision, had something of God, or Jah, in them: *Daniel—God is my Judge; Hananiah—The grace of the Lord; Mishael—He that is the strong God; Azariah—The Lord is a help.* To make them forget the God of their fathers, the guide of their youth, they give them names that savour of the Chaldean idolatry. *Belteshazzar* signifies the *keeper of the hidden treasures of Bel; Shadrach*—The *inspiration of the sun*, which the Chaldeans worshipped; *Meshach—Of the goddess Shach*, under which name Venus was worshipped; *Abed-nego*, The *servant of the shining fire*, which they worshipped also.

Verses 8–16

II. Daniel was still firm to his religion. They had changed his name, but they could not change his nature. Whatever they pleased to call him, he still retained the spirit of an Israelite indeed. He was resolved that *he would not defile himself with the portion of the king's meat*, he would not meddle with it, nor *with the wine which he drank*, *v.* 8. His fellows concurred in the same resolution, *v.* 11. This was from a principle of conscience. It was not in itself unlawful for them to *eat of the king's meat* or to *drink of his wine*. But, 1. They were scrupulous concerning the meat, lest it should be sinful. Sometimes such meat would be set before them as was forbidden by their law, as swine's flesh; or they were afraid lest it should have been offered in sacrifice to an idol, or blessed in the name of an idol. The Jews were distinguished from other nations very much by their meats (Lev. xi. 45, 46). If the command be against it, they must abide by that. 2. They were jealous lest, though it should not be sinful in itself, it should be an *occasion of sin* to them. 3. Jerusalem was in distress, and they themselves were in captivity. They had no heart *to drink wine in bowls*, so much were they *grieved for the affliction of Joseph.*

JAMIESON, FAUSSET, BROWN

18, 19; 36:30), and his dead body, as was foretold, was dragged out of the gates by the Chaldean besiegers, and left unburied. The second deportation under Jehoiachin was eight years later. **2. Shinar**—the old name of Babylonia (Gen. 11:2; 14:1; Isa. 11:11; Zech. 5:11). Nebuchadnezzar took only "part of the vessels," as he did not intend wholly to overthrow the state, but to make it tributary, and to leave such vessels as were absolutely needed for the public worship of Jehovah. Subsequently all were taken away and were restored under Cyrus (Ezra 1:7). **his god**—Bel. His temple, as was often the case among the heathen, was made "treasure-house" of the king. **3. master of . . . eunuchs**—called in Turkey the *kislar aga.* **of the king's seed**—cf. the prophecy, II Kings 20:17, 18. **4. no blemish**—A handsome form was connected, in Oriental ideas, with mental power. "Children" means youths of twelve or fourteen years old. **teach . . . tongue of . . . Chaldeans**—their language and literature, the Aramaic-Babylonian. That the heathen lore was not altogether valueless appears from the Egyptian magicians who opposed Moses; the Eastern Magi who sought Jesus, and who may have drawn the tradition as to the "King of the Jews" from Daniel 9:24, etc., written in the East. As Moses was trained in the learning of the Egyptian sages, so Daniel in that of the Chaldeans, to familiarize his mind with mysterious lore, and so develop his heaven-bestowed gift of understanding in visions (vss. 4, 5, 17). **5. king's meat**—It is usual for an Eastern king to entertain, from the food of his table, many retainers and royal captives (Jer. 52:33, 34). The *Hebrew* for "meat" implies *delicacies.* **stand before the king**—as attendant courtiers; not as eunuchs. **6. children of Judah**—the most noble tribe, being that to which the "king's seed" belonged (cf. vs. 3). **7. gave names**—designed to mark their new relation, that so they might forget their former religion and country (Gen. 41:45). But as in Joseph's case (whom Pharaoh called Zaphnath-paaneah), so in Daniel's, the name indicative of his relation to a heathen court ("Belteshazzar," i.e., "Bel's prince"), however flattering to him, is not the one retained by Scripture, but the name marking his relation to God ("Daniel," *God my Judge*, the theme of his prophecies being *God's judgment* on the heathen world powers). **Hananiah**—i.e., "whom Jehovah hath favored." **Shadrach**—from *Rak,* in Babylonian, "the King," i.e., "the Sun"; the same root as in *Abrech* (*Margin,* Gen. 41:43), inspired or illumined by the Sun-god." **Mishael**—i.e., "who is what God is?" *Who is comparable to God*? **Meshnach**—The Babylonians retained the first syllable of Mishael, the *Hebrew* name; but for *El,* i.e., GOD, substituted *Shak,* the Babylonian goddess, called Sheshach (Jer. 25:26; 51:41), answering to the Earth, or else Venus, the goddess of love and mirth; it was during her feast that Cyrus took Babylon. **Azariah**—i.e., "whom Jehovah helps." **Abednego**—i.e., "servant of the shining fire." Thus, instead of to Jehovah, these His servants were dedicated by the heathen to their four leading gods [HERODOTUS, *Clio*]; Bel, the Chief-god, the Sun-god, Earth-god, and Fire-god. To the last the three youths were consigned when refusing to worship the golden image (ch. 3). The *Chaldee version* translates "Lucifer," in Isaiah 14:12, *Nogea,* the same as *Nego.* The names thus at the outset are significant of the seeming triumph, but sure downfall, of the heathen powers before Jehovah and His people. **8. Daniel . . . would not defile himself with . . . king's meat**—Daniel is specified as being the leader in the "purpose" (the word implies a *decided* resolution) to abstain from defilement, thus manifesting a character already formed for prophetical functions. The other three youths, no doubt, shared in his purpose. It was the custom to throw a small part of the viands and wine upon the earth, as an initiatory offering to the gods, so as to consecrate to them the whole entertainment (cf. Deut. 32:38). To have partaken of such a feast would have been to sanction idolatry, and was forbidden even after the legal distinction of clean and unclean meats was done away (I Cor. 8:7, 10; 10:27, 28). Thus the faith of these youths was made instrumental in overruling the evil foretold against the Jews (Ezek. 4:13; Hos. 9:3), to the glory of God. Daniel and his three friends, says AUBERLEN, stand out like an oasis in the desert. Like Moses, Daniel "chose rather to suffer affliction with the people of God, than to enjoy the pleasures of sin for a season" (see ch. 9). He who is to interpret divine revelations must not feed on the dainties, nor drink from the intoxicating cup, of this world. This made him as dear a name to his countrymen as Noah and Job, who also stood alone in their piety among a perverse generation (Ezek. 14:14; 28:3).

ADAM CLARKE

from him and formed an alliance with the king of Egypt, sent Nebuchadnezzar, his son, whom he invested with the authority of king, to reduce those provinces, as was customary among the easterns when the heir presumptive was sent on any important expedition or embassy. This young prince, having quelled the insurrection in those parts, marched against Jerusalem about the end of the third or beginning of the fourth year of the reign of Jehoiakim, king of Judah. He soon took the city, and put Jehoiakim in chains with the design of carrying him to Babylon; but, changing his mind, he permitted him to resume the reins of government under certain oppressive conditions. At this year, the seventy years of the Babylonish captivity commence. Nabopolassar dying in the interim, Nebuchadnezzar was obliged to return speedily to Babylon, leaving his generals to conduct the Jewish captives to Babylon, among whom were Daniel and his companions.

2. *Part of the vessels of the house of God.* He took the richest and finest of them for the service of his god Bel, and left what were necessary for carrying on the public worship of Jehovah; for leaving Jehoiakim on the throne, he only laid the land under tribute. *The land of Shinar.* This was the ancient name of Babylon. See Gen. xi. 2. *The treasure house of his god.* This was Bel, who had a splendid temple in Babylon, and was the tutelar god of the city and empire.

3. *Master of his eunuchs.* This word *eunuchs* signifies officers about or in the palace, whether literally eunuchs or not.

4. *Children.* "Youths, young men"; and so the word should be rendered throughout this book. *Skilful in all wisdom.* Rather, persons capable of every kind of literary accomplishment, that they might be put under proper instruction.

6. *Now among these.* There were no doubt several noble youths from other provinces; but the four mentioned here were Jews, and are supposed to have all been of royal extraction.

7. *Unto whom the prince of the eunuchs gave names.* This change of names was a mark of dominion and authority. It was customary for masters to impose new names upon their slaves; and rulers often, on their ascending the throne, assumed a name different from that which they had before. *Daniel* signifies "God is my Judge." This name they changed into *Belteshatstsar;* in Chaldee, "The treasure of Bel." *Hananiah* signifies "The Lord has been gracious to me," or "He to whom the Lord is gracious." This name was changed into *Shadrach,* Chaldee, which has been variously translated: "The inspiration of the sun"; "God, the author of evil, be propitious to us"; "Let God preserve us from evil." *Mishael* signifies "He who comes from God." Him they called *Meshach,* which in Chaldee signifies "He who belongs to the goddess Sheshach," a celebrated deity of the Babylonians, mentioned by Jeremiah, chap. xxv. 26. *Azariah,* which signifies "The Lord is my Helper they changed into *Abed-nego,* which in Chaldee is "The servant of Nebo," who was one of their divinities.

MATTHEW HENRY

I. Daniel was a favourite with the *prince of the eunuchs* (*v.* 9), as Joseph was with the keeper of the prison.

III. When Daniel requested that he might have none of the king's meat or wine, the prince of the eunuchs objected that, if he and his fellows were not in as good case as their companions, he would be in danger of losing his head, *v.* 10. Daniel desires the matter might be put to a trial. He applies to the under-officer, Melzar: "*Prove us for ten days;* let us have nothing but *pulse to eat*, nothing but herbs and fruits, parched peas or lentils, and nothing but *water to drink*, and see how we can live upon that," *v.* 13. Trial was accordingly made. Daniel and his fellows lived for ten days upon *pulse and water*. *At the end of the ten days* they were found *fairer and fatter in flesh* than *all those who did eat the portion of the king's meat*, *v.* 15. This was in part a natural effect of their temperance, but it must be ascribed to the special blessing of God, which will make a little to go a great way.

IV. The steward did not force them to eat against their consciences, but, as they desired, *gave them pulse and water* (*v.* 16). This abstemiousness fitted them for their eminent services. Hereby they kept their minds clear and unclouded. Those that had thus inured themselves to hardship, and lived a life of self-denial, could the more easily venture upon the fiery furnace and the den of lions.

Verses 17–21

The great learning which God gave Daniel and his fellows was, 1. A balance for their losses. They had, for the iniquity of their fathers, been deprived of honours and pleasures, but to make them amends for that, God, in giving them learning, gave them better honours and pleasures. 2. A recompence for their integrity. They kept to their religion, even in the minutest instances. God rewarded them. To Daniel he gave a double portion; he had *understanding in visions and dreams* by a divine sagacity and wisdom which God gave him. After *three years* spent in their education they were presented to the king, *v.* 18. And the king examined them and *communed with them* himself, *v.* 19. The king examined them *in all matters of wisdom and understanding*, and found that they had *more understanding than the ancients*. He freely owned that, upon trial, he found those poor young captive Jews wiser and *better than all the magicians that were in all his realm*, *v.* 20. These four young students were *ten times* better than all the old practitioners. This judgment being given, they *stood before the king* (*v.* 19).

JAMIESON, FAUSSET, BROWN

requested—While decided in principle, we ought to seek our object by gentleness, rather than by an ostentatious testimony, which, under the plea of faithfulness, courts opposition. **9. God . . . brought Daniel into favour**—The favor of others towards the godly is the doing of God. So in Joseph's case (Gen. 39:21). Especially towards Israel (Ps. 106: 46; cf. Prov. 16:7). **10. worse liking**—looking less healthy. **your sort**—of *your age,* or *class;* lit., "circle." **endanger my head**—An arbitrary Oriental despot could, in a fit of wrath at his orders having been disobeyed, command the offender to be instantly decapitated. **11. Melzar**—rather, the steward, or chief butler, entrusted by Ashpenaz with furnishing the daily portion to the youths [GESENIUS]. The word is still in use in Persia. **12. pulse**—The *Hebrew* expresses any vegetable grown from *seeds*, i.e., vegetable food in general [GESENIUS]. **13-15.** Illustrating Deuteronomy 8:3, "Man doth not live by bread only, but by every word that proceedeth out of the mouth of the Lord." **17. God gave them knowledge**—(Exod. 31:2, 3; I Kings 3:12; Job. 32:8; Jas. 1:5, 17). **Daniel had understanding in . . . dreams**—God thus made one of the despised covenant people eclipse the Chaldean sages in the very science on which they most prided themselves. So Joseph in the court of Pharaoh (Gen. 40:5; 41:1-8). Daniel, in these praises of his own "understanding," speaks not through vanity, but by the direction of God, as one transported out of himself. See my *Introduction,* "CONTENTS OF THE BOOK." **18. brought them in**—i.e., not only Daniel and his three friends, but other youths (vs. 3; and vs. 19, "among *them all*). **19. stood . . . before the king**—i.e., were advanced to a position of favor near the throne. **20. ten times**—lit., "ten hands." **magicians**—properly, "sacred scribes, skilled in the sacred writings, a class of Egyptian priests" [GESENIUS]; from a *Hebrew* root, "a pen." The word in our *English Version,* "magicians," comes from *mag,* i.e., "a priest." The Magi formed one of the six divisions of the Medes. **astrologers**—*Hebrew,* "enchanters," from a root, "to conceal," practisers of the occult arts. **21. Daniel continued . . . unto . . . first year of Cyrus**—(II Chron. 36:22; Ezra 1:1). Not that he did not continue *beyond* that year, but the expression is designed to mark the fact that he who was one of the first captives taken to Babylon, lived to see the end of the captivity. See my *Introduction,* "SIGNIFICANCE OF THE BABYLONIAN EXILE." In ch. 10:1 he is mentioned as living "in the third year of Cyrus." See *Margin Note,* on the use of "till," (Ps. 110:1, 112:8).

ADAM CLARKE

11. *Then said Daniel to Melzar.* Melzar was an officer under Ashpenaz, whose office it was to attend to the food, clothing, etc., of these royal captives.

12. *Give us pulse to eat.* Seeds or grain, such as barley, wheat, rye, peas, etc. Though a vegetable diet might have produced that healthiness of the system in general, and of the countenance particularly, as mentioned here, yet we are to understand that there was an especial blessing of God in this, because this spare diet was taken on a religious account.

21. *The first year of king Cyrus.* That is, to the end of the Chaldean empire. And we find Daniel alive in the third year of Cyrus; see chap. x. 1.

MATTHEW HENRY

CHAPTER 2

Verses 1–13

There is difficulty in the date of this story; it is said to be in the second year of the reign of Nebuchadnezzar, *v.* 1. Now Daniel was carried to Babylon in his first year, and, it should seem, he was three years under tutors before he was presented to the king, *ch.* i. 5. How then could this happen in *the second year?* Perhaps Daniel had been but one year at school. Some make it to be the second year after he began to reign alone, but the fifth or sixth year since he began to reign in partnership with his *father*. Some read it, *and in the second year* (the second after Daniel and his fellows stood before the king), *in the kingdom of Nebuchadnezzar*, or *in his reign*, this happened. It appears in Ezekiel, that Daniel was soon famous both for wisdom and prevalence in prayer. He came to be eminent for both these early in Nebuchadnezzar's reign.

I. The perplexity that Nebuchadnezzar was in by reason of a dream which he had forgotten (*v.* 1). There was something in the impression it made upon him which was evidence of its divine origin and its prophetic significance. Nebuchadnezzar was a troubler of God's Israel, but God here troubled him. All the treasures and delights which this mighty monarch had could not procure him a little repose, when by reason of the trouble of his mind his *sleep broke from him.*

JAMIESON, FAUSSET, BROWN

CHAPTER 2

VSS. 1-49. NEBUCHADNEZZAR'S DREAM: DANIEL'S INTERPRETATION OF IT, AND ADVANCEMENT. **1. second year of . . . Nebuchadnezzar**—Ch. 1:5 shows that "three years" had elapsed since Nebuchadnezzar had taken Jerusalem. The solution of this difficulty is: Nebuchadnezzar first ruled as subordinate to his father Nabopolassar, to which time ch. 1 refers; whereas "the second year" in ch. 2 is dated from his sole sovereignty. The very difficulty is a proof of genuineness; all was clear to the writer and the original readers from *their* knowledge of the circumstances, and so he adds no explanation. A forger would not *introduce* difficulties; the author did not *then* see any difficulty in the case. Nebuchadnezzar is called "king" (ch. 1:1), *by anticipation.* Before he left Judea, he became actual king by the death of his father, and the Jews always called him "king," as commander of the invading army. **dreams**—It is significant that not to Daniel, but to the-then-world-ruler, Nebuchadnezzar, the dream is vouchsafed. It was from the first of its representatives who had conquered the theocracy, that the world power was to learn its doom, as about to be in its turn subdued, and for ever, by the kingdom of God. As this vision opens, so that in ch. 7 developing the same truth more fully, closes the first part. Nebuchadnezzar, as vicegerent of God (vs. 37; cf. Jer. 25:9; Ezek. 28:12-15; Isa. 44:28; 45:1; Rom. 13:1), is honored with the revelation in the form of a dream, the appropriate form to one outside the kingdom of God. So in the cases of Abimelech, Pharaoh, etc. (Gen. 20 and 41), especially as the heathen attached such importance to dreams. Still it is not he, but an Israelite, who interprets it. Heathendom is passive, Israel active, in divine things, so that the glory redounds to "the God of heaven." **2. Chaldeans**—here, a certain order of priest-magicians, who wore a peculiar dress, like that seen on the gods and deified men in the Assyrian sculptures. Probably they belonged exclusively to the Chaldeans, the original tribe of the Bab-

ADAM CLARKE

CHAPTER 2

1. *The second year of the reign of Nebuchadnezzar.* That is, the second year of his reigning alone, for he was king two years before his father's death. This was therefore the fifth year of his reign, and the fourth of the captivity of Daniel.

Nebuchadnezzar dreamed dreams, wherewith his spirit was troubled. The dream had made a deep and solemn impression upon his mind; and, having forgotten all but general circumstances, his mind was distressed.

2. *The Chaldeans.* Who these were is difficult to be ascertained. They might be a college of learned men, where all arts and sciences were professed and taught.

MATTHEW HENRY

II. The trial that he made of his magicians and astrologers. They were immediately sent for, to *show the king his dreams, v.* 2. His dream had slipped out of his mind, and he could not possibly recollect it. The magicians were proud of being sent for into the king's bed-chamber. He tells them that he had *dreamed a dream, v.* 3. They desired him to tell his dream, and undertook with all possible assurance to interpret it, *v.* 4.

But the king insisted that they must tell him the dream. And, if they could not do this, they should all be put to death as deceivers (*v.* 5), themselves *cut to pieces* and *their houses made a dunghill.*

If they could, they should be rewarded, *v.* 6. The magicians insist that the king must tell them the dream, and then, if they do not tell him the interpretation of it, it is their fault, *v.* 7. But arbitrary power is deaf to reason. The king falls into a passion, gives them hard words, and charges them with trying to affront him: *You have prepared lying and corrupt words to speak before me.* He tells them that they did but dally with him, to gain time (*v.* 8), *till the time be changed* (*v.* 9), either till the king's desire to know his dream be over, or till they may hope he has so perfectly forgotten his dream that they may tell him what they please. And therefore, without delay, they must tell him the dream. In vain do they plead, 1. That there is *no man on earth* that can retrieve the king's dream, *v.* 10. They acknowledge that the gods may indeed *declare unto man what is his thought* (Amos iv. 13). But those who can do this are gods (*v.* 11), and it is they alone that can do this. See here an instance of the ignorance of these magicians, that they speak of many gods, whereas there is but one and can be but one infinite; yet see their knowledge that there is a God, who is a Spirit, and perfectly knows the spirits of men and all their thoughts. 2. That there is no king on earth that would expect or require such a thing, *v.* 10.

III. The doom passed upon all the magicians of Babylon. There is but *one decree for them all* (*v.* 9).

They must every man of them be slain (*v.* 13), Daniel and his fellows (though they knew nothing of the matter) not excepted. Nebuchadnezzar is here a tyrant in true colours, speaking death when he cannot speak sense.

Verses 14–23

When the king sent for his wise men to tell them his dream (*v.* 2), Daniel was not summoned to appear. How miserable is the case of those who live under an arbitrary government, as this of Nebuchadnezzar's! Daniel was famous both for prudence and prayer; as a prince he had power with God and man; by prayer he had power with God, by prudence he had power with man, and in both he prevailed. In these verses we have a remarkable instance of both.

I. Daniel by prudence knew how to deal with men. When *Arioch, the captain of the guard,* appointed to slay all the wise men of Babylon, seized Daniel, he *answered with counsel and wisdom* (*v.* 14); he did not fall into a passion, but mildly asked, *Why is the decree so hasty? v.* 15. Daniel undertakes, if he may but have a little time to give the king all the satisfaction he desired, *v.* 16.

JAMIESON, FAUSSET, BROWN

ylonian nation, just as the Magians were properly Medes. **3. troubled to know the dream**—He awoke in alarm, remembering that something solemn had been presented to him in a dream, without being able to recall the form in which it had clothed itself. His thoughts on the unprecedented greatness to which his power had attained (vs. 29) made him anxious to know what the issue of all this should be. God meets this wish in the way most calculated to impress him. **4.** Here begins the Chaldee portion of Daniel, which continues to the end of ch. 7. In it the course, character, and crisis of the Gentile power are treated; whereas, in the other parts, which are in Hebrew, the things treated apply more particularly to the Jews and Jerusalem. **Syriac**—the Aramean Chaldee, the vernacular tongue of the king and his court; the prophet, by mentioning it here, hints at the reason of his own adoption of it from this point. **live for ever**—a formula in addressing kings, like our "Long live the king!" Cf. I Kings 1:31. **5. The thing**—i.e., The dream, "is gone from me." GESENIUS translates, "The *decree* is gone forth from me," irrevocable (cf. Isa. 45:23); viz., that you shall be executed, if you do not tell both the dream and the interpretation. *English Version* is simpler, which supposes the king himself to have forgotten the dream. Pretenders to supernatural knowledge often bring on themselves their own punishment. **cut in pieces**—(I Sam. 15:33). **houses . . . dunghill**—rather, "a morass heap." The Babylonian houses were built of sun-dried bricks; when demolished, the rain dissolves the whole into a mass of mire, in the wet land, near the river [STUART]. As to the consistency of this cruel threat with Nebuchadnezzar's character, see ch. 4:17, "basest of men"; Jeremiah 39:5, 6; 52:9-11. **6. rewards**—lit., "presents *poured out in* lavish profusion." **8. gain . . . time**—lit., "buy." Cf. Ephesians 5:16; Colossians 4:5, where the sense is somewhat different. **the thing is gone from me**—(See *Note,* vs. 5). **9. one decree**—There can be no second one reversing the first (Esther 4:11). **corrupt**—deceitful. **till the time be changed**—till a new state of things arrive, either by my ceasing to trouble myself about the dream, or by a change of government (which perhaps the agitation caused by the dream made Nebuchadnezzar to forebode, and so to suspect the Chaldeans of plotting). **tell . . . dream, and I shall know . . . ye can show . . . interpretation**—If ye cannot tell the past, a dream actually presented to me, how can ye know, and show, the future events prefigured in it? **10. There is not a man . . . that can show**—God makes the heathen, out of their own mouth, condemn their impotent pretensions to supernatural knowledge, in order to bring out in brighter contrast His power to reveal secrets to His servants, though but "men upon the earth" (cf. vss. 22, 23). **therefore . . .**—i.e., If such things could be done by men, other absolute princes would have required them from their magicians; as they have not, it is proof such things cannot be done and cannot be reasonably asked from us. **11. gods, whose dwelling is not with flesh**—answering to "no man *upon the earth*"; for there were, in their belief, "men *in heaven,*" viz., men deified; e.g., Nimrod. The *supreme* gods are referred to here, who alone, in the Chaldean view, could solve the difficulty, but who do not communicate with men. The *inferior* gods, intermediate between men and the supreme gods, are unable to solve it. Contrast with this heathen idea of the utter severance of God from man, John 1:14, "The Word was made *flesh,* and *dwelt* among us"; Daniel was in this case made His representative. **12, 13.** Daniel and his companions do not seem to have been actually numbered among the Magi or Chaldeans, and so were not summoned before the king. Providence ordered it so that all mere human wisdom should be shown vain before His divine power, through His servant, was put forth. Verse 24 shows that the decree for slaying the wise men had not been actually executed when Daniel interposed. **14. captain of the king's guard**—commanding the executioners (see *Margin;* and Gen. 37:36, *Margin*). **15. Why is the decree so hasty**—Why were not all of us consulted before the decree for the execution of all was issued? **the thing**—the agitation of the king as to his dream, and his abortive consultation of the Chaldeans. It is plain from this that Daniel was till now ignorant of the whole matter. **16. Daniel went in**—perhaps not in person, but by the mediation of some courtier who had access to the king. His first direct interview seems to have been verse 25 [BARNES]. **time**—The king granted "time" to Daniel, though he would not do so to the Chaldeans because they betrayed their lying purpose by requiring him to tell the dream, which Daniel did

ADAM CLARKE

4. *Then spake the Chaldeans to the king in Syriack. Aramith,* the language of Aram or Syria. What has been generally called the Chaldee.

O king, live for ever. With these words the Chaldee part of Daniel commences; and continues to the end of the seventh chapter.

5. *Ye shall be cut in pieces.* This was arbitrary and tyrannical in the extreme; but, in the order of God's providence, it was overruled to serve the most important purpose.

F. B. MEYER:

The forgotten dream. This was the second year of Nebuchadnezzar's sole reign. At first he was joint-governor with his father. From v. 4b to 7:28 the Syriac or Aramaic language is employed, and as this was the vernacular tongue of the king and his court, it is possible that this part of Daniel's record is based upon documents of state. The king's argument throughout his discussion with the magicians and astrologers was that if they could not recall the past, they certainly could not be trusted to foretell the future; the failure of the wise men provided the opportunity for the greater triumph of the servant of God. The wise men of Babylon said truly that only the gods, whose dwelling is not with flesh, could recover lost dreams. Daniel thought so, too, only he looked to the Lord God of his fathers. Irresponsible power is a temptation to the ruler and perilous to the ruled. No mortal should have despotic power over life and death.
—*Bible Commentary*

14. *Captain of the king's guard.* Chief of the king's executioners or slaughter men.

MATTHEW HENRY

II. Daniel knew how by prayer to converse with God.

1. His humble petition that God would discover to him what was the king's dream, and the interpretation of it. He *went to his house* to be alone with his God, for from him alone, the Father of lights, he expected this great gift. He engaged his companions to pray for it too, *v.* 17, 18. St. Paul often entreats his friends to pray for him. Thus we must show that we put a value upon our friends, upon their prayers. He was particular in this prayer: *That they would desire mercies of the God of heaven concerning this secret, v.* 18. Whatever is the matter of our care must be the matter of our prayer; we must desire mercy of God concerning this thing and the other thing that occasions us trouble and fear. God gives us leave to be humbly free with him. We may in faith pray to him who has all hearts in his hand, and who in his providence does wonders, for the discovery of that which is out of our view and the obtaining of that which is out of our reach. The mercy which Daniel and his fellows prayed for was bestowed. The *secret* was *revealed unto Daniel* in a *night-vision, v.* 19. Some think he dreamed the same dream, when he was asleep, that Nebuchadnezzar had dreamed.

2. His grateful thanksgiving for this mercy, *v.* 19. As he had prayed in a full assurance that God would do this for him, so he gave thanks in a full assurance that he had done it. *Blessed be the name of God for ever and ever.* There is that *for ever* in God which is to be blessed and praised; it is unchangeably and eternally in him. His companions were present with Daniel when the discovery was made, or as soon as he knew it he told them that those who had assisted him with their prayers might assist him in their praises; his joining them with him is an instance of his humility. Thus St. Paul sometimes joins Sylvanus, Timotheus, or some other minister, with himself in the inscriptions to many of his epistles.

Verses 24–30

The introduction to Daniel's declaring the dream, and the interpretation of it.

I. He immediately bespoke the reversing of the sentence against the wise men of Babylon, *v.* 24. He went with all speed to Arioch: *Destroy not the wise men of Babylon.*

II. He offered his service, with great assurance, to go to the king, and tell him his dream and the interpretation of it, *v.* 24, 25.

III. He contrived to give honour to God, upon this occasion. The king owned that it was a bold undertaking (*v.* 26): *Art thou able to make known unto me the dream?* The less likely it appeared to the king that Daniel should do this the more God was glorified in enabling him to do it.

JAMIESON, FAUSSET, BROWN

not. Providence doubtless influenced his mind, already favorable (ch. 1:19, 20), to show special favor to Daniel. **17.** Here appears the reason why Daniel sought "time" (vs. 16), viz., he wished to engage his friends to join him in prayer to God to reveal the dream to him. **18.** An illustration of the power of united prayer (Matt. 18:19). The same instrumentality rescued Peter from his peril (Acts 12:5-12). **19. revealed . . . in . . . night vision**—(Job 33:15, 16). **20. answered**—responded to God's goodness by praises. **name of God**—*God in His revelation of Himself* by acts of love, "wisdom, and might" (Jer. 32:19). **21. changeth . . . times . . . seasons**— "He herein gives a general preparatory intimation, that the dream of Nebuchadnezzar is concerning the changes and successions of kingdoms" [JEROME]. The "times" are the *phases* and periods of *duration* of empires (cf. ch. 7:25; I Chron. 12:32; 29:30; the "seasons" the *fitting* times for their culmination, decline, and fall (Eccles. 3:1; Acts 1:7; I Thess. 5:1). The vicissitudes of states, with their times and seasons, are not regulated by chance or fate, as the heathen thought, but by God. **removed kings**—(Job 12:18; Ps. 75:6, 7; Jer. 27:5; cf. I Sam. 2:7, 8). **giveth wisdom**—(I Kings 3:9-12; Jas. 1:5). **22. revealeth**—(Job 12:22). So spiritually (Eph. 1:17, 18). **knoweth what is in . . . darkness**—(Ps. 139: 11, 12; Heb. 4:13). **light . . . him**—(Jas. 1:17; I John 1:4). *Apocalypse* (or "revelation") signifies a divine, *prophecy* a human, activity. Cf. I Corinthians 14:6, where the two are distinguished. The prophet is connected with the outer world, addressing to the congregation the words with which the Spirit of God supplies him; he *speaks* in the Spirit, but the apocalyptic seer *is in* the Spirit in his whole person (Rev. 1:10; 4:2). The form of the apocalyptic revelation (the very term meaning that the *veil* that hides the invisible world is *taken off*) is subjectively either the *dream,* or, higher, the *vision.* The interpretation of Nebuchadnezzar's dream was a preparatory education to Daniel himself. By gradual steps, each revelation preparing him for the succeeding one, God fitted him for disclosures becoming more and more special. In chs. 2 and 4 he is but an interpreter of Nebuchadnezzar's dreams; then he has a dream himself, but it is only a vision in a dream of the night (ch. 7:1, 2); then follows a vision in a waking state (ch. 8:1-3); lastly, in the two final revelations (chs. 9 and 10-12) the ecstatic state is no longer needed. The progression in the *form* answers to the progression in the *contents* of his prophecy; at first general *outlines,* and these afterwards filled up with minute chronological and historical *details,* such as are not found in the Revelation of John, though, as became the New Testament, the form of revelation is the highest, viz., clear waking visions [AUBERLEN]. **23. thee . . . thee**—He ascribes all the glory to God. **God of my fathers**—Thou hast shown Thyself the same God of grace to me, a captive exile, as Thou didst to Israel of old and this on account of the *covenant* made with our "fathers" (Luke 1:54, 55; cf. Ps. 106:45). **given me wisdom and might**—Thou being the fountain of both; referring to vs. 20. Whatever *wise ability* I have to stay the execution of the king's cruel decree, is Thy gift. **me . . . we . . . us**—The revelation was given to Daniel, as "me" implies; yet with just modesty he joins his friends with him; because it was to their joint prayers, and not to his individually, that he owed the revelation from God. **known . . . the king's matter**—the very words in which the Chaldeans had denied the *possibility* of *any man on earth* telling the dream ("not a man upon the earth can show *the king's matter,"* (vs. 10). Impostors are compelled by the God of truth to eat up their own words. **24. Therefore**—because of having received the divine communication. **bring me in before the king**—implying that he had not previously been in person before the king (*Note,* vs. 16). **25. I have found a man**—Like all courtiers, in announcing agreeable tidings, he ascribes the merit of the discovery to himself [JEROME]. So far from it being a discrepancy, that he says nothing of the previous understanding between him and Daniel, or of Daniel's application to the king (vss. 15, 16), it is just what we should expect. Arioch would not dare to tell an absolute despot that he had stayed the execution of his sanguinary decree, on his own responsibility; but would, in the first instance, secretly stay it until Daniel had got, by application from the king, the time required, without Arioch seeming to know of Daniel's application as the cause of the respite; then, when Daniel had received the revelation, Arioch would in trembling haste bring him in, as if then for the first time he had "found" him. The very difficulty when cleared up is a proof of genuineness, as it never would be *introduced* by a

ADAM CLARKE

19. ***Then was the secret revealed . . . in a night vision.*** **Daniel either dreamed it or it was represented to his mind by an immediate inspiration.**

20. ***Wisdom and might are his.*** **He knows all things, and can do all things.**

F. B. MEYER:

"Then was the secret revealed in a night vision" (v. 19). This prayer-meeting, called hurriedly, must have been very intense. There was no knowing whether it might not be interrupted before it was completed by the guards of the palace summoning the supplicants to die. These two or three were gathered in the name of God, in rooms which never before had heard his name. But when their prayers had been offered, such serene peace resulted that Daniel was able to sleep with the utmost composure; and his mind, like a mirror, received upon its placid depths the impression of God's thoughts.

It is a test of prayer having attained its object, when the praying soul feels there is no need to wrestle longer, and the sweet assurance is borne in that God has received our supplication, and that further words are needless. This serenity of heart shows itself in the unruffled calm of the commercial man in a time of panic; in the quietness of the soul under provocation; in the stayedness of the heart on God, while storms sweep earth and sky.

It has been pointed out that there are three New Testament words for prayer to which we do well to take heed. Be sober unto prayer (1 Peter 4:7). Do not be drunk with worldly vanity, business, or gaiety; but bring a humble, penitent, clear, and sound mind. Be at leisure when you pray (1 Cor. 7:5). The word means that prayer is not to be hurried; that nothing should interfere with its leisurely enjoyment. Labor at prayer (Col. 1:29; or 4:12). As a man labors at his daily work, or strives on the battlefield, or agonizes to preserve a beloved friend from danger. It was thus that Jesus labored in the Garden of Gethsemane. And it was thus that these faithful souls must have prayed.

—Great Verses Through the Bible

24. ***Destroy not the wise men.*** **The decree was suspended till it should be seen whether Daniel could tell the dream and give its interpretation.**

MATTHEW HENRY

Daniel puts the king out of conceit with his soothsayers (*v.* 27): "*This secret they cannot show to the king.* Therefore let not the king be angry with them for not doing that which they cannot do; but rather cast them off, because they cannot do it. Though they cannot find out the secret, let not the king despair of having it found out, for *there is a God in heaven that reveals secrets,*" *v.* 28.

IV. He confirmed the king in his opinion that the dream was of great value. It was a divine discovery, a ray of light darted into his mind from the upper world, relating to the great affairs of this lower world. God in it *made known to the king what should be in the latter days* (*v.* 28). Some think that the *thoughts* which are said to have *come into the king's mind upon his bed, what should come to pass hereafter,* were his own thoughts when he was awake. Just before he fell asleep he was musing what would be the issue of his growing greatness, what his kingdom would herafter come to; and so the dream was an answer to those thoughts.

V. He solemnly professes that he could not pretend to have merited from God the favour of this discovery (*v.* 30): "*But, as for me,* this secret is not found out by me, but is *revealed to me,* and that *not for any wisdom that I have* to qualify me for the receiving of such a discovery." The secret was made known to him for the sake of his people, his brethren and companions in tribulation. God revealed this thing to Daniel that he might make it known to the king. Prophets receive that they may give, that the discoveries made to them may be communicated to the persons that are concerned.

Verses 31–45

Daniel here gives full satisfaction to Nebuchadnezzar concerning his dream and the interpretation. And now the king is abundantly repaid, and for receiving this prophet, though not in the name of a prophet, he had a prophet's reward.

I. The dream itself, *v.* 31, 45. Nebuchadnezzar was a worshipper of images, and now behold a *great image* is set before him in a dream. This was the image of a man erect: *It stood before him,* as a living man; and, because those monarchies represented by it were admirable in the eyes of their friends, the *brightness* of this image *was excellent*; and because they were formidable to their enemies, the *form* of this image is said to be *terrible*; both the features of the face and the postures of the body made it so. But that which was most remarkable was the different metals of which it was composed—the *head of gold* (the richest and most durable metal), the *breast and arms of silver* (the next to it in worth), the *belly and sides* (or *thighs*) *of brass,* the *legs of iron* (still baser metals), and lastly the feet *part of iron and part of clay.* See what the things of this world are; the further we go in them the less valuable they appear. Some observe that in Daniel's visions the monarchies were represented by four beasts (*ch.* vii), for he looked upon that wisdom from beneath, to be earthly, and a tyrannical power, to have more in it of the beast than of the man. But to Nebuchadnezzar, a heathen prince, they were represented by a gay and pompous image of a man, for he was an admirer of the *kingdoms of this world and the glory of them.*

JAMIESON, FAUSSET, BROWN

forger. **27. cannot**—Daniel, being learned in all the lore of the Chaldeans (ch. 1:4), could authoritatively declare the *impossibility* of mere man solving the king's difficulty. **soothsayers**—from a root, "to cut off"; referring to their *cutting* the heavens into divisions, and so guessing at men's destinies from the place of the stars at one's birth. **28. God**—in contrast to "the wise men," etc. (vs. 27). **revealeth secrets**—(Amos 3:7; 4:13). Cf. Genesis 41:45, *Zaphnath-paaneah,* "revealer of secrets," the title given to Joseph. **the latter days**—lit., "in the after days" (vs. 29); "hereafter" (Gen. 49:1). It refers to the whole future, including the Messianic days, which is the final dispensation (Isa. 2:2). **visions of thy head**—conceptions formed in the brain. **29.** God met with a revelation Nebuchadnezzar, who had been meditating on the future destiny of his vast empire. **30. not . . . for any wisdom that I have**—not *on account* of any previous wisdom which I may have manifested (ch. 1:17, 20). The specially-favored servants of God in all ages disclaim merit in themselves and ascribe all to the grace and power of God (Gen. 41:16; Acts 3:12). The "as for me," disclaiming extraordinary merit, contrasts elegantly with "as for thee," whereby Daniel courteously, but without flattery, implies, that God honored Nebuchadnezzar, as His vicegerent over the world kingdoms, with a revelation on the subject uppermost in his thoughts, the ultimate destinies of those kingdoms. **for their sakes that shall make known . . .**—a Chaldee idiom for, "to the intent that the interpretation may be made known to the king." **the thoughts of thy heart**—thy subject of thought before falling asleep. Or, perhaps the *probation of Nebuchadnezzar's character* through this revelation may be the meaning intended (cf. II Chron. 32:31; Luke 2:35). **31.** The world power in its totality appears as a colossal human form: Babylon the head of gold, Medo-Persia the breast and *two* arms of silver, Græco-Macedonia the belly and *two* thighs of brass, and Rome, with its Germano-Slavonic offshoots, the legs of iron and feet of iron and clay, the fourth still existing. Those kingdoms only are mentioned which stand in some relation to the kingdom of God; of these none is left out; the final establishment of that kingdom is the aim of His moral government of the world. The colossus of metal stands on weak feet, of clay. All man's glory is as ephemeral and worthless as chaff (cf. I Pet. 1:34). But the kingdom of God, small and unheeded as a "stone" on the ground is compact in its homogeneous unity; whereas the world power, in its heterogeneous constituents successively supplanting one another, contains the elements of decay. The relation of the stone to the mountain is that of the kingdom of the cross (Matt. 16:23; Luke 24:26) to the kingdom of glory, the latter beginning, and the former ending when the kingdom of God breaks in pieces the kingdoms of the world (Rev. 11:15). Christ's contrast between the two kingdoms refers to this passage. **a great image**—lit., "*one* image that was great." Though the kingdoms were different, it was essentially *one* and the same world power under different phases, just as the image was *one,* though the parts were of different metals. **32.** On ancient coins states are often represented by human figures. The head and higher parts signify the earlier times; the lower, the later times. The metals become successively baser and baser, implying the growing degeneracy from worse to worse. Hesiod, 200 years before Daniel, had compared the four ages to the four metals in the same order; the idea is sanctioned here by Holy Writ. It was perhaps one of those fragments of revelation among the heathen, derived from the tradition as to the fall of man. The metals lessen in *specific gravity,* as they go downwards; silver is not so heavy as gold, brass not so heavy as silver, and iron not so heavy as brass, the *weight* thus being arranged in the reverse of stability [Tregelles]. Nebuchadnezzar derived his authority from God, not from man, nor as responsible to man. But the Persian king was so far dependent on others that he could not deliver Daniel from the princes (ch. 6:14, 15); contrast ch. 5:18, 19, as to Nebuchadnezzar's power from God, whom he would he slew, and whom he would he kept alive" (cf. Ezra 7:14; Esther 1:13-16). Græco-Macedonia betrays its deterioration in its divisions, not united as Babylon and Persia. Iron is stronger than brass, but inferior in other respects; so Rome hardy and strong to tread down the nations, but less kingly and showing its chief deterioration in its last state. Each successive kingdom incorporates its predecessor (cf. ch. 5:28). Power that in Nebuchadnezzar's hands was a God-derived (vss. 37, 38) autocracy, in the Persian king's was a rule resting on his nobility of person and birth,

ADAM CLARKE

27. *Cannot the wise men.* Cannot your own able men, aided by your gods, tell you the secret? This question was necessary in order that the king might see the foolishness of depending on the one or worshipping the other. *The soothsayers.* One of our old words: "The tellers of truth."

28. *There is a God in heaven.* To distinguish Him from those idols, the works of men's hands, and from the false gods in which the Chaldeans trusted. *In the latter days.* A phrase which, in the prophets, generally means the times of the Messiah.

KEIL-DELITZSCH:

To the question of the king, whether he was able to show the dream with its interpretation, Daniel replies by directing him from man, who is unable to accomplish such a thing, to the living God in heaven, who alone reveals secrets. The expression, *whose name was Belteshazzar* (v. 26), intimates that he who was known among the Jews by the name Daniel was known to the Chaldean king only under the name given to him by the conqueror—that Nebuchadnezzar knew of no Daniel, but only of Belteshazzar. The question, *"art thou able?"* i.e. hast thou ability? does not express the king's ignorance of the person of Daniel, but only his amazement at his ability to make known the dream, in the sense, "art thou really able?" This amazement Daniel acknowledges as justified, for he replies that no wise man was able to do this thing. "But there is a God in heaven." Daniel "declares in the presence of the heathen the existence of God, before he speaks to him of His works." Klief. But when he testifies of a God in heaven as One who is able to reveal hidden things, he denies this ability *eo ipso* to all the so-called gods of the heathen. Thereby he not only assigns the reason of the inability of the heathen wise men, who knew not the living God in heaven, to show the divine mysteries, but he refers also all the revelations which the heathen at any time receive to the one true God.

—*Commentary on the Old Testament*

31. *A great image.* Representing the four great monarchies.

32. *Head was of fine gold.* The Babylonish empire, the first and greatest. *Breast and his arms of silver.* The Medo-Persian empire, under Cyrus, etc.

His belly and his thighs of brass. The Macedonian empire, under Alexander the Great, and his successors.

MATTHEW HENRY

ALEXANDER MACLAREN:

The Image. It was a human form of strangely mingled materials, of giant size no doubt, and of majestic aspect. Barbarous enough it would have looked beside the marble lovelinesses of Greece, but it was quite like the coarser art which sought for impressiveness through size and costliness. Other people than Babylonian sculptors think that bigness is greatness, and dearness preciousness.

This image embodied what is now called a philosophy of history. It set forth the fruitful idea of a succession and unity in the rise and fall of conquerors and kingdoms. The four empires represented by it are diverse, and yet parts of a whole, and each following on the other. So the truth is taught that history is an organic whole, however unrelated its events may appear to a superficial eye. The writer of this book had learned lessons far in advance of his age, and not yet fully grasped by many so-called historians.—*Expositions of Holy Scripture*

But what became of this image? The next part of the dream shows it calcined, and brought to nothing. He saw a stone cut out of the quarry by an unseen power, and this stone fell upon the *feet of the image,* that were of *iron and clay,* and *broke them to pieces*; and then the image must fall and the gold, and silver, and brass, and iron, were all broken to pieces, beaten so small that they became like the *chaff of the summer threshing-floors*: but the stone *cut out of the mountain* became itself a *great mountain, and filled the earth.*

JAMIESON, FAUSSET, BROWN

the nobles being his equals in rank, but not in office; in Greece, an aristocracy not of birth, but individual influence, in Rome, lowest of all, dependent entirely on popular choice, the emperor being appointed by popular military election. **33.** As the two arms of silver denote the kings of the Medes and Persians [JOSEPHUS]; and the two thighs of brass the Seleucidæ of Syria and Lagidæ of Egypt, the two leading sections into which Græco-Macedonia parted, so the two legs of iron signify the two Roman consuls [NEWTON]. The clay, in verse 41, "potter's clay," verse 43, "miry clay," means "earthenware," hard but brittle (cf. Ps. 2:9; Rev. 2:27, where the same image is used of the same event); the feet are stable while bearing only direct pressure, but easily broken to pieces by a blow (vs. 34), the iron intermixed not retarding, but hastening, such a result. **34. stone**—Messiah and His kingdom (Gen. 49:24; Ps. 118:22; Isa. 28:16). In its relations to Israel, it is a "stone of stumbling" (Isa. 8:14; Acts 4:11; I Pet. 2:7, 8) on which both houses of Israel are broken, not destroyed (Matt. 21:32). In its relation to the Church, the same stone which destroys the image is the foundation of the Church (Eph. 2:20). In its relation to the Gentile world power, the stone is its destroyer (vss. 35, 44; cf. Zech. 12:3). Christ saith (Matt. 21:44, referring to Isa. 8:14, 15), "Whosoever shall fall on this stone [i.e., stumble, and be offended, at Him, as the *Jews* were, from whom, therefore, He says, 'The kingdom shall be taken'] shall be *broken;* but [referring to vss. 34, 35] on whomsoever it shall fall [referring to *the world power* which had been the instrument of *breaking* the Jews], it will [not merely *break,* but] *grind him to powder*" (I Cor. 15:24). The falling of the stone of the feet of the image cannot refer to Christ at His first advent, for the fourth kingdom was not then as yet divided—no toes were in existence (see *Note,* vs. 44). **cut out**—viz., from "the mountain" (vs. 45); viz., Mount Zion (Isa. 2:2), and antitypically, the heavenly mount of the Father's glory, from whom Christ came. **without hands**—explained in vs. 44, "The *God of heaven* shall set up a kingdom," as contrasted with the image which was made *with hands* of man. Messiah not created by human agency, but conceived by the Holy Ghost (Matt. 1:20; Luke 1:35; cf. Zech. 4:6; Mark 14:58; Heb. 9:11, 24). So "not made with hands," i.e., *heavenly,* II Corinthians 5:1; *spiritual,* Colossians 2:11. The world kingdoms were reared by *human* ambition: but this is the "kingdom of *heaven*"; "not of this world" (John 18:36). As the fourth kingdom, or Rome, was represented in a twofold state, first strong, with legs of iron, then weak, with toes part of iron, part of clay; so this fifth kingdom, that of Christ, is seen conversely, first insignificant as a "stone," then as a "mountain" filling the whole earth. The ten toes are the ten lesser kingdoms into which the Roman kingdom was finally to be divided; this tenfold division here hinted at is not specified in detail till the seventh chapter. The fourth empire originally was bounded in Europe pretty nearly by the line of the Rhine and Danube; in Asia by the Euphrates. In Africa it possessed Egypt and the north coasts; South Britain and Dacia were afterwards added but were ultimately resigned. The ten kingdoms do not arise until a deterioration (by mixing clay with the iron) has taken place; they are in existence when Christ comes in glory, and then are broken in pieces. The ten have been sought for in the invading hosts of the fifth and sixth century. But though many provinces were then severed from Rome as independent kingdoms, the dignity of emperor still continued, and the imperial power was exercised over Rome itself for two centuries. So the tenfold divisions cannot be looked for before A.D. 731. But the East is not to be excluded, five toes being on each foot. Thus no point of time before the overthrow of the empire at the taking of Constantinople by the Turks (A.D. 1453) can be assigned for the division. It seems, therefore, that the definite ten will be the ultimate development of the Roman empire just before the rise of Antichrist, who shall overthrow three of the kings, and, after three and a half years, he himself be overthrown by Christ in person. Some of the ten kingdoms will, doubtless, be the same as some past and present divisions of the old Roman empire, which accounts for the *continuity* of the connection between the toes and legs, a gap of centuries not being interposed, as is objected by opponents of the futurist theory. The lists of the ten made by the latter differ from one another; and they are set aside by the fact that they include countries which were never Roman, and exclude one whole section of the empire, viz., the East

ADAM CLARKE

33. *His legs of iron.* The Roman government. *His feet part of iron and part of clay.* The same, mixed with the barbaric nations, and divided into ten kingdoms.

34. *A stone was cut out.* The fifth monarchy; the spiritual kingdom of the Lord Jesus, which is to last forever, and diffuse itself over the whole earth.

JOSEPH PARKER:

"Without hands." That is the mysterious element in life. If all things were done with hands we could arrange by careful calculation what could be done under given circumstances. It is the unknown quantity that troubles our arithmetic. The fool wrote upon his slate so many thousand bushels of grain, so may scores of years, so many necessities provided for by so many supplies; then, having added the thing up, he said, "Soul, thou hast much goods laid up for many years; take thine ease," and a voice without shape said, "Thou fool! this night thy soul shall be required of thee." The calculator had set down in his calculation everything but God, which means that he had filled his slate with ciphers. All great things are done "without hands." The sun, to use popular language, is rolled up in the east morning by morning without hands, and the least flower warms itself at the great fire, erects itself without hands, and is painted without hands. It is the handless ministry that is so mysterious and sublime. We were delivered by a hand unseen; we were reared from our cradle by influences that only embodied themselves in father and mother and home agency. The real Father we have not seen; he is father-mother-nurse, shepherd-lover-friend; hyphen all these great, sweet words, and so link them into eternal wedlock, and they will stand a poor symbol of the thing that never can be fully spoken.—*The People's Bible*

MATTHEW HENRY

II. The interpretation of this dream.

1. This image represented the kingdoms of the earth that should successively bear rule among the nations and have influence on the affairs of the Jewish church. The four monarchies were not represented by four distinct statues, but by one image, because they were all of one and the same spirit, and all more or less against the church. It was the same power, only lodged in four different nations. (1) The *head of gold* signified the Chaldean monarchy, which was now in being (*v.* 37, 38): Thou art the *highest of kings* on earth at this time. It is *the God of heaven* that has *given thee a kingdom, power, and strength, and glory*, a kingdom that exercises great authority, stands firmly.

The extent of his dominion is set forth (*v.* 38), that *wheresoever the children of men dwell* in all the nations of that part of the world, he was *ruler over them all*. Thus "*thou art the head of gold*; thou, and thy son, and thy son's son, for seventy years." Compare this with Jer. xxv. 9, 11, especially Jer. xxvii. 5-7. There were other powerful kingdoms in the world at this time, as that of the Scythians; but it was the kingdom of Babylon that reigned over the Jews. It is called a *head*, for its wisdom, and absolute power, a head of *gold* for its wealth (Isa. xiv. 4). Some make this monarchy to begin in Nimrod, and so bring into it all the Assyrian kings. But it had not been so long a monarchy of such vast extent, therefore others make only Nebuchadnezzar, Evil-merodach, and Belshazzar, to belong to this *head of gold*. (2) The *breast and arms of silver* signified the monarchy of the Medes and Persians. *There shall arise another kingdom inferior to thee* (*v.* 39), not so rich, powerful, or victorious. This kingdom was founded by Darius the Mede and Cyrus the Persian, in alliance and therefore represented by two arms. Cyrus was himself a Persian by his father, a Mede by his mother. (3) The *belly and thighs of brass* signified the monarchy of the Grecians, founded by Alexander, who conquered Darius, the last of the Persian emperors. This is the *third kingdom, of brass*, inferior in wealth and extent to the Persian monarchy, but in Alexander himself it shall by the power of the sword *bear rule over all the earth*; for Alexander boasted that he had conquered the world.

(4) The *legs and feet of iron* signified the Roman monarchy. It was in the time of that monarchy, when it was at its height, that the kingdom of Christ was set up in the world by the preaching of the everlasting gospel. The Roman kingdom strong as iron (*v.* 40), *broke in pieces* the Grecian empire and afterwards destroyed the nation of the Jews. Towards the latter end of the Roman monarchy it grew weak, and branched into ten kingdoms, which were as the toes of these feet. Some of these were weak as clay, others strong as iron, *v.* 42. *They shall not cleave one to another*, *v.* 43. This empire divided the government for a long time between the senate and the people, the nobles and the commons, but they did not coalesce. There were civil wars between Marius and Sulla, Caesar and Pompey, whose parties were as iron and clay.

JAMIESON, FAUSSET, BROWN

[TREGELLES]. **upon his feet**—the last state of the Roman empire. Not "upon his *legs*." Cf. "in the days of these kings" (*Note*, vs. 44). **35. broken . . . together**—excluding a contemporaneous existence of the kingdom of the world and the kingdom of God (in its *manifested*, as distinguished from its *spiritual*, phase). The latter is not gradually to wear away the former, but to destroy it at once, and utterly (II Thess. 1:7-10; 2:8). However, the *Hebrew* may be translated, "in one discriminate mass." **chaff**—image of the ungodly, as they shall be dealt with in the judgment (Ps. 1:4, 5; Matt. 3:12). **summer threshing-floors**—Grain was winnowed in the East on an elevated space in the open air, by throwing the grain into the air with a shovel, so that the wind might clear away the chaff. **no place . . . found for them**—(Rev. 20:11; cf. Ps. 37:10, 36; 103:16). **became . . . mountain**—cut out of the mountain (vs. 45) originally, it ends in *becoming a mountain*. So the kingdom of God, coming from heaven originally, ends in heaven being established on earth (Rev. 21:1-3). **filled . . . earth**—(Isa. 11:9; Hab. 2:14). It is to do so in connection with Jerusalem as the mother Church (Ps. 80:9; Isa. 2:2, 3). **36. we**—Daniel and his three friends. **37. Thou . . . art a king of kings**—The committal of power in fullest plenitude belongs to Nebuchadnezzar personally, as having made Babylon the mighty empire it was. In twenty-three years after him the empire was ended: with him its greatness is identified (ch. 4:30), his successors having done nothing notable. Not that he actually ruled every part of the globe, but that God granted him illimitable dominion *in whatever direction his ambition led him*, Egypt, Nineveh, Arabia, Syria, Tyre, and its Phœnician colonies (Jer. 27:5-8). Cf. as to Cyrus, Ezra 1:2. **38. men . . . beasts . . . fowls**—the dominion originally designed for man (Gen. 1:28; 2:19, 20), forfeited by sin; temporarily delegated to Nebuchadnezzar and the world powers; but, as they abuse the trust for self, instead of for God, to be taken from them by the Son of man, who will exercise it for God, restoring in His person to man the lost inheritance (Ps. 8:4-6). **Thou art . . . head of gold**—alluding to the riches of Babylon, hence called "the golden city" (Isa. 14:4; Jer. 51:7; Rev. 18:16). **39.** That Medo-Persia is the second kingdom appears from ch. 5:28 and 8:20. Cf. II Chronicles 36:20; Isaiah 21:2. **inferior**—"The kings of Persia were the worst race of men that ever governed an empire" [PRIDEAUX]. Politically (which is the main point of view here) the power of the central government in which the nobles shared with the king, being weakened by the growing independence of the provinces, was inferior to that of Nebuchadnezzar, whose sole word was law throughout his empire. **brass**—The Greeks (the third empire, ch. 8:21; 10:20; 11:2-4) were celebrated for the *brazen* armor of their warriors. JEROME fancifully thinks that the brass, as being a *clear-sounding* metal, refers to the *eloquence* for which Greece was famed. The "belly," in verse 32, may refer to the drunkenness of Alexander and the luxury of the Ptolemies [TIRINUS]. **over all the earth**—Alexander commanded that he should be called "king of all the world" [JUSTIN, 12. sec. 16. 9; ARRIAN, Exp. Alex. 7. sec. 15]. The four successors (*diadochi*) who divided Alexander's dominions at his death, of whom the Seleucidæ in Syria and the Lagidæ in Egypt were chief, held the same empire. **40. iron**—This vision sets forth the *character* of the Roman power, rather than its territorial extent [TREGELLES]. **breaketh in pieces**—So, in righteous retribution, itself will at last be *broken in pieces* (vs. 44) by the kingdom of God (Rev. 13:10). **41-43. feet . . . toes . . . part . . . clay . . . iron**—explained presently, "the kingdom shall be partly strong, partly broken" (rather, "brittle," as earthenware); and verse 43, "they shall mingle . . . with the seed of men," i.e., there will be power (in its deteriorated form, *iron*) mixed up with that which is wholly of man, and therefore brittle; power in the hands of the people having no internal stability, though something is left of the strength of the iron [TREGELLES]. NEWTON, who understands the Roman empire to be parted into the ten kingdoms already (whereas TREGELLES makes them *future*), explains the "clay" mixture as the blending of barbarous nations with Rome by intermarriages and alliances, in which there was no stable amalgamation, though the ten kingdoms retained much of Rome's strength. The "mingling with the seed of men" (vs. 44) seems to refer to Genesis 6:2, where the marriages of the seed of godly Seth with the daughters of ungodly Cain are described in similar words. The reference, therefore, seems to be to the blending of the Christianized Roman empire with the pagan nations, a deterioration being the result. Ef-

ADAM CLARKE

37. *The God of heaven.* **Not given by your own gods, nor acquired by your own skill and prowess; it is a divine gift. *Power.* To rule this kingdom. *And strength.* To defend it against all foes. *And glory.* Great honor and dignity.**

ALEXANDER MACLAREN:

Again, the kingdoms are seen in their brilliancy, as they would naturally appear to the thoughts of a conqueror, whose highest notion of glory was earthly dominion, and who was indifferent to the suffering and blood through which he waded to a throne. When the same kingdoms are shown to Daniel in chapter seven they are represented by beasts. Their cruelty and the destruction of life which they caused were uppermost in a prophet's view; their vulgar splendor dazzled a king's sleeping eyes, because it had intoxicated his waking thoughts. Much worldly glory and many of its aims appear as precious metal to dreamers, but are seen by an illuminated sight to be bestial and destructive.

Once more there is a steady process of deterioration in the four kingdoms. Gold is followed by silver, and that by brass, and that by the strange combination of iron and clay. This may simply refer to the diminution of worldly glory, but it may also mean deterioration, morally and otherwise. Is it not the teaching of Scripture that, unless God interpose, society will steadily slide downwards? And has not the fact been so, wherever the brake and lever of revelation have not arrested the decline and effected elevation? We are told nowadays of evolution, as if the progress of humanity were upwards; but if you withdraw the influence of supernatural revelation, the evidence of power in manhood to work itself clear of limitations and lower forms is very ambiguous at the best—in reference to morals, at all events. Evil is capable of development, as well as good; and perhaps Nebuchadnezzar's colossus is a truer representation of the course of humanity than the dreams of modern thinkers who see manhood becoming steadily better by its own effort, and think that the clay and iron have inherent power to pass into fine gold.

—Expositions of Holy Scripture

MATTHEW HENRY

2. The stone *cut out without hands* represented the kingdom of Jesus Christ, for it should be neither raised nor supported by human power or policy. (1) The gospel-church is a kingdom *not of this world*, and yet set up in it; it is the kingdom of God among men. (2) The *God of heaven* was to set up this kingdom, to give authority to Christ, to set him as *King upon his holy hill of Zion*. It is often in the *New Testament* called the *kingdom of heaven*, for its origin is from above and its tendency is upwards. (3) It was to be set up *in the days of these kings*, the kings of the fourth monarchy, of which particular notice is taken (Luke ii. 1). When these kings are contesting with each other, God will do his own work and fulfil his own counsels. (4) It is a kingdom that knows no decay, and will not admit any succession or revolution. As Christ is a monarch that has no successor (for he himself shall reign for ever), so his kingdom is a monarchy that has no revolution. The kingdom of God was indeed taken from the Jews and given to the Gentiles (Matt. xxi. 43), but still it was Christianity that ruled, the kingdom of the Messiah. (5) It is a kingdom that shall be victorious. It shall *break in pieces and consume all those kingdoms*, as the *stone cut out of the mountain without hands* broke in pieces the image, *v.* 44, 45. And in the kingdoms that submit to the kingdom of Christ tyranny, and idolatry, and everything that is their reproach, shall, as far as the gospel of Christ gets ground, be broken. Our Saviour seems to refer to this (Matt. xxi. 44) when he says, *On whomsoever* this stone *shall fall, it will grind him to powder*. (6) It shall be an everlasting kingdom. *The Lord shall reign for ever*, not only to the end of time, but when time and days shall be no more, and *God shall be all in all* to eternity.

III. Daniel having thus interpreted the dream, to the satisfaction of Nebuchadnezzar, closes with a solemn assertion, 1. Of the divine origin of this dream: *The great God* has *made known to the king what shall come to pass hereafter*, which the gods of the magicians could not do. 2. Of the undoubted certainty of the things foretold by this dream. Whatever God has made known we may depend upon.

Verses 46–49

Instead of resenting it as an affront, the king received it as an oracle, and here we are told what the expressions were of the impressions it made upon him. 1. He was ready to look upon Daniel as a little god. He concluded that he had certainly a divinity lodged in him, worthy his adoration; and therefore he *fell upon his face and worshipped Daniel*, *v.* 46. Thus did God magnify divine revelation *and make it honourable*. And that Daniel did say something to him which turned his eyes and thoughts another way is intimated in what follows (*v.* 47), *The king answered Daniel*. 2. He readily acknowledged the God of Daniel to be the great God. If Daniel will not suffer himself to be worshipped, he will *worship God*, by confessing (*v.* 47), *Of a truth your God is a God of gods*, over all gods in dominion. 3. He preferred Daniel, made him a great man, *v.* 48. The king *gave him many great gifts*. He made him *ruler over the whole province of Babylon*, he made him chancellor of the university, *chief of the governors over all the wise men of Babylon*. 4. He preferred his companions for his sake, and upon his request, *v.* 49. Daniel himself *sat in the gate of the king*, and procured places in the government for Shadrach, Meshach, and Abednego. And these pious Jews, being thus preferred in Babylon, had opportunity of serving their brethren in captivity.

JAMIESON, FAUSSET, BROWN

forts have been often made to reunite the parts into one great empire, as by Charlemagne and Napoleon, but in vain. Christ alone shall effect that. **44. in the days of these kings**—in the days of these kingdoms, i.e., of the last of the four. So Christianity was set up when Rome had become mistress of Judea and the world (Luke 2:1, etc.) [NEWTON]. Rather, "in the days of these kings," answers to "upon his feet" (vs. 34); i.e., the ten *toes* (vs. 42), or ten kings, the final state of the Roman empire. For "these kings" cannot mean the four successional monarchies, as they do not *coexist* as the holders of power; if the fourth had been meant, the *singular*, not the *plural*, would be used. The falling of the stone on the image must mean, *destroying judgment* on the fourth Gentile power, not gradual evangelization of it by grace; and the destroying judgment cannot be dealt by Christians, for they are taught to submit to the powers that be, so that it must be dealt by Christ Himself at His coming again. We live under the divisions of the Roman empire which began 1400 years ago, and which at the time of His coming shall be definitely *ten*. All that had failed in the hand of man shall then pass away, and that which is kept in His own hand shall be introduced. Thus the second chapter is the alphabet of the subsequent prophetic statements in Daniel [TREGELLES]. **God of heaven . . . kingdom**—hence the phrase, "the kingdom of heaven" (Matt. 3:2). **not . . . left to other people**—as the Chaldees had been forced to leave their kingdom to the Medo-Persians, and these to the Greeks, and these to the Romans (Mic. 4:7; Luke 1:32, 33). **break . . . all**—(Isa. 60: 12; I Cor. 15:24). **45. without hands**—(*Note*, vs. 35). **46. fell upon . . . face, and worshipped Daniel**—worshipping God in the person of Daniel. Symbolical of the future prostration of the world power before Messiah and His kingdom (Phil. 2:10). As other servants of God refused such honors (Acts 10: 25, 26; 14:13-15; Rev. 22:8, 9), and Daniel (ch. 1:8) would not taste defiled food, nor give up prayer to God at the cost of his life (ch. 6), it seems likely that Daniel rejected the proffered divine honors. The word "answered" (vs. 47) implies that Daniel had objected to these honors; and in compliance with his objection, "the king *answered*, Of a truth, your God is a God of gods." Daniel had disclaimed all personal merit in vs. 30, giving GOD all the glory (cf. vs. 45). **commanded . . . sweet odours**—divine honors (Ezra 6:10). It is not said his command was executed. **47. Lord of kings**—The world power shall at last have to acknowledge this (Rev. 17:14; 19:16); even as Nebuchadnezzar, who had been the God-appointed "king of kings" (vs. 37), but who had abused the trust, is constrained by God's servant to acknowledge that God is the true "Lord of kings." **48.** One reason for Nebuchadnezzar having been vouchsafed such a dream is here seen; viz., that Daniel might be promoted, and the captive people of God be comforted: the independent state of the captives during the exile and the alleviation of its hardships, were much due to Daniel. **49. Daniel requested**—Contrast this honorable remembrance of his humble friends in his elevation with the spirit of the children of the world in the chief butler's case (Gen. 40:23; Eccles. 9:15, 16; Amos 6:6). **in the gate**—the place of holding courts of justice and levees in the East (Esther 2:19; Job 29:7). So "the Sublime *Porte*," or "Gate," denotes the sultan's government, his counsels being formerly held in the entrance of his palace. Daniel was a chief counsellor of the king, and president over the governors of the different orders into which the Magi were divided.

ADAM CLARKE

44. *A kingdom, which shall never be destroyed*. The extensive and extending empire of Christ. *Shall not be left to other people*. All the preceding empires have swallowed up each other successively, but this shall remain to the end of the world.

45. *The dream is certain*. It contains a just representation of things as they shall be. *And the interpretation thereof sure*. The parts of the dream being truly explained.

46. *The king . . . fell upon his face*. Prostrated himself; this was the fullest act of adoration among the ancients. *Worshipped Daniel*. Supposing him to be a god, or divine being. No doubt Daniel forbade him, for to receive this would have been gross idolatry.

47. *Your God is a God of gods*. He is greater than all others. *And a Lord of kings*. He governs in both heaven and earth.

48. *Made Daniel a great man*. (1) By giving him many rich gifts, (2) By making him governor over the whole province of Babylon, and (3) By making him the chief or president over all the wise men.

49. *Daniel requested of the king, and he set Shadrach, Meshach, and Abed-nego, over the affairs of the province of Babylon*. He wished his three companions promoted who had shared his anxieties and helped him by their prayers. They all had places of trust, in which they could do much good, and prevent much evil. *Daniel sat in the gate of the king*. That is, was the chief officer in the palace, and the greatest confidant and counsellor of the king.

CHAPTER 3 (MATTHEW HENRY)

CHAPTER 3 (JAMIESON, FAUSSET, BROWN)

VSS. 1-30. NEBUCHADNEZZAR'S IDOLATROUS IMAGE; SHADRACH, MESHACH, AND ABED-NEGO ARE DELIVERED FROM THE FURNACE. Between the vision of Nebuchadnezzar in the second chapter and that of Daniel in the seventh, four narratives of Daniels and his friends' personal history are introduced. As chapters 2 and 7 go together, so chapters 3 and 6 (the deliverance from the lions' den), and chapters 4 and 5. Of these last two pairs, the former shows God's nearness to save His saints when faithful to Him, at the very time they seem to be crushed by the world power. The second pair shows, in the case of the two kings of the first monarchy, how God can suddenly humble the world power in the height of its insolence. The latter advances from mere self-glorification, in the fourth chapter, to open opposition to God in the fifth. Nebuchadnezzar demands homage to be paid to his image (ch. 3), and boasts of his

CHAPTER 3 (ADAM CLARKE)

MATTHEW HENRY

Verses 1–7

I. A *golden image set up* to be worshipped. Babylon was full of idols, but those who have forsaken the one only living God, and begin to set up many gods, will find the gods they set up so unsatisfying, that they will multiply them without measure. It was *an image of gold.* It was *threescore cubits high and six cubits broad,* as if its being monstrous would make amends for its being lifeless. Perhaps he set it up as an image of himself, and designed to be himself worshipped in it. The good impressions made upon him were quite lost, and quickly. He had acknowledged that the God of Israel is a *God of gods* and a *Lord of kings*; yet now, in defiance of the express law of that God, he sets up an image to be worshipped. The very dream and the interpretation of it, which made such good impressions upon him, now had a quite contrary effect. Now it made him set up for a bold competitor with God.

II. The states summoned to attend the dedication of this image, *v.* 2, 3. Long journeys many took upon a foolish errand; but, as the idols are senseless things, such are the worshippers.

III. A proclamation made, commanding all persons present to fall down and worship the image.

It was proclaimed, That whosoever would not *worship this golden image* should be immediately thrown *into the midst of a burning fiery furnace,* ready prepared for that purpose, *v.* 6.

JAMIESON, FAUSSET, BROWN

power (ch. 4). But Belshazzar goes further, blaspheming God by polluting His holy vessels. There is a similar progression in the conduct of God's people. Shadrach, Meshach, and Abednego refuse *positive* homage to the image of the world power (ch. 3); Daniel will not yield it even a *negative* homage, by omitting for a time the worship of God (ch. 6). Jehovah's power manifested for the saints against the world in individual histories (ch. 3-6) is exhibited in chapters 2 and 7, in worldwide prophetical pictures; the former heightening the effect of the latter. The miracles wrought in behalf of Daniel and his friends were a manifestation of God's glory in Daniel's person, as the representative of the theocracy before the Babylonian king, who deemed himself almighty, at a time when God could not manifest it in His people as a body. They tended also to secure, by their impressive character, that respect for the covenant people on the part of the heathen powers which issued in Cyrus' decree, not only restoring the Jews, but ascribing honor to the God of heaven, and commanding the building of the temple (Ezra 1:1-4) [AUBERLEN]. **1. image**—Nebuchadnezzar's confession of God did not prevent him being a worshipper of idols, besides. Ancient idolaters thought that each nation had its own gods, and that, in addition to these, foreign gods might be worshipped. The Jewish religion was the only exclusive one that claimed *all* homage for Jehovah as the *only* true God. Men will in times of trouble confess God, if they are allowed to retain their favorite heart-idols. The image was that of Bel, the Babylonian tutelary god; or rather, Nebuchadnezzar *himself,* the personification and representative of the Babylonian empire, as suggested to him by the dream (ch. 2:38), "*Thou* art this head *of gold.*" The interval between the dream and the event here was about nineteen years. Nebuchadnezzar had just returned from finishing the Jewish and Syrian wars, the spoils of which would furnish the means of rearing such a colossal statue [PRIDEAUX]. The colossal size makes it likely that the frame was wood, overlaid with gold. The "height," 60 cubits, is so out of proportion with the "breadth," exceeding it ten times, that it seems best to suppose the *thickness* from breast to back to be intended, which is exactly the right proportion of a well-formed man [AUGUSTINE, *De Civitate Dei,* 15. 20]. PRIDEAUX thinks the 60 cubits refer to *the image and pedestal together,* the image being 27 cubits high, or 40 feet, the pedestal 33 cubits, or 50 feet. HERODOTUS (1. 183) confirms this by mentioning a *similar* image, 40 *feet high,* in the temple of Belus at Babylon. It was not the *same* image, for the one here was on the plain of Dura, not in the city. **2. princes**—"satraps" of provinces [GESENIUS]. **captains**—*rulers,* not exclusively military. **sheriffs**—men learned in the law, like the Arab *mufti* [GESENIUS]. **3. stood before the image**—in an attitude of devotion. Whatever the king approved of, they all approve of. There is no stability of principle in the ungodly. **4.** The arguments of the persecutor are in brief, Turn or burn. **5. cornet**—A wind instrument, like the French horn, is meant. **flute**—a pipe or pipes, not blown transversely as our "flute," but by mouthpieces at the end. **sackbut**—a triangular stringed instrument, having short strings, the sound being on a high sharp key. **psaltery**—a kind of harp. **dulcimer**—a bagpipe consisting of two pipes, thrust through a leathern bag, emitting a sweet plaintive sound. *Chaldee sumponya,* the modern Italian *zampogna,* Asiatic *zambonja.* **fall down**—that the recusants might be the more readily detected. **6.** No other nation but the Jews would feel this edict oppressive; for it did not prevent them worshipping their own gods *besides.* It was evidently aimed at the Jews by those jealous of their high position in the king's court, who therefore induced the king to pass an edict as to all recusants, representing such refusal of homage as an act of treason to Nebuchadnezzar as civil and religious "head" of the empire. So the edict under Darius (6th ch.) was aimed against the Jews by those jealous of Daniel's influence. The literal image of Nebuchadnezzar is a typical prophecy of "the image of the beast," connected with mystical Babylon, in Revelation 13:14. The second mystical beast there causeth the earth, and them that dwell therein, to worship the first beast, and that as many as would not, should be killed (Rev. 13:12, 15). **furnace**—a common mode of punishment in Babylon (Jer. 29:22). It is not necessary to suppose that the furnace was made for the occasion. Cf. "brick kiln," II Samuel 12:31. Any furnace for common purposes in the vicinity of Dura would serve. CHARDIN, in his travels (A.D. 1671-1677), mentions that in Persia, to terrify those who took

ADAM CLARKE

1. *Nebuchadnezzar the king made an image of gold.* It is supposed that the history given here did not occur till the close, or near the end, of Nebuchadnezzar's reign. For it was after his insanity, as we see chap. iv. 33-36, and this happened near the close of his reign. A few observations on this image may be necessary: (1) It is not likely that this image was in human form—the dimensions show the improbability of this. (2) It is not likely that this image was all of gold. (3) It might have been a pillar on which an image of the god *Bel* was erected. The image itself might be of gold, or more probably gilt, that is, covered with thin plates of gold, and on this account it might be called the golden image. *The plain of Dura.* The situation of this place is not exactly known; there was a town or city called *Dura,* or *Doura,* in Mesopotamia, near the Tigris.

2. *Sent to gather together the princes.* It is not easy to show what these different offices were, as it is difficult to ascertain the meaning of the Chaldee words.

4. *Then a herald cried aloud.* "A crier called with might."

5. *The sound of the cornet.* There is not less difficulty in ascertaining the precise meaning of these musical instruments than there is in the offices in v. 2.

6. *Shall the same hour.* This is the first place in the Old Testament where we find the division of time into hours. The Greeks say that Anaximander was the inventor. He had it probably from the Chaldeans, among whom this division was in use long before Anaximander was born.

MATTHEW HENRY

IV. The general compliance of the assembly with this command, *v.* 7.

Verses 8–18

It was strange that Shadrach, Meshach, and Abednego, would be present at this assembly. Surely because they would obey the king's orders and be ready to bear a public testimony against this gross idolatry.

I. Information is brought to the king by *certain Chaldeans* against these three, *v.* 8. Perhaps these that accused them were some of those *magicians or astrologers* that were particularly called *Chaldeans* (*ch.* ii. 2, 4). Perhaps they were such of the Chaldeans as envied them their preferments; *and who can stand before envy?* They appeal to the king, 1. To put him in mind of the law he had lately made, That all manner of persons, without exception of nation or language, should *fall down and worship this golden image*, *v.* 10, 11. 2. To inform him that these three men, Shadrach, Meshach, and Abednego, had not conformed to this edict, *v.* 12. To incense the king the more against them, (1) They put him in mind of the dignity to which the criminals had been preferred. It was therefore an insufferable piece of insolence, for them to disobey the king's command. The high station they were in would make their refusal the more scandalous. (2) They suggest that it was done in contempt of him and his authority.

II. These three pious Jews are brought before the king, and examined upon this information. Nebuchadnezzar fell into a great passion, and *in his rage and fury commanded* them to be seized, *v.* 13.

III. The king asked them whether it was true that they had not worshipped the golden image when others did, *v.* 14. It may be, upon second thoughts, they will change their minds. The king is willing that if they will *worship the golden image*, well and good; their former omission shall be pardoned. The king is resolved, if they persist in their refusal, that they shall immediately be *cast into the fiery furnace. Turn, or burn;* and, because he knew they buoyed themselves up in their refusal with a confidence in their God, he set him at defiance: "*And who is that God that shall deliver you out of my hands?* Let him, if he can."

IV. They answer that they still adhere to their resolution not to worship the golden image, *v.* 16–18. We call these the *three children* (they were indeed *young men*), but we should rather call them the three champions, the *first three* of the *worthies* of God's *kingdom among men.* They did not go out of their way to court martyrdom; but, when they were duly called to the fiery trial, they acquitted themselves bravely.

1. Their contempt of death, and the noble negligence with which they look upon the dilemma: *O Nebuchadnezzar! we are not careful to answer thee in this matter*. They do not in sullenness deny him an answer, but they tell him that they are in no care about it. They needed no time to deliberate concerning their answer; for they did not hesitate whether they should comply or no. But the sin and duty in the case were determined by the letter of the second commandment, and no room was left to question what was right. They were not contriving an evasive answer, when a direct answer was expected from them.

2. Their confidence in God and their dependence upon him, *v.* 17. They trusted in the living God, and by that faith chose rather to suffer than to sin. "If we must be thrown into the fiery furnace unless we serve thy gods, know then, though we worship not *thy gods* yet we are not atheists; there is a God whom we call ours. We serve this God. We are well assured that this God is *able to deliver us from the burning fiery furnace*. If he do not deliver us from the fiery furnace, he will *deliver us out of thy hand*." Nebuchadnezzar can but torment and kill the body, and, after that, there is no more than he can do. God will deliver us either from death or in death.

3. Their firm resolution to adhere to their principles, whatever might be the consequence (*v.* 18). They were not required to abjure their own God, or to renounce his worship. It was but one single act that was required of them, which would be done in a minute, and they might afterwards declare their sorrow for it. They might be excused if they should go down the stream, when it is so strong. Did not all the ten tribes, for many ages, worship gods of gold at Dan and Bethel? If they should comply, they would save their lives and so be in a capacity to do a great deal of service to their brethren. But there is enough in that one word of God wherewith to answer and silence these and many more such like carnal reasonings: *Thou shalt not bow down thyself to any images, nor worship them.* They must rather suffer than sin, and must not do evil that good may come. And truly,

JAMIESON, FAUSSET, BROWN

advantage of scarcity to sell provisions at exorbitant prices, the cooks were roasted over a slow fire, and the bakers cast into a burning oven. **7.** None of the Jews seem to have been present, except the *officers,* summoned specially.

8. accused the Jews—lit., "ate the rent limbs," or flesh of the Jews (cf. Job 31:31; Ps. 14:4; 27:2; Jer. 10:25). Not probably in general, but as verse 12 states, Shadrach, Meshach, and Abednego. Why Daniel was not summoned does not appear. Probably he was in some distant part of the empire on state business, and the general summons (vs. 2) had not time to reach him before the dedication. Also, the Jews' enemies found it more politic to begin by attacking Shadrach, Meshach, and Abed-nego, who were nearer at hand, and had less influence, before they proceeded to attack Daniel. **9. live for ever**—A preface of flattery is closely akin to the cruelty that follows. So Acts 24:2, 3, etc., Tertullus in accusing Paul before Felix. **12. serve not thy gods**—not only not the golden image, but also *not any* of Nebuchadnezzar's *gods.*

13. bring—Instead of commanding their immediate execution, as in the case of the Magi (ch. 2:12), Providence inclined him to command the recusants to be *brought* before him, so that their noble "testimony" for God might be given before the world powers "against them" (Matt. 10:18), to the edification of the Church in all ages. **14. Is it true**—rather, as *Margin* [THEODOTION], "Is it *purposely* that . . . ?" Cf. the *Hebrew*, Numbers 35:20, 22. Notwithstanding his "fury," his past favor for them disposes him to give them the opportunity of excusing themselves on the ground that their disobedience had not been *intentional;* so he gives them another trial to see whether they would still worship the image. **15. who is that God**—so Sennacherib's taunt (II Kings 18:35), and Pharaoh's (Exod. 5:2).

16. not careful to answer thee—rather, "We have *no need* to answer thee"; thou art determined on thy side, and our mind is made up not to worship the image: there is therefore no use in our arguing as if we could be shaken from our principles. Hesitation, or parleying with sin, is fatal; unhesitating decision is the only safety, where the path of duty is clear (Matt. 10:19, 28).

17. If it be so—VATABLUS translates, "Assuredly." *English Version* agrees better with the original. The sense is, *If it be* our lot to be cast into the furnace, *our God* (quoted from Deut. 6:4) is able to deliver us (a reply to Nebuchadnezzar's challenge, "Who is that God that shall deliver you?"); and He will deliver us (either *from* death, or *in* death, II Tim. 4:17, 18). He will, *we trust,* literally deliver us, but certainly He will do so spiritually.

18. But if not . . .—connected with vs. 18. "Whether our God deliver us, as He is able, or do not, we will not serve thy gods." Their service of God is not mercenary in its motive. Though He slay them, they will still trust in Him (Job 13:15). Their deliverance from sinful compliance was as great a miracle in the kingdom of grace, as that from the furnace was in the kingdom of nature. Their youth, and position as captives and friendless exiles, before the absolute world potentate and the horrid death awaiting them if they should persevere in their faith, all enhance the grace of God, which carried them through such an ordeal.

ADAM CLARKE

8. *Accused the Jews.* That is, Shadrach, Meshach, and Abed-nego. The other Jews were left unnoticed, and probably at this time Daniel was too high to be touched, but we may rest assured that he was not found among these idolaters.

16. *We are not careful.* We have no need to put you to any further trouble; we have made up our minds on this subject, and have our answer ready: "Be it known unto thee . . . we will not serve thy gods." This was as honest as it was decisive.

MATTHEW HENRY

the saving of them from this sinful compliance was as great a miracle as the saving of them out of the fiery furnace.

Verses 19–27

I. The casting of these three faithful servants of God into the fiery furnace. Nebuchadnezzar, instead of being convinced by what they said, was exasperated, and made more outrageous, *v.* 19. It made him *full of fury*, and the *form of his visage was changed* against these men. Nebuchadnezzar, in this heat, exchanged the awful majesty of a prince for the frightful fury of a *wild bull in a net*. Instead of mitigating their punishment, he ordered it to be heightened, that they should *heat the furnace seven times more than it was wont to be heated* for other malefactors. He ordered them to be bound in their clothes, and cast into the midst of the burning fiery furnace, which was done accordingly, *v.* 20, 21. God's providence ordered it for the increase of the miracle, in that their clothes were not so much as singed. The men that bound them, and threw them into the furnace, were themselves consumed or suffocated by the flame, *v.* 22. But these men were only the instruments of cruelty; he that bade them do it had the greater sin. Nebuchadnezzar himself was reserved for a further reckoning.

II. The deliverance of these three faithful servants of God out of the furnace.

1. Nebuchadnezzar finds them walking in the fire. *He was astonished, and rose up in haste*, *v.* 24. In his astonishment he calls his counsellors. *Did we not cast three men bound into the fire? "True, O king!"* say they. "But now," says the king, "I have been looking into the furnace, and *I see four men, loose, walking in the midst of the fire*," *v.* 25. They were loosed from their bonds. The fire that did not so much as singe their clothes burnt the cords wherewith they were bound, and set them at liberty. They *walked in the midst of the fire*. The furnace was large, so that they had room to walk; they were unhurt, so that they were able to walk; their minds were easy, so that they were disposed to walk, as in a paradise or garden of pleasure. There was a fourth seen with them in the fire, whose form, in Nebuchadnezzar's judgment, was *like the Son of God*; he appeared as a divine person, a messenger from heaven, not as a servant, but as a son. In the apocryphal narrative of this story it is said, *The angel of the Lord came down into the furnace*; and Nebuchadnezzar here says (*v.* 28), God *sent his angel and delivered them*; and it was an angel that shut the lions' mouths when Daniel was in the den, *ch.* vi. 22. But some think it was the eternal Son of God. Those that suffer for Christ have his gracious presence with them in their sufferings, even in the fiery furnace, even in the valley of the shadow of death, and therefore even there they need *fear no evil*.

2. Nebuchadnezzar calls them out of the furnace (*v.* 26): He *comes near to the mouth of the burning fiery furnace*, and bids them *come forth and come hither*. He is convinced by their miraculous preservation that he did evil in casting them into the furnace. The *fourth*, whose *form was like the Son of God*, withdrew, but the other three *came forth out of the midst of the fire*, as brands out of the burning. They had not received the least damage by the fire, *v.* 27. There was not so much as *a hair of their head singed*. Their clothes did not change colour, nor smell of fire, much less were their bodies scorched or blistered; no, *the fire had no power on them*. The Chaldeans worshipped the fire, as a sort of image of the sun, so that, in restraining the fire now, God put contempt, not only upon their king, but upon their god too.

Verses 28–30

The effect it had upon Nebuchadnezzar.

I. He gives glory to the God of Israel as a God able and ready to protect his worshippers (*v.* 28): *Blessed be the God of Shradrach, Meshach, and Abednego*. God can extort confessions of his blessedness even from those that have been ready to curse him to his face. 1. He gives him the glory of his power: *There is no other God that can deliver after this sort* (*v.* 29). If God can work such deliverance as no other can, he may demand such obedience as no other may. 2. He gives him the glory that he was ready to do it (*v.* 28): *He has sent his angel and delivered his servants*. Bel could not save his worshippers from being burnt at the mouth of the furnace, but the God of Israel saved his from being burnt when they were cast into the midst of the furnace because they refused to *worship any other god*.

II. He applauds the constancy of these three men in their religion, and describes it to their honour, *v.* 28. They *yielded their* own *bodies* to be cast into the fiery furnace rather than forsake their God. They *changed the king's word*, that is, they went

JAMIESON, FAUSSET, BROWN

19. visage . . . changed—He had shown forbearance (vss. 14, 15) as a favor to them, but now that they despise even his forbearance, anger "fills" him, and is betrayed in his whole countenance. **seven times more than it was wont**—lit., "than it was (ever) *seen* to be heated." *Seven* is the perfect number; i.e., it was made *as hot as possible*. Passion overdoes and defeats its own end, for the hotter the fire, the sooner were they likely to be put out of pain. **21. coats . . . hosen . . . hats**—HERODOTUS (1. 195) says that the Babylonian costume consisted of three parts: 1. wide, long pantaloons; 2. a woollen *shirt;* 3. an outer *mantle* with a girdle round it. So these are specified [GESENIUS], "their pantaloons, inner tunics (*hosen*, or stockings, are not commonly worn in the East), and outer mantles." Their being cast in so hurriedly, with all their garments on, enhanced the miracle in that not even the smell of fire passed on their clothes, though of delicate, inflammable material. **22. flame . . . slew those men**—(ch. 6:24; Ps. 7:16). **23. fell down**—not *cast down;* for those who brought the three youths to the furnace, perished by the flames themselves, and so could not *cast* them in. Here follows an addition in LXX, *Syrian, Arabic*, and *Vulgate versions*. "The Prayer of Azarias," and "The Song of the Three Holy Children." It is not in the *Chaldee*. The hymn was sung throughout the whole Church in their liturgies, from the earliest times (RUFINUS *in Symb. Ap.*, and ATHANASIUS). The "astonishment" of Nebuchadnezzar in verse 24 is made an argument for its genuineness, as if it explained the cause of his astonishment, viz., "they walked in the midst of the fire praising God, but the angel of the Lord came down into the oven" (vs. 1 and vs. 27 of the Aprocryphal addition). But verse 25 of *English Version* explains his astonishment, without need of any addition. **24. True, O king**—God extorted this confession from His enemies' own mouths. **25. four**—whereas but three had been cast in. **loose**—whereas they had been cast in "bound." Nebuchadnezzar's question, in verse 24, is as if he can scarcely trust his own memory as to a fact so recent, now that he sees through an aperture in the furnace what seems to contradict it. **walking in . . . midst of . . . fire**—image of the godly unhurt, and at large (John 8:36), "in the midst of trouble" (Ps. 138:7; cf. Ps. 23:3, 4). They walked up and down in the fire, not leaving it, but waiting for God's time to bring them out, just as Jesus waited in the tomb as God's prisoner, till God should let Him out (Acts 2:26, 27). So Paul (II Cor. 12:8, 9). So Noah waited in the ark, after the flood, till God brought him forth (Gen. 8:12-18). **like the Son of God**—Unconsciously, like Saul, Caiaphas (John 11:49-52), and Pilate, he is made to utter divine truths. "Son of God" in *his* mouth means only an "angel" from heaven, as verse 28 proves. Cf. Job 1:6; 38:7; Psalm 34:7, 8; and the probably heathen centurion's exclamation (Matthew 27:54). The Chaldeans believed in *families* of gods: Bel, the supreme god, accompanied by the goddess Mylitta, being the father of the gods; thus the expression *he* meant: *one sprung from and sent by the gods*. *Really* it was the "messenger of the covenant," who herein gave a prelude to His incarnation. **26. the most high God**—He acknowledges Jehovah to be supreme above other gods (not that he ceased to believe in these); so he returns to his original confession, "your God is a God of gods" (ch. 2:47), from which he had swerved in the interim, perhaps intoxicated by his success in taking Jerusalem, whose God he therefore thought unable to defend it. **27. nor . . . an hair**—(Luke 12:7; 21:18). **fire had no power**—fulfilling Isaiah 43:2; cf. Hebrews 11:34. God alone is a "consuming fire" (Heb. 12:29). **nor . . . smell of fire**—cf. spiritually, I Thess. 5:22. **28.** In giving some better traits in Nebuchadnezzar's character, Daniel agrees with Jeremiah 39:11; 42:12. **changed the king's word**—have made the king's attempt to coerce into obedience vain. Have set aside his word (so "alter . . . word," Ezra 6:11) from regard to God. Nebuchadnezzar now admits that God's law should be obeyed, rather than his (Acts 5:29). **yielded . . . bodies**—viz., to the fire. **not serve**—by sacrificing. **nor worship**—by prostration of the body. Decision for God at last gains the respect even of the worldly (Prov. 16:7).

ADAM CLARKE

20. *The most mighty men.* The generals, or chief officers of his army.

21. *Their hats.* This word "hat" is found only in this place in the Old Testament. The word *sarbal* properly means an outer garment.

25. *Is like the Son of God.* A most improper translation. What notion could this idolatrous king have of the Lord Jesus Christ? for so the place is understood by thousands. *Bar elahin* signifies "a son of the gods," that is, a divine person or angel; and so the king calls him in v. 28: "God . . . hath sent his angel, and delivered his servants."

28. *Blessed be the God of Shadrach.* Here is a noble testimony from a heathen. And what produced it? The intrepidly pious conduct of these three noble Jews.

MATTHEW HENRY

contrary to it, and thereby made him repent. They did it with confidence in their God. They *trusted* that he would either bring them out of the fiery furnace on earth or lead them through the fiery furnace forward to their place in heaven; and in this confidence they became regardless of their own lives.

III. He issues a royal edict, strictly forbidding any to speak evil of the God of Israel, *v.* 29. The miracle now wrought by the power of this God in defence of his worshippers, publicly in the sight of the thousands of Babylon, was a sufficient justification of this edict. It is a great mercy to the church when its enemies, though they have not their hearts turned, yet have their mouths stopped and their tongues tied.

IV. He not only reverses the attainder of these three men, but restores them to their places in the government (*makes them to prosper*, so the word is).

JAMIESON, FAUSSET, BROWN

29. This decree promulgated throughout the vast empire of Nebuchadnezzar must have tended much to keep the Jews from idolatry in the captivity and thenceforth (Ps. 76:10).

ADAM CLARKE

29. *Speak any thing amiss.* Though by the decree the king does not oblige the people to worship the true God, yet he obliges them to treat Him with reverence.

30. *Then the king promoted.* He restored them to the offices which they held before the charge of disobedience and treason was brought against them.

At the end of this verse the Septuagint add, "And he advanced them to be governors over all the Jews that were in his kingdom." This may be the meaning of the latter verse. They were more likely to be set over the Jews than over the Chaldeans.

MATTHEW HENRY — CHAPTER 4

Verses 1–3

I. The form, which was usual in proclamations issued by the king, *v.* 1. The royal style is short, and unaffected—*Nebuchadnezzar the king.* The declaration is directed *to all people, nations, and languages, that dwell in all the earth.* He salutes those to whom he writes, in the usual form, *Peace be multiplied unto you.*

II. He writes this, 1. To acquaint others with the providences of God that had related to him (*v.* 2): *I thought it good to show the signs and wonders that the high God* (so he calls the true God) *has wrought towards me.* It was a debt he owed to God and the world, now that he had recovered from his distraction, to relate how justly God had humbled him and how graciously he had at length restored him. We ought to give glory to God, not only by praising him for his mercies, but by confessing our sins, accepting the punishment of our iniquity. 2. To show how much he was himself convinced by them, *v.* 2. He admires God's doings. Nebuchadnezzar was now old, had reigned above forty years, and had seen much of the world and revolutions, yet never till now was he brought to admire God's signs and his wonders. Now, *How great, how mighty*, are they! He thence infers God's dominion. *His kingdom is an everlasting kingdom;* and not like his own kingdom, which he saw, in a dream, hastening towards a period. Other reigns are confined to one generation, and other dynasties to a few generations, but God's *dominion is from generation to generation.*

Verses 4–18

Nebuchadnezzar, before he relates the judgments of God wrought upon him for his pride, gives an account of the fair warning he had of them before they came.

I. This alarm was given to him (*v.* 4), when he was *at rest in his house, and flourishing in his palace.* He had lately conquered Egypt, and with it completed his victories, and ended his wars, about the thirty-fourth or thirty-fifth year of his reign, Ezek. xxix. 17. Then he had this dream, which was accomplished about a year after. Seven years of his distraction continued, upon his recovery from which he penned this declaration, lived about two years after, and died in his forty-fifth year.

II. The impression it made upon him (*v.* 5): *I saw a dream which made me afraid.* His *thoughts upon his bed* made him uneasy, and the *visions of his head*, the creatures of his own imagination, *troubled him.*

III. His consulting, in vain, with the magicians and astrologers. He had not now forgotten the dream, as before, *ch.* ii. He wanted to know the interpretation of it, *v.* 6. Orders are immediately given to summon *all the wise men of Babylon* to see if any could interpret the king's dream. His expectation from them was disappointed: He *told them the dream* (*v.* 7), but they *could not tell him the interpretation of it*, though they had boasted, with great assurance (*ch.* ii. 4, 7). Now was fulfilled what Isaiah foretold (*ch.* xlvii. 12, 13), that when the ruin of Babylon was drawing on her *enchantments* and *sorceries*, her *astrologers* and *star-gazers*, should not be able to do her any service.

IV. *At the last Daniel came in*, *v.* 8. Many make God's word their last refuge, and never have recourse to it till they are driven off from all other succours. He compliments Daniel very highly. He applauds his rare endowments: He has *the spirit of the holy gods*, so he tells him to his face (*v.* 9). Here is a strange medley in Nebuchadnezzar, but such as is common in those that side with their corruptions against their convictions. 1. He is an idolater, and his speech betrayeth him. He speaks of many gods. And some think, when he speaks of *the spirit of the holy gods*,

JAMIESON, FAUSSET, BROWN — CHAPTER 4

VSS. 1-37. EDICT OF NEBUCHADNEZZAR CONTAINING HIS SECOND DREAM, RELATING TO HIMSELF. Punished with insanity for his haughtiness, he sinks to the level of the beasts (illustrating Ps. 49:6, 12). The opposition between bestial and human life, set forth here, is a key to interpret the symbolism in the seventh chapter concerning the beasts and the Son of man. After his conquests, and his building in fifteen days a new palace, according to the heathen historian, ABYDENUS (268 B.C.), whose account confirms Daniel, he ascended upon his palace roof (see vs. 29, *Margin*), whence he could see the surrounding city which he had built, and seized by some deity, he predicted the Persian conquest of Babylon, adding a prayer that the Persian leader might on his return be borne where there is no path of men, and where the wild beasts graze (*language* evidently derived by tradition from vss. 32, 33, though the *application* is different). In his insanity, his excited mind would naturally think of the coming conquest of Babylon by the Medo-Persians, already foretold to him in ch. 2. **1. Peace**—the usual salutation in the East, *shalom*, whence "salaam." The primitive revelation of the fall, and man's alienation from God, made "peace" to be felt as the first and deepest want of man. The Orientals (as the East was the cradle of revelation) retained the word by tradition. **2. I thought it good**—"It was seemly before me" (Ps. 107:2-8). **signs**—tokens significant of God's omnipotent agency. The *plural* is used, as it comprises the marvellous dream, the marvellous interpretation of it, and its marvellous issue. **4. I was . . . at rest**—my wars over, my kingdom at peace. **flourishing**—"green." Image from a tree (Jer. 17:8). Prosperous (Job 15:32).

6. It may seem strange that Daniel was not first summoned. But it was ordered by God's providence that he should be reserved to the last, in order that all mere human means should be proved vain, before God manifested His power through His servant; thus the haughty king was stripped of all fleshly confidences. The Chaldees were the king's recognized interpreters of dreams; whereas Daniel's interpretation of the one in ch. 2 had been a peculiar case, and very many years before; nor had he been consulted on such matters since.

8. Belteshazzar—called so from the god Bel or Belus (see *Note*, ch. 1:7). **9. spirit of the holy gods**—Nebuchadnezzar speaks as a heathen, who yet has imbibed some notions of the true God. Hence he speaks of "gods" in the *plural* but gives the epithet "holy," which applies to Jehovah alone, the heathen gods making no pretension to purity, even in the opinion of their votaries (Deut. 32:31; cf. Isa. 63:11). "I know" refers to his knowledge of Daniel's skill many years before (ch. 2); hence he calls him "master of the magicians." **troubleth**—gives thee difficulty in explaining it.

ADAM CLARKE — CHAPTER 4

1. *Nebuchadnezzar the king, unto all people.* This is a regular decree, and is one of the most ancient on record, and no doubt was copied from the state papers of Babylon. Daniel has preserved it in the original language.

2. *I thought it good to shew.* A part of the decree was a recital of the wonders wrought by the hand of the true God in his kingdom and on his person.

4. *I . . . was at rest.* I had returned to my palace in Babylon after having subdued Syria, Phoenicia, Judea, Egypt, and Arabia. It was probably these great conquests that puffed him up with pride, and brought that chastisement upon him which he afterwards describes.

MATTHEW HENRY

that he supposes there are some evil malignant deities, and some who are good beneficent deities, and that by the spirit of the latter Daniel was animated. He also applauds Daniel, not as *a servant of God*, but as *master of the magicians* (*v.* 9). How loose his convictions sat, and how easily he had dropped them! He once called the God of Israel a *God of gods*, *ch.* ii. 47. Now he sets him upon a level with the rest of those whom he calls the *holy gods*. Nebuchadnezzar, not going forward with acknowledgments of the sovereignty of the true God, soon *went backwards*, yet professes a great opinion of Daniel, whom he knows to be a servant of the true God.

V. The account he gives him of his dream.

1. He saw a stately flourishing tree *planted in the midst of the earth* (*v.* 10), fitly representing him who reigned in Babylon, the midst of the then known world. His dignity was signified by the height of this tree, which was *exceedingly great*; it *reached unto heaven*. He over-topped those about him, and aimed to have divine honours given him. This tree had everything in it that was pleasant to the eye and good for food (*v.* 12): *The leaves thereof were fair*, denoting the pomp and splendour of Nebuchadnezzar's court. This tree was, (1) For protection; the boughs of it were for shelter. Princes should be a screen to their subjects *from the heat* and *from the storm*. (2) For provision. The Assyrian was compared to a *cedar* (Ezek. xxxi. 6), which affords shadow only; but this tree here had much fruit—in it was *meat for all* and *all flesh was fed of it*. This mighty monarch, it should seem by this, not only was great, but did good.

2. He heard the doom of this tree read. The sentence was passed upon it by an angel, whom he saw *come down from heaven*, and heard proclaim this sentence aloud. This angel is here called a *watcher*, or *watchman*. This angel was a *messenger*, or *ambassador* (so some read it), and *a holy one*.

(1) Orders are given that it be cut down (*v.* 14).

(2) Care is taken that the root be preserved (*v.* 15): "*Leave the stump of it in the earth*, exposed to all weathers. Let it be hooped round with *a band of iron and brass*, to keep it firm." God in judgment remembers mercy; and may yet have good things in store for those whose condition seems most forlorn. There is *hope of a tree, if it be cut down, that it will sprout again, that through the scent of water it will bud*, Job xiv. 7–9.

(3) The meaning of this is explained by the angel himself to Nebuchadnezzar, *v.* 16. Whoever is the person signified by this tree he is sentenced to be deposed from the dignity of a man, to be deprived of his reason, and to live like a brute, till *seven times pass over him. Let a beast's heart be given unto him*. This is surely the saddest and sorest of all temporal judgments. Those proud tyrants who *set their heart as the heart of God* (Ezek. xxviii. 2) may justly be deprived of the heart of man, and have a beast's heart given them.

(4) The truth of it is confirmed (*v.* 17). The angels of heaven have subscribed to it. It is by *the decree of the watchers*. Such was Nebuchadnezzar's doom; it was by the *decree of the watchers*. The saints on earth petitioned for it, as well as the angels in heaven: *The demand is by the word of the holy ones*. God's suffering people, that had long groaned under the heavy yoke of Nebuchadnezzar's tyranny, made the demand, and God gave this answer to it.

(5) The design of it is declared. Orders are given for the cutting down of this tree, *to the intent that the living may know that the Most High rules*.

Thus has Nebuchadnezzar fully and faithfully related his dream, what he saw and what he heard, and now demands of Daniel the interpretation of it (*v.* 18).

JAMIESON, FAUSSET, BROWN

10. tree—So the Assyrian is compared to a "cedar" (Ezek. 31:3; cf. Ezek. 17:24). **in the midst of the earth**—denoting its conspicuous position as the center whence the imperial authority radiated in all directions. **12. beasts . . . shadow under it**—implying that God's purpose in establishing empires in the world is that they may be as trees affording men "fruits" for "meat," and a "shadow" for rest (cf. Lam. 4:20). But the world powers abuse their trust for self; therefore Messiah comes to plant the tree of His gospel kingdom, which alone shall realize God's purpose (Ezek. 17:23; Matt. 13:32). HERODOTUS (7. 19) mentions a dream (probably suggested by the tradition of this dream of Nebuchadnezzar in Daniel) which Xerxes had; viz., that he was crowned with olive, and that the branches of the olive filled the whole earth, but that afterwards the crown vanished from his head: signifying his universal dominion soon to come to an end. **13. watcher and an holy one**—rather, "even an holy one." Only *one* angel is intended, and he not one of the bad, but of the *holy* angels. Called a "watcher," because ever on the watch to execute God's will [JEROME], (Ps. 103:20, 21). Cf. as to their watchfulness, Revelation 4:8, "*full of eyes* within . . . they rest not day *and night*." Also they watch good men committed to their charge (Ps. 34:7; Heb. 1:14); and watch over the evil to record their sins, and at God's bidding at last punish them (Jer. 4:16, 17), "watchers" applied to *human* instruments of God's vengeance. As to GOD (ch. 9:14; Job 7:12; 14:16; Jer. 44:27). In a good sense (Gen. 31:49; Jer. 31:28). The idea of heavenly "watchers" under the supreme God (called in the *Zendavesta* of the Persian Zoroaster, *Ormuzd*) was founded on the primeval revelation as to evil angels having *watched* for an opportunity until they succeeded in tempting man to his ruin, and good angels ministering to God's servants (as Jacob, Gen. 28:15; 32:1, 2). Cf. the watching over Abraham for good, and over Sodom for wrath after long watching in vain for good men it it, for whose sake He would spare it, Genesis 18; and over Lot for good, Genesis 19. Daniel fitly puts in Nebuchadnezzar's mouth the expression, though not found elsewhere in Scripture, yet substantially sanctioned by it (II Chron. 16:9; Prov. 15:3, Jer. 32:19), and natural to him according to Oriental modes of thought. **14. Hew down**—(Matt. 3:10; Luke 13:7). The holy (Jude 14) one incites his fellow angels to God's appointed work (cf. Rev. 14:15, 18). **beasts get away from under it**—It shall no longer afford them shelter (Ezek. 31:12). **15. stump**—The kingdom is still reserved secure for him at last, as a tree stump secured by a hoop of brass and iron from being split by the sun's heat, in the hope of its growing again (Isa. 11:1; cf. Job 14:7-9). BARNES refers it to the chaining of the royal maniac. **16. heart**—understanding (Isa. 6:10). **times**—i.e., "years" (ch. 12:7). "Seven" is the perfect number: a week of years: a complete revolution of time accompanying a complete revolution in his state of mind. **17. demand**—i.e., determination; viz., as to the change to which Nebuchadnezzar is to be doomed. A solemn council of the heavenly ones is supposed (cf. Job 1:6; 2:1), over which God presides supreme. His "decree" and "word" are therefore said to be theirs (cf. vs. 24, "decree of the Most High"); "the decree of the watchers," "the word of the holy ones." For He has placed particular kingdoms under the administration of angelic beings, subject to Him (ch. 10:13, 20; 12:1). The word "demand," in the second clause, expresses a distinct idea from the first clause. Not only as members of God's council (ch. 7:10; I Kings 22:19; Ps. 103:21; Zech. 1:10) do they subscribe to His "decree," but that decree is in answer to their prayers, wherein they *demand* that every mortal who tries to obscure the glory of God shall be humbled [CALVIN]. Angels are grieved when God's prerogative is in the least infringed. How awful to Nebuchadnezzar to know that angels plead against him for his pride, and that the decree has been passed in the high court of heaven for his humiliation in answer to angels' *demands!* The conceptions are moulded in a form peculiarly adapted to Nebuchadnezzar's modes of thought. **the living**—not as distinguished from the dead, but from the inhabitants of heaven, who "know" that which the men of the world need to the taught (Ps. 9:16); the ungodly confess there is a God, but would gladly confine Him to heaven. But, saith Daniel, God ruleth not merely there, but "in the kingdom of men." **basest**—the lowest in condition (I Sam. 2:8; Luke 1:52). It is not one's talents, excellency, or noble birth, but God's will, which elevates to the throne. Nebuchadnezzar abased to the dunghill,

ADAM CLARKE

10. *I saw . . . a tree.* This vision Nebuchadnezzar says made him afraid. What a mercy it is that God has hidden futurity from us! Were he to show every man the lot that is before him, the misery of the human race would be complete. Great men and princes are often represented, in the language of the prophets, under the similitude of trees; see **Ezek. xvii. 5-6; xxxi. 3, etc.; Jer. xxii. 15; Ps. i. 3; xxxvii. 35.**

13. *A watcher and an holy one.* These are both angels but, according to the Chaldean oracles, of different orders. They appear, according to their opinions, to be a kind of judges of human actions who had the power of determining the lot of men; see v. 17.

14. *Hew down the tree.* As the tree was to be cut down, the beasts are commanded to flee away from under his branches. His courtiers, officers, all abandoned him as soon as his insanity appeared; but he soon fled from the society of men.

15. *Leave the stump.* Let him not be destroyed, nor his kingdom alienated.

16. *Let his heart be changed.* Let him conceive himself to be a beast, and act as such, herding among the beasts of the field. *Let seven times pass over him.* Let him continue in this state for seven years.

MATTHEW HENRY

Verses 19–27

The interpretation of Nebuchadnezzar's dream; and when once it is declared that he is the tree in the dream, when once it is said, *Thou art the man,* there needs little more to be said for the explication of the dream. The thing was so plain that Daniel, upon hearing the dream, was *astonished for one hour, v.* 19. He was struck with amazement and terror at so great a judgment coming upon so great a prince. He was likewise struck with confusion when he found himself the man that must bring to the king *these heavy tidings.*

I. The king observed him stand as one astonished, and thinking he was loth to speak out for fear of offending him, encouraged him to deal plainly with him: *Let not the dream, nor the interpretation thereof, trouble thee.* This he speaks either, 1. As one that sincerely desired to know the truth. Or, 2. As one that despised the truth, and set it at defiance. Daniel is concerned for him, and therefore wishes, "*The dream be to those that hate thee.* Let the ill it bodes light on the head of thy enemies, not on thy head." Though Nebuchadnezzar was an oppressor of the people of God, yet he was, at present, Daniel's prince.

II. The interpretation itself is only a repetition of the dream, with application to the king. "As for *the tree* which thou sawest *flourishing* (*v.* 20, 21), *it is thou, O king*!" *v.* 22. He shows the king his present prosperous state in the glass of his own dream, *ch.* ii. 37, 38. "As for the doom passed upon the tree (*v.* 23), it is *the decree of the Most High, which comes upon my lord the king,*" *v.* 24.

He must be deposed from his throne, *driven from men,* and being deprived of his reason, and having a beast's heart given him, his dwelling shall be *with the beasts of the field*; he shall *eat grass as oxen,* and, like them, lie out all weathers, till *seven times* pass over him, that is, *seven years*; and then he shall know that the *Most High rules,* and when he is brought to know and own this he shall be restored to his dominion again (*v.* 26). God is here called *the heavens,* and the influence which the visible heavens have upon this earth is intended as a faint representation of the dominion the God of heaven has over this lower world; we are said to *sin against heaven,* Luke xv. 18.

III. The close of the interpretation which Daniel, as a prophet, gave the king, *v.* 27. 1. How humbly he gives his advice, and with what tenderness and respect: "*O king! let my counsel be acceptable unto thee.*" 2. He does not counsel him to enter into a course of physic, for the preventing of the distemper, but to break off a course of sin. He wronged his own subjects, and dealt unfairly with his allies. He had been cruel to the poor.

3. The motive with which he backs this advice: *If it may be a lengthening of thy tranquillity.*

Verses 28–33

Nebuchadnezzar's dream accomplished, and Daniel's application of it to him justified and confirmed.

I. God's patience with him: *All this came upon him,* but not till *twelve months after* (*v.* 29), so long there was a *lengthening of his tranquillity,* though it does not appear that he *broke off his sins,* or showed any *mercy to the poor* captives. God gave him space to repent; he *let him alone this year also,* this *one* year more.

JAMIESON, FAUSSET, BROWN

and then restored, was to have in himself an experimental proof of this (vs. 37). **19. Daniel . . . Belteshazzar**—The use of the Hebrew as well as the Chaldee name, so far from being an objection, as some have made it, is an undesigned mark of genuineness. In a proclamation to "*all* people," and one designed to honor the God of the Hebrews, Nebuchadnezzar would naturally use the Hebrew name (derived from *El,* "God," the name by which the prophet was best known among his countrymen), as well as the Gentile name by which he was known in the Chaldean empire. **astonied**—overwhelmed with awe at the terrible import of the dream. **one hour**—the original means often "a moment," or "short time," as in ch. 3:6, 15. **let not the dream . . . trouble thee**—Many despots would have punished a prophet who dared to foretell his overthrow. Nebuchadnezzar assures Daniel he may freely speak out. **the dream be to them that hate thee**—We are to desire the prosperity of those under whose authority God's providence has placed us (Jer. 29:7). The wish here is not so much against others, as for the king: a common formula (II Sam. 18:32). It is not the language of uncharitable hatred. **20.** The *tree* is the king. The *branches,* the princes. The *leaves,* the soldiers. The *fruits,* the revenues. The *shadow,* the protection afforded to dependent states. **22. It is thou**—He speaks pointedly, and without circumlocution (II Sam. 12:7). While pitying the king, he uncompromisingly pronounces his sentence of punishment. Let ministers steer the mean between, on the one hand, fulminations against sinners under the pretext of zeal, without any symptom of compassion; and, on the other, flattery of sinners under the pretext of moderation. **to the end of the earth**—(Jer. 27:6-8). To the Caspian, Euxine, and Atlantic seas. **24. decree of the Most High**—What was termed in vs. 17 by Nebuchadnezzar, "the decree *of the watchers,*" is here more accurately termed by Daniel, "the decree *of the Most High.*" They are but His ministers. **25. they shall drive thee**—a Chaldee idiom for "thou shalt be driven." Hypochondriacal madness was his malady, which "drove" him under the fancy that he was a beast, to "dwell with the beasts"; verse 34 proves this, "mine understanding returned." The regency would leave him to roam in the large beast-abounding parks attached to the palace. **eat grass**—i.e., vegetables, or herbs in general (Gen. 3:18). **they shall wet thee**—i.e., thou shalt be wet. **till thou know . . .**—(Ps. 83: 17, 18; Jer. 27:5). **26. thou shalt have known . . .**—a promise of spiritual grace to him, causing the judgment to humble, not harden, his heart. **heavens do rule**—The plural is used, as addressed to Nebuchadnezzar, the head of an organized earthly kingdom, with various principalities under the supreme ruler. So "the kingdom of heaven" (Matt. 4:17; *Greek,* "kingdom of the *heavens*") is a *manifold* organization, composed of various orders of angels, under the Most High (Eph. 1:20, 21; 3:10; Col. 1:16). **27. break off**—as a galling yoke (Gen. 27:40); sin is a heavy load (Matt. 11:28). LXX and *Vulgate* translate not so well, "redeem," which is made an argument for Rome's doctrine of the expiation of sins by meritorious works. Even translate it so, it can only mean; Repent and show the reality of thy repentance by works of justice and charity (cf. Luke 11:41); so God will remit thy punishment. The trouble will be longer before it comes, or shorter when it does come. Cf. the cases of Hezekiah, Isa. 38:1-5; Nineveh, Jonah 3:5-10; Jeremiah 18:7, 8. The change is not in God, but in the sinner who repents. As the king who had provoked God's judgments by sin, so he might avert it by a return to righteousness (cf. Ps. 41:1, 2; Acts 8:22). Probably, like most Oriental despots, Nebuchadnezzar had oppressed the poor by forcing them to labor in his great public works without adequate remuneration. **if . . . lengthening of . . . tranquillity**—if haply thy present prosperity shall be prolonged. **29. twelve months**—This respite was granted to him to leave him without excuse. So the 120 years granted before the flood (Gen. 6:3). At the first announcement of the coming judgment he was alarmed, as Ahab (I Kings 21:27), but did not thoroughly repent; so when judgment was not executed at once, he thought it would never come, and so returned to his former pride (Eccles. 8:11). **in the palace**—rather, upon the (flat) palace roof, whence he could contemplate the splendor of Babylon. So the heathen historian, ABYDENUS, records. The palace roof was the scene of the fall of another king (II Samuel 11:2). The outer wall of Nebuchadnezzar's new palace embraced six miles; there were two other embattled walls within, and a great tower, and three brazen gates. **30. Babylon, that I have built**—HERODOTUS ascribes the building of

ADAM CLARKE

19. *Daniel . . . was astonied for one hour.* He saw the design of the dream, and he felt the great delicacy of interpreting it. He was not puzzled by the difficulties of it. He felt for the king, and for the nation; and with what force and delicacy does he express the general portent: "The dream . . . to them that hate thee, and the interpretation thereof to thine enemies"!

20. *The tree that thou sawest.* The dream is so fully interpreted in the following verses that it needs no comment.

26. *Thy kingdom shall be sure unto thee.* No new king was set up; Evil-merodach, his son, was regent during his father's insanity.

MATTHEW HENRY

II. His pride, and haughtiness, and abuse of that patience. He walked *in the palace of the kingdom of Babylon*, in pomp and pride. Everything in Babylon he thinks looks great; "and this *great Babylon I have built*." Babylon was built many ages before he was born, but he boasts that he has built it, as Augustus Caesar boasted concerning Rome, *I found it brick, but I left it marble*. He boasts that he built it *for the house of the kingdom*, the metropolis of his empire.

III. His punishment. The powerful word came from heaven, by which he was immediately deprived, 1. Of his honour as a king: *The kingdom has departed from thee*. 2. He is deprived of his honour as a man. He loses his reason, and by that means loses his dominion: *They shall drive thee from men*, *v*. 32. And it was fulfilled (*v*. 33): he was *driven from men the same hour*. On a sudden he fell stark mad. His understanding and memory were gone, and all the faculties of a rational soul broken. He went naked, and on all fours, like a brute, and ran wild into the fields and woods. He was made to *eat grass as oxen*. Nebuchadnezzar would be more than a man, and therefore God justly makes him less than a man, and puts him upon a level with the beasts who set up for a rival with his Maker. See Job xl. 11–13.

Verses 34–37

We have here Nebuchadnezzar's recovery from his distraction, and his return to his right mind, *at the end of the days*, that is, of the seven years. *At the end of the days* (says he), *I lifted up my eyes unto heaven* (*v*. 34), looked no longer down towards the earth as a beast, but began to look up as a man. But there was more in it than this; he looked up as a penitent, as a humble petitioner for mercy.

I. He has the use of his reason so far restored to him that with it he glorifies God, and humbles himself. Men never rightly use their reason till they begin to be religious, nor live as men till they live to the glory of God. His folly was the means whereby he became wise. To bring him to himself, he must first be *beside himself*. His flatterers often complimented him with, *O king! live for ever*. But he is now convinced that no king lives for ever, but the God of Israel only. God's kingdom is like himself, *everlasting*, and his *dominion from generation to generation*; there is no succession, no revolution, in his kingdom. *All nations* before him are *as nothing*. His power is irresistible, for he *does according to his will*. Everything which God does is well done: His *works are truth*, for they all agree with his word. *His ways are judgment*, both wise and righteous, consonant to the rules of prudence and equity. *Those that walk in pride he is able to abase* (*v*. 37).

II. He has the use of his reason restored to him (*v*. 36). He is now established in his kingdom as firmly as if there had been no interruption. Afflictions shall last no longer than till they have done the work for which they were sent. When Nebuchadnezzar is restored to his kingdom he *praises, and extols*, and *honours the King of heaven* (*v*. 37).

It was not long after this that Nebuchadnezzar ended his life and reign. Abydenus, quoted by Eusebius (*Praep. Evang*. i. 9), reports that upon his death-bed he foretold the taking of Babylon by Cyrus. Whether he continued in the same good mind that here he seems to have been in we are not told. If our charity may reach so far as to hope he did, we must admire free grace, by which he lost his wits for a while, that he might save his soul for ever.

JAMIESON, FAUSSET, BROWN

Babylon to Semiramis and Nitocris, his informant under the *Persian* dynasty giving him the Assyrian and Persian account. BEROSUS and ABYDENUS give the *Babylonian* account, viz., that Nebuchadnezzar added much to the old city, built a splendid palace and city walls. HERODOTUS, the so-called "father of history," does not even mention Nebuchadnezzar. (Nitocris, to whom he attributes the beautifying of Babylon, seems to have been Nebuchadnezzar's wife.) Hence infidels have doubted the Scripture account. But the latter is proved by thousands of bricks on the plain, the inscriptions of which have been deciphered, each marked "Nebuchadnezzar, the son of Nabopolassar." "Built," i.e., restored and enlarged (II Chron. 11:5, 6). It is curious, all the bricks have been found with the stamped face downwards. Scarcely a figure in stone, or tablet, has been dug out of the rubbish heaps of Babylon, whereas Nineveh abounds in them; fulfilling Jer. 51:37, "Babylon shall become *heaps*." The "*I*" is emphatic, by which he puts himself in the place of God; so the "my . . . my." He impiously opposes *his* might to God's, as though God's threat, uttered a year before, could never come to pass. He would be more than man; God, therefore, justly, makes him less than man. An acting over again of the fall; Adam, once lord of the world and the very beasts (Gen. 1:28; so Nebuchadnezzar ch. 2:38), would be a god (Gen. 3:5); therefore he must die like the beasts (Ps. 82:6; 49:12). **31. While . . .**—in the very act of speaking, so that there could be no doubt as to the connection between the crime and the punishment. So Luke 12:19, 20. **O king . . . to thee it is spoken**—Notwithstanding thy *kingly* power, to thee thy doom *is* now *spoken*, there is to be no further respite. **33. driven from men**—as a maniac fancying himself a wild beast. It is possible, a conspiracy of his nobles may have cooperated towards his having been "driven" forth as an outcast. **hairs . . . eagles' feathers**—matted together, as the hair-like, thick plumage of the ossifraga eagle. The "nails," by being left uncut for years, would become like "claws." **34. lifted up mine eyes unto heaven**—whence the "voice" had issued (vs. 31) at the beginning of his visitation. Sudden mental derangement often has the effect of annihilating the whole interval, so that, when reason returns, the patient remembers only the event that immediately preceded his insanity. Nebuchadnezzar's looking up towards heaven was the first symptom of his "understanding" having "returned." Before, like the beasts, his eyes had been downward to the earth. Now, like Jonah's (Jonah 2:1, 2, 4) out of the fish's belly, they are lifted up to heaven in prayer. He turns to Him that smiteth him (Isa. 9:13), with the faint glimmer of reason left to him, and owns God's justice in punishing him. **praised . . . him**—Praise is a sure sign of a soul spiritually healed (Ps. 116:12, 14; Mark 5:15, 18, 19). **I . . . honoured him**—implying that the cause of his chastisement was that he had before robbed God of His honor. **everlasting dominion**—not temporary or mutable, as a human king's dominion. **35. all . . . as nothing**—(Isa. 40:15, 17). **according to his will in . . . heaven**—(Ps. 115:3; 135:6; Matt. 6:10; Ephesians 1:11). **army**—the heavenly hosts, angels and starry orbs (cf. Isa. 24:21). **none . . . stay his hand**—lit., "strike His hand." Image from striking the hand of another, to check him in doing anything (Isa. 43:13; 45:9). **What doest thou**—(Job 9:12; Rom. 9:20). **36.** An inscription in the East India Company's Museum is read as describing the period of Nebuchadnezzar's insanity [G. V. SMITH]. In the so-called standard inscription read by Sir H. Rawlinson, Nebuchadnezzar relates that during four (?) years he ceased to lay out buildings, or to furnish with victims Merodach's altar, or to clear out the canals for irrigation. No other instance in the cuneiform inscriptions occurs of a king recording his own inaction. **my counsellors . . . sought unto me**—desired to have me, as formerly, to be their head, wearied with the anarchy which prevailed in my absence (cf. *Note*, vs. 33); the likelihood of a conspiracy of the nobles is confirmed by this verse. **majesty was added**—My authority was greater than ever before (Job 42:12; Prov. 22:4; Matt. 6:33, "added"). **37. praise . . . extol . . . honour**—He heaps word on word, as if he cannot say enough in praise of God. **all whose works . . . truth . . . judgment**—i.e., are true and just (Rev. 15: 3; 16:7). God has not dealt unjustly or too severely with me; whatever I have suffered, I deserved it all. It is a mark of true contrition to condemn one's self, and justify God (Ps. 51:4). **those that walk in pride . . . abase**—exemplified in me. He condemns himself before the whole world, in order to glorify God.

ADAM CLARKE

30. *Is not this great Babylon?* Here his heart was inflated with pride; he attributed everything to himself, and acknowledged God in nothing. The walls, hanging gardens, temple of Bel, and the royal palace, all built by Nebuchadnezzar, made it the greatest city in the world.

31. *While the word was in the king's mouth*. How awful to a victorious and proud king: "The kingdom is departed from thee"! All your goods and gods are gone in a moment!

36. *My reason returned*. Everything was fulfilled that was exhibited by the dream and its interpretation. It is very likely that this unfortunate king had so concealed himself that the place of his retreat was not found out; and the providence of God had so watched over everything that, on his return to his palace, he found his counsellors and his lords, who received him gladly, and cleaved to and served him as they had formerly done.

MATTHEW HENRY

CHAPTER 5

Verses 1–9

Belshazzar the king very gay, but all of a sudden very gloomy. He affronts God, and God affrights him.

I. He *made a great feast*, or *banquet of wine*; probably it was some anniversary. Historians say that Cyrus, who was now besieging Babylon, knew of this feast, and presuming that they then would be off their guard, *buried in sleep and wine*, took that opportunity to attack the city, and so made himself master of it. Belshazzar invited *a thousand of his lords to come and drink with him*. In this sumptuous feast, 1. He bade defiance to God's judgments. His city was now besieged; his life and kingdom lay at stake. He should therefore have proclaimed a fast; but, as one resolved to walk contrary to God, he proclaims a feast. 2. He put an affront upon the temple of God, *v.* 2. *While he tasted the wine, he commanded to bring the vessels* of the temple, that they might drink in them.

3. He put an affront upon God himself, and bade defiance to his deity; for *they drank wine, and praised the gods of gold and silver*, *v.* 4.

II. How God affrighted the king, and struck a terror upon him. Belshazzar and his lords are in the midst of their revels, but the hour had come when that must be fulfilled which had been long ago said of the king of Babylon, Isa. xxi. 2–4. *The night of my pleasures has he turned into fear to me*. 1. *There* appear the *fingers of a man's hand writing on the plaster of the wall*, before the king's face (*v.* 5).

JAMIESON, FAUSSET, BROWN

CHAPTER 5

VSS. 1-31. BELSHAZZAR'S IMPIOUS FEAST; THE HANDWRITING ON THE WALL INTERPRETED BY DANIEL OF THE DOOM OF BABYLON AND ITS KING. 1.**Belshazzar**—RAWLINSON, from the Assyrian inscriptions, has explained the seeming discrepancy between Daniel and the heathen historians of Babylon, BEROSUS and ABYDENUS, who say the last king (Nabonidus) surrendered in Borsippa, after Babylon was taken, and had an honorable abode in Caramania assigned to him. *Belshazzar was joint king with his father* (called *Minus* in the inscriptions), *but subordinate to him;* hence the *Babylonian* account suppresses the facts which cast discredit on Babylon, viz., that Belshazzar shut himself up in that city and fell at its capture; while it records the surrender of the principal king in Borsippa (see my *Introduction* to Daniel). The heathen XENOPHON's description of Belshazzar accords with Daniel's; he calls him "impious," and illustrates his cruelty by mentioning that he killed one of his nobles, merely because, in hunting, the noble struck down the game before him; and unmanned a courtier, Gadates, at a banquet, because one of the king's concubines praised him as handsome. Daniel shows none of the sympathy for him which he had for Nebuchadnezzar. XENOPHON confirms Daniel as to Belshazzar's end. WINER explains the "shazzar" in the name as meaning "fire." **made . . . feast**—heaven-sent infatuation when his city was at the time being besieged by Cyrus. The fortifications and abundant provisions in the city made the king despise the besiegers. It was a festival-day among the Babylonians [XENOPHON]. **drank . . . before the thousand**—The king, on this extraordinary occasion, departed from his usual way of feasting apart from his nobles (cf. Esther 1:3). **2. whiles he tasted the wine**—While under the effects of wine, men will do what they dare not do when sober. **his father Nebuchadnezzar**—i.e., his forefather. So "Jesus . . . the *son* of David, the *son* of Abraham." Daniel does not say that the other kings mentioned in other writers did not reign between Belshazzar and Nebuchadnezzar, viz., Evil-merodach (Jer. 52:31), Neriglissar, his brother-in-law, and Laborasoarchod (nine months). BEROSUS makes Nabonidus, the last king, to have been *one of the people,* raised to the throne by an insurrection. As the inscriptions show that Belshazzar was distinct from, and joint king with, him, this is not at variance with Daniel, whose statement that Belshazzar was *son* (grandson) *of Nebuchadnezzar* is corroborated by Jeremiah (Jer. 27:7). Their joint, yet independent, testimony, as contemporaries, and having the best means of information, is more trustworthy than any of the heathen historians, if there were a discrepancy. Evilmerodach, son of Nebuchadnezzar (according to BEROSUS), reigned but a short time (one or two years), having, in consequence of his bad government, been dethroned by a plot of Neriglissar, his sister's husband; hence Daniel does not mention him. At the elevation of Nabonidus as supreme king, Belshazzar, the grandson of Nebuchadnezzar, was doubtless suffered to be subordinate king and successor, in order to conciliate the legitimate party. Thus the seeming discrepancy becomes a confirmation of genuineness when cleared up, for the real harmony must have been undesigned. **wives . . . concubines**—not usually present at feasts in the East, where women of the harem are kept in strict seclusion. Hence Vashti's refusal to appear at Ahasuerus' feast (Esther 1). But the Babylonian court, in its reckless excesses, seems not to have been so strict as the Persian. XENOPHON (*Cyrop.* 5.2, 28) confirms Daniel, representing a feast of Belshazzar where the concubines are present. At the beginning "the lords" (vs. 1), for whom the feast was made, alone seem to have been present; but as the revelry advanced, the women were introduced. Two classes of them are mentioned, those to whom belonged the privileges of "wives," and those strictly concubines (II Sam. 5:13; I Kings 11:3; Song of Sol. 6:8). **3.** This act was not one of necessity, or for honor's sake, but in reckless profanity. **4. praised**—sang and shouted praises to "gods," which being of gold, "are their own witnesses" (Isa. 44:9), confuting the folly of those who fancy such to be gods. **5. In the same hour**—that the cause of God's visitation might be palpable, viz., the profanation of His vessels and His holy name. **fingers of . . . hand**—God admonishes him, not by a dream (as Nebuchadnezzar had been warned), or by a voice, but by "fingers coming forth," the invisibility of Him who moved them heightening the awful impressiveness of the scene, the hand of the Unseen One attesting his doom before the eyes of himself and his guilty fellow revel-

ADAM CLARKE

CHAPTER 5

1. *Belshazzar the king made a great feast.* After the death of Nebuchadnezzar, Evil-merodach, his son, ascended the throne of Babylon. Having reigned about two years, he was slain by his brother-in-law, Neriglissar. He reigned four years, and was succeeded by his son Leborosoarchod, who reigned only nine months. At his death Belshazzar, the son of Evil-merodach, was raised to the throne, and reigned seventeen years, and was slain, as we read here, by Cyrus, who surprised and took the city on the night of this festivity. But the Scripture mentions only Nebuchadnezzar, Evil-merodach, and Belshazzar, by name; and Jeremiah, chap. xxvii. 7, expressly says, "All nations shall serve him [Nebuchadnezzar], and his son [Evil-merodach], and his son's son [Belshazzar] until the very time of his land come"; i.e., till the time in which the empire should be seized by Cyrus. Here there is no mention of Neriglissar nor Laborosoarchod; but as they were usurpers, they might have been purposely passed by. But there remains one difficulty still: Belshazzar is expressly called the son of Nebuchadnezzar by the queen mother, v. 11. The solution of this difficulty is that in Scripture the name of "son" is indifferently given to sons and grandsons, and even to great-grandsons.

To a thousand of his lords. Perhaps this means lords or satraps, that were each over 1,000 men.

TODAY'S DICTIONARY OF THE BIBLE:

Belshazzar—*Bel protect the king!*—the last of the kings of Babylon (Dan. 5:1). He was the son of Nabonidus by Nitocris, who was the daughter of Nebuchadnezzar and the widow of Nergal-sharezer. When still a young man he made a great feast to a thousand of his lords, and when heated with wine sent for the sacred vessels his "father" (Dan. 5:2)—or grandfather—Nebuchadnezzar had carried away from the temple in Jerusalem, and he and his princes drank out of them. In the midst of their mad revelry a hand was seen by the king, tracing on the wall the announcement of God's judgment, which that night fell upon him. At the insistence of the queen (i.e., his mother) Daniel was brought in, and he interpreted the writing. That night the kingdom of the Chaldeans came to an end, and the king was slain (Dan. 5:30).

The absence of the name of Belshazzar on the monuments was long regarded as an argument against the genuineness of the Book of Daniel. In 1854 Sir Henry Rawlinson found an inscription of Nabonidus which referred to his eldest son. More recently, the side of a ravine undermined by heavy rains fell at Hillah, a suburb of Babylon. A number of huge, coarse earthenware vases were laid bare. These were filled with tablets, the receipts and contracts of a firm of Babylonian bankers, which showed that Belshazzar had a household, with secretaries and stewards. One was dated in the third year of the king Marduk-sar-uzur. As Marduk was another name for Baal, this Marduk-sar-uzur was found to be the Belshazzar of Scripture. In one of these contract tablets, dated in the July after the defeat of the army of Nabonidus, we find him paying tithes for his sister to the temple of the sungod at Sippar.

MATTHEW HENRY

Here was no destroying angel with his sword drawn—only a pen in the hand, writing upon the wall, *over-against the candlestick*, where they might all see it by the light of their own candle. The king saw *the part of the hand that wrote*, but saw not the person whose hand it was. What we see of God, the part of the hand that writes in the book of the scriptures, may serve to possess us with awful thoughts concerning that of God which we do not see. If this be *the finger of God*, what is his arm made bare? 2. The king is immediately seized with a panic (*v.* 6): *His countenance was changed* (his colour went and came); *the joints of his loins were loosed, his knees smote one against another*. Why is he in such a fright? *His thoughts troubled him;* his own guilty conscience told him that he had no reason to expect any good news from Heaven. God can soon make the heart of the stoutest sinner to tremble; and there needs no more than to let loose his own thoughts upon him. 3. The wise men of Babylon are called in, to see what they can make of this writing upon the wall, *v.* 7. Whoever will may read the mind of God in the scriptures. The king promised that whoever would give him a satisfactory account of this writing should be dignified with the highest honours. 4. The king is disappointed; they can none of them *read the writing*, much less interpret it (*v.* 8), which increases the king's confusion, *v.* 9.

Verses 10–29

I. The information given to the king, by the queen-mother, concerning Daniel, how fit he was to be consulted in this difficult case. It is supposed that this queen was the widow of Evil-Merodach, that famous Nitocris whom Herodotus mentions as a woman of extraordinary prudence. Tidings being brought to her apartment, she came herself to the banqueting-house, to recommend to the king a physician for his melancholy. She could not read the writing herself, but directed him to one that could; let *Daniel be called* now, who should have been called first. He is a *man in whom is the spirit of the holy gods*, who has something in him more than human. She speaks honourably of him as a man that had *light, and understanding, and wisdom*. It was evident he was divinely inspired; he had *knowledge* and *understanding* beyond all the other wise men for *interpreting dreams*. He had an admirably good heart: *An excellent spirit was found in him*. *"The king thy father,"* that is, thy grandfather, *"made him master of the magicians."* He *named him Belteshazzar*, according to the name of his god, thinking thereby to put honour upon him. *Let Daniel be called, and he will show the interpretation.*

II. Daniel was *brought in before the king*, *v.* 13. The king asks, with an air of haughtiness: *Art thou that Daniel who art of the children of the captivity?* He acknowledges that all the wise men of Babylon were baffled; they could not *read this writing*, nor *show the interpretation*, *v.* 16. But he promises him the same rewards that he had promised them if he would do it, *v.* 16.

III. The interpretation which Daniel gave of these mystic characters, was far from easing the king of his fears. Daniel was now in years, and Belshazzar was young; and therefore he seems to take a greater liberty of dealing plainly and roundly with him than he had done upon the like occasions with Nebuchadnezzar.

1. He undertakes to read the writing which gave them this alarm, and to show them the interpretation of it, *v.* 17. He slights the offer of rewards, for he is not one of those that *divine for money*. *Let thy gifts be to thyself*, for they will not be long thine, and *give thy fee to another*. Let us do our duty in the world, read God's writing and make known the interpretation of it.

2. He recounts to the king God's dealings with his father Nebuchadnezzar, *v.* 18, 21. He describes the great dignity and power to which the divine Providence had advanced Nebuchadnezzar, *v.* 18, 19. His ability was so strong that it was irresistible. His authority was so absolute that it was uncontrollable. *Whom he would he slew, and whom he would he saved alive*, though both were equally innocent or equally guilty. *Whom he would he set up, and whom he would he put down*. He sets before him the sins which Nebuchadnezzar had been guilty of, whereby he had provoked God against him. The description given of his power intimates his abuse of his power. He behaved insolently towards the God above him, and grew proud and haughty (*v.* 20). He reminds him of the judgments of God that were brought upon him for his pride and obstinacy, how he was deprived of his reason, and so *deposed from his kingly throne* (*v.* 20), *driven from among men, to dwell with the wild asses*, *v.* 21.

JAMIESON, FAUSSET, BROWN

lers. **against the candlestick**—the candelabra; where the mystic characters would be best seen. BARNES makes it the candlestick taken from the temple of Jerusalem, the nearness of the writing to it intimating that the rebuke was directed against the sacrilege. **upon the plaster of the wall of the king's palace**—Written in cuneiform letters on slabs on the walls, and on the very bricks, are found the perpetually recurring recital of titles, victories, and exploits, to remind the spectator at every point of the regal greatness. It is significant, that on the same wall on which the king was accustomed to read the flattering legends of his own magnificence, he beholds the mysterious inscription which foretells his fall (cf. Prov. 16:18; Acts 12:21-23). **part of the hand**—the anterior part, viz., the fingers. **6. countenance**—lit., "brightness," i.e., his bright look. **joints of his loins**—"the vertebræ of his back" [GESENIUS]. **7.** He calls for the magicians, who more than once had been detected in imposture. He neglects God, and Daniel, whose fame as an interpreter was then well established. The world wishes to be deceived and shuts its eyes against the light [CALVIN]. The Hebrews think the words were Chaldee, but in the old Hebrew character (like that now in the Samaritan Pentateuch). **third ruler**—The first place was given to the king; the second, to the son of the king, or of the queen; the third, to the chief of the satraps. **8.** The words were in such a character as to be illegible to the Chaldees, God reserving this honor to Daniel.

10. queen—the queen mother, or *grandmother*, Nitocris, had not been present till now. She was wife either of Nebuchadnezzar or of Evil merodach; hence her acquaintance with the services of Daniel. She completed the great works which the former had begun. Hence HERODOTUS attributes them to her alone. This accounts for the deference paid to her by Belshazzar. (See *Note*, ch. 4:36.) Cf. similar rank given to the queen mother among the Hebrews (I Kings 15:13). **11. spirit of the holy gods**—She remembers and repeats Nebuchadnezzar's language (ch. 4:8, 9, 18). As Daniel was probably, according to Oriental custom, deprived of the office to which Nebuchadnezzar had promoted him, as "master of the magicians" (ch. 4:9), at the king's death, Belshazzar might easily be ignorant of his services. **the king . . . thy father the king . . . thy father**—The repetition marks with emphatic gravity both the excellencies of Daniel, and the fact that Nebuchadnezzar, whom Belshazzar is bound to reverence as his father, had sought counsel from him in similar circumstances. **13. the captivity of Judah**—the captive Jews residing in Babylon.

17. Not inconsistent with verse 29. For here he declares his interpretation of the words is not from the *desire* of reward. The honors in verse 29 were doubtless *urged* on him, without his wish, in such a way that he could not with propriety refuse them. Had he refused them after announcing the doom of the kingdom, he might have been suspected of cowardice or treason. **18. God gave**—It was not his own birth or talents which gave him the vast empire, as he thought. To make him unlearn his proud thought was the object of God's visitation on him. **majesty**—in the eyes of his subjects. **glory**—from his victories. **honour**—from the enlargement and decoration of the city. **19.** A purely absolute monarchy (Jer. 27:7).

21. heart was made like . . . beasts—lit., "he made his heart like the beasts," i.e., he desired to dwell with them.

ADAM CLARKE

8. *They could not read the writing.* Because it was in the pure Hebrew, not the Chaldean, character.

10. *The queen . . . came.* This is generally allowed to have been the widow of Nebuchadnezzar.

16. *Dissolve doubts.* Untie knots—unbind what is bound. An expression used in the East to signify a judge of eminent wisdom and skill.

17. *Let thy gifts be to thyself.* They could be of little use to any, as the city was in a few hours to be taken and pillaged.

18. *Nebuchadnezzar thy father.* Or "grandfather." See the notes on v. 1.

19. *Whom he would he slew.* The genuine character of a despot, whose will is the only rule of his conduct.

20. *He was desposed from his kingly throne.* Became insane, and the reins of government were taken out of his hands.

MATTHEW HENRY

3. In God's name, he exhibits articles of impeachment against Belshazzar. Before he reads him his doom, from the hand-writing on the wall, he shows him his crime. He had not taken warning by the judgments of God upon his father (*v.* 22): "*Thou his son, O Belshazzar! hast not humbled thy heart, though thou knewest all this.* He had affronted God more impudently than Nebuchadnezzar himself had done, witness the revels of this very night (*v.* 23): "*Thou hast lifted up thyself against the Lord of heaven,* thou hast profaned the *vessels of his house*, and made the utensils of his sanctuary instruments of thy iniquity, and hast *praised the gods of silver and gold, which see not, nor hear, nor know* anything, as if they were to be preferred before the God that sees, and hears, and knows everything." He had not answered the end of his creation and maintenance: *The God in whose hand thy breath is, and whose are all thy ways, hast thou not glorified.* This is a general charge, which stands good against us all. Our dependence upon God as our Creator, preserver, benefactor, owner, and ruler; not only from his hand our breath was at first, but *in his hand our breath is* still; it is he that *holds our souls in life*, and, if he *take away our breath, we die.* We ought to glorify him, to devote ourselves to his honour and employ ourselves in his service. We have *all sinned, and have come short of the glory of God.* This is the indictment against Belshazzar.

4. He now proceeds to read the sentence, as he found it *written upon the wall*: "*Then*" (says Daniel) "when thou hast come to such a height of impiety as thus to trample upon the most sacred things, *then* when thou wast in the midst of thy sacrilegious idolatrous feast, then was *the part of the hand*, the writing fingers, sent *from him*, from God; he *sent them*, and *this writing*, thou now seest, *was written*, *v.* 24. Now the writing was, *Mene, Mene, Tekel, Upharsin*, *v.* 25. The signification of them is, *He has numbered, he has weighed, and they divide.* (1) *Mene;* repeated, for the thing is certain—*Mene, mene;* that signifies, both in Hebrew and Chaldee, *He has numbered and finished*, which Daniel explains thus (*v.* 26): "*God has numbered thy kingdom.* Here is an end of thy kingdom." (2) *Tekel;* signifies, in Chaldee, *Thou art weighed*, and, in Hebrew, *Thou art too light.* God does not give judgment against him till he has first pondered his actions, and considered the merits of his case. (3) *Upharsin* (*v.* 28): "*Thy kingdom is divided*, is rent from thee, and *given to the Medes and Persians*, as a prey to be divided among them." Belshazzar was so far convicted by his own conscience of the reasonableness of all he said that he gave Daniel the reward he promised him, put on him the *scarlet gown* and the *gold chain*, and proclaimed him the *third ruler in the kingdom* (*v.* 29).

Verses 30–31

1. The death of the king. Heathen writers speak of Cyrus's taking Babylon by surprise, with the assistance of two deserters that showed him the best way into the city. 2. The transferring of the kingdom into other hands. From the head of gold we now descend to the breast and arms of silver. *Darius the Mede took the kingdom* in partnership with, and by the consent of Cyrus, who had conquered it, *v.* 31.

JAMIESON, FAUSSET, BROWN

22. Thou hast erred not through ignorance, but through deliberate contempt of God, notwithstanding that thou hadst before thine eyes the striking warning given in thy grandfather's case. **23. whose are all thy ways**—(Jer. 10:23). **24. Then**—When thou liftedst up thyself against the Lord. **the part of the hand**—the fore part, the fingers. **was . . . sent from him**—i.e., from God. **25. Mene, Mene, Tekel, Upharsin**—lit., "numbered, weighed, and dividers." **26.** God hath fixed the number of years of thine empire, and that number is now complete. **27. weighed in the balances**—The Egyptians thought that Osiris weighed the actions of the dead in a literal balance. The Babylonians may have had the same notion, which would give a peculiar appropriateness to the image here used. **found wanting**—too light before God, the weigher of actions (I Sam. 2:3; Ps. 62:9). Like spurious gold or silver (Jer. 6:30). **28. Peres**—the explanation of "dividers" (vs. 25), the *active participle plural* there being used for the *passive participle singular*, "dividers" for "divided." The word *Peres* alludes to the similar word "Persia." **divided**—viz., among the Medes and Persians [MAURER]; or, "severed" from thee [GROTIUS]. **29. Belshazzar . . . clothed Daniel with scarlet**—To come from the presence of a prince in a dress presented to the wearer as a distinction is still held a great honor in the East. Daniel was thus restored to a similar rank to what he had held under Nebuchadnezzar (ch. 2:48). Godly fidelity which might be expected to bring down vengeance, as in this case, is often rewarded even in this life. The king, having promised, was ashamed before his courtiers to break his word. He perhaps also affected to despise the prophecy of his doom, as an idle threat. As to Daniel's reasons for now accepting what at first he had declined, cf. *Note*, vs. 17. The insignia of honor would be witnesses for God's glory to the world of his having by God's aid interpreted the mystic characters. The *cause* of his elevation too would secure the favor of the new dynasty (ch. 6:2) for both himself and his captive countrymen. As the capture of the city by Cyrus was not till near daylight, there was no want of *time* in that eventful night for accomplishing all that is here recorded. The capture of the city so immediately after the prophecy of it (following Belshazzar's sacrilege), marked most emphatically to the whole world the connection between Babylon's sin and its punishment. **30.** HERODOTUS and XENOPHON confirm Daniel as to the *suddenness* of the event. Cyrus diverted the Euphrates into a new channel and, guided by two deserters, marched by the dry bed into the city, while the Babylonians were carousing at an annual feast to the gods. See also Isaiah 21:5; 44:27; and Jer. 50:38, 39; and 51:36. As to Belshazzar's being slain, cf. Isaiah 14:18-20; 21:2-9; Jeremiah 50:29-35; 51:57. **31. Darius the Median**—i.e., Cyaxares II, the son and successor of Astyages, 569-536 B.C. Though Koresh, or Cyrus, was leader of the assault, yet all was done in the name of Darius; therefore, he alone is mentioned here; but ch. 6:28 shows Daniel was not ignorant of *Cyrus'* share in the capture of Babylon. Isaiah 13:17 and 21:2, confirm Daniel in making the *Medes* the leading nation in destroying Babylon. So also Jeremiah 51:11, 28. HERODOTUS, on the other hand, omits mentioning Darius, as that king, being weak and sensual, gave up all the authority to his energetic nephew, Cyrus (XENOPHON, *Cyrop.* 1.5; 8.7). **threescore and two years old**—This agrees with XENOPHON, Cyrop. 8.5, 19, as to Cyaxares II.

ADAM CLARKE

22. *Hast not humbled thine heart.* These judgments and mercies have had no good effect upon thee.

23. *But hast lifted up thyself against the Lord.* And the highest evidence of this rebellion was the profaning the sacred vessels of the Lord's house.

24. *Then was the part of the hand sent.* This was the filling up of the cup of your iniquity; this last act made you ripe for destruction.

25. It should be observed that each word stands for a short sentence: *mene* signifies "numeration"; *tekel*, "weighing"; and *peres*, "division." All the ancient versions, except the Syriac, read the words simply *Mene, Tekel, Phares*, as they are explained in the following verses, without the repetition of *Mene*.

29. *Clothed Daniel with scarlet.* More probably with "purple." The gold chain about the neck was an emblem of magisterial authority. It is often thus mentioned in Scripture.

30. *In that night was Belshazzar . . . slain.* Xenophon says he was dispatched by two lords, Gadatas and Gobrias, who went over to Cyrus to avenge themselves of certain wrongs which Belshazzar had done them. We have already seen that Cyrus entered the city by the bed of the Euphrates, which he had emptied, by cutting a channel for the waters and directing them into the marshy country.

31. *Darius the Median took the kingdom.* This is supposed to be the same as Cyaxares, son of Astyages and maternal uncle of Cyrus, to whom he gave the throne of Babylon after himself had had the honor of taking the city.

Daniel speaks nothing of the war that raged between the Babylonians and the Medes; but Isaiah speaks particularly of it, chaps. xiii—xiv; xlv—xlvli; and so does Jeremiah, chaps. l—li. I need not add that it is largely spoken of by profane authors. The Medes and Persians were confederates in the war; the former under Darius, the latter under Cyrus. Both princes are supposed to have been present at the taking of this city.

MATTHEW HENRY — CHAPTER 6

Verses 1–5

Concerning Daniel,

I. What a *great man* he was. When Darius, upon his accession to the crown of Babylon by conquest, new-modelled the government, he made Daniel prime-minister of state. Darius *set over the kingdom* 120 *princes* (*v.* 1), and appointed them their districts. Over these princes there was a *triumvirate*, or *three presidents*, who were to take and state the public accounts *that the king should have no damage* (*v.* 2), that he should not sustain loss in his revenue. Of these three Daniel was the chief, *preferred above the presidents and princes* (*v.* 3). Daniel had been a great man in the kingdom that was conquered, and for that reason, one would think, should have been imprisoned or banished. He was a native of a foreign kingdom, and a ruined one, and might have been despised as a stranger and captive. But Darius was soon aware that Daniel had something extraordinary

JAMIESON, FAUSSET, BROWN — CHAPTER 6

VSS. 1-28. DARIUS' DECREE: DANIEL'S DISOBEDIENCE, AND CONSEQUENT EXPOSURE TO THE LION'S: HIS DELIVERANCE BY GOD, AND DARIUS' DECREE. **1. Darius**—GROTEFEND has read it in the cuneiform inscriptions at Persepolis, as *Darheush*, i.e., "Lord-King," a name applied to many of the Medo-Persian kings in common. Three of that name occur: Darius Hystaspes, 521 B.C., in whose reign the decree was carried into effect for rebuilding the temple (Ezra 4:5; Hag. 1:1); Darius Codomanus, 336 B.C., whom Alexander overcame, called "the Persian" (Neh. 12:22), an expression used after the rule of Macedon was set up; and Darius Cyaxares II, between Astyages and Cyrus (ÆSCHYLUS, Pers. 762, 763). **hundred and twenty**—satraps; set over the conquered provinces (including Babylon) by Cyrus (XENOPHON, *Cyrop.* 8. 6. 1). No doubt Cyrus acted *under Darius*, as in the capture of Babylon; so that Daniel rightly attributes the appointment to *Darius*. **3. Daniel was preferred**—probably because of his

ADAM CLARKE — CHAPTER 6

1. *An hundred and twenty princes.* A chief or satrap over every province which belonged to the Medo-Persian empire. Afterwards we find it enlarged to 127 provinces, by the victories of Cambyses and Darius Hystaspes. See Esther i. 1.

2. *Three presidents.* Each having forty of these presidents accountable to him for their administration. *Daniel was first.* As being established over that part where was the seat of government. He was confirmed in his offices by Darius.

MATTHEW HENRY

in him, and therefore, finding Daniel excel in prudence and virtue, and probably having heard of his being divinely inspired, he made him his right hand. Though Daniel was now very old yet he was as able as ever for business, and won respect from all by being an oak, not by being a willow, by a constancy in virtue, not by a pliableness to vice.

II. *An excellent spirit was in him, v.* 3. There was *no error*, or *fault, to be found in him, v.* 4.

III. The presidents and princes envied him because he was advanced above them. 1. The cause of envy is everything that is good. The better a man is the worse he is thought of by his rivals. 2. The effect of envy is everything that is bad. Those that envied Daniel sought no less than his ruin. His enemies set spies upon him; they *sought to find occasion against him.* They concluded, at length, that they should not find any occasion against him except *concerning the law of his God, v.* 5. It seems then that Daniel kept up the profession of his religion, and there was no law that required him to be of the king's religion, or incapacitated him to bear office in the state unless he were. He was at the king's service *usque ad aras—as far as the altars*; but there he left him. In this matter therefore his enemies hoped to ensnare him.

Verses 6–10

Daniel's adversaries contrive a new law, by which they hope to ensnare him, and such was his fidelity to his God that they gained their point.

I. Darius's impious law—*Darius's*, because he gave the royal assent to it. The presidents and princes framed the edict. They intimate to the king that it was carried *unanimously*: "*All the presidents* are of this mind"; and yet we are sure that Daniel, the chief of the three presidents. did not agree to it. These designing men, under colour of doing honour to the king, press him to pass this into a law, and make it a royal statute, that *whosoever shall ask a petition of any god or man for thirty days, save of the king, shall be cast into the den of lions, v.* 7. All men must be made to believe that the king is so ready to all petitioners, that none in any distress need to apply either to God or man for relief, but to him only. And for thirty days together he will be ready to give audience to all that have any petition to present to him. There is a great deal in it that is apparently evil. Must not a beggar ask an alms, or one neighbour beg a kindness of another? If the child want bread, must he not ask it of his parents, or be cast into the den of lions if he do? But it was an impudent affront to all religion, to forbid asking a petition *of any god.* To interdict prayer for thirty days is to rob God of all the tribute he has from man and to rob man of all the comfort he has in God. Does not every man's heart direct him, when he is in want or distress, to call upon God, and must this be made high treason? Had they proposed only to prohibit the Jews from praying to their God, Daniel would have been as effectually ensnared; but they knew the king would not pass such a law, and therefore made it general.

II. Daniel's pious disobedience to this law, *v.* 10. He did not retire into the country, but stood his ground, knowing that he had now a fair opportunity of honouring God before men.

1. Daniel *prayed in his house*, sometimes himself alone and sometimes with his family about him, and made a solemn business of it. Every house not only may be, but ought to be, a house of prayer; where we have a tent God must have an altar, and on it we must offer spiritual sacrifices. In every prayer he gave thanks. When he prayed and gave thanks he *kneeled upon his knees*. Kneeling is a begging posture, and we come to God as beggars, beggars for our lives. He *opened the windows of his chamber*, that the sight of the visible heavens might affect his heart with awe. He *opened them towards Jerusalem*, the holy city, though now in ruins, to signify the affection he had for its very stones and dust (Ps. cii. 14). He did this *three times a day*. It is good to have our hours of prayer, not to bind, but to remind conscience; and, if we think our bodies require refreshment by food thrice a day, can we think seldomer will serve our souls? All who knew him knew it to be his practice; and he was not ashamed of it.

2. Daniel's constant adherence to this practice, even when it was made by the law a capital crime. When he knew that *the writing was signed* he continued to do *as he did aforetime*. Many a man, yea, and many a good man, would have thought it prudence to omit it for these thirty days, when he could not do it without hazard of his life; but Daniel, who had so many eyes upon him, must act with courage. And we must take heed lest, under pretence of discretion, we be found guilty of cowardice in the cause of God.

JAMIESON, FAUSSET, BROWN

having so wonderfully foretold the fall of Babylon. Hence the very expression used by the queen mother on that occasion (ch. 5:12) is here used, "because *an excellent spirit was in him.*" **king thought to set him over the whole realm**—Agreeing with Darius' character, weak and averse to business, which he preferred to delegate to favorites. God overruled this to the good both of Daniel, and, through him, of His people.

4. occasion . . . concerning the kingdom—pretext for accusation in his administration (Eccles. 4:4). **5.** It is the highest testimony to a godly man's walk, when his most watchful enemies can find no ground of censure save in that he walks according to the law of God even where it opposes the ways of the world. **6. assembled together**—lit., "assembled hastily and tumultuously." Had they come more deliberately, the king might have refused their grant; but they gave him no time for reflection, representing that their *test-decree* was necessary for the safety of the king. **live for ever**—ARRIAN (4) records that Cyrus was the first before whom prostration was practised. It is an undesigned mark of genuineness that Daniel should mention no prostration before Nebuchadnezzar or Darius (see *Note,* ch. 3:9). **7.** The Persian king was regarded as representative of the chief god, Ormuzd; the seven princes near him represented the seven Amshaspands before the throne of Ormuzd; hence Mordecai (Esther 3:4) refused such homage to Haman, the king's prime minister, as inconsistent with what is due to God alone. A weak despot, like Darius, much under the control of his princes, might easily be persuaded that such a decree would test the obedience of the Chaldeans just conquered, and tame their proud spirits. So absolute is the king in the East, that he is regarded not merely as the ruler, but the owner, of the people. **All . . . governors . . . counsellors . . .**—Several functionaries are here specified, not mentioned in verses 4, 6. They evidently exaggerated the case of the weak king, as if *their* request was that of *all* the officers in the empire. **den of lions**—an underground cave or pit, covered with a stone. It is an undesigned proof of genuineness, that the "fiery furnace" is not made the means of punishment here, as in ch. 3; for the Persians were *fire-worshippers,* which the Babylonians were not. **8. decree**—or, "interdict." **that it be not changed**—(Esther 1:19; 8:8). This immutability of the king's commands was peculiar to the Medes and Persians: it was due to their regarding him infallible as the representative of Ormuzd; it was not so among the Babylonians. **Medes and Persians**—The order of the names is an undesigned mark of genuineness. Cyrus the Persian reigned subordinate to Darius the Mede as to dignity, though exercising more real power. After Darius' death, the order is "the Persians and Medes" (Esther 1:14, 19, etc.). **9.** Such a despotic decree is quite explicable by remembering that the king, as the incarnation of Ormuzd, might demand such an act of religious obedience as a *test of loyalty*. Persecuting laws are always made on false pretenses. Instead of bitter complaints against men, Daniel prays to God. Though having vast business as a ruler of the empire, he finds time to pray thrice a day. Daniel's three companions (ch. 3), are not alluded to here, nor any other Jew who conscientiously may have disregarded the edict, as the conspirators aimed at Daniel alone (vs. 5). **10. when Daniel knew. . . writing . . . signed**—and that, therefore, the power of advising the king against it was taken from him. **went into his house**—withdrawing from the God-dishonoring court. **windows . . . open**—not in vainglory, but that there might be no obstruction to his view of the direction in which Jerusalem, the earthly seat of Jehovah under the Old Testament, lay; and that the sight of heaven might draw his mind off from earthly thoughts. To Christ in the heavenly temple let us turn our eyes in prayer, from this land of our captivity (I Kings 8:44, 48; II Chron. 6:29, 34, 38; Ps. 5:7). **chamber**—the upper room, where prayer was generally offered by the Jews (Acts 1:13). Not on the housetop (Acts 10:9), where he would be conspicuous. **upon his knees**—Humble attitudes in prayer become humble suppliants. **three times a day**—(Ps. 55:17). The third, sixth, and ninth hour; our nine, twelve, and three o'clock (Acts 2:15; 10:9; 3:1; 10:30; cf. ch. 9:21). **as . . . aforetime**—not from contempt of the king's command.

ADAM CLARKE

3. *The king thought to set him over the whole realm.* Intended to make him grand vizier. This partiality of the king made Daniel the object of the other presidents, and the grandees of the kingdom.

4. *Sought to find occasion against Daniel.* But they found no blemish in his administration, for he was faithful to his king; this was a virtue. But he was also faithful to his God; this they hoped to construe into a crime, and make it the cause of his ruin.

7. *Whosoever shall ask a petition.* What pretense could they urge for so silly an ordinance? Probably to flatter the ambition of the king, they pretend to make him a god for thirty days, so that the whole empire should make prayer and supplication to him, and pay him divine honors! This was the bait; but their real object was to destroy Daniel.

10. *Now when Daniel knew that the writing was signed.* He saw what was designed, and he knew whom he served. *His windows being open.* He would not shut them to conceal himself, but "kneeled down with his face turned toward Jerusalem, and prayed thrice each day, giving thanks to God as usual." When the Jews were in distant countries, in prayer they turned their faces towards Jerusalem; and when in Jerusalem, they turned their faces towards the Temple. Solomon, in his prayer at the dedication of the Temple, 1 Kings viii. 48, had entreated God to hear the prayers of those who might be in strange lands, or in captivity, when they should turn their faces towards their own land, which God gave unto their fathers; and towards the city which He had chosen, and the house which was dedicated to His name. It was in reference to this that Daniel turned his face towards Jerusalem when he prayed.

MATTHEW HENRY

Verses 11–17

Proof made of Daniel's praying to his God, notwithstanding the late edict to the contrary (*v.* 11): *These men assembled; they came tumultuously together*, so the word is, the same that was used *v.* 6. They came together to visit Daniel, perhaps under pretence of business, at that time which they knew to be his usual hour of devotion; and they *found him on his knees praying* and *making supplication before his God.* They lost no time, but applied to the king (*v.* 12), and proceeded to accuse Daniel, *v.* 13. They so describe him as to exasperate the king and incense him the more against him: "He is *of the children of the captivity of Judah*; and a captive in a despicable state, that can call nothing his own but what he has by the king's favour, and yet *he regards not thee, O king! nor the decree that thou hast signed.*" They do not say, He makes his petition to his God, lest Darius should take notice of that to his praise, but only, *He makes his petition*, which is the thing the law forbids. The king now perceived that, whatever they pretended, it was not to honour him, but to spite Daniel, *v.* 14. Now the king *sets his heart to deliver Daniel*; both by argument and by authority he labours *till the going down of the sun* to *deliver him*, that is, to persuade his accusers not to insist upon his prosecution. The prosecutors demanded judgment, *v.* 15. We are not told what Daniel said; the king himself is his advocate. But the prosecutors insist upon it that the law must have its course. The Persians magnified the wisdom of their king, by supposing that whatever law he solemnly ratified it was so well made that there could be no occasion to alter it. The king himself, with the utmost reluctance, and against his conscience, signs the warrant for his execution; and Daniel, that venerable grave man, who carried such a mixture of majesty and sweetness in his countenance, is purely for worshipping his God, *thrown into the den of lions*, to be devoured by them, *v.* 16. To make sure work, the stone *laid upon the mouth of the den* is *sealed* (*v.* 17). The encouragement which Darius gave to Daniel to trust in God: *Thy God whom thou servest continually, he will deliver thee*, *v.* 16. He justifies Daniel from guilt, owning all his crime to be serving his God continually. He leaves it to God to free him: *He will deliver thee.*

Verses 18–24

I. The melancholy night which the king had, upon Daniel's account, *v.* 18. He could not forgive himself for throwing him into the danger. He *passed the night fasting*. He forbade the music.

II. The early enquiry he made concerning Daniel the next morning, *v.* 19, 20. He *went in haste to the den of lions.* When he comes to the den, he cries, *with a lamentable voice, O Daniel! servant of the living God*, has *thy God whom thou servest* made it to appear that he is *able to deliver thee from the lions?*

III. Daniel is alive, is safe, and well, and unhurt in the lions' den, *v.* 21, 22. Daniel knew the king's voice: *O king! live for ever.* He does not reproach him, but has heartily forgiven him. The account Daniel gives the king is triumphant. 1. God has preserved his life by a miracle. He is *my God*, whom I own, and who owns me, for *he has sent his angel.* The same that was seen in *the form of the Son of God* with the three children in the fiery furnace had visited Daniel, and had *shut the lions' mouths.* See the care God takes of his faithful worshippers. He does in effect *stop the lions' mouths*, that they cannot hurt them. 2. Daniel was represented to the king as disaffected to him and his government. We do not find that he said anything in his own vindication, but left it to God to establish his integrity, and he did it effectually, by working a miracle for his preservation.

IV. The discharge of Daniel from his confinement. His prosecutors cannot but own that the law is satisfied, though they are not. No cause can be shown why Daniel should not be fetched out of the den (*v.* 23).

V. The committing of his prosecutors to the same prison, *v.* 24. Darius is animated by this miracle wrought for Daniel, and now begins to take courage and act like himself. Daniel's accusers, now that his innocency is cleared, have the same punishment inflicted upon them which they designed against him.

JAMIESON, FAUSSET, BROWN

11. assembled—as in vs. 6, "assembled" or "ran hastily," so as to come upon Daniel suddenly and detect him in the act. **12.** They preface their attack by alleging the king's edict, so as to get him again to confirm it unalterably, before they mention *Daniel's* name. Not to break a wicked promise, is not firmness, but guilty obstinacy (Matt. 14:9; Mark 6:26). **13. That Daniel**—contemptuously. **of . . . captivity of Judah**—recently a captive among thy servants, the Babylonians—one whom humble obedience most becomes. Thus they aggravate his guilt, omitting mention of his being prime minister, which might only remind Darius of Daniel's state services. **regardeth not thee**—because he regarded God (Acts 4:19; 5:29). **14. displeased with himself**—for having suffered himself to be entrapped into such a hasty decree (Prov. 29:20). On the one hand he was pressed by the immutability of the law, fear that the princes might conspire against him, and desire to consult for his own reputation, not to seem fickle; on the other, by regard for Daniel, and a desire to save him from the effects of his own rash decree. **till . . . going down of . . . sun**—The king took this time to deliberate, thinking that after sunset Daniel would be spared till morning, and that meanwhile some way of escape would turn up. But (vs. 15) the conspirators "assembled tumultuously" (lit.) to prevent this delay in the execution, lest the king should meantime change his decree. **16. Thy God . . . will deliver thee**—The heathen believed in the interposition of the gods at times in favor of their worshippers. Darius recognized Daniel's God as a god, but not *the only true* God. He had heard of the deliverance of the three youths in ch. 3 and hence augurs Daniel's deliverance. I am not my own master, and cannot deliver thee, however much I wish it. "Thy God will." Kings are the slaves of their flatterers. Men admire piety to God in others, however disregarding Him themselves. **17. stone . . . sealed**—typical of Christ's entombment under a seal (Matt. 27:66). Divinely ordered, that the deliverance might be the more striking. **his own signet, and . . . of his lords**—The *concurrence* of the lords was required for making laws. In this, kingly power had fallen since it was in Nebuchadnezzar's hands. The Median king is a puppet in his lords' hands; they take the security of their own seal as well as his, that he should not release Daniel. The king's seal guaranteed Daniel from being killed by them, should he escape the lions. **18. neither were instruments of music . . .**—GESENIUS translates, "concubines." Daniel's mentioning to us as an extraordinary thing of Darius, that he neither approached his table nor his harem, agrees with XENOPHON'S picture of him as devoted to wine and women, vain, and without self-control. He is sorry for the evil which he himself had caused, yet takes no steps to remedy it. There are many such halters between good and bad, who are ill at ease in their sins, yet go forward in them, and are drawn on by others. **19.** His grief overcame his fear of the nobles. **20. living God**—having life Himself, and able to preserve thy life; contrasted with the lifeless idols. Darius borrowed the phrase from Daniel; God extorting from an idolater a confession of the truth. **thou servest continually**—in times of persecution, as well as in times of peace. **is thy God . . . able**—the language of doubt, yet hope. **21.** Daniel might have indulged in anger at the king, but does not; his sole thought is, God's glory has been set forth in his deliverance. **22. his angel**—the instrument, not the author, of his deliverance (Ps. 91:11; 34:7). **shut . . . lions' mouths**—(Heb. 11:33). So spiritually, God will shut the roaring lion's mouth (I Pet. 5:8) for His servants. **forasmuch as before him innocency**—not absolutely (in ch. 9:7, 18 he disclaims such a plea), but relatively to this case. God has attested the justice of my cause in standing up for His worship, by delivering me. Therefore, the "forasmuch" does not justify Rome's doctrine of works meriting salvation. **before thee**—Obedience to God is in strictest compatibility with loyalty to the king (Matt. 22:21; I Pet. 2:17). Daniel's disobedience to the king was seeming, not real, because it was not from contempt of the king, but from regard to the King of kings (cf. Acts 24:16). **23. because he believed**—"Faith" is stated in Hebrews 11:33 to have been his actuating principle: a prelude to the Gospel. His belief was not with a view to a miraculous deliverance. He shut his eyes to the event, committing the keeping of his soul to God, in well-doing, as unto a faithful Creator (I Pet. 4:19), sure of deliverance in a better life, if not in this. **24.** (Deut. 19:19; Prov. 19:5.) **accused**—lit., "devoured the bones and flesh." It was just that they who had torn Daniel's character, and

ADAM CLARKE

14. *The king . . . was sore displeased with himself.* And well he might, when through his excessive folly he passed a law that, for its ostensible object, would have been a disgrace almost to an idiot. *And set his heart on Daniel.* He strove by every means to get the law annulled. He had no doubt spoken to several of his lords in private, and had gone from one to another till the going down of the sun.

15. *Then these men assembled.* Having got favorable answers, as we may presume, from many individuals, he called a parliament; but they now collectively joined to urge the execution of the law, not its repeal.

16. *Then the king commanded.* With a heavy heart he was obliged to warrant this murderous conspiracy. But when passing sentence his last words were affecting: "Thy God whom thou servest continually, he will deliver thee."

17. *A stone was brought.* All this *precaution* served the purposes of the Divine Providence. There could be no trick nor collusion here; if Daniel be preserved, it must be by the power of the Supreme God. The same precaution was taken by the Jews in the case of the burial of our blessed Lord; and this very thing has served as one of the strongest proofs of the certainty of His resurrection and their unmixed wickedness.

18. *Passed the night fasting.* He neither ate nor drank, had no music to solace, nor sweet odors burnt or brought before him, and he passed the night without sleep. All this points out his great sincerity; and when it is considered that Darius could not be less than sixty-two or sixty-three years of age at this time, it shows more fully the depth of his concern.

22. *My God hath sent his angel.* Such a one as that who attended Shadrach, Meshach, and Abed-nego in the fiery furnace, and blew inside the flames, so that they could not hurt them. *Before him innocency was found in me.* Because I was innocent God has preserved me; and now that I am preserved, my innocence is fully proved.

MATTHEW HENRY

Verses 25–28

Darius here studies to make amends for the dishonour he had done both to God and Daniel.

I. He gives honour to God by a decree published to all nations, by which they are required to fear before him. He sends this decree—*to all people, nations, and languages, that dwell in all the earth, v.* 25. The decree is—that *men tremble and fear before the God of Daniel.* This goes further than Nebuchadnezzar's decree, for that only restrained people from *speaking amiss* of this God, but this requires them to *fear before him.* But, though this decree goes far, it does not go far enough; had he come up to his present convictions, he would have commanded all men not only to fear before this God, but to love him and trust in him, to forsake the service of their idols, and to worship him only. There is good reason why all men should fear before this God, for, 1. His being is transcendent. 2. His government is incontestable. 3. Both his being and his government are unchangeable. 4. He has ability sufficient to support such an authority, *v.* 27. He delivers his faithful servants from trouble and rescues them out of trouble. 5. He has given a fresh proof of all this in *delivering* his servant *Daniel from the power of the lions.*

II. He puts honour upon Daniel (*v.* 28): *So this Daniel prospered.*

JAMIESON, FAUSSET, BROWN

sought the tearing of his person, should be themselves given to be torn in pieces (Prov. 11:8). **their children**—Among the Persians, all the kindred were involved in the guilt of one culprit. The Mosaic law expressly forbade this (Deut. 24:16; II Kings 14:6). **or ever**—i.e., "before ever." The lions' sparing Daniel could not have been because they were full, as they showed the keenness of their hunger on the accusers. **26.** Stronger than the decree (ch. 3:29). That was negative; this, positive; not merely men must say "nothing amiss of," but must "fear before God."

28. It was in the third year of Cyrus that Daniel's visions (ch. 10-12) were given. Daniel "prospered" because of his prophecies (Ezra 1:1, 2).

ADAM CLARKE

26. *I make a decree, That . . . man tremble and fear before the God of Daniel.* As in the case of the three Hebrews, chap. iii. **29.** The true God was known by His servants, and by the deliverances He wrought for them.

28. *So this Daniel prospered.* He had served five kings: Nebuchadnezzar, Evil-merodach, Belshazzar, Darius, and Cyrus. Few courtiers have had so long a reign, served so many masters with out flattering any, been more successful in their management of public affairs, been so useful to the states where they were in office, been more owned of God, or have left such an example to posterity.

MATTHEW HENRY

CHAPTER 7

F. B. MEYER:

God's everlasting dominion (7:1–14). This chapter enumerates the succession of world empires and rulers which bridge the gulf of centuries from the Captivity to the Second Advent. The lion represents Babylon, whose cruel and mighty kingdom was animated by marvelous intelligence; the bear, Persia; the leopard, Greece under Alexander the Great; and the fourth beast, with great iron teeth, Rome. The ten horns are ten kings, and these probably represent great European kingdoms which have succeeded, or may yet succeed, to the heritage of the Roman Empire. The Ancient of Days is sitting today upon his throne, his snow-white raiment betokening his purity, the fire of his throne bespeaking his antagonism to all things that offend and work iniquity. The government of the world is on shoulders which are well able to carry it, and he will cause all things to work out his purpose, which is to promote and assure the glory of Christ.—*Bible Commentary*

Verses 1–8

The date of this chapter places it before *ch.* v, which was in the last year of Belshazzar, and *ch.* vi, which was in the first of Darius. Belshazzar's name here is, in the original, spelt *Bel-eshe-zar—Bel is on fire by the enemy.* Bel the god of the Chaldeans had prospered, but is now to be consumed.

Daniel's vision of the four monarchies that were oppressive to the Jews.

I. The circumstances of this vision (*v.* 1): He *had visions of his head upon his bed,* when he was asleep; so God sometimes revealed his mind to men, when deep sleep fell upon them (Job xxxiii. 15). When he was awake he *wrote the dream,* and *told the sum of the matters* to his brethren, and gave it to them in writing, that it might be preserved for their children, who shall see these things accomplished. The Jews, misunderstanding Jeremiah and Ezekiel, flattered themselves that, after their return, they should enjoy uninterrupted tranquillity. God by this prophet lets them know that they shall have tribulation.

JAMIESON, FAUSSET, BROWN

CHAPTER 7

Vss. 1-28. VISION OF THE FOUR BEASTS. This chapter treats of the same subject as the second chapter. But there the four kingdoms, and Messiah's final kingdom, were regarded according to their *external* political aspect, but here according to the mind of God concerning them, and their *moral* features. The outward political history had been shown in its general features to the world ruler, whose position fitted him for receiving such a revelation. But God's prophet here receives disclosures as to the characters of the powers of the world, in a religious point of view, suited to *his* position and receptivity. Hence in the second chapter the images are taken from the inanimate sphere; in the seventh chapter they are taken from the animate. Nebuchadnezzar saw superficially the world power as a splendid human figure, and the kingdom of God as a mere stone at the first. Daniel sees the world kingdoms in their inner essence as of an *animal* nature lower than human, being estranged from God; and that only in the kingdom of God ("the Son of *man,*" the representative-man) is the true dignity of man realized. So, as contrasted with Nebuchadnezzar's vision, the kingdom of God appears to Daniel, *from the very first,* superior to the world kingdom. For though in *physical* force the beasts excel man, man has essentially *spiritual* powers. Nebuchadnezzar's colossal image represents mankind in its own strength, but only the outward man. Daniel sees man spiritually degraded to the beast level, led by blind impulses, through his alienation from God. It is only from above that the perfect Son of man comes, and in His kingdom man attains his true destiny. Cf. Psalm 8 with Genesis 1:26-28. Humanity is impossible without divinity: it sinks to bestiality (Ps. 32:9; 49:20; 73:22). Obstinate heathen nations are compared to "bulls" (Ps. 68:30); Egypt to the dragon in the Nile (Isa. 27:1; 51:9; Ezek. 29:3). The animal with all its sagacity looks always to the ground, without consciousness of relation to God. What elevates man is communion with God, in willing subjection to Him. The moment he tries to exalt himself to independence of God, as did Nebuchadnezzar (ch. 4: 30), he sinks to the beast's level. Daniel's acquaintance with the animal colossal figures in Babylon and Nineveh was a psychological preparation for his animal visions. Hosea 13:7, 8 would occur to him while viewing those ensigns of the world power. Cf. Jeremiah 2:15; 4:7: 5:6. **1. Belshazzar**—Good *Hebrew* MSS. have "Belshazzar"; meaning "Bel is to be burnt with hostile fire" (Jer. 50:2; 51:44). In the *history* he is called by his ordinary name; in the *prophecy,* which gives his true destiny, he is called a corresponding name, by the change of a letter. **visions of his head**—not *confused* "dreams," but distinct images seen *while his mind was collected.* **sum**—a "summary." In predictions, generally, details are not given so fully as to leave no scope for free agency, faith, and patient waiting for God manifesting His will in the event. He "wrote" it for the Church in all ages; he "told" it for the comfort of his captive fellow countrymen. **2. the four winds**—answering to the "four beasts"; their several *conflicts in the four quarters or directions of the world.* **strove**—burst forth (from the abyss) [MAUR-

ADAM CLARKE

CHAPTER 7

KEIL-DELITZSCH:

After presenting to view (ch. 3, 4) in concrete delineation, partly in the prophetically significant experiences of Daniel and his friends, and partly in the typical events which befell the world-rulers, the position and conduct of the representatives of the world-power in relation to the worshipers of the living God, there follows in this chapter the record of a vision seen by Daniel in the first year of Belshazzar. In this vision the four world-monarchies which were shown to Nebuchadnezzar in a dream in the form of an image are represented under the symbol of beasts; and there is a further unfolding not only of the nature and character of the four successive world-kingdoms, but also of the everlasting kingdom of God established by the judgment of the world-kingdoms. With this vision, recorded like the preceding chapters in the Chaldean language, the first part of this work, treating of the development of the world-power in its four principal forms, is brought to a conclusion suitable to its form and contents.

This chapter is divided, according to its contents, into two equal portions. Verses 1–14 contain the vision, and verses 15–28 its interpretation.—*Commentary on the Old Testament*

1. *In the first year of Belshazzar.* This is the same Belshazzar who was slain at the taking of Babylon, as we have seen at the conclusion of chap. v.

MATTHEW HENRY

II. The vision itself: 1. He observed the *four winds to strive upon the great sea, v.* 2. They strove which should blow strongest, and, at length, blow alone. This represents the contests among princes for empire. The four winds strive for mastery! That is what the kings of the nations are contending for in their wars, which are as noisy and violent as the battle of the winds.

2. He saw *four great beasts come up from the sea,* from the *troubled waters.* The monarchs and monarchies are represented by *beasts.* These beasts were *diverse one from another* (*v.* 3), to denote the different genius of the nations.

The first beast *was like a lion, v.* 4. This was the Chaldean monarchy, fierce and strong, and the kings absolute. This lion had *eagle's wings,* denoting the speed that Nebuchadnezzar made in his conquest of kingdoms. But Daniel soon sees the *wings plucked.*

Divers countries that had been tributaries revolt; so that this winged lion is made to *stand upon the feet as a man, and a man's heart is given to it.* It has lost the heart of a lion (one of our English kings was called *Coeur de Lion—Lion-heart*), has become feeble, dreading everything and daring nothing.

The *second* beast was *like a bear, v.* 5. This was the Persian monarchy, less strong and generous, but no less ravenous.

This bear *raised up itself on one side* against the lion, and soon mastered it. It *raised up one dominion*; so some read it. Persia and Media now set up a joint government.

This bear had *three ribs in the mouth of it between the teeth,* the remains of those nations it had devoured; some ribs still stuck in the teeth of it, which it could not conquer. Whereupon it was said, "*Arise, devour much flesh;* set upon that which will be an easier prey." The princes will push on their conquests, and let nothing stand before them. The *third* beast was *like a leopard, v.* 6. This was the Grecian monarchy, founded by *Alexander the Great,* active, crafty, and cruel, like a *leopard.*

He had *four wings of a fowl*; for though Nebuchadnezzar made great despatch in his conquests Alexander made much greater. In six years' time he gained the whole empire of Persia, a great part of Asia, made himself master of Syria, Egypt, India, and other nations.

JAMIESON, FAUSSET, BROWN

ER]. **sea**—The world powers rise out of the agitations of the political *sea* (Jer. 46:7, 8; Luke 21:25; cf. Rev. 13:1; 17:15; 21:1); the kingdom of God and the Son of man from the *clouds of heaven* (vs. 13; cf. John 8:23). TREGELLES takes "the great sea" to mean, as always elsewhere in Scripture (Josh. 1:4; 9:1), *the Mediterranean,* the center territorially of the four kingdoms of the vision, which all border on it, and have Jerusalem subject to them. *Babylon* did not border on the Mediterranean, nor rule Jerusalem, till Nebuchadnezzar's time, when both things took place simultaneously. *Persia* encircled more of this sea, viz., from the Hellespont to Cyrene. *Greece* did not become a monarchy before Alexander's time, but then, succeeding to Persia, it became mistress of Jerusalem. It surrounded still more of the Mediterranean, adding the coasts of Greece to the part held by Persia. *Rome,* under Augustus, realized three things at once—it became a monarchy; it became mistress of the last of the four parts of Alexander's empire (symbolized by the four heads of the third beast), and of Jerusalem; it surrounded *all* the Mediterranean. **3. beasts**—not *living animals,* as the cherubic four in Revelation 4:7 (for the original is a different word from "beasts," and ought to be there translated, "living animals"). The cherubic *living animals* represent redeemed man, combining in himself the highest forms of animal life. But the "beasts" here represent the world powers, in their beastlike, grovelling character. It is on the fundamental harmony between nature and spirit, between the three kingdoms of nature, history, and revelation, that Scripture symbolism rests. The selection of symbols is not arbitrary, but based on the essence of things. **4. lion**—the symbol of *strength and courage;* chief among the kingdoms, as the lion among the beasts. Nebuchadnezzar is called "the lion" (Jer. 4:7). **eagle's wings**—denoting a widespread and rapidly acquired (Isa. 46:11; Jer. 4:13; Lam. 4:19; Hab. 1:6) empire (Jer. 48:40). **plucked**—Its ability for widespread conquests passed away under Evil-merodach, etc. [GROTIUS]; rather, during Nebuchadnezzar's privation of his throne, while deranged. **it was lifted up from the earth**—i.e., from its grovelling bestiality. **made stand . . . as a man**—So long as Nebuchadnezzar, in haughty pride, relied on his own strength, he forfeited the true dignity of man, and was therefore degraded to be with the beasts. Ch. 4:16: "Let his *heart* be changed from *man's,* and let a beast's *heart* be given unto him." But after he learned by this sore discipline that "the Most High ruleth in the kingdom of men" (ch. 4:35, 36), the change took place in him, "a *man's* heart is given to him; instead of his former beast's heart, he attains man's true position, viz., to be consciously dependent on God." Cf. Psalm 9:20. **5. bear**—symbolizing the austere life of the Persians in their mountains, also their cruelty (Isa. 13:17, 18; Cambyses, Ochus, and other of the Persian princes were notoriously cruel; the Persian laws involved, for one man's offense, the whole kindred and neighborhood in destruction, ch. 6:24) and rapacity. "A bear is an *all-devouring* animal" [ARISTOTLE, 8. 5], (Jeremiah 51:48, 56). **raised . . . itself on one side**—but the *Hebrew,* "It raised up one *dominion.*" The Medes, an ancient people, and the Persians, a modern tribe, formed *one united sovereignty* in contrast to the third and fourth kingdoms, each originally one, afterwards divided. *English Version* is the result of a slight change of a *Hebrew* letter. The idea then would be, "It lay on one of its fore feet, and stood on the other"; a figure still to be seen on one of the stones of Babylon (MUNTER, *Relig. Babyl.,* 112); denoting a kingdom that had been at rest, but is now rousing itself for conquest. Media is the lower side, passiveness; Persia, the upper, active element [AUBERLEN]. The three ribs in its mouth are *Media, Lydia, and Babylon,* brought under the Persian sway. Rather, *Babylon, Lydia, and Egypt,* not properly parts of its body, but seized by Medo-Persia [SIR I. NEWTON]. Called "ribs" because they strengthened the Medo-Persian empire. "Between its teeth," as being much grinded by it. **devour much flesh**—i.e., subjugate many nations. **6. leopard**—smaller than the lion; swift (Hab. 1:8); cruel (Isa. 11:6), the opposite of tame; springing suddenly from its hiding-place on its prey (Hos. 13:7); spotted. So Alexander, a small king, of a small kingdom, Macedon, attacked Darius at the head of the vast empire reaching from the Ægean Sea to the Indies. In twelve years he subjugated part of Europe, and all Asia from Illyricum and the Adriatic to the Ganges, not so much fighting as conquering [JEROME]. Hence, whereas Babylon is represented with *two* wings, Macedon has *four,* so rapid were its conquests. The various spots denote the various nations incorporated into his empire

ADAM CLARKE

2. *The four winds of the heaven strove upon the great sea.* The idea of strife is taken here from the effects that must be produced were the east, the west, the north, and the south winds to rise tempestuously, and meet on the surface of the sea. By the great sea, the Mediterranean is meant. This dream is the same in meaning, under different emblems, as that of Nebuchadnezzar's metallic image; but in Daniel's dream several circumstances are added. It is supposed that Daniel had this dream about forty-eight years after Nebuchadnezzar had the vision of the great image.

3. *Four great beasts came up from the sea.* The term *sea,* in Hebrew *yam,* from *hamah,* "to be tumultuous, agitated," seems to be used here to point out the then known globe, because of its generally agitated state; and the four winds striving point out those predatory wars that prevailed almost universally among men, from the days of Nimrod, the founder of the Assyrian or Babylonish monarchy, down to that time, and in the end gave birth to the four great monarchies which are the subject of this vision.

4. *The first was like a lion, and had eagle's wings.* The beast like a lion is the kingdom of the Babylonians; and the king of Babylon is compared to a lion, Jer. iv. 7; Isa. v. 29; and is said to fly as an eagle, Jer. xlviii. 40; Ezek. xvii. 3, 7. The lion is considered the king of the beasts, and the eagle the king of the birds; and therefore the kingdom of Babylon, which was signified by the golden head of the great image, was the first and noblest of all the kingdoms; and was the greatest then in being. The wings of the eagle denote the rapidity with which the lion, Nebuchadnezzar, made his conquests. For in a few years, by his own arms, he brought his empire to such an extent, and raised it to such a degree of eminence, as was truly surprising; and all tended to show with what propriety this eagle-winged lion is here made his emblem. *The wings thereof were plucked.* Lydia, Media, and Persia, which had been provinces of the Babylonish empire, cast off the yoke, and put themselves under kings of their own. Besides, the rapidity of its conquests was stopped by its wars with the Medes and Persians; by whom it was at last conquered, and divided between Darius and Mede and Cyrus the Persian. *And made stand upon the feet as a man.* This I think refers to the taming of Nebuchadnezzar's pride. He had acted like a fierce and ravening lion. God struck him with insanity; he then lived the life of a beast, and had a beast's heart—disposition and habits. At last God restored him. *And a man's heart was given to it.* He became humane, humble, and pious; and in this state he appears to have died.

5. *Another beast . . . like to a bear.* This was the Medo-Persian empire, represented here under the symbol of the bear, as the largest species of these animals was found in *Media,* a mountainous, cold, and rough country, covered with woods. The Medes and Persians are compared to a *bear* on account of their *cruelty* and *thirst after blood,* a bear being a most voracious and cruel animal. The bear is termed by Aristotle an all-devouring animal; and the Medo-Persians are known to have been great robbers and spoilers. See Jer. li. 48-56. The Persians were notorious for the cruelty of their punishments. *Raised up itself on one side.* Cyrus arose on the borders of Chaldea, and thus the bear appeared to put itself in the position to attack the lion. *It had three ribs in the mouth of it.* The ribs being between the teeth of the bear may show how Babylon, Lydia, and Egypt were ground and oppressed by the bear—the Persians; though, as ribs strengthen the body, they were a powerful support to their conquerors.

6. *Another, like a leopard . . . four wings . . . four heads.* This was the Macedonian or Greek empire, and Alexander the Great its king. *Four wings of a fowl.* The Babylonian empire was represented with two wings; and they sufficiently marked the rapidity of Nebuchadnezzar's conquests. But the Macedonian has here four wings; for nothing, in the history of the world, was equal to the conquests of Alexander, who ran through all the countries from Illyricum and the Adriatic Sea to the Indian Ocean and the River Ganges; and in twelve years subdued part of Europe and all Asia.

MATTHEW HENRY

This beast had *four heads*; upon Alexander's death his conquests were divided among his four chief captains; Seleucus Nicanor had Asia the Great; Perdiccas, and after him Antigonus, had Asia the Less; Cassander had Macedonia; and Ptolemeus had Egypt.

The *fourth* beast was more fierce and formidable than any of them. *v.* 7. The learned are not agreed concerning this anonymous beast; some make it to be the Roman empire, which comprehended ten kingdoms, Italy, France, Spain, Germany, Britain, Sarmatia, Pannonia, Asia, Greece, and Egypt; and then the little horn which rose by the fall of three of the other horns (*v.* 8) they make to be the Turkish empire, which rose in the room of Asia, Greece, and Egypt. Others make this fourth beast to be the kingdom of Syria, the family of the Seleucidae, which was very cruel to the Jews, as we find in Josephus and the history of the Maccabees. Their armies were the *great iron teeth* with which they *devoured and broke in pieces* the people of God, and *trampled upon the residue* of them. The *ten horns* are then supposed to be ten kings that reigned successively in Syria; and then the *little horn* is Antiochus Epiphanes, the last of the ten, who undermined three of the kings, and got the government.

JAMIESON, FAUSSET, BROWN

[BOCHART]; or Alexander's own variation in character, at one time mild, at another cruel, now temperate, and now drunken and licentious. **four heads**—explained in chapter 8:8, 22; the four kingdoms of the *Diadochi* or "successors" into which the Macedonian empire was divided at the death of Alexander, viz., Macedon and Greece under Cassander, Thrace and Bithynia under Lysimachus, Egypt under Ptolemy, and Syria under Seleucus. **dominion . . . given to it**—by God; not by Alexander's own might. For how unlikely it was that 30,000 men should overthrow several hundreds of thousands! JOSEPHUS (*Antiquities,* 11.6) says that Alexander adored the high priest of Jerusalem, saying that he at Dium in Macedonia had seen a vision of God so habited, inviting him to go to Asia, and promising him success. **7.** As Daniel lived under the kingdom of the first beast, and therefore needed not to describe it, and as the second and third are described fully in the second part of the book, the chief emphasis falls on the fourth. Also prophecy most dwells on the *end,* which is the consummation of the preceding series of events. It is in the fourth that the world power manifests fully its God-opposing nature. Whereas the three former kingdoms were designated respectively, as a lion, bear, and leopard, no particular beast is specified as the image of the fourth; for Rome is so terrible as to be not describable by any one, but combines in itself all that we can imagine inexpressibly fierce in all beasts. Hence *thrice* (vss. 7, 19, 23) it is repeated, that the fourth was "diverse from all" the others. The formula of introduction, "I saw in the night visions," occurs here, as at vs. 2, and again at vs. 13, thus dividing the whole vision into three parts—the first embracing the three kingdoms, the second the fourth and its overthrow, the third Messiah's kingdom. The first three together take up a few centuries; the fourth, thousands of years. The whole lower half of the image in ch. 2 is given to it. And whereas the other kingdoms consist of only one material, this consists of two, iron and clay (on which much stress is laid, ch. 2:41-43); the *"iron* teeth" here allude to one material in the fourth kingdom of the image. **ten horns**—It is with the *crisis,* rather than the *course,* of the fourth kingdom that this seventh chapter is mainly concerned. The ten *kings* (vs. 24, the "horns" representing *power*), i.e., *kingdoms,* into which Rome was divided on its incorporation with the Germanic and Slavonic tribes, and again at the Reformation, are thought by many to be here intended. But the variation of the list of the ten, and their ignoring the eastern half of the empire altogether, and the existence of the Papacy *before* the breaking up of even the *Western* empire, instead of being the "little horn" springing up *after* the other ten, are against this view. The Western Roman empire continued till A.D. 731, and the Eastern, till A.D. 1453. The ten kingdoms, therefore, prefigured by the ten "toes" (ch. 2:41; cf. Rev. 13:1; 17:12), are the ten kingdoms into which Rome shall be found finally divided when Antichrist shall appear [TREGELLES]. These, probably, are prefigured by the number *ten* being the prevalent one at the chief turning points of Roman history. **8. little horn**—*little* at first, but afterwards waxing greater than all others. He must be sought "among them," viz., the ten horns. The Roman empire did not represent itself as a continuation of Alexander's; but the Germanic empire calls itself "the holy Roman empire." Napoleon's attempted universal monarchy was avowedly Roman: his son was called king of Rome. The czar (*Cæsar*) also professes to represent the eastern half of the Roman empire. The Roman civilization, church, language, and law are the chief elements in Germanic civilization. But the Romanic element seeks universal empire, while the Germanic seeks individualization. Hence the universal monarchies attempted by the Papacy, Charlemagne, Charles V, and Napoleon have failed, the iron not amalgamating with the clay. In the king symbolized by "the little horn," the God-opposing, haughty spirit of the world, represented by the fourth monarchy, finds its intensest development. "The man of sin," "the son of perdition" (II Thess. 2). Antichrist (I John 2: 18, 22; 4:3). It is the complete evolution of the evil principle introduced by the fall. **three of the first horns plucked up**—the exarchate of Ravenna, the kingdom of the Lombards and the state of Rome, which constituted the Pope's dominions at the first; obtained by Pope Zachary and Stephen II in return for acknowledging the usurper Pepin lawful king of France [NEWTON]. See TREGELLES' objections, vs. 7, "ten horns," *Note.* The "little horn," in his view, is to be Antichrist rising three and a half years before Christ's second advent, having first

ADAM CLARKE

The beast had also four heads. Signifying the empire after the death of Alexander, divided between his four generals: Cassander reigning over Macedon and Greece; Lysimachus, over Thrace and Bithynia; Ptolemy, over Egypt; and Seleucus, over Syria.

Dominion was given to it. It was not owing to the skill, courage, or valor of Alexander and his troops that he made those wondrous conquests; the nations were given to him. For, as Bishop Newton says, had he not been assisted by the mighty power of God, how could he, with only 30,000 men, have overcome Darius with 600,000; and in so short a time have brought the countries from Greece as far as India into subjection?

7. *I saw . . . a fourth beast . . . it had great iron teeth.* This is allowed, on all hands, to be the Roman empire. It was dreadful, terrible, and exceeding strong; *it devoured and brake in pieces, and stamped the residue,* that is, the remains of the former kingdoms, with its feet. It reduced Macedon into a Roman province about one hundred and sixty-eight years before Christ; the kingdom of Pergamos, about one hundred and thirty-three years; Syria, about sixty-five; and Egypt, about thirty years before Christ. And, besides the remains of the Macedonian empire, it subdued many other provinces and kingdoms; so that it might, by a very usual figure, be said to devour the whole earth, to tread it down, and break it to pieces; and became in effect, what the Roman writers delight to call it, "the empire of the whole world." *It had ten horns.* The ten kingdoms into which the Roman empire was afterwards divided.

8. *Another little horn.* Among Protestant writers this is considered to be the popedom.

MATTHEW HENRY

He was a man of great ingenuity, and therefore is said to have eyes *like the eyes of a man.*

Verses 9–14

Whether we understand the fourth beast to signify the Syrian empire, or the Roman, it is plain that these verses are intended for the comfort of the people of God in the persecutions they were likely to sustain. Three things are here discovered that are encouraging:

I. That there is a judgment to come, and God is the Judge. Now men have their day. *I beheld* (*v.* 9) *till the thrones were cast down,* not only the thrones of these beasts, but *all rule, authority, and power,* that are set up in opposition to the kingdom of God among men (1 Cor. xv. 24): such are the thrones of the kingdoms of the world, in comparison with God's kingdom. *I beheld till thrones were set up* (so it may as well be read), Christ's throne and the throne of his Father. It is the *judgment* that is here *set, v.* 10. This is intended to proclaim God's wise and righteous government of the world by his providence. Perhaps it points at the destruction brought upon Syria, or Rome, for their tyrannizing over the people of God. It seems principally designed to describe the last judgment. Many of the New Testament predictions of the judgment to come have a plain allusion to this vision, especially St. John's vision of it, Rev. xx. 11, 12. The Judge is *the Ancient of days* himself, *God the Father.* He is called *the Ancient of days,* because he is God *from everlasting to everlasting.* The glory of the Judge is set forth by his garment, *white as snow,* denoting his splendour and purity; and the *hair of his head as the pure wool,* white and venerable. The throne is *like the fiery flame,* dreadful to the wicked. The *wheels* thereof are *as burning fire,* to devour the adversaries. This is enlarged upon, *v.* 10. The attendants are numerous. The Shechinah is always attended with angels; it is so here (*v.* 10): *Thousand thousands minister to him,* and *ten thousand times ten thousand stand before him. The judgment is set,* publicly, and *the books are opened.*

II. That the cruel enemies of the church of God will be brought down in due time, *v.* 11, 12. This is here represented, 1. In the destroying of the fourth

JAMIESON, FAUSSET, BROWN

overthrown three of the ten contemporaneous kingdoms, into which the fourth monarchy, under which we live, shall be finally divided. Popery seems to be *a* fulfilment of the prophecy in many particulars, the Pope claiming to be God on earth and above all earthly dominions; but the spirit of Antichrist prefigured by Popery will probably culminate in ONE *individual,* to be destroyed by Christ's coming; He will be the product of the political *world* powers, whereas Popery which prepares His way, is a *Church* become worldly. **eyes of man**—Eyes express intelligence (Ezek. 1:18); so (Gen. 3:5) the serpent's promise was, man's "eyes should be opened," if he would but rebel against God. Antichrist shall consummate the self-apotheosis, begun at the fall, high intellectual culture, independent of God. The metals representing Babylon and Medo-Persia, gold and silver, are more precious than brass and iron, representing Greece and Rome; but the latter metals are more useful to civilization (Gen. 4:22). The clay, representing the Germanic element, is the most plastic material. Thus there is a progress in *culture;* but this is not a progress *necessarily* in man's truest dignity, viz., union and likeness to God. Nay, it has led him farther from God, to self-reliance and world-love. The beginnings of civilization were among the children of Cain (Gen. 4:17-24; Luke 16:8). Antiochus Epiphanes, the first Antichrist, came from civilized Greece, and loved art. As Hellenic civilization produced the *first,* so modern civilization under the fourth monarchy will produce the *last* Antichrist. The "mouth" and "eyes" are those of a man, while the symbol is otherwise brutish, i.e., it will assume man's true dignity, viz., wear the guise of the kingdom of God (which comes as the "Son of *man*" from above), while it is really bestial, viz., severed from God. Antichrist promises the same things as Christ, but in an opposite way: a caricature of Christ, offering a regenerated world without the cross. Babylon and Persia in their religion had more reverence for things divine than Greece and Rome in the imperial stages of their history. Nebuchadnezzar's human *heart,* given him (ch. 4:16) on his repentance, contrasts with the human *eyes* of Antichrist, the pseudo son of man, viz., intellectual culture, while heart and mouth blaspheme God. The deterioration politically corresponds: the first kingdom, an organic unity; the second, divided into Median and Persian; the third branches off into four; the fourth, into ten. The two eastern kingdoms are marked by nobler metals; the two western, by baser; individualization and division appear in the latter, and it is they which produce the two Antichrists. **9. I beheld till**—I continued looking till. **thrones . . . cast down**—rather, "thrones were *placed*" [*Vulgate* and LUTHER], viz., for the saints and elect angels to whom "judgment is given" (vs. 22), as assessors with the Judge. Cf. vs. 10, "thousand thousands ministered unto Him" (Matt. 19:28; Luke 22:30; I Cor. 6:2, 3; I Tim. 5:21; Rev. 2:26; 4:4). In *English Version* the thrones *cast down* are those of the previously mentioned kings who give place to Messiah. **Ancient of days**—"The everlasting Father" (Isa. 9:6). HE is the Judge here, as THE SON does not judge in His own cause, and it is His cause which is the one at issue with Antichrist. **sit**—the attitude of a judge about to pass sentence. **white**—The judicial purity of the Judge, and of all things round Him, is hereby expressed (Rev 1:14). **wheels**—as Oriental thrones move on wheels. Like the rapid flame, God's judgments are most swift in falling where He wills them (Ezek. 1:15, 16). The judgment here is not the last judgment, for *then* there will be no beast, and heaven and earth shall have passed away; but it is that on Antichrist (the last development of the fourth kingdom), typical of the last judgment: "Christ coming to substitute the millennial kingdom of *glory* for that of *the cross* (Rev. 17:12-14; 19:15-21; 11:15). **10 thousand . . . ministered unto him**—so at the giving of the law (Deut. 33:2; Ps. 68:17; Heb. 12:22; Jude 14). **ten . . . thousand before him**—image from the Sanhedrin, in which the father of the consistory sat with his assessors on each side, in the form of a semicircle, and the people standing before him. **judgment was set**—The judges sat (Rev. 20:4). **books . . . opened**—(Rev. 20:12). Forensic image; all the documents of the cause at issue, connected with the condemnation of Antichrist and his kingdom, and the setting up of Messiah's kingdom. *Judgment* must pass on the world as being under the curse, before the glory comes; but Antichrist offers glory without the cross, a renewed world without the world being *judged.* **11.** Here is set forth the execution on earth of the judgment pronounced in the unseen heavenly court of judicature (vss.

ADAM CLARKE

KEIL-DELITZSCH:

Verse 8. Here a new event is brought under our notice. While continuing to contemplate the horns, Daniel sees another little horn rise up among them, which uproots, i.e. destroys, three of the other horns that were already there. He observes that this horn had the eyes of a man, and a mouth which spake great things. The eye and the mouth suggest a human being as represented by the horn. Eyes and seeing with eyes are the symbols of insight, circumspection, prudence. This king will thus excel the others in point of wisdom and circumspection. But why the eyes of a *man*? Certainly this is not merely to indicate to the reader that the horn signified a man. This is already distinctly enough shown by the fact that eyes, a mouth, and speech were attributed to it. The eyes of a man were not attributed to it in opposition to a beast, but in opposition to a higher celestial being, for whom the ruler denoted by the horn might be mistaken on account of the terribleness of his rule and government.

Verses 9, 10. "One advanced in days, very old," is not the Eternal; for although God is meant, yet Daniel does not see the everlasting God, but an old man, or a man of grey hairs, in whose majestic form God makes himself visible (Ezek. 1:26). When Daniel represents the true God as an aged man, he does so not in contrast with the recent gods of the heathen which Antiochus Epiphanes wished to introduce, or specially with reference to new gods, by reference to Deut. 32:17 and Jer. 23:23; for God is not called the old God, but appears only as an old man, because age inspires veneration and conveys the impression of majesty. This impression is heightened by the robe with which He is covered, and by the appearance of the hair of His head, and also by the flames of fire which are seen to go forth from His throne. His robe is white as snow, and the hair of His head is white like pure wool (Rev. 1:14). Both are symbols of spotless purity and holiness. Flames of fire proceed from His throne as if it consisted of it, and the wheels of His throne scatter forth fire. One must not take the fire exclusively as a sign of punishment. Fire and the shining of fire are the constant phenomena of a manifestation of God in the world, as the earthly elements most fitting for the representation of the burning zeal with which the holy God not only punishes and destroys sinners, but also purifies and renders glorious His own people (Ex. 3:3).

—*Commentary on the Old Testament*

10. *A fiery stream issued.* This is not spoken of the final judgment; but of that which He was to execute upon this fourth beast, the Roman empire; and the little boasting horn, which is a part of the fourth beast, and must fall when the other falls.

MATTHEW HENRY

beast. God's quarrel with this beast is *because of the voice of the great words which the horn spoke*, bidding defiance to Heaven. The Syrian empire, after Antiochus, was destroyed. He himself died of a miserable disease, his family was rooted out, the kingdom wasted by the Parthians and Armenians, and at length made a province of the Roman empire by Pompey. And the Roman empire itself (if we take that for the fourth beast), after it began to persecute Christianity, declined and wasted away, and was destroyed. 2. In the weakening of the other three beasts (*v.* 12): They had *their dominion taken away*, and so were disabled from doing mischiefs to the people of God; but *a prolonging in life was given them, for a time and a season.* The power of the foregoing kingdoms was broken, but the people still remained in a mean, weak condition. And thus God deals with his church's enemies; sometimes he crushes the persecution, but reprieves the persecutors, that they may have space to repent.

III. That the kingdom of the Messiah shall be set up in the world, in spite of all the opposition of the powers of darkness. Daniel sees this in vision, and comforts his friends. 1. The Messiah is here called the Son of man—*one like unto the Son of man;* for he was *made in the likeness of sinful flesh*, was *found in fashion as a man. I saw one like unto the Son of man.* Our Saviour seems plainly to refer to this vision when he says (John v. 27) that the *Father* has therefore *given him authority to execute judgment* because he is *the Son of man.* 2. He is said to *come with the clouds of heaven.* Some refer this to his incarnation. I think it is rather to be referred to his ascension, Acts i. 9. When the cloud received him out of the sight of his disciples, it is worth while to enquire whither it carried him; and here we are told he ascended to *his Father and our Father*, to *his God and our God* (John xx. 17). He was *brought near*, as our high priest, who for us enters within the veil, and as our forerunner.

He is represented as having a mighty influence upon this earth, *v.* 14. When he went to be glorified with his Father he had a *power given him over all flesh*, John xvii. 2, 5. With the prospect of this Daniel and his friends are comforted, that not only the dominion of the church's enemies shall be taken away (*v.* 12), but the church's head shall have *the dominion given him*; to him *every knee shall bow* and *every tongue confess*, Phil. ii. 9, 10. His *dominion* shall not *pass away.* The church shall continue militant to the end of time, and triumphant to the endless ages of eternity.

Verses 15–28

I. The deep impressions which these visions made upon the prophet (*v.* 15): *I Daniel was grieved in my spirit, in the midst of my body.* The word here used for the *body* properly signifies a *sheath* or *scabbard*, for the body is no more to the soul. The *visions of my head troubled me*, and again (*v.* 28), *my cogitations much troubled me.* The manner in which these things were discovered to him quite overwhelmed him.

II. His earnest desire to understand the meaning (*v.* 16).

III. The key that was given him.

1. *The great beasts* are great *kings* and their kingdoms, *which shall arise out of the earth*, as those beasts did *out of the sea*, *v.* 17.

JAMIESON, FAUSSET, BROWN

9, 10). **body . . . given to . . . flame**—(Rev. 19:20). **12.** "The rest of the beasts," i.e., the three first, had passed away not by *direct* destroying judgments, such as consumed the little horn, as being the finally matured evil of the fourth beast. They had continued to exist, but their "*dominion* was taken away"; whereas the fourth beast shall cease utterly, superseded by Messiah's kingdom. **for a season . . . time**—Not only the triumph of the beasts over the godly, but their very existence is limited to a *definite time,* and that time the *exactly suitable* one (cf. Matt. 24:22). Probably a definite period is meant by a "season and time" (cf. vs. 25; Rev. 20:3). It is striking, the fourth monarchy, though Christianized for 1500 years past, is not distinguished from the previous heathen monarchies, or from its own heathen portion. Nay, it is represented as the most God-opposed of all, and culminating at last in blasphemous Antichrist. The reason is: Christ's kingdom *now* is not of this world (John 18:36); and only at the second advent of Christ does it become an external power of the world. **13. Son of man**—(See *Note,* Ezek. 2:1). Not merely Son of David, and King of Israel, but Head of restored *humanity* (corresponding to the world-wide horizon of Daniel's prophecy); the seed of the woman, crushing Antichrist, the seed of the serpent, according to the Protevangel in Paradise (Gen. 3). The Representative Man shall then realize the original destiny of man as Head of the creation (Gen. 1:26, 28); the center of unity to Israel and the Gentiles. The beast, which taken conjointly represents the four beasts, ascends from the sea (ch. 7:2; Rev. 13:1); the Son of man descends *from "heaven."* Satan, as the serpent, is the representative head of all that is bestial; man, by following the serpent, has become bestial. God must, therefore, become man, so that man may cease to be beastlike. Whoever rejects the incarnate God will be judged by the Son of man just because He is the Son of man (John 5:27). This title is always associated with His coming again, because the kingdom that then awaits Him is that which belongs to Him as the Saviour of man, the Restorer of the lost inheritance. "Son of man" expresses His VISIBLE state, formerly in His humiliation, hereafter in His exaltation. He "comes to the Ancient of days" to be invested with the kingdom. Cf. Psalm 110:2: "The Lord shall send the rod of thy strength [Messiah] out of Zion." This investiture was at His ascension "with the clouds of heaven" (Acts 1:9; 2:33, 34; Ps. 2:6-9; Matt. 28:18), which is a pledge of His return "in like manner" in the clouds" (Acts 1:11; Matt. 26:64), and "with clouds" (Rev. 1:7). The kingdom then was given to Him in *title* and *invisible* exercise; at His second coming it shall be in *visible* administration. He will vindicate it from the misrule of those who received it to hold for and under God, but who ignored His supremacy. The Father will assert His right by the Son, the heir, who will hold it for Him (Ezek. 1:27; Heb. 1:2; Rev. 19:13-16). TREGELLES thinks the investiture here *immediately precedes* Christ's coming forth; because He sits at God's right hand *until* His enemies are made His footstool, *then* the kingdom is given to the Son in actual investiture, and He comes to crush His so prepared footstool under His feet. But the words, "with the clouds," and the universal power actually, though invisibly, given Him then (Eph. 1:20-22), agree best with His investiture at the ascension, which, in the prophetic view that overleaps the interval of ages, is the precursor of His coming visibly to reign; no event of equal moment taking place in the interval. **15. body**—lit., "sheath": the body being the "sheath" of the soul. **17. kings**—i.e., kingdoms. Cf. vs. 23, "fourth kingdom"; ch. 2: 38; 8:20-22. Each of the four kings represents a dynasty. Nebuchadnezzar, Alexander, Antiochus, and Antichrist, though *individually* referred to, are representatives of characteristic tendencies. **18. the Most High**—the emphatic title of God in this prophecy, who delegates His power first to Israel; then to the Gentiles (ch. 2:37, 38) when Israel fails to realize the idea of the theocracy; lastly, to Messiah, who shall rule truly for God, taking it from the Gentile world powers, whose history is one of continual degeneracy culminating in the last of the kings, Antichrist. Here, in the interpretation, "the saints," but in the vision (vss. 13, 14), "the Son of man," takes the kingdom; for Christ and His people are one in suffering, and one in glory. TREGELLES translates, "most high places" (Eph. 1:3; 2:6). Though oppressed by the beast and little horn, they belong not to the earth from which the four beasts arise, but to the most high places. **19.** Balaam, an Aramean, dwelling on the Euphrates, at the be-

ADAM CLARKE

11. *I beheld then because of the voice* (or, *the beast will be destroyed because*) *of the great words which the horn spake . . . his body destroyed.* When the dominion was taken from the rest of the beasts, their bodies were not destroyed, but suffered to continue still in being; but when the dominion shall be taken away from this beast, his body shall be totally destroyed; because other kingdoms succeeded to those, but no other earthly kingdom shall succeed to this (Bishop Newton).

13. *One like the Son of man came with the clouds of heaven.* This most certainly points out the Lord Jesus, who took our nature upon Him that He might redeem us unto himself. To prove himself to be the Messiah, He applies, before the high priests, these words of the Prophet Daniel to himself, Matt. xxiv. 30.

14. *And there was given him dominion.* This also is applied to our Lord Jesus by himself after His resurrection, Matt. xxviii. 18. *His dominion is an everlasting dominion.* Christianity shall increase, and prevail to the end of the world. See the parallel passages in the margin.

15. *I Daniel was grieved.* The words in the original are uncommonly emphatic. "My spirit was grieved (or sickened) within its sheath (or scabbard)."

MATTHEW HENRY

2. Daniel understands the first three beasts, but concerning the fourth he desires to be better informed, *v.* 19.

But especially he desired to know what the *little horn* was, that *had eyes*, and a *mouth that spoke very great things*, *v.* 20. It was this horn that *made war with the saints, and prevailed against them*, *v.* 21.

It is time to ask, "What is the meaning of this? What is this same horn that shall prevail so far against the saints?" To this his interpreter answers (*v.* 23–25) that this *fourth beast* is a *fourth kingdom*, that *shall devour the whole earth*, or (as it may be read) *the whole land*. That the *ten horns are ten kings*, and the *little horn* is another king that shall subdue three kings, and shall be very abusive to God and his people. He shall *wear out the saints of the Most High.*

He shall *think to change times and laws*, to abolish all the ordinances and institutions of religion.

And in these daring attempts he shall for a time prosper and have success; they shall be given into his hand *until time, times, and half a time* (that is, for three years and a half).

JAMIESON, FAUSSET, BROWN

ginning of Israel's independent history, and Daniel at the close of it, prophetically exhibit to the hostile world powers Israel as triumphant over them at last, though the world powers of the East (Asshur) and the West (Chittim) carry all before them and afflict Eber (Israel) for a time (Num. 23:8-10, 28; 24:2, 7-9, 22-24). To Balaam's "Asshur" correspond Daniel's two eastern kingdoms, Babylon and Medo-Persia; to "Chittim," the two western kingdoms, Greece and Rome (cf. Gen. 10:4, 11, 22). In Babel, Nimrod the hunter (revolter) founds the first kingdom of the world (Gen. 10:8-13). The Babylonian world power takes up the thread interrupted at the building of Babel, and the kingdom of Nimrod. As at Babel, so in Babylon the world is united against God; Babylon, the first world power, thus becomes the type of the God-opposed world. The fourth monarchy consummates the evil; it is "diverse" from the others only in its more unlimited universality. The three first were not in the full sense universal monarchies. The fourth is; so in it the God-opposed principle finds its full development. All history moves within the Romanic, Germanic, and Slavonic nations; it shall continue so to Christ's second advent. The fourth monarchy represents universalism externally; Christianity, internally. Rome is Babylon fully developed. It is the world power corresponding in contrast to Christianity, and therefore contemporary with it (Matt. 13:38; Mark 1:15; Luke 2:1; Gal. 4:4). **20. look . . . more stout than . . . fellows**—viz., than that of the other horns. **21. made war with the saints**—persecuted the Church (Rev. 11:7; 13:7). **prevailed**—but not ultimately. The limit is marked by "until" (vs. 22). The little horn continues, *without intermission,* to persecute up to Christ's second advent (Rev. 17:12, 14; 19:19, 20). **22. Ancient of days came**—The title applied to the Father in vs. 13 is here applied to the Son; who is called "the everlasting Father" (Isa. 9:6). The Father is never said to "come"; it is the Son who *comes.* **judgment was given to . . . saints**—*Judgment* includes *rule*; "kingdom" in the end of this verse (I Cor. 6:2; Rev. 1:6, 5:10; 20:4). Christ first receives "judgment" and the "kingdom," then the saints with Him (vss. 13, 14). **24. ten horns**—answering to the ten "toes" (ch. 2:41). **out of this kingdom**—It is *out of* the fourth kingdom that ten others arise, whatever exterior territory any of them possess (Rev. 13:1; 17: 12). **rise after them**—yet contemporaneous with them; the ten are contemporaries. Antichrist rises after their rise, at first "little" (vs. 8); but after destroying three of the ten, he becomes greater than them all (vss. 20, 21). The three being gone, he is the eighth (cf. Rev. 17:11); a distinct head, and yet "of the seven." As the previous world kingdoms had their representative heads (Babylon, Nebuchadnezzar; Persia, Cyrus; Greece, Alexander), so the fourth kingdom and its Antichrists shall have their evil concentrated in the one final Antichrist. As Antiochus Epiphanes, the Antichrist of the third kingdom in ch. 8, was the personal enemy of God, so the final Antichrist of the fourth kingdom, his antitype. The Church has endured a pagan and a papal persecution; there remains for her an infidel persecution, general, purifying, and cementing [CECIL]. He will not merely, as Popery, *substitute* himself for Christ *in Christ's name,* but *"deny* the Father and the Son" (I John 2:22). The persecution is to continue *up to Christ's second coming* (vss. 21, 22); the horn of blasphemy cannot therefore be past; for now there is almost a general cessation of persecution. **25.** Three attributes of Antichrist are specified: (1) The highest worldly wisdom and civilization. (2) The uniting of the whole civilized world under his dominion. (3) Atheism, antitheism, and autotheism in its fullest development (I John 2:22). Therefore, not only is power taken from the fourth beast, as in the case of the other three, but God destroys it and the world power in general by a final judgment. The present external Christianity is to give place to an almost universal apostasy. **think**—lit., "carry within him as it were the burden of the thought." **change times**—the prerogative of God alone (ch. 2:21); blasphemously assumed by Antichrist. The "times and laws" here meant are those of religious ordinance; *stated times of feasts* [MAURER]. Perhaps there are included the *times assigned by God to the duration of kingdoms.* He shall set Himself above all that is called God (II Thess. 2:4), putting his own "will" above God's times and laws (ch. 11:36, 37). But the "times" of His wilfulness are limited for the elect's sake (Matt. 24:22). **they**—the saints. **given into his hand**—to be persecuted. **time . . . times and . . . dividing of time**—one year, two years, and half a year: 1260 days (Rev. 12:6, 14); forty-two months (Rev. 11:2,

ADAM CLARKE

19. *His nails of brass.* This is not mentioned in the seventh verse, where the description of the beast is given.

21. *The same horn made war with the saints, and prevailed against them.* Those who make Antiochus the little horn make the saints the Jewish people. Those who understand the popedom by it see this as referring to the cruel persecutions of the popes of Rome against the Waldenses and Albigenses, and the Protestant church in general.

25. *He shall speak great words against the most High.* "He shall speak as if he were God." So St. Jerome quotes from Symmachus. To none can this apply so well or so fully as to the popes of Rome. They have assumed infallibility, which belongs only to God. They profess to forgive sins, which belongs only to God. They profess to open and shut heaven, which belongs only to God. They profess to be higher than all the kings of the earth, which belongs only to God. And they go beyond God in pretending to loose whole nations from their oath of allegiance to their kings, when such kings do not please them! *And shall wear out the saints.* By wars, crusades, massacres, inquisitions, and persecutions of all kinds. What in this way have they not done against all those who have protested against their innovations, and refused to submit to their idolatrous worship? Witness the exterminating crusades published against the Waldenses and Albigenses. Witness John Huss, and Jerome of Prague. *And think to change times and laws.* Appointing fasts and feasts; canonizing persons whom he chooses to call saints; granting pardons and indulgences for sins; instituting new modes of worship utterly unknown to the Christian Church; new articles of faith; new rules of practice; and reversing, with pleasure, the laws both of God and man (Dodd). *Until a time and times and the dividing of time.* In prophetic language a *time* signifies a "year"; and a prophetic year has a year for each

MATTHEW HENRY

But at the end of that time the *judgment shall sit and take away his dominion* (*v.* 26), which he expounds (*v.* 11) of the beast being *slain and his body destroyed.* And (as Mr. Mede reads *v.* 12) *as to the rest of the beast*, the ten horns, especially the little *ruffling* horn, they had their dominion taken away. Now the question is, Who is this enemy? Interpreters are not agreed. Some will have the fourth kingdom to be that of the Seleucidae, and the little horn to be Antiochus, and show the accomplishment of all this in the history of the Maccabees; but others will have the fourth kingdom to be that of the Romans, and the *little horn* to be Julius Caesar, and the succeeding emperors (says Calvin), the antichrist, the papal kingdom. Others make the *little horn* to be the *Turkish empire*; so Luther, Vatablus, and others. Since prophecies sometimes have many fulfillings, I am willing to allow that they are both in the right, and that this prophecy has primary reference to the Syrian empire, and was intended for the encouragement of the Jews who suffered under Antiochus. But yet it has a further reference, and foretells the persecuting power in Rome, against the Christian religion. And St. John in his visions, which point primarily at Rome, has reference to these visions of Daniel.

3. He has a joyful prospect given him of God's kingdom among men, and its victory over all opposition at last. This is brought in abruptly (*v.* 18 and again *v.* 22), before it comes, in the course of the vision, to be interpreted, *v.* 26, 27. And this also refers, (1) To the prosperous days of the Jewish church, after it had weathered the storm under Antiochus. (2) To the setting up of the kingdom of the Messiah in the world by the preaching of his gospel. (3) To the second coming of Jesus Christ. *The Ancient of days shall come*, *v.* 22. God shall judge the world by his Son, to whom he has *committed all judgments. The judgment shall sit*, *v.* 26. God *judges in the earth*, both in wisdom and in equity. The *dominion* of the enemy shall be *taken away*, *v.* 26. All Christ's enemies shall be made his footstool. *Judgment is given to the saints of the Most High.* The apostles are entrusted with the preaching of a gospel by which the *world shall be judged.* That which is most insisted upon is that *the saints of the Most High shall take the kingdom, and possess the kingdom for ever*, *v.* 18. And again (*v.* 22), The *time came that the saints possessed the kingdom.* And again (*v.* 27), The *kingdom and dominion, and the greatness of the kingdom under the whole heavens, shall be given to the people of the saints of the Most High.* This intimates the spiritual dominion of the saints over their own lusts and corruptions, their victories over Satan and his temptations, and the triumphs of the martyrs over death and its terrors. It likewise promises that the gospel kingdom shall be set up, a kingdom of light, holiness, and love. The saints shall possess the kingdom for *ever, even for ever and ever*; and the reason is because he whose saints they are is the *Most High* and *his kingdom is an everlasting kingdom*, *v.* 27. *Because I live, you shall live also*, John xiv. 19. His kingdom is theirs.

JAMIESON, FAUSSET, BROWN

3). That literally three and a half years are to be the term of Antichrist's persecution is favored by ch. 4:16, 23, where the year-day theory would be impossible. If the Church, moreover, had been informed that 1260 years must elapse before the second advent, the attitude of expectancy which is inculcated (Luke 12:38; I Cor. 1:7; I Thess. 1:9, 10; II Pet. 3:12) on the ground of the uncertainty of the time, would be out of place. The original word for "time" denotes *a stated period* or *set feast;* or the interval from one set feast to its recurrence, i.e., a year [TREGELLES]; Leviticus 23:4, "seasons"; Leviticus 23:44, "feasts." The passages in favor of the year-day theory are Ezekiel 4:6, where each day of the forty during which Ezekiel lay on his right side is defined by God as meaning a year. Cf. Numbers 14:34, where a year of wandering in the wilderness was appointed for each day of the forty during which the spies searched Canaan; but the days were, in these two cases, merely the type or reason for the years, which were *announced as they were to be fulfilled.* In the prophetic part of Numbers 14:34 *years* are literal. If the year-day system was applied to them, they would be 14,400 years! In Ezekiel 4:4-6, if *day* meant *year,* Ezekiel would have lain on his right side forty years! The context here in vss. 24, 25, is not symbolical. Antichrist is no longer called a horn, but a *king* subduing three out of ten *kings* (no longer horns. vss. 7, 8). So in ch. 12:7, where "time, times, and half a time," again occurs, nothing symbolic occurs in the context. So that there is no reason why the three and a half years should be so. For the first four centuries the "days" were interpreted literally; a mystical meaning of the 1260 days then began. WALTER BRUTE first suggested the year-day theory in the end of the fourteenth century. The *seventy years* of the Babylonian captivity foretold by Jeremiah (Jer. 25:12; 29:10) were understood by Daniel (ch. 9:2) as literal years, not symbolical, which would have been 25,200 years! [TREGELLES]. It is possible that the year-day and day-day theories are *both* true. The seven (symbolical) times of the Gentile monarchies (Lev. 26:24) during Israel's casting off will end in the seven years of Antichrist. The 1260 years of papal misrule in the name of Christ may be represented by three and a half years of open Antichristianity and persecution before the millennium. Witnessing churches may be succeeded by witnessing individuals, the former occupying the longer, the latter the shorter period (Rev. 11:3). The beginning of the 1260 years is by ELLIOTT set at A.D. 529 or 533, when Justinian's edict acknowledged Pope John II to be head of the Church; by LUTHER, at 606, when Phocas confirmed Justinian's grant. But 752 is the most likely date, when the *temporal* dominion of the popes began by Pepin's grant to Stephen II (for Zachary, his predecessor's recognition of his title to France), confirmed by Charlemagne. For it was then first that the little horn plucked up three horns, and so became the prolongation of the fourth *secular* kingdom [NEWTON]. This would bring us down to about A.D. 2000, or the seventh thousand millenary from creation. But CLINTON makes about 1862 the seventh millenary, which may favor the dating from A.D. 529. **26. consume . . . destroy**—a twofold operation. Antichrist is to be *gradually* "consumed," as the Papacy has been consuming for 400 years past, and especially of late years. He is also to be "destroyed" *suddenly* by Christ at His coming; the fully developed man of sin (II Thess. 2:3) or false prophet making a last desperate effort in confederacy with the "beast" (Rev. 16:13, 14, 16) or secular power of the Roman empire (some conjecture Louis Napoleon): destroyed at Armageddon in Palestine. **27. greatness of the kingdom under . . . whole heaven**—The power, which those several kingdoms had possessed, shall all be conferred on Messiah's kingdom. "Under . . . heaven," shows it is a kingdom *on earth,* not in heaven. **people of . . . saints of . . . Most High**—"the people of the saints, or holy ones" (*Margin,* ch. 8:24): the Jews, the people to whom the saints stand in a peculiar relation. The saints are gathered out of Jews and Gentiles, but the stock of the Church is Jewish (Rom. 9:24; 11:24); God's faithfulness to this election Church is thus virtually faithfulness to Israel, and a pledge of their future national blessing. Christ confirms this fact, while withholding the date (Acts 1:6, 7). **everlasting kingdom**—If *everlasting,* how can the kingdom here refer to the millennial one? Answer: Daniel saw the whole time of future blessedness as *one period.* The clearer light of the New Testament distinguishes, in the whole period, the millennium and the time of the new heaven and new earth (cf. Rev. 20:4 with 21:1 and 22:5).

ADAM CLARKE

day. Three years and a half (a day standing for a year, as in chap. ix. 24) will amount to 1,260 years, if we reckon 30 days to each month, as the Jews do. If the papal power, as a horn or temporal power, be intended here, which is most likely (and we know that that power was given in 755 to Pope Stephen II by *Pepin,* king of France), counting 1,260 years from that, we are brought to A.D. 2015. But I neither lay stress upon nor draw conclusions from these dates. If the church of Rome will reform itself, it will then be the true Christian Church, and will never be destroyed. Let it throw aside all that is ritually Jewish, all that is heathen, all that which pretends to be of God and which is only of man, all doctrines that are not in the Bible, and all rites and ceremonies which are not of the appointment of Christ and His apostles; and then, all hail the once Roman, but now, after such a change, the holy, Catholic Church! Every true Protestant would wish rather the reform than the extinction of this church.

JOHN GILL:

Verse 26. "But the judgment shall sit." As in verse 10; the court shall sit, the Judge shall take the bench, and all things be prepared for the arraignment, trial, condemnation, and punishment, of the little horn or antichrist, when the above time is up; God the Father, the Ancient of Days, and Christ, said to be like the Son of Man, brought near to him, shall sit as Judges, attended by the holy angels: "and they shall take away his dominion, to consume and to destroy it unto the end"; either the angels, or rather the saints of the Most High; particularly the Christian princes, into whose hearts God will put it to hate the whore, eat her flesh, and burn her with fire; so that there shall be an utter end of antichrist; he shall be stripped of all his power and authority; his destruction will be inevitable and irrecoverable; he shall never come out of it; it shall continue to the end of the world, to the end of time.

Verse 27. "And the kingdom and dominion, and the greatness of the kingdom under the whole heaven, shall be given to the people of the saints of the Most High." Not only the dominion that shall be taken away from the little horn or antichrist, and from all the antichristian states, but the dominion of all others throughout all the earth, and under the whole heaven, shall be given to the people of God, and the true professors of faith in Christ. The kingdoms of this world will become Christ's, and Christian princes will be kings of them everywhere; and not only the royal power and authority will be vested with them, but all the grandeur and state belonging to them will be theirs; as well as all the saints in general shall reign in a spiritual manner with Christ, enjoying all ordinances, and all religious liberties, as well as civil, and be free from all persecutions. "Whose kingdom is an everlasting kingdom, and all dominions shall serve and obey him"; the people of the saints of the Most High, all shall be subject to them, all dominions, and the governors of them; or Christ the head of them, under and with whom they reign.—*Gill's Commentary*

MATTHEW HENRY

Daniel, in the close, tells us what impressions this vision made upon him; it overwhelmed his spirits to such a degree that his *countenance* was *changed*, but he *kept the matter in his heart*. Daniel kept *the matter in his heart*, with a design, not to keep it from the church, but to keep it for the church.

CHAPTER 8

Verses 1–14

I. The date of this vision, *v*. 1. It was *in the third year of the reign of Belshazzar*, his last year, as many reckon; so that this chapter should be before the fifth. That Daniel might not be surprised at the destruction of Babylon, now at hand. God gives him a foresight of the destruction of other kingdoms hereafter. And this vision puts him in mind of a former vision which *appeared to him at the first*, and is an explication and confirmation of it, and points at many of the same events.

II. The scene of this vision. The place where that was laid was in *Shushan the palace*, situated in the province of Elam, that part of Persia next to Babylon. Daniel was not there in person, for he was now in Babylon, a captive. But he was there in vision; as Ezekiel, when a captive in Babylon, was often brought, in the spirit, to the land of Israel. The soul may be at liberty when the body is in captivity; for, when we are bound, the Spirit of the Lord is not bound.

III. The vision itself.

1. He saw a *ram* with *two horns*, *v*. 3. This was the second monarchy, of which the kingdoms of Media and Persia were the two horns. The horns were *very high*; but that which came up last was the higher. The kingdom of Persia, which rose last, in Cyrus, became more eminent than that of the Medes.

2. He saw this *ram pushing* all about him with his horns (*v*. 4), *westward* (towards Babylon, Syria, Greece, and Asia the less), *northward* (towards the Lydians, Armenians, and Scythians), and *southward* (towards Arabia, Ethiopia, and Egypt), for all these nations did the Persian empire make attempts upon for the enlarging of their dominion. And at last he became so powerful that *no beasts might stand before him*. The kings of Persia did according *to their will*, and *became great*.

3. He was considering the *ram* and, *behold*, *a he-goat came*, *v*. 5. This was Alexander the Great, the son of Philip king of Macedonia. He *came from the west*, from Greece. He did in effect conquer the world. He *touched not the ground*, so lightly did he move; that is, he met with little or no opposition. This *he-goat*, or buck, had a *notable horn between his eyes*. He had strength, and knew his own strength. Alexander pushed his conquests on so fast, and with so much fury, that none had courage to make a stand. This *he-goat* came to the *ram that had two horns*, *v*. 6. Alexander with his victorious army attacked the kingdom of Persia, an army consisting of no more than 30,000 foot and 5,000 horse. Alexander with his army came up with Darius Codomannus, then emperor of Persia, being *moved with choler against him*, *v*. 7. Alexander was too hard for him whenever he engaged him, *smote him*, *cast him down to the ground*, and *stamped upon him*, which three expressions some think, refer to the three famous victories that Alexander obtained over Darius, at Granicus, at Issus, and at Arbela, by which he was at length totally routed, having, in the last battle, had 600,000 men killed, so that Alexander became absolute master of all the Persian empire, *broke his two horns*, the kingdoms of Media and Persia.

4. He saw the he-goat made very considerable; but the *great horn*, that had done all this execution, *was broken*, *v*. 8. Alexander was twenty years old when

JAMIESON, FAUSSET, BROWN

Christ's kingdom is "everlasting." Not even the last judgment shall end it, but only give it a more glorious appearance, the new Jerusalem coming down from God out of heaven, with the throne of God and the Lamb in it (cf. Rev. 5:9, 10; 11:15). **28. cogitations . . . troubled me**—showing that the Holy Spirit intended much more to be understood by Daniel's words than Daniel himself understood. We are not to limit the significance of prophecies to what the prophets themselves understood (I Pet. 1: 11, 12).

CHAPTER 8

Vss. 1-27. Vision of the Ram and He-goat: the 2300 Days of the Sanctuary Being Trodden Down. With this chapter the Hebrew part of the book begins and continues to be the language of the remainder; the visions relating wholly to the Jews and Jerusalem. The scene here narrows from world-wide prophecies to those affecting the one covenant people in the five centuries between the exile and the advent. Antichrist, like Christ, has a more immediate future, as well as one more remote. The vision, ch. 8, begins, and that, chs. 10-12, concludes, the account of the Antichrist of the third kingdom. Between the two visions ch. 9 is inserted, as to Messiah and the covenant people at the end of the half millennium (seventy weeks of years). **1. vision**—a higher kind of revelation than a dream. **after that . . . at the first**—that in ch. 7:1. **2. Shushan**—Susa. Though then comparatively insignificant, it was destined to be the capital of Persia after Cyrus' time. Therefore Daniel is transported into it, as being the capital of the kingdom signified by the two-horned ram (Neh. 1:1; Esther 1:2-5). **Elam**—west of Persia proper, east of Babylonia, south of Media. Daniel was not present there personally, but *in vision*. **Ulai**—called in Pliny Eulœus; by the Greeks, Choaspes. Now Kerah, or Karasu. So in ch. 10:4 he receives a vision near another river, the Hiddekel. So Ezekiel (Ezek. 1:1) at the Chebar. Perhaps because synagogues used to be built near rivers, as before praying they washed their hands in the water [Rosenmuller], (Ps. 137:1). **3.** *two* **horns**—The *"two"* ought not to be in italics, as if it were not in the original; for it is expressed by the *Hebrew* dual. "Horn" in the East is the symbol of power and royalty. **one . . . higher than . . . other . . . the higher came up last**—Persia, which was of little note till Cyrus' time, became then ascendant over Media, the more ancient kingdom. Darius was sixty-two years old (ch. 5:31) when he began to reign; during his short reign of two years, being a weak king (ch. 6), the government was almost entirely in Cyrus' hands. Hence Herodotus does not mention Darius; but Xenophon does under the name of Cyaxares II. The "ram" here corresponds to the "bear" (ch. 7:5), symbolizing *clumsy firmness*. The king of Persia wore a jewelled ram's head of gold instead of a diadem, such as are seen on the pillars at Persepolis. Also the *Hebrew* for "ram" springs from the same root as "Elam," or Persia [Newton]. The "one horn higher than the other" answers to the bear "raising itself *on one side*" (cf. *Note*, ch. 7:5). **4. ram pushing westward**—Persia conquered westward Babylon, Mesopotamia, Syria, Asia Minor. **northward**—Colchis, Armenia, Iberia, and the dwellers on the Caspian Sea. **southward**—Judea, Egypt, Ethiopia, Libya; also India, under Darius. He does not say *eastward*, for the Persians themselves came from the east (Isa. 46:11). **did according to his will**—(Ch. 11:3, 16; cf. ch. 5:19). **5. he-goat**—Græco-Macedonia. **notable horn**—Alexander. "Touched not . . . ground," implies the incredible swiftness of his conquests; he overran the world in less than twelve years. The he-goat answers to the leopard (ch. 7:6). Caranus, the first king of Macedonia, was said to have been led by *goats* to Edessa, which he made the seat of his kingdom, and called Æge, i.e., "goat-city." **6. standing before the river**—Ulai. It was at the "river" Granicus that Alexander fought his first victorious battle against Darius, 334 B.C. **7. moved with choler**—Alexander represented the concentrated wrath of Greece against Persia for the Persian invasions of Greece; also for the Persian cruelties to Greeks, and Darius' attempts to seduce Alexander's soldiers to treachery [Newton]. **stamped upon him**—In 331 B.C. he defeated Darius Codomanus, and in 330 B.C. burned Persepolis and completed the conquest of Persia. **none . . . could deliver**—Not the immense hosts of Persia could save it from the small army of Alexander (Ps. 33:16). **8. when he was strong . . . great horn was broken**—The empire was in full strength at Alexander's death by fever at Babylon,

ADAM CLARKE

CHAPTER 8

1. *In the third year of the reign of . . . Belshazzar*. We now come once more to the Hebrew, the Chaldee part of the book being finished. As the Chaldeans had a particular interest in both the history and prophecies from chap. ii. 4 to the end of chap. vii, the whole is written in Chaldee. But as the prophecies which remain concern times posterior to the Chaldean monarchy, and principally relate to the Church and people of God generally, they are written in the Hebrew language, this being the tongue in which God chose to reveal all His counsels given under the Old Testament relative to the New.

2. *I saw in a vision*. Daniel was at this time in Shushan, which appears to have been a strong place, where the kings of Persia had their summer residence. It was the capital of the province of Elam, which was most probably added to the Chaldean territories by Nebuchadnezzar; see Jer. xlix. 34-35. Here was Daniel's ordinary residence; and though here at this time, he, in vision, saw himself on the banks of the river Ulai. This is the same as the river Euleus, which divided Shushan or Susiana from Elymais.

3. *A ram which had two horns*. In the former vision there were four beasts, pointing out four empires; in this we have but two, as only two empires are concerned here, viz., the Grecian and the Persian. The Babylonish empire is not mentioned; its fate was before decided, and it was now at its close. By the *ram*, the empire of the Medes and Persians was pointed out, as explained by the angel Gabriel, v. 20; and particularly Cyrus, who was the founder of that empire. A *ram* was the symbol of the Persians; and a ram's head with two horns, one higher than the other, appears as such in different parts of the ruins of Persepolis. This ram had two horns; that is, two kingdoms, viz., Media and Persia; but one was higher than the other, and the higher came up last. Media, signified by the shorter horn, was the more ancient of the two kingdoms. Persia, the higher horn, had come up but lately, and was of little historic or political consequence till the time of Cyrus. But in the reigns of this prince and his immediate successors, Persia attained a political consequence greatly superior to that possessed at any time by the kingdom of Media; therefore it is said to have been the higher, and to have come up last.

4. *I saw the ram pushing westward*. The Persians, who are signified by the ram, as well as their founder, Cyrus, pushed their conquests west, north, and south. The principal theatre of their wars, says Calmet, was against the Scythians, northward; against the Greeks, westward; and against the Egyptians, southward. *He did according to his will*. There was no other nation at that time that could stay the progress of the Persian arms.

5. *Behold an he goat*. This was Alexander the Great; and a goat was a very proper symbol of the Grecian or Macedonian people. *Came from the west*. Europe lies westward of Asia. *On the face of the whole earth*. Carrying everything before him. *Touched not the ground*. Seemed to fly from conquest to conquest. By the time Alexander was thirty years of age he had conquered all Asia: and, because of the rapidity of his conquests, he is represented as a leopard with four wings, in the preceding vision.

6. *And he came to the ram*. This and the following verse give an account of the overthrow of the Persian empire by Alexander and ran unto him in the fury of his power. The conflicts between the Greeks and the Persians were excessively severe. Alexander first

MATTHEW HENRY

he began his wars. When he was twenty-six he conquered Darius, and became master of the whole Persian empire; but when he was thirty-two *years of age*, in his full strength, he was *broken*. He died of a drunken surfeit, or, as some suspect, by poison, and left no child living.

5. He saw this kingdom divided into four parts, and instead of one great horn there came up *four notable ones*, Alexander's four captains. These *four notable horns* were towards the *four winds of heaven*, the kingdoms of Syria and Egypt, Asia and Greece.

6. He saw a *little horn* which became a great persecutor of the church and people of God; *ch*. xi. 30, &c. All agree that this was *Antiochus Epiphanes*. He is called here (as before. *ch*. vii. 8) a *little horn*, because he was in origin contemptible; there were others between him and the kingdom, and he had been a hostage and prisoner at Rome, whence he made his escape, and got the kingdom.

He seized Egypt, and invaded Persia and Armenia. But that which is here noted is the mischief that he did to the Jews. (1) He set himself against *the pleasant land*, the land of Israel. Mount Zion was *beautiful for situation*, and the *joy of the whole earth*, Ps. xlviii. 2. We reckon that a pleasant place which is a holy place, in which God dwells, and where we may have opportunity of communing with him. (2) He fought against the *host of heaven*, that is, the people of God, the church-militant here on earth.

(3) He *cast down some of the host to the ground, and stamped upon them*. Some of those most eminent in church and state, burning and shining lights in their generation, he either forced to comply with his idolatries or put them to death, as good old Eleazar, and the *seven brethren*, whom he put to death with cruel tortures, because they would not eat swine's flesh, 2 Mac. vi. 7. (4) He *magnified himself even to the prince of the host*. He set himself against the high priest, Onias, or against God himself. (5) He *took away the daily sacrifice*. The morning and evening lamb, which God appointed to be offered upon his altar, Antiochus forbade. (6) He *cast down the place of his sanctuary*. He did not burn

JAMIESON, FAUSSET, BROWN

and seemed then least likely to fall. Yet it was then "broken." His natural brother, Philip Aridœus, and his two sons, Alexander Ægus and Hercules, in fifteen months were murdered. **four . . . toward . . . four winds**—Seleucus, in the east, obtained Syria, Babylonia, Media, etc.; Cassander, in the west, Macedon Thessaly, Greece; Ptolemy, in the south, Egypt, Cyprus, etc.; Lysimachus, in the north, Thrace, Cappadocia, and the north parts of Asia Minor. **9. little horn**—not to be confounded with the little horn of the fourth kingdom in ch. 7:8. The little horn in ch. 7 comes as an eleventh horn after ten preceding horns. In ch. 8 it is not an independent fifth horn, after the four previous ones, but it arises out of one of the four existing horns. This horn is explained (vs. 23) to be "a king of fierce countenance," etc. Antiochus Epiphanes is meant. Greece with all its refinement produces the first, i.e., the Old Testament Antichrist. Antiochus had an extraordinarly love of art, which expressed itself in grand temples. He wished to substitute Zeus Olympius for Jehovah at Jerusalem. Thus first heathen civilization from below, and revealed religion from above, came into collision. Identifying himself with Jupiter, his aim was to make *his own* worship universal (cf. vs. 25 with ch. 11:36); so mad was he in this that he was called Epimanes (maniac) instead of Epiphanes. None of the previous world rulers, Nebuchadnezzar (ch. 4:31-34), Darius (ch. 6:27, 28), Cyrus (Ezra 1:2-4), Artaxerxes Longimanus (Ezra 7:12), had systematically opposed the Jews' religious worship. Hence the need of prophecy to prepare them for Antiochus. The struggle of the Maccabees was a fruit of Daniel's prophecy (I Maccabees 2:59). He is the forerunner of the final Antichrist, standing in the same relation to the first advent of Christ that Antichrist does to His second coming. The sins in Israel which gave rise to the Greek Antichrist were that some Jews adopted Hellenic customs (cf. ch. 11:30, 32), erecting theaters, and regarding all religions alike, sacrificing to Jehovah, but at the same time sending money for sacrifices to Hercules. Such shall be the state of the world when ripe for Antichrist. At vs. 9 and vs. 23 the description passes from the literal Antiochus to features which, though partially attributed to him, hold good in their fullest sense only of his antitype, the New Testament Antichrist. The Mohammedan Antichrist may also be included; answering to the Euphratean (Turk) horsemen (Rev. 9:14-21), loosed "an hour, a day, a month, a year" (391 years, in the year-day theory), to scourge corrupted idolatrous Christianity. In A.D. 637 the Saracen Moslem mosque of Omar was founded on the site of the temple, "treading under foot the sanctuary" (vss. 11-13); and there it still remains. The first conquest of the Turks over Christians was in A.D. 1281; and 391 years after they reached their zenith of power and began to decline, Sobieski defeating them at Vienna. Mohammed II, called "the conqueror," reigned A.D. 1451-1481, in which period Constantinople fell; 391 years after brings us to our own day, in which Turkey's fall is imminent. **waxed . . . great, toward . . . south**—(ch. 11:25). Antiochus fought against Ptolemy Philometer and Egypt, i.e., the south. **toward the east**—He fought against those who attempted a change of government in Persia. **toward the pleasant land**—Judea, "the glorious land" (ch. 11:16, 41, 45; cf. Ps. 48:2; Ezek. 20:6, 15). Its chief *pleasantness* consists in its being God's chosen land (Ps. 132:13; Jer. 3:19). Into it Antiochus made his inroad after his return from Egypt. **10. great, even to . . . host of heaven**—explained in vs. 24, "the mighty and holy people," i.e., the Jews (ch. 7:21) and their priests (cf. Isa. 24:21). The Levites' service is called "a *warfare*" (*Margin*, Num. 8:24, 25). Great civil and religious powers are symbolized by "stars" (Matt. 24:29). See I Maccabees 1:25, etc.; 2:35, etc.; 5:2, 12, 13. TREGELLES refers "stars" to those Jews whose portion from God is heavenly glory (ch. 12:3), being believers in Him who is above at God's right hand: not the blinded Jews. **cast . . . stars to the ground**—So Babel, as type of Antichrist, is described (Isa. 14: 13, 14), "I will exalt my throne above the stars of God." Cf. Revelation 12:4; II Maccabees 9:10, as to Antiochus. **11. to the prince of the host**—i.e., God Himself, the Lord of Sabaoth, the hosts in heaven and earth, stars, angels, and earthly ministers. So vs. 25, "he shall stand up against the *Prince of princes*"; "against the God of gods" (ch. 11:36; cf. ch. 7:8). He not only opposes God's ancient people, but also God Himself. **daily sacrifice**—offered morning and evening (Exod. 29:38, 39). **taken away**—by Antiochus (I Maccabees 1:20-50). **sanctuary . . . cast down**—Though robbed of its

ADAM CLARKE

vanquished the generals of Darius, at the river Granicus, in Phrygia; he next attacked and totally routed Darius, at the straits of Issus, in Cilicia; and afterwards at the plains of Arbela, in Assyria.

7. *And brake his two horns.* Subdued Persia and Media; sacked and burnt the royal city of Persepolis, the capital of the Persian empire and, even in its ruins, one of the wonders of the world to the present day. This he did because "he was moved with choler" against Darius, who had endeavored to draw off his captains with bribes, and had labored to induce some of his friends to assassinate him. Alexander, finding this, would listen to no proposals of peace, and was determined never to rest till he had destroyed Darius and his whole empire. In Media, Darius was seized and made prisoner by some of his own treacherous subjects, and afterwards basely murdered. *He cast him down to the ground, and stamped upon him.* Totally destroyed the family, and overturned the whole monarchy.

8. *The he goat waxed very . . . strong.* He had subdued nearly the whole of the then known world. *The great horn was broken.* Alexander died in the height of his conquests, when he was but about thirty-three years of age. His natural brother, Philip Aridaeus, and his two sons, Alexander Aegus and Hercules, kept up the show and name of the Macedonian kingdom for a time, but they were all murdered within fifteen years; and thus the great horn, the Macedonian kingdom, was broken, Alexander's family being now cut off. *And for it came up four notable ones.* The regal family being all dead, the governors of provinces usurped the title of kings; and Antigonus, one of them, being slain at the battle of Ipsus, they were reduced to four, as we have already seen: (1) Seleucus, who had Syria and Babylon, from whom came the *Seleucidae*, famous in history; (2) Lysimachus, who had Asia Minor; (3) Ptolemy, son of Lagus, who had Egypt; and (4) Cassander, who had Greece and the neighboring countries. These held dominion towards the four winds of heaven. Cassander had the western parts, Lysimachus had the northern regions, Ptolemy possessed the southern countries, and Seleucus had the eastern provinces.

9. *Out of one of them came forth a little horn.* Some think that Antiochus Epiphanes is meant.

Toward the pleasant land. Judea, so called in Ps. cvi. 24; Jer. iii. 19; Dan. xi. 16, 41.

10. *The host of heaven.* The Jewish hierarchy. *The stars*, the priests and Levites. The powers or *host of heaven* are probably intended by our Lord, Matt. xxiv. 29, to signify the whole Jewish hierarchy.

MATTHEW HENRY

the temple, but made it the temple of Jupiter Olympus, and set up his image in it.

He also *cast down the truth to the ground,* trampled upon the book of the law, and burnt it. God would not have permitted it if his people had not provoked him to do so. It is *by reason of transgression,* the transgression of Israel, that Antiochus is employed to give them all this trouble. The great transgression of the Jews after the captivity was a contempt and profanation of the holy things, *snuffing* at the service of God, *bringing the torn and the lame for sacrifice,* as if the *table of the Lord* were a *contemptible* thing (Mal. i. 7, 8, &c.), and therefore God sent Antiochus to *take away the daily sacrifice* and *cast down the place of his sanctuary.* 7. He heard the time of this calamity limited, *how long it should last,* that, when they had no more any *prophets to tell them how long,* they might have this prophecy to give them a prospect of deliverance. The question was asked: "*How long shall be the vision concerning the daily sacrifice?* How long shall the prohibition of it continue?"

The answer was given to Daniel, because for his sake the question was asked: *He said unto me, v.* 14. Christ assures him that the trouble shall end; it shall continue 2,300 *days and no longer,* so many *evenings and mornings.* Understand them of so many natural days; 2,300 days make *six years* and *three months,* and about eighteen days; and just so long they reckon from the defection of the people, procured by Menelaus the high priest in the 142nd year of the kingdom of the Seleucidae, the sixth month of that year, and the 6th day of the month (so Josephus dates it), to the cleansing of the sanctuary, and the re-establishment of religion among them, which was in the 148th year, the 9th month, and the 25th *day of the month,* 1 Mac. iv. 52.

Verses 15–27

I. Daniel's earnest desire to have this vision explained to him (*v.* 15): *I sought the meaning.*

II. One *in the appearance of a man* (who, some think, was Christ himself), orders Gabriel to *make Daniel understand this vision.*

III. The consternation that Daniel was in upon the approach of his instructor (*v.* 17): *When he came near I was afraid.* Prostrate upon the ground, he *fell into a deep sleep* (*v.* 18).

IV. The relief which the angel gave to Daniel. 1. He *touched him,* and *set him upon his feet, v.* 18. He promised to inform him: "*Understand, O son of man! v.* 17. Thou shalt understand, if thou wilt but apply thy mind to understand."

JAMIESON, FAUSSET, BROWN

treasures, it was not strictly "cast down" by Antiochus. So that a fuller accomplishment is future. Antiochus took away the daily sacrifice for a few years; the Romans, for many ages, and "cast down" the temple; and Antichrist, in connection with Rome, the fourth kingdom, shall do so again after the Jews in their own land, still unbelieving, shall have rebuilt the temple, and restored the Mosaic ritual: God giving them up to him "by reason of transgression" (vs. 12), i.e., not owning the worship so rendered [TREGELLES]; and then the opposition of the horn to the "truth" is especially mentioned. **12. an host**—rather, "*the* host was given *up* to him," i.e., *the holy people* were given into his hands. So in vs. 10 "the host" is used; and again in vs. 13, where also "give" is used as here for *"giving up"* for destruction (cf. ch. 11:6) [MAURER]. **against . . . daily sacrifice**—rather (the host was given up for him to tread upon), *"together* with the daily sacrifice" (cf. vs. 13). **by reason of transgression**—I Maccabees 1:11-16 traces all the calamities suffered under Antiochus to the *transgression* of certain Jews who introduced heathen customs into Jerusalem just before. But *transgression* was not *at the full* (vs. 23) under Antiochus; for Onias the high priest administered the laws in godliness at the time (II Maccabees 3:1). Therefore the "transgression" must refer to that of the Jews hereafter restored to Palestine in unbelief. **the truth**—the worship of the true God. Isaiah 59:14, "Truth is fallen in the street." **practised, and prospered**—Whatever he undertook succeeded (vs. 4; ch. 11:28, 36). **13. that certain saint**—Daniel did not know the names of these two holy angels, but saw only that one was speaking to the other. **How long shall be the vision** *concerning* . . . **daily sacrifice**—How long shall the daily sacrifice be suspended? **transgression of desolation—lit.,** "making desolate," i.e., Antiochus' *desolating profanation* of the temple (ch. 11:31; 12:11). Cf. as to Rome and the last Antichrist, Matthew 24:15. **14. unto me**—The answer is to *Daniel,* not to the inquirer, for the latter had asked in Daniel's name; as vice versa the saint or angel (Job 15:15; Ps. 89:6, 7) speaks of the vision granted to Daniel, as if it had been granted to himself. For holy men are in Scripture represented as having attendant angels, with whom they are in a way identified in interests. If the conversation had been limited to the angels, it could have been of no use to us. But God conveys it to prophetical men, for our good, through the ministry of angels. **two thousand . . . three hundred days**—lit., "mornings and evenings," specified in connection with the *morning and evening* sacrifice. Cf. Genesis 1:5. Six years and 110 days. This includes not only the three and a half years during which the daily sacrifice was *forbidden* by Antiochus (JOSEPHUS, B. J. 1. 1. sec. 1), but the whole series of events whereby it was practically interrupted: beginning with the "little horn waxing great toward the pleasant land," and "casting down some of the host" (vss. 9, 10); viz., when in 171 B.C., or the month Sivan in the year 142 of the era of the Seleucidæ, the sacrifices began to be neglected, owing to the high priest Jason introducing at Jerusalem Grecian customs and amusements, the palæstra and gymnasium; ending with the death of Antiochus, 165 B.C., or the month Shebath, in the year 148 of the Seleucid era. Cf. I Maccabees 1:11-15; II Maccabees 4:9, etc. The reason for the greater minuteness of historical facts and dates, given in Daniel's prophecies, than in those of the New Testament, is that Israel, not having yet the clear views which Christians have of immortality and the heavenly inheritance, could only be directed to the earthly future: for it was on earth the looked-for Messiah was to appear, and the sum and subject of Old Testament prophecy was *the kingdom of God upon earth.* The minuteness of the revelation of Israel's earthly destiny was to compensate for the absence, in the Old Testament, of views of heavenly glory. Thus, in ch. 9, the times of Messiah are foretold to the very year; in ch. 8 the times of Antiochus, even to the day; and in ch. 11 the Syro-Egyptian struggles in most minute detail. **cleansed**—lit., "justified," vindicated from profanation. Judas Maccabeus celebrated the feast of dedication after the cleansing, on the twenty-fifth of the ninth month, Kisleu (I Maccabees 4:51-58; II Maccabees 10:1-7; John 10:22). As to the antitypical dedication of the new temple, see Ezekiel 43, etc.; also Amos 9:11, 12. **16. Gabriel**—meaning, "the strength of God." **17. the time of the end**—so vs. 19; ch. 11:35, 36, 40. The event being to take place at "the time of the end" makes it likely that the Antichrist ultimately referred to (besides the immediate reference to Antiochus) in this chapter, and the one in ch. 7:8, are one and the

ADAM CLARKE

F. B. MEYER:

God's sanctuary dishonored (8:1–14). At Shushan, in the palace, by the river Ulai, the prophet beheld in vision the attack which would subsequently be made on the Medo-Persian kingdom by Alexander. The great horn which was broken is, of course, Alexander, and the four notable ones are his four generals who after his death divided up his conquests. The little horn is referred by many to Antiochus, whose conflict with the Maccabees was one of the most significant in later Jewish history. Others refer it to Mohammed and his followers, who have reigned over the same regions. In this case the little horn would stand for the eastern apostasy as distinguished from the western, which is said to be represented by the little horn of the fourth beast, 7:8. The Books of the Maccabees, included in the Apocrypha, should be studied to understand more clearly the history behind vv. 11, 12. The explanation of these obscure verses is also given in vv. 24, 25. Antiochus was obsessed with hatred against the spiritual worship of the Jews and their refusal to admit his image into the Temple. He stopped their sacrifices, though they were restored for a season, to be finally suspended during the present age. The day for a year system, v. 14, may refer to the desolations of the Turkish or Ottoman Empire, of which Antiochus was the representative.

—*Bible Commentary*

14. *Unto two thousand and three hundred days.* Though literally it be 2,300 evenings and mornings, yet I think the prophetic day should be understood here, as in other parts of this prophet, and must signify so many years. If we date these years from the vision of the he-goat (Alexander's invading Asia) this was 334 B.C.; and 2,300 years from that time will reach to A.D. 1966.

MATTHEW HENRY

He assures him that he shall be made to know *what shall be in the last end of the indignation*, *v.* 19. Let it be a comfort to those who live to see these calamitous times that there shall be an end of them; *the indignation shall cease* (Isa. x. 25); it *shall be overpast*, Isa. xxvi. 20. Good will be brought out of it. He tells him (*v.* 17), "*At the time of the end shall be the vision;* when the last end of the indignation comes, when the course of this providence is completed, then the vision shall be made plain and intelligible by the event."

V. The exposition which he gave him of the vision.

1. Concerning the two monarchies of Persia and Greece, *v.* 20–22. The *ram* signified the succession of the kings of Media and Persia; the *rough goat* signified the kings of Greece; the *great horn* was Alexander; the *four horns* that rose in his room were the four kingdoms of which we read, *v.* 8. Josephus relates that when Alexander had taken Tyre, and was upon his march to Jerusalem Jaddas, then high priest, fearing his rage, had recourse to God by prayer, and was warned in a dream that upon Alexander's approach he should open the gates of the city, and that he and the rest of the priests should go forth to meet him in their habits, and all the people in white. Alexander, seeing this company at a distance, went alone to the high priest, and, having prostrated himself, saluted him; and, being asked by one of his own captains why he did so, he said that while he was yet in Macedon, musing on the conquest of Asia, there appeared to him a man thus attired, who invited him into Asia, and assured him of success in the conquest of it. The priests led him to the temple, where he offered sacrifice to the God of Israel as they directed him; and they showed him this book of the prophet Daniel, where it was foretold that a Grecian should destroy the Persians, which cheered him in the expedition against Darius. Hereupon he took the Jews and their religion under his protection, promised to be kind to those of their religion in Babylon and Media, whither he was now marching. *Joseph. lib.* 11.

2. Concerning Antiochus, and his oppression of the Jews. This is said to be in the *latter time of the* kingdom of the Greeks, *when the transgressors are come to the full* (*v.* 23), He shall be a *king of fierce countenance*, neither fearing God nor regarding man, *understanding dark sentences*, or (rather) *versed in dark practices*, the *hidden things of dishonesty*. He shall make havoc of the nations: *His power shall be mighty*, bearing down all before it (*v.* 24), by the assistance of his allies Eumenes and Attalus, partly by the baseness and treachery of many of the Jews. The princes of Egypt cannot stand before him with all their forces. He destroys the *holy people*, or *the people of the holy ones*; their sacred character does not deter him. He will gain this success by *craft* (*v.* 25), by deceit, and serpentine subtlety: He shall *cause craft to prosper*; he shall gain his point by the art of wheedling. *By peace he shall destroy many*, as others do by war; under the pretence of treaties, leagues, and alliances, he shall trick them into subjection to him. Sometimes what a nation truly brave has gained in a righteous war a nation truly base has regained in a treacherous peace. *He shall magnify himself in his heart*, so that he shall *stand up against the Prince of princes*, that is, against God himself. He will profane his temple and altar, and persecute his worshippers. The ruin that he shall be brought to at last: *He shall be broken without hand*. He shall not be slain in war, nor shall he be assassinated, but he shall fall into the hand of the living God and die. He, hearing that the Jews had cast the image of Jupiter Olympius out of the temple, where he had placed it, was so enraged that he vowed he would make Jerusalem *a common burial-place*, but no sooner had he spoken these proud words than he was struck with an incurable plague. He continued in this misery. At first he persisted in his menaces against the Jews; but at length, despairing of his recovery, he acknowledged the injuries he had done to the Jews and his profaning the temple at Jerusalem. Then he wrote courteous letters, and vowed that if he recovered he would let them have the free exercise of their religion. But, finding his disease grow upon him, he said, *It is meet to submit to God, and for man who is mortal not to set himself in competition with God*, and so died in a strange land, on the mountains of Pacata near Babylon.

VI. Here is the conclusion of this vision, and the charge given to Daniel to keep it private for the present: *Shut thou up the vision; for it shall be for many days*. Let it be kept for the generations that should live about the time of the accomplishment of it, for to them it would be most serviceable.

JAMIESON, FAUSSET, BROWN

same. The objection that the one in ch. 7 springs out of the ten divisions of the Roman earth, the fourth kingdom, the one in ch. 8 and ch. 11 from one of the four divisions of the third kingdom, Greece, is answered thus: The four divisions of the Grecian empire, having become parts of the Roman empire, shall at the end form four of its ten final divisions [TREGELLES]. However, the origin from one of the four parts of the third kingdom may be *limited to Antiochus*, the immediate subject of ch. 8 and ch. 11, while the ulterior typical reference of these chapters (viz., Antichrist) may belong to one of the ten Roman divisions, not *necessarily* one formerly of the four of the third kingdom. The event will tell. "Time of the end" may apply to the time of Antiochus. For it is the prophetic phrase for the time of fulfilment, seen always at the end of the prophetic horizon (Gen. 49:1; Num. 24:14). **19. the last end of the indignation**—God's displeasure against the Jews for their sins. For their comfort they are told, the calamities about to come are not to be for ever. The "time" is limited (ch. 9:27; 11:27, 35, 36; 12:7; Hab. 2:3). **21. the first king**—Philip was king of Macedon before Alexander, but the latter was the first who, as a generalissimo of Greece, subdued the Persian empire. **22. not in his power**—not with the power which Alexander possessed [MAURER]. An empire united, as under Alexander, is more powerful than one divided, as under the four Diadochi.

23. transgressors are come to the full—This does not hold good of the times of Antiochus, but of the closing times of the Christian era. Cf. Luke 18:8, and II Timothy 3: 1-9, as to the wickedness of the world in general just before Christ's second coming. *Israel's* guilt, too, shall then be at the full, when they who rejected Christ shall receive Antichrist; fulfilling Jesus' words, "I am come in My Father's name, and ye receive Me not; if another shall come in his own name, him ye will receive" (cf. Gen. 15:16; Matt. 23:32; I Thess. 2:16). **of fierce countenance**—(Deut. 28:50); one who will spare neither old nor young. **understanding dark sentences**—rather, "artifices" [GESENIUS]. Antiochus made himself master of Egypt and Jerusalem successively by *craft* (I Maccabees 1:30, etc.; II Maccabees 5:24, etc.). **24. not by his own power**—which in the beginning was "little" (vs. 9; ch. 7:8); but by gaining over others through craft, the once *little* horn became "mighty" (cf. vs. 25; ch. 11:23). To be fully realized by Antichrist. He shall act by the power of Satan, who shall then be permitted to work through him in unrestricted license, such as he has not now (Rev. 13:2; hence the ten kingdoms shall give the beast their power (II Thess. 2:9-12; Rev. 17:13). **prosper and practise**—prosper in all that he attempts (vs. 12). **holy people**—His persecutions are especially directed against the *Jews*. **25. by peace**—by pretending "peace" and friendship; *in the midst of security* [GESENIUS], suddenly striking his blow (cf. *Note*, Jer. 15:8). "A spoiler *at noon-day*." **also . . . against the Prince of princes**—not merely against the Jews (vs. 11; ch. 11:36). **broken without hand**—by God's special visitation. The stone "cut out of the mountain without hands," i.e., Christ is to smite the world-power image *on his feet* (ch. 2:34), i.e., in its last development (cf. ch. 7:11). Antiochus' horrible death by worms and ulcers, when on his way to Judea, intending to take vengeance for the defeat of his armies by the Maccabees, was a primary fulfilment, foreshadowing God's judgment on the last enemy of the Jewish Church. **26. shut . . . up . . . vision**—implying the vision was *not to be understood* for the present. In Revelation 22:10 it is said, "*Seal not* the vision, for the time is at hand." What in Daniel's time was hidden was more fully explained in Revelation, and as the time draws nearer, it will be clearer still. **it shall be for many days**—It refers to remote times (Ezek. 12:27). **27. I . . . was sick**—through grief at the calamities coming on my people and the Church of God (cf. Ps. 102:14). **afterward I . . . did the king's business**—He who holds nearest communion with heaven can best discharge the duties of common life. **none understood it**—He had heard of kings, but knew not their names; He foresaw the events, but not the time when they were to take place; thereupon he could only feel "astonished," and leave all with the omniscient God [JEROME].

ADAM CLARKE

KEIL-DELITZSCH:

Daniel must close the prophecy, because it extends into a long time. The Hebrew is not equivalent to *to seal up,* but it means *to stop, to conclude, to hide* (2 Kings 3:19; Ezek. 28:3), but not in the sense of keeping secret, or because it would be incomprehensible for the nearest times; for to seal or to shut up has nothing in common with incomprehensibility, but is used in the sense of *keeping*. "A document is sealed up in the original text, and laid up in archives (shut up), that it may remain preserved for remote times, but not that it may remain secret, while copies of it remain in public use" (Kliefoth). The meaning of the command, then, is simply this: "Preserve the revelation, not because it is not yet to be understood, also not for the purpose of keeping it secret, but that it may remain preserved for distant times" (Kliefoth). The reason assigned for the command only agrees with this interpretation. *To many days* designates only *a long time*; and this indefinite expression is here used because it was not intended to give exactly again the termination according to verses 17 and 19, but only to say that the time of the end was not near.

In verse 27 the influence of this vision on Daniel is mentioned (7:28). It so deeply agitated the prophet that he was sick certain days, and not till after he had recovered from this sickness could he attend to the king's business. The contents of the vision remained fixed in his mind; the scene filled him with amazement, and no one understood it. Maurer, Hitzig, and Kranichfeld interpret *I understood it not,* supplying the pronoun of the first person from the connection. But even though the construction of the words should admit of this supplement, for which a valid proof is not adduced, yet it would be here unsuitable, and is derived merely from giving to the false interpretation of *to conceal.* If Daniel had been required to keep the prophecy secret according to the command in verse 26, then the remark "no one understood it" would have been altogether superfluous. But if he was required only to preserve the prophecy, and it deeply moved him, then those around him must have had knowledge of it, and the amazement of Daniel would become the greater when not only he but all others failed to understand it. The fulfilment of this vision can alone lead to its full understanding.

—*Commentary on the Old Testament*

MATTHEW HENRY

CHAPTER 9

Verses 1–3

Daniel here employed in better business than any the king had for him, speaking to God and hearing from him, not for himself only, but for the church. Daniel had this communion with God (*v.* 1), *in the first year of Darius the Mede*, who was newly made king of the Chaldeans, Babylon being conquered by him and his nephew, or grandson, Cyrus. In this year the seventy years of the Jews' captivity ended. He *understood by books* that seventy years was the time fixed for the continuance of *the desolations of Jerusalem*, *v.* 2. The *book* by which he understood this was the book of Jeremiah, in which he found it expressly foretold (Jer. xxix. 10), *After seventy years be accomplished in Babylon I will visit you, and perform my good word towards you.* It was likewise said (Jer. xxv. 11). *This whole land shall be seventy years a desolation* (*chorbath*), the same word that Daniel here uses for the *desolations of Jerusalem*, which shows that he had that prophecy before him when he wrote this. Now *Daniel sought by prayer and supplications* that the people might be prepared by the grace of God for the deliverance that God was about to work out for them. This prayer: *I set my face unto the Lord God to seek him*, denotes the fixedness of his thoughts, the firmness of his faith, in the duty. Probably, in token of his setting his face towards God, he set his face towards Jerusalem. In token of his deep humiliation before God for his own sins, and the sins of his people, when he prayed he *fasted* and put on *sackcloth* and *ashes*.

Verses 4–19

Daniel's prayer to God as his God, and the confession which he joined with that prayer: I *prayed, and made my confession.* In every prayer we must make confession, not only of our sins, but of our faith in God.

I. His humble, reverent address in which he gives glory to God, 1. As a God to be feared: "*O Lord! the great and dreadful God*, that art able to deal with the greatest and most terrible of the church's enemies."

2. As a God to be trusted: *Keeping the covenant and mercy to those that love him*, and, as a proof of their love to him, *keep his commandments*. He will be better than his word, for he keeps mercy to them, something more than was in the covenant. It was proper for Daniel to think of God's mercy now that he was to lay before him the miseries of his people, and to sue for the performance of a promise.

II. Here is a penitent confession of sin, *v.* 5, 6. When we seek for national mercies we ought to humble ourselves for national sins. Two things aggravated their sins: 1. That they had violated the laws God had given them by Moses. 2. That they had slighted the fair warnings God had given them by the prophets (*v.* 6): "*We have not hearkened to thy servants the prophets*, who have put us in mind of thy laws."

JAMIESON, FAUSSET, BROWN

CHAPTER 9

VSS. 1-27. DANIEL'S CONFESSION AND PRAYER FOR JERUSALEM: GABRIEL COMFORTS HIM BY THE PROPHECY OF THE SEVENTY WEEKS. The world powers here recede from view; Israel, and the salvation by Messiah promised to it, are the subject of revelation. Israel had naturally expected salvation at the end of the captivity. Daniel is therefore told, that, after the seventy years of the captivity, seventy times seven must elapse, and that even then Messiah would not come in glory as the Jews might through misunderstanding expect from the earlier prophets, but by dying would put away sin. This ninth chapter (Messianic prophecy) stands between the two visions of the Old Testament Antichrist, to comfort "the wise." In the interval between Antiochus and Christ, no further revelation was needed; therefore, as in the first part of the book, so in the second, Christ and Antichrist in connection are the theme. **1. first year of Darius**—Cyaxares II, in whose name Cyrus, his nephew, son-in-law, and successor, took Babylon, 538 B.C. The date of this chapter is therefore 537 B.C., a year before Cyrus permitted the Jews to return from exile, and sixty-nine years after Daniel had been carried captive at the beginning of the captivity, 606 B.C. **son of Ahasuerus**—called Astyages by XENOPHON. Ahasuerus was a name common to many of the kings of Medo-Persia. **made king**—The phrase implies that Darius owed the kingdom not to his own prowess, but to that of another, viz., Cyrus. **2. understood by books**—rather, letters, i.e., Jeremiah's letter (Jer. 29:10) to the captives in Babylon; also Jeremiah 25:11, 12; cf. II Chronicles 36:21; Jeremiah 30:18; 31:38. God's promises are the ground on which we should, like Daniel, rest sure hope; not so as to make our prayers needless, but rather to encourage them. **3. prayer . . . supplications**—lit., "intercessions . . . entreaties *for mercy*." Praying for *blessings*, and deprecating evils. **4. my confession**—according to God's promises in Leviticus 26:39-42, that if Israel in exile for sin should repent and *confess,* God would remember for them His covenant with Abraham (cf. Deut. 30:1-5; Jer. 29:12-14; Jas. 4:10). God's promise was absolute, but prayer also was ordained as about to precede its fulfilment, this too being the work of God *in* His people, as much as the *external* restoration which was to follow. So it shall be at Israel's final restoration (Ps. 102:13-17). Daniel takes his countrymen's place of confession of sin, identifying himself with them, and, as their representative and intercessory priest, "accepts the punishment of their iniquity." Thus he typifies Messiah, the Sin-bearer and great Intercessor. The prophet's own life and experience form the fit starting point of the prophecy concerning the sin-atonement. He prays for Israel's restoration as associated in the prophets (cf. Jer. 31:4, 11, 12, 31, etc.) with the hope of Messiah. The revelation, now granted, analyzes into its successive parts that which the prophets, in prophetical perspective, heretofore saw together in one; viz., the redemption from captivity, and the full Messianic redemption. God's servants, who, like Noah's father (Gen. 5:29), hoped many a time that now the Comforter of their afflictions was at hand, had to wait from age to age, and to view preceding fulfilments only as pledges of the coming of Him whom they so earnestly desired to see (Matt. 13:17); as now also Christians, who believe that the Lord's second coming is nigh, are expected to continue waiting. So Daniel is informed of a long period of seventy prophetic weeks before Messiah's coming, instead of seventy years, as *he* might have expected (cf. Matt. 18:21, 22) [AUBERLEN]. **great and dreadful God**—as we know to our cost by the calamities we suffer. The *greatness* of God and His *dreadful* abhorrence of sin should prepare sinners for reverent, humble acknowledgment of the justice of their punishment. **keeping . . . covenant and mercy**—i.e., the covenant of Thy mercy, whereby Thou hast promised to deliver us, not for our merits, but of Thy mercy (Ezek. 36:22, 23). So weak and sinful is man that any covenant for good on God's part with him, to take effect, must depend solely on His grace. If He be a God to be *feared* for His justice, He is one to be *trusted* for His "mercy." **love . . . keep his commandments**—Keeping His commandments is the only sure test of love to God (John 14:15). **5.** Cf. Nehemiah's confession (Nehemiah 9). **sinned . . . committed iniquity . . . done wickedly . . . rebelled**—a climax. Erred in *ignorance* . . . sinned by *infirmity* . . . *habitually and wilfully* done wickedness . . . as *open and obstinate rebels* set ourselves against God. **6. prophets . . . spake . . . to our kings . . . to all the people**—They fearlessly warned all

ADAM CLARKE

CHAPTER 9

1. *In the first year of Darius.* This is the same Darius the Mede spoken of before, who succeeded Belshazzar, king of the Chaldeans. See chap. v. 31.

2. *I Daniel understood by books.* The prophecy referred to here is found Jer. xxv. 12; xxix. 10. The people must have been satisfied of the divine inspiration of Jeremiah or his prophecies would not have been so speedily collected nor so carefully preserved. It appears that there was a copy of them then in Daniel's hands.

3. *I set my face . . . to seek by prayer.* He found that the time of the promised deliverance could not be at any great distance; and as he saw nothing that indicated a speedy termination of their oppressive captivity, he was very much afflicted, and earnestly besought God to put a speedy end to it; and how earnestly he sought, his own words show. He prayed, he supplicated, he fasted, he put sackcloth upon his body, and he put ashes upon his head. He used that kind of prayer prescribed by Solomon in his prayer at the dedication of the Temple. See 1 Kings viii. 47-48.

4. *Keeping the covenant.* Fidelity and truth are characteristics of God. He had never yet broken His engagements to His followers, and was ever showing mercy to men.

MATTHEW HENRY

III. Here is a self-abasing acknowledgment of the righteousness of God in all the judgments brought upon them. He acknowledges that it was sin that plunged them in all these troubles. Israel is *dispersed* through *all the countries* about, and so weakened, impoverished, and exposed. It is *because of their trespass that they have trespassed* (*v.* 7); they mingled themselves with the nations that they might be debauched by them, and now God mingles them with the nations that they might be stripped by them. He takes notice of the fulfilling of the scripture in what was brought upon them. *The curse is poured upon us and the oath*, that is, the curse that was ratified by an oath in the law of Moses, *v.* 11. God did but inflict the penalty of the law. "It is not some of the common troubles of life that we are complaining of, but that which has in it special marks of divine displeasure; for *under the whole heaven has not been done as has been done upon Jerusalem*," *v.* 12. It is Jeremiah's lamentation in the name of the church, *Was ever sorrow like unto my sorrow?* which must suppose another similar question, *Was ever sin like unto my sin?* He puts shame upon the whole nation, from the highest to the lowest. If Israel had continued a holy people, they would have been *high above all nations in praise, and name, and honour* (Deut. xxvi. 19); but now that they have *sinned and done wickedly* confusion and disgrace belong to them, to *the men of Judah and the inhabitants of Jerusalem*, to *all Israel*, both to the two tribes, *that are near*, by the rivers of Babylon, and to the ten tribes, *that are afar off*, in the land of Assyria. He imputes the continuance of the judgment to their incorrigibleness (*v.* 13, 14). *We have not entreated the face of the Lord our God* (so the word is); "we have taken no care to make our peace with God and reconcile ourselves to him." If men were brought rightly to *understand God's truth*, and to submit to the power and authority of it, they would turn from the error of their ways. Now the first step towards this is to *make our prayer before the Lord our God*, that the affliction may be sanctified before it is removed.

IV. Here is a believing appeal to the mercy of God. 1. God has been always ready to pardon sin (*v.* 9). He is a *God of pardons* (Neh. ix. 17, marg.); he *multiplies to pardon*, Isa. lv. 7. 2. Daniel looks back for the encouragement of his faith (*v.* 15): "*Thou hast* formerly *brought thy people out of Egypt with a mighty hand*, and wilt thou not now with the same mighty hand bring them out of Babylon? And has not God said that their deliverance out of Babylon shall outshine even that out of Egypt?" Jer. xvi. 14, 15.

V. Here is a pathetic complaint of the reproach that God's people lay under, and the ruins that God's sanctuary lay in. Their neighbours laugh them to scorn, and triumph in their disgrace. God's holy place was desolate. Jerusalem, the holy city, was a reproach (*v.* 16), the holy house was desolate (*v.* 17), the altars were demolished, and all the buildings laid in ashes.

VI. Here is an importunate request to God for the restoring of the captive Jews. "*O Lord! I beseech thee*, *v.* 16. *Now therefore, O our God! hear the prayer of thy servant and his supplication* (*v.* 17)." Now what are his petitions? What are his requests? 1. That God would turn away his wrath from them; that is it which all the saints dread and deprecate more than any thing: O let *thy anger be turned away from thy Jerusalem, thy holy mountain!* (*v.* 16). He does not pray for the turning again of their captivity (let the Lord do with them as seems good in his eyes), but he prays first for the *turning away of God's wrath*. Take away the cause, and the effect will cease. 2. That he would lift up the light of his countenance upon them (*v.* 17): *Cause thy face to shine upon thy sanctuary that is desolate*. The shining of God's face upon the desolations of the sanctuary is all in all towards the repair of it; and upon that foundation it must be rebuilt. If therefore its friends would begin their work at the right end, they must first be earnest with God in prayer for his favour.

VII. Here are several pleas and arguments to enforce the petitions. God gives us leave not only to pray, but to plead, not to move him (he himself knows what he will do), but to move ourselves, and encourage our faith. 1. They disdain a dependence upon any righteousness of their own; they pretend not to merit anything at God's hand but wrath and the curse (*v.* 18). Moses had told Israel that, whatever God did for them, it was *not for their righteousness*, Deut. ix. 4, 5. 2. They take their encouragement in prayer from God only, as knowing they are suing for grace and mercy from him. (1) "Do it *for thy own sake* (*v.* 19), for the accomplishment of thy own counsel, the performance of thy own promise." (2) "Do it for the Lord's sake." Christ is *the Lord*; he is Lord of all. It is for his sake that God causes his face to shine upon sinners when

JAMIESON, FAUSSET, BROWN

without respect of persons. **7. confusion of faces, as at this day**—Shame at our guilt, betrayed in our countenance, is what belongs to us; as our punishment "at this day" attests. **near, and . . . far off**—the chastisement, however varied, some Jews not being cast off so far from Jerusalem as others, all alike were sharers in the guilt. **9. mercies**—The *plural* intensifies the force; mercy manifold and exhibited in countless ways. As it is humbling to recollect "*righteousness* belongeth unto God," so it is comforting, that "*mercies* belong to the Lord OUR God." **though we have rebelled**—rather, "since . . ." [*Vulgate*], (Ps. 25:11). Our punishment is not inconsistent with His "mercies," *since* we have rebelled against Him. **10. set before us**—not ambiguously, but plainly, so that we were without excuse. **11. all**—(Ps. 14:3; Rom. 3:12). **the curse . . . and . . . oath . . . in . . . law**—the *curse* against Israel, if disobedient, which God ratified by *oath* (Lev. 26:14-39; Deut; 27:15-26; 28:15-68; 29). **12. confirmed his words**—showed by the punishments we suffer, that His words were no idle threats. **under . . . heaven hath not been done as . . . upon Jerusalem**—(Lam. 1:12). **13. yet made we not our prayer before**—lit., "soothed not the face of." Not even our chastisement has taught us penitence (Isa. 9:13; Jer. 5:3; Hos. 7:10). Diseased, we spurn the healing medicine. **that we might turn . . .**—Prayer can only be accepted when joined with the desire to *turn* from sin to God (Ps. 66:18; Prov. 28:9). **understand thy truth**—"attentively regard Thy faithfulness" in fulfilling Thy promises, and also Thy threats [CALVIN]. *Thy law* (ch. 8:12), [MAURER]. **14. watched upon the evil**—expressing ceaseless vigilance that His people's sins might not escape His judgment, as a watchman on guard night and day (Job 14:16; Jer. 31:28; 44:27). God *watching* upon the Jews' punishment forms a striking contrast to the Jews' slumbering in their sins. **God is righteous**—True penitents "justify" God, "ascribing righteousness to Him," instead of complaining of their punishment as too severe (Neh. 9:33; Job 36:3; Ps. 51:4; Lam. 3:39-42). **15. brought thy people . . . out of . . . Egypt**—a proof to all ages that the seed of Abraham is Thy covenant people. That ancient benefit gives us hope that Thou wilt confer a like one on us now under similar circumstances (Ps. 80:8-14; Jer. 32:21; 23:7, 8). **as at this day**—is known. **16. thy righteousness**—not stern *justice* in punishing, but Thy *faithfulness* to Thy promises of mercy to them who trust in Thee (Ps. 31:1; 143:1). **thy city**—chosen as *Thine* in the election of grace, which changes not. **for . . . iniquities of . . . fathers**—(Exod. 20:5). He does not impugn God's justice in this, as did the murmurers (Ezek. 18:2, 3; cf. Jer. 31:29). **thy people . . . a reproach**—which brings reproach on Thy name. "All the nations that are about us" will say that Thou, Jehovah, wast not able to save Thy peculiar people. So vs. 17, "for the Lord's sake"; vs. 19, "for Thine own sake" (Isa. 48:9, 11). **17. cause thy face to shine**—metaphor from the sun, which gladdens all that it beams upon (Num. 6:25; Mal. 4:2). **18. present . . . supplications**—lit., "cause to fall . . . " (cf. *Note*, Jer. 36:7). **19.** The short broken ejaculations and repetitions show the intense fervor of his supplications. **defer not**—He implies that the seventy years are now all but complete. **thine own sake**—often repeated, as being the strongest plea (Jer. 14:21). **20. whiles I was speaking**—repeated in vs. 21; emphatically marking that the answer was given before the prayer was completed, as God promised (Isa. 30:19; 65:24; cf. Ps. 32:5). **21. I had seen in the vision at the beginning**—viz., in the former vision by the river Ulai (ch. 8:1, 16). **fly swiftly**—lit., "with weariness," i.e., move swiftly as one breathless and wearied out with quick running [GESENIUS]. *English Version* is better (Isa. 6:2; Ezek. 1:6; Rev. 14:6). **time of . . . evening oblation**—the ninth hour, three o'clock (cf. I Kings 18:36). As formerly, when the temple stood, this hour was devoted to sacrifices, so now to prayer. Daniel, during the whole captivity to the very last, with pious patriotism never forgot God's temple-worship, but speaks of its rites long abolished, as if still in use. **22. to give thee . . . understanding**—Ch. 8:16; vs. 26 in that chapter shows that the symbolical vision had not been understood. God therefore now gives "information" directly, instead of by symbol, which required interpretation. **23. At the beginning of thy supplications . . .**—The promulgation of the divine decree was made in heaven to the angels as soon as Daniel began to pray. **came forth**—from the divine throne; so vs. 22. **thou art greatly beloved**—lit., "a man of desires" (cf. Ezek. 23:6,12); the object of God's delight. As the apocalyptic prophet of the New Testament was "the disciple whom Jesus loved," so

ADAM CLARKE

7. *All Israel, that are near, and that are far off.* He prays both for Judah and Israel. The latter were more dispersed, and had been much longer in captivity.

9. *Mercies and forgivenesses.* From God's goodness flow God's mercies; from His mercies, forgivenesses.

11. *Therefore the curse is poured upon us.* It is probable that he alludes here to the punishment of certain criminals by pouring melted metal upon them; therefore he uses the word *tittach*, "it is poured out," like melted metal.

14. *The Lord watched upon the evil.* In consequence of our manifold rebellions He hath now watched for an opportunity to bring these calamities upon us.

17. *And cause thy face to shine.* Give us proof that Thou art reconciled to us.

19. *Thy city and thy people are called by thy name.* The Holy City, the city of the great King. I think it scarcely possible for any serious man to read these impressive and pleading words without feeling a measure of the prophet's earnestness.

21. *The man Gabriel.* Or the angel Gabriel, who had appeared to me as a "man." *Being caused to fly swiftly.* God hears with delight such earnest, humble, urgent prayers; and sends the speediest answer. Gabriel himself was ordered on this occasion to make more than usual speed.

MATTHEW HENRY

they repent and turn to him, because of the satisfaction he has made. (3) "Do it *according to all thy righteousness* (*v.* 16), that is, plead for us against our persecutors and oppressors *according to thy righteousness.*" (4) "Do it *for thy great mercies* (*v.* 18), to make it to appear that thou art a merciful God." (5) "Do it for the sake of the relation we stand in to thee. The sanctuary that is desolate is thy sanctuary (*v.* 17). Jerusalem is *thy* city and *thy holy mountain* (*v.* 16); it is *the city which is called by thy name,*" *v.* 18. "The people that have *become a reproach* are *thy people*, they are *called by thy name* (*v.* 19). They are *thine, save them,*" Ps. cxix. 94.

Verses 20–27

The answer that was immediately sent to Daniel's prayer, contains the most illustrious prediction of Christ and gospel-grace that is extant in all the *Old Testament.*

I. The time when this answer was given.

1. It was while Daniel was at prayer. This he observed and laid a strong emphasis upon: *While I was speaking in prayer* (*v.* 21), before he rose from his knees, and while there was yet more which he intended to say. He was confessing sin and lamenting *my sin and the sin of my people Israel.* Now was fulfilled what God had spoken Isa. lxv. 24, *While they are yet speaking, I will hear.* Daniel grew very fervent in prayer, *v.* 18, 19. And, *while he was speaking* the angel came to him with a gracious answer. We cannot now expect that God should send us answers to our prayer by angels, but, if we pray with fervency for that which God has promised, we may by faith take the promise as an immediate answer to the prayer: for *he is faithful that has promised.* He had a discovery made to him of a far greater and more glorious redemption which God would work out for his church in the latter days.

2. It was *about the time of the evening oblation, v.* 21. The altar was in ruins, and there was no oblation offered upon it, but the pious Jews in their captivity were daily thoughtful of the time when it should have been offered, and hoped that their prayer should be *set forth before God as incense*, and the *lifting up of their hands*, and their hearts with their hands, should be acceptable in his sight *as the evening-sacrifice*, Ps. cxli. 2. The evening oblation was a type of the great sacrifice which Christ was to offer in the evening of the world, and it was in the virtue of that sacrifice that Daniel's prayer was accepted when he prayed *for the Lord's sake.*

II. The messenger by whom this answer was sent. It was not given him in a dream, nor by a voice from heaven, but an angel was sent on purpose, appearing in a human shape, to give this answer to Daniel. Gabriel is the only created angel that is named in scripture. It was he *whom I had seen in the vision at the beginning.* Daniel heard him called by his name, and thence learned it (Dan. viii. 16). This angel said to *Zacharias, I am Gabriel* (Luke i. 19). Note instructions received from the Father of lights to whom Daniel prayed (*v.* 23): *At the beginning of thy supplications* the word, *the commandment, came forth* from God. Perhaps it was *at the beginning of Daniel's supplications* that *Cyrus's word*, or *commandment, went forth to restore and to build Jerusalem, v.* 25. "The thing was done *this very day*; the proclamation of liberty to the Jews was signed this morning, just when thou wast praying for it." He *touched him* (*v.* 21) to give him a hint to break off his prayer. He *talked with him* (*v.* 22), familiarly, that *his terror might not make him afraid.* "*I have come to show thee*" (*v.* 23). He had shown him the troubles of the church under Antiochus, and the period of those troubles (*ch.* viii. 19); but now he has greater things to show him. "Nay, *I have now come forth to give thee skill and understanding* (*v.* 22), not only to show thee these things, but to *make thee understand* them." He assured him that he was a favourite of Heaven. *I have come to show thee, for thou art greatly beloved.* Those may reckon themselves greatly beloved of God to whom, and in whom, he *reveals his Son.*

III. The message itself was recorded with great exactness; but in it there are things dark and hard to be understood. Daniel, who understood by the prophet Jeremiah the expiration of the seventy years of the captivity, is now employed to make known to the church another more glorious release, at the end of seventy, not years, but weeks of years.

1. The times here determined are somewhat hard to be understood. In general, it is *seventy weeks*, that is, *seventy times seven years*, which makes just 490 years. The great affairs that are yet to come concerning the people of Israel, and the city of Jerusalem, will lie within the compass of these years. The land had *enjoyed its sabbaths*, in a melancholy sense, seventy years, Lev. xxvi. 34. But now the

JAMIESON, FAUSSET, BROWN

the apocalyptic prophet of the Old Testament was "greatly beloved" of God. **the vision**—the further revelation as to Messiah in connection with Jeremiah's prophecy of seventy years of the captivity. The charge to "understand" is the same as in Matthew 24:15, where Rome primarily, and Antichrist ultimately, is referred to (cf. *Note*, vs. 27, below). **24. Seventy weeks**—viz., of years; lit., Seventy sevens"; seventy heptads or hebdomads; 490 years; expressed in a form of "*concealed* definiteness" [HENGSTENBERG], a usual way with the prophets. The Babylonian captivity is a turning point in the history of the kingdom of God. It terminated the free Old Testament theocracy. Up to that time Israel, though oppressed at times, was, as a rule, free. From the Babylonian captivity the theocracy never recovered its full freedom down to its entire suspension by Rome; and this period of Israel's subjection to the Gentiles is to continue till the millennium (Rev. 20), when Israel shall be restored as head of the New Testament theocracy, which will embrace the whole earth. The free theocracy ceased in the first year of Nebuchadnezzar, and the fourth of Jehoiakim; the year of the world 3338, the point at which the seventy years of the captivity begin. Heretofore Israel had a right, if subjugated by a foreign king, to shake off the yoke (Judg. 4 and 5; II Kings 18:7) as an unlawful one, at the first opportunity. But the prophets (Jer. 27:9-11) declared it to be *God's will* that they should submit to Babylon. Hence every effort of Jehoiakim, Jeconiah, and Zedekiah to rebel was vain. The period of the world-times, and of Israel's depression, from the Babylonian captivity to the millennium, though abounding more in afflictions (e.g., the two destructions of Jerusalem, Antiochus' persecution, and those which Christians suffered), contains all that was good in the preceding ones, summed up in Christ, but in a way visible only to the eye of faith. Since He came as a servant, He chose for His appearing the period darkest of all as to His people's temporal state. Always fresh persecutors have been rising, whose end is destruction, and so it shall be with the last enemy, Antichrist. As the Davidic epoch is the point of the covenant people's highest glory, so the captivity is that of their lowest humiliation. Accordingly, the people's sufferings are reflected in the picture of the suffering Messiah. He is no longer represented as the theocratic King, the Antitype of David, but as the Servant of God and Son of man; at the same time the cross being the way to glory (cf. ch. 9 with ch. 2:34, 35, 44, and ch. 12:7). In the second and seventh chapters, Christ's first coming is not noticed, for Daniel's object was to prophesy to his nation as to the whole period from the destruction to the re-establishment of *Israel;* but this ninth chapter minutely predicts Christ's first coming, and its effects on the covenant people. *The seventy weeks date thirteen years before the rebuilding of Jerusalem;* for then the re-establishment of the theocracy began, viz., at *the return of Ezra to Jerusalem,* 457 B.C. So Jeremiah's seventy years of the captivity begin 606 B.C., eighteen years before the destruction of Jerusalem, for then Judah ceased to exist as an independent theocracy, having fallen under the sway of Babylon. Two periods are marked in Ezra: (1) The return from the captivity under Jeshua and Zerubbabel, and rebuilding of the *temple,* which was the first anxiety of the theocratic nation. (2) The return of Ezra (regarded by the Jews as a second Moses) from Persia to Jerusalem, the restoration of *the city, the nationality,* and the law. Artaxerxes, in the *seventh* year of his reign, gave him the commission which virtually includes permission to rebuild the city, afterwards confirmed to, and carried out by, Nehemiah in the *twentieth* year (Ezra 9:9; 7, 11, etc.); vs. 25, "from the going forth of the commandment *to build Jerusalem,*" proves that the second of the two periods is referred to. The words in verse 24 are not, "are determined upon the holy city," but "*upon thy people* and thy holy city"; thus the restoration of the religious *national polity* and the law (the inner work fulfilled by Ezra the priest), and the rebuilding of the *houses and walls* (the outer work of Nehemiah, the governor), are both included in vs. 25, "restore and build Jerusalem." "Jerusalem" represents both the city, the body, and the congregation, the soul of the state. Cf. Psalms 46, 48, 87. The starting point of the seventy weeks dated from eighty-one years after Daniel received the prophecy: the object being not to fix *for him* definitely the time, but for the Church: the prophecy taught *him* that the Messianic redemption, which he thought near, was separated from him by at least a half millennium. Expectation was sufficiently kept alive by the *general* conception of the

ADAM CLARKE

CHARLES H. SPURGEON:

Verse 24. The Lord God appointed a set time for the coming of His Son into the world; nothing was left to chance. Infinite wisdom dictated the hour at which the Messiah should be born, and the moment at which he should be cut off. His advent and His work are the highest point of the purpose of God, the hinge of history, the center of providence, the crowning of the edifice of grace, and therefore peculiar care watched over every detail. Once in the end of the world hath the Son of God appeared to put away sin by the sacrifice of Himself, and this is *the* event before which all other events must bow. The studious mind will be delighted to search out the reasons why the Messiah came not before, and why He did not tarry till yet later ages. Prophecies declared the date; but long before infallible wisdom had settled it for profoundest reasons. It was well that the Redeemer came: it was well that He came in what Scripture calls the fullness of time, even in these last days.

Note, again, that the Lord told His people somewhat darkly, but still with a fair measure of clearness, when the Christ would come. Thus He cheered them when the heavy clouds of woe hung over their path. This prophecy shone like a star in the midst of the sorrows of Israel: so bright was it that at the period when Christ came there was a general expectation of Him. Holy men and women, diligent in the study of the Scriptures, were waiting for Him: Simeon was waiting for the consolation of Israel, and Anna looked for redemption in Jerusalem with others of like mind. Not only the Jews, but the Samaritans expected Him, for the woman at the well exclaimed, "I know that Messias cometh, which is called Christ." Even in heathen lands there was a remarkable cessation from stir and battle; and unusual peace reigned over all the nations, and the hush of expectation ruled the hour. Men were looking for the coming One; for the corn of earth was ripe for the reaper. Men were on the tiptoe of expectation, and wondered when the promised Prince would arrive. Alas, they knew Him not when He appeared. After this fashion are things at the present moment with regard to the Second Advent of our Lord Jesus Christ. "Of that day and of that hour knoweth no man"; but it is known unto God, and fixed in the roll of His eternal purposes. "Known unto God are all His works from the creation of the world," and especially those grand works which concern the Person of our adorable Lord Jesus. He shall come as God hath appointed: the vision of His glory shall not tarry. He has given us suggestive hints as to that glorious appearing; and He has plainly taught us to be looking for and hastening unto the day of the Lord. Among His last words are these, "Surely I come quickly": these are words of consolation as well as of warning.—*The Treasury of the Old Testament*

MATTHEW HENRY

people of the Lord shall enjoy their sabbaths seven times seventy years, and in them seventy sabbatical years, which makes ten jubilees.

Difficulties arise about these seventy weeks concerning the time when they commence and whence they are to be reckoned. They are here dated *from that going forth of the commandment to restore and to build Jerusalem*, *v.* 25. I should most incline to understand this of the edict of Cyrus mentioned Ezra i. 1. And it looks as though the seventy weeks should begin immediately upon the expiration of the seventy years, but by this reckoning the *Persian monarchy*, from the taking of Babylon by Cyrus to Alexander's conquest of Darius, lasted but 130 years; whereas, by the particular account given of the reigns of the Persian emperors, it is computed that it continued 230 years. So Thucydides, Xenophon, and others reckon. Mr. Poole, in his Latin Synopsis, has a vast and most elaborate collection of what has been said, *pro* and *con*, concerning the different beginnings of these weeks. Concerning the termination of them, interpreters are not agreed. Some make them to end at the death of Christ. But others think, because it is said that *in the midst of the weeks* (that is, the last of the seventy weeks) he *shall cause the sacrifice and the oblation to cease*, they end *three years and a half* after the death of Christ. Concerning the division of them into seven weeks, and sixty-two weeks, and one week, the reason is as hard to account for as anything else. In the first seven weeks, or forty-nine years, the temple and city were built: and in the last single week Christ preached his gospel, by which the foundations were laid of the gospel city and temple. But, whatever uncertainty we may labour under concerning the exact fixing of these times, there is enough certain to answer the two great ends. (1) It did serve them to raise and support the expectations of believers. By the light of this prophecy they were directed about what time to expect him. (2) It does serve still to refute and silence the expectations of unbelievers, who will not own that Jesus is he who *should come*, but still *look for another*. Reckon these seventy weeks from which of the commandments to build Jerusalem we please, it is certain that they have expired above 1,500 years ago. We are confirmed in our belief of the Messiah's being come, and that our Jesus is he.

2. The events here foretold are more easy to be understood.

(1) Concerning the return of the Jews now speedily to their own land, and their settlement again there: Let this be a comfort to the pious Jews, that a *commandment* shall *go forth to restore and to build Jerusalem, v.* 25. God will carry on his own work, will build up his Jerusalem, will beautify it, will fortify it, *even in troublous times*.

JAMIESON, FAUSSET, BROWN

time; not only the Jews, but many Gentiles looked for some great Lord of the earth to spring from Judea *at that very time* (TACITUS, *Hist.* 5.13; SUETONIUS, *Vesp.* 4). Ezra's placing of Daniel in the canon immediately before his own book and Nehemiah's was perhaps owing to his feeling that he himself brought about the beginning of the fulfilment of the prophecy (ch. 9) [AUBERLEN]. **determined**—*lit.*, "cut out," viz., from the whole course of time, for God to deal in a particular manner with Jerusalem. **thy . . . thy**—Daniel had in his prayer often spoken of Israel as "*Thy* people, *Thy* holy city"; but Gabriel, in reply, speaks of them as *Daniel's* ("thy" . . . "thy") people and city, God thus intimating that until the "everlasting righteousness" should be brought in by Messiah, He could not fully own them as *His* [TREGELLIS] (cf. Exod. 32:7). Rather, as God is wishing to console Daniel and the godly Jews, "the people whom *thou* art so anxiously praying for"; such weight does God give to the intercessions of the righteous (Jas. 5:16-18). **finish**—lit., "shut up"; remove from God's sight, i.e., abolish (Ps. 51:9) [LENGKERKE]. The seventy years' exile was a punishment, but not a full atonement, for the sin of the people; this would come only after seventy prophetic weeks, through Messiah. **make an end of**—The *Hebrew* reading, "to steal," i.e., to hide out of sight (from the custom of *sealing* up things to be concealed, cf. Job 9:7), is better supported. **make reconciliation for**—lit., "to cover," to overlay (as with pitch, Gen. 6:14). Cf. Psalm 32:1. **bring in everlasting righteousness**—viz., the restoration of the normal state between God and man (Jer. 23:5, 6); to continue eternally (Heb. 9: 12; Rev. 14:6). **seal up . . . vision . . . prophecy**—lit., "prophet." To give the seal of confirmation to the prophet and his vision by the fulfilment. **anoint the Most Holy**—primarily, to "anoint," or to *consecrate* after its pollution "the Most Holy" *place* but mainly *Messiah*, the antitype to the Most Holy place (John 2:19-22). The propitiatory in the temple (the same Greek word expresses *the mercy seat* and *propitiation*, Rom. 3:25), which the Jews looked for at the restoration from Babylon, shall have its true realization only in Messiah. For it is only when sin is "made an end of" that God's presence can be perfectly manifested. As to "anoint," cf. Exodus 40:9, 34. Messiah was *anointed* with the Holy Ghost (Acts 4:27; 10:38). So hereafter, God-Messiah will "anoint" or consecrate with His presence the holy place at Jerusalem (Jer. 3:16, 17; Ezek. 37:27, 28), after its pollution by Antichrist, of which the feast of dedication after the pollution by Antiochus was a type. **25. from the going forth of the commandment**—viz., the command from God, whence originated the command of the Persian king (Ezra 6:14). AUBERLEN remarks, there is but one Apocalypse in each Testament. Its purpose in each is to sum up all the preceding prophecies, previous to the "troublous times" of the Gentiles, in which there was to be no revelation. Daniel sums up all the previous Messianic prophecy, separating into its individual phases what the prophets had seen in one and the same perspective, the temporary deliverance from captivity and the antitypical final Messianic deliverance. The seventy weeks are separated (vss. 25-27) into three unequal parts, seven, sixty-two, one. The seventieth is the consummation of the preceding ones, as the Sabbath of God succeeds the working days; an idea suggested by the division into *weeks*. In the sixty-nine weeks Jerusalem is restored, and so a place is prepared for Messiah wherein to accomplish His sabbatic work (vss. 25, 26) of "confirming the covenant" (vs. 27). The Messianic time is the Sabbath of Israel's history, in which it had the offer of all God's mercies, but in which it was cut off for a time by its rejection of them. As the seventy weeks end with seven years, or a week, so they begin with seven times seven, i.e., seven weeks. As the seventieth week is separated from the rest *as a period of revelation*, so it may be with the seven weeks. The number *seven* is associated with revelation; for the *seven* spirits of God are the mediators of all His revelations (Rev. 1:4; 3:1; 4:5). *Ten* is the number of what is human; e.g., the world power issues in *ten heads* and *ten horns* (ch. 2:42; 7:7). *Seventy* is *ten* multiplied by *seven*, the human moulded by the divine. The *seventy* years of exile symbolize the triumph of the world power over Israel. In the seven times seventy years the world number ten is likewise contained, i.e., God's people is still under the power of the world ("troublous times"); but the number of the divine is multiplied by itself; seven times seven years, at the beginning a period of Old Testament revelation to God's people by Ezra, Nehemiah, and Malachi, whose

ADAM CLARKE

24. *Seventy weeks are determined.* This is a most important prophecy, and has given rise to a variety of opinions relative to the proper mode of explanation; but the chief difficulty, if not the only one, is to find out the time from which these seventy weeks should be dated. What is here said by the angel is not a direct answer to Daniel's prayer. He prays to know when the seventy weeks of the Captivity are to end. Gabriel shows him that there are seventy weeks determined relative to a redemption from another sort of captivity, which shall commence with the going forth of the edict to restore and rebuild Jerusalem, and shall terminate with the death of Messiah, the Prince, and the total abolition of the Jewish sacrifices. In the following four verses he enters into the particulars of this most important determination, and leaves them with Daniel for his comfort, who has left them to the Church of God for the confirmation of its faith, and a testimony to the truth of divine revelation. Of all the writers I have consulted on this most noble prophecy, Dean Prideaux appears to me the most clear and satisfactory. I shall therefore follow his method in my explanation, and often borrow his words. *Seventy weeks are determined*—The Jews had sabbatic years, Lev. xxv. 8, by which their years were divided into weeks of years, as in this important prophecy, each week containing 7 years. The 70 weeks therefore here spoken of amount to 490 years. In v. 24 there are six events mentioned which should be the consequences of the incarnation of our Lord: (I) *To finish* ("to restrain") *the transgression,* which was effected by the preaching of the gospel, and pouring out of the Holy Ghost among men. (II) *To make an end of sins;* rather "to make an end of sin offerings," which our Lord did when He offered His spotless soul and body on the Cross once for all. (III) *To make reconciliation* ("to make atonement or expiation") *for iniquity.* (IV) *To bring in everlasting righteousness,* "the righteousness, or righteous One, of ages." (V) *To seal up* ("to finish or complete") *the vision and prophecy*; that is, to put an end to the necessity of any further revelations, by completing the canon of Scripture, and fulfilling the prophecies which related to His person, sacrifice, and the glory that should follow. (VI) *And to anoint the most Holy, kodesh kodashim,* "the holy of holies." *Mashach,* "to anoint" (from which comes *mashiach,* "the Messiah," the Anointed One), signifies in general to consecrate or appoint to some special office. Here it means the consecration or appointment of our blessed Lord, the Holy One of Israel, to be the Prophet, Priest, and King of mankind.

The above 70 weeks, or 490 years, are divided in v. 25 into three distinct periods, to each of which particular events are assigned. The 3 periods are—(I) *Seven weeks,* that is, 49 years. (II) *Sixty-two weeks,* that is, 434 years. (III) *One week,* that is, 7 years. To the first period of 7 weeks the restoration and repairing of Jerusalem are referred; and so long were Ezra and Nehemiah employed in restoring the sacred constitutions and civil establishments of the Jews, for this work lasted 49 years after the commission was given by Artaxerxes.

MATTHEW HENRY

(2) Concerning the Messiah. The carnal Jews looked for a Messiah that should deliver them from the Roman yoke and give them temporal power and wealth, whereas they were here told that the Messiah should come upon another errand, purely spiritual. Christ came to *take away sin.* Sin had made a quarrel between God and man, had alienated man from God and provoked God against man; it was this that brought misery upon mankind. Christ undertakes to *destroy the works of the devil.* He does not say to *finish your* transgressions and your sins, but *transgression* and *sin* in general, for he is the propitiation *for the sins of the whole world.* He came, *First,* To *finish transgression,* to *restrain* it (so some), to break the power of it, and to set up a kingdom of holiness and love in the hearts of men. *Secondly,* To *make an end of sin,* to abolish it, to *seal up sins* (so the margin reads it), that they may not break out against us. *Thirdly,* To *make reconciliation for iniquity,* as by a sacrifice, to *make peace* and bring God and man together. He is not only the *peace-maker,* but the *peace.* He is the *atonement.* God might justly have made an end of the sin by making an end of the sinner; but Christ found out another way, and so made an end of sin as to save the sinner, by providing a righteousness for him. The merit of his sacrifice is *our righteousness.* By faith we apply this to ourselves and plead it with God, and our *faith is imputed to us for righteousness,* Rom. iv. 3, 5. He came to *seal up the vision and prophecy,* all the prophetical visions of the Old Testament, which had reference to the Messiah. He *sealed them up,* that is, he accomplished them. He is called *Messiah* (*v.* 25, 26), which signifies *Christ—Anointed* (John i. 41), because he received the unction both for himself and for all that are his. When Paul preaches the death of Christ, he says that he preached nothing but *what the prophet said should come,* Acts xxvi. 22, 23. And *thus it behoved Christ to suffer.* He must be *cut off, but not for himself.* It was to atone for our sins, and to purchase life for us, that he was *cut off.* He must *cause the sacrifice and oblation to cease.* By offering himself a sacrifice once for all he shall put an end to all the Levitical sacrifices.

(3) Concerning the final destruction of Jerusalem, and of the Jewish church and nation; this follows immediately upon the cutting off of the Messiah, because it was the *just punishment* of those that put him to death. He died to take away the ceremonial law, to abolish *that law of commandments.* But the Jews would not be persuaded to quit it; they stoned Stephen for saying that Jesus should *change the customs which Moses delivered them* (Acts vi. 14). It is here foretold that *the people of the prince that shall come* shall be the instruments of this destruction, that is, the Roman armies, belonging to a monarchy yet to come. The *city* and *sanctuary* shall in a particular manner be *destroyed* and laid waste. Titus the Roman general would fain have saved the temple, but his soldiers were so enraged against the Jews that he could not restrain them from burning it to the ground.

JAMIESON, FAUSSET, BROWN

labors extend over about half a century, or *seven weeks,* and whose writings are last in the canon; and in the end, seven years, the period of New Testament revelation in Messiah. The commencing seven weeks of years of Old Testament revelation are hurried over, in order that the chief stress might rest on the Messianic week. Yet the seven weeks of Old Testament revelation are marked by their separation from the sixty-two, to be above those sixty-two wherein there was to be none. **Messiah the Prince**—*Hebrew, Nagid. Messiah* is Jesus' title in respect to *Israel* (Ps. 2:2; Matt. 27:37, 42). *Nagid,* as Prince of the *Gentiles* (Isa. 55:4). *Nagid* is applied to Titus, only as representative of Christ, who designates the Roman destruction of Jerusalem as, in a sense, His coming (Matt. 24; John 21:22). *Messiah* denotes His calling; *Nagid,* His power. He is to "be cut off, and there shall be nothing for Him." (So the *Hebrew* for "not for Himself," vs. 26, ought to be translated). Yet He is "the Prince" who is to "come," by His representative at first, to inflict judgment, and at last in person. **wall**—the "trench" or "scarped rampart" [TREGELLES]. The *street and trench* include the complete restoration of the city externally and internally, which was during the sixty-nine weeks. **26. after threescore and two weeks**—rather, *the* threescore and two, etc. In this verse, and in verse 27, Messiah is made the prominent subject, while the fate of the city and sanctuary are secondary, being mentioned only in the second halves of the verses. Messiah appears in a twofold aspect, salvation to believers, judgment on unbelievers (Luke 2:34; cf. Mal. 3:1-6; 4:1-3). He repeatedly, in Passion week, connects His being "cut off" with *the destruction of the city,* as cause and effect (Matt. 21:37-41; 23:37, 38; Luke 21:20-24; 23:28-31). Israel might naturally expect Messiah's kingdom of glory, if not after the seventy years' captivity, at least at the end of the sixty-two weeks; but, instead of that, shall be His death, and the consequent destruction of Jerusalem. **not for himself**—rather, "there shall be nothing to Him" [HENGSTENBERG]; not that the real object of His first coming (His *spiritual* kingdom) should be frustrated; but the *earthly* kingdom anticipated by the Jews should, for the present, *come to naught,* and not *then* be realized. TREGELLES refers the title, "the Prince" (vs. 25), to the time of His entering Jerusalem on an ass's colt, His only appearance as a king, and six days afterwards put to death as "King of the Jews." **the people of the prince**—the Romans, led by Titus, the representative of the world power, ultimately to be transferred to Messiah, and so called by Messiah's title, "the Prince"; as also because sent by Him, as His instrument of judgment (Matt. 22:7). **end thereof**—of the sanctuary. TREGELLES takes it, "the end of the Prince," the last head of the Roman power, Antichrist. **with a flood**—viz., of war (Ps. 90:5; Isa. 8:7, 8; 28:18). Implying the completeness of the catastrophe, "not one stone left on another." **unto the end of the war**—rather, "unto the end *there* is war." **determined**—by God's decree (Isa. 10:23; 28:22). **27. he shall confirm the covenant**—Christ. The confirmation of the covenant is assigned to Him also elsewhere. Isaiah 42:6, "I will give thee for a *covenant* of the people" (i.e., He in whom the covenant between Israel and God is personally expressed); cf. Luke 22:20, "The new testament in My blood"; Malachi 3:1, "the angel of the covenant"; Jeremiah 31:31-34, describes the Messianic covenant in full. Contrast ch. 11:30, 32, "forsake the covenant," "do wickedly against the covenant." The prophecy as to Messiah's *confirming the covenant with many* would comfort the faithful in Antiochus' times, who suffered partly from persecuting enemies, partly from false friends (ch. 11:33-35). Hence arises the similarity of the language here and in ch. 11:30, 32, referring to Antiochus, the type of Antichrist. **with many**—(Isa. 53:11; Matt. 20:28; 26:28; Rom. 5:15, 19; Heb. 9:28). **in . . . midst of . . . week**—The seventy weeks extend to A.D. 33. Israel was not actually destroyed till A.D. 79, but it was so virtually, A.D. 33, about three or four years after Christ's death, during which the Gospel was preached exclusively to the Jews. When the Jews persecuted the Church and stoned Stephen (Acts 7), the respite of grace granted to them was at an end (Luke 13:7-9). Israel, having rejected Christ, was rejected by Christ, and henceforth is counted dead (cf. Gen. 2:17 with 5:5; Hos. 13:1, 2), its actual destruction by Titus being the consummation of the removal of the kingdom of God from Israel to the Gentiles (Matt. 21:43), which is not to be restored until Christ's second coming, when Israel shall be at the head of humanity (Matt. 23:39; Acts 1:6, 7; Rom. 11:25-31; 15). The interval forms for the

ADAM CLARKE

From the above 7 weeks the second period of 62 weeks, or 434 years more, commences, at the end of which the prophecy says *Messiah the Prince* should come. That is, **7 weeks, or 49 years,** should be allowed for the restoration of the Jewish state; from which time till the public entrance of the Messiah on the work of the ministry should be 62 weeks, or 434 years—in all, 483 years. From the coming of our Lord, the third period is to be dated, viz., "He shall confirm the covenant with many for one week," that is, *seven* years, v. 27. This confirmation of the covenant must take in the ministry of John the Baptist with that of our Lord, comprehending the term of 7 years, during the whole of which He might be well said to confirm or ratify the new covenant with mankind. Our Lord says, "The law was until John"; but from his first public preaching the kingdom of God, or gospel dispensation, commenced. Dean Prideaux thinks that the whole refers to our Lord's preaching connected with that of the Baptist. *Vachatsi,* says he, signifies in the "half part" of the week; that is, in the latter 3½ years in which He exercised himself in the public ministry, He caused, by the sacrifice of himself, all other sacrifices and oblations to cease, which were instituted to signify His. In the latter parts of vv. 26 and 27 we find the third part of this great prophecy, which refers to what should be done after the completion of these 70 weeks.

26. *And the people of the prince that shall come shall destroy the city and the sanctuary.* By the "prince" Titus, the son of Vespasian, is plainly intended; and "the people" of that prince are no other than the Romans, who, according to the prophecy, destroyed the sanctuary, *hakkodesh,* "the holy place" or Temple, and, as a flood, swept away all, till the total destruction of that obstinate people finished the war.

MATTHEW HENRY

The *sacrifice and oblation* shall be *made to cease.*

There shall be *an overspreading of abominations,* to be understood of the armies of the Romans. These are the words which Christ refers to, Matt. xxiv. 15, *When you shall see the abomination of desolation, spoken of by Daniel, stand in the holy place, then let those who shall be in Judæa flee,* which is explained Luke xxi. 20.

H. DEANE:

"And for the overspreading" (v. 27). As the text stands it can be literally translated only as follows, "and upon the wing of abominations is a desolator." The desolator, of course, is the person who causes the desolation mentioned in verse 26. But what is meant by the "wing of abominations?" The language is without parallel in the Old Testament, unless such passages as Ps. 18:10, 104:3 are adduced, where, however, the plural "wings," and not the singular, is used. If the number is disregarded, the words before us are explained to mean that "the abomination" or idolatry is the power by which the desolator accomplishes his purposes. He comes riding on the wings of abominations, using them for his ministers as God does the winds or the cherubim. As it appears decisive against this interpretation that Daniel has written "wing," and not "wings," it is better to explain the words as referring to the "sanctuary" spoken of in the last verse. The sense is in that case, "and upon the wing"—i.e., the pinnacle of the abominations is a desolator. The Temple is thus called on account of the extent to which it had been desecrated by Israel.

—*Ellicott's Commentary on the Whole Bible*

JAMIESON, FAUSSET, BROWN

covenant people a great parenthesis. **he shall cause the sacrifice . . . oblation to cease**—distinct from the temporary "*taking away*" of "the daily" (sacrifice) by Antiochus (ch. 8:11; 11:31). Messiah was to cause all sacrifices and oblations in general to "*cease*" utterly. There is here an *allusion* only to Antiochus' act; to comfort God's people when sacrificial worship was to be trodden down, by pointing them to the Messianic time when salvation would fully come and yet temple sacrifices cease. This is the same consolation as Jeremiah and Ezekiel gave under like circumstances, when the destruction of Jerusalem by Nebuchadnezzar was impending (Jer. 3:16; 31:31; Ezek. 11:19). Jesus died in the middle of the last week, A.D. 30. His prophetic life lasted three and a half years; the very time in which "the saints are given into the hand" of Antichrist (ch. 7: 25). Three and a half does not, like ten, designate the power of the world in its fulness, but (while opposed to the divine, expressed by *seven*) broken and defeated in its seeming triumph; for immediately after the three and a half times, judgment falls on the victorious world powers (ch. 7:25, 26). So Jesus' death seemed the triumph of the world, but was really its defeat (John 12:31). The rending of the veil marked the cessation of sacrifices through Christ's death (Lev. 4:6, 17; 16:2, 15; Heb. 10:14-18). There cannot be a covenant without sacrifice (Gen. 8:20; 9:17; 15:9, etc.; Heb. 9:15). Here the old covenant is to be confirmed, but in a way peculiar to the New Testament, viz., by the one sacrifice, which would terminate all sacrifices (Ps. 40:6, 11). Thus as the Levitical rites approached their end, Jeremiah, Ezekiel, and Daniel, with ever increasing clearness, oppose the spiritual new covenant to the transient earthly elements of the old. **for the overspreading of abominations**—*On account of the abominations* committed by the unholy people against the Holy One, He shall not only destroy the city and sanctuary (vs. 25), but shall continue its desolation until the time of the consummation "determined" by God (the phrase is quoted from Isa. 10:22, 23), when at last the world power shall be judged and dominion be given to the saints of the Most High (ch. 7:26, 27). AUBERLEN translates, "On account of the desolating *summit* of abominations (cf. ch. 11:31; 12:11; thus the repetition of the same thing as in vs. 26 is avoided), and till the consummation which is determined, it (the curse, vs. 11, foretold by Moses) will pour on the desolated." Israel reached the summit of abominations, which drew down desolation (Matt. 24:28), nay, which is the desolation itself, when, after murdering Messiah, they offered sacrifices, Mosaic indeed in form, but heathenish in spirit (cf. Isa. 1:13; Ezek. 5:11). Christ refers to this passage (Matt. 24:15), "When ye see the abomination of desolation, spoken of by Daniel the prophet, stand *in the holy place*" (the latter words being *tacitly implied* in "abominations" as being such as are committed *against the sanctuary*). TREGELLES translates, "upon the *wing* of abominations shall be that which causeth desolation"; viz., an idol set up on a wing or pinnacle of the temple (cf. Matt. 4:5) by Antichrist, who makes a covenant with the restored Jews for the last of the seventy weeks of years (fulfilling Jesus' words, "If another shall come in his own name, him ye will receive"), and for the first three and a half years keeps it, then in the midst of the week breaks it, causing the daily sacrifices to cease. TREGELLES thus identifies the last half week with the time, times, and a half of the persecuting little horn (ch. 7:25). But thus there is a gap of at least 1830 years put between the sixty-nine weeks and the seventieth week. SIR ISAAC NEWTON explains the wing ("overspreading") of abominations to be the Roman ensigns (eagles) brought to the east gate of the temple, and there sacrificed to by the soldiers; the war, ending in the destruction of Jerusalem, lasted from spring A.D. 67 to autumn A.D. 70, i.e., just three and a half years, or the last half week of years (JOSEPHUS, *B.J.* 6. 6). **poured upon the desolate**—TREGELLES translates, "the *causer* of desolation," viz., Antichrist. Cf. "abomination *that maketh* desolate" (ch. 12:11). Perhaps *both* interpretations of the whole passage may be in part true; the Roman desolator, Titus, being a type of Antichrist, the final desolator of Jerusalem. BACON (*Adv. Learn.* 2. 3) says, "Prophecies are of the nature of the Author, with whom a thousand years are as one day; and therefore are not fulfilled punctually at once, but have a springing and germinant accomplishment through many years, though the height and fulness of them may refer to one age."

ADAM CLARKE

27. *And for the overspreading of abominations he shall make it desolate.* This clause is remarkably obscure. "And upon the wing of abominations causing amazement." This is a literal translation of the place; but still there is no determinate sense. A Hebrew MS., written in the thirteenth century, has preserved a very remarkable reading here, which frees the place from all embarrassment. Instead of the above reading, this valuable MS. has, "And in the temple [of the Lord] there shall be abomination." This makes the passage plain, and is strictly conformable to the facts themselves, for the Temple was profaned; and it agrees with the prediction of our Lord, who said that the abomination that maketh desolate should stand in the holy place, Matt. xxiv. 15, and quotes the words as spoken by Daniel, the prophet. That the above reading gives the true sense, there can be little doubt, because it is countenanced by the most eminent ancient versions. The Vulgate reads, "And in the temple there shall be abomination." The Septuagint, "And upon the temple there shall be the abomination of desolation."

MATTHEW HENRY

CHAPTER 10

Verses 1–9

This vision is dated in the *third year of Cyrus*, that is, of his reign after the conquest of Babylon, his third year since Daniel became acquainted with him.

I. A general idea of this prophecy (*v.* 1): *The thing was true. But the time appointed was long;* to the end of the reign of Antiochus was 300 years. This prophecy looks in type as far forward as the end of the world and the resurrection of the dead; and then he might well say, *The time appointed was long.*

II. An account of Daniel's mortification of himself before he had this vision. He *was mourning full three weeks* (*v.* 2), for his own sins and the sins of his people, and their sorrows. Some think that the occasion of his mourning was the slothfulness of many of the Jews, who, though they had liberty to return to their own land, continued still in the land of their captivity. Others think that it was because he heard of the obstruction given to the building of the temple by the enemies of the Jews, who *hired counsellors against them, to frustrate their purpose* (Ezra iv. 4, 5), *all the days of Cyrus. Daniel ate no flesh, drank no wine, nor anointed himself*, for these three weeks' time, *v.* 3.

III. A description of that glorious person whom Daniel saw in vision, which, it is generally agreed, could be no other than Christ himself, the eternal Word. He was by the side of the river Hiddekel (*v.* 4), probably walking in contemplation, as Isaac walked in the field, to meditate. There he *looked up* and saw even *the man Christ Jesus* (*v.* 5–6). His attendants *saw not the vision.* Paul's companions were aware of the *light*, but *saw no man*, Acts ix. 7; xxii. 9. But, though they saw not the vision, *a great quaking fell upon them, so that they fled to hide themselves*, probably among the willows that grew by the river's side. Daniel saw it alone, but he was not able to bear the sight of it. It overwhelmed his spirit, so that *there remained no strength in him*, *v.* 8. But, though Daniel was thus dispirited with the vision of Christ, yet he *heard the voice of his words* and knew what he said. When the vision of Christ terrified Daniel the voice of his words composed him, and laid him to sleep in a holy security and serenity of mind: *When I heard the voice of his words I fell into a slumber*, a sweet slumber, *on my face*, and *my face towards the ground.*

Verses 10–21

Daniel is by degrees brought to himself.

I. The hand that *touched him* set him at first *upon his knees and the palms of his hands*, *v.* 10. Afterwards

JAMIESON, FAUSSET, BROWN

CHAPTER 10

Vss. 1-21. Daniel Comforted by an Angelic Vision. Chapters 10 through 12 more fully describe the vision in chapter 8 by a second vision on the same subject, just as the vision in the seventh chapter explains more fully that in the second. The tenth chapter is the prologue; the eleventh, the prophecy itself; and the twelfth, the epilogue. The tenth chapter unfolds the spiritual worlds as the background of the historical world (Job 1:7; 2:1, etc.; Zech. 3:1, 2; Rev. 12:7), and angels as the ministers of God's government of men. As in the world of nature (John 5:4; Rev. 7:1-3), so in that of history here; Michael, the champion of Israel, and with him another angel, whose aim is to realize God's will in the heathen world, resist the God-opposed spirit of the world. These struggles are not merely symbolical, but real (I Sam. 16:13-15; I Kings 22:22; Eph. 6:12). **1. third year of Cyrus**—two years after Cyrus' decree for the restoration of the Jews had gone forth, in accordance with Daniel's prayer in ch. 9. This vision gives not merely general outlines, or symbols, but minute details of the future, in short, anticipative history. It is the expansion of the vision in ch. 8. That which then "none understood," he says here, "he understood"; the messenger being sent to him for this (vss. 11, 14), to make him understand it. Probably Daniel was no longer in office at court; for in ch. 1:21, it is said, "Daniel continued even unto the first year of King Cyrus"; not that he *died* then. See *Note* there. **but the time appointed was long**—rather, "it (i.e., the prophecy) referred to *great calamity*" [Maurer]; or, "long and calamitous warfare" [Gesenius]. Lit., "host going to war"; hence, warfare, calamity. **2. mourning**—i.e., afflicting myself by fasting from "pleasant bread, flesh and wine" (vs. 3), as a sign of sorrow, not for its own sake. Cf. Matthew 9:14, "fast," answering to "mourn" (vs. 15). Cf. I Corinthians 8:8; I Timothy 4:3, which prove that "fasting" is not an indispensable Christian obligation; but merely an outward expression of sorrow, and separation from ordinary worldly enjoyments, in order to give one's self to prayer (Acts 13:2). Daniel's mourning was probably for his countrymen, who met with many obstructions to their building of the temple, from their adversaries in the Persian court. **3. no pleasant bread**—"unleavened bread, even the bread of affliction" (Deut. 16:3). **anoint**—The Persians largely used unguents. **4. first month**—Nisan, the month most suited for considering Israel's calamity, being that in which the feast of unleavened bread reminded them of their Egyptian bondage. Daniel mourned not merely for the *seven* days appointed (Exod. 12:18), from the evening of the fourteenth to the twenty-first of Nisan, but *thrice seven* days, to mark extraordinary sorrow. His mourning ended on the twenty-first day, the closing day of the passover feast; but the vision is not till the twenty-fourth, because of the opposition of "the prince of Persia" (vs. 13). **I was by . . . the . . . river**—in waking reality, not a trance (vs. 7); when younger, he saw the future in images, but now when old, he receives revelations from angels in common language, i.e., in the *apocalyptic mode.* In the patriarchal period God often appeared *visibly,* i.e., theophany. In the *prophets,* next in the succession, the *inward* character of revelation is prominent. The consummation is when the seer looks up from earth into the unseen world, and has the future shown to him by angels, i.e., apocalypse. So in the New Testament there is a parallel progression: God in the flesh, the spiritual activity of the apostles and the apocalypse [Auberlen]. **Hiddekel**—the Tigris. **5. lifted up mine eyes**—from the ground on which they had been fixed in his mourning. **certain man**—lit., "one man." An angel of the highest order; for in ch. 8:16 he commands Gabriel to make Daniel to understand the vision, and in ch. 12:6 one of the two angels inquires of him how long it would be till the end predicted. **linen**—the raiment of priests, being the symbol of sanctity, as more pure than wool (Exod. 28:42); also of *prophets* (Jer. 13:1); and of *angels* (Rev. 15:6). **girded with . . . gold**—i.e., with a girdle interwoven with gold (Rev. 1:13). **6. beryl**—lit., "Tarshish," in Spain. The beryl, identical with the chrysolite or topaz, was imported into the East from Tarshish, and therefore is called "the Tarshish stone." **7. they fled**—terrified by the presence of the angel. **8. comeliness**—lit., "vigor," i.e., lively expression and color. **into corruption**—"deadliness," i.e., death-like paleness (ch. 5:6; 7:28). **9. voice of his words**—the *sound* of his words. **was I in a deep sleep**—"I *sank* into a deep sleep" [Lengkerke]. **10. an hand**—viz., of Gabriel, who inter-

ADAM CLARKE

CHAPTER 10

1. *In the third year of Cyrus.* Which answers to the first year of Darius the Mede.

The time appointed was long. But the "warfare long"; there will be many contentions and wars before these things can be accomplished.

2. *I . . . was mourning three full weeks.* The weeks are most probably dated from the time of the termination of the last vision.

3. *I ate no pleasant bread.* This fast was rather a general abstinence, living all the while on coarse and unsavory food, drinking nothing but water, not using the bath, and most probably wearing haircloth next the skin, during the whole of the time.

4. *By the side of . . . Hiddekel.* The same as the Tigris, the great river of Assyria.

5. *Clothed in linen.* The description is intended to point out the splendor of the garments. *Gold of Uphaz.* The same as Ophir.

6. *His body also was like the beryl.* The description of this person is very similar to that of our Lord in Rev. i. 13-15.

7. *The men that were with me saw not the vision.* An exactly parallel case with what occurred at the conversion of Saul of Tarsus, Acts ix. 7. There was a divine influence which they all felt, but only Daniel saw the corporeal appearance.

9. *Was I in a deep sleep.* I fell into a swoon.

10. *An hand touched me.* Nothing was appar-

MATTHEW HENRY

he is helped up, but he *stands trembling* (*v.* 11), for fear lest he fall again. Before God *gives strength and power unto his people* he makes them sensible of their own weakness. At length he recovered, not only the use of his feet, but the use of his tongue; and, when he *opened his mouth* (*v.* 16), that which he had to say was to excuse his having been so long silent. "*My sorrows are turned upon me.*" And again (*v.* 17), half dead with fright, "As for me, *straightway there remained no strength in me* to receive these displays of the divine glory and these discoveries of the divine will; nay, *there is no breath left in me.*"

II. The angel that was employed by Christ to converse with him gave him all the encouragement and comfort that could be. Christ himself comforted John when he in a like case *fell at his feet as dead* (Rev. i. 17); but here he did it by *the angel.*

1. He lent him his hand to help him (*v.* 10), else he would still have lain grovelling, *touched his lips* (*v.* 16), else he would have been still dumb; again he *touched him* (*v.* 18), and put strength into him. One touch from heaven brings us to our knees, sets us on our feet, opens our lips, and strengthens us; for it is God that works on us, and *works in us, both to will and to do* that which is good.

2. He assured him of the favour God had for him: Thou art *a man greatly beloved* (*v.* 11); and again (*v.* 19), *O man greatly beloved!* Those are greatly beloved indeed whom God loves; and it is comfort enough to know it.

3. He silenced his fears, and encouraged his hopes, with good words and comfortable words. *Fear not, Daniel* (*v.* 12); and again (*v.* 19), *O man greatly beloved! fear not; peace be unto thee; be strong, yea, be strong.* And now that Daniel has experienced the efficacy of God's strengthening word and grace, he is ready for anything.

4. He assured him that his fastings and prayers had come up for a memorial before God, *Fear not, Daniel, v.* 12. From the first day that we begin to look towards God in a way of duty he is ready to meet us in a way of mercy.

5. On what errand did this angel come to Daniel? He tells him (*v.* 14): *I have come to make thee understand what shall befall thy people in the latter days.* That which the angel is entrusted to communicate to Daniel, and which Daniel is encouraged to expect from him, is not speculation, though he is an angel, but what he has *received from the Lord.* It was the *revelation of Jesus Christ* that the angel gave to St. John to be *delivered to the churches,* Rev. i. 1. So here (*v.* 21): *I will show thee what is written in the scriptures of truth.* The *decree of God* is a thing written, it is a *scripture* which remains and cannot be altered.

6. He gave him a general account of the adversaries of the church's cause. (1) The *kings of the earth* are and will be its adversaries, Ps. ii. 2. The angel told Daniel that the *prince of the kingdom of Persia withstood him one and twenty days,* just the three weeks that Daniel had been fasting and praying. This new king of Persia, by hindering the temple, had hindered those good tidings which otherwise he should have brought him. "When *I have gone forth* from the kings of Persia, when their monarchy is brought down for their unkindness to the Jews, then *the prince of Grecia shall come,*" *v.* 20. The Grecian monarchy, though favourable to the Jews at first, as the Persian was, will yet come to be vexatious to them. (2) The *God of heaven* is, and will be, its protector. Gabriel resolves, when he has despatched this errand to Daniel, that he will return *to fight with the prince of Persia,* and will at length bring down that proud monarchy (*v.* 20). Here is Michael our prince, the great protector of the church: *The first of the chief princes, v.* 13. Some understand it of a created angel. Others think that *Michael the archangel* is no other than Christ himself, *v.* 5. He *came to help me* (*v.* 13); and there is *none but he that holds with me in these things, v.* 21. Christ is the church's prince; angels are not, Heb. ii. 5.

JAMIESON, FAUSSET, BROWN

preted other revelations to Daniel (ch. 8:16) [THEODORET]. **set me upon my knees**—GESENIUS translates, "cause me to reel on my knees . . . ." **11. man . . . beloved**—(ch. 9:23, *Note*). **understand**—"attend to." See ch. 8:17, 18. **12. Fear not**—Be not affrighted at my presence. **didst set thine heart to understand**—what shall come to pass to thy people at the last times (cf. vs. 14). **chasten thyself**—(vss. 2, 3). **thy words were heard**—(Acts 10:4). Prayer is heard at once in heaven, though the sensible answer may *seem* to be delayed. God's messenger was detained on the way (vs. 13) by the opposition of the powers of darkness. If in our prayers amidst long protracted sorrows we believed God's angel is on his way to us, what consolation it would give us! **for thy words**—because of thy prayers. **13. prince of . . . Persia**—the angel of darkness that represented the Persian world power, to which Israel was then subject. This verse gives the reason why, though Daniel's "words were heard from the first day" (vs. 12), the good angel did not come to him until more than three weeks had elapsed (vs. 4). **one and twenty days**—answering to the three weeks of Daniel's mourning (vs. 2). **Michael**—i.e., "Who is like God?" Though an archangel, "one of the chief princes," Michael was not to be compared to God. **help me**—Michael, as patron of Israel before God (vs. 21; 12:1), "helped" to influence the Persian king to permit the Jews' return to Jerusalem. **I remained**—*I was detained* there with the kings of Persia, i.e., with the angel of the Persian rulers, with whom I had to contend, and from whom I should not have got free, but for the help of Michael. GESENIUS translates, "I obtained the ascendency," i.e., I gained my point against the adverse angel of Persia, so as to influence the Persian authorities to favor Israel's restoration. **14. what shall befall thy people in the latter days**—an intimation that the prophecy, besides describing the doings of Antiochus, reaches to the concluding calamities of Israel's history, prior to the nation's full restoration at Christ's coming—calamities of which Antiochus' persecutions were the type. **vision is for many days**—i.e., extends far into the future. **15. face toward the ground**—in humble reverence (Gen. 19:1). **dumb**—with overwhelming awe. **16. touched my lips**—the same significant action wherewith the Son of man accompanied His healing of the dumb (Mark 7:33). He alone can give spiritual utterance (Isa. 6:6, 7; Eph. 6:19), enabling one to "open the mouth boldly." The same one who makes dumb (vs. 15) opens the mouth. **sorrows**—lit., "writhings" as of a woman in travail. **17. this . . . this my lord**—to avoid the tautology in *English Version,* join rather "this," with *servant,* "How can *this servant* of my lord (i.e., how can I who am *so feeble*) talk with this my lord (who is *so majestic*)?" Thus Daniel gives the reason why he is so overwhelmed with awe [MAURER]. **18. again . . . touched me**—It was gradually that Daniel recovered his strength. Hence there was need of the second touch, that he might hear the angel with composure. **19. peace be unto thee**—God is favorable to thee and to thy people Israel. See Judges 13:21, 22, as to the fear of some evil resulting from a vision of angels. **20. Knowest thou wherefore**—The angel asks, after Daniel had recovered from his fright, whether he has understood what was revealed (vs. 13). On Daniel, by his silence, intimating that he did understand, the angel declares he will return to renew the fight with the evil angel, the prince of Persia. This points to new difficulties to the Jews' restoration which would arise in the Persian court, but which would be counteracted by God, through the ministry of angels. **prince of Grecia shall come**—Alexander the Great, who conquered Persia, and favored the Jews [CALVIN]. Rather, as the prince of Persia is an angel, representing the hostile world power, so the prince of Grecia is a fresh angelic adversary, representing Greece. When I am gone forth from conquering the Persian foe, a fresh one starts up, viz., the world power that succeeds Persia, Greece; Antiochus Epiphanes, and his antitype Antichrist, but him, too, with the help of Michael, Israel's champion, I shall overcome [GEJER]. **21. noted in the scripture of truth**—in the secret book of God's decrees (Ps. 139: 16; Rev. 5:1), which are truth, i.e., the things which shall most surely come to pass, being determined by God (cf. John 17:17). **none . . . but Michael**—To him alone of the angels the office of protecting Israel, in concert with the angelic speaker, was delegated; all the world powers were against Israel.

ADAM CLARKE

ent or palpable but a hand. A hand had written Belshazzar's fate upon the wall, and the hand is frequently mentioned when the power or majesty of God is intended. Perhaps by "hand" God himself may be meant.

12. *I am come for thy words.* On account of your prayers I am sent to comfort and instruct you.

13. *But the prince of the kingdom of Persia withstood me.* I think it would go far to make a legend or a precarious tale of this important place to endeavor to maintain that either a good or evil angel is intended here. Cyrus alone was the *prince of Persia,* and God had destined him to be the deliverer of his people; but there were some matters, of which we are not informed, that caused him to hesitate for some time. Fearing, probably, the greatness of the work, and not being fully satisfied of his ability to execute it, he therefore for a time resisted the secret inspirations which God had sent him. The opposition might be in reference to the building of the Temple. *But, lo, Michael.* Gabriel, who speaks, did not leave Cyrus till Michael came to take his place. Michael, "he who is like God," sometimes appears to signify the Messiah, at other times the highest or chief archangel. Indeed there is no archangel mentioned in the whole Scripture but this one. See Jude 9; Rev. xii. 7.

14. *For yet the vision is for many days.* There are many things which remain yet to be revealed, and the time of their accomplishment is very distant.

15. *I set my face toward the ground.* He was standing upright, v. 11, and he now bent his body in reverence, and looked down upon the ground.

16. *Like the similitude of the sons of men.* I think Gabriel is here meant, who appeared to Daniel in a human form; and so in v. 18, and see also chap. ix. 21. *Touched my lips.* Before this he was unable to speak. *By the vision.* The vision that I have already had, and of which I have not a proper knowledge, has greatly afflicted me, because I see it intimates grievous calamities to my people. See chap. ix. 26.

17. *Neither is there breath.* He could not breathe freely; he was almost suffocated with sorrow.

19. *O man greatly beloved.* "Man of delights." *Let my lord speak.* I am now so strengthened and encouraged that I shall be able to bear any revelation that you may make.

20. *Knowest thou wherefore I come?* So high are you in the favor of God that He hath sent me unto you to give you further satisfaction, though I was elsewhere employed upon a most important mission, and I must speedily return to accomplish it, viz., *To fight with the prince of Persia.* To remove all the scruples of Cyrus, and to excite him to do all that God designs him to do for the restoration of my people, and the rebuilding of the city and Temple of Jerusalem. Nothing less than a supernatural agency in the mind of Cyrus can account for his decree in favor of the Jews. He had no natural, no political inclination to it; and his reluctance to obey the heavenly motions is here represented as a fight between him and the angel. *The prince of Grecia shall come.* I believe this refers to Alexander the Great, who was to destroy the Persian empire. See the second and third verses of the following chapter.

21. *Noted in the scripture of truth.* Perhaps this refers to what he had already written down. See the preceding visions, which Daniel did not fully understand, though a general impression from them had filled his heart with sorrow. *Michael your prince.* The archangel mentioned before, v. 13, and who has been always supposed to be appointed by God as the guardian of the Jewish nation. It appears that God chose to make use of the ministry of angels in this work; that angels, as they could be in only one place at one time, could not produce influence where they were not; and that, to carry on the operation on the mind of the Persian king, it was necessary that either Gabriel or Michael should be present with him, and when one went on another commission another took his place; see v. 13. But we know so little of the invisible world that we cannot safely affirm anything positively.

MATTHEW HENRY

CHAPTER 11

Verses 1–4

1. The angel Gabriel lets Daniel know the good service he has done to the Jewish nation (*v.* 1). Thus by the angel, and at the request of *the watcher*, the golden head was broken, and the axe laid to the root of the tree. God's care of his church formerly encourages us to depend upon him in further straits and difficulties. 2. He foretells the reign of four Persian kings (*v.* 2). (1) There shall stand up *three kings in Persia*, besides Darius, in whose reign this prophecy is dated, *ch.* ix. 1. Mr. Broughton makes these three to be Cyrus, Artaxasta or Artaxerxes, called by the Greeks *Cambyses*, and Ahasuerus that married Esther, called *Darius son of Hystaspes*. To these three the Persians gave these attributes—Cyrus was a father, Cambyses a master, and Darius a hoarder up. So Herodotus. (2) There shall be a fourth, *far richer than them all*, that is, Xerxes, of whose wealth the Greek authors take notice. By *his strength* (his vast army, consisting of 800,000 men at least) and *his riches* he *stirred up all* against *the realm of Greece*. Xerxes's expedition against Greece ended in shameful defeat. About thirty years after the first return from captivity, Darius, a young king, revived the building of the temple, owning the hand of God against his predecessors for hindering it, Ezra vi. 7.

3. He foretells Alexander's conquests and the partition of his kingdom, *v.* 3. He is that *mighty king* that shall *stand up* against the kings of Persia, shall *rule with great dominion*, and with despotic power, for he shall *do according to his will*.

But (*v.* 4) his *kingdom* shall soon be *broken*, and *divided* into four parts, *but not to his posterity*. His *kingdom was plucked up for others besides those* of his own family. Arideus, his brother, was made king in Macedonia; Olympias, Alexander's mother, killed him, and poisoned Alexander's two sons, Hercules and Alexander. Thus was his family rooted out by its own hands.

Verses 5–20

I. The rise and power of two great kingdoms out of the remains of Alexander's conquests, *v.* 5. 1. Egypt was made considerable by Ptolemaeus Lagus, one of Alexander's captains. He is called the king of the *south*, that is, Egypt, *v.* 8, 42, 43. The countries that at first belonged to Ptolemy are Egypt, Phoenicia, Arabia, Libya, Ethiopia, &c. 2. The kingdom of Syria was set up by Seleucus Nicanor, or the *conqueror*; he was one of Alexander's princes, and the most powerful of all Alexander's successors. Ptolemy invaded Judæa, and took Jerusalem *on a sabbath*, pretending a friendly visit. Seleucus also gave disturbance to Judæa.

II. The fruitless attempt to unite these two kingdoms as iron and clay in Nebuchadnezzar's image (*v.* 6): "*At the end of certain years*, about seventy after Alexander's death, the Lagidae and the Seleucidae shall associate, but not in sincerity. Ptolemy Philadelphus, king of Egypt, shall marry his daughter Berenice to Antiochus Theos, king of Syria," who had already a wife called *Laodice*. "Berenice shall come to the *king of the north*, to make an agreement, but

JAMIESON, FAUSSET, BROWN

CHAPTER 11

Vss. 1-45. This chapter is an enlargement of the eighth: THE OVERTHROW OF PERSIA BY GRECIA: THE FOUR DIVISIONS OF ALEXANDER'S KINGDOM: CONFLICTS BETWEEN THE KINGS OF THE SOUTH AND OF THE NORTH, THE PTOLEMIES AND SELEUCIDÆ: ANTIOCHUS EPIPHANES. **1. I**—the angel (ch. 10:18). **first year of Darius**—Cyaxares II; the year of the conquest of Babylon (ch. 5:31). Cyrus, who wielded the real power, though in name subordinate to Darius, in that year promulgated the edict for the restoration of the Jews, which Daniel was at the time praying for (ch. 9:1, 2, 21, 23). **stood**—implying promptness in helping (Ps. 94:16). **strengthen him**—viz., Michael; even as Michael (ch. 10:21, "*strengtheneth* himself with me") helped the angel, both joining their powers in behalf of Israel [ROSENMULLER]. Or, *Darius*, the angel "confirming him" in his purpose of kindness to Israel. **2. three kings in Persia**—Cambyses, Pseudo-Smerdis, and Darius Hystaspes. (Ahasuerus, Artaxerxes, and Darius, in Ezra 4:6, 7, 24.) The Ahasuerus of *Esther* (see *Note*, ch. 9:1) is identified with Xerxes, both in Greek history and in Scripture, appearing proud, self-willed, careless of contravening Persian customs, amorous, facile, and changeable (vs. 2). **fourth ... riches ... against ... Grecia**—Xerxes, whose riches were proverbial. Persia reached its climax and showed its greatest power in his invasion of Greece, 480 B.C. After his overthrow at Salamis, Persia is viewed as politically dead, though it had an *existence*. Therefore, the third verse, without noticing Xerxes' successors, proceeds at once to Alexander, under whom, first, the third world kingdom, Grecia, reached its culmination, and assumed an importance as to the people of God. **stir up all**—Four years were spent in gathering his army out of all parts of his vast empire, amounting to two millions six hundred and forty-one thousand men. [PRIDEAUX, *Connex.* 1. 4. 1. 410]. **3. mighty king ... do according to his will**—answering to the he-goat's "notable horn" (ch. 8:6, 7, 21). Alexander invaded Persia 334 B.C., to avenge the wrongs of Greece on Persia for Xerxes' past invasion (as Alexander said in a letter to Darius Codomanus, ARRIAN, *Alex.* 2. 14. 7). **4. kingdom ... divided toward ... four winds**—the fourfold division of Alexander's kingdom at his death (ch. 8:8, 22), after the battle of Ipsus, 301 B.C. **not to his posterity**—(*Notes*, ch. 8:8, 22). **nor according to his dominion**—None of his successors had so wide a dominion as Alexander himself. **others besides those**—besides *Alexander's sons*, Hercules by Barsine, Darius' daughter, and Alexander by Roxana, who were both slain [MAURER]. Rather, besides *the four successors* to the four chief divisions of the empire, there will be other lesser chiefs who shall appropriate smaller fragments of the Macedonian empire [JEROME]. **5.** Here the prophet leaves Asia and Greece and takes up Egypt and Syria, these being in continual conflict under Alexander's successors, entailing misery on Judea, which lay between the two. Holy Scripture handles external history only so far as it is connected with God's people, Israel [JEROME]. TREGELLES puts a chasm between vs. 4 and vs. 5, making the transition to the final Antichrist here, answering to the chasm (in his view) at ch. 8:22, 23. **king of ... south**—lit., "of midday": Egypt (vss. 8, 42), Ptolemy Soter, son of Lagus. He took the title "king," whereas Lagus was but "governor." **one of his princes**—Seleucus, at first a satrap of Ptolemy Lagus, but from 312 B.C. king of the largest empire after that of Alexander (Syria, Babylon, Media, etc.), and called therefore *Nicator*, i.e., "conqueror." Connect the words thus, "And one of his (Ptolemy's) princes, *even* he (Seleucus) shall be strong above him" (above Ptolemy, his former master). **6. in ... end of years**—when the predicted time shall be consummated (vs. 13, *Margin;* ch. 8:17; 12:13). **king's daughter of the south**—Berenice, daughter of Ptolemy Philadelphus of Egypt. The latter, in order to end his war with Antiochus Theus, "king of the north" (lit., "midnight": the prophetical phrase for the region whence came affliction to Israel, Jer. 1:13-15; Joel 2:20), i.e., Syria, gave Berenice to Antiochus, who thereupon divorced his former wife, Laodice, and disinherited her son, Seleucus Callinicus. The designation, "king of the north" and "of the south," is given in relation to Judea, as the standpoint. Egypt is mentioned by name (vss. 8, 42), though Syria is not; because the former was in Daniel's time a flourishing kingdom, whereas Syria was *then* a mere dependency of Assyria and Babylon: an undesigned proof of the genuineness of the Book of Daniel. **agreement**—lit., "rights," i.e., to put things to rights

ADAM CLARKE

CHAPTER 11

1. *In the first year of Darius the Mede.* This is a continuation of the preceding discourse.

2. *There shall stand up yet three kings.* Gabriel had already spoken of Cyrus, who was now reigning; and after him three others should arise. These were: Cambyses, the son of Cyrus; Smerdis, the Magian, who was an impostor, who pretended to be another son of Cyrus; and Darius, the son of Hystaspes, who married Mandane, the daughter of Cyrus. *The fourth shall be far richer than they all.* This was Xerxes, the son of Darius, of whom Justin says: "He had so great an abundance of riches in his kingdom, that although rivers were dried up by his numerous armies, yet his wealth remained unexhausted."

3. *A mighty king shall stand up.* This was Alexander the Great. It is not said that this mighty king shall stand up against Xerxes, for he was not born till one hundred years after that monarch; but simply that he should "stand up," i.e., that he should reign in Greece.

4. *His kingdom shall be broken.* Shall, after his death, be divided among his four chief generals, as we have seen before. See chap. viii. 22. *And not to his posterity.* The family of Alexander had a most tragical end, so that in fifteen years after his death not one of his family or posterity remained alive! "Blood calls for blood." He (Alexander) was the great butcher of men. He was either poisoned or killed himself by immoderate drinking when he was only thirty-two years and eight months old; and a retributive Providence destroyed all his posterity, so that neither root nor branch of them was left on the face of the earth. Thus ended Alexander, the great butcher; and thus ended his family and posterity.

5. *The king of the south.* This was Ptolemy Lagus, one of his generals, who had the government of Egypt, Libra, etc., which are on the south of Judea. He was strong, for he had added Cyprus, Phoenicia, Caria, etc., to his kingdom of Egypt. *And one of his princes . . . shall be strong above him.* This was Seleucus Nicator, who possessed Syria, Babylon, Media, and the neighboring countries. This was "the king of the north," for his dominions lay north of Judea.

6. *In the end of years.* Several historical circumstances are here passed by. *The king's daughter of the south.* Berenice, daughter of Ptolemy Philadelphus, king of Egypt, was married to Antiochus Theos, king of Syria. These two sovereigns had a bloody war for some years; and they agreed to terminate it by the above marriage, on condition that Antiochus would put away his wife, Laodice, and her children, which he did; and Berenice having brought an immense fortune to her husband, all things appeared to go on well for a time.

MATTHEW HENRY

she shall not retain the power of the arm; neither she nor her posterity shall establish themselves in the kingdom of the north, but *she shall be given up and those that brought her*." Antiochus divorced Berenice, took his former wife Laodice again, who poisoned him, procured Berenice and her son to be murdered, and set up her own son by Antiochus to be king, who was called *Seleucus Callinicus*.

III. A war between the two kingdoms, *v.* 7, 8. A branch from the same root with Berenice *shall stand up in his estate*. Ptolemaeus Euergetes, the son of Ptolemaeus Philadelphus, shall come against Seleucus Callinicus, king of Syria, to avenge his sister's quarrel, and shall prevail; and shall carry away rich booty into Egypt, and shall *continue more years than the king of the north*.

But (*v.* 9) he shall be forced to *come into his kingdom* and *return into his own land*, to keep peace there.

IV. The long reign of *Antiochus the Great*, king of Syria. Seleucus Callinicus, that king of the north that was overcome (*v.* 7) and died miserably, left two sons, Seleucus and Antiochus; these are the sons of the *king of the north*, that shall be *stirred up, and shall assemble a multitude of great forces*, to recover what their father had lost, *v.* 10. But Seleucus the elder was poisoned, and reigned only two years; and his brother Antiochus succeeded him, who reigned thirty-seven years, and was called *the Great*.

1. The *king of the south*, in this war, shall at first have great success. Ptolemaeus Philopater, moved with indignation at the indignities done by *Antiochus the Great*, shall *come forth, and fight with him*, and shall bring a vast army.

And the *other multitude*, the army of Antiochus, shall *be given into his hand*. Ptolemaeus Philopater, having gained this victory, *his heart was lifted up*; he went into the temple at Jerusalem, and entered the most holy place.

2. The *king of the north*, *Antiochus the Great*, shall *return* with a *greater army* than *the former*; and, at the *end of times* (*that is, years*) he shall *come with a mighty army, and great riches*, against the *king of the south*, that is, Ptolemaeus Epiphanes, who succeeded Ptolemaeus Philopater his father. In this expedition he had powerful allies (*v.* 14): Philip of Macedon was confederate with Antiochus against the king of Egypt. Antiochus routed him, destroyed a great part of his army; whereupon the Jews joined with him, helped him to besiege Ptolemaeus's garrisons. Then *the robbers of thy people shall exalt themselves to establish the vision*, but *they shall fall, and shall come to nothing*, *v.* 14.

JAMIESON, FAUSSET, BROWN

between the belligerents. **she shall not retain the power of the arm**—She shall not be able to effect the purpose of the alliance, viz., that she should be the *mainstay* of peace. Ptolemy having died, Antiochus took back Laodice, who then poisoned him, and caused Berenice and her son to be put to death, and raised her own son, Seleucus Nicator, to the throne. **neither shall he stand**—The king of Egypt shall not gain his point of setting his line on the throne of Syria. **his arm**—that on which he relied. Berenice and her offspring. **they that brought her**—her attendants from Egypt. **he that begat her**—rather as *Margin*, "the child *whom she brought forth*" [EWALD]. If *English Version* (which MAURER approves) be retained, as Ptolemy died a natural death, "given up" is not in his case, as in Berenice's, to be understood of giving up *to death*, but in a general sense, of his plan proving abortive. **he that strengthened her in these times**—Antiochus Theus, who is to *attach himself to her* (having divorced Laodice) at the times predicted [GEJER]. **7. a branch of her roots . . . in his estate**—Ptolemy Euergetes, brother of Berenice, succeeding *in the place* (see *Margin*) of Philadelphus, avenged her death by overrunning Syria, even to the Euphrates. **deal against them**—He shall deal with the Syrians at his own pleasure. He slew Laodice. **8. carry . . . into Egypt their gods . . .**—Ptolemy, on hearing of a sedition in Egypt, returned with 40,000 talents of silver, precious vessels, and 2400 images, including Egyptian idols, which Cambyses had carried from Egypt into Persia. The idolatrous Egyptians were so gratified, that they named him Euergetes, or "benefactor." **continue more years**—Ptolemy survived Seleucus four years, reigning in all forty-six years. MAURER translates, "Then he for several years shall *desist from* (contending with) the king of the north" (cf. vs. 9). **9. come into his kingdom**—Egypt: not only with impunity, but with great spoil. **10. his sons**—the two sons of the king of the north, Seleucus Callinicus, upon his death by a fall from his horse, viz., Seleucus Ceraunus and Antiochus the Great. **one shall . . . come**—Ceraunus having died, Antiochus alone prosecuted the war with Ptolemy Philopater, Euergetes' son, until he had recovered all the parts of Syria subjugated by Euergetes. **pass through**—like an "overflowing" torrent (vss. 22, 26, 40; Isa. 8:8). Antiochus penetrated to Dura (near Cæsarea), where he gave Ptolemy a four months' truce. **return**—renew the war at the expiration of the truce (so vs. 13). **even to his fortress**—Ptolemy's; Raphia, a border-fortress of Egypt against incursions by way of Edom and Arabia Petræa, near Gaza; here Antiochus was vanquished.

11. the king of the south . . . moved with choler—at so great losses, Syria having been wrested from him, and his own kingdom imperilled, though otherwise an indolent man, to which his disasters were owing, as also to the odium of his subjects against him for having murdered his father, mother, and brother, whence in irony they called him *Philopater*, "father-lover." **he shall set forth a great multitude**—Antiochus, king of Syria, whose force was 70,000 infantry and 5000 cavalry. **but . . . multitude . . . given into his hand**—into Ptolemy's hands; 10,000 of Antiochus' army were slain, and 4000 made captives.

12. when he hath taken away—i.e., *subdued* "the multitude" of Antiochus. **heart . . . lifted up**—instead of following up his victory by making himself master of the whole of Syria, as he might, he made peace with Antiochus, and gave himself up to licentiousness (POLYB. 87; JUSTIN. 30.4], and *profaned the temple of God* by entering the holy place [GROTIUS]. **not be strengthened by it**—He shall lose the power gained by his victory through his luxurious indolence. **13. return**—renew the war. **after certain years**—*fourteen years* after his defeat at Raphia. Antiochus, after successful campaigns against Persia and India, made war with Ptolemy Epiphanes, son of Philopater, a mere child. **14. many stand up against the king of the south**—Philip, king of Macedon, and rebels in Egypt itself, combined with Antiochus against Ptolemy. **robbers of thy people**—i.e., factious men of the Jews shall exalt themselves, so as to revolt from Ptolemy, and join themselves to Antiochus; the Jews helped Antiochus' army with provisions, when on his return from Egypt he besieged the Egyptian garrison left in Jerusalem (JOSEPHUS, *Antiquities*, 12.3.3). **to establish the vision**—Those turbulent Jews unconsciously shall help to fulfil the purpose of God, as to the trials which await Judea, according to this

ADAM CLARKE

But she shall not retain the power of the arm. "Her posterity" shall not reign in that kingdom. *But she shall be given up.* Antiochus recalled his former wife, Laodice, and her children; and she, fearing that he might recall Berenice, caused him to be poisoned and her to be murdered, and set her son Callinicus upon the throne. *And they that brought her.* Her Egyptian women, striving to defend their mistress, were many of them killed. *And he that begat her.* Or, as the margin, "he whom she brought forth"; the son being murdered, as well as the mother, by order of Laodice. *And he that strengthened her.* Probably her father, Ptolemy, who was excessively fond of her, and who had died a few years before.

7. *But out of a branch of her roots.* A branch from the same root from which she sprang. This was Ptolemy Euergetes, her brother, who, to avenge his sister's death, marched with a great army against Seleucus Callinicus, took some of his best places, indeed all Asia, from Mount Taurus to India, and returned to Egypt with an immense booty, 40,000 talents of silver, precious vessels, and 2,500 images of their gods, without Callinicus daring to offer him battle.

8. *He shall continue more years.* Seleucus Callinicus died (an exile) by a fall from his horse, and Ptolemy Euergetes survived him four or five years.

9. *So the king of the south*—Ptolemy Euergetes—*shall come into his kingdom*—that of Seleucus Callinicus. *And shall return.* Having heard that a sedition had taken place in Egypt, Ptolemy Euergetes was obliged to return speedily in order to repress it; else he had wholly destroyed the kingdom of Callinicus.

10. *But his sons shall be stirred up.* That is, the sons of Callinicus, who were Seleucus Ceraunus and Antiochus, afterwards called the Great. *Shall assemble a multitude.* Seleucus Ceraunus did assemble a multitude of forces in order to recover his father's dominions; but, not having money to pay them, they became mutinous, and he was poisoned by two of his own generals. His brother Antiochus was then proclaimed king; so that one only of the sons did *certainly come, and overflow, and pass through;* he retook Seleucia, and regained Syria. He then returned, and overcame Nicolaus, the Egyptian general; and seemed disposed to invade Egypt, as he came even to his fortress, to the frontiers of Egypt.

11. *The king of the south.* Ptolemy Philopater, who succeeded his father, Euergetes. *Shall come forth and fight with him.* He did come forth to Raphia, where he was met by Antiochus, when a terrible battle was fought between these two kings. *And he* (Antiochus, the king of the north) *shall set forth a great multitude.* Amounting to 62,000 foot, 6,000 horse, and 102 elephants; but yet the multitude was *given into his hand,* the hand of the king of the south; for Ptolemy gained a complete victory. Raphia and other neighboring towns declared for the victor, and Antiochus was obliged to retreat with his scattered army to Antioch, from which he sent to solicit a peace. See Polybius. lib. v.

12. *His heart shall be lifted up.* Had Ptolemy improved his victory, he might have dispossessed Antiochus of his whole empire; but giving way to pride, and a criminally sensual life, he made peace on dishonorable terms; and though he had gained a great victory, yet his kingdom was not *strengthened by it,* for his subjects were displeased and rebelled against him, or at least became considerably disaffected.

13. *The king of the north shall return . . . after certain years.* In about fourteen years Antiochus did return, Philopater being dead, and his son Ptolemy Epiphanes being then a minor. He brought a much larger army and more riches; these he had collected in a late eastern expedition.

14. *Many stand up against the king of the south.* Antiochus, and Philip, king of Macedon, united together to overrun Egypt. *Also the robbers of thy people.* The Jews, who revolted from their religion, and joined Ptolemy, under Scopas. *Shall exalt themselves to establish the vision.* That is, to build a temple like that of Jerusalem, in Egypt, hoping thereby to fulfill a prediction of Isaiah, chap. xxx. 18-25, which seemed to intimate that the Jews and the

MATTHEW HENRY

Hereupon (*v.* 15) the *king of the north,* this same Antiochus, shall carry on his design against the king of the south another way. (1) He shall surprise his strongholds; all that he has got in Syria and Samaria, and the king of Egypt, shall not be able to withstand him.

(2) He shall make himself master of the land of Judæa (*v.* 16): *He that comes against him* (that is, the king of the north) shall carry all before him; so the land of Israel was wasted and consumed. The land of Judæa lay between these two potent kingdoms of Egypt and Syria, so that in all the struggles between them that was sure to suffer.

(3) He shall still push on his war against the king of Egypt, and *set his face to enter with the strength of his whole kingdom,* taking advantage of the infancy of Ptolemy Epiphanes, *v.* 17.

(4) His war with the Romans (*v.* 18): He shall *turn his face to the isles* (*v.* 18), Greece and Italy. He took many of the isles about the Hellespont, but a *prince,* or *state* (so some), shall *return his reproach upon himself.* This was fulfilled when the two Scipios were sent with an army against Antiochus, and gave him a total defeat. Thus he caused the *reproach offered by him to cease.* (5) His fall. When he was routed by the Romans, and was forced to abandon to them all he had in Europe, he *turned to his own land,* and, to raise money to pay his tribute, he plundered a temple of Jupiter, which so incensed his own subjects against him that they killed him; so he *fell,* and *was no more found, v.* 19.

(6) His next successor, *v.* 20. There rose up one in his place, a *raiser of taxes,* a *sender forth of the extortioner.* Seleucus Philopater, the elder son of Antiochus the Great, was a great oppressor of his subjects, and exacted abundance of money from them. He likewise attempted to rob the temple at Jerusalem.

JAMIESON, FAUSSET, BROWN

vision. **but they shall fall**—Though helping to fulfil the vision, they shall fail in their aim, of making Judea independent.

15. king of . . . north—Antiochus the Great. **take . . . fenced cities**—Scopas, the Egyptian general, met Antiochus at Paneas, near the sources of the Jordan, and was defeated, and fled to Sidon, a strongly "fenced city," where he was forced to surrender. **chosen people**—Egypt's choicest army was sent under Eropus, Menocles, and Damoxenus, to deliver Scopas, but in vain [JEROME]. **16. he that cometh against him**—Antiochus coming against Ptolemy Epiphanes. **glorious land**—Judea (vss. 41, 45; ch. 8:9; Ezek. 20:6, 15). **by his hand shall be consumed**—lit., "perfected," i.e., completely brought under his sway. JOSEPHUS (*Antiquities,* 12. 3. 3) shows that the meaning is not, that the Jews should be utterly consumed: for Antiochus favored them for taking his part against Ptolemy, but that their land should be *subjected* to him [LENGKERKE]. GROTIUS translates, "shall be perfected by him," i.e., shall flourish under him. *English Version* gives a good sense; viz., that Judea was much "*consumed*" or *desolated* by being the arena of conflict between the combatants, Syria and Egypt. TREGELLES refers (vs. 14), "robbers of thy people," to the Gentiles, once oppressors, attempting to restore the Jews to their land by mere human effort, whereas this is to be effected only by divine interposition: their attempt is frustrated (vs. 16) by the wilful king, who makes Judea the scene of his military operations. **17. set his face**—*purpose* steadfastly. Antiochus' purpose was, however, turned from open assault to wile, by his war with the Romans in his endeavor to extend his kingdom to the limits it had under Seleucus Nicator. **upright one**—*Jasher,* or *Jeshurun* (Deut. 32:15; Isa. 44:2); the epithet applied by the Hebrews to their nation. It is here used not in praise; for in vs. 14 (see *Note*) they are called "robbers," or "men of violence, factious": it is the general designation of Israel, as *having God for their God.* Probably it is used to rebuke those who ought to have been God's "upright ones" for confederating with godless heathen in acts of *violence* (the contrast to the term in vs. 14 favors this). **thus shall he do**—Instead of at once invading Ptolemy's country with his "whole strength," he prepares his way for doing so by the following plan: he gives to Ptolemy Epiphanes his daughter Cleopatra in marriage, promising Cœlo-Syria and Judea as a dowry, thus securing his neutrality in the war with Rome: he hoped through his daughter to obtain Syria, Cilicia, and Lycia, and even Egypt itself at last; but Cleopatra favored her husband rather than her father, and so defeated his scheme [JEROME]. "She shall not stand on his side." **18. isles**—He "took many" of the isles in the Ægean in his war with the Romans, and crossed the Hellespont. **prince for his own behalf shall cause the reproach . . . to cease**—Lucius Scipio Asiaticus, the Roman general, by routing Antiochus at Magnesia (190 B.C.), caused the reproach which he offered Rome by inflicting injuries on Rome's allies, to cease. He did it *for his own glory.* **without his own reproach**—with untarnished reputation. **19. Then he shall turn . . . toward . . . his own land**—Compelled by Rome to relinquish all his territory west of the Taurus, and defray the expenses of the war, he garrisoned the cities left to him. **stumble . . . not be found**—Attempting to plunder the temple of Jupiter at Elymais by night, whether through avarice, or the want of money to pay the tribute imposed by Rome (a thousand talents), he was slain with his soldiers in an insurrection of the inhabitants [JUSTIN 32. 2]. **20. in his estate**—in Antiochus' stead: his successor, Seleucus Philopater, his son. **in the glory of the kingdom**—i.e., inheriting it by hereditary right. MAURER translates, "one who shall cause the taxgatherer (Heliodorus) to pass through the glory of the kingdom," i.e., *Judea,* "the glorious land" (vss. 16, 41; ch. 8:9). Simon, a Benjamite, in spite against Onias III, the high priest, gave information of the treasures in the Jewish temple; and Seleucus having reunited to Syria Cœlo-Syria and Palestine, the dowry formerly given by Antiochus the Great to Cleopatra, Ptolemy's wife, sent Heliodorus to Jerusalem to plunder the temple. This is narrated in II Maccabees 3:4, etc. Contrast Zechariah 9:8, "No oppressor shall pass through . . . any more."

ADAM CLARKE

Egyptians should be one people. They now revolted from Ptolemy and joined Antiochus, and this was the means of contributing greatly to the accomplishment of prophecies that foretold the calamities that should fall upon the Jews. *But they shall fall.* For Scopas came with a great army from Ptolemy and, while Antiochus was engaged in other parts, reduced Caelesyria and Palestine, subdued the Jews, placed guards on the coasts of Jerusalem, and returned with great spoils to Egypt.

15. *So the king of the north.* Antiochus came to recover Judea. Scopas was sent by Ptolemy to oppose him; but he was defeated near the fountains of Jordan, and was obliged to take refuge in Sidon with 10,000 men. Antiochus pursued and besieged him, and he was obliged by famine to surrender at discretion, and their lives only were spared. Antiochus afterwards besieged several of the fenced cities and took them; in short, carried all before him; so that the king of the south, Ptolemy, and *his chosen people,* his ablest generals, were not able to oppose him.

16. *He shall stand in the glorious land.* Judea. For he reduced Palestine; and the Jews supplied him with provisions, and assisted him to reduce the garrison that Scopas had left in the citadel of Jerusalem. *Which by his hand shall be consumed.* Or, "which shall be perfected in his hand." For Antiochus showed the Jews great favor: he brought back those that were dispersed, and reestablished them in the land; freed the priests and Levites from all tribute.

17. *He shall also set his face to enter.* Antiochus purposed to have marched his army into Egypt; but he thought it best to proceed by fraudulence, and therefore proposed a treaty of marriage between him and his daughter Cleopatra, called here *the daughter of women,* because of her great beauty and accomplishments. And this he appeared to do, having *upright ones with him.* Or, as the Septuagint have it, "And he will make all things straight with him"; that is, he acted as if he were influenced by nothing but the most upright views. But he intended his daughter to be a snare to Ptolemy, and therefore purposed to corrupt her that she might betray her husband. *But she shall not stand on his side.* On the contrary, her husband's interests became more dear to her than her father's, and by her means Ptolemy was put upon his guard against the intentions of Antiochus.

18. *Shall he turn his face unto the isles.* Antiochus had fitted out a great fleet of 100 large ships and 200 smaller, and with this fleet subdued most of the maritime places on the coast of the Mediterranean, and took many of the isles, Rhodes, Samos, Eubaea, Colophon, and others. *But a prince for his own behalf.* Or, "a captain." The consul Acilius Glabrio caused *the reproach . . . to cease*" beat and routed his army at the straits of Thermopylae, and expelled him from Greece. So he obliged him to pay the tribute which he hoped to impose on others, for he would grant him peace only on condition of paying the expense of the war, 15,000 talents. *Without his own reproach.* Without losing a battle, or taking a false step, Acilius caused the reproach which he was bringing upon the Romans to turn upon himself.

19. *He shall turn his face toward the fort of his own land.* After this shameful defeat, Antiochus fled to Sardis, thence to Apamea, and the next day got into Syria, and to Antioch, his own fort, whence he sent ambassadors to treat for peace; and was obliged to engage to pay the immense sum of money mentioned above. *But he shall stumble and fall.* Being under the greatest difficulties how to raise the stipulated sums, he marched into his eastern provinces to exact the arrears of taxes; and, attempting to plunder the temple of Jupiter Belus at Elymais, he was opposed by the populace, and he and his attendants slain. This is the account that Diodorus Siculus, Strabo, and Justin give of his death.

20. *Then shall stand up in his estate a raiser of taxes.* Seleucus Philopater succeeded his father, Antiochus. He sent his treasurer, Heliodorus, to seize the money deposited in the Temple of Jerusalem, which is here called *the glory of the kingdom;* see 2 Macc. ix. 23. He was so

MATTHEW HENRY

But *within a few days he shall be destroyed, neither in anger nor in battle*, but poisoned by Heliodorus, one of his own servants.

V. From all this let us learn, 1. That God in his providence sets up one, and pulls down another, as he pleases. Some have called great men the *foot-balls of fortune*; or, rather, they are the *tools of Providence*. 2. This world is full of *wars and fightings*, which come *from men's lusts*.

Verses 21–45

All this is a prophecy of the reign of Antiochus Epiphanes, the *little horn* (*ch.* viii. 9); a sworn enemy to the Jewish religion, and a bitter persecutor. Some things in this prediction concerning Antiochus are alluded to in the New Testament predictions of the antichrist, especially *v.* 36, 37.

I. His character: He called himself *Epiphanes—the illustrious*. The heathen writers describe him as an *odd-humoured* man, boisterous, base and sordid. He would sometimes steal out of the court into the city, and herd with any infamous company *in disguise*; some took him to be silly, others to be mad. He is called a *vile person*, for he had been a hostage at Rome for the fidelity of his father when the Romans had subdued him.

II. His accession to the crown. By a trick he got his elder brother's son, Demetrius, to be sent a hostage to Rome, in exchange for him, and his elder brother being killed by Heliodorus (*v.* 20), he took the kingdom. The states of Syria did not *give it to him* (*v.* 21), but he *came in peaceably*, pretending to reign for his brother's son, Demetrius, then a hostage at Rome. But *by flatteries he obtained the kingdom*, crushed Heliodorus; even to *the prince of the covenant*, his nephew, the rightful heir, he pretended to covenant that he would resign whenever he should return, *v.* 22.

But (*v.* 23) *after the league made with him he shall work deceitfully*, as one whose avowed maxim it is that princes ought not to be bound by their word any longer than it is for their interest. And *with a small people*, that at first cleave to him, he shall *become strong*, and (*v.* 24) *he shall enter peaceably upon the fattest places* of the kingdom of Syria, shall *scatter* among the people the *prey, and the spoil, and riches*, to insinuate himself into their affections; but, at the same time, he shall *forecast his devices against the strongholds*, to make himself master of them. When he has got the garrisons into his hands he will scatter his spoil no more, but rule by force.

III. His war with Egypt, his second expedition thither, is described, *v.* 25, 27. Antiochus shall *stir up his power and courage* against Ptolemaeus Philometer king of Egypt.

Ptolemy, thereupon, shall *be stirred up to battle* against him. Antiochus's army shall *overthrow* the Egyptian army.

JAMIESON, FAUSSET, BROWN

within few days . . . destroyed—after a reign of twelve years, which were "few" compared with the thirty-seven years of Antiochus' reign. Heliodorus, the instrument of Seleucus' sacrilege, was made by God the instrument of his punishment. Seeking the crown, in the absence at Rome of Seleucus' only son and heir, Demetrius, he poisoned Seleucus. But Antiochus Epiphanes, Seleucus' brother, by the help of Eumenes, king of Pergamos, succeeded to the throne, 175 B.C. **neither in anger, nor in battle** —not in a popular outbreak, nor in open battle. **21. vile**—Antiochus called Epiphanes, i.e., "the illustrious," for vindicating the claims of the royal line against Heliodorus, was nicknamed, by a play of sounds, Epimanes, i.e., "the madman," for his mad freaks beneath the dignity of a king. He would carouse with the lowest of the people, bathe with them in the public baths, and foolishly jest and throw stones at passers-by [POLYB. 26. 10]. Hence, as also for his crafty supplanting of Demetrius, the rightful heir, from the kingdom, he is termed "vile." **they shall not give . . . kingdom: but . . . by flatteries** —The nation shall not, by a public act, confer the kingdom on him, but he shall obtain it by artifice, "flattering" Eumenes and Attalus of Pergamos to help him, and, as he had seen candidates at Rome doing, canvassing the Syrian people high and low, one by one, with embraces [LIVY, 41. 20]. **22. shall they be overflown . . . before him**—Antiochus Epiphanes shall invade Egypt with overwhelming forces. **prince of the covenant**—Ptolemy Philometer, the son of Cleopatra, Antiochus' sister, who was joined in covenant with him. Ptolemy's guardians, while he was a boy, sought to recover from Epiphanes Cœlo-Syria and Palestine, which had been promised by Antiochus the Great as Cleopatra's dowry in marrying Ptolemy Epiphanes. Hence arose the war. Philometer's generals were vanquished, and Pelusium, the key of Egypt, taken by Antiochus, 171 B.C. **23.** TREGELLES notes three divisions in the history of the "vile person," which is continued to the end of the chapter: (1) His rise (vs. 21, 22). (2) The time from his making the covenant to the taking away of the daily sacrifice and setting up of the abomination of desolation (vss. 23-31). (3) His career of blasphemy, to his destruction (vss. 32-45); the latter two periods answering to the "week" of years of his "covenant with many" (viz., in Israel) (ch. 9:27), and the last being the closing half week of ch. 9. But the context so accurately agrees with the relations of Antiochus to Ptolemy that the primary reference seems to be to the "league" between them. *Antitypically*, Antichrist's relations towards *Israel* are probably delineated. Cf. ch. 8:11, 25, with vs. 22 here, "prince of the covenant." **work deceitfully**—Feigning friendship to young Ptolemy, as if he wished to order his kingdom for him, he took possession of Memphis and all Egypt ("the fattest places," vs. 34) as far as Alexandria. **with a small people**—At first, to throw off suspicion, his forces were small. **24. peaceably**—lit., "unexpectedly"; under the guise of friendship he seized Ptolemy Philometer. **he shall do that which his fathers have not done**—His predecessors, kings of Syria, had always coveted Egypt, but in vain: he alone made himself master of it. **scatter among them . . . prey**—among his followers (I Maccabees 1: 19). **forecast his devices against . . . strongholds**— He shall form a studied scheme for making himself master of the Egyptian fortresses. He gained them all except Alexandria, which successfully resisted him. Retaining to himself Pelusium, he retired to Judea, where, in revenge for the joy shown by the Jews at the report of his death, which led them to a revolt, he subdued Jerusalem by storm or stratagem. **for a time**—His rage shall not be for ever; it is but for a time limited by God. CALVIN makes "for a time" in antithesis to "unexpectedly," in the beginning of the verse. He *suddenly* mastered the weaker cities: he had to "forecast his plans" more *gradually* ("for a time") as to how to gain the stronger fortresses. **25.** A fuller detail of what was summarily stated (vss. 22-24). This is the first of Antiochus' three (vs. 29) open invasions of Egypt. **against the king of the south**—against Ptolemy Philometer. Subsequently, Ptolemy Physcon (the Gross), or Euergetes II, was made king by the Egyptians, as Ptolemy Philometer was in Antiochus' hands. **great army**—as distinguished from the "small people" (vs. 23) with which he first came. This was his first *open* expedition; he was emboldened by success to it. Antiochus "entered Egypt with an overwhelming multitude, with chariots, elephants, and cavalry" (I Maccabees 1:17). **stirred up**—by the necessity, though naturally indolent. **not stand**—Philometer was defeated. **they shall forecast . . .**—*His own nobles* shall frame

ADAM CLARKE

cramped to pay the annual tax to the Romans that he was obliged to burden his subjects with continual taxes. *He shall be destroyed, neither in anger*—fighting against an enemy, *nor in battle*—at the head of his troops; but basely and treacherously by the hand of Heliodorus, his treasurer, who hoped to reign in his stead.

21. *In his estate shall stand up a vile person.* This was Antiochus, surnamed Epiphanes—"the Illustrious." They did not give him the honor of the kingdom; he was at Athens, on his way from Rome, when his father died; and Heliodorus had declared himself king, as had several others. But Antiochus came in peaceably, for he obtained the kingdom by flatteries. He flattered Eumenes, king of Pergamus, and Attalus, his brother, and got their assistance. He flattered the Romans, and sent ambassadors to court their favor, and pay them the arrears of the tribute. He flattered the Syrians, and gained their concurrence; and as he flattered the Syrians, so they flattered him, giving him the epithet of Epiphanes—"the Illustrious." But that he was what the prophet here calls him, *a vile person*, is fully evident from what Polybius says of him, from *Athenaeus*, lib. v: "He was every man's companion: he resorted to the common shops, and prattled with the workmen: he frequented the common taverns, and ate and drank with the meanest fellows, singing debauched songs." On this account a contemporary writer, and others after him, instead of *Epiphanes*, called him *Epimanes*—"the Madman."

22. *And with the arms of a flood. The arms* which were *overflown . . . before him* were his competitors for the crown. They were vanquished by the forces of Eumenes and Attalus, and were dissipated by the arrival of Antiochus from Athens, whose presence disconcerted all their measures. *The prince of the covenant.* This was Onias, the high priest, whom he removed, and put Jason in his place, who had given him a great sum of money; and then put wicked Menelaus in his room, who had offered him a larger sum. Thus he acted deceitfully in the league made with Jason.

23. *He shall come up.* From Rome, where he had been a hostage for the payment of the tax laid on his father. *Shall become strong with a small people.* At first he had but few to espouse his cause when he arrived at Antioch, the people having been greatly divided by the many claimants of the crown; but being supported by Eumenes and Attalus, his few people increased, and he became strong.

24. *He shall enter peaceably even upon the fattest places.* The very richest provinces—Coelesyria and Palestine. *He shall do that which his fathers have not done, nor his fathers' fathers.* He became profuse in his liberalities, and scattered among them the prey of his enemies, the spoil of temples, and the riches of his friends, as well as his own revenues. He spent much in public shows, and bestowed largesses among the people. We are told in 1 Macc. iii. 30, that "in the liberal giving of gifts he abounded above all the kings that went before him." These are nearly the words of the prophet. *He shall forecast his devices.* As Eulaeus and Lenaeus, who were the guardians of the young Egyptian king Ptolemy Philometor, demanded from Antiochus the restitution of Coelesyria and Palestine, which he refused, he foresaw that he might have a war with that kingdom; and therefore "he forecast devices"—fixed a variety of plans to prevent this, visited the strongholds and frontier places to see that they were in a state of defense. And this he did *for a time*—he employed some years in hostile preparations against Egypt.

25. *He shall stir up his power.* Antiochus marched against Ptolemy, *the king of the south* (Egypt), with a great army; and the Egyptian generals had raised a mighty force. *Stirred up to battle.* The two armies met between Pelusium and Mount Casius; but he (the king of the south) could not stand—the Egyptian army was defeated. The next campaign he had greater success; he routed the Egyptian army, took Memphis, and made himself master of all Egypt, except Alexandria; see 1 Macc. i. 16-19. And all these advantages he gained by "forecasting devices," probably by corrupting his ministers and captains. Ptolemy Macron gave up Cyprus to

MATTHEW HENRY

The king of Egypt shall be betrayed by his own counsellors.

After the battle, a treaty of peace shall be set on foot, and these two kings shall meet but they shall neither of them be sincere in it. And then no marvel that *it shall not prosper*. The peace shall not last.

IV. Another expedition against Egypt. From the former he *returned with great riches* (*v.* 28), and therefore took the first occasion to invade Egypt again, two years after, *v.* 29.

But this attempt shall not succeed, for (*v.* 30) *the ships of Chittim shall come against him*, that is, the navy of the Romans, or ambassadors from the Roman senate, who came in ships. Ptolemaeus Philometer, king of Egypt, being now in a strict alliance with the Romans, craved their aid against Antiochus, who had besieged him and his mother Cleopatra in the city of Alexandria. The Roman senate thereupon sent an embassy to Antiochus, to command him to raise the siege, and, fearing the Roman power, he was forced to give orders for the raising of the siege and the retreat of his army out of Egypt. So Livy and others relate the story.

V. In his return from his expedition into Egypt, *v.* 28, he *did exploits* against the Jews; then he spoiled the city and temple. But the most terrible storm was in his return from Egypt, two years after, *v.* 30. Then he took Judæa in his way home; and, because he could not gain his point in Egypt by reason of the Romans interposing, he wreaked his revenge upon the Jews.

1. He had a rooted antipathy to the Jews' religion: *His heart* was *against the holy covenant*, *v.* 28. And (*v.* 30) *he had indignation against the holy covenant*. He hated the law of Moses and the worship of the true God, and was vexed at the privileges of the Jewish nation and the promises made to them.

2. He carried on his malicious designs against the Jews by the assistance of some apostate Jews. He kept up *intelligence with those that forsook the holy covenant* (*v.* 30). We read much in the book of the Maccabees of the mischief done to the Jews by these treacherous men of their own nation, Jason and Menelaus, and their party. "*Such as do wickedly against the covenant*, he shall *corrupt with flatteries*, to make use of them as decoys to draw in others," *v.* 32.

JAMIESON, FAUSSET, BROWN

treacherous "devices" against him (see vs. 26). Eulœus and Lenœus maladministered his affairs. Antiochus, when checked at last at Alexandria, left Ptolemy Philometer at Memphis as king, pretending that his whole object was to support Philometer's claims against the usurper Physcon. **26. they that feed of . . . his meat**—those from whom he might naturally have looked for help, his intimates and dependents (Ps. 41:9; John 13:18); his ministers and guardians. **his army shall overflow**—Philometer's army shall be dissipated as water. The phrase is used of overflowing *numbers,* usually in a victorious sense, but here in the sense of *defeat,* the very numbers which ordinarily ensure victory, hastening the defeat through mismanagement. **many shall fall down slain**—(I Maccabees 1:18, "many fell wounded to death"). Antiochus, when he might have slain all in the battle near Pelusium, rode around and ordered the enemy to be taken alive, the fruit of which policy was, he soon gained Pelusium and all Egypt [DIODORUS SICULUS, 26.77]. **27. both . . . to do mischief**—each to the other. **speak lies at one table**—They shall, under the semblance of intimacy, at Memphis try to deceive one another (*Notes,* vss. 3, 25). **it shall not prosper**—Neither of them shall carry his point at this time. **yet the end shall be**—"the end" of the contest between them is reserved for "the time appointed" (vss. 29, 30). **28.** (I Maccabees 1:19, 20, etc.). **against the holy covenant**—On his way back to Syria, he attacked Jerusalem, the metropolis of Jehovah's covenant people, slew 80,000, took 40,000 prisoners, and sold 40,000 as slaves (II Maccabees 5:5-14). **he shall do exploits**—He shall effect his purpose. Guided by Menelaus, the high priest, he entered the sanctuary with blasphemies, took away the gold and silver vessels, sacrificed swine on the altar, and sprinkled broth of the flesh through the temple (II Maccabees 5:15-21). **29. At the time appointed**—"the time" spoken of in vs. 27. **return**—his second open invasion of Egypt. Ptolemy Philometer, suspecting Antiochus' designs with Physcon, hired mercenaries from Greece. Whereupon Antiochus advanced with a fleet and an army, demanding the cession to him of Cyprus, Pelusium, and the country adjoining the Pelusiac mouth of the Nile. **it shall not be as the former**—not successful as the former expedition. Popilius Lœnas, the Roman ambassador, met him at Eleusis, four miles from Alexandria, and presented him the decree of the senate; on Antiochus replying that he would consider what he was to do, Popilius drew a line round him with a rod and said, "I must have a reply to give to the senate before you leave this circle." Antiochus submitted, and retired from Egypt; and his fleets withdrew from Cyprus. **or as the latter**—that mentioned in vss. 42, 43 [TREGELLES]. Or, making this the *third* expedition, the sense is "not as the first or as the second" expeditions [PISCATOR]. Rather "not as the former, *so* shall be *this* latter" expedition [GROTIUS]. **30. ships of Chittim**—the Roman ambassadors arriving in *Macedonian Grecian* vessels (see *Note,* Jer. 2:10). *Chittim,* properly *Cyprian,* so called from a Phœnician colony in Cyprus; then the islands and coasts of the Mediterranean in general. **grieved**—humbled and dispirited through fear of Rome. **indignation against the holy covenant**—Indignant that meantime God's worship had been restored at Jerusalem, he gives vent to his wrath at the check given him by Rome, on the Jews. **intelligence with them that forsake the . . . covenant**—viz., with the apostates in the nation (I Maccabees 1:11-15). Menelaus and other Jews instigated the king against their religion and country, learning from Greek philosophy that all religions are good enough to keep the masses in check. These had cast off circumcision and the religion of Jehovah for Greek customs. Antiochus, on his way home, sent Apollonius (167 B.C.) with 22,000 to destroy Jerusalem, two years after its capture by himself. Apollonius slew multitudes, dismantled and pillaged the city. They then, from a fortress which they built commanding the temple, fell on and slew the worshippers; so that the temple service was discontinued. Also, Antiochus decreed that all, on pain of death, should conform to the Greek religion, and the temple was consecrated to Jupiter Olympius. Identifying himself with that god, with fanatical haughtiness he wished to make his own worship universal (I Maccabees 1:41; II Maccabees 6:7). This was the gravest peril which ever heretofore threatened revealed religion, the holy people, and the theocracy on earth, for none of the previous world rulers had interfered with the religious worship of the covenant people, when subject to them (ch. 4:31-34; 6:27, 28; Ezra 1:2, 4; 7:12; Neh. 2:18). Hence arose the need of such a

ADAM CLARKE

Antiochus; and the Alexandrians were led to renounce their allegiance to Ptolemy Philometor, and took Euergetes, or Physcon, his younger brother, and made him king in his stead. All this was doubtless by the corruptions of Antiochus.

26. *Yea, they that feed of the portion of his meat.* This is the proof of what has been last noted, that the intrigues of Antiochus, corrupting the ministers and officers of Ptolemy, were the cause of all the disasters that fell on the Egyptian king. *They that feed of the portion of his meat*—who were in his confidence and pay, and possessed the secrets of the state—betrayed him; and these were the means of destroying him and his army, so that he was defeated, as was before observed.

27. *And both these kings' hearts shall be to do mischief.* That is, Antiochus and Ptolemy Philometor, who was nephew to the former, and whose interest he now pretended to have much at heart, since the Alexandrians had renounced their allegiance to him, and set his younger brother, Euergetes, upon the throne. When Antiochus came to Memphis, he and Philometor had frequent conferences at the same table; and at these times they spoke lies to each other, Antiochus professing great friendship to his nephew and concern for his interests, yet in his heart designing to ruin the kingdom by fomenting the discords which already subsisted between the two brothers. On the other hand, Philometor professed much gratitude to his uncle for the interest he took in his affairs, and laid the blame of the war upon his minister, Eulaeus; while at the same time he spoke lies, determining as soon as possible to accommodate matters with his brother, and join all their strength against their deceitful uncle. *But it shall not prosper.* Neither succeeded in his object, for the end of the appointed time was not yet come.

28. *Then shall he return into his land with great riches.* Antiochus did return, laden with riches, from the spoils that he took in Egypt; see 1 Macc. i. 19-20. And hearing that there had been a report of his death, at which the citizens of Jerusalem had made great rejoicings—*his heart shall be against the holy covenant.* He was determined to take a severe revenge, and he had an ostensible pretext for it; for Jason, who had been deprived of the high priesthood, hearing the report of the death of Antiochus, raised forces, marched against Jerusalem, took it, and obliged Menelaus, the high priest, to shut himself up in the castle. Antiochus brought a great army against Jerusalem; took it by storm; slew 40,000 of the inhabitants; sold as many more for slaves; boiled swine's flesh, and sprinkled the Temple and the altar with the broth; broke into the holy of holies; took away the golden vessels and other sacred treasures, to the value of 1,800 talents; restored Menelaus to his office; and made one Philip, a Phrygian, governor of Judea (1 Macc. i. 24; 2 Macc. v. 21).

29. *At the time appointed he shall return.* Finding that his treachery was detected, and that the two brothers had united their counsel and strength for their mutual support, he threw off the mask; and having collected a great army early in the spring, he passed through Coelesyria; entered Egypt; and the inhabitants of Memphis having submitted to him, he came by easy marches to Alexandria. But, says the prophet, *it shall not be as the former, or as the latter.* He had not the same success as the former, when he overthrew the Egyptian army at Pelusium; nor as the latter, when he took Memphis, and subdued all Egypt, except Alexandria.

30. *For the ships of Chittim shall come against him. Chittim* is well known to mean the Roman empire. Antiochus, being now in full march to besiege Alexandria, and within seven miles of that city, heard that ships were arrived there from Rome, with legates from the senate. He went to salute them. They delivered to him the letters of the senate, in which he was commanded, on pain of the displeasure of the Roman people, to put an end to the war against his nephews. Antiochus said he would go and consult his friends; on which Popilius, one of the legates, took his staff, and instantly drew a circle round Antiochus on the sand where he

MATTHEW HENRY

3. He profaned the temple. *Arms stand on his part* (*v.* 31), not only his own army, but deserters from the Jewish religion, and they *polluted the sanctuary of strength.* The story of this we have, 1 Mac. i. 21, &c. And (2 Mac. v. 15, &c.) *Antiochus went into the most holy temple, Menelaus, that traitor to the laws and to his own country, being his guide.* Antiochus *took away the daily sacrifice*, *v.* 31.

Then he *set up the abomination of desolation upon the altar* (1 Mac. i. 54), even an *idol altar* (*v.* 59), and called the temple the temple of *Jupiter Olympius*, 2 Mac. vi. 2.

4. He persecuted those who retained their integrity. Though there are many who *forsake the covenant*, yet there is a people who do *know their God*, and *they shall be strong and do exploits*, *v.* 32. Good old Eleazar, one of the *principal scribes*, when he had swine's flesh thrust into his mouth, did bravely spit it out again, though he knew he must be tormented to death for so doing, 2 Mac. vi. 19. The mother and her seven sons were put to death for adhering to their religion, 2 Mac. vii. This might well be called *doing exploits*; for to choose suffering rather than sin is a great exploit. The right knowledge of God is the strength of the soul, and, in the strength of that, gracious souls do exploits. Concerning this people that knew their God, we are here told *they shall instruct many*, *v.* 33. They shall show others what they have learned of the difference between truth and falsehood, good and evil. Some understand this of a society newly erected for the propagating of divine knowledge, called *Assideans, pietists* (so the name signifies). *They shall fall* by the cruelty of Antiochus, shall be put to death by his rage. Their sufferings *for righteousness' sake* would try and purge the nation of the Jews. *When they shall fall* they shall not be utterly cast down, but *they shall be holpen with a little help*, *v.* 34.

JAMIESON, FAUSSET, BROWN

forewarning of the covenant people as to him—so accurate, that PORPHYRY, the adversary of revelation, saw it was hopeless to deny its correspondence with history, but argued from its accuracy that it must have been written *subsequent* to the event. But as Messianic events are foretold in Daniel, the Jews, the adversaries of Jesus, would never have forged the prophecies which confirm His claims. The ninth chapter was to comfort the faithful Jews, in the midst of the "abominations" against "the covenant," with the prospect of Messiah who would "confirm the covenant." He would show by bringing salvation, and yet abolishing sacrifices, that the temple service which they so grieved after, was not absolutely necessary; thus the correspondence of phraseology would suggest comfort (cf. ch. 9:27 with ch. 11:30, 31). **31. arms**—viz., of the human body; not *weapons;* human forces. **they**—Antiochus' hosts confederate with the apostate Israelites; these latter attain the climax of guilt, when they not only, as before, "*forsake* the covenant" (vs. 30), but "*do wickedly against*" it (vs. 32), turning complete heathens. Here Antiochus' actings are described in language which reach beyond him the type to Antichrist the antitype [JEROME] (just as in Ps. 72 many things are said of Solomon the type, which are only applicable to Christ the Antitype); including perhaps Rome, Mohammed, and the final personal Antichrist. SIR ISAAC NEWTON refers the rest of the chapter from this verse to the Romans, translating, "*after him* arms (i.e., the Romans) shall stand up"; at the very time that Antiochus left Egypt, the Romans conquered Macedon, thus finishing the reign of Daniel's third beast; so here the prophet naturally proceeds to the fourth beast. JEROME'S view is simpler; for the narrative seems to continue the history of Antiochus, though with features only in type applicable to him, fully to Antichrist. **sanctuary of strength**—not only naturally a place of strength, whence it held out to the last against the besiegers, but chiefly the *spiritual* stronghold of the covenant people (Ps. 48:1-3, 12-14). Apollonius "polluted" it with altars to idols and sacrifices of swine's flesh, after having "taken away the daily sacrifice" (see *Note*, ch. 8:11). **place . . . abomination that maketh desolate**—i.e., that pollutes the temple (ch. 8:12, 13). Or rather, "the abomination *of the desolater,*" Antiochus Epiphanes (I Maccabees 1:29, 37-49). Cf. ch. 9:27, wherein the antitypical *desolating abomination* of Rome (the eagle standard, the bird of Jupiter, sacrificed to by Titus' soldiers within the sacred precincts, at the destruction of Jerusalem), of Mohammed and of the final Antichrist, is foretold. I Maccabees 1:54, uses the very phrase, "the fifteenth day of the month Casleu, in the 145th year, they set up the *abomination of desolation* on the altar"; viz., an idol-altar and image of Jupiter Olympius, erected upon Jehovah's altar of burnt offerings. "Abomination" is the common name for an *idol* in the Old Testament. The Roman emperor Adrian's erection of a temple to Jupiter Capitolinus where the temple of God had stood, A.D. 132; also the erection of the Mohammedan mosque of Omar in the same place (it is striking, Mohammedanism began to prevail in A.D. 610, only about three years of the time when Popery assumed the temporal power); and the idolatry of the Church of Rome in the spiritual temple, and the final blasphemy of the personal Antichrist in the literal temple (II Thess. 2) may all be antitypically referred to here under Antiochus the type, and the Old Testament Antichrist. **32.** (I Maccabees 1:52.) **corrupt**—seduce to apostasy. **by flatteries**—promises of favor. **people that . . . know their God**—the Maccabees and their followers (I Maccabees 1:62, 63). **33. they that understand**—who know and keep the truth of God (Isa. 11:2). **instruct many**—in their duty to God and the law, not to apostatize. **yet they shall fall**—as Eleazar (II Maccabees 6:18, etc.). They shall be sorely persecuted, even to death (Heb. 11:35, 36, 37; II Maccabees 6, 7). Their enemies took advantage of the Sabbath to slay them on the day when they would not fight. TREGELLES thinks, from comparison with vs. 35, it is *the people* who "fall," not *those of understanding*. But vs. 35 makes *the latter* "fall," not an unmeaning repetition; in vs. 33 they fall (die) by persecution; in vs. 35 they fall (spiritually) for a time by their own weakness. **flame**—in caves, whither they had retired to keep the Sabbath. Antiochus caused some to be roasted alive (II Maccabees 7:3-5). *many* **days**—rather, "*certain* days," as in ch. 8:27. JOSEPHUS (*Antiquities*, 12. 7. 6, 7) tells us the persecution lasted for three years (I Maccabees 1:59; 4:54; II Maccabees 10:1-7). **34. a little help**—The liberty obtained by the Maccabean heroes for the Jews was of but short duration.

ADAM CLARKE

stood, and commanded him not to pass that circle till he had given a definitive answer. Antiochus, intimidated, said, he would do whatever the senate enjoined; and in a few days after began his march, and returned to Syria. *Therefore he shall be grieved.* "Grieving and groaning," says Polybius; both mortified, humbled, and disappointed. *Have indignation against the holy covenant.* For he vented his rage against the Jews; and he sent his general, Apollonius, with 22,000 men against Jerusalem, plundered and set fire to the city, pulled down the houses round about it, slew much of the people, and built a castle on an eminence that commanded the Temple, and slew multitudes of the poor people who had come up to worship, polluted every place, so that the Temple service was totally abandoned, and all the people fled from the city. And when he returned to Antioch he published a decree that all should conform to the Grecian worship; and the Jewish worship was totally abrogated, and the Temple itself consecrated to Jupiter Olympius. How great must the wickedness of the people have been when God could tolerate this! In the transacting of these matters he had *intelligence with them that forsake the holy covenant;* with wicked Menelaus, the high priest; and the apostate Jews united with him, who gave from time to time such information to Antiochus as excited him against Jerusalem, the Temple, and the people. See 1 Macc. i. 41, 62; confirmed by Josephus, *War*, book i, chap. 1, s. 1.

31. *And arms shall stand on his part.* After Antiochus, *arms*, that is, the Romans, *shall stand* up: for "arms" in this prophecy everywhere denote military power; and "standing up," the power in activity and conquering.

CHARLES H. SPURGEON:

Verses 32, 33. The uninspired book of the Maccabees is perhaps the best interpreter of this passage in Daniel. The prophet, we think, refers to the great persecution under Antiochus, when the followers of Judas Maccabeus, knowing their God and keeping close to Him amid general defection, refused to bow before the idols of Syria; these were strong by God's grace, and did great exploits: wonders of valor we read of in the history of Judas and his brethren, and wonders of heroic suffering never surpassed are recounted of the mother and the sons and those other martyrs who, under tortures of the most amazing character, held fast their faith even to the end. In that age there were some who were stoned, who were sawn asunder, who felt the violence of fire, and yet were not separated from their God by all that the foe could do. We have a lesson to learn from the text before us, and we therefore leave the historical references and proceed to enter into the teaching of the text. It appears that the people who did all this were a knowing people and an understanding people. Those by whom the exploits were performed were not ignorant, but a people who did know their God; and those who helped to keep up the light of Israel in the midst of the thick darkness were not uninstructed themselves, but they were a people who did understand.

—*The Treasury of the Old Testament*

MATTHEW HENRY

It is likewise foretold that *many shall cleave to them with flatteries*; when they see the Maccabees prosper some Jews shall join with them, but will only pretend friendship either with design to *betray them* or in hope to *rise with them*; but the *fiery trial* (*v.* 35) will separate between the *precious and the vile.* Though these troubles may continue long, yet they will have *an end.*

5. He grew insolent, and profane, and, being puffed up with his conquests, bade defiance to Heaven, and trampled upon everything that was sacred, *v.* 36. He shall impiously dishonour the God of Israel, called here the *God of gods.* He shall, in defiance of him, *do according to his will* against his people and his holy religion. This was fulfilled when Antiochus forbade *sacrifices* to be *offered* in God's temple, and ordered the *sabbaths* to be *profaned*, the *sanctuary* and the *holy people* to be *polluted*, &c., to *the end that they might forget the law and change all the ordinances*, and this upon pain of death, 1 Mac. i. 45. Antiochus did not *regard any god*, but *magnified himself above all*, *v.* 37. Thus he carried all before him, *till the indignation was accomplished* (*v.* 36). Antiochus shall not *regard the god of his fathers*; he made laws to abolish the religion of his country, and to bring in the idols of the Greeks.

He shall set up an unknown god, a new god, *v.* 38. *In his estate* he shall *honour the god of forces*, a supposed deity of power, a *god whom his fathers knew not*, nor worshipped. This seems to be Jupiter Olympius, but never introduced among the Syrians till Antiochus introduced it.

Thus shall he do *in the most strongholds*, in the temple of Jerusalem, which is called *the sanctuary of strength* (*v.* 31), and here the *fortresses of munitions*; *there* he shall set up the image of this *strange god.* Some by the *Mahuzzim*, or *god of forces*, that Antiochus shall worship, understand *money*, which is said to *answer all things.*

VI. Here seems to be another expedition into Egypt. Ptolemy, *king of the south, pushes at him* (*v.* 40), makes an attempt upon some of his territories, whereupon Antiochus, the *king of the north, comes against him like a whirlwind*, with incredible

JAMIESON, FAUSSET, BROWN

They soon fell under the Romans and Herodians, and ever since every attempt to free them from Gentile rule has only aggravated their sad lot. The period of the world times (Gentile rule) is the period of depression of the theocracy, extending from the exile to the millennium [Roos]. The more immediate reference seems to be, the forces of Mattathias and his five sons were originally *few* (I Maccabees 2). **many shall cleave to them**—as was the case under Judas Maccabeus, who was thus able successfully to resist Antiochus. **with flatteries**—Those who had deserted the Jewish cause in persecution, now, when success attended the Jewish arms, joined the Maccabean standard, (e.g., Joseph, the son of Zecharias, Azarias, etc. (I Maccabees 5:55-57; II Maccabees 12:40; 13:21). MAURER explains it, of those who through fear of the Maccabees' severity against apostates joined them, though ready, if it suited their purpose, to desert them (I Maccabees 2:44; 3:58). **35. to try them**—the design of affliction. Image from *metals* tried with fire. **to purge**—Even in the elect there are dregs which need to be purged out (I Pet. 1:7). Hence they are allowed to fall for a time; not finally (II Chron. 32:31; Luke 22:31). Image from wheat cleared of its chaff by the wind. **make . . . white**—image from cloth (Rev. 7:9). **to . . . time of . . . end**—God will not suffer His people to be persecuted without limitation (I Cor. 10:13). The godly are to wait patiently for "the end" of "the time" of trial; "for it is (to last) yet for a time appointed" by God. **36.** The wilful king here, though primarily Antiochus, is antitypically and mainly Antichrist, the seventh head of the seven-headed and ten-horned beast of Revelation 13, and the "beast" of Armageddon (Rev. 16: 13, 16; 19:19). Some identify him with the revived French emperorship, the eighth head of the beast (Rev. 17:11), who is to usurp the kingly, as the Pope has the priestly, dignity of Christ—the false Messiah of the Jews, who will "plant his tabernacle between the seas in the holy mountain," "exalting himself above every god" (II Thess. 2:4; Rev. 13:5, 6). This last clause only in part holds good of Antiochus; for though he assumed divine honors, identifying himself with Jupiter Olympius, yet it was for that god he claimed them; still it applies to him as *the type.* **speak marvellous things against . . . God of gods**—so ch. 7:25, as to the "little horn," which seemingly identifies the two (cf. ch. 8:25). Antiochus forbade the worship of Jehovah by a decree "marvellous" for its wickedness: thus he was a type of Antichrist. Cf. ch. 7:8, "a mouth speaking great things." **indignation . . . accomplished**—God's visitation of wrath on the Jews for their sins (ch. 8:19). **that . . . determined**—(ch. 9:26, 27; 10: 21). **37. Neither . . . regard . . . the desire of women**—(Cf. Ezek. 24:16, 18). The wife, as the *desire* of man's eyes, is the symbol of the tenderest relations (II Samuel 1:26). Antiochus would set at naught even their entreaties that he should cease from his attack on Jehovah's worship [POLANUS]. MAURER refers it to Antiochus' attack on the temple of *the Syrian Venus, worshipped by women* (I Maccabees 6:1, etc.; II Maccabees 1:13). NEWTON refers it to Rome's "forbidding to marry." ELLIOTT rightly makes the antitypical reference be to *Messiah.* Jewish women desired to be mothers with a view to Him, the promised seed of the woman (Gen. 30:23; Luke 1:25, 28). **nor regard any god**—(II Thess. 2:4). **38. God of forces**—probably Jupiter Capitolinus, to whom Antiochus began to erect a temple at Antioch [LIVY 41. 20]. Translate, "He shall honor the god of *fortresses on his basis,*" i.e., the base of the statue. NEWTON translates, "And the god 'Mahuzzim' (*guardians,* i.e., saints adored as '*protectors*' in the Greek and Roman churches) shall he honor." **honour with gold . . .**—Cf. Revelation 17:4 as to Antiochus' antitype, Antichrist. **39.** NEWTON translates, *"to be defenders of Mahuzzim* (the monks and priests who uphold saint-worship), together with the strange god whom he shall acknowledge, he shall multiply honor." *English Version* is better: He shall do (exploits) in the most strongholds (i.e., shall succeed against them) with a strange god (under the auspices of a god which he worshipped not before, viz., Jupiter Capitolinus, whose worship he imported into his empire from Rome). Antiochus succeeded against Jerusalem, Sidon, Pelusium, Memphis. **cause them**—Antiochus "caused" his *followers and the apostates* "to rule over many" Jews, having "divided their land" (Judea), "for gain" (i.e., as a *reward* for their compliance). **40.** The difficulty of reconciling this with Antiochus' history is that no historian but PORPHYRY mentions an expedition of his into *Egypt* towards the close of his reign. This vs. 40, therefore, may be a recapitulation summing up the facts

ADAM CLARKE

36. *And the king shall do according to his will.* This may apply to Antiochus, who exalted himself above every god, called himself a god, sported with all religion, profaned the Temple. But others think an antichristian power in the Church is intended; for in the language of this prophecy *king* is taken for power, a kingdom, etc. That such a power did spring up in the Church that acted in an arbitrary manner against all laws, human and divine, is well-known. This power showed itself in the Greek emperors in the East, and in the bishops of Rome in the West.

MATTHEW HENRY

swiftness and fury, *with chariots, and horses, and many ships*, a great force. He shall *come through countries, and shall overflow and pass over*. In this flying march *many countries shall be overthrown by him*; and he shall enter into *the glorious land*, the land of Israel.

Some shall escape his fury, particularly Edom and Moab, and *the chief of the children of Ammon*, *v.* 41. But the land of Egypt *shall not escape. He shall have power over the treasures of gold and silver, and all the precious things of Egypt*, *v.* 43.

VII. Here is a prediction of the fall and ruin of Antiochus, as before (*ch.* viii. 25), when he is in the height of his honour, tidings *out of the east* and *out of the north* shall trouble him, *v.* 44. This obliged him to drop the enterprises he had in hand, and to go against the Persians and Parthians. Now comes the last effort of his rage against the Jews. When he finds himself perplexed and embarrassed in his affairs he shall *go forth with great fury to destroy and utterly to make away many*, *v.* 44. When impiety grows very impudent we may see its ruin near. *He shall come to his end and none shall help him.* This is the same with that which was foretold *ch.* viii. 25 (*He shall be broken without hand*).

JAMIESON, FAUSSET, BROWN

of the first expedition to Egypt (171-170 B.C., in vss. 22, 25; and vs. 41, the former invasion of Judea, in vs. 28; vss. 42, 43, the second and third invasions of Egypt (169 and 168 B.C.) in vss. 23, 24, 29, 30. AUBERLEN takes rather PORPHYRY'S statement, that Antiochus, in the eleventh year of his reign (166-165 B.C.), invaded Egypt again, and took Palestine on his way. The "tidings" (vs. 44) as to the revolt of tributary nations then led him to the East. PORPHYRY'S statement that Antiochus starting from Egypt took Arad in Judah, and devastated all Phœnicia, agrees with vs. 45; then he turned to check Artaxias, king of Armenia. He died in the Persian town Tabes, 164 B.C., as both POLYBIUS and PORPHYRY agree. Doubtless, antitypically, the final Antichrist, and its predecessor Mohammed, are intended, to whom the language may be more fully applicable than to Antiochus the type. The Saracen Arabs "of the south" "pushed at" the Greek emperer Heraclius, and deprived him of Egypt and Syria. But the Turks of "the north" not merely *pushed at*, but destroyed the Greek empire; therefore more is said of them than of the Saracens. Their "horsemen" are specfied, being their chief strength. Their standards still are *horse tails.* Their "ships," too, often gained the victory over Venice, the great naval power of Europe in that day. They "overflowed" Western Asia, and then "passed over" into Europe, fixing their seat of empire at Constantinople under Mohammed II [NEWTON]. **41.** Antiochus, according to PORPHYRY, marching against Ptolemy, though he turned from his course to wreak his wrath on the Jews, did not meddle with Edom, Moab, and Ammon on the side of Judea. In I Maccabees 4:61; 5:3 etc., it is stated that he used their help in crushing the Jews, of whom they were the ancient enemies. Cf. Isaiah 11:14, as to Israel's future retribution, just as the Maccabees made war on them as the friends of Antiochus (I Maccabees 5). Antitypically, the Turks under Selim entered Jerusalem on their way to Egypt, and retain "the glorious land" of Palestine to this day. But they never could conquer the Arabs, who are akin to Edom, Moab, and Ammon (Gen. 16:12). So in the case of the final Antichrist. **42, 43. Egypt . . . Libyans . . . Ethiopians**—The latter two, being the allies of the first, served under Antiochus when he conquered Egypt. Antitypically, Egypt, though it held out long under the Mamelukes, in A.D. 1517 fell under the Turks. Algiers, Tunis, and other parts of Africa, are still under them. **at his steps**—following him (*Margin*, Exod. 11:8; Judg. 4:10). **44. tidings out of the east and out of the north**—Artaxias, king of Armenia, his vassal, had revolted in the north, and Arsaces, leader of the Parthians, in the east (I Maccabees 3:10, etc., 37; TACITUS, *H.* 5. 8). In 147 B.C. Antiochus went on the expedition against them, on the return from which he died. **great fury**—at the Jews, on account of their successes under Judas Maccabeus, whence he desired to replenish his treasury with means to prosecute the war with them; also at Artaxias and Arsaces, and their respective followers. DE BURGH makes the "tidings" which rouse his fury, to be concerning the Jews' restoration; such may be the antitypical reference. **45. plant . . . between the seas**—the Dead Sea and the Mediterranean. **tabernacles of . . . palace**—his palace-like military tents, such as Oriental princes travel with. See *Note*, vs. 40, as to the time of Antiochus' attack on Judea, and his subsequent "end" at Tabes, which was caused by chagrin both at hearing that his forces under Lysias were overcome by the Jews, and at the failure of his expedition against the temple of Elymais (II Maccabees 9:5). **holy mountain**—Jerusalem and Mount Zion. The desolation of the sanctuary by Antiochus, and also the desecration of the consecrated ground round Jerusalem by the idolatrous Roman ensigns, as also by the Mohammedan mosque, and, finally, by the last Antichrist, are referred to. So the last Antichrist is to sit upon "the *mount* of the congregation" (Isa. 14:13), but "shall be brought down to hell" (cf. *Note*, ch. 7:26; II Thess. 2:8).

ADAM CLARKE

H. DEANE:

Verse 40. "At the time of the end." These verses speak of the last expedition of the northern king, and of the disappearance of the king of the south. The portrait of Antiochus, as noticed in verse 36, was gradually fading away, and now not a line of it remains. No such invasion of Egypt as that mentioned here is mentioned in history. From the time mentioned in verse 30 he appears to have abstained from approaching too closely to the Roman authorities. The story related in 1 Macc. 3:27–37 states that on hearing of the successes of the Maccabee princes he went into Persia on a plundering expedition, leaving Lysias his representative in Palestine. Lysias was defeated at Bethsur, and the news of the overthrow of his army was brought to Antiochus while he was in Persia. So appalling was the effect upon him of these tidings, that "he fell sick for grief" (1 Macc. 6:8), and died. It is unnecessary to suppose that the revelation resumes the narrative from verse 29 after a parenthetic passage (verses 30–39), or to assume that we have a general recapitulation of the wars of Antiochus, described in verses 22–39, without distinguishing the different campaigns.

"Time of the end" (8:17). The words mean the end of the world, with which (verse 45) the end of this king coincides. The word "push" occurs also in 8:4, and from the context it may be inferred that the southern king begins the last conflict, in the course of which both kings come to an end.

Verse 41. "The glorious land." On the occasion of his hasty march against Egypt, while passing through Palestine, the king takes the shortest route, avoiding the three tribes which had been distinguished by their hostility towards the people of Israel. It is remarkable that these nations (two of which appear as figures of Antichrist, Isa. 25:10; 63:1) should escape, while other nations fell before Antichrist.

Verse 44. "He shall go forth." The end of the northern king. While in Egypt he has bad news brought to him from the north and from the east, which stirs up feelings of revenge. Once again he halts in Palestine, where he comes to an end. That this cannot apply to Antiochus is evident from the following facts—(1) Antiochus was in Persia when the news of the defeat of Lysias reached him; (2) Judea and Jerusalem cannot in any sense be regarded as either east or north of Persia; (3) Antiochus died in Persia, and not near Jerusalem.

—*Ellicott's Commentary of the Whole Bible*

CHAPTER 12 (Matthew Henry)

CHAPTER 12 (Jamieson, Fausset, Brown)

Vss. 1-13. CONCLUSION OF THE VISION (chs. 10-12) AND EPILOGUE TO THE BOOK. Cf. vss. 4, 13; as vss. 6, 7 refer to ch. 7:25, i.e., to the time of Antichrist, so the subsequent vss. 8-12 treat of the time of Antiochus (cf. vs. 11 with ch. 11:31), thus putting together in one summary view the two great periods of distress. The political resurrection of the Jews under the Maccabees is the starting point of transition to the literal resurrection about to follow the destruction of Antichrist by Christ's com-

CHAPTER 12 (Adam Clarke)

MATTHEW HENRY

Verses 1–4

I. Jesus Christ shall appear his church's patron and protector: *At that time*, when the persecution is at the hottest, *Michael shall stand up*, *v*. 1. Christ is *that great prince. At that time* Michael shall stand up for the working out of our eternal salvation; the Son of God shall be incarnate, shall be *manifested to destroy the works of the devil.* Christ *stood for the children of our people* when he was made sin and a curse for them, stood in their stead as a sacrifice, bore the curse for them, to bear it from them.

II. When Christ appears he will recompense tribulation to those that trouble his people. There shall *be a time of trouble*, threatening to all. This is applicable, 1. To the destruction of Jerusalem, which Christ calls such a *great tribulation as was not since the beginning of the world to this time*, Matt. xxiv. 21. Or, 2. To the judgment of the great day, that will be such a *day of trouble* as never was to all those whom Michael our prince stands against.

III. He will work salvation for his people: "*At that time thy people shall be delivered* from the mischief and ruin designed them by Antiochus."

IV. There shall be a resurrection of those that *sleep in the dust*, *v*. 2. 1. When God works deliverance for his people from persecution it is a kind of resurrection; so the Jews' release out of Babylon was represented in vision (Ezek. xxxvii) and so the deliverance of the Jews from Antiochus, they were as *life from the dead*. 2. When, upon the appearing of Michael our prince, his gospel is preached, many of those who *sleep in the dust*, both Jews and Gentiles, shall be awakened by it to take upon them a profession of religion. But, 3. It must be meant of the general resurrection at the last day: *The multitude of those that sleep in the dust shall awake*.

V. There shall be glorious reward conferred on those who, in the day of trouble and distress, being themselves *wise*, did *instruct many*. They should do eminent service, and yet should *fall by the sword and by flame*; now, if there were not another life after this, they would be *of all men most miserable*, and therefore we are here assured that they shall be recompensed *in the resurrection of the just* (*v*. 3). Those that turn *men to righteousness*, that *turn sinners from the errors of their ways* and help to *save their souls from death* (Jas. v. 20), will share in the glory of those they have helped to heaven, which will be a great addition to their own glory.

VI. This prophecy of those times, though sealed up now, would be of great use to those that should live then, *v*. 4. Daniel must now *shut up the words and seal the book* because the *time would be long* ere these things would be accomplished. He must keep it safely, as a treasure of great value, laid up for the ages to come. Those things of God which are now dark and obscure will hereafter be made clear, and easy to be understood. *Truth is the daughter of time.* Scripture prophecies will be expounded by the accomplishment of them.

JAMIESON, FAUSSET, BROWN

ing in glory. The language passes here from the nearer to the more remote event, to which alone it is fully applicable. **1. at that time**—*typically*, towards the close of Antiochus' reign; *antitypically*, the time when Antichrist is to be destroyed at Christ's coming. **Michael**—the guardian angel of Israel ("thy people"), (ch. 10:13). The transactions on earth affecting God's people have their correspondences in heaven, in the conflict between good and bad angels; so at the last great contest on earth which shall decide the ascendency of Christianity (Rev. 12:7-10). An archangel, not the Lord Jesus; for he is distinguished from "the Lord" in Jude 9. **there shall be**—rather, "it shall be." **time of trouble, such as never was**—partially applicable to the time of Antiochus, who was the first subverter of the Jews' religion, and persecutor of its professors, which no other world power had done. Fully applicable to the last times of Antichrist, and his persecutions of Israel restored to Palestine. Satan will be allowed to exercise an unhindered, unparalleled energy (Isa. 26:20, 21; Jer. 30:7; Matt. 24:21; cf. ch. 8:24, 25; 11:36). **thy people shall be delivered**—(Rom. 11:26). The same deliverance of Israel as in Zechariah 13:8, 9, "the third part . . . brought through the fire . . . refined as silver." The remnant in Israel spared, as not having joined in the Antichristian blasphemy (Rev. 14:9, 10); not to be confounded with those who have confessed Christ before His coming, "the remnant according to the election of grace" (Rom. 11:5), part of the Church of the first-born who will share His millennial reign in glorified bodies; the spared remnant (Isa. 10:21) will only know the Lord Jesus when they see Him, and when the spirit of grace and supplication is poured out on them [TREGELLES]. **written in the book**—viz., of God's secret purpose, as destined for deliverance (Ps. 56:8; 69:28; Luke 10:20; Rev. 20: 15; 21:27). Metaphor from a muster-roll of citizens (Neh. 7:5). **2. many . . . that sleep**—"many *from among* the sleepers . . . *these* shall be unto everlasting life; but *those* (the rest of the sleepers who do not awake at this time) shall be unto shame" [TREGELLES]. Not the *general* resurrection, but that of those who share in the first resurrection; the rest of the dead being not to rise till the end of the thousand years (Rev. 20:3, 5, 6; cf. I Cor. 15:23; I Thess. 4:16). Israel's national resurrection, and the first resurrection of the elect Church, are similarly connected with the Lord's coming forth out of His place to punish the earth in Isaiah 26:19, 21; 27:6. Cf. Isaiah 25:6-9. The Jewish commentators support TREGELLES. AUBERLEN thinks the sole purpose for which the resurrection is introduced in this verse is an incitement to faithful perseverance in the persecutions of Antiochus; and that there is no *chronological* connection between the time of trouble in vs. 1 and the resurrection in vs. 2; whence the phrase, "at that time," twice occurs in vs. 1, but no fixing of time in vss. 2, 3; II Maccabees 7:9, 14, 23, shows the fruit of this prophecy in animating the Maccabean mother and her sons to brave death, while confessing the resurrection in words like those here. Cf. Hebrews 11:35. NEWTON's view that "many" means *all*, is not so probable; for Romans 5:15, 19, which he quotes, is not in point, since the *Greek* is "*the* many," i.e., all, but there is no article in the *Hebrew* here. Here only *in the Old Testament* is "everlasting life" mentioned. **3. wise**—(Prov. 11:30). Answering to "they that understand" (ch. 11:33, 35), the same *Hebrew, Maskilim*; Israelites who, though in Jerusalem when wickedness is coming to a head, are found intelligent witnesses against it. As *then* they appeared worn out with persecutions (typically, of Antiochus; antitypically, of Antichrist); so *now* in the resurrection they "shine as the brightness of the firmament." The design of past afflictions here appears "to make them white" (Matt. 13:43; Rev. 7:9, 14). **turn . . . to righteousness**—lit., "justify," i.e., convert many to justification through Christ (Jas. 5:20). **stars**—(I Cor. 15:41, 42). **4. shut up . . . seal the book**—John, on the contrary, is told (Rev. 22:10) not to seal his visions. Daniel's prophecy refers to a *distant* time, and is therefore obscure for the immediate future, whereas John's was to be *speedily* fulfilled (Rev. 1:1, 3; 22:6). *Israel*, to whom Daniel prophesied after the captivity, with premature zeal sought after signs of the predicted period: Daniel's prophecy was designed to restrain this. The *Gentile* Church, on the contrary, for whom John wrote, needs to be impressed with the shortness of the period, as it is, owing to its Gentile origin, apt to conform to the world, and to forget the coming of the Lord (cf. Matt. 25:13, 19; Mark 13:32-37; II Pet. 3:8, 12; Rev. 22:20). **run to and fro**—not referring to the modern rapidity of loco-

ADAM CLARKE

1. *And at that time Michael shall stand up.* Michael, the archangel, as has already been observed, was ever reputed the guardian of the Jewish people.

Every one that shall be found written in the book. All that truly fear, love, and obey the Lord.

2. *Many of them that sleep in the dust of the earth.* This prophecy has been referred to the future restoration of the Jews. It will be also true of the state of mankind at the general judgment.

3. *And they that be wise.* Those who are thoroughly instructed in Christ's word and doctrine *shall shine*—shall be eminently distinguished in the Christian Church by the holiness of their lives and the purity of their creed.

And they that turn many to righteousness. They who, by preaching Christ crucified among their brethren, shall be the means of converting them to the Christian faith, shall be *as the stars*—bright luminaries in the gospel kingdom of Jesus Christ.

4. *Shut up the words, and seal the book.* When a prophet received a prediction concerning what was at a considerable distance of time, he shut his book, did not communicate his revelation for some time after. This Daniel was commanded to do, chap. viii. 26. See also Isa. **xxix. 10-11; Rev. xxii. 10.** Among the ancients, those were said to "seal" who in the course of their reading stamped the places of which they were yet doubtful, in order to keep them in memory, that they might refer to them again, as not yet fully understood. *Many shall run to and fro.* Many shall endeavor to search out the

MATTHEW HENRY

Verses 5–13

Daniel had been made to foresee the amazing revolutions of states and kingdoms, as far as the Israel of God was concerned in them; in them he foresaw troublous times to the church. *When* shall the *end be?* And, *What* shall the *end be?*

I. The question, *When shall the end be?* is asked by an angel, *v.* 5, 6. Daniel had had discourse with the angel Gabriel, and now he *looks*, and *behold other two* (*v.* 5), two angels that he had not seen before, *one upon the bank of the river on one side and the other on the other side.* Christ stood *on the waters of the river* (*v.* 6), *between the banks of Ulai.* Daniel had not seen them before, but now, when they began to speak, he looked up, and saw them. The question was put, to the *man clothed in linen*, of whom we read before (*ch.* x. 5), to Christ our great high priest, *who was upon the waters of the river.* The angel asked as one concerned, *How long shall it be?* What is the time for the *end of these wonders,* these suffering trying times, that are to pass over the people of God? Here is a general account given to the angel that made the enquiry (*v.* 7). They shall continue *for a time, times, and a half*, that is, a year, two years, and half a year, as was before intimated (*ch.* vii. 25). Some understand it indefinitely, a certain time for an uncertain; it shall be *for a time* (a considerable time), for *times* (a longer time yet), and yet but *half a time*; when it is over it shall seem not half so much as was feared. But it is rather to be taken for a certain time; we meet with it in the Revelation, sometimes of three days and a half, put for three years and a half, sometimes forty-two months, sometimes 1,260 days. This Mighty One that Daniel saw stood with *both feet* on the water, and swore with *both hands* lifted up. God's time to succour and relieve his people is when their affairs are brought to the last extremity; *in the mount of the Lord it shall be seen* that Isaac is saved just when he lies ready to be sacrificed. Now the event answered the prediction; Josephus says that Antiochus surprised Jerusalem *and held it three years and six months*, and was then *cast out of the country* by the Maccabees. Christ's public ministry continued *three years and a half*, during which time he endured the contradiction of sinners against himself, and lived in poverty and disgrace; and then, when at his death, his enemies triumphed over him, he obtained the most glorious victory and said, *It is finished.*

II. The question, *What shall the end be?* is asked by Daniel. Daniel asked this question because, though he *heard what was said* to the angel, yet he did not *understand* it, *v.* 8. He directs his enquiry not to the angel that talked with him, but immediately to Christ. When we take a view of the affairs of this world, and of the church of God in it, we see things move as if they would end in the utter ruin of God's kingdom among men. When we see vice and impiety, the decay of religion, the sufferings of the righteous, and the triumphs of the ungodly, we may well ask, *O my Lord! what will be the end of these things?* Daniel must content himself with the discoveries that had been made to him: "*Go thy way, Daniel. Go thy way, and record what thou hast seen* and heard, for the benefit of posterity, and covet not to see and hear more at present." He must not expect that what had been said to him would be fully understood till it was accomplished. As long as the world stands, there will still be in it a mixture of good and bad, *v.* 10. Bad men will do bad things; and a *corrupt tree* will *never bring forth good fruit.* Wicked practices are the natural products of wicked principles and dispositions. We are told, before, that the *wicked will do wickedly.* They *will not understand*; they shut their eyes against the light, and none so blind as those that will not see. Wilful sin is the effect of wilful ignorance; they *will not understand* because *they are wicked*; they *hate the light*, and come not to the light, *because their deeds are evil*, John iii. 19. Yet, bad as the world is, God will secure to himself a remnant of good people in it. There shall be many, to whom the providences and ordinances of God shall be *a savour of life unto life. Many shall be purified, and made white, and tried*, by their troubles (compare *ch.* xi. 35). The word of God shall do them good. When the *wicked understand not*, but stumble at the word, the *wise shall understand.* Those who are governed by the divine law and love shall be illuminated with a divine light. For if any man will *do his will* he shall *know the truth*, John vii. 17.

JAMIESON, FAUSSET, BROWN

motion, as some think, nor to Christian missionaries going about to preach the Gospel to the world at large [BARNES], which the context scarcely admits; but, whereas now but few care for this prophecy of God, "at the time of the end," i.e., near its fulfilment, "many shall run to and fro," i.e., scrutinize it, running through every page. Cf. Habak kuk 2:2 [CALVIN]: it is thereby that "*the* knowledge (viz., of God's purposes as revealed in prophecy) shall be increased." This is probably being now fulfilled. **5.** A vision of two other angels, one on one side of the Hiddekel or Tigris, the other on the other side, implying that on all sides angels attend to execute God's commands. The angel addressing Daniel had been *over* the river "from above" (vs. 6, *Margin*). **6. one**—viz., of the two (vs. 5). **man . . . in linen**—who had spoken up to this point. God impelled the angel to ask in order to waken us out of our torpor, seeing that the very "angels desire to look into" the things affecting man's redemption (I Pet. 1:12), as setting forth the glory of their Lord and ours (Eph. 3:10). **How long . . . to the end of these wonders**—This question of the angel refers to the final dealings of God in general, Antichrist's overthrow, and the resurrection. Daniel's question (vs. 8) refers to the more immediate future of his nation [AUBERLEN]. **7. held up . . . right . . . and . . . left hand**—Usually the right hand was held up in affirmation as an appeal to heaven to attest the truth (Deut. 32:40; Rev. 10:5, 6). Here *both* hands are lifted up for the fuller confirmation. **time, times, and a half**—(See *Note*, ch. 7:25). NEWTON, referring this prophecy to the Eastern apostasy, Mohammedanism, remarks that the same period of three and a half years, or 1260 prophetic days, is assigned to it as the Western apostasy of the little horn (ch. 7:25); and so, says PRIDEAUX, Mohammed began to forge his imposture, retiring to his cave, A.D. 606, the very year that Phocas made the grant to the bishop of Rome, whence he assumed the title, The Universal Pastor; Antichrist thus setting both his feet on Christendom together, the one in the East, and the other in the West. Three and a half is the time of the world power, in which the earthly kingdoms rule over the heavenly [AUBERLEN]. "Three and a half" represents *the idea of spiritual trial;* (besides this certain *symbolical* meaning, there is doubtless an accurate *chronological* meaning, which is as yet to us uncertain): it is half of "seven," the complete number, so a semi-perfect state, one of probation. The holy city is trodden by the Gentiles forty-two months (Rev. 11:2), so the exercise of the power of the beast (Rev. 13:5). The two witnesses preach in sackcloth 1260 days, and remained unburied *three days and a half:* so the woman in the wilderness: also the same for a "time, times, and a half" (Rev. 11:3, 9, 11; 12:6, 14). *Forty-two* connects the Church with Israel, whose haltings in the wilderness were *forty-two* (Num. 33: 1-50). The famine and drought on Israel in Elijah's days were for "three years and six months" (Luke 4:25; Jas. 5:17); there same period as Antiochus' persecution: so the ministry of the Man of Sorrows, which ceased in the midst of a week (ch. 9:27) [WORDSWORTH, *Apocalypse*]. **scatter . . . holy people**—"accomplished" here answers to "the consummation" (ch. 9:27), viz., the "pouring out" of the last dregs of the curse on the "desolated holy people." Israel's lowest humiliation (the utter "scattering of her power") is the precursor of her exaltation, as it leads her to seek her God and Messiah (Matt. 23:39). **8. understood not**—Daniel "understood" the main features of the vision as to Antiochus (ch. 10:1, 14), but not as to the *times.* I Peter 1:10-12 refers mainly to Daniel: for it is he who foretells "the sufferings of Christ and the glory that should follow"; it is he who prophesies "not unto himself, but unto us"; it is he who "searched what, or what manner of *time* the Spirit of Christ in him did signify." **9.** Daniel's desire of knowing more is thus deferred "till the time of the end." John's Revelation in part reveals what here is veiled (*Note*, vs. 4, and ch. 8:26). **10.** There is no need of a fuller explanation as to the *time;* for when the predictions so far given shall have come to pass, the godly shall be "purified" by the foretold trials and shall understand that the end is at hand; but the wicked shall not understand, and so shall rush on to their own ruin (ch. 11:33-35) [MAURER]. The "end" is primarily, of Antiochus' persuasion; antitypically, the end of Antichrist's. It is the very clearness in the main which renders necessary the obscurity. The fulfilment of God's decree is not a mere arithmetical problem which the profane may understand by arithmetical calculations, but a holy enigma to stimulate to a faithful observance of God's ways, and to a diligent study of the history of God's peo-

ADAM CLARKE

sense, *and knowledge shall be increased* by these means, though the meaning shall not be fully known till the events take place. Then the seal shall be broken, and the sense become plain. This seems to be the meaning of this verse, though another has been put on it, viz., "Many shall run to and fro preaching the Gospel of Christ, and therefore religious knowledge and true wisdom shall be increased." This is true in itself, but it is not the meaning of the prophet's words.

5. *Behold, there stood other two.* Probably two angels. We know no more of them, unless they be the same as those called "saints," chap. viii. 13, which see. The *river* was most likely the Tigris.

6. *The man clothed in linen.* Gabriel, in a human form. Thus he is represented, chap. x. 5.

7. *Which was upon the waters.* By this description, he was standing on the water. This is very similar to the description of the angel, Rev. x. 5-6, and in the seventh verse there seems to be a reference to this prophecy, *a time, times, and an half.* See the note on chap. vii. 25.

9. *The words are closed up.* The prophecy shall not be understood, but in its accomplishment; and then the depth of the wisdom and providence of God will be clearly seen in these matters. See on v. 4. We must wait *till the time of the end.*

10. *Many shall be purified.* During the interim the great work of God's providence and grace shall be carried on in the salvation of men; who, in the midst of trials, temptations, and difficulties, shall be *purified, and made white*—be fully saved from their sins. *None of the wicked shall understand.* Because they are wicked, and will continue in their sins, the eyes of their understanding shall be closed, and their hearts hardened, so that they shall not see the light of the glorious gospel. *But the wise.* Those who open their hearts to God, that He may pour in His light, *shall understand* the things that make for their peace.

MATTHEW HENRY

Here is something added more particularly concerning the time of the continuance of those troubles, in what is said to Daniel, *v.* 11, 12. The time of the trouble is to be dated, from the *taking away of the daily sacrifice* by Antiochus, and the *setting up* of the image of Jupiter upon the altar, which was the *abomination of desolation.*

Their trouble shall last 1,290 days, *three years* and *seven months*, or (as some reckon) *three years, six months*, and *fifteen days*; and then it is probable, the daily sacrifice was restored, and the abomination of desolation taken away. It appears that the beginning of the trouble was in the 145th year of the Seleucidae, and the end of it in the 148th year. Thus we may learn, *First*, That there is a time fixed for the termination of the church's troubles, and the bringing about of her deliverance. *Secondly*, That this time must be waited for with faith and patience. *Thirdly*, That, when it comes, it will abundantly recompense us for our long expectation.

Time and days will have an end; not only our time and days will end very shortly, but all times and days will have an end at length; yet a little while, and time shall be no more, but all its revolutions will be numbered and finished. It was a comfort to Daniel, it is a comfort to all the saints, that, whatever their lot is in the days of time, they shall have a happy lot in *the end of the days*. A believing hope and prospect of a blessed lot in the heavenly Canaan, at the end of the days, will furnish us with living comforts in dying moments.

JAMIESON, FAUSSET, BROWN

ple [AUBERLEN]. To this Christ refers (Matt. 24: 15), "Whose readeth, let him *understand.*" **11. from . . . sacrifice . . . taken way . . . abomination**—(ch. 11:31). As to this epoch, which probably is prophetically germinant and manifold; the profanation of the temple *by Antiochus* (in the month Ijar of the year 145 B.C.. till the restoration of the worship by Judas Maccabeus on the twenty-fifth day of the ninth month (Chisleu) of 148 B.C., according to the Seleucid era, 1290 days; forty-five days more elapsed before Antiochus' death in the month Shebat of 148 B.C., so ending the Jews' calamities [MAURER]); *by pagan Rome,* after Christ's death; *by Mohammed; by Antichrist,* the culmination of apostate Rome. The "abomination" must reach its climax (see AUBERLEN's translation, "summit," ch. 9:27), and the measure of iniquity be full, before Messiah comes. **thousand two hundred and ninety days**—a month beyond the "time, times, and a half" (vs. 7). In vs. 12, forty-five days more are added, in all 1335 days. TREGELLES thinks Jesus at His coming will deliver the Jews. An interval elapses, during which their consciences are awakened to repentance and faith in Him. A second interval elapses in which Israel's outcasts are gathered, and then the united blessing takes place. These stages are marked by the 1260, 1290, and 1335 days. CUMMING thinks the 1260 years begin when Justinian in A.D. 533 subjected the Eastern churches to John II, bishop of Rome; ending in 1792, when the Code Napoleon was established and the Pope was dishonored. 1290 reach to 1822, about the time of the waning of the Turkish power, the successor to Greece in the empire of the East. Forty-five years more end in 1867, the end of "the times of the Gentiles." See Leviticus 26:24, "seven times," i.e., 7×360, or 2520 years: 652 B.C. is the date of Judah's captivity, beginning under Manasseh; 2520 from this date end in 1868, thus nearly harmonizing with the previous date, 1867. See *Note,* also ch. 8:14. The seventh millenary of the world [CLINTON] begins in 1862. Seven years to 1869 (the date of the second advent) constitute the reign of the personal Antichrist; in the last three and a half, the period of final tribulation, Enoch (or else Moses) and Elijah, the two witnesses, prophesy in sackcloth. This theory is very dubious (cf. Matt. 24:36; Acts 1:7; I Thess. 5:2; II Pet. 3:10); still the event alone can tell whether the chronological coincidences of such theories are fortuitous, or solid data on which to fix the future times. HALES makes the periods 1260, 1290, 1335, begin with the Roman destruction of Jerusalem and end with the precursory dawn of the Reformation, the preaching of Wycliffe and Huss. **13. rest**—in the grave (Job 3:17; Isa. 57:2). He, like his people Israel, was to wait patiently and confidently for the blessing till God's time. He "received not the promise," but had to wait until the Christian elect saints should be brought in, at the first resurrection, that he and the older Old Testament saints "without us should not be made perfect" (Heb. 11:40). **stand**—implying *justification* unto life, as opposed to condemnation (Ps. 1:5). **thy lot**—image from the *allotment* of the earthly Canaan.

ADAM CLARKE

12. *Blessed is he that waiteth.* He who implicitly depends on God, expecting, as His truth cannot fail, that these predictions shall be accomplished in due time. *And cometh to the thousand three hundred and five and thirty days.* This is 75 days more than what is included in the 3½ years, or the time, times, and a half in the seventh verse; and as we have met with so many instances of prophetical days and years, this undoubtedly is another instance; and as a day stands for a year, this must mean a period of 1,335 years, which period is to bring all these wonders to an end, v. 6. But we are left totally in the dark relative to the time from which these 1,335 years are to be reckoned.

THE BOOK OF HOSEA

I. The training of the prophet (1:1-3:5)
A. His domestic life and national conscience (1:1-2:1)
1. The word of the Lord at first (1:1, 2)
2. The marriage (1:3)
3. The domestic life and the national conscience (1:4-9)
4. The vision of hope (1:10-2:1)

B. His home tragedy, a revelation (2:2-23)
1. The charge—Hosea and Jehovah (2:2-5)
2. The severity of love—Jehovah only (2:6-13)
3. The tenderness of love—Jehovah only (2:14-23)

C. His dealing with Gomer—a command and a revelation (3:1-5)
1. The instruction of Jehovah (3:1)
2. Hosea's obedience (3:2, 3)
3. The national interpretation (3:4, 5)

II. The teaching of the prophet (4:1-14:9)
A. Pollution and its cause (4:1-6:3)
1. The general charge (4:1-3)
2. The cause declared and results described (4:4-19)
3. Special message to priest, people, and king (5:1-15)
4. The plaintive plea of the prophet (6:1-3)

B. Pollution and its punishment (6:4-10:15)
1. The case stated (6:4-7:16)
2. The judgment pronounced (8:1-9:17)
3. Recapitulation and appeal (10:1-15)

C. The love of Jehovah (11:1-14:8)
1. The message of Jehovah with prophetic interpolations (11:1-13:16)
2. The final call of the prophet with the promise of Jehovah (14:1-8)

D. Epilogue (14:9)

I. The twelve minor prophets were sometimes grouped together as "one book." They are called the minor prophets not because their writings are of less authority than those of the greater prophets, but only because they are shorter. These prophets preached as much as the others, but did not write so much. These twelve, Josephus says, were put into one volume by the "men of the great synagogue" in Ezra's time. These are the fragments of prophecy carefully gathered up by the divine Providence and the care of the church. Nine of these prophets prophesied before the captivity, and the last three after the return of the Jews to their own land. Some difference there is in the order of these books. We place them as the ancient Hebrew did; and all agree to put Hosea first; but the ancient Septuagint places the first six in this order—Hosea, Amos, Micah, Joel, Obadiah, and Jonah. The thing is not material.

II. The prophecy of Hosea, who was the first of all the writing prophets. The ancients say he was of Bethshemesh and of the tribe of Issachar. He continued very long a prophet; so that, as Jerome observes, he prophesied of the destruction of the kingdom of the ten tribes and lived to see and lament it. The scope of his prophecy is to discover sin and to denounce the judgments of God against a people that would not be reformed. The style is concise and in some places it seems like the book of Proverbs, without connection, and rather to be called Hosea's "sayings" than Hosea's "sermons."

MATTHEW HENRY

CHAPTER 1

Verse 1

1. The prophet's name, which he prefixes to his prophecy. His name, *Hosea*, or *Hoshea* (the same as Joshua's original name), signifies a *saviour*. His surname was *Ben-Beeri*, or *the son of Beeri*. *Beeri* signifies a *well*, which may put us in mind of living waters from which prophets must be continually drawing. 2. His authority and commission: *The word of the Lord came to him*. What he said and wrote was by divine inspiration. Therefore this book was received among the canonical books of the Old Testament, which is confirmed by what is quoted out of it in the New Testament, Matt. ii. 15; ix. 13; xii. 7; Rom. ix. 25, 26; 1 Pet. ii. 10. 3. Here is a particular account of the times in which he prophesied—*in the days of Uzziah, Jotham, Ahaz, and Hezekiah, kings of Judah, and in the days of Jeroboam the son of Joash, king of Israel*. Now by this account given of the reigns in which Hosea prophesied it appears that he prophesied a long time, that he began when he was young, and that he continued till he was very old. And yet the longer they enjoyed him the less they regarded him; they despised his youth first, and afterwards his age. Some of these kings were good, and encouraged him; others were bad, and frowned upon him and discouraged him; and yet he was still the same. He began to prophesy in Israel at a time when their kingdom was in a prosperous condition, as in the reign of Jeroboam the second, 2 Kings xiv. 25, yet then Hosea boldly tells them of their sins and foretells their destruction.

Verses 2–7

The beginning of the word of the Lord by Hosea, may refer either, 1. To that glorious set of prophets which was raised up. About this time there lived and prophesied Joel, Amos, Micah, Jonah, Obadiah, and Isaiah; but Hosea was the first of them that foretold the destruction of Israel. Or, rather, 2. To Hosea's own prophecies. This was the first message God sent him upon to this people, to tell them that they were *an evil and an adulterous generation*. He

JAMIESON, FAUSSET, BROWN

CHAPTER 1

Vss. 1-11. INSCRIPTION. Spiritual whoredom of Israel set forth by symbolical acts; Gomer taken to wife at God's command: Jezreel, Lo-ruhamah, and Lo-ammi, the children. Yet a promise of Judah and Israel's restoration. **1.** See *Introduction*. **Jeroboam**—the second; who died in the fifteenth year of Uzziah's forty-one years' reign. From his time forth *all* Israel's kings worshipped false gods: Zachariah (II Kings 15:9), Menahem (II Kings 15:18), Pekahiah (II Kings 15:24), Pekah (II Kings 15:28), Hoshea (II Kings 17:2). As Israel was most flourishing externally under Jeroboam II, who recovered the possessions seized on by Syria, Hosea's prophecy of its downfall at that time was the more striking as it could not have been foreseen by mere human sagacity. Jonah the prophet had promised success to Jeroboam II from God, not for the king's merit, but from God's mercy to Israel; so the coast of Israel was restored by Jeroboam II from the entering of Hamath to the sea of the plain (II Kings 14:23-27).

2. beginning—not of the prophet's predictions generally, but of those spoken by *Hosea*.

ADAM CLARKE

CHAPTER 1

TODAY'S DICTIONARY OF THE BIBLE:

Hosea, Prophecies of. This book stands first in order among the "Minor Prophets." "The probable cause of the location of Hosea may be the thoroughly national character of his oracles, their length, their earnest tone, and vivid representations." This was the longest of the prophetic books written before the Captivity. Hosea prophesied in a dark and melancholy period of Israel's history—the period of Israel's decline and fall. Their sins had brought upon them great national disasters. "Their homicides and fornication, their perjury and theft, their idolatry and impiety, are censured and satirized with a faithful severity." He was a contemporary of Isaiah.

His service occurred at the same time as Amos, Isaiah, and Micah. Hosea writes from personal experience, for he was married to a harlot, Gomer, and knew what it meant to live with a faithless woman (2:3).

MATTHEW HENRY

might have desired to be excused till he had gained authority and some interest in their affections. No; he must *begin with this*, that they might know what to expect from a prophet of the Lord.

I. The prophet must, as it were in a looking-glass, show them *their sin*. The prophet is ordered to *take unto him a wife of whoredoms and children of whoredoms, v.* 2. And he did so, *v.* 3. He married a woman of ill fame, *Gomer the daughter of Diblaim*, one that had lived scandalously in the single state. To marry such a one was not prudent, and therefore forbidden to the priests, and would be an affliction to the prophet, but not a sin. But most commentators think that it was done *in vision*, or that it is no more than a parable. He must take *a wife of whoredoms*, and have such children by her as everyone would suspect, though born in wedlock, to be *children of whoredoms*. "Now" (saith God) "Hosea, this people is to me such a dishonour, and such a grief and vexation, as a *wife of whoredoms* and *children of whoredoms* would be to thee. *For the land has committed great whoredoms*." Their idolatry especially is the whoredom they are here charged with. *Idolatry* is *great whoredom*, worse than any other; it is departing from *the Lord*. *The land has committed whoredom*; the whole land is polluted with it. Is it not offensive to the *holy God* to have such a people as this to be called by his name and have a place in his house? It was as if he should have married Gomer the daughter of Diblaim, a noted harlot. The land of Israel was like Gomer the daughter of Diblaim. *Gomer* signifies *corruption; Diblaim* signifies *two cakes*, or *lumps of figs;* this denotes that Israel was near to ruin, and that their luxury and sensuality were the cause of it. It intimates sin to be the daughter of plenty and destruction the daughter of the abuse of plenty.

II. The prophet must, as it were through a perspective glass, show them their ruin; and this he does in the names given to the children born of this adulteress.

1. He foretells the fall of the royal family in the name he is appointed to give to his first child, which was a son: *Call his name Jezreel, v.* 4. Jezreel signifies *the seed of God*, but it signifies also the *scattered of God. Call them not Israel*, which signifies *dominion*, but call them Jezreel, which signified *dispersion. I will revenge the blood of Jezreel upon the house of Jehu*, the blood which Jehu shed when he destroyed the house of Ahab, with all the worshippers of Baal. God approved of what he did (2 Kings x. 30). Yet here God will avenge that *blood upon the house of Jehu*, when the time has expired during which it was promised that his family should reign. It was the execution of a righteous sentence passed upon the house of Ahab, and, as such, it was rewarded; but Jehu did it not in a right manner. He did it with a malice against the sinners, but not with any antipathy to the sin; for he kept up the worship of the golden calves, 2 Kings x. 31. And therefore when God came to reckon with them, the first article in the account is for the blood of the house of Ahab, here called the *blood of Jezreel*. Some make those words, *I will visit, or appoint, the blood of Jezreel upon the house of Jehu*, to signify, not the revenging of that bloodshed, but the repeating of that bloodshed: "I will punish the house of Jehu, as I punished the house of Ahab." After the death of Zechariah, the last of the house of Jehu, the kingdom of the ten tribes went to decay. And, in order to the ruin of it, it is threatened (*v.* 5), *I will break the bow of Israel in the valley of Jezreel. The breaking of the bow* intimates a sinking ruined power.

2. He foretells God's abandoning the whole nation in the name he gives to the second child. Call the name of this daughter *Lo-ruhamah—not beloved*, Rom. ix. 25, or *not having obtained mercy*, 1 Pet. ii. 10. This intimates that God had shown them great mercy, but they had abused his favours, and forfeited them. Though God has borne long, he will not bear always, with a people that hate to be reformed.

III. He must show them what mercy God had in store for the house of Judah, at the same time that he was thus contending with the house of Israel (*v.* 7): *But I will have mercy upon the house of Judah.* When the Assyrian armies had destroyed Samaria, and carried the ten tribes away into captivity, they proceeded to besiege Jerusalem; but God had mercy on the house of Judah, and saved them by the vast slaughter which an angel made, in one night, in the camp of the Assyrians; then they were *saved by the Lord their God*, and not by sword or bow. This may refer also to the salvation of Judah from idolatry, which qualified and prepared them for their other salvations. Just at the time that the kingdom of Israel was *utterly taken away*, under Hoshea, the kingdom of Judah was gloriously reformed, under

JAMIESON, FAUSSET, BROWN

take . . . wife of whoredoms—not externally acted, but internally and in vision, as a pictorial illustration of Israel's unfaithfulness [HENGSTENBERG]. Cf. Ezekiel 16:8, 15, etc. Besides the loathsomeness of such a marriage, if an external act, it would require years for the birth of three children, which would weaken the symbol (cf. Ezek. 4:4). HENDERSON objects that there is no hint of the transaction being fictitious: Gomer fell into lewdness *after* her union with Hosea, not before; for thus only she was a fit symbol of Israel, who lapsed into spiritual whoredom *after* the marriage contract with God on Sinai, and made even before at the call of the patriarchs of Israel. Gomer is called "a wife of whoredoms," anticipatively. **children of whoredoms**—The kingdom collectively is viewed as a *mother*; the individual subjects of it are spoken of as her *children*. "Take" being applied to both implies that they refer to the same thing viewed under different aspects. The "children" were not the prophet's own, but born of adultery, and presented to him as his [KITTO, *Biblical Cyclopœdia*]. Rather, "children of whoredoms" means that the children, like their mother, fell into spiritual fornication. Cf. "bare *him* a son" (see ch. 2:4, 5). Being children of a spiritual whore, they naturally fell into her whorish ways. **3. Gomer . . . daughter of Diblaim**—symbolical names; lit., "completion, daughter of grape-cakes"; the dual expressing the double layers in which these dainties were baked. So, *one completely given up to sensuality.* MAURER explains "Gomer" as lit., "a burning coal." Cf. Proverbs 6: 27, 29, as to an adulteress; Job 31:9, 12.

4. Jezreel—i.e., "God will scatter" (cf. Zech. 10:9). It was the royal city of Ahab and his successors, in the tribe of Issaschar. Here Jehu exercised his greatest cruelties (II Kings 9:16, 25, 33; 10:11, 14, 17). There is in the name an allusion to "Israel" by a play of letters and sounds.

5. bow—the prowess (Jer. 49:35; cf. Gen. 49:24). **valley of Jezreel**—afterwards called Esdraelon, extending ten miles in breadth, and in length from Jordan to the Mediterranean near Mount Carmel, the great battlefield of Palestine (Judg. 6:33; I Sam. 29:1). **6. Lo-ruhamah**—i.e., "not an object of mercy or gracious favor." **take . . . away**—Israel, as a kingdom, was never restored from Assyria, as Judah was from Babylon after seventy years. MAURER translates according to the primary meaning, "No more will I have mercy on the house of Israel, so as to *pardon* them." **7.** *Judah* is only incidentally mentioned to form a contrast to *Israel.* **by the Lord their God**—more emphatic than "by Myself"; by that Jehovah (Me) whom they worship as *their God*, whereas ye despise Him. **not . . . by bow**—on which ye Israelites rely (vs. 5, "the bow of Israel"); Jeroboam II was famous as a warrior (II Kings 14:25). Yet it was not by their warlike power Jehovah would save Judah (I Sam. 17:47; Ps. 20:7). The deliverance of Jerusalem from Sennacherib (II Kings 19:35), and the restoration from Babylon, are herein predicted.

ADAM CLARKE

2. *A wife of whoredoms.* That is, says Newcome, a wife from among the Israelites, who were remarkable for spiritual fornication, or idolatry. God calls himself the Husband of Israel; and this chosen nation owed Him the fidelity of a wife. See Exod. xxxiv. 15; Deut. xxxi. 16; Judge. ii. 17; Isa. liv. 5; Jer. iii. 14; xxxi. 32; Ezek. xvi. 17; xxiii. 5, 27; Hos. ii. 2, 5; Rev. xvii. 1-2. He therefore says, with indignation, Go join thyself in marriage to one of those who have committed fornication against Me, and raise up children who, by the power of example, will themselves swerve to idolatry.

3. *He went and took Gomer.* All this appears to be a real transaction, though having a typical meaning.

4. *Call his name Jezreel.* That is, "God will disperse." This seems to intimate that a dispersion or sowing of Israel shall take place; which happened under Shalmaneser, king of Assyria, 2 Kings xvii. 5-6. But the word refers also to the name of a city, where Jehu slew Jezebel and all the children of Ahab, 2 Kings ix. 10, 36 and x. 6. *The blood of Jezreel.* Not Jehu's vengeance on Ahab's family, but his acts of cruelty while he resided at Jezreel, a city in the tribe of Issachar, Josh. xix. 18, where the kings of Israel had a palace, 1 Kings xxi. 1. *Will cause to cease the kingdom.* Either relating to the cutting off of the kingdom of Israel by the Assyrians, see v. 6, or to the ceasing of the kingdom of Israel from the house of Jehu, 2 Kings x. 30, and which was fulfilled, 2 Kings xv. 10.

5. *In the valley of Jezreel.* This also is supposed to relate either to some signal defeat of the Israelites by the Assyrians, which took place in the valley of Jezreel; or to the death of Zechariah, the fourth lineal descendant of Jehu, which may have happened here. See 2 Kings xv. 10.

6. *Call her . . . Lo-ruhamah.* "Not having obtained mercy." This also was a prophetic or typical name; and the reason of its imposition is immediately given: *For I will no more have mercy.* "For I will no more add to have mercy upon the house of Israel." This refers to the total destruction of that kingdom.

7. *But I will have mercy upon the house of Judah.* I will spare them as a kingdom after Israel has been carried away into captivity by the Assyrians. *And will save them by the Lord their God.* Remarkably fulfilled in the supernatural defeat of the army of the Assyrians, see 2 Kings xix. 35; and so they were saved, not by *bow*, nor by *sword*, nor by *battle*, nor by *horses*, nor by *horsemen*.

MATTHEW HENRY

Hezekiah; and in Babylon God saved them from their idolatry first, and then from their captivity. Some make this promise to look forward to the great salvation which, in the fulness of time, was to be wrought out *by the Lord our God*, Jesus Christ.

Verses 8–11

I. The rejection of Israel for a time is signified by the name of another child that Hosea had by his adulterous spouse, *v.* 8, 9. *When she had weaned* her daughter, *she conceived and bore a son.* Some think that her bearing another son signifies that people's persisting in their wickedness; lust still *conceived* and *brought forth sin.* The name given him: *Call him Lo-ammi—Not my people.* When they were told that God would *no more have mercy on them* they regarded it not, but buoyed up themselves with this conceit, that they were God's people, whom he could not but have mercy on. And therefore he plucks that staff from under them, and disowns all relation to them: *You are not my people,* and *I will not be your God.* This was fulfilled in Israel when they were *utterly taken away* into the *land of Assyria.* They were no longer *God's people*; no prophets were sent to them, no promises made to them, as were to the two tribes in their captivity.

II. Of the reduction and restoration of Israel in the fulness of time. Here, as before, mercy is remembered in the midst of wrath; the rejection, as it shall not be total, so it shall not be final (*v.* 10, 11).

1. Some think that these promises had their accomplishment in the return of the Jews out of their captivity in Babylon, when many of the ten tribes joined themselves to Judah, and came out of the countries into which they were dispersed, to their own land, appointed Zerubbabel, their head, and coalesced into one people. And in their own land God would by his prophets own them as his children.

2. Some think that these promises will not have their accomplishment in full, till the general conversion of the Jews in the latter days.

3. This promise had its accomplishment in the setting up of the kingdom of Christ, and the bringing in both of Jews and Gentiles (Rom. ix. 25, 26 and 1 Pet. ii. 10). This Israel shall greatly multiply. Though Israel according to the flesh be diminished, the spiritual Israel shall be innumerable. In the multitudes that by the preaching of the gospel have been brought to Christ, in the first ages of Christianity and ever since, this promise is fulfilled, Rev. vii. 4, 9; Gal. iv. 27. God will renew his covenant with the gospel-Israel, and will incorporate it a church by as full a charter as that whereby the Old Testament church was incorporated. The *abandoned Gentiles* in their respective places, and the *rejected Jews* in theirs, shall be blessed. There, where the fathers were cast off for their unbelief, the children, upon their believing, shall be taken in. The privilege is enlarged; now it is not only, *You are my people,* as formerly, but *You are the sons of the living God,* whether by birth you were Jews or Gentiles. They were as children *under age*; now, under the gospel, they have grown up to greater understanding and greater liberty, Gal. iv. 1, 2. The sonship of believers shall be acknowledged; *You are the sons of the living God.* It will add to their honour, when they are dignified with the tokens of God's favour in that very place where they had long lain under the tokens of his displeasure. Those who had been at variance should be happily brought together (*v.* 11): *Then shall the children of Judah and the children of Israel be gathered together.* This uniting of Judah and Israel is mentioned only as a specimen, or one instance, of the happy effect of the setting up of Christ's kingdom in the world. The first disciples were partly Jews and partly Galileans. When the Samaritans believed, though between them and the Jews there was a much greater enmity, yet in Christ there was a perfect unanimity, Acts viii. 14. By the death of Christ, the partition-wall of the ceremonial law was taken down. See Eph. ii. 14–16. Jesus Christ should be the centre of unity to all God's spiritual Israel. To believe in Christ is to appoint him our head, that is, to consent to God's appointment, and willingly commit ourselves to his guidance and government; all good Christians that make him their head, though they are many, yet in him they are one, and so become one with each other. Having appointed Christ for their head, *they shall come up out of the land*; they shall come, some of all sorts, from all parts. It denotes not a local remove (for they are said to be in the same place, *v.* 10), but a change of their mind, a spiritual ascent to Christ. When all this comes to pass, *great shall be the day of Jezreel.* Israel is here called *Jezreel,* the *seed of God.* This seed is now sown in the earth, and buried; but great shall be its day when the harvest comes.

JAMIESON, FAUSSET, BROWN

8. weaned—said to complete the symbolical picture, not having any special signification as to Israel [HENDERSON]. Israel was bereft of all the privileges which were as needful to them as milk is to infants (cf. Ps. 131:2; I Pet. 2:2) [VATABLUS]. Israel was *not suddenly,* but *gradually* cast off; God bore with them with long-suffering, until they were incurable [CALVIN]. But as it is not God, but *Gomer* who weans Loruhamah, the weaning may imply the lust of Gomer, who was hardly weaned when she is again pregnant [MANGER]. **9. Lo-ammi**—once "My people," but henceforth *not* so (Ezek. 16:8). The intervals between the marriage and the successive births of the three children, imply that three successive generations are intended. Jezreel, the first child, represents the dynasty of Jeroboam I and his successors, ending with Jehu's shedding the blood of Jeroboam's line in Jezreel; it was there that Jezebel was slain, in vengeance for Naboth's blood shed in the same Jezreel (I Kings 16:1; II Kings 9: 21, 30). The scenes of Jezreel were to be enacted over again on Jehu's degenerate race. At Jezreel Assyria routed Israel [JEROME]. The child's name associates past sins, intermediate punishments, and final overthrow. Lo-ruhamah ("not pitied"), the second child, is a *daughter,* representing the effeminate period which followed the overthrow of the first dynasty, when Israel was at once abject and impious. Lo-ammi ("not my people"), the third child, a *son,* represents the vigorous dynasty (II Kings 14:25) of Jeroboam II; but, as prosperity did not bring with it revived piety, they were still *not God's people.*

10. Literally fulfilled *in part* at the return from Babylon, in which many Israelites joined with Judah. Spiritually, the believing seed of Jacob or Israel, Gentiles as well as Jews, numerous "as the sand" (Gen. 32:12); the Gentiles, once not God's people, becoming His "sons" (John 1:12; Rom. 9:25, 26; I Pet. 2:10; I John 3:1). To be fulfilled in its literal *fulness* hereafter in Israel's restoration (Rom. 11:26). **the living God**—opposed to their *dead* idols.

11. Judah . . . Israel . . . together—(Isa. 11:12, 13; Jer. 3:18; Ezek. 34:23; 37:16-24). **one head**—Zerubbabel typically; Christ antitypically, under whom alone Israel and Judah are joined, the "Head" of the Church (Eph. 1:22; 5:23), and of the hereafter united kingdom of Judah and Israel (Jer. 34:5, 6; Ezek. 34:23). Though "appointed" by the Father (Ps. 2:6), Christ is in another sense "appointed" as their Head by His people, when they accept and embrace Him as such.

out of the land—of the Gentiles among whom they sojourn. **the day of Jezreel**—"The day of one" is the time of God's special visitation of him, either in wrath or in mercy. Here "Jezreel" is in a different sense from that in vs. 4, "God will sow," not "God will scatter"; they shall be *the seed of God,* planted by God again in their own land (Jer. 24:6; 31:28; 32: 41; Amos 9:15).

ADAM CLARKE

9. *Call his name Lo-ammi.* "Not My people."

10. *Yet the number of the children of Israel.* God had promised that the children of Israel should be as the sand of the sea. See Gen. xxxii. 12; Rom. ix. 25-26. And though for their iniquities He had thinned and scattered them, yet the spirit and design of His promise and covenant shall be fulfilled. An Israel there shall be. In the place of the reprobated people, who were now no longer His people, there shall be found an Israel that shall be the children "of the living God." See the above scriptures, and 1 Pet. ii. 10. This must mean either the Israelites after their conversion to Christianity, or even the Gentiles themselves converted to God, and now become the true Israel.

11. *The children of Judah and the children of Israel.* After the return from Babylon, the distinction between Israel and Judah was entirely destroyed; and those of them that did return were all included under one denomination, "Jews." The *one head* may refer to Zerubbabel, their leader, and afterwards under Ezra and Nehemiah. In the more extensive view of the prophet the "one head" may mean Jesus Christ, under whom the true Israel, Jews and Gentiles, shall be finally gathered together; so that there shall be one flock, and one Shepherd over that flock. *They shall come up out of the land.* Assyria and Chaldea in particular, but also from the various places of their dispersions in general. *Great shall be the day of Jezreel.* He alludes to the meaning of the word, the "seed of God." God, who has dispersed—sown—them in different lands, shall gather them together; and that day of God's power shall be great and glorious. It was a wonderful seedtime in the divine justice; it shall then be a wonderful harvest in the divine mercy. He sowed them among the nations in His wrath; He shall reap them and gather them in His bounty.

MATTHEW HENRY

CHAPTER 2

Verses 1–5

The first words of this chapter some make the close of the foregoing chapter. When they shall have appointed Christ their head, "say to them, *Ammi*, and *Ruhamah*; call them so again, for they shall no longer lie under the reproach and doom of *Lo-ammi* and *Lo-ruhamah*; they shall now be *my people* again, and shall *obtain mercy*." The *mother* (*v.* 2) seems to be the same with the *brethren* and *sisters* (*v.* 1), the church of the ten tribes, and in a special manner the heads and leaders, who were as the mother by whom the rest were brought up and nursed. But who are the children that must *plead with their mother* thus? Either, 1. The godly that were among them, that witnessed against the iniquities of the times: let those that had not bowed the knee to Baal reason the case with those that had. Or, 2. The sufferers among them, that shared in the calamities of the times: let them not complain of God, nor lay the blame on him, as if he had dealt hardly with them, and not like a tender father. No; let them *plead with their mother*, and lay the fault on her, where it ought to be laid; compare Isa. l. 1.

I. They must put her in mind of the relation wherein she had stood to God, the kindness he had had for her. Let them tell their *brethren* and *sisters* that they had been *Ammi* and *Ruhamah*, God's people and vessels of his mercy.

II. They must charge her with the violation of the marriage-covenant between her and God. Tell her (*v.* 2) that *she is not my wife, neither am I her husband*, that by her spiritual whoredom she has forfeited her relation to God. They must charge this home upon her (*v.* 5): *Their mother has played the harlot; their congregation has run after idols*, wherein they were encouraged by their false prophets.

III. They must upbraid her with her ingratitude to God her benefactor, in ascribing to her idols the glory of the gifts he had given her, *v.* 5. *She said*, Whatever is offered to the contrary, *I will go after my lovers*, or *those that cause me to love them*. The Chaldee understands it of the nations whose alliance Israel courted, who supplied them with what they needed. "I will go after my lovers, because they give me my *bread and my water*, which are necessary to sustain the body, *my wool and my flax*, which are necessary to clothe the body, and pleasant things, *my oil*, and *my drink*, my liquors" (so the word is), "wine and strong drink." The idolaters made Ceres the goddess of their corn, Bacchus the god of their wine, &c., and then foolishly fancied they had their corn and wine from these, forgetting the Lord their God, who both gave them that good land and *gave them power to get wealth* out of it.

IV. God will disown her if she persist in her whoredoms, *v.* 2. Let her be convinced that it is possible for her to reform. True penitents will forsake both open sins and secret sins. They will both avoid the outward occasions of sin and mortify the inward disposition to it.

V. They must show her the utter ruin that will certainly be the consequence of her sin if she do not repent and reform (*v.* 3). She shall be starved, shall be deprived of her honours, her comforts and necessary supports. She shall be famished, shall be made *as a wilderness* and *a dry land*, and *slain with thirst*. Some understand it thus: *I will make her as* she was in the *wilderness*, and set her as she was *in the desert land*, where she was sometimes ready to perish *for thirst*. I will set her *as in the day that she was born*; for it was in the vast howling wilderness that Israel was first formed into a people.

Verses 6–13

I. They shall be perplexed and embarrassed in their counsels, and disappointed in their expectations. This is threatened, *v.* 6, 7. But to the threatening is annexed a promise that this shall be a means to convince them of their folly, and bring them home to their duty.

1. God will raise up difficulties and troubles: *I will hedge up thy way with thorns*. She said, "*I will go after my lovers;* I will pursue my leagues and alliances with foreign powers, and depend upon them." But God says, "She shall be frustrated in these projects, and not be able to proceed in them." She shall be as a traveller that finds no way at all to go forward. And then *she shall follow after her lovers, but shall not overtake them;* she shall endeavour to make an interest in the Assyrians and Egyptians, and to have them for her protectors, but she shall not gain her point. This is such a mercy, as Balaam met when the angel stood in his way, to hinder his going forward to *curse Israel*, Num. xxii. 22. Crosses and obstacles in an evil course are great blessings. They

JAMIESON, FAUSSET, BROWN

CHAPTER 2

Vss. 1-23. Application of the Symbols in Chapter I. Israel's spiritual fornication, and her threatened punishment: yet a promise of God's restored favor, when chastisements have produced their designed effect. **1. Say . . . unto . . . brethren, Ammi . . .**–i.e., When the prediction (ch. 1:11) shall be accomplished, then ye will call one another, as *brothers* and *sisters* in the family of God, Ammi and Ruhamah. **2. Plead**–expostulate. **mother**–i.e., the nation *collectively*. The address is to "her children," i.e., to the *individual* citizens of the state (cf. Isa. 50:1).

for she is not my wife–She has deprived herself of her high privilege by spiritual adultery.

5. I will go after–The *Hebrew* expresses a *settled determination*. **lovers**–the idols which Israel fancied to be the givers of all their goods, whereas God gave all these goods (vss. 8-13; cf. Jer. 44:17-19). **bread and . . . water**– the *necessaries* of life in food. **wool . . . flax**–clothing. **oil . . . drink**–perfumed unguents and palatable drinks: the *luxuries* of Hebrew life.

out of her sight–rather, "from her face." Her very countenance unblushingly betrayed her lust, as did also her exposed "breasts."

3. set her as in the day . . . born–(Ezek. 16:4; 23:25, 26, 28, 29). The day of her political "birth" was when God delivered her from the bondage of Egypt, and set up the theocracy. **make her as a wilderness**–(Jer. 6:8; Zeph. 2:13). Translate, "make her as the wilderness," viz., that in which she passed forty years on her way to her goodly possession of Canaan. With this agrees the mention of "thirst" (cf. Jer. 2:6). **4. her children**–Not even her *individual* members shall escape the doom of the nation collectively, for they are individually guilty.

6, 7. thorns . . . wall–(Job 19:8; Lam. 3:7, 9). The hindrances which the captivity interposed between Israel and her idols. As she attributes all her temporal blessings to idols, I will reduce her to straits in which, when she in vain has sought help from false gods, she will at last seek Me as her only God and Husband, as at the first (Isa. 54:5; Jer. 3:14; Ezek. 16:8). **then**–before Israel's apostasy, under Jeroboam. The way of duty is hedged *about* with thorns; it is the way of sin that is hedged *up* with thorns. Crosses in an evil course are God's hedges to turn us from it. Restraining grace and restraining providences (even sicknesses and trials) are great blessings when they stop us in a course of sin.

ADAM CLARKE

CHAPTER 2

1. *Say ye unto your brethren, Ammi.* I prefer the interpretation of these proper names. *Say ye unto your brethren,* "My people"; *and to your sisters,* who have "obtained mercy."

2. *Plead with your mother.* People of Judah, accuse your mother (Jerusalem), who has abandoned My worship and is become idolatrous; convince her of her folly and wickedness, and let her return to Him from whom she has so deeply revolted.

5. *That give me my bread.* See the note on Jer. xliv. 17-18. where nearly the same words are found and illustrated.

3. *Lest I strip her naked.* Lest I expose her to infamy, want, and punishment. The punishment of an adulteress among the ancient Germans was this: "They shaved off her hair, stripped her naked in the presence of her relatives, and in this state drove her from the house of her husband." See on Isa. iii. 17; and see also Ezek. xvi. 39; xxiii. 26. *And set her like a dry land.* The Israelites, if obedient, were promised a land flowing with milk and honey; but, should they be disobedient, the reverse. And this is what God here threatens against disobedient Israel.

4. *They be the children of whoredoms.* They are all idolaters; and have been consecrated to idols, whose marks they bear.

6. *I will hedge up thy way with thorns.* I will put it out of your power to escape the judgments I have threatened; and, in spite of all your attachment to your idols, you shall find that they can give you neither bread, nor water, nor wool, nor flax, nor oil, nor drink. And he shall be brought into such circumstances that the pursuit of your expensive idolatry shall be impossible. And she shall be led so deep into captivity as never to find the road back to her own land. And this is the fact; for those who were carried away into Assyria have been lost among the nations, few of them having ever returned to Judea. And, if in being, where they are now is utterly unknown.

MATTHEW HENRY

are God's hedges to restrain us from wandering, and to make the way of sin difficult.

2. These difficulties that God raises up in their way shall raise up in their minds thoughts of turning back. Two things are here extorted from this degenerate apostate people: (1) A just acknowledgment of the folly of their apostasy. (2) A good purpose, to come back again to their duty: *I will go, and return to my first husband;* and she knows so much of his goodness and readiness to forgive that she speaks without any doubt of his receiving her again.

II. The necessary supports and comforts of life shall be taken from them, because they had dishonoured God with them, *v.* 8, 9.

1. How graciously their plenty was given to them. God gave them not only corn but he *multiplied their silver and gold,* wherewith to traffic with other nations. He gave them *wool* and *flax* too, to *cover their nakedness,* Ezek. xvi. 10.

2. How basely their plenty was abused by them. (1) They robbed God of the honour of his gifts: *She did not know that I gave her corn and wine;* she did not remember it. (2) They served and honoured his enemies with them: *They prepared them for Baal;* they adorned their images with *gold and silver* (Jer. x. 4), and adorned themselves for the worship of their images, *v.* 13.

3. How justly their plenty should be taken from them: "*Therefore will I return;* I will alter my dealings with them, will take another course, *and will take away my corn* and other good things that I gave her." Those that abuse the mercies God gives them, to his dishonour, cannot expect to enjoy them long.

III. They shall lose *all their honour,* and be exposed to contempt (*v.* 10): "*I will discover her lewdness,* will bring to light her secret wickedness, to her shame. And this *in the sight of her lovers,* in the sight of the neighbouring nations, with whom she courted an alliance, and on whom she had a dependence; they shall not think her any longer worthy of their friendship." Those who will not deliver themselves into the hand of God's mercy cannot be delivered out of the hand of his justice.

IV. They shall lose all their pleasure, and shall be left melancholy (*v.* 11): *I will cause her mirth to cease.*

1. God will take away the occasions of their sacred mirth—*their feast-days, their new moons, their sabbaths, and all their solemn feasts.* These God instituted to be observed in a religious manner, and they were to be observed with rejoicing. They kept up the observance of these, not at God's temple at Jerusalem, for they had long since forsaken that, but probably at Dan and Bethel, where the calves were. Thus, when they had lost the power of godliness, yet, for the pleasing of a carnal mind, they kept up the form of it; and by this means their new-moons and their sabbaths became an iniquity which God *could not away with,* Isa. i. 13.

2. God will take away their provisions for these solemnities (*v.* 12): *I will destroy her vines and her fig-trees.* He will wither them with a blast, or bring in a foreign enemy that shall lay the country waste, so that their vineyards shall become *a forest;* the enclosures shall be thrown down, so that the *beasts of the field* shall eat their grapes and their figs. This shall be the ruin of their mirth: God will *cause all her mirth to cease.* "I will *destroy her vines and her fig-trees,* will take away her sensual pleasures, and then she will think herself undone indeed." This shall be the punishment of her idolatry (*v.* 13): "*I will visit upon her the days of Baalim.*" The *days of Baalim* are the solemn festival days which they kept in honour of their idols. These were the days wherein she *burnt incense* to idols, and *decked herself with her ear-rings and her jewels,* that the honour she did to Baal might be thought the greater.

Verses 14–23

The state of Israel, restrained by the divine grace, looks bright and pleasant here, and the more surprisingly so as the promises follow thus close upon the threatenings. When it was said, *She forgot me,* one would think it should have followed, "Therefore I will abandon her, I will never look after her more." No, *Therefore I will allure her.* God's thoughts and ways of mercy are infinitely above ours, Isa. lvii. 17, 18. Because she will not be restrained by the denunciations of wrath, God will try whether she will be wrought upon by the offers of mercy. Some think it may be translated, *Afterwards,* or *nevertheless,* I will allure her. It comes all to one; the design is plainly to magnify free grace to those on whom God will have mercy purely for mercy's sake.

I. Though now Israel was ready to despair it should again be revived with comforts and hopes, *v.* 14, 15. This is expressed here with an allusion to God's dealings

JAMIESON, FAUSSET, BROWN

Cf. Luke 15:14-18, "I will arise, and go to my father." So here, "I will go, and return . . ."; crosses in the both cases being sanctified to produce this effect.

8. she did not know that I—not the idols, as she thought: the "lovers" alluded to in vs. 5. **which they prepared for Baal**—i.e., of which they made images of Baal, or at least the plate-covering of them (ch. 8:4). Baal was the Phœnician sun-god: answering to the female Astarte, the moon-goddess. The name of the idol is found in the Phœnician Hannibal, Hasdrubal. Israel borrowed it from the Tyrians. **9. my corn . . . my wool . . . my flax**—in contrast to "*my* bread . . . *my* wool . . . *my* flax," (vs. 5). Cf. also vss. 21-23, on God as the great First Cause giving these through secondary instruments in nature. "Return, and take away," is equivalent to, "I will take back again," viz., by sending storms, locusts, Assyrian enemies, etc. "Therefore," i.e., because she did not acknowledge Me as the Giver. **in the time thereof**—in the harvest time. **10. lewdness**—rather, "the shame of her nakedness"; laying aside the figure, "I will expose her in *her state, bereft of every necessary,* before her lovers," i.e., the idols (personified, as if they could see), who, nevertheless, can give her no help. "Discover" is appropriate to stripping off the self-flatteries of her hypocrisy.

11. her feast days—of Jeroboam's appointment, distinct from the Mosaic (I Kings 12:32). However, most of the Mosaic feasts, "new moons" and "sabbaths" to Jehovah, remained, but to degenerate Israel worship was a weariness; they cared only for the carnal indulgence on them (Amos 8:5).

12. my rewards—my hire as a harlot (Isa. 23:17, 18). **lovers**—idols. **destroy . . . vines . . . make . . . forest**—(Isa. 5:6; 7:23, 24). Fulfilled in the overthrow of Israel by Assyria (ch. 9:4, 5).

13. days of Baalim—the days consecrated to the Baals, or various images of Baal in different cities, whence the names *Baal-gad, Baal-hermon,* etc. **decked herself with . . . earrings**—rather, "nose-rings" (Isa. 3:21; *Margin,* Ezek. 16:12), with which harlots decked themselves to attract admirers: answering to the ornaments in which the Israelites decked themselves on the idols' feasts. **forgat me**—worse than the nations which had never known God. Israel *wilfully apostatized* from Jehovah, whom she had known.

14. Therefore—rather, "Neverthless" [HENDERSON]. *English Version* gives a more lovely idea of God. That

ADAM CLARKE

8. *For she did not know that I gave her corn.* How often are the gifts of God's immediate bounty attributed to fortuitous causes—to any cause but the right one! *Which they prepared for Baal.* And how often are the gifts of God's bounty perverted into means of dishonoring Him! God gives us wisdom, strength, and property; and we use them to sin against Him with the greater skill, power, and effect!

9. *Therefore will I return, and take away.* In the course of My providence I will withhold those benefits which she has prostituted to her idolatrous services. And I will neither give the land rain nor fruitful seasons.

10. *In the sight of her lovers.* Her idols, and her faithful or faithless allies.

12. *These are my rewards.* They attributed all the blessings of Providence as rewards received from the idols which they worshipped.

13. *Days of Baalim.* To *visit* signifies to "inflict punishment"; *the days* are taken for the acts of idolatrous worship committed on them; and *Baalim* means the multitude of false gods worshipped by them. *Baal* was a general name for a male idol, as *Astarte* was for a female. *Baalim* includes all the male idols, as *Ashtaroth* all those that were female. *Her earrings. Nizmah* signifies rather a "nose jewel." These are worn by females in the East to the present day, in great abundance. *And her jewels.* Rings, armlets, bracelets, ankle rings, and ornaments of this kind.

MATTHEW HENRY

with that people when he brought them out of Egypt, through the wilderness to Canaan, *in the day that they were born, v.* 3. They shall be new-formed by such miracles of love and mercy as they were first-formed by. He will *bring them into the wilderness,* as he did when he brought them out of Egypt. The land of their captivity shall be to them now, as that wilderness was then, the *furnace of affliction,* in which God will *choose them.* When God delivered Israel out of Egypt he led them into the wilderness, to *humble them and prove them, that he might do them good* (Deut. viii. 2, 3, 15, 16), and so he will do again. Those whom God has mercy in store for he first *brings into a wilderness*—into solitude and retirement, that they may the more freely converse with him out of the noise of this world, and sometimes into outward distress and trouble, thereby to open the ear to discipline. He will then *allure them and speak comfortably to them,* will *persuade them* and *speak to their hearts,* that is, he will by his word and Spirit incline their hearts to return to him, and encourage them to do so. *By the hand of my servants the prophets I will speak comfort to her heart;* so the **Chaldee.** This refers to the offers of divine grace in the gospel, by which we are allured to forsake our sins and to turn to God. By the promise of rest in Christ we are invited to take his yoke upon us; and the work of conversion may be forwarded by comforts as well as by convictions. From that time and from that place where he has afflicted her, and brought her to see her folly, thenceforward he will *do her good.* He had *destroyed her vines* (*v.* 12), but now he will give her whole *vineyards,* and so she will be repaid; she shall not only have corn for necessity, but vineyards for delight. These denote the privileges and comforts of the gospel, which are prepared for those that *come up out of the wilderness leaning upon* Christ as *their beloved,* Cant. viii. 5. He will give her *the valley of Achor for a door of hope. The valley of Achor* was that in which Achan was stoned; it signifies *the valley of trouble,* because he troubled Israel, and there God troubled him. So when God returns to his people in mercy, and they to him in duty, it will be to them as happy an omen as anything. If they put away the accursed thing from among them, if by mortifying sin they stone the Achan that has troubled their camp, their subduing that enemy within themselves is an earnest to them of victory over all the kings of Canaan. *She shall sing there as in the days of her youth.* This plainly refers to that triumphant and prophetic song which Moses and the children of Israel sang at the *Red Sea,* Exod. xv. 1. When they are delivered out of captivity they shall repeat that song, and to them it shall be a new song.

II. Though they had been much addicted to the worship of Baal, they should now abandon all appearances of idolatry, and cleave to God only, *v.* 16, 17. The very *names of Baalim* shall be *taken out of their mouths.* Thus the apostle expresses the abhorrence we ought to have of all fleshly lusts: *Let them not be once named among you,* Eph. v. 3. God's grace in the heart will change the language by making that iniquity to be loathed which was beloved. The very word Baal shall be laid aside, even in its innocent signification. God says, *Thou shalt call me Ishi, and call me no more Baali;* both signify *my husband,* and both had been made use of concerning God. Isa. liv. 5, *Thy Maker is thy husband,* thy *Baal* (so the word is), thy patron, and protector.

III. Though they had been in continual troubles, as if the whole creation had been at war with them, now they shall enjoy perfect peace and tranquillity, as if they were in a league of friendship with the whole creation (*v.* 18). The inferior creatures shall do them no harm, as they had done when the *beasts of the field* ate up their vineyards (*v.* 12). God can make *the beasts of the field* to *honour* him (so he has promised, Isa. xliii. 20) and to contribute to his people's comfort. And it is our part of the covenant not to abuse them. But this is not all; men are more in danger from one another than from the brute beast, and therefore it is further promised that God will *make wars to cease,* will disarm the enemy: *I will break the bow, and sword, and battle.* He will do it for those whose *ways please him,* for he *makes even their enemies to be at peace with them,* Prov. xvi. 7. This agrees with the promise that in gospel-times *swords shall be beaten into ploughshares,* Isa. ii. 4.

IV. Though God had given them a bill of divorce for their whoredoms, yet, upon their repentance, he would again take them into a marriage-covenant, *v.* 19, 20. *I will betroth thee unto me;* and again, and a third time, *I will betroth thee.* All that are sincerely devoted to God are betrothed to him; God will love them, protect them, and provide for them. The covenant itself shall be inviolable; God will not break it on his part, and you shall not on yours; and the

JAMIESON, FAUSSET, BROWN

which would provoke all others to unappeasable wrath, Israel's perversity and consequent punishment, is made a reason why God should at last have mercy on her. As the "therefore" (vs. 9) expresses Israel's punishment as the *consequence* of Israel's guilt, so "therefore" here, as in vs. 6, expresses, that when that punishment has effected its designed end, the hedging up her way with thorns so that she returns to God, her first love, the *consequence* in God's wondrous grace is, He "speaks comfortably" (lit., "speaks to her heart"; cf. Judg. 19:8; Ruth 2: 13). So obstinate is she that God has to "allure her," i.e., so to temper judgment with unlooked-for grace as to *win* her to His ways. For this purpose it was necessary to "bring her into the wilderness" (i.e., into temporal want and trials) first, to make her sin hateful to her by its bitter fruits, and God's subsequent grace the more precious to her by the contrast of the "wilderness." JEROME makes the "bringing into the wilderness" to be rather a *deliverance from her enemies,* just as ancient Israel was brought into the wilderness from the bondage of Egypt; to this the phrase here alludes (cf. vs. 15). The wilderness sojourn, however, is not literal, but moral: while still in the land of their enemies *locally,* by the discipline of the trial rendering the word of God sweet to them, they are to be brought *morally* into the wilderness state, i.e., into a state of preparedness for returning to their temporal and spiritual privileges in their own land; just as the literal wilderness prepared their fathers for Canaan: thus the bringing of them into the *wilderness state* is *virtually* a deliverance from their enemies. **15. from thence**—returning from the wilderness. God gives Israel a fresh grant of Canaan, which she had forfeited; so of her vineyards, etc. (vss. 9, 12). **Achor**—i.e. "trouble." As formerly Israel, after their tedious journey through the wilderness, met with the *trouble* resulting from Achan's crime in this valley, on the very threshold of Canaan, and yet that *trouble* was presently turned into *joy* at the great victory at Ai, which threw all Canaan into their hands (Josh. 7, 8); so the very trouble of Israel's wilderness state will be the "door of hope" opening to better days. The valley of Achor, near Jericho, was specially fruitful (Isa. 65:10); so "trouble" and "hope" are rightly blended in connection with it. **sing . . . as . . . when she came . . . out of . . . Egypt**—It shall be a second exodus song, such as Israel sang after the deliverance at the Red Sea (Exod. 15; cf. Isa. 11:15, 16); and "the song of Moses" (Rev. 15:2, 3) sung by those who through the Lamb overcome the beast, and so stand on the sea of glass mingled with fire, emblems of fiery trial, such as that of Israel at the Red Sea.

16. Ishi . . . no more Baali—"my *Husband* . . . no more my *Lord.*" *Affection* is the prominent idea in "Husband"; *rule,* in "Lord." The chief reason for the substitution of *Husband* for *Lord appears* in the next verse; viz., *Baali,* the *Hebrew* for *my Lord,* had been perverted to express the images of Baal, whose name ought not to be taken on their lips (Exod. 23:13; Zech. 13:2). **17. Baalim**—*plural,* expressing the various images of Baal, which, according to the places of their erection, received various names, Baal-gad, Baal-ammon, etc. **18. for them**—for their benefit. **covenant . . . with the beasts**—not to hurt them (Job 5:23). They shall fulfil the original law of their creation by becoming subject to man, when man fulfils the law of his being by being subject to God. To be realized fully in millennial times (Isa. 11:6-9). **break the bow . . . out of the earth**—rather, "out of the *land";* i.e., I will break *and remove* war out of the earth (Ps. 46:9); and "out of the *land" of Israel* first (Isa. 2:4; Ezek. 39:9, 10; Zech. 9:9, 10). **lie down**—A reclining posture is the usual one with Orientals when not in action. **safely**—(Jer. 23:6).

19, 20. "Betroth" is *thrice* repeated, implying the intense love of God to His people; and perhaps, also, *the three Persons* of the *Triune God,* severally engaging to make good the betrothal. The marriage covenant will be as it were renewed from the beginning, on a different

ADAM CLARKE

14. *I will allure her, and bring her into the wilderness, and speak comfortably unto her.* After inflicting many judgments upon her, I will restore her again. I will deal with her as a very affectionate husband would do to an unfaithful wife. Instead of making her a public example, he takes her in private, talks to and reasons with her; puts her on her good behavior; promises to pass by all, and forgive all, if she will now amend her ways. In the meantime he provides what is necessary for her wants and comfortable support; and thus, opening a door of hope for her, she may be fully reconciled; rejoice as at the beginning, when he first took her by the hand, and she became his bride.

15. *She shall sing there.* There she shall sing the responsive song, as on high festival occasions, and in marriage ceremonies. The Book of Canticles is of this sort.

16. *Thou shalt call me Ishi.* That is, "My Man," or, "My Husband," a title of love and affection; *and not Baali,* "My master," a title exciting fear and apprehension; which, howsoever good in itself, was now rendered improper to be applied to Jehovah, having been prostituted to false gods. This intimated that they should scrupulously avoid idolatry; and they had such a full proof of the inefficacy of their idolatrous worship that, after their captivity, they never more served idols.

18. *Will I make a covenant for them.* I will make an agreement between them and the birds, beasts, and reptiles, so that they shall not be injured by those; their flocks shall not be destroyed, nor their crops spoiled. I will also prevent every species of war, that they may no more have the calamities that arise from that source. They shall also be safe from robbers and nightly alarms; for *I will make them to lie down* in safety.

19. *I will betroth thee unto me.* The people are always considered under the emblem of a wife unfaithful to her husband.

MATTHEW HENRY

blessings of it shall be everlasting. "And," says God, **"I will renew the covenant *in righteousness*."** Will it not reflect upon his wisdom? "No," says God; "I will do it *in judgment*." *In loving kindness and in mercies*—God will deal tenderly and graciously in covenanting with them. It shall be a covenant of grace, made in a compassionate consideration of their infirmities. *Thou shalt know the Lord.* This is not only a promise that God will reveal himself to them more fully than ever, but that he will give them *a heart to know him*; they shall know him in another manner. They shall all be *taught of God* to know him.

V. Though the heavens had been to them as brass, and the earth as iron, now the heavens shall yield their dews, and by that means the earth its fruits, *v.* 21, 22. This promise of *corn and wine* is to be taken also in a spiritual sense: it is an effusion of those blessings and graces which relate to the soul that is here promised under the metaphor of temporal blessings, the dew of heaven, as well as the fatness of the earth, and that put first, as in the blessing of Jacob, Gen. xxvii. 28. "But," say the heavens, "we have no rain to give unless he who has the key of the clouds unlock them, and open these bottles; so that, *if the Lord do not help you*, we cannot." God will graciously take notice of their addresses to him. And then *I will hear the heavens*; I will *answer them* (so it may be read); and then they shall *hear and answer the earth*, and pour down seasonable rain upon it. See here the coherence of second causes with one another, as links in a chain, and the necessary dependence they all have upon God, the first Cause.

VI. That whereas they were now divided and scattered all the world over, God will turn this curse into a blessing: "I will not only water the earth for her, but will *sow her unto me in the earth*; like that of the seed in the field, wherever they are scattered they shall *take root downward and bear fruit upward. The good seed are the children of the kingdom. I will sow her unto me*." When in all parts of the world Christianity got footing, then this promise was fulfilled.

VII. That, whereas they had been *Lo-ammi—not a people*, and *Lo-ruhamah—not finding mercy* with God, now they shall be restored to his favour (*v.* 23). God had mercy on those who *had not obtained mercy*. God's mercy must not be despaired of anywhere on this side hell. He says to them, "*Thou art my people*, whom I will own and bless," and they shall say, "*Thou art my God*, whom I will serve and worship, and to whose honour I will be for ever devoted."

JAMIESON, FAUSSET, BROWN

footing; not for a time only, as before, through the apostasy of the people, but "forever" through the grace of God writing the law on their hearts by the Spirit of Messiah (Jer. 31:31-37). **righteousness . . . judgment**—in rectitude and truth. **loving-kindness . . .**—Hereby God assures Israel, who might doubt the possibility of their restoration to His favor; low, sunk, and unworthy as thou art. I will restore thee from a regard to My own "loving-kindness," not thy merits. **faithfulness**—to My new covenant of grace with thee (I Thess. 5:24; Heb. 10:23).

21. in that day—of grace to Israel. **heavens . . . hear the earth**—personification. However many be the intermediate instruments, God is the Great First Cause of all nature's phenomena. God had threatened (vs. 9) He would *take back His corn, His wine, etc.* Here, on the contrary, God promises to *hearken to the skies*, as it were, supplicating Him to fill them with rain to pour on the earth; and that the skies again would hearken to the earth begging for a supply of the rain it requires; and again, that the earth would hearken to the corn, wine, and oil, begging it to bring them forth; and these again would hear Jezreel, i.e., would fulfil Israel's prayers for a supply of them. Israel is now no longer "Jezreel" in the sense, *God will* SCATTER (ch. 1:4), but in the sense, "*God will* PLANT" (ch. 1:11). **23. I will sow her**—referring to the meaning of *Jezreel* (vs. 22).

ADAM CLARKE

In righteousness. According to law, reason, and equity. *In judgment.* According to what is fit and becoming. *In lovingkindness.* Having the utmost affection and love for you. *In mercies.* Forgiving and blotting out all past miscarriages.

20. *In faithfulness.* You shalt no more prostitute yourself to idols, but be faithful to Him who calls himself your Husband. *Thou shalt know the Lord.* There shall be no more infidelity on your part nor divorce on Mine.

21. *I will hear, saith the Lord.* The sentence is repeated, to show how fully the thing was determined by the Almighty, and how implicitly they might depend on the divine promise.

22. *Shall hear the corn, and the wine.* When they seem to express a desire to supply the wants of man. *And they shall hear Jezreel.* The destitute people who are in want of the necessaries of life.

23. *I will sow her.* Alluding to the import of the name *Jezreel*, "the seed of God." Then shall it appear that God has shown mercy to them that had not obtained mercy. Then the covenant of God will be renewed; for He will call them His people who were not His people; and they shall call Jehovah their God, who before had Him not for the object of their worship.

The sentences in the latter part of this verse are very abrupt, but exceedingly expressive; leaving out those words supplied by the translators and which unnerve the passage, it stands thus: "I will say to not my people, Thou my people; and they shall say, My God."

MATTHEW HENRY — CHAPTER 3

Verses 1–5

Some think that this chapter refers to Judah, the two tribes, as the adulteress the prophet married (*ch.* i. 3) represented the *ten tribes*. But the *children of Israel* were the ten tribes, and therefore it is more probable that of them this parable is to be understood.

I. In this parable we may observe, God's goodness and Israel's badness serving for a foil to each other, *v.* 1. Israel is as a woman *beloved of her friend*, and *yet an adulteress*; such is the case between God and Israel. If they were restrained from bowing the knee to idols, yet they had *eyes full of that* spiritual *adultery*. And they loved *flagons of wine*; they joined with idolaters because they lived merrily and drank hard. Idolatry and sensuality commonly go together. Their badness had not put an end to God's goodness. Such is my *love to the children of Israel*; it is love to the loveless, to the unlovely, to those that have a thousand times forfeited it. God humbles them (*v.* 2): *I bought her to me for fifteen pieces of silver, and a homer and a half of barley*, that is, I courted her to return to her first husband, as *ch.* ii. 14. But the present which the prophet brought her for the purchasing of her favour is a very small one; and in it she is reduced to a short allowance, and, to punish her for her pride, is made to look very mean. The prophet here visited his wife with *fifteen pieces of silver*, a small sum, till her husband thought fit to restore her to her first estate. She shall also have *a homer and a half of barley*, for bread-corn, and that is all she must expect till she be sufficiently humbled. God had given Egypt for Israel's ransom once, Isa. xliii. 3, 4. But now that they have gone a-whoring from him he will give but fifteen pieces of silver for them, so much have they lost in their value by their iniquity. Now see the new terms upon which God is willing to come (*v.* 3). They must be to him a people, and he will be to them a God. They must take to themselves the shame of their apostasy from him: *Thou shalt abide for me many days* in *solitude* and *silence*, as a widow that is *desolate* and in sorrow; they must *lay aside their ornaments*, and wait with

JAMIESON, FAUSSET, BROWN — CHAPTER 3

Vss. 1-5. ISRAEL'S CONDITION IN THEIR PRESENT DISPERSION, SUBSEQUENT TO THEIR RETURN FROM BABYLON, SYMBOLIZED. The prophet is to take back his wife, though unfaithful, as foretold in ch. 1:2. He purchases her from her paramour, stipulating she should wait for a long period before she should be restored to her conjugal rights. So Israel is to live for a long period without her ancient rites of religion, and yet be free from idolatry; then at last she shall acknowledge Messiah, and know Jehovah's goodness restored to her. **1. Go yet**—"Go *again*," referring to ch. 1:2 [HENDERSON]. **a woman**—purposely indefinite, for *thy wife*, to express the *separation* in which Hosea had lived from Gomer for her unfaithfulness. **beloved of her friend**—used for "her *husband*," on account of the estrangement between them. She was still beloved of her husband, though an adulteress; just as God still loved Israel, though idolatrous (Jer. 3:20). Hosea is told, not as in ch. 1:2, "*take* a wife," but "*love*" her, i.e., renew thy conjugal kindness to her. **who look to other gods**—i.e., have done so heretofore, but henceforth (from the return from Babylon) shall do so no more (vs. 4). **flagons of wine**—rather, pressed cakes of dried grapes, such as were offered to idols (Jer. 7:18) [MAURER]. **2. I bought her**—The price paid is too small to be a probable dowry wherewith to buy *a wife* from her parents; but it is just half the price of a female *slave*, in money, the rest of the price being made up in grain (Exod. 21:32). Hosea pays this for the redemption of his wife, who has become the *slave of her paramour*. The price being *half grain* was because the latter was the allowance of food for the slave, and of the coarsest kind, not *wheat*, but *barley*. Israel, as *committing sin*, was *the slave of sin* (John 8:34; Rom. 6:16-20; II Pet. 2:19). The low price expresses Israel's *worthlessness*. **3. abide for me**—separate from intercourse with any other man, and *remaining* for me who have redeemed thee (cf. Deut. 21:13). **so will I also be for thee**—*remain for thee*, not taking any other consort. As Israel should long *remain*

ADAM CLARKE — CHAPTER 3

1. *Go yet, love a woman.* This is a different command from that mentioned in the first chapter. That denoted the infidelity of the kingdom of Israel and God's divorce of them. He gave them up to their enemies, and caused them to be carried into captivity. The *woman* mentioned here represents one who was a lawful wife joining herself to a paramour; then divorced by her husband; afterwards repenting, and desirous to be joined to her spouse; ceasing from her adulterous commerce, but not yet reconciled to him. This was the state and disposition of the Jews under the Babylonish captivity. Though separated from their own idols, they continued separated from their God. He is still represented as having affectionate feelings towards them; awaiting their full repentance and contrition, in order to renew the marriage covenant. These things are pointed out by the symbolical actions of the prophet.

Beloved of her friend. Or "a lover of evil." *According to the love of the Lord.* This woman, who had proved false to her husband, was still beloved by him, though he could not acknowledge her; as the Israelites were beloved by the Lord, while they were looking after other gods. The *flagons of wine* were probably such as were used for libations, or drunk in idol feasts.

2. *Fifteen pieces of silver.* If they were shekels, the price of this woman was about two pounds five shillings. *An homer* of barley. As the homer was about eight bushels, the homer and half was about twelve or thirteen bushels.

3. *Thou shalt abide for me many days.* He did not take her home, but made a contract with her that, if she would abstain from her evil ways, he would take her to himself after a sufficient trial. In the meantime he gave her

MATTHEW HENRY

patience and submission to know what God will do with them. It is not enough to take shame to ourselves for the sins we have committed, and to justify God in correcting us for them, but we must resolve, in the strength of God's grace, that we will not offend any more. In the land of their captivity they would be courted to worship the idols of the country; that would be a trial for them, a *long* trial, many days: "But if thou keep thy ground, and hold fast thy integrity, if, when *all this comes upon thee*, thou dost not *stretch out thy hand to a strange god*, thou wilt be qualified for the returns of God's favour."

II. In the last two verses we have the interpretation of the parable and the application of it to Israel. *They shall abide many days without a king, and without a prince;* and a nation in this condition may well be called *a widow. They shall* abide *without a sacrifice*, and *without an image* (or a *statue*, or *pillar;* the word is used concerning the pillars Jacob erected, Gen. xxviii. 18; xxxi. 45; xxxv. 20), and *without an ephod and teraphim.* The meaning is that in their captivity they should have no face of a nation upon them, no face of a church. They shall have *no ephod*, nor *teraphim*, no legal priesthood. This was the case of the Jews in their captivity; and it is so far the case of the scattered Jews at this day that, though they have their synagogues, they have no temple-service.

They shall at length be received again as a wife (*v.* 5): *Afterwards*, in process of time, when they have gone through this discipline, *they shall return.* The Chaldee reads it, They shall *seek the service of the Lord their God*, and *shall obey Messiah, the Son of David their king*. Compare this with Jer. xxx. 9; Ezek. xxxiv. 23; xxxvii. 25.

They shall fear the Lord and his goodness. Some by his *goodness* here understand the temple, towards which they shall look, in worshipping God. The Jews say, There were three things—which Israel cast off in the days of Rehoboam—the *kingdom of heaven*, the *family of David*, and the *house of the sanctuary*. But it is rather to be taken for that attribute of God which he showed as his glory, and by which he proclaimed his name. It is not only the Lord and his greatness that we are to fear, but the Lord and his goodness, not only his majesty, but his mercy.

JAMIESON, FAUSSET, BROWN

without serving other gods, yet separate from Jehovah; so Jehovah on His part, in this long period of estrangement, would form no marriage covenant with any other people (cf. vs. 4). He would not *immediately* receive her to marriage privileges, but would test her repentance and discipline her by the long probation; still the marriage covenant would hold good, she was to be kept separated for but a time, not divorced (Isa. 50:1); in God's good time she shall be restored. **4.** The long period here foretold was to be one in which Israel should have no civil polity, king, or prince, no sacrifice to Jehovah, and yet no idol, or false god, no ephod, or teraphim. Exactly describing their state for the last nineteen centuries, separate from idols, yet without any legal sacrifice to Jehovah, whom they profess to worship, and without being acknowledged by Him as His Church. So KIMCHI, a Jew, explains it. The ephod was worn by the high priest above the tunic and robe. It consisted of two finely wrought pieces which hung down, the one in front over the breast, the other on the back, to the middle of the thigh; joined on the shoulders by golden clasps set in onyx stones with the names of the twelve tribes, and fastened round the waist by a girdle (Exod. 28:6-12). The *common* ephod worn by the lower priests, Levites, and any person performing sacred rites, was of linen (II Sam. 6:14; I Chron. 15:27). In the breast were the Urim and Thummim by which God gave responses to the Hebrews. The latter was one of the five things which the second temple lacked, and which the first had. It, as representing the divinely constituted priesthood, is opposed to the idolatrous "teraphim," as "sacrifice" (to Jehovah) is to "an [idolatrous] image." "Abide" answers to "thou shalt *abide* for me" (vs. 3). *Abide* in solitary isolation, as a separated wife. The teraphim were tutelary household gods, in the shape of human busts, cut off at the waist (as the root of the *Hebrew* word implies) [MAURER], (Gen. 31:19, 30-35). They were supposed to give responses to consulters (II Kings 23: 24; *Margin,* Ezek. 21:21; Zech. 10:2). Saul's daughter, Michal, putting one in a bed, as if it were David, proves the shape to have been that of a man. **5. Afterward**—after the long period ("many days," vs. 4) has elapsed. **return**—from their idols to "their God," from whom they had wandered. **David their king**—Israel had forsaken the worship of Jehovah at the same time that they forsook their allegiance to David's line. Their repentance towards God is therefore to be accompanied by their return to the latter. So Judah and Israel shall be one, and under "one head," as is also foretold (ch. 1:11). That representative and antitype of David is Messiah. "David" means "the beloved." Cf. as to Messiah, Matthew 3:17; Ephesians 1:6. Messiah is called David (Isa. 55:3, 4; Jer. 30:9; Ezek. 34:23, 24; 37: 24, 25). **fear the Lord and his goodness**—i.e., tremblingly flee to the Lord, to escape from the wrath to come; and to His goodness," as manifested in Messiah, which attracts them to Him (Jer. 31:12). The "fear" is not that which "hath torment" (I John 4:18), but *reverence* inspired by His goodness realized in the soul (Ps. 130:4). **the latter days**—those of Messiah [KIMCHI].

ADAM CLARKE

the money and the barley to subsist upon, that she might not be under the temptation of becoming again unfaithful. *So will I also be for thee.* That is, if you, Israel, will keep yourself separate from your idolatry, and give Me proof, by your total abstinence from idols, that you will be My faithful worshipper, I will receive you again, and in the meantime support you with the necessaries of life while you are in the land of your captivity.

4. *Many days without a king.* Hitherto this prophecy has been literally fulfilled. Since the destruction of the Temple by the Romans they have had neither king nor prince. *Without an image . . . ephod . . . teraphim.* The Septuagint, "Without a sacrifice, without an altar, without a priesthood, and without oracles."

5. *Afterward shall the children of Israel return.* Shall repent of their iniquities, *and seek the Lord;* lay aside their mock worship, and serve the true God in spirit and in truth. *And David their king.* Or as the Targum, "They shall obey the Messiah, the Son of David, their King"; and thus look believingly upon Him whom they have pierced, and mourn.

MATTHEW HENRY

CHAPTER 4

Verses 1-5

I. The court set, and attention demanded: "*Hear the word of the Lord, you children of Israel.*" They will be ready enough to hear when God speaks comfortably to them; but are they willing to hear when he has a controversy with them?

II. The indictment read, by which the whole nation stands charged with crimes by which God is highly provoked. 1. They are charged with national omissions of the most important duties. The people seemed to have no sense at all of honesty. Much less had they any sense of mercy, or any obligation they were under to pity and help the poor. What good can be expected where there is no knowledge of God? Hence follow national commissions of enormous sins against both the first and second table. *Swearing*, and *lying*, and *killing*, and *stealing*, and *committing adultery*, against the third, ninth, sixth, eighth, and seventh commandments, were to be found in all corners of the land, *v.* 2. They *break out*, that is, they transgress all bounds of reason and conscience, and the divine law. When they break out thus *blood touches blood*, murders are committed in all parts of the country. It was about this time that there was so much blood shed in grasping at the crown.

III. Sentence passed upon this guilty land, *v.* 3.

JAMIESON, FAUSSET, BROWN

CHAPTER 4

VSS. 1-19. HENCEFORTH THE PROPHET SPEAKS PLAINLY AND WITHOUT SYMBOL, IN TERSE, SENTENTIOUS PROPOSITIONS. In this chapter he reproves the people and priests for their sins in the interregnum which followed Jeroboam's death; hence there is no mention of the king or his family; and in vs. 2 bloodshed and other evils usual in a civil war are specified. **1. Israel**—the ten tribes. **controversy**—judicial ground of complaint (Isa. 1:18; Jer. 25:31; Mic. 6:2).

no . . . knowledge of God—exhibited in practice (Jer. 22:16). **2. they break out**—bursting through every restraint.

blood toucheth blood—lit., "bloods." One act of bloodshed follows another without any interval between (see II Kings 15:8-16, 25; Mic. 7:2).

ADAM CLARKE

CHAPTER 4

1. *The Lord hath a controversy.* What we should call a "lawsuit," in which God is Plaintiff, and the Israelites defendants. It is Jehovah *versus* Israel and Judah.

2. *Blood toucheth blood.* Murders are not only frequent, but assassinations are mutual.

MATTHEW HENRY

It shall be utterly laid waste. The valleys are said to *mourn* when by war and famine they are made desolate. The destruction of the fruits of the earth shall be so great that there shall not be picking for the *fowls of the air*.

IV. The order (*v.* 4): *Yet let no man strive nor reprove another*, intimates that as long as there is any hope we ought to reprove sinners for their sins. Yet sometimes they are so hardened in sin that it will be to little purpose either to deal with them or to deal with God for them. *Thy people are as those that strive with the priests.* Those who rebel against ministerial reproof, which is an ordinance of God for their reformation, have forfeited the benefit of brotherly reproof too. Perhaps this may refer to the late wickedness of Joash king of Judah, and his people, who stoned Zechariah, 2 Chron. xxiv. 21. "*Therefore*, because thou wilt take no reproof, *thou shalt* stumble and *fall in the day*, and *the prophet*, the false prophet that flattered thee, shall *fall with thee in the night*; the darkness of the night shall not help to cover thee from trouble nor the light of the day help thee to flee from it." And did the children think that when they were in danger of falling their mother would help them? It shall be in vain to expect it, for *I will destroy thy mother*, Samaria, the mother-city, which is as a mother to every part. It shall all be *made silent*.

Verses 6–11

I. The people *strove with the priests*; justly therefore were they *destroyed for lack of knowledge*, *v.* 6. Those that rebel against the light can expect no other than to perish in the dark. Or it is a charge upon the priests, who should have been still *teaching the people knowledge* (Eccles. xii. 9), but they did not.

II. Both priests and people rejected knowledge; and justly therefore will God *reject them*. The reason why the people did not learn, and the priests did not teach, was not because they had not the light, but because they hated it.

III. They *forgot the law of God*, nor desired to transmit the remembrance of it to their posterity, and therefore will God *forget* them and *their children*, the people's children. Or it may be meant of the priests' children; they shall not succeed them in the priests' office, 1 Sam. ii. 20.

IV. They dishonoured God, *v.* 7. It was their honour that they were increased in number, wealth, power, and dignity. The beginning of their nation was small, but it *greatly increased*. But, *as they were increased, so they sinned* against God. Their wealth, honour, and power, did but make them the more daring in sin. Therefore, says God, *will I change their glory into shame.*

V. The priests ate up the sin of God's people, and therefore *they shall eat and not have enough.* They abused the maintenance that was allowed to the priests (*v.* 8). They *set their hearts* upon the people's *iniquities*; they *lifted up their soul* to them, that is, they were glad when people did commit iniquity, that they might be obliged to bring an offering to make atonement for it, of which they should have their share. God will therefore deny them his blessing upon their maintenance (*v.* 10): *They shall eat and not have enough.* Though they have great plenty by the abundance of offerings, yet they shall have no satisfaction in it.

VI. The more they increased the more they sinned (*v.* 7), and therefore though they *commit whoredom*, though they take the most wicked methods to multiply their people, yet *they shall not increase.*

VII. The people and the priests did harden one another in sin; and therefore justly shall they be sharers in the punishment (*v.* 9): *There shall be, like people, like priest.*

VIII. They indulged themselves in the delights of sense, to hold up their hearts; but they shall find that they *take away their hearts* (*v.* 11): *Whoredom, and wine, and new wine take away the heart.*

Verses 12–19

I. The sins charged upon the people of Israel.

1. Spiritual whoredom, or idolatry. They have in them a *spirit of whoredoms*, a strong inclination to that sin. So (*v.* 15) Israel has *played the harlot*; their conduct in the worship of their idols was like that of a harlot, wanton and impudent. And (*v.* 16). *Israel slideth back as a backsliding heifer*, as an *untamed* heifer (so some), or as a *perverse* or *refractory* one (so others), as a heifer that is turned loose runs madly about the pasture, or, if put under the yoke (which seems rather to be alluded to here), will draw back instead of going forward, will struggle to get her neck out of the yoke and her feet out of the furrow. Thus unruly, ungovernable, untractable, were the

JAMIESON, FAUSSET, BROWN

3. land . . . languish—(Isa. 19:8; 24:4; Joel 1:10, 12). **sea**—including all bodies of water, as pools and even rivers (*Note*, Isa. 19:5). A general drought, the greatest calamity in the East, is threatened.

4. let no man . . . reprove—Great as is the sin of Israel, it is hopeless to reprove them; for their presumptuous guilt is as great as that of one who refuses to obey the priest when giving judgment in the name of Jehovah, and who therefore is to be put to death (Deut. 17:12). They rush on to their own destruction as wilfully as such a one. **thy people**—the ten tribes of Israel; distinct from Judah (vs. 1). **5. fall in the day**—in broad *daylight*, a time when an attack would not be expected (*Notes*, Jer. 6:4, 5; 15:8). **in . . . night**—No time, night or day, shall be free from the slaughter of individuals of the people, as well as of the false prophets. **thy mother**—the Israelitish state, of which the citizens are the children (ch. 2:2). **6. lack of knowledge**—"of God" (vs. 1), i.e., lack of piety. Their ignorance was wilful, as the epithet, "*My* people," implies; they *ought* to have known, having the opportunity, as the people of God. **thou**—O priest, so called. Not regularly constituted, but still bearing the name, while confounding the worship of Jehovah and of the calves in Beth-el (I Kings 12:29, 31). **I will . . . forget thy children**—Not only those who then were alive should be deprived of the priesthood, but their children who, in the ordinary course would have succeeded them, should be set aside. **7. As they were increased**—in numbers and power. Cf. vs. 6, "thy children," to which their "increase" in *numbers* refers. **so they sinned**—(Cf. ch. 10:1 and 13:6). **will I change their glory into shame**—i.e., I will strip them of all they now *glory* in (their numbers and power), and give them *shame* instead. A just retribution: as they changed their glory into shame, by idolatry (Ps. 106:20; Jer. 2:11; Rom. 1: 23; Phil. 3:19). **8. eat . . . sin of my people**—i.e., the sin offerings (Lev. 6:26; 10:17). The priests greedily devoured them. **set their heart on their iniquity**—lit., "lift up the animal soul to lust after," or strongly desire. Cf. *Margin*, Deuteronomy 24: 15; Psalm 24:4; Jeremiah 22:27. The priests set *their own* hearts on the iniquity *of the people*, instead of trying to suppress it. For the more the people sinned, the more sacrificial victims in atonement for sin the priests gained. **9. like people, like priest**—They are one in guilt; therefore they shall be one in punishment (Isa. 24:2). **reward them their doings**—in homely phrase, "pay them back in their own coin" (Prov. 1:31). **10. eat, and not have enough**—just retribution on those who "eat up [greedily] the sin of My people" (vs. 8; Mic. 6:14; Hag. 1:6). **whoredom, and . . . not increase**—lit., "break forth"; used of *giving birth to children* (Gen. 28:14, *Margin;* cf. Gen. 38:29). Not only their wives, but their concubines, shall be barren. To be childless was considered a great calamity among the Jews. **11.** A moral truth applicable to all times. The special reference here is to the licentious orgies connected with the Syrian worship, which lured Israel away from the pure worship of God (Isa. 28:1, 7; Amos 4:1). **take away the heart**—i.e., the understanding; make men blind to their own true good (Eccles. 7:7). **12.** Instances of their understanding ("heart") being "taken away." **stocks**—wooden idols (Jer. 2:27; Hab. 2:19). **staff**—alluding to divination by rods (*Notes*, Ezek. 21:21, 22). The diviner, says ROSENMULLER, threw a rod from him, which was stripped of its bark on one side, not on the other: if the bare side turned uppermost, it was a good omen; if the side with the bark, it was a bad omen. The Arabs used two rods, the one marked *God bids*, the other, *God forbids;* whichever came out first, in drawing them out of a case, gave the omen for, or against, an undertaking. **declareth**—i.e., is consulted to inform them of future events. **spirit of whoredoms**—a general *disposition* on the part of all *towards idolatry* (ch. 5:4). **err**—go astray from the true God. **from under their God**—They have gone away from God *under* whom they were, as a wife is under the dominion of her husband.

15. Though *Israel's* ten tribes indulge in spiritual harlotry, at least thou, *Judah*, who hast the legal priesthood, and the temple rites, and Jerusalem, do not follow her bad example.

16. backsliding—Translate, "Israel is refractory, as a refractory heifer," viz., one that throws the yoke off her neck. Israel had represented God under the form of "calves" (I Kings 12:28); but it is she herself who is one.

ADAM CLARKE

4. *Yet let no man strive.* Or, "No man contendeth." All these evils stalk abroad unreproved, for all are guilty. *For thy people are.* The *people* and the *priest* are alike rebels against the Lord, the priests having become idolaters as well as the people. Bishop Newcome renders this clause, "And as is the provocation of the priest, so is that of my people."

5. *Therefore shalt thou fall in the day.* In the most open and public manner. *And the prophet also shall fall . . . in the night.* The false prophet, when employed in taking prognostications from stars. *And I will destroy thy mother.* The metropolis or mother city. Jerusalem or Samaria is meant.

7. *Will I change their glory into shame.* As the idolaters at Dan and Bethel have changed My glory into the similitude of an ox that eateth grass (Rom. i. 23), so will I change their glory into shame or ignominy.

8. *They eat up the sin of my people. Chattath*, the "sin offering."

12. *At their stocks.* They consult their wooden gods. *And their staff declareth.* They use divination by rods; see Ezekiel xxi.

16. *Israel slideth back.* They are untractable, like an unbroken *heifer* or steer, that pulls back, rather than draw in the yoke.

MATTHEW HENRY

people of Israel. *My people ask counsel at their stocks*, their wooden gods. They *say to a stock, Thou art my father* (Jer. ii. 27). (It is probable that this refers to wicked methods of divination by a *piece of wood*, or by *a staff*, like Nebuchadnezzar's divining by *his arrows*, Ezek. xxi. 21.) They offered sacrifice to them as gods (*v.* 13): to atone and pacify them, and *burn incense* to them, to please and gratify them. They chose places, *upon the tops of the mountains* and *upon the hills*, foolishly imagining that the height of the ground gave them some advantage in their approaches towards heaven; places, *under oaks, and poplars, and elms, because the shadow thereof* is pleasant to them, and they fancied that a thick shade possesses the mind with something of awe, and therefore is proper for devotion.

2. Corporal whoredom is another crime here charged upon them: *They have committed whoredom continually*, *v.* 18. They drove a trade of uncleanness. Their false gods drew them to it; for the devil whom they worshipped, though a spirit, is an unclean spirit. To punish them for that God gave up their wives and daughters to the like vile affections.

3. The perverting of justice, *v.* 18. *Their rulers do love, Give ye*, that is, they love bribes, and have it continually in their mouths. Justice, duly administered, is refreshing, like drink to the thirsty, but when it is perverted, and rulers take rewards either to acquit the guilty or to condemn the innocent, the *drink is sour*.

II. The tokens of God's wrath against them for their sins. *I will not punish your daughters;* and, not being punished for their sin, they would go on in it. The impunity of one sinner is sometimes made the punishment of another.

They themselves should prosper for a while, but their prosperity should help to destroy them (*v.* 16): *The Lord will feed them as a lamb in a large place;* but it shall be only to prepare them for the slaughter, as a lamb is that is so fed. But others make them feed as *a lamb on the common*, a large place indeed, but where it has short grass and lies exposed. The Shepherd of Israel will turn them both out of his pastures and out of his protection.

"*Ephraim is joined to idols*, is in love with them and addicted to them, and therefore *let him alone*, as *v.* 4 and *v.* 17, *Let no man reprove* him." The father corrects not the rebellious son any more when he determines to disinherit him. Those that are not disturbed in their sin will be destroyed for their sin.

They should be hurried away with a swift and shameful destruction (*v.* 19).

III. The warning given to Judah not to sin after the similitude of Israel's transgression. *Though thou, Israel, play the harlot, yet let not Judah offend.* This was a very needful caution. The men of Israel were near neighbours, more numerous, and prosperous. Judah has greater means of knowledge than Israel, has the temple and priesthood, and a king of the house of David; from Judah Shiloh is to come; therefore *let not Judah offend*, for more is expected from them than from Israel, and from them God will take it more unkindly. If *Israel play the harlot*, let not Judah do so too, for then God will have no professing people in the world. *Come not you unto Gilgal*, where *all their wickedness was* (*ch.* ix. 15; xii. 11); there they *multiplied transgression* (Amos iv. 4). And for the same reason they must *not go up to Bethel*, here called the *house of vanity*, for so *Bethaven* signifies, not the *house of God*, as *Bethel* signifies.

CHAPTER 5

JAMIESON, FAUSSET, BROWN

13. upon . . . mountains—High places were selected by idolaters on which to sacrifice, because of their greater nearness to the heavenly hosts which they worshipped (Deut. 12:2). **elms**—rather, "terebinths" [MAURER]. **shadow . . . good**—screening the lascivious worshippers from the heat of the sun. **daughters . . . commit whoredom . . . spouses . . . adultery**—in the polluted worship of Astarte, the Phœnician goddess of love.

18. Their drink is sour—metaphor for *utter degeneracy* of principle (Isa. 1:22). Or, *unbridled licentiousness;* not mere ordinary sin, but as abandoned as drunkards who vomit and smell sour with wine potations [CALVIN]. MAURER not so well translates, "When their drinking *is over*, they commit whoredoms," viz., in honor of Astarte (vss. 13, 14). **her rulers**—Israel's; lit., "shields" (cf. Ps. 47:9). **with shame . . . love, Give ye**—(Prov. 30:15). No remedy could be effectual against their corruptions since the very rulers sold justice for gifts [CALVIN]. MAURER translates, "The rulers are marvelously enamored of shame." *English Version* is better. **14. I will not punish . . . daughters**—I will visit with the heaviest punishments "not" the unchaste "daughters and spouses," but the fathers and husbands; for it is these who "themselves" have set the bad example, so that as compared with the punishment of the latter, that of the former shall seem as nothing [MUNSTER]. **separated with whores**—withdrawn from the assembly of worshippers to some receptacle of impurity for carnal connection with *whores.* **sacrifice with harlots**—They commit lewdness with *women* who *devote their persons* to be violated in honor of Astarte. (So the *Hebrew* for "harlots" means, as distinguished from "whores.") Cf. Numbers 25:1-3; and the prohibition, Deuteronomy 23:18. **not understand**—(Isa. 44:18; 45:20). **shall fall**—shall be cast down.

lamb in a large place—not in a good sense, as in Isaiah 30:23. Here there is irony: lambs like a large pasture; but it is not so safe for them as a small one, duly fenced from wild beasts. God will "feed" them, but it shall be with the "rod" (Mic. 7:14). It shall be no longer in the narrow territory of Israel, but "in a large place," viz., they shall be scattered in exile over the wide realm of Assyria, a prey to their foes; as lambs, which are timid, gregarious, and not solitary, are a prey when scattered asunder to wild beasts. **17. Ephraim**—the ten tribes. Judah was at this time not so given to idolatry as afterwards. **joined to idols**—closely and voluntarily; identifying themselves with them as a whoremonger becomes one flesh with the harlot (Num. 25:3; I Cor. 6:16, 17). **idols**—The *Hebrew* means also "sorrows," "pains," implying the pain which idolatry brings on its votaries. **let him alone**—Leave him to himself. Let him reap the fruits of his own perverse choice; his case is desperate; say nothing to him (cf. Jer. 7:16). Here vs. 15 shows the address is to *Judah*, to avoid the contagion of Israel's bad example. He is bent on his own ruin; leave him to his fate, lest, instead of saving him, thou fall thyself (Isa. 48:20; Jer. 50:8; 51:6, 45; II Cor. 6:17).

19. Israel shall be swept away from her land (vs. 16) suddenly and violently as if by "the wings of the wind" (Ps. 18:10; 104:3; Jer. 4:11, 12). **ashamed . . . of their sacrifices**—disappointed to their shame in their hope of help through their sacrifices to idols. **Gilgal**—situated between Jordan and Jericho on the confines of Samaria; once a holy place to Jehovah (Josh. 5:10-15; I Sam. 10:8; 15:21); afterwards desecrated by idol-worship (ch. 9:15; 12-11; Amos 4:4; 5:5; cf. Judg. 3:19, *Margin*). **Beth-aven**—i.e., "house of vanity" or idols: a name substituted in contempt for *Beth-el*, "the house of God"; once sacred to Jehovah (Gen. 28:17, 19; 35:7), but made by Jeroboam the seat of the worship of the calves (I Kings 12:28-33; 13:1; Jer. 48:13; Amos 3:14; 7:13). "Go *up*" refers to the fact that Beth-el was on a hill (Josh. 16:1). **nor swear, The Lord liveth**—This formula of oath was appointed by God Himself (Deut. 6:13; 10:20; Jer. 4:2). It is therefore here forbidden not absolutely, but in conjunction with idolatry and falsehood (Isa. 48:1; Ezek. 20:39; Zeph. 1:5).

CHAPTER 5

Vss. 1-5. GOD'S JUDGMENTS ON THE PRIESTS, PEOPLE, AND PRINCES OF ISRAEL FOR THEIR SINS. Judah, too, being guilty shall be punished; nor shall Assyria, whose aid they both sought, save them; judgments shall at last lead them to repentance. **1.**

ADAM CLARKE

13. *The shadow thereof is good.* Their "*daughters* committed *whoredom*, and their *spouses* committed *adultery*." (1) Their deities were worshipped by prostitution. (2) They *drank* much in their idol worship, v. 11, and thus their passions became inflamed. (3) The *thick groves* were favorable to the whoredoms and adulteries mentioned here. In imitation of these, some nations have their public gardens.

18. *Their drink is sour.* Or rather, "He is gone after their wine." The enticements of idolatry have carried them away.

Her rulers with shame do love. Rather, "have loved shame"; they glory in their abominations. *Give ye.* Perhaps it would be better to read, "Her rulers have committed, etc. They have loved gifts. What a shame!"

14. *I will not punish.* "Why should ye be stricken any more? ye will revolt more and more." When God, in judgment, removes His judgments, the case of that people is desperate. While there is *hope*, there is *correction. Themselves are separated.* There is a reference here to certain debaucheries which should not be described. The state of the people at this time must have been abominable beyond all precedent—animal, sensual, bestial, diabolical: women consecrating themselves to serve their idols by public prostitution; boys dismembered like the *Galli* or priests of Cybele; men and women acting unnaturally; and all conjoining to act diabolically.

Will feed them as a lamb in a large place. A species of irony. You shall go to Assyria, and be scattered among the nations; you may sport yourselves in the extensive empire, whither you shall be carried captives.

17. *Ephraim.* The ten tribes. *Let him alone.* They are irreclaimable; leave them to the consequences of their vicious conduct.

15. *Let not Judah offend.* Israel was totally dissolute; Judah was not so. Here she is exhorted to maintain her integrity. If the former will go to what was once Bethel, the "house of God," now *Beth-aven*, the "house of iniquity," because Jeroboam has set up his calves there, let not Judah imitate them. *Gilgal* was the place where the covenant of circumcision was renewed when the people passed over Jordan; but was rendered infamous by the worship of idols, after Jeroboam had set up his idolatry.

CHAPTER 5

MATTHEW HENRY

Verses 1–7

I. All orders and degrees of men are cited (*v.* 1): *Hear you this, O priests!* "Hearken, *you house of Israel*, the common people, and *give ear, O house of the king!*" Let them all take notice, for they have all contributed to the national guilt, and shall share in the national judgments.

III. They had been industrious to draw people either into sin or into trouble: You have been *a snare on Mizpah, and a net spread upon Tabor* (*v.* 1).

They had been both crafty and cruel in carrying on their designs (*v.* 2): *The revolters are profaned to make slaughter.*

They had *committed whoredom*, defiled their own bodies with fleshly lusts, defiled their own souls with the worship of idols, *v.* 3.

II. Witness is produced against them; it is God's omniscience (*v.* 3): *I know Ephraim, and Israel is not hidden from me.* They have *not known the Lord* (*v.* 4), but the Lord has known them.

They had no disposition at all to come into acquaintance and communion with God. The *spirit of whoredoms*, having *caused them to err* from him, keeps them wandering endlessly, *v.* 4. It is true we cannot by our own power, without the special grace of God, turn to him; but we may by the due improvement of our own faculties, and the common aids of his Spirit, *frame our doings* to turn to him.

They were guilty of notorious arrogance, and insolence in sin (*v.* 5): *The pride of Israel doth testify to his face* in the gaiety and gaudiness of their worship, as a harlot is known by her attire, Prov. vii. 10.

IV. "*Judgment is towards you.* God is coming forth to contend with you, and to testify his displeasure against you for your sins." They shall *fall in their iniquity*. This follows upon their *pride testifying to their face* (*v.* 5). *Therefore shall Israel and Ephraim fall in their iniquity.* They shall fall short of God's favour when they profess to seek it (*v.* 6): *They shall go with their flocks and with their herds to seek the Lord*, but in vain; *they shall not find him.* This seems to be spoken principally of Judah. They went as usual, at the solemn feasts, *with their flocks and herds to seek the Lord*; but their hearts were not *entire for him*. Those that go *with their flocks and their herds* only to seek the Lord, and not with their hearts and souls, cannot expect to find him, for his favour is not to be purchased with *thousands of rams.*

They departed from God to idols, and bred up their children in idolatry (*v.* 7). Those deal treacherously with God indeed who not only turn from following him themselves but train up their children in wicked ways.

They and their portions shall all be swallowed up. They have *dealt treacherously against the Lord*, but *now shall a month devour them with their portions.* By their *portions* is meant their idols, whom they chose for their portion instead of God. A *month* shall *devour* them. The judgments of God sometimes make quick work with a sinful people. A month devours more, and more portions, than many years can repair.

JAMIESON, FAUSSET, BROWN

the king—probably Pekah; the contemporary of Ahaz, king of Judah, under whom idolatry was first carried so far in Judah as to call for the judgment of the joint Syrian and Israelite invasion, as also that of Assyria. **judgment is towards you**—i.e., threatens you from God. **ye have been a snare on Mizpah . . . net . . . upon Tabor**—As hunters spread their net and snares on the hills, Mizpah and Tabor, so ye have snared the people into idolatry and made them your prey by injustice. As *Mizpah* and *Tabor* mean a "watch tower," and a "lofty place," a fit scene for hunters, playing on the words, the prophet implies, in the lofty place in which I have set you, whereas ye ought to have been the *watchers* of the people, guarding them from evil, ye have been as *hunters entrapping* them into it [JEROME]. These two places are specified, Mizpah in the east and Tabor in the west, to include the *high places* throughout the *whole* kingdom, in which Israel's rulers set up idolatrous altars. **2. revolters**—apostates. **profound**—*deeply* rooted [CALVIN] and sunk to the lowest depths, *excessive* in their idolatry (ch. 9:9; Isa. 31:6) [HENDERSON]. From the antithesis (vs. 3), "not hid from me," I prefer explaining, *profoundly cunning* in their idolatry. Jeroboam thought it a *profound* piece of policy to set up golden calves to represent God in Dan and Beth-el, in order to prevent Israel's heart from turning again to David's line by going up to Jerusalem to worship. So Israel's subsequent idolatry was grounded by their leaders on various pleas of state expediency (cf. Isa. 29:15). **to . . . slaughter**—He does not say "to *sacrifice*," for their so-called sacrifices were *butcheries* rather than sacrifices; there was nothing sacred about them, being to idols instead of to the holy God. **though**—MAURER translates, "*and* [in spite of their hope of safety through their slaughter of victims to idols] *I will be* a chastisement to them all." *English Version* is good sense: They have deeply revolted, *notwithstanding* all my prophetical warnings. **3. Ephraim**—the tribe so called, as distinguished from "Israel" here, the other nine tribes. It was always foremost of the tribes of the northern kingdom. For 400 years in early history, it, with Manasseh and Benjamin, its two dependent tribes, held the pre-eminence in the whole nation. Ephraim is here addressed as foremost in idolatry. **I know . . . not hid from me**—notwithstanding their supposed *profound* cunning (vs. 2; Rev. 2:2, 9, 13, 19). **now**—"though I have been a rebuker of all them" (vs. 2) who *commit* such spiritual *whoredoms*, thou art *now* continuing in them. **4. They**—Turning from a direct address to Ephraim, he uses the third person *plural* to characterize the people in general. The *Hebrew* is against the *Margin*, their doings will not suffer *them*" the omission of "them" in the *Hebrew* after the verb being unusual. The sense is, they are incurable, for they will not *permit* (as the *Hebrew* lit. means) their doings to be framed so as to turn unto God. Implying that they *resist* the Spirit of God, not *suffering* Him to renew them; and give themselves up to "the spirit of whoredoms" (in antithesis to "the Spirit of God" implied in "suffer" or "permit") (ch. 4:12; Isa. 63:10; Ezek. 16:43; Acts 7:51). **5. the pride of Israel**—wherewith they reject the warnings of God's prophets (vs. 2), and prefer their idols to God (ch. 7:10; Jer. 13:17). **testify to his face**—openly *to his face* he shall be convicted of the pride which is so palpable in him. Or, "*in* his face," as in Isaiah 3:9. **Judah . . . shall fall with them**—This prophecy is later than ch. 4:15, when Judah had not gone so far in idolatry; now her imitation of Israel's bad example provokes the threat of her being doomed to share in Israel's punishment. **6. with . . . flocks**—to propitiate Jehovah (Isa. 1:11-15). **seek . . . not find**—because it is slavish fear that leads them to seek Him; and because it then shall be too late (Prov. 1:28; John 7:34). **7. treacherously**—as to the marriage covenant (Jer. 3:20). **strange children**—alluding to "children of whoredoms" (ch. 1:2; 2:4). "Strange" or *foreign* implies that their idolatry was imported from abroad [HENDERSON]. Or rather, "regarded by God as strangers, not His," as being reared in idolatry. The case is desperate, when not only the existing, but also the rising, generation is reared in apostasy. **a month**—*a very brief space of time* shall elapse, and then punishment shall overtake them (Zech. 11:8). The allusion seems to be to money loans, which were *by the month*, not as with us by the year. You cannot put it off; the time of your destruction is immediately and suddenly coming on you; just as the debtor must meet the creditor's demand at the expiration of the month. The prediction is of the invasion of Tiglath-pileser, who carried away Reuben, Gad, Naphtali, and the half tribe of Manasseh. **portions**—i.e., possessions.

ADAM CLARKE

1. *Hear ye this, O priests.* A process is instituted against the priests, the Israelites, and the *house of the king;* and they are called on to appear and defend themselves. The accusation is that they have ensnared the people, caused them to practice idolatry, at both *Mizpah* and *Tabor*. Mizpah was situated beyond Jordan, in the mountains of Gilead; see Judg. xi. 29. And Tabor was a beautiful mountain in the tribe of Zebulum. Both these places are said to be eminent for hunting, and hence the natural occurrence of the words *snare* and *net* in speaking of them.

2. *The revolters are profound to make slaughter.* Here may be a reference to the practice of hunters making deep pits in the ground, and lightly covering them over, that the beasts, not discovering them, might fall in, and become a prey.

Though I have been a rebuker. "I will bring chastisement on them all."

6. *They shall go with their flocks.* They shall offer many sacrifices, professing to seek and be reconciled to the Lord, but they shall not find Him. As they still retain the spirit of their idolatry, He has withdrawn himself from them.

7. *Now shall a month devour them.* In a month's time the king of Assyria shall be upon them, and oblige them to purchase their lives and liberties by a grievous tax of fifty shekels per head. This Menahem, king of Israel, gave to Pul, king of Assyria, 2 Kings xv. 16-20. Instead of *month*, some translate the original "locust." "The locusts shall devour them."

MATTHEW HENRY

Verses 8–15

I. A loud alarm sounded, giving notice of judgments coming (*v.* 8): *Blow you the cornet in Gibeah* and *in Ramah*, two cities in the confines of the two kingdoms of Judah and Israel, Gibeah a frontier-town of the kingdom of Judah, Ramah of Israel; so that the warning is hereby sent into both kingdoms. "*Cry aloud at Beth-aven*, or Bethel." He had before spoken of the judgments as certain; here he speaks of them as near.

The blowing of this cornet is explained, *v.* 9. *Among the tribes of Israel have I made known that which shall surely be*, that which is *true* or *certain*, so the word is.

II. The ground of God's controversy. He has a quarrel with *the princes of Judah*, because they were daring leaders in sin, *v.* 10. They have encroached even upon God's rights, have trampled upon the distinctions between good and evil. Some have observed that the princes of Judah were more absolute, and assumed a more arbitrary power, than the princes of Israel did; now, for this, God has a controversy with them: *I will pour out my wrath upon them like water.* He has a quarrel with the *people of Ephraim*, because they were sneaking followers in sin (*v.* 11): *He willingly walked after the commandment*, that is, the commandment of Jeroboam and the succeeding kings of Israel, who obliged all their subjects by a law to worship the calves at Dan and Bethel, and never to go up to Jerusalem to worship. It is for this that *Ephraim is oppressed and broken in judgment*, has his civil rights and liberties broken. Nothing gives greater advantage to a mastiff-like tyranny, that is fierce and furious, than a spaniel-like submission, that is fawning and flattering.

III. The different methods that God would take both with Judah and Ephraim.

1. He would begin with less judgments, which should sometimes work silently and insensibly (*v.* 12): *I will be unto Ephraim as a moth;* they *are unto Ephraim as a moth*, for it is such a *sickness* as Ephraim now sees, *v.* 13. The judgments of God are sometimes to a sinful people *as a moth*, and *as rottenness*, or as *a worm.* Silently, so as they themselves shall not be sensible of it; they shall think themselves safe and thriving, but shall find themselves wasting and decaying. Slowly, and with long delays and intervals, that he may give them *space to repent.*

2. When it appeared that those had not done their work he would come upon them with greater (*v.* 14): *I will be unto Ephraim as a lion, and to the house of Judah as a young lion.* If less judgments prevail not to do their work, it may be expected that God will send greater. There is a more immediate work of God in some judgments than in others. *I will tear, and go away.*

IV. The different effects of those different methods. When God contended with them by less judgments they sought to creatures for relief, but sought in vain, *v.* 13. Then they sent *to the Assyrian*, to come to their assistance, made their court to king Jareb, which, some think, was one of the names of Tiglathpileser, king of Assyria, to whom both Israel and Judah applied for relief in their distress, hoping by an alliance to re-establish their declining interests. Carnal hearts, in time of trouble, see their sickness, but do not see the sin that is the cause of it. Instead of going the next way to the Creator, who could relieve them, they go to creatures, who can do them no service. The kings of Assyria, whom Judah and Israel sought unto, *distressed them* and *helped them not*, 2 Chron. xxviii. 16, 28. They had sent him *a present* (*ch.* x. 6), and, having so retained him, they doubted not of his fidelity to them; but he deceived them, Jer. xvii. 5, 6. When God brought greater judgments upon them, then they would at length be forced to apply to him, *v.* 15. *I will go and return to my place*, to heaven, or to the mercy-seat, the throne of grace. When God punishes sinners he *comes out of his place* (Isa. xxvi. 21); but, when he designs them favour, he *returns to his place*, where he *waits to be gracious.* He will bring them home to himself, by their afflictions, no longer withdraw from them. Two things are instances of their return: 1. Their penitent confession of sin: *Till they acknowledge their offence;* marg. *Till they be guilty*,

JAMIESON, FAUSSET, BROWN

Their resources and garrisons will not avail to save them. HENDERSON explains from Isaiah 57:6, "portions" as *their idols;* the context favors this, "the Lord" the true "*portion* of His people" (Deut. 32:9), being in antithesis to "their portions," the idols. **8.** The arrival of the enemy is announced in the form of an injunction to *blow an alarm.* **cornet . . . trumpet**—The "cornet" was made of the curved horn of animals and was used by shepherds. The "trumpet" was of brass or silver, straight, and used in wars and on solemn occasions. The *Hebrew* is *hatzotzerah,* the sound imitating the trumpet note (ch. 8:1; Num. 10:2; Jer. 4:5; Joel 2:1). **Gibeah . . . Ramah**—both in Benjamin (Isa. 10:29). **Beth-aven**—in Benjamin; not as in ch. 4:15; *Beth-el,* but a town east of it (Josh. 7:2). "Cry aloud," viz., to raise the alarm. "Benjamin" is put for the whole southern kingdom of Judah (cf. vs. 5), being the first part of it which would meet the foe advancing from the north. "After thee, O Benjamin," implies the position of Beth-aven, *behind* Benjamin, at the borders of Ephraim. When the foe is at Beth-aven, he is at Benjamin's rear, close upon thee, O Benjamin (Judg. 5:14). **9, 10.** Israel is referred to in vs. 9, Judah in vs. 10. **the day of rebuke**—the day when I shall chastise him. **among the tribes of Israel have I made known**—proving that the scene of Hosea's labor was among the ten tribes. **that which shall surely be**—viz., the coming judgment here foretold. It is no longer a conditional decree, leaving a hope of pardon on repentance; it is absolute, for Ephraim is hopelessly impenitent. **remove the bound**—(Deut. 19:14; 27:17; Job 24:2; Prov. 22:28; 23:10). Proverbial for the rash setting aside of the ancestral laws by which men are kept to their duty. Ahaz and his courtiers ("the princes of Judah"), setting aside the ancient ordinances of God, removed the borders of the bases and the laver and the sea and introduced an idolatrous altar from Damascus (II Kings 16:10-18); also he burnt his children in the valley of Hinnom, after the abominations of the heathen (II Chron. 28:3). **11. broken in judgment**—viz., the "judgment" of God on him (vs. 1). **walked after the commandment**—Jeroboam's, to worship the calves (II Kings 10:28-33). Cf. Micah 6:16, "the *statutes* of Omri," viz., idolatrous statutes. We ought to obey God rather than men (Acts 5:29). Jerome reads "filthiness." LXX gives the sense, not the literal translation: "after *vanities.*" **12. as a moth**—consuming a garment (Job 13:28; Ps. 39:11; Isa. 50:9). **Judah . . . rottenness**—Ephraim, or the ten tribes, are as a *garment* eaten by the moth; Judah as the *body* itself consumed by rottenness (Prov. 12:4). Perhaps alluding to the superiority of the latter in having the house of David, and the temple, the religious center of the nation [GROTIUS]. As in vss. 13, 14, the violence of the calamity is prefigured by the "wound" which "a lion" inflicts, so here its long protracted duration, and the certainty and completeness of the destruction from small unforeseen beginnings, by the images of a slowly but surely consuming *moth* and *rottenness.* **13. wound**—lit., "bandage"; hence a *bandaged wound* (Isa. 1:6; Jer. 30:12). "Saw," i.e., felt its weakened state politically, and the dangers that threatened it. It aggravates their perversity, that, though aware of their unsound and calamitous state, they did not inquire into the cause or seek a right remedy. **went . . . to the Assyrian**—First, Menahem (II Kings 15:19) applied to Pul; again, Hoshea to Shalmaneser (II Kings 17:3). **sent to King Jareb**—Understand *Judah* as the nominative to "sent." Thus, as "Ephraim saw his sickness" (the first clause) answers in the parallelism to "Ephraim went to the Assyrian" (the third clause), so "Judah saw his wound" (the second clause) answers to (*Judah*) "sent to King Jareb" (the fourth clause). *Jareb* ought rather to be translated, "their *defender,*" lit., "avenger" [JEROME]. The Assyrian "king," ever ready, for his own aggrandizement, to mix himself up with the affairs of neighboring states, professed to *undertake* Israel's and Judah's *cause;* in Judges 6:32, *Jerub,* in Jerub-baal is so used, viz., "*plead* one's cause." Judah, under Ahaz, applied to Tiglath-pileser for aid against Syria and Israel (II Kings 16:7, 8; II Chron. 28:16-21); the Assyrian "distressed him, but strengthened him not," fulfilling the prophecy here, "he could not heal your, nor cure you of your wound. **14. lion**—The *black lion* and the *young lion* are emblems of strength and ferocity (Ps. 91:13). **I, even I**—emphatic; when I, even I, the irresistible God, tear in pieces (Ps. 50: 22), no Assyrian power can rescue. **go away**—as a lion stalks leisurely back with his prey to his lair. **15. return to my place**—i.e., withdraw My favor. **till they acknowledge their offence**—The *Hebrew* is, "till they suffer the penalty of their guilt." Prob-

ADAM CLARKE

8. *Blow ye the cornet in Gibeah. Gibeah* and *Ramah* were cities of Judah, in the tribe of Benjamin. *After thee, O Benjamin.* An abrupt call of warning. "Benjamin, fly for your life! The enemy is just behind you!" This is a prediction of the invasion of the Assyrians and the captivity of the ten tribes.

9. *Among the tribes of Israel have I made known.* They have got sufficient warning; it is their own fault that they have not taken it.

10. *Like them that remove the bound.* As execrable as they who remove the landmark. They have leaped over law's enclosure, and scaled all the walls of right; they have despised and broken all laws, human and divine.

11. *Walked after the commandment.* Jeroboam's commandment to worship his calves at Dan and Bethel. Many of them were not forced to do this; they did it willingly.

12. *Unto Ephraim as a moth.* I will consume them by little and little, as a moth frets a garment.

13. *When Ephraim saw his sickness.* When both Israel and Judah felt their own weakness to resist their enemies, instead of calling upon and trusting in Me, they sought sinful alliances, and trusted in their idols. *King Jareb.* This name occurs nowhere in Scripture but here and in chap. x. 6. The Vulgate and Targum render *yareb*, an "avenger," a person whom they thought able to save them from their enemies. It is well-known that Menahem, king of Israel, sought alliance with Pul and Tiglath-pileser, kings of Assyria, and Ahaz, king of Judah. These were the protectors that Ephraim sought after. See 2 Kings xv and xvi. But far from healing them by making them tributary, the Assyrians made their wound more dangerous.

15. *I will go and return to my place.* I will abandon them till they acknowledge their offenses. This had the wished-for effect, as we

MATTHEW HENRY

that is, till they be sensible of their guilt, and humble themselves before God for it. When men begin to complain more of their sins than of their afflictions then there begins to be some hope of them. 2.Their humble petition for the favour of God: Till they *seek my face*. If they seek him thus, though it might be called seeking him late, yet it is not too late.

CHAPTER 6

Verses 1–3

These may be taken either as the words of the prophet to the people, calling them to repentance, or as the words of the people to one another.

I. Let us go no more to the Assyrian, nor send to king Jareb; let us *return to the Lord*, return to the worship of him, and to our hope in him.

II. "Let us return to him, for *he has torn, he has smitten. Therefore* let us return to him, because it is for our revolts from him that he has smitten us, and we cannot expect that he should be reconciled to us till we return to him. He that has torn will *heal us*, he that has smitten will *bind us up*," as the skilful surgeon with a tender hand binds up the broken bone or bleeding wound. Of his mercy he will do it; nay, *therefore* he has torn that he may heal. Some think this points particularly to the return of the Jews out of Babylon. They promise themselves that their deliverance out of their troubles shall be to them as *life from the dead* (*v.* 2): "*After two days he will revive us* (that is, in a short time, in a day or two), *and the third day*, when it is expected that the dead body should be buried *out of our sight*, then will he *raise us up*, and *we shall live in his sight*, and it shall be reviving to us. Though he *forsake* for *a small moment*, he will *gather* with *everlasting kindness*." But this seems to have a further reference to the resurrection of Jesus Christ; and the time may be a figure of Christ's rising the *third day*, for all the prophets testified of *the sufferings of Christ and the glory that should follow*. Though they might not be aware of this mystery in the words, yet now that they are fulfilled to the letter in the resurrection of Christ it is a confirmation that *this is he that should come*, and we are to *look for no other*. And it is suitable that a prophecy of Christ's rising should be thus expressed, "He will raise *us* up, and *we* shall live," for Christ rose as the first-fruits, and we revive with him, we live through him. *Then shall we know, if we follow on to know, the Lord*, *v.* 3. When God returns in mercy to his people, he will give them more knowledge of himself; the earth shall be *full of that knowledge*, Isa. xi. 9. It may be taken as the fruit of Christ's resurrection, and the life we live by him, that we shall have not only greater means of knowledge, but grace to improve in knowledge. Our knowledge shall be perfected, and yet be eternally increasing. *His going forth is prepared as the morning*, that is, the returns of his favour, which he had withdrawn from us when he *returned to his place. He shall come to us*, and be welcome to us, *as the rain, as the latter and former rain unto the earth*, which refreshes it and makes it fruitful. Now this looks further than their deliverance out of captivity, and was to have its full accomplishment in Christ, and the grace of the gospel. *His going forth was prepared as the morning*, for he came in the fulness of time; *John Baptist* was himself the *bright and morning star. He shall come down as the rain upon the mown grass*, Ps. lxxii. 6. The grace of God in Christ is both the *latter and the former rain*, for by it the good work of our fruit-bearing is both begun and carried on.

Verses 4–11

Two evil things, both Judah and Ephraim are here charged with,

I. That they were unsteady, *unstable as water*, *v.* 4, 5. *O Ephraim! what shall I do unto thee? O Judah! what shall I do unto thee?* God speaks after the manner of men, to show how absurd and unreasonable they were. God would have done them good, but they were not qualified for it: "*What shall I do unto thee?* What else can I do but cast thee off, when I cannot in honour save thee?" See here their conduct towards God: *Their goodness*, or *kindness*, was *as the morning cloud*. What good appeared in them sometimes soon vanished *as the morning cloud and the early dew*. Shall he accept their goodness? No, for it *passes away*. That goodness will never be either pleasing to God or profitable to ourselves which is as the morning cloud and the early dew. When men promise fair and do not perform, when they are unsteady, uneven, and inconstant, then is their *goodness as the morning cloud and the early dew*. "*Therefore*, because they were so, *I have hewn them by the prophets*, as timber or

JAMIESON, FAUSSET, BROWN

ably "*accepting* the punishment of their guilt" (cf. Zech. 11:5) is included in the idea, as *English Version* translates. Cf. Leviticus 26:40, 41; Jeremiah 29:12, 13; Ezekiel 6:9; 20:43; 36:31. **seek my face**—i.e., seek My favor (Prov. 29:26, *Margin*). **in . . . affliction . . . seek me early**—i.e., diligently; rising up before dawn to seek Me (Ps. 119:147; cf. Ps. 78:34).

CHAPTER 6

VSS. 1-11. THE ISRAELITES' EXHORTATION TO ONE ANOTHER TO SEEK THE LORD. At vs. 4 a new discourse, *complaining of them,* begins; for vss. 1-3 evidently belong to vs. 15, of ch. 5, and form the *happy* termination of Israel's *punishment:* primarily, the return from Babylon; ultimately, the return from their present long dispersion. The eighth verse perhaps refers to the murder of Pekahiah; the discourse cannot be later than Pekah's reign, for it was under it that *Gilead* was carried into captivity (II Kings 15:29). **1. let us return**—in order that God who has "returned to His place" may return to us (ch. 5:15). **torn, and . . . heal**—(Deut. 32:39; Jer. 30:17). They ascribe their punishment not to fortune, or man, but to God, and acknowledge that none (not the Assyrian, as they once vainly thought, ch. 5:13) but God can heal their wound. They are at the same time persuaded of the mercy of God, which persuasion is the starting-point of true repentance, and without which men would not seek, but hate and flee from God. Though our wound be severe, it is not past hope of recovery; there is room for grace, and a hope of pardon. He hath smitten us, but not so badly that He cannot heal us (Ps. 130:4). **2.** Primarily, in type, Israel's national revival, *in a short period* ("*two or three*" being used to denote a *few* days, Isa. 17:6; Luke 13:32, 33); antitypically the language is so framed as to refer in its *full accuracy* only to Messiah, the ideal Israel (Isa. 49:3; cf. Matt. 2:15, with ch. 11:1), raised on the third day (John 2:19; I Cor. 15.4; cf. Isa. 53:10). "He shall *prolong* His *days.*" Cf. the similar use of Israel's political resurrection as the type of the general resurrection of which "Christ is the first fruits" (Isa. 26:19; Ezek. 37:1-14; Dan. 12:2). **live in his sight**—enjoy His countenance shining on us, as of old; in contrast to ch. 5:6, 15, "Withdrawn Himself from them." **3. know, if we follow on to know the Lord**—The result of His recovered favor (vs. 2) will be onward growth in saving knowledge of God, as the result of perseverance in following after Him (Ps. 63:8; Isa. 54:13). "Then" implies the consequence of the revival in vs. 2. The "if" is not so much *conditional,* as expressive of the *means* which God's grace will sanctify to the full enlightenment of Israel in the knowledge of Him. As want of "knowledge of God" has been the source of all evils (ch. 4:1; 5:4), so the knowledge of Him will bring with it all blessings; yea, it is "life" (John 17:3). This knowledge is practice, not mere theory (Jer. 22:15, 16). Theology is life, not science; realities, not words. This onward progress is illustrated by the light of "morning" increasing more and more "unto the perfect day" (Prov. 4:18). **prepared**—"is sure," lit., "fixed," ordered in His everlasting purposes of love to His covenant people. Cf. "prepared of God" (*Margin,* Gen. 41:32; Rev. 12:6). Jehovah shall surely come to the relief of His people after their dark night of calamity. **as the morning**—(II Sam. 23:4). **as the rain . . . latter . . . former**—(Job 29:23; Joel 2:23). First, "the rain" generally is mentioned; then the two rains (Deut. 11:14) which caused the fertility of Palestine, and the absence of which was accounted the greatest calamity: "the latter rain" which falls in the latter half of February, and during March and April, just before the harvest whence it takes its name, from a root meaning "*to gather*"; and "the former rain," lit., "the darting rain," from the middle of October to the middle of December. As the rain fertilizes the otherwise barren land, so God's favor will restore Israel long nationally lifeless. **4. what shall I do unto thee**—to bring thee back to piety. What more could be done that I have not done, both in mercies and chastenings (Isa. 5:4)? At this verse a new discourse begins, resuming the threats (ch. 5:14). See opening remarks on this chapter. **goodness**—godliness. **morning cloud**—soon dispersed by the sun (ch. 13:3). There is a tacit contrast here to the promise of God's grace to Israel hereafter, in vs. 3. *His* going forth is "as the morning," shining more and more unto the perfect day; *your* goodness is "as a morning cloud," soon vanishing. His coming to His people is "as the [fertilizing] latter and former rains"; your coming to Him "as the early dew goeth away." **5. I hewed them by the prophets**

ADAM CLARKE

shall see in the following chapter; for they repented and turned to God, and He had mercy upon them.

CHAPTER 6

1. *Come, and let us return unto the Lord.* When God had purposed to abandon them, and they found that He had returned to His place—to His temple, where alone He could be successfully sought—they, feeling their weakness, and the fickleness, weakness, and unfaithfulness of their idols and allies, now resolve to *return unto the Lord;* and referring to what He said, chap. v. 14: "I will tear and go away," they say, He "hath torn," but "he will heal us." Their allies had torn, but they gave them no healing.

2. *After two days will he revive.* Such is His power that in two or three days He can restore us. He can realize all our hopes, and give us the strongest token for good. *In the third day he will raise us up.* In so short a time can He give us complete deliverance. These words are supposed to refer to the death and resurrection of our Lord; and it is thought that the apostle refers to them, 1 Cor. xv. 4: Christ "rose again the third day according to the scriptures"; and this is the only place in the Scriptures, i.e., of the Old Testament, where His resurrection on the third day seems to be hinted at. The original, *yekimenu*, has been translated, "He will raise him up."

3. *Then shall we know.* We shall have the fullest evidence that we have not believed in vain. *If we follow on to know the Lord.* If we continue to be as much in earnest as we now are.

His going forth. The manifestation of His mercy to our souls is as certain as the rising of the sun at the appointed time.

And he shall come unto us as the rain. As surely as the early and the latter rain come. The first, to prepare the earth for the seed—this fell in autumn; the second, to prepare the full ear for the harvest—this fell in spring.

4. *O Ephraim, what shall I do unto thee?* This is the answer of the Lord to the above pious resolutions; sincere while they lasted, but frequently forgotten, because the people were fickle. Their *goodness* was like the *morning cloud* that fadeth away before the rising sun, or like *the early dew* which is speedily evaporated by heat.

MATTHEW HENRY

stone is hewn for use; *I have slain them by the words of my mouth.*" They were ready to say that the prophets killed them, when they dealt faithfully with them. They were uneven in religion (*v.* 4), therefore God hewed them. The hearts of sinners are as rough stone, which requires a great deal of pains to bring it into shape, or as knotty timber, that is not squared without a great deal of difficulty. And there are those whom ministers must rebuke sharply; every word should cut, though the reproved fly in the face of the reprover and reckon him an enemy because he tells the truth.

God accomplished that which was foretold: "*I have slain them* by my judgments, according to the words of my mouth." The word of God will be the death either of the sin or of the sinner. His prophets had taken great pains with them, but the means used had not the desired effect. Now they cannot charge God with severity if he bring upon them the miseries threatened. The prophet acknowledges, *Thy judgments are as the light that goes forth,* evidently just and righteous.

II. That they were not faithful to God's covenant with them, *v.* 6, 7.

1. The covenant that God made with them (*v.* 6): *I desired mercy and not sacrifice,* and insisted upon *the knowledge of God more than* upon *burnt-offerings. Mercy* here is the same word which in *v.* 4 is rendered *goodness—chesed—piety, sanctity;* it is put for all practical religion; it is the same with *charity* in the New Testament, the reigning love of God and our neighbour. This is fully explained, Jer. vii. 22, 23. Perhaps this is mentioned here to show a difference between the God whom they deserted and the gods to whom they went. The *power of godliness* is the main thing God looks at and requires, and without it the *form of godliness* is of no avail.

2. How little they had regarded this covenant! There were *good things committed* to them to keep, the jewels of mercy and piety, and the knowledge of God, in the cabinet of sacrifice and burnt-offering, but they betrayed their trust, kept the cabinet, but pawned the jewels for the gratification of a base lust, and this is that for which God has justly a quarrel with them (*v.* 7). *They, like Adam, have transgressed the covenant* (so it might very well be read); as he transgressed the covenant of innocency, so they transgressed the covenant of grace. Dealing treacherously with God is here called dealing treacherously against him, for it is both an affront and an opposition. Look on the other side Jordan, to the country most exposed to neighbouring nations, and where therefore the people were concerned to keep themselves under the divine protection, and there you will find the most daring provocations of the divine Majesty, *v.* 8. Gilead, which lay in the lot of Gad and the half tribe of Manasseh, was *a city of the workers of iniquity.* Ramoth Gilead is one of the three cities of refuge on the other side Jordan, and a Levites' city; the inhabitants, though of the sacred tribe, were *workers of iniquity.* They would, for a bribe, protect those that were guilty of wilful murder. Those whose business it was to minister in holy things were as bad as the worst (*v.* 9). The *companies of priests* were cruel and bloodthirsty. They were cunning. *They murder in the way to Shechem* (so the margin reads it, as a proper name) such as were going to Jerusalem (for that way Shechem lay) to worship. Or *in the way to Shechem* (some think) means in the same manner that their father Levi, with Simeon his brother, murdered the Shechemites (Gen. xxxiv), by fraud and deceit. *There is the whoredom of Ephraim,* both corporal and spiritual whoredom; too plain to be denied. Look into Judah, and you find them sharing with Israel (*v.* 11): *Also, O Judah! he has set a harvest for thee;* thou that hast *ploughed iniquity,* and *sown wickedness,* shalt *reap the same.*

JAMIESON, FAUSSET, BROWN

—i.e., I *announced* by the prophets that they should be hewn asunder, like trees of the forest. God identifies His act with that of His prophets; the word being His instrument for executing His will (Jer. 1:10; Ezek. 43:3). **by . . . words of my mouth**—(Isa. 11:4; Jer. 23:29; Heb. 4:12). **thy judgments**—the judgments which I will inflict on thee, Ephraim and Judah (vs. 4). So "*thy* judgments," i.e., those inflicted *on thee* (Zeph. 3:15). **are as the light . . .**—like the light, palpable to the eyes of all, as coming from God, the punisher of sin. HENDERSON translates, "lightning" (cf. *Margin,* Job 37:3, 15). **6. mercy**—put for *piety* in general, of which *mercy* or *charity* is a branch. **not sacrifice**—i.e., "*rather than* sacrifice." So "not" is merely comparative (Exod. 16:8; Joel 2:13; John 6:27; I Tim. 2:14). As God Himself instituted sacrifices, it cannot mean that He desired them not absolutely, but that even in the Old Testament, He valued *moral obedience* as the only end for which *positive* ordinances, such as sacrifices, were instituted—as of more importance than a mere external ritual obedience (I Sam. 15: 22; Ps. 50:8, 9; 51:16; Isa. 1:11, 12; Mic. 6:6-8; Matt. 9:13; 12:7). **knowledge of God**—experimental and practical, not merely theoretical (vs. 3; Jer. 22:16; I John 2:3, 4). "Mercy" refers to the *second* table of the law, our duty to our fellow man; "the knowledge of God" to the *first* table, our duty to God, including inward spiritual worship. The second table is put first, not as superior in dignity, for it is secondary, but in the order of our understanding. **7. like men**—the common sort of men (Ps. 82:7). Not as *Margin,* "like Adam," Job 31:33. For the *expression* "covenant" is not found elsewhere applied to Adam's relation to God; though the *thing* seems implied (Rom. 5:12-19). Israel "transgressed the covenant" of God as lightly as men break everyday compacts with their fellow men. **there**—in the northern kingdom, Israel. **8. Gilead . . . city**—probably Ramoth-gilead, metropolis of the hilly region beyond Jordan, south of the Jabbok, known as "Gilead" (I Kings 4:13; cf. Gen. 31:21-25). **work iniquity**—(ch. 12:11). **polluted with blood**—"marked with blood traces [MAURER]. Referring to Gilead's complicity in the regicidal conspiracy of Pekah against Pekahiah (II Kings 15: 25). See *Note,* on vs. 1. Many homicides were there, for there were beyond Jordan more cities of refuge, in proportion to the extent of territory, than on this side of Jordan (Num. 35:14; Deut. 4:41-43; Josh. 20:8). Ramoth-gilead was one. **9. company**—"association" or guild of priests. **murder . . . by consent**—lit., "with one shoulder" (cf. Zeph. 3:9, *Margin*). The image is from oxen putting their *shoulders together* to pull the same yoke [RIVETUS]. MAURER translates, "in the way *towards Shechem.*" It was a city of refuge between Ebal and Gerizim; on Mount Ephraim (Josh. 20:7; 21:21), long the civil capital of Ephraim, as Shiloh was the religious capital; now called Naploos; for a time the residence of Jeroboam (I Kings 12:25). The priests there became so corrupted that they waylaid and murdered persons fleeing to the asylum for refuge [HENDERSON]; the sanctity of the place enhanced the guilt of the priests who abused their priestly privileges, and the right of asylum to perpetrate murders themselves, or to screen those committed by others [MAURER]. **commit lewdness**—*deliberate* crime, presumptuous wickedness, from an *Arabic* root, "to form a deliberate purpose." **10. horrible thing**—(Jer. 5:30; 18:13; 23:14). **whoredom**—idolatry. **11. an harvest**—viz., of judgments (as in Jer. 51:33; Joel 3:13; Rev. 14:15). Called a "harvest" because it is the fruit of the seed which Judah herself had sown (ch. 8:7; 10:12; Job 4:8; Prov. 22:8). Judah, under Ahaz, lost 120,000 "slain in one day (by Israel under Pekah), because they had forsaken the Lord God of their fathers.' **when I returned the captivity of my people**—when I, by Oded My prophet, caused 200,000 women, sons, and daughters, of Judah to be restored from captivity by Israel (II Chron. 28:6-15). This prophecy was delivered under Pekah [LUDOVICUS DE DIEU]. MAURER explains, When Israel shall have been exiled for its sins, and has been subsequently restored by Me, thou, Judah, also shalt be exiled for thine. But as Judah's punishment was not at the time *when* God restored Israel, LUDOVICUS DE DIEU's explanation must be taken. GROTIUS translates, "When I *shall have returned to make captive* (i.e., when I shall have again made captive) My people." The first captivity of Israel under Tiglath-pileser was followed by a *second* under Shalmaneser. Then came the siege of Jerusalem, and the capture of the fenced cities of Judah, by Sennacherib, the forerunner of other attacks, ending in Judah's captivity.

ADAM CLARKE

5. *Therefore have I hewed them by the prophets.* I have sent My prophets to testify against their fickleness. They have smitten them with the most solemn and awful threatenings; they have, as it were, *slain them by the words of my mouth.* But to what purpose? *Thy judgments are as the light that goeth forth.* The proper reading is, most probably, "And My judgment is as the light going forth." It shall be both evident and swift.

7. *But they like men* (*keadam,* "like Adam") *have transgressed the covenant.* They have sinned against light and knowledge as he did. This is sense; the other is scarcely so. There was a striking similarity in the two cases. Adam, in paradise, transgressed the commandment, and I cast him out; Israel, in possession of the Promised Land, transgressed My covenant, and I cast them out, and sent them into captivity.

8. *Gilead is a city of them that work iniquity.* In this place Jacob and Laban made their covenant, and set up a heap of stones, which was called *Galeed,* the "heap of testimony"; and most probably idolatry was set up here. Perhaps the very heap became the object of superstitious adoration.

9. *As troops of robbers.* What a sad picture is this of the state of the priesthood! The country of Gilead was infamous for its robberies and murders. The idolatrous priests there formed themselves into companies, and kept possession of the roads and passes; and if they found any person going to Jerusalem to worship the true God, they put him to death.

10. *I have seen an horrible thing.* That is, the idolatry that prevailed in *Israel* to such a degree that the whole land was *defiled.*

11. *O Judah, he hath set an harvest for thee.* You also have transgressed; your harvest will come; you shall be reaped down and sent into captivity.

When I returned the captivity of my people. Bishop Newcome translates, "Among those who lead away the captivity of my people."

MATTHEW HENRY

CHAPTER 7

Verses 1–7

I. A general idea given of the present state of Israel, *v.* 1, 2.

1. God graciously designed to do well for them: *I would have healed Israel.* He would have reformed them, would have purged out the corruptions that were among them. He would have delivered them out of their troubles, and restored to them their peace and prosperity. Their own folly put them back again.

2. They stood in their own light and put a bar in their own door. When God *would have healed them* that wickedness which had been concealed was *found out.* When endeavours were used to reform them vice grew more outrageous. They dissemble with God in their professions of repentance.

3. A practical disbelief of God's omniscience and government was at the bottom of all their wickedness (*v.* 2): "*They consider not in their hearts,* they never say it to their own hearts, never think of this, *that I remember all their wickedness.*" This is the sinner's atheism; as good say that there is *no God* as say that he is either ignorant or forgetful. But the time will come when those who thus deceive themselves shall be undeceived: *Now their own doings have beset them about.*

4. God had begun his judgments: *The thief comes in, and the troop of robbers spoils without.* Some take this as an instance of their wickedness, that they robbed and spoiled one another. It seems rather to be a punishment of their sin; they were infested with secret thieves among themselves, and *troops of robbers,* foreign invaders, that with open violence *spoiled abroad.*

II. A particular account of the sins of the court, of the king and princes, who were pleased with the wickedness of their subjects (*v.* 3): *They make the king and princes glad with their wickedness.* Drunkenness and revelling abound much at the court, *v.* 5. The *day of our king* was a merry day with them, and they *made him sick with bottles of wine.* When he was thus intoxicated, he *stretched out his hand with scorners;* then he that was entrusted with the government of a kingdom lost the government of himself. Adultery and uncleanness prevailed much among the courtiers. This is spoken of *v.* 4, 6, 7, and the charge of drunkenness comes in in the midst of this article; for wine is oil to the fire of lust, Prov. xxiii. 33. *Adulterers* (*v.* 4) are here again and again compared to an oven heated by the baker (*v.* 4): *They have made ready their heart like an oven* (*v.* 6); *they are all hot as an oven, v.* 7. An unclean heart is like an oven heated. The baker kindled a fire in his oven and laid sufficient fuel to it. In the morning he finds his oven well heated, and ready for his purpose. So these wicked people, when they have formed a design for the gratifying of some covetous or unclean lusts, have their hearts so fully set in them to do evil that, though they may stifle them for a while, yet the fire is still glowing within, and, as soon as there is an opportunity for it, their purposes break out into overt acts, as a fire flames out when it has vent given it. *They have devoured their judges,* those few good judges that were among them, that would have put out these fires with which they were heated. *All their kings* have *fallen* one after another, and their families with them, which could not but put the kingdom into confusion. There are heart-burnings; they are *hot as an oven* with rage and malice at one another, and this occasions the *devouring of their judges,* the *falling* of their *kings.* But in the midst of all this disorder *there is none among them that calls unto God.*

Verses 8–16

The *iniquity of Ephraim is discovered,* as well as *the sin of Samaria,* of the people as well as the princes.

I. They did not distinguish themselves from the heathen, as God had distinguished them: *Ephraim, he has mingled himself among the people,* has associated with them, and conformed himself to them, and lost his character among them. They went up and down among the heathen, to beg help of one of them against another. They were not entirely devoted to God: *Ephraim is a cake not turned,* and so is burnt on one side and dough on the other side, but good for nothing on either side.

II. They were strangely insensible of the judgments of God, *v.* 9. They were slowly drawing towards the ruin of their state partly by the encroachments of foreigners: *Strangers have devoured his strength,* and eaten him up. Some devoured them by open wars (as 2 Kings xiii. 7, when the king of Syria made them *like the dust by threshing*), others by pretending treaties of peace, in which they made them pay dearly for that which did them no good, as 2 Kings xvi. 9. They were reduced partly by their own mal-

JAMIESON, FAUSSET, BROWN

CHAPTER 7

Vss. 1-16. REPROOF OF ISRAEL. Probably delivered in the interreign and civil war at Pekah's death; for vs. 7, "all their kings . . . fallen," refers to the murder of Zechariah, Shallum, Menahem, Pekahiah, and Pekah. In vs. 8 the reference seems to be to Menahem's payment of tribute to Pul, in order to secure himself in the usurped throne, also to Pekah's league with Rezin of Syria, and to Hoshea's connection with Assyria during the interregnum at Pekah's death [MAURER]. **1. I would have healed Israel**–Israel's restoration of the 200,000 Jewish captives at God's command (II Chron. 28:8-15) gave hope of Israel's reformation [HENDERSON]. Political, as well as moral, healing is meant. When I would have healed Israel in its calamitous state, then their iniquity was discovered to be so great as to preclude hope of recovery. Then he enumerates their wickedness: "The thief cometh in [indoors stealthily], and the troop of robbers spoileth without" (out-of-doors with open violence). **2. consider not in their hearts**–lit., "say not to . . ." (Ps. 14:1). **that I remember**–and will punish. **their own doings have beset them about**–as so many witnesses against them (Ps. 9:16; Prov. 5:22). **before my face**–(Ps. 90:8).

3. Their princes, instead of checking, "have pleasure in them that do" such crimes (Rom. 1:32). **4. who ceaseth from raising**–rather, "heating" it, from an *Arabic* root, "to be hot." So LXX. Their adulterous and idolatrous lust is inflamed as the oven of a baker who has it at such a heat that he ceaseth from heating it only from the time that he hath kneaded the dough, until it be leavened; he only needs to omit feeding it during the short period of the fermentation of the bread. Cf. II Peter 2:14, "that cannot cease from sin" [HENDERSON]. **5. the day of our king**–his birthday or day of inauguration. **have made *him* sick**–viz., the king. MAURER translates, "make themselves sick." **with bottles of wine**–drinking not merely glasses, but *bottles.* MAURER translates, "owing to the heat of wine." **he stretched out his hand with scorners**–the gesture of revellers in holding out the cup and in drinking to one another's health. Scoffers were the king's boon companions. **6. they have made ready**–rather, "they make their heart approach," viz., their king, in going to drink with him. **like an oven**–following out the image in vs. 4. As it conceals the lighted fire all night while the baker sleeps but in the morning burns as a flaming fire, so they brood mischief in their hearts while conscience is lulled asleep, and their wicked designs wait only for a fair occasion to break forth [HORSLEY]. Their heart is the oven, their baker the ringleader of the plot. In vs. 7 their plots appear, viz., the intestine disturbances and murders of one king after another, after Jeroboam II. **7. all hot**–All burn with eagerness to cause universal disturbance (II Kings 15). **devoured their judges**–magistrates; as the fire of the oven devours the fuel. **all their kings . . . fallen**–See *Notes* at the beginning of this chapter. **none . . . calleth unto me**–Such is their perversity that amid all these national calamities, none seeks help from Me (Isa. 9:13; 64:7).

8. mixed . . . among the people–by leagues with idolaters, and the adoption of their idolatrous practices (vss. 9, 11; Ps. 106:35).

Ephraim . . . cake not turned–a cake burnt on one side and unbaked on the other, and so uneatable; an image of the *worthlessness* of Ephraim. The Easterners bake their bread on the ground, covering it with embers (I Kings 19:6), and *turning* it every ten minutes, to bake it thoroughly without burning it. **9. Strangers**–foreigners: the Syrians and Assyrians (II Kings 13:7; 15:19, 20; 17:3-6).

ADAM CLARKE

CHAPTER 7

1. *When I would have healed Israel.* As soon as one wound was healed, another was discovered. Scarcely was one sin blotted out till another was committed. *The thief cometh in.* Their own princes spoil them. *The troop of robbers spoileth without.* The Assyrians, under different leaders, waste and plunder the country.

3. *They make the king glad.* They pleased Jeroboam by coming readily into his measures, and heartily joining with him in his idolatry.

4. *As an oven heated by the baker.* Calmet's paraphrase on this and the following verses expresses pretty nearly the sense: Hosea makes a twofold comparison of the Israelites: to an *oven,* and to *dough.* Jeroboam set fire to his own oven—his kingdom—and put the leaven in his dough; and afterwards went to rest, that the fire might have time to heat his oven, and the leaven to raise his dough, that the false principles which he introduced might infect the whole population. This fire spread very rapidly, and the dough was very soon impregnated by the leaven. All Israel was seen running to this feast, and partaking in these innovations. But what shall become of the oven—the kingdom; and the bread—the people? The *oven* shall be consumed by these flames; the king, the princes, and the people shall be enveloped in the burning, v. 7. Israel was put under the ashes, as a loaf well-kneaded and leavened; but not being carefully turned, it was burnt on one side before those who prepared it could eat of it; and enemies and strangers came and carried off the loaf. See vv. 8-9. Their lasting captivity was the consequence of their wickedness and their apostasy from the religion of their fathers.

7. *All their kings are fallen.* There was a pitiful slaughter among the idolatrous kings of Israel; four of them had fallen in the time of this prophet. Zechariah was slain by Shallum; Shallum, by Menahem; Pekahiah, by Pekah; and Pekah, by Hoshea, 2 Kings xv. All were idolaters, and all came to an untimely death.

8. *A cake not turned.* In the East, having heated the hearth, they sweep one corner, put the cake upon it, and cover it with embers; in a short time they turn it, cover it again, and continue this several times, till they find it sufficiently baked.

MATTHEW HENRY

administrations: *Yea, gray hairs are here and there upon him,* that is, the sad symptoms of a decaying declining state, which is *waxing old* and *ready to vanish away.*

III. They went on in their wicked ways (*v.* 10): *The pride of Israel* still *testifies to his face,* as it had done before (*ch.* v. 5); their hearts were still unhumbled; they *do not return to the Lord their God,* though they suffer for going astray, yet they think not of applying to God.

IV. They took wrong methods when they were in distress (*v.* 11, 12): *Ephraim is like a silly dove without heart.* To be harmless as a dove is commendable; but to be sottish as a dove is shame. This dove laments not the loss of her young that are taken from her, but will make her nest again in the same place; so they have their people carried away by the enemy, but continue their dealings with those that deal barbarously with them. She is easily enticed into the net, and has *no heart,* no understanding, to discern her danger. So they were drawn into leagues with neighbouring nations that were their ruin. When she is frightened, she has not courage to stay where she is safe, under the careful protection of her owner, but hovers, seeking shelter first in one place, then in another, and exposes herself the more. So this people in distress did not fly *like the doves to their windows,* where they might have been secured from the birds of prey, but threw themselves out of God's protection, and *called to Egypt* to help them, and went *to Assyria,* to seek that aid which they might, by repentance, and prayer, have found in their God. They are ensnared: "*I will spread my net upon them,* bring them into straits, that they may see their folly and think of returning." They soar upward, proud of their foreign alliances; but *I will bring them down. I will chastise them as their congregation has heard;* they have been many a time told that *vain is the help of man,* that *in the son of man there is no help;* they have heard both from the law and from the prophets, and *as they have heard* now *they shall see,* they shall feel.

V. They revolted from God notwithstanding the methods he took to retain them, *v.* 13–15. God, as a gracious sovereign towards a people dear unto him, had *redeemed them* (*v.* 13), and delivered them out of many a distress. He had *bound and strengthened their arms, v.* 15. When their power was weakened, like an arm broken, God set it again. He had given Israel victories over the Syrians (2 Kings xiii. 16, 17), had *restored their coast* (2 Kings xiv. 25, 26), had *girded them with strength for battle.* He had taken them into covenant but *they fled from him,* as if he had been their dangerous enemy. He had given them his laws, which were all holy, just, and good, by which he designed to keep them in the right way; but they *transgressed against him.* They rejected his messages sent them by his prophets. In their hypocritical professions of religion, and promises of amendment, they lied to the Lord. He designed well for them, but they *imagined mischief against him, v.* 15. Sin is a mischievous thing; it is mischief against God, it is treason. They shall be punished for this (*v.* 13): *Woe unto them! for they have fled from me.*

VI. Their shows of devotion were but shows, *v.* 14. When they were under personal troubles, and called upon God, they were not sincere. They used many good words, but they did not *cry with their heart,* and therefore God reckons it as no crying to him. Moses is said to *cry unto God* when he spoke not a word, only his heart prayed with faith, Exod. xiv. 15. These made a great noise, and yet did not *cry to God,* because their hearts were not *right with him.* God is so far from approving their prayer and accepting it that he calls it *howling.* Some think it intimates the *noisiness* of their prayers as they used to cry to Baal. They did not pray for the grace of God or that God would pardon their sins, but only that he would not take away from them *their corn and wine.* Carnal hearts covet temporal mercies only, and dread no other but temporal judgments. They pretended reformation, but neither was that sincere, *v.* 16. *They return,* that is, they make as if they would return; whereas God says (Jer. iv. 1), *If thou wilt return, O Israel! return to me;* do not only *turn towards me,* but *return to me.* This dissimulation of theirs makes them like a *deceitful bow,* which is bent and drawn, but when strength comes to be laid to it, either the bow or the string breaks. The sin of the princes of Israel is *the rage of their tongue,* quarrelling with God and with all about them. The princes shall *fall by the sword* either of their enemies or of their own people, and *this shall be their derision, v.* 16.

JAMIESON, FAUSSET, BROWN

gray hairs—i.e., symptoms of approaching national dissolution. **are here and there upon**—lit., "are sprinkled on" him. **yet he knoweth not**—Though old age ought to bring with it wisdom, he neither knows of his senile decay, nor has the true knowledge which leads to reformation. **10.** Repetition of ch. 5:5. **not return to . . . Lord . . . for all this**—notwithstanding all their calamities (Isa. 9:13).

11. like a silly dove—a bird proverbial for simplicity: easily deceived.

without heart—i.e., understanding. **call to Egypt**—Israel lying between the two great rival empires Egypt and Assyria, sought each by turns to help her against the other. As this prophecy was written in the reign of Hoshea, the allusion is probably to the alliance with So or Sabacho II (of which a record has been found on the clay cylindrical seals in Koyunjik), which ended in the overthrow of Hoshea and the deportation of Israel (II Kings 17:3-6). As the dove betrays its foolishness by fleeing in alarm from its nest only to fall into the net of the fowler, so Israel, though warned that foreign alliances would be their ruin, rushed into them. **12. When they shall go**—to seek aid from this or that foreign state. **spread my net upon them**—as on birds taken on the ground (Ezek. 12:13), as contrasted with "*bringing them down* as the fowls *of the heavens,* viz., by the use of missiles. **as their congregation hath heard**—viz., by My prophets through whom I threatened "chastisement" (ch. 5:9; II Kings 17:13-18).

13. fled—as birds from their nest (Prov. 27:8; Isa. 16:2). **me**—who both could and would have healed them (vs. 1), had they applied to Me. **redeemed them**—from Egypt and their other enemies (Mic. 6:4). **lies**—(Ps. 78: 36; Jer. 3:10). Pretending to be My worshippers, when they all the while worshipped idols (vs. 14; ch. 12:1); also defrauding Me of the glory of their deliverance, and ascribing it and their other blessings to idols [CALVIN]. **14. not cried unto me**—but unto other gods [MAURER], (Job 35:9, 10). Or, they did indeed cry unto Me, but not "with their heart": answering to "lies," vs. 13 (see *Note*). **when they howled upon their beds**—sleepless with anxiety; image of *deep affliction.* Their cry is termed "howling," as it is the cry of anguish, not the cry of repentance and faith. **assemble . . . for corn . . .**—viz., in the temples of their idols, to obtain from them a good harvest and vintage, instead of coming to Me, the true Giver of these (ch. 2:5, 8, 12), proving that their cry to God was "not with their heart." **rebel against me**—lit., "withdraw themselves *against* Me," i.e., not only withdraw *from* Me, but also rebel *against* Me. **15. I . . . bound**—when I saw their arms as it were relaxed with various disasters, I bound them so as to strengthen their sinews; image from surgery [CALVIN]. MAURER translates, "I *instructed* them" to war (Ps. 18:34; 144:1), viz., under Jeroboam II (II Kings 14:25). GROTIUS explains, "Whether I chastised them (*Margin*) or strengthened their arms, they imagined mischief against Me." *English Version* is best.

16. return, but not to the Most High—or, "to one who is *not the Most High,*" one very different from Him, a stock or a stone. So LXX. **deceitful bow**—(Ps. 78:57). A bow which, from its faulty construction, shoots wide of the mark. So Israel pretends to seek God, but turns aside to idols. **for the rage of their tongue**—their boast of safety from Egyptian aid, and their "lies" (vs. 13), whereby they pretended to serve God, while worshipping idols; also their perverse defense for their idolatries and blasphemies against God and His prophets (Ps. 73: 9; 120:2, 3). **their derision in . . . Egypt**—Their "fall" shall be the subject of "derision" to Egypt, to whom they had applied for help (ch. 9:3, 6; II Kings 17:4).

ADAM CLARKE

9. *Gray hairs are here and there upon him, yet he knoweth not.* The kingdom is grown old in iniquity; the time of their captivity is at hand, and they are apprehensive of no danger.

11. *Ephraim also is like a silly dove without heart.* A bird that has little understanding, that is easily snared and taken.

They call to Egypt, they go to Assyria. They strive to make these their allies and friends. But in this they showed that they were without heart, had not a sound understanding; for these were rival nations, and Israel could not attach itself to the one without incurring the jealousy and displeasure of the other. Thus, like the silly dove, they were constantly falling into snares; sometimes of the Egyptians, at others of the Assyrians. By the former they were betrayed; by the latter, ruined.

12. *When they shall go*—to those nations for help—*I will spread my net upon them.* I will cause them to be taken by those in whom they trusted.

13. *Though I have redeemed them.* Out of Egypt; and given them the fullest proof of My love and power. *Yet they have spoken lies against me.* They have represented Me as rigorous and cruel, and My service as painful and unprofitable.

16. *They return, but not to the most High.* They go to their idols. *They are like a deceitful bow.* Which, when it is reflexed, in order to be strung, suddenly springs back into its quiescent curve. This bending of the bow requires both strength and skill; and if not properly done, it will fly back, and regain its former position; and in this recoil endanger the archer—may even break an arm. I have been in this danger myself in bending the Asiatic bow. *Shall fall by the sword. Their tongue* has been enraged against Me; the *sword* shall be enraged against them. They have *mocked* Me (v. 5) and their fall is now a subject of *derision in the land of Egypt.* What they have sown, that do they now reap.

MATTHEW HENRY

CHAPTER 8

Verses 1–7

The prophet must sound an alarm. An enemy is coming to seize their land.

I. The people have *transgressed my covenant, v.* 1. They have not only done foolishly, but have dealt deceitfully. They have *trespassed against my law.* They have cast off *the thing that is good*; the service and worship of God, which is, in effect, *casting God off.*

II. *The enemy shall come as an eagle against the house of the Lord,* and (*v.* 3) *shall pursue him.* If by *the house of the Lord* we understand the temple at Jerusalem, by the eagle we must suppose to be meant either Sennacherib, or Nebuchadnezzar, who burnt the temple. But, if we make it to point at the destruction of the kingdom of the ten tribes by the king of Assyria, we must reckon it is the body of that people which, as Israelites, is here called the *house of the Lord.* Those who break their covenant of friendship with God make themselves a cheap and easy prey.

III. The people's hypocritical claim of relation to God (*v.* 2): *Israel shall cry unto me;* and in their distress will pretend to that knowledge of God's ways which in their prosperity they *desired not,* but *despised.* But what stead will it stand a man in to be able to say, *My God, I know thee,* when he cannot say, "My God, I love thee"?

IV. The prophet's expostulation (*v.* 5): *How long will it be ere they attain to innocency?* It is not meant of absolute innocency, but how long will it be ere they become innocent and free from the sin of idolatry? In trouble they cry, *How long* will it be ere God return to us in a way of mercy? but they do not hear him ask, *How long* will it be ere they return to God in a way of duty?

V. Some particular sins.

1. In their civil affairs. They *set up kings without God, v.* 4. So they did when they rejected Samuel and chose Saul. So they did when they set up Jeroboam. So they did now about the time when Hosea prophesied, when it seems to have grown fashionable to *set up kings,* and depose them again, 2 Kings xv. 8, &c.

2. In their religious matters they did much worse; for they *set up calves against God.* They called them *gods* (1 Kings xii. 28, *Behold thy gods, O Israel!*) but God calls them *idols*; the word signifies *griefs,* or *troubles,* because they are offensive to God and will be ruining to those that worship them. Trace them to their original, and they will be found the creatures of their fancies and the work of their hands, *v.* 6. The calf they worshipped is here called *the calf of Samaria,* because it is probable that when Samaria, in Ahab's time, became the metropolis of the kingdom, a calf was set up there to be near the court. It was a device of their own (some think), not borrowed from the Egyptians, for, though they worshipped Apis in a living cow, they never worshipped a *golden calf.* The gold and silver of which it was made were collected from the people of Israel: it was a poor god that was framed by contribution. *The workmen made it, therefore it is not God, v.* 6. A made god is no God. If they are not gods, they will not last. *They have* made to themselves idols, *that they may be cut off* (*v.* 4) from God, from their own land, from the land of the living. Those that suffer themselves to be deceived into any idolatries will certainly find themselves deceived in them. Their disappointment in their idols is illustrated (*v.* 7) by a similitude: *They have sown the wind.* They have put themselves to a great deal of trouble and expense to make and worship their idols, as the husbandman does by sowing his corn, in expectation of reaping advantage from it. They did it to be as prosperous as the neighbouring nations were, that worshipped idols. But it is like *sowing the wind,* which can yield no increase. They shall *reap the whirlwind,* a *great whirlwind.* They have not their false gods for them, but they set the true God against them. The service of idols is an unprofitable service, and the works of darkness are unfruitful; Rom. vi. 21, *The end of those things is death.*

Verses 8–14

I. They multiplied their alliances (*v.* 9): *They have hired lovers.* They were at great expense to purchase the friendship of the nations about them. Those surely have behaved ill among their neighbours who have no lovers, but what they hire. *Israel is swallowed up,* devoured by strangers, their land eaten up (*v.* 7), and being impoverished, they have lost their reputation, like a merchant that has become a bankrupt. Israel made court to the nations notwithstanding (*v.* 9): They have *gone to Assyria* to help them; and herein they are as a *wild ass alone by himself,* headstrong, and unruly. *Though they have hired among the nations,* what they provided for their own safety shall

JAMIESON, FAUSSET, BROWN

CHAPTER 8

Vss. 1-14. Prophecy of the Irruption of the Assyrians, in Punishment for Israel's Apostasy, Idolatry, and Setting Up of Kings without God's Sanction. In vs. 14, *Judah* is said to multiply fenced cities; and in vss. 7-9, Israel, to its great hurt, is said to have gone up to Assyria for help. This answers best to the reign of Menahem. For it was then that Uzziah of Judah, his contemporary, built fenced cities (II Chron. 26:6, 9, 10). Then also Israel turned to Assyria and had to pay for their sinful folly a thousand talents of silver (II Kings 15: 19) [Maurer]. **1. Set the trumpet . . .**—to give warning of the approach of the enemy: "To thy *palate* (i.e., "mouth," Job 31:30, *Margin*) the trumpet"; the abruptness of expression indicates the suddenness of the attack. So ch. 5:8. **as . . . eagle**—the Assyrian (Deut. 28:49; Jer. 48:40; Hab. 1:8). **against . . . house of . . . Lord**—not the temple, but Israel viewed as *the family of God* (ch. 9:15; Num. 12:7; Zech. 9:8; Heb. 3:2; I Tim. 3:15; I Pet. 4:17). **2. My God, we know thee**—the singular, "My," is used distributively, each one so addressing God. They, in their hour of need, plead their knowledge of God as the covenant people, while in their *acts* they acknowledge Him not (cf. Matt. 7:21, 22; Titus 1:16; also Isa. 29:13; Jer. 7:4). The *Hebrew* joins "Israel," not as *English Version,* with "shall cry," but "*We, Israel,* know thee"; God denies the claim thus urged on the ground of their descent from Israel. **3. Israel**—God repeats the name in opposition to *their* use of it (vs. 2). **the thing that is good**—Jerome translates, "God" who is good and doing good (Ps. 119: 68). He is the chief object rejected, but with Him also all that is good. **the enemy shall pursue him**—in just retribution from God. **4. kings . . . not by me**—not with My sanction (I Kings 11:31; 12:20). Israel set up Jeroboam and his successors, whereas God had appointed the house of David as the rightful kings of the whole nation. **I knew it not**—I *approved* it not (Ps. 1:6). **of . . . gold . . . idols**—(Ch. 2:8; 13:2). **that they may be cut off**—i.e., though warned of the consequences of idolatry, as it were with open eyes they rushed on their own destruction. So Jeremiah 27:10, 15; 44:8. **5. hath cast thee off**—As the ellipsis of *thee* is unusual, Maurer translates, "thy calf *is abominable.*" But the antithesis to vs. 3 establishes *English Version,* "Israel *hath cast off* the thing that is good"; therefore, in just retribution, "thy calf hath *cast thee off,*" i.e., is made by God the cause of thy being cast off (ch. 10:15). Jeroboam, during his sojourn in Egypt, saw Apis worshipped at Memphis, and Mnevis at Heliopolis, in the form of an ox; this, and the temple cherubim, suggested the idea of the calves set up at Dan and Beth-el. **how long . . . ere they attain to innocency?**—How long will they be incapable of bearing innocency? [Maurer]. **6. from Israel was it**—i.e., the calf originated with them, not from Me. "It also," as well as their "kings set up" by them, "but not by Me" (vs. 4).

7. sown . . . reap—(Prov. 22:8; Gal. 6:7). "Sow . . . wind," i.e., to make the vain show of worship, while faith and obedience are wanting [Calvin]. Rather, to offer senseless supplications to the calves for good harvests (cf. ch. 2: 8); the result being that God will make them "reap no stalk," i.e., "standing corn." Also, the phraseology proverbially means that all their undertakings shall be profitless (Prov. 11:29; Eccles. 5:16). **the bud**—or, "growth." **strangers**—foreigners (ch. 7: 9). **8. vessel wherein is no pleasure**—(Ps. 41:12; Jer. 22:28; 48:38). **9. gone . . . to Assyria**—referring to Menahem's application for Pul's aid in establishing him on the throne (cf. ch. 5:13; 7:11). Menahem's name is read in the inscriptions in the southwest palace of Nimrod, as a tributary to the Assyrian king in his eighth year. The dynasty of Pul, or Phalluka, was supplanted at Nineveh by that of Tiglath-pileser, about 768 (or 760) B.C. Semiramis seems to have been Pul's wife, and to have withdrawn to Babylon in 768; and her son, Nabonassar, succeeding after a period of confusion, originated "the era of Nabonassar," 747 B.C. [G. V. Smith]. Usually foreigners coming to Israel's land were said to go *up*"; here it is the reverse, to intimate Israel's *sunken* state, and Assyria's superiority. **wild ass**—a figure of Israel's headstrong perversity in following her own bent (Jer. 2:24). **alone by himself**—characteristic of Israel in all ages: "lo, the people shall dwell alone" (Num. 23:9; cf. Job 39: 5-8). **hired lovers**—reversing the ordinary way, viz., that lovers should hire her (Ezek. 16:33, 34).

ADAM CLARKE

CHAPTER 8

1. *Set the trumpet to thy mouth.* Sound another alarm. Let them know that an enemy is fast approaching. *As an eagle against the house of the Lord.* Shalmaneser, king of Assyria, who, for his rapidity, avarice, rapacity, and strength, is fitly compared to this royal bird. He is represented here as hovering over the house of God, as the eagle does over the prey which he has just espied, and on which he is immediately to pounce.

2. *Israel shall cry.* The rapidity of the eagle's flight is well imitated in the rapidity of the sentences in this place. *My God, we know thee.* The same sentiment, from the same sort of persons, under the same feelings, as that in the Gospel of St. Matthew, chap. vii. 22-23: "Lord, have we not prophesied in thy name? and in thy name have cast out devils? . . . then will I profess unto them, I never knew you."

4. *They have set up kings, but not by me.* Properly speaking, not one of the kings of Israel, from the defection of the ten tribes from the house of David, was the anointed of the Lord. *I knew it not.* It had not My approbation. In this sense the word "know" is frequently understood. *That they may be cut off.* That is, They shall be cut off in consequence of their idolatry.

5. *Thy calf, O Samaria, hath cast thee off.* Bishop Newcome translates: "Remove far from thee thy calf, O Samaria!" Abandon your idolatry; for My anger is kindled against you.

7. *They have sown the wind, and they shall reap the whirlwind.* As the husbandman reaps the same kind of grain which he has sown, but in far greater abundance, so he who sows the wind shall have a whirlwind to reap. *It hath no stalk.* Nothing that can yield a blossom. If it have a blossom, that blossom shall not yield fruit; if there be fruit, the sower shall not enjoy it, for strangers shall eat it. The meaning is, the labors of this people shall be utterly unprofitable and vain.

8. *Now shall they be among the Gentiles.* They shall be carried into captivity, and there be as a vessel wherein there is no pleasure; one soiled, unclean, infectious, to be despised, abhorred, not used. The allusion is to a rotten, corrupted skin-bottle.

9. *They are gone up to Assyria.* For succor.

A wild ass alone by himself. Like that animal, jealous of its liberty, and suffering no rival. *Ephraim hath hired lovers.* Hath subsidized the neighboring heathen states.

MATTHEW HENRY

but make them easier prey to their enemies. The king of Assyria, whose friendship they courted, laid *burdens* upon Israel, levied taxes upon them, 2 Kings xv. 19, 20. And for these *they shall sorrow a little. They have begun to be diminished* (so some read it), *by the burden of the king of princes* (see Isa. x. 8).

II. They multiplied their altars and temples. They denied *the power of godliness* (*v.* 12): *I have written to him the great things of my law.* The things of God's law are *magnalia Dei—the great things of God.* They are things that proclaim the greatness of the Law-maker, things of great importance to us; they are our life, and our eternal welfare depends upon our observance of them and obedience to them. It is a great privilege to have the things of God's law written. Moses and the prophets were his amanuenses, and holy men wrote as they were moved by the Holy Ghost. And, if those were happy who had the *great things of God's law* written to them, how much happier are we who have the much greater things of his gospel written to us! But these great things of the law were *counted as a strange thing*, as unintelligible and unreasonable. *We desire not the knowledge of thy ways.* They kept up the form of godliness notwithstanding to little purpose. They multiplied their altars (*v.* 11): *Ephraim made many altars to sin.* Their multiplying of altars dedicated to the God of Israel would introduce altars dedicated to other gods. They multiplied their sacrifices, *v.* 13. Their altars were smoking altars: They *sacrificed flesh for the sacrifices of God's offerings*, as if they hoped by their observing a ceremonial law of their own to excuse themselves from the obligation of all God's moral precepts. *The Lord accepts them not.* How should he, when they only sacrificed flesh, but not the spiritual sacrifice of a penitent believing heart? A petition for leave to sin amounts to an imprecation of the curse for sin, and so it shall be answered, *according to the multitude of the idols. Israel has forgotten his Maker, v.* 14, *and builds temples.* Some by temples here understand *palaces*, which defy God's judgments. Judah is likewise charged with *multiplying fenced cities*, and trusting in them for safety, when the judgments of God were abroad.

JAMIESON, FAUSSET, BROWN

10. will I gather them—viz., the *nations* (Assyria, etc.) against Israel, instead of their assisting her as she had wished (Ezek. 16:37). **a little**—rather, "in a little" [HENDERSON]. *English Version* gives good sense: They shall sorrow *a little* at the imposition of the tribute; God suspended yet the *great* judgment, viz., their deportation by Assyria. **the burden of the king of princes**—the tribute imposed on Israel (under Menahem) by the Assyrian king Pul, (II Kings 15:19-22), who had many "princes" under his sway (Isa. 10:8). **11.** God in righteous retribution gives them up to their own way; the sin becomes its own punishment (Prov. 1:31). **many altars**—in opposition to God's law (Deut. 12:5, 6, 13, 14). **to sin . . . to sin**—Their altars which were "sin" (whatever religious intentions they might plead) should be treated as such, and be the source of their punishment (I Kings 12:30; 13:34). **12. great things of . . . law**—(Deut. 4:6, 8; Ps. 19:8; 119:18, 72; 147:19, 20). MAURER not so well translates, "*the many* things of My law." **my law**—as opposed to their inventions. This reference of Hosea to the Pentateuch alone is against the theory that some earlier written prophecies have not come down to us. **strange thing**—as if a thing with which they had nothing to do. **13. sacrifices of mine offerings**—i.e., which they offer to Me. **eat it**—Their own carnal gratification is the object which they seek, not My honor. **now**—i.e., "speedily." **shall return to Egypt**—(ch. 9:3, 6; 11:11). The same threat as in Deuteronomy 28:68. They fled thither to escape from the Assyrians (cf. as to *Judah*, Jer. 42-44), when these latter had overthrown their nation. But see *Note*, ch. 9:3. **14. forgotten . . . Maker**—(Deut. 32:18). **temples**—to idols. **Judah . . . fenced cities**—Judah, though less idolatrous than Israel, betrayed lack of faith in Jehovah by trusting more to its fenced cities than to Him; instead of making peace with God, Judah multiplied human defenses (Isa. 22:8; Jer. 5:17; Mic. 5:10, 11). **I will send . . . fire upon . . . cities**—Sennacherib burned all Judah's fenced cities except Jerusalem (II Kings 18:13). **palaces thereof**—viz., of the land. Cf. as to Jerusalem, Jeremiah 17:27.

ADAM CLARKE

10. *For the burden of the king of princes.* The exactions of the Assyrian king, and the princes of the provinces.

11. *Many altars to sin.* Though it does not appear that the Jews in Babylon were obliged to worship the idols of the country except in the case mentioned by Daniel, yet it was far otherwise with the Israelites in Assyria, and the other countries of their dispersion. Because they had made many altars to sin while they were in their own land, they were obliged to continue in the land of their captivity a similar system of idolatry against their will. Thus they felt and saw the evil of their idolatry, without power to help themselves.

13. *They sacrifice flesh.* Bishop Newcome translates thus: "They sacrifice gifts appointed unto me, and eat flesh." They offer to their idols the things which belong to Jehovah; or, while pretending to offer unto the Lord, they eat and drink idolatrously; and therefore the Lord will not accept them. *They shall return to Egypt.* Many of them did return to Egypt after the conquest of Palestine by Shalmaneser, and many after the ruin of Jerusalem by Nebuchadnezzar; but they had in effect returned to Egypt by setting up the worship of the golden calves, which were in imitation of the Egyptian Apis.

MATTHEW HENRY — CHAPTER 9

Verses 1–6

I. The people of Israel are charged with spiritual adultery: *O Israel! thou hast gone a whoring from thy God, v.* 1. When they set up idols and worshipped them, they *went a whoring from God* as their God, and honoured the pretenders with the affection, adoration, and confidence, which were due to God only. *They loved a reward upon every corn-floor*, to give to their idols the offerings and first-fruits. Or, they loved to receive rewards from their idols; and such they reckoned the fruits of the earth to be.

II. They are forbidden to rejoice: "*Rejoice not, O Israel! for joy. What peace*, what joy, what hast thou to do with either, while thy whoredoms and witchcrafts are so many?" (2 Kings ix. 19–22). Some think that they had at this time particular occasions for joy, probably upon the account of some league made with a potent ally.

III. They are threatened with judgments for their spiritual whoredoms. Their land shall not yield its wonted increase. Canaan, that *fruitful land*, shall be *turned into barrenness for the wickedness of those that dwell therein* (*v.* 2). *The floor and the winepress shall not feed them*, much less feast them. Their land shall not only cease to feed them, but cease to be a habitation for them; it shall *spue them out*, as it had done the Canaanites before them (*v.* 3). It was a sad and sore judgment to be driven out from such a land as this; it was like driving our first parents out of the garden of Eden. Note, Those cannot expect to dwell in the Lord's land that will not be subject to the Lord's laws. They shall have no rest nor satisfaction in any other land. Some shall *return into Egypt*, the old house of bondage; thither they shall flee from the Assyrian (*ch.* viii. 13). Others shall be carried captives to Assyria and there shall be forced to *eat unclean things*—things not fit for Jews to eat, being prohibited by their law. In the land of their enemies they shall have no opportunity either of giving honour to God or obtaining favour with God, by offering any acceptable sacrifice to him. They shall have no sacrifices to offer, nor any altar. They shall not so much as *offer drink-offerings* to the Lord, much less any other sacrifices. Instead of sacrifices of joy they shall *eat the bread of mourners.* Their *bread for their soul*, the bread which they shall have for the support of their lives, *shall not come into the house of the Lord.* The return of the days of their

JAMIESON, FAUSSET, BROWN — CHAPTER 9

Vss. 1-17. WARNING AGAINST ISRAEL'S JOY AT PARTIAL RELIEF FROM THEIR TROUBLES: THEIR CROPS SHALL FAIL, AND THE PEOPLE LEAVE THE LORD'S LAND FOR EGYPT AND ASSYRIA, WHERE THEY CANNOT, IF SO INCLINED, SERVE GOD ACCORDING TO THE ANCIENT RITUAL: FOLLY OF THEIR FALSE PROPHETS. **1. Rejoice not . . . for joy**—lit., "to exultation." Thy exultation at the league with Pul, by which peace seems secured, is out of place: since thy idolatry will bring ruin on thee. **as other people**—the Assyrians for instance, who, unlike thee, are in the height of prosperity. **loved a reward upon every corn-floor**—Thou hast desired, in *reward* for thy homage to idols, abundance of corn on every threshing-floor (ch. 2:12).

2. (Ch. 2:9, 12.) **fail**—disappoint her expectation. **3. return to Egypt**—(*Note*, ch. 8:13). As in ch. 11:5 it is said, "He shall *not* return into . . . Egypt." FAIRBAIRN thinks it is not the exact country that is meant, but the *bondage state* with which, from past experience, Egypt was identified in their minds. Assyria was to be a second Egypt to them. Deuteronomy 28:68, though threatening a return to Egypt, speaks (vs. 36) of their being brought to a nation which *neither they nor their fathers had known*, showing that it is not the literal Egypt, but a second Egypt-like bondage that is threatened. **eat unclean things in Assyria**—reduced by necessity to eat meats pronounced unclean by the Mosaic law (Ezek. 4:13). See II Kings 17:6. **4. offer wine offerings**—lit., "pour as a libation (Exod. 30:9; Lev. 23:13). **neither shall they be pleasing unto him**—as being offered on a profane soil. **sacrifices . . . as the bread of mourners**—which was unclean (Deut. 26:14; Jer. 16:7; Ezek. 24:17). **their bread for their soul**—their offering for the expiation of their soul [CALVIN], (Lev. 17:11). Rather, "their bread for their sustenance ('soul' being often used for *the animal life*, Gen. 14:21, *Margin*) shall not come into the Lord's house"; it shall only subserve their own uses, not My worship. **5.** (Ch. 2:11.)

ADAM CLARKE — CHAPTER 9

1. *Rejoice not.* Do not imitate the heathen, nor serve their idols. Do not prostitute your soul and body in practicing their impurities. Hitherto you have acted as a common harlot, who goes even to the common threshing places; connects herself with the meanest, in order to get a hire even of the grain there threshed out.

4. *As the bread of mourners.* By the law, a dead body, and everything that related to it, the house where it lay, and the persons who touched it, were all polluted and unclean, and whatever they touched was considered as defiled. See Deut. xxvi. 14; Num. xix. 11, 13-14.

5. *What will ye do in the solemn day?* When ye shall be despoiled of everything by the Assyrians; for the Israelites who remained in the land after its subjection to the Assyrians did worship the true God, and offer unto Him the sacrifices appointed by the law, though in an imperfect and schismatic manner; and it was a great mortification to them to be deprived of their religious festivals in a land of strangers.

MATTHEW HENRY

sacred feasts would therefore be uncomfortable to them (*v.* 5). They should perish in the land of their dispersion (*v.* 6): *For, lo, they have gone* out of the Lord's land, *gone because of destruction,* gone to Egypt because of the destruction of their own country by the Assyrians, flattering themselves that they shall return when the storm is over; but they shall find there are *graves in Egypt,* as their murmuring ancestors said (Exod. xiv. 11). As for *their tabernacles,* where they formerly dwelt and kept their stores, *the pleasant places for their silver,* they shall be laid in ruins, be overgrown with *nettles.*

Verses 7–10

I. The destruction spoken of shall come speedily. It is at the door (*v.* 7): *The days of visitation have come, the days of recompence have come,* and the time of the divine patience has expired.

II. Hereby they shall be made ashamed of their sentiments concerning their prophets. 1. They shall know then that the pretenders to prophecy, who flattered them in their sins, and rocked them asleep in their security (as Ahab's prophets did, 1 Kings xxii. 24), were *fools* and *madmen.* 2. They shall know then the *true prophets,* God's faithful ambassadors to them. Mocking the messengers of the Lord was the sin for which they were punished.

III. The wickedness of the false prophets themselves shall be manifested to their shame (*v.* 8). "The *watchman of Ephraim* pretends to have been *with my God,* and prefaces his lies with, *Thus saith the Lord*; but he is *a snare of a fowler in all his ways. The best things, when corrupted, become the worst.*

IV. God will now reckon with them for the sins of their fathers, *v.* 9, 10. They were as bad as their fathers: *They have deeply corrupted themselves;* they are far gone in the *depths of Satan* (Isa. xxxi. 6). Lewdness and wickedness were as impudent and daring now as in the days of Gibeah; and therefore what can be expected but such a vengeance as was then taken on Gibeah? Hence God takes occasion to upbraid them with the degeneracy of their ancestors, *v.* 10. God first formed them into a people: *I found Israel like grapes in the wilderness.* He took as much delight in them as a poor traveller would if he found grapes in a wilderness. God set them apart for himself as a peculiar people, but they went to Baal-peor, joined with the Moabites in sacrificing to that dirty dunghill deity (Num. xxv. 2, 3), and they *separated themselves unto that shame,* that shameful idol. This was the way of their fathers; God had done well for them, but they had acted ungratefully towards him, and in the same manner had the present generation *deeply corrupted themselves.*

Verses 11–17

I. The sin of Ephraim. Their worship was corrupt (*v.* 15): *All their wickedness is in Gilgal,* a place infamous for idolatry, as appears, *ch.* iv. 15; xii. 11; Amos iv. 4; v. 5. That place had been famous in other ages for solemn transactions between God and Israel, as Joshua v. 2, 10; 1 Sam. x. 8; xi. 15. Grotius conjectures that there is a mystical sense here. Golgotha in Syriac is the same with Gilgal in Hebrew, and therefore he thinks this may have reference to the putting of Christ to death at Golgotha, which was the greatest sin of the Jewish nation, and of which it might truly be said, *All their wickedness* was summed up in that.

II. The displeasure of God against Ephraim. He *departs from them, v.* 12. He hates them. *In Gilgal,* where *all their wickedness is, there I hated them.* There, where the abominations of sin are committed, there God abominates the sinners. *For the wickedness of their doings, I will drive them out of my house.* They shall be *castaways.*

III. The fruits of this displeasure comes in the cutting off and abandoning of their posterity. The name *Ephraim* is derived from *fruitfulness,* Gen. xli. 52. Moses's blessing foretold the *ten thousands of Ephraim,* Deut. xxxiii. 17. This was his glory, *v.* 11. Ephraim is as strong and rich as ever Tyre was, and as proud and secure. *Their glory shall fly away like a bird* (*v.* 11); their children shall be taken away and the hopes of their families cut off. *Ephraim is smitten; their root is dried up; they shall bear no fruit, v.* 16. They shall perish of themselves (*v.* 11): They shall *fly away from the birth, and from the womb, and from the conception.* They shall perish by the hand of their enemies; they shall die violent deaths (*v.* 12). Again (*v.* 13), *Ephraim shall bring forth his children to the murderer.* The mothers shall travail with pain to bear their children, and a cruel enemy comes and puts all to the sword. The Chaldee-paraphrase, and many of the rabbin, by the *murderers* to whom the children were brought forth, understand those that sacrificed their children to Moloch. Those few that

JAMIESON, FAUSSET, BROWN

6. because of destruction—to escape from the devastation of their country. **Egypt shall gather them up**—i.e., into its sepulchres (Jer. 8:2; Ezek. 29: 5). Instead of returning to Palestine, they should die in Egypt. **Memphis**—famed as a necropolis. **the pleasant** *places* **for their silver**—i.e., their desired treasuries for their money. Or, "whatever precious thing they have of silver" [MAURER]. **nettles**—the sign of desolation (Isa. 34:13). **7. visitation**—vengeance: punishment (Isa. 10:3). **Israel shall know it**—to her cost experimentally (Isa. 9:9). **the prophet is a fool**—The false prophet who foretold prosperity to the nation shall be convicted of folly by the event. **the spiritual man**—the man pretending to inspiration (Lam. 2:14; Ezek. 13:3; Mic. 3: 11; Zeph. 3:4). **for the multitude of thine iniquity . . .**—Connect these words with, "the days of visitation . . . are come"; "the prophet . . . is mad," being parenthetical. **the great hatred**—or, "the great provocation" [HENDERSON]; or, (thy) "great apostasy" [MAURER]. *English Version* means Israel's "*hatred*" of God's prophets and the law. **8. The watchman . . . was with my God**—The spiritual watchmen, the true prophets, formerly consulted my God (Jer. 31:6; Hab. 2:1); but their so-called *prophet* is a snare, entrapping Israel into idolatry. **hatred**—rather, (a cause of) "apostasy" (see vs. 7) [MAURER]. **house of his God**—i.e., the state of Ephraim, as in ch. 8:1 [MAURER]. Or, "the house of his (false) god," the calves [CALVIN]. Jehovah, "*my* God," seems contrasted with "*his* God." CALVIN's view is therefore preferable. **9. as in the days of Gibeah**—as in the day of the perpetration of the atrocity of Gibeah, narrated in Judges 19:16-22, etc. **10.** As the traveller in a wilderness is delighted at finding grapes to quench his thirst, or the early fig (esteemed a great delicacy in the East, Isa. 28:4; Jer. 24:2; Mic. 7:1); so it was My delight to choose your fathers as My peculiar people in Egypt (ch. 2:15). **at her first time**—when the first fruits of the tree become ripe. **went to Baal-peor**—(Num. 25:3): the Moabite idol, in whose worship young women prostituted themselves; the very sin Israel latterly was guilty of. **separated themselves**—consecrated themselves. **unto that shame**—to that shameful or foul idol (Jer. 11:13). **their abominations were according as they loved**—rather, as *Vulgate,* "they became abominable like the object of their love" (Deut. 7:26; Ps. 115:8). *English Version* gives good sense, "their abominable idols they followed after, according as their lusts prompted them" (*Margin,* Amos 4:5). **11. their glory shall fly away**—fit retribution to those who "separated themselves unto that *shame*" (vs. 10). Children were accounted the *glory* of parents; sterility, a reproach. "Ephraim" means "fruitfulness" (Gen. 41:52); this its name shall cease to be its characteristic. **from the birth . . . womb . . . conception**—Ephraim's children shall perish in a threefold gradation; (1) From the time of birth. (2) From the time of pregnancy. (3) From the time of their first conception. **12.** Even though they should rear their children, yet will I bereave them (the Ephraimites) of them (Job 27:14). **woe . . . to them when I depart**—Yet the ungodly in their madness desire God to depart from them (Job 21:14; 22:17; Matt. 8:34). At last they know to their cost how awful it is when God has departed (Deut. 31:17; I Sam. 28:15, 16; cf. vs. 11, and I Sam. 4:21). **13. Ephraim, as I saw Tyrus . . . in a pleasant place**—i.e., in looking towards Tyrus (on whose borders Ephraim lay) I saw Ephraim beautiful in situation like her (Ezek. 26, 27 and 28). **is planted**—as a *fruitful* tree; image suggested by the meaning of "Ephraim" (vs. 11). **bring forth his children to the murderer**—(vs. 16; ch. 13:16). With all his fruitfulness, his children shall only be brought up to be slain. **14. what wilt thou give?**—As if overwhelmed by feeling, he deliberates with God what is most desirable. **give . . . a miscarrying womb**—Of two evils he chooses the least. So great will be the calamity, that barrenness will be a blessing, though usually counted a great misfortune (Job 3:3; Jer. 20:14; Luke 23:29). **15. All their wickedness**—i.e., their chief guilt. **Gilgal**—(see *Note,* ch. 4:15). This was the scene of their first contumacy in rejecting God and choosing a king (I Sam. 11:14, 15; cf. I Sam. 8:7), and of their subsequent idolatry. **there I hated them**—not with the human passion, but holy hatred of their sin, which required punishment to be inflicted on themselves (cf. Mal. 1:3). **out of mine house**—as in ch. 8:1: out of the land holy unto ME. Or, as "love" is mentioned immediately after, the reference may be to the Hebrew mode of divorce, the husband (God) putting the wife (Israel) out of the house. **princes . . . revolters**—"*Sarim . . . Sorerim*" (*Hebrew*), a play on similar sounds. **16.** The figures "root," "fruit," are suggested by the

ADAM CLARKE

6. *For, lo, they are gone.* Many of them fled to Egypt to avoid the destruction, but they went there only to die. *The pleasant places for their silver.* The fine estates or villas which they had purchased by their money, being now neglected and uninhabited, are covered with *nettles*; and even *in their tabernacles,* thorns and brambles of different kinds grow.

7. *The days of visitation.* Of punishment. *The prophet is a fool.* Who has pretended to foretell, on divine authority, peace and plenty; for, behold, all is desolation. *The spiritual man. Ish haruach,* "the man of spirit," who was ever pretending to be under a divine afflatus. *Is mad.* He is now enraged to see everything falling out contrary to his prediction.

8. *The watchman of Ephraim.* The true prophet, *was with,* faithful to, *God. The prophet.* The false prophet is the *snare of a fowler;* is continually deceiving the people, and leading them into snares.

9. *They have deeply corrupted themselves, as in the days of Gibeah.* This relates to that shocking rape and murder of the Levite's wife mentioned in Judg. xix. 16, etc.

10. *I found Israel like grapes in the wilderness.* While they were faithful, they were as acceptable to Me as ripe grapes would be to a thirsty traveller in the desert.

And their abominations were according as they loved. Or, "They became as abominable as the object of their love."

11. *Their glory shall fly away.* It shall suddenly spring away from them, and return no more. *From the birth.* "So that there shall be no birth, no carrying in the womb, no conception."—Newcome.

13. *Ephraim, as I saw Tyrus.* Tyre was strongly situated on a rock in the sea; Samaria was on a mountain, both strong and pleasant. But the strength and beauty of those cities shall not save them from destruction. *Ephraim shall bring forth his children to the murderer.* The people shall be destroyed, or led into captivity by the Assyrians.

14. *Give them, O Lord: what wilt thou give?* There is an uncommon beauty in these words. The prophet, seeing the evils that were likely to fall upon his countrymen, begins to make intercession for them; but when he had formed the first part of his petition, "Give them, O Lord," the prophetic light discovered to him that the petition would not be answered, and that God was about to give them something widely different. Then changing his petition, which the Divine Spirit had interrupted, by signifying that he must not proceed in his request, he asks the question, then, "What wilt Thou give them?" and the answer is, "Give them a miscarrying womb and dry breasts." And this he is commanded to announce. It is probable that the Israelites had prided themselves in the fruitfulness of their families and the numerous population of their country. God now tells them that this shall be no more; their wives shall be barren, and their land cursed.

15. *All their wickedness is in Gilgal.* Though we are not directly informed of the fact, yet we have reason to believe they had been guilty of some scandalous practices of idolatry in *Gilgal.* See chap. iv. 15.

16. *Ephraim is smitten.* The thing being determined, it is considered as already done. *Their root is dried up.* They shall nevermore be a kingdom. And they never had any political form from their captivity by the Assyrians to the present day. *Yea, though they bring forth.* See the note on vv. 11-12.

MATTHEW HENRY

escape shall be dispersed (*v.* 17): They shall be *wanderers among the nations*. The prophet's prayer relating to it (*v.* 14): *Give them, O Lord! what wilt thou give?* Rather let them have no children than have them to be made miserable. Christ said, *Blessed is the womb that never bore and the paps that never gave suck*, Luke xxiii. 29. "Give therefore *a miscarrying womb and dry breasts*; for it is better to fall into the hands of the Lord, whose mercies are great, than into the hands of man."

CHAPTER 10

Verses 1–8

I. National sins bring down national judgment.

1. They were not fruitful in the fruits of righteousness. Here all their wickedness began (*v.* 1): *Israel is an empty vine*. A vine is of all trees least serviceable if it do not bear fruit. It is thenceforth good for nothing, Ezek. xv. 3, 5.

2. They multiplied their altars and images, and the more bountiful God's providence was to them the more prodigal they were in serving their idols.

3. Their hearts were divided, *v.* 2. They were at variance about their idols, at variance about their kings, and alienated one from another, and there was no such thing as friendship among them. They *halted between God and Baal*, that was the dividing of their heart.

4. They made no conscience of what they said and what they did in the most solemn manner, *v.* 4. They *swore falsely in making a covenant*; subjects violated their oaths of allegiance and kings their coronation-oaths; they broke their leagues with the nations. God is greatly offended with corruptions, not only in his own worship, but in the administration of justice between man and man.

II. They shall have no joy of their kings and of their government. *Now they shall say*, "*We have no king*, that is, we are as if we had none, none to preserve the public peace nor to fight our battles; and justly has this come to us." Those that keep themselves in the fear and favour of God may say, "What can the greatest of men do against us?" But those that throw themselves out of his protection must say, with despair, "What can the greatest of men do for us?" Their civil government shall not only be weakened, but quite destroyed (*v.* 7): *As for Samaria*, the royal city, *her king is cut off as the foam from the water*. The foam makes a great show upon the face of the water, yet it is but a heap of bubbles. Such were the kings of Israel, after their revolt from the house of David, a mere scum; their government had no foundation. He *shall break down their altars*. God shall do it by the hand of the Assyrians: the Assyrians shall do it by order from God. *He shall spoil their images*, *v.* 2. If the grace of God prevail not to destroy the love of sin in us, it is just that the providence of God should destroy the food and fuel of sin about us. *The thorn and the thistle* shall *come up on their altars*, that is, they shall lie in ruins. Thus idolaters are brought in trembling when God arises to *shake terribly the earth*, Isa. ii. 21.

And here (*v.* 8), *They shall say to the mountains, Cover us; and to the hills, Fall on us*.

Verses 9–15

I. They are put in mind of the sins of their fathers. It was told them (*ch.* ix. 9) that they had *corrupted themselves, as in the days of Gibeah*, and here (*v.* 9), *O Israel! thou hast sinned from the days of Gibeah*. The wickedness that was committed in that age is revived in this, and reacted. It has been continued in a constant series and succession through all the intervening ages. The case was bad then, for *there they stood*; and *the battle in Gibeah against the*

JAMIESON, FAUSSET, BROWN

word "Ephraim," i.e., *fruitful*" (*Notes*, vss. 11, 12). "Smitten," viz., with a blight (Ps. 102:4). **17. My God**—"My," in contrast to "them," i.e., the people, whose God Jehovah no longer is. Also Hosea appeals to God as supporting his authority against the whole people. **wanderers among . . . nations**—(II Kings 15:29; I Chron. 5:26).

CHAPTER 10

Vss. 1-15. ISRAEL'S IDOLATRY, THE SOURCE OF PERJURIES AND UNLAWFUL LEAGUES, SOON DESTINED TO BE THE RUIN OF THE STATE, THEIR KING AND THEIR IMAGES BEING ABOUT TO BE CARRIED OFF; A JUST CHASTISEMENT, THE REAPING CORRESPONDING TO THE SOWING. The prophecy was uttered between Shalmaneser's first and second invasions of Israel. Cf. vs. 14; also vs. 6, referring to Hoshea's calling So of Egypt to his aid; also vss. 4, 13. **1. empty**—stripped of its fruits [CALVIN], (Nah. 2:2); compelled to pay tribute to Pul (II Kings 15:20). MAURER translates, "A *widespreading* vine"; so LXX. Cf. Genesis 49:22; Psalm 80:9-11; Ezekiel 17:6. **bringeth forth fruit unto himself**—not unto ME. **according to . . . multitude of . . . fruit . . . increased . . . altars**—In proportion to the abundance of their prosperity, which called for fruit unto God (cf. Rom. 6:22), was the abundance of their idolatry ch. 8:4, 11). **2. heart . . . divided**—(I Kings 18:21; Matt. 6:24; Jas. 4:8). **now**—i.e., soon. **he**—Jehovah. **break down**—"cut off," viz., the heads of the victims. Those altars, which were the scene of *cutting off* the victims' heads, shall be themselves cut off. **3. now . . .**—Soon they, deprived of their king, shall be reduced to say, We have no king (vss. 7, 15), for Jehovah deprived us of him, because of our not fearing God. What then (seeing God is against us) should a king be able to do for us, if we had one? As they rejected the heavenly King, they were deprived of their earthly king. **4. words**—mere empty words. **swearing falsely in making a covenant**—breaking their engagement to Shalmaneser (II Kings 17:4), and making a covenant with So, though covenants with foreigners were forbidden. **judgment . . . as hemlock**—i.e., divine judgment shall spring up as rank, and as deadly, as hemlock in the furrows (Deut. 29:18; Amos 5:7; 6:12). GESENIUS translates, "poppy." GROTIUS, "darnel." **5. fear because of the calves**—i.e., shall fear *for* them. **Beth-aven**—substituted for Beth-el in contempt (ch. 4:15). **it**—*singular*, the *one* in Beth-el; after the pattern of which the other "calves" (*plural*) were made. "Calves" in the *Hebrew* is *feminine*, to express contempt. **priests**—The *Hebrew* is only used of *idolatrous priests* (II Kings 23:5; Zeph. 1:4), from a root meaning either "the black garment" in which they were attired; or, "to resound," referring to their howling cries in their sacred rites [CALVIN]. *that* **rejoiced on it**—because it was a source of gain to them. MAURER translates, "Shall leap in trepidation on account of it"; as Baal's priests did (I Kings 18:26). **the glory thereof**—the magnificence of its ornaments and its worship. **6. It . . . also**—The calf, so far from saving its worshippers from deportation, itself shall be carried off; hence "Israel shall be ashamed" of it. **Jareb**—(*Note*, ch. 5:13). "A present to the king (whom they looked to as) their *defender*," or else *avenger*, whose wrath they wished to appease, viz., Shalmaneser. The minor states applied this title to the Great King, as the avenging Protector. **his own counsel**—the calves, which Jeroboam set up as a stroke of policy to detach Israel from Judah. Their severance from Judah and Jehovah proved now to be not politic, but fatal to them. **7.** (Vss. 3, 15.) **foam**—denoting short-lived existence and speedy dissolution. As the foam, though seeming to be eminent raised on the top of the water, yet has no solidity, such is the throne of Samaria. MAURER translates, "a chip" *or broken branch* that cannot resist the current. **8. Aven**—i.e., Beth-aven. **the sin**—i.e., the occasion of sin (Deut. 9:21; I Kings 12:30). **they shall say to . . . mountains, Cover us**—So terrible shall be the calamity, that men shall prefer death to life (Luke 23:30; Rev. 6:16; 9:6). Those very hills on which were their idolatrous altars (one source of their confidence, as their "king," vs. 7, was the other), so far from helping them, shall be called on by them to overwhelm them. **9. Gibeah**—(ch. 9:9; Judg. 19 and 20). They are singled out as a specimen of the whole nation. **there they stood**—The Israelites have, as there and then, so ever since, *persisted* in their sin [CALVIN]. Or, better, "they stood their

ADAM CLARKE

17. *My God will cast them away*. Here the prophet seems to apologize for the severity of these denunciations; and to vindicate the divine justice, from which they proceeded. It is *because they did not hearken unto him* that *my God*, the Fountain of mercy and kindness, *will cast them away*. *And they shall be wanderers among the nations*. And where they have wandered to, who can tell? and in what nations to be found, no man knows.

CHAPTER 10

1. *Israel is an empty vine*. Or, "a vine that casteth its grapes." *He bringeth forth fruit*. Or, "He laid up fruit for himself." He abused the blessings of God to the purposes of idolatry. He was prosperous, but his prosperity corrupted his heart. *According to the multitude of his fruit*. He became idolatrous in proportion to his prosperity; and in proportion to their wealth was the costliness of their images, and the expensiveness of their idol worship.

2. *Their heart is divided*. They wish to serve God and mammon, Jehovah and Baal; but this is impossible.

4. *They have spoken words*. Vain, empty, deceitful words. *Swearing falsely*. This refers to the alliances made with strange powers, to whom they promised fidelity without intending to be faithful.

5. *The inhabitants of Samaria shall fear*. According to Calmet, shall worship the calves of Beth-aven; those set up by Jeroboam at Bethel. *Fear* is often taken for religious reverence. *The people thereof shall mourn*. On seeing the object of their worship carried into captivity, as well as themselves. *And the priests thereof*. *Kemarim*. The priests of Samaria, says Calmet, are here called *kemarim*, that is, "black coats" or "shouters," because they made loud cries in their sacrifices.

6. *A present to king Jareb*. See on chap. v. 13. If this be a proper name, the person intended is not known in history: but it is most likely that Pul, king of Assyria, is intended, to whom Menahem, king of Israel, appears to have given one of the golden calves, to insure his assistance.

7. *Her king is cut off as the foam*. As lightly as a puff of wind blows off the foam that is formed below by a fall of water, so shall the kings of Israel be cut off. We have already seen that not less than four of them died by assassination in a very short time. See on chap. vii. 7.

8. *The high places*. Idol temples. *Of Aven*. Beth-aven. *The thorn and the thistle shall come up on their altars*. Owing to the uncultivated and unfrequented state of the land, and of their places of idol worship, the people being all carried away into captivity. *And they shall say to the mountains, Cover us; and to the hills, Fall on us*. "This sublime description of fear and distress our Lord had in view, Luke xxiii. 30, which may be a reference, and not a quotation. However, the Septuagint, in the Codex Alexandrinus, has the same order of words as occurs in the evangelist" (Newcome).

9. *Thou hast sinned from the days of Gibeah*. This is another reference to the horrible rape and murder of the Levite's wife, Judg. xix. 13-14. *There they stood*. Only one tribe was nearly destroyed, viz., that of Benjamin.

MATTHEW HENRY

children of iniquity did not overtake them till the third engagement, and then did not overtake them all, for 600 made their escape. But thy sin is worse than theirs.

II. They have warning given them of the judgments of God that were coming upon them, *v.* 10. God had hitherto pitied and spared them. Because God does not desire the death and ruin of sinners, therefore he does desire their chastisement. "Because they receive not chastisement from me by my prophets, who in my name rebuke them, I will chastise them by the hands of the people who shall be *gathered against them, when they shall bind themselves in their two furrows,*" that is, within a double entrenchment. Or, *When I shall bind them for their two transgressions* (so the margin reads it), meaning their corporal and spiritual whoredom. Or, *When I shall bind them to their two furrows*, that is, bring them into servitude to the Assyrians, as oxen in the plough, who are bound to the two furrows up the field and down it. Thus those that would not be God's freemen shall be their enemies' slaves.

III. Ephraim is *as a heifer that is taught to tread out the corn, and loves* that work, because, not muzzled, she has liberty to eat at pleasure, *v.* 11. "But," says God, "I have a yoke to put upon *her fair neck. I will make Ephraim to ride*, I will cause them to be ridden by the Assyrians and other conquerors that shall rule them with rigour, as men do the beasts they ride upon (Ps. lxvi. 12); and *Judah* shall be made to *plough*, and *Jacob to break the clods*," that is, they shall be used hardly, but not so hardly as Ephraim. Dr. Pocock inclines to another sense of these words, as intimating the gentle methods God took with this people, to bring them into obedience to his law; he had managed them as the husbandman does his cattle that he trains up for service. Ephraim a docile heifer, fit to be employed, God took hold of *her fair neck*, to accustom her to the hand, *harnessed her*, or put the yoke of his commandment upon her, gave his people Israel a law, that they might not be tempted by the usages of the heathen. He had used all fair and likely means with them to keep them in their obedience, had set *Judah to plough* and *Jacob to break the clods*, and yet they would not be retained in their obedience, but started aside.

IV. They are invited and encouraged to return to God by prayer, repentance, and reformation, *v.* 12, 13. They are *God's husbandry* (1 Cor. iii. 9), and the duties are expressed in language borrowed from the husbandman's calling. Let them *break up the fallow ground*; let them cleanse their hearts from all corrupt affections and lusts, which are as weeds and thorns, and let them be of a broken and contrite spirit; let them prepare to receive the divine precepts, as the ground that is ploughed is to receive the seed, that it may take root. See Jer. iv. 3. Let them *sow to themselves in righteousness*; let them return to the practice of good works, and let them *sow to the Spirit*, as the apostle speaks, Gal. vi. 7, 8. Let them *seek the Lord*; let them look up to him for his grace, and beg of him to bless the *seed sown.* It is time to do it; it is *high time.* If we *sow to ourselves in righteousness* —if we be careful and diligent to do our duty, in a dependence upon his grace—he will shower down his grace upon us, will *rain righteousness*, the very thing that those need most who are to sow *in righteousness.* We have *ploughed wickedness and reaped iniquity*; and the time *past of our life may suffice* that we have done so, *v.* 13. "You have taken a great deal of pains in the service of sin, and will you grudge to bear the burden and heat of the day in God's service? You have done much to damn your souls; will you not undo it again, and do something to save them?" "*Thou didst trust in thy ways, in the multitude of thy mighty men;* thou hast stayed thyself upon creatures, thy own power and policy, and thy hopes have deceived thee; come therefore, and seek the Lord, and thy hope in him shall not deceive thee."

V. They are threatened with utter destruction, both for their carnal practices and for their carnal confidences, *v.* 14, 15. *Therefore, a tumult shall arise among thy people*, either by insurrections at home or invasions from abroad. The *fortresses* which they confided in, shall be seized and rifled, as *Shalman spoiled Beth-arbel in the day of battle.* This refers to some event that had lately happened, and probably Shalman is the same with Shalmaneser king of Assyria, who had lately sacked some town, or castle (*Beth-arbel is the house of Arbel*), to terrify other garrisons into a speedy surrender. God tells them that thus Samaria should be *spoiled.* The inhabitants shall be put to the *sword*, as it was at *Beth-arbel. In a morning shall the king of Israel utterly be cut off*, *v.* 15. Hoshea was the last king of Israel; in him the whole kingdom was *cut off*; it may refer to him or to some of his predecessors that were cut off by treach-

JAMIESON, FAUSSET, BROWN

ground," i.e., did not perish then [MAURER]. **the battle . . . did not overtake them**—Though God spared you then, He will not do so now; nay, the battle whereby God punished the Gibeonite "children of iniquity," shall the more heavily visit you for your continued impenitence. Though "they stood" then, it shall not be so now. The change from "thou" to "they" marks God's alienation from them; they are, by the use of the third person, put to a greater distance from God. **10. my desire . . . chastise**—expressing God's *strong inclination* to vindicate His justice against sin, as being the infinitely holy God (Deut. 28:63). **the people**—*Foreign invaders* "shall be gathered against them." **when they shall bind themselves in their two furrows**—image from two oxen ploughing together side by side, in two contiguous furrows: so the Israelites shall join themselves, to unite their powers against all dangers, but it will not save them from My destroying them [CALVIN]. Their "two furrows" may refer to their *two places of setting up the calves,* their ground of confidence, Dan and Beth-el; or, the two divisions of the nation, *Israel and Judah,* "in their two furrows," i.e., in their respective two places of habitation; vs. 11, which specifies the two, favors this view. HENDERSON prefers the *Keri* (*Hebrew Margin*) reading, "for their two *iniquities*"; and translates, "when they are bound" in captivity. *English Version* is best, as the image is carried out in vs. 11; only it is perhaps better to translate, "the people (the invaders) *binding them,*" i.e., making them captives; and so vs. 11 alludes to the yoke being put on the neck of Ephraim and Judah. **11. taught**—i.e., accustomed. **loveth to tread out . . . corn**—a far easier and more self-indulgent work than ploughing. In treading corn, cattle were not bound together under a yoke, but either trod it singly with their feet, or drew a threshing sledge over it (Isa. 28:27, 28): they were free to eat some of the corn from time to time, as the law required they should be unmuzzled (Deut. 25: 4), so that they grew fat in this work. An image of Israel's freedom, prosperity, and self-indulgence heretofore. But now God will put the Assyrian yoke upon her, instead of freedom, putting her to servile work. **I passed over upon**—I put the yoke upon. **make . . . to ride**—as in Job 30:22; i.e., *hurry* Ephraim *away* to a distant region [CALVIN]. LYRA translates, "I will make (the Assyrian) to ride upon Ephraim." MAURER, "I will make Ephraim to carry," viz., a charioteer. **his clods**—"the clods before him." **12.** Continuation of the image in vs. 11 (Prov. 11:18). Act righteously and ye shall reap the reward; a reward not of debt, but of grace. **in mercy**—according to the measure of the divine "mercy," which over and above repays the *goodness* or "mercy" which we show to our fellow man (Luke 6:38). **break . . . fallow ground**—Remove your superstitions and vices, and be renewed. **seek . . . Lord, till he come**—Though not answered immediately, persevere unceasingly "*till* He come." **rain**—send down as a copious shower. **righteousness**—the reward of righteousness, i.e., *salvation,* temporal and spiritual (I Sam. 26:23; cf. Joel 2:23).

13. reaped iniquity—i.e., the *fruit* of iniquity; as "righteousness" (vs. 12) is "the *fruit* of righteousness" (Job 4:8; Prov. 22:8; Gal. 6:7, 8). **lies**—false and spurious worship.

trust in thy way—thy perverse way (Isa. 57:10; Jer. 2:23), thy worship of false gods. This was their internal safeguard, as their external was "the multitude of their mighty men."

14. tumult—a tumultuous war. **among thy people**—lit., "peoples": the war shall extend to the whole people of Israel, through all the tribes, and the peoples allied to her. **Shalman spoiled Beth-arbel**—i.e., Shalmaneser, a compound name, in which the part common to it and the names of three other Assyrian kings, is omitted; Tiglath-pileser, Esar-haddon, Shar-ezer. So Jeconiah is abbreviated to Coniah. Arbel was situated in Naphtali in Galilee, on the border nearest Assyria. Against it Shalmaneser, at his first invasion of Israel (II Kings 17:3), vented his chief rage. God threatens Israel's fortresses with the same fate as Arbel suffered "in the day [on the occasion] of the battle" then well known, though not mentioned elsewhere (cf. II Kings 18:34). This event, close on the reign of Hezekiah, shows the inscription of Hosea (ch. 1:1) to be correct.

ADAM CLARKE

They were the criminals, *the children of iniquity;* the others were faultless, and stood only for the rights of justice and mercy.

10. *When they shall bind themselves in their two furrows.* "When they are chastised for their two iniquities," i.e., the calves in Dan and Bethel (Newcome). But this double iniquity may refer to what Jeremiah says, chap. ii. 13: "My people have committed two evils"—(1) "They have forsaken me"; (2) They have joined themselves to idols.

11. *Ephraim is as an heifer that is taught.* One thoroughly broken in to the yoke. *Loveth to tread out.* Goes peacably in the yoke; and is pleased because, not being muzzled, she eats of the corn.

I passed over upon her fair neck. I brought the yoke upon it, that she should not tread out the corn merely, but draw the plough and drag the harrow. *Jacob shall break his clods.* Harrow.

12. *Break up your fallow ground.* Do not be satisfied with a slight furrow; let the land that was fallowed (slightly ploughed) be broken up again with a deep furrow.

13. *Ye have ploughed wickedness.* You have labored sinfully. *Ye have reaped iniquity.* The punishment due to your iniquity. *Ye have eaten the fruit of lies.* Your false worship and your false gods have brought you into captivity and misery.

Because thou didst trust in thy way. Didst confide in your own counsels, and in *thy mighty men*, and not in the God who made you.

14. *Shall a tumult arise.* The enemy shall soon fall upon your people, and take all your fortified places. *As Shalman spoiled Beth-arbel.* Some think that an allusion is made here to the destruction of Arbela, a city of Armenia, by Shalmaneser, here called *Shalman;* and this while he was only general of the Assyrian forces, and not yet king. I think the history to which this refers is unknown.

MATTHEW HENRY

ery. It shall be done *in a morning*, as suddenly as the dawning of the morning. What is the spring of this bloodshed? He tells us (*v.* 15): *So shall Bethel do unto you.* Bethel was the place where one of the calves was; Gilgal, where *all their wickedness* is said to have been, was hard by; there was their *great wickedness*, the *evil of their evil* (so the word is), the sum and quintessence of their sin. He does not say, "So shall the *king of Assyria* do to you"; but, "So shall *Bethel* do to you." Whatever mischief is done to us it is sin that does it.

CHAPTER 11

Verses 1–7

I. God very gracious to Israel. 1. He had a kindness for them when they were young (*v.* 1): *When Israel was a child then I loved him;* when they first began to multiply into a nation in Egypt God then *set his love upon them*, and *chose them because he loved them*, Deut. vii. 7, 8. When they were helpless as children, foolish as children, when they were outcasts, and children exposed, then God *loved them.* Those that have grown up, nay, those that have grown old, ought often to reflect upon the goodness of God to them in their childhood. 2. He delivered them out of the house of bondage: *I called my son out of Egypt*, because a beloved son. These words are said to have been fulfilled in Christ, when, upon the death of Herod, he and his parents were *called out of Egypt* (Matt. ii. 15). The calling of Christ out of Egypt was a figure of the calling of all that are his, through him, out of spiritual slavery.

I taught Ephraim also to go, as a child in leading-strings is taught. *He taught them to go* in the way of his commandments, by the institutions of the ceremonial law, which were as tutors. When anything was amiss with them he was their physician: *I healed them.* He brought them into his service by mild and gentle methods (*v.* 4): *I drew them with cords of a man, with bands of love.* He draws, (1) *With the cords of a man*, with such cords as men draw with that have a principle of humanity. (2) *With bands of love*, or *cart-ropes* of love. This word signifies stronger cords than the former. He eased them of burdens: *I was to them as those that take off the yoke on their jaws*, alluding to the care of the good husbandman, who is merciful to his beast, and will not tire him with hard and constant labour. In Egypt they fared hard, but, when God brought them out, he *laid meat unto them*, as the husbandman, when he has unyoked his cattle, fodders them. God rained manna about their camp, bread from heaven, angels' food.

II. Israel ungrateful to God. They were deaf and disobedient to his voice. They were fond of idols, and worshipped them. Idolatry was the sin which from the beginning, and all along, had most easily beset them. They were regardless of God, and of his favours to them: *They knew not that I healed them.* Ignorance is at the bottom of ingratitude, *ch.* ii. 8. They were strongly inclined to apostasy. This is the blackest article in the charge (*v.* 7): *My people are bent to backsliding from me.* They are *bent to backslide*; they are ready to sin. It also intimates that they are resolute in sin; their hearts are *fully set in them to do evil.* They were strangely averse to repentance and reformation. *They refused to return, v.* 5. God's prophets and ministers called them to return to the God from whom they had revolted, to the most high God, from whom they had sunk into this wretched degeneracy; but they called in vain.

III. God had brought them out of Egypt to take them for a people to himself but they would not be faithful to him (*v.* 5): "*Therefore Israel shall not return into the land of Egypt*, though that was a house of bondage grievous enough; but he shall go into a harder service, for *the Assyrian shall be his king*, who will use him worse than ever Pharaoh did." God, who gave them Canaan, shall bring his judgments upon them there (*v.* 6): *The sword* shall come upon them, the sword of a foreign enemy, triumphing over them. They continued their rebellions against God, and therefore God continued his judgments on them.

JAMIESON, FAUSSET, BROWN

15. So shall Beth-el do unto you—Your idolatrous calf at Beth-el shall be the cause of a like calamity befalling you. **your great wickedness**—lit., "the wickedness of your wickedness." **in a morning**—speedily as quickly as the dawn is put to flight by the rising sun (ch. 6:4; 13:3; Ps. 30:5). **king**—Hoshea.

CHAPTER 11

Vss. 1-12. God's Former Benefits, and Israel's Ingratitude Resulting in Punishment, Yet Jehovah Promises Restoration at Last. Verse 5 shows this prophecy was uttered after the league made with Egypt (II Kings 17:4). **1. Israel . . . called my son out of Egypt**—Bengel translates, "*From* the time that he [Israel] was *in* Egypt, I called him My son," which the parallelism proves. So ch. 12:9 and 13:4 use "from . . . Egypt," for "from the time that thou didst sojourn *in* Egypt." Exodus 4:22 also shows that Israel was called by God, "My son," from the time of his Egyptian sojourn (Isa. 43:1). God is always said to have *led* or *brought forth,* not to have "called," Israel from Egypt. Matthew 2: 15, therefore, in quoting this prophecy (typically and primarily referring to Israel, antitypically and fully to Messiah), applies it to Jesus' sojourn *in* Egypt, not His return *from* it. Even from His infancy, partly spent in Egypt, God called Him His son. God included Messiah, and Israel for Messiah's sake, in one common love, and therefore in one common prophecy. Messiah's people and Himself are one, as the Head and the body. Isaiah 49:3 calls Him "Israel." The same general reason, danger of extinction, caused the infant Jesus, and Israel in its national infancy (cf. Gen. 42:43; 45:18; 46:3, 4; Ezek. 16:4-6; Jer. 31:20) to sojourn in Egypt. So He, and His spiritual Israel, are already called "God's sons" while yet in the Egypt of the world. **2. As they called them**—"they," viz., monitors sent by Me. "Called," in vs. 1, suggests the idea of the many subsequent calls by the prophets. **went from them**—turned away in contempt (Jer. 2: 27). **Baalim**—images of Baal, set up in various places. **3. taught . . . to go**—lit., "to use his feet." Cf. a similar image, Deuteronomy 1:31; 8:2, 5, 15; 32:10, 11; Nehemiah 9:21; Isaiah 63:9; Amos 2:10. God bore them as a parent does an infant, unable to supply itself, so that it has no anxiety about food, raiment, and its going forth. Acts 13:18, which probably refers to this passage of Hosea; He took them by the arms, to guide them that they might not stray, and to hold them up that they might not stumble. **knew not that I healed them**—i.e., that My design was to restore them spiritually and temporally (Exod. 15:26). **4. cords of a man**—parallel to "bands of love"; not such cords as oxen are led by, but *humane methods,* such as men employ when inducing others, as for instance, a father drawing his child, by leading-strings, teaching him to go (vs. 1). **I was . . . as they that take off the yoke on their jaws . . . I laid meat**—as the humane husbandman occasionally loosens the straps under the jaws by which the yoke is bound on the neck of oxen and lays food before them to eat. An appropriate image of God's deliverance of Israel from the Egyptian yoke, and of His feeding them in the wilderness. **5. He shall not return into . . . Egypt**—viz., to seek help against Assyria (cf. ch. 7:11), as Israel lately had done (II Kings 17:4), after having revolted from Assyria, to whom they had been tributary from the times of Menahem (II Kings 15: 19). In a *figurative* sense, "he *shall* return to Egypt" (ch. 9:3), i.e., to Egypt-like bondage; also many Jewish fugitives were literally to *return* to Egypt, when the Holy Land was to be in Assyrian and Chaldean hands. **Assyrian shall be his king**—instead of having kings of their own, and Egypt as their auxiliary. **because they refused to return**—just retribution. They would not return (spiritually) to God, therefore they shall not return (corporally) to Egypt, the object of their desire. **6. abide**—or, "fall upon" [Calvin]. **branches**—villages, which are the branches or dependencies of the cities [Calvin]. Grotius translates, "his bars" (so Lam. 2:9), i.e., the warriors who were the bulwarks of the state. Cf. ch. 4:18, "rulers" (*Margin*), "shields" (Ps. 47:9). **because of their own counsels**—in worshipping idols, and relying on Egypt (cf. ch. 10: 6). **7. bent to backsliding**—Not only do they *backslide,* and that too *from* ME, their "chief good,"

ADAM CLARKE

15. *So shall Beth-el do unto you.* This shall be the consequence of your idolatry. *In a morning shall the king of Israel be cut off.* Suddenly, unexpectedly. Hoshea, the king of Israel, shall be cut off by the Assyrians.

CHAPTER 11

1. *When Israel was a child.* In the infancy of his political existence.

3. *I taught Ephraim also to go.* An allusion to a mother or nurse teaching a child to walk, directing it how to lift and lay its feet, and supporting it in the meantime by the arms, that it may use its feet with the greater ease. This is a passage truly pathetic.

4. *I drew them with cords of a man.* This is a reference to leading strings, one end of which is held by the child, the other by the nurse, by which the little one, feeling some support, and gaining confidence, endeavors to walk. *That take off the yoke on their jaws.* There appears to be here an allusion to the moving and pulling forward the collar or yoke of beasts which have been hard at work, to let in the cool air between it and their neck, so as to refresh them, and prevent that heat which with the sweat would scald their necks. I have often done this at the land ends, in ploughing. *And I laid meat unto them.* Giving them at the same time a bite of grass or hay, to encourage them to go on afresh.

5. *He shall not return into . . . Egypt.* I have brought them thence already, with the design that the nation should never return thither again. But as they have sinned, and forfeited My favor and protection, they shall go to Assyria; and this because they refused to return to Me.

6. *The sword shall abide on his cities.* Israel was agitated with external and intestine wars from the time of Jeroboam II. Although Zechariah, his son, reigned twelve years, yet it was in continual troubles; and he was at last slain by the rebel Shallum, who, having reigned one month, was slain by Menahem. Pekahiah succeeded his father, Menahem, and reigned two years, and was killed by Pekah, son of Remaliah. He joined Rezin, king of Syria, and made an irruption into the land of Judah. But Ahaz having obtained succor from Tiglath-pileser, king of Assyria, Pekah was defeated, and the tribes of Reuben, Gad, Naphtali, and the half-tribe of Manasseh were carried away captives by the Assyrian king. In a short time after, Hoshea, son of Elah, slew Pekah, and usurped the kingdom, which he could not possess without the assistance of Shalmaneser, who for his services imposed a tribute on the Israelitish king. Wishing to rid himself of this yoke, he applied to the king of Egypt; but this being known to Shalmaneser, he came against Samaria and after a three years' siege took and destroyed it. Thus the sword rested on their cities; it continued in the land till all was ruined.

MATTHEW HENRY

Verses 8–12

I. God's debate within himself concerning Israel's case, a debate between justice and mercy, in which victory plainly inclines to mercy's side. Not that there are such struggles in God as there are in us, but they are expressions after the manner of men, to show what severity the sin of Israel had deserved, and yet how divine grace would spare them notwithstanding. *How shall I give thee up?* 1. The proposals that justice makes concerning Israel. Let Ephraim be given up, as an incorrigible son. Let Israel be delivered into the enemy's hand, as a lamb to the lion to be torn in pieces; let them be made as Admah and set as Zeboim, the two cities that with Sodom and Gomorrah were destroyed. Ephraim and Israel deserve to be thus abandoned, and God will do them no wrong if he deal thus with them. 2. The opposition that mercy makes to these proposals: *How shall I do it?* As the tender father reasons with himself, "How can I cast off my untoward son? for he is my son. I cannot do it. They have been a people near unto me; there are yet some good among them; it may be they will yet repent and reform; and therefore how can I do it?" God speaks as if he were conscious to himself of a strange striving of affections in compassion to Israel: *My repentings are kindled together.* After a long contest mercy rejoices against judgment, and carries the day, *v.* 9. It is decreed that the reprieve shall be lengthened out yet longer, and *I will not* now *execute the fierceness of my anger.* They shall be corrected, but not consumed. The reason for this determination: *For I am God and not man, the Holy One of Israel.* He is *Lord of his anger*, whereas men's anger commonly lords it over them. It is a great encouragement to our hope in God's mercies to remember that he is *God, and not man.*

II. He will qualify them to receive the good he designs for them (*v.* 10, 11): *They shall walk after the Lord.* It is spoken of the ten tribes, and had its accomplishment, in part, in the return of some of them with those of the two tribes in Ezra's time; but it had its more full accomplishment in God's spiritual Israel, the gospel-church, brought together by the gospel of Christ. They were to be called and brought together. This call should make such an impression as the roaring of a lion makes upon all the beasts of the forest: *When he shall roar then the children shall tremble.* When those whose hearts the gospel reached trembled, and cried out, *What shall we do?*—when they were working out their salvation, and worshipping God with fear and trembling, then this promise was fulfilled. *The children shall tremble from the west.* This seems to have reference to the calling of the Gentiles that lay westward from Canaan, for that way especially the gospel spread. The apostle speaks of *mighty signs and wonders* that were wrought by the preaching of the gospel from *Jerusalem round about to Illyricum*, Rom. xv. 19. Then the children trembled from the west. And, whereas Israel after the flesh was dispersed in Egypt and Assyria, it is promised that they shall be effectually summoned thence (*v.* 11): *They shall tremble;* they shall come with all haste, *as a bird* upon the wing, *out of Egypt*, and *as a dove out of the land of Assyria.* Those that lay most remote from each other shall meet in Christ, and be incorporated in the church. Our holy trembling at the word of Christ will draw us to him, not drive us from him. When he *roars like a lion* the slaves tremble and flee from him, the children tremble and flee to him. At their return (*v.* 11): *I will place them in their houses*; all those that come at the gospel-call shall have a place and a name in the gospel-church. They shall dwell in God, and be at home in him as a man in his own house; they shall have mansions, for there are many in *our Father's house.*

III. The treachery of Ephraim and Israel may be an intimation that it is not Israel after the flesh, but the spiritual Israel, to whom the foregoing promises belong, for as for this Ephraim, this Israel, they *compass God about with lies and deceit.*

IV. A pleasant commendation of the integrity of the two tribes comes as an aggravation of the perfidiousness of the ten tribes, and a reason why God had that mercy in store for Judah which he had not for Israel (*ch.* i. 6, 7). *Judah rules with God*, that is, he serves God, and the service of God is dignity and dominion. They *walk in the way of good men*; and those that do so *rule with God*, they have a mighty interest in Heaven.

JAMIESON, FAUSSET, BROWN

but they are *bent upon it.* Though they (the prophets) called them (the Israelites) to the Most High (from their idols), "none would exalt (i.e., extol or honor) Him." To exalt God, they must cease to be "*bent on* backsliding," and *must* lift themselves upwards. **8. as Admah . . . Zeboim**—among the cities, including Sodom and Gomorrah, irretrievably overthrown (Deut. 29:23). **heart is turned within me**—with the deepest compassion, so as not to execute My threat (Lam. 1:20; cf. Gen. 43:30; I Kings 3:26). So the phrase is used of a new turn given to the feeling (Ps. 105:25). **repentings**—God speaks according to *human* modes of thought (Num. 23:19). God's *seeming* change is in accordance with His secret everlasting purpose of love to His people, to magnify His grace after their desperate rebellion. **9. I will not return to destroy Ephraim**—i.e., I will no more, as in past times, destroy Ephraim. The destruction primarily meant is probably that by Tiglath-pileser, who, as the Jewish king Ahaz' ally against Pekah of Israel and Rezin of Syria, deprived Israel of Gilead, Galilee, and Naphtali (II Kings 15: 29). The ulterior reference is to the long dispersion hereafter, to be ended by God's covenant mercy restoring His people, not for their merits, but of His grace. **God, . . . not man**—not dealing as man would, with implacable wrath under awful provocation (Isa. 55:7-9; Mal. 3:6). I do not, like man, change when once I have made a covenant of everlasting love, as with Israel (Num. 23:19). We measure God by the human standard, and hence are slow to credit fully His promises; these, however, belong to the faithful remnant, not to the obstinately impenitent. **in the midst of thee**—as peculiarly thy God (Exod. 19:5, 6). **not enter into the city**—as an enemy: as I entered Admah, Zeboim, and Sodom, utterly destroying them, whereas I will not utterly destroy thee. Somewhat similarly JEROME: "I am *not one such as human dwellers in a city*, who take cruel vengeance; I save those whom I correct." Thus "not man," and "in the midst of thee," are parallel to "into the city." Though I am in the midst of thee, it is not as man entering a rebellious city to destroy utterly. MAURER needlessly translates, "I will not come *in wrath.*"

10. he shall roar like a lion—by awful judgments on their foes (Isa. 31:4; Jer. 25:26-30; Joel 3:16), calling His dispersed "children" from the various lands of their dispersion. **shall tremble**—shall flock in eager agitation of haste. **from the west**—(Zech. 8:7). Lit., "the sea." Probably the Mediterranean, including its "isles of the sea," and maritime coast. Thus as vs. 11 specifies regions of Africa and Asia, so here Europe. Isaiah 11:11-16, is parallel, referring to the very same regions. On "children," see ch. 1:10.

11. tremble—flutter in haste. **dove**—no longer "a silly dove" (ch. 7:11), but as "doves flying to their windows" (Isa. 60:8).

in their houses—(Ezek. 28: 26). Lit., "upon," for the Orientals live almost as much *upon* their flat-roofed houses as *in* them. **12.** MAURER joins this verse with ch. 12. But as this verse praises Judah, whereas ch. 12:2 censures him, it must belong rather to ch. 11 and a new prophecy begins at ch. 12. To avoid this, MAURER translates this verse as a censure, "Judah wanders with God," i.e., though having the true God, he wanders after false gods. **ruleth with God**—to serve God is to reign. Ephraim wished to rule *without God* (cf. I Cor. 4:8); nay, even, in order to rule, cast off God's worship [RIVETUS]. In Judah was the legitimate succession of kings and priests. **with the saints**—the holy priests and Levites [RIVETUS]. With the fathers and prophets who handed down the pure worship of God. Israel's apostasy is the more culpable, as he had before him the good example of Judah, which he set at naught. The parallelism ("with GOD") favors *Margin*, "With THE MOST HOLY ONE."

ADAM CLARKE

7. *Though they called them to the most High.* Newcome is better: "And though they call on him together because of the yoke, he will not raise it. He shall receive no refreshment." See the metaphor, v. 4.

8. *How shall I give thee up?* See the notes on chap. vi. 4, where we have similar words from similar feeling. *Mine heart is turned within me.* Justice demands your punishment; Mercy pleads for your life. As you change, Justice resolves to destroy, or Mercy to save. My heart is oppressed, and I am weary with repenting—with so frequently changing My purpose. All this, though spoken after the manner of men, shows how merciful, compassionate, and loath to punish, the God of heaven is.

9. *I will not execute.* Here is the issue of this conflict in the divine mind. Mercy triumphs over Judgment; Ephraim shall be spared. He is God, and not man. He cannot be affected by human caprices. They are now penitent, and implore mercy; He will not, as *man* would do, punish them for former offenses, when they have fallen into His hand.

10. *They shall walk after the Lord.* They shall discern the operations of His providence, when *he shall roar like a lion.* When He shall utter His majestic voice, Cyrus shall make his decree. *The people shall tremble*—be in a state of commotion, everyone hurrying to avail himself of the opportunity to return to his own land.

11. *They shall tremble as a bird.* Those of them that are in Egypt shall also be called thence, and shall speed hither *as a bird.* Those in Assyria shall also be called to return, and they shall flee as doves to their windows.

12. *Ephraim compasseth me about with lies.* I think this verse does not well unite with the above; it belongs to another subject, and should begin the following chapter, as in the Hebrew.

Judah yet ruleth with God. There is an allusion here to Gen. xxxii. 24, where Jacob, having wrestled with the Angel, had his name changed to Israel, one that "rules with God." That glory the Israelites had lost by their idolatry; but Judah still retained the true worship, and alone deserved the name of Israel.

MATTHEW HENRY

CHAPTER 12

Verses 1–6

I. Ephraim is convicted of folly, in staying himself upon Egypt and Assyria, when he was in straits (*v.* 1): *Ephraim feeds on wind.*

The men of Ephraim thought to secure the Assyrians in their interests by a *solemn league*: *They make a covenant with the Assyrians*, but they will find that potent prince will be a slave to his word no longer than he pleases. They thought to secure the Egyptians for their confederates by a rich present: *Oil is carried into Egypt.* But the Egyptians, when they had got the bribe, dropped the cause.

II. *The Lord has also a controversy with Judah;* for though he had awhile ago *ruled with God*, and been *faithful with the saints*, yet now he begins to degenerate.

III. Both Ephraim and Judah are put in mind of their father Jacob, that they might be encouraged to return to God. He had called this people Jacob (*v.* 2), threatening to punish them; but *how shall I give them up*?

How shall that dear name be forgotten? From what passed between God and Jacob we may learn that *Jehovah, the Lord God of hosts*, is *the God of Israel*; he was the God of Jacob, and this is *his memorial* throughout all the generations of the seed of Jacob (*v.* 5). Here are two memorials by which he is distinguished from all others, and is to be acknowledged by us. The first denotes his *existence of himself*. He is Jehovah, much the same with *I AM*, the same that *was, and is, and is to come*, infinite, eternal, and unchangeable. Jehovah is *his memorial*, his peculiar name. The second denotes his dominion over all: He is the *God of hosts*, that has all the hosts of heaven and earth at his command. God's names, titles, and attributes, are the memorials of him; there is no need for images to be such.

JAMIESON, FAUSSET, BROWN

CHAPTER 12

VSS. 1-14. REPROOF OF EPHRAIM AND JUDAH: THEIR FATHER JACOB OUGHT TO BE A PATTERN TO THEM. This prophecy was delivered about the time of Israel's seeking the aid of the Egyptian king So, in violation of their covenant with Assyria (see vs. 1). He exhorts them to follow their father Jacob's persevering prayerfulness, which brought God's favor upon him. As God is unchangeable, He will show the same favor to Jacob's posterity as He did to Jacob, if, like him, they seek God. **1. feedeth on wind**–(Prov. 15:14; Isa. 44:20). Followeth after vain objects, such as alliances with idolaters and their idols (cf. ch. 8:7). **east wind**–the simoon, blowing from the desert east of Palestine, which not only does not benefit, but does injury. Israel follows not only things vain, but things pernicious (cf. Job 15:2). **increaseth lies**–accumulates lie upon lie, i.e., impostures wherewith they deceive themselves, forsaking the truth of God. **desolation** –*violent oppressions* practised by Israel [MAURER]. Acts which would prove the *cause* of Israel's own *desolation* [CALVIN]. **covenant with . . . Assyrians** –(ch. 5:13; 7:11). **oil . . . into Egypt**–as a present from Israel to secure Egypt's alliance (Isa. 30:6; 57: 9; cf. II Kings 17:4). Palestine was famed for oil (Ezek. 27:17). **2. controversy with Judah**–(ch. 4:1; Mic. 6:2). Judah, under Ahaz, had fallen into idolatry (II Kings 16:3, etc.). **Jacob**–i.e., the ten tribes. If Judah, the favored portion of the nation, shall not be spared, much less degenerate Israel. **3. He**–Jacob, contrasted with his degenerate descendants, called by his name, Jacob (vs. 2; cf. Mic. 2:7). *He* took Esau by the heel in the womb in order to obtain, if possible, the privileges of the first-born (Gen. 25:22-26), whence he took his name, Jacob, meaning "supplanter"; and again, by his strength, prevailed in wrestling with God for a blessing (Gen. 32:24-29); whereas ye disregard My promises, putting your confidence in idols and foreign alliances. *He* conquered God, *ye* are the slaves of idols. Only have Jehovah on your side, and ye are stronger than Edom, or even Assyria. So the spiritual Israel lays hold of the heel of Jesus, "the First-born of many brethren," being born again of the Holy Spirit. Having no right in themselves to the inheritance, they lay hold of the bruised heel, the humanity of Christ crucified, and let not go their hold of Him who is not, as Esau, a curse (Heb. 12: 16, 17), but, by becoming a curse for us, is a blessing to us. **power with God**–referring to his name, "Israel," *prince of God,* acquired on that occasion (cf. Matt. 11:12). As the promised Canaan had to be gained forcibly by Israel, so heaven by the faithful (Rev. 3:21; cf. Luke 13:24). "Strive," lit., "as in the agony of a contest." So the Canaanitess (Matt. 15:22). **his strength**–which lay in his conscious weakness, whence, when his thigh was put out of joint by God, he *hung upon Him.* To seek strength was his object; to grant it, God's. Yet God's mode of procedure was strange. In human form He tries as it were to throw Jacob down. When simple wrestling was not enough, He does what seems to ensure Jacob's fall, dislocating his thigh joint, so that he could no longer stand. Yet it was then that Jacob prevailed. Thus God teaches us the irresistible might of conscious weakness. For when weak in ourselves, we are strong by His strength put in us (Job 23:6; Isa. 27:5; II Cor. 12:9, 10). **4. the angel**–the uncreated Angel of the Covenant, as God the Son appears in the Old Testament (Mal. 3:1). **made supplication**–Genesis 32:26; I will not let thee go, except thou bless me." **he found him**–The angel found Jacob, when he was fleeing from Esau into Syria: the Lord appearing to him "in Beth-el" (Gen. 28:11-19; 35:1). What a sad contrast, that in this same Beth-el now Israel worships the golden calves! **there he spake with us** –"with *us,"* as being in the loins of our progenitor Jacob (cf. Ps. 66:6, "They . . . *we*"; Heb. 7:9, 10). What God there spoke to Jacob appertains to us. God's promises to him belong to all his posterity who follow in the steps of his prayerful faith. **5. Lord God**–JEHOVAH, a name implying His *immutable constancy to His promises.* From the *Hebrew* root, meaning "existence." "He that is, was, and is to be," always the same (Heb. 13:8; Rev. 1:4, 8; cf. Exod. 3:14, 15; 6:3). As He was unchangeable in His favor to Jacob, so will He be to His believing posterity. **of hosts**–which Israel foolishly worshipped. Jehovah has all the hosts (*saba*) or powers of heaven and earth at His command, so that He is as all-powerful, as He is faithful, to fulfil His promises (Ps. 135:6; Amos 5:27). **memorial**–the name expressive of the character in which God was ever to be remembered (Ps. 135:13). **6. thou**–who

ADAM CLARKE

CHAPTER 12

1. *Ephraim feedeth on wind.* He forms and follows empty and unstable counsels.

Followeth after the east wind. They are not only empty, but dangerous and destructive. The *east wind* was a parching, wasting, injurious wind. *He daily increaseth lies.* He promises himself safety from foreign alliances.

He made *a covenant with the Assyrians,* and sent a subsidy of *oil* to *Egypt.* The latter abandoned him; the former oppressed him.

2. *The Lord hath also a controversy with Judah.* The rest of the prophecy belongs to both Judah and Israel. He reproaches both with their ingratitude, and threatens them with God's anger.

3. *He took his brother by the heel.* See on Gen. xxv. 26 and xxxii. 24, etc.

4. *He had power over the angel.* Who represented the invisible Jehovah. *He wept, and made supplication.* He entreated with tears that God would bless him, and he prevailed. The circumstance of his weeping is not mentioned in Genesis. *He found him in Beth-el.* It was there that God made those glorious promises to Jacob relative to his posterity. See in Gen. xxviii. 13-15.

5. *The Lord is his memorial.* He is the same God as when Jacob so successfully wrestled with Him.

MATTHEW HENRY

"*Therefore turn thou to thy God.* He that was the God of Jacob is the God of Israel, is *thy God*; from him thou hast revolted; therefore turn thou to him by repentance and faith, turn to him as thine, to love him, obey him, and depend upon him. *Keep mercy and judgment,* mercy in relieving and succouring the poor and distressed, judgment in rendering to all their due; be kind to all."

Verses 7–14

I. Reproofs for sin. Ephraim is charged with turning from his God by idolatry, and breaking the laws of justice and judgment.

1. *He is a merchant.* The margin reads it as a proper name, *He is Canaan,* or a Canaanite, unworthy to be dominated from Jacob and Israel. See Amos ix. 7. But Canaan sometimes signifies *a merchant*, and here Ephraim is charged with deceit in trade. Though God had given his people a land flowing with milk and honey, yet he did not forbid them to enrich themselves by merchandise. And, if they had been fair merchants, it would have been no reproach at all. But he is such a merchant as the Canaanites were, who cheated all they dealt with. Ephraim deceives and thereby oppresses. With a great deal of art and cunning: *The balances of deceit are in his hand.*

2. He justifies himself in this sin, *v.* 8. Ephraim stands indicted for a common cheat. He does not deny the charge, but insists upon his own justification. Suppose he did use balances of deceit, yet he had got a good estate. Let the prophet say what he pleased of his deceit, he could not be convinced there was any harm in it: "*Yet I have become rich, I have found me out substance.*" Carnal hearts are often confirmed in their evil ways by their worldly prosperity and success in those ways. But it is a great mistake. Every word in what Ephraim says here proclaims his folly. It is folly to call the riches of this world substance, for they are things that are not, Prov. xxiii. 5. It is folly to think that what we have is for ourselves. *I have found me out substance*, as if we had it for our own use, whereas we hold it in trust, only as stewards. It is folly to think that growing rich in a sinful way makes us innocent, or will make us safe. See Isa. xlvii. 10; Prov. i. 32. He pleads that he had kept a good reputation. Carnal hearts are apt to build a good opinion of themselves upon the fair character they have among their neighbours. He excused the fraud, so that none condemned it: "*They shall find no iniquity in me that were sin*, nothing very bad, nothing but what is very excusable." It is a fashionable iniquity; it is customary; it is what everybody does; nobody will think the worse of them for it. But God sees not as man sees; he judges not as man judges. He is also charged with idolatry, with the making and worshipping of images, which are vanities (*v.* 11): *Surely they are vanity;* they do not profit, but deceive. The prophet mentions two places notorious for idolatry: (1) Gilead on the other side Jordan, which had been branded for it before (*ch.* vi. 8): *Is there iniquity in Gilead?* It is a thing to be wondered at; it is a thing to be sadly lamented. (2) And in Gilgal too; there they *sacrifice bullocks* (*ch.* ix. 15), and there *their altars* are as thick *as heaps* of manure *in the furrows of the field* that is to be sown, *ch.* viii. 11.

II. Threatenings of wrath for sin. Some make that to be so (*v.* 9), *I will make thee to dwell in tabernacles as in the days of the appointed time*, as did the Israelites when they dwelt in tents and wandered for forty years; that was the *time appointed in the wilderness.* Ephraim thought that there was no iniquity in him that deserved to be called sin (*v.* 8); but God told him that there was that in him which was sin, and would be found so if he did not repent and reform. *Ephraim provoked him to anger most bitterly.* He shall take away his forfeited life: *He shall leave his blood upon him*, that is, he shall not hold him guiltless. *His blood shall be upon his own head* (2 Sam. i. 16). *His reproach shall his Lord return upon him.*

III. Here are memorials of former mercy, which come in to convict them of base ingratitude.

1. That God had raised them from meanness. When Ephraim had become rich he forgot that which God obliged them every year to acknowledge (Deut. xxvi. 5), *A Syrian ready to perish was my father.* But God here puts them in mind of it, *v.* 12. Let them remember, not only the honours of their father Jacob, *v.* 3, but what a poor servant he was to Laban. *Jacob fled into Syria* from a malicious brother, and there served a covetous uncle *for a wife* and *for a wife he kept sheep*, because he had no estate. He was a plain man, dwelling in tents, and keeping sheep; therefore *balances of deceit* ill became them. God wonderfully preserved him, which magnifies the goodness of God both to him and them and leaves

JAMIESON, FAUSSET, BROWN

dost wish to be a true descendant of Jacob. **to THY God**—who is therefore bound by covenant to hear thy prayers. **keep mercy and judgment**—(Mic. 6: 8). These two include the second-table commandments, duty towards one's neighbor, the most visible test of the sincerity on one's repentance. **wait on thy God**—alone, not on thy idols. Including all the duties of the first table (Ps. 37:3, 5, 7; 40:1).

7. merchant—a play on the double sense of the *Hebrew,* "Canaan," i.e., a Canaanite and a "merchant" Ezekiel 16:3: "Thy birth is . . . of Canaan." They who naturally were descendants of pious *Jacob* had become virtually *Canaanites,* who were proverbial as cheating *merchants* (cf. Isa. 23:11, *Margin*), the greatest reproach to Israel, who despised Canaan. The Phœnicians called themselves *Canaanites* or *merchants* (Isa. 23:8). **oppress**—*open* violence: as the "balances of deceit" imply *fraud.* **8. And**—i.e., Notwithstanding. **Yet I am . . . rich**—I regard not what the prophets say: I am content with my state, as I am rich (Rev. 3:17). Therefore, in just retribution, this is the very language of the enemy in being the instrument of Israel's punishment. Zechariah 11:5: "They that sell them say . . . *I am rich.*" Far better is poverty with honesty, than riches gained by sin. **my labours**—my gains by labor. **they shall find none**—i.e., none, shall find any. **iniquity . . . that were sin**—iniquity that would bring down the penalty of sin. Ephraim argues, My success in my labors proves that I am not a guilty sinner as the prophets assert. Thus sinners pervert God's long-suffering goodness (Matt. 5:45) into a justification of their impenitence (cf. Eccles. 8:11-13). **9. And**—rather, "And yet." Though Israel deserves to be cast off for ever, yet I am still what I have been from the time of My delivering them out of Egypt, their covenant God; therefore, "I will yet make thee to dwell in tabernacles," i.e., to keep the feast of tabernacles again in remembrance of a new deliverance out of bondage. Fulfilled primarily at the return from Babylon (Neh. 8:17). Fully and antitypically to be fulfilled at the final restoration from the present dispersion (Zech. 14:16; cf. Lev. 23:42, 43). **10. by . . . the prophets**—lit., "upon," i.e., My spirit resting *on* them. I deposited *with them* My instructions which ought to have brought you to the right way. An aggravation of your guilt, that it was not through ignorance you erred, but in defiance of God and His prophets [CALVIN]. Ahijah the Shilonite, Shemaiah, Iddo, Azariah, Hanani, Jehu, Elijah, Elisha, Micaiah, Joel, and Amos were "the prophets" before Hosea. **visions . . . similitudes**—I adopted such modes of communication, adapted to man's capacities, as were calculated to arouse attention: I left no means untried to reform you. Chs. 1, 2, 3 contain examples of "similitudes." **11. Is there iniquity in Gilead?**—He asks the question, not as if the answer was doubtful, but to strengthen the affirmation: "Surely they are vanity"; or as MAURER translates, "They are *nothing but* iniquity." *Iniquity,* especially idolatry, in Scripture is often termed "vanity." Proverbs 13:11: "Wealth gotten by *vanity,*" i.e., *iniquity.* Isaiah 41:29: "They are all *vanity . . . images.*" "Gilead" refers to Mizpah-gilead, a city representing the region beyond Jordan (ch. 6:8; Judg. 11:29); as "Gilgal," the region on this side of Jordan (ch. 4:15). In all quarters alike they are utterly vile. **their altars are as heaps in the furrows**—i.e., as numerous as such heaps: viz., the heaps of stones cleared out of a stony field. An appropriate image, as at a distance they look like altars (cf. ch. 10:1, 4, and 8:11). As the third member in the parallelism answers to the first, "Gilgal" to "Gilead," so the fourth to the second, "altars" to "vanity." The word "heaps" alludes to the name "Gilgal," meaning "a heap of stones." The very scene of the general circumcision of the people, and of the solemn passover kept after crossing Jordan, is now the stronghold of Israel's idolatry. **12. Jacob fled . . . served**—Though ye pride yourselves on the great name of "Israel," forget not that your progenitor was the same Jacob who was a fugitive, and who served for Rachel fourteen years. *He* forgot not ME who delivered him when fleeing from Esau, and when oppressed by Laban (Gen. 28:5; 29:20, 28; Deut. 26:5). *Ye,* though delivered from Egypt (vs. 13), and loaded with My favors, are yet unwilling to return to Me. **country of Syria**—the champaign region of Syria, the portion lying between the Tigris and Euphrates, hence called Mesopotamia. Padan-aram means the same, i.e., "Low Syria," as opposed to Aramea (meaning the "high country") or Syria (Gen. 48:7).

ADAM CLARKE

6. *Therefore turn thou to thy God.* Because He is the same and cannot change. Seek Him as faithfully and as fervently as Jacob did, and you will find Him the same merciful and compassionate Being.

7. *He is a merchant.* Or a "Canaanite," referring to the Phoenicians, famous for their traffic. Ephraim is as corrupt as those heathenish traffickers were. He kept, as many in all ages have done, a weight and a weight—a heavy one to buy with and a light one to sell by.

8. *I am become rich.* They boasted in their riches, notwithstanding the unjust manner in which they were acquired.

9. *And I . . . the Lord thy God.* I, who brought you out of the land of Egypt, will again make you *to dwell in tabernacles.* This appears to be a threatening. I will reduce you to as miserable a state in the land of your captivity as you often were through your transgressions in the wilderness.

10. *I have also spoken.* I have used every means and employed every method to instruct and save you. I have sent *prophets,* who spoke plainly, exhorting, warning, and beseeching you to return to Me. They have had divine *visions,* which they have declared and interpreted. They have *used similitudes,* "symbols, metaphors, allegories," in order to fix your attention and bring you back to your duty and interest.

11. *Iniquity in Gilead.* Gilgal and Gilead are equally iniquitous and equally idolatrous. Gilead, which was beyond Jordan, had already been brought under subjection by Tiglath-pileser. Gilgal, which was on this side Jordan, shall share the same fate, because it is now as idolatrous as the other.

Their altars are as heaps. They occur everywhere. The whole land is given to idolatry.

12. *Served for a wife.* Seven years for Rachel. *For a wife he kept sheep.* Seven years for Leah, having been cheated by Laban, who gave him first Leah instead of Rachel, and afterwards made him serve seven years more before he would confirm his first engagement. Critics complain of want of connection here. Why is this isolated fact predicted? Thus, in a detached sentence, the prophet speaks of the low estate of their ancestors and how amply the providence of God had preserved and provided for them. This is all the connection the place requires.

MATTHEW HENRY

them under the stain of base ingratitude to God who was their founder and benefactor.

2. That God had rescued them from misery, raised them out of poverty and slavery (*v.* 13). God *brought Israel out of Egypt by a prophet*, Moses, who, though he is called *king in Jeshurun* (Deut. xxxiii. 5), yet did what he did for Israel *as a prophet*, by direction from God and by the power of his word. This shows how ungrateful this people were in rejecting their God. They should have loved and valued his prophets and have studied to answer God's end in sending them, for the sake of that prophet by whom God had brought them out of Egypt.

3. That God had taken care of their education as they grew up. This instance of God's goodness we have, *v.* 10. As by a prophet he delivered them, so *by prophets* he still continued to speak to them.

IV. Here are intimations of further mercy in the midst of sin and wrath (as some understand *v.* 9): "*I that am the Lord thy God from the land of Egypt*, who then and there took thee to be my people, and have approved myself thy God ever since, in a constant series of merciful providences, have yet a kindness for thee, bad as thou art; and I will *make thee to dwell in tabernacles*, not as in the wilderness, but *as in the days of the solemn feast*," the feast of tabernacles, which was celebrated with great joy, Lev. xxiii. 40.

JAMIESON, FAUSSET, BROWN

13. by a prophet—Moses (Num. 12:6-8; Deut. 18:15, 18). **preserved**—Translate, "kept"; there is an allusion to the same *Hebrew* word in vs. 12, "*kept* sheep"; Israel was *kept* by God as *His flock*, even as *Jacob kept sheep* (Ps. 80:1; Isa. 63:11). **14. provoked him**—i.e., God. **leave his blood upon him**—not take away the guilt and penalty of the innocent blood shed by Ephraim in general, and to Molech in particular. **his reproach shall his Lord return unto him** Ephraim's dishonor to God in worshipping idols, God will repay to him. That God is "*his* Lord" by right redemption and special revelation to Ephraim only aggravates his guilt, instead of giving him hope of escape. God does not give up His claim to them as *His*, however they set aside His dominion.

ADAM CLARKE

13. *By a prophet* (Moses) *the Lord brought Israel out of Egypt, and by a prophet* (Joshua) *was he preserved.* Joshua succeeded Moses, and brought the Israelites into the Promised Land; and when they passed the Jordan at Gilgal, he received the covenant of circumcision—and yet this same place was now made by them the seat of idolatry!

14. *Therefore shall he leave his blood upon him.* He will not remove his guilt.

MATTHEW HENRY — CHAPTER 13

Verses 1–4

Idolatry was the sin that did most easily beset the Jewish nation till after the captivity; the ten tribes from the first were guilty of it, but especially after the days of Ahab.

I. The provision that God made to prevent their falling into idolatry. This we have, *v.* 4. He made himself known to them as *the Lord their God*. He told them so from heaven at Mount Sinai. This he continued to prove to them by his prophets and by his providences. He gave them a law forbidding them to worship any other: "*Thou shalt know no God but me.*" He gave them a good reason for it: *There is no saviour besides me*.

II. The honour that Ephraim had, while he kept himself clear from idolatry (*v.* 1): *While Ephraim spoke trembling*, or *with trembling*, so long *he exalted himself in Israel. Those that humble themselves*, especially that humble themselves before God, *shall be exalted*.

III. The lamentable growth of idolatry among them (*v.* 2): *Now they sin more and more*. They made themselves *molten images*. They made them of *their silver*. They made them *according to their own understanding*, according to their own fancy. Or *according to their own likeness*, in the form of a man. Though they were thus the work of their hands, yet they were the beloved of their souls; for they say of them, *Let the men that sacrifice kiss the calves*.

IV. Threatenings of wrath for their idolatry. Because they are so fond of kissing their calves, therefore God will give them sensible convictions of their folly, *v.* 3. God tells them that they shall be disappointed, and *driven away in their wickedness*. They shall be like the *morning cloud* or the *early dew*. Both *pass away*, and the day proves as dry and hot as ever; so their prosperity should be, and so their expectations from their idols. They are *as the chaff*, light and worthless. They are *as the smoke*, noisome and offensive (see Isa. lxv. 5), and they shall be driven away *as the smoke out of the chimneys*.

Verses 5–8

1. The plentiful provision God had made for Israel (*v.* 5): "*I did know thee in the wilderness*, made provision for thee, even in *a land of great drought*, when no relief was to be had in an ordinary way." The God that knew them and fed them there, was a *friend indeed*. 2. Their unworthy ungrateful abuse of God's favour to them. God not only took care of them in the wilderness, but put them in possession of Canaan (*v.* 6), *according to their pasture so were they filled*. When they came into Canaan they fed themselves *to the full*. It would have promised better, if they had been more moderate in the use of their plenty. *They were filled, and their heart was exalted.* Their luxury and sensuality made them proud, insolent, and secure. The best comment upon this is that of Moses, Deut. xxxii. 13–15. But *Jeshurun waxed fat and kicked*. They began to think they had no further need of God: *Their heart was exalted, therefore have they forgotten me*. We ought to know that we live upon God when we live upon common providence, though we do not, as Israel in the wilder-

JAMIESON, FAUSSET, BROWN — CHAPTER 13

VSS. 1-16. EPHRAIM'S SINFUL INGRATITUDE TO GOD, AND ITS FATAL CONSEQUENCE; GOD'S PROMISE AT LAST. This chapter and chapter 14 probably belong to the troubled times that followed Pekah's murder by Hoshea (cf. ch. 13:11; II Kings 15:30). The subject is the idolatry of Ephraim, notwithstanding God's past benefits, destined to be his ruin. **1. When Ephraim spake trembling**—rather, "When Ephraim [the tribe most powerful among the twelve in Israel's early history] spake [authoritatively] there was trembling"; all reverentially feared him [JEROME], (cf. Job 29:8, 9, 21). **offended in Baal**—i.e., *in respect to* Baal, by worshipping him (I Kings 16:31), under Ahab; a more heinous offense than even the calves. Therefore it is at this climax of guilt that Ephraim "died." Sin has, in the sight of God, within itself the germ of death, though that death may not visibly take effect till long after. Cf. Romans 7:9, "Sin revived, and I *died*." So Adam in the day of his sin was to die, though the sentence was not visibly executed till long after (Gen. 2:17; 5:5). Israel is similarly represented as politically dead in Ezekiel 37. **2. according to their own understanding**—i.e., their arbitrary devising. Cf. "will-worship," Colossians 2:23. Men are not to be "wise above that which is written," or to follow their own understanding, but God's command in worship. **kiss the calves**—an act of adoration to the golden calves (cf. I Kings 19:18; Job 31:27; Ps. 2:12). **3. they shall be as the morning cloud . . . dew**—(ch. 6:4). As their "goodness" soon vanished like the morning cloud and dew, so they shall perish like them. **the floor**—the threshing-floor, generally an open area, on a height, exposed to the winds. **chimney**—generally in the East an orifice in the wall, at once admitting the light, and giving egress to the smoke. **4.** (Ch. 12:9; Isa. 43:11.) **no saviour** [temporal as well as spiritual] **besides me**—(Isa. 45:21).

5. I did know thee—did acknowledge thee as Mine, and so took care of thee (Ps. 144:3; Amos 3:2). As *I knew* thee as Mine, so *thou* shouldest *know* no God but Me (vs. 4). **in . . . land of . . . drought**—(Deut. 8:15). **6.** Image from cattle, waxing wanton in abundant pasture (cf. ch. 2:5, 8; Deut. 32:13-15). In proportion as I fed them to the full, they were so satiated that "their heart was exalted"; a sad contrast to the time when, by God's blessing, Ephraim truly "exalted himself in Israel" (vs. 1).

therefore have they forgotten me—the very reason why men should remember God (viz., prosperity, which comes from Him) is the cause often of their forgetting Him. God had warned them of this danger (Deut. 6:11, 12).

ADAM CLARKE — CHAPTER 13

1. *When Ephraim spake trembling.* When he was meek and humble, of a broken heart and contrite spirit. *He exalted himself in Israel.* He became great in God's sight; he rose in the divine esteem in proportion as he sank in his own. *He offended in Baal.* He became an idolater. *He died.* The sentence of death from the divine justice went out against him.

3. *Therefore they shall be as the morning cloud . . . as the early dew . . . as the chaff . . . as the smoke.* Four things, most easy to be driven about and dissipated, are employed here to show how they should be scattered among the nations, and dissipated by captivity.

4. *I am the Lord thy God.* This was the first discovery I made of myself to you, and the first commandment I gave; and I showed you that besides Me there was *no saviour*.

5. *I did know thee.* I approved of you.

MATTHEW HENRY

ness, live upon miracles. 3. God's just resentment of their base ingratitude, *v.* 7, 8. *I will be unto them as a lion* and *as a leopard.* Some read it (and the original will bear it), *I will be as a leopard in the way of Assyria.* The judgments of God shall surprise them just when they are going to the Assyrians to seek for protection and help from them. He will *rend the caul of their heart.* The lion is observed to aim at the heart of the beasts he preys upon, and thus will God *devour them like a lion.* The judgments of God against impenitent sinners will be terrible. They will *rend the caul of the heart,* will fill the soul with confusion.

Verses 9–16

The first of these verses is the summary, or contents, of all the rest (*v.* 9). 1. All the blame of Israel's ruin laid upon themselves: *O Israel! thy perdition is thence;* it is of and from thyself; or, "*It has destroyed thee, O Israel!*" 2. All the glory of Israel's relief ascribed to God: *But in me is thy help.* It may be: "Thy case is bad, but it is not desperate. *Thou hast destroyed thyself;* but come to me, and I will help thee."

1. They treasure up wrath against the day of wrath, and so they destroy themselves. Their former sins contributed to their present destruction; for they were *laid up in store with God,* Deut. xxxii. 34, 35; Job xiv. 17. The sin of sinners is not forgotten till it is pardoned.

II. How God was the help of this self-destroying people, their only help (*v.* 10): *I will be thy King,* to rule and save thee. Though they had rebelled against him, yet he would still be their King. Our case would be sad indeed if God were not better to us than we are to ourselves.

1. God will be their King when they have no other king. "*Where is the king that may save thee in all thy cities? Where are thy judges,* who by administering public justice should preserve the public peace?" They rejected Samuel when they said, *Give us a king* like the nations, whereas the *Lord was their King.* The ten tribes desired a kingly government different from that of the house of David, because they thought that bore too hard upon them, and they hoped to better themselves by setting up Jeroboam. Providence gave them Saul first, and afterwards Jeroboam. And what better were they for them? Saul was *given in anger* (given in *thunder,* 1 Sam. xii. 18, 19) and soon after was *taken away in wrath,* upon Mount Gilboa. The kingly government of the ten tribes was given in anger against the ten tribes, for their disaffection to the house of David; and God was now about to take that away in wrath by the power of the king of Assyria.

2. They are their own ruin because they will not do what they should do towards their own salvation, *v.* 13. They shall be thrown into pangs and agonies, very sharp and severe, and yet, like the pains of a woman in labour, in order to deliverance; and by these, though God corrects them, yet he designs their good. They are chastened, that they may not be destroyed. But they do not repent and so cannot expect the joy of deliverance, *v.* 13. Those are in danger of miscarrying in conversion who delay it.

2. God will do that for them which no other king could do if they had one (*v.* 14): *I will ransom them from the power of the grave.* Their deliverance shall be by ransom; and we know who it was that paid their ransom, and what the ransom was, for it was the Son of man that *gave his life a ransom for many,* Matt. xx. 28. Christ has abolished death, has broken the power of it and altered the property of it, and so enabled us to triumph over it. Thanks be to God therefore who gives us the victory.

Here is a sad description of the desolation they are doomed to, *v.* 15, 16. It is taken for granted that *Ephraim* is *fruitful among his children*; but sin turns this fruitful tribe into barrenness. The instrument is an *east wind,* representing a foreign enemy that should invade it. It is called the *wind of the Lord.*

JAMIESON, FAUSSET, BROWN

7. (Ch. 5, 14; Lam. 3:10). **leopard**—The *Hebrew* comes from a root meaning "spotted" (cf. Jer. 13:23). Leopards lurk in thickets and thence spring on their victims. **observe**—i.e., *lie in wait* for them. Several MSS., LXX, *Vulgate, Syriac,* and *Arabic* read, by a slight change of the *Hebrew* vowel pointing, "by the way *of Assyria,*" a region abounding in leopards and lions. *English Version* is better. **8.** "Writers on the natures of beasts say that none is more savage than a *she bear,* when *bereaved of her whelps*" [JEROME]. **caul of . . . heart**—the membrane enclosing it: the pericardium. **there**—"by the way" (vs. 7). **9. thou . . . in me**—in contrast. **hast destroyed thyself**—i.e., thy destruction is of thyself (Prov. 6:32; 8:36). **in me is thine help**—lit., "in thine help" (cf. Deut. 33:26). Hadst thou rested thy hope *in Me,* I would have been always ready at hand *for thy help* [GROTIUS]. **10. I will be thy king; where**—rather, as *Margin* and LXX, *Syriac, Vulgate,* "Where now is thy king?" [MAURER]. *English Version* is, however, favored both by the *Hebrew,* by the antithesis between Israel's self-chosen and *perishing kings,* and God, Israel's *abiding King* (cf. ch. 3:4, 5). **where . . . Give me a king**—Where now is the king whom ye substituted in My stead? Neither Saul, whom the whole nation begged for, not contented with Me their true king (I Sam. 8:5, 7, 19, 20; 10:19), nor Jeroboam, whom subsequently the ten tribes chose instead of the line of David My anointed, can save thee now. They had expected from their kings what is the prerogative of God alone, viz., the power of saving them. **judges**—including all civil authorities under the king (cf. Amos 2:3). **11. I gave . . . king in . . . anger . . . took . . . away in . . . wrath**—true both of Saul (I Sam. 15:22, 23; 16:1) and of Jeroboam's line (II Kings 15:30). Pekah was taken away through Hoshea, as he himself took away Pekahiah; and as Hoshea was soon to be taken away by the Assyrian king. **12. bound up . . . hid**—Treasures, meant to be kept, are bound up and hidden; i.e., do not flatter yourselves, because of the delay, that I have forgotten your sin. Nay (ch. 9:9), Ephraim's iniquity is kept as it were safely sealed up, until the due time comes for bringing it forth for punishment (Deut. 32:34; Job 14:17; 21:19; cf. Rom. 2:5). Opposed to "blotting out the handwriting against" the sinner (Col. 2:14). **13. sorrows of a travailing woman**—calamities sudden and agonizing (Jer. 30:6). **unwise**—in not foreseeing the impending judgment, and averting it by penitence (Prov. 22:3). **he should not stay long in the place of the breaking forth of children**—When Israel might deliver himself from calamity by the pangs of penitence, he brings ruin on himself by so long deferring a new birth unto repentance, like a child whose mother has not strength to bring it forth, and which therefore remains so long in the passage from the womb as to run the risk of death (II Kings 19:3; Isa. 37:3; 66:9). **14.** Applying primarily to God's restoration of Israel from Assyria partially, and, in times yet future, fully from all the lands of their present long-continued dispersion, and political *death* (cf. ch. 6:2; Isa. 25:8; 26:19; Ezek. 37:12). God's power and grace are magnified in quickening what to the eye of flesh seems dead and hopeless (Rom. 4:17, 19). As Israel's history, past and future, has a representative character in relation to the Church, this verse is expressed in language alluding to Messiah's (who is the ideal Israel) grand victory over the grave and death, the first fruits of His own resurrection, the full harvest to come at the general resurrection; hence the similarity between this verse and Paul's language as to the latter (I Cor. 15:55). That similarity becomes more obvious by *translating* as LXX, from which Paul plainly quotes; and as the same *Hebrew* word is translated in vs. 10, "O death, *where* are thy plagues (paraphrased by LXX, 'thy victory')? O grave, where is thy destruction" (rendered by LXX, 'thy sting')?" The question is that of one triumphing over a foe, once a cruel tyrant, but now robbed of all power to hurt. **repentance shall be hid from mine eyes**—i.e., I will not change My purpose of fulfilling My promise by delivering Israel, on the condition of their return to Me (cf. ch. 14:2-8; Num. 23:19; Rom. 11:29). **15. fruitful**—referring to the meaning of "Ephraim," from a *Hebrew* root, "to be fruitful" (Gen. 41:52). It was long the most numerous and flourishing of the tribes (Gen. 48:19). **wind of the Lord**—i.e., sent by the Lord (cf. Isa. 40:7), who has His instruments of punishment always ready. The Assyrian, Shalmaneser, etc., is meant (Jer. 4:11; 18:17; Ezek. 19:12). **from the wilderness**—i.e., the desert part of Syria (I Kings 19:15), the route from Assyria into Israel. **he**—the Assyrian invader. Shalmaneser began the siege of

ADAM CLARKE

7. *Will I observe them.* The *leopard,* tiger, and panther will hide themselves in thick bushwood, near where they expect any prey to pass; and as soon as it comes near, spring suddenly upon it.

8. *As a bear . . . bereaved.* This is a figure to denote excessive ferocity. See 2 Sam. xvii. 8. *And will rend the caul of their heart.* Every savage beast goes first to the seat of the blood when it has seized its prey, as in this fluid they delight more than in the most delicate parts of the flesh.

10. *Give me a king and princes.* Referring to the time in which they cast off the divine theocracy and chose Saul in the place of Jehovah.

11. *I gave thee a king in mine anger.* Such was Saul, for they highly offended God when they clamored to have a king like the heathen nations that were around them. *Took him away in my wrath.* Permitted him and the Israelites to fall before the Philistines.

12. *The iniquity of Ephraim is bound up.* It is registered in My court of justice; the death warrant is in store, and will be produced in due time.

13. *The sorrows of a travailing woman.* These judgments shall come suddenly and unavoidably.

14. *I will ransom them from the power of the grave.* In their captivity they are represented as dead and buried, which is a similar view to that taken of the Jews in the Babylonish captivity by Ezekiel in his vision of the valley of dry bones. *O grave, I will be thy destruction. Sheol,* which we translate *grave,* is the "state of the dead." *Maveth,* which we translate *death,* is the "principle of corruption" that renders the body unfit to be longer the tenement of the soul, and finally decomposes it. *Sheol* shall be destroyed, for it must deliver up all its dead. *Maveth* shall be annihilated, for the body shall be raised incorruptible. See the use which the apostle makes of this passage, 1 Cor. xv. 54-55.

Repentance shall be hid from mine eyes. On these points I will not "change my purpose"; this is the signification of repentance when attributed to God.

15. *Though he be fruitful. Yaphri;* a paronomasia on the word *ephrayim,* which comes from the same root, *parah,* "to be fruitful, to sprout, to bud." *An east wind shall come.* As the east wind parches and blasts all vegetation, so shall Shalmaneser blast and destroy the Israelitish state.

MATTHEW HENRY | JAMIESON, FAUSSET, BROWN | ADAM CLARKE

Was it a rich tribe? The foreign enemy shall make it poor enough and shall exhaust the sources of its wealth. Was it a populous tribe, and numerous? The enemy shall depopulate it and make its men few: *Samaria shall become desolate*, without inhabitants.

I. Israel destroyed themselves. It is said (*v*. 16), They *rebelled against God*.

CHAPTER 14

Verses 1–3

I. A kind invitation given to sinners to repent, *v*. 1. It is directed to Israel, God's professing people. They are called to *return*. Conversion must be preached even to those that are within the pale of the church as well as to heathen. *"Thou hast fallen by thy iniquity." Thou hast stumbled;* so some read it. Their idols were their *stumbling-blocks*. Sin is a fall; and it concerns those that have fallen by sin to get up again by repentance. *"Return to the Lord thy God;* return to him as *the Lord* whom thou hast a dependance upon, *as thy God*." Return *even to the Lord*, or *quite home* to the Lord. The ancient Jews had a saying, grounded on this, *Repentance is a great thing, for it brings men quite up to the throne of glory*.

II. How to repent. 1. They must bethink themselves what to say to God when they come to him: *Take with you words*. They are required to bring, not sacrifices and offerings, but penitential prayers, the *fruit* not of the lips only, but of the heart. The heart must dictate to the tongue. 2. They must bethink themselves what to do. They must not only take with them words, but must *turn to the Lord;* inwardly in their hearts, outwardly in their lives.

III. For their assistance and encouragement, God is pleased to put words into their mouths, to teach them what they shall say. They are,

1. Petitioning words. Two things we are here directed to petition for: (1) To be acquitted from guilt. When we return to the Lord we must say to him, "Lord, *take away all iniquity*. Lift it off as a *burden* or as the stumbling-block which we have often fallen over. Take it all away by a free and full remission, for we cannot strike it off by a satisfaction of our own." (2) To be accepted as righteous in God's sight: "*Receive us graciously*. Let us have thy favour and love. Receive our prayer graciously; be well pleased with that good which by thy grace we are enabled to do." *Take good* (so the word is); take it to bestow upon us, so the margin reads it—*Give good*. This follows upon the petition for the taking away of iniquity; for, till iniquity is taken away, we have no reason to expect any good from God. *Give good*, that good which will make us good and keep us from returning to iniquity again.

2. Promising words. These also are put into their mouths, not to move God, but to move themselves. Two things they are to promise and vow: (1) Thanksgiving. "Pardon our sins, and accept of us, so *will we render the calves of our lips*," The *fruit of our lips* (so the LXX), a word they used for *burnt-offerings*, and so it agrees with the Hebrew. The apostle quotes this phrase (Heb. xiii. 15). (2) Amendment of life. They are taught to promise, not only verbal acknowledgments, but a real reformation. They will not trust to their alliances abroad: *Asshur* (that is, Assyria) *shall not save us*. "We will not court the help of the Assyrians when we are in distress, as we have done (*ch*. v. 13; vii. 11; viii. 9); we will scorn to be beholden to the Assyrians for help. *We will not ride upon horses*," that is, we will not make court to Egypt," for thence they fetched their horses, Deut. xvii. 16; Isa. xxx. 16; xxxi. 1, 3. We must promise that we will not set our hearts upon the gains of this world, nor pride ourselves in our external performances in religion, for that is, in effect, to say to the work of our hands, *You are our gods*.

3. Pleading words are here put into their mouths: For *in thee the fatherless find mercy*. Those may expect to find help in God that are truly sensible of their helplessness in themselves and are willing to acknowledge it. They plead God's wonted lovingkindness to such as were in that condition: *With thee the fatherless* not only may find, but *does find*, and shall find, *mercy*.

Samaria in 723 B.C. Its close was in 721 B.C., the first year of Sargon, who seems to have usurped the throne of Assyria while Shalmaneser was at the siege of Samaria. Hence, while II Kings 17:6 states, "the *king of Assyria* took Samaria," II Kings 18:10 says, "at the end of three years *they* took it." In Sargon's magnificent palace at Khorsabad, inscriptions mention the number—27,280—of Israelites carried captive from Samaria and other places of Israel by the founder of the palace [G. V. SMITH]. **16.** This verse and vs. 15 foretell the calamities about to befall Israel before her restoration (vs. 14), owing to her impenitence. **her God**—the greatest aggravation of her rebellion, that it was against *her* God (vs. 4). **infants . . . dashed in pieces . . .**—(II Kings 8:12; 15:16; Amos 1:13).

CHAPTER 14

VSS. 1-9. GOD'S PROMISE OF BLESSING, ON THEIR REPENTANCE: THEIR ABANDONMENT OF IDOLATRY FORETOLD: THE CONCLUSION OF THE WHOLE, THE JUST SHALL WALK IN GOD'S WAYS, BUT THE TRANSGRESSOR SHALL FALL THEREIN. **1. fallen by thine iniquity**—(ch. 5:5; 13:9).

2. Take with you words—instead of sacrifices, viz., the words of penitence here put in your mouths by God. "Words," in *Hebrew*, mean "realities," there being the same term for "words" and "things"; so God implies, He will not accept empty professions (Ps. 78:36; Isa. 29:13). He does not ask costly sacrifices, but *words* of heartfelt penitence.

receive us graciously—lit. (for) "good."

calves of our lips—i.e., instead of sacrifices of *calves*, which we cannot offer to Thee in exile, we present the praises of our *lips*. Thus the exile, wherein the temple service ceased, prepared the way for the gospel time when the types of the animal sacrifices of the Old Testament being realized in Christ's perfect sacrifice once for all, "the sacrifice of praise to God continually that is *the fruit of our lips*" (Heb. 13:14) takes their place in the New Testament. **3.** Three besetting sins of Israel are here renounced, trust in Assyria, application to Egypt for its cavalry (forbidden, Deut. 17:16; cf. ch. 7:11; 11:5; 12:1; II Kings 17:4; Ps. 33:17; Isa. 30:2, 16; 31:1), and idolatry.

fatherless—descriptive of the *destitute* state of Israel, when severed from God, their true Father. We shall henceforth trust in none but Thee, the only Father of the fatherless, and Helper of the destitute (Ps. 10:14; 68:5); our nation has experienced Thee such in our helpless state in Egypt, and now in a like state again our only hope is Thy goodness.

---

16. *Samaria shall become desolate*. This was the capital of the Israelitish kingdom. What follows is a simple prophetic declaration of the cruelties which should be exercised upon this hapless people by the Assyrians in the sackage of the city.

CHAPTER 14

1. *O Israel, return unto the Lord*. These words may be considered as addressed to the people now in captivity; suffering much, but having still much more to suffer if they did not repent. But it seems all these evils might yet be prevented, though so positively predicted, if the people would repent and return; and the very exhortation to this repentance shows that they still had power to repent, and that God was ready to save them and avert all these evils.

3. *We will not ride upon horses*—We shall no more fix our hopes on the proud Egyptian cavalry, to deliver us out of the hands of enemies to whom Thy divine justice has delivered us.

MATTHEW HENRY

Verses 4–7

An answer of peace to the prayers of returning Israel. They seek God's face, and they shall not *seek in vain.*

I. Do they dread and deprecate God's displeasure, and therefore return to him? He assures them that, upon their submission, his *anger is turned away from them.* This is laid as the ground of all the other favours here promised.

II. Do they pray for the *taking away of iniquity*? He assures them that he will *heal their backslidings*; so he promised, Jer. iii. 22.

III. Do they pray that God will receive them graciously? In answer to that, behold, it is promised, *I will love them freely.*

IV. Do they pray that God will *give good,* will make them good? In answer to that, behold, it is promised, *I will be as the dew unto Israel, v.* 5. This ensures *spiritual blessings in heavenly things*; and it follows upon the healing of their backslidings, for pardoning mercy is always accompanied with renewing grace. The bad being by the grace of God made good, they shall by the same grace be made better; for grace, wherever it is true, is growing. They *shall grow as the lily.* The growth of the lily is very speedy. The root of the lily seems lost in the ground all winter, but, when it is refreshed with the dews of the spring, it starts up in a little time; so the grace of God improves young converts sometimes very fast. They shall grow downwards, and be more firm. The lily indeed grows fast, and grows fine, but it soon fades and is easily plucked up; and therefore it is here promised to Israel that with the flower of the lily he shall have the root of the cedar: He shall *cast forth his roots as Lebanon,* as the *trees of Lebanon,* which, having taken deep root, cannot be plucked up, Amos ix. 15. Spiritual growth consists most in the growth of the root, which is out of sight. The more we depend upon Christ and draw sap and virtue from him, the more we act in religion from a principle and the more steadfast and resolved we are in it, the more we *cast forth our roots.* They shall grow round about (*v.* 6): *His branches shall spread* on all sides. And (*v.* 7) he shall *grow as the vine,* whose branches extend furthest of any tree. They shall be graceful and acceptable both to God and man. They are here compared to such trees as are pleasant, 1. To the sight: *His beauty shall be as the olive-tree,* which is always green, Jer. xi. 16. Ordinances are the beauty of the church. Holiness is the beauty of a soul. 2. To the smell: *His smell* shall be *as Lebanon* (*v.* 6) and his *scent* as *the wine of Lebanon, v.* 7. The church is compared to a *garden of spices* (Cant. iv. 12, 14). Grace is the perfume of the soul, Eccles. vii. 1. *The memorial thereof shall be as the wine of Lebanon* (so the margin reads it), their surviving honours when they are gone, shall be as *the wine of Lebanon,* that has a delicate flavour.

I. Concerning Ephraim, *v.* 8.

1. His repentance and reformation: *Ephraim shall say, What have I to do any more with idols?* As some read it, God here reasons and argues with him, why he should renounce idolatry: "*O Ephraim! what to me and idols? What concord* or agreement can there be *between me and idols?*" As we read it, God promises to bring Ephraim and keep him to this: *Ephraim shall say, What have I to do any more with idols?* He had promised (*v.* 3) not to *say any more to the works of his hands, You are my gods.* Ephraim had been *joined to idols* (*ch.* iv. 17), and yet God will work such a change in him that he shall loathe them as much as ever he loved them.

2. The gracious notice God is pleased to take of it: *I have heard him, and observed him. I have heard, and will look upon him;* so some read it. God *observed* Ephraim, to see whether he would bring forth fruits meet for this profession of repentance.

3. Before, Israel was compared to a tree, now God compares himself to one. "*I am like a green fir-tree,* and will be so to thee." He will be either *a sun and a shield* or a *shade and a shield,* according as their case requires. As the root of a tree: *From me is thy fruit found*—from him we receive grace and strength to enable us to do our duty. Whatever fruits of righteousness we bring forth, all the praise of them is due to God.

II. Concerning everyone that reads the words of the prophecy of this book (*v.* 9): *Who is wise? and he shall understand these things.* Those that are wise in the doing of their duty, that are prudent in practical religion, are most likely to know and understand the truths and providences of God, which are a mystery to others, John vii. 17. The right ways of God to those that are good are, and will be, a savour of life unto life: *The just shall walk in them. The transgressors shall fall* not only in their own wrong ways, but even *in the right ways of the Lord.*

JAMIESON, FAUSSET, BROWN

4. God's gracious reply to their self-condemning prayer. **backsliding**—*apostasy;* not merely occasional backslidings. God can heal the most desperate sinfulness [CALVIN]. **freely**—with a gratuitous, unmerited, and abundant love (Ezek. 16:60-63). So as to the spiritual Israel (John 15:16; Rom. 3:24; 5:8; I John 4:10). **5. as the dew**—which falls copiously in the East, taking the place of the more frequent rains in other regions. God will not be "as the early dew that goeth away," but constant (ch. 6:3, 4; Job 29:19; Prov. 19:12). **the lily**—No plant is more productive than the lily, one root often producing fifty bulbs [PLINY, H. N. 21. 5]. The common lily is white, consisting of six leaves opening like bells. The royal lily grows to the height of three or four feet; Matthew 6:29 alludes to the beauty of its flowers. **roots as Lebanon**—i.e., as the trees of Lebanon (especially the cedars), which cast down their roots as deeply as is their height upwards; so that they are immovable [JEROME], (Isa. 10:34). Spiritual growth consists most in the growth of the root which is out of sight. **6. branches**—shoots, or suckers. **beauty . . . as the olive**—which never loses its verdure. One plant is not enough to express the graces of God's elect people. The *lily* depicts its lovely growth; but as it wants duration and firmness, the deeply rooted cedars of Lebanon are added; these, however, are fruitless, therefore the fruitful, peace-bearing, fragrant, ever green *olive* is added. **smell as Lebanon**—which exhaled from it the fragrance of odoriferous trees and flowers. So Israel's name shall be in good savor with all (Gen. 27:27; Song of Sol. 4:11). **7.** *They that* used to *dwell under* Israel's *shadow* (but who shall have been forced to leave it), shall *return,* i.e., be restored (Ezek. 35:9). Others take "*His* shadow" to mean *Jehovah's* (cf. Ps. 17:8; 91:1; Isa. 4:6), which vss. 1, 2 ("*return* unto *the Lord* . . .") favor. But the "his" in vs. 6 refers to Israel, and therefore must refer to the same here. **revive as . . . corn**—As the corn long buried in the earth springs up, with an abundant produce, so shall they revive from their calamities, with a great increase of offspring (cf. John 12:24). **scent thereof**—i.e., Israel's *fame.* Cf. vs. 6, "His smell as Lebanon"; Song of Solomon 1:3: "Thy *name* is as ointment poured forth." LXX favors *Margin,* "memorial." **as the wine of Lebanon**—which was most celebrated for its aroma, flavor, and medicinal restorative properties. **8. Ephraim** *shall say*—being brought to penitence by God's goodness, and confessing and abhorring his past madness. **I have heard . . . and observed him**—I Jehovah have *answered* and *regarded* him *with favor;* the opposite of God's "hiding His face from" one (Deut. 31:17). It is the experience of God's favor, in contrast to God's wrath heretofore, that leads Ephraim to abhor his past idolatry. Jehovah *heard* and answered: whereas the idols, as Ephraim now sees, could not *hear,* much less answer. **I am . . . a green fir**—or cypress; ever green, winter and summer alike; the leaves not falling off in winter. **From me is thy fruit found**—"From Me," as the root. Thou needest go no farther than Me for the supply of all thy wants; not merely the *protection* implied by the *shadow* of the cypress, but that which the cypress has not, viz., *fruit,* all spiritual and temporal blessings. It may be also implied, that whatever spiritual graces Ephraim seeks for or may have, are not of themselves, but of God (Ps. 1:3; John 15:4, 5, 8; Jas. 1:17). God's promises to us are more our security for mortifying sin than our promises to God (Isa. 27:9). **9. EPILOGUE,** summing up the whole previous teaching. Here alone Hosea uses the term "righteous," so rare were such characters in his day. There is enough of saving truth clear in God's Word to guide those humbly seeking salvation, and enough of difficulties to confound those who curiously seek them out, rather than practically seek salvation. **fall**—stumble and are offended at difficulties opposed to their prejudices and lusts, or above their self-wise understanding (cf. Prov. 10:29; Mic. 2:7; Matt. 11:19; Luke 2:34; John 7:17; I Pet. 2:7, 8). To him who sincerely seeks the *agenda,* God will make plain the *credenda.* Christ is the foundation-stone to some: a stone of stumbling and rock of offense to others. The same sun softens wax and hardens clay. But their fall is the most fatal who fall in the ways of God, split on the Rock of ages, and suck poison out of the Balm of Gilead.

ADAM CLARKE

4. *I will heal their backsliding.* Here is the answer of God to these prayers and resolutions.

8. *What have I to do any more with idols?* The conversion of Ephraim is now as complete as it was sincere. God hears and observes this.

I am like a green fir tree. Perhaps these words should be joined to the preceding, as Newcome has done, and be a part of God's speech to Ephraim. "I have heard him; and I have seen him as a flourishing fir tree."

ALEXANDER MACLAREN:

"His beauty shall be as the olive-tree." Anybody that has ever seen a grove of olives knows that their beauty is not such as strikes the eye. If it was not for the blue sky overhead, that rays down glorifying light, they would not be much to look at or talk about. The tree has a gnarled, grotesque trunk which divides into insignificant branches, bearing leaves mean in shape, harsh in texture, with a silvery underside. It gives but a quivering shade and has no massiveness, nor symmetry. Ay! but there are olives on the branches. And so the beauty of the humble tree is in what it grows for man's good. After all, it is the outcome in fruitfulness which is the main thing about us. God's meaning, in all His gifts of dew, and beauty, and purity, and strength, is that we should be of some use in the world.

—*Expositions of Holy Scripture*

THE BOOK OF JOEL

I. Things present (1:1-2:27)
A. Locust plague and first meaning (1:1-20)
1. The call to contemplation (1:1-12)
2. The call to humiliation (1:13-20)
B. Locust plague and deeper teaching (2:1-27)
1. The trumpet of alarm and answer of God (2:1-14)
2. The trumpet of repentance and answer of God (2:15-27)

II. Things to come (2:28-3:21)
A. The dispensation of the Spirit (2:28-32)
1. Initiation and characteristics (2:28, 29)
2. Signs of ending and coming of the Day of the Lord (2:30, 31)
3. Deliverance from terrors of that Day (2:32)
B. The Day of the Lord (3:1-21)
1. God's dealing with His ancient people (3:1-8)
2. God's judgment of the nations (3:9-16)
3. The restoration of Israel (3:17-21)

We are uncertain concerning the time when this prophet prophesied; it is probable that it was about the same time that Amos prophesied. Hosea and Obadiah prophesied about the same time; and it appears that Amos prophesied in the days of Jeroboam II, king of Israel (Amos 7:10). God sent a variety of prophets, that they might strengthen the hands one of another.

In this prophecy:

I. The desolations made by hosts of noxious insects is described (ch. 1 and part of ch. 2).

II. The people are called to repentance (ch. 2).

III. Promises are made of the return of mercy upon their repentance (ch. 2), and promises of the pouring out of the Spirit in the latter days.

IV. The cause of God's people is pleaded against their enemies, whom God would in due time reckon with (ch. 3); and glorious things are spoken of Jerusalem and of the prosperity and perpetuity of it.

MATTHEW HENRY

CHAPTER 1

Verses 1–7

Joel here speaks of a sore judgment which was now brought, or to be brought, upon Judah, for their sins.

I. The judgment was such as could not be paralleled in the ages that were past, or in the memory of any living, *v.* 2. Those that outdo their predecessors in sin may expect to fall under greater judgments than any of their predecessors knew. It was such as would not be forgotten in the ages to come (*v.* 3): "*Tell you your children of it;* that they may take warning, and learn obedience by the things which you have suffered. Yea, let *your children tell their children, and their children another generation;* let them tell it to *teach their children* to stand in awe of God and of his judgments, and to tremble before him."

II. The judgment is an invasion of the country of Judea by a great army. Many interpreters both ancient and modern understand it of armies of men, the forces of the Assyrians, which, under Sennacherib, *took all the defended cities of Judah,* and made havoc of the country. Some make the four sorts of animals here named (*v.* 4) to signify the four monarchies which, in their turns, were oppressive to the Jews, one destroying what had escaped the fury of the other. But it seems much rather to be understood literally of armies of insects coming upon the land and eating up the fruits of it. The plague of locusts in Egypt lasted but for a few days; this seems to have continued for four years successively (as some think), because here are four sorts of insects mentioned (*v.* 4), but others think they came all in one year. Though a devastation by these insects is primarily intended here, yet it is expressed in language applicable to the destruction of the country by a foreign enemy. If this nation of worms do not subdue them, another nation shall come to ruin them. These animals are *locusts* and *caterpillars, palmer-worms* and *canker-worms, v.* 4. They were all little insects, but when they came in vast swarms they were formidable and ate up all before them. The weaker the instrument is that God employs the more is his power magnified.

III. A call to the drunkards to lament this judgment (*v.* 5): *Awake and weep, all you drinkers of wine.* It should touch them in a tender part; the *new wine* which they loved so well should be *cut off from their mouth.* The more men place their happiness in the gratifications of sense the more pressing temporal afflictions are upon them. The drinkers of water needed not to care when the vine was laid waste; they could live as well without it as they had done.

JAMIESON, FAUSSET, BROWN

CHAPTER 1

Vss. 1-20. The Desolate Aspect of the Country through the Plague of Locusts; the People Admonished to Offer Solemn Prayers in the Temple; for This Calamity Is the Earnest of a Still Heavier One. **1. Joel**—meaning, "Jehovah is God." **son of Pethuel**—to distinguish Joel the prophet from others of the name. Persons of eminence also were noted by adding the father's name. **2, 3.** A spirited introduction calling attention. **old men**—the best judges in question concerning the past (Deut. 32:7; Job 32:7). **Hath this been . . .**—i.e., Hath any *so grievous* a calamity *as this* ever been before? No such plague of locusts had been since the ones *in Egypt.* Exodus 10:14 is not at variance with this verse, which refers to *Judea,* in which Joel says there had been no such devastation before. **3. Tell ye your children**—in order that they may be admonished by the severity of the punishment to fear God (Ps. 78:6-8; cf. Exod. 13:8; Josh. 4:7). **4.** This verse states the subject on which he afterwards expands. Four species or stages of locusts, rather than four different insects, are meant (cf. Lev. 11:22). Lit., (1) the *gnawing* locust; (2) the *swarming* locust; (3) the *licking* locust; (4) the *consuming* locust; forming a climax to the most destructive kind. The last is often three inches long, and the two antennæ, each an inch long. The two hinder of its six feet are larger than the rest, adapting it for leaping. The first "kind" is that of the locust, having just emerged from the egg in spring, and without wings. The second is when at the end of spring, still in their first skin, the locusts put forth little ones without legs or wings. The third, when after their third casting of the old skin, they get small wings, which enable them to leap the better, but not to fly. Being unable to go away till their wings are matured, they devour all before them, grass, shrubs, and bark of trees: translated "rough caterpillars" (Jer. 51:27). The fourth kind, the matured winged locusts (see *Note,* Nah. 3:16). In ch. 2:25 they are enumerated in the reverse order, where the restoration of the devastations caused by them is promised. The Hebrews make the first species refer to Assyria and Babylon; the second species, to Medo-Persia; the third, to Greco-Macedonia and Antiochus Epiphanes; the fourth, to the Romans. Though the primary reference be to literal locusts, the Holy Spirit doubtless had in view the successive empires which assailed Judea, each worse than its predecessor, Rome being the climax. **5. Awake**—out of your ordinary state of drunken stupor, to realize the cutting off from you of your favorite drink. Even the drunkards (from a *Hebrew* root, "any strong drink") shall be forced to "howl," though usually laughing in the midst of the greatest national calamities, so palpably and universally shall the calamity affect all. **wine . . . new wine**—"New" or "fresh wine," in *Hebrew,* is the unfermented, and therefore unintoxicating, *sweet juice* extracted by pressure from grapes or other fruit, as *pomegranates* (Song of Sol. 8:2).

ADAM CLARKE

CHAPTER 1

2. *Hath this been in your days?* He begins very abruptly; and before he proposes his subject, excites attention and alarm by intimating that he is about to annnounce disastrous events, such as the oldest man among them has never seen, nor any of them learned from the histories of ancient times.

3. *Tell ye your children of it.* To heighten the effect, he still conceals the subject, and informs them that it is such as should be handed down from father to son through all generations.

4. *That which the palmerworm hath left.* Here he begins to open his message, and the words he chooses show that he is going to announce a devastation of the land by locusts, and a famine consequent on their depredations. What the different insects may be which he specifies is not easy to determine. I shall give the words of the original, with their etymology. The *palmerworm, gazam,* from the same root, "to cut short"; probably the caterpillar, from its cutting the leaves of the trees into pieces for its nourishment. The *locust, arbeh,* from *rabah,* "to multiply," from the immense increase and multitude of this insect. *Cankerworm, yelek,* from *lak,* "to lick or lap" with the tongue. *Caterpillar, chasil,* from *chasal,* "to consume, to eat up"; the consumer. Bishop Newcome translates the first "grasshopper"; the second, "locust"; the third, "devouring locust"; and the fourth, "consuming locust." After all that has been said by interpreters concerning these four animals, I am fully of opinion that the *arbeh,* or locust himself, is the *gazam,* the *yelek,* and the *chasil;* and that these different names are used here by the prophet to point out the locust in its different states, or progress from embryo to full growth. See the note on chap. ii. 2.

5. *Awake, ye drunkards.* The general destruction of vegetation by these devouring creatures has totally prevented both harvest and vintage. It is well-known that the ruin among the vines by locusts prevents the vintage for several years after.

MATTHEW HENRY

They are here called a *nation* (*v.* 6), because they act as it were with a common design; for, though *the locusts have no king, yet go they forth all of them by bands* (Prov. xxx. 27). They are said to have the *teeth of a lion* because of the great and terrible execution they do. Locusts become as lions when they come armed with a divine commission. They destroy not only the grass and corn, but the trees (*v.* 7): The *vine is laid waste.* These vermin eat the leaves which should be a shelter to the fruit while it ripens. They eat the very bark of the fig-tree, and so kill it. Thus the *fig-tree does not blossom,* nor is there *fruit in the vine.*

Verses 8–13

They are called to lament (*v.* 8), as a virgin laments the death of her lover to whom she was espoused, or as a young woman lately married, from whom the *husband of her youth,* or the husband to whom she was married when she was young, is suddenly taken away by death.

I. Let the husbandmen and vine-dressers lament, *v.* 11. They shall see the fruit of their labour eaten up before their eyes, and shall not be able to save any of it. *The field is laid waste* (*v.* 10); all is consumed that it produced; *the land mourns;* the ground has a melancholy aspect.

They are justly brought to lament the loss and want of the *wheat and barley.*

The trees are destroyed, not only the *vine and the fig-tree* (as before, *v.* 7), but the *pomegranate, palm-tree,* and *apple-tree,* all the *trees of the field,* as well as those of the orchard, timber-trees as well as fruit-trees. See what need we have to live in a continual dependence upon God and his providence, for our own hands are not sufficient for us.

II. Let the priests, the Lord's ministers, lament, for they share deeply in the calamity: *Gird yourselves* with sackcloth (*v.* 13). The ministers of the altar must *lament and howl.* "He is your God in a particular manner, and therefore it is expected that you should be more concerned than others for that which is a hindrance to the service of his sanctuary." As far as any public trouble is an obstruction to the course of religion it is to be upon that account, more than any other, sadly lamented, especially by the priests, the Lord's ministers.

JAMIESON, FAUSSET, BROWN

"Wine" is the produce of the grape alone, and is intoxicating (see *Note,* vs. 10). **6. nation**—applied to the locusts, rather than "people" (Prov. 30:25, 26), to mark not only their *numbers,* but also their *savage hostility;* and also to prepare the mind of the hearer for the transition to the figurative locusts in ch. 2, viz., the "nation" or *Gentile* foe coming against Judea. (cf. ch. 2:2). **my land**—i.e., Jehovah's; which never would have been so devastated were *I* not pleased to inflict punishment (ch. 2: 18; Isa. 14:25; Jer. 16:18; Ezek. 36:5; 38:16). **strong**—as irresistibly sweeping away before its compact body the fruits of man's industry. **without number**—so Judges 6:5; 7:12, "like grasshoppers (or "locusts") for multitude" (Jer. 46:23; Nah. 3:15). **teeth . . . lion**—i.e., the locusts are as destructive as a lion; there is no vegetation that can resist their bite (cf. Rev. 9:8). PLINY says "they gnaw even the doors of houses." **7. barked**—BOCHART, with LXX and *Syriac,* translates, from an *Arabic* root, "hath broken," viz., the topmost shoots, which locusts most feed on. CALVIN supports *English Version.* **my vine . . . my fig tree**—being in "My land," i.e., Jehovah's (vs. 6). As to the vine-abounding nature of ancient Palestine, see Numbers 13:23, 24. **cast it away**—down to the ground. **branches . . . white**—both from the bark being stripped off (Gen. 30:37), and from the branches drying up through the trunk, both bark and wood being eaten up below by the locusts. **8. Lament**—O "my land" (vs. 6; Isa. 24:4). **virgin . . . for the husband**—A virgin betrothed was regarded as married (Deut. 22:23; Matt. 1:19). The *Hebrew* for "husband" is "lord" or "possessor," the husband being considered the master of the wife in the East. **of her youth**—when the affections are strongest and when sorrow at bereavement is consequently keenest. Suggesting the thought of what Zion's grief ought to be for her separation from Jehovah, the betrothed husband of her early days (Jer. 2:2; Ezek. 16:8; Hos. 2:7; cf. Prov. 2:17; Jer. 3:4). **9.** The greatest sorrow to the mind of a religious Jew, and what ought to impress the whole nation with a sense of God's displeasure, is the cessation of the usual temple worship. **meat offering**—*Hebrew, mincha;* "meat" not in the English sense "flesh," but the unbloody offering made of flour, oil, and frankincense. As it and the drink offering or libation *poured out* accompanied every sacrificial *flesh* offering, the latter is included, though not specified, as being also "cut off," owing to there being no food left for man or beast. **priests . . . mourn**—not for their own loss of sacrificial perquisites (Num. 18:8-15), but because they can no longer offer the appointed offerings to Jehovah, to whom they minister. **10. field . . . land** differing in that "field" means the open, unenclosed country; "land," the rich *red* soil (from a root "to be red") fit for cultivation. Thus, "a man of the field," in *Hebrew,* is a hunter; a "man of the ground" or "land," an agriculturist (Gen. 25:27). "Field" and "land" are here personified. **new wine**—from a *Hebrew* root implying that it *takes possession* of the brain, so that a man is not master of himself. So the *Arabic* term is from a root "to hold captive." It is already fermented, and so intoxicating, unlike the *sweet fresh wine,* in vs. 5, called also "new wine," though a different *Hebrew* word. It and "the oil" stand for the vine and the olive tree, from which the "wine" and "oil" are obtained (vs. 12). **dried up**—not "ashamed," as *Margin,* as is proved by the parallelism to "languisheth," i.e., droopeth. **11. Be . . . ashamed**—i.e., Ye shall have the *shame* of disappointment on account of the failure of "the wheat" and "barley" "harvest." **howl . . . vine dressers**—The semicolon should follow, as it is the "husbandmen" who are to be "ashamed" "for the wheat." The reason for the "vine dressers" being called to "howl" does not come till vs. 12, "The vine is dried up." **12. pomegranate**—a tree straight in the stem growing twenty feet high; the fruit is of the size of an orange, with blood-red colored pulp. **palm tree**—The dates of Palestine were famous. The palm is the symbol of Judea on coins under the Roman emperor Vespasian. It often grows a hundred feet high. **apple tree**—The *Hebrew* is generic, including the orange, lemon, and pear tree. **joy is withered away**—such as is felt in the harvest and the vintage seasons (Ps. 4:7; Isa. 9:3). **13. Gird yourselves**—viz., with sackcloth; as in Isaiah 32:11, the ellipsis is supplied (cf. Jer. 4:8). **lament, ye priests**—as it is your duty to set the example to others; also as the guilt was greater, and a greater scandal was occasioned, by your sin to the cause of God. **come**—LXX, "enter" *the house of God* (cf. vs. 14). **lie all night in sackcloth**—so Ahab (I Kings 21:27). **ministers of my God**—(I Cor. 9: 13). Joel claims authority for his doctrine; it is

ADAM CLARKE

6. *A nation is come up upon my land.* That real locusts are intended there can be little doubt; but it is thought that this may be a double prophecy, and that the destruction by the Chaldeans may also be intended, and that the four kinds of locusts mentioned above may mean the four several attacks made on Judea by them: the first in the last year of Nabonassar (father of Nebuchadnezzar), which was the third of Jehoiakim; the second when Jehoiakim was taken prisoner in the eleventh year of his reign; the third in the ninth year of Zedekiah; and the fourth three years after, when Jerusalem was destroyed by Nebuchadnezzar. Others say that they mean four powers which have been enemies of the Jews: (1) The *palmerworm,* the Assyrians and Chaldeans. (2) The *locust,* the Persians and Medes. (3) The *cankerworm,* the Greeks, and particularly Antiochus Epiphanes. (4) The *caterpillar,* the Romans.

7. *He hath laid my vine waste.* The locusts have eaten off both leaves and bark. *Chasoph chasaphah, he hath made it clean bare; suddad sadeh,* "the field is laid waste," v. 10; and *kesod mishshaddai, a destruction from the Almighty,* v. 15, are all paronomasias, in which this prophet seems to delight.

8. *Lament like a virgin . . . for the husband of her youth. Virgin* is a very improper version here. The original is *bethulah,* which signifies a young woman or bride, not a virgin.

9. *The meat offering and the drink offering is cut off.* The crops and the vines being destroyed by the locusts, the total devastation in plants, trees, corn, etc., is referred to and described with a striking variety of expression in this and the following verses.

JOSEPH PARKER:

We need a Joel today. For his wages we would award him starvation. He would not live in kings' houses. There is nothing today in Church or state that does not need pulling to pieces, cross-examination, analysis, that all that is good therein—and there is much good—may be brought into new cohesion, and set to new and fuller uses. Men are bribing men, and then going to the Sunday school; many are saying, If you will get this property on these terms through my hands it will be on the understanding that—And the all but silent reply is, That will, of course, be understood. And then they go to church! If some Joel were to come he would be starved—he must be starved. No one ever came to do Messianic work who was not nailed and pierced and crucified. It is in vain to preach peace until we have first preached repentance; it is mischievous to say, Peace, peace, where there is no peace; it is iniquity in the sight of God to daub the wall with untempered mortar. Nothing is settled until it is settled at the foundations.

—*The People's Bible*

MATTHEW HENRY

Verses 14–20

Abundance of tears were shed for the destruction of the fruits of the earth by the locusts; now those tears must be turned into the right channel, that of repentance and humiliation before God.

I. A proclamation issued for a general fast. The priests are ordered to appoint one. Under public judgments there ought to be public humiliations. 1. A day is to be appointed for this purpose, a *day of restraint* (so the margin reads it), a day in which people must be restrained from their ordinary business. 2. It must be a *fast*, a religious abstaining from meat and drink, further than is of absolute necessity. Hereby we own ourselves unworthy of our necessary food, and that we have forfeited it. We punish ourselves and mortify the body. 3. There must be a solemn assembly. All had contributed to the national guilt, all shared in the national calamity, and therefore they must all join in the professions of repentance. 4. They must come together in the temple, *the house of the Lord* their *God*, because that was the house of prayer, and there they might hope to meet with God because it was the place which he had *chosen to put his name there*. 5. They must *sanctify* this fast, must observe it with sincere devotion.

II. Some considerations suggested to induce them to proclaim this fast and to observe it strictly.

1. God was beginning a controversy with them. It is time to *cry unto the Lord*, for *the day of the Lord is at hand*, *v.* 15. "The day of his judgment is very near, it is *at hand*; it *will not slumber*, and therefore you should not." It will be terrible. There is no fleeing from him but by fleeing to him.

2. They saw themselves already under the tokens of his displeasure. It is time to fast and pray, for their distress is very great, *v.* 16. Let them look into God's house, and see the effects of the judgment there; joy and gladness were *cut off from the house of God*.

3. The prophet returns to describe the grievousness of the calamity, in some particulars. Corn and cattle are the husbandman's staple commodities; now here he is deprived of both these. (1) The caterpillars have devoured the corn, *v.* 17. *The seed is rotten under the clods*, either through too much rain or for want of rain, or perhaps some insects underground ate it up. (2) The cattle perish too for want of grass (*v.* 18): *How do the beasts groan!* Even *the flocks of sheep*, which will live upon very short grass, *are made desolate*.

III. The prophet stirs them up to cry to God.

1. His own example (*v.* 19): *O Lord! to thee will I cry*. That which engaged him to *cry to God* was, not so much any personal affliction, as the national calamity: The *fire has devoured the pastures of the wilderness*, which seems to be meant of some parching scorching heat of the sun, which consumed them all.

2. The example of the inferior creatures: "*The beasts of the field* do not only *groan*, but *cry unto thee*, *v.* 20." The complaints of the brute-creatures here are for want of water, and for want of grass.

JAMIESON, FAUSSET, BROWN

in God's name and by His mission I speak to you.

14. Sanctify . . . a fast—Appoint a solemn fast. **solemn assembly**—lit., a "day of restraint" or cessation from work, so that all might give themselves to supplication (ch. 2:15, 16; I Sam. 7:5, 6; II Chron. 20:3-13). **elders**—The contrast to "children" (ch. 2:16) requires age to be intended, though probably elders in *office* are included. Being the people's leaders in guilt, they ought to be their leaders also in repentance.

15. day of the Lord—(ch. 2:1, 11); i.e., the day of His anger (Isa. 13:9; Obad. 15; Zeph. 1:7, 15). It will be a foretaste of the coming day of the Lord as Judge of all men, whence it receives the same name. Here the transition begins from the plague of locusts to the worse calamities (ch. 2) from invading armies about to come on Judea, of which the locusts were the prelude. **16.** Cf. vs. 9, and latter part of vs. 12. **joy**—which prevailed at the annual feasts, as also in the ordinary sacrificial offerings, of which the offerers ate before the Lord with gladness and thanksgivings (Deut. 12:6, 7, 12; 16:11, 14, 15). **17. is rotten**—"is dried up," "vanishes away," from an *Arabic* root [MAURER]. "Seed," lit., "grains." The drought causes the seeds to lose all their vitality and moisture. **garners**—granaries; generally underground, and divided into separate receptacles for the different kinds of grain. **18. cattle . . . perplexed**—implying the restless gestures of the dumb beasts in their inability to find food. There is a tacit contrast between the sense of the brute creation and the insensibility of the people. **yea, the . . . sheep**—*Even the sheep,* which are content with less rich pasturage, cannot find food. **are made desolate**—lit., "suffer punishment." The innocent brute shares the *punishment* of guilty man (Exod. 12:29; Jonah 3:7; 4:11). **19. to thee will I cry**—Joel here interposes, As this people is insensible to shame or fear and will not hear, I will leave them and address myself directly to Thee (cf. Isa. 15:5; Jer. 23:9). **fire**—i.e., the parching heat. **pastures**—"grassy places"; from a *Hebrew* root "to be pleasant." Such places would be selected for "habitations." But the *English Version* rendering is better than *Margin*. **20. beasts . . . cry . . . unto thee**—i.e., look up to heaven with heads lifted up, as if their only expectation was from God (Job 38:41; Ps. 104:21; 145:15; 147:9; cf. Ps. 42:1). They tacitly reprove the deadness of the Jews for not even now invoking God.

ADAM CLARKE

14. *Call a solemn assembly.* The clause should be translated—"Consecrate a fast, proclaim a time of restraint"; that is, of total abstinence from food, and from all secular employment. All the elders of the land and the representatives of the people were to be collected at the Temple to cry unto the Lord, to confess their sins, and pray for mercy. The Temple was not yet destroyed. This prophecy was delivered before the captivity of Judah.

18. *How do the beasts groan!* How do the horses *neigh!* How do the asses *bray!*

19. *O Lord, to thee will I cry.* Let this calamity come as it may, we have sinned, and should humble ourselves before God. *The fire hath devoured the pastures.* This may refer either to a drought or to the effects of the locusts.

20. *The beasts of the field cry also unto thee.* Even the cattle, wild and tame, are represented as supplicating God to have mercy upon them and send them provender! There is a similar affecting description of the effects of a drought in Jeremiah, chap. xiv. 6.

MATTHEW HENRY — CHAPTER 2

Verses 1–11

God contending with his own professing people for their sins and executing upon them the judgment written in the law (Deut. xxviii. 42), *The fruit of thy land shall the locust consume*, *v.* 60.

I. The war proclaimed (*v.* 1): *Blow the trumpet in Zion* to give notice to Judah and Jerusalem of the approach of the judgment, that they might *prepare to meet their God* by prayers and tears. It was the priests' business to sound the trumpet (Num. x. 8), both as an appeal to God in the day of their distress, and a summons to the people to come together to seek his face. It is the work of ministers to give warning from the word of God of the fatal consequences of sin.

II. A general idea given of the day of battle which is *nigh at hand*. It is the *day of the Lord*, the day of his judgment, *a day of darkness and gloominess* (*v.* 2), literally so, the swarms of locusts and caterpillars being so large and so thick as to darken the sky (Exod. x. 15). The darkness of this day will come as suddenly as the morning light, as irresistibly.

III. The army drawn up in array (*v.* 2): They are a *great people, and a strong*.

JAMIESON, FAUSSET, BROWN — CHAPTER 2

VSS. 1-32. THE COMING JUDGMENT A MOTIVE TO REPENTANCE. PROMISE OF BLESSINGS IN THE LAST DAYS. A more terrific judgment than that of the locusts is foretold, under imagery drawn from that of the calamity then engrossing the afflicted nation. He therefore exhorts to repentance, assuring the Jews of Jehovah's pity if they would repent. Promise of the Holy Spirit in the last days under Messiah, and the deliverance of all believers in Him. **1. Blow . . . trumpet**—to sound an alarm of coming war (Num. 10; Hos. 5:8; Amos 3:6); the office of the priests. Ch. 1:15 is an anticipation of the fuller prophecy in this chapter. **2. darkness . . . gloominess . . . clouds . . . thick darkness**—accumulation of synonyms, to intensify the picture of *calamity* (Isa. 8:22). Appropriate here, as the swarms of locusts intercepting the sunlight suggested *darkness* as a fit image of the coming visitation. **as the morning spread upon the mountains: a great people**—Substitute a comma for a colon after mountains: As the morning light spreads itself over the mountains, so a people *numerous* [MAURER] and strong shall spread themselves. The *suddenness* of the rising of the morning light, which gilds the mountain tops first, is less probably thought by others to be the point of comparison to the sudden inroad of the foe. MAURER refers it to the *yellow splendor* which arises from the reflection of the sunlight on the wings of the immense hosts of locusts as they approach. This is likely; understanding, however, that the locusts are only the symbols of human foes. The immense Assyrian host of invaders under Sennacherib (cf. Isa. 37:36) destroyed by God (vss. 18,

ADAM CLARKE — CHAPTER 2

1. *Blow ye the trumpet in Zion.* This verse also shows that the Temple was still standing. All assemblies of the people were collected by the sound of the trumpet. *The day of the Lord cometh.* This phrase generally means a day of judgment or punishment.

2. *A day of darkness,* etc. The depredations of the locusts are described from the second to the eleventh verses, and their destruction in the twentieth. Dr. Shaw, who saw locusts in Barbary in 1724 and 1725, thus describes them: "Those which I saw in 1724 and 1725 were much bigger than our common grasshopper; and had brown spotted wings, with legs and bodies of a bright yellow. Their first appearance was toward the latter end of March, the wind having been for some time south. In the middle of April their numbers were so vastly increased that, in the heat of the day, they formed themselves into large and numerous swarms; flew in the air like a succession of clouds; and as the prophet Joel expresses it (ii. 10), they darkened the sun. In the month of May, when the ovaries of those insects were ripe and turgid, each of these swarms began gradually to disappear; and retired into the plains, where they deposited their eggs. These were no sooner hatched in June than each of these broods collected itself into a compact body of a furlong or more square; and, marching immediately forward in the direction of the sea, they let nothing escape them; eating up everything that was green and juicy,

MATTHEW HENRY

The army is here described to be daring: They *are as horses*, as war-horses, and *as horsemen*, carried on with martial fire and fury, *so they shall run*, *v*. 4. Some of the ancients have observed that the head of a locust is very like, in shape, to the head of a horse.

They are loud and noisy—*like the noise of chariots* when driven furiously over rough ground, *on the tops of the mountains*, *v*. 5. The noise is like the *noise of a flame* that *devours the stubble*. When God's judgments are abroad they make a great noise. They are very regular, and keep ranks *as a strong people set in battle array* (*v*. 5). *They shall not break their ranks, nor one thrust another*, *v*. 7, 8.

IV. The terrible execution done by this formidable army, 1. In the country, *v*. 3. Look upon the fields that they have eaten up and they are *as a desolate wilderness*. 2. In the city. They shall *climb the wall* (*v*. 7), they shall *run upon the houses*, and *enter in at the windows like a thief* (*v*. 9).

V. The impressions upon the people. These enemies are invulnerable and therefore irresistible, *v*. 8. "One is in pain for his field, another for his vineyard, *and all faces gather blackness*." When God frowns upon men the lights of heaven will be small joy to them.

VI. The commander-in-chief of this formidable army is God himself, *v*. 11. And this makes the *great day* of the Lord *very terrible*.

Verses 12–17

God brings us into straits, that he may bring us to repentance and so bring us to himself. Here is a gracious invitation.

I. To a personal repentance, exercised in the soul. Everyone must mend one and mourn for one, and then we should all be mended.

1. What it is to repent, for it is the same that the Lord our God still requires of us. (1) We must be truly humbled for our sins, must be sorry we have by sin offended God, and ashamed we have by sin wronged ourselves. There must be outward expressions of sorrow and shame, *fasting*, and *weeping*, and *mourning*. But the outward expressions of sorrow must spring from within. And therefore it follows, *Rend your heart, and not your garments*. Rending the heart is that which God looks for and requires; that is the *broken and contrite heart* which he *will not despise*, Ps. li. 17. (2) We must be thoroughly converted to our God, and come home to him when we fall out with sin. *Turn you even to me, saith the Lord* (*v*. 12), and again (*v*. 13), *Turn unto the Lord your God*.

2. Arguments used to persuade this people thus to turn to the Lord *with all their hearts*. We are sure that he is a good God. We must *turn to the Lord our God*, not only because he has been just and righteous in punishing us for our sins, but because he is *gracious and merciful*, in receiving us upon our repentance. *He repents him of the evil*, not that he changes his mind, but, when the sinner's mind is changed, God's way towards him is changed; the sentence is reversed, and the curse of the law is taken off. There is no question at all but that if we truly repent of our sins God will forgive them, and be reconciled to us; but whether he will remove this or the other affliction which we are under may well be questioned, and yet the probability of it should encourage us to repent.

JAMIESON, FAUSSET, BROWN

20, 21), may be the primary objects of the prophecy; but ultimately the last antichristian confederacy, destroyed by special divine interposition, is meant (*Note*, ch. 3:2).

there hath not been ever the like–(Cf. ch. 1:2 and Exod. 10:14). **3. before . . . behind**–i.e., *on every side* (I Chron. 19:10). **fire . . . flame**–destruction . . . desolation (Isa. 10:17). **as . . . Eden . . . wilderness**–conversely (Isa. 51:3; Ezek. 36: 35). **4. appearance . . . of horses**–(Rev. 9:7). Not literal, but figurative locusts. The fifth trumpet, or first woe, in the parallel passage (Rev. 9), cannot be literal: for in Revelation 19:11 it is said, "they had *a king* over them, the angel of the bottomless pit–in the *Hebrew, Abaddon* ("destroyer"), but in the *Greek, Apollyon*"–and (Rev. 9:7) "on their heads were as it were *crowns* like gold, and their faces were as the faces of *men*." Cf. vs. 11, "the day of the Lord . . . great and very terrible"; implying their ultimate reference to be connected with Messiah's second coming in judgment. The locust's head is so like that of a horse that the Italians call it *cavalette*. Cf. Job 39:20, "the horse . . . as the grasshopper," or *locust*. **run**–The locust *bounds*, not unlike the horse's gallop, raising and letting down together the two front feet. **5. Like the noise of chariots**–referring to the loud sound caused by their wings in motion, or else the movement of their hind legs. **on the tops of mountains**–MAURER connects this with "they," i.e., the locusts, which first occupy the higher places, and thence descend to the lower places. It may refer (as in *English Version*) to "chariots," which make most noise in crossing over rugged heights. **6. much pained**–viz., with terror. The Arab proverb is, "More terrible than the locusts." **faces shall gather blackness**–(Isa. 13:8; Jer. 30:6; Nah. 2:10). MAURER translates, "withdraw their brightness," i.e., wax pale, lose color (cf. vs. 10 and ch. 3:15). **7-9.** Depicting the regular military order of their advance, "One locust not turning a nail's breadth out of his own place in the march" [JEROME]. Cf. Proverbs 30:27, "The locusts have no king, yet go they forth all of them *by bands*." **8. Neither shall one thrust another**–i.e., press upon so as to thrust his next neighbor out of his place, as usually occurs in a large multitude. **when they fall upon the sword**–i.e., among *missiles*. **not be wounded**–because they are protected by defensive armor [GROTIUS]. MAURER translates, "Their (the locusts') ranks are *not broken* when they rush among missiles" (cf. Dan. 11:22). **9. run to and fro in the city**–greedily seeking what they can devour. **the wall**–surrounding each house in Eastern buildings. **enter in at the windows**–though barred. **like a thief**–(John 10:1; cf. Jer. 9:21). **10. earth . . . quake before them**–i.e., the inhabitants of the earth quake with fear of them. **heavens . . . tremble**–i.e., the powers of heaven (Matt. 24:29); its illumining powers are disturbed by the locusts which intercept the sunlight with their dense flying swarms. These, however, are but the images of revolutions of states caused by such foes as were to invade Judea. **11. Lord . . . his army**–So among Mohammedans, "Lord of the locusts" is a title of God. **his voice**–His word of command to the locusts, and to the antitypical human foes of Judea, as "His army." **strong that executeth his word**–(Rev. 18: 8). **12.** With such judgments impending over the Jews, Jehovah Himself urges them to repentance. **also now**–*Even now*, what none could have hoped or believed possible, God still invites you to the hope of salvation. **fasting . . . weeping . . . mourning**–Their sin being most heinous needs extraordinary humiliation. The outward marks of repentance are to signify the depth of their sorrow for sin. **13.** Let there be the inward sorrow of heart, and not the mere outward manifestation of it by "rending the garment" (Josh. 7:6). **the evil**–the calamity which He had threatened against the impenitent. **14. leave . . . a meat offering and a drink offering**–i.e., give plentiful harvests, out of the first fruits of which we may offer the meat and drink offering, now "cut off" through the famine (ch. 1:9, 13, 16). "Leave *behind Him*": as God in visiting His people now has left behind Him a curse, so He will, on returning to visit them, leave behind Him a blessing.

ADAM CLARKE

not only the lesser kinds of vegetables, but the vine likewise; the fig tree, the pomegranate, the palm, and the apple tree, even all the trees of the field, Joel i. 12; in doing which they kept their ranks like men of war; climbing over, as they advanced, every tree or wall that was in their way. Nay, they entered into our very houses and bedchambers, like so many thieves. The inhabitants, to stop their progress, made a variety of pits and trenches all over their fields and gardens, which they filled with water; or else they heaped up in them heath, stubble, and suchlike combustible matter, which were severally set on fire upon the approach of the locusts. But this was all to no purpose, for the trenches were quickly filled up, and the fires extinguished, by infinite swarms succeeding one another; while the front was regardless of danger, and the rear pressed on so close that a retreat was altogether impossible. A day or two after one of these broods was in motion, others were already hatched to march and glean after them; gnawing off the very bark, and the young branches, of such trees as had before escaped with the loss only of their fruit and foliage. So justly have they been compared by the prophet Joel (chap. ii. 3) to a great army; who further observes, that 'the land is as the garden of Eden before them, and behind them a desolate wilderness.'" *A day of darkness.* They sometimes obscure the sun. *As the morning spread upon the mountains.* They appeared suddenly, as the sun, in rising behind the mountains, shoots his rays over them.

3. *A fire devoureth before them.* They consume like a general conflagration. "They destroy the ground, not only for the time, but burn trees for two years after" (Sir Hans Sloane, *Nat. Hist. of Jamaica*, I., 29). *Behind them a flame burneth.* "Wherever they feed," says Ludolf, in his *History of Ethiopia*, "their leavings seem as if parched with fire." *Nothing shall escape them.* "After devouring the herbage," says Adanson, "with the fruits and leaves of trees, they attacked even the buds and the very bark; they did not so much as spare the reeds with which the huts were thatched."

4. *The appearance of horses.* The head of the locust is remarkably like that of the horse. On this account the Italians call them *cavaletta*, cavalry.

5. *Like the noise of chariots.* Bochart remarks: "The locusts fly with a great noise, so as to be heard six miles off, and while they are eating the fruits of the earth, the sound of them is like that of a flame driven by the wind."

6. *All faces shall gather blackness.* Universal mourning shall take place, because they know that such a plague is irresistible.

7. *Like mighty men . . . like men of war* (*and as horsemen*, v. 4). The prophet does not say they are such, but they resemble. *They shall not break their ranks.* See the account on v. 2, from Dr. Shaw.

8. *They shall not be wounded.* They have hard scales like a coat of mail; but the expression refers to the utter uselessness of all means to prevent their depredations. See Shaw's account above.

10. *The earth shall quake . . . the heavens shall tremble.* Poetical expressions, to point out universal consternation and distress. *The sun and the moon shall be dark.* Bochart relates that "their multitude is sometimes so immense as to obscure the heavens for the space of twelve miles!"

11. *The Lord shall utter his voice.* Such a mighty force seems as if summoned by the Almighty, and the noise they make in coming announces their approach, while yet afar off.

12. *Turn ye even to me.* Three means of turning are recommended: *fasting, weeping, mourning*, i.e., continued sorrow.

13. *Rend your heart.* Let it not be merely a rending of your garments, but let your hearts be truly contrite. *And repenteth him of the evil.* Is ever ready to "change His purpose" to destroy, when He finds the culprit willing to be saved.

14. *Who knoweth if he will return?* He may yet interpose and turn aside the calamity threatened, and so far preserve the land from these ravagers that there will be food for men

MATTHEW HENRY

II. They are here called to a public national repentance, as a national act, for the glory of God, and that the neighbouring nations might know what it was that qualified them for God's gracious returns in mercy to them. The congregation must be called together, *v.* 15, 16. The trumpet was blown (*v.* 1), to sound an *alarm of war*; but now it must be blown in order to a treaty of peace. What was said *ch.* i. 14 is here repeated: "*Call a solemn assembly; gather the people; sanctify the congregation;* appoint a time for solemn preparation beforehand and put them in mind to prepare themselves. Let not the greatest be excused, but *assemble the elders,* the judges and magistrates. Let not the meanest be passed by, but *gather the children, and those that suck the breasts.*" Private joys must give way to public sorrows, both those for affliction and those for sin. The priests, *the Lord's ministers,* must preside in the congregation, and be God's mouth to the people, and theirs to God. They must officiate *between the porch and the altar.* There the people must see them weeping and wrestling, like their father Jacob, and be helped into the same devout frame. Their petition must be, *Spare thy people, O Lord!* "Let not the heathen make them *a proverb,* or a *by-word*" (so some read it); "let it never be said, *As poor and beggarly as an Israelite.*"

Verses 18–27

They prayed that God would *spare them,* and see here with what *good words and comfortable words* he answered them; for God's promises are real answers to the prayers of faith.

I. Whence this mercy promised shall take rise (*v.* 18): God will be *jealous for his land* and *pity his people.* He will restore them their forfeited comforts.

II. Instances of his mercy: 1. The destroying army shall be dispersed and defeated (*v.* 20): "*I will remove far off from you the northern army,* that army of locusts and caterpillars that invaded you from the north. Nothing shall remain of these swarms of insects but the ill savour of them. "Many interpreters, by this northern army, understand that of Sennacherib, which was dispersed when God by it had *accomplished his whole work upon Mount Zion and upon Jerusalem,* Isa. x. 12.

It is promised (*v.* 22) that *the pastures of the wilderness,* the pastures which the locusts had left as bare as the wilderness, shall again *spring* and the *trees shall again bear their fruit,* particularly the *fig-tree and the vine.* It shall be, for (*v.* 23) *the Lord has given* and will give you *the former rain and the latter rain,* and will give them moderately, and in due season, the *latter rain in the first month,* when it was wanted and expected.

III. What use shall be made of these returns of God's mercy.

1. God shall have the glory for they shall *rejoice in the Lord their God* (*v.* 23), and not praise their idols, nor call their corn and wine the *rewards that their lovers had given them.*

JAMIESON, FAUSSET, BROWN

15. Blow the trumpet—to convene the people (Num. 10:3). Cf. ch. 1:14. The nation was guilty, and therefore there must be a national humiliation. Cf. Hezekiah's proceedings before Sennacherib's invasion (II Chron. 30). **16. sanctify the congregation**—viz., by expiatory rites and purification with water [CALVIN], (Exod. 19:10, 22). MAURER translates, "appoint a solemn assembly," which would be a tautological repetition of vs. 15. **elders . . . children**—No age was to be excepted (II Chron. 20:13). **bridegroom**—ordinarily exempted from public duties (Deut. 24: 5; cf. I Cor. 7:5, 29). **closet**—or, nuptial bed, from a *Hebrew* root "to cover," referring to the canopy over it. **17. between the porch and . . . altar**—the porch of Solomon's temple on the east (I Kings 6:3); the altar of burnt offerings in the court of the priests, before the porch (II Chron. 8:12; cf. Ezek. 8:16; Matt. 23:35). The suppliants thus were to stand with their backs to the altar on which they had nothing to offer, their faces towards the place of the Shekinah presence. **heathen should rule over them**—This shows that not locusts, but human foes, are intended. The *Margin* translation, "use a byword against them," is not supported by the *Hebrew.* **wherefore should they say . . . , Where is their God?**—i.e., do not for thine own honor's sake, let the heathen sneer at the God of Israel, as unable to save His people (Ps. 79:10; 115:2). **18. Then**—when God sees His people penitent. **be jealous for his land**—as a husband *jealous* of any dishonor done to the wife whom he loves, as if done to himself. The *Hebrew* comes from an *Arabic* root, "to be flushed in face" through indignation. **19. corn . . . wine . . . oil**—rather, as *Hebrew,* "*the* corn . . . *the* wine . . . *the* oil," viz., which the locusts have destroyed [HENDERSON]. MAURER not so well explains, "the corn, etc., necessary for your sustenance." "The Lord will *answer,*" viz., the prayers of His people, priests, and prophets. Cf. in the case of Sennacherib, II Kings 19:20, 21. **20. the northern** *army*—The *Hebrew* expresses that the *north* in relation to Palestine is not merely the quarter whence the invader comes, but is his native land, "the Northlander"; viz., the Assyrian or Babylonian (cf. Jer. 1:14, 15; Zeph. 2:13). The locust's native country is not the *north,* but the *south,* the deserts of Arabia, Egypt, and Libya. Assyria and Babylon are the type and forerunner of all Israel's foes (Rome, and the final Antichrist), from whom God will at last deliver His people, as He did from Sennacherib (II Kings 19:35). **face . . . hinder part**—more applicable to a human army's *van* and *rear,* than to locusts. The northern invaders are to be dispersed in every other direction but that from which they had come: "a land barren and desolate," i.e., Arabia Deserta: "the eastern (or *front*) sea," i.e., the Dead Sea: "the utmost (or *hinder*) sea," i.e., the Mediterranean. *In front* and *behind* mean east and west; as, in marking the quarters of the world, they *faced* the east, which was therefore "in front"; the west was *behind* them; the south was on their *right,* and the north on their *left.* **stink**—metaphor from *locusts,* which perish when blown by a storm into the sea or the desert, and emit from their putrefying bodies such a stench as often breeds a pestilence. **because he hath done great things**—i.e., because the invader hath *haughtily magnified himself in his doings.* Cf. as to Sennacherib, II Kings 19:11-13, 22, 28. This is quite inapplicable to the locusts, who merely seek food, not self-glorification, in invading a country. **21-23.** In an ascending gradation, the *land* destroyed by the enemy, *the beasts of the field,* and the *children of Zion,* the land's inhabitants, are addressed. the former two by personification. **Lord will do great things**—In contrast to the "great things" done by the haughty foe (vs. 20) to the hurt of Judah stand the "great things" to be done by Jehovah for her benefit (cf. Ps. 126:2, 3). **22.** (Zech. 8:12). As before (ch. 1:18, 20) he represented the beasts as *groaning* and *crying* for want of food in the "pastures," so now he reassures them by the promise of *springing pastures.* **23. rejoice in the Lord**—not merely *in the springing pastures,* as the brute "beasts" which cannot raise their thoughts higher (Isa. 61:10; Hab. 3:18). **former rain . . . the rain . . . the former . . . the latter rain**—The autumnal, or "former rain," from the middle of October to the middle of December, is put first, as Joel prophesies in summer when the locusts' invasion took place, and therefore looks to the time of early sowing in autumn, when the autumnal rain was indispensably required. Next, "the rain," *generically,* lit., "the showering" or "heavy rain." Next, the two species of the latter, "the former and the latter rain" (in March and April). The repetition of the "former rain" implies that He will give it not merely for the

ADAM CLARKE

and cattle, and a sufficiency of offerings for the Temple service. Therefore—

15. *Blow the trumpet.* Let no time be lost, let the alarm be sounded.

16. *Gather the children.* Let all share in the humiliation, for all must feel the judgment, should it come. Let no state nor condition among the people be exempted. The elders, the young persons, the infants, the bridegroom, and the bride; let all leave their houses, and go to the temple of God.

17. *Let the priests . . . weep between the porch and the altar.* The altar of burnt offerings stood before the porch of the Temple, 1 Chron. viii. 12, and between them there was an open space of fifteen or twenty cubits. It was there that the priests prostrated themselves on such occasions. *Let them say.* The following was the form to be used on this occasion, *Spare thy people.* And if this be done with a rent heart, "then will the Lord be jealous for his land, and pity his people," v. 18. He will surely save if you seriously return to and penitently seek Him.

20. *I will remove far off from you the northern army.* "That is, the *locusts;* which might enter Judea by the *north.* Or the locusts may be thus called, because they spread terror like the *Assyrian* armies, which entered Judea by the *north.* See Zeph. ii. 13."—Newcome. Syria, which was northward of Judea, was infested with them; and it must have been a northern wind that brought them into Judea in the time of Joel; as God promises to change this wind, and carry them into a barren and desolate land, Arabia Deserta. *His face toward the east sea,* i.e., the Dead Sea, which lay eastward of Jerusalem. *His hinder part toward the utmost sea,* the western sea, i.e., the Mediterranean. and his stink shall come up. After having been drowned by millions in the Mediterranean, the reflux of the tide has often brought them back and thrown them in heaps upon the shore, where they putrefied in such a manner as to infect the air and produce pestilence, by which both men and cattle have died in great multitudes. See Bochar, *Hieroz.,* ii, 481. Livy, and St. Augustine after him, relate that there was such an immense crowd of locusts in Africa that, having eaten up every green thing, a wind arose that carried them into the sea, where they perished; but being cast upon the shore, they putrefied, and bred such a pestilence that 80,000 men died of it in the kingdom of Massinissa, and 30,000 in the garrison of Utica, in which only 10 remained alive. See Livy, lib. xc, and August. *De Civitate Dei,* lib. iv, c. 31. *Because he hath done great things.* Or, *ki,* "although" he have done great things, or, "after" he has done them, i.e., in almost destroying the whole country.

21. *Fear not . . . for the Lord will do great things.* The words are repeated from the preceding verse; Jehovah will do great things in driving them away, and supernaturally restoring the land to fertility.

MATTHEW HENRY

All their losses shall be repaired (*v.* 25): "*I will restore to you the years that the locust has eaten;* you shall be comforted according to the time that you have been afflicted, and shall have years of plenty to balance the years of famine." Look into the stores and you shall find *the floors full of wheat, and the vats overflowing with wine and oil* (*v.* 24), whereas, in the day of their distress, the *wine and oil languished* and *the barns were broken down, ch.* i. 10, 17. Some expositors understand these promises figuratively, as pointing at gospel-grace. When God sends us his promises to be the matter of our comfort, his graces to be the grounds of it, and his Spirit to be the author of it, he has sent us (according to his promise here, *v.* 19) *corn, and wine, and oil,* or that which is unspeakably better.

2. They shall have the comfort, and spiritual benefit, thereof. Their reputation shall be retrieved (*v.* 19): "*I will no more make you a reproach among the heathen,* that triumphed in your calamities and insulted over you; and *v.* 26, 27. Their joys shall be revived (*v.* 23). They shall *rejoice in the Lord their God,* not so much in the good things themselves that are given them as in the good hand that gives them. The *joy of harvest* and the joy of a feast must both terminate in God, whose love we should taste in all the gifts of his bounty, that we may make him our chief joy, as he is our chief good, and the fountain of all good to us. Their faith in God shall be confirmed and increased. This is promised here (*v.* 27): *You shall know that I am in the midst of Israel,* the *Holy One in the midst of thee* (Hos. xi. 9), *and that I am the Lord your God, and none else.* We should labour to grow in our acquaintance with God by all providences, both merciful and afflictive.

Verses 28–32

The promises of corn, and wine, and oil, would be acceptable to a wasted country; but we must not rest in those things. These verses have reference to better things, both the kingdom of grace and the kingdom of glory.

I. How the kingdom of grace shall be introduced by a plentiful *effusion of the Spirit, v.* 28, 29. The apostle Peter has given us an assurance that when the Spirit was poured out upon the apostles, on the day of Pentecost (Acts ii. 1, &c.), that was the very thing *which was spoken of here by the prophet Joel, v.* 16, 17. We often read in the Old Testament of the Spirit of the Lord coming by drops, as it were, upon the judges and prophets whom God raised up for extraordinary services; but now the Spirit shall be poured out plentifully in a full stream, as was promised, Isa. xliv. 3. The time fixed for this is *afterwards*; after the fulfilling of the foregoing promises this shall be fulfilled. The Spirit shall be *poured out upon all flesh,* not as hitherto upon Jews only, but upon Gentiles also; for in Christ there is no distinction between Jew and Greek, Rom. x. 11, 12. The Jews understand it of all flesh in the land of Israel, and Peter himself did not fully understand it as speaking of the Gentiles till he saw it accomplished in the descent of the Holy Ghost upon Cornelius and his friends, who were Gentiles (Acts x. 44, 45), which was but a continuation of the same gift which was bestowed on the day of Pentecost. "*Your old men,* who are past their vigour and whose spirits begin to decay, *your young men,* who have yet but little experience of divine things, shall yet *dream dreams* and *see visions*; God will reveal himself by dreams and visions both to young and old.

JAMIESON, FAUSSET, BROWN

exigence of that particular season when Joel spake, but also for the future in the regular course of nature, the autumn and the spring rain; the former being put first, in the order of nature, as being required for the sowing in autumn, as the latter is required in spring for maturing the young crop. The *Margin,* "a teacher of righteousness," is wrong. For the same *Hebrew* word is translated "former rain" in the next sentence, and cannot therefore be differently translated here. Besides, Joel begins with the inferior and temporal blessings, and not till vs. 28 proceeds to the higher and spiritual ones, of which the former are the pledge. **moderately**—rather, "in due measure," as much as the land requires; lit., "according to right"; neither too much nor too little, either of which extremes would hurt the crop (cf. Deut. 11:14; Prov. 16:15; Jer. 5:24; *Note,* Hos. 6:3). The phrase, "in due measure," in this clause is parallel to "in the first month," in the last clause (i.e., "*in the month* when *first* it is needed," each rain in its proper season). Heretofore the *just* or *right* order of nature has been interrupted through your sin; now God will restore it. **24.** The effect of the seasonable rains shall be abundance of all articles of food. **25. locust . . . cankerworm . . . caterpiller . . . palmer worm**—the reverse order from ch. 1:4, where (see *Note*) God will restore not only what has been lost by the full-grown *consuming locust,* but also what has been lost by the less destructive *licking locust,* and *swarming locust,* and *gnawing locust.* **26. never be ashamed**—shall no longer endure the "reproach of the heathen (vs. 17), [Maurer]; or rather, "shall not bear the shame of disappointed hopes," as the husbandmen had heretofore (ch. 1: 11). So spiritually, waiting on God, His people shall not have the shame of disappointment in their expectations from Him (Rom. 9:33). **27. know that I am in the midst of Israel**—As in the Old Testament dispensation God was present by the Shekinah, so in the New Testament first, for a brief time by the Word made flesh dwelling among us (John 1:14), and to the close of this dispensation by the Holy Spirit in the Church (Matt. 28:20), and probably in a more perceptible manner with Israel when restored (Ezek. 37:26-28). **never be ashamed**—not an unmeaning repetition from vs. 26. The twice-asserted truth enforces its unfailing certainty. As the "shame" in vs. 26 refers to temporal blessings, so in this verse it refers to the spiritual blessings flowing from the presence of God with His people (cf. Jer. 3:16, 17; Rev. 21:3). **28. afterward**—"in the last days" (Isa. 2:2) under Messiah *after* the invasion and deliverance of Israel from the *northern army.* Having heretofore stated the outward blessings, he now raises their minds to the expectation of extraordinary spiritual blessings, which constitute the true restoration of God's people (Isa. 44:3). Fulfilled in earnest (Acts 2:17) on Pentecost; among the Jews and the subsequent election of a people among the Gentiles; hereafter more fully at the restoration of Israel (Isa. 54:13; Jer. 31:9, 34; Ezek. 39:29; Zech. 12:10) and the consequent conversion of the whole world (Isa. 2:2; 11:9; 66:18-23; Mic. 5:7; Rom. 11:12, 15). As the Jews have been the seedmen of the elect Church gathered out of Jews and Gentiles, the first Gospel preachers being Jews from Jerusalem, so they shall be the harvest-men of the coming world-wide Church, to be set up at Messiah's appearing. That the promise is not *restricted* to the first Pentecost appears from Peter's own words: "The promise is [not only] unto you and to your children, [but also] to *all that are afar off* [both in space and in time], even as many as the Lord our God shall call" (Acts 2:39). So here "upon *all* flesh." I will *pour out*—under the new covenant: not merely, *let fall drops,* as under the Old Testament (John 7:39). **my spirit**—the Spirit "proceeding from the Father and the Son," and at the same time one with the Father and the Son (cf. Isa. 11:2). **sons . . . daughters . . . old . . . young**—not merely on a privileged few (Num. 11:29) as the prophets of the Old Testament, but men of all ages and ranks. See Acts 21:9, and I Corinthians 11: 5, as to "daughters," i.e., women, prophesying. **dreams . . . visions**—(Acts 9:10; 16:9). The "dreams" are attributed to the "old men," as more in accordance with their years; "visions" to the "young men," as adapted to their more lively minds. The three modes whereby God revealed His will under the Old Testament (Num. 12:6), "prophecy, dreams, and visions," are here made the symbol of the full manifestation of Himself to all His people, not only in miraculous gifts to some, but by His indwelling Spirit to all in the New Testament (John 14:21, 23; 15:15). In Acts 16:9, and 18:9, the term used is "vision," though in the night, not a *dream.*

ADAM CLARKE

23. *The former rain moderately. Hammoreh litsedakah,* "the former rain in righteousness," that is, in due time and in just proportion. This rain fell after autumn, the other in spring. See Hos. vi. 3. *In the first month. Barishon,* "as aforetime."

25. *I will restore . . . the years.* It has already been remarked that the locusts not only destroyed the produce of that year, but so completely ate up all buds, and barked the trees, that they did not recover for some years. Here God promises that He would either prevent or remedy that evil; for He would restore the years that the locusts, cankerworm, caterpillar, and palmerworm had eaten.

26. *Praise the name of the Lord your God, that hath dealt wondrously with you.* In so destroying this formidable enemy; and so miraculously restoring the land to fertility, after so great a devastation.

28. *Shall come to pass afterward.* "After this"; the same, says Kimchi, as "in the latter days," which always refers to the "days of the Messiah"; and thus this prophecy is to be interpreted. We have the testimony of St. Peter, Acts ii. 17, that this prophecy relates to that mighty effusion of the Holy Spirit which took place after the Day of Pentecost.

Your sons and your daughters shall prophesy. Shall "preach"—exhort, pray, and instruct, so as to benefit the Church.

MATTHEW HENRY

They shall prophesy; they shall receive new discoveries of divine things, and that not for their own use only, but for the benefit of the church. They shall interpret scripture, and speak of things distant, and future. By these extraordinary gifts the Christian church was first founded and set up, and the scriptures were written, and the ministry settled.

II. How the kingdom of glory shall be introduced by the change of nature, *v.* 30, 31. The pouring out of the Spirit will be very comfortable to the righteous; but let the unrighteous hear this and tremble. There is a great and terrible day of the Lord coming. It will be accomplished in full at the end of time. It was accomplished in part in the death of Christ (which is called the *judgment of this world,* when the earth quaked and the sun was darkened), and in the destruction of Jerusalem, which was a figure of the general judgment. The judgments of God upon a sinful world, and the frequent destruction of wicked kingdoms by fire and sword, are presages of the judgment of the world in the last day.

III. The safety and happiness of all true believers both in the first and second coming of Jesus Christ, *v.* 32. This speaks of particular persons, for to them the New Testament has more respect, and less to kingdoms and nations, than the Old. Though the day of the Lord will be great and terrible, yet *in Mount Zion and in Jerusalem there shall be deliverance* from the terror of it. Christ is himself not only the *Saviour,* but *the salvation;* he is so *to the ends of the earth.* This deliverance, laid up for us in the covenant of grace, is in performance of the promises made to the fathers. See Luke i. 72. There is a remnant interested in this salvation, and for whom the deliverance is wrought. *Christ in you, the hope of glory.* Those that sincerely call upon God: *Whosoever shall call on the name of the Lord,* whether Jew or Gentile, Rom. x. 13, *shall be delivered.* This calling on God supposes knowledge of him, faith in him, desire towards him, dependence on him, and a conscientious obedience to him; for, without that, crying *Lord, Lord,* will not stand us in any stead.

JAMIESON, FAUSSET, BROWN

No other dream is mentioned in the New Testament save those given to Joseph in the very beginning of the New Testament, before the full Gospel had come; and to the wife of Pilate, a *Gentile* (Matt. 1:20; 2:13; 27:19). "Prophesying" in the New Testament is applied to all speaking under the enlightenment of the Holy Spirit, and not merely to foretelling events. All true Christians are "priests" and "ministers" of our God (Isa. 61:6), and have the Spirit (Ezek. 36:26, 27). Besides this, probably, a special gift of prophecy and miracle-working is to be given at or before Messiah's coming again. **29. And also**—"And even." The very slaves by becoming the Lord's servants are His freemen (I Cor. 7:22; Gal. 3:28; Col. 3:11; Philemon 16). Therefore, in Acts 2:18 it is quoted, "*My* servants" and "*My* handmaidens"; as it is only by becoming *the Lord's* servants they are spiritually free, and partake of the same spirit as the other members of the Church. **30, 31.** As Messiah's manifestation is full of joy to believers, so it has an aspect of wrath to unbelievers, which is represented here. Thus when the Jews received Him not in His coming of grace, He came in judgment on Jerusalem. Physical prodigies, massacres, and conflagrations preceded its destruction [JOSEPHUS, J. B.]. To these the language here may allude; but the figures chiefly symbolize political revolutions and changes in the ruling powers of the world, prognosticated by previous disasters (Amos 8:9; Matt. 24:29; Luke 21:25-27), and convulsions such as preceded the overthrow of the Jewish polity. Such shall probably occur in a more appalling degree before the final destruction of the ungodly world ("the great and terrible day of Jehovah," cf. Mal. 4:5), of which Jerusalem's overthrow is the type and earnest. **32. call on . . . name of . . . Lord**—*Hebrew,* JEHOVAH. Applied to Jesus in Romans 10:13 (cf. Acts 9:14; I Cor. 1:2). Therefore, Jesus is JEHOVAH; and the phrase means, "Call on Messiah in His divine attributes." **shall be delivered**—as the Christians were, just before Jerusalem's destruction, by retiring to Pella, warned by the Saviour (Matt. 24:16); a type of the spiritual deliverance of all believers, and of the last deliverance of the elect "remnant" of Israel from the final assault of Antichrist. "In Zion and Jerusalem" the Saviour first appeared; and there again shall He appear as the *Deliverer* (Zech. 14:1-5). **as the Lord hath said**—Joel herein refers, not to the other prophets, but to his own words preceding. **call**—metaphor from an invitation to a feast, which is an act of gratuitous kindness (Luke 14:16). So the remnant called and saved is according to the election of grace, not for man's merits, power, or efforts (Rom. 11:5).

ADAM CLARKE

29. *And also upon the servants and upon the handmaids.* The gifts of teaching and instructing men shall not be restricted to any one class or order of people. And this God has done, and is still doing. He left the line of Aaron, and took His apostles indiscriminately from any tribe. He passed by the regular order of the priesthood, and the public schools of the most celebrated doctors, and took His evangelists from among fishermen, tentmakers, and even the Roman taxgatherers. And He, lastly, passed by the Jewish tribes, and took the Gentile converts, and made them preachers of righteousness to the inhabitants of the whole earth.

30. *Wonders in the heavens and in the earth.* This refers to those dreadful sights, dreadful portents, and destructive commotion by which the Jewish polity was finally overthrown, and the Christian religion established in the Roman empire. See how our Lord applies this prophecy, Matt. xxiv. 29.

31. *The sun shall be turned into darkness.* The Jewish polity, civil and ecclesiastical, shall be entirely destroyed. *Before the great and the terrible day of the Lord come.* In the taking and sacking of Jerusalem, and burning of the Temple, by the Romans, under Titus, the son of Vespasian.

32. *For in Mount Zion and in Jerusalem.* Our blessed Lord first began to preach the gospel in Mount Zion, in the Temple, and throughout Jerusalem. There He formed His Church, and thence He sent His apostles and evangelists to every part of the globe.

MATTHEW HENRY — CHAPTER 3

Verses 1-8

The *year of the redeemed,* and the *year of recompences for the controversy of Zion.* A prophecy of what shall be done whenever it comes, for it comes often, and at the end of time it will come once for all.

I. It shall be the *year of the redeemed,* for God will *bring again the captivity of Judah and Jerusalem, v.* 1. Though the bondage of God's people may be grievous and long, yet it shall not be everlasting. That in Egypt ended at length. *Let my son go, that he may serve me.* That in Babylon shall likewise end well. And the Lord Jesus will provide for the effectual redemption of enslaved souls from under the dominion of sin and Satan, and will proclaim that *acceptable year,* and the *opening of the prison to those that were bound.*

II. It shall be the *year of recompences for the controversy of Zion.* God will lead captivity captive (Ps. lxviii. 18), will lead those captive that led his people captive, Rev. xiii. 10. All nations had made themselves liable to the judgment of God for wrong done to his people. Whatsoever nation injured God's nation, they should not go unpunished; for he that touches the Israel of God shall be made to know that he touches the apple of his eye.

They shall all be *gathered* (*v.* 2). They shall be *brought down into the valley of Jehoshaphat,* which lay near Jerusalem, and there *God will plead with them.* It was in this valley of Jehoshaphat (as Dr. Lightfoot suggests) that Sennacherib's army, or part of it, lay, when it was destroyed by an angel. This prosecution is set on foot *for my people,* and *for my heritage Israel.*

JAMIESON, FAUSSET, BROWN — CHAPTER 3

Vss. 1-21. GOD'S VENGEANCE ON ISRAEL'S FOES IN THE VALLEY OF JEHOSHAPHAT. HIS BLESSING ON THE CHURCH. **1. bring again the captivity**—i.e., reverse it. The Jews restrict this to the return from Babylon. Christians refer it to the coming of Christ. But the prophet comprises the whole redemption, beginning from the return out of Babylon, then continued from the first advent of Christ down to the last day (His second advent), when God will restore His Church to perfect felicity [CALVIN]. **2.** Parallel to Zechariah 14:2, 3, 4, where the "Mount of Olives" answers to the "Valley of Jehoshaphat" here. The latter is called "the valley of blessing (*Berachah*) (II Chron. 20:26). It lies between Jerusalem and the Mount of Olives and has the Kedron flowing through it. As Jehoshaphat overthrew the confederate foes of Judah, viz., Ammon, Moab, etc. (Ps. 83:6-8), in this valley, so God was to overthrow the Tyrians, Zidonians, Philistines, Edom, and Egypt, with a similar utter overthrow (vss. 4, 19). This has been long ago fulfilled; but the ultimate event shadowed forth herein is still future, when God shall specially interpose to destroy Jerusalem's last foes, of whom Tyre, Zidon, Edom, Egypt, and Philistia are the types. As "Jehoshaphat" means "the judgment of Jehovah," *the valley of Jehoshaphat* may be used as a *general* term for the theater of God's final judgments on Israel's foes, with an allusion to the judgment inflicted on them by Jehoshaphat. The definite mention of the Mount of Olives in Zechariah 14, and the fact that this was the scene of the ascension, makes it likely the same shall be the scene of Christ's coming again: cf. "this same Jesus . . . shall so come *in like manner* as ye have seen Him go into heaven" (Acts 1:11). **all nations**—viz., which have maltreated Judah. **plead with them**—(Isa. 66:16; Ezek. 38:22). **my heritage Israel**—

ADAM CLARKE — CHAPTER 3

1. *For, behold, in those days.* According to the preceding prophecy, these days should refer to gospel times, or to such as should immediately precede them. *I shall bring again the captivity of Judah and Jerusalem.* This may refer to the return from the Babylonish captivity.

2. *The valley of Jehoshaphat.* There is no such valley in the land of Judea, and hence the word must be symbolical. It signifies the "judgment of God," or "Jehovah judgeth"; and may mean someplace where Nebuchadnezzar should gain a great battle, which would utterly discomfit the ancient enemies of the Jews, and resemble the victory which Jehoshaphat gained over the Ammonites, Moabites, and Edomites, 2 Chron. xx. 22-26. *And parted my land.* The above nations had frequently entered into the territories of Israel, and divided among themselves the lands they had thus overrun. While the Jews were in captivity, much of the land of Israel was seized on, and occupied by the Philistines and other nations that bordered on Judea.

MATTHEW HENRY

Many affronts they had put upon God by their idolatries, but that for which God has a quarrel with them is the affront they have put upon his people and upon the vessels of his sanctuary. They had been abusive to the people of Israel, had *scattered them among the nations.* They *parted their land,* and have *cast lots for my people,* and *sold them.* When they had taken them prisoners they did *not increase their wealth by their price,* but sold them for pleasure rather than profit; they *gave a boy* taken in war for the *hire of a harlot,* and *a girl* for so many bottles of wine as would serve them for one sitting, a *goodly price* for a son and daughter of Israel to be a slave and a drudge in a tavern or a brothel. That which is got by one sin is commonly spent upon another. But the neighbouring nations shall be particularly reckoned with—*Tyre, and Sidon, and all the coasts of Palestine,* or the Philistines, who have been troublesome neighbours to the Israel of God, *v.* 4.

The Tyrians and Philistines, when they seized any of the children of Judah and Jerusalem, sold them to the Grecians, that they *might remove them far from their* own *border, v.* 6. They had unjustly seized *God's silver and gold* (*v.* 5), by which some understand the wealth of Israel. But it seems rather to be meant of the *vessels* and *treasures of the temple,* which God here calls his *goodly pleasant things.* These they *carried into their temples* as trophies of their victory over God's Israel, thinking that therein they triumphed over Israel's God, and that their idols triumphed over him. Thus the ark was put in Dagon's temple. Can they pretend that either God or his people have done them any injury, for which they may justify themselves in doing them these mischiefs? Those that contend with God will find themselves unable to make their part good with him. He will recompense them *suddenly.* They shall not gain their end in the mischief they designed against God's people. They thought to *remove them so far from their border* that they should never return to it again, *v.* 6. But (says God) "*I will raise them out of the place whither you have sold them,* and they shall not, as you intended, be buried alive there." The sellers shall be paid in their own coin. They shall justly be *sold to the Sabeans,* to a *people far off.* This (some think) had its accomplishment in the victories obtained by the Maccabees over the enemies of the Jews; others think it looks as far forward as the last day.

Verses 9–17

The notice of God's judging the nations may have reference to the destruction of Sennacherib, Nebuchadnezzar, Antiochus, and to the Antichrist especially, and all the proud enemies of the Christian church; but some of the best interpreters, ancient and modern, think the scope of these verses is to set forth the day of the last judgment.

I. A challenge given to all the enemies of God's kingdom, *v.* 9–11. It seems to be here spoken ironically: "*Proclaim you this among the Gentiles;* let all the forces of the nations be summoned to join in confederacy against God and his people." Thus does a God of almighty power bid defiance to all the opposition of the powers of darkness.

II. A charge given to the ministers of God's justice to appear and act against these enemies of his kingdom among men: And therefore *cause thy mighty ones to come down, O Lord! v.* 11. Some think the words (*v.* 9, 10), *Prepare war, wake up the mighty men,* are not a challenge to the enemies' hosts, but a charge to God's hosts.

JAMIESON, FAUSSET, BROWN

(Deut. 32:9; Jer. 10:16). Implying that the source of Judah's redemption is God's free love, wherewith He chose Israel as *His peculiar heritage,* and at the same time assuring them, when desponding because of trials, that He would plead their cause as His own, and as if He were injured in their person. **3. cast lots for my people**—i.e., divided among themselves My people as their captives by lot. Cf. as to the distribution of captives by lot (Obad. 11; Nah. 3:10). **given a boy for . . . harlot**—Instead of paying a harlot for her prostitution in money, they gave her a Jewish captive boy as a slave. **girl for wine**—So valueless did they regard a Jewish girl that they would sell her for a draught of wine. **4. what have ye to do with me**—Ye have no connection with Me (i.e., with My people: God identifying Himself with Israel; I (i.e., My people) have given you no cause of quarrel, why then do ye trouble Me (i.e., My people)? (Cf. the same phrase, Josh. 22:24; Judg. 11:12; II Sam. 16:10; Matt. 8:29). **Tyre . . . Zidon . . . Palestine**—(Amos 1:6, 9). **if ye recompense me**—If *ye injure Me* (My people), *in revenge* for fancied wrongs (Ezek. 25:15-17), I will requite you in your own coin swiftly and speedily. **5. my silver . . . my gold**—i.e., the gold and silver of My people. The Philistines and Arabians had carried off all the treasures of King Jehoram's house (II Chron. 21:16, 17). Cf. also I Kings 15:18; II Kings 12:18; 14:14, for the spoiling of the treasures of the temple and the king's palace in Judah by Syria. It was customary among the heathen to hang up in the idol temples some of the spoils of war as presents to their gods. **6. Grecians**—lit., Javanites, i.e., the Ionians, a Greek colony on the coast of Asia Minor who were the first Greeks known to the Jews. The Greeks themselves, however, in their *original descent* came from Javan (Gen. 10:2, 4). Probably the germ of Greek civilization in part came through the Jewish slaves imported into Greece from Phœnicia by traffickers. Ezekiel 27:13 mentions *Javan* and Tyre as trading in the persons of men. **far from their border**—far from Judea; so that the captive Jews were cut off from all hope of return. **7. raise them**—i.e., I will *rouse* them. Neither sea nor distance will prevent My bringing them back. Alexander, and his successors, restored to liberty many Jews in bondage in Greece (JOSEPHUS 13.5; J. B. 9, 2). **8. sell them to . . . Sabeans**—The Persian Artaxerxes Mnemon and Darius Ochus, and chiefly the Greek Alexander, reduced the Phœnician and Philistine powers. Thirty thousand Tyrians after the capture of Tyre by the last conqueror, and multitudes of Philistines on the taking of Gaza, were sold as slaves. The Jews are here said to do that which the God of Judah does in vindication of their wrong, viz., sell the Phœnicians who sold them, to a people "far off," as was Greece, whither the Jews had been sold. The Sabeans at the most remote extremity of Arabia Felix are referred to (cf. Jer. 6:20; Matt. 12:42). **9.** The nations hostile to Israel are summoned by Jehovah to "come up" (this phrase is used because Jerusalem was on a *hill*) against Jerusalem, not that they may destroy it, but to be destroyed by the Lord (Ezek. 38:7-23; Zech. 12:2-9; 14:2, 3). **Prepare war**—lit., *sanctify* war: because the heathen always began war with religious ceremonies. The very phrase used of Babylon's *preparations* against Jerusalem (Jer. 6:4) is now used of the final foes of Jerusalem. As Babylon was then desired by God to advance against her for her destruction, so now all her foes, of whom Babylon was the type, are desired to advance against her for *their own* destruction. **10. Beat your ploughshares into swords**—As the foes are desired to "beat their *ploughshares into swords,* and *their pruning hooks into spears,*" that so they may perish in their unhallowed attack on Judah and Jerusalem, so these latter, and the nations converted to God by them, after the overthrow of the antichristian confederacy, shall, on the contrary, "beat their *swords into ploughshares,* and their *spears into pruning hooks,*" when under Messiah's coming reign there shall be war no more (Isa. 2:4; Hos. 2:18; Mic. 4:3). **let the weak say, I am strong**—So universal shall be the rage of Israel's foes for invading her, that even the *weak* among them will fancy themselves *strong* enough to join the invading forces. Age and infirmity were ordinarily made valid excuses for exemption from service, but so mad shall be the fury of the world against God's people, that even the feeble will not desire to be exempted (cf. Ps. 2:1-3). **11. Assemble**—"Hasten" [MAURER]. **thither**—to the valley of Jehoshaphat. **thy mighty ones**—the warriors who fancy themselves "mighty ones," but who are on that very spot to be overthrown by Jehovah [MAURER]. Cf. "the mighty men" (vs. 9). Rather, Joel speaks of God's really

ADAM CLARKE

3. *Have given a boy for an harlot.* To such wretched circumstances were the poor Jews reduced in their captivity that their children were sold by their oppressors, and both males and females used for the basest purposes. Or this may refer to the issue of the Chaldean war in Judea, where the captives were divided among the victors. And being set in companies, they *cast lots* for them. And those to whom they fell sold them for various purposes: the boys to be slaves and catamites, the girls to be prostitutes; and in return for them they got *wine* and such things. I think this is the meaning of the text.

4. *What have ye to do with me?* Why have the Tyrians and Sidonians joined their other enemies to oppress My people? *Will ye render me a recompence?* Do you think by this to avenge yourselves upon the Almighty? to retaliate upon God!

5. *Ye have taken my silver and my gold.* The Chaldeans had spoiled the Temple, and carried away the sacred vessels, and put them in the temple of their own god in Babylon.

6. *Sold unto the Grecians.* These were the descendants of Javan, Gen. x. 2-5. And with them the Tyrians trafficked, Ezek. xxvii. 19.

That ye might remove them far from their border. Intending to send them as far off as possible, that it might be impossible for them to get back to reclaim the land of which you had dispossessed them.

7. *I will raise them.* I shall find means to bring them back from the place whither you have sold them, and they shall retaliate upon you the injuries they have sustained. It is said that Alexander and his successors set at liberty many Jews that had been sold into Greece. And it is likely that many returned from different lands, on the publication of the edict of Cyrus.

8. *I will sell your sons.* When Alexander took Tyre, he reduced into slavery all the lower people, and the women.

9. *Prepare war.* Let all the enemies of God and of His people join together; let them even call all the tillers of the ground to their assistance, instead of laboring in the field; let every peasant become a soldier.

Let them turn their agricultural implements into offensive weapons, so that the weak, being well-armed, may confidently say, "I am strong."

Yet, when thus collected and armed, "Jehovah will bring down *thy mighty ones*"; for so the clause in v. 11 should be rendered.

MATTHEW HENRY

The heathen must *come up to the valley of Jehoshaphat*, to receive their doom (*v.* 12). Jehoshaphat signifies *the judgment of the Lord*. Let them come to the place of God's judgment, which perhaps is the chief reason for the using of this name. The challenge (*v.* 9) is turned into a summons, *v.* 12. However, it is plain that to them the charge is given (*v.* 13), *Put you in the sickle, for the harvest is ripe;* that is, *their wickedness is great*, they are ripe for ruin.

III. The vast appearance that shall be in that solemn day (*v.* 14): *Multitudes, multitudes, in the valley of decision*, the same which before was called the *valley of Jehoshaphat*. The day of judgment will be the *day of decision*. *The valley of the distribution of judgment* (so the Chaldee), when *every man shall receive according to the things done in the body*. *The valley of threshing* (so the margin), carrying on the metaphor of the *harvest*, *v.* 13. The proud enemies of God's people will then be made as the *dust of the summer threshing-floors*.

IV. The amazing change that shall then be made in the kingdom of nature (*v.* 15): *The sun and moon shall be darkened*, as before, *ch.* ii. 31. Their glory and lustre shall be eclipsed by the far greater brightness of that glory in which the Judge shall then appear.

V. The different impressions which that day will make. 1. To the wicked it will be a terrible day. *The Lord* shall then speak *from Zion and Jerusalem*, from the throne of his glory. His speaking will be to the wicked, terrible as the roaring of a lion (for so the word signifies). 2. To the righteous it will be a joyful day. Their longings shall be satisfied: *The Lord will be the hope of his people*. He will be the *harbour* of his people (so the word is), their home. Their happiness shall be confirmed. Their holiness shall be completed (*v.* 17): *Then shall Jerusalem be holy*, the *holy city* indeed. The gospel-church is a holy society, even in its militant state, but will never be holiness itself till it comes to be triumphant. There shall not enter into the New Jerusalem anything that defiles or works iniquity. *So shall you know that I am the Lord your God*. It is an experimental knowledge. They shall find him their *hope and strength* in the worst of times, and so they shall *know that he is the Lord their God*.

Verses 18–21

These promises have their accomplishment in part in the kingdom of grace, but will have their full accomplishment in the kingdom of glory.

I. It is promised that the enemies of the church shall be vanquished and brought down, *v.* 19. Egypt, that old enemy of Israel, and Edom, which had an inveterate enmity to Israel, these *shall be a desolation*, no more to be inhabited. The quarrel God has with these kingdoms is for their *violence against the children of Judah*; see Ezek. xxv. 3, 8, 12, 15; xxvi. 2.

II. It is promised that the church shall be very happy in spiritual privileges, even during its militant state, but much more when it comes to be triumphant. Three things are promised:

1. Purity. This is put last here, as a reason for the rest (*v.* 21); but we may consider it first, as the ground and foundation of the rest: *I will cleanse their blood that I have not cleansed*. That shall be cleansed by the blood of Christ which could not be cleansed by the sacrifices and purifications of the ceremonial law. Though the refining and reforming of the church is work that goes on slowly, and still there is something that is *not cleansed*, yet there is a day coming when everything that is amiss shall be amended.

2. Plenty, *v.* 18. It intimates the abundance of vineyards, and of cattle in the pastures. And, to make the corn-land fruitful, the *rivers of Judah shall flow with water*, so that the country shall be like the garden of Eden, Ps. lxv. 9. But this seems to be meant spiritually; the graces and comforts of the new covenant are compared to *wine and milk* (Isa. lv. 1), and the Spirit to *rivers of living water*, John vii. 38. And these gifts abound much more under the New Testament than they did under the Old. The fountain of this plenty is in the *house of God*, whence the streams take their rise, as those *waters of the sanctuary* (Ezek. xlvii. 1) from *under the threshold of the house*. Christ himself is this fountain; his merit and grace cleanse and refresh us. This is said to water *the valley of Shittim*, which lay on the other side of Jordan, a barren valley, which intimates that gospel-grace, flowing from Christ, shall reach far, even to the Gentile world.

3. Perpetuity. This crowns all the rest (*v.* 20): *Judah shall dwell for ever*, and Jerusalem shall continue *from generation to generation*. The church of Christ shall continue in the world to the end of time.

JAMIESON, FAUSSET, BROWN

"mighty ones" in contrast to the self-styled "mighty men" (vs. 9; Ps. 103:20: Isa. 13:3; cf. Dan. 10:13). **12.** See vs. 2. **judge all the heathen round about**—i.e., all the nations from all parts of the earth which have maltreated Israel; not merely, as HENDERSON supposes, the nations *round about* Jerusalem (cf. Ps. 110:6; Isa. 2:4; Mic. 4:3, 11-13; Zeph. 3:15-19; Zech. 12:9; 14:3-11; Mal. 4:1-3). **13.** Direction to the ministers of vengeance to execute God's wrath, as the enemy's wickedness is come to its full maturity. God does not cut off the wicked at once, but waits till their guilt is at its *full* (so as to the Amorites' iniquity, Gen. 15:16), to show forth His own long-suffering, and the justice of their doom who have so long abused it (Matt. 13:27-30, 38, 40; Rev. 14:15-19). For the image of a harvest to be threshed, cf. Jeremiah 51:33; and a wine press, Isaiah 63:3 and Lamentations 1:15. **14.** The prophet in vision seeing the immense array of nations congregating, exclaims, "Multitudes, multitudes!" a Hebraism for *immense multitudes*. **valley of decision**—i.e., the valley in which they are to meet their *determined doom*. The same as "the valley of Jehoshaphat," i.e., "the valley *of judgment*" (*Note*, vs. 2). Cf. vs. 12, "there will I sit to *judge*," which confirms *English Version* rather than *Margin*, "threshing." The repetition of "valley of decision" heightens the effect and pronounces the awful *certainty* of their doom. **15.** (*Notes*, ch. 2:10, 31). **16.** (Cf. Ezek. 38:18-22.) The victories of the Jews over their cruel foe Antiochus, under the Maccabees, may be a reference of this prophecy; but the ultimate reference is to the last Antichrist, of whom Antiochus was the type. Jerusalem being the central seat of the theocracy (Ps. 132:13), it is from thence that Jehovah discomfits the foe. **roar**—as a lion (Jer. 25:30; Amos 1:2; 3:8). Cf. as to Jehovah's voice thundering, Psalm 18:13; Habakkuk 3: 10, 11. **Lord . . . the hope of his people**—or, "their refuge" (Ps. 46:1). **17. shall ye know**—experimentally by the proofs of favors which I shall vouchsafe to you. So "know" (Isa. 60:16; Hos. 2:20). **dwelling in Zion**—as peculiarly *your God*. **holy . . . no strangers pass through**—to attack, or to defile, the holy city (Isa. 35:8; 52:1; Zech. 14:21). *Strangers*, or Gentiles, shall come to Jerusalem, but it shall be in order to worship Jehovah there (Zech. 14: 16). **18. mountains . . . drop . . . wine**—figurative for *abundance of vines*, which were cultivated in terraces of earth between the rocks on the sides of the hills of Palestine (Amos 9:13). **hills . . . flow with milk**—i.e., they shall abound in flocks and herds yielding milk plentifully, through the richness of the pastures. **waters**—the great desideratum for fertility in the parched East (Isa. 30:25). **fountain . . . of . . . house of . . . Lord . . . water . . . valley of Shittim**—The blessings, temporal and spiritual, issuing from Jehovah's house at Jerusalem, shall extend even to Shittim, on the border between Moab and Israel, beyond Jordan (Num. 25:1; 33:49; Josh. 2:1; Mic. 6:5). Shittim means "acacias," which grow only in arid regions: implying that even *the arid desert* shall be fertilized by the blessing from Jerusalem. So Ezekiel 47:1-12 describes the waters issuing from the threshold of the house as flowing into the Dead Sea, and purifying it. Also in Zechariah 14:8 the waters flow on one side into the Mediterranean, on the other side into the Dead Sea, near which latter Shittim was situated (cf. Ps. 46: 4; Rev. 22:1). **19. Edom**—It was subjugated by David, but revolted under Jehoram (II Chron. 21: 8-10); and at every subsequent opportunity tried to injure Judah. Egypt under Shishak spoiled Jerusalem under Rehoboam of the treasures of the temple and the king's house; subsequently to the captivity, it inflicted under the Ptolemies various injuries on Judea. Antiochus spoiled Egypt (Dan. 11:40-43). Edom was made "desolate" under the Maccabees (JOSEPHUS 12.11, 12). The low condition of the two countries for centuries proves the truth of the prediction (cf. Isa. 19:1, etc. Jer. 49:17; Obad. 10). So shall fare all the foes of Israel, typified by these two (Isa. 63:1, etc.). **20. dwell for ever**—(Amos 9:15), i.e., be established as a flourishing state. **21. cleanse . . . blood . . . not cleansed**—I will purge away from Judah the extreme guilt (represented by "blood," the shedding of which was the climax of her sin, Isa. 1:15) which was for long not purged away, but visited with judgments (Isa. 4:4). Messiah saves from guilt, in order to save from punishment (Matt. 1:21).

ADAM CLARKE

12. *Let the heathen be wakened.* The heathen "shall be wakened." *The valley of Jehoshaphat.* Any place where God may choose to display His judgments against His enemies.

13. *Put ye in the sickle.* The destruction of His enemies is represented here under the metaphor of reaping down the harvest; and of gathering the grapes, and treading them in the winepresses.

14. *Multitudes, multitudes. Hamonim, hamonim,* "crowds upon crowds," *in the valley of decision*—the same as the valley of Jehoshaphat, the place where God is to execute judgment on His enemies.

15. *The sun and the moon shall be darkened.* High and mighty states shall be eclipsed, and brought to ruin, and the *stars*—petty states, princes, and governors—*shall withdraw their shining;* withhold their influence and tribute from the kingdoms to which they have belonged, and set up themselves as independent governors.

16. *The Lord also shall roar, out of Zion.* His temple and worship shall be reestablished there, and He will thence denounce His judgments against the nations. *The heavens and the earth shall shake.* There shall be great commotions in powerful empires and their dependencies; but in all these things His own people shall be unmoved, for God shall be their *hope* and *strength.*

17. *So shall ye know.* By the judgments I execute on your enemies, and the support I give to yourselves, that I am the all-conquering Jehovah, and that I have again taken up My residence in Jerusalem. All this may refer, ultimately, to the restoration of the Jews to their land; when "holiness to the Lord" shall be their motto; and no strange god, nor impure people, shall be permitted to enter the city, or even pass through it. This, I think, must refer to gospel times.

18. *In that day.* After their return from their captivities. *The mountains shall drop down new wine.* A poetic expression for great fertility. *And all the rivers of Judah,* far from being generally dry in the summer, shall have their channels always full of water.

And a fountain shall come forth of the house of the Lord. See the account of the typical waters in Ezekiel, chap. xlvii, to which this seems to have a reference. At least the subject is the same, and seems to point out the grace of the gospel, the waters of salvation, that shall flow from Jerusalem, and *water the valley of Shittim.* Shittim was in the plains of Moab beyond Jordan (Num. xxxiii. 49; Josh. iii. 1); but as no stream of water could flow from the Temple, pass across Jordan, or reach this plain, *the valley of Shittim* must be considered symbolical, as the valley of Jehoshaphat. But as *Shittim* may signify "thorns," it may figuratively represent the most uncultivated and ferocious inhabitants of the earth receiving the gospel of Christ, and being civilized and saved by it. We know that briers and thorns are emblems of bad men; see Ezek. ii. 6. Thus all the figures in this verse will point out the happy times of the gospel.

19. *Egypt shall be a desolation.* While peace, plenty, and prosperity of every kind shall crown My people, all their enemies shall be as a *wilderness*; and those who have used *violence* against the saints of God, and shed the blood of innocents (of the holy martyrs) in their land, when they had political power, these and all such shall fall under the just judgments of God.

20. *But Judah shall dwell for ever.* The true Church of Christ shall be supported, while all false and persecuting churches shall be annihilated. The promise may also belong to the full and final restoration of the Jews, when they dwell at Jerusalem as a distinct people professing the faith of our Lord Jesus Christ.

21. *For I will cleanse their blood.* "I will avenge" the slaughter and martyrdom of My people, which I have not yet avenged.

THE BOOK OF AMOS

I. Declamations (1:1-2:16)
A. Damascus (1:1-5)
B. Gaza (1:6-8)
C. Tyre (1:9, 10)
D. Edom (1:11, 12)
E. Children of Ammon (1:13-15)
F. Moab (2:1-3)
G. Judah (2:4, 5)
H. Israel (2:6-16)

II. Proclamations (3:1-6:14)
A. Jehovah's verdict and sentence (3:1-15)
1. Privileged people to be punished (3:1, 2)
2. The prophet's vindication of himself (3:3-8)
3. Reason of punishment (3:9-15)
B. Jehovah's summons (4:1-13)
1. Indictment of the women (4:1-3)
2. Final summons to the people (4:4-13)
C. Lamentation and its causes (5:1-6:14)
1. The lamentation (5:1, 2)
2. The sequence of explanations (5:3-17)
3. The double woe (5:18-6:14)

III. Revelations (7:1-9:10)
A. The locusts—judgment threatened and restrained (7:1-3)
B. The fire—judgment threatened and restrained (7:4-6)
C. The plumbline—judgment determined (7:7-9)
D. Historical interpolation (7:10-17)
E. The basket of summer fruit—judgment at hand (8:1-14)
F. Jehovah—judgment executed (9:1-10)

IV. Restorations (9:11-15)
A. Restoration—preliminary (9:11-13)
1. "I will" (9:11)
2. "They shall" (9:12, 13)
B. Restoration—progressive (9:14)
1. "I will" (9:14a)
2. "They shall" (9:14b)
C. Restoration—permanent (9:15)
1. "I will" (9:15a)
2. "They shall (9:15b)

Amos was a country farmer. Amos signifies a *burden*, whence the Jews have a tradition that he spoke with stammering lips; we may say that his speech was *weighty* and his word the *burden of the Lord.* He was (as most think) of Judah, yet prophesied chiefly against Israel and at Bethel (7:13). Some think his style is plain and rustic.

It appears by his contest with Amaziah the priest of Bethel that he met with opposition, but was faithful and bold in reproving sin and pressing in his exhortations to repentance and reformation. He begins with threatenings against the neighboring nations that were enemies to Israel (chs. 1, 2). He then calls Israel to account and judges them for their idolatry and their incorrigibleness under God's judgments (chs. 3, 4). He calls them to repentance (ch. 5), foretells the desolations that were coming upon them notwithstanding their security (ch. 6), some particular judgments (ch. 7), particularly on Amaziah; and, after other reproofs and threatenings (chs. 8, 9), concludes with a promise of the setting up of the Messiah's kingdom and the happiness of God's spiritual Israel.

MATTHEW HENRY

CHAPTER 1

Verses 1–2

I. The general character of this prophecy. It consists of *the words which the prophet saw.* The prophet saw these words, that is they were revealed to him in a *vision*, as John is said to see *the voice* that spoke to him, Rev. i. 12.

II. The person by whom this prophecy was sent—*Amos, who was among the herdmen of Tekoa*, and was one of them. Some think he was a rich dealer in cattle. Others think he was a poor keeper of cattle, for we find (*ch.* vii. 14, 15) that he was withal a *gatherer of wild figs*, by which we may suppose he could but just get his bread. When God would send a prophet to reprove and warn his people, he employed a shepherd.

III. The persons concerned in the prophecy of this book; the *ten tribes*, who were now ripening apace for ruin. God had raised them up prophets among themselves (*ch.* ii. 11), but they regarded them not; therefore God sends them one from Tekoa, in the land of Judah.

IV. The book is dated by the reigns of the kings under whom the prophet prophesied. It was in the days of *Uzziah king of Judah*, when the affairs of that kingdom went very well, and of Jeroboam II, king of Israel, when the affairs of that kingdom went pretty well; yet then they must both be told of their sins and of the judgments that were coming upon them, that they might not with the present gleam of prosperity flatter themselves into a confidence of their perpetual security. It was *two years before the earthquake*, that earthquake which is mentioned to have been *in the days of Uzziah* (Zech. xiv. 5).

V. The introduction to these prophecies, containing the general scope of them (*v.* 2): *The Lord will roar from Zion.* His threatenings by his prophets will be as terrible as the roaring of a lion is to the shepherds and their flocks. See Hosea (*ch.* xi. 10) and Joel, *ch.* iii. 16.

Verses 3–15

What the Lord says here may be explained by what he says Jer. xii. 14. Damascus was a near

JAMIESON, FAUSSET, BROWN

CHAPTER 1

Vss. 1-15. God's Judgments on Syria, Philistia, Tyre, Edom, and Ammon. **1. The words of Amos**—i.e., Amos' *oracular communications.* A heading found only in Jeremiah 1:1. **among the herdmen**—rather, "shepherds"; both owning and tending sheep; from an *Arabic* root, "to mark with pricks," viz., to select the best among a species of sheep and goats *ill-shapen and short-footed* (as others explain the name from an *Arabic* root), but distinguished by their wool [Maurer]. God chooses "the weak things of the world to confound the mighty," and makes a humble shepherd reprove the arrogance of Israel and her king arising from prosperity (cf. I Sam. 17:40). **which he saw**—in supernatural *vision* (Isa. 1:1). **two years before the earthquake**—mentioned in Zechariah 14:5. The earthquake occurred in Uzziah's reign, at the time of his being stricken with leprosy for usurping the priest's functions [Josephus, *Antiquities* 9. 10. 4]. This clause must have been inserted by Ezra and the compilers of the Jewish canon. **2. will roar**—as a **lion** (Joel 3:16). Whereas Jehovah is there represented roaring in Israel's behalf, here He roars against her (cf. Ps. 18:13; Jer. 25:30). **from Zion . . . Jerusalem**—the seat of the theocracy, from which ye have revolted; not from Dan and Bethel, the seat of your idolatrous worship of the calves. **habitations . . . mourn**—poetical personification. Their *inhabitants* shall mourn, imparting a sadness to the very *habitations.* **Carmel**—the mountain promontory north of Israel, in Asher, abounding in rich pastures, olives, and vines. The name is the symbol of *fertility.* When Carmel itself "withers," how utter the desolation! (Song of Sol. 7:5; Isa. 33:9; 35:2; Jer. 50:19; Nah. 1:4). **3.** Here begins a series of threatenings of vengeance against six other states, followed by one against Judah, and ending with one against Israel, with whom the rest of the prophecy is occupied. The eight predictions are in symmetrical stanzas, each prefaced by "Thus saith the Lord." Beginning with the sin of others, which Israel would be ready enough to recognize, he proceeds to bring home to

ADAM CLARKE

CHAPTER 1

1. *The words of Amos.* This person and the father of Isaiah, though named alike in our translation, were as different in their names as in their persons. The father of Isaiah, *Amots;* the prophet before us, *Amos.* The first, *aleph, mem, vau, tsaddi;* the second, *ain, mem, vau, samech. Among the herdmen.* He seems to have been among the very lowest orders of life, a herdsman, one who tended the flocks of *others* in the open fields, and "a gatherer of sycomore fruit." Of whatever species this was, whether a kind of fig, it is evident that it was wild fruit; and he probably collected it for his own subsistence, or to dispose of either for the service of his employer, or to increase his scanty wages.

Before the earthquake. Probably the same as that referred to in Zech. xiv. 5.

2. *The Lord will roar from Zion.* It is a pity that our translators had not followed the hemistich form of the Hebrew:

Jehovah from Zion shall roar,
And from Jerusalem shall give forth his voice;
And the pleasant dwellings of the shepherds shall mourn,
And the top of mount Carmel shall wither.

Carmel was a very fruitful mountain in the tribe of Judah, Josh. xv. 55; Isa. xxxv. 2. This introduction was natural in the mouth of a herdsman who was familiar with the roaring of lions, the bellowing of bulls, and the lowing of kine. The roaring of the lion in the forest is one of the most terrific sounds in nature; when near, it strikes terror into the heart of both man and beast.

MATTHEW HENRY

neighbour to Israel on the north, Tyre and Gaza on the west, Edom on the south, Ammon and Moab on the east; and all had been evil neighbours.

I. Though those nations will not worship him as their God, yet they shall be made to know that they are accountable to him as their Judge.

1. The indictment drawn up against them all is thus far the same, (1) That they are charged in general with *three transgressions, and with four*, that is, with many transgressions (as by one or two we mean *a few*, so by three or four we mean many), where we read of *three things, yea, four*, generally one seems to be more especially intended. (2) That the particular sin which is the fourth, is the sin of persecution.

2. The judgment given against them all is thus far the same, (1) That, their sin having risen to such a height, *God will not turn away the punishment thereof*. Justice shall take its course. (2) That God will *kindle a fire* among them; this is said concerning all these *evil neighbours, v.* 4, 7, 10, 12, 14. God will *send a fire* into their cities.

II. What is peculiar to each of them.

1. Concerning Damascus, the capital of Syria, a kingdom that was often vexatious to Israel. (1) The peculiar sin of Damascus: *They threshed Gilead with threshing-instruments of iron* (*v.* 3), which may be understood literally of their putting to the torture the inhabitants of Gilead whom they got into their hands, as David put the Ammonites under *saws and harrows*, 2 Sam. xii. 31. Or it may be taken figuratively. 2 Kings xiii. 7, He *destroyed them, and made them like the dust by threshing*. (2) The peculiar punishment of Damascus is, [1] That fire shall fasten not on the chief city, but on *the house of Hazael*, which he built; and *it shall devour the palaces of Ben-hadad*.

[2] That the enemy shall force his way into the city (*v.* 5): *I will break the bar of Damascus* may be understood figuratively: the strength and safety of that great city shall fail, and prove insufficient. [3] That the people shall be destroyed with the sword: *I will cut off the inhabitant from the plain of Aven*, the *valley of idolatry* (1 Kings xx. 23).

[4] That the body of the nation shall be carried off. The *people shall go into captivity unto Kir*, which was in the country of the Medes. We find this fulfilled (2 Kings xvi. 9) about fifty years after.

2. Concerning Gaza, a city of the Philistines. (1) The peculiar sin of the Philistines was *carrying away captive the whole captivity*, either of Israel or Judah, which some think refers to that inroad made upon Jehoram (2 Chron. xxi. 17), or, perhaps, to their seizing those that fled to them for shelter when Sennacherib invaded Judah, and *selling them to the Grecians* (Joel iii. 4–6), or to the Edomites.

JAMIESON, FAUSSET, BROWN

Israel her own guilt. Israel must not think hereafter, because she sees others visited similarly to herself, that such judgments are matters of chance; nay, they are divinely foreseen and foreordered, and are confirmations of the truth that God will not clear the guilty. If God spares not the nations that know not the truth, how much less Israel that sins wilfully (Luke 12:47, 48; Jas. 4:17)! **for three transgressions . . . and for four**—If Damascus had only sinned once or twice, I would have spared them, but since, after having been so often pardoned, they still persevere *so continually,* I will no longer "turn away" *their punishment*. The *Hebrew* is simply, "I will not reverse *it,*" viz., the sentence of punishment which follows; the negative expression implies more than it expresses; i.e., "I will *most surely execute* it"; God's fulfilment of His threats being more awful than human language can express. "Three and four" imply sin *multiplied on sin* (cf. Exod. 20:5; Prov. 30:15, 18, 21; "six and seven," Job 5:19; "once and twice," Job 33:14; "twice and thrice," *Margin;* "oftentimes," *English Version,* Job 33:29; "seven and also eight," Eccles. 11:2). There may be also a reference to *seven,* the product of *three* and *four* added; *seven* expressing the *full completion* of the measure of their guilt (Lev. 26: 18, 21, 24; cf. Matt. 23:32). **threshed**—the very term used of the Syrian king Hazael's oppression of Israel under Jehu and Jehoahaz (II Kings 10:32, 33; 13:7). The victims were thrown before the threshing-sledges, the teeth of which tore their bodies. So David to Ammon (II Sam. 12:31; cf. Isa. 28:27). **4. Hazael . . . Ben-hadad**—A black marble obelisk found in the central palace of Nimroud, and now in the British Museum, is inscribed with the names of Hazael and Ben-hadad of Syria, as well as Jehu of Israel, mentioned as tributaries of "Shalmanubar," king of Assyria. The kind of tribute from Jehu is mentioned: gold, pearls, precious oil, etc. [G. V. SMITH]. The Ben-hadad here is the son of Hazael (II Kings 13:3), not the Ben-hadad supplanted and slain by Hazael (II Kings 8:7, 15). The phrase, "I will send a fire," i.e., the flame of war (Ps. 78:63), occurs also in vss. 7, 10, 12, 14, and ch. 2:2, 5; Jeremiah 49:27; Hosea 8:14. **5. bar of Damascus**—i.e., the bar of its gates (cf. Jer. 51:30). **the inhabitant**—*singular* for *plural,* "inhabitants." HENDERSON, because of the parallel, "him that holdeth the scepter," translates, "the ruler." But the parallelism is that of one clause complementing the other, "the inhabitant" or *subject* here answering to "him that holdeth the scepter" or *ruler* there, both ruler and subject alike being cut off. **Aven**—the same as *Oon* or *Un,* a delightful valley, four hours' journey from Damascus, towards the desert. Proverbial in the East as a place of delight [JOSEPHUS ABASSUS]. It is here parallel to "Eden," which also means "pleasantness"; situated at Lebanon. As JOSEPHUS ABASSUS is a doubtful authority, perhaps the reference may be rather to the valley between Lebanon and Anti-Lebanon, called *El-Bekaa,* where are the ruins of the Baalbek temple of the sun; so the LXX renders it *On,* the same name as the city in Egypt bears, dedicated to the sun-worship (Gen. 41:45; *Margin,* Ezek. 30:17, *Heliopolis,* "the city of the sun"). It is termed by Amos "the valley of Aven," or "vanity," from the worship of idols in it. **Kir**—a region subject to Assyria (Isa. 22:6) in Iberia, the same as that called now in *Armenian Kur,* lying by the river Cyrus which empties itself into the Caspian Sea. Tiglath-pileser fulfilled this prophecy when Ahaz applied for help to him against Rezin king of Syria, and the Assyrian king took Damascus, slew Rezin, and carried away its people captive to Kir. **6. Gaza**—the southernmost of the five capitals of the five divisions of Philistia, and the key to Palestine on the south: hence put for the whole Philistine nation. Uzziah commenced the fulfilment of this prophecy (see II Chron. 26:6). **because they carried away . . . the whole captivity**—i.e., they left none. Cf. with the phrase here, Jeremiah 13:19, "Judah . . . carried captive *all* of it . . . *wholly* carried away." Under Jehoram already the Philistines had carried away all the substance of the king of Judah, and his wives and his sons, "so that there was never a son left to him, save Jehoahaz"; and after Amos' time (if the reference includes the *future,* which to the prophet's eye is as if already done), under Ahaz (II Chron. 28:18), they seized on all the cities and villages of the low country and south of Judah. **to deliver them up to Edom**—Judah's bitterest foe; as slaves (vs. 9; cf. Joel 3:1, 3, 6). GROTIUS refers it to the fact (Isa. 16:4) that on Sennacherib's invasion of Judah, many fled for refuge to neighboring countries; the Philistines, instead of hospitably sheltering the refugees, sold them, as if captives in war,

ADAM CLARKE

3. *For three transgressions of Damascus, and for four.* These expressions of *three* and *four,* so often repeated in this chapter, mean repetition, abundance, and anything that goes towards excess. "Very, very exceedingly"; and so it was used among the ancient Greek and Latin poets. See the passionate exclamation of Ulysses, in the storm, *Odyss.*, lib. v, v. 306.

THRICE *happy Greeks! and* FOUR *times who were slain*
In Atreus' cause, upon the Trojan plain.

Damascus was the capital of Syria.

4. *Ben-hadad.* He was son and successor of Hazael. See the cruelties which they exercised upon the Israelites, 2 Kings x. 32; xiii. 7, etc.; and see especially 2 Kings viii. 12, where these cruelties are predicted. The *fire* threatened here is the war so successfully carried on against the Syrians by Jeroboam II, in which he took Damascus and Hamath, and reconquered all the ancient possessions of Israel. See 2 Kings xiv. 25-26, 28.

5. *The bar of Damascus.* The gates, whose long traverse bars, running from wall to wall, were their strength. I will throw it open; and the gates were forced, and the city taken, as above.

The plain of Aven . . . the house of Eden. The plain of Aven, or *Birkath-Aven,* Calmet says, is a city of Syria, at present called Baal-Bek, and by the Greeks Heliopolis; and is situated at the end of that long valley which extends from south to north, between Libanus and Anti-Libanus.

The people of Syria shall go into captivity unto Kir. Kir is supposed to be the country of Cyrene in Albania, on the river Cyrus, which empties itself into the Caspian Sea. The fulfillment of this prophecy may be seen in 2 Kings xvi. 1-9.

6. *They carried away captive.* Gaza is well know to have been one of the five lordships of the Philistines; it lay on the coast of the Mediterranean Sea, near to Egypt. The *captivity* mentioned here may refer to inroads and incursions made by the Philistines in times of peace. See 2 Chron. xxi. 16.

MATTHEW HENRY

(2) The peculiar punishment of the Philistines is that fire shall devour the palaces of Gaza, and that the *inhabitants* of the other cities of the Philistines, Ashdod (or Azotus), Ashkelon, and Ekron, shall all be *cut off.*

3. Concerning Tyre, that famous city, that was itself a kingdom, *v.* 9. (1) The peculiar sin of Tyre is *delivering up the whole captivity to Edom,* that is, selling to the Edomites those of Israel that fled to them for shelter. (2) In the punishment of Tyrus *the palaces thereof* shall be *devoured,* which was done when Nebuchadnezzar took it after thirteen years' siege.

4. Concerning Edom, the posterity of Esau. (1) Their peculiar sin was an unmerciful pursuit of the people of God to do them a mischief, *v.* 11. He did *pursue his brother with the sword,* not only of old (Num. xx. 18), but ever since. Whenever any other enemy had put Judah or Israel to flight, then the Edomites fell upon the rear, slew those that were half dead already, and did *cast off all pity.* (2) In their punishment a *fire* shall be *sent to devour their palaces.*

5. Concerning the Ammonites, *v.* 13-15. The fire of their anger turned against the people of God; they *ripped up the women with child of Gilead.* It was done with a devilish design to extirpate the race of Israel by killing not only all that were born, but all that were to be born. It was *that they might enlarge their border,* that they might make the land of Gilead their own. We find (Jer. xlix. 1) that the Ammonites inherited *Gad* (that is, Gilead) under pretence that Israel had no heirs. (2) See how violently the fire of God's anger burned against them. *Shall not his soul be avenged.* The fire shall be kindled *with shouting in the day of battle,* that is, war shall kindle the fire. It is particularly threatened that *their king and his princes shall go together into captivity,* carried away by the king of Babylon. *Milchom shall go into captivity;* some understand it of the god of the Ammonites, whom they called *Moloch—a king.*

CHAPTER 2

Verses 1-8

I. The judgment of Moab. 1. Moab's fourth transgression was cruelty. The instance given refers not to the people of God: The king of Moab *burnt the bones of the king of Edom into lime.* There was war between the Edomites and the Moabites, in which the king of Moab offered his own son for a burnt-offering, to appease his deity, 2 Kings iii. 26, 27. Afterwards he, or his successors, having an advantage against the *king of Edom,* seized him alive and burnt him to

JAMIESON, FAUSSET, BROWN

to their enemies, the Idumeans. **7. fire**—i.e., the flame of war (Num. 21:28; Isa. 26:11). Hezekiah fulfilled the prophecy, smiting the Philistines unto Gaza (II Kings 18:8). Foretold also by Isaiah 14: 29, 31. **8. Ashdod...**—Gath alone is not mentioned of the five chief Philistine cities. It had already been subdued by David; and it, as well as Ashdod, was taken by Uzziah (II Chron. 26:6). Gath perhaps had lost its position as one of the five primary cities before Amos uttered this prophecy, whence arose his omission of it. So Zephaniah 2:4, 5. Cf. Jeremiah 47:4; Ezekiel 25:16. Subsequently to the subjugation of the Philistines by Uzziah, and then by Hezekiah, they were reduced by Psammetichus of Egypt, Nebuchadnezzar, the Persians, Alexander, and lastly the Asmoneans. **9. Tyrus... delivered up the... captivity to Edom**—the same charge as against the Philistines (vs. 6). **remembered not the brotherly covenant**—the league of Hiram of Tyre with David and Solomon, the former supplying cedars for the building of the temple and king's house in return for oil and corn (II Sam. 5:11; I Kings 5: 2-6; 9:11-14, 27; 10-22; I Chron. 14:1; II Chron. 8: 18; 9:10). **10. fire**—(Cf. vss. 4, 7; *Notes,* Isa. 23: Ezek. 26, 27, and 28). Many parts of Tyre were burnt by fiery missiles of the Chaldeans under Nebuchadnezzar. Alexander of Macedon subsequently overthrew it. **11. Edom... did pursue his brother**—(Isa. 34:5). The chief aggravation to Edom's violence against Israel was that they both came from the same parents, Isaac and Rebekah (cf. Gen. 25:24-26; Deut. 23:7, 8; Obad. 10, 12; Mal. 1:2). **cast off all pity**—lit., "destroy compassions," i.e., did suppress all the natural feeling of pity for a brother in distress. **his wrath for ever**—As Esau kept up his grudge against Jacob, for having twice supplanted him, viz., as to the birthright and the blessing (Gen. 27:41), so Esau's posterity against Israel (Num. 20:14, 21). Edom first showed his spite in not letting Israel pass through his borders when coming from the wilderness, but threatening to "come out against him with the sword"; next, when the Syrians attacked Jerusalem under Ahaz (cf. II Chron. 28:17, with II Kings 16:5); next, when Nebuchadnezzar assailed Jerusalem (Ps. 137:7, 8). In each case Edom chose the day of Israel's calamity for venting his grudge. This is the point of Edom's guilt dwelt on in Obadiah 10-13. God punishes the children, not for the sin of their fathers, but for their own filling up the measure of their fathers' guilt, as children generally follow in the steps of, and even exceed, their fathers' guilt (cf. Exod. 20:5). **12. Teman**—a city of Edom, called from a grandson of Esau (Gen. 36:11, 15; Obad. 8, 9); situated five miles from Petra; south of the present Wady Musa. Its people were famed for wisdom (Jer. 49:7). **Bozrah**—a city of Edom (Isa. 63: 1). Selah or Petra is not mentioned, as it had been overthrown by Amaziah (II Kings 14:7). **13. Ammon**—The Ammonites under Nahash attacked Jabesh-gilead and refused to accept the offer of the latter to save them, unless the Jabesh-gileadites would put out all their right eyes (I Sam. 11:1, etc.). Saul rescued Jabesh-gilead. The Ammonites joined the Chaldeans in their invasion of Judea for the sake of plunder. **ripped up... women with child**—as Hazael of Syria also did (II Kings 8:12; cf. Hos. 13: 16). Ammon's object in this cruel act was to leave Israel without "heir," so as to seize on Israel's inheritance (Jer. 49:1). **14. Rabbah**—the capital of Ammon: meaning "the Great." Distinct from Rabbah of Moab. Called *Philadelphia,* afterwards, from Ptolemy Philadelphus. **tempest**—i.e., with an onset swift, sudden, and resistless as a *hurricane.* **day of the whirlwind**—parallel to "the day of battle"; therefore meaning "the day of the foe's *tumultuous assault.*" **15. their king... princes**—or else, "their Molech [the idol of Ammon] and his priests" [GROTIUS and LXX]. Isaiah 43:28 so uses "princes" for *priests.* So ch. 5:26, "your Molech"; and Jeremiah 49:3, *Margin. English Version,* however, is perhaps preferable both here and in Jeremiah 49:3; see *Notes* there.

CHAPTER 2

Vss. 1-16. CHARGES AGAINST MOAB, JUDAH, AND LASTLY ISRAEL, THE CHIEF SUBJECT OF AMOS' PROPHECIES. **1. burned... bones of... king of Edom into lime**—When Jehoram of Israel, Jehoshaphat of Judah, and the king of Edom, combined against Mesha king of Moab, the latter failing in battle to break through to the king of Edom, took the oldest son of the latter and offered him as a burnt offering on the wall (II Kings 3:27) [MICHAELIS]. Thus, "*king* of Edom" is taken as *the heir to*

ADAM CLARKE

9. *Tyrus.* See Ezekiel xxvi; xxvii; and xxviii. *The brotherly covenant.* This possibly refers to the very friendly league made between Solomon and Hiram, king of Tyre, 1 Kings v. 12; but some contend that the brotherly covenant refers to the two people having descended from the two brothers, Jacob and Esau.

10. *I will send a fire on the wall of Tyrus.* The destructive fire or siege by Nebuchadnezzar, which lasted thirteen years, and ended in the destruction of this ancient city; see Ezekiel, chap. xxvi. 7-14. It was finally ruined by Alexander.

11. *For three transgressions of Edom.* That the Edomites were always implacable enemies of the Jews is well-known; but most probably that which the prophet has in view was the part they took in distressing the Jews when Jerusalem was besieged, and finally taken, by the Chaldeans. See Obad. 11-14; Ezek. xxv. 12; xxxv. 5; Ps. cxxxvii. 7.

12. *Teman . . . Bozrah.* Principal cities of Idumea.

13. *The children of Ammon.* The country of the Ammonites lay to the east of Jordan, in the neighborhood of Gilead. *Rabbah* was its capital.

Because they have ripped up. This refers to some barbarous transaction well-known in the time of this prophet, but of which we have no distinct mention in the sacred historians.

14. *With shouting in the day of battle.* They shall be totally subdued. This was done by Nebuchadnezzar. See Jer. xxvii. 3, 6.

15. *Their king shall go into captivity.* Probably *malcham* should be Milcom, who was a chief god of the Ammonites; and the following words, *he and his princes,* may refer to the body of his priesthood. See 1 Kings xi. 33. All these countries were subdued by Nebuchadnezzar.

CHAPTER 2

1. *For three transgressions of Moab, and for four.* See an explanation of this form, chap. i. 2. The land of the Moabites lay to the east of the Dead Sea. For the origin of this people, see Gen. xix. 37. *He burned the bones of the king of Edom into lime.* Possibly referring to some brutality, such as opening the grave of one of the Idumean kings, and calcining his bones. It is supposed by some to refer to the fact mentioned in 2 Kings iii. 26, when the kings of Judah,

MATTHEW HENRY

ashes, or slew him and burnt his body, or dug up the bones and *burnt them to lime.*

2. Moab's doom for this transgression is death. *Moab shall die;* the Moabites shall be cut off with the sword. The king, judges and princes, shall be cut off together.

II. Judah also is a near neighbour to Israel, and had made itself like the heathen and mingled with them, and therefore the indictment here runs in the same form: *For three transgressions of Judah, and for four, I will not turn away the punishment thereof.*

The sentence is the same (*v.* 5): "***I will send a fire upon Judah,*** and it shall ***devour the palaces of Jerusalem,*** though it is the holy city, and God has formerly been *known in its palaces for a refuge.*" But the sin charged upon Judah is different from all the rest. The other nations were reckoned with for injuries done to men, but Judah is reckoned with for indignities done to God, *v.* 4. *They have despised the law of the Lord,* and herein they despised the wisdom, justice, and goodness, as well as the authority and sovereignty, of the Lawmaker. They put honour upon his rivals, their idols, here called *their lies,* which *caused them to err.*

III. *The words* which *Amos saw concerning Israel.* He begins with them as with the rest: *For three transgressions of Israel, and for four, I will not turn away the punishment thereof.* Their sins were, 1. Perverting justice. They made nothing of selling a righteous man for a piece of silver; the bribe always turned the scale. Those who will wrong their consciences for anything will come at length to sell justice for a pair of old shoes. 2. Oppressing the poor: *They pant after the dust of the earth on the head of the poor;* they make a prey of those that are in sorrow with dust on their heads, poor orphans in mourning for their parents; to get their estates. 3. Abominable uncleanness, even incest itself. 4. Regaling themselves, and yet pretending to honour their God with that which they had got by oppression and extortion, *v.* 8. They *lay themselves down* at ease upon *clothes laid to pledge,* which they ought to have restored the same night, according to the law, Deut. xxiv. 12, 13. And they *drink the wine of the condemned,* of such as they have fined, spending that in sensuality which they have got by injustice. They think to make atonement for this by *drinking this wine in the house of their God,* in the temples where they worshipped their calves.

Verses 9–16

I. God puts his people Israel in mind of the great things he had done for them, *v.* 9, 10. "Israel, remember God brought thee out of *Egypt,* where thou wouldst otherwise have perished in slavery. He *led thee forty years* through a desert land, and fed thee in a *wilderness.*" He made room for them in Canaan: *I destroyed the Amorite before them.* They were of great stature (*whose height was like the height of the cedars*) and the people of Israel were as shrubs to them; and they were *strong as the oaks. I destroyed his fruit from above and his roots from beneath,* so that the Amorites were no more a nation. Thus highly did God value Israel. How ungrateful then were those who put such contempt upon him!

JAMIESON, FAUSSET, BROWN

the throne of Edom. But "his son" is rather the *king of Moab's own son,* whom the father offered to Molech [JOSEPHUS, *Antiquities,* 9. 3]. Thus the reference here in Amos is not to that fact, but to the revenge which probably the king of Moab took on the king of Edom, when the forces of Israel and Judah had retired after their successful campaign against Moab, leaving Edom without allies. The Hebrew tradition is that Moab in revenge tore from their grave and burned the bones of the king of Edom, the ally of Jehoram and Jehoshaphat, who was already buried. Probably the "burning of the bones" means, "he burned the king of Edom alive, reducing his very bones to lime" [MAURER]. **2. Kirioth**—the chief city of Moab, called also Kir-Moab (Isa. 15:1). The form is *plural* here, as including both the acropolis and town itself (see Jer. 48:24, 41, *Margin*). **die with tumult**—i.e., amid the tumult of battle (Hos. 10:14). **3. the judge**—the chief magistrate, the supreme source of justice. "King" not being used, it seems likely a change of government had before this time substituted for *kings,* supreme *judges.* **4.** From foreign kingdoms he passes to Judah and Israel, lest it should be said, he was strenuous in denouncing sins abroad, but connived at those of his own nation. Judah's guilt differs from that of all the others, in that it was directly against God, not merely against man. Also because Judah's sin was wilful and wittingly against light and knowledge. **law**—the Mosaic code in general. **commandments**—or *statutes,* the ceremonies and civil laws. **their lies**—their lying idols (Ps. 40:4; Jer. 16:19), from which they drew false hopes. The order is to be observed. The Jews first cast off the divine *law,* then fall into *lying errors;* God thus visiting them with a righteous retribution (Rom. 1:25, 26, 28; II Thess. 2:11, 12). The pretext of a *good intention* is hereby refuted: the "lies" that mislead them are "*their* [own] lies" [CALVIN]. **after . . . which their fathers . . . walked**—We are not to follow the fathers in error, but must follow the word of God alone. It was an aggravation of the Jews' sin that it was not confined to preceding generations; the sins of the sons rivalled those of their fathers (Matt. 23:32; Acts 7:51) [CALVIN]. **5. a fire**—Nebuchadnezzar. **6. Israel**—the ten tribes, the main subject of Amos' prophecies. **sold the righteous**—Israel's judges for a bribe are induced to condemn in judgment him who has a righteous cause; in violation of Deuteronomy 16:19. **the poor for a pair of shoes**—lit., "sandals" of wood, secured on the foot by leather straps; less valuable than shoes. Cf. the same phrase, for "the most paltry bribe," ch. 8:6; Ezekiel 13:19; Joel 3:3. They were not driven by poverty to such a sin; beginning with suffering themselves to be tempted by a large bribe, they at last are so reckless of all shame as to prostitute justice for the merest trifle. Amos convicts them of injustice, incestuous unchastity, and oppression first, as these were so notorious that they could not deny them, before he proceeds to reprove their contempt of God, which they would have denied on the ground that they worshipped God in the form of the calves. **7. pant after . . . dust of . . . earth on . . . head of . . . poor**—i.e., eagerly thirst for this object, by their oppression to prostrate the poor so as to cast the dust on their heads in mourning on the earth (cf. II Sam. 1:2; Job 2:12; Ezek. 27:30). **turn aside . . . way of. . . meek**—pervert their cause (ch. 5:12; Job 24:4 [GROTIUS]; Isa. 10:2). **a man and his father**—a crime "not so much as named among the Gentiles" (I Cor. 5:1). When God's people sin in the face of light, they often fall lower than even those who know not God. **go in unto the same maid**—from vs. 8 it seems likely "the damsel" meant is one of the prostitutes attached to the idol Astarte's temple: prostitution being part of her filthy worship. **to profane my . . . name**—Israel in such abominations, as it were, *designedly* seeks to insult God. **8. lay themselves . . . upon clothes laid to pledge**—the *outer garment,* which Exodus 22:25-27 ordered to be restored to the poor man before sunset, as being his only covering. **It** aggravated the crime that they lay on these clothes in an idol temple. **by every altar**—They partook in a recumbent posture of their idolatrous feasts; the ancients being in the habit of reclining at full length in eating, the upper part of the body resting on the left elbow, not sitting as we do. **drink . . . wine of the condemned**—i.e., wine bought with the money of those whom they unjustly fined. **9. Yet**—My former benefits to you heighten your ingratitude. **the Amorite**—the most powerful of all the Canaanite nations, and therefore put for them all (Gen. 15:16; 48:22; Deut. 1:20; Josh. 7:7). **height . . . like . . . cedars**—(Num. 13:32, 33). **destroyed his fruit. . . above . . . roots . . . beneath**—i.e.,

ADAM CLARKE

Israel, and Idumea joined together to destroy Moab. The king of it, despairing to save his city, took 700 men, and made a desperate sortie on the quarter where the king of Edom was; and, though not successful, took prisoner the son of the king of Edom; and, on their return into the city, offered him as a burnt offering upon the wall, so as to terrify the besieging armies, and cause them to raise the siege. Others understand the son that was sacrificed to be the king of Moab's own son.

2. *The palaces of Kirioth.* This was one of the principal cities of the Moabites. *Moab shall die with tumult.* All these expressions seem to refer to this city's being taken by storm, which was followed by a total slaughter of its inhabitants.

3. *I will cut off the judge. Shophet* may signify the chief magistrate.

4. *For three transgressions of Judah.* We may take the *three* and *four* here to any latitude; for this people lived in continual hostility to their God, from the days of David to the time of Uzziah, under whom Amos prophesied. Their iniquities are summed up under three general heads: (1) They *despised,* or rejected, *the law of the Lord.* (2) They kept not His statutes. (3) They followed *lies,* were idolaters, and followed false prophets rather than those sent by Jehovah.

5. *I will send a fire upon Judah.* This fire was the war made upon the Jews by Nebuchadnezzar, which terminated with the sackage and burning of Jerusalem and its palace, the Temple.

6-8. *For three transgressions of Israel.* To be satisfied of the exceeding delinquency of this people, we have only to open the historical and prophetic books in any part, for the whole history of the Israelites is one tissue of transgression against God. Their crimes are enumerated under the following heads: (1) Their judges were mercenary and corrupt.

(2) They were unmerciful to the poor generally. They *pant after the dust of the earth on the head of the poor;* or, to put it on the head of the poor; or, they bruise the head of the poor against the dust of the earth. (3) They *turn aside the way of the meek.* They are peculiarly oppressive to the weak and afflicted. (4) They were licentious to the uttermost abomination; for in their idol feasts, where young women prostituted themselves publicly in honor of Astarte, the father and son entered into impure connections with the same female. (5) They were cruel in their oppressions of the poor; for the garments or beds which the poor had pledged they retained contrary to the law, Exod. xxii. 7-26, which required that such things should be restored before the setting of the sun. (6) They punished the people by unjust and oppressive fines, and served their tables with wine bought by such fines. Or it may be understood of their appropriating to themselves that wine which was allowed to criminals to mitigate their sufferings in the article of death.

MATTHEW HENRY

II. He upbraids them with the spiritual privileges they enjoyed as a holy nation, *v.* 11. They had prophets divinely inspired, and commissioned to make known the mind of God to them. It was an honour that they had children of their own to be God's messengers to them. They had Nazarites that were bright examples of piety. These God raised up to be his witnesses against the impieties of that degenerate age.

III. He charges them with the abuse of the means of grace they enjoyed, *v.* 12. They did what they could to debauch good people: *You gave the Nazarites wine to drink*, contrary to their vow. They did what they could to silence good ministers, and to stop their mouths: *You commanded the prophets, saying, Prophesy not*, and threatened them if they did prophesy (*ch.* vii. 12).

IV. He complains of the wrong they did him by their sins (*v.* 13): "*I am pressed under you*, I am *straitened* by you (Hos. xi. 8, 9). I am loaded and burdened by you (Isa. i. 24). *I am pressed under you* and the load of your sins *as a cart is pressed that is full of sheaves*, is loaded with corn, in the midst of the *joy of harvest*."

V. He threatens them with unavoidable ruin. And so some read, *v.* 13, "*Behold I will press*, or straiten, *your place, as a cart full of sheaves presses;* they shall be loaded with judgments till they sink." If God load us daily with his benefits, and we, notwithstanding that, load him with our sins, how can we expect any other than that he should load us with his judgments? When the Assyrian army comes to lay the country waste by sword and captivity none shall escape. *He that is swift of foot shall not deliver himself*, *v.* 15. Or do they say, *We will flee upon horses*, and *we will ride upon the swift*? Yet they shall be overtaken. It will be in vain to think of fighting it out. *The strong shall not strengthen his force*. And *the mighty* shall not be able to *deliver himself*. And, as the bodily strength shall fail, so shall the weapons of war. *Neither shall he stand that handles the bow. He that is courageous among the mighty*, that used to look danger in the face, shall *flee away naked in that day*.

JAMIESON, FAUSSET, BROWN

destroyed him *utterly* (Job 18:16; Ezek. 17:9; Mal. 4:1). **10. brought you up from . . . Egypt**—"brought up" is the phrase, as Egypt was low and flat, and Canaan hilly. **to possess the land of the Amorite**—The Amorites strictly occupied both sides of the Jordan and the mountains afterward possessed by Judah; but they here, as in vs. 9, stand for *all* the Canaanites. God kept Israel forty years in the wilderness, which tended to discipline them in His statutes, so as to be the better fitted for entering on the possession of Canaan. **11.** Additional obligations under which Israel lay to God; the *prophets* and *Nazarites,* appointed by Him, to furnish religious instruction and examples of holy self-restraint. **of your young men**—It was a specimen of Israel's highly favored state, that, of the class most addicted to pleasures, God chose those who by a solemn vow bound themselves to abstinence from all produce of the vine, and from all ceremonial and moral defilement. The Nazarite was not to shave (Num. 6:2, etc.). God left nothing undone to secure the purity of their worship and their faithfulness to it (Lam. 4:7). The same comes from a *Hebrew* root, *nazar,* "to set apart." Samson, Samuel, and John the Baptist were Nazarites. **Is it not even thus**—Will any of you dare to deny it is so? **12.** Ye so despised these My favors, as to tempt the Nazarite to break his vow; and forbade the prophets prophesying (Isa. 30:10). So Amaziah forbade Amos (ch. 7:12, 13, 14). **13. I am pressed under you**—so CALVIN (cf. Isa. 1:14). *Margin* translates actively, "I will depress your place," i.e., "I will make it narrow," a metaphor for *afflicting* a people; the opposite of *enlarging,* i.e., relieving (Ps. 4:1; Prov. 4:12). MAURER translates, "I will press you *down*" (not as *Margin,* "your place"; so the *Hebrew,* Job 40:12; or vs. 7 in *Hebrew* text). Amos, as a shepherd, appropriately draws his similes from rustic scenes. **14. flight shall perish from . . . swift**—Even the swift shall not be able to escape. **strong shall not strengthen his force**—i.e., shall not be able to use his strength. **himself**—lit., "his life." **16. flee . . . naked**—If any escape, it must be with the loss of accoutrements, and all that would impede rapid flight. They must be content with saving their life alone.

ADAM CLARKE

12. *But ye gave the Nazarites wine.* This was expressly forbidden in the laws of their institution. See Num. vi. 1-3.

13. *Behold, I am pressed under you.* The marginal reading is better: "Behold, I will press your place, as a cart full of sheaves presseth."

15. *Neither shall he that rideth the horse deliver himself.* I believe all these sayings, from verse 13 to 16 inclusive, are proverbs, to show the inutility of all attempts, even in the best circumstances, to escape the doom now decreed, because the cup of their iniquity was full.

MATTHEW HENRY — CHAPTER 3

Verses 1-8

The *children of Israel* would not regard the words of counsel that God had spoken to them, and now they shall be made to hear the word of reproof.

I. The gracious cognizance God had taken of them, and the favours he had bestowed, should not exempt them from the punishment due for their sins. Israel is a *family* that God *brought up out of the land of Egypt* (*v.* 1), and it was no more than a family when it went thither; thence God delivered it. It is a family that God has owned in a peculiar manner. *In Judah is God known*, and therefore Judah is known of God. God has covenanted with them, and conversed with them. *Therefore I will punish you for all your iniquities*. The favours of God, if they do not restrain us from sin, shall not exempt us from punishment. It is necessary that God should vindicate his own honour by making it appear that he hates sin and hates it most in those that are nearest to him.

II. They could not expect any comfortable communion with God unless they first made their peace with him (*v.* 3): *Can two walk together except they be agreed?* Where there is not friendship, there cannot be fellowship.

JAMIESON, FAUSSET, BROWN — CHAPTER 3

VSS. 1-15. GOD'S EXTRAORDINARY LOVE, BEING REPAID BY ISRAEL WITH INGRATITUDE, OF NECESSITY CALLS FOR JUDGMENTS, WHICH THE PROPHETS ANNOUNCE, NOT AT RANDOM, BUT BY GOD'S COMMISSION, WHICH THEY CANNOT BUT FULFIL. THE OPPRESSION PREVALENT IN ISRAEL WILL BRING DOWN RUIN ON ALL SAVE A SMALL REMNANT. **1. children of Israel**—not merely the ten tribes, but "the *whole family* brought up from Egypt"; all the descendants of Jacob, including Judah and Benjamin. Cf. Jeremiah 8:3, and Micah 2:3, on "family" for the nation However, as the prophecy following refers to the ten tribes, *they* must be chiefly, if not solely, meant: they were the majority of the nation; and so Amos concedes what they so often boasted, that they were the elect people of God [CALVIN], *but* implies that this only heightens their sins. **2. You only have I known**—i.e., acknowledged as My people, and treated with peculiar favor (Exod. 19:5; Deut. 4:20). Cf. the use of "know," Psalm 1:6; 144:3; John 10: 14; II Timothy 2:19. **therefore I will punish**—the greater the privileges, the heavier the punishment for the abuse of them; for to the other offenses there is added, in this case, ingratitude. When God's people do not glorify Him, He glorifies Himself by punishing them. **3.** Here follow several questions of a parable-like kind, to awaken conviction in the people. **Can two walk together, except they be agreed?**—Can God's prophets be so unanimous in prophesying against you, if God's Spirit were not joined with them, or if their prophecies were false? The Israelites were "at ease," not believing that God was with the prophets in their denunciations of coming ruin to the nation (ch. 6:1, 3; cf. I Kings 22:18, 24, 27; Jer. 43:2). This accords with vss. 7, 8. So "I will be with thy mouth" (Exod. 4:12; Jer. 1:8; Matt. 10:20). If the prophets and God were not agreed, the former could not predict the future as they do. In ch. 2:12 He had said, the Israelites forbade the prophets prophesying; therefore, in vss. 3, 8, He asserts the agreement between the prophets and God who spake by them against Israel [ROSENMULLER]. Rather, I once walked with you (Lev. 26:12) as a Father and Husband (Isa. 54:5; Jer. 3:14); but now your way and Mine are utterly diverse; there can therefore be no fellowship between us such as there was (vs. 2); I

ADAM CLARKE — CHAPTER 3

1. *Against the whole family.* That is, all, both the kingdoms of Israel and Judah. In this all the twelve tribes are included.

2. *You only have I known.* I have taken no other people to be My own people. I have approved of you, loved you, fed, sustained, and defended you; but because you have forsaken Me, have become idolatrous and polluted, therefore will I punish you. And the punishment shall be in proportion to the privileges you have enjoyed, and the grace you have abused.

MATTHEW HENRY

III. The warnings God gave them of judgments approaching were not groundless (*v.* 4): "*Will a lion roar in the forest when he has no prey* in view? No; he roars upon his prey. Nor would God thus give you warning if he were not really about to fall upon you with judgments." The threatenings of the word and providence of God are not bugbears, to frighten children and fools, but are inferences from the sin of man and presages of the judgments of God.

IV. Their own wickedness was the cause of these judgments, *v.* 5. It is their own sin that has entangled them; for *can a bird fall in a snare upon the earth where no gin is for him?* Nothing but their own repentance can disentangle them.

V. All their troubles came from the hand of God's providence (*v.* 6).

VI. Their prophets, who give them warning of judgments approaching, deliver nothing to them but what they have *received from the Lord* (*v.* 7): *Surely the Lord Jehovah will do nothing*, none of that evil in the city spoken of (*v.* 6), *but he reveals it to his servants the prophets.* The *secret* of God is in a peculiar manner with the prophets, to whom the Spirit of prophecy is a Spirit of revelation. The prophets cannot but make that known to the people which God has made known to them (*v.* 8): *The Lord God has spoken; who can but prophesy?* They received a command from God to deliver what they had been charged with; and they would have been false to their trust if they had not done it.

VII. They ought to tremble before God as they would on the sounding of a trumpet. *Shall a trumpet be blown in the city, and the people not be afraid,* or *run together?* (so some read it, *v.* 6). Yet when God by his prophets gives them notice of their danger it makes no impression.

Verses 9–15

The Israelites are again convicted and condemned.

I. Notice is given of it to their neighbours. The prophet is ordered to *publish it in the palaces of Ashdod*, one of the chief cities of the Philistines; the summons must go even to *the palaces in the land of Egypt*. God's controversies with sinners do not fear a scrutiny; even Philistines and Egyptians will be made to see that *the ways of the Lord are equal,* but *our ways are unequal.*

1. Let them observe the behaviour of the inhabitants of Samaria; and they may see how boisterous they are, and hear how loud the cry of their sin is, as was that of Sodom.

In their streets you will see *great tumults in the midst thereof*; reason and justice run down by the fury of an outrageous mob. *The oppressed* are *in the midst thereof,* thrown down and crushed by their oppressors. In their courts of justice, those who preside *know not to do right*; they act as if they had no notion at all of justice. Their treasures and stores are replenished with *violence and robbery*, with that which was unjustly got and unjustly kept.

2. Let them see how heavy the doom is, *v.* 11, 12. Their country shall be invaded and ruined. The Assyrian forces shall surround it and break in on every side. They *stored up robbery in their palaces*, and therefore their *palaces shall be spoiled.* Their countrymen shall not escape, *v.* 12. They shall be in the hands of the enemy, as a lamb in the mouth of a lion, devoured and eaten up, and if any do escape,

JAMIESON, FAUSSET, BROWN

will walk with you only to "punish you"; as a "lion" walks with his "prey" (vs. 4), as a bird-catcher with a bird [TARNOVIUS]. The prophets, and all servants of God, can have no fellowship with the ungodly (Ps. 119:63; II Cor. 6:16, 17; Eph. 5:11; Jas. 4:4). **4.** The same idea as in Matthew 34:28. Where a corrupt nation is, there God's instruments of punishment are sure also to be. The lion roars loudly only when he has prey in sight. **Will a young lion cry out . . . if he**—the "lion," not the "young lion"—**have taken nothing?**—The young lion just weaned lies silent, until the old lion brings the prey near; then the scent rouses him. So, the prophet would not speak against Israel, if God did not reveal to him Israel's sins as requiring punishment. **5.** When a bird trying to fly upwards is made to fall upon the earth-snare, it is a plain proof that the snare is there; so, Israel, now that thou art falling, infer thence, that it is in the snare of the divine judgment that thou art entangled [LUDOVICUS DE DIEU]. **shall** *one* **take up a snare from the earth, and have taken nothing**—The bird-catcher does not remove his snare off the ground till he has caught some prey; so God will not withdraw the Assyrians, etc., the instruments of punishment, until they have had the success against you which God gives them. The foe corresponds to the "snare," suddenly *springing* from the ground and enclosing the bird on the latter touching it; the *Hebrew* is lit., "Shall the snare *spring* from the earth?" Israel entangled in judgments answers to the bird "taken." **6.** When the sound of alarm is trumpeted by the watchman in the city, the people are sure to *run to and fro in alarm* (*Hebrew* lit.). Yet Israel is not alarmed, though God threatens judgments. **shall there be evil in a city, and the Lord hath not done it?**—This is the explanation of the preceding similes: God is the Author of all the calamities which come upon you, and which are foretold by His prophets. The evil of sin is from ourselves; the evil of trouble is from God, whoever be the instruments. **7. his secret**—viz., His purpose hidden from all, until it is revealed to His prophets (cf. Gen. 18:17). In a wider sense, God's will is revealed to all who love God, which it is not to the world (Ps. 25:14; John 15:15; 17:25, 26). **unto his servants**—who being *servants* cannot but obey their Lord in setting forth His purpose (viz., that of judgment against Israel) (Jer. 20:9; Ezek. 9:11). Therefore the fault which the ungodly find with them is groundless (I Kings 18:17). It aggravates Israel's sin, that God is not about to inflict judgment, without having fully warned the people, if haply they might repent. **8.** As when "the lion roars" (cf. ch. 1:2; and vs. 4 above), none can help but "fear," so when Jehovah communicates His awful message, the prophet cannot but prophesy. Find not fault with me for prophesying; I must obey God. In a wider sense true of all believers (Acts 4:20; 5:29). **9. Publish in . . . palaces**—as being places of greatest resort (cf. Matt. 10:27); and also as it is the sin of *princes* that he arraigns, he calls on princes (the occupants of the "palaces") to be the witnesses. **Ashdod**—put for all Philistia. Convene the Philistine and the Egyptian magnates, from whom I have on various occasions rescued Israel. (The opposite formula to "Tell it not in Gath," viz., lest the heathen should glory over Israel). Even these idolaters, in looking on your enormities, will condemn you; how much more will the holy God? **upon the mountains of Samaria**—on the hills surrounding and commanding the view of Samaria, the metropolis of the ten tribes, which was on a lower hill (ch. 4:1; I Kings 16:24). The mountains are to be the tribunal on which the Philistines and Egyptians are to sit aloft to have a view of your crimes, so as to testify to the justice of your punishment (vs. 13). **tumults**—caused by the violence of the princes of Israel in "oppressions" of the poor (Job 35:9; Eccles. 4:1). **10. know not to do**—Their moral corruption blinds their power of discernment so that they cannot do right (Jer. 4;22). Not simple intellectual ignorance; the defect lay in the heart and will. **store up violence and robbery**—i.e., treasures obtained by "violence and robbery" (Prov. 10:2). **11.** Translate, "An adversary [the abruptness produces a startling effect]! *and that too,* from every side of the land." So in the fulfilment, II Kings 17:5: "The king of Assyria [Shalmaneser] came up *throughout all the land,* and went up to Samaria, and besieged it three years." **bring down thy strength from thee**—i.e., bring thee down from thy strength (the strength on which thou didst boast thyself): all thy resources (Prov. 10:15). **palaces shall be spoiled**—a just retribution in kind (vs. 10). *The palaces* in which spoils of *robbery* were *stored up,* "shall be spoiled." **12. shepherd**—a pastoral image, appropriately used by Amos, a shepherd him-

ADAM CLARKE

5. *Can a bird fall in a snare?* Can you, as a sinful people, fall into calamities which I have not appointed? *Shall one take up a snare . . . and have taken nothing?* Will the snare be removed before it has caught the expected prey? Shall I remove My judgments till they are fully accomplished?

6. *Shall a trumpet be blown?* The sign of alarm and invasion. *Shall there be evil in a city?* Shall there be any public calamity on the wicked that is not an effect of My displeasure? The word does not mean moral evil, but punishment for sin.

8. *The lion hath roared.* God hath sent forth a terrible alarm. *Who will not fear?* Can any hear such denunciations of divine wrath and not tremble? *Who can but prophesy?* Who can help proclaiming at large the judgment threatened against the nation? But I think *naba,* here, is to be taken in its natural and ideal signification, to "pray, supplicate." The Lord hath spoken of punishment—who can help supplicating His mercy, that His judgments may be averted?

12. *As the shepherd taketh out of the mouth of the lion.* Scarcely any of you shall escape;

MATTHEW HENRY

yet they shall be very few, and those of the meanest and least considerable, like *two legs*, or *shanks*, of a lamb, *or a piece of an ear*, which the lion drops, or *the shepherd* takes from him, when he has eaten the body; so, perhaps, here and there one may escape from Samaria and from Damascus, but those shall do so with the utmost hazard, by hiding themselves in the *corner of a bed* or under the *bed's feet*, which intimates that their spirits shall be quite cowed and broken.

II. Notice is given to themselves, *v.* 13. Let this be *testified*, and *heard, in the house of Jacob*, for it is spoken *by the Lord God, the God of hosts.*

1. Woe to *their altars*, for God will *visit* them. He will bring into the account all their superstition and idolatry—*the horns of the altar shall be cut off*, and *fall to the ground*, and with them the altar itself broken to pieces. Some make *the horns of the altar* to signify all those things which they flee to for refuge; they shall all be cut off, so that they shall have nothing to take hold of. 2. Woe to their houses, for God will visit them too. He will enquire into the robbery they have stored up in their houses, and the luxury in which they lived: *and I will smite the winter-house with the summer-house*, *v.* 15. *The houses of ivory shall perish*, shall be burnt or pulled down; *and the great houses shall have an end;* their extravagance about them will be put to the score of their sins and follies.

JAMIESON, FAUSSET, BROWN

self. **piece of . . . ear**—brought by the shepherd to the owner of the sheep, so as not to have to pay for the loss (Gen. 31:39; Exod. 22:13). So if aught of Israel escapes, it shall be a miracle of God's goodness. It shall be but a scanty remnant. There is a kind of goat in the East the ears of which are a foot long, and proportionally broad. Perhaps the reference is to this. Cf. on the image I Samuel 17:34, 35; II Timothy 4:17. **that dwell in Samaria in the corner of a bed**—i.e., that live luxuriously in Samaria (cf. ch. 6:1, 4). "A bed" means here the Oriental divan, a raised part of the room covered with cushions. **in Damascus in a couch**—Jeroboam II had lately restored Damascus to Israel (II Kings 14:25, 28). So the Israelites are represented as not merely in "the corner of a bed," as in Samaria, but "in a [whole] couch," at Damascus, living in luxurious ease. Of these, now so luxurious, soon but a remnant shall be left by the foe. The destruction of Damascus and that of Samaria shall be conjoined; as here their luxurious lives, and subsequently under Pekah and Rezin their inroads on Judah, were combined (Isa. 7:1-8; 8:4, 9; 17:3). The parallelism of "Samaria" to "Damascus," and LXX favor *English Version* rather than GESENIUS: "on a *damask* couch." The *Hebrew* pointing, though generally expressing *damask*, may express the city "Damascus"; and many MSS. point it so. Cf. for Israel's overthrow, II Kings 17:5, 6; 18:9-12. **13. testify in the house . . .**—i.e., *against* the house of Jacob. God calls on the same persons as in vs. 9, viz., the heathen Philistines and the Egyptians to witness with their own eyes Samaria's corruptions above described, so that none may be able to deny the justice of Samaria's punishment [MAURER]. **God of hosts**—having all the powers of heaven and earth at His command, and therefore One calculated to strike terror into the hearts of the guilty whom He threatens. **14. That**—rather, "since," or "for." This verse is not, as *English Version* translates, the thing which the witnesses cited are to "testify" (vs. 13), but the reason why God calls on the heathen to witness Samaria's guilt; viz., in order to justify the punishment which He declares He will inflict. **I will also visit . . . Beth-el**—the golden calves which were the source of all "the transgressions of Israel" (I Kings 12:32; 13:2; II Kings 23:15, 16), though Israel thought that by them their transgressions were atoned for and God's favor secured. **horns of the altar**—which used to be sprinkled with the blood of victims. They were horn-like projecting points at the corners of ancient altars. The *singular*, "altar," refers to the great altar erected by Jeroboam to the calves. The "altars," *plural*, refer to the lesser ones made in imitation of the great one (II Chron. 34:5, cf. with I Kings 13:2; Hos. 8: 11;; 10:1). **15. winter . . . summer house**—(Judg. 3: 20; Jer. 36:22). Winter houses of the great were in sheltered positions facing the south to get all possible sunshine, summer houses in forests and on hills, facing the east and north. **houses of ivory**—having their walls, doors, and ceilings inlaid with ivory. So Ahab's house (I Kings 22:39; Ps. 45:8).

ADAM CLARKE

and those that do shall do so with extreme difficulty, just as a shepherd, of a whole sheep carried away by a lion, can recover no more than two of its legs or a piece of its ear, just enough to prove by the marks on those parts that they belonged to a sheep which was his own. *So shall the children of Israel be taken out.* Those of them that escape these judgments shall escape with as great difficulty, and be of as little worth, as the two legs and piece of an ear that shall be snatched out of the lion's mouth. *In the corner of a bed.* The *corner* is the most honorable place in the East, and a *couch* in the corner of a room is the place of the greatest distinction.

13. *Hear ye.* This is an address to the prophet.

14. *In the day that I shall visit.* When Josiah made a reformation in the land he destroyed idolatry, pulled down the temples and altars that had been consecrated to idol worship, and even burnt the bones of the priests of Baal and the golden calves upon their own altars. See 2 Kings xxiii. 15-16, etc.

15. *I will smite the winter house with the summer house.* I will not only destroy the poor habitations and villages in the country, but I will destroy those of the nobility and gentry; as well the lofty palaces in the fortified cities in which they dwell in the winter season, as those light and elegant seats in which they spend the summer season. *And the houses of ivory.* Those remarkable for their magnificence and their ornaments, not built of ivory, but in which ivory vessels, ornaments, and inlaying abounded.

MATTHEW HENRY — CHAPTER 4

Verses 1–5

Oppressors shall be humbled and idolaters shall be hardened.

I. Proud oppressors shall be humbled for their oppressions; for *he that does wrong shall receive according to the wrong that he has done.*

1. How their sin is described, *v.* 1. They are compared to the *kine of Bashan*, a breed of cattle very strong, especially if they were fed upon *the mountain of Samaria.* Amos had been a herdsman, and he speaks in the dialect of his calling, comparing the rich men, that lived in luxury and wantonness, to the *kine of Bashan*, which were wanton and unruly, broke through the hedges, and trespassed upon the neighbouring grounds; and not only so, but pushed and gored the smaller cattle. Those that had their summer-houses upon the mountains of Samaria were as mischievous as the kine upon the mountains of Bashan and as injurious to those about them. They oppress the poor and *crush* them, to squeeze something out of them. They are in confederacy with those that do so. They *say to their masters* (to the masters of the poor, that take from them what they have, when they ought to relieve them), "*Bring, and let us drink;* let us feast with you upon the gains of your oppression, and then we will protect you, and stand by you in it, and reject the appeals of the poor against you."

2. How their punishment is described, *v.* 2, 3. God will *take them away with hooks, and their pos-*

JAMIESON, FAUSSET, BROWN — CHAPTER 4

Vss. 1-13. DENUNCIATION OF ISRAEL'S NOBLES FOR OPPRESSION; AND OF THE WHOLE NATION FOR IDOLATRY; AND FOR THEIR BEING UNREFORMED EVEN BY GOD'S JUDGMENTS: THEREFORE THEY MUST PREPARE FOR THE LAST AND WORST JUDGMENT OF ALL. **1. kine of Bashan**—fat and wanton cattle such as the rich pasture of Bashan (east of Jordan, between Hermon and Gilead) was famed for (Deut. 32:14; Ps. 22:12; Ezek. 39:18). Figurative for those luxurious nobles mentioned, ch. 3:9, 10, 12, 15. The feminine, *kine*, or *cows*, not *bulls*, expresses their effeminacy. This accounts for masculine forms in the *Hebrew* being intermixed with feminine; the latter being figurative, the former the real persons meant. **say to their masters**—i.e., to *their king*, with whom the princes indulged in potations (Hos. 7:5), and whom here they importune for more wine. "Bring" is *singular*, in the *Hebrew* implying that *one* "master" alone is meant. **2. The Lord**—the same *Hebrew* as "masters" (vs. 1). Israel's nobles say to their master or lord, Bring us drink: but "the Lord" of him and them "hath sworn . . . ." **by his holiness**—which binds Him to punish the guilty (Ps. 89:35). **he will take you away**—i.e., God by the instrumentality of the enemy. **with hooks**—lit., "thorns" (cf.II Chron. 33:11). As fish are taken out of the water by hooks, so the Israelites are to be taken out of their cities by the enemy (Ezek. 29: 4; cf. Job 41:1, 2; Jer. 16:16; Hab. 1:15). The image is the more appropriate, as anciently cap-

ADAM CLARKE — CHAPTER 4

1. *Hear this word, ye kine of Bashan.* Such an address was quite natural from the herdsman of Tekoa. *Bashan* was famous for the fertility of its soil, and its flocks and herds; and the prophet here represents the iniquitous, opulent, idle, lazy drones, whether men or women, under the idea of fatted bullocks, which were shortly to be led out to the slaughter.

2. *He will take you away with hooks.* Two modes of fishing are here alluded to: (1) angling with rod, line, and baited hook; (2) that with the gaff, eel-spear, harpoon, or suchlike—the first used in catching small fish, by which the common people may be here represented; the second, for catching large fish. Some understand the latter word as meaning a sort of fishnets.

MATTHEW HENRY

terity with fish-hooks; he will send the Assyrian army upon them, that shall not only enclose the body of the nation in their net, but shall angle for particular persons, and take them prisoners as with fish-hooks, shall draw them out of their own land as fish are drawn out of the water. Some shall attempt to escape by flight: *You shall go out at the breaches* made in the wall of the city, *every cow at that which is before her*, to shift for her own safety, and now the unruly kine of Bashan are themselves crushed, as they crushed the poor and needy. Others shall think to shelter themselves: *You shall throw yourselves* (so some read it), or *throw them* (that is your children) *into the palace*, where the enemy will find them ready to be seized.

3. How their sentence to this punishment is ratified: *The Lord God has sworn it by his holiness.* He swears by *his holiness*, that attribute of his which is so much his glory.

II. Obstinate idolaters shall be hardened in their idolatries (*v.* 4, 5): *Come to Bethel, and transgress.* It is spoken ironically: "*Do* so; take your course; *multiply* your *transgressions* by multiplying your sacrifices, *for this liketh you*; but what will you do in the end?" They mimicked God's institutions.

They had their *daily sacrifice* at the altar of Bethel, as God had at his altar; they had their *thank-offerings* as God had, only they allowed *leaven* in them. Holy bread would not serve them, unless it were pleasant bread. They are upbraided with it. "Your foolish hearts shall be more and more darkened and besotted, and you shall be quite *given up to* these *strong delusions, to believe a lie.*" Thus Christ said to the Jews, *Fill you up the measure of your fathers*, Matt. xxiii. 32.

Verses 6–13

I. God had by several tokens intimated to them his displeasure, but it had no effect.

1. It is five times repeated in these verses, as the burden of the charge, "*Yet have you not returned unto me, saith the Lord;* there is no sign of amendment. This intimates that that which God designed in all his rebukes was to influence them to return to him. If they had returned to their God, they would have been accepted. It is no *pleasure to the Almighty that he should afflict.*

2. He recounts the less judgments with which he had tried to bring them to repentance. There had sometimes been a scarcity of provisions (*v.* 6): "*I have given you cleanness of teeth in all your cities*, for you had no meat to chew." Or, *I have given you emptiness of teeth*, nothing to fill your mouths with. Some think this refers to that *seven years' famine* that was in Elisha's time, which we read of 2 Kings viii. 1. *I have withholden the rain from you.* The rain was withheld *when there were yet three months to the harvest.*

Sometimes the fruits of their ground were eaten up by caterpillars, or blasted with mildew, *v.* 9. But they did not take warning: *Yet have you not returned unto me.*

Sometimes the plague had raged among them, and the sword of war had cut off multitudes, *v.* 10. It was a *pestilence after the manner of Egypt. In the way of Egypt* (so the margin); when they were making their escape to Egypt, or going thither to seek for aid, the pestilence seized them by the way.

JAMIESON, FAUSSET, BROWN

tives were led by their conquerors by a hook made to pass through the nose (II Kings 19:28), as is to be seen in the Assyrian remains. **3. go out at the breaches**—viz., of the city walls broken by the enemy. **every** *cow at that which is* **before her**—figurative for *the once luxurious nobles* (cf. vs. 1, "kine of Bashan") shall go out *each one right before her;* not through the gates, but *each at the breach before him*, not turning to the right or left, apart from one another. **ye shall cast** *them* **into the palace**—"them," i.e., "your posterity," from vs. 2. You yourselves shall escape through the breaches, after having cast your little children into the palace, so as not to see their destruction, and to escape the more quickly. Rather, "ye shall cast *yourselves* into the palace," so as to escape from it out of the city [CALVIN]. The palace, the scene of the princes' riots (ch. 3:10, 15; 4:1), is to be the scene of their ignominious flight. Cf. in the similar case of *Jerusalem's* capture, the king's escape by way of the palace, through a breach in the wall (Ezek. 12:5, 12). GESENIUS translates, "Ye shall be cast [as captives] into the [enemy's] stronghold"; in this view, the enemy's stronghold is called "palace," in retributive contrast to the "palaces" of Israel's nobles, the *store houses* of their *robberies* (ch. 3:10). **4.** God gives them up to their self-willed idolatry, that they may see how unable their idols are to save them from their coming calamities. So Ezekiel 20: 39. **Beth-el**—(ch. 3:14). **Gilgal**—(Hos. 4:15; 9:15; 12:11). **sacrifices every morning**—as commanded in the law (Num. 28:3, 4). They imitated the letter, while violating by calf worship the spirit, of the Jerusalem temple worship. **after three years**—every third year; lit., "after three [years of] days" (i.e., the fullest complement of days, or *a year*); "after three *full* years." Cf. Leviticus 25:20; Judges 17:10, and "the days" for the *years,* Joel 1:2. So *a month of days* is used for *a full month*, wanting no day to complete it (*Margin*, Gen. 29:14; Num. 11:20, 21). The Israelites here also kept to the letter of the law in bringing in the tithes of their increase every third year (Deut. 14:28; 26:12). **5. offer**—lit., "burn incense"; i.e., "offer a sacrifice of thanksgiving with *burnt incense* and with leavened bread." The frankincense was laid on the meat offering, and taken by the priest from it to burn on the altar (Lev. 2:1, 2, 8-11). Though *unleavened cakes* were to accompany the peace offering sacrifice of animals, *leavened bread* was also commanded (Lev. 7:12, 13), but not as a "meat offering" (Lev. 2:11). **this liketh you**—i.e., this is what ye like. **6-11.** Jehovah details His several chastisements inflicted with a view to reclaiming them: but adds to each the same sad result, "yet have ye not returned unto Me" (Isa. 9:13; Jer. 5:3; Hos. 7:10); the monotonous repetion of the same burden marking their pitiable obstinacy. **cleanness of teeth**—explained by the parallel, "want of bread." The famine alluded to is that mentioned in II Kings 8:1 [GROTIUS]. Where there is no food to masticate, the teeth are free from uncleanness, but it is the cleanness of want. Cf. Proverbs 14:4, "Where no oxen are, the crib is clean." So spiritually, where all is outwardly smooth and clean, it is often because there is no solid religion. Better fighting and fears with real piety, than peace and respectable decorum without spiritual life. **7. withholden . . . rain . . . three months to . . . harvest**—the time when rain was most needed, and when usually "the latter rain" fell, viz., in spring, the latter half of February, and the whole of March and April (Hos. 6:3; Joel 2:23). The drought meant is that mentioned in I Kings 17:1 [GROTIUS]. **rain upon one city . . . not . . . upon another**—Any rain that fell was only partial. **8. three cities wandered**—i.e., *the inhabitants of* three cities (cf. Jer. 14:1-6). GROTIUS explains this verse and vs. 7, "The rain fell on neighboring countries, but not on Israel, which marked the drought to be, not accidental, but the special judgment of God." The Israelites were obliged to leave their cities and homes to seek water at a distance [CALVIN]. **9. blasting**—the blighting influence of the east wind on the corn (Gen. 41:6). **when . . . gardens . . . increased**—In vain ye multiplied your gardens, etc., for I destroyed their produce. BOCHART supports *Margin*, "the *multitude* of your gardens." **palmer worm**—A species of *locust* is here meant, hurtful to fruits of trees, not to herbage or corn. The same east wind which brought the drought, blasting, and mildew, brought also the locusts into Judea [BOCHART], (Exod. 10:13). **10. pestilence after the manner of Egypt**—such as I formerly sent on the Egyptians (Exod. 9:3, 8, etc.; 12:29; Deut. 28:27, 60). Cf. the same phrase, Isaiah 10:24. **have taken away your horses**—lit., "accompanied with the captivity of your horses"; I have given up your young men to be slain, and their

ADAM CLARKE

3. *And ye shall go out at the breaches.* Probably the metaphor is here kept up. They shall be caught by the hooks, or by the nets; and though they may make breaches in the latter by their flouncing, when caught they shall be taken out at these very breaches.

4. *Come to Beth-el, and transgress.* Spoken ironically. Go on to worship your calves at Bethel; and multiply your transgressions at Gilgal, the very place where I rolled away the reproach of your fathers, by admitting them there into My covenant by circumcision—a place that should have ever been sacred to Me, but you have now desecrated it by enormous idolatries. Let your morning and evening sacrifices be offered still to your senseless gods, and continue to support your present vicious priesthood by the regular triennial tithes which should have been employed in My service.

5. *Offer a sacrifice of thanksgiving.* To the senseless metal, from which ye never did and never could receive any help. Proceed yet further, and bring freewill offerings; testify superabundant gratitude to your metallic gods, to whom ye are under such immense imaginary obligations! *Proclaim and publish* these *offerings*, and set forth the perfections of the subjects of your worship; and see what they can do for you, when I, Jehovah, shall send drought, and blasting, and famine, and pestilence, and the sword among you.

6. *Cleanness of teeth.* Scarcity of bread, as immediately explained. *Yet have ye not returned unto me, saith the Lord.* This reprehension is repeated five times in this chapter; and in it are strongly implied God's long-suffering, His various modes of fatherly chastisement, the ingratitude of the people, and their obstinate wickedness.

7. *When there were yet three months to the harvest.* St. Jerome says, from the end of April, when the latter rain falls, until harvest, there are three months, May, June, and July, in which no rain falls in Judea. The rain, therefore, that God had withheld from them was that which was usual in the spring months, particularly in April. *I caused it to rain upon one city.* To prove to them that this rain did not come fortuitously or of necessity, God was pleased to make these most evident distinctions.

MATTHEW HENRY

The dead carcases of those that were slain either with sword or pestilence were so many that the *stench of their camps came up into their nostrils*. And yet this did not prevail to make them religious. In these judgments some were remarkably cut off, and made monuments of justice, others were remarkably spared, and made monuments of mercy, but it had no effect, *v.* 11. *I have overthrown some of you, as God overthrew Sodom and Gomorrah.*

Others very narrowly escaped: "You *were* many of you as a *firebrand plucked out of the burning*, like Lot out of Sodom, and yet you hate sin never the more, nor love God ever the more for the deliverance he wrought for you."

II. God calls upon his people, now in this their day, to understand the things that belong to their peace, before they were hidden from their eyes, *v.* 12, 13. He threatens them with sorer judgments than any they had yet been under. Nothing but reformation will prevent the ruin of a sinful people. *I will punish you yet seven times more, if you will* not *be reformed* (Lev. xxvi. 23, 24). "Resolve therefore to meet him as a humble suppliant, to meet him as *thy God*, in covenant with thee, to submit, and stand it out no longer." Since we cannot flee from God we are concerned to prepare to meet him; and therefore he gives us warning, that we may prepare. He sets forth the greatness and power of God as a reason why we should prepare to meet him, *v.* 13. He that formed the *great mountains* can *make them plain*, when they stand in the way of his people's salvation. He *declares unto man what is his thought*. He makes known by his servants the prophets the thought of his justice against impenitent sinners, and the thought of good he thinks towards those that repent. He knows the thought that is in man's heart; he *understands it afar off*. He *treads upon the high places of the earth*, tramples upon proud men, and upon the idols that were worshipped in the highest places. *Jehovah the God of hosts is his name*, for he has his being of himself, and is the fountain of all being, and all the hosts of heaven and earth are at his command. Let us humble ourselves before this God.

JAMIESON, FAUSSET, BROWN

horses to be taken by the foe (cf. II Kings 13:7). **stink of your camps**—i.e., of your slain men (cf. Isa. 34:3; Joel 2:20). **to come up unto your nostrils**—The *Hebrew* is more emphatic, "to come up, *and that* unto your nostrils." **11. some of you**—some parts of your territory. **as God overthrew Sodom**—(Deut. 29:23; Isa. 13:19; Jer. 49:18; 50:40; II Peter 2:6; Jude 7). "God" is often repeated in *Hebrew* instead of *"I."* The earthquake here apparently alluded to is not that in the reign of Uzziah, which occurred "two years" later (ch. 1:1). Traces of earthquakes and volcanic agency abound in Palestine. The allusion here is to some of the effects of these in previous times. Cf. the prophecy, Deuteronomy 28:15-68, with vss. 6-11 here. **as a firebrand plucked out of . . . burning**—(Cf. Isa. 7:4; Zech. 3:2). The phrase is proverbial for a narrow escape from utter extinction. Though Israel revived as a nation under Jeroboam II, it was but for a time, and that after an almost utter destruction previously (II Kings 14:26). **12. Therefore**—as all chastisements have failed to make thee "return unto Me." **thus will I do unto thee**—as I have threatened (vss. 2, 3). **prepare to meet thy God**—God is about to inflict the last and worst judgment on thee, the extinction of thy nationality; consider then what preparation thou canst make for encountering Him as thy foe (Jer. 46:14; Luke 14:31, 32). But as that would be madness to think of (Isa. 27:4; Ezek. 22:14; Heb. 10:31), see what can be done towards mitigating the severity of the coming judgment, by penitence (Isa. 27:5; I Cor. 11:31). This latter exhortation is followed up in ch. 5:4, 6, 8, 14, 15. **13.** The God whom Israel is to "prepare to meet" (vs. 12) is here described in sublime terms. **wind**—not as *Margin*, "spirit." The God with whom thou hast to do is the Omnipotent Maker of things *seen*, such as the stupendous mountains, and of things *too subtle* to be seen, though of powerful agency, as the "wind." **declareth unto man . . . his thought**—(Ps. 139:2). Ye think that your secret thoughts escape My cognizance, but I am the searcher of hearts. **maketh . . . morning darkness**—(ch. 5:8; 8:9). Both literally turning the sunshine into darkness, and figuratively turning the prosperity of the ungodly into sudden adversity (Ps. 73:12, 18, 19; cf. Jer. 13:16). **treadeth upon . . . high places**—God treadeth down the proud of the earth. He subjects to Him all things however high they be (Mic. 1:3). Cf. Deuteronomy 32:13; 33:29, where the same phrase is used of God's people, elevated by God above every other human height.

ADAM CLARKE

12. *Therefore thus will I do unto thee.* I will continue My judgments, I will fight against you; and, because I am thus determined, *prepare to meet thy God, O Israel.* This is a military phrase, and is to be understood as a challenge to come out to battle. As if the Lord had said, I will attack you immediately. Throw yourselves into a posture of defense, summon your idols to your help, and try how far your strength, and that of your gods, will avail you against the unconquerable arm of the Lord of hosts!

13. *He that formeth the mountains.* Here is a powerful description of the majesty of God. He formed the earth; He created the wind; He knows the inmost thoughts of the heart; He is the Creator of darkness and light; He steps from mountain to mountain, and has all things under His feet! Who is He who hath done and can do all these things? *JEHOVAH ELOHIM TSEBAOTH,* that is His name. (1) Being. (2) The God who is in covenant with mankind. (3) The universal Commander of all the hosts of earth and heaven. This name is further illustrated in the following chapter.

MATTHEW HENRY — CHAPTER 5

Verses 1–3

This chapter begins with *Hear this word.* It is the *word which I take up*—not the prophet only, but the God that sent him. It is *the word that the Lord has spoken, ch.* iii. 1, a lamentable account of the present state of the kingdom of Israel, and a prediction of its destruction. *The virgin of Israel has fallen* (*v.* 2), *she has fallen* into contempt, and is universally slighted. *She shall no more rise*, shall never recover her former dignity again. *She is forsaken upon her land.* Those she was in alliance with abroad failed her, but friends at home deserted her; she would not have been carried captive into a strange land if she had not first been *forsaken upon her own land.* Their people, that should have helped them up, were diminished, *v.* 3. The city that had a militia, 1,000 strong, after the battle, shall find but 100 *left*; and, in proportion, the city that sent out 100 shall have but *ten* come back.

Verses 4–15

A message from God to the house of Israel.

1. They are exhorted to be sincere and devout in their addresses to God, *v.* 4. God is not sought truly if he be not sought exclusively: "*Seek you the Lord, and seek not Bethel* (*v.* 5), for you *forsake your own mercies* if you observe those *lying vanities.* But *seek the Lord* (*v.* 6, 8); enquire after him; seek to know his mind as your rule." Seeking God will be *our life.* So he tells them (*v.* 4): *Seek you me, and you shall live.*

II. They are told of what judgments they lay exposed to for their sins. The places of their idolatry are in danger of being ruined, *v.* 5. *Gilgal*, the headquarters of idolatry, *shall go into captivity, and Bethel* with its golden calf *shall come to nought.*

JAMIESON, FAUSSET, BROWN — CHAPTER 5

Vss. 1-27. Elegy over the Prostrate Kingdom: Renewed Exhortations to Repentance: God Declares that the Coming Day of Judgment Shall Be Terrible to the Scorners Who Despise It: Ceremonial Services Are Not Acceptable to Him Where True Piety Exists Not: Israel Shall Therefore Be Removed Far Eastward. **1. lamentation**—an elegy for the destruction coming on you. Cf. Ezekiel 32:2, "take up," viz., as a mournful *burden* (Ezek. 19:1; 27:2). **2. virgin of Israel**—the Israelite state heretofore unsubdued by foreigners. Cf. Isaiah 23:12; Jeremiah 18:13; 31:4, 21; Lamentations 2:13; may be interpreted, Thou who wast once the "virgin daughter of Zion." Rather, "virgin" as applied to a state implies its beauty, and the delights on which it prides itself, its luxuries, power, and wealth [Calvin]. **no more rise**—in the existing order of things: in the Messianic dispensation it is to rise again, according to many prophecies. Cf. II Kings 6:23; 24:7, for the restricted sense of "no more." **forsaken upon her land**—or, "prostrated upon . . ." (cf. Ezek. 29:5; 32:4) [Maurer]. **3. went out by a thousand**—i.e., "the city from which there used to go out a thousand" equipped for war. "City" is put for "the inhabitants of the city," as in ch. 4:8. **shall leave . . . hundred**—shall have only a hundred left, the rest being destroyed by sword and pestilence (Deut. 28:62). **4. Seek ye me, and ye shall live**—lit., "Seek . . . Me, and *live.*" The second imperative expresses the *certainty* of "life" (escape from judgment) resulting from obedience to the precept in the first imperative. If they perish, it is their own fault; God would forgive, if they would repent (Isa. 55:3, 6). **5. seek not Beth-el**—i.e., the calves at Beth-el. **Gilgal**—(*Note*, ch. 4:4). **Beer-sheba**—in Judah on the southern frontier towards Edom. Once "the well of the oath" by Jehovah, ratifying Abraham's covenant with Abimelech, and the scene of his calling on "the Lord, the everlasting God" (Gen. 21:31, 33), now a stronghold of idolatry (ch. 8:14). **Gilgal shall sure-**

ADAM CLARKE — CHAPTER 5

1. *Hear ye this word.* Attend to this doleful song which I make for the house of Israel.

2. *The virgin of Israel.* The kingdom of Israel, or the ten tribes, which were carried into captivity, and are now totally lost in the nations of the earth.

3. *The city that went out by a thousand.* The city that could easily have furnished, on any emergency, 1,000 fighting men, can now produce scarcely 100; and now of the 100 scarcely 10 remain. So reduced was Israel when Shalmaneser besieged and took Samaria, and carried the residue into captivity.

4. *Seek ye me, and ye shall live.* Cease your rebellion against Me; return to Me with all your heart; and though consigned to death, you shall be rescued and live.

5. *But seek not Beth-el.* There was one of Jeroboam's golden calves, and at *Gilgal* were carved images; both were places in which idolatry was triumphant. The prophet shows them that all hope from those quarters is utterly vain;

MATTHEW HENRY

The body of the kingdom is in danger of being ruined with them, *v.* 6. There is danger lest, if you seek not God, he *break out like a fire in the house of Joseph and devour it. And there shall be none to quench it in Bethel.* God tells them that when the fire of his judgments should kindle upon them all the gods they served at Bethel should not be able to quench it. So the prophet tells them (*v.* 6): *Seek the Lord, and you shall live.* "You shall be delivered from the judgments you are threatened with; your nation shall live, shall recover from its present languishings; your souls shall live; you shall be sanctified and comforted, and made for ever blessed. *You shall live.*" God whom we are to *seek* (*v.* 8, 9) is a God of almighty power. Divers instances are here given of God's power as Creator. Compare *ch.* iv. 13. *First,* The stars are the work of his hands (*v.* 26), the *stars of your god,* those stars are God's creatures and servants. He *makes the seven stars and Orion,* two constellations, which Amos, a herdsman, while he kept his cattle by night, had particularly observed. He made them and either *binds* or *looses* the *sweet influences* of *Pleiades* and *Orion,* the two constellations mentioned. See Job xxxviii. 31; ix. 9. *Secondly,* The constant succession of day and night is under his direction. It is he that *turns* the night *into the morning* by the rising of the sun, and by the setting of the sun *makes the day dark with night*; and the same power can, for humble penitents, easily turn affliction and sorrow into prosperity and joy, but can as easily turn the prosperity of presumptuous sinners into darkness. *Thirdly,* The rain rises and falls as he appoints. He *calls for the waters of the sea*; out of them vapours are drawn up by the heat of the sun, which gather into clouds, and are *poured out upon the face of the earth,* to make it fruitful. It is God that has *made these things*; *Jehovah is his name.* As he is a God of almighty power himself, so he *gives strength and power unto his people* that seek him, and *renews strength* to those that had lost it, if they *wait upon him* for it; for (*v.* 9) he *strengthens the spoiled against the strong.* This is an encouragement to the people to *seek the Lord,* that, if they do so, they shall find him able to retrieve their affairs.

I. They are told of their faults. God tells them, in general (*v.* 12), "*I know your manifold transgressions, and your mighty sins;* and you shall be made to know them too." What a multitude of vain and vile thoughts lodge within us! What a multitude of idle, wicked words have been spoken by us! In what a multitude of instances have we indulged our corrupt appetites and passions! And how many are our omissions of duty. He specifies some of these mighty sins. They corrupted the worship of God, and turned to idols; this is implied, *v.* 5. They had *sought to Bethel,* where one of the golden calves was; they had frequented Gilgal, a place where they chose to set up idols. Beer-sheba, famous in the days of the patriarchs, was now another rendezvous of idols. They perverted justice among themselves (*v.* 7): "*You turn judgment to wormwood,* that is, you make your administrations of justice bitter and displeasing to God and man." They trod upon the poor (*v.* 11), and such as they could get nothing by. The judges aimed at nothing but to enrich themselves; and therefore they *took from* the poor *burdens of wheat* by extortion. The poor had no other way to save themselves than by presenting to them horse-loads of corn which they and their families should have had to subsist upon. They took from the poor *debts of wheat,* so some read it. This sin of oppression they are again charged with (*v.* 12): *They afflict the just,* by turning the law against those that are innocent and *quiet in the land*; and he that *departed from evil* thereby *made himself a prey* to them. They take a bribe from the rich to patronise and protect them in oppressing the poor. Thus they *turn aside the poor in the gate,* in the courts of justice, *from their right.* Furthermore they were malicious persecutors of God's faithful ministers and people, *v.* 10. They could not bear to be reproved by the reading and expounding of the law, and the messages which the prophets delivered to them in the name of the Lord. *They hate him that rebukes in the gate.* Though things were generally very bad, yet there were some among them that *spoke uprightly,* and condemned them. For that reason *they abhorred them*; they were such inveterate enemies to honesty that they could not endure the sight of an honest man. Prophets cannot keep silence; the impulse they are under will not allow them to act on prudential considerations; they must *cry aloud, and not spare. The prudent,* who were *wise as serpents,* because they knew not how what they said might be misrepresented, were so cautious as to say nothing. The cautious men will say to a bold reprover, as Erasmus to Luther: "*Abi in cellam, et*

JAMIESON, FAUSSET, BROWN

ly go into captivity—a play on similar sounds in the *Hebrew, Gilgal, galoh, yigleh:* "Gilgal (the place of *rolling*) shall rolling be rolled away." **Beth-el shall come to naught**—Beth-el (i.e., the "house of God"), called because of its vain idols Beth-aven (i.e., "the house of vanity," or "naught," Hos. 4:15; 10:5, 8), shall indeed "come to naught." **6. break out like fire**—bursting through everything in His way. God is "a consuming fire" (Deut. 4:24; Isa. 10:17; Lam. 2:3). **the house of Joseph**—the kingdom of Israel, of which the tribe of Ephraim, Joseph's son, was the chief tribe (cf. Ezek. 37:16). **none to quench it in Beth-el**—i.e., none in Beth-el to quench it; none of the Beth-el idols on which Israel so depended, able to remove the divine judgments. **7. turn judgment to wormwood**—i.e., pervert it to most bitter wrong. As justice is sweet, so injustice is bitter to the injured. "Wormwood" is from a *Hebrew* root, to "execrate," on account of its noxious and bitter qualities. **leave on righteousness in . . . earth**—Maurer translates, "*cast* righteousness *to the ground,*" as in Isaiah 28:2; Daniel 8:12. **8. the seven stars**—lit., the *heap* or cluster of *seven* larger stars and others smaller (Job 9:9; 38:31). The former whole passage seems to have been in Amos' mind. He names the stars well known to shepherds (to which class Amos belonged), Orion as the precursor of the tempests which are here threatened, and the Pleiades as ushering in spring. **shadow of death**—Hebraism for *the densest darkness.* **calleth for the waters of the sea**—both to send *deluges* in judgment, and the ordinary *rain* in mercy (I Kings 18:44). **9. strengtheneth the spoiled**—lit., "spoil" or "devastation": hence the "person spoiled." Winer, Maurer, and the best modern critics translate, "*maketh devastation* (or *destruction*) *suddenly to arise,*" lit., maketh it to gleam forth like the dawn. Ancient versions support *English Version.* The *Hebrew* is elsewhere used, *to make, to shine, to make glad:* and as *English Version* here (Ps. 39:13), "recover *strength.*" **the spoiled shall come**—"devastation," or "destruction shall come upon" [Maurer]. *English Version* expresses that, strong as Israel fancies herself after the successes of Jeroboam II (II Kings 14:25), even the *weakest* can be made by God to prevail against the strong. **10. him that rebuketh in the gate**—the *judge* who condemns their iniquity *in the place of judgment* (Isaiah 29:21). **abhor him that speaketh uprightly**—the *prophet* telling them the unwelcome truth: answering in the parallelism to the *judge* "that rebuketh in the gate" (cf. I Kings 22:8; Prov. 9:8; 12:1; Jer. 36:23). **11. burdens of wheat**—*burdensome taxes* levied in kind from the *wheat* of the needy, to pamper the lusts of the great [Henderson]. Or wheat advanced in time of scarcity, and exacted again at a burdensome interest [Rabbi Salomon]. **built houses . . . but not dwell in them . . . vineyards, . . . but not drink wine of them**—according to the original prophecy of Moses (Deut. 28:30, 38, 39). The converse shall be true in restored Israel (ch. 9:14; Isa. 65:21, 22). **12. they afflict . . . they take**—rather, "(ye) who afflict . . . take." **bribe**—lit., a *price* with which one who has an unjust cause *ransoms* himself from your sentence (I Sam. 12:3, *Margin;* Prov. 6:35). **turn aside the poor in the gate**—refuse them their right *in the place of justice* (ch. 2:7; Isa. 29:21).

13. the prudent—the spiritually wise. **shall keep silence**—not mere silence of tongue, but the prudent shall keep himself quiet from taking part in any public or private affairs which he can avoid: as it is "an evil time," and one in which all law is set at naught. Ephesians 5:16 refers to this. Instead of impatiently agitating against irremediable evils, the godly wise will not cast pearls before swine, who would trample these, and rend the offerers (Matt. 7:6), but will patiently wait for God's time of deliverance in silent submission (Ps. 39:9).

ADAM CLARKE

for Gilgal shall . . . go into captivity, and Beth-el be brought *to nought.* There is a play or paronomasia on the letters and words in this clause: *haggilgal galoh yigleh, ubeith el yiheyeh leaven.* "This Gilgal shall go captive into captivity; and Beth-el [the house of God] shall be for Beth-aven" (the house of iniquity).

6. *Seek the Lord, and ye shall live.* Repeated from v. 4. *In the house of Joseph.* The Israelites of the ten tribes, of whom Ephraim and Manasseh, sons of Joseph, were the chief.

7. *Ye who turn judgment to wormwood.* Who pervert judgment; causing him who obtains his suit to mourn sorely over the expenses he has incurred in gaining his right.

8. *That maketh the seven stars and Orion.* See Job. ix. 9 and xxxviii. 32.

9. *That strengtheneth the spoiled.* Who takes the part of the poor and oppressed against the oppressor; and, in the course of His providence, sets up the former and depresses the latter.

10. *They hate him that rebuketh in the gate.* They cannot bear an upright magistrate, and will not have righteous laws executed.

11. *Your treading is upon the poor.* You tread them under your feet. *Ye take from him burdens of wheat.* You will have his bread for doing him justice.

12. *I know your manifold transgressions.* I have marked the multitude of your smaller crimes, as well as your mighty offenses.

13. *The prudent shall keep silence.* A wise man will consider that it is useless to complain. He can have no justice without bribes; and he has no money to give: consequently, in such an evil time, it is best to keep silence.

MATTHEW HENRY

dic, Miserere mei, Domine—Away to thy cell, and cry, Have mercy on me, O Lord!" *Evil times* will not bear plain dealing, that is, *evil men* will not.

What they have got by extortion shall be taken from them (*v.* 11): "*You have built houses of hewn stone,* which you thought would be lasting; *but you shall not dwell in them,* for your enemies shall burn them down, or take you into captivity. *You have planted pleasant vineyards,* but you shall never *drink wine of them.*"

III. They are told their duty, and have great encouragement to set about it. The duties here prescribed are godliness and honesty, seriousness in their applications to God and justice in their dealings with men.

2. They are exhorted to be honest and just in their dealings with men, *v.* 14, 15: *Seek good, and not evil. Hate the evil, and love the good, and establish judgment in the gate;* re-establish it there, whence it has been banished, *v.* 7. If the right course be taken grievances may be redressed and abuses rectified: justice may yet triumph where injustice tyrannizes. In order to this, good must be loved and sought, evil must be hated. We must love good principles, love to do good, love good people; and, whatever good we do, we must do it from a principle of love, and with delight. "He will be with you *as you have spoken,* that is, as you have *gloried.*" Or, "As you have prayed when *you sought the Lord.* Live up to your prayers, and you shall have what you pray for." This is the likeliest way to make the nation happy: "If you seek and love that which is good, you may contribute to the saving of the land from ruin."

Verses 16–20

I. A terrible threatening of destruction approaching, *v.* 16, 17. The threatening is introduced with more than ordinary solemnity, to strike an awe upon them; it is not the word of the prophet only, but it is the *Lord Jehovah,* it is the *God of hosts,* and it is *Adonai—the Lord,* who has an absolute sovereignty; it is he who can and will make his words good. The land of Israel shall be put in mourning. Look into the cities, and *wailing shall be in all streets.* Look into the country, and *they shall say in all the highways, Alas! alas!* The husbandman shall be called from the plough by the calamities of his country. Even in all vineyards, where there used to be nothing but mirth and pleasure, there shall be general wailing, when a foreign force invades the country. *I will pass through thee,* as the destroying angel passed through the land of Egypt.

II. A reproof to those who made light of these threatenings, *v.* 18. Woe unto you that *desire the day of the Lord,* that really wish for times of war and confusion, as some do who have restless spirits, and long for changes. Or it is spoken to those who, in their lamentations for the calamities, wished they might die. Or, rather, it is spoken to those who speak jestingly of the day of the Lord. Let him do his worst; *let him make speed,* and *hasten his work,* Isa. v. 19. In answer to this, 1. He shows the folly of those who impudently wished for God's judgments: "*To what end is it for you* that the day of the Lord should come? You will find it not a thing to be bantered. *The day of the Lord is darkness, and not light, v.* 18. And, when God makes a day dark, all the world cannot make it light." He shows the folly of those who desire *the day of the Lord,* in hope to better themselves, or, at least, to know the worst. But the prophet tells them that they know not what they ask, *v.* 19. It is *as if a man did flee from a lion and a bear met him,* or as if a man, to escape all dangers abroad, *went into the house for security,* and *leaned his hand on the wall* to rest himself, and there a *serpent bit him.*

Verses 21–27

These verses show how little God valued their shows of devotion while they went on in their sins.

I. How displeasing their hypocritical services were to God. They had their *feast-days* at Bethel, in imitation of those at Jerusalem. They had their *solemn assemblies* for religious worship. They offered to God *burnt-offerings,* to the honour of God, together with the *meat-offerings;* they offered the *peace-offerings,* to implore the favour of God, and they offered the *fat beasts* they had, *v.* 21, 22. In imitation likewise of the temple-music, they had the *noise of their songs* and the *melody of their viols* (*v.* 23). With these services they hoped to obtain leave to go on in sin. He *hated,* he *despised,* their *feast-days.* Nothing more hateful, more despicable, than hypocrisy. God will not *smell* in *their solemn assemblies,* for there is nothing in them that is grateful to him, but a great deal that is offensive. He will not accept them. Now this intimates, 1. That sacrifice itself is of small

JAMIESON, FAUSSET, BROWN

your "seeking good." **14. and so**—on condition of **shall be with you, as ye have spoken**—as ye have boasted; viz., that God is with you, and that you are His people (Mic. 3:11). **15. Hate . . . evil . . . love . . . good**—(Isa. 1:16, 17; Rom. 12:9). **judgment in the gate**—*justice* in the place where causes are tried. **it may be that the Lord . . . will be gracious**—so, "peradventure" (Exod. 32:30). Not that men are to come to God with an *uncertainty* whether or no He will be gracious: the expression merely implies the difficulty in the way, because of the want of true repentance on man's part, so as to stimulate the zealous earnestness of believers in seeking God (cf. Gen. 16:2; Joel 2:14; Acts 8:22). **the remnant of Joseph**—(see vs. 6). Israel (represented by "Ephraim," the leading tribe, and descendant of Joseph) was, as compared to what it once was, now but a remnant, Hazael of Syria having smitten all the coasts from Jordan eastward, Gilead and Bashan, Gad, Reuben, and Manasseh (II Kings 10:32, 33) [HENDERSON]. Rather, "the remnant of Israel that shall have been left after the wicked have been destroyed" [MAURER]. **16. Therefore**—resumed from vs. 13. God foresees they will not obey the exhortation (vss. 14, 15), but will persevere in the unrighteousness stigmatized (vss. 7, 10, 12). **the Lord** [JEHOVAH], **the God of hosts, the Lord**—an accumulation of titles, of which His lordship over all things is the climax, to mark that from His judgment there is no appeal. **streets . . . highways**—the *broad open spaces* and the *narrow streets* common in the East. **call the husbandman to mourning**—The citizens shall call the inexperienced *husbandmen* to act the part usually performed by professional mourners, as there will not be enough of the latter for the universal mourning which prevails. **such as are skilful of lamentation**—professional mourners hired to lead off the lamentations for the deceased; alluded to in Ecclesiastes 12:5; generally women (Jer. 9:17-19). **17. in all vineyards . . . wailing**—where usually songs of joy were heard. **pass through thee**—taking vengeance (Exod. 12:12, 23; Nah. 1:12). "Pass *over*" and "pass by," on the contrary, are used of God's *forgiving* (Exod. 12:23; Mic. 7:18; cf. ch. 7:8). **18.** Woe unto you who do not scruple to say in irony, "We desire that the day of the Lord would come," i.e., "Woe to you who treat it as if it were a mere dream of the prophets" (Isa. 5:19; Jer. 17:15; Ezek. 12:22). **to what end is it for you!**—Amos taking their ironical words in earnest: for God often takes the blasphemer at his own word, in righteous retribution making the scoffer's jest a terrible reality against himself. Ye have but little reason to desire the day of the Lord; for it will be to you calamity, and not joy. **19. As if a man did flee . . . a lion, and a bear met him**—Trying to escape one calamity, he falls into another. This perhaps implies that in vs. 18 their ironical desire for the day of the Lord was as if it would be an escape from existing calamities. The coming of the day of the Lord would be good news to us, if true: for we have served God (i.e., the golden calves). So do hypocrites flatter themselves as to death and judgment, as if these would be a relief from existing ills of life. The lion may from generosity spare the prostrate, but the *bear* spares none (cf. Job 20:24; Isa. 24:18). **leaned . . . on the wall**—on the side wall of the house, to support himself from falling. Snakes often hid themselves in fissures in a wall. Those not reformed by God's judgments will be pursued by them: if they escape one, another is ready to seize them. **21. I hate, I despise**—The two verbs joined without a conjunction express God's strong abhorrence. **your feast days**—*yours;* not *Mine;* I do not acknowledge them: unlike those in Judah, yours are of human, not divine institution. **I will not smell**—i.e., I will take *no delight in* the sacrifices offered (Gen. 8:21; Lev. 26:31). **in your solemn assemblies**—lit., "days of restraint." Isaiah 1: 10-15 is parallel. Isaiah is fuller; Amos, more condensed. Amos condemns Israel not only on the ground of their thinking to satisfy God by sacrifices without obedience (the charge brought by Isaiah against the Jews), but also because even their external ritual was a mere corruption, and unsanctioned by God. **22. meat offerings**—flour, etc. Unbloody offerings. **peace offerings**—offerings for obtaining from God peace and prosperity. *Hebrew,* "thank offerings." **23. Take . . . away from me**—lit., "Take away, *from upon* Me"; the idea being that of a *burden* pressing *upon* the bearer. So Isaiah 1:14, "They are a trouble unto Me (lit., a burden *upon* Me): I am weary to bear them." **the noise of thy songs**—The hymns and instrumental music on sacred occasions are to Me nothing but a disagreeable *noise.* **I will not hear**—Isaiah sub-

ADAM CLARKE

16. *They shall call the husbandman to mourning.* Because the crops have failed, and the ground has been tilled in vain.

17. *And in all vineyards shall be wailing.* The places where festivity especially used to prevail. *I will pass through thee.* As I passed, by the ministry of the destroying angel, through Egypt, not to spare, but to destroy.

18. *Woe unto you that desire the day of the Lord!* The prophet had often denounced the coming of God's day, that is, of a time of judgment; and the unbelievers had said, "Let His day come, that we may see it." Now the prophet tells them that that day would be to them *darkness,* calamity, *and not light,* not prosperity.

19. *As if a man did flee from a lion, and a bear met him.* The Israelites, under their king Menahem, wishing to avoid a civil war, called in Pul, king of Assyria, to help them. This led to a series of evils inflicted by the Syrian and Assyrian kings, till at last Israel was ravaged by Shalmaneser, and carried into captivity. Thus, in avoiding one evil they fell into another still more grievous.

21. *I hate, I despise your feast days.* I abominate those sacrificial festivals where there is no piety, and I despise them because they pretend to be what they are not.

23. *The noise of thy songs . . . the melody of thy viols.* They had both vocal and instrumental music in those sacrificial festivals, and God hated the noise of the one and shut His ears against the melody of the other.

MATTHEW HENRY

account with God in comparison with moral duties; to love God and our neighbour is *better than all burnt-offering and sacrifice.* 2. That the sacrifice of the wicked is really an abomination to him, Prov. xv. 8. Dissembled piety is double iniquity.

II. What it was that he required without which no sacrifice would be acceptable (*v.* 24): *Let judgment run down as waters,* among you, *and righteousness as a mighty stream,* that is, "Let there be a general reformation of manners among you; let religion (God's *judgment*) and *righteousness* have their due influence upon you; let your land be watered with it, and let it bear down all vice and profaneness; let it run wide as overflowing waters, and strong as a mighty stream. Let justice be duly administered, let not the current of it be stopped by partiality and bribery; let it be pure as running waters, not muddied with corruption; let it run *like a mighty stream.*

III. What little stress God had laid upon the law of sacrifices, in comparison with the moral precepts (*v.* 25): "*Did you offer unto me sacrifices in the wilderness forty years?* No, you did not." For part of that time sacrifice was neglected; after the second year, the passover was not kept till they came into Canaan; and yet he never imputed the omission to them as their fault, but continued his kindness to them: it was their murmuring and unbelief for which God was displeased with them. But, though ritual sacrifices may thus be dispensed with, spiritual sacrifices will not; even justice and honesty will not excuse for the want of prayer and praise, a broken heart and the love of God.

IV. What little reason they had to expect that their sacrifices should be acceptable to God, when they and their fathers had been all along addicted to the worship of other gods. So some take *v.* 25, "*Did you offer to me sacrifices,* that is, to me only? No, and therefore not at all to me acceptably." "*But you have borne the tabernacle of your Moloch* (*v.* 26), little shrines that you made to carry. You have had the images of your *Moloch—your king*" (probably representing *the sun,* that sits king among the heavenly bodies), "and *Chiun,* or *Remphan*" (as Stephen calls it, Acts vii. 43, after the LXX), which, it is supposed, represented Saturn. The worship of the sun, moon, and stars, was the most ancient, and most plausible idolatry.

They *made to themselves* the *star of their God,* the name of which they gave to their god.

V. What punishment God would inflict upon them for their persisting in idolatry (*v.* 27): *I will cause you to go into captivity beyond Damascus.* Their captivity by the Assyrians was far beyond that by the Syrians. Or the captivity of Israel under Shalmaneser was far beyond that of Damascus under Tiglath-pileser, and much more grievous, which was foretold, *ch.* i. 5.

JAMIESON, FAUSSET, BROWN

stitutes "prayers" (Isa. 1:15) for the "songs" and "melody" here; but, like Amos, closes with "I will not hear." **24. judgment**—justice. **run down**—lit., "roll," i.e., flow abundantly (Isa. 48:18). Without the desire to fulfil righteousness in the offerer, the sacrifice is hateful to God (I Sam. 15:22; Ps. 66:18; Hos. 6:6; Mic. 6:8). **25, 26. Have ye offered . . .**—Yes: ye have. "But (all the time with strange inconsistency) ye have borne (aloft in solemn pomp) the tabernacle (i.e., the portable shrine, or model *tabernacle:* small enough not to be detected by Moses; cf. Acts 19:24) of your Molech" (that idol is "*your*" god; I am not, though ye go through the form of presenting offerings to Me). The question, "Have ye," is not a denial (for they *did* offer in the wilderness to Jehovah sacrifices of the cattle which they took with them in their nomad life there, Exodus 24:4; Numbers 7 and 9:1, etc.), but a strong affirmation (cf. I Sam. 2:27, 28; Jer. 31:20; Ezek. 20:4). The sin of Israel in Amos' time is the very sin of their forefathers, mocking God with worship, while at the same time worshipping idols (cf. Ezek. 20:39). It was clandestine in Moses' time, else he would have put it down; he was aware generally of their unfaithfulness, though not knowing the particulars (Deut. 31:21, 27). **Molech . . . Chiun**—Molech means "king" answering to *Mars* [BENGEL], *the Sun* [JABLONSKI]; *Saturn,* the same as "Chiun" [MAURER]. The LXX translates "Chiun" into *Remphan,* as Stephen quotes it (Acts 7:42, 43). The same god often had different names. *Molech* is the Ammonite name; *Chiun,* the Arabic and Persian name, written also *Chevan.* In an Arabic lexicon *Chiun* means "austere"; so astrologers represented *Saturn* as a planet baleful in his influence. Hence the Phœnicians offered human sacrifices to him, children especially; so idolatrous Israel also. *Rimmon* was the Syrian name (II Kings 5:18); pronounced as *Remvan,* or "Remphan," just as *Chiun* was also *Chevan.* Molech had the form of a king; Chevan, or Chiun, of a star [GROTIUS]. Remphan was the Egyptian name for *Saturn:* hence the LXX translator of Amos gave the Egyptian name for the Hebrew, being an Egyptian. [HODIUS II: *Bibl.* 4. 115.] The same as the Nile, of which the Egyptians made the star *Saturn* the representative [HARENBERG]. BENGEL considers *Remphan* or *Rephan* akin to *Teraphim* and *Remphis,* the name of a king of Egypt. The Hebrews became infected with Sabeanism,the oldest form of idolatry, the worship of the *Saba* or starry hosts, in their stay in the Arabian desert, where Job notices its prevalence (Job 31: 26); in opposition, in vs. 27, Jehovah declares Himself "the God of *hosts.*" **the star of your god**—R. ISAAC CARO says all the astrologers represented Saturn as *the star of Israel.* Probably there was a figure of a star on the head of the image of the idol, to represent the planet Saturn; hence "images" correspond to "star" in the parallel clause. A star in hieroglyphics represents God (Num. 24:17). "Images" are either a Hebraism for "image," or refer to the many images made to represent Chiun. **27. beyond Damascus**—In Acts 7:43 it is "beyond *Babylon,*" which includes *beyond Damascus.* In Amos' time, Damascus was the object of Israel's fear because of the Syrian wars. Babylon was not yet named as the place of their captivity. Stephen supplies this name. Their place of exile was in fact, as he states, "*beyond* Babylon," in Halah and Habor by the river Gozan, and in the cities of the Medes (II Kings 17:6; cf. here ch. 1:5; 4:3; 6:14). The road to Assyria lay through "Damascus." It is therefore specified, that not merely shall they be carried captives to Damascus, as they had been by Syrian kings (II Kings 10:32, 33; 13:7), but, beyond that, to a region whence a return was not so possible as from Damascus. They were led captive by Satan into idolatry, therefore God caused them to go captive among idolaters. Cf. II Kings 15:29; 16:9; Isa. 8:4, whence it appears Tiglath pileser attacked Israel and Damascus at the same time at Ahaz' request (Amos 3:11).

ADAM CLARKE

24. *Let judgment run down.* Let the execution of justice be everywhere like the showers that fall upon the land to render it fertile; and *let righteousness* in heart and life be like a mighty river, or the Jordan, that shall wind its course through the whole nation, and carry every abomination into the Dead Sea.

25. *Have ye offered unto me sacrifices?* Did you offer to Me, during forty years in the wilderness, sacrifices in such a way as was pleasing to Me? Ye did not; for your hearts were divided, and ye were generally in a spirit of insurrection or murmuring.

26. *But ye have borne.* The preceding verse spoke of their fathers; the present verse speaks of the Israelites then existing, who were so grievously addicted to idolatry that they not only worshipped at stated public places the idols set up by public authority, but they carried their gods about with them everywhere. *The tabernacle of your Moloch.* Probably a small portable shrine, with an image of their god in it, such as *Moloch;* and the star or representative of their god *Chiun* (see Acts vii. 42).

27. *Will I cause you to go into captivity beyond Damascus.* That is, into Assyria, the way to which from Judea was by Damascus.

MATTHEW HENRY — CHAPTER 6

Verses 1–7

The first words of the chapter are the contents of these verses: *Woe to those that are at ease!*

I. A description of their pride, security, and sensuality, for which God would reckon with them.

1. They were vainly conceited of their own dignities, and thought those would secure them from the judgments threatened. (1) Those that dwelt in Zion thought that was honour and protection enough. Those that dwelt there doubted not but that God's sanctuary would be a sanctuary to them and would

JAMIESON, FAUSSET, BROWN — CHAPTER 6

VSS. 1-14. DENUNCIATION OF BOTH THE SISTER NATIONS (ESPECIALLY THEIR NOBLES) FOR WANTON SECURITY—ZION, AS WELL AS SAMARIA: THREAT OF THE EXILE: RUIN OF THEIR PALACES AND SLAUGHTER OF THE PEOPLE: THEIR PERVERSE INJUSTICE. **1. named chief of the nations**—i.e., you nobles, so eminent in influence, that your names are celebrated among the chief nations [LUDOVICUS DE DIEU]. *Hebrew,* "Men designated by name among the first fruits of the nations," i.e., men of note in Israel, the people chosen by God as first of the nations (Exod.

ADAM CLARKE — CHAPTER 6

1. *Woe to them that are at ease in Zion!* For *hashshaanannim,* "who dwell at ease," it has been proposed to read *hashshaananim,* "who confidently lean," the two words differing in only one letter, an *ain* for an *aleph.* They leaned confidently on Zion, supposing that, notwithstanding their iniquities, they should be saved for Zion's sake. Thus the former clause will agree better with the latter, "leaning upon Zion," and "trusting in the mountain of Samaria." *Are named chief.* See Isa. xliv. 5. They call

MATTHEW HENRY

shelter them from his judgments. (2) Those that dwelt *in the mountain of Samaria*, trusted in it, because it was the metropolis of a potent kingdom, and the headquarters of its religion. (3) Both these two kingdoms valued themselves upon their relation to Israel, which they looked upon as making them the *chief of the nations.* The *house of Israel* came to them, that is, was divided into those kingdoms, of which Zion and Samaria were the mother cities. Those that were at ease were the princes and rulers. Great nations and great men are apt to overvalue themselves. But, for a check to their pride, the prophet bids them take notice of those cities that had been as illustrious in their time as ever Zion or Samaria was, and yet were destroyed, *v.* 2. "Go *to Calneh* (an ancient city built by Nimrod, Gen. x. 10), it is now in ruins; so is *Hamath the great*, one of the chief cities of Syria. Gath was likewise made desolate by Hazael, 2 Kings xii. 17. Now *were they better than these kingdoms* of Judah and Israel? Yes, and *their border greater than your border*, so they had more reason than you to be confident of their safety; yet you see what has become of them, and dare you be secure?"

2. They persisted in their wicked courses upon a presumption that they should never be called to an account for them (*v.* 3). You *put it far away*, and therefore you *cause the seat of violence to draw near.*

3. They indulged themselves in all manner of sensual pleasures and delights, *v.* 4–6. That which they are here charged with is not in itself sinful (these things might be soberly and moderately used), but they placed their happiness in the gratification of their carnal appetites. They were extravagant. They were lazy. They *abound in superfluities* (so the margin reads it), when many of their poor brethren wanted necessaries. They must have everything of the best and abundance of it: They ate *the lambs out of the flock* and the *calves out of the midst of the stall.* Some men never show their ingenuity but in their luxury; on that they bestow all their faculty of invention. Or it intimates their profaneness in their mirth; they mimicked the temple-music, and made a jest of that, because, it may be, it was old-fashioned, and they took a pride in bantering it. They drank to excess. They affected the strongest perfumes to make them more in love with their own bodies.

4. They had no concern at all for the interests of the church of God, and of the nation: *They are not grieved for the affliction of Joseph;* the church of God, including both the kingdoms of Judah and Israel (which are called *Joseph*, Ps. lxxx. 1), was in distress, invaded. As to their own kingdom, great breaches were made upon it, upon its peace and welfare; and they were so besotted that they were not aware of them. It is all one to them whether the nation sink or swim, so that they can but live in pleasure. Some think that, in calling the afflicted church *Joseph*, there is an allusion to the story of Pharaoh's butler, who *remembered not Joseph, but forgot him*, Gen. xl. 21, 23. Thus they *drank wine in bowls*, but *were not grieved for the affliction of Joseph.*

II. The doom passed upon them (*v.* 7): *Therefore now shall they go captive with the first that go captive.* Those who lived in luxury shall lose even their liberty. Those who *stretched themselves* shall be made to contract themselves, and to come into a less compass.

Verses 8–14

I. This burden is bound on by *the Lord the God of hosts.*

II. How heavily this burden lies! 1. God will abhor and abandon them, and that implies misery enough. Their temple, altar, and priesthood, were the excellencies of Jacob; but, when these were polluted by sin, God abhorred them, *ch.* v. 21. And, if God abhor them, He will *deliver up the city with all that is therein*, into the hands of the enemy, that will lay it waste, and make a prey of all its wealth. 2. There shall be a great and general mortality among them (*v.* 9). That which makes this judgment the more grievous is that their hearts seem to be hardened under it.

JAMIESON, FAUSSET, BROWN

19:5; cf. Num. 24:20) [PISCATOR]. **to whom . . . Israel came**—i.e., the princes to whom the Israelites used to repair for the decision of controversies, recognizing their authority [MAURER]. I prefer to refer "which" to the antecedent "Zion" and "Samaria"; these were esteemed "chief" strongholds among the heathen nations "to whom . . . Israel came" when it entered Canaan; vs. 2 accords with this. **2. Calneh**—on the east bank of the Tigris. Once powerful, but recently subjugated by Assyria (Isa. 10:9; about 794 B.C.). **Hameth**—subjugated by Jeroboam II (II Kings 14:25). Also by Assyria subsequently (II Kings 18:34). Cf. vs. 14, below. **Gath**—subjugated by Uzziah (II Chron. 26:6). **be they better**—no. Their so recent subjugation renders it needless for Me to tell you they *are* not. And yet they *once were;* still they could not defend themselves against the enemy. How vain, then, *your* secure confidence in the strength of Mounts Zion and Samaria! He takes cities respectively east, north, south, and west of Israel (cf. Nah. 3:8). **3.** Ye persuade yourselves that "the evil day" foretold by the prophets is "far off," though they declare it near (Ezek. 12:22, 27). Ye in your imagination put it far off, and therefore bring near *violent oppression,* suffering it to *sit enthroned,* as it were, among you (Ps. 94:20). The notion of judgment being far off has always been an incentive to the sinner's recklessness of living (Eccles. 8:12, 13; Matt. 24:48). Yet that very recklessness brings near the evil day which he puts far off. "Ye bring on fever by your intemperance, and yet would put it far off" [CALVIN]. **4.** (See ch. 2:8.) **beds of ivory**—i.e., adorned, or inlaid, with ivory (ch. 3:15). **stretch themselves**—in luxurious self-indulgence. **lambs out of the flock**—picked out as the choicest, for their owners' selfish gratification. **5. chant**—lit., "mark distinct sounds and tones." **viol**—the lyre, or lute. **invent . . . instruments . . . like David**—They fancy they equal David in musical skill (I Chron. 23:5; Neh. 12:36). They defend their luxurious passion for music by his example: forgetting that *he* pursued this study when at peace and free from danger, and that for the praise of God; but *they* pursue for their own self-gratification, and that when God is angry and ruin is imminent. **6. drink . . . in bowls**—in the *large vessels* or basins in which wine was mixed; not satisfied with the smaller *cups* from which it was ordinarily drunk, after having been poured from the large mixer. **chief ointments**—i.e., the most costly: not for health or cleanliness, but wanton luxury. **not grieved for the affliction of Joseph**—lit., "the breach," i.e., the national wound or calamity (Ps. 60:2; Ezek. 34:4) of the house of *Joseph* (ch. 5:6); resembling in this the heartlessness of their forefathers, the sons of Jacob, towards Joseph, "eating bread" while their brother lay in the pit, and then selling him to Ishmaelites. **7. Therefore . . . shall they go captive with the first**—As they were first among the people in rank (vs. 1), and anointed themselves "with the chief ointments" (vs. 6), so shall they be among the foremost in going into captivity. **banquet**—lit., the "merry-making shout of revellers"; from an *Arabic* root, "to cry out." In the *Hebrew, marzeach;* here, there is an allusion to *mizraqu,* "bowls" (vs. 6). **them that stretched themselves**—on luxurious couches (vs. 4). **8. the excellency of Jacob**—(Ps. 47:4). The *sanctuary* which was the great glory of the covenant people [VATABLUS], (Ezek. 24:21). The priesthood, and kingdom, and dignity, conferred on them by God. These, saith God, are of no account in My eyes towards averting punishment [CALVIN]. **hate his palaces**—as being the storehouses of "robbery" (ch. 3:10, 15). How sad a change from God's *love* of Zion's gates (Ps. 87:2) and palaces (Ps. 48:3, 13), owing to the people's sin! **the city**—collectively: both Zion and Samaria (vs. 1). **all that is therein**—lit., "its fulness"; the *multitude* of men and of riches in it (cf. Ps. 24:1). **9.** If as many as *ten* (Lev. 26:26; Zech. 8:23) remain in a house (a rare case, and only in the scattered villages, as there will be scarcely a house in which the enemy will leave any), they shall all, to a man, die of the plague, a frequent concomitant of war in the East (Jer. 24:10; 44:13; Ezek. 6:11). **10. a man's uncle**—The nearest relatives had the duty of burying the dead (Gen. 25: 9; 35:29; Judg. 16:31). No nearer relative was left of this man than an *uncle.* **and he that burneth him**—the uncle, who is *also* at the same time the one that burneth him (one of the "ten," vs. 9). Burial was the usual Hebrew mode of disposing of their dead. But in cases of necessity, as when the men of Jabesh-gilead took the bodies of Saul and his three sons from the walls of Beth-shan and burned them to save them from being insulted by the Philistines, burning was practised. So in this case, to prevent contagion.

ADAM CLARKE

themselves not after their ancestors, but after the chief of the idolatrous nations with whom they intermarry, contrary to the law.

2. *Pass ye unto Calneh.* This is, says Calmet, the Ctesiphon on the river Tigris. *Hamath.* A city on the Orontes, in Syria. *Gath.* A well-known town, and head of one of the five seignories of the Philistines. *Be they better?* You have no more reason to expect exemption from the consequences of your sins than they had. They have been punished; so shall you.

4. *That lie upon beds of ivory.* The *beds* mentioned here may be either sofas to recline on at table or beds to sleep on, and these among the ancients were ornamented with ivory inlaid.

7. *With the first that go captive.* The house of Israel shall be carried into captivity before the house of Judah.

9. *Ten men . . . they shall die.* All shall be cut off by the sword, or by captivity, or by famine.

10. *A man's uncle shall take him up.* Bishop Newcome says this obscure verse seems to describe the effects of famine and pestilence during the siege of Samaria. The carcass shall be burnt, and the bones removed with no ceremony of funeral rites, and without the assistance of the nearest kinsman. Solitude shall reign in the house; and if one is left, he must be silent (see chap. viii. 3) and retired, lest he be plundered of his scanty provision!

MATTHEW HENRY

3. Their houses shall be destroyed, *v.* 11. God *will smite the great house with breaches, and the little house with clefts.*

III. How justly they are thus burdened. If we understand the matter aright, we shall say, *The Lord is righteous.* God had sent them his prophets, to *break up their fallow-ground*; but they found them as hard as the rock.

Though they are the house of Israel, yet he will *raise up against them a nation* which they had many a time hoped in, even the Assyrians, and this nation shall *afflict them,* from the *entering in of Hamath,* in the north, to *the river of the wilderness,* the river of Egypt, Sihor or Nile, in the south.

JAMIESON, FAUSSET, BROWN

the bones—i.e., the dead *body* (Gen. 50:25). Perhaps here there is an allusion in the phrase to the *emaciated* condition of the body, which was little else but skin and bones. **say unto him that is by the sides of the house**—i.e., to the only one left of the ten *in the interior of the house* [MAURER] (cf. *Note,* Isa. 14:13). **Hold thy tongue . . . we may not . . . mention . . . the Lord**—After receiving the reply, that none is left besides the one addressed, when the man outside fancies the man still surviving inside to be on the point, as was customary, of expressing devout gratitude to God who spared him, the man outside interrupts him, "Hold thy tongue! for there is not now cause for mentioning with praise (Josh. 23:7) the name of Jehovah"; for *thou* also must die; as all the ten are to die to the last man (vs. 9; cf. ch. 8:3). Formerly ye boasted in the name of Jehovah, as if ye were His peculiar people; now ye shall be silent and shudder at His name, as hostile to you, and as one from whom ye wish to be hidden (Rev. 6:16), [CALVIN]. **11. commandeth, and he will smite**—His word of command, when once given, cannot but be fulfilled (Isa. 55:11). His mere word is enough to smite with destruction. **great house . . . little house**—He will spare none, great or small (ch. 3:15). JEROME interprets "the great house" as Israel, and "the small house" as Judah: the former being reduced to branches or ruins, lit., "small drops"; the latter, though injured with "clefts" or rents, which threaten its fall, yet still permitted to stand. **12.** In turning "judgment [justice] into gall [poison], and . . . righteousness into hemlock" [or wormwood, bitter and noxious], ye act as perversely as if one were to make "horses run upon the rock" or to "plough with oxen there" [MAURER]. As horses and oxen are useless on a rock, so ye are incapable of fulfilling justice [GROTIUS]. Ye impede the course of God's benefits, because ye are as it were a hard rock on which His favor cannot run. "Those that will not be tilled as fields, shall be abandoned as rocks" [CALVIN]. **13. rejoice in a thing of naught**—i.e., in your vain and fleeting riches. **Have we not taken to us horns**—i.e., acquired power, so as to conquer our neighbors (II Kings 14:25). *Horns* are the Hebrew symbol of *power,* being the instrument of strength in many animals (Ps. 75:10). **14. from the entering in of Hamath**—the point of entrance for an invading army (as Assyria) into Israel from the north; specified here, as Hamath had been just before subjugated by Jeroboam II (vs. 2). Do not glory in your recently acquired city, for it shall be the starting-point for the foe to afflict you. How sad the contrast to the feast of Solomon attended by a congregation *from* this same *Hamath,* the most northern boundary of Israel, *to* the Nile, the *river of Egypt,* the most southern boundary! **unto the river of the wilderness**—i.e., to Kedron, which empties itself into the north bay of the Dead Sea below Jericho (II Chron. 28:15), the southern boundary of the ten tribes (II Kings 14:25, "from the entering of Hamath unto the sea of the plain") [MAURER]. *To the river Nile,* which skirts the Arabian wilderness and separates Egypt from Canaan [GROTIUS]. If this verse includes Judah, as well as Israel (cf. vs. 1, "Zion" and "Samaria"), GROTIUS' view is correct; and it agrees with I Kings 8:65.

ADAM CLARKE

11. *He will smite the great house with breaches.* The great and small shall equally suffer; no distinction shall be made; rich and poor shall fall together. Death has received his commission, and he will spare none.

12. *Shall horses run upon the rock?* First, they could not do it, because they were unshod; for the shoeing of horses with iron was not then known. Secondly, if they did run on the rock, it would be useless to their owner, and hurtful to themselves. Thirdly, and it would be as useless to plough on the rock with oxen, for there it would be impossible to sow with any advantage.

13. *Ye which rejoice in a thing of nought.* In your idols, for an idol is nothing in the world. *Have we not taken to us horns?* We have arrived to power and dignity by our strength. *Horns* were the symbols of power and authority.

14. *I will raise up against you a nation.* The Assyrians under Pul, Tiglath-pileser, and Shalmaneser, who subdued the Israelites at various times, and at last carried them away captive in the days of Hoshea, the last king of Israel in Samaria. *From the entering in of Hemath* (on the north) *unto the river of the wilderness.* Besor, which empties itself into the sea, not far from Gaza, and was in the southern part of the tribe of Simeon.

MATTHEW HENRY — CHAPTER 7

God bears long, but he will not bear always, with a provoking people.

I. Two instances of God's sparing mercy.

1. God is here coming against this sinful nation, first by one judgment and then by another. (1) He begins with the judgment of famine. The prophet saw this in vision. He saw God *forming grasshoppers,* or *locusts, v.* 1. God formed these grasshoppers (and the wisdom and power of God appears in the structure of an ant as of an elephant), as instruments of his wrath. These grasshoppers were sent *in the beginning of the shooting up of the latter growth, after the king's mowings.* The judgment was mitigated by the mercy that went before it. God could have sent these insects to eat up the grass at the beginning of the first growth, in the spring, when the grass was most needed; but God suffered that to grow, and suffered them to gather it in. The grasshoppers were commissioned to eat up only the *latter growth* (the edgrew we call it in the country), the after-grass, is of little value in comparison with the former. The remembrance of the mercies of the former growth should make us submissive to the will of God when we meet with disappointments in the latter growth Some understand this figuratively of a wasting destroying army brought upon them.

JAMIESON, FAUSSET, BROWN — CHAPTER 7

Vss. 1-9. Chapters 7, 8, 9, contain VISIONS, WITH THEIR EXPLANATIONS. Ch. 7 consists of two parts. First (vss. 1-9): PROPHECIES ILLUSTRATED BY THREE SYMBOLS: (1) A vision of *grasshoppers* or young locusts, which devour the grass, but are removed at Amos' entreaty; (2) *Fire* drying up even the deep, and withering part of the land, but removed at Amos' entreaty; (3) A *plumb-line* to mark the buildings for destruction. Secondly (vss. 10-17): NARRATIVE OF AMAZIAH'S INTERRUPTION OF AMOS IN CONSEQUENCE OF THE FOREGOING PROPHECIES, AND PREDICTION OF HIS DOOM. **1. showed . . . me; and, behold**—The same formula prefaces the three visions in this chapter, and the fourth in ch. 8:1. **grasshoppers**—rather, "locusts" in the caterpillar state, from a *Hebrew* root, "to creep forth." In the autumn the eggs are deposited in the earth; in the spring the young come forth [MAURER]. **the latter growth**—viz., of grass, which comes up after the mowing. They do not in the East mow their grass and make hay of it, but cut it off the ground as they require it. **the king's mowings**—the first fruits of the mown grass, tyrannically exacted by the king from the people. The literal locusts, as in Joel, are probably symbols of human foes: thus the "growth" of grass "after the king's mowings" will

ADAM CLARKE — CHAPTER 7

1. *Behold, he formed grasshoppers.* "Locusts."

The shooting up of the latter growth. The early crop of grass had been already mowed and housed. The second crop was not yet begun.

By *the king's mowings* we may understand the first crop, a portion of which the king probably claimed as being the better hay.

MATTHEW HENRY

2. The prophet, by prayer, seeks to turn away his wrath, *v.* 2. It was the business of prophets to pray for those to whom they prophesied, and so to show they did not *desire the woeful day.*

(1) The prophet's prayer: *O Lord God! Forgive, I beseech thee,* and take away the sin, *v.* 2. He sees sin at the bottom of the trouble, and that the pardon of sin must be at the bottom of the deliverance. *Cease, I beseech thee,* and take away the judgment; *cause thy anger towards us to cease.* Take away the cause and the effect will cease.

(2) The prophet's plea to enforce this prayer: *By whom shall Jacob arise, for he is small? v.* 2. And it is repeated (*v.* 5). It is Jacob that he is interceding for, the professing people of God, called by his name. *Jacob is small,* weakened and brought low by former judgments; if these come, he will be brought to nothing. The people are unable to help themselves or one another. Sin will soon diminish the numerous and weaken the courageous. *By whom shall he arise?* He has no friend to help him, none to raise him, unless the hand of God do it.

3. In answer to the prophet's prayer (*v.* 3): *The Lord repented for this.* He did not change his mind; he changed his way, took another course in mercy. He said, *It shall not be.* And again (*v.* 6), *This also shall not be.* This was not the first time that Israel's life was begged, and so saved. What a blessing praying people, praying prophets, are to a land. Amos moves for a reprieve, and obtains it, because God inclines to grant it. It is the glory of God that he *multiplies to pardon,* that he spares, and forgives, to more than seventy times seven times.

(2) He proceeds to the judgment of fire (*v.* 4): *The Lord God called to contend by fire.* A fire was kindled among them, by which perhaps is meant a great drought (the heat of the sun scorched it, and burnt up the roots of the grass which the locusts had eaten the spires of), or a raging fever, which was as a fire in their bones, or lightning, fire from heaven, which consumed their houses, as Sodom and Gomorrah were consumed (*ch.* iv. 11), or it was the burning of their cities, either by accident or by the hand of the enemy. Thus were the towns wasted, as the country was by the grasshoppers. This fire *devoured the great deep,* as the fire that fell from heaven on Elijah's altar licked up the water that was in the trench.

II. The rejection of those at last who had been often reprieved, and yet never reduced to their duty. This is represented to the prophet by a vision (*v.* 7, 8).

1. The vision is of a *plumb-line,* a line with a plummet at the end of it, such as masons and bricklayers use to run up a wall by, that they may work it straight and true. Israel was a wall which God had reared, as a bulwark to his sanctuary. This wall was *made by a plumb-line,* exact and firm. It had long stood fast as a wall of brass. But God now *stands upon it with a plumb-line in his hand,* to take measure of it. Thus God would bring the people of Israel to the trial, would show wherein they erred; and he would set a *plumb-line in the midst of them,* to mark how far their wall must be pulled down.

2. The prediction is of utter ruin, *v.* 9. (1) The body of the people shall be destroyed. They are here called *the house of Isaac* (*v.* 16), some think in allusion to the signification of Isaac's name; it is *laughter;* they shall become a jest among all their neighbours. Their castles they thought safe, and their temples sanctuaries. These shall be *laid waste,* to punish them for their idolatry and their carnal confidences.

(2) The royal family shall sink first: Jeroboam the second, was now king of the ten tribes; his family was extirpated in his son Zecharias, 2 Kings xv. 10.

Verses 10–17

Amos is persecuted.

I. The malicious information brought to the king against the prophet Amos, *v.* 10, 11. The informer was *Amaziah the priest of Bethel,* the chief of the priests that ministered to the golden calf there, the *president of Bethel* (so some read it). He complained against Amos because he prophesied against his altars, which would soon be deserted if Amos' preaching could but gain credit. Priests have been bitter persecutors. Amaziah brings an information to Jeroboam against Amos.

JAMIESON, FAUSSET, BROWN

mean the political revival of Israel under Jeroboam II (II Kings 14:25), after it had been mown down, as it were, by Hazael and Ben-hadad of Syria (II Kings 13:3), [GROTIUS]. **2. by whom shall Jacob arise?**—If Thou, O God, dost not spare, how can *Jacob maintain his ground,* reduced as he is by repeated attacks of the Assyrians, and erelong about to be invaded by the Assyrian Pul (II Kings 15:19, 20)? Cf. Isaiah 51:19. The mention of "Jacob" is a plea that God should "remember for them His covenant" with their forefather, the patriarch (Ps. 106:45). **he is small**—reduced in numbers and in strength. **3. repented for this**—i.e., of this. The change was not in the mind of God (Num. 2:19; Jas. 1:17), but in the effect outwardly. God unchangeably does what is just; it is just that He should hear intercessory prayer (Jas. 5:16-18), as it would have been just for Him to have let judgment take its course at once on the guilty nation, but for the prayer of one or two righteous men in it (cf. Gen. 18:23-33; I Sam. 15:11; Jer. 42:10). The repentance of the sinner, and God's regard to His own attributes of mercy and covenanted love, also cause God outwardly to deal with him as if he repented (Jonah 3:10), whereas the change in outward dealing is in strictest harmony with God's own unchangeableness. **It shall not be**—Israel's utter overthrow now. Pul was influenced by God to accept money and withdraw from Israel. **4. called to contend**—i.e., with Israel judicially (Job 9:3; Isa. 66:16; Ezek. 38:22). He ordered to come at His call the infliction of punishment by "fire" on Israel, i.e., drought (cf. ch. 4:6-11), [MAURER]. Rather, *war* (Num. 21:28), viz., Tiglath-pileser [GROTIUS]. **devoured the . . . deep**—i.e., a great part of Israel, whom he carried away. *Waters* are the symbol for *many people* (Rev. 17:15). **did eat up a part**—viz., all the *land* (cf. ch. 4:7) of Israel east of Jordan (I Chron. 5:26; Isa. 9:1). This was a worse judgment than the previous one: the locusts ate up the grass: the fire not only affects the surface of the ground, but burns up the very roots and reaches even to the deep. **7. wall made by a plumb-line**—viz., perpendicular. **8. plumb-line in . . . midst of . . . Israel**—No longer are the symbols, as in the former two, stated generally; this one is expressly applied to Israel. God's long-suffering is worn out by Israel's perversity: so Amos ceases to intercede (cf. Gen. 18:33). The plummet-line was used not only in building, but in destroying houses (II Kings 21:13; Isa. 28:17; 34:11; Lam. 2:8). It denotes that God's judgments are measured out by the most exact rules of justice. Here it is placed "in the midst" of Israel, i.e., the judgment is not to be confined to an outer part of Israel, as by Tiglath-pileser; it is to reach the very center. This was fulfilled when Shalmaneser, after a three years' siege of Samaria, took it and carried away Israel captive finally to Assyria (II Kings 17:3, 5, 6, 23). **not . . . pass by . . . any more**—not forgive them any more (ch. 8:2; Prov. 19:11; Mic. 7:18). **9. high places**—dedicated to idols. **of Isaac**—They boasted of their following the example of their forefather Isaac, in erecting high places at Beer-sheba (ch. 5:5; cf. Gen. 26:23, 24; 46:1); but he and Abraham erected them before the temple was appointed at Jerusalem—and to God; whereas they did so, after the temple had been fixed as the only place for sacrifices—and to idols. In the *Hebrew* here "Isaac" is written with *s,* instead of the usual *ts;* both forms mean "laughter"; the change of spelling perhaps expresses that their "high places of Isaac" may be well so called, but not as they meant by the name; for they are only fit to be *laughed at* in scorn. Probably, however, the mention of "Isaac" and "Israel" simply expresses that these names, which their degenerate posterity boasted in as if ensuring their safety, will not save them and their idolatrous "sanctuaries" on which they depended from ruin (cf. ch. 8:14). **house of Jeroboam with . . . sword**—fulfilled in the extinction of Zachariah, son of Jeroboam II, the last of the descendants of Jeroboam I, who had originated the idolatry of the calves (II Kings 15:8-10).

10-17. AMAZIAH'S CHARGE AGAINST AMOS: HIS DOOM FORETOLD. **10. priest of Beth-el**—chief priest of the royal sanctuary to the calves at Beth-el. These being a device of state policy to keep Israel separate from Judah. Amaziah construes Amos' words against them as treason. So in the case of Elijah and Jeremiah (I Kings 18:17; Jer. 37:13, 14). So the antitype Jesus was charged (John 19:12); political expediency being made in all ages the pretext for dishonoring God and persecuting His servants (John 11:48-50). So in the case of Paul (Acts 17:6, 7; 24:5). **in the midst of . . . Israel**—probably alluding to Amos' own words, "in the midst of . . . Israel" (vs. 8), foretelling the state's

ADAM CLARKE

2. *By whom shall Jacob arise?* The locusts, the symbols of the many enemies that had impoverished Jerusalem, having devoured much of the produce of the land, were proceeding, till, at the intercession of the prophet, they were removed.

3. *The Lord repented.* Changed His purpose of destroying them by the locusts. See v. 6.

4. *The Lord God called to contend by fire.* Permitted war, both civil and foreign, to harass the land, after the death of Jeroboam II. These wars would have totally destroyed it had not the prophet interceded.

7. *With a plumbline in his hand.* This appears to be intended as an emblem of strict justice, and intimated that God would now visit them according to their iniquities.

8. *I will set a plumbline.* I will visit them by justice without any mixture of mercy.

9. *And the high places of Isaac shall be desolate.* Their total destruction is at hand. The *high place of Isaac* was Beersheba, where Isaac had built an altar to the Lord, Gen. xxvi. 25. This high place, which had been abused to idolatrous uses, was demolished by Josiah, king of Judah, as we read in 2 Kings xxiii. 8, for he "defiled the high places . . . from Geba to Beersheba."

I will rise against the house of Jeroboam. The Lord had promised to Jehu, the ancestor of Jeroboam, that his family should sit on the throne of Israel to the fourth generation. Zechariah, the son of Jeroboam, was the fourth in order after Jehu; and on him the threatening in this verse fell; for he was murdered by Shallum after he had reigned six months, and in him the family became extinct. See 2 Kings x. 30 and xv. 8-10.

10. *Amaziah the priest of Beth-el.* The idolatrous priest who had been established by the king to maintain the worship of the golden calves which Jeroboam the elder had set up at this place.

MATTHEW HENRY

1. The crime he is charged with is treason: "*Amos has conspired against thee,* to depose and murder thee; he aims at succeeding thee. *The land is not able to bear his words.*" It is slyly insinuated that the country was exasperated against him. It is no new thing for the accusers of the brethren to misrepresent them as enemies to the king and kingdom, when really they are the best friends to both. 2. The words laid in the indictment for the support of this charge (*v.* 11): *Amos says* (and they have witnesses ready to prove it) *Jeroboam shall die by the sword, and Israel shall be led away captive.* He does not tell the king how Amos had interceded for Israel, and by his intercession had turned away first one judgment and then another. He does not tell him that he had often assured them that if they would repent the ruin should be prevented. It does not appear that Jeroboam took any notice of this information; perhaps he reverenced a prophet, and stood more in awe of the divine authority than Amaziah his priest did.

II. The method he used to persuade Amos to quit the country (*v.* 12, 13); he insinuated himself into his acquaintance, and endeavoured to persuade him to go and prophesy in the *land of Judah,* and not at Bethel. He suggests to him,

1. That Bethel was not a proper place for him to exercise his ministry in, for it was *the king's chapel,* or *sanctuary,* and it was *the king's court,* or *the house of the kingdom,* where the royal family resided and where were set the thrones of judgment. And why not? (1) Because Amos is too plain and blunt a preacher for the court and the king's chapel. (2) Because the worship that is in the king's chapel will be a continual vexation to Amos. (3) Because it was not fit that the king and his house should be affronted in their own court and chapel by reproofs and threatenings in the name of the Lord. (4) Because he could not expect any encouragement there, but, on the contrary, to be ridiculed and threatened. He could not think to persuade any from that idolatry which was supported by the authority and example of the king. To preach his doctrine there was but (as we say) to run his head against a post.

2. He persuades him that the land of Judah was the fittest place for him. *Flee thee away* thither with all speed, and *there eat bread,* and *prophesy there.* There thou wilt be safe; there thou wilt be welcome. (1) How willing wicked men are to get clear of their reprovers. (2) How apt worldly men are to measure others by themselves. Amaziah, as a priest, aimed at nothing but the profits of his place, and he thought Amos, as a prophet, had the same views.

III. The reply which Amos made to these suggestions of Amaziah's. He did not *consult with flesh and blood,* nor was it his care to enrich himself, but to *make full proof of his ministry,* not to sleep in a whole skin, but to keep a good conscience; and therefore he resolved to abide by his post, and, in answer to Amaziah,

1. He justified himself in his adherence to his work and his place (*v.* 14, 15). He had a divine commission: "*I was no prophet, nor prophet's son,* neither born nor bred to the office, as Samuel and Jeremiah, but *I was a herdman,* a keeper of cattle, and *a gatherer of sycamore-fruit.*" He was a plain country-man, bred up and employed in country work and used to country fare. God made him a prophet, and a prophet to them, appointed him his work and his post. Therefore he ought not to be silenced, for, (1) He could produce a divine commission for what he did. Men will find it is at their peril if they oppose any that come in God's name. An affront done to an ambassador is an affront to the prince that sends him. (2) The mean character he wore before he received that commission strengthened his warrant. [1] He had no thoughts at all of ever being a prophet, and therefore his prophesying was due to a divine impulse. [2] He was not instructed in the art of prophesying, and therefore he must have his abilities for it immediately from God, an undeniable proof that he had his mission from him. The apostles, being originally unlearned and ignorant men, evidenced that they owed their knowledge to their having *been with Jesus,* Acts iv. 13. [3] He had an honest calling, by which he could comfortably maintain himself and his family, and therefore did not need to prophesy for bread, as Amaziah suggested (*v.* 12). If God, that sent him, had not strengthened him, he could not thus have *set his face as a flint,* Isa. l. 7. A herdman of Tekoa puts to shame a priest of Bethel, when he receives from God authority to act for him.

2. He condemns Amaziah for the opposition he gave him in the name of the Lord and by authority from him, *v.* 16, 17.

(1) For the opposition he gave to Amos God will bring ruin upon himself and his family. He shall

JAMIESON, FAUSSET, BROWN

overthrow *to the very center.* Not secretly, or in a corner, but openly, in *the very center of the state,* so as to upset the whole utterly. **land is not able to bear all his words**—They are so many and so intolerable. A sedition will be the result. The mention of his being "priest of Beth-el" implies that it was for his own priestly gain, not for the king or state, he was so keen. **11. Jeroboam shall die . . .**—Amos had not said this: but that "the *house* of Jeroboam" should fall "with the sword" (vs. 9). But Amaziah exaggerates the charge, to excite Jeroboam against him. The king, however, did not give ear to Amaziah, probably from religious awe of the prophet of Jehovah. **12. Also**—Besides informing the king against Amos, lest that course should fail, as it did, Amaziah urges the troublesome prophet himself to go back to his own land Judah, pretending to advise him in friendliness. **seer**—said contemptuously in reference to Amos' *visions* which precede. **there eat bread**—You can earn a livelihood there, whereas remaining here you will be ruined. He judges of Amos by his own selfishness, as if regard to one's own safety and livelihood are the paramount considerations. So the false prophets (Ezek. 13:19) were ready to say whatever pleased their hearers, however false, for "handfuls of barley and pieces of bread." **13. prophesy not again**—(ch. 2:12). **at Beth-el**—Amaziah wants to be let alone at least in his own residence. **the king's chapel**—Beth-el was preferred by the king to Dan, the other seat of the calf worship, as being nearer Samaria, the capital, and as hallowed by Jacob of old (Gen. 28:16, 19; 35:6, 7). He argues by implication against Amos' presumption, as a private man, in speaking against the worship sanctioned by the king, and that in the very place consecrated to it for the king's own devotions. **king's court**—i.e., residence: the seat of empire, where the king holds his court, and which thou oughtest to have reverenced. Samaria was the usual king's residence: but for the convenience of attending the calf worship, a royal palace was at Beth-el also. **14. I** *was* **no prophet**—in answer to Amaziah's insinuation (vs. 12), that he discharged the prophetical office to earn his "bread" (like Israel's mercenary prophets). So far from being rewarded, Jehovah's prophets had to expect imprisonment and even death as the result of their prophesying in Samaria or Israel: whereas the prophets of Baal were maintained at the king's expense (cf. I Kings 18:19). I was not, says Amos, of the order of prophets, or educated in their schools, and deriving a livelihood from exercising the public functions of a prophet. I am a *shepherd* (cf. vs. 15, "flock"; the *Hebrew* for "herdsman" includes the meaning, *shepherd,* cf. ch. 1:1) in humble position, who did not even think of prophesying among you, until a divine call impelled me to it. **prophet's son**—i.e., disciple. Schools of prophets are mentioned first in I Samuel; in these youths were educated to serve the theocracy as public instructors. Only in the kingdom of the ten tribes is the continuance of the schools of the prophets mentioned. They were missionary stations near the chief seats of superstition in Israel, and associations endowed with the Spirit of God; none were admitted but those to whom the Spirit had been previously imparted. Their spiritual fathers travelled about to visit the training schools, and cared for the members and even their widows (II Kings 4:1, 2). The pupils had their common board in them, and after leaving them still continued members. The offerings which in Judah were given by the pious to the Levites, in Israel went to the schools of the prophets (II Kings 4:42). Prophecy (e.g., Elijah and Elisha) in Israel was more connected with extraordinary events than in Judah, inasmuch as, in the absence of the legal hierarchy of the latter, it needed to have more palpable divine sanction. **sycamore**—abounding in Palestine. The fruit was like the fig, but inferior; according to PLINY, a sort of compound, as the name expresses, of the fig and the mulberry. It was only eaten by the poorest (cf. I Kings 10:27). **gatherer**—one occupied with their cultivation [MAURER]. To cultivate it, an incision was made in the fruit when of a certain size, and on the fourth day afterwards it ripened (PLINY, H. N. 13. 7, 14). GROTIUS from JEROME says, if it be not plucked off and "gathered" (which favors *English Version*), it is spoiled by gnats. **15. took me as I followed the flock**—So David was taken (II Sam. 7:8; Ps. 78: 70, 71). Messiah is the antitypical *Shepherd* (Ps. 23; John 10). **unto my people**—"against" [MAURER]; so vs. 16. Jehovah claims them still as *His* by right, though slighting His authority. God would recover them to His service by the prophet's ministry. **16. drop**—distil as the refreshing drops of rain (Deut.

ADAM CLARKE

Amos hath conspired against thee. This was truly a lying prophet; there is not one word of truth in this message which he sent to Jeroboam. Amos had not conspired against the king—had not said that Jeroboam should die by the sword—and had not said that Israel should be carried away captive, though this last was implied in God's threatenings, and afterwards delivered by this prophet; see v. 17.

JOSEPH PARKER:

Verse 14. Read it emphatically: "No prophet I, no prophet's son I." The emphasis is intense. ". . . But I was an herdman, and a gatherer of sycamore fruit." Amos always kept good hold of his history. Because we let our personal history slip from the memory we lose a great deal of power. Remember your poverty; remember early hardships; remember through what difficulty you had to fight for every inch of foothold you have secured; remember how you were sustained in weakness; recall the time when men were so savage against you that you were not certain whether you would end your days in the workhouse or in the madhouse; recall your history, have it as a daily companion, because keeping fellowship with your memories you can take the next step upward and a step heavenward.

Verse 15. "The Lord took me": I was passive, I was never expecting such election and elevation—an elevation that brought danger; an election that was charged with solemn responsibility. It is the Lord's doing; if I am a prophet at all it is because the Lord has anointed me. How he lifts the subject to a new level! With Amaziah he is a conspirator, a man arranging a policy of selfishness, talking mysteries that he may bewilder the people. When Amos stands upon the scene he changes the whole perspective, he elevates the entire level; he says, If I am anything at all, I am God's chosen servant; I have only spoken what I was told, I have simply delivered a message; I never sat down in my life to write a sentence, saying, This is shapely, this is classical; the people of Israel will consider this a very polished composition; I never made a sentence in my life. When I opened my mouth the Lord's thunder escaped my lips, and I heard it with surprise, and knew it was the tempest of judgment. How his face burns; how his port dignifies; how he conquers a space for himself; and how the caitiff Amaziah, the mimicking priest, falls back into his proper shadow. You know the true man when you see him. If people will listen with their hearts they can easily tell which is the true voice and which is the false voice.

—*The People's Bible*

16. *Now therefore hear thou the word of the Lord.* While he was speaking in his own vindication, God seems to have inspired him with the awful prediction which he immediately delivers.

MATTHEW HENRY

have no comfort in his relations: *His wife shall be a harlot.* His *sons and his daughters shall fall by the sword* of war. He shall be stripped of all his estate. He shall himself perish in a strange country, in a *polluted land*, a heathen country.

(2) Amos was accused for saying, *Israel shall be led away captive* (*v.* 11), but he stands to it, and repeats it. The *burden of the word of the Lord* cannot be shaken off. Stopping the mouths of God's ministers will not stop the progress of God's word, for it shall not return void.

CHAPTER 8

Verses 1–3

I. The approach of the threatened ruin is represented by *a basket of summer-fruit* which Amos saw in vision (*v.* 1 and 2). He saw *a basket of summer-fruit* gathered and ready to be eaten, which signified, 1. That they were ripe for destruction, they lay ready to be eaten up. 2. That the year of God's patience was drawing toward a conclusion; it was autumn with them. 3. Those we call *summer-fruits* will not keep till winter, must be used immediately, an emblem of this people, that had nothing consistent in them.

II. The intent and meaning of this vision is no more than this: It signifies that *the end has come upon my people Israel.* What was said *ch.* vii. 8 is here repeated as God's determined resolution, *I will not again pass by them any more.*

III. The consequence of this shall be a universal desolation (*v.* 3). Here in a sinful world, in a sinful nation, 1. Sorrow reigns, reigns to such a degree that *the songs of the temple shall be howlings.* When God's judgments are abroad, they will turn the joy into heaviness, the temple-songs, which used to sound so pleasantly, into loud howlings. 2. Death reigns. There shall be *many* dead bodies *in every place* (Ps. cx. 6), slain by sword or pestilence. They shall not so much as have the bell tolled, but they shall *cast them forth with silence.*

Verses 4–10

I. They had the character of the unjust judge (Luke xviii. 2) that neither *feared God nor regarded man.*

They do indeed keep up a show of godliness; they observe the *sabbath* and the *new moon*; but they were soon weary of them. They said, *When will the sabbath be gone, that we may sell corn?* They were weary of the restraints of the sabbaths and the new-moons, and wished them over. They were fond of market-days; they longed to be *selling corn* and *setting forth wheat.* Those are strangers to God, and enemies to themselves, that love market days better than sabbath days, that would rather be selling corn than worshipping God. They neither *do justly* nor *love mercy.* When they *sell their corn* they impose upon the buyer. They measure him the corn by their own measure, but they *make the ephah small.* When they receive his money they weigh it in their own scales, by their own weights. They *make the shekel great,* so that the money, being found too light, must have more added to it. They have in their hearts neither the fear nor the love of that God who has so plainly said that *false weights and balances are an abomination to him.* Another instance of their fraudulent dealing is that they *sell the refuse of the wheat*, and, taking advantage of their neighbours' ignorance or necessity, make them take it at the same price at which they sell the *finest of the wheat.* They are barbarous and unmerciful to the poor: They *swallow up the needy*, and *make the poor of the land to fail.* But he who thus *reproaches the poor despises his Maker,* in whose hands *rich and poor meet together.* They swallowed up the poor by making them hard bargains, and bring them so low that they may have their labour for next to nothing. Thus *they buy the poor for silver*; they bring them and their *children into bondage.* You might buy a poor man to be your slave *for a pair of shoes.* Property was first invaded and then liberty; it is the method of oppressors first to make men beggars and then to make them their vassals.

II. The punishment that shall be inflicted on them for this sin. God will remember their sin against them. He swears, *Surely I will never forget any of their works. I will never forget them* is as much as to say, *I will never forgive them.* He will bring ruin and confusion upon them. There shall be universal terror and consternation (*v.* 8). When God comes forth against them the waters of trouble and calamity shall *rise up wholly as a flood*, that swells, when it is dammed up, and soon overflows its banks. The whole land *shall be cast out, and drowned,* and laid under water, as the land of Egypt is every year by the overflowing

JAMIESON, FAUSSET, BROWN

32:2; Ezek. 21:2; cf. Mic. 2:6, 11). **17. Thy wife shall be an harlot in the city**—i.e., shall be forced by the enemy, while thou art looking on, unable to prevent her dishonor (Isa. 13:16; Lam. 5:11). The words, "saith the LORD," are in striking opposition to "*Thou* sayest (vs. 16). **divided by line**—among the foe. **a polluted land**—Israel regarded every foreign land as that which really her own land was now, "polluted" (Isa. 24:5; Jer. 2:7).

CHAPTER 8

Vss. 1-14. VISION OF A BASKET OF SUMMER FRUIT SYMBOLICAL OF ISRAEL'S END. RESUMING THE SERIES OF SYMBOLS INTERRUPTED BY AMAZIAH, AMOS ADDS A FOURTH. THE AVARICE OF THE OPPRESSORS OF THE POOR: THE OVERTHROW OF THE NATION: THE WISH FOR THE MEANS OF RELIGIOUS COUNSEL, WHEN THERE SHALL BE A FAMINE OF THE WORD. **1. summer fruit**—*Hebrew, kitz.* In vs. 2 "end" is in *Hebrew, keetz.* The similarity of sounds implies that, as the *summer* is the *end* of the year and the time of the ripeness of fruits, so Israel is *ripe* for her *last* punishment, *ending* her national existence. As the fruit is plucked when ripe from the tree, so Israel from her land. **2. end**—(Ezek. 7:2, 6). **3. songs of . . . temple**—(ch. 5:23). The joyous hymns in the temple of Judah (or rather, in the *Beth-el* "royal temple," ch. 7:13; for the allusion is to *Israel,* not Judah, throughout this chapter) shall be changed into "howlings." GROTIUS translates, "palace"; cf. ch. 6:5, as to the songs there. But ch. 5:23, and 7:13, favor *English Version.* **they shall cast them forth with silence**—not as *Margin,* "be silent." It is an adverb, "silently." There shall be such great slaughter as even to prevent the bodies being buried [CALVIN]. There shall be none of the usual professional mourners (ch. 5: 16), but the bodies will be cast out in silence. Perhaps also is meant that terror, both of God (cf. ch. 6:10) and of the foe, shall close their lips. **4. Hear**—The nobles needed to be urged thus, as hating to *hear* reproof. **swallow up the needy**—or, "gape after," i.e., pant for their goods; so the word is used, Job 7:2, *Margin.* **to make the poor . . . to fail**—"that they (themselves) may be placed alone in the midst of the earth" (Isa. 5:8). **5.** So greedy are they of unjust gain that they cannot spare a single day, however sacred, from pursuing it. They are strangers to God and enemies to themselves, who love market days better than sabbath days; and they who have lost piety will not long keep honesty. The new moons (Num. 10:10) and sabbaths were to be kept without working or trading (Neh. 10:31). **set forth wheat**—lit., "open out" stores of wheat for sale. **ephah**—containing three seahs, or above three pecks. **making . . . small**—making it below the just weight to purchasers. **shekel great**—taking from purchasers a greater weight of money than was due. Shekels used to be *weighed out* in payments (Gen. 23:16). Thus they committed a double fraud against the law (Deut. 25:13, 14). **6. buy . . . poor for silver . . . pair of shoes**—i.e., that we may compel the needy for money, or any other thing of however little worth, to sell themselves to us as bondmen, in defiance of Leviticus 25:39; the very thing which brings down God's judgment (ch. 2:6). **sell the refuse of . . . wheat**—which contains no nutriment, but which the poor eat at a low price, being unable to pay for flour.

7. Lord hath sworn by the excellency of Jacob—i.e., by Himself, in whom Jacob's seed glory [MAURER]. Rather, by the spiritual privileges of Israel, the adoption as His peculiar people [CALVIN], the temple, and its Shekinah symbol of His presence. Cf. ch. 6:8, where it means Jehovah's *temple* (cf. ch. 4:2). **never forget**—not *pass by* without punishing (vs. 2; Hos. 8:13; 9:9). **8. the land . . . rise up wholly as a flood**—The land will, as it were, be wholly turned into a flooding river (a flood being the image of overwhelming calamity, Dan. 9:26). **cast out and drowned . . .**—swept away and overwhelmed, as the land adjoining the Nile is by it, when flooding (ch. 9:5). The Nile rises generally twenty feet. The waters then "cast out" mire and dirt (Isa. 57:20).

ADAM CLARKE

17. *Thy wife shall be an harlot.* As this was the word of the Lord, so it was fulfilled; but as we have no further account of this idolatrous priest, so we cannot tell in what circumstances these threatenings were executed. *Israel shall surely go into captivity.* He now declares fully what he had not declared before, though Amaziah had made it a subject of accusation. This particular was probably revealed at this instant, as well as those which concerned Amaziah and his family.

CHAPTER 8

1. *A basket of summer fruit.* As summer fruit was not proper for preserving, but must be eaten as soon as gathered, so the Lord intimates by this symbol that the kingdom of Israel was now ripe for destruction, and that punishment must descend upon it without delay.

2. *A basket of summer fruit. Kelub kayits; the end is come—bahakkets;* here is a paronomasia or play upon the words *kayits,* "summer fruit," and *kets,* "the end," both coming from similar roots. See Ezek. vii. 2, where there is a similar play on the same word.

5. *Making the ephah small, and the shekel great.* Giving short measure, and taking full price; or buying with a heavy weight, and selling with one that was light.

6. *That we may buy the poor for silver.* Buying their services for such a time, with just money enough to clear them from other creditors. *And the needy for a pair of shoes.* See chap. ii. 6. *And sell the refuse of the wheat.* Selling bad wheat and damaged flour to poor people as good, knowing that such cannot afford to prosecute them.

7. *By the excellency of Jacob.* By the state of eminence to which He had raised the descendants of Jacob; or by the "excellent One of Jacob," that is, himself. The meaning is: "As surely as I have raised you to such a state of eminence, so surely will I punish you in proportion to your advantages and your crimes."

MATTHEW HENRY

of its river Nile. It shall come upon them when they little think of it (*v.* 9): "*I will cause the sun to go down at noon*, when it is in its full strength and lustre. The *earth* shall be *darkened in the clear day*, when everything looks pleasant and hopeful." It shall change their note, and mar all their mirth (*v.* 10): *I will turn your feasts into mourning*, as (*v.* 3) the *songs of the temple into howlings*. The state of impenitent sinners grows worse and worse, and the last of all will be the worst of all.

Verses 11–14

I. A spiritual famine coming upon the whole land, a *famine of the word of God*, the failing of oracles and the scarcity of good preaching. *The days come* when another kind of darkness shall come upon that land of light. When Amos prophesied, and for a considerable time after, they had great plenty of prophets, abundant opportunities of *hearing the word of God*. God threatens that hereafter he will deprive them of this privilege. They should have plenty of bread and water, and yet their teachers should be removed. Their nation had been great and high, for *to them were committed the oracles of God*; but, when these were taken from them, their beauty was stained and their honour laid in the dust. This was a token of God's highest displeasure against them. We should say at any time that a famine of the word of God is the sorest famine, the heaviest judgment.

They shall wander from sea to sea, from the sea of Tiberias to the Great Sea, to see if God will send them prophets (*v.* 12). And *in the day* of this famine *the fair virgins and the young men shall faint for thirst* (*v.* 13). The *Jewish churches*, and the *masters of their synagogues*, some take to be meant by the *virgins* and the *young men*. Those that trust in their own merit and think they have no need of Christ, others take to be meant by the *fair virgins* and the *choice young men*; they shall *faint for thirst*, when those that *hunger and thirst after the righteousness* of Christ shall be filled.

II. The particular destruction of those that were ringleaders in idolatry, *v.* 14. They *swear by the sin of Samaria*, that is, by the god of Samaria, the idol that was worshipped at Bethel, not far off from Samaria. They say, *Thy God, O Dan! liveth;* that was the other golden calf, a dumb dead idol, and yet caressed as if it had been the living God. They say, *The manner*, or way, of *Beer-sheba liveth*; they swore by the *religion* of Beer-sheba. Those who thus give that honour to idols which is due to God alone *shall fall*, and the gods cannot stand their friends, so they shall *never rise again*.

CHAPTER 9

Verses 1–10

I. Sentence is passed. The prophet saw in vision *the Lord standing upon the altar* (*v.* 1), the altar of burnt-offerings. He is removed from the *mercy-seat* between the *cherubim*. He stands on the altar, to prohibit sacrifice.

Now the order given is, *Smite the lintel of the door* of the temple with such a blow *that the posts may shake*, and *cut them*, wound them *in the head, all of them*; break down the door of God's

JAMIESON, FAUSSET, BROWN

9. "Darkness" made to rise "at noon" is the emblem of great calamities (Jer. 15:9; Ezek. 32:7-10). **10. baldness**—a sign of mourning (Isa. 15:2; Jer. 48:37; Ezek. 7:18). **I will make it as . . . mourning of an only son**—"it," i.e., "the earth" (vs. 9). I will reduce the land to such a state that there shall be the same occasion for mourning as when parents mourn for an only son (Jer. 6:26; Zech. 12:10). **11. famine of . . . hearing the words of the Lord**—a just retribution on those who now will not hear the Lord's prophets, nay even try to drive them away, as Amaziah did (ch. 7:12); they shall look in vain, in their distress, for divine counsel, such as the prophets now offer (Ezek. 7:26; Mic. 3:7). Cf. as to the Jews' rejection of Messiah, and their consequent rejection by Him (Matt. 21:43); and their desire for Messiah too late (Luke 17:22; John 7:34; 8:21). So, the prodigal when he had sojourned awhile in the "far-off country, began to be in want" in the "mighty famine" which arose (Luke 15:14; cf. I Sam. 3:1; 7:2). It is remarkable that the Jews' religion is almost the only one that *could* be abolished *against the will of the people themselves,* on account of its being dependent on a particular *place*, viz., the temple. When that was destroyed, the Mosaic ritual, which could not exist without it, necessarily ceased. Providence designed it, that, as the law gave way to the Gospel, so all men should perceive it was so, in spite of the Jews' obstinate rejection of the Gospel. **12. they shall wander from sea to sea**—i.e., from the Dead Sea to the Mediterranean, from east to west. **from . . . north . . . to . . . east**—where we might expect "from north to south." But so alienated was Israel from Judah, that no Israelite even then would think of repairing *southward*, i.e., to Jerusalem for religious information. The circuit is traced as in Numbers 34:3, etc., except that the south is omitted. Their "seeking the word of the Lord" would not be from a sincere desire to obey God, but under the pressure of punishment. **13. faint for thirst**—viz., thirst for hearing the words of the Lord, being destitute of all other comfort. If even the young and strong faint, how much more the infirm (Isa. 40:30, 31)! **14. swear by the sin of Samaria**—viz., the calves (Deut. 9:21; Hos. 4:15). "Swear by" means to *worship* (Ps. 63:11). **The manner**—i.e., as "the way" is used (Ps. 139:24; Acts 9:2), *the mode of worship*. **Thy god, O Dan**—the other golden calf at Dan (I Kings 22:26-30). **liveth . . . liveth**—rather, "May thy god . . . live . . . may the manner . . . live." Or, "As (surely as) thy god, O Dan, liveth." This is their formula when they swear; not "May Jehovah live!" or, "As Jehovah liveth!"

CHAPTER 9

Vss. 1-15. Fifth and Last Vision. *None can escape the coming judgment in any hiding-place: for God is omnipresent and irresistible* (vss. 1-6). *As a kingdom, Israel shall perish as if it never was in covenant with Him: but as individuals the house of Jacob shall not utterly perish, nay, not one of the least of the righteous shall fall, but only all the sinners* (vss. 7-10). *Restoration of the Jews finally to their own land after the re-establishment of the fallen tabernacle of David; consequent conversion of all the heathen* (vss. 11-15). **1. Lord . . . upon the altar**—viz., in the idolatrous temple at Beth-el; the calves which were spoken of in the verse just preceding, of ch. 8. Hither they would flee for protection from the Assyrians, and would perish in the ruins, with the vain object of their trust [Henderson]. Jehovah stands here to direct the destruction of it, them, and the idolatrous nation. He demands many victims on the altar, but they are to be human victims. Calvin and Fairbairn, and others, make it in the *temple at Jerusalem*. Judgment was to descend both on Israel and Judah. As the services of both alike ought to have been offered on the Jerusalem temple-altar, it is there that Jehovah ideally stands, as if the whole people were assembled there, their abominations lying unpardoned there, and crying for vengeance, though in fact committed elsewhere (cf. Ezek. 8:1-18). This view harmonizes with the similarity of the vision in Amos to that in Isaiah 6, *at Jerusalem*. Also with the end of this chapter (vss. 11-15), which applies both to *Judah* and Israel: "the tabernacle of David," viz., at Jerusalem. His attitude, "standing," implies fixity of purpose. **lintel**—rather, the spherelike *capital* of the column [Maurer]. **posts**—rather, thresholds, as in Isaiah 6:4, *Margin*. The temple is to be smitten below as well as above, to ensure utter destruction. **cut them in the head**—viz., with the

ADAM CLARKE

F. B. MEYER:

"I will send a famine in the land . . . of hearing the words of the Lord" (Amos 8:11). Israel will not listen to God's prophets, and their voices would be silenced. This was a just retribution. As they were not willing to have the word of God, so there should be a famine of that word. The word of God was precious in the days of Samuel, because there was no open vision; so should it be again. And perhaps this privation will one day be meted out to our beloved country. There is a much larger proportion of our population outside than inside our churches; and men proudly eschew God's Word. It may be that the message of the Gospel will almost cease from among them, and be replaced—as in so many instances is now the case—by the dry husks of morality and ceremonialism. Then they shall run to and fro to seek the word of the Lord, and shall not find it.

—*Great Verses Through the Bible*

12. *They shall wander from sea to sea.* From the Mediterranean to the Dead Sea or from west to east, and from north to south, *to seek the word of the Lord;* to find a prophet, or any person authorized by God to show them the end of their calamities. In this state they shall continue, because they have rejected Him who is the Bread of Life.

14. *By the sin of Samaria.* Baal, who was worshipped here. *Thy god, O Dan.* The golden calf, or ox, the representative of the Egyptian god Apis, or Osiris. *The manner of Beer-sheba.* The worship or object of worship. Another of the golden calves which Jeroboam had set up there.

CHAPTER 9

1. *I saw the Lord standing upon the altar.* As this is a continuation of the preceding prophecy, the *altar* here may be one of those at either Dan or Beersheba.

Smite the lintel. Either the piece of timber that binds the wall above the door or the upper part of the doorframe.

MATTHEW HENRY

house, in token that he is going out from it, and forsaking it. "Smite the king, who is as the lintel of the door, that the princes, who are as *the posts,* may *shake*; *cut them in the head,* cleave them down, *all of them,* and *I will slay the last of them.*"

II. God's judgments will overtake the swiftest that think to out-run them, *v.* 2. "Though *they dig into hell,* into the centre of the earth, yet *thence shall my hand take them.*" The grave is a hiding-place to the righteous from the malice of the world (Job. iii. 17), but it shall be no hiding-place to the wicked from the justice of God. *The top of Carmel* shall not protect them: "*Though they hide themselves there,* where they imagine nobody will look for them, *I will search, and take them out thence.*" The *bottom of the sea* shall not serve to conceal them. *Thence will I command the serpent, and he shall bite them,* the *crooked serpent,* even *the dragon that is in the sea,* Isa. xxvii. 1. Remote countries will not befriend them, nor less judgments excuse them from greater (*v.* 4). Threatenings are more or less formidable according to the power of him that threatens. We laugh at impotent wrath; but the wrath of God is not so; it is omnipotent wrath. Those who have the Lord of hosts against them, have the whole creation at war with them. He is the Creator and governor of the upper world: *It is he that builds his stories in the heavens,* the celestial orbs, or spheres, one over another as so many stories in a high and stately palace. He has the command of this lower world too, both *earth* and *sea.* Do they think to make a land-fight of it? He *has founded his troop in the earth,* his troop of guards, for the protection of his subjects and the punishment of his enemies. All the creatures on earth make one bundle (as the margin reads it), one bundle of arrows, out of which he takes what he pleases to discharge against the persecutors, Ps. vii. 13. Do they think to make a sea-fight of it? He has the waters of the sea at command; even its waves, the most tumultuous rebellious waters, do obey him. How justly God passes this sentence upon the people of Israel. He does not destroy them by an act of sovereignty, but by an act of righteousness. *Are you not as children of the Ethiopians unto me, O children of Israel?* A sad change! Those that were trained up in the knowledge and fear of God, and promised fair, throw off their profession and become as bad as the worst. This is an intimation of the rejection of the unbelieving Jews in the days of the Messiah; because they embraced not the doctrine of Christ, the kingdom of God was taken from them, they were unchurched, and cast out of covenant. They thought he would not cast them off, and put them upon a level with other nations, because he had done that for them which he had not done for other nations. "No," says he, "the favours shown to you are not so distinguishing as you think they are: *Have not I brought up Israel out of the land of Egypt?* I have also brought the *Philistines from Caphtor,* or *Cappadocia.*" In like manner the Syrians were brought up from Kir when they had been carried away thither, 2 Kings xvi. 9. If God's Israel lose the peculiarity of their holiness, they lose the peculiarity of their privileges. Though the wicked Israelites shall be as the wicked Ethiopians, and their being called Israelites shall stand them in no stead, yet the pious Israelites shall not be as the *wicked ones.* I will distinguish, as becomes a righteous judge. The house of Israel shall be *sifted as corn is sifted*; but still in the hands of God, as the sieve in the hands of him that sifts (*v.* 9): *I will sift the house of Israel among all nations.* The righteous ones among them, that are as the solid wheat, shall none of them perish; *not the least grain shall fall on the earth,* so as to be lost and forgotten—not the least *stone* (so the word is), for the good corn is weighty as a stone in comparison with that which we call *light corn.*

Verses 11–15

To him to whom all the prophets bear witness this prophet here bears his testimony, and speaks of *that day* in which God will do great things for his church, by the setting up of the kingdom of the Messiah. The promise here may refer to the planting of the Christian church, Acts xv. 15–17. It is promised,

I. That in the Messiah the kingdom of David shall be restored (*v.* 11). The church militant, in its present state, dwelling as in shepherds' tents to feed, as in soldiers' tents to fight, is the *tabernacle of David.* The royal family was so impoverished, its power abridged, for many of that race degenerated, and in the captivity it lost the imperial dignity. So it was with the church of the Jews; in the latter days its glory departed; it was like a tabernacle brought to ruin. By Jesus Christ these tabernacles were raised and rebuilt. In him God's covenant with David had its accomplishment; and the glory of that house revived

JAMIESON, FAUSSET, BROWN

broken fragments of the capitals and columns (cf. Ps. 68:21; Hab. 3:13). **slay the last of them**—their posterity [HENDERSON]. The survivors [MAURER]. Jehovah's directions are addressed to His angels, ministers of judgment (cf. Ezek. 9). **he that fleeth . . . shall not flee away**—He who fancies himself safe and out of reach of the enemy shall be taken (ch. 2: 14). **2. Though they dig into hell**—though they hide ever so deeply in the earth (Ps. 139:8). **though they climb up to heaven**—though they ascend the greatest heights (Job 20:6, 7; Jer. 51:53; Obad. 4). **3. Carmel**—where the forests, and, on the west side, the caves, furnished hiding-places (ch. 1:2; Judg. 6:2; I Sam. 13:6). **the sea**—the Mediterranean, which flows at the foot of Mount Carmel; forming a strong antithesis to it. **command the serpent**—the sea-serpent, a term used for any great water-monster (Isa. 27:1). The symbol of *cruel and oppressive kings* (Ps. 74:13, 14). **4. though they go into captivity**—hoping to save their lives by voluntarily surrendering to the foe. **5.** As Amos had threatened that nowhere should the Israelites be safe from the divine judgments, he here shows God's omnipotent ability to execute His threats. So in the case of the threat in ch. 8:8, God is here stated to be the first cause of the mourning of "all that dwell" in the land, and of its rising "like a flood," and of its being "drowned, as by the flood of Egypt." **6. stories**—lit., "ascents," i.e., upper chambers, to which the ascent is by steps [MAURER]; evidently referring to the words in Psalm 104:3, 13. GROTIUS explains it, *God's royal throne,* expressed in language drawn from Solomon's throne, to which the ascent was by steps (cf. I Kings 10:18, 19). **founded his troop**—viz., all animate creatures, which are God's *troop,* or *host* (Gen. 2:1), doing His will (Ps. 103:20, 21; Joel 2:11). MAURER translates, "His *vault,*" i.e., the vaulted sky, which seems to rest on the earth supported by the horizon. **7. unto me**—however great ye seem *to yourselves.* Do not rely on past privileges, and on My having delivered you from Egypt, as if therefore I never would remove you from Canaan. I make no more account of you than of "the Ethiopian" (cf. Jer. 13:23). "Have not I (who) brought you out of Egypt," done as much for other peoples? For instance, did I not bring "the Philistines (*Notes,* Isa. 14:29, etc.) from Caphtor (cf. Deut. 2:23; *Note,* Jer. 47:4), where they had been bond-servants, and the Syrians from Kir?" It is appropriate, that as the Syrians migrated into Syria from Kir (cf. *Note,* Isa. 22:6), so they should be carried back captive into the same land (*Note,* ch. 1:15; II Kings 16:9), just as elsewhere Israel is threatened with a return to Egypt whence they had been delivered. The "Ethiopians," *Hebrew,* "Cushites," were originally akin to the race that founded Babylon: the cuneiform inscriptions in this confirming independently the Scripture statement (Gen. 10: 6, 8, 10). **8. eyes . . . upon the sinful kingdom**—i.e., I am watching all its sinful course in order to punish it (cf. vs. 4; Ps. 34:15, 16). **not utterly destroy the house of Jacob**—Though as a "kingdom" the nation is now utterly to perish, a remnant is to be spared for "Jacob," their forefather's sake (cf. Jer. 30:11); to fulfil the covenant whereby "the seed of Israel" is hereafter to be "a nation for ever" (Jer. 31:36). **9. sift**—I will cause the Israelites to be tossed about through all nations as corn is shaken about in a sieve, in such a way, however, that while the chaff and dust (the wicked) fall through (perish), all the solid grains (the godly elect) remain (are preserved), (Rom. 11:26; cf. *Note,* Jer. 3:14). So spiritual Israel's final safety is ensured (Luke 22:32; John 10:28; 6:39). **10. All the sinners**—answering to the chaff in the image in vs. 9, which falls on the earth, in opposition "to the grain" that does not "fall." **overtake . . . us**—"come on us from behind" [MAURER]. **11. In that day**—quoted by James (Acts 15: 16, 17), "After this," i.e., in the dispensation of Messiah (Gen. 49:10; Hos. 3:4, 5; Joel 2:28; 3:1). **tabernacle of David**—not "the *house* of David," which is used of his affairs when prospering (II Sam. 3:1), but the *tent* or *booth,* expressing the low condition to which his kingdom and family had fallen in Amos' time, and subsequently at the Babylonian captivity before the restoration; and secondarily, in the last days preceding Israel's restoration under Messiah, the antitype to David (Ps. 102:13, 14; *Note,* Isa. 12:1; Jer. 30:9; Ezek. 34:24; 37:24). The type is taken from architecture (Eph. 2:20). The restoration under Zerubbabel can only be a partial, temporary fulfilment; for it did not include Israel, which nation is the main subject of Amos' prophecies, but only Judah; also Zerubbabel's kingdom was not independent and settled; also all the prophets end their prophecies with Messiah, whose advent is the cure of all previous disorders. "Tab-

ADAM CLARKE

3. *Though they hide themselves.* All these are metaphorical expressions, to show the impossibility of escape.

4. *I will set mine eyes upon them for evil.* I will use that very providence against them which before worked for their good.

7. *Children of the Ethiopians.* Or Cushites. Cush was the son of Ham, Gen. x. 6; and his descendants inhabited a part of Arabia Petraea and Arabia Felix. All this stock was universally despised. *The Philistines from Caphtor.* The island of Crete, the people of which were the Cherethim. See 1 Sam. xxx. 14; Ezek. xxv. 16; Zeph. ii. 5. *The Syrians from Kir.* Perhaps a city of the Medes, Isa. xxii. 6. Aram, from whom Syria had its name, was the son of Shem, Gen. x. 22. The meaning of the verse is this: Do not presume on My having brought you out of the land of Egypt and house of bondage into a land flowing with milk and honey. I have brought other nations, and some of your neighbors, who are your enemies, from comparatively barren countries into fruitful territories.

8. *The eyes of the Lord God are upon the sinful kingdom.* The kingdom of Israel, peculiarly sinful; and therefore to be signally destroyed by the Assyrians.

11. *Will I raise up the tabernacle of David.* It must refer to their restoration under the gospel, when they shall receive the Lord Jesus as their Messiah, and be by Him restored to their own land. See these words quoted by James, Acts xv. 17. Then indeed it is likely that they shall possess the "remnant of Edom," and have the whole length and breadth of Immanuel's land, v. 12.

MATTHEW HENRY

again. The spiritual glory of the family of Christ far exceeded the temporal glory of the family of David. In him also God's covenant with Israel had its accomplishment, and in the gospel-church the tabernacle of God was set up among men again. This is quoted in the first council at Jerusalem as referring to the calling in of the Gentiles and God's *taking out of them a people for his name.*

II. That that kingdom shall be enlarged (*v.* 12), that the house of David may possess the *remnant of Edom, and of all the heathen,* that is, that Christ may have them given him for his *inheritance,* Ps. ii. 8. Christ died to *gather together in one the children of God that were scattered abroad,* here said to be those that were *called by his name.*

III. That in the kingdom of the Messiah there shall be great plenty (*v.* 13): *The ploughman shall overtake the reaper,* that is there shall be such a plentiful harvest every year, that it shall last all summer, even till autumn, when it is time to begin to plough again. The hills that were dry and barren shall be moistened and shall melt with the *fatness* or *mellowness* (as we call it) of *the soil.* This must be understood of the spiritual blessings with which all those are blessed who are in sincerity added to Christ and his church; they shall have the bread of life, to *strengthen their hearts,* and the wine of divine consolations to *make them glad—meat indeed* and *drink indeed*—all the benefit that comes to the souls of men from the word and Spirit of God. When great multitudes were converted and when the preachers of the gospel were *always caused to triumph in* the success of their preaching, then the *ploughman overtook the reaper.*

IV. That the kingdom of the Messiah shall be well peopled; there shall be mouths for this meat, *v.* 14. Those that take pains in religion, as men must do about their vineyards and gardens, shall have both the pleasure and the profit of it. The *bringing again* of the *captivity* of God's Israel, which is here promised, may refer to the cancelling of the ceremonial law, and the investing of them in the liberty wherewith Christ came to make his church free, Gal. v. 1.

V. That the kingdom of the Messiah shall take such deep rooting in the world as never to be rooted out of it (*v.* 15): *I will plant them upon their land.* The church may be corrupted, but shall not quite forsake God, may be persecuted, but shall not quite be forsaken of God. Two things secure the perpetuity of the church: 1. God's grants to it: It is *the land which I have given them.* 2. Its interest in him: He is *the Lord thy God,* who has said it, and will make it good, who shall *reign for ever unto all generations.* And because he lives the church shall live also.

JAMIESON, FAUSSET, BROWN

ernacle" is appropriate to Him, as His human nature is the tabernacle which He assumed in becoming Immanuel, "God with us" (John 1:14). "Dwelt," lit., *tabernacled* "among us" (cf. Rev. 21: 3). Some understand "the tabernacle of David" as that which David pitched for the ark in Zion, after bringing it from Obededom's house. It remained there all his reign for thirty years, till the temple of Solomon was built, whereas the "tabernacle of the congregation" remained at Gibeon (II Chron. 1:3), where the priests ministered in sacrifices (I Chron. 16:39). Song and praise was the service of David's attendants before the ark (Asaph, etc.): a type of the gospel separation between the sacrificial service (*Messiah's* priesthood now *in heaven*) and the access of *believers on earth* to the presence of God, apart from the former (cf. II Sam. 6:12-17; I Chron. 16: 37-39; II Chron. 1:3). **breaches thereof**—lit., "of them," i.e., of the *whole* nation, Israel as well as Judah. **as in . . . days of old**—as it was formerly in the days of David and Solomon, when the kingdom was in its full extent and undivided. **12. That they may possess . . . remnant of Edom, and of all the heathen**—"Edom," the bitter foe, though the brother, of Israel; therefore to be punished (ch. 1:11, 12). Israel shall be lord of the "remnant" of Edom left after the punishment of the latter. James quotes it, "That *the residue of men* might *seek after the Lord, and all the Gentiles . . . .*" For "all the heathen" nations stand on the same footing as *Edom:* Edom is the representative of them all. The *residue* or *remnant* in both cases expresses those left after great antecedent calamities (Rom. 9:27; Zech. 14: 16). Here the conversion of "*all* nations" (of which the earnest was given in James's time) is represented as only to be realized on the re-establishment of the theocracy under Messiah, the Heir of the throne of David (vs. 11). The possession of the heathen nations by Israel is to be spiritual, the latter being the ministers to the former for their conversion to Messiah, King of the Jews; just as the first conversions of pagans were through the ministry of the apostles, who were Jews. Cf. Isaiah 54:3, "thy seed shall *inherit the Gentiles*" (cf. Isa. 49:8; Rom. 4:13). A remnant of Edom became Jews under John Hyrcanus, and the rest amalgamated with the Arabians, who became Christians subsequently. **which are called by my name**—i.e., who belong to Me, whom I claim as Mine (Ps. 2:8); in the purposes of electing grace, God terms them already *called by His name.* Cf. the title, "the children," applied by anticipation, Hebrews 2:14. Hence as an act of sovereign grace, fulfilling His promise, it is spoken of God. Proclaim His title as sovereign, "the Lord that doeth this" ("all these things," Acts 15:17, viz., all these and such like acts of sovereign love). **13. the days come**—at the future restoration of the Jews to their own land. **ploughman shall overtake . . . reaper . . . treader of grapes him that soweth**—fulfilling Leviticus 26:5. Such shall be the abundance that the harvest and vintage can hardly be gathered before the time for preparing for the next crop shall come. Instead of the greater part of the year being spent in war, the whole shall be spent in sowing and reaping the fruits of earth. Cf. Isaiah 65:21-23, as to the same period. **soweth seed**—lit., "draweth it forth," viz., from the sack in order to sow it. **mountains . . . drop sweet wine**—an appropriate image, as the vines in Palestine were trained on *terraces at the sides of the hills.* **14. build the waste cities**—(Isa. 61:4; Ezek. 36:33-36). **15. plant them . . . no more be pulled up**—(Jer. 32:41). **thy God**—Israel's; this is the ground of their restoration, God's original choice of them as His.

ADAM CLARKE

CHARLES H. SPURGEON:

"Behold, the days come, saith the Lord, that the plowman shall overtake the reaper, and the treader of grapes him that soweth seed; and the mountains shall drop sweet wine, and all the hills shall melt" (Amos 9:13).

God's promises are not exhausted when they are fulfilled, for when once performed, they stand just as good as they did before, and we may await a second accomplishment of them. Man's promises even at the best, are like a cistern which holds but a temporary supply; but God's promises are as a fountain, never emptied, ever overflowing, so that you may draw from them the whole of that which they apparently contain, and they shall be still as full as ever. Hence it is that you will frequently find a promise containing both a literal and spiritual meaning. In the literal meaning it has already been fulfilled to the letter; in the spiritual meaning it shall also be accomplished, and not a jot or tittle of it shall fail. This is true of the particular promise which is before us. Originally, as you are aware, the land of Canaan was very fertile; it was a land that flowed with milk and honey. Even where no tillage had been exercised upon it the land was so fruitful, that the bees who sucked the sweetness from the wild flowers produced such masses of honey that the very woods were sometimes flooded with it. It was "A land of wheat, and barley, and vines, and fig trees, and pomegranates; a land of olive oil, and honey." When, however, the children of Israel thrust in the ploughshare and began to use the divers arts of agriculture, the land became exceedingly fat and fertile, yielding so much corn, that they could export through the Phoenicians both corn, and wine, and oil, even to the pillars of Hercules, so that Palestine became, like Egypt, the granary of the nations. It is somewhat surprising to find that now the land is barren, that its valleys are parched, and that the inhabitants gather miserable harvests from the arid soil. Yet the promise stands true, that one day, in the very letter, Palestine shall be as rich and fruitful as ever it was. There be those who understand the matter, who assert that if the man who sowed could reap, and keep the corn which his own industry had sown and gathered, the land might yet again laugh in the midst of the nations, and become the joyous mother of children. There is no reason *in the soil* for its barrenness. It is simply the neglect that has been brought on from the fact, that when a man has been industrious, his savings are taken from him by the hand of rapine, and the very harvest for which he toiled is often reaped by another, and his own blood, spilt upon the soil.

—*The Treasury of the Old Testament*

THE BOOK OF OBADIAH

I. The judgment of Edom (1-16)
A. Explanatory introduction (1)
B. The doom declared (2-9)
C. The reason assigned (10-16)

II. The restoration of Israel (17-21)
A. The delivered remnant (17)
B. The victorious people (18)
C. The conquering people (19)
D. The returning captives (20)
E. The final issue (21)

This is the shortest of all the books of the Old Testament, and yet is not to be passed by, for this penny has Caesar's image and superscription upon it; it is stamped with a divine authority. This book is entitled, "The Vision of Obadiah." Who this Obadiah was does not appear. Some of the ancients imagined him to be the same with that Obadiah that was steward to Ahab's household (1 Kings 18:3); and, if so, he that hid and fed the prophets had indeed a prophet's reward, when he was himself made a prophet. But that is a conjecture which has no ground. This Obadiah, it is probable, was of a later date, some think contemporary with Hosea, Joel, and Amos; others think he lived about the time of the destruction of Jerusalem, when the children of Edom so barbarously triumphed in that destruction. However, what he wrote was what he saw; it is his *vision*. It is a foolish fancy of some of the Jews that because he prophesies only concerning Edom that he was himself an Edomite by birth, but a proselyte to the Jewish religion. Other prophets prophesied against Edom, and some of them seem to have borrowed from him in their predictions against Edom (Jer. 49:7; Ezek. 25:12).

MATTHEW HENRY

CHAPTER 1

Verses 1–9

Edom is the nation against which this prophecy is levelled, and which, some think, is put for all the enemies of Israel. Though Edom was mortified in the times of the Maccabees, as it had been before by Jehoshaphat, yet its destruction seems to have been typical, as their father Esau's rejection, and to have had further reference to the destruction of the enemies of the gospel-church. Some have well observed that it could not but be a great trial to the people of Israel, when they saw themselves, the children of beloved Jacob, in trouble, and the Edomites, the seed of hated Esau, triumphing over them in their troubles; and therefore God gives them a prospect of the destruction of Edom, and of a happy issue of their own correction.

I. A declaration of war against Edom (*v.* 1): "*We have heard a rumour*, or rather *an order*, *from the Lord*, the God of hosts; he has given the word of command that all who do mischief to his people shall certainly bring mischief upon themselves. We have heard a report that God is preparing his throne for judgment; and an *ambassador is sent among the heathen*," a *herald* rather, to alarm the nations. *Arise ye*, stir up yourselves and one another, and let *us rise up against Edom in battle*. The confederate forces under Nebuchadnezzar prepare to make a descent upon that country: *Gather yourselves together, and come against her*.

II. A prediction of the success of that war. Edom shall certainly be subdued. "*Behold, I have made thee small among the heathen*, so that none of thy neighbours will court an alliance with thee; *thou art greatly despised* among them, as an unfaithful nation." And thus (*v.* 3) *the pride of thy heart has deceived thee*. The fortifications of their country shall deceive them. They *dwelt in the clefts of the rock*, as an eagle in her nest, and their *habitation* was *high*, fortified against their enemies, so high as to be out of the reach of danger. Edom says in the pride of his heart: *Who shall bring me down to the ground?* He speaks with a confidence of his own strength, and a contempt of God's judgments. Carnal security is a sin that most easily besets men in the day of their pomp, power, and prosperity. If men will dare to challenge Omnipotence, their challenge shall be taken up: *Who shall bring me down?* says Edom. "*I will*," says God. "*Though thou exalt thyself as the eagle* that soars high and builds high, nay, *though thou set thy nest among the stars*, it is but in thy own imagination, and *thence will I bring thee down*." This we had Jer. xlix. 15, 16. Their money shall rather expose them than protect them; it shall be made a prey to the enemy, and they for the sake of it, *v.* 5, 6. How art thou fallen, and how great is thy fall! *How art thou stupefied!* so the Chaldee words it. The prophet shows that it should be an utter ruin, not a usual calamity; for it is indeed usual for those that have wealth to have it stolen, and to lose a little out of their great deal. *Thieves come to them* and steal no more than they think they can carry away, and out of a great stock it is scarcely missed. It shall not be so with Edom; his wealth shall all be taken away, and nothing shall escape the hands of the destroying army, *v.* 6. *How are his hidden things*, his hidden treasures, plundered, rifled,

JAMIESON, FAUSSET, BROWN

CHAPTER 1

VSS.1-21. DOOM OF EDOM FOR CRUELTY TO JUDAH, EDOM'S BROTHER; RESTORATION OF THE JEWS. **1. Obadiah**—i.e., servant of Jehovah; same as *Abdeel* and *Arabic Abd-allah*.

We—I and my people. **heard**—(Isa. 21:10). **and an ambassador is sent**—Yea, an ambassador is *already* sent, viz., an angel, to stir up the Assyrians (and afterwards the Chaldeans) against Edom. The result of the ambassador's message on the heathen is, they simultaneously exclaim, "Arise ye, and let us [with united strength] rise . . . ." Jeremiah 49:14 quotes this. **2. I have made thee small**—Thy reduction to insignificance is *as sure as if it were already accomplished;* therefore the past tense is used [MAURER]. Edom then extended from Dedan of Arabia to Bozrah in the north (Jer. 49:8, 13). CALVIN explains it, "Whereas thou wast made by Me an insignificant people, why art thou so *proud*" (vs. 3)? But if so, why should the heathen peoples be needed to subdue one so insignificant? Jeremiah 49:15, confirms MAURER'S view. **3. clefts of . . . rock**—(Song of Sol. 2:14; Jer. 48:28). The cities of Edom, and among them Petra (*Hebrew, sela*, meaning "rock," II Kings 14:7, *Margin*), the capital, in the Wady Musa, consisted of houses mostly cut in the rocks. **4. exalt** *thyself*—or supply from the second clause, "thy nest" [MAURER] (cf. Job 20:6; Jer. 49:16; Amos 9:2). **set . . . nest among . . . stars**—viz., on the loftiest hills which seem to reach the very stars. Edom is a type of Antichrist (Isa. 14:13; Dan. 8:10; 11:37). **thence will I bring thee down**—in spite of thy boast (vs. 3), "*Who* shall bring me down?" **5. The spoliation** which thou shalt suffer shall not be such as that which thieves cause, bad as that is, for these when they have seized enough, or all they can get in a hurry, leave the rest—nor such as grape-gatherers cause in a vineyard, for they, when they have gathered most of the grapes, leave gleanings behind—but it shall be utter, so as to leave thee nothing. The exclamation; "How art thou cut off!" bursting in amidst the words of the image, marks strongly excited feeling. The contrast between Edom where no gleanings shall be left, and Israel where at the worst a gleaning is left (Isa. 17:6; 24:13), is striking.

6. How are *the things of* **Esau searched out!**—by hostile soldiers seeking booty. Cf. with vss. 5, 6 here, Jer. 49:9, 10. **hidden things**—or *places*. Edom abounded in such hiding-places, as caves, clefts in the rock, etc. None of these would be left unexplored by the foe.

ADAM CLARKE

CHAPTER 1

Who was this prophet? where born? of what country? at what time did he prophesy? who were his parents? when and where did he die? are questions which have been asked from the remotest antiquity; and which, to this day, have received no answer worthy of recording. All that seems probable is that, as he prophesied concerning the destruction of Edom, he flourished a little before, or a little after, the taking of Jerusalem by Nebuchadnezzar, which happened about five hundred and eight-eight years before Christ; and the destruction of Idumea by the same monarch, which took place a short time after; probably between 588 B.C. and 575 B.C., in the interval of the thirteen years which Nebuchadnezzar employed in the siege of Tyre, which he undertook immediately after the capture of Jerusalem.

Obadiah foretells the subduction of the Idumeans by the Chaldeans, and finally by the Jews, whom they had used most cruelly when brought low by other enemies. These prophecies have been literally fulfilled, for the Idumeans, as a nation, are totally extinct.

Whoever will be at the trouble to collate this short prophecy with the forty-ninth chapter of Jeremiah will find a remarkable similarity, not only in the sentiments and words, but also in whole verses. In the above chapter Jeremiah predicts the destruction of the Idumeans. Whether he copied Obadiah, or Obadiah copied him, cannot be determined; but it would be very strange if two prophets, unacquainted with each other, should speak of the same event precisely in the same terms.

1. *We have heard a rumour.* See Jer. xlix. 14, where the same expressions are found. The prophet shows that the enemies of Idumea had confederated against it, and that Jehovah is now summoning them to march directly against it.

3. *The pride of thine heart.* St. Jerome observes that all the southern part of Palestine, from Eleutheropolis to Petra and Aialath, was full of caverns hewn out of the rocks, and that the people had subterranean dwellings similar to ovens. Here they are said to dwell *in the clefts of the rock*, in reference to the caverns above mentioned. Some think that by *sena*, "rock," Petra, the capital of Idumea, is intended.

4. *Though thou exalt thyself as the eagle.* Though like this bird you get into the highest cliff of the highest rock, it will not avail you. See Jer. xlix. 16.

5. *If thieves came to thee.* That is, if *thieves* entered your dwellings, they would not have taken everything; they would have laid hold on your wealth, and carried off as much as they could escape with conveniently. If *grapegatherers* entered your vineyards, they would not have taken every bunch; some gleanings would have been left. But the Chaldeans have stripped you bare; they have searched out all your "hidden things," v. 6; they have left you nothing.

MATTHEW HENRY

and *sought up!* Their alliances with neighbouring states and potentates shall fail them (*v.* 7): "The *men of thy confederacy*, all of them, the Ammonites and Moabites, and other allies that were at *peace with thee, did eat thy bread*, were entertained by thee, lived upon thee; they *brought thee even to the border* of thy land, were respectful to thy ambassadors, and brought them on their way home; but then they have *deceived thee;* they flew back and retreated when thou wast in extremity. They have *prevailed against thee;* they were too hard for thee in the treaty imposed upon thee, brought thee into danger, and there left thee an easy prey to thy enemy. They have *laid a wound under thee*; that is, they have laid that under thee for a support, which will prove a wound to thee; not as thorns only, but as swords." If God lay under us the arms of his power and love, these will be firm under us; the God of our covenant will never deceive us. But if we trust to *the men of our confederacy*, and what they will lay under us, it may prove to us a *wound* and *dishonour*. Just censure is passed upon Edom for trusting to those who played tricks with him: "*There is no understanding in him*, or else he would never have put it into their power to betray him by putting such a confidence in them. The politics of their counsellors shall fail them, *v.* 8. Edom had been famous for great statesmen, but now the *counsellors* have become *fools. Shall I not in that day destroy the wise men out of Edom?* This was just punishment of their folly in trusting to an arm of flesh; *There is no understanding in them, v.* 7. It was the forerunner of their destruction. A nation is certainly marked for ruin when God hides the things that belong to its peace from the eyes of those that are entrusted with its counsels. Do they depend upon the strength and courage of their soldiers?

They are able-bodied men of spirit and courage, but now (*v.* 9), *Thy mighty men, O Teman! shall be dismayed;* their courage shall fail them, *to the end that every one of the mount of Esau may be cut off by slaughter*, and none escape.

Verses 10–16

Many things were amiss in Edom; they were a sinful people, and *a people laden with iniquity.* But that one single crime which is laid to their charge, as bringing this ruin upon them, is the injury they had done to the people of God (*v.* 10): "It is *for thy violence against thy brother Jacob*, that ancient grudge which thou hast borne to the people of Israel, that all this *shame shall cover thee* and *thou shalt be cut off for ever.*" It is violence *against thy brother*, to whom thou shouldst be a *goël—a redeemer*, whom it is thy duty to right if others wronged him. Thou *slanderest* and *abusest thy own mother's son.* Much more if it is done against one of God's people; "it is thy brother Jacob that is in covenant with God, and dear to him. Thou hatest him whom God has loved."

I. The violence which Edom did against his brother Jacob. That which is laid to their charge is their barbarous conduct towards Judah and Jerusalem when they were in distress, and ready to be destroyed, probably by the Chaldeans. See this is charged upon the Edomites (Ps. cxxxvii. 7), that *in the day of Jerusalem they said, Rase it, rase it*, and Ezek. xxv. 12. Thou *shouldst not have looked*, thou *shouldst not have entered;* but thou didst do so. (*v.* 12–14). Let us see,

1. The case of Judah and Jerusalem when the Edomites insulted over them. With the Edomites it was a day of prosperity when with the Israelites it was a day of calamity, for judgment commonly *begins at the house of God.* Children are corrected when strangers are let alone. It was the day *of their destruction* (*v.* 12), when *foreigners entered into the gates of Jerusalem*, when the great officers of the king of Babylon's army sat in the gates, as judges of the land. It was a day when the *strangers carried away captive his forces* (*v.* 11). The Edomites, their neighbours and brethren, should have pitied them and helped them.

2. The Edomites are here condemned. They looked with pleasure upon the affliction of God's people (*v.* 12, 13), unconcerned. Those have a great deal to answer for that are idle spectators of the troubles and afflictions of their neighbours, when they are capable of being their active helpers. They *rejoiced over the children of Judah in the day of their destruction.*

JAMIESON, FAUSSET, BROWN

7. Men of thy confederacy—i.e., thy confederates. **brought thee . . . to the border**—i.e., when Idumean ambassadors shall go to confederate states seeking aid, these latter shall conduct them with due ceremony to their border, giving them empty compliments, but not the aid required [DRUSIUS]. This view agrees with the context, which speaks of false friends *deceiving* Edom: i.e., failing to give help in need (cf. Job 6:14, 15). CALVIN translates, "have *driven,*" i.e., *shall drive thee;* shall help to drive thee *to thy border* on thy way into captivity in foreign lands. **the men that were at peace with thee**—lit., "the men of thy peace." Cf. Psalm 41:9; Jeremiah 38:22 (*Margin*), where also the same formula occurs, "prevailed against thee." **they that eat thy bread**—the poorer tribes of the desert who subsisted on the bounty of Edom. Cf. again Psalm 41:9, which seems to have been before Obadiah's mind, as his words were before Jeremiah's. **have laid a wound under thee**—"laid" implies that their intimacy was used as a SNARE *laid* with a view to wound; also, these guest friends of Edom, instead of the cushions ordinarily *laid* under guests at table, *laid* snares to wound, i.e., had a secret understanding with Edom's foe for that purpose. MAURER translates, "a snare." But *English Version* agrees with the *Hebrew,* which means, lit., "a bandage for a wound." **none understanding**—none of the wisdom for which Edom was famed (see vs. 8) to extricate him from his perilous position. **in him**—instead of "in thee." The change implies the alienation of God from Edom: Edom has so estranged himself from God, that He speaks now *of* him, not *to* him. **8.** (Isa. 49:7; cf. Job 5:12, 13; Isa. 19:3; Jer. 19:7). **in that day . . . even destroy**—Heretofore Edom, through its intercourse with Babylon and Egypt, and from its means of information through the many caravans passing to and fro between Europe and India, has been famed for knowledge; but in that day *at last* ("even") I will destroy its wise men. **mount of Esau**—i.e., Idumea, which was a mountainous region. **9. cut off by slaughter**—MAURER translates, "on account of the slaughter," viz., that inflicted on Judea by Edom (cf. vs. 14). LXX, *Syriac,* and *Vulgate* connect these words with vs. 10, "for the slaughter, for the violence (of which thou art guilty) against thy brother Jacob." *English Version,* "cut off *by slaughter*" (i.e., an *utter* cutting off), answers well to "cut off *for ever*" (vs. 10). However, the arrangement of LXX gives a better parallelism in vs. 10. "For the *slaughter*" (1) being balanced in just retribution by "thou shalt be *cut off* for ever" (4); as "For thy *violence* (not so bad as *slaughter*) against thy brother Jacob" (2) is balanced by "*shame* (not so bad as being *cut off*) shall cover thee" (3). Shame and extinction shall repay violence and slaughter (Matt. 26:52; Rev. 13:10). Cf. as to Edom's violence, Ps. 137:7; Ezek. 25:12; Amos 1:11. **10. against thy brother**—This aggravates the sin of Esau, that it was against him who was his brother by birth and by circumcision. The posterity of Esau followed in the steps of their father's hatred to Jacob by violence against Jacob's seed (Gen. 27:41). **Jacob**—not merely his own brother, but his *twin* brother; hence the name *Jacob,* not Israel, is here put emphatically. Cf. Deuteronomy 23:7 for the opposite feeling which Jacob's seed was commanded to entertain towards Edom's. **shame . . . cover thee**—(Ps. 35:26; 69:7). **for ever**—(Isa. 34:10; Ezek. 35:9; Mal. 1:4). Idumea, *as a nation,* should be "cut off for ever," though the land should be again inhabited. **11. thou stoodest on the other side**—in an attitude of hostility, rather than the sympathy which became a brother, feasting thine eyes (see vs. 12) with the misery of Jacob, and eagerly watching for his destruction. So Messiah, the antitype to Jerusalem, abandoned by His kinsmen (Ps. 38:11). **strangers**—the Philistines, Arabians in the reign of Jehoram, etc. (II Chron. 21:16); the Syrians in the reign of Joash of Judah (II Chron. 24:24); the Chaldeans (II Chron. 36). **carried . . . captive his forces**—his "host" (vs. 20): the multitude of Jerusalem's inhabitants. **cast lots upon Jerusalem**—(Joel 3:3). So Messiah, Jerusalem's antitype, had lots cast for His only earthly possessions (Ps. 22:18). **12. looked on**—with malignant pleasure, and a brutal stare. So the antitypes, Messiah's foes (Ps. 22:17). MAURER translates, as *Margin,* "thou shouldest not look" any more. *English Version* agrees with the context better. **the day of thy brother**—his day of calamity. **became a stranger**—i.e., was banished as an alien from his own land. God sends heavy calamities on those who rejoice in the calamities of their enemies (Prov. 17:5; 24:17, 18). Contrast the opposite conduct of David and of the divine Son of David in a like case (Ps. 35:13-15). **spoken proudly**—lit.,

ADAM CLARKE

7. *All the men of thy confederacy.* The Chaldeans are here intended, to whom the Idumeans were attached, and whose agents they became in exercising cruelties upon the Jews. *Have brought thee even to the border.* Have hemmed you in on every side, and reduced you to distress. Or, they have driven you to your border; cast you out of your own land into the hands of your enemies.

The men that were at peace with thee. The men of your covenant, with whom you had made a league. *That eat thy bread.* That professed to be your firmest friends.

8. *Shall I not . . . destroy the wise men?* It appears, from Jer. xlix. 7, that the Edomites were remarkable for wisdom, counsel, and prudence.

9. *Thy mighty men, O Teman.* This was one of the strongest places in Idumea; and is put here, as in Amos i. 2, and elsewhere, for Idumea itself. *Mount of Esau.* Mount Seir.

10. *For thy violence against thy brother Jacob.* By this term the Israelites in general are understood; for the two brothers—Jacob, from whom sprang the Jews; and Esau, from whom sprang the Idumeans or Edomites—are here put for the whole people or descendants of both.

11. *Thou stoodest on the other side.* You not only did not help your brother when you might, but you did assist his foes against him.

And cast lots. When the Chaldeans cast lots on the spoils of Jerusalem, you did come in for a share of the booty; *thou wast as one of them.*

12. *Thou shouldest not have looked.* The Edomites triumphed when they saw the judgments of God fall upon the Jews. This the Lord severely reprehends in vv. 12-15.

MATTHEW HENRY

They went further, for they *entered into the gate* of God's people and *laid hands on their substance.* Though they did not help to conquer them, they helped to plunder them, *v.* 13. They not only robbed their brethren, but murdered them, *v.* 14. When the victorious sword of the Chaldeans was making bloody work among the Jews many made their escape, but the Edomites basely intercepted them, *stood in the cross-way*; some they barbarously cut off; others they delivered up to the pursuers. In all this they joined with the open enemies and persecutors of Israel: *Even thou wast as one of them.*

II. The shame that shall cover them for this violence. When they come to be in the same calamitous condition that Israel is now in, they will be ashamed (*v.* 15): *The day of the Lord is near upon all the heathen,* when God will recompense tribulation to the troublers of his church.

As you have drunk upon my holy mountain (*v.* 16), that is, as God's professing people have drunk deeply of the cup of affliction, *so shall all the heathen drink* of the same bitter cup. They may expect their case to be worse in the day of distress than that of Israel was in their day. The afflictions of God's people were but for a moment, but their enemies shall *drink continually* the *wine of God's wrath,* Rev. xiv. 10. The dregs of the cup are reserved for the *wicked of the earth* (Ps.lxxv. 8); they shall *drink and swallow down,* or *sup up* (as the margin reads it), shall drink it to the bottom.

Verses 17–21

Precious promises of salvation with which this prophecy concludes, as those of Joel and Amos did, which, however they might be in part fulfilled in the return of the Jews out of Babylon, are yet, doubtless, to have their full accomplishment in that great salvation wrought out by Jesus Christ.

I. There shall be salvation upon Mount Zion: *Upon Mount Zion shall be deliverance, v.* 17. A remnant of Israel, *upon the holy mountain,* shall be saved, *v.* 16.

II. Where there is salvation, there shall be sanctification: *And there shall be holiness,* to prepare and qualify the children of Zion for this deliverance; for wherever God designs glory he gives grace.

III. This salvation and sanctification shall spread, and prevail: The *house of Jacob,* even this *Mount Zion,* with the deliverance and the holiness there wrought, shall *possess their possessions*; that is, the gospel-church shall be set up among the heathen, and shall replenish the earth. When they possess their hearts they shall *possess their possessions,* for those who have given up themselves to the Lord give up all they have to him.

1. How this possession shall be *gained* (*v.* 18): *The house of Jacob shall be a fire, and the house of Joseph a flame,* for their God is a *consuming fire*; and the house of Esau shall be for *stubble.* The gospel, preached in the house of Jacob and Joseph, shall be as a fire and a flame to melt hard hearts, to burn up the dross, that they may be purified with the *spirit of judgment and* the *spirit of burning.* The word of God in the mouth of his ministers is said to be like fire, and the people as wood to be devoured by it, Jer. v. 14. Those that are not refined as gold by the fire of the gospel shall be consumed as dross by it.

2. How far this possession shall extend, *v.* 19, 20. The *captivity of this host of Israel,* that are still called the *children of the captivity,* these shall recover their own land, and gain ground upon their neighbours adjoining them. Some shall become proselytes and shall incorporate with the Jews, who, by possessing them in a holy communion, possess their land.

JAMIESON, FAUSSET, BROWN

"made great the mouth"; proudly insulting the fallen (Ezek. 35:13, *Margin;* cf. I Sam. 2:8 Rev. 13:6). **13. substance**—translated "forces" in vs. 11. **14. stood in the crossway, to cut off those of his** [Judah's] **that did escape**—The Jews naturally fled by the crossways. (MAURER translates, "narrow mountain passes") well known to them, to escape to the desert, and through Edom to Egypt; but the Edomites stood ready to intercept the fugitives and either kill or "deliver them up" to the foe. **15. For**—resumptive in connection with vs. 10, wherein Edom was threatened with *cutting off for ever.* **the day of the Lord**—the day in which He will manifest Himself as the Righteous Punisher of the ungodly peoples (Joel 3:14). The "all" shows that the fulfilment is not exhausted in the punishment inflicted on the surrounding nations by the instrumentality of Nebuchadnezzar; but, as in Joel 3:14, and Zechariah 12:3, that the last judgment to come on the nations confederate against Jerusalem is referred to. **as thou hast done, it shall be done unto thee**—the righteous principle of retribution in kind (Lev. 24:17; Matt. 7:2; cf. Judg. 1:6, 7; 8:19; Esther 7:10). **thy reward**—the reward of thy deed (cf. Isa. 3:9-11). **16. ye . . . upon my holy mountain**—a periphrasis for, "ye Jews" [MAURER], whom Obadiah now by a sudden apostrophe addresses. The clause, "upon My holy mountain," expresses the reason of the vengeance to be taken on Judah's foes; viz., that Jerusalem is God's holy mountain, the seat of His temple, and Judah His covenant people. Jeremiah 49:12, which is copied from Obadiah, establishes this view (cf. I Pet. 4:17). **as ye have drunk . . .** viz., the cup of wrath, being dispossessed of your goods and places as a nation, by Edom and all the heathen; so shall all the heathen (Edom included) drink the same cup (Ps. 60:3; Isa. 51:17, 22; Jer. 13:12, 13; 25:15-33; 49:12; 51:7; Lam 4:21, 22; Nah. 3:11; Hab. 2:16). **continually**—whereas Judah's calamity shall be temporary (vs. 17). The foes of Judah shall never regain their former position (vs. 18, 19). **swallow down**—so as not to leave anything in the cup of calamity; not merely "drink" (Ps. 75:8). **be as though they had not been**—not a trace left of their national existence (Job 10:19; Ps. 37:36; Ezek. 26:21). **17. upon . . . Zion . . . deliverance**—both in the literal sense and spiritual sense (Joel 2:32; Isa. 46:16; 59:20; Rom. 11:26). MAURER as *Margin* explains it, "there shall be a remnant that shall escape." Cf. Isaiah 37:32; to the deliverance from Sennacherib there described GROTIUS thinks Obadiah here refers. "Jerusalem shall not be taken, and many of the neighboring peoples also shall find deliverance there." Unlike Judah's heathen foes of whom no remnant shall escape (vss. 9, 16), a remnant of Jews shall escape when the rest of the nation has perished, and shall regain their ancient "possessions." **there shall be holiness**—i.e., Zion shall be sacrosanct or inviolable: no more violated by foreign invaders (Isa. 42:1; Joel 3:17). **18. fire**—See the same figure, Numbers 21:28; Isaiah 5:24; 10:17. **house of Jacob . . . Joseph**—i.e., the two kingdoms, Judah and Ephraim or Israel [JEROME]. The two shall form one kingdom, their former feuds being laid aside (Isa. 11:12, 13; 37:22-28; Jer. 3:18; Hos. 1:11). The Jews returned with some of the Israelites from Babylon; and, under John Hyrcanus, so subdued and, compelling them to be circumcised, incorporated the Idumeans with themselves that they formed part of the nation [JOSEPHUS, 13. 17, and 12. 11]. This was but an earnest of the future union of Israel and Judah in the possession of the enlarged land as one kingdom (Ezek. 37:16, etc.). **stubble**—(Mal. 4:1). **19. they of the south**—The Jews who in the coming time are to occupy the south of Judea shall possess, in addition to their own territory, the adjoining *mountainous region of Edom.* **they of the plain**—The Jews who shall occupy the low country along the Mediterranean, south and southwest of Palestine, shall possess, in addition to their own territory, the land of "the Philistines," which runs as a long strip between the hills and the sea. **and they shall possess the fields of Ephraim**—i.e., the rightful owners shall be restored, the Ephraimites to the fields of Ephraim. **Benjamin shall possess Gilead**—i.e., the region east of Jordan, occupied formerly by Reuben, Gad, and half Manasseh. Benjamin shall possess besides its own territory the adjoining territory eastward, while the two and a half tribes shall in the redistribution occupy the adjoining territory of Moab and Ammon. **20. the captivity of this host**—i.e., the captives of this multitude of Israelites. **shall possess that of the Canaanites**—MAURER translates, "the captives . . . whom the Canaanites (carried away captive into Phœnicia) even unto Zarephath, shall possess the south," viz., Idumea as well

ADAM CLARKE

14. *Neither shouldest thou have stood in the crossway.* They are represented here as having stood in the passes and defiles to prevent the poor Jews from escaping from the Chaldeans. By stopping these passes, they threw the poor fugitives back into the teeth of their enemies. They had gone so far in this systematic cruelty as to deliver up the few that had taken refuge among them.

17. *But upon mount Zion shall be deliverance.* Here is a promise of the return from the Babylonish captivity. They shall come to Zion, and there they shall find safety; and it is remarkable that after their return they were greatly befriended by the Persian kings, and by Alexander the Great and his successors; so that, whilst they ravaged the neighboring nations, the Jews were unmolested.

And there shall be holiness. They shall return to God, separate themselves from their idols, and become a better people than they were when God permitted them to be carried into captivity.

18. *The house of Jacob shall be a fire.* After their return from captivity, the Jews, called here the *house of Jacob* and the *house of Joseph,* did break out as *a flame* upon the Idumeans; they reduced them into slavery, and obliged them to receive circumcision, and practice the rites of the Jewish religion. See 1 Macc. v. 3, etc,; and Joseph. *Antiq.,* lib. xiii, c. 17. *There shall not be any remaining.* As a people and a nation they shall be totally destroyed. This is the meaning; it does not signify that every individual shall be destroyed.

19. *They of the south.* The Jews who possessed the southern part of Palestine should render themselves masters of the mountains of Idumea which were contiguous to them. *They of the plain.* From Eleutheropolis to the Mediterranean Sea. In this and the following verse the prophet shows the different districts which should be occupied by the Israelites after their return from Babylon. *The fields of Samaria.* Alexander the Great gave Samaria to the Jews, and John Hyrcanus subdued the same country after his wars with the Syrians. See Josephus, *contra. App.* lib. ii, and *Antiq.* lib. xiii, c. 18. *Benjamin shall possess Gilead.* Edom lay to the south, the Philistines to the west, Ephraim to the north, and Gilead to the east. Those who returned from Babylon were to extend themselves everywhere. See, for the fulfilment, 1 Macc. v. 9, 35, 45 and ix. 35-36.

MATTHEW HENRY

The kingdom of Israel shall join with that of Judah both in civil and sacred interests, and, as friends and brethren, shall mutually possess and enjoy one another; and both together shall *possess the Canaanites*, even to Zarephath, which *belongeth to Zidon*; and Jerusalem shall possess the *cities of the south*, even to Sepharad. Thus did the Jews enlarge their borders on all sides. But the promise here, no doubt, has a spiritual signification, and had its accomplishment in the setting up of the Christian church, the gospel-Israel, in the world, and shall have its accomplishment more and more in the enlargement of it, till the mystical body is completed.

IV. The kingdom of the Redeemer shall be erected to the comfort of his loyal subjects and the shame of his enemies (*v.* 21): *The kingdom shall be the Lord's*, the Lord Christ's. The mountain of Zion shall be saved; on it *saviours* shall *come*, the preachers of the gospel, called saviours, because their business is to save themselves and those that hear them; and in this they are *workers together with Christ*.

The mountain of Esau shall be judged; and the same that come as saviours on Mount Zion shall *judge* the *mountain of Esau*; for the word of the gospel in their mouth, that convinces and condemns them. And in the course of God's providence his scripture is fulfilled; when God raises up friends to the church in her distress, then *saviours come on Mount Zion*, to save it; and when the enemies of the church are brought down, then is the *mount of Esau judged*; and this shall be done in every age in such a way as God thinks best.

JAMIESON, FAUSSET, BROWN

as the south (vs. 19). HENDERSON, similarly, "the captives that are among the Canaanites . . . ." But the corresponding clauses of the parallelism are better balanced in *English Version*, "the ten tribes of Israel shall possess the territory of the Canaanites," viz., Western Palestine and Phœnicia (Judg. 3:3). "And the captives of Jerusalem (and Judah) shall possess the southern cities," viz., Edom, etc. Each has the region respectively adjoining assigned to it; Israel has the western Canaanite region; Judah, the southern. **even unto Zarephath**—near Zidon; called Sarepta in Luke 4:26. The name implies it was a place for smelting metals. From this quarter came the "woman of Canaan" (Matt. 15:21, 22). Captives of the Jews had been carried into the coasts of Palestine or Canaan, about Tyre and Zidon (Joel 3:3, 4; Amos 1:9). The Jews when restored shall possess the territory of their ancient oppressors. **in Sepharad**—i.e., the Bosphorus [JEROME, *from his Hebrew instructor*]. Sephar, according to others (Gen. 10:30). Palæography confirms JEROME. In the cuneiform inscription containing a list of the tribes of Persia [NIEBUHR, *Tab.* 31.1], before Ionia and Greece, and after Cappadocia, comes the name CPaRaD. It was therefore a district of Western Asia Minor, about Lydia, and near the Bosphorus. It is made an appellative by MAURER. "The Jerusalem captives *of the dispersion*" (cf. Jas. 1:1), wherever they be dispersed, shall return and possess the southern cities. Sepharad, though literally the district near the Bosphorus, represents the Jews' far and wide dispersion. JEROME says the name in Assyrian means a *boundary*, i.e., "the Jews scattered in all boundaries and regions." **21. saviours**—There will be in the kingdom yet to come no king, but a prince; the sabbatic period of the judges will return (cf.the phrase so frequent in Judges, only once found in the times of the kings, II Chronicles 14:1, "the land had *rest*"), when there was no visible king, but God reigned in the theocracy. Israelites, not strangers, shall dispense justice to a God-fearing people (Isa. 1:26; Ezek. 45). The judges were not such a burden to the people as the kings proved afterwards (I Sam. 8:11-20). In their time the people more readily repented than under the kings (cf. II Chron. 15:17), [Roos]. Judges were from time to time raised up as *saviours* or *deliverers* of Israel from the enemy. These, and the similar deliverers in the long subsequent age of Antiochus, the Maccabees, who conquered the *Idumeans* (as here foretold, cf. II Maccabees 10:15, 23), were types of the peaceful period yet to come to Israel. **to judge . . . Esau**—*to punish* (so "judge," I Sam. 3:13) . . . Edom (cf. vss. 1-9, 15-19). Edom is the type of Israel's and God's last foes (Isa. 63:1-4). **kingdom shall be the Lord's**—under Messiah (Dan. 2:44; 7:14, 27; Zech. 14:9; Luke 1:33; Rev. 11:15; 19:6).

ADAM CLARKE

20. *Zarephath.* Sarepta, a city of the Sidonians, 1 Kings xvii. 9. That is, they should possess the whole city of Phoenicia, called here *that of the Canaanites. Which is in Sepharad.* This is a difficult word.

21. *And saviours shall come up.* Certain persons whom God may choose to be deliverers of His people; such as Zerubbabel, Ezra, Nehemiah, and the Maccabees.

THE BOOK OF JONAH

I. The first commission (1:1-2:10)
A. The prophet's commission and disobedience (1:1-3)
B. Jehovah's interposition (1:4-2:10)
1. The tempest (1:4-14)
2. Jonah cast out (1:15-17)
3. The experience of the deep (2:1-9)
4. The deliverance (2:10)

II. The second commission (3:1-4:11)
A. The prophet's commission and obedience (3:1-11)
1. The commission (3:1, 2)
2. The obedience (3:3, 4)
3. The result (3:5-10)
B. The prophet and Jehovah (4:1-11)
1. Jonah displeased (4:1-3)
2. Jehovah (4:4-7)
3. Jonah distressed (4:8)
4. Jehovah (4:9-11)

This book of Jonah, though it be placed in the midst of the prophetical books, is rather a history than a prophecy; one line of prediction there is in it, "Yet forty days, and Nineveh shall be overthrown"; the rest of the book is a narrative of the preface to and the consequences of that prediction. Probably Jonah was himself the penman of this book, and he, as other inspired penmen, records his own faults, which is an evidence that in these writings they designed God's glory and not their own. We read of this same Jonah (2 Kings 14:25), where we find that he was of Gath-hepher in Galilee, a city that belonged to the tribe of Zebulun, in a remote corner of the land of Israel. He was a messenger of mercy to Israel in the reign of Jeroboam the second; for the "restoring of the coast of Israel," is said to be "according to the word of the Lord which he spoke by the hand of his servant Jonah the prophet." This story contains remarkable instances of human infirmity in Jonah; and of God's mercy in pardoning repenting sinners, witness Nineveh; and in bearing with complaining saints, witness Jonah.

MATTHEW HENRY

CHAPTER 1

Verses 1–3

1. The honour God put upon Jonah, in giving him a commission to go and prophesy against Nineveh. *Jonah* signifies *a dove*, a proper name for all God's prophets, all his people, who ought to be *harmless as doves*, and to *mourn as doves* for the sins and calamities of the land. His father's name was *Amittai—My truth*; for God's prophets should be sons of truth. To him *the word of the Lord came*—to him it was (so the word signifies). The orders now given were, *Arise, go to Nineveh, that great city, v.* 2. Nineveh was the metropolis of the Assyrian monarchy (Gen. x. 11), *a great city*, great in the number of the inhabitants, great in power and dominion; it was the city that for some time *ruled over the kings of the earth.* But great cities, as well as great men, are under God's government. Nineveh was a heathen city, without the knowledge and worship of the true God. This great city was a wicked city: *Their wickedness has come up before me*; and they sinned with *a high hand.* Jonah must *cry against it*; he must witness against their great wickedness, and must warn them of the destruction that was coming upon them for it. *Cry aloud, spare not.* He must not whisper his message, but publish it in the streets of Nineveh; *he that has ears to hear let him hear* what God has to say by his prophet against that wicked city. He must *go to Nineveh*, and cry there upon the spot against the wickedness of it. Other prophets were ordered to send messages to the neighbouring nations, but Jonah must go and carry the message himself. The dishonour Jonah did to God in refusing to go (*v.* 3): *But Jonah*, instead of rising to go to Nineveh, *rose up to flee to Tarshish*, to *the sea*, not bound for any port, but desirous to get away *from the presence of the Lord.* He *consulted with flesh and blood*, and declined the embassy because he was jealous for the prerogatives of his country, and not willing that any other nation should share in the honour of divine revelation. He owns himself (*ch.* iv. 2) that the reason of his aversion was because he foresaw that the Ninevites would repent, and God would forgive them and take them into favour, which would be a slur upon the people of Israel, who had been so long a peculiar people to God. He went to Joppa, a famous seaport in the land of Israel, in quest of a ship bound for Tarshish, and there he found one. Providence seemed to give him an opportunity to escape. The ready way is not always the right way. He found the ship and set sail for Tarshish. So he *paid the fare thereof.* He went *with them*, the mariners, the passengers, the merchants, whoever they were that were going to Tarshish. Jonah, forgetting his dignity as well as duty, herded with them.

Verses 4–10

I. God sends a pursuer after him, *a mighty tempest in the sea, v.* 4. The effect of this wind was *a mighty tempest*; for when the winds rise the waves rise. The tempest prevailed to such a degree that *the ship was likely to be broken.* This wind was sent after Jonah,

JAMIESON, FAUSSET, BROWN

CHAPTER 1

Vss. 1-17. Jonah's Commission to Nineveh, Flight, Punishment, and Preservation by Miracle. **1. Jonah**—meaning in *Hebrew*, "dove." Cf. Genesis 8:8, 9, where the dove in vain seeks rest after flying from Noah and the ark: so Jonah. Grotius not so well explains it, "one sprung from Greece" or Ionia, where there were prophets called *Amythaonidæ*. **Amittai**—*Hebrew* for "truth," "truth-telling"; appropriate to a prophet. **2. to Nineveh**—east of the Tigris, opposite the modern Mosul. The only case of a prophet being sent to the heathen. Jonah, however, is sent to Nineveh, not solely for Nineveh's good, but also to shame *Israel*, by the fact of a heathen city repenting at the first preaching of a single stranger, Jonah, whereas God's people will not repent, though preached to by their many national prophets, late and early. Nineveh means "the residence of Ninus," i.e., Nimrod. Genesis 10:11, where the translation ought to be, *"He* [Nimrod] went forth *into Assyria* and builded Nineveh." Modern research into the cuneiform inscriptions confirms the Scripture account that Babylon was founded earlier than Nineveh, and that both cities were built by descendants of Ham, encroaching on the territory assigned to Shem (Gen. 10:5, 6, 8, 10, 25). **great city**—480 stadia in circumference, 150 in length, and 90 in breadth (Diodorus Siculus, 2. 3). Taken by Arbaces the Mede, in the reign of Sardanapalus, about the seventh year of Uzziah; and a second time by Nabopolassar of Babylon and Cyaxares the Mede in 625 B.C. See my *Note*, ch. 3:3. **cry**—(Isa. 40:6; 58:1). **come up before me**—(Gen. 4:10; 6:13; 18:21; Ezra 9:6; Rev. 18:5); i.e., their wickedness is so great as to require My open interposition for punishment. **3. flee**—Jonah's motive for flight is hinted at in ch. 4:2: fear that after venturing on such a dangerous commission to so powerful a heathen city, his prophetical threats should be set aside by God's "repenting of the evil," just as God had so long spared Israel notwithstanding so many provocations, and so he should seem a false prophet. Besides, he may have felt it beneath him to discharge a commission to a foreign idolatrous nation, whose destruction he desired rather than their repentance. This is the only case of a prophet, charged with a prophetical message, concealing it. **from the presence of the Lord**—(Cf. Gen. 4:16). Jonah thought in fleeing from the land of Israel, where Jehovah was peculiarly present, that he should escape from Jehovah's prophecy-inspiring influence. He probably knew the truth stated in Psalm 139:7-10, but virtually ignored it (cf. Gen. 3:8-10; Jer. 23:24). **went down**—appropriate in going from land to the sea (Ps. 107:23). **Joppa**—now Jaffa, in the region of Dan; a harbor as early as Solomon's time (II Chron. 2: 16). **Tarshish**—Tartessus in Spain; in the farthest west at the greatest distance from Nineveh in the east. **4. sent out**—lit., *caused* a wind *to burst forth.* Coverdale translates, "hurled a greate wynde into the see."

ADAM CLARKE

CHAPTER 1

1. *Now the word of the Lord came unto Jonah.* He was of Gath-hepher, in the tribe of Zebulun, in lower Galilee, Josh. xix. 13; and he prophesied in the reigns of Jeroboam II and Joash, kings of Israel. Jeroboam came to the throne 823 years before the Christian era, and reigned in Samaria 41 years, 2 Kings xiv. 23-25. As a prophet, it is likely that he had but this one mission.

2. *Go to Nineveh.* This was the capital of the Assyrian empire, and one of the most ancient cities of the world, Gen. x. 10; and one of the largest, as it was three days' journey in circumference. It is reported to have had walls 100 feet high, and so broad that three chariots might run abreast upon them. It was situated on the Tigris, or a little to the west, or on the west side of that river. It was well peopled, and had at this time 120,000 persons in it reputed to be in a state of infancy, which on a moderate computation would make the whole number 600,000 persons.

3. *To flee unto Tarshish.* Tartessus, in Spain, near the straits of Gibraltar. *And went down to Joppa.* The nearest port to Jerusalem on that side of the Mediterranean. *And he found a ship.* The Phoenicians carried on a considerable trade with Tartessus, Ezek. xxvii. 12, and it was probably in one of their ships that Jonah embarked.

MATTHEW HENRY

to fetch him back again to God and to his duty; and it is a great mercy to be reclaimed and called home when we go astray, though it be by a tempest.

II. The ship's crew were alarmed by this mighty tempest, but Jonah only was unconcerned, *v.* 5. The mariners were *afraid*; though, their business leading them to dangers of this kind, they used to make light of them; yet the oldest and stoutest of them began to tremble, being apprehensive that there was something more than ordinary in this tempest, so suddenly did it rise, so strongly did it rage. They *cried every man unto his god.* Many will not be brought to prayer till they are frightened to it; he that would learn to pray, let him go to sea. Having called upon their gods to help them, they did what they could to help themselves. They *cast forth the wares that were in the ship into the sea, to lighten it of them*, as Paul's mariners in a like case, Acts xxvii. 18, 19, 38. But where is Jonah all this while? One would have expected him busier than any, but we find him gone down into *the hold, between the sides of the ship*, and there he lies, and is *fast asleep*; neither the noise without, nor the sense of guilt within, awoke him.

III. The master of the ship called Jonah up to his prayers, *v.* 6. The *ship-master came to him*, and bade him for shame get up, both to *pray for life* and to *prepare for death. What meanest thou, O sleeper?* We commend the ship-master. We pity Jonah, who needed this reproof; as a prophet of the Lord, if he had been in his place, he might have been reproving the king of Nineveh, but, being out of the way of his duty, he is open to the reproofs of a sorry ship-master. Yet we must admire God's goodness in sending him this seasonable reproof, for it was the first step towards his recovery, as the crowing of the cock was to Peter. "*Arise, call upon thy God;* we are here crying every man to his god, why dost not thou get up and cry to thine?" *If so be that God will think upon us, that we perish not.* It should seem, the many gods they called upon were considered by them only as mediators between them and the supreme God, for the ship-master speaks of one God still, from whom he expected relief.

IV. Jonah is found out to be the cause of the storm. The mariners observed so much peculiar and uncommon in the storm that they concluded it was a messenger of divine justice sent to arrest someone of those that were in that ship, as having been guilty of some enormous crime (Acts xxviii. 4), and it is for his sake they suffer. *Let us cast lots, that we may know for whose cause this evil is upon us.* They suspected one another, and would find out the man. These mariners desired to know the person that was the dead weight in their ship, that that one man might *die for the people* and that the whole ship *might not be lost.* In order to this they cast lots, by which they appealed to the judgment of God. The *lot fell upon Jonah*, who could have saved them this trouble if he would but have told them what his own conscience told him, *Thou art the man.* We may suppose there were those in the ship who were greater sinners than Jonah, and yet he is the man that the tempest pursues. The storm is sent after Jonah, because God has work for him to do, and it is sent to fetch him back to it. Jonah is brought under examination before the master and mariners. He was a stranger; none of them had anything to lay to his charge, and therefore they must extort a confession from him and judge him *out of his own mouth.* They did not fly outrageously upon him, but calmly enquired into his case. There is a compassion due to offenders when they are discovered and convicted. "*Tell us for whose cause this evil is upon us;* is it indeed for thy cause, and, if so, *for what cause?* What is the offence for which thou art thus prosecuted?" They enquire concerning his calling: *What is thy occupation? Whence comest thou?* In answer Jonah tells them he is *a Hebrew* (*v.* 9), and therefore is the more ashamed to own that he is a criminal; for the sins of Hebrews, that make such a profession of religion, are exceedingly sinful. He gives an account of his religion, for that was his calling: "*I fear the Lord Jehovah;* that is the God I worship, even *the God of heaven*, the sovereign Lord of all, that has *made the sea and the dry land* and has the command of both." He owns that he *fled from the presence of the Lord*, that he was here running away from his duty, and that he was sent to fetch him back. *The men were exceedingly afraid*, and justly, for they perceived that God was angry with one that feared and worshipped him, for running from his work in a particular instance. "If a prophet of the Lord be thus severely punished for one offence, what will become of us that have been guilty of so many, and great, and heinous offences?" They said to him, "*Why hast thou done this?* Why hast thou involved us in the prosecution?"

JAMIESON, FAUSSET, BROWN

5. mariners were afraid—though used to storms; the danger therefore must have been extreme.

cried every man unto his god—The idols proved unable to save them, though each, according to Phœnician custom, called on his tutelary god. But Jehovah proved able: and the heathen sailors owned it in the end by sacrificing to Him (vs. 16).

into the sides—i.e., the interior recesses (cf. I Sam. 24:3; Isa. 14:13, 15). Those conscious of guilt shrink from the presence of their fellow man into concealment. **fast asleep**—Sleep is no necessary proof of innocence; it may be the fruit of carnal security and a seared conscience. How different was Jesus' sleep on the Sea of Galilee! (Mark 4:37-39). Guilty Jonah's indifference to fear contrasts with the unoffending mariners' alarm. The original therefore is in the nominative absolute: "But *as for Jonah*, he. . . ." Cf. spiritually, Ephesians 5: 14. **6. call upon thy God**—The ancient heathen in dangers called on foreign gods, besides their national ones (cf. Ps. 107:28). MAURER translates the preceding clause, "What is the reason that thou sleepest?" **think upon us**—for good (cf. Gen. 8:1; Exod. 2:25; 3:7, 9; Ps. 40:17).

7. cast lots—God sometimes sanctioned this mode of deciding in difficult cases. Cf. the similar instance of Achan, whose guilt involved Israel in suffering, until God revealed the offender, probably by the casting of lots (Prov. 16:33; Acts 1:26). Primitive tradition and natural conscience led even the heathen to believe that one guilty man involves all his associates, though innocent, in punishment. So CICERO (*Nat. Deorum*, 3. 37) mentions that the mariners sailing with Diagoras, an atheist, attributed a storm that overtook them to his presence in the ship (cf. *Hor. Od.* 3. 2. 26).

8. The guilty individual being discovered is interrogated so as to make full confession with his own mouth. So in Achan's case (Josh. 7:19). **9. I am an Hebrew**—He does not say "an Israelite." For this was the name used among themselves; "Hebrew," among foreigners (Gen. 40:15; Exod. 3:18). **I fear the Lord**—in profession: his practice belied his profession: his profession aggravated his guilt. **God . . . which . . . . made the sea**—appropriately expressed, as accounting for the tempest sent on the *sea*. The heathen had distinct gods for the "heaven," the "sea," and the "land." Jehovah is the one and only true God of all alike. Jonah at last is awakened by the violent remedy from his lethargy. Jonah was but the reflection of Israel's backsliding from God, and so must bear the righteous punishment. The guilt of the minister is the result of that of the people, as in Moses' case (Deut. 4:21). This is what makes Jonah a suitable type of Messiah, who bore the *imputed* sin of the people. **10.** "The men were exceedingly afraid," when made aware of the wrath of so powerful a God at the flight of Jonah. **Why hast thou done this?**—If professors of religion do wrong, they will hear of it from those who make no such profession.

ADAM CLARKE

CHARLES H. SPURGEON:

Verses 5, 6. Of all the men in the ship, Jonah was the person who ought most to have been awake; but nevertheless, he was not only asleep, but *fast* asleep; all the creaking of the cordage, the dashing of the waves, the howling of the winds, the straining of the timbers and the shouting of the mariners, did not arouse him; he was fast locked in the arms of sleep. See here, in Jonah's heavy slumber, the effect of sin. No noxious drug can give such deadly sleep as sin. The body never knows so dread a sleep when under the influence of opiates, as the soul does when sin has cast it into a slumber. If men could be awake to the evils, to the danger, to the desperate punishment of sin, sin were not half so deadly as it is; but when it puts its sweet cup of nightshade to the lip, that cup soon blinds the eye and "steeps the senses in forgetfulness," and man knows not what or where he is. Nor is sin the only cradle in which evil rocks the soul, the world too, casts men into slumber. I do not know that Jonah ever slept so soundly anywhere as when he had gotten into the midst of busy mariners who were going to Tarshish. Ah, it is comparatively easy for us to maintain our stedfastness and integrity when we meet with those who rejoice in His name; but the world is an enchanted ground, and happy is that Christian who is able to survive the deadening influence of business, the soporific influence which creeps over the houses are filled with the riches of nations. What downy pillows does the world sew to all armholes! What beds of ease she spreads for those whom she entraps.

—The Treasury of the Old Testament

7. *Come, and let us cast lots.* This was a very ancient mode of endeavoring to find out the mind of Divine Providence; and in this case it proves that they supposed the storm to have arisen on account of some hidden crime of some person aboard. *The lot fell upon Jonah.* In this case God directed the lot.

9. *I fear the Lord.* In this Jonah was faithful. He gave an honest testimony concerning the God he served, which placed Him before the eyes of the sailors as infinitely higher than the objects of their adoration.

MATTHEW HENRY

Verses 11–17

Something more was to be done, for still *the sea wrought and was tempestuous* (*v.* 11), and (*v.* 13), it *grew more and more tempestuous* (so the margin reads it).

I. They enquired of Jonah himself what he thought they must do with him (*v.* 11). He appears to be a delinquent, but he appears also to be a penitent. They would not *cast him into the sea* if he could think of any other expedient by which to *save the ship.*

II. Jonah reads his own doom (*v.* 12): *Take me up, and cast me forth into the sea.* This is the language of true penitents, who earnestly desire that none but themselves may fare the worse, for their sins and follies. How ready Jonah is to take all the guilt upon himself, and to look upon all the trouble as theirs. "If it is I that have raised the storm, it is not casting the wares into the sea that will lay it again; no, you must cast me thither." When conscience is awakened, and a storm raised, nothing will turn it into a calm but parting with the sin that occasioned the disturbance.

III. The poor mariners did what they could to save throwing Jonah into the sea, but all in vain (*v.* 13): *They rowed hard to bring the ship to the land,* that, if they must part with Jonah, they might set him safely on shore; *but they could not.*

IV. When they cast Jonah into the sea they first prayed to God that his blood might not lie upon them, *v.* 14. They prayed to the *God of Israel,* being now convinced, by the providences of God concerning Jonah and the information he had given them, that he is God *alone.* "*Lord,*" say they, "*let us not perish for this man's life.*"

V. Having deprecated the guilt (*v.* 15): *They took up Jonah,* and cast *him forth into the sea.* When sin is the Jonah that raises the storm, it must thus be cast forth into the sea; we must drown that which otherwise will *drown us.*

VI. The throwing of Jonah into the sea immediately put an end to the storm. If we turn from our sins, God will soon turn from his anger.

VII. The mariners were hereby more confirmed in their belief that Jonah's God was the only true God (*v.* 16). As evidence they *offered sacrifice* to him when they came ashore again in the land of Israel, and for the present made vows that they would do so, in thankfulness for their deliverance.

VIII. Jonah's life is saved by a miracle. In the midst of judgment God *remembers mercy.* Though he flees from the presence of the Lord, and seems to fall into his avenging hands, yet God has more work for him to do, and therefore has *prepared a great fish to swallow up Jonah* (*v.* 17), *a whale* our Saviour calls it (Matt. xii. 40), one of the largest sorts of whales, that have wider throats than others, in the belly of which has sometimes been found the dead body of a man in armour. It was of the Lord's mercies that Jonah was not now consumed. Jonah by this preservation was designed to be made, 1. A monument of divine mercy. 2. A successful preacher to Nineveh.

3. An illustrious type of Christ, who was buried and rose again according to the scriptures (1 Cor. xv. 4), for, *as Jonah was three days and three nights in the whale's belly, so was the Son of man three days and three nights in the heart of the earth,* Matt. xii. 40. Was Jonah's grave a strange one, a new one? So was Christ's, one in which never man before was laid. Was Jonah there the best part of three days and three nights? So was Christ; but both in order to their rising again for the bringing of the doctrine of repentance to the Gentile world.

JAMIESON, FAUSSET, BROWN

11. What shall we do unto thee?—They ask this, as Jonah himself must best know how his God is to be appeased. "We would gladly save thee, if we can do so, and yet be saved ourselves" (vss. 13, 14). **12. cast me . . . into the sea**—Herein Jonah is a type of Messiah, the one man who offered Himself to die, in order to allay the stormy flood of God's wrath (cf. Ps. 69:1, 2, as to Messiah), which otherwise must have engulfed all other men. So Caiaphas by the Spirit declared it expedient that one man should die, and that the whole nation should not perish (John 11:50). Jonah also herein is a specimen of true repentance, which leads the penitent to "accept the punishment of his iniquity" (Lev. 26:41, 43), and to be more indignant at his sin than at his suffering. **13. they could not**—(Prov. 21:30). Wind and tide—God's displeasure and God's counsel—were against them. **14. for this man's life**—i.e., for taking this man's life. **innocent blood**—Do not punish us as Thou wouldst punish the shedders of innocent blood (cf. Deut. 21: 8). In the case of the Antitype, Pontius Pilate washed his hands and confessed Christ's *innocence,* "I am innocent of the blood of this *just* person." But whereas Jonah the victim was guilty and the sailors innocent, Christ our sacrificial victim was innocent and Pontius Pilate and all of us men were guilty. But by *imputation* of our guilt to Him and His righteousness to us, the spotless Antitype exactly corresponds to the guilty type. **thou . . . Lord, hast done as it pleased thee**—That Jonah has embarked in this ship, that a tempest has arisen, that he has been detected by casting of lots, that he has passed sentence on himself, is all Thy doing. We reluctantly put him to death, but it is Thy pleasure it should be so. **15. sea ceased . . . raging**—so at Jesus' word (Luke 8:24). God spares the prayerful penitent, a truth illustrated now in the case of the sailors, presently in that of Jonah, and thirdly, in that of Nineveh. **16. offered a sacrifice**—They offered some sacrifice of thanksgiving at once, and vowed more when they should land. GLASSIUS thinks it means only, "They *promised* to offer a sacrifice." **17. prepared a great fish**—not *created* specially for this purpose, but appointed in His providence, to which all creatures are subservient. The fish, through a mistranslation of Matthew 12:40, was formerly supposed to be a whale; there, as here, the original means "a great fish." The whale's neck is too narrow to receive a man. BOCHART thinks, the *dogfish,* the stomach of which is so large that the body of a man in armor was once found in it (HIEROZO. 2. 5. 12). Others, the *shark* [JEBB]. The *cavity in the whale's throat,* large enough, according to Captain SCORESBY, to hold a ship's jolly-boat full of men. A *miracle* in any view is needed, and we have no data to speculate further. A "sign" or miracle it is expressly called by our Lord in Matthew 12. Respiration in such a position could only be by miracle. The miraculous interposition was not without a sufficient reason; it was calculated to affect not only Jonah, but also Nineveh and Israel. The life of a prophet was often marked by experiences which made him, through sympathy, best suited for discharging the prophetical function to his hearers and his people. The infinite resources of God in mercy as well as judgment are prefigured in the devourer being transformed into Jonah's preserver. Jonah's condition under punishment, shut out from the outer world, was rendered as much as possible the emblem of death, a present type to Nineveh and Israel, of the death in sin, as his deliverance was of the spiritual resurrection on repentance; as also, a future type of Jesus' literal death for sin, and resurrection by the Spirit of God. **three days and three nights**—probably, like the Antitype, Christ, Jonah was cast forth on the land on the *third* day (Matt. 12:40); the Hebrew counting the first and third parts of days as whole twenty-four hour days.

ADAM CLARKE

ALEXANDER MACLAREN:

Jonah's conduct in the storm is no less noble than his former conduct had been base. The burst of the tempest blew away all the fog from his mind, and he saw the stars again. His confession of faith; his calm conviction that he was the cause of the storm; his quiet, unhesitating command to throw him into the wild chaos foaming about the ship; his willing acceptance of death as the wages of sin, all tell how true a saint he was in the depth of his soul. Sorrow and chastisement turn up the subsoil. If a man has any good in him, it generally comes to the top when he is afflicted and looks death in the face. If there is nothing but gravel beneath, it too will be brought up by the plough. There may be much selfish unfaithfulness overlying a real devoted heart.

—*Expositions of Holy Scripture*

17. *Now the Lord had prepared a great fish.* This could not have been a whale, for the throat of that animal can scarcely admit a man's leg; but it might have been a shark, which abounds in the Mediterranean, and whose mouth and stomach are exceedingly capacious. In several cases they have been known to swallow a man when thrown overboard. That days and nights do not, among the Hebrews, signify complete days and nights of twenty-four hours, see Esther iv. 16, compared with chap. v. 1; Judg. xiv. 17-18. Our Lord lay in the grave one natural day, and part of two others; and it is most likely that this was the precise time that Jonah was in the fish's belly.

MATTHEW HENRY

CHAPTER 2

Verses 1–9

God and his servant Jonah had parted in anger, and the quarrel began on Jonah's side; he fled from his country that he might outrun his work. The reconciliation begins on God's side. In the close of the foregoing chapter we found God returning to Jonah in a way of mercy, *delivering him from going down to the pit,* having *found a ransom*; in this chapter we find Jonah returning to God in a way of duty.

I. When he prayed (*v.* 1): *Then Jonah prayed;* when he was in trouble, under the sense of sin, then he prayed. Then when he was in a hopeful way of deliverance, being preserved alive by miracle, then he

JAMIESON, FAUSSET, BROWN

CHAPTER 2

Vss. 1-10. JONAH'S PRAYER OF FAITH AND DELIVERANCE.

ADAM CLARKE

CHAPTER 2

MATTHEW HENRY

prayed.

II. Where he prayed—in *the fish's belly.* No place is amiss for prayer. Wherever God casts us we may find a way open heavenward. He that has Christ dwelling in his heart by faith, wherever he goes carries his altar along with him, that *sanctifies the gift,* and is himself a *living temple.* Men may shut us out from communion with one another, but not from communion with God. Jonah was now in the bottom of the sea, yet *out of the depths he cries to God.*

III. To whom he prayed—*to the Lord his God.* He had been fleeing from God, but now he sees the folly of it, and returns to him.

IV. What his prayer was. He reflects upon the workings of his heart towards God when he was in distress, and the conflict that was then in his breast between faith and sense, between hope and fear. He said, *I cried, by reason of my affliction, unto the Lord.* "*Out of the belly of hell* and the grave *cried I.*" And it was not in vain: *God heard him, heard the voice* of his affliction. How low he was thrown (*v.* 3): *Thou hadst cast me into the deep.* The mariners cast him there; but he saw the hand of God casting him there. How terribly he was beset: *The floods compassed me about.* The channels and springs of the waters of the sea surrounded him on every side; it was high-water with him. *All thy billows and thy waves passed over me.* These words are plainly quoted by Jonah from Ps. xlii. 7, where in the original David's complaint is the same *verbatim.* If ever any man's case was singular, surely Jonah's was, and yet, to his great satisfaction, he finds even the man after God's own heart making the same complaint of God's *waves and billows going over him.* Our path of trouble is no untrodden path. To the same purport, *v.* 5, *The waters compassed me about even to the soul.* And this also is borrowed from David's complaint, Ps. lxix. 1, The *waters have come in unto my soul.* How fast he was held (*v.* 6): *He went down to the bottom of the mountains*; the *earth with her bars was about him*; it was likely to be about him for ever. He began to sink into despair. When the *waters compassed him about even to the soul* no marvel that *his soul fainted within him.* What hopes could he have of deliverance out of a trouble which his *own ways and doings* had *procured to himself*? He says, *I am cast out of thy sight.* Sometimes the condition of God's people may be such in this world that they may think themselves excluded from God's presence, so as no more to see him. But it is only the surmise of unbelief, for God has not *cast away his people whom he has chosen.* He recovered himself from sinking into despair, with some comfortable prospects of deliverance. Faith corrected and controlled the surmises of fear and distrust. Here was a fierce struggle between sense and faith, but faith had the last word and came off conqueror. Jonah's faith said, *Yet I will look again towards thy holy temple.* When Hezekiah desired that he might be assured of his recovery, he asked, *What is the sign that I shall go up to the house of the Lord?* (Isa. xxxviii. 22), as if that were the only thing for the sake of which he wished for health; so Jonah here hopes he shall *look again towards the temple.* How modestly Jonah expresses himself; as one conscious to himself of guilt and unworthiness, he dares not speak of dwelling in God's house, but he hopes he may be admitted to look towards it. Or these words may be taken as Jonah's vow when he was in distress, and he speaks (*v.* 9) of paying what he vowed. His sin for which God pursued him was *fleeing from the presence of the Lord.* He will never again look towards Tarshish, but will again look towards the temple, and will go *from strength to strength* till he appear before God there. When our souls faint we must remember God; and when we think on his name we should call on his name. He reflects upon the favour of God to him when in his distress he sought and trusted him. God graciously accepted his prayer (*v.* 7): *My prayer,* being sent to him, *came in unto him,* even *into his holy temple*; it was heard in the highest heavens, though it was prayed in the lowest deeps. He wonderfully wrought deliverance for him (*v.* 6): *Yet hast thou brought up my life from corruption, O Lord my God!* Some think he said this when he was vomited up on dry ground. *The earth with her bars was about me for ever,* and yet *thou hast brought up my life from the pit,* from the *bars of the pit.* Or we may suppose it spoken while he was yet in the fish's belly, and then it is the language of his faith: "Thou hast kept me alive in the pit, and therefore thou canst, thou wilt, *bring up my life from the pit*"; and he speaks of it with as much assurance as if it were done already: *Thou hast brought up my life.* If the Lord be our God, he will be to us the *resurrection and the life,* will redeem our lives from destruction, from the power of the grave. He gives warning to others to keep close to

JAMIESON, FAUSSET, BROWN

1. his God—"his" still, though Jonah had fled from Him. Faith enables Jonah now to feel this; just as the returning prodigal says of the Father, from whom he had wandered, "I will arise and go to *my* Father" (Luke 15:18). **out of the fish's belly**—Every place may serve as an oratory. No place is amiss for prayer. Others translate, "when (delivered) out of the fish's belly." *English Version* is better. **2.** His prayer is partly descriptive and precatory, partly eucharistical. Jonah incorporates with his own language inspired utterances familiar to the Church long before in vs. 2, Psalm 120:1; in vs. 3, Psalm 42:7; in vs. 4, Psalm 31:22; in vs. 5, Psalm 69:1; in vs. 7, Psalm 142:3, and 18:6; in vs. 8, Psalm 31:6; in vs. 9, Psalm 116:17, 18, and 3:8. Jonah, an inspired man, thus attests both the antiquity and inspiration of the Psalms. It marks the spirit of faith, that Jonah identifies himself with the saints of old, appropriating their experiences as recorded in the Word of God (Ps. 119:50). Affliction opens up the mine of Scripture, before seen only on the surface. **out of the belly of hell**—*Sheol,* the unseen world, which the belly of the fish resembled. **3. thou hadst cast . . . thy billows . . . thy waves**—Jonah recognizes the source whence his sufferings came. It was no mere chance, but *the hand of God* which sent them. Cf. Job's similar recognition of God's hand in calamities, Job 1:21; 2:10; and David's, II Samuel 16:5-11. **4. cast out from thy sight**—i.e., from Thy favorable regard. A just retribution on one who had fled "*from the presence* of the Lord" (ch. 1:3). Now that he has got his desire, he feels it to be his bitterest sorrow to be deprived of God's presence, which once he regarded as a burden, and from which he desired to escape. He had turned his back on God; so God turned His back on him, making his sin his punishment. **toward thy holy temple**—In the confidence of faith he anticipates yet to see the temple at Jerusalem, the appointed place of worship (I Kings 8:38), and there to render thanksgiving [HENDERSON]. Rather, I think, "Though cast out of Thy sight, I will still *with the eye of faith* once more *look in prayer* towards Thy temple at Jerusalem, whither, as Thy earthly throne, Thou hast desired Thy worshippers to direct their prayers." **5. even to the soul**—i.e., threatening to extinguish the *animal life.* **weeds**—He felt as if the seaweeds through which he was dragged were wrapped about his head. **6. bottoms of . . . mountains**—their *extremities* where they *terminate* in the hidden depths of the sea. Cf. Psalm 18:7, "the foundations of the hills" (Ps. 18:15). **earth with her bars was about me**—Earth, the land of the living, is (not "was") shut against me. **for ever**—so far as any effort of *mine* can deliver me.

7. soul fainted . . . I remembered the Lord—beautifully exemplifying the triumph of spirit over flesh, of faith over sense (Ps. 73:26; 42:6). For a time troubles shut out hope; but faith revived when Jonah "remembered the Lord," what a gracious God He is, and how now He still preserves his life and consciousness in his dark prison house. **into thine holy temple**—the temple at Jerusalem (vs. 4). As there he looks in believing prayer towards it, so here he regards his prayer as already heard. **yet hast thou brought up my life from corruption**—rather, "Thou *bringest* . . . from the pit" [MAURER]. As in the previous clauses he expresses the hopelessness of his state, so in this, his sure hope of deliverance through Jehovah's infinite resources. "Against hope he believes in hope," and speaks as if the deliverance were actually being accomplished. **Hezekiah seems** to have incorporated Jonah's very words in his prayer (Isa. 38:17), just as Jonah appropriated the language of the Psalms.

ADAM CLARKE

1. *Then Jonah prayed . . . out of the fish's belly.* It may be asked, "How could Jonah either pray or breathe in the stomach of the fish?" Very easily, if God willed it. And let the reader keep this constantly in view; the whole is a miracle, from Jonah's being swallowed by the fish till he was cast ashore by the same animal. It was God that had prepared the great fish. It was the Lord that spake to the fish, and caused it to vomit Jonah upon the dry land. All is miracle.

2. *Out of the belly of hell.* Among the Hebrews *sheol* means the "grave," and deep pit, the place of separate spirits. Here the prophet represents himself as in the bottom of the sea, for so *sheol* must be understood in this place.

3. *All thy billows and thy waves passed over me.* This may be understood literally; while the fish, in whose belly he was, sought its pleasure or sustenance in the paths of the deep, the waves and billows of the sea were rolling above. This line seems borrowed from Ps. xlii. 7.

4. *I am cast out of thy sight.* See Ps. xxxi. 22.

5. *The waters compassed me about, even to the soul.* So as to seem to deprive me of life. I had no hope left. *The weeds were wrapped about my head.* This may be understood literally also. He found himself in the fish's stomach, together with seaweeds, and suchlike marine substances, which the fish had taken for its aliment.

6. *Yet hast thou brought up my life.* The substance of this poetic prayer was composed while in the fish's belly. But afterwards the prophet appears to have thrown it into its present poetic form, and to have added some circumstances, such as that before us; for he now speaks of his deliverance from this imminent danger of death. Thou hast *brought up my life from corruption.*

MATTHEW HENRY

God (*v.* 8): *Those that observe lying vanities forsake their own mercy.* Those that worship other gods, as the heathen mariners did, and expect relief and comfort from them, *forsake their own mercy*; they turn their back upon their own happiness. Or, those that follow their own inventions, as Jonah himself had done when he *fled from the presence of the Lord* to go to Tarshish, *forsake their own mercy*, that mercy which they might find if they would but keep close to God and their duty. He solemnly binds his soul with a bond that, if God work deliverance for him, the God of his mercies shall be the God of his praises, *v.* 9. Jonah promises, that with the sacrifice of thanksgiving he will *mention the lovingkindness of the Lord*, to his glory, and the encouragement of others. He will honour him by a punctual performance of his vows. Probably his vow was that if God would deliver him he would readily go wherever he should please to send him, though it were to Nineveh. He concludes with an acknowledgement of God as the Saviour of his people: *Salvation is of the Lord;* it *belongs to the Lord*, Ps. iii. 8. Jonah's experience shall encourage others, in all ages, to trust in God as the God of their salvation.

Verse 10

Jonah's discharge from his imprisonment, and his deliverance from death may be considered as an instance of God's mercy to a poor penitent, that in his distress prays to him. When God had him at his mercy he showed him mercy, and did not *contend for ever.* It seems a type and figure of Christ's resurrection. He died and was buried, to lay the storm which our sin had raised, and lay in the grave, as Jonah did, three days and three nights, a prisoner for our debt; but the third day he came forth, by his messengers to preach repentance, and remission of sins, even to the Gentiles.

JAMIESON, FAUSSET, BROWN

8. observe lying vanities—regard or reverence idols, powerless to save (Ps. 31:6). **mercy**—Jehovah, the very idea of whom is identified now in Jonah's mind with mercy and loving-kindness. As the Psalmist (Ps. 144:2) styles Him, "my goodness"; God who is to me all beneficence. Cf. Psalm 59:17, "the God of my mercy," lit., "my kindness-God." Jonah had "forsaken His own mercy," God, to flee to heathen lands where "lying vanities" (idols) were worshipped. But now, taught by his own preservation in conscious life in the fish's belly, and by the inability of the mariners' idols to lull the storm (ch. 1:5), estrangement from God seems estrangement from his own happiness (Jer. 2:13; 17:13). Prayer has been restrained in Jonah's case, so that he was "fast asleep" in the midst of danger, heretofore; but now prayer is the sure sign of his return to God. **9. I will sacrifice . . . thanksgiving**—In the believing anticipation of sure deliverance, he offers thanksgivings already. So Jehoshaphat (II Chron. 20:21) appointed singers to *praise* the Lord in front of the army before the battle with Moab and Ammon, as if the victory was already gained. God honors such confidence in Him. There is also herein a mark of sanctified affliction, that he vows amendment and thankful obedience (Ps. 119:67). **10. upon the dry land**—probably on the coast of Palestine.

ADAM CLARKE

10. *And the Lord spake unto the fish.* That is, by His influence the fish swam to shore, and cast Jonah on the dry land.

MATTHEW HENRY

CHAPTER 3

Verses 1–4

I. Jonah's commission is renewed and readily obeyed.

God was perfectly reconciled to Jonah, and the commission anew given him was an evidence of the remission of his former disobedience. *The word of the Lord came unto Jonah the second time* (*v.* 1). After he has been thrown into the sea, and thrown out of it again, God comes and asks him, "Jonah, wilt thou go to Nineveh now?" Jonah shall be trusted. God might justly have said as we should concerning one that had dealt treacherously with us, that though we would not proceed to the rigour of the law against him, yet we would never again repose confidence in him. But, behold! the word of the Lord comes to him again, to show that when God forgives he forgets, and whom he forgives he receives into his family again, and restores them to their former estate. God's making use of us is the best evidence of his being at peace with us. Jonah was reconciled to God, not now *disobedient to the heavenly vision.* He neither endeavoured to avoid hearing the command, nor did he decline obeying it. But now, without murmuring and disputing, *Jonah arose, and went unto Nineveh, according to the word of the Lord*, *v.* 3. He went directly to Nineveh, though it was a great way off, and a place where, it is likely, he never was before; yet thither he took his journey, *according to the word of the Lord.*

II. The command given him. He was sent in the name of the God of heaven, to proclaim war with Nineveh (*v.* 2): "*Arise, go up to Nineveh, that great city,*" that metropolis, and *preach unto it*, preach *against it*, so the Chaldee. Jonah is sent to Nineveh, which was at this time the chief city of the Gentile world, as an indication of God's gracious intentions to make the light of divine revelation to shine in those dark regions. God knew that if Sodom and Gomorrah, Tyre and Sidon, had had the means of grace, they would have repented, Matt. xi. 21, 23. He knew that if Nineveh had now the means of grace they would repent, and he gave them those means and sent Jonah. Go, and preach (says God) *the preaching that I bid thee.* Tell the men of Nineveh that their wickedness has come up to God, and God's vengeance is coming down upon them. This was the message Jonah was loth to deliver, and flew off and went to Tarshish; but, when he is brought to it the second time, God does not alter the message, to gratify him, or make it the more passable; no, he must now preach the very same that he was then ordered to preach and would not. It was an encouragement to him that God would go with him, that the Spirit of prophecy should abide upon him, when he was at Nineveh, to give him further instructions.

JAMIESON, FAUSSET, BROWN

CHAPTER 3

VSS. 1-10. JONAH'S SECOND COMMISSION TO NINEVEH: THE NINEVITES REPENT OF THEIR EVIL WAY: SO GOD REPENTS OF THE EVIL THREATENED. **2. preach . . . the preaching**—lit., "proclaim the proclamation." On the former occasion the specific object of his commission to Nineveh was declared; here it is indeterminate. This is to show how freely he yields himself, in the spirit of unconditional obedience, to speak whatever God may please. **3. arose and went**—like the son who was at first disobedient to the father's command, "Go work in my vineyard," but who afterwards "repented and went" (Matt. 21:28, 29). Jonah was thus the fittest instrument for proclaiming judgment, and yet hope of mercy on repentance to Nineveh, being himself a living exemplification of both—judgment in his entombment in the fish, mercy on repentance in his deliverance. Israel professing to obey, but not obeying, and so doomed to exile in the same Nineveh, answers to the son who said, "I go, sir, and went not." In Luke 11:30 it is said that Jonas was not only a sign to the men in Christ's time, but also "unto the Ninevites." On the latter occasion (Matt. 16:1-4) when the Pharisees and Sadducees tempted Him, asking a sign *from heaven,* He answered, "No sign shall be given, but the sign of the prophet Jonas." Thus the sign had a *twofold* aspect, a direct bearing on the Ninevites, an indirect bearing on the Jews in Christ's time. To the Ninevites he was not merely a prophet, but himself a wonder in the earth, as one who had tasted of death, and yet had not seen corruption, but had now returned to witness among them for God. If the Ninevites had indulged in a captious spirit, they never would have inquired and so known Jonah's wonderful history; but being humbled by God's awful message, they learned from Jonah himself that it was the previous concealing in his bosom of the same message of their own doom that caused him to be entombed as an outcast from the living. Thus he was a "sign" to them of wrath on the one hand, and, on the other, of mercy. Guilty Jonah saved from the jaws of death gives a ray of hope to guilty Nineveh. Thus God, who brings good from evil, made Jonah in his fall, punishment, and restoration, a sign (an *embodied lesson* or *living symbol*) through which the Ninevites were roused to hear and repent, as they would not have been likely to do, had he gone on the first commission before his living entombment and resurrection. To do evil that good may come, is a policy which can only come from Satan; but from evil already done to extract an instrument against the kingdom of darkness, is a triumphant display of the grace and wisdom of God. To the Pharisees in Christ's time, who, not content with the

ADAM CLARKE

CHAPTER 3

1. *And the word of the Lord.* The same oracle as that before given; and which, from what he had felt and seen of the justice and mercy of the Lord, he was now prepared to obey.

2. *And preach unto it the preaching.* "And cry the cry that I bid you." Be My herald, and faithfully deliver My message.

ALEXANDER MACLAREN:

Note the renewed charge to the penitent Prophet, and his new eagerness to fulfill it. His deliverance and second commission are put as if all but simultaneous, and his obedience was swift and glad. Jonah did not venture to take for granted that the charge which he had shirked was still continued to him. If God commands to take the trumpet, and we refuse, we dare not assume that we shall still be honored with the delivery of the message. The punishment of dumb lips is often dumbness. Opportunities of service, slothfully or faintheartedly neglected, are often withdrawn. We can fancy how Jonah, brought back to the better mind which breathes in his psalm, longed to be honored by the trust of preaching once more, and how rapturously his spirit would address itself to the task. Duties once unwelcome become sweet when we have passed through the experience of the misery that comes from neglecting them. It is God's mercy that gives us the opportunity of effacing past disobedience by new alacrity.

—*Expositions of Holy Scripture*

MATTHEW HENRY

Jonah must go with an implicit faith. Admirals, sometimes, when they are sent abroad, are not to open their commission till they have got so many leagues off at sea; so Jonah must go to Nineveh, and, when he comes there, shall be told what to say.

III. He faithfully and boldly delivered his errand. When he came to Nineveh he found it was an *exceedingly great city of three days' journey* (v. 3); a city *great to God*, so the Hebrew phrase is, meaning no more than as we render it, *exceedingly great*. The greatness of Nineveh consisted chiefly in the extent of it; it was much larger than Babylon, such a city, says Diodorus Siculus, as no man ever after built.

When he came thither he lost no time; but opened his commission immediately, according to his instructions, and he *cried, and said, Yet forty days, and Nineveh shall be overthrown*. This was the purport of his message. He meant, and they understood him, that it should be overthrown, not by an war, but by some immediate stroke, either by an earthquake or by fire and brimstone as Sodom was. So long God will wait to see if, upon this alarm given, they will humble themselves and amend their doings, and so prevent the ruin threatened. But he will wait no longer. Forty days is a long time for a righteous God to defer his judgments, yet it is but a little time for an unrighteous people to repent and reform. The fixing of the day thus, with all possible assurance, would help to convince them that it was a message from God.

Verses 5–10

I. A wonder of divine grace in the repentance and reformation of Nineveh, upon the warning given them of their destruction approaching. It will *rise up in judgment against the men of* the gospel-*generation, and condemn them; for the Ninevites repented at the preaching of Jonas, but behold, a greater than Jonas is here*, Matt. xii. 41. It did condemn the impenitence and obstinacy of Israel at that time. God sent many prophets to Israel, well known to be *mighty in word and deed*; but to Nineveh he sent only one, and him a stranger, whose aspect was mean, and his *bodily presence weak*, after so long a journey; and yet they repented, but Israel repented not. Jonah preached but one sermon, and we do not find that he gave them any sign or wonder, and yet they were wrought upon, while Israel continued obstinate. Jonah only threatened wrath and ruin; we do not find that he gave them any encouragements to hope that they should find mercy if they did repent, and yet they repented; but Israel persisted in impenitence, though the prophets sent to them drew them *with cords of a man, and with bands of love*.

JAMIESON, FAUSSET, BROWN

many signs exhibited by Him, still demanded a sign *from heaven,* He gave a sign in the opposite quarter, viz., Jonah, who came "out of the belly of *hell*" (the unseen region). They looked for a Messiah gloriously coming in the clouds of *heaven;* the Messiah, on the contrary, is to pass through a like, though a deeper, humiliation than Jonah; He is to lie "in the heart of *the earth.*" Jonah and his Antitype alike appeared low and friendless among their hearers; both victims to death for God's wrath against sin, both preaching repentance. Repentance derives all its efficacy from the death of Christ, just as Jonah's message derived its weight with the Ninevites from his entombment. The Jews stumbled at Christ's death, the very fact which ought to have led them to Him, as Jonah's entombment attracted the Ninevites to his message. As Jonah's restoration gave hope of God's placability to Nineveh, so Christ's resurrection assures us God is fully reconciled to man by Christ's death. But Jonah's entombment only had the effect of a *moral suasive*; Christ's resurrection assures us God is fully reconciliation between God and man [FAIRBAIRN]. **Nineveh was an exceeding great city**—lit., "great to God," i.e., before God. All greatness was in the Hebrew mind associated with GOD; hence arose the idiom (cf. Ps. 36:6; 80:10), "great mountains," *Margin*, "mountains of God"; "goodly cedars," *Margin*, "cedars of God," Genesis 10:9, "a mighty hunter *before the Lord*." **three days' journey**—i.e., about sixty miles, allowing about twenty miles for a day's journey. Jonah's statement is confirmed by heathen writers, who describe Nineveh as 480 stadia in circumference [DIODORUS SICULUS, 2. 3]. HERODOTUS defines a day's journey to be 150 stadia; so three days' journey will not be much below DIODORUS' estimate. The parallelogram in Central Assyria covered with remains of buildings has Khorsabad northeast; Koyunjik and Nebbi Yunus near the Tigris, northwest; Nimroud, between the Tigris and the Zab, southwest; and Karamless, at a distance inward from the Zab, southeast. From Koyunjik to Nimroud is about eighteen miles; from Khorsabad to Karamless, the same; from Koyunjik to Khorsabad, thirteen or fourteen miles; from Nimroud to Karamless, fourteen miles. The length thus was greater than the breadth; cf. vs. 4, "a day's journey," which is confirmed by heathen writers and by modern measurements. The walls were 100 feet high, and broad enough to allow three chariots abreast, and had moreover 1500 lofty towers. The space between, including large parks and arable ground, as well as houses, was Nineveh in its full extent. The oldest palaces are at Nimroud, which was probably the original site. LAYARD latterly has thought that the name Nineveh belonged originally to Koyunjik, rather than to Nimroud. Jonah (ch. 4:11) mentions the children as numbering 120,000, which would give about a million to the whole population. Existing ruins show that Nineveh acquired its greatest extent under the kings of the second dynasty, i.e., the kings mentioned in Scripture; it was then that Jonah visited it, and the reports of its magnificence were carried to the west [LAYARD]. **4. a day's journey**—not going straight forward without stopping: for the city was but eighteen miles in length; but stopping in his progress from time to time to announce his message to the crowds gathering about him. **Yet forty days, and Nineveh shall be overthrown**—The commission, given indefinitely at his setting out, assumes now on his arrival a definite form, and that severer than before. It is no longer a cry against the sins of Nineveh, but an announcement of its ruin in forty days. This number is in Scripture associated often with humiliation. It was forty days that Moses, Elijah, and Christ fasted. Forty years elapsed from the beginning of Christ's ministry (the antitype of Jonah's) to the destruction of Jerusalem. The more definite form of the denunciation implies that Nineveh has now almost filled up the measure of her guilt. The change in the form which the Ninevites would hear from Jonah on anxious inquiry into his history, would alarm them the more, as implying the increasing nearness and certainty of their doom, and would at the same time reprove Jonah for his previous guilt in delaying to warn them. The very solitariness of the one message announced by the stranger thus suddenly appearing among them, would impress them with the more awe. Learning from him, that so far from lightly prophesying evil against them, he had shrunk from announcing a less severe denunciation, and therefore had been cast into the deep and only saved by miracle, they felt how imminent was their peril, threatened as they now were by a prophet whose fortunes were so closely bound up with theirs. In

ADAM CLARKE

3. *Nineveh was an exceeding great city, of three days' journey*. See on chap. i. 2. Strabo says, lib. xvi, "It was much larger than Babylon"; and Ninus, the builder, not only proposed to make it the largest city of the world, but the largest that could be built by man. See Diodor. *Sic. Bib*. l. ii. And as we find, from the lowest computation, that it was at least fifty-four or sixty English miles in circumference, it would take the prophet three days to walk round and announce the terrible message, "Yet forty days, and Nineveh will be destroyed!"

TODAY'S DICTIONARY OF THE BIBLE:

Before this century our knowledge of the great Assyrian empire and of its magnificent capital was almost wholly a blank. Vague memories had indeed survived of its power and greatness, but little was definitely known about it. Other cities which had perished—i.e., Palmyra, Persepolis, and Thebes—had left ruins to mark their sites and tell of their former greatness; but of this city, imperial Nineveh, not a single vestige seemed to remain, and the very place on which it had stood was only a matter of conjecture. In fulfillment of prophecy, God made "an utter end of the place." It became a "desolation."

In the days of the Greek historian Herodotus, 400 B.C., it had become a thing of the past; and when Xenophon the historian passed the place in the "Retreat of the Ten Thousand," the very memory of its name had been lost. It was buried out of sight, and no one knew its grave. It is never again to rise from its ruins.

At length, after being lost for more than two thousand years, the city was disentombed. Excavations have uncovered a mound of accumulated debris some 90 feet thick. At this point, evidence points to a beginning of occupation around 4500 B.C. Most of the archaeological work done to date has been on the northern mound of Quyunjiq, as the mound Nebi Yunus is covered by a modern village, cemetery, mosque and other hindrances to excavation. Work was begun on the site by Paul Emile Botta in 1842, but abandoned shortly thereafter because of his failure to uncover monumental art. Botta's work was resumed in 1849 by Austen Henry Layard who, excavating in Botta's footsteps uncovered the magnificent palace of Sennacherib, the "Taylor Prism" and, in the following year, the library of Ashurbanipal, one of Near Eastern archaeology's more significant finds. The Taylor Prism is of special interest to readers of Scripture, for it contains the account of Sennacherib's assault on Judah and the siege of Jerusalem. He brags that he conquered "46 walled cities" and "shut up Hezekiah the Jew . . . like a bird in a cage" (2 Kings 18—20; Isa. 36—39). Later, another Englishman, George Smith, discovered the Babylonian creation myth and portions of the *Gilgamesh Epic* containing the Mesopotamian flood story in the ruins of Nineveh.

MATTHEW HENRY

The men of Nineveh *believed God*; they gave credit to the word which Jonah spoke to them in the name of God: they believed that there was but *one living and true God*—that to him they were accountable—that they had sinned against him—that this notice sent them of ruin approaching came from him—that he is a merciful God, and there might be some hopes of the turning away of the wrath threatened, if they did turn away from the sins for which it was threatened. They brought word to the king of Nineveh, who, some think, was at this time Sardanapalus. Jonah is not sent to the court, but to the streets of Nineveh, to make his proclamation. However, an account is brought to the king of Nineveh, not by way of information against Jonah, as a disturber of the public peace, but as a message from heaven, by some that were concerned for the public welfare. The king set them a good example of humiliation, *v.* 6. When he heard of the *word of God* sent to him he *rose from his throne* in sorrow and shame for sin, by which he and his people had become obnoxious. He laid aside his royal robe, the badge of his imperial dignity, as an acknowledgment that, having not used his power as he ought for the restraining of violence and wrong, and the maintaining of right, he had forfeited his throne and robe to the justice of God. Even the king himself disdained not to put on the garb of a penitent, for he *covered himself with sackcloth, and sat in ashes.* The people *put on sackcloth, from the greatest of them even to the least of them, v.* 5. Though bodily exercise alone profits nothing, and a man's *spreading sackcloth and ashes under him,* if that be all, is but a jest (it is the heart that God looks at, Isa. lviii. 5), yet when God *calls to mourning and girding with sackcloth,* we must by outward expressions of inward sorrow *glorify God with our bodies,* at least by laying aside their ornaments. A general fast was observed throughout that great city, *v.* 7–9. On the day appointed *let neither man nor beast taste anything*; nor so much as *drink water.* Let them make themselves uneasy in body, to show how uneasy they are in mind, through sorrow for sin and the fear of divine wrath. With their fasting and mourning they must join prayer and supplication to God; for the fasting is designed to fit the body for the service of the soul in the duty of prayer. In prayer we must cry mightily, with a fixedness of thought, firmness of faith, and fervour of pious and devout affections. Yet this is not all. They must to their fasting and praying add reformation and amendment of life: *Let them turn everyone from his evil way,* and particularly *from the violence that is in their hands*; let them restore what they have unjustly taken, and make reparation for what wrong they have done. It is not enough to fast for sin, but we must fast from sin. This fast is proclaimed and religiously observed (*v.* 9). They hope that God will, upon their repenting and turning, revoke his sentence against them. As when we pray for the favour of God we pray for all good, so when we pray against the wrath of God we pray against all evil. Jonah had not told them; they had not among them any other prophets to tell them, yet they had a general notion of the goodness of God's nature, his mercy to man, and from this they raised some hopes that he would spare them; they dare not presume, but they will not despair.

II. Here is a wonder of divine mercy in the sparing of these Ninevites upon their repentance (*v.* 10). God saw that they *turned from their evil way,* and that was the thing he looked for and required. Here were no sacrifices offered to God, that we read of, to make atonement for sin, but the *sacrifice of God is a broken spirit; a broken and contrite heart,* such as the Ninevites now had, is what he *will not despise;* it is what he will give countenance to and put honour upon.

JAMIESON, FAUSSET, BROWN

Noah's days 120 years of warning were given to men, yet they repented not till the flood came, and it was too late. But in the case of Nineveh, God granted a double mercy: first, that its people should repent immediately after threatening; second, that pardon should immediately follow their repentance. **5. believed God**—gave credit to Jonah's message from God; thus recognizing Jehovah as the true God. **fast . . . sackcloth**—In the East outward actions are often used as symbolical expressions of inward feelings. So fasting and clothing in sackcloth were customary in humiliation. Cf. in Ahab's case, parallel to that of Nineveh, both receiving a *respite* on penitence (I Kings 21:27; 20:31, 32; Joel 1:13). **from the greatest . . . to the least**—The penitence was not partial, but pervading all classes. **6. in ashes**—emblem of the deepest humiliation (Job 2:8; Ezek. 27:30). **7. neither . . beast . . . taste any thing**—The brute creatures share in the evil effects of man's sin (ch. 4:11; Rom. 8:20, 22); so they here according to Eastern custom, are made to share in man's outward indications of humiliation. "When the Persian general Masistias was slain, the horses and mules of the Persians were shorn, as well as themselves" [NEWCOME from PLUTARCH; also HERODOTUS, 9.24]. **8. cry . . . turn**—Prayer without reformation is a mockery of God (Ps. 66:18; Isa. 58: 6). Prayer, on the other hand, must precede true reformation, as we cannot turn to God from our evil way unless God first turns us (Jer. 31:18, 19). **9. Who can tell**—(Cf. Joel 2:14). Their acting on a vague possibility of God's mercy, without any special ground of encouragement, is the more remarkable instance of faith, as they had to break through long-rooted prejudices in giving up idols to seek Jehovah at all. The only ground which their ready faith rested on, was the fact of God sending one to warn them, instead of destroying them at once; this suggested the thought of a possibility of pardon. Hence they are cited by Christ as about to condemn in the judgment those who, with much greater light and privileges, yet repent not (Matt. 12:41). **11. God repented of the evil**—When the message was sent to them, they were so ripe for judgment that a purpose of destruction to take effect in forty days was the only word God's righteous abhorrence of sin admitted of as to them. But when they repented, the position in which they stood towards God's righteousness was altered. So God's mode of dealing with them must alter accordingly, if God is not to be inconsistent with His own immutable character of dealing with men according to their works and state of heart, taking vengeance at last on the hardened impenitent, and delighting to show mercy on the penitent. Cf. Abraham's reasoning, Gen. 18:25; Ezek. 18:21-25; Jer. 18:7-10. What was really a change *in them* and in God's corresponding dealings is, in condescension to human conceptions, represented as a change in God (cf. Exod. 32:14), who, in His essential righteousness and mercy, changeth not (Num. 23:19; I Sam. 15:29; Mal. 3:6; Jas. 1:17). The reason why the announcement of destruction was made absolute, and not dependent on Nineveh's continued impenitence, was that this form was the only one calculated to rouse them; and at the same time it was a *truthful* representation of God's purpose towards Nineveh under its existing state, and of Nineveh's due. When that state ceased, a new relation of Nineveh to God, not contemplated in the message, came in, and room was made for the word to take effect, "the curse causeless shall not come" [FAIRBAIRN]. Prophecy is not merely for the sake of proving God's omniscience by the verification of predictions of the future, but is mainly designed to vindicate God's justice and mercy in dealing with the impenitent and penitent respectively (Rom. 11: 22). The Bible ever assigns the first place to the eternal principles of righteousness, rooted in the character of God, subordinating to them all divine arrangements. God's sparing Nineveh, when in the jaws of destruction, on the first dawn of repentance encourages the timid penitent, and shows beforehand that Israel's doom, soon after accomplished, is to be ascribed, not to unwillingness to forgive on God's part, but to their own obstinate impenitence.

ADAM CLARKE

8. *Let man and beast be covered.* This was done that every object which they beheld might deepen the impression already made, and cause them to mourn after a godly sort. Virgil tells us that the mourning for the death of Julius Caesar was so general that the cattle neither ate nor drank.

10. *And God saw their works.* They repented, and brought forth fruits meet for repentance, works which showed that they did most earnestly repent. He therefore changed His purpose, and the city was saved. The purpose was: If the Ninevites do not return from their evil ways, and the violence that is in their hands, within forty days I will destroy the city. The Ninevites did return, and therefore escaped the threatened judgment. Thus we see that the threatening was conditional.

MATTHEW HENRY — CHAPTER 4

Verses 1–4

I. Jonah quarrelled with God for his mercy to Nineveh. This gives us occasion to suspect that Jonah had only delivered the message of wrath against the Ninevites, and had not assisted them in their repentance.

Jonah grudged them the mercy they found (*v.* 1):

JAMIESON, FAUSSET, BROWN — CHAPTER 4

VSS. 1-11. JONAH FRETS AT GOD'S MERCY TO NINEVEH: IS REPROVED BY THE TYPE OF A GOURD. **1. angry**—lit., "hot," probably, with *grief* or *vexation,* rather than *anger* [FAIRBAIRN]. How sad the contrast between God's feeling on the repentance of Nineveh towards Him, and Jonah's feeling on the repentance of God towards Nineveh. Strange in

ADAM CLARKE — CHAPTER 4

1. *But it displeased Jonah exceedingly.* This hasty, and indeed inconsiderate prophet, was vexed because his prediction was not fulfilled. He had more respect to his high sense of his own honor than he had to the goodness and mer-

MATTHEW HENRY

It displeased Jonah exceedingly; and *he was very angry.* Whatever pleases God should please us, and, though we cannot account for it, yet we must acquiesce in it. He had so little affection to men as to be angry at the conversion of the Ninevites and their reception into the divine favour. It was a point of honour that Jonah stood upon and that made him angry. He was jealous for the honour of his country; the repentance and reformation of Nineveh shamed the obstinacy of Israel that repented not, but *hated to be reformed;* and the favour God had shown to these Gentiles, upon their repentance, was an ill omen to the Jewish nation. He was jealous for his own honour, fearing lest, if Nineveh was not destroyed within forty days, he should be accounted a false prophet, and stigmatized accordingly.

He quarrelled with God about it. When his heart was not within him, he *spoke unadvisedly with his lips;* and here he tells us what he said (*v.* 2, 3): He *prayed unto the Lord,* but it is a very awkward prayer. Being in discontent, his corruptions got head of his graces, and, when he should have been praying for benefit by the mercy of God himself, he was complaining of the benefit others had by that mercy. He now begins to justify himself in fleeing *from the presence of the Lord* when he was first ordered to go to Nineveh: "*Lord,*" said he, "*was not this my saying when I was in my own country?* Did I not foresee that if I went to preach to Nineveh they would repent, and thou wouldst forgive them?" What a strange sort of man was Jonah, to dread the success of his ministry! It is unaccountable that that which all the saints had made the matter of their joy and praise Jonah should make the matter of reflection upon God, as if that were an imperfection of the divine nature which is indeed the greatest glory of it—that God is *gracious and merciful.* In a passion, he wishes for death (*v.* 3), "*Now, O Lord! take, I beseech thee, my life from me.* If Nineveh must live, let me die, rather than see thy word and mine disproved, rather than see the glory of Israel transferred to the Gentiles," as if there were not grace enough in God both for Jews and Gentiles. It was very absurd for him to wish he might die when he had a prospect of living to so good a purpose and could be so ill spared. Our business is to get ready to die by doing the work of life, and then to refer ourselves to God to take away our life when and how he pleases.

II. See how justly God reproved Jonah for this heat that he was in (*v.* 4): The Lord said, *Doest thou well to be angry?* See how mildly the great God speaks to this foolish man, to teach us to restore those that have fallen with a *spirit of meekness,* and with *soft answers* to *turn away wrath. Doest thou well?* We should often put this question to ourselves. When passion is up, let it meet with this check, "Do I well to be so soon angry, so often angry, so long angry, to put myself into such a heat, and to give others such ill language in my anger?"

Verses 5–11

Jonah persists here in his discontent.

I. Jonah's sullen expectation of the fate of Nineveh. He retires, *goes out of the city,* sits alone, and keeps silence, because he sees the Ninevites repent and reform, *v.* 5. The forty days were now expiring, or had expired, and Jonah hoped that, if Nineveh was not overthrown, yet some judgment or other would come upon it, sufficient to save his credit. He *made himself a booth* of the boughs of trees.

II. God's gracious provision for his shelter and refreshment when he thus foolishly afflicted himself, *v.* 6. Jonah was sitting in his booth, fretting at the cold of the night and the heat of the day. God looked on him with compassion, as the tender mother does on the froward child. He *prepared a gourd,* a plant with broad leaves, that suddenly grew up, and covered his hut or booth. It was *a shadow over his head, to*

JAMIESON, FAUSSET, BROWN

one who was himself a monument of mercy on his repentance! We all, like him, need the lesson taught in th parable of the unforgiving, though forgiven, debtor (Matt. 18:23-35). Jonah was grieved because Nineveh's preservation, after his denunciation, made him seem a false prophet [CALVIN]. But it would make Jonah a demon, not a man, to have preferred the destruction of 600,000 men rather than that his prophecy should be set aside through God's mercy triumphing over judgment. And God in that case would have severely chastised, whereas he only expostulates mildly with him, and by a mode of dealing, at once gentle and condescending, tries to show him his error. Moreover, Jonah himself, in apologizing for his vexation, does not mention *the failure of his prediction* as the cause: but solely the thought of God's *slowness to anger.* This was what led him to flee to Tarshish at his first commission; not the likelihood *then* of his prediction being falsified; for in fact his commission then was not to foretell Nineveh's downfall, but simply to "cry against" Nineveh's "wickedness" as having "come up before God." Jonah could hardly have been so vexed for the letter of his prediction failing, when the end of his commission had virtually been gained in leading Nineveh to repentance. This then cannot have been regarded by Jonah as the *ultimate* end of his commission. If Nineveh had been the prominent object with him, he would have rejoiced at the result of his mission. But Israel was the prominent aim of Jonah, as a prophet of the elect people. Probably then he regarded the destruction of Nineveh as fitted to be an example of God's judgment at last suspending His long forbearance so as to startle Israel from its desperate degeneracy, heightened by its new prosperity under Jeroboam II at that very time, in a way that all other means had failed to do. Jonah, despairing of anything effectual being done for God in Israel, unless there were first given a striking example of severity, thought when he proclaimed the downfall of Nineveh in forty days, that now at last God is about to give such an example; so when this means of awakening Israel was set aside by God's mercy on Nineveh's repentance, he was bitterly disappointed, not from pride or mercilessness, but from hopelessness as to anything being possible for the reformation of Israel, now that his cherished hope is baffled. But GOD's plan was to teach Israel, by the example of Nineveh, how inexcusable is their own impenitence, and how inevitable their ruin if they persevere. Repenting Nineveh has proved herself more worthy of God's favor than apostate Israel; the children of the covenant have not only fallen down to, but actually below, the level of a heathen people; Israel, therefore, must go down, and the heathen rise above her. Jonah did not know the important lessons of hope to the penitent, and condemnation to those amidst outward privileges impenitent, which Nineveh's preservation on repentance was to have for aftertimes, and to all ages. He could not foresee that Messiah Himself was thus to apply that history. A lesson to us that if we *could* in any particular alter the plan of Providence, it would not be for the better, but for the worse [FAIRBAIRN]. **2. my saying**—my thought, or feeling. **fled before**—*I anticipated by fleeing,* the disappointment of my design through Thy long-suffering mercy. **gracious . . . and merciful . . .**—Jonah here has before his mind Exodus 34: 6; as Joel (Joel 2:13) in his turn quotes from Jonah. **3.** Jonah's impatience of life under disappointed hopes of Israel's reformation through the destruction of Nineveh, is like that of Elijah at his plan for reforming Israel (I Kings 18) failing through Jezebel (I Kings 19:4). **4. Doest thou well to be angry?**—or *grieved;* rather as *Margin,* "Art thou *much* angry," or "grieved?" [FAIRBAIRN with LXX and *Syriac*]. But *English Version* suits the spirit of the passage, and is quite tenable in the *Hebrew* [GESENIUS]. **5. made him a booth**—i.e., a temporary hut of branches and leaves, so slightly formed as to be open to the wind and sun's heat. **see what would become of the city**—The term of forty days had not yet elapsed, and Jonah did not know that anything more than a suspension, or mitigation, of judgment had been granted to Nineveh. Therefore, not from sullennesss, but in order to watch the event from a neighboring station, he lodged in the booth. As a stranger, he did not know the depth of Nineveh's repentance; besides, from the Old Testament standpoint he knew that chastening judgments often followed, as in David's case (II Sam. 12:10-12, 14), even where sin had been repented of. To show him what he knew not, the largeness and completeness of God's mercy to penitent Nineveh, and the reasonableness of it, God made his booth a

ADAM CLARKE

cy of God. *And he was very angry.* Because the prediction was not literally fulfilled, for he totally lost sight of the condition.

KEIL-DELITZSCH:

The prayer which follows, *"Take my life from me,"* calls to mind the similar prayer of Elijah in 1 Kings 19:4; but the motive assigned is a different one. While Elijah adds, "for I am not better than my fathers," Jonah adds, *"for death is better to me than life."* This difference must be distinctly noticed, as it brings out the difference in the state of mind of the two prophets. In the inward conflict that had come upon Elijah he wished for death, because he did not see the expected result of his zeal for the Lord of Sabaoth; in other words, it was from spiritual despair, caused by the apparent failure of his labors. Jonah, on the other hand, did not wish to live any longer, because God had not carried out His threat against Nineveh. His weariness of life arose, not like Elijah's from stormy zeal for the honor of God and His kingdom, but from vexation at the non-fulfilment of his prophecy. This vexation was not occasioned, however, by offended dignity, or by anxiety or fear lest men should regard him as a liar or babbler; nor was he angry, as Calvin supposes, because he associated his office with the honor of God, and was unwilling that the name of God should be exposed to the scoffing of the heathen, or "because he saw that it would furnish material for impious blasphemies if God changed His purpose, or if He did not abide by His word;" but, as Luther observes (in his remarks on Jonah's flight), "he was hostile to the city of Nineveh, and still held a Jewish and carnal view of God." That this was really Jonah's view, is proved by Luther from the fact that God reproves his displeasure and anger in these words, "Should I not spare Nineveh?" etc. (v. 11). "He hereby implies that Jonah was displeased at the fact that God had spared the city, and was angry because He had not destroyed it as he had preached, and would gladly have seen." Offended vanity or unintelligent zeal for the honor of God would have been reproved by God in different terms from those in which Jonah was actually reproved, according to the next verse (v. 4), where Jehovah asks the prophet, *"Is thine anger justly kindled?"*

—Commentary on the Old Testament

3. *Take, I beseech thee, my life from me.* "Take, I beseech Thee, even my soul."

4. *Doest thou well to be angry?* "Is anger good for you?" Dr. Taylor renders the clause, "Art thou very much grieved?"

5. *So Jonah went out of the city.* I believe this refers to what had already passed; and I therefore agree with Bishop Newcome, who translates, "Now Jonah had gone out of the city, and had sat."

MATTHEW HENRY

deliver him from his grief, that, being refreshed in body, he might the better guard against the uneasiness of his mind. A gourd, one would think, was but a slender fortification at the best, yet Jonah *was exceedingly glad of the gourd.* A gourd in the right place may do us more service than a cedar. A small toy will serve sometimes to pacify a cross child, as the gourd did Jonah.

III. The sudden loss of this provision which God had made for his refreshment, and the return of his trouble, *v.* 7, 8. God *prepared a worm* to destroy the gourd. The gourd withered the next day after it sprang up; our comforts *come forth like flowers and are soon cut down.* A little thing withers them; a small worm at the root destroys a large gourd. Something unseen and undiscerned does it. God did not send an angel to pluck up Jonah's gourd, but sent a worm to smite it. He *prepared a wind* to make Jonah feel the want of the gourd, *v.* 8. It was a *vehement east wind*, which drove the heat of the rising sun violently upon the head of Jonah. Thus poor Jonah lay open to sun and wind.

IV. The further fret that this put Jonah into (*v.* 8). "If the gourd be killed, if the gourd be dead, kill me too, *let me die with the gourd.*" It is just that those who love to complain should never be left without something to complain of, that their folly may be manifested and corrected, and, if possible, cured.

V. The rebuke God gave him for this; he again reasoned with him: *Doest thou well to be angry for the gourd? v.* 9. When afflicting providences deprive us of our relations, possessions, and enjoyments, we must bear it patiently, must not be angry at God, must not be angry *for the gourd.* It is comparatively but a small loss, the loss of a shadow. That which should especially silence our discontent is that though our gourd be gone our God is not gone.

VI. His justification of his passion and discontent is strange, *v.* 9. He said, *I do well to be angry, even unto death.* Passion often over-rules conscience, and forces it to give a false judgment, as Jonah here did. He has so little regard to himself as to abandon his own life, to kill himself with fretting.

VII. He did ill to murmur at the sparing of Nineveh. Out of his own mouth God will judge him; he made no reply, but, we hope, returned to his right mind and recovered his temper. 1. God argued (*v.* 10, 11): "*Thou hast had pity on the gourd,* hast *spared* it, and saidst, *What a pity it is* that this gourd should ever wither! and *should not I then spare Nineveh*? The gourd thou hadst pity on was but one; but the inhabitants of Nineveh, whom I have pity on, are numerous." It is very populous, as appears by the number of the infants, two years old and under, of which there are 120,000 in Nineveh. So many there were in Nineveh not guilty of any transgression, and consequently had not contributed to the common guilt, and yet, if Nineveh had been overthrown, they would all have been involved in the common calamity; "and *shall not I spare* Nineveh then, with an eye to them?" God took notice of the abundance of cattle too that were in Nineveh, which he had more reason to pity and spare than Jonah had to pity and to spare the gourd, inasmuch as the animal life is more excellent than the vegetable. 2. The gourd which Jonah was concerned for was none of his own; which he made not to grow; but the persons in Nineveh whom God had compassion on were all the *work of his own hands*, he made them, and his they were, and therefore he had much more reason to have compassion on them. 3. The gourd which Jonah had pity on was of a sudden growth, and therefore of less value; it *came up in a night, it was the son of a night* (so the word is); but Nineveh is an ancient city, of many ages standing, and therefore cannot be so easily given up. 4. The gourd which Jonah had pity on *perished in a night*; it withered, and there was an end of it. But the precious souls in Nineveh that God had pity on are immortal. One soul is of more value than the whole world, surely then one soul is of more value than many gourds. It may be that Jonah, after this was well reconciled to the sparing of Nineveh, and was as well pleased with it as ever he had been displeased. Jonah had said, *I do well to be angry*, but he could not prove it. God says and proves it, *I do well to be merciful*; and it is a great encouragement to poor sinners to hope that they shall find mercy with him. Such murmurers shall be made to understand this doctrine, that, how narrow soever their souls, their principles are, and how willing soever they are to engross divine grace to themselves and those of their own way, there is one *Lord over all, that is rich in mercy to all that call upon him*, and in *every nation*, in Nineveh as well as in Israel, *he that fears God and works righteousness is accepted of him*; he that repents, and turns from his evil way, shall find mercy with him.

JAMIESON, FAUSSET, BROWN

school of discipline to give him more enlightened views. **6. gourd**—*Hebrew, kikaion*; the Egyptian *kiki*, the "ricinus" or castor-oil plant, commonly called "palm-christ" (*palma christi*). It grows from eight to ten feet high. Only one leaf grows on a branch, but that leaf being often more than a foot large, the collective leaves give good shelter from the heat. It grows rapidly, and fades as suddenly when injured. **to deliver him from his grief**—It was therefore *grief*, not selfish anger, which Jonah felt (*Note*, vs. 1). Some external comforts will often turn the mind away from its sorrowful bent. **7. a worm**—of a particular kind, deadly to the ricinus. A small worm at the root destroys a large gourd. So it takes but little to make our creature comforts wither. It should silence discontent to remember, that when our gourd is gone, our God is not gone. **the next day**—after Jonah was so "exceeding glad" (cf. Ps. 80:7). **8. vehement**—rather, "scorching"; *Margin, silent*, expressing sultry *stillness*, not *vehemence*. **9.** (*Note*, vs. 4). **I do well to be angry, even unto death**—"I am very much grieved, even to death" [Fairbairn]. So the Antitype (Matt. 26:38). **10, 11.** The main lesson of the book. If Jonah so pities a plant which cost him no toil to rear, and which is so short lived and valueless, much more must Jehovah pity those hundreds of thousands of immortal men and women in great Nineveh whom He has made with such a display of creative power, especially when many of them repent, and seeing that, if all in it were destroyed, "more than six score thousand" of *unoffending* children, besides "much cattle," would be involved in the common destruction. Cf. the same argument drawn from God's justice and mercy in Genesis 18:23-33. A similar illustration from the insignificance of a plant, which "to-day is and tomorrow is cast into the oven," and which, nevertheless, is clothed by God with surpassing beauty, is given by Christ to prove that God will care for the infinitely more precious bodies and souls of men who are to live for ever (Matt. 6:28-30). One soul is of more value than the whole world; surely, then, one soul is of more value than many gourds. The point of comparison spiritually is the *need* which Jonah, for the time being, had of the foliage of the gourd. However he might dispense with it at other times, now it was necessary for his comfort, and almost for his life. So now that Nineveh, as a city, fears God and turns to Him, God's cause needs it, and would suffer by its overthrow, just as Jonah's material well-being suffered by the withering of the gourd. If there were any hope of Israel's being awakened by Nineveh's destruction to fulfil her high destination of being a light to surrounding heathenism, then there would not have been the same need to God's cause of Nineveh's preservation, (though there would have always been need of saving the penitent). But as Israel, after judgments, now with returning prosperity turns back to apostasy, the means *needed* to vindicate God's cause, and provoke Israel, if possible, to jealousy, is the example of the great capital of heathendom suddenly repenting at the first warning, and consequently being spared. Thus Israel would see the kingdom of heaven transplanted from its ancient seat to another which would willingly yield its spiritual fruits. The tidings which Jonah brought back to his countrymen of Nineveh's repentance and rescue, would, if believingly understood, be far more fitted than the news of its overthrow to recall Israel to the service of God. Israel failed to learn the lesson, and so was cast out of her land. But even this was not an unmitigated evil. Jonah was a type, as of Christ, so also of Israel. Jonah, though an outcast, was highly honored of God in Nineveh; so Israel's outcast condition would prove no impediment to her serving God's cause still, if only she was faithful to God. Ezekiel and Daniel were so at Babylon; and the Jews, scattered in all lands as witnesses for the one true God, pioneered the way for Christianity, so that it spread with a rapidity which otherwise was not likely to have attended it [Fairbairn]. **that cannot discern between their right hand and their left**—children under three of four years old (Deut. 1:39). *Six score thousand* of these, allowing them to be a fifth of the whole, would give a *total* population of 600,000. **much cattle**—God cares even for the brute creatures, of which man takes little account. These in wonderful powers and in utility are far above the shrub which Jonah is so concerned about. Yet Jonah is reckless as to their destruction and that of innocent children. The abruptness of the close of the book is more strikingly suggestive than if the thought had been followed out in detail.

ADAM CLARKE

6. *And the Lord God prepared a gourd.* I believe this should be rendered in the preterpluperfect tense. The Lord had prepared this plant.

7. *But God prepared a worm.* By being eaten through the root, the plant, losing its nourishment, would soon wither; and this was the case in the present instance.

8. *A vehement east wind.* Which was of itself of a parching, withering nature; and the sun, in addition, made it intolerable. These winds are both scorching and suffocating in the East, for deserts of burning sand lay to the east or southeast, and the easterly winds often brought such a multitude of minute particles of sand on their wings as to add greatly to the mischief.

9. *I do well to be angry, even unto death.* Many persons suppose that the gifts of prophecy and working miracles are the highest that can be conferred on man; but they are widely mistaken, for the gifts change not the heart. Jonah had the gift of prophecy, but had not received that grace which destroys the old man.

11. *And should not I spare Nineveh?* In v. 10 it is said, "Thou hast had pity on the gourd," *attah chasta;* and here the Lord uses the same word, *veani lo achus*, "And shall not I have pity upon Nineveh?" How much is the city better than the shrub?

CHARLES H. SPURGEON:

Do you not see that *God was teaching Jonah by the eye and by experience*? Unless the Lord had put Jonah through this process, He could not so well have argued with His servant. So the gourd must go, and the wind must come, and the sun must beat upon the fainting prophet, and Jonah in his angry temper must get to feel great grief over his poor gourd which had met with such an untimely death, and then God comes to him, and says, "Art thou troubled about thy gourd? Hast thou pity upon a gourd, and should not I have pity upon a great city with more than a hundred and twenty thousand helpless children within its walls, and all those thousands of unsinning cattle? Should not I spare these, when thou wouldst have spared this tender plant, which sprang up in a night, and withered in a night?" Sometimes God puts us through an unusual experience in order that we may the better understand Him; and sometimes that we may the better know ourselves. Men who are of a hard nature must have hard usage, diamond must cut diamond, that at last the purpose of the great Owner of the jewels may be accomplished.

—*The Treasury of the Old Testament*

THE BOOK OF MICAH

I. To the nations—concerning the chosen (1:1-2:13)
- *A. The summons (1:1-4)*
- *B. The proclamation of Jehovah (1:5-7)*
- *C. The prophetic message (1:8-2:5)*
  - 1. Lamentation of the prophet (1:8-10)
  - 2. A wailing description of the judgment (1:11-16)
  - 3. The cause stated (2:1-5)
- *D. The false prophets (2:6-11)*
- *E. The promise of deliverance (2:12-13)*

II. To the rulers concerning the coming one (3:1-5:15)
- *A. Sin and consequent judgment (3:1-12)*
  - 1. The princes (3:1-4)
  - 2. The prophets (3:5-8)
  - 3. All ruling classes (3:9-12)
- *B. The coming one and consequent deliverance (4:1-5:15)*
  - 1. The vision of restored order (4:1-5:1)
  - 2. The deliverer and the deliverance (5:2-15)

III. To the chosen concerning the controversy (6:1-7:20)
- *A. The prophet—the summons (6:1, 2)*
- *B. Jehovah—a plaintive appeal (6:3-5)*
- *C. The people—questions of conviction (6:6, 7)*
- *D. The prophet—the answer (6:8, 9)*
- *E. Jehovah—a terrible charge (6:10-16)*
- *F. The people—confession and hope (7:1-10)*
- *G. The prophet—the answer to hope (7:11-13)*
- *H. The people—at prayer (7:14)*
- *I. Jehovah—the answer of peace (7:15)*
- *J. The prophet—faith expressing the promise (7:16, 17)*
- *K. The people—the final doxology (7:18-20)*

There is a resemblance between Isaiah's prophecy and this (cf. Isa. 2:2, 3, with Mic. 4:1, 2). Isaiah's prophecy is said to be concerning "Judah and Jerusalem," but Micah's concerning "Samaria and Jerusalem"; for, though this prophecy be dated only by the reigns of the kings of Judah, yet it refers to the kingdom of Israel, the approaching ruin of which, in the captivity of the ten tribes, he foretells and laments:

I. To convince sinners of their sins, by charging both Israel and Judah with idolatry, covetousness, oppression, contempt of the word of God, and their rulers both in church and state with the abuse of their power; and also by showing them the judgments of God.

II. To comfort God's people with promises of mercy and deliverance, especially with an assurance of the coming of the Messiah and of the grace of the gospel through him.

Two quotations out of it were made publicly upon very solemn occasions and both refer to very great events. One is a prediction of the destruction of Jerusalem (3:12), which we find quoted in the Old Testament, by "the elders of the land" (Jer. 16:17, 18), in justification of Jeremiah. "Micah [say they] foretold that Zion should be ploughed as a field, and Hezekiah did not put him to death; why then should we punish Jeremiah for saying the same?" Another is a prediction of the birth of Christ (5:2) which we find quoted in the New Testament, by the "chief priests and scribes of the people," in answer to Herod's inquiry, "where Christ should be born" (Matt. 2:5, 6).

MATTHEW HENRY

CHAPTER 1

Verses 1-7

I. A general account of this prophet and his prophecy, *v.* 1. The prophecy is the *word of the Lord*; a divine revelation. This word of the Lord came to the prophet, and he saw the vision, saw the things themselves which he foretold, as if they had been already accomplished. The prophet is Micah the Morasthite; his name *Micah* is a contraction of Micaiah; his surname, the *Morasthite*, signifies that he was born, or lived, at Moresheth, which is mentioned (*v.* 14), or Mareshah, which is mentioned *v.* 15, and Joshua xv. 44. The date of his prophecy is in the reigns of three kings of Judah—Jotham, Ahaz, and Hezekiah. Ahaz was one of the worst of Judah's kings, and Hezekiah one of the best. The promises and threatenings of this book are interwoven; even in the wicked reign he preached comfort; and in the pious reign he preached conviction, for, however the times change, the word of the Lord is still the same. The prophecy is *concerning Samaria and Jerusalem*, the head cities of the two kingdoms of Israel and Judah.

II. A solemn introduction to the following prophecy (*v.* 2), in which, 1. The people are summoned to draw near. "*Hear you people*" (*all of them*, so the margin reads it). It is an unusual construction; but those words with which Micah begins his prophecy are the same in the original with those wherewith Micaiah ended his, 1 Kings xxii. 28. 2. The earth is called upon, with *all that therein is*, to hear what the prophet has to say: *Hearken, O earth!* If the church, and those in it, will not hear, the earth, and those in it, shall, and shame them. 3. God himself is appealed to in testimony against this people: "*Let the Lord God be witness against you*, a witness that you had fair warning given but you would not take the warning; let the accomplishment of the prophecy prove that it was the word of God, and no word of his shall fall to the ground." He will be a witness *from his holy temple* in heaven, when he comes down to execute judgment (*v.* 3) against those that turned a deaf ear to his oracles.

JAMIESON, FAUSSET, BROWN

CHAPTER 1

Vss. 1-16. God's Wrath against Samaria and Judah; the Former Is to Be Overthrown; Such Judgments in Prospect Call for Mourning.

2.
all that therein is—*Hebrew*, "whatever fills it." Micaiah, son of Imlah, begins his prophecy similarly, "Hearken, O people, every one of you." Micah designedly uses the same preface, implying that his ministrations are a continuation of his predecessor's of the same name. Both probably had before their mind Moses' similar attestation of heaven and earth in a like case (Deut. 31:28; 32:1; cf. Isa. 1:2). **God be witness against you**—viz., that none of you can say, when the time of your punishment shall come, that you were not forewarned. The punishment denounced is stated in vs. 3, etc. **from his holy temple**—i.e., heaven (I Kings 8:30; Ps. 11:4; Jonah 2:7; cf. Rom. 1:18).

ADAM CLARKE

CHAPTER 1

1. *In the days of Jotham, Ahaz, and Hezekiah.* These three kings reigned about threescore years, and Micah is supposed to have prophesied about forty or fifty years; but no more of his prophecies have reached posterity than what are contained in this book, nor is there any evidence that any more was written. His time appears to have been spent chiefly in preaching and exhorting, and he was directed to write those parts only that were calculated to profit succeeding generations.

2. *Hear, all ye people.* The very commencement of this prophecy supposes preceding exhortations and predictions. *Hearken, O earth. Arets*, here, should be translated "land," the country of the Hebrews being only intended.

MATTHEW HENRY

III. A terrible prediction of judgments which should come upon Judah and Israel, which had its accomplishment soon after in Israel, and at length in Judah; for it is foretold, 1. That God himself will appear against them, *v.* 3. God's way towards this people had long been a way of mercy, but now he changes his way, he *comes out of his place*, and will come down. 2. That when the Creator appears against them it shall be in vain for any creature to appear for them. High places, set up for the worship of idols or for military fortifications, shall all be trampled into the dust. Neither men of *high degree*, as the mountains, nor *men of low degree*, as the valleys, shall secure either themselves or the land from the judgments of God, when they are sent with commission to lay all waste. This is applied particularly to the head city of Israel (*v.* 6): I *will make Samaria*, that is now a rich and populous city, as *a heap of the field*, as a heap of stones gathered together to be carried away, and *as plantings of a vineyard*, as hillocks of earth raised to plant vines in. Their *altars* had been as *heaps in the furrows of the fields* (Hos. xii. 11) and now their houses shall be as ruinous heaps.

IV. A charge of sin upon them, as the cause of these judgments (*v.* 5): *For the transgression of Jacob is all this.* All the calamities of Jacob and Israel are owing to their transgressions. But it is asked, *What is the transgression of Jacob?* It is idolatry; it is the *high places.* It is the idolatry of Samaria and Jerusalem, the royal cities of those two kingdoms. These were the places that had the greatest influence upon the country, by authority and example. If the transgression of Jacob is Samaria, therefore shall *Samaria become a heap.* Let the ringleaders in sin hear this and fear.

V. The punishment made to answer the sin, *v.* 7. 1. The gods they worshipped shall be destroyed: *The graven images shall be beaten to pieces* by the army of the Assyrians, *and all the idols shall be laid desolate. Samaria and her idols* were ruined together by Sennacherib (Isa. x. 11), and *their gods cast into the fire*, for *they were no gods* (Isa. xxxvii. 19). The gifts that passed between them and their gods shall be destroyed; for *all the hires thereof shall be burnt with fire.* And all this wealth shall become a prey to the idolatrous nations, and so be the *hire of a harlot* again, wages to an army of idolaters.

Verses 8–16

The funeral of a ruined kingdom.

I. The prophet is himself chief mourner (*v.* 8, 9). The prophets usually expressed their own grief for public grievances. It was not out of ill-will that they denounced the judgments of God. They dreaded it more than anything. We ought to lament the punishments of sinners as well as the sufferings of saints in this world; the weeping prophet did so (Jer. ix. 1); so did this prophet. He *makes a wailing like the dragons*, or the *jackals*, ravenous beasts that meet in the night, and *howl*, and make *hideous noises*; he mourns *as the owls*, the *screech-owls*, or *ostriches*, as some read it. Israel's case is desperate: Her *wound is incurable.* She will not by repentance and reformation help herself. There is indeed balm in Gilead and a physician there; but they will not apply to the physician. Judah likewise is in danger. The cup is going round, and is now put into Judah's hand: *The enemy has come to the gate of Jerusalem.* Soon after the destruction of Samaria the Assyrian army, under Sennacherib, laid siege to Jerusalem, came to the gate, but could not force its way any further.

II. Several places are here called upon to mourn; but they must not let the Philistines hear them (*v.* 10): *Declare it not in Gath;* this is borrowed from David's

JAMIESON, FAUSSET, BROWN

3. tread upon the high places of the earth—He shall destroy the fortified heights (cf. Deut. 32 13; 33:29) [GROTIUS]. **4.** Imagery from earthquak s and volcanic agency, to describe the terrors which attend Jehovah's coming in judgment (cf. Judg. 5:5). Neither men of high degree, as the mountains, nor men of low degree, as the valleys, can secure themselves or their land from the judgments of God. **as wax**—(Ps. 97:5; cf. Isa. 64: 1-3). The third clause, "as wax . . . ," answers to the first in the parallelism, "the mountains shall be molten"; the fourth, "as the waters . . . ," to the second, "the valleys shall be cleft." As wax melts by fire, so the mountains before God, at His approach; and as waters poured down a steep cannot stand but are diffused abroad, so the valleys shall be cleft before Jehovah. **5. For the transgression of Jacob is all this**—All these terrors attending Jehovah's coming are caused by the sins of Jacob or Israel, i.e., the whole people. **What is the transgression of Jacob?**—Taking up the question often in the mouths of the people when reproved, "What is our transgression?" (cf. Mal. 1:6,7), He answers, Is it not Samaria? Is not that city (the seat of the calf worship) the cause of Jacob's apostasy (I Kings 14: 16; 15:26, 34; 16:13, 19, 25, 30)? **and what are the high places of Judah?**—What city is the cause of the idolatries on the high places of Judah? Is it not Jerusalem (cf. II Kings 18:4)? **6.** Samaria's punishment is mentioned first, as it was to fall before Jerusalem. **as an heap of the field**—(ch. 3:12). Such a heap of stones and rubbish as is gathered out of fields, to clear them (Hos. 12:11). Palestine is of a soil abounding in stones, which are gathered out before the vines are planted (Isa. 5:2). **as plantings of a vineyard**—as a place where vines are planted. Vineyards were cultivated on the sides of hills exposed to the sun. The hill on which Samaria was built by Omri, had been, doubtless, planted with vines originally; now it is to be reduced again to its original state (I Kings 16:24). **pour down**—*dash down* the stones of the city into the valley beneath. A graphic picture of the present appearance of the ruins, which is as though "the buildings of the ancient city had been thrown down from the brow of the hill" [SCOTTISH MISSION OF INQUIRY, pp. 293, 294]. **discover the foundations**—destroy it so utterly as to lay bare its foundations (Ezek. 13:14). Samaria was destroyed by Shalmaneser. **7. all the hires**—the wealth which Israel boasted of receiving from her idols as the "rewards" or "hire" for worshipping them (Hos. 2:5, 12). **idols . . . will I . . . desolate**—i.e., give them up to the foe to strip off the silver and gold with which they are overlaid. **she gathered it of the hire of an harlot, and they shall return to the hire of an harlot**—Israel gathered (made for herself) her idols from the gold and silver received from false gods, as she thought, the "hire" of her worshipping them; and they shall again become what they had been before, the hire of spiritual harlotry, i.e., the prosperity of the foe, who also being worshippers of idols will ascribe the acquisition to their idols [MAURER]. GROTIUS explains it, *The offerings sent to Israel's temple by the Assyrians,* whose idolatry Israel adopted, shall go back to the Assyrians, her teachers in idolatry, as the hire or *fee for having taught it.* The image of a *harlot's hire* for the supposed temporal reward of spiritual fornication, is more common in Scripture (Hos. 9: 1). **8. Therefore I will wail**—The prophet first shows how the coming judgment affects himself, in order that he might affect the minds of his countrymen similarly. **stripped**—i.e., *of shoes,* or *sandals,* as the LXX translates. Otherwise "naked" would be a tautology. "Naked" means *divested of the upper garment* (Isa. 20:2). "Naked and barefoot," the sign of mourning (II Sam. 15:30). The prophet's upper garment was usually rough and coarse-haired (II Kings 1:8; Zech. 13:4). **like the dragons**—so JEROME. Rather, "the wild dogs," jackals or wolves, which wail like an infant when in distress or alone [MAURER]. (See *Note,* Job 30: 29.) **owls**—rather, "ostriches," which give a shrill and long-drawn, sigh-like cry, especially at night. **9. wound . . . incurable**—Her case, politically and morally, is desperate (Jer. 8:22). **it is come**—the wound, or impending calamity (cf. Isa. 10:28). **he is come . . . even to Jerusalem**—The evil is no longer limited to Israel. The prophet foresees Sennacherib coming even "to the gate" of the principal city. The use of "it" and "he" is appropriately distinct. "It," the calamity, "came unto" Judah, many of the inhabitants of which suffered, but did not reach the citizens of Jerusalem, "the gate" of which the foe ("he") "came unto," but did not enter (Isa. 36:1; 37:33-37). **10. Declare ye it not at Gath**—on the borders of Judea, one of the five cities of the Phi-

ADAM CLARKE

3. *For, behold, the Lord cometh forth.* See this clause, Amos iv. 13. He represents Jehovah as a mighty Conqueror, issuing from His pavilion, stepping from mountain to mountain, which rush down and fill the valleys before Him; a consuming fire accompanying Him, that melts and confounds every hill and dale, and blends all in universal confusion. *And why is all this mighty movement?* Verse 5, "For the transgression of Jacob is all this, and for the sins of the house of Israel."

5. *What is the transgression of Jacob?* Is it not something extremely grievous? Is it not that of *Samaria?* Samaria and Jerusalem, the chief cities, are infected with idolatry. Each has its high places and its idol worship, in opposition to the worship of the true God. That there was idolatry practiced by the elders of Israel, even in the temple of Jehovah, see Ezek. viii. 1, etc. As the royal cities in both kingdoms gave the example of gross idolatry, no wonder that it spread through the whole land of both Israel and Judah.

6. *I will make Samaria.* I will bring it to desolation: and, instead of being a royal city, it shall be a place for vineyards.

I will discover the foundations thereof. I will cause its walls and fortifications to be razed to the ground.

7. *All the hires thereof shall be burned.* Multitudes of women gave the money they gained by their public prostitution at the temples for the support of the priesthood, the ornamenting of the walls, altars, and images. So that these things, and perhaps several of the images themselves, were literally the hire of the harlots. God threatens here to deliver all into the hands of enemies who should seize on this wealth, and literally spend it in the same way in which it was acquired; so that *to the hire of an harlot* these things should *return.*

9. *Her wound is incurable.* Nothing shall prevent their utter ruin, for they have filled up the measure of their iniquity. *He is come . . . even to Jerusalem.* The desolation and captivity of Israel shall first take place; that of Judah shall come after.

10. *Declare ye it not at Gath.* Do not let this prediction be known among the Philistines, else they will glory over you.

MATTHEW HENRY

lamentation for Saul and Jonathan (2 Sam. i. 20), for the uncircumcised will triumph in Israel's tears. One would not gratify those that make merry with the sins or the sorrows of God's Israel. But, though it may be prudent not to give way to a noisy sorrow, yet it is duty to admit a silent one when the church of God is in distress.

"*Roll thyself in the dust* and so let the house of Judah and every house in Jerusalem become a *house of Aphrah*, a *house of dust*." Other places are here named that should be sharers in this universal mourning, the names of some of which we do not find elsewhere. Sennacherib's invasion is described by the impressions of terror it should make upon the several cities that fell in his way, Isa. x. 28, 29, &c. 1. *The inhabitants of Saphir*, which *signifies* neat and *beautiful* (*thou that dwellest fairly*, so the margin reads it), shall *pass away* into captivity, or be forced to flee, stripped of all their ornaments *and having their shame naked.*

2. *The inhabitants of Zaanan*, which signifies the *country of flocks*, a populous country, where the people are as numerous as flocks of sheep, shall yet be so taken up with their own calamities, that they shall *not come forth in the mourning of Bethezel*, which signifies a *place near*, shall not bring succour to their neighbours in distress; for *he shall receive of you his standing*; the enemy shall find footing among you.

3. As for *the inhabitants of Maroth* (which, some think, is put for Ramoth, others that it signifies the *rough places*), they *waited carefully for good*, but were disappointed; for *evil came from the Lord unto the gate of Jerusalem*, when the Assyrian army besieged it, *v.* 12.

4. Lachish was a city of Judah, which Sennacherib laid siege to, Isa. xxxvi. 1, 2. The inhabitants of that city are called to *bind the chariot to the swift beast*, to prepare for a speedy flight. God's quarrel with Lachish is that she is *the beginning of sin*, the sin of idolatry, *to the daughter of Zion* (*v.* 13); they had learned it from the ten tribes, their near neighbours, and so infected the two tribes with it.

Lachish, having been so much accessory to the sin of Israel, shall certainly be reckoned with: *Thou shalt give presents to Moresheth-gath*, a city of the Philistines, to assist thee, but it shall be in vain, for (*v.* 14) *the houses of Achzib* (a city which joined to Mareshah, or Moresheth, and is mentioned with it, Joshua xv. 44) *shall be a lie to the kings of Israel. Achzib* signifies *a lie.*

JAMIESON, FAUSSET, BROWN

listines, who would exult at the calamity of the Hebrews (II Sam. 1:20). Gratify not those who exult over the falls of the Israel of God. **weep ye not at all**—Do not betray your inward sorrow by outward weeping, within the cognizance of the enemy, lest they should exult at it. RELAND translates, "Weep not *in Acco*," i.e., Ptolemais, now St. Jean d'Acre, near the foot of Mount Carmel; allotted to Asher, but never occupied by that tribe (Judg. 1:31); Acco's inhabitants would, therefore, like Gath's, rejoice at Israel's disaster. Thus the parallelism is best carried out in all the three clauses of the verse, and there is a similar play on sounds in each, in the *Hebrew Gath*, resembling in sound the *Hebrew* for "declare"; *Acco*, resembling the *Hebrew* for "weep"; and *Aphrah*, meaning "dust." While the Hebrews were not to expose their misery to foreigners, they ought to bewail it in their own cities, e.g., Aphrah or Ophrah (Josh. 18:23; I Sam. 13:17), in the tribe of Benjamin. To "roll in the dust" marked deep sorrow (Jer. 6:26; Ezek. 27:30). **11. Pass ye away**—i.e., Thou shalt go into captivity. **inhabitant of Saphir**—a village amidst the hills of Judah, between Eleutheropolis and Ascalon, called so, from the *Hebrew* word for "beauty". Though thy name be "beauty," which heretofore was thy characteristic, thou shalt have thy "shame" made "naked." This city shall be dismantled of its walls, which are the garments, as it were, of cities; its citizens also shall be hurried into captivity, with persons exposed (Isa. 47:3; Ezek. 16:37; Hos. 2:10). **the inhabitant of Zaanan came not forth**—Its inhabitants did not come forth to console the people of Beth-ezel in their mourning, because the calamity was universal; none was exempt from it (cf. Jer. 6:25). "Zaanan" is the same as Zenan, in Judah (Josh. 15:37), meaning the "place of flocks." The form of the name used is made like the *Hebrew* for "came forth." Though in name seeming to imply that thou dost *come forth*, thou "camest not forth." **Beth-ezel**—perhaps Azal (Zech. 14:5), near Jerusalem. It means a "house on the side," or "near." Though *so near*, as its name implies, to Zaanan, Beth-ezel received no succor or sympathy from Zaanan. **he shall receive of you his standing**—"he," i.e., the foe; "his standing," i.e., his sustenance [PISCATOR]. Or, "he shall be caused a delay by you, Zaanan." He shall be brought to a stand for a time in besieging you; hence it is said just before, "Zaanan came not forth," i.e., shut herself up within her walls to withstand a siege. But it was only for a time. She, too, fell like Beth-ezel before her [VATABLUS]. MAURER construes thus: "The inhabitant of Zaanan came not forth; the mourning of Beth-ezel *takes away from* you her shelter." Though Beth-ezel be *at your side* (i.e., near), according to her name, yet as she also mourns under the oppression of the foe, she cannot give you shelter, or be *at your side* as a helper (as her name might lead you to expect), if you come forth and be intercepted by him from returning to Zaanan. **12. Maroth**—possibly the same as Maarath (Josh. 15:59). Perhaps a different town, lying between the previously mentioned towns and the capital, and one of those plundered by Rabshakeh on his way to it. **waited carefully for good**—i.e., for better fortune, but in vain [CALVIN]. GESENIUS translates, "*is grieved* for her goods" *taken away* from her. This accords with the meaning of Maroth, "bitterness," to which allusion is made in "is grieved." But the antithesis favors *English Version*, "waited carefully (i.e., anxiously) for *good;* but *evil* came down." **from the Lord**—not from *chance*. **unto the gate of Jerusalem**—after the other cities of Judah have been taken. **13.** "Bind the chariot to the swift *steed*," in order by a hasty flight to escape the invading foe. Cf. *Note*, Isaiah 36:2, on "Lachish," at which Sennacherib fixed his headquarters (II Kings 18:14, 17; Jer. 34:7). **she is the beginning of the sin to . . . Zion**—Lachish was the first of the cities of Judah, according to this passage, to introduce the worship of false gods, imitating what Jeroboam had introduced in Israel. As lying near the border of the north kingdom, Lachish was first to be infected by its idolatry, which thence spread to Jerusalem. **14. shalt thou give presents to Moresheth-gath**—that its inhabitants may send thee help. MAURER explains it, "thou shalt give a writing of renunciation to Moresheth-gath," i.e., thou shalt renounce all claim to it, being compelled to yield it up to the foe. "Thou," i.e., Judah. "Israel" in this verse is used for the kingdom of *Judah*, which was the chief representative of the whole nation of Israel. Moresheth-gath is so called because it had fallen for a time under the power of the neighboring Philistines of *Gath*. It was the native town of Micah (vs. 1). **Achzib**—meaning "lying." Achzib, as its name implies, shall prove a "lie to . . . Israel," i.e., shall dis-

ADAM CLARKE

House of Aphrah. Or "Beth-aphrah." This place is mentioned in Josh. xviii. 23, as in the tribe of Benjamin. There is a paronomasia, or play on words, here: *bebeith leaphrah aphar, "Roll thyself in the dust* in the house of dust."

11. *Inhabitant of Saphir. Sapher,* "Sephoris." *Zaanan.* Another city in the tribe of Judah, Josh. xv. 13.

Beth-ezel. A place near Jerusalem, Josh. xiv. 5. Some think that Jerusalem itself is intended by this word.

12. *The inhabitant of Maroth.* There was a city of a similar name in the tribe of Judah, Josh. xv. 59.

13. *Inhabitant of Lachish.* This city was in the tribe of Judah, Josh. xv. 39, and was taken by Sennacherib when he was coming against Jerusalem, 2 Kings xviii. 13, etc., and it is supposed that he wished to reduce this city first, that, possessing it, he might prevent Hezekiah's receiving any help from Egypt. *She is the beginning of the sin.* This seems to intimate that Lachish was the first city in Judah which received the idolatrous worship of Israel.

14. *Give presents to Moresheth-gath.* Calmet says that Moresa or Morashti, and *Achzib*, were cities not far from Gath. It is possible that when Ahaz found himself pressed by Pekah, king of Israel, he might have sent to these places for succor, that by their assistance he might frustrate the hopes of the king of Israel; and this may be the meaning of *The houses of Achzib shall be a lie to the kings of Israel.* In these verses there are several instances of the paronomasia. See v. 10, *aphar,* "dust," and *aphrah,* the name of the city. Verse 11, *tsaanan,* the city, and *yatsah,* "to go out." Verse 13, *lachish,* the

MATTHEW HENRY

5. Mareshah, that could not, or would not, help Israel, shall herself be made a prey (*v.* 15): "*I will bring an heir* (that is, an enemy) that shall take possession of thy lands, with as much assurance as if he were heir to them, and *The glory of Israel* shall come to be as Adullam, a poor despicable place."

6. The whole land of Judah seems (*v.* 16) called to weeping and mourning: "*Make thee bald*, by tearing thy hair and shaving thy head; *poll thee for thy delicate children*, that had been tenderly and nicely brought up; *enlarge thy baldness as the eagle* when she casts her feathers and is all over bald; *for they have gone into captivity from thee*, and their captivity will be the more grievous to them because they have not been inured to hardship."

JAMIESON, FAUSSET, BROWN

appoint Israel's hopes of succor from her (cf. Job 6:15-20; Jer. 15:18). Achzib was in Judah between Keilah and Mareshah (Josh. 15:44). Perhaps the same as Chezib (Gen. 38:5). **15. Yet will I bring an heir unto thee**—rather, "*the* heir." As thou art now occupied by possessors who expelled the former inhabitants, so will I bring "yet" again *the* new *possessor*, viz., the Assyrian foe. Other heirs will supplant us in every inheritance but that of heaven. There is a play upon the meaning of Mareshah, "an inheritance": there shall come the new *heir* of the *inheritance*. **Adullam the glory of Israel**—so called as being superior in situation; when it and the neighboring cities fell, Israel's glory was gone. MAURER, as *Margin*, translates, "the glory of Israel" (her chief citizens: answering to "thy delicate children," vs. 16) "shall come in flight to Adullam." *English Version* better preserves the parallelism, "the heir" in the first clause answering to "he" in the second. **16. Make thee bald, . . .**—a token of deep mourning (Erza 9:3; Job 1:20). Mourn, O land, for thy darling children. **poll**—shave off thy hair. **enlarge thy baldness**—Mourn grievously. The land is compared to a mother weeping for her children. **as the eagle**—the bald eagle, or the dark-winged vulture. In the moulting season all eagles are comparatively bald (cf. Ps. 103:5).

ADAM CLARKE

city, and *rechesh*, "the swift beast." Verse 14, *achzib*, the city, and *achzab*, "a lie." Such paronomasias were reputed ornaments by the prophets. They occur in Isaiah with great effect. See Isa. v. 7.

15. *Yet will I bring an heir unto thee, O . . . Mareshah.* Here is another instance, *haiyeresh*, "to bring an heir," and *mareshah*, the city, the name of which signifies "heirship." *Adullam the glory of Israel.* This was a fenced city in the south of Judah (see 2 Chron. xi. 7) towards the Dead Sea.

16. *Make thee bald.* Cutting off the hair was a sign of great distress, and was practiced on the death of near relatives; see Amos viii. 10. The desolation should be so great that Israel should feel it to her utmost extent, and the mourning should be like that of a mother for the death of her most delicate children. *Enlarge thy baldness as the eagle.* Referring to the molting of this bird, when in casting its feathers and breeding new ones it is very sickly, and its strength wholly exhausted. *They are gone into captivity.* This is a prediction of the captivity by Shalmaneser. Samaria, the chief city, is called on to deplore it, as then fast approaching.

MATTHEW HENRY — CHAPTER 2

Verses 1–5

I. The injustice of man contriving the evil of sin, *v.* 1, 2. It is the sin of oppression. 1. They desire that which is not their own—that is the *root of bitterness*, the root of all evil, *v.* 2. They *covet fields and houses*, as Ahab did Naboth's vineyard. 2. They invent ways of accomplishing their desire (*v.* 4). It is bad to do mischief upon a sudden thought, but much worse to do it with deliberation. They devised it *upon their beds*, when they should have been asleep. 3. They practise the iniquity they have devised, *because it is in the power of their hand*; by the help of their wealth, and the authority and interest they have. 4. They are industrious and as soon as the *morning is light* they practise it. 5. They stick at nothing to compass their designs; what they *covet* they *take away*—men's fields by violence, not only by fraud, and colour of law, but by force and with a high hand. They care not to whom they do wrong. They *oppress a man and his house*; they rob those that have families to maintain, though they send them and their wives and children begging. They *oppress a man and his heritage*; take away from men that which they have received from their ancestors, and which they have but in trust, to transmit it to their posterity.

II. The justice of God contriving punishment for this sin (*v.* 3): *Therefore thus saith the Lord, Behold, against this family do I devise an evil*, that is, against the whole kingdom, the *house of Israel*, and particularly those families in it that were cruel and oppressive. 1. He finds them very confident that they shall in some way or other escape judgment, and therefore he tells them, It is *an evil from which they shall not remove their neck*. They were children of *Belial*, that would not endure the easy yoke of God's righteous commands, but *broke those bonds* asunder, and therefore God will lay upon them the heavy yoke of his righteous judgments. 2. He finds them proud, and therefore tells them they shall not go haughtily, with *stretched-forth necks and wanton eyes, walking and mincing as they go* (Isa. iii. 16); for *this time is evil*, and the events of it are very humbling. 3. He finds them jovial, and tells them their laughter shall be turned into mourning and their joy into heaviness (*v.* 4): *In that day*, when God comes to punish you for your oppression, *shall one take up a parable against you*, and *lament with a doleful lamentation*, with a *lamentation of lamentations* (so the word is). Their enemies shall insult over them, and make a jest of their griefs, for they shall *take up a parable against them*. 4. He finds them rich in houses and lands, gained by oppression, and therefore tells them that they shall be stripped of all. They shall say, *We are utterly spoiled; he has changed the portion of my people*, so that it is now in the possession of their enemies: *How has he removed it from me! Turning away* from us in wrath, he *has divided our fields*, and given them into the hands of strangers. The margin reads it, "*Instead of restoring, he has divided our fields.*" God shall ratify what they say (*v.* 5): *Thou shalt have none to cast a cord by lot in the congregation of the Lord*, none to divide inheritances, because there shall be no inheritances to divide. It was God's land, a holy land, and therefore it was the more grievous to them to be turned out of it.

JAMIESON, FAUSSET, BROWN — CHAPTER 2

VSS. 1-13. DENUNCIATION OF THE EVILS PREVALENT: THE PEOPLE'S UNWILLINGNESS TO HEAR THE TRUTH: THEIR EXPULSION FROM THE LAND THE FITTING FRUIT OF THEIR SIN: YET JUDAH AND ISRAEL ARE HEREAFTER TO BE RESTORED. **1. devise . . . work . . . practise**—They do evil not merely on a sudden impulse, but with deliberate design. As in the former chapter sins against the first table are reproved, so in this chapter sins against the second table. A gradation: "devise" is the *conception* of the evil purpose; "work" (Ps. 58:2), or "fabricate," the *maturing* of the scheme; "practise," or "effect," the *execution* of it. **because it is in the power of their hand**—for the phrase see Genesis 31:29; Proverbs 3:27. Might, not right, is what regulates their conduct. Where they can, they commit oppression; where they do not, it is because they cannot. **2.** Parallelism, "Take by violence," answers to "take away"; "fields" and "houses," to "house" and "heritage" (i.e., one's land). **3. against this family**—against the nation, and especially against those reprobates in vss. 1, 2. **I devise an evil**—a happy antithesis between God's dealings and the Jews' dealings (vs. 1). Ye "devise evil" against your fellow countrymen; I devise evil against you. Ye devise it wrongfully, I by righteous retribution in kind. **from which ye shall not remove your necks**—as ye have done from the law. The yoke I shall impose shall be one which ye cannot shake off. They who will not bend to God's "easy yoke" (Matt. 11:29, 30), shall feel His iron yoke. **go haughtily**—(Cf. *Note*, Jer. 6:28). Ye shall not walk as now with neck haughtily uplifted, for the yoke shall press down your "neck." **this time is evil**—rather, "for *that* time shall be an evil time," viz., the time of the carrying away into captivity (cf. Amos 5:13; Eph. 5:16). **4. one take up a parable against you**—i.e., Some of your foes shall do so, taking in derision from your own mouth your "lamentation," viz., "We be spoiled . . . ." **lament with a doleful lamentation**—lit., "lament with a lamentation of lamentations." *Hebrew, naha, nehi, nihyah*, the repetition representing the continuous and monotonous wail. **he hath changed the portion of my people**—a charge of injustice against Jehovah. He transfers to other nations the sacred territory assigned as the rightful portion of our people (ch. 1:15). **turning away he hath divided our fields**—Turning away from us to the enemy, He hath divided among them our fields. CALVIN, as *Margin*, explains, "*Instead of restoring* our territory, He hath divided our fields among our enemies, each of whom henceforward will have an interest in keeping what he hath gotten: so that we are utterly shut out from hope of restoration." MAURER translates as a noun, "He hath divided our fields *to a rebel*," i.e., to the foe who is a rebel against the true God, and a worshipper of idols. So "backsliding," i.e., backslider (Jer. 49:4). *English Version* gives a good sense; and is quite tenable in the *Hebrew*. **5. Therefore**—resumed from vs. 3. On account of your crimes described in vss. 1, 2. **thou**—the ideal individual ("me," vs. 4), representing the guilty people in whose name he spoke. **none that . . . cast a cord by lot**—none who shall have any possession *measured out*. **in the congregation of the Lord**—among

ADAM CLARKE — CHAPTER 2

1. *Woe to them that devise iniquity!* Who lay schemes and plans for transgressions; and make these things their nocturnal meditations, that, having fixed their plan, they may begin to execute it as soon as it is light in the morning.

2. *They covet fields.* These are the rich and mighty in the land; and, like Ahab, they will take the vineyard or inheritance of any poor Naboth on which they may fix their covetous eye, so that they take away even the heritage of the poor.

3. *Against this family* (the Israelites) *do I devise an evil.* You have devised the evil of plundering the upright; I will devise the evil to you of punishment for your conduct; you shall have your *necks* brought under the yoke of servitude. Tiglath-pileser ruined this kingdom, and transported the people to Assyria, under the reign of Hezekiah, king of Judah; and Micah lived to see this catastrophe. See on v. 9.

4. *Take up a parable against you.* Your wickedness and your punishment shall be subjects of common conversation, and a "funeral dirge" shall be composed and sung for you as for the dead. The lamentation is that which immediately follows: *We be utterly spoiled;* and ends, "Are these his doings?" v. 7

5. *None that shall cast a cord.* You will no more have your inheritance divided to you by lot, as it was to your fathers; you shall have neither fields nor possessions of any kind.

MATTHEW HENRY

Verses 6–11

Two sins charged upon the people of Israel, and judgments for each—persecuting God's prophets and oppressing God's poor.

I. Persecuting God's prophets, suppressing and silencing them, is a sin that provokes God, for his sending prophets to us is a sure token of his goodwill.

1. The opposition which this people gave to God's prophets: They *said to those that prophesy, Prophesy ye not*, as Isa. xxx. 10. They *said to the seers, "See not;* do not trouble us with accounts of what you have seen, nor bring us any such frightful messages." They must either not prophesy at all or prophesy only what is pleasing. Some read it, *Prophesy not; let these prophesy.* Let not those prophesy that tell us of our faults, and threaten us, but *let those prophesy* that will flatter us in our sins, and cry peace to us. If a prophet will but tell them that it is lawful for them to drink as much as they please of their wine and strong drink, that they *shall have peace though they go on and add drunkenness to thirst*, this is a man after their own heart. *He shall even be the prophet of this people;* such a man will not only associate with them in their rioting and revellings, but will pretend to consecrate their sensualities by his prophecies.

2. They are here reproved (*v.* 7): "*O thou that art named the house of Jacob*, wilt thou silence those that prophesy, and forbid them to speak in God's name? *Is the Lord's Spirit straitened?* In silencing the Lord's prophets you do what you can to silence his Spirit too. Can you make the Spirit of God your servant? Will you forbid him to say what is displeasing to you? If you silence the prophets, yet the Spirit of the Lord will find out other ways to reach your consciences? Can your unbelief frustrate the divine counsels?" As Jews: "You are *named the house of Jacob*, and this is your honour; but *are these* the doings of your father Jacob?" Consider how unreasonable the thing is in itself: *Do not my words do good to those that walk uprightly?* God owns the words of the prophets to be his words (they are *my words*) and by them aims and designs to do good to mankind (Ps. cxix. 68); and will you hinder the great benefactor from doing good? It is certainly for the common good of states and kingdoms that religion should be encouraged.

3. They are threatened with punishment for this sin. They shall be deprived of the benefit of a faithful ministry. Since they say, *Prophesy not*, God will take them at their word, and *they shall not prophesy to them.* Let the physician no longer attend the patient that will not be healed, for he will not be ruled. They shall be given up to the blind guidance of an unfaithful ministry.

II. Oppressing God's poor is another sin they are charged with (*v.* 1, 2),

The sin is described, *v.* 8, 9. Those who formerly rose up against the enemies of the nation, now of late *rose up as enemies of the nation*, and, instead of defending it, destroyed it. They made a prey of men, that were travelling on the way, that *pass by securely as men averse from war*, about their lawful occasions. Those they set upon, and *pulled off the robe with the garment from them*, that is, they stripped them. Of women (*v.* 9): *The women of my people have you cast out from their pleasant houses. They devoured widows' houses* (Matt. xxiii. 14), turned them out of the possession of them. Of children, whose age entitles them to a tender usage: *From their children have you taken away my glory for ever.* It was the glory of the Israelites' children that they were free, but they enslaved them, sold them to strangers, sent them into idolatrous countries. The sentence is passed upon them for it (*v.* 10): "*Arise ye, and depart;* prepare to quit this land. You shall have neither contentment nor continuance in it, *because it is polluted* by your wickedness. You shall not only be obliged to depart out of this land, but *it shall destroy you even with a sore destruction*; you shall either be turned out of it or you shall be ruined in it."

JAMIESON, FAUSSET, BROWN

the people consecrated to Jehovah. By covetousness and violence (vs. 2) they had forfeited "the portion of Jehovah's people." This is God's implied answer to their complaint of injustice (vs. 4). **6. Prophesy ye not, say they**—viz., the Israelites say to the true prophets, when announcing unwelcome truths. Therefore God judicially abandons them to their own ways: "The prophets, by whose ministry they might have been saved from *shame* (ignominious captivity), shall not (i.e., no longer) prophesy to them" (Isa. 30:10; Amos 2:12; 7:16). MAURER translates the latter clause, "they shall not prophesy *of such things*" (as in vss. 3-5, these being rebellious Israel's words); "let them not prophesy"; "they never cease from insult" (from prophesying insults to us). *English Version* is supported by the parallelism: wherein the similarity of sound and word implies how exactly God makes their punishment answer to their sin, and takes them at their own word. "Prophesy," lit., "drop" (Deut. 32:2; Ezek. 21:2). **7. O thou . . . named the house of Jacob**—priding thyself on the *name*, though having naught of the spirit, of thy progenitor. Also, bearing the name which ought to remind thee of God's favors granted to thee because of His covenant with Jacob. **is the Spirit of the Lord straitened?**—Is His *compassion* contracted within narrower limits now than formerly, so that He should delight in your destruction (cf. Ps. 77:7-9; Isa. 59:1, 2)? **are these his doings?**—i.e., Are such threatenings His delight? Ye dislike the prophets' threatenings (vs. 6): but who is to blame? Not God, for He delights in blessing, rather than threatening; but yourselves (vs. 8) who provoke His threatenings [GROTIUS]. CALVIN translates, "Are your doings such as are prescribed by Him?" Ye boast of being God's peculiar people: Do ye then conform your lives to God's law? **do not my words do good to him that walketh uprightly**—Are not My words good to the upright? If your ways were upright, My words would not be threatening (cf. Ps. 18:26; Matt. 11:19; John 7:17). **8.** Your ways are not such that I can deal with you as I would with the upright. **Even of late**—lit., "yesterday," "long ago." So "of old." *Hebrew*, "yesterday" (Isa. 30:33); "heretofore," *Hebrew*, "since yesterday" (Josh. 3:4). **my people is risen up as an enemy**—i.e., has rebelled against My precepts; also has become *an enemy* to the unoffending passers-by. **robe with the garment**—Not content with the outer "garment," ye greedily rob passers-by of the ornamental "robe" fitting the body closely and flowing down to the feet [LUDOVICUS DE DIEU] (Matt. 5:40). **as men averse from war**—in antithesis to (*My people*) "as an enemy." Israel treats the innocent passers-by, though "averse from war," as an enemy" would treat captives in his power, stripping them of their habiliments as lawful spoils. GROTIUS translates, "as men *returning* from war," i.e., as captives over whom the right of war gives the victors an absolute power. *English Version* is supported by the antithesis. **9. The women of my people**—i.e., the *widows* of the men slain by you (vs. 2) ye cast out from their homes which had been their delight, and seize on them for yourselves. **from their children**—i.e., from the orphans of the widows. **taken away my glory**—viz., their substance and raiment, which, being the fruit of God's blessing on the young, reflected *God's glory.* Thus Israel's crime was not merely robbery, but sacrilege. Their sex did not save the women, nor their age the children from violence. **for ever**—There was no repentance. They persevered in sin. The pledged garment was to be restored to the poor before sunset (Exod. 22:26, 27); but these *never* restored their unlawful booty. **10. Arise ye, and depart**—not an exhortation to the children of God to depart out of an ungodly world, as it is often applied; though that sentiment is a scriptural one. This world is doubtless not our "rest," being "polluted" with sin: it is our passage, not our portion; our aim, not our home (II Cor. 6:17; Heb. 13:14). The imperatives express the *certainty* of the *future* event *predicted.* "Since such are your doings (cf. vss. 7, 8, etc.), My sentence on you is irrevocable (vss. 4, 5), however distasteful to you (vs. 6); ye who have *cast out* others from their homes and possessions (vss. 2, 8, 9) must *arise, depart*, and be cast out of your own (vss. 4, 5): *for this is not your rest*" (Num. 10:33; Deut. 12:9; Ps. 95:11). Canaan was designed to be a *rest* to them after their wilderness fatigues. But it is to be so no longer. Thus God refutes the people's self-confidence, as if God were bound to them inseparably. The promise (Ps. 132:14) is quite consistent with temporary withdrawal of God from Israel for their sins. **it shall destroy you**—*The land* shall spew you out, because of the defilements wherewith ye "polluted" it (Lev. 18:25, 28; Jer. 3:2;

ADAM CLARKE

6. *Prophesy ye not.* Do not predict any more evils—we have as many as we can bear. We are utterly ruined—shame and confusion cover our faces. The original is singular, and expressive of sorrow and sobbing. Literally, "Do not cause it to rain; they will cause it to rain; they cannot make it rain sooner than this; confusion shall not depart from us." To "rain" often means to "preach," to "prophesy"; Ezek. xxv. 46; xxi. 2; Amos vii. 16; Deut. xxxii. 2; Job xxix. 22; Prov. v. 3. The last line Bishop Newcome translates, "For he shall not remove from himself reproaches"; and paraphrases, "The true prophet will subject himself to public disgrace by exercising his office."

8. *My people is risen up as an enemy.* You are not only opposed to Me, but you are enemies to each other. You rob and spoil each other. You plunder the peaceable passenger, depriving him of both his upper and under garment.

9. *The women of my people.* These two verses may probably relate to the war made on Ahaz by Rezin, king of Syria, and Pekah, king of Israel. They fell suddenly upon the Jews; killed in one day 120,000, took 200,000 captive, and carried away much spoil. Thus they rose up against them as enemies, when there was peace between the two kingdoms; spoiled them of their goods, carried away men, women, and children, till at the remonstrances of the prophet Oded they were released. See 2 Chron. xxviii. 6, etc. Micah lived in the days of Ahaz, and might have seen the barbarities which he here describes.

10. *Arise ye, and depart.* Prepare for your captivity; you shall have no resting place here. The very land is *polluted* by your iniquities, and shall vomit you out, and it shall be destroyed; and the destruction of it shall be great and sore. Some think this is an exhortation to the godly to leave a land that was to be destroyed so speedily.

MATTHEW HENRY

We may understand *v.* 11 as a threatening: *If a man be found walking in the spirit of falsehood,* he *shall be the prophet of this people.* Since they will not admit the *truth in the love of it,* God will send them *strong delusions to believe a lie,* 2 Thess. ii. 10, 11.

Verses 12–13

The chapter concludes, as is usual in the prophets, with promises of mercy, which were in part fulfilled when the Jews returned out of Babylon, and had their full accomplishment in the kingdom of the Messiah. 1. Whereas they were dispersed, they shall be brought together again (*v.* 12): "*I will surely assemble, O Jacob! all of thee,* all that are *named of the house of Jacob* (*v.* 7) now expelled your country, *v.* 10. *I will surely gather the remnant of Israel. I will put them together as the sheep of Bozrah.*" Sheep are sociable creatures; they shall be *as the flock in the midst of their fold,* their own fold, where they are safe under the shepherd's eye and care; and *they shall make great noise* (as numerous flocks and herds do, with their bleatings and lowing) *by reason of the multitude of men,* not by reason of their strifes and contentions, but by reason of their great numbers. This was accomplished when Christ by his gospel gathered together in one *all the children of God that were scattered abroad,* and united both Jews and Gentiles in one fold, and under one Shepherd. 2. Whereas God had seemed to desert them, and cast them off, now he will help them through all the difficulties in the way of their return and deliverance (*v.* 13): *The breaker has come up before them,* to break down all opposition, and clear the road for them; and under his guidance *they have broken up, and have passed through the gate,* the door of escape out of their captivity. *Their king shall pass before them,* to head them in the way, even Jehovah (he is their king) *on the head of them,* as he was on the head of the armies of Israel through the wilderness. Christ is the church's King; he is Jehovah; he passes before them, brings them out of the land of their captivity, into the land of their rest. Bishop Pearson applies it to the resurrection of Christ. *The breaker has gone up before us* out of the grave, and has carried away its gates, and by that breach we go out.

JAMIESON, FAUSSET, BROWN

Ezek. 36:12-14). **11. walking in the spirit**—The *Hebrew* means also "wind." "If a man professing to have the 'spirit' of inspiration (Ezek. 13:3; so 'man of the spirit,' i.e., one claiming inspiration, Hos. 9:7), but really walking in 'wind' (prophecy void of nutriment for the soul, and unsubstantial as the *wind*) and falsehood, do lie, saying (that which ye like to hear), I will prophesy. . . .," even such a one, however false his prophecies, since he flatters your wishes, shall be your prophet (cf. vs. 6; Jer. 5:31). **prophesy . . . of wine**—i.e., of an abundant supply of wine. **12.** A sudden transition from threats to the promise of a glorious restoration. Cf. a similar transition in Hos. 1:9, 10. Jehovah, too, prophesies of good things to come, but not like the false prophets, "of wine and strong drink" (vs. 11). After I have sent you into captivity as I have just threatened, I will thence assemble you again (cf. ch. 4:6, 7). **all of thee**—The restoration from Babylon was partial. Therefore that here meant must be still future, when "*all* Israel shall be saved" (Rom. 11:26). The restoration from "Babylon" (specified (ch. 4:10) is the type of the future one. **Jacob . . . Israel**—the ten tribes' kingdom (Hos. 12:2) and Judah (II Chron. 19:8; 21:2, 4). **remnant**—the elect remnant, which shall survive the previous calamities of Judah, and from which the nation is to spring into new life (Isa. 6:13; 10:20-22). **as the sheep of Bozrah**—a region famed for its rich pastures (cf. II Kings 3:4). GESENIUS for Bozrah translates, "sheepfold." But thus there will be tautology unless the next clause be translated, "in the midst of their *pasture.*" *English Version* is more favored by the *Hebrew.* **13. The breaker**—Jehovah Messiah, who *breaks* through every obstacle in the way of their restoration: not as formerly *breaking forth* to destroy them for transgression (Exod. 19:22; Judg. 21:15), but breaking a way for them through their enemies. **they**—the returning Israelites and Jews. **passed through the gate**—i.e., through the gate of the foe's city in which they had been captives. So the image of the resurrection (Hos. 13:14) represents Israel's restoration. **their king**—"the Breaker," peculiarly "*their* king" (Hos. 3:5; Matt. 27:37). **pass before them**—as He did when they went up out of Egypt (Exod. 13:21; Deut. 1:30, 33). **the Lord on the head of them**—Jehovah at their head (Isa. 52:12). Messiah, the second person, is meant (cf. Exod. 23:20; 33:14; Isa. 63:9).

ADAM CLARKE

11. *If a man walking in the spirit and falsehood.* The meaning is: If a man who professes to be divinely inspired do lie, by prophesying of plenty, then such a person shall be received as a true prophet by this people.

12. *I will surely assemble.* This is a promise of the restoration of Israel from captivity. He compares them to a flock of sheep rushing together to their fold, the hoofs of which make a wonderful noise or clatter.

13. *The breaker is come up.* He who is to give them deliverance, and lead them out on the way of their return. He who takes down the hurdles, or makes a gap in the wall or hedge, to permit them to pass through. This may ap[ply] to those human agents that shall permit and order their return. And Jehovah being at their *head* may refer to their final restoration, when the Lord Jesus shall become their Leader, they having returned unto Him as the Shepherd and Bishop of their souls, and they and the Gentiles forming one fold under one Shepherd, to go no more out into captivity forever.

MATTHEW HENRY — CHAPTER 3

Verses 1–7

I. Let the princes hear their charge and their doom. The *heads of Jacob,* and the *princes of the house of Israel,* are called upon to *hear* what the prophet has to say to them, *v.* 1. The prophet faithfully discharged his trust: "*And I said, Hear, O princes!* Is it not your business to administer justice impartially, and not to *know faces*" (as the Hebrew phrase for partiality and respect of persons is), "but to *know judgment,* and the merits of every cause?" Therefore stand still, and hear your own judgment.

2. They had transgressed the rules of judgment, though they knew what they were. They *hate the good and love the evil.* This being their principle, their practice is according to it; they are cruel towards those that are under their power, and whoever lies at their mercy will find that they have none. They fleece the flock they should feed; instead of feeding it, they feed upon it, Ezek. xxxiv. 2. They *eat the flesh of my people.* It is fit that they should be clothed with the wool, but that will not serve: They *flay the skin from them, v.* 3. By imposing heavier taxes and exacting them with rigour, by fines, and corporal punishments, for pretended crimes, they ruined their subjects, took away from some their lives, from others their livelihoods, and were as beasts of prey, rather than shepherds. "They *break their bones* to come at the marrow, and *chop* the flesh *in pieces as for the pot.*"

3. How they might expect that God should deal with them. The rule is fixed, Those shall have judgment without mercy that have shown no mercy (*v.* 4). *With the froward God will show himself froward,* and often gives us cruel and unmerciful men into the hands of those who are cruel and unmerciful themselves.

II. Let the prophets hear their charge too; they were such as prophesied falsely, and the princes bore rule by their means.

1. Their sin: They made it their business to flatter and deceive the people. "They make them to err by crying peace, by telling them that all shall be well with them; whereas they are in the paths of sin, and within a step of ruin. They *cry peace,* but they *bite*

JAMIESON, FAUSSET, BROWN — CHAPTER 3

VSS. 1-12. THE SINS OF THE PRINCES, PROPHETS, AND PRIESTS: THE CONSEQUENT DESOLATION OF ZION. **1. princes**—magistrates or judges. **Is it not for you?**—Is it not your special function (Jer. 5:4, 5)?

judgment—justice. Ye sit in judgment on others; surely then ye ought to know the judgment for injustice which awaits yourselves (Rom. 2:1).

2. pluck off their skin . . . flesh—rob their fellow countrymen of all their substance (Ps. 14:4; Prov. 30:14).

3. pot . . . flesh within . . . caldron—manifold species of cruel oppressions. Cf. Ezekiel 24:3, etc., containing, as to the coming punishment, the same figure as is here used of the sin: implying that the sin and punishment exactly correspond. **4. Then**—at the time of judgment, which Micah takes for granted, so certain is it (cf. ch. 2:3). **they cry. . . . but he will not hear**—just as those oppressed by them had formerly cried, and they would not hear. Their prayer shall be rejected, because it is the mere cry of nature for deliverance from pain, not that of repentance for deliverance from sin. **ill in their doings**—Men cannot expect to do ill and fare well. **5.** Here he attacks the false prophets, as before he had attacked the "princes." **make my people err**—knowingly mislead My people by not denouncing their sins as incurring judgment.

ADAM CLARKE — CHAPTER 3

1. *Hear . . . O heads of Jacob.* The metaphor of the flock is still carried on. The chiefs of Jacob, and the princes of Israel, instead of taking care of the flocks, defending them, and finding them pasture, oppressed them in various ways. They are like wolves, who tear the skin of the sheep and the flesh off their bones. This applies to all unjust and oppressive rulers. Suetonius tells us, in his *Life of Tiberius,* that when the governors of provinces wrote to the emperor, entreating him to increase the tributes, he wrote back: "It is the property of a good shepherd to shear his sheep, not to skin them."

4. *Then shall they cry.* When calamity comes upon these oppressors, they shall cry for deliverance: but they shall not be heard because, in their unjust exactions upon the people, they went on ruthlessly, and would not hear the cry of the oppressed.

MATTHEW HENRY

with their teeth," which perhaps is meant of their biting their own lips, as we are apt to do when we would suppress something. They *bite with their teeth, and cry peace*; that is, they flatter and compliment those that will feed them with good bits, but as for those that *put not into their mouths,* they look upon them as their enemies. They preach either comfort or terror to men, not according as they are to God, but as they are to them.

2. The sentence passed upon them for this sin, *v.* 6, 7 *Night shall be upon them,* a dark cold night of calamity, such as they, in their flattery, led the people to hope would never come. *It shall be dark unto you; the sun shall go down over the prophets;* All comfort shall depart and all hope. Their mind shall be full of confusion, their heads shall be clouded, and their own thoughts shall trouble them. They kept others in the dark, and now God will bring them into the dark. Thereby they shall be silenced, and all their pretensions to prophecy for ever shamed. They never had any true vision; it was all a sham, and they were cheats and impostors. They shall not have so much as a counterfeit vision to produce, they shall be *ashamed,* and *confounded,* and *cover their lips.*

Verses 8–12

I. The prophet experiences a divine power going along with him in his work. He could not but speak the word that God put into his mouth. The false prophets were *sensual, not having the Spirit,* but truly (says Micah) *I am full of power by the Spirit of the Lord, v.* 8. The qualifications with which this prophet was endued: He was *full of power and of judgment, and of might*; he had an ardent love to God and to the souls of men, a deep concern for his glory and their salvation, and a flaming zeal against sin. He had likewise courage to reprove it and witness against it. He was a man of wisdom as well as courage; in all his preaching there was light as well as heat, and a spirit of wisdom as well as of zeal. Those who act honestly may act boldly; and those who are sure that they have a commission from God need not be afraid of opposition from men. He *declared to Jacob his transgression and to Israel his sin.* Since few have meekness enough to receive reproof, those have need of a great deal of boldness, who are to give reproofs, and must pray for a spirit both of wisdom and might.

II. The prophet exerts this power in dealing with the *heads of the house of Jacob.* He repeats the summons (*v.* 9), the same that we had *v.* 1, to *the princes of the house of Israel,* yet he means those of *Judah*; for it appears (Jer. xxvi. 18, 19, where *v.* 12 is quoted) that this was spoken in Hezekiah's kingdom; but, the ten tribes being gone into captivity, Judah is all that is now left of Jacob and Israel. He gives them their titles of *heads* and *princes.* Ministers must be faithful to great men, but they must not be rude and uncivil to them.

1. The great wickedness of the *princes, priests,* and *prophets*; they were covetous, and prostituted their offices to their love of money. (1) The *princes abhorred all judgment*; they *perverted all equity,* when it could not be made pliable to their secular interests. It is laid to their charge (*v.* 10) that *they build up Zion with blood.* "They pretend, in justification of their extortion, that they add new streets and squares to the holy cities, and adorn them. But it is *with blood* and *with iniquity,* and therefore it cannot prosper; nor will their intentions of good to the city of God justify their contradictions to the law of God." *They judge for reward* (*v.* 11). The most righteous cause shall not be carried without a fee, and for a fee the most unrighteous cause shall be carried. The priests' work was to teach the people, but they *teach for hire,* and will be hired to teach anything, which they know will please. The prophets *divine for money.* A man might have what oracle he would from them if he would but pay them for it.

2. They *lean upon the Lord,* and because they are, in profession, his people, think there is neither harm nor danger in their wicked practices. Faith builds upon the Lord, rests in him, and relies upon him, as the soul's foundation; presumption only *leans upon the Lord* as a prop, makes use of him to serve a turn, while still the world is the foundation that is built upon. "*Is not the Lord among us?* Have we not the tokens of his presence with us, his temple, his ark, his lively oracles?" They are *haughty because of the holy mountain* (Zeph. iii. 11), as if their church privileges would palliate the worst of practices. They are confident of their own safety: *No evil can come upon us.* Many are rocked asleep in a fatal security by their church-privileges, as if those would protect them in sin.

3. The doom passed upon them for their wickedness, notwithstanding (*v.* 12): *Therefore shall Zion*

JAMIESON, FAUSSET, BROWN

bite with . . . teeth, and cry, Peace—i.e., who, so long as they are supplied with food, promise *peace* and prosperity in their prophecies. **he that putteth not into their mouths, they . . . prepare war against him**—Whenever they are not supplied with food, they foretell war and calamity. **prepare war**—lit., "sanctify war," i.e., proclaim it as a *holy* judgment of God because they are not fed (*Note,* Jer. 6:4; cf. Isa. 13:3; Joel 1:14). **6 night . . . dark**—Calamities shall press on you so overwhelming as to compel you to cease pretending to *divine* (Zech. 13:4). Darkness is often the image of calamity (Isa. 8:22; Amos 5:18; 8:9). **7. cover their lips**—The Orientals prided themselves on the moustache and beard (*Margin,* "upper lip"). To *cover* it, therefore, was a token of shame and sorrow (Lev. 13:45; Ezek. 24:17, 22). "They shall be so ashamed of themselves as *not to dare to open their mouths* or boast of the name of prophet" [CALVIN]. **there is no answer of God**—They shall no more profess to have responses from God, being struck dumb with calamities (vs. 6).

8. I—in contrast to the false prophets (vss. 5, 7). **full of power**—that which "the Spirit of Jehovah" imparts for the discharge of the prophetical function (Luke 1:17; 24:49; Acts 1:8). **judgment**—a sense of *justice* [MAURER]; as opposed to the false prophets' speaking to please men, not from a regard to truth. Or, "judgment" to discern between graver and lighter offenses, and to denounce punishments accordingly [GROTIUS]. **might**—moral *intrepidity* in speaking the truth at all costs (II Tim. 1:7).

to declare unto Jacob his . . . sin—(Isa. 58:1). Not to flatter the sinner as the false prophets do with promises of peace.

9. Hear—resumed from vs. 1. Here begins the leading subject of the prophecy: a demonstration of his assertion that he is "full of power by the Spirit of Jehovah" (vs. 8).

10. They—change of person from "ye" (vs. 9); the third person puts them to a greater distance as estranged from Him. It is, lit., "*Whosoever* builds," *singular.* **build up Zion with blood**—build on it stately mansions with wealth obtained by the condemnation and murder of the innocent (Jer. 22:13; Ezek. 22:27; Hab. 2:12).

11. heads thereof—the princes of Jerusalem. **judge for reward**—take bribes as judges (ch. 7:3). **priests teach for hire**—It was their duty to teach the law and to decide controversies gratuitously (Lev. 10:11; Deut. 17:11; Mal. 2:7; cf. Jer. 6:13; Jude 11). **prophets . . . divine**—i.e., false prophets.

Is not the Lord among us?—viz., in the temple (Isa. 48:2; Jer. 7:4, 8-11).

ADAM CLARKE

5. *That bite with their teeth.* That eat to the full; that are well provided for, and as long as they are so, prophesy smooth things, *and cry, Peace;* i.e., You shall have nothing but peace and prosperity. Whereas the true prophet, who *putteth not into their mouths,* who makes no provision for their evil propensities, they *prepare war against him.*

6. *Night shall be unto you.* You shall have no spiritual light, nor will God give you any revelation of His will. *The sun shall go down over the prophets.* They prospered for a while, causing the people to err; but they shall also be carried into captivity, and then the sun of their prosperity shall go down forever.

7. *Shall the seers be ashamed.* For the false visions of comfort and prosperity which they pretended to see. *And the diviners confounded.* Who pretended to foretell future prosperity; for they themselves are now enthralled in that very captivity which the true prophets foretold, and which the false prophets said should not happen.

10. *They build up Zion with blood.* They might cry out loudly against that butchery practiced by Pekah, king of Israel, and Pul, coadjutor of Rezin, against the Jews. See on chap. ii. 9. But these were by no means clear themselves; for if they strengthened the city, or decorated the Temple, it was by the produce of their exactions and oppressions of the people.

12. *Therefore shall Zion . . . be plowed as a field.* Thus did the Romans treat Jerusalem

MATTHEW HENRY

for your sake be ploughed as a field. This passage is quoted as a bold word spoken by Micah (Jer. xxvi. 18), which yet Hezekiah and his princes took well; they repented and reformed, and so the execution of this threatening did not come in those days. It is Zion that shall be ploughed as a field, the building burnt to the ground and levelled with it. Some observe that this was literally fulfilled in the destruction of Jerusalem by the Romans, when the ground on which the city stood was ploughed up in token of its utter desolation. The wickedness of those who preside in them brings the ruin: "It is *for your sake* that *Zion shall be ploughed as a field*; you pretend to build up Zion, but doing it by blood and iniquity, you pull it down."

CHAPTER 4

Verses 1–7

It is a very comfortable *but* with which this chapter begins. When we sometimes see the corruptions of the church, *Zion ploughed as a field*, we are ready to fear that it will one day perish. But let not our faith fail; out of the ashes of the church another phoenix shall arise. The first words of this chapter bring in *the mountain of the Lord's house* as much dignified by being frequented as ever it had been disgraced by being deserted. Though Zion be ploughed as a field, yet God has not *cast off his people*, but by the fall of the Jews salvation has come to the Gentiles, Rom. xi. 11, 12. This is the mystery which God by the prophet here shows us, the same in the first three verses of this chapter which another prophet said (Isa. ii. 2–4).

I. There shall be a church for God set up in the world, after the defection and destruction of the Jewish church, *in the days of the Messiah.* The people of God shall be incorporated by a new charter, a new spiritual way of worship shall be enacted; better privileges shall be granted by this new charter, and better provision made for establishing the kingdom of God among men than had been made by the Old Testament constitution: *The mountain of the house of the Lord* shall again appear firm ground, *v.* 1. A church shall be set up in the world, to which the Lord will be daily *adding such as shall be saved.*

II. This church shall be firmly founded and well-built: It *shall be established in the top of the mountains*; Christ himself will build it upon a rock.

III. It shall become eminent and conspicuous: It *shall be exalted above the hills*, observed with wonder for its growing greatness from small beginnings. The glory of this latter house is greater than that of the former, Hag. ii. 9. See 2 Cor. iii. 7, 8, &c.

IV. There shall be a great accession of converts to it and succession of converts in it. *People shall flow unto it* as a constant stream of believers flowing in from all parts into the church. In gospel-times many nations shall flow into the church. Ministers shall be sent forth to *disciple all nations*, and they shall not *labour in vain.* "*He will teach us of his ways*, what is the way in which he would have us to walk with him and in which we may depend upon him to meet us graciously."

V. A new revelation shall be published to the world, on which the church shall be founded, and by which multitudes shall be brought into it: *For the law shall go forth of Zion, and the word of the Lord from Jerusalem.* The gospel is here called *the word of the Lord.* It began to be spoken by the Lord Christ himself, Heb. ii. 3. And it is *a law*, a law of faith; we are *under the law to Christ.* This was to go *forth from Jerusalem, from Zion.* Thence the gospel must take rise, to show the connection between the Old Testament and the New, that the gospel is not set up in opposition to the law, but is an explication and illustration of it, and a *branch growing out of its roots.* It was in Jerusalem that Christ preached and wrought miracles; there he died, rose again, and ascended; there the Spirit was poured out; and those that were to preach repentance and remission of sins to all nations were ordered to *begin at Jerusalem.*

VI. A convincing power should go along with the gospel of Christ, in all places where it should be preached (*v.* 3): *He shall judge among many people.*

VII. A disposition to mutual peace and love shall be the happy effect of the setting up of the kingdom of the Messiah, Tit. iii. 2, 3. Those who, before their conversion, did injuries, and would bear none, after their conversion can bear injuries, but will do none. As far as the gospel prevails it makes men peaceable, for such is *the wisdom from above*; it is *gentle and easy to be entreated*; and, if nations were but leavened by it, there would be universal peace. The art of war, instead of being improved (which some reckon the glory of a kingdom), shall be forgotten and laid

JAMIESON, FAUSSET, BROWN

12. Jeremiah 26:18 quotes this verse. The Talmud and Maimonides record that at the destruction of Jerusalem by the Romans under Titus, Terentius Rufus, who was left in command of the army, with a ploughshare tore up the foundations of the temple. **mountain of the house**—the height on which the temple stands. **as the high places of the forest**—shall become as heights in a forest overrun with wild shrubs and brushwood.

CHAPTER 4

VSS. 1-13. TRANSITION TO THE GLORY, PEACE, KINGDOM, AND VICTORY OF ZION. **1-3.** Almost identical with Isaiah 2:2-4.

the mountain of the house of the Lord—which just before (ch. 3:12) had been doomed to be a wild forest height. Under Messiah, its elevation is to be not that of situation, but of moral dignity, as the seat of God's universal empire.

people shall flow into it—In Isaiah it is "all nations": a more universal prophecy.

3. rebuke—convict of sin (John 16:8, 9); and subdue with judgments (Ps. 2:5, 9; 110:5, 6; Rev. 2:27; 12:5). **many people . . . strong nations afar off**—In Isaiah 2:4 it is "the nations . . . many people."

ADAM CLARKE

when it was taken by Titus. Turnus Rufus caused a plough to be drawn over all the courts of the Temple to signify that it should never be rebuilt, and the place serve only for agricultural purposes. See Matt. xxiv. 2. Thus *Jerusalem* became *heaps*, an indiscriminate mass of ruins and rubbish; and *the mountain of the house*, Mount Moriah, on which the Temple stood, became so much neglected after the total destruction of the Temple that it soon resembled the *high places of the forest.* What is said here may apply also to the ruin of the Temple by Nebuchadnezzar in the last year of the reign of Zedekiah, the last king of the Jews.

CHAPTER 4

1-4. *But in the last days it shall come to pass.* These four verses contain, says Bishop Newcome, a prophecy that was to be fulfilled by the coming of the Messiah, when the Gentiles were to be admitted into covenant with God, and the apostles were to preach the gospel, beginning at Jerusalem, Luke xxiv. 47; Acts ii. 14, etc.; when Christ was to be the spiritual Judge and King of many people, was to convince many nations of their errors and vices, and was to found a religion which had the strongest tendency to promote peace. See Isa. ii. 2, etc.

F. B. MEYER:

"In the latter days it shall come to pass" (v. 1). These words are repeated in Isa. 2:2–4. The holy men that wrote of their predecessors. Amid the dark night this promise of God shone like binary stars.

No doubt they have been fulfilled in the Gospel dispensation. In a deep and true sense it has come to pass that the Lord's house has been established in the top of the mountains, and has been exalted above the hills. The Church is a conspicuous and influential object among the forces of the world; and peoples are flowing towards it. In very many cases whole nations have flung away the religion of their ancestors, and gathered within that Christian temple which has been built upon the foundations of Judaism. Out of Zion there has gone forth the law; and from Jerusalem the Word of the Lord. In Jesus, the Jew is still the center of the world's vision.

But the full accomplishment of these words waits behind the curtain that is so soon to be rent at the coming of our Lord. Then holy influences will proceed from the chosen people who shall have been led to recognize Christ as their Messiah. From these the Gospel shall go forth unto all the world. Beneath the hallowing influences of that age swords shall be beaten into ploughshares, and spears into pruning hooks; the cannon shall be as obsolete as the tomahawk; the explosives of war shall be stored in museums; while schools for training the art of war shall be used as missionary seminaries.

There shall be no war, because there shall be no fear. "None shall make them afraid." And there shall be no fear, because universal love shall reign towards God and man.

—Great Verses Through the Bible

MATTHEW HENRY

aside as useless. The gospel men peaceable (*v.* 4): *They shall sit* safely, and none shall disturb them; they shall sit securely, and shall not disturb themselves, every man *under his vine and under his fig-tree*, enjoying the fruit of them, and needing no other shelter than the leaves of them. *None shall make them afraid;* they shall not be disposed to fear.

VIII. The churches shall be constant in their duty, *v.* 5. Peace is a blessing indeed when it strengthens our resolutions to cleave to the Lord. How constant God's people now resolve to be to him: "*We will walk in the name of the Lord our God*, will acknowledge him in all our ways."

IX. Notwithstanding the dispersions, distress, and infirmities of the church, it shall be formed and established, *v.* 6, 7. 1. The state of the church had been low, and very helpless, in the latter times of the Old Testament, partly through the corruptions of the Jewish nation, and partly through the oppressions under which they groaned. They were like *a flock of sheep* that were *maimed*, *worried*, and *scattered*, Ezek. xxxiv. 16; Jer. l. 6, 17. It is promised that these grievances shall be redressed. Christ will come himself (Matt. xv. 24), and send his apostles to *the lost sheep of the house of Israel*, Matt. x. 6. From among the Jews God gathered a remnant (*v.* 7). And from among the Gentiles he raised a strong nation. And such a strong nation the gospel-church is, that the gates of hell shall never be able to prevail against it.

X. The *Messiah* shall be the king of this kingdom to the end of time.

Verses 8–13

These verses relate to Zion and Jerusalem, here called the *tower of the flock*, or the *tower of Edor*; we read of such a place (Gen. xxxv. 21) near Bethlehem; and some conjecture it is the same place where the shepherds were keeping their flocks when the angels brought them tidings of the birth of Christ, and some think Bethlehem itself is here spoken of, as *ch.* v. 2. Some think it is a tower at that gate of Jerusalem which is called the *sheep-gate* (Neh. iii. 32), and conjecture that through that gate Christ rode in triumph into Jerusalem. However, it seems to be put for Jerusalem itself, or for Zion the *tower of David*.

I. A promise of the glories of the spiritual Jerusalem, the gospel-church, which is the tower of the flock, that one fold in which all the sheep of Christ are protected under one Shepherd: "*Unto thee shall it come; even the first dominion*, a dignity and power equal to that of David and Solomon, that *kingdom* shall again *come to the daughter of Jerusalem*, which it was deprived of at the captivity." Now this had by no means its accomplishment in Zerubbabel; and therefore it must refer to the kingdom of the *Messiah* and had its accomplishment when God gave to our Lord Jesus *the throne of his father David* (Luke i. 32).

II. This is illustrated by a prediction of the calamities of the literal Jerusalem, to which some favour and relief should be granted, as a type and figure of what God would do for the gospel-Jerusalem.

1. Jerusalem put in pain by the providences of God. "She *cries out aloud*, because there is *no king in her*, none of that honour she used to have. Instead of ruling the nations, she is ruled by them, and has become a captive. Her *counsellors* have *perished. Pangs have taken her*." She is carried captive to Babylon. "She *goes forth out of the city*, and is constrained to *dwell in the field*, exposed to all manner of inconveniences; she *goes even to Babylon*, and there wears out *seventy tedious* years in a miserable captivity, *in pain, as a woman in travail*, waiting to be delivered."

When she is delivered out of Babylon, still she is in fear; for *now also*, when Jerusalem is in

JAMIESON, FAUSSET, BROWN

4. sit every man under his vine . . .—i.e., enjoy the most prosperous tranquillity (I Kings 4:25; Zech. 3:10). The "vine"and "fig tree" are mentioned rather than a *house,* to signify, there will be no need of a covert; men will be safe even in the fields and open air. **Lord of hosts hath spoken it**—Therefore it must come to pass, however unlikely now it may seem. **5. For**—rather, *Though it be that* all people walk after their several gods, yet we (the Jews in the dispersion) will walk in the name of the Lord. So the *Hebrew* particle means in *Margin,* Genesis 8:21; Exodus 13:17; Joshua 17:18. The resolution of the exile Jews is: As Jehovah gives us hope of so glorious a restoration, notwithstanding the overthrow of our temple and nation, we must in confident reliance on His promise persevere in the true worship of Him, however the nations around, our superiors now in strength and numbers, walk after their gods [ROSENMULLER]. As the Jews were thoroughly weaned from idols by the Babylonian captivity, so they shall be completely cured of unbelief by their present long dispersion (Zech. 10:8-12). **6. assemble her that halteth**—feminine for neuter in *Hebrew* idiom, "*whatever* halteth": metaphor from sheep wearied out with a journey: all the suffering exiles of Israel (Ezek. 34:16; Zeph. 3:19). **her . . . driven out**—all Israel's outcasts. Called "the Lord's flock' (Jer. 13:17; Ezek. 34:13; 37:21). **7. I will make her that halted a remnant**—I will cause a remnant to remain which shall not perish. **Lord shall reign . . . in . . . Zion**—David's kingdom shall be restored in the person of Messiah, who is the seed of David and at the same time Jehovah (Isa. 24:23). **for ever**—(Isa. 9:6, 7; Dan. 7:14, 27; Luke 1:33; Rev. 11:15). **8. tower of the flock**—following up the metaphor of *sheep* (*Note,* vs. 6). Jerusalem is called the "tower," from which the King and Shepherd observes and guards His flock: both the spiritual Jerusalem, the Church now whose tower-like elevation is that of doctrine and practice (Song of Sol. 4:4, "Thy neck is like the *tower* of David"), and the literal hereafter (Jer. 3:17). In large pastures it was usual to erect a high wooden tower, so as to oversee the flock. JEROME takes the *Hebrew* for "flock," *Eder* or *Edar*, as a proper name, viz., a village near Bethlehem, for which it is put, Bethlehem being taken to represent the *royal stock of David* (ch. 5:2; cf. Gen. 35:21). But the explanatory words, "the stronghold of the daughter of Zion," confirm *English Version.* **stronghold**—*Hebrew,* "Ophel"; an impregnable height on Mount Zion (II Chron. 27:3; 33:14; Neh. 3:26, 27). **unto thee shall . . . come . . . the first dominion**—viz., the dominion formerly exercised by thee shall come back to thee. **kingdom shall come to the daughter of Jerusalem**—rather, "the kingdom *of* the daughter of Jerusalem shall come (again)"; such as it was under David, before its being weakened by the secession of the ten tribes. **9.** Addressed to the daughter of Zion, in her consternation at the approach of the Chaldeans. **is there no king in thee?**—asked tauntingly. There *is* a king in her; but it is the same as if there were none, so helpless to devise means of escape are he and his counsellors [MAURER]. Or, Zion's pains are because her king *is* taken away from her (Jer. 52:9; Lam. 4:20; Ezek. 12:13) [CALVIN]. The former is perhaps the preferable view (cf. Jer. 49:7). The latter, however, describes better Zion's kingless state during her present long dispersion (Hos. 3:4, 5). **10. Be in pain, and labour**—carrying on the metaphor of a pregnant woman. Thou shalt be affected with bitter sorrows before thy deliverance shall come. I do not forbid thy grieving, but I bring thee consolation. Though God cares for His children, yet they must not expect to be exempt from trouble, but must prepare for it. **go forth out of the city**—on its capture. So "come out" is used II Kings 24:12; Isaiah 36:16. **dwell in the field**—viz., in the open country, defenseless, instead of their fortified *city.* Beside the Chebar (Ps. 137:1; Ezek. 3:15). **Babylon**—Like Isaiah, Micah looks beyond the existing Assyrian dynasty to the Babylonian, and to Judah's captivity under it, and restoration (Isa. 39:7; 43:14; 48:20). Had they been, as rationalists represent, merely sagacious politicians, they would have restricted their prophecies to the sphere of the existing *Assyrian* dynasty. But their seeing into the far-off future of *Babylon's* subsequent supremacy, and Judah's connection with her, proves them to be inspired prophets. **there . . . there**—emphatic repetition. The very scene of thy calamities is to be the scene of thy deliverance. In the midst of enemies, where all hope seems cut off, *there* shall Cyrus, the deliverer, appear (cf. Judg. 14:14). Cyrus again being the type of the greater Deliverer, who shall

ADAM CLARKE

4. *Under his vine and under his fig tree.* A proverbial expression, indicative of perfect peace, security, and rural comfort. See on Isa. ii. 1. This verse is an addition to the prophecy as it stands in Isaiah.

5. *Every one in the name of his god.* This shall be the state of the Gentile world; but after the Captivity, the Jews walked in the name of Jehovah alone.

6-7. *Will I assemble her that halteth . . . driven out . . . afflicted.* Under these epithets, the state of the Jews, who were to be gathered into the Christian Church, is pointed out.

They *halted* between the true God and idols; they were *driven out* into captivity, because of this idolatry; and they were variously *afflicted*, because they would not return unto the Lord that bought them.

8. *O tower of the flock.* I think the Temple is meant, or Jerusalem; the place where the *flock,* the whole congregation of the people, assembled to worship God.

Even the first dominion. The divine theocracy under Jesus Christ; this former, this *first dominion,* was to be restored.

MATTHEW HENRY

the rebuilding, *many nations are gathered against her*, *v.* 11. They were so in Ezra's and Nehemiah's time, and did all they could to obstruct the building of the temple and the wall. They were so in the time of the Maccabees; they said, *Let her be defiled.*

2. Jerusalem made easy by the promises of God: "*Why dost thou cry out aloud?*" Jerusalem's pangs are not dying agonies, but travailing throes, which after a while will be forgotten, for joy that a child is born into the world. Let the literal Jerusalem comfort herself with this, that, she shall continue until the coming of the Messiah, for there his kingdom must be first set up, and when at length she is ploughed as a field (as is threatened, *ch.* iii. 12), yet her privileges shall be resigned to the spiritual Jerusalem, and the promises made to her shall be fulfilled. Let Jerusalem be easy then, for, her captivity in Babylon shall have a happy end (*v.* 10). This was done by Cyrus, who acted therein as God's servant; and that deliverance was typical of our redemption by Jesus Christ. The designs of her enemies against her afterwards shall be baffled, *v.* 12, 13. Their coming together against Zion shall be the occasion of their ruin. Zion shall have the honour of being victorious over them, *v.* 13. "*Arise, and thresh, O daughter of Zion!* God will make *thy horn iron*, to push them down, and *thy hoofs brass*, to tread upon them when they are down; and thus thou shalt *beat in pieces many people*, that have long been beating thee in pieces." Thus, when God pleases, *the daughter of Babylon is made a threshing floor*, and the *worm Jacob* is made *a threshing instrument*, with which God will *thresh the mountains, and make them as chaff*, Isa. xli. 14, 15. How strangely are the tables turned, since Jacob was the threshing-floor and Babylon the threshing instrument! Isa. xxi. 10. The spoils gained by Zion's victory shall be brought into the sanctuary, and devoted to God, either in part, as those of Midian (Num. xxxi. 28), or in whole, as those of Jericho, Joshua vi. 17. Some make all this to point at the defeat of Sennacherib when he besieged Jerusalem, others to the destruction of Babylon, others to the successes of the Maccabees; but others think it had its full accomplishment in the Spiritual victories obtained by the gospel of Christ over the powers of darkness that fought against it. The nations thought to ruin Christianity in its infancy, but it was victorious over them.

CHAPTER 5

Verses 1–6

I. The abasement and distress of Zion, *v.* 1. The Jewish nation, for many years before the captivity, dwindled: *Now gather thyself in troops, O daughter of troops!* It is a summons to Zion's enemies. Let them *gather in troops*, for, says the prophet, in the name of the inhabitants of Jerusalem, *He has laid siege against us;* the king of Assyria has, the king of Babylon has, and prevail so far as *to smite the judge of Israel*—the king, the chief justice, and the other inferior judges—*with a rod upon the cheek*, having made them prisoners. Complaint had been made of the judges of Israel (*ch.* iii. 11) that they were corrupt and took bribes, and this disgrace came justly upon them for abusing their power.

II. The advancement of Zion's King. Having shown how low the house of David should be brought to encourage the faith of God's people, he adds an illustrious prediction of the Messiah in whom that covenant should be established, and the honours of that house should be revived.

1. How the Messiah is here described. It is he that is to be *ruler in Israel, whose goings forth have been from of old, from everlasting*, from the *days of eternity*, as the word is. This description of Christ's eternal generation, or his going forth as the Son of God, begotten of his Father before all worlds, shows that this prophecy must belong only to him, and could never be verified of any other. The *going forth* is used (Deut. viii. 3) for a *word* which *proceeds out of the mouth*, and is therefore very fitly used to signify the eternal generation of him who is called the *Word of God*, that was *in the beginning with God*, John i. 1, 2. His office as Mediator; he was to be *ruler in Israel*, king of his church; he was to *reign over the house of Jacob for ever*, Luke i. 32, 33. It is a spiritual Israel that he reigns over. In the hearts of these he reigns by his Spirit and grace, and in the society of these by his word and ordinances.

2. What is here foretold concerning him.

(1) That Bethlehem should be the place of his nativity, *v.* 2. *Beth-lehem* signifies *the house of bread*, the fittest place for him to be born in who is *the bread of life*. And, because it was the city of David, by a special providence it was ordered that he should

JAMIESON, FAUSSET, BROWN

finally restore Israel. **11. many nations**—the subject peoples composing Babylon's armies: and also Edom, Ammon, etc., who exulted in Judah's fall (Lam. 2:16; Obad. 11-13). **defiled**—metaphor from a virgin. Let her be defiled (i.e., outraged by violence and bloodshed), and let our eye gaze insultingly on her shame and sorrow (ch. 7:10). Her foes desired to feast their *eyes* on her calamities. **12. thoughts of the Lord**—Their *unsearchable wisdom*, overruling seeming disaster to the final good of His people, is the very ground on which the restoration of Israel hereafter (of which the restoration from Babylon is a type) is based in Isaiah 55:8; cf. with vss. 3, 12, 13, which prove that *Israel*, not merely the Christian Church, is the ultimate subject of the prophecy; also in Romans 11:13. God's counsel is to discipline His people for a time with the foe as a scourge; and then to destroy the foe by the hands of His people. **gather them as . . . sheaves**—them who "gathered" themselves for Zion's destruction (vs. 11) the Lord "shall gather" for destruction by Zion (vs. 13), like *sheaves gathered to be threshed* (cf. Isa. 21:10; Jer. 51:33). The *Hebrew* is *singular*, "sheaf." However great the numbers of the foe, they are all but as *one sheaf* ready to be threshed [CALVIN]. Threshing was done by treading with the feet: hence the propriety of the image for treading under foot and breaking asunder the foe. **13. thresh**—destroy thy foes "gathered" by Jehovah as "sheaves" (Isa. 41:15, 16). **thine horn**—Zion being compared to an ox treading corn, and an ox's strength lying in the horns, her *strength* is implied by giving her a *horn of iron* (cf. Kings 22:11). **beat in pieces many**—(Dan. 2:44). **I will consecrate their gain unto the Lord**—God subjects the nations to Zion, not for her own selfish aggrandizement, but for His glory (Isa. 60:6, 9; Zech. 14:20, with which cf. Isa. 23:18) and for their ultimate good; therefore He is here called, not merely God of Israel, but "Lord of the whole earth."

CHAPTER 5

Vss. 1-15. THE CALAMITIES WHICH PRECEDE MESSIAH'S ADVENT. HIS KINGDOM, CONQUEST OF JACOB'S FOES, AND BLESSING UPON HIS PEOPLE. **1. gather thyself in troops**—i.e., thou shalt do so, to resist the enemy. Lest the faithful should fall into carnal security because of the previous promises, he reminds them of the calamities which are to precede the prosperity. **daughter of troops**—Jerusalem is so called on account of her numerous *troops*. **he hath laid siege**—*the enemy* hath. **they shall smite the judge of Israel with a rod upon the cheek**—the greatest of insults to an Oriental. Zedekiah, the judge (or *king*, Amos 2:3) of Israel, was loaded with insults by the Chaldeans; so also the other princes and judges (Lam. 3:30). HENGSTENBERG thinks the expression, "the judge," marks a time when no king of the house of David reigned. The smiting on the cheek of other judges of Israel was a type of the same indignity offered to Him who nevertheless is the Judge, not only of Israel, but also of the world, and who is "from everlasting" (vs. 2; Isa. 50:6; Matt. 26:67; 27:30). **2. Beth-lehem Ephratah**—(Gen. 48:7), or, Beth-lehem Judah; so called to distinguish it from Beth-lehem in Zebulun. It is a few miles southwest of Jerusalem. Beth-lehem means "the house of bread"; *Ephratah* means "fruitful": both names referring to the fertility of the region. **though thou be little among**—*though thou be scarcely large enough to be reckoned among . . . .* It was insignificant in size and population; so that in Joshua 15:21, etc., it is not enumerated among the cities of Judah; nor in the list in Nehemiah 11:25, etc. Under Rehoboam it became a city: II Chronicles 11:6, "He *built* Beth-lehem." Matthew 2:6 seems to contradict Micah, "thou art *not* the least." But really he, by an independent testimony of the Spirit, confirms the prophet, Little in *worldly* importance, thou art not least (i.e., far from least, yea, *the very greatest*) among the thousands, of princes of Judah, in the spiritual significance of being the birthplace of Messiah (John 7:42). God chooses the little things of the world to eclipse in glory its greatest things (Judg. 6:15; John 1:46; I Cor. 1:27, 28). The low state of David's line when Messiah was born is also implied here. *thousands*—Each tribe

ADAM CLARKE

11. *Many nations are gathered against thee.* The Chaldeans, who were composed of many nations. And, we may add, all the surrounding nations were their enemies; and rejoiced when the Chaldean army had overthrown Jerusalem, destroyed the Temple, and led the people away captive. *Let her be defiled.* Let Jerusalem be laid as low as she can be, like a thing defiled and cast away with abhorrence; that their eyes might look upon Zion with scorn, contempt, and exultation.

12. *But they know not the thoughts of the Lord.* These think that God has utterly rejected His people, and they shall have a troublesome neighbor no more. But this is not His design. He will afflict them for a time; but these, the enemies of His people, He will gather as *sheaves* into the threshing floor, there to be trodden, and the wheel to go over them. This is the *counsel*, the "purpose" of God, which these do not understand. The persons here referred to are not only the Chaldeans, which were threshed by the Persians and Medes; but the Idumeans, Ammonites, Moabites, and Philistines, which the Jews afterwards subdued.

13. *Arise and thresh, O daughter of Zion.* This refers to the subject of the preceding verse. When God shall have gathered together all your enemies, as into the threshing floor, He will give you commission and power to get a complete victory over them, and reduce them to servitude. And that you may be able to do this, He will be on your side as a powerful Helper; here signified by the metaphors, iron horns, and brazen hoofs. You shall have power, authority, and unconquerable strength. *I will consecrate their gain unto the Lord.* What they have taken from you in the way of spoil shall be restored, and again consecrated unto the service of Him who will show himself to be *the Lord*, the Supreme Governor of the *whole earth*. Was not this prediction fulfilled when Cyrus gave the Jews permission to return to their own land, and gave them back the sacred vessels of the Temple which Nebuchadnezzar had carried away?

CHAPTER 5

1. *O daughter of troops.* The Chaldeans, whose armies were composed of troops from various nations. *He* (Nebuchadnezzar) *hath laid siege against us* (Jerusalem): *they shall smite the judge of Israel* (Zedekiah) *with a rod upon the cheek.* They shall offer him the greatest indignity. They slew his sons before his face; and then put out his eyes, loaded him with chains, and carried him captive to Babylon.

2. *But thou, Beth-lehem Ephratah.* To distinguish it from another Bethlehem, which was in the tribe of Zebulun, Josh. xix. 15.

MATTHEW HENRY

be born there. It is called *Bethlehem-Ephratah*, both names of the same city, as appears Gen. xxxv. 19. It was *little among the thousands of Judah*, not considerable either for the number of the inhabitants or the figure they made. Christ would give honour to the place of his birth, and not derive honour from it.

CHARLES H. SPURGEON:

"Out of thee," said Jehovah, speaking by the mouth of Micah, "out of thee shall he come forth unto *me*." It is a sweet thought that Jesus Christ did not come forth without His Father's permission, authority, consent, and assistance. He was sent of the Father, that he might be the Savior of men. We are, alas! too apt to forget, that while there are distinctions as to the Persons in the Trinity, there are no distinctions of honor; and we do very frequently ascribe the honor of our salvation, or at least the depths of its mercy and the extremity of its benevolence, more to Jesus Christ than we do to the Father. This is a very great mistake. What if Jesus came? Did not His Father send Him? If He was made a Child did not the Holy Ghost beget Him? If He spake wondrously, did not His Father pour grace into His lips, that He might be an able minister of the new covenant? If His Father did forsake Him when He drank the bitter cup of gall, did He not love Him still? and did He not, by-and-by, after three days, raise Him from the dead, and at last receive Him up on high, leading captivity captive? Ah! beloved, he who knows the Father, and the Son, and the Holy Ghost as he should know them, never setteth one before another; he is not more thankful to one than the other; he sees them at Bethlehem, at Gethsemane, and on Calvary, all equally engaged in the work of salvation. "He shall come forth unto *me*."—*The Treasury of the Old Testament*

(2) That in the fulness of time he should be born of a woman (*v.* 3). Though the out-goings of the Messiah were *from everlasting*, yet the *redemption in Jerusalem*, the *consolation of Israel*, must be *waited for* (Luke ii. 25–38) until the time that *she who should bring forth* (so the virgin Mary is called, as Christ is himself called, *He that shall come*) shall *bring forth*; and in the meantime *he will give them up*. Divine salvations must be waited for until the time fixed for the bringing of them forth.

(3) That *the remnant of his brethren shall then return to the children of Israel*. The remnant of the Jewish nation shall return to the spirit of the true children of Israel, a people in covenant with God. Some understand it of all believers, Gentiles as well as Jews; they shall all be incorporated into the commonwealth of Israel; and, as they are all brethren to one another, so *he is not ashamed to call them brethren*, Heb. ii. 11.

(4) That he shall be a glorious prince, and his subjects shall be happy under his government (*v.* 4): *He shall stand and feed*, that is, he shall both teach and rule. He shall do this, not as an ordinary man, but *in the strength of the Lord*, as one clothed with a divine power to go through his work. The prophets prefaced their messages with, *Thus saith the Lord;* but Christ spoke, not as a servant, but as a Son—*Verily, verily, I say unto you*. This was feeding *in the majesty of the name of the Lord his God*. Christ's government shall be happy for his subjects, for *they shall abide*.

JAMIESON, FAUSSET, BROWN

was divided into *clans* or "thousands" (each thousand containing a thousand families), which had their several heads or "princes"; hence in Matthew 2:6 it is quoted "princes," substantially the same as in Micah, and authoritatively explained in Matthew. It is not so much this thousand that is preferred to the other thousands of Judah, but the Governor or Chief Prince out of it, who is preferred to the governors of all the other thousands. It is called a "town" (rather in the *Greek*, "village"), John 7:42; though scarcely containing a thousand inhabitants, it is ranked among the "thousands" or larger divisions of the tribe, because of its being the cradle of David's line, and of the Divine Son of David. Moses divided the people into thousands, hundreds, fifties, and tens, with their respective "rulers" (Exod. 18:25; cf. I Sam. 10:19). **unto me**—unto God the Father (Luke 1:32): to fulfil all the Father's will and purpose from eternity. So the Son declares (Ps. 2:7; 40:7, 8; John 4:34); and the Father confirms it (Matt. 3:17; 12:18, cf. with Isa. 42:1). God's glory is hereby made the ultimate end of redemption. **ruler**—the "Shiloh," "Prince of peace," "on whose shoulders the government is laid" (Gen. 49: 10; Isa. 9:6). In II Samuel 23:3, "*He that ruleth* over men must be just," the same *Hebrew* word is employed; Messiah alone realizes David's ideal of a ruler. Also in Jeremiah 30:21, "*their governor* shall proceed from the midst of them"; answering closely to "out of thee shall come forth *the ruler,*" here (cf. Isa. 11:1-4). **goings forth . . . from everlasting**—The plain antithesis of this clause, to "come forth out of thee" (*from Beth-lehem*), shows that the eternal generation of the Son is meant. The terms convey the strongest assertion of infinite duration of which the *Hebrew* language is capable (cf. Ps. 90:2; Prov. 8:22, 23; John 1:1). Messiah's generation as man coming forth unto God to do His will on earth is *from Beth-lehem;* but as Son of God, His goings forth are *from everlasting*. The promise of the Redeemer at first was vaguely general (Gen. 3:15). Then the Shemitic division of mankind is declared as the quarter in which He was to be looked for (Gen. 9:26, 27); then it grows clearer, defining the race and nation whence the Deliverer should come, viz., the seed of Abraham, the Jews (Gen. 12:3); then the particular tribe, Judah (Gen. 49:10); then the family, that of David (Ps. 89:19, 20); then the very town of His birth, here. And as His coming drew nigh, the very parentage (Matt. 1; Luke 1 and 2); and then all the scattered rays of prophecy concentrate in Jesus, as their focus (Heb. 1:1, 2). **3.** "*Therefore* (because of His settled plan) *will* God *give up* to their foes His people Israel, *until* . . . ." **she which travaileth hath brought forth**—viz., "the virgin" mother, mentioned by Micah's contemporary, Isaiah 7:14. *Zion* "in travail" (ch. 4:9, 10) answers to the *virgin* in travail of Messiah. Israel's deliverance from her long travail pains of sorrow will synchronize with the appearance of Messiah as her Redeemer (Rom. 11:26) in the last days, as the Church's spiritual deliverance synchronized with the virgin's giving birth to Him at His first advent. The ancient *Church's* travail-like waiting for Messiah is represented by *the virgin's* travail. Hence, *both* may be meant. It cannot be *restricted* to the Virgin Mary: for Israel is still "given up," though Messiah has been "brought forth" almost two thousand years ago. But the Church's throes are included, which are only to be ended when Christ, having been preached for a witness to all nations, shall at last appear as the Deliverer of Jacob, and when the times of the Gentiles shall be fulfilled, and Israel as a nation shall be born in a day (Isa. 66:7-11; Luke 21:24; Rev. 12:1, 2, 4: cf. Rom. 8:22). **the remnant of his brethren shall return unto the children of Israel**—(Cf. ch. 4:7). The remainder of the Israelites dispersed in foreign lands shall return to join their countrymen in Canaan. The *Hebrew* for "unto" is, lit, "upon," implying superaddition to those already gathered. **4. he shall stand**—i.e., persevere: implying the endurance of His kingdom [CALVIN]. Rather, His sedulous care and pastoral circumspection, as a shepherd *stands* erect to survey and guard His flock on every side (Isa. 61:5) [MAURER]. **feed**—i.e., rule: as the Greek word similarly in Matthew 2:6 (*Margin*), means both "feed" and "rule" (Isa. 40:11; 49:10; Ezek. 34:23; cf. II Sam. 5:2; 7:8). **in the majesty of the name of the Lord**—possessing the majesty of all Jehovah's *revealed attributes* ("name") (Isa. 11:2; Phil. 2:6, 9; Heb. 2:7-9). **his God**—God is "*His* God" in a oneness of relation distinct from the sense in which God is *our* God (John 20:17). **they shall abide**—the Israelites ("they," viz., the *returning remnant* and the "children of Israel" previously in Canaan) shall *dwell in permanent*

ADAM CLARKE

Thousands of Judah. The tribes were divided into small portions called "thousands."

From everlasting. "From the days of all time"; from time as it came out of eternity. That is, there was no time in which He has not been going forth—coming in various ways to save men.

3. *Therefore will he give them up*. Jesus Christ shall give up the disobedient and rebellious Jews into the hands of all the nations of the earth, till "she which travaileth hath brought forth"; that is, till the Christian Church, represented in Rev. xii. 1 under the notion of a woman in travail, shall have had the fullness of the Gentiles brought in.

Then the remnant of his brethren shall return. The Jews also shall be converted unto the Lord; and thus "all Israel shall be saved," according to Rom. xi. 26.

4. *He shall stand and feed*. The Messiah shall remain with His followers, supporting and governing them in the strength and majesty of the Lord.

MATTHEW HENRY

Now shall he be great to the ends of the earth. Now that he stands and feeds his flock, *now shall he be great.* For Christ reckons it his greatness to do good.

(5) That he shall secure the peace and welfare of his church and people against all the attempts of his and their enemies (*v.* 5, 6): *This man,* as king and ruler, *shall be the peace when the Assyrians shall come into our land.* This refers to the deliverance of Hezekiah and his kingdom from the power of Sennacherib, who invaded them, in the type; but, under the shadow of that, it is a promise of the safety of the gospel-church and of all believers from the designs and attempts of the powers of darkness, Satan and all his instruments, the dragon and his angels, that seek to devour the church of the first-born and all that belong to it. When the Assyrian comes with such a force into a land, can there be any other peace than a tame submission and an unresisted desolation? Yes, even then. Christ is our peace, as a priest, making atonement for sin, and reconciling us to God; and he is our peace as a king, conquering our enemies and commanding down disquieting fears and passions; he *creates the fruit of the lips, peace.* He will find out proper instruments to be employed for their protection and deliverance, and the defeat of their enemies: *Then shall we raise against him seven shepherds and eight principal men, that is, a competent number of persons,* men that shall have the care and tenderness of shepherds and the courage and authority of *principal men,* or *princes of men. Seven* and *eight* are a certain number for an uncertain. Magistrates and ministers are shepherds and principal men, raised in defence of religion's righteous cause against the powers of sin and Satan in the world. The opposition given to the church shall be got over, and the opposers brought down. This is represented by the laying of Assyria and Chaldea waste, which two nations were the most formidable enemies to the Israel of God of any, and the destruction of them signified the making of Christ's enemies his footstool: *They shall waste the land of Assyria with the sword, and the land of Nimrod in the entrance thereof.*

Verses 7–15

Glorious things are here spoken of *the remnant of Jacob,* that remnant which was raised of *her that halted* (*ch.* iv. 7), and it seems to be that *remnant which the Lord our God shall call* (Joel ii. 32), on whom the Spirit shall be poured out, the remnant that shall be saved, Rom. ix. 27.

I. They shall be *as a dew* in the midst of the nations, *v.* 7. God's church is dispersed all the world over; it is *in the midst of many people,* as gold in the ore, wheat in the heap. Israel according to the flesh dwelt alone, but the spiritual Israel lies scattered *in the midst of many people,* as the *salt of the earth,* or as seed sown in the ground, here a grain and there a grain, Hos. ii. 23. Now this remnant shall be *as dew from the Lord, born from above,* not of the earth, savouring the things of the earth. They shall be numerous as the drops of dew in a summer's morning, pure and clear. They shall be as the dew that distils insensibly, such is the way of the Spirit. They shall rely on divine grace, for they are no more than what the free grace of God makes them every day. They shall be great blessings to those among whom they live, as the dew and the showers are to the grass. They shall be mild and gentle in their behaviour, like their Master, who comes down *like rain upon the new-mown grass,* Ps. lxxii. 6.

II. That they shall be *as a lion among the beasts of the forest,* that *treads down and tears in pieces, v.* 8. As they shall be silent, and gentle, and communicative of all good, to those that receive the truth in the love of it, so they shall be bold as a lion in witnessing against the corruptions of the times and places they live in, and strong as a lion, in the strength of God, to resist and overcome their spiritual enemies.

III. That they shall be brought off from all carnal confidences, which they have relied on, by the providence of God they shall enjoy such a security that they shall not need them. They had trusted in chariots and horses, and multiplied them (Ps. xx. 7); but now God will *cut off their horses,* and *destroy their chariots* (*v.* 10). They depended upon their fortified cities for their security; but God will take care that they be demolished (*v.* 11). They shall have them for habitations, but not for garrisons. Many of them depended much upon the advice of their diviners and fortune-tellers; and those God will cut off (*v.* 12). Many of them had said to the work of their hands, *You are our gods;* but now idolatry shall be abolished and abandoned (*v.* 13). Among other monuments of idolatry, *I will pluck up thy groves out of the midst of thee, v.* 14. These were planted and preserved in honour of their

JAMIESON, FAUSSET, BROWN

security and prosperity (ch. 4:4; Isa. 14:30). **unto the ends of the earth**—(ch. 4:1; Ps. 72:8; Zech. 9:10). **5. this man**—in *Hebrew* simply "This." The One just mentioned; He and He alone. Emphatical for Messiah (cf. Gen. 5:29). **the peace**—the fountain-head of peace between God and man, between Israel and Israel's justly offended God (Gen. 49:10; Isa. 9:6; Eph. 2:14, 17; Col. 1:20), and, as the consequence, the fountain of "peace on earth," where heretofore all is strife (ch. 4:3; Hos. 2:18; Zech. 9: 10; Luke 2:14). **the Assyrian**—Being Israel's most powerful foe at that time, Assyria is made the representative of all the foes of Israel in all ages, who shall receive their final destruction at Messiah's appearing (Ezek. 38). **seven shepherds, and eight**—"Seven" expresses perfection; "seven and eight" is an idiom for *a full and sufficient number* (Job 5:19; Prov. 6:16; Eccles. 11:2). **principal men**—lit., "anointed (humble) men" (Ps. 62:9), such as the apostles were. Their anointing, or consecration and qualification to office, was by the Holy Spirit [CALVIN] (I John 2:20, 27). "Princes" also were anointed, and they are mentioned as under Messiah (Isa. 32:1). *English Version* therefore gives the probable sense. **6. waste**—lit., "eat up": following up the metaphor of "shepherds" (cf. Num. 22:4; Jer. 6:3). **land of Nimrod**—Babylon (ch. 4:10; Gen. 10: 10); or, including Assyria also, to which he extended his borders (Gen. 10:11). **in the entrances**—the passes into Assyria (II Kings 3:21). The *Margin* and JEROME, misled by a needless attention to the parallelism, "with the sword," translate, "with her own naked swords"; as in Psalm 55:21 the *Hebrew* is translated. But "in the entrances" of Assyria, answers to, "within our borders." As the Assyrians invade *our borders,* so shall *their own* borders or "entrances" be invaded. **he . . . he**– *Messiah* shall deliver us, when the *Assyrian* shall come. **7. remnant of Jacob**—already mentioned in vs. 3. It in comparative smallness stands in antithesis to the "many people." Though Israel be but a remnant amidst many nations after her restoration, yet she shall exercise the same blessed influence in quickening them spiritually that the small imperceptible dew exercises in refreshing the grass (Deut. 32:2; Ps. 72: 6; 110:3). The influence of the Jews restored from Babylon in making many Gentile proselytes is an earnest of a larger similar effect hereafter (Isa. 66: 19; Zech. 8:13). **from the Lord**—Israel's restoration and the consequent conversion of the Gentiles are solely of grace. **tarrieth not for man**—entirely God's work, as independent of human contrivance as the dew and rains that fertilize the soil. **8. as a lion**—In vs. 7 Israel's benignant influence on the nations is described; but here her vengeance on the godless hosts who assail her (Isa. 66:15, 16, 19, 24; Zech. 12:3, 6, 8, 9; 14:17, 18). Judah will be "as as lion," not in respect to its cruelty, but in its power of striking terror into all opponents. Under the Maccabees, the Jews acquired Idumea, Samaria, and parts of the territory of Ammon and Moab [GROTIUS]. But this was only the earnest of their future glory on their coming restoration. **9. Thine hand shall be lifted up**—In Isaiah 26:11 it is *Jehovah's* hand that is lifted up; here *Israel's* as vs. 8 implies, just as "Zion" is addressed and directed to "beat in pieces many people" (ch. 4:13; cf. Isa. 54: 15, 17). For Israel's foes are Jehovah's foes. When her hand is said to be lifted up, it is Jehovah's hand that strikes the foe by her (cf. Exod. 13:9, with 14:8). **10. cut off thy horses . . . chariots**—viz., those used for the purposes of war. Israel had been forbidden the use of cavalry, or to go to Egypt for horses (Deut. 17:16), lest they should trust in worldly forces, rather than in God (Ps. 20:7). Solomon had disregarded this command (I Kings 10:26, 28). Hereafter, saith God, I will remove these impediments to the free course of My grace: horses, chariots, etc., on which ye trust. The Church will never be safe, till she is stripped of all creature-trusts, and rests on Jehovah alone [CALVIN]. The universal peace given by God shall cause warlike instruments to be needless. He will *cut* them *off* from Israel (Zech. 9:10); as she will cut them off from Babylon, the representative of the nations (Jer. 50:37; 51:21). **11. cut off . . . cities . . . strongholds**—such as are fortified for war. In that time of peace, men shall live in unwalled villages (Ezek. 38:11; cf. Jer. 23:6; 49:31; Zech. 2:8). **12. witchcrafts out of thine hand**—i.e., which thou now usest. **13. graven images . . . cut off**—(Cf. Isa. 2:8, 18-21; 30:22; Zech. 13:2). **standing images**—statues. **14. groves . . . cities**—The "groves" are the idolatrous symbol of Astarte (Deut. 16:21; II Kings 21:7). "Cities" being parallel to "groves," must mean cities in or near which such idolatrous groves existed. Cf. "city of the house of Baal" (II Kings 10:25), i.e.,

ADAM CLARKE

For now shall he be great. The Messiah shall be *great,* as bringing salvation to *the ends of the earth.* All nations shall receive His religion, and He shall be universal King.

5. *And this man shall be the peace.* This clause should be joined to the preceding verse, as it finishes the prophecy concerning our blessed Lord, who is the Author and Prince of Israel; and shall finally give peace to all nations, by bringing them under His yoke. *When the Assyrian shall come.* This is a new prophecy, and relates to the subversion of the Assyrian empire. *Then shall we raise against him seven shepherds.* Supposed to mean the seven Maccabees, Mattathias, and his five sons, and Hyrcanus, the son of Simon. *Eight principal men.* "Eight princes, the Asmonean race; beginning with Aristobulus, and ending with Herod, who was married to Mariamme."—Sharpe. Perhaps *seven* and *eight* are a definite for an indefinite number, as Eccles. xi. 2; Job v. 19.

6. *The land of Nimrod.* Assyria, and Nineveh, its capital; and Babylon, which was also built by Nimrod, who was its first king, Gen. x. 11-12, in the margin. *In the entrances thereof.* At its water gates; for it was by rendering themselves masters of the Euphrates that the Medes and Persians took the city, according to the prediction of Jeremiah, chap. li. 32, 36.

7. *The remnant of Jacob.* "From the reign of Darius Hystaspes (Ahasuerus, husband of Esther) the Jews were greatly favoured. Those who continued in Persia and Chaldea were greatly honoured under the protection of Mordecai and Esther."—Calmet. But others consider this as applying to the Maccabees. *As a dew from the Lord.* Even during their captivity many of the Jews were the means of spreading the knowledge of the one true God; see Dan. ii. 47; iii. 29; iv. 34; vi. 26. This may be the *dew from the Lord* mentioned here. When the Messiah appeared, the gospel was preached by them; and it shall again be propagated by their future glorious restoration, Rom. xi. 12, 25. *The grass, that tarrieth not for man.* Which grass springs up without the attention and culture of man. *Nor waiteth for the sons of men. Libney adam,* for the "sons of Adam," the first transgressor. The *dew* and the *showers* descend on the earth and water it, in order to render it fruitful; and the *grass* springs up independently of either the worth or the wickedness of man.

8. *As a lion.* In this and the following verse the victories of the Maccabees are supposed to be foretold.

9. *All thine enemies shall be cut off.* The Assyrians, who had destroyed Israel; and the Babylonians, who had ruined Judah.

10. *I will cut off thy horses.* You shall have no need of cavalry in your armies; God will fight for you.

11. *I will . . . throw down all thy strong holds.* You shall have no need of fortified cities; I will be your Defense.

12. *I will cut off witchcrafts.* You shall seek help only in Jehovah, your God. They have had neither soothsayers, images, groves, nor high places from the Captivity to the present day.

13. *Thy graven images also will I cut off.* You shall be no more an idolatrous people.

MATTHEW HENRY

idols, and used in the worship of them. And so *will I destroy their cities*, meaning the cities that were dedicated to the idols.

IV. That those who stand it out against the gospel of Christ, and continue in league with their idolatries and witchcrafts, shall fall under the wrath of God (*v.* 15).

JAMIESON, FAUSSET, BROWN

a portion of the city sacred to Baal.

15. vengeance . . . such as they have not heard—or, as the *Hebrew order* favors, "the *nations* that have not hearkened to My warnings." So LXX (Ps. 149:7).

ADAM CLARKE

15. *I will execute vengeance . . . upon the heathen.* And He did so; for the empires of the Assyrians, Chaldeans, and others, the sworn enemies of the Jews, have long since been utterly destroyed.

MATTHEW HENRY — CHAPTER 6

Verses 1–5

Here, I. The prefaces to the message are very solemn. *Hear you now what the Lord says. Arise, contend thou before the mountains*, or *with the mountains*, and *let the hills hear thy voice.* Contend with the mountains and hills of Judæa, that is, with the inhabitants of those mountains and hills; some think, reference is to those mountains on which they worshipped idols. It is to be taken more generally, as appears by his call, not only to the mountains, but to the *strong foundations of the earth.* He must speak as vehemently as if to make even the hills hear him. "*Let the hills hear thy voice*, for this senseless, careless people will not hear it. Let the rocks, the *foundations of the earth*, that have no ears, hear, since Israel, will not hear."

II. The message itself is to let all the world know that God has a quarrel with his people. God will plead with his people Israel, that they may be convinced and that he may be justified. In the close of the foregoing chapter he pleaded with the heathen in anger, but here he pleads with Israel in compassion and tenderness, to bring them to repentance, *Come now, and let us reason together.* They had revolted from God and rebelled against him; but had they any cause to do so? (*v.* 3): "*O my people! what have I done unto thee?*" Here is a challenge to all that ever were in God's service to testify against him if they have found him, in anything, a hard Master, or if they have found his demands unreasonable. He brought them out of Egypt, the land of their bondage, *v.* 4. They were content with their slavery, and almost in love with their chains, for the sake of the garlic and onions they had plenty of; but God *brought them up*, inspired them with an ambition of liberty and animated them with a resolution to shake off their fetters. The Egyptians held them fast, but God *redeemed them* by force, *out of the house of servants, the house of bondage.* When he brought them out of Egypt into a howling wilderness, he sent before them *Moses, Aaron, and Miriam, three prophets* (says the Chaldee paraphrase). We must not forget the mercy of good teachers when we were young. It was God that sent them before us, to prepare the way. God no less glorified himself, and honoured them when he brought them into the land of their rest than when he brought them out of the land of their servitude. Let them remember now what God did for them in baffling and defeating the designs of Balak and Balaam; in bringing them *from Shittim*, their last lodgment out of Canaan, *unto Gilgal*, their first lodgment in Canaan. There it was, between Shittim and Gilgal, that, upon the death of Moses, Joshua, a type of Christ, was raised up to put Israel in possession of the land of promise.

Verses 6–8

The proposal for accommodation between God and Israel. Judgment is given against Israel, and therefore,

I. They express their desires to be at peace with God upon any terms (*v.* 6, 7). Knowing everyone the plague of his own heart, they ask not, *What shall this man do?* But, *What shall I do? What will the Lord be pleased with? What shall I give for my transgressions?*

II. They make proposals such as betray their ignorance, though they show their zeal.

1. They bid high. They offer *thousands of rams.* God required one ram for a sin-offering; they proffer their whole stock, so that they may but be at peace with God. They could be content to part with *their first-born for their transgressions*, if that would be accepted as an atonement, and the *fruit of their body for the sin of their soul.* To those that had become *vain in their imaginations* this seemed a probable expedient of making satisfaction for sin, because our children are pieces of ourselves.

2. Yet they do not bid right. It is true some of these things were instituted by the ceremonial law, but these alone would not recommend them to God. The legal sacrifices had their virtue from the reference they had to Christ the great propitiation; but otherwise, of themselves, it was *impossible that the blood of bulls and goats should take away sin.* All the proposals of peace but those that are according to the

JAMIESON, FAUSSET, BROWN — CHAPTER 6

Vss. 1-16. APPEAL BEFORE ALL CREATION TO THE ISRAELITES TO TESTIFY, IF THEY CAN, IF JEHOVAH EVER DID AUGHT BUT ACTS OF KINDNESS TO THEM FROM THE EARLIEST PERIOD: GOD REQUIRES OF THEM NOT SO MUCH SACRIFICES, AS REAL PIETY AND JUSTICE: THEIR IMPIETIES AND COMING PUNISHMENT. **1. contend thou**—Israel is called by Jehovah to plead with Him in controversy. Ch. 5:11-13 suggested the transition from those happy times described in ch. 4 and 5, to the prophet's own degenerate times and people. **before the mountains**—in their presence; personified as if witnesses (cf. ch. 1: 2; Deut. 32:1; Isa. 1:2). Not as *Margin*, "with"; as God's controversy is with Israel, not *with* them.

2. Lord's controversy—How great is Jehovah's condescension, who, though the supreme Lord of all, yet wishes to prove to worms of the earth the equity of His dealings (Isa. 5:3; 43:26).

3. my people—the greatest aggravation of their sin, that God always treated them, and still treats them, as *His people.* **what have I done unto thee?**—save kindness, that thou revoltest from Me (Jer. 2:5, 31). **wherein have I wearied thee?**—What commandments have I enjoined that should have wearied thee as irksome (I John 5:3)? **4. For**—*On the contrary*, so far from doing anything harsh, I did thee every kindness from the earliest years of thy nationality. **Miriam**—mentioned, as being the prophetess who led the female chorus who sang the song of Moses (Exod. 15:20). God sent Moses to give the best laws; Aaron to pray for the people; Miriam as an example to the women of Israel. **5. what Balak . . . consulted**—how Balak plotted to destroy thee by getting Balaam to curse thee (Num. 22:5). **what Balaam . . . answered**—how the avaricious prophet was constrained against his own will, to bless Israel whom he had desired to curse for the sake of Balak's reward (Num. 24:9-11) [MAURER]. GROTIUS explains it, "how Balaam *answered*, that the only way to injure thee was by tempting thee to idolatry and whoredom" (Num. 31:16). The mention of "Shittim" agrees with this: as it was the scene of Israel's sin (Num. 25:1-5; II Pet. 2:15; Rev. 2:14). **from Shittim unto Gilgal**—not that Balaam accompanied Israel from Shittim *to Gilgal*: for he was slain in Midian (Num. 31:8). But the clause, "from Shittim," alone applies to Balaam. "Remember" God's kindnesses "from Shittim," the scene of Balaam's wicked counsel taking effect in Israel's sin, whereby Israel merited utter destruction but for God's sparing mercy, "to Gilgal," the place of Israel's first encampment in the promised land between Jericho and Jordan, where God renewed the covenant with Israel by circumcision (Josh. 5:2-11). **know the righteousness**—Recognize that, so far from God having treated thee harshly (vs. 3), His dealings have been kindness itself (so "righteous acts" for *gracious* Judg. 5:11; Ps. 24:5, 112:9). **6. Wherewith shall I come before the Lord?**—The people, convicted by the previous appeal of Jehovah to them, ask as if they knew not (cf. vs. 8) what Jehovah requires of them to appease Him, adding that they are ready to offer an immense heap of sacrifices, and those the most costly, even to the fruit of their own body. **burnt offerings**—(Lev. 1). **calves of a year old**—which used to be offered for a priest (Lev. 9:2, 3). **7. rivers of oil**—used in sacrifices (Lev. 2:1, 15). Will God be appeased by my offering so much oil that it shall flow in myriads of torrents?

ADAM CLARKE — CHAPTER 6

1. *Arise, contend thou.* This chapter is a sort of dialogue between God and the people. God speaks the first five verses, and convicts the people of sin, righteousness, and judgment. The people, convinced of their iniquity, deprecate God's judgments, in the sixth and seventh verses. In the eighth verse God prescribes the way in which they are to be saved; and then the prophet, by the command of God, goes on to remonstrate from the ninth verse to the end of the chapter.

2. *Hear ye, O mountains.* Micah, as God's advocate, summons this people into judgment, and makes an appeal to inanimate creation against them.

4. *I brought thee up out of the land of Egypt.* Where you were slaves, and grievously oppressed; from all this I redeemed you. *I sent before thee Moses,* My chosen servant, and instructed him that he might be your leader and lawgiver. I sent with him *Aaron,* that he might be your priest. I sent *Miriam,* to whom I gave the spirit of prophecy, that she might be the director of your females.

5. *Remember now what Balak king of Moab consulted.* He sent for Balaam to curse your fathers, but by My influence he was obliged to bless them. See Numbers xxii and xxiii.

From Shittim unto Gilgal. From the encampment at Shittim, Num. xxv. 1, on the way to that of Gilgal, Josh. iv. 19. Balaam gave different answers in the interval between these places.

6. *Wherewith shall I come before the Lord?* Now the people, as defendants, appear; but instead of vindicating themselves, or attempting to dispute what has been alleged against them, they seem at once to plead guilty; and now anxiously inquire how they shall appease the wrath of the Judge, how they shall make atonement for the sins already committed.

MATTHEW HENRY

gospel are absurd. Some of them are wicked things, as to give our *first-born* and the *fruit of our body* to death. Do they not belong to God? Are they not his already, and born to him? How then can they be a ransom? They could not answer the demands of divine justice, nor would they serve in lieu of the sanctification of the heart and the reformation of the life.

III. God tells them plainly what he demands, *v.* 8. We need not trouble ourselves to make proposals, the terms are already settled and laid down. He whom we have offended has shown it, not only to thee, *O Israel!* but *to thee, O man!* Gentiles as well as Jews—to men, who are rational creatures. What is spoken to *all men everywhere* in general, must by faith be applied to ourselves in particular, as if it were spoken *to thee, O man!* by name, and to no other. The good which God requires of us is not the paying of a price for the pardon of sin. (1) We must *do justly*, must *render to all their due*, according as our relation and obligation to them are; we must do wrong to none, but do right to all, in their bodies, goods, and good name. (2) We must *love mercy*, not only be just to all we deal with, but kind to all that need us. Nor must we only show mercy, but we must *love mercy*. (3) We must *walk humbly with our God*. This includes all the duties of the first table, as the two former include all the duties of the second table. Enoch's walking with God is interpreted (Heb. xi. 5) his *pleasing God*. We must, in the whole course of our conversation, conform ourselves to the will of God, keep up our communion with God, and study to approve ourselves to him. We must *humble ourselves to walk with God* (so the margin reads it); every thought within us must be brought down, to be brought into obedience to God. This is that which God requires, and without which the most costly services are *vain oblations*; this is more than *all burnt-offerings and sacrifices*.

Verses 9–16

God, having shown them how necessary it was that they should do justly, here shows them how plain it was that they had done unjustly.

I. The action is entered against them, *v.* 9. God speaks to *the city*, to Jerusalem, to Samaria. When the sin of a city cries to God his voice cries against the city. He warns before he wounds, because he is *not willing that any should perish*. 1. How the voice of God is discerned by some: *The man of wisdom will see thy name*. 2. What this voice of God says to all: "*Hear you the rod, and who hath appointed it*. Hear the rod when it is coming; hear it at a distance, before you see it and feel it. Hear the rod when it has come, and you are sensible of the smart of it; hear what cautions it speaks to you." Every rod has a voice, and it is the voice of God that is to be heard in the rod of God. God in every affliction *performs the thing that is appointed for us* (Job xxiii. 14).

II. What is the ground of the action, and the things that are laid to their charge.

1. They are charged with injustice, a sin against the second table. After all the methods that God has taken to teach them to do justly, will they yet deal unjustly? It seems, they will, *v.* 10. And *shall I count them pure? v.* 11. Those that are dishonest in their dealings shall never be reckoned pure. *Treasures of wickedness profit nothing*. A *scant measure*, by which they sold to the poor, cheated them. They had *wicked balances and a bag of false weights*. Those that had wealth and power in their hands abused it. They are *full of violence*, that is, they have their houses full of that which is got by violence. *The inhabitants thereof have spoken lies*; if they are not able to use force and violence, they use fraud and deceit.

2. They are charged with idolatry (*v.* 6): *The statutes of Omri are kept, and all the work of the house of Ahab*. Both these kings were wicked, and the wickedness which they established by a law, was idolatry. The wickedness which they established by their laws and examples remained. Those that make corrupt laws, and bring in corrupt usages, are doing that which perhaps may prove the ruin of the child unborn.

III. The sentence which God had given them warning of (*v.* 9) shall be brought upon them (*v.* 13): *Therefore also I will make thee sick, in smiting thee*. As they had smitten the poor with the rod of their oppressions, so would God in like manner smite them, so as to make them sick of the gains they had unjustly gotten.

1. What they have shall do them no good. Their food shall not nourish them: *Thou shalt eat, but not be satisfied*. Men may be surfeited with the good things of this world and yet not satisfied, Eccles. v. 10; Isa. lv. 2. Their country shall not harbour and protect them: "*Thy casting down shall be in the midst*

JAMIESON, FAUSSET, BROWN

my first-born—(II Kings 3:27). As the king of Moab did. **fruit of my body**—*my children*, as an atonement (Ps. 132:11). The Jews offered human sacrifices in the valley of Hinnom (Jer. 19:5; 32:35; Ezek. 23:27).

8. He—Jehovah. **hath showed thee**—long ago, so that thou needest not ask the question as if thou hadst never heard (vs. 6; cf. Deut. 10:12; 30:11-14). **what is good**—"the good things to come" under Messiah, of which "the law had the shadow." The Mosaic sacrifices were but suggestive foreshadowings of His *better* sacrifice (Heb. 9:23; 10:1). To have this "good" first "showed," or *revealed* by the Spirit, is the only basis for the superstructure of the moral requirements which follow. Thus the way was prepared for the Gospel. The banishment of the Jews from Palestine is designed to preclude the possibility of their looking to the Mosaic rites for redemption, and shuts them up to Messiah. **justly . . . mercy**—preferred by God to sacrifices. For the latter being *positive* ordinances, are only *means* designed with a view to the former, which being *moral* duties are the *ends*, and of everlasting obligation (I Sam. 15:22; Hos. 6:6; 12:6; Amos 5:22, 24). Two duties towards *man* are specified—*justice*, or strict equity; and *mercy*, or a kindly abatement of what we might justly demand, and a hearty desire to do good to others. **to walk humbly with thy God**—passive and active obedience towards God. The three moral duties here are summed up by our Lord (Matt. 23:23), "judgment, mercy, and faith" (in Luke 11:42, "the love of God"). Cf. James 1: 27. *To walk with God* implies constant prayer and watchfulness, familiar yet "humble" converse with God (Gen. 5:24; 17:1). **9. unto the city**—Jerusalem. *the man of* **wisdom**—As in Proverbs 13: 6, *Hebrew*, "sin" is used for "*a man of* sin," and in Psalm 109:4, "prayer" for "*a man of* prayer"; so here "wisdom" for "*the man of* wisdom." **shall see thy name**—shall regard Thee, in Thy revelations of Thyself. Cf. the end of ch. 2, vs. 7. God's "name" expresses the sum total of His revealed attributes. Contrast with this Isaiah 26:10, "will not behold the majesty of the Lord." Another reading is adopted by LXX, *Syriac*, and *Vulgate*, "there is deliverance for those who *fear* Thy name." *English Version* is better suited to the connection; and the rarity of the *Hebrew* expression, as compared with the frequency of that in the other reading, makes it less likely to be an interpolation. **hear . . . the rod . . .**—Hear what punishment (cf. vs. 13, etc.; Isa. 9:3; 10:5, 24) awaits you, and from whom. I am but a man, and so ye may disregard me; but remember my message is not mine, but God's. Hear the rod when it is come, and you feel its smart. Hear what counsels, what cautions it speaks. **appointed it**—(Jer. 47:7). **10. Are there yet**—notwithstanding all My warnings. Is there to be no end of acquiring treasures by wickedness? Jehovah is speaking (vs. 9). **scant measure . . . abominable**—(Prov. 11:1; Amos 8:5). **11. Shall I count them pure**—lit., "Shall I be pure with . . . ?" *With the pure God shows Himself pure;* but *with the froward* God *shows Himself froward* (Ps. 18:26). Men often are changeable in their judgments. But God, in the case of the impure who use "wicked balances," cannot be pure, i.e., cannot deal with them as He would with the pure. VATABLUS and HENDERSON make the "I" to be "any one"; "Can I (i.e., one) be innocent with wicked balances?" But as "I," in vs. 13, refers to Jehovah, it must refer to Him also here. **the bag**—in which weights used to be carried, as well as money (Deut. 25:13; Prov. 16:11). **12. For**—rather, "Inasmuch as"; the conclusion "therefore . . . , following in vs. 13. **thereof**—of Jerusalem. **13. make *thee* sick in smiting**—(Lev. 26:16, to which perhaps the allusion here is, as in vs. 14; Ps. 107:17, 18; Jer. 13:13). **14. eat . . . not be satisfied**—fulfilling the threat, Leviticus 26:26. **thy casting down shall be in the midst of thee**—Thou shalt be cast down, not merely on My borders, but in the midst of thee, thy metropolis and temple being overthrown [TIRINUS]. Even though there should be no enemy, yet thou shalt be consumed with intestine evils [CALVIN]. MAURER translates as from an *Arabic* root, "there shall be *emptiness* in thy belly." Similarly GROTIUS, "there shall be a sinking of thy belly (once filled with food), through hunger." This suits the parallelism to the first clause. But *English Version* maintains the parallelism sufficiently. The casting down in the midst of the land, including the failure of food, through the invasion thus answering to, "Thou shalt eat, and not be satisfied."

ADAM CLARKE

7. *Shall I give my firstborn for my transgression?* See some cases of such offerings, 2 Kings iii. 27; Lev. xx. 27. *The fruit of my body for the sin of my soul?* Shall I make the firstborn *chattah*, a "sin offering," for my soul?

9. *The Lord's voice crieth unto the city*. No man is found to hear; but the *man of wisdom* will hear, *tushiyah;* a word frequent in the writings of Solomon and Job, signifying wisdom, wealth, substance, reason, essence, happiness—anything that is complete; or that which is substantial, in opposition to vanity, emptiness, mere show, unsubstantiality. When God speaks, the man of common sense, who has any knowledge of God or his own soul, will *see thy name;* but instead of *yireh*, "will see," the Septuagint, Syriac, Vulgate, and Arabic have read *yirey*, "they that fear." The Vulgate reads: "And thou shalt be salvation to them that fear thy name." The Septuagint, "And he shall save those who fear his name."

13. *Will I make thee sick in smiting thee*. Perhaps better, "I also am weary with smiting you, in making you desolate for your sins."

14. *Thou shalt eat, but not be satisfied*. All your possessions are cursed, because of your sins; and you have no real good in all your enjoyments.

MATTHEW HENRY

of thee, that is, thou shalt be ruined by mischiefs at home, though thou shouldst not be invaded by a foreign force." They shall not be able to preserve what they have from a foreign force: "*Thou shalt take hold* of what is about to be taken from thee, but thou shalt not hold it fast, shalt not retrieve it." Their wives and children whom they resolved not to part with, must go into captivity. What they save for a time shall be reserved for a future stroke: *That which thou deliverest* out of the hand of one enemy *will I give up to the sword* of another enemy. What they have laboured for they shall not enjoy (*v.* 15): "*Thou shalt sow, but thou shalt not reap;* it shall be withered, or an enemy shall reap it for himself, or thou shalt be carried into captivity, and leave it to be reaped by thou knowest not whom. Thou shalt *tread the olives*, but *thou shalt not anoint thyself with oil*, having no heart when all is going to ruin. Thou shalt tread out *the sweet wine*, but *shalt not drink wine*, for many things may fall between the cup and the lip."

2. All they have shall at length be taken from them (*v.* 13): *Thou shalt be made desolate because of thy sins;* and *v.* 16, *a desolation and a hissing.* When a people that have been flourishing are made desolate it is the astonishment of some and the triumph of others. Thus *you shall bear the reproach of my people.* Now that their sins and God's judgments have made their land desolate, their having been once the people of God does but turn so much the more to their reproach; their enemies will say, *These are the people of the Lord*, Ezek. xxxvi. 20.

JAMIESON, FAUSSET, BROWN

thou shalt take hold, but . . . not deliver—Thou shalt take hold (with thine arms), in order to save [CALVIN] thy wives, children and goods. MAURER, from a different root, translates, "thou shalt remove them," in order to save them from the foe. But thou shalt fail in the attempt to deliver them (Jer. 50:37). **that which thou deliverest**—If haply thou dost rescue aught, it will be for a time: I will give it up to the foe's sword. **15. sow . . . not reap**—fulfilling the threat (Lev. 26:16; Deut. 28:38-40; Amos 5:11). **16. statutes of Omri**—the founder of Samaria and of Ahab's wicked house; and a supporter of Jeroboam's superstitions (I Kings 16:16-28). This verse is a recapitulation of what was more fully stated before, Judah's sin and consequent punishment. Judah, though at variance with Israel on all things else, imitated her impiety. **works of . . . Ahab** (I Kings 21:25, 26). **ye walk in their counsels**—Though these superstitions were the fruit of their king's "counsels" as a master stroke of state policy, yet these pretexts were no excuse for setting at naught the counsels and will of God. **that I should make thee a desolation**—Thy conduct is framed so, as if it was thy set purpose "that I should make thee a desolation." **inhabitants thereof**—viz., of Jerusalem. **hissing**—(Lam. 2:15). **the reproach of my people**—The very thing ye boast of, viz., that ye are "My people," will only increase the severity of your punishment. The greater My grace to you, the greater shall be your punishment for having despised it, Your being God's people in name, while walking in His love, was an honor; but now the name, without the reality, is only a "reproach" to you.

ADAM CLARKE

16. *The statutes of Omri are kept.* Omri, king of Israel, the father of Ahab, was one of the worst kings the Israelites ever had; and Ahab followed in his wicked father's steps. The *statutes* of those kings were the very grossest idolatry.

MATTHEW HENRY

CHAPTER 7

Verses 2–6

This description of bad times some take as a prediction of what should be in the reign of Manasseh. But we rather suppose it to be in the reign of Ahaz, or in the beginning of Hezekiah's time, in the best of his days, when he had done his best to purge out corruptions, but still there was much amiss. The prophet bemoans himself that his lot was cast in such a degenerate age, among a people that were ripening apace for a ruin which many a good man would unavoidably be involved in. He laments, 1. That there were so few good people to be found, even among those that were God's people: *The good man has perished out of the earth*, or *out of the land*, *v.* 2. The *good man* is a *godly man* and a *merciful man;* the word signifies both. Those are completely good men that are devout towards God and compassionate and beneficent towards men, that love mercy and walk with God. There is no such thing as a good man to be met with. This is illustrated by a comparison (*v.* 1): They were *as when they have gathered the summer fruits*; it was as hard a thing to find a good man as to find any of the summer-fruits, the choicest and best, when the harvest is over. You can find no societies of them as bunches of grapes: *There is no cluster to eat;* and the best and fullest grapes are those that grow in large clusters. When we read of the devotion and charity, of the professors of religion in former ages, and see the reverse of this in the present age, we cannot but wish, with a sigh, *O for primitive Christianity again!* 2. That there were so many wicked people that did all the hurt they could: "*They all lie in wait for blood*, and *hunt every man his brother.* They act as if mankind were in a state of war, and force were the only right. They are as beasts of prey to their neighbours, for *they all lie in wait for blood* as lions for their prey." 3. That the magistrates, who by their office ought to have been the patrons and protectors of right, were the practisers and promoters of wrong: *That they may do evil with both hands earnestly, the prince asketh, and the judge asketh for a reward*, for a bribe, with which they will be hired for carrying on any wicked design *with both hands. So they wrap it up;* they make it intricate (so some understand it), that they may lose equity in a mist, and so make the cause turn which way they please. A sad character is given of them (*v.* 4), *the best of them is as a brier, and the most upright is sharper than a thorn-hedge.* And, when things have come to this pass, *the day of thy watchmen comes*, that is *the day of thy visitation*, when God will reckon with thee for all this wickedness, which is called *the day of the watchmen*, because their prophets, whom God set as watchmen over them, had often warned them of that day. 4. That there was no faith in man; people had grown universally treacherous, *v.* 5. "Those that have any sense of honour remaining in them, have a firm regard to the laws of friendship; they would not

JAMIESON, FAUSSET, BROWN

CHAPTER 7

Vss. 1-20. THE UNIVERSALITY OF THE CORRUPTION; THE CHOSEN REMNANT, DRIVEN FROM EVERY HUMAN CONFIDENCE, TURNS TO GOD; TRIUMPHS BY FAITH OVER HER ENEMIES; IS COMFORTED BY GOD'S PROMISES IN ANSWER TO PRAYER, AND BY THE CONFUSION OF HER ENEMIES, AND SO BREAKS FORTH INTO PRAISES OF GOD'S CHARACTER. **1. I am as when . . .**—It is the same with me as with one seeking fruits after the harvest, grapes after the vintage. "There is not a cluster" to be found: no "first-ripe fruit" (or early fig. *Note*, Isa. 28:4) which "my soul desireth" [MAURER]. So I look in vain for any good men left (vs. 2). **2.** (Ps. 12:1). **good man**—The *Hebrew* expresses "one *merciful and good* in relation to man," rather than to God. **3. That they may do evil with both hands earnestly**—lit., "Their hands are for evil that they may do it well" (i.e., cleverly and successfully). **the great man, he**—emphatic repetition. *As for the great man, he* no sooner has expressed his bad desire (lit., the "mischief or lust of his soul), than the venal judges are ready to wrest the decision of the case according to his wish. **so they wrap it up**—The *Hebrew* is used of *intertwining cords together.* The "threefold cord is not quickly broken" (Eccles. 4:12); here the "prince," the "judge," and the "great man" are the three in guilty complicity. "They wrap it up," viz., they conspire to carry out the great man's desire at the sacrifice of justice. **4. as a brier**—or *thorn;* pricking with injury all who come in contact with them (II Sam. 23:6, 7; Isa. 55:13; Ezek. 2:6). **the day of thy watchmen**—the day foretold by thy (true) prophets, as the time of "thy visitation" in wrath [GROTIUS]. Or, "the day of thy *false* prophets being punished"; they are specially threatened as being not only blind themselves, but leading others blindfold [CALVIN]. **now**—at the time foretold, "at that time"; the prophet transporting himself into it. **perplexity**—(Isa. 22:5). They shall not know whither to turn. **5. Trust ye not in a friend**—Faith is kept nowhere: all to a man are treacherous (Jer. 9:2-6). When justice is perverted by the great, faith nowhere is safe. So, in gospel times of persecution, "a man's foes are they of his own household" (Matt. 10:35, 36; Luke 12:53). **guide**—a counsellor [CALVIN] able to help and advise (cf. Ps. 118:8, 9; 146:3). *The head of your family,* to whom all the members of the family would naturally repair in emergencies. Similarly the *Hebrew* is translated in Joshua 22:14 and "chief friends" in Proverbs 16:28 [GROTIUS]. **her that lieth in thy bosom**—thy wife (Deut. 13:6). **6. son dishonoureth the father**—The state of unnatural lawlessness in all relations of life is here described which is to characterize the last times, before Messiah comes to punish the ungodly and save Israel (cf. Luke 21:16; II Tim. 3:1-3).

ADAM CLARKE

CHAPTER 7

1. *Woe is me!* This is a continuation of the preceding discourse. And here the prophet points out the small number of the upright to be found in the land. He desired to see *the firstripe fruit*—distinguished and eminent piety; but he found nothing but a very imperfect or spurious kind of godliness.

2. *The good man is perished out of the earth.* A similar sentiment may be found in Ps. xii. 1; Isa. lvii. 1.

3. *That they may do evil with both hands.* That is, *earnestly*, greedily, to the uttermost of their power. *The prince asketh* a bribe, to forward claims in his court. *The judge asketh for a reward.* That he may decide the cause in favor of him who gives most money, whether the cause be good or evil. *The great man, he uttereth his mischievous desire.* Such consider themselves above law, and they make no secret of their unjust determinations. And *so they wrap it up*—they all conjoin in doing evil in their several offices, and oppressing the poor.

4. *The best of them is as a brier.* They are useless in themselves, and cannot be touched without wounding him that comes in contact with them. *The day of thy watchmen.* The day of vengeance, which the prophets have foreseen and proclaimed, is at hand.

6. *For the son dishonoureth the father.* See the use our Lord has made of these words, where He quotes them, Matt. x. 21, 25, 36.

MATTHEW HENRY

discover what passed in private conversation, nor divulge secrets, to the prejudice of a friend. But those things are now made a jest of. Wise men take it for a rule, *Trust you not in a friend*, for you will find him false. As for him that undertakes to be *your guide* in any business which he professes to understand better than you, you cannot *put a confidence* in him, for he will mislead you if he can get anything by it." Some by a guide understand a husband, who is called *the guide of thy youth*; and that agrees with what follows, "*Keep the doors of thy lips from her that lieth in thy bosom*, from thy own wife; take heed what thou sayest before her, lest she betray thee. 5. That children were abusive to their parents, *v.* 6. It is sad when a man's betrayers and worst enemies are his own children and his best friends.

Verses 7–13

The prophet, having sadly complained of the wickedness of the times, fastens upon some considerations for comfort. The case is bad, but it is not desperate.

I. "Though God be now displeased he shall be reconciled to us, and then all will be well," *v.* 7, 9. At such a time, 1. We must have recourse to God under our troubles (*v.* 7): *Therefore I will look unto the Lord.* All may look bright above him when all looks dark about him. The prophet had been complaining that there was no confidence to be put in friends and relations, and this drives him to his God: *Therefore I will look unto the Lord.* 2. We must submit to the will of God in our troubles: "*I will bear the indignation of the Lord* patiently, without murmuring and repining, *because I have sinned against him.*" When we complain to God of the badness of the times we ought to complain against ourselves for the badness of our own hearts. 3. We must depend upon God to work deliverance for us. When things are brought to the last extremity: *My God will hear me;* if the Lord be our God, he will hear our prayers, and grant an answer of peace to them. "*When I sit in darkness*, disconsolate and perplexed, then *the Lord shall be a light to me*, as a light to my eyes, a light to my feet, a light *in a dark place.*" *He will plead my cause, and execute judgment for me*, *v.* 9. "He *will bring me forth to the light*. The morning of comfort shall shine forth out of the long and dark night of trouble. *I shall behold his righteousness;* the performance of his promises to me."

II. Though enemies triumph, they shall be put to shame, *v.* 8, 10. The enemies of God's people said, *Where is the Lord their God?* As if because they were afflicted God had forsaken them, and they knew not where to find him with their prayers, and he knew not how to help them with his favours. The people of God by faith bear up under these insults (*v.* 8): "*Rejoice not against me, O my enemy!* I am now down, but shall not be always so, and when my God appears for me then *she that is my enemy shall see it, and be ashamed.*" The deliverance of the church will be the confusion of her enemies.

III. Though the land continue a great while desolate, yet it shall at length be replenished again. Its salvation shall not come *till after it has been desolate*; so the margin reads it, *v.* 13. It must lie long under his rebukes, *because of those that dwell therein.* For this they must expect to smart a great while. When it does come it shall be a complete salvation; and it seems to refer to their deliverance out of Babylon by Cyrus. *The decree shall be far removed.* God's decree concerning their captivity, and Nebuchadnezzar's decree, his resolution never to release them shall be set aside. Jerusalem and the cities of Judah shall be again reared: Then *thy walls shall be built.* All that belong to the land of Israel, whithersoever dispersed, far and wide, shall come flocking to it again (*v.* 12): *He shall come even to thee.* They shall come from all the remote parts, *from sea to sea and from mountain to mountain*, not turning back till they come to Zion.

Verses 14–20

I. The prophet's prayer to God to take care of his own people, *v.* 14. When we see God coming towards us in ways of mercy, we must go forth to meet him by prayer. It is a prophetic prayer, which amounts to a promise of the good prayed for; what God directed his prophet to ask no doubt he designed to give. The people of Israel are here called the *flock of God's heritage*. This flock *dwells solitarily in the wood*, or *forest, in the midst of Carmel*, a high mountain. Israel was a peculiar people, *that dwelt alone*, like a flock of sheep in a wood. They were now a desolate people (*v.* 13), in the land of their captivity as sheep in a forest, in danger from the beasts of the forest. He prays that God would *feed them there with his rod*, that is, that he would take care of them

JAMIESON, FAUSSET, BROWN

7. Therefore I will look unto the Lord—as if no one else were before mine eyes. We must not only "look *unto* the Lord," but also "wait *for* Him." Having no hope from man (vss. 5, 6), Micah speaks in the name of Israel, who herein, taught by chastisement (vs. 4) to feel her sin (vs. 9), casts herself on the Lord as her only hope," in patient waiting (Lam. 3:26). She did so under the Babylonian captivity; she shall do so again hereafter when the spirit of grace shall be poured on her (Zech. 12:10-13). **8. Rejoice not**—at my fall. **when I fall, I shall arise**—(Ps. 37:24; Prov. 24:16). **when I sit in darkness, the Lord shall be a light**—Israel reasons as her divine representative, Messiah, reasoned by faith in His hour of darkness and desertion (Isa. 50:7, 8, 10). Israel addresses Babylon, her triumphant foe (or Edom), as *a female;* the type of her last and worst foes (Ps. 137:7, 8). "Mine enemy," in *Hebrew,* is feminine. **9. bear**—patiently. **the indignation of the Lord**—His punishment inflicted on me (Lam. 3:39). The true penitent "accepts the punishment of his iniquity" (Lev. 26:41, 43); they who murmur against God, do not yet know their guilt (Job 40:4, 5). **execute judgment for me**—against my foe. God's people plead guilty before God; but, in respect to their human foes, they are innocent and undeserving of their foes' injuries. **bring me forth to the light**—to the temporal and spiritual redemption. **I shall behold his righteousness**—His gracious faithfulness to His promises (Ps. 103:17). **10. shame shall cover her**—in seeing how utterly mistaken she was in supposing that I was utterly ruined. **Where is . . . thy God**—(Ps. 42:3, 10). If He be "*thy* God," as thou sayest, let Him come now and deliver thee. So as to Israel's representative, Messiah (Matt. 27:43). **mine eyes shall behold her**—a just retribution in kind upon the foe who had said, "Let our *eye look upon* Zion." Zion shall behold her foe prostrate, not with the carnal joy of revenge, but with spiritual joy in God's vindicating His own righteousness (Isa. 66:24; Rev. 16:5-7). **shall she be trodden down**—herself, who had trodden down me. **11. thy walls . . . be built**—under Cyrus, after the seventy years' captivity; and again, hereafter, when the Jews shall be restored (Amos 9:11; Zech. 12:6). **shall the decree be far removed**—viz., thy tyrannical decree or rule of Babylon shall be put away from thee, "the statutes that were not good" (Ezek. 20:25) [CALVIN]. Psalm 102:13-16; Isaiah 9:4. The *Hebrew* is against MAURER's translation, "the boundary of the city shall be *far extended,*" so as to contain the people flocking into it from all nations (vs. 12; Isa. 49:20; 54:2). **12. In that day also**—rather, an answer to the supposed question of Zion, When shall my walls be built? "The day (of thy walls being built) is the day when he (i.e., many) shall come to thee from Assyria . . ." [LUDOVICUS DE DIEU]. The Assyrians (including the Babylonians) who spoiled thee shall come. **and** *from* **the fortified cities**—rather, to suit the parallelism, "from Assyria *even to Egypt.*" (*Matzor* may be so translated.) So Assyria and Egypt are contrasted in Isaiah 19:23 [MAURER]. CALVIN agrees with *English Version,* "from all fortified cities." **from the fortress even to the river**—"from *Egypt* even to the river" Euphrates (answering in parallelism to "Assyria") [MAURER]. Cf. Isaiah 11:15, 16; 19:23-25; 27:13; Hosea 11:11; Zechariah 10:10. **13.** However glorious the prospect of restoration, the Jews are not to forget the visitation on their "land" which is to intervene for the "fruit of (evil caused by) their doings" (cf. Prov. 1:31; Isa. 3:10, 11; Jer. 21:14). **14. Feed thy people**—Prayer of the prophet, in the name of his people to God, which, as God fulfils believing prayer, is prophetical of what God *would* do. When God is about to deliver His people, He stirs up their friends to pray for them. **Feed**—including the idea of both pastoral *rule* and care over His people (*Margin,* ch. 5:4), regarded as a flock (Ps. 80:1; 100:3). Our calamity must be fatal to the nation, unless Thou of Thy unmerited grace, remembering Thy covenant with "Thine heritage" (Deut. 4:20; 7:6; 32:9), shalt restore us. **thy rod**—the shepherd's rod, wherewith He directs the flock (Ps. 23:4). No longer the rod of punishment (ch. 6:9). **which dwell solitarily in the wood, in . . . Carmel**—Let Thy people who have been dwelling as it were in a solitude of woods (*in* the world, but not *of* it), scattered among various nations, dwell in Carmel, i.e., where there are fruit-bearing lands and vineyards [CALVIN]. Rather, "which are about to dwell (i.e., that they may dwell) separate in the wood, in . . . Carmel" [MAURER], which are to be no longer mingled with the heathen, but are to dwell as a distinct people in their own land. Micah has here Balaam's prophecy in view (cf. ch. 6:5, where

ADAM CLARKE

8. *Rejoice not against me, O mine enemy.* The captive Israelites are introduced as speaking here and in the preceding verse. The *enemy* are the Assyrians and Chaldeans; the *fall* is their idolatry and consequent captivity; the *darkness,* the calamities they suffered in that captivity; their rise and *light,* their restoration and consequent blessedness.

9. *I will bear the indignation of the Lord.* The words of the penitent captives, acknowledging their sins and praying for mercy.

10. *Then she that is mine enemy.* This may refer particularly to the city of Babylon. *Shall she be trodden down.* Literally fulfilled in the sackage of that city by the Persians, and its consequent total ruin.

11. *In the day that thy walls are to be built.* This refers to Jerusalem; *the decree,* to the purpose of God to deliver the people into captivity. The restoration of Jerusalem is certainly what the prophet describes.

12. *In that day also he shall come.* The Israelites were to return from their captivity, and reoccupy their ancient country from Assyria to Egypt; that is, from the river Euphrates to the river Nile, and from the Mediterranean Sea to the ocean, and from Mount Libanus to the mountains of Arabia Petraea, or Mount Seir. See Amos viii. 12. This prediction was literally fulfilled under the Asmoneans. The Jewish nation was greatly extended and very powerful under Herod, at the time that our Lord was born.

13. *Notwithstanding the land shall be desolate.* This should be translated in the preter tense, "Though the land had been desolate"; that is, the land of Israel had been desolate during the Captivity.

14. *Feed thy people with thy rod.* "With thy crook." The shepherd's crook is most certainly designed, as the word *flock* immediately following shows. No rod of correction or affliction is here intended, nor does the word mean such.

Solitarily. They have been long without a shepherd or spiritual governor. *In the midst of Carmel.* Very fruitful in vines.

MATTHEW HENRY

in their captivity, and do the part of a good shepherd to them. "Let them be governed by thy rod, not the rod of their enemies, for they are thy people." He prays that God would in due time bring them back to feed in the plains of Bashan and Gilead. *Let them feed* in their own country again, *as in the days of old.* Some apply this spiritually, and make it either the prophet's prayer to Christ or his Father's charge to him, to take care of his church, as the great Shepherd of the sheep.

II. God's promise, in answer to this prayer. God answers that he *will show them marvellous things* (*v.* 15), will out-do their hopes and expectations. He will do that which shall be the repetition of the wonders and miracles of former ages—*according to the days of thy coming out of the land of Egypt.* He will do that for them which shall be matter of amazement to the present age, *v.* 16, 17. The *nations about* shall take notice of it. They shall be *confounded at all the might* with which the captives shall now exert themselves, whom they thought for ever disabled. They shall now *lay their hands upon their mouths,* as being ashamed of what they have said. They shall stop their ears, not willing to hear any more of God's wonders wrought for people, whom they had so despised.

Those that had impudently confronted God himself shall now be brought, in profession at least, to submit to him (*v.* 17): *They shall lick the dust like a serpent,* as if they were sentenced to the same curse the serpent was laid under (Gen. iii. 14).

III. The prophet's thankful acknowledgment of God's mercy, *v.* 18–20. Pardoning mercy was at the bottom of it. As it was their sin that brought them into bondage, so it was God's pardoning their sin that brought them out of it; Ps. lxxxv. 1, 2, and Isa. xxxiii. 24; xxxviii. 17; xl. 1, 2. This the prophet stands amazed at, while the surrounding nations stood amazed only at those deliverances which were but the fruits of this. The reasons why God pardons sin, and keeps not his anger for ever, are all taken from within himself; it is *because he delights in mercy,* and the salvation of sinners is what he has pleasure in, not their death and damnation. There is *no God like unto him;* no magistrate forgives as God does. In this his thoughts and ways are infinitely above ours; in this he is *God, and not man.* His mercy *endures for ever,* and therefore as he has *shown mercy* so he will, *v.* 19, 20. He will renew us, to prepare and qualify us for his favour: *He will subdue our iniquities;* when he takes away the guilt of sin, that it may not damn us, he will break the power of sin, that it may not have dominion over us. *Thou wilt cast all their sins into the depth of the sea,* as when he brought them out of Egypt he subdued Pharaoh and the Egyptians, and cast them into the depth of the sea. It intimates that when God forgives sin he *remembers it no more.* He casts them into the sea, not near the shore-side, where they may appear again next low water, but into *the depth of the sea,* never to rise again. *All their sins* shall be cast there without exception, for when God forgives sin he forgives all. He with this good work will do all that our case requires and which he has promised (*v.* 20).

JAMIESON, FAUSSET, BROWN

also Balaam is referred to). "Lo, the people shall dwell *alone*" (Num. 23:9; cf. Deut. 33:28). To "feed in the wood in Carmel," is to feed in the rich pastures among its woods. To "sleep in the woods," is the image of *most perfect security* (Ezek. 34:25). So that the Jews' *security,* as well as their *distinct nationality,* is here foretold. Also Jeremiah 49:31. **Bashan**—famed for its cattle (Ps. 22:12; Amos 4:1). Parallel to this passage is **Jeremiah** 50:19. Bashan and Gilead, east of Jordan, were chosen by Reuben, Gad, and half Manasseh, as abounding in pastures suited for their many cattle (Num. 32; Deut. 3:12-17). **15. thy . . . him**—both referring to Israel. So in vs. 19 the person is changed from the first to the third, "us . . . our . . . their." Jehovah here answers Micah's prayer in vs. 14, assuring him, that as He delivered His people from Egypt by miraculous power, so He would again "show" it in their behalf (Jer. 16:14, 15). **16. shall see**—the "marvellous things" (vs. 15; Isa. 26: 11). **confounded at all their might**—having so suddenly proved unavailing: that might wherewith they had thought that there is nothing which they could not effect against God's people. **lay . . hand upon . . . mouth**—the gesture of silence (Job 21:5; 40:4; Ps. 107:42; Isa. 52:15). They shall be struck dumb at Israel's marvellous deliverance, and no longer boast that God's people is destroyed. **ears . . . deaf**—They shall stand astounded so as not to hear what shall be said [GROTIUS]. Once they had eagerly drunk in all rumors as so many messages of victories; but then they shall be afraid of hearing them, because they continually fear new disasters, when they see the God of Israel to be so powerful [CALVIN]. They shall close their ears so as not to be compelled to hear of Israel's successes. **17. lick the dust**—in abject prostration as suppliants (Ps. 72: 9; cf. Isa. 49:23; 65:25). **move out of their holes**—As reptiles from their holes, they shall come forth from their hiding-places, or fortresses (Ps. 18:45), to give themselves up to the conquerors. More lit., "they shall tremble from," i.e., tremblingly come forth from their coverts. **like worms**—reptiles or crawlers (Deut. 32:24). **they shall be afraid of the Lord**—or, they shall *in fear turn with haste to* the Lord. Thus the antithesis is brought out. They shall tremble forth *from* their holes: they shall in trepidation turn *to* the Lord for salvation (cf. *Note,* Hos. 3:5, and Jer. 33:9). **fear because of thee**—shall fear Thee, Jehovah [and so fear Israel as under Thy guardianship]. There is a change here from speaking *of* God to speaking *to* God [MAURER]. Or rather, "shall fear thee, Israel" [HENDERSON]. **18.** Grateful at such unlooked-for grace being promised to Israel, Micah breaks forth into praises of Jehovah. **passeth by the transgression**—not conniving at it, but forgiving it; leaving it unpunished, as a traveller *passes by* what he chooses not to look into (Prov. 19:11). Contrast Amos 7: 8, and "*mark* iniquities," Ps. 130:3. **the remnant**—who shall be permitted to survive the previous judgment: the elect remnant of grace (ch. 4:7; 5:3, 7, 8). **retaineth not . . . anger**—(Ps. 103:9). **delighteth in mercy**—God's forgiving is founded on His nature, which delights in loving-kindness, and is averse from wrath. **19. turn again**—to us, from having been turned away from us. **subdue our iniquities**—lit., "tread under foot," as being hostile and deadly to us. Without subjugation of our bad propensities, even pardon could not give us peace. When God takes away the guilt of sin that it may not condemn us, He takes away also the power of sin that it may not rule us. **cast . . . into . . . depths of the sea**—never to rise again to view, buried out of sight in eternal oblivion: not merely at the shore side, where they may rise again. **our . . . their**—change of person. Micah in the first case identifying himself and his sins with his people and their sins; in the second, speaking *of* them and their sins. **20. perform the truth**—the faithful promise. **to Jacob . . . Abraham**—Thou shalt make good to their posterity the promise made to the patriarchs. God's promises are called "mercy," because they flow slowly from grace; "truth," because they will be surely performed (Luke 1:72, 73; I Thess. 5:24). **sworn unto our fathers**—(Ps. 105:9, 10). The promise to Abraham is in Genesis 12:2; to Isaac, in Genesis 26:24; to Jacob, in Genesis 28:13. This unchangeable promise implied an engagement that the seed of the patriarchs should never perish, and should be restored to their inheritance as often as they turned wholly to God (Deut. 30:1, 2).

ADAM CLARKE

Bashan and Gilead. Proverbially fruitful in pasturages.

15. *According to the days.* This is the answer to the prophet's prayer; and God says He will protect, save, defend, and work miracles for them in their restoration, such as He wrought for their fathers in their return from Egypt to the Promised Land.

16. *The nations shall see and be confounded.* Whether the words in these verses (15-17) be applied to the return from the Babylonish captivity or to the prosperity of the Jews under the Maccabees, they may be understood as ultimately applicable to the final restoration of this people, and their lasting prosperity under the gospel.

S. L. WARREN:

"Who is a God like unto thee?" Micah, with an allusion to the significance of his own name, concludes his book with a burst of enthusiastic homage to the God of gods. The gracious character here ascribed to Jehovah is unparalleled in the Bible in human utterances; it is the response of the prophet to the glorious works spoken by Jehovah of Himself (Exod. 34:6, 7). The promise there made to Moses is here extended by the inspiration of the prophet to the Gentiles. The "remnant" refers to the returned from the captivity.

Verse 20. "Thou wilt perform." The closing words in the prophecy of Micah are gloriously taken up some centuries later by Zechariah: "As he spake by the mouth of his holy prophets, which have been since the world began: that we should be saved from our enemies, and from the hand of all that hate us, to perform the mercy promised to our fathers, and to remember his holy covenant, the oath which he sware to our father Abraham, that he would grant unto us, that we being delivered out of the hand of our enemies, might serve him without fear, in holiness and righteousness before him, all the days of our life" (Luke 1:54, 55).

—*Ellicott's Commentary on the Whole Bible*

20. *Thou wilt perform the truth to Jacob.* The promises which He has made to Jacob and His posterity. Not one of them can ever fall to the ground.

And the mercy to Abraham, which thou hast sworn; viz., that in his Seed all the families of the earth should be blessed, that the Messiah should come from Abraham.

THE BOOK OF NAHUM

I. Verdict and vengeance (1:1-15)
A. Subject and method (1:1)
B. Jehovah (1:2-8)
C. The verdict (1:9-14)
D. The cry to Judah (1:15)

II. Vision of vengeance (2:1-13)
A. Preliminary declaration (2:1, 2)
B. The vision of vengeance (2:3-10)
C. The prophet's exultation (2:11-13)

III. Vindication of vengeance (3:1-19)
A. Vice declared and vengeance (3:1-3)
B. Vice described and vengeance (3:4-7)
C. Vice dissected and vengeance (3:8-17)
D. Vice destroyed (3:18, 19)

The name of this prophet signifies a *comforter;* for it was a charge given to all the prophets. "Comfort you, comfort you, my people"; and even this prophet, though wholly taken up in foretelling the destruction of Nineveh, is, even that, comforter to the ten tribes of Israel, who, it is probable, were lately carried captives into Assyria. It is uncertain, but probable that he lived in the time of Hezekiah, and prophesied against Nineveh after the captivity of Israel by the king of Assyria, which was in the ninth year of Hezekiah and before Sennacherib's invading Judah, which was in the fourteenth year of Hezekiah—for to that attempt and the defeat of it, it is supposed, the first chapter has reference. It is the conjecture of Huetius that the two other chapters of this book were delivered by Nahum some years after, perhaps in the reign of Manasseh, and in that reign the Jewish chronologies generally place him, some time before the captivity of Judah.

MATTHEW HENRY

CHAPTER 1

Verse 1

Nineveh was the place concerned, and the Assyrian monarchy had the royal seat there. Jonah had, in God's name, foretold the speedy overthrow of this great city; but then the Ninevites repented and were spared. The Ninevites then saw clearly how to turn from their evil way; it was the saving of their city; and yet, soon after, they returned to it again; it became worse than ever. Then God sent them this prophecy, to read them their doom, which was now irreversible. It is *the book of the vision of Nahum the Elkoshite.* The burden of Nineveh was what the prophet plainly foresaw, for it was his vision. When he was gone, the event might be compared with the prediction. All the account we have of the prophet himself is that he was an *Elkoshite,* of the town called *Elkes,* which, Jerome says, was in Galilee.

Verses 2-8

Nineveh knows not God, and therefore is here told what a God he is. This glorious description of the Sovereign of the world, like the pillar of cloud and fire, has a bright side towards Israel and a dark side towards the Egyptians.

I. He is a God of inflexible justice; let Nineveh know this, and tremble before him. Their idols are insignificant things; there is nothing formidable in them. But the God of Israel is greatly to be feared. He resents the indignities done him by those that deny his being or any of his perfections, that set up other gods in competition with him, that destroy his laws, ridicule his word, or are abusive to his people. Let such know that Jehovah is jealous for his own honour in the matters of his worship, and will not endure a rival; he is jealous for the comfort of his worshippers, *jealous for his land* (Joel ii. 18), and will not have that injured. He *has fury* (so the word is) not as man has it, in whom it is an ungoverned passion, but he has it in such a way as becomes the righteous God. He is *Lord of anger* (so the Hebrew phrase is for that which we read, *he is furious*); he has anger, but he has it at command and under government. Our anger is often lord over us, as theirs that have *no rule over their own spirits,* but God is always *Lord of his anger* and *weighs a path to it,* Ps. lxxviii. 50. Whoever are his adversaries and enemies among men, he will make them feel his resentments in the day of wrath. He *will not at all acquit the wicked* that sin, and stand to it, and do not repent, *v.* 3. This revelation of the wrath of God against his enemies is applied to Nineveh (*v.* 8), and should be applied by all those who go on still in their trespasses: *With an over-running flood he will make an utter end of the place thereof. Darkness shall pursue his enemies;* terror and trouble shall follow them, whithersoever they go; if they think to flee from the darkness which pursues them they will but fall into that which is before them.

II. He is a God of irresistible power. If we look up into the regions of the air, there we shall find proofs of his power, for *he has his ways in the whirlwind and the storm.* He spoke to Job out of the whirlwind, and even *stormy winds fulfil his word.* If we cast our eye upon the great deeps, we find that the sea is his, for, when he pleases, *he rebukes the sea and*

JAMIESON, FAUSSET, BROWN

CHAPTER 1

Vss. 1-15. JEHOVAH'S ATTRIBUTES AS A JEALOUS JUDGE OF SIN, YET MERCIFUL TO HIS TRUSTING PEOPLE, SHOULD INSPIRE THEM WITH CONFIDENCE. HE WILL NOT ALLOW THE ASSYRIANS AGAIN TO ASSAIL THEM, BUT WILL DESTROY THE FOE. **1. burden of Nineveh**—the *prophetic doom* of Nineveh. Nahum prophesied against that city 150 years after Jonah. **2. jealous**—In this there is sternness, yet tender affection. We are jealous only of those we love: a husband, of a wife; a king, of his subjects' loyalty. God is jealous of men because He loves them. God will not bear a rival in His claims on them. His burning jealousy for His own wounded honor and their love, as much as His justice, accounts for all His fearful judgments: the flood, the destruction of Jerusalem, that of Nineveh. His jealousy will not admit of His friends being oppressed, and their enemies flourishing (cf. Exod. 20:5; I Cor. 16: 22; II Cor. 11:2). *Burning zeal* enters into the idea in "jealous" here (cf. Num. 25:11, 13; I Kings 19: 10). **the Lord revengeth . . . Lord revengeth**—The repetition of the incommunicable name JEHOVAH, and of His *revenging,* gives an awful solemnity to the introduction. **furious**—lit., "a master of fury." So *a master of the tongue,* i.e., "eloquent." "One who, if He pleases, can most readily give effect to His fury" [GROTIUS]. Nahum has in view the provocation to fury given to God by the Assyrians, after having carried away the ten tribes, now proceeding to invade Judea under Hezekiah. **reserveth wrath for his enemies**—*reserves it* against His own appointed time (II Pet. 2:9). After long waiting for their repentance in vain, at length punishing them. A wrong estimate of Jehovah is formed from His suspending punishment: it is not that He is insensible or dilatory, but He reserves wrath for His own fit time. In the case of the penitent, He does not *reserve* or retain His anger (Ps. 103:9; Jer. 3:5, 12; Mic. 7:18). **3. slow to anger, and great in power**—i.e., *but* great in power, so as to be able in a moment, if He pleases, to destroy the wicked. His long-suffering is not from want of power to punish (Exod. 34:6, 7). **not at all acquit**—lit., "will not acquitting acquit," or treat as innocent. **Lord hath his way in the whirlwind**—From this to vs. 5, inclusive, is a description of His power exhibited in the phenomena of nature, especially when He is wroth. His vengeance shall sweep away the Assyrian foe like a whirlwind (Prov. 10:25). **clouds are the dust of his feet**—Large as they are, He treads on them, as a man would on the small dust; He is Lord of the clouds, and uses them as He pleases. **4. rebuketh the sea**—as Jesus did (Matt. 8:26), proving Himself God (cf. Isa. 50:2). **Bashan languisheth**—through drought; ordinarily it was a region famed for its rich pasturage (cf. Joel 1:10). **flower of Lebanon**—*its bloom;* all that blooms so luxuriantly on Lebanon (Hos. 14:7). As Bashan was famed for its pastures, Carmel for its cornfields and vineyards, so Lebanon for its forests (Isa. 33:9). There is nothing in the world so blooming that God cannot change it when He is wroth. **5. earth is burned**—so GROTIUS. Rather, "lifts itself," i.e., "heaveth" [MAURER]: as the *Hebrew* is translated in Psalm 89:

ADAM CLARKE

CHAPTER 1

1. *The burden of Nineveh. Massa* not only signifies a *burden,* but also a thing "lifted up, pronounced, or proclaimed"; also a "message." It is used by the prophets to signify the revelation which they have received from God to deliver to any particular people: the "oracle"—the prophecy. Here it signifies the declaration from God relative to the overthrow of Nineveh, and the commission of the prophet to deliver it. As the Assyrians under Pul, Tiglath-pileser, and Shalmaneser, three of their kings, had been employed by a just God for the chastisement His disobedient people, the end being now accomplished by them, God is about to burn the rod wherewith He corrected Israel; and Nineveh, the capital of the Assyrian empire, is to be destroyed. This prediction appears to have been accomplished a short time after this by Nebuchadnezzar and Cyaxares, the Ahasuerus of Scripture. *Nahum* signifies "comforter." The name was very suitable, as he was sent to comfort the people, by showing them that God was about to destroy their adversaries.

3. *The clouds are the dust of his feet.* This is spoken in allusion to a chariot and horses going on with extreme rapidity; they are all enveloped in a cloud of dust. So Jehovah is represented as coming through the circuit of the heavens as rapidly as lightning, the clouds surrounding Him as the dust does the chariot and horses.

4. *He rebuketh the sea,* the Red Sea, and *the rivers;* probably an allusion to the passage of the Red Sea and Jordan. The description of the coming of Jehovah, from the third to the sixth verse, is dreadfully majestic.

MATTHEW HENRY

makes it dry, drying up all the rivers. If we look round on this earth, we find proofs of his power, when, either by the extreme heat and drought of summer or the cold and frost of winter, *Bashan languishes, and Carmel, and the flower of Lebanon languishes.* Earthquakes shake the mountains (*v.* 5), melt the hills, and level them with the plains. When he pleases *the earth is burnt at his presence* by the scorching heat of the sun. If God be an almighty God, we may thence infer (*v.* 6), *Who can stand before his indignation?* The Ninevites had once found God *slow to anger* (*v.* 3), and perhaps presumed upon the mercy they had then experienced. It is in vain for the stoutest and strongest of sinners to think to make their part good against the power of God's anger. God's anger is so fierce that it beats down all before it: *The rocks are thrown down on him.* The eruption of subterraneous fires is a faint resemblance of the fierceness of God's anger against sinners whose hearts are rocky. Sinners as stubble before the fire, the wrath of God. *Who can abide in the fierceness of his anger?* Some of the effects of God's displeasure in this world a man may bear up under, but the *fierceness of his anger*, when it fastens immediately upon the soul, who can bear? Let us *fear before him;* let us *stand in awe, and not sin.*

III. He is a God of infinite mercy. *Let the sinners in Zion be afraid*, that go on still in their transgressions, but let not those that trust in God tremble before him. He is *slow to anger* (*v.* 3), ready to show mercy. When the tokens of his rage against the wicked are abroad he takes care of his own people (*v.* 7): *The Lord is good* to those that are *good*, and to them he will be *a stronghold in the day of trouble.*

Verses 9–15

These verses seem to point at the destruction of the army of the Assyrians under Sennacherib, which may well be reckoned a part of the burden of Nineveh, the head city of the Assyrian empire, and a pledge of the destruction of Nineveh itself about 100 years after.

I. The great provocation which the Assyrians gave to God, the just and jealous God, for which, though *slow to anger*, he would take vengeance (*v.* 11): *There is one come out of thee, that imagines evil against the Lord*—Sennacherib, and his spokesman Rabshakeh. They framed an evil letter and an evil speech, not only against Hezekiah and his people, but against God himself, as level with the gods of the heathen, and unable to protect his worshippers, urging his people to put themselves under the protection of the *great king, the king of Assyria.* To this evil counsel he says (*v.* 9): "*What do you imagine against the Lord?* What a foolish wicked thing it is for you to plot against God, as if you could outwit divine wisdom and overpower omnipotence itself!"

II. The great destruction which God would bring upon them for it, not immediately upon the whole monarchy (the ruin of that was deferred) but,

1. Upon the army; God will *make an utter end* of that; it shall be totally cut off and ruined at one blow. They have laid themselves open to divine wrath by their own act and deed, *v.* 10. They are *as thorns* that entangle one another, and are *folded together.* They make one another worse. God will do with them as the husbandmen does with a bush of thorns when he cannot part them: he puts them all into the fire together. They are *as drunken men*, intoxicated with pride and rage; and such as they shall be destroyed. They shall be *devoured as stubble fully dry*, which is irresistibly and irrecoverably consumed by the flame.

JAMIESON, FAUSSET, BROWN

9; Hosea 13:1; cf. *Margin,* II Samuel 5:21. **6. fury is poured out like fire**—like the liquid fire poured out of volcanoes in all directions (see Jer. 7:20) **rocks are thrown down**—or, "are burnt asunder"; the usual effect of volcanic fire (Jer. 51:25, 56). As Hannibal burst asunder the Alpine rocks by fire to make a passage for his army [GROTIUS]. **7.** Here Nahum enters on his special subject, for which the previous verses have prepared the way, viz., to assure his people of safety in Jehovah under the impending attack of Sennacherib (vs. 7), and to announce the doom of Nineveh, the capital of the Assyrian foe (vs. 8). The contrast of vss. 7 and 8 heightens the force. **he knoweth**—recognizes as His own (Hos. 13:5; Amos 3:2); and so, cares for and guards (Ps. 1:6; II Tim. 2:19). **8. with an overrunning flood**—i.e., with irresistible might which *overruns* every barrier like a flood. This image is often applied to overwhelming *armies* of invaders. Also of *calamity* in general (Ps. 32:6; 42:7; 90:5). There is, perhaps, a special allusion to the mode of Nineveh's capture by the Medo-Babylonian army; viz., through a *flood* in the river which broke down the wall twenty furlongs (see *Note,* ch. 2:6; Isa. 8: 8; Dan. 9:26; 11:10, 22:40). **end of the place thereof**—Nineveh is personified as a queen; and "*her* place" of residence (the *Hebrew* for "thereof" is feminine) is *the city itself* (ch. 2:8), [MAURER]. Or, He shall so utterly destroy Nineveh that its place cannot be found; ch. 3:17 confirms this (cf. Ps. 37:36; Dan. 2:35; Rev. 12:8 and 20:11). **darkness**—the severest calamities. **9. What do ye imagine against the Lord?**—abrupt address to the Assyrians. How mad is your attempt, O Assyrians, to resist so powerful a God! What can ye do against such an adversary, successful though ye have been against all other adversaries? Ye *imagine* ye have to *do* merely with mortals and with a weak people, and that so you will gain an easy victory; but you have to encounter God, the protector of His people. Parallel to Isaiah 37:23-29; cf. Psalm 1:1. **he will make an utter end**—The utter overthrow of Sennacherib's host, soon about to take place, is an earnest of the "utter end" of Nineveh itself. **affliction shall not rise up the second time**—Judah's "affliction" caused by the invasion shall never rise again. So vs. 12. But CALVIN takes the "affliction" to be that *of Assyria*: "There will be no need of His inflicting on you a second blow: He will make an utter end of you once for all" (I Sam. 3:12; 26:8; II Sam. 20:10). If so, this verse, in contrast to vs. 12, will express, Affliction shall visit the Assyrian no more, in a sense very different from that in which God will afflict Judah no more. In the Assyrian's case, because the blow will be fatally final; the latter, because God will make lasting blessedness in Judah's case succeed temporary chastisement. But it seems simpler to refer "affliction" here, as in vs. 12, to Judah; indeed *destruction*, rather than *affliction*, applies to the Assyrian. **10. while they are folden together as thorns**—lit., "*to the same degree* as thorns" (cf. *Margin,* I Chron. 4:27). As thorns, so folded together and entangled that they cannot be loosed asunder without trouble, are thrown by the husbandmen all in a mass into the fire, so the Assyrians shall all be given together to destruction. Cf. II Samuel 23:6, 7, where also "thorns" are the image of the wicked. As this image represents the speediness of their destruction *in a mass,* so that of "drunkards," their rushing as it were *of their own accord* into it; for drunkards fall down without any one pushing them [KIMCHI]. CALVIN explains, *Although* ye be *dangerous to touch* as thorns (i.e., full of rage and violence), yet the Lord can easily consume you. But "although" will hardly apply to the next clause. *English Version* and KIMCHI, therefore, are to be preferred. The comparison to drunkards is appropriate. For drunkards, though exulting and bold, are weak and easily thrown down by even a finger touching them. So the insolent self-confidence of the Assyrians shall precipitate their overthrow by God. The *Hebrew* is "*soaked,*" or "drunken as with their own wine." Their drunken revelries are perhaps *alluded to,* during which the foe (according to DIODORUS SICULUS, 2) broke into their city, and Sardanapalus *burned* his palace; though the main and ultimate destruction of Nineveh referred to by Nahum was long subsequent to that under Sardanapalus. **11.** The cause of Nineveh's overthrow: Sennacherib's plots against Judah. **out of thee**—O Nineveh. From thyself shall arise the source of thy own ruin. Thou shalt have only thyself to blame for it. **imagineth evil**—Sennacherib carried out the *imaginations* of his countrymen (vs. 9) against the Lord and His people (II Kings 19:22, 23). **a wicked counsellor**

ADAM CLARKE

8. *But with an overrunning flood.* Bishop Newcome thinks this may refer to the manner in which Nineveh was taken. The Euphrates overflowed its banks, deluged a part of the city, and overturned twenty stadia of the wall; in consequence of which the desponding king burned himself, and his palace, with his treasures.

Darkness shall pursue. All kinds of calamity shall pursue them till they are destroyed.

9. *Affliction shall not rise up the second time.* There shall be no need to repeat the judgment; with one blow God will make a full end of the business.

11. *Imagineth evil against the Lord.* Such were Pul, 2 Kings xv. 10; Tiglath-pileser, 2 Kings xv. 29; Shalmaneser, 2 Kings xvii. 6; and Sennacherib, 2 Kings xviii. 17 and xix. 23. *A wicked counsellor.* Sennacherib and Rabshakeh.

MATTHEW HENRY

This great army (*v.* 12), *though they be quiet and likewise many,* very secure, because *they are numerous,* yet shall they be cut down, as grass and corn when *he shall pass through.*

2. Upon the king. He *imagined evil against the Lord,* and shall he escape? (*v.* 14): "*The Lord has given a commandment concerning thee;* the decree has gone forth, *that thy name be no more sown,* that thy memory perish." The images he worshipped should be cut off from their temple, which, some think, was fulfilled when Sennacherib was slain by his *two sons, as he was worshipping in the house of Nisroch his god.* The temple was looked upon as defiled, and was therefore disused, and the images were cut off. Sennacherib's grave shall be made there, some think in the house of his god; there he is slain, and there he shall be buried, for *he is vile.* Or it may be meant of the ignominious fall of the Assyrian monarchy itself, upon the ruins of which that of Babylon was raised.

III. The great deliverance which God would hereby work for his own people and the city that was called by his name. The siege shall be raised: "*Now will I break his yoke from off thee,* by which thou art kept in servitude, and *will burst thy bonds asunder,* by which thou seemest bound to the Assyrian's wrath." This was a figure of the great salvation, by which the Jerusalem that is above is made free. The enemy shall be so weakened and dispirited that they shall never make any such attempt again. The enemy shall not dare again to attack Jerusalem (*v.* 15): *The wicked shall no more pass through thee as* they have done, to lay all waste. His army is cut off, his spirit cut off, and at length he himself is cut off. The tidings of this great deliverance will be welcomed throughout the kingdom, *v.* 15. While Sennacherib prevailed, and carried all before him, every day brought bad news; but now, *behold, upon the mountains, the feet of him that bringeth good tidings,* the *feet of the evangelist;* he is seen coming at a distance upon the mountains, as fast as his feet will carry him; and how pleasant a sight is it once more to see a messenger of peace, after we have received so many of Job's messengers! These words are also quoted by the apostle, both from Isaiah and Nahum, and applied to the great redemption wrought for us by our Lord Jesus, and the publishing of it to the world by the everlasting gospel, Rom. x. 15. Christ's ministers are those messengers of good tidings, that preach *peace by Jesus Christ.* During the trouble ordinary feasts had been intermitted. While Jerusalem was *encompassed with armies* they could not go thither to worship; but now they must return to the observance of their feasts. Now that the deliverance is wrought they are called upon to perform their vows.

JAMIESON, FAUSSET, BROWN

—lit., "a counsellor of Belial." Belial means "without profit," worthless, and so bad (I Sam. 25:25; II Cor. 6:15). **12-14.** The same truths repeated as in vss. 9-11, Jehovah here being the speaker. He addresses Judah, prophesying good to it, and evil to the Assyrian. **Though they be quiet**—i.e., without fear, and tranquilly secure. So *Chaldee* and CALVIN. Or, "entire," "complete"; "Though their power be *unbroken* [MAURER], and though they be *so many, yet even so* they shall be cut down" (lit., "shorn"; as *hair shaved off closely by a razor,* Isa. 7:20). As the Assyrian was a razor shaving others, so shall he be shaven himself. Retribution in kind. In the height of their pride and power, they shall be clean cut off. The same *Hebrew* stands for "likewise" and "yet thus." So *many* as they are, *so* many shall they perish. **when he shall pass through**—or, "and he shall pass away," viz., "the wicked counsellor" (vs. 11), Sennacherib. The change of number to the *singular* distinguishes *him* from *his host. They* shall be cut down, *he* shall pass away home (II Kings 19:35, 36) [HENDERSON]. *English Version* is better, "they shall be cut down, *when* He [Jehovah] shall pass through," destroying by one stroke the Assyrian host. This gives the reason why they with all their numbers and power are to be so utterly cut off. Cf. "pass through," i.e., in destroying power (Ezek. 12:12, 23; Isa. 8:8; Dan. 11:10). **Though I have afflicted thee**—Judah, "I will afflict thee no more" (Isa. 40:1, 2; 52:1, 2). The contrast is between "they," the Assyrians, and "thee," Judah. *Their* punishment is fatal and final. Judah's was temporary and corrective. **13. will I break his yoke**—the Assyrian's yoke, viz., the tribute imposed by Sennacherib on Hezekiah (II Kings 18: 14). **from off thee**—O Judah (Isa. 10:27). **14. that no more of thy name be sown**—that no more of thy seed, bearing thy name, as kings of Nineveh, be propagated; that thy dynasty become extinct, viz., on the destruction of Nineveh here foretold; "thee" means the *king of Assyria.* **will I cut off . . . graven image**—The Medes under Cyaxares, the joint destroyers of Nineveh with the Babylonians, hated idolatry, and would delight in destroying its idols. As the Assyrians had treated the gods of other nations, so their own should be treated (II Kings 19:18). The Assyrian palaces partook of a sacred character [LAYARD]; so that "house of thy gods" *may* refer to the *palace.* At Khorsabad there is remaining a representation of a man cutting an idol to pieces. **I will make thy grave**—rather, "I will make it (viz., 'the house of thy gods,' i.e., Nisroch) thy grave" (II Kings 19:37; Isa. 37:38). Thus, by Sennacherib's being slain in it, Nisroch's house should be defiled. Neither thy gods, nor thy temple, shall save thee; but the latter shall be thy sepulchre. **thou art vile**—or, thou art lighter than due weight (Dan. 5:27; cf. Job 31:6) [MAURER]. **15.** This verse is joined in the *Hebrew* text to ch. 2. It is nearly the same as Isaiah 52:7, referring to the similar deliverance from Babylon. **him that bringeth good tidings**—announcing the overthrow of Sennacherib and deliverance of Jerusalem. The "mountains" are those round Jerusalem, on which Sennacherib's host had so lately encamped, preventing Judah from keeping her "feasts," but on which messengers now speed to Jerusalem, publishing his overthrow with a loud voice where lately they durst not have opened their mouths. A type of the far more glorious spiritual deliverance of God's people from Satan by Messiah, heralded by ministers of the Gospel (Rom. 10:15). **perform thy vows**—which thou didst promise if God would deliver thee from the Assyrian. **the wicked**—lit., "Belial"; the same as the "counsellor of Belial" (*Margin,* ch. 1: 11); viz., Sennacherib.

ADAM CLARKE

12. *Though they be . . . many.* Sennacherib invaded Judea with an army of nearly 200,000 men. *Thus shall they be cut down.* The angel of the Lord (a suffocating wind) slew of them in one night 185,000, 2 Kings xix. 35.

13. *Now will I break his yoke from off thee.* This refers to the tribute which the Jews were obliged to pay to the Assyrians, 2 Kings xvii. 14.

14. *No more of thy name be sown.* No more of you shall be carried away into captivity.

I will make thy grave; for thou art vile. I think this is an address to the Assyrians, and especially to Sennacherib. The house of his gods is to be his grave; and we know that while he was worshipping in the house of his god Nisroch, his two sons, Adrammelech and Sharezer, smote him there that he died, 2 Kings xix. 37.

15. *Behold upon the mountains.* Borrowed probably from Isa. lii. 7, but applied here to the messengers who brought the good tidings of the destruction of Nineveh. Judah might then keep her solemn feasts, for the wicked Assyrian should pass through the land no more, being entirely cut off, and the imperial city razed to its foundations.

MATTHEW HENRY — CHAPTER 2

Verses 1–10

I. An alarm of war went to Nineveh, *v.* 1. The prophet speaks of it as just at hand: "Look about thee, and see, *he that dashes in pieces has come up before thy face.* Nebuchadnezzar is noted for dashing nations in pieces, and will disperse thee." The attempt of Nebuchadnezzar upon Nineveh is bold, and daring: "He *has come up before thy face,* avowing his design to ruin thee; therefore stand to thy arms, *O Nineveh! keep the munition;* secure thy towers and magazines: *watch the way;* set guards upon all the avenues to the city; *make thy loins strong;* encourage thy soldiers; animate thyself and them; *fortify thy power mightily*" (this is spoken ironically); "do the utmost thou canst, yet *there is no counsel or strength against the Lord.*"

JAMIESON, FAUSSET, BROWN — CHAPTER 2

Vss. 1-13. THE ADVANCE OF THE DESTROYING FORCES AGAINST NINEVEH, AFTER IT WAS USED AS GOD'S ROD FOR A TIME TO CHASTISE HIS PEOPLE: THE CAPTURE OF THAT LION'S DWELLING, ACCORDING TO THE SURE WORD OF JEHOVAH. **1. He that dasheth in pieces**—God's "battle-axe," wherewith He "breaks in pieces" His enemies. Jeremiah 51: 20 applies the same *Hebrew* term to Nebuchadnezzar (cf. Prov. 25:18; Jer. 50:23, "the hammer of the whole earth"). Here the Medo-Babylonian army under Cyaxares and Nabopolassar, that destroyed Nineveh, is prophetically meant. **before thy face**—before Nineveh. *Openly,* so that the work of God may be manifest. **watch the way**—by which the foe will attack, so as to be ready to meet him. Ironical advice; equivalent to a prophecy, Thou shalt have need to use all possible means of defense;

ADAM CLARKE — CHAPTER 2

1. *He that dasheth in pieces.* Or "scattereth." The Chaldeans and Medes. *Keep the munition.* Guard the fenced places, From this to the end of the fifth verse, the preparations made at Nineveh to repel their enemies are described. The description is exceedingly picturesque.

Watch the way. By which the enemy is most likely to approach.

MATTHEW HENRY

II. The causes of the war (*v.* 2): *The Lord has turned away the excellency of Jacob, as the excellency of Israel.* The Assyrians have been abusive to Jacob, the two tribes as well as to Israel, the ten tribes, *have emptied them, and marred their vine-branches.* For this God will reckon with them; though done long since. Or, It may mean God is now by Nebuchadnezzar about *to turn away the pride of Jacob* by the captivity of the two tribes, as he did the pride of Israel by their captivity. The enemy that is to do it must begin with Nineveh. God is looking upon proud cities, and abasing them. Samaria is humbled, and Jerusalem is to be humbled, and shall not Nineveh, that proud city, he brought down too? *Emptiers have emptied* the cities, *and marred the vine-branches* in the country of Jacob and Israel.

III. A particular account given of the terrors wherein the invading enemy shall appear against Nineveh. 1. *The shields of his mighty men are made red* as if they were already tinctured with the blood they had shed.

2. *The valiant men are in scarlet;* rich clothes, to intimate the wealth of the army.

3. *The chariots shall be with flaming torches in the day of his preparation;* the wheels shall strike fire upon the stones. Or they carried flaming torches with them in the open chariots, when they made their approach in the night, to be both a guide to themselves to set all on fire wherever they went.

4. *The fir-trees shall be terribly shaken;* the great men of Nineveh, that overtop their neighbours, as the stately firs do the shrubs; or the standing trees shall be made to shake by the concussions which that great army shall cause. 5. The chariots of war shall be very terrible (*v.* 4): *They shall rage in the streets,* that is, those that drive them shall rage. Even *in the broad ways,* where, one would *think,* there should be room enough, they shall *jostle one another*; and these iron chariots shall be made so bright that in the beams of the sun *shall they seem like torches* in the night.

Nebuchadnezzar's commanders are here called his *worthies,* his *gallants* (so the margin reads it). *His worthies shall remember* (so some read it); they shall be mindful of duty, and the charge they have received, and be so intent upon their business that they *shall stumble in their walks,* for *they shall make haste to the wall thereof,* and the defence, or the covered way, shall be prepared (something to shelter them from the darts of the besieged), and they shall carry on the siege, and with so much vigour, that the *gates of the rivers shall be opened* (*v.* 6); those gates of Nineveh which open upon the river Tigris (on which Nineveh was built) shall be first forced by the enemy, and by those gates they shall enter.

JAMIESON, FAUSSET, BROWN

but use what thou wilt, all will be in vain. **make thy loins strong**—The loins are the seat of strength; to gird them up is to prepare all one's strength for conflict (Job 40:7). Also gird on thy sword (II Sam. 20:8; II Kings 4:29). **2. For the Lord hath turned away the excellency of Jacob**—i.e., the time for Nineveh's overthrow is ripe, because Jacob (Judah) and Israel (the ten tribes) have been sufficiently chastised. The Assyrian rod of chastisement, having done its work, is to be thrown into the fire. If God chastised Jacob and Israel with all their "excellency" (Jerusalem and the temple, which was their pre-eminent excellency above all nations in God's eyes, Ps. 47:4; 87:2; Ezek. 24:21; *Note,* Amos 6:8), how much more will He punish fatally Nineveh, an alien to Him, and idolatrous? MAURER, not so well, translates, "restores," or "will restore the excellency of Jacob." **emptiers**—the Assyrian spoilers. **have emptied them out**—have spoiled the Israelites and Jews (Hos. 10:1). Cf. Psalm 80:8-16, on "vine branches," as applied to Israel. **3. his mighty men**—the Medo-Babylonian general's *mighty men* attacking Nineveh. **made red**—The ancients dyed their bull's-hide shields *red,* partly to strike terror into the enemy, chiefly lest the blood from wounds which they might receive should be perceived and give confidence to the foe [CALVIN]. G. V. SMITH conjectures that the reference is to the red reflection of the sun's rays from shields of bronze or copper, such as are found among the Assyrian remains. **in scarlet**—or *crimson* military tunics (cf. Matt. 27:28). Xenophon mentions that the Medes were fond of this color. The Lydians and Tyrians extracted the dye from a particular worm. **chariots . . . with flaming torches**—i.e, the chariots shall be like flaming torches, their wheels in lightning-like rapidity of rotation flashing light and striking sparks from the stones over which they pass (cf. Isa. 5:28). *English Version* supposes a transposition of the *Hebrew* letters. It is better to translate the *Hebrew* as it is, "the chariots (shall be furnished) with fire-flashing *scythes*" (lit., "with the fire," or glitter, *of iron weapons*). Iron scythes were fixed at right angles to the axles and turned down, or parallel to it, inserted into the felly of the wheel. The Medes, perhaps, had such chariots, though no traces of them are found in Assyrian remains. On account of the latter fact, it may be better to translate, "the chariots (shall come) with the glitter of *steel weapons*" [MAURER and G. V. SMITH]. **in the day of his preparation**—JEHOVAH'S (Isa. 13:3). Or, *"Medo-Babylonian commander's* day of preparation for the attack" (vs. 1). "He" confirms this, and "his" in this verse. **the fir trees**—their fir-tree lances. **terribly shaken**—branded so as to strike terror. Or, "shall be tremulous with being brandished" [MAURER]. **4. rage**—are driven in furious haste (Jer. 46:9). **justle one against another**—run to and fro [MAURER]. **in the broad ways**—(II Chron. 32:6). Large open spaces in the suburbs of Nineveh. **they shall seem like torches**—lit., "their (feminine in *Hebrew*) appearance" (is): viz., the appearance of *the broad places* is like that of torches, through the numbers of chariots in them flashing in the sun (*Margin,* Prov. 8:26). **run like the lightnings**—with rapid violence (Matt. 24:27; Luke 10:18). **5.** The Assyrian preparations for defense. **He**—the Assyrian king. **shall recount his worthies**—(ch. 3:18). *Review,* or *count over in his mind,* his nobles, choosing out the bravest to hasten to the walls and repel the attack. But in vain; for "they shall stumble in their *advance*" through fear and hurry. **the defence shall be prepared**—rather, *the covering machine* used *by besiegers* to protect themselves in advancing to the wall. Such sudden transitions, as here from the besieged to the besiegers, are frequent (cf. Ezek. 4:2), [MAURER]. Or, used *by the besieged Assyrians* [CALVIN]. **6. The gates of the rivers . . . opened**—The river wall on the Tigris (the west defense of Nineveh) was 4,530 yards long. On the north, south, and east sides, there were large moats, capable of being easily filled with water from the Khosru. Traces of dams ("gates," or sluices) for regulating the supply are still visible, so that the whole city could be surrounded with a water barrier (vs. 8). Besides, on the east, the weakest side, it was further protected by a lofty double rampart with a moat 200 feet wide between its two parts, cut in the rocky ground. The moats or canals, flooded by the Ninevites before the siege to repel the foe, were made a dry bed to march into the city, by the foe turning the waters into a different channel: as Cyrus did in the siege of Babylon [MAURER]. In the earlier capture of Nineveh by Arbaces the Mede, and Belesis the Babylonian, DIODORUS SICULUS, *l.* 2. 80, states that there was an old prophecy that it should not be taken till the river

ADAM CLARKE

Make thy loins strong. Take courage. *Fortify thy power.* Muster your troops; call in all your allies.

F. B. MEYER:

"The Lord bringeth again the excellency of Jacob" (v. 2). Too long Nineveh had exerted her malign influence upon the fortunes of the chosen people; that, to use the expressive simile of the eleventh verse, it had resembled a den of lions, whence ravenous beasts prowl forth to devour the villagers. The Assyrians, pouring forth from their mighty metropolis, had devastated the excellency of Jacob, the cry of the land had gone up to Jehovah; and He here declares his determination to quell the enemy and avenger, and to bring again the excellency of the people whom He loved.

It may be that you, too, have been carried into captivity, or devastated by strongly besetting sins; though you pray and yearn for emancipation, still you are kept low by the depredations of the power of evil. But be of good cheer; God is moving to your help. He is against those who are against you; He will bring again your excellency. He resembles the mother, whose child is smitten with smallpox. Does she love it less? Nay, but comes nearer, that they may fight the disease together.

You shall excel in faith when the hindrance is removed. The faith that once characterized you shall arouse with its former vigor, and make an open pathway down which heaven's best blessings may enter your life. At its summons the unseen will become more real than the seen, and God will be all in all. You shall excel also in hope. This is the realizing faculty, accepting the assurances of faith following them as the beacon-lights that guide weary sailors; for hope is more than faith, as the artist is more than the preparer of colors. You shall also excel in love. When self-will looses its hold upon the soul, love springs spontaneously from its soil.

—*Great Verses Through the Bible*

4. *The chariots shall rage.* Those of the besiegers and the besieged, meeting in the streets, producing universal confusion and carnage.

5. *He shall recount his worthies.* Muster up his most renowned warriors and heroes. *Shall make haste to the wall.* Where they see the enemies making their most powerful attacks, in order to get possession of the city.

6. *The gates of the rivers shall be opened.* The account given by Diodorus Siculus, lib. ii, is very surprising. He begins thus: "There was a prophecy received from their forefathers, that Nineveh should not be taken till the river first became an enemy to the city. It happened in the third year of the siege, that the Euphrates [query, Tigris] being swollen with continued rains, overflowed part of the city, and threw down twenty stadia of the wall. The king, then imagining that the oracle was accomplished, and that the river was now manifestly become an enemy to the city, casting aside all hope of safety, and lest he should fall into the hands of the enemy, built a large funeral pyre in the palace, and having collected all his gold and silver and royal vestments, together with his concubines and eunuchs, placed himself with them in a little apartment built in the pyre; burnt them, himself, and the palace together.

MATTHEW HENRY

And then the *palace shall be dissolved*, either the king's house or the house of Nisroch his god; the same word signifies both a palace and a temple.

IV. A prediction of the consequences of this. 1. The queen shall fall into the hands of the enemy (*v.* 7): *Huzzub shall be led away captive;* she that was *established* (so some read it), thought herself safe because she was concealed, shall be *discovered* (so the margin reads it) and shall be led *away captive*, in disgrace.

She shall be *brought up* in a mock state, *and her maids* of honour *shall lead her*, because she is weak and faint. They shall be *tabering upon their breasts*, beating their own breasts in grief, as if they were *drumming* upon them, for so the word signifies. 2. The inhabitants, shall none of them be able to stand their ground (*v.* 8): *Nineveh is of old like a pool of water*, replenished with people as a pool with water. It was long ago a populous city; in Jonah's time there were 120,000 little children in it (Jonah iv. 11).

Their commanders shall cry, "*Stand, stand*, have a good heart on it, and we shall do well enough." They shall not have the least spark of courage remaining. They shall not so much as look back to see who calls for them. 3. The wealth of the city shall become a prey, and all its rich furniture shall fall into the hands of the victorious enemy (*v.* 9).

Thus this rich city is empty, and void, and waste, *v.* 10. 4. The soldiers and people shall have no heart to appear for the defence of the city. *Much pain* shall be *in all loins*, as is the case in extreme frights, so that they shall not be able to hold up their backs. And the *faces of them all shall gather blackness*, like that of a pot that is every day over the fire; so the word signifies.

Verses 11–13

Nineveh's ruin, 1. Its neighbours now remember against it all the oppressions it had been guilty of in its pomp and prosperity (*v.* 11, 12): *Where is the dwelling of the lions? Where is the feeding place of the young lions*, where they glutted themselves with prey? The princes of Nineveh had been as lions, beasts of prey. Though nobody loved them, everybody feared them, and that was all they desired. The king made it his business, by violence and extortion to enrich himself and raise his family; he did *tear in pieces enough for his whelps* and he *strangled for his lionesses*. 2. It is avowed by the righteous Judge (*v.* 13): *Behold, I am against thee, saith the Lord of hosts*. The oppressors in Nineveh thought they only set their neighbours against them, but they set God against them, who is the asserter of right and the avenger of wrong. These military preparations will stand them in no stead: *I will burn their chariots in the smoke;* he does not say *in the fire*, but, in contempt of them, the very *smoke* of God's indignation shall serve to burn their chariots. Their children the hopes of their families, shall be cut off: *The sword shall devour the young lions*. The wealth they have heaped up by fraud and violence shall not be enjoyed by them: thou shalt not be the better for it and no one else shall. *The voice of thy messengers shall no more be heard*, no more be heeded, which some think refers to Rabshakeh.

JAMIESON, FAUSSET, BROWN

became its enemy; so in the third year of the siege, the river by a flood broke down the walls twenty furlongs, and the king thereupon burnt himself and his palace and all his concubines and wealth together, and the enemy entered by the breach in the wall. Fire and water were doubtless the means of the second destruction here foretold, as of the first. **dissolved**—by the inundation [HENDERSON]. Or, those in the palace shall melt with fear, viz., the king and his nobles [GROTIUS]. **7. Huzzab**—the name of the queen of Nineveh, from a *Hebrew* root implying that she *stood by* the king (Ps. 45:9), [VATABLUS]. Rather, Nineveh personified as a queen. She who had long *stood* in the most supreme prosperity. Similarly CALVIN. MAURER makes it not a proper name, and translates, "It is established," or "determined" (cf. Gen. 41:32). *English Version* is more supported by the parallelism. **led away captive**—The *Hebrew* requires rather, "she *is laid bare*"; brought forth from the apartments where Eastern women remained secluded, and is stripped of her ornamental attire. Cf. Isaiah 47:2, 3, where the same image of a woman with face and legs exposed is used of a city captive and dismantled (cf. ch. 3:5), [MAURER]. **brought up**—Her people shall be *made to go up* to Babylon. Cf. the use of "go up" for *moving from* a place in Jeremiah 21:2. **her maids . . . as . . . doves**—As Nineveh is compared to a queen dethroned and dishonored, so she has here assigned to her in the image *handmaids attending her with dove-like plaints* (Isa. 38:14; 59:11. The image implies *helplessness and grief suppressed, but at times breaking out*). The minor cities and dependencies of Nineveh may be meant, or her captive women [JEROME]. GROTIUS and MAURER translate, for "lead *her*," "*moan*," or "*sigh*." **tabering**—*beating* on their breasts *as on a tambourine*. **8. But**—rather, "Though" [G. V. SMITH]. **of old**—rather, "*from the days* that she hath been"; from the earliest period of her existence. Alluding to Nineveh's antiquity (Gen. 10:11). "Though Nineveh has been of old defended by water surrounding her, yet her inhabitants shall flee away." GROTIUS, less probably (cf. ch. 3:8-12), interprets, the "waters" of her *numerous population* (Isa. 8:7; Jer. 51:13; Rev. 17:15). **Stand, stand,** *shall they cry*—i.e., the few patriotic citizens *shall cry* to their *fleeing* countrymen; "but none looketh back," much less stops in flight, so panic-stricken are they. **9. silver . . . gold**—The conquerors are summoned to plunder the city. Nineveh's riches arose from the annual tribute paid by so many subject states, as well as from its extensive merchandise (ch. 3:16; Ezek. 27:23, 24). **store**—accumulated by the plunder of subject nations. It is remarkable, that while small articles of value (bronze inlaid with gold, gems, seals, and alabaster *vases*) are found in the ruins of Nineveh, there are none of *gold* and *silver*. These, as here foretold, were "taken for spoil" before the palaces were set on fire. **glory out of all the pleasant furniture**—or, "there is abundance of precious vessels of every kind" [MAURER]. **10.** Lit., "emptiness, and emptiedness, and devastation." The accumulation of substantives without a verb (as in ch. 3:2), the two first of the three being derivatives of the same root, and like in sound, and the number of syllables in them increasing in a kind of climax, intensify the gloomy effectiveness of the expression.

faces of all gather blackness—(*Note*, Joel 2:6). CALVIN translates, "withdraw (lit., 'gather up') their glow," or flush, i.e. grow pale. This is probably the better rendering. So MAURER. **11. dwelling of . . . lions**—Nineveh, the seat of empire of the rapacious and destructive warriors of various ranks, typified by the "lions," "young lions," "old lion" (or *lioness* [MAURER]), "the lion's whelp." The image is peculiarly appropriate, as lions of every form, winged, and sometimes with the head of a man, are frequent in the Assyrian sepulchres. It was as full of spoils of all nations as a lion's den is of remains of its prey. The question, "Where . . ." implies that Jehovah "would make an utter end of *the place*," so that its very site could not be found (ch. 1:8). It is a question expressing wonder, so incredible did it then seem. **12. prey . . . ravin**—different kinds of prey. Cf. Isaiah 3:1, "the stay and the staff." **13. burn . . . in the smoke**—or (so as to pass) "*into* smoke," i.e., "entirely" [MAURER], (Ps. 37:20; 46:9). CALVIN, like *English Version*, explains, As soon as the flame catches, and the fire smokes, by the mere smoke I will burn her chariots. **cut off thy prey from the earth**—Thou shalt no more carry off prey from the nations of the earth. **the voice of thy messengers . . . no more . . . heard**—No more shall thy emissaries be heard throughout thy provinces conveying thy king's commands, and exacting tribute of subject nations.

ADAM CLARKE

When the death of the king was announced by certain deserters, the enemy entered in by the breach which the waters had made, and took the city."

7. *And Huzzab shall be led away captive*. Perhaps *Huzzab* means the queen of Nineveh, who had escaped the burning mentioned above by Diodorus. As there is no account of the queen being burnt, but only of the king, the concubines, and the eunuchs, we may therefore naturally conclude that the queen escaped; and is represented here as *brought up* and delivered to the conqueror, her maids at the same time bewailing her lot. Some think *Huzzab* signifies Nineveh itself.

8. *But Nineveh is of old like a pool of water*. Bishop Newcome translates the line thus: "And the waters of Nineveh are a pool of waters."

Stand, stand. Consternation shall be at its utmost height; the people shall flee in all directions; and though quarter is offered, and they are assured of safety if they remain, yet not one looketh back.

9. *Take ye the spoil*. Though the king burnt his treasures, vestments, he could not totally destroy the silver and the gold. Nor did he burn the riches of the city; these fell a prey to the conquerors; and there was no end of the store of glorious garments, and the most costly vessels and furniture.

10. *She is empty, and void, and waste*. The original is strongly emphatic. The words are of the same sound, and increase in their length as they point out great, greater, and greatest desolation. *Bukah, umebukah, umebullakah*. "She is void, empty, and desolate."

11. *Where is the dwelling of the lions?* Nineveh, the habitation of bold, strong, and ferocious men. *The feedingplace of the young lions*. Whither her victorious and rapacious generals frequently returned to consume the produce of their success. Here they walked at large, *and none made them afraid*. Wheresoever they turned their arms they were victors, and all nations were afraid of them.

12. *The lion did tear*. This verse gives us a striking picture of the manner in which the Assyrian conquests and depredations were carried on. How many people were spoiled to enrich his *whelps*—his sons, princes, and nobles! How many women were stripped and slain, whose spoils went to decorate his *lionesses*—his queen, concubines, and mistresses! And they had even more than they could assume; their *holes* and *dens*—treasure-houses, palaces, and wardrobes—were filled *with ravin*, the riches which they got by plunder.

13. *Behold, I am against thee*. Assyria, and Nineveh, its capital. I will deal with you as you have dealt with others. *The voice of thy messengers*. Announcing your splendid victories, and the vast spoils taken.

MATTHEW HENRY

CHAPTER 3

Verses 1–7

I. Nineveh arraigned and indicted. 1. It is a *city of blood.* 2. *It is all full of lies;* truth is banished from among them; there is no such thing as honesty. 3. It is all full of *robbery* and rapine. 4. There is a *multitude of whoredoms* in it, that is, idolatries, spiritual whoredoms. 5. She is a *mistress of witchcrafts,* and by them she *sells families, v.* 4. That which Nineveh aimed at was a universal monarchy, to be the metropolis of the world, compelling some, deluding others, into subjection to her, and wheedling them as a harlot by her charms. These were her witchcrafts, with which she unaccountably gained dominion.

II. Nineveh condemned to ruin upon this indictment, *v.* 1.

1. Nineveh had with her cruelties been a terror and destruction to others, and therefore destruction and terror shall be brought upon her. Hear the alarm with which Nineveh shall be terrified, *v.* 2. It is a formidable army that advances against it; you may hear them at a distance, the *noise of the whip,* the *rattling of the wheels, the prancing horses, and the jumping chariots;* the very noise is frightful. Nineveh shall be laid waste (*v.* 3), the sword drawn, *the bright sword lifted up and the glittering spear,* the dazzling brightness of which is terrible. See what havoc these make when they are commissioned to slay! The destruction of Sennacherib's army, which, in the morning, were *all dead corpses,* is perhaps looked upon here as a figure of the like destruction that should afterwards be in Nineveh.

2. Nineveh had drawn others to shameful wickedness, and therefore God will load her with contempt (*v.* 5–7): *The Lord of hosts* is *against her.* When it shall be seen that while she courted her neighbours it was with design to ruin their liberty and property, then her *shame is discovered to the nations.* When her proud pretensions are baffled, then *to see the nakedness of the land do they come,* and it appears ridiculous. Then do they *cast abominable filth upon her,* as upon a carted strumpet, and *make her vile.* Those that formerly looked upon her in hopes of protection from her, now *look upon her and flee from her,* for fear of being ruined with her. When Nineveh is laid waste *who will bemoan her?* Those that showed no pity in the day of their power can expect to find no pity in the day of their fall.

Verses 8–19

I. Nineveh shall fall unpitied and uncomforted and she shall not be able to help herself: *Art thou better than populous No? v.* 8. He quotes precedents. The city mentioned is *No,* a great city in the land of Egypt (Jer. xlvi. 25), *No-Ammon,* so some read it. Some think it was *Diospolis,* others *Alexandria.* As God said to Jerusalem, *Go, see what I did to Shiloh* (Jer. vii. 12), so to Nineveh, *Go, see what I did to populous No.*

Now, concerning No, 1. How firm her standing, *v.* 8. She was fortified both by nature and art, was *situate among the rivers.*

JAMIESON, FAUSSET, BROWN

CHAPTER 3

Vss. 1-19. Repetition of Nineveh's Doom, with New Features; the Cause Is Her Tyranny, Rapine, and Cruelty: No-ammon's Fortifications Did Not Save Her; It Is Vain, Therefore, for Nineveh to Think Her Defenses Will Secure Her against God's Sentence. **1. the bloody city!**—lit., "city of blood," viz., shed by Nineveh; just so now her own blood is to be shed. **robbery**—violence [Maurer]. Extortion [Grotius]. **the prey departeth not**—Nineveh never ceases to live by rapine. Or, the *Hebrew* verb is transitive, "she (Nineveh) does not make the prey depart"; she ceases not to plunder. **2.** The reader is transported into the midst of the fight (cf. Jer. 47:3). The "noise of the whips" urging on the horses (in the chariots) is heard, and of "the rattling of the wheels" of war-chariots, and the "horses" are seen "prancing," and the "chariots jumping," etc. **3. horseman**—distinct from "the horses" (in the chariots, vs. 2). **lifteth up**—denoting readiness for fight [Ewald]. Gesenius translates, "lifteth up (lit., makes to ascend) his horse." Similarly Maurer, "makes his horse to rise up on his hind feet." *Vulgate* translates, "ascending," i.e., making his horse to advance up to the assault. This last is perhaps better than *English Version.* **the bright sword and the glittering spear**—lit., "the glitter of the sword and the flash of the spear!" This, as well as the translation, "the horseman advancing up," more graphically presents the battle scene to the eye. **they stumble upon their corpses**—The *Medo-Babylonian* enemy stumble upon the *Assyrian corpses.* **4. Because of the multitude of the whoredoms**—This assigns the reason for Nineveh's destruction. **whoredoms of the well-favoured harlot**—As Assyria was not a worshipper of the true God, "whoredoms" cannot mean, as in the case of Israel, apostasy to the worship of false gods; but, her *harlot-like artifices* whereby she allured neighboring states so as to subject them to herself. As the unwary are allured by the "well-favored harlot's" looks, so Israel, Judah (e.g., under Ahaz, who, calling to his aid Tiglath-pileser, was made tributary by him, II Kings 16:7-10), and other nations, were tempted by the plausible professions of Assyria, and by the lure of commerce (Rev. 18:2, 3), to trust her. **witchcrafts**—(Isa. 47:9, 12). Alluding to the love incantations whereby harlots tried to dement and ensnare youths; answering to the subtle machinations whereby Assyria attracted nations to her. **selleth**—deprives of their liberty; as slaves used to be *sold:* and in other property also *sale* was a usual mode of transfer. Maurer understands it of depriving nations of their freedom, and literally *selling* them as slaves to distant peoples (Joel 3:2, 3, 6-8). But elsewhere there is no evidence that the Assyrians did this. **families**—peoples. **5. I will discover thy skirts upon thy face**—i.e., discover thy nakedness by *throwing up thy skirts upon thy face* (the greatest possible insult), pulling them up as as high as thy head (Jer. 13:22; Ezek. 16:37-41). I will treat thee not as a matron, but as a harlot whose shame is exposed; her gaudy finery being lifted up off her (Isa. 47:2, 3). So Nineveh shall be stripped of all her glory and defenses on which she prides herself. **6. cast abominable filth upon thee**—as infamous harlots used to be treated. **gazing-stock**—exposed to public ignominy as a warning to others (Ezek. 28:17). **7. all . . . that look upon thee**—when thou hast been made "a gazing-stock" (vs. 6). **shall flee from thee**—as a thing horrible to look upon. Cf. "standing *afar off,*" Rev. 18:10. **whence shall I seek comforters for thee?**—Cf. Isaiah 51:19, which Nahum had before his mind. **8. populous No**—rather, as *Hebrew,* "No-ammon," the Egyptian name for Thebes in Upper Egypt; meaning the *portion* or *possession of Ammon,* the Egyptian Jupiter (whence the Greeks called the city Diospolis), who was especially worshipped there. The Egyptian inscriptions call the god *Amon-re,* i.e., "*Amon the Sun*"; he is represented as a human figure with a ram's head, seated on a chair (Jer. 46:25; Ezek. 30:14-16). The blow inflicted on No-ammon, described in vs. 10, was probably by the Assyrian Sargon (cf. *Notes* on Isa. 18 and 20). As Thebes, with all her resources, was overcome by Assyria, so Assyrian Nineveh, notwithstanding all her might, in her turn, shall be overcome by Babylon. *English Version,* "populous," if correct, implies that No's large population did not save her from destruction. **situate among the rivers**—probably the *channels* into which the Nile here divides (cf. Isa. 19:6-8). Thebes lay on both sides of the river. It was famed in Homer's time for its hundred gates (*Illiad,* 9.381). Its ruins still describe a circumference of twenty-seven miles. Of them the

ADAM CLARKE

CHAPTER 3

1. *Woe to the bloody city!* Nineveh, the threatenings against which are continued in a strain of invective, astonishing for its richness, variety, and energy. One may hear and see the whip cracking, the horses prancing, the wheels rumbling, the chariots bounding after the galloping steeds; the reflection from the drawn and highly polished swords; and the hurled spears, like flashes of lightning, dazzling the eyes; the slain lying in heaps, and horses and chariots stumbling over them!

4. *Because of the multitude of the whoredoms.* Above, the Ninevites were represented under the emblem of a lion tearing all to pieces; here they are represented under the emblem of a beautiful harlot or public prostitute, enticing all men to her, inducing the nations to become idolatrous; and, by thus perverting them, rendering them also objects of the divine wrath.

Mistress of witchcrafts, that selleth nations through her whoredoms. Using every means to excite to idolatry; and being, by menace or wiles, successful in all.

8. *Art thou better than populous No?* No-Ammon, in the Delta, on one branch of the Nile, which had been lately destroyed, probably by the Chaldeans.

MATTHEW HENRY

Nile watered her fields, guarded her wall. *Her rampart was the sea,* the *lake of Mareotis.*

It was also supported by alliances abroad, *v.* 9. *Ethiopia,* or Arabia, *was her strength,* either by trade or by forces furnished for military service. The whole country of Egypt contributed to this populous city; so that it was *infinite, and there was no end of it* (so it might be rendered); she set no bounds to her ambition and knew no end of her wealth and strength; but it is God's prerogative to be infinite. *Put and Lubim were thy helpers,* two neighbouring countries of Africa, Mauritania and Libya, that is, Libya Cyrenica. 2. How fatal her fall proved to be (*v.* 10): *Yet was she carried away,* and her strength failed her; even she that was so strong, so secure, yet *went into captivity. Her young children* were *dashed in pieces at the top of all the streets* by the merciless conquerors. *They cast lots for her honourable men* that were made prisoners of war, to be slaves. What a mortification was this to *populous No.* Hence he infers against Nineveh (*v.* 11), "Thou also shalt be intoxicated, drunk with the cup of the Lord's fury, that shall be put into thy hand" (see Jer. xxv. 17, 27). *Thou shalt fall and rise no more.*

II. He shows them that all those things in which they reposed confidence should fail them. 1. Did the men of Nineveh trust to their own bravery? Their hearts should sink and fail them. *They shall be hid,* shall abscond for shame. They shall *seek strength,* shall come sneaking to their neighbours to beg assistance. 2. Did they depend upon the garrisons and strongholds they had? Those shall prove but paper-walls, and *like the first-ripe figs,* which, if you give the tree but a little shake, will *fall into the mouth of the eater* that gapes for them, *v.* 12. They make their strongholds as strong as possible, and are challenged to do their utmost to make them tenable against the invader (*v.* 14): *Draw thee water for the siege;* it is put here for all manner of provision, with which Nineveh is ironically told to furnish herself, in expectation of a siege. "*Go into clay, and tread the mortar,* and *make strong the brick-kiln;* take all the pains thou canst in erecting new fortifications; but it shall be all in vain, for (*v.* 15) there shall *the fire devour thee* if the stronghold be burnt, or *the sword cut thee off* if it be taken by storm." 3. Did they put confidence in the multitude of their inhabitants? They shall but sink the sooner under the weight of their own numbers (*v.* 13): *Thy people in the midst of thee are women;* they shall be fickle, and fainthearted in danger and distress; adding to their fears by the power of their own imagination. Though they *make themselves many* (*v.* 15), as the *cankerworm* and *as the locust,* that come in vast swarms, *though thou hast multiplied thy merchants above the stars of heaven,* though thy exchange be thronged with wealthy traders, yet their hearts shall fail them too; though they be numerous as caterpillars, yet the fire and sword shall eat them up irresistibly as the cankerworm, *v.* 15. He adds (*v.* 16), *The canker-worm spoils,* or *spreads herself, and flies away.* Both the merchants and the enemies were compared to canker-worms. The enemies shall spoil Nineveh, and carry away the spoil without opposition. Or the rich merchants, who have come from abroad to settle in Nineveh, when they see the country invaded and the city likely to be besieged, will remove to some other place, will *spread their wings* and *fly away* where they may be safe. 4. Did they put a confidence in the strength of their gates and bars? (*v.* 13). *The gates of thy land shall be set wide open unto thy enemies,* the gates of thy rivers (*ch.* ii. 6), the flood-gates, or the passes. *The fire shall devour thy bars,* and they shall fly open.

JAMIESON, FAUSSET, BROWN

temples of Luxor and Karnak, east of the river, are most famous. The colonnade of the former, and the grand hall of the latter, are of stupendous dimensions. One wall still represents the expedition of Shishak against Jerusalem under Rehoboam (I Kings 14:25; II Chron. 12:2-9). **whose . . . wall was from the sea**—i.e., *rose up* "from the sea." MAURER translates, "whose wall consisted *of the sea.*" But this would be a mere repetition of the former clause. The Nile is called a *sea,* from its appearance in the annual flood (Isa. 19:5). **9. Ethiopia**—*Hebrew, Cush.* Ethiopia is thought at this time to have been mistress of Upper Egypt. **Egypt** —Lower Egypt. **her strength**—her safeguard as an ally. **it was infinite**—The resources of these, her allies, were endless. **Put**—or Phut (Gen. 10:6); descended from Ham (Ezek. 27:10). From a root meaning a *bow;* as they were famed as archers [GESENIUS]. Probably west of Lower Egypt. JOSEPHUS (*Antiquities,* 1. 6. 2) identifies it with Mauritania (cf. *Margin,* Jer. 46:9; Ezek. 38:5). **Lubim**—the Libyans, whose capital was Cyrene; extending along the Mediterranean west of Egypt (II Chron. 12:3; 16:8; Acts 2:10). As, however, the *Lubim* are always connected with the Egyptians and Ethiopians, they are perhaps distinct from the *Libyans.* The Lubim were probably at first wandering tribes, who afterwards were settled under Carthage in the region of Cyrene, under the name Libyans. **thy**—No's. **helpers**—lit., "in thy help," i.e., among thy auxiliaries. **10.** Notwithstanding all her might, she was overcome. **cast lots for her honourable men**—They divided them among themselves by lot, as slaves (Joel 3:3). **11. drunken**—made to drink of the cup of Jehovah's wrath (Isa. 51:17, 21; Jer. 25: 15). **hid**—covered out of sight: a prediction remarkably verified in the state in which the ruins of Nineveh have been found [G. V. SMITH]. But as "hid" precedes "seek strength . . . ," it rather refers to Nineveh's state when attacked by her foe: "Thou who now so vauntest thyself, shalt be compelled to seek a hiding-place from the foe" [CALVIN]; or, shalt be neglected and slighted by all [MAURER]. **seek strength because of the enemy**—Thou too, like Thebes (vs. 9), shalt have recourse to other nations for help against thy Medo-Babylonian enemy. **12. thy strongholds**—on the borders of Assyria, protecting the approaches to Nineveh: "the gates of thy land" (vs. 13). **fig trees with the first ripe figs**—expressing the rapidity and ease of the capture of Nineveh (cf. Isa. 28.4; Rev. 6.13). **13. thy people**—thy soldiers. **women**—unable to fight for thee (Isa. 19:16; Jer. 50: 37; 51:30). **gates on thy land**—the fortified passes or entrances to the region of Nineveh (cf. Jer. 15:7). Northeast of Nineveh there were hills affording a natural barrier against an invader; the guarded passes through these are probably "the gates of the land" meant. **fire shall devour thy bars**—the "bars" of the fortresses at the passes into Assyria. So in Assyrian remains the Assyrians themselves are represented as setting fire to the gates of a city [BONOMI, *Nin.* pp. 194, 197]. **14.** Ironical exhortation to Nineveh to defend herself. **Draw . . . waters**—so as not to be without water for drinking, in the event of being cut off by the besiegers from the fountains. **make strong the brick-kiln**—or "repair" [MAURER]; so as to have a supply of bricks formed of kiln-burnt clay, to repair breaches in the ramparts, or to build new fortifications inside when the outer ones are taken by the foe. **15. There**—in the very scene of thy great preparations for defense; and where thou now art so secure. **fire**—even as at the former destruction; Sardanapalus (Pul?) perished with all his household in the conflagration of his palace, having in despair set it on fire, the traces of which are still remaining. **cankerworm**—"the licking locust" [HENDERSON]. **make thyself many as the locusts**—"the swarming locusts" [HENDERSON]; i.e., however "many" be thy forces, like those of "the swarming locusts," or the "licking locusts," yet the foe shall consume thee as the "licking locust" licks up all before it. **16. multiplied thy merchants**—(Ezek. 27: 23, 24). Nineveh, by large canals, had easy access to Babylon; and it was one of the great routes for the people of the west and northwest to that city; lying on the Tigris it had access to the sea. The Phœnicians carried its wares everywhere. Hence its merchandise is so much spoken of. **the cankerworm spoileth, and fleeth away**—i.e., **spoiled** *thy merchants.* The "cankerworm," or licking locust, answers to the Medo-Babylonian invaders of Nineveh [G. V. SMITH]. CALVIN explains less probably, "Thy merchants spoiled many regions; but the same shall befall them as befalls locusts, they in a moment shall be scattered and flee away." MAURER, somewhat similarly, "The licking locust puts off (the en-

ADAM CLARKE

The waters round about it. Being situated in the Delta, it had the fork of two branches of the Nile to defend it by land; and its barrier or *wall* was the *sea,* the Mediterranean, into which these branches emptied themselves: so that this city, and the place it stood on, were wholly surrounded by the waters.

9. *Put and Lubim.* A part of Africa and Libya, which were all within reach of forming alliances with No-Ammon.

10. *They cast lots for her honourable men.* This refers still to the city called "populous No." And the custom of casting *lots* among the commanders, for the prisoners which they had taken, is here referred to. *Great men were bound in chains.* These were reserved to grace the triumph of the victor.

12. *Thy strong holds.* The effects of the consternation into which the Ninevites were cast by the assault on their city are here pointed out by a very expressive metaphor. The *firstripe figs,* when at full maturity, fell from the tree with the least shake; and so, at the first shake or consternation, all the fortresses of Nineveh were abandoned; and the king, in despair, burnt himself and household in his own palace.

13. *Thy people . . . are women.* They lost all courage, and made no resistance.

14. *Draw thee waters for the siege.* The Tigris ran near to Nineveh, and here they are exhorted to lay in plenty of fresh water, lest the siege should last long, and lest the enemy should cut off this supply. *Go into clay, and tread the morter.* This refers to the manner of forming bricks anciently in those countries; they digged up the clay, kneaded it properly by treading, mixed it with straw or coarse grass, molded the bricks, and dried them in the sun.

16. *Thou hast multiplied thy merchants.* Like Tyre, this city was a famous resort for merchants; but the multitudes which were there previously to the siege, like the locusts, took the alarm, and fled away.

MATTHEW HENRY

5. Did they put a confidence in their king and princes? They should do them no service (*v.* 17): *Thy crowned heads are as the locusts;* those that had pomp and power, as crowned heads, were enfeebled. "*Thy captains*, that should lead thy forces look great, but they are as the great *grasshoppers*, they are but grasshoppers, worthless things, that can do no service. *They encamp in the hedges, in the cold day*, the cold weather, *but, when the sun arises, they flee away*, nobody knows whither. So these mercenary soldiers, when any trouble arises, flee away, and shift for their own safety. *The hireling flees, because he is a hireling*." The *king of Assyria* is told that *his shepherds slumber*; they have no spirit to appear for the flock. The *nobles shall dwell in the dust*, and be buried in silence. 6. Did they hope that they should yet rally? In this also they should be disappointed; for, when the shepherds are smitten, the *sheep are scattered*; the people are dispersed *upon the mountains* and *no man gathers them*. The judgment they are under is as a wound, and it is incurable; thy case is desperate (*v.* 19) and thy neighbours shall *clap their hands over thee*, and triumph in thy fall. *Upon whom has not thy wickedness passed continually?* Thou hast been always doing mischief to those about thee; and therefore they shall be far from pitying thee. *The troublers shall be troubled* will be the burden of many, as it is here the burden of Nineveh.

JAMIESON, FAUSSET, BROWN

velope in which his wings had been folded), and fleeth away" (ch. 2:9; cf. Joel 1:4). The *Hebrew* has ten different names for the locust, so destructive was it. **17. Thy crowned**—Thy princes (Rev. 9:7). The king's nobles and officers wore the tiara, as well as the king; hence they are called here "thy crowned ones." **as the locusts**—as many as ***the swarming locusts.*** **thy captains**—*Tiphsar*, an Assyrian word; found also in Jeremiah 51:27, meaning *satraps* [MICHAELIS]; or rather, "military leaders" [MAURER]. The last syllable, *sar* means a "prince," and is found in *Belshaz-zar, Nabopolas-sar, Nebuchadnez-zar*. **as the great grasshoppers**—lit., as the locust of locusts, i.e., the largest locust. MAURER translates, "as many as *locusts upon locusts,*" i.e., swarms of locusts. *Hebrew* idiom favors *English Version*. **in the hedges in the cold**—Cold deprives the locust of the power of flight; so they alight in cold weather and at night, but when warmed by the sun soon "flee away." So shall the Assyrian multitudes suddenly disappear, not leaving a trace behind (cf. PLINY *Hist. Nat.* 11. 29). **18. Thy shepherds**—i.e., Thy leaders. **slumber**—are carelessly secure [MAURER]. Rather, "lie in death's sleep, having been slain" [JEROME] (Exod. 15:16; Ps. 76:6). **shall dwell** *in the dust* (Ps. 7:5; 94:17). **thy people is scattered**—the necessary consequence of their leaders being laid low (I Kings 22:17). **19. bruit**—the report. **clap the hands**—with joy at thy fall. The sole descendants of the ancient Assyrians and Babylonians in the whole country are the Nestorian Christians, who speak a Chaldean language [LAYARD]. **upon whom hath not thy wickedness passed continually?**—implying God's long forbearance, and the consequent enormity of Assyria's guilt, rendering her case one that admitted no hope of restoration.

ADAM CLARKE

17. *Thy crowned are as the locusts.* You have numerous princes and numerous commanders.

Which camp in the hedges in the cold day. The locusts are said to lie in shelter about the hedges of fertile spots when the weather is cold, or during the night; but as soon as the sun shines out and is hot, they come out to their forage, or take to their wings.

18. *Thy shepherds slumber.* That is, the rulers and tributary princes, who, as Herodotus informs us, deserted Nineveh in the day of her distress, and came not forward to her succor.

19. *There is no healing of thy bruise.* You shall never be rebuilt. *All that hear the bruit of thee.* The report or acccount. *Shall clap the hands.* Shall exult in your downfall. *For upon whom hath not thy wickedness passed?* You have been a universal oppressor, and therefore all nations rejoice at your fall and utter desolation.

THE BOOK OF HABAKKUK

I. The prophet's problems (1:1-2:4)
A. The first problem and answer (1:1-11)
1. The problem (1:2-4)
2. The answer (1:5-11)
B. The second problem and answer (1:12-2:4)
1. The problem (1:12-17)
2. The prophet's attitude (2:1)
3. The answer (2:2-4)

II. The prophet's proclamations (2:5-3:19)
A. Of the puffed-up (2:5-20)
1. Description (2:5)
2. Woes (2:6-19)
3. Final statement (2:20)
B. Of the righteous (3:1-19)
1. The initial prayer (3:1, 2)
2. The God in whom faith is centered (3:3-15)
3. The fear and faith of the just (3:16-19)

It is a foolish fancy of some of the Jewish rabbis that this prophet was the son of the Shunamite woman that was miraculously raised to life by Elisha (2 Kings 4), as they say also that the prophet Jonah was the son of the widow of Zaraphath. It is a more probable conjecture that he lived and prophesied in the reign of king Manasseh, when wickedness abounded and destruction was hastening on, destruction by the Chaldeans whom this prophet mentions as the instruments of God's judgments; and Manasseh was himself carried to Babylon, as an earnest of what should come afterwards. In the apocryphal story of Bel and the Dragon mention is made of Habakkuk the prophet in the land of Judah, who was carried thence by an angel to Babylon to feed Daniel in the den; those who give credit to that story take pains to reconcile our prophet's living before the captivity and foretelling it with that. And some have imagined that Habakkuk's feeding Daniel in the den is to be understood mystically, that Daniel then "lived by faith," as Habakkuk had said "the just should do"; he was "fed" by that word (Hab. 2:4). The prophecy of this book is a mixture of the prophet's addresses to God in the people's name and to the people in God's name; for it is the office of the prophet to carry messages both ways. It is the interaction and communion between a gracious God and a gracious soul. The whole refers particularly to the invasion of the land of Judah by the Chaldeans.

MATTHEW HENRY

CHAPTER 1

Verses 1–4

The penman was *a prophet*, a man divinely inspired and commissioned, and the book itself is *the burden which* he *saw*; he was as sure of the truth of it as if he had seen it with his bodily eyes already accomplished. The prophet sadly laments the iniquity of the times. The land was *full of violence*, as the old world was, Gen. vi. 11. The prophet *cries out of violence* (*v.* 2), *iniquity* and *grievance*, *spoil* and *violence*. It does not appear that the prophet himself had any great wrong done him (in losing times it fared best with those that had nothing to lose), but it grieved him to see other people wronged. He complains (*v.* 4) that *the wicked doth compass about the righteous.* One honest man, one honest cause, shall have enemies besetting it on every side. The kingdom was broken into parties and factions that were continually biting and devouring one another. *There are that raise up strife and contention* (*v.* 3), that foment divisions, and sow discord among brethren. And, if *blessed are the peace-makers*, cursed are such peace-breakers. The torrent of violence and strife ran so strongly as to bid defiance to laws and the administration of justice, *v.* 4. Because God did not appear against them, nobody else would; *therefore the law is slacked*, is silent; *its pulse beats not* (so, it is said, the word signifies); *and judgment does not go forth.* He complained of this to God, but could not obtain a redress of those grievances: "*Lord,*" says he, "*why dost thou show me iniquity?* Why hast thou cast my lot in a time and place when and where it is to be seen?" When God seems to connive at the wickedness of the wicked, and to countenance it, by suffering them to prosper in their wickedness, it shocks the faith of good men. God has reasons for the reprieves of bad men and the rebukes of good men; and therefore we must believe the day will come when the cry of sin will be heard against those that do wrong and the cry of prayer for those that suffer it.

Verses 5–11

An answer to the prophet's complaint. Though God bore long, he would not bear always with this provoking people.

I. The preamble to the sentence (*v.* 5): *Behold,* you *among the heathen, and regard.* Since they will not be brought to repentance by the long-suffering of God, he will inflict upon them, 1. A public punishment, at which the neighbouring nations shall stand amazed, see Deut. xxix. 24, 25. Israel will be made a spectacle to the world. 2. An amazing punishment, so strange that it shall not be credited even by those that were eye-witnesses of it when it comes: *You will not believe it; though it be told you.* The punishment of God's professing people cannot but be the astonishment of all about them. 3. A speedy punishment: "*I will work a work in your days,* now

JAMIESON, FAUSSET, BROWN

CHAPTER 1

Vss. 1-17. Habakkuk's Expostulation with Jehovah on Account of the Prevalence of Injustice: Jehovah Summons Attention to His Purpose of Sending the Chaldeans as the Avengers. The Prophet Complains, that These Are Worse than Those on Whom Vengeance Was to Be Taken. **1. burden**—the prophetic sentence. **2, 3. violence . . . Why dost thou show me iniquity?**—Similar language is used of the Chaldeans (vss. 9, 13), as here is used of the Jews: implying, that as the Jews sinned by *violence* and *injustice,* so they should be punished by *violence* and *injustice* (Prov. 1:31). Jehoiakim's reign was marked by injustice, treachery, and bloodshed (Jer. 22:3, 13-17). Therefore the Chaldeans should be sent to deal with him and his nobles according to their dealings with others (vss. 6, 10, 11, 17). Cf. Jeremiah's expostulation with Jehovah, Jeremiah 12:1; 20:8; and Job 19:7, 8. **3. cause me to behold grievance**—Maurer denies that the *Hebrew* verb is ever *active;* he translates," (Wherefore) dost Thou behold (without doing aught to check) grievance?" The context favors *English Version.* **there are that raise up strife and contention**—so Calvin. But Maurer, not so well, translates, "There is strife, and contention raises *itself*. **4. Therefore**—because Thou dost suffer such crimes to go unpunished. **law is slacked**—is chilled. It has no authority and secures no respect. **judgment**—justice. **wrong judgment proceedeth**—Decisions are given contrary to right. **5. Behold . . . marvellously . . . a work**—(Cf. Isa. 29:14). Quoted by Paul (Acts 13:41). **among the heathen**—In Acts 13:41, "ye despisers," from the LXX. So the *Syriac* and *Arabic* versions; perhaps from a different *Hebrew* reading. In the *English Version* reading of Habakkuk, God, in reply to the prophet's expostulation, addresses the Jews as about to be punished, "Behold ye *among the heathen* (with whom ye deserve to be classed, and by whom ye shall be punished, as despisers; the sense *implied,* which Paul *expresses*): learn from them what ye refused to learn from Me!" For "wonder marvellously," Paul, in Acts 13:41, has, "wonder *and perish,*" which gives the *sense,* not the literal wording, of the *Hebrew,* "Wonder, wonder," i.e., be overwhelmed in wonder. The despisers are to be given up to their own stupefaction, and so perish. The Israelite unbelievers would not credit the prophecy as to the fearfulness of the destruction to be wrought by the Chaldeans, nor afterwards the deliverance promised from that nation. So analogously, in Paul's day, the Jews would not credit the judgment coming on them by the Romans, nor the salvation proclaimed through Jesus. Thus the same Scripture applied to both. **ye will not believe, though it be told you**—i.e,, ye will not believe *now that I foretell it.*

ADAM CLARKE

CHAPTER 1

We know little of this prophet. He was probably of the tribe of Simeon, and a native of Beth-zacar. It is very likely that he lived after the destruction of Nineveh, as he speaks of the Chaldeans, but makes no mention of the Assyrians. And he appears also to have prophesied before the Jewish captivity; see chap. i. 5; ii. 1; iii. 2, 16-19; and therefore Archbishop Newcome thinks he may be placed in the reign of Jehoiakim, between the years 606 B.C. and 598 B.C.

As a poet, Habakkuk holds a high rank among the Hebrew prophets. The beautiful connection between the parts of his prophecy, its diction, imagery, spirit, and sublimity, cannot be too much admired; and his hymn, chap. iii, is allowed by the best judges to be a masterpiece of its kind.

1. *The burden.* The word signifies an "oracle" or revelation in general; but chiefly one relative to future calamities.

2. *O Lord, how long shall I cry!* The prophet feels himself strongly excited against the vices which he beheld; and which, it appears from this verse, he had often declaimed against, but in vain. The people continued in their vices, and God in His long-suffering.

3. *And cause me to behold grievance. Amal,* labor, toil, distress, misery—the common fruits of sin.

5. *Behold ye among the heathen.* Instead of *baggoyim,* among the "nations" or *heathen,* some critics think we should read *bogedim,* "transgressors"; and to the same purpose the Septuagint, Syriac, and Arabic have read; and thus it is quoted by St. Paul, Acts xiii. 41. Newcome translates, "See, ye transgressors, and behold a wonder, and perish." *I will work a work in your days.* As he is speaking of the desolation that should be produced by the Chaldeans, it follows that the *Chaldeans* invaded Judah whilst those were living whom the prophet addressed.

MATTHEW HENRY

quickly; this generation shall not pass till the judgment threatened be accomplished." 4. It shall be a punishment in which the hand of God shall appear. *This is the Lord's doing*. 5. It shall be such a punishment as will typify the destruction to be brought upon the despisers of Christ and his gospel. The ruin of Jerusalem by the Chaldeans for their idolatry was a figure of their ruin by the Romans for rejecting Christ and his gospel.

II. The sentence itself is dreadful and particular (*v.* 6): *Lo, I raise up the Chaldeans.* When God's professing people quarrel among themselves, snarl, and devour one another, it is just with God to bring the common enemy upon them, that shall make peace by making a devastation. The contending parties in Jerusalem were divided one against another, when the Romans came and *took away their place and nation.*

1. The people that shall be raised up against Israel, to be a scourge to them, are *a bitter and hasty nation,* cruel and fierce. They show no mercy and they spare no pains. *They are terrible and dreadful, famed* for the troops they bring into the field (*v.* 8); *their horses are swifter than leopards, more fierce* than the *evening wolves;* and wolves are observed to be the most ravenous towards the evening, waiting for darkness under which *all beasts of the forest creep forth,* Ps. civ. 20. "*Their horsemen shall spread themselves* a great way, for they shall *come from far*, from all parts of their own country. Their own will is a law to them, and they will not be governed by any laws of humanity, equity, or honour: *Their judgment and their dignity shall proceed of themselves,*" *v.* 7. Appetite and passion rule them, and not reason nor conscience.

2. A prophecy of the terrible execution that shall be made by this nation: *They shall march through the breadth of the earth.* The Chaldean forces subdued all the nations in those parts, so that they seemed to have conquered the world. Or, through the breadth of *the land* of Israel, which was wholly laid waste by them. *Their faces shall sup up as the east wind;* their very countenances shall be so fierce and frightful that a look will serve to make them masters of all they have a mind to; so that they shall *swallow up* all, as the east wind nips and blasts the buds and flowers. They shall take a vast number of prisoners, and send them into Babylon: *They shall gather the captivity as the sand* for multitude. *They shall scoff* (he shall, so it is in the original, meaning Nebuchadnezzar, who, being puffed up with his successes, shall scoff) *at the kings* and commanders, and *the princes shall be a scorn to them. He shall deride every stronghold,* for to him it shall be weak, and *he shall heap dust, and take it;* a little soil, thrown up for ramparts, shall serve to give him all the advantage that he can desire; he shall make a sport of taking them. By all this he shall be puffed up with an intolerable pride, which shall be his destruction (*v.* 11): *Then shall his mind change* for the worse. *Bel* and *Nebo* were the gods of the Chaldeans, and to them they gave the glory of their successes; they were hardened in their idolatry, and blasphemously argued that because they had conquered Israel their gods were too strong for the God of Israel.

Verses 12–17

The prophet now turns to God, and again addresses him for the ease of his own mind under the burden which he saw. If he look about him, he sees nothing but violence done by Israel; if he look before him, he sees nothing but violence done against Israel. The prospect of the prevalence of the Chaldeans drives the prophet to his knees to plead with God concerning it.

I. The truths which he resolves to abide by, to comfort himself and his friends, under the threatening of the Chaldeans.

1. God is *the Lord our God,* and *our Holy One.* He is *Jehovah,* the fountain of all being, power, and perfection. *Our rock* is not *as theirs.* "He is *my God.*" He speaks in the people's name; every Israelite may say, "He is *mine.* Though *all this has come upon us, yet have we not forgotten the name of our God.* We will not entertain any hard thoughts of him, nor of his service, for all this."

2. Our God is from everlasting. If he is from everlasting, he will be to everlasting, and we must have recourse to this first principle, when things seen, which are temporal, are discouraging, that we have hope and help sufficient in a God that is eternal. "Art thou not *from of old,* a God in covenant with thy people?" (so some understand it). "Art thou not the same God still? Thou art God, *and changest not.*"

3. While the world stands God will have a church in it. The prophet infers the perpetuity of the church from the eternity of God; for Christ has said, *Because*

JAMIESON, FAUSSET, BROWN

6. I raise up—not referring to God's having brought the Chaldeans from their original seats to Babylonia (*Note,* Isa. 23:13), for they had already been upwards of twenty years (since Nabopolassar's era) in political power there; but to His being about now to raise them up as the instruments of God's "work" of judgment on the Jews (II Chron. 36:6). The *Hebrew* is *future,* "I will raise up." **bitter**—i.e., cruel (Jer. 50:42; cf. *Margin,* Judg. 18:25; I Sam. 17:8). **hasty**—not *passionate,* but "impetuous." **7. their judgment and . . . dignity . . . proceed of themselves**—i.e., they recognize no *judge* save themselves, and they get for themselves and keep their own "dignity" without needing others' help. It will be vain for the Jews to complain of their tyrannical *judgments;* for whatever the Chaldeans decree they will do according to their own will, they will not brook anyone attempting to interfere. **8. swifter than the leopards**—OPPIAN (*Cyneg.* 3. 76), says of the leopard, "It runs most swiftly straight on: you would fancy it was flying through the air." **more fierce**—rather, "more keen"; lit., "sharp." **evening wolves**—wolves famished with fasting all day and so most keen in attacking the fold under covert of the approaching night (Jer. 5:6; Zeph. 3:3; cf. Gen. 49:27). Hence "twilight" is termed in *Arabic* and *Persian* "the wolf's tail"; and in French, *entre chien et loup.* **spread themselves**—proudly; as in Jeremiah 50:11, and Malachi 4:2, it implies *strength* and *vigor.* So also the *Arabic* cognate word [MAURER]. **their horsemen . . . come from far**—and yet are not wearied by the long journey. **9. all for violence**—The sole object of all is not to establish just rights, but to get all they can by violence. **their faces shall sup up as the east wind**—i.e., they shall, as it were, *swallow up* all before them; so the horse in Job 39:24 is said to "*swallow* the ground with fierceness and rage." MAURER takes it from an *Arabic* root, "the *desire* of their faces," i.e., the eager desire expressed by their faces. HENDERSON, with SYMMACHUS and *Syriac,* translates, "the aspect." **as the east wind**—the simoon, which spreads devastation wherever it passes (Isa. 27:8). GESENIUS translates, "(is) forwards." The rendering proposed, *eastward,* as if it referred to the Chaldeans' return home *eastward* from Judea, laden with spoils, is improbable. Their "gathering the sand" accords with the simoon being meant, as it carries with it whirlwinds of sand collected in the desert. **10. scoff at . . . kings**—as unable to resist them. **they shall heap dust, and take it**—"they shall heap" earth mounds outside, and so "take every stronghold" (cf. II Sam. 20:15; II Kings 19:32) [GROTIUS]. **11. Then**—when elated by his successes. **shall his mind change**—He shall lose whatever of reason or moderation ever was in him, with pride. **he shall pass over**—all bounds and restraints: his pride preparing the sure way for his destruction (Prov. 16:18). The language is very similar to that describing Nebuchadnezzar's "change" from man's heart (understanding) to that of a beast, because of pride (Dan. 4:16, 30-34; see *Notes* there). An undesigned coincidence between the two sacred books written independently. *imputing* **this his power unto his god**—(Dan. 5:4). Sacrilegious arrogance, in ascribing to his idol Bel the glory that belongs to God [CALVIN]. GROTIUS explains, "(saying that) his power is his own as one who is a god to himself" (cf. vs. 16, and Dan. 3). So MAURER, "He shall offend as one to whom his power is his god" (Job 12:6; *Note,* Mic. 2:1). **12.** In opposition to the impious deifying of the Chaldeans' power as their god (MAURER, or, as *English Version,* their attributing of their successes to their idols), the prophet, in an impassioned address to Jehovah, vindicates His being "from everlasting," as contrasted with the Chaldean so-called "god." **my God, mine Holy One**—Habakkuk speaks in the name of his people. God was "the Holy One of *Israel,*" against whom the Chaldean was setting up himself (Isa. 37:23).

ADAM CLARKE

6. *That bitter and hasty nation.* Cruel and oppressive in their disposition, and prompt and speedy in their assaults and conquests.

7. *Their judgment . . . shall proceed of themselves.* By revolting from the Assyrians, they have become a great nation. Thus their judgment and excellence were the result of their own valor. Other meanings are given to this passage.

8. *Their horses also are swifter than the leopards.* The Chaldean cavalry are proverbial for swiftness, courage, etc. In Jeremiah, chap. iv. 13, it is said, speaking of Nebuchadnezzar, "His chariots shall be as a whirlwind; his horses are swifter than eagles."

10. *They shall scoff at the kings.* No power shall be able to stand before them. They will have no need to build formidable ramparts; by sweeping the *dust* together they shall make mounts sufficient to pass over the walls and take the city.

11. *Then shall his mind change.* This is thought to relate to the change which took place in Nebuchadnezzar, when "a beast's heart was given to him," and he was "driven from the dwellings of men." And this was because of his offending—his pride and arrogance—and his attributing all his success to his idols.

12. *Art thou not from everlasting?* The idols change, and their worshippers change and fail; but Thou, Jehovah, art eternal; Thou canst not change, and they who trust in Thee are safe.

MATTHEW HENRY

I live, and therefore as long as I live, *you shall live also*, John xiv. 19. *We shall not die.*

3. It was God that gave the Chaldeans their power. He gave them their commission *to take the spoil and to take the prey*, Isa. x. 6. Herein God appears a mighty God, that the power of mighty men is derived from him, and is under his cheek; *Hitherto shall it come, and no further.* Those whom God ordains shall do no more than what God has ordained. And he has *ordained them for judgment*, and *for correction.* God's people need correction, and deserve it; but it is for their correction, to drive out the foolishness that is found in their hearts.

5. Though the wicked may prosper for a while, yet God is a holy God, and does not approve of that wickedness (*v.* 13): *Thou art of purer eyes than to behold evil.* The prophet, observing how vicious the Chaldeans were, and yet what great success they had against God's Israel, found a temptation to say it was vain to serve God. But he suppresses the thought, by having recourse to his first principle, That God is not the author or patron of sin; he is *of purer eyes than to behold it* with approbation. There is in the nature of God an antipathy to those practices that are contrary to his holy law; and, though an expedient is happily found out for his being reconciled to sinners, yet he never will, nor can, be reconciled to sin. The mischief done to God's people by their persecutors; though God sees cause to permit it, yet he does not approve of it.

II. The grievances he finds hard to reconcile with these truths: "Since we are sure that thou art a holy God, *Wherefore lookest thou upon the Chaldeans* that *deal treacherously* with thy people and givest them success? Why dost thou suffer thy sworn enemies, to deal thus cruelly with thy sworn subjects, who desire to fear thy name? What shall we say to this?" This was a temptation to Job (*ch.* xxi. 7; xxiv. 1), to David (Ps. lxxiii. 2, 3), to Jeremiah, *ch.* xii. 1, 2. 1. That God permitted sin, and was patient with the sinners. 2. That his patience was abused, and *because sentence* against these evil works and workers *was not executed speedily*, therefore *their hearts* were the more *fully set in them to do evil.* They were false and deceitful. They hated and persecuted men because they were better than themselves, as Cain hated Abel because *his own works were evil and his brother's righteous.* They made no more of killing men than of catching fish. The prophet complains that, Providence having delivered up the weaker to be a prey to the stronger, they were, in effect, made as *the fishes of the sea v.* 14. So they had been among themselves, preying upon one another as the greater fishes do upon the less (*v.* 3). They were *as the creeping things*, or *swimming things* (for the word is used for *fish*, Gen. i. 20), *that have no ruler* over them. They are given up to the Chaldeans as fish to the fishermen. Those proud oppressors make no conscience of killing them, any more than men do of pulling fish out of the water. They have various ways of spoiling and destroying, as men have of taking fish. Some they *take up with the angle* (*v.* 15), one by one; others *they catch* in shoals, wholesale, *in their net*, and *gather them in their drag*, their enclosing net. *Their portion is fat, and their meat plenteous.* They live merrily (*v.* 15): *Therefore they rejoice and are glad*, because their wealth is great, and their projects succeed. They are great admirers of their own ingenuity: They *sacrifice to their own net, and burn incense to their own drag.*

III. The prophet, in the close, humbly expresses his hope that God will not suffer these destroyers of mankind always to go on and prosper thus (*v.* 17): "*Shall they therefore empty their net?* Shall they empty their net of what they have caught, that they may cast it into the sea again, to catch more? Must the numbers and wealth of nations be sacrificed to their net? Is not God the king of nations, and will he not assert their rights? Is he not jealous for his own honour, and will he not maintain that?" The prophet lodges the matter in God's hand, and leaves it with him, as the psalmist does. Ps. lxxiv. 22, *Arise, O God! plead thy own cause.*

JAMIESON, FAUSSET, BROWN

we shall not die—Thou, as being *our* God, wilt not permit the Chaldeans utterly to destroy us. This reading is one of the eighteen called by the Hebrews "the appointment of the scribes"; the Rabbis think that Ezra and his colleagues corrected the old reading, "*Thou shalt* not die." **thou hast ordained them for judgment**—i.e., to execute Thy judgments. **for correction**—to chastise transgressors (Isa. 10:5-7). But not that they may deify their own power (vs. 11, for their power is from Thee, and but for a time); nor that they may destroy utterly Thy people. The *Hebrew* for "mighty God" is *Rock* (Deut. 32:4). However the world is shaken, or man's faith wavers, God remains unshaken as the Rock of Ages (*Margin,* Isa. 26:4). **13. purer . . . than to behold evil**—without being displeased at it. **canst not look on iniquity**—unjust injuries done to Thy people. The prophet checks himself from being carried too far in his expostulatory complaint, by putting before himself honorable sentiments of God.

them that deal treacherously—the Chaldeans, once allies of the Jews, but now their violent oppressors. Cf. "treacherous dealers," (Isa. 21:2; 24:16). Instead of speaking evil against God, he goes to God Himself for the remedy for his perplexity (Ps. 73:11-17).

devoureth the man that is more righteous—The Chaldean oppresses the Jew, who with all his faults, is better than his oppressor (cf. Ezek. 16:51, 52). **14. And**—i.e., And *so,* by suffering oppressors to go unpunished, "Thou makest men as the fishes . . . that have no ruler"; i.e., no defender. All may fish in the sea with impunity; so the Chaldeans with impunity afflict Thy people, as these have no longer the God of the theocracy, their King, to defend them. Thou reducest men to such a state of anarchy, by wrong going unpunished, as if there were no God. He compares the world to the *sea*; men to *fishes*; Nebuchadnezzar to a *fisherman* (vss. 15-17). **15. they take up all of them**—all kinds of fishes, i.e., *men*, as captives, and all other prey that comes in their way. **with the angle**—i.e., the hook. Some they take up as with the hook, one by one; others in shoals, as in a "net" and "drag" or enclosing net. **therefore**—because of their successes. **they rejoice**—They glory in their crimes because attended with success (cf. vs. 11). **16. sacrifice unto their net**—i.e., their arms, power, and military skill, wherewith they gained their victories; instead of to God. Cf. vs. 11, MAURER'S interpretation. They idolize themselves for their own cleverness and might (Deut. 8:17; Isa. 10:13; 37:24, 25). **by them**—by their net and dragnet. **their portion**—image from a banquet: the prey which they have gotten. **17. Shall they . . . empty their net?**—Shall they be allowed without interruption to enjoy the fruits of their violence? **therefore**—seeing that they attribute all their successes to themselves, and not to Thee. The answer to the prophet's question, he by inspiration gives himself in ch. 2.

ADAM CLARKE

Thou art infinite in Thy mercy; therefore, *we shall not die*, shall not be totally exterminated.

Thou hast ordained them for judgment. Thou hast raised up the Chaldeans to correct and punish us, but Thou hast not given them a commission to destroy us totally.

13. *Thou art of purer eyes.* Seeing Thou art so pure, and *canst not look on iniquity*—it is so abominable—how canst Thou bear with them who *deal treacherously, and holdest thy tongue when the wicked devoureth the . . . righteous?"* All such questions are easily solved by a consideration of God's ineffable mercy, which leads Him to suffer long and be kind. He has no pleasure in the death of a sinner.

14. *Makest men as the fishes of the sea.* Easily are we taken and destroyed. We have no leader to guide us, and no power to defend ourselves. Nebuchadnezzar is here represented as a fisherman, who is constantly casting his nets into the sea, and enclosing multitudes of fishes; and, being always successful, he sacrifices to his own net—attributes all his conquests to his own power and prudence; not considering that he is only like a net that, after having been used for a while, shall at last be thrown by as useless, or burnt in the fire.

MATTHEW HENRY — CHAPTER 2

Verses 1–4

I. The prophet humbly gives his attendance upon God (*v.* 1): "*I will stand upon my watch*, as a sentinel on the walls of a besieged city. I will look up, will look round, will look within, *and watch to see what he will say unto me. I will watch to see what he will say in me*" (so it may be read), "what the Spirit of prophecy in me will dictate to me, by way of answer to my complaints." God not only speaks to us by his word, but speaks in us by our own consciences,

JAMIESON, FAUSSET, BROWN — CHAPTER 2

Vss. 1-20. THE PROPHET, WAITING EARNESTLY FOR AN ANSWER TO HIS COMPLAINTS (ch. 1), RECEIVES A REVELATION, WHICH IS TO BE FULFILLED, NOT IMMEDIATELY, YET IN DUE TIME, AND IS THEREFORE TO BE WAITED FOR IN FAITH: THE CHALDEANS SHALL BE PUNISHED FOR THEIR CRUEL RAPACITY, NOR CAN THEIR FALSE GODS AVERT THE JUDGMENT OF JEHOVAH, THE ONLY TRUE GOD. **1. stand upon . . . watch**—i.e., watch-post. The prophets often compare themselves, awaiting the revelations of Je-

ADAM CLARKE — CHAPTER 2

1. *I will stand upon my watch.* The prophets are always represented as watchmen, watching constantly for the comfort, safety, and welfare of the people; and watching also to receive information from the Lord.

MATTHEW HENRY

whispering to us, *This is the way, walk in it.* Those that expect to hear from God must withdraw from the world, and get above it, must raise their attention, fix their thought, study the scriptures, consult experiences and the experienced, continue instant in prayer, and thus set themselves *upon the tower.* 1. When we are perplexed with doubts concerning the methods of Providence, are tempted to think that it is fate, and not a wise God, that governs the world, then we must set ourselves upon the tower, to see if we can discover that which will silence the temptation and solve the difficulties, must go into the sanctuary of God, and there labour to understand the end of these things. 2. When we have been at prayer, pouring out our complaints and requests before God, we must carefully observe what answers God gives by his word, his Spirit, and his providences.

II. The prophet had complained of the prevalence of the Chaldeans; now, to pacify him concerning it, he here gives him a prospect of their fall and ruin, as Isaiah, before this, when he had foretold the captivity in Babylon, foretold also the destruction of Babylon.

1. The prophet must *write the vision, v.* 2. We have reason to bless God for written visions, that God has written to us the great things of his prophets as well as of his law. He must *write the vision,* and *make it plain upon tables,* must write it legibly, in large characters, so that *he who runs may read it.* God himself has prefixed his *imprimatur* to them; he has said, *Make them plain.*

2. The people must wait for the accomplishment of the *vision* (*v.* 3): "*The vision is yet for an appointed time* to come. You shall now be told of your deliverance by the breaking of the Chaldeans' power, and that the time of it is fixed in the counsel and decree of God." God has an appointed time for his appointed work, and will be sure to do the work when the time comes; it is not for us to anticipate his appointments, but to wait his time.

3. This vision will be such an exercise of faith and patience as will try and discover men what they are, *v.* 4. There are some who will proudly disdain this vision; they think *their own hands sufficient for them,* and God's promise is to them an insignificant thing. Those who are truly good, and whose hearts are upright with God, will value the promise, and venture their all upon it; and will keep close to God and duty in the most difficult trying times, and live comfortably in communion with God, dependence on him, and expectation of him.

Verses 5–14

The prophet having had orders to *write the vision,* the vision itself reads the doom, some think, of Nebuchadnezzar, who was principally active in the destruction of Jerusalem, or of all such proud and oppressive powers as bear hard, especially upon God's people.

I. The charge laid down against this enemy, *v.* 5. The *lusts of the flesh, the lusts of the eye,* and *the pride of life,* are snares; and we find him that led Israel captive, himself led captive by each of these. 1. He is sensual and voluptuous, and given to his pleasures: *He transgresses by wine.* Drunkenness is the cause of abundance of transgression. 2. He is haughty and imperious: *He is a proud man,* and his pride is a certain presage of his fall. When a man is drunk, though he makes himself as a beast, yet he thinks himself as great as a king, and prides himself in that by which he shames himself, Isa. xxviii. 1.

JAMIESON, FAUSSET, BROWN

hovah with earnest patience, to watchmen on an eminence watching with intent eye all that comes within their view (Isa. 21:8, 11; Jer. 6:17; Ezek. 3:17; 33:2, 3; cf. Ps. 5:3; 85:8). The "watch-post" is the withdrawal of the whole soul from earthly, and fixing it on heavenly, things. The accumulation of synonyms, "stand open . . . watch . . . set me upon . . . tower . . . watch to see" implies persevering fixity of attention. **what he will say unto me**—in answer to my complaints (ch. 1:13). Lit., "in me," God speaking, not to the prophet's outward ear, but *inwardly.* When we have prayed to God, we must observe what answers God gives by His word, His Spirit, and His providences. **what I shall answer when I am reproved**—what answer I am to make to the *reproof* which I anticipate from God on account of the liberty of my expostulation with Him. MAURER translates, "What I am to answer in respect to my complaint against Jehovah" (ch. 1:12-17). **2. Write the vision**—which I am about to reveal to thee. **make it plain**—(Deut. 27:8). In large legible characters. **upon tables**—boxwood tables covered with wax, on which national affairs were engraved with an iron pen, and then hung up in public, at the prophets' own houses, or at the temple, that those who passed might read them. Cf. Luke 1:63, "writing-table," i.e., tablet. **that he may run that readeth it**—commonly explained, "so intelligible as to be easily read by any one running past"; but then it would be, "that he that runneth may read it." The true sense is, "so legible *that whoever readeth it, may run* to tell all whom he can the good news of the foe's coming doom, and Judah's deliverance." Cf. Daniel 12:4, "many shall *run* to and fro," viz., with the explanation of the prophecy, then unsealed; also, Revelation 22:17, "let him that heareth [the good news] say [to every one within his reach], Come." "Run" is equivalent to *announce the divine revelation* (Jer. 23:21); as everyone who becomes informed of a divine message is bound to *run,* i.e., use all despatch to make it known to others [HENDERSON]. GROTIUS, LUDOVICUS DE DIEU, and MAURER interpret it: "Run" is not literal *running,* but "that he who reads it may run through it," i.e., read it *at once without difficulty.* **3. for**—assigning the cause why it ought to be *committed to writing: because* its fulfilment belongs to the future. **the vision is yet for an appointed time**—(Dan. 10:14; 11:27, 35). Though the time appointed by God for the fulfilment be yet future, it should be enough for your faith that God hath spoken it (Lam. 3:26). **at the end it shall speak**—MAURER translates, "it *pants for* the end." But the antithesis between, "it shall *speak,*" and "not be silent," makes *English Version* the better rendering. So the *Hebrew* is translated in Proverbs 12:17. Lit., "breathe out words," "break forth as a blast." **though it tarry, wait for it**—(Gen. 49:18). **4. his soul which is lifted up**—the Chaldean's [MAURER]. The unbelieving Jew's [HENDERSON]. **is not upright in him**—i.e., is not accounted upright in God's sight; in antithesis to "shall live." So Hebrew 10:38, which with inspired authority applies the general sense to the particular case which Paul had in view, "If any man *draw back* (one result of being "lifted up" with overweening arrogancy), *my soul shall have no pleasure* in him." **the just shall live by his faith**—the *Jewish nation,* as opposed to the unbelieving Chaldean (cf. vs. 5, etc.; ch. 1:6, etc., 13) [MAURER]. HENDERSON'S view is that the *believing* Jew is meant, as opposed to the unbelieving Jew (cf. Rom. 1:17; Gal. 3:11). The believing Jew, though God's promise tarry, will wait for it; the unbelieving "draws back," as Hebrews 10:38 expresses it. The sense, in MAURER'S view, which accords better with the context (vs. 5, etc.) is: the Chaldean, though for a time seeming to prosper, yet being lifted up with haughty unbelief (ch. 1:11, 16), is not upright; i.e., has *no right* stability of soul resting on God, to ensure permanence of prosperity; hence, though for a time executing God's judgments, he at last becomes "lifted up" so as to attribute to his own power what is the work of God, and in this sense "draws back" (Heb. 10:38), becoming thereby a type of all backsliders who thereby incur God's displeasure; as the believing Jew is of all who *wait* for God's promises with patient *faith,* and so "live" (stand accepted) before God. The *Hebrew* accents induce BENGEL to translate, "he who is just by his faith shall live." Other MSS. read the accents as *English Version,* which agrees better with *Hebrew* syntax. **5. Yea also, because**—additional reason why the Jews may look for God punishing their Chaldean foe, viz., *because . . . he is* **a proud man**—rather, this clause continues the reason for the Jews expecting the punishment of the Chaldeans, "because he transgresseth by wine

ADAM CLARKE

What he will say unto me. "In me"—in my understanding and heart.

And what I shall answer when I am reproved. What I shall say to God in behalf of the people, and what the Lord shall command me to say to the people. Some translate, "And what he will answer for my conviction." Or, "what shall be answered to my pleading."

2. *Write the vision.* Carefully take down all that I shall say.

That he may run that readeth it. That he who attentively peruses it may speed to save his life from the irruption of the Chaldeans, by which so many shall be cut off. The prophet does not mean that the words are to be made so plain that a man running by may easily read them, and catch their meaning.

3. *The vision is yet for an appointed time.* The Chaldeans, who are to ruin Judea, shall afterwards be ruined themselves. But they must do this work before they receive their wages; therefore the vision is for an appointed time. *But at the end it shall speak.* When his work of devastation is done, his day of retribution shall take place. *Though it tarry.* Though it appear to be long, do not be impatient; *it will surely come, it will not tarry* longer than the prescribed time, and this time is not far distant. *Wait for it.*

4. *Behold, his soul which is lifted up.* He that presumes on his safety without any special warrant from God is a proud man; and whatever he may profess, or think of himself, his mind *is not upright in him.* But he that is "just by faith shall live"—he that believes what God hath said relative to the Chaldeans besieging Jerusalem shall make his escape from the place, and consequently shall save his life. The words in the New Testament are accommodated to the salvation which believers in Christ shall possess.

5. *Because he transgresseth by wine.* Nebuchadnezzar is here represented in his usual character, proud, haughty, and ambitious; inebriated with his successes, and determined on more extensive conquests; and, like the "grave," can never have enough. Yet, after the subjuga-

MATTHEW HENRY

3. He is covetous and greedy of wealth, and this is the effect of his pride. The Chaldean monarchy aimed to be a universal one. He *keeps not at home*, is not content with his own, but thinks it too little. His ambition is his perpetual uneasiness. Though the home be a palace, yet to a discontented mind it is a prison. He *enlarges his desire as hell*, or *the grave*, which daily receives, and yet still cries, *Give, give*. And it is just with God that the desires which are insatiable should still be unsatisfied.

II. The sentence passed upon him (*v.* 6): *Shall not all these take up a parable against him?*

1. Since pride has been his sin, disgrace and dishonour shall be his punishment, and he shall be laughed at and despised by all about him.

2. Since he has been abusive to his neighbours, those very persons whom he has abused shall be the instruments of his disgrace: *All those shall take up a taunting proverb against him. He shall say* (he that draws up the insulting ditty shall say thus), *Ho, he that increases that which is not his! Aha!* what has become of him now? So it may be read in a taunting way.

Woe against him for increasing his own possessions by invading his neighbour's rights, *v.* 6–8. He is *lading himself with thick clay*. Riches are but clay, thick clay; what are gold and silver but white and yellow earth? People cry to God, "How long wilt thou suffer this proud oppressor to trouble the nations?" Or they say to one another, "See how long it will last, how long he will be able to keep what he gets thus dishonestly?" What he has got by violence from others, others shall take by violence from him. The Medes and Persians shall make a prey of the Chaldeans, as they have done of other nations, *v.* 7, 8. "There shall be those that will *bite thee* and *vex thee*; those that seemed *asleep*, shall *rise up* and *awake* to be a plague to thee. They shall rise up *suddenly* when thou art most secure. According to the law of retaliation, as *thou hast spoiled many nations* so thou shalt thyself be *spoiled* (*v.* 8); *all the remnant of the people shall spoil thee*."

Woe against him for coveting still more, and aiming to be still higher, *v.* 9–11. *Woe to him that gains an evil gain;* so the margin reads it. There is a lawful gain, which by the blessing of God may be a comfort to a house (*a good man leaves an inheritance to his children's children*), but what is got by fraud and injustice is ill-got, and will be poor gain, will bring poverty and ruin upon it.

Thou hast consulted, not safety, but *shame, to thy house, by cutting off many people*, *v.* 10. An estate raised by iniquity is a scandal to a family. "*Thou hast sinned against thy own soul*, and endangered that." But if the sinner pleads, Not guilty, and thinks his frauds cannot be proved upon him, let him know that *the stone shall cry out of the wall* against him, and *the beam out of the timber* in the roof *shall answer it*, *v.* 11. Woe against him for building a town and a city by blood and extortion (*v.* 12). So Nebuchadnezzar did (Dan. iv. 30): *Is not this great Babylon that I have built for the house of the kingdom?* But it is built with the blood of his own subjects, whom he has oppressed, and the blood of his neighbours, whom he has invaded; it is *established by iniquity*. The shame of the Chaldeans, who had taken so much pains, and were at such a vast expense, to fortify it (*v.* 13): *Is it not of the Lord of hosts that the people* who have laboured so hard to defend that city shall *labour in the very fire*, shall labour in vain to save it? There is not a greater drudge in the world than he that is under the power of reigning covetousness. They are but poorly paid for it; for, after all, *they weary themselves for very vanity*; it is worse than vanity, it is *vexation of spirit*.

JAMIESON, FAUSSET, BROWN

(a besetting sin of Babylon, cf. Dan. 5, and CURTIUS, 5.1), *being* a proud man." Love of wine often begets a *proud* contempt of divine things, as in Belshazzar's case, which was the immediate cause of the fall of Babylon (Dan. 5:2-4, 30; cf. Prov. 20:1; 30:9; 31:5). **enlargeth his desire as hell**—the grave, or the unseen world, which is "never full" (Prov. 27:20; 30:16; Isa. 5:14). The Chaldeans under Nebuchadnezzar were filled with an insatiable desire of conquest. Another reason for their punishment. **6. Shall not all these**—the "nations" and "peoples" (vs. 5) "heaped unto him" by the Chaldean. **take up a parable**—a derisive song. Habakkuk follows Isaiah (Isa. 14:4) and Micah (Mic. 2:4) in the phraseology. **against him**—when dislodged from his former eminence. **Woe**—The "derisive song" here begins, and continues to the end of the chapter. It is a symmetrical whole, and consists of five stanzas, the first three consisting of three verses each, the fourth of four verses, and the last of two. Each stanza has its own subject, and all except the last begin with "Woe"; and all have a closing verse introduced with "for," "because," or "but." **how long?**—*how long* destined to retain his ill-gotten gains? But for a short time, as his fall now proves [MAURER]. "Covetousness is the greatest bane to men. For they who invade others' goods, often lose even their own" [MENANDER]. CALVIN makes "how long?" to be the cry of those groaning under the Chaldean oppression while it still lasted: How long shall such oppression be permitted to continue? But it is plainly part of the *derisive song*, after the Chaldean tyranny had passed away. **ladeth himself with thick clay**—viz., gold and silver dug out of the "clay," of which they are a part. The covetous man in heaping them together is only lading himself with a clay burden, as he dares not enjoy them, and is always anxious about them. LEE and FULLER translate the *Hebrew* as a reduplicated single noun, and not two words, "an accumulation of pledges" (Deut. 24:10-13). The Chaldean is compared to a harsh usurer, and his ill-gotten treasures to heaps of pledges in the hands of a usurer. **7. suddenly**—the answer to the question, "How long?" (vs. 6). **bite**—often used of *usury*; so favoring LEE's rendering (vs. 6). As the Chaldean, like a usurer, oppressed others, so other nations shall, like usurers, *take pledges of*, i.e., spoil, him. **8. the remnant of the people**—Those remaining of the peoples spoiled by thee, though but a remnant, will suffice to inflict vengeance on thee. **the violence of the land . . . city**—i.e., on account of *thy violent oppression of the lands and cities* of the earth [GROTIUS] (cf. vss. 5, 6, 12). The same phrase occurs in vs. 17, where the "land" and "city" are Judea and Jerusalem. **9. coveteth an evil covetousness**—i.e., a covetousness so surpassingly evil as to be fatal to himself. **to his house**—greedily seizing enormous wealth, not merely for himself, but for his family, to which it is destined to be fatal. The very same "evil covetousness" that was the cause of Jehoiakim's being given up to the Chaldean oppressor (Jer. 22:13) shall be the cause of the Chaldean's own destruction. **set his nest on high**—(Num. 24:21; Jer. 49:16; Obad. 4). The image is from an eagle (Job 39:27). The *royal citadel* is meant. The Chaldean built high towers, like the Babel founders, to "be delivered from the power of evil" (Gen. 11:4). **10. Thou hast consulted shame . . . by cutting off many**—MAURER, more lit., "Thou hast consulted shame . . . to destroy many," i.e., in consulting (determining) to cut off many, thou hast consulted shame to thy house. **sinned against thy soul**—i.e., against thyself; thou art the guilty cause of thine own ruin (Prov. 8:36; 20:2). They who wrong their neighbors, do much greater wrong to their own souls. **11. stone . . . cry out**—personification. The very stones of thy palace built by rapine shall testify against thee (Luke 19:40). **the beam out of the timber**—the crossbeam or main rafter connecting the timbers in the walls. **shall answer it**—viz., the stone. The stone shall begin and the crossbeam continue the cry against thy rapine. **12. buildeth a town with blood**—viz., Babylon rebuilt and enlarged by blood-bought spoils (cf. Dan. 4:30). **13. is it not of the Lord of hosts**—JEHOVAH, who has at His command all the *hosts* of heaven and earth, is the righteous author of Babylon's destruction. "Shall not God have His turn, when cruel rapacious men have triumphed so long, though He seem now to be still?" [CALVIN]. **people . . . labour in the . . . fire . . . weary themselves for . . . vanity**—The Chaldeans labor at what is to be food for the fire, viz., their city and fortresses which shall be burnt. Jeremiah 51:58 adopts the same phraseology to express the vanity of the Chaldean's labor on Babylon, as doomed to the flames. **14.** Adapted from Isaiah

ADAM CLARKE

tion of many peoples and nations, he shall be brought down, and become so despicable that he shall be a proverb or reproach, and be taunted and scorned by all those whom he had before enslaved.

6. *Shall not all these take up a parable against him?* His ambition, derangement, and the final destruction of his mighty empire by the Persians shall form the foundation of many sententious sayings among the people.

7. *Shall they not rise up suddenly?* Does not this refer to the sudden and unexpected taking of Babylon by Cyrus, whose troops entered into the city through the bed of the Euphrates, whose waters they had diverted by another channel; so that the Babylonians knew nothing of the matter till they saw the Persian soldiers rise up as in a moment, in the very heart of their city?

8. *For the violence of the land.* Or "for the violence done to the land" of Judea, and to *the city* of Jerusalem.

9. *An evil covetousness to his house.* Nebuchadnezzar wished to aggrandize his family, and make his empire permanent; but both family and empire were soon cut off by the death of his son Belshazzar, and the consequent destruction of the Chaldean empire.

10. *Hast sinned against thy soul.* Your life is forfeited by your crimes.

11. *The stone shall cry out of the wall, and the beam out of the timber shall answer it.* This appears to refer to the ancient mode of building walls: two or three courses of stone, and then one course of timber. See 1 Kings vi. 36; thus was the palace of Solomon built. The splendid and costly buildings of Babylon have been universally celebrated. But how were these buildings erected? By the spoils of conquered nations, and the expense of the blood of multitudes; therefore the stones and the timber are represented as calling out for vengeance against this ruthless conqueror.

12. *Woe to him that buildeth a town with blood!* At the expense of much slaughter. This is the answer of the *beam* to the *stone*.

13. *The people shall labour in the very fire.* All these superb buildings shall be burnt down. See the parallel passage, Jer. li. 58. *Shall weary themselves for very vanity.* For the gratification of the wishes of ambition, and in buildings which shall be brought to naught.

MATTHEW HENRY

Verses 15–20

The foregoing articles, upon which the woes here are grounded, are very near akin to each other.

But here are two articles more, of a different nature, which carry a *woe* to those in general to whom they belong, and particularly to the Babylonian monarchs, by whom the people of God were taken and held captives.

I. The promoters of drunkenness stand here condemned. Belshazzar was one of those; he was so, remarkably that very night that the prophecy of this chapter was fulfilled, when he *drank wine before a thousand* of his lords (Dan. v. 1), and forced them to pledge him. The succeeding monarchs of Persia (as we find, Esther i. 8) had seen in the kings of Babylon the mischievous consequences of forcing healths and making people drunk. But the woe here stands firm and fearful against all those, whoever they are, who are guilty of this sin at any time and in any place.

1. The sinner here articled against is he that *makes his neighbour drunk*, *v.* 15. To give a neighbour drink with design to intoxicate him, that he may expose himself, may make himself ridiculous, may disclose his own secret concerns—this is abominable wickedness; and those who are guilty of it are rebels against God in heaven, and his sacred laws, factors for the devil in hell, and enemies to men on earth.

2. Sentence is here passed upon him. There is a woe to him (*v.* 15), and a punishment (*v.* 16) that shall answer to the sin. (1) Does he put the cup of drunkenness into the hand of his neighbour? The *cup of the Lord's right hand*, shall be *turned unto him*; shall at length be put into the hand of the king of Babylon, as was foretold, Jer. xxv. 15, 16, 18, 26, 27. Does he take a pleasure in putting his neighbour to shame? He shall himself be loaded with contempt: "*Thou art filled with shame for glory, with shame instead of glory.* Thou *also shalt drink* of the cup of trembling, and shalt expose thyself by thy cowardice, which shall be as the *uncovering of thy nakedness*, to thy shame. For *the violence of Lebanon shall cover thee, and the spoil of beasts* (*v.* 17); thou shalt be hunted with as much violence as ever any wild beasts in Lebanon were."

II. The promoters of idolatry stand condemned. Belshazzar, in his revels, *praised his idols*. They are *mad upon their idols*; so the Chaldeans are said to be, Jer. l. 38. They have a great variety of idols, *graven images* and *molten images*. The *maker of the work* has performed his part admirably well, the *fashioner of his fashion* (so it is in the margin). *They lay them over with gold and silver. The maker of the work trusts therein* as his god. They pray to them: *They say to the wood, Awake* for our relief, and to the dumb stone, "*Arise*, and save us." They consult them as oracles, and expect to be directed by them. The folly of this is exposed. Their images are wholly void both of sense and reason, lifeless and speechless, so that the most minute animal, that has but breath and motion, is more excellent than they. It is not in their power to do their worshippers any good (*v.* 18): *What profits the graven image?* It is so far from profiting them that it keeps them under the power of a strong delusion; they say, *It shall teach*, but it is a *teacher of lies*; for it represents God as having a body, as being finite, visible, and dependent, whereas he is a Spirit, infinite, invisible, and independent.

JAMIESON, FAUSSET, BROWN

11:9. Here the sense is, "The Jews shall be restored and the temple rebuilt, so that God's glory in saving His people, and punishing their Chaldean foe, shall be manifested throughout the world," of which the Babylonian empire formed the greatest part; a type of the ultimate full manifestation of His glory in the final salvation of Israel and His Church, and the destruction of all their foes. **waters cover the sea**—viz., the bottom of the sea; the sea-bed. **15. giveth . . . neighbour drink . . . puttest . . . bottle to him**—lit., "skin," as the Easterns use "bottles" of skin for wine. MAURER, from a different *Hebrew* root, translates, "that pourest in thy *wrath*." *English Version* keeps up the metaphor better. It is not enough for thee to be "drunken" thyself, unless thou canst lead others into the same state. The thing meant is, that the Chaldean king, with his insatiable desires (a kind of *intoxication*), allured neighboring states into the same mad thirst for war to obtain booty, and then at last exposed them to loss and shame (cf. Isa. 51:17; Obad. 16). An appropriate image of Babylon, which at last fell during a drunken revel (Dan. 5). **that thou mayest look on their nakedness!**—with light, like Ham of old (Gen. 9:22). **16. art filled**—now that thou art fallen. "Thou art filled" indeed (though so insatiable), but it is "with shame." **shame for glory**—instead of thy former glory (Hos. 4:7). **drink thou also**—The cup of sorrow is now in thy turn to pass to thee (Jer. 25:15-17; Lam. 4:21). **thy foreskin**—expressing in Hebrew feeling the most utter contempt. So of Goliath (I Sam. 17:36). It is not merely thy "nakedness," as in vs. 15, that shall be "uncovered," but the foreskin, the badge of thy being an uncircumcised alien from God. The same shall be done to thee, as thou didst to others, and worse. **cup . . . shall be turned unto thee**—lit., shall *turn itself*, viz., from the nations whom thou hast made to drink it. "Thou shalt drink it *all*, so that it may be *turned* as being drained" [GROTIUS]. **shameful spewing**—i.e., vomiting; viz., that of the king of Babylon, compelled to disgorge the spoil he had swallowed. It expresses also the ignominious state of Babylon in its calamity (Jer. 25:27). "Be drunken, spew, and fall." Less appropriately it is explained *of the foe* spewing in the face of the Babylonian king. **17. the violence of Lebanon**—thy "violence" against "Lebanon," i.e., Jerusalem (Isa. 37:24; Jer. 22:23; Ezek. 17:3, 12; for Lebanon's cedars were used in building the temple and houses of Jerusalem; and its beauty made it a fit type of the metropolis), shall fall on thine own head. **cover**—i.e., *completely* overwhelm. **the spoil of beasts, which made them afraid**—MAURER explains, "*the spoiling* inflicted on *the beasts* of Lebanon (i.e., on the people of Jerusalem, of which city 'Lebanon' is the type), *which made them afraid* (shall cover thee)." But it seems inappropriate to compare the elect people to "beasts." I therefore prefer explaining, "the spoiling of beasts," i.e., such as is inflicted on beasts caught in a net, and "which makes them afraid" (shall cover thee). Thus the Babylonians are compared to wild beasts terrified at being caught suddenly in a net. In cruel rapacity they resembled wild beasts. The ancients read, "the spoiling of wild beasts *shall make* THEE *afraid*." Or else explain, "the spoiling of beasts (the Medes and Persians) which (*inflicted by thee*) made them afraid (shall in turn cover thyself—revert on thyself from them)." This accords better with the parallel clause, "the violence of Lebanon," i.e., inflicted by thee on Lebanon. As thou didst hunt men as wild beasts, so shalt thou be hunted thyself as a wild beast, which thou resemblest in cruelty. **because of men's blood**—shed by thee; repeated from vs. 8. But here the "land" and "city" are used of *Judea* and *Jerusalem:* not of the *earth* and cities *generally*, as in vs. 8. **the violence of the land . . .**—i.e., inflicted *on the* land by thee. **18.** The powerlessness of the idols to save Babylon from its doom is a fitting introduction to the last stanza (vs. 19), which, as the former four, begins with "Woe." **teacher of lies**—its priests and prophets uttering lying oracles, as if from it. **make dumb idols**—Though men can "make" idols, they cannot *make them speak*. **19. Awake**—Arise to my help. **it shall teach!**—rather, An exclamation *of the prophet*, implying an ironical question to which a negative answer must be given. What! "It teach?" Certainly not [MAURER]. Or, "It (the idol itself) shall (i.e., ought to) teach you that it is deaf, and therefore no God" [CALVIN]. Cf. "they are their own witnesses" (Isa. 44:9). **Behold**—The *Hebrew* is nominative, "There it is" [HENDERSON]. **it is laid over with gold . . . no breath . . . in the midst**—Outside it has some splendor, within none. **20. But the Lord**—JEHOVAH; in striking contrast with the idols. **in**

ADAM CLARKE

14. *For the earth shall be filled.* This is a singular and important verse. It may be first applied to Babylon. God's power and providence shall be widely displayed in the destruction of this city and empire. Secondly, it may be applied to the glorious days of the Messiah. Thirdly, it may be applied to the universal spread of the gospel over the habitable globe.

15. *Woe unto him that giveth his neighbour drink!* This has been considered as applying to Pharaoh-hophra, king of Egypt, who enticed his neighbors Jehoiachin and Zedekiah to rebel against Nebuchadnezzar, whereby the nakedness and imbecility of the poor Jews was soon discovered; for the Chaldeans soon took Jerusalem, and carried its kings, princes, and people into captivity.

16. *The cup of the Lord's right hand.* Among the ancients, all drank out of the same cup; it was passed from hand to hand, and each drank as much as he chose. The Chaldeans gave to the neighboring nations the cup of idolatry and of deceitful alliance, and in return they received from the Lord the cup of His fury.

17. *For the violence of Lebanon.* Or the violence done to Lebanon; to men, to cattle, to Judea, and to Jerusalem. See the parallel place, v. 8. This may be a threatening against Egypt, as the former was against Chaldea.

18. *What profiteth the graven image?* This is against idolatry in general, and every species of it, as well as against those princes, priests, and people who practice it, and encourage others to do the same. *Dumb idols? Elilim illemim*, "dumb nothings." This is exactly agreeable to St. Paul, 1 Cor. viii. 4, who says, "An idol is nothing in the world."

MATTHEW HENRY

The people of God triumph in him when the idolaters thus shame themselves (*v.* 20): *Our rock is not as their rock*, Deut. xxxii. 31. Theirs are dumb idols; ours is Jehovah, a living god, who is what he is, and not, as theirs, what men please to make him. They have laid waste his temple at Jerusalem; but he has a temple above that is out of the reach of their rage and malice, but within the reach of his people's faith and prayers.

CHAPTER 3

Verses 1–2

This chapter is entitled *a prayer of Habakkuk*. It is an intercession for the church. Prophets were praying men, and sometimes they prayed for even those whom they prophesied against.

1. The prophet owns the receipt of God's answer to his former representation, and the impression it made upon him (*v.* 2): "*O Lord! I have heard thy speech, thy hearing*" (so some read it). Those that would rightly order their speech to God must carefully observe his speech to them. The matter of this message made the prophet afraid, when he heard how low the people of God should be brought, under the Chaldeans, and he was afraid lest their spirits should fail, and lest the church should be utterly rooted out and lost at length. 2. He earnestly prays that these *days of trouble* might be *shortened* or moderated, or the people of God supported. He thinks it very long to wait till the *end of the years*; perhaps he refers to the seventy years of the captivity, and therefore, "Lord," says he, "do something on our behalf *in the midst of the years*, though we be not delivered, yet let us not be abandoned and cast off." *Revive thy work*, thy church even when it *walks in the midst of trouble*, Ps. cxxxviii. 7, 8. *Revive the work of thy grace* in us, by sanctifying the trouble to us and supporting us under it, though the time be not yet come for our deliverance out of it. *In the midst of the years make known*, make thyself known, make known thy power, thy pity, thy promise, thy providence, in the government of the world, for the safety and welfare of thy church. When *in the midst of the years* of the captivity God miraculously owned the three children in the fiery furnace, and humbled Nebuchadnezzar, this prayer was answered.

Verses 3–15

God's people, when in distress, help themselves by recollecting their experiences, *considering the days of old*. The prophet here looks as far back as the miracles in Egypt, and through the wilderness. He that thus brought them at first into Canaan can now bring them out of Babylon.

I. God appeared in his glory (*v.* 3, 4): *He came from Teman, even the Holy One from Mount Paran*. This refers to the visible display of the glory of God when he gave the law upon Mount Sinai, Deut. xxxiii. 2.

JAMIESON, FAUSSET, BROWN

his holy temple—"His place" (Isa. 26:21); heaven (Ps. 11:4; Jonah 2:7; Mic. 1:2). The temple at Jerusalem is a type of it, and there God is to be worshipped. He does not lie hid under gold and silver, as the idols of Babylon, but reigns in heaven and fills heaven, and thence succors His people. **keep silence**—in token of reverent submission and subjection to His judgments (Job 40:4; Ps. 76:8; Zeph. 1:7; Zech. 2:13).

CHAPTER 3

Vss. 1-19. Habakkuk's Prayer to God: God's Glorious Revelation of Himself at Sinai and at Gibeon, a Pledge of His Interposing Again in Behalf of Israel against Babylon, and All Other Foes; Hence the Prophet's Confidence amid Calamities. This sublime ode begins with an exordium (vss. 1, 2), then follows the main subject, then the peroration (vss. 16-19), a summary of the practical truth, which the whole is designed to teach. (Deut. 33:2-5; Ps. 77:13-20 are parallel odes). This was probably designed by the Spirit to be a fit formula of prayer for the people, first in their Babylonian exile, and now in their dispersion, especially towards the close of it, just before the great Deliverer is to interpose for them. It was used in public worship, as the musical term, Selah! (vss. 3, 9, 13), implies. **1. prayer**—the only strictly called prayers are in vs. 2. But all devotional addresses to God are called "prayers" (Ps. 72:20). The *Hebrew* is from a root "to apply to a judge for a favorable decision." *Prayers* in which *praises* to God for deliverance, anticipated in the sure confidence of faith, are especially calculated to enlist Jehovah on His people's side (II Chron. 20:20-22, 26). **upon Shigionoth**—a musical phrase, "after the manner of elegies," or mournful odes, from an *Arabic* root [Lee]; the phrase is *singular* in Psalm 7, title. More simply, from a *Hebrew* root to "err," "on account of *sins of ignorance*." Habakkuk thus teaches his countrymen to confess not only their more grievous sins, but also their *errors* and *negligences*, into which they were especially likely to fall when in exile away from the Holy Land [Calvin]. So *Vulgate* and Aquila, and Symmachus. "For voluntary transgressors" [Jerome]. Probably the subject would regulate the kind of music. Delitzsch and Henderson translate, "With triumphal music," from the same root "to err," implying its enthusiastic irregularity. **2. I have heard thy speech**—Thy revelation to me concerning the coming chastisement of the Jews [Calvin], and the destruction of their oppressors. This is Habakkuk's reply to God's communication [Grotius]. Maurer translates, "the report of Thy coming," lit., "Thy report." **and was afraid**—reverential fear of God's judgments (vs. 16). **revive thy work**—Perfect the *work* of delivering *Thy* people, and do not let Thy promise lie as if it were dead, but *give it new life* by performing it [Menochus]. Calvin explains "thy work" to be *Israel;* called "the work of My hands" (Isa. 45:11). God's elect people are peculiarly His work (Isa. 43:1), pre-eminently illustrating His power, wisdom, and goodness. "Though we seem, as it were, dead nationally, *revive* us" (Ps. 85:6). However (Ps. 64:9), where "the work of God" refers to *His judgment on their enemies*, favors the former view (Ps. 90:16, 17; Isa. 51:9, 10). **in the midst of the years**—viz., of calamity in which we live. Now that our calamities are at their height; during our seventy years' captivity. Calvin more fancifully explains it, in the midst of the years of Thy people, extending from Abraham to Messiah; if they be cut off before His coming, they will be cut off as it were *in the midst of their years*, before attaining their maturity. So Bengel makes *the midst of the years* to be the middle point of the years of the world. There is a strikingly similar phrase (Dan. 9:27), "*In the midst of the week.*" The parallel clause, "in wrath" (i.e., *in the midst* of wrath), however, shows that "in the midst of the years" means "in the years of our present exile and calamity." **make known**—Made *it* (*Thy* work) known by experimental proof; show in very deed, that this is Thy work. **3. God**—*singular* in the *Hebrew*, "Eloah," instead of "Elohim," *plural*, usually employed. The *singular* is not found in any other of the minor prophets, or Jeremiah, or Ezekiel; but it is in Isaiah, Daniel, Job, and Deuteronomy. **from Teman**—the country south of Judea and near Edom, in which latter country Mount Paran was situated [Henderson]. "Paran" is the desert region, extending from the south of Judah to Sinai. Seir, Sinai, and Paran are adjacent to one another, and are hence associated together, in respect to God's giving of the

ADAM CLARKE

CHAPTER 3

1. *A prayer of Habakkuk . . . upon Shigionoth.* See the note on the title of Psalm vii, where the meaning of *Shiggaion* is given.

2. *In the midst of the years.* "As the years approach." The nearer the time, the clearer and fuller is the prediction; and the signs of the times show that the complete fulfilment is at hand.

3. *Teman.* This was a city, the capital of a province of Idumea, to the south of the land of Canaan, Num. xx. 21; Jer. xlix. 7. *Paran* was a city which gave its name to a province in Arabia Petraea, Gen. xxi. 21; Deut. xxxiii. 2.

MATTHEW HENRY

Then *his glory covered the heavens.* The *earth also* was *full of his praise*, or of his *splendour*, as some read it. Or the earth was full of those works of God which were to be praised. Some by the horns, the *two horns* (for the word is dual), *coming out of his hand*, understand the *two tables of the law.* It is added,

And there was the hiding of his power. The operations of his power, compared with what he could have done, were rather the hiding of it than the discovery of it.

II. God sent plagues on Egypt, for the humbling of proud Pharaoh (*v.* 5): *Before him went the pestilence*, which slew all the first-born of Egypt in one night; and *burning coals went forth at his feet*, when, in the plague of hail, there was *fire mingled with hail—burning diseases* (so the margin reads it). These were *at his feet*, that is, at his coming, for they are at his command; he says to them, Go, and they go, Come, and they come, Do this, and they do it.

III. He divided the land of Canaan to his people Israel, and expelled the heathen (*v.* 6): *He stood, and measured the earth*, measured that land, to assign it for an inheritance to Israel his people, Deut. xxxii. 8, 9. *He beheld, and drove asunder the nations*, though they combined together against Israel. Then *the everlasting mountains were scattered, and the perpetual hills did bow*; the mighty princes of Canaan, that seemed as high and as firmly fixed, as the mountains, were broken to pieces.

When he *drove asunder the nations of Canaan* one might have seen the *tents of Cushan in affliction, the curtains of the land of Midian trembling*, and all the inhabitants of the neighbouring countries, *v.* 7.

JAMIESON, FAUSSET, BROWN

law (Deut. 33:2). Teman is so identified with Seir or *Edom*, as here to be substituted for it. Habakkuk appeals to God's glorious manifestations to His people at Sinai, as the ground for praying that God will "revive His work" (vs. 2) now. For He is the same God now as ever. **Selah**—a musical sign, put at the close of sections and strophes, always at the end of a verse, except thrice; viz., here, and vs. 9. and Psalm 55:19; 57:3, where, however, it closes the hemistich. It implies a change of the modulation. It comes from a root to "rest" or "pause" [GESENIUS]; implying a cessation of the chant, during an instrumental interlude. The solemn pause here prepares the mind for contemplating the glorious description of Jehovah's manifestation which follows. **earth . . . full of his praise**—i.e., of His glories which were calculated to call forth universal *praise;* the parallelism to "glory" proves this to be the sense. **4. as the light**—viz., of the sun (Job 37:21; Prov. 4:18). **horns**—the emblem of *power* wielded by "His hand" [LUDOVICUS DE DIEU]. "Rays" emanating from "His hand," compared by the Arabs to the horns of the gazelle (cf. "hind of the morning," Ps. 22, title, *Margin*). The *Hebrew* verb for to "emit rays," is from the root meaning "horns" (Exod. 34:29, 30, 35) [GROTIUS]. The rays are His *lightnings* (Ps. 18:8), [MAURER]. **there**—*in that "brightness." In it,* notwithstanding its brilliancy, there was but the veil (*"the hiding*) of His power." Even "light," God's "garment," covers, instead of revealing fully, His surpassing glory (Ps. 104:2) [HENDERSON]. Or, *on Mount Sinai* [DRUSIUS]. (Cf. Exod. 24:17.) LXX and *Syriac* versions read for "there," *He made* a hiding, etc.; He hid Himself with clouds. *English Version* is better, which CALVIN explains, there is said to be "a hiding of God's power," because God did not reveal it indiscriminately to all, but specially to His people (Ps. 31:20). The contrast seems to me to be between the "horns" or *emanations* out of His power ("hand"), and that "power" itself. The latter was *hidden,* whereas the "horns" or *emanations* alone were manifested. If the mere scintillations were so awfully overwhelming, how much more so the hidden power itself! This was especially true of His manifestation at Sinai (Ps. 18:11; cf. Isa. 45:15, 17). **5. pestilence**—to destroy His people's foes (I Sam. 5:9, 11). As Jehovah's advent is glorious to His people, so it is terrible to His foes. **burning coals**—Psalm 18:8 favors *English Version.* But the parallelism requires, as *Margin* translates, "burning disease" (cf. Deut. 32:24; Ps. 91:6). **went . . . at his feet**—i.e., after Him, as His attendants (Judg. 4:10). **6. He stood, and measured the earth**—Jehovah, in His advance, is represented as stopping suddenly, and *measuring* the earth with His all-seeing glance, whereat there is universal consternation. MAURER, from a different root, translates, "*rocked* the earth"; which answers better to the parallel "drove asunder"; the *Hebrew* for which latter, however, may be better translated, "made to tremble." **everlasting mountains**—which have ever been remembered as retaining the same place and form from the foundation of the world. **did bow**—as it were, in reverent submission. **his ways are everlasting**—His marvellous ways of working for the salvation of His people mark His everlasting character: such as He was in His workings for them formerly, such shall He be now. **7. the tents**—i.e, the dwellers. **Cushan** the same as *Cush;* made Cush-*an* to hamonize with Midi-*an* in the parallel clause. So *Lotan* is found in the *Hebrew* of Genesis for *Lot.* BOCHART therefore considers it equivalent to Midian, or a part of Arabia. So in Numbers 12:1, Moses' Midianite wife is called an Ethiopian (*Hebrew, Cushite*). MAURER thinks *the dwellers on both sides of the Arabian Gulf,* or *Red Sea,* are meant; for in the preceding verse God's *everlasting* or ancient *ways* of delivering His people are mentioned; and in the following verse, the dividing of the Red Sea for them. Cf. Miriam's song as to the *fear* of Israel's foes far and near caused thereby (Exod. 15:14-16). Hebrew expositors refer it to Cushan-rishathaim, king of Mesopotamia, or Syria, the first oppressor of Israel (Judg. 3:8, 10), from whom Othniel delivered them. Thus the second hemistich of the verse will refer to the deliverance of Israel from Midian by Gideon (Judg. 6 and 7) to which vs. 11 plainly refers. Whichever of these views be correct, the general reference is to God's interpositions against Israel's foes of old. **in affliction**—rather, "*under* affliction" (regarded) as a heavy burden. Lit., "vanity" or "iniquity," hence the *punishment* of it (cf. Num. 25:17, 18). **curtains**—the coverings of their tents; the shifting habitations of the nomad tribes, which resembled the modern Bedouins. **tremble**—viz., at Jehovah's terrible interposition for

ADAM CLARKE

Selah. This word is not well-known; probably it means a pause or alteration in the music. See it in the Psalms.

4. *He had horns coming out of his hand.* "Rays." *His hand*—His power—was manifested in a particular place, by the sudden issuing out of rays, which diverged in coruscations of light, so as to illuminate the whole hemisphere.

Yet *there was the hiding of his power.* His majesty could not be seen, nor any kind of image, because of the insufferable splendor.

5. *Before him went the pestilence.* This plague was several times inflicted on the disobedient Israelites in the wilderness; see Num. xi. 33; xiv. 37; xvi. 46; and was always the proof that the just God was then manifesting His power among them. *Burning coals went forth at his feet.* Newcome translates, "And flashes of fire went forth after him." The disobedient Israelites were consumed by a fire that went out from Jehovah; see Lev. x. 2; Num. xi. 1; xvi. 35. And the burnt offering was consumed by a fire which came out from before Jehovah, Lev. xi. 24.

6. *He stood, and measured the earth. Erets,* "the land"; He divided the Promised Land among the twelve tribes. *He beheld, and drove asunder the nations.* The nations of Canaan, the Hittites, Hivites, Jebusites, etc., and all who opposed His people. Even His look dispersed them. *The everlasting mountains were scattered.* Or "broken asunder." This may refer to the convulsions on Mount Sinai, and to the earthquake which announced the descent of the Most High. See Exod. xix. 18.

7. *I saw the tents of Cushan in affliction. Cush* is Arabia. The Arabians dwelt in *tents.* When the Lord appeared on Mount Sinai, the Arabs of the Red Sea abandoned their tents, being terror-struck; and the Midianites also were seized with fear.

MATTHEW HENRY

IV. He divided the Red Sea and Jordan, and yet fetched a river out of a rock when Israel wanted it, *v.* 8. God *rode upon his horses and chariots of salvation,* as a general at the head of his forces, mighty to save.

VI. He completed Israel's victories over the nations of Canaan and their kings. This is a plea with God that he would restore them again to that land.

1. Many expressions are here used to set forth the conquest of Canaan. God's *bow was made quite naked,* taken out of the case, to be employed for Israel; *we should say,* his *sword was quite unsheathed.*

2. God would hereby make good his promise to the fathers; it was *according to the oaths of the tribes, even his word, v.* 9. He had sworn to give this land to the *tribes of Israel.*

Thou didst cleave the earth with rivers; channels in the wilderness, for the waters out of the rock, to supply the camp of Israel.

When they came to enter Canaan, the *overflowing of the water passed by,* that is, Jordan, which at that time overflowed all his banks, was divided, Joshua iii. 15. Then *the deep uttered his voice,* when, the Red Sea and Jordan being divided, the waters roared. They *lifted up their hands,* or sides, *on high* (for the waters *stood up on a heap,* Joshua iii. 16).

V. He arrested the motion of the sun and moon, to befriend Israel's victories (*v.* 11). *At the light,* at the direction, *of thy arrows, they went,* and at *the shining of thy glittering spear;* his spear pointed (the glittering light of which they acknowledged to outshine theirs) that way they directed their march, as when *the stars in their courses fought against Sisera.*

He *marched through the land* from end to end, *in indignation,* as scorning to let that wicked generation of Canaanites any longer possess so good a land. He *threshed the heathen in anger,* trod them out, as corn in the floor. He would hereby show his kindness to *his people,* because of their relation to him, and his interest in them: *Thou wentest forth for the salvation of thy people, v.* 13. He would hereby give a type and figure of the redemption of the world by Jesus Christ. It is *for salvation with thy anointed,* with Joshua, who was a figure of him whose name he bore, even Jesus our Joshua.

He *wounded the heads out of the house of the wicked;* he destroyed their princes, cut off the heads, and so *discovered the foundations of them,* even *to the neck.* Some apply this to Christ's victories over Satan and the powers of darkness, in which he *wounded the heads over many countries,* Ps. cx. 6.

JAMIESON, FAUSSET, BROWN

Israel against them. **8. Was the Lord displeased against the rivers?**—"Was the cause of His dividing the Red Sea and Jordan His displeasure against these waters?" The answer to this is tacitly implied in "Thy chariots *of salvation.*" "Nay; it was not displeasure against the waters, but His pleasure in interposing for His people's *salvation*" (cf. vs. 10). **thy chariots**—in antithesis to Thy foe, *Pharaoh's* chariots," which, notwithstanding their power and numbers, were engulfed in the waters of *destruction.* God can make the most unlikely means work for His people's salvation (Exod. 14:7, 9, 23, 25-28; 15: 3-8, 19). Jehovah's chariots are His angels (Ps. 68:17), or the cherubim, or the ark (Josh. 3:13 and 4:7; cf. Song of Solomon 1:9). **9. bow . . . made . . . naked**—i.e., was drawn forth from its cover, in which bows usually were cased when not in use. Cf. Isaiah 22:6, "Kir uncovered the shield." *according* **to the oaths of the tribes** *even thy* **word**—i.e., Thy *oaths* of promise to *the tribes* of Israel (Ps. 77:8; Luke 1:73, 74). Habakkuk shows that God's miraculous interpositions for His people were not limited to one time, but that God's *oaths* to His people are sure ground for their always expecting them. The mention of the *tribes,* rather than *Abraham* or Moses, is in order that they may not doubt that to them belongs this grace of which Abraham was the depository [CALVIN and JEROME]. MAURER translates, "The spears were glutted with blood, the triumphal song!" i.e., no sooner did Jehovah begin the battle by baring His bow, than the spears were glutted with blood and the triumphal song sung. **Thou didst cleave the earth with rivers**—the result of the earthquake caused by God's approach [MAURER]. GROTIUS refers it to the bringing forth water from the rock (Exod. 17:6; Num. 20:10, 11; Ps. 78: 15, 16; 105:4). But the context implies not the giving of water to His people to drink, but the fearful physical phenomena attending Jehovah's attack on Israel's foes. **10. The mountains**—repetition with increased emphasis of some of the tremendous phenomena mentioned in vs. 6. **overflowing of the water passed by**—viz., of the Red Sea; and again, of the Jordan. God marked His favor to His people in all the elements, causing every obstacle, whether mountains or waters, which impeded their progress, to *pass away* [CALVIN]. MAURER, not so well, translates, "torrents (rains) of water rush down." **lifted . . . hands on high**—viz., its billows *lifted on high* by the tempest. Personification. As men signify by *voice* or gesture of *hand* that they will do what they are commanded, so these parts of nature testified their obedience to God's will (Exod. 14:22; Josh. 3: 16; Ps. 77:17, 18; 114:4). **11. sun . . . moon stood still**—at Joshua's command (Josh. 10:12, 13). MAURER wrongly translates, "stand" (*withdrawn,* or *hidden from view,* by the clouds which covered the sky during the thunders). **light of thine arrows**—hail mixed with lightnings (Josh. 10:10, 11). **they went**—The *sun* and *moon* "went," not as always heretofore, but according to the light and direction of Jehovah's arrows, viz., His lightnings hurled in defense of His people; astonished at these they stood still [CALVIN]. MAURER translates, "At the light of Thine arrows (which) went" or flew. **12. march**—implying Jehovah's majestic and irresistible progress before His people (Judg. 5:4; Ps. 68:7). Israel would not have dared to attack the nations, unless Jehovah had gone before. **thresh**—(Mic. 4:13). **13. with thine anointed**—with Messiah; of whom Moses, Joshua, and David, God's anointed leaders of Israel, were the types (Ps. 89:19, 20, 38). God from the beginning delivered His people in person, or by the hand of a Mediator (Isa. 63:11). Thus Habakkuk confirms believers in the hope of their deliverance, as well because God is always the same, as also because the same anointed Mediator is ready now to fulfil God's will and interpose for Israel, as of old [CALVIN]. MAURER translates to suit the parallelism, "for salvation to Thine anointed," viz., Israel's *king* in the abstract, answering to the "people" in the former clause (cf. Ps. 28:8; Lam. 4:20). Or Israel is meant, the *anointed,* i.e., consecrated people of Jehovah (Ps. 105:15). **woundedst the head out of the house of the wicked**—probably an allusion to Psalm 68:21. Each *head person* sprung from and belonging to *the house of* Israel's *wicked* foes; such as Jabin, whose city Hazor was "the head of all the kingdoms" of Canaan (Josh. 11:10; cf. Judg. 4:2, 3, 13). **discovering the foundation**—Thou destroyedst high and low. As the *head* of the house" means the prince, so the "foundation" means the general *host* of the enemy. **unto the neck**—image from a flood reaching *to the neck* (Isa. 8:8; 30:28). So God, by His wrath overflowing on the foe, caused their princes' *necks* to be trodden under foot by Israel's leaders (Josh. 10:24; 11:8, 12). **14. strike**

ADAM CLARKE

8. *Was the Lord displeased against the rivers?* Floods; here is a reference to the passage of the Red Sea. The Lord is represented as heading His troops, riding in His chariot, and commanding the sea to divide, that a free passage might be left for His army to pass over.

9. *Thy bow was made quite naked.* That is, it was drawn out of its case; as the arrows had their quiver, so the bows had their cases. This verse appears to be an answer to the questions in the preceding: "Was the Lord displeased?" The answer is, All this was done *according to the oaths of the tribes;* the covenant of God, frequently repeated and renewed, which He made with the tribes, to give them the land of the Canaanites for their inheritance.

Thou didst cleave the earth with rivers. Or, "Thou didst cleave the streams of the land." Or, "Thou cleavedst the dry land into rivers." This may be a reference to the passage of Jordan, and transactions at Arnon and the brook Jabbok. See Num. xxi. 13-15.

10. *The mountains saw thee.* This is the continued answer to the questions in v. 8. These are figures highly poetic, to show with what ease God accomplished the most arduous tasks in behalf of His people. As soon as the *mountains* saw Him, they trembled, they were in pangs. When He appeared, the sea fled to right and left, to give Him a passage.

11. *The sun and moon stood still.* This was at the prayer of Joshua, when he fought against the Amorites. See Josh. x. 11-12. *At the light of thine arrows they went.* I think we should translate:

By their light, thine arrows went abroad;
By their brightness, the lightning of Thy spear.

Calvin very justly remarks that the arrows and spears of the Israelites are called those of God, under whose auspices the people fought. The meaning is that, by the continuation of the course, the Israelites saw how to continue the battle, till their enemies were all defeated.

12. *Thou didst march through the land.* This refers to the conquest of Canaan. God is represented as going at the head of His people as general in chief; and leading them on from conquest to conquest—which was the fact. *Thou didst thresh the heathen in anger.* Thou didst tread them down, as the oxen do the sheaves on the threshing floor.

13. *Thou wentest forth for the salvation of thy people.* Their deliverance would not have been effected but through Thy interference. *For salvation with thine anointed.* That is, with Joshua, whom God had anointed, or solemnly appointed to fill the place of Moses, and lead the people into the Promised Land. *Thou woundedst the head out of the house of the wicked.* This alludes to the slaying of the firstborn through all the land of Egypt. *By discovering the foundation unto the neck.* The general meaning of this clause is sufficiently plain: the government of these lands should be utterly subverted; the very foundations of it should be razed. "Thou hast wounded the head even unto the neck, in the house of the wicked, by laying bare the foundation." There was no hope left to the Egyptians, because the firstborn of every family was cut off, so that the very foundation was laid bare, no firstborn being left to continue the heirship of families.

MATTHEW HENRY

He *struck through with his staves the head of the villages* (*v.* 14). Staves shall do the same execution as swords. Pharaoh, when he pursued Israel to the Red Sea, *came out as a whirlwind*; so did the kings of Canaan against Israel. *Their rejoicing was as to devour the poor secretly;* they were as confident of success in their enterprise as ever any great man was of devouring a poor man. But God disappointed them, and their pride did but make their fall more shameful and God's care of his poor more illustrious. He *walked to the sea with his horses* (so some read it, *v.* 15), that is, he carried Israel's victories to the Great Sea, which was opposite to that side of Canaan at which they entered. This seems to be referred to again (*v.* 15). *Thou didst walk through the heap*, or mud, *of great waters*, slowly as the children and cattle walked.

Verses 16–19

I. The prophet had foreseen the prevalence of the church's enemies and the sight made him tremble, *v.* 16. Here he goes on with what he had said *v.* 2, "*I have heard thy speech and was afraid. When I heard* what sad times were coming *my belly trembled, my lips quivered at the voice.*"

It was no reproach to his courage. *I tremble in myself, that I might rest in the day of trouble.* He that has joy in store for those that *sow in tears* has rest in store for those that tremble before him. *Good hope through grace* is founded in a *holy fear.*

II. He had looked back upon the church in former ages, and had observed what great things God had done for them, and so fell into a transport of holy joy.

1. He supposes the ruin not only of the delights of this life, but even of the necessary supports of it, *v.* 17. Famine is one of the ordinary effects of war. He supposes the fruit-tree to be withered and barren; the *fig-tree* (which used to furnish them with much of their food); he supposes *the labour of the olive* to *fail*, their oil, which was to them as butter is to us; *the fields shall yield no meat. The flock is cut off from the fold, and there is no herd in the stall.*

2. He resolves to delight and triumph in God notwithstanding; when all is gone his God is not gone (*v.* 18): "*Yet will I rejoice in the Lord.*" Those who, when they were full, enjoyed God in all, when they are emptied can *enjoy all in God*, and can sit down upon a melancholy heap of the ruins and even then sing to the praise and glory of God. This is the principal ground of our joy in God, that he is the God of our eternal salvation, the salvation of the soul; and, if he be so, we may rejoice in him in our greatest distresses, since by them our salvation cannot be hindered, but may be furthered. Joy in God is never out of season, nay, it is in a special manner seasonable when we meet with losses and crosses in the world, that it may then appear that our hearts are not set upon these things, nor our happiness bound up in them. He that is the *God of salvation* in another world will be our strength in this world, to carry us on in our journey thither, and help us over the difficulties and oppositions we meet with in our way. Thus the prophet, who began his prayer with fear and trembling, concludes it with joy and triumph, for prayer is heart's ease to a gracious soul. He set his song upon *Shigionoth* (*v.* 1), wandering tunes, *according to the variable songs*, and upon *Neginoth* (*v.* 19), *the stringed instruments.* He that is afflicted, and has prayed aright, may then be so easy, may then be so merry, as to sing psalms.

JAMIESON, FAUSSET, BROWN

. . . with his staves–with the "wicked" (vs. 13) foe's own sword (MAURER translates, "spears") (Judg. 7: 22). **head of his villages**–Not only kings were overthrown by God's hand, but His vengeance passed through the foe's *villages* and dependencies. A just retribution, as the foe had made "the inhabitants of Israel's villages to cease" (Judg. 5:7). GROTIUS translates, "of his warriors"; GESENIUS, "the chief of his captains." **to scatter me**–*Israel,* with whom Habakkuk identifies himself (cf. ch. 1:12). **rejoicing . . . to devour the poor secretly**–"The poor" means the *Israelites,* for whom in their helpless state the foe lurks *in his lair,* like a wild beast, to pounce on and *devour* (Ps. 10:9; 17:12). **15. Thou didst walk through the sea with thine horses**–(*V.* 8). No obstacle could prevent Thy progress when leading Thy people in safety to their inheritance, whether the Red Sea, Jordan, or the figurative waves of foes raging against Israel (Ps. 65:7; 77:19). **16. When I heard . . . trembled**–viz., at the judgments which God had declared (ch. 1) were to be inflicted on Judea by the Chaldeans. **belly**–The *bowels* were thought by the Hebrews to be the seat of yearning compassion (Jer. 31:20). Or "heard" may refer to vs. 2 of this ch. 3, "When I *heard* as to Jehovah's coming interposition for Israel against the Chaldeans being still at some distance" (ch. 2: 3); so also the voice" [MAURER]. **at the voice**–of the divine threatenings (ch. 1:6). The faithful tremble at the *voice* alone of God before He inflicts punishment. Habakkuk speaks in the person of all the faithful in Israel. **trembled in myself**–i.e., I trembled all over [GROTIUS]. **that I might rest in the day of trouble**–The true and only path to *rest* is through such fear. Whoever is securely torpid and hardened towards God, will be tumultuously agitated in the day of affliction, and so will bring on himself a worse destruction; but he who in time meets God's wrath and trembles at His threats, prepares the best *rest* for himself in the day of affliction [CALVIN]. HENDERSON translates, "Yet I shall have rest." Habakkuk thus consoling his mind, Though trembling at the calamity coming, yet I shall have rest in God (Isa. 26:3). But that sentiment does not seem to be directly asserted till vs. 17, as the words following at the close of this verse imply. **when he cometh unto the people, he will invade**–rather (as *English Version* is a mere truism), connected with the preceding clause, "that I might rest . . . when he (the Chaldean foe) cometh up unto the people (the Jews), *that he may cut them off*" [CALVIN]. The *Hebrew* for "invade" means, *to rush upon, or to attack and cut off with congregated troops.* **17.** Destroy the "vines" and "fig trees" of the carnal heart, and his mirth ceases. But those who when full enjoyed God in all, when emptied can enjoy all in God. They can sit down upon the heap of ruined creature comforts, and rejoice in Him as the "God of their salvation." Running in the way of His commandments, we outrun our troubles. Thus Habakkuk, beginning his prayer with trembling, ends it with a song of triumph (Job 13:15; Ps. 4:7; 43:3, 5). **labour of the olive**–i.e., the *fruit* expected from the olive. **fail**–lit., "lie", i.e., disappoint the hope (*Margin,* Isa. 58:11). **fields**–from a *Hebrew* root meaning "to be yellow"; as they look at harvest-time. **meat**–food, grain. **cut off**–i.e., cease. **18. yet I will rejoice**–The prophet speaks in the name of his people. **19. hinds' feet . . . walk upon . . . high places**–Habakkuk has here before his mind Psalm 18:33, 34; Deuteronomy 32:13. "Hinds' (gazelles') feet" imply the *swiftness* with which God enables him (the prophet and his people) to escape from his enemies, and return to his native land. The "high places" are called "mine," to imply that Israel shall be restored to *his own* land, a land of hills which are places of safety and of eminence (cf. Gen. 19: 17, and Matt. 24:16). Probably not only the *safety,* but the *moral elevation,* of Israel above all the lands of the earth is implied (Deut. 33:29). **on my stringed instruments**–*neginoth.* This is the prophet's direction to the *precentor* ("chief singer") as to how the preceding ode (ch. 3) is to be performed (cf. Ps. 4 and 6, titles). The prophet had in mind a certain form of stringed instrument adapted to certain numbers and measures. This formula at the end of the ode, directing the kind of instrument to be used, agrees with that in the beginning of it, which directs the kind of melody (cf. Isa. 38:20).

ADAM CLARKE

14. *Thou didst strike through.* The Hebrew will bear this sense: "Thou hast pierced amidst their tribes the head of their troops," referring to Pharaoh and his generals, who came like a whirlwind to fall upon the poor Israelites when they appeared to be hemmed in by sea, and no place for their escape.

16. *When I heard, my belly trembled.* The prophet, having finished his account of the wonders done by Jehovah, in bringing their fathers from Egypt into the Promised Land, now returns to the desolate state of his countrymen, who are shortly to be led into captivity, and suffer the most grievous afflictions.

When he (Nebuchadnezzar) *cometh up unto the people* (the Jews), *he will invade them* (overpower and carry them away captive) *with his troops.*

17. *Although the fig tree shall not blossom.* "Shall not flourish," shall not put forth its young figs, for the fig tree does not blossom.

These two verses give the finest display of resignation and confidence that I have ever met with. He saw that evil was at hand, and unavoidable; he submitted to the dispensation of God, whose Spirit enabled him to paint it in all its calamitous circumstances. He knew that God was merciful and gracious. He trusted to His promise, though all appearances were against its fulfillment; for he knew that the word of Jehovah could not fail, and therefore his confidence is unshaken.

19. *The Lord God is my strength.* This is an imitation, if not a quotation, from Ps. xviii. 32-33. *Will make me to walk upon mine high places.* This last verse is spoken in the person of the people, who seem to anticipate their restoration, and that they shall once more rejoice in the hills and mountains of Judea. *To the chief singer on my stringed instruments.* This line, which is evidently a superscription, leads me to suppose that, when the prophet had completed his short ode, he folded it up, with the above direction to the master singer, or leader of the choir, to be sung in the Temple service. Many of the psalms are directed in the same way. "To the master singer" or "chief musician"; to be sung, according to their nature, on different kinds of instruments, or with particular airs or tunes. *Neginoth,* which we translate "stringed instruments," means such as were struck with a plectrum, or excited by some kind of friction or pulsation; as violins and cymbals, or tambourines are. I do not think that the line makes any part of the prophecy, but merely the superscription or direction of the work when it was finished. The ending will appear much more dignified, this line being separated from it.

THE BOOK OF ZEPHANIAH

I. The day of wrath with an appeal (1:1-2:15)
- *A. The day of wrath (1:1-18)*
  1. Announced in general terms (1:1-6)
  2. Described particularly (1:7-13)
  3. Described as to character (1:14-18)
- *B. The appeal (2:1-15)*
  1. The cry of the nations (2:1, 2)
  2. The call to the remnant (2:3)
  3. The argument (2:4-15)

II. The day of wrath and its issue (3:1-20)
- *A. The day of wrath (3:1-8)*
  1. The woe declared (3:1)
  2. The reasons declared (3:2-7)
  3. The final word (3:8)
- *B. The issue of the day (3:9-20)*
  1. The gathering of a remnant (3:9-13)
  2. The remnant addressed (3:14-20)

This prophet is placed last of all the minor prophets before the captivity, and not long before Jeremiah who lived at the time of the captivity. He foretells the general destruction of Judah and Jerusalem by the Chaldeans, and sets their sins before them, calls them to repentance, threatens the neighboring nations with the like destructions, and gives encouraging promises of their joyful return out of captivity in due time.

MATTHEW HENRY

CHAPTER 1

Verses 1–6

I. The title-page of this book (*v.* 1); it is from heaven, and not of men: It is *the word of the Lord. Zephaniah* signifies the *servant of the Lord,* for God *revealed his secrets to his servants the prophets.* The pedigree of Zephaniah goes back four generations, and the highest mentioned is *Hizkiah*; it is the same name in the original with that of Hezekiah king of Judah (2 Kings xviii. 1). This prophet prophesied *in the days of Josiah king of Judah,* who in the twelfth year of his reign carried on a work of reformation, in which he destroyed idols. Now it does not appear whether Zephaniah prophesied in the beginning of his reign; if so, we may suppose his prophesying had a great influence on that reformation.

II. The summary of this book. The general proposition contained in it is, That utter destruction is coming apace upon Judah and Jerusalem for sin. He begins abruptly (*v.* 2): *By taking away I will make an end of all things from off the face of the land, saith the Lord. I will consume the beasts, the fowls of the heaven, and the fishes of the sea* (*v.* 3). The expressions are figurative, denoting universal desolation. Those that fly ever so high, those that hide ever so close, shall yet become a prey to them, and be utterly consumed. *"I will consume man; I will cut off man from the land.* The land shall be dispeopled and left uninhabited; I will destroy, not only Israel, but *man.* Though they shall not be cut off from the Lord, yet they shall be *cut off from the land."* Even Judah, where God is known, and Jerusalem, where his dwelling-place is, if they revolt from him and rebel against him, shall have his hand stretched out against them. *"I will consume the stumbling-blocks with the wicked,* the idols with the idolaters, the offences with the offenders." The Chaldeans would spare none of the images of Baal, or the worshippers of those images. The *Chemarim* shall be *cut off*; we read of them in the history of Josiah's reformation. 2 Kings xxiii. 5, *He put down the idolatrous priests:* the word is the *Chemarim.* The word signifies *black men,* some think because they wore black clothes, others because their faces were black with attending the altars, the fires in which they burnt their children to Moloch. They seem to have been immediate attendants upon the service of Baal. And, among other idolaters, the *worshippers of the host of heaven upon the house-tops* shall be cut off (*v.* 5). It will appear as great an offence to God to give divine honours to a star as to give them to a stone or a stock. Those also shall be consumed that halt between God and Baal, and worship between Jehovah and Moloch, and *swear by both*; or, as it might better be read, swear *to the Lord and to Malcham.* Those also shall be consumed that have apostatized from God, together with those that never gave up their names to him, *v.* 6.

JAMIESON, FAUSSET, BROWN

CHAPTER 1

VSS. 1-18. GOD'S SEVERE JUDGMENT ON JUDAH FOR ITS IDOLATRY AND NEGLECT OF HIM: THE RAPID APPROACH OF THE JUDGMENT, AND THE IMPOSSIBILITY OF ESCAPE. **1. days of Josiah**—Had their idolatries been under former kings, they might have said, Our kings have forced us to this and that. But under Josiah, who did all in his power to reform them, they have no such excuse. **son of Amon**—the idolater, whose bad practices the Jews clung to, rather than the good example of Josiah, his son; so incorrigible were they in sin. **Judah**—Israel's ten tribes had gone into captivity before this. **2. utterly consume**—from a root to "sweep away," or "scrape off utterly." See the *Margin,* Jeremiah 8:13, and here. **from off the land**—of Judah. **3.** Enumeration in detail of the "all things" (vs. 2; cf. Jer. 9:10; Hos. 4:3). **the stumbling blocks**—idols which cause Judah to offend or stumble (Ezek. 14:3, 4, 7). **with the wicked**—The idols and their worshippers shall be involved in a common destruction. **4. stretch out mine hand**—indicating some remarkable and unusual work of vengeance (Isa. 5:25; 9:12, 17, 21). **Judah**—including Benjamin. These two tribes are to suffer, which thought themselves perpetually secure, because they escaped the captivity in which the ten tribes were involved. **Jerusalem**—the fountain-head of the evil. God begins with His sanctuary (Ezek. 9:6), and those who are nigh Him (Lev. 10:3). **the remnant of Baal**—the remains of Baal-worship, which as yet Josiah was unable utterly to eradicate in remote places. Baal was the Phœnician tutelary god. From the time of the Judges (Judg. 2:13), Israel had fallen into this idolatry; and Manasseh lately had set up this idol within Jehovah's temple itself (II Kings 21:3, 5, 7). Josiah began his reformation in the twelfth year of his reign (II Chron. 34:4, 8), and in the eighteenth had as far as possible completed it. **Chemarims**—idol priests, who had not reached the age of puberty; meaning "ministers of the gods" (SERVIUS on *Æneid,* 11), the same name as the Tyrian *Camilli, r* and *l* being interchangeable (cf. *Margin,* Hos. 10:5). Josiah is expressly said (*Margin,* II Kings 23:5) to have "put down the Chemarim." The *Hebrew* root means "black" (from the *black garments* which they wore or the *marks* which they branded on their foreheads); or "zealous", from their idolatrous fanaticism. The very "name," as well as themselves, shall be forgotten. **the priests**—of Jehovah, of Aaronic descent, who ought to have used all their power to eradicate, but who secretly abetted, idolatry (cf. ch. 3:4; Ezek. 8; 22:26; 44:10). From the *priests* Zephaniah passes to the *people.* **5. worship the host of heaven**—*Saba:* whence, in contrast to Sabeanism, Jehovah is called *Lord of Sabaoth.* **upon the housetops**—which were flat (II Kings 23:5, 6, 12; Jer. 19:13; 32:29). **swear by the Lord**—rather, "swear *to* JEHOVAH" (II Chron. 15:14); solemnly dedicating themselves to Him (cf. Isa. 48:1; Hos. 4:15). **and**—*"and yet* (with strange inconsistency, I Kings 18:21; Ezek. 20:39; Matt. 6:24) swear by Malcham," i.e., *"their king"* [MAURER]: the same as Molech (*Note,* Amos 5:26), and "Milcom the god of . . . Ammon" (I Kings 11:33). If Satan have half the heart, he will have all; if the Lord have but half offered to Him, He will have none. **6.** This verse describes more comprehensively those guilty of defection from Jehovah in any way (Jer. 2:13,

ADAM CLARKE

CHAPTER 1

1. *The word of the Lord which came unto Zephaniah.* Though this prophet has given us so large a list of his ancestors, yet little concerning him is known, because we know nothing certain relative to the persons of the family whose names are here introduced. He prophesied *in the days of Josiah the son of Amon, king of Judah;* and from the description which he gives of the disorders which prevailed in Judea in his time, it is evident that he must have prophesied before the reformation made by Josiah, which was in the eighteenth year of his reign. And as he predicts the destruction of Nineveh, chap. ii. 13, which could not have taken place before the sixteenth of Josiah, allowing with Berosus twenty-one years for the reign of Nabopolassar over the Chaldeans; we must, therefore, place this prophecy about the beginning of the reign of Josiah, or from 640 B.C. to 609 B.C.

2. *I will utterly consume all things.* All being now ripe for destruction, I will shortly bring a universal scourge upon the land. He speaks particularly of the idolaters.

3. *I will consume man and beast.* By *war,* and by *pestilence.* Even the waters shall be infected, and the fish destroyed; the air become contaminated, and the fowls die.

4. *I will cut off the remnant of Baal.* I think he refers here, partly at least, to the reformation which Josiah was to bring about. See the account, 2 Kings xxiii. 5. *The Chemarims.* The black-robed priests of different idols. See 2 Kings xxiii. 5. These were put down by Josiah.

5. *The host of heaven.* Sun, moon, planets, and stars. This worship was one of the most ancient and the most common of all species of idolatry; and it had a greater semblance of reason to recommend it. See 2 Kings xxiii. 5, 12; Jer. xix. 13; xxxii. 29. *That swear by the Lord, and that swear by Malcham.* Associating the name of an idol with that of the Most High. For *Malcham,* see Hos. iv. 15 and Amos v. 26.

6. *Them that are turned back.* Who have forsaken the true God, and become idolaters. *Nor enquired for him.* Have not desired to know His will.

MATTHEW HENRY

Verses 7–13

Notice is given to Judah and Jerusalem that God is coming against them; *his day*, the day of his judgment is not far off, *v.* 7. Men have their day now, when they do what they please; but *God's day is at hand*; it is here called his *sacrifice*, reparation to his injured honour.

II. God will punish these sinners. He will silence them (*v.* 7): *Hold thy peace at the presence of the Lord.* He will *sacrifice* them, for it is *the day of the Lord's sacrifice* (*v.* 8); he will give them into the hands of their enemies.

I. Those that shall be punished in this day of reckoning: The royal family for their pride and affectation (*v.* 8). They shall be punished, and all such as, like them, are clothed *with strange apparel. The princes and the king's children* send abroad to strange countries for their clothes, which would not please unless they were far-fetched and dear-bought. Pride in apparel is displeasing to God, and a symptom of the degeneracy of a people.

In the same day will I punish those that leap on the threshold, a phrase which probably signified the invading of their neighbour's rights. They *leap on the threshold*, as much as to say that the house is their own, and, accordingly, they make all in it their own, and so *fill their masters' houses* with goods gotten *by violence and deceit.*

In that day there shall be a noise of a cry from the fish-gate, so called because near to the fish-market.

And a howling from the second, which was next to that *fish-gate.*

The alarm shall go round the walls of Jerusalem from gate to gate; and there shall be *a great crashing from the hills*, from the mountains round about Jerusalem, from the acclamations of the invaders, and the lamentations of the invaded. The inhabitants of the city, even of the closest safest part of the city, shall *howl* (*v.* 11), so clamorous shall the grief be.

Iniquity is found among *the inhabitants of Maktesh*, a low part of Jerusalem, deep like a mortar (for so the word signifies); the *goldsmiths* lived there (Neh. iii. 32) and the merchants; and they are now *cut down*, have shut up their shops, and become bankrupts.

JAMIESON, FAUSSET, BROWN

17). **7. Hold thy peace at the presence of the Lord**—(Hab. 2:20). Let the *earth* be silent at His approach [MAURER]. Or, "Thou whosoever hast been wont to speak against God, as if He had no care about earthly affairs, cease thy murmurs and self-justifications; submit thyself to God, and repent in time" [CALVIN]. **Lord . . .prepared a sacrifice**—viz., a slaughter of the guilty Jews, the victims due to His justice (Isa. 34:6; Jer. 46:10; Ezek. 39:17). **bid his guests**—lit., "sanctified His called ones" (cf. Isa. 13:3). It enhances the bitterness of the judgment that the heathen Chaldeans should be *sanctified*, or consecrated as it were, by God as His priests, and be *called* to eat the flesh of the elect people; as on feast days the priests used to feast among themselves on the remains of the sacrifices [CALVIN]. *English Version* takes it not of the *priests*, but the *guests bidden*, who also had to "sanctify" or purify themselves before coming to the sacrificial feast (I Sam. 9:13, 22; 16:5). Nebuchadnezzar was *bidden* to come to take vengeance on guilty Jerusalem (Jer. 25:9). **8. the princes**—who ought to have been an example of good to others, but were ringleaders in all evil. **the king's children**—fulfilled on Zedekiah's children (Jer. 39:6); and previously, on Jehoahaz and Eliakim, the sons of Josiah (II Kings 23:31, 36; II Chron. 36:6; cf. also II Kings 20:18; 21:13). Huldah the prophetess (II Kings 22:20) intimated that which Zephaniah now more expressly foretells. **all such as are clothed with strange apparel**—the *princes* or *courtiers* who attired themselves in costly garments, imported from abroad; partly for the sake of luxury, and partly to ingratiate themselves with foreign great nations whose costume as well as their idolatries they imitated, [CALVIN]; whereas in costume, as in other respects, God would have them to be separate from the nations. GROTIUS refers the "strange apparel" to garments forbidden by the law, e.g., men's garments worn by women, and vice versa, a heathen usage in the worship of Mars and Venus (Deut. 22: 5). **9. those that leap on the threshold**—the servants of the princes, who, after having gotten prey (like hounds) for their masters, leap exultingly on their masters' thresholds; or, on the thresholds of the houses which they break into [CALVIN]. JEROME explains it of those *who walk up the steps into the sanctuary with haughtiness.* ROSENMULLER translates, "Leap *over* the threshold"; viz., in imitation of the Philistine custom of not treading on the threshold, which arose from the head and hands of Dagon being broken off on the threshold before the ark (I Sam. 5:5). Cf. Isa. 2:6, "thy people . . . are soothsayers *like the Philistines.*" CALVIN'S view agrees best with the latter clause of the verse. **fill . . . masters' houses with violence . . .**—i.e., with goods obtained *with violence. . . .* **10. fish gate**—(II Chron. 33:14; Neh. 3:3; 12:39). Situated on the east of the lower city, north of the sheep gate [MAURER]: near the stronghold of David in Milo, between Zion and the lower city, towards the west [JEROME]. This verse describes the state of the city when it was besieged by Nebuchadnezzar. It was through the fish gate that he entered the city. It received its name from the fish market which was near it. Through it passed those who used to bring fish from the lake of Tiberias and Jordan. It answers to what is now called the Damascus gate [HENDERSON]. **the second**—viz., the gate which was *second* in dignity [CALVIN]. Or, *the second* or lower part of the city. Appropriately, the fish gate, or extreme end of the lower part of the city, first resounds with the cries of the citizens as the foe approaches; then, as he advances further, that part of the city itself, viz., its inner part; lastly, when the foe is actually come and has burst in, the hills, the higher ones, especially Zion and Moriah, on which the upper city and temple were founded [MAURER]. The *second*, or lower city, answers to Akra, north of Zion, and separated from it by the valley of Tyropœon running down to the pool of Siloam [HENDERSON]. The *Hebrew* is translated "college," II Kings 22:14; so VATABLUS would translate here. **hills**—not here those outside, but those within the walls: Zion, Moriah, and Ophel. **11. Maktesh**—rather, "the mortar," a name applied to the valley of Siloam from its hollow shape [JEROME]. The valley between Zion and Mount Olivet, at the eastern extremity of Mount Moriah, where the merchants dwelt. Zechariah 14:21, "The Canaanite," viz., merchant [*Chaldee Version*]. The Tyropœon (i.e., *cheese-makers'*) valley below Mount Akra [ROSENMULLER]. Better *Jerusalem itself*, so called as lying in the midst of hills (Isa. 22:1; Jer. 21:13) and as doomed to be the scene of its people being destroyed as corn or drugs are pounded in a *mortar* (Prov. 27:22) [MAURER]. Cf. the similar

ADAM CLARKE

7. *Hold thy peace at the presence of the Lord God.* Remonstrances are now useless.

The Lord hath prepared a sacrifice. A slaughter of the people. *He hath bid his guests.* The Babylonians, to whom He has given a commission to destroy you.

8. *I will punish the princes, and the king's children.* After the death of Josiah the kingdom of Judah saw no prosperity, and every reign terminated miserably; until at last King Zedekiah and the king's children were cruelly massacred at Riblah, when Nebuchadnezzar had taken Jerusalem.

Strange apparel. I really think this refers more to their embracing idolatrous customs and heathen usages than to their changing their dress.

9. *That leap on the threshold.* Or "that leap over the threshold." It is most probable that the Philistines are here meant. After the time that Dagon fell before the ark, and his hands were broken off on the threshold of his temple, his worshippers would no more set a foot upon the threshold, but stepped or leaped over it, when they entered into his temple.

10. *A cry from the fish gate.* This gate, which is mentioned in Neh. iii. 3, was opposite to Joppa; and perhaps the way in which the news came of the irruption of the Chaldean army, the *great crashing from the hills.*

The second, or second city, may here mean a part of Jerusalem, mentioned in 2 Kings xxii. 14; 2 Chron. xxxiv. 22.

11. *Maktesh.* Calmet says this signifies a "mortar," or a rock in form of a mortar, and was the name of a quarter of Jerusalem where they hulled rice, corn, etc., according to St. Jerome. Some think the city of Jerusalem is meant, where the inhabitants should be beat and pounded to death as grain is pounded in a mortar.

MATTHEW HENRY

All those that bear silver are cut off by the invaders. All the careless people that live a loose idle life are next reckoned with (*v.* 12). God will find them out, and punish them: *At that time I will search Jerusalem with candles*, to discover them. God will punish not only the secret idolaters, but the secret epicures and profane. Their dispositions are sensual: They *are settled on their lees*, intoxicated with their pleasures. Their notions are atheistical. They could not live such loose lives but that they say *in their heart, The Lord will not do good, neither will he do evil*; that is, *He will do nothing*. They deny his providential government of the world. If they were not drowned in sense, they could not be thus senseless.

They shall be stripped of all they have; it shall be a prey to the enemy (*v.* 13): *Their household goods*, and *shop-goods*, shall *become a booty*, and a rich booty they shall be; *their houses shall be* levelled with the ground and be *a desolation*; those of them that have *built* new houses *shall not inherit them*, but the invaders shall get and keep possession of them. And the *vineyards* they have planted they shall not *drink the wine of*, but, instead of having it for the relief of their friends that faint among them, they shall part with it for the animating of their foes that fight against them, Deut. xxviii. 30.

Verses 14–18

The warning given to Judah and Jerusalem of the approaching destruction by the Chaldeans. It is *the great day of the Lord*, a kind of doom's-day, as the last destruction of Jerusalem by the Romans is represented to be in our Saviour's prediction concerning it, Matt. xxiv. 27.

I. This *day of the Lord* is here spoken of as very near. The prophet gives the alarm like one that awakens a family with the cry of *Fire! fire!* when it is at the next door.

II. It is spoken of as a very dreadful day. The very *voice* of this *day of the Lord*, shall make *the mighty men cry there bitterly*. It will be a day of *trouble and distress* to the sinners; they shall see no ways of easing or helping themselves. It is *a day of clouds and thick darkness*; the thick clouds are big with storms and tempests.

III. It is spoken of as a destroying day, *v.* 16, 17. What forts, what fences, can hold out against the wrath of God? "*I will bring distress upon men*, the strongest and stoutest of men; they shall *walk like blind men*, wandering endlessly, *because they have sinned against the Lord*." Those that walk as bad men will justly be left to walk as blind men, always in doubt and danger.

IV. The destruction of that day will be unavoidable and universal, *v.* 18. There shall be no escaping it by ransom: *Neither their silver nor their gold shall be able to deliver them in the day of the Lord's wrath*. There shall be no escaping it by flight or concealment; for the *whole land shall be devoured by the fire of his jealousy*, and where then can a hiding-place be found?

JAMIESON, FAUSSET, BROWN

image of a "pot" (Ezek. 24:3, 6). The reason for the destruction is subjoined, viz., its *merchant people's* greediness of gain. **all the merchant people**—lit., the "Canaanite people": irony: all the merchant people of Jerusalem are very *Canaanites* in greed for gain and in idolatries (*Note,* Hos. 12:7). **all . . . that bear silver**—loading themselves with that which will prove but a *burden* (Hab. 2:6). **12. search . . . with candles**—or lamps; so as to leave no dark corner in it wherein sin can escape the punishment, of which the Chaldeans are My instruments (cf. vs. 13; Luke 15:8). **settled on their lees**—"hardened" or crusted; image from the crust formed at the bottom of wines long left undisturbed (Jer. 48:11). The effect of *wealthy undisturbed ease* ("lees") on the ungodly is *hardening:* they become stupidly secure (cf. Ps. 55:19; Amos 6:1). **Lord will not do good . . . evil**—They deny that God regards human affairs, or renders good to the good; or evil to the evil, but that all things go haphazard (Ps. 10: 4; Mal. 2:17). **13.** Fulfilling the prophecy in Deuteronomy 28:30, 39 (cf. Amos 5:11).

14. voice of . . . day of . . . Lord—i.e., Jehovah ushering in that day with a roar of vengeance against the guilty (Jer. 25:30; Amos 1:2). They who will not now heed (vs. 12) His voice by His prophets, must heed it when uttered by the avenging foe. **mighty . . . shall cry . . . bitterly**—in hopeless despair; the might on which Jerusalem now prides itself, shall then fail utterly. **15. wasteness . . . desolation**—The *Hebrew* terms by their similarity of sounds, *Shoah, Umeshoah*, express the dreary monotony of desolation (cf. *Note,* Nah. 2:10). **16. the trumpet**—viz., of the besieging enemy (Amos 2:2). **alarm**—the war shout [MAURER]. **towers**—lit., "angles"; for city walls used not to be built in a direct line, but with sinuous curves and angles, so that besiegers advancing might be assailed not only in front, but on both sides, caught as it were in a cul-de-sac; towers were built especially at the angles. So TACITUS describes the walls of Jerusalem (*Hist.* 5. 11. 7). **17. like blind men**—unable to see whither to turn themselves so as to find an escape from existing evils. **flesh**—*Hebrew,* "bread"; so the *Arabic* term for "bread" is used for "flesh" (Matt. 26:26). **18. Neither . . . silver nor . . . gold shall . . . deliver them . . .**—(Prov. 11:4). **fire of his jealousy**—(Ezek. 38:19); His wrath jealous for His honor consuming the guilty like fire. **make even a speedy riddance of all**—rather, a consummation (complete destruction: "full end," Jer. 46:28; Ezek. 11:13) *altogether* sudden" [MAURER]. "A consumption, *and that* a sudden one" [CALVIN].

ADAM CLARKE

12. *I will search Jerusalem with candles.* I will make a universal and thorough search.

That are settled on their lees. Those who are careless, satisfied with the goods of this life.

14. *The great day of the Lord is near.* It commenced with the death of the good king Josiah, who was slain by Pharaoh-necho at Megiddo, and continued to the destruction of Jerusalem by Nebuchadnezzar.

15. *That day is a day of wrath.* From the fourteenth to the sixteenth verse inclusive there is amplification of the disasters that were coming on Jerusalem; the invasion, incursion, attack, carnage, confusion, horrible din occasioned by the sound of the trumpet, the cries of the people, and the shrieks and groans of the dying, are pointed out with great force and mighty effect.

17. *They shall walk like blind men.* Be in the most perplexing doubt and uncertainty; and while in this state, have their blood poured out by the sword of their enemies, and their flesh trodden underfoot.

MATTHEW HENRY — CHAPTER 2

Verses 1–3

The prophet meant in that terrible description of approaching judgments not to drive the people to despair, but to drive them to God and to their duty—not to frighten them out of their wits, but to frighten them out of their sins.

I. The summons to a national assembly (*v.* 1): *Gather yourselves together*. The summons is given to a *nation not desired*. The word signifies either, 1. *Not desiring*, that has not any desire towards God. "Yet *come together*, and see if you can stir up desires in one another." Or, 2. *Not desirable*, nor having anything which might recommend them to God. God says, "*Gather together*, that you may in a body humble yourselves." Some read it, "*Enquire into yourselves;* examine your consciences; look into your hearts; search and try your ways; *enquire into yourselves*, that you may find out the sin by which God has been provoked."

II. Arguments urged to press them to expedition herein (*v.* 2): "Do it in earnest; do it with all speed before it is too late, *before the decree bring forth, before the day pass*."

JAMIESON, FAUSSET, BROWN — CHAPTER 2

VSS. 1-15. EXHORTATION TO REPENT BEFORE THE CHALDEAN INVADERS COME. DOOM OF JUDAH'S FOES, THE PHILISTINES, MOAB, AMMON, WITH THEIR IDOLS, AND ETHIOPIA AND ASSYRIA. **1. Gather yourselves**—*to a religious assembly*, to avert the judgment by prayers (Joel 2:16) [GROTIUS]. Or, so as not to be dissipated "as chaff" (vs. 2). The *Hebrew* is akin to a root meaning "chaff." Self-confidence and corrupt desires are the dissipation from which they are exhorted to *gather themselves* [CALVIN]. The foe otherwise, like the wind, will scatter you "as the chaff." Repentance is the *gathering of themselves* meant. **nation not desired**—(Cf. II Chron. 21:20), i.e., not desirable; unworthy of the grace or favor of God; and yet God so magnifies that grace as to be still solicitous for their safety, though they had destroyed themselves and forfeited all claims on His grace [CALVIN]. *Margin* from *Chaldee Version* has, "not desirous," viz., of returning to God. MAURER and GESENIUS translate, "Not waxing pale," i.e., dead to shame. *English Version* is best. **2. Before the decree bring forth**—i.e., Before God's decree against you announced by me (ch. 1) *have its fulfilment*. As the embryo lies hid in the womb, and then emerges to light in its own due time, so though God for a time hides His vengeance, yet He *brings* it *forth* at the proper season. **before the day pass as the chaff**—i.e., before *the day* for repentance *pass*, and with it you, the ungodly, pass away *as the chaff* (Job 21:18; Ps. 1:4). MAURER puts it parenthetically, "the day (i.e., time) passes as the chaff" (i.e., most quickly). CALVIN, "before

ADAM CLARKE — CHAPTER 2

1. *Gather yourselves.* The Israelites are addressed.

MATTHEW HENRY

III. Directions prescribed. They are not to gather together in a consternation, but seriously and calmly (*v.* 3): *Seek you the Lord.* If the land be saved, it must be by the intercession of the pious few, *the meek of the earth,* or of *the land.* They must *seek the Lord,* seek his favour and grace. Seek God for the performance of his promises to you, and see to it that you abound yet more in duty to him.

IV. Encouragements given to take these directions: *It may be, you shall be hid in the day of the Lord's anger. "Verily it shall be well with thy remnant,* Jer. xv. 11. *It may be, you shall be hid:* if any be hid, you shall." They shall be hid (as Luther says) *aut in cœlo, aut sub cœlo—either in heaven or under heaven,* either in the possession of heaven or under the protection of heaven.

Verses 4–7

The prophet foretells what share the neighbouring nations should have in the destruction made by Nebuchadnezzar. The *day of the Lord* might appear the more dreadful, but though God had seemed to be their enemy, and to fight against them, yet he was still so far their friend, and an enemy to their enemies, that he resented, and would revenge, the indignities done them.

In these verses we have the doom of the Philistines, neighbours, and old enemies, to the people of Israel. They were the *inhabitants of the sea-coasts* (*v.* 5), for their country lay upon the Great Sea. The *nation of the Cherethites* is here joined with them, which bordered upon them (1 Sam. xxx. 14) and fell with them. The Philistines' land is here called *Canaan,* for it belonged to that country which God gave to his people Israel, Joshua xiii. 3. This land is yet to be possessed for so that they wrongfully kept Israel out of the possession of it (Judges iii. 3).

I. It is here foretold that the Philistines, the usurpers, shall be dispossessed and quite extirpated. *Gaza shall be forsaken,* though now a populous city. It was foretold (Jer. xlvii. 5) that *baldness* should come upon Gaza; Alexander the Great razed that city, and we find (Acts viii. 26) that Gaza was a desert. *Ashkelon* shall be *a desolation. Ashdod shall be driven out at noon-day;* in the extremity of the scorching heat. They shall be forced away into captivity. *Ekron* likewise shall be *rooted up,* that had been long taking root. The land of the Philistines shall be dispeopled, *v.* 5. The sea-coast, which used to be a harbour for ships and a habitation for merchants, shall now be deserted, and be only *cottages for shepherds* and *folds for flocks* (*v.* 6).

II. It is here foretold that the house of Judah, the rightful owners, shall recover the possession of it, *v.* 7. The remnant of those that shall *return out of captivity* shall *lie down* in safety *in the houses of Ashkelon.*

Verses 8–11

The Moabites and Ammonites were both of the posterity of Lot; their countries joined.

I. They are both charged with reviling the people of God and triumphing in their calamities (*v.* 8). They have *spoken big* (so some read it, *magna locuti sunt—they have spoken great things*) *against their border* (*v.* 8), against those of them that bordered upon their country; they *spoke big against the people of the Lord of hosts* as a deserted abandoned people. "But *I have heard them*" (says God).

II. They are both laid under the same doom. Sentence is pronounced upon them, *v.* 9. The Moabites and Ammonites *shall be as Sodom and Gomorrah,* the marks of whose ruins in the Dead Sea lay near adjoining to the countries of Moab and Ammon; they shall be laid waste; not again to be inhabited, or not of a long time. The country shall produce *nettles,* instead of corn; and there shall be *brine-pits,* instead of fountains of water. Israel shall *spoil them* of their goods and *possess* their country. And *this shall they have for their pride.*

III. Other nations shall in like manner be humbled. Heathen gods must be abolished. Their worshippers have gloried in them. But *the Lord* will *famish all the gods of the earth,* will starve them out of their strongholds.

JAMIESON, FAUSSET, BROWN

the decree bring forth" (the predicted vengeance), (then) the chaff (the Jews) shall pass in a day, i.e., in a moment, though they thought that it would be long before they could be overthrown. *English Version* is best; the latter clause being explanatory of the former, and so the *before* being understood, not expressed. **3.** As in vs. 1 (cf *Note,* ch. 1:12) he had warned the hardened among the people to humble themselves, so now he admonishes "the meek" to proceed in their right course, that so they may escape the general calamity (Ps. 76:9). The *meek* bow themselves under God's chastisements to God's will, whereas the ungodly become only the more hardened by them. **Seek ye the Lord**—in contrast to those that "sought not the Lord" (ch. 1: 6). The *meek* are not to regard what the multitudes do, but seek God at once. **his judgment**—i.e., law. The true way of "seeking the Lord" is to "work judgment," not merely to be zealous about outward ordinances. **seek meekness**—not perversely murmuring against God's dealings, but patiently submitting to them, and composedly waiting for deliverance. **it may be ye shall be hid**—(Isa. 26:20; Amos 5:6). This phrase does not imply doubt of the deliverance of the godly, but expresses the difficulty of it, as well that the ungodly may see the certainty of their doom, as also that the faithful may value the more the grace of God in their case (I Pet. 4:17-19) [CALVIN]. Cf. II Kings 25:12. **4. For**—He makes the punishment awaiting the neighboring states an argument why the ungodly should repent (vs. 1) and the godly persevere, viz., that so they may escape from the general calamity. **Gaza shall be forsaken**—In the *Hebrew* there is a play of similar sounds, *Gaza Gazubah;* Gaza shall be forsaken, as its name implies. So the *Hebrew* of the next clause, *Ekron teeakeer.* **at the noonday**—when on account of the heat Orientals usually sleep, and military operations are suspended (II Sam. 4:5). Hence an attack *at noon* implies one sudden and unexpected (Jer. 6:4, 5; 15:8). **Ekron**—*Four* cities of the Philistines are mentioned, whereas *five* was the normal number of their leading cities. Gath is omitted, being at this time under the Jews' dominion. David had subjugated it (I Chron. 18:1). Under Joram the Philistines almost regained it (II Chron. 21:16), but Uzziah (II Chron. 26:6) and Hezekiah (II Kings 18:8) having conquered them, it remained under the Jews. Amos 1:6, Zechariah 9:5, 6, Jeremiah 25:20, similarly mention only *four* cities of the Philistines. **5. inhabitants of the seacoast**—the Philistines dwelling on the strip of seacoast southwest of Canaan. Lit., the "cord" or "line" of sea (cf. Jer. 47:7; Ezek. 25:16). **the Cherethites**—the Cretans, a name applied to the Philistines as sprung from Crete (Deut. 2:23; Jer. 47:4; Amos 9:7). *Philistine* means "an emigrant." **Canaan . . . land of the Philistines**—They occupied the southwest of *Canaan* (Josh. 13:2, 3); a name which hints that they are doomed to the same destruction as the early occupants of the land. **6. dwellings** *and* **cottages for shepherds**—rather, "dwellings with cisterns" (i.e., water-tanks *dug* in the earth) *for shepherds.* Instead of a thick population and tillage, the region shall become a pasturage for nomad shepherds' flocks. The *Hebrew* for "dug cisterns," *Ceroth,* seems a play on sounds, alluding to their name Cherethites (vs. 5): Their land shall become what their national name implies, a land of *cisterns.* MAURER translates, *"Feasts* for shepherds' (flocks)," i.e., one wide pasturage. **7. remnant of . . . Judah**—those of the Jews who shall be left after the coming calamity, and who shall return from exile. **feed thereupon**—viz., in the pastures of that seacoast region (vs. 6). **visit**—in mercy (Exod. 4:31). **8. I have heard**—A seasonable consolation to Judah when wantonly assailed by Moab and Ammon with impunity: God saith, "I have heard it all, though I might seem to men not to have observed it because I did not immediately inflict punishment." **magnified themselves**—acted haughtily, invading the territory of Judah (Jer. 48:29; 49:1; cf. vs. 10; Ps. 35: 26; Obad. 12). **9. the breeding of nettles**—or, *the overspreading* of nettles, i.e., a place overrun with them. **salt pits**—found at the south of the Dead Sea. The water overflows in the spring, and salt is left by the evaporation. Salt land is barren (Judg. 9:45; *Margin,* Ps. 107:34). **possess them**—i.e., their land; in retribution for their having occupied Judah's land. **10.** (Cf. vs. 8.) **their pride**—in antithesis to the *meek* (vs. 3). **11. famish**—bring low by taking from the idols their former fame; as beasts are famished by their food being withheld. Also by destroying the kingdoms under the tutelage of idols (Ps. 96:4; Isa. 46:1). **gods of the earth**—who have their existence only *on earth,* not in heaven as the true God. **every one from his place**

ADAM CLARKE

3. *Ye meek of the earth.* Ye oppressed and humbled of the land.

It may be ye shall be hid. The sword has not a commission against you. Ask God, and He will be a Refuge to you from the storm and from the tempest.

4. *Gaza shall be forsaken.* This prophecy is against the Philistines. They had been greatly harassed by the kings of Egypt; but were completely ruined by Nebuchadnezzar, who took all Phoenicia from the Egyptians; and about the time of his taking Tyre, devastated all the seignories of the Philistines.

5. *The sea coast, the nation of the Cherethites.* The *sea coast* means all the country lying on the Mediterranean coast from Egypt to Joppa and Gaza. The *Cherethites*—the Cretans, who were probably a colony of the Phoenicians. See 1 Sam. xxx. 14 and Amos ix. 7.

6. *And the sea coast shall be dwellings.* Newcome considers *keroth* as a proper name, not *cottages* or *folds.* The Septuagint have "Crete," and so has the Syriac.

7. *The coast shall be for the remnant.* Several devastations fell on the Philistines. Gaza was ruined by the army of Alexander the Great, and the Maccabees finally accomplished all that was predicted by the prophets against this invariably wicked people. They lost their polity, and were at last obliged to receive circumcision.

8. *I have heard the reproach of Moab.* God punished them for the curel part they had taken in the persecutions of the Jews; for when they lay under the displeasure of God, these nations insulted them in the most provoking manner. See Amos i. 13.

11. *He will famish all the gods of the earth.* They shall have no more sacrifices; their worship shall be entirely destroyed.

MATTHEW HENRY

When the gospel gets ground, by it men shall be brought to worship him who lives for ever, *everyone from his place*; they shall not need to go up to Jerusalem to worship the God of Israel, but, wherever they are, they may have access to him.

Verses 12–15

The Ethiopians, or Arabians, that had sometimes been a terror to Israel (as in Asa's time, 2 Chron. xiv. 9), *shall be slain by my sword, v.* 12. Nebuchadnezzar was God's sword, the instrument with which these enemies were punished, Ps. xvii. 14. The Assyrians, and Nineveh the head city of their monarchy, are next to receive their doom: *He* that is God's sword *will stretch out his hand against the north and destroy Assyria.* Assyria had been the rod of God's anger against Israel, and now Babylon is the rod of God's anger against Assyria, Isa. x. 5. Nineveh was so strong that she feared no evil. She shall be made *a desolation, v.* 13.

The melancholy birds, as the *cormorant and bittern*, shall make their nests in what remains of the houses. The *lintels*, or *chapiters* of the pillars, the *windows* and *thresholds*, and all the fine *cedar-work*, shall lie exposed; and on them these rueful ominous birds shall perch, and their *voice shall sing.*

Everyone that passes by shall hiss at her, and *wag his hand*—"There is an end of proud Nineveh."

JAMIESON, FAUSSET, BROWN

—each *in his own* Gentile *home*, taught by the Jews in the true religion: not in Jerusalem alone shall men worship God, but everywhere (Ps. 68:29, 30; Mal. 1:11; John 4:21; I Cor. 1:2; I Tim. 2:8). It does not mean, as in Isaiah 2:2; Micah 4:1, 2; Zechariah 8:22; 14:16 that they shall come *from* their several *places* to Jerusalem to worship [MAURER]. **all . . . isles of . . . heathen**—i.e., all the maritime regions, especially the west, now being fulfilled in the gathering in of the Gentiles to Messiah. **12.** Fulfilled when Nebuchadnezzar (God's *sword*, Isa. 10:5) conquered Egypt, with which Ethiopia was closely connected as its ally (Jer. 46:2-9; Ezek. 30:5-9). **Ye**—lit., "They." The third person expresses estrangement; while doomed before God's tribunal in the second person, they are spoken of in the third as aliens from God. **13.** Here he passes suddenly to the north. Nineveh was destroyed by Cyaxares and Nabopolassar, 625 B.C. The Scythian hordes, by an inroad into Media and thence in the southwest of Asia (thought by many to be the forces described by Zephaniah, as the invaders of Judea, rather than the Chaldeans), for a while interrupted Cyaxares' operations; but he finally succeeded. Arbaces and Belesis previously subverted the Assyrian empire under Sardanapalus (i.e., Pul?), 877 B.C. **14. flocks**—of sheep; answering to "beasts" in the parallel clause. Wide pastures for sheep and haunts for wild beasts shall be where once there was a teeming population (cf. vs. 6). MAURER, needlessly for the parallelism, makes it "flocks *of savage animals*." **beasts of the nations**—i.e., beasts of the earth (Gen. 1:24). Not as ROSENMULLER, "all kinds of beasts that form a nation," i.e., gregarious beasts (Prov. 30:25, 26). **cormorant**—rather, the pelican (so Ps. 102:6; *Margin*, Isa. 34:11). **bittern**—(Isa. 14:23). MAURER translates, "the hedgehog"; HENDERSON, "the porcupine." **upper lintels**—rather, "*the capitals* of her columns," viz., in her temples and palaces [MAURER]. Or, "on the pomegranate-like knops at the tops of the houses" [GROTIUS]. **their voice shall sing in the windows**—The desert-frequenting birds' "voice in the windows" implies desolation reigning in the upper parts of the palaces, answering to "desolation . . . in the thresholds," i.e., in the lower. **he shall uncover the cedar work**—laying the cedar wainscoting on the walls, and beams of the ceiling, bare to wind and rain, the roof being torn off, and the windows and doors broken through. All this is designed as a consolation to the Jews that they may bear their calamities patiently, knowing that God will avenge them. **15.** Nothing then seemed more improbable than that the capital of so vast an empire, a city sixty miles in compass, with walls 100 feet high, and so thick that three chariots could go abreast on them, and with 1500 towers, should be so totally destroyed that its site is with difficulty discovered. Yet so it is, as the prophet foretold. **there is none beside me**—This peculiar phrase, expressing self-gratulation as if peerless, is plainly adopted from Isaiah 47:8. The later prophets, when the spirit of prophecy was on the verge of departing, leaned more on the predictions of their predecessors. **hiss**—in astonishment at a desolation so great and sudden (I Kings 9:8); also in derision (Job 27:23; Lam. 2:15; Ezek. 27:36).

ADAM CLARKE

12. *Ye Ethiopians also.* Nebuchadnezzar subdued these. See Jer. xlvi. 2, 9; Ezek. xxx. 4, 10. See also Amos ix. 17.

13. *He will . . . destroy Assyria.* He will overthrow the empire, and Nineveh, their metropolitan city. See on Jonah and Nahum.

TODAY'S DICTIONARY OF THE BIBLE:

Nineveh. First mentioned in Gen. 10:11, which is rendered in the Revised Version, "He [i.e., Nimrod] went into Assyria, and built Nineveh." It is not again mentioned till the days of Jonah, when it is described (Jonah 3:3; 4:11) as a great and populous city, the flourishing capital of the Assyrian empire (2 Kings 19:36; Isa. 37:37). The book of the prophet Nahum is almost exclusively taken up with prophetic denunciations against this city. Its ruin and utter desolation are foretold (Nah. 1:14; 3:19, etc.). Zephaniah also (2:13–15) predicts its destruction along with the fall of the empire of which it was the capital. From this time there is no mention of it in Scripture till it is named in gospel history (Matt. 12:41; Luke 11:32, Nineve).

This "exceeding great city" lay on the eastern or left bank of the river Tigris. The city proper is buried beneath two mounds, Quyunjiq (many sheep) and Nebi Yunus (prophet Jonah) opposite modern Mosul. The mounds are surrounded by the remains of a wall eight miles in circumference. It occupies a central position on the great highway between the Mediterranean and the Indian Ocean, thus uniting the East and the West. Wealth, therefore, flowed into it from many sources, so that it became one of the greatest of all ancient cities.

About 633 B.C. the Assyrian empire began to show signs of weakness, and Nineveh was attacked by the Medes (612 B.C.) and the Babylonians. When it fell, it was burned to the ground. The Assyrian empire came to an end (605 B.C.), and the Medes and Babylonians divided its provinces between them.

MATTHEW HENRY

CHAPTER 3

Verses 1–7

I. A very bad character given of Jerusalem in general. She shames herself; she is *filthy and polluted* (*v.* 1), has made herself *infamous* (so some read it), *the gluttonous* city (so the margin), always making provision for the flesh.

She wrongs her neighbours and inhabitants; she is *the oppressing city*. She is provoking to her God, *v.* 2. He had given his law, but *she obeyed not his voice*. Her confidence was placed in her alliances with the nations more than in her covenant with God.

JAMIESON, FAUSSET, BROWN

CHAPTER 3

VSS. 1-20. RESUMPTION OF THE DENUNCIATION OF JERUSALEM, AS BEING UNREFORMED BY THE PUNISHMENT OF OTHER NATIONS: AFTER HER CHASTISEMENT JEHOVAH WILL INTERPOSE FOR HER AGAINST HER FOES; HIS WORSHIP SHALL FLOURISH IN ALL LANDS, BEGINNING AT JERUSALEM, WHERE HE SHALL BE IN THE MIDST OF HIS PEOPLE, AND SHALL MAKE THEM A PRAISE IN ALL THE EARTH. **1. filthy**—MAURER translates from a different root, "rebellious," "contumacious." But the following term, "polluted," refers rather to her inward moral *filth*, in spite of her outward ceremonial purity [CALVIN]. GROTIUS says, the *Hebrew* is used of women who have prostituted their virtue. There is in the *Hebrew Moreah;* a play on the name *Moriah*, the hill on which the temple was built; implying the glaring contrast between their *filthiness* and the holiness of the worship on Moriah in which they professed to have a share. **oppressing**—viz., the poor, weak, widows, orphans and strangers (Jer. 22:3). **2. received not correction**—Jerusalem is incurable, obstinately rejecting salutary admonition, and refusing to be reformed by "correction" (Jer. 5:3). **trusted not in . . . Lord**—Distrust in the Lord as if He were insufficient, is the parent of all superstitions and wickednesses [CALVIN]. **drew not near**

ADAM CLARKE

CHAPTER 3

1. *Woe to her that is filthy!* This is a denunciation of divine judgment against Jerusalem.

2. *She obeyed not the voice.* Of conscience, of God, and of His prophets. *She received not correction.* Did not profit by His chastisements.

MATTHEW HENRY

She *drew not near to her God.* She stood at a distance, and *said to the Almighty, Depart.*

II. The leading men in it are the great patrons of wickedness, and those that should be her physicians are really her worst disease. *Her princes are* barbarous as *roaring lions,* and are universally hated. *Her judges are evening wolves,* rapacious, their cruelty and covetousness insatiable: *They gnaw not the bones till the morrow;* they take delight in oppression that when they have devoured a good man they reserve the bones, as it were, for a sweet morsel, Job xxxi. 31. *Her prophets,* who pretend to be special messengers from heaven to them, *are light and treacherous persons,* men of no consistency, in whom one can put no confidence. *Her priests* are false to their trust and betray it. They were to preserve the purity of the *sanctuary,* but they themselves *pollute* it. They *did violence to the law;* they corrupted the sense of it. By forced constructions, they made the law to speak what they pleased, and so, in effect, *made void the law.*

III. General corruption in Jerusalem. They had the tokens of God's presence yet they persisted in their disobedience, *v.* 5. "*The just Lord is in the midst of thee* as a holy God, and therefore thy pollutions are the more offensive," Deut. xxiii. 14. "A just God will punish the affronts you put upon him, and the wrongs you do to one another." He sent to them his prophets, rising up early and sending them: *Every morning he brings his judgment to light.* He wakens his prophets with the rising sun, to bring to light the things which belong to their peace.

God had set before their eyes monuments of his justice, designed for warning (*v.* 6): *I have cut off the nations,* the seven nations of Canaan, Lev. xviii. 28. Or it may refer to some of the neighbouring nations made desolate for their wickedness. *Their towers were desolate,* their *streets were wasted, their cities* were *destroyed* and laid in ruins; *no man* was to be found in them. The enemies did it, but God avows it: *I cut them off,* says he. And God designed this for an admonition to Jerusalem.

He had assured them of the continuance of their prosperity if they would fear him and receive instruction, for so *their dwelling would not be cut off* as their neighbour's was.

He had made them feel the smart of the rod, though he reprieved them from the sword.

They were more resolute and eager in their wicked courses than ever. God *rose up early,* to send them his *prophets,* but they were *up before him,* to shut and bolt the door against them.

Verses 8–13

Things looked bad. Jerusalem has got a very bad name, and seems to be incorrigible, incurable, mercy-proof and judgment-proof. But behold the riches of divine grace. They still grew worse and worse, *therefore wait you upon me, saith the Lord, v.* 8. "Since the *law,* it seems, will *make nothing perfect,* the *bringing in of a better hope shall.* Let those that lament the corruptions of the church *wait upon God,* till he send his Son into the world, to *save his people from their sins,* and to purify to himself a peculiar people both of Jews and Gentiles." And there were those who *waited for redemption* in Jerusalem; and long-looked-for, it came at last, Luke ii. 38.

I. By the gospel of Christ preached to every creature all nations are summoned, as it were, to appear in a body before the Lord Jesus, who is about to set up his kingdom in the world. But, since the greatest part of mankind will not obey the summons, he will *pour upon them his indignation,* for he that *believes not is condemned already.* Then *all the earth shall be devoured with the fire of his jealousy;* both Jews and Gentiles shall be reckoned with for their enmity to the gospel.

JAMIESON, FAUSSET, BROWN

to her God—Though God was specially near to her (Deut. 4:7) as "her God," yet she drew not near to Him, but gratuitously estranged herself from Him. **3. roaring**—for prey (Prov. 28:15; Ezek. 22:27; Amos 3:4; Mic. 2:2). **evening wolves**—which are most ravenous at evening after being foodless all day (Jer. 5:6; Hab. 1:8). **they gnaw not the bones till the morrow**—rather, "they put not off till tomorrow to gnaw the bones"; but devour all at once, bones and flesh, so ragingly ravenous are they [CALVIN]. **4. light**—in whose life and teaching there is no truth, gravity, or steadiness. **treacherous**—false to Jehovah, whose prophets they profess to be (Jer. 23:32; Ezek. 22:28). **polluted . . . sanctuary**—by their profane deeds. **5-7.** The Jews regard not God's justice manifested in the midst of them, nor His judgments on the guilty nations around. **5. The just Lord**—Why then are ye so unjust? **is in the midst thereof**—He retorts on them their own boast, "Is not the Lord among us" (Mic. 3:11)? True He is, but it is for another end from what ye think [CALVIN]; viz., to lead you *by the example of His righteousness* to be righteous. Leviticus 19:2, "Ye shall be holy: for I the Lord your God am holy" [MAURER]. But CALVIN, "That ye may feel His hand to be the nearer *for taking vengeance for your crimes:* 'He will not do iniquity' by suffering your sins to go unpunished" (Deut. 32:4). **every morning**—lit., "morning by morning." The time in the sultry East for dispensing justice. **bring . . . to light**—publicly and manifestly by the teaching of His prophets, which aggravates their guilt; also by samples of His judgments on the guilty. **he faileth not**—He is continually setting before you samples of His justice, sparing no pains. Cf. Isaiah 5:4; 50:4, "he wakeneth *morning by morning.*" **knoweth no shame**—The unjust Jews are not shamed by His justice into repentance. **6.** I had hoped that My people by My judgments on other nations would be led to amendment; but they are not, so blinded by sin are they. **towers**—lit., "angles" or "corners"; hence the *towers* built at the angles of their city walls. Under Josiah's long and peaceful reign the Jews were undisturbed, while the great incursion of Scythians into Western Asia took place. The judgment on the ten tribes in a former reign also is here alluded to. **7. I said, Surely . . .**—God speaks after the manner of men in condescension to man's infirmity; not as though God was ignorant of the future contingency, but in their sense, *Surely one might have expected* ye would under such circumstances repent: but no! **thou**—at least, O Jerusalem! Cf. "*thou, even thou,* at least in this thy day" (Luke 19:42). **their dwelling**—the *sanctuary* [BUXTORF]. Or, the *city.* Cf. Jesus' words (Luke 13:35), "Behold, *your house* is left unto you desolate" (Lev. 26:31, 32; Ps. 69:25); and used as to *the temple* (Mic. 3:12). "Their" is used instead of "thy"; this change of person implies that God puts them to a greater distance. **howsoever I punished them**—Howsoever I might have punished them, I would not have *cut off their dwelling.* CALVIN, "Howsoever I had marked them out for punishment" because of their provocations, still, if even then they had repented, taught by My corrections, I was ready to have pardoned them. MAURER, "Altogether in accordance with what I had long ago decreed (ordained) concerning you" (Deut. 28:1-14, and, on the other hand, 15-68; 27:15-26). *English Version,* or CALVIN's view, is better. **rose early, and corrupted . . .**—Early morning is in the East the best time for transacting serious business, before the relaxing heat of midday comes on. Thus it means, With the greatest earnestness they set themselves to "corrupt *all* their doings" (Gen. 6:12; Isa. 5:11; Jer. 11:7; 25:3). **8. wait ye upon me**—Here Jehovah turns to the pious Jews. Amidst all these judgments on the Jewish nation, look forward to the glorious time of restoration to be ushered in by God's precious outpouring of wrath on all nations, Isaiah 30:18-33; where the same phrase, "blessed are all they that *wait for* Him," is used as to the same great event. CALVIN erroneously makes this verse an address to the ungodly; and so MAURER, "Ye shall not have to wait for Me in vain"; I will presently come armed with indignation: I will no longer contend with you by My prophets. **until the day**—i.e., waiting for the day (Hab. 2:3). **rise up to the prey**—like a savage beast rising from his lair, greedy for the prey (cf. Matt. 24:28). Or rather, as a warrior leading Israel to *certain victory,* which is expressed by "the prey," or *booty,* which is the reward of victory. LXX and *Syriac* versions read the *Hebrew,* "I rise up as a *witness*" (cf. Job 16:8; Mal. 3:5). Jehovah being in this view *witness,* accuser, and judge. *English Version* is better (cf. Isa. 33:23). **gather the nations**—against Jerusalem (Zech. 14:2), to pour

ADAM CLARKE

3. *Her princes . . . are roaring lions.* Tearing all to pieces without shadow of law, except their own despotic power. *Her judges are evening wolves.* Being a little afraid of the lion-like princes, they practice their unjust dealings from evening to morning, and take the day to find their rest. *They gnaw not the bones till the morrow.* They devour the flesh in the night, and gnaw the bones and extract the marrow afterwards.

4. *Her prophets are light and treacherous persons.* They betray the souls of the people for the sake of worldly honor, pleasure, and profit.

5. *The just Lord is in the midst thereof.* He sees, marks down, and will punish all these wickednesses.

Every morning doth he bring his judgment to light. The sense is, says Bishop Newcome, "Not a day passes but we see instances of his goodness to righteous men, and of his vengeance on the wicked."

6. *I have cut off the nations.* Syria, Israel, and those referred to, Isa. xxxvi. 18, 20.

7. *Surely thou wilt fear me.* After so many displays of My sovereign power and judgments.

But they rose early. And instead of returning to God, they practiced every abomination. They were diligent to find out times and places for their iniquity. This is the worst state of man.

8. *Wait ye upon me.* Expect the fulfillment of all My promises and threatenings; I am God, and change not. *For all the earth.* All the land of Judah.

MATTHEW HENRY

II. When God intends the restoration of Israel he makes way for their reformation and the revival of their virtue and piety; for this is God's method, first to make them holy and then to make them happy. These promises were in part accomplished after the return of the Jews out of Babylon. It is promised that there shall be a reformation in men's discourse, which had been generally corrupt, but should now be with grace seasoned with salt (*v.* 9): "*Then will I turn to the people a pure language.*" Converting grace refines the language, not by making the phrases witty, but the substance wise. The Jews, after the captivity, had mingled the language of Canaan with that of Ashdod (Neh. xiii. 24). But that is not all: their language shall be purified from all profaneness, filthiness, and falsehood. I will turn them to a *choice language* (so some read it). Instead of sacrifice and incense, they shall *call upon the name of the Lord.* Prayer is the spiritual offering with which God must be honoured.

They shall serve God *with one consent,* with *one shoulder* (so the word is), alluding to oxen in the yoke, that draw even. When Christians are unanimous in the service of God the work goes on cheerfully. Purity is the way to unity; the reformation of manners is the way to a comprehension. Those that were driven from God shall return to him and be accepted of him (*v.* 10). *From beyond the rivers of Ethiopia,* or from some other remote country, they shall be put in mind of him, as the prodigal son was of his father's house, in the far country. The *daughter of his dispersed,* that is *afar off,* will be found among those whom *the Lord our God shall call.* Wherever they are, though *beyond the rivers of Ethiopia,* a great way from his house of prayer, they still are his suppliants.

They shall bring my offering, shall bring themselves as spiritual sacrifices to God (Rom. xii. 1).

In that day shalt thou not be ashamed for all thy doings. They shall be ashamed as penitents (see Ezek. xvi. 63), but they shall not be ashamed as sinners that return to folly again. "*I will take away out of the midst of thee,* not only the profane, but the hypocrites, who appear beautiful outwardly, and *rejoice in thy pride,* in the holy city, the holy house." These were *haughty because of the holy mountain,* were conceited, scornful and set even the judgments of God at defiance. That haughtiness is the most offensive to God which is fed by the pretensions of holiness. God will have a remnant of holy, humble, serious people (*v.* 12): *I will leave in the midst of thee an afflicted and poor people.* This select remnant shall be blessed with purity and peace, *v.* 13, both in words and actions: They *shall neither do iniquity nor speak lies.*

Verses 14–20

After the promises of the taking away of sin, here follow promises of the taking away of trouble; for when the cause is removed the effect will cease. Rejoice and sing (*v.* 14): *Sing, O daughter of Zion!* sing for joy; *shout, O Israel!* Those that love God with all their heart have occasion with all their heart to rejoice in him. *In that day it shall be said to Jerusalem* (God will say it by his prophets, by his providences, their neighbours shall say it, they shall say it to one another), "*Fear thou not.* Lift up thy hands in prayer to God; lift up thy hands to help thyself."

JAMIESON, FAUSSET, BROWN

out His indignation upon them there (Joel 3:2; Zech. 12:2, 3). **9. For**—The blessed things promised in this and vs. 10 are the immediate results of the punishment inflicted on the nations, mentioned in vs. 8 (cf. vs. 19). **turn to the people a pure language**—i.e., *changing* their impure language I will *give* to them again *a pure language* (lit., "lip"). Cf. for this *Hebrew* idiom, *Margin,* I Samuel 10:9. The confusion of languages was of the penalty sin, probably idolatry at Babel (*Margin,* Gen. 11:1-6, where also "lip" expresses *language,* and perhaps also *religion*; vs. 4, "a tower whose top *may reach* unto heaven," or rather, *points to heaven,* viz., dedicated to *the heavens* idolized, or Bel); certainly, of rebellion against God's will. An earnest of the removal of this penalty was the gift of tongues on pentecost (Acts 2). The full restoration of the earth's unity of language and of worship is yet future, and is connected with the restoration of the Jews, to be followed by the conversion of the world. Cf. Isaiah 19:18; Zechariah 14:9; Romans 15:6, "with one mind and *one mouth* glorify God." The Gentiles' *lips* have been rendered impure through being the instruments of calling on idols and dishonoring God (cf. Ps. 16:4; Hos. 2:17). Whether Hebrew shall be the one universal language or not, the God of the Hebrews shall be the one only object of worship. Until the Holy Ghost purify the *lips,* we cannot rightly call upon God (Isa. 6:5-7). **serve him with one consent**—lit., "shoulder" or "back"; metaphor from a yoke, or burden, borne between two (Num. 13:23); helping one another with conjoint effort. If one of the two bearers of a burden, laid on both conjointly, give way, the burden must fall to the earth [CALVIN]. Christ's rule is called a *burden* (Matt. 11:30; Acts 15:28; Rev. 2:24; cf. II Cor. 6:14 for the same image). **10. From beyond . . . Ethiopia my suppliants**—lit., "burners of incense" (cf. Ps. 141:2; Rev. 5:8, and 8: 3, 4). The Israelites are meant, called "the daughter of My dispersed," a *Hebrew* idiom for *My dispersed people.* "The rivers of Ethiopia" are those which enclose it on the north. In the west of Abyssinia there has long existed a people called *Falashas,* or "emigrants" (akin to the synonym "Philistine"). These trace their origin to Palestine and profess the Jewish religion. In physical traits they resemble the Arabs. When Bruce was there, they had a Jewish king, Gideon, and his queen, Judith. Probably the Abyssinian Christians were originally in part converted Jews. They are here made the representatives of all Israel which is to be restored. **shall bring mine offering**—i.e., the *offering* that is *My right.* I prefer, with DE WETTE and *Chaldee Version,* making "suppliants" the objective case, not the nominative. The *peoples* (vss. 8, 9), brought to fear Me by My judgments, "shall bring as Mine offering My suppliants (an appropriate term for the Jews, on whom then there shall have been poured the spirit of *supplications,* Zech. 12:10), the daughter of My dispersed." So Isaiah 66:20, "they shall bring all your brethren for an *offering* unto the Lord." Cf. HORSLEY's view of Isaiah 18:1, 2, 7. England in this view may be the naval power to restore Israel to Palestine (Isa. 60:9). The *Hebrew* for Ethiopia is *Cush,* which may include not only Ethiopia, but also the region of the Tigris and Babylon, where Nimrod, Cush's son (Gen. 10:8-12), founded Nineveh and acquired Babylon, and where the ten tribes are mentioned as being scattered (I Peter 1:1; 5:13; cf. Isa. 11:11). The restoration under Cyrus of the Jews transported under Pharaohnecho to Egypt and Ethiopia, was an earnest of the future restoration under Christ. **11. shalt thou not be ashamed**—Thou shalt then have no cause to be ashamed; for I will then *take away out of the midst of thee* those who by their sins gave thee cause for shame (vs. 7). **them that rejoice in thy pride**—those priding themselves *on that which thou boastest of,* thy temple ("My holy mountain"), thy election as God's people, etc., in the Pharisaic spirit (Jer. 7:4; Mic. 3:11; Matt. 3:9). Cf. Jeremiah 13:17, "mine eyes shall weep for *your pride.*" The converted remnant shall be of a humble spirit (vs. 12; Isa. 66: 2, 10). **12. afflicted . . . they shall trust in . . . Lord**—the blessed effect of sanctified affliction on the Jewish remnant. Entire trust in the Lord cannot be, except where all cause for boasting is taken away (Isa. 14:32; Zech. 11:11). **13. nor speak lies**—worshipping God in truth, and towards man having love without dissimulation. The characteristic of the 144,000 *sealed of Israel.* **none shall make them afraid**—either foreign foe, or unjust prince (vs. 3), prophet, or priest (vs. 4). **14.** The prophet in mental vision sees the joyful day of Zion present, and bids her rejoice at it. **15.** The cause for joy: "The Lord hath taken away thy judgments," viz., those

ADAM CLARKE

9. *Will I turn to the people.* This promise must refer to the conversion of the Jews under the gospel. The *pure language* may here mean the form of religious worship. They had been before idolaters; now God promises to restore His pure worship among them.

10. *From beyond the rivers of Ethiopia.* This may denote both Africa and southern Arabia.

14. *Sing, O daughter of Zion.* Here is not only a gracious prophetic promise of their restoration from captivity, but of their conversion to God through Christ.

MATTHEW HENRY

I. An end shall be put to all their troubles and distresses (*v.* 15): "*The Lord has taken away thy judgments*, has removed all the calamities which were the punishments of thy sin; the noise of war shall be silenced, the reproach of famine done away, and the captivity brought back. *He has cast out thy enemy*, that has thrust himself into thy land. He has *swept out thy enemy*" (so some read it). The way to get clear of the evil of trouble is to keep clear from the evil of sin; and to those that do so trouble has no real evil in it.

II. God will give them the tokens of his presence with them. "*The Lord is in the midst of thee, O Zion!* of thee, *O Jerusalem!* as the sun in the centre of the universe, to diffuse his light and influence upon every part. He (*v.* 15) is in the midst of thee as a king in the midst of his people. He is the Lord thy God, thine in covenant, in the midst of thee as thy God, whose thou art. *He will save. He will be Jesus*, will answer the name, for he will save his people from their sins."

III. God will take delight in doing them good. *He will rejoice over thee with joy.* The conversion of sinners and the consolation of saints are the joy of angels, for they are the joy of God himself. He will *rest in his love*, will be *silent in his love*, so the word is.

IV. God will comfort Zion's mourners and will wipe away their tears (*v.* 18): *I will gather those who are sorrowful for the solemn assemblies, to whom the reproach of it was a burden.* Zion is in mourning. Many are her calamities. The city is ruined, and the palaces are demolished; trade is at an end, but all these are nothing to them in comparison with the destruction of the temple and the altar, to attend on which, in solemn feasts, all Israel used to come together three times a year. It is for those sacred solemn assemblies that they are sorrowful. The restraining of public assemblies for religious worship, the scattering of them by their enemies, or the forsaking of them by their friends, is a sorrowful thing to all good people. The reproach of the solemn assemblies is a burden to them.

V. God will recover the captives and bring home the banished that seemed to be expelled, *v.* 19, 20. "*At that time I will undo all that afflict thee*, will break their power, and blast their counsels, so that they shall be forced to surrender the prey they have taken." One act of mercy and grace shall serve both to collect them out of their dispersions and to conduct them to their own land. When the *people's hearts are prepared*, the work will be done suddenly.

VI. God will by all this gain them respect from all about them. When God returns, in mercy, to his church, it is here promised that she shall regain her credit. "*I will get them praise and fame in every land, where they have been put to shame.*" Those that said, "This is Zion whom no man looks after," shall say, "This is Zion whom the great God looks after." So the Jewish church was when *the fear of the Jews* fell upon their neighbours (Esther viii. 17). So the Christian church was when it was made to flourish in the world, for there is that in it which may justly recommend it to the esteem of all people.

JAMIESON, FAUSSET, BROWN

sent by Him upon thee. After the taking away of sin (vs. 13) follows the taking away of trouble. When the cause is removed, the effect will cease. Happiness follows in the wake of holiness.

the Lord is in the midst of thee—Though He seemed to desert thee for a time, He is now present as thy safeguard (vs. 17). **not see evil any more**—Thou shalt not *experience* it (Jer. 5:12; 44:17). **16. Let not thine hands be slack**—(Heb. 12:12). Do not faint in the work of the Lord. **17. he will rest in his love**—content with it as His supreme delight (cf. Luke 15:7, 10) [CALVIN], (Isa. 62:5; 55:19). Or, *He shall be silent*, viz. as to thy faults, not imputing them to thee [MAURER] (Ps. 32:2; Ezek. 33:16). I prefer explaining it of that calm *silent* joy in the possession of the object of one's love, too great for words to express: just as God after the six days of creation *rested* with silent satisfaction in His work, for "behold it was very good" (Gen. 1:31; 2:2). So the parallel clause by contrast expresses the joy, not kept silent as this, but uttered in "singing." **18. sorrowful for the solemn assembly**—pining after the solemn assembly which they cannot celebrate in exile (Lam. 1:4; 2:6). **who are of thee**—i.e., of thy true citizens; and whom therefore I will restore. **to whom the reproach of it was a burden**—i.e., to whom *thy* reproach ("the reproach of My people," Mic. 6:16; their ignominious captivity) was a burden. "Of it" is put *of thee*, as the person is often changed. Those who shared in the burden of reproach which fell on My people. Cf. Isaiah 25:8, "the rebuke of His people shall He take away from off all the earth." **19. undo**—MAURER translates, "I will deal with," i.e., as they deserve. Cf. Ezek. 23:25, where the *Hebrew* is similarly translated. The destruction of Israel's foes precedes Israel's restoration (Isa. 66:15, 16). **her that halteth**—all that are helpless. Their weakness will be no barrier in the way of My restoring them. So in Psalm 35:15 (*Margin*), "halting" is used for *adversity*. Also Ezekiel 34:16; Micah 4:6, 7. **I will get them praise . . .**—lit., "I will make them (to become) a praise and a name. . . ." **shame**—(Ezek. 34:29). **20. make you a name . . . praise**—make you to become celebrated and praised. **turn back your captivity**—bring back your captives [MAURER]. The *Hebrew* is *plural*, "captivities"; to express the captivities of different ages of their history, as well as the diversity of places in which they were and are dispersed. **before your eyes**—Incredible as the event may seem, *your own eyes* with delight shall see it. You will scarcely believe it for joy, but the testimony of your own eyes shall convince you of the delightful reality (cf. Luke 24:41).

ADAM CLARKE

15. *The king of Israel, even the Lord, is in the midst of thee.* They have never had a king since the death of Zedekiah, and never shall have one till they have the King Messiah to reign among them; and this promise refers to that event.

16. *Fear thou not.* You shall have no more captivities nor national afflictions. *Let not thine hands be slack.* This may refer, first, to the rebuilding of the Temple of God, after the return from Babylon; and, secondly, to their diligence and zeal in the Christian Church.

17. *The Lord thy God. Yehovah Eloheycha*, "The self-existent and eternal Being, who is in covenant with you"; the character of God in reference to the Jews when standing in the nearest relation to them. *Is mighty. Gibbor*, is the "prevailing One," the "all-conquering Hero." The character which is given to Christ, Isa. ix. 6: "His name shall be called *El gibbor*, the prevailing Almighty God." *He will save.* "Deliver" you from all the power, from all the guilt, and from all the pollution of your sins; and when thus saved, *he will rejoice over thee with joy*, with peculiar gladness. *He will rest in his love*—He will renew His love. He will show the same love to you that He did of old to Abraham, Isaac, and Jacob.

18. *I will gather . . . sorrowful.* This may refer to those who, during the Captivity, mourned for their former religious assemblies; and who were reproached by their enemies because they could not enjoy their religious solemnities. See Psalm cxxxvii: "By the rivers of Babylon, there we sat down, yea, we wept, when we remembered Zion. . . . For there they that carried us away captive required of us a song," etc. This very circumstance may be the reference here.

19. *I will undo all that afflict thee.* They who have persecuted you shall be punished for it. It shows much malignity and baseness of mind to afflict or reproach those who are lying under the chastising hand of God. This was the conduct of the Edomites, Moabites, and Ammonites when the Jews were in adversity; and how severely did the Lord punish them for it! *I will save her that halteth.* See Mic. iv. 6, where there is a parallel place.

20. *At that time.* First, when the seventy years of the Babylonish captivity shall terminate. I will *bring you again* to your own land; and this restoration shall be a type of their redemption from sin and iniquity; and, at this time, and at this only, will they have *a name and a praise among all people of the earth*, not only among the Jews, but the Gentiles.

THE BOOK OF HAGGAI

I. First prophecy (1:1-11)
- *A. Introduction (1:1)*
- *B. The reason—neglect of the Lord's House and time not yet come (1:2)*
- *C. The message (1:3-11)*
  1. Their own houses (1:3, 4)
  2. Consider your ways (1:5-7)
  3. The reason of failure (1:8-11)
- *D. Historic interlude (1:12-15)*
  1. Obedience (1:12)
  2. Encouragement (1:13)
  3. Enthusiasm (1:14, 15)

II. Second prophecy (2:1-9)
- *A. Introduction (2:1, 2)*
- *B. The reason—the old men of disappointment (2:3)*
- *C. The message (2:4-9)*
  1. The call (2:4a)
  2. The immediate promise (2:4b, 5)
  3. The larger promise (2:6-9)

III. Third prophecy (2:10-19)
- *A. Introduction (2:10)*
- *B. The message (2:11-19)*
  1. Appeal to priests and principles deduced (2:11-13)
  2. Application of principles (2:14-18)
- *C. The reason—the delay of blessing, disappointment (2:19a)*
- *D. The promise (2:19b)*

IV. Fourth prophecy (2:20-23)
- *A. Introduction (2:20, 21a)*
- *B. The message (2:21b-23)*
  1. The shaking of false authority (2:21b, 22)
  2. The establishment of true authority (2:23)

The captivity in Babylon gave a very remarkable turn to the affairs of the Jewish church both in history and prophecy. Nine of the twelve minor prophets lived and preached before that captivity. But the last three lived and preached after the return out of captivity. Haggai and Zechariah appeared eighteen years after the return, when the building of the temple was both retarded by its enemies and neglected by its friends. "Then the prophets, Haggai the prophet and Zechariah the son of Iddo, prophesied unto the Jews that were in Jerusalem, in the name of the God of Israel, even unto them" (Ezra 5:1), to encourage them to revive that good work when it had stood still for some time. Haggai began two months before Zechariah. But Zechariah continued longer at the work; for all Haggai's prophecies that are recorded were delivered within four months, in the second year of Darius. But we have Zechariah's prophecies dated above two years after (Zech. 7:1). The Jews ascribe to these two prophets the honor of being members of the great synagogue, which was formed after the return out of captivity; we think it more certain and a much greater honor, that they prophesied of Christ. Haggai spoke of him as the "glory of the latter house," and Zechariah as "the man, the branch." In them the light of that morning star shone more brightly as they now began to see his day approaching. The LXX make Haggai and Zechariah to be the penmen of Psalm 138 and of Psalms 147—148.

MATTHEW HENRY

CHAPTER 1

Verses 1–11

It was the complaint of the Jews in Babylon that they *saw not their signs*, and there was *no more any prophet* (Ps. lxxiv. 9), which was a judgment for mocking the prophets. We read of no prophets they had in their return. But the lamp of Old Testament prophecy shall yet make some glorious efforts before it expire; and Haggai is the first that appears under the character of a special messenger from heaven. In the reign of Darius Hystaspes, the third of the Persian kings, in the second year of his reign, this prophet was sent; and the word of the Lord came to him, and by him to the leading men among the Jews, *v.* 1.

The chief governor was *Zerubbabel, the son of Shealtiel*, of the house of David, who was commander-in-chief of the Jews, in their return out of captivity.

JAMIESON, FAUSSET, BROWN

CHAPTER 1

Vss. 1-15. HAGGAI CALLS THE PEOPLE TO CONSIDER THEIR WAYS IN NEGLECTING TO BUILD GOD'S HOUSE: THE EVIL OF THIS NEGLECT TO THEMSELVES: THE HONOR TO GOD OF ATTENDING TO IT: THE PEOPLE'S PENITENT OBEDIENCE UNDER ZERUBBABEL FOLLOWED BY GOD'S GRACIOUS ASSURANCE. **1. second year of Darius**—Hystaspes, the king of Medo-Persia, the second of the world-empires, Babylon having been overthrown by the Persian Cyrus. The Jews having no king of their own, dated by the reign of the world-kings to whom they were subject. Darius was a common name of the Persian kings, as Pharaoh of those of Egypt, and Cæsar of those of Rome. The name in the cuneiform inscriptions at Persepolis is written *Daryawus*, from the root *Darh*, "to preserve," the *Conservator* [LASSEN]. HERODOTUS, 6.98, explains it *Coercer*. Often opposite attributes are assigned to the same god; in which light the Persians viewed their king. Erza 4:24 harmonizes with Haggai in making this year the date of the resumption of the building. **sixth month**—of the Hebrew year, not of Darius' reign (cf. Zech. 1:7; 7:1, 3; 8:19). Two months later (the eighth month," Zech. 1:1) Zechariah began to prophesy, seconding Haggai. **the Lord**—*Hebrew*, JEHOVAH: God's covenant title, implying His unchangeableness, the guarantee of His faithfulness in keeping His promises to His people. **by Haggai**—*Hebrew*, "in the hand of Haggai"; God being the real speaker, His prophet but the instrument (cf. Acts 7:35; Gal. 3:19). **Zerubbabel**—called also Shesh-bazzar in Ezra 1:8; 5:14, 16, where the same work is attributed to Shesh-bazzar that in ch. 3:8 is attributed to Zerubbabel. Shesh-bazzar is probably his Chaldean name; as Belteshazzar was that of Daniel. Zerubbabel, his *Hebrew* name, means "one born in Babylon." **son of Shealtiel**—or Salathiel. But I Chronicles 3:17, 19 makes Pedaiah his father. Probably he was adopted by his *uncle* Salathiel, or

ADAM CLARKE

CHAPTER 1

1. *In the sixth month.* Called *Elul* by the Hebrews. It was the sixth month of the ecclesiastical year, and the last of the civil year, and answered to a part of our September.

Zerubbabel the son of Shealtiel. Who was son of Jeconiah, king of Judah, and of the family of David, and exercised the post of a governor among the people, but not over them, for both he and they were under the Persian government. But they were permitted to have Zerubbabel for their own governor, and Joshua for their high priest; and these regulated all matters relative to their peculiar political and ecclesiastical government.

MATTHEW HENRY

In the church was *Joshua the son of Josedech*, who was now *high priest*. They were great men and good men. The prophets, who were extraordinary messengers, did not set aside the institutions of magistracy and ministry, but endeavoured to render both more effectual.

I. The sin of the Jews at this time, *v.* 2. As soon as they came up out of captivity they set up an altar for sacrifice, and within a year after laid the foundations of a temple, Ezra iii. 10. They then seemed very forward in it, but, being served with a prohibition from the Persian court, and charged not to go on with it, they not only yielded to the force, when they were actually under it, but afterwards, when the violence of the opposition had abated, they had no spirit to set about it again, but let it stand still. These Jews continued loitering until they were reminded of their duty. They suggested one to another, "*The time has not come, the time that the Lord's house should be built*. Our losses are not repaired. It is too great an undertaking for beginners as we are; let us first get our own houses up, before we talk of building churches, and in the mean time let a bare altar serve us, as it did our father Abraham." They did not say that they would not build a temple at all, but, "Not yet; it is all in good time."

III. The reproof which the prophet gives them for their neglect of the temple-work (*v.* 4): "*Is it time for you, O you! to dwell in your ceiled houses*, to have them beautified and adorned, and your families settled in them?" They were not content with walls and roofs for necessity. "It is high time," says one, "that my house were wainscoted." "It is high time," says another, "that mine were painted." And God's house, all this time, *lies waste*, and nothing is done at it.

IV. The good counsel which the prophet gives to those who thus despised God. *Now therefore consider your ways*, *v.* 5 and again *v.* 7.

II. The judgments of God by which they were punished for this neglect, *v.* 6, 9–11. That the punishment might answer to the sin, God by his providence kept them still behind-hand, and that poverty which they thought to prevent by not building the temple God brought upon them for not building it. We need the help of God's prophets and ministers to expound, not only the judgments of God's mouth, but the judgments of his hands, that we may understand his mind and meaning in his rod as well as in his word.

1. God did not send them into captivity again, nor bring a foreign enemy upon them, as they deserved, but denied his blessing upon the *seed sown*, and then it never prospered. *They sowed much* (*v.* 6), kept a great deal of ground in tillage, because their land had long *lain fallow* and had *enjoyed its sabbaths*. Having sown much, they looked for much from it, but they were disappointed: *They bring in little*, very little (*v.* 6); when they have made the utmost of it, *it comes to little* (*v.* 9). When they had it upon the board it was not that to them that they expected: "*You eat, but you have not enough. You clothe yourselves, but there is none warm. He that earns wages* by hard labour, and has it paid him in ready current money, *puts it into a bag with holes*; it drops through, and wastes away insensibly. Everything is so scarce and dear that they spend their money as fast as they get it." Think what you have done that has provoked God and think what you will do to testify your repentance. He would have them reform (*v.* 8): "*Go up to the mountain*, to Lebanon, *and bring wood*, and other materials, *and*

JAMIESON, FAUSSET, BROWN

Shealtiel, at the death of his father (cf. Matt. 1:12; Luke 3:27). **governor of Judah**—to which office Cyrus had appointed him. The *Hebrew Pechah* is akin to the original of the modern Turkish *Pasha*; one ruling a region of the Persian empire of less extent than that under a satrap. **Joshua**—called Jeshua (Ezra 2:2); so the son of Nun in Nehemiah 8:17. **Josedech**—or Jehozadak (I Chron. 6:15), one of those carried captive by Nebuchadnezzar. Haggai addresses the civil and the religious representatives of the people, so as to have them as his associates in giving God's commands; thus priest, prophet, and ruler jointly testify in God's name. **2. the Lord of hosts**—Jehovah, Lord of the powers of heaven and earth, and therefore requiring implicit obedience. **This people**—"This" sluggish and selfish "people." He does not say, *My* people, since they had neglected the service of God. **The time**—the proper time for building the temple. Two out of the seventy predicted years of captivity (dating from the destruction of the temple, 558 B.C., (II Kings 25:9) were yet unexpired; this they make their plea for delay [HENDERSON]. The seventy years of captivity were completed long ago in the first year of Cyrus, 536 B.C. (Jer. 29:10); dating from 606 B.C., Jehoiakim's captivity (II Chron. 36:6). The seventy years to the completion of the temple (Jer. 25:12) were completed this very year, the second of Darius [VATABLUS]. Ingenious in excuses, they pretended that the interruption in the work caused by their enemies proved it was *not yet the proper time;* whereas their real motive was selfish dislike of the trouble, expense, and danger from enemies. "God," say they, "hath interposed many difficulties to punish our rash haste" [CALVIN]. Smerdis' interdict was no longer in force, now that Darius the rightful king was on the throne; therefore they had no real excuse for not beginning at once to build. AUBERLEN denies that by "Artaxerxes" in Ezra 4:7-22 is meant Smerdis. Whether Smerdis or Artaxerxes Longimanus be meant, the interdict referred only to the rebuilding of the *city,* which the Persian kings feared might, if rebuilt, cause them trouble to subdue; not to the rebuilding of the *temple.* But the Jews were easily turned aside from the work. Spiritually, like the Jews, men do not say they will never be religious, but, It is not time yet. So the great work of life is left undone. **4. Is it time**—It is not time (vs. 2), ye say, to build Jehovah's house; yet how is it that ye make it a fit time not only to *build,* but to "dwell" at ease in your own houses? **you, O ye**—rather, for "you, you"; the repetition marking the shameful contrast between their concern for *themselves,* and their unconcern for God [MAURER]. Cf. a similar repetition in I Samuel 25:24; Zechariah 7:5. **ceiled**—rather, "wainscoted," or "paneled," referring to the walls as well as the ceilings; furnished not only with comfort but luxury, in sad contrast to God's house not merely unadorned, but the very walls not raised above the foundations. How different David's feelings (II Sam. 7:2)! **5. Consider your ways**—lit., "Set your heart" on your ways. The *plural* implies, Consider both what ye have done (actively, Lam. 3:40) and what ye have suffered (passively) [JEROME]. Ponder earnestly whether ye have gained by seeking self at the sacrifice of God. **6.** Nothing has prospered with you while you neglected your duty to God. The punishment corresponds to the sin. They thought to escape poverty by not building, but keeping their money to themselves; God brought it on them *for* not building (Prov. 13:7; 11:24; Matt. 6:33). Instead of cheating God, they had been only cheating themselves. **ye clothe . . . but . . . none warm**—through insufficiency of clothing; as ye are unable through poverty from failure of your crops to purchase sufficient clothing. The verbs are infinitive, implying a *continued state:* "Ye have sown, and *been bringing in* but little; ye have *been eating,* but not to *being satisfied;* ye have *been drinking,* but not to *being filled;* ye have been *putting* on clothes, but not to *being warmed"* [MOORE]. Careful consideration of God's dealings with us will indicate God's will regarding us. The events of life are the hieroglyphics in which God records His feelings towards us, the key to which is found in the Bible [MOORE]. **wages . . . put . . . into a bag with holes**—proverbial for labor and money spent profitlessly (Zech. 8:10; cf. Isa. 55:2; Jer. 2:13). Contrast, spiritually, the "bags that wax not old, the treasure in heaven that faileth not" (Luke 12:33). Through the high cost of necessaries, those who wrought for a day's wages parted with them at once, as if they had put them into a bag with holes. **8. Go up to the mountain**—Moriah [ROSENMULLER]; Lebanon [HENDERSON]. Rather, generally, *the mountains* around, now covered with wood, the growth of the

ADAM CLARKE

Joshua the son of Josedech. And son of Seraiah, who was high priest in the time of Zedekiah, and was carried into captivity by Nebuchadnezzar, 1 Chron. vi. 15. But Seraiah was slain at Riblah, by order of Nebuchadnezzar, 2 Kings xxv. 18-21.

2. *The time is not come.* They thought that the seventy years spoken of by Jeremiah were not yet completed, and it would be useless to attempt to rebuild until that period had arrived.

4. *Is it time for you?* If the time be not come to rebuild the Temple, it cannot be come for you to build yourselves comfortable houses. The foundation of the Temple had been laid fourteen years before, and some considerable progress made in the building, and it had been lying waste in that unfinished state to the present time.

5. *Consider your ways.* Is it fit that you should be building yourselves elegant houses, and neglect a place for the worship of that God who has restored you from captivity?

6. *Ye have sown much.* God will not bless you in any labor of your hands unless you rebuild His temple and restore His worship. This verse contains a series of proverbs, no less than five in the compass of a few lines.

MATTHEW HENRY

build the house with all speed." He assures them: *Build the house, and I will take pleasure in it;* and that was encouragement enough for them to go through with it, whatever it cost them. Those who have long deferred their return to God, if at length they return with all their heart, must not despair of his favour.

2. God thus stopped the current of the favours promised them at their return (Joel ii. 24); they provoked him to do it: *It is because of my house that is waste.* The foundation of the temple is laid, but the building does not go on. "Every man *runs to his own house,* to finish that, and no care is taken about the Lord's house." If God cross us in our temporal affairs, and we meet with trouble and disappointment, we shall find this is the cause of it, the work we have to do for God is left undone, and we *seek our own things more than the things of Jesus Christ,* Phil. ii. 21.

We are here told how they came to be disappointed (*v.* 10): *The heaven over you is stayed from dew;* he that has the key of the clouds in his hands shut them up, and withheld the rain, and then of course *the earth is stayed from her fruit*; for, if the heaven be as brass, the earth is as iron. God will make us sensible of our necessary and constant dependence upon him, throughout all the links in the chain of second causes, so that we can at no time say, "Now we have no further occasion for God and his providence." See Hos. ii. 21. *I called for a drought upon the land,* ordered the weather to be extremely hot, and then the fruits of the earth were burnt up. The heat of the sun puts life into the plants and *renews the face of the earth at* spring. And yet, if that go into an extreme, it undoes all again. This drought was *upon the mountains,* which, lying high, were first affected with it. The mountains were their pasture-grounds, and used to be *covered over with flocks,* but now there was no grass for them. It was *upon the corn, the new wine, and the oil*; all failed through the extremity of the hot weather. It inflamed men and put them into fevers. It brought diseases upon cattle too. The bread they ate did not nourish them. When they had the corn in the barn they were not sure of it: *I did blow upon it, saith the Lord of hosts* (*v.* 9), and it withered.

Verses 12–15

The foregoing sermon met with the desired success among the people, and their obedience met with due encouragement from God.

I. All those to whom that sermon was preached were wrought upon by it. Zerubbabel, the chief governor, was a man that had been eminently useful in his day, and did not plead his former merits in answer to this reproof for his present remissness. Joshua also, as high priest, willingly received admonition and instruction. *The remnant of the people* all *obeyed the voice of the Lord their God,* and bowed to the yoke of his commands, *v.* 12. They looked upon the prophet to be the Lord's messenger, and the word he delivered to be the Lord's message; and therefore received it *not as the word of man, but as the word of* Almighty God, *v.* 12. Prophecy was a new thing with them; they had had no special messenger from heaven for a great while, and now that they had one, they paid extraordinary regard to him. It is sometimes so; when good preaching is most scarce it does most good, whereas the manna that is rained in plenty is loathed as *light bread.* And, because they so readily received this prophet, God, within a month or two after, raised them up another, Zech. i. 1. When they saw their own sin to be the cause of those judgments, then they feared. *The Lord stirred up* their spirits, *v.* 14. He encouraged them, and with those encouragements enlarged their hearts, Ps. cxix. 32. Lest they should sink under the weight of fear, God stirred them up, and made them cheerful and bold. They applied to their work with all possible vigour. Everyone, according to his capacity or ability, lent a hand, to further that good work. The consideration of God's covenant-relation to his people by his grace should stir up our spirits to act for him, and for the advancement of the interest of his kingdom among men. It was but on the first day of the sixth month that Haggai preached this sermon, and little more than three weeks after, they were all busy working in the house of the Lord their God, *v.* 15. Those that have lost time have need to redeem time.

II. How God met them in mercy. The same prophet that brought them the reproof brought them a comforting encouraging word (*v.* 13): *Then spoke Haggai, the Lord's messenger, in the Lord's message, saying, I am with you, saith the Lord.* That is all he has to say, and that is enough. *I am with you,* that is, I will forgive your neglects hitherto. *I am with you* to protect you against your enemies, and to prosper you, to strengthen your hands, and bless the work.

JAMIESON, FAUSSET, BROWN

long period of the captivity. So Nehemiah 8:15, "Go forth unto *the mount,*" i.e., the neighboring hills [MAURER]. **wood**–Haggai specifies this as being the first necessary; not to the exclusion of other materials. *Stones* also were doubtless needed. That the old walls were not standing, as the Hebrew interpreters quoted by JEROME state, or the new walls partly built, appears from ch. 2: 18, where express mention is made of *laying the foundations.* **I will take pleasure in it, and I will be glorified**–I will be propitious to suppliants in it (I Kings 8:30), and shall receive the honor due to Me which has been withheld. In neglecting the temple, which is the mirror of My presence, ye dishonor Me [CALVIN]; in its being built, ye shall glorify Me. **9. Ye looked for much**–lit., "looked" so as to turn your eyes "to much." The *Hebrew* infinitive here expresses *continued* looking. Ye hoped to have your store made "much" by neglecting the temple. The greater was your greediness, the more bitter your disappointment in being poorer than ever. **when ye brought it home, I did blow upon it**–even the little crop brought into your barns I *dissipated.* "I did blow upon," i.e., I scattered and caused to perish with My mere breath, as scattered and blighted corn. **mine house . . . his own house**–in emphatic antithesis. **ye run**–expressing the keenness of everyone of them in pursuing their own selfish interests. Cf. "run," Psalm 119:32; Proverbs 1:16, contrasted with their apathy about God's house. **10. heaven . . . is stayed from dew**–lit., stays itself. Thus heaven or the sky is personified: implying that inanimate nature obeys Jehovah's will; and, shocked at His people's disobedience, withholds its goods from them (cf. Jer. 2:12, 13). **11. I called**–what the "heaven" and "earth," the second causes, were said to do (vs. 10), being the *visible* instruments, Jehovah, in this verse, the invisible first cause, declares to be His doing. He "calls for" famine, etc., as instruments of His wrath (II Kings 8:1; Ps. 105:16). The contrast is striking between the prompt obedience of these material agencies, and the slothful disobedience of living men, His people. **drought**–*Hebrew, Choreb,* like in sound to *Chareeb,* "waste" (vss. 4, 9), said of God's house; implying the correspondence between the sin and its punishment. Ye have let My house be *waste,* and I will send on all that is yours a *wasting drought.* This would affect not merely the "corn," etc., but also "men" and "cattle," who must perish in the absence of the "corn," etc., lost by the drought. **labour of the hands**–all the fruits of lands, gardens, and vineyards, obtained by labor of the hands (Deut. 28:33; Ps. 78:46). **12. remnant of the people**–all those who have returned from the exile (Zech. 8:6). **as . . . God sent him**–according to all that Jehovah had enjoined him to speak. But as it is not till vs. 14 after Haggai's second message (vs. 13) that the people actually *obeyed,* MAURER translates here, *"hearkened to* the voice of the Lord," and instead of "as," "*because* the Lord had sent him." However, *English Version* rightly represents their *purpose* of obedience as obedience in God's eyes already, though not carried into effect till vs. 14. **13. the Lord's messenger**–so the priests (Mal. 2:7) are called (cf. Gal. 4:14; II Pet. 1:21). **in the Lord's message**–by the Lord's authority and commission: on the Lord's embassage. **I** *am* **with you**–(Matt. 28:20). On the people showing the mere disposition to obey, even before they actually set to work, God passes at once from the reproving tone to that of tenderness. He hastens as it were to forget their former unfaithfulness, and to assure them, when obedient, that He *both is and will be* with them: *Hebrew,* "I with you!" God's presence is the best of blessings, for it includes all others. This is the sure guarantee of their success no matter how many their foes might be (Rom. 8:31). Nothing more inspirits men and rouses them from torpor, than, when relying on the promises of divine aid, they have a sure hope of a successfull issue [CALVIN]. **14. Lord stirred up the spirit of . . .**–God gave them alacrity and perseverance in the good work, though slothful in themselves. Every good impulse and revival of religion is the direct work of God by His Spirit. **came and did work**–collected the wood and stones and other materials (cf. vs. 8) for the work. Not actually built or "laid the (secondary) foundations" of the temple, for this was not done till three months after, viz., the twenty-fourth day of the *ninth* month (ch. 2:18) [GROTIUS]. **15. four and twentieth day**–twenty-three days after the first message of Haggai (vs. 1).

ADAM CLARKE

8. *Go up to the mountains, and bring* wood. Go to Lebanon, and get timber. In the second year of the return from the Captivity, they had procured cedar trees from Lebanon, and brought them to Joppa, and had hired masons and carpenters from the Tyrians and Sidonians; but that labor had been nearly lost by the long suspension of the building. Ezra iii. 7.

9. *Ye looked for much.* You made great pretensions at first, but they have come to nothing. You did a little in the beginning, but so scantily and unwillingly that I could not but reject it.

Ye run every man unto his own house. To rebuild and adorn it; and God's house is neglected!

10. *Therefore the heaven over you is stayed from dew.* It appears from the following verse that God had sent a drought upon the land, which threatened them with scarcity and famine.

12. *Then Zerubbabel.* The threatening of Haggai had its proper effect. The civil governor, the high priest, and the whole of the people united together to do the work. When the authority of God is acknowledged, His words will be carefully obeyed.

13. *Then spake Haggai.* He was the *Lord's messenger,* and he came with *the Lord's message,* and consequently he came with authority. *I am with you, saith the Lord.* Here was high encouragement. What may not a man do when God is his Helper?

15. *In the four and twentieth day.* Haggai received his commission on the first day of this month, and by the twenty-fourth day he had so completely succeeded that he had the satisfaction of seeing the whole people engaged heartily in the Lord's work; they left their own houses to build that of the Lord.

MATTHEW HENRY

CHAPTER 2

Verses 1–9

I. The date of this message, *v.* 1. It was sent on the twenty-first day of the seventh month, when the builders had been about a month at work. Those that are hearty in the service of God shall receive fresh encouragements from him to proceed in it. Set the wheels going, and God will oil them.

II. The direction of this message, *v.* 2. *Speak to Zerubbabel, and Joshua, and the residue of the people*, the very same that *obeyed the voice of the Lord* (*ch.* i. 12) and whose spirits God stirred up to do so (*ch.* i. 14); to them are sent these words of comfort.

III. The message itself. That which was such a damp upon them, when the foundation of the temple was laid, was still a clog upon them—that they could not build such a temple now as Solomon built, *v.* 3. This fetched tears from the eyes of many, when the dimensions of it were first laid (Ezra iii. 12). It was now about seventy years since Solomon's temple was destroyed, so that there might be some yet alive who could remember to have seen it. One could remember the gold with which it was overlaid, another the precious stones, the porch, the pillars—and where are these now? It is sometimes the fault of old people to discourage the services of the present age by crying up too much the performances and attainments of the former age. *Say not thou that the former days were better than these* (Eccles. vii. 10), but thank God that there is any good in these, bad as they are. The encouragement that is given them to go on in the work, notwithstanding (*v.* 4): *Yet now*, though this house is likely to be inferior to the former, *be strong, O Zerubbabel! and be strong, O Joshua!* Let leading men do as well as they can, when they cannot do so well as they would. The grounds of these encouragements. God himself says to them, *Fear you not* (*v.* 5). The presence of God with us, as the *Lord of hosts*, is enough to silence all our fears. The Jews had hosts against them, but they had the Lord of hosts with them. Though *he chastens them for their transgressions with the rod*, yet he will not make his faithfulness to fail. It was the Spirit of God that stirred up their spirits to come out of Babylon (Ezra i. 5), and now to build the temple, Hag. i. 14.

They shall have the Messiah among them shortly—*him that should come*, *v.* 6, 7. Let the Son of man, when he comes, find faith on the earth. Concerning his coming it is here foretold it shall be introduced by a general shaking (*v.* 6): *I will shake the heavens, and the earth, and the sea, and the dry land.* This is applied to the setting up of Christ's kingdom in the world. God will once again do for his church as he did when he brought them out of Egypt; he shook the heavens and earth at Mount Sinai. This shall be done again when at the birth of Christ, Herod and all *Jerusalem are troubled* (Matt. ii. 3), and he is *set for the fall and rising again of many.*

JAMIESON, FAUSSET, BROWN

CHAPTER 2

Vss. 1-9. SECOND PROPHECY. *The people, discouraged at the inferiority of this temple to Solomon's, are encouraged nevertheless to persevere, because God is with them, and this house by its connection with Messiah's kingdom shall have a glory far above that of gold and silver.* **1. seventh month**—of the Hebrew year; in the second year of Darius' reign (ch. 1:1); not quite a month after they had begun the work (ch. 1:15). This prophecy was very shortly before that of Zechariah. **3. Who is left . . . that saw . . . first glory**—Many elders present at the laying of the foundation of the second temple who had seen the first temple (Ezra 3:12, 13) in all its glory, wept at the contrast presented by the rough and unpromising appearance of the former in its beginnings. From the destruction of the first temple to the second year of Darius Hystaspes, the date of Haggai's prophecy, was a space of seventy years (Zech. 1:12); and to the first year of Cyrus, or the end of the captivity, fifty-two years; so that the elders might easily remember the first temple. The Jews note five points of inferiority: The absence from the second temple of (1) the sacred fire; (2) the Shekinah; (3) the ark and cherubim; (4) the Urim and Thummim; (5) the spirit of prophecy. The connection of it with Messiah more than counterbalanced all these; for He is the antitype to all the five (vs. 9). **how do ye see it now?**—God's estimate of things is very different from man's (Zech. 8:6; cf. I Sam. 16:7). However low their estimate of the present temple ("it") from its outward inferiority, God holds it superior (Zech. 4:10; I Cor. 1:27, 28). **4. be strong . . . for I am with you**—The greatest *strength* is to have Jehovah *with* us as our strength. Not in man's "might," but in that of God's Spirit (Zech. 4:6). **5.** *According to* **the word that**—lit., "(I am with you) the word (or *thing*) which I covenanted"; i.e., I am with you as I covenanted with you when ye came out of Egypt (Exod. 19:5, 6; 34:10, 11). The *covenant* promise of God to the elect people at Sinai is an additional motive for their persevering. The *Hebrew* for to "covenant" is lit. "to cut," alluding to the sacrificial victims *cut* in ratification of a covenant. **so**—or, "and." **my Spirit remaineth among you**—to strengthen you for the work (ch. 1:14; Zech. 4:6). The inspiration of Haggai and Zechariah at this time was a specimen of the presence of God's *Spirit* remaining still *with* His people, as He had been with Moses and Israel of old (Ezra 5:1; Isa. 63:11). **6. Yet once, it** *is* **a little while**—or, "(it is) yet *a* little while." The *Hebrew* for "once" expresses the indefinite article "a" [MAURER]. Or, "it is yet *only* a little while"; lit., one little, i.e., a single brief space till a series of movements is to begin; viz., the shakings of nations soon to begin which are to end in the advent of Messiah, "the desire of all nations" [MOORE]. The *shaking of nations* implies judgments of wrath on the foes of God's people, to precede the reign of the Prince of peace (Isa. 13:13). The kingdoms of the world are but the scaffolding for God's spiritual temple, to be thrown down when their purpose is accomplished. The transitoriness of all that is earthly should lead men to seek "peace" in Messiah's everlasting kingdom (vs. 9; Heb. 12:27, 28) [MOORE]. The Jews in Haggai's times hesitated about going forward with the work, through dread of the world power, Medo-Persia, influenced by the craft of Samaria. The prophet assures them this and all other world powers are to fall before Messiah, who is to be associated with this temple; therefore they need fear naught. So Hebrews, 12:26, which quotes this passage; the apostle compares the heavier punishment which awaits the disobedient under the New Testament with that which met such under the Old Testament. At the establishment of the Sinaitic covenant, only the earth was shaken to introduce it, but now heaven and earth and all things are to be shaken, i.e., along with prodigies in the world of nature, all kingdoms that stand in the way of Messiah's kingdom, "which cannot be shaken," are to be upturned (Dan. 2:35, 44; Matt. 21:44). Hebrews 12:27, "Yet *once more,*" favors *English Version.* Paul condenses together the two verses of Haggai (vss. 6, 7, and vss. 21, 22), implying that it was one and the same shaking, of which the former verses of Haggai denote the beginning, the latter the end. The shaking began introductory to the first advent; it will be finished at the second. Concerning the former, cf. Matthew 3:17; 27:51; 28:2; Acts 2:2; 4: 31; concerning the latter, Matthew 24:7; Revelation 16:20; 18:20; 20:11 [BENGEL]. There is scarcely a prophecy of Messiah in the Old Testament which does not, to some extent at least, refer to His second

ADAM CLARKE

CHAPTER 2

1. *In the seventh month.* This was a new message, and intended to prevent discouragment, and excite them to greater diligence in their work.

3. *Who is left among you that saw this house in her first glory?* Who of you has seen the Temple built by Solomon? The foundation of the present house had been laid about fifty-three years after the destruction of the Temple built by Solomon, and though this prophecy was uttered fifteen years after the foundation of this second Temple, yet there might still survive some of those who had seen the Temple of Solomon.

Is it not in your eyes? Most certainly the Jews at this time had neither men nor means to make any such splendid building as that erected by Solomon. The present was as nothing when compared with the former.

4. *Yet now be strong.* Do not let this discourage you. The chief glory of the Temple is not its splendid building, but My presence; and as I covenanted to be with you when you came out of Egypt, so I will fulfill My covenant, for "my spirit remaineth among you: fear ye not," v. 5.

6. *Yet once, it is a little while, and I will shake the heavens.* "The political or religious revolutions which were to be effected in the world, or both," says Archbishop Newcome, "are here referred to; compare vv. 21-22; Matt. xxiv. 29; Heb. xii. 26-28."

MATTHEW HENRY

When his kingdom was set up it was with a shock to the nations. The shaking of the nations is often in order to the settling of the church and the establishing of the things that cannot be shaken.

CHARLES H. SPURGEON:

Verse 7. The second temple was never intended to be as magnificent as the first. The first was to be the the embodiment of the full-glory of the dispensation of symbols and types, and soon to pass away. This comparative feebleness had been proved by the idolatry and apostasy of the people of Israel, and when they returned to Jerusalem they were to have a structure that would be sufficient for the purposes of their worship, but they were not again to be indulged with the splendors of the former house which God had erected by the hand of Solomon. Had it been God's providence that a temple equally magnificent as the first should be erected, it might have been very readily accomplished. Cyrus appears to have been obedient to the divine will, and to have been a great favorer of the Jews, but he expressly by edict diminished the length of the walls and gave express command that the walls should never be erected so high as before. We have also evidence that a like decree was made by Darius, an equally great friend of the Jews, who could with the lifting of his finger have outdone the glory of Solomon's temple, but in God's providence it was not arranged that so it should be. And though Herod, not a Jew, and only a Jew by religious pretence to suit his own particular purpose, lavished a good deal of treasure upon the second temple, for the pleasure of the nation he ruled, and to gain some favor from them, yet he rather profaned than adorned the temple, since he did not follow the prescribed architecture by which it ought to have been built, and he had not the divine approval upon his labors. No prophet ever commanded, and no prophet ever sanctioned, the labors of such a horrible wretch as that Herod. The reason seems to me to be this. In the second temple, during the time it should stand, the dispensation of Christ was softly melted into the light of spiritual truth. The outward worship was to cease there. It seems right that it should cease in a temple that had not the external glory of the first. God intended there to light up the first beams of the spiritual splendor of the second temple, namely, His true temple, the Church, and He would put a sign of decay on the outward and visible in the temple of the first.

—*The Treasury of the Old Testament*

The house they are now building shall be filled with glory to such a degree that its glory shall exceed that of Solomon's temple. It is God's prerogative to fill with glory; the glory that comes from him is satisfying, and not vain glory. Moses's tabernacle and Solomon's temple were filled with glory when God in a cloud took possession of them; but this house shall be filled with glory of another nature.

Let them not be concerned because this house will not have so much silver and gold about it as Solomon's temple had, *v.* 8.

JAMIESON, FAUSSET, BROWN

coming [SIR I. NEWTON]. Psalm 68:8 mentions the *heavens* dropping near the mountain (Sinai); but Haggai speaks of the whole created heavens: "Wait only *a little while,* though the promised event is not apparent yet; for soon will God change things for the better: do not stop short with these preludes and fix your eyes on the present state of the temple [CALVIN]. God shook the *heaven* by the lightnings at Sinai; the *earth,* that it should give forth waters; the *sea,* that it should be divided asunder. In Christ's time God *shook the heaven,* when He spake from it; the *earth,* when it quaked; the *sea,* when He commanded the winds and waves [GROTIUS]. CICERO records at the time of Christ the silencing of the heathen oracles; and DIO, the fall of the idols in the Roman capitol. **7. shake**—not *convert;* but cause that agitation which is to precede Messiah's coming as the healer of the nations' agitations. The previous shaking shall cause the yearning *"desire"* for the Prince of peace. MOORE and others translate "the beauty," or "the desirable things (the precious gifts) of all nations shall come" (Isa. 60:5, 11; 61:6). He brings these objections to applying "the desire of all nations" to Messiah: (1) The *Hebrew* means the *quality,* not the *thing* desired, viz., its *desirableness* or beauty, But the abstract is often put for the concrete. So "a man of desires," i.e., *one desired* or *desirable* (*Margin,* Dan. 9:23; 10:3, 11). (2) Messiah was not desired by all nations, but "a root out of a dry ground," having "no beauty that we should *desire* Him" (Isa. 53:2). But what is implied is not that the nations definitely desired *Him,* but that He was the only one to satisfy the yearning desires which all felt unconsciously for a Saviour, shown in their painful rites and bloody sacrifices. Moreover, while the Jews as a nation desired Him not (to which people Isa. 53:2 refers), the Gentiles, who are plainly pointed out by "all nations," accepted Him; and so to them He was peculiarly desirable. (3) The verb, "shall come," is *plural,* which requires the noun to be understood in the *plural,* whereas if Messiah be intended, the noun is *singular.* But when two nouns stand together, of which one is governed by the other, the verb agrees sometimes *in number* with the latter, though it really has the former as its nominative, i.e., the *Hebrew* "come" is made *in number* to agree with "nations," though really agreeing with "the desire." Besides, Messiah may be described as realizing in Himself at His coming *"the desires* (the noun expressing collectively the *plural*) of all nations"; whence the verb is *plural.* So in Song of Solomon, 5:16, "He is altogether lovely," in the *Hebrew* the same word as here, "all *desires,*" i.e., altogether desirable, or the object of desires. (4) Verse 8, "The silver is mine . . ." accords with the translation, "the choice things of all nations" shall be brought in. But the eighth verse harmonizes quite as well with *English Version* of vs. 7, as the *Note* on vs. 8 will show. (5) LXX and *Syriac* versions agree with MOORE'S translation. But *Vulgate* confirms *English Version.* So also early Jewish Rabbis before JEROME'S time. PLATO, *Alcibiades* 2, shows the yearning of the Gentiles after a spiritual deliverer: "It is therefore necessary," says Alcibiades on the subject of acceptable worship, "to wait until One teach us how we ought to behave towards the gods and men." Alcibiades replies, "When shall that time arrive, and who shall that Teacher be? For most glad would I be to see such a man." The "good tidings of great joy" were "to all people" (Luke 2:10). The Jews, and those in the adjoining nations instructed by them, looked for *Shiloh* to *come unto whom the gathering of the people was to be,* from Jacob's prophecy (Gen. 49:10). The early patriarchs, Job (Job 19:25-27; 33:23-26) and Abraham (John 8:56), *desired Him.* **fill this house with glory**—(vs. 9). As the first temple was filled with the cloud of glory, the symbol of God (I Kings 8:11; II Chron. 5:14), so this second temple was filled with the "glory" of God (John 1:14) *veiled* in the flesh (as it were in the cloud) at Christ's first coming, when He entered it and performed miracles there (Matt. 21:12-14); but that "glory" is to be *revealed* at His second coming, as this prophecy in its ulterior reference foretells (Mal. 3:1). The Jews before the destruction of Jerusalem all expected Messiah would appear in the second temple. Since that time they invent various forced and false interpretations of such plain Messianic prophecies. **8. The silver is mine**—(Job 41:11; Ps. 50:12). Ye are disappointed at the absence of these precious metals in the adorning of this temple, as compared with the first temple: If I pleased I could adorn this temple with them, but I will adorn it with a "glory" (vss. 7, 9) far more precious; viz., with the presence of My divine Son in His veiled glory first, and

ADAM CLARKE

7. *And the desire of all nations shall come.* This is a difficult place if understood of a person; but *chemdath,* "desire," cannot well agree with *bau,* "they shall come." It is true that some learned men suppose that *chemdoth,* "desirable things," may have been the original reading; but this is supported by no MS. It is generally understood of the desirable or valuable things which the different nations should bring into the Temple, and it is certain that many rich presents were brought into this Temple. All are puzzled with it. But the principal difficulty lies in the verb *ubau,* "they shall come." God says He will *shake* or stir up *all nations;* that these nations shall bring their desirable things; that the house shall be filled with God's glory; that the silver and gold, which these nations are represented as bringing by way of gifts, are the Lord's; and that the glory of this latter house shall exceed the former. I cannot see how the words can apply to Jesus Christ, even if the construction were less embarrassed than it is, because I cannot see how He could be called the Desire of all nations. The whole seems to be a metaphorical description of the Church of Christ, and of His filling it with all the excellences of the Gentile world, when the fullness of the Gentiles shall be brought in.

MATTHEW HENRY

Let them be comforted with this, that, though this temple have less gold in it, it shall have more glory than Solomon's (*v.* 9): *The glory of this latter house shall be greater than of the former.* The presence of the Messiah will be in it, the Son of God presented there, attending there at twelve years old, and afterwards his preaching and working miracles there, and his driving the buyers and sellers out of it. It was necessary, then, that the Messiah should come while the second temple stood; but, that being long since destroyed, we must conclude that our Lord Jesus is the Christ, is *he that should come*, and we are to *look for no other.* It was the *glory of this latter house*, that before the coming of Christ, it was always kept free from idols and idolatries. The purity of the church, and the strict adherence to divine institutions, are much more its glory than external pomp and splendour. After Christ, the gospel was preached in it by the apostles, even all the words of this life, Acts v. 20. In the temple Jesus Christ was daily preached, Acts v. 42. Where Christ is, *behold a greater than Solomon is there*, so the heart in which he dwells, and makes a living temple, is more glorious than Solomon's temple, and will be so to eternity. *In this place will I give peace, saith the Lord of hosts.* But the Jews under the latter temple had so much trouble that we must conclude this promise to have its accomplishment in that spiritual peace which Jesus Christ bequeathed to all believers (John xiv. 27). God will *give peace in this place*; he will give his Son to be the peace, Eph. ii. 14.

Verses 10–19

This sermon was preached two months after that in the former part of the chapter. The people were now going on vigorously with the building of the temple.

I. God sees there are many among them that spoil this good work, by going about it with unsanctified hearts and hands. All are warned thereby to purify the hands they employ in this work. A spiritual use is to be made of the ceremonial law; it was intended, not only as a divine ritual to the Jews, but for *instruction in righteousness* to all. The prophet is ordered to enquire of the priests concerning it (*v.* 11). Haggai himself, though a prophet, must *ask the priests concerning the law.* It was their duty to expound the ordinances of God, and to give the general rules for the observance of them. The rules of the law, in the cases propounded, are that he that has holy flesh in his clothes cannot by the touch of his clothes communicate holiness (*v.* 12), but he that is ceremonially unclean by the touch of a dead body does by his touch communicate that uncleanness. The law is express (Num. xix. 22). The sum of these two rules is that pollution is more easily communicated than sanctification. The law is here applied (*v.* 14): *So is this people, and so is this nation, before me.* They thought their offering sacrifices on the altar would sanctify them, and excuse their neglect to build the temple. "No," says God, "your holy flesh and your altar will be so far from sanctifying your meat and drink, your wine and oil, to you, that your contempt of God's temple will bring a pollution, not only on your common enjoyments, but even on your sacrifices too." If they be sensual, and morally impure, though they work hard at the temple while it is building, and though they offer many and costly sacrifices there when it is built, yet that shall not serve to sanctify their meat and drink to them; the impurity of their hearts and lives shall make even that work of their hands, and all their offerings, unclean, and an abomination to God.

JAMIESON, FAUSSET, BROWN

at His second coming with His revealed glory, accompanied with outward adornment of gold and silver, of which the golden covering within and without put on by Herod is the type. Then shall the nations bring offerings of those precious metals which ye now miss so much (Isa. 2:3; 60:3, 6, 7; Ezek. 43:2, 4, 5; 44:4). The heavenly Jerusalem shall be similarly adorned, but shall need "no temple" (Rev. 21:10-22). Cf. I Corinthians 3:12, where *gold* and *silver* represent the most precious things (Zech. 2:5). The inward glory of New Testament redemption far exceeds the outward glory of the Old Testament dispensation. So, in the case of the individual poor believer, God, if He pleased, could bestow gold and silver, but He bestows far better treasures, the possession of which might be endangered by that of the former (Jas. 2:5). **9. The glory of this latter house . . . greater than of the former**—viz., through the presence of Messiah, *in* whose *face is given the light of the knowledge of the glory of God* (II Cor. 4:6; cf. Heb. 1:2), and who said of Himself, "in this place is one greater than the temple" (Matt. 12:6), and who "sat daily teaching in it" (Matt. 26:55). Though Zerubbabel's temple was taken down to the foundations when Herod rebuilt the temple, the latter was considered, in a religious point of view, as not a *third* temple, but virtually the second temple. **in this place . . . peace**—viz., at Jerusalem, the metropolis of the kingdom of God, whose seat was the temple: where Messiah "made peace through the blood of His cross" (Col. 1:20). Thus the "glory" consists in this "peace." This peace begins by the removal of the difficulty in the way of the just God accepting the guilty (Ps. 85:8, 10; Isa. 9:6, 7; 53:5; Zech. 6:13; II Cor. 5:18, 19); then it creates peace in the sinner's own heart (Isa. 57:19; Acts 10:36; Rom. 5:1; 14:17; Eph. 2:13-17; Phil. 4:7); then peace in the whole earth (Mic. 5:5; Luke 2:14).

10-19. THIRD PROPHECY. *Sacrifices without obedience (in respect to God's command to build the temple) could not sanctify. Now that they are obedient, God will bless them, though no sign is seen of fertility as yet.* **10. four and twentieth day . . . ninth month**—three days more than two months from the second prophecy (vs. 1); in the month Chisleu, the lunar one about the time of our December. The Jews seem to have made considerable progress in the work in the interval (vss. 15-18). **11. Ask . . . the priests**—Propose this question to them on the law. The priests were the authorized expounders of the law (Lev. 10:11; Deut. 33:10; Ezek. 44:23; Mal. 2:7). **12.** "Holy flesh" (i.e., the flesh of a sacrifice, Jer. 11:15), indeed, makes holy the "skirt" in which it is carried; but that "skirt" cannot impart its sanctity to any thing beyond, as "bread," etc. (Lev. 6:27). This is cited to illustrate the principle, that a sacrifice, holy, as enveloping divine things (just as the "skirt" is "holy" which envelops "holy" flesh), cannot by its inherent or *opus operatum* efficacy make holy a person whose disobedience, as that of the Jew while neglecting God's house, made him unholy. **13.** On the other hand, a legally "unclean" person imparts his uncleanness to any thing, whereas a legally holy thing cannot confer its sanctity on an "unclean" person (Num. 19:11, 13, 22). Legal sanctity is not so readily communicated as legal impurity. So the paths to sin are manifold: the paths to holiness one, and that one of difficult access [GROTIUS]. One drop of filth will defile a vase of water: many drops of water will not purity a vase of filth [MOORE]. **14. Then answered Haggai**—rather, "Then Haggai answered (in rejoinder to the priests' answer) and said" [MAURER]. **so is this people**—heretofore not in such an obedient state of mind as to deserve to be called *My* people (Titus 1:15). Here he applies the two cases just stated. By the first case, "this people" is not made "holy" by their offerings "there" (viz., on the altar built in the open air, under Cyrus, Ezra 3:3); though the ritual sacrifice can ordinarily sanctify outwardly so far as it reaches (Heb. 9:13), as the "holy flesh" sanctified the "skirt," yet it cannot make the offerers in their persons and all their works acceptable to God, because lacking the spirit of obedience (I Sam. 15:22) so long as they neglected to build the Lord's house. On the contrary, by the second case, they made "unclean" their very *offerings* by being unclean through "dead works" (disobedience), just as the person unclean by contact with a dead body imparted his uncleanness to all that he touched (cf. Heb. 9:14). This all applies to them as they had been, not as they are now that they have begun to obey; the design is to guard them against falling back again. The "there" points to the altar, probably in view of the audience which the prophet ad-

ADAM CLARKE

9. *And in this place will I give peace. Shalom,* "a peace offering," as well as *peace* itself; or Jesus Christ, who is called the "Prince of Peace," through whom peace is proclaimed between God and man. But it is said that *the glory of this latter house shall be greater than of the former,* because under it the grand scheme of human salvation was exhibited, and the redemption price paid down for a lost world. As all probably applies to the Christian Church, the real house of God, its glory was most certainly greater than any glory which was ever possessed by that of the Jews.

10. *In the four and twentieth day of the ninth month.* Three months after they had begun to rebuild the Temple, Haggai is ordered to go and put two questions to the priests.

(1) "If one bear holy flesh in the skirt of his garment," and he touch anything with his skirt, is that thing made holy? The priests answered, No! v. 12.

(2) If one has touched a dead body, and thereby become unclean, does he communicate his uncleanness to whatever he may touch? And the priests answered, Yes! v. 13.

14. *Then answered Haggai . . . So is this people.* As an unclean man communicates his uncleanness to everything he touches, so are you unclean, and whatever you have hitherto done is polluted in the sight of God.

MATTHEW HENRY	JAMIESON, FAUSSET, BROWN	ADAM CLARKE

II. Comfort and encouragement. If their hearts be right with God, and their eye single, God will take away the judgment of famine, and will restore them great plenty. On the twenty-fourth day of the sixth month they began to prepare materials (*ch.* i. 15), and now on the twenty-fourth day of the ninth month they began to *lay a stone upon a stone in the temple of the Lord.* They had gone behind-hand before this day. Let them remember the time when there was waste and decay in all they had, *v.* 16. A man went to his garner, expecting to find *a heap of twenty measures* of corn, but he found it unaccountably diminished, and, when he came to measure it, *there were but ten* measures; it had dried away in the keeping, or vermin had eaten it, or it was stolen. In like manner he went to *the wine-press,* expecting to draw *fifty vessels* of wine; they did not yield as usual, for he could get *but twenty.* *I smote you with blastings,* winds and frosts, which made every green thing to wither, *and with mildew,* which choked the corn when it was knitting, *and with hail,* which battered it down when it had grown to some maturity; thus they were disappointed *in all the labour of their hands,* while they neglected to lay their hands to the work of God. As long as they continued in neglect of the temple work all their affairs went backward. But they should find that from this day forward God would bless them (*v.* 18, 19): "*Consider now* whether when you begin to change your way towards God you do not find God changing his way towards you." He does not say what they shall be, but, in general, *I will bless you;* they can desire no more to make them happy.

Verses 20–23

After Haggai's sermon *to the people,* here follows one, the same day, *to the magistrates,* particularly to *Zerubbabel* (*v.* 21): *Speak to Zerubbabel, governor of Judah,* speak to him by himself. Zerubbabel is concerned about the community, about the neighbouring nations, and their governments, and what will become of the few and feeble Jews, and how such a poor prince as he should be able to keep his ground and serve his country. "Go to him," says God, "and tell him it shall be well with him and his remnant."

I. Let him expect to hear of great commotions in the nations (*v.* 21, 22): *I will shake the heavens and the earth.* The world is like the sea, like the wheel, always in motion, but sometimes in a special manner turbulent. But, blessed be God, if the earth be shaken, it is to *shake the wicked out of it,* Job xxxviii. 13. In the apocalyptic visions earthquakes bode no ill to the church. The Chaldean monarchy, which had been the throne of kingdoms was already overthrown; and the powers that are yet to come, shall in like manner be overthrown; their day will come to fall. They *trust in chariots and horses* (Ps. xx. 7), but their *chariots* shall be *overthrown,* and *those that ride in them.* This reads the doom of all the enemies of God's church, and seems likewise designed as a promise of Christ's victory over the powers of darkness; his overthrow of Satan's throne, that *throne of kingdoms.* All opposing *rule, principality,* and *power,* shall be put down, that the *kingdom* may be *delivered up to God, even the Father.*

II. He shall be safe under the divine protection in the midst of all these commotions, *v.* 23. Zerubbabel was active to build God a house, and therefore God makes the same promise to him as he did to David—that he would *build him a house,* and establish it, even *in that day* when heaven and earth are shaken. His successors likewise in the government of Judah might take encouragement from it. But this promise has special reference to Christ, who lineally descended from Zerubbabel, and is the sole builder of the gospel-temple. Zerubbabel is here owned as *God's servant. I have chosen thee* to this office. It is promised that, being chosen, God will make him *as a signet.* Jeconiah had been as the *signet on God's right hand,* but was *plucked thence* (Jer. xxii. 24). He shall be near and dear to God, and his family shall continue till the Messiah spring out of it, who is *the signet on God's right hand.* Princes sign their edicts, grants, and commissions, with their signet-rings, Esther iii. 10. Our Lord Jesus is the signet on God's right hand, for all power is given to him and derived from him. By him the great charter of the gospel is signed and ratified, and it is in him that all the promises of God are yea and amen.

dressed. **15. consider**—lit., "lay it to heart." Ponder earnestly, retracing the past *upward* (i.e., backward), comparing what evils heretofore befell you before ye set about this work, with the present time when you have again commenced it, and when in consequence I now engage to "bless you." Hence ye may perceive the evils of disobedience and the blessing of obedience. **16. Since those** *days* **were**—from the time that those days of your neglect of the temple work have been. **when** *one* **came to an heap of twenty** *measures*—i.e., to a heap *which he had expected would be one* of twenty measures, there were but ten. **fifty** *vessels* **out of the press**—As LXX translates "measure," and *Vulgate* "a flagon," and as we should rather expect *vat* than *press.* MAURER translates (omitting *vessels,* which is not in the original), "*purahs,*" or "wine-measures." **17.** Appropriated from Amos 4:9, whose canonicity is thus sealed by Haggai's inspired authority; in the last clause, "*turned,*" however, has to be supplied, its omission marking by the elliptical abruptness ("yet ye not to Me!") God's displeasure. Cf. (*let him come*) unto Me!" Moses in excitement omitting the bracketed words (Exod. 32:26). "Blasting" results from excessive drought; "mildew," from excessive moisture. **18.** Resumed from vs. 15 after vss. 16, 17, that the blessing in vs. 19 may stand in the more marked contrast with the curse in vss. 16, 17. Affliction will harden the heart, if not referred to God as its author [MOORE]. **even from the day that the foundation of . . . temple was laid**—The first foundation beneath the earth had been long ago laid in the second year of Cyrus, 535 B.C. (Ezra 3:10, 11); the foundation now laid was the secondary one, which, above the earth, was laid on the previous work [TIRINUS]. Or, translate, "From this day on which the temple is being *begun,*" viz., on the foundations long ago laid [GROTIUS]. MAURER translates, "Consider . . . from the four and twentieth day . . . *to* (the time which has elapsed) from the day on which the foundation . . . was laid." The *Hebrew* supports *English Version.* **19. Is the seed yet in the barn?**—implying, It is *not.* It has been already sown this month, and there are no more signs of its bearing a good crop, much less of its being safely stored *in the barn,* than there were in the past season, when there was such a failure; yet I promise to you *from this day* (emphatically marking by the repetition the connection of the blessing with *the day* of their obedience) a *blessing* in an abundant harvest. So also the vine, etc., which heretofore have borne little or nothing, shall be *blessed* with productiveness. Thus it will be made evident that the blessing is due to Me, not to nature. We may trust God's promise to bless us, though we see no visible sign of its fulfilment (Hab. 2:3).

20-23. FOURTH PROPHECY. *God's promise through Zerubbabel to Israel of safety in the coming commotions.* **20. the month**—the ninth in the second year of Darius. The same date as Prophecy III (vs. 10). **21. to Zerubbabel**—Perhaps Zerubbabel had asked as to the convulsions foretold (vss. 6, 7). This is the reply: The Jews had been led to fear that these convulsions would destroy their national existence. *Zerubbabel,* therefore, as their civil leader and representative is addressed, not Joshua, their religious leader. Messiah is the antitypical Zerubbabel, their national Representative and King, with whom God the Father makes the covenant wherein they, as identified with Him, are assured of safety in God's electing love (cf. vs. 23, "will make thee as a signet"; "I have chosen thee"). **shake . . . heavens**—(*Note,* vss. 6, 7); violent political convulsions accompanied with physical prodigies (Matt. 24:7, 29). **22.** All other world kingdoms are to be overthrown to make way for Christ's universal kingdom (Dan. 2:44). War chariots are to give place to His reign of peace (Mic. 5:10; Zech. 9:10). **23. take thee**—under My protection and to promote thee and thy people to honor (Ps. 78:70). **a signet**—(Song of Sol. 8:6; Jer. 22:24). A ring with a seal on it; the legal representative of the owner; generally of precious stones and gold, etc., and much valued. Being worn on the finger, it was an object of constant regard. In all which points of view the theocratic people, and their representative, Zerubbabel the type, and Messiah his descendant the Antitype, are regarded by God. The safety of Israel to the end is guaranteed in Messiah, in whom God hath chosen them as His own (Isa. 42:1; 43:10; 44:1; 49:3). So the spiritual Israel is sealed in their covenant head by His Spirit (II Cor. 1:20, 22; Eph. 1:4, 13, 14). All is ascribed, not to the merits of Zerubbabel, but to God's gratuitous *choice.* The signet of an Eastern monarch was the sign of *delegated authority;* so Christ (Matt. 28:18; John 5:22, 23).

16. *Since those days were.* I have shown My displeasure against you, by sending blasting and mildew; and so poor have been your crops that *an heap* of corn which should have produced *twenty measures* produced only *ten;* and that quantity of grapes which in other years would have produced *fifty* measures, through their poverty, smallness, etc., produced only *twenty.*

And this has been the case ever since the first stone was laid in this Temple; for your hearts were not right with Me, and therefore I blasted you "in all the labours of your hands; yet ye turned not to me," v. 17.

18. *Consider now from this day.* I will now change My conduct towards you; *from this day* that you have begun heartily to rebuild My temple and restore My worship, I will bless you. Whatever you sow, whatever you plant, shall be blessed; your land shall be fruitful, and you shall have abundant crops of all sorts.

20. *Again the word of the Lord came.* This was a second communication in the same day.

23. *And will make thee as a signet.* I will exalt you to high dignity, power, and trust, of which the seal was the instrument or sign in those days. You shall be under My peculiar care, and shall be to Me very precious. See Jer. xxii. 24; Cant. viii. 6. *For I have chosen thee.* He had an important and difficult work to do, and it was necessary that he should be assured of God's especial care and protection during the whole.

THE BOOK OF ZECHARIAH

I. Messages during building of Temple (1:1-8:23)
A. The first message (1:1-6)
B. The second message—visions (1:7-6:8)
1. Of myrtle trees—picture of Israel today (1:7-17)
2. Of horns and smiths—overthrow of Israel's enemies (1:18-21)
3. Of measuring line—resultant condition of Jerusalem (2:1-13)
4. Of Joshua—Israel as a priest cleansed (3:1-10)
5. Of candlestick—Israel according to ideal (4:1-14)
6. Of flying roll—government of the earth (5:1-4)
7. Of Ephah—restriction of wickedness (5:5-11)
8. Of chariots (6:1-8)
C. Historic interlude—great symbolic act (6:9-15)
D. The third message—voices (7:1-8:23)
1. The question asked (7:1-3)
2. The fourfold answer (7:4-8:23)

II. Messages after building of Temple (9:1-14:21)
A. The burden of Hadrach—The anointed King rejected (9:1-11:17)
1. The King announced (9:1-10)
2. The King's program (9:11-10:12)
3. The King rejected (11:1-17)
B. The burden of Israel—The rejected King enthroned (12:1-14:21)
1. Final victories—as to the nations and Israel (12:1-13:6)
a. As to the nations (12:1-6)
b. As to Israel (12:7-13:6)
2. Final victories—as to the King (13:7-14:21)
a. His rejection (13:7-9)
b. His day (14:1-8)
c. His process (14:9-15)
d. His Kingdom (14:16-21)

This prophet was colleague with the prophet Haggai, and a worker together with him in forwarding the building of the second temple (Ezra 5:1). Zechariah began to prophesy some time after Haggai. But he continued longer, soared higher in visions and revelations, and prophesied more particularly concerning Christ, than Haggai had done. He begins with a sermon, expressive of that which was the scope of his prophesying, in the first five verses; but afterwards, to the end of chapter 6, he relates the visions he saw, and the instructions he received from heaven by them. At chapter 7, from an inquiry made by the Jews concerning fasting, he takes occasion to show them the duty of their present day, and to encourage them to hope for God's favor, after which there are two sermons, both called "burdens of the word of the Lord" (one begins with chapter 9, the other with chapter 12). The scope of them is to reprove for sin, and threaten God's judgment against the impenitent, and to encourage those that feared God with assurances of the mercy God had in store for his church, and especially of the coming of the Messiah and the setting up of his kingdom in the world.

MATTHEW HENRY

CHAPTER 1

Verses 1–6

I. The foundation of Zechariah's ministry: *The word of the Lord came to him.* He received a divine commission to be God's mouth to the people. It came in the evidence and demonstration of the Spirit, as a real thing, and not a fancy. The word of the Lord came first to him *in the second year of Darius.* Before the captivity the prophets dated their writings by the reigns of the kings of Judah and Israel; but now by the reigns of the kings of Persia, to whom they were subjects. Zechariah preached his first sermon in the *eighth month* of this *second year* of Darius; Haggai preached his in the sixth month of the same year, Hag. i. 1. *Zechariah was the son of Barachiah, the son of Iddo,* and he was *the prophet,* as Haggai is called *the prophet,* Hag. i. 1.

II. The first-fruits of Zechariah's ministry. Before he published the promises of mercy, he published calls to repentance, for thus *the way of the Lord* must be *prepared.* Law must be first preached, and then gospel. The prophet puts them in mind of the controversy God had had with their fathers (*v.* 2): "*The Lord has been sorely displeased with your fathers.* You have seen with your eyes the woeful remains of it." The judgments of God, which those that went before us were under, should be taken as calls to repentance, that we may cut off the curse and get it turned into a blessing. He calls them, in God's name, to return and make their peace with him, *v.* 3. Let the rebels return to their allegiance, and they shall enjoy all the privileges of good subjects. But that which is most observable here is that God is called here the *Lord of hosts* three times: *Thus saith the Lord of hosts. Turn you to me, saith the Lord of hosts* (this intimates the authority and obligation of the command), *and I will turn to you, saith the Lord of hosts*—this intimates the validity and value of the promise; so that it is no vain repetition. He warns them not to persist in their impenitence, as their fathers had done (*v.* 4): *Be you not as your fathers.* We are apt to be governed very much by precedent. Some argued, "Shall we be wiser than our fathers? They never minded the prophets, and why then should we mind them? They made laws against them, and why should we tolerate them?" But they are here taught how they should argue: "Our fathers slighted the prophets, and God was sorely displeased with

JAMIESON, FAUSSET, BROWN

CHAPTER 1

VSS. 1-17. INTRODUCTORY EXHORTATION TO REPENTANCE. THE VISIONS—*The man among the myrtles: Comforting explanation by the angel, an encouragement to the Jews to build the city and temple: The four horns and four artificers.*

2. God fulfilled His threats against your fathers; beware, then, lest by disregarding His voice by me, as they did in the case of former prophets, *ye* suffer like them. The special object Zechariah aims at is that they should awake from their selfish negligence to obey God's command to rebuild His temple (Hag. 1:4-8). **sore displeased**—*Hebrew,* "displeased with a displeasure," i.e., vehemently, with no common displeasure, exhibited in the destruction of the Jews' city and in their captivity. **3. saith the Lord of hosts**—a phrase frequent in Haggai and Zechariah, implying God's boundless resources and universal power, so as to inspire the Jews with confidence to work. **Turn ye unto me . . . and I will turn**—i.e., *and then,* as the sure consequence, "I will turn unto you" (Mal. 3:7; Jas. 4:8; cf. also Jer. 3:12; Ezek. 18:30; Mic. 7:19). Though God hath brought you back from captivity, yet this state will not last long unless ye are really converted. God has heavier scourges ready, and has begun to give symptoms of displeasure [CALVIN]. (Hag. 1:6). **4. Be ye not as your fathers**—The Jews boasted of their *fathers;* but he shows that their fathers were refractory, and that ancient example and long usage will not justify disobedience (II Chron. 36:15, 16).

ADAM CLARKE

CHAPTER 1

1. *In the eighth month, in the second year of Darius.* This was Darius Hystaspes, and from this date we find that Zechariah began to prophesy just two months after Haggai.

3. *Turn ye unto me.* This shows that they had power to return, if they would but use it.

MATTHEW HENRY

them for it; therefore let us regard what God says to us by his prophets." "*The former prophets cried to your fathers* as men in earnest, in the name of *the Lord of hosts;* and this was the substance of what they said—*Turn you now from your evil ways, and from your evil doings;* the very same that we now preach to you. A speedy reformation is the only way to prevent an approaching ruin." "What has become both of your fathers and of the prophets that preached to them? They are all dead and gone," *v.* 5. In another world both we and our prophets shall live for ever; and to prepare for that world ought to be our great care and business in this. "The preachers died, and the hearers died, but the word of God died not; that took effect, and not one iota or tittle of it fell to the ground." Though God's prophets could not fasten convictions upon them, the calamities threatened overtook them, and they could not escape them. The unbelief of man cannot make the threatenings of God's word of no effect, but, sooner or later, they will take place, if the prescribed course be not taken to prevent them. *They returned, and said* (they changed their mind, and when it was too late to prevent the ruin of their nation they acknowledged), *Like as the Lord of hosts thought to do unto us according to our ways and doings, so has he dealt with us,* and we must acknowledge both his truth and his justice.

Verses 7–17

Visions and revelations of the Lord; for in that way God chose to speak by Zechariah, to awaken the people's attention. Most of the following visions seem designed for the comfort of the Jews, newly returned out of captivity, and their encouragement to go on with the building of the temple. The scope of this vision (which is an introduction to the rest) is to assure the Jews of the care God took of them, now they seem deserted, and their case deplorable. The vision is dated (*v.* 7) *the twenty-fourth day of the eleventh month,* three months after he preached that sermon (*v.* 1), in which he calls them to repentance. Finding it had a good effect, and that they returned to God in a way of duty, the assurances are confirmed, that God would return to them in a way of mercy.

I. The prophet saw a grove of *myrtle-trees,* a dark shady grove, down *in a bottom,* hidden by the adjacent hills. This represented the low, dark, solitary, melancholy condition of the Jewish church at this time. He saw *a man* mounted upon *a red horse,* standing in the midst of this shady myrtle-grove. This man is no other than the *man Christ Jesus,* the same that appeared to Joshua with *his sword drawn in his hand* as *captain of the host of the Lord* (Joshua v. 13, 14). Though the church was in a low condition, yet Christ was present in the midst of it. He was *riding,* as a man of war, as a man in haste, *riding on the heavens for the help* of his people, Deut. xxxiii. 26. He rode on a *red horse,* as this same victorious prince appeared *red in his apparel,* Isa. lxiii. 1, 2. Red is a fiery colour, denoting that he is *jealous for Jerusalem* (*v.* 14), and angry at her enemies. Christ, under the law, appeared on a red horse, denoting that he had yet his conflict before him, when he was to *resist unto blood.* But, under the gospel, he appears on *a white horse* (Rev. vi. 2, and again *ch.* xix. 11), denoting that he has now gained the victory. *Behind him there were some red horses, and* some *speckled, and* some *white,* angels attending the Lord Jesus, ready to be employed by him for the service of his church, some in acts of judgment, others of mercy, others in varied events.

He had an angel talking with him, as his instructor. Zechariah asked him (*v.* 9), *O my Lord! what are these?* The account given him was, *These are those whom the Lord has sent;* they are his messengers.

JAMIESON, FAUSSET, BROWN

the former prophets—those who lived before the captivity. It aggravated their guilt that, not only had they the law, but they had been often called to repent by God's *prophets.* **5. Your fathers . . . and the prophets, do they live for ever?**—In contrast to "*My* words" (v. 6), which "endure for ever" (I Pet. 1:25). "Your fathers have perished, as was foretold; and their fate ought to warn you. But you may say, The prophets too are dead. I grant it, but still My words do not die: though dead, their prophetical words from Me, fulfilled against *your fathers,* are not dead with them. Beware, then, lest ye share their fate." **6. statutes**—My determined purposes to punish for sin. **which I commanded my servants**—viz., to announce to your fathers. **did they not take hold**—i.e., overtake, as a foe overtakes one fleeing. **they returned**—*Turning* from their former self-satisfaction, they recognized their punishment as that which God's prophets had foretold. **thought to do**—i.e., decreed to do. Cf. with this verse Lamentations 2:17. **our ways**—evil ways (Jer. 4:18; 17:10; 23:2). **7.** The general plan of the nine following visions (ch. 1:8 to end of ch. 6) is first to present the symbol; then, on a question being put, to subjoin the interpretation. Though the visions are distinct, they form one grand whole, presented in one night to the prophet's mind, two or three months after the prophet's first commission (vs. 1). **Sebat**—the eleventh month of the Jewish year, from the new moon in February to the new moon in March. The term is Chaldee, meaning a "shoot," viz., the month when trees begin to shoot or bud. **8. by night**—The Jews begin their day with sunset; therefore the night which preceded the twenty-fourth day of the month is meant (vs. 7). **a man**—Jehovah, the second person of the Trinity, manifested in *man's* form, an earnest of the incarnation; called the "angel of Jehovah" (vss. 11, 12), "Jehovah the angel of the covenant" (Mal. 3: 1; cf. Gen. 16:7 with vs. 13; 22:11 with vs. 12; Exodus 3:2 with vs. 4). Being at once divine and human, He must be God and man in one person. **riding**—implying swiftness in executing God's will in His providence; hastening to help His people. **red horse**—the color that represents *bloodshed:* implying vengeance to be inflicted on the foes of Israel (cf. II Kings 3:22; Isa. 63:1, 2; Rev. 6.4); also *fiery zeal.* **among the myrtle trees**—symbol of the Jewish Church: not a stately cedar, but a lowly, though fragrant, myrtle. It was its depressed state that caused the Jews to despond; this vision is designed to cheer them with better hopes. The uncreated angel of Jehovah's presence *standing* (as His abiding-place, Ps. 122:14) *among* them, is a guarantee for her safety, lowly though she now be. **in the bottom**—in a low place or bottom of a river; alluding to Babylon near the rivers Euphrates and Tigris, the scene of Judah's captivity. The myrtle delights in low places and the banks of waters [PEMBELLUS]. MAURER translates, from a different root, "in a *shady* place." **red horses**—i.e., *horsemen* mounted *on red horses;* vss. 10, 11, confirm this view. **speckled . . . white**—The "white" implies triumph and victory for Judah; "speckled" (from a root "to intertwine"), a combination of the two colors *white* and *red* (bay [MOORE]), implies a state of things mixed, partly prosperous, partly otherwise [HENDERSON]; or, the connection of the wrath (answering to the "red") about to fall on the Jews' foes, and triumph (answering to the "white") to the Jews themselves in God's arrangements for His people [MOORE]. Some angels ("the red horses") exercised offices of vengeance; others ("the white"), those of joy; others ("the speckled"), those of a mixed character (cf. ch. 6:2, 3). God has ministers of every kind for promoting the interests of His Church. **9. the angel that talked with me**—not the "man upon the red horse," as is evident from the tenth verse, where he (the Divine Angel) is distinguished from the "angel that talked with me" (the phrase used of him, vs. 13, 14; ch. 2:3; 4:1, 4, 5; 5:5, 10; 6:4), i.e., the interpreting angel. The *Hebrew* for "*with* me," or, "*in* me" (Num. 12:8), implies *internal, intimate* communication [JEROME]. **show thee**—reveal to thy mental vision. **10. answered**—The "angel of the covenant" here gives the reply instead of the interpreting angel, to imply that all communications through the interpreting angel come from Him as their source. **Lord hath sent to walk to and fro through the earth**—If "Satan walks to and fro in the earth" (implying *restless activity*) on errands of mischief to God's people (Job 1:7), the Lord *sends* other angels to "walk to and fro" with unceasing activity everywhere to counterwork Satan's designs, and to defend His people (Ps. 34:7; 91:11; 103:20, 21; Heb. 1:41). **11.** The attendant

ADAM CLARKE

5. *Your fathers, where are they?* Israel has been destroyed and ruined in the bloody wars with the Assyrians; and Judah, in those with the Chaldeans. *The prophets, do they live for ever?* They also, who spoke unto your fathers, are dead; but their predictions remain; and the events which have taken place according to those predictions prove that God sent them.

6. *Did they not take hold of your fathers?* Everything happened according to the predictions, and they were obliged to acknowledge this; and yet they would not turn from their evil way.

7. *Upon the four and twentieth day of the eleventh month.* This revelation was given about three months after the former, and two months after they had recommenced the building of the Temple. *Sebat* answers to a part of our February. See Hag. ii. 18.

8. *I saw by night.* The time was emblematical of the affliction under which the Jews groaned. *A man.* An angel in the form of a man; supposed to have been the Lord Jesus, who seems to have appeared often in this way, as a prelude to His incarnation; see Josh. v. 13; Ezek. i. 26; Dan. vii. 13; and x. 5. The same, probably, that appeared to Joshua with a drawn sword, as the captain of the Lord's host, Josh. v. 13-15. *A red horse.* An emblem of war and bloodshed.

Among the myrtle trees. This tree was an emblem of peace, intimating that all war was shortly to end.

9. *O my lord, what are these?* The angel here mentioned was distinct from those mentioned in the eighth verse; he who talked with the prophet, v. 13.

10. *The man that stood among the myrtle trees.* The angel of the covenant, as above, v. 11. *Whom the Lord hath sent.* Who are constituted guardians of the land.

MATTHEW HENRY

II. What the prophet heard, and what instructions were thereby given him. He heard the report which the angels made, *v.* 11. They had been out abroad, as flying posts, and, having returned, they give this account to the *Angel that stood among the myrtle-trees*: *We have walked to and fro through the earth, and, behold, all the earth sits still and is at rest.* We find the world of mankind here very careless: *All the earth sits still, and is at rest*, while all the church is made uneasy, *tossed with tempests and not comforted.* Those that are strangers to the church are secure; those that are enemies to it are successful. The Chaldeans and Persians dwell at ease, while the poor Jews are continually alarmed. He heard Christ's intercession with the Father for his afflicted Church, *v.* 12. The angels related the posture of affairs in this world, but we read not of any prayers they made for the redress of the grievances. It is *the Angel among the myrtle-trees* who is the great intercessor. Upon the report of the angels he immediately turned heavenward, and said, *Lord, wilt thou not have mercy* on thy church? *How long wilt thou not have mercy!* The objects of compassion are Jerusalem, the holy city, and the other cities of Judah that were now in ruins; for God had had *indignation against them* now *threescore and ten years.* So long the indignation lasted, and though *now for a little space grace* had been *shown them from the Lord their God*, to *give them some reviving* (Ezra ix. 8), yet the scars of those seventy years' captivity still remained deep. The captivity went off, as it came on, gradually. "Lord, we are still under the burden of the seventy years' wrath, *and wilt thou be angry with us for ever*?" He heard a gracious reply given to this intercession (*v.* 13): *The Lord answered the angel*, this angel of the covenant, *with good words and comfortable words*, with promises of mercy and deliverance, and the perfecting of what he had begun. He heard that reply which was given to the angel repeated to himself, with a commission to publish it to the children of his people, for their comfort. Now that God would *speak comfortably to Jerusalem*, Zechariah is *the voice of one crying in the wilderness, Prepare you the way of the Lord. The voice said, Cry.* The prophets must now cry as loudly to show God's people their comforts as ever they did formerly to show them *their transgressions*, Isa. xl. 2, 3, 6. He must proclaim the wrath God has in store for the enemies of Jerusalem, *v.* 14. The earth *sat still and was at rest* (*v.* 11), not relenting at all for all the mischief they had done to Jerusalem (*v.* 15). God is displeased with those who help forward the affliction even of such as suffer justly; for true humanity, in such a case, is good divinity. He must cry, "*Thus saith the Lord, I have returned to Jerusalem with mercies* (*v.* 16).

I was going away in wrath, but I am now returning in love" (*v.* 17). *The Lord*, even the Lord of hosts, assures them, the temple, though it meet with much discouragement, shall be perfected, and they shall have the tokens of God's presence. Jerusalem shall again be *built as a city compact together. A line shall be stretched forth upon Jerusalem*, in order to the rebuilding of it with exactness and uniformity. The nation shall again become populous and rich. Not only Jerusalem, but other cities that are reduced, shall yet *spread abroad.* The cities that should thus increase God calls his cities; they are *blessed* by him, and they are *fruitful and multiply, and replenish the land.* God has comforts in reserve for Zion and all her mourners. As he first built them up into a people when he brought them out of Egypt, so he will now rebuild them, when he brings them out of Babylon.

Verses 18–21

In this vision (the second which this prophet had), we have an illustration of God's Spirit making a stand, and making head, against the formidable power of the church's adversaries.

I. We have here the enemies of the church threatening to be its death: *I looked and behold four horns* (*v.* 18), which are explained *v.* 19.

JAMIESON, FAUSSET, BROWN

angels report to the Lord of angels, "the earth . . . is at rest." The flourishing state of the heathen "earth," while Judah was desolate and its temple not yet restored, is the powerful plea in the Divine Angel's intercession with God the Father in vs. 12. When Judah was depressed to the lowest point, and the heathen elated to the highest, it was time for Jehovah to work for His people. **sitteth still**—dwells surely. **12.** Not only does Messiah *stand among* His people (the "myrtles," vs. 8), but intercedes for them with the Father ("Lord," or "Jehovah of hosts") effectively (vs. 13; Heb. 7:25). Cf. Psalm 102:13-20; Isaiah 62:6, 7, as to Judah's restoration in answer to prayer. **answered and said**—said *in continuation* of the discourse: *proceeded to say.* **how long**—Messiah's people pray similarly to their Head. Revelation 6:10, "How long. . . ." Heretofore it was vain to pray, but now that the divinely appointed "threescore and ten years" (Jer. 25:11; 29:10) are elapsed, it is time to pray to Thee for the fulfilment of Thy promise, seeing that Thy grace is not yet fully manifested, nor Thy promise fulfilled. God's promises are not to make us slothful, but to quicken our prayers. HENDERSON, dating the seventy years from the destruction of Jerusalem (588 B.C.), supposes two years of the seventy had yet to run (520 B.C.). **13. the Lord**—JEHOVAH, called "the angel of the Lord (Jehovah)" (vs. 12). **good words** *and* **comfortable words**—lit., "words, consolations." The subject of these consolatory words is stated in vs. 14, etc.; the promise of full re-establishment, Jeremiah 29:10, 11 (cf. Isa. 57:18; Hos. 11:8). **14. Cry**—Proclaim so as to be heard clearly by all (Isa. 40:6; 58:1). **I am jealous for Jerusalem**—As a husband jealous for his wife, wronged by others, so Jehovah is for Judah, who has been injured wantonly by the heathen (ch. 8:2; Num. 25:11, 13; I Kings 19:10; Joel 2:18). **15. very sore displeased with the heathen**—in contrast with "I was *but a little* displeased" with My people. God's displeasure with His people is temporary and for their chastening; with the heathen oppressors, it is final and fatal (Jer. 30:11). God's instruments for chastising His people, when He has done with them, He casts into the fire. **are at ease**—carnally secure. A stronger phrase than "is at rest" (vs. 11). They are "at ease," but as I am "sore displeased" with them, their ease is accursed. Judah is in "affliction," but as I love her and am jealous for her, she has every reason to be encouraged in prosecuting the temple work. **helped forward the affliction**—afflicted My people more than I desired. The heathen sought the utter extinction of Judah to gratify their own ambition and revenge (Isa. 47:6; Ezek. 25:3, 6; Obad. 10-17). **16. I am returned**—whereas in anger I had before withdrawn from her (Hos. 5:15). **with mercies**—not merely of one kind, nor once only, but repeated mercies. **my house shall be built**—which at this time (the second year of Darius, ch. 1:1) had only its foundations laid (Hag. 2:18). It was not completed till the sixth year of Darius (Ezra 6:15). **line**—(Job 38:5). The measuring-line for building, not hastily, but with measured regularity. Not only the temple, but *Jerusalem* also was to be rebuilt (Neh. 2:3, etc.; cf. ch. 2:1, 2). Also, as to the future temple and city, Ezekiel 41:3; 42; 43; 44; 45:6. **17. yet**—though heretofore lying in abject prostration. **My cities**—not only Jerusalem, but the subordinate *cities* of Judah. God claims them all as peculiarly *His*, and therefore will restore them. **through prosperity . . . spread abroad**—or *overflow;* metaphor from an overflowing vessel or fountain (cf. Prov. 5:16) [PEMBELLUS]. Abundance of fruits of the earth, corn and wine, and a large increase of citizens, are meant; also spiritual prosperity. **comfort Zion**—(Isa. 40:1, 2; 51:3). **choose**—(ch. 2:12; 3:2; Isa. 14:1). Here meaning, "*show by acts of loving-kindness* that He has chosen." His immutable *choice* from everlasting is the fountain whence flow all such particular acts of love.

18-21. SECOND VISION. *The power of the Jews' foes shall be dissipated.* **18. four horns**—To a pastoral people like the Jews the *horns* of the strongest in the herd naturally suggested a symbol of *power* and *pride* of conscious strength: hence *the ruling powers of the world* (Rev. 17:3, 12). The number *four* in Zechariah's time referred to the four cardinal points of the horizon. Wherever God's people turned, there were foes to encounter (Neh. 4:7); the Assyrian, Chaldean, and Samaritan on the north; Egypt and Arabia on the south; Philistia on the west; Ammon and Moab on the east. But the Spirit in the prophet looked farther; viz., to the *four* world powers, the only ones which were, or are, to rise till the kingdom of Messiah, the fifth, overthrows and absorbs all others in its universal

ADAM CLARKE

11. *All the earth sitteth still, and is at rest.* There is general peace through the Persian empire, and other states connected with Judea; but the Jews are still in affliction; their city is not yet restored, nor their Temple built.

12. *Then the angel of the Lord.* He who was among the myrtles—the Lord Jesus. *O Lord of hosts, how long?* Jesus Christ was not only the "Lamb slain from the foundation of the world," but was always the sole Mediator and Intercessor between God and man. *These threescore and ten years.* The time that had elapsed from the destruction of the Temple to the time in which the angel spoke.

13. *The Lord answered the angel.* And the angel told the prophet that the answer was gracious and comfortable. This answer is given in the next verse.

14. *I am jealous for Jerusalem.* I have for them a strong affection, and indignation against their enemies.

15. *I was but a little displeased.* I was justly displeased with My people, and I gave their enemies a commission against them; but they carried this far beyond My design by oppression and cruelty, and now they shall suffer in their turn.

16. *I am returned to Jerusalem with mercies.* Before, He came to them in judgments; and the principal mercy is, the house of the Lord shall be rebuilt, and the ordinances of the Lord re-established.

And a line shall be stretched forth. The circuit shall be determined, and the city built according to the line marked out.

17. *My cities . . . shall yet be spread abroad.* The whole land of Judea shall be inhabited, and the ruined cities restored.

18. *And behold four horns.* Denoting four powers by which the Jews had been oppressed: the Assyrians, Persians, Chaldeans, and Egyptians.

MATTHEW HENRY

They *are the horns which have scattered Judah, Israel, and Jerusalem,* that is, the Jews both in the country and in the city. They have *tossed them* (so some read it), as furious bulls with their horns toss. They have scattered them, *so that no man did lift up his head, v.* 21. They are *four horns,* for the Jews are surrounded with them on every side. The men of Judah and of Jerusalem, and many of Israel that joined themselves to them, set about building the temple; but enemies from all sides drove them from it. Rehum, and Shimshai, and the other Samaritans that opposed the building of the temple, were these horns, Ezra iv. 8. So were Sanballat and Tobiah, and the Ammonites and Arabians, that opposed the building of the wall, Neh. iv. 7.

II. The friends of the church active and prevailing. The prophet did himself see the four horns, but *the Lord* then *showed him four carpenters,* or *smiths,* who were empowered to cut off these horns, *v.* 20, 21. With an eye of sense we see the power of the enemies of the church; but it is with an eye of faith that we see it safe, notwithstanding. *Carpenters* or *smiths* (for they are supposed by some to have been horns of iron) were the men who had skill and ability to break the horns. Some by these four carpenters understand Zerubbabel and Joshua, Ezra and Nehemiah, who carried on the work of God in spite of the opposition.

JAMIESON, FAUSSET, BROWN

dominion. Babylon and Medo-Persia alone had as yet risen, but soon Græco-Macedonia was to succeed (as ch. 9:13 foretells), and Rome the fourth and last, was to follow (Daniel, chs. 2 and 7). The fact that the repairing of the evils caused to Judah and Israel by *all four* kingdoms is spoken of here, proves that the exhaustive fulfilment is yet future, and only the earnest of it given in the overthrow of the two world powers which up to Zechariah's time had "scattered" Judah (Jer. 51:2; Ezek. 5:10, 12). That only two of the four had as yet risen, is an argument having no weight with us, as we believe God's Spirit in the prophets regards the future as present; we therefore are not to be led by Rationalists who on such grounds deny the reference here and in ch. 6:1 to the four world kingdoms. **19. Judah, Israel**—Though some of the ten tribes of *Israel* returned with *Judah* from Babylon, the full return of the former, as of the latter, is here foretold and must be yet future. **20. four carpenters**—or "artificers." The several instrumentalities employed, or to be employed, in crushing the "Gentile" powers which "scattered" Judah, are hereby referred to. For every one of the *four horns* there was a cleaving "artificer" to beat it down. For every enemy of God's people, God has provided a counteracting power adequate to destroy it. **21. These are the horns**—rather, *Those* . . . viz., the horns being distinguished from the "carpenters," or destroying workmen ("skilful to destroy," Exod. 21:31), intended in the "these" of the question. **no man . . . lift up his head**—so depressed were they with a heavy weight of evils (Job 10:15). **to fray**—*to strike terror into* them (Ezek. 30:9). **lifted up . . . horn**—in the haughtiness of conscious strength (Ps. 75:4, 5) tyrannizing over Judah (Ezek. 34:21).

ADAM CLARKE

20. *Four carpenters.* Four other powers, who should defeat the powers intended by the horns. These are the same as the four chariots mentioned in chap. vi. 1-3, 6-7. The first was Nabopolassar, father of Nebuchadnezzar, who overturned the empire of the Assyrians. The second was Cyrus, who destroyed the empire of the Chaldeans. The third was Alexander the Great, who destroyed the empire of the Persians. And the fourth was Ptolemy, who rendered himself master of Egypt.

21. *These are come to fray them.* To break, pound, and reduce them to powder. *Charashim* signifies either "carpenters" or "smiths"; probably the latter are here intended, who came with hammers, files, and suchlike, to destroy these horns, which no doubt seemed to be of iron.

MATTHEW HENRY

CHAPTER 2

Verses 1–5

This prophet was to assure the people (*ch.* i. 16) that a *line should be stretched forth upon Jerusalem.*

I. He sees, in a vision, a man going to measure Jerusalem (*v.* 1, 2): *He lifted up his eyes again, and looked.* In the close of the foregoing chapter he had seen Jerusalem's enemies baffled and broken, so now he begins to hope she shall not be ruined. *The man Christ Jesus,* whom the prophet sees *with a measuring line in his hand,* is the master builder of his church (Heb. iii. 3), and he builds exactly by line and level. Zechariah asked him *whither he was going* with that measuring line. And he readily told him that he was going to *measure Jerusalem,* to take account of the dimensions of it each way, that it might be computed what was necessary for the making of a wall about it, and by comparing its dimensions with the vast numbers that should inhabit it, what additions were necessary to be made. When multitudes flock to Jerusalem (Isa. lx. 4) it is time for her to *enlarge the place of her tent,* Isa. liv. 2.

II. He is informed that this vision means well to Jerusalem. The *angel that talked with* the prophet *went forth,* but *another angel went out to meet him,* to desire that he would first explain this vision to the prophet for his encouragement (*v.* 4): *Jerusalem shall be inhabited as towns without walls;* it shall extend itself far beyond the present dimensions. It shall be extended as freely as if it had no walls at all, and yet shall be as safe as if it had the strongest walls, such a *multitude of men* (which are the best walls of a city) *shall there be therein.* It shall be safe, for God himself will be a *wall of fire round about it.* Jerusalem had no walls about it at this time, but now God will be unto her a wall of fire. Some think it alludes to shepherds that made fires about their flocks, or travellers that made fires about their tents in desert places, to frighten wild beasts from them. He will himself be such a wall; a wall of fire round about on every side. God himself *will be the glory in the midst of it.* Now all this was fulfilled in part in Jerusalem, which in process of time became a very flourishing city, beyond what could have been expected, considering how low it was brought and how long it was ere it recovered itself.

Verses 6–9

One would have thought that Cyrus's proclamation, which gave liberty to the captive Jews to return to their own land, would suffice to bring them all back, but it had not that effect. There were about 40,000

JAMIESON, FAUSSET, BROWN

CHAPTER 2

Vss. 1-13. THIRD VISION. *The man with the measuring line.* The city shall be fully restored and enlarged (vss. 2-5). Recall of the exiles (vss. 6, 7). Jehovah will protect His people and make their foes a spoil unto them (vss. 8, 9). The nations shall be converted to Jehovah, as the result of His dwelling manifestly amidst His people (vss. 10-13). **1. man with a measuring-line**—the same image to represent the same future fact as in Ezekiel 40:3; 41, 42. The "man" is Messiah (*Note,* ch. 1:8), who, by measuring Jerusalem, is denoted as the Author of its coming restoration. Thus the Jews are encouraged in Zechariah's time to proceed with the building. Still more so shall they be hereby encouraged in the future restoration. **2. To measure Jerusalem**—(Cf. Rev. 11:1; 21:15, 16). **to see what** *is* **the breadth . . . what** *is* **the length**—rather, what *is to be the due* breadth and length. **3. angel that talked with me . . . another angel**—The interpreting angel is met by another angel sent by the measuring Divine Angel to "run" to Zechariah (vs. 4). Those who perform God's will must not merely creep, nor walk, but *run* with alacrity. **went forth**—viz., from me (Zechariah). **went out**—from the measuring angel. **4. this young man**—So Zechariah is called as being still a *youth* when prophetically inspired [GROTIUS]. Or, he is so called in respect to his *ministry* or *service* (cf. Num. 11:27; Josh. 1:1) [VATABLUS]. Naturally the "angel that talked with" Zechariah is desired to "speak to" him the further communications to be made from the Divine Being. **towns without walls for the multitude . . . cattle**—So many shall be its inhabitants that all could not be contained within the walls, but shall spread out in the open country around (Esther 9:19); and so secure shall they be as not to need to shelter themselves and their cattle behind walls. So hereafter Judea is to be "the land of unwalled villages" (Ezek. 38:11). Spiritually, now the Church has extended herself beyond the walls (Eph. 2:14, 15) of Mosaic ordinances and has spread from cities to country villages, whose inhabitants gave their Latin name (*pagani*) to *pagans,* as being the last in parting with heathenism. **5. I . . . wall of fire round**—Cf. vs. 4. Yet as a city needs some wall, I JEHOVAH will act as one of fire which none durst approach (ch. 9:8; Isa. 26:1). **glory in the midst**—not only a defense from foes outside, but a *glory* within (Isa. 60:19; Rev. 21:23). The same combination of "glory and defense" is found in Isaiah 4: 5, alluding to the pillar of cloud and fire which defended and enlightened Israel in the desert. Cf. Elisha in Dothan (II Kings 6:17). As God is to be her "glory," so she shall be His "glory" (Isa. 62:3). **6. flee from the land of the north**—i.e., from Babylon: a type of the various Gentile lands, from which the Jews are to be recalled hereafter; hence "the four winds of

ADAM CLARKE

CHAPTER 2

1. *A man with a measuring line in his hand.* Probably a representation of Nehemiah, who got a commission from Artaxerxes Longimanus to build up the walls of Jerusalem; for hitherto it had remained without being enclosed.

4. *Run, speak to this young man.* Nehemiah must have been a *young man* when he was cupbearer to Artaxerxes.

As towns without walls. It shall be so numerously inhabited as not to be contained within its ancient limits. Josephus, speaking of this time, says, *Wars* v. iv. 2, "The city, overflowing with inhabitants, by degrees extended itself beyond its walls."

5. *I . . . will be unto her a wall of fire.* Her safety shall consist in My defense. I shall be as *fire round about* her. No adversary shall be permitted to touch her. Much of this must refer to the New Jerusalem.

6. *Flee from the land of the north.* From Chaldea, Persia, and Babylon, where several of the Jews still remained. See v. 7.

MATTHEW HENRY

whose spirits God stirred up to go, and they went; but many stayed behind. The land of their captivity was to most of them the land of their nativity; they had taken root there. They had no great affection to their own land, and apprehended the difficulties insuperable. This proceeded from a distrust of the power and promise of God, a love of ease and worldly wealth, and an indifference to the religion of their country and to the God of Israel himself; and it was a tacit censure of those that did return. Here is therefore another proclamation by the God of Israel, commanding all his free-born subjects, wherever dispersed, speedily to return into their own land. They are loudly summoned (*v.* 6): *Ho! ho! come forth, and flee from the land of the north, saith the Lord.* This fitly follows upon the promise of the rebuilding of Jerusalem. If God will build it for them they must come and inhabit it for him and his glory, and not continue sneaking in Babylon. They are now dispersed, but should unite for their mutual common defence (*v.* 6): "*I have spread you abroad as the four winds of heaven*, some into one corner of the world and some into another, and you should now think of coming together again, to help one another." They are now to assert their liberty: "*Deliver thyself, O Zion!*" When Christ has proclaimed that deliverance to the captives which he has himself wrought, it concerns each of us to *deliver ourselves*, and, since we are under grace, to resolve that *sin shall not have dominion over us. Deliver thyself, O Zion!* by a speedy return to thy own land, and do not destroy thyself by continuing in that polluted land. God now espouses their cause and will plead it with jealousy, *v.* 8, 9. The *angel that talked with* the prophet (that is, Jesus Christ) tells him what he had commission to do for their protection and the perfecting of their salvation. Christ, who is the *Lord of hosts, says, He* (that is, the Father) *has sent me.* He is sent *after the glory.* Christ is sent, in the first place, to the nation and people of the Jews, *to whom pertained the glory*, Rom. ix. 4. But *after the glory*, after his care of them, he is *sent to the nations, to be a light to lighten the Gentiles*, by the power of his gospel to captivate them, and bring them into obedience to himself. He is *sent to the nations that spoiled them*, to take vengeance on them for the wrongs done to Zion. *They shall be a spoil to their servants*, shall be enslaved to those whom they had enslaved. The promise is fulfilled in Christ's victory over our spiritual enemies, his *spoiling principalities and powers and making a show of them openly*, Col. ii. 15. What he will do for his church shall be proof of God's affection for it: *He that touches you touches the apple of his eye.* He takes what is done against her as done against the very apple of his eye, the tenderest part, which nature has put a double guard upon. See (Ps. xvii. 8), *Keep me as the apple of the eye;* and (Prov. vii. 2), *Keep his law as the apple of thy eye.*

Verses 10–13

Joy proclaimed to the church of God, to the *daughter of Zion*, that had separated herself from the *daughter of Babylon.* The Jews that had returned were in distress, their enemies in the neighbourhood were spiteful, their friends that remained in Babylon were cool and declined coming in to their assistance; and yet they are directed to *sing*, and to *rejoice* even in tribulation.

I. God will have a people among them. If their brethren in Babylon will not come to them, those of other nations shall: *Many nations shall be joined to the Lord in that day.* The Jewish nation, after the captivity, multiplied very much, by the accession of proselytes to it, that were naturalized, and entitled to the privileges of native Israelites. It was strange that that should be so great an offence to the Jews in the apostles' times, which was promised as a blessing in the prophets' times.

II. They shall have his presence among them: *Sing and rejoice, for I come.* 1. In the dedication of the temple, in their regularly observing all God's institutions there. Those have God *dwelling in the midst of them.* 2. In the incarnation of Christ. He that promises to dwell among them is that *Lord whom the Lord of hosts has sent* (*v.* 11), and therefore must be the *Lord Jesus*, the eternal *Word*, that was *made flesh, and dwelt among us.*

III. They shall have all their ancient dignities and privileges restored to them again, *v.* 12. Canaan shall be a holy land again. Judah shall be in this holy land, and no longer be scattered in Babylon. Judah shall be God's portion in which he will be glorified. God will protect his people and govern them as a man does his inheritance. He will *choose Jerusalem again*, will continue it a chosen place, till it must resign its honours to the Jerusalem that is from above.

IV. Here is silence proclaimed to all the world

JAMIESON, FAUSSET, BROWN

heaven" are specified, implying that they are to return from all quarters (Deut. 28:64; Jer. 16:15; Ezek. 17:21). The reason why they should flee from Babylon is: (1) because of the blessings promised to God's people in their own land; (2) because of the evils about to fall on their foe (vss. 7-9). Babylon was soon to fall before Darius, and its inhabitants to endure fearful calamities (Isa. 48: 20; Jer. 50:8; 51:6, 45). Many of the Jews in Zechariah's time had not yet returned to Judea. Their tardiness was owing to (1) unbelief; (2) their land had long lain waste, and was surrounded with bitter foes; (3) they regarded suspiciously the liberty of return given by Cyrus and Darius, as if these monarchs designed suddenly to crush them; (4) their long stay in Babylon had obliterated the remembrance of their own land; (5) the wealth and security there contrasted with Judea, where their temple and city were in ruins. All this betrayed foul ingratitude and disregard of God's extraordinary favor, which is infinitely to be preferred to all the wealth of the world [CALVIN and PEMBELLUS]. **for I have spread you abroad**—The reasoning is: I who scattered you from your land to all quarters, can also gather you again to it. **7. O Zion . . . daughter of Babylon**—Thou whose only sure dwelling is "Zion," inseparably connected with the temple, art altogether out of thy place in "dwelling with the daughter of Babylon" (i.e., Babylon and her people, Ps. 137:8; Isa. 1:8). **After the glory**—*After* restoring the "glory" (vs. 5; Isa. 4:5; Rom. 9:4) of Jehovah's presence to Jerusalem, He (God the Father) hath commissioned ME (God the Son, Isa. 48:16, the Divine Angel: God thus being at once the Sender and the Sent) to visit in wrath "the nations which spoiled you." Messiah's twofold office from the Father is: (1) to glorify His Church; (2) to punish its foes (II Thess. 1:7-10). Both offices manifest His *glory* (Prov. 16:4). **toucheth . . . the apple of his eye**—viz., of Jehovah's eye (Deut. 32:10; Ps. 17:8; Prov. 7:2). The pupil, or aperture, through which rays pass to the retina, is the tenderest part of the eye; the member which we most sedulously guard from hurt as being the dearest of our members; the one which feels most acutely the slightest injury, and the loss of which is irreparable. **9. shake . . . hand**—A mere wave of God's hand can prostrate all foes (cf. Ruth 1:13; Job 31:21; Isa. 11:15; 19:16; Acts 13:11). **a spoil to their servants**—to the Jews whom they had once as their slaves (cf. Isa. 14:2). As the Jews' state between the return from Babylon and Christ's coming was checkered with much adversity, this prophecy can only have its fulfilment under Christ. **sent me**—(Isa. 48:16; 61:1; John 10:36). **10. I will dwell in . . . midst of thee**—primarily at Messiah's first advent (Ps. 40:7; John 1:14; Col. 2:9; I Tim. 3:16); more fully at His second advent (Isa. 40:10). So ch. 9:9 where see the *Note* (Isa. 12:6; Ezek. 37:27; Zeph. 3:14). Meanwhile God dwells spiritually in His people (II Cor. 6:16). **11. many nations . . . joined to the Lord in that day**—The result of the Jews' exile in Babylon was that, at their subsequent return, through the diffusion of knowledge of their religion, many Gentiles became proselytes, worshipping in the court of the Gentiles (I Kings 8:41). Cyrus, Darius, Alexander, Ptolemy Philadelphus, Augustus, and Tiberius, paid respect to the temple by sending offerings [GROTIUS]. But all this is but a shadow of the future conversion of the Gentiles which shall result from Jehovah dwelling in Jerusalem (Ps. 102:15, 16; Phil. 2:10, 11). **sent me unto thee**—"unto thee" is here added to the same formula (vs. 9). Zion first shall "know (generally) that Jehovah of hosts hath sent" Messiah, by the judgments inflicted by Him on her foes. Subsequently, she shall know experimentally the particular *sending* of Messiah *unto her.* Jehovah here says, "*I* will dwell," and then that JEHOVAH of hosts sent Him; therefore Jehovah the Sender and Jehovah the Sent must be One. **12. Judah his portion in the holy land**—Lest the joining of the Gentile "nations to Jehovah" (vs. 11) should lead the Jews to fear that their peculiar relation to Him (Deut. 4:20; 9: 29; 32:9) as "His inheritance" should cease, this verse is added to assure them of His making them so hereafter "again." **choose Jerusalem again**—The course of God's grace was interrupted for a time, but His covenant was not set aside (Rom. 11:28, 29); the election was once for all, and therefore shall hold good for ever. **13. Be silent, O all flesh**—(Hab. 2:20.) "Let all in silent awe and reverence await the Lord's coming interposition in behalf of His people!" The address is both to the Gentile foes, who prided themselves on their power as if irresistible, and to the unbelieving Jews, who distrusted God's promises as incredible. Three rea-

ADAM CLARKE

8. *After the glory.* After your glorious deliverance from the different places of your dispersion. He hath *sent me unto the nations which spoiled you*, that they may fall under grievous calamities, and be punished in their turn. On Babylon a great calamity fell, when besieged and taken by the Persians.

9. *I will shake mine hand upon them.* I will threaten first, and then stretch out My hand of judgment against them. *A spoil to their servants.* To those whom they had formerly subjected to their sway. As the Babylonians to the Medes and Persians; and so of the rest in the subversion of empires.

10. *I will dwell in the midst of thee, saith the Lord.* This must chiefly refer to the Christian Church, in which God ever dwells by the power of His Spirit, as He had done by the symbol of His presence in the first Jewish temple.

11. *Many nations shall be joined to the Lord.* This most certainly belongs to the Christian Church. No nation or people ever became converts to the Jewish religion, but whole nations have embraced the faith of our Lord Jesus Christ.

12. *The Lord shall inherit Judah his portion in the holy land.* This is a promise of the final restoration of the Jews, and that they should be God's portion in their own land.

13. *Be silent, O all flesh.* Let all the nations of the world be astonished at this. God will arise, and deliver this ancient people, and bring them into the glorious liberty of the sons of God.

MATTHEW HENRY

besides, *v.* 13. The daughter of Zion must sing, but *all flesh* must *be silent.* God is about to do something unexpected and to plead his people's cause, which had long seemed neglected. Leave it to God to take his own way, and neither prescribe to him what he should do nor quarrel with him whatever he does. *Be still, and know that he is God. Stand still, and see his salvation.*

CHAPTER 3

Verses 1–7

There was a Joshua that was a principal agent in the first settling of Israel in Canaan; here is another of the same name very active in their second settlement there after the captivity; Jesus is the same name, and it signifies *Saviour*; they were both figures of him that was to come, our chief captain and our chief priest. The angel that talked with *Zechariah showed him Joshua the high priest*; it is probable that the prophet saw him frequently, and that there was a great intimacy between them; but then he only saw how he appeared before men; how he stands before the Lord must be shown him in vision. He *stood before the angel of the Lord*, to execute his office. He stood to consult the oracle on behalf of Israel. Guilt and corruption are our two great discouragements when we stand before God obnoxious to his justice and odious to his holiness.

I. Joshua is accused as a criminal, but is justified. 1. A violent opposition is made to him. *Satan stands at his right hand to resist him* as the prosecutor or witness. When God is about to re-establish the priesthood Satan objects the sins that were found among the priests. It is by our own folly that we give Satan advantage against us. We must expect to meet with all the resistance that Satan's subtlety and malice can give us. Let us then resist him and he shall flee from us.

2. A victorious defence is made (*v.* 2): *The Lord* (that is, the Lord Christ) *said unto Satan, The Lord rebuke thee.* It is the happiness of the saints that the Judge is their friend. Satan is here checked by one that has authority. *The Lord said* (that is, the Lord our Redeemer), *The Lord rebuke thee*, that is, the Lord the Creator. The power of God is engaged for the making of the grace of Christ effectual. Satan resists the priest, but his resistance will be to no purpose against Jerusalem, for *the Lord has chosen.* He knew the worst when he chose them. *Is not this a brand plucked out of the fire?* Joshua is so, and the priesthood, and the people, whose representative he is. Christ has that to say for them for which they are to be pitied. One can expect no other than that those who but the other day were captives in Babylon should appear mean and despicable. They have been wonderfully delivered out of the fire, that God might be glorified in them; will he then abandon them?

JAMIESON, FAUSSET, BROWN

sons why they must be silent are implied: (1) they are but "flesh," weak and ignorant; (2) He is JEHOVAH, all-wise and all-powerful; (3) He is already "raised up out of His place," and who can stand before Him? [PEMBELLUS], (Ps. 76:8, 9). **he is raised up out of his holy habitation**–i.e., out of *heaven* (Deut. 26:15; II Chron. 30:27; Isa. 63:15), to judge and avenge His people (Isa. 26:21); or, "out of His holy" *temple*, contemptible and incomplete as it looked then when Zechariah urged them to rebuild it [CALVIN]. But the call to all to "be silent" is rather when God has come forth from heaven where so long He has dwelt unseen, and is about to inflict vengeance on the foe, *before* taking up His dwelling in Zion and the temple. However, Psalm 50:1, 2 ("Out of Zion"), 3 (cf. Hab. 2:3), 4, favors CALVIN's view. God is now "silent" while the Gentile foe speaks arrogance against His people; but "our God shall come and *no longer keep silence*"; then in turn must all flesh "be silent" before Him.

CHAPTER 3

Vss. 1-10. FOURTH VISION. *Joshua the high priest before the angel of Jehovah; accused by Satan, but justified by Jehovah through Messiah the coming Branch.* **1.** Joshua as high priest (Hag. 1:1) represents "Jerusalem" (vs. 2), or the elect people, put on its trial, and "plucked" narrowly "out of the fire." His attitude, "standing before the Lord," is that of a high priest ministering before the altar erected previously to the building of the temple (Ezra 3:2, 3, 6; Ps. 135:2). Yet, in this position, by reason of his own and his people's sins, he is represented as on his and their trial (Num. 35:12). **he showed me**–"He" is *the interpreting angel.* Jerusalem's (Joshua's) "filthy garments" (vs. 3) are its sins which had hitherto brought down God's judgments. The "change of raiment" implies its restoration to God's favor. Satan suggested to the Jews that so consciously polluted a priesthood and people could offer no acceptable sacrifice to God, and therefore they might as well desist from the building of the temple. Zechariah encourages them by showing that their demerit does not disqualify them for the work, as they are accepted in the righteousness of another, their great High Priest, the Branch (vs. 8), a scion of their own royal line of David (Isa. 11:1). The full accomplishment of Israel's justification and of Satan the accuser's being "rebuked" finally, is yet future (Rev. 12:10). Cf. Revelation 11:8, wherein "Jerusalem," as here, is shown to be meant primarily, though including the whole Church in general (cf. Job 1:9). **Satan**–the *Hebrew* term meaning "adversary" in a law court: as *devil* is the *Greek* term, meaning *accuser.* Messiah, on the other hand, is "advocate" for His people in the court of heaven's justice (I John 2:1). **standing at his right hand**–the usual position of a *prosecutor* or *accuser* in court, as the left hand was the position of the defendant (Ps. 109:6). The "angel of the Lord" took the same position just before another high priest was about to beget the forerunner of Messiah (Luke 1:11), who supplants Satan from his place as accuser. Some hence explain Jude 9 as referring to this passage: "the body of Moses" being thus *the Jewish Church*, for which Satan contended as his by reason of its sins; just as the "body of Christ" is *the Christian Church.* However, Jude 9 plainly speaks of the literal body of Moses, the resurrection of which at the transfiguration Satan seems to have opposed on the ground of Moses' error at Meribah; the same divine rebuke, "the Lord rebuke thee," checked Satan in contending for judgment against Moses' body, as checked him when demanding judgment against the Jewish Church, to which Moses' body corresponds. **2. the Lord**–JEHOVAH, hereby identified with the "angel of the Lord (Jehovah)" (vs. 1). **rebuke thee**–twice repeated to express the certainty of Satan's accusations and machinations against Jerusalem being frustrated. Instead of lengthened argument, Jehovah *silences* Satan by the one plea, viz., God's *choice.* **chosen Jerusalem**–(Rom. 9:16; 11:5). The conclusive answer. If the issue rested on Jerusalem's merit or demerit, condemnation must be the award; but Jehovah's "choice" (John 15:16) rebuts Satan's charge against Jerusalem (ch. 1:17; 2:16; Rom. 8:33, 34, 37), represented by Joshua (cf. in the great atonement, Lev. 16:6-20, etc.), not that she may continue in sin, but be freed from it (vs. 7). **brand plucked out of . . . fire**–(Amos 4:11; I Pet. 4:18; Jude 23). Herein God implies that His acquittal of Jerusalem is not that He does not recognize her sin (vss. 3, 4, 9), but that having punished

ADAM CLARKE

CHAPTER 3

1. *And he shewed me Joshua the high priest.* The Angel of the Lord is the Messiah, as we have seen before. Joshua, the high priest, may here represent the whole Jewish people; and *Satan*, the grand accuser of the brethren.

There is a paraonomasia here: *Satan standing at his right hand to resist him.* Satan signifies an "adversary." *Lesiteno*, "to be his adversary," or accuser.

2. *Is not this a brand plucked out of the fire?* The Jews were nearly destroyed because of their sins; a remnant of them is yet left, and God is determined to preserve them. He has had mercy upon them, and forgiven them their sins. Would you have them destroyed?

MATTHEW HENRY

II. Joshua appears as one polluted, but is purified; for he represents the Israel of God, who are all *as an unclean thing. He was clothed,* not only in coarse, but in *filthy garments,* such as did very ill become the dignity of his office, and the sanctity of his work, Exod. xxviii. 2. Joshua's garments were a shame and reproach; yet in them *he stood before the angel of the Lord;* he had no clean linen wherein to minister. This intimates, not only that the priesthood was poor and despised, and loaded with contempt, but that there was iniquity cleaving to the holy things. The returned Jews, because they were free from idolatry, thought themselves chargeable with no iniquity. But God showed them there were many things amiss in them. There were spiritual enemies warring against them, Ezra x. 18. Yet Joshua was permitted to *stand before the angel of the Lord.* Provision was made for his cleansing. Two things are done for Joshua, representing a double work of divine grace wrought in and for believers: (1) His filthy garments are taken from him, *v.* 4. The meaning of this is given us in what Christ said, and he said it as one having authority, *Behold, I have caused thy iniquity to pass from thee.* When God forgives our sins he *causes our iniquity to pass from us,* he sanctifies the nature and enables us to *put off the old man,* to cast away from us the filthy rags of our corrupt affections and lusts. (2) He is clothed anew, has not only the shame of his filthiness removed, but the shame of his nakedness covered: *I will clothe thee with change of raiment.* Joshua had no clean linen of his own, but he shall appear as lovely as ever he appeared loathsome. Thus those whom Christ makes spiritual priests are clothed with the spotless robe of his righteousness and appear before God in that, and with the graces of his Spirit, which are ornaments to them.

III. Joshua is re-installed and established in his office. 1. The crown of the priesthood is put upon him, *v.* 5. This was done at the request of the prophet. When God designs the restoring or reviving of religion he stirs up his prophets and people to pray for it, and does it in answer to their prayers. Zechariah prayed that the angels might be ordered to set the mitre on Joshua's head, and they did it immediately, and *clothed him with* the priestly *garments.* 2. The covenant of the priesthood is renewed with him, which is called God's *covenant of peace,* Num. xxv. 12. It is *the patent of his office,* which is here declared and delivered to him before witnesses, *v.* 6, 7. Joshua must *walk in God's ways,* must go before the people in the paths of God's commandments, and walk circumspectly.

He must also *keep God's charge,* and must see to it that the inferior priests performed the duties of their place. Let him be sure to do his part, and God will own him. The high priest might not make any new laws for God's house, nor ordain any other rites of worship; but he must judge God's house, that is, he must see to it that God's laws and ordinances were observed.

"Thou shalt also keep my courts; thou shalt have oversight of all the courts of the temple, and keep them in good order for worship to be performed in them." *I will give thee places to walk among those that stand by.* Those that *walk in God's ways* may be said to *walk among the angels* themselves, for they do the will of God as the angels do it that are in heaven, and are their *fellow-servants,* Rev. xix. 10.

Verses 8–10

As the promises made to David often slide insensibly into promises of the Messiah, whose kingdom David's was a type of, so the promises here made to Joshua rise as far upward, and look as far forward, as to Christ, of whose priesthood Joshua's was now a shadow. Christ is a high priest, as Joshua was, for sinners and sufferers.

I. The promise of Christ (*v.* 8): *"Hear now, O Joshua!* Thou hast heard what belongs to thyself; but, behold, a greater than Joshua is at hand. *Hear now* concerning him, *thou* and the rest of the priests, *thy fellows, who sit before thee* as learners."

JAMIESON, FAUSSET, BROWN

her people for it with a seventy years' captivity, He on the ground of His *electing* love has delivered her from the fiery ordeal; and when once He has begun a deliverance, as in this case, He will perfect it (Ps. 89:30-35; Phil. 1:6). **3. filthy garments**—symbol of sin (Prov. 30:12; Isa 4:4; 64:6); proving that it is not on the ground of His people's righteousness that He accepts them. Here primarily the "filthy garments" represent the abject state temporally of the priesthood and people at the return from Babylon. Yet he "stood before the angel." Abject as he was, he was *before Jehovah's eye,* who graciously accepts His people's services, though mixed with sin and infirmity. **4. those that stood before him**—the ministering angels (cf. the phrase in I Kings 10:8; Dan. 1:5). **Take away the filthy garments**—In vs. 9 it is "remove the iniquity of *that land";* therefore Joshua represents the land. **from him**—lit., "from upon him"; pressing upon him as an overwhelming burden. **change of raiment**—festal robes of the high priest, most costly and gorgeous; symbol of Messiah's imputed righteousness (Matt. 22:11). The restoration of the glory of the priesthood is implied: first, partially, at the completion of the second temple; fully realized in the great High Priest *Jesus,* whose name is identical with *Joshua* (Heb. 4:8), the Representative of Israel, the "kingdom of priests" (Exod. 19:6); once clad in the filthy garments of our vileness, but being the chosen of the Father (Isa. 42:1; 44:1; 49:1-3), He hath by death ceased from sin, and in garments of glory entered the heavenly holy place as our High Priest (Heb. 8:1; 9:24). Then, as the consequence (I Pet. 2:5), realized in the Church generally (Luke 15:22; Rev. 19:8), and in Israel in particular (Isa. 61:10, cf. 3:6; 66:21). **5. And I said**—Here the prophet, rejoicing at the change of raiment so far made, interposes to ask for the crowning assurance that the priesthood would be fully restored, viz., the putting *the miter* or priestly turban on Joshua: its *fair* color symbolizing the official purity of the order restored. He does not command, but prays; not "Set," but "Let them set." *Vulgate* and *Syriac* version read it, *"He* then said," which is the easier reading; but the very difficulty of the present *Hebrew* reading makes it less likely to come from a modern corrector of the text. **angel of . . . Lord stood by**—the Divine Angel had been sitting (the posture of a judge, Dan. 7:9); now He "stands" to see that Zechariah's prayer be executed, and then to give the charge (vss. 6, 7). **6. protested**—proceeded *solemnly to declare.* A forensic term for an affirmation on oath (Heb. 6:17, 18). God thus solemnly states the end for which the priesthood is restored to the people, His own glory in their obedience and pure worship, and their consequent promotion to heavenly honor. **7.** God's *choice* of Jerusalem (vs. 2) was unto its sanctification (John 15:16; Rom. 8:29); hence the charge here which connects the promised blessing with obedience. **my charge**—the ordinances, ritual and moral (Num. 3:28, 31, 32, 38; Josh. 1:7-9; I Kings 2:3; Ezek. 44:16). **judge my house**—Thou shalt long preside over the temple ceremonial as high priest (Lev. 10:10; Ezek. 44:23; Mal. 2:7) [GROTIUS]. Or, rule over My house, i.e., My people [MAURER] (Num. 12:7; Hos. 8:1). We know from Deuteronomy 17:9 that the priest judged cases. He was not only to obey the Mosaic institute himself, but to see that it was obeyed by others. God's people are similarly to exercise judgment hereafter, as the reward of their present faithfulness (Dan. 7:18, 22; Luke 19:17; I Cor. 6:2); by virtue of their royal priesthood (Rev. 1:6). **keep my courts**—guard My house from profanation. **places to walk**—free ingress and egress (I Sam. 18:16; I Kings 3:7; 15:17), so that thou mayest go through these ministering angels who stand by Jehovah (ch. 4:14; 6:5; I Kings 23:19) into His presence, discharging thy priestly function. In Ezekiel 42:4 the same *Hebrew* word is used of a *walk* before the priests' chambers in the future temple. Zechariah probably refers here to such a *walk* or *way;* Thou shalt not merely walk among priests like thyself, as in the old temple *walks,* but among the very angels as thine associates. HENGSTENBERG translates, "I will give thee *guides* (from) among these . . . ." But there is no "from" in the *Hebrew; English Version* is therefore better. Priests are called *angels* or "messengers" (Mal. 2:7); they are therefore thought worthy to be associated with heavenly angels. So these latter are present at the assemblies of true Christian worshippers (I Cor. 11:10; cf. Eccles. 5:6; Eph. 3:10; Rev. 22:9). **8. Hear**—On account of the magnitude of what He is about to say, He at once demands solemn attention. **thy fellows that sit before thee**—thy subordinate colleagues in the priesthood; not that they were

ADAM CLARKE

3. *Joshua was clothed with filthy garments.* The Jewish people were in a most forlorn, destitute, and to all human appearance despicable, condition; and besides all, they were sinful, and the priesthood defiled by idolatry; and nothing but the mercy of God could save them.

4. *Take away the filthy garments.* The Jews wore sackcloth in times of public calamity; probably the filthy garments refer to this. Let their clothing be changed. I have turned again their captivity; I will fully restore them, and blot out all their iniquities.

5. *A fair mitre upon his head.* To signify that he had renewed to him the office of the high priesthood, which had been defiled and profaned before. The *mitre* was the bonnet which the high priest put on his head when he entered into the sanctuary, Exod. xxviii. 4, etc. *Clothed him with garments.* Referring to the vestments of the high priest.

ALEXANDER MACLAREN:

There are two images blended together in the great words of my text; the one is that of the king's court, the other is that of a temple. With regard to the former it is a privilege given to the highest nobles of a kingdom—or it was so in old days—to have the right of *entrée,* at all moments and in all circumstances, to the monarch. With regard to the latter, the prerogative of the high priest, who was the recipient of this promise, as to access to the Temple, was a very restricted one. Once a year, with the blood that prevented his annihilation by the brightness of the Presence into which he ventured, he passed within the veil, and stood before that mysterious Light that coruscated in the darkness of the Holy of Holies. But this High Priest is promised an access on all days and at all times; and that He may stand there, beside and like the seraphim, who with one pair of wings veiled their faces in token of the incapacity of the creature to behold the Creator; "with twain veiled their feet" in token of the unworthiness of creatural activities to be set before Him, "and with twain did fly" in token of their willingness to serve him with all their energies. This Priest passes within the veil when He will. Or, to put away the two metaphors, and to come to the reality far greater than either of them, we can, whensoever we please, pass into the presence before which the splendors of an earthly monarch's court shrink into vulgarity, and attain to a real reception of the light that irradiates the true Holy Place, before which that which shone in the earthly shrine dwindles and darkens into a shadow.

—*Expositions of Holy Scripture*

MATTHEW HENRY

They are set *for signs*, for types and figures of Christ's priesthood. They are *men of wonder*; they are amazed to think how happily their condition is altered.

II. The promise itself consists of several parts designed for the encouragement of Joshua and his friends in that great work of building the temple. 1. The Messiah shall come: *Behold, I will bring forth my servant the branch.* He is the branch; so he was called; Isa. iv. 2, *The branch of the Lord.* Isa. xi. 1, *A branch out of the roots of Jesse.* His beginning was small, as a tender branch, but in time he should become a great tree, Isa. liii. 2, the branch from which all our fruit must be gathered. He is *the stone laid before Joshua*, alluding to the foundation, or chief corner-stone, of the temple, which probably was laid, with great solemnity, in the presence of Joshua. Christ is not only the branch, which is the beginning of a tree, but the foundation, which is the beginning of a building.

Seven eyes shall be upon him. The eye of his Father was upon him, to protect him, especially in his sufferings. The eyes of all the prophets and Old Testament saints were upon this one stone. The eyes of all believers are upon him; they look unto him and are saved.

I will engrave the graving thereof, saith the Lord of hosts. This stone the builders refused, as rough and unsightly; but God undertakes to smooth and polish it and to carve it so that it shall be the *head stone of the corner.* This stone is a *precious stone*, though laid for a *foundation*; and the *graving* of it seems to allude to the precious stones in the breastplate of the high priest, Exod. xxviii. 21, 22. By him sin shall be taken away, both the guilt and the dominion of it: *I will remove the iniquity of that land in one day.* When the high priest had the names of Israel engraven on the precious stones he was adorned with he is said to *bear the iniquity of the holy things* (Exod. xxviii. 38). He bore the iniquity of the land, as a type of Christ; but he could not remove it; the doing of that was reserved for Christ, that blessed *Lamb of God, that takes away the sin of the world.* Some make the engravings wherewith God engraved him to signify the wounds and stripes which were given to his blessed body, which he underwent for our *transgression*, and *by which we are healed.* The effect of all this shall be (*v.* 10): *In that day you shall call every man his neighbour under the vine and fig tree.* When iniquity is taken away we repose in tranquillity and are quiet from the fear of evil. We sit down under Christ's shadow with delight, and by it are sheltered from the scorching heat of the curse of the law.

JAMIESON, FAUSSET, BROWN

actually then *sitting before him;* but their usual posture in consultations was on chairs or benches before him, while he sat on an elevated seat as their president. **they are**—From speaking to Joshua He passes to speaking *of him and them,* in the third person, to the attendant angels (cf. vs. 9). **men wondered at**—*Hebrew,* "men of wonder," i.e., having a typical character (Isa. 8:18; 20:3; Ezek. 12:11; 24:24). Joshua the high priest typifies Messiah, as Joshua's "fellows" typify believers whom Messiah admits to share His Priesthood (I Pet. 2:5; Rev. 5:10). This, its typical character, then, is a pledge to assure the desponding Jews that the priesthood shall be preserved till the great Antitype comes. There may be also an indirect reproof of the unbelief of the multitude who "wonder" at God's servants and even at God's Son incredulously (Ps. 71:7; Isa. 8:18; 53:1, etc.). **behold**—marking the greatness of what follows. **my servant**—the characteristic title of Messiah (Isa. 42:1; 49:3; 50:10; 52:13; 53:11; Ezek. 34:23, 24). **the Branch**—Messiah, a tender branch from the almost extinct royal line of David (ch. 6:12; Isa. 4:2; 11:1; Jer. 23:5; 33:15). Luke 1:78, where for "day spring," "branch" may be substituted (Mal. 4:2, however, favors *English Version*). The reference cannot be to Zerubbabel (as GROTIUS thinks), for *he* was then in the full discharge of his office, whereas "the Branch" here is regarded as future. **9. For**—expressing the ground for encouragement to the Jews in building the temple: I (Jehovah) have laid the (foundation) stone as the chief architect, before (in the presence of) Joshua, by "the hand of Zerubbabel" (ch. 4:10; Ezra 3:8-13), so that your labor in building shall not be vain. Antitypically, the (foundation) stone alluded to is Christ, before called "the Branch." Lest any should think from that term that His kingdom is weak, He now calls it "the stone," because of its solidity and strength whereby it is to be the foundation of the Church, and shall crush all the world kingdoms (Ps. 118:22; cf. Isa. 28:16; Dan. 2:45; Matt. 21:42; I Cor. 3:11; I Pet. 2:6, 7). The angel pointing to the chief stone lying before Him, intimates that a deeper mystery than the material temple is symbolized. MOORE thinks the "stone" is *the Jewish Church,* which Jehovah engages watchfully to guard. *The temple,* rather, is that symbolically. But the antitype of the foundation *stone* is Messiah. **upon one stone shall be seven eyes**—viz., the watchful "eyes" of Jehovah's care ever fixed "upon" it (ch. 4:10) [MAURER]. The eye is the symbol of *Providence:* "seven," of *perfection* (Rev. 5:6; cf. II Chron. 16:9; Ps. 32:8). Antitypically, "the seven eyes upon the stone" are the eyes of all angels (I Tim. 3:16), and of all saints (John 3:14, 15; 12:32), and of the patriarchs and prophets (John 8:56; I Pet. 1:10, 11), fixed on Christ; above all, the eyes of the Father ever rest with delight on Him. CALVIN (perhaps better) considers *the seven eyes* to be *carved on the stone,* i.e., not the eyes of the Father and of angels and saints ever *fixed on* Him, but *His own* sevenfold (perfect) fullness of grace, and of gifts of the Spirit (Isa. 11:2, 3; John 1:16; 3:34; Col. 1:19; 2:9), and *His* watchful providence now for the Jews in building the temple, and always for His Church, His spiritual temple. Thus the "stone" is not as other stones senseless, but *living* and full of eyes of perfect intelligence (I Pet. 2:4, "a *living* stone"), who not only attracts the eyes (John 12:32) of His people, but emits illumination so as to direct them to Him. **engrave . . . graving**—implying Messiah's exceeding beauty and preciousness; alluding to the polished stones of the temple: Christ excelled them, as much as God who "prepared His body" (Heb. 10:5; cf. John 2:21) is superior to all human builders. **remove . . . iniquity of that land in one day**—i.e., the iniquity and its consequences, viz., the punishment to which the Jews heretofore had been subjected (Hag. 1:6, 9-11). The remission of sin is the fountain of every other blessing. The "one day" of its *removal* is primarily the day of national atonement celebrated after the completion of the temple (Lev. 23:27) on the tenth day of the seventh month. Antitypically, the atonement by Messiah for all men, *once for all* ("one day") offered, needing no repetition like the Mosaic sacrifices (Heb. 10:10, 12, 14). **10. under . . . vine . . . fig tree**—emblem of tranquil prosperity (I Kings 4:25). Type of spiritual *peace* with God through Christ (Rom. 5:1); and of millennial blessedness (Mic. 4:4).

ADAM CLARKE

9. *For behold the stone that I have laid.* Alluding no doubt to the foundation stone of the Temple. But this represented Christ Jesus: "Behold, I lay in Zion for a foundation a stone, a tried stone, a precious corner stone, a sure foundation," Isa. xxviii. 16.

Upon one stone shall be seven eyes. This is supposed to mean the providence of God, as under it all the work should be completed.

I will engrave the graving thereof. This is an allusion to engraving precious stones, in which the ancients greatly excelled. But what was *this* engraving? Was it not the following words? "I will remove the iniquity of that land in one day"; and was not this when Jesus Christ expired upon the Cross?

10. *Shall ye call every man his neighbour.* See Isa. xxxvi. 16. Everyone shall be inviting and encouraging another to believe on the Lord Jesus Christ, and thus taste and see that God is good. See Isa. ii. 2-3. And there shall be the utmost liberty to preach, believe on, and profess the faith of our Lord Jesus Christ.

MATTHEW HENRY

CHAPTER 4

Verses 1–10

I. The prophet prepared to receive the discovery: *The angel that talked with him came and waked him, v.* 1.

II. The discovery was made to him when he was prepared. He saw a *golden candlestick.* The church is a candlestick for the enlightening of this dark world and the holding of the light of divine revelation to it. The candle is God's; the church is but the candlestick. This golden candlestick had *seven lamps* branching out from it, so many sockets, in each of which was a burning and shining light. The Jewish church was but one, but now, under the gospel, Christ is the centre of unity, and not Jerusalem, or any place. This candlestick had one *bowl,* on the top, into which oil was continually dropping, and from it, by seven pipes, it was diffused to the seven lamps, so that, without any further care, they received oil as fast as they wasted it. They never wanted, nor were ever glutted, and so kept always burning clear. And the bowl too was continually supplied: without any man; for (*v.* 3) he saw *two olive-trees,* one on each side the candlestick, that of their own accord poured oil continually into the bowl, which by two larger pipes (*v.* 12) dispersed the oil to smaller ones and so to the lamps; so that nobody needed to attend this candlestick, which is to show that God easily can, and often does, accomplish his gracious purposes concerning his church, without the aid of man.

III. The enquiry which the prophet made concerning the meaning of this (*v.* 4): *I answered and spoke to the angel,* saying, *What are these, my lord?* He saw what these *were,* but asked what they *signified.* The angel answered him with a question, *Knowest thou not what these be?* He knew there was a golden candlestick in the tabernacle, which it was the priests' constant business to supply with oil. When therefore he saw such a candlestick, with lamps always kept burning, and yet no priests to attend it, he might discern the meaning of this to be that though God had set up the priesthood again, yet he could carry on his work for his people without them.

IV. The general intention of this vision is to assure the prophet that this work of building the temple should, by Providence, and divine grace, be brought to a happy issue, though the enemies of it were many and the friends few. This vision was to illustrate a word to Zerubbabel, to encourage him to go on with the building of the temple. Let him know that he is a worker together with God, and that it is a work which God will own and crown.

1. God will carry on this work, not by external force, but by internal influences upon the minds of men. He will do it, *not by* human *might or power,* but *by his own Spirit.* It was by the *Spirit of the Lord of hosts* that the people were excited and animated to build the temple; and *therefore* they are said to be *helped by the prophets of God,* because they, as the Spirit's mouth, spoke to their hearts, Ezra v. 2. It was by the same Spirit that the heart of Darius was inclined to favour that good work and that the enemies of it were infatuated so that they could not hinder it. When instruments fail, let us therefore leave it to God to do his work himself by his own Spirit.

2. All the difficulties and oppositions that lie in the way shall be removed, even those that seem insuperable (*v.* 7): *Who art thou, O great mountain? Before Zerubbabel thou shalt become a plain.* The enemies of the Jews are proud and hard as great mountains; but, when God has work to do, the mountains dwindle into mole-hills. Faith will remove mountains and make them plains. Christ is our Zerubbabel; nothing is too hard for his grace to do.

JAMIESON, FAUSSET, BROWN

CHAPTER 4

Vss. 1-14. FIFTH VISION. *The golden candlestick and the two olive trees. The temple shall be completed by the aid of God's Spirit.* **1. waked me**—The prophet was lying in a state of ecstatic slumber with astonishment at the previous vision. "Came again, and waked me," does not imply that the angel had departed and now returned, but is an idiom for "waked me again." **2. candlestick**—symbolizing the Jewish theocracy; and ultimately, the Church of which the Jewish portion is to be the head: the *light-bearer* (so the original is of "lights," Matt. 5:14, 16; Phil. 2:15) to the world. **all . . . gold**—all pure in doctrine and practice, precious and indestructible; such is the true ideal of the Church; such she shall be (Ps. 45:13). **bowl upon the top**—In the candlestick of the tabernacle the *plural* is used, *bowls* (Exod. 25-31). The *Hebrew* implies that it was the *fountain* of supply of oil to the lamps. Christ at the head ("on the top") of the Church is the true fountain, *of* whose *fulness of the Spirit all we receive grace* (John 1:16). **his seven lamps**—united in one stem; so in Exodus 25:32. But in Revelation 1:12 the seven candlesticks are separate. The Gentile churches will not realize their unity till the Jewish Church as the stem unites all the lamps in one candlestick (Rom. 11:16-24). The "seven lamps," in Revelation 4:5, are the "seven Spirits of God." **seven pipes**—feeding tubes, seven apiece from the "bowl" to each lamp (see *Margin*) [MAURER and CALVIN]; lit., "seven and seven": forty-nine in all. The greater the number of oil-feeding pipes, the brighter the light of the lamps. The explanation in vs. 6 is, that man's power by itself can neither retard nor advance God's work, that the real motive-power is God's *Spirit.* The seven times seven imply the manifold modes by which the Spirit's grace is imparted to the Church in her manifold work of enlightening the world. **3. two olive trees**—supplying oil to the bowl. The Holy Ghost, who fills with His fulness Messiah (the *anointed:* the "bowl"), from whom flow supplies of grace to the Church. **by it**—lit., "upon it," i.e., growing so as somewhat to overtop it. For the explanation of the "two" see vss. 12, 14. **4.** The prophet is instructed in the truths meant, that we may read them with the greater reverence and attention [CALVIN]. **5. Knowest thou not . . .**—Not a reproof of his ignorance, but a stimulus to reflection on the mystery. **No, my lord**—ingenious confession of ignorance; as a little child he casts himself for instruction at the feet of the Lord. **6. Not by might . . . but by my Spirit**—As the lamps burned continually, supplied with oil from a source (the living olive trees) which man did not make, so Zerubbabel need not be disheartened because of his weakness; for as the work is one to be effected by the living Spirit (cf. Hag. 2:5) of God, man's weakness is no obstacle, for God's might will perfect strength out of weakness (Hos. 1:7; II Cor. 12: 10; Heb. 11:34). "Might and power" express human strength of every description, physical, mental, moral. Or, "might" is the strength *of many* (an "army,"); "power," that *of one man* [PEMBELLUS]. God can save, "whether with many, or with them that have no power" (II Chron. 14:11; cf. I Sam. 14:6). So in the conversion of sinners (I Cor. 3:6; II Cor. 10:4). "Zerubbabel" is addressed as the chief civil authority in directing the work. **7.** All *mountain*-like obstacles (Isa. 40:4; 49:11) in *Zerubbabel's* way shall be removed, so that the crowning topstone shall be put on, and the completion of the work be acknowledged as wholly of "grace." Antitypically, the antichristian last foe of Israel, the obstacle preventing her establishment in Palestine, about to be crushed before Messiah, is probably meant (Jer. 51:25; Dan. 2:34, 44; Matt. 21:44). **bring forth the headstone**—Primarily, bring it forth from the place where it was chiselled and give it to the workmen to put on the top of the building. It was customary for chief magistrates to lay the foundation, and also the crowning top-stone (cf. Ezra 3:10). Antitypically, the reference is to the time when the full number of the spiritual Church shall be completed, and also when "all Israel shall be saved" (cf. Rom. 11:26; Heb. 11:40; 12:22, 23; Rev. 7:4–9). **Grace, grace**—The repetition expresses, *Grace* from first to last (*Margin,* Isa. 26: 3). Thus the Jews are urged to pray perseveringly and earnestly that the same grace which completed it may always preserve it. "Shoutings" of acclamation accompanied the foundation of the literal temple (Ezra 3:11, 13). So shoutings of "Hosanna" greeted the Saviour in entering Jerusalem (Matt. 21:9), when about to complete the purchase of salvation by His death: His Body being the second

ADAM CLARKE

CHAPTER 4

1. *The angel . . . came again, and waked me.* Archbishop Newcome considers this vision as represented on the same night, chap. i. 8, with the preceding ones. See the latter part of v. 10 compared with chap. iii. 9. After some interval the prophet, overpowered with the vision which had been presented to him, was awakened from his prophetic trance as from a sleep.

2-3. *A candlestick all of gold.* This candlestick is formed in some measure after that of the sanctuary, Exod. xxv. 31-32. The *two olive trees* were to supply the bowl with oil; the *bowl* was to communicate the oil to the *seven pipes;* and the seven pipes were to supply the *seven lamps.* In general, the candlestick, its bowl, pipes, lamps, and olive trees, are emblems of the pure service of God, and the grace and salvation to be enjoyed by His true worshippers.

6. *This is the word of the Lord unto Zerubbabel.* This prince was in a trying situation, and he needed especial encouragement from God; and here it is: *Not by might* (of your own), *nor by power* (authority from others), *but by my spirit*—the providence, authority, power, and energy of the Most High. In this way shall My temple be built; in this way shall My Church be raised and preserved.

7. *O great mountain.* The hindrances which were thrown in the way, the regal prohibition to discontinue the building of the Temple. *Before Zerubbabel . . . a plain.* The sovereign power of God shall remove them. March on, Zerubbabel; all shall be made plain and smooth before you. *He shall bring forth the headstone.* As he has laid the foundation stone, so shall he put on the headstone; as he has begun the building, so shall he finish it!

MATTHEW HENRY

3. The same hand that has begun this good work will perform it: *He shall bring forth the head-stone* (*v.* 7); and again (*v.* 9), *The hands of Zerubbabel have laid the foundation of this house*, and *his hands shall also finish it;* herein he is a type of Christ, who is both the *author* and the *finisher of our faith.* When the work is finished it must be thankfully acknowledged that it was not by any power of our own, but that it was grace that did it—God's goodwill towards us and his good work in us and for us.

4. This shall be a full ratification of the prophecies which went before concerning the Jews' return. When the temple is finished then *thou shalt know that the Lord of hosts has sent me unto you.*

5. This shall effectually silence those that looked with contempt upon the beginning of this work, *v.* 10. In God's work the day of small things is not to be despised. A grain of mustard-seed may become a great tree.

6. Those that despaired of the finishing of the work shall rejoice when they *see the plummet in the hand of Zerubbabel.*

7. This shall magnify God's providence, which is always employed for the good of his church. Zerubbabel does his part, but it is *with those seven, those seven eyes of the Lord* which we read of *ch.* iii. 9. He could do nothing if the gracious providence of God did not go before him and go along with him in it.

Those *seven eyes* that *run through the earth* are all *upon the stone* that Zerubbabel is laying straight with his plummet. And those that have the plummet in their hand must have a constant regard to divine Providence, and act in dependence upon its guidance.

Verses 11–14

Enough is said to Zechariah to encourage him, and to enable him to encourage others, and that was the principal intention of the vision he saw; but still he is inquisitive about the particulars.

I. His enquiry. He understood the meaning of the candlestick with its lamps: It is Jerusalem, it is the temple, and their salvation that is to *go forth as a lamp that burns;* but he wants to know what are these *two olive-trees* (*v.* 11), these *two olive-branches? v.* 12. He took notice not only that the two olive-trees grew, one *on the right side and the other on the left side of the candlestick* (so nigh, so ready, is divine grace to the church), but that the *two olive-branches*, from which in particular the candlestick did receive of *the root and fatness of the olive*, did empty the *golden oil out of themselves through the two golden pipes*, into the *golden bowl* on the head of the candlestick. Our Lord Jesus emptied himself, to fill us; his precious blood is the golden oil in which we are supplied with all we need.

II. Now again the angel obliged him to his own ignorance, before he informed him (*v.* 13): "*Knowest thou not what these are?* If thou knowest the church to be the candlestick, canst thou think the olive-trees, that supply it with oil, to be any other than the grace of God?" 1. If by the candlestick we understand the visible church, particularly that of the Jews at that time, for whose comfort it was primarily intended, these *sons of oil*, that *stand before the Lord of the whole earth*, are the two great ordinances and offices of the magistracy and ministry, at that time lodged in the hands of those two great and good men Zerubbabel and Joshua. Kings and priests were anointed with oil. Their wisdom, courage, and zeal, were continually emptying themselves into the golden bowl, to keep the lamps burning. 2. If by the candlestick we understand the church of the first-born, of true believers, these sons of oil may be meant of Christ and the Spirit, the Redeemer and the Comforter. From Christ, the *olive tree*, by the *Spirit*, *the olive branch*, all the golden oil of grace is communicated to believers, which keeps their lamps burning.

JAMIESON, FAUSSET, BROWN

temple, or place of God's inhabitation (John 2:20, 21). So when the full number of the saints and of Israel is complete, and God shall say, "It is done," then again shall "a great voice of much people in heaven" attribute all to the "grace" of God, saying, "Alleluia! Salvation, and glory, and honor, and power, unto the Lord our God" (Rev. 19:1, 6). Psalm 118:22 regards Him as "the headstone of the corner," i.e., the *foundation*-stone. Cf. the angels' acclamations at His birth, Luke 2:14. Here it is the *top-stone.* Messiah is not only the "Author," but also the Finisher (Heb. 12:2). "Grace" is ascribed "unto it," i.e. the stone, Messiah. Hence the benediction begins, "The *grace* of the Lord Jesus Christ" (II Cor. 13:14). **9. Zerubbabel . . . shall . . . finish it**—(Ezra 6:15) in the sixth year of Darius' reign. **Lord . . . sent me unto you**—(ch. 2:9). The Divine Angel announces that in what He has just spoken, He has been commissioned by God the Father. **10. who . . . despised . . . small things**—He reproves their ungrateful unbelief, which they felt because of the humble beginning, compared with the greatness of the undertaking; and encourages them with the assurance that their progress in the work, though small, was an earnest of great and final success, because Jehovah's eye is upon Zerubbabel and the work, to support Him with His favor. Contrast, "great is *the day* of Jezreel" (Hos. 1:11) with "the day of *small* things" here. **they shall rejoice . . .** *with* **those seven; they** *are* **the eyes of the Lord**—rather, "they, *even* those seven eyes of the Lord (cf. ch. 3:9), which . . . shall rejoice and see (i.e., rejoicingly see) the plummet (lit., the "stone of tin") in the hand of Zerubbabel" [MOORE]; the plummet in his hand indicating that the work is going forward to its completion. The *Hebrew* punctuation, however, favors *English Version*, of which the sense is, They who incredulously "despised" such "small" beginnings of the work as are made now, shall rejoicingly see its going on to completion under Zerubbabel, "with (*the aid of*) those seven," viz., the "seven eyes upon one stone" (ch. 3:9): which are explained, "They are the eyes of the Lord which . . . " [PEMBELLUS]. So differently do men and Jehovah regard the "small" beginnings of God's work (Ezra 3:12; Hag. 2:3). Men "despised" the work in its early stage: God rejoicingly regards it, and shall continue to do so. **run to and fro . . .**—Nothing in the whole earth escapes the eye of Jehovah, so that He can ward off all danger from His people, come from what quarter it may, in prosecuting His work (Prov. 15:3; I Cor. 16:9). **11, 12.** Zechariah three times (vss. 4, 11, 12) asks as to the two olives before he gets an answer; the question becomes more minute each time. What he at first calls "two olive trees," he afterwards calls "branches," as on closer looking he observes that the "branches" of the trees are the channels through which a continual flow of oil dropped into the bowl of the lamps (vs. 2), and that this is the purpose for which the two olive trees stand beside the candlestick. Primarily, the "two" refer to Joshua and Zerubbabel. God, says AUBERLEN, at each of the transition periods of the world's history has sent great men to guide the Church. So the two witnesses shall appear before the destruction of Antichrist. Antitypically, "the two anointed ones" (vs. 14) are the twofold supports of the Church, the civil power (answering to Zerubbabel) and the ecclesiastical (answering to Joshua, the high priest), which in the restored Jewish polity and temple shall "stand by," i.e., minister to "the Lord of the whole earth," as He shall be called in the day that He sets up His throne in Jerusalem (ch. 14:9; Dan. 2:44; Rev. 11:15). Cf. the description of the offices of the "priests" and the "prince" (Isa. 39:23 and Ezek. 44, 45, 46). As in Revelation 11:3, 4, the "two witnesses" are identified with the two olive trees and the two candlesticks. WORDSWORTH explains them to mean the Law and the Gospel: the two Testaments that *witness* in the Church for the truth of God. But this is at variance with the sense here, which requires Joshua and Zerubbabel to be primarily meant. **through**—lit., "by the hand of," i.e., by the agency of. **branches**—lit., "ears"; so the olive branches are called, because as ears are full of grain, so the olive branches are full of olives. **golden** *oil*—lit., "gold," i.e., goldlike liquor. **out of themselves**—Ordinances and ministers are channels of grace, not the grace itself. The supply comes not from a dead reservoir of oil, but through living olive trees (Ps. 52:8; Rom. 12:1) fed by God. **13. Knowest thou not**—God would awaken His people to zeal in learning His truth. **14. anointed ones**—lit., "sons of oil" (*Margin*, Isa. 5:1). Joshua the high priest, and Zerubbabel the

ADAM CLARKE

10. *Who hath despised the day of small things?* The poverty, weakness, and unbefriended state of the Jews. *And shall see the plummet in the hand of Zerubbabel.* He is master builder under God, the grand Architect.

Those seven . . . are the eyes of the Lord. Either referring to His particular and especial providence or to those ministering spirits whom He has employed in behalf of the Jews, to dispense the blessings of that providence.

14. *These are the two anointed ones.* Joshua, the high priest; and Zerubbabel, the governor. These are *anointed*—appointed by the Lord; and *stand by* Him, the one to minister in the ecclesiastical, the other in the civil state.

MATTHEW HENRY

JAMIESON, FAUSSET, BROWN

ADAM CLARKE

civil ruler, must first be anointed with grace themselves, so as to be the instruments of furnishing it to others (cf. I John 2:20, 27).

MATTHEW HENRY — CHAPTER 5

Verses 1–4

We do not find that the prophet now needed to be awakened, as he did *ch.* iv. 1.

I. He looked up into the air, and *behold a flying roll.* The angel asks him *what he sees?* And he gives him this account of it: *I see a flying roll,* and as near as he can guess by his eye it is *twenty cubits long* (that is ten yards) and *ten cubits broad,* that is five yards. The scriptures of the Old Testament and the New are *rolls,* in which God has *written to us the great things of his law* and gospel. Christ is the Master of the rolls. They are *flying* rolls. God's word *runs very swiftly,* Ps. cxlvii. 15.

II. This flying roll is a *curse*; it contains a declaration of the righteous wrath of God against those who by swearing affront God's majesty or by stealing invade their neighbours' property. This curse *goes forth over the face of the whole earth,* not only of the land of Israel. All mankind are liable to the judgment of God. How welcome then the tidings of a Saviour who came to *redeem us from the curse of the law* by being himself *made a curse for us,* and, like the prophet, *eating this roll!* The world is full of sin: so was the Jewish church at this time. But two sorts of sinners are here specified: (1) Thieves; it is *for everyone that steals,* especially that converts to his own use what was devoted to God, Mal. iii. 8; Neh. xiii. 10. Sacrilege is, without doubt, the worst kind of thievery. (2) Swearers. Sinners of the former class offend against the second table, these against the first. He that swears profanely shall not be held guiltless, much less he that swears falsely (*v.* 4). He that pronounces the sentence will take care to see it executed. Who can put by or resist the curse which a God of almighty power brings forth? The effect is very dreadful: *Everyone that steals shall be cut off,* not corrected, but cut off. He shall be cut off *as on this side* (cut off from this place, that is, from Jerusalem). God will not spare the sinners he finds among his own people, nor shall the holy city be a protection to the unholy. *It shall enter into the house of the thief and of him that swears.* God's curse cannot be kept out by bars or locks. Unless he repent and reform, there is no way to throw it out. It shall *consume it with the timber thereof, and the stones thereof.* Sin is the ruin of houses and families, especially the sins of injury and perjury.

Verses 5–11

The foregoing vision was very plain, but in this are things *dark and hard to be understood.* Some think that it is to foretell the final destruction of the Jewish nation and the dispersion of the Jews, when, by crucifying Christ and persecuting his gospel, they should have filled up the measure of their iniquities.

JAMIESON, FAUSSET, BROWN — CHAPTER 5

Vss. 1-4. Sixth Vision. The Flying Roll. *The fraudulent and perjuring transgressors of the law shall be extirpated from Judea.* **1. flying roll**—of papyrus, or dressed skins, used for writing on when paper was not known. It was inscribed with the words of the curse (Deut. 27:15-26; 28:15-68). Being written implied that its contents were beyond all escape or repeal (Ezek. 2:9). Its "flying" shows that its curses were ready swiftly to visit the transgressors. It was unrolled, or else its dimensions could not have been seen (vs. 2). Being open to all, none could say in excuse he knew not the law and the curses of disobedience. As the previous visions intimated God's favor in restoring the Jewish state, so this vision announces judgment, intimating that God, notwithstanding His favor, did not approve of their sins. Being written on both sides, "on this and on that side" (vs. 3), Vatablus connects it with the two tables of the law (Exod. 32:15), and implies its comprehensiveness. One side denounced "him that sweareth falsely (vs. 4) by God's name," according to the third commandment of *the first table,* duty to God; the other side denounced *theft,* according to the eighth commandment, which is in *the second table,* duty to one's neighbor. **2. length . . . twenty cubits . . . breadth . . . ten cubits**—thirty feet by fifteen, the dimensions of the temple porch (I Kings 6:3), where the law was usually read, showing that it was divinely authoritative in the theocracy. Its large size implies the great number of the curses contained. The *Hebrew* for "roll" or "volume" is used of the law (Ps. 40:7). **3. curse . . . earth**—(Mal. 4:6). The Gentiles are amenable to the curse of the law, as they have its substance, so far as they have not seared and corrupted conscience, written on their hearts (Rom. 2:15). **cut off**—lit., "cleared away." **as on this side . . . as on that side**—both sides of the *roll* [Vatablus]. From this place . . . from this place (repeated twice, as "the house" is repeated in vs. 4) [Maurer]; so "hence" is used, Gen. 37:17 (or, "on this and on that side," i.e., *on every side*) [Henderson]. None can escape, sin where he may: for God from one side to the other shall call all without exception to judgment [Calvin]. God will not spare even "this place," Jerusalem, when it sins [Pembellus]. *English Version* seems to take Vatablus' view. **according to it**—according as it is written. **4.** The "theft" immediately meant is similar sacrilege to that complained of in Nehemiah 13:10; Malachi 3:8. They robbed God by neglecting to give Him His due in building His house, while they built their own houses, forswearing their obligations to Him; therefore, the "houses" they build shall be "consumed" with God's "curse." Probably literal theft and perjury accompanied their virtual theft and perjury as to the temple of God (Mal. 3:5). Stealing and perjury go together; for the covetous and fraudulent perjure themselves by God's name without scruple (see Prov. 30:9). **enter . . . the house**—In vain they guard and shut themselves up who incur the curse; it will inevitably enter even when they think themselves most secure. **consume . . . timber . . . stones**—not leaving a vestige of it. So the "stones" and "timber" of the house of a leper (type of the sinner) were to be utterly removed (Lev. 14:15; cf. I Kings 18:38).

5-11. Seventh Vision. The Woman in the Ephah. *Wickedness and idolatry removed from the Holy Land to Babylon, there to mingle with their kindred elements.* The "ephah" is the Hebrew dry measure containing about 37 quarts. Alluding to the previous vision as to theft and perjury: the ephah which, by falsification of the measure, they made the instrument of defrauding, shall be made the instrument of their punishment [Grotius]. Cf. "this is their resemblance" (vs. 6), i.e., this is a representation of what the Jews have done, and what they shall suffer. Their total dispersion ("the land of Shinar" being the emblem of the various Gentile lands of their present dispersion) is herein foretold, when the *measure* (to which the ephah alludes) of their sins should be full. The former vision denounces judgment on individuals; this one, on the whole state: but enigmatically, not to discourage their present building [Pembellus]. Rather, the vision is consolatory after the preceding one [Calvin]. Idolatry and its kindred sins, covetousness and fraud (denounced in the vision of the roll), shall be removed far out of the Holy Land to

ADAM CLARKE — CHAPTER 5

1. *Behold a flying roll.* This was twenty cubits long, and ten cubits broad; the prophet saw it expanded, and flying. Itself was the catalogue of the crimes of the people, and the punishment threatened by the Lord. Some think the crimes were those of the Jews; others, those of the Chaldeans. The *roll* is mentioned in allusion to those large rolls on which the Jews write the Pentateuch. One now lying before me is 153 feet long, by 21 inches wide, written on fine brown goatskin; some time since brought from Jerusalem, supposed to be 400 years old.

3. *Every one that stealeth . . . and every one that sweareth.* It seems that the roll was written on both the front and back. Stealing and swearing are supposed to be two general heads of crimes: the former comprising sins against men; the latter, sins against God. It is supposed that the roll contained the sins and punishments of the Chaldeans.

4. *Into the house of him.* Babylon, the house or city of Nebuchadnezzar, who was a public plunderer, and a most glaring idolater.

MATTHEW HENRY

The prophet was told to turn and he should see greater desolations, *v.* 5. *What is this that goeth forth?* The prophet now, through either the distance or the dimness of his sight, could not well tell what it was, *v.* 6. And the angel tells him both what it is and what it means.

I. He sees an *ephah*, a measure wherewith they measured corn. And *this is their resemblance*, the resemblance of the Jewish nation *over all the earth*, wherever they are now dispersed. And some think that the mentioning of an ephah, which is used in buying and selling, intimates that fraud, and extortion in commerce, were sins abounding among them.

II. He sees a *woman sitting in the midst of the ephah*, representing the sinful church and nation of the Jews in their latter and degenerate age. He that weighs the hills in a balance measures nations and churches as in an ephah; so exact is he in his judicial dealings with them. God's people are called *the corn of his floor*, Isa. xxi. 10. And here he puts this corn into the bushel. The angel says of the woman in the *ephah, This is wickedness;* it is a wicked nation, else God would not have rejected it thus; it is as wicked as *wickedness* itself.

III. He sees the woman thrust down into the ephah, and a *talent*, or large weight, *of lead*, cast upon the *mouth* of it, by which she is made a prisoner in the *ephah*. This is designed to show that the wrath of God against impenitent sinners is what they cannot escape. It is insupportable. Guilt is upon the sinner as a talent of lead.

IV. He sees the ephah, with the woman in it, carried away into some far country. The instruments employed to do it were *two women*, who had *wings like* those *of a stork*, and, to make them fly the more swiftly, they had the *wind in their wings*, denoting the expedition with which the Romans destroyed the Jewish nation. They *lifted it up between the earth and the heaven*, as unworthy of either and abandoned by both.

When the prophet enquired whither they carried their prisoner (*v.* 10) he was told that they designed *to build it a house in the land of Shinar*. This intimates that the punishment of the Jews should be a final dispersion; they should be forced to dwell in far countries. There the *ephah* shall *be established, and set upon her own base*. Their calamity shall continue from generation to generation. Their iniquity shall continue too, and their hearts shall be hardened in it.

JAMIESON, FAUSSET, BROWN

their own congenial soil, never to return (so ch. 3: 9; Isa. 27:9; 52:1; 60:21; Jer. 50:20; Zeph. 3:13). For more than 2000 years, ever since the Babylonian exile, the Jews have been free from *idolatry;* but the full accomplishment of the prophecy is yet future, when *all* sin shall be purged from Israel on their return to Palestine, and conversion to Christ. **5. went forth**—The interpreting angel had withdrawn after the vision of the roll to receive a fresh revelation from the Divine Angel to communicate to the prophet. **6. This is their resemblance**—lit., "eye" (cf. Ezek. 1:4, 5, 16). HENGSTENBERG translates, "Their (the people's) eye" was all directed to evil. But *English Version* is better. "This is the appearance (i.e., an image) of the Jews in all *the land*" (not as *English Version*, "in all *the earth*"), i.e., of the wicked Jews. **This**—Here used of what was *within* the ephah, not the ephah itself. **7. lifted up**—The cover is lifted off the ephah to let the prophet see the female personification of "wickedness" within, about to be removed from Judea. The cover being "of lead," implies that the "woman" cannot escape from the ponderous load which presses her down. **talent**—lit., "a round piece": hence a talent, a weight of 125 pounds troy. **woman**—cf. for comparison of "wickedness" to a *woman,* Proverbs 2:16; 5:3, 4. In personifying abstract terms, the feminine is used, as the idea of giving birth to life is associated with woman. **8. wickedness**—lit., *the* wickedness: implying wickedness in its peculiar development. Cf. "*the* man of sin," II Thessalonians 2:3. **cast it**—i.e, her, Wickedness, who had moved more freely while the heavy lid was partially lifted off. **weight**—lit., "stone," i.e., round mass. **9.** The agents to carry away the "woman," are, consistently with the image, "women." God makes the wicked themselves the agents of punishing and removing wickedness. "Two" are employed, as one is not enough to carry such a load [MAURER]. Or, the Assyrians and Babylonians, who carried away idolatry in the persons, respectively, of Israel and Judah [HENDERSON]. As two "anointed ones" (ch. 4:14) stand by the Lord as His ministers, so *two* winged women execute His purpose here in removing the embodiment of "wickedness": answering to the "mystery of iniquity" (the LXX here in Zechariah uses the same words as Paul and "the man of sin," whom the Lord shall destroy with the spirit of His mouth and the brightness of His coming, II Thess. 2:3, 7, 8). Their "wings" express velocity. The "stork" has long and wide wings, for which reason it is specified; also it is a migratory bird. The "wind" helps the rapid motion of the wings. The being "lifted up between heaven and earth" implies open execution of the judgment before the eyes of all. As the "woman" here is removed to Babylon as her own dwelling, so the woman in the Apocalypse of St. John is Babylon (Rev. 17:3-5). **11. To build . . . house in . . . Shinar**—Babylonia (Gen. 10:10), the capital of the God-opposed world kingdoms, and so representing in general the seat of irreligion. As the "building of houses" in Babylon (Jer. 29:5, 28) by the Jews themselves expressed their long exile there, so the building of an house for "wickedness" there implies its permanent stay. **set . . . upon her own base**—fixed there as in its proper place. "Wickedness" being cast out of Judah, shall for ever dwell with the antichristian apostates (of whom Babylon is the type), who shall reap the fruit of it, which they deserve.

ADAM CLARKE

6. *This is an ephah that goeth forth.* This, among the Jews, was the ordinary measure of grain. The woman in the *ephah* is supposed to represent Judea, which shall be visited for its sins; the talent of lead on the ephah, within which the woman was enclosed, the wrath of God, bending down this culprit nation, in the measure of its sins. For the angel said, "This is wickedness"; that is, the woman represents the mass of iniquity of this nation.

9. *There came out two women.* As the one woman represented the impiety of the Jewish nation, so these two women who were to carry the ephah, in which the woman "iniquity" was shut up, under the weight of a talent of lead, may mean the desperate unbelief of the Jews in rejecting the Messiah; and that impiety, or universal corruption of manners, which was the consequence of their unbelief, and brought down the wrath of God upon them. The strong *wings,* like those of *a stork,* may point out the power and swiftness with which Judea was carried on to fill up the measure of her iniquity, and to meet the punishment which she deserved. *Between the earth and the heaven.* Sins against God and man, sins which heaven and earth contemplated with horror. Or the Babylonians and Romans may be intended by the two women who carried the Jewish ephah to its final punishment. The Chaldeans ruined Judea before the advent of our Lord; the Romans, shortly after.

11. *To build it an house in the land of Shinar.* The land of *Shinar* means Babylon; and Babylon means Rome, in the Apocalypse. The building the house for the woman imprisoned in the ephah may signify that there should be a long captivity under the Romans, as there was under that of Shinar or Babylon.

MATTHEW HENRY — CHAPTER 6

Verses 1–8

The prophet *turned and lifted up his eyes and looked.* This was the seventh vision he had had. The sight that the prophet had of *four chariots* drawn by horses of divers colours, *v.* 1–5.

JAMIESON, FAUSSET, BROWN — CHAPTER 6

Vss. 1-8. EIGHTH VISION. THE FOUR CHARIOTS. **1. four chariots**—symbolizing the various dispensations of Providence towards the Gentile nations which had been more or less brought into contact with Judea; especially in punishing Babylon. Cf. vs. 8 ("the north country," i.e., Babylon); ch. 1:15; 2:6. The number "four" is specified not merely in reference to the four quarters of the horizon (implying *universal* judgments), but in allusion to the *four* world kingdoms of Daniel. **from between two mountains**—the valley of Jehoshaphat, between Moriah and Mount Olivet [MOORE]; or the valley between Zion and Moriah, where the Lord is (ch. 2:10), and whence He sends forth His ministers of judgment on the heathen [MAURER]. The temple on Mount Moriah is the symbol of the theocracy; hence the nearest spot accessible to chariots in the valley below is the most suitable for a vision affecting Judah in relation to the Gentile world powers. The chariot is the symbol of war, and so of judgments. **of brass**—the metal among the ancients representing hard solidity; so the immovable and

ADAM CLARKE — CHAPTER 6

1. *There came four chariots.* Four monarchies or empires. This is supposed to mean the same with the vision of the four horns, in chap. i.

Mountains of brass. The strong barriers of God's purposes, which restrained those powers within the times and limits appointed by Jehovah.

MATTHEW HENRY

Some by the *four chariots* understand the four monarchies; and then they read (*v.* 5), *These are the four winds of the heavens*, and suppose that therein reference is had to Dan. vii. 2. The Babylonian monarchy, they think, is here represented by the *red horses*. The second chariot with the *black horses* is the Persian monarchy, which went forth northward against the Babylonians, and *quieted God's Spirit in the north country*, by executing his judgments on Babylon and freeing the Jews from their captivity. The *white*, the Grecians, go *forth after them* in the north, for they overthrow the Persians. The *grizzled*, the Romans, who conquercd the Grecian empire, are said to *go forth towards the south country*, because Egypt, which lay southward was subdued by the Romans. The *bay horses* had been with the *grizzled*, but afterwards went forth by themselves; and by these they understand the Goths and Vandals.

But I incline rather to understand this vision more generally to represent the administration of the kingdom of Providence in the government of this lower world. The *angels* are often called the *chariots of God*, as Ps. lxviii. 17. The various providences of God concerning nations and churches are represented by the different colours of horses, Rev. vi. 2, 4, 5, 8. And so here the counsels and decrees of God are the spring of all events, immovable, as *mountains of brass*. The *chariots* came *from between the two mountains*; for God *performs the thing that is appointed for us*. We could as soon grasp the mountains in our arms as comprehend the divine counsels in our finite understandings, and as soon remove *mountains of brass* as alter any of God's purposes. The works of Providence are as chariots, in which he rides as a prince. His providences move swiftly as chariots, directed by his infinite wisdom as chariots by their drivers. The holy angels are the ministers of God's providence, and are employed by him, as *the armies of heaven*. They are the *chariots* or the horses that draw the chariots, great in power and might, to carry one prophet to heaven and guard another on earth. The *horses* in the *first chariot* were *red*, signifying war and bloodshed. Those in the *second chariot* were *black*, signifying the dismal melancholy consequences of war. Those in the *third chariot* were *white*, signifying the return of comfort, and peace, and prosperity, after these dark and dismal times. Those in the *fourth chariot* were of a mixed colour, *grizzled* and *bay*; signifying events interwoven, a day of prosperity and a day of adversity set *the one over against the other*. *These are the four spirits of heaven, the four winds* (so some), which seem to blow as they list, from the various points of the compass. Or, rather, These are *the angels* that *go forth from standing before the Lord of all the earth*, to behold his glory in the upper world, which is their blessedness, and to serve his glory in this lower world, which is their business. There is an admirable beauty in Providence, and one event serves for a balance to another (*v.* 6): *The black horses went forth*, carrying with them very dark and melancholy events, but presently *the white went forth after them*, carrying joy to those that mourned. Such are God's dealings with his church and people: if the black horses go forth, the white ones presently go after them; for *as affliction abounds consolation much more abounds*. The *grizzled* and *bay horses* were both in the *fourth chariot* (*v.* 3), and though they went forth, at first, towards the *south country*, yet afterwards they *sought to walk to and fro through the earth*, *v.* 7. If we go to and fro through the earth, we shall find the events of Providence neither all black nor all white, but ash-coloured, or grey, mixed of black and white. Such is the world we live in. God is well-pleased with all the operations of his providence (*v.* 8): *These have quieted my spirit*, these *black horses* which denote extraordinary judgments, and the *white* ones which denote extraordinary deliverances, both which *went towards the north country*. These have *quieted my spirit in the north-country*, which had of late been the most remarkable scene of action with reference to the church.

Verses 9–15

God did not only at *sundry times*, but *in divers manners*, speak in time past by the prophets to his church. In the former part of this chapter he spoke by a vision, which only the prophet himself saw; here, in this latter part, he speaks by a sign, or type, which many saw, and which was a prediction of the Messiah as the priest and king of his church.

JAMIESON, FAUSSET, BROWN

resistless firmness of God's people (cf. Jer. 1:18). CALVIN explains the "two mountains" thus: The secret purpose of God from eternity does not come forth to view before the execution, but is hidden and kept back irresistibly till the fit time, as it were *between* lofty *mountains;* the *chariots* are the various changes wrought in nations, which, as swift heralds, announce to us what before we knew not. The "two" may thus correspond to the number of the "olive trees" (ch. 4:3); the *allusion* to the "two mountains" near the temple is not necessarily excluded in this view. HENDERSON explains them to be the Medo-Persian kingdom, represented by the "two horns" (Dan. 8:3, 4), now employed to execute God's purpose in punishing the nations; but the prophecy reaches far beyond those times. **2. red**—implying carnage. **black**—representing sorrow; also famine (Rev. 6:5, 6; cf. ch. 1:8). **3. white**—implying joy and victory [CALVIN]. **grizzled**—piebald. Implying a *mixed* dispensation, partly prosperity, partly adversity. All four dispensations, though various in character to the Gentile nation, portended alike good to God's people. **bay**—rather, "strong" or "fleet"; so *Vulgate* [GESENIUS]. The horses have this epithet, whose part it was to "walk to and fro through the earth" (vs. 7). However, LXX and *Chaldee* agree with *English Version* in referring the *Hebrew* to *color*, not strength. **4.** The prophet humbly and teachably seeks instruction from God, and therefore seeks not in vain. **5. four spirits of the heavens**—heavenly spirits who "stand before Jehovah" to receive God's commands (ch. 4:14; I Kings 22:19; Job 2:1; Luke 1:19) in heaven (of which Zion is the counterpart on earth, *Note*, vs. 1), and proceed with chariot speed (II Kings 6:17; Ps. 68:17) to execute them on earth in its four various quarters (Ps. 104: 4; Heb. 1:7, 14) [PEMBELLUS]. Or, the secret impulses of God which emanate from His counsel and providence; the prophet implies that all the revolutions in the world are from the Spirit of God and are as it were, His messengers or spirits [CALVIN]. **6. north country**—Babylon (*Note*, Jer. 1:14). The north is the quarter specified in particular whence Judah and Israel are hereafter to return to their own land (ch. 2:6; Jer. 3:18). "The black horses" go to Babylon, primarily to represent the awful desolation with which Darius visited it in the fifth year of his reign (two years after this prophecy) for revolting [HENDERSON]. The "white" go after the "black" horses to the same country; *two* sets being sent to it because of its greater cruelty and guilt in respect to Judea. The white represent Darius' triumphant subjugation of it [MOORE]. Rather, I think, the white are sent to victoriously subdue Medo-Persia, the second world kingdom, lying in the same quarter as Babylon, viz., north. **grizzled . . . toward the south**—i.e., to Egypt, the other great foe of God's people. It, being a part of the Græco-Macedonian kingdom, stands for the whole of it, the third world kingdom. **7. bay**—rather, the "fleet" (or "strong"). As the "red" are not otherwise mentioned, the epithet "fleet" (as the *Hebrew* for "bay" ought to be translated) in vs. 3 seems to apply to all four, and here especially to the "red." Their office is to complete hereafter the work already in part executed by the previous three who have stilled Babylon, Medo-Persia, and Græco-Macedonia; viz., to punish finally the last great foe of Israel, the final form assumed by the fourth world kingdom, Rome, which is to continue down to the second advent of Christ. Hence they "walk to and fro through the earth," counterworking Satan's "going to and fro in the earth" (Job 1:7; II Thess. 2:8, 9; I Tim. 4:1), in connection with the last awful development of the fourth world kingdom. Their "fleetness" is needed to counteract his restless activity; their red color implies the final great carnage (Ezek. 39; Rev. 19:17, 18, 21). **8. north . . . quieted . . . my spirit**—i.e., caused My *anger* to rest (*Margin*, Judg. 8:3; Eccles. 10:4; Ezek. 5:13; 16:42). Babylon alone of the four great world kingdoms had in Zechariah's time been finally punished; therefore, in its case alone does God now say His anger is satisfied; the others had as yet to expiate their sin; the fourth has still to do so.

9-15. NINTH VISION. THE CROWNING OF JOSHUA. The double crown is placed on Joshua's head, symbolizing that the true priesthood and the kingdom shall be conferred on the one Messiah. Cf. Hebrews 6:20; 7:1-21, on Melchizedek, who similarly combined the kingdom and priesthood as type of Messiah. **10. Take of** *them of* **the captivity**—Take *silver and gold* (vs. 11) *from* them. The three named came from Babylon (where some of the exiled Jews still were left) to present gifts of silver and gold towards the building of the temple. But

ADAM CLARKE

2. *In the first chariot were red horses.* The empire of the Chaldeans, which overthrew the empire of the Assyrians. *The second chariot black horses.* The empire of the Persians, founded by Cyrus, which destroyed the empire of the Chaldeans.

3. *The third chariot white horses.* The empire of the Greeks, founded by Alexander the Great, which destoyed the empire of the Persians. *The fourth chariot grisled and bay horses.* That is, party-colored horses; or with horses, some grisled and some bay. The empire of the Romans or of the Greeks. The Greeks divided after the death of Alexander: one part pointing out the Lagidae, who attacked and subdued Egypt; and the other, the Seleucidae, who subdued Syria under Seleucus.

5. *The four spirits of the heavens.* Ministers of God's wrath against the sinful nations of the world.

6. *The black horses.* This refers to the second chariot; of the first the angel makes no mention, because the empire designed by it had ceased to exist. This had red horses, to show the cruelty of the Chaldeans towards the Jews, and the carnage they committed in the land of Judea. *The black.* Cyrus, at the head of the Persians and Medes, bringing devastation and death among the Chaldeans, called the "north" in many parts of Scripture. *The white.* Alexander, who was splendid in his victories, and mild towards all that he conquered. *The grisled.* The Lagidae or Ptolemies, who founded an empire in Egypt; of these some were good, some bad, some despotic, some moderate, some cruel, and some mild; represented by the party-colored horses.

7. *And the bay went forth.* The Seleucidae, who conquered Syria and the upper provinces, and who wished to extend their conquests, and *sought to go, that they might walk to and fro through the earth*, were of unbounded ambition, and sought universal empire; such as Antiochus the Great. *So they walked to and fro,* did extend their conquests, and harassed many countries by their vexatious and almost continual wars.

8. *Have quieted my spirit in the north country.* They have fulfilled my judgments on Assyria and Chaldea. Nabopolassar and Cyrus first, against the Assyrians and Chaldeans; and Alexander next, against the Persians.

10. *Take of them of the captivity.* The names that follow were probably those to whom the silver and golden vessels of the Temple were instrusted.

MATTHEW HENRY

I. The *coronation of Joshua* the high priest, *v.* 10, 11. There are two types of Christ in the Old Testament—Joshua the chief captain, a type of Christ the captain of our salvation, and Joshua the chief priest, a type of Christ the high priest of our profession, and both in their day saviours and leaders into Canaan. Joshua was far from being ambitious of a crown, and the people of having a crowned head over them; but the prophet is ordered to crown Joshua as if he had been a king. And Zerubbabel's prudence and piety kept this from being any affront to him. Jews from Babylon brought an offering to the house of God, *some of the captivity* that *came from Babylon* on a visit to Jerusalem. Perhaps they came hearing that the building of the temple went on slowly for want of money, with an offering of gold and silver for the service of the house of God. They thought to bring their present to the priest, but God has a prophet ready to receive them and it, which would be an encouragement to them, who, in their captivity, had so often complained, *We see not our signs, there is no more any prophet.* He was to meet them in the house of Josiah, the son of Zephaniah, who probably kept the treasures of the temple. Crowns are to be *made*, and *put upon the head of Joshua, v.* 11. It is supposed that there were two crowns provided, one of silver and the other of gold; the former (as some think) denoting his priestly dignity, the latter his kingly dignity. The sun shines as gold, when he *goes forth in his strength*; and the beams of the moon, when she *walks in brightness*, we call *silver beams.* Those that worshipped the sun and moon shall now fall down before the golden and silver crowns of the Redeemer, before whom the sun shall be ashamed and the moon confounded.

II. "What is the meaning of Joshua's being crowned thus?" The prophet is ready to tell them.

1. God will, in the fulness of time, raise up a great high priest, like Joshua. Joshua is but the figure of one that is to come, a faint shadow of him (*v.* 12): *Speak unto him* in the name of *the Lord of hosts*, that *the man whose name is The BRANCH* shall *grow up out of his place*, out of the city of David. Though the family be a root in a dry ground, yet this branch shall spring out of it, as when the sun returns, the flowers spring out of the roots, in which they lay buried out of sight and out of mind.

2. Joshua was active in building the temple, so *the man, the branch*, shall be the sole builder of the spiritual temple, the gospel-church. He *shall build the temple of the Lord.*

3. Christ shall bear the glory. Glory is a burden, but not too heavy for him to bear who upholds all things. The cross was his glory, and he bore that; so was the crown *an exceeding weight of glory*, and he bears that. That which he shall undertake, shall be indeed the *glory of Israel.* He shall *lift up the glory* (so it may be read); he shall raise it out of the dust.

4. He shall have a throne, and be both priest and king upon his throne. A throne denotes both dignity and dominion, an exalted honour with an extensive power. Christ, as a priest, ever lives to make intercession for us; but he does it sitting at his Father's right hand, as one having authority, Heb. viii. 1. Christ, who is ordained to offer sacrifices for us, is authorized to give law to us. He will not save us unless we be willing that he should govern us. God has prepared him a throne *in the heavens*; and, if we would have any benefit by that, we must prepare him a throne in our hearts. This king shall be a *priest upon his throne.* With the majesty and power of a king, he shall have the tenderness and simplicity of a priest.

5. *The counsel of peace shall be between them both.* That is, Between *Jehovah* and the *man the branch*, between the Father and the Son; concerning the peace to be made between God and man, by the mediation of Christ. Some think it alludes to the former government of the Jews' state, wherein the king and priest, separate officers, did take counsel one with another, for the maintenance of peace and prosperity in church and state, as did Zerubbabel and Joshua now.

JAMIESON, FAUSSET, BROWN

in vss. 11, 14, "crowns" are directed to be made of them, then to be set on Joshua's head, and to be deposited in the temple as a memorial of the donors, until Messiah shall appear. **Heldai**—meaning "robust." Called *Helem* below. **Tobijah**—i.e., "the goodness of God." **Jedaiah**—i.e., "God knows." **which are come from Babylon**—This clause in the *Hebrew* comes after "Josiah son of Zephaniah." Therefore, MOORE thinks Josiah as well as the three "came from Babylon." But as he has a "house" at Jerusalem, he is plainly a resident, not a visitor. Therefore *English Version* is right; or MAURER, "Josiah son of Zephaniah, to *whom* they are come (as guests) from Babylon." **the same day**—No time was to be lost to mark the significancy of their coming from afar to offer gifts to the temple, typifying, in the double crown made of their gifts and set on Joshua's head, the gathering in of Israel's outcasts to Messiah hereafter, who shall then be recognized as the true king and priest. **11.** The high priest wore a crown above the miter (ch. 3:5; Lev. 8:9). Messiah shall wear many *crowns,* one surmounting the other (Rev. 19:12). It was a thing before unknown in the Levitical priesthood that the same person should wear at once the crown of a king and that of a high priest (Ps. 110:4; Heb. 5:10). Messiah shall be revealed fully in this twofold dignity when He shall "restore the kingdom to Israel" (Acts 1:6). **12. Behold, the man**—viz., shall arise. Pilate unconsciously spake God's will concerning Him, "*Behold* the man" (John 19:5). The sense here is, "Behold in Joshua a remarkable shadowing forth of Messiah." It is not for his own sake that the crown is placed on him, but as type of Messiah about to be at once king and priest. Joshua could not personally be crowned king, not being of the royal line of David, but only in his *representative* character. **Branch**—(*Note,* ch. 3:8; Isa. 4:2; Jer. 23:5; 33:15). **he shall grow up out of his place**—retaining the image of a "Branch"; "He shall sprout up from His place," i.e., the place peculiar to Him: not merely from Bethlehem or Nazareth, but by His own power, without man's aid, in His miraculous conception [HENDERSON]; a sense brought out in the original, "from under Himself," or "from (of) Himself" [CALVIN]. MOORE makes it refer to His growing lowly *in His place* of obscurity, "as a tender plant and a root out of a dry ground" (Isa. 53:2), for thirty years unknown except as the son of a carpenter. MAURER translates, "Under Him there shall be growth (in the Church)." *English Version* accords better with the *Hebrew* (cf. Exod. 10:23). The idea in a Branch is that Christ's glory is growing, not yet fully manifested as a full-grown tree. Therefore men reject Him now. **build the temple**—The promise of the future true building of the spiritual temple by Messiah (Matt. 16:18; I Cor. 3:17; II Cor. 6:16; Eph. 2:20-22; Heb. 3:3) is an earnest to assure the Jews, that the material temple will be built by Joshua and Zerubbabel, in spite of all seeming obstacles. It also raises their thoughts beyond the material to the spiritual temple, and also to the future glorious temple, to be reared in Israel under Messiah's superintendence (Ezek. 40, 41, 42, 43). The repetition of the same clause (vs. 13) gives emphasis to the statement as to Messiah's work. **13. bear the glory**—i.e., wear the insignia of the kingly glory, "the crowns" (Ps. 21:5; 102:16; Isa. 52:13). *He himself* shall bear the glory, not thou, Joshua, though thou dost bear the crowns. The Church's dignity is in her head alone, Christ. So Eliakim, type of Messiah, was to have "all the glory of his father's house hung upon him" (Isa. 22:24). **sit**—implying security and permanence. **priest . . . throne**—(Gen. 14:18; Ps. 110:4; Heb. 5:6, 10; 6:20; 7). **counsel of peace . . . between . . . both**—Joshua and Zerubbabel, the religious and civii authorities co-operating in the temple, typify the *peace,* or harmonious union, *between both* the kingly and priestly offices. The kingly majesty shall not depress the priestly dignity, nor the priestly dignity the kingly majesty [JEROME]. The peace of the Church, formerly sought for in the mutual "counsels" of the kings and the priests, who had been always distinct, shall be perfectly ensured by the concurrence of the two offices in the one Messiah, who by His mediatorial priesthood purchases it, and by His kingly rule maintains it. VITRINGA takes "*His* throne" to be Jehovah the Father's. Thus it will be, "there shall be . . . peace between the Branch and Jehovah" [LUDOVICUS DE DIEU]. The other view is better, viz., "*Messiah's* throne." As Priest He expiates sin; as King, extirpates it. "*Counsel* of peace," implies that it is the plan of infinite "wisdom," whence Messiah is called "Counsellor" (Isa. 9:6; Eph. 1:8, 11; Heb. 6:17). Peace between the kingly and priestly attributes of Mes-

ADAM CLARKE

The house of Josiah. Probably an artificer in silver, gold, etc.

12. *Behold the man whose name is The BRANCH.* I cannot think that Zerubbabel is here intended; indeed, he is not so much as mentioned in chap. iii. 8. Joshua and his companions are called "figurative" or "typical" men. The crowning therefore of Joshua in this place, and calling him the branch, was most probably in reference to that glorious Person, the Messiah, of whom he was the type or figure. *And he shall grow up out of his place.* That is, out of David's root, tribe, and family.

And he shall build the temple of the Lord. This cannot refer to the building of the Temple then in hand, for Zerubbabel was its builder; but to that temple, the Christian Church, that was typified by it. For Zerubbabel is not named here, and only "Joshua" or Jesus (the name is the same) is the Person who is to be crowned and to build this spiritual temple.

13. *Even he shall build the temple.* Joshua, not Zerubbabel. *He shall bear the glory.* Have all the honor of it, for none can do this but himself. The Messiah is still intended.

And shall sit and rule upon his throne. For the government of the Church shall be upon His shoulder. *And he shall be a priest upon his throne.* He shall, as the great High Priest, offer the only available offering and atonement; and so He shall be both King and Priest, a royal King and a royal Priest, for even the *priest* is here stated to sit *upon his throne. And the counsel of peace shall be between them both.* The purpose to establish peace between heaven and earth must be between the Father and the Son.

MATTHEW HENRY

III. *The crowns* that were used were not given to Joshua, but must be *kept for a memorial in the temple of the Lord, v.* 14. Either they were laid up in the temple treasury or (as the Jews' tradition is) they were hung up in the windows of the temple, in the view of all for evidence of the promise of the Messiah.

6. There shall be a happy coalition between Jews and Gentiles in the gospel-church, and they shall both meet in Christ, the priest upon his throne, as the centre of their unity (*v.* 15): *Those that are far off shall come and build in the temple of the Lord.*

7. This will be confirmation of the truth of God's word: *You shall know that the Lord of hosts has sent me unto you.* That promise, that those that were afar off should assist them in *building the temple of the Lord,* was *a sign.* This should be fulfilled now very speedily; see Ezra vi. 13, 14. *"For this shall come to pass if you will diligently obey the voice of the Lord your God.* You shall have the help of foreigners in building the temple, if you will but set about it in good earnest yourselves."

JAMIESON, FAUSSET, BROWN

siah implies the harmonizing of the conflicting claims of God's justice as a King, and His love as a Father and Priest. Hence is produced peace to man (Luke 2:14; Acts 10:36; Eph. 2:13-17). It is only by being pardoned through His atonement and ruled by His laws, that we can find "peace." The royal "throne" was always connected with the "temple," as is the case in the Apocalypse (Rev. 7: 15), because Christ is to be a king on His throne and a priest, and because the people, whose "king" the Lord is, cannot approach Him except by a priestly mediation [Roos]. Jesus shall come to effect, by His presence (Isa. 11:4; Dan. 7:17), that which in vain is looked for, in His absence, by other means. He shall exercise His power mediatorially as priest on His throne (vs. 13); therefore His reign is for a limited period, which it could not be if it were the final and everlasting state of glory. But being for a special purpose, to reconcile all things in this world, now disordered by sin, and so present it to God the Father that He may again for the first time since the fall come into direct connection with His creatures; therefore it is limited, forming the dispensation in the fulness of times (Eph. 1:10), when God shall gather in one all things in Christ, the final end of which shall be, "God all in all" (I Cor. 15:24-28). **14. the crowns shall be to Helem . . . a memorial**—deposited in the temple, to the honor of the donors; a memorial, too, of the coronation of Joshua, to remind all of Messiah, the promised antitypical king-priest, soon to come. Helem, the same as Heldai above. So Hen (i.e., "favor") is another name for Josiah (i.e., "God founds") above. The same person often had two names. **15. they . . . far off shall . . . build**—The reason why the crowns were made of gold received from afar, viz., from the Jews of Babylon, was to typify the conversion of the Gentiles to Messiah, King of Israel. This, too, was included in the "peace" spoken of in vs. 13 (Acts 2:39; Eph. 2:12-17). Primarily, however, the return of the dispersed Israelites "from afar" (Isa. 60:9) to the king of the Jews at Jerusalem is intended, to be followed, secondly, by the conversion of the Gentiles from "far off" (ch. 2:11; 8:22, 23; Isa. 60:10; 57:19). **build in the temple**—Christ "builds the temple" (vss. 12, 13; Heb. 3:3, 4): His people "build *in* the temple." Cf. Hebrews 3:2, "Moses *in* His house." **ye shall know . . .**—when the event corresponds to the prediction (ch. 2:9; 4:9). **this shall come to pass, if ye . . . obey . . .**—To the Jews of Zechariah's day a stimulus is given to *diligent* prosecution of the temple building, the work which it was meanwhile their duty to fulfil, relying on the hope of the Messiah afterwards to glorify it. The completion of the temple shall "come to pass," if ye diligently on your part "obey the Lord." It is not meant that their unbelief could set aside God's gracious purpose as to Messiah's coming. But there is, secondarily, meant, that Messiah's glory as priest-king of Israel shall not be manifested to the Jews till they turn to Him with obedient penitence. They meanwhile are cast away "branches" until they be grafted in again on the Branch and their own olive tree (ch. 38; 12:10-12; Matt. 23:39; Rom. 11:16-24).

ADAM CLARKE

JOHN GILL:

Verse 14. "And the crowns shall be to Helem." The same with Heldai, verse 10; "and to Tobijah, and to Jedaiah, and to Hen the son of Zephaniah"; the same with Josiah, verse 10; "for a memorial in the temple of the Lord"; the crowns, after they had been put upon the head of Joshua, were taken off, and laid up in some part of the temple, of which the Jews make mention in their Misna: and say there were golden chains fixed to the beams of the porch (of the temple), by which the young priests went up, and saw the crowns; as it is said, Zech. 6:14; "and the crowns shall be to Helem," these were laid up for a memorial of the liberality and generosity of those men, as Jarchi interprets it, who had so freely and largely offered towards the building of the temple; or rather as Alshec, another Jewish commentator, observes, they were for a memorial of something future, even of the Messiah, who was typified by Joshua, when he had those crowns upon him; for those crowns respected the glory of Christ's government in future times; and being made both of silver and gold, and put upon the head of the high-priest Joshua, denoted the union of the kingly and priestly offices in the Messiah.

—*Gill's Commentary*

15. *And they that are far off shall come.* The Gentiles shall come to the Saviour of the world; and *build*—become a part of this new *temple;* for they, as living stones, shall become "an holy temple . . . an habitation of God through the Spirit."

Ye shall know that the Lord of hosts hath sent me. These predictions, relative to the regal and sacerdotal offices of the Messiah, shall be so circumstantially fulfilled that you, Jews, shall be obliged to acknowledge that the Lord of hosts hath sent me with this message.

MATTHEW HENRY

CHAPTER 7

Verses 1–7

I. Some persons were sent to enquire of the priests and prophets whether they should continue to observe their yearly fasts, particularly that in the fifth month, as they had done. It is uncertain whether the case was put by those that yet remained in Babylon, or by those that had returned, called the *people of the land, v.* 5.

They were *Sherezer* and *Regem-melech,* persons of some rank and figure, for they came *with their men.*

JAMIESON, FAUSSET, BROWN

CHAPTER 7

Vss. 1-14. II. Didactic Part, chaps. 7, 8. Obedience, rather than Fasting, Enjoined: Its Reward. **1. fourth year of . . . Darius**—two years after the previous prophecies (ch. 1:1, etc.). **Chisleu**—meaning "torpidity," the state in which nature is in November, answering to this month. **2. they . . . sent unto . . . house of God**—*The Jews* of the country sent to the house of God or congregation at Jerusalem. The altar was long since reared (Ezra 3:3), though the temple was not completed till two years afterwards (Ezra 6:15). The priests' duty was to give decision on points of the law (Deut. 17:9; Matt. 2:4). *Beth-el* is here used instead of *Beth-Jehovah,* because the religious authorities, rather than the house itself (designated Beth-Jehovah in next verse), are intended. The old Beth-el had long ceased to be the seat of idol worship, so that the name had lost its opprobrious meaning. "The house of the Lord" is used for the congregation of worshippers headed by their priests (ch. 3:7; Hos. 8:1). Maurer makes the "house of God" nominative to "sent." Henderson makes "Beth-el" so. **Sherezer**—an Assyrian name meaning, "Prefect of the treasury." **Regemmelech**—meaning, "The king's official." These names perhaps intimate the semi-heathen character of the inquirers, which may also be implied in the name "Beth-el" (*Hebrew* for "house of God"), so notorious once for its calf wor-

ADAM CLARKE

CHAPTER 7

1. *The fourth year of King Darius.* Two years after they began to rebuild the Temple, see chap. i. 1. *The ninth month, even in Chisleu.* This answers to a part of our November and December. The names of the month appear only under and after the Captivity.

2. *When they had sent . . . Sherezer and Regem-melech.* To inquire whether the fasts should be continued, which they had hitherto observed on account of their ruined Temple; and the reason why they inquired was that they were rebuilding that Temple, and were likely to bring it to a joyful issue.

MATTHEW HENRY

They were sent perhaps not with *gold and silver* (as those, *ch.* vi. 10, 11), but upon the two great errands which should bring us all to the house of God, (1) To intercede with God for his mercy. They were sent to *pray before the Lord*, and to *offer sacrifice*. The Jews, in captivity, prayed towards the temple (as appears Dan. vi. 10); but now that it was to be rebuilt they sent their representatives to pray in it. (2) To enquire of God concerning his mind. They spoke *to the priests that were in the house of the Lord and to the prophets*. The priests and the prophets were not jealous one of another, nor had any difference among themselves; let not the people then make differences between them, but thank God they had both. They asked (*v.* 3): *Should I weep in the fifth month, separating myself, as I have done these so many years*. They kept up solemn stated fasts for humiliation and prayer. They mention only one, that of the fifth month; but it appears, *ch.* viii. 19, that they observed four anniversary fasts, one in the fourth month (*June* 17), in remembrance of the breaking up of the wall of Jerusalem (Jer. lii. 6), another in the fifth month (*July* 4), in remembrance of the burning of the temple (Jer. lii. 12, 13), another in the seventh month (*September* 3), in remembrance of the killing of Gedaliah, and another in the tenth month (*December* 10), in remembrance of the beginning of the siege of Jerusalem, 2 Kings xxv. 1. Their present doubt was whether they should continue these fasts or no. The case is put as by a single person: *Should I weep?* A religious fast must be solemnized, not only by abstinence but by a godly sorrow for sin, here expressed by weeping. "Should I still keep such *days to afflict the soul* as *I have done these so many years*?" It is said (*v.* 5) to be seventy years. Something is to be said for the continuance of these fasts. They were still under the tokens of God's displeasure; and it is unwise for the patient to break off his course of physic while he is sensible of remains of his distemper. But there is something to be said for the letting fall of these fasts. God had returned in mercy to them. Now that the bridegroom has returned, why should the *children of the bride-chamber fast*? And as to the fast of the fifth month, that, being kept in remembrance of the burning of the temple, might seem to be superseded because the temple was now in a fair way to be rebuilt.

II. Though the question looked plausible enough, those who proposed it were not conscientious in it, for they were more concerned about the ceremony than about the substance. And therefore the first answer to their enquiry is a very sharp reproof of their hypocrisy. *Did you at all fast unto me, even to me?* He appeals to their own consciences. Was it *to me, even to me?* The repetition intimates what a great deal of stress is laid upon this as the main matter. To fast, and not fast to God, was to mock him and provoke him. If the solemnities of our fasting, though frequent, long, and severe, do not serve to quicken prayer, and to alter the temper of our minds and the course of our lives for the better, God will not accept them as performed to him. They had the same eye to themselves in their fasting that they had in their eating and drinking (*v.* 6). The thing they should have done was left undone (*v.* 7): "*Should you not hear the words which the Lord has cried by the former prophets?* You must do that which you have not yet done; you must repent of your sins and reform your lives. This is what we now call you to, and it is the same that the former prophets called your fathers to." He puts them in mind of the former flourishing state of their country: Jerusalem *was* then *inhabited and in prosperity*, that is now desolate and in distress. But then God *by the prophets cried* to them to amend their ways or else their prosperity would soon be at an end. "Now," says the prophet, "you should have taken notice of that, and, if you do not, all your fasting and weeping signify nothing."

Verses 8–14

Warning to these hypocritical enquirers, who continued their sins when they asked with great preciseness whether they should continue their fasts.

I. This prophet here repeats what former prophets preached to their fathers (*v.* 9, 10). The duties required are not keeping fasts and offering sacrifices, but *doing justly* and *loving mercy*. Magistrates must administer justice impartially. Neighbours must have a tender concern for one another. The infirmities of others, as well as their calamities, are to be looked upon with compassion. *Let none of you imagine evil against his brother in your heart*.

II. He describes the wilfulness and disobedience of their fathers (*v.* 11, 12). If they did hear what was said to them, and seemed inclined at first to comply with it, yet like a bullock unaccustomed to the yoke,

JAMIESON, FAUSSET, BROWN

ship. They sent to *Jehovah's house* as their forefathers sent to old *Beth-el*, not in the spirit of true obedience. **pray before the Lord**—lit., "to entreat the face of," i.e., to offer sacifices, the accompaniment of prayers, to conciliate His favor (I Sam. 13:12).

3. Should I weep in the fifth month—"I" represents here the people of God (cf. ch. 8:21). This rather favors MAURER'S view, taking "the house of God," *the congregation*, as nominative to "sent.' Their hypocrisy appeared because they showed more concern about a ceremony of human institution (not improper in itself) than about moral obedience. If, too, they had trusted God's promise as to the restoration of Church and State, the fast would have now given place to joy, for which there was more cause than for grief [PEMBELLUS]. **to the prophets**—Haggai and Zechariah especially. *The tenth day of the fifth month* was kept a fast, being the anniversary of the destruction of Jerusalem (Jer. 52:12-14). They ask, Should the fast *be continued*, now that the temple and city are being restored? **separating myself**—sanctifying myself by separation, not only from food, but from all defilements (cf. Joel 2:16) as was usual in a solemn fast. **5. Speak unto all**—The question had been asked in the name of the people in general by Sherezer and Regemmelech. The self-imposed fast they were tired of, not having observed it in the spirit of true religion. **seventh month**—This fast was in memory of the murder of Gedaliah and those with him at Mizpah, issuing in the dispersion of the Jews (II Kings 25: 25, 26; Jer. 41:1-3). **did ye . . . fast unto me?**—No; it was to gratify yourselves in hypocritical will-worship. If it had been "unto *Me*," ye would have "separated yourselves" not only from food, but from your sins (Isa. 58:3-7). They falsely made the fast an end intrinsically meritorious in itself, not a means towards God's glory in their sanctification. The true principle of piety, *reference to God*, was wanting: hence the emphatic repetition of "unto Me." Before settling questions as to the outward forms of piety (however proper, as in this case), the great question was as to piety itself; that being once settled, all their outward observances become sanctified, being "unto the Lord" (Rom. 14:6). **6. did not ye eat** *for yourselves*?—lit., "Is it not *ye* who eat?" i.e., it is not unto Me and My glory. It tends no more to My glory, your feasting than your fasting. **7.** *Should ye* **not** *hear* **the words**—rather, "Should *ye* not *do* the words," as their question naturally was as to what they should do (vs. 3); "hearing" is not mentioned till vs. 12. The sense is, It is not fasts that Jehovah requires of you, but that ye should keep His precepts given to you at the time when Jerusalem was in its integrity. Had ye done so then, ye would have had no occasion to institute fasts to commemorate its destruction, for it would never have been destroyed (vss. 9-14) [MAURER]. Or, as *Margin*, "*Are* not *these* the words" of the older prophets (Isa. 58:3; Jer. 14:12) which threatened a curse for disobedience, which the event has so awfully confirmed. If ye follow them in sin, ye must follow them in suffering. *English Version* is good sense: Ye inquire anxiously about the fasts, whereas ye ought to be anxious about *hearing* the lesson taught by the former prophets and verified in the nation's punishment; penitence and obedience are required rather than fasts. **the plain**—southwest of Jerusalem. They then inhabited securely the region most unguarded.

9. speaketh—implying that these precepts addressed to their ancestors were the requirements of Jehovah not merely then, but *now*. We must not only not hurt, but we must help our fellow men. God is pleased with such loving obedience, rather than with empty ceremonies. **10. imagine evil**—i.e., devise evil. LXX takes it, Harbor not the desire of revenge (Lev. 19:18). "Devise evil against one another" is simpler (Ps. 36:4; Mic. 2:1). **11. pulled away the shoulder**—lit., "presented a refractory shoulder"; an image from beasts refusing to bear the yoke (*Margin*, Neh. 9:29). **stopped . . . ears**—

ADAM CLARKE

F. B. MEYER:

The penalty of injustice and cruelty. During their captivity the Jews observed four feasts. That of the tenth month recalled the first enclosure of Jerusalem by the enemies' lines; of the fourth the capture of the city; of the fifth the destruction by fire of the Temple; of the seventh the murder of Gedaliah. The national life was depressed by this constant memory of disaster. It seemed incongruous to act thus, when the Holy City was rising from the dust. Surely the lamentations which were befitting in Babylon were out of place now. A deputation was therefore sent to inquire the views of the leaders. Zechariah gave four separate answers to the request. In vv. 4–7 he suggests that as these fasts had been set up by themselves, they were at liberty to discontinue them, and the main question was whether they were pondering the teachings and warnings of the older prophets.
—*Bible Commentary*

5. *When ye fasted and mourned in the fifth . . . month.* This they did in the remembrance of the burning of the Temple, on the tenth day of that month; and in the seventh month, on the third of which month they observed a fast for the murder of Gedaliah, and the dispersion of the remnant of the people which were with him. See Jer. xli. 1 and 2 Kings xxv. 25.

7. *The words which the Lord hath cried by the former prophets. Nebiim harishonim* is the title which the Jews give to Joshua, Judges, the two Books of Samuel, and the two Books of Kings. The "latter prophets," *nebiim acharonim,* are Isaiah, Jeremiah, Ezekiel, and the twelve minor prophets.

The south and the plain. The *south* was the wilderness and mountainous parts of Judea; and the *plain,* the plains of Jericho.

11. *Pulled away the shoulder.* From under the yoke of the law, like an unbroken or restive bullock in the plough.

MATTHEW HENRY

they pulled away the shoulder, and would not submit to the *easy yoke and light burden* of God's commandments. *They gave a withdrawing shoulder* (so the word is); they seemed to lay their shoulder to the work, but they presently withdrew it again, as those Jer. xxxiv. 10, 11. *They made their hearts as an adamant-stone*, as a *diamond*, the hardest of stones to be wrought upon, or as a *flint*. Nothing is so hard, so unmalleable as the heart of a presumptuous sinner. The reason why men are not good is because they will not be so; they will not consider, will not comply; and therefore God says, *if thou scornest, thou alone shalt bear it*.

III. He shows the fatal consequences to their fathers: *Therefore came great wrath from the Lord of hosts*. As they had turned a deaf ear to God's word, so God turned a deaf ear to their prayers, *v.* 13. As they flew from their allegiance to God, so God dissipated them and threw them about as chaff before a whirlwind: *He scattered them among all the nations whom they knew not*, *v.* 14. As they violated all the laws of their land, so God took away all the glories of it: *Their land was desolate after them, and no man passed through or returned*. It was not so much the Chaldeans that did it. No; they did it themselves.

JAMIESON, FAUSSET, BROWN

(Isa. 6:10; Jer. 7:26; Acts 7:57). **12. hearts . . . adamant**–(Ezek. 3:9; 11:19). **Lord . . . sent in his Spirit by . . . prophets**–i.e., sent by the former prophets *inspired with His Spirit*. **therefore . . . great wrath**–(II Chron. 36:16). As they pushed from them the yoke of obedience, God laid on them the yoke of oppression. As they made their heart hard as adamant, God brake their hard hearts with judgments. Hard hearts must expect hard treatment. The harder the stone, the harder the blow of the hammer to break it. **3. he cried**–by His prophets. **they cried**–in their calamities. **I . . . not hear**–retribution in kind (Prov. 1:24-26; Isa. 1:15; Mic. 3:4) **14. whirlwind**–of wrath (Nah. 1:3). **nations whom they knew not**–foreign and barbarous. **desolate after them**–after their expulsion and exile. It was ordered remarkably by God's providence, that no occupants took possession of it, but that during the Jews' absence it was reserved for them against their return after seventy years. **they laid . . . desolate**–The Jews did so by their sins. The blame of their destruction lay with themselves, rather than with the Babylonians (II Chron. 36:21). **pleasant land**–Canaan. Lit., "the land of desire" (Jer. 3:19).

ADAM CLARKE

14. *I scattered them with a whirlwind*. This refers to the swift victories and cruel conduct of the Chaldeans towards the Jews. They came upon them like a whirlwind; they were tossed to and fro, and up and down, everywhere scattered and confounded.

MATTHEW HENRY — CHAPTER 8

Verses 1–8

The prophet designed to bring them to repentance not to drive them to despair, so here sets before them the great things God had in store for them.

I. God will appear for Jerusalem, and will be revenged on Zion's enemies (*v.* 2). The great wrath that was against her (*ch.* vii. 12) now turns against her adversaries. "*I have returned to Zion*, after I had seemed so long to stand at a distance, and I will again *dwell in the midst of Jerusalem* as formerly." This secures to them the tokens of his presence in his ordinances and in his providences.

II. There shall be a wonderful reformation in Jerusalem, and religion shall flourish there. *Jerusalem*, that has dealt treacherously both with God and man, shall become so famous for fidelity and honesty that it *shall be called* and known by the name of *a city of truth*, and the inhabitants of it shall be called *children that will not lie*.

III. There shall be in Jerusalem a great increase of people, and all the marks of a profound tranquillity. *In the streets of Jerusalem*, that had been filled with the bodies of the slain, shall now dwell *old men* and *old women*, who have not been cut off by untimely deaths, but have the even thread of their days spun out to a full length; they shall go to their grave in a full age, as a *shock of corn in his season*. The hoary head, as it is a crown of glory to those that wear it, so it is to the places where they live. It is a graceful thing to a city to see abundance of old people in it; it is a sign, not only of the healthfulness of the air, but of the prevalence of virtue and the banishment of vices, a sign, not only that the climate is temperate, but that the people are so. You may look with as much pleasure upon the generation that is rising up in their room (*v.* 5): *The streets of the city shall be full of boys and girls playing in the streets*. Their children shall be healthful, and strong, shall be hearty and cheerful. It is their pleasant playing age; let us not grudge it to them; much good may it do them and no harm. They shall not be terrified with the alarms of war, but enjoy a perfect security.

IV. The scattered Israelites shall be brought together again from all parts whither they were dispersed (*v.* 7): "*I will save my people from the east country, and from the west*; I will save them from being lost, or losing themselves, in Babylon, or in Egypt, or in any other country whither they were driven."

V. God would renew his covenant with them: *They shall be my people and I will be their God*. That is the foundation and crown of all these promises, and is inclusive of all happiness. God will never leave nor forsake them in a way of mercy, as he has promised them; and they shall never leave nor forsake him in a way of duty, as they have promised him. These promises were fulfilled in the flourishing state of the Jewish church, between the captivity and Christ's time; they were to have a further and a fuller accomplishment in the gospel-church, but the fullest accomplishment of all will be in the future state.

All doubts of God's people are silenced with that question (*v.* 6): "*If it be marvellous in the eyes of this people, should it be marvellous in my eyes?* If it seem unlikely to you that ever Jerusalem should be thus repaired, should be thus replenished, is it therefore impossible with God?"

JAMIESON, FAUSSET, BROWN — CHAPTER 8

Vss. 1-23. Continuation of the Subject in Chap. 7. *After urging them to obedience by the fate of their fathers, he urges them to it by promises of coming prosperity*. **2. jealous for Zion**–(ch. 1:14). **with great fury**–against her oppressors. **3. I am returned**–i.e., I am determined to return. My decree to that effect is gone forth.

Jerusalem . . . city of truth–i.e., faithful to her God, who is the God of truth (Isa. 1:21, 26; John 17:17). Never yet fully fulfilled, therefore still to be so. **the mountain of the Lord**–(Isa. 2:2, 3). **holy mountain**–(Jer. 31:23).

4. So tranquil and prosperous shall the nation be that wars shall no longer prematurely cut off the people: men and women shall reach advanced ages. The promise of long life was esteemed one of the greatest blessings in the Jewish theocracy with its temporal rewards of obedience (Exod. 20:12; Deut. 4:40). Hence this is a leading feature in millennial blessedness (Isa. 65:20, 22). **for very age**–lit., "for multitude of days." **5. boys and girls playing**–implying security and a numerous progeny, accounted a leading blessing among the Jews. Contrast Jeremiah 6:11; 9:21. **6.** However impossible these things just promised by Me seem to you, they are not so with God. The "remnant" that had returned from the captivity, beholding the city desolate and the walls and houses in ruins, could hardly believe what God promised. The expression "remnant" glances at their ingratitude in rating so low God's power, though they had experienced it so "marvellously" displayed in their restoration. A great source of unbelief is, men "limit" God's power by their own (Ps. 78:19, 20, 41). **these days**–"of small things" (ch. 4:10), when such great things promised seemed incredible. Maurer, after Jerome, translates, "in *those* days"; i.e., if the thing which I promised to do in *those* days, seems "marvellous . . . ." **7. save my people from . . . east . . . west**–i.e., from every region (cf. Ps. 50:1; the "West" is lit., "the going down of the sun") to which they are scattered; they are now found especially in countries west of Jerusalem. The dispersion under Nebuchadnezzar was only to the east, viz., to Babylonia. The restoration, including a spiritual return to God (vs. 8), here foretold, must therefore be still future (Isa. 11:11, 12; 43:5, 6; Ezek. 37:21; Amos 9:14, 15; also ch. 13:9; Jer. 30:22; 31:1, 33). **8. in truth**–in good faith, both on their side and Mine: God being faithful to His everlasting covenant and enabling them by His Spirit to be faithful to Him.

ADAM CLARKE — CHAPTER 8

2. *I was jealous*. Some refer this to the Jews themselves. They were as the spouse of Jehovah; but they were unfaithful, and God punished them as an injured husband might be expected to punish an unfaithful wife. Others apply it to the enemies of the Jews. Though I gave them a commission to afflict you, yet they exceeded their commission. I will therefore deal with them in *fury*—in vindictive justice.

3. *I am returned unto Zion*. I have restored her from her captivity. I will dwell among them. The Temple shall be rebuilt, and so shall Jerusalem; and instead of being false, unholy, and profligate, it shall be the *city of truth*, and My *holy mountain*.

6. *If it be marvellous*. You may think that this is impossible, considering your present low condition. But suppose it be impossible in your eyes, should it be so in Mine? *saith the Lord of hosts*.

7. *I will save my people from the east country, and from the west*. From every land in which any of them may be found. But these promises principally regard the Christian Church, or the bringing in the Jews with the fullness of the Gentiles.

MATTHEW HENRY

Verses 9–17

God, by the prophet, here gives further assurances of the mercy he had in store for Judah and Jerusalem. These verses contain strong encouragements.

I. These encouragements belong—to those who, in obedience to the call of God by his prophets, applied in good earnest to the building of the temple (*v.* 9). Those, and those only, that are employed for God, may expect to be encouraged by him; those who lay their hands to the plough of duty shall have them strengthened with the promises of mercy.

II. The discouragements they had hitherto laboured under, *v.* 10, are mentioned as a foil to the blessings God was now about to bestow upon them. *Before these days* of reformation began *there was no hire for man, nor any hire for beasts.* The fruits of the earth were thin and poor. Merchants had no goods to export, so that they needed not to hire either men or beasts.

There was no such thing as friendship or good neighbourship among them: *I set all men everyone against his neighbour.* In this there was a great deal of sin, for these wars and fightings came from men's lust.

III. "Thus and thus you have been harassed and afflicted, but now God will change his way towards you, *v.* 11. Now that you return to your duty the ebbing tide shall flow again." They shall have great plenty and abundance of all good things (*v.* 12). The *heavens shall give their dew,* without which the earth would not yield her increase, which is a constant intimation to us of the beneficence of the God of heaven to men on earth and of their dependence on him. They shall recover their credit among their neighbours (*v.* 13).

The blessed of the Lord are the blessing of the land, and should be so accounted. God himself will determine to do them good, *v.* 14, 15.

IV. Let them take comfort in these promises: *Fear you not* (*v.* 15); *let your hands be strong* (*v.* 9 and *v.* 13). Let them do the duty which those promises call for from them, *v.* 16, 17. "Leave it to God to perform for you what he has promised, in his own way and time, but upon condition that you make conscience of your duty. *These are the things then that you shall do.* You must never tell a lie, but *Speak you every man the truth to his neighbour. Execute the judgment of truth and peace in your gates.* Let the judges that sit in the gates have regard both to truth and to peace. No man must bear malice against his neighbour. Great reverence must be had for an oath, and conscience made of it." The things there forbidden are all of them found among the *seven things which the Lord hates,* Prov. vi. 16–19.

Verses 18–23

These verses contain two precious promises, for the further encouragement of those Jews that were building the temple.

I. Their fasts should be converted into thanksgiving days, *v.* 19. Joyous times will come to the church after troublous times; if weeping endure for more than a night, and joy come not next morning, yet the morning will come that will introduce it at length. Let the truths of God rule in your heads, and let the peace of God rule in your hearts.

JAMIESON, FAUSSET, BROWN

9-13. All adversities formerly attended them when neglecting to build the temple: but now God promises all blessings, as an encouragement to energy in the work. **hands . . . strong**–be of courageous mind (II Sam. 16:21), not merely in building, but in general, as having such bright prospects (vs. 13, etc.). **these days**–the time that had elapsed between the prophet's having spoken "these words" and the time (vs. 10; cf. Hag. 2:15-19) when they set about in earnest restoring the temple. **the prophets**–Haggai and Zechariah himself (Ezra 5:1, 2). The same prophets who promised prosperity at the foundation of the temple, now promised still greater blessings hereafter. **10. before these days**–before the time in which ye again proceeded with the building of the temple (vs. 9), viz., at the time that the temple lay neglected. **no hire for man . . . beast**–i.e., no produce of the field to repay the labor of man and beast on it (Hag. 1:6, 9, 10; 2:16). **neither . . . peace to him that went out or came in**–(II Chron. 15:5). No one could in safety do his business at home or abroad, in the city or in the country, whether going or returning. **because of the affliction**–so *sorely pressed* were they by the foe outside. MAURER translates, "Because of *the foe*" (Ezra 4:1). **every one against . . . neighbour**–There was internal discord, as well as foes from without. **11.** "But now that the temple has been built, I will not do as I had formerly done to those who returned from Babylon" [JEROME]. Henceforth I will bless you. **12. seed . . . prosperous**–i.e., shall not fail to yield abundantly (Hos. 2:21,22; Hag. 2:19). Contrast with this verse Haggai 1:6, 9-11; 2:16. **dew**–especially beneficial in hot countries where rain is rare. **13. a curse**–As the heathen have made you another name for "a curse," wishing to their foes as bad a lot as yours (Jer. 24:9; 29:18); so your name shall be a formula of blessing, so that men shall say to their friend, May thy lot be as happy as that of Judah (Gen. 48:20). Including also the idea of the Jews being a source of blessing to the Gentile nations (Mic. 5:7; Zeph. 3:20). The distinct mention of "Judah" and "Israel" proves that the prophecy has not yet had its full accomplishment, as *Israel* (the ten tribes) has never yet been restored, though *individuals* of Israel returned with Judah. **14. I thought**–I determined. **you**–i.e., your fathers, with whom ye are one; the Jewish Church of all ages being regarded as an organic whole (cf. Hag. 2:5; Matt. 23:31, 32). **repented not**–I changed not My purpose, because they changed not their mind (II Chron. 36:16). With the froward God shows Himself froward (Ps. 18:26). If the threatened punishment has been so unchangeably inflicted, much more will God surely give the promised blessing, which is so much more consonant to His nature (Jer. 31:28). **16, 17.** The promised blessings are connected with obedience. God's covenanted grace will lead those truly blessed by it to holiness, not licentiousness. **truth to . . . neighbour**–not that the truth should not be spoken to foreigners too; but He makes it an aggravation of their sin, that they spared not even their brethren. Besides, and above all outward ordinances (ch. 7:3), God requires truth and justice. **judgment of . . . peace**–Equitable decisions tend to allay feuds and produce peace. **gates**–the place where courts of judicature in the East were held. **17. all these . . . I hate**–therefore ye too ought to hate them. Religion consists in conformity to God's nature, that we should love what God loves and hate what God hates. **18, 19.** The prophet answers the query (ch. 7:3) as to the fast in the fifth month, by a reply applying to all their fasts: these are to be turned into days of rejoicing. So Jesus replied to His disciples when similarly consulting Him as to why fasting was not imposed by Him, as it was by John the Baptist. When the Sun of righteousness shines, tears are dried up (Matt. 9:15). So hereafter (Isa. 35:10). **fast of . . . fourth month**–On the fourth month of the eleventh year of Zedekiah's reign, on the ninth day, Jerusalem was taken (Jer. 39:2; 52:6, 7). It was therefore made a fast day. **fifth . . . seventh**–(*Notes,* ch. 7:3-5). **tenth**–On the tenth month and tenth day, in the ninth year of Zedekiah, the siege began (Jer. 52:4). **therefore love the truth**–or, "*only* love." *English Version* is better. God's blessing covenanted to Israel is not made to depend on Israel's goodness: but Israel's goodness should follow as the consequence of God's gracious promises (vss. 16, 17; ch. 7:9, 10). God will bless, but not those who harden themselves in sin. **20.** (Isa. 2:3; Mic. 4:2.) **Thus saith the Lord of hosts**–a preface needed to assure the Jews, now disheartened by the perils surrounding them, and by the humble aspect of the temple. "Unlikely as what follows may seem to you, *Jehovah of hosts,* boundless in

ADAM CLARKE

9. *By the mouth of the prophets.* The day or time of the foundation was about two years before, as this discourse of the prophet was in the fourth year of Darius.

KEIL-DELITZSCH:

This phrase does not refer specially to their courageous continuation of the building of the temple, but has the more general meaning of taking courage to accomplish what the calling of each required, as verses 10–13 show. The persons addressed are those who hear the words of the prophets in these days. This suggests a motive for taking courage. Because they hear these words, they are to look forward with comfort to the future, and do what their calling requires. The words of the prophets are the promises which Zechariah announced in verses 2–8, and his contemporary Haggai in ch. 2. It will not do to take the plural in a general sense, as referring to Zechariah alone. For if there had been no prophet at that time beside Zechariah, he could not have spoken in general terms of prophets. But the defining phrase, who are or who rose up at the time when the foundation of the temple was laid, these prophets are distinguished from the earlier ones before the captivity (7:7, 12; 1:4), and their words are thereby limited to what Haggai and Zechariah prophesied from that time downwards.

—*Commentary on the Old Testament*

19. *The fast of the fourth month.* To commemorate the taking of Jerusalem, 2 Kings xxv. 3; Jer. xxxix. 2; and lii. 6-7. *The fast of the fifth.* In memory of the ruin of the Temple, 2 Kings xxv. 8; Jer. lii. 12-13. *The fast of the seventh.* For the murder of Gedaliah, Jer. xli. 1-17. *The fast of the tenth.* In commemoration of the siege of Jerusalem, which began on the tenth day of the tenth month, 2 Kings xxv. 1; Jer. lii. 4; Ezek. xxiv. 1-2; and see on chap. vii. 3, 5.

MATTHEW HENRY

II. A great accession should be made to the church by the conversion of many foreigners, *v.* 20–23. This was fulfilled in part when, in the latter times of the Jewish church, there were many proselytes from countries nearby or remote, who came yearly to worship at Jerusalem, which added to the grandeur and wealth of that city, making it considerable before our Saviour's time, though now it was but just peeping out of its ruins. But it would be accomplished much more fully in the conversion of the Gentiles to the faith of Christ, and incorporating them with the believing Jews in one body, under Christ the head (Rom. xvi. 26). The inhabitants of many cities shall embrace the gospel of Christ; *yea, many people and strong nations* (*v.* 22), some of *all languages, v.* 23. They shall come *to pray before the Lord and to seek the Lord of hosts* (*v.* 21). Converts to God and members of the church are such as *seek the Lord of hosts,* such as enquire for *God their Maker,* and are sincerely devoted to his honour and glory. They are such as *pray before the Lord.* They shall be zealous in exciting one another to it (*v.* 21): *The inhabitants of one city shall go to another,* and they shall say, *Let us go speedily to pray before the Lord; I will go also.* Those who are brought into an acquaintance with Christ themselves should do all they can to bring others; thus Andrew invited Peter to Christ and Philip invited Nathanael. True grace hates monopolies. As iron sharpens iron, so may good men sharpen the countenances and spirits one of another in that which is good. They shall join themselves to the church, not for the church's sake, but for his sake who dwells in it (*v.* 23). This intimates the great honour they have for a Jew, as one of the chosen people of God. *We will go with you, for we have heard that God is with you.*

JAMIESON, FAUSSET, BROWN

resources, *saith* it, therefore it shall be so." Just before Christ's coming, a feeling grew up among the heathen of the unsatisfactoriness of their systems of religion and philosophy; this disposed them favorably towards the religion of the Jew, so that proselytes embraced the worship of Jehovah from various parts of Asia; these again were predisposed to embrace Christianity when it was preached to them (Acts 2:9-12, 41). But the full accomplishment of the conversion of the Gentiles foretold here is reserved till "Jerusalem" (vs. 22) becomes the center of Christianized Jewry (Rom. 11:12, 15). **21. Let us . . . I**—manifesting zeal and love: converted themselves, they seek the conversion of others (Song of Sol. 1:4). To exhortation in *general* ("Let us go"), they add *individual* example ("I will go"). Or, the change from *plural* to *singular* implies that the *general* consent in religious earnestness leads *each individual* to decide for God. **go speedily**—lit., "go, going"; implying intense earnestness. **pray**—*Hebrew, entreat the face* (ch. 7:2); entreat His favor and grace. **22. many . . . strong nations . . . in Jerusalem**—In contrast to the few and weak Jews now building the temple and city, then such shall be their influence that *many and strong nations* shall come to worship Jehovah their God in Jerusalem (Isa. 60: 3; 66:23). **23. ten**—a definite number for an indefinite. So in Leviticus 22:26; Numbers 14:22. **of all languages of the nations**—i.e., of nations of all languages (cf. Isa. 66:18; Rev. 7:9). **take hold of the skirt**—a gesture of suppliant entreaty as to a superior. Cf. Isa. 3:6; 4:1, on a different occasion. The Gentiles shall eagerly seek to share the religious privileges of the Jew. The skirt with a fringe and blue ribbon upon it (Num. 15:38; Deut. 22:12) was a distinguishing badge of a Jew. **God is with you**—the effect produced on unbelievers in entering the assemblies of the Church (I Cor. 14:25). But primarily, that produced on the nations in witnessing the deliverance of the Jews by Cyrus. Finally, that to be produced on the nations by the future grand interposition of Messiah in behalf of His people.

ADAM CLARKE

20. *There shall come people.* Similar promises to those in Isa. ii. 3 and in Mic. iv. 1-2.

23. *Ten men . . . shall take hold of the skirt of him that is a Jew.* The converts from among the Gentiles shall be to the Jews as ten to one. But *ten* may here signify a great number, without comparison.

MATTHEW HENRY — CHAPTER 9

Verses 1–8

I. The Syrians had been bad neighbours to Israel. The word of the Lord shall be a *burden in the land of Hadrach,* that is, of *Syria.* Damascus is the metropolis of that kingdom, and the judgments here threatened shall lie upon it.

And the reason of this burden's resting on Damascus is because *the eyes of man, as of all the tribes of Israel* (or rather, *even of all the tribes of Israel*), are *towards the Lord,* because the people of God by faith and prayer look up to him for succour and relief against their enemies. When St. Paul was converted at Damascus, and preached there, and disputed with the Jews, then the word of the Lord might be said to rest there, and then *the eyes of men,* of other men besides *the tribes of Israel,* began to be *towards the Lord*; see Acts ix. 22.

JAMIESON, FAUSSET, BROWN — CHAPTER 9

Vss. 1-17. Chaps. 9 to 14 Are Prophetical. Written long after the previous portions of the book, whence arise the various features which have been made grounds for attacking their authenticity, notwithstanding the testimony of the LXX and of the compilers of the Jewish canon in their favor. See *Introduction.* Alexander's Conquests in Syria (vss. 1-8). God's People Safe because Her King Cometh Lowly, but a Saviour (vss. 9-10). The Maccabean Deliverance a Type Thereof (vss. 11-17). **1. in . . . Hadrach**—rather, *concerning* or *against* Hadrach (cf. Isa. 21:13). "Burden" means a *prophecy* burdened *with wrath against the guilty.* Maurer, not so well, explains it, *What is taken up and uttered, the utterance, a solemn declaration.* **Hadrach**—a part of Syria, near Damascus. As the name is not mentioned in ancient histories, it probably was the less-used name of a region having two names (Hadrach and Bikathaven, *Margin,* Amos 1: 5); hence it passed into oblivion. An ancient Rabbi Jose is, however, stated to have expressly mentioned it. Ant Arab, Jos. Abassi, in 1768 also declared to Michaelis that there was then a town of that name, and that it was capital of the region Hadrach. The name means "enclosed" in Syrian, i.e., the west interior part of Syria, *enclosed* by hills, the Cœlo-Syria of Strabo [Maurer]. Jerome considers Hadrach to be the metropolis of Cœlo-Syria, as Damascus was of the region about that city. Hengstenberg regards Hadrach as a symbolical name of Persia, which Zechariah avoids designating by its proper name so as not to offend the government under which he lived. But the context seems to refer to the Syrian region. Gesenius thinks that the name is that of a Syrian king, which might more easily pass into oblivion than that of a region. Cf. the similar "land of Sihon," Nehemiah 9:22. **Damascus . . . rest thereof**—i.e., the place on which the "burden" of the Lord's wrath shall rest. It shall permanently settle on it until Syria is utterly prostrate. Fulfilled under Alexander the Great, who overcame Syria [Curtius, B. 3 and 4]. **eyes of man, as of all . . . Israel . . . toward the Lord**—The eyes of men in general, and of all Israel in particular, through consternation at the victorious progress of Alexander, shall be directed to Jehovah. The Jews, when threatened by him because of Jaddua the high priest's refusal to swear fealty to him, prayed earnestly to the Lord, and so were delivered (II Chron. 20:12; Ps. 23:2). Typical of the effect of God's judgments hereafter on all men, and espe-

ADAM CLARKE — CHAPTER 9

1. *The burden of the word of the Lord.* The oracle contained in the word which Jehovah now speaks. This is a prophecy against Syria, the Philistines, Tyre, and Sidon, which were to be subdued by Alexander the Great. After this the prophet speaks gloriously concerning the coming of Christ, and redemption by Him.

Most learned men are of opinion that this and the succeeding chapters are not the work of Zechariah, but rather of Jeremiah, Hosea, or someone before the Captivity. It is certain that chap. xi. 12-13 is quoted in Matt. xxvii. 9-10, as the language of Jeremiah, the prophet. The first eight chapters appear by the introductory parts to be the prophecies of Zechariah. They stand in connection with each other, are pertinent to the time when they were delivered, are uniform in style and manner, and constitute a regular whole. But the last six chapters are not expressly assigned to Zechariah, and are unconnected with those that precede. The first three of them are unsuitable in many parts to the time when Zechariah lived; all of them have a more adorned and poetical turn of composition than the first eight chapters, and they manifestly break the unity of the prophetical book.

I conclude, from internal marks, that these three chapters (ix; x; xi) were written much earlier than the time of Jeremiah, and before the captivity of the ten tribes. They seem to suit Hosea's age and manner; but whoever wrote them, their divine authority is established by the two quotations from them, chap. ix. 9 and xi. 12-13.

The twelfth, thirteenth, and fourteenth chapters form a distinct prophecy, and were written after the death of Josiah, chap. xii. 11; but whether before or after the Captivity, and by what prophet, is uncertain, although I incline to think that the author lived before the destruction of Jerusalem by the Babylonians. See on chap. xiii. 2-6. They are twice quoted in the New Testament, chap. xii. 10 and xiii. 7 (Newcome).

My own opinion is that these chapters form not only a distinct work, but belong to a different author. If they do not belong to Jeremiah, they form a thirteenth book in the minor prophets, but the inspired writer is unknown.

The land of Hadrach. The valley of Damascus,

MATTHEW HENRY

II. Tyre and Zidon come next to be called to account as in other prophecies, *v.* 2–4. Tyrus flourishing, thinking herself very safe, is ready to set God's judgments at defiance. She is *very wise.* It is spoken ironically; she thinks herself very wise!

But there is no *wisdom* nor *counsel against the Lord*; nay, it is his honour to take the wise in their own craftiness. *Tyrus did build herself a stronghold,* which she thought could never be brought down nor got over. By her vast trade she has *heaped up silver as the dust,* as common as heaps of sand. Tyre made *fine gold* to be as *the mire of the streets.*

Her wisdom, and wealth, and strength, shall not be able to secure her (*v.* 4): *The Lord will cast her out* of that stronghold wherein she has fortified herself, will *make her poor.*

God will *smite her power in the sea*; her being surrounded by the water shall not secure her, but *she shall be devoured with fire,* and burnt down to the ground.

III. God next contends with the Philistines, with their great cities that bordered southward upon Israel. Now *Ashkelon shall see* the ruin of her friends and allies, and shall *fear*; *Gaza also shall see it, and be very sorrowful, and Ekron.* What will become of their house when their neighbour's is on fire? They shall themselves be ruined and wasted.

The king shall perish from Gaza. Ashkelon shall not be inhabited. Foreigners shall take possession of their land (*v.* 6): *A bastard shall dwell in Ashdod.* And thus God will *cut off the pride of the Philistines.* This prophecy of the destruction of the Philistines, and of Damascus, and Tyre, was accomplished, not long after this, by Alexander the Great, who ravaged all these countries, took the cities, and planted colonies in them. Some understand *v.* 7 as a promise that God would take away the sins of these nations—*their blood* and *their abominations,* their cruelties and their idolatries. He would preserve a remnant even of these nations, that should be monuments of his mercy and grace.

JAMIESON, FAUSSET, BROWN

cially on the Jews in turning them to Him. MAURER, PEMBELLUS and others, less probably translate, "The eyes of the Lord are upon man, as they are upon all Israel," viz., to punish the ungodly and to protect His people. He, who has chastised His people, will not fail to punish men for their sins severely. The "all," I think, implies that whereas men's attention generally (whence "man" is the expression) was directed to Jehovah's judgments, *all* Israel especially looks to Him. **2. Hamath**—a Syrian kingdom with a capital of the same name, north of Damascus. **shall border thereby**—shall be joined to Damascus in treatment, as it is in position; shall share in the burden of wrath of which Damascus is the resting-place. MAURER understands "which"; "Hamath, which borders on Damascus, also *shall be the resting-place of Jehovah's wrath*" (the latter words being supplied from vs. 1). Riblah, the scene of the Jews' sufferings from their foe, was there: it therefore shall suffer (II Kings 23: 33; 25:6, 7, 20, 21). **Tyrus . . . Zidon**—lying in the conqueror's way on his march along the Mediterranean to Egypt (cf. Isa. 23). Zidon, the older city, surrendered, and Abdolonymus was made its viceroy. **very wise**—in her own eyes. Referring to Tyre: vs. 3 shows wherein her *wisdom* consisted, viz., *in building a stronghold,* and *heaping up gold and silver* (Ezek. 38:3, 5, 12, 17). On Alexander's expressing his wish to sacrifice in Hercules' temple in New Tyre on the island, she showed her wisdom in sending a golden crown, and replying that the true and ancient temple of Hercules was at Old Tyre on the mainland. With all her wisdom she cannot avert her doom. **3.** The heathen historian, DIODORUS SICULUS (17. 40), confirms this. "Tyre had the greatest confidence owing to her insular position and fortifications, and the abundant stores she had prepared." New Tyre was on an island 700 paces from the shore. As Isaiah's and Ezekiel's (Ezekiel 27) prophecies were directed against Old Tyre on the mainland and were fulfilled by Nebuchadnezzar, so Zechariah's are against New Tyre, which was made seemingly impregnable by a double wall 150 feet high, as well as the sea on all sides. **4.** (Ezek. 26:4, 12; 27:27). **cast her out**—*Hebrew,* "dispossess her," i.e., will cast her inhabitants into exile [GROTIUS]. Alexander, though without a navy, by incredible labor constructed a mole of the ruins of Old Tyre (fulfilling Ezek. 26:4-12, etc., by "scraping her dust from her," and "laying her stones, timber, and dust in the midst of the water"), from the shore to the island, and, after a seven months' siege, took the city by storm, slew with the sword about 8000, enslaved 13,000, crucified 2000, and set the city on "fire," as here foretold [CURTIUS, B. 4]. **smite her power in the sea**—situated though she be *in the sea,* and so seeming impregnable (cf. Ezek. 28:2, "I sit in the seat of God, *in the midst of the sea*"). "Her power" includes not only her fortifications, but her fleet, all of which Alexander sank *in the sea* before her very walls [CURTIUS, B. 4]. Ezekiel 26:17 corresponds, "How art thou destroyed which wast strong in the sea!" **5. Ashkelon . . .**—Gath alone is omitted, perhaps as being somewhat inland, and so out of the route of the advancing conqueror. **Ekron . . . expectation . . . ashamed**—Ekron, the farthest north of the Philistine cities, had *expected* Tyre would withstand Alexander, and so check his progress southward through Philistia to Egypt. This hope being confounded ("put to *shame*"), Ekron shall "fear." **king shall perish from Gaza**—Its government shall be overthrown. In literal fulfilment of this prophecy, after a two month's siege, Gaza was taken by Alexander, 10,000 of its inhabitants slain, and the rest sold as slaves. Betis the satrap, or petty "king," was bound to a chariot by thongs thrust through the soles of his feet, and dragged round the city. **6. bastard**—not the rightful heir; vile and low men, such as are bastards (Deut. 23:2) [GROTIUS]. *An alien*; so LXX; implying the desolation of the region wherein men shall not settle, but sojourn in only as aliens passing through [CALVIN]. **7. take . . . his blood out of . . . mouth**—*Blood* was forbidden as food (Gen. 9:4; Lev. 7:26). **abominations**—things sacrificed to idols and then partaken of by the worshippers (Num. 25:2; Acts 15:29). The sense is, "I will cause the Philistines to cease from the worship of idols." **even he** *shall be* **for our God**—"even he," like Hamath, Damascus, Tyre, etc., which, these words imply, shall also be converted to God (Isa. 56:3. "son of the stranger joined himself to the Lord") [ROSENMULLER]. The "even," however, may mean, *Besides the Hebrews,* "even" the Philistine shall worship Jehovah (so Isa. 56:8) [MAURER]. **he shall be as a governor in Judah**—On the conversion of the Philistine prince, he shall have

ADAM CLARKE

or a place near to Damascus. Alexander the Great gained possession of Damascus, and took all its treasures; but it was without blood; the city was betrayed to him. *Damascus shall be the rest thereof.* The principal part of this calamity shall fall on this city. God's anger "rests" on those whom He punishes, Ezek. v. 13; xvi. 42; xxiv. 13. *When the eyes of man.* Newcome translates thus: "For the eye of Jehovah is over man, and over all the tribes of Israel." This is an easy sense, and is followed by the versions.

2. *And Hamath also shall border thereby. Hamath* on the river Orontes; and Tyre and Sidon, notwithstanding their political wisdom, address, and cunning, shall have a part in the punishment. These prophecies are more suitable to the days of Jeremiah than to those of Zechariah; for there is no evidence—although Alexander did take Damascus, but without bloodshed—that it was destroyed from the times of Zechariah to the advent of our Lord. And as Tyre and Sidon were lately destroyed by Nebuchadnezzar, it is not likely that they could soon undergo another devastation.

3. *And Tyrus did build herself.* The rock on which Tyre was built was strongly fortified; and that she had abundance of riches has been already seen, Ezek. xxviii. 1, etc.

4. *Will smite her power in the sea.* See Ezek. xxvi. 17. Though Alexander did take Tyre, Sidon, Gaza, etc., yet it seems that the prediction relative to their destruction was fulfilled by Nebuchadnezzar. See Amos i. 6-8; Zeph. ii. 4, 7.

5. *Ashkelon shall see it, and fear.* All these prophecies seem to have been fulfilled before the days of Zechariah—another evidence that these last chapters were not written by him. *Her expectation shall be ashamed.* The expectation of being succored by Tyre.

7. *I will take away his blood out of his mouth.* The Philistines, when incorporated with the Israelites, shall abstain from blood, and everything that is abominable.

MATTHEW HENRY

Their birth shall be no bar to their acceptance with God, but a Philistine shall be as acceptable to God, upon gospel-terms, as one of Judah, and a man of Ekron shall be as a Jebusite, or a man of Jerusalem.

IV. In all this God intends mercy for Israel, and it is in kindness to them that God will deal thus with the neighbouring nations. Thus some understand the seventh verse. God would deliver his people from their bloody adversaries, when they were just ready to devour them and make a prey of them: I will *take away his blood* (that is, the blood of Israel) out of the mouth of the Philistines and *from between their teeth* (Amos iii. 12). And *he that remains* (that is, the remnant of Israel) *shall be for our God*, shall be taken into his favour, shall own him and be owned by him, and *he shall be as a governor in Judah*. However it is plainly the sense of *v.* 8 that God will take his people under his special protection, and *therefore* will weaken their neighbours, that it may not be in their power to do them a mischief: *I will encamp about my house because of the army*. When the times are perilous, when armies are marching, and all bearing ill-will to Zion, then Providence will as it were double its guards upon the church of God, *because of him that passes by and because of him that returns*, that whether he return a conqueror or conquered he may do it no harm. This was fulfilled when, for some time after the struggles of the Maccabees, Judæa was a free and flourishing state, or perhaps when Alexander the Great, struck with an awe of Jaddus the high priest, favoured the Jews, and took them under his protection, when he wasted the neighbouring countries.

Verses 9–11

Here begins a prophecy of the Messiah and his kingdom with express application to Christ's riding in triumph into *Jerusalem*, Matt. xxi. 6; John xii. 15.

I. The approach of the Messiah promised, as matter of great joy to the Old Testament church: *Behold, thy king cometh unto thee*. Christ is a king, a sovereign prince, having all power both in heaven and on earth. In the gospel-church his spiritual kingdom is administered. "This King has been long in coming, but now, *behold, he cometh*; he is at the door. There are but a few ages more to run out, and he that shall come will come."

II. Here is such a description of him as renders his coming to them very acceptable. 1. He is a righteous ruler; *he is just*. 2. He is a powerful protector to all those that bear faith and true allegiance to him, for he *has salvation*; he has it in his power to bestow upon all his subjects.

He is a *meek, humble, tender Father* to all his subjects as his children; he is *lowly*; he is *poor* and *afflicted* (so the word signifies); having *emptied himself*, he was *despised and rejected of men*. He is *meek*, not taking state upon him, nor resenting injuries, but *humbling himself* from first to last. (Matt. xi. 29, *Learn of me, for I am meek and lowly in heart*.)

JAMIESON, FAUSSET, BROWN

the same dignity "in Judah as a governor"; there shall be no distinction [HENDERSON]. The Philistine princes with their respective states shall equally *belong to the Jews' communion, as if* they were among the "governors" of states "in Judah" [MAURER]. **Ekron as a Jebusite**—The Jebusites, the original inhabitants of Jerusalem, who, when subjugated by David, were incorporated with the Jews (II Sam. 24:16, etc.), and enjoyed their privileges: but in a subordinate position *civilly* (I Kings 9:20, 21). The Jebusites' condition under Solomon being that of bond-servants and tributaries, CALVIN explains the verse differently: "I will rescue the Jew *from the teeth* of the Philistine foe (image from wild beasts rending their prey with their *teeth*), who would have devoured him, as he would devour *blood* or flesh of his *abominable* sacrifices to idols: and *even he*, the seemingly ignoble remnant of the Jews, shall be sacred to *our God* (consecrated by His favor); and though so long bereft of dignity, I will make them to be *as governors* ruling others, and Ekron shall be a tributary bond-servant as the Jebusite." Thus the antithesis is between the Jew *that remaineth* (the elect remnant) and the Ekronite. **8. encamp about**—(Ps. 34:7). **mine house**—viz., the Jewish people (ch. 3:7; Hos. 8:1) [MAURER]. Or, *the temple:* reassuring the Jews engaged in building, who might otherwise fear their work would be undone by the conqueror [MOORE]. The Jews were, in agreement with this prophecy, uninjured by Alexander, though he punished the Samaritans. Typical of their final deliverance from every foe. **passeth by . . . returneth**—Alexander, when advancing against Jerusalem, was arrested by a dream, so that neither in "passing by" to Egypt, nor in "returning," did he injure the Jews, but conferred on them great privileges. **no oppressor . . . . pass through . . . any more**—The prophet passes from the immediate future to the final deliverance to come (Isa. 60:18; Ezek. 28:24). **seen with mine eyes**—viz., how Jerusalem has been oppressed by her foes [ROSENMULLER] (Exod. 3:7; 2:25). God is said *now* to have *seen*, because He now begins to bring the foe to judgment, and manifests to the world His sense of His people's wrongs. **9.** From the coming of the Grecian conqueror, Zechariah makes a sudden transition, by the prophetical law of suggestion, to the coming of King Messiah, a very different character. **daughter of Zion**—The theocratic people is called to "rejoice" at the coming of her King (Ps. 2:11). **unto thee**—He comes not for His own gain or pleasure, as earthly kings come, but for the sake of His Church: especially for the Jews' sake, at His second coming (Rom. 11:26). **he is just**—*righteous:* an attribute constantly given to Messiah (Isa. 45:21; 53:11; Jer. 23:5, 6) in connection with *salvation*. He does not merely pardon by conniving at sin, but He *justifies* by becoming the Lord our righteousness-fulfiller, so that not merely mercy, but justice, requires the justification of the sinner who by faith becomes one with Christ. God's justice is not set aside by the sinner's salvation, but is magnified and made honorable by it (Isa. 42:1, 21). His future *reign* "in righteousness," also, is especially referred to (Isa. 32:1). **having salvation**—not passively, as some interpret it, "saved," which the context, referring to a "king" coming to reign, forbids; also the old versions, LXX, *Syriac*, and *Vulgate*, give *Saviour*. The *Hebrew* is reflexive in sense, "showing Himself a Saviour;" "having salvation in Himself" for us. Endowed with a salvation which He bestows as a king. Cf. *Margin*, "saving Himself." Cf. Matthew 1:21, in the *Greek*, "*Himself* shall save His people"; i.e., not by any other, but by Himself shall He save [PEARSON *on the Creed*]. His "having salvation" for others manifested that He had in Himself that righteousness which was indispensable for the justification of the unrighteous (I Cor. 1:30; II Cor. 5:21; I John 2:1). This contrasts beautifully with the haughty Grecian conqueror who came to destroy, whereas Messiah came to save. Still, Messiah shall come to take "just" vengeance on His foes, previous to His reign of peace (Mall. 4:1, 2). **lowly**—mild, gentle: corresponding to His "riding on an ass" (not a despised animal, as with us; nor a badge of humiliation, for princes in the East rode on asses, as well as low persons, Judg. 5:10), i.e., coming as "Prince of *peace*" (vs. 10; Isa. 9:6); the "horse," on the contrary is the emblem of *war*, and shall therefore be "cut off." Perhaps the *Hebrew* includes both the "lowliness" of His *outward* state (which applies to His first coming) and His "meekness" *of disposition*, as Matt. 21:5 quotes it (cf. Matt. 11:29), which applies to both His comings. Both adapt Him for loving sympathy with us men; and at the same time

ADAM CLARKE

And Ekron as a Jebusite. As an inhabitant of Jerusalem. Many of the Philistines became proselytes to Judaism, and particularly the cities of Gaza and Ashdod. See Joseph. *Antiq*. lib. xiii, c. 15, s. 4.

8. *I will encamp about mine house*. This may apply to the conquests in Palestine by Alexander, who, coming with great wrath against Jerusalem, was met by Jaddua, the high priest, and his fellows in their sacred robes, who made intercession for the city and the Temple; and, in consequence, Alexander spared both, which he had previously purposed to destroy. He showed the Jews also much favor, and remitted the tax every seventh year, because the law on that year forbade them to cultivate their ground. See this extraordinary account in Joseph. *Antiq*., lib. xi, c. 8, s. 5.

9. *Rejoice greatly, O daughter of Zion*. See this prophecy explained on Matt. xxi. 5. *Behold, thy King cometh*. Not Zerubbabel, for he was never king; nor have they had a king, except Jesus, the Christ, from the days of Zedekiah to the present time. *He is just*. The righteous One, and the Fountain of righteousness.

MATTHEW HENRY

When he made his public entry into his own city (and it was the only passage of his life that had anything in it magnificent in the eye of the world), he chose to ride, not upon a stately horse, or in a chariot, as great men used to ride, but *upon an ass*, nor was it an ass fitted for use, but an *ass's colt*, a little foolish unmanageable thing, likely to disgrace his rider. He had no saddle, no trappings, no equipage, but his disciples' clothes thrown upon the colt; for he *made himself of no reputation* when he visited us in great humility.

III. His kingdom is here set forth in the glory of it. This king has a kingdom, not of this world, but a spiritual kingdom, a *kingdom of heaven*. It shall not be set up by carnal weapons of warfare. No; he *will cut off the chariot from Ephraim and the horses from Jerusalem* (*v.* 10), in kindness to his people, that they may not cut themselves off from God by putting confidence in them which they should put in the power of God only. He will establish his kingdom by proclaiming peace on earth goodwill towards men. As far as it prevails in the minds of men and has the ascendant over them, it will make them peaceable, and slay all enmities; it will cut off the battle-bow, and *beat swords into plough-shares*. The preachers of the gospel shall carry it from one country to another till the remotest corners of the world are enlightened by it.

IV. The great benefit procured for mankind by the Messiah, is redemption from extreme misery, typified by the deliverance of the Jews out of their captivity in Babylon (*v.* 11). *I have sent forth thy prisoners*, thy captives out of Babylon, which was to them as *a pit* in which was *no water*. It was part of the covenant that, if in the land of their captivity, they sought the Lord, he would be found of them, Lev. xxvi. 42, 44, 45; Deut. xxx. 4. It was *by the blood of that covenant*, typifying the blood of Christ, in whom all God's covenants with man are yea and amen, that they were released out of captivity; and this was but a shadow of the great salvation wrought out by *thy King, O daughter of Zion*!

Verses 12–17

The prophet, having taught those that had returned out of captivity to attribute their deliverance to the *blood of the covenant* and to the promise of the Messiah, now cheers them with the prospect of a joyful and happy settlement; but these promises have their full accomplishment in the spiritual blessings of the gospel which we enjoy by Jesus Christ.

I. They are invited to look unto Christ, and flee unto him as their city of refuge (*v.* 12): *Turn you to the stronghold, you prisoners of hope*. The Jews that had returned out of captivity into their own land were *prisoners of hope*, or *expectation*, for God had given them a *little reviving in their bondage*, Ezra ix. 8, 9. Those that continued in Babylon yet lived in hope some time or other to see their own land again. Now both these are directed to turn their eyes upon the Messiah. The promise of the Messiah was the stronghold of the faithful long before his coming; they saw his day at a distance and were glad, Luke ii. 25, 28. This invitation to the stronghold speaks the language of the gospel-call, *v.* 12. Sinners are prisoners, but they are prisoners of hope; Christ is a stronghold for them.

II. They are assured of God's favour to them: "*I will render double unto thee*, to everyone of you prisoners of hope." As a pledge of this, in the fulness of time God here promises to the Jews victory, plenty, and joy, in their own land, which should be but a type of more glorious victories, riches, and joys, in the kingdom of Christ.

1. They shall triumph over their enemies. The Jews, after their return, were surrounded with enemies on all sides. But it is here promised that the Lord would deliver them. They shall be instruments in God's hand for the defeating and baffling of their persecutors: "I *have bent Judah for me*, as my bow of steel; that *bow I have filled with Ephraim* as my arrows, have drawn it up to its full bent, till the arrow be at the head." But let them not think that they gain their successes by their own bow, for they themselves are no more than God's bow and his arrows, tools in his hands, which he manages as he pleases. The following words explain this: *I have raised up* and animated *thy sons, O Zion! against thy sons, O Greece!* This was fulfilled when *against Antiochus*, one of the kings of the Grecian monarchy, the people that knew their God were *strong* and *did exploits*, Dan. xi. 32. God will be commander-in-chief in every engagement (*v.* 14): *The Lord shall be seen over them*. Is their army to be mustered, and brought into the field? *The Lord shall blow the trumpet*, to gather the forces together, and to give directions. Whatever enterprise the campaign is opened with,

JAMIESON, FAUSSET, BROWN

are the ground of His coming manifested exaltation (John 5:27; Phil. 2:7-9). **colt**—untamed, "whereon yet never man sat" (Luke 19:30). The symbol of a triumphant conqueror and judge (Judg. 5:10; 10:4; 12:14). **foal of an ass**—lit., "asses": in *Hebrew* idiom, the indefinite *plural* for *singular* (so Gen. 8:4, "*mountains* of Ararat," for *one* of the mountains). The dam accompanied the colt (Matt. 21:2). The entry of Jesus into Jerusalem at His first coming is a pledge of the full accomplishment of this prophecy at His second coming. It shall be "the day of the Lord" (Ps. 118:24), as that first Palm *Sunday* was. The Jews shall then *universally* (Ps. 118:26) say, what *some* of them said then, "Blessed is He that cometh in the name of the Lord" (cf. Matt. 21:9, with 23:39); also "Hosanna," or "Save now, I beseech thee." "Palms," the emblem of triumph, shall then also be in the hands of His people (cf. John 12:13, with Rev. 7:9, 10). Then also, as on His former entry, shall be the feast of tabernacles (at which they used to draw water from Siloam, quoting Isaiah 12:3). Cf. Psalm 118:15, with ch. 14:16. **10.** (Isa. 2:4; Hos. 2:18; Mic. 5:10). **Ephraim . . . Jerusalem**—the ten tribes, and Judah and Benjamin; both alike to be restored hereafter. **speak peace**—command it authoritatively. **dominion . . . from sea . . . river . . . ends of . . . earth**—fulfilling Genesis 15:18; Exodus 23:31; and Psalm 72: 8. "Sea . . . sea," are the Red Sea and Mediterranean. The "river" is the Euphrates. Jerusalem and the Holy Land, extended to the limits promised to Abraham, are to be the center of His future dominion; whence it will extend to the remotest parts of the earth. **11. As for thee also**—i.e., the daughter of Zion," or "Jerusalem" (vs. 9): the theocracy. The "thee also," in contradistinction to *Messiah* spoken of in vs. 10, implies that besides *cutting off the battle-bow* and extending MESSIAH'S "dominion to the ends of the earth," God would *also* deliver *for* her *her* exiled people from their foreign captivity. **by the blood of thy covenant**—i.e., according to the covenant vouchsafed to thee on Sinai, and ratified by the blood of sacrifices (Exod. 24:8; Heb. 9:18-20). **pit wherein . . . no water**—Dungeons were often pits without water, miry at the bottom, such as Jeremiah sank in when confined (Gen. 37:24; Jer. 38:6). An image of the misery of the Jewish exiles in Egypt, Greece, etc., under the successors of Alexander, especially under Antiochus Epiphanes, who robbed and profaned the temple, slew thousands, and enslaved more. God delivered them by the Maccabees. A type of the future deliverance from their last great persecutor hereafter (Isa. 51:14; 60:1). **12. stronghold**—in contrast to the "pit" (vs. 11); lit., "a place *cut off* from access." MAURER thinks, "*a height*" (Ps. 18: 33). An image for the *security* which the returning Jews shall have in Messiah (vs. 8) *encamped about* His people (Ps. 46:1, 5; cf. Isa. 49:9; Prov. 18:10). **prisoners of hope**—i.e., who in spite of afflictions (Job 13:15; Ps. 42:5, 11) maintain hope in the covenant-keeping God; in contrast to unbelievers, who say, "There is no hope" (Jer. 2:25; 18:12). Especially those *Jews* who believe God's word to Israel (Jer. 31:17), "there is hope in the end, that thy children shall come again to their own border," and do not say, as in Ezekiel 37:11, "Our hope is lost." Primarily, the Jews of Zechariah's time are encouraged not to be dispirited in building by their trials; secondarily, the Jews before the coming restoration are encouraged to look to Messiah for deliverance from their last oppressors. **even to-day**—when your circumstances seem so unpromising; in contrast with the "day of the Lord," when Zion's King shall come to her deliverance (vs. 9). **I will render double**—Great as has been thy adversity, thy prosperity shall be *doubly* greater (Isa. 61:7). **13. bent Judah**—made Judah as it were My bow, and "filled" it "with Ephraim," as My arrow, wherewith to overcome the successor of the Grecian Alexander, Antiochus Epiphanes (cf. *Notes*, Dan. 8 and 11:32; I Maccabees 1:62; 2:41-43), the oppressor of Judah. Having spoken (vss. 1-8) of Alexander's victories, after the parenthesis (vss. 9, 10) as to Messiah the infinitely greater King coming, he passes to the victories which God would enable Judah to gain over Alexander's successor, after his temporary oppression of them. **O Zion . . . O Greece**—God on one hand addresses Zion, on the other Greece, showing that He rules all people. **14.** Another image: "Jehovah shall be seen (conspicuously manifesting His power) over them" (i.e., in behalf of the Jews and against their foes), as formerly He appeared in a cloud over the Israelites against the Egyptians (Exod. 14:19, 24). **his arrow . . . as . . . lightning**—flashing forth instantaneous destruction to the foe (Ps. 18:14). **blow . . . trumpet**—to summon and in-

ADAM CLARKE

Riding upon an ass. God had commanded the kings of Israel not to multiply horses. The kings who broke this command were miserable themselves, and scourgers to their people. Jesus came to fulfill the law. Had He in His title of King ridden upon a horse, it would have been a breach of a positive command of God; therefore He rode upon an ass, and thus fulfilled the prophecy, and kept the precept unbroken.

10. *I will cut off the chariot from Ephraim, and the horse from Jerusalem.* No wars shall be employed to spread the kingdom of the Messiah; for it shall be founded and established, "not by might, nor by power," but by the Spirit of the Lord of hosts, chap. iv. 6.

11. *As for thee also* (Jerusalem), *by the blood of thy covenant.* The covenant made with Abraham, Isaac, Jacob, and the Israelites in general, and ratified by the blood of many victims; until the time should come in which the Messiah should shed His blood, as typified by the ancient sacrifices. *I have sent forth thy prisoners.* Those who were under the arrest of God's judgments; the human race, fast bound in sin and misery, and who by the pitifulness of His tender mercy were loosed, He dying in their stead.

12. *Turn you to the strong hold.* Ye who feel your sins, and are shut up under a sense of your guilt, look up to Him who was delivered for your offenses, and rose again for your justification.

I will render double unto thee. Give you an abundance of peace and salvation.

13. *When I have bent Judah.* Judah is the bow, and Ephraim is the arrows, and these are to be shot against the Greeks.

14. *The Lord shall be seen over them.* Shadowing and refreshing them, as the cloud did the camp in the wilderness.

MATTHEW HENRY

God shall go forth at the head *with whirlwinds of the south*, which were of incredible swiftness and before these whirlwinds thy sons, O Greece! shall be as chaff. Is the army actually engaged? God's *arrows shall go forth as lightning*. He *sent out his arrows* and *scattered them*. This alludes to that which God had done for Israel of old when he brought them out of Egypt, and into Canaan, and had its accomplishment partly in the wonderful successes which the Jews had in the time of the Maccabees, but perfectly in the glorious victories gained by the cross of Christ over Satan and all the powers of darkness. Did their enemies hope to swallow them up? It shall be turned upon them, and they shall *devour* their enemies, and shall *subdue with sling-stones*. The *stones of the brook*, when God pleases, shall do as great execution as the best train of artillery.

2. They shall triumph in their God. They shall take the comfort and give God the glory of their successes. So some read *v.* 15. *They shall eat* (that is, they shall quietly enjoy) what they have got. And, in the fulness of their joy, they shall offer abundance of sacrifices to the honour of God, so that *they shall fill both the bowls and the corners of the altar* with the fat and blood of their sacrifices. They shall triumph in the relation wherein they stand to him, that they are *the flock of his people* and he is their Shepherd, and that they are to him *as the stones of a crown*, very precious and of great value, and kept under a strong guard. And *they shall be lifted up as an ensign upon his land*, as the royal standard is displayed in token of triumph and joy. *For how great is his goodness and how great is his beauty!* This is the burden of the songs wherewith they shall *make a noise* before the Lord. This may refer to the Messiah, to Zion's *King* that *cometh*. See *that king in his beauty* (Isa. xxxiii. 17), who is the *fairest of ten thousand*, and *altogether lovely*. Though, in the eye of the world, he had no form or comeliness, in the eye of faith how great is his beauty! *How great is his goodness!* How rich in mercy is he! Here is an instance of his goodness to his people: *Corn shall make the young men cheerful and new wine the maids;* that is, God will bless his people with an abundance of the fruits of the earth.

JAMIESON, FAUSSET, BROWN

cite His people to battle for the destruction of their foe. **go with whirlwinds of the south**–i.e., go forth in the most furious storm, such as is one from the south (Isa. 21:1). Alluding, perhaps, to Jehovah's ancient miracles at Sinai coming "from Teman" (*"the south,"* in *Margin*). **15. devour**–the flesh of their foes. **drink**–the blood of their foes; i.e., utterly destroy them. Image (as Jer. 46:10) from a sacrifice, wherein part of the flesh was eaten, and the blood poured in libation (cf. Isa. 63:1, etc.). **subdue with sling-stones**–or, "tread under foot the sling-stones" hurled by the foe at them; i.e., will contemptuously trample on the hostile missiles which shall fall harmless under their feet (cf. Job 41:28). Probably, too, it is implied that *their foes* are as impotent as the common *stones* used in *slinging* when they have fallen under foot: in contrast to the people of God (vs. 16), "the (precious) stones of a crown" (cf. I Sam. 25:29) [MAURER]. *English Version* is good sense: The Jews shall subdue the foe *at the first onset*, with the mere *slingers* who stood in front of the line of battle and began the engagement. Though armed with but sling-stones, like David against Goliath, they shall subdue the foe (Judg. 20:16; I Chron. 12:2) [GROTIUS]. **noise**–the battle shout. **through wine**–(Ch. 10:7). The Spirit of God fills them with triumph (Eph. 5:18). **filled**–with blood. **like bowls**–the bowls used to receive the blood of the sacrifices. **as . . . corners**–or "horns" of the altar, which used to be sprinkled with blood from the bowls (Exod. 29:12; Lev. 4:18). **16. save them . . . as the flock of his people**–as the flock of His people ought to be saved (Ps. 77:20). Here the image of *war* and *bloodshed* (vs. 15) is exchanged for the *shepherd* and *flock*, as God will give not only victory, but afterwards safe and lasting peace. In contrast to the worthless *sling-stones* trodden under foot stand the (gems) "stones of the crown (Isa. 62:3; Mal. 3:17), lifted up as an ensign," that all may flock to the Jewish Church (Isa. 11: 10, 12; 62:10). **17. his goodness . . . his beauty**–the goodness and beauty which Jehovah Messiah bestows on His people. Not as MAURER thinks, the goodness, etc., of *His land* or *His people* (Ps. 31:19; Jer. 31:12). **make . . . cheerful**–lit., *make it grow.* **new wine the maids**–supply, "shall make . . . to grow." *Corn* and *wine* abundant indicate peace and plenty. The new wine gladdening the maids is peculiar to this passage. It confutes those who interdict the use of wine as food. The Jews, heretofore straitened in provisions through pressure of the foe, shall now have abundance to cheer, not merely the old, but even the youths and maidens [CALVIN].

ADAM CLARKE

16. *Shall save them in that day.* They are His flock, and He is their Shepherd; and, as His own, He shall save and defend them. *As the stones of a crown.* "Crowned stones erecting themselves"; i.e., being set up by themselves, as monuments of some deliverance, they seem to be lifting themselves up, offering themselves to the attention of every passenger.

MATTHEW HENRY — CHAPTER 10

Verses 1–4

Gracious things and glorious were promised to this poor afflicted people in the foregoing chapter. God intimates to them that he expects they should acknowledge him in all their ways and in all his ways towards them.

I. The prophet directs them to apply to God by prayer for rain in the season thereof. *"Ask you of the Lord rain.* Do not pray to the clouds, nor to the stars, for rain, but *to the Lord."* The former rain fell at the seed-time, in autumn, the latter fell in the spring, between March and May, which brought the corn to an ear and filled it. If either of these rains failed, it was very bad with that land. We must, in our prayers dutifully attend the course of Providence; we must ask for mercies in their proper time, and not expect that God should go out of his usual way and method for us. *So the Lord shall make bright clouds* (which, though they are without rain themselves, are yet presages of rain)—*lightnings* (so the margin reads it), for *he maketh lightnings for the rain.*

II. He shows them the folly of making their addresses to idols (*v.* 2): *The idols have spoken vanity.*

JAMIESON, FAUSSET, BROWN — CHAPTER 10

Vss. 1-12. PRAYER AND PROMISE. Call to prayer to Jehovah, as contrasted with the idol worship which had brought judgments on the princes and people. Blessings promised in answer to prayer: (1) rulers of themselves; (2) conquest of their enemies; (3) restoration and establishment of both Israel and Judah in their own land in lasting peace and piety. **1. Ask . . . rain**–on which the abundance of "corn" promised by the Lord (ch. 9:17) depends. Jehovah alone can give it, and will give it on being asked (Jer. 10:13; 14:22). **rain in . . . time of . . . latter rain**–i.e., the latter rain in its due time, viz., in spring, about February or March (Job 29:23; Joel 2:23). The latter rain ripened the grain, as the former rain in October tended to fructify the seed. Including *all* temporal blessings; these again being types of spiritual ones. Though God has begun to bless us, we are not to relax our prayers. The former rain of conversion may have been given, but we must also ask for the latter rain of ripened sanctification. Though at Pentecost there was a former rain on the Jewish Church, a latter rain is still to be looked for, when the full harvest of the nation's conversion shall be gathered in to God. The spirit of prayer in the Church is an index at once of her piety, and of the spiritual blessings she may expect from God. When the Church is full of prayer, God pours out a full blessing. **bright clouds**–rather, "lightnings," the precursors of rain [MAURER]. **showers of rain**–lit., "rain of heavy rain." In Job 37:6 the same words occur in inverted order [HENDERSON]. **grass**–a general term, including both *corn* for men and *grass* for cattle. **2. idols**–lit., "the teraphim," the household gods, consulted in divination (*Note*, Hos. 3:4). Derived by GESENIUS from an *Arabic* root, "comfort," indicating them as the givers of comfort. Or an Ethiopian root, "relics." Herein Zechariah shows that the Jews by their own idolatry had

ADAM CLARKE — CHAPTER 10

W. H. LOWE:

Verse 2. "Idols." Better, as in margin, *teraphim.* Against the post-exilian origin of this passage, and of 13:2, it has been objected that *idols and false prophets harmonise only with a time prior to the exile.* It is true that after the captivity idolatry was not the sin to which the people were especially inclined, as they were in former times. Still, even if the prophet was not speaking of sins of the past, rather than those of his own day, it must be remembered that the marriage with heathen women, which is so often spoken of after the captivity, must have been, as was the case with Solomon, a continual source of danger in that respect. Moreover, idolatry, soothsaying, etc., were actually practiced up to the time of the destruction of Jerusalem by Titus. Thus we read of false prophets who opposed Nehemiah (Neh. 6:10–14), and of "sorcerers" in Mal. 3:5, and so, too, of false prophets in Acts 5:36, 37; 13:6.

—*Ellicott's Commentary on the Whole Bible*

2. *The idols have spoken vanity.* This is spoken of the Jews, and must refer to their idolatry practiced before the Captivity, for there were no idols after.

MATTHEW HENRY

The *diviners*, who were the prophets of those idols, *have seen a lie* (their visions were all a cheat and a sham); and *they have told false dreams*, which proved that they were not from God. They not only got nothing by the false gods, but they lost the favour of the true God, for *therefore they went their way* into captivity *as a flock*, and *they were troubled* as scattered sheep are, *because there was no shepherd*. Those that wandered after strange gods were made to wander into strange nations.

III. He shows them the hand of God in events, both those that made against them and those that made for them, *v.* 3. When everything went cross it was God that walked contrary to them (*v.* 3): "*My anger was kindled against the shepherds* that should have fed the flock, but neglected it, and starved it. I was displeased at the wicked magistrates and ministers, the idol-shepherds." The captivity in Babylon was a token of God's anger against them; in it likewise he *punished the goats*, those of the flock that were filthy and mischievous. When things began to change for the better it was God that gave them the happy turn. "He has now *visited his flock* with favour, and has made them *as his goodly horse in the battle*, managed and made use of them, as a man does the horse he rides on, has made them valuable in themselves and formidable to those about them, *as his goodly horse*."

IV. He shows them that every creature is to them what God makes it to be (*v.* 4): *Out of him came forth the corner, out of him the nails. Out of him* came the combined force of their enemies; nor could they have had such power unless it had been given them from above. All the power likewise that was engaged for them was derived from him. Out of him came forth *the corner-stone* of the building, the power of magistrates, which keeps the several parts of the state together. Out of him came forth *the nail* that fixed the state (Isa. xxii. 23), the *nail in his holy place*, Ezra ix. 8. Out of him came forth *the battle-bow*, the military power, and out of him *every oppressor*.

Verses 5–12

Precious promises made to the people of God, which look further than to the state of the Jews, and have certain reference to the spiritual Israel of God, the gospel-church, and all true believers.

I. They shall have God's favour and presence, and shall be owned and accepted of him. This is the foundation of all the rest: *The Lord is with them*, *v.* 5. Again (*v.* 6), *I have mercy upon them*. All their dignity and joy are owing purely to God's mercy; and mercy, as it supposes misery, so it excludes merit. *They shall be as though I had not cast them off*. Such favour does God show to returning repenting sinners, such fellowship are they admitted into, and such freedom does he use with them, that they are *as though they had never been cast off*. *I am the Lord their God*, according to the original contract, the covenant made with their fathers.

II. They shall be victorious over their enemies. (*v.* 5): *They shall be as mighty men*, that are both strong in body and bold in spirit, effective men. They shall, as mighty men, *tread down their enemies in the battle because the Lord is with them*. Some would argue that they may *therefore* sit still, and do nothing, because the Lord is with them, who can and will do all. No; God's gracious presence with us to help us must not supersede, but quicken and animate, our endeavours to help ourselves. Then *the riders on horses shall be confounded*. The preachers of the gospel of Christ went forth to war a good warfare; they charged bravely, because God was with them; and the *riders on horses* that opposed them *were confounded*. But whence have they all this might? It is in the Lord, and in the power of his might, that they are so (*v.* 6). God saves us by strengthening us, and works out our happiness by working in us to do our duty.

III. Those of them that are dispersed shall be gathered together into one body (*v.* 6): *I will bring them again to place them*, bring them from other lands to place them in their own land. In order to this (*v.* 8) *I will hiss for them*, or, rather, *whistle* for them, as the shepherd with his pipe calls his sheep together, that *know his voice*; and so *I will gather them. I will gather them, for I have redeemed them*. It has its spiritual accomplishment in the gathering in of precious souls out of a bondage worse than that in

JAMIESON, FAUSSET, BROWN

stayed the grace of God heretofore, which otherwise would have given them all those blessings, temporal and spiritual, which they are now (vs. 1) urged to "ask" for. **diviners**—who gave responses to consulters of the teraphim: opposed to Jehovah and His true prophets. **seen a lie**—pretending to see what they saw not in giving responses. **comfort in vain**—lit., "give *vapor* for comfort"; i.e., give comforting promises to consulters which are sure to come to naught (Job 13:4; 16:2; 21:34). **therefore they went their way**—i.e., Israel and Judah were led away captive. **as a flock . . . no shepherd**—As sheep wander and are a prey to every injury when without a shepherd, so the Jews had been while they were without Jehovah, the true shepherd; for the false prophets whom they trusted were no shepherds (Ezek. 34:5). So now they are scattered, while they know not Messiah their shepherd; typified in the state of the disciples, when they had forsaken Jesus and fled (Matt. 26:56; cf. ch. 13:7). **3. against the shepherds**—the civil rulers of Israel and Judah who abetted idolatry. **punished**—lit., "visited *upon*." The same word "visited," without the "upon," is presently after used in a good sense to heighten the contrast. **goats**—he-goats. As "shepherds" described what they *ought* to have been, so "he-goats" describes what they *were*, the emblem of headstrong wantonness and offensive lust (*Margin*, Isa. 14:9; Ezek. 34:17; Dan. 8:5; Matt. 25:33). The he-goats head the flock. They who are first in crime will be first in punishment. **visited**—in mercy (Luke 1:68). **as his goodly horse**—In ch. 9:13 they were represented under the image of *bows and arrows*, here under that of their commander-in-chief, Jehovah's *battle horse* (Song of Sol. 1:9). God can make His people, timid though they be as sheep, courageous as the charger. The general rode on the most beautiful and richly caparisoned, and had his horse tended with the greatest care. Jehovah might cast off the Jews for their vileness, but He regards His election or adoption of them: whence He calls them here "*His* flock," and therefore saves them. **4. Out of him**—*Judah* is to be no more subject to foreigners, but *from itself* shall come its rulers. **the corner**—stone, Messiah (Isa. 28:16). "Corners" simply express *governors* (*Margin*, I Sam. 14:38; *Margin*, Isa. 19:13). The Maccabees, Judah's governors and deliverers from Antiochus the oppressor, are primarily meant; but Messiah is the Antitype. Messiah supports and binds together the Church, Jews and Gentiles. **the nail**—(Judg. 4:21; Isa. 22:23). The large peg inside an Oriental tent, on which is hung most of its valuable furniture. On Messiah hang all the glory and hope of His people. **bow**—(ch. 9:13). Judah shall not need foreign soldiery. Messiah shall be her battle bow (Ps. 45:4, 5; Rev. 6:2). **every oppressor**—rather, in a good sense, *ruler*, as the kindred Ethiopic term means. So "exactor," in Isaiah 60:17, viz., one who exacts the tribute from the nations made tributary to Judah [LUDOVICUS DE DIEU]. **5. riders on horses**—viz., the enemy's horsemen. Though the Jews were forbidden by the law to multiply horses in battle (Deut. 17:16), they are made Jehovah's war horse (vs. 3; Ps. 20:7), and so tread down on foot the foe with all his cavalry (Ezek. 38:4; Dan. 11:40). Cavalry was the chief strength of the Syro-Grecian army (I Maccabees 3:39). **6. Judah . . . Joseph**—i.e., the ten tribes. The distinct mention of both Judah and Israel shows that there is yet a more complete restoration than that from Babylon, when Judah alone and a few Israelites from the other tribes returned. The Maccabean deliverance is here connected with it, just as the painter groups on the same canvas objects in the foreground and hills far distant; or as the comparatively near planet and the remote fixed star are seen together in the same firmament. Prophecy ever hastens to the glorious final consummation under Messiah. **bring them again to place them**—viz., securely in their own land. The *Hebrew* verb is compounded of two, "I will bring again," and "I will place them" (Jer. 32:37) MAURER, from a different form, translates, "I will make them to dwell." **7. like a mighty man**—in the battle with the foe (vss. 3, 5). **rejoice**—at their victory over the foe. **children shall see it**—who are not yet of age to serve. To teach patient waiting for God's promises. If ye do not at present see the fulfilment, your *children* shall, and their joy shall be complete. **rejoice in the Lord**—the Giver of such a glorious victory. **8. hiss for them**—Keepers of bees by a whistle call them together. So Jehovah by the mere word of His call shall gather back to Palestine His scattered people (vs. 10; Isa. 5:26; Ezek. 36:11). The multitudes mentioned by JOSEPHUS (B. 3. ch. 3:2), as peopling Galilee 200 years after this time, were a

ADAM CLARKE

Therefore they went their way. They were like a flock that had no shepherd, shifting from place to place.

3. *Mine anger was kindled against the shepherds.* Bad kings and bad priests. *I punished the goats;* these were the wicked priests, who were shepherds by their office, and goats by the impurity of their lives.

4. *Out of him came forth the corner.* This is spoken of the tribe of Judah; all strength, counsel, and excellence came from that tribe. The cornerstone, the ornament and completion of the building; *the nail,* by which the tents were fastened, and on which they hung their clothes, armor, etc.; *the battle bow,* the choicest archers.

Every oppressor together. Those heroes and generals by whom, under God, their foes should be totally routed. Perhaps all this is spoken of the Messiah.

5. *They shall be as mighty men.* The Maccabees and their successors. *Riders on horses.* The Macedonians, who opposed the Maccabees, and had much cavalry; whereas the Jews had none, and even few weapons of war, yet they overcame these horsemen.

6. *I will strengthen the house of Judah.* I doubt whether the sixth, seventh, eighth, and ninth verses are not to be understood of the future ingathering of the Jews in the times of the gospel. See Jer. iii. 14; xxiii. 6; Hos. i. 2; vi. 11.

7. *Ephraim shall be like a mighty man.* This tribe was always distinguished for its valor.

8. *I will hiss for them.* "I will shriek for them"; call them with such a shrill, strong voice that they shall hear Me, and find that it is the voice of their redemption.

MATTHEW HENRY

Egypt or Assyria, and the bringing of them into the glorious liberties of the children of God. All the land of promise is theirs, even Gilead and Lebanon. How shall a people so dispersed be got together? The difficulties seem insuperable, but they shall be got over as effectually as those that lay in the way of their deliverance out of Egypt and their entrance into Canaan: *He shall pass through the sea with affliction*, as of old through the Red Sea. And *all the deeps of the river shall dry up*, as Jordan did to make way for Israel's passage into that good land which God had given them. Does *the pride of Assyria* stand in the way of their deliverance? He shall give check to it who sets bounds to the *proud waves of the sea*. Does the sceptre of Egypt oppose it? That shall *depart away*. When the gospel-church was to be gathered out of all nations by the preaching of the gospel, great opposition was given to it by the enraged powers of earth and hell. But, by divine power it became *mighty to the pulling down of strongholds*, and the conversion and salvation of thousands. Then the sea fled, and Jordan was *driven back at the presence of the Lord*.

IV. They shall greatly multiply, and the church, that new world, shall be replenished (*v.* 8): *They shall increase as they have increased* formerly in Egypt. *In Judah* only *God* had been *known*, and his *name was great in Israel* only; here only he revealed his *statutes* and *judgments*. But in gospel-times that place shall be much too strait; the church's tent must be enlarged. Then *I will sow them among the people*, *v.* 9. Their scattering shall be like the scattering of seed in the ground, not to bury it, but to increase it. The Jews that came from all parts to worship at Jerusalem fetched thence the gospel light and fire to their own countries, as those Acts ii, and the eunuch, Acts viii. And their own synagogues in the several cities of the Gentiles were the first receptacles of the apostles and their preaching. Thus when God *sowed them among the people* he took care that they should *remember him*, and make mention of his name *in far countries*; and, by keeping up the knowledge of God among them as he had revealed himself in the Old Testament, they would be the more ready to admit the knowledge of Christ as he has revealed himself in the New Testament.

V. God himself will be both their strength and their song. In him they shall be comforted, and shall have abundant satisfaction (*v.* 7). When we resolutely resist, and so overcome, our spiritual enemies, then our hearts shall rejoice. And with graces joys shall be propagated: *Their children shall see it and be glad, and their hearts* also *shall rejoice in the Lord*. It is good to acquaint children betimes with the delights of religion, and to make the services of it pleasant, that, learning betimes to rejoice in the Lord, they may cleave to him.

If God strengthen us (*v.* 12) we must bestir ourselves, must *walk up and down* in all the duties of the Christian life. To us to live must be Christ; and, *whatever we do in word or deed*, we must *do all in the name of the Lord Jesus*, that we receive not the strengthening grace of God in vain. See Ps. lxxx. 17, 18.

JAMIESON, FAUSSET, BROWN

pledge of the future more perfect fulfilment of the prophecy. **for I have redeemed them**—viz., in My covenant purpose "redeemed" both temporally and spiritually. **as they have increased**—in former times. **9. sow them among . . . people**—Their dispersion was with a special design. Like seed sown far and wide, they shall, when quickened themselves, be the fittest instruments for quickening others (cf. Mic. 5:7). The slight hold they have on every soil where they now live, as also the commercial and therefore cosmopolitan character of their pursuits, making a change of residence easy to them, fit them peculiarly for missionary work [MOORE]. The wide dispersion of the Jews just before Christ's coming prepared the way similarly for the apostles' preaching in the various Jewish synagogues throughout the world; everywhere some of the Old Testament seed previously sown was ready to germinate when the New Testament light and heat were brought to bear on it by Gospel preachers. Thus the way was opened for entrance among the Gentiles. "*Will sow*" is the *Hebrew* future, said of that which has been done, is being done, and may be done afterwards [MAURER], (cf. Hos. 2:23). **shall remember me in far countries**—(Deut. 30:1; II Chron. 6:37). Implying the Jews' return to a right mind in "all the nations" where they are scattered simultaneously. Cf. Luke 15:17, 18, with Psalm 22:27, "All the ends of the world *remembering* and turning unto the Lord," preceded by the "seed of Jacob . . . Israel . . . fearing and glorifying Him"; also Psalm 102:13-15. **live**—in political and spiritual life. **10. Egypt . . . Assyria**—the former the first, the latter among the last of Israel's oppressors (or *representing the four great world kingdoms*, of which it was the first): types of the present *universal* dispersion, Egypt being south, Assyria north, opposite ends of the compass. MAURER *conjectures* that many Israelites fled to "Egypt" on the invasion of Tiglath-pileser. But Isaiah 11: 11 and this passage rather accord with the view of the *future* restoration. **Gilead . . . Lebanon**—The whole of the Holy Land is described by two of its boundaries, the eastern ("Gilead" beyond Jordan) and the northern ("Lebanon"). **place shall not be found for them**—i.e., there shall not be room enough for them through their numbers (Isa. 49:20; 54:3). **11. pass . . . sea with affliction**—Personifying the "sea"; He shall afflict the sea, i.e., cause it to cease to be an obstacle to Israel's return to Palestine (Isa. 11:15, 16). *Vulgate* translates, "The strait of the sea." MAURER, "He shall *cleave* and smite." *English Version* is best (Ps. 114:3). As Jehovah smote the Red Sea to make a passage for His people (Exod. 14:16, 21), so hereafter shall He make a way through every obstacle which opposes Israel's restoration. **the river**—the Nile (Amos 8:8; 9:5), or the Euphrates. Thus the Red Sea and the Euphrates in the former part of the verse answer to "Assyria" and "Egypt" in the latter. **sceptre of Egypt . . . depart**—(Ezek. 30:13). **12. I . . . strengthen them in . . . Lord**—(Hos. 1:7). I, the Father, will strengthen them in the name, i.e., the manifested power, of the Lord, Messiah, the Son of God. **walk . . . in his name**—i.e., live everywhere and continually under His protection, and according to His will (Gen. 5:22; Ps. 20:1, 7; Mic. 4:5).

ADAM CLARKE

TODAY'S DICTIONARY OF THE BIBLE:

Redemption, the purchase back of something that had been lost, by the payment of a ransom. The Greek word so rendered is *apolutrōsis,* a word occurring nine times in Scripture, and always with the idea of a ransom or price paid—i.e., redemption by a *lutron* in man's relation to man (Ex. 21:30; Lev. 19:20; 25:51; Num. 35:31, 32; Prov. 6:35; Isa. 45:13), and in the same sense of man's relation to God (Num. 3:49; 18:15).

There are many passages in the New Testament which represent Christ's sufferings under the idea of a ransom or price, and the result thereby secured by a purchase or *redemption* (comp. Acts 20:28; 1 Cor. 6:19, 20; Gal. 3:13; 4:4, 5; Eph. 1:7; Col. 1:14; 1 Tim. 2:5, 6; Titus 2:14; Heb. 9:12; 1 Pet. 1:18, 19; Rev. 5:9). The idea running through all these texts, however various their reference, is that of *payment* made for our redemption. The debt against us is not viewed as simply canceled, but is fully paid. Christ's blood or life, which he surrendered for them, is the "ransom" by which the deliverance of his people from the servitude of sin and from its penal consequences is secured. It is the plain doctrine of Scripture that "Christ saves us neither by the mere exercise of power, nor by his doctrine, nor by his example, nor by the moral influence which he exerted, nor by any subjective influence on his people, whether natural or mystical, but as a satisfaction to divine justice, as an expiation for sin, and as a ransom from the curse and authority of the law, thus reconciling us to God by making it consistent with his perfection to exercise mercy toward sinners" (Hodge's *Systematic Theology*).

11. *And he shall pass through the sea.* Here is an allusion to the passage of the Red Sea on their coming out of Egypt, and to their crossing Jordan when they went into the Promised Land. The waves or waters of both were dried up, thrown from side to side, till all the people passed safely through. When they shall return from the various countries in which they now sojourn, God will work, if necessary, similar miracles to those which He formerly worked for their forefathers; and the people shall be glad to let them go, however much they may be profited by their operations in the state. Those that oppose, as Assyria and Egypt formerly did, shall be brought down, and their sceptre broken.

MATTHEW HENRY — CHAPTER 11

Verses 1–3

In dark and figurative expressions, as is usual in the scripture predictions of things at a great distance, that destruction of Jerusalem and of the Jewish church and nation is here foretold which our Lord Jesus, when the time was at hand, prophesied of very plainly and expressly. 1. Preparation made for that destruction (*v.* 1): "*Open thy doors, O Lebanon!* Thou wouldst not open them to let thy king in. Now thou must open them to let thy ruin in. Some by Lebanon here understand the temple, which was built of cedars from Lebanon. It was burnt with fire by the Romans, and its gates were forced open by the fury of the soldiers. Others understand it of Jerusalem, or rather of the whole land of Canaan, to which Lebanon was an inlet on the north.

All shall lie open to the invader, and the cedars, the mighty and eminent men, shall be devoured, which cannot but alarm those of an inferior rank, *v.* 2. If *the cedars* have *fallen* let the *fir-tree howl*. How can the slender fir-trees stand if stately cedars fall? And let the *oaks of Bashan*, that lie exposed to every injury, *howl, for the forest of the vintage* (or the

JAMIESON, FAUSSET, BROWN — CHAPTER 11

VSS. 1-17. DESTRUCTION OF THE SECOND TEMPLE AND JEWISH POLITY FOR THE REJECTION OF MESSIAH. **1. Open thy doors, O Lebanon**—i.e., the temple so called, as being constructed of cedars of Lebanon, or as being lofty and conspicuous like that mountain (cf. Ezek. 17:3; Hab. 2:17). Forty years before the destruction of the temple, the tract called "Massecheth Joma" states, its doors of their own accord opened, and Rabbi Johanan in alarm said, I know that thy desolation is impending according to Zechariah's prophecy. CALVIN supposes Lebanon to refer to *Judea*, described by its north boundary: "Lebanon," the route by which the Romans, according to JOSEPHUS, gradually advanced towards Jerusalem. MOORE, from HENGSTENBERG, refers the passage to the civil war which caused the calling in of the Romans, who, like a storm sweeping through the land from Lebanon, deprived Judea of its independence. Thus the passage forms a fit introduction to the prediction as to Messiah born when Judea became a Roman province. But the weight of authority is for the former view. **2. fir tree . . . cedar**—if even the *cedars* (the highest in the state) are not spared, how much less *the fir trees* (the lowest)! **forest of . . . vintage**—As the vines are stripped of their grapes in the vintage (cf. Joel 3:13),

ADAM CLARKE — CHAPTER 11

1. *Open thy doors, O Lebanon. Lebanon* signifies the Temple, because built of materials principally brought from that place.

2. *Howl, fir tree.* This seems to point out the fall and destruction of all the mighty men.

MATTHEW HENRY

flourishing vineyard, that used to be guarded with a particular care) has come down, or (as some read it) when the *defenced forests*, such as Lebanon was, have come down. 2. Lamentation made for the destruction (*v.* 3): *There is a voice of howling*. Those who have fallen howl for grief and shame, and those who see their own turn coming howl for fear. The great men especially receive the alarm with the utmost confusion. Those great men were by office shepherds, and such should have protected God's flock committed to their charge; it is the duty both of princes and priests. But they were as *young lions*, that made themselves a terror to the flock. The *young lions howl*, for *the pride of Jordan is spoiled*. The pride of Jordan was the thickets on the banks, in which the lions reposed when the river overflowed, the lions came up from them (as we read Jer. xlix. 19), and they came up roaring.

Verses 4–14

The prophet here is made a type of Christ, as the prophet Isaiah sometimes was; and the scope of these verses is to show that *for judgment Christ came into this world* (John ix. 39), for judgment to the Jewish church and nation, which were, about the time of his coming, corrupted by the worldliness and hypocrisy of their rulers. Christ would have healed them, but they would not be healed.

1. The charge he received from his Father to try what might be done with this flock (*v.* 4); *Thus saith the Lord my God, Feed the flock of the slaughter*. The Jews were God's flock, but they were *the flock of slaughter*, for their enemies had killed them all the day long.

I. The desperate case of the Jewish church, under the tyranny of their own governors, *v.* 5. In Zechariah's time we find the rulers and the nobles justly rebuked for *exacting usury of their brethren*, Neh. v. 7, 15. In Christ's time the Sadducees, who were deists, corrupted their judgments. The Pharisees, who were bigots for superstition, corrupted their morals, by making void the commandments of God, Matt. xv. 16. Thus they slew the sheep of the flock, thus they sold them. They affronted God, by giving him thanks. They said, *Blessed be the Lord, for I am rich*, as if, because they prospered in their wickedness God had made himself patron of their unjust practices. Christ had compassion on *the multitude because they fainted and were scattered abroad, as if they had no shepherd* (as really they had worse than none). It is ill for a church when its pastors can look upon the ignorant, the foolish, the wicked, the weak, without pity.

II. The sentence of God's wrath passed upon them for their stupidity. And, as their shepherds pitied them not, so they did not bemoan themselves; therefore God says (*v.* 6), "*I will no more pity the inhabitants of the land.*" Those who are willing to have their consciences oppressed by those who *teach for doctrines the commandments of men* are often punished by oppression in their civil interests, and justly, for those forfeit their own rights who tamely give up God's rights. He will deliver them into the hand of oppressors, *everyone into his neighbour's hand*. They shall be delivered everyone *into the hand of his king*, whom they chose to submit to rather than to Christ.

III. A trial yet made whether their ruin might be prevented by sending Christ among them as a shepherd, Matt. xxi. 37. Divers of the prophets had spoken of him as the *Shepherd of Israel*, Isa. xl. 11; Ezek. xxxiv. 23. He himself told the Pharisees that he was the *Shepherd of the sheep* (John x. 1, 2, 11), apparently referring to this passage, where we have,

2. His acceptance of this charge, *v.* 7. Christ will care for these lost sheep; he will go about among them, *teaching* and *healing even you, O poor of the flock*! His disciples, who were his constant attendants, were of the poor of the flock.

JAMIESON, FAUSSET, BROWN

so the forest of Lebanon "is come down," stripped of all its beauty. Rather, "*the fortified*" or "*inaccessible* forest" [MAURER]; i.e., Jerusalem dense with houses as a thick forest is with trees, and "fortified" with a wall around. Cf. Micah. 3:12, where its desolate state is described as a forest. **3. shepherds**—the Jewish rulers. **their glory**—*their* wealth and magnificence; or that *of the temple*, "their glory" (Mark 13:1; Luke 21:5). **young lions**—the princes, so described on account of their cruel rapacity. **pride of Jordan**—its thickly wooded banks, the lair of "lions" (Jer. 12:5; 49:19). Image for Judea "spoiled" of the magnificence of its rulers ("the young lions"). The valley of the Jordan forms a deeper gash than any on the earth. The land at Lake Merom is on a level with the Mediterranean Sea; at the Sea of Tiberias it falls 650 feet below that level, and to double that depression at the Dead Sea, i.e., in all, 1950 feet below the Mediterranean; in twenty miles' interval there is a fall of from 3000 to 4000 feet. **4.** The prophet here proceeds to show the cause of the destruction just foretold, viz., the rejection of Messiah. **flock of . . . slaughter**—(Ps. 44:22). God's people doomed to slaughter by the Romans. Zechariah here represents typically Messiah, and performs in vision the actions enjoined: hence the language is in part appropriate to him, but mainly to the Antitype, Messiah. A million and a half perished in the Jewish war, and one million one hundred thousand at the fall of Jerusalem. "Feed" implies that the Jews could not plead ignorance of God's will to execute their sin. Zechariah and the other prophets had by God's appointment "fed" them (Acts 20:28) with the word of God, teaching and warning them to escape from coming wrath by repentance: the type of Messiah, the chief Shepherd, who receives the commission of the Father, with whom He is one (vs. 4); and Himself says (vs. 7), "*I* will feed the flock of slaughter." Zechariah did not live to "feed" literally the "flock of slaughter"; Messiah alone "fed" those who, because of their rejection of Him, were condemned to slaughter. Jehovah-Messiah is the speaker. It is He who threatens to inflict the punishments (vss. 6, 8). The typical breaking of the staff, performed in vision by Zechariah (vs. 10), is fulfilled in His breaking the covenant with Judah. It is He who was sold for thirty pieces of silver (vss. 12, 13). **5. possessors**—The *buyers* [MAURER], their Roman oppressors, contrasted with "they that sell men." The instruments of God's righteous judgment, and therefore "not holding themselves guilty" (Jer. 50:7). It is meant that they *might* use this plea, not that they actually used it. Judah's adversaries felt no compunction in destroying them; and God in righteous wrath against Judah allowed it. **they that sell them**—(Cf. vs. 12). The rulers of Judah, who by their avaricious rapacity and selfishness (John 11:48, 50) virtually sold their country to Rome. Their covetousness brought on Judea God's visitation by Rome. The climax of this was the sale of the innocent Messiah for thirty pieces of silver. They thought that Jesus was thus sold and their selfish interest secured by the delivery of Him to the Romans for crucifixion; but it was themselves and their country that they thus sold to the Roman "possessors." **I am rich**—by selling the sheep (Deut. 29:19; Hos. 12:8). In short-sighted selfishness they thought they had gained their object, covetous self-aggrandizement (Luke 16:14), and hypocritically "thanked" God for their wicked gain (cf. Luke 18:11). **say . . . pity**—In *Hebrew* it is *singular:* i.e., *each* of those that sell them *saith:* Not *one* of their own shepherds *pitieth* them. An emphatical mode of expression by which each individual is represented as doing, or not doing, the action of the verb [HENDERSON]. HENGSTENBERG refers the *singular* verbs to JEHOVAH, the true actor; the wicked shepherds being His unconscious instruments. Cf. vs. 6, "For *I* will no more pity," with the *Hebrew* "*pitieth* not" here. **6.** Jehovah, in vengeance for their rejection of Messiah, gave them over to intestine feuds and Roman rule. The Zealots and other factious Jews expelled and slew one another by turns at the last invasion by Rome. **his king**—Vespasian or Titus: they themselves (John 19:15) had said, unconsciously realizing Zechariah's words, identifying Rome's king with Judah's ("his") king, "We have no king but Cæsar." God took them at their word, and gave them the Roman king, who "smote (lit., dashed in pieces) their land," breaking up their polity, when they rejected their true King who would have saved them. **7. And**—rather, *Accordingly:* implying the motive cause which led Messiah to assume the office, viz., the will of the Father (vss. 4, 5), who pitied the sheep without any true shepherd. **I will feed**—"I fed" [CALVIN],

ADAM CLARKE

3. *Young lions*. Princes and rulers. By *shepherds*, kings or priests may be intended.

4. *Feed the flock of the slaughter*. This people resemble a flock of sheep fattened for the shambles; *feed*, instruct, this people who are about to be slaughtered.

5. *Whose possessors*. Governors and false prophets, *slay them*, by leading them to those things that will bring them to destruction. *And they that sell them*. Give them up to idolatry.

6. *For I will no more pity*. I have determined to deliver them into the hands of the Chaldeans.

7. *And I will feed the flock of slaughter*. I showed them what God had revealed to me relative to the evils coming upon the land; and I did this the more especially for the sake of the poor of the flock.

MATTHEW HENRY

I *took unto me two staves*, pastoral staves; other shepherds have but one crook, but Christ had two, denoting what he did both for the souls and for the bodies of men. David speaks of God's *rod* and his *staff* (Ps. xxiii. 4), a correcting rod and a supporting staff. One staff he called Beauty, denoting the Temple; the other he called *Bands*, denoting their civil state. Christ, in his gospel, and in all he did consulted the advancement both of their civil and of their sacred interests.

The chief Shepherd *fed the flock* (*v.* 7), and displaced those under-shepherds that were false to their trust (*v.* 8): *Three shepherds I cut off in one month.*

IV. Their enmity to Christ. He came to the sheep of his own pasture; it might have been expected that between them and him there would be affection, but they conducted themselves so ill that *his soul loathed them*, was *straitened* towards them (so it may be read). Whatever estrangement there is between God and man, it begins on man's side.

V. The sentence of their rejection passed (*v.* 9): "*Then said I, I will not feed you.* That which will make itself a prey to the wolf, let it be a prey, and let the rest so far forget their own gentle nature as to *eat the flesh of one another;* let these sheep fight like dogs."

A sign of it given (*v.* 10): *I took my staff, even Beauty, and cut it asunder.* The breaking of this staff signified the breaking of God's covenant which he had *made with all the people*, the covenant of peculiarity made with all the tribes of *Israel*. When Christ told them plainly that the *kingdom of God* should be *taken from them*, and *given to another people*, then he broke the *staff of Beauty*, Matt. xxi. 43. Though Jerusalem and the Jewish nation held up forty years longer, yet from that day we may reckon the staff of Beauty broken, *v.* 11.

JAMIESON, FAUSSET, BROWN

which comes to the same thing, as the past tense must in Zechariah's time have referred to the event of Messiah's advent then future: the prophets often speaking of the future in vision as already present. It was not My fault, Jehovah implies, that these sheep were not fed; the fault rests solely with you, because ye rejected the grace of God [CALVIN]. **even you, O poor of the flock**—rather, "in order that (I might feed, i.e., save) the poor (humble; cf. vs. 11; Zeph. 3:12; Matt. 5:3) of the flock"; lit., (not "*you,*" but), "*therefore* (I will feed)" [MOORE]. See *Margin, "Verily* the poor." It is for the sake of the believing remnant that Messiah took charge of the flock, though He would have saved all, if they would have come to Him. They would not come; therefore, *as a nation,* they are "the flock of (i.e., doomed to) slaughter." **I took . . .two staves**—i.e., shepherds' staves or rods (Ps. 23:4). Symbolizing His assumption of the pastor's office. **Beauty**—The Jews' peculiar *excellency* above other nations (Deut. 4:7), God's special manifestation to them (Ps. 147: 19, 20), the glory of the temple ("the *beauty* of holiness," Ps. 29:2; cf. Ps. 27:4, and 90:17; II Chron. 20:21), the "pleasantness" of their land (Gen. 49: 15; Dan. 8:9; 11:16), "the glorious land." **Bands**—implying the *bond* of "brotherhood" between Judah and Israel. "Bands," in Psalm 119:61 (*Margin*), is used for confederate *companies:* The Easterns in making a confederacy often tie a cord or band as a symbol of it, and untie it when they dissolve the confederacy [LUDOVICUS DE DIEU]. Messiah would have joined Judah and Israel in the *bonds* of a common faith and common laws (vs. 14), but they would not; therefore in just retribution He broke "His covenant which He had made with all the people." Alexander, Antiochus Epiphanes, and Pompey were all kept from marring utterly the distinctive "beauty" and "brotherhood" of Judah and Israel, which subsisted more or less so long as the temple stood. But when Jehovah brake the staves, not even Titus could save the temple from his own Roman soldiery, nor was Jurian able to restore it. **8. Three shepherds . . . I cut off**—lit., to cause to disappear, to destroy so as not to leave a vestige of them. The three shepherds whom Messiah removes are John, Simon, and Eleazar, three leaders of factions in the Jewish war [DRUSIUS]. Or, as Messiah, the Antitype, was at once *prophet, priest, and king,* so He by the destruction of the Jewish polity destroyed these *three* orders for the unbelief of both the rulers and people [MOORE]. If they had accepted Messiah, they would have had all three combined in Him, and would have been themselves spiritually prophets, priests, and kings to God. Refusing Him, they lost all three, in every sense. **one month**—a brief and fixed space of time (Hos. 5:7). Probably alluding to the last period of the siege of Jerusalem, when all authority within the city was at an end [HENDERSON]. **loathed them**—lit., "was straitened" as to them; instead of being *enlarged* towards them in love (II Cor. 6:11, 12). The same *Hebrew* as in Numbers 21:4, *Margin.* No room was left by them for the grace of God, as His favors were rejected [CALVIN]. The mutual distaste that existed between the holy Messiah and the guilty Jews is implied. **9. Then said I**—at last when all means of saving the nation had been used in vain (John 8:24). **I will not**—i.e., *no more* feed you. The last rejection of the Jews is foretold, of which the former under Nebuchadnezzar, similarly described, was the type (Jer. 15:1-3; 34:17; 43:11; Ezek. 6:12). Perish those who are doomed to perish, since they reject Him who would have saved them! Let them rush on to their own ruin, since they will have it so. **eat . . . flesh of another**—Let them madly perish by mutual discords. JOSEPHUS attests the fulfilment of this prophecy of *threefold calamity:* pestilence and famine ("dieth . . . die"), war ("cut off . . . cut off"), intestine discord ("eat . . . one . . . another"). **10. covenant which I made with all the people**—The covenant made with the *whole nation* is to hold good no more except to the elect remnant. This is the force of the clause, not as MAURER, and others translate. The covenant which I made with all the *nations* (not to hurt My elect people, Hos. 2:18). But the *Hebrew* is the term for *the elect people* (*Ammim*), not that for *the Gentile nations* (*Goiim*). The *Hebrew plural* expresses the great numbers of the Israelite people formerly (I Kings 4:20). The article is, in the *Hebrew*, all *the* or *those* peoples. His cutting asunder the staff "Beauty," implies the setting aside of the outward symbols of the Jews' distinguishing excellency above the Gentiles (*Note,* vs. 7) as God's own people. **11. poor . . . knew**-The humble, godly remnant knew by the event the truth of the prediction and of Messiah's mission.

ADAM CLARKE

Two staves. Two shepherd's crooks. *One I called Beauty*—that probably by which they marked the sheep, dipping the end into vermillion, or some red liquid. And this was done when they were to mark every tenth sheep, as it came out of the field, when the tithe was to be set apart for the Lord. *The other I called Bands.* Probably that with the hook or crook at the head of it, by which the shepherd was wont to catch the sheep by the horns or legs when he wished to bring any to hand. *And I fed the flock.* These two rods show the beauty and union of the people, while under God as their Shepherd.

8. *Three shepherds also I cut off in one month.* Perhaps three orders may be intended: (1) The priesthood. (2) The dictatorship, including the scribes, Pharisees, etc. (3) The magistracy, the great Sanhedrin, and the smaller councils. These were all annihilated by the Roman conquest.

10. *I took my staff . . . Beauty, and cut it asunder.* And thus I showed that I determined no longer to preserve them in their free and glorious state. And thus I brake My covenant with them, which they had broken on their part already.

11. *So the poor of the flock.* The pious, who attended to My teaching, saw that this was *the word*—the "design," of God.

MATTHEW HENRY

It was said before, *Their souls abhorred him;* and here we have an instance of it, their buying and selling him for thirty pieces of silver. This is here foretold in somewhat obscure expressions, lest otherwise the plainness of the prophecy might prevent the accomplishment of it. The Shepherd comes to them for his wages (*v.* 12): '*If you think good, give me my price;* you are weary of me, pay me off and discharge me; and, *if not, forbear.*"

Compare with this what Christ said to Judas when he was going to sell him, "*What thou doest do quickly;* let them either take the bargain or leave it," John xiii. 27. They value him at *thirty pieces of silver*. It was the ordinary price of a slave, Exod. xxi. 32. The silver being no way proportionable to his wrath, it is *thrown to the potter* with disdain: "Let him take it to buy clay with."

So the prophet *cast the thirty pieces of silver to the potter in the house of the Lord*. There is a particular accomplishment of this in the history of Christ's sufferings, Matt. xxvii. 9, 10. *Thirty pieces of silver* was the very sum for which Christ was sold to the chief priests; the money was laid out in the purchase of *the potter's field*. The completing of their rejection was the cutting asunder of the other staff, *v.* 14. The former denoted the ruin of their church, by breaking the covenant between God and them—that defaced their *beauty*; this denotes the ruin of their state, by breaking the brotherhood between Judah and Israel. They shall be crumbled into parties and factions, being thus divided, shall be *brought to desolation*. Nothing ruins a people so inevitably, as the breaking of *the staff of Bands*, and the weakening of the brotherhood among them.

Verses 15–17

God, having shown this people justly abandoned by the good Shepherd, here shows their further misery in being shamefully abused by a foolish shepherd. The prophet is himself to personate this pretended shepherd (*v.* 15): *Take unto thee the instruments* or accoutrements *of a foolish shepherd*, such a shepherd's coat, and bag, and staff, as a foolish shepherd would appear in; for such a shepherd shall be set over them (*v.* 16), who, instead of protecting them, shall do them mischief. The description here given of the foolish shepherd suits the character Christ gives of the scribes and Pharisees, Matt. xxiii. They shall be under the tyranny of unmerciful princes. They shall be imposed upon by false Christs and false prophets, as our Saviour foretold, Matt. xxiv. 5.

JAMIESON, FAUSSET, BROWN

He had, thirty-seven years before the fall of Jerusalem, forewarned His disciples when they should see the city compassed with armies, to "flee unto the mountains." Accordingly, Cestius Gallus, when advancing on Jerusalem, unaccountably withdrew for a brief space, giving Christians the opportunity of obeying Christ's words by fleeing to Pella. **waited upon me**—looked to the hand of God in all these calamities, not blindly shutting their eyes to the true cause of the visitation, as most of the nation still do, instead of referring it to their own rejection of Messiah. Isaiah 30:18-21 refers similarly to the Lord's return in mercy to the remnant that "wait for Him" and "cry" to Him (Zeph. 3:12, 13). **12. I said**—The prophet here represents the person of Jehovah-Messiah. **If ye think good**—lit., "If it be good in your eyes." Glancing at their self-sufficient pride in not *deigning* to give Him that return which His great love in coming down to them from heaven merited, viz., their love and obedience. "My price"; my reward for pastoral care, both during the whole of Israel's history from the Exodus, and especially the three and a half years of Messiah's ministry. He speaks as their "servant," which He was to them in order to fulfil the Father's will (Phil. 2:7). **if not, forbear**—They withheld that which He sought as His only reward, their love; yet He will not force them, but leave His cause with God (Isa. 49:4, 5). Cf. the type Jacob cheated of his wages by Laban, but leaving his cause in the hands of God (Gen. 31:41, 42). **So . . . thirty pieces of silver**—*thirty shekels*. They not only refused Him His due, but added insult to injury by giving for Him the price of a gored bondservant (Exod. 21:32; Matt. 26:15). A freeman was rated at twice that sum. **13. Cast it unto the potter**—proverbial: Throw it to the temple-potter, the most suitable person to whom to cast the despicable sum, plying his trade as he did in the polluted valley (II Kings 23:10) of Hinnom, because it furnished him with the most suitable clay. This same valley, and the potter's shop, were made the scene of symbolic actions by Jeremiah (ch. 18 and 19) when prophesying of this very period of Jewish history. Zechariah connects his prophecy here with the older one of Jeremiah: showing the further application of the same divine threat against his unfaithful people in their destruction under Rome, as before in that under Nebuchadnezzar. Hence Matthew 27:9, in *English Version,* and in the oldest authorities, quotes Zechariah's words as *Jeremiah's*, the latter being the original author from whom Zechariah derived the groundwork of the prophecy. Cf. the parallel case of Mark 1:2, 3 in the oldest MSS. (though not in *English Version*), quoting Malachi's words as those of "Isaiah," the original source of the prophecy. Cf. my *Introduction* to Zechariah. The "potter" is significant of God's absolute power over the clay framed by His own hands (Isa. 45:9; Jer. 18:6; Rom. 9:20,21). **in the house of the Lord**—The thirty pieces are thrown down *in the temple,* as the house of Jehovah, the fit place for the money of Jehovah-Messiah being deposited, in the treasury, and the very place accordingly where Judas "cast them down." The thirty pieces were cast "to the potter," because it was to him they were "appointed by the Lord" ultimately to go, as a worthless price (cf. Matt. 27:6, 7, 10). For "I took," "I threw," here Matthew has "*they* took," "*they* gave them"; because their (the Jews' and Judas') act was all *His "appointment"* (which Matthew also expresses), and therefore is here attributed to Him (cf. Acts 2:23; 4:28). It is curious that some old translators translate, for "to the potter," "*to the treasury*" (so MAURER), agreeing with Matthew 27:6. But *English Version* agrees better with *Hebrew* and Matthew 27:10. **14.** The breaking of the bond of union between Judah and Israel's ten tribes under Rehoboam is here the image used to represent the *fratricidal discord of factions* which raged within Jerusalem on the eve of its fall, while the Romans were thundering at its gates without. See JOSEPHUS, J. B. Also the continued *severance of the tribes* till their coming reunion (Rom. 11:15). **15. yet**—"take *again*"; as in vs. 7 previously he had taken other implements. **instruments**—the accoutrements, viz., the shepherd's crook and staff, wallet, etc. Assume the character of a bad ("foolish" in Scripture is synonymous with *wicked,* Ps. 14:1) shepherd, as before thou assumedst that of a good shepherd. Since the Jews would not have Messiah, "the Good Shepherd" (John 10:11), they were given up to Rome, heathen and papal, both alike their persecutor, especially the latter, and shall be again to Antichrist, the "man of sin," the instrument of judgment by Christ's permission. Antichrist will first make a covenant with them as their ruler, but

ADAM CLARKE

12. *If ye think good, give me my price.* "Give me my hire." And we find they rated it contemptuously, thirty pieces of silver being the price of a slave, Exod. xxi. 32.

13. *And the Lord said unto me, Cast it unto the potter.* Jehovah calls the price of His prophet His own price; and commands that it should not be accepted, but given to a potter, to foreshadow the transaction related in Matt. xxvii. 7.

W. H. LOWE:

"A goodly price . . . of them." Better, *O, the magnificence of the price that I was appraised at of them!* That is to say, "What a price!" ironically. The prophet—in imagination, no doubt—goes into the Temple, and there before God and Israel, in the place where the covenant had been so often ratified by sacrifice, he meets "a potter," and there flings to him the "goodly price," and so pronounces the divorce between God and the congregation of Israel. The prophet, in his symbolical act, represented God (Ezek. 34:5), but at the same time he might well (or must) have represented God's vice-gerent, "my servant David," or, in other words, the Messiah. Thus, though this prophecy received, no doubt, numerous fulfilments in the oft-recurring ingratitude of Israel, yet we can well, with St. Matthew, see its most remarkable and complete fulfilment in Him who was in every sense "the Good Shepherd," and in whose rejection the ingratitude of the chosen nation culminated. The citation in the New Testament is a free paraphrase of the original, made, probably, from memory, and agrees in all the main points with the original. The introduction of the word "field" (Matt. 27:10) was made, probably inadvertently, by an unconscious act of a mind which wished to find an excellent parallel between the prophecy and its fulfilment; but the price, thirty pieces of silver, does not seem to have been a mere coincidence. May not the "chief priests" have viciously proposed to Judas this price of a slave (the same that Hosea paid for the adulterous woman, half in money, and half in kind, 2:1, 2)? and may not the wretched Judas have maliciously accepted this very sum from the same motives which the prophet supposes to have actuated the people to whom he prophesies? Such a fulfilment would be a fulfilment indeed; while a mere chance coincidence between the sum mentioned in one case and that mentioned in another, apart from any agreement in the latter with the spirit of the former, would, in our estimation, amount to no fulfilment at all.

—Ellicott's Commentary on the Whole Bible

MATTHEW HENRY

I. What a curse this foolish shepherd should be to the people, *v.* 16. He will not *visit those that are cut off*, will take no care of the *young ones*, nor *heal that* which was *broken*, but let it die of its bruises, when a little thing, in time, would have saved it. He will never do anything to *support the weak* and comfort the *feeble-minded*. Foolish shepherds *eat of the flesh of the fat*; they will have of the best for themselves; when they are in a rage against any of the flock, they *tear their* very *claws in pieces* by overdriving them.

II. What a curse this foolish shepherd should bring upon himself (*v.* 17): *Woe to the idol-shepherd.* His doom is that *the sword* of God's justice shall be *upon his arm* and *his right eye*, so that he shall quite lose the use of both. This was fulfilled when Christ said to the Pharisees, *I have come that those who see may be made blind*, John ix. 39.

JAMIESON, FAUSSET, BROWN

then will break it, and they shall feel the iron yoke of his tyranny as the false Messiah, because they rejected the light yoke of the true Messiah (Dan. 11:35-38; 12:1; 9:27; II Thess. 2:3-12). But at last he is to perish utterly (vs. 17), and the elect remnant of Judah and Israel is to be saved gloriously. **16. in the land**—Antichrist will probably he a Jew, or at least one in Judea. **not visit . . . neither . . . seek . . . heal . . . broken, nor feed . . . but . . . eat . . . flesh . . . tear**—Cf. similar language as to the unfaithful shepherds of Israel in Ezekiel 34: 2-4. This implies, they shall be paid in kind. Such a shepherd in the worst type shall "tear" them for a limited time. **those . . . cut off**—"those perishing" [LXX], i.e., those sick unto death, as if already cut off. **the young**—The *Hebrew* is always used of human youths, who are really referred to under the image of the young of the flock. Ancient expositors [*Chaldee Version*, JEROME, etc.] translate, "*the straying*," "the dispersed"; so GESENIUS. **broken**—the wounded. **standeth still**—with faintness lagging behind. **tear . . . claws**—expressing cruel voracity; tearing off the very hoofs (cf. Exod. 10:26), giving them excruciating pain, and disabling them from going in quest of pasture. **17. the idol**—The *Hebrew* expresses both *vanity* and *an idol*. Cf. Isaiah 14:13; Daniel 11:36; II Thessalonians 2:4; Revelation 13:5, 6, as to the idolatrous and blasphemous claims of Antichrist. The "idol shepherd *that leaveth the flock*" cannot apply to Rome, but to some ruler among the Jews themselves, at first cajoling, then "leaving" them, nay, destroying them (Dan. 9:27; 11:30-38). God's sword shall descend on his "arm," the instrument of his tyranny towards the sheep (II Thess. 2:8); and on his "right eye," wherewith he ought to have watched the sheep (John 10:12, 13). However, Antichrist shall *destroy*, rather than "*leave* the flock." Perhaps, therefore, the reference is to the shepherds who *left the flock* to Antichrist's rapacity, and who, in just retribution, shall feel his "sword" on their "arm," which ought to have protected the flock but did not, and on their "eye," which had failed duly to watch the sheep from hurt. The blinding of "the *right* eye" has attached to it the notion of ignominy (I Sam. 11:2).

ADAM CLARKE

17. *Woe to the idol shepherd!* "The worthless" or "good for nothing" shepherd. The shepherd in name and office, but not performing the work of one. See John x. 11. *The sword shall be upon his arm.* Punishment shall be executed upon the wicked Jews, and especially their wicked kings and priests. See v. 16. *Arm*—the secular power; *right eye*—the ecclesiastical state. *His arm shall be clean dried up.* The secular power shall be broken, and become utterly inefficient. *His right eye shall be utterly darkened.* Prophecy shall be restrained; and the whole state, ecclesiastical and civil, shall be so completely eclipsed that none of their functions shall be performed.

MATTHEW HENRY

CHAPTER 12

Verses 1–8

I. The title of this charter of promises made to God's Israel; it is the *burden of the word of the Lord*, a divine prediction. But it is *for Israel*; for their comfort and benefit.

II. The title of him that grants this charter: he is the Creator of the world and our Creator, and therefore has irresistible dominion. He *stretches out the heavens* and keeps them stretched out *like a curtain*, and will do so till the end come. He *lays the foundation of the earth*, and keeps it fixed on its own axis, though it is *founded on the seas* (Ps. xxiv. 1, 2), nay, though it is *hung upon nothing*, Job xxvi. 7. He *forms the spirit of man within him.* He *made us these souls*, Jer. xxxviii. 16. He not only breathed into the first man, but still breathes into every man the breath of life.

III. The promises by which the church shall be secured. Whatever attacks the enemies of the church may make upon her purity or peace, they will certainly issue in their own confusion. Jerusalem is in safety, and those are in danger who fight against it. This is here illustrated by three comparisons: 1. *Jerusalem* shall be *a cup of trembling* to all that lay siege to it, *v.* 2. Thus Alexander the Great was struck with amazement when he met Jaddas the high priest, and was deterred from offering any violence to Jerusalem. When Sennacherib laid siege *against Judah* and *Jerusalem* he found them such a cup of stupefying wine as laid all his mighty men asleep, Ps. lxxvi. 5, 6.

2. *Jerusalem* shall be *a burdensome stone* to all that attempt to remove it or carry it away, *v.* 3. Those that are for advancing the kingdom of sin in the world look upon Jerusalem, even the church of God, as the great obstacle to their design, and they must have it out of the way; but they cannot remove it. God will have a church in the world, in spite of them; it is *built upon a rock*, and is as *Mount Zion*, Ps. cxxv. 1. This *stone, cut out of the mountain without hands*, will *break in pieces all that burden themselves* with it, as that stone *smote the image*, Dan. ii. 45. Our Saviour seems to allude to these words when he speaks of himself as a burdensome stone to those that will not have him for their foundation-stone, which shall *fall upon them and grind them to powder*, Matt. xxi. 44.

JAMIESON, FAUSSET, BROWN

CHAPTER 12

VSS. 1-14. JERUSALEM THE INSTRUMENT OF JUDGMENT ON HER FOES HEREAFTER; HER REPENTANCE AND RESTORATION. **1. burden**—"weighty prophecy"; fraught with destruction to Israel's foes; the expression may also refer to the distresses of Israel *implied* as about to precede the deliverance. **for Israel**—*concerning* Israel [MAURER]. **stretcheth forth**—present; *now*, not merely "*hath* stretched forth," as if God only created and then left the universe to itself (John 5:17). To remove all doubts of unbelief as to the possibility of Israel's deliverance, God prefaces the prediction by reminding us of His creative and sustaining power. Cf. a similar preface in Isaiah 42:5; 43:1; 65:17, 18. **formeth . . . spirit of man**—(Num. 16:22; Heb. 12:9). **2. cup of trembling**—a cup causing those who drink it to *reel* (from a *Hebrew* root "to reel"). Jerusalem, who drank the "cup of trembling" herself, shall be so to her foes (Isa. 51:17, 22; Jer. 13:13). CALVIN with LXX translates, "*threshold* of destruction," on which they shall stumble and be crushed when they attempt to cross it. *English Version* is better. **both against Judah**—The *Hebrew* order of words is lit., "And also against Judah shall he (the foe) be in the siege against Jerusalem"; implying virtually that Judah, as it shares the invasion along with Jerusalem, so it shall, like the metropolis, prove a cup of trembling to the invaders. MAURER with JEROME translates, "Also upon Judah shall be (the cup of trembling); i.e., some Jews forced by the foe shall join in the assault on Jerusalem, and shall share the overthrow with the besiegers. But vss. 6, 7 show that Judah escapes and proves the scourge of the foe. **3.** (Cf. 14:4, 6-9, 13.) JEROME states it was a custom in Palestine to test the strength of youths by their lifting up a massive stone; the phrase, "burden themselves with it," refers to this custom. Cf. Matthew 21:44: The Jews "fell" on the rock of offense, Messiah, and were "broken"; but the rock shall fall on Antichrist, who "burdens himself with it" by his assault on the restored Jews, and "grind him to powder." **all . . . people of . . . earth**—The Antichristian confederacy against the Jews shall be almost universal.

ADAM CLARKE

CHAPTER 12

1. *The burden of the word of the Lord.* This is a new prophecy. It is directed to both Israel and Judah, though Israel alone is mentioned in this verse.

2. *Jerusalem a cup of trembling.* The Babylonians, who captivated and ruined the Jews, shall in their turn be ruined. I incline to think that what is spoken in this chapter about the Jews and Jerusalem belongs to the "glory of the latter times."

MATTHEW HENRY

3. The governors of Judah shall be among their enemies like *a hearth of fire among the wood, and a torch of fire in a sheaf*, *v.* 6. Those that contend with them will find it is like an opposition given by briers and thorns to a consuming fire, Isa. xxvii. 4. It will go through them, and burn them together. The enemies thought to be as water to this fire, but God will make them as wood, nay, as a sheaf of corn (which is more combustible), to this fire. The persecutors of the primitive church found this fulfilled in it, witness the confession of Julian the apostate at last, *Thou hast overcome me, O thou Galilean! If you are weary of your life, persecute the Christians*, was once a proverb. It is promised that God will infatuate the counsels and enfeeble the courage of the church's enemies (*v.* 4). The church's infantry shall be too hard for the enemy's cavalry. It is promised that Jerusalem shall be re-peopled and replenished (*v.* 6). They shall have a new Jerusalem upon the same foundation, the same spot of ground. They had so after their return out of captivity, but the gospel-church is a Jerusalem inhabited *in its own place*; for, the gospel being preached to all the world, it may call every place its own. It is promised that the inhabitants of Jerusalem shall be enabled to defend themselves under the divine protection, *v.* 8. God will not only be a *wall of fire* about the city, but he will encompass particular persons with his favour *as with a shield.* He does it by giving them strength and courage to help themselves. In that day the feeblest of the inhabitants of Jerusalem *shall be as David*, as skilful and strong, as serviceable to Jerusalem in guarding it as David himself was in founding it. *The house of David shall be as God*, that is, *as the angel of the Lord, before them.* Zerubbabel was now the top-branch of the house of David; he shall be endued with wisdom and grace, and shall go before the people as an angel, Exod. xxiii. 20. But this was to have its full accomplishment in Christ; now the house of David looked little and mean, and its glory was eclipsed, but in Christ the house of David shone more brightly than ever. It is promised that there shall be a very good understanding between the city and the country. *The governors of Judah*, the magistrates of the country, shall think honourably of the citizens, *the inhabitants of Jerusalem.* It is well with a kingdom when its great men know how to value its good men. God will put signal honour upon Judah, and so save them from the contempt of their brethren. God says (*v.* 4), *I will open my eyes upon the house of Judah*, and (*v.* 7), *the Lord shall save the tents of Judah first.* Those that dwell in tents lie most exposed; but God will deliver them before those that dwell in Jerusalem. Courtiers and citizens ought not to despise country people, those whom God *opens his eyes upon* and who are *first saved.* This promise has a further reference to the gospel-church, in which no difference shall be made between high and low, rich and poor, bond and free, circumcision and uncircumcision, Col. iii. 11.

Verses 9–14

The *day* here spoken of is the day of Jerusalem's defence and deliverance, that glorious day, which, if it refer to the successes which the Jews had against their enemies in the time of the Maccabees, yet certainly looks further, to the *gospel-day*, to Christ's victories over the powers of darkness and the great salvation he has wrought.

I. A glorious work of God to be wrought for his people: "*I will seek to destroy all the nations that come against Jerusalem*, *v.* 9. Nations come against Jerusalem, but they shall all be destroyed." In Christ's first coming, he *sought to destroy him that had the power of death*, and did destroy him. In his second coming, he will complete their destruction, and *death* itself shall be *swallowed up in* that *victory.*

II. A gracious work of God to be wrought in his people. When he seeks to destroy their enemies he will *pour upon them the Spirit of grace and supplication.* When God intends great mercy for his people the first thing he does is to set them praying. But this promise has reference to the graces of the Spirit given to all believers, as that Isa. xliv. 3, *I will pour my Spirit upon thy seed*, which was fulfilled when *Jesus was glorified*, John vii. 39. These blessings are poured on *the house of David*, on the great men; for they are no more, and no better, than the grace of God makes them. But it was given also to *the inhabitants of Jerusalem*, the common people. The church is Jerusalem, the heavenly Jerusalem; all true believers, that have their conversation in heaven, are inhabitants of this Jerusalem, and to them this promise belongs. God will *pour his Spirit upon them*: 1. As a *Spirit of grace*, to sanctify and to make gracious. 2. As a *Spirit of supplications*, instructing and assisting us in the duty of prayer. *I will pour upon them the Spirit of grace.* One effect of the gift is

JAMIESON, FAUSSET, BROWN

4. I will smite . . . horse—The arm of attack especially formidable to Judah, who was unprovided with cavalry. So in the overthrow of Pharaoh (Exod. 15:19, 21). **open mine eyes upon . . . Judah**—to watch over Judah's safety. Heretofore Jehovah seemed to have shut His eyes, as having no regard for her. **blindness**—so as to rush headlong on to their own ruin (cf. ch. 14:12, 13). **5. shall say**—when they see the foe divinely smitten with "madness." **Judah . . . Jerusalem**—here distinguished as the country and the metropolis. Judah recognizes her "strength" to be "Jerusalem and its inhabitants" as the instrument, and "Jehovah of hosts their God" (dwelling especially there) as the author of all power (Joel 3:16). My strength is the inhabitants of Jerusalem, who have the Lord their God as their help. The repulse of the foe by the metropolis shall assure the Jews of the country that the same divine aid shall save them. **6.** On "governors of Judah," see *Note*, ch. 9:7. **hearth**—or pan. **torch . . . in a sheaf**—Though small, it shall consume the many foes around. One prophet supplements the other. Thus Isaiah 29, Joel 3, and Zechariah 12, 13, 14, describe more Antichrist's *army* than himself. Daniel represents him as a horn growing out of the fourth beast or fourth kingdom; St. John, as a separate beast having an individual existence. Daniel dwells on his worldly conquests as a king; St. John, more on his spiritual tyranny, whence he adds a second beast, the false prophet coming in a semblance of spirituality. What is briefly described by one is more fully prophesied by the other [Roos]. **7.** Judah is to be "first saved," because of her meek acknowledgment of dependence on Jerusalem, subordinate to Jehovah's aid. **tents**—shifting and insecure, as contrasted with the solid fortifications of Judah. But God chooses the weak to confound the mighty, that all human glorying may be set aside. **8.** Jerusalem, however, also shall be specially strengthened against the foe. **feeble . . . shall be as David**—to the Jew, the highest type of strength and glory on earth (II Sam. 17:8; 18:3; Joel 3:10. **angel of the Lord before them**—the divine angel that went "before them" through the desert, the highest type of strength and glory in heaven (Exod. 23:20; 32:34). "The house of David" is the "prince," and his family sprung from David (Ezek. 45:7, 9). David's house was then in a comparatively weak state.

9. I will seek to destroy—I will set Myself with determined earnestness to destroy . . . (Hag. 2:22). **10.** Future conversion of the Jews is to flow from an extraordinary outpouring of the Holy Spirit (Jer. 31:9, 31-34; Ezek. 39:29). **spirit of grace . . . supplications**—"spirit" is here not the spirit produced, but THE HOLY SPIRIT *producing* a "*gracious*" disposition, and inclination for "*supplications.*" CALVIN explains "spirit of grace" as *the grace of God* itself (whereby He "pours" out His bowels of mercy), "conjoined with the sense of it in man's heart." The "spirit of supplications" is the mercury whose rise or fall is an unerring test of the state of the Church [MOORE]. In *Hebrew*, "grace" and "supplications" are kindred terms; translate, therefore, "*gracious* supplications." The *plural* implies suppliant prayers "without ceasing." Herein not merely external help against the foe, as before, but internal grace is promised subsequently. **look upon me**—with profoundly earnest regard, as the Messiah whom they so long denied. **pierced**—implying Messiah's humanity: as "*I* will pour . . . spirit" implies His divinity. **look . . . mourn**—True repentance arises from the sight by faith of the crucified Saviour. It is the tear that drops from the eye of faith looking on Him. Terror only produces remorse. The true penitent weeps over his sins in love to Him who in love has suffered for them. **me . . . him**—The change of person is due to Jehovah-Messiah speaking *in His own person* first, then the prophet speaking *of Him.* The Jews, to avoid the conclusion that He whom they have "pierced" is Jehovah-Messiah, who says, "I will pour out . . . spirit," altered "me" into "him," and represent the "pierced" one to be Messiah Ben (son of) Joseph, who was to suffer in the battle with Gog, before Messiah Ben David should come to reign. But *Hebrew, Chaldee, Syriac*, and *Arabic* oppose this; and the ancient Jews interpreted it of Messiah. Psalm 22:16 also refers to His being "pierced." So John 19:37; Revelation 1:7. The actual piercing of His side was the culminating point of all

ADAM CLARKE

5. *The governors of Judah.* This supposes a union between the two kingdoms of Israel and Judah.

6. *Jerusalem shall be inhabited again.* This seems to refer to the future conversion of the Jews, and their return to their own land.

7. *The Lord also shall save the tents of Judah first.* This, I suppose, refers to the same thing. The gospel of Christ shall go from the least to the greatest. Eminent men are not the first that are called; the poor have the gospel preached to them. And this is done in the wise providence of God, that the *glory of the house of David*, etc., that secular influence may appear to have no hand in the matter; and that God does not send His gospel to a great man because he is such.

10. *I will pour upon the house of David.* This is the way in which the Jews themselves shall be brought into the Christian Church.

MATTHEW HENRY

that they shall mourn, for there is a mourning that will end in rejoicing and has a blessing upon it. This mourning is a fruit of the Spirit, an evidence of a work of grace in the soul. It is a mourning grounded upon a sight of Christ: *They shall look on him whom they have pierced, and shall mourn for him.* It is foretold that Christ should be pierced, and this scripture is quoted as that which was fulfilled when Christ's side was pierced upon the cross; see John xix. 37. He is spoken of as one whom we have pierced; it is spoken primarily of the Jews, yet it is true of us all as sinners. Those that truly repent of sin look upon Christ as one who was pierced for their sins and is pierced by them. They shall mourn for sin *as one mourns for an only son.* The sorrow of parents for a child, for a first-born, is natural; it is secret and lasting; such are the sorrows of a true penitent, flowing purely from love to Christ above any other. It shall be *like the mourning of Hadadrimmon in the valley of Megiddon,* where good king Josiah was slain, for whom there was a general lamentation (*v.* 11). They cried out, *The crown has fallen from our head. Woe unto us, for we have sinned!* Lam. v. 16. Christ is our King; our sins were his death, and, for that reason, ought to be our grief. There shall be not only a mourning of *the land,* by its representatives in a general assembly (as Judges ii. 5, when the place was called *Bochim—A place of weepers*), but: *Every family apart* shall mourn (*v.* 12), *all the families that remain, v.* 14. Four several families are here specified as examples to others: (1) Two of them are royal families; the *house of David,* in Solomon, and the *house of Nathan,* another son of David, Luke iii. 27–31. (2) Two of them are sacred families (*v.* 13), *the family of the house of Levi,* which was God's tribe, and in it particularly the family of Shimei, which was a branch of the tribe of Levi (1 Chron. vi. 17). As the princes must mourn for the sins of the magistracy, so must the priests for the *iniquity of the holy things.*

JAMIESON, FAUSSET, BROWN

their insulting treatment of Him. The act of the Roman soldier who pierced Him was their act (Matt. 27:25), and is so accounted here in Zechariah. The *Hebrew* word is always used of a literal piercing (so ch. 13:3); not of a metaphorical *piercing,* "insulted," as MAURER and other Rationalists (from the LXX) represent. **as one mourneth for . . . son** —(Jer. 6:26; Amos 8:10). A proverbial phrase peculiarly forcible among the Jews, who felt childlessness as a curse and dishonor. Applied with peculiar propriety to mourning for Messiah, "the *first-born* among many brethren" (Rom. 8:29). **11.** As in vs. 10 the bitterness of their mourning is illustrated by a private case of mourning, so in this verse by a public one, the greatest recorded in Jewish history, that for the violent death in battle with Pharaoh-necho of the good King Josiah, whose reign had been the only gleam of brightness for the period from Hezekiah to the downfall of the state; lamentations were written by Jeremiah for the occasion (II Kings 23:29, 30; II Chron. 35:22-27). **Hadad-rimmon**—a place or city in the great plain of Esdraelon, the battlefield of many a conflict, near Megiddo; called so from the Syrian idol Rimmon. the Syrians (MACROB, *Saturnalia,* 1.23). **12-14.** A Hadad also was the name of the sun, a chief god of universal and an individual mourning at once. **David . . . Nathan**—representing the highest and lowest of the royal order. Nathan, not the prophet, but a younger son of David (II Sam. 5:14; Luke 3:31). **apart**—Retirement and seclusion are needful for deep personal religion. **wives apart**—Jewish females worship separately from the males (Exod. 15:1, 20). **13. Levi . . . Shimei**—the highest and lowest of the priestly order (Num. 3:18, 21). Their example and that of the royal order would of course influence the rest. **14. All . . . that remain**—after the fiery ordeal, in which two-thirds fall (ch. 13: 8, 9).

ADAM CLARKE

11. *A great mourning.* A universal repentance. *As the mourning of Hadad-rimmon.* They shall mourn as deeply for the crucified Christ as their forefathers did for the death of Josiah, who was slain at *Hadad-rimmon in the valley of Megiddon.* See 2 Chron. xxxv. 24-25.

MATTHEW HENRY — CHAPTER 13

Verses 1–6

Behold the Lamb of God *taking away the sin of the world,* 1 John iii. 5.

I. He takes away the guilt of sin by the blood of his cross (*v.* 1): *In that day,* in the gospel-day, *there shall be a fountain opened,* that is, provision made for the cleansing of all those from the pollutions of sin who truly repent. *In that day,* when the Spirit of grace is poured out to set them a mourning for their sins, their consciences shall be purified and pacified by the *blood of Christ, which cleanses from all sin,* 1 John i. 7. This *fountain opened* is the pierced side of Jesus Christ, spoken of just before (*ch.* xii. 10), for thence there came there out *blood and water,* and both for cleansing. Sin is uncleanness; it defiles the mind and conscience, renders us odious to God and uneasy in ourselves, unfit to be employed in the service of God. There is mercy enough in God, and merit enough in Christ, for the forgiving of the greatest sins and sinners, 1 Cor. vi. 11. Under the law there were a brazen laver and a brazen sea to wash in; those were but vessels, but we have a fountain overflowing, ever-flowing. It is a *fountain opened*; it is opened, not only to *the house of David,* but to *the inhabitants of Jerusalem,* to the poor and mean as well as to the rich and great.

II. He takes away the dominion of sin by the power of his grace. Those that are washed, as they are justified, so they are sanctified. In that day (*v.* 2): *I will cut off the names of the idols out of the land.* This was fulfilled in the rooted aversion which the Jews had, after the captivity, to idols and idolatry, and still retain to this day; it was fulfilled also in the conversion of many to the faith of Christ, by which they were taken off from making an idol of the ceremonial law. False prophecy shall also be brought to an end. The devil is an *unclean* spirit; and he has his prophets. It is here foretold that false prophets should be brought to punishment even by their nearest relations (*v.* 3). Holy zeal for God and godliness will make us hate sin, and dread temptation, most in those whom naturally we love best.

False prophets should be themselves convinced of their sin (*v.* 4): "*The prophets shall be ashamed everyone*

JAMIESON, FAUSSET, BROWN — CHAPTER 13

VSS. 1-9. CLEANSING OF THE JEWS FROM SIN; ABOLITION OF IDOLATRY; THE SHEPHERD SMITTEN: THE PEOPLE OF THE LAND CUT OFF, EXCEPT A THIRD PART REFINED BY TRIALS. **1.** Connected with the close of ch. 12. The mourning penitents are here comforted. **fountain opened**—It has been long opened, but then first it shall be so "*to the house of David . . .*" (representing all Israel) after their long and weary wanderings. Like Hagar in the wilderness they remain ignorant of the refreshment near them, until God "*opens* their eyes" (Gen. 21:19) [MOORE]. It is not the fountain, but their eyes that need to be opened. It shall be a "fountain" ever flowing; not a laver needing constantly to be replenished with water, such as stood between the tabernacle and altar (Exod. 30:18). **for sin . . . uncleanness**—i.e., judicial guilt and moral impurity. Thus justification and sanctification are implied in this verse as both flowing from the blood of Christ, not from ceremonial sacrifices (I Cor. 1:30; Heb. 9:13, 14; I John 1:7; cf. Ezek. 36:25). *Sin* in *Hebrew* is literally *a missing the mark* or *way.* **2.** Consequences of pardon; not indolence, but the extirpation of sin. **names of . . . idols**—Their very names were not to be mentioned; thus the Jews, instead of Mephi-baal, said Mephibosheth (*Bosheth* meaning a contemptible thing) (Exod. 23:13; Deut. 12:3; Ps. 16:4). **out of the land**—Judea's two great sins, idolatry and false prophecy, have long since ceased. But these are types of all sin (e.g., covetousness, Eph. 5:5, a besetting sin of the Jews now). Idolatry, combined with the "spirit" of "Satan," is again to be incarnated in "the man of sin," who is to arise in Judea (II Thess. 2:3-12), and is to be "consumed with the Spirit of the Lord's mouth." Cf. as to Antichrist's papal precursor, "seducing spirits . . . doctrines of devils," etc., I Timothy 4:1-3; II Peter 2:1. **the unclean spirit**—*Hebrew, spirit of uncleanness* (cf. Rev. 16:13); opposed to "the Spirit of holiness" (Rom. 1:4), "spirit of error" (I John 4:6). One assuming to be divinely inspired, but in league with Satan. **3.** The form of phraseology here is drawn from Deuteronomy 13:6-10; 18:20. The substantial truth expressed is that false prophecy shall be utterly abolished. If it were possible for it again to start up, the very parents of the false prophet would not let parental affection interfere, but would be the first to thrust him through. Love to Christ must be paramount to the tenderest of natural ties (Matt. 10:37). Much as the godly love their children, they love God and His honor more. **4. prophets . . . ashamed**—of the false prophecies which they have uttered in times past, and which the event has confuted. **rough garment**—sackcloth.

ADAM CLARKE — CHAPTER 13

1. *In that day there shall be a fountain opened.* This chapter is a continuation of the preceding, and should not have been separated from it. *A fountain.* The source of mercy in Christ Jesus; perhaps referring to the death He should die, and the piercing of His side, when blood and water issued out. *To the house of David.* To David's family, and suchlike persons as it included. *Inhabitants of Jerusalem.* Suchlike persons as the Jews were in every part of their history. *For sin and for uncleanness.* For the removal of the guilt of sin, and for the purification of the soul from the uncleanness or pollution of sin.

2. *I will cut off the names of the idols.* There shall not only be no idolatry, but the very *names of the idols* shall be forgotten, or be held in such abhorrence that no person shall mention them. This prophecy seems to be ancient, and to have been delivered while idolatry had prevalence in Israel and Judah. *I will cause the prophets.* All false teachers.

MATTHEW HENRY

of his vision; because God has by his grace awakened their consciences and shown them their error, or because the event disproves their predictions. And therefore they shall no longer *wear a rough garment*, or *garment of hair*, as the true prophets used to do, in imitation of Elijah." Let men be really as good as they seem to be, but not seem to be better than really they are.

The pretender, as a true penitent *shall say*, "*I am no prophet*, as I have pretended to be. *I am a husbandman;* I was never taught of God to prophesy, but *taught of man to keep cattle*." We must evince the truth of our repentance by returning to our duty again, though it be the severest mortification to us.

"Hast thou not been beaten into this acknowledgment? Was it not the rod and reproof that gave thee this wisdom?" And he shall own, "Yes, it was; these are the *wounds with which I was wounded in the house of my friends*, who bound me, and brought me to my senses." Reduced by stripes, he had the sense and honesty to own that they were his friends, his real friends, who thus wounded him, that they might reclaim him. Some good interpreters think that these are the words of Christ who was wounded in his hands, when they were nailed to the cross. After his resurrection, he had the marks of these wounds; and here he tells how he came by them; he received them as a false prophet, for the chief priests called him a deceiver, but he received them in the house of the Jews, who should have been his friends.

Verses 7–9

Here is a prophecy,

I. Of the sufferings of Christ who was to be pierced, and was to be the fountain opened. *Awake, O sword! against my Shepherd, v.* 7. These are the words of God the Father, giving commission to the sword of his justice to awake against his Son, when he had voluntarily made his soul an offering for sin; for it *pleased the Lord to bruise him* and *put him to grief*; and *he was stricken, smitten of God, and afflicted*, Isa. liii. 4, 10. Observe, 1. How he calls him. "As God, he is *my fellow*"; for he thought it *no robbery to be equal with God.* He and *the Father* are *one.* "As Mediator, he is *my Shepherd*, the Shepherd that was to lay down his life for the sheep." 2. How he uses him: *Awake, O sword! against him.* If he will be a sacrifice, he must be slain, for without the shedding of blood, the life-blood, there was no remission. It is not a charge given to a rod to correct him, but to a sword to slay him; for God *spared not his own Son.*

II. Of the dispersion of the disciples thereupon: *Smite the Shepherd, and the sheep shall be scattered.* This our Lord Jesus himself declares to have been fulfilled when *all his disciples were offended because of him* in the night wherein he was betrayed, Matt. xxvi. 31; Mark xiv. 27. They all *forsook him and fled.* They were *scattered everyone to his own, and left him alone*, John xvi. 32. Some think this refers to Christ the *Shepherd* of the Jewish nation; he was smitten; they themselves smote him; and therefore they were dispersed among the nations. These words, *I will turn my hand upon the little ones*, may be understood either as a threatening (as Christ suffered, so shall his disciples), or as a promise that God would gather Christ's scattered disciples together again, and give them the meeting in Galilee.

JAMIESON, FAUSSET, BROWN

The badge of a prophet (II Kings 1:8; Isa. 20:2), to mark their frugality alike in food and attire (Matt. 3:4); also, to be consonant to the mournful warnings which they delivered. It is not the dress that is here condemned, but the purpose for which it was worn, viz., to conceal wolves under sheep's clothing [CALVIN]. The monkish hair-shirt of Popery, worn to inspire the multitude with the impression of superior sanctity, shall be then cast aside. **5, 6.** The detection of one of the false prophets dramatically represented. He is seized by some zealous vindicator of the law, and in fear cries out, "I am no prophet." **man**—i.e., one. **taught me to keep cattle**—As "keeping cattle" is not the same as to be "an husbandman," translate rather, "Has used (or 'appropriated') me as a servant," viz., *in husbandry* [MAURER]. However, husbandry and keeping cattle might be regarded as jointly the occupation of the person questioned: then Amos 7:14, "herdman," will accord with *English Version.* A *Hebrew* kindred word means "cattle." Both occupations, the respondent replies, are inconsistent with my being a "prophet." **6. wounds in thine hand**—The interrogator still suspects him: "If so, if you have never pretended to be a prophet, whence come those wounds?" The *Hebrew* is literally, "*between* thine hands." The hands were naturally held up to ward off the blows, and so were "thrust through" (vs. 3) "between" the bones of the hand. *Stoning* was the usual punishment; "thrusting through" was also a fit retribution on one who tried to "thrust Israel away" from the Lord (Deut. 13:10); and perfects the type of Messiah, condemned as a false prophet, and pierced with "wounds *between* His hands." Thus the transition to the direct prophecy of Him (vs. 7) is natural, which it would not be if He were not indirectly and in type alluded to. **wounded in . . . house of my friends**—an implied admission that he had pretended to prophecy, and that his friends had wounded him for it in zeal for God (vs. 3). The Holy Spirit in Zechariah alludes indirectly to Messiah, the Antitype, wounded by those whom He came to befriend, who ought to have been His "friends," who were His kinsmen (cf. vs. 3, as to the false prophet's friends, with Mark 3:21, "His friends," *Margin,* "kinsmen"; John 7:5; "His own," John 1:11; *the Jews,* "of whom as concerning the flesh He came," Rom. 9:5), but who wounded Him by the agency of the Romans (ch. 12:10). **7.** Expounded by Christ as referring to Himself (Matt. 26: 31, 32). Thus it is a resumption of the prophecy of His betrayal (ch. 11:4, 10, 13, 14), and the subsequent punishment of the Jews. It explains the mystery why He, who came to be a blessing, was cut off while bestowing the blessing. God regards sin in such a fearful light that He spared not His own co-equal Son in the one Godhead, when that Son bore the sinner's guilt. **Awake**—Cf. a similar address to the sword of justice personified (Jer. 46:6, 7). For "smite" (imperative), Matthew 26:31 has "I will smite." The act of the sword, it is thus implied, is GOD's act. So the prophecy in Isaiah 6:9, "Hear ye," is imperative; the fulfilment as declared by Jesus is future (Matt. 13:14), "ye shall hear." **sword**—the symbol of judicial power, the highest exercise of which is to take away the life of the condemned (Ps. 17:13; Rom. 13:4). Not merely a show, or expression, of justice (as Socinians think) is distinctly implied here, but an actual execution of it on Messiah the shepherd, the substitute for the sheep, by God as judge. Yet God in this shows His love as gloriously as His justice. For God calls Messiah "*My* shepherd," i.e., provided (Rev. 13:8) for sinners by My love to them, and ever the object of My love, though judicially smitten (Isa. 53:4) for their sins (Isa. 42:1; 59:16). **man that is my fellow**—lit., *the "man of my union."* The *Hebrew* for "man" is "a mighty man," one peculiarly man in his noblest ideal. "My fellow," i.e., "my associate." "My equal" ([DE WETTE]; a remarkable admission from a Rationalist). "My nearest kinsman" [HENGSTENBERG], (John 10:30; 14: 10, 11; Phil. 2:6). **sheep shall be scattered**—The scattering of Christ's disciples on His apprehension was the partial fulfilment (Matt. 26:31), a pledge of the dispersion of the Jewish nation (once the Lord's *sheep,* Ps. 100:3) consequent on their crucifixion of Him. The Jews, though "scattered," are still the Lord's "sheep," awaiting their being "gathered' 'by Him (Isa. 40:9, 11). **I will turn . . . hand upon . . . little ones**—i.e., I will interpose in favor of (cf. the phrase in a good sense, Isa. 1:25) "the little ones," viz., the humble followers of Christ from the Jewish Church, despised by the world: "the poor of the flock" (ch. 11:7, 11); comforted after His crucifixion at the resurrection (John 20:17-20); saved again by a special interposition from the destruction of Je-

ADAM CLARKE

4. *Neither shall they wear a rough garment.* A *rough garment* made of goats' hair, coarse wool, or the coarse pile of the camel, was the ordinary garb of God's prophets. And the false prophets wore the same; for they pretended to the same gifts, and the same spirit, and therefore they wore the same kind of garments. John Baptist had a garment of this kind.

6. *What are these wounds in thine hands?* Marks which he had received in honor of his idols.

But he shall excuse himself by stating that he had received these marks in his own family; when, most probably, they had been dedicated to some of those idols. I do not think that these words are spoken at all concerning Jesus Christ. I have heard them quoted in this way, but I cannot hear such an application of them without horror. In quoting from the Old Testament in reference to the New, we cannot be too cautious. We may wound the truth instead of honoring it.

7. *Awake, O sword, against my shepherd.* This is generally understood of Jesus Christ. The sword is that of divine justice, which seemed to have been long asleep, and should long ago have struck either man or his Substitute, the Messiah. Jesus is here called God's *shepherd*, because He had appointed Him to feed and govern, as well as to save, the whole lost world.

The man that is my fellow. "Upon the strong man" or "the hero that is with me"; my neighbor.

Smite the shepherd, and the sheep shall be scattered. This is quoted by our Lord, Matt. xxvi. 31, in relation to His disciples, who should be scattered on His crucifixion. And they were so; for every one, giving up all for lost, went to his own house. *And I will turn mine hand upon the little ones.* I will take care of the little flock, and preserve them from Jewish malice and Gentile persecution. And so this little flock was most wondrously preserved, and has been increasing from year to year from that time to the present day.

MATTHEW HENRY

III. Of the rejection and ruin of the unbelieving Jews (*v.* 8); and this shall have its accomplishment, in the destruction of the corrupt and hypocritical part of the church.

IV. Of the reformation of the chosen remnant, those of them that believed, and the Christian church in general (*v.* 9): *The third part shall be left.* When Jerusalem and Judæa were destroyed, all the Christians in that country, having the warning Christ gave them to *flee to the mountains*, shifted for their own safety, and were sheltered in a city called *Pella*, on the other side Jordan. *I will bring* that *third part through the fire* of affliction, *and will refine* and *try them* as *silver and gold are refined and tried.* This was fulfilled in the persecutions of the primitive church, the *fiery trial*, 1 Pet. iv. 12. Their communion with God is their triumph: *They shall call on my name, and I will hear them.* They write to God by prayer, and receive from him answers of peace. Their covenant with God is their triumph: "*I will say, It is my people*, whom I have chosen and loved, and will own; *and they shall say, The Lord is my God*, all-sufficient to me."

CHAPTER 14

Verses 1–7

God's providences concerning his church are here represented as strangely changing and strangely mixed.

I. As strangely changing. Sometimes the tide runs high and strong against them, but presently it turns.

1. God here appears against Jerusalem. When the *day of the Lord comes* (*v.* 1) Jerusalem must pass through the fire to be refined. The *city shall be taken by the* Romans, the houses shall be rifled, and *the women* shall *be ravished. One-half of the city* shall then be carried *into captivity*, to be sold or enslaved.

2. He presently changes his way, and appears for Jerusalem; for, though judgment begin at the house of God, yet, it shall not end there. A remnant shall be spared. *One-half shall go into captivity*, whence they may be fetched back, *and the residue of the people shall not* be cut off *from the city.* Many of the Jews shall receive the gospel, and so shall prevent their being cut off from the city of God, his church upon earth. *Then*, when God has made use of these nations as a scourge to his people, he shall *go forth* and *fight against them* by his judgments. The Roman empire never flourished after the destruction of Jerusalem as it had done before, but in many instances God fought against it. Though Jerusalem and the temple be destroyed, yet God will have a church in the world, into which Gentiles shall be admitted, and with whom the believing Jews shall be incorporated, *v.* 4, 5. God will carefully inspect Jerusalem, even when the enemies of it are laying it waste: *His feet shall stand in that day upon the mount of Olives*, Mark xiii. 3. When the refiner puts his gold into the furnace he stands by to see that it receive no damage; so when Jerusalem, God's gold, is to be refined, he will stand by *upon the mount of Olives*; this was literally fulfilled when our Lord Jesus was often upon this mountain. Thence he *ascended up into heaven*, Acts i. 12. It was the last place on which his feet stood on this earth. By the destruction of Jerusalem this mountain shall be made to *cleave in the midst*, and the Gentiles made one with the Jews by the breaking down of this *middle wall of partition*, Eph. ii. 14. A great mountain the ceremonial law was in the way of the Jews' conversion, yet before Christ and his gospel it was made plain. A new and living way shall be opened to the new Jerusalem. The mountain being divided, one-half *towards the north* and the other half *towards the south*, there shall be *a very great valley*, a broad way of communication between Jerusalem and the Gentile world, by which the Gentiles shall have free admission into the gospel-Jerusalem, and the word of the Lord, that *goes forth from Jerusalem*, shall have a *free course* into the Gentile world. The *valley of the mountains* is the gospel-church, to which there were added of the Jews daily *such as should be saved.* God *makes his mountains a way* (Isa. xlix. 11), by making them a valley. To those that are now separated from God this valley shall reach; for the Gentiles, who are afar off, shall be made nigh, with the Jews, who are a *people near unto him*, and both have a mutual access to each other and a joint access to God as a Father by one Spirit, Eph. ii. 18.

JAMIESON, FAUSSET, BROWN

rusalem, having retired to Pella when Cestius Gallus so unaccountably withdrew from Jerusalem. Ever since there has been a Jewish "remnant" of "the little ones" "according to the election of grace." The hand of Jehovah was laid in wrath on the Shepherd that His *hand might be turned* in grace *upon the little ones.* **8, 9.** Two-thirds of the Jewish nation were to perish in the Roman wars, and a third to survive. Probably from the context (ch. 14:2-9), which has never yet been fulfilled, the destruction of the two-thirds (lit., "the proportion of two," or "portion of two") and the saving of the remnant, the one-third, are still future, and to be fulfilled under Antichrist. **9. through . . . fire**—of trial (Ps. 66:10; Amos 4:11; I Cor. 3:15; I Peter 1: 6, 7). It hence appears that the Jews' conversion is not to precede, but to follow, their external deliverance by the special interposition of Jehovah; which latter shall be the main cause of their conversion, combined with a preparatory inward shedding abroad in their hearts of the Holy Spirit (ch. 12:10-14); and here, "they shall call on My name," in their trouble, which brings Jehovah to their help (Ps. 50: 15). **my people**—(Jer. 30:18-22; Ezek. 11:19, 20; Hos. 2:23).

CHAPTER 14

Vss. 1-21. LAST STRUGGLE WITH THE HOSTILE WORLD POWERS: MESSIAH-JEHOVAH SAVES JERUSALEM AND DESTROYS THE FOE, OF WHOM THE REMNANT TURNS TO THE LORD REIGNING AT JERUSALEM. **1. day of the Lord**—in which He shall vindicate His justice by punishing the wicked and then saving His elect people (Joel 2:31; 3:14; Mal. 4:1, 5). **thy spoil . . . divided in the midst of thee**—by the foe; secure of victory, they shall not divide the spoil taken from thee in their camp outside, but "in the midst" of the city itself. **2. gather all nations . . .**—The prophecy seems literal (cf. Joel 3:2). If Antichrist be the leader of the nations, it seems inconsistent with the statement that he will at this time be sitting in the temple as God at Jerusalem (II Thess. 2:4); thus Antichrist outside would be made to besiege Antichrist within the city. But difficulties do not set aside revelations: the event will clear up seeming difficulties. Cf. the complicated movements, Daniel 11. **half . . . the residue**—In ch. 13: 8, 9, it is "two-thirds" that perish, and "the *third*" escapes. There, however, it is "in *all the land*"; here it is "half *of the city*." Two-thirds of the *whole people* perish, one-third survives. One-half of the *citizens* are led captive, the residue are not cut off. Perhaps, too, we ought to translate, "a (not 'the') residue." **3. Then**—In Jerusalem's extremity. **as . . . in . . . day of battle**—as when Jehovah fought for Israel against the Egyptians at the Red Sea (Exod. 14:14; 15:3). As He then made a way through the divided sea, so will He now divide in two "the Mount of Olives" (vs. 4). **4.** The object of the cleaving of the mount in two by a fissure or valley (a prolongation of the valley of Jehoshaphat, and extending from Jerusalem on the west towards Jordan, eastward) is to open a way of escape to the besieged (ch. Joel 3:12, 14). Half the divided mount is thereby forced northward, half southward; the valley running between. **The place of His departure at His ascension shall be the place of His** return: and the "manner" of His return also shall be similar (Acts 1:11). He shall probably "come from the east" (Matt. 24:27). He so made His triumphal entry into the city from the Mount of Olives from the east (Matt. 21:1-10). This was the scene of His agony: so it shall be the scene of His glory. Cf. Ezekiel 11:23, with 43:2, "from the way of the east." **5. ye shall flee *to* the valley**—rather "*through* the valley," as in II Samuel 2:29. The valley made by the cleaving asunder of the Mount of Olives (vs. 4) is designed to be their way of escape, not their place of refuge [MAURER]. JEROME is on the side of *English Version.* If it be translated so, it will mean, Ye shall flee *to* the valley, not to hide there, but as the passage through which an escape may be effected. The same divinely sent earthquake which swallows up the foe, opens out a way of escape to God's people. The earthquake in Uzziah's days is mentioned (Amos 1:1) as a recognized epoch in Jewish history. Cf. also Isaiah 6:1: perhaps the same year that Jehovah held His heavenly court and gave commission to Isaiah for the Jews, an earthquake in the physical world, as often happens (Matt. 24:7), marked momentous movements in the unseen spiritual world. **of the mountains**—rather, "of *My* mountains," viz., Zion and Moriah, peculiarly sacred to Jehovah [MOORE]. Or, the mountains formed by *My* cleaving Olivet into two [MAURER].

ADAM CLARKE

8. *Two parts therein shall be cut off.* In the war with the Romans. *But the third shall be left.* Those who believe on the Lord Jesus Christ shall be preserved alive; and not one of these perished in the siege, or afterwards, by those wars.

9. *I will bring the third part through the fire.* The Christian Church shall endure a great fight of afflictions, by which they shall be refined—not consumed.

I will say, It is my people. The Church that I have chosen.

CHAPTER 14

1. *Behold, the day of the Lord cometh.* This appears to be a prediction of that war in which Jerusalem was finally destroyed, and the Jews scattered all over the face of the earth, and of the effects produced by it.

2. *I will gather all nations.* The Romans, whose armies were composed of all the nations of the world. In this verse there is a pitiful account given of the horrible outrages which should be committed during the siege of Jerusalem and at its capture.

The residue of the people shall not be cut off. Many were preserved for slaves, and for exhibition in the provincial theatres.

3. *Then shall the Lord go forth, and fight against those nations.* Against the Romans, by means of the northern nations, who shall destroy the whole empire of this once mistress of the world. But this is an obscure place.

4. *And his feet shall stand.* He shall appear in full possession of the place, as a mighty Conqueror. *And the mount of Olives shall cleave.* God shall display His miraculous power as fully in the final restoration of the Jews as He did when He divided the Red Sea, that their forefathers might pass through dry-shod. Some refer this to the destruction of the city by the Romans. It was on the Mount of Olives that Titus posted his army to batter Jerusalem. *And half of the mountain shall remove.* I really think that these words refer to the intrenchments, redoubts, etc., which the Romans made while carrying on the siege of this city; and particularly the lines or trenches which the army made on Mount Olivet itself.

5. *Ye shall flee to the valley.* Some think this refers to the valley through which Zedekiah and others endeavored to escape when Nebuchadnezzar pressed the siege of Jerusalem, but it appears to speak only of the Jewish wars of the Romans.

MATTHEW HENRY

God shall appear in his glory for the accomplishing of all this: *The Lord my God shall come, and all the saints with thee*; which may refer to his coming to destroy Jerusalem, or to destroy the enemies of Jerusalem; or his coming to set up his kingdom in the world, which is called the *coming of the son of Man* (Matt. xxiv. 37); or to his last coming, at the end of time; however, it teaches us that the Lord will come. Some think that *v.* 5 may be read as a prayer, *Yet, O Lord my God! come, and bring all the saints with thee.*

II. God's providences appear here strangely mixed (*v.* 6, 7): *In that day* of the Lord the *light shall not be clear nor dark, not day* nor *night;* but *at evening time it shall be light.* Some refer this to all the time from hence to the coming of the Messiah; the Jewish church had neither perfect peace nor constant trouble, but a cloudy day. But it may be taken more generally to represent the method God usually takes in the administration of the kingdom both of providence and grace. It is so with the church of God in this world; where the Sun of righteousness has risen it cannot be dark night, and yet short of heaven it will not be clear day. *It shall be one day which shall be known to the Lord.* This intimates beauty and harmony in such mixed events; there is one and the same design in all. *At evening-time it shall be light;* it shall be clear light, and no longer dark; we are sure of it in the other world, and we hope for it in this world—at *evening-time,* when things are at the worst and the case of the church is most deplorable.

Verses 8–15

I. Blessings promised to Jerusalem, the gospel-Jerusalem, in the day of the Messiah, and to all the earth.

1. Jerusalem shall be a spring of living waters to the world; it was made so when there the Spirit was poured out upon the apostles, and thence the word of the Lord diffused itself to the nations about (*v.* 8). It was the honour of Jerusalem that *thence the word of the Lord went forth* (Isa. ii. 3). Half of these waters shall go *towards the former sea* and *half towards the hinder sea,* as all rivers bend their course towards some sea or other, some eastward, others westward. The gospel shall spread into all parts of the world. The knowledge of God shall diffuse itself every way and every day. In *summer and in winter it shall be.* And such a divine power goes along with these living waters that they shall not be dried up, either by the droughts in summer or by the frosts in winter.

2. The kingdom of God among men shall be a universal and united kingdom, *v.* 9. *The Lord shall be King over all the earth. There shall be one Lord, and his name one.* All false gods shall be abandoned, and all false ways of worship abolished; and as God shall be the centre of their unity, so the scripture shall be the rule of their unity.

JAMIESON, FAUSSET, BROWN

Azal—the name of a place *near* a gate east of the city. The *Hebrew* means "adjoining" [Henderson]. Others give the meaning, "departed," "ceased." The valley reaches up to the city gates, so as to enable the fleeing citizens to betake themselves immediately to it on leaving the city. **Lord my God . . . with thee**—The mention of the "Lord my God" leads the prophet to pass suddenly to a direct address to Jehovah. It is as if "lifting up his head" (Luke 21:28), he suddenly sees in vision the Lord coming, and joyfully exclaims, "All the saints with Thee!" So Isaiah 25:9. **saints**—*holy angels* escorting the returning King (Matt. 24:30, 31; Jude 14); and redeemed men (I Cor. 15:23; I Thess. 3:13; 4: 14). Cf. the similar mention of the "saints" and "angels" at His coming on Sinai (Deut. 32:2, 3; Acts 7:53; Gal. 3:19; Heb. 2:2). Phillips thinks Azal is Ascalon on the Mediterranean. An earthquake beneath Messiah's tread will divide Syria, making from Jerusalem to Azal a valley which will admit the ocean waters from the west to the Dead Sea. The waters will rush down the valley of Arabah, the old bed of the Jordan, clear away the sand-drift of 4000 years, and cause the commerce of Petra and Tyre to center in the holy city. The Dead Sea rising above its shores will overflow by the valley of Edom, completing the straits of Azal into the Red Sea. Thus will be formed the great pool of Jerusalem (cf. vs. 8; Ezek. 47:1, etc.; Joel 3:18). Euphrates will be the north boundary, and the Red Sea the south. Twenty-five miles north and twenty-five miles south of Jerusalem will form one side of the fifty miles square of the Lord's Holy Oblation (Ezek. 48). There are seven spaces of fifty miles each from Jerusalem northward to the Euphrates, and five spaces of fifty miles each southward to the Red Sea. Thus there are thirteen equal distances on the breadth of the future promised land, one for the oblation and twelve for the tribes, according to Ezekiel 48. That the Euphrates north, Mediterranean west, the Nile and Red Sea south, are to be the future boundaries of the holy land, which will include Syria and Arabia, is favored by Genesis 15:8; Exodus 23:31; Deuteronomy 11:24; Joshua 1: 4; I Kings 4:21; II Chronicles 9:26; Isaiah 27:12; all which was partially realized in Solomon's reign, shall be antitypically so hereafter. The theory, if true, will clear away many difficulties in the way of the literal interpretation of this chapter and Ezekiel 48. **6. light . . . not . . . clear . . . dark**—Jerome, *Chaldee, Syriac,* and LXX *translate,* "There shall not be light, but cold and ice"; i.e., a day full of horror (Amos 5:18). But the *Hebrew* for "clear" does not mean "cold," but "precious," "splendid" (cf. Job 31:26). Calvin translates, "The light shall not be clear, *but* dark" (lit., "condensation," i.e., thick mist); like a dark day in which you can hardly distinguish between day and night. *English Version* accords with vs. 7: "There shall not be altogether light nor altogether darkness," but an intermediate condition in which sorrows shall be mingled with joys. **7. one day**—a day altogether *unique,* different from all others [Maurer]. Cf. "one," i.e., unique (Song of Sol. 6:9; Jer. 30:7). Not as Henderson explains, "One continuous day, without night" (Rev. 22:5, 25); the millennial period (Rev. 20:3-7). **known to . . . Lord**—This truth restrains man's curiosity and teaches us to wait the Lord's own time (Matt. 24:36). **not day, nor night**—answering to "not . . . clear nor . . . dark" (vs. 6); not altogether daylight, yet not the darkness of night. **at evening . . . shall be light**—Towards the close of this twilight-like time of calamity, "light" shall spring up (Ps. 97:11; 112:4; Isa. 30:26; 60:19, 20). **8. living waters**—(Ezek. 47:1; Joel 3:18). **former sea**—i.e., the *front,* or east, which Orientalists face in taking the points of the compass; the Dead Sea. **hinder sea**—the west or Mediterranean. **summer . . . winter**—neither dried up by heat, nor frozen by cold; ever flowing. **9. king over all . . . earth**—Isaiah 54:5 implies that this is to be the consequence of Israel being again recognized by God as His own people (Dan. 2:44; Rev. 11:15). **one Lord . . . name one**—Not that He is not so already, but He shall then be *recognized by all unanimously* as "One." Now there are "gods many and lords many." Then Jehovah alone shall be worshipped. The *manifestation* of the unity of the Godhead shall be simultaneous with that of the unity of the Church. Believers are one in spirit already, even as God is one (Eph. 4:3-6). But externally there are sad divisions. Not until these disappear, shall God reveal fully His unity to the world (John 17:21, 23). Then shall there be "a pure language, that all may call upon the name of the Lord with one consent" (Zeph. 3:9). The Son too shall at last give up His mediatorial kingdom to the Father, when the pur-

ADAM CLARKE

Azal. This, as a place, is not known. If a place, it was most probably near to Jerusalem, and had its name from that circumstance.

6. *The light shall not be clear, nor dark.* Metaphorically, there will be a mixture of justice and mercy in all this.

7. *At evening time it shall be light.* At the close of this awful visitation, there shall be light.

8. *Living waters shall go out.* There shall be a wide diffusion of divine knowledge, and of the plan of human salvation, which shall go out by apostles and preachers, first from Jerusalem. *The former sea, and . . . the hinder sea.* The Dead Sea and the Mediterranean; see Joel ii. 20. These are metaphors. *In summer.* In time of drought; or in the countries where there was no knowledge of God, there shall these waters flow. The stream shall never cease; it shall run in *summer* as well as *winter.*

9. *And the Lord shall be king.* When this universal diffusion of divine knowledge shall take place. Wherever it goes, the laws of God shall be acknowledged; and, consequently, He shall be King over the whole earth.

MATTHEW HENRY

3. The land of Judea, and Jerusalem, its mother-city, shall be repaired and taken under the special protection of Heaven, *v.* 10, 11. Some think this denotes particular favour to the people of the Jews, but it is rather to be understood figuratively of the gospel-church, typified by Judah and Jerusalem. The church shall be like a fruitful country, abounding in all the rich products of the soil. The whole land of Judæa, naturally uneven and hilly, shall be *turned as a plain*; it shall become a smooth level valley, from Gibeah, its utmost border north, to Rimmon, *south of Jerusalem*. The gospel of Christ, where it comes in its power, levels the ground, that the Lord alone may be exalted. As the holy land shall be levelled, so the holy city shall be peopled. *Jerusalem shall be lifted* up out of its low estate, shall be raised out of its ruins. The whole city shall be inhabited. The utmost limits of it are here mentioned, all built upon, from *Benjamin's-gate* north-east to the *corner-gate* north-west and *from the tower of Hananeel* in the south to the *king's wine-presses* in the north.

Those that dwell in it shall dwell securely, and there shall be no more anathema (as some read it), no more curse.

II. Judgments threatened against the enemies of the church, that *have fought*, or do fight, against Jerusalem. Those that fight against the city of God, and his people, will be found fighting against God, *v.* 12. They shall waste away under grievous and languishing diseases. They shall be dashed in pieces one against another (*v.* 13): *A great tumult from the Lord shall be among them.* Those that are combined against the church will justly be separated, and set against one another; and their tumults raised against God will be avenged in tumults among themselves. Some think this was fulfilled in the factions and dissensions that were among the Jews, when the Romans were destroying them all. The plunder of their camp shall greatly enrich the people of God, or the spoils of their country (*v.* 14): *Judah also shall eat at Jerusalem* (so one learned interpreter reads it); people shall come from all parts to share in the prey. The *wealth of the sinner is* often *laid up for the just*, and the Israel of God enriched with the spoil of the Egyptians. The very cattle shall share in the plague with which the enemies of God's church shall be cut off (*v.* 15).

Verses 16–21

Three things are here foretold:

I. Those that were left of the enemies of religion shall be so sensible of the mercy of God to them in their narrow escape that they shall apply themselves to the worship of the God of Israel, and pay their homage to him, *v.* 16. As some of Christ's foes shall be made his footstool, so others of them shall be made his friends. They shall *go up to worship* at Jerusalem, because that was the place which God had chosen, and there the temple was, which was a type of Christ and his mediation. Gospel-worship is here represented by the *keeping of the feast of tabernacles*, for the sake of those two great graces which were in a special manner *acted* and *signified* in that feast—contempt of the world, and joy in God, Neh. viii. 17. We must go to Christ our temple with all our offerings, for in him only our *spiritual sacrifices* are acceptable to God, 1 Pet. ii. 5. They shall go up *from year to year*, at the times appointed for this solemn feast. Every day of a Christian's life is a day of the *feast of tabernacles*, and every Lord's day especially.

II. Those who neglect the duties of gospel-worship shall be reckoned with for their neglect. *Upon them there shall be no rain, v.* 17. Some understand it figuratively; the rain of heavenly doctrine shall be withheld, and of the heavenly grace, which should accompany that doctrine. It is a righteous thing with God to withhold the blessings of grace from those that do not attend the means of grace, to deny the *green pastures* to those that attend not the *shepherd's tents*. If we be barren and unfruitful towards

JAMIESON, FAUSSET, BROWN

poses for which it was established shall have been accomplished, "that God may be all in all" (I Cor. 15:24). **10. turned**—or, "changed round about": lit., "to make a circuit." The whole hilly land *round* Jerusalem, which would prevent the free passage of the living waters, shall be *changed* so as to be "as a [or *the*] plain" (Isa. 40:4). **from Geba to Rimmon**—Geba (II Kings 23:8) in Benjamin, the north border of Judah. Rimmon, in Simeon (Josh. 15:32), the south border of Judah; not the Rimmon northeast of Michmash. "*The* plain from Geba to Rimmon" (i.e., from one boundary to the other) is the Arabah or plain of the Jordan, extending from the Sea of Tiberias to the Elanitic Gulf of the Red Sea. **it shall be lifted up**—viz., Jerusalem shall be exalted, the hills all round being lowered (Mic. 4:1). **inhabited in her place**—(ch. 12:6). **from Benjamin's gate**—leading to the territory of Benjamin. The same as Ephraim's gate, the north boundary of the city (II Kings 14:13). **the first gate**—west of the city [GROTIUS]. "The place of . . ." implies that the gate itself was then not in existence. "The old gate" (Neh. 3:6). **the corner gate**—east of the city [GROTIUS]. Or the "corner" joining the north and west parts of the wall [VILLALPANDUS]. GROTIUS thinks "corners" refers to the *towers* there built (cf. *Margin*, Zeph. 3:6). **tower of Hananeel**—south of the city, near the sheep gate (Neh. 3:1; 12:39; Jer. 31:38) [GROTIUS]. **king's winepresses**—(Song of Sol. 8:11). In the interior of the city, at Zion [GROTIUS]. **11. no more utter destruction**—(Jer. 31:40). Lit., "no more *curse*" (Rev. 22:3; cf. Mal. 4:6), for there will be no more sin. Temporal blessings and spiritual prosperity shall go together in the millennium: long life (Isa. 65:20-22), peace (Isa. 2:4), honor (Isa. 60:14-16), righteous government (Isa. 54:14; 60:18). Judgment, as usual, begins at the house of God, but then falls fatally on Antichrist, whereon the Church obtains perfect liberty. The last day will end everything evil (Rom. 8:21) [AUBERLEN]. **12.** Punishment on the foe, the last Antichristian confederacy (Isa. 59:18; 66:24; Ezek. 38, 39; Rev. 19:17-21). A living death: the *corruption* (Gal. 6:8) of death combined in ghastly union with the conscious sensibility of life. Sin will be felt by the sinner in all its loathsomeness, inseparably clinging to him as a festering, putrid body. **13. tumult**—consternation (ch. 12:4; I Sam. 14:15, 20). **lay hold . . . on . . . hand of . . . neighbour**—instinctively grasping it, as if thereby to be safer, but in vain [MENOCHIUS]. Rather, in order to assail "his neighbor" [CALVIN], (Ezek. 38:21). Sin is the cause of all quarrels on earth. It will cause endless quarrels in hell (Jas. 3:15, 16). **14. Judah . . . fight at Jerusalem**—viz., against the foe: not against Jerusalem, as MAURER translates in variance with the context. As to the spoil gained from the foe, cf. Ezekiel 39:10, 17. **15.** The plague shall affect the very beasts belonging to the foe. A typical foretaste of all this befell Antiochus Epiphanes and his host at Jerusalem (I Maccabees 13:49; II Maccabees 9:5). **16. every one . . . left**—(Isa. 66:19, 23). God will conquer all the foes of the Church. Some He will destroy; others He will bring into willing subjection. **from year to year**—lit., "from the sufficiency of a year in a year." **feast of tabernacles**—The other two great yearly feasts, passover and pentecost, are not specified, because, their antitypes having come, the types are done away with. But the feast of tabernacles will be commemorative of the Jews' sojourn, not merely forty years in the wilderness, but for almost 2000 years of their dispersion. So it was kept on their return from the Babylonian dispersion (Neh. 8:14-17). It was the feast on which Jesus made His triumphal entry into Jerusalem (Matt. 21:8); a pledge of His return to His capital to reign (cf. Lev. 23:34, 39, 40, 42; Rev. 7:9; 21:3). A feast of peculiar joy (Ps. 118:15; Hos. 12:9). The feast on which Jesus gave the invitation to the living waters of salvation ("Hosanna," *save us now*, was the cry, Matt. 21:9; cf. Ps. 118:25, 26) (John 7:2, 37). To the Gentiles, too, it will be significant of perfected salvation after past wanderings in a moral wilderness, as it originally commemorated the ingathering of the harvest. The seedtime of tears shall then have issued in the harvest of joy [MOORE]. "All the nations" could not possibly in person go up to the feast, but they may do so by representatives. **17. no rain**—including every calamity which usually follows in the East from want of rain, viz., scarcity of provisions, famine, pestilence, etc. Rain is the symbol also of God's favor (Hos. 6:3). That there shall be unconverted men under the millennium appears from the outbreak of God and Magog at the end of it (Rev. 20:7-9); but they, like Satan their master, shall be restrained during the thousand years. Note, too,

ADAM CLARKE

10. *All the land shall be turned as a plain.* Or rather, "He shall encompass the whole land as a plain." He shall cast His defense all around it; from *Geba*, in Benjamin, north of Jerusalem (Josh. xxi. 17), to *Rimmon* in Judah, to the *south of Jerusalem*, Josh. xv. 32.

It shall be lifted up. The city shall be exalted. *And inhabited in her place.* Jerusalem shall be rebuilt in the very place in which it originally stood. *From Benjamin's gate,* which was probably on the north side of Jerusalem, *unto the place of the first gate,* supposed to be that called "the old gate," Neh. iii. 6; xii. 39, placed by Lightfoot towards the southwest. *Unto the corner gate.* See 2 Kings xiv. 13.

The tower of Hananeel. This tower and the corner gate seem to be placed as two extremities of the city.

16. *Shall even go up from year to year.* The Jews had three grand original festivals, which characterized different epochs in their history, viz.: (1) The Feast of the Passover, in commemoration of their departure from Egypt. (2) The Feast of Pentecost, in commemoration of the giving of the law upon Mount Sinai. (3) The Feast of Tabernacles, in commemoration of their wandering forty years in the wilderness. This last feast is very properly brought in here to point out the final restoration of the Jews, and their establishment in the light and liberty of the gospel of Christ, after their long wandering in vice and error.

MATTHEW HENRY

God, justly is the earth made so to us. But what shall be done to the defaulters of the land of Egypt, to whom the threatening is no threatening, for they have no rain at any time; the river Nilus waters their land, and makes it fruitful, *v.* 18, 19. There shall be, in effect, the same plague. God can restrain the overflowing of the river, which was equivalent to the shutting up of the clouds. It does not follow that those who can live without rain can therefore live without God. Omissions are sins, and those contract guilt that *go not up to worship* at the times appointed, as they have opportunity.

III. The name and character of holiness shall not be so confined as formerly. *Holiness to the Lord* had been written only upon the high priest's forehead, but now it shall not be so appropriated. All Christians shall be *living temples*, and *spiritual priests*, dedicated to the honour of God and employed in his service. There shall be a more plentiful effusion of the Spirit of holiness and sanctification after Christ's ascension than ever before. There shall be holiness introduced into common things. The furniture of their horses shall be consecrated to God. "*Upon the bells of the horses* shall be engraven *Holiness to the Lord*, or upon the *bridles* of the horses (so the margin) or the *trappings*. Travellers shall have it upon their bridles, with which they guide their horses, to guide themselves by this rule. The furniture of their houses too shall be consecrated to God, to be employed in his service. The common drinking cups they used shall be *like the bowls before the altar*, that were used either to receive the blood of the sacrifices or to present the wine and oil for the *drink-offerings*. The vessels which they used for their own tables shall be used to the glory of God, and their meals shall look like sacrifices; they shall eat and drink, not to themselves, but to him that spread their tables and fills their cups. "*Every pot in Jerusalem and in Judah shall be holiness to the Lord*—the pots in which they boil their meat, the cups out of which they drink. What they eat and drink out of these shall nourish their bodies for the service of God; and out of these they shall give liberally for the relief of the poor"; then are they *Holiness to the Lord*. When there shall be such real holiness people shall not be so concerned about ceremonial holiness: "*Those that sacrifice shall come and take* of these common vessels, *and seethe* their sacrifices *therein*, making no distinction between them and the *bowls before the altar*." In gospel-times the true worshippers shall worship God *in spirit and in truth*, John iv. 21. One place shall be as acceptable to God as another, and one vessel shall be as acceptable as another. There shall be no unholiness introduced into their sacred things, to corrupt them: *In that day there shall be no more the Canaanite in the house of the Lord of hosts*. Some read it, There shall be no more *the merchant*, for so a Canaanite sometimes signifies; and they think it was fulfilled when Christ once and again drove the buyers and sellers out of the temple. At the end of time, and not before, Christ shall gather out of his kingdom everything that offends.

JAMIESON, FAUSSET, BROWN

from this verse that the Gentiles shall come up to Jerusalem, rather than the Jews go as missionaries to the Gentiles (Isa. 2:2; Mic. 5:7). However, Isaiah 66:19 *may* imply the converse. **18. if . . . Egypt go not up**—specified as Israel's ancient foe. If Egypt go not up, and so there be no rain on them (a judgment which Egypt would condemn, as depending on the Nile's overflow, not on rain), there shall be the plague . . . . Because the guilty are not affected by one judgment, let them not think to escape, for God has other judgments which shall plague them. MAURER translates, "If Egypt go not up, upon them also there shall be none" (no rain). Psalm 105:32 mentions "rain" in Egypt. But it is not their main source of fertility. **19. punishment**—lit., "sin"; i.e., "punishment for sin."

20. shall there be upon the bells—viz., this inscription, "Holiness to the Lord," the same as was on the miter of the high priest (Exod. 28:36). This implies that all things, even the most common, shall be sacred to Jehovah, and not merely the things which under the law had peculiar sanctity attached to them. The "bells" were metal plates hanging from the necks of horses and camels as ornaments, which *tinkled* (as the *Hebrew* root means) by striking against each other. Bells attached to horses are found represented on the walls of Sennacherib's palace at Koyunjik. **pots . . . like . . . bowls**—the vessels used for boiling, for receiving ashes, etc., shall be as holy as the bowls used for catching the blood of the sacrificial victims (*Note*, ch. 9:15; I Sam. 2:14). The priesthood of Christ will be explained more fully both by the Mosaic types and by the New Testament in that temple of which Ezekiel speaks. Then the Song of Solomon, now obscure, will be understood, for the marriage feast of the Lamb will be celebrated in heaven (Rev. 19), and on earth it will be a Solomonic period, peaceful, glorious, and nuptial. There will be no king but a prince; the sabbatic period of the judges will return, but not with the Old Testament, but New Testament glory (Isa. 1:26; Ezek. 45) [ROOS]. **21. every pot**—even in private houses, as in the temple, shall be deemed holy, so universal shall be the consecration of all things and persons to Jehovah. **take of them**—as readily as they would take of the pots of the temple itself, whatever number they wanted for sacrifice. **no . . . Canaanite**—no unclean or ungodly person (Isa. 35:8; 52:1; Joel 3:17). Cf. as to the final state subsequent to the millennium, Revelation 21:27; 22:15. MAURER not so well translates "merchant" here, as in Proverbs 31:24. If a man would have the beginnings of heaven, it must be by absolute consecration of everything to God on earth. Let his life be a liturgy, a holy service of acted worship [MOORE].

ADAM CLARKE

20. *Holiness unto the Lord*. As the gospel is a holy system, preaching holiness and producing holiness in those who believe, so all without, as well as within, shall bear this impress; and even a man's labor shall be begun and continued and ended in the Lord; yea, and the animals He uses, and the instruments He works with, shall be all consecrated to God through Christ.

THE BOOK OF MALACHI

I. Fundamental affirmation (1:1-5)
A. The sensitive word of Jehovah (1:1-2a)
B. The skeptical question (1:2b)
C. The answer in proof (1:2c-5)

II. Formal accusations (1:6-2:17)
A. Against the priests (1:6-2:9)
1. Their corruption declared (1:6-14)
2. The punishment threatened (2:1-9)
B. Against the people (2:10-16)
C. Against all (2:17)

III. Final annunciations (3:1-4:6)
A. The coming one (3:1-18)
1. Announcement of advent (3:1-6)
2. Appeal to the nation (3:7-15)
3. Attitude of the remnant (3:16-18)
B. The coming day (4:1-3)
C. The closing words (4:4-6)

God's prophets were his witnesses to his church, each in his day, for several ages; witnesses for him and his authority; witnesses against sin and sinners, attesting God's providences in his dealings with his people then and his grace concerning his church in the days of the Messiah. The Jews say prophecy continued forty years after the second temple and this prophet they call the "seal of prophecy," because in him the series or succession of prophets broke off and came to a period.

I. The person of the prophet. We have only his name, *Malachi,* and no account of his country or parentage. Malachi signifies *my angel.* Prophets were messengers, God's messengers; his name is in the original (3:1) *my messenger.* The tradition of some of the ancients is that he was of the tribe of Zebulun, and that he died young.

II. The scope of the prophecy. Haggai and Zechariah were sent to reprove the people for delaying to build the temple; Malachi was sent to reprove them for the neglect of it when it was built, and for their profanation of the temple service (for from idolatry and superstition they ran into the other extreme of impiety and irreligion). And now that prophecy was to cease he speaks more clearly of the Messiah as nigh at hand, and concludes with a direction to the people of God to keep in remembrance the law of Moses, while they were in expectation of the gospel of Christ.

MATTHEW HENRY

CHAPTER 1

Verses 1–5

The prophecy of this book is entitled, *The burden of the word of the Lord* (*v.* 1), which intimates, 1. That it was of great weight and importance. 2. That it ought to be often repeated as the burden of a song. 3. That there were those to whom it was a burden and a reproach. 4. That to them it would prove a burden indeed, to sink them, unless they repented.

This *burden of the word of the Lord* was sent, 1. To Israel. Many prophets God had sent to Israel, and now he will try them with one more. 2. *By Malachi, by the hand of Malachi.*

In these verses, they are charged with ingratitude.

I. God asserts the great kindness he had for them (*v.* 2): *I have loved you, saith the Lord.* Thus abruptly, thus kindly does the sermon begin. In this one word God sums up all his gracious dealings with them.

II. They question his love, *Yet you say, Wherein hast thou loved us?* As God traces up all his favours to them to the fountain, which was his love, so he traces up all their sins against him to the fountain, which was their contempt of his love. "Have we not been wasted, impoverished, and carried captive; and wherein then *hast thou loved us?*"

III. He makes it out, beyond contradiction, that he has loved them. Some read their question, *Wherefore hast thou loved us?* as if they did indeed own that he had loved them, but insinuate that he loved them because their father Abraham had loved him, so that it was not a free love, but a love of debt, to which he replies, "*Was not Esau* as near akin to Abraham as you are? And therefore, if there were any right to a recompence for Abraham's love, Esau had it, and yet *I hated Esau* and *loved Jacob.*" What a difference God had made between Jacob and Esau! Esau was Jacob's brother, his twin-brother: "*Yet I loved Jacob* and *I hated Esau,* that is, took Jacob into covenant. but refused and rejected Esau." The apostle quotes this (Rom. ix. 13). Esau was justly hated, but Jacob freely loved.

1. The Edomites shall be made the monuments of God's justice. For *Esau have I hated; I laid his*

JAMIESON, FAUSSET, BROWN

CHAPTER 1

Vss. 1-14. God's Love: Israel's Ingratitude: The Priests' Mercenary Spirit: A Gentile Spiritual Priesthood Shall Supersede Them. **1. burden**—heavy sentence. **to Israel**—represented now by the two tribes of Judah and Benjamin, with individuals of the ten tribes who had returned with the Jews from Babylon. So "Israel" is used, Ezra 7:10. Cf. II Chronicles 21:2, "Jehoshaphat king of *Israel,*" where Judah, rather than the ten tribes, is regarded as the truest representative of Israel (cf. II Chronicles 12:6; 28:19). **Malachi**—see *Introduction.* God sent no prophet after him till John the Baptist, the forerunner of Christ, in order to enflame His people with the more ardent desire for Him, the great antitype and fulfiller of prophecy. **2. I have loved you**—above other men; nay, even above the other descendants of Abraham and Isaac. Such gratuitous love on My part called for love on yours. But the return ye make is sin and dishonor to Me. This which is to be supplied is left unexpressed, sorrow as it were breaking off the sentence [Menochius], (Deut. 7:8; Hos. 11:1). **Wherein hast thou loved us?**—In painful contrast to the tearful tenderness of God's love stands their insolent challenge. The root of their sin was insensibility to God's *love,* and to their own wickedness. Having had prosperity taken from them, they imply they have no tokens of God's love; they look at what God had taken, not at what God had left. God's love is often least acknowledged where it is most manifested. We must not infer God does not love us because He afflicts us. Men, instead of referring their sufferings to their proper cause, their own sin, impiously accuse God of indifference to their welfare [Moore]. Thus the four first verses form a fit introduction to the whole prophecy. **Was not Esau Jacob's brother?**—and so, as far as dignity went, as much entitled to God's favor as Jacob. My adoption of Jacob, therefore, was altogether by gratuitous favor (Rom. 9:13). So God has passed by our elder brethren, the angels who kept not their first estate, and yet He has provided salvation for man. The perpetual rejection of the fallen angels, like the perpetual desolations of Edom, attests God's severity to the lost, and goodness to those gratuitously saved. The sovereign eternal purpose of God is the only ground on which He bestows on one favors withheld from another. There are difficulties in referring salvation to the election of God, there are greater in referring it to the election of man [Moore]. Jehovah illustrates His condescension and patience in arguing the case with them. **3. hated**—not positively, but relatively; i.e., did not

ADAM CLARKE

CHAPTER 1

1. *The burden of the word of the Lord to Israel by Malachi.* This prophet is undoubtedly the *last* of the Jewish prophets. He lived after Zechariah and Haggai; for we find that the Temple, which was begun in their time, was standing complete in his. See chap. iii. 10. Some have thought that he was contemporary with Nehemiah; indeed, several have supposed that Malachi is no other than Ezra under the feigned name of "angel of the Lord" or "my angel." John the Baptist was the link that connected Malachi with Christ. According to Archbishop Ussher, he flourished in 416 B.C.; but the Authorized Version, which we have followed in the margin, states this even to have happened nineteen years later.

2. *Was not Esau Jacob's brother?* Have I not shown a greater partiality to the Israelites than I have to the Edomites? *I loved Jacob.* My love to Jacob has been proved by giving him greater privileges and a better inheritance than what I have given to Esau.

3. *And I hated Esau.* I have shown him less love, Gen. xxix. 30-31. I comparatively hated

MATTHEW HENRY

mountains waste, the mountains of Seir, which were *his heritage*. When all that part of the world was ravaged by the Chaldean army the country of Edom was laid in ruins, Isa. xxxiv. 6, 11. The Edomites had triumphed in Jerusalem's overthrow (Ps. cxxxvii. 7), and therefore it was just to put the same cup of trembling into their hands. Jacob's cities are laid waste, but they are rebuilt; Edom's are laid waste, and never rebuilt. The sufferings of the righteous will end well; their grievances will be redressed, and their sorrow turned into joy; but the sufferings of the wicked will be as Edom's desolations, *v.* 4. The vain hopes of the Edomites had no promise to build upon. They say, "It is true, *we are impoverished*; it is the common chance, and there is no remedy; but *we will return and build the desolate places*; we are resolved we will" (not so much as asking God leave). They build presumptuously, as Hiel built Jericho in direct contradiction to the word of God (1 Kings xvi. 34), and it shall speed accordingly. They say, *We will build;* but what says *the Lord of hosts*? *They shall build, but I will throw down.* All that see them shall call them *the border of wickedness*, a sinful nation, incurably so, and therefore *the people against whom the Lord has indignation for ever*. Since their wickedness is such as will never be reformed, their desolations shall be such as are never to be repaired.

2. The Israelites shall be made the monuments of his mercy, *v.* 5. "The Edomites shall be stigmatized as a people hated of God, *but your eyes shall see* your doubts concerning his love to you silenced; for you shall have cause to say, *The Lord will be magnified from* every part and border of the land of Israel." When the border of Edom still remains desolate, and the border of Israel is repaired and replenished, then it will appear that God has loved Jacob. God's goodness being his glory, when he does us good we must proclaim him great, for that is magnifying him.

Verses 6–14

The prophet is here calling the priests to account, though they were themselves appointed judges, to call the people to an account. Thus *saith the Lord of hosts to you, O priests! v.* 6.

I. What it was that God expected from them (*v.* 6): *A son honours his father*, because he is his father; nature has written this law in the hearts of children, before God wrote it at Mount Sinai; *a servant*, though his obligation to his master is by voluntary compact, yet thinks it his duty to honour him. But the priests, who are God's children and his servants, do not fear and honour him. They were *fathers* and *masters* to the people, and expected to be called so (Judges xviii. 19, Matt. xxii. 7, 10); but they forgot their Father and Master in heaven, and the duty they owed to him. Our relation to God as our Father and Master strongly obliges us to fear and honour him. If we honour and fear the fathers of our flesh, much more the Father and Master of our spirits, Heb. xii. 9.

II. What the contempt was which the priests put upon God. They despised God's name, his word and ordinances, causing even the *sacrifices of the Lord to be abhorred*, as Eli's sons did. They *profaned God's name*, *v.* 12. They *polluted* it, *v.* 7. They not only made no account of sacred things, but they perverted them to the service of the worst purposes—their own pride, covetousness, and luxury. This is the general charge against them. To this they plead *Not guilty*, and challenge God to prove it upon them. *You say, Wherein have we despised thy name?* (*v.* 6), and *wherein have we polluted thee? v.* 7. Their defence was their offence, and their saying, *Wherein have we despised thy name?* proved them proud and perverse. Justly might they have been condemned upon the general charge, but God shows them very particularly wherein they had despised his name.

1. They despised God's name in what they said: "*You say* in your hearts, *The table of the Lord is contemptible*" (*v.* 7), and again (*v.* 12), "You say, *The table of the Lord is polluted;* it is to be no more regarded than any other table." Either the table in the temple on which the show-bread was placed, is that which they reflect upon, or rather the altar of burnt-offerings is here called the table. This they thought was contemptible in comparison with their own tables, and those of their great men: *The fruit thereof, even his meat, is contemptible.*

2. They despised God's name in what they did, which was of a piece with what they said. They thought anything would serve for a sacrifice, though ever so coarse and mean. With every sacrifice they were to bring a meat-offering of *fine flour mingled with oil*; but they brought *polluted bread* (*v.* 7). And as to the beasts they offered, though the law was express that what was offered in sacrifice should not have a blemish, yet they brought *the blind, and the lame,*

JAMIESON, FAUSSET, BROWN

choose him out to be the object of gratuitous favor, as I did Jacob (cf. Luke 14:26, with Matt. 10:37; Gen. 29:30, 31; Deut. 21:15, 16). **laid his mountains . . . waste**—i.e., his territory which was generally mountainous. Israel was, it is true, punished by the Chaldeans, but Edom has been utterly destroyed; viz., either by Nebuchadnezzar [ROSENMULLER], or by the neighboring peoples, Egypt, Ammon, and Moab [JOSEPHUS, *Antiquities,* 10.9, 7; MAURER], (Jer. 49:18). **dragons**—jackals [MOORE] (cf. Isa. 34: 13). MAURER translates, "*Abodes* of the wilderness," from an *Arabic* root "*to stop,*" or "to abide." *English Version* is better. **4. Whereas**—*But if* Edom say [MAURER]. Edom may strive as she may to recover herself, but it shall be in vain, for I doom her to perpetual desolation, whereas I restore Israel. This Jehovah states, to illustrate His gratuitous love to Israel, rather than to Edom. **border of wickedness**—a region given over to the curse of reprobation [CALVIN]. For a time Judea seemed as desolate as Idumea; but though the latter was once the highway of Eastern commerce, now the lonely rock-houses of Petra attest the fulfilment of the prophecy. It is still "the border of wickedness," being the resort of the marauding tribes of the desert. Judea's restoration, though delayed, is yet certain. **the Lord hath indignation**—"the people of My curse" (Isa. 34:5). **5. from the border of Israel**—Ye, restored to your own "borders" in Israel, "from" them shall raise your voices to "magnify the Lord," acknowledging that Jehovah has shown to you a gratuitous favor not shown to Edom, and so ought to be especially "magnified from the borders of Israel."

6. Turning from the people to the priests, Jehovah asks, whereas His love to the people was so great, where was their love towards Him? If the priests, as they profess, regard Him as their Father (Isa. 63:16) and Master, let them show the reality of their profession by *love and reverential fear* (Exod. 20:12; Luke 6:46). He addresses the priests because they ought to be leaders in piety to the rest of the people, whereas they are foremost in "despising His name."

Wherein have we despised . . .—The same captious spirit of self-satisfied insensibility as prompted their question (vs. 2), "Wherein hast Thou loved us?" They are blind alike to God's love and their own guilt.

7. ye offer . . .—God's answer to their challenge (vs. 6), "Wherein have we despised?" **polluted bread**—viz., blemished sacrifices (vs. 8, 13, 14; Deut. 15:21). So "the *bread* of thy God" is used for "*sacrifices* to God" (Lev. 21:8). **polluted thee**—i.e., offered to thee "polluted bread." **table of the Lord**—i.e., the altar (Ezek. 41:22) (not the table of shewbread). Just as the sacrificial *flesh* is called "bread." **contemptible**—(vss. 12, 13). Ye sanction the niggardly and blemished offerings of the people on the altar, to gain favor with them. Darius, and probably his successors, had liberally supplied them with victims for sacrifice, yet they presented none but the worst. A cheap religion, costing little, is rejected by God, and so is worth nothing. It costs more than it is worth, for it is worth nothing, and so proves really dear. God despises not the widow's mite, but he does despise the miser's mite [MOORE].

ADAM CLARKE

him by giving him an inferior lot. And now I have not only laid waste the dwelling place of the Edomites, by the incursions of their enemies, but (v. 4) they shall remain the perpetual monuments of My vengeance.

4. *They shall build, but I will throw down.* We have already seen enough of the wickedness of the Edomites to justify the utmost severity of divine justice against them. The pulling down predicted here was by Judas Maccabeus; see 1 Macc. v. 65; and by John Hyrcanus; see Joseph. *Antiq.*, lib. xiii, c. 9, x. 1. *They shall call them, The border of wickedness.* A wicked land. Among this people scarcely any trace of good could ever be noted.

5. *Your eyes.* You Israelites shall see, in your succeeding generations, that *the Lord will be magnified*. By His kindness in Israel, and His judgments beyond.

6. *A son honoureth his father.* I am your Father—*where, then, is mine honour?* Where your filial obedience? *If I be a master, where is my fear?* The respect due to Me.

7. *Ye offer polluted bread.* The priests, probably to ingratiate themselves with the people, took the refuse beasts, etc., and offered them to God; and thus the sacrificial ordinances were rendered *contemptible*.

MATTHEW HENRY

and the sick (*v.* 8), and again (*v.* 13), *the torn, and the lame, and the sick*, that was ready to die of itself. Some make *v.* 8 to be a continuation of what the priests profanely said *v.* 7, *You say* to the people, *If you offer the blind for sacrifice, it is not evil; or the lame and the sick, it is not evil.* If we worship God ignorantly, and without understanding, we bring the blind for sacrifice; if we do it carelessly, if we are cold, and dull, and dead, in it, we bring the sick; if we rest in the bodily exercise, and do not make heart-work of it, we bring the *lame*; and, if we suffer vain thoughts and distractions to lodge within us, we bring the torn. Is it not a great affront to God and a great wrong and injury to our own souls? They would do no more of their work than what they were paid for. There is not a man among the priests that would *shut the doors*, or *kindle a fire, for nought.* Their work was a perfect drudgery to them (*v.* 13): *You said also, Behold, what a weariness is it!* They thought the duty of their office toilsome and troublesome, and *snuffed at it* as unreasonable.

III. God expostulates and reasons the case with them. 1. Would they affront an earthly prince thus? You offer to God *the lame and the sick*; *offer it now unto thy governor* (*v.* 8), either as tribute or as a present, *will he be pleased with thee?* 2. Could they imagine that such sacrifices as these would be pleasing to God? "*Should I accept this at your hand, saith the Lord?*" (*v.* 13). If God has no pleasure in the person, if the person be not in a justified state, if he be not sanctified, God will not accept the offering. God had respect to Abel first and then to his sacrifice. 3. How could they expect to prevail with God in their intercessions for the people when they thus affronted God in their sacrifices? 4. Had God deserved this at their hands? No, he had provided comfortably for them, and had given them such encouragement in their work as might have engaged them to do it cheerfully and well.

IV. He calls them to repentance for their profanations of his holy name. So we may understand *v.* 9, "*Now, I pray you, beseech God that he will be gracious to us.* Humble yourselves for your sin, cry mightily to God for pardon; for all the rebukes of Providence we are under *are by your means.*"

V. He declares his resolution both to secure the glory of his own name and to reckon with those who profane it. God will magnify his law and make it honourable, though they vilify it and make it contemptible; for (*v.* 11) *from the rising of the sun to the going down of the same my name shall be great among the Gentiles.* Instead of those carnal ordinances, which they profaned, a spiritual way of worship shall be introduced and established: *Incense shall be offered to God's name* (which signifies prayer and praise, Ps. cxli. 2; Rev. viii. 3), instead of the blood and fat of bulls and goats. Instead of his being worshipped and served among the Jews only, a small people in a corner of the world, he will be served and worshipped in all places, *from the rising of the sun to the going down of the same*; *in every place*, in every part of the world, *incense shall be offered to his name*; nations shall speak of the wonderful works of God, and have them spoken to them in their own language. This is a plain prediction of that great revolution by which the Gentiles, who had been *strangers and foreigners*, came to be *fellow-citizens with the saints and of the household of God*, and welcome to the throne of grace. Profane and careless worshippers are such as *vow and sacrifice to the Lord a corrupt thing* when they have *in their flock a male.* The priests would accept it, though God would not, pretending to be more indulgent than he was. They are *deceivers*; they deal falsely and fraudulently with God. Hypocrites are deceivers, and they will prove self-deceivers, and so self-destroyers. They are *cursed*; they expect a blessing, but will meet with a curse. The heathen paid more respect to their gods, though idols, than the Jews did to theirs, though the only true and living God.

JAMIESON, FAUSSET, BROWN

8. Your earthly ruler would feel insulted, if offered by you the offering with which ye put off God (see Lev. 22:22, 24). **is it not evil?**—MAURER translates, "There is no evil," in your opinion, in such an offering; it is quite good enough for such a purpose. 9. **now . . . beseech God that he will be gracious**—Ironical. Think you that God will be persuaded by such polluted gifts to be gracious to you? Far from it. **this hath been by your means**—lit., "hand." These contemptible offerings are your doing, as being the priests mediating between God and the people; and think you, will God pay any regard to you (cf. vss. 8, 10)? "Accept thy person" ("face"), vs. 8, answers to "regard your persons," in this verse. **10. Who . . . for naught**—Not one even of the least priestly functions (as shutting the doors, or kindling a fire on the altar) would ye exercise without pay, therefore ye ought to fulfil them faithfully (I Cor. 9:13). DRUSIUS and MAURER translate, "Would that there were absolutely some one of you who would shut the doors of the temple (i.e., of the inner court, in which was the altar of burnt offerings), and that ye would not kindle fire on My altar in vain!" Better no sacrifices than vain ones (Isa. 1:11-15). It was the duty of some of the priests to stand at the doors of the court of the altar of burnt offerings, and to have excluded blemished victims [CALVIN]. **11. For**—Since ye Jewish priests and people "despise My name" (vs. 6), I shall find others who will magnify it (Matt. 3:9). Do not think I shall have no worshippers because I have not you; for from the east to the west My name shall be great among the Gentiles (Isa. 66:19, 20), those very peoples whom ye look down upon as abominable. **pure offering**—not "the blind, the lame, and the sick," such as ye offer (vs. 8). "In every place," implies the catholicity of the Christian Church (John 4:21, 23; I Tim. 2:8). The "incense" is figurative of *prayers* (Ps. 141:2; Rev. 8:3). "Sacrifice" is used metaphorically (Ps. 51:17; Heb. 13:10, 15, 16; I Pet. 2:5, 12). In this sense the reference to the Lord's Supper, maintained by many of the fathers, may be admitted; it, like prayer, is a spiritual offering, accepted through the literal offering of the "Lamb without blemish," once for all slain. 12. Renewal of the charge in vs. 7. **fruit . . . meat**—the offerings of the people. The "fruit" is the *produce* of the altar, on which the priests subsisted. They did not literally say, The Lord's table is contemptible; but their *acts* virtually said so. They did not act so as to lead the people to reverence, and to offer their best to the Lord on it. The people were poor, and put off God with the worst offerings. The priests let them do so, for fear of offending the people, and so losing all gains from them. **13. what a weariness is it!**—Ye regard God's service as irksome, and therefore try to get it over by presenting the most worthless offerings. Cf. Micah 6:3, where God challenges His people to show wherein is the "weariness" or hardship of His service. Also Isaiah 43:22-24, wherein He shows that it is they who have "wearied" Him, not He who has wearied them. **snuffed at**—despised. **it**—the table of the Lord, and the meat on it (vs. 12). **torn**—viz., by beasts, which it was not lawful to eat, much less to offer (Exod. 22:31). **thus . . . offering**—*Hebrew, "mincha"*; the *unbloody offering* of flour, etc. Though this may have been of ordinary ingredients, yet the *sacrifices* of blemished animals accompanying it rendered it unacceptable. **14. deceiver**—hypocrite. Not poverty, but avarice was the cause of their mean offerings. **male**—required by law (Lev. 1:3, 10). **great King**—(Ps. 48:2; Matt. 5:35). **my name . . . dreadful among . . . heathen**—Even the heathen dread Me because of My judgments; what a reproach this is to you, My people, who fear Me not (vs. 6)! Also it may be translated, "*shall be* feared among . . . ," agreeing with the prophecy of the call of the Gentiles (vs. 11).

ADAM CLARKE

11. *From the rising of the sun.* The total abolition of the Mosaic sacrifices, and the establishment of a spiritual worship over the whole earth, is here foretold.

12. *Ye have profaned it.* You have desecrated God's worship; is it any wonder that God should cast you off, and follow you with His judgments?

13. *Ye have snuffed at it.* A metaphor taken from cattle which do not like their fodder. They blow strongly through their noses upon it, and after this neither they nor any other cattle will eat it.

MATTHEW HENRY — CHAPTER 2

Verses 1-9

What was said in the foregoing chapter was directed to the priests (*ch.* i. 6): *Thus saith the Lord of hosts to you, O priests! that despise my name.* They might think it some excuse that they offered what the people brought. If the priests had given the people better instructions, the people would have brought better offerings; and therefore the blame returns upon the priests: *And now, O you priests! this commandment is* purely *for you* (*v.* 1).

V. A sentence of wrath passed upon them, *v.* 2, 3. But it is conditional: *If you will not lay it to heart*, implying, "If you will, God's anger shall be turned

JAMIESON, FAUSSET, BROWN — CHAPTER 2

VSS. 1-17. REPROOF OF THE PRIESTS FOR VIOLATING THE COVENANT; AND THE PEOPLE ALSO FOR MIXED MARRIAGES AND UNFAITHFULNESS **1. for you**—The priests in particular are reproved, as their part was to have led the people aright, and reproved sin, whereas they encouraged and led them into sin. Ministers cannot sin or suffer alone. They drag down others with them if they fall [MOORE]. **2. lay . . . to heart**—My commands. **send a curse**—rather, as *Hebrew, "the curse"*; viz., that denounced in Deuteronomy 27:15-26; 28:15-68. **curse your blessings**—turn the blessings you enjoy into curses (Ps. 106:15). **cursed them**—*Hebrew, them several-*

ADAM CLARKE — CHAPTER 2

2. *Yea, I have cursed them already.* This may refer, generally, to unfruitful seasons; or, particularly, to a dearth that appears to have happened about this time. See Hag. i. 6-11.

MATTHEW HENRY

away." *I will send a curse upon you*, so that you shall neither be blessed yourselves nor blessings to the people, but even your plenty shall be a plague to you and you shall be plagues to your generation." The fruits of the earth should be no comfort to them: "*Behold, I will corrupt your seed;* the corn you sow shall rot under ground." Or it may be understood of the seed of the word which they preached. *Bring no more vain oblations;* your *incense is an abomination* to me.

I. A recital of the covenant God made with that sacred tribe, which was their commission for their work: The *Lord of hosts sent a commandment* to them, for the establishing of this covenant (*v.* 4). Let the sons of Levi know then (and particularly the sons of Aaron) what honour God put upon their family (*v.* 5): *My covenant was with him of life and peace.* This is called *his covenant of life and peace* because it was intended for the support of religion, which brings life and peace to the souls of men. What is here said of the covenant of priesthood is true of the covenant of grace made with all believers, as spiritual priests; it assures all believers of everlasting peace, everlasting life, all happiness both in this world and in that to come. This covenant was made with the whole tribe of Levi when they were distinguished from the rest of the tribes. These great blessings of life and peace, contained in that covenant, God *gave to him*, to Levi, to Aaron, to Phinehas; he entrusted them with these benefits for the use and behoof of God's Israel; they received that they might give. The tribe of Levi gave a signal proof of their holy fear of God when they appeared so bravely against the worshippers of the golden calf (Exod. xxxii. 26); and for their zeal in that matter God bestowed this blessing upon them. Some read *v.* 5 not as the consideration of the grant, but as the condition of it: *I gave them to him, provided* that he should *fear before me.* They were hereby made *the messengers of the Lord of hosts*, messengers of that covenant of life and peace, not mediators of it, but only messengers, or ambassadors, employed to treat of the terms of peace between God and Israel. The priests were *God's mouth* to his people. *The priests' lips should keep knowledge*, not keep it from the people, but keep it for them. Ministers must be men of knowledge; they must not only have it, but they must have it ready to be communicated to others as there is occasion. The people *should seek the law at his mouth*; they should consult the priests as God's messengers.

II. The fidelity and zeal of many of their predecessors in the priest's office, are mentioned as an aggravation of their sin in degenerating from such honourable ancestors. The good priest (*v.* 6) was ready and mighty in the scriptures: *The law of truth was in his mouth*, for the use of those that *asked the law at his mouth.* Truth is a law, it has a commanding power. It is by truth that Christ rules. He lived like a priest that was chosen to *walk before God*, 1 Sam. ii. 30. He walked with God in peace, *in equity. He did turn many away from iniquity*, and God crowned his endeavours with wonderful success; he helped to save many a soul from death, and there are multitudes now in heaven blessing God that ever they knew him. *When the priest is upright many will be upright.*

III. A high charge drawn up against the priests who violated the covenant. Many corruptions had crept into the church of the Jews at this time, mixed marriages, admitting strangers into the house of God, profanation of the sabbath-day, which were all owing to the carelessness and unfaithfulness of the priests. 1. They transgressed the rule: "*You have not kept my ways*, not kept in them yourselves, nor done your part to keep others in them," *v.* 9. 2. They betrayed their trust: "*You have corrupted the covenant of Levi.* You have managed your office as if it were designed only to feed you fat and make you great, and not for the glory of God and the good of the souls of men." Another instance of their betraying their trust was that they were *partial in the law, v.* 9. In the law they were to lay down to the people they *knew faces* (so the word is); they *accepted persons.* 3. They did mischief to the souls of men, which they should have helped to save: *You have caused many to stumble at the law.* 4. When they were under the rebukes of the word and of the providence of God, they *would not hear.*

IV. The judgments God had brought upon these priests. They had lost their comfort (*v.* 2): *I have already cursed your blessings.* They had not the comfort of their work, which is the satisfaction of doing good. They had lost their credit (*v.* 9): *Therefore have I also made you contemptible and base before all the people.* When they forsook the ways of God, and corrupted the covenant of Levi, they

JAMIESON, FAUSSET, BROWN

ly; i.e., I have cursed each one of your blessings. **3. corrupt . . .**—lit., "rebuke," answering to the opposite prophecy of blessing (ch. 3:11), "I will *rebuke* the devourer." To rebuke the seed is to forbid its growing. **your**—lit., "*for you*"; i.e., to your hurt. **dung of . . . solemn feasts**—The dung in the maw of the victims sacrificed on the feast days; the maw was the perquisite of the priests (Deut. 18:3), which gives peculiar point to the threat here. You shall get the dung of the maw as your perquisite, instead of the maw. **one shall take you away with it**—i.e., ye shall be taken away with it; it shall cleave to you wherever ye go [MOORE]. Dung shall be thrown on your faces, and ye shall be taken away as dung would be, dung-begrimed as ye shall be (I Kings 14:10; cf. Jer. 16:4; 22:19). **4. ye shall know**—by bitter experience of consequences, that it was with this design I admonished you, in order "that My covenant with Levi might be" maintained; i.e., that it was for your own good (which would be ensured by your maintaining the Levitical command) I admonished you, that ye should return to your duty [MAURER] (cf. vss. 5, 6). Malachi's function was that of a reformer, leading back the priests and people to the law (ch. 4:4). **5-9.** He describes the promises, and also the conditions of the covenant; Levi's observance of the conditions and reward (cf. Num. 25:11-13, Phinehas' zeal); and on the other hand the violation of the conditions, and consequent punishment of the present priests. "Life" here includes the *perpetuity* implied in Numbers 25:13, "*everlasting* priesthood." "Peace" is specified both here and there. MAURER thus explains it; the *Hebrew* is, lit., "My covenant was with him, *life* and *peace* (to be given him on My part), and I gave them to him: (and on his part) fear (i.e., reverence), and he did fear Me . . . ." The former portion of the verse expresses the *promise*, and Jehovah's fulfilment of it; the latter, the *condition*, and Levi's steadfastness to it (Deut. 33:8, 9). The Jewish priests self-deceivingly claimed the privileges of the covenant, while neglecting the conditions of it, as if God were bound by it to bless them, while they were free from all the obligation which it imposed to serve Him. The covenant is said to be not merely "*of* life and peace," but "life and peace"; for the keeping of God's law is its own reward (Ps. 19:11).

6. law of truth was in his mouth—He taught the people the truths of the law in all its fulness (Deut. 33:10). The priest was the ordinary expounder of the law; the prophets were so only on special occasions. **iniquity . . . not found**—no injustice in his judicial functions (Deut. 17:8, 9; 19:17). **walked with me**—by faith and obedience (Gen. 5:22). **in peace**—viz., the "peace" which was the fruit of obeying the covenant (vs. 5). Peace with God, man, and one's own conscience, is the result of "walking with God" (cf. Job 22:21; Isa. 27:5; Jas. 3:18). **turn many . . . from iniquity**—both by positive precept and by tacit example "walking with God" (Jer. 23:22; Dan. 12:3; Jas. 5:20). **7.** In doing so (vs. 6) he did his duty as a priest, "for . . . ." **knowledge**—of the law, its doctrines, and positive and negative precepts (Lev. 10:10, 11; Deut. 24:8; Jer. 18:18; Hag. 2:11). **the law**—i.e., its true sense. **messenger of . . . Lord**—the interpreter of His will; cf. as to the prophets, Haggai 1:13. So ministers are called "ambassadors of Christ" (II Cor. 5:20); and the bishops of the seven churches in Revelation, "angels" or messengers (cf. Gal. 4:14). **8. out of the way**—i.e., from the covenant. **caused many to stumble**—By scandalous example, the worse inasmuch as the people look up to you as ministers of religion (I Sam. 2:17; Jer. 18:15; Matt. 18:6; Luke 17:1). **at the law**—i.e., in respect to the observances of the law. **corrupted . . . covenant**—made it of none effect, by not fulfilling its conditions, and so forfeiting its promises (Zech. 11:10; Neh. 13:29). **9.** Because ye do not keep the condition of the covenant, I will not fulfil the promise. **partial in the law**—having respect to persons rather than to truth in the interpretation and administration of the law (Lev. 19:15).

ADAM CLARKE

3. *Behold, I will corrupt your seed.* So as to render it unfruitful.

4. *This commandment.* That in the first verse; to drive such priests from His presence and His service. *That my covenant might be with Levi.* I gave the priesthood and the service of My altar to that tribe.

5. *My covenant was with him of life and peace.* These are the two grand blessings given to men by the new covenant, which was shadowed by the Old. To man, excluded from the favor of God, and sentenced to death because of sin, God gave *berith*, a "covenant sacrifice," and this secured *life*—exemption from the death deserved by transgressors; communication of that inward spiritual life given by Christ, and issuing in that eternal life promised to all His faithful disciples. And, as it secured life, so it gave *peace*, prosperity, and happiness; peace between God and man, between man and man, and between man and his own conscience.

8. *But ye are departed out of the way.* You have become impure yourselves, and you have led others into iniquity.

9. *Therefore have I also made you contemptible.* The people despised you because they saw that you acted contrary to your functions.

MATTHEW HENRY

thereby made themselves not only mean, but vile, in the eyes even of the common people.

Verses 10–17

Corrupt practices are the genuine fruit and product of corrupt principles. In these verses we find men dealing falsely with one another, and it is because they think falsely of their God.

I. In general, they *dealt treacherously every man against his brother, v.* 10. It cannot be expected that he who is false to his God should be true to his friend. Two things they are here charged with—taking strange wives of heathen nations, and abusing and putting away the wives they had of their own nation; in both these they violated a sacred covenant. They married strange wives, which was expressly prohibited, and provided against, in that covenant, Deut. vii. 3. God engaged to do them good upon this condition, that they should not mingle with the heathen; this was the covenant made with their fathers, the great charter by which that nation was incorporated. *Have we not all one Father?* Yes, we have, for *has not one God created us?* Are we not all *his offspring?* Here it seems to refer to the Jewish nation: *Have we not all one father,* Abraham, or Jacob? This they prided themselves in, *We have Abraham to our father.* "*Has not one God created us,* that is, formed us into a people, made us a nation by ourselves, and put a life into us, distinct from that of other nations? And should not this oblige us to maintain the dignity of our character?" They were dedicated to God, as well as distinguished from the neighbouring nations. *Israel was holiness to the Lord* (Jer. ii. 3), but by marrying strange wives they profaned this holiness, and laid the honour of it in the dust. *Judah has married the daughter of a strange god.* The harm was not so much that she was the daughter of a strange nation, but that she was the daughter of a strange God. God would reckon with them for it (*v.* 12): *The Lord will cut off the man that doeth this,* that marries the daughter of a strange god. He has, in effect, cut himself off from the holy nation, and *God will cut him off, him and all that belongs to him;* so the original intimates. God will no more own them as belonging to his nation; and the priest that *offers an offering to the Lord,* if he marry a strange wife (as we find many of the priests did, Ezra x. 18), shall not escape. He shall be cut off from the temple of the Lord, as others from the tabernacles of Jacob. In contempt of the marriage-covenant, which God instituted for the common benefit of mankind, they abused and put away the wives they had of their own nation (*v.* 13). They did not behave as they ought to have done towards their wives. The wives, not daring to make their case known to any other, complained to God, and *covered the altar of the Lord with tears, with weeping, and with crying.* The good Master we serve will not have his altar covered with tears, but compassed with songs. It is a reason given why yoke-fellows should live in holy love and joy—*that their prayers may not be hindered,* 1 Pet. iii. 7. They dealt treacherously with them, *v.* 14–16. They did not perform their promises to them, but took in concubines to share in the affection that was due to their wives only. They *put them away,* gave them a bill of divorce, and turned them off. In all this *they covered violence with their garment;* they abused their wives, and yet, in the sight of others, they pretended to be very loving to them. "*The Lord has been witness between thee and the wife of thy youth* (*v.* 14), has been witness to the marriage-covenant between thee and her, for to him you appealed concerning your sincerity and fidelity. She is *thy wife*; thy own, bone of thy bone and flesh of thy flesh, the nearest to thee of all the relations thou hast in the world, and to cleave to whom thou must quit the rest. She is *the wife of thy youth,* who had thy affections when they were at the strongest. Let not the darling of thy youth be the scorn and loathing of thy age. She is *thy companion*; she has long been an equal sharer with thee in thy cares, and griefs, and joys." The wife is to be looked upon, not as a servant, but as a companion to the husband. "She is *the wife of thy covenant* to whom thou art so firmly bound that, while she continues faithful, thou canst not be loosed from her, for it was a covenant for life." Man and wife should continue together, to their lives' end, in holy love and peace, and neither quarrel with each other nor separate from each other. God has joined them together (*v.* 15): *Did not he make one,* one Eve for one Adam, that Adam might never *take another to her to vex her* (Lev. xviii. 18), nor put her away to make room for another? Designing *Adam a help meet for him,* he made him *one wife*; had he made him more, he would not have had a *meet help.* And wherefore did he make but one woman for one man? It was *that he might seek a godly seed—a seed of God* (so the word is), a seed that should bear the image of

JAMIESON, FAUSSET, BROWN

10-16. Reproof of those who contracted marriages with foreigners and repudiated their Jewish wives. **10. Have we not all one father?**—Why, seeing we all have one common origin, "do we deal treacherously against *one another*" ("His brother" being a general expression implying that all are "brethren" and sisters as children of the same Father above, II Thess. 4:6 and so including the *wives* so injured)? viz., by putting away our Jewish wives, and taking foreign women to wife (cf. vs. 14 and vs. 11; Ezra 9:1-9), and so violating "the covenant" made by Jehovah with "our fathers," by which it was ordained that we should be a people separated from the other peoples of the world (Exod. 19:5; Lev. 20:24, 26; Deut. 7:3). To intermarry with the heathen would defeat this purpose of Jehovah, who was the common Father of the Israelites in a peculiar sense in which He was not Father of the heathen. The "one Father" is Jehovah (Job 31:15; I Cor. 8:6; Eph. 4:6). "Created us": not merely physical creation, but "created us" to be His peculiar and chosen people (Ps. 102:18; Isa. 43:1; 45:8; 60:21; Eph. 2:10), [CALVIN]. How marked the contrast between the honor here done to the female sex, and the degradation to which Oriental women are generally subjected! **11. dealt treacherously**—viz., in respect to the Jewish wives who were put away (vs. 14; also vss. 10, 15, 16). **profaned the holiness of . . . Lord**—by ill-treating the Israelites (viz., the wives), who were set apart as a people *holy unto the Lord:* "the holy seed" (Ezra 9:2; cf. Jer. 2:3). Or, "the holiness of the Lord" means His holy ordinance and covenant (Deut. 7:3). But "which He loved," seems to refer to *the holy people,* Israel, whom God so gratuitously loved (ch. 1:2), without merit on their part (Ps. 47:4). **married . . .**—(Ezra 9:1, 2; 10: 2; Neh. 13:23, etc.). **daughter of a strange god**—women worshipping idols: as the worshipper in Scripture is regarded in the relation of a child to a father (Jer. 2:27). **12. master and . . . scholar**—lit., "him that watcheth and him that answereth." So "wakeneth" is used of *the teacher* or "master" (Isa. 50:4); masters are *watchful* in guarding their scholars. The reference is to the priests, who ought to have taught the people piety, but who led them into evil. "Him that answereth" is the *scholar* who has to answer the questions of his teacher (Luke 2: 47) [GROTIUS]. The Arabs have a proverb, "None calling and none answering," i.e., there being *not one alive.* So GESENIUS explains it of the Levite watches in the temple (Ps. 134:1), one *watchman* calling and another *answering.* But the scholar is rather the *people,* the pupils of the priests "in doing this," viz., forming unions with foreign wives. "Out of the tabernacles of Jacob" proves it is not the priests alone. God will spare neither priests nor people who act so. **him that offereth**—His offerings will not avail to shield him from the penalty of his sin in repudiating his Jewish wife and taking a foreign one. **13. done again**—"a second time": an aggravation of your offense (Neh. 13:23-31), in that it is a relapse into the sin already checked once under Ezra (Ezra 9:10) [HENDERSON]. Or, "the second time" means this: Your first sin was your blemished offerings to the Lord: now "again" is added your sin towards your wives [CALVIN]. **covering . . . altar . . . with tears**—shed by your unoffending wives, repudiated by you that ye might take foreign wives. CALVIN makes the "tears" to be those of all the people on perceiving their sacrifices to be sternly rejected by God. **14. Wherefore?**—Why does God reject our offerings? **Lord . . . witness between thee and . . . wife**—(so Gen. 31:49, 50). **of thy youth**—The Jews still marry very young, the husband often being but thirteen years of age, the wife younger (Prov. 5:18; Isa. 54:6). **wife of thy covenant**—not merely joined to thee by the marriage covenant generally, but by *the covenant between God and Israel,* the covenant people, whereby a sin against a wife, a daughter of Israel, is a sin against God [MOORE]. Marriage also is called "the covenant of God" (Prov. 2:17), and to it the reference may be (Gen. 2:24; Matt. 19:6; I Cor. 7:10). **15.** MAURER and HENGSTENBERG explain the verse thus: The Jews had defended their conduct by the precedent of Abraham, who had taken Hagar to the injury of Sarah, his lawful wife; to this Malachi says now, "No one (ever) did so in whom there was a residue of intelligence (discriminating between good and evil); and what did the one (Abraham, to whom you appeal for support) do, seeking a godly seed?" His object (viz., not to gratify passion, but to obtain the seed promised by God) makes the case wholly inapplicable to defend your position. MOORE (from FAIRBAIRN) better explains, in accordance with vs. 10, "Did not He make (us Israelites) one? Yet He had the residue of the Spirit (i.e., His

ADAM CLARKE

10. *Have we not all one father?* From this to v. 16 the prophet censures the marriages of Israelites with strange women, which the law had forbidden, Deut. vii. 3. And also divorces, which seem to have been multiplied for the purpose of contracting these prohibited marriages. *Why do we deal treacherously?* Gain the affections of the daughter of a brother Jew, and then profane the covenant of marriage, held sacred among our fathers, by putting away this same wife and daughter!

11. *Daughter of a strange god.* Of a man who worships an idol.

12. *The master and the scholar.* He who teaches such doctrine, and he who follows this teaching, the Lord will cut off both the one and the other.

13. *Covering the altar of the Lord with tears.* Of the poor women who, being divorced by cruel husbands, come to the priests, and make an appeal to God at the altar; and you do not speak against this glaring injustice.

14. *Ye say, Wherefore?* Is the Lord angry with us? Because you have been *witness* of the contract made between the parties; and when the lawless husband divorced his wife, the wife of his youth, his companion, and the wife of his covenant, you did not execute on him the discipline of the law.

15. *And did not he make one?* One of each kind, Adam and Eve. *Yet had the residue of the spirit;* He could have made millions of pairs, and inspired them all with living souls. Then wherefore one? He made one pair from whom all the rest might proceed, that He might have a holy offspring; that children being a marked property of one man and one woman, proper care might be taken that they should be brought up in the discipline of the Lord. Perhaps the holy or *godly seed, zera Elohim,* "a seed of God," may refer to the Messiah.

MATTHEW HENRY

God, that *every man having his own wife*, and *but one*, according to the law (1 Cor. vii. 2), they might live in chaste and holy love, and not, as brute beasts, that the children, being born in holy matrimony, which is an ordinance of God, might thus be made a *seed to serve him.*

God is much displeased with those who go about to put asunder *what he has joined together* (*v.* 16). The caution inferred from all this (*v.* 15): *Therefore take heed to your spirit, and let none deal treacherously against the wife of his youth;* and again, *v.* 16.

II. How corrupt their principles were, to which were owing all these corrupt practices! Let us trace up the streams to the fountain (*v.* 17): *You have wearied the Lord with your words.* It is a wearisome thing, even to God himself, to hear people insist upon their own justification in their corrupt and wicked practices. They had denied him to be a holy God, and had the impudence to say, *Every one that does evil is good in the sight of the Lord, and he delights in them.* This wicked inference they drew, without any reason, from the prosperity of sinners in their sinful courses (see *ch.* iii. 15). Under pretence of making God not so severe as he was commonly represented, they said he was *altogether such a one as themselves.* They said, "*Where is the God of judgment?* We may do what we please; he sees us not, nor will regard us."

JAMIESON, FAUSSET, BROWN

isolating us from other nations was not because there was no residue of the Spirit left for the rest of the world). And wherefore (i.e., *why then* did He thus isolate us as) the one (people; the *Hebrew* is '*the* one')? In order that He might seek a godly seed"; i.e., that He might have "a seed of God," a nation the repository of the covenant. and the stock of the Messiah, and the witness for the one God amidst the surrounding polytheisms. Marriage with foreign women, and repudiation of the wives wedded in the Jewish covenant, utterly set aside this divine purpose. CALVIN thinks "the one" to refer to the conjugal one body formed by the original pair (Gen. 2). God might have joined many wives as one with the one husband, for He had no lack of spiritual being to impart to others besides Eve; the design of the restriction was to secure a pious offspring: but cf. *Note*, vs. 10. One object of the marriage relation is to raise a seed for God and for eternity. **16. putting away**—i.e., divorce. **for one coveteth violence with . . . garment**—MAURER translates, "And (Jehovah hateth him who) covereth his garment (i.e., his *wife*, in *Arabic* idiom; cf. Genesis 20:16, 'He is to thee a *covering* of thy eyes'; the husband was so to the wife, and the wife to the husband; also Deuteronomy 22:30; Ruth 3:9; Ezekiel 16:8) with injury." The *Hebrew* favors "garment," being accusative of the *thing covered.* Cf. with *English Version,* Psalm 73:6, "violence covereth them as a garment." Their "violence" is the putting away of their wives; the "garment" with which they try to cover it is the plea of Moses' permission (Deut. 24:1; cf. Matt. 19:6-9). **17. wearied . . . Lord**—(Isa. 43:24). This verse forms the transition to ch. 3:1, etc. The Jewish skeptics of that day said virtually, God delighteth in evil-doers (inferring this from the prosperity of the surrounding heathen, while they, the Jews, were comparatively not prosperous: forgetting that their attendance to minor and external duties did not make up for their neglect of the weightier duties of the law; e.g., the duty they owed their wives, just previously discussed); or (if not) Where (is the proof that He is) the God of judgment? To this the reply (ch. 3:1) is, "The Lord whom ye seek, and whom as messenger of the covenant (i.e., divine ratifier of God's covenant with Israel) ye delight in (thinking He will restore Israel to its proper place as first of the nations), shall suddenly come," not as a Restorer of Israel temporally, but as a consuming *Judge* against Jerusalem (Amos 5:18, 19, 20). The "suddenly" implies the unpreparedness of the Jews, who, to the last of the siege, were expecting a temporal deliverer, whereas a temporal judgment was about to destroy them. So skepticism shall be rife before Christ's second coming. He shall suddenly and unexpectedly come then also as a consuming Judge to unbelievers (II Pet. 3:3, 4). Then, too, they shall affect to seek His coming, while really denying it (Isa. 5:19; Jer. 17:15; Ezek. 12:22, 27).

ADAM CLARKE

16. *For the Lord . . . hateth putting away.* He abominates all such divorces, and him that makes them. *Covereth violence with his garment.* And He also notes those who frame idle excuses to cover the violence they have done to the wives of their youth, by putting them away, and taking others in their place, whom they now happen to like better, when their own wives have been worn down in domestic services.

17. *Ye have wearied the Lord.* He has borne with you so long, and has been provoked so often, that He will bear it no longer. It is not fit that He should.

MATTHEW HENRY

CHAPTER 3

Verses 1–6

The first words of this chapter seem a direct answer to the profane atheistical demand of the scoffers: *Where is the God of judgment?* "Here he is; he is just at the door; the long-expected Messiah is ready to appear; and he says, *For judgment have I come into this world.*"

I. A prophecy of the appearing of his forerunner John the Baptist, which the prophet Isaiah had foretold (*ch.* xl. 3), as the *preparing* of the *way of the Lord.* 1. He is *God's messenger.* John Baptist had his commission *from heaven, and not of men.* All held John Baptist for a prophet, for he was God's messenger, as the prophets were, to call men to repentance and reformation. 2. He is Christ's harbinger: He *shall prepare the way before me*, by taking them off from a confidence in their relation to Abraham *as their father* (which, they thought, would serve their turn without a saviour), and by giving notice that the Messiah was now at hand.

JAMIESON, FAUSSET, BROWN

CHAPTER 3

Vss. 1-18. MESSIAH'S COMING, PRECEDED BY HIS FORERUNNER, TO PUNISH THE GUILTY FOR VARIOUS SINS, AND TO REWARD THOSE WHO FEAR GOD. **1. Behold**—Calling especial attention to the momentous truths which follow. Ye unbelievingly ask, Where is the God of judgment (ch. 2:7)? "Behold," therefore, "I send . . . " Your unbelief will not prevent My keeping My covenant, and bringing to pass in due time that which ye say will never be fulfilled. **I will** *send* **. . . he shall** *come*—The Father *sends* the Son: the Son *comes.* Proving the distinctness of personality between the Father and the Son. **my messenger**—John the Baptist; as Matthew 3:3; 11:10; Mark 1:2, 3; Luke 1:76; 3:4; 7:26, 27; John 1:23, prove. This passage of Malachi evidently rests on that of Isaiah his predecessor (Isa. 40:3-5). Perhaps also, as HENGSTENBERG thinks, "messenger" includes *the long line of prophets* headed by *Elijah* (whence his name is put in ch. 4:5 as a representative name), and terminating in John, the last and greatest of the prophets (Matt. 11:9-11). John as the representative prophet (the forerunner of Messiah the representative God-man) gathered in himself all the scattered lineaments of previous prophecy (hence Christ terms him "much more than a prophet," Luke 7:26), reproducing all its awful and yet inspiriting utterances: his coarse garb, like that of the old prophets, being a visible exhortation to repentance; the wilderness in which he preached symbolizing the lifeless, barren state of the Jews at that time, politically and spiritually; his topics sin, repentance, and salvation, presenting for the last time the condensed epitome of all previous teach-

ADAM CLARKE

CHAPTER 3

1. *Behold, I will send my messenger. Malachi*, the very name of the prophet. But this speaks of John the Baptist. I, the Messiah, the Seed of God, mentioned above, *will send my messenger*, John the Baptist.

MATTHEW HENRY

II. A prophecy of the appearing of the Messiah himself: "*The Lord, whom you seek, shall suddenly come to his temple*, even *the God of judgment*, who, you think, has forsaken the earth. The Messiah has been long called *he that should come*, now shortly he will come." 1. He is *the Lord—Adonai*, the basis and foundation on which the world is founded, that one *Lord over all* (Acts x. 36) that has all power committed to him (Matt. xxviii. 18) and is to *reign over the house of Jacob for ever*, Luke i. 33. 2. He is the *Messenger of the covenant*, or the *angel of the covenant*, *sent* from heaven to negotiate a peace between God and man. Christ is the *angel of this covenant*, by whose mediation it is brought about and established. That covenant which is all our *salvation began to be spoken by the Lord*, Heb. ii. 3. Though he is the *prince of the covenant* (as some read this) yet he condescended to be the *messenger of it*. 3. He it is *whom you seek, whom you delight in*, whom the pious Jews expect and desire. In looking and waiting for him, they *looked for redemption in Jerusalem* and *waited for the consolation of Israel*, Luke ii. 25, 38. Those that seek Jesus shall find pleasure in him. If he be our heart's desire he will be our heart's delight.

4. He *shall suddenly come*; his coming draws nigh, and we see it not at so great a distance as the patriarchs saw it at. 5. He *shall come to his temple*, this temple at Jerusalem, which was lately built. It is his temple, for it is *his Father's house*, John ii. 16.

III. The great ends and intentions of his coming, *v.* 2. He is one whom they seek, and yet *who may abide the day of his coming*, though he comes not to condemn the world, but that the world through him might have life? Even in the days of his flesh there were some emanations of his glory and power, such as none could stand before, witness his transfiguration. The Jewish doctors speak of the *pangs* or *griefs* of the Messiah, meaning (they say) the great afflictions that should be to Israel at the time of his coming. *He shall be like a refiner's fire*, which separates between the gold and the dross by melting the ore, or *like fuller's soap*, which with much rubbing fetches the spots out of the cloth. Christ came to discover men, *that the thoughts of many hearts might be revealed* (Luke ii. 35), to separate between the precious and the vile, for *his fan is in his hand* (Matt. iii. 12).

1. The gospel shall work good upon those that are disposed to be good, to them it shall be a savour of life unto life (*v.* 3): *He shall sit as a refiner*. He will *purge them as gold and silver*, that is, he will sanctify them inwardly.

JAMIESON, FAUSSET, BROWN

ings of God by His prophets; so that he is called pre-eminently God's "messenger." Hence the oldest and true reading of Mark 1:2 is, "as it is written in *Isaiah* the prophet"; the difficulty of which is, How can the prophecy of Malachi be referred to Isaiah? The explanation is: the passage in Malachi rests on that in Isaiah 40:3, and therefore the *original source* of the prophecy is referred to in order to mark this dependency and connection. **the Lord**—*Ha-Adon* in *Hebrew*. The article marks that it is JEHOVAH (Exod. 23:17; 34:23; cf. Josh. 3:11, 13). Cf. Daniel 9:17, where the Divine Son is meant by "for THE *Lord's* sake." God the speaker makes "the Lord," the "messenger of the covenant," one with Himself: "I will send . . . before Me," adding, "THE LORD . . . shall . . . come"; so that *the Lord* must be one with the "Me," i.e., He must be GOD, "before" whom John was *sent*. As the divinity of the Son and His oneness with the Father are thus proved, so the distinctness of personality is proved by "I send" and He "shall come," as distinguished from one another. He also comes to the temple as "His temple": marking His divine lordship *over* it, as contrasted with all creatures, who are but "servants *in*" it (Hag. 2:7; Heb. 3:2, 5, 6). **whom ye seek . . . whom ye delight in**—(see *Note*, ch. 2:17). At His first coming they "sought" and "delighted in" the hope of a *temporal* Saviour: not in what He then was. In the case of those whom Malachi in his time addresses, "whom ye seek . . . delight in," is ironical. They unbelievingly asked, When will He come at last? Ch. 2:17, "Where is the God of judgment" (Isa. 5:19; Amos 5:18; II Pet. 3:3, 4)? In the case of the godly the desire for Messiah was sincere (Luke 2:25, 28). He is called "Angel of God's presence" (Isa. 63:9), also Angel of Jehovah. Cf. His appearances to Abraham (Gen. 18:1, 2, 17, 33), to Jacob (Gen. 31:11; 48:15, 16), to Moses in the bush (Exod. 3:2-6); He went before Israel as the Shekinah (Exod. 14:19), and delivered the law at Sinai (Acts 7:38). **suddenly**—This epithet marks the second coming, rather than the first; the earnest of that unexpected coming (Luke 12:38-46; Rev. 16:15) to judgment was given in the judicial expulsion of the money-changing profaners from the temple by Messiah (Matt. 21:12, 13), where also as here He calls the temple *His temple*. Also in the destruction of Jerusalem, most unexpected by the Jews, who to the last deceived themselves with the expectation that Messiah would suddenly appear as a temporal Saviour. Cf. the use of "suddenly" in Numbers 12:4-10, where He appeared in wrath. **messenger of the covenant**—viz., of the ancient covenant with Israel (Isa. 63:9) and Abraham, in which the promise to the Gentiles is ultimately included (Gal. 4:16, 17). The gospel at the first advent began with Israel, then embraced the Gentile world: so also it shall be at the second advent. All the manifestations of God in the Old Testament, the Shekinah and human appearances, were made in the person of the Divine Son (Exod. 23:20, 21; Heb. 11:26; 12:26). He was the messenger of the old covenant, as well as of the new. **2.** (Ch. 4:1; Rev. 6:16, 17.) The Messiah would come, not, as they expected, to flatter the theocratic nation's prejudices, but to subject their principles to the fiery test of His heart-searching truth (Matt. 3:10-12), and to destroy Jerusalem and the theocracy after they had rejected Him. His mission is here regarded as a whole from the first to the second advent: the process of refining and separating the godly from the ungodly beginning during Christ's stay on earth, going on ever since, and about to continue till the final separation (Matt. 25:31-46). The refining process, whereby a third of the Jews is refined as silver of its dross, while two-thirds perish, is described, Zechariah 13:8, 9 (cf. Isa. 1:25). **3. sit**—The purifier *sits* before the crucible, fixing his eye on the metal, and taking care that the fire be not too hot, and keeping the metal in, only until he knows the dross to be completely removed by his seeing his own image reflected (Rom. 8:29) in the glowing mass. So the Lord in the case of His elect (Job 23:10; Ps. 66:10; Prov. 17:3; Isa. 48:10; Heb. 12:10; I Pet. 1:7). He will *sit* down to the work, not perfunctorily, but with patient love and unflinching justice. The Angel of the Covenant, as in leading His people out of Egypt by the pillar of cloud and fire, has an aspect of terror to His foes, of love to His friends. The same separating process goes on in the world as in each Christian. When the godly are completely separated from the ungodly, the world will end. When the dross is taken from the gold of the Christian, he will be for ever delivered from the furnace of trial. The purer the gold, the hotter the fire now; the whiter the garment, the harder the

ADAM CLARKE

And the Lord, whom ye seek. The Messiah, whom ye expect, from the account given by the prophet Daniel, chap. ix. 24.

Shall suddenly come to his temple. Shall soon be presented before the Lord in His temple, cleanse it from its defilement, and fill it with His teaching and His glory.

The messenger of the covenant. He that comes to fulfill the great design, in reference to the covenant made with Abram, that in his seed all the families of the earth should be blessed.

3. *He shall sit as a refiner.* Alluding to the case of a refiner of metals, sitting at his fire; increasing it when he sees necessary, and watching the process of his work.

MATTHEW HENRY

He will purge them with fire, *as gold and silver are purged*, for he *baptizes with the Holy Ghost and with fire* (Matt. iii. 11), with the Holy Ghost working like fire. *That they may offer unto the Lord an offering in righteousness*, that is, that they may be in sincerity converted to God and consecrated. He makes the tree good that the fruit may be good. And then it follows (*v.* 4), *The offering of Judah and Jerusalem shall be pleasant unto the Lord*. It shall no longer be offensive, as when they brought the torn, and the lame, and the sick, for sacrifice; but it shall be *acceptable*. The Messiah will, by his grace in them, make them acceptable; when he has purified and refined them, then they shall offer such sacrifices as God requires and will accept. He will, by his intercession for them, make them accepted.

2. It shall turn for a testimony against those that are resolved to go on in their wickedness, *v.* 5. This is the direct answer to their challenge, "*Where is the God of judgment?* You shall know where he is, and shall know it to your terror and confusion, for *I will come near to you to judgment*." The sinners that must appear to be judged by the gospel of Christ are the *sorcerers*, who deal in spiritual wickedness, and the *adulterers*, who wallow in the lusts of the flesh; and the *false swearers*, who profane God's name by calling him to witness to a lie; and the oppressors, who *defraud the hireling in his wages* and crush *the widow and fatherless*. That which is at the bottom of all this is, *They fear not me, saith the Lord of hosts*. *I will come near and will be a swift witness against* them.

IV. The ratification of all this (*v.* 6): *For I am the Lord; I change not; therefore you sons of Jacob are not consumed.* Though the sentence passed against evil works (*v.* 5) be not executed speedily, yet it will be executed for he is *the Lord*; he *changes not*. The people of Israel had reason to say that he was an unchangeable God, for he had been faithful to his covenant with them and their fathers. They had been false and fickle in their conduct to him, and he might justly have abandoned them; but because he *remembered his covenant*, they were preserved. We may apply this to ourselves; because we have to do with a God that *changes not*, therefore it is that *we are not consumed*.

Verses 7–12

God's controversy with the men of that generation for deserting his service and robbing him.

I. They had run away from their Master, and quitted the work he gave them to do (*v.* 7): *You have gone away from my ordinances and have not kept them.* What a gracious invitation God gives them to return and repent: "*Return unto me*, and to your duty, return to your allegiance, return as a traveller that has missed his way, as a soldier that has run his colours, as a treacherous wife that has gone away from her husband; return to me; and then *I will return to you* and will remove the judgments you are under and prevent those you fear." What a peevish answer they return! "*But you said* with disdain to the prophets, to one another, to your own hearts, to stifle the convictions you were under: you said, *Wherein shall we return?*" They take it as an affront to be *told of their faults*, and called upon to amend them. They are so ignorant of themselves, and of the strictness, extent, and spiritual nature, of the divine law, that they think they need no repentance. They are firmly resolved to go on in sin.

II. They had robbed their Master, and embezzled his goods. They stand indicted for robbery, for sacrilege, the worst of robberies: *You have robbed me. Will a man* be so daringly impudent as to *rob God*? *Will a man do violence to God?* so some read it. *Will a man stint or straighten him?* so others read it. The people plead *Not guilty*, and put God upon the proof of it. They rob God, and know not what they do. They rob him of his honour, rob him of that which is devoted to him, to be employed in his service, rob him of themselves, rob him of sabbath-time, rob him of that which is given for the support of religion, and give him not his dues out of their estates; and yet they ask, *Wherein have we robbed thee?* It is *in tithes and offerings*. They detained them, defrauded the priests of them, would not pay their tithes. They brought not the offerings which God required, or brought the torn, and lame, and sick which were not fit for use. For this they were *cursed with a curse*, *v.* 9. God punished them with famine and scarcity, through unseasonable weather, or insects that ate up the fruits of the earth. Because God had punished them with scarcity of bread, they made that a pretence for robbing him—that now, being impoverished, they could not afford to bring their tithes and offerings. They are urged to reform in this matter, with a promise that if they did the

JAMIESON, FAUSSET, BROWN

washing [MOORE]. **purify ... sons of Levi**—of the sins specified above. The very Levites, the ministers of God, then needed cleansing, so universal was the depravity. **that they may offer ... in righteousness**—as originally (ch. 2:6), not as latterly (ch. 1:7-14). So believers, the spiritual priesthood (I Pet. 2:5). **4. as in the days of old**—(ch. 1:11; 2:5, 6). The "offering" (*Mincha, Hebrew*) is not expiatory, but prayer, thanksgiving, and self-dedication (Rom. 12:1; Heb. 13:15; I Pet. 2:5). **5. I ... come near ... to judgment**—*I* whom ye challenged, saying, "Where is the God of judgment?" (ch. 2:17). I whom ye think far off, and to be slow in judgment, am "near," and will come as a "swift witness"; not only a judge, but also an eye-*witness* against sorcerers; for Mine eyes see every sin, though ye think I take no heed. Earthly judges need witnesses to enable them to decide aright: I alone need none (Ps. 10:11; 73:11; 94:7, etc.). **sorcerers**—a sin into which the Jews were led in connection with their foreign idolatrous wives. The Jews of Christ's time also practised sorcery (Acts 8:9; 13:6; Gal. 5: 20; JOSEPHUS, *Antiquities*, 20. 6; B. Jud. 2; 12.23). It shall be a characteristic of the last Antichristian confederacy, about to be consumed by the brightness of Christ's coming (Matt. 24:24; II Thess. 2:9; Rev. 13:13, 14; 16:13, 14; also 9:21; 18:23; 21:8; 22:15). Romanism has practised it; an order of *exorcists* exists in that Church. **adulterers**—(ch. 2:15, 16). **fear not me**—the source of all sins. **6. the Lord**—Jehovah: a name implying His immutable faithfulness in fulfilling His promises: the covenant name of God to the Jews (Exod. 6:3), called here "the sons of Jacob," in reference to God's covenant with that patriarch. **I change not**—Ye are mistaken in inferring that, because I have not yet executed judgment on the wicked, I am changed from what I once was, viz., a God of judgment. **therefore ye ... are not consumed**—Ye yourselves being "not consumed," as ye have long ago deserved, are a signal proof of My unchangeableness. Romans 11:29: cf. the whole chapter, in which God's mercy in store for Israel is made wholly to flow from God's unchanging faithfulness to His own covenant of love. So here, as is implied by the phrase "sons of *Jacob*" (Gen. 28:13; 35:12). They are spared because I am JEHOVAH, and they *sons of Jacob*; while I spare them, I will also punish them; and while I punish them, I will not wholly consume them. The unchangeableness of God is the sheet-anchor of the Church. The perseverance of the saints is guaranteed, not by their unchangeable love to God, but by His unchangeable love to them, and His eternal purpose and promise in Christ Jesus [MOORE]. **He** upbraids their ingratitude that they turn His very long-suffering (Lam. 3:22) into a ground for skeptical denial of His coming as a Judge at all (Ps. 50: 1, 3, 4, 21; Eccles. 8:11, 12; Isa. 57:11; Rom. 2: 4-10). **7-12.** Reproof for the non-payment of tithes and offerings, which is the cause of their national calamities, and promise of prosperity on their paying them. **7. from ... days of your fathers**—Ye live as your fathers did when they brought on themselves the Babylonian captivity, and ye wish to follow in their steps. This shows that nothing but God's unchanging long-suffering had prevented their being long ago "consumed" (vs. 6). **Return unto me**—in penitence. **I will return unto you**—in blessings. **Wherein ...**—(*V.* 16). The same insensibility to their guilt continues: they speak in the tone of injured innocence, as if God calumniated them. **8. rob**—lit., "cover": hence, defraud. Do ye call defrauding God no sin to be "returned" from (vs. 7)? Yet ye have done so to Me in respect to the tithes due to Me, viz., the tenth of all the remainder after the first fruits were paid, which tenth was paid to the Levites for their support (Lev. 27:30-33): a tenth paid by the Levites to the priests (Num. 18:26-28): a second tenth paid by the people for the entertainment of the Levites, and their own families, at the tabernacle (Deut. 12:18): another tithe every third year for the poor, etc. (Deut. 14:28, 29). **offerings**—the first fruits, not less than one-sixtieth part of the corn, wine, and oil (Deut. 18:4; Neh. 13:10, 12). The priests had this perquisite also, the tenth of the tithes which were the Levites' perquisite. But they appropriated all the tithes, robbing the Levites of their due nine-tenths; as they did also, according to JOSEPHUS, before the destruction of Jerusalem by Titus. Thus doubly God was defrauded, the priests not discharging aright their sacrificial duties, and robbing God of the services of the Levites, who were driven away by destitution [GROTIUS]. **9. cursed**—(ch. 2:2). As ye despoil Me, so I despoil you, as I threatened I would, if ye continued to disregard Me. In trying to defraud God we only defraud ourselves. The eagle who

ADAM CLARKE

The sons of Levi. Those who minister in their stead under the new covenant, for the old Levitical institutions shall be abolished.

6. *I am the Lord, I change not.* The new dispensation of grace and goodness, which is now about to be introduced, is not the effect of any change in My counsels. It is, on the contrary, the fulfillment of My everlasting purposes; as is also the throwing aside of the Mosaic ritual, which was intended only to introduce the great and glorious gospel of My Son. And because of this ancient covenant, you Jews are not totally consumed; but you are now, and shall be still, preserved as a distinct people—monuments of both My justice and mercy.

8. *Will a man rob God?* Here is one point on which you are guilty; you withhold the *tithes* and *offerings* from the temple of God, so that the divine worship is neglected.

9. *Ye are cursed with a curse.* The whole nation is under My displeasure. The curse of God is upon you.

MATTHEW HENRY

judgments should be removed. *Bring you all the tithes into the storehouse.* "Bring in the full tithes to the utmost that the law requires, *that there may be meat in God's house* for those that serve at the altar, whether there be meat in your houses or no." "Let God be first served, and then *prove me herewith, saith the Lord of hosts, whether I will not open the windows of heaven.*" The expression is figurative; every good gift coming from above, thence God will plentifully pour out upon them the bounties of his providence. Very sudden plenty is expressed by *opening the windows of heaven,* 2 Kings vii. 2. Here they are opened to *pour down blessings,* to such a degree that there should not be *room enough to receive* them. God will not only be reconciled to sinners that repent and reform, but he will be a bountiful benefactor, to them. God has blessings ready to bestow upon us, but, through the weakness of our faith and narrowness of our desires, we have not room to receive them. Whereas the fruits of their ground had been eaten up by locusts and caterpillars God would now remove that judgment (*v.* 11). Whereas they had lain under the *reproach of famine,* now *all nations shall call them blessed.*

Verses 13–18

I. The angry notice God takes of the impudent blasphemous talk of the sinners in Zion. *Your words have been stout against me, saith the Lord.* They came from their pride, and haughtiness, and contempt of God. They spoke it proudly, and with disdain, scorning to be under the divine check and government. *What have we spoken so much against thee,* so much that there needs all this ado about it? They cannot deny that they have spoken against God, but they make a light matter of it. They said, *It is vain to serve God,* or, "*He is vain that serves God,* that is, he labours in vain and to no purpose; he has his labour for his pains, and therefore is a fool for his labour. We have walked *mournfully,* or *in black,* with great gravity and great grief, *before the Lord of hosts,* have afflicted our souls, and yet we are never the better." They would have it thought that they had served God and had kept his ordinances, whereas it was only the external observance of them that they had kept up, and therefore might say, It is *in vain.* They had *walked mournfully* before God, whereas God had required them to serve him with gladness, and to walk cheerfully before him. They by their own superstitions made the service of God a task and drudgery to themselves, and then complained of it as a hard service. They complained that they had got nothing by their religion; they were still in poverty and affliction. Perhaps this refers to the errors of the Sadducees. They denied a future state, and then said, It is *vain to serve God,* which has indeed some colour in it, for, *if in this life only we had hope in Christ, we were of all men most miserable,* 1 Cor. xv. 19. They maintained that wickedness was the way of prosperity, *v.* 15. The outward prosperity of sinners in their sins, as it has weakened the hands of the godly in their godliness (Ps. lxxiii. 13), so it has strengthened the hands of the wicked in their wickedness. Wait awhile, and you shall see *those that work wickedness set up* as a mark to the arrows of God's vengeance, and *those that tempt God delivered* to the tormentors.

II. Even in this corrupt and degenerate age, when there was so great a decay, so great a contempt, of serious godliness, there were yet some that retained their integrity and zeal for God. They *feared the Lord*—that is the beginning of wisdom and the root of all religion; they reverenced the majesty of God, submitted to his authority. In every age there has been a remnant that feared the Lord, though sometimes but a little remnant. They *thought upon his name*; and meditated upon the discoveries God has made of himself in his word and by his providences. They *spoke often one to another* concerning the God they feared. *Those that feared the Lord* kept together; they spoke kindly one to another, for the promoting of mutual love, that might not *wax cold* when *iniquity* did thus *abound.* They spoke intelligently to one another, for the increasing of faith and holiness. Then, when iniquity was bold and barefaced, the people of God took courage, and stirred up themselves, *the innocent against the hypocrite,* Job xvii. 8. When religion was misrepresented, its friends did all they could to support the credit of it. When seducers were busy to deceive unwary souls with prejudices against religion, those that feared God were industrious to strengthen one another's hands. God countenanced them: *The Lord hearkened and heard it,* and was well pleased with it. When the two disciples, going to Emmaus, were discoursing concerning Christ, he hearkened and heard, and joined himself to them, and made a third, Luke xxiv. 15. *A book of remem-*

JAMIESON, FAUSSET, BROWN

robbed the altar set fire to her nest from the burning coal that adhered to the stolen flesh. So men who retain God's money in their treasuries will find it a losing possession. No man ever yet lost by serving God with a whole heart, nor gained by serving Him with a half one. We may compromise with conscience for half the price, but God will not endorse the compromise; and, like Ananias and Sapphira, we shall lose not only what we thought we had purchased so cheaply, but also the price we paid for it. If we would have God "open" His treasury, we must open ours. One cause of the barrenness of the Church is the parsimony of its members [MOORE]. **10.** (Prov. 3:9, 10.) **storehouse**—(*Margin,* II Chron. 31:11; cf. I Chron. 26:20; Neh. 10:38; 13:5, 12). **prove me . . . herewith**—with this; by doing so. Test Me whether I will keep My promise of blessing you, on condition of your doing your part (II Chron. 31:10). **pour . . . out**—lit., "empty out": image from a vessel completely emptied of its contents: no blessing being kept back. **windows of heaven**—(II Kings 2:7). **that . . . not . . . room enough . . .**—lit., "even to not . . . sufficiency," i.e., either, as *English Version.* Or, even so as that there should be "*not merely*" "sufficiency" but *superabundance* [JEROME, MAURER]. GESENIUS not so well translates, "Even to a failure of sufficiency," which in the case of God could never arise, and therefore means *for ever, perpetually:* so Psalm 72: 5, "as long as the sun and moon endure"; lit., "until a failure of the sun and moon," which is never to be; and therefore means, *for ever.* **11. I will rebuke**—(*Note,* ch. 2:3). I will no longer "rebuke [*English Version,* 'corrupt'] the seed," but will rebuke every agency that could hurt it (Amos 4:9). **12.** Fulfilling the blessing (Deut. 33:29; Zech. 8:13). **delightsome land**—(Dan. 8:9). **13-18.** He notices the complaint of the Jews that it is of no profit to serve Jehovah, for that the ungodly proud are happy; and declares He will soon bring the day when it shall be known that He puts an everlasting distinction between the godly and the ungodly. **words . . . stout**—*Hebrew,* "hard"; so "the *hard* speeches which ungodly sinners have spoken against Him" (Jude 15) [HENDERSON]. **have we spoken**—The *Hebrew* expresses at once their *assiduity* and *habit* of speaking against God [VATABLUS]. The niphal form of the verb implies that these things were said, not directly *to* God, but *of* God, to one another (Ezek. 33:20) [MOORE]. **14. what profit . . . that we . . . kept . . .**—(*Note,* ch. 2:17). They here resume the same murmur against God. Job 21:14, 15; 22:17 describe a further stage of the same skeptical spirit, when the skeptic has actually ceased to keep God's service. Psalm 73:1-14 describes the temptation to a like feeling in the saint when seeing the really godly suffer and the ungodly prosper in worldly goods now. The Jews here mistake utterly the nature of God's service, converting it into a mercenary bargain; they attended to outward observances, not from love to God, but in the hope of being well paid for in outward prosperity; when this was withheld, they charged God with being unjust, forgetting alike that God requires very different motives from theirs to accompany outward observances, and that God rewards even the true worshipper not so much in this life, as in the life to come. **his ordinance**—lit., what He requires to be kept, "His observances." **walked mournfully**—*in mournful garb,* sackcloth and ashes, the emblems of penitence; they forget Isaiah 58:3-8, where God, by showing what is true fasting, similarly rebukes those who then also said, Wherefore have we fasted and Thou seest not? etc. They mistook the outward show for real humiliation. **15. And now**—Since we who serve Jehovah are not prosperous and "the proud" heathen flourish in prosperity, we must pronounce them the favorites of God (ch. 2:17; Ps. 73:12). **set up**—lit., "built up": metaphor from architecture (Prov. 24:3; cf. *Margin,* Gen. 16:2; *Margin,* 30:3). **tempt God**—dare God to punish them, by breaking His laws (Ps. 95:9). **16.** "Then," when the ungodly utter such blasphemies against God, the godly hold mutual converse, defending God's righteous dealings against those blasphemers (Heb. 3:13). The "often" of *English Version* is not in the *Hebrew.* There has been always in the darkest times a remnant that feared God (I Kings 19: 18; Rom. 11:4). **feared the Lord**—reverential and loving fear, not slavish terror. When the fire of religion burns low, true believers should draw the nearer together, to keep the holy flame alive. Coals separated soon go out. **book of remembrance . . . for them**—for their advantage, against the day when those found faithful among the faithless shall receive their final reward. The kings of Persia kept

ADAM CLARKE

10. *Bring ye all the tithes.* They had so withheld these that the priests had not food enough to support life, and the sacred service was interrupted. See Neh. xiii. 10.

ALEXANDER MACLAREN:

The returning exiles had not had the prosperity which they had hoped. So many of them, even of those who had served God, began to let doubts darken their trust, and to listen to the whispers of their own hearts, reinforced by the mutterings of others, and to ask: "What is the use of religion? Does it make any difference to a man's condition?" Here they had been keeping God's charge, and going in black garments "before the Lord," in token of penitence, and no good had come to them, while arrogant neglect of His commandments did not seem to hinder happiness, and "they that work wickedness are built up." Sinful lives appeared to have a firm foundation, and to rise high and palace-like, while righteous ones were like huts. Goodness seemed to spell ruin.

What was wrong in these "stout words"? It was wrong to attach such worth to external acts of devotion, as if these were deserving of reward. It was wrong to suspend the duty of worship on the prosperity resulting from it, and to seek "profit" from "keeping his charge." Such religion was shallow and selfish, and had the evils of the later Pharisaism in germ in it. It was wrong to yield to the doubts which the apparently unequal distribution of worldly prosperity stirred in their hearts. But the doubts themselves were almost certain to press on Old Testament believers, as well as on Old Testament scoffers, especially under the circumstances of Malachi's time. The fuller light of Christianity has eased their pressure, but not removed it, and we have all had to face them, both when our own hearts have ached with sorrow and when pondering on the perplexities of this confused world. We look around, and, like the psalmist, see "the prosperity of the wicked," and, like him, have to confess that our "steps had wellnigh slipped" at the sight. The old, old question is ever starting up.

—*Expositions of Holy Scripture*

16. *They that feared the Lord.* There were a few godly in the land, who, hearing the language and seeing the profligacy of the rebels above, concluded that some signal mark of God's vengeance must fall upon them; they, therefore, as the corruption increased, cleaved the closer to their Maker. There are three characteristics given of this people: (1) They *feared the Lord.* They had that reverence for Jehovah that caused them to depart from evil, and to keep His ordinances. (2) They *spake often one to another.* They kept up the communion of saints. By mutual exhortation they strengthened each each other's hands in the Lord. (3) They *thought upon his name.* His name was sacred to them; it was a fruitful source of profound and edifying meditation.

MATTHEW HENRY

brance was written before him. God remembers the services of his people, that he may say, *Well done; enter thou into the joy of thy Lord.* God has a book for the sighs and tears of his mourners (Ps. lvi. 8). Never was any good word spoken of God, or for God, but it was registered, that it might be recompensed. He promises them a share in his glory hereafter (*v.* 17): *They shall be mine, saith the Lord of hosts, in that day when I make up my jewels. They shall be my segullah—my peculiar treasure* (it is the word used, Exod. xix. 5), *in the day when I make* or *do* what I have said and designed to do; so some read it. The saints are God's jewels; they are a *royal diadem* in his hand, Isa. lxii. 3. There is a day coming when God will *make up his jewels.* They shall be gathered up out of the dirt into which they are now thrown, from all places to which they are now scattered. He promises them a share in his grace now: *I will spare them as a man spares his own son that serves him.* The word usually signifies to spare with compassion, *as a father pities his children,* Ps. ciii. 13. It is our duty to serve God with the disposition of children. We must be his sons, must by a new birth partake of a divine nature. And we must be his servants; God will not have his children trained up in idleness; they must do him service, from a principle of love, with cheerfulness and delight. Nehemiah, when he had done much good, yet, knowing there is not a *just man on earth,* that *does good and sins not,* prays, *Lord, spare me according to the greatness of thy mercy;* Neh. xiii. 22. And God as a Father, will show them this mercy. They will thus be distinguished from the children of this world (*v.* 18). You that now speak against God as making no difference between good and bad, and say, *It is in vain to serve him* (*v.* 14), you shall be made to see your error. This manifest difference that was made between the believing Jews and those that persisted in their infidelity, at the time of the destruction of Jerusalem, and of the Jewish church and nation, by the Romans. But it is to have its full accomplishment at the second coming of Jesus Christ. All the children of men are either such as serve God or such as serve him not. In this world it is often hard to *discern between the righteous and the wicked.* There are many who, we think, serve God, who, having not their hearts right with him, will be found none of his servants; and, on the other hand, many will be found his faithful servants, who, because they followed not with us, did not, as we thought, serve him. At the bar of Christ, in the last judgment, it will be easy to *discern between the righteous and the wicked;* for then every man's character will be both perfected and perfectly discovered, every man will then appear in his true colours, and his disguises will be taken off.

JAMIESON, FAUSSET, BROWN

a record of those who had rendered services to the king, that they might be suitably rewarded (Esther 6:1, 2; cf. Esther 2:23; Ezra 4:15; Ps. 56:8; Isa. 65:6; Dan. 7:10; Rev. 20:12). CALVIN makes the fearers of God to be those awakened from among the ungodly mass (before described) to true repentance; the *writing* of the book thus will imply that some were reclaimable among the blasphemers, and that the godly should be assured that, though no hope appeared, there would be a door of penitence opened for them *before* God. But there is nothing in the context to support this view. **17. jewels**—(Isa. 62:3). Lit., "My peculiar treasure" (Exod. 19: 5; Deut. 7:6; 14:2; 26:18; Ps. 135:4; Titus 2:14; I Pet. 2:9; cf. Eccles. 2:8). CALVIN translates more in accordance with *Hebrew* idiom, "They shall be My peculiar treasure *in the day in which I will do it*" (i.e., fulfil My promise of gathering My completed Church; or, "make" those things come to pass foretold in vs. 5 above [GROTIUS]); so in ch. 4:3 "do" is used absolutely, "in the day that I shall do *this.*" MAURER, not so well, translates, "in the day which I shall make," i.e., appoint as in Psalm 118:24. **as . . . man spareth . . . son**—(Ps. 103:18).

18. Then shall ye . . . discern—Then shall ye see the falseness of your calumny against God's government (vs. 15), that the "proud" and wicked prosper. Do not judge before the time till My work is complete. It is in part to test your disposition to trust in God in spite of perplexing appearances, and in order to make your service less mercenary, that the present blended state is allowed; but at last *all* ("ye," both godly and ungodly) shall see the eternal difference there really is "between him that serveth God and him that serveth Him not" (Ps. 58:11). **return**—Ye shall turn to a better state of mind on this point.

ADAM CLARKE

17. *They shall be mine.* I will acknowledge them as My subjects and followers; in the day, especially, when I come to punish the wicked and reward the righteous. *When I make up my jewels.* My peculium, my "proper treasure"; that which is a man's own, and most prized by him.

MATTHEW HENRY

CHAPTER 4

Verses 1–3

The great and terrible day of the Lord, like the pillar of cloud and fire, shall have a dark side turned towards the Egyptians that fight against God, and a bright side towards the faithful Israelites that follow him: *The day cometh,* has reference both to the first and to the second coming of Jesus Christ.

I. In both Christ is a consuming fire to those that rebel against him. The day of his coming *shall burn as an oven;* it shall be a day of wrath, of *fiery indignation.* God, that has perfect knowledge of everyone's character, knows who are *the proud,* and of everyone's actions, knows who they are that *do wickedly;* and they shall be as *stubble* to this fire; they shall be consumed by it, and it is wholly owing to themselves that they shall be so, for they make themselves stubble, that is, combustible matter, to this fire. Those that by their unbelief oppose Christ thereby set themselves as *briers and thorns* before a *devouring fire,* Isa. xxvii. 4, 5. *The day that cometh shall burn them up,* and shall *leave them neither root nor branch.* Now this was fulfilled when Christ spoke terror and condemnation to the proud Pharisees and the other Jews that did wickedly, when he sent that fire on the earth which burnt up the chaff of the traditions of the elders and the corrupt glosses they had put upon the law of God. Jerusalem was destroyed by the Romans, and the nation of the Jews, as a nation, blotted out. This seems to be principally intended here; our Saviour says that those should be the *days of vengeance,* Luke xxi. 22. It is certainly applicable also to the day of judgment.

II. In both Christ is a rejoicing light to those who serve him faithfully (*v.* 2). Here are mercy and comfort kept in store for all those who fear the Lord and think on his name. *To you that fear my name shall the Sun of righteousness arise, with healing in*

JAMIESON, FAUSSET, BROWN

CHAPTER 4

Vss. 1-6. GOD'S COMING JUDGMENT: TRIUMPH OF THE GODLY: RETURN TO THE LAW THE BEST PREPARATION FOR JEHOVAH'S COMING: ELIJAH'S PREPARATORY MISSION OF REFORMATION. **1. the day cometh . . . burn**—(ch. 3:2; II Peter 3:7). Primarily is meant the judgment coming on Jerusalem; but as this will not exhaust the meaning, without supposing what is inadmissible in Scripture—exaggeration—the final and full accomplishment, of which the former was the earnest, is the day of general judgment. This principle of interpretation is not double, but *successive fulfilment.* The language is abrupt, "Behold, the day cometh! It burns like a furnace." The abruptness imparts terrible reality to the picture, as if it suddenly burst on the prophet's view. **all the proud**—in opposition to the cavil above (ch. 3:15), "now we call the *proud* (haughty despisers of God) happy." **stubble**—(Obad. 18; Matt. 3:12). As Canaan, the inheritance of the Israelites, was prepared for their possession by purging out the heathen, so judgment on the apostates shall usher in the entrance of the saints upon the Lord's inheritance, of which Canaan is the type—not heaven, but earth to its utmost bounds (Ps. 2:8) purged of all things that offend (Matt. 13:41), which are to be "gathered *out of His kingdom,*" the scene of the judgment being that also of the kingdom. The present dispensation is a spiritual kingdom, parenthetical between the Jews' literal kingdom and its antitype, the coming literal kingdom of the Lord Jesus. **neither root nor branch**—proverbial for *utter* destruction (Amos 2:9). **2.** The effect of the judgment on the righteous, as contrasted with its effect on the wicked (vs. 1). To the wicked it shall be as an oven that consumes the stubble (Matt. 6:30); to the righteous it shall be the advent of the gladdening Sun, not of condemnation, but "of righteousness"; not destroying, but "heal-

ADAM CLARKE

CHAPTER 4

1. *Behold, the day cometh, that shall burn as an oven.* The destruction of Jerusalem by the Romans.

And all the proud. This is in reference to v. 15 of the preceding chapter. *The day that cometh shall burn them up.* Either by famine, by sword, or by captivity. All those rebels shall be destroyed.

It shall leave them neither root nor branch. A proverbial expression for total destruction.

MATTHEW HENRY

his wings. The day that comes will be a fair and bright day to those who fear God, and reviving as the rising sun is to the earth; and particular notice is taken of the rising of the sun upon Zoar when that was mercifully distinguished from the cities of the plain, Gen. xix. 23. When the hearts of others *fail for fear* let them *lift up their heads for joy,* for *their redemption draws nigh,* Luke xxi. 28. By the *Sun of righteousness* here we are certainly to understand Jesus Christ. But it is to be applied to the coming of Christ in the flesh to seek and save those that were lost. Christ is the *light of the world.* He is the *light of men* (John i. 4), is to men's souls as the sun is to the visible world, which without the sun would be a dungeon; so would mankind be darkness itself without the *light of the glory of God* shining *in the face of Christ.* He is the *Sun of righteousness,* for he is himself a righteous Saviour. Righteousness sometimes signifies mercy or benignity, and it was in Christ that the *tender mercy of our God* visited us. Those that are governed by a holy fear of God shall have his *love* also *shed abroad in their hearts by the Holy Ghost.* Christ's second coming will be a glorious and welcome sun-rising to all that *fear his name.* Christ came, as *the sun,* to bring not only light to a dark world, but health to a diseased distempered world. The Jews have a proverbial saying, *As the sun riseth, infirmities decrease.* Christ came into the world to be the great physician, and the great medicine too, both the balm in Gilead, and the physician there. When he was upon earth, he went about as the sun in his circuit, doing this good; he *healed all manner of sicknesses and diseases among the people.* His healing bodily diseases was a specimen of his great design in coming into the world to heal the diseases of men's souls. "*You shall go forth,* as those that are healed go abroad and return to their business." The souls shall go forth out of their bodies at death, and the bodies out of their graves at the resurrection, as prisoners out of their dungeons, to see the light and be set at liberty. "You shall likewise *grow up*; being restored to health and liberty, you shall increase in knowledge, and grace, and spiritual strength." Those that by the grace of God are made wise and good are by the same grace made wiser and better. Their growth is compared to that of *the calves of the stall,* which is a quick, strong, and useful growth. Some read it, instead of *You shall grow up,* You shall *move yourselves,* or *leap for joy,* shall be as frolicsome as calves of the stall, when they are let loose in the open field. It shall make them victorious over their enemies (*v.* 3): *You shall tread down the wicked.* When believers by faith *overcome the world,* when they suppress their own corrupt appetites and passions, when the God of peace bruises Satan under their feet, then they *tread down the wicked.* The saints' triumphs are all owing to God's victories; it is not they that do this, but God that does it for them.

Verses 4–6

This is doubtless intended for a solemn conclusion. They were not to expect any more of the dictates of the Spirit of prophecy, till the beginning of the gospel of the Messiah.

Now there are two things required.

I. They must keep up an obedient veneration for the law of Moses (*v.* 4): *Remember the law of Moses my servant,* and observe to do according to it, even that law which *I commanded unto him in Horeb.* Honourable mention is made of *Moses.* God by Malachi calls him *Moses my servant*; for the righteous shall be had in everlasting remembrance. Honourable mention is made of the *law of Moses*; it was what God himself *commanded.* We are concerned to keep the law because God has commanded it and commanded it for us, for we are the spiritual Israel; and, if we expect the benefit of the covenant with Israel (Heb. viii. 10), we must observe the commands given to Israel, those of them that were intended to be of perpetual obligation. The office of conscience is to bid us *remember the law.* Even when we have made considerable advances in knowledge we must still retain the first principles of practical religion and resolve to abide by them. Those that study the writings of the prophets, and the apocalypse, must still remember the law of Moses and the four gospels. Prophecy was now to cease in the church for some ages, and the Spirit of prophecy not to return till the *beginning of the gospel,* and now they are told to *remember the law of Moses*; let them live by the rules and live upon the promises. As long as we have Bibles, we may keep our communion with God, and keep ourselves in his way. They were to expect the coming of the Messiah, the preaching of his gospel, and the setting up of his kingdom. Let them observe the law of Moses, and then they might expect the benefit of the gospel of Christ, for *to him that has,*

JAMIESON, FAUSSET, BROWN

ing" (Jer. 23:6). **you that fear my name**—The same as those in ch. 3:16, who confessed God amidst abounding blasphemy (Isa. 66:5; Matt. 10:32). The spiritual blessings brought by Him are summed up in the two, "righteousness" (I Cor. 1:30) and spiritual "healing" (Ps. 103:3; Isa. 57:19). Those who walk in the dark now may take comfort in the certainty that they shall walk hereafter in eternal light (Isa. 50:10). **in his wings**—implying the *winged swiftness* with which He shall appear (cf. "suddenly," ch. 3:1) for the relief of His people. The *beams* of the Sun are His "wings." Cf. "wings of the morning," Psalm 139:9. The "Sun" gladdening the righteous is suggested by the previous "day" of terror consuming the wicked. Cf. as to Christ, II Sam. 23:4; Ps. 84:11; Luke 1:78; John 1:9; 8:12; Eph. 5:14; and in His second coming, II Peter 1:19. The Church is the *moon* reflecting His light (Rev. 12:1). The righteous shall by His righteousness "shine as the Sun in the kingdom of the Father" (Matt. 13:43).

ye shall go forth—from the straits in which you were, as it were, held captive. An earnest of this was given in the escape of the Christians to Pella before the destruction of Jerusalem.

grow up—rather, "leap" as frisking calves [CALVIN]; lit., "spread," "take a wide range." **as calves of the stall**—which when set free from the stall disport with joy (Acts 8:8; 13:52; 20:24; Rom. 14:17; Gal. 5:22; Phil. 1:4, I Pet. 1:8). Especially the godly shall rejoice at their final deliverance at Christ's second coming (Isa. 61:10). **3.** Solving the difficulty (ch. 3:15) that the wicked often now prosper. Their prosperity and the adversity of the godly shall soon be reversed. Yea, the righteous shall be the army attending Christ in His final destruction of the ungodly (II Sam. 22:43; Ps. 49:14; 47:3; Mic. 7:10; Zech. 10:5; I Cor. 6:2 Rev. 2:26, 27; 19:14, 15). **ashes**—after having been burnt with the fire of judgment (vs. 1).

4. Remember . . . law—"The law and all the prophets" were to be in force until John (Matt. 11:13), no prophet intervening after Malachi; therefore they are told, "Remember the law," for in the absence of living prophets, they were likely to forget it. The office of Christ's forerunner was to bring them back to the law, which they had too much forgotten, and so "to make ready a people prepared for the Lord" at His coming (Luke 1: 17). God withheld prophets for a time that men might seek after Christ with the greater desire [CALVIN]. The history of human advancement is marked by periods of rest, and again progress. So in Revelation: it is given for a time; then during its suspension men live on the memories of the past. After Malachi there was a silence of 400 years; then a harbinger of light in the wilderness, ushering in the brightest of all the lights that had been manifested, but short-lived; then eighteen centuries during which we have been guided by the light which shone in that last manifestation. The silence has been longer than before, and will be succeeded by a more glorious and awful revelation than ever. John the Baptist was to "restore" the defaced image of "the law," so that the original might be recognized when it appeared among men [HINDS]. Just as "Moses" and "Elias" are here connected with the Lord's coming, so at the transfiguration they converse with Him, implying that the law and prophets which had prepared His way were now fulfilled in Him. **statutes . . . judgments**—*ceremonial* "statutes": "judgments" in civil questions at issue. "The law" refers to *morals* and *religion.*

ADAM CLARKE

2. *You that fear my name.* The persons mentioned in the sixteenth verse of the preceding chapter; you that look for redemption through the Messiah. *The Sun of righteousness.* The Lord Jesus, the promised Messiah, the Hope of Israel.

With healing in his wings. As the sun, by the rays of light and heat, revives, cheers, and fructifies the whole creation, giving, through God, light and life everywhere; so Jesus Christ, by the influences of His grace and Spirit, shall quicken, awaken, enlighten, warm, invigorate, heal, purify, and refine every soul that believes in Him; and, by His wings or rays, diffuse these blessings from one end of heaven to another.

F. B. MEYER:

"The Sun of Righteousness shall arise with healing in his wings" (v. 2). At the end of the Old Testament it is meet that the sun should break out. The morning that broke on Paradise was clear enough. It was without clouds. But the sky soon became darkened, and at last veiled, with only here and there a chink of blue sky left. All through the dark succeeding centuries there have been gleams of sunshine to let men know that the sun was shining still. Every precious promise, every solemn type, every holy life, that was bathed in supernatural beauty, was like a shining forth of the sun through the bars of human darkness and sin. But evidently more was in store than Old Testament saints had dreamed; and the time was coming when the reign of type, symbol, and parable, would be succeeded by the clear vision of the face of God.

We live in the days of open vision. Let us go forth and exult. We are to rejoice in every good thing He gives us. As the young calves of the early spring manifest their exuberant life in their caperings and gambols in the pastures, so let us give expression to our joy. Exult because of the clear shining of God's love: exult because the darkness is past, and the true light now shines: exult because He is coming again, as surely as He came once. Wake up, my soul, take psaltery and harp, and sing. The Bridegroom is at hand. Hark! are those his chariot wheels reverberating through the air? Even so! Lord Jesus, come quickly!

—*Great Verses Through the Bible*

MATTHEW HENRY

and uses what he has well, *more shall be given*, and *he shall have abundance*.

II. They must keep up a believing expectation of the gospel of Christ, and must look for the beginning of it in the appearing of Elijah the prophet (*v.* 5, 6). The *law and the prophets were until John* (Luke xvi. 16); they continued to be the only lights of the church till that morning-star appeared. The Jewish doctors will have it to be the same Elijah that prophesied in Israel in the days of Ahab—that he shall come again to be the forerunner of the Messiah; yet others of them say not the same person, but another of the same spirit. But we Christians know very well that John Baptist was the Elias that was to come, Matt. xvii. 10–13; and very expressly, Matt. xi. 14, *This is Elias that was to come;* and *v.* 10, the same of whom it is written, *Behold, I send my messenger*, *ch.* iii. 1. Elijah was a man of great austerity, bold in reproving sin. John Baptist was animated by the same spirit and power, and preached repentance and reformation, as Elias had done. John Baptist gave them fair warning when he told them of the *wrath to come*, and put them into a way of escape from it, and when he told them of the *fan in Christ's hand*, with which Christ would thoroughly purge his floor; see Matt. iii. 7, 10, 12.

John Baptist *shall turn the heart of the fathers to their children, and the heart of the children to their fathers;* so *making ready a people prepared for him* (Luke i. 16, 17). It is promised concerning John, 1. That he shall make a bold stand against the strong torrent of sin and impiety. This is called his *coming to restore all things* (Matt. xvii. 11). 2. That he shall preach a doctrine that shall reach men's hearts. Many had their consciences awakened by his ministry. 3. That he shall turn the hearts of the fathers with the children, and of the children with the fathers (for so some read it), to God and to their duty. 4. That thus he shall be an instrument to bind them faster to each other, by bringing and binding them all to their God. He shall prepare the way for that kingdom of heaven which will make all its faithful subjects of *one heart* and *one soul* (Acts iv. 32), which will be a kingdom of love, and will slay all enmities. The body of the Jewish nation, by their impiety and impenitence in it, had laid themselves open to the curse of God. God was ready to smite them with that curse, but he will yet once more try them, and therefore he sends John Baptist to preach repentance to them, that their conversion might prevent their confusion; so unwilling is God that any should perish. Some observe that the last word of the Old Testament is a curse, that we may bid Christ welcome, who comes with a blessing; and it is with a blessing, with the choicest of blessings, that the New Testament ends, and with it let us arm ourselves, or rather let God arm us, against this curse. *The grace of our Lord Jesus Christ be with us all. Amen.*

JAMIESON, FAUSSET, BROWN

5. I send you Elijah—as a means towards your "remembering the law" (vs. 4). **the prophet**—emphatical; not "the Tishbite"; for it is **in his official, not his personal** capacity, that his coming is here predicted. In this sense, John the Baptist was *an* Elijah in spirit (Luke 1:16, 17), but not *the literal* Elijah; whence when asked, "Art thou Elias?" (John 1:21), He answered, "I am not." "Art thou that prophet?" "No." This implies that John, though knowing from the angel's announcement to his father that he was referred to by Malachi 4:5 (Luke 1:17), whence he wore the costume of Elijah, yet knew by inspiration that he did not exhaustively fulfil *all* that is included in this prophecy: that there is a further fulfilment (cf. *Note*, ch. 3:1). As Moses in vs. 4 represents the law, so Elijah represents the prophets. The Jews always understood it of the literal Elijah. Their saying is, "Messiah must be anointed by Elijah." As there is another consummating advent of Messiah Himself, so also of His forerunner Elijah; perhaps in person, as at the transfiguration (Matt. 17:3; cf. 11). He in his appearance at the transfiguration in that body on which death had never passed is the forerunner of the saints who shall be found alive at the Lord's second coming. Revelation 11:3 may refer to the same witnesses as at the transfiguration, Moses and Elijah; Revelation 11:6 identifies the latter (cf. I Kings 17:1; Jas. 5:17). Even after the transfiguration Jesus (Matt. 17:11) speaks of Elijah's coming "to restore all things" as still future, though He adds that Elijah (in the person of John the Baptist) is come already *in a sense* (cf. Acts 3:21). However, the future forerunner of Messiah at His second coming may be a prophet or number of prophets clothed with Elijah's power, who, with zealous upholders of "the law" clothed in the spirit of "Moses," may be the forerunning witnesses alluded to here and in Revelation 11:2-12. The words "before the . . . *dreadful* day of the Lord," show that John cannot be exclusively meant; for he came before the day of Christ's coming in grace, not before His coming in terror, of which last the destruction of Jerusalem was the earnest (vs. 1; Joel 2:31). **6. turn . . . heart of . . . fathers to . . . children . . .**—Explained by some, that John's preaching should restore harmony in families. But Luke 1:16, 17 substitutes for "the heart of the children to the fathers," "the disobedient to the wisdom of the just," implying that the reconciliation to be effected was that between the unbelieving disobedient children and the believing ancestors, Jacob, Levi, "Moses," and "Elijah" (just mentioned) (cf. ch. 1:2; 2:4, 6; 3:3, 4). The threat here is that, if this restoration were not effected, Messiah's coming would prove "a curse" to the "earth," not a blessing. It proved so to guilty Jerusalem and the "earth," i.e., the *land* of Judea when it rejected Messiah at His first advent, though He brought blessings (Gen. 12:3) to those who accepted Him (John 1:11-13). Many were delivered from the common destruction of the nation through John's preaching (Rom. 9:29; 11:5). It will prove so to the disobedient at His second advent, though He comes to be glorified in His saints (II Thess. 1:6-10). **curse**—*Hebrew, Cherem,* "a ban"; the fearful term applied by the Jews to the extermination of the guilty Canaanites. Under this ban Judea has long lain. Similar is the awful curse on all of Gentile churches who love not the Lord Jesus now (I Cor. 16:22). For if God spare not the natural branches, the Jews, much less will He spare unbelieving professors of the Gentiles (Rom. 11:20, 21). It is deeply suggestive that the last utterance from heaven for 400 years before Messiah was the awful word "curse." Messiah's first word on the mount was "Blessed" (Matt. 5:3). The law speaks wrath; the Gospel, blessing. Judea is now under the "curse" because it rejects Messiah; when the spirit of Elijah, or a literal Elijah, shall bring the Jewish children back to the Hope of their "fathers," blessing shall be theirs, whereas the apostate "earth" shall be "smitten with the curse" previous to the coming restoration of all things (Zech. 12:13, 14).

May the writer of this Commentary and his readers have grace "to take heed to the sure word of prophecy as unto a light shining in a dark place, until the day dawn!" To the triune Jehovah be all glory ascribed for ever!

ADAM CLARKE

5. *Behold, I will send you Elijah the prophet.* This is meant alone of John the Baptist, as we learn from Luke i. 17, in whose spirit and power he came.

6. *And he shall turn* (convert) *the heart of the fathers to the children.* Or, together with the children; both old and young. *Lest I come and,* finding them unconverted, *smite the earth with a curse, cherem,* "utter extinction." So we find that, had the Jews turned to God, and received the Messiah at the preaching of John the Baptist and that of Christ and His apostles, the awful *cherem* of final excision and execration would not have been executed upon them.

There are three remarkable predictions in this chapter: (1) The advent of John Baptist, in the spirit and authority of Elijah. (2) The manifestation of Christ in the flesh, under the emblem of the Sun of righteousness. (3) The final destruction of Jerusalem, represented under the emblem of a burning oven, consuming everything cast into it.

In most of the Masoretic Bibles the fifth verse is repeated after the sixth—"Behold, I send unto you Elijah the prophet, before the great and terrible day of Jehovah come"; for the Jews do not like to let their sacred book end with a *curse;* and hence, in reading, they immediately subjoin the above verse, or else the fourth—"Remember ye the law of Moses my servant."

In most MSS. and printed Masoretic Bibles there are only three chapters in this prophet, the fourth being joined to the third, making it twenty-four verses. In the Jewish reckonings the Twelve Minor Prophets make but one book.

I have this day completed this commentary, on which I have labored above thirty years; and which, when I began, I never expected to live long enough to finish. May it be a means of securing glory to God in the highest, and peace and goodwill among men upon earth! Amen, Amen.

ADAM CLARKE

Heydon Hall, Middlesex,
Monday, March 28, A.D. 1825.

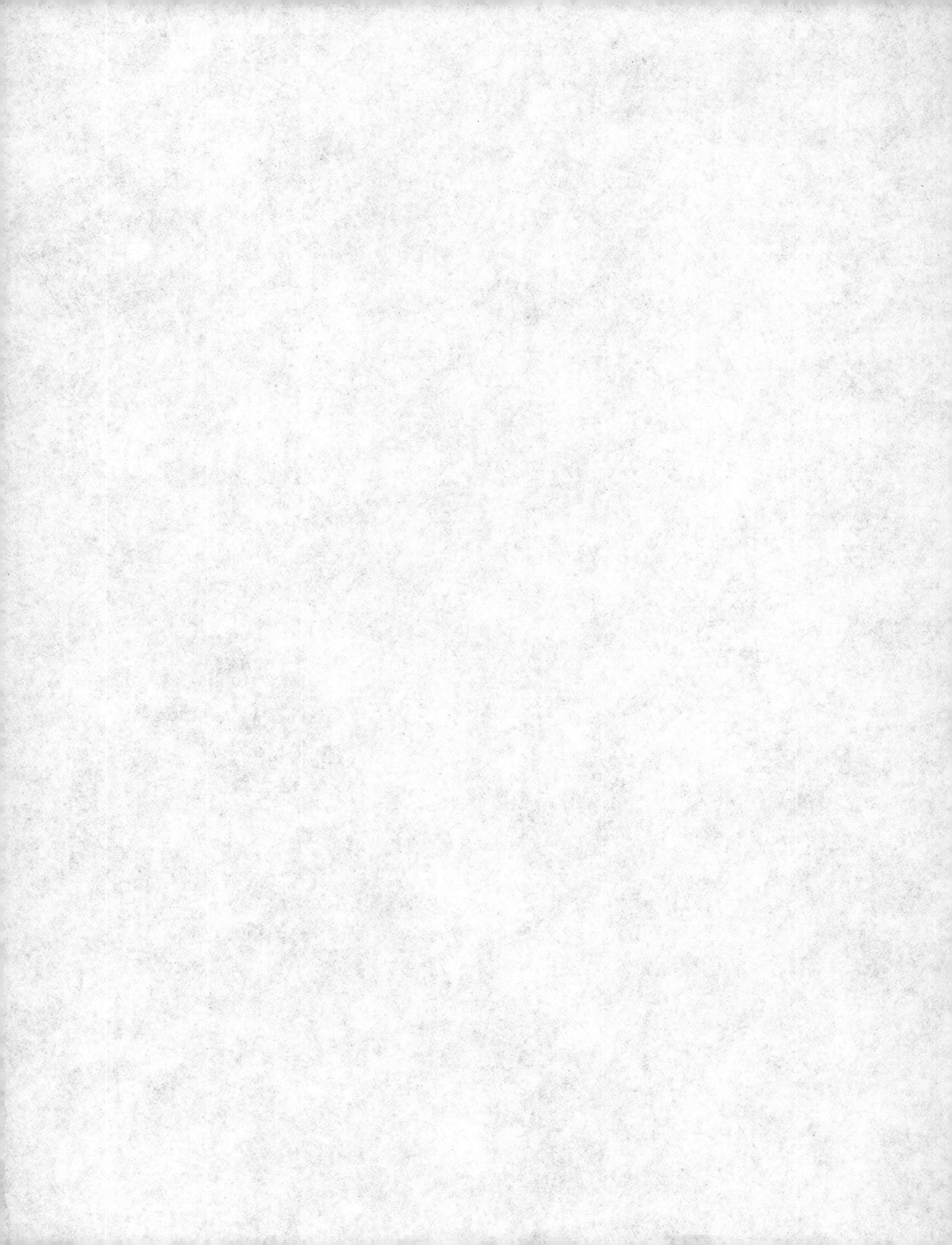